sky SPORTS FOOTBALL YEARBOOK 2017–2018

Compiled by
John Anderson

First published in 2017
by HEADLINE PUBLISHING GROUP

1

Front cover photographs:
(left) Kevin De Bruyne (Manchester City) – *Laurence Griffiths/Getty Images*; (centre and background) N'Golo Kanté (Chelsea) – *Adam Davy/Empics Sport/Press Association Images*; (right) Philippe Coutinho (Liverpool) – *Clive Brunskill/Getty Images*

Spine photograph:
Chelsea manager Antonio Conte with the Premier League trophy, May 2017 – *Darren Walsh/Getty Images*

Back cover photographs:
(above) Gabi (Atletico Madrid) and Shinji Okazaki (Leicester City), UEFA Champions League Quarter-Final Second Leg – *Action Images via Reuters/Carl Recine Livepic*; (below) Myles Beerman (Rangers) and Patrick Roberts (Celtic) – *Kirk O'Rourke/Rangers FC/Press Association Images*

Cataloguing in Publication Data is available from the British Library

ISBN 978 1 4722 3396 7 (Hardback)
ISBN 978 1 4722 3397 4 (Trade Paperback)

Typeset by Wearset Ltd, Boldon, Tyne and Wear

Printed and bound in the UK by CPI Mackays, Chatham ME5 8TD

Headline's policy is to use papers that are natural, renewable and recyclable products and made from wood grown in sustainable forests.

HEADLINE PUBLISHING GROUP
An Hachette UK Company
Carmelite House
50 Victoria Embankment
London EC4Y 0DZ

www.headline.co.uk
www.hachette.co.uk

CONTENTS

INTERNATIONAL FOOTBALL

NON-LEAGUE FOOTBALL

INFORMATION AND RECORDS

WELCOME

Welcome to the *Sky Sports Football Yearbook 2017–2018.*

Last season was our biggest ever season of Premier League football on Sky Sports: we brought fans more games than ever before, Ultra High-Definition coverage for the first time, and goals as they go in on the Football Score Centre app.

Right from the opening game there was drama and the unexpected, with Hull City beating Leicester City and putting an instant dent in the title defence; that would be the story of another thrilling season.

With more games on Sky Sports, it gave our expert analysts even more to tackle, and we were also able to introduce more technology to take viewers closer to the action. For the first time in the Premier League, we were able to use Spidercam for a number of matches, as well as UHD for every match.

We also brought fans a wide range of review and preview shows, Game of the Day, Match Choice, and, of course, our daily rolling news coverage on Sky Sports News.

When Gary Neville, Jamie Carragher, Thierry Henry, Jamie Redknapp and Graeme Souness return refreshed from their summer break I know they will be itching to get started again.

Because I'm sure that's the feeling you will have, waiting for the fixtures to be announced and then starting to plan and get excited for a new campaign. That enthusiasm runs right through Sky Sports as we prepare for a huge season.

Looking at how the teams develop over the summer provides endless excitement, but that moment when the season begins is when it all becomes real.

Two new teams will grace the Premier League: our cameras will show newly promoted Brighton & Hove Albion and Huddersfield Town and, of course, the returning Newcastle United.

Sky Sports followed the Championship story last season, so those teams are not new to our screens, but the Premier League will head to the Amex Stadium and the John Smith's Stadium for the first time.

The EFL houses some big names, from Aston Villa to Sunderland to Sheffield Wednesday, and it looks set to be another unpredictable battle for promotion across another packed season.

As the exclusive home of live EFL football – including the Carabao Cup all the way through to February's final at Wembley – as well as dedicated match highlights On Demand and online, Sky Sports will again bring fans across the EFL into closer contact with their clubs.

And north of the border, we'll have the full story too – with SPFL Premiership action throughout the season, including every league Old Firm derby meeting exclusively live, and the Scottish Cup.

We can't wait to get started, and we hope you'll share in what is sure to be a great season on Sky Sports. Anything is possible.

Barney Francis

FOREWORD

Time to go again – another new season means more excitement and more drama.

There is so much to look forward to in the year ahead – an intriguing season in the top flight has set the stage for a thrilling battle at the top of the football pyramid, but there are great stories right throughout the Premier League and EFL.

Chelsea electrified the top flight last year. After a pre-season dominated by the stories of Jose and Pep's rivalry resuming in Manchester, of the big-money move for Paul Pogba and the speculation about how Leicester would fare, Antonio Conte stole the headlines.

After switching to that 3-4-3 formation following their defeat at Arsenal, Chelsea never looked back. They marched away with the title in emphatic fashion, driven again – like Leicester last season – by the midfield dynamo of N'Golo Kanté, and propelled by the attacking verve and class of Eden Hazard.

But many of the sides below the Blues enjoyed positive seasons too – Pochettino's young and vibrant Spurs had a fine final year at White Hart Lane, and Manchester United, though disappointed by a sixth-place finish in the league, walked away with a pair of trophies.

It means this season's title race looks set to be one of the most open in years. With Conte, Mourinho and Guardiola looking settled, Pochettino building real signs of a sustained title-challenging side at Spurs, and with Klopp continuing to lead Liverpool forward, it's anyone's guess as to who will be Premier League champions come May 2018.

Throughout the league, though, I'm fascinated to see how many teams will manage in the year ahead. Huddersfield – three times champions of the English game in the 1920s – are back in the top flight for the first time since the early 1970s, after their maverick manager David Wagner led them to that dramatic play-off final win.

Brighton, too, return to the top flight for the first time in 34 years, with Chris Hughton continuing to rise in reputation after another fine season on the south coast saw them finally seal promotion.

Then we have the continuing remarkable stories of clubs like Bournemouth, who under the energetic and talented Eddie Howe, are now playing their third consecutive season in the Premier League.

The presence of some of those traditionally 'smaller' clubs in the top flight means that the Championship is a league packed with big names.

Aston Villa, Leeds United, Nottingham Forest, Sheffield Wednesday and Sunderland – to name just a few – are all enormous clubs with huge followings. All of them – and others like Fulham, QPR and Wolves – will feel that the top flight is where they belong.

But the beauty of that league – and indeed of the whole of the English Football League – is that anyone can beat anyone on their day.

From the 6,972 capacity of Burton Albion's Pirelli Stadium to the 49,000 that can be packed into the Stadium of Light in Sunderland, the Championship is a league with clubs of varying sizes and with different budgets – but despite all of that, it is arguably the most competitive league in all of Europe.

It means a fascinating race for promotion, and to beat the drop, will again be on the cards – and it's anyone's guess who'll do it. Very few would have put Huddersfield down as one of their three promoted sides at the start of last season.

Heading down into League One, former Premier League champions Blackburn Rovers will be forced to face up to the realities of life in the third tier, but they'll have to adapt fast – like the Championship, League One is uncompromising and consistently competitive.

League One also welcomes back some sides in the ascendancy – Portsmouth, Plymouth, Doncaster and Blackpool – who will all feel confident of doing well following promotion from League Two. The recent successes of clubs like Burton in building solid foundations following promotion will provide ample inspiration.

Down in League Two – well, where do I begin but with Hartlepool? My beloved club dropped out of the EFL last year for the first time in the club's history. It was a difficult end to a painful season.

But where the league lost a club for the first time, so it gained a brand new one in Forest Green Rovers, who continued their remarkable rise with victory in the play-offs, and will play league football for the very first time. There, they'll be in with sides like Coventry City, FA Cup champions in 1987 and in the Premier League as recently as 2001. Across the league, another intriguing year lies in store.

And what about in Scotland?

After walking to the title unbeaten in Brendan Rodgers' first season as boss, few would bet against Celtic retaining their SPFL Premiership crown, and making it seven on the bounce.

But that would discount the continued excellence of Aberdeen, and a Rangers side now settled back in Scotland's top flight. It will be interesting to see how that next chapter in the Old Firm rivalry develops, and whether Aberdeen, Rangers, or someone else, somewhere, can present a meaningful challenge.

Across the board, there are many questions to be answered, many dramatic chapters in a sporting saga to unfold – I just can't wait for it all to begin again!

Jeff Stelling

INTRODUCTION

The 48th edition of the Yearbook is our fifteenth with sponsors Sky Sports and includes every game so far of the European Qualifying campaign for the 2018 World Cup in Russia. Full match line-ups and league tables are included for all of the European qualifiers up to the end of the 2016–17 campaign. The quest for a place in the World Cup Finals in Russia begins again in September 2017. Other international football at various levels is also well catered for in this edition.

The concise feature entitled Cups and Ups and Downs Diary is included with dates of those events affecting cup finals, plus promotion and relegation issues. In a season where a record number of managerial changes were made, the Managers In and Out section is once again included, with a diary of managerial changes throughout the year. As women's football continues to grow, the Super League and Premier Leagues are included, together with the UEFA Women's Championship and UEFA Champions League.

At European level, both the Champions League and Europa League have their usual comprehensive details included, with results, goalscorers, attendances, full line-ups and formations from the qualifying rounds onwards and also including all the league tables from the respective group stages.

The 2016–17 season ended with Chelsea triumphant in the Premier League with Tottenham Hotspur improving on their third-place finish of last season to complete the season as runners-up. Antonio Conte was voted Manager of the Year by his peers at the League Managers Association, N'Golo Kanté followed up his Premier League success of last season with another league title for Chelsea and also won the Football Writers' Footballer of the Year award and the PFA Player of the Year award. The Championship season ended with Newcastle United and Brighton & Hove Albion promoted automatically, with the Magpies taking the Championship title on a dramatic last day, joined by Huddersfield Town who defeated Reading on penalties in the play-off final.

All of these statistics are reproduced in the pages devoted not only to the Premier League, but the three Football League competitions too, as well as all major allied cup competitions.

While transfer fees are invariably those reported at the time and rarely given as official figures, the edition reflects those listed at the time.

In the club-by-club pages that contain the line-ups of all league matches, appearances are split into starting and substitute appearances. In the Players Directory the totals show figures combined.

The Players Directory and its accompanying A to Z index enables the reader to quickly find the club of any specific player.

Throughout the book players sent off are designated with ■, substitutes in the club pages are 12, 13 and 14. Included again in main cup competitions are the formations for each team.

In addition to competitions already mentioned there is full coverage of Scottish Premiership and Scottish League and cup competitions. There are also sections devoted to Welsh, Irish, Women's football, the Under-21s and various other UEFA youth levels, schools, reserve team, academies, referees and the leading non-league competitions as well as the work of club chaplains. The chief tournaments outside the UK at club and national level are not forgotten. The International Directory itself features Europe in some depth as well as every FIFA-affiliated country's international results for the year since July 2016; for the first time every reigning league and cup champion worldwide is listed.

Naturally there are international appearances and goals scored by players for England, Scotland, Northern Ireland, Wales and the Republic. For easy reference, those players making appearances and scoring goals in the season covered are picked out in bold type.

The Yearbook would like to extend its appreciation to the publishers Headline for excellent support in the preparation of this edition, particularly Jonathan Taylor for photographic selection throughout the book and to Graham Green for his continued support.

ACKNOWLEDGEMENTS

In addition the Yearbook is also keen to thank the following individuals and organisations for their co-operation.

Special thanks to Barney Francis, Jeff Stelling, Gary Neville and Peter Smith from Sky Sports for their pieces, and to Jamie Carragher for his Sky Sports Team of the Season.

Thanks are also due to Ian Nannestad for the Obituaries, Did You Know? and Fact File features in the club section. Many thanks also to John English for his conscientious proof reading and compilation of the International Directory.

The Yearbook is grateful to the Football Association, the Scottish Professional Football League, the Football League, Rev. Nigel Sands for his contribution to the Chaplain's page and Bob Bannister, Kenny Holmes and Martin Cooper for their help.

Sincere thanks to George Schley and Simon Dunnington for their excellent work on the database, and to Andy Cordiner, Geoff Turner, Brian Tait, Mick Carruthers, Robin Middlemiss and the staff at Wearset for their much appreciated efforts in the production of the book throughout the year.

EDITORIAL

Well, another year, another season done, another treble for Manchester United.

Of course, I'd be wrong to start anywhere really but with Chelsea. Antonio Conte's side provided a masterclass last season, looking assured, confident and in command.

The Italian manager's tactical nous shone through, nowhere more clearly than when he made that switch to a defensive three after his side were embarrassed at Arsenal, a change that saw the Blues start a 13-match winning run and put themselves in control in the title race.

Tottenham impressed – and they'll go on to challenge again next year with a young and exciting squad driven forward by the verve and skill of Dele Alli and the finishing ability of Harry Kane. With goals, pace and youth, Spurs – if they can keep Pochettino and the squad together – could challenge for years to come.

The Manchester rivalry was given another dimension last year with the arrival of Jose Mourinho and Pep Guardiola at United and City respectively. In the league, both clubs would be willing to admit they enjoyed mixed campaigns, but with each manager now seemingly settled at his new home, the two clubs could really mount a challenge for the title in the coming season.

That's without mentioning Liverpool, who returned to the top four last year. With Klopp's energy, they are again back in the reckoning at the top of the tree.

It makes for a fascinating mix heading into next year's title race – it's anyone's guess as to who will walk away with that trophy come May.

Chelsea would make themselves favourites after this season. But then you would have said that at the start of the 2015–16 season, and look what happened there with Leicester.

One of the beautiful things about the Premier League is how competitive it is throughout. Covering it for Sky Sports over the last season, we've seen how sides throughout the league mix it with the very best.

Bournemouth took four points from Liverpool over the course of last season, and Manchester City were held to draws home and away by relegated Middlesbrough. Manchester United drew 10 times at Old Trafford in the league last season. Any side, anywhere in the league, can compete in any game.

I can't wait to see how the league shapes up in the coming year. Anything is possible.

I have to mention the fans. Across the season, one of the things we always notice at Sky Sports is the unbelievable support throughout English football. Week in, week out, through thick and thin, you all turn up to watch and support in your droves.

It's amazing, the dedication shown to the sport in this country – the fans provide a constant source of inspiration, a reminder of what this game means, and how important it is to communities across the country.

Football is emotional, it is beautiful, and it can be painful – but that's what makes it so exciting. I can't wait to get cracking, covering it all for Sky Sports in the year ahead.

Bring it on!

Gary Neville

SKY SPORTS TEAM OF THE SEASON

JAMIE CARRAGHER'S SKY SPORTS TEAM OF THE SEASON 2016–17

Thibaut Courtois
(Chelsea)

Cesar Azpilicueta *(Chelsea)* — Toby Alderweireld *(Tottenham H)* — David Luiz *(Chelsea)* — Danny Rose *(Tottenham H)*

Kevin De Bruyne *(Manchester C)* — N'Golo Kanté *(Chelsea)* — Dele Alli *(Tottenham H)* — Eden Hazard *(Chelsea)*

Diego Costa *(Chelsea)* — Harry Kane *(Tottenham H)*

EUROPEAN GOLDEN SHOE

The European Golden Shoe award is presented to the leading goalscorer in European League football. However, the determination of the winner comes from a points system which depends on the status of the country involved. The goals total is multiplied by a factor of either two, one and a half, or just by one.

The top 30 places were as follows:

	Scorer	*Team*	*Country*	*Goals*	*Factor*	*Points*
1	Lionel Messi	Barcelona	Spain	37	2	74
2	Bas Dost	Sporting Lisbon	Portugal	34	2	68
3	Pierre-Emerick Aubameyang	Borussia Dortmund	Germany	31	2	62
4	Robert Lewandowski	Bayern Munich	Germany	30	2	60
5	Harry Kane	Tottenham H	England	29	2	58
6	Edin Dzeko	Roma	Italy	28	2	56
7	Luis Suarez	Barcelona	Spain	28	2	56
8	Dries Mertens	Napoli	Italy	27	2	54
9	Edison Cavani	Paris Saint-Germain	France	35	1.5	52.5
10	Andrea Belotti	Torino	Italy	25	2	50
11	Anthony Modeste	FC Cologne	Germany	25	2	50
12	Cristiano Ronaldo	Real Madrid	Spain	25	2	50
13	Romalu Lukaku	Everton	England	25	2	50
14	Gonzalo Higuain	Juventus	Italy	24	2	48
15	Mauro Icardi	Inter Milan	Italy	24	2	48
16	Alexis Sanchez	Arsenal	England	24	2	48
17	Ciro Immobile	Lazio	Italy	22	2	44
18	Timo Werner	RB Leipzig	Germany	21	2	42
19	Alexandre Lacazette	Lyon	France	28	1.5	42
20	Diego Costa	Chelsea	England	20	2	40
21	Sergio Aguero	Manchester C	England	20	2	40
22	Tiquinho Soares	Porto	Portugal	19	2	38
23	Iago Aspas	Celta Vigo	Spain	19	2	38
24	Dele Alli	Tottenham H	England	18	2	36
25	Matt Derbyshire	Omonia Nicosia	Cyprus	24	1.5	36
26	Marcus Berg	Panathinaikos	Greece	23	1.5	34.5
27	Lorenzo Insigne	Napoli	Italy	17	2	34
28	Zlatan Ibrahimovic	Manchester U	England	17	2	34
29	Marcus Ingvartsen	Nordsjaelland	Denmark	22	1.5	33
30	Marco Boriello	Cagliari	Italy	16	2	32

FOOTBALL AWARDS 2016–17

FOOTBALLER OF THE YEAR

The Football Writers' Association Sir Stanley Matthews Trophy for the Footballer of the Year was awarded to N'Golo Kanté of Chelsea and France. Eden Hazard (Chelsea and Belgium) was runner-up and Dele Alli (Tottenham H and England) came third.

Past Winners

1947–48 Stanley Matthews (Blackpool), 1948–49 Johnny Carey (Manchester U), 1949–50 Joe Mercer (Arsenal), 1950–51 Harry Johnston (Blackpool), 1951–52 Billy Wright (Wolverhampton W), 1952–53 Nat Lofthouse (Bolton W), 1953–54 Tom Finney (Preston NE), 1954–55 Don Revie (Manchester C), 1955–56 Bert Trautmann (Manchester C), 1956–57 Tom Finney (Preston NE), 1957–58 Danny Blanchflower (Tottenham H), 1958–59 Syd Owen (Luton T), 1959–60 Bill Slater (Wolverhampton W), 1960–61 Danny Blanchflower (Tottenham H), 1961–62 Jimmy Adamson (Burnley), 1962–63 Stanley Matthews (Stoke C), 1963–64 Bobby Moore (West Ham U), 1964–65 Bobby Collins (Leeds U), 1965–66 Bobby Charlton (Manchester U), 1966–67 Jackie Charlton (Leeds U), 1967–68 George Best (Manchester U), 1968–69 Dave Mackay (Derby Co) shared with Tony Book (Manchester C), 1969–70 Billy Bremner (Leeds U), 1970–71 Frank McLintock (Arsenal), 1971–72 Gordon Banks (Stoke C), 1972–73 Pat Jennings (Tottenham H), 1973–74 Ian Callaghan (Liverpool), 1974–75 Alan Mullery (Fulham), 1975–76 Kevin Keegan (Liverpool), 1976–77 Emlyn Hughes (Liverpool), 1977–78 Kenny Burns (Nottingham F), 1978–79 Kenny Dalglish (Liverpool), 1979–80 Terry McDermott (Liverpool), 1980–81 Frans Thijssen (Ipswich T), 1981–82 Steve Perryman (Tottenham H), 1982–83 Kenny Dalglish (Liverpool), 1983–84 Ian Rush (Liverpool), 1984–85 Neville Southall (Everton), 1985–86 Gary Lineker (Everton), 1986–87 Clive Allen (Tottenham H), 1987–88 John Barnes (Liverpool), 1988–89 Steve Nicol (Liverpool), 1989–90 John Barnes (Liverpool), 1990–91 Gordon Strachan (Leeds U), 1991–92 Gary Lineker (Tottenham H), 1992–93 Chris Waddle (Sheffield W), 1993–94 Alan Shearer (Blackburn R), 1994–95 Jurgen Klinsmann (Tottenham H), 1995–96 Eric Cantona (Manchester U), 1996–97 Gianfranco Zola (Chelsea), 1997–98 Dennis Bergkamp (Arsenal), 1998–99 David Ginola (Tottenham H), 1999–2000 Roy Keane (Manchester U), 2000–01 Teddy Sheringham (Manchester U), 2001–02 Robert Pires (Arsenal), 2002–03 Thierry Henry (Arsenal), 2003–04 Thierry Henry (Arsenal), 2004–05 Frank Lampard (Chelsea), 2005–06 Thierry Henry (Arsenal), 2006–07 Cristiano Ronaldo (Manchester U), 2007–08 Cristiano Ronaldo (Manchester U), 2008–09 Ryan Giggs (Manchester U), 2009–10 Wayne Rooney (Manchester U), 2010–11 Scott Parker (West Ham U), 2011–12 Robin van Persie (Arsenal), 2012–13 Gareth Bale (Tottenham H), 2013–14 Luis Suarez (Liverpool), 2014–15 Eden Hazard (Chelsea), 2015–16 Jamie Vardy (Leicester C), 2016–17 N'Golo Kanté (Chelsea and France).

THE PFA AWARDS 2017

Player of the Year: N'Golo Kanté, Chelsea and France
Young Player of the Year: Dele Alli, Tottenham H and England
Women's Player of the Year: Lucy Bronze, Manchester C and England
Women's Young Player of the Year: Jess Carter, Birmingham C and England
PFA Merit Award: David Beckham
PFA Special Achievement Award: Kelly Smith, Arsenal and England

PFA Premier League Team of the Year 2017
David de Gea (Manchester U); Kyle Walker (Tottenham H), David Luiz (Chelsea), Gary Cahill (Chelsea), Danny Rose (Tottenham H), Dele Alli (Tottenham H), Eden Hazard (Chelsea), N'Golo Kanté (Chelsea), Sadio Mane (Liverpool), Harry Kane (Tottenham H), Romelu Lukaku (Everton).

PFA Championship Team of the Year 2017
David Stockdale (Brighton & HA); Bruno Saltor (Brighton & HA), Lewis Dunk (Brighton & HA), Jamaal Lascelles (Newcastle U), Ryan Sessegnon (Fulham), Tom Cairney (Fulham), Anthony Knockaert (Brighton & HA), Aaron Mooy (Huddersfield T), Jonjo Shelvey (Newcastle U), Dwight Gayle (Newcastle U), Chris Wood (Leeds U).

PFA League 1 Team of the Year 2017
Simon Moore (Sheffield U); Kieron Freeman (Sheffield U), Mark Beevers (Bolton W), David Wheater (Bolton W), James Meredith (Bradford C), Mark Duffy (Sheffield U), John Fleck (Sheffield U), Josh Morris (Scunthorpe U), Erhun Oztumer (Walsall), Billy Sharp (Sheffield U), James Vaughan (Bury).

PFA League 2 Team of the Year 2017
Luke McCormick (Plymouth Arg); Kelvin Mellor (Blackpool), Sonny Bradley (Plymouth Arg), Christian Burgess (Portsmouth), Enda Stevens (Portsmouth), Nicky Adams (Carlisle U), Luke Berry (Cambridge U), James Coppinger (Doncaster R), Graham Carey (Plymouth Arg), Danny Hylton (Luton T), John Marquis (Doncaster R).

SCOTTISH AWARDS 2016–17

SCOTTISH PFA PLAYER OF THE YEAR AWARDS 2017

Player of the Year: Scott Sinclair, Celtic
Young Player of the Year: Kieran Tierney, Celtic and Scotland
Manager of the Year: Brendan Rodgers, Celtic
Championship Player of the Year: John McGinn, Hibernian and Scotland
League One Player of the Year: Liam Buchanan, Livingston
League Two Player of the Year: Shane Sutherland, Elgin C
Goal of the Season: Moussa Dembele, Celtic (vs St Johnstone), Scottish Premiership, 5 February 2017
Special Merit Award: Scotland Women's National Team

SCOTTISH FOOTBALL WRITERS' ASSOCIATION 2017

Player of the Year: Scott Sinclair, Celtic
Young Player of the Year: Kieran Tierney, Celtic and Scotland
Manager of the Year: Brendan Rodgers, Celtic

PREMIER LEAGUE AWARDS 2016–17

	PLAYER OF THE MONTH AWARDS 2016–17	MANAGER OF THE MONTH AWARDS 2016–17
August	Raheem Sterling (Manchester C)	Mike Phelan (Hull C)
September	Son Heung-Min (Tottenham H)	Jürgen Klopp (Liverpool)
October	Edin Hazard (Chelsea)	Antonio Conte (Chelsea)
November	Diego Costa (Chelsea)	Antonio Conte (Chelsea)
December	Zlatan Ibrahimovic (Manchester U)	Antonio Conte (Chelsea)
January	Dele Alli (Tottenham H)	Paul Clement (Swansea C)
February	Harry Kane (Tottenham H)	Pep Guardiola (Manchester C)
March	Romalu Lukaku (Everton)	Eddie Howe (Bournemouth)
April	Heung-Min Son (Tottenham H)	Mauricio Pochettino (Tottenham H)

SKY BET LEAGUE AWARDS 2016–17

SKY BET FOOTBALL LEAGUE PLAYER OF THE MONTH AWARDS 2016–17

	Championship	*League 1*	*League 2*
August	Conor Hourihane (Barnsley)	Josh Morris (Scunthorpe U)	James Coppinger (Doncaster R)
September	Scott Hogan (Brentford)	Josh Morris (Scunthorpe U)	Jon Stead (Notts Co)
October	Sone Aluko (Fulham)	Zac Clough (Bolton W)	Jason Kennedy (Carlisle U)
November	Henri Lansbury (Nottingham F)	Jay O'Shea (Chesterfield)	Omar Bogle (Grimsby T)
December	Sam Winnall (Barnsley)	Matty Lund (Rochdale)	Scott Kashket (Wycombe W)
January	Chris Woods (Leeds U)	James Vaughan (Bury)	Ollie Watkins (Exeter C)
February	Aiden McGeady (Preston NE)	Billy Sharp (Sheffield U)	Matt Godden (Stevenage)
March	Tom Barkhuizen (Preston NE)	Filipe Morais (Bolton W)	Shay McCartan (Accrington S)
April	Yann Kermorgant (Reading)	Leon Clarke (Sheffield U)	Micky Demetriou (Newport Co)
Player of the Season			
	Antony Knockaert (Brighton & HA)	Billy Sharp (Sheffield U)	John Marquis (Doncaster R)

SKY BET FOOTBALL LEAGUE MANAGER OF THE MONTH AWARDS 2016–17

	Championship	*League 1*	*League 2*
August	David Wagner (Huddersfield T)	Phil Parkinson (Bolton W)	Jim Bentley (Morecambe)
September	Alex Neil (Norwich C)	David Flitcroft (Bury)	Derek Adams (Plymouth Arg)
October	Rafael Benitez (Newcastle U)	Phil Parkinson (Bolton W)	Keith Curle (Carlisle U)
November	Steve McClaren (Derby Co)	Graham Alexander (Scunthorpe U)	Gareth Ainsworth (Wycombe W)
December	Chris Hughton (Brighton & HA)	Keith Hill (Rochdale)	John McGreal (Colchester U)
January	Jaap Stam (Reading)	Uwe Rosler (Fleetwood T)	Darren Ferguson (Doncaster R)
February	David Wagner (Huddersfield T)	Neil Harris (Millwall)	Darren Sarll (Stevenage)
March	Paul Lambert (Wolverhampton W)	Phil Parkinson (Bolton W)	John Coleman (Accrington S)
April	Carlos Carvalhal (Sheffield W)	Chris Wilder (Sheffield U)	Paul Cook (Portsmouth)
Manager of the Year			
	David Wagner (Huddersfield T)	Chris Wilder (Sheffield U)	Darren Ferguson (Doncaster R)

LEAGUE MANAGERS ASSOCIATION AWARDS 2016–17

LMA MANAGER OF THE YEAR SPONSORED BY EVEREST
Antonio Conte (Chelsea)

PREMIER LEAGUE MANAGER OF THE YEAR SPONSORED BY BARCLAYS
Antonio Conte (Chelsea)

SKY BET FOOTBALL LEAGUE CHAMPIONSHIP MANAGER OF THE YEAR
Chris Hughton (Brighton & HA)

SKY BET FOOTBALL LEAGUE 1 MANAGER OF THE YEAR
Chris Wilder (Sheffield U)

SKY BET FOOTBALL LEAGUE 2 MANAGER OF THE YEAR
Paul Cook (Portsmouth)

LMA SPECIAL ACHIEVEMENT AWARD SPONSORED BY PROSTATE CANCER UK
Danny Cowley (Lincoln C)

LMA SERVICE TO FOOTBALL AWARD
Tony Collins

OTHER AWARDS

EUROPEAN FOOTBALLER OF THE YEAR 2016
Cristiano Ronaldo, Real Madrid and Portugal

EUROPEAN WOMEN'S PLAYER OF THE YEAR 2016
Ada Hegerberg, Lyon and Norway

FIFA BALLON D'OR PLAYER OF THE YEAR 2016
Cristiano Ronaldo, Real Madrid and Portugal

FIFA BALLON D'OR WOMEN'S PLAYER OF THE YEAR 2016
Carli Lloyd, Houston Dash and USA

FIFA PUSKAS AWARD GOAL OF THE YEAR 2016
Mohd Faiz Subri, Penang v Pahang, Malaysian Super League, 16 February 2016

PREMIER LEAGUE 2016–17

(P) *Promoted into division at end of 2015–16 season.*

			Home					*Away*					*Total*						
		P	*W*	*D*	*L*	*F*	*A*	*W*	*D*	*L*	*F*	*A*	*W*	*D*	*L*	*F*	*A*	*GD*	*Pts*
1	Chelsea	38	17	0	2	55	17	13	3	3	30	16	30	3	5	85	33	52	93
2	Tottenham H	38	17	2	0	47	9	9	6	4	39	17	26	8	4	86	26	60	86
3	Manchester C	38	11	7	1	37	17	12	2	5	43	22	23	9	6	80	39	41	78
4	Liverpool	38	12	5	2	45	18	10	5	4	33	24	22	10	6	78	42	36	76
5	Arsenal	38	14	3	2	39	16	9	3	7	38	28	23	6	9	77	44	33	75
6	Manchester U	38	8	10	1	26	12	10	5	4	28	17	18	15	5	54	29	25	69
7	Everton	38	13	4	2	42	16	4	6	9	20	28	17	10	11	62	44	18	61
8	Southampton	38	6	6	7	17	21	6	4	9	24	27	12	10	16	41	48	–7	46
9	Bournemouth	38	9	4	6	35	29	3	6	10	20	38	12	10	16	55	67	–12	46
10	WBA	38	9	2	8	27	22	3	7	9	16	29	12	9	17	43	51	–8	45
11	West Ham U	38	7	4	8	19	31	5	5	9	28	33	12	9	17	47	64	–17	45
12	Leicester C	38	10	4	5	31	25	2	4	13	17	38	12	8	18	48	63	–15	44
13	Stoke C	38	7	6	6	24	24	4	5	10	17	32	11	11	16	41	56	–15	44
14	Crystal Palace	38	6	2	11	24	25	6	3	10	26	38	12	5	21	50	63	–13	41
15	Swansea C	38	8	3	8	27	34	4	2	13	18	36	12	5	21	45	70	–25	41
16	Burnley (P)	38	10	3	6	26	20	1	4	14	13	35	11	7	20	39	55	–16	40
17	Watford	38	8	4	7	25	29	3	3	13	15	39	11	7	20	40	68	–28	40
18	Hull C (P)	38	8	4	7	28	35	1	3	15	9	45	9	7	22	37	80	–43	34
19	Middlesbrough (P)	38	4	6	9	17	23	1	7	11	10	30	5	13	20	27	53	–26	28
20	Sunderland	38	3	5	11	16	34	3	1	15	13	35	6	6	26	29	69	–40	24

PREMIER LEAGUE LEADING GOALSCORERS 2016–17

	League	*FA Cup*	*EFL Cup*	*Other*	*Total*
Harry Kane *(Tottenham H)*	29	4	0	2	35
Sergio Aguero *(Manchester C)*	20	5	0	8	33
Alexis Sanchez *(Arsenal)*	24	2	0	3	29
Zlatan Ibrahimovic *(Manchester U)*	17	1	4	6	28
Romelu Lukaku *(Everton)*	25	1	0	0	26
Dele Alli *(Tottenham H)*	18	3	0	1	22
Diego Costa *(Chelsea)*	20	1	0	0	21
Heung-min Son *(Tottenham H)*	14	6	0	1	21
Theo Walcott *(Arsenal)*	10	5	0	4	19
Eden Hazard *(Chelsea)*	16	1	0	0	17
Christian Benteke *(Crystal Palace)*	15	2	0	0	17
Joshua King *(AFC Bournemouth)*	16	0	0	0	16
Jamie Vardy *(Leicester C)*	13	0	0	3	16
Olivier Giroud *(Arsenal)*	12	2	0	2	16
Jermain Defoe *(Sunderland)*	15	0	0	0	15
Fernando Llorente *(Swansea C)*	15	0	0	0	15
Philippe Coutinho *(Liverpool)*	13	0	1	0	14
Sadio Mane *(Liverpool)*	13	0	0	0	13
Pedro *(Chelsea)*	9	4	0	0	13
Roberto Firmino *(Liverpool)*	11	0	1	0	12
Sam Vokes *(Burnley)*	10	2	0	0	12
Troy Deeney *(Watford)*	10	0	0	0	10
Alvaro Negredo *(Middlesbrough)*	9	1	0	0	10
Andre Gray *(Burnley)*	9	1	0	0	10
Gylfi Sigurdsson *(Swansea C)*	9	0	1	0	10
Michail Antonio *(West Ham U)*	9	0	0	0	9

Other matches consist of European games, Community Shield.

PREMIER LEAGUE – RESULTS 2016–17

	Arsenal	Bournemouth	Burnley	Chelsea	Crystal Palace	Everton	Hull C	Leicester C	Liverpool	Manchester C	Manchester U	Middlesbrough	Southampton	Stoke C	Sunderland	Swansea C	Tottenham H	Watford	WBA	West Ham U
Arsenal	—	3-1	2-1	3-0	2-0	3-1	2-0	1-0	3-4	2-2	2-0	0-0	2-1	3-1	2-0	3-2	1-1	1-2	1-0	3-0
Bournemouth	3-3	—	2-1	1-3	0-2	1-0	6-1	1-0	4-3	0-2	1-3	4-0	1-3	2-2	1-2	2-0	0-0	2-2	1-0	3-2
Burnley	0-1	3-2	—	1-1	3-2	2-1	1-1	1-0	2-0	1-2	0-2	1-0	1-0	1-0	4-1	0-1	0-2	2-0	2-2	1-2
Chelsea	3-1	3-0	3-0	—	1-2	5-0	2-0	3-0	1-2	2-1	4-0	3-0	4-2	4-2	5-1	3-1	2-1	4-3	1-0	2-1
Crystal Palace	3-0	1-1	0-2	0-1	—	0-1	4-0	2-2	2-4	1-2	1-2	1-0	3-0	4-1	0-4	1-2	0-1	1-0	0-1	0-1
Everton	2-1	6-3	3-1	0-3	1-1	—	4-0	4-2	0-1	4-0	1-1	3-1	3-0	1-0	2-0	1-1	1-1	1-0	3-0	2-0
Hull C	1-4	3-1	1-1	0-2	3-3	2-2	—	2-1	2-0	0-3	0-1	4-2	2-1	0-2	0-2	2-1	1-7	2-0	1-1	2-1
Leicester C	0-0	1-1	3-0	0-3	3-1	0-2	3-1	—	3-1	4-2	0-3	2-2	0-0	2-0	2-0	2-1	1-6	3-0	1-2	1-0
Liverpool	3-1	2-2	2-1	1-1	1-2	3-1	5-1	4-1	—	1-0	0-0	3-0	0-0	4-1	2-0	2-3	2-0	6-1	2-1	2-2
Manchester C	2-1	4-0	2-1	1-3	5-0	1-1	3-1	2-1	1-1	—	0-0	1-1	1-1	0-0	2-1	2-1	2-2	2-0	3-1	3-1
Manchester U	1-1	1-1	0-0	2-0	2-0	1-1	0-0	4-1	1-1	1-2	—	2-1	2-0	1-1	3-1	1-1	1-0	2-0	0-0	1-1
Middlesbrough	1-2	2-0	0-0	0-1	1-2	0-0	1-0	0-0	0-3	2-2	1-3	—	1-2	1-1	1-0	3-0	1-2	0-1	1-1	1-3
Southampton	0-2	0-0	3-1	0-2	3-1	1-0	0-0	3-0	0-0	0-3	0-0	1-0	—	0-1	1-1	1-0	1-4	1-1	1-2	1-3
Stoke C	1-4	0-1	2-0	1-2	1-0	1-1	3-1	2-2	1-2	1-4	1-1	2-0	0-0	—	2-0	3-1	0-4	2-0	1-1	0-0
Sunderland	1-4	0-1	0-0	0-1	2-3	0-3	3-0	2-1	2-2	0-2	0-3	1-2	0-4	1-3	—	0-2	0-0	1-0	1-1	2-2
Swansea C	0-4	0-3	3-2	2-2	5-4	1-0	0-2	2-0	1-2	1-3	1-3	0-0	2-1	2-0	3-0	—	1-3	0-0	2-1	1-4
Tottenham H	2-0	4-0	2-1	2-0	1-0	3-2	3-0	1-1	1-1	2-0	2-1	1-0	2-1	4-0	1-0	5-0	—	4-0	4-0	3-2
Watford	1-3	2-2	2-1	1-2	1-1	3-2	1-0	2-1	0-1	0-5	3-1	0-0	3-4	0-1	1-0	1-0	1-4	—	2-0	1-1
WBA	3-1	2-1	4-0	0-1	0-2	1-2	3-1	0-1	0-1	0-4	0-2	0-0	0-1	1-0	2-0	3-1	1-1	3-1	—	4-2
West Ham U	1-5	1-0	1-0	1-2	3-0	0-0	1-0	2-3	0-4	0-4	0-2	1-1	0-3	1-1	1-0	1-0	1-0	2-4	2-2	—

SKY BET CHAMPIONSHIP 2016–17

(P) *Promoted into division at end of 2015–16 season.* (R) *Relegated into division at end of 2015–16 season.*

		Home						*Away*					*Total*						
		P	*W*	*D*	*L*	*F*	*A*	*W*	*D*	*L*	*F*	*A*	*W*	*D*	*L*	*F*	*A*	*GD*	*Pts*
1	Newcastle U (R)	46	15	3	5	49	23	14	4	5	36	17	29	7	10	85	40	45	94
2	Brighton & HA	46	17	3	3	46	14	11	6	6	28	26	28	9	9	74	40	34	93
3	Reading	46	16	5	2	35	16	10	2	11	33	48	26	7	13	68	64	4	85
4	Sheffield W	46	15	2	6	36	22	9	7	7	24	23	24	9	13	60	45	15	81
5	Huddersfield T¶	46	15	2	6	34	26	10	4	9	22	32	25	6	15	56	58	–2	81
6	Fulham	46	10	8	5	45	32	12	6	5	40	25	22	14	10	85	57	28	80
7	Leeds U	46	14	4	5	32	16	8	5	10	29	31	22	9	15	61	47	14	75
8	Norwich C (R)	46	15	4	4	55	22	5	6	12	30	47	20	10	16	85	69	16	70
9	Derby Co	46	11	8	4	33	20	7	5	11	21	30	18	13	15	54	50	4	67
10	Brentford	46	11	5	7	42	25	7	5	11	33	40	18	10	18	75	65	10	64
11	Preston NE	46	11	6	6	40	26	5	8	10	24	37	16	14	16	64	63	1	62
12	Cardiff C	46	11	4	8	31	26	6	7	10	29	35	17	11	18	60	61	–1	62
13	Aston Villa (R)	46	12	8	3	33	20	4	6	13	14	28	16	14	16	47	48	–1	62
14	Barnsley (P)	46	6	11	6	32	33	9	2	12	32	34	15	13	18	64	67	–3	58
15	Wolverhampton W	46	8	4	11	25	30	8	6	9	29	28	16	10	20	54	58	–4	58
16	Ipswich T	46	8	10	5	30	24	5	6	12	18	34	13	16	17	48	58	–10	55
17	Bristol C	46	11	4	8	33	26	4	5	14	27	40	15	9	22	60	66	–6	54
18	QPR	46	9	4	10	30	32	6	4	13	22	34	15	8	23	52	66	–14	53
19	Birmingham C	46	8	5	10	25	31	5	9	9	20	33	13	14	19	45	64	–19	53
20	Burton Alb (P)	46	9	4	10	28	30	4	9	10	21	33	13	13	20	49	63	–14	52
21	Nottingham F	46	12	4	7	42	30	2	5	16	20	42	14	9	23	62	72	–10	51
22	Blackburn R	46	8	8	7	29	30	4	7	12	24	35	12	15	19	53	65	–12	51
23	Wigan Ath (P)	46	5	8	10	19	26	5	4	14	21	31	10	12	24	40	57	–17	42
24	Rotherham U	46	5	6	12	23	34	0	2	21	17	64	5	8	33	40	98	–58	23

¶Huddersfield T promoted via play-offs.

SKY BET CHAMPIONSHIP LEADING GOALSCORERS 2016–17

	League	*FA Cup*	*EFL League Cup*	*Play-Offs*	*Total*
Chris Wood *(Leeds U)*	27	0	3	0	30
Tammy Abraham *(Bristol C)*	23	0	3	0	26
Dwight Gayle *(Newcastle U)*	23	0	0	0	23
Glenn Murray *(Brighton & HA)*	23	0	0	0	23
Jonathan Kodjia *(Aston Villa)*	19	0	0	0	19
Yann Kermorgant *(Reading)*	18	0	0	1	19
Cameron Jerome *(Norwich C)*	16	0	0	0	16
Lasse Vibe *(Brentford)*	15	1	0	0	16
Matt Ritchie *(Newcastle U)*	12	2	2	0	16
Scott Hogan *(Aston Villa)*	15	0	0	0	15
(Includes 14 League goals for Brentford.)					
Anthony Knockaert *(Brighton & HA)*	15	0	0	0	15
Thomas Ince *(Derby Co)*	14	1	0	0	15
Britt Assombalonga *(Nottingham F)*	14	0	0	0	14
Sam Winnall *(Sheffield W)*	14	0	0	0	14
(Includes 11 League goals for Barnsley.)					
Tomer Hemed *(Brighton & HA)*	11	1	2	0	14
Tom Cairney *(Fulham)*	12	0	0	1	13
Danny Graham *(Blackburn R)*	12	1	0	0	13
Jordan Hugill *(Preston NE)*	12	0	1	0	13
Elias Kachunga *(Huddersfield T)*	12	0	1	0	13
Stefan Johansen *(Fulham)*	11	2	0	0	13
Fernando Forestieri *(Sheffield W)*	12	0	0	0	12
Jota *(Brentford)*	12	0	0	0	12
Kenneth Zohore *(Cardiff C)*	12	0	0	0	12
Sam Gallagher *(Blackburn R)*	11	1	0	0	12
Lukas Jutkiewicz *(Birmingham C)*	11	1	0	0	12
Nelson Oliveira *(Norwich C)*	11	0	1	0	12
(Also 2 goals in EFL Trophy for Norwich C U21.)					
Danny Ward *(Rotherham U)*	11	1	0	0	12

SKY BET CHAMPIONSHIP – RESULTS 2016–17

	Aston Villa	Barnsley	Birmingham C	Blackburn R	Brentford	Brighton & HA	Bristol C	Burton Alb	Cardiff C	Derby Co	Fulham	Huddersfield T	Ipswich T	Leeds U	Newcastle U	Norwich C	Nottingham F	Preston NE	QPR	Reading	Rotherham U	Sheffield W	Wigan Ath	Wolverhampton W
Aston Villa	—	1-3	1-0	2-1	1-1	1-1	2-0	2-1	3-1	1-0	1-0	1-1	0-1	1-1	1-1	2-0	2-2	2-2	1-0	1-3	3-0	2-0	1-0	1-1
Barnsley	1-1	—	2-2	2-0	1-1	0-2	2-2	1-1	0-0	2-0	2-4	1-1	1-1	3-2	0-2	2-1	2-5	0-0	3-2	1-2	4-0	1-1	0-0	1-3
Birmingham C	1-1	0-3	—	1-0	1-3	1-2	1-0	0-2	0-0	1-2	1-0	2-0	2-1	1-3	0-0	3-0	0-0	2-2	1-4	0-1	4-2	2-1	0-1	1-3
Blackburn R	1-0	0-2	1-1	—	3-2	2-3	1-1	2-2	1-1	1-0	0-1	1-1	0-0	1-2	1-0	1-4	2-1	2-2	1-0	2-3	4-2	0-1	1-0	1-1
Brentford	3-0	0-2	1-2	1-3	—	3-3	2-0	2-1	2-2	4-0	0-2	0-1	2-0	2-0	1-2	0-0	1-0	5-0	3-1	4-1	4-2	1-1	0-0	1-2
Brighton & HA	1-1	2-0	3-1	1-0	0-2	—	0-1	4-1	1-0	3-0	2-1	1-0	1-1	2-0	1-2	5-0	3-0	2-2	3-0	3-0	3-0	2-1	2-1	1-0
Bristol C	3-1	3-2	0-1	1-0	0-1	0-2	—	0-0	2-3	1-1	0-2	4-0	2-0	1-0	0-1	1-1	2-1	1-2	2-1	2-3	1-0	2-2	2-1	3-1
Burton Alb	1-1	0-0	2-0	1-1	3-5	0-1	1-2	—	2-0	1-0	0-2	0-1	1-2	2-1	1-2	2-1	1-0	0-1	1-1	2-4	2-1	3-1	0-2	2-1
Cardiff C	1-0	3-4	1-1	2-1	2-1	0-0	2-1	1-0	—	0-2	2-2	3-2	3-1	0-2	0-2	0-1	1-0	2-0	0-2	0-1	5-0	1-1	0-1	2-1
Derby Co	0-0	2-1	1-0	1-2	0-0	0-0	3-3	0-0	3-4	—	4-2	1-1	0-1	1-0	0-2	1-0	3-0	1-1	1-0	3-2	3-0	2-0	0-0	3-1
Fulham	3-1	2-0	0-1	2-2	1-1	1-2	0-4	1-1	2-2	2-2	—	5-0	3-1	1-1	1-0	2-2	3-2	3-1	1-2	5-0	2-1	1-1	3-2	1-3
Huddersfield T	1-0	2-1	1-1	1-1	2-1	3-1	2-1	0-1	0-3	1-0	1-4	—	2-0	2-1	1-3	3-0	2-1	3-2	2-1	1-0	2-1	0-1	1-2	1-0
Ipswich T	0-0	4-2	1-1	3-2	1-1	0-0	2-1	2-0	1-1	0-3	0-2	0-1	—	1-1	3-1	1-1	0-2	1-0	3-0	2-2	2-2	0-1	3-0	0-0
Leeds U	2-0	2-1	1-2	2-1	1-0	2-0	2-1	2-0	0-2	1-0	1-1	0-1	1-0	—	0-2	3-3	2-0	3-0	0-0	2-0	3-0	1-0	1-1	0-1
Newcastle U	2-0	3-0	4-0	0-1	3-1	2-0	2-2	1-0	2-1	1-0	1-3	1-2	3-0	1-1	—	4-3	3-1	4-1	2-2	4-1	4-0	0-1	2-1	0-2
Norwich C	1-0	2-0	2-0	2-2	5-0	2-0	1-0	3-1	3-2	3-0	1-3	1-2	1-1	2-3	2-2	—	5-1	0-1	4-0	7-1	3-1	0-0	2-1	3-1
Nottingham F	2-1	0-1	3-1	0-1	2-3	3-0	1-0	4-3	1-2	2-2	1-1	2-0	3-0	3-1	2-1	1-2	—	1-1	1-1	3-2	2-0	1-2	4-3	0-2
Preston NE	2-0	1-2	2-1	3-2	4-2	2-0	5-0	1-1	3-0	0-1	1-2	3-1	1-1	1-4	1-2	1-3	1-1	—	2-1	3-0	1-1	1-1	1-0	0-0
QPR	0-1	2-1	1-1	1-1	0-2	1-2	1-0	1-2	2-1	0-1	1-1	1-2	2-1	3-0	0-6	2-1	2-0	0-2	—	1-1	5-1	1-2	2-1	1-2
Reading	1-2	0-0	0-0	3-1	3-2	2-2	2-1	3-0	2-1	1-1	1-0	1-0	2-1	1-0	0-0	3-1	2-0	1-0	0-1	—	2-1	2-1	1-0	2-1
Rotherham U	0-2	0-1	1-1	1-1	1-0	0-2	2-2	1-2	1-2	1-1	0-1	2-3	1-0	1-2	0-1	2-1	2-2	1-3	1-0	0-1	—	0-2	3-2	2-2
Sheffield W	1-0	2-0	3-0	2-1	1-2	1-2	3-2	1-1	1-0	2-1	1-2	2-0	1-2	0-2	2-1	5-1	2-1	2-1	1-0	0-2	1-0	—	2-1	0-0
Wigan Ath	0-2	3-2	1-1	3-0	2-1	0-1	0-1	0-0	0-0	0-1	0-0	0-1	2-3	1-1	0-2	2-2	0-0	0-0	0-1	0-3	3-2	0-1	—	2-1
Wolverhampton W	1-0	0-4	1-2	0-0	3-1	0-2	3-2	1-1	3-1	2-3	4-4	0-1	0-0	0-1	0-1	1-2	1-0	1-0	1-2	2-0	1-0	0-2	0-1	—

SKY BET LEAGUE 1 2016–17

(P) *Promoted into division at end of 2015–16 season.* (R) *Relegated into division at end of 2015–16 season.*

			Home					Away					Total						
		P	W	D	L	F	A	W	D	L	F	A	W	D	L	F	A	GD	Pts
1	Sheffield U	46	17	3	3	42	16	13	7	3	50	31	30	10	6	92	47	45	100
2	Bolton W (R)	46	13	7	3	35	16	12	4	7	33	20	25	11	10	68	36	32	86
3	Scunthorpe U	46	14	6	3	46	22	10	4	9	34	32	24	10	12	80	54	26	82
4	Fleetwood T	46	12	8	3	34	20	11	5	7	30	23	23	13	10	64	43	21	82
5	Bradford C	46	11	12	0	36	17	9	7	7	26	26	20	19	7	62	43	19	79
6	Millwall¶	46	13	6	4	34	17	7	7	9	32	40	20	13	13	66	57	9	73
7	Southend U	46	11	7	5	39	27	9	5	9	31	26	20	12	14	70	53	17	72
8	Oxford U (P)	46	11	4	8	33	27	9	5	9	32	25	20	9	17	65	52	13	69
9	Rochdale	46	13	7	3	48	25	6	5	12	23	37	19	12	15	71	62	9	69
10	Bristol R (P)	46	13	6	4	42	26	5	6	12	26	44	18	12	16	68	70	–2	66
11	Peterborough U	46	9	6	8	39	33	8	5	10	23	29	17	11	18	62	62	0	62
12	Milton Keynes D (R)	46	7	6	10	29	37	9	7	7	31	21	16	13	17	60	58	2	61
13	Charlton Ath (R)	46	9	8	6	31	19	5	10	8	29	34	14	18	14	60	53	7	60
14	Walsall	46	11	5	7	34	29	3	11	9	17	29	14	16	16	51	58	–7	58
15	AFC Wimbledon (P)	46	8	8	7	34	25	5	10	8	18	30	13	18	15	52	55	–3	57
16	Northampton T (P)	46	9	5	9	35	29	5	6	12	25	44	14	11	21	60	73	–13	53
17	Oldham Ath	46	8	9	6	19	18	4	8	11	12	26	12	17	17	31	44	–13	53
18	Shrewsbury T	46	10	5	8	26	26	3	7	13	20	37	13	12	21	46	63	–17	51
19	Bury	46	9	3	11	36	33	4	8	11	25	40	13	11	22	61	73	–12	50
20	Gillingham	46	8	9	6	32	30	4	5	14	27	49	12	14	20	59	79	–20	50
21	Port Vale	46	10	6	7	32	31	2	7	14	13	39	12	13	21	45	70	–25	49
22	Swindon T	46	7	6	10	23	24	4	5	14	21	42	11	11	24	44	66	–22	44
23	Coventry C	46	8	7	8	22	24	1	5	17	15	44	9	12	25	37	68	–31	39
24	Chesterfield	46	7	5	11	26	39	2	5	16	17	39	9	10	27	43	78	–35	37

¶*Millwall promoted via play-offs.*

SKY BET LEAGUE 1 LEADING GOALSCORERS 2016–17

	League	FA Cup	EFL League Cup	EFL Trophy	Play-Offs	Total
Billy Sharp *(Sheffield U)*	30	0	0	0	0	30
James Vaughan *(Bury)*	24	0	0	0	0	24
Josh Morris *(Scunthorpe U)*	19	0	1	0	0	20
Matt Taylor *(Bristol R)*	17	2	0	1	0	20
(Includes 1 goal in EFL Championship for Bristol C.)						
Ian Henderson *(Rochdale)*	15	2	1	1	0	19
Steve Morison *(Millwall)*	11	2	1	2	3	19
Lee Gregory *(Millwall)*	17	0	0	0	1	18
Chris Maguire *(Oxford U)*	13	1	0	3	0	17
Simon Cox *(Southend U)*	16	0	0	0	0	16
Erhun Oztumer *(Walsall)*	15	0	0	0	0	15
Alex Jones *(Bradford C)*	14	1	0	0	0	15
(Includes 1 goal in FA Cup for Port Vale.)						
Aiden O'Brien *(Millwall)*	13	1	1	0	0	15
David Ball *(Fleetwood T)*	14	0	0	0	0	14
Josh Wright *(Gillingham)*	13	0	0	1	0	14
Kieran Agard *(Milton Keynes D)*	12	1	0	1	0	14
Ivan Toney *(Scunthorpe U)*	12	0	0	1	1	14
(Includes 6 League goals and 1 EFL Trophy goal for Shrewsbury T.)						
Billy Bodin *(Bristol R)*	13	0	0	0	0	13
Ricky Holmes *(Charlton Ath)*	13	0	0	0	0	13
Nicky Ajose *(Charlton Ath)*	11	0	0	1	0	12
(Includes 5 League goals for Swindon T.)						
Tony Wordsworth *(Southend U)*	11	0	0	1	0	12
Paddy Madden *(Scunthorpe U)*	11	0	0	0	0	11

SKY BET LEAGUE 1 – RESULTS 2016–17

	AFC Wimbledon	Bolton W	Bradford C	Bristol R	Bury	Charlton Ath	Chesterfield	Coventry C	Fleetwood T	Gillingham	Millwall	Milton Keynes D	Northampton T	Oldham Ath	Oxford U	Peterborough U	Port Vale	Rochdale	Scunthorpe U	Sheffield U	Shrewsbury T	Southend U	Swindon T	Walsall
AFC Wimbledon	—	1-2	2-3	0-1	5-1	1-1	2-1	1-1	2-2	2-0	2-2	2-0	0-1	0-0	2-1	0-0	4-0	3-1	1-2	2-3	1-1	0-2	0-0	1-0
Bolton W	1-1	—	0-0	1-1	0-0	1-2	0-0	1-0	2-1	4-0	2-0	1-1	2-1	2-0	0-2	3-0	3-1	1-0	2-1	1-0	2-1	1-1	1-2	4-1
Bradford C	3-0	2-2	—	1-1	1-1	0-0	2-0	3-1	2-1	2-2	1-1	2-2	1-0	1-1	1-0	1-0	0-0	4-0	0-0	3-3	2-0	1-1	2-1	1-0
Bristol R	2-0	1-2	1-1	—	4-2	1-5	2-1	4-1	2-1	2-1	3-4	0-0	5-0	1-0	2-1	1-2	2-1	2-2	1-1	0-0	2-0	2-0	1-0	1-1
Bury	1-2	0-2	0-2	3-0	—	2-0	2-1	2-1	0-0	1-2	2-3	0-0	3-0	0-1	2-3	5-1	4-1	0-1	1-2	1-3	2-1	1-4	1-0	3-3
Charlton Ath	1-2	1-1	1-1	4-1	0-1	—	1-0	3-0	1-1	3-0	0-0	0-2	1-1	1-1	0-1	0-2	2-0	0-1	2-1	1-1	3-0	2-1	3-0	1-1
Chesterfield	0-0	1-0	0-1	3-2	1-2	1-2	—	1-0	0-1	3-3	1-3	0-0	3-1	0-1	0-4	3-3	1-0	1-3	0-3	1-4	1-1	0-4	3-1	2-0
Coventry C	2-2	2-2	0-2	1-0	0-0	1-1	2-0	—	0-1	2-1	0-2	1-2	1-1	0-0	2-1	1-0	2-1	2-0	0-1	1-2	0-0	0-2	1-3	1-0
Fleetwood T	0-0	2-4	2-1	3-1	0-0	2-2	2-1	2-0	—	2-1	1-0	1-4	3-0	1-0	2-0	2-0	0-0	0-0	2-2	1-1	3-0	1-1	0-1	2-1
Gillingham	2-2	0-4	1-1	3-1	2-1	1-1	1-1	2-1	2-3	—	1-1	1-0	2-1	1-2	0-1	0-1	1-1	3-0	3-2	1-2	1-1	2-1	1-1	1-1
Millwall	0-0	0-2	1-1	4-0	0-0	3-1	0-0	1-1	2-1	2-1	—	2-1	3-0	3-0	0-3	1-0	2-0	2-3	3-1	2-1	0-1	1-0	2-0	0-0
Milton Keynes D	1-0	1-1	1-2	3-3	1-3	0-1	2-3	1-0	0-1	3-2	2-2	—	5-3	1-0	0-0	0-2	0-1	2-2	0-1	0-3	2-1	0-3	3-2	1-1
Northampton T	0-0	0-1	1-2	2-3	3-2	2-1	3-1	3-0	1-1	0-0	1-3	3-2	—	1-2	0-0	0-1	2-1	2-3	1-2	1-2	1-1	4-0	2-1	2-0
Oldham Ath	0-0	1-0	1-2	0-2	0-0	1-0	0-0	3-2	2-0	1-0	0-0	0-2	0-0	—	2-1	2-0	0-0	1-1	2-0	1-1	2-3	0-2	0-2	0-0
Oxford U	1-3	2-4	1-0	0-2	5-1	1-1	1-1	4-1	1-3	1-0	1-2	1-0	0-1	1-1	—	2-1	2-0	1-0	2-1	2-3	2-0	0-2	2-0	0-0
Peterborough U	0-1	1-0	0-1	4-2	3-1	2-0	5-2	1-1	1-2	1-1	5-1	0-4	3-0	1-1	1-2	—	2-2	3-1	0-2	0-1	2-1	1-4	2-2	1-1
Port Vale	2-0	0-2	1-2	1-1	2-2	1-1	1-0	0-2	2-1	2-1	3-1	0-0	2-3	2-2	2-2	0-3	—	1-0	3-1	0-3	2-1	2-0	3-2	0-1
Rochdale	1-1	1-0	1-1	0-0	2-0	3-3	3-0	2-0	2-1	4-1	3-3	0-1	1-1	1-0	0-4	2-3	3-0	—	3-2	3-3	2-1	3-0	4-0	4-0
Scunthorpe U	1-2	1-0	3-2	3-1	3-2	0-0	3-1	3-1	0-2	5-0	3-0	2-1	1-1	1-0	1-1	1-1	3-2	2-1	—	2-2	0-1	4-0	4-1	0-0
Sheffield U	4-0	2-0	3-0	1-0	1-0	2-1	3-2	2-0	0-2	2-2	2-0	2-1	1-0	2-0	2-1	1-0	4-0	1-1	1-1	—	2-1	0-3	4-0	0-1
Shrewsbury T	2-1	0-2	1-0	2-0	2-1	4-3	2-1	0-0	0-1	2-3	1-2	0-1	2-4	1-0	2-0	1-1	0-0	1-0	0-1	0-3	—	1-0	1-1	1-1
Southend U	3-0	0-1	3-0	1-1	1-0	1-1	1-0	3-1	0-2	1-3	3-1	1-2	2-2	3-0	2-1	1-1	1-1	2-1	3-1	2-4	1-1	—	1-1	3-2
Swindon T	0-0	0-1	1-0	1-2	1-2	3-0	0-1	1-0	1-1	3-1	1-0	1-1	1-3	0-0	1-2	0-1	1-0	3-0	1-2	2-4	1-1	0-0	—	0-2
Walsall	3-1	1-0	1-1	3-1	3-3	1-2	1-0	1-1	0-1	1-2	2-1	1-4	2-1	2-0	1-1	2-0	0-1	0-2	1-4	4-1	3-2	0-0	1-0	—

SKY BET LEAGUE 2 2016–17

(P) *Promoted into division at end of 2015–16 season.* (R) *Relegated into division at end of 2015–16 season.*

			Home					*Away*					*Total*						
		P	*W*	*D*	*L*	*F*	*A*	*W*	*D*	*L*	*F*	*A*	*W*	*D*	*L*	*F*	*A*	*GD*	*Pts*
1	Portsmouth	46	14	4	5	48	19	12	5	6	31	21	26	9	11	79	40	39	87
2	Plymouth Arg	46	13	3	7	41	29	13	6	4	30	17	26	9	11	71	46	25	87
3	Doncaster R (R)	46	14	6	3	40	22	11	4	8	45	33	25	10	11	85	55	30	85
4	Luton T	46	11	7	5	38	26	9	10	4	32	17	20	17	9	70	43	27	77
5	Exeter C	46	8	5	10	36	29	13	3	7	39	27	21	8	17	75	56	19	71
6	Carlisle U	46	10	7	6	34	34	8	10	5	35	34	18	17	11	69	68	1	71
7	Blackpool (R)¶	46	10	9	4	40	24	8	7	8	29	22	18	16	12	69	46	23	70
8	Colchester U (R)	46	14	4	5	43	27	5	8	10	24	30	19	12	15	67	57	10	69
9	Wycombe W	46	11	6	6	29	21	8	6	9	29	32	19	12	15	58	53	5	69
10	Stevenage	46	11	1	11	42	33	9	6	8	25	30	20	7	19	67	63	4	67
11	Cambridge U	46	9	5	9	30	26	10	4	9	28	24	19	9	18	58	50	8	66
12	Mansfield T	46	9	7	7	31	21	8	8	7	23	29	17	15	14	54	50	4	66
13	Accrington S	46	10	7	6	36	29	7	7	9	23	27	17	14	15	59	56	3	65
14	Grimsby T (P)	46	9	6	8	32	31	8	5	10	27	32	17	11	18	59	63	–4	62
15	Barnet	46	6	9	8	27	31	8	6	9	30	33	14	15	17	57	64	–7	57
16	Notts Co	46	7	7	9	25	30	9	1	13	29	46	16	8	22	54	76	–22	56
17	Crewe Alex (R)	46	8	7	8	35	26	6	6	11	23	41	14	13	19	58	67	–9	55
18	Morecambe	46	6	4	13	24	38	8	6	9	29	35	14	10	22	53	73	–20	52
19	Crawley T	46	8	7	8	29	30	5	5	13	24	41	13	12	21	53	71	–18	51
20	Yeovil T	46	8	8	7	25	24	3	9	11	24	40	11	17	18	49	64	–15	50
21	Cheltenham T (P)	46	8	7	8	27	25	4	7	12	22	44	12	14	20	49	69	–20	50
22	Newport Co	46	6	8	9	26	35	6	4	13	25	38	12	12	22	51	73	–22	48
23	Hartlepool U	46	7	8	8	28	30	4	5	14	26	45	11	13	22	54	75	–21	46
24	Leyton Orient	46	4	1	18	19	40	6	5	12	28	47	10	6	30	47	87	–40	36

¶*Blackpool promoted via play-offs.*

SKY BET LEAGUE 2 LEADING GOALSCORERS 2016–17

	League	*FA Cup*	*EFL League Cup*	*EFL Trophy*	*Play-Offs*	*Total*
Danny Hylton *(Luton T)*	21	3	0	2	1	27
John Akinde *(Barnet)*	26	0	0	0	0	26
John Marquis *(Doncaster R)*	26	0	0	0	0	26
Charlie Wyke *(Carlisle U)*	21	0	1	2	0	24
(Includes 7 League goals in EFL 1 for Bradford C.)						
Omar Bogle *(Grimsby T)*	22	0	0	0	0	22
(Includes 3 League goals in EFL Championship for Wigan Ath.)						
James Collins *(Crawley T)*	20	0	0	2	0	22
Luke Berry *(Cambridge U)*	17	4	1	0	0	22
Matt Godden *(Stevenage)*	20	0	0	1	0	21
David Wheeler *(Exeter C)*	17	0	0	2	2	21
Adebayo Akinfenwa *(Wycombe W)*	12	2	0	4	0	18
Chris Dagnall *(Crewe Alex)*	14	0	2	1	0	17
Chris Porter *(Colchester U)*	16	0	0	0	0	16
Ollie Watkins *(Exeter C)*	13	0	0	1	2	16
Graham Carey *(Plymouth Arg)*	14	1	0	0	0	15
Billy Kee *(Accrington S)*	13	2	0	0	0	15
Kal Naismith *(Portsmouth)*	13	0	1	1	0	15
Billy Waters *(Cheltenham T)*	12	2	0	1	0	15
Padraig Amond *(Hartlepool U)*	14	0	0	0	0	14
Jon Stead *(Notts Co)*	14	0	0	0	0	14
Reuben Reid *(Exeter C)*	13	1	0	0	0	14
Jabo Ibehre *(Carlisle U)*	12	2	0	0	0	14
Tommy Rowe *(Doncaster R)*	13	0	0	0	0	13
Jake Jervis *(Plymouth Arg)*	12	0	0	1	0	13
Kyle Vassell *(Blackpool)*	11	0	0	2	0	13
Brennan Dickenson *(Colchester U)*	12	0	0	0	0	12
Kurtis Guthrie *(Colchester U)*	12	0	0	0	0	12
Andy Williams *(Doncaster R)*	11	0	0	1	0	12
Shay McCartan *(Accrington S)*	11	0	0	0	0	11

SKY BET LEAGUE 2 – RESULTS 2016–17

	Accrington S	Barnet	Blackpool	Cambridge U	Carlisle U	Cheltenham T	Colchester U	Crawley T	Crewe Alex	Doncaster R	Exeter C	Grimsby T	Hartlepool U	Leyton Orient	Luton T	Mansfield T	Morecambe	Newport Co	Notts Co	Plymouth Arg	Portsmouth	Stevenage	Wycombe W	Yeovil T
Accrington S	—	1-0	2-1	2-0	1-1	1-1	2-1	1-0	3-2	3-2	1-2	1-1	2-2	5-0	1-4	1-1	2-3	1-3	2-0	0-1	1-0	0-1	2-2	1-1
Barnet	2-0		1-1	0-1	0-1	3-1	1-1	2-2	0-0	1-3	1-4	3-1	3-2	0-0	0-1	0-2	2-2	0-0	3-2	1-0	1-1	1-2	0-2	2-2
Blackpool	0-0	2-2	—	1-1	2-2	3-0	1-1	0-0	2-2	4-2	2-0	1-3	2-1	3-1	0-2	0-1	3-1	4-1	4-0	0-1	3-1	1-0	0-0	2-2
Cambridge U	2-1	1-1	0-0	—	2-2	3-1	1-1	2-0	2-1	2-3	1-0	0-1	0-1	3-0	0-3	1-3	1-2	3-2	4-0	0-1	0-1	0-0	1-2	1-0
Carlisle U	1-1	1-1	1-4	0-3	—	1-1	2-0	3-1	0-2	2-1	3-2	1-3	3-2	2-2	0-0	5-2	1-1	2-1	1-2	1-0	0-3	1-1	1-0	2-1
Cheltenham T	3-0	1-2	2-2	0-1	1-0	—	0-3	2-1	2-0	0-1	1-3	2-1	1-0	1-1	1-1	0-0	3-1	1-1	2-3	1-2	1-1	0-0	0-1	2-0
Colchester U	1-2	2-1	3-2	2-0	4-1	2-0	—	2-3	4-0	1-1	2-3	3-2	2-1	0-3	2-1	2-0	2-2	0-0	2-1	0-0	0-4	4-0	1-0	2-0
Crawley T	0-0	1-1	1-0	1-3	3-3	0-0	1-1	—	0-3	0-0	1-2	3-2	1-0	3-0	2-0	2-2	1-3	3-1	1-3	1-2	0-2	1-2	1-0	2-0
Crewe Alex	0-1	4-1	1-1	1-2	1-1	0-0	2-0	0-2	—	2-1	2-0	5-0	3-3	3-0	1-2	1-1	2-1	1-2	2-2	1-2	0-0	1-2	2-1	0-1
Doncaster R	2-2	3-2	0-1	1-0	2-2	2-0	1-0	1-1	3-1	—	1-3	1-0	2-1	3-1	1-1	1-0	1-1	2-0	3-1	0-1	3-1	1-0	2-2	4-1
Exeter C	0-2	2-1	2-2	1-2	2-3	3-0	3-0	0-1	4-0	1-3	—	0-0	1-2	4-0	0-0	2-0	3-1	0-1	0-2	0-2	0-1	1-1	4-2	3-3
Grimsby T	2-0	2-2	0-0	2-1	2-2	0-1	1-0	1-1	0-2	1-5	0-3	—	0-3	1-2	1-1	3-0	2-0	1-0	2-0	1-1	0-1	5-2	1-2	4-2
Hartlepool U	2-0	0-2	0-1	0-5	1-1	2-0	1-1	1-1	4-0	2-1	3-1	0-1	—	1-3	1-1	0-0	3-2	2-2	1-2	1-1	0-2	2-0	0-2	1-1
Leyton Orient	1-0	1-3	1-2	1-1	1-2	0-1	1-3	3-2	0-2	1-4	0-1	0-3	2-1	—	1-2	1-2	0-1	0-1	2-3	0-2	0-1	3-0	0-2	0-1
Luton T	1-0	3-1	1-0	2-0	1-1	2-3	0-1	2-1	1-1	3-1	1-1	1-2	3-0	2-2	—	1-1	3-1	2-1	2-1	1-1	1-3	0-2	4-1	1-1
Mansfield T	4-4	0-1	1-0	0-0	2-0	1-1	0-0	3-1	3-0	1-1	1-2	0-1	4-0	2-0	1-1	—	0-1	2-1	3-1	0-2	0-1	1-2	1-1	1-0
Morecambe	1-2	0-1	2-1	2-0	0-3	1-2	1-1	2-3	0-0	1-5	0-3	1-0	1-1	1-2	0-2	1-3	—	0-1	4-1	2-1	2-0	0-2	1-1	1-3
Newport Co	1-0	2-2	1-3	1-2	2-0	2-2	1-1	1-0	1-1	0-0	1-4	0-0	3-1	0-4	1-1	2-3	1-1	—	2-1	1-3	2-3	0-2	0-1	1-0
Notts Co	0-2	1-0	1-0	0-1	2-3	2-1	3-1	2-1	1-1	0-1	2-2	2-2	2-1	3-1	0-0	0-0	1-2	0-3	—	1-2	1-3	1-1	0-2	0-0
Plymouth Arg	0-1	0-2	0-3	2-1	2-0	1-0	2-1	2-0	2-1	2-0	3-0	0-3	1-1	2-3	0-3	2-0	1-0	6-1	0-1	—	2-2	4-2	3-3	4-1
Portsmouth	2-0	5-1	2-0	2-1	1-1	6-1	2-0	3-0	0-1	1-2	0-1	4-0	0-0	2-1	1-0	4-0	1-1	2-1	1-2	1-1	—	1-2	4-2	3-1
Stevenage	0-3	1-0	0-2	1-2	1-2	2-1	2-4	2-1	1-2	3-4	0-2	2-0	6-1	4-1	2-1	0-1	0-1	3-1	3-0	1-2	3-0	—	3-0	2-2
Wycombe W	1-1	0-2	0-0	1-0	1-2	3-3	0-2	1-2	5-1	2-1	1-0	2-1	2-0	1-0	1-1	0-1	2-0	2-1	0-1	1-1	1-0	1-0	—	1-1
Yeovil T	1-1	0-1	0-3	1-1	0-2	4-2	2-1	5-0	3-0	0-3	0-0	0-0	1-2	1-1	0-4	0-0	0-1	1-0	2-0	2-1	0-0	1-1	1-0	—

FOOTBALL LEAGUE PLAY-OFFS 2016–17

SKY BET CHAMPIONSHIP SEMI-FINALS FIRST LEG

Saturday, 13 May 2017

Fulham (0) 1 *(Cairney 65)*

Reading (0) 1 *(Obita 53)* 23,717

Fulham: (4231) Bettinelli; Fredericks, Kalas, Ream, Malone; McDonald, Johansen; Aluko (Cyriac 87), Cairney, Ayite; Martin (Kebano 61).
Reading: (3421) Al Habsi; McShane■, Moore, Blackett; Gunter, Williams, Evans, Obita; Grabban (Mendes 68 (Tiago Ilori 82)), Swift (van den Berg 74); Kermorgant.
Referee: Stuart Attwell.

Sunday, 14 May 2017

Huddersfield T (0) 0

Sheffield W (0) 0 20,357

Huddersfield T: (4231) Coleman; Smith, Hefele, Schindler, Lowe (Holmes-Dennis 90); Hogg, Mooy; Kachunga (Quaner 78), Brown, van La Parra; Wells (Cranie 90).
Sheffield W: (442) Westwood; Hunt, Lees, Loovens, Pudil; Wallace (Jones 63), Lee, Bannan, Reach; Fletcher (Rhodes 69), Forestieri (Winnall 73).
Referee: Paul Tierney.

SKY BET CHAMPIONSHIP SEMI-FINALS SECOND LEG

Tuesday, 16 May 2017

Reading (0) 1 *(Kermorgant 49 (pen))*

Fulham (0) 0 22,044

Reading: (3412) Al Habsi; Tiago Ilori, Moore, van den Berg; Gunter, Evans, Williams, Blackett (McCleary 66); Swift (Kelly 75); Kermorgant (Mendes 89), Grabban.
Fulham: (433) Bettinelli; Fredericks, Kalas, Ream, Malone (Martin 73); Cairney, McDonald, Johansen; Kebano (Piazon 58), Aluko, Ayite (Sessegnon 58).
Reading won 2-1 on aggregate.
Referee: Martin Atkinson.

Wednesday, 17 May 2017

Sheffield W (0) 1 *(Fletcher 51)*

Huddersfield T (0) 1 *(Lees 73 (og))* 32,625

Sheffield W: (442) Westwood; Hunt, Lees, Loovens, Pudil (Nuhiu 108); Wallace (Reach 5), Lee, Hutchinson, Bannan; Fletcher (Rhodes 61), Forestieri.
Huddersfield T: (4231) Ward; Smith, Hefele, Schindler, Lowe; Hogg, Mooy; Kachunga (Quaner 72), Brown (Payne 97), van La Parra (Holmes-Dennis 105); Wells.
aet; Huddersfield T won 4-3 on penalties.
Referee: Andre Marriner.

SKY BET CHAMPIONSHIP FINAL

Monday, 29 May 2017

Huddersfield T (0) 0

Reading (0) 0 76,682

Huddersfield T: (4231) Ward; Smith (Cranie 88), Hefele, Schindler, Lowe; Hogg, Mooy; Kachunga (Quaner 66), Brown (Palmer 98), van La Parra; Wells.
Reading: (3412) Al Habsi; Tiago Ilori, Moore, van den Berg (Obita 64); Gunter, Evans, Williams, Blackett; Swift (Kelly 100); Kermorgant, Grabban (McCleary 74).
aet; Huddersfield T won 4-3 on penalties.
Referee: Neil Swarbrick.

SKY BET LEAGUE ONE SEMI-FINALS FIRST LEG

Thursday, 4 May 2017

Bradford C (0) 1 *(McArdle 77)*

Fleetwood T (0) 0 15,696

Bradford C: (4411) Doyle; McMahon, McArdle, Knight-Percival, Meredith; Marshall, Vincelot, Cullen, Law (Dieng 88); Clarke B (Hiwula 69); Wyke.
Fleetwood T: (352) Cairns; Eastham, Pond, Davies; McLaughlin, Dempsey, Schwabl (Glendon 46), Grant, Bell; Ball (Burns 81), Cole (Hunter 66).
Referee: Oliver Langford.

Millwall (0) 0

Scunthorpe U (0) 0 12,568

Millwall: (442) Archer; Cummings (Romeo 62), Webster, Hutchinson, Craig; Wallace, Abdou, Williams, Ferguson (O'Brien 74); Gregory, Morison.
Scunthorpe U: (442) Anyon; Clarke, Mirfin, Wallace, Townsend; Dawson (Mantom 90), Bishop, Ness, Morris; Toney, Madden.
Referee: Andrew Madley.

SKY BET LEAGUE ONE SEMI-FINALS SECOND LEG

Sunday, 7 May 2017

Fleetwood T (0) 0

Bradford C (0) 0 5076

Fleetwood T: (352) Cairns; Eastham (Brannagan 71), Bolger, Davies; McLaughlin, Dempsey, Glendon (Cole 58), Grant, Bell; Ball, Hunter (Burns 79).
Bradford C: (4411) Doyle; McMahon, McArdle, Knight-Percival, Meredith; Marshall (Darby 86), Vincelot, Cullen, Law (Gilliead 70); Clarke B (Dieng 62); Wyke.
Bradford C won 1-0 on aggregate.
Referee: David Coote.

Huddersfield Town's Christopher Schindler scores the winning penalty to win the shoot-out in the Championship Play-Off final against Reading and send his team into the Premier League. The game had finished 0-0 after extra time. (Reuters/John Sibley Livepic)

Millwall beat Bradford City in the League One Play-Off final at Wembley Stadium on 20 May. Club legend Steve Morison scores the only goal of the game in the 85th minute. (Mike Egerton/PA Wire/PA Images)

Scunthorpe U (1) 2 *(Toney 19, Dawson 81)*
Millwall (1) 3 *(Morison 45, 58, Gregory 52)* 7190
Scunthorpe U: (442) Anyon; Clarke, Mirfin, Wallace, Townsend (Davies 74); Dawson, Bishop, Ness (Holmes 65), Morris; Toney, Madden (van Veen 59).
Millwall: (442) Archer; Romeo, Webster, Hutchinson, Craig; Wallace, Abdou, Williams, O'Brien (Ferguson 69); Gregory (Butcher 80), Morison.
Millwall won 3-2 on aggregate.
Referee: Chris Kavanagh.

SKY BET LEAGUE ONE FINAL

Saturday, 20 May 2017

Bradford C (0) 0
Millwall (0) 1 *(Morison 85)* 53,320
Bradford C: (3412) Doyle; McArdle, Vincelot, Knight-Percival; McMahon, Cullen, Law (Dieng 74), Meredith; Clarke B (Jones 74); Marshall, Wyke.
Millwall: (442) Archer; Romeo, Webster, Hutchinson, Craig; Wallace (Onyedinma 89), Abdou, Williams, O'Brien (Ferguson 70); Gregory (Butcher 90), Morison.
Referee: Simon Hooper.

SKY BET LEAGUE TWO SEMI-FINALS FIRST LEG

Sunday, 14 May 2017

Blackpool (1) 3 *(Cullen 19, 47, 67 (pen))*
Luton T (2) 2 *(Potts 26, Vassell 28)* 3882
Blackpool: (352) Slocombe; Aimson, Aldred, Robertson; Mellor, Danns (Flores 80), Payne, Potts, Taylor; Cullen (Black 85), Vassell (Delfouneso 68).
Luton T: (352) Moore; Rea, Cuthbert, Sheehan; Justin, D'Ath (Palmer 86), Lee, Ruddock, Potts; Hylton, Vassell (Marriott 74).
Referee: Nigel Miller.

Carlisle U (1) 3 *(Moore-Taylor 32 (og), O'Sullivan 71, Miller S 73)*
Exeter C (2) 3 *(Grant 15, Harley 45, Wheeler 56)* 9708
Carlisle U: (451) Gillespie; Miller T, Raynes (Miller S 61), Liddle, Grainger; Devitt (O'Sullivan 56), Bailey (Waring 68), Lambe, Joyce, Adams; Proctor.
Exeter C: (451) Olejnik; Sweeney, Brown, Moore-Taylor, Woodman (Reid 69); Wheeler (Stacey 77), Taylor, James, Harley, Grant (Holmes 78); Watkins.
Referee: David Webb.

SKY BET LEAGUE TWO SEMI-FINALS SECOND LEG

Thursday, 18 May 2017

Exeter C (1) 3 *(Watkins 10, 79, Stacey 90)*
Carlisle U (0) 2 *(Kennedy 81, O'Sullivan 90)* 7450
Exeter C: (4411) Olejnik; Stacey, Brown, Moore-Taylor, Woodman; Wheeler, Taylor, Tillson, Holmes (Grant 58); Harley; Watkins.
Carlisle U: (4231) Gillespie; Miller T, Raynes (Kennedy 75), Liddle, Grainger; Joyce, Bailey; Devitt (Miller S 57), Lambe (O'Sullivan 63), Adams; Proctor.
Exeter C won 6-5 on aggregate.
Referee: Dean Whitestone.

Luton T (2) 3 *(Mellor 36 (og), Cuthbert 45, Hylton 57 (pen))*
Blackpool (1) 3 *(Delfouneso 22, Gnanduillet 76, Moore 90 (og))* 10,032
Luton T: (352) Moore; Justin, Cuthbert, Sheehan; Lee (Cook 82), Rea, D'Ath, Ruddock, Potts; Vassell, Hylton.
Blackpool: (352) Slocombe; Aimson, Aldred, Robertson; Mellor, Danns, Payne (Black 46), Potts, Taylor (Samuel 74); Cullen, Delfouneso (Gnanduillet 57).
Blackpool won 6-5 on aggregate.
Referee: Darren Deadman.

SKY BET LEAGUE TWO FINAL

Sunday, 28 May 2017

Blackpool (1) 2 *(Potts 3, Cullen 64)*
Exeter C (1) 1 *(Wheeler 40)* 23,380
Blackpool: (3142) Slocombe; Aimson, Aldred (Samuel 31), Robertson; Payne (Black 62); Mellor, Danns, Potts, Daniel; Cullen (Flores 75), Vassell.
Exeter C: (433) Pym; Stacey, Brown (Sweeney 58), Moore-Taylor, Woodman (Holmes 71); Taylor, James, Harley; Wheeler, Watkins, Grant (Reid 57).
Referee: Darren England.

REVIEW OF THE SEASON 2016–17

Antonio Conte won what was billed as the battle of the super managers by returning Chelsea to the top of the Premier League table and clinching the 2016–17 title in his first season in England.

The Italian had been victorious in his previous three league campaigns in Italy with Juventus and made it four in a row with the help of a tactical intervention that transformed the style of teams across the division.

Chelsea, who finished tenth in their Premier League title defence in 2015–16, switched to a 3-4-3 formation after defeats to Liverpool and Arsenal in September and embarked on a record-equalling 13-game winning streak.

The system was so successful that 17 of the other 19 Premier League teams experimented with three-man defences at some point during the season, but none mastered the set-up quite like Chelsea.

In attack, Eden Hazard and Diego Costa were back to their best, directly contributing to 48 goals between them. N'Golo Kanté, a summer signing from Leicester City, made it two title wins in two seasons, with his award-winning performances in central midfield.

Defensively, ever-present Cesar Azpilicueta, returning Brazilian David Luiz and stand-in skipper Gary Cahill impressed, while rarely-used club captain John Terry waved goodbye to Stamford Bridge with his fifth league-winner's medal.

Despite Chelsea's dominance – they set a record for Premier League wins in a season (30) and posted the second-highest points total seen in the competition (93) – it was Tottenham Hotspur, for a second year in a row, who registered the league's best figures for goals for and against. Since the start of 2015–16, no team has won more points than Mauricio Pochettino's men.

But a run of two wins from eight games from mid-October proved costly. Striker Harry Kane was absent for three of those fixtures and Spurs missed their star man. The England international finished the season with a flourish, netting seven goals in four days to take his tally to 29 and retain the golden boot. His partnership with attacking midfielder Dele Alli (18 goals) was thrilling.

Kane also had the honour of scoring the final goal at White Hart Lane, where Spurs went undefeated for an entire league campaign for the first time since 1964–65. After 118

Tottenham Hotspur's Dele Alli had another stellar season in the Premier League, contributing 18 goals and 7 assists and helping Spurs to second place. For good measure, he won the PFA Young Player of the Year award. Here he is scoring his side's opening goal away at Manchester City which resulted in a 2-2 draw in January.
(Dave Howarth/EMPICS)

Eden Hazard scores Chelsea's second goal in their 3-1 defeat of Arsenal at Stamford Bridge in February. Hazard's 16 goals and 5 assists helped drive Antonio Conte's side to the Premier League title. (Reuters/Jon Sibley Livepic)

years at The Lane, they will play at Wembley Stadium next season while work on their new ground is completed. They will hope to improve on their poor record at the national stadium, which included just one win in five appearances there during the season.

At Manchester City, the eagerly anticipated Pep Guardiola era began in mouth-watering style, with the Spaniard overseeing 10 straight wins across all competitions at the start of the season. But after a six-game stutter, City struggled to re-find that early form and Guardiola earned a heap of unwanted records.

Guardiola's first trophy-less campaign as a manager also saw him experience his most ever league losses (six), his heaviest league defeat (4-0 at Everton), suffer his first double defeat to the same manager (Conte) and finish outside of the top two for the first time. Significant transfer spending is anticipated this summer.

Jurgen Klopp, meanwhile, led Liverpool to Champions League qualification in his first full season in charge. But for a bad habit of dropping points to teams in the lower half of the table, Liverpool – who went unbeaten against the rest of the top seven – could have challenged for the title. Philippe Coutinho enjoyed his best season for Liverpool while new arrival Sadio Mane also starred.

Liverpool's success meant Arsenal finished outside of the top four for the first time since 1996 and for the first time under Arsène Wenger. The under-fire Frenchman was targeted by a 'Wenger out' campaign throughout the season, as a promising start petered out and an end-of-season surge came too late.

Wenger will point to a record seventh FA Cup win and a haul of 75 points, which was enough for Manchester United to win the title in 1996–97, as reasons for hope. But after being handed a new two-year contract, the manager will know far more is expected next time around.

Jose Mourinho may have finished in the lowest position of the six superstar managers but three pieces of silverware from Manchester United's marathon 64-game season – the Community Shield, the EFL Cup and a Europa League triumph, which earned Champions League qualification – was hardly a poor return.

United – lining up with the world's most expensive player, Paul Pogba, and 17-goal Zlatan Ibrahimovic – also went on a club-record 25-game unbeaten run in the league. However, 10 home draws left many Old Trafford fans frustrated by what could have been.

Captain Wayne Rooney was increasingly marginalised but broke United's goal-scoring record, passing Bobby Charlton's mark of 249 and finishing the season with 253 in total.

His former club, Everton, finished seventh, with Ronald Koeman's first season in charge lit up by the 25 goals of Romelu Lukaku, now the club's top scorer in Premier League history.

Fifteen points further down the table, Southampton took eighth and reached the EFL Cup final under Claude Puel (who was then fired in June), while Bournemouth achieved their highest league finish in ninth, out-scoring Manchester United.

Tony Pulis led West Bromwich Albion to another mid-table finish and took points off Tottenham, Manchester United and Arsenal, but there was frustration at the London Stadium as crowd trouble and heavy defeats featured in West Ham United's first season away from Upton Park. The acrimonious sale of ace Dimitri Payet in January made Slaven Bilic's task even tougher.

Leicester City fans were treated to another season to remember as the Foxes managed to combine a worst-ever Premier League title defence with a run to the quarter-finals of the Champions League. That league form controversially cost Claudio Ranieri his job in February, nine months after lifting the Premier League trophy.

Stoke City's progress stalled – their final-day win over Southampton was the first time they beat a team above them in the table all season – while Crystal Palace looked set for the drop before Sam Allardyce, who had started the season as England manager, stepped in to replace Alan Pardew and inspire a surge for survival which included wins over Chelsea, Arsenal and Liverpool before resigning at the end of the season.

Swansea City had three managers in the space of the season, with American Bob Bradley lasting just three months after replacing Francesco Guidolin, before Paul Clement impressively oversaw a turnaround by harnessing the creative talents of Gylfi Sigurdsson (13 assists) and goal-scoring of Fernando Llorente (15 goals).

Burnley turned Turf Moor into a fortress, winning 33 of their 40 points on home territory to retain PL status for the first time, while Watford once again secured Premier League survival – and once again sacked their manager after doing so. Walter Mazzarri

David Silva of Manchester City shoots for goal against Swansea City at the Etihad Stadium in February. The game finished 2-1 but City finished a disappointing third in the Premier League in Pep Guardiola's first season in charge. (Martin Rickett/PA Wire/PA Images)

Blackpool's Brad Potts celebrates scoring his side's first goal in their 2-1 victory over Exeter City in the League Two Play-Off final. (Action Images/Tony O'Brien Livepic)

paid the price for an uninspiring campaign which saw the Hornets finish 17th – albeit just six points off eighth.

Despite making a fast start to the season, including an opening-day win over defending champions Leicester, Hull City made an immediate return to the Championship with Mike Phelan and then Marco Silva unable to keep them up, following Steve Bruce's summer exit.

Middlesbrough also dropped back into the second tier after scoring just 27 times all season under Aitor Karanka and then Steve Agnew, while David Moyes resigned after his poor Sunderland team finished bottom of the table – the place they had occupied since February 1st.

In the Championship, an 89th-minute equaliser by Aston Villa on the final day of the season meant Brighton & Hove Albion were promoted to the Premier League for the first time in their history as runners-up, rather than champions, with Rafa Benitez's Newcastle United taking the crown. Huddersfield Town will also be Premier League new boys, after beating Reading on penalties in the play-off final.

At the other end of the table, Rotherham United, Wigan Athletic and 1994–95 Premier League winners Blackburn Rovers slipped into League One. They will be replaced by third-tier champions Sheffield United, Bolton Wanderers and Millwall, who achieved play-off success over Bradford City, a year on from their play-off final defeat to Barnsley.

Relegated Port Vale, Swindon Town, Coventry City and Chesterfield will be playing League Two football next season, while Portsmouth, Plymouth Argyle, Doncaster Rovers and play-off winners Blackpool earned promotion to League One.

An unhappy season for Leyton Orient, which saw the club dogged by financial problems, ended with them finishing rock bottom of the EFL pile and relegated along with Hartlepool United. Lincoln City, who enjoyed a fairytale run to the quarter-finals of the FA Cup, and Forest Green Rovers, who will make their first-ever appearance in the Football League, will take their place.

Peter Smith

CUPS AND UPS AND DOWNS DIARY

AUGUST 2016
2 FA Community Shield: Manchester U 2 Leicester C 1.

SEPTEMBER 2016
25 Manchester C Champions of Women's Super League.

OCTOBER 2016
2 Women's Continental Cup Final: Manchester C 1 Birmingham C 0 *(aet)*.

NOVEMBER 2016
27 Betfred Scottish League Cup Final: Celtic 3 Aberdeen 0.

JANUARY 2017
21 Nathaniel MG Welsh League Cup Final: The New Saints 4 Barry T 0.

FEBRUARY 2017
18 JBE Northern Irish League Cup Final: Ballymena T 2 Carrick Rangers 0.
26 EFL Cup Final: Manchester U 3 Southampton 2.

MARCH 2017
25 Irn-Bru Scottish League Challenge Cup Final: Dundee U 2 St Mirren 1.

APRIL 2017
1 Rotherham U relegated from EFL Championship to EFL League One. Celtic Champions of Scottish Premiership.
3 EFL Trophy Final: Coventry C 2 Oxford U 1.
8 Sheffield U promoted from EFL League One to EFL Championship. Doncaster R promoted from EFL League Two to EFL League One. Livingston promoted from Scottish League One to Scottish Championship. FA County Youth Cup Final: Middlesex 2 Cornwall 1.
14 Coventry C relegated from EFL League One to EFL League Two.
15 Sheffield U Champions of EFL League One. Southport relegated from National League.
17 Brighton & HA promoted from EFL Championship to Premier League. Chesterfield relegated from EFL League One to EFL League Two. Plymouth Arg promoted from EFL League Two to EFL League One. Portsmouth promoted from EFL League Two to EFL League One. North Ferriby U relegated from National League.
19 FA Youth Cup Final First Leg: Manchester C 1 Chelsea 1.
22 Swindon T relegated from EFL League One to EFL League Two. Leyton Orient relegated from EFL League Two to National League. Lincoln C promoted from National League to EFL League Two.
24 Newcastle U promoted from EFL Championship to Premier League.
26 FA Youth Cup Final Second Leg: Chelsea 5 Manchester C 1.
29 Sunderland relegated from Premier League to EFL Championship. Wigan Ath relegated from EFL Championship to EFL League One. Braintree T relegated from National League. York C relegated from National League.
30 Bolton W promoted from EFL League One to EFL Championship. Port Vale relegated from EFL League One to EFL League Two. Welsh FA Cup Final: Bala Town 2 The New Saints 1.

MAY 2017
6 Portsmouth Champions of EFL League Two. Hartlepool U relegated from EFL League Two to National League. Stenhousemuir relegated from Scottish League One to Scottish League Two. Arbroath promoted from Scottish League Two to Scottish League One. Ayr U relegated from Scottish Championship to Scottish League One. Tennent's Northern Irish FA Cup Final: Linfield 3 Coleraine 0.
7 Newcastle U Champions of EFL Championship. Blackburn R relegated from EFL Championship to EFL League One. FA Sunday Cup Final: Hardwick Social 1 New Salamis 1 *(aet; Hardwick Social won 3-1 on penalties)*.
8 Middlesbrough relegated from Premier League to EFL Championship.
12 Chelsea Champions of Premier League.
13 Raith R relegated from Scottish Championship to Scottish League One. SSE FA Women's Cup Final: Manchester C 4 Birmingham C 1.
14 Hull C relegated from Premier League to EFL Championship. National League Play-Off Final: Forest Green R 3 Tranmere R 1 *(Forest Green R promoted to EFL League Two)*.
20 EFL League 1 Play-Off Final: Millwall 1 Bradford C 0. *(Millwall promoted to EFL Championship)*. Inverness CT relegated from Scottish Premiership to Scottish League One. Scottish Championship Play-Off: Brechin C promoted from Scottish League One to Scottish Championship after beating Alloa Ath 5-4 on penalties (aggregate 4-4). Scottish League One Play-Off: Forfar Ath promoted from Scottish League Two to Scottish League One after beating Peterhead 7-2 on aggregate. Peterhead relegated from Scottish League One to Scottish League Two. Scottish League Two Play-Off: Cowdenbeath remain in Scottish League Two after beating East Kilbride 5-3 on penalties (aggregate 1-1).
21 FA Trophy Final: York C 3 Macclesfield T 2. FA Vase Final: South Shields 4 Cleethorpes T 0.
24 UEFA Europa League Final: Manchester United 2 Ajax 0.
27 Emirates FA Cup Final: Arsenal 2 Chelsea 1. William Hill Scottish FA Cup Final: Celtic 2 Aberdeen 1.
28 EFL League 2 Play-Off Final: Blackpool 2 Exeter C 1 *(Blackpool promoted to EFL League 1)*. Scottish Premiership Play-Off: Hamilton A retain their Scottish Premiership status after beating Dundee U (aggregate 1-0).
29 EFL Championship Play-Off Final: Huddersfield T 0 Reading 0 *(aet; Huddersfield T won 4-3 on penalties) (Huddersfield T promoted to Premier League)*.

JUNE 2017
1 UEFA Women's Champions League Final: Lyon 0 Paris Saint-Germain 0 *(Lyon won 7-6 on penalties)*.
3 UEFA Champions League Final: Real Madrid 4 Juventus 1.

THE FA COMMUNITY SHIELD WINNERS 1908–2016

CHARITY SHIELD 1908–2001

1908	Manchester U v QPR	1-1
Replay	Manchester U v QPR	4-0
1909	Newcastle U v Northampton T	2-0
1910	Brighton v Aston Villa	1-0
1911	Manchester U v Swindon T	8-4
1912	Blackburn R v QPR	2-1
1913	Professionals v Amateurs	7-2
1920	WBA v Tottenham H	2-0
1921	Tottenham H v Burnley	2-0
1922	Huddersfield T v Liverpool	1-0
1923	Professionals v Amateurs	2-0
1924	Professionals v Amateurs	3-1
1925	Amateurs v Professionals	6-1
1926	Amateurs v Professionals	6-3
1927	Cardiff C v Corinthians	2-1
1928	Everton v Blackburn R	2-1
1929	Professionals v Amateurs	3-0
1930	Arsenal v Sheffield W	2-1
1931	Arsenal v WBA	1-0
1932	Everton v Newcastle U	5-3
1933	Arsenal v Everton	3-0
1934	Arsenal v Manchester C	4-0
1935	Sheffield W v Arsenal	1-0
1936	Sunderland v Arsenal	2-1
1937	Manchester C v Sunderland	2-0
1938	Arsenal v Preston NE	2-1
1948	Arsenal v Manchester U	4-3
1949	Portsmouth v Wolverhampton W	1-1*
1950	English World Cup XI v FA Canadian Touring Team	4-2
1951	Tottenham H v Newcastle U	2-1
1952	Manchester U v Newcastle U	4-2
1953	Arsenal v Blackpool	3-1
1954	Wolverhampton W v WBA	4-4*
1955	Chelsea v Newcastle U	3-0
1956	Manchester U v Manchester C	1-0
1957	Manchester U v Aston Villa	4-0
1958	Bolton W v Wolverhampton W	4-1
1959	Wolverhampton W v Nottingham F	3-1
1960	Burnley v Wolverhampton W	2-2*
1961	Tottenham H v FA XI	3-2
1962	Tottenham H v Ipswich T	5-1
1963	Everton v Manchester U	4-0
1964	Liverpool v West Ham U	2-2*
1965	Manchester U v Liverpool	2-2*
1966	Liverpool v Everton	1-0
1967	Manchester U v Tottenham H	3-3*
1968	Manchester C v WBA	6-1
1969	Leeds U v Manchester C	2-1
1970	Everton v Chelsea	2-1
1971	Leicester C v Liverpool	1-0
1972	Manchester C v Aston Villa	1-0
1973	Burnley v Manchester C	1-0
1974	Liverpool v Leeds U	1-1
	Liverpool won 6-5 on penalties.	
1975	Derby Co v West Ham U	2-0
1976	Liverpool v Southampton	1-0
1977	Liverpool v Manchester U	0-0*
1978	Nottingham F v Ipswich T	5-0
1979	Liverpool v Arsenal	3-1
1980	Liverpool v West Ham U	1-0
1981	Aston Villa v Tottenham H	2-2*
1982	Liverpool v Tottenham H	1-0
1983	Manchester U v Liverpool	2-0
1984	Everton v Liverpool	1-0
1985	Everton v Manchester U	2-0
1986	Everton v Liverpool	1-1*
1987	Everton v Coventry C	1-0
1988	Liverpool v Wimbledon	2-1
1989	Liverpool v Arsenal	1-0
1990	Liverpool v Manchester U	1-1*
1991	Arsenal v Tottenham H	0-0*
1992	Leeds U v Liverpool	4-3
1993	Manchester U v Arsenal	1-1
	Manchester U won 5-4 on penalties.	
1994	Manchester U v Blackburn R	2-0
1995	Everton v Blackburn R	1-0
1996	Manchester U v Newcastle U	4-0
1997	Manchester U v Chelsea	1-1
	Manchester U won 4-2 on penalties.	
1998	Arsenal v Manchester U	3-0
1999	Arsenal v Manchester U	2-1
2000	Chelsea v Manchester U	2-0
2001	Liverpool v Manchester U	2-1

COMMUNITY SHIELD 2002–16

2002	Arsenal v Liverpool	1-0
2003	Manchester U v Arsenal	1-1
	Manchester U won 4-3 on penalties.	
2004	Arsenal v Manchester U	3-1
2005	Chelsea v Arsenal	2-1
2006	Liverpool v Chelsea	2-1
2007	Manchester U v Chelsea	1-1
	Manchester U won 3-0 on penalties.	
2008	Manchester U v Portsmouth	0-0
	Manchester U won 3-1 on penalties.	
2009	Chelsea v Manchester U	2-2
	Chelsea won 4-1 on penalties.	
2010	Manchester U v Chelsea	3-1
2011	Manchester U v Manchester C	3-2
2012	Manchester C v Chelsea	3-2
2013	Manchester U v Wigan Ath	2-0
2014	Arsenal v Manchester C	3-0
2015	Arsenal v Chelsea	1-0
2016	Manchester U v Leicester C	2-1

* *Each club retained shield for six months.*

THE FA COMMUNITY SHIELD 2016

Manchester U (1) 2, Leicester C (0) 1

at Wembley, Sunday 7 August 2016, attendance 85,437

Manchester U: (4-3-3) de Gea; Valencia, Bailly, Blind, Shaw (Rojo 69); Lingard (Mata 63 (Mkhitaryan 90)), Fellaini, Carrick (Herrera 61); Martial (Rashford 70), Rooney (Schneiderlin 88), Ibrahimovic.
Scorers: Lingard 32, Ibrahimovic 83.

Leicester C: (4-4-2) Schmeichel; Simpson (Hernandez 63), Morgan, Huth (Ulloa 89), Fuchs (Schlupp 80); Albrighton (Gray 46), Drinkwater, King (Mendy 62), Mahrez; Vardy, Okazaki (Musa 46).
Scorer: Vardy 52.

Referee: Craig Pawson.

ACCRINGTON STANLEY

FOUNDATION

Accrington Football Club, founder members of the Football League in 1888, were not connected with Accrington Stanley. In fact both clubs ran concurrently between 1891 when Stanley were formed and 1895 when Accrington FC folded. Actually Stanley Villa was the original name, those responsible for forming the club living in Stanley Street and using the Stanley Arms as their meeting place. They became Accrington Stanley in 1893. In 1894–95 they joined the Accrington & District League, playing at Moorhead Park. Subsequently they played in the North-East Lancashire Combination and the Lancashire Combination before becoming founder members of the Third Division (North) in 1921, two years after moving to Peel Park. In 1962 they resigned from the Football League, were wound up, re-formed in 1963, disbanded in 1966 only to restart as Accrington Stanley (1968), returning to the Lancashire Combination in 1970.

Wham Stadium, Livingstone Road, Accrington, Lancashire BB5 5BX.

Telephone: (01254) 356 950. ***Fax:*** (01254) 356 951.

Website: www.accringtonstanley.co.uk

Email: info@accringtonstanley.co.uk

Ground Capacity: 6,217.

Record Attendance: 13,181 v Hull C, Division 3 (N), 28 September 1948 (at Peel Park); 4,634 v AFC Wimbledon, FL 2 Play-Offs, 18 May 2016 (at Wham Stadium).

Pitch Measurements: 101.5m × 65m (111yd × 71yd).

Chairman: Andy Holt.

Managing Director: David Burgess.

Manager: John Coleman.

Assistant Manager: Jimmy Bell.

Colours: Red and white striped shirts, white shorts, red socks with white trim.

Year Formed: 1891, reformed 1968.

Turned Professional: 1919.

Club Nickname: 'The Reds', 'Stanley'.

Previous Names: 1891, Stanley Villa; 1893, Accrington Stanley.

Grounds: 1891, Moorhead Park; 1897, Bell's Ground; 1919, Peel Park; 1970, Crown Ground (renamed Interlink Express Stadium, Fraser Eagle Stadium, Store First Stadium 2013, Wham Stadium 2015).

First Football League Game: 27 August 1921, Division 3 (N), v Rochdale (a) L 3-6 – Tattersall; Newton, Baines, Crawshaw, Popplewell, Burkinshaw, Oxley, Makin, Green (1), Hosker (2), Hartles.

Record League Victory: 8–0 v New Brighton, Division 3 (N), 17 March 1934 – Maidment; Armstrong (pen), Price, Dodds, Crawshaw, McCulloch, Wyper, Lennox (2), Cheetham (4), Leedham (1), Watson.

Record Cup Victory: 7–0 v Spennymoor U, FA Cup 2nd rd, 8 December 1938 – Tootill; Armstrong, Whittaker, Latham, Curran, Lee, Parry (2), Chadwick, Jepson (3), McLoughlin (2), Barclay.

Record Defeat: 1–9 v Lincoln C, Division 3 (N), 3 March 1951.

HONOURS

League Champions: Conference – 2005–06.

Runners-up: Division 3N – 1954–55, 1957–58.

FA Cup: 4th rd – 1927, 1937, 1959, 2010, 2017.

League Cup: 3rd rd – 2016–17.

sky SPORTS FACT FILE

Billy Robinson played at outside-left for Accrington Stanley in the final match of the 1952–53 season. Three weeks later he was shot dead. John Waddington, a Salford man, was found guilty of manslaughter and sentenced to five years' imprisonment.

Most League Points (2 for a win): 61, Division 3 (N), 1954–55.

Most League Points (3 for a win): 85, FL 2, 2015–16.

Most League Goals: 96, Division 3 (N), 1954–55.

Highest League Scorer in Season: George Stewart, 35, Division 3 (N), 1955–56; George Hudson, 35, Division 4, 1960–61.

Most League Goals in Total Aggregate: George Stewart, 136, 1954–58.

Most League Goals in One Match: 5, Billy Harker v Gateshead, Division 3 (N), 16 November 1935; George Stewart v Gateshead, Division 3 (N), 27 November 1954.

Most Capped Player: Romuald Boco, 19 (48), Benin.

Most League Appearances: Andy Procter, 275, 2006–12, 2014–16.

Youngest League Player: Ian Gibson, 15 years 358 days, v Norwich C, 23 March 1959.

Record Transfer Fee Received: £50,000 (rising to £250,000) from Blackpool for Brett Ormerod, March 1997.

Record Transfer Fee Paid: £85,000 (rising to £150,000) to Swansea C for Ian Craney, January 2008.

Football League Record: 1921 Original Member of Division 3 (N); 1958–60 Division 3; 1960–62 Division 4; 2006– FL 2.

LATEST SEQUENCES

Longest Sequence of League Wins: 7, 27.12.1954 – 5.2.1955.

Longest Sequence of League Defeats: 9, 8.3.1930 – 21.4.1930.

Longest Sequence of League Draws: 4, 10.9.1927 – 27.9.1927.

Longest Sequence of Unbeaten League Matches: 15, 14.2.2016 – 17.4.2017.

Longest Sequence Without a League Win: 18, 17.9.1938 – 31.12.1938.

Successive Scoring Runs: 22 from 14.11.1936.

Successive Non-scoring Runs: 5 from 15.3.1930.

MANAGERS

William Cronshaw *c.*1894
John Haworth 1897–1910
Johnson Haworth *c.*1916
Sam Pilkingson 1919–24
(*Tommy Booth p-m 1923–24*)
Ernie Blackburn 1924–32
Amos Wade 1932–35
John Hacking 1935–49
Jimmy Porter 1949–51
Walter Crook 1951–53
Walter Galbraith 1953–58
George Eastham snr 1958–59
Harold Bodle 1959–60
James Harrower 1960–61
Harold Mather 1962–63
Jimmy Hinksman 1963–64
Terry Neville 1964–65
Ian Bryson 1965
Danny Parker 1965–66
Gerry Keenan
Gary Pierce
Dave Thornley
Phil Staley
Eric Whalley
Stan Allen 1995–96
Tony Greenwood 1996–98
Billy Rodaway 1998
Wayne Harrison 1998–99
John Coleman 1999–2012
Paul Cook 2012
Leam Richardson 2012–13
James Beattie 2013–14
John Coleman September 2014–

TEN YEAR LEAGUE RECORD

		P	W	D	L	F	A	Pts	Pos
2007-08	FL 2	46	16	3	27	49	83	51	17
2008-09	FL 2	46	13	11	22	42	59	50	16
2009-10	FL 2	46	18	7	21	62	74	61	15
2010-11	FL 2	46	18	19	9	73	55	73	5
2011-12	FL 2	46	14	15	17	54	66	57	14
2012-13	FL 2	46	14	12	20	51	68	54	18
2013-14	FL 2	46	14	15	17	54	56	57	15
2014-15	FL 2	46	15	11	20	58	77	56	17
2015-16	FL 2	46	24	13	9	74	48	85	4
2016-17	FL 2	46	17	14	15	59	56	65	13

DID YOU KNOW ?

On 1 April 2017, Accrington Stanley played their 500th Football League game since returning to the competition in the 2006–07 season. The near 500-mile round trip to Plymouth Argyle proved to be a successful occasion with an early goal by Jordan Clarke clinching a 1-0 victory.

ACCRINGTON STANLEY – SKY BET LEAGUE TWO 2016–17 LEAGUE RECORD

Match No.	Date	Venue	Opponents	Result	H/T Score	Lg Pos.	Goalscorers	Attendance
1	Aug 6	H	Doncaster R	W 3-2	2-1	5	Boco [8], Pearson [29], McConville [90]	2647
2	13	A	Barnet	L 0-2	0-1	14		1501
3	16	A	Wycombe W	D 1-1	0-1	15	McConville [48]	2747
4	20	H	Exeter C	L 1-2	0-0	18	Davies [70]	1300
5	27	H	Morecambe	L 2-3	2-1	20	Kee 2 [27, 34]	1763
6	Sept 3	A	Carlisle U	D 1-1	0-0	21	Kee [58]	5128
7	10	A	Notts Co	W 2-0	1-0	16	O'Sullivan [17], Boco [67]	3988
8	17	H	Portsmouth	W 1-0	0-0	10	Lacey [52]	2461
9	24	A	Colchester U	W 2-1	0-1	9	Boco [59], Kee [68]	3109
10	27	H	Mansfield T	D 1-1	0-1	7	Gornell [56]	1134
11	Oct 1	A	Cambridge U	L 1-2	0-1	12	Kee [51]	3765
12	8	H	Cheltenham T	D 1-1	0-0	10	Gornell [74]	1637
13	15	H	Blackpool	W 2-1	0-0	7	Boco 2 (1 pen) [89 (p), 90]	2754
14	22	A	Crawley T	D 0-0	0-0	7		2092
15	29	H	Newport Co	L 1-3	0-0	9	Donacien [79]	1251
16	Nov 12	A	Luton T	L 0-1	0-0	10		8008
17	19	H	Stevenage	L 0-1	0-0	15		1283
18	22	A	Hartlepool U	L 0-2	0-0	18		2514
19	26	H	Yeovil T	D 1-1	0-0	20	Boco [90]	1263
20	Dec 10	A	Leyton Orient	L 0-1	0-0	22		3964
21	17	H	Plymouth Arg	L 0-1	0-0	22		1573
22	26	A	Grimsby T	L 0-2	0-1	22		5782
23	31	A	Crewe Alex	W 1-0	1-0	21	Kee [43]	3471
24	Jan 2	H	Hartlepool U	D 2-2	0-0	21	Kee (pen) [57], Pearson [70]	1590
25	14	A	Cheltenham T	L 0-3	0-0	21		2854
26	21	H	Carlisle U	D 1-1	1-1	20	McCartan [21]	2634
27	Feb 4	H	Notts Co	W 2-0	1-0	19	Rodgers [45], Husin [80]	1731
28	11	A	Portsmouth	L 0-2	0-1	21		15,955
29	14	A	Mansfield T	D 4-4	3-2	20	Beckles [5], McCartan [29], Kee 2 (1 pen) [43, 66 (p)]	3226
30	18	H	Colchester U	W 2-1	2-0	19	Kee [18], Pearson [32]	1310
31	25	A	Doncaster R	D 2-2	1-1	20	McCartan [4], Edwards [81]	5272
32	28	H	Wycombe W	D 2-2	1-0	21	Clare [45], Pearson [63]	1045
33	Mar 4	H	Barnet	W 1-0	0-0	20	McCartan [54]	1236
34	11	A	Exeter C	W 2-0	1-0	18	McCartan [11], Pearson [71]	3897
35	14	H	Leyton Orient	W 5-0	1-0	16	Kee [44], Pearson 2 [51, 90], McConville 2 [84, 85]	1306
36	18	A	Yeovil T	D 1-1	0-0	16	Beckles [51]	2991
37	21	A	Morecambe	W 2-1	1-0	14	McCartan 2 [45, 66]	1506
38	25	H	Grimsby T	D 1-1	0-0	15	McCartan [89]	2312
39	28	H	Cambridge U	W 2-0	1-0	13	McConville [19], McCartan [54]	1333
40	Apr 1	A	Plymouth Arg	W 1-0	1-0	13	Clark [8]	9708
41	8	H	Crewe Alex	W 3-2	0-2	11	Hughes 2 [57, 79], McCartan [61]	1720
42	14	A	Blackpool	D 0-0	0-0	11		4300
43	17	H	Crawley T	W 1-0	0-0	9	McCartan [48]	1652
44	22	A	Newport Co	L 0-1	0-0	13		3719
45	29	H	Luton T	L 1-4	1-1	13	Pearson [39]	2150
46	May 6	A	Stevenage	W 3-0	0-0	13	Kee 2 (1 pen) [72 (p), 79], Conneely (pen) [90]	3517

Final League Position: 13

GOALSCORERS

League (59): Kee 13 (3 pens), McCartan 11, Pearson 8, Boco 6 (1 pen), McConville 5, Beckles 2, Gornell 2, Hughes 2, Clare 1, Clark 1, Conneely 1 (1 pen), Davies 1, Donacien 1, Edwards 1, Husin 1, Lacey 1, O'Sullivan 1, Rodgers 1.
FA Cup (7): Kee 2, Beckles 1, Boco 1, Clark 1, McConville 1, O'Sullivan 1.
EFL Cup (1): Pearson 1.
EFL Checkatrade Trophy (4): Gornell 2, Clark 1, Taylor-Fletcher 1.

Chapman A 15	Donacien J 30 + 5	Beckles O 40 + 1	Hughes M 36	Pearson M 43	Conneely S 38	Brown S 27 + 1	Clark J 35 + 7	Boco R 12 + 17	McConville S 41	Gornell T 10 + 9	McCartan S 26 + 8	Eagles C 2 + 4	Jones C — + 2	O'Sullivan J 18 + 1	Hewitt S 4 + 5	Hery B — + 1	Davies A 4	Kee B 37 + 2	Parish E 11	Lacey P 7 + 4	Vyner Z 16	Taylor-Fletcher G — + 4	Edwards J 2 + 8	Rodak M 20	Rodgers H 19	Clare S 6 + 2	Husin N 7 + 4	Shaw B — + 2	Ogle R — + 1	*Match No.*
1	2^{2}	3	4	5	6	7	8^{3}	9^{1}	10	11	12	13	14																	1
1	2	3	4	5	8		14	12^{3}	9	11^{2}		10		6	7^{1}	13														2
1	5	4	3	2	8			12	6			10^{1}		9^{2}	13		7	11												3
1	2	3	4	5	8		10^{1}		9			12		6	13		7^{2}	11												4
	2	3	4■	5	8			12	9		10^{1}			6	7^{2}			11	1	13										5
1	2	4		5	7		12	10^{2}	9	13				6	8			11^{1}			3									6
1	5	4		3	8	7^{1}	10	12	9					6^{2}	13			11			2									7
1	5	3		4	7		9	12	10					8^{2}	13			11		6^{1}	2									8
	5	4		3		6■	8	9	10	12					13			11	1	7^{2}	2^{1}									9
	5	3		4			6	12	9	11^{1}					8			10	1	7	2									10
1	5^{2}	3		4		6	9^{1}	8	10	12		13						11		7	2									11
1		4	3^{3}	5	8	7	9^{2}	10		11		14	13	6^{1}				12			2									12
	5	3		4	7	8	10	13	9	11^{1}	14			6^{3}					1		2^{2}	12								13
	5	3		4		8	10	12	9	11				6^{1}					1	7	2									14
	5	3		4	7	8	10^{2}	13	9	11	14			6^{1}					1		2^{3}	12								15
		4	3	5	7	8	9	10	6	11									1	2^{1}		12								16
		3		4	7	8^{3}	9^{1}	6	5	11^{2}	10			12				13	1	14	2									17
		3	5■		8^{2}	7	6	13	9		11			2				10^{1}	1	12	4									18
			3	4	8	7	9	13	5		10^{2}			6				11^{1}	1	12	2^{3}	14								19
1		4	3	2		8	9	12	5■	11^{1}	13			10			7^{2}			6										20
		3	4	5	8	7	9	10^{2}		13	12			6				11	1		2^{1}									21
1		3^{2}	4	5	10	8^{1}	6	9		13	12			7				11			2									22
1	5		4	3	8	7	12	13	9		10^{2}			6^{1}				11			2									23
1	5	3	4	2	7	8	13		9^{2}		10^{1}			6				11					12							24
	5	3	4	2	8	7■	6^{2}		9	13	12							11					10^{1}	1						25
	12	3	4	2■	6			9	5		10^{2}						7^{1}	11						1	8	13				26
	5	3	4		9			6	7		11^{1}							10					13	1	2	8^{2}	12			27
	5	4	3		7		13	14	9		12							10					11	1	2^{3}	6^{1}	8^{2}			28
	5	4	3	2	7	8	6	12	9^{2}		11^{3}							10^{1}					13	1		14				29
		3■	4	5	7	8	6	12	9		10^{1}							11						1	2					30
			4	3	8	7^{1}	6	2^{3}			10							11					13	1	5	9^{2}	12	14		31
	5		4	3	7	8	9			12	6							11						1	2	10^{1}				32
	5		4	2	8	7	12		9		10							11						1	3	6^{1}				33
	5	13	4	2	8	7	12		9^{1}		10							11						1	3	6^{2}				34
		3	4	5	8	7^{3}	6^{2}		9		10^{1}							11					13	1	2		12	14		35
	13	3	4	5	7	8■	6^{1}	14	9^{3}		10^{2}							11						1	2		12			36
	12	4	3	5	7^{1}		9		6		11							10						1	2		8			37
1	5^{1}	3	4	6			8		10		9							11					12		2		7			38
1	5	3	4	8			6		9		10							11							2		7			39
	12	3	4	5	8		6		9		10							11						1	2^{1}		7			40
	12	3	4	5	8		6		9		10							11						1	2		7^{1}			41
	7	3	4	5	8		6		9		10							11						1	2					42
	5	3	4	8	7		6		9		10							11						1	2					43
	5	3	4^{2}	7		12	6^{3}		9	14	10							11					13	1	2		8^{1}			44
	3	4	5	7	8		6^{2}		9		10^{1}							11					12	1	2				13	45
	5	3	4	2	7	8	6		9	12	10							11^{1}						1						46

FA Cup

First Round	Bradford C	(a)	2-1
Second Round	Woking	(a)	3-0
Third Round	Luton T	(h)	2-1
Fourth Round	Middlesbrough	(a)	0-1

EFL Cup

First Round	Bradford C	(h)	0-0
(*aet; Accrington S won 11-10 on penalties*)			
Second Round	Burnley	(h)	1-0
(*aet*)			
Third Round	West Ham U	(a)	0-1

EFL Checkatrade Trophy

Northern Group B	Crewe Alex	(h)	0-3
Northern Group B	Chesterfield	(a)	4-1
Northern Group B	Wolverhampton W U21	(a)	0-4

AFC WIMBLEDON

FOUNDATION

While the history of AFC Wimbledon is straightforward since it was a new club formed in 2002, there were in effect two clubs operating for two years with Wimbledon connections. The other club was MK Dons, of course. In August 2001, the Football League had rejected the existing Wimbledon's application to move to Milton Keynes. In May 2002, they rejected local sites and were given permission to move by an independent commission set up by the Football League. AFC Wimbledon was founded in the summer of 2002 and held its first trials on Wimbledon Common. In subsequent years, there was considerable debate over the rightful home of the trophies obtained by the former Wimbledon football club. In October 2006, an agreement was reached between Milton Keynes Dons FC, its Supporters Association, the Wimbledon Independent Supporters Association and the Football Supporters Federation to transfer such trophies and honours to the London Borough of Merton.

The Cherry Red Records Stadium, Kingsmeadow, Jack Goodchild Way, 422a Kingston Road, Kingston-upon-Thames, Surrey KT1 3PB.

Telephone: (0208) 547 3528.

Fax: (0808) 2800 816.

Website: www.afcwimbledon.co.uk

Email: info@afcwimbledon.co.uk

Ground Capacity: 5,027.

Record Attendance: 4,870 v Accrington S, FL 2 Play-Offs, 14 May 2016.

Pitch Measurements: 104m × 66m (113.5yd × 72yd).

President: Dickie Guy.

Chief Executive: Erik Samuelson.

Manager: Neal Ardley.

Assistant Manager: Neil Cox.

First-Team Coach: Simon Bassey.

Club Nickname: 'The Dons'.

Colours: Blue shirts with yellow trim, black shorts with yellow trim, blue socks with yellow trim.

Year Formed: 2002.

Turned Professional: 2002.

Grounds: 2002, Kingsmeadow (renamed The Cherry Red Records Stadium).

First Football League Game: 6 August 2011, FL 2 v Bristol R (h) L 2–3 – Brown; Hatton, Gwillim (Bush), Porter (Minshull), Stuart (1), Johnson B, Moore L, Wellard, Jolley (Ademeno (1)), Midson, Yussuff.

HONOURS

League: *Runners-up:* FL 2 – (7th) 2015–16 *(promoted via play-offs)*; Conference – (2nd) 2010–11 *(promoted via play-offs)*.

FA Cup: 3rd rd – 2015, 2017.

League Cup: never past 1st rd.

sky SPORTS FACT FILE

Up to the end of the 2016–17 season, AFC Wimbledon had played six Football League Cup games and lost every one of them. They have lost four times by a single goal margin and the closest they have come to progressing to the second round came in 2016–17 when they went down to injury time defeat at Peterborough United.

MANAGERS

Terry Eames 2002–04
Nicky English *(Caretaker)* 2004
Dave Anderson 2004–07
Terry Brown 2007–12
Neal Ardley October 2012–

Record League Victory: 5–1 v Bury, FL 2, 19 November 2016 – Shea; Fuller, Robertson, Robinson (Taylor), Owens, Francomb (2 (1 pen)), Reeves, Parrett, Whelpdale (1), Elliott (1) (Nightingale), Poleon (1), (Barrett).

Record Cup Victory: 5–0 v Bury, FA Cup 1st rd replay, 5 November 2016 – Shea; Fuller (Owens), Robertson, Robinson (1), Francomb. Parrett (1), Reeves, Bulman (Beere), Whelpdale, Barcham (Poleon (2)), Taylor (1).

Record Defeat: 2–6 v Burton Alb, FL 2, 25 August 2012.

Most League Points (3 for a win): 75, FL 2, 2015–16.

Most League Goals: 64, FL 2, 2015–16.

Highest League Scorer in Season: Lyle Taylor, 20, 2015–16.

Most League Goals in Total Aggregate: Kevin Cooper, 107, 2002–04.

Most League Goals in One Match: Not more than two goals by one player.

Most Capped Player: Shane Smeltz, 5 (51), New Zealand.

Most League Appearances: Sammy Moore, 139, 2011–15.

Youngest League Player: Ben Harrison, 17 years 195 days v Accrington S, 13 September 2014.

Record Transfer Fee Received: £120,000 from Coventry C for Chris Hussey, January 2010.

Record Transfer Fee Paid: £25,000 (in excess of) to Stevenage for Byron Harrison, January 2012.

Football League Record: 2011 Promoted from Conference Premier; 2011–16 FL 2; 2016– FL 1.

LATEST SEQUENCES

Longest Sequence of League Wins: 5, 2.4.2016 – 23.4.2016.
Longest Sequence of League Defeats: 6, 26.11.2011 – 2.1.2012.
Longest Sequence of League Draws: 3, 12.1.2013 – 2.2.2013.
Longest Sequence of Unbeaten League Matches: 8, 17.9.2016 – 22.10.2016.
Longest Sequence Without a League Win: 12, 15.10.2011 – 2.1.2012.
Successive Scoring Runs: 10 from 28.12.2016.
Successive Non-scoring Runs: 6 from 1.4.2017.

TEN YEAR LEAGUE RECORD

		P	*W*	*D*	*L*	*F*	*A*	*Pts*	*Pos*
2007-08	Isth PR	42	22	9	11	81	47	75	3
2008-09	Conf S	42	26	10	6	86	36	88	1
2009-10	Conf P	44	18	10	16	61	47	64	8
2010-11	Conf P	46	27	9	10	83	47	90	2
2011-12	FL 2	46	15	9	22	62	78	54	16
2012-13	FL 2	46	14	11	21	54	76	53	20
2013-14	FL 2	46	14	14	18	49	57	53*	20
2014-15	FL 2	46	14	16	16	54	60	58	15
2015-16	FL 2	46	21	12	13	64	50	75	7
2016-17	FL 1	46	13	18	15	52	55	57	15

** 3 pts deducted.*

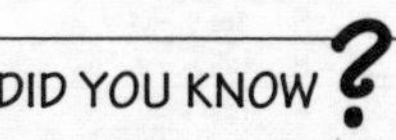

The largest attendance AFC Wimbledon have played in front of to date was for the League Two Play-Off final in May 2016. A crowd of 57,956 turned out at Wembley Stadium to see them beat Plymouth Argyle 2-0 and clinch a place in League One for the first time.

AFC WIMBLEDON – SKY BET LEAGUE ONE 2016–17 LEAGUE RECORD

Match No.	*Date*	*Venue*	*Opponents*	*Result*	*H/T Score*	*Lg Pos.*	*Goalscorers*	*Attendance*
1	Aug 6	A	Walsall	L 1-3	0-2	20	Taylor (pen) [90]	5845
2	13	H	Bolton W	L 1-2	1-1	23	Barcham [16]	4619
3	16	H	Scunthorpe U	L 1-2	0-2	24	Charles [61]	4163
4	20	A	Northampton T	D 0-0	0-0	23		5185
5	27	A	Rochdale	D 1-1	1-0	24	Barcham [12]	2274
6	Sept 3	H	Chesterfield	W 2-1	0-1	19	Robinson [53], Poleon [90]	4425
7	10	H	Sheffield U	L 2-3	1-2	21	Poleon [37], Elliott [72]	4810
8	17	A	Charlton Ath	W 2-1	0-1	17	Poleon [78], Barnett [85]	11,927
9	24	H	Shrewsbury T	D 1-1	1-0	20	Taylor [6]	4318
10	28	A	Coventry C	D 2-2	1-1	20	Meades [37], Taylor [83]	8030
11	Oct 1	H	Gillingham	W 2-0	2-0	15	Poleon [20], Parrett (pen) [45]	4653
12	9	A	Oxford U	W 3-1	3-0	10	Elliott [20], Charles [42], Barcham [45]	7742
13	15	H	Swindon T	D 0-0	0-0	12		4800
14	18	A	Bury	W 2-1	1-1	9	Taylor [39], Meades [90]	2211
15	22	A	Peterborough U	W 1-0	1-0	6	Elliott [10]	6642
16	29	H	Bradford C	L 2-3	1-1	8	Elliott [18], Taylor (pen) [68]	4826
17	Nov 12	A	Oldham Ath	D 0-0	0-0	9		3856
18	19	H	Bury	W 5-1	4-1	6	Whelpdale [26], Poleon [27], Elliott [28], Francomb 2 (1 pen) [36 (p), 57]	4141
19	22	A	Millwall	D 0-0	0-0	7		8614
20	26	H	Fleetwood T	D 2-2	0-1	7	Poleon [47], Parrett (pen) [75]	4023
21	Dec 10	A	Milton Keynes D	L 0-1	0-0	9		11,185
22	17	H	Port Vale	W 4-0	0-0	9	Poleon [53], Elliott [58], Barnett [85], Robertson [89]	4291
23	26	A	Southend U	L 0-3	0-2	11		8493
24	31	A	Bristol R	L 0-2	0-0	11		10,093
25	Jan 2	H	Millwall	D 2-2	1-2	11	Taylor [12], Elliott [51]	4742
26	14	H	Oxford U	W 2-1	2-1	12	Parrett [12], Kelly [28]	4808
27	21	A	Chesterfield	D 0-0	0-0	11		6379
28	Feb 4	A	Sheffield U	L 0-4	0-2	14		20,549
29	11	H	Charlton Ath	D 1-1	0-1	15	Elliott [90]	4595
30	14	H	Coventry C	D 1-1	0-0	14	Robinson [90]	4022
31	18	A	Shrewsbury T	L 1-2	0-0	15	Barcham [68]	5751
32	21	A	Gillingham	D 2-2	1-2	14	Taylor [17], Barcham [69]	4956
33	25	H	Walsall	W 1-0	0-0	13	Taylor [68]	4586
34	28	A	Scunthorpe U	W 2-1	0-0	12	Parrett [60], Poleon [69]	3368
35	Mar 4	A	Bolton W	D 1-1	1-1	13	Elliott [39]	13,599
36	11	H	Northampton T	L 0-1	0-0	13		4512
37	14	H	Milton Keynes D	W 2-0	0-0	12	Reeves [62], Taylor [68]	4112
38	18	A	Fleetwood T	D 0-0	0-0	13		2802
39	25	H	Southend U	L 0-2	0-1	13		4803
40	28	H	Rochdale	W 3-1	0-0	12	Kelly [53], Taylor [55], Parrett (pen) [58]	3812
41	Apr 1	A	Port Vale	L 0-2	0-1	12		4308
42	8	H	Bristol R	L 0-1	0-1	13		4742
43	14	A	Swindon T	D 0-0	0-0	13		7716
44	17	H	Peterborough U	D 0-0	0-0	12		4294
45	22	A	Bradford C	L 0-3	0-2	15		18,615
46	30	H	Oldham Ath	D 0-0	0-0	15		4867

Final League Position: 15

GOALSCORERS

League (52): Taylor 10 (2 pens), Elliott 9, Poleon 8, Barcham 5, Parrett 5 (3 pens), Barnett 2, Charles 2, Francomb 2 (1 pen), Kelly 2, Meades 2, Robinson 2, Reeves 1, Robertson 1, Whelpdale 1.
FA Cup (12): Elliott 4, Poleon 3, Taylor 2, Barnett 1, Parrett 1, Robinson 1.
EFL Cup (2): Taylor 1, Whelpdale 1.
EFL Checkatrade Trophy (6): Barnett 2, Poleon 2, Barcham 1, Taylor 1.

Clarke R 7	Fuller B 28	Robinson P 43	Charles D 32 + 2	Kelly S 22 + 4	Whelpdale C 8 + 9	Bulman D 31 + 7	Reeves J 46	Elliott T 30 + 9	Taylor L 36 + 7	Barcham A 32 + 5	Barnett T 11 + 25	Poleon D 19 + 22	Parrett D 20 + 12	Beere T 3 + 5	Meades J 22 + 2	Francomb G 31 + 3	Shea J 36	Egan A 3 + 6	Robertson C 13	Nightingale W 10 + 2	Owens S 2 + 1	Oakley G — + 2	Soares T 15	Fitzpatrick D 2 + 4	Antwi J — + 1	McDonnell J 3	Sibbick T 1 + 1	Kaja E — + 1	*Match No.*
1	2	3	4	5	6^1	7	8	9^2	10	11^3	12	13	14																1
1	2	4	3	5		7	8	9^1	11	10^2	12	13	6^3	14															2
1	2	4	3	5	6^1	7	8	12	11^2	9^3	10	14	13																3
1	2	4	3	5	6	7	8	10^2	11^1	9	12	13																	4
1	2	4	3		6^2	7	8	10^1	11^3	9	12		13		5	14													5
1	5	3	4			8	7	13	10^1	6^3	11	14	12		2	9^2													6
1	2	4	3^1		14		8	13	12	9	10^2	11	7		5	6^3													7
	2	4	3		14	7	8	12	11^1	9^3	13	10			5	6^2	1												8
	2	4	3		14	7	8	10^3	11^1	13	12	9	6^2		5		1												9
	2	4	3			7	8	12	11	9^3	10^2	14	6^1	13	5		1												10
	2	4	3	14		13	8	11	12	9		10^1	6	7^2	5^3		1												11
	2	4	3			7	8	11^1	10^2	9	12	14	6^3		5		1	13											12
	2	4	3		14	8	7	10^1	11^2	9^3	13	12	6		5		1												13
	2	3	4			7^3	8	14	11^2	9	10^1	13	6		5		1	12											14
	2				6^3	14	7	11	12	10			13	9^2	4	8^1	1		3	5									15
	2	3			14	6	7	10^3	9^2	11	12			13	5	8^1	1			4									16
	2	3			12	7	8	10^1	9	11^3	14	13	6^2			5	1		4										17
	2	4^2			9		7	10^1	13		14	11^3	8			6	1		3	12	5								18
	2	4			12	7	8	10	9^3			11^2		13	5■	6^1	1		3		14								19
		3		12	9	6	7	13			10^2	11	8^1	14		2	1		4		5^3								20
	2	4			13	7	8	10^2	12		14	11^3	9^1		5	6	1		3										21
	2	4		3		8	7	10^2	11	13	14	9^1	12			6^3	1		5										22
	2	3		5		7	8	10	9■	13	12	11^2				6^1	1		4										23
	2	4	14			8^2	7	10		9^3	11^1	13	12		5	6	1		3										24
	2	4	3	5		14	8	10^3	11		12	13	7		9^2	6^1	1												25
	2	4	3	5	13	7	8	10^3	11^1		12	9	6^2				1	14											26
	2		3	5	6	14	8				10^2	9		7^3		13	1	11^1	4			12							27
	2	3	4	5		7^2	8	10	11	9^1		13				12	1						6						28
	2^1	4		5			8	10■	9	12	13	11^2				6	1		3				7						29
		4		5		7^3	8		10^2	11	14	9^1				2	1		3			13	6	12					30
		3	4	5			7	10	11^2	9	13	12				2	1						8	6^1					31
		3	4	5^2			8	10^1	11	9	14	13				2	1			12			7	6^3					32
		4	3	5		7	6	10	11^1	9		12				2	1						8						33
		2	3			14	8	12	10^1	9		11^2	7			5^3	1			4			6	13					34
		3	2	14		4	7	11^3	12		13	10^1			9^2	5	1			6			8						35
			10			12	9	13	4^1	6		11	8		14	5^3	1		3	2			7^2						36
		4	5	3		6	7	11^1	10^2	9	14	13	12		2		1						8^3						37
		3	4			7	8	11	12	9	10^2		6^1		13	5	1			2									38
		2	4				7	10^2	9^1	11	13	14	12		6	5	1			3			8^3						39
		4	3	5			7	10^2	9^3	11^1	12	14	6			2	1						8	13					40
		3	5	4			7	10^1	11	6^2		12	8^3			9	1	14					2		13				41
		4	14	5		7^3	6		11		12	10^1			8	2	1	9^2		3				13					42
		3	4	5		8	7		10	13	11^2		12		2	6^3		14					9^1			1			43
		4	3	5		14	7		10	9^3	11^1	12	13			6^2							8			1	2		44
		4	3^3	12		8	9		11	6		13	7^1		5^2	10		14		2						1			45
		4		3		6^1	7		11	9		10^2	14			2	1	8^3		5							12	13	46

FA Cup

First Round	Bury	(a)	2-2
Replay	Bury	(h)	5-0
Second Round	Curzon Ashton	(a)	4-3
Third Round	Sutton U	(a)	0-0
Replay	Sutton U	(h)	1-3

EFL Cup

First Round	Peterborough U	(a)	2-3

EFL Checkatrade Trophy

Southern Group B	Swansea C U21	(h)	3-0
Southern Group B	Plymouth Arg	(h)	2-1
Southern Group B	Newport Co	(a)	0-2
Second Round South	Brighton & HA U21	(h)	1-2

ARSENAL

FOUNDATION

Formed by workers at the Royal Arsenal, Woolwich in 1886, they began as Dial Square (name of one of the workshops), and included two former Nottingham Forest players, Fred Beardsley and Morris Bates. Beardsley wrote to his old club seeking help and they provided the new club with a full set of red jerseys and a ball. The club became known as the 'Woolwich Reds' although their official title soon after formation was Woolwich Arsenal.

Emirates Stadium, Highbury House, 75 Drayton Park, Islington, London N5 1BU.

Telephone: (020) 7619 5003.

Fax: (020) 7704 4001.

Ticket Office: (020) 7619 5000.

Website: www.arsenal.com

Email: ask@arsenal.co.uk

Ground Capacity: 60,260.

Record Attendance: 73,295 v Sunderland, Div 1, 9 March 1935 (at Highbury); 73,707 v RC Lens, UEFA Champions League, 25 November 1998 (at Wembley); 60,162 v Manchester U, FA Premier League, 3 November 2007 (at Emirates).

Pitch Measurements: 105m × 68m (114yd × 74yd).

Chairman: Sir John 'Chips' Keswick.

Chief Executive: Ivan Gazidis.

Manager: Arsène Wenger.

Assistant Manager: Steve Bould.

Colours: Red shirts with white sleeves, white shorts with red trim, red socks with white trim.

Year Formed: 1886.

Turned Professional: 1891.

Previous Names: 1886, Dial Square; 1886, Royal Arsenal; 1891, Woolwich Arsenal; 1914, Arsenal.

Club Nickname: 'The Gunners'.

Grounds: 1886, Plumstead Common; 1887, Sportsman Ground; 1888, Manor Ground; 1890, Invicta Ground; 1893, Manor Ground; 1913, Highbury; 2006, Emirates Stadium.

First Football League Game: 2 September 1893, Division 2, v Newcastle U (h) D 2–2 – Williams; Powell, Jeffrey; Devine, Buist, Howat; Gemmell, Henderson, Shaw (1), Elliott (1), Booth.

HONOURS

League Champions: FA Premier League – 1997–98, 2001–02, 2003–04; Division 1 – 1930–31, 1932–33, 1933–34, 1934–35, 1937–38, 1947–48, 1952–53, 1970–71, 1988–89, 1990–91. *Runners-up:* FA Premier League – 1998–99, 1999–2000, 2000–01, 2002–03, 2004–05, 2015–16; Division 1 – 1925–26, 1931–32, 1972–73; Division 2 – 1903–04.

FA Cup Winners: 1930, 1936, 1950, 1971, 1979, 1993, 1998, 2002, 2003, 2005, 2014, 2015, 2017. *Runners-up:* 1927, 1932, 1952, 1972, 1978, 1980, 2001.

League Cup Winners: 1987, 1993. *Runners-up:* 1968, 1969, 1988, 2007, 2011.

Double performed: 1970–71, 1997–98, 2001–02.

European Competitions
European Cup: 1971–72 *(qf)*, 1991–92.
UEFA Champions League: 1998–99, 1999–2000, 2000–01, 2001–02, 2002–03, 2003–04, 2004–05, 2005–06 *(runners-up)*, 2006–07, 2007–08 *(qf)*, 2008–09 *(sf)*, 2009–10*(qf)*, 2010–11, 2011–12, 2012–13, 2013–14, 2014–15, 2015–16, 2016–17.
Fairs Cup: 1963–64, 1969–70 *(winners)*, 1970–71.
UEFA Cup: 1978–79, 1981–82, 1982–83, 1996–97, 1997–98, 1999–2000 *(runners-up)*.
European Cup-Winners' Cup: 1979–80 *(runners-up)*, 1993–94 *(winners)*, 1994–95 *(runners-up)*.
Super Cup: 1994 *(runners-up)*.

sky SPORTS FACT FILE

Arsenal manager Herbert Chapman was a great supporter of floodlit football. The Gunners and Rangers (cup holders in England and Scotland) had planned to meet each other in floodlit matches at Wembley Stadium and Ibrox during the 1930–31 season but the FA stepped in and issued a ban on member clubs taking part in the games.

Record League Victory: 12–0 v Loughborough T, Division 2, 12 March 1900 – Orr; McNichol, Jackson; Moir, Dick (2), Anderson (1); Hunt, Cottrell (2), Main (2), Gaudie (3), Tennant (2).

Record Cup Victory: 11–1 v Darwen, FA Cup 3rd rd, 9 January 1932 – Moss; Parker, Hapgood; Jones, Roberts, John; Hulme (2), Jack (3), Lambert (2), James, Bastin (4).

Record Defeat: 0–8 v Loughborough T, Division 2, 12 December 1896.

Most League Points (2 for a win): 66, Division 1, 1930–31.

Most League Points (3 for a win): 90, FA Premier League, 2003–04.

Most League Goals: 127, Division 1, 1930–31.

Highest League Scorer in Season: Ted Drake, 42, 1934–35.

Most League Goals in Total Aggregate: Thierry Henry, 175, 1999–2007; 2011–12.

Most League Goals in One Match: 7, Ted Drake v Aston Villa, Division 1, 14 December 1935.

Most Capped Player: Thierry Henry, 81 (123), France.

Most League Appearances: David O'Leary, 558, 1975–93.

Youngest League Player: Jack Wilshere, 16 years 256 days v Blackburn R, 13 September 2008.

Record Transfer Fee Received: £25,400,000 (rising to £29,800,000) from Barcelona for Cesc Fabregas, August 2011.

Record Transfer Fee Paid: £45,000,000 (rising to £52,000,000) to Lyon for Alexandre Lacazette, July 2017.

Football League Record: 1893 Elected to Division 2; 1904–13 Division 1; 1913–19 Division 2; 1919–92 Division 1; 1992– FA Premier League.

MANAGERS

Sam Hollis 1894–97
Tom Mitchell 1897–98
George Elcoat 1898–99
Harry Bradshaw 1899–1904
Phil Kelso 1904–08
George Morrell 1908–15
Leslie Knighton 1919–25
Herbert Chapman 1925–34
George Allison 1934–47
Tom Whittaker 1947–56
Jack Crayston 1956–58
George Swindin 1958–62
Billy Wright 1962–66
Bertie Mee 1966–76
Terry Neill 1976–83
Don Howe 1984–86
George Graham 1986–95
Bruce Rioch 1995–96
Arsène Wenger September 1996–

LATEST SEQUENCES

Longest Sequence of League Wins: 14, 10.2.2002 – 18.8.2002.

Longest Sequence of League Defeats: 7, 12.2.1977 – 12.3.1977.

Longest Sequence of League Draws: 6, 4.3.1961 – 1.4.1961.

Longest Sequence of Unbeaten League Matches: 49, 7.5.2003 – 24.10.2004.

Longest Sequence Without a League Win: 23, 28.9.1912 – 1.3.1913.

Successive Scoring Runs: 55 from 19.5.2001.

Successive Non-scoring Runs: 6 from 25.2.1987.

TEN YEAR LEAGUE RECORD

		P	W	D	L	F	A	Pts	Pos
2007-08	PR Lge	38	24	11	3	74	31	83	3
2008-09	PR Lge	38	20	12	6	68	37	72	4
2009-10	PR Lge	38	23	6	9	83	41	75	3
2010-11	PR Lge	38	19	11	8	72	43	68	4
2011-12	PR Lge	38	21	7	10	74	49	70	3
2012-13	PR Lge	38	21	10	7	72	37	73	4
2013-14	PR Lge	38	24	7	7	68	41	79	4
2014-15	PR Lge	38	22	9	7	71	36	75	3
2015-16	PR Lge	38	20	11	7	65	36	71	2
2016-17	PR Lge	38	23	6	9	77	44	75	5

DID YOU KNOW?

The first-ever football match to be broadcast on radio was between Arsenal and Sheffield United. The game took place at Highbury on 22 January 1927 and ended in a 1-1 draw. Radio coverage included the community singing that preceded the match as well as the full 90 minutes' play. Commentators were Teddy Wakelam and C.A. Lewis.

ARSENAL – PREMIER LEAGUE 2016–17 LEAGUE RECORD

Match No.	*Date*	*Venue*	*Opponents*	*Result*	*H/T Score*	*Lg Pos.*	*Goalscorers*	*Attendance*
1	Aug 14	H	Liverpool	L 3-4	1-1	15	Walcott [31], Oxlade-Chamberlain [64], Chambers [75]	60,033
2	20	A	Leicester C	D 0-0	0-0	14		32,008
3	27	A	Watford	W 3-1	3-0	7	Cazorla (pen) [9], Sanchez [40], Ozil [45]	20,545
4	Sept 10	H	Southampton	W 2-1	1-1	4	Koscielny [29], Cazorla (pen) [90]	59,962
5	17	A	Hull C	W 4-1	1-0	3	Sanchez 2 [17, 83], Walcott [55], Xhaka [90]	22,536
6	24	H	Chelsea	W 3-0	3-0	2	Sanchez [11], Walcott [14], Ozil [40]	60,028
7	Oct 2	A	Burnley	W 1-0	0-0	2	Koscielny [90]	20,982
8	15	H	Swansea C	W 3-2	2-1	1	Walcott 2 [26, 33], Ozil [57]	60,007
9	22	H	Middlesbrough	D 0-0	0-0	1		59,982
10	29	A	Sunderland	W 4-1	1-0	1	Sanchez 2 [19, 78], Giroud 2 [71, 76]	44,322
11	Nov 6	H	Tottenham H	D 1-1	1-0	3	Wimmer (og) [42]	60,039
12	19	A	Manchester U	D 1-1	0-0	4	Giroud [89]	75,264
13	27	H	Bournemouth	W 3-1	1-1	4	Sanchez 2 [12, 90], Walcott [53]	59,978
14	Dec 3	A	West Ham U	W 5-1	1-0	2	Ozil [24], Sanchez 3 [72, 80, 86], Oxlade-Chamberlain [84]	56,980
15	10	H	Stoke C	W 3-1	1-1	1	Walcott [42], Ozil [49], Iwobi [75]	59,964
16	13	A	Everton	L 1-2	1-1	2	Sanchez [20]	39,510
17	18	A	Manchester C	L 1-2	1-0	4	Walcott [5]	54,409
18	26	H	WBA	W 1-0	0-0	3	Giroud [86]	59,925
19	Jan 1	H	Crystal Palace	W 2-0	1-0	3	Giroud [17], Iwobi [56]	59,975
20	3	A	Bournemouth	D 3-3	0-2	4	Sanchez [70], Lucas Perez [75], Giroud [90]	11,202
21	14	A	Swansea C	W 4-0	1-0	2	Giroud [37], Cork (og) [54], Naughton (og) [67], Sanchez [73]	20,875
22	22	H	Burnley	W 2-1	0-0	2	Mustafi [59], Sanchez (pen) [90]	59,955
23	31	H	Watford	L 1-2	0-2	2	Iwobi [58]	60,035
24	Feb 4	A	Chelsea	L 1-3	0-1	3	Giroud [90]	41,490
25	11	H	Hull C	W 2-0	1-0	3	Sanchez 2 (1 pen) [34, 90 (p)]	59,962
26	Mar 4	A	Liverpool	L 1-3	0-2	5	Welbeck [57]	53,146
27	18	A	WBA	L 1-3	1-1	5	Sanchez [15]	24,065
28	Apr 2	H	Manchester C	D 2-2	1-2	6	Walcott [40], Mustafi [53]	60,001
29	5	H	West Ham U	W 3-0	0-0	5	Ozil [58], Walcott [68], Giroud [83]	59,961
30	10	A	Crystal Palace	L 0-3	0-1	6		25,648
31	17	A	Middlesbrough	W 2-1	1-0	6	Sanchez [42], Ozil [71]	31,298
32	26	H	Leicester C	W 1-0	0-0	6	Huth (og) [86]	59,829
33	30	A	Tottenham H	L 0-2	0-0	6		31,811
34	May 7	H	Manchester U	W 2-0	0-0	6	Xhaka [54], Welbeck [57]	60,055
35	10	A	Southampton	W 2-0	0-0	5	Sanchez [60], Giroud [83]	31,474
36	13	A	Stoke C	W 4-1	1-0	5	Giroud 2 [42, 80], Ozil [55], Sanchez [76]	27,535
37	16	H	Sunderland	W 2-0	0-0	5	Sanchez 2 [72, 81]	59,510
38	21	H	Everton	W 3-1	2-0	5	Bellerin [8], Sanchez [27], Ramsey [90]	59,976

Final League Position: 5

GOALSCORERS

League (77): Sanchez 24 (2 pens), Giroud 12, Walcott 10, Ozil 8, Iwobi 3, Cazorla 2 (2 pens), Koscielny 2, Mustafi 2, Oxlade-Chamberlain 2, Welbeck 2, Xhaka 2, Bellerin 1, Chambers 1, Lucas Perez 1, Ramsey 1, own goals 4.
FA Cup (18): Walcott 5, Ramsey 3, Sanchez 3, Giroud 2, Welbeck 2, Lucas Perez 1, Monreal 1, own goal 1.
EFL Cup (6): Oxlade-Chamberlain 3, Lucas Perez 2 (1 pen), Xhaka 1.
UEFA Champions League (20): Ozil 4 ,Walcott 4, Lucas 3, Sanchez 3, Giroud 2 (1 pen), Iwobi 1, Oxlade-Chamberlain 1, Xhaka 1, own goal 1.

Cech P 35	Bellerin H 27 + 6	Holding R 9	Chambers C 1	Monreal N 35 + 1	Coquelin F 22 + 7	El-Nenny M 8 + 6	Walcott T 23 + 5	Ramsey A 13 + 10	Iwobi A 18 + 8	Sanchez A 36 + 2	Oxlade-Chamberlain A 16 + 13	Cazorla S 7 + 1	Xhaka G 28 + 4	Koscielny L 33	Ozil M 32 + 1	Wilshere J — + 2	Giroud O 11 + 18	Gibbs K 8 + 3	Mustafi S 26	Lucas Perez M 2 + 9	Maitland-Niles A — + 1	Jenkinson C 1	Debuchy M 1	Gabriel A 15 + 4	Welbeck D 8 + 8	Ospina D 1 + 1	Martinez D 2	Mertesacker P — + 1	*Match No.*
1	2	3	4	5	6	7^{2}	8	9^{1}	10^{3}	11	12	13	14																1
1	2	3		5	6		8			11	10^{1}	9^{2}	7^{3}	4	12	13	14												2
1	2	3		5^{3}		12	8			11	10^{1}	6	7	4	9^{2}	13		14											3
1	2			5	7		8^{2}		14	13	10^{1}	6		4	9		12		3	11^{3}									4
1	2			5	6	13	8^{1}		10^{3}	11		7^{2}	12	4	9				3	14									5
1	2			5	7^{2}		8		10^{3}	11^{1}		6	12	4	9		14	13	3										6
1	2			5		12	8		10^{1}	11	13	6	7^{2}	4	9				3										7
1	2			5	12		8		10^{3}	11^{2}	13	6	7■	4	9^{1}			14	3										8
1	2			5	7	6^{2}	8		10^{1}	11	13			4	9				3	12									9
1	2				6^{3}	7		13	10^{1}	11	8^{2}			4	9		12	5	3		14								10
1	2			5	6^{3}		8^{2}	12	10^{1}	11	14		7	4	9		13		3										11
1				5	6^{2}	7^{1}	8	10		11	14		13	4	9		12		3			2^{3}							12
1				5		6	8^{2}	13		11	10^{3}		7	4	9		14		3				2^{1}	12					13
1				5	6^{1}	13	8^{2}	12	14	11	10		7	4	9^{3}				3					2					14
1	12			5	6		8		13	11^{2}	10^{3}		7	4	9		14		3^{1}					2					15
1	2			5	6^{1}		8^{2}		13	11	10^{3}		7	4	9		12			14				3					16
1	2			5	6^{1}	14	8		10^{2}	11	12^{3}		7	4	9		13							3					17
1	2			12	6^{1}			14	8^{3}	10			7	4	9		11	5^{2}		13				3					18
1	2			5	12	6^{1}		13	9^{3}	10	14		7	4			11			8^{2}				3					19
1	2			5	6^{1}			9	8^{2}	10	12		7	4^{3}			11		3	13				14					20
1				5				6	8	10^{3}	12		7	4	9^{2}		11^{1}		3	14				2	13				21
1	14			5	12			6	8^{2}	10			7■	4	9^{1}		11^{3}		3					2	13				22
1				5	7^{2}		13	6^{3}	8	10	12			4	9		11^{1}		3	14				2					23
1	2^{3}			5	7^{1}		8^{2}		10	11	6			4	9		13		3					12	14				24
1	2				7	12	8^{2}		10^{3}	11	6^{1}			4	9			5	3	14					13				25
1	2			5	6^{3}		13		9	12	8		7	4			11^{2}		3	14					10^{1}				26
1^{2}	2			5			9^{1}	6	14	11^{3}	8		7	4			13		3						10	12			27
	2			5	6		8^{3}		14	10			7	4^{1}	9		13		3					12	11^{2}	1			28
	2			5		6^{2}	8^{3}	13		10	14		7		9		12		3					4	11^{1}		1		29
	2			5		7^{1}	8^{3}	12		10	14		6		9		13		3					4	11^{2}		1		30
1	13	4		8	12			6		10^{2}	5		7	3	9^{1}		11							2					31
1	5			4	6^{1}		9^{2}	14		11			7	3	10		13	8^{3}						2	12				32
1	13			4			14	6		10	5		7^{3}	3	9		11^{2}	8						2^{1}	12				33
1	14	2		4	12			6		10	5^{1}		7^{3}	3	9		13	8							11^{2}				34
1	12	2		4	14			6		10	5^{2}		7		9^{3}		13	8	3						11^{1}				35
1	5	2		8	6		14	12		10^{1}			7	4	9^{2}		11^{3}		3						13				36
1	5	2		4			14	6^{2}	13	10			7		9		11^{1}	8^{3}	3						12				37
1	5	4		8	13			6	14	10^{2}			7^{3}	3■	9									2^{1}	11			12	38

FA Cup

Third Round	Preston NE	(a)	2-1
Fourth Round	Southampton	(a)	5-0
Fifth Round	Sutton U	(a)	2-0
Sixth Round	Lincoln C	(h)	5-0
Semi-Final (*aet*)	Manchester C	(h)	2-1
Final	Chelsea	(Wembley)	2-1

EFL Cup

Third Round	Nottingham F	(a)	4-0
Fourth Round	Reading	(h)	2-0
Quarter-Final	Southampton	(h)	0-2

UEFA Champions League

Group A	Paris Saint-Germain	(a)	1-1
Group A	Basel	(h)	2-0
Group A	Ludogorets	(h)	6-0
Group A	Ludogorets	(a)	3-2
Group A	Paris Saint-Germain	(h)	2-2
Group A	Basel	(a)	4-1
Round of 16 1st leg	Bayern Munich	(a)	1-5
Round of 16 2nd leg	Bayern Munich	(h)	1-5

Bayern Munich won 10-2 on aggregate.

ASTON VILLA

FOUNDATION

Cricketing enthusiasts of Villa Cross Wesleyan Chapel, Aston, Birmingham decided to form a football club during the winter of 1874–75. Football clubs were few and far between in the Birmingham area and in their first game against Aston Brook St Mary's rugby team they played one half rugby and the other soccer. In 1876 they were joined by Scottish soccer enthusiast George Ramsay who was immediately appointed captain and went on to lead Aston Villa from obscurity to one of the country's top clubs in a period of less than ten years.

Villa Park, Trinity Road, Birmingham B6 6HE.

Telephone: (0121) 327 2299.

Fax: (0121) 322 2107.

Ticket Office: (0333) 323 1874.

Website: www.avfc.co.uk

Email: postmaster@avfc.co.uk

Ground Capacity: 42,786.

Record Attendance: 76,588 v Derby Co, FA Cup 6th rd, 2 March 1946.

Pitch Measurements: 105m × 68m (114yd × 74yd).

Chairman: Dr Tony Xia.

Chief Executive: Keith Wyness.

Manager: Steve Bruce.

Assistant Manager: Colin Calderwood.

Colours: Claret shirts with thin sky blue stripes and sky blue sleeves, white shorts with claret trim, sky blue socks with claret trim.

Year Formed: 1874.

Turned Professional: 1885.

Club Nickname: 'The Villans'.

Grounds: 1874, Wilson Road and Aston Park (also used Aston Lower Grounds for some matches); 1876, Wellington Road, Perry Barr; 1897, Villa Park.

First Football League Game: 8 September 1888, Football League, v Wolverhampton W (a) D 1–1 – Warner; Cox, Coulton; Yates, Harry Devey, Dawson; Albert Brown, Green (1), Allen, Garvey, Hodgetts.

Record League Victory: 12–2 v Accrington S, Division 1, 12 March 1892 – Warner; Evans, Cox; Harry Devey, Jimmy Cowan, Baird; Athersmith (1), Dickson (2), John Devey (4), Lewis Campbell (4), Hodgetts (1).

HONOURS

League Champions: Division 1 – 1893–94, 1895–96, 1896–97, 1898–99, 1899–1900, 1909–10, 1980–81; Division 2 – 1937–38, 1959–60; Division 3 – 1971–72.
Runners-up: FA Premier League – 1992–93; Division 1 – 1902–03, 1907–08, 1910–11, 1912–13, 1913–14, 1930–31, 1932–33, 1989–90; Football League 1888–89; Division 2 – 1974–75, 1987–88.

FA Cup Winners: 1887, 1895, 1897, 1905, 1913, 1920, 1957.
Runners-up: 1892, 1924, 2000, 2015.

League Cup Winners: 1961, 1975, 1977, 1994, 1996.
Runners-up: 1963, 1971, 2010.

Double Performed: 1896–97.

European Competitions
European Cup: 1981–82 *(winners)*, 1982–83 *(qf)*.
UEFA Cup: 1975–76, 1977–78 *(qf)*, 1983–84, 1990–91, 1993–94, 1994–95, 1996–97, 1997–98 *(qf)*, 1998–99, 2001–02, 2008–09.
Europa League: 2009–10, 2010–11.
Intertoto Cup: 2000, 2001 *(winners)*, 2002 *(sf)*, 2008 *(qualified for UEFA Cup)*.
Super Cup: 1982 *(winners)*.
World Club Championship: 1982.

sky SPORTS FACT FILE

A total of 73 Aston Villa players had been capped for England up to the end of the 2016–17 season. The first to receive international honours were Arthur Brown and Howard Vaughton who appeared against Ireland in February 1882. England won 13-0 with Brown scoring four times and Vaughton five. This was Ireland's first-ever international match.

Record Cup Victory: 13–0 v Wednesbury Old Ath, FA Cup 1st rd, 30 October 1886 – Warner; Coulton, Simmonds; Yates, Robertson, Burton (2); Richard Davis (1), Albert Brown (3), Hunter (3), Loach (2), Hodgetts (2).

Record Defeat: 0–8 v Chelsea, FA Premier League, 23 December 2012.

Most League Points (2 for a win): 70, Division 3, 1971–72.

Most League Points (3 for a win): 78, Division 2, 1987–88.

Most League Goals: 128, Division 1, 1930–31.

Highest League Scorer in Season: 'Pongo' Waring, 49, Division 1, 1930–31.

Most League Goals in Total Aggregate: Harry Hampton, 215, 1904–15.

Most League Goals in One Match: 5, Harry Hampton v Sheffield W, Division 1, 5 October 1912; 5, Harold Halse v Derby Co, Division 1, 19 October 1912; 5, Len Capewell v Burnley, Division 1, 29 August 1925; 5, George Brown v Leicester C, Division 1, 2 January 1932; 5, Gerry Hitchens v Charlton Ath, Division 2, 18 November 1959.

Most Capped Player: Steve Staunton 64 (102), Republic of Ireland.

Most League Appearances: Charlie Aitken, 561, 1961–76.

Youngest League Player: Jimmy Brown, 15 years 349 days v Bolton W, 17 September 1969.

Record Transfer Fee Received: £32,500,000 from Liverpool for Christian Benteke, July 2015.

Record Transfer Fee Paid: £18,000,000 (rising to £24,000,000) to Sunderland for Darren Bent, January 2011.

Football League Record: 1888 Founder Member of the League; 1936–38 Division 2; 1938–59 Division 1; 1959–60 Division 2; 1960–67 Division 1; 1967–70 Division 2; 1970–72 Division 3; 1972–75 Division 2; 1975–87 Division 1; 1987–88 Division 2; 1988–92 Division 1; 1992–2016 FA Premier League; 2016– FL C.

MANAGERS

George Ramsay 1884–1926
(*Secretary-Manager*)
W. J. Smith 1926–34
(*Secretary-Manager*)
Jimmy McMullan 1934–35
Jimmy Hogan 1936–44
Alex Massie 1945–50
George Martin 1950–53
Eric Houghton 1953–58
Joe Mercer 1958–64
Dick Taylor 1964–67
Tommy Cummings 1967–68
Tommy Docherty 1968–70
Vic Crowe 1970–74
Ron Saunders 1974–82
Tony Barton 1982–84
Graham Turner 1984–86
Billy McNeill 1986–87
Graham Taylor 1987–90
Dr Jozef Venglos 1990–91
Ron Atkinson 1991–94
Brian Little 1994–98
John Gregory 1998–2002
Graham Taylor OBE 2002–03
David O'Leary 2003–06
Martin O'Neill 2006–10
Gerard Houllier 2010–11
Alex McLeish 2011–12
Paul Lambert 2012–15
Tim Sherwood 2015
Remi Garde 2015–16
Roberto Di Matteo 2016
Steve Bruce October 2016–

LATEST SEQUENCES

Longest Sequence of League Wins: 9, 15.10.1910 – 10.12.1910.

Longest Sequence of League Defeats: 11, 14.2.2016 – 30.4.2016.

Longest Sequence of League Draws: 6, 12.9.1981 – 10.10.1981.

Longest Sequence of Unbeaten League Matches: 15, 12.3.1949 – 27.8.1949.

Longest Sequence Without a League Win: 19, 14.8.2015 – 2.1.2016.

Successive Scoring Runs: 35 from 10.11.1895.

Successive Non-scoring Runs: 6 from 26.12.2014.

TEN YEAR LEAGUE RECORD

		P	W	D	L	F	A	Pts	Pos
2007-08	PR Lge	38	16	12	10	71	51	60	6
2008-09	PR Lge	38	17	11	10	54	48	62	6
2009-10	PR Lge	38	17	13	8	52	39	64	6
2010-11	PR Lge	38	12	12	14	48	59	48	9
2011-12	PR Lge	38	7	17	14	37	53	38	16
2012-13	PR Lge	38	10	11	17	47	69	41	15
2013-14	PR Lge	38	10	8	20	39	61	38	15
2014-15	PR Lge	38	10	8	20	31	57	38	17
2015-16	PR Lge	38	3	8	27	27	76	17	20
2016-17	FL C	46	16	14	16	47	48	62	13

DID YOU KNOW ?

Aston Villa were the second best supported team in England in both 1936–37 and 1937–38 despite the fact that they were playing in Division Two. In 1937–38 Villa were Second Division champions, thus returning to the top flight after a two-year absence.

ASTON VILLA – SKY BET CHAMPIONSHIP 2016–17 LEAGUE RECORD

Match No.	Date	Venue	Opponents	Result		H/T Score	Lg Pos.	Goalscorers	Attendance
1	Aug 7	A	Sheffield W	L	0-1	0-0	19		30,060
2	13	H	Rotherham U	W	3-0	2-0	7	Gestede 2 [21, 45], Grealish [84]	33,286
3	16	H	Huddersfield T	D	1-1	1-0	11	McCormack [25]	34,924
4	20	A	Derby Co	D	0-0	0-0	11		31,205
5	27	A	Bristol C	L	1-3	1-0	16	Grealish [5]	21,099
6	Sept 11	H	Nottingham F	D	2-2	0-0	17	McCormack [72], Gestede [74]	30,619
7	14	H	Brentford	D	1-1	1-0	17	Kodjia [19]	29,752
8	17	A	Ipswich T	D	0-0	0-0	18		19,249
9	24	H	Newcastle U	D	1-1	0-1	18	Tshibola [88]	32,062
10	27	A	Barnsley	D	1-1	0-0	17	Ayew [61]	15,830
11	Oct 1	A	Preston NE	L	0-2	0-2	19		17,696
12	15	H	Wolverhampton W	D	1-1	1-1	19	Kodjia (pen) [15]	32,533
13	18	A	Reading	W	2-1	1-0	17	Kodjia [38], Ayew (pen) [90]	20,331
14	22	H	Fulham	W	1-0	0-0	15	Kodjia [80]	32,201
15	30	A	Birmingham C	D	1-1	1-0	15	Gardner [29]	29,656
16	Nov 5	H	Blackburn R	W	2-1	0-0	12	Kodjia 2 (1 pen) [58 (p), 70]	29,712
17	18	A	Brighton & HA	D	1-1	1-1	13	Baker [20]	30,107
18	26	H	Cardiff C	W	3-1	2-1	10	Adomah [24], Kodjia [39], Gestede (pen) [90]	31,484
19	Dec 3	A	Leeds U	L	0-2	0-0	15		32,648
20	10	H	Wigan Ath	W	1-0	0-0	12	Grealish [88]	29,392
21	13	A	Norwich C	L	0-1	0-0	13		26,044
22	18	A	QPR	W	1-0	0-0	13	Kodjia [75]	16,285
23	26	H	Burton Alb	W	2-1	1-1	9	Bacuna [15], McCormack [78]	41,337
24	29	H	Leeds U	D	1-1	0-0	9	Kodjia (pen) [86]	37,078
25	Jan 2	A	Cardiff C	L	0-1	0-1	12		21,391
26	14	A	Wolverhampton W	L	0-1	0-1	13		27,255
27	21	H	Preston NE	D	2-2	2-0	12	Adomah 2 (1 pen) [22, 36 (p)]	32,415
28	31	A	Brentford	L	0-3	0-2	14		10,016
29	Feb 4	A	Nottingham F	L	1-2	1-1	14	Kodjia [19]	19,866
30	11	H	Ipswich T	L	0-1	0-0	16		30,796
31	14	H	Barnsley	L	1-3	1-2	16	Kodjia [44]	26,435
32	20	A	Newcastle U	L	0-2	0-1	17		50,024
33	25	H	Derby Co	W	1-0	1-0	17	Chester [25]	30,935
34	28	H	Bristol C	W	2-0	0-0	15	Kodjia [54], Hourihane [59]	28,119
35	Mar 4	A	Rotherham U	W	2-0	0-0	13	Vaulks (og) [68], Kodjia [87]	10,720
36	7	A	Huddersfield T	L	0-1	0-0	15		20,584
37	11	H	Sheffield W	W	2-0	1-0	12	Kodjia 2 [34, 79]	31,143
38	18	A	Wigan Ath	W	2-0	0-0	12	Chester [73], Hogan [84]	14,811
39	Apr 1	H	Norwich C	W	2-0	1-0	11	Kodjia 2 [25, 87]	32,605
40	4	H	QPR	W	1-0	1-0	11	Kodjia [5]	27,154
41	8	A	Burton Alb	D	1-1	1-0	11	Kodjia [3]	6716
42	15	H	Reading	L	1-3	1-1	12	Chester [14]	30,742
43	17	A	Fulham	L	1-3	0-1	12	Grealish [50]	23,891
44	23	H	Birmingham C	W	1-0	0-0	12	Agbonlahor [68]	40,884
45	29	A	Blackburn R	L	0-1	0-0	12		21,884
46	May 7	H	Brighton & HA	D	1-1	0-0	13	Grealish [89]	32,856

Final League Position: 13

GOALSCORERS

League (47): Kodjia 19 (3 pens), Grealish 5, Gestede 4 (1 pen), Adomah 3 (1 pen), Chester 3, McCormack 3, Ayew 2 (1 pen), Agbonlahor 1, Bacuna 1, Baker 1, Gardner 1, Hogan 1, Hourihane 1, Tshibola 1, own goal 1.
FA Cup (0).
EFL Cup (1): Ayew 1.

Gollini P 20	Hutton A 31 + 3	Elphick T 20 + 6	Baker N 31 + 1	Cissokho A 11 + 1	Bacuna L 22 + 8	Gardner G 18 + 8	Westwood A 18 + 5	Ayew J 17 + 4	McCormack R 13 + 7	Gestede R 8 + 10	Tshibola A 5 + 3	Grealish J 20 + 11	Green A 4 + 11	Chester J 45	Traore A — + 1	Kozak L — + 2	Amavi J 26 + 8	De Laet R 3	Jedinak M 33	Kodjia J 36	Bunn M 5 + 1	Richards M 1 + 1	Adomah A 30 + 8	Hepburn-Murphy R — + 3	Agbonlahor G 4 + 9	Johnstone S 21	Davis K — + 6	Lansbury H 17 + 1	Hourihane C 13 + 4	Bjarnason B 5 + 3	Bree J 6 + 1	Hogan S 9 + 4	Taylor N 14	Taylor C — + 1	*Match No.*
1	2	3	4	5	6^3	7^2	8	9	10^1	11	12	13	14																						1
1		3		5	2	13	7	6^3	10^2	11	8	9^1	14	4	12																				2
1		3		5	2	13	7	6	11^1	10	8^2	9	12	4																					3
1		3		5	2	8	7	6	11	10^1		9^2	13	4		12^3	14																		4
1		3		5^2	6		8^1	11	10			9	14	4		13	12	2^3	7																5
1^2		3		5		7^1	8	6	11	13		9		4				2		10	12														6
1		3		5	13	14	7	9	10^3	11^1				4			12	2^2	8	6															7
1		3	4^2	13	5^1		6	11				8		2			9^3		7	10		12	14												8
1		3	4^1		9		6^2	11		13	12			2			8		7	10			5^3	14											9
1		3		5	2		12	10		13	9^2	7		4					8	11			6^1												10
	2	3		5^1			7^3	10	12	13		9^2		4			14		6	11	1		8												11
1	13	3^3	14	5			12		11		8	9		4					7^2	10		2^1	6												12
1	2		4	5^2	7	9		12	14	11^3				3			13		8	10^1			6												13
1	2		4		6	8	14	11^2	13	10^1				3			5		7^3	9			12												14
1	2		4			8	6^1	11^3	12	14				3			5		7	10			9^2		13										15
1	2	14	4			7	13		11^3			9^2		3			5		6	10^1			8		12										16
1	2		4			8^2	6	12				13		3			5		7	11			9		10^1										17
1	2	12	4^3				7	10^2		14		9		3			5		6	11			8^1		13										18
1	2	3				8^2	6	13		10^1		12		4			5		7	11			9^3		14										19
1	2	3			14	6^2		10	12	13		9^1		4			5		7	11			8^3												20
1	2	3					6	9^1	12	14		8^3		4			5		7	11			13		10^2										21
	2		4		9	8^3	14		10^2	13				3			5		7	11^1	1		6		12										22
	2		4		9	7^1		13	10			12		3			5		8^3	11^2	1		6		14										23
	2		4		10		7	8^3	12	14		9^1		3			5		6^2	11	1		13												24
	2		4		10	6^3	7^2		11^1		12	9		3			5				1		8	14	13										25
	2	3			9				10		8^1	12	13	4			5		7^2				6^3		11	1	14								26
	2		4		12	13	7					9^2	10	3			5^3						8		11	1	14	6^1							27
	2		4		12							13	11	3			5			10			9			1		7^1	6	8^2					28
		3	4		12							9■	14	2						10^2			13			1		7^1	6	8	5	11^3			29
	2^3	4^2	5		14								13	3						10			12			1		8	7	9		11	6^1		30
	2^1		4		14							9^3	12	3			5			10			8			1		6^2	7	13		11			31
	2	4			14	13								3					6^2	10^1			12			1		8	9	7^3		11	5		32
	2		4		6■	14							10^2	3			12		7	11^1			8^3			1		9		13			5		33
	2		4			6^3							11^2	3					7	10			9^1			1		8	12	14	13		5		34
	2		4									12^3		3			13		6	11^2			7			1	14	8	9	10^1			5		35
			4											3			10^1		6	11			7			1	12	8	9		2		5^2	13	36
	12	13	4^1			9								3			10		6	11^2			8^3			1	14		7		2		5		37
	6	14				7^2								3			9		4	11			10^1			1		13	8		2^3	12	5		38
	2		4			13							14	3			12		8	11			6			1		7^2	9^1			10^3	5		39
	2	14	4		8								13	3			10^3		6	11^1			9^2			1		7				12	5		40
	2		4		6							13		3			11		7	10^3			9^2			1		8^1	14			12	5		41
	2		4^2		9							13		3			5^1		7	10			11			1		8	6			12			42
	12	3	4			6						8		2			9^3		7	11■				13		1			14		5^2	10^1			43
	2		4		8	13						11^3		3					7				9^1		12	1		6	14			10^2	5		44
	2		4		6	8						13		3						10^2			14		12	1		9^1	7^3			11	5		45
		14	4■		6							13		3			11^3						9^1			1	12	8	7		2	10^2	5		46

FA Cup
Third Round Tottenham H (a) 0-2

EFL Cup
First Round Luton T (a) 1-3

BARNET

FOUNDATION

Barnet Football Club was formed in 1888 as an amateur organisation and they played at a ground in Queen's Road until they disbanded in 1901. A club known as Alston Works FC was then formed and they played at Totteridge Lane until changing to Barnet Alston FC in 1906. They moved to their present ground a year later, combining with The Avenue to form Barnet and Alston in 1912. The club progressed to senior amateur football by way of the Athenian and Isthmian Leagues, turning professional in 1965. It was as a Southern League and Conference club that they made their name.

The Hive Stadium, Camrose Avenue, Edgware HA8 6AG.

Telephone: (020) 831 3800.

Ticket Office: (020) 831 3800 (ext. 1700)

Website: www.barnetfc.com

Email: tellus@barnetfc.com

Ground Capacity: 5,454.

Record Attendance: 11,026 v Wycombe Wanderers, FA Amateur Cup 4th rd, 1951–52.

Pitch Measurements: 102m × 65m (111.5yd × 71yd).

Chairman: Anthony Kleanthous.

Finance Director: Andrew Adie.

Head Coach: Rossi Eames.

Colours: Black shirts with amber trim, black shorts, black socks with amber trim.

Year Formed: 1888.

Turned Professional: 1965.

Previous Name: 1906, Barnet Alston FC; 1919, Barnet.

Club Nickname: 'The Bees'.

Grounds: 1888, Queen's Road; 1901, Totteridge Lane; 1907, Barnet Lane; 2013, The Hive.

First Football League Game: 17 August 1991, Division 4, v Crewe Alex (h) L 4–7 – Phillips; Blackford, Cooper (Murphy), Horton, Bodley (Stein), Johnson, Showler, Carter (2), Bull (2), Lowe, Evans.

Record League Victory: 7–0 v Blackpool, Division 3, 11 November 2000 – Naisbitt; Stockley, Sawyers, Niven (Brown), Heald, Arber (1), Currie (3), Doolan, Richards (2) (McGleish), Cottee (1) (Riza), Toms.

Record Cup Victory: 6–1 v Newport Co, FA Cup 1st rd, 21 November 1970 – McClelland; Lye, Jenkins, Ward, Embery, King, Powell (1), Ferry, Adams (1), Gray, George (3), (1 og).

Record Defeat: 1–9 v Peterborough U, Division 3, 5 September 1998.

HONOURS

League Champions: Conference – 1990–91, 2004–05, 2014–15.
Runners-up: Conference – 1986–87, 1987–88, 1989–90. Division 3 – (3rd) 1992–93 *(promoted)*.

FA Cup: 4th rd – 2007, 2008.

League Cup: 3rd rd – 2006.

FA Amateur Cup Winners: 1946.

sky SPORTS FACT FILE

Barnet narrowly missed out on becoming the first non-league team to gain automatic promotion in 1987–88. The Bees led the Conference table for most of the season but a loss of form in the closing stages saw them win just once in the last six games, allowing Lincoln City to overtake them and win the title by a margin of two points.

Most League Points (3 for a win): 79, Division 3, 1992–93.

Most League Goals: 81, Division 4, 1991–92.

Highest League Scorer in Season: John Akinde, 26, FL 2, 2016–17.

Most League Goals in Total Aggregate: John Akinde, 49, 2015–17.

Most League Goals in One Match: 4, Dougie Freedman v Rochdale, Division 3, 13 September 1994; 4, Lee Hodges v Rochdale, Division 3, 8 April 1996.

Most Capped Player: Luke Gambin 7 (9), Malta.

Most League Appearances: Lee Harrison, 270, 1996–2002, 2006–09.

Youngest League Player: Kieran Adams, 17 years 71 days v Mansfield T, 31 December 1994.

Record Transfer Fee Received: £800,000 from Crystal Palace for Dougie Freedman, September 1995.

Record Transfer Fee Paid: £130,000 to Peterborough U for Greg Heald, August 1997.

Football League Record: 1991 Promoted to Division 4 from Conference; 1991–92 Division 4; 1992–93 Division 3; 1993–94 Division 2; 1994–2001 Division 3; 2001–05 Conference; 2005–13 FL 2; 2013–15 Conference Premier; 2015– FL 2.

LATEST SEQUENCES

Longest Sequence of League Wins: 6, 28.8.1993 – 25.9.1999.

Longest Sequence of League Defeats: 11, 8.5.1993 – 2.10.1993.

Longest Sequence of League Draws: 4, 22.1.1994 – 12.2.1994.

Longest Sequence of Unbeaten League Matches: 12, 5.12.1992 – 2.3.1993.

Longest Sequence Without a League Win: 14, 11.12.1993 – 8.3.1994.

Successive Scoring Runs: 12 from 19.3.1995.

Successive Non-scoring Runs: 5 from 12.2.2000.

MANAGERS

Lester Finch
George Wheeler
Dexter Adams
Tommy Coleman
Gerry Ward
Gordon Ferry
Brian Kelly
Bill Meadows 1976–79
Barry Fry 1979–85
Roger Thompson 1985
Don McAllister 1985–86
Barry Fry 1986–93
Edwin Stein 1993
Gary Phillips (*Player-Manager*) 1993–94
Ray Clemence 1994–96
Alan Mullery (*Director of Football*) 1996–97
Terry Bullivant 1997
John Still 1997–2000
Tony Cottee 2000–01
John Still 2001–02
Peter Shreeves 2002–03
Martin Allen 2003–04
Paul Fairclough 2004–08
Ian Hendon 2008–10
Mark Stimson 2010–11
Martin Allen 2011
Lawrie Sanchez 2011–12
Mark Robson 2012
Edgar Davids 2012–14
Ulrich Landvreugd and Dick Schreuder 2014
Martin Allen 2014–16
Kevin Nugent 2017
Rossi Eames May 2017–

TEN YEAR LEAGUE RECORD

		P	W	D	L	F	A	Pts	Pos
2007-08	FL 2	46	16	12	18	56	63	60	12
2008-09	FL 2	46	11	15	20	56	74	48	17
2009-10	FL 2	46	12	12	22	47	63	48	21
2010-11	FL 2	46	12	12	22	58	77	48	22
2011-12	FL 2	46	12	10	24	52	79	46	22
2012-13	FL 2	46	13	12	21	47	59	51	23
2013-14	Conf P	46	19	13	14	58	53	70	8
2014-15	Conf P	46	28	8	10	94	46	92	1
2015-16	FL 2	46	17	11	18	67	68	62	15
2016-17	FL 2	46	14	15	17	57	64	57	15

DID YOU KNOW ?

Barnet played in three FA Amateur Cup finals, winning the trophy in 1945–46 when they defeated Bishop Auckland at Stamford Bridge. They lost to Leytonstone in the 1949 final (also played at Chelsea's ground) and in 1959 went down 3-2 to Crook Town in front of a crowd of 60,000 at Wembley Stadium.

BARNET – SKY BET LEAGUE TWO 2016–17 LEAGUE RECORD

Match No.	Date	Venue	Opponents	Result		H/T Score	Lg Pos.	Goalscorers	Attendance
1	Aug 6	A	Cambridge U	D	1-1	0-0	9	Nicholls [75]	4873
2	13	H	Accrington S	W	2-0	1-0	2	Akinde, J [33], Akpa Akpro [60]	1501
3	16	H	Blackpool	D	1-1	0-1	1	Akinde, J [90]	1502
4	20	A	Crawley T	D	1-1	1-0	8	Akinde, J [3]	1929
5	27	H	Carlisle U	L	0-1	0-1	13		1620
6	Sept 10	A	Mansfield T	W	1-0	0-0	13	Akinde, J [57]	2523
7	17	H	Colchester U	D	1-1	0-1	15	Weston [82]	2158
8	24	A	Portsmouth	L	1-5	1-1	17	Akinde, J (pen) [27]	16,280
9	27	H	Morecambe	D	2-2	2-1	15	Akinde, J 2 [7, 31]	1164
10	Oct 1	H	Leyton Orient	D	0-0	0-0	18		2682
11	8	A	Doncaster R	L	2-3	0-2	19	Dembele [63], Gambin [86]	4861
12	15	H	Exeter C	L	1-4	1-1	23	Akinde, J [11]	1640
13	22	A	Wycombe W	W	2-0	0-0	20	Vilhete [65], Akinde, J [90]	3596
14	25	A	Newport Co	D	2-2	0-1	18	Akinde, J 2 [76, 85]	2381
15	29	H	Hartlepool U	W	3-2	0-1	14	Akinde, J (pen) [68], Gambin [76], Batt [79]	1690
16	Nov 12	A	Grimsby T	D	2-2	0-2	11	Akinde, J 2 (2 pens) [50, 55]	5519
17	19	H	Crewe Alex	D	0-0	0-0	14		1603
18	22	A	Plymouth Arg	W	2-0	2-0	11	Dembele [7], Akinde, J [45]	7188
19	26	H	Notts Co	W	3-2	1-1	8	Dembele [30], Gambin 2 [64, 74]	1958
20	Dec 10	A	Yeovil T	W	1-0	0-0	8	Nicholls [84]	3254
21	17	H	Stevenage	L	1-2	0-1	10	Akinde, J (pen) [47]	3228
22	26	A	Cheltenham T	W	2-1	1-1	8	Weston [8], Akinde, J [51]	3441
23	31	A	Luton T	L	1-3	1-1	9	Dembele [37]	8262
24	Jan 2	H	Plymouth Arg	W	1-0	1-0	9	Vilhete [14]	3045
25	7	A	Leyton Orient	W	3-1	0-0	7	Santos 2 [63, 66], Weston [90]	4642
26	14	H	Doncaster R	L	1-3	1-3	9	Akinde, J [13]	2582
27	21	H	Newport Co	D	0-0	0-0	8		2623
28	28	A	Carlisle U	D	1-1	0-1	8	Akinde, J (pen) [77]	4547
29	Feb 4	H	Mansfield T	L	0-2	0-1	10		1859
30	11	A	Colchester U	L	1-2	0-2	12	Akinde, J [86]	3606
31	14	A	Morecambe	W	1-0	0-0	11	Champion [65]	1100
32	18	H	Portsmouth	D	1-1	0-0	10	Vilhete [82]	4571
33	25	H	Cambridge U	L	0-1	0-0	12		2396
34	28	A	Blackpool	D	2-2	1-0	13	Akinde, J [13], Clough [47]	2094
35	Mar 4	A	Accrington S	L	0-1	0-0	14		1236
36	11	H	Crawley T	D	2-2	1-1	14	Akinola [39], Campbell-Ryce [88]	1701
37	15	H	Yeovil T	D	2-2	1-1	14	Nelson [30], Watson [85]	1525
38	19	A	Notts Co	L	0-1	0-0	14		7178
39	25	H	Cheltenham T	W	3-1	0-1	14	Weston [70], Akinde, J 2 [77, 79]	1861
40	Apr 1	A	Stevenage	L	0-1	0-1	15		3657
41	8	H	Luton T	L	0-1	0-0	16		3313
42	14	A	Exeter C	L	1-2	0-2	16	Akinde, J [69]	4780
43	17	H	Wycombe W	L	0-2	0-1	16		2507
44	22	A	Hartlepool U	W	2-0	0-0	15	Akinde, J [66], Akinola [71]	4208
45	29	H	Grimsby T	W	3-1	2-0	15	Akinde, J [21], Tutonda [40], Weston [53]	3247
46	May 6	A	Crewe Alex	L	1-4	0-2	15	Weston [64]	4587

Final League Position: 15

GOALSCORERS

League (57): Akinde, J 26 (6 pens), Weston 6, Dembele 4, Gambin 4, Vilhete 3, Akinola 2, Nicholls 2, Santos 2, Akpa Akpro 1, Batt 1, Campbell-Ryce 1, Champion 1, Clough 1, Nelson 1, Tutonda 1, Watson 1.
FA Cup (0).
EFL Cup (0).
EFL Checkatrade Trophy (3): Amaluzor 1, Nicholls 1, Weston 1.

Vickers J 22 + 1	Taylor H 22 + 3	Nelson M 43	Dembele B 23	Johnson E 33 + 3	Watson R 15 + 4	Weston C 36 + 4	Togwell S 11 + 1	Gambin L 13 + 6 / Akinde S — + 1	Gash M 2	Akinde J 46	Akpa Akpro J 7 + 16	Nicholls A 11 + 6	Campbell-Ryce J 23 + 9	Vilhete M 36 + 4	Champion T 22 + 4	Batt S 3 + 8	Muggleton S 5 + 8	Stephens J 18	N'Gala B 9 + 1	Sesay A 2 + 3 / Fonguck W 2 + 1	Amaluzor J — + 11	Hoyte G 2	Kyei N 6 + 6	Tomlinson B 1 + 2	Mason-Clark E 3 + 3	Taylor J 13 + 1	Santos R 15	Akinola S 14 + 5	Sweeney D — + 4	Tutonda D 6 + 1	Coulson L 4 + 7	Clough C 18	Ruben Bover I 10 + 4	Burgoyne H 2	Buchel B 4	Cojocarel S 1 + 2	Shomotun F 3 + 1	Match No.
1	2^{2}	3	4	5	6	7	8	9^{3}	10^{1}	11	12	13	14																									1
1	2	3	4	5	6^{3}	7	8		10^{1}	11	12	9^{2}		13	14																							2
1	2^{1}	3	4	5	6^{3}	7	8^{2}	12		11	10	9				13	14																					3
1	2	4	3	5	7^{1}	9	8			11	10^{3}	6^{2}		12		14	13																					4
	2	4		5	8^{3}	9	7	14		10	11^{2}	6^{1}		13		12		1	3																			5
1		3		5		8	7	9^{2}		11	12	6^{1}	13	2		10^{3}			4	14																		6
1		3		5	14	8	7^{1}	9		10	13	6^{3}	12	2		11^{2}			4																			7
1	2	3	4■	5	8^{1}	7		12		11	9^{3}		10^{2}	6		13			14																			8
		4		2		6	7	13		11	8^{1}	9^{2}	10	5		12		1	3																			9
1	7^{2}	4	3	5		12	8	9		11	14	13	6^{1}	2		10^{3}																						10
1		4	5		7		8^{1}	13		10	11^{3}	14	6^{2}	2			9		3		12																	11
	2	3	4		7	8		14		11	12	6^{3}	10^{1}	5		13	9^{2}	1																				12
1	13	4				10^{3}		9^{1}		11^{2}	12			6	8		5		3	7		2	14															13
1		4			12	9^{2}				11	14	10		6	8	13	5		3^{1}	7		2^{3}																14
1	7^{3}	4	5			12		9		11	14			2	8	13			3				6^{2}	10^{1}														15
	2^{3}	4	3	5^{1}	7	10^{2}				11	12		6	9	8		13	1		14■																		16
		4		9	7^{2}	10		6		11	12			2	8		5^{1}	1	3						13													17
	2^{3}	4	3	5	7^{2}	10	14	9^{1}		11		13		6	8			1						12														18
		4	3	5		8	7	6^{1}		10^{2}	12			2	11		13	1						14	9^{3}													19
		4	3	5		8		9^{3}		10	13	12		6	7^{1}		14	1							11^{2}	2												20
		3	4	5	8^{1}	7		9^{3}		11	13	12		6				1					14		10^{2}	2												21
		4	3	5		7		9^{3}		10	11^{1}	6^{2}	12	2			13	1		14						8												22
		3	4	5		7		6^{1}		11	12	9^{2}	10^{3}	2			14	1					13			8												23
	2^{1}	3		5		7				11			12	6			14	1					9^{3}			8	4	10^{2}	13									24
12	2	3		5		7				11			13	6	14			1^{3}					9^{1}			8	4	10^{2}										25
1	2^{2}	3		5		8				11			10^{1}	7	6^{3}								12			9	4	13		14								26
1	2^{1}	3		5		7				10				6									9			8	4	11			12							27
1		4		5						10	12		6^{2}	9	7								13				3	11■			8^{1}	2						28
1		4		5		8				11			10^{2}	6	7^{1}								9		12		3^{3}				14	2	13					29
1		3	4	5		8^{2}				11			12	10	7						13		9^{3}								6^{1}	2	14					30
1	12	3		5		10^{1}				11			9^{2}	6	8						14						4		13			2	7^{3}					31
1		3		5		9				11				6	8						13						4	10^{2}	12			2	7^{1}					32
		3		5		9				11			12	6	8						13						4	10^{2}				2	7^{1}	1				33
	12	3	5			9^{2}				11			10	6	8												4^{3}	13	14			2	7^{1}	1				34
	2	4	5		14					11			9^{1}	6	8^{2}						12		13					10^{3}				3	7		1			35
		3		5	12					11			9	6^{2}	8												4	10^{3}			14	2	7^{1}		1	13		36
		3	4	14	8					11			9^{3}	6	7						12							10^{1}		5^{2}	13	2			1			37
		3	4^{3}		8					11			9	6	7^{2}												2	10^{1}		5	14		13		1	12		38
		3	4		8	13				11			9		7^{2}			1			14							12		5	6^{1}	2				10^{3}		39
		3	4			10				11			6	12	7^{1}			1			14							9^{3}		5		2	8^{2}				13	40
	2			5		7				11			9	6^{1}				1			13					12	4	14				3	8^{2}				10^{3}	41
	2			5		13				11			12	6				1			14					7	4	10^{2}			9^{3}	3	8^{1}					42
	2			5		8		13		10			6	9^{1}				1								7	4					3	12				11^{2}	43
1	2	3		5		7				11			6		12					14						8^{3}		13				4	9^{1}				10^{2}	44
1	4	3		14		7				10			6		13					8^{3}						9		11^{2}		2^{1}	12	5						45
1	2	3		12		7				11			10^{1}							8^{2}					13	9		6		5^{3}	14	4						46

FA Cup
First Round — Shrewsbury T — (a) — 0-3

EFL Cup
First Round — Millwall — (h) — 0-4

EFL Checkatrade Trophy
Southern Group F — Milton Keynes D — (a) — 2-2
(Milton Keynes D won 5-3 on penalties)
Southern Group F — Norwich C U21 — (h) — 0-5
Southern Group F — Peterborough U — (h) — 1-2

BARNSLEY

FOUNDATION

Many clubs owe their inception to the Church and Barnsley are among them, for they were formed in 1887 by the Rev. T. T. Preedy, curate of Barnsley St Peter's, and went under that name until it was dropped in 1897 a year before being admitted to the Second Division of the Football League.

Oakwell Stadium, Grove Street, Barnsley, South Yorkshire S71 1ET.

Telephone: (01226) 211 211.

Fax: (01226) 211 444.

Ticket Office: (01226) 211 183.

Website: www.barnsleyfc.co.uk

Email: thereds@barnsleyfc.co.uk

Ground Capacity: 23,287.

Record Attendance: 40,255 v Stoke C, FA Cup 5th rd, 15 February 1936.

Pitch Measurements: 100.5m × 67m (110yd × 73yd).

Chairman: Maurice Watkins.

Finance Director: Robert Zuk.

Head Coach: Paul Heckingbottom.

First-Team Coach: Jamie Clapham.

Colours: Red shirts with white trim, white shorts with red trim, red socks with white hoops.

Year Formed: 1887.

Turned Professional: 1888.

Previous Name: 1887, Barnsley St Peter's; 1897, Barnsley.

Club Nickname: 'The Tykes', 'The Reds', 'The Colliers'.

Ground: 1887, Oakwell.

First Football League Game: 1 September 1898, Division 2, v Lincoln C (a) L 0–1 – Fawcett; McArtney, Nixon; King, Burleigh, Porteous; Davis, Lees, Murray, McCullough, McGee.

Record League Victory: 9–0 v Loughborough T, Division 2, 28 January 1899 – Greaves; McArtney, Nixon; Porteous, Burleigh, Howard; Davis (4), Hepworth (1), Lees (1), McCullough (1), Jones (2). 9–0 v Accrington S, Division 3 (N), 3 February 1934 – Ellis; Cookson, Shotton; Harper, Henderson, Whitworth; Spence (2), Smith (1), Blight (4), Andrews (1), Ashton (1).

Record Cup Victory: 6–0 v Blackpool, FA Cup 1st rd replay, 20 January 1910 – Mearns; Downs, Ness; Glendinning, Boyle (1), Utley; Bartrop, Gadsby (1), Lillycrop (2), Tufnell (2), Forman. 6–0 v Peterborough U, League Cup 1st rd 2nd leg, 15 September 1981 – Horn; Joyce, Chambers, Glavin (2), Banks, McCarthy, Evans, Parker (2), Aylott (1), McHale, Barrowclough (1).

Record Defeat: 0–9 v Notts Co, Division 2, 19 November 1927.

Most League Points (2 for a win): 67, Division 3 (N), 1938–39.

Most League Points (3 for a win): 82, Division 1, 1999–2000.

HONOURS

League Champions: Division 3N – 1933–34, 1938–39, 1954–55.
Runners-up: First Division – 1996–97; Division 3 – 1980–81; Division 3N – 1953–54; Division 4 – 1967–68.

FA Cup Winners: 1912.
Runners-up: 1910.

League Cup: quarter-final – 1982.

League Trophy Winners: 2016.

sky SPORTS FACT FILE

Barnsley reached the FA Cup final in both 1910 and 1912 as a Second Division team, winning the trophy on the latter occasion. In the season in between, 1910–11, they finished second to bottom in the table and had to seek re-election at the League's Annual General Meeting.

Most League Goals: 118, Division 3 (N), 1933–34.

Highest League Scorer in Season: Cecil McCormack, 33, Division 2, 1950–51.

Most League Goals in Total Aggregate: Ernest Hine, 123, 1921–26 and 1934–38.

Most League Goals in One Match: 5, Frank Eaton v South Shields, Division 3 (N), 9 April 1927; 5, Peter Cunningham v Darlington, Division 3 (N), 4 February 1933; 5, Beau Asquith v Darlington, Division 3 (N), 12 November 1938; 5, Cecil McCormack v Luton T, Division 2, 9 September 1950.

Most Capped Player: Gerry Taggart, 35 (51), Northern Ireland.

Most League Appearances: Barry Murphy, 514, 1962–78.

Youngest League Player: Reuben Noble-Lazarus, 15 years 45 days v Ipswich T, 30 September 2008.

Record Transfer Fee Received: £5,500,000 from Swansea C for Alfie Mawson, August 2016.

Record Transfer Fee Paid: £1,500,000 to Partizan Belgrade for Georgi Hristov, July 1997; £1,500,000 to QPR for Mike Sheron, January 1999.

Football League Record: 1898 Elected to Division 2; 1932–34 Division 3 (N); 1934–38 Division 2; 1938–39 Division 3 (N); 1946–53 Division 2; 1953–55 Division 3 (N); 1955–59 Division 2; 1959–65 Division 3; 1965–68 Division 4; 1968–72 Division 3; 1972–79 Division 4; 1979–81 Division 3; 1981–92 Division 2; 1992–97 Division 1; 1997–98 FA Premier League; 1998–2002 Division 1; 2002–04 Division 2; 2004–06 FL 1; 2006–14 FL C; 2014–16 FL 1; 2016– FL C.

LATEST SEQUENCES

Longest Sequence of League Wins: 10, 5.3.1955 – 23.4.1955.

Longest Sequence of League Defeats: 9, 14.3.1953 – 25.4.1953.

Longest Sequence of League Draws: 7, 28.3.1911 – 22.4.1911.

Longest Sequence of Unbeaten League Matches: 21, 1.1.1934 – 5.5.1934.

Longest Sequence Without a League Win: 26, 13.12.1952 – 26.8.1953.

Successive Scoring Runs: 44 from 2.10.1926.

Successive Non-scoring Runs: 6 from 27.11.1971.

MANAGERS

Arthur Fairclough 1898–1901 (*Secretary-Manager*)
John McCartney 1901–04 (*Secretary-Manager*)
Arthur Fairclough 1904–12
John Hastie 1912–14
Percy Lewis 1914–19
Peter Sant 1919–26
John Commins 1926–29
Arthur Fairclough 1929–30
Brough Fletcher 1930–37
Angus Seed 1937–53
Tim Ward 1953–60
Johnny Steele 1960–71 (*continued as General Manager*)
John McSeveney 1971–72
Johnny Steele (*General Manager*) 1972–73
Jim Iley 1973–78
Allan Clarke 1978–80
Norman Hunter 1980–84
Bobby Collins 1984–85
Allan Clarke 1985–89
Mel Machin 1989–93
Viv Anderson 1993–94
Danny Wilson 1994–98
John Hendrie 1998–99
Dave Bassett 1999–2000
Nigel Spackman 2001
Steve Parkin 2001–02
Glyn Hodges 2002–03
Gudjon Thordarson 2003–04
Paul Hart 2004–05
Andy Ritchie 2005–06
Simon Davey 2007–09 (*Caretaker from November 2006*)
Mark Robins 2009–11
Keith Hill 2011–12
David Flitcroft 2012–13
Danny Wilson 2013–15
Lee Johnson 2015–16
Paul Heckingbottom June 2016–

TEN YEAR LEAGUE RECORD

		P	*W*	*D*	*L*	*F*	*A*	*Pts*	*Pos*
2007-08	FL C	46	14	13	19	52	65	55	18
2008-09	FL C	46	13	13	20	45	58	52	20
2009-10	FL C	46	14	12	20	53	69	54	18
2010-11	FL C	46	14	14	18	55	66	56	17
2011-12	FL C	46	13	9	24	49	74	48	21
2012-13	FL C	46	14	13	19	56	70	55	21
2013-14	FL C	46	9	12	25	44	77	39	23
2014-15	FL 1	46	17	11	18	62	61	62	11
2015-16	FL 1	46	22	8	16	70	54	74	6
2016-17	FL C	46	15	13	18	64	67	58	14

DID YOU KNOW ?

The Northern Intermediate League was the idea of Barnsley manager Angus Seed. Launched in the 1949–50 season as a competition for former schoolboys aged 15 to 17, the competition ran until a reorganisation of youth football in the 1990s.

BARNSLEY – SKY BET CHAMPIONSHIP 2016–17 LEAGUE RECORD

Match No.	*Date*	*Venue*	*Opponents*	*Result*	*H/T Score*	*Lg Pos.*	*Goalscorers*	*Attendance*
1	Aug 6	A	Ipswich T	L 2-4	0-0	23	Hourihane [49], Watkins [74]	17,370
2	13	H	Derby Co	W 2-0	1-0	12	Carson (og) [11], Mawson [47]	15,049
3	17	H	QPR	W 3-2	1-0	7	Watkins [4], Hourihane [77], Scowen [89]	11,613
4	20	A	Huddersfield T	L 1-2	0-1	9	Mawson [47]	20,001
5	27	H	Rotherham U	W 4-0	0-0	3	Roberts [54], Hammill [57], Bradshaw [86], Kent [90]	15,283
6	Sept 10	A	Preston NE	W 2-1	1-0	3	Winnall [27], Armstrong [79]	11,852
7	13	A	Wolverhampton W	W 4-0	0-0	3	Hourihane [73], Hammill [83], Janko [85], Bradshaw [90]	18,668
8	17	H	Reading	L 1-2	0-2	3	Armstrong [81]	12,675
9	24	A	Brighton & HA	L 0-2	0-1	7		26,018
10	27	H	Aston Villa	D 1-1	0-0	10	Winnall [90]	15,830
11	Oct 1	A	Leeds U	L 1-2	0-1	10	Taylor (og) [70]	27,350
12	15	H	Fulham	L 2-4	2-2	11	Watkins [4], Winnall [41]	11,974
13	18	H	Newcastle U	L 0-2	0-0	14		18,597
14	22	A	Brentford	W 2-0	1-0	10	Armstrong [29], Winnall [67]	10,417
15	29	H	Bristol C	D 2-2	1-0	10	Watkins [21], Hammill [90]	11,869
16	Nov 5	A	Burton Alb	D 0-0	0-0	13		4913
17	19	H	Wigan Ath	D 0-0	0-0	14		12,181
18	25	H	Nottingham F	L 2-5	2-3	17	Winnall [5], Watkins [14]	13,180
19	Dec 3	A	Birmingham C	W 3-0	1-0	12	Roberts [38], Winnall 2 [84, 87]	17,072
20	10	H	Norwich C	W 2-1	2-0	11	Bradshaw [12], Hourihane [40]	12,306
21	13	A	Sheffield W	L 0-2	0-1	11		27,248
22	17	A	Cardiff C	W 4-3	3-1	12	Winnall 2 [19, 32], Scowen [43], Williams [90]	14,754
23	26	H	Blackburn R	W 2-0	1-0	8	Winnall [14], Watkins [90]	14,192
24	31	H	Birmingham C	D 2-2	2-1	9	Bradshaw [24], Winnall [28]	13,397
25	Jan 2	A	Nottingham F	W 1-0	0-0	8	Hourihane [88]	22,105
26	14	A	Fulham	L 0-2	0-1	10		18,010
27	21	H	Leeds U	W 3-2	1-1	7	Bradshaw [45], Kent [48], Hourihane [54]	17,817
28	28	A	Rotherham U	W 1-0	0-0	7	Armstrong [70]	11,050
29	31	H	Wolverhampton W	L 1-3	0-2	8	Roberts [80]	11,808
30	Feb 4	H	Preston NE	D 0-0	0-0	9		12,590
31	11	A	Reading	D 0-0	0-0	10		16,222
32	14	A	Aston Villa	W 3-1	2-1	9	Armstrong (pen) [25], Bradshaw 2 [43, 58]	26,435
33	18	H	Brighton & HA	L 0-2	0-0	9		12,743
34	25	H	Huddersfield T	D 1-1	0-1	9	Watkins [75]	18,075
35	Mar 4	A	Derby Co	L 1-2	0-0	11	James [52]	30,280
36	7	A	QPR	L 1-2	0-1	11	Bradshaw [79]	11,635
37	11	H	Ipswich T	D 1-1	0-0	11	Watkins [58]	11,836
38	18	A	Norwich C	L 0-2	0-1	11		26,105
39	Apr 1	H	Sheffield W	D 1-1	0-0	12	MacDonald [90]	18,003
40	4	H	Cardiff C	D 0-0	0-0	13		10,814
41	8	A	Blackburn R	W 2-0	2-0	13	Roberts [3], Watkins [10]	12,347
42	13	A	Wigan Ath	L 2-3	1-0	13	Armstrong [42], Kent [59]	10,838
43	17	H	Brentford	D 1-1	1-1	14	Watkins [28]	13,935
44	22	A	Bristol C	L 2-3	1-0	14	Mowatt [37], Moncur [64]	18,617
45	29	H	Burton Alb	D 1-1	1-0	14	Moncur [38]	12,952
46	May 7	A	Newcastle U	L 0-3	0-1	14		52,276

Final League Position: 14

GOALSCORERS

League (64): Winnall 11, Watkins 10, Bradshaw 8, Armstrong 6 (1 pen), Hourihane 6, Roberts 4, Hammill 3, Kent 3, Mawson 2, Moncur 2, Scowen 2, James 1, Janko 1, MacDonald 1, Mowatt 1, Williams 1, own goals 2.
FA Cup (1): MacDonald 1.
EFL Cup (1): Scowen 1.

Davies A 46	Yiadom A 31 + 1	Roberts M 40	Mawson A 4	White A 10	Kent R 38 + 6	Scowen J 38 + 3	Hourihane C 25	Hammill A 22 + 15	Bradshaw T 28 + 14	Winnall S 20 + 2	Watkins M 34 + 8	Payne S — + 7	Moncur G 8 + 4	Bree J 18 + 1	D'Almeida S — + 3	Lee E — + 6	MacDonald A 39	Armstrong A 21 + 13	Morsy S 12 + 2	Kpekawa C 4 + 3	Janko S 7 + 7	Jackson A 9 + 1	Williams R 4 + 12	Brown J — + 2	Kay J 1	Jones G 16 + 1	James M 17 + 1	Evans C 1 + 2	Mowatt A 6 + 5	Elder C 5	Hedges R 2 + 6	*Match No.*
1	2	3	4	5	6^2	7	8	9	10^1	11^3	12	13	14																			1
1		3	4	5	6	7	8	9^1	10^2		11^3	12		2	13	14																2
1		3	4	5	6	7	8	9	11^1		10^2	12		2	13																	3
1	14	3	4	5	6^1	7	8	9	10^3		11	12		2^2	13																	4
1	2	3		5	6	7	8	9^1	13	11^2	10	12^3				14	4															5
1	2	3		5	6^2	8	7	9^1		10^3	11						4	12	13	14												6
1	2	3		5	6^2	8	7	9	12	11^3	13						4	10^1			14											7
1	2	3		5^3	6^2	7	8	9	13	11^1							4	10		12	14											8
1	2	3			12	7^1	8	9	14	10^3	6^2						4	11	13	5												9
1	2	3			10	9	8	14	11^3	13	6^1						4	12	7^2	5												10
1	2	3			6^1	8	7	9	13	11	12						4	10^2		5												11
1	2	3			6	8■		9	13	11^3	10^2			14			4	12	7^1	5												12
1	5	3			6		7	9^3	12	11	10^1			2^2		13			8	14		4										13
1	5				9^1		7	13		10^3	6			2			3	11^2	8			4	12	14								14
1	5				9			12		10	6^1			2			3	11	7			4	13		8^2							15
1	5				9^2	12	8	13		10	6			2			3	11^1	7			4										16
1	5	3			9^1	7	8	12	13	10^3	6			2				11^2			14	4										17
1	5	3				7	8	9	12	10^2	6■			2^3				11^1			13	4	14									18
1	5	3			9^2	6	7	13	10	11^3				2			4		8^1		14		12									19
1	5	3			9^2	6	8	12	11^1	10^3		13		2			4		7		14											20
1	5	3			9^2	6	7	13■	10^1	11		12		2			4		8^3		14											21
1	5	3			9^2	6	7		11^1	10	12			2			4		8				13									22
1	5	3			9^2	6	7		10^3	11^1	12			2			4	13	8					14								23
1	5	3■			9^2	12	8		11^1	10	6			2			4		7			13										24
1	5				6^3	8	7	9	11^1	13	12			2			4	14				3	10^2									25
1		3		5	13	7	8	9^1	11^3		6		14	2			4	12					10^2									26
1		3			9	7	8	12	10^2		6			2			4	11^1					13			5						27
1		3		5^2	9^3	8		14	11		6						4	10^1					13			2	7	12				28
1		3			6^3	8		9	14		11^2						4	13					10^1			2	12	5	7■			29
1		3			9^1	8		12	11^2		6						4	10								2	7			5	13	30
1	5	3			14	7^2		9^3	11		10		12				4	13					6^1			2	8					31
1	2	3			9^3			13	11^2		6		7				4	10					14			12	8			5^1		32
1	5	3			9^1			12	10^2		6		7^3				4	11					13			2	8		14			33
1	2	3			9^3	7		12	13		10						4	11^1					14			5	8		6^2			34
1	5	3			12	7^1		9	10^3		6					14	4	11^2								2	8		13			35
1	2	3			9^3	6		14	12		10^1						4	11									7		8^2	5	13	36
1	2	3				8		9	10		6						4	11^1					12			5	7					37
1	2	3			12	8		9^3	11		6^2						4	10^1								5	7		13		14	38
1	5^2	3			10	6		8	11^1		14		12				4	13			2						7		9^3			39
1		3			12	9		10^3	11^1		6						4	13			2					5	8		7^2		14	40
1		3			10^1	9			12		11		7^3				4	13			2					5	8		14		6^2	41
1		3			9	12			10		6		7				4	11^1			2					5	8					42
1		3			11	6			10^1		9		8^2				4	12			2					5	7				13	43
1		3^3			10	6			13		8		7			14	4	11^2			2					5		12	9^1			44
1					9	6			10		11		8^3				4	13				3				2^2	7		12	5^1	14	45
1					10^3	8			11^2		12		9			14	4				2	3	13				6			5	7^1	46

FA Cup

Third Round	Blackpool	(a)	0-0
Replay	Blackpool	(h)	1-2
(*aet*)			

EFL Cup

First Round	Northampton T	(h)	1-2
(*aet*)			

BIRMINGHAM CITY

FOUNDATION

In 1875, cricketing enthusiasts who were largely members of Trinity Church, Bordesley, determined to continue their sporting relationships throughout the year by forming a football club which they called Small Heath Alliance. For their earliest games played on waste land in Arthur Street, the team included three Edden brothers and two James brothers.

St Andrew's Stadium, Cattell Road, Birmingham B9 4RL.

Telephone: (0121) 772 0101.

Fax: (0121) 766 7866.

Ticket Office: (0121) 772 0101 (option 2).

Website: www.bcfc.com

Email: reception@bcfc.com

Ground Capacity: 29,409.

Record Attendance: 66,844 v Everton, FA Cup 5th rd, 11 February 1939.

Pitch Measurements: 100m × 67.5m (109.5yd × 74yd).

Directors: Panos Paviakis, Wenqing Zhao, Chun Kong Yiu, Kai Zhu, Gannan Zheng, Yao Weng.

Manager: Harry Redknapp.

Assistant Manager: Kevin Bond.

Colours: Blue shirts with white trim, white shorts, blue socks.

Year Formed: 1875.

Turned Professional: 1885.

Previous Names: 1875, Small Heath Alliance; 1888, dropped 'Alliance'; 1905, Birmingham; 1945, Birmingham City.

Club Nickname: 'Blues'.

Grounds: 1875, waste ground near Arthur St; 1877, Muntz St, Small Heath; 1906, St Andrew's.

First Football League Game: 3 September 1892, Division 2, v Burslem Port Vale (h) W 5–1 – Charsley; Bayley, Speller; Ollis, Jenkyns, Devey; Hallam (1), Edwards (1), Short (1), Wheldon (2), Hands.

Record League Victory: 12–0 v Walsall T Swifts, Division 2, 17 December 1892 – Charsley; Bayley, Jones; Ollis, Jenkyns, Devey; Hallam (2), Walton (3), Mobley (3), Wheldon (2), Hands (2). 12–0 v Doncaster R, Division 2, 11 April 1903 – Dorrington; Goldie, Wassell; Beer, Dougherty (1), Howard; Athersmith, Leonard (4), McRoberts (1), Wilcox (4), Field (1), (1 og).

Record Cup Victory: 9–2 v Burton W, FA Cup 1st rd, 31 October 1885 – Hedges; Jones, Evetts (1); Fred James, Felton, Arthur James (1); Davenport (2), Stanley (4), Simms, Figures, Morris (1).

Record Defeat: 1–9 v Blackburn R, Division 1, 5 January 1895; 1–9 v Sheffield W, Division 1, 13 December 1930; 0–8 v Bournemouth, FLC, 25 October 2014.

HONOURS

League Champions: Division 2 – 1892–93, 1920–21, 1947–48, 1954–55; Second Division – 1994–95.
Runners-up: FL C – 2006–07, 2008–09; Division 2 – 1893–94, 1900–01, 1902–03; 1971–72, 1984–85; Division 3 – 1991–92.

FA Cup: *Runners-up:* 1931, 1956.

League Cup Winners: 1963, 2011.
Runners-up: 2001.

League Trophy Winners: 1991, 1995.

European Competitions
Fairs Cup: 1955–58, 1958–60 *(runners-up)*, 1960–61 *(runners-up)*, 1961–62.
Europa League: 2011–12.

sky SPORTS FACT FILE

Birmingham City jointly hold the record number of promotions to the top flight having achieved this on 12 occasions, most recently in 2008–09. Ironically when they won the old Second Division in 1892–93 they were not promoted after losing out to Newton Heath in the end-of-season 'Test Match'.

Most League Points (2 for a win): 59, Division 2, 1947–48.

Most League Points (3 for a win): 89, Division 2, 1994–95.

Most League Goals: 103, Division 2, 1893–94 (only 28 games).

Highest League Scorer in Season: Walter Abbott, 34, Division 2, 1898–99 (Small Heath); Joe Bradford, 29, Division 1, 1927–28 (Birmingham City).

Most League Goals in Total Aggregate: Joe Bradford, 249, 1920–35.

Most League Goals in One Match: 5, Walter Abbott v Darwen, Division 2, 26 November, 1898; 5, John McMillan v Blackpool, Division 2, 2 March 1901; 5, James Windridge v Glossop, Division 2, 23 January 1915.

Most Capped Player: Maik Taylor, 58 (including 8 on loan at Fulham) (88), Northern Ireland.

Most League Appearances: Frank Womack, 491, 1908–28.

Youngest League Player: Trevor Francis, 16 years 139 days v Cardiff C, 5 September 1970.

Record Transfer Fee Received: £6,700,000 (rising to £8,000,000) from Liverpool for Jermaine Pennant, July 2006.

Record Transfer Fee Paid: £6,000,000 to Valencia for Nikola Zigic, May 2010.

Football League Record: 1892 Elected to Division 2; 1894–96 Division 1; 1896–1901 Division 2; 1901–02 Division 1; 1902–03 Division 2; 1903–08 Division 1; 1908–21 Division 2; 1921–39 Division 1; 1946–48 Division 2; 1948–50 Division 1; 1950–55 Division 2; 1955–65 Division 1; 1965–72 Division 2; 1972–79 Division 1; 1979–80 Division 2; 1980–84 Division 1; 1984–85 Division 2; 1985–86 Division 1; 1986–89 Division 2; 1989–92 Division 3; 1992–94 Division 1; 1994–95 Division 2; 1995–2002 Division 1; 2002–06 FA Premier League; 2006–07 FL C; 2007–08 FA Premier League; 2008–09 FL C; 2009–11 FA Premier League; 2011– FL C.

MANAGERS

Alfred Jones 1892–1908 (*Secretary-Manager*)
Alec Watson 1908–10
Bob McRoberts 1910–15
Frank Richards 1915–23
Billy Beer 1923–27
William Harvey 1927–28
Leslie Knighton 1928–33
George Liddell 1933–39
William Camkin and Ted Goodier 1939–45
Harry Storer 1945–48
Bob Brocklebank 1949–54
Arthur Turner 1954–58
Pat Beasley 1959–60
Gil Merrick 1960–64
Joe Mallett 1964–65
Stan Cullis 1965–70
Fred Goodwin 1970–75
Willie Bell 1975–77
Sir Alf Ramsay 1977–78
Jim Smith 1978–82
Ron Saunders 1982–86
John Bond 1986–87
Garry Pendrey 1987–89
Dave Mackay 1989–91
Lou Macari 1991
Terry Cooper 1991–93
Barry Fry 1993–96
Trevor Francis 1996–2001
Steve Bruce 2001–07
Alex McLeish 2007–11
Chris Hughton 2011–12
Lee Clark 2012–14
Gary Rowett 2014–16
Gianfranco Zola 2016–17
Harry Redknapp April 2017–

LATEST SEQUENCES

Longest Sequence of League Wins: 13, 17.12.1892 – 16.9.1893.

Longest Sequence of League Defeats: 8, 28.9.1985 – 23.11.1985.

Longest Sequence of League Draws: 8, 18.9.1990 – 23.10.1990.

Longest Sequence of Unbeaten League Matches: 20, 3.9.1994 – 2.1.1995.

Longest Sequence Without a League Win: 17, 28.9.1985 – 18.1.1986.

Successive Scoring Runs: 24 from 24.9.1892.

Successive Non-scoring Runs: 6 from 11.2.1989.

TEN YEAR LEAGUE RECORD

		P	W	D	L	F	A	Pts	Pos
2007-08	PR Lge	38	8	11	19	46	62	35	19
2008-09	FL C	46	23	14	9	54	37	83	2
2009-10	PR Lge	38	13	11	14	38	47	50	9
2010-11	PR Lge	38	8	15	15	37	58	39	18
2011-12	FL C	46	20	16	10	78	51	76	4
2012-13	FL C	46	15	16	15	63	69	61	12
2013-14	FL C	46	11	11	24	58	74	44	21
2014-15	FL C	46	16	15	15	54	64	63	10
2015-16	FL C	46	16	15	15	53	49	63	10
2016-17	FL C	46	13	14	19	45	64	53	19

DID YOU KNOW 

Birmingham City were the first team to win a Wembley cup final as a result of a 'golden goal'. The 1995 Auto Windscreens Shield final against Carlisle United was goalless after 90 minutes and was decided by Paul Tait's strike after 103 minutes' play.

BIRMINGHAM CITY – SKY BET CHAMPIONSHIP 2016–17 LEAGUE RECORD

Match No.	Date	Venue	Opponents	Result	H/T Score	Lg Pos.	Goalscorers	Attendance
1	Aug 6	H	Cardiff C	D 0-0	0-0	10		19,833
2	13	A	Leeds U	W 2-1	1-1	4	Maghoma 15, Morrison 55	27,392
3	16	A	Wigan Ath	D 1-1	1-0	9	Davis 44	11,182
4	20	H	Wolverhampton W	L 1-3	1-0	11	Adams 24	18,569
5	27	H	Norwich C	W 3-0	1-0	7	Davis 22, Donaldson 2 (1 pen) 68 (p), 83	16,295
6	Sept 10	A	Fulham	W 1-0	0-0	4	Donaldson (pen) 49	17,603
7	13	A	Reading	D 0-0	0-0	5		14,602
8	17	H	Sheffield W	W 2-1	0-0	4	Donaldson (pen) 81, Jutkiewicz 90	16,786
9	24	A	QPR	D 1-1	1-1	6	Jutkiewicz 23	13,693
10	27	H	Preston NE	D 2-2	1-2	6	Shotton 30, Adams 68	15,779
11	Oct 1	H	Blackburn R	W 1-0	0-0	4	Gleeson 64	16,781
12	14	A	Nottingham F	L 1-3	0-1	6	Jutkiewicz 71	19,208
13	18	H	Rotherham U	W 4-2	3-1	5	Morrison 15, Jutkiewicz 35, Maghoma 43, Cotterill (pen) 84	16,404
14	21	A	Burton Alb	L 0-2	0-1	5		5818
15	30	H	Aston Villa	D 1-1	0-1	7	Davis 71	25,696
16	Nov 5	A	Huddersfield T	D 1-1	0-0	7	Jutkiewicz 73	20,200
17	19	H	Bristol C	W 1-0	0-0	4	Adams 81	18,586
18	26	A	Brentford	W 2-1	1-0	4	Donaldson (pen) 14, Shotton 63	10,925
19	Dec 3	H	Barnsley	L 0-3	0-1	4		17,072
20	10	A	Newcastle U	L 0-4	0-2	7		52,145
21	13	H	Ipswich T	W 2-1	1-0	7	Donaldson (pen) 41, Morrison 53	15,212
22	17	H	Brighton & HA	L 1-2	0-0	8	Jutkiewicz 52	17,287
23	27	A	Derby Co	L 0-1	0-0	11		32,616
24	31	A	Barnsley	D 2-2	1-2	11	Maghoma 33, Jutkiewicz (pen) 52	13,397
25	Jan 2	H	Brentford	L 1-3	1-0	13	Jutkiewicz 23	18,030
26	14	H	Nottingham F	D 0-0	0-0	12		18,041
27	21	A	Blackburn R	D 1-1	1-1	12	Jutkiewicz (pen) 3	12,035
28	28	A	Norwich C	L 0-2	0-2	12		25,678
29	31	H	Reading	L 0-1	0-0	12		16,672
30	Feb 4	H	Fulham	W 1-0	0-0	12	Jutkiewicz 75	17,426
31	10	A	Sheffield W	L 0-3	0-1	12		24,805
32	14	A	Preston NE	L 1-2	0-1	14	Adams 47	10,233
33	18	H	QPR	L 1-4	0-1	14	Nsue 90	20,265
34	24	A	Wolverhampton W	W 2-1	2-0	13	Kieftenbeld 27, Davis 32	27,541
35	Mar 3	H	Leeds U	L 1-3	0-1	14	Gardner 63	20,321
36	7	H	Wigan Ath	L 0-1	0-1	17		15,596
37	11	A	Cardiff C	D 1-1	0-0	17	Jutkiewicz 89	20,334
38	18	H	Newcastle U	D 0-0	0-0	17		19,796
39	Apr 1	A	Ipswich T	D 1-1	0-0	17	Grounds 48	16,667
40	4	A	Brighton & HA	L 1-3	0-1	18	Adams 85	28,654
41	8	H	Derby Co	L 1-2	0-1	18	Adams 68	19,381
42	14	A	Rotherham U	D 1-1	0-0	19	Frei 73	10,160
43	17	H	Burton Alb	L 0-2	0-1	20		19,794
44	23	A	Aston Villa	L 0-1	0-0	21		40,884
45	29	H	Huddersfield T	W 2-0	1-0	20	Grounds 41, Gardner (pen) 76	26,914
46	May 7	A	Bristol C	W 1-0	1-0	19	Adams 16	25,404

Final League Position: 19

GOALSCORERS

League (45): Jutkiewicz 11 (2 pens), Adams 7, Donaldson 6 (5 pens), Davis 4, Maghoma 3, Morrison 3, Gardner 2 (1 pen), Grounds 2, Shotton 2, Cotterill 1 (1 pen), Frei 1, Gleeson 1, Kieftenbeld 1, Nsue 1.
FA Cup (2): Cotterill 1, Jutkiewicz 1.
EFL Cup (0).

Kuszczak T 38	Spector J 22	Morrison M 30 + 1	Shotton R 43	Grounds J 42	Gleeson S 25 + 4	Davis D 40 + 1	Cotterill D 19 + 6	Fabbrini D 2 + 5	Maghoma J 20 + 7	Donaldson C 16 + 7	Storer J — + 4	Brown R 1 + 7	Tesche R 19 + 5	Kieftenbeld M 33 + 6	Robinson P 13 + 9	Adams C 28 + 12	Stewart G 6 + 15	Solomon-Otabor V — + 3	Jutkiewicz L 31 + 7	Legzdins A 8 + 2	Wiggins R 1 + 1	Dacres-Cogley J 9 + 5	O'Keeffe C — + 1	Gardner C 19 + 1	Frei K 3 + 10	Nsue E 18	Keita C 9 + 1	Sinclair J 3 + 2	Bielik K 8 + 2	Match No.
1	2	3	4	5	6	7^2	8^1	9^3	10	11	12	13	14																	1
1	2	3	4	5	8^1	9^2	7		10	11			12	6	13															2
1	2	3	4	5	9	8^3	7^2		10^1	11				6		12	13	14												3
1	2^1	3	4	5	7	6	8		10^2	11	13■		12			9^3	14													4
1	2	3	4	5		6	13		9^1	10		12	8	7		11^2														5
1	2	3	4	5		6^1	13		9	10^2			7	8		11^3	14		12											6
	2	3	4	5		10	8	14	12	13			7^3	6		9^2			11^1	1										7
	2	3	4	5	7^2	6^1			9	10		12		8^3		11	13		14	1										8
	2	3	4	5	6	8^2			10		14			7	13	9^3	12		11^1	1										9
	2	3	4	5		13	10		9^2			8^3		6		12	7^1	14	11	1										10
	2	3	4	5	7	8^1	6	12	9^3						14	10^2			11	1	13									11
		3	2	5	7	6^3	8	12	10^2	13		14			4	9^1			11	1										12
	2	3	4	5	7		6^3		9	10^1		12		8	14	13			11^2	1										13
	2	3	4	5	7	9^2	8^1		10^3	13				6		12	14		11	1										14
1	2	3	4		8	6	13		9	11				7^3	14	10^1			12		5^2									15
1	2	3	4	5	8	9^1	6^2	12		10				7			13		11											16
1	2■	3	4	5	7^2	9	6^3		13	11^1				8		12	14		10											17
1		3	4	5		6	9^3			11		13	7^2	8	14	12			10^1			2								18
1		3	4	5		9■	6^1			11		14	7	8^3		12	13		10^2			2								19
1		3	4	5	7		10^1			11			6^3	13		9	8^2		12			2	14							20
1	2	3	4	5	8	9^1	6^2		13	10^3				7	14	12			11											21
1	2^3	3	4	5	7^2	8	11						13	6	14		9^1		10			12								22
1	2	3	4	5	6	8		13	10^2					9^1		12	7		11											23
1	2	3	4	5	6	9	13		10					8^2		11	7^1		12											24
1	2	3	4	5		7	8^3		10^2				6^1	12		9	13	14	11											25
1	2	3	4	5	7	8	13	9^1						6^2		11			10					12						26
1^2		3	4	5	6	8^3	7^1							13		10			11	12		2		9	14					27
1		3	4	5		6^1	12						7^2	13		11			10			14		8	9	2^3				28
1		12	3^2	5	7	6^1									4	9	13		10			2		8	11					29
1				4	7	8^1							13	6	3	12			10					9		2	5	11^2		30
1				4	7	8^1								6^3	3	13	14		10					9	12	2	5	11^2		31
1				4	7^2									6		10	13		11			12		8■	9^3	2	5^1	14	3	32
1			4	5							14		8^3	7	12	10	9					3^2			13	2	6^1	11		33
1			3			6							7	8	4■	11	13					2		10^1		5^2	9		12	34
1			3			6							7	8^3	4	11^1			12			2		10	13	5	9^2	14		35
1			3			6^1			14				7	8^2	4	11			13			2^3		10	12	5	9			36
1			3	9		6^1							7	8	4^2	12			11			14		10	13	5			2^3	37
1			3	9	13	6				12			7	8	4				11^2					10^1		5			2	38
1			3	9	13	8^1				12			7	6^2	4				11					10		5			2	39
1			3	4	7				14	11^2			6^3	13		10								8^1	12	5	9		2	40
1			3	9	14	7^2				13			6^3		4	10			11^1					8	12	5			2	41
1			3	9		6			14				7^2	13	4^3	10			11					8^1	12	5			2	42
1^3			3	4		6			14				7			10			11	13				8^2	12	5^1	9		2	43
1			3	5		9			10^2					6^1	4	8	12		11					7		2	13			44
1		3	4	5		6			9					7		10■			11^1			12		8		2				45
1		3	4	5	14	6			9^3	13				8		10^2			11^1					7		2			12	46

FA Cup

Third Round	Newcastle U	(h)	1-1
Replay	Newcastle U	(a)	1-3

EFL Cup

First Round	Oxford U	(h)	0-1
(*aet*)			

BLACKBURN ROVERS

FOUNDATION

It was in 1875 that some public school old boys called a meeting at which the Blackburn Rovers club was formed and the colours blue and white adopted. The leading light was John Lewis, later to become a founder of the Lancashire FA, a famous referee who was in charge of two FA Cup finals, and a vice-president of both the FA and the Football League.

Ewood Park, Blackburn, Lancashire BB2 4JF.

Telephone: (01254) 372 001.

Fax: (01254) 671 042.

Ticket Office: (01254) 372 000.

Website: www.rovers.co.uk

Email: (via website)

Ground Capacity: 31,154.

Record Attendance: 62,522 v Bolton W, FA Cup 6th rd, 2 March 1929.

Pitch Measurements: 105m × 66m (115yd × 72yd).

Finance Director: Mike Chesterton.

Directors: Robert Coar, Gandhi Babu.

Manager: Tony Mowbray.

Assistant Manager: David Lowe.

Colours: Blue and white halved shirts, white shorts, blue socks.

Year Formed: 1875.

Turned Professional: 1880.

Club Nickname: 'Rovers'.

Grounds: 1875, all matches played away; 1876, Oozehead Ground; 1877, Pleasington Cricket Ground; 1878, Alexandra Meadows; 1881, Leamington Road; 1890, Ewood Park.

First Football League Game: 15 September 1888, Football League, v Accrington (h) D 5–5 – Arthur; Beverley, James Southworth; Douglas, Almond, Forrest; Beresford (1), Walton, John Southworth (1), Fecitt (1), Townley (2).

Record League Victory: 9–0 v Middlesbrough, Division 2, 6 November 1954 – Elvy; Suart, Eckersley; Clayton, Kelly, Bell; Mooney (3), Crossan (2), Briggs, Quigley (3), Langton (1).

Record Cup Victory: 11–0 v Rossendale, FA Cup 1st rd, 13 October 1884 – Arthur; Hopwood, McIntyre; Forrest, Blenkhorn, Lofthouse; Sowerbutts (2), Jimmy Brown (1), Fecitt (4), Barton (3), Birtwistle (1).

HONOURS

League Champions: FA Premier League – 1994–95; Division 1 – 1911–12, 1913–14; Division 2 – 1938–39; Division 3 – 1974–75.
Runners-up: FA Premier League – 1993–94; First Division – 2000–01; Division 2 – 1957–58; Division 3 – 1979–80.

FA Cup Winners: 1884, 1885, 1886, 1890, 1891, 1928.
Runners-up: 1882, 1960.

League Cup Winners: 2002.

Full Members' Cup Winners: 1987.

European Competitions
European Cup: 1995–96.
UEFA Cup: 1994–95, 1998–99, 2002–03, 2003–04, 2006–07, 2007–08.
Intertoto Cup: 2007.

sky SPORTS FACT FILE

Despite creating three club goalscoring records during the 1954–55 season, Blackburn Rovers only finished in sixth place in Division Two. The team scored a best-ever tally of 114 goals including a record 9-0 victory over Middlesbrough, while there were also wins over Bristol Rovers 8-3 (when Tommy Briggs netted a record seven goals) and Doncaster Rovers 7-2.

Record Defeat: 0–8 v Arsenal, Division 1, 25 February 1933; 0-8 v Lincoln C, Division 2, 29 August 1953.

Most League Points (2 for a win): 60, Division 3, 1974–75.

Most League Points (3 for a win): 91, Division 1, 2000–01.

Most League Goals: 114, Division 2, 1954–55.

Highest League Scorer in Season: Ted Harper, 43, Division 1, 1925–26.

Most League Goals in Total Aggregate: Simon Garner, 168, 1978–92.

Most League Goals in One Match: 7, Tommy Briggs v Bristol R, Division 2, 5 February 1955.

Most Capped Player: Morten Gamst Pedersen, 70 (83), Norway.

Most League Appearances: Derek Fazackerley, 596, 1970–86.

Youngest League Player: Harry Dennison, 16 years 155 days v Bristol C, 8 April 1911.

Record Transfer Fee Received: £18,000,000 from Manchester C for Roque Santa Cruz, June 2009.

Record Transfer Fee Paid: £8,000,000 to Manchester U for Andy Cole, December 2001; £8,000,000 to Huddersfield T for Jordan Rhodes, August 2012.

Football League Record: 1888 Founder Member of the League; 1936–39 Division 2; 1946–48 Division 1; 1948–58 Division 2; 1958–66 Division 1; 1966–71 Division 2; 1971–75 Division 3; 1975–79 Division 2; 1979–80 Division 3; 1980–92 Division 2; 1992–99 FA Premier League; 1999–2001 Division 1; 2001–12 FA Premier League; 2012–17 FL C; 2017– FL 1.

LATEST SEQUENCES

Longest Sequence of League Wins: 8, 1.3.1980 – 7.4.1980.

Longest Sequence of League Defeats: 7, 12.3.1966 – 16.4.1966.

Longest Sequence of League Draws: 5, 11.10.1975 – 1.11.1975.

Longest Sequence of Unbeaten League Matches: 23, 30.9.1987 – 27.2.1988.

Longest Sequence Without a League Win: 16, 11.11.1978 – 24.3.1979.

Successive Scoring Runs: 32 from 24.4.1954.

Successive Non-scoring Runs: 4 from 14.12.2015.

MANAGERS

Thomas Mitchell 1884–96
(*Secretary-Manager*)
J. Walmsley 1896–1903
(*Secretary-Manager*)
R. B. Middleton 1903–25
Jack Carr 1922–26
(*Team Manager under Middleton to 1925*)
Bob Crompton 1926–31
(*Hon. Team Manager*)
Arthur Barritt 1931–36
(*had been Secretary from 1927*)
Reg Taylor 1936–38
Bob Crompton 1938–41
Eddie Hapgood 1944–47
Will Scott 1947
Jack Bruton 1947–49
Jackie Bestall 1949–53
Johnny Carey 1953–58
Dally Duncan 1958–60
Jack Marshall 1960–67
Eddie Quigley 1967–70
Johnny Carey 1970–71
Ken Furphy 1971–73
Gordon Lee 1974–75
Jim Smith 1975–78
Jim Iley 1978
John Pickering 1978–79
Howard Kendall 1979–81
Bobby Saxton 1981–86
Don Mackay 1987–91
Kenny Dalglish 1991–95
Ray Harford 1995–96
Roy Hodgson 1997–98
Brian Kidd 1998–99
Graeme Souness 2000–04
Mark Hughes 2004–08
Paul Ince 2008
Sam Allardyce 2008–10
Steve Kean 2010–12
Henning Berg 2012
Michael Appleton 2013
Gary Bowyer 2013–15
Paul Lambert 2015–16
Owen Coyle 2016–17
Tony Mowbray February 2017–

TEN YEAR LEAGUE RECORD

		P	W	D	L	F	A	Pts	Pos
2007-08	PR Lge	38	15	13	10	50	48	58	7
2008-09	PR Lge	38	10	11	17	40	60	41	15
2009-10	PR Lge	38	13	11	14	41	55	50	10
2010-11	PR Lge	38	11	10	17	46	59	43	15
2011-12	PR Lge	38	8	7	23	48	78	31	19
2012-13	FL C	46	14	16	16	55	62	58	17
2013-14	FL C	46	18	16	12	70	62	70	8
2014-15	FL C	46	17	16	13	66	59	67	9
2015-16	FL C	46	13	16	17	46	46	55	15
2016-17	FL C	46	12	15	19	53	65	51	22

DID YOU KNOW ?

Blackburn Rovers led the Division Two table by four points on Boxing Day 1984 but failed to get promotion, finishing in fifth position. A poor run of results in the second half of the season including a spell with just one win from nine led to them missing out on a place in the top flight.

BLACKBURN ROVERS – SKY BET CHAMPIONSHIP 2016–17 LEAGUE RECORD

Match No.	*Date*	*Venue*	*Opponents*	*Result*		*H/T Score*	*Lg Pos.*	*Goalscorers*	*Attendance*
1	Aug 6	H	Norwich C	L	1-4	0-3	24	Stokes [67]	12,641
2	13	A	Wigan Ath	L	0-3	0-2	24		12,216
3	17	A	Cardiff C	L	1-2	0-2	24	Graham [77]	14,041
4	20	H	Burton Alb	D	2-2	1-1	23	Conway [25], Gallagher [61]	10,356
5	27	H	Fulham	L	0-1	0-0	24		10,464
6	Sept 10	A	QPR	D	1-1	0-0	24	Gallagher [73]	13,210
7	13	A	Leeds U	L	1-2	0-0	24	Emnes [77]	19,009
8	17	H	Rotherham U	W	4-2	2-1	23	Conway [22], Emnes [29], Marshall [46], Gallagher [90]	10,699
9	24	A	Derby Co	W	2-1	0-0	20	Emnes [70], Graham [73]	26,602
10	27	H	Sheffield W	L	0-1	0-1	22		12,844
11	Oct 1	A	Birmingham C	L	0-1	0-0	22		16,781
12	15	H	Ipswich T	D	0-0	0-0	23		10,820
13	18	H	Nottingham F	W	2-1	2-0	20	Gallagher 2 [11, 44]	10,462
14	22	A	Bristol C	L	0-1	0-0	21		21,452
15	29	H	Wolverhampton W	D	1-1	1-0	22	Gallagher [13]	10,652
16	Nov 5	A	Aston Villa	L	1-2	0-0	23	Gallagher [54]	29,712
17	19	H	Brentford	W	3-2	3-2	22	Graham 2 (1 pen) [15, 20 (p)], Dean (og) [38]	10,506
18	26	A	Newcastle U	W	1-0	0-0	20	Mulgrew [75]	52,092
19	Dec 3	H	Huddersfield T	D	1-1	1-1	21	Graham (pen) [34]	12,034
20	10	A	Preston NE	L	2-3	1-2	21	Graham 2 [22, 70]	14,527
21	13	H	Brighton & HA	L	2-3	0-1	22	Gallagher 2 [66, 90]	9976
22	17	H	Reading	L	2-3	1-1	22	Graham [44], Brown, W [73]	10,982
23	26	A	Barnsley	L	0-2	0-1	22		14,192
24	31	A	Huddersfield T	D	1-1	0-0	22	Graham [81]	21,311
25	Jan 2	H	Newcastle U	W	1-0	0-0	22	Mulgrew [74]	18,524
26	14	A	Ipswich T	L	2-3	1-1	22	Akpan [43], Graham (pen) [74]	15,009
27	21	H	Birmingham C	D	1-1	1-1	22	Graham [45]	12,035
28	Feb 1	H	Leeds U	L	1-2	0-0	23	Bennett [83]	17,026
29	4	H	QPR	W	1-0	0-0	22	Gallagher [90]	10,846
30	11	A	Rotherham U	D	1-1	0-0	22	Kelly (og) [85]	9438
31	14	A	Sheffield W	L	1-2	1-2	23	Hutchinson (og) [20]	24,603
32	24	A	Burton Alb	D	1-1	1-0	23	Palmer (og) [31]	5496
33	28	H	Derby Co	W	1-0	0-0	22	Conway (pen) [58]	10,536
34	Mar 4	H	Wigan Ath	W	1-0	0-0	20	Emnes [58]	13,165
35	7	H	Cardiff C	D	1-1	0-1	19	Williams [90]	10,645
36	11	A	Norwich C	D	2-2	0-1	22	Lucas Joao 2 [73, 78]	26,224
37	14	A	Fulham	D	2-2	0-1	21	Conway (pen) [79], Lucas Joao [90]	15,487
38	18	H	Preston NE	D	2-2	1-1	22	Bennett [43], Conway [56]	18,435
39	Apr 1	A	Brighton & HA	L	0-1	0-0	22		30,216
40	4	A	Reading	L	1-3	0-2	22	Bennett [77]	15,353
41	8	H	Barnsley	L	0-2	0-2	22		12,347
42	14	A	Nottingham F	W	1-0	0-0	22	Hoban [78]	26,279
43	17	H	Bristol C	D	1-1	0-1	22	Gallagher [71]	13,935
44	22	A	Wolverhampton W	D	0-0	0-0	22		20,249
45	29	H	Aston Villa	W	1-0	0-0	22	Graham [54]	21,884
46	May 7	A	Brentford	W	3-1	2-0	22	Mulgrew [10], Guthrie [16], Conway (pen) [83]	11,969

Final League Position: 22

GOALSCORERS

League (53): Graham 12 (3 pens), Gallagher 11, Conway 6 (3 pens), Emnes 4, Bennett 3, Lucas Joao 3, Mulgrew 3, Akpan 1, Brown, W 1, Guthrie 1, Hoban 1, Marshall 1, Stokes 1, Williams 1, own goals 4.
FA Cup (5): Bennett 1, Feeney 1, Gallagher 1, Graham 1, own goal 1.
EFL Cup (7): Duffy 2, Stokes 2, Akpan 1, Conway 1, Wharton 1.
EFL Checkatrade Trophy (2): Feeney 1, Stokes 1.

Steele J 41	Lowe J 43	Duffy S 3	Ward E 6	Henley A 2	Feeney L 21 + 13	Lenihan D 32 + 8	Akpan H 16 + 9	Bennett E 18 + 7	Graham D 28 + 7	Marshall B 22	Greer G 19 + 2	Stokes A 2 + 6	Byrne J 3 + 1	Hendrie S 2 + 2	Conway C 34 + 8	Gallagher S 35 + 8	Wharton S 1 + 1	Hoban T 15 + 1	Williams D 39	Guthrie D 22 + 2	Mulgrew C 26 + 2	Evans C 16 + 3	Emnes M 22 + 13	Samuelsen M 1 + 2	Nyambe R 22 + 3	Brown W 3 + 2	Lucas Joao E 3 + 10	Mahoney C 4 + 10	Tomlinson W — + 1	Raya D 5	*Match No.*
1	2	3	4^{2}	5	6	7	8^{1}	9^{3}	10	11	12	13	14																		1
1	2	3		5^{2}	6^{1}	7			10^{3}	11	4	9	8	12	13	14															2
1	2	3■			14	13	8^{3}		10	6^{2}	4	11^{1}	7	5	9	12															3
1	2				14	12	8		10^{3}	9^{2}	3	13	7^{1}	5	6	11	4														4
1	2				14	12	8		10	6^{3}	3	13			9	11^{2}		4	5	7^{1}											5
1	2						7		10^{2}	9	3				6	11^{3}		4	5		8^{1}	12	13	14							6
1	2				13	14	7^{3}		10^{1}	9	3				6	11		4^{2}	5			8	12								7
1	2					13				6	3^{2}				9^{1}	11	12	4	5	8		7^{3}	10	14							8
1	2					13			12	6	3				9	10^{1}		4	5	7		8	11^{2}								9
1	2^{1}				14	13			12	6	3				9	11^{3}		4	5	7^{2}		8	10								10
1	2					7		14	10^{2}	6	3				9	12		4	5	13		8^{3}	11^{1}								11
1						12	14	13		2	3^{2}				6	10		4	5	7		8^{3}	11	9^{1}							12
1	2				13	3				6^{1}					9	10		4	5	7	12	8	11^{2}								13
1	2					3	13			6					9	11		4	5^{2}	7^{1}	12	8	10								14
1	2					4				6	3	13		12	9	10				7	5^{1}	8	11^{2}								15
1	2				13	4	14		12	6	3				9^{2}	10				7^{1}	5	8	11^{3}								16
1	7				6	3		13	10^{2}	2					9	11			5		4	8^{1}			12						17
1	7				6	3			11	2					9	10^{1}			5		4	8	12								18
1	7				6	3		13	10^{2}						9^{1}	11			5		4	8	12		2						19
1	7				6^{1}	3			10	2	13	14			9^{2}	11			5		4^{3}	8	12								20
1	6				13	4	12		11	2	3■				8	10			5			7^{2}	9^{1}								21
1	7					4	8^{1}		11	2					6	9			5				10		12	3					22
1					13	4■	7		10						6^{2}	9			5		8	12	11		2	3^{1}					23
1					6		7	12	10^{2}		3				9	11			5		4	8^{1}			2	13					24
1	7				6		8		10		3				9^{2}	12			5		4	13	11^{1}		2^{3}	14					25
1	7				6	3	8	9^{1}	11	2						10			5		4		12								26
1	7				6	2	8^{1}	9	11		3				13	10^{2}			5	14	4^{3}				12						27
1	7^{2}				6^{1}	4		9	11		3				12	10			5		8				2		13				28
1	5				6	4	14	7	11^{3}		3^{2}				9^{1}	10					8		12		2			13			29
1	7				6^{2}	3	12	8	11						9^{1}	10			5		4		13		2^{3}			14			30
1	2				14	3	8■	9	10						12	11^{3}			5	7^{2}	4		13					6^{1}			31
1	7				6^{2}	3			10^{1}						9	13			5	8	4		11^{3}		2		12	14			32
1	7				6^{2}	3		12							9	11			5	8^{1}	4		10^{3}		2			13	14		33
1	7				6^{1}	3		14	12						9^{3}	11			5	8	4		10^{2}		2			13			34
1	7				6	3	14		13						9^{1}	11^{2}			5	8^{3}	4		10		2			12			35
1	7				9^{2}	3	13	6	10									4	5	8^{3}			11		2^{1}		14	12			36
1	7				14	3		6^{2}	10^{3}						9^{1}			4	5	8			11		2		12	13			37
1	7				14	3		6^{2}							9^{1}	13			5	8	4		10^{3}		2		11	12			38
1	7				13	3		9							6^{1}	12			5	8	4		11^{3}		2		10^{2}	14			39
1	7				10	3^{2}	8	9							6^{1}	11		12	5		4^{3}		13		2		14				40
1	7							9	12^{3}						14	13		4	5	8^{2}			10^{1}		2	3	11	6			41
	7		3		9^{2}		8	10				12				11^{1}		4	5						2		13	6		1	42
	7		3^{3}		9^{1}		8	10							12	11		4	5				14		2^{2}		13	6		1	43
	8		4			3		7^{1}	12						10^{2}	11^{3}			6	9	5		14		2		13			1	44
	6^{3}		3			2	13	11	10^{1}						12	9^{2}			8	7	4				5		14			1	45
	6		3^{1}			2		11	10^{3}						12	9			8	7^{2}	4		14		5		13			1	46

FA Cup

Third Round	QPR	(a)	2-1
Fourth Round	Blackpool	(h)	2-0
Fifth Round	Manchester U	(h)	1-2

EFL Cup

First Round	Mansfield T	(a)	3-1
Second Round (*aet*)	Crewe Alex	(h)	4-3
Third Round	Leeds U	(a)	0-1

EFL Checkatrade Trophy (Blackburn R U21)

Northern Group D	Fleetwood T	(a)	0-1
Northern Group D	Carlisle U	(a)	0-2
Northern Group D	Oldham Ath	(h)	2-2

(Oldham Ath won 5-4 on penalties)

BLACKPOOL

FOUNDATION

Old boys of St John's School, who had formed themselves into a football club, decided to establish a club bearing the name of their town and Blackpool FC came into being at a meeting at the Stanley Arms Hotel in the summer of 1887. In their first season playing at Raikes Hall Gardens, the club won both the Lancashire Junior Cup and the Fylde Cup.

Bloomfield Road, Seasiders Way, Blackpool, Lancashire FY1 6JJ.

Telephone: (01253) 685 000.

Fax: (01253) 405 011.

Ticket Office: (0844) 847 1953.

Website: www.blackpoolfc.co.uk

Email: secretary@blackpoolfc.co.uk

Ground Capacity: 16,476.

Record Attendance: 38,098 v Wolverhampton W, Division 1, 17 September 1955.

Pitch Measurements: 100m × 64m (109.5yd × 70yd).

Chairman: Karl Oyston.

Manager: Gary Bowyer.

First-Team Coach: Richie Kyle.

HONOURS

League Champions: Division 2 – 1929–30.
Runners-up: Division 1 – 1955–56; Division 2 – 1936–37, 1969–70; Division 4 – 1984–85.

FA Cup Winners: 1953.
Runners-up: 1948, 1951.

League Cup: semi-final – 1962.

League Trophy Winners: 2002, 2004.

Anglo-Italian Cup Winners: 1971.
Runners-up: 1972.

Colours: Tangerine shirts with white trim, white shorts with tangerine trim, tangerine socks with white hoops.

Year Formed: 1887.

Turned Professional: 1887.

Previous Name: 'South Shore' combined with Blackpool in 1899, twelve years after the latter had been formed on the breaking up of the old 'Blackpool St John's' club.

Club Nickname: 'The Seasiders'.

Grounds: 1887, Raikes Hall Gardens; 1897, Athletic Grounds; 1899, Raikes Hall Gardens; 1899, Bloomfield Road.

First Football League Game: 5 September 1896, Division 2, v Lincoln C (a) L 1–3 – Douglas; Parr, Bowman; Stuart, Stirzaker, Norris; Clarkin, Donnelly, Robert Parkinson, Mount (1), Jack Parkinson.

Record League Victory: 7–0 v Reading, Division 2, 10 November 1928 – Mercer; Gibson, Hamilton, Watson, Wilson, Grant, Ritchie, Oxberry (2), Hampson (5), Tufnell, Neal. 7–0 v Preston NE (away), Division 1, 1 May 1948 – Robinson; Shimwell, Crosland; Buchan, Hayward, Kelly; Hobson, Munro (1), McIntosh (5), McCall, Rickett (1). 7–0 v Sunderland, Division 1, 5 October 1957 – Farm; Armfield, Garrett, Kelly J, Gratrix, Kelly H, Matthews, Taylor (2), Charnley (2), Durie (2), Perry (1).

Record Cup Victory: 7–1 v Charlton Ath, League Cup 2nd rd, 25 September 1963 – Harvey; Armfield, Martin; Crawford, Gratrix, Cranston; Lea, Ball (1), Charnley (4), Durie (1), Oates (1).

sky SPORTS FACT FILE

The first Blackpool player to play for England was Harry Bedford who played in the 4-2 win away to Sweden in May 1923. The most recent player to be capped was Alan Ball, whose final appearance for England while on the Seasiders' books was the World Cup final against West Germany in July 1966.

Record Defeat: 1–10 v Small Heath, Division 2, 2 March 1901 and v Huddersfield T, Division 1, 13 December 1930.

Most League Points (2 for a win): 58, Division 2, 1929–30 and Division 2, 1967–68.

Most League Points (3 for a win): 86, Division 4, 1984–85.

Most League Goals: 98, Division 2, 1929–30.

Highest League Scorer in Season: Jimmy Hampson, 45, Division 2, 1929–30.

Most League Goals in Total Aggregate: Jimmy Hampson, 248, 1927–38.

Most League Goals in One Match: 5, Jimmy Hampson v Reading, Division 2, 10 November 1928; 5, Jimmy McIntosh v Preston NE, Division 1, 1 May 1948.

Most Capped Player: Jimmy Armfield, 43, England.

Most League Appearances: Jimmy Armfield, 568, 1952–71.

Youngest League Player: Matty Kay, 16 years 32 days v Scunthorpe U, 13 November 2005.

Record Transfer Fee Received: £6,750,000 from Liverpool for Charlie Adam, July 2011.

Record Transfer Fee Paid: £1,250,000 to Leicester C for D.J. Campbell, August 2010.

Football League Record: 1896 Elected to Division 2; 1899 Failed re-election; 1900 Re-elected; 1900–30 Division 2; 1930–33 Division 1; 1933–37 Division 2; 1937–67 Division 1; 1967–70 Division 2; 1970–71 Division 1; 1971–78 Division 2; 1978–81 Division 3; 1981–85 Division 4; 1985–90 Division 3; 1990–92 Division 4; 1992–2000 Division 2; 2000–01 Division 3; 2001–04 Division 2; 2004–07 FL 1; 2007–10 FL C; 2010–11 FA Premier League; 2011–15 FL C; 2015–16 FL 1; 2016–17 FL 2; 2017– FL 1.

MANAGERS

Tom Barcroft 1903–33
(*Secretary-Manager*)
John Cox 1909–11
Bill Norman 1919–23
Maj. Frank Buckley 1923–27
Sid Beaumont 1927–28
Harry Evans 1928–33
(*Hon. Team Manager*)
Alex 'Sandy' Macfarlane 1933–35
Joe Smith 1935–58
Ronnie Suart 1958–67
Stan Mortensen 1967–69
Les Shannon 1969–70
Bob Stokoe 1970–72
Harry Potts 1972–76
Allan Brown 1976–78
Bob Stokoe 1978–79
Stan Ternent 1979–80
Alan Ball 1980–81
Allan Brown 1981–82
Sam Ellis 1982–89
Jimmy Mullen 1989–90
Graham Carr 1990
Bill Ayre 1990–94
Sam Allardyce 1994–96
Gary Megson 1996–97
Nigel Worthington 1997–99
Steve McMahon 2000–04
Colin Hendry 2004–05
Simon Grayson 2005–08
Ian Holloway 2009–12
Michael Appleton 2012–13
Paul Ince 2013–14
José Riga 2014
Lee Clark 2014–15
Neil McDonald 2015–16
Gary Bowyer June 2016–

LATEST SEQUENCES

Longest Sequence of League Wins: 9, 21.11.1936 – 1.1.1937.

Longest Sequence of League Defeats: 8, 26.11.1898 – 7.1.1899.

Longest Sequence of League Draws: 5, 4.12.1976 – 1.1.1977.

Longest Sequence of Unbeaten League Matches: 17, 6.4.1968 – 21.9.1968.

Longest Sequence Without a League Win: 23, 7.2.2015 – 29.8.2015.

Successive Scoring Runs: 33 from 23.2.1929.

Successive Non-scoring Runs: 5 from 25.11.1989.

TEN YEAR LEAGUE RECORD

		P	*W*	*D*	*L*	*F*	*A*	*Pts*	*Pos*
2007-08	FL C	46	12	18	16	59	64	54	19
2008-09	FL C	46	13	17	16	47	58	56	16
2009-10	FL C	46	19	13	14	74	58	70	6
2010-11	PR Lge	38	10	9	19	55	78	39	19
2011-12	FL C	46	20	15	11	79	59	75	5
2012-13	FL C	46	14	17	15	62	63	59	15
2013-14	FL C	46	11	13	22	38	66	46	20
2014-15	FL C	46	4	14	28	36	91	26	24
2015-16	FL 1	46	12	10	24	40	63	46	22
2016-17	FL 2	46	18	16	12	69	46	70	7

DID YOU KNOW?

Blackpool's matches in the post-war period were enlivened by the presence of the 'Atomic Boys', a group of fans who dressed exotically and followed the team to away games. They brought with them a live duck as a mascot.

BLACKPOOL – SKY BET LEAGUE TWO 2016–17 LEAGUE RECORD

Match No.	Date	Venue	Opponents	Result	H/T Score	Lg Pos.	Goalscorers	Atten-dance
1	Aug 6	H	Exeter C	W 2-0	1-0	2	Vassell [20], Brown (og) [52]	3754
2	13	A	Morecambe	L 1-2	1-1	10	Potts [23]	3676
3	16	A	Barnet	D 1-1	1-0	5	Cullen [24]	1502
4	20	H	Wycombe W	D 0-0	0-0	12		3144
5	27	H	Plymouth Arg	L 0-1	0-0	17		3085
6	Sept 3	A	Yeovil T	W 3-0	0-0	11	Daniel 2 [59, 83], Gnanduillet [87]	3108
7	10	A	Colchester U	L 2-3	1-1	15	Gnanduillet [13], Potts [89]	3077
8	17	H	Carlisle U	D 2-2	0-0	17	Vassell [59], Gnanduillet [74]	5471
9	24	A	Crewe Alex	D 1-1	1-0	14	Guthrie (og) [10]	4185
10	27	H	Portsmouth	W 3-1	1-1	13	Mellor [18], Potts [49], Vassell [65]	3055
11	Oct 1	A	Crawley T	L 0-1	0-0	16		2300
12	8	H	Cambridge U	D 1-1	0-1	14	Taylor [90]	3070
13	15	A	Accrington S	L 1-2	0-0	17	Cain [81]	2754
14	22	H	Doncaster R	W 4-2	2-1	14	Potts 2 [25, 47], Mellor [39], Vassell [48]	3623
15	29	A	Cheltenham T	D 2-2	1-2	15	Vassell 2 [45, 47]	3162
16	Nov 12	H	Notts Co	W 4-0	1-0	9	Vassell 2 [20, 87], Daniel [48], Matt [52]	3443
17	19	A	Leyton Orient	W 2-1	1-0	7	Matt [30], Aldred [57]	4376
18	22	A	Mansfield T	L 0-1	0-0	10		2801
19	26	H	Newport Co	W 4-1	1-1	7	Potts [4], Payne [61], Vassell [72], Mellor [83]	3062
20	Dec 10	A	Stevenage	W 2-0	0-0	7	Samuel [77], Cullen [84]	2513
21	17	H	Luton T	L 0-2	0-1	8		3992
22	26	A	Hartlepool U	W 1-0	0-0	7	Cullen [64]	3767
23	31	A	Grimsby T	D 0-0	0-0	7		5637
24	Jan 2	H	Mansfield T	L 0-1	0-1	10		2948
25	14	A	Cambridge U	D 0-0	0-0	12		4248
26	21	H	Yeovil T	D 2-2	0-1	13	Mellor [70], Delfouneso [90]	2885
27	Feb 4	H	Colchester U	D 1-1	1-1	14	Matt [12]	2772
28	7	H	Crawley T	D 0-0	0-0	14		2080
29	11	A	Carlisle U	W 4-1	1-0	11	Potts [33], Flores [56], Odelusi [83], Delfouneso [86]	6170
30	14	A	Portsmouth	L 0-2	0-1	12		15,132
31	18	H	Crewe Alex	D 2-2	2-0	14	Delfouneso [8], Aldred [27]	3389
32	25	A	Exeter C	D 2-2	2-1	15	Daniel [18], Potts [39]	4125
33	28	H	Barnet	D 2-2	0-1	15	Delfouneso [59], Vassell [90]	2094
34	Mar 4	H	Morecambe	W 3-1	1-0	11	Cullen [14], Potts [54], Edwards (og) [80]	3453
35	7	A	Plymouth Arg	W 3-0	2-0	10	Cullen [27], Potts [30], Flores [62]	10,568
36	11	A	Wycombe W	D 0-0	0-0	9		3774
37	14	H	Stevenage	W 1-0	1-0	8	Cullen (pen) [15]	2456
38	18	A	Newport Co	W 3-1	1-0	8	Samuel 2 [16, 90], Cullen (pen) [68]	2427
39	25	H	Hartlepool U	W 2-1	1-1	5	Samuel [21], Vassell [80]	5374
40	Apr 1	A	Luton T	L 0-1	0-0	8		7968
41	8	H	Grimsby T	L 1-3	1-2	8	Boyce (og) [43]	4668
42	14	H	Accrington S	D 0-0	0-0	8		4300
43	17	A	Doncaster R	W 1-0	0-0	7	Flores (pen) [90]	6914
44	22	H	Cheltenham T	W 3-0	2-0	6	Cullen [28], Delfouneso [34], Danns [62]	3775
45	29	A	Notts Co	L 0-1	0-1	7		7108
46	May 6	H	Leyton Orient	W 3-1	2-0	7	Danns [11], Cullen [36], Taylor [65]	3602

Final League Position: 7

GOALSCORERS

League (69): Vassell 11, Potts 10, Cullen 9 (2 pens), Delfouneso 5, Daniel 4, Mellor 4, Samuel 4, Flores 3 (1 pen), Gnanduillet 3, Matt 3, Aldred 2, Danns 2, Taylor 2, Cain 1, Odelusi 1, Payne 1, own goals 4.
FA Cup (5): Matt 2, Mellor 1, Potts 1, Samuel 1.
EFL Cup (4): Herron 1, McAlister 1, Mellor 1, Potts 1.
EFL Checkatrade Trophy (5): Gnanduillet 2, Vassell 2, Mellor 1.
League Two Play-Offs (8): Cullen 4 (1 pen), Delfouneso 1, Gnanduillet 1, Potts 1, own goal 1.

Slocombe S 34	Mellor K 44	Aldred T 44	Aimson W 15 + 3	Taylor A 38	Potts B 42	McAlister J 18 + 4	Pugh D 18	Samuel B 13 + 18	Philliskirk D 10 + 8	Vassell K 27 + 7	Daniel C 27 + 7	Yeates M 2 + 3	Matt J 14 + 18	Robertson C 44	Cain M 2 + 4	Cullen M 17 + 10	Gnanduillet A 9 + 10	Payne J 32 + 3	Lyness D 12 + 1	Boney M — + 1	Nolan E 1 + 2	Delfouneso N 16 + 2	Odelusi S 1 + 6	Danns N 11 + 2	Flores J 14 + 5	Black I 1 + 9	Match No.
1	2	3	4	5	6	7	8	9^{3}	10^{2}	11^{1}	12	13	14														1
1	2	4		5^{3}	6	7	8	9^{1}		11	12	14		3	10^{2}	13											2
1	2	3	13	5	9	7	8	6			11^{1}			4	12	10^{2}											3
1	2	3		5	9	7	8	6^{1}			10			4		11	12										4
1	2	3		5	6^{3}	7^{1}	8	14		12	9			4		11^{2}	10	13■									5
1	2	4		5	6^{1}	7	8	12		10^{2}	9	13		3			11										6
1	2	4		5	7	8^{1}	6	12	13	11^{2}	9^{3}			3			10	14									7
1	2	3		5	9	8			6^{1}	10	13		12	4			11^{2}	7									8
1^{1}	2	4		5		7			6	10^{2}	14	9^{3}	13	3			11	8	12								9
	2	3	12	5	6^{3}	7			9	10			13	4^{2}	14		11^{1}	8	1								10
	2	3	4	5^{3}	6	8		14	9^{2}	11^{1}	12		13				10	7	1								11
	2	3		5	9	8		12	6^{1}	10				4		13	11^{2}	7	1^{3}	14							12
1	2	4		3	9	7^{3}				11^{1}	6		10^{2}	5	13	12	14	8									13
1	2	3		5	6		8			10	9		11^{1}	4		12		7									14
1	2	4		5	6		8			11	9		10^{1}	3			12	7									15
1	2	3		5	6^{1}	13	8	14		10	9		11^{2}	4			12	7^{3}									16
1	2	3		5	6	12	7		14	10^{2}	9^{3}		11^{1}	4			13	8									17
1	2	4		5	6		8		13		9		11^{2}	3		10^{1}	12	7									18
1	2	3		5	6	13	8	12	14	10	9^{3}		11^{2}	4				7^{1}									19
1	2	3		5	6	14	8	13	9^{3}	10^{1}			11^{2}	4		12		7									20
1		3		5	6		8	12	9^{2}	10			11^{3}	4		13	14	7			2^{1}						21
1	2	3		5	7	8	9	6^{1}	12	10				4		11											22
1	2	4		5	8	7		6^{3}	13	10			14	3	12	11^{1}		9^{2}									23
1	2	3		5	6		8	13	9^{3}	10^{1}			12	4	7	14	11^{2}										24
1	5	3■	2	8	9^{2}	7		12	13	10^{1}			14	4		11^{3}		6									25
1	2	3	4			7	8	6	10^{1}			9^{2}	11	5								12	13				26
1		3	2	9	7^{2}	5^{1}					12		10	4							13	11		6	8		27
1	5	3	2	9						13	14		10^{2}	4				6				11^{3}	12	7^{1}	8		28
1	2	3	5		9^{3}					11^{2}	7		14	4				12				10	13	8^{1}	6		29
1	2	4	3		7^{2}			13		10^{1}	6		12	5				8^{3}				11	14		9		30
1	2	3^{1}	6	5	9			14		10^{3}	7^{2}		13	4							12	11			8		31
1	2		3	5	6			9^{3}	13		8		10^{2}	4		14							11^{1}		7	12	32
	2		3	5^{3}	6^{1}			14		13	9		11^{2}	4			12	7	1			10			8		33
	5	3	2		6			12			9			4		10^{2}	13	7^{3}	1			11			8^{1}	14	34
	2	3		5	6			12			9^{3}		14	4		10^{2}		7	1			11			8^{1}	13	35
	2	6	4	5	8								12	3		10^{2}		9	1			11		13	7^{1}		36
	2	3		5	6^{3}						9		14	4		11^{1}		8	1			10		12	7^{2}	13	37
	2	3	14					11			5		12	4		10^{1}		8	1			9		6^{3}	7^{2}	13	38
	2	3			10			9		14	5			4		11^{3}		8	1			6^{1}		7^{2}	12	13	39
	2	3			10^{3}			9^{1}		13	5			4		11^{2}		8	1			12	14	7	6		40
	2	3		5^{3}	9			11		10^{1}	6		12	4		14		7	1						8^{2}	13	41
1	2	3			6^{3}			9^{2}		10^{1}	5		14	4				8				11	13	7	12		42
1	2	3	4	6	7								14	5		13		8^{3}				11^{2}		9^{1}	12	10	43
1	2	3		5	10			13		12	9^{2}			4		11^{3}		8				6		7^{1}		14	44
1	2	3		5^{2}	10			12		13	9			4		11^{1}		8				6		7^{3}	14		45
1	5	3	2	9	7^{2}					11				4		10^{3}	14	8						6^{1}	13	12	46

FA Cup

First Round	Kidderminster H	(h)	2-0
Second Round	Brackley T	(h)	1-0
Third Round	Barnsley	(h)	0-0
Replay	Barnsley	(a)	2-1
(*aet*)			
Fourth Round	Blackburn R	(a)	0-2

EFL Cup

First Round	Bolton W	(h)	4-2
(*aet*)			
Second Round	Crystal Palace	(a)	0-2

EFL Checkatrade Trophy

Northern Group A	Cheltenham T	(h)	2-1
Northern Group A	Bolton W	(a)	0-1
Northern Group A	Everton U21	(a)	1-1
(*Blackpool won 5-4 on penalties*)			
Second Round North	Doncaster R	(a)	1-1
(*Blackpool won 8-7 on penalties*)			
Third Round	Wycombe W	(h)	1-1
(*Wycombe W won 5-4 on penalties*)			

League Two Play-Offs

Semi-Final 1st leg	Luton T	(h)	3-2
Semi-Final 2nd leg	Luton T	(a)	3-3
Final	Exeter C	(Wembley)	2-1

BOLTON WANDERERS

FOUNDATION

In 1874 boys of Christ Church Sunday School, Blackburn Street, led by their master Thomas Ogden, established a football club which went under the name of the school and whose president was vicar of Christ Church. Membership was 6d (two and a half pence). When their president began to lay down too many rules about the use of church premises, the club broke away and formed Bolton Wanderers in 1877, holding their earliest meetings at the Gladstone Hotel.

Macron Stadium, Burnden Way, Lostock, Bolton BL6 6JW.

Telephone: (01204) 673 673. ***Fax:*** (01204) 673 773.

Ticket Office: (0844) 871 2932.

Website: www.bwfc.co.uk

Email: reception@bwfc.co.uk

Ground Capacity: 28,049.

Record Attendance: 69,912 v Manchester C, FA Cup 5th rd, 18 February 1933 (at Burnden Park); 28,353 v Leicester C, FA Premier League, 23 December 2003 (at The Reebok Stadium).

Pitch Measurements: 102m × 65m (112yd × 71yd).

Chairman: Ken Anderson.

Director: Patricia Anderson.

Manager: Phil Parkinson.

Assistant Manager: Steve Parkin.

Colours: White shirts with blue trim, blue shorts with white trim, white socks with blue and red hoops.

Year Formed: 1874.

Turned Professional: 1880.

Previous Name: 1874, Christ Church FC; 1877, Bolton Wanderers.

Club Nickname: 'The Trotters'.

Grounds: Park Recreation Ground and Cockle's Field before moving to Pike's Lane ground 1881; 1895, Burnden Park; 1997, Reebok Stadium (renamed Macron Stadium 2014).

First Football League Game: 8 September 1888, Football League, v Derby Co (h) L 3–6 – Harrison; Robinson, Mitchell; Roberts, Weir, Bullough, Davenport (2), Milne, Coupar, Barbour, Brogan (1).

Record League Victory: 8–0 v Barnsley, Division 2, 6 October 1934 – Jones; Smith, Finney; Goslin, Atkinson, George Taylor; George T. Taylor (2), Eastham, Milsom (1), Westwood (4), Cook, (1 og).

Record Cup Victory: 13–0 v Sheffield U, FA Cup 2nd rd, 1 February 1890 – Parkinson; Robinson (1), Jones; Bullough, Davenport, Roberts; Rushton, Brogan (3), Cassidy (5), McNee, Weir (4).

HONOURS

League Champions: First Division – 1996–97; Division 2 – 1908–09, 1977–78; Division 3 – 1972–73.
Runners-up: Division 2 – 1899–1900, 1904–05, 1910–11, 1934–35; Second Division – 1992–93; FL 1 – 2016–17.

FA Cup Winners: 1923, 1926, 1929, 1958.
Runners-up: 1894, 1904, 1953.

League Cup: *Runners-up:* 1995, 2004.

League Trophy Winners: 1989.
Runners-up: 1986.

European Competitions
UEFA Cup: 2005–06, 2007–08.

sky SPORTS FACT FILE

Bolton Wanderers recorded their largest ever away win at Villa Park on Boxing Day 1914. The home team played all but the opening minutes of the game with 10 men, but briefly led 1-0 before Wanderers replied with goals from Smith (4), Roberts (2) and Hilton to finish 7-1 winners.

Record Defeat: 1–9 v Preston NE, FA Cup 2nd rd, 5 November 1887.

Most League Points (2 for a win): 61, Division 3, 1972–73.

Most League Points (3 for a win): 98, Division 1, 1996–97.

Most League Goals: 100, Division 1, 1996–97.

Highest League Scorer in Season: Joe Smith, 38, Division 1, 1920–21.

Most League Goals in Total Aggregate: Nat Lofthouse, 255, 1946–61.

Most League Goals in One Match: 5, Tony Caldwell v Walsall, Division 3, 10 September 1983.

Most Capped Player: Ricardo Gardner, 72 (112), Jamaica.

Most League Appearances: Eddie Hopkinson, 519, 1956–70.

Youngest League Player: Ray Parry, 15 years 267 days v Wolverhampton W, 13 October 1951.

Record Transfer Fee Received: £15,000,000 from Chelsea for Nicolas Anelka, January 2008.

Record Transfer Fee Paid: £8,200,000 to Toulouse for Johan Elmander, July 2008.

Football League Record: 1888 Founder Member of the League; 1899–1900 Division 2; 1900–03 Division 1; 1903–05 Division 2; 1905–08 Division 1; 1908–09 Division 2; 1909–10 Division 1; 1910–11 Division 2; 1911–33 Division 1; 1933–35 Division 2; 1935–64 Division 1; 1964–71 Division 2; 1971–73 Division 3; 1973–78 Division 2; 1978–80 Division 1; 1980–83 Division 2; 1983–87 Division 3; 1987–88 Division 4; 1988–92 Division 3; 1992–93 Division 2; 1993–95 Division 1; 1995–96 FA Premier League; 1996–97 Division 1; 1997–98 FA Premier League; 1998–2001 Division 1; 2001–12 FA Premier League; 2012–16 FL C; 2016–17 FL 1; 2017– FL C.

LATEST SEQUENCES

Longest Sequence of League Wins: 11, 5.11.1904 – 2.1.1905.

Longest Sequence of League Defeats: 11, 7.4.1902 – 18.10.1902.

Longest Sequence of League Draws: 6, 25.1.1913 – 8.3.1913.

Longest Sequence of Unbeaten League Matches: 23, 13.10.1990 – 9.3.1991.

Longest Sequence Without a League Win: 26, 7.4.1902 – 10.1.1903.

Successive Scoring Runs: 24 from 22.11.1996.

Successive Non-scoring Runs: 5 from 27.4.2015.

MANAGERS

Tom Rawthorne 1874–85 (*Secretary*)
J. J. Bentley 1885–86 (*Secretary*)
W. G. Struthers 1886–87 (*Secretary*)
Fitzroy Norris 1887 (*Secretary*)
J. J. Bentley 1887–95 (*Secretary*)
Harry Downs 1895–96 (*Secretary*)
Frank Brettell 1896–98 (*Secretary*)
John Somerville 1898–1910
Will Settle 1910–15
Tom Mather 1915–19
Charles Foweraker 1919–44
Walter Rowley 1944–50
Bill Ridding 1951–68
Nat Lofthouse 1968–70
Jimmy McIlroy 1970
Jimmy Meadows 1971
Nat Lofthouse 1971 (*then Admin. Manager to 1972*)
Jimmy Armfield 1971–74
Ian Greaves 1974–80
Stan Anderson 1980–81
George Mulhall 1981–82
John McGovern 1982–85
Charlie Wright 1985
Phil Neal 1985–92
Bruce Rioch 1992–95
Roy McFarland 1995–96
Colin Todd 1996–99
Roy McFarland and Colin Todd 1995–96
Sam Allardyce 1999–2007
Sammy Lee 2007
Gary Megson 2007–09
Owen Coyle 2010–12
Dougie Freedman 2012–14
Neil Lennon 2014–16
Phil Parkinson June 2016–

TEN YEAR LEAGUE RECORD

		P	W	D	L	F	A	Pts	Pos
2007-08	PR Lge	38	9	10	19	36	54	37	16
2008-09	PR Lge	38	11	8	19	41	53	41	13
2009-10	PR Lge	38	10	9	19	42	67	39	14
2010-11	PR Lge	38	12	10	16	52	56	46	14
2011-12	PR Lge	38	10	6	22	46	77	36	18
2012-13	FL C	46	18	14	14	69	61	68	7
2013-14	FL C	46	14	17	15	59	60	59	14
2014-15	FL C	46	13	12	21	54	67	51	18
2015-16	FL C	46	5	15	26	41	81	30	24
2016-17	FL 1	46	25	11	10	68	36	86	2

DID YOU KNOW ?

Jimmy McIlroy had one of the shortest spells on record as manager of a Football League club after his appointment at Bolton Wanderers in November 1970. He stayed just 18 days before resigning, with the club losing both games during his period in charge.

BOLTON WANDERERS – SKY BET LEAGUE ONE 2016–17 LEAGUE RECORD

Match No.	Date	Venue	Opponents	Result	H/T Score	Lg Pos.	Goalscorers	Atten-dance
1	Aug 6	H	Sheffield U	W 1-0	1-0	7	Spearing [37]	17,050
2	13	A	AFC Wimbledon	W 2-1	1-1	2	Madine [34], Trotter [70]	4619
3	17	A	Bristol R	W 2-1	2-0	1	Vela [6], Spearing [26]	9169
4	20	H	Fleetwood T	W 2-1	0-1	1	Madine [51], Vela [84]	13,524
5	27	A	Charlton Ath	D 1-1	0-0	1	Madine [53]	10,926
6	Sept 3	H	Southend U	D 1-1	0-1	1	Anderson [48]	13,519
7	10	H	Milton Keynes D	D 1-1	1-0	1	Beevers [7]	12,727
8	17	A	Walsall	L 0-1	0-1	2		5962
9	24	H	Bradford C	D 0-0	0-0	3		17,486
10	27	A	Rochdale	L 0-1	0-0	7		6011
11	Oct 1	H	Oxford U	L 0-2	0-0	8		14,207
12	8	A	Swindon T	W 1-0	0-0	4	Ormonde-Ottewill (og) [86]	7023
13	15	H	Oldham Ath	W 2-0	1-0	3	Clough 2 [10, 77]	14,891
14	18	A	Millwall	W 2-0	1-0	3	Ameobi [3], Wheater [86]	7898
15	24	A	Bury	W 2-0	1-0	2	Clough 2 (2 pens) [13, 56]	8007
16	29	H	Port Vale	W 3-1	3-0	2	Clough [7], Vela [11], Wilson [16]	13,937
17	Nov 13	A	Peterborough U	L 0-1	0-1	4		4780
18	19	H	Millwall	W 2-0	1-0	3	Vela [17], Thorpe [57]	13,110
19	22	H	Coventry C	W 1-0	1-0	2	Clough [11]	12,290
20	26	A	Northampton T	W 1-0	1-0	2	Clough [25]	7018
21	Dec 12	H	Gillingham	W 4-0	2-0	2	Madine 2 [14, 65], Vela [28], Ameobi [80]	13,861
22	17	A	Chesterfield	L 0-1	0-1	3		6924
23	26	H	Shrewsbury T	W 2-1	2-0	3	Wheater 2 [24, 28]	16,238
24	31	H	Scunthorpe U	W 2-1	1-0	1	Vela [17], Henry [90]	17,062
25	Jan 2	A	Coventry C	D 2-2	0-1	2	Clough (pen) [67], Clayton [90]	8397
26	14	H	Swindon T	L 1-2	0-0	3	Wheater [48]	13,955
27	28	H	Charlton Ath	L 1-2	1-2	3	Clough [13]	13,265
28	Feb 4	A	Milton Keynes D	D 1-1	1-0	3	Spearing [45]	21,545
29	11	H	Walsall	W 4-1	3-1	3	Madine [15], O'Connor (og) [26], Trotter [30], Long [87]	13,610
30	14	H	Rochdale	W 1-0	0-0	3	Beevers [82]	13,313
31	18	A	Bradford C	D 2-2	0-2	3	Wheater [62], Madine [74]	21,190
32	25	A	Sheffield U	L 0-2	0-1	4		27,165
33	28	H	Bristol R	D 1-1	1-0	4	Vela [7]	13,383
34	Mar 4	H	AFC Wimbledon	D 1-1	1-1	4	Madine [15]	13,599
35	11	A	Fleetwood T	W 4-2	2-1	3	Le Fondre 2 [17, 78], Wheater [20], Beevers [48]	5123
36	14	A	Gillingham	W 4-0	3-0	3	Wheater [3], Le Fondre [15], Beevers [45], Vela [49]	5199
37	18	H	Northampton T	W 2-1	0-0	2	Le Fondre (pen) [75], Morais [82]	14,255
38	21	A	Oxford U	W 4-2	2-1	2	Morais [4], Beevers [23], Dunkley (og) [60], Vela [90]	7146
39	25	A	Shrewsbury T	W 2-0	0-0	2	Beevers [51], Le Fondre [66]	7532
40	Apr 1	H	Chesterfield	D 0-0	0-0	2		23,376
41	4	A	Southend U	W 1-0	0-0	2	Beevers [90]	9340
42	8	A	Scunthorpe U	L 0-1	0-1	2		6149
43	15	A	Oldham Ath	L 0-1	0-0	2		8788
44	18	H	Bury	D 0-0	0-0	2		18,223
45	22	A	Port Vale	W 2-0	0-0	2	Wheater [66], Madine [82]	8890
46	30	H	Peterborough U	W 3-0	1-0	2	Karacan [22], Wheater [53], Le Fondre [75]	22,590

Final League Position: 2

GOALSCORERS

League (68): Clough 9 (3 pens), Madine 9, Vela 9, Wheater 9, Beevers 7, Le Fondre 6 (1 pen), Spearing 3, Ameobi 2, Morais 2, Trotter 2, Anderson 1, Clayton 1, Henry 1, Karacan 1, Long 1, Thorpe 1, Wilson 1, own goals 3.
FA Cup (5): Ameobi 1, Henry 1, Madine 1, Trotter 1, Vela 1.
EFL Cup (2): Proctor 1, Woolery 1.
EFL Checkatrade Trophy (1): Ameobi 1.

Howard M 26 + 1	Wilson L 18	Beevers M 45	Wheater D 43	Moxey D 16 + 3	Taylor C 3 + 13	Spearing J 36 + 1	Vela J 45 + 1	Buxton L 9	Pratley D 11 + 1	Madine G 36	Davies M 4 + 1	Proctor J 7 + 14	Trotter L 17 + 3	Clough Z 17 + 6	Taylor A 31 + 3	Wilkinson C 2 + 7	Woolery K — + 1	Henry J 12 + 18	Anderson K 3 + 5	Ameobi S 15 + 5	Thorpe T 16 + 5	Osede D 19 + 6	Alnwick B 20 + 1	Clayton M — + 10	Morais F 19	Long C 3 + 7	Solomon-Otabor V — + 4	Le Fondre A 17 + 2	Dervite D 13 + 1	Wabara R 1	Karacan J 2 + 3	*Match No.*
1	2	3	4	5	6^{2}	7^{3}	8	9	10	11^{1}	12	13	14																			1
1		4	3	5	13	7	8^{1}	2		10	9^{2}	11	6^{3}	12	14																	2
1		4	3	5	12	6	9	2		10^{1}	8	11^{2}	7^{3}	13		14																3
1		4	3	5		7	6	2		11^{2}	10		8	9^{1}		13	12															4
1		4	3	5	12	8	7	2		10^{1}	9^{3}	11^{2}	6		13	14																5
1		3	4	5^{3}		8	7	2		11^{2}		12	9		14			6^{1}	10	13												6
1		4	3		13	6	7^{2}	2				11	8		5			9^{3}	10^{1}	12	14											7
1		3	4	14	9^{1}		7	2^{3}				11	8	12	5^{2}			6	13■	10												8
1		4	3	5	14	6	8	2				10	7^{3}	13				9^{1}		11^{2}	12											9
1	2^{3}		4	5	8^{1}	6	14					10	9	12				7	11^{2}	13	3											10
1		3	4	5		6	2			11^{1}		14	9	10^{3}	8			7^{2}	13	12												11
1	5	4	3			6	7			11^{3}		13		9^{2}	10			8^{1}	14	12	2											12
1	2	4	3			7	8			11^{2}		12		10	5			14		9^{1}	6^{3}	13										13
1	5	3	4			7	10			11		14		6^{2}	2			13		9^{3}	8^{1}	12										14
1	2	4	3		14	7	10			11^{3}		12		9^{1}	5			13		6^{2}		8										15
1	2	4	3		12		8^{2}			10			7	11	5			13		9^{1}		6										16
1^{3}	6	3	4		13		7			10			8	11	5			14		9^{1}	2^{2}		12									17
	2	3				6	7			11^{2}		14	8^{3}	10^{1}	5			13		9	12	4	1									18
	2	4			13	6	8			11^{1}		14		10^{2}	5			12		9^{3}	7	3	1									19
	2	4			14	7	8			11^{2}		13		10^{1}	5			12		9^{3}	6	3	1									20
	2	4	3		12	6	8^{2}			11				10^{1}	5			13	14	9^{3}	7		1									21
	2^{1}	3	4		12	8	7			11		14		10^{2}	5				13	6	9^{3}		1									22
	2	4	3		13	6^{2}	7			10				11^{1}	5					9	8	12	1									23
	2^{1}	4	3			6	9			11				10^{2}	5			13		8	7	12	1									24
		4	3			6	9			11		14	7^{1}	12	5			8^{2}		10		2^{3}	1	13								25
	2^{2}	4	3			6	9			11		13		10	5			8			7^{1}		1	12								26
	2	4^{1}	3			6	9			11		14		10	5	13		8^{2}			7^{3}		1	12								27
	2	4	3	5		6	9			11												7^{2}	1	12	8^{1}	10^{3}	13	14				28
		4	3			8	10			11			7^{3}		5						13	2	1		6^{2}	12	14	9^{1}				29
		4	3	12		7	8			11			6^{3}		9^{1}						14	2	1		5	13		10^{2}				30
		3	2	5^{3}			7			10			6^{2}			14		13			8	4	1		9		12	11^{1}				31
1		4	3	9			7									11^{2}		5			8^{1}	2		14	6	13		10^{3}	12			32
1		3	4			7^{2}	9						12		5			8^{3}				6			10	11■	13	14		2^{1}		33
		4	2				7			10					9			12			8^{1}	6	1		5			11	3			34
		3	4				8^{1}		7^{2}	10			13		9							6	1		5			11	2		12	35
		4	3				8		7^{2}	10^{3}					9			14				6	1	13	5^{1}			11	2		12	36
		3	2			12	7		8	10					9							6^{1}	1		5			11	4			37
		4	3			6^{1}	9		7^{3}	10					8							14	1		5	12		11^{2}	2		13	38
14		2	3	13			8		6	11^{2}					9^{3}							7	1^{1}		5	12		10	4			39
1		3	4	9^{2}		6	7		8									13						12	5	11^{1}		10	2			40
1		3	4	9		6	7		8	11^{1}														12	5			10	2			41
1		4	3	9		6	7		8^{1}							11^{2}		12						13	5			10	2			42
1		2	3	9^{1}		7	10		6^{2}									13				8^{3}		12	5	14		11	4			43
1		3	4			9	10		7^{2}						6			12				8^{1}			2	13		11	5			44
1		3	2			7^{1}	8			11^{2}					4	14		12				13			5			10	6		9^{3}	45
1		3	2			7	9		12	10^{1}					8	13									5			11	4		6^{2}	46

FA Cup

First Round	Grimsby T	(h)	1-0
Second Round	Sheffield U	(h)	3-2
Third Round	Crystal Palace	(h)	0-0
Replay	Crystal Palace	(a)	1-2

EFL Cup

First Round (*aet*)	Blackpool	(a)	2-4

EFL Checkatrade Trophy

Northern Group A	Everton U21	(h)	0-2
Northern Group A	Blackpool	(h)	1-0
Northern Group A	Cheltenham T	(a)	0-1

AFC BOURNEMOUTH

FOUNDATION

There was a Bournemouth FC as early as 1875, but the present club arose out of the remnants of the Boscombe St John's club (formed 1890). The meeting at which Boscombe FC came into being was held at a house in Gladstone Road in 1899. They began by playing in the Boscombe and District Junior League.

Vitality Stadium, Dean Court, Kings Park, Bournemouth, Dorset BH7 7AF.

Telephone: (0344) 576 1910.

Fax: (01202) 726 373.

Ticket Office: (0344) 576 1910.

Website: www.afcb.co.uk

Email: enquiries@afcb.co.uk

Ground Capacity: 11,464.

Record Attendance: 28,799 v Manchester U, FA Cup 6th rd, 2 March 1957.

Pitch Measurements: 105m × 68m (115yd × 74.5yd).

Chairman: Jeff Mostyn.

Chief Executive: Neill Blake.

Manager: Eddie Howe.

Assistant Manager: Jason Tindall.

Colours: Red and black striped shirts, black shorts with red trim, black socks with red trim.

Year Formed: 1899.

Turned Professional: 1910.

Previous Names: 1890, Boscombe St John's; 1899, Boscombe FC; 1923, Bournemouth & Boscombe Ath FC; 1972, AFC Bournemouth.

Club Nickname: 'Cherries'.

Grounds: 1899, Castlemain Road, Pokesdown; 1910, Dean Court (renamed Fitness First Stadium 2001, Seward Stadium 2011, Goldsands Stadium 2012, Vitality Stadium 2015).

First Football League Game: 25 August 1923, Division 3 (S), v Swindon T (a) L 1–3 – Heron; Wingham, Lamb; Butt, Charles Smith, Voisey; Miller, Lister (1), Davey, Simpson, Robinson.

Record League Victory: 8–0 v Birmingham C, FL C, 25 October 2014 – Boruc; Francis, Elphick, Cook, Daniels; Ritchie (1), Arter (Gosling), Surman, Pugh (3); Pitman (1) (Rantie 2 (1 pen)), Wilson (1) (Fraser). 10–0 win v Northampton T at start of 1939–40 expunged from the records on outbreak of war.

Record Cup Victory: 11–0 v Margate, FA Cup 1st rd, 20 November 1971 – Davies; Machin (1), Kitchener, Benson, Jones, Powell, Cave (1), Boyer, MacDougall (9 incl. 1p), Miller, Scott (De Garis).

Record Defeat: 0–9 v Lincoln C, Division 3, 18 December 1982.

HONOURS

League Champions: FL C – 2014–15; Division 3 – 1986–87.
Runners-up: FL 1 – 2012–13; Division 3S – 1947–48; FL 2 – 2009–10; Division 4 – 1970–71.

FA Cup: 6th rd – 1957.

League Cup: quarter-final – 2015.

League Trophy Winners: 1984.
Runners-up: 1998.

sky SPORTS FACT FILE

Goalkeeper Tommy Godwin made 178 consecutive Football League appearances for Bournemouth between January 1953 and November 1956, a run of almost four years without an absence. He also won five caps for the Republic of Ireland during his time at Dean Court.

Most League Points (2 for a win): 62, Division 3, 1971–72.

Most League Points (3 for a win): 97, Division 3, 1986–87.

Most League Goals: 98, FL C, 2014–15.

Highest League Scorer in Season: Ted MacDougall, 42, 1970–71.

Most League Goals in Total Aggregate: Ron Eyre, 202, 1924–33.

Most League Goals in One Match: 4, Jack Russell v Clapton Orient, Division 3 (S), 7 January 1933; 4, Jack Russell v Bristol C, Division 3 (S), 28 January 1933; 4, Harry Mardon v Southend U, Division 3 (S), 1 January 1938; 4, Jack McDonald v Torquay U, Division 3 (S), 8 November 1947; 4, Ted MacDougall v Colchester U, 18 September 1970; 4, Brian Clark v Rotherham U, 10 October 1972; 4, Luther Blissett v Hull C, 29 November 1988; 4, James Hayter v Bury, Division 2, 21 October 2000.

Most Capped Player: Tokelo Rantie, 24 (38), South Africa.

Most League Appearances: Steve Fletcher, 628, 1992–2007; 2008–13.

Youngest League Player: Jimmy White, 15 years 321 days v Brentford, 30 April 1958.

Record Transfer Fee Received: £12,000,000 from Newcastle U for Matt Ritchie, July 2016.

Record Transfer Fee Paid: £20,000,000 to Chelsea for Nathan Ake, June 2017.

Football League Record: 1923 Elected to Division 3 (S) and remained a Third Division club for record number of years until 1970; 1970–71 Division 4; 1971–75 Division 3; 1975–82 Division 4; 1982–87 Division 3; 1987–90 Division 2; 1990–92 Division 3; 1992–2002 Division 2; 2002–03 Division 3; 2003–04 Division 2; 2004–08 FL 1; 2008–10 FL 2; 2010–13 FL 1; 2013–15 FL C; 2015– FA Premier League.

MANAGERS

Vincent Kitcher 1914–23
(*Secretary-Manager*)
Harry Kinghorn 1923–25
Leslie Knighton 1925–28
Frank Richards 1928–30
Billy Birrell 1930–35
Bob Crompton 1935–36
Charlie Bell 1936–39
Harry Kinghorn 1939–47
Harry Lowe 1947–50
Jack Bruton 1950–56
Fred Cox 1956–58
Don Welsh 1958–61
Bill McGarry 1961–63
Reg Flewin 1963–65
Fred Cox 1965–70
John Bond 1970–73
Trevor Hartley 1974–75
John Benson 1975–78
Alec Stock 1979–80
David Webb 1980–82
Don Megson 1983
Harry Redknapp 1983–92
Tony Pulis 1992–94
Mel Machin 1994–2000
Sean O'Driscoll 2000–06
Kevin Bond 2006–08
Jimmy Quinn 2008
Eddie Howe 2008–11
Lee Bradbury 2011–12
Paul Groves 2012
Eddie Howe October 2012–

LATEST SEQUENCES

Longest Sequence of League Wins: 8, 12.3.2013 – 20.4.2013.

Longest Sequence of League Defeats: 7, 13.8.1994 – 13.9.1994.

Longest Sequence of League Draws: 5, 25.4.2000 – 19.8.2000.

Longest Sequence of Unbeaten League Matches: 18, 6.3.1982 – 28.8.1982.

Longest Sequence Without a League Win: 14, 6.3.1974 – 27.4.1974.

Successive Scoring Runs: 31 from 28.10.2000.

Successive Non-scoring Runs: 6 from 1.2.1975.

TEN YEAR LEAGUE RECORD

		P	W	D	L	F	A	Pts	Pos
2007-08	FL 1	46	17	7	22	62	72	48*	21
2008-09	FL 2	46	17	12	17	59	51	46†	21
2009-10	FL 2	46	25	8	13	61	44	83	2
2010-11	FL 1	46	19	14	13	75	54	71	6
2011-12	FL 1	46	15	13	18	48	52	58	11
2012-13	FL 1	46	24	11	11	76	53	83	2
2013-14	FL C	46	18	12	16	67	66	66	10
2014-15	FL C	46	26	12	8	98	45	90	1
2015-16	PR Lge	38	11	9	18	45	67	42	16
2016-17	PR Lge	38	12	10	16	55	67	46	9

**10 pts deducted; †17 pts deducted.*

DID YOU KNOW ?

Bournemouth made their first trip abroad in October 1927 when they travelled to Rotterdam to play the Netherlands national team. The Cherries lost 1-0 in a match played at the Sparta ground, which acted as a warm up for the hosts' forthcoming fixture against France.

AFC BOURNEMOUTH – PREMIER LEAGUE 2016–17 LEAGUE RECORD

Match No.	Date	Venue	Opponents	Result	H/T Score	Lg Pos.	Goalscorers	Attendance
1	Aug 14	H	Manchester U	L 1-3	0-1	20	Smith, A [69]	11,355
2	21	A	West Ham U	L 0-1	0-0	20		56,977
3	27	A	Crystal Palace	D 1-1	1-0	18	King [11]	23,503
4	Sept 10	H	WBA	W 1-0	0-0	12	Wilson, C [79]	11,184
5	17	A	Manchester C	L 0-4	0-2	16		54,335
6	24	H	Everton	W 1-0	1-0	13	Stanislas [23]	11,291
7	Oct 1	A	Watford	D 2-2	1-0	12	Wilson, C [31], King [62]	20,575
8	15	H	Hull C	W 6-1	3-1	9	Daniels [5], Cook, S [41], Stanislas 2 (1 pen) [45 (p), 65], Wilson, C [83], Gosling [88]	11,029
9	22	H	Tottenham H	D 0-0	0-0	9		11,201
10	29	A	Middlesbrough	L 0-2	0-1	10		29,600
11	Nov 5	H	Sunderland	L 1-2	1-1	11	Gosling [11]	11,084
12	19	A	Stoke C	W 1-0	1-0	8	Ake [26]	27,815
13	27	A	Arsenal	L 1-3	1-1	10	Wilson, C (pen) [23]	59,978
14	Dec 4	H	Liverpool	W 4-3	0-2	10	Wilson, C (pen) [56], Fraser [76], Cook, S [78], Ake [90]	11,183
15	10	A	Burnley	L 2-3	1-2	10	Afobe [45], Daniels [90]	19,680
16	13	H	Leicester C	W 1-0	1-0	8	Pugh [34]	11,068
17	18	H	Southampton	L 1-3	1-1	10	Ake [6]	11,113
18	26	A	Chelsea	L 0-3	0-1	11		41,384
19	31	A	Swansea C	W 3-0	2-0	10	Afobe [25], Fraser [45], King [88]	20,316
20	Jan 3	H	Arsenal	D 3-3	2-0	9	Daniels [16], Wilson, C (pen) [20], Fraser [58]	11,202
21	14	A	Hull C	L 1-3	1-1	10	Stanislas (pen) [3]	17,963
22	21	H	Watford	D 2-2	0-1	10	King [48], Afobe [82]	11,123
23	31	H	Crystal Palace	L 0-2	0-0	14		11,286
24	Feb 4	A	Everton	L 3-6	0-3	14	King 2 [59, 70], Arter [90]	39,026
25	13	H	Manchester C	L 0-2	0-1	14		11,129
26	25	A	WBA	L 1-2	1-2	14	King (pen) [5]	24,162
27	Mar 4	A	Manchester U	D 1-1	1-1	14	King (pen) [40]	75,245
28	11	H	West Ham U	W 3-2	1-1	14	King 3 [31, 48, 90]	11,369
29	18	H	Swansea C	W 2-0	1-0	12	Mawson (og) [31], Afobe [72]	11,240
30	Apr 1	A	Southampton	D 0-0	0-0	11		31,847
31	5	A	Liverpool	D 2-2	1-1	12	Afobe [7], King [87]	53,292
32	8	H	Chelsea	L 1-3	1-2	14	King [42]	11,283
33	15	A	Tottenham H	L 0-4	0-2	16		31,943
34	22	H	Middlesbrough	W 4-0	2-0	12	King [2], Afobe [16], Pugh [65], Daniels [70]	10,890
35	29	A	Sunderland	W 1-0	0-0	10	King [88]	38,394
36	May 6	H	Stoke C	D 2-2	0-1	10	Stanislas [62], Shawcross (og) [81]	11,046
37	13	H	Burnley	W 2-1	1-0	9	Stanislas [25], King [85]	11,388
38	21	A	Leicester C	D 1-1	1-0	9	Stanislas [1]	32,000

Final League Position: 9

GOALSCORERS

League (55): King 16 (2 pens), Stanislas 7 (2 pens), Afobe 6, Wilson, C 6 (3 pens), Daniels 4, Ake 3, Fraser 3, Cook, S 2, Gosling 2, Pugh 2, Arter 1, Smith, A 1, own goals 2.
FA Cup (0).
EFL Cup (4): Gosling 1, Grabban 1 (1 pen), Gradel 1, Wilson, M 1.

Boruc A 35	Smith A 34 + 2	Francis S 34	Cook S 38	Daniels C 34	Cook L 4 + 2	Surman A 21 + 1	Arter H 33 + 2	Ibe J 13 + 12	Wilson C 16 + 4	King J 31 + 5	Grabban L — + 3	Afobe B 14 + 17	Gradel M — + 11	Fraser R 19 + 9	Ake N 8 + 2	Gosling D 14 + 13	Stanislas J 18 + 3	Wilshere J 22 + 5	Mousset L 3 + 8	Federici A 2	Pugh M 16 + 5	Smith B 3 + 2	Mings T 5 + 2	Cargill B — + 1	Allsop R 1	Worthington M — + 1	Match No.
1	2	3	4	5	6¹	7	8	9²	10³	11	12	13	14														1
1	2	3	4	5		8	7■	6²	11¹	10	12			9³	13	14											2
1	2	3	4	5		6	7	9³	10²	11	13			8¹	14	12											3
1	2	3	4	5		8	7	6³	11	10²			13			14	9¹	12									4
1	2	3	4	5		8	9	6²	12	11			14			13	10³	7¹									5
1	2	3	4	5		6	7	10¹	11²			14	12			13	8	9³									6
1	2	3	4	5		6	7	10²	11³	12		14				13	8	9¹									7
1	2	3	4	5		6	7	10²	11¹	12		14				13	8	9³									8
1	2	3	4	5			7	10²	11³	8¹		13	12	14		6		9									9
1	2	3	4	5		6	7²	10¹	11³	8		13		12		14		9									10
1	2	3	4	5			7³	10¹		11		12		14		6	8²	9	13								11
		2	3	5			7		11²	8¹		12			4	6	10	9		1	13						12
	8	2	3				7	13	11³	9		12			4	6	10¹		14	1		5²					13
1	5	2	3				6	12	11	8³		14		13	4	7¹	10²	9									14
1	6	2	3	5			8		11²	13		10		9³	4	7¹		12			14						15
1	8	2	3	5			6		12³	9²		11¹			4	13		7			10		14				16
1	8	2	3	5			7	14	11²	9³		13		12	4			6			10¹						17
1	5	2	3	4		7²	8	14		11³		13				6	12	10				9¹					18
1	13	2	3	5		7²	6			12		11		10¹	4	14	8³	9									19
1	13	2■	3	5		12	6		11²	9¹				10³	4	7	8					14					20
1	2		3	5		6	7		13	12		11¹		10²			8³	9			14		4				21
1	2		3	5		6		12	11	9³		13		10²			8¹	7			14		4				22
1	2	3	4			6	14	12	13	9		11³		10			8²	7				5¹					23
1		2³	3			7	6	12		11		14		5		8²		10			9¹	13	4				24
1	2	3¹	4	5		6	9	7²		11		13		10				8³			14		12				25
1	2		3	5		7	6³			11		12		8		13		9²	14		10¹		4				26
1	2		3	5		6■	7			9¹		11	14	8		12					10³		4²	13			27
1	2	3	4	5			6			9		11²		8¹		7		12	13		10						28
1	2	3	4	5		7		13		10²		11	14	6³		8		12			9¹						29
1	2	3	4	5		7²	12			11¹		10		6		8		13			9						30
1	2	3	4	5			7	6²		10		11	13	12				8			9¹						31
1	2	3	4	5			7	12		11		10²	14	6¹				8	13		9³						32
1	2	3	4	5	12		7			10		11³		13			6²	8¹	14		9						33
1	2	3	4	5	12		7			10³		11		6¹		8²	13		14		9						34
1	2	3	4	5	8		7			10		11¹	14	6²			12		13		9³						35
1	2	3	4	5	6		7	14		9			13	12			8²		11³		10¹						36
1	2	3	4	5	8		7²	14		10				12		13	6¹		11³		9						37
	2	3	4	5		8		13				12		10¹		7	6		11²		9³				1	14	38

FA Cup

Third Round	Millwall	(a)	0-3

EFL Cup

Second Round	Morecambe	(a)	2-1
Third Round	Preston NE	(h)	2-3
(*aet*)			

BRADFORD CITY

FOUNDATION

Bradford was a rugby stronghold around the turn of the 20th century but after Manningham RFC held an archery contest to help them out of financial difficulties in 1903, they were persuaded to give up the handling code and turn to soccer. So they formed Bradford City and continued at Valley Parade. Recognising this as an opportunity to spread the dribbling code in this part of Yorkshire, the Football League immediately accepted the new club's first application for membership of the Second Division.

Northern Commercials Stadium, Valley Parade, Bradford, West Yorkshire BD8 7DY.

Telephone: (0871) 978 1911.

Fax: (01274) 773 356.

Ticket Office: (0871) 978 8000.

Website: www.bradfordcityfc.co.uk

Email: (via website).

Ground Capacity: 25,137.

Record Attendance: 39,146 v Burnley, FA Cup 4th rd, 11 March 1911.

Pitch Measurements: 103.5m × 64m (113yd × 70yd).

Joint Owners: Stefan Rupp and Edin Rahic.

Chief Operating Officer: James Mason.

Manager: Stuart McCall.

Assistant Manager: Kenny Black.

Colours: Claret and amber shirts, black shorts with amber trim, black socks with amber trim.

Year Formed: 1903.

Turned Professional: 1903.

Club Nickname: 'The Bantams'.

Ground: 1903, Valley Parade (renamed Bradford & Bingley Stadium 1999, Intersonic Stadium 2007, Coral Windows Stadium 2007, Northern Commercials Stadium 2016).

First Football League Game: 1 September 1903, Division 2, v Grimsby T (a) L 0–2 – Seymour; Wilson, Halliday; Robinson, Millar, Farnall; Guy, Beckram, Forrest, McMillan, Graham.

Record League Victory: 11–1 v Rotherham U, Division 3 (N), 25 August 1928 – Sherlaw; Russell, Watson; Burkinshaw (1), Summers, Bauld; Harvey (2), Edmunds (3), White (3), Cairns, Scriven (2).

Record Cup Victory: 11–3 v Walker Celtic, FA Cup 1st rd (replay), 1 December 1937 – Parker; Rookes, McDermott; Murphy, Mackie, Moore; Bagley (1), Whittingham (1), Deakin (4 incl. 1p), Cooke (1), Bartholomew (4).

HONOURS

League Champions: Division 2 – 1907–08; Division 3 – 1984–85; Division 3N – 1928–29.
Runners-up: First Division – 1998–99; Division 4 – 1981–82.

FA Cup Winners: 1911.

League Cup: *Runners-up:* 2013.

European Competitions:
Intertoto Cup: 2000.

sky SPORTS FACT FILE

Harold Walden, who played for Bradford City between 1911 and 1920, won an Olympic gold medal for the Great Britain team in 1912. He scored nine goals in the tournament including six in a 7-0 rout of Hungary. Walden later became a well-known music hall entertainer.

Record Defeat: 1–9 v Colchester U, Division 4, 30 December 1961.

Most League Points (2 for a win): 63, Division 3 (N), 1928–29.

Most League Points (3 for a win): 94, Division 3, 1984–85.

Most League Goals: 128, Division 3 (N), 1928–29.

Highest League Scorer in Season: David Layne, 34, Division 4, 1961–62.

Most League Goals in Total Aggregate: Bobby Campbell, 121, 1981–84, 1984–86.

Most League Goals in One Match: 7, Albert Whitehurst v Tranmere R, Division 3 (N), 6 March 1929.

Most Capped Player: Jamie Lawrence, 19 (24), Jamaica.

Most League Appearances: Cec Podd, 502, 1970–84.

Youngest League Player: Robert Cullingford, 16 years 141 days v Mansfield T, 22 April 1970.

Record Transfer Fee Received: £2,000,000 from Newcastle U for Des Hamilton, March 1997; £2,000,000 from Newcastle U for Andrew O'Brien, March 2001.

Record Transfer Fee Paid: £2,500,000 to Leeds U for David Hopkin, July 2000.

Football League Record: 1903 Elected to Division 2; 1908–22 Division 1; 1922–27 Division 2; 1927–29 Division 3 (N); 1929–37 Division 2; 1937–61 Division 3; 1961–69 Division 4; 1969–72 Division 3; 1972–77 Division 4; 1977–78 Division 3; 1978–82 Division 4; 1982–85 Division 3; 1985–90 Division 2; 1990–92 Division 3; 1992–96 Division 2; 1996–99 Division 1; 1999–2001 FA Premier League; 2001–04 Division 1; 2004–07 FL 1; 2007–13 FL 2; 2013– FL 1.

LATEST SEQUENCES

Longest Sequence of League Wins: 10, 26.11.1983 – 3.2.1984.

Longest Sequence of League Defeats: 8, 21.1.1933 – 11.3.1933.

Longest Sequence of League Draws: 6, 30.1.1976 – 13.3.1976.

Longest Sequence of Unbeaten League Matches: 21, 11.1.1969 – 2.5.1969.

Longest Sequence Without a League Win: 16, 28.8.1948 – 20.11.1948.

Successive Scoring Runs: 30 from 26.12.1961.

Successive Non-scoring Runs: 7 from 18.4.1925.

MANAGERS

Robert Campbell 1903–05
Peter O'Rourke 1905–21
David Menzies 1921–26
Colin Veitch 1926–28
Peter O'Rourke 1928–30
Jack Peart 1930–35
Dick Ray 1935–37
Fred Westgarth 1938–43
Bob Sharp 1943–46
Jack Barker 1946–47
John Milburn 1947–48
David Steele 1948–52
Albert Harris 1952
Ivor Powell 1952–55
Peter Jackson 1955–61
Bob Brocklebank 1961–64
Bill Harris 1965–66
Willie Watson 1966–69
Grenville Hair 1967–68
Jimmy Wheeler 1968–71
Bryan Edwards 1971–75
Bobby Kennedy 1975–78
John Napier 1978
George Mulhall 1978–81
Roy McFarland 1981–82
Trevor Cherry 1982–87
Terry Dolan 1987–89
Terry Yorath 1989–90
John Docherty 1990–91
Frank Stapleton 1991–94
Lennie Lawrence 1994–95
Chris Kamara 1995–98
Paul Jewell 1998–2000
Chris Hutchings 2000
Jim Jefferies 2000–01
Nicky Law 2001–03
Bryan Robson 2003–04
Colin Todd 2004–07
Stuart McCall 2007–10
Peter Taylor 2010–11
Peter Jackson 2011
Phil Parkinson 2011–16
Stuart McCall June 2016–

TEN YEAR LEAGUE RECORD

		P	W	D	L	F	A	Pts	Pos
2007-08	FL 2	46	17	11	18	63	61	62	10
2008-09	FL 2	46	18	13	15	66	55	67	9
2009-10	FL 2	46	16	14	16	59	62	62	14
2010-11	FL 2	46	15	7	24	43	68	52	18
2011-12	FL 2	46	12	14	20	54	59	50	18
2012-13	FL 2	46	18	15	13	63	52	69	7
2013-14	FL 1	46	14	17	15	57	54	59	11
2014-15	FL 1	46	17	14	15	55	55	65	7
2015-16	FL 1	46	23	11	12	55	40	80	5
2016-17	FL 1	46	20	19	7	62	43	79	5

DID YOU KNOW ?

Bradford City's inaugural match in the Football League against Grimsby Town in September 1903 was also the club's first-ever fixture of any sort. Never before had a club played the very first game of its existence at this level.

BRADFORD CITY – SKY BET LEAGUE ONE 2016–17 LEAGUE RECORD

Match No.	Date	Venue	Opponents	Result		H/T Score	Lg Pos.	Goalscorers	Attendance
1	Aug 6	H	Port Vale	D	0-0	0-0	14		18,558
2	13	A	Peterborough U	W	1-0	1-0	9	Hiwula [11]	5906
3	16	A	Milton Keynes D	W	2-1	2-0	5	Cullen [12], Clarke, B [17]	8166
4	20	H	Coventry C	W	3-1	0-1	3	McMahon 2 (2 pens) [67, 75], Marshall [69]	17,595
5	27	H	Oldham Ath	D	1-1	0-1	2	Clarke, B (pen) [57]	17,793
6	Sept 3	A	Millwall	D	1-1	1-0	2	Webster (og) [42]	9067
7	10	A	Gillingham	D	1-1	1-1	3	Hiwula [29]	5079
8	17	H	Bristol R	D	1-1	0-0	4	Meredith [73]	17,489
9	24	A	Bolton W	D	0-0	0-0	4		17,486
10	27	H	Fleetwood T	W	2-1	1-1	3	Morais [45], Clarke, B (pen) [62]	16,759
11	Oct 1	A	Chesterfield	W	1-0	1-0	2	Clarke, B [26]	6997
12	8	H	Shrewsbury T	W	2-0	1-0	2	Law [21], Vuckic (pen) [90]	17,703
13	15	A	Oxford U	L	0-1	0-0	2		8245
14	18	H	Southend U	D	1-1	1-0	2	McNulty [36]	16,112
15	22	H	Sheffield U	D	3-3	1-1	2	Clarke, B [35], Hiwula [60], Dieng [68]	20,972
16	29	A	AFC Wimbledon	W	3-2	1-1	3	Hiwula [3], Hanson, James 2 (1 pen) [78 (p), 90]	4826
17	Nov 12	H	Rochdale	W	4-0	2-0	2	Clarke, B [41], Dieng [44], Hanson, James [59], Marshall [63]	18,205
18	19	A	Southend U	L	0-3	0-1	4		7005
19	22	H	Northampton T	W	1-0	0-0	4	Hanson, James [56]	15,935
20	26	A	Swindon T	L	0-1	0-1	4		6344
21	Dec 10	H	Charlton Ath	D	0-0	0-0	4		17,968
22	17	A	Walsall	D	1-1	0-0	4	Hiwula [53]	5148
23	26	H	Scunthorpe U	D	0-0	0-0	5		21,874
24	31	H	Bury	D	1-1	0-1	5	Law [52]	18,012
25	Jan 2	A	Northampton T	W	2-1	0-1	5	Marshall [73], Hiwula [86]	6931
26	7	H	Chesterfield	W	2-0	2-0	4	Marshall [22], Hiwula [45]	17,416
27	14	A	Shrewsbury T	L	0-1	0-1	4		5590
28	21	H	Millwall	D	1-1	0-0	5	Meredith [60]	17,712
29	28	A	Oldham Ath	W	2-1	1-1	5	Vincelot [14], McArdle [76]	6516
30	Feb 4	H	Gillingham	D	2-2	2-1	5	Wyke [15], McMahon [38]	18,840
31	11	A	Bristol R	D	1-1	1-1	5	Law [26]	9043
32	14	A	Fleetwood T	L	1-2	1-0	5	Hiwula [43]	3418
33	18	H	Bolton W	D	2-2	2-0	5	Wyke 2 [10, 16]	21,190
34	25	A	Port Vale	W	2-1	1-0	5	Vincelot [41], Jones [74]	4953
35	28	H	Milton Keynes D	D	2-2	2-2	5	McMahon (pen) [22], Wyke [43]	16,725
36	Mar 4	H	Peterborough U	W	1-0	1-0	5	Jones [24]	17,220
37	11	A	Coventry C	W	2-0	0-0	4	Jones [51], Hiwula [56]	9150
38	14	A	Charlton Ath	D	1-1	1-1	5	Dieng [42]	9326
39	18	H	Swindon T	W	2-1	0-0	4	Wyke 2 [85, 90]	17,916
40	26	A	Scunthorpe U	L	2-3	2-1	5	Toner [14], Jones [16]	5247
41	Apr 1	H	Walsall	W	1-0	0-0	4	Clarke, B [58]	17,880
42	8	A	Bury	W	2-0	0-0	4	Marshall [56], Wyke [84]	5268
43	14	H	Oxford U	W	1-0	0-0	4	Law [61]	19,346
44	17	A	Sheffield U	L	0-3	0-3	5		26,838
45	22	H	AFC Wimbledon	W	3-0	2-0	5	McMahon 2 (1 pen) [29 (p), 85], Marshall [45]	18,615
46	30	A	Rochdale	D	1-1	1-0	5	Jones [9]	6876

Final League Position: 5

GOALSCORERS

League (62): Hiwula 9, Clarke, B 7 (2 pens), Wyke 7, Marshall 6, McMahon 6 (4 pens), Jones 5, Hanson, James 4 (1 pen), Law 4, Dieng 3, Meredith 2, Vincelot 2, Cullen 1, McArdle 1, McNulty 1, Morais 1, Toner 1, Vuckic 1 (1 pen), own goal 1.
FA Cup (1): own goal 1.
EFL Cup (0).
EFL Checkatrade Trophy (8): Hiwula 3, Vuckic 3, Dieng 1, Law 1.
League One Play-Offs (1): McArdle 1.

Doyle C 44	Meredith J 41	Knight-Percival N 42	Vincelot R 45	McMahon T 25	Marshall M 38 + 4	Law N 37 + 3	Devine D 8 + 3	Morais F 4 + 13	Hanson James 13 + 4	Clarke B 25 + 8	Anderson P — + 3	Hiwula J 26 + 15	Cullen J 40	Dieng T 28 + 11	Webb-Foster R — + 1	Rabiega V — + 1	Darby S 19 + 3	McNulty M 5 + 10	Vuckic H 4 + 6	Kilgallon M 6 + 1	McArdle R 22 + 2	Sattelmaier R 2	Jones A 9 + 6	Gilliead A 5 + 4	Wyke C 16	Toner K 2	Hudson E — + 1	Penney M — + 1	Pybus D — + 1	Match No.
1	2	3	4	5	6	7	8	9^{2}	10	11^{1}	12	13																		1
1	5	4	3	2	9^{1}	6	8		10	12	13	11^{2}	7																	2
1	2	3	4	5	6^{2}	8	9			10^{1}	12	11	7	13																3
1	5	3	4	2^{3}	6	9	7^{2}	13		10^{1}		11	8	12	14															4
1	5	4	3		6	9	2			10		11^{1}	8	7		12														5
1	5	4	3		9	8	6	12		10		11^{1}		7			2													6
1	5	4	3		6^{3}	9		13	14	10^{1}		11^{2}	7	8			2	12												7
1	5	4	3		9^{2}	6^{1}		13	11	10^{3}			8	7			2	14	12											8
1	5	4	3		6	9				11		12	7	8			2	10^{1}												9
1	5	4	3		14	13		6^{2}		12		10	7	8			2	9^{1}	11^{3}											10
1	5	4	3		6	9^{1}		13		10^{2}		11	8	7			2		12											11
1	5	4	3		6	7	12	9^{2}		10^{3}		11^{1}		8			2	13	14											12
1	5^{2}	4	3		6^{1}	9		13		10		11^{3}	8	7			2	14		12										13
1		4	3		6	8		14	12			13	9^{2}				2	7^{1}	11^{3}	5	10									14
1		4	3			8			10	9		11	7	6						5	2									15
1		3	5		13	8		14	10	11^{3}		6^{1}	7^{2}	9			2	12		4										16
	5	3	4		6^{1}	9	14	13	11	10^{3}		12	8	7^{2}			2					1								17
1	5	4	3		6	9		13	10			11^{2}	7	8			2^{1}	12												18
1	5	4	3		9	7		12	11			13	8^{1}				2	6^{3}	10^{2}		14									19
1	5	4	3		6^{2}	9		13	10			14	8	7			2^{1}	11^{3}	12											20
1	2	3	4		9^{2}	6		13	10			11^{1}	8	7			5	12												21
1	5	3	4		9	7			10			11^{2}	6	8			2^{1}	12	13											22
1	5	3	4	2	9	10		6^{1}	11				8	7				12												23
1		4	3	2	6^{2}	9	8^{3}		10			11^{1}	7	13				12	14	5										24
1	5	3	6^{2}		13	8			12			10	9	7			2		11^{1}		4									25
1	5	4	3	2	6	9						10	7	8			12						11^{1}							26
1	5^{1}	3	4	2	6	9			12			10^{2}	8	7^{3}							14		11	13						27
1	9	2	7	5	10	6^{3}				14		13	8	12						4^{1}	3		11^{2}							28
1	5		4	2	6	9				11^{2}		10^{1}	7	8							3		12	13						29
1	5		4	2	6	9				10		12	8^{1}	7							3				11					30
1	5	4	8	2	6	9				10^{1}		12		7							3				11					31
1	5	4	7		12	8				13		11^{1}	6^{2}				2				3			9	10					32
1	5	9	4	2	6^{1}	7^{2}				11^{3}		14	8	12							3			13	10					33
1	5	4	6	2		8^{2}				7^{3}		11	9	14							3		13	12	10^{1}					34
1	5	4	8	2		9				10^{1}			7								3		12	6	11					35
1	5	4	8	2	9^{2}							12	7	13							3		11^{1}	6	10					36
1	5	4	8	2	9					13		11	7								3		12^{2}	6^{1}	10					37
1	2	4	3	6	8					11^{1}		12	7	9							5				10					38
1	5	4	8	2	6^{1}					12		10^{3}	9	7^{2}			14				3		13		11					39
1	5		6	2	10		13			9^{2}		12		7							4		8^{1}		11	3				40
1	5	4	8	2	6	13				9^{2}			7	12							3		10^{1}		11					41
1	5	4	6	2	10^{3}	12				9^{1}		13	7	14							3		8^{2}		11					42
1	5	3	7	2	6^{2}	9^{3}				14		10^{1}	8	12			13				4				11					43
1	8	4	3	5	10	9							6	7^{1}							2		12		11					44
1	5	4	7^{3}	2	9	8^{1}				13		14	6	12							3		11^{2}		10					45
							6			9^{1}		8		7			2			4	3	1	11^{3}	10^{2}		5	12	13	14	46

FA Cup

First Round	Accrington S	(h)	1-2

EFL Cup

First Round	Accrington S	(a)	0-0

(*aet; Accrington S won 11-10 on penalties*)

League One Play-Offs

Semi-Final 1st leg	Fleetwood T	(h)	1-0
Semi-Final 2nd leg	Fleetwood T	(a)	0-0
Final	Millwall	(Wembley)	0-1

EFL Checkatrade Trophy

Northern Group C	Stoke C U21	(h)	1-0
Northern Group C	Bury	(h)	2-1
Northern Group C	Morecambe	(a)	2-3
Second Round North	Cambridge U	(h)	1-0
Third Round	Cheltenham T	(a)	1-0
Quarter-Final	Oxford U	(a)	1-2

BRENTFORD

FOUNDATION

Formed as a small amateur concern in 1889 they were very successful in local circles. They won the championship of the West London Alliance in 1893 and a year later the West Middlesex Junior Cup before carrying off the Senior Cup in 1895. After winning both the London Senior Amateur Cup and the Middlesex Senior Cup in 1898 they were admitted to the Second Division of the Southern League.

Griffin Park, Braemar Road, Brentford, Middlesex TW8 0NT.

Telephone: (0845) 3456 442.

Ticket Office: (0208) 847 2511 (option 1).

Website: www.brentfordfc.co.uk

Email: enquiries@brentfordfc.co.uk

Ground Capacity: 12,802.

Record Attendance: 38,678 v Leicester C, FA Cup 6th rd, 26 February 1949.

Pitch Measurements: 101m × 67m (110yd × 73yd).

Chairman: Cliff Crown.

Chief Executive: Mark Devlin.

Head Coach: Dean Smith

Assistant Head Coach: Richard O'Kelly.

Colours: Red and white striped shirts with black trim, black shorts with white trim, black socks with white trim.

Year Formed: 1889.

Turned Professional: 1899.

Club Nickname: 'The Bees'.

Grounds: 1889, Clifden Road; 1891, Benns Fields, Little Ealing; 1895, Shotters Field; 1898, Cross Road, S. Ealing; 1900, Boston Park; 1904, Griffin Park.

First Football League Game: 28 August 1920, Division 3, v Exeter C (a) L 0–3 – Young; Hodson, Rosier, Jimmy Elliott, Levitt, Amos, Smith, Thompson, Spreadbury, Morley, Henery.

Record League Victory: 9–0 v Wrexham, Division 3, 15 October 1963 – Cakebread; Coote, Jones; Slater, Scott, Higginson; Summers (1), Brooks (2), McAdams (2), Ward (2), Hales (1), (1 og).

Record Cup Victory: 7–0 v Windsor & Eton (away), FA Cup 1st rd, 20 November 1982 – Roche; Rowe, Harris (Booker), McNichol (1), Whitehead, Hurlock (2), Kamara, Joseph (1), Mahoney (3), Bowles, Roberts. *N.B.* 8–0 v Uxbridge: Frail, Jock Watson, Caie, Bellingham, Parsonage (1), Jay, Atherton, Leigh (1), Bell (2), Buchanan (2), Underwood (2), FA Cup, 3rd Qual rd, 31 October 1903.

Record Defeat: 0–7 v Swansea T, Division 3 (S), 8 November 1924; v Walsall, Division 3 (S), 19 January 1957; v Peterborough U, 24 November 2007.

Most League Points (2 for a win): 62, Division 3 (S), 1932–33 and Division 4, 1962–63.

HONOURS

League Champions: Division 2 – 1934–35; Division 3 – 1991–92; Division 3S – 1932–33; FL 2 – 2008–09; Third Division – 1998–99; Division 4 – 1962–63.
Runners-up: FL 1 – 2013–14; Second Division – 1994–95; Division 3S – 1929–30, 1957–58.

FA Cup: 6th rd – 1938, 1946, 1949, 1989.

League Cup: 4th rd – 1983, 2011.

League Trophy: *Runners-up:* 1985, 2001, 2011.

sky SPORTS FACT FILE

Percy Saunders joined Brentford from Sunderland in the summer of 1939 and featured for the Bees in the abandoned 1939–40 season. Soon afterwards he enlisted in the Royal Army Ordnance Corps. Evacuated following the Japanese invasion of Singapore in 1942, Saunders was one of those killed when the SS *Roosebaum* was torpedoed en route to Colombo (Sri Lanka).

Most League Points (3 for a win): 94, FL 1, 2013–14.

Most League Goals: 98, Division 4, 1962–63.

Highest League Scorer in Season: Jack Holliday, 38, Division 3 (S), 1932–33.

Most League Goals in Total Aggregate: Jim Towers, 153, 1954–61.

Most League Goals in One Match: 5, Jack Holliday v Luton T, Division 3 (S), 28 January 1933; 5, Billy Scott v Barnsley, Division 2, 15 December 1934; 5, Peter McKennan v Bury, Division 2, 18 February 1949.

Most Capped Player: John Buttigieg, 22 (98), Malta.

Most League Appearances: Ken Coote, 514, 1949–64.

Youngest League Player: Danis Salman, 15 years 248 days v Watford, 15 November 1975.

Record Transfer Fee Received: £12,000,000 from Aston Villa for Scott Hogan, January 2017.

Record Transfer Fee Paid: £2,500,000 to Norwich C for Sergi Canos, January 2017.

Football League Record: 1920 Original Member of Division 3; 1921–33 Division 3 (S); 1933–35 Division 2; 1935–47 Division 1; 1947–54 Division 2; 1954–62 Division 3 (S); 1962–63 Division 4; 1963–66 Division 3; 1966–72 Division 4; 1972–73 Division 3; 1973–78 Division 4; 1978–92 Division 3; 1992–93 Division 1; 1993–98 Division 2; 1998–99 Division 3; 1999–2004 Division 2; 2004–07 FL 1; 2007–09 FL 2; 2009–14 FL 1; 2014– FL C.

LATEST SEQUENCES

Longest Sequence of League Wins: 9, 30.4.1932 – 24.9.1932.

Longest Sequence of League Defeats: 9, 20.10.1928 – 25.12.1928.

Longest Sequence of League Draws: 5, 16.3.1957 – 6.4.1957.

Longest Sequence of Unbeaten League Matches: 26, 20.2.1999 – 16.10.1999.

Longest Sequence Without a League Win: 18, 9.9.2006 – 26.12.2006.

Successive Scoring Runs: 26 from 4.3.1963.

Successive Non-scoring Runs: 7 from 7.3.2000.

MANAGERS

Will Lewis 1900–03 (*Secretary-Manager*)
Dick Molyneux 1902–06
W. G. Brown 1906–08
Fred Halliday 1908–12, 1915–21, 1924–26 (*only Secretary to 1922*)
Ephraim Rhodes 1912–15
Archie Mitchell 1921–24
Harry Curtis 1926–49
Jackie Gibbons 1949–52
Jimmy Bain 1952–53
Tommy Lawton 1953
Bill Dodgin Snr 1953–57
Malcolm Macdonald 1957–65
Tommy Cavanagh 1965–66
Billy Gray 1966–67
Jimmy Sirrel 1967–69
Frank Blunstone 1969–73
Mike Everitt 1973–75
John Docherty 1975–76
Bill Dodgin Jnr 1976–80
Fred Callaghan 1980–84
Frank McLintock 1984–87
Steve Perryman 1987–90
Phil Holder 1990–93
David Webb 1993–97
Eddie May 1997
Micky Adams 1997–98
Ron Noades 1998–2000
Ray Lewington 2000–01
Steve Coppell 2001–02
Wally Downes 2002–04
Martin Allen 2004–06
Leroy Rosenior 2006
Scott Fitzgerald 2006–07
Terry Butcher 2007
Andy Scott 2007–11
Nicky Forster 2011
Uwe Rosler 2011–13
Mark Warburton 2013–15
Marinus Dijkhuizen 2015
Dean Smith December 2015–

TEN YEAR LEAGUE RECORD

		P	W	D	L	F	A	Pts	Pos
2007-08	FL 2	46	17	8	21	52	70	59	14
2008-09	FL 2	46	23	16	7	65	36	85	1
2009-10	FL 1	46	14	20	12	55	52	62	9
2010-11	FL 1	46	17	10	19	55	62	61	11
2011-12	FL 1	46	18	13	15	63	52	67	9
2012-13	FL 1	46	21	16	9	62	47	79	3
2013-14	FL 1	46	28	10	8	72	43	94	2
2014-15	FL C	46	23	9	14	78	59	78	5
2015-16	FL C	46	19	8	19	72	67	65	9
2016-17	FL C	46	18	10	18	75	65	64	10

DID YOU KNOW 

Brentford finished in 21st place in Division Three South at the end of 1920–21, their first season of League football, and therefore had to seek re-election. As the division was expanded to 24 clubs neither the Bees nor bottom club Gillingham were required to submit to a ballot, both being readmitted automatically.

BRENTFORD – SKY BET CHAMPIONSHIP 2016–17 LEAGUE RECORD

Match No.	Date	Venue	Opponents	Result		H/T Score	Lg Pos.	Goalscorers	Attendance
1	Aug 6	A	Huddersfield T	L	1-2	0-0	19	Yennaris 77	18,479
2	13	H	Ipswich T	W	2-0	0-0	8	Egan 2 48, 56	10,089
3	16	H	Nottingham F	W	1-0	1-0	6	Hogan 29	10,004
4	20	A	Rotherham U	L	0-1	0-1	8		8367
5	27	H	Sheffield W	D	1-1	0-0	11	Vibe 54	9677
6	Sept 10	A	Brighton & HA	W	2-0	1-0	3	Hogan 2 29, 70	26,388
7	14	A	Aston Villa	D	1-1	0-1	8	Egan 88	29,752
8	17	H	Preston NE	W	5-0	1-0	5	Hogan 3 34, 84, 87, Dean 74, Humphrey (og) 85	9920
9	24	A	Wolverhampton W	L	1-3	0-0	9	KaiKai 67	20,637
10	27	H	Reading	W	4-1	2-0	4	Clarke 41, Vibe 44, Colin 58, Hogan 86	9679
11	Oct 1	H	Wigan Ath	D	0-0	0-0	6		9547
12	15	A	Newcastle U	L	1-3	0-2	8	Hogan 52	51,885
13	18	A	Derby Co	D	0-0	0-0	8		26,707
14	22	H	Barnsley	L	0-2	0-1	9		10,417
15	28	A	QPR	W	2-0	1-0	8	Clarke 42, Sawyers 74	16,888
16	Nov 4	H	Fulham	L	0-2	0-1	11		12,052
17	19	A	Blackburn R	L	2-3	2-3	13	Hogan 2 1, 30	10,506
18	26	H	Birmingham C	L	1-2	0-1	16	Hogan 77	10,925
19	Dec 3	A	Norwich C	L	0-5	0-2	18		26,076
20	10	H	Burton Alb	W	2-1	1-1	16	Hogan 2 11, 53	9035
21	13	A	Bristol C	W	1-0	0-0	14	Colin 68	16,444
22	17	A	Leeds U	L	0-1	0-0	14		25,134
23	26	H	Cardiff C	D	2-2	0-1	14	KaiKai 2 83, 90	11,098
24	31	H	Norwich C	D	0-0	0-0	15		9377
25	Jan 2	A	Birmingham C	W	3-1	0-1	14	Hogan 54, Davis (og) 73, Yennaris 87	18,030
26	14	H	Newcastle U	L	1-2	0-1	14	Vibe 52	11,435
27	21	A	Wigan Ath	L	1-2	0-2	15	Jota 86	10,244
28	31	H	Aston Villa	W	3-0	2-0	13	Vibe 2 25, 65, Yennaris 38	10,016
29	Feb 5	H	Brighton & HA	D	3-3	2-0	13	Jota 15, Dean 22, Kerschbaumer 90	10,433
30	11	A	Preston NE	L	2-4	1-1	15	Field 12, Colin 89	10,130
31	14	A	Reading	L	2-3	0-1	15	Jota 63, Vibe 66	15,710
32	21	A	Sheffield W	W	2-1	2-0	14	Egan 35, Dean 44	25,014
33	25	H	Rotherham U	W	4-2	1-0	13	Jota 3 (1 pen) 13, 90, 90 (p), Yennaris 78	9918
34	Mar 4	A	Ipswich T	D	1-1	1-1	14	Yennaris 44	15,863
35	7	A	Nottingham F	W	3-2	1-0	12	Vibe 2 17, 55, Jota 68	16,903
36	11	H	Huddersfield T	L	0-1	0-1	14		11,278
37	14	H	Wolverhampton W	L	1-2	1-0	14	Colin 31	8732
38	18	A	Burton Alb	W	5-3	1-3	13	Canos 2 10, 61, Vibe 2 51, 85, Jota 86	4549
39	Apr 1	H	Bristol C	W	2-0	2-0	12	Canos 18, Vibe 26	11,360
40	4	H	Leeds U	W	2-0	2-0	12	Sawyers 18, Vibe 34	10,759
41	8	A	Cardiff C	L	1-2	1-0	12	Canos 42	15,861
42	14	H	Derby Co	W	4-0	1-0	11	Vibe 2 32, 82, Jota 2 70, 90	11,133
43	17	A	Barnsley	D	1-1	1-1	10	Jozefzoon 41	13,935
44	22	H	QPR	W	3-1	1-0	9	Barbet 31, Jota 2 (1 pen) 60 (p), 64	11,888
45	29	A	Fulham	D	1-1	1-1	10	Yennaris 34	24,594
46	May 7	H	Blackburn R	L	1-3	0-2	10	Vibe 56	11,969

Final League Position: 10

GOALSCORERS

League (75): Vibe 15, Hogan 14, Jota 12 (2 pens), Yennaris 6, Canos 4, Colin 4, Egan 4, Dean 3, KaiKai 3, Clarke 2, Sawyers 2, Barbet 1, Field 1, Jozefzoon 1, Kerschbaumer 1, own goals 2.
FA Cup (5): Field 2, Barbet 1 (1 pen), Sawyers 1, Vibe 1.
EFL Cup (0).

Bentley D 45	Clarke J 19 + 11	Dean H 42	Egan J 34	Elder C 6	McEachran J 14 + 13	Woods R 42	Sawyers R 39 + 4	Kerschbaumer K 9 + 11	Macleod L 10 + 3	Hogan S 25	Saunders S 2 + 6	Yennaris N 39 + 7	Hofmann P — + 10	Colin M 38	Vibe L 30 + 4	Ledesma E — + 1	Bjelland A 25 + 3	KaiKai S 6 + 12	Barbet Y 15 + 8	McCormack A 2 + 9	Field T 13 + 2	Jota R 19 + 2	Jozefzoon F 6 + 13	Canos S 13 + 5	Henry R 12	Shaibu J — + 4	Cole R — + 1	Bonham J 1	Westbrooke Z — + 1	*Match No.*
1	2	3	4	5	6^1	7	8	9^2	10^3	11	12	13	14																	1
1	8	4	3	5	14	7	10	13	9^3	11	12	6^1		2^2																2
1	8	3	4	5		7	9		10^1	11	12	6		2																3
1		3	4	5	14	7	9^3		10^2	11	12	6		2	8^1	13														4
1		3	4	5		7	9^1		10^2	11	12	6		2	8■		13													5
1	8^1	3	4	5^2		7	9		10^3	11	14	6		2			12	13												6
1	8^3	3	4		14	7	9		10^2	11		6^1		2	13		5	12												7
1	14	3	4		12	7	9		8	11		6^1		2			5^3	10^2	13											8
1		3	4		7^1	6	9		8^2	11		12		2	13			10	5											9
1	8	3	4		13		9			11		7		2	10^3		5^2	14	12	6^1										10
1	8^2	3	4		14		10		13	11		7		2	9^3		5	12		6^1										11
1	8	3	4			7	10		9^3	11		6^2		2			5^1	12	13	14										12
1	12		3		13	6	9		14	11	8^1	7^2		2			4	10^3	5											13
1	12		3		13	6	9^1			11	8^3	7	14	2			4	10^2	5											14
1	8^2	3	4		9^1	6	10	14	12^3	11		7		2			5	13												15
1	9^2	3	4		8^3	7	11^1			10		6	14	2	13		5	12												16
1	6	3	4			7	12			11		8		2	10^2		5^1	9	13											17
1	13	3	2		14	6	9^3			11		7		5	10^2		4	12	8^1											18
1	8	3	4		13	7^3	9^2			11		6	14	2	10^1			12	5											19
1		4	3		7^2	8	10			11		9		2	12		5		6^1		13									20
1		3	2		12	6	11			10		7^3		5	9^2		4	14	13		8^1									21
1		3	2		12	8	7			11		6^3		5	10^2		4	13	14		9^1									22
1		3	2		13	6	11^3			10		7	14	5	9^2		4^1	12			8									23
1		3	2^3		7^1	8	12			10		6	14	5			4	11	13		9^2									24
1		3	2		7^3	6	9	13		11^1		12	14	5	10^2		4		8											25
1	14	3	2^2		7^3	8	10^1					6	13	5	11		4				9	12								26
1	14	3	2^3		6^1	7	10^2					8	13	5	11		4				9	12								27
1	12	3			7^2	8		13				6^3		2	10		4			14	5	9	11^1							28
1	2	3			7	6		14				8^1			10		4			13	5^2	9	11^3	12						29
1		3			8^1	7	13	14				6^3		2	10		4				5	9	11^2	12						30
1	13	3			7	8		14				6^2		2	10		4				5	9^3	12	11^1						31
1		3	4		7^1	8	10	12				6		2							14	9	13	11^2	5^3					32
1			3			7	10	6^2				8		2			4					9	11^1	12	5	13				33
1			3			6	9					7		2	11^2		4^3		12			8	13	10^1	5	14				34
1		3	4			7	9					6^3		2	11^2							8^1	12	10	5	13	14			35
1		3	4			6	9^3	13				7^2	14	2	11							8	10^1	12	5					36
1	13	3	4			7	14	9^3				6		2	11^2							8^1	12	10	5					37
1		3				7	9^3	6^1				12		2	11				4	14	5	8	13	10^2						38
1	13	3				6	9	7^2				14		2^1	11				4			8	12	10^3	5					39
1	2	3				6^2	9	14				7^3			11				4	12		8	13	10^1	5					40
1	2	3				6	9^2	7^3				12			11				4	14		8	13	10^1	5					41
1	2	3				6^1	9^2	14				7			11				4	13		8	12	10^3	5					42
	2	3	4			6^1	9	7^3				13			11^2					14		8	10	12	5			1		43
1	13	3				6	9					7		2^3	11^1				4			8	12	10^2	5	14				44
1	2	3					9	7^2				6			11				4		5	8	12	10^1					13	45
1	2	3■					9	7^2				6			11		12		4	13	5^1	8	14	10^3						46

FA Cup

Third Round	Eastleigh	(h)	5-1
Fourth Round	Chelsea	(a)	0-4

EFL Cup

First Round	Exeter C	(a)	0-1
(*aet*)			

BRIGHTON & HOVE ALBION

FOUNDATION

A professional club Brighton United was formed in November 1897 at the Imperial Hotel, Queen's Road, but folded in March 1900 after less than two seasons in the Southern League at the County Ground. An amateur team Brighton & Hove Rangers was then formed by some prominent United supporters and after one season at Withdean, decided to turn semi-professional and play at the County Ground. Rangers were accepted into the Southern League but folded in June 1901. John Jackson, the former United manager, organised a meeting at the Seven Stars public house, Ship Street on 24 June 1901 at which a new third club Brighton & Hove United was formed. They took over Rangers' place in the Southern League and pitch at County Ground. The name was changed to Brighton & Hove Albion before a match was played because of objections by Hove FC.

American Express Community Stadium, Village Way, Falmer, Brighton BN1 9BL.

Telephone: (01273) 878 288.

Fax: (01273) 878 241.

Ticket Office: (0844) 327 1901.

Website: www.seagulls.co.uk

Email: supporter.services@bhafc.co.uk

Ground Capacity: 30,750.

Record Attendance: 36,747 v Fulham, Division 2, 27 December 1958 (at Goldstone Ground); 8,691 v Leeds U, FL 1, 20 October 2007 (at Withdean); 30,338 v Bristol C, FL C, 29 April 2017 (at Amex).

Pitch Measurements: 105m × 68m (115yd × 74.5yd).

Chairman: Tony Bloom.

Chief Executive: Paul Barber.

Manager: Chris Hughton.

Assistant Manager: Paul Trollope.

Colours: Blue and white striped shirts with blue sleeves, blue shorts, blue socks with white trim.

Year Formed: 1901.

Turned Professional: 1901.

Club Nickname: 'The Seagulls'.

Grounds: 1901, County Ground; 1902, Goldstone Ground; 1997, groundshare at Gillingham FC; 1999, Withdean Stadium; 2011, American Express Community Stadium.

First Football League Game: 28 August 1920, Division 3, v Southend U (a) L 0–2 – Hayes; Woodhouse, Little; Hall, Comber, Bentley; Longstaff, Ritchie, Doran, Rodgerson, March.

Record League Victory: 9–1 v Newport Co, Division 3 (S), 18 April 1951 – Ball; Tennant (1p), Mansell (1p); Willard, McCoy, Wilson; Reed, McNichol (4), Garbutt, Bennett (2), Keene (1). 9–1 v Southend U, Division 3, 27 November 1965 – Powney; Magill, Baxter; Leck, Gall, Turner; Gould (1), Collins (1), Livesey (2), Smith (3), Goodchild (2).

HONOURS

League Champions: FL 1 – 2010–11; Second Division – 2001–02; Division 3S – 1957–58; Third Division – 2000–01; Division 4 – 1964–65.
Runners-up: FL C – 2016–17; Division 2 – 1978–79; Division 3 – 1971–72, 1976–77, 1987–88; Division 3S – 1953–54, 1955–56.

FA Cup: *Runners-up:* 1983.

League Cup: 5th rd – 1979.

sky SPORTS FACT FILE

Brighton & Hove Albion's first-ever game in the top flight took place at the Goldstone Ground on 18 August 1979 when they went down to a 4-0 defeat to Arsenal in front of a crowd of 28,347. Their biggest top-flight victory to date is 4-1, achieved against Coventry City (1979–80) and Manchester City (1980–81).

Record Cup Victory: 10–1 v Wisbech, FA Cup 1st rd, 13 November 1965 – Powney; Magill, Baxter; Collins (1), Gall, Turner; Gould, Smith (2), Livesey (3), Cassidy (2), Goodchild (1), (1 og).

Record Defeat: 0–9 v Middlesbrough, Division 2, 23 August 1958.

Most League Points (2 for a win): 65, Division 3 (S), 1955–56 and Division 3, 1971–72.

Most League Points (3 for a win): 95, FL 1, 2010–11.

Most League Goals: 112, Division 3 (S), 1955–56.

Highest League Scorer in Season: Peter Ward, 32, Division 3, 1976–77.

Most League Goals in Total Aggregate: Tommy Cook, 114, 1922–29.

Most League Goals in One Match: 5, Jack Doran v Northampton T, Division 3 (S), 5 November 1921; 5, Adrian Thorne v Watford, Division 3 (S), 30 April 1958.

Most Capped Player: Steve Penney, 17, Northern Ireland.

Most League Appearances: Ernie 'Tug' Wilson, 509, 1922–36.

Youngest League Player: Ian Chapman, 16 years 259 days v Birmingham C, 14 February 1987.

Record Transfer Fee Received: £8,000,000 from Leicester C for Leonardo Ulloa, July 2014.

Record Transfer Fee Paid: £6,000,000 to Valencia for Mathew Ryan, June 2017.

Football League Record: 1920 Original Member of Division 3; 1921–58 Division 3 (S); 1958–62 Division 2; 1962–63 Division 3; 1963–65 Division 4; 1965–72 Division 3; 1972–73 Division 2; 1973–77 Division 3; 1977–79 Division 2; 1979–83 Division 1; 1983–87 Division 2; 1987–88 Division 3; 1988–96 Division 2; 1996–2001 Division 3; 2001–02 Division 2; 2002–03 Division 1; 2003–04 Division 2; 2004–06 FL C; 2006–11 FL 1; 2011–17 FL C; 2017– FA Premier League.

MANAGERS

John Jackson 1901–05
Frank Scott-Walford 1905–08
John Robson 1908–14
Charles Webb 1919–47
Tommy Cook 1947
Don Welsh 1947–51
Billy Lane 1951–61
George Curtis 1961–63
Archie Macaulay 1963–68
Fred Goodwin 1968–70
Pat Saward 1970–73
Brian Clough 1973–74
Peter Taylor 1974–76
Alan Mullery 1976–81
Mike Bailey 1981–82
Jimmy Melia 1982–83
Chris Cattlin 1983–86
Alan Mullery 1986–87
Barry Lloyd 1987–93
Liam Brady 1993–95
Jimmy Case 1995–96
Steve Gritt 1996–98
Brian Horton 1998–99
Jeff Wood 1999
Micky Adams 1999–2001
Peter Taylor 2001–02
Martin Hinshelwood 2002
Steve Coppell 2002–03
Mark McGhee 2003–06
Dean Wilkins 2006–08
Micky Adams 2008–09
Russell Slade 2009
Gus Poyet 2009–13
Óscar Garcia 2013–14
Sammi Hyypia 2014
Chris Hughton December 2014–

LATEST SEQUENCES

Longest Sequence of League Wins: 9, 2.10.1926 – 20.11.1926.

Longest Sequence of League Defeats: 12, 17.8.2002 – 26.10.2002.

Longest Sequence of League Draws: 6, 16.2.1980 – 15.3.1980.

Longest Sequence of Unbeaten League Matches: 22, 2.5.2015 – 15.12.2015.

Longest Sequence Without a League Win: 15, 21.10.1972 – 27.1.1973.

Successive Scoring Runs: 31 from 4.2.1956.

Successive Non-scoring Runs: 6 from 23.9.1970.

TEN YEAR LEAGUE RECORD

		P	*W*	*D*	*L*	*F*	*A*	*Pts*	*Pos*
2007-08	FL 1	46	19	12	15	58	50	69	7
2008-09	FL 1	46	13	13	20	55	70	52	16
2009-10	FL 1	46	15	14	17	56	60	59	13
2010-11	FL 1	46	28	11	7	85	40	95	1
2011-12	FL C	46	17	15	14	52	52	66	10
2012-13	FL C	46	19	18	9	69	43	75	4
2013-14	FL C	46	19	15	12	55	40	72	6
2014-15	FL C	46	10	17	19	44	54	47	20
2015-16	FL C	46	24	17	5	72	42	89	3
2016-17	FL C	46	28	9	9	74	40	93	2

DID YOU KNOW?

Brighton & Hove Albion briefly adopted the nickname 'The Dolphins' in the early 1970s. In 1977 they became known as 'The Seagulls' and this has remained the case ever since. Previous nicknames have included 'Albion' and 'The Seasiders'.

BRIGHTON & HOVE ALBION – SKY BET CHAMPIONSHIP 2016–17 LEAGUE RECORD

Match No.	Date	Venue	Opponents	Result		H/T Score	Lg Pos.	Goalscorers	Attendance
1	Aug 6	A	Derby Co	D	0-0	0-0	11		28,749
2	12	H	Nottingham F	W	3-0	1-0	1	Knockaert [36], Murray 2 [68, 82]	25,748
3	16	H	Rotherham U	W	3-0	2-0	1	Knockaert [23], Murray [26], Hemed (pen) [58]	25,128
4	20	A	Reading	D	2-2	1-1	2	Baldock [8], Knockaert [46]	16,781
5	27	A	Newcastle U	L	0-2	0-1	6		49,196
6	Sept 10	H	Brentford	L	0-2	0-1	11		26,388
7	13	H	Huddersfield T	W	1-0	0-0	6	Knockaert [80]	24,166
8	17	A	Burton Alb	W	1-0	0-0	6	Hemed (pen) [88]	4756
9	24	H	Barnsley	W	2-0	1-0	3	Murray 2 [12, 48]	26,018
10	27	A	Ipswich T	D	0-0	0-0	3		15,228
11	Oct 1	A	Sheffield W	W	2-1	1-0	3	Baldock [26], Knockaert [73]	25,605
12	15	H	Preston NE	D	2-2	0-1	4	Baldock [54], Murray [65]	27,606
13	18	H	Wolverhampton W	W	1-0	1-0	3	Baldock [14]	25,231
14	22	A	Wigan Ath	W	1-0	0-0	2	Stephens [68]	10,430
15	29	H	Norwich C	W	5-0	1-0	2	Murray 3 [6, 60, 73], Dunk [64], Knockaert [84]	29,469
16	Nov 5	A	Bristol C	W	2-0	2-0	2	Sidwell [13], Murphy [20]	19,096
17	18	H	Aston Villa	D	1-1	1-1	2	Murray [45]	30,107
18	26	H	Fulham	W	2-1	0-1	2	Baldock [52], Murray [79]	29,445
19	Dec 3	A	Cardiff C	D	0-0	0-0	2		16,168
20	9	H	Leeds U	W	2-0	1-0	1	Murray (pen) [23], Hemed (pen) [82]	28,206
21	13	A	Blackburn R	W	3-2	1-0	1	Duffy [16], Stephens [61], Murray [79]	9976
22	17	A	Birmingham C	W	2-1	0-0	1	Knockaert [82], Murray [90]	17,287
23	27	H	QPR	W	3-0	1-0	1	Baldock [11], Murray (pen) [53], Knockaert [69]	30,176
24	Jan 2	A	Fulham	W	2-1	0-0	1	Hemed (pen) [74], Dunk [75]	24,300
25	14	A	Preston NE	L	0-2	0-1	2		11,391
26	20	H	Sheffield W	W	2-1	1-1	1	Knockaert 2 [34, 85]	27,162
27	24	H	Cardiff C	W	1-0	0-0	1	Hemed [73]	26,688
28	Feb 2	A	Huddersfield T	L	1-3	1-3	1	Hemed [20]	20,104
29	5	A	Brentford	D	3-3	0-2	2	March [75], Duffy [78], Hemed [90]	10,433
30	11	H	Burton Alb	W	4-1	1-0	1	Hemed 2 (1 pen) [12, 57 (p)], Baldock [47], Murray [83]	29,464
31	14	H	Ipswich T	D	1-1	1-1	2	Hemed (pen) [29]	26,360
32	18	A	Barnsley	W	2-0	0-0	1	Baldock 2 [53, 68]	12,743
33	25	H	Reading	W	3-0	1-0	1	Baldock [35], Murphy [56], Knockaert [80]	29,613
34	28	H	Newcastle U	L	1-2	1-0	2	Murray (pen) [14]	30,230
35	Mar 4	A	Nottingham F	L	0-3	0-0	2		22,020
36	7	A	Rotherham U	W	2-0	0-0	2	Knockaert [48], March [79]	8366
37	10	H	Derby Co	W	3-0	2-0	2	Knockaert [5], Baldock [43], Murray [78]	27,552
38	18	A	Leeds U	L	0-2	0-0	2		29,767
39	Apr 1	H	Blackburn R	W	1-0	0-0	2	Murray [67]	30,216
40	4	H	Birmingham C	W	3-1	1-0	1	Murray [2], Hemed [48], Hunemeier [54]	28,654
41	7	A	QPR	W	2-1	0-0	1	Murray [58], Pocognoli [64]	16,503
42	14	A	Wolverhampton W	W	2-0	1-0	1	Knockaert 2 [45, 82]	23,221
43	17	H	Wigan Ath	W	2-1	1-0	1	Murray [37], March [65]	29,940
44	21	A	Norwich C	L	0-2	0-2	1		26,932
45	29	H	Bristol C	L	0-1	0-1	1		30,338
46	May 7	A	Aston Villa	D	1-1	0-0	2	Murray (pen) [64]	32,856

Final League Position: 2

GOALSCORERS

League (74): Murray 23 (4 pens), Knockaert 15, Baldock 11, Hemed 11 (6 pens), March 3, Duffy 2, Dunk 2, Murphy 2, Stephens 2, Hunemeier 1, Pocognoli 1, Sidwell 1.
FA Cup (3): Hemed 1, Kayal 1, Towell 1.
EFL Cup (9): Hemed 2, Manu 2, Murphy 2, Adekugbe 1, Baldock 1, LuaLua 1.
EFL Checkatrade Trophy (5): Towell 2 (1 pen), Ince 1, Manu 1, Starkey 1.

Stockdale D 45	Rosenior L 9 + 1	Saltor B 42	Dunk L 43	Bong G 24	Knockaert A 44 + 1	Sidwell S 26 + 8	Kayal B 17 + 3	Skalak J 24 + 7	Murray G 39 + 6	Hemed T 20 + 17	Baldock S 27 + 4	Murphy J 20 + 15	LuaLua K — + 3	Stephens D 33 + 6	Norwood O 16 + 17	Maenpaa N 1	Duffy S 31	Manu E — + 2	Hunt R — + 1	Pocognoli S 17 + 3	Goldson C 4 + 1	March S 9 + 16	Adekugbe S 1	Akpom C 1 + 9	Hunemeier U 11	Tomori F 2 + 7	Towell R — + 1	Match No.
1	2	3	4	5	6[3]	7	8	9[2]	10	11[1]	12	13	14															1
1	2	3	4	5	6	7	8[2]	9[3]	10	11[1]	12			13	14													2
	2	3	4	5	6[1]				11[2]	10	12	9	13	7	8	1												3
1	2	3	4	5	6	7	8	9[1]	10[2]	14	11[3]	13			12													4
1		2	4	5	6	7[1]	8	9[2]	10[3]	12	11■		14		13		3											5
1		2	4	5	6		8	14	10	11[2]		9[3]		13	7[1]		3	12										6
1		2	4	5	10[3]	13	8	6[1]	12	11[2]		9		7			3	14										7
1		2[2]	4	5	6		7[1]	9	12	11		10[3]		8	14		3		13									8
1		2	4	5	6	14	8[1]	9[2]	11	10[3]	13			7	12		3											9
1		2	4		6	13		9[2]	10	11[1]		12		7■	8		3			5								10
1		2	4	5	6	8		12	11[2]	13	10[1]	9			7		3											11
1		2	4	5	6	7			10		11[1]	9		12	8		3											12
1		2[1]	4	5	6[3]	8		9	11		10[2]			13	7		3			14	12							13
1		2		5	6[1]	8		9	10		11[3]	13		12	7[2]		4			14	3							14
1		2	4	5	6[1]	8		9	10[2]	12	11[3]	14		7	13		3											15
1		2	4	5		8		6[1]	10[2]	13	11[3]	9		7	12		3					14						16
1		2	4	5	6[1]	8		9	10		11[2]	12		7	13		3											17
1		2	4	5	6[2]	8		12	10		11[1]	9		7	13		3											18
1		2	4	5■	12	8		6[2]	10		11[1]	9		7			3			13								19
1		2	4		6[1]			14	10[3]	13	11	9[2]		7	8		3			5		12						20
1		2	4		6[2]	13		9	12	11[1]	10[3]			7	8		3			5		14						21
1		2	4	5	6	8[3]		9[1]	10	14	11[2]			7	12		3					13						22
1		2	4	5	6			14	10[1]	13	11[2]	12		7	8		3					9[3]						23
1		2	4	5	6[3]			9[1]	10	13	11[2]	14		7	8		3					12						24
1		2			6	7[3]	14	9[2]	11	13	10[1]	12			8		4				3		5					25
1			4		6[3]	12		14	10■	11		9[1]		7	8[2]		3			5	2	13						26
1			4		8[1]	13	7[2]	14		11		10		6	12		3			5	2	9[3]						27
1		2	4■		6	12	7[1]		10	11[2]		9[3]			8		3			5		13		14				28
1		2			6	7		9[3]	11[1]	14		10[2]			8		3			5		12		13	4			29
1		2	4		6	7	12		14	10[2]	11[1]			8[3]			3			5		9		13				30
1		2	4		6	8			12	11[3]	10[2]	13		7			3			5		9[1]		14				31
1		2	4		6[2]	8			11[1]		10	9		7			3			5				12		13		32
1		2	4		6	8			10[2]	12	11[1]	9		7			3			5[3]				13		14		33
1		2	4		6[1]	8	13		11		10[3]	9		7			3			5[2]		14				12		34
1	5	2	4		6	8[1]			11	14	10[2]	9[3]		7	13		3					12						35
1	5	2	4		6[1]		7	9	13	11[2]	10[3]			8								12			3		14	36
1	5	2[1]	4		6[3]		8	9	10[2]	13	11			7								14			3	12		37
1	5		4		6		8[3]	9[2]	11		10[1]			7	14							12		13	3	2		38
1	2		4		6[2]		8	9[3]	10	12		14		7						5		13		11[1]	3			39
1		2	4[2]	5	6[3]		8		10	11		13		7[1]	14							9			3	12		40
1		2	4[3]		6[1]	8			10	11[2]		13		7	14					5		9			3	12		41
1		2	4		6	8			10	11[2]		12		7	13					5		9[1]			3			42
1		2	4	5	6		8[3]		10	11[1]		12		7	13							9[2]		14	3			43
1		2	4		6[1]	8			11[3]	12		10		13	7[2]					5		9		14	3			44
1		2	4[2]	5	6	13	8[1]	9[3]	10	11				7								12			3	14		45
1	13	2[1]	4		6	8			11	14	10[3]	9[2]		7						5		12				3		46

FA Cup

Third Round	Milton Keynes D	(h)	2-0
Fourth Round	Lincoln C	(a)	1-3

EFL Cup

First Round	Colchester U	(h)	4-0
Second Round	Oxford U	(a)	4-2
Third Round	Reading	(h)	1-2

EFL Checkatrade Trophy (Brighton & HA U21)

Southern Group G	Southend U	(a)	0-2
Southern Group G	Stevenage	(a)	2-2
(Brighton & HA won 4-3 on penalties)			
Southern Group G	Leyton Orient	(h)	1-0
Second Round South	AFC Wimbledon	(a)	2-1
Third Round	Coventry C	(a)	0-3

BRISTOL CITY

FOUNDATION

The name Bristol City came into being in 1897 when the Bristol South End club, formed three years earlier, decided to adopt professionalism and apply for admission to the Southern League after competing in the Western League. The historic meeting was held at the Albert Hall, Bedminster. Bristol City employed Sam Hollis from Woolwich Arsenal as manager and gave him £40 to buy players. In 1900 they merged with Bedminster, another leading Bristol club.

Ashton Gate Stadium, Ashton Road, Bristol BS3 2EJ.

Telephone: (0117) 963 0600.

Fax: (0117) 963 0700.

Ticket Office: (0117) 963 0600 (option 1).

Website: www.bcfc.co.uk

Email: enquiries@bcfc.co.uk

Ground Capacity: 26,478.

Record Attendance: 43,335 v Preston NE, FA Cup 5th rd, 16 February 1935.

Pitch Measurements: 105m × 68.5m (115yd × 75yd).

Chairman: Keith Dawe.

Chief Operating Officer: Mark Ashton.

Head Coach: Lee Johnson.

First-Team Coach: Dean Holden.

Colours: Red shirts with white trim, red shorts with white trim, red socks with white trim.

Year Formed: 1894.

Turned Professional: 1897.

Previous Name: 1894, Bristol South End; 1897, Bristol City.

Club Nickname: 'Robins'.

Grounds: 1894, St John's Lane; 1904, Ashton Gate.

First Football League Game: 7 September 1901, Division 2, v Blackpool (a) W 2–0 – Moles; Tuft, Davies; Jones, McLean, Chambers; Bradbury, Connor, Boucher, O'Brien (2), Flynn.

Record League Victory: 9–0 v Aldershot, Division 3 (S), 28 December 1946 – Eddols; Morgan, Fox; Peacock, Roberts, Jones (1); Chilcott, Thomas, Clark (4 incl. 1p), Cyril Williams (1), Hargreaves (3).

Record Cup Victory: 11–0 v Chichester C, FA Cup 1st rd, 5 November 1960 – Cook; Collinson, Thresher; Connor, Alan Williams, Etheridge; Tait (1), Bobby Williams (1), Atyeo (5), Adrian Williams (3), Derrick, (1 og).

Record Defeat: 0–9 v Coventry C, Division 3 (S), 28 April 1934.

HONOURS

League Champions: Division 2 – 1905–06; FL 1 – 2014–15; Division 3S – 1922–23, 1926–27, 1954–55.
Runners-up: Division 1 – 1906–07; Division 2 – 1975–76; FL 1 – 2006–07; Second Division – 1997–98; Division 3 – 1964–65, 1989–90; Division 3S – 1937–38.

FA Cup: *Runners-up:* 1909.

League Cup: semi-final – 1971, 1989.

League Trophy Winners: 1986, 2003, 2015.
Runners-up: 1987, 2000.

Welsh Cup Winners: 1934.

Anglo-Scottish Cup Winners: 1978.

sky SPORTS FACT FILE

Former England international striker Joe Royle had the distinction of scoring four goals on his debut for Bristol City against Middlesbrough after joining on loan from Manchester City in November 1977. The Robins won 4-1 and, not surprisingly, the move was made permanent the following month.

Most League Points (2 for a win): 70, Division 3 (S), 1954–55.

Most League Points (3 for a win): 99, FL 1, 2014–15.

Most League Goals: 104, Division 3 (S), 1926–27.

Highest League Scorer in Season: Don Clark, 36, Division 3 (S), 1946–47.

Most League Goals in Total Aggregate: John Atyeo, 314, 1951–66.

Most League Goals in One Match: 6, Tommy 'Tot' Walsh v Gillingham, Division 3 (S), 15 January 1927.

Most Capped Player: Billy Wedlock, 26, England.

Most League Appearances: John Atyeo, 596, 1951–66.

Youngest League Player: Marvin Brown, 16 years 105 days v Bristol R, 17 October 1999.

Record Transfer Fee Received: £11,000,000 from Aston Villa for Jonathan Kodjia, August 2016.

Record Transfer Fee Paid: £5,300,000 to Angers for Famara Diedhiou, June 2017.

Football League Record: 1901 Elected to Division 2; 1906–11 Division 1; 1911–22 Division 2; 1922–23 Division 3 (S); 1923–24 Division 2; 1924–27 Division 3 (S); 1927–32 Division 2; 1932–55 Division 3 (S); 1955–60 Division 2; 1960–65 Division 3; 1965–76 Division 2; 1976–80 Division 1; 1980–81 Division 2; 1981–82 Division 3; 1982–84 Division 4; 1984–90 Division 3; 1990–92 Division 2; 1992–95 Division 1; 1995–98 Division 2; 1998–99 Division 1; 1999–2004 Division 2; 2004–07 FL 1; 2007–13 FL C; 2013–15 FL 1; 2015– FL C.

LATEST SEQUENCES

Longest Sequence of League Wins: 14, 9.9.1905 – 2.12.1905.

Longest Sequence of League Defeats: 8, 10.12.2016 – 21.1.2017.

Longest Sequence of League Draws: 4, 6.11.1999 – 27.11.1999.

Longest Sequence of Unbeaten League Matches: 24, 9.9.1905 – 10.2.1906.

Longest Sequence Without a League Win: 21, 16.3.2013 – 22.10.2013.

Successive Scoring Runs: 25 from 26.12.1905.

Successive Non-scoring Runs: 6 from 20.12.1980.

MANAGERS

Sam Hollis 1897–99
Bob Campbell 1899–1901
Sam Hollis 1901–05
Harry Thickett 1905–10
Frank Bacon 1910–11
Sam Hollis 1911–13
George Hedley 1913–17
Jack Hamilton 1917–19
Joe Palmer 1919–21
Alex Raisbeck 1921–29
Joe Bradshaw 1929–32
Bob Hewison 1932–49 (*under suspension 1938–39*)
Bob Wright 1949–50
Pat Beasley 1950–58
Peter Doherty 1958–60
Fred Ford 1960–67
Alan Dicks 1967–80
Bobby Houghton 1980–82
Roy Hodgson 1982
Terry Cooper 1982–88 (*Director from 1983*)
Joe Jordan 1988–90
Jimmy Lumsden 1990–92
Denis Smith 1992–93
Russell Osman 1993–94
Joe Jordan 1994–97
John Ward 1997–98
Benny Lennartsson 1998–99
Tony Pulis 1999–2000
Tony Fawthrop 2000
Danny Wilson 2000–04
Brian Tinnion 2004–05
Gary Johnson 2005–10
Steve Coppell 2010
Keith Millen 2010–11
Derek McInnes 2011–13
Sean O'Driscoll 2013
Steve Cotterill 2013–16
Lee Johnson February 2016–

TEN YEAR LEAGUE RECORD

		P	W	D	L	F	A	Pts	Pos
2007-08	FL C	46	20	14	12	54	53	74	4
2008-09	FL C	46	15	16	15	54	54	61	10
2009-10	FL C	46	15	18	13	56	65	63	10
2010-11	FL C	46	17	9	20	62	65	60	15
2011-12	FL C	46	12	13	21	44	68	49	20
2012-13	FL C	46	11	8	27	59	84	41	24
2013-14	FL 1	46	13	19	14	70	67	58	12
2014-15	FL 1	46	29	12	5	96	38	99	1
2015-16	FL C	46	13	13	20	54	71	52	18
2016-17	FL C	46	15	9	22	60	66	54	17

DID YOU KNOW ?

Bristol City lost the opening game of the 1905–06 season 5-1 away to Manchester United. They then lost just one more League game and finished the campaign as Division Two champions, four points clear of United.

BRISTOL CITY – SKY BET CHAMPIONSHIP 2016–17 LEAGUE RECORD

Match No.	Date	Venue	Opponents	Result	H/T Score	Lg Pos.	Goalscorers	Attendance
1	Aug 6	H	Wigan Ath	W 2-1	0-1	4	Magnusson [81], Reid [90]	17,635
2	13	A	Burton Alb	W 2-1	1-0	1	Abraham 2 [44, 90]	4579
3	16	A	Norwich C	L 0-1	0-1	7		26,297
4	20	H	Newcastle U	L 0-1	0-1	10		22,512
5	27	H	Aston Villa	W 3-1	0-1	4	Abraham [59], Bryan [61], Tomlin [81]	21,099
6	Sept 10	A	Rotherham U	D 2-2	0-1	9	Abraham [74], Reid [83]	8559
7	13	A	Sheffield W	L 2-3	2-0	12	Abraham 2 [33, 39]	24,151
8	17	H	Derby Co	D 1-1	0-1	10	Wilbraham [90]	19,451
9	24	A	Fulham	W 4-0	1-0	10	Abraham [10], Freeman [60], Reid [68], Flint [83]	20,585
10	27	H	Leeds U	W 1-0	0-0	5	Pack [59]	19,699
11	Oct 1	H	Nottingham F	W 2-1	0-1	2	Abraham [65], Paterson [68]	18,922
12	14	A	Cardiff C	L 1-2	0-1	5	Tomlin [69]	22,776
13	18	A	QPR	L 0-1	0-0	6		12,552
14	22	H	Blackburn R	W 1-0	0-0	5	Wilbraham [88]	21,452
15	29	A	Barnsley	D 2-2	0-1	5	Tomlin (pen) [58], Abraham [76]	11,869
16	Nov 5	H	Brighton & HA	L 0-2	0-2	7		19,096
17	19	A	Birmingham C	L 0-1	0-0	10		18,586
18	26	A	Reading	L 1-2	0-2	13	O'Neil [87]	18,778
19	Dec 3	H	Ipswich T	W 2-0	1-0	9	Tomlin (pen) [31], Freeman [72]	18,309
20	10	A	Huddersfield T	L 1-2	1-1	13	Abraham [33]	18,333
21	13	H	Brentford	L 0-1	0-0	15		16,444
22	17	H	Preston NE	L 1-2	0-1	16	Wilbraham [78]	18,619
23	26	A	Wolverhampton W	L 2-3	2-1	17	Abraham [38], Flint [44]	24,669
24	30	A	Ipswich T	L 1-2	0-1	17	Abraham [52]	15,640
25	Jan 2	H	Reading	L 2-3	1-0	18	Abraham 2 (1 pen) [27, 47 (p)]	20,074
26	14	H	Cardiff C	L 2-3	0-0	19	Murphy (og) [51], Abraham [78]	19,452
27	21	A	Nottingham F	L 0-1	0-0	20		17,418
28	31	H	Sheffield W	D 2-2	1-1	20	Tomlin (pen) [31], Abraham [70]	17,438
29	Feb 4	H	Rotherham U	W 1-0	0-0	20	Djuric [73]	18,737
30	11	A	Derby Co	D 3-3	3-0	20	Taylor [14], Abraham 2 [27, 38]	28,043
31	14	A	Leeds U	L 1-2	0-1	20	Taylor [90]	22,402
32	22	H	Fulham	L 0-2	0-1	21		17,272
33	25	A	Newcastle U	D 2-2	2-0	21	Wilbraham [11], Cotterill [21]	52,131
34	28	A	Aston Villa	L 0-2	0-0	21		28,119
35	Mar 4	H	Burton Alb	D 0-0	0-0	22		17,914
36	7	H	Norwich C	D 1-1	0-1	22	Wright [78]	17,035
37	11	A	Wigan Ath	W 1-0	0-0	21	Flint [88]	10,787
38	17	H	Huddersfield T	W 4-0	2-0	19	Tomlin [30], Abraham [45], Flint [79], Cotterill (pen) [83]	16,984
39	Apr 1	A	Brentford	L 0-2	0-2	21		11,360
40	4	A	Preston NE	L 0-5	0-1	21		10,224
41	8	H	Wolverhampton W	W 3-1	2-0	21	Paterson [33], Abraham 2 (1 pen) [39 (p), 49]	20,323
42	14	H	QPR	W 2-1	2-0	18	Pack [14], Paterson [40]	20,404
43	17	A	Blackburn R	D 1-1	1-0	18	Abraham [14]	13,935
44	22	H	Barnsley	W 3-2	0-1	17	Abraham [53], Paterson [69], Flint [74]	18,617
45	29	A	Brighton & HA	W 1-0	1-0	17	Brownhill [43]	30,338
46	May 7	H	Birmingham C	L 0-1	0-1	17		25,404

Final League Position: 17

GOALSCORERS

League (60): Abraham 23 (2 pens), Tomlin 6 (3 pens), Flint 5, Paterson 4, Wilbraham 4, Reid 3, Cotterill 2 (1 pen), Freeman 2, Pack 2, Taylor 2, Brownhill 1, Bryan 1, Djuric 1, Magnusson 1, O'Neil 1, Wright 1, own goal 1.
FA Cup (1): Paterson 1.
EFL Cup (6): Abraham 3, Reid 1, Tomlin 1, Wilbraham 1.

O'Donnell R 8	Ayling L 1	Flint A 46	Magnusson H 26 + 2	Bryan J 39 + 5	Pack M 29 + 4	O'Neil G 22 + 7	O'Dowda C 15 + 19	Brownhill J 19 + 8	Tomlin L 30 + 8	Kodjia J 4	Abraham T 40 + 1	Reid B 18 + 12	Freeman L 14 + 4	Little M 26 + 2	Wilbraham A 8 + 23	Matthews A 11 + 1	Golbourne S 17 + 2	Paterson J 16 + 6	Ekstrand J 1 + 1	Smith K 21 + 2	Fielding F 27	Moore T 1 + 4	Engvall G — + 2	Lucic I 1 + 1	Hegeler J 8 + 4	Wright B 21	Djuric M 3 + 8	Giefer F 10	Cotterill D 12 + 1	Taylor M 9 + 6	Vyner Z 3	Match No.
1	2	3	4	5	6^{3}	7	8^{1}	9^{2}	10	11	12	13	14																			1
1		3	4	5	14	7	9^{1}	8^{2}	6^{3}	10	11	12		2	13																	2
1		3	4	5	6^{1}	7	10^{2}		9	8	11	14	12	2^{3}		13																3
1		3	4			6	13		9	8	11^{1}	7	10	12	14	2^{2}	5^{3}															4
1		3	4	10^{3}	13	6	12		9		11^{2}	7	8^{1}	2	14		5															5
1		3	4	10		6	12		9		11	7	8^{3}	2^{1}			5^{2}	13	14													6
1		3	4	5	9	6■	7^{2}	8^{1}	10^{3}		11	14		2			12			13												7
		3	4	8^{1}	6^{3}				9		10	7	13	5	14		12	11	2^{2}		1											8
		3	4	5	6		14	13	9^{2}		11^{1}	7	10^{3}	2	12			8			1											9
		3	4	5	6	13			9^{3}		11^{2}	7	10	2^{1}	14			8			1	12										10
		3	4	14	6^{1}	13	10	7			11	9^{2}			12		5	8			1	2^{3}										11
		3	4	5	7^{3}	6	14		9		11^{1}	13	10	2	12			8^{2}			1											12
		3	4	5	13	7	8^{3}	6^{2}	10		11	9^{1}	14		12	2					1											13
		3	4	14		7			9		11		10^{3}		12	2^{2}	5	8^{1}		6	1	13										14
		3	4	13		6		14	9		11	7^{3}			10	2^{1}	5^{2}			8	1	12										15
1		3	4	10^{2}		6	14		9		11	13		2	12		5^{3}	8		7^{1}												16
		3	4	5	6	7^{2}	14		10		11	9		2^{3}	13			8^{1}		12	1											17
		3	4	5	6	7	13		10^{3}		11	9		2^{2}	12			8^{1}			1		14									18
		3	4		7	14		12	9^{2}		10	13	6^{3}		11	2	5			8^{1}	1											19
		3	4	12	8^{2}	13			9		10	14	6^{3}		11^{1}	2	5			7	1											20
		3	4	10	6^{1}				13		11	9	8			2	5^{3}			7	1^{2}		14	12								21
		3	4	5	6^{1}	7		13	9		11	10^{3}	8^{2}		12	2		14						1								22
		3	4	5	7		12	6	9		11	10^{1}	8^{2}	13	14	2^{3}					1											23
		3	4^{1}	13	8		14	7	9		11		6	2^{2}	10		5^{3}				1	12										24
		3		9			7^{1}	8			11	12	10^{2}	2	13	4	5			6	1											25
		3		8	7		9^{1}	6^{3}	14		11			5	12			13			1				2	4	10^{2}					26
		3	4	8		6^{1}	13	12	14		11			5^{3}				9							7	2	10^{2}	1				27
		3		9		13	10^{1}	7	8^{2}		11			2			5								6	4	12	1				28
		3		10	7				9^{1}		11^{3}			2^{2}			5	13							6	4	14	1	8	12		29
		3		9			13	8			11^{2}			2			5								7	4	12	1	6	10^{1}		30
		3		9		14		8	10		11^{1}			2^{3}			5^{2}								7	4	13	1	6	12		31
		3		9		14		7^{2}	13			12				2^{3}	5								8^{1}	4	11	1	6	10		32
		3	12	5^{1}	13	6	10					9			11					8^{2}					14	4		1	7^{3}		2	33
		3		5		7	10^{1}		14			9			11^{3}			13		6^{2}						4		1	8	12	2	34
		3	4	8		7			11^{2}			9^{3}			10^{1}			14		6						2	13	1	5	12		35
		3		5	7		10		14			9^{1}			11^{3}					6	1					4	13		8	12	2^{2}	36
		3		5	8^{3}	7	13	14	9		10				12					2	1					4			6^{1}	11^{2}		37
		3		5	7	6^{1}	10	12	9^{3}		11^{2}				14					2	1				13	4			8			38
		3		5	7^{2}	6^{3}	10		9		11	13								2	1				14	4			8^{1}	12		39
		3	13	5	7^{2}		10^{1}	14	9		11				12					2	1				6^{3}	4			8			40
		3		5	8		13	6			10^{1}			2	12			9^{3}		7	1				14	4				11^{2}		41
		3		5	8		13	6	14		10^{3}			2	12			9^{1}		7	1					4				11^{2}		42
		3		5	8		12	6			10			2^{2}	14			9^{3}		7	1					4			13	11^{1}		43
		3		5	8		12	6			10			2				9^{1}		7	1					4				11		44
		3		5	8		14	6			11^{3}	12		2				9^{2}		7	1					4	13			10^{1}		45
		3		5	8		14	6	12		10			2^{3}				9^{2}		7						4	13	1		11^{1}		46

FA Cup

Third Round	Fleetwood T	(h)	0-0
Replay	Fleetwood T	(a)	1-0
Fourth Round	Burnley	(a)	0-2

EFL Cup

First Round	Wycombe W	(a)	1-0
Second Round	Scunthorpe U	(a)	2-1
(*aet*)			
Third Round	Fulham	(a)	2-1
Fourth Round	Hull C	(h)	1-2

BRISTOL ROVERS

FOUNDATION

Bristol Rovers were formed at a meeting in Stapleton Road, Eastville, in 1883. However, they first went under the name of the Black Arabs (wearing black shirts). Changing their name to Eastville Rovers in their second season in 1888–89, they won the Gloucestershire Senior Cup. Original members of the Bristol & District League in 1892, this eventually became the Western League and Eastville Rovers adopted professionalism in 1897.

The Memorial Stadium, Filton Avenue, Horfield, Bristol BS7 0BF.

Telephone: (0117) 909 6648.

Fax: (0117) 907 4312.

Ticket Office: (0117) 909 6648 (option 1).

Website: www.bristolrovers.co.uk

Email: dave@bristolrovers.co.uk

Ground Capacity: 12,296.

Record Attendance: 38,472 v Preston NE, FA Cup 4th rd, 30 January 1960 (at Eastville); 9,464 v Liverpool, FA Cup 4th rd, 8 February 1992 (at Twerton Park); 12,011 v WBA, FA Cup 6th rd, 9 March 2008 (at Memorial Stadium).

HONOURS

League Champions: Division 3 – 1989–90; Division 3S – 1952–53.
Runners-up: Division 3 – 1973–74; Conference – (2nd) 2014–15 *(promoted via play-offs)*.

FA Cup: 6th rd – 1951, 1958, 2008.

League Cup: 5th rd – 1971, 1972.

League Trophy: *Runners-up:* 1990, 2007.

Pitch Measurements: 100m × 64m (109.5yd × 70yd).

Chairman: Steve Hamer.

Manager: Darrell Clarke.

Assistant Manager: Marcus Stewart.

Physio: Paul Maxwell.

Colours: Blue and white quartered shirts, blue shorts with white trim, white socks with blue trim.

Year Formed: 1883.

Turned Professional: 1897.

Previous Names: 1883, Black Arabs; 1884, Eastville Rovers; 1897, Bristol Eastville Rovers; 1898, Bristol Rovers. ***Club Nicknames:*** 'The Pirates', 'The Gas'.

Grounds: 1883, Purdown; Three Acres, Ashley Hill; Rudgeway, Fishponds; 1897, Eastville; 1986, Twerton Park; 1996, The Memorial Stadium.

First Football League Game: 28 August 1920, Division 3, v Millwall (a) L 0–2 – Stansfield; Bethune, Panes; Boxley, Kenny, Steele; Chance, Bird, Sims, Bell, Palmer.

Record League Victory: 7–0 v Brighton & HA, Division 3 (S), 29 November 1952 – Hoyle; Bamford, Fox; Pitt, Warren, Sampson; McIlvenny, Roost (2), Lambden (1), Bradford (1), Petherbridge (2), (1 og). 7–0 v Swansea T, Division 2, 2 October 1954 – Radford; Bamford, Watkins; Pitt, Muir, Anderson; Petherbridge, Bradford (2), Meyer, Roost (1), Hooper (2), (2 og). 7–0 v Shrewsbury T, Division 3, 21 March 1964 – Hall; Hillard, Gwyn Jones; Oldfield, Stone (1), Mabbutt; Jarman (2), Brown (1), Biggs (1p), Hamilton, Bobby Jones (2).

Record Cup Victory: 7–1 v Dorchester, FA Cup 4th qualifying rd, 25 October 2014 – Midenhall; Locyer, Trotman (McChrystal), Parkes, Monkhouse (2), Clarke, Mansell (1) (Thomas), Brown, Gosling, Harrison (3), Taylor (1) (White).

Record Defeat: 0–12 v Luton T, Division 3 (S), 13 April 1936.

sky SPORTS FACT FILE

Bristol Rovers played a number of home games at Ashton Gate, the home of rivals Bristol City, in the 1939–40 season. Attendances were so poor that matches were subsequently switched to the Aero Engine Ground in Kingswood in the second half of the season.

Most League Points (2 for a win): 64, Division 3 (S), 1952–53.
Most League Points (3 for a win): 93, Division 3, 1989–90.
Most League Goals: 92, Division 3 (S), 1952–53.
Highest League Scorer in Season: Geoff Bradford, 33, Division 3 (S), 1952–53.
Most League Goals in Total Aggregate: Geoff Bradford, 242, 1949–64.
Most League Goals in One Match: 4, Sidney Leigh v Exeter C, Division 3 (S), 2 May 1921; 4, Jonah Wilcox v Bournemouth, Division 3 (S), 12 December 1925; 4, Bill Culley v QPR, Division 3 (S), 5 March 1927; 4, Frank Curran v Swindon T, Division 3 (S), 25 March 1939; 4, Vic Lambden v Aldershot, Division 3 (S), 29 March 1947; 4, George Petherbridge v Torquay U, Division 3 (S), 1 December 1951; 4, Vic Lambden v Colchester U, Division 3 (S), 14 May 1952; 4, Geoff Bradford v Rotherham U, Division 2, 14 March 1959; 4, Robin Stubbs v Gillingham, Division 2, 10 October 1970; 4, Alan Warboys v Brighton & HA, Division 3, 1 December 1973; 4, Jamie Cureton v Reading, Division 2, 16 January 1999; 4, Ellis Harrison v Northampton T, FL 1, 7 January 2017.
Most Capped Player: Vitalijs Astafjevs, 31 (167), Latvia.
Most League Appearances: Stuart Taylor, 546, 1966–80.
Youngest League Player: Ronnie Dix, 15 years 173 days v Charlton Ath, 25 February 1928.
Record Transfer Fee Received: £2,100,000 from Fulham for Barry Hayles, November 1998; £2,100,000 from WBA for Jason Roberts, July 2000.
Record Transfer Fee Paid: £375,000 to QPR for Andy Tillson, November 1992.
Football League Record: 1920 Original Member of Division 3; 1921–53 Division 3 (S); 1953–62 Division 2; 1962–74 Division 3; 1974–81 Division 2; 1981–90 Division 3; 1990–92 Division 2. 1992–93 Division 1; 1993–2001 Division 2; 2001–04 Division 3; 2004–07 FL 2; 2007–11 FL 1; 2011–14 FL 2; 2014–15 Conference Premier; 2015–16 FL 2; 2016– FL 1.

MANAGERS

Alfred Homer 1899–1920 (*continued as Secretary to 1928*)
Ben Hall 1920–21
Andy Wilson 1921–26
Joe Palmer 1926–29
Dave McLean 1929–30
Albert Prince-Cox 1930–36
Percy Smith 1936–37
Brough Fletcher 1938–49
Bert Tann 1950–68 (*continued as General Manager to 1972*)
Fred Ford 1968–69
Bill Dodgin Snr 1969–72
Don Megson 1972–77
Bobby Campbell 1978–79
Harold Jarman 1979–80
Terry Cooper 1980–81
Bobby Gould 1981–83
David Williams 1983–85
Bobby Gould 1985–87
Gerry Francis 1987–91
Martin Dobson 1991
Dennis Rofe 1992
Malcolm Allison 1992–93
John Ward 1993–96
Ian Holloway 1996–2001
Garry Thompson 2001
Gerry Francis 2001
Garry Thompson 2001–02
Ray Graydon 2002–04
Ian Atkins 2004–05
Paul Trollope 2005–10
Dave Penney 2011
Paul Buckle 2011–12
Mark McGhee 2012
John Ward 2012–14
Darrell Clarke March 2014–

LATEST SEQUENCES

Longest Sequence of League Wins: 12, 18.10.1952 – 17.1.1953.
Longest Sequence of League Defeats: 8, 26.10.2002 – 21.12.2002.
Longest Sequence of League Draws: 6, 4.2.2017 – 28.2.2017.
Longest Sequence of Unbeaten League Matches: 32, 7.4.1973 – 27.1.1974.
Longest Sequence Without a League Win: 20, 5.4.1980 – 1.11.1980.
Successive Scoring Runs: 26 from 26.3.1927.
Successive Non-scoring Runs: 6 from 14.10.1922.

TEN YEAR LEAGUE RECORD

		P	W	D	L	F	A	Pts	Pos
2007-08	FL 1	46	12	17	17	45	53	53	16
2008-09	FL 1	46	17	12	17	79	61	63	11
2009-10	FL 1	46	19	5	22	59	70	62	11
2010-11	FL 1	46	11	12	23	48	82	45	22
2011-12	FL 2	46	15	12	19	60	70	57	13
2012-13	FL 2	46	16	12	18	60	69	60	14
2013-14	FL 2	46	12	14	20	43	54	50	23
2014-15	Conf P	46	25	16	5	73	34	91	2
2015-16	FL 2	46	26	7	13	77	46	85	3
2016-17	FL 1	46	18	12	16	68	70	66	10

DID YOU KNOW ?

Bristol Rovers' 1973–74 strike force of Alan Warboys and Bruce Bannister were widely known as 'Smash and Grab'. Between them they scored 40 of Rovers' 65 League goals to ensure promotion from the Third Division that season.

BRISTOL ROVERS – SKY BET LEAGUE ONE 2016–17 LEAGUE RECORD

Match No.	Date	Venue	Opponents	Result		H/T Score	Lg Pos.	Goalscorers	Attendance
1	Aug 6	A	Scunthorpe U	L	1-3	1-0	21	Taylor [31]	4636
2	14	H	Oxford U	W	2-1	1-1	12	Easter [25], Taylor [70]	10,053
3	17	H	Bolton W	L	1-2	0-2	17	Harrison [57]	9169
4	20	A	Southend U	D	1-1	0-0	18	Hartley [61]	6084
5	Sept 10	H	Rochdale	D	2-2	1-2	19	Taylor 2 [21, 49]	8057
6	13	H	Walsall	D	1-1	1-1	19	Taylor (pen) [27]	7805
7	17	A	Bradford C	D	1-1	0-0	21	Colkett [86]	17,489
8	20	A	Swindon T	W	2-1	0-1	15	Taylor (pen) [83], Branco (og) [84]	6760
9	24	H	Port Vale	W	2-1	1-1	9	Harrison [44], Easter (pen) [63]	9088
10	27	A	Sheffield U	L	0-1	0-0	10		19,196
11	Oct 1	A	Northampton T	W	3-2	0-1	7	Gaffney [60], Hartley [71], Colkett [90]	6642
12	15	H	Gillingham	W	2-1	0-0	8	Lines [82], Harrison [90]	9489
13	18	A	Milton Keynes D	D	3-3	0-2	10	Taylor 3 [46, 87, 88]	8366
14	22	A	Oldham Ath	W	2-0	1-0	5	Colkett [25], Clarke-Salter [87]	4394
15	29	H	Peterborough U	L	1-2	0-0	7	Taylor (pen) [57]	9839
16	Nov 1	H	Fleetwood T	W	2-1	0-1	5	Taylor [61], Montano [73]	10,088
17	12	A	Millwall	L	0-4	0-1	5		9645
18	19	H	Milton Keynes D	D	0-0	0-0	8		9031
19	22	H	Charlton Ath	L	1-5	0-2	10	Taylor (pen) [90]	8089
20	26	A	Chesterfield	L	2-3	1-2	13	Hartley [3], Bodin [76]	6330
21	Dec 10	H	Bury	W	4-2	2-1	7	Gaffney [32], Taylor [45], Clarke, O [67], Hartley [82]	7843
22	17	A	Shrewsbury T	L	0-2	0-1	11		6139
23	26	H	Coventry C	W	4-1	1-0	10	Hartley [18], Bodin 3 (1 pen) [54, 74, 83 (p)]	11,200
24	31	H	AFC Wimbledon	W	2-0	0-0	10	Taylor 2 [61, 70]	10,093
25	Jan 2	A	Charlton Ath	L	1-4	1-1	10	Easter [12]	12,252
26	7	H	Northampton T	W	5-0	4-0	8	Bodin [7], Harrison 4 [17, 21, 24, 54]	8424
27	14	A	Fleetwood T	L	1-3	0-2	9	Bodin [54]	3728
28	21	A	Walsall	L	1-3	0-1	10	Taylor [82]	6029
29	28	H	Swindon T	W	1-0	1-0	8	Bodin [29]	10,557
30	Feb 4	A	Rochdale	D	0-0	0-0	10		3168
31	11	H	Bradford C	D	1-1	1-1	10	Lines [15]	9043
32	14	H	Sheffield U	D	0-0	0-0	10		9175
33	18	A	Port Vale	D	1-1	0-0	10	Bodin [78]	4460
34	25	H	Scunthorpe U	D	1-1	1-0	11	Clarke, O [39]	8784
35	28	A	Bolton W	D	1-1	0-1	11	Moore [75]	13,383
36	Mar 4	A	Oxford U	W	2-0	2-0	8	Clarke, O [16], Sinclair [36]	9862
37	11	H	Southend U	W	2-0	2-0	8	Bodin [1], Gaffney [31]	9274
38	14	A	Bury	L	0-3	0-0	8		2535
39	18	H	Chesterfield	W	2-1	2-0	8	Clarke, O [1], Gaffney [18]	8524
40	25	A	Coventry C	L	0-1	0-0	9		11,946
41	Apr 1	H	Shrewsbury T	W	2-0	0-0	8	Bodin 2 (1 pen) [54 (p), 83]	9498
42	8	A	AFC Wimbledon	W	1-0	1-0	8	Moore [1]	4742
43	14	A	Gillingham	L	1-3	0-0	9	Bodin (pen) [73]	5916
44	17	H	Oldham Ath	W	1-0	0-0	9	Harrison [75]	9083
45	22	A	Peterborough U	L	2-4	0-2	10	Gaffney 2 [85, 90]	5498
46	30	H	Millwall	L	3-4	2-3	10	Easter [33], Lines [42], Bodin [74]	11,750

Final League Position: 10

GOALSCORERS

League (68): Taylor 16 (4 pens), Bodin 13 (3 pens), Harrison 8, Gaffney 6, Hartley 5, Clarke, O 4, Easter 4 (1 pen), Colkett 3, Lines 3, Moore 2, Clarke-Salter 1, Montano 1, Sinclair 1, own goal 1.
FA Cup (6): Gaffney 3, Taylor 2 (1 pen), Brown 1.
EFL Cup (3): Harrison 1 (1 pen), Hartley 1, Lines 1.
EFL Checkatrade Trophy (2): Easter 1, Taylor 1.

Mildenhall S 4	Leadbitter D 28 + 2	Lockyer T 46	Clarke J 19 + 3	Hartley P 17 + 1	Brown L 41	Clarke O 30	Sinclair S 37 + 1	Lines C 40 + 4	Taylor M 23 + 4	Gaffney R 22 + 12	Harrison E 25 + 12	Montano C 12 + 13	Bodin B 28 + 8	McChrystal M 3 + 1	Easter J 9 + 12	James L 10 + 14	Roos K 16	Boateng H 9	Colkett C 8 + 7	Moore B 12 + 15	Clarke-Salter J 9 + 3	Roberts C 2	Puddy W 7	Mansell L 4 + 5	Lawrence L 1 + 3	Partington J 4 + 3	Lumley J 19	Broom R — + 5	Sweeney R 16	Lucas J — + 1	Harris R 4 + 1	Burn J 1 + 1	Match No.
1	2	3	4^{1}	5	6	7	8^{2}	9	10	11^{3}	12	13	14																				1
1		4	5		2	7		8	12	10^{2}	13	6	9^{3}	3	11^{1}	14																	2
1	5^{2}	2	3	4	9^{3}	6^{1}	8	7	10		11	14	12		13																		3
1	2	4	3	5	6	7	9	8	10^{1}	13	11^{2}				12																		4
		3	2	4	5		7	8	10		12		11^{1}		9^{2}	14	1	6^{3}	13														5
	2	3		4	5		9	12	10	13	11^{1}		7				1	6^{2}	14	8^{3}													6
	2	3		4	5		8	14	11		10		6^{2}			12	1	7^{1}	13	9^{3}													7
	2	3	4		5	7	6^{3}	8	11	10^{1}	13		9^{2}		14		1		12														8
	2	4		3	5	8^{1}	7	6		11^{2}	10		13		9^{3}	14	1			12													9
	2	4	3^{1}		6^{2}	7		8			11		13		10■	14	1	9^{3}		12	5												10
		3		4	5	7^{1}	8^{2}	6	14	11	10^{3}		13				1		9	12		2											11
	5	3	2^{2}	4	8		7^{1}	6	11	10^{3}	13	14	12				1		9														12
		3			5	6^{1}	8	7	11	14	9^{3}	13	10^{2}				1		12		4	2											13
		3	2	4^{2}	5		7	6	11	10		13					1	8^{1}	9^{3}	14	12												14
	2	3			5	7^{2}	6	8	11	10^{1}	12				13		1		9		4												15
	2	3			5		8	7	11^{1}	12	10^{3}	9^{2}			14		1		13	6	4												16
	2■	3		4	5		6	7	11^{1}		10	13		12	14		1	8^{2}	9^{3}														17
	2	3			5	6	7	13	12	14	10^{2}				11		1	8^{1}	9^{3}		4												18
	2	3		13	5		8^{1}	7	11	10	14	9^{3}					1		12	6^{2}	4												19
	2	3		4	5	6	8^{3}	7	10	9^{2}	14	12	13		11^{1}		1																20
	12	3	2	4	5	6	9		10^{1}	11						13		7^{3}	8^{2}				1	14									21
		3	2	4	5	6	7^{1}	13	11	10	12		14					8^{2}	9^{3}				1										22
	2	3		4	5	8		7^{2}	11	10^{1}	12	9^{3}	6										1	14	13								23
	2	3		4	5	7		8	10	13	11^{3}	9^{1}	6^{2}							12			1		14								24
	2^{2}	3	14	4	5		7		12	11^{3}	13				10^{1}					6			1	8	9								25
		4	5		2	8		7	10^{2}		11	6^{1}	9^{3}	3	13					12			1		14								26
		4	2		5^{1}	7		8	11^{3}		10		6	3^{2}	12	14				9			1			13							27
	2^{1}	3	4		5	7	9	8	10	11^{2}			6^{3}			12				13							1	14					28
	2	3			5	7	8	9	11^{2}	13	10^{1}		6^{3}			14				12							1		4				29
		3			5	7	8	9		12	11^{2}	13	6^{1}			10										2	1		4				30
	2	4			5	8	7	9		13	11^{1}	6^{2}				10^{3}											1	12	3	14			31
		3			5	9	7^{2}	8		11	10^{1}	12	6							13						2	1		4				32
		3^{3}				7	9	8		11	10^{2}	12	6			14										2^{1}	1		4		5	13	33
	2	3	13			8	9	7		10	12		6			11^{2}											1		4		5^{1}		34
	2	3	5			7	9	6			11^{1}	10^{2}	8			12				13							1		4				35
		3	2		5	8^{2}	7	6		12		13	9^{1}			10^{3}				11				14			1		4				36
	2^{2}	3	13		5			7		10^{3}		9^{1}	6			11				12	14			8			1		4				37
		3	2^{1}		5^{3}		9■	7		13		14	6^{2}			10				11	12			8			1		4				38
	2	3			5	7^{3}		8		10		9^{1}	6		13	11^{2}				12				14			1		4				39
	12	3	2^{2}		5	7	9	8		11^{1}			6			10				13							1				14	4^{3}	40
	2	3			5	7^{2}	12	8		10		9^{3}	6		14	11^{1}				13							1		4				41
	5^{1}	4			8		6	7			10^{2}		9			14				11	2^{3}			13		12	1		3				42
		2			8		5	6			10^{2}	14	11		13	12				9^{3}	4			7^{1}			1		3				43
		3					7	8			10	9^{2}	6		13	11^{1}				12						2^{3}	1	14	4		5		44
		3	2^{1}				7	8		13	10^{2}		6		11					9						12	1	14	4		5^{3}		45
	2	3			5		7	8			10^{2}		6		11^{1}	12				9	4						1	13					46

FA Cup

First Round	Crawley T	(a)	1-1
Replay	Crawley T	(h)	4-2
(*aet*)			
Second Round	Barrow	(h)	1-2

EFL Cup

First Round	Cardiff C	(h)	1-0
(*aet*)			
Second Round	Chelsea	(a)	2-3

EFL Checkatrade Trophy

Southern Group A	Reading U21	(h)	2-3
Southern Group A	Yeovil T	(h)	0-0
(*Bristol R won 5-3 on penalties*)			
Southern Group A	Portsmouth	(a)	0-1

BURNLEY

FOUNDATION

On 18 May 1882 Burnley (Association) Football Club was still known as Burnley Rovers as members of that rugby club had decided on that date to play Association Football in the future. It was only a matter of days later that the members met again and decided to drop Rovers from the club's name.

Turf Moor, Harry Potts Way, Burnley, Lancashire BB10 4BX.

Telephone: (0871) 221 1882.

Fax: (01282) 700 014.

Ticket Office: (0871) 221 1914.

Website: www.burnleyfootballclub.com

Email: info@burnleyfc.com

Ground Capacity: 21,940.

Record Attendance: 54,775 v Huddersfield T, FA Cup 3rd rd, 23 February 1924.

Pitch Measurements: 103m × 65m (112.5yd × 71yd).

Chairman: Mike Garlick.

Chief Executive: Dave Baldwin.

Manager: Sean Dyche.

Assistant Manager: Ian Woan.

Colours: Claret shirts with sky blue trim, white shorts with sky blue trim, white socks with claret trim.

Year Formed: 1882.

Turned Professional: 1883.

Previous Name: 1882, Burnley Rovers; 1882, Burnley.

Club Nickname: 'The Clarets'.

Grounds: 1882, Calder Vale; 1883, Turf Moor.

First Football League Game: 8 September 1888, Football League, v Preston NE (a) L 2–5 – Smith; Lang, Bury, Abrahams, Friel, Keenan, Brady, Tait, Poland (1), Gallocher (1), Yates.

Record League Victory: 9–0 v Darwen, Division 1, 9 January 1892 – Hillman; Walker, McFettridge, Lang, Matthews, Keenan, Nicol (3), Bowes, Espie (1), McLardie (3), Hill (2).

Record Cup Victory: 9–0 v Crystal Palace, FA Cup 2nd rd (replay), 10 February 1909 – Dawson; Barron, McLean; Cretney (2), Leake, Moffat; Morley, Ogden, Smith (3), Abbott (2), Smethams (1). 9–0 v New Brighton, FA Cup 4th rd, 26 January 1957 – Blacklaw; Angus, Winton; Seith, Adamson, Miller; Newlands (1), McIlroy (3), Lawson (3), Cheesebrough (1), Pilkington (1). 9–0 v Penrith, FA Cup 1st rd, 17 November 1984 – Hansbury; Miller, Hampton, Phelan, Overson (Kennedy), Hird (3 incl. 1p), Grewcock (1), Powell (2), Taylor (3), Biggins, Hutchison.

Record Defeat: 0–11 v Darwen, FA Cup 1st rd, 17 October 1885.

Most League Points (2 for a win): 62, Division 2, 1972–73.

HONOURS

League Champions: Division 1 – 1920–21, 1959–60; FL C – 2015–16; Division 2 – 1897–98, 1972–73; Division 3 – 1981–82; Division 4 – 1991–92.
Runners-up: Division 1 – 1919–20, 1961–62; FL C – 2013–14; Division 2 – 1912–13, 1946–47; Second Division – 1999–2000.

FA Cup Winners: 1914.
Runners-up: 1947, 1962.

League Cup: semi-final – 1961, 1969, 1983, 2009.

League Trophy: *Runners-up:* 1988.

Anglo-Scottish Cup Winners: 1979.

European Competitions
European Cup: 1960–61 *(qf)*.
Fairs Cup: 1966–67.

sky SPORTS FACT FILE

In the years leading up to the First World War, Burnley fans adapted the popular song 'It's a long way to Tipperary' to cheer their team on to success. 'It's a long way to Crystal Palace' inspired the Clarets to a semi-final place in 1913 and to win the trophy 12 months later.

Most League Points (3 for a win): 93, FL C, 2013–14; FL C, 2015–16.

Most League Goals: 102, Division 1, 1960–61.

Highest League Scorer in Season: George Beel, 35, Division 1, 1927–28.

Most League Goals in Total Aggregate: George Beel, 179, 1923–32.

Most League Goals in One Match: 6, Louis Page v Birmingham C, Division 1, 10 April 1926.

Most Capped Player: Jimmy McIlroy, 51 (55), Northern Ireland.

Most League Appearances: Jerry Dawson, 522, 1907–28.

Youngest League Player: Tommy Lawton, 16 years 174 days v Doncaster R, 28 March 1936.

Record Transfer Fee Received: £30,000,000 from Everton for Michael Keane, July 2017.

Record Transfer Fee Paid: £13,000,000 to Norwich C for Robbie Brady, January 2017.

Football League Record: 1888 Original Member of the Football League; 1897–98 Division 2; 1898–1900 Division 1; 1900–13 Division 2; 1913–30 Division 1; 1930–47 Division 2; 1947–71 Division 1; 1971–73 Division 2; 1973–76 Division 1; 1976–80 Division 2; 1980–82 Division 3; 1982–83 Division 2; 1983–85 Division 3; 1985–92 Division 4; 1992–94 Division 2; 1994–95 Division 1; 1995–2000 Division 2; 2000–04 Division 1; 2004–09 FL C; 2009–10 FA Premier League; 2010–14 FL C; 2014–15 FA Premier League; 2015–16 FL C; 2016– FA Premier League.

MANAGERS

Harry Bradshaw 1894–99
(*Secretary-Manager from 1897*)
Club Directors 1899–1900
J. Ernest Mangnall 1900–03
(*Secretary-Manager*)
Spen Whittaker 1903–10
(*Secretary-Manager*)
John Haworth 1910–24
(*Secretary-Manager*)
Albert Pickles 1925–31
(*Secretary-Manager*)
Tom Bromilow 1932–35
Selection Committee 1935–45
Cliff Britton 1945–48
Frank Hill 1948–54
Alan Brown 1954–57
Billy Dougall 1957–58
Harry Potts 1958–70
(*General Manager to 1972*)
Jimmy Adamson 1970–76
Joe Brown 1976–77
Harry Potts 1977–79
Brian Miller 1979–83
John Bond 1983–84
John Benson 1984–85
Martin Buchan 1985
Tommy Cavanagh 1985–86
Brian Miller 1986–89
Frank Casper 1989–91
Jimmy Mullen 1991–96
Adrian Heath 1996–97
Chris Waddle 1997–98
Stan Ternent 1998–2004
Steve Cotterill 2004–07
Owen Coyle 2007–10
Brian Laws 2010
Eddie Howe 2011–12
Sean Dyche October 2012–

LATEST SEQUENCES

Longest Sequence of League Wins: 10, 16.11.1912 – 18.1.1913.

Longest Sequence of League Defeats: 8, 2.1.1995 – 25.2.1995.

Longest Sequence of League Draws: 6, 21.2.1931 – 28.3.1931.

Longest Sequence of Unbeaten League Matches: 30, 6.9.1920 – 25.3.1921.

Longest Sequence Without a League Win: 24, 16.4.1979 – 17.11.1979.

Successive Scoring Runs: 27 from 13.2.1926.

Successive Non-scoring Runs: 6 from 21.3.2015.

TEN YEAR LEAGUE RECORD

		P	W	D	L	F	A	Pts	Pos
2007-08	FL C	46	16	14	16	60	67	62	13
2008-09	FL C	46	21	13	12	72	60	76	5
2009-10	PR Lge	38	8	6	24	42	82	30	18
2010-11	FL C	46	18	14	14	65	61	68	8
2011-12	FL C	46	17	11	18	61	58	62	13
2012-13	FL C	46	16	13	17	62	60	61	11
2013-14	FL C	46	26	15	5	72	37	93	2
2014-15	PR Lge	38	7	12	19	28	53	33	19
2015-16	FL C	46	26	15	5	72	35	93	1
2016-17	PR Lge	38	11	7	20	39	55	40	16

DID YOU KNOW

Burnley had to wait until match 15 of the 1970–71 season before achieving their first League win. Fielding six players from the team that had won the FA Youth Cup in 1967–68, they beat Crystal Palace 2-1 at Turf Moor on 31 October.

BURNLEY – PREMIER LEAGUE 2016–17 LEAGUE RECORD

Match No.	Date	Venue	Opponents	Result	H/T Score	Lg Pos.	Goalscorers	Attendance
1	Aug 13	H	Swansea C	L 0-1	0-0	19		19,126
2	20	H	Liverpool	W 2-0	2-0	2	Vokes [2], Gray [37]	21,313
3	27	A	Chelsea	L 0-3	0-2	12		41,607
4	Sept 10	H	Hull C	D 1-1	0-0	13	Defour [72]	18,803
5	17	A	Leicester C	L 0-3	0-1	15		31,916
6	26	H	Watford	W 2-0	1-0	13	Hendrick [38], Keane [50]	18,519
7	Oct 2	H	Arsenal	L 0-1	0-0	14		20,982
8	16	A	Southampton	L 1-3	0-0	14	Vokes (pen) [72]	29,040
9	22	H	Everton	W 2-1	1-0	14	Vokes [39], Arfield [90]	21,416
10	29	A	Manchester U	D 0-0	0-0	13		75,325
11	Nov 5	H	Crystal Palace	W 3-2	2-0	9	Vokes [2], Gudmundsson [14], Barnes [90]	19,196
12	21	A	WBA	L 0-4	0-3	12		23,016
13	26	H	Manchester C	L 1-2	1-1	12	Marney [14]	21,794
14	Dec 3	A	Stoke C	L 0-2	0-2	14		27,306
15	10	H	Bournemouth	W 3-2	2-1	13	Hendrick [13], Ward [16], Boyd [75]	19,680
16	14	A	West Ham U	L 0-1	0-1	13		56,990
17	18	A	Tottenham H	L 1-2	1-1	16	Barnes [21]	31,467
18	26	H	Middlesbrough	W 1-0	0-0	13	Gray [80]	21,562
19	31	H	Sunderland	W 4-1	1-0	10	Gray 3 [31, 51, 53], Barnes (pen) [67]	21,124
20	Jan 2	A	Manchester C	L 1-2	0-0	11	Mee [70]	54,463
21	14	H	Southampton	W 1-0	0-0	9	Barton [78]	20,254
22	22	A	Arsenal	L 1-2	0-0	12	Gray (pen) [90]	59,955
23	31	H	Leicester C	W 1-0	0-0	9	Vokes [87]	19,202
24	Feb 4	A	Watford	L 1-2	0-2	12	Barnes (pen) [78]	20,178
25	12	H	Chelsea	D 1-1	1-1	12	Brady [24]	21,744
26	25	A	Hull C	D 1-1	0-0	11	Keane [76]	20,156
27	Mar 4	A	Swansea C	L 2-3	1-1	12	Gray 2 (1 pen) [20 (p), 61]	20,679
28	12	A	Liverpool	L 1-2	1-1	12	Barnes [7]	53,145
29	18	A	Sunderland	D 0-0	0-0	13		41,518
30	Apr 1	H	Tottenham H	L 0-2	0-0	14		21,684
31	4	H	Stoke C	W 1-0	0-0	11	Boyd [58]	19,881
32	8	A	Middlesbrough	D 0-0	0-0	12		29,547
33	15	A	Everton	L 1-3	0-0	13	Vokes (pen) [52]	39,328
34	23	H	Manchester U	L 0-2	0-2	15		21,870
35	29	A	Crystal Palace	W 2-0	1-0	12	Barnes [7], Gray [85]	25,013
36	May 6	H	WBA	D 2-2	0-0	14	Vokes 2 [56, 86]	20,825
37	13	A	Bournemouth	L 1-2	0-1	14	Vokes [83]	11,388
38	21	H	West Ham U	L 1-2	1-1	16	Vokes [23]	21,634

Final League Position: 16

GOALSCORERS

League (39): Vokes 10 (2 pens), Gray 9 (2 pens), Barnes 6 (2 pens), Boyd 2, Hendrick 2, Keane 2, Arfield 1, Barton 1, Brady 1, Defour 1, Gudmundsson 1, Marney 1, Mee 1, Ward 1.
FA Cup (4): Vokes 2, Defour 1, Gray 1.
EFL Cup (0).

Heaton T 35	Lowton M 36	Keane M 35	Mee B 34	Ward S 37	Boyd G 33 + 3	Marney D 21	Jones D 1	Arfield S 23 + 8	Gray A 26 + 6	Vokes S 21 + 16	Gudmundsson J 10 + 10	Jutkiewicz L — + 2	Defour S 16 + 5	O'Neill A — + 3	Tarkowski J 4 + 15	Hendrick J 31 + 1	Bamford P — + 6	Kightly M 1 + 4	Flanagan J 3 + 3	Barnes A 20 + 8	Robinson P 3	Barton J 12 + 2	Brady R 7 + 7	Westwood A 6 + 3	Agyei D — + 3	Long K 3	Match No.
1	2	3	4	5	6	7	8^{1}	9^{2}	10	11	12	13															1
1	2	3	4	5	6	7		9	10^{3}	11^{1}	12	13	8^{2}	14													2
1	2	3	4	5	6	7^{3}		9^{2}	10	11	12		8^{1}	13	14												3
1	2	3	4	5	6	8		13	10^{1}	11	9^{2}		7^{3}			12	14										4
1	2	3	4	5	10	8		6^{2}	11^{3}	13	12		7^{1}			9	14										5
1	2	3	4	5	10	8		12		11	6^{1}		9^{2}			7		13									6
1	2	3	4	5	10	8		12		11	6		9^{1}			7											7
1	2	3	4	5	10^{2}	8				11	6^{3}		9^{1}	12		7	14	13									8
1	2	3	4	5^{2}		7		10		11^{3}	6				12	8	14	9^{1}	13								9
1	2	3	4	5^{1}	14	8		9	10^{2}	11	6^{3}					7			12	13							10
1	2	3	4		12	7		9^{2}		11	6		8^{3}		13	10^{1}			5	14							11
1	2	3	4	5	14	7		9	13	11^{2}	6^{3}		8^{1}			10				12							12
	2	3	4	5	9	7^{3}		12		11	6^{2}		8^{1}		13	10				14	1						13
		3	4	5	6^{2}	7		9^{3}	11	12					13	8		14	2^{1}	10	1						14
1	2	3	4	5	10^{1}	7		8	12	11^{2}			6^{3}		14	9				13							15
1	2	3	4	5	6^{1}	8		9^{2}	11	10						7	13			12							16
1	2	3	4	5	6^{1}	7^{3}		9	11	12			14			8		13		10^{2}							17
1		3	4	5	6	7^{1}		9^{3}	10	12	14		13			8			2	11^{2}							18
1	2	3	4	5	6	7		9	11^{1}	13	12		8^{3}		14					10^{2}							19
1	2	3	4	5	6			7^{3}	10	13	9^{2}		12			8	14			11^{1}							20
1	2	3	4	5	6	7^{2}			11^{1}	13			9^{3}		14	8				10		12					21
1	2	3	4	5	6	7^{3}			10	14			9^{1}		13	8^{2}				11		12					22
1	2	3	4	5	9			12	11	13			6^{1}		14	7^{2}				10^{3}		8					23
1	2	3	4	5	6^{2}			9^{3}	11^{1}	14						8■				10		7	12	13			24
1	2	3	4	5	6			12	10^{1}	13										11		7	9^{2}	8			25
1	2	3	4	5	6			14	11^{2}	12					13					10■		8	9^{1}	7^{3}			26
	2	3	4	5	6			12	11	10^{3}					13	8					1	7^{2}	9^{1}	14			27
1	2	3	4	5	6^{2}			9^{3}	11^{1}	13						8				10		7	12		14		28
1	2	3	4	5	6^{2}			9	11	12						8				10^{1}		7	13				29
1	2	3	4	5	6^{3}			9^{1}	10^{2}	12			14			7				11		8	13				30
1	2	3	4	5	6				11^{3}	10^{1}			9^{2}		14	8				13		7	12				31
1	2	3	4	5	6				11^{1}	12					13	8				10^{2}		7	9				32
1	2	3	4	5	6				12	10^{3}						7^{1}				11^{2}		8	9	14	13		33
1	2	3	4^{1}	5	6^{2}				10		13				12	8				11^{3}		7	9		14		34
1	2	3		5^{2}	6			9	13	10					4	8			12	11^{1}				7			35
1	2			5	6^{3}			9^{2}	12	10	13				4	8				11^{1}			14	7		3	36
1	2			5	6^{3}			9^{2}	12	11	14				4	8				10^{1}			13	7		3	37
1	2			5				6	11^{1}	10	12		13		4	7				14			9^{3}	8^{2}		3	38

FA Cup

Third Round	Sunderland	(a)	0-0
Replay	Sunderland	(h)	2-0
Fourth Round	Bristol C	(h)	2-0
Fifth Round	Lincoln C	(h)	0-1

EFL Cup

Second Round	Accrington S	(a)	0-1
(*aet*)			

BURTON ALBION

FOUNDATION

Once upon a time there were three Football League clubs bearing the name Burton. Then there was none. In reality it had been two. Originally Burton Swifts and Burton Wanderers competed in it until 1901 when they amalgamated to form Burton United. This club disbanded in 1910. There was no senior club representing the town until 1924 when Burton Town, formerly known as Burton All Saints, played in the Birmingham & District League, subsequently joining the Midland League in 1935–36. When the Second World War broke out the club fielded a team in a truncated version of the Birmingham & District League taking over from the club's reserves. But it was not revived in peacetime. So it was not until a further decade that a club bearing the name of Burton reappeared. Founded in 1950 Burton Albion made progress from the Birmingham & District League, too, then into the Southern League and because of its geographical situation later had spells in the Northern Premier League. In April 2009 Burton Albion restored the name of the town to the Football League competition as champions of the Blue Square Premier League.

Pirelli Stadium, Princess Way, Burton-on-Trent, Staffordshire DE13 0AR.

Telephone: (01283) 565 938.

Fax: (01283) 523 199.

Ticket Office: (01283) 565 938.

Website: www.burtonalbionfc.co.uk

Email: bafc@burtonalbionfc.co.uk

Ground Capactiy: 6,972.

Record Attendance: 5,806 v Weymouth, Southern League Cup final 2nd leg 1964 (at Eton Park); 6,746 v Derby Co, FL C, 26 August 2016 (at Pirelli Stadium).

Pitch Measurements: 100m × 68.5m (109.5yd × 75yd).

Chairman: Ben Robinson.

Manager: Nigel Clough.

Assistant Manager: Gary Crosby.

Colours: Yellow and black striped shirts, black shorts with yellow trim, black socks with yellow trim.

Year Formed: 1950.

Turned Professional: 1950.

Club Nickname: 'The Brewers'.

Grounds: 1950, Eton Park; 2005, Pirelli Stadium.

HONOURS

League Champions: FL 2 – 2014–15; Conference – 2008–09.
Runners-up: FL 1 – 2015–16.

FA Cup: 4th rd – 2011.

League Cup: 3rd rd – 2013, 2015.

sky SPORTS FACT FILE

Burton Albion won 12 consecutive Conference games between November 2008 and January 2009. However, a poor run into the end of the season saw them gain just three points from the final five fixtures. This was still enough to win them the title and automatic promotion to the Football League.

First Football League Game: 8 August 2009, FL 2, v Shrewsbury T (a) L 1–3 – Redmond; Edworthy, Boertien, Austin, Branston, McGrath, Maghoma, Penn, Phillips (Stride), Walker, Shroot (Pearson) (1).

Record League Victory: 6-1 v Aldershot T, FL 2, 12 December 2009 – Krysiak; James, Boertien, Stride, Webster, McGrath, Jackson, Penn, Kabba (2), Pearson (3) (Harrad) (1), Gilroy (Maghoma).

Record Cup Victory: 12–1 v Coalville T, Birmingham Senior Cup, 6 September 1954.

Record Defeat: 0–10 v Barnet, Southern League, 7 February 1970.

Most League Points (3 for a win): 94, FL 2, 2014–15.

Most League Goals: 71, FL 2, 2009–10; 2012–13.

Highest League Scorer in Season: Shaun Harrad, 21, 2009–10.

Most League Goals in Total Aggregate: Billy Kee, 39, 2011–15.

Most League Goals in One Match: 3, Greg Pearson v Aldershot T, FL 2, 12 December 2009; 3, Shaun Harrad v Rotherham U, FL 2, 11 September 2010; 3, Lucas Akins v Colchester U, FL 1, 23 April 2016.

Most Capped Player: Irvine Jackson 8 (12), Australia.

Most League Appearances: Damien McCrory, 170, 2012–17.

Youngest League Player: Sam Austin, 17 years 310 days v Stevenage, 25 October 2014.

Record Transfer Fee Received: Reported £390,000 (undisclosed) from QPR for Nasser El Khayati, January 2016.

Record Transfer Fee Paid: £500,000 to Ross Co for Liam Boyce, June 2017.

Football League Record: 2009 Promoted from Blue Square Premier; 2009–15 FL 2; 2015–16 FL 1; 2016– FL C.

MANAGERS

Reg Weston
Sammy Crooks 1957
Eddie Shimwell 1958
Bill Townsend 1959–62
Peter Taylor 1962–65
Richie Norman
Reg Gutteridge
Harold Bodle 1974–76
Ian Storey-Moore 1978–81
Neil Warnock 1981–86
Brian Fidler 1986–88
Vic Halom 1988
Bobby Hope 1988
Chris Wright 1988–89
Ken Blair 1989–90
Steve Powell 1990–91
Brian Fidler 1991–92
Brian Kenning 1992–94
John Barton 1994–98
Nigel Clough 1998–2009
Roy McFarland 2009
Paul Peschisolido 2009–12
Gary Rowett 2012–14
Jimmy Floyd Hasselbaink 2014–15
Nigel Clough December 2015–

LATEST SEQUENCES

Longest Sequence of League Wins: 4, 24.11.2015 – 12.12.2015.

Longest Sequence of League Defeats: 8, 25.2.2012 – 24.3.2012.

Longest Sequence of League Draws: 6, 25.4.2011 – 16.8.2011.

Longest Sequence of Unbeaten League Matches: 13, 7.3.2015 – 8.8.2015.

Longest Sequence Without a League Win: 16, 31.12.2011 – 24.3.2012.

Successive Scoring Runs: 18 from 16.4.2011 – 8.10.2011.

Successive Non-scoring Runs: 5 from 25.2.2012 – 10.3.2012.

TEN YEAR LEAGUE RECORD

		P	W	D	L	F	A	Pts	Pos
2007-08	Conf P	46	23	12	11	79	56	81	5
2008-09	Conf P	46	27	7	12	81	52	88	1
2009-10	FL 2	46	17	11	18	71	71	62	13
2010-11	FL 2	46	12	15	19	56	70	51	19
2011-12	FL 2	46	14	12	20	54	81	54	17
2012-13	FL 2	46	22	10	14	71	65	76	4
2013-14	FL 2	46	19	15	12	47	42	72	6
2014-15	FL 2	46	28	10	8	69	39	94	1
2015-16	FL 1	46	25	10	11	57	37	85	2
2016-17	FL C	46	13	13	20	49	63	52	20

DID YOU KNOW ?

Burton Albion's first home was at Wellington Street, formerly the ground of Lloyd's Foundry, a local works' team who played in the Burton & District League. It was not until joining the Southern League in 1958–59 that they moved to Eton Park which was on the other side of the town.

BURTON ALBION – SKY BET CHAMPIONSHIP 2016–17 LEAGUE RECORD

Match No.	Date	Venue	Opponents	Result	H/T Score	Lg Pos.	Goalscorers	Attendance
1	Aug 6	A	Nottingham F	L 3-4	2-2	18	Akins[27], Dyer[30], Naylor[90]	23,012
2	13	H	Bristol C	L 1-2	0-1	21	Naylor[88]	4579
3	16	H	Sheffield W	W 3-1	2-1	15	McFadzean[7], Irvine[45], Dyer[77]	4997
4	20	A	Blackburn R	D 2-2	1-1	14	Irvine[43], Naylor[88]	10,356
5	26	H	Derby Co	W 1-0	1-0	6	Irvine[12]	6746
6	Sept 10	A	Wolverhampton W	D 1-1	0-0	14	Miller[90]	22,049
7	13	A	Fulham	D 1-1	0-0	15	Irvine[51]	15,288
8	17	H	Brighton & HA	L 0-1	0-0	15		4756
9	24	A	Norwich C	L 1-3	0-1	18	Akins[46]	26,104
10	27	H	QPR	D 1-1	0-0	18	Ward[58]	3725
11	Oct 1	H	Cardiff C	W 2-0	1-0	13	Irvine[12], Akins[49]	4426
12	15	A	Wigan Ath	D 0-0	0-0	16		10,430
13	18	A	Ipswich T	L 0-2	0-1	17		15,816
14	21	H	Birmingham C	W 2-0	1-0	13	Dyer[32], Ward[62]	5818
15	29	A	Leeds U	L 0-2	0-0	18		24,220
16	Nov 5	H	Barnsley	D 0-0	0-0	17		4913
17	19	A	Reading	L 0-3	0-2	20		15,545
18	26	A	Preston NE	D 1-1	1-1	19	Irvine[23]	10,696
19	Dec 3	H	Rotherham U	W 2-1	1-0	19	Irvine[15], Palmer[62]	4446
20	10	A	Brentford	L 1-2	1-1	19	Ward[27]	9035
21	13	H	Huddersfield T	L 0-1	0-0	21		4564
22	17	H	Newcastle U	L 1-2	1-2	21	Dyer[20]	6665
23	26	A	Aston Villa	L 1-2	1-1	21	Ward[31]	41,337
24	29	A	Rotherham U	W 2-1	2-1	19	O'Grady[36], Irvine[41]	9806
25	Jan 2	H	Preston NE	L 0-1	0-1	21		5144
26	14	H	Wigan Ath	L 0-2	0-1	21		4411
27	21	A	Cardiff C	L 0-1	0-0	21		15,543
28	28	A	QPR	W 2-1	1-0	20	Murphy[11], Dyer[52]	12,116
29	Feb 1	H	Fulham	L 0-2	0-0	21		3725
30	4	H	Wolverhampton W	W 2-1	0-1	21	Kightly[60], Woodrow[90]	5608
31	11	A	Brighton & HA	L 1-4	0-1	21	Kightly[75]	29,464
32	18	H	Norwich C	W 2-1	1-0	20	Woodrow[25], Kightly[56]	5263
33	21	A	Derby Co	D 0-0	0-0	20		31,081
34	24	H	Blackburn R	D 1-1	0-1	19	Sordell[54]	5496
35	Mar 4	A	Bristol C	D 0-0	0-0	19		17,914
36	7	A	Sheffield W	D 1-1	1-1	19	Irvine[24]	24,929
37	11	H	Nottingham F	W 1-0	1-0	18	Woodrow[26]	6115
38	18	H	Brentford	L 3-5	3-1	20	Sordell 2[21, 23], Woodrow[41]	4549
39	Apr 1	A	Huddersfield T	W 1-0	0-0	19	Irvine[90]	20,154
40	5	A	Newcastle U	L 0-1	0-0	19		48,814
41	8	H	Aston Villa	D 1-1	0-1	20	Dyer[61]	6716
42	14	H	Ipswich T	L 1-2	0-0	21	Akins (pen)[86]	5236
43	17	A	Birmingham C	W 2-0	1-0	19	Dyer[36], Akins[52]	19,794
44	22	H	Leeds U	W 2-1	0-0	18	Sordell[75], Kightly[77]	6073
45	29	A	Barnsley	D 1-1	0-1	17	Varney[52]	12,952
46	May 7	H	Reading	L 2-4	0-2	20	Turner[69], Woodrow[72]	6264

Final League Position: 20

GOALSCORERS

League (49): Irvine 10, Dyer 7, Akins 5 (1 pen), Woodrow 5, Kightly 4, Sordell 4, Ward 4, Naylor 3, McFadzean 1, Miller 1, Murphy 1, O'Grady 1, Palmer 1, Turner 1, Varney 1.
FA Cup (0).
EFL Cup (3): Beavon 1, Butcher 1, Reilly 1.

McLaughlin J 43	Flanagan T 22 + 8	Mousinho J 28 + 4	McFadzean K 29 + 2	Turner B 38 + 1	Dyer L 37 + 5	Palmer M 31 + 5	Choudhury H 6 + 7	Williamson L 8 + 6	O'Grady C 22 + 4	Akins L 30 + 8	Naylor T 23 + 10	Beavon S 5 + 5	McCrory D 11 + 5	Irvine J 41 + 1	Butcher C — + 1	Brayford J 33	Miller W 4 + 11	Harness M — + 10	Barker S — + 5	Ward J 15 + 3	Fox B — + 1	Sordell M 19 + 2	Murphy L 18 + 1	Bywater S 3 + 2	Christensen L 15 + 1	Woodrow C 11 + 3	Kightly M 10 + 2	Varney L 4 + 11	Sbarra J — + 1	Match No.
1	2¹	3	4	5	6	7	8	9²	10³	11	12	13	14																	1
1	2¹	3	4	5	6	7		8²	10	11	13	12		9																2
1	12	2	3	4	9	7²	13		11	5	6	10¹		8																3
1		2¹	3	4	9	7	14	12	11²	5	6	10³		8	13															4
1			3	4	9	7²		13	11	5	6³			8		2	10¹	12	14											5
1			3	4	9	7	12		10	5³	6²			8		2	13	14		11¹										6
1				12	9	7	8²	6	10		3	11¹	5³	2		4			14	13										7
1	4				9	7	6¹	5			3			8		2	10²	12		11	13									8
1	12■	2			9	7	6			5	3	10³		8		4¹	13		14	11²										9
1		2	3	4	9	7		5¹		10	6			8				12		11										10
1	13	14	3	4	9	7	6²		10³	5	2			8			12			11¹										11
1			3	4	9	7	13		11	5	6²			8		2	10¹			12										12
1	14	2¹	3	4	8	6		13	11	10				7²		5³		12		9										13
1			3	4	9	7¹	14	13	11	5	6²			8		2	12			10³										14
1			3	4	9	7		6²	10	5	13	12		8		2				11¹										15
1	12		3	4	9	7		6³	10¹	5	13	14		8		2				11²										16
1	14	3		4¹	9	7		6³	11²	5	13	10		8		2	12													17
1		3		4	9	7			11¹	6	8		5	10		2		12												18
1	14	3		4	9	7	12		10²	5	6¹			8		2	13			11³										19
1		3		4	9	7			11¹	6	14		5³	8		2	12	13		10²										20
1			3		9	7	6¹	13	10	5			4	8		2	12			11²										21
1		2	3		9	7¹			11	10²	6		4	8		5	13			12										22
1		2	3³		9	7		13	12	10	6	14	4²	8		5				11¹										23
1	12	2	3		9	7¹			11³	10	6		4	8		5²		13	14											24
1		2³	3		9	7	14		10¹	5	6		4	8				13		11²		12								25
1³			3	4	8²	6			11	5	14		13			2				9		10	7¹	12						26
1	5		3	4	10	7²			13	6	8¹					2		12				11	9							27
1	2	12		4	10	9				13			5	7		3³						11¹	8		6²	14				28
1	2	3		4	10³	6			12	8	13		5	9			14					11¹	7²							29
1	2	3		4		14				13	12		5²	8								11	7		6¹	10	9³			30
1	5	3		4		12				6	2			10			14					11¹	8³		7²		9	13		31
1	5	3		4	12						2			9					14			6	8		7²	11¹	10³	13		32
1	5	3		4	10	8			14		2			9¹								13	12		7	11³		6²		33
1	5	3	14	4	13	7³					2											11	8		6	10²	9¹	12		34
1	5	3	13	4	10³	14								9		2						6¹	8²		7	11		12		35
1	5		6	4	10	12					3			9		2						7²			8	13		11¹		36
1	5		3	4	9					13	14			8		2						11²	7		6	10¹		12³		37
1	5		3	4	12	13				14				9		2²						6	8³		7	11	10¹			38
1	6	3	4	5						14				12		2						11	8		7²	10³	9¹	13		39
1	6	3		5	13					2¹				9		4						10³	8		7²	14	12	11		40
1	5	13	3	4	9					12				8		2						6¹	7			11³	10²	14		41
1	5	3		4	9					14				8		2						6¹	7		13	11³	10²	12		42
1²	5	13	3	4	9³					10			14	8		2							7	12	6			11¹		43
	5	8	3	4	10²					6			13	9		2³						11¹		1	7		12	14		44
	9¹	2	3	4						12			14	8²		5						10	7	1	6		11³	13		45
		6	3	4	12									9		2	11¹					5	7³	1		10	8²	14	13	46

FA Cup

Third Round	Watford	(a)	0-2

EFL Cup

First Round (*aet*)	Bury	(h)	3-2
Second Round	Liverpool	(h)	0-5

BURY

FOUNDATION

A meeting at the Waggon & Horses Hotel, attended largely by members of Bury Wesleyans and Bury Unitarians football clubs, decided to form a new Bury club. This was officially formed at a subsequent gathering at the Old White Horse Hotel, Fleet Street, Bury on 24 April 1885.

Gigg Lane, Bury, Lancashire BL9 9HR.

Telephone: (0161) 764 5521.

Fax: (0161) 764 5521.

Ticket Office: (0161) 764 5521 (option 1).

Website: www.buryfc.co.uk

Email: info@buryfc.co.uk

Ground Capacity: 11,376.

Record Attendance: 35,000 v Bolton W, FA Cup 3rd rd, 9 January 1960.

Pitch Measurements: 102.5m × 67m (112yd × 73yd).

Chairman: Stewart Day.

Chief Executive: Karl Evans.

Manager: Lee Clark.

Assistant Manager: Alan Thompson.

Colours: White shirts with blue trim, blue shorts with white trim, blue socks.

Year Formed: 1885.

Turned Professional: 1885.

Club Nickname: 'The Shakers'.

Ground: 1885, Gigg Lane (renamed JD Stadium 2013); 2015 Gigg Lane.

First Football League Game: 1 September 1894, Division 2, v Manchester C (h) W 4–2 – Lowe; Gillespie, Davies; White, Clegg, Ross; Wylie, Barbour (2), Millar (1), Ostler (1), Plant.

Record League Victory: 8–0 v Tranmere R, Division 3, 10 January 1970 – Forrest; Tinney, Saile; Anderson, Turner, McDermott; Hince (1), Arrowsmith (1), Jones (4), Kerr (1), Grundy, (1 og).

Record Cup Victory: 12–1 v Stockton, FA Cup 1st rd (replay), 2 February 1897 – Montgomery; Darroch, Barbour; Hendry (1), Clegg, Ross (1); Wylie (3), Pangbourn, Millar (4), Henderson (2), Plant, (1 og).

Record Defeat: 0–10 v Blackburn R, FA Cup pr rd, 1 October 1887. 0–10 v West Ham U, Milk Cup 2nd rd 2nd leg, 25 October 1983.

Most League Points (2 for a win): 68, Division 3, 1960–61.

Most League Points (3 for a win): 85, FL 2, 2014–15.

Most League Goals: 108, Division 3, 1960–61.

HONOURS

League Champions: Division 2 – 1894–95; Second Division – 1996–97; Division 3 – 1960–61.
Runners-up: Division 2 – 1923–24; Division 3 – 1967–68; FL 2 – 2010–11.

FA Cup Winners: 1900, 1903.

League Cup: semi-final – 1963.

sky SPORTS FACT FILE

Bury walked away with the Second Division title in 1894–95, their first season as Football League members, finishing nine points clear of their closest rivals. It still wasn't enough to gain automatic promotion and the Shakers only sealed their top flight place with a 1-0 win over Liverpool at Ewood Park in the end-of-season 'Test Match'.

Highest League Scorer in Season: Craig Madden, 35, Division 4, 1981–82.

Most League Goals in Total Aggregate: Craig Madden, 129, 1978–86.

Most League Goals in One Match: 5, Eddie Quigley v Millwall, Division 2, 15 February 1947; 5, Ray Pointer v Rotherham U, Division 2, 2 October 1965.

Most Capped Player: Bill Gorman, 11 (13), Republic of Ireland and (4), Northern Ireland.

Most League Appearances: Norman Bullock, 505, 1920–35.

Youngest League Player: Brian Williams, 16 years 133 days v Stockport Co, 18 March 1972; Callum Styles, 16 years 41 days v Southend U, 8 May 2016 (later found to be an ineligible player).

Record Transfer Fee Received: £1,100,000 from Ipswich T for David Johnson, November 1997.

Record Transfer Fee Paid: £200,000 to Ipswich T for Chris Swailes, November 1997; £200,000 to Swindon T for Darren Bullock, February 1999.

Football League Record: 1894 Elected to Division 2; 1895–1912 Division 1; 1912–24 Division 2; 1924–29 Division 1; 1929–57 Division 2; 1957–61 Division 3; 1961–67 Division 2; 1967–68 Division 3; 1968–69 Division 2; 1969–71 Division 3; 1971–74 Division 4; 1974–80 Division 3; 1980–85 Division 4; 1985–96 Division 3; 1996–97 Division 2; 1997–99 Division 1; 1999–2002 Division 2; 2002–04 Division 3; 2004–11 FL 2; 2011–13 FL 1; 2013–15 FL 2; 2015– FL 1.

LATEST SEQUENCES

Longest Sequence of League Wins: 9, 26.9.1960 – 19.11.1960.

Longest Sequence of League Defeats: 12, 1.10.2016 – 17.12.2016.

Longest Sequence of League Draws: 6, 6.3.1999 – 3.4.1999.

Longest Sequence of Unbeaten League Matches: 18, 4.2.1961 – 29.4.1961.

Longest Sequence Without a League Win: 19, 1.4.1911 – 2.12.1911.

Successive Scoring Runs: 24 from 1.9.1894.

Successive Non-scoring Runs: 6 from 11.1.1969.

MANAGERS

T. Hargreaves 1887 (*Secretary-Manager*)
H. S. Hamer 1887–1907 (*Secretary-Manager*)
Archie Montgomery 1907–15
William Cameron 1919–23
James Hunter Thompson 1923–27
Percy Smith 1927–30
Arthur Paine 1930–34
Norman Bullock 1934–38
Charlie Dean 1938–44
Jim Porter 1944–45
Norman Bullock 1945–49
John McNeil 1950–53
Dave Russell 1953–61
Bob Stokoe 1961–65
Bert Head 1965–66
Les Shannon 1966–69
Jack Marshall 1969
Colin McDonald 1970
Les Hart 1970
Tommy McAnearney 1970–72
Alan Brown 1972–73
Bobby Smith 1973–77
Bob Stokoe 1977–78
David Hatton 1978–79
Dave Connor 1979–80
Jim Iley 1980–84
Martin Dobson 1984–89
Sam Ellis 1989–90
Mike Walsh 1990–95
Stan Ternent 1995–98
Neil Warnock 1998–99
Andy Preece 1999–2003
Graham Barrow 2003–05
Chris Casper 2005–08
Alan Knill 2008–11
Richie Barker 2011–12
Kevin Blackwell 2012–13
David Flitcroft 2013–16
Chris Brass 2016–17
Lee Clark February 2017–

TEN YEAR LEAGUE RECORD

		P	W	D	L	F	A	Pts	Pos
2007-08	FL 2	46	16	11	19	58	61	59	13
2008-09	FL 2	46	21	15	10	63	43	78	4
2009-10	FL 2	46	19	12	15	54	59	69	9
2010-11	FL 2	46	23	12	11	82	50	81	2
2011-12	FL 1	46	15	11	20	60	79	56	14
2012-13	FL 1	46	9	14	23	45	73	41	22
2013-14	FL 2	46	13	20	13	59	51	59	12
2014-15	FL 2	46	26	7	13	60	40	85	3
2015-16	FL 1	46	16	12	18	56	73	57*	16
2016-17	FL 1	46	13	11	22	61	73	50	19

3 pts deducted.

DID YOU KNOW ?

A total of six Bury players have won full international honours for England. The first player capped was inside-forward Jimmy Settle who scored a hat-trick as England demolished Ireland 13-2 at Sunderland's Roker Park in February 1899.

BURY – SKY BET LEAGUE ONE 2016–17 LEAGUE RECORD

Match No.	Date	Venue	Opponents	Result	H/T Score	Lg Pos.	Goalscorers	Attendance
1	Aug 6	H	Charlton Ath	W 2-0	0-0	5	Danns (pen) [71], Etuhu [87]	4037
2	13	A	Gillingham	L 1-2	0-1	10	Pope [66]	5324
3	16	A	Coventry C	D 0-0	0-0	9		9098
4	20	H	Oldham Ath	L 0-1	0-1	14		4479
5	27	A	Walsall	D 3-3	0-3	14	Barnett [47], Vaughan [49], Mayor [66]	4393
6	Sept 3	H	Port Vale	W 4-1	3-0	9	Vaughan 2 [6, 30], Mellis [22], Hope [73]	4042
7	10	H	Shrewsbury T	W 2-1	0-0	7	Mayor 2 [65, 90]	2990
8	17	A	Swindon T	W 2-1	2-0	3	Hope 2 [13, 45]	6931
9	24	H	Chesterfield	W 2-1	1-1	2	Ismail [41], Pope [87]	3494
10	27	A	Milton Keynes D	W 3-1	1-0	2	Vaughan 2 [8, 68], Ismail [90]	7652
11	Oct 1	H	Scunthorpe U	L 1-2	0-1	3	Soares [58]	5355
12	8	A	Peterborough U	L 1-3	1-1	3	White (og) [2]	3964
13	15	A	Rochdale	L 0-2	0-1	6		5344
14	18	H	AFC Wimbledon	L 1-2	1-1	8	Danns (pen) [27]	2211
15	24	H	Bolton W	L 0-2	0-1	11		8007
16	29	A	Northampton T	L 2-3	0-1	13	Miller, G [74], Ismail [82]	5739
17	Nov 12	H	Southend U	L 1-4	1-2	16	Vaughan (pen) [20]	3033
18	19	A	AFC Wimbledon	L 1-5	1-4	18	Vaughan [40]	4141
19	22	A	Sheffield U	L 0-1	0-0	19		19,022
20	26	H	Millwall	L 2-3	0-0	20	Vaughan 2 [61, 67]	3028
21	Dec 10	A	Bristol R	L 2-4	1-2	20	Burgess, S [25], Miller, G [75]	7843
22	17	H	Oxford U	L 2-3	2-2	22	Vaughan [5], Pope [39]	2986
23	26	A	Fleetwood T	D 0-0	0-0	20		4017
24	31	A	Bradford C	D 1-1	1-0	20	Burgess, S [39]	18,012
25	Jan 2	H	Sheffield U	L 1-3	1-1	20	Mellis [12]	6123
26	7	A	Scunthorpe U	L 2-3	1-3	21	Miller, G [41], Etuhu [67]	5173
27	14	H	Peterborough U	W 5-1	4-1	20	Vaughan 4 [7, 16, 24, 27], Miller, G [71]	2820
28	20	A	Port Vale	D 2-2	1-2	20	Vaughan 2 [40, 55]	4338
29	28	H	Walsall	D 3-3	2-0	21	Vaughan [22], Brown, R [45], Soares [90]	3280
30	Feb 4	A	Shrewsbury T	L 1-2	0-0	22	Mellis [87]	5368
31	11	H	Swindon T	W 1-0	1-0	21	Vaughan (pen) [37]	2713
32	14	H	Milton Keynes D	D 0-0	0-0	21		2005
33	18	A	Chesterfield	W 2-1	0-1	20	Tutte [80], Miller, G [90]	5582
34	25	A	Charlton Ath	W 1-0	1-0	19	Lowe [21]	14,640
35	28	H	Coventry C	W 2-1	2-0	18	Vaughan [16], Pope [40]	2611
36	Mar 4	H	Gillingham	L 1-2	0-1	19	Vaughan [75]	3203
37	11	A	Oldham Ath	D 0-0	0-0	19		5776
38	14	H	Bristol R	W 3-0	0-0	18	Vaughan (pen) [50], Leigh [65], Miller, G [75]	2535
39	18	A	Millwall	D 0-0	0-0	17		9049
40	25	H	Fleetwood T	D 0-0	0-0	17		4174
41	28	A	Oxford U	L 1-5	0-3	17	Vaughan [59]	6552
42	Apr 8	H	Bradford C	L 0-2	0-0	18		5268
43	13	H	Rochdale	L 0-1	0-1	18		4850
44	18	A	Bolton W	D 0-0	0-0	20		18,223
45	22	H	Northampton T	W 3-0	1-0	19	Vaughan 2 [3, 90], Miller, G [72]	5190
46	30	A	Southend U	L 0-1	0-1	19		9245

Final League Position: 19

GOALSCORERS

League (61): Vaughan 24 (3 pens), Miller, G 7, Pope 4, Hope 3, Ismail 3, Mayor 3, Mellis 3, Burgess, S 2, Danns 2 (2 pens), Etuhu 2, Soares 2, Barnett 1, Brown, R 1, Leigh 1, Lowe 1, Tutte 1, own goal 1.
FA Cup (2): Hope 2.
EFL Cup (2): Maher 1, Pope 1.
EFL Checkatrade Trophy (6): Pope 2, Ismail 1 (1 pen), Kay 1, Miller 1, Walker 1.

Williams B 22	Jones C 12 + 1	Kay A 42	Cameron N 3 + 1	Leigh G 45	Hope H 17 + 16	Soares T 26	Mellis J 31 + 4	Danns N 13 + 5	Pope T 33 + 4	Clark N 2 + 1	Ismail Z 12 + 4	Mayor D 17 + 4	Etuhu K 11 + 9	Maher N 14 + 3	Barnett L 24	Vaughan J 36 + 1	Dudley A — + 3	Bryan K 6 + 6	Walker T 1 + 10	Tutte A 10 + 7	Miller I — + 3	Miller G 5 + 23	Burgess S 14 + 2	Bedeau J 6 + 1	Rachubka P 1	Lainton R 7	Styles C 12 + 1	Mackreth J 1 + 2	Moore T 18 + 1	Brown R 7	Burgess C 18	Lowe R 7 + 5	Pennant J 2 + 5	Murphy J 16	Caddis P 13	Beadling T 2	*Match No.*
1	2	3	4	5	6^1	7	8^2	9	10	11^3	12	13	14																								1
1	2^2	3	4	5	10^1	6	8	9	11	7^3	12	13		14																							2
1	2	4	3	5	10^2	7	12	8^1	11		13	9	6																								3
1	2	4		5	12	7	8^2		9	13	6	11	3^1		10																						4
1	7	3		5	9^3	6	13		12		10^1	8		2^2	4	11	14																				5
1		3		5	12	8	7		10^2		6	9		2^1	4	11^3		13	14																		6
1	12	3		5	13	8	7^1		10		6^2	9		2^3	4	11■		14																			7
1	5	3		2	10^3	8	7^1		11		9	6^2		4			14		12	13																	8
1	2	3		5	9^2	8^3	7^1	12	10		6		14	4		11			13																		9
1	2^3	4		5	14	8	7	9	10^2		6		13	3^1		11		12																			10
1		3		5	11^2	8	7	9^3	10		6		14	2^1			13	4	12																		11
1		4		5	12			8^1	10^2		9	6	7	2		11		3	13																		12
1		3		5	12	7	9■	8^2			10^1	6		2		11		4■			13																13
1		3		5	11^2	8		7^3			6^1	9	2	4		10			13	12	14																14
1		4		5	12	7	10	9^2			6	8	13	2^3	3^1	11				14																	15
1		4		5	13	7^3	9	10			12	8		2		11			3^2	6^1		14															16
1		3		4	11	7	8^1	6				5			2	10			12	9^2		13															17
1		4		5	10^3	7	8	13	12			9		2	3	11^1				6^2		14															18
1	2	3		5■		8	7■	14	10^1			9	12		4^2	11				13			6^3														19
1	5^1	3				4		6^2	10			9	7	2■		11				12			8	13													20
1	2^1			5		3		7■	10			9	8			11						12	6	4													21
		3		5	14	2			11			8^1	7	13		10^3			12			9	6	4^2	1												22
		3		5	9	2			11				7									10	6	4		1	8										23
		3		5	9	2	13		10				7			12						11^2	6^1	4		1	8										24
1		3		5		2	7^1	12	13				8			11						14	10	4			9^2	6^3									25
		4		5					10^1				13			11					14	9	8^2	3		1	6^3	12	2	7							26
		3		5	9		8^3	12	11^1				14			10						13	6			1			2^2	7	4						27
		4		5	6	2	9		10^1			13	12			11						14	7^3			1				8^2	3						28
		4		2	9^1	7	6^3		10^2							11						12				1			5	8	3	13	14				29
		4		5	9^2		14		10				7^1			11						13				1		12	2	8	3		6^3				30
		4		6	14		9		10^3						5	11^1				12		13	7^2						2	8	3			1			31
		4		6			8		10^2						3	11^1				7		12	9^3						2		5	14	13	1			32
		3		8	14		6		11^2						4					9		12	7^3				13		5		2	10^1		1			33
		3		6	11^2		9		13						5							12					7		2		4	10^1		1	8		34
				9	13		8		10^1					14	2	11^2						12					7^3		5		3			1	6	4	35
				9			6		10^3						2	11						12					8		5^2		3	13	14	1	7^1	4	36
		4		9			8^1								3	11		13		12		14					7^2		5		2	10^3		1	6		37
		4		6					11						3	10^2		13		8^3		12					9^1		2		5		14	1	7		38
		4		6	13		7								3	10		12		9^2									2		5	11^1		1	8		39
		4		6	14		9		11^2						3	10^1		5				13					8		2^3				12	1	7		40
		3		9	14		8								5	10		4^3	13			12							2			11^2	6^1	1	7		41
	2^1	4		6			9^2								3	11						10	14				7		12^3		5	13		1	8		42
				5	12		8^2		10^3						4	11		2^1	14			13					9			6	3			1	7		43
		4		6					10^1						3	11				9		12	8^2						2		5	13		1	7		44
		4	14	6					11^2						3	10^1				7		12	13						2		5	8^3		1	9		45
		3		9					11^1			13			2	10				6		12							5		4	8^2		1	7		46

FA Cup

First Round	AFC Wimbledon	(h)	2-2
Replay	AFC Wimbledon	(a)	0-5

EFL Cup

First Round (*aet*)	Burton Alb	(a)	2-3

EFL Checkatrade Trophy

Northern Group C	Morecambe	(h)	4-1
Northern Group C	Bradford C	(a)	1-2
Northern Group C	Stoke C U21	(a)	1-1

(*Stoke C U21 won 4-3 on penalties*)

CAMBRIDGE UNITED

FOUNDATION

The football revival in Cambridge began soon after World War II when the Abbey United club (formed 1912) decided to turn professional in 1949. In 1951 they changed their name to Cambridge United. They were competing in the United Counties League before graduating to the Eastern Counties League in 1951 and the Southern League in 1958.

Cambs Glass Stadium, Newmarket Road, Cambridge CB5 8LN.

Telephone: (01223) 566 500.

Ticket Office: (01223) 566 500.

Website: www.cambridge-united.co.uk

Email: info@cambridge-united.co.uk

Ground Capacity: 7,897.

Record Attendance: 14,000 v Chelsea, Friendly, 1 May 1970.

Pitch Measurements: 100.5m × 67.5m (110yd × 74yd).

Chairman: Dave Doggett.

Vice-chairman: Eddie Clarke.

Manager: Shaun Derry.

Assistant Manager: Joe Dunne.

Colours: Amber shirts with thin black stripes, black shorts with amber trim, amber socks with black trim.

Year Formed: 1912.

Turned Professional: 1949.

Ltd Co.: 1948.

Previous Name: 1919, Abbey United; 1951, Cambridge United.

Club Nickname: The 'U's'.

Grounds: 1932, Abbey Stadium (renamed R Costings Abbey Stadium 2009, Cambs Glass Stadium 2016).

First Football League Game: 15 August 1970, Division 4, v Lincoln C (h) D 1–1 – Roberts; Thompson, Meldrum (1), Slack, Eades, Hardy, Leggett, Cassidy, Lindsey, McKinven, Harris.

Record League Victory: 7–0 v Morecambe, FL 2, 19 April 2016 – Norris; Roberts (1), Coulson, Clark, Dunne (Williams), Ismail (1), Berry (2 pens), Ledson (Spencer), Dunk (2), Williamson (1) (Simpson).

Record Cup Victory: 5–1 v Bristol C, FA Cup 5th rd second replay, 27 February 1990 – Vaughan; Fensome, Kimble, Bailie (O'Shea), Chapple, Daish, Cheetham (Robinson), Leadbitter (1), Dublin (2), Taylor (1), Philpott (1).

Record Defeat: 0–7 v Sunderland, League Cup 2nd rd, 1 October 2002.

Most League Points (2 for a win): 65, Division 4, 1976–77.

HONOURS

League Champions: Division 3 – 1990–91; Division 4 – 1976–77.
Runners-up: Division 3 – 1977–78; Fourth Division – (6th) 1989–90 *(promoted via play-offs)*; Third Division – 1998–99; Conference – (2nd) 2013–14 *(promoted via play-offs)*.

FA Cup: 6th rd – 1990, 1991.

League Cup: quarter-final – 1993.

League Trophy: *Runners-up:* 2002.

sky SPORTS FACT FILE

Cambridge United came close to qualifying for the inaugural Premier League competition, reaching the Division Two play-offs in 1991–92 only to be defeated at the semi-final stage by Leicester City. The average home attendance at the Abbey Stadium that season was a record 7,078.

Most League Points (3 for a win): 86, Division 3, 1990–91.

Most League Goals: 87, Division 4, 1976–77.

Highest League Scorer in Season: David Crown, 24, Division 4, 1985–86.

Most League Goals in Total Aggregate: John Taylor, 86, 1988–92; 1996–2001.

Most League Goals in One Match: 5, Steve Butler v Exeter C, Division 2, 4 April 1994.

Most Capped Player: Tom Finney, 7 (15), Northern Ireland.

Most League Appearances: Steve Spriggs, 416, 1975–87.

Youngest League Player: Andy Sinton, 16 years 228 days v Wolverhampton W, 2 November 1982.

Record Transfer Fee Received: £1,300,000 from Leicester C for Trevor Benjamin, July 2000.

Record Transfer Fee Paid: £192,000 to Luton T for Steve Claridge, November 1992.

Football League Record: 1970 Elected to Division 4; 1973–74 Division 3; 1974–77 Division 4; 1977–78 Division 3; 1978–84 Division 2; 1984–85 Division 3; 1985–90 Division 4; 1990–91 Division 3; 1991–92 Division 2; 1992–93 Division 1; 1993–95 Division 2; 1995–99 Division 3; 1999–2002 Division 2; 2002–04 Division 3; 2004–05 FL2; 2005–14 Conference Premier; 2014– FL 2.

MANAGERS

Bill Whittaker 1949–55
Gerald Williams 1955
Bert Johnson 1955–59
Bill Craig 1959–60
Alan Moore 1960–63
Roy Kirk 1964–66
Bill Leivers 1967–74
Ron Atkinson 1974–78
John Docherty 1978–83
John Ryan 1984–85
Ken Shellito 1985
Chris Turner 1985–90
John Beck 1990–92
Ian Atkins 1992–93
Gary Johnson 1993–95
Tommy Taylor 1995–96
Roy McFarland 1996–2001
John Beck 2001
John Taylor 2001–04
Claude Le Roy 2004
Herve Renard 2004
Steve Thompson 2004–05
Rob Newman 2005–06
Jimmy Quinn 2006–08
Gary Brabin 2008–09
Martin Ling 2009–11
Jez George 2011–12
Richard Money 2012–15
Shaun Derry November 2015–

LATEST SEQUENCES

Longest Sequence of League Wins: 7, 19.2.1977 – 1.4.1977.

Longest Sequence of League Defeats: 7, 8.4.1985 – 30.4.1985.

Longest Sequence of League Draws: 6, 6.9.1986 – 30.9.1986.

Longest Sequence of Unbeaten League Matches: 14, 9.9.1972 – 10.11.1972.

Longest Sequence Without a League Win: 31, 8.10.1983 – 23.4.1984.

Successive Scoring Runs: 26 from 9.4.2002.

Successive Non-scoring Runs: 5 from 29.9.1973.

TEN YEAR LEAGUE RECORD

		P	W	D	L	F	A	Pts	Pos
2007-08	Conf P	46	25	11	10	68	41	86	2
2008-09	Conf P	46	24	14	8	65	39	86	2
2009-10	Conf P	44	15	14	15	65	53	59	10
2010-11	Conf P	46	11	17	18	53	61	50	17
2011-12	Conf P	46	19	14	13	57	41	71	9
2012-13	Conf P	46	15	14	17	68	69	59	14
2013-14	Conf P	46	23	13	10	72	35	82	2
2014-15	FL 2	46	13	12	21	61	66	51	19
2015-16	FL 2	46	18	14	14	66	55	68	9
2016-17	FL 2	46	19	9	18	58	50	66	11

DID YOU KNOW ?

Cambridge United gained their first-ever Football League victory at the third time of asking on 29 August 1970. They defeated Oldham Athletic at the Abbey Stadium by a 3-1 margin, the goals coming from Peter Leggett, George Harris and Bill Cassidy.

CAMBRIDGE UNITED – SKY BET LEAGUE TWO 2016–17 LEAGUE RECORD

Match No.	*Date*	*Venue*	*Opponents*	*Result*	*H/T Score*	*Lg Pos.*	*Goalscorers*	*Attendance*
1	Aug 6	H	Barnet	D 1-1	0-0	10	Mingoia [61]	4873
2	13	A	Colchester U	L 0-2	0-1	21		4521
3	16	A	Doncaster R	L 0-1	0-0	22		4768
4	20	H	Carlisle U	D 2-2	2-1	24	Legge [7], Berry (pen) [41]	4139
5	27	H	Luton T	L 0-3	0-0	24		5606
6	Sept 3	A	Mansfield T	D 0-0	0-0	24		2981
7	10	A	Plymouth Arg	L 1-2	0-1	24	Elito [79]	7068
8	17	H	Morecambe	L 1-2	1-0	24	Mingoia [36]	4110
9	24	A	Newport Co	W 2-1	0-1	24	Ikpeazu [61], Berry [83]	2225
10	27	H	Yeovil T	W 1-0	0-0	21	Roberts [65]	3556
11	Oct 1	H	Accrington S	W 2-1	1-0	19	Legge [14], Mingoia [81]	3765
12	8	A	Blackpool	D 1-1	1-0	17	Berry [17]	3070
13	15	H	Grimsby T	L 0-1	0-1	21		5121
14	22	A	Exeter C	W 2-1	2-0	18	Berry [7], Dunk [10]	3485
15	29	H	Portsmouth	L 0-1	0-1	22		6397
16	Nov 12	A	Crawley T	W 3-1	2-1	17	Taylor [19], Ikpeazu [28], Berry [51]	2408
17	19	H	Wycombe W	L 1-2	0-1	19	Maris [87]	4139
18	22	A	Notts Co	W 1-0	1-0	14	Newton [26]	2736
19	26	H	Cheltenham T	W 3-1	1-0	11	Ikpeazu [7], Berry 2 [56, 74]	4606
20	Dec 10	A	Hartlepool U	W 5-0	0-0	9	Dunne [51], Berry [62], Legge [66], Ikpeazu [70], Clark [88]	3261
21	17	H	Crewe Alex	W 2-1	0-0	6	Ikpeazu [51], Taylor [60]	4167
22	26	A	Stevenage	W 2-1	1-0	7	Legge [21], Mingoia [82]	3957
23	31	A	Leyton Orient	D 1-1	1-0	7	Dunk [21]	5897
24	Jan 2	H	Notts Co	W 4-0	1-0	7	Berry 2 [18, 61], Ikpeazu [57], Mingoia [69]	4981
25	14	H	Blackpool	D 0-0	0-0	8		4248
26	21	H	Mansfield T	L 1-3	1-1	10	Maris [8]	4211
27	28	A	Luton T	L 0-2	0-1	11		8917
28	Feb 4	H	Plymouth Arg	L 0-1	0-1	12		5084
29	11	A	Morecambe	L 0-2	0-0	14		2162
30	14	A	Yeovil T	D 1-1	0-0	14	Corr [89]	2847
31	18	H	Newport Co	W 3-2	0-1	13	Corr [63], Legge [72], Roberts [90]	4175
32	25	A	Barnet	W 1-0	0-0	10	Berry [65]	2396
33	28	H	Doncaster R	L 2-3	0-2	12	Maris [78], Berry [90]	4236
34	Mar 4	H	Colchester U	D 1-1	1-0	12	McDonagh [20]	5708
35	11	A	Carlisle U	W 3-0	0-0	12	Elito 3 (2 pens) [66 (p), 71 (p), 90]	4427
36	14	H	Hartlepool U	L 0-1	0-0	12		3824
37	18	A	Cheltenham T	W 1-0	1-0	12	Elito [2]	2905
38	25	H	Stevenage	D 0-0	0-0	12		5520
39	28	A	Accrington S	L 0-2	0-1	12		1333
40	Apr 1	A	Crewe Alex	W 2-1	1-0	10	Berry 2 [37, 72]	3759
41	8	H	Leyton Orient	W 3-0	2-0	9	Berry [31], O'Neil [41], Maris [53]	4681
42	14	A	Grimsby T	L 1-2	0-0	10	Halliday [90]	5166
43	17	H	Exeter C	W 1-0	1-0	8	Legge [29]	6130
44	22	A	Portsmouth	L 1-2	0-1	11	Berry [80]	18,165
45	29	H	Crawley T	W 2-0	1-0	9	Wharton [35], Berry (pen) [90]	5675
46	May 6	A	Wycombe W	L 0-1	0-0	11		6313

Final League Position: 11

GOALSCORERS

League (58): Berry 17 (2 pens), Ikpeazu 6, Legge 6, Elito 5 (2 pens), Mingoia 5, Maris 4, Corr 2, Dunk 2, Roberts 2, Taylor 2, Clark 1, Dunne 1, Halliday 1, McDonagh 1, Newton 1, O'Neil 1, Wharton 1.
FA Cup (10): Berry 4 (1 pen), Elito 1, Ikpeazu 1, Legge 1, Mingoia 1, Roberts 1, Williamson 1.
EFL Cup (3): Berry 1, Elito 1, Mingoia 1.
EFL Checkatrade Trophy (3): Ikpeazu 1, Pigott 1, own goal 1.

Norris W 45	Long S 5 + 2	Dallison T 5	Legge L 43 + 1	Adams B 4 + 2	Mingoia P 40	Dunne J 28 + 5	Berry L 45	Clark M 17 + 10	Dunk H 23 + 15	Pigott J 5 + 5	Williamson B 17 + 16	Elito M 12 + 11	Maris G 17 + 6	Taylor G 34 + 2	Roberts M 26 + 1	Newton C 17 + 10	Coulson J 6 + 1	Keane K 1	Gosling J 3 + 1	Ikpeazu U 20 + 9	Halliday B 30	McGurk A 7 + 8	Gregory D 1	Davies L 3 + 2	Carroll J 19 + 1	McDonagh G 5 + 8	Lewis P 5 + 8	Wharton S 9	O'Neil L 13	Corr B 1 + 6	*Match No.*
1	2	3	4	5	6	7^3	8	9^1	10^2	11	12	13	14																		1
1	2	4^1	3		6	8	7			11	10^2	14	9^3	5	12	13															2
1	2	4			8	6^2	9	5		13	11	10				12	3	7^1													3
1	2		5		6	7^2	8			11	12	10^1		3		13	4		9												4
1			3	2^2	6	8	7	9^1		12	11^3	10		5			4		14	13											5
1		4	3		8	6^3	10	14		11^1	12	9		5		7^2					2	13									6
1		4	3		7		8	6^3	13	11^2		10		5^1		9				14	2	12									7
1			4		6		7	13	5		10^2	9^1		14		8^3	3			12	2	11									8
1			3				7	8	5		10^1	6		12	4		14		9^2	13^3	2	11									9
1			4				7	8	9		10			5	3	13			6^2	12	2	11^1									10
1			3■		6	12	8	7^3	9		10^2			5	4	14				13	2■	11^1									11
1	5				6	7	8	13	9		10^1			2	3		4			12		11^2									12
			4		6	7^1	8	12	9	14	10^3			5^2	3	13					2	11	1								13
1	14		3		8	6	9	7	10^1		13			5	4					11^2	2^3	12									14
1			3		6	8		7^3	9	14	12			5	4	13				11	2^1	10^2									15
1			4	13	8	6	9	7	10^3		14	12		5^1	3					11^2	2										16
1			12	5	6^2		8	9			11		10		3	7	4^1			13	2										17
1			4		8^2	6	9	13	12		14		10^1	5	3	7^3				11	2										18
1	14		3		8^3	6	9^1	7	13		12		10^2	5	4					11	2										19
1			4		6^3	7	8	13	12		14		10^2	2	3	9^1				11	5										20
1			3		8	7	9^2	12	10^1		14		13	5	4	6				11^3	2										21
1			3		8	6	9	13	10^2				12	5	4	7^1				11	2										22
1			3		8	6	9	12	10^1	14	13			5	4	7^3				11^2	2										23
1			3	5	8^3	6	9	7	12		10^1			2	4	14				11^2				13							24
1			3	12	8	6	9	7^3			14		10^2	2^1	4	13				11					5						25
1			3		8	6	9	7^1					10^2		4					11				2	5	12	13				26
1			3		7^3	6^2	9		10^1		12				4	8				11	2				5	14	13				27
1			2		5	8^3	7		12		11^1				3					10					9^2	14	13	4	6		28
1			4		9	6	10		12		14				3	7^3				11^1					5			2^2	8	13	29
1			4		6		10	12	14				9^2		3					11^1				2	5		8^3		7	13	30
1			3		8		9		10		11^1		14		4									2	5^2	13	7^3		6	12	31
1			4		6^2	12	10		9^1			13	14	2	3										5	11	8^3		7		32
1			3		8	6^1	9		14		11^3	13	10	2	4										5^2	12			7		33
1			4		6	12	8		9^2			14	10^1	2^3										13	5	11		3	7		34
1			4		6	7	9	8^2	14			12	10^1	5							3					11^3	13	2			35
1			3		7	8^3	9	5■	10^2			12	14								2				6	11^1	13	4			36
1			4		6		8		13		10^2	11^3		5							2				9	12	7^1	3		14	37
1			3		6^1		10		14		11^2		9	7							2	12			5		8^3	4		13	38
1			4				9		10		11^2		8^1	6^3	3	14					2				5	13			7	12	39
1			4				9		10			13	8^1	3		7^2				12	2				5		14■		6	11^3	40
1			3				9		10			12	8^1	4		7^3				11^2	2	13			5		14		6		41
1			3				9		10			12	8^2	4		7^3				11	2	13			5		14		6^1		42
1			3		6	12	10		13			9^1		4		8^3				11	2	14			5				7^2		43
1			3		6	13	7		12			10		4		9^1				11^2	2	14			5				8^3		44
1			7		6	3	10		9		13	11^2		5		8^1					2					12		4			45
1			3		6	7^2	8		12		13	11	9^3	5							2				14	10		4^1			46

FA Cup

First Round	Dover Ath	(h)	1-1
Replay	Dover Ath	(a)	4-2
(*aet*)			
Second Round	Coventry C	(h)	4-0
Third Round	Leeds U	(h)	1-2

EFL Cup

First Round	Sheffield W	(h)	2-1
(*aet*)			
Second Round	Wolverhampton W	(a)	1-2

EFL Checkatrade Trophy

Northern Group G	Shrewsbury T	(a)	1-0
Northern Group G	Middlesbrough U21	(h)	2-1
Northern Group G	Scunthorpe U	(h)	0-2
Second Round North	Bradford C	(a)	0-1

CARDIFF CITY

FOUNDATION

Credit for the establishment of a first class professional football club in such a rugby stronghold as Cardiff is due to members of the Riverside club formed in 1899 out of a cricket club of that name. Cardiff became a city in 1905 and in 1908 the South Wales and Monmouthshire FA granted Riverside permission to call themselves Cardiff City. The club turned professional under that name in 1910.

Cardiff City Stadium, Leckwith Road, Cardiff CF11 8AZ.

Telephone: (0845) 365 1115. ***Fax:*** (0845) 365 1116.

Ticket Office: (0845) 345 1400.

Website: www.cardiffcityfc.co.uk

Email: club@cardiffcityfc.co.uk

Ground Capacity: 33,280.

Record Attendance: 57,893 v Arsenal, Division 1, 22 April 1953 (at Ninian Park); 28,680 v Derby Co, FL C, 2 April 2016 (at Cardiff City Stadium).

Ground Record Attendance: 62,634, Wales v England, 17 October 1959 (at Ninian Park); 33,280, Wales v Belgium, 12 June 2015 (at Cardiff City Stadium).

Pitch Measurements: 105m × 68m (115yd × 74.5yd).

Chairman: Mehmet Dalman.

Chief Executive: Ken Choo.

Manager: Neil Warnock

Assistant Manager: Kevin Blackwell

Colours: Blue shirts with white trim, blue shorts with white trim, blue socks with white trim.

Year Formed: 1899.

Turned Professional: 1910.

Previous Names: 1899, Riverside; 1902, Riverside Albion; 1908, Cardiff City.

Club Nickname: 'The Bluebirds'.

Grounds: Riverside, Sophia Gardens, Old Park and Fir Gardens; 1910, Ninian Park; 2009, Cardiff City Stadium.

First Football League Game: 28 August 1920, Division 2, v Stockport Co (a) W 5–2 – Kneeshaw; Brittan, Leyton; Keenor (1), Smith, Hardy; Grimshaw (1), Gill (2), Cashmore, West, Evans (1).

Record League Victory: 9–2 v Thames, Division 3 (S), 6 February 1932 – Farquharson; Eric Morris, Roberts; Galbraith, Harris, Ronan; Emmerson (1), Keating (1), Jones (1), McCambridge (1), Robbins (5).

Record Cup Victory: 8–0 v Enfield, FA Cup 1st rd, 28 November 1931 – Farquharson; Smith, Roberts; Harris (1), Galbraith, Ronan; Emmerson (2), Keating (3); O'Neill (2), Robbins, McCambridge.

HONOURS

League Champions: FL C – 2012–13; Division 3S – 1946–47; Third Division – 1992–93.
Runners-up: Division 1 – 1923–24; Division 2 – 1920–21, 1951–52, 1959–60; Division 3 – 1975–76, 1982–83; Third Division – 2000–01; Division 4 – 1987–88.

FA Cup Winners: 1927.
Runners-up: 1925, 2008.

League Cup: *Runners-up:* 2012.

Welsh Cup Winners: 22 times (joint record).

European Competitions
European Cup-Winners' Cup: 1964–65 *(qf)*, 1965–66, 1967–68 *(sf)*, 1968–69, 1969–70, 1970–71 *(qf)*, 1971–72, 1973–74, 1974–75, 1976–77, 1977–78, 1988–89, 1992–93, 1993–94.

sky SPORTS FACT FILE

Enthusiastic walker and Cardiff City supporter Charles Manley walked some 350 miles to see the team play at Newcastle in April 1922, while the following season he went on a four-month trek around the country covering 3,500 miles while watching the Bluebirds away from home. He was also holder of the world record time for walking 1,000 miles.

Record Defeat: 2–11 v Sheffield U, Division 1, 1 January 1926.

Most League Points (2 for a win): 66, Division 3 (S), 1946–47.

Most League Points (3 for a win): 87, FL C, 2012–13.

Most League Goals: 95, Division 3, 2000–01.

Highest League Scorer in Season: Robert Earnshaw, 31, Division 2, 2002–03.

Most League Goals in Total Aggregate: Len Davies, 128, 1920–31.

Most League Goals in One Match: 5, Hugh Ferguson v Burnley, Division 1, 1 September 1928; 5, Walter Robbins v Thames, Division 3 (S), 6 February 1932; 5, William Henderson v Northampton T, Division 3 (S), 22 April 1933.

Most Capped Player: Aron Gunnarsson, 48 (71), Iceland.

Most League Appearances: Phil Dwyer, 471, 1972–85.

Youngest League Player: Bob Adams, 15 years 355 days v Southend U, 18 February 1933.

Record Transfer Fee Received: £10,000,000 from Internazionale for Gary Medel, August 2014.

Record Transfer Fee Paid: £11,000,000 to Sevilla for Gary Medel, August 2013.

Football League Record: 1920 Elected to Division 2; 1921–29 Division 1; 1929–31 Division 2; 1931–47 Division 3 (S); 1947–52 Division 2; 1952–57 Division 1; 1957–60 Division 2; 1960–62 Division 1; 1962–75 Division 2; 1975–76 Division 3; 1976–82 Division 2; 1982–83 Division 3; 1983–85 Division 2; 1985–86 Division 3; 1986–88 Division 4; 1988–90 Division 3; 1990–92 Division 4; 1992–93 Division 3; 1993–95 Division 2; 1995–99 Division 3; 1999–2000 Division 2; 2000–01 Division 3; 2001–03 Division 2; 2003–04 Division 1; 2004–13 FL C; 2013–14 FA Premier League; 2014– FL C.

LATEST SEQUENCES

Longest Sequence of League Wins: 9, 26.10.1946 – 28.12.1946.

Longest Sequence of League Defeats: 7, 4.11.1933 – 25.12.1933.

Longest Sequence of League Draws: 6, 29.11.1980 – 17.1.1981.

Longest Sequence of Unbeaten League Matches: 21, 21.9.1946 – 1.3.1947.

Longest Sequence Without a League Win: 15, 21.11.1936 – 6.3.1937.

Successive Scoring Runs: 24 from 25.8.2012.

Successive Non-scoring Runs: 8 from 20.12.1952.

MANAGERS

Davy McDougall 1910–11
Fred Stewart 1911–33
Bartley Wilson 1933–34
B. Watts-Jones 1934–37
Bill Jennings 1937–39
Cyril Spiers 1939–46
Billy McCandless 1946–48
Cyril Spiers 1948–54
Trevor Morris 1954–58
Bill Jones 1958–62
George Swindin 1962–64
Jimmy Scoular 1964–73
Frank O'Farrell 1973–74
Jimmy Andrews 1974–78
Richie Morgan 1978–81
Graham Williams 1981–82
Len Ashurst 1982–84
Jimmy Goodfellow 1984
Alan Durban 1984–86
Frank Burrows 1986–89
Len Ashurst 1989–91
Eddie May 1991–94
Terry Yorath 1994–95
Eddie May 1995
Kenny Hibbitt (*Chief Coach*) 1995–96
Phil Neal 1996
Russell Osman 1996–97
Kenny Hibbitt 1997–98
Frank Burrows 1998–2000
Billy Ayre 2000
Bobby Gould 2000
Alan Cork 2000–02
Lennie Lawrence 2002–05
Dave Jones 2005–11
Malky Mackay 2011–13
Ole Gunnar Solskjaer 2014
Russell Slade 2014–16
Paul Trollope 2016
Neil Warnock October 2016–

TEN YEAR LEAGUE RECORD

		P	*W*	*D*	*L*	*F*	*A*	*Pts*	*Pos*
2007-08	FL C	46	16	16	14	59	55	64	12
2008-09	FL C	46	19	17	10	65	53	74	7
2009-10	FL C	46	22	10	14	73	54	76	4
2010-11	FL C	46	23	11	12	76	54	80	4
2011-12	FL C	46	19	18	9	66	53	75	6
2012-13	FL C	46	25	12	9	72	45	87	1
2013-14	PR Lge	38	7	9	22	32	74	30	20
2014-15	FL C	46	16	14	16	57	61	62	11
2015-16	FL C	46	17	17	12	56	51	68	8
2016-17	FL C	46	17	11	18	60	61	62	12

DID YOU KNOW ?

Cardiff City's former ground at Ninian Park hosted two world title boxing bouts, both involving Welshmen. In 1946 Swansea's Ronnie James was defeated by Ike Williams for the world lightweight crown, while in 1967 Howard Winstone lost a points decision to Vicente Salvador for the featherweight title in front of around 25,000 fans.

CARDIFF CITY – SKY BET CHAMPIONSHIP 2016–17 LEAGUE RECORD

Match No.	*Date*	*Venue*	*Opponents*	*Result*		*H/T Score*	*Lg Pos.*	*Goalscorers*	*Attendance*
1	Aug 6	A	Birmingham C	D	0-0	0-0	12		19,833
2	14	H	QPR	L	0-2	0-0	17		15,869
3	17	H	Blackburn R	W	2-1	2-0	14	Duffy (2 ogs) 14, 20	14,041
4	20	A	Fulham	D	2-2	0-1	14	Ralls 60, Pilkington 65	15,401
5	27	H	Reading	L	0-1	0-0	17		15,013
6	Sept 10	A	Norwich C	L	2-3	0-1	18	Pilkington 2 86, 90	25,519
7	13	A	Preston NE	L	0-3	0-2	21		9216
8	17	H	Leeds U	L	0-2	0-0	23		16,608
9	24	A	Rotherham U	W	2-1	0-0	21	Lambert 2 73, 79	8348
10	27	H	Derby Co	L	0-2	0-0	23		14,131
11	Oct 1	A	Burton Alb	L	0-2	0-1	23		4426
12	14	H	Bristol C	W	2-1	1-0	19	Whittingham (pen) 25, Bamba 67	22,776
13	19	H	Sheffield W	D	1-1	1-0	22	Whittingham 9	15,887
14	22	A	Nottingham F	W	2-1	2-0	20	Gunnarsson 28, Ralls 39	16,539
15	29	H	Wigan Ath	L	0-1	0-0	21		15,969
16	Nov 5	A	Newcastle U	L	1-2	0-2	21	Whittingham 77	51,257
17	19	H	Huddersfield T	W	3-2	3-1	19	Morrison 15, Hoilett 17, Lambert 33	15,930
18	26	A	Aston Villa	L	1-3	1-2	22	Lambert 28	31,484
19	Dec 3	H	Brighton & HA	D	0-0	0-0	22		16,168
20	10	A	Ipswich T	D	1-1	1-0	22	Gunnarsson 38	15,042
21	13	H	Wolverhampton W	W	2-1	0-1	19	Connolly 68, Pilkington 86	14,853
22	17	H	Barnsley	L	3-4	1-3	20	Morrison 3, Whittingham 79, Pilkington 89	14,754
23	26	A	Brentford	D	2-2	1-0	19	Whittingham (pen) 24, Zohore 89	11,098
24	Jan 2	H	Aston Villa	W	1-0	1-0	19	Ralls 16	21,391
25	14	A	Bristol C	W	3-2	0-0	17	Pilkington 2 (1 pen) 74 (p), 85, Harris, K 82	19,452
26	21	H	Burton Alb	W	1-0	0-0	16	Healey 90	15,543
27	24	A	Brighton & HA	L	0-1	0-0	16		26,688
28	28	A	Reading	L	1-2	1-1	16	Ralls (pen) 45	18,558
29	31	H	Preston NE	W	2-0	2-0	15	Whittingham (pen) 18, Zohore 28	13,894
30	Feb 4	H	Norwich C	L	0-1	0-1	16		15,901
31	11	A	Leeds U	W	2-0	0-0	14	Morrison 53, Zohore 71	31,516
32	14	A	Derby Co	W	4-3	1-2	12	Harris, K 2 41, 47, Noone 57, Ralls (pen) 90	26,541
33	18	H	Rotherham U	W	5-0	2-0	12	Harris, K 11, Hoilett 45, Noone 49, Zohore 2 54, 83	15,650
34	25	H	Fulham	D	2-2	1-1	12	Zohore 2 24, 56	15,656
35	Mar 4	A	QPR	L	1-2	1-0	12	Bamba 45	15,103
36	7	A	Blackburn R	D	1-1	1-0	13	Zohore 38	10,645
37	11	H	Birmingham C	D	1-1	0-0	13	Ralls (pen) 53	20,334
38	18	H	Ipswich T	W	3-1	1-1	12	Zohore 2 36, 50, Bennett 63	15,182
39	Apr 1	A	Wolverhampton W	L	1-3	1-2	14	Zohore 12	20,519
40	4	A	Barnsley	D	0-0	0-0	14		10,814
41	8	H	Brentford	W	2-1	0-1	14	Morrison 47, Whittingham 76	15,861
42	14	A	Sheffield W	L	0-1	0-0	14		28,007
43	17	H	Nottingham F	W	1-0	0-0	13	Gunnarsson 70	16,413
44	22	A	Wigan Ath	D	0-0	0-0	12		10,875
45	28	H	Newcastle U	L	0-2	0-0	13		23,153
46	May 7	A	Huddersfield T	W	3-0	2-0	12	Zohore 7, Bennett 2 29, 71	20,583

Final League Position: 12

GOALSCORERS

League (60): Zohore 12, Pilkington 7 (1 pen), Whittingham 7 (3 pens), Ralls 6 (3 pens), Harris, K 4, Lambert 4, Morrison 4, Bennett 3, Gunnarsson 3, Bamba 2, Hoilett 2, Noone 2, Connolly 1, Healey 1, own goals 2.
FA Cup (1): Pilkington 1.
EFL Cup (0).

Marshall D 4	Peltier L 28	Ecuele Manga B 16 + 5	Connolly M 26 + 2	Richards A 25 + 1	Ralls J 39 + 3	Whittingham P 28 + 9	John D 9 + 6	Pilkington A 21 + 13	Immers L 10 + 3	Gounongbe F 3 + 8	Zohore K 24 + 5	Noone C 17 + 17	O'Keefe S 3 + 5	Huws E 1 + 2	Morrison S 43 + 1	Gunnarsson A 40	Harris K 22 + 15	Wilson B 3	Lambert R 13 + 5	Amos B 16	Bamba S 26	Bennett J 23 + 1	Hoilett J 29 + 4	Chamakh M — + 2	Richardson K 2 + 4	Murphy B 4 + 1	Halford G 9 + 7	McGregor A 19	Kennedy M — + 2	Healey R 2 + 5	Harris M 1 + 1	Meite I — + 1	Match No.
1	2	3	4	5	6²	7	8	9¹	10	11³	12	13	14																				1
1	2	3	4	5³	8	7	9	11	6¹	10²	13	14		12																			2
1	5²	2	4		8	7	9	11³	10¹	13				14	3	6	12																3
1	2	14	4	5²	8	7¹	9	11³	10	13					3	6	12																4
	2³	12	4	5	7	8		11	10²	13		14			3	9¹	6	1															5
	2		4²	5	7	13	8¹	10	9³			14			3	6	12	1	11														6
	2	4			8¹	13	9³	10		14		12		6²	3	7	5	1	11														7
	2		4²	5	8³	7		11¹	14	13		9			3	6	12		10	1													8
	2¹	13	4	5	10²	9			8			7	6		3		12		11	1													9
		14	4▮	2	10¹	6	5		9²		12	8	7		3		13		11³	1													10
	2	4			10²	6	5		9¹	13	14	8	7		3		12		11³	1													11
	2				9	8²		14	12			6			3	7	13		11³	1	4	5	10¹										12
	2				9	7¹		12				6²	14		3	8			11³	1	4	5	10	13									13
			2		9	7¹		6				12	14		3	8			11²	1	4	5	10³		13								14
	2				9	7¹		11	14			6³	13		3	8	12			1	4	5	10²										15
	2				9	13						6¹			3	8	14		11³	1	4	5	10	12	7²								16
	2				6	8		5		12					3	7			11¹	1	4	9	10²		13								17
	2▮				8²	9		6³		13		12			3	7			11¹	1	4	5	10		14								18
			2		9	7		12		11²					3	8	6			1	4	5	10¹		13								19
	5	14	2			8		12				13			3	7	6³		11²	1	4▮	9¹	10										20
	5	4	2		14	7¹		11	10³		13	12			3	8				1			6		9²								21
	5	4	2			7		10			11	6¹			3	8	12		13	1			9²										22
	2³	5	3		9	8²		13			10	14	12		4	7						6	11¹			1							23
	2	5	13		9						11	12			4	8	7				3	6²	10¹			1							24
	2		3		9	7¹		10³			11				4	8	12				5	6²	13			1	14						25
	5		2		8			10¹			11²				3	7	6		13		4		9³					1	12	14			26
	2			5	9³	14					11	12			3	8	7				4		10¹				6²	1		13			27
	5			8	6³	14					11²				3	7	12				4		9				2¹	1	13	10			28
	2²		12	5	9	7³					11				3	8	6				4¹		10				13	1		14			29
			2³	5	9	7²	14				11	12			3	8	6				4		10¹					1		13			30
			2	5	6						11¹	8			3	9	10²		12		4		13				7	1					31
			2	5	9		14				11	7¹			3	8	10³				4		13				6²	1		12			32
			2	5	8		14	13			11	6²			3	7	9³				4		12					1		10¹			33
			2	5	8		12				11	6¹			3	7	9				4		10					1					34
			2²	5	8			12			11	6¹			3	7³	9				4	13	10				14	1					35
				2	9	8	12	14			11³	13			3		7¹				4	5	10²				6	1					36
				2	9	12		7			11				3	8	13				4	5	10¹				6²	1					37
				2		8	14	13			11²	6³			3	7	9¹				4	5	10				12	1					38
		4		2	9²	13		14			11	12			3	8	10³				6	5	7¹					1					39
		4	3				2³	10			11	7			13	8	14				6²	5				12	9	1¹					40
		4		2	8	10¹		12			11²				3	7	9					5	6				13	1					41
		4		2	9¹	14		12			11	13			3	8	10					5	7³				6²	1					42
	2²	4		12	13	8¹		10³			11				3	7	9					5	6				14	1					43
		4	2		9			11				7¹			3	6	10²		12	1		5					14				8³	13	44
		4		2	13	9³		14			11	12			3	8	10¹					5	7				6²	1					45
	2		4	5	7	12		9²			10³				3	6			14			8	11¹			1					13		46

FA Cup
Third Round — Fulham — (h) — 1-2

EFL Cup
First Round (*aet*) — Bristol R — (a) — 0-1

CARLISLE UNITED

FOUNDATION

Carlisle United came into being when members of Shaddongate United voted to change its name on 17 May 1904. The new club was admitted to the Second Division of the Lancashire Combination in 1905–06, winning promotion the following season. Devonshire Park was officially opened on 2 September 1905, when St Helens Town were the visitors. Despite defeat in a disappointing 3–2 start, a respectable mid-table position was achieved.

Brunton Park, Warwick Road, Carlisle, Cumbria CA1 1LL.

Telephone: (01228) 526 237.

Fax: (01228) 554 141.

Ticket Office: (0844) 371 1921.

Website: www.carlisleunited.co.uk

Email: enquiries@carlisleunited.co.uk

Ground Capacity: 17,792.

Record Attendance: 27,500 v Birmingham C, FA Cup 3rd rd, 5 January 1957 and v Middlesbrough, FA Cup 5th rd, 7 February 1970.

Pitch Measurements: 102.5m × 67.5m (112yd × 74yd).

Chairman: Andrew Jenkins.

Chief Executive: Nigel Clibbens.

Manager: Keith Curle.

Assistant Manager: Colin West.

Colours: Blue shirts with white and red trim, white shorts with blue and red trim, red socks.

Year Formed: 1904. ***Turned Professional:*** 1921.

Previous Name: 1904, Shaddongate United; 1904, Carlisle United.

Club Nicknames: 'The Cumbrians', 'The Blues'.

Grounds: 1904, Milholme Bank; 1905, Devonshire Park; 1909, Brunton Park.

First Football League Game: 25 August 1928, Division 3 (N), v Accrington S (a) W 3–2 – Prout; Coulthard, Cook; Harrison, Ross, Pigg; Agar (1), Hutchison, McConnell (1), Ward (1), Watson.

Record League Victory: 8–0 v Hartlepool U, Division 3 (N), 1 September 1928 – Prout; Smiles, Cook; Robinson (1) Ross, Pigg; Agar (1), Hutchison (1), McConnell (4), Ward (1), Watson. 8–0 v Scunthorpe U, Division 3 (N), 25 December 1952 – MacLaren; Hill, Scott; Stokoe, Twentyman, Waters; Harrison (1), Whitehouse (5), Ashman (2), Duffett, Bond.

Record Cup Victory: 6–0 v Shepshed Dynamo, FA Cup 1st rd, 16 November 1996 – Caig; Hopper, Archdeacon (pen), Walling, Robinson, Pounewatchy, Peacock (1), Conway (1) (Jansen), Smart (McAlindon (1)), Hayward, Aspinall (Thorpe), (2 og). 6–0 v Tipton T, FA Cup 1st rd, 6 November 2010 – Collin; Simek, Murphy, Chester, Cruise, Robson (McKenna), Berrett, Taiwo (Hurst), Marshall, Zoko (Curran) (2), Madine (4).

HONOURS

League Champions: Division 3 – 1964–65; FL 2 – 2005–06; Third Division – 1994–95.
Runners-up: Division 3 – 1981–82; Division 4 – 1963–64; Conference – (3rd) 2004–05 *(promoted via play-offs)*.

FA Cup: 6th rd – 1975.

League Cup: semi-final – 1970.

League Trophy Winners: 1997, 2011.
Runners-up: 1995, 2003, 2006, 2010.

sky SPORTS FACT FILE

Bill Shankly began his career as a manager with Carlisle United in March 1949. His first major success came when his Division Three North team drew 0-0 at Highbury in an FA Cup tie in January 1951. A crowd of 20,000 welcomed the team home after their rail journey north, but the Cumbrians lost the replay at Brunton Park 4-1.

Record Defeat: 1–11 v Hull C, Division 3 (N), 14 January 1939.

Most League Points (2 for a win): 62, Division 3 (N), 1950–51.

Most League Points (3 for a win): 91, Division 3, 1994–95.

Most League Goals: 113, Division 4, 1963–64.

Highest League Scorer in Season: Jimmy McConnell, 42, Division 3 (N), 1928–29.

Most League Goals in Total Aggregate: Jimmy McConnell, 124, 1928–32.

Most League Goals in One Match: 5, Hugh Mills v Halifax T, Division 3 (N), 11 September 1937; 5, Jim Whitehouse v Scunthorpe U, Division 3 (N), 25 December 1952.

Most Capped Player: Eric Welsh, 4, Northern Ireland.

Most League Appearances: Allan Ross, 466, 1963–79.

Youngest League Player: John Slaven, 16 years 162 days v Scunthorpe U, 16 March 2002.

Record Transfer Fee Received: £1,000,000 from Crystal Palace for Matt Jansen, February 1998.

Record Transfer Fee Paid: £140,000 to Blackburn R for Joe Garner, August 2007.

Football League Record: 1928 Elected to Division 3 (N); 1958–62 Division 4; 1962–63 Division 3; 1963–64 Division 4; 1964–65 Division 3; 1965–74 Division 2; 1974–75 Division 1; 1975–77 Division 2; 1977–82 Division 3; 1982–86 Division 2; 1986–87 Division 3; 1987–92 Division 4; 1992–95 Division 3; 1995–96 Division 2; 1996–97 Division 3; 1997–98 Division 2; 1998–2004 Division 3; 2004–05 Conference; 2005–06 FL 2; 2006–14 FL 1; 2014– FL 2.

LATEST SEQUENCES

Longest Sequence of League Wins: 7, 18.2.2006 – 8.4.2006.

Longest Sequence of League Defeats: 12, 27.9.2003 – 13.12.2003.

Longest Sequence of League Draws: 6, 11.2.1978 – 11.3.1978.

Longest Sequence of Unbeaten League Matches: 19, 1.10.1994 – 11.2.1995.

Longest Sequence Without a League Win: 15, 12.4.2014 – 20.9.2014.

Successive Scoring Runs: 26 from 23.8.1947.

Successive Non-scoring Runs: 7 from 25.2.2017.

MANAGERS

Harry Kirkbride 1904–05 (*Secretary-Manager*)
McCumiskey 1905–06 (*Secretary-Manager*)
Jack Houston 1906–08 (*Secretary-Manager*)
Bert Stansfield 1908–10
Jack Houston 1910–12
Davie Graham 1912–13
George Bristow 1913–30
Billy Hampson 1930–33
Bill Clarke 1933–35
Robert Kelly 1935–36
Fred Westgarth 1936–38
David Taylor 1938–40
Howard Harkness 1940–45
Bill Clark 1945–46 (*Secretary-Manager*)
Ivor Broadis 1946–49
Bill Shankly 1949–51
Fred Emery 1951–58
Andy Beattie 1958–60
Ivor Powell 1960–63
Alan Ashman 1963–67
Tim Ward 1967–68
Bob Stokoe 1968–70
Ian MacFarlane 1970–72
Alan Ashman 1972–75
Dick Young 1975–76
Bobby Moncur 1976–80
Martin Harvey 1980
Bob Stokoe 1980–85
Bryan 'Pop' Robson 1985
Bob Stokoe 1985–86
Harry Gregg 1986–87
Cliff Middlemass 1987–91
Aidan McCaffery 1991–92
David McCreery 1992–93
Mick Wadsworth (*Director of Coaching*) 1993–96
Mervyn Day 1996–97
David Wilkes and John Halpin (*Directors of Coaching*), and **Michael Knighton** 1997–99
Nigel Pearson 1998–99
Keith Mincher 1999
Martin Wilkinson 1999–2000
Ian Atkins 2000–01
Roddy Collins 2001–02; 2002–03
Paul Simpson 2003–06
Neil McDonald 2006–07
John Ward 2007–08
Greg Abbott 2008–13
Graham Kavanagh 2013–14
Keith Curle September 2014–

TEN YEAR LEAGUE RECORD

		P	W	D	L	F	A	Pts	Pos
2007-08	FL 1	46	23	11	12	64	46	80	4
2008-09	FL 1	46	12	14	20	56	69	50	20
2009-10	FL 1	46	15	13	18	63	66	58	14
2010-11	FL 1	46	16	11	19	60	62	59	12
2011-12	FL 1	46	18	15	13	65	66	69	8
2012-13	FL 1	46	14	13	19	56	77	55	17
2013-14	FL 1	46	11	12	23	43	76	45	22
2014-15	FL 2	46	14	8	24	56	74	50	20
2015-16	FL 2	46	17	16	13	67	62	67	10
2016-17	FL 2	46	18	17	11	69	68	71	6

DID YOU KNOW?

Carlisle United gained just 5 points from their first 21 games of the 2004–05 season, leaving them 15 points adrift at the bottom of the table. The 40 points they achieved from the remaining 25 games was almost promotion form but insufficient to avoid relegation to the Football Conference.

CARLISLE UNITED – SKY BET LEAGUE TWO 2016–17 LEAGUE RECORD

Match No.	Date	Venue	Opponents	Result		H/T Score	Lg Pos.	Goalscorers	Attendance
1	Aug 6	A	Portsmouth	D	1-1	1-1	11	Lambe [14]	17,570
2	13	H	Plymouth Arg	W	1-0	1-0	7	Lambe [37]	5129
3	16	H	Cheltenham T	D	1-1	0-0	9	Kennedy [89]	4203
4	20	A	Cambridge U	D	2-2	1-2	10	Kennedy [23], Wyke [59]	4139
5	27	A	Barnet	W	1-0	1-0	6	Ibehre [21]	1620
6	Sept 3	H	Accrington S	D	1-1	0-0	9	Adams [65]	5128
7	10	H	Leyton Orient	D	2-2	0-1	9	Wyke [46], Grainger (pen) [87]	4465
8	17	A	Blackpool	D	2-2	0-0	7	Wyke [51], Raynes [58]	5471
9	24	H	Wycombe W	W	1-0	0-0	5	Miller, S [57]	4354
10	27	A	Doncaster R	D	2-2	1-2	7	Miller, S [15], Ibehre [79]	4773
11	Oct 1	H	Colchester U	W	2-0	0-0	3	Kennedy [51], Ibehre [79]	4516
12	8	A	Morecambe	W	3-0	1-0	3	Grainger [15], Kennedy [72], McGowan (og) [78]	3773
13	15	H	Hartlepool U	W	3-2	1-0	3	Ibehre [20], Grainger [68], Raynes [79]	7333
14	22	A	Stevenage	W	2-1	1-1	2	Kennedy [16], Grainger (pen) [57]	2720
15	29	H	Crawley T	W	3-1	3-0	2	Ibehre [5], Kennedy [28], Joyce [45]	5619
16	Nov 12	A	Newport Co	L	0-2	0-1	2		2521
17	19	H	Exeter C	W	3-2	1-1	2	Wyke 2 [9, 90], Miller, S [89]	5058
18	22	A	Grimsby T	D	2-2	1-0	2	Wyke [44], Mills (og) [67]	4818
19	26	H	Mansfield T	W	5-2	1-1	1	Kennedy [13], Wyke 3 (1 pen) [49, 62, 80 (p)], Lambe [90]	4822
20	Dec 10	A	Luton T	D	1-1	1-1	2	Kennedy [5]	7953
21	17	H	Yeovil T	W	2-1	2-0	2	Brisley [10], Wyke [36]	4646
22	26	A	Crewe Alex	D	1-1	1-1	2	Miller, S [35]	4962
23	31	A	Notts Co	W	3-2	2-2	2	Wyke [10], Ibehre [45], Kennedy [65]	3825
24	Jan 2	H	Grimsby T	L	1-3	1-0	3	Wyke [31]	6865
25	7	A	Colchester U	L	1-4	1-2	3	Brisley [28]	3525
26	14	H	Morecambe	D	1-1	0-1	3	Wyke [74]	5524
27	21	A	Accrington S	D	1-1	1-1	3	Beckles (og) [20]	2634
28	28	H	Barnet	D	1-1	1-0	3	Wyke [29]	4547
29	Feb 4	A	Leyton Orient	W	2-1	1-1	3	Liddle [34], Proctor [68]	4306
30	11	H	Blackpool	L	1-4	0-1	3	Ibehre [69]	6170
31	14	H	Doncaster R	W	2-1	1-0	3	Adams [34], Mason (og) [85]	4527
32	18	A	Wycombe W	W	2-1	2-1	3	Proctor [9], Lambe [34]	3858
33	25	H	Portsmouth	L	0-3	0-0	3		7197
34	28	A	Cheltenham T	L	0-1	0-0	3		2433
35	Mar 4	A	Plymouth Arg	L	0-2	0-2	3		10,381
36	11	H	Cambridge U	L	0-3	0-0	5		4427
37	14	H	Luton T	D	0-0	0-0	4		4052
38	18	A	Mansfield T	L	0-2	0-0	6		4463
39	25	H	Crewe Alex	L	0-2	0-1	8		4695
40	Apr 1	A	Yeovil T	W	2-0	1-0	7	O'Sullivan [16], Lambe [55]	3145
41	8	H	Notts Co	L	1-2	0-0	7	Ibehre [57]	4361
42	14	A	Hartlepool U	D	1-1	1-0	7	Ibehre [7]	5011
43	17	H	Stevenage	D	1-1	0-0	7	Ibehre [72]	4572
44	22	A	Crawley T	D	3-3	2-2	10	Ibehre [29], Proctor [42], Lambe [59]	2003
45	29	H	Newport Co	W	2-1	0-1	6	Ibehre [58], Adams [60]	5402
46	May 6	A	Exeter C	W	3-2	1-2	6	Grainger 2 (2 pens) [30, 72], Proctor [75]	6774

Final League Position: 6

GOALSCORERS

League (69): Wyke 14 (1 pen), Ibehre 12, Kennedy 9, Grainger 6 (4 pens), Lambe 6, Miller, S 4, Proctor 4, Adams 3, Brisley 2, Raynes 2, Joyce 1, Liddle 1, O'Sullivan 1, own goals 4.
FA Cup (5): Ibehre 2, Grainger 1 (1 pen), Kennedy 1, Lambe 1.
EFL Cup (3): Jones 1, Miller, S 1, Wyke 1.
EFL Checkatrade Trophy (13): Wyke 3, Grainger 2 (2 pens), Miller, S 2, Lambe 1, McKee 1, Miller, T 1, Raynes 1, Salkeld 1, own goal 1.
League Two Play-Offs (5): O'Sullivan 2, Kennedy 1, Miller, S 1, own goal 1.

Gillespie M 46	Miller T 38 + 3	Raynes M 40 + 1	Gillesphey M 31 + 1	Grainger D 31	Kennedy J 23 + 4	Jones M 26 + 2	Devitt J 17 + 18	Adams N 41 + 1	Lambe R 27 + 11	Miller S 19 + 11	Joyce L 42 + 3	Ellis M 5 + 2	Atkinson D — + 1	Wyke C 19 + 7	Ibehre J 20 + 18	Brisley S 22 + 6	Penn R — + 1	McKee J 1 + 3	Asamoah D — + 8	Brough P — + 1	Wright K — + 2	McQueen A 1 + 3	Liddle G 21	O'Sullivan J 10 + 7	Proctor J 16 + 1	Waring G 2 + 7	Bailey J 8 + 4	Hooper J — + 1	Joachim J — + 2	Nabi S — + 1	Tomlinson B — + 2	*Match No.*
1	2	3	4	5	6^1	7	8■	9	10^3	11^2	12	13	14																			1
1	2	3		5	14	8	13	9	6^2	10^1	7	4		11^3	12																	2
1	2	3		5	14	7	12	9	6^2	11^3	8	4^1		10	13																	3
1	2	3	4	5	9^1	8	13	10	6^2		7			12	11																	4
1	2	3	4	5		8	10^1	9^2	6		7			12	11^3	13	14															5
1	2	3	4	5	14	7	9^1	10	8	13	6^2			12	11^3																	6
1	2	4	3	5		7	9^1	8	13	11^2	6	10^3		12	14																	7
1	2	3	4^2	5	7	8		9	6^1		12	13		10	11^3	14																8
1	2	3	4	5	6	7	14	9	12	10^3	8^2			11^1	13																	9
1	2^3	4	3	5	11	6	7^2	9	14	10^1	8			13	12																	10
1	2	3	4	5	6	8^2	14	9^3	12	10^1	7			11	13																	11
1	2	3	4	5	6	8^3	12	9		10^2	7^1				11	14		13														12
1	2	3	4	5	6	7		9^1		11■	8			12	10^2	14			13^3													13
1	2	3	4	5^2	6	7		9	12		8			10^3	11^1	13			14													14
1	2^1	3			6	7	13	9		14	8	4		10^2	11^3	5				12												15
1	2	3	4	5	6	8		9	13	10^2	7^3			12	11^1				14													16
1	2^2	3		5	6^3	8	13■	9	12	14	7			10	11^1	4																17
1	2	4		5	6	8^3		11^1	9^2		7			10	12	3		13	14													18
1	2	3		5	7^2	9		10^1	6	13	8			11^3		4		12	14													19
1	2	3■	13	5^2	6	8^1	14	9	12	11^3	7			10		4																20
1	2	3	5		7		12	9	6	10^1	8			11^2	13	4																21
1	2	3	5		8		12	9	6^2	11^1	7			10^3	13	4					14											22
1	2	3	5		6		9^2	8	12	13	7			10^3	11^1	4			14													23
1	2^3	3	5		7		12	9	6^1	11^2	8			10	13	4			14													24
1	2^2		5^1		8		6	9		13	7^3	4		11	10	3					14	12										25
1	3^2	13	5		7		10	9	6^3	12	8			11					14			2^1	4									26
1	5^2	3	4		8		13	9		11	7			10	12			6^1					2									27
1	2^3	3	5		6^2		13	9	12	14	8			10	11	4^1							7									28
1	5	3	4			13	6	8^1			7				10^2								2	9^3	11■	12	14					29
1	2^3	3	5			13	7^1	9		10^2	8				12								4	6		11	14					30
1		3	5			6	12	10^3	8		7				13	4							2	9^1	11^2		14					31
1		3	5			6	12	10^3	9		7				13	4							2	8^1	11^2	14						32
1	12	3^1	5			7		10	9		6				14	4^2						13	2	8^3	11							33
1	14		4			8		9	5^3		7				12	3							2	13	11	10^1	6^2					34
1	2			5		7	12	10	6^3		9^2				13	4							3	14	11		8^1					35
1	2^2			5		7		10	9^3	13					11^1	4							3	8	14	12	6■					36
1	2			5				8	9	10^1	6					4							3	7^2	11	13		12				37
1	2^2	4		5				10	6	11	7					8						12^3	3	14	9^1				13			38
1	2	4^2		5			6^1	9^3	7	10■	8												3	14	11	13			12			39
1	2	4		5			12		10		9^2					3							7	6^1	11^3	13	8			14		40
1	2	3		5	13		8^2		9^3		14				12	4							6	10	11^1		7					41
1		4		5			9		12		7				11	2							3	8^2	10^1	13	6					42
1		3	4^3	5			6	13	9^2		8				11								2	12	10		7^1				14	43
1		3	4	9			7^3		5^1		6				11	14							2	13	10^2		8				12	44
1	13	3	4	5			6	9^1	7	12	8				11								2		10^2							45
1	2	4	5^2	6			8	9		13	7^3				10^1								3	14	11		12					46

FA Cup

First Round	St Albans C	(a)	5-3
Second Round	Rochdale	(h)	0-2

EFL Cup

First Round	Port Vale	(h)	2-1
Second Round	Derby Co	(a)	1-1

(*aet; Derby Co won 14-13 on penalties*)

EFL Checkatrade Trophy

Northern Group D	Oldham Ath	(a)	5-4
Northern Group D	Blackburn R U21	(h)	2-0
Northern Group D	Fleetwood T	(h)	4-2
Second Round North	Mansfield T	(h)	2-3

League Two Play-Offs

Semi-Final 1st leg	Exeter C	(h)	3-3
Semi-Final 2nd leg	Exeter C	(a)	2-3

CHARLTON ATHLETIC

FOUNDATION

The club was formed on 9 June 1905, by a group of 14- and 15-year-old youths living in streets by the Thames in the area which now borders the Thames Barrier. The club's progress through local leagues was so rapid that after the First World War they joined the Kent League where they spent a season before turning professional and joining the Southern League in 1920. A year later they were elected to the Football League's Division 3 (South).

The Valley, Floyd Road, Charlton, London SE7 8BL.

Telephone: (020) 8333 4000.

Fax: (020) 8333 4001.

Ticket Office: (03330) 144 444.

Website: www.cafc.co.uk

Email: info@cafc.co.uk

Ground Capacity: 27,111.

Record Attendance: 75,031 v Aston Villa, FA Cup 5th rd, 12 February 1938 (at The Valley).

Pitch Measurements: 101.5m × 66m (111yd × 72yd).

Chairman: Roland Duchatelet.

Chief Executive: Katrien Meire.

Manager: Karl Robinson.

Assistant Manager: Lee Bowyer.

Colours: Red shirts with white trim, white shorts, red socks.

Year Formed: 1905.

Turned Professional: 1920.

Club Nickname: 'The Addicks'.

Grounds: 1906, Siemen's Meadow; 1907, Woolwich Common; 1909, Pound Park; 1913, Horn Lane; 1920, The Valley; 1923, Catford (The Mount); 1924, The Valley; 1985, Selhurst Park; 1991, Upton Park; 1992, The Valley.

First Football League Game: 27 August 1921, Division 3 (S), v Exeter C (h) W 1–0 – Hughes; Johnny Mitchell, Goodman; Dowling (1), Hampson, Dunn; Castle, Bailey, Halse, Green, Wilson.

Record League Victory: 8–1 v Middlesbrough, Division 1, 12 September 1953 – Bartram; Campbell, Ellis; Fenton, Ufton, Hammond; Hurst (2), O'Linn (2), Leary (1), Firmani (3), Kiernan.

Record Cup Victory: 7–0 v Burton A, FA Cup 3rd rd, 7 January 1956 – Bartram; Campbell, Townsend; Hewie, Ufton, Hammond; Hurst (1), Gauld (1), Leary (3), White, Kiernan (2).

Record Defeat: 1–11 v Aston Villa, Division 2, 14 November 1959.

Most League Points (2 for a win): 61, Division 3 (S), 1934–35.

HONOURS

League Champions: First Division – 1999–2000; FL 1 – 2011–12; Division 3S – 1928–29, 1934–35.
Runners-up: Division 1 – 1936–37; Division 2 – 1935–36, 1985–86.

FA Cup Winners: 1947.
Runners-up: 1946.

League Cup: quarter-final – 2007.

Full Members' Cup:
Runners-up 1987.

sky SPORTS FACT FILE

A group of Charlton Athletic fans campaigning for the club to return to their traditional home at The Valley set up The Valley Party which contested seats for Greenwich Council in the May 1990 local elections. They secured 14,838 votes (10.9%) and although not winning any seats the group paved the way for the club to return home two years later.

Most League Points (3 for a win): 101, FL 1, 2011–12.

Most League Goals: 107, Division 2, 1957–58.

Highest League Scorer in Season: Ralph Allen, 32, Division 3 (S), 1934–35.

Most League Goals in Total Aggregate: Stuart Leary, 153, 1953–62.

Most League Goals in One Match: 5, Wilson Lennox v Exeter C, Division 3 (S), 2 February 1929; 5, Eddie Firmani v Aston Villa, Division 1, 5 February 1955; 5, John Summers v Huddersfield T, Division 2, 21 December 1957; 5, John Summers v Portsmouth, Division 2, 1 October 1960.

Most Capped Player: Jonatan Johansson, 42 (106), Finland.

Most League Appearances: Sam Bartram, 579, 1934–56.

Youngest League Player: Jonjo Shelvey, 16 years 59 days v Burnley, 26 April 2008.

Record Transfer Fee Received: £16,500,000 from Tottenham H for Darren Bent, May 2007.

Record Transfer Fee Paid: £4,750,000 to Wimbledon for Jason Euell, January 2001.

Football League Record: 1921 Elected to Division 3 (S); 1929–33 Division 2; 1933–35 Division 3 (S); 1935–36 Division 2; 1936–57 Division 1; 1957–72 Division 2; 1972–75 Division 3; 1975–80 Division 2; 1980–81 Division 3; 1981–86 Division 2; 1986–90 Division 1; 1990–92 Division 2; 1992–98 Division 1; 1998–99 FA Premier League; 1999–2000 Division 1; 2000–07 FA Premier League; 2007–09 FL C; 2009–12 FL 1; 2012–16 FL C; 2016– FL 1.

LATEST SEQUENCES

Longest Sequence of League Wins: 12, 26.12.1999 – 7.3.2000.

Longest Sequence of League Defeats: 10, 11.4.1990 – 15.9.1990.

Longest Sequence of League Draws: 6, 13.12.1992 – 16.1.1993.

Longest Sequence of Unbeaten League Matches: 15, 4.10.1980 – 20.12.1980.

Longest Sequence Without a League Win: 18, 18.10.2008 – 17.1.2009.

Successive Scoring Runs: 25 from 26.12.1935.

Successive Non-scoring Runs: 5 from 17.10.2015.

MANAGERS

Walter Rayner 1920–25
Alex Macfarlane 1925–27
Albert Lindon 1928
Alex Macfarlane 1928–32
Albert Lindon 1932–33
Jimmy Seed 1933–56
Jimmy Trotter 1956–61
Frank Hill 1961–65
Bob Stokoe 1965–67
Eddie Firmani 1967–70
Theo Foley 1970–74
Andy Nelson 1974–79
Mike Bailey 1979–81
Alan Mullery 1981–82
Ken Craggs 1982
Lennie Lawrence 1982–91
Steve Gritt and Alan Curbishley 1991–95
Alan Curbishley 1995–2006
Iain Dowie 2006
Les Reed 2006
Alan Pardew 2006–08
Phil Parkinson 2008–11
Chris Powell 2011–14
José Riga 2014
Bob Peeters 2014–15
Guy Luzon 2015
Karel Fraeye 2015–16
José Riga 2016
Russell Slade 2016
Karl Robinson November 2016–

TEN YEAR LEAGUE RECORD

		P	*W*	*D*	*L*	*F*	*A*	*Pts*	*Pos*
2007-08	FL C	46	17	13	16	63	58	64	11
2008-09	FL C	46	8	15	23	52	74	39	24
2009-10	FL 1	46	23	15	8	71	48	84	4
2010-11	FL 1	46	15	14	17	62	66	59	13
2011-12	FL 1	46	30	11	5	82	36	101	1
2012-13	FL C	46	17	14	15	65	59	65	9
2013-14	FL C	46	13	12	21	41	61	51	18
2014-15	FL C	46	14	18	14	54	60	60	12
2015-16	FL C	46	9	13	24	40	80	40	22
2016-17	FL 1	46	14	18	14	60	53	60	13

DID YOU KNOW ?

The highest average home attendance achieved by Charlton Athletic was 40,126 in the 1948–49 season. They were the 11th best supported team in the country. In pre-war years they had twice made the top ten but with lower attendances.

CHARLTON ATHLETIC – SKY BET LEAGUE ONE 2016–17 LEAGUE RECORD

Match No.	Date	Venue	Opponents	Result		H/T Score	Lg Pos.	Goalscorers	Attendance
1	Aug 6	A	Bury	L	0-2	0-0	23		4037
2	13	H	Northampton T	D	1-1	0-1	20	Jackson 57	11,567
3	16	H	Shrewsbury T	W	3-0	3-0	8	Holmes 2 22, 31, Jackson 24	9174
4	20	A	Walsall	W	2-1	1-0	5	Ajose 2 42, 74	4586
5	27	H	Bolton W	D	1-1	0-0	9	Lookman 90	10,926
6	Sept 10	A	Fleetwood T	D	2-2	1-2	13	Magennis 32, Novak 87	3371
7	17	H	AFC Wimbledon	L	1-2	1-0	14	Lookman 8	11,927
8	20	A	Scunthorpe U	D	0-0	0-0	14		3801
9	24	A	Oxford U	D	1-1	0-0	16	Jackson (pen) 54	8847
10	27	H	Oldham Ath	D	1-1	1-0	12	Magennis 22	8745
11	Oct 1	H	Rochdale	L	0-1	0-1	18		14,460
12	15	H	Coventry C	W	3-0	1-0	15	Holmes 32, Lookman 78, Magennis 88	11,406
13	18	A	Port Vale	D	1-1	1-0	15	Ulvestad 30	3494
14	22	A	Gillingham	D	1-1	0-1	17	Ajose (pen) 90	8670
15	29	H	Chesterfield	W	1-0	0-0	12	Novak 86	10,153
16	Nov 12	A	Swindon T	L	0-3	0-1	15		6599
17	19	H	Port Vale	W	2-0	2-0	14	Magennis 30, Ajose 44	8992
18	22	A	Bristol R	W	5-1	2-0	11	Lookman 26, Magennis 44, Bauer 50, Chicksen 77, Ajose 85	8089
19	26	H	Sheffield U	D	1-1	0-1	11	Bauer 90	12,580
20	Dec 10	A	Bradford C	D	0-0	0-0	10		17,968
21	17	H	Peterborough U	L	0-2	0-1	13		10,193
22	21	A	Millwall	L	1-3	0-2	14	Ajose 49	14,395
23	26	A	Milton Keynes D	W	1-0	1-0	12	Lookman 38	10,257
24	31	A	Southend U	D	1-1	0-1	12	Crofts 89	10,329
25	Jan 2	H	Bristol R	W	4-1	1-1	11	Magennis 3 41, 50, 73, Teixeira 61	12,252
26	14	H	Millwall	D	0-0	0-0	11		15,315
27	28	A	Bolton W	W	2-1	2-1	10	Bauer 23, Byrne 45	13,265
28	Feb 4	H	Fleetwood T	D	1-1	1-0	12	Holmes 37	9916
29	11	A	AFC Wimbledon	D	1-1	1-0	13	Holmes 8	4595
30	14	A	Oldham Ath	L	0-1	0-1	13		2946
31	18	A	Rochdale	D	3-3	1-1	13	Botaka 41, Teixeira 2 67, 88	2842
32	21	H	Oxford U	L	0-1	0-1	13		9109
33	25	H	Bury	L	0-1	0-1	14		14,640
34	28	A	Shrewsbury T	L	3-4	2-1	15	Holmes 3 24, 44, 70	4913
35	Mar 4	A	Northampton T	L	1-2	1-1	16	Botaka 36	7118
36	7	H	Scunthorpe U	W	2-1	1-0	14	Jackson 33, Watt (pen) 90	9088
37	11	H	Walsall	D	1-1	0-1	14	Watt 61	9900
38	14	H	Bradford C	D	1-1	1-1	15	Teixeira 35	9326
39	18	A	Sheffield U	L	1-2	1-1	15	Holmes 3	23,308
40	Apr 1	A	Peterborough U	L	0-2	0-0	16		5482
41	4	H	Milton Keynes D	L	0-2	0-1	16		10,943
42	8	H	Southend U	W	2-1	1-1	16	Holmes 6, Thompson (og) 74	11,730
43	14	A	Coventry C	D	1-1	0-1	15	Bauer 54	9479
44	17	H	Gillingham	W	3-0	2-0	15	Pearce 20, Holmes 31, Magennis 54	12,449
45	22	A	Chesterfield	W	2-1	1-0	14	Forster-Caskey 37, Holmes 57	5657
46	30	H	Swindon T	W	3-0	2-0	13	Magennis 14, Forster-Caskey 43, Holmes 66	11,932

Final League Position: 13

GOALSCORERS

League (60): Holmes 13, Magennis 10, Ajose 6 (1 pen), Lookman 5, Bauer 4, Jackson 4 (1 pen), Teixeira 4, Botaka 2, Forster-Caskey 2, Novak 2, Watt 2 (1 pen), Byrne 1, Chicksen 1, Crofts 1, Pearce 1, Ulvestad 1, own goal 1.
FA Cup (4): Lookman 2, Chicksen 1, Jackson 1.
EFL Cup (0).
EFL Checkatrade Trophy (1): Ajose 1.

Rudd D 38	Solly C 27	Pearce J 23	Johnson R 1 + 1	Fox M 24	Holmes R 31 + 4	Crofts A 41 + 4	Foley K 12 + 3	Jackson J 22 + 8	Ajose N 17 + 4	Novak L 13 + 16	Lookman A 15 + 6	Hanlan B — + 9	Konsa E 30 + 2	Magennis J 36 + 3	Botaka J 8 + 18	Holmes-Dennis T — + 1	Bauer P 34 + 2	Ulvestad F 26 + 1	Lennon H 2	Chicksen A 15 + 6	Phillips D 8	Teixeira J 15 + 5	Aribo J 13 + 6	Ahearne-Grant K 1 + 7	Umerah J — + 1	Page L 8	Byrne N 16 + 1	Watt T 9 + 7	Dasilva J 6 + 4	Forster-Caskey J 12 + 3	Mavididi S 3 + 2	Barnes A — + 1	*Match No.*
1	2	3	4	5	6	7	8[2]	9	10[1]	11	12	13																					1
1	2	3		5	6[3]	8	7[2]	9	10	14	12		4	11[1]	13																		2
1	2	4		5	9[1]	7	6	8[2]	11	13	12		3	10[3]	14																		3
1	5	3		2	9[2]	7	8	6[3]	10[1]		12		4	11		13	14																4
1	2	3		5	6	7	8[1]	9[2]	10		13	14	4	11[3]			12																5
1	2	4		5	6[1]	8	13		11[2]	12	9		3	10	14			7[3]															6
1	2	4		5	6	8			11[1]	12	9		3	10				7															7
1	2	4		5		8	6[1]	9			10			11	12		3	7															8
1	2			5	12	6	7[1]	9[2]		13	10[3]			11	14		4	8	3■														9
1	2			5	6	7[3]	13	9[2]	14	11[1]	12		3	10			4	8															10
1		4		5	6[1]	7[2]	2	9	12	13	11			10[3]	14		3	8															11
1	2	4		5	6[1]	7		12		10[2]	9	13		11			3	8															12
1	3			5	10[2]	8		7		13	9[1]	12		11[3]			4	6	2	14													13
1	2	4		5	6	8		9[1]	12	13	10		3	11[2]				7															14
1	2	4		5	6	7			11[1]	13	9[2]			10	12		3	8															15
1	2	4		5		7	6[2]	9[1]	11	10		12					3	8		13													16
1		4		5		7	2	9[3]	11		6[2]	13	14	10[1]	12		3	8															17
		4		5		7	2	14	10		6[3]	12		11[2]	13		3	8		9[1]	1												18
		4		5		8[2]	2	9[3]	11[1]	13	6			10	14		3	7		12	1												19
		4[2]				8		13	6[1]	11		14	5	10	9[3]		3■	7		2	1	12											20
				5[1]		8			11		9	14	2	10	6[2]		3	7[3]		12	1	4	13										21
				5		7		8[1]	10		6		2	11	12		3			9[2]	1	4		13									22
			14	2		6		7[1]	11[2]		9[3]		5	10			4	8		13	1	3	12										23
				5[1]		7			10[3]				2	11	12		3	8[2]		9	1	4	6	13	14								24
	2[2]			5		6	14		13				7[1]	11	10		4	12		9	1	3	8[3]										25
1	2				14	7							6	10[2]			3			11		4■	8			5[1]	9	12	13[3]				26
1	3				13	6		14		12			8				4			10			9[3]			5■	2[2]	11[1]		7			27
1	2				11[3]	7		12		13			4				3			5[2]		14	6				9■	10		8[1]			28
1	2				9[1]	7				10[2]			6	12	13		3			5		4	8					11[3]			14		29
1	2				12	8				14			3	11	6[3]		4			5			9					13		7[1]	10[2]		30
1	2				10	6				14			3[2]	11	8[3]		4					12				5		9[1]		7	13		31
1	11■				4	7[1]								3	14		5					9	13			2	10[2]	12		8[3]	6		32
1					9	12				10[3]			6	13			3[1]					4	7			5	2	14		8[2]	11		33
1					6	7		5[3]		11			4	10[1]	9[2]							3	8	12			2	13	14				34
1					6	8				10[3]			3	11	9		4[2]	7		13		12				5[1]	2	14					35
1					9[3]	12		6		11[1]			3	10[2]				8		5		4	7	14			2	13					36
1					10	8		12		13			4[1]					7		5		3	9	14		2[2]	6	11[3]					37
1					6[1]	7[3]		2		10			13				3	8		9		4				5[2]		11	12	14			38
1					7	12				10			3		13		4	9[1]		6[3]		5					2	11	14	8[2]			39
1					9	13		6[3]		11[2]				12	14		4	7		5		3					2	10[1]		8			40
1	2	4			9			6[1]						10	13		3						8				12	11[2]	5	7			41
1	2	4			11[1]	6							7[2]	10			3	8				13					9		5	12			42
1	2	4			11[1]	6							7[2]	10			3	8					13				9		5	12			43
1		4			11	6		13					7[2]	10	9[3]		3						14	12			2		5	8[1]			44
1		4			10	6		14		12			3	11[1]	13								9[2]	8[3]			2		5	7			45
1	2[1]	4			6	9		8[2]						11			3						13	12			10[3]		5	7		14	46

FA Cup

First Round	Scunthorpe U	(h)	3-1
Second Round	Milton Keynes D	(h)	0-0
Replay (*aet*)	Milton Keynes D	(a)	1-3

EFL Cup

First Round	Cheltenham T	(a)	0-1

EFL Checkatrade Trophy

Southern Group E	Southampton U21	(h)	0-0
(*Charlton Ath won 5-4 on penalties*)			
Southern Group E	Crawley T	(h)	0-2
Southern Group E	Colchester U	(a)	1-1
(*Colchester U won 5-4 on penalties*)			

CHELSEA

FOUNDATION

Chelsea may never have existed but for the fact that Fulham rejected an offer to rent the Stamford Bridge ground from Mr H. A. Mears who had owned it since 1904. Fortunately he was determined to develop it as a football stadium rather than sell it to the Great Western Railway and got together with Frederick Parker, who persuaded Mears of the financial advantages of developing a major sporting venue. Chelsea FC was formed in 1905 and applications made to join both the Southern League and Football League. The latter competition was decided upon because of its comparatively meagre representation in the south of England.

Stamford Bridge, Fulham Road, London SW6 1HS.
Telephone: (0371) 811 1955. ***Fax:*** (020) 7381 4831.
Ticket Office: (0371) 811 1905.
Website: www.chelseafc.com
Email: enquiries@chelseafc.com
Ground Capacity: 41,631.
Record Attendance: 82,905 v Arsenal, Division 1, 12 October 1935.
Pitch Measurements: 103m × 67.5m (112yd × 74yd).
Chairman: Bruce Buck.
Chief Executive: Marina Granovskaia.
Manager: Antonio Conte.
Technical Director: Michael Emenalo.
Assistant First-Team Coach: Steve Holland.
Colours: Reflex blue shirt with white trim, reflex blue shorts with white trim, white socks with reflex blue trim.
Year Formed: 1905. ***Turned Professional:*** 1905.
Club Nickname: 'The Blues'.
Ground: 1905, Stamford Bridge.
First Football League Game: 2 September 1905, Division 2, v Stockport Co (a) L 0–1 – Foulke; Mackie, McEwan; Key, Harris, Miller; Moran, Jack Robertson, Copeland, Windridge, Kirwan.
Record League Victory: 8–0 v Wigan Ath, FA Premier League, 9 May 2010 – Cech; Ivanovic (Belletti), Ashley Cole (1), Ballack (Matic), Terry, Alex, Kalou (1) (Joe Cole), Lampard (pen), Anelka (2), Drogba (3, 1 pen), Malouda; 8–0 v Aston Villa, FA Premier League, 23 December 2012 – Cech; Azpilicueta, Ivanovic (1), Cahill, Cole, Luiz (1), Lampard (1) (Ramirez (2)), Moses, Mata (Piazon), Hazard (1), Torres (1) (Oscar (1)).

HONOURS

League Champions: FA Premier League – 2004–05, 2005–06, 2009–10, 2014–15, 2016–17; Division 1 – 1954–55; Division 2 – 1983–84, 1988–89.
Runners-up: FA Premier League – 2003–04, 2006–07, 2007–08, 2010–11; Division 2 – 1906–07, 1911–12, 1929–30, 1962–63, 1976–77.

FA Cup Winners: 1970, 1997, 2000, 2007, 2009, 2010, 2012.
Runners-up: 1915, 1967, 1994, 2002, 2017.

League Cup Winners: 1965, 1998, 2005, 2007, 2015.
Runners-up: 1972, 2008.

Full Members' Cup Winners: 1986, 1990.

European Competitions
Champions League: 1999–2000, 2003–04 *(sf)*, 2004–05 *(sf)*, 2005–06, 2006–07 *(sf)*, 2007–08 *(runners-up)*, 2008–09 *(sf)*, 2009–10, 2010–11 *(qf)*, 2011–12 *(winners)*, 2012–13, 2013–14 *(sf)*, 2014–15, 2015–16.
Fairs Cup: 1958–60, 1965–66, 1968–69.
UEFA Cup: 2000–01, 2001–02, 2002–03.
Europa League: 2012–13 *(winners)*.
European Cup-Winners' Cup: 1970–71 *(winners)*, 1971–72, 1994–95 *(sf)*, 1997–98 *(winners)*, 1998–99 *(sf)*.
Super Cup: 1998 *(winners)*, 2012, 2013.
Club World Cup: 2012 *(runners-up)*.

sky SPORTS FACT FILE

Chelsea created a record aggregate score for European competitions in the 1971–72 season when they defeated Jeunesse Hautcharage 21-0 in the European Cup Winners' Cup first round, with Peter Osgood scoring eight of their goals. The margin has been equalled since but never beaten.

Record Cup Victory: 13–0 v Jeunesse Hautcharage, ECWC, 1st rd 2nd leg, 29 September 1971 – Bonetti; Boyle, Harris (1), Hollins (1p), Webb (1), Hinton, Cooke, Baldwin (3), Osgood (5), Hudson (1), Houseman (1).

Record Defeat: 1–8 v Wolverhampton W, Division 1, 26 September 1953; 0–7 v Nottingham F, Division 1, 20 April 1991.

Most League Points (2 for a win): 57, Division 2, 1906–07.

Most League Points (3 for a win): 99, Division 2, 1988–89.

Most League Goals: 103, FA Premier League, 2009–10.

Highest League Scorer in Season: Jimmy Greaves, 41, 1960–61.

Most League Goals in Total Aggregate: Bobby Tambling, 164, 1958–70.

Most League Goals in One Match: 5, George Hilsdon v Glossop, Division 2, 1 September 1906; 5, Jimmy Greaves v Wolverhampton W, Division 1, 30 August 1958; 5, Jimmy Greaves v Preston NE, Division 1, 19 December 1959; 5, Jimmy Greaves v WBA, Division 1, 3 December 1960; 5, Bobby Tambling v Aston Villa, Division 1, 17 September 1966; 5, Gordon Durie v Walsall, Division 2, 4 February 1989.

Most Capped Player: Frank Lampard, 104 (106), England.

Most League Appearances: Ron Harris, 655, 1962–80.

Youngest League Player: Ian Hamilton, 16 years 138 days v Tottenham H, 18 March 1967.

Record Transfer Fee Received: £60,000,000 from Shanghai SIPG for Oscar, January 2017.

Record Transfer Fee Paid: £50,000,000 to Liverpool for Fernando Torres, January 2011.

Football League Record: 1905 Elected to Division 2; 1907–10 Division 1; 1910–12 Division 2; 1912–24 Division 1; 1924–30 Division 2; 1930–62 Division 1; 1962–63 Division 2; 1963–75 Division 1; 1975–77 Division 2; 1977–79 Division 1; 1979–84 Division 2; 1984–88 Division 1; 1988–89 Division 2; 1989–92 Division 1; 1992– FA Premier League.

MANAGERS

John Tait Robertson 1905–07
David Calderhead 1907–33
Leslie Knighton 1933–39
Billy Birrell 1939–52
Ted Drake 1952–61
Tommy Docherty 1961–67
Dave Sexton 1967–74
Ron Suart 1974–75
Eddie McCreadie 1975–77
Ken Shellito 1977–78
Danny Blanchflower 1978–79
Geoff Hurst 1979–81
John Neal 1981–85 (*Director to 1986*)
John Hollins 1985–88
Bobby Campbell 1988–91
Ian Porterfield 1991–93
David Webb 1993
Glenn Hoddle 1993–96
Ruud Gullit 1996–98
Gianluca Vialli 1998–2000
Claudio Ranieri 2000–04
Jose Mourinho 2004–07
Avram Grant 2007–08
Luiz Felipe Scolari 2008–09
Guus Hiddink 2009
Carlo Ancelotti 2009–11
Andre Villas-Boas 2011–12
Roberto Di Matteo 2012
Rafael Benitez 2012–13
Jose Mourinho 2013–15
Guus Hiddink 2015–16
Antonio Conte June 2016–

LATEST SEQUENCES

Longest Sequence of League Wins: 13, 1.10.2016 – 31.12.2016.

Longest Sequence of League Defeats: 7, 1.11.1952 – 20.12.1952.

Longest Sequence of League Draws: 6, 20.8.1969 – 13.9.1969.

Longest Sequence of Unbeaten League Matches: 40, 23.10.2004 – 29.10.2005.

Longest Sequence Without a League Win: 21, 3.11.1987 – 2.4.1988.

Successive Scoring Runs: 27 from 29.10.1988.

Successive Non-scoring Runs: 9 from 14.3.1981.

TEN YEAR LEAGUE RECORD

		P	*W*	*D*	*L*	*F*	*A*	*Pts*	*Pos*
2007-08	PR Lge	38	25	10	3	65	26	85	2
2008-09	PR Lge	38	25	8	5	68	24	83	3
2009-10	PR Lge	38	27	5	6	103	32	86	1
2010-11	PR Lge	38	21	8	9	69	33	71	2
2011-12	PR Lge	38	18	10	10	65	46	64	6
2012-13	PR Lge	38	22	9	7	75	39	75	3
2013-14	PR Lge	38	25	7	6	71	27	82	3
2014-15	PR Lge	38	26	9	3	73	32	87	1
2015-16	PR Lge	38	12	14	12	59	53	50	10
2016-17	PR Lge	38	30	3	5	85	33	93	1

DID YOU KNOW ?

Chelsea are the only team to score eight goals on two separate occasions in Premier League matches. They defeated Wigan Athletic 8-0 in May 2010 and Aston Villa by the same score in December 2012. Frank Lampard scored in both games.

CHELSEA – PREMIER LEAGUE 2016–17 LEAGUE RECORD

Match No.	Date	Venue	Opponents	Result	H/T Score	Lg Pos.	Goalscorers	Attendance
1	Aug 15	H	West Ham U	W 2-1	0-0	3	Hazard (pen) [47], Costa [89]	41,521
2	20	A	Watford	W 2-1	0-0	4	Batshuayi [80], Costa [87]	20,772
3	27	H	Burnley	W 3-0	2-0	1	Hazard [9], Willian [41], Moses [89]	41,607
4	Sept 11	A	Swansea C	D 2-2	1-0	2	Costa 2 [18, 81]	20,865
5	16	H	Liverpool	L 1-2	0-2	3	Costa [61]	41,514
6	24	A	Arsenal	L 0-3	0-3	6		60,028
7	Oct 1	A	Hull C	W 2-0	0-0	6	Willian [61], Costa [67]	21,257
8	15	H	Leicester C	W 3-0	2-0	5	Costa [7], Hazard [33], Moses [80]	41,547
9	23	H	Manchester U	W 4-0	2-0	4	Pedro [1], Cahill [21], Hazard [62], Kante [70]	41,424
10	30	A	Southampton	W 2-0	1-0	4	Hazard [6], Costa [55]	31,827
11	Nov 5	H	Everton	W 5-0	3-0	1	Hazard 2 [19, 56], Alonso [20], Costa [42], Pedro [65]	41,429
12	20	A	Middlesbrough	W 1-0	1-0	1	Costa [41]	32,704
13	26	H	Tottenham H	W 2-1	1-1	1	Pedro [45], Moses [51]	41,513
14	Dec 3	A	Manchester C	W 3-1	0-1	1	Costa [60], Willian [70], Hazard [90]	54,457
15	11	H	WBA	W 1-0	0-0	1	Costa [76]	41,622
16	14	A	Sunderland	W 1-0	1-0	1	Fabregas [40]	41,008
17	17	A	Crystal Palace	W 1-0	1-0	1	Costa [43]	25,259
18	26	H	Bournemouth	W 3-0	1-0	1	Pedro [24], Hazard (pen) [49], Cook, S (og) [90]	41,384
19	31	H	Stoke C	W 4-2	1-0	1	Cahill [34], Willian 2 [57, 65], Costa [85]	41,601
20	Jan 4	A	Tottenham H	L 0-2	0-1	1		31,491
21	14	A	Leicester C	W 3-0	1-0	1	Alonso 2 [6, 51], Pedro [71]	32,066
22	22	H	Hull C	W 2-0	1-0	1	Costa [45], Cahill [81]	41,605
23	31	A	Liverpool	D 1-1	1-0	1	Luiz [24]	53,157
24	Feb 4	H	Arsenal	W 3-1	1-0	1	Alonso [13], Hazard [53], Fabregas [85]	41,490
25	12	A	Burnley	D 1-1	1-1	1	Pedro [7]	21,744
26	25	H	Swansea C	W 3-1	1-1	1	Fabregas [19], Pedro [72], Costa [84]	41,612
27	Mar 6	A	West Ham U	W 2-1	1-0	1	Hazard [25], Costa [50]	56,984
28	18	A	Stoke C	W 2-1	1-1	1	Willian [13], Cahill [87]	27,724
29	Apr 1	H	Crystal Palace	L 1-2	1-2	1	Fabregas [5]	41,489
30	5	H	Manchester C	W 2-1	2-1	1	Hazard 2 [10, 35]	41,528
31	8	A	Bournemouth	W 3-1	2-1	1	Smith, A (og) [17], Hazard [20], Alonso [68]	11,283
32	16	A	Manchester U	L 0-2	0-1	1		75,272
33	25	H	Southampton	W 4-2	2-1	1	Hazard [5], Cahill [45], Costa 2 [53, 89]	41,168
34	30	A	Everton	W 3-0	0-0	1	Pedro [66], Cahill [79], Willian [86]	39,595
35	May 8	H	Middlesbrough	W 3-0	2-0	1	Costa [23], Alonso [34], Matic [65]	41,500
36	12	A	WBA	W 1-0	0-0	1	Batshuayi [82]	25,367
37	15	H	Watford	W 4-3	2-1	1	Terry [22], Azpilicueta [36], Batshuayi [49], Fabregas [88]	41,473
38	21	H	Sunderland	W 5-1	1-1	1	Willian [8], Hazard [61], Pedro [77], Batshuayi 2 [90, 90]	41,618

Final League Position: 1

GOALSCORERS

League (85): Costa 20, Hazard 16 (2 pens), Pedro 9, Willian 8, Alonso 6, Cahill 6, Batshuayi 5, Fabregas 5, Moses 3, Azpilicueta 1, Kante 1, Luiz 1, Matic 1, Terry 1, own goals 2.
FA Cup (16): Pedro 4, Willian 4 (1 pen), Batshuayi 2 (1 pen), Costa 2, Hazard 1, Ivanovic 1, Kante 1, Matic 1.
EFL Cup (8): Batshuayi 2, Cahill 2, Fabregas 2, Azpilicueta 1, Moses 1.
EFL Checkatrade Trophy (4): Ugbo 2, Ali 1, Quintero 1.

Courtois T 36	Ivanovic B 6 + 7	Cahill G 36 + 1	Terry J 6 + 3	Azpilicueta C 38	Kante N 35	Willian d 15 + 19	Oscar E 5 + 4	Matic N 30 + 5	Hazard E 36	Costa D 35	Pedro R 26 + 9	Moses V 29 + 5	Batshuayi M 1 + 19	Fabregas F 13 + 16	Luiz D 33	Alonso M 30 + 1	Chalobah N 1 + 9	Aina O — + 3	Loftus-Cheek R — + 6	Zouma K 3 + 6	Begovic A 2	Ake N 1 + 1	Kenedy R 1	Match No.
1	2	3	4	5	6	7^{1}	8^{2}	9	10^{3}	11	12	13	14											1
1	2	3	4	5	6		8^{2}	9^{1}	10	11	7^{3}	12	13	14										2
1	2	3	4	5	6	7^{1}	8	9	10^{3}	11^{2}	14	12	13											3
1	2	3	4	5	6	7^{2}	8^{1}	9^{3}	10	11		13	14	12										4
1	2	3		5	6	8^{3}	9^{2}	7^{1}	10	11	14	12		13	4									5
1	2	3		5	6	7^{1}		9	10^{3}	11	13		14	8^{2}	4	12								6
1		4		2	7	9^{1}	12	6	11^{3}	10	13	5^{2}			3	8	14							7
1		4		2	6			7	11^{3}	10	9^{2}	5^{1}			3	8	12	13	14					8
1		4		2	6	13		7	11^{2}	10^{1}	9^{3}	5	14		3	8	12							9
1	13	4		2	6	12		7	11	10^{3}	9^{2}	5^{1}	14		3	8								10
1		4^{3}	14	2	6		12	7	11^{2}	10	9^{1}	5	13		3	8								11
1	13	4		2	6		14	7	11^{1}	10	9^{3}	5^{2}			3	8	12							12
1	13	4		2	6	12	14	7	11^{3}	10	9^{1}	5^{2}			3	8								13
1		4		2	6	12			11^{1}	10^{2}	9^{3}	5	14	7	3	8	13							14
1	14	4		2	6	12		7	11^{1}	10	9^{3}	5^{2}		13	3	8								15
1	14	4		2	6	9^{3}		12		10	11^{2}	5^{1}		7	3	8	13							16
1	13	4		2	6	9^{1}		7	11	10^{3}		5^{2}	14	12	3	8								17
1		4		2		9^{3}		7	10^{1}		11	5^{2}	14	6	3	8	12	13						18
1	13	4		2	7	9^{1}		12	11	10		5^{3}		6^{2}	3	8	14							19
1		4		2	7^{1}	12		6	11	10	9	5^{2}	14	13	3	8^{3}								20
1		4		2	6	9^{3}		7	10^{2}		11^{1}	5	14	12	3	8			13					21
1		4		2	6	12		7	11^{3}	10^{1}	9^{2}	5	14	13	3	8								22
1		4		2	6	9^{3}		7	11^{2}	10^{1}	12	5	14	13	3	8								23
1		4		2	6	12		7	11^{3}	10	9^{2}	5^{1}		13	3	8				14				24
1		4		2	6	13		7^{2}	11	10	9^{1}	5^{3}	14	12	3	8								25
1		4		2	6	13		12	11^{1}	10	9^{3}	5^{2}		7	3	8				14				26
1		4		2	7	13		12	11^{2}	10	9^{3}	5^{1}		6	3	8				14				27
1		4		2	6	9^{3}		7^{2}		10	11	5^{1}		12	3	8			13	14				28
1		4		2	6	12		7^{3}	10	11	5		13	9^{1}	3	8^{2}			14					29
1		4		5	7	13		12	10^{3}	11	9			6^{1}	3	8			14	2^{2}				30
1		4		2	6	13		7	10^{1}	11	9^{2}	5^{3}		12	3	8				14				31
		4		8	6	13		7^{1}	10	11	9	5^{2}		12	3				14	2^{3}	1			32
1		4	13	2	6	14		7	10^{2}	11	12	5^{1}		9^{3}	3	8								33
1		4		2	6	14		7	10^{2}	11	9^{3}	5		13	3^{1}	8						12		34
1		4	14	2		12		7	10^{1}	11	9^{3}	5		6	3^{2}	8	13							35
1		4		2		12		7	10^{3}	11	9^{2}	5^{1}	13	6	3	8				14				36
			3	5	6	9			10		14		11^{3}	13			7^{1}	12		2	1	4	8^{2}	37
1		12	4^{3}	2	7	9			10^{1}	11^{2}	14	5	13	6	3	8								38

FA Cup

Third Round	Peterborough U	(h)	4-1
Fourth Round	Brentford	(h)	4-0
Fifth Round	Wolverhampton W	(a)	2-0
Sixth Round	Manchester U	(h)	1-0
Semi-Final	Tottenham H	(h)	4-2
Final	Arsenal	(Wembley)	1-2

EFL Cup

Second Round	Bristol R	(h)	3-2
Third Round (*aet*)	Leicester C	(a)	4-2
Fourth Round	West Ham U	(a)	1-2

EFL Checkatrade Trophy (Chelsea U21)

Southern Group C	Swindon T	(a)	1-2
Southern Group C	Exeter C	(a)	2-3
Southern Group C	Oxford U	(h)	1-1

(*Chelsea U21 won 13-12 on penalties*)

CHELTENHAM TOWN

FOUNDATION

Although a scratch team representing Cheltenham played a match against Gloucester in 1884, the earliest recorded match for Cheltenham Town FC was a friendly against Dean Close School on 12 March 1892. The School won 4–3 and the match was played at Prestbury (half a mile from Whaddon Road). Cheltenham Town played Wednesday afternoon friendlies at a local cricket ground until entering the Mid Gloucester League. In those days the club played in deep red coloured shirts and were nicknamed 'the Rubies'. The club moved to Whaddon Lane for season 1901–02 and changed to red and white colours two years later.

World of Smile Stadium, Whaddon Road, Cheltenham, Gloucestershire GL52 5NA.

Telephone: (01242) 573 558.

Fax: (01242) 224 675.

Ticket Office: (01242) 573 558 (option 1).

Website: www.ctfc.com

Email: info@ctfc.com

Ground Capacity: 7,027.

Record Attendance: 10,389 v Blackpool, FA Cup 3rd rd, 13 January 1934 (at Cheltenham Athletic Ground); 8,326 v Reading, FA Cup 1st rd, 17 November 1956 (at Whaddon Road).

Pitch Measurements: 102.5m × 66m (112yd × 72yd)

Chairman: Paul Baker.

Vice-chairman: David Bloxham.

Manager: Gary Johnson.

Assistant Manager: Russell Milton.

Colours: Red and white striped shirts, black shorts with white trim, black socks with red trim.

Year Formed: 1892.

Turned Professional: 1932.

Club Nickname: 'The Robins'.

Grounds: Pre-1932, Agg-Gardner's Recreation Ground; Whaddon Lane; Carter's Lane; 1932, Whaddon Road (renamed The Abbey Business Stadium 2009, World of Smile Stadium 2015).

First Football League Game: 7 August 1999, Division 3, v Rochdale (h) L 0–2 – Book; Griffin, Victory, Banks, Freeman, Brough (Howarth), Howells, Bloomer (Devaney), Grayson, Watkins (McAuley), Yates.

Record League Victory: 5–0 v Mansfield T, FL 2, 6 May 2006 – Higgs; Gallinagh, Bell, McCann (1) (Connolly), Caines, Duff, Wilson, Bird (1p), Gillespie (1) (Spencer), Guinan (Odejayi (1)), Vincent (1).

Record Cup Victory: 12–0 v Chippenham R, FA Cup 3rd qual. rd, 2 November 1935 – Bowles; Whitehouse, Williams; Lang, Devonport (1), Partridge (2); Perkins, Hackett, Jones (4), Black (4), Griffiths (1).

HONOURS

League Champions: Conference – 1998–99, 2015–16.
Runners-up: Conference – 1997–98.

FA Cup: 5th rd – 2002.

League Cup: never past 2nd rd.

sky SPORTS FACT FILE

Prior to turning professional in 1932 Cheltenham Town regularly entered the FA Amateur Cup. In 1919–20 they reached the first round proper of the competition for the first time, but went down to a 2-0 defeat at home to Clandown.

Record Defeat: 1–8 v Crewe Alex, FL 2, 2 April 2011; 0–7 v Crystal Palace, League Cup 2nd rd, 2 October 2002.
N.B. 1–10 v Merthyr T, Southern League, 8 March 1952.

Most League Points (2 for a win): 60, Southern League Division 1, 1963–64.

Most League Points (3 for a win): 78, Division 3, 2001–02.

Most League Goals: 66, Division 3, 2001–02; 66, FL 2, 2011–12.

Highest League Scorer in Season: Julian Alsop, 20, Division 3, 2001–02.

Most League Goals in Total Aggregate: Julian Alsop, 39, 2000–03; 2009–10.

Most League Goals in One Match: 3, Martin Devaney v Plymouth Arg, Division 3, 23 September 2000; 3, Neil Grayson v Cardiff C, Division 3, 1 April 2001; 3, Damien Spencer v Hull C, Division 3, 23 August 2003; 3, Damien Spencer v Milton Keynes D, FL 1, 31 January 2009; 3, Michael Pook v Burton Alb, FL 2, 13 March 2010.

Most Capped Player: Grant McCann, 7 (40), Northern Ireland.

Most League Appearances: David Bird, 288, 2001–11.

Youngest League Player: Kyle Haynes, 17 years 85 days v Oldham Ath, 24 March 2009.

Record Transfer Fee Received: £400,000 from Colchester U for Steve Gillespie, July 2008.

Record Transfer Fee Paid: £60,000 to Aldershot T for Jermaine McGlashan, January 2012.

Football League Record: 1999 Promoted to Division 3; 2002 Division 2; 2003–04 Division 3; 2004–06 FL 2; 2006–09 FL 1; 2009–15 FL 2; 2015–16 National League; 2016– FL 2.

MANAGERS

George Blackburn 1932–34
George Carr 1934–37
Jimmy Brain 1937–48
Cyril Dean 1948–50
George Summerbee 1950–52
William Raeside 1952–53
Arch Anderson 1953–58
Ron Lewin 1958–60
Peter Donnelly 1960–61
Tommy Cavanagh 1961
Arch Anderson 1961–65
Harold Fletcher 1965–66
Bob Etheridge 1966–73
Willie Penman 1973–74
Dennis Allen 1974–79
Terry Paine 1979
Alan Grundy 1979–82
Alan Wood 1982–83
John Murphy 1983–88
Jim Barron 1988–90
John Murphy 1990
Dave Lewis 1990–91
Ally Robertson 1991–92
Lindsay Parsons 1992–95
Chris Robinson 1995–97
Steve Cotterill 1997–2002
Graham Allner 2002–03
Bobby Gould 2003
John Ward 2003–07
Keith Downing 2007–08
Martin Allen 2008–09
Mark Yates 2009–14
Paul Buckle 2014–15
Gary Johnson March 2015–

LATEST SEQUENCES

Longest Sequence of League Wins: 5, 29.10.2011 – 10.12.2011.

Longest Sequence of League Defeats: 7, 27.1.2009 – 28.2.2009.

Longest Sequence of League Draws: 5, 5.4.2003 – 21.4.2003.

Longest Sequence of Unbeaten League Matches: 16, 1.12.2001 – 12.3.2002.

Longest Sequence Without a League Win: 14, 20.12.2008 – 7.3.2009.

Successive Scoring Runs: 17 from 16.2.2008.

Successive Non-scoring Runs: 5 from 10.3.2012 – 30.3.2012.

TEN YEAR LEAGUE RECORD

		P	W	D	L	F	A	Pts	Pos
2007-08	FL 1	46	13	12	21	42	64	51	19
2008-09	FL 1	46	9	12	25	51	91	39	23
2009-10	FL 2	46	10	18	18	54	71	48	22
2010-11	FL 2	46	13	13	20	56	77	52	17
2011-12	FL 2	46	23	8	15	66	50	77	6
2012-13	FL 2	46	20	15	11	58	51	75	5
2013-14	FL 2	46	13	16	17	53	63	55	17
2014-15	FL 2	46	9	14	23	40	67	41	23
2015-16	NL	46	30	11	5	87	30	101	1
2016-17	FL 2	46	12	14	20	49	69	50	21

DID YOU KNOW ?

After a 2-1 win over Cambridge United on 21 October, Cheltenham Town registered just three more League Two victories in their remaining 32 fixtures in the 2014–15 season and were relegated to the Football Conference.

CHELTENHAM TOWN – SKY BET LEAGUE TWO 2016–17 LEAGUE RECORD

Match No.	Date	Venue	Opponents	Result		H/T Score	Lg Pos.	Goalscorers	Attendance
1	Aug 6	H	Leyton Orient	D	1-1	0-1	12	Waters [76]	3912
2	13	A	Mansfield T	D	1-1	0-0	16	O'Shaughnessy [79]	2884
3	16	A	Carlisle U	D	1-1	0-0	17	Pell [57]	4203
4	20	H	Doncaster R	L	0-1	0-0	22		2923
5	27	H	Crewe Alex	W	2-0	2-0	14	Dickie [16], Dayton [22]	2623
6	Sept 3	A	Plymouth Arg	L	0-1	0-0	17		7552
7	10	A	Newport Co	D	2-2	2-2	19	Hall [11], Wright (pen) [34]	2656
8	17	H	Notts Co	L	2-3	1-2	19	Wright [24], Pell [55]	3067
9	24	A	Yeovil T	L	2-4	1-3	22	Downes [41], Waters [57]	3448
10	27	H	Stevenage	D	0-0	0-0	23		2238
11	Oct 1	H	Luton T	D	1-1	0-0	22	O'Shaughnessy [64]	3660
12	8	A	Accrington S	D	1-1	0-0	21	Dickie [89]	1637
13	15	H	Crawley T	W	2-1	1-0	19	Waters [3], Munns [62]	2678
14	22	A	Grimsby T	W	1-0	1-0	16	Waters [9]	4809
15	29	H	Blackpool	D	2-2	2-1	16	Dayton [18], Wright [45]	3162
16	Nov 12	A	Hartlepool U	L	0-2	0-1	20		3316
17	19	H	Portsmouth	D	1-1	0-0	21	O'Shaughnessy [65]	4702
18	22	H	Colchester U	L	0-3	0-0	23		2276
19	26	A	Cambridge U	L	1-3	0-1	23	Waters [85]	4606
20	Dec 10	H	Exeter C	L	1-3	0-0	23	Waters [70]	3113
21	17	A	Morecambe	W	2-1	0-1	23	Waters [70], Pell [71]	1297
22	26	H	Barnet	L	1-2	1-1	23	Wright [44]	3441
23	30	H	Wycombe W	L	0-1	0-1	23		3761
24	Jan 2	A	Colchester U	L	0-2	0-1	23		3840
25	14	H	Accrington S	W	3-0	0-0	22	Wright [55], De Girolamo [74], Waters [78]	2854
26	21	H	Plymouth Arg	L	1-2	0-1	22	Holman [85]	4729
27	28	A	Crewe Alex	D	0-0	0-0	22		3373
28	31	A	Luton T	W	3-2	2-1	20	Boyle [5], Barthram [28], Waters [60]	6708
29	Feb 4	H	Newport Co	D	1-1	0-0	20	Wootton [62]	3763
30	11	A	Notts Co	L	1-2	0-2	20	Onariase [87]	7910
31	14	A	Stevenage	L	1-2	0-1	22	Wootton [82]	1930
32	18	H	Yeovil T	W	2-0	0-0	21	Plavotic [48], Waters (pen) [63]	3347
33	25	A	Leyton Orient	W	1-0	1-0	19	Winchester [21]	4747
34	28	H	Carlisle U	W	1-0	0-0	18	Wright [85]	2433
35	Mar 4	H	Mansfield T	D	0-0	0-0	18		2941
36	11	A	Doncaster R	L	0-2	0-1	20		5737
37	14	A	Exeter C	L	0-3	0-1	22		3539
38	18	H	Cambridge U	L	0-1	0-1	22		2905
39	25	A	Barnet	L	1-3	1-0	22	Wright [16]	1861
40	Apr 1	H	Morecambe	W	3-1	1-0	21	Pell 2 [33, 57], Wright (pen) [48]	2751
41	8	A	Wycombe W	D	3-3	2-2	21	Waters 2 [7, 83], Pell [13]	3596
42	14	A	Crawley T	D	0-0	0-0	21		2008
43	17	H	Grimsby T	W	2-1	2-0	20	Boyle [34], Pell [39]	3550
44	22	A	Blackpool	L	0-3	0-2	21		3775
45	29	H	Hartlepool U	W	1-0	1-0	20	Wright [18]	5606
46	May 6	A	Portsmouth	L	1-6	0-1	21	Dayton [77]	17,956

Final League Position: 21

GOALSCORERS

League (49): Waters 12 (1 pen), Wright 9 (2 pens), Pell 7, Dayton 3, O'Shaughnessy 3, Boyle 2, Dickie 2, Wootton 2, Barthram 1, De Girolamo 1, Downes 1, Hall 1, Holman 1, Munns 1, Onariase 1, Plavotic 1, Winchester 1.
FA Cup (6): Waters 2, Barthram 1, Holman 1, Pell 1, Wright 1.
EFL Cup (1): Pell 1.
EFL Checkatrade Trophy (10): De Girolamo 3, Morgan-Smith 2 (1 pen), Waters 2, Jennings 1, O'Shaughnessy 1, Wright 1 (1 pen).

Griffiths R 24	Suliman E 5 + 4	Parslow D 19 + 2	O'Shaughnessy D 26 + 1	Jennings J 2 + 1	Rowe J 26 + 6	Pell H 42	Whitehead D 5 + 1	Morgan-Smith A 4 + 13	Holman D 16 + 8	Wright D 34 + 7	Cranston J 30 + 8	Barthram J 22 + 7	Waters B 41 + 5	Hall A 8 + 2	Dayton J 10 + 18	Arthur K 1 + 4	Smith J 2 + 3	Dickie R 20	Downes A 15 + 5	Munns J 8 + 10	Cooper A 1	Storer K 18 + 5	Onariase M 22	De Girolamo D 4 + 1	Brown S 21	Boyle W 21	Pike A 5	Winchester C 20	Wootton K 10 + 6	Davis L 13 + 3	Plavotic T 10 + 1	Lainton R 1	*Match No.*
1	2^1	3	4	5^2	6^3	7	8	9	10	11	12	13	14																				1
1	2	3	4	5^3	14	9	7^1	8	11	10	12	13	6^2																				2
1	2	4	3		13	10	9			11	5	6^2	7^1	8	12																		3
1	2^2	3	4	13		8	7^3			10	5		6	12	9	11^1	14																4
1		4	3		9^1	7	12	14		11^3	5	13	10	8	6^2			2															5
1		3	4		7	6	8	12		11	9		10^1	5				2															6
1		4	5		7^3	8				11	6	2^1	10^2	9	13		12	3	14														7
1		4	5^1		7^2	8				11	10		13	6^3	12		9	2	3	14													8
1	2^3	5	3			7				10	6		13	14	8^1		11^2	9	4	12													9
1		14	5			8		12		11	6^3	2^2	10	7	13			3	4	9^1													10
1			4			6		12		11	9	5	10^2	7	13			2	3	8^1													11
1		12	4■			8				11		5	10^1	7	13		14	2	3	6^3	9^2												12
1	13	4						12		11	9	5	10^2		6^1			2	3	8		7											13
1		3				10^1		12			9	5	11		6			4	2	7		8											14
1		4				6		12		10	9	5^1	11		8^2			2	3	13		7											15
1		3	4			6		13	12	11	9		10^1		7^2	14		5	2	8^3													16
1	13	4	8^1		6	7			10	11	12	5^2	9					2	3														17
1		4	3		6^1	7■		12	11^2	10	5		9			13		2		14		8^3											18
1	13	3^1			6			14	11^3	10	9	5^2	7		12			2	4			8											19
1	13	3^2	12			7		9^3		11	5		10		6	14		2	4			8^1											20
1		3	4^2			7		12		10^1	9	14	11			13		5	2	8^3		6											21
1		4^3				8		14	12	10^2	9	5	11		13			2	3	6^1		7											22
1			3		9	8		13	10	11^2	2	14	6		12			5	4^3			7^1											23
1			4		8	7		9^3	10^2	13	5		6		12			2		14			3	11^1									24
			4		7^3					10	8		9		14					12		13	2	11^1	1	3	5	6^2					25
			4		8				13	10		9	7									12	2	11^1	1	3	5^2	6					26
			5		6	7			14	10^3	12		8										4	11^2	1	3	2	9^1	13				27
			4		7	6				13	9^2	5	12									14	2		1	3		10^1	11^3	8			28
					7	6			10^2	13		5	9										2	12	1	3			11^1	8	4		29
					9	8^1			12	14	6		13										5		1	3	2^3	7^2	11	10	4		30
					8	7			12		5		11^1		13					14			3		1	4	2	6^2	10	9^3			31
			9		8	7						5	11									12	2		1	3		6^1	10		4		32
					8^1	7						5	10									12	4		1	3		6	11	9	2		33
						7			13	12		5	11^3		14							6^1	2		1	3		8	10^2	9	4		34
			4		14	7				12	13	5	11^2									6■	2		1	3		8^3	10^1	9			35
					6	8^2			14		12	5	10		13								2		1	3■		7^1	11	9^3	4		36
			4^2		13	8				14	6	2	10		7					12			3		1			9^3	11^1		5		37
						7			11^1	10		5^3	9^2		13				14				2		1	3		6	12	8	4		38
					13	7				10^1	14	2	8		11^3								3		1	4		9^2	12	6	5		39
					7^2	6			11	10	5		9^1		13							8	3		1	4		2		12			40
					8^2	6			10	11	5■	12^3	9						14			7	4			3		2^1			13	1	41
					12	6			11	10^2			9									7	2		1	4		8	13	5	3^1		42
					8^3	6			10^2	11^1	5		9						13			7	4		1	3		2	14	12			43
					8	6^1			11	10	5^2		9^3		13					14		7	4		1	3		2		12			44
					6	7			10^2	11^3	12		9						13			3	5		1	4		8^1	14	2			45
			4		7	6^1			10^2	11	2^3	13	9		12					14		8			1	3				5			46

FA Cup

First Round	Crewe Alex	(h)	1-1
Replay	Crewe Alex	(a)	4-1
Second Round	Sutton U	(a)	1-2

EFL Cup

First Round	Charlton Ath	(h)	1-0
Second Round	Newcastle U	(a)	0-2

EFL Checkatrade Trophy

Northern Group A	Blackpool	(a)	1-2
Northern Group A	Everton U21	(h)	2-1
Northern Group A	Bolton W	(h)	1-0
Second Round North	Leicester C U21	(h)	6-1
Third Round	Bradford C	(h)	0-1

CHESTERFIELD

FOUNDATION

Chesterfield are fourth only to Stoke, Notts County and Nottingham Forest in age for they can trace their existence as far back as 1866, although it is fair to say that they were somewhat casual in the first few years of their history, playing only a few friendlies a year. However, their rules of 1871 are still in existence, showing an annual membership of 2s (10p), but it was not until 1891 that they won a trophy (the Barnes Cup) and followed this a year later by winning the Sheffield Cup, Barnes Cup and the Derbyshire Junior Cup.

The Proact Stadium, 1866 Sheffield Road, Whittington Moor, Chesterfield, Derbyshire S41 8NZ.

Telephone: (01246) 269 300.

Fax: (01246) 556 799.

Ticket Office: (01246) 269 300.

Website: www.chesterfield-fc.co.uk

Email: reception@chesterfield-fc.co.uk

Ground Capacity: 10,401.

Record Attendance: 30,968 v Newcastle U, Division 2, 7 April 1939 (at Saltergate); 10,089 v Rotherham U, FL 2, 18 March 2011 (at b2net Stadium (now called the Proact Stadium)).

Pitch Measurements: 103m × 67m (112.5yd × 73.5yd).

Chairman: Mike Warner.

Director of football: Chris Turner.

Manager: Gary Caldwell.

First-Team Coach: Steve Eyre.

Colours: Blue shirts with white trim, white shorts with blue trim, blue socks with white trim.

Year Formed: 1866.

Turned Professional: 1891.

Previous Name: 1867, Chesterfield Town; 1919, Chesterfield.

Club Nicknames: 'The Blues', 'The Spireites'.

Grounds: 1867, Drill Field; 1871, Recreation Ground, Saltergate; 2010, b2net Stadium (renamed The Proact Stadium 2012).

First Football League Game: 2 September 1899, Division 2, v Sheffield W (a) L 1–5 – Hancock; Pilgrim, Fletcher; Ballantyne, Bell, Downie; Morley, Thacker, Gooing, Munday (1), Geary.

Record League Victory: 10–0 v Glossop NE, Division 2, 17 January 1903 – Clutterbuck; Thorpe, Lerper; Haig, Banner, Thacker; Tomlinson (2), Newton (1), Milward (3), Munday (2), Steel (2).

Record Cup Victory: 6–0 v Braintree T (a), FA Cup 1st rd, 8 November 2014 – Lee; Darikwa, Evatt, Raglan, Jones (Humpreys), Morsy, Ryan, O'Shea (1) (Gardner), Clucas (1), Roberts (1) (Boco), Doyle (2), own goal (1).

Record Defeat: 0–10 v Gillingham, Division 3, 5 September 1987.

HONOURS

League Champions: Division 3N – 1930–31, 1935–36; FL 2 – 2010–11, 2013–14; Division 4 – 1969–70, 1984–85.
Runners-up: Division 3N – 1933–34.

FA Cup: semi-final – 1997.

League Cup: 4th rd – 1965, 2007.

League Trophy Winners: 2012.
Runners-up: 2014.

Anglo-Scottish Cup Winners: 1981.

sky SPORTS FACT FILE

William Thomas Hickinson who played regularly for Chesterfield reserves in the Midland League in 1908–09 went on to become a well-known artist. After studying at the Royal College of Art and in Paris he became an official government artist in the First World War before emigrating to the United States.

Most League Points (2 for a win): 64, Division 4, 1969–70.

Most League Points (3 for a win): 91, Division 4, 1984–85.

Most League Goals: 102, Division 3 (N), 1930–31.

Highest League Scorer in Season: Jimmy Cookson, 44, Division 3 (N), 1925–26.

Most League Goals in Total Aggregate: Ernie Moss, 162, 1969–76, 1979–81 and 1984–86.

Most League Goals in One Match: 4, Jimmy Cookson v Accrington S, Division 3 (N), 16 January 1926; 4, Jimmy Cookson v Ashington, Division 3 (N), 1 May 1926; 4, Jimmy Cookson v Wigan Borough, Division 3 (N), 4 September 1926; 4, Tommy Lyon v Southampton, Division 2, 3 December 1938.

Most Capped Player: Walter McMillen, 4 (7), Northern Ireland; Mark Williams, 4 (36), Northern Ireland; Liam Graham, 4, New Zealand.

Most League Appearances: Dave Blakey, 617, 1948–67.

Youngest League Player: Dennis Thompson, 16 years 160 days v Notts Co, 26 December 1950.

Record Transfer Fee Received: £1,300,000 from Hull C for Sam Clucas, July 2015.

Record Transfer Fee Paid: £250,000 to Watford for Jason Lee, August 1998.

Football League Record: 1899 Elected to Division 2; 1909 failed re-election; 1921–31 Division 3 (N); 1931–33 Division 2; 1933–36 Division 3 (N); 1936–51 Division 2; 1951–58 Division 3 (N); 1958–61 Division 3; 1961–70 Division 4; 1970–83 Division 3; 1983–85 Division 4; 1985–89 Division 3; 1989–92 Division 4; 1992–95 Division 3; 1995–2000 Division 2; 2000–01 Division 3; 2001–04 Division 2; 2004–07 FL 1; 2007–11 FL 2; 2011–12 FL 1; 2012–14 FL 2; 2014–17 FL 1; 2017– FL 2.

LATEST SEQUENCES

Longest Sequence of League Wins: 10, 6.9.1933 – 4.11.1933.

Longest Sequence of League Defeats: 9, 22.10.1960 – 27.12.1960.

Longest Sequence of League Draws: 8, 26.11.2005 – 2.1.2006.

Longest Sequence of Unbeaten League Matches: 21, 26.12.1994 – 29.4.1995.

Longest Sequence Without a League Win: 18, 11.9.1999 – 3.1.2000.

Successive Scoring Runs: 46 from 25.12.1929.

Successive Non-scoring Runs: 7 from 23.9.1977.

MANAGERS

E. Russell Timmeus 1891–95
(*Secretary-Manager*)
Gilbert Gillies 1895–1901
E. F. Hind 1901–02
Jack Hoskin 1902–06
W. Furness 1906–07
George Swift 1907–10
G. H. Jones 1911–13
R. L. Weston 1913–17
T. Callaghan 1919
J. J. Caffrey 1920–22
Harry Hadley 1922
Harry Parkes 1922–27
Alec Campbell 1927
Ted Davison 1927–32
Bill Harvey 1932–38
Norman Bullock 1938–45
Bob Brocklebank 1945–48
Bobby Marshall 1948–52
Ted Davison 1952–58
Duggie Livingstone 1958–62
Tony McShane 1962–67
Jimmy McGuigan 1967–73
Joe Shaw 1973–76
Arthur Cox 1976–80
Frank Barlow 1980–83
John Duncan 1983–87
Kevin Randall 1987–88
Paul Hart 1988–91
Chris McMenemy 1991–93
John Duncan 1993–2000
Nicky Law 2000–01
Dave Rushbury 2002–03
Roy McFarland 2003–07
Lee Richardson 2007–09
John Sheridan 2009–12
Paul Cook 2012–15
Dean Saunders 2015
Danny Wilson 2015–17
Gary Caldwell January 2017–

TEN YEAR LEAGUE RECORD

		P	*W*	*D*	*L*	*F*	*A*	*Pts*	*Pos*
2007-08	FL 2	46	19	12	15	76	56	69	8
2008-09	FL 2	46	16	15	15	62	57	63	10
2009-10	FL 2	46	21	7	18	61	62	70	8
2010-11	FL 2	46	24	14	8	85	51	86	1
2011-12	FL 1	46	10	12	24	56	81	42	22
2012-13	FL 2	46	18	13	15	60	45	67	8
2013-14	FL 2	46	23	15	8	71	40	84	1
2014-15	FL 1	46	19	12	15	68	55	69	6
2015-16	FL 1	46	15	8	23	58	70	53	18
2016-17	FL 1	46	9	10	27	43	78	37	24

DID YOU KNOW ?

Chesterfield lost their first and last Division Three North home games of the 1929–30 season, but won 18 and drew one of the games in between. It was not enough to win promotion, however, and the Spireites finished in fourth place.

CHESTERFIELD – SKY BET LEAGUE ONE 2016–17 LEAGUE RECORD

Match No.	Date	Venue	Opponents	Result	H/T Score	Lg Pos.	Goalscorers	Attendance
1	Aug 6	A	Oxford U	D 1-1	0-1	10	Evans [76]	8679
2	13	H	Swindon T	W 3-1	2-0	5	Liddle [22], O'Shea (pen) [45], Evans [64]	5378
3	16	H	Walsall	W 2-0	0-0	1	Evans 2 [75, 79]	5406
4	20	A	Shrewsbury T	L 1-2	1-1	4	O'Shea [14]	4936
5	27	H	Millwall	L 1-3	0-3	10	Hird [65]	5630
6	Sept 3	A	AFC Wimbledon	L 1-2	1-0	11	Charles (og) [35]	4425
7	10	A	Oldham Ath	D 0-0	0-0	14		3457
8	17	H	Northampton T	W 3-1	1-0	10	Wilkinson 2 [7, 49], Dennis [70]	5910
9	24	A	Bury	L 1-2	1-1	15	Dennis [44]	3494
10	27	H	Gillingham	D 3-3	1-0	11	Wilkinson 2 [2, 72], Dennis (pen) [52]	4714
11	Oct 1	H	Bradford C	L 0-1	0-1	17		6997
12	15	A	Southend U	L 0-1	0-1	21		6004
13	18	H	Fleetwood T	L 0-1	0-1	22		4598
14	22	H	Scunthorpe U	L 0-3	0-0	23		6328
15	29	A	Charlton Ath	L 0-1	0-0	23		10,153
16	Nov 1	A	Coventry C	L 0-2	0-0	23		7941
17	13	H	Sheffield U	L 1-4	1-0	24	Nolan [2]	8451
18	19	A	Fleetwood T	L 1-2	0-1	24	O'Shea (pen) [66]	2901
19	22	A	Milton Keynes D	W 3-2	1-0	23	O'Shea (pen) [32], Dennis [77], Gardner [80]	7429
20	26	H	Bristol R	W 3-2	2-1	22	Evatt [28], O'Shea 2 [37, 50]	6330
21	Dec 10	A	Peterborough U	L 2-5	2-2	23	Evans [22], O'Neil [25]	5120
22	17	H	Bolton W	W 1-0	1-0	20	O'Neil [26]	6924
23	26	A	Rochdale	L 0-3	0-1	22		3863
24	30	A	Port Vale	L 0-1	0-0	22		4027
25	Jan 2	H	Milton Keynes D	D 0-0	0-0	21		5554
26	7	A	Bradford C	L 0-2	0-2	22		17,416
27	14	H	Coventry C	W 1-0	0-0	22	Gardner [77]	5896
28	21	H	AFC Wimbledon	D 0-0	0-0	22		6379
29	Feb 4	H	Oldham Ath	L 0-1	0-0	23		6375
30	11	A	Northampton T	L 1-3	0-2	23	Faupala [54]	5824
31	14	A	Gillingham	D 1-1	0-0	23	Anderson [90]	4595
32	18	H	Bury	L 1-2	1-0	23	Dennis [32]	5582
33	21	A	Millwall	D 0-0	0-0	23		9005
34	25	H	Oxford U	L 0-4	0-2	23		5901
35	Mar 4	A	Swindon T	W 1-0	0-0	23	Mitchell [90]	6691
36	7	A	Walsall	L 0-1	0-0	23		3963
37	11	H	Shrewsbury T	D 1-1	1-1	23	Evatt [42]	6317
38	14	H	Peterborough U	D 3-3	2-3	23	Ebanks-Blake [4], Dennis [27], Donohue [54]	5048
39	18	A	Bristol R	L 1-2	0-2	23	Ebanks-Blake [85]	8524
40	25	H	Rochdale	L 1-3	0-3	23	Dennis [51]	5927
41	Apr 1	A	Bolton W	D 0-0	0-0	23		23,376
42	8	H	Port Vale	W 1-0	0-0	23	Rowley [54]	5527
43	14	H	Southend U	L 0-4	0-1	23		5529
44	17	A	Scunthorpe U	L 1-3	0-2	23	Anderson [90]	4636
45	22	H	Charlton Ath	L 1-2	0-1	24	Mitchell [90]	5657
46	30	A	Sheffield U	L 2-3	1-1	24	Dennis (pen) [45], McGinn [65]	31,003

Final League Position: 24

GOALSCORERS

League (43): Dennis 8 (2 pens), O'Shea 6 (3 pens), Evans 5, Wilkinson 4, Anderson 2, Ebanks-Blake 2, Evatt 2, Gardner 2, Mitchell 2, O'Neil 2, Donohue 1, Faupala 1, Hird 1, Liddle 1, McGinn 1, Nolan 1, Rowley 1, own goal 1.
FA Cup (2): Evans 1, O'Shea 1.
EFL Cup (1): McGinn 1.
EFL Checkatrade Trophy (7): Dennis 2, Dimaio 1 (1 pen), Ebanks-Blake 1, Evans 1, Maguire 1, O'Shea 1.

Fulton R 26	McGinn P 17 + 1	Raglan C 1	Donohue D 36 + 1	Evatt I 29 + 1	Gardner D 22 + 12	Nolan J 28 + 2	Liddle G 26	Ariyibi G 24 + 4	Evans C 20 + 5	O'Shea J 23 + 4	Simons R 6 + 13	Dennis K 26 + 9	Hird S 35	Jones D 11 + 3	Mitchell R 16 + 12	Morrison C — + 1	Wilkinson C 6 + 6	Anderson T 34 + 1	Dimaio C 17 + 6	German R 1 + 6	Brownell J — + 1	Graham L 4	Maguire L 10 + 1	O'Neil L 17	Humphreys R — + 2	Allinson L 5	Beesley J 4 + 3	Daley D — + 1	El Fitouri S 2	Grimshaw L 10 + 3	Faupala D 7 + 7	Martinez A 5 + 4	Brown R — + 2	Kakay O 7 + 1	Ebanks-Blake S 9 + 4	Stuckmann T 15	Rowley J 7	Wakefield C — + 1	*Match No.*
1	2	3	4	5	6^{2}	7	8	9	10^{1}	11	12	13																										1
1	2		5	4	10^{2}	7	6	8	11^{1}	9^{3}		14	3	12	13																							2
1	2		5	4	10	7	6	8	11^{1}	9	12		3																										3
1	2		7	5	8^{1}	6	4	10	11	9^{2}		13	3			12																						4
1	2		5	4	10^{1}	7	6	8	11	9^{2}		13	3		12																							5
1	5		2	3		6^{2}	7	10	11	9			4		8^{1}		12	13																				6
1	2		5		10^{2}		7	8	11	12		13	3				9^{1}	4	6																			7
1	2		5		12	8	7	6		9		10^{2}	3				11^{1}	4		13																		8
1	2^{2}			14	13	8	7	9		6^{1}		10	3				11^{3}	4	12			5																9
1			14			8	7	6		12		10	3		9^{2}		11^{1}	4	13			2	5^{3}															10
1						8^{3}	7	6		12		11^{1}	3		9^{2}		10	4	13	14		2	5															11
1			5			7	8	9		6^{2}		10^{1}	3		13		11^{3}	4	14	12				2														12
1	14		5			8	7	6	13	11		10^{3}	3		9^{2}			4		12				2^{1}														13
1			5		12	8	7	6	10	9^{2}	14		3		13			4		11^{1}				2^{3}														14
1			5	4	8^{3}		6	10	11^{2}	12		14	3						9	13		7^{1}		2														15
1			5	4			7	6	10	9^{1}		11^{2}	3		13				8	12				2														16
1			5	3		8^{1}	7	6	10^{2}	11		12						4	9					2	13													17
			9	3			2	6		11		10^{1}			5			4	8^{2}				13	7		1	12											18
1			5	2	13	14	4	9		8^{2}		12			10^{3}			3	7					6			11^{1}											19
1			8	3	14	12	2	11	13	9^{2}					5			4	7^{3}					6			10^{1}											20
1				3			6	12	11	10	8^{1}						14	4	7				5^{2}	2			9^{3}	13										21
			9	3			2	11	10	8			5					4	7					6		1												22
			9	3			2	5	10	11			7				12	4	6^{1}					8		1												23
1			5	4	14	7	2	9^{2}	11	10^{3}	12		3		6^{1}		13							8														24
1			5	3		7	8	13	11	9					6^{2}		12	4						2			10^{1}											25
1			5	4	14	9	8	12	11		6^{3}		7		10^{2}		13	3						2^{1}														26
1			5	4	7	8		12	10	9		11	6					3^{1}						2														27
1			5	4	8	6		7	10	9^{1}	11^{2}	13	3		12									2														28
1			9	3	6	8^{2}			10		14			5^{1}				4											2	7^{3}	11	12	13						29
			9	3	6^{2}	8			14			11^{3}		5^{1}	13			4								1			2	7	10	12							30
			4	3	7^{1}	6^{3}					13	10^{2}			9			2								1				8	11	12		5	14				31
				2	6^{2}						14	11^{3}	3	8	13			4■												7	10		12	5	9^{1}	1			32
				2	6^{2}						12	11	3	4	5^{1}				13								14			7	10	8			9^{3}	1			33
				2	8^{3}				13		14	11	3	4^{2}	5															6	9^{1}	7		12	10	1			34
			4	3	14				12			10^{2}	8	9^{3}	13			2												6		7		5	11^{1}	1			35
			4	3	12							11^{2}	7	9^{3}	13			2												8	14	6^{1}		5	10	1			36
			5	3^{2}	6							11	2	13	9^{3}			4	8											7^{1}	14	12			10	1			37
			4		13	6					9^{2}	10^{3}	2	8^{1}	14			3	7												12			5	11	1			38
	6		7		14	8					9^{2}	11^{1}	3	2				4	12												13			5^{3}	10	1			39
	2		8		14	6					12	10						3					4								13■	7		5^{2}	11^{3}	1	9^{1}		40
	2		8		5^{1}	9■					12	11^{3}	3				4	6				10							13					14	1	7^{2}		41
	5		8^{3}		6^{1}						12	11^{2}	3	9				2	7				4							13					14	1	10		42
	5		8■		6^{3}						12	11^{1}	3	9				2	7				4							13					14	1	10^{2}		43
	5				6						9^{1}	10	3	13	12			2	7				4								11^{2}					1	8^{3}	14	44
	5				7^{2}	6						10	2		8			3	9^{1}		13		4								12					1	11		45
	5				6■	8						11^{2}	2		9^{1}			3					4		13		14			7	12					1	10^{3}		46

FA Cup

First Round	Colchester U	(a)	2-1
Second Round	Wycombe W	(h)	0-5

EFL Cup

First Round	Rochdale	(a)	1-3

EFL Checkatrade Trophy

Northern Group B	Wolverhampton W U21	(h)	2-1
Northern Group B	Accrington S	(h)	1-4
Northern Group B	Crewe Alex	(a)	2-0
Second Round North	Rochdale	(a)	2-0
Third Round	Luton T	(a)	0-4

COLCHESTER UNITED

FOUNDATION

Colchester United was formed in 1937 when a number of enthusiasts of the much older Colchester Town club decided to establish a professional concern as a limited liability company. The new club continued at Layer Road which had been the amateur club's home since 1909.

Weston Homes Community Stadium, United Way, Colchester, Essex CO4 5UP.

Telephone: (01206) 755 100.

Fax: (01206) 715 327.

Ticket Office: (01206) 755 161.

Website: www.cu-fc.com

Email: media@colchesterunited.net

Ground Capacity: 10,105.

Record Attendance: 19,072 v Reading, FA Cup 1st rd, 27 November 1948 (at Layer Road); 10,064 v Norwich C, FL 1, 16 January 2010 (at Community Stadium).

Pitch Measurements: 100.5m × 65m (110yd × 71yd).

Executive Chairman: Robbie Cowling.

Manager: John McGreal.

Assistant Manager: Steve Ball.

Colours: Royal blue and white striped shirts, royal blue shorts with white trim, white socks with royal blue trim.

Year Formed: 1937.

Turned Professional: 1937.

Club Nickname: 'The U's'.

Grounds: 1937, Layer Road; 2008, Weston Homes Community Stadium.

First Football League Game: 19 August 1950, Division 3 (S), v Gillingham (a) D 0–0 – Wright; Kettle, Allen; Bearryman, Stewart, Elder; Jones, Curry, Turner, McKim, Church.

Record League Victory: 9–1 v Bradford C, Division 4, 30 December 1961 – Ames; Millar, Fowler; Harris, Abrey, Ron Hunt; Foster, Bobby Hunt (4), King (4), Hill (1), Wright.

Record Cup Victory: 9-1 v Leamington, FA Cup 1st rd, 5 November 2005 – Davison; Stockley (Garcia), Duguid, Brown (1), Chilvers, Watson (1), Halford (1), Izzet (Danns) (2), Iwelumo (1) (Williams), Cureton (2), Yeates (1).

Record Defeat: 0–8 v Leyton Orient, Division 4, 15 October 1988.

Most League Points (2 for a win): 60, Division 4, 1973–74.

HONOURS

League Champions: Conference – 1991–92.
Runners-up: FL 1 – 2005–06; Division 4 – 1961–62; Conference – 1990–91.

FA Cup: 6th rd – 1971.

League Cup: 5th rd – 1975.

League Trophy: *Runners-up:* 1997.

sky SPORTS FACT FILE

Colchester United's first manager was Ted Davis who was appointed in time for their first season of competitive football. A former goalkeeper with Blackburn Rovers and Huddersfield Town, he led the U's to the Southern League Cup in 1937–38, their inaugural season, and the Southern League title the following season.

Most League Points (3 for a win): 81, Division 4, 1982–83.

Most League Goals: 104, Division 4, 1961–62.

Highest League Scorer in Season: Bobby Hunt, 38, Division 4, 1961–62.

Most League Goals in Total Aggregate: Martyn King, 130, 1956–64.

Most League Goals in One Match: 4, Bobby Hunt v Bradford C, Division 4, 30 December 1961; 4, Martyn King v Bradford C, Division 4, 30 December 1961; 4, Bobby Hunt v Doncaster R, Division 4, 30 April 1962.

Most Capped Player: Bela Balogh, 2 (9), Hungary.

Most League Appearances: Micky Cook, 613, 1969–84.

Youngest League Player: Lindsay Smith, 16 years 218 days v Grimsby T, 24 April 1971.

Record Transfer Fee Received: £2,500,000 from Reading for Greg Halford, January 2007.

Record Transfer Fee Paid: £400,000 to Cheltenham T for Steve Gillespie, July 2008.

Football League Record: 1950 Elected to Division 3 (S); 1958–61 Division 3; 1961–62 Division 4; 1962–65 Division 3; 1965–66 Division 4; 1966–68 Division 3; 1968–74 Division 4; 1974–76 Division 3, 1976–77 Division 4; 1977–81 Division 3; 1981–90 Division 4; 1990–92 Conference; 1992–98 Division 3; 1998–2004 Division 2; 2004–06 FL 1; 2006–08 FL C; 2008–16 FL 1; 2016– FL 2.

MANAGERS

Ted Fenton 1946–48
Jimmy Allen 1948–53
Jack Butler 1953–55
Benny Fenton 1955–63
Neil Franklin 1963–68
Dick Graham 1968–72
Jim Smith 1972–75
Bobby Roberts 1975–82
Allan Hunter 1982–83
Cyril Lea 1983–86
Mike Walker 1986–87
Roger Brown 1987–88
Jock Wallace 1989
Mick Mills 1990
Ian Atkins 1990–91
Roy McDonough 1991–94
George Burley 1994
Steve Wignall 1995–99
Mick Wadsworth 1999
Steve Whitton 1999–2003
Phil Parkinson 2003–06
Geraint Williams 2006–08
Paul Lambert 2008–09
Aidy Boothroyd 2009–10
John Ward 2010–12
Joe Dunne 2012–14
Tony Humes 2014–15
Kevin Keen 2015–16
John McGreal May 2016–

LATEST SEQUENCES

Longest Sequence of League Wins: 7, 31.12.2005 – 7.2.2006.

Longest Sequence of League Defeats: 9, 31.10.2015 – 28.12.2015.

Longest Sequence of League Draws: 6, 21.3.1977 – 11.4.1977.

Longest Sequence of Unbeaten League Matches: 20, 22.12.1956 – 19.4.1957.

Longest Sequence Without a League Win: 20, 2.3.1968 – 31.8.1968.

Successive Scoring Runs: 24 from 15.9.1962.

Successive Non-scoring Runs: 5 from 11.2.2006.

TEN YEAR LEAGUE RECORD

		P	*W*	*D*	*L*	*F*	*A*	*Pts*	*Pos*
2007-08	FL C	46	7	17	22	62	86	38	24
2008-09	FL 1	46	18	9	19	58	58	63	12
2009-10	FL 1	46	20	12	14	64	52	72	8
2010-11	FL 1	46	16	14	16	57	63	62	10
2011-12	FL 1	46	13	20	13	61	66	59	10
2012-13	FL 1	46	14	9	23	47	68	51	20
2013-14	FL 1	46	13	14	19	53	61	53	16
2014-15	FL 1	46	14	10	22	58	77	52	19
2015-16	FL 1	46	9	13	24	57	99	40	23
2016-17	FL 2	46	19	12	15	67	57	69	8

DID YOU KNOW ?

Colchester United attracted a record attendance of 19,072 to Layer Road for their FA Cup tie with Reading in November 1948. The match was abandoned at half-time due to dense fog with the teams level at 1-1. There was another bumper crowd of 13,371 for the replayed match which Reading won 4-2.

COLCHESTER UNITED – SKY BET LEAGUE TWO 2016–17 LEAGUE RECORD

Match No.	Date	Venue	Opponents	Result	H/T Score	Lg Pos.	Goalscorers	Attendance
1	Aug 6	A	Hartlepool U	D 1-1	1-1	13	Eastman [4]	4055
2	13	H	Cambridge U	W 2-0	1-0	3	Dickenson [8], Johnstone [82]	4521
3	16	H	Grimsby T	W 3-2	3-0	2	Dickenson 2 [10, 39], Guthrie [34]	3287
4	20	A	Portsmouth	L 0-2	0-0	5		15,967
5	27	A	Wycombe W	W 2-0	0-0	4	Porter [63], Szmodics [82]	3439
6	Sept 3	H	Exeter C	L 2-3	2-1	8	Szmodics [13], Guthrie [38]	3364
7	10	H	Blackpool	W 3-2	1-1	5	Szmodics [36], Porter 2 [56, 84]	3077
8	17	A	Barnet	D 1-1	1-0	5	Fosu [6]	2158
9	24	H	Accrington S	L 1-2	1-0	8	Drey Wright [7]	3109
10	27	A	Crawley T	D 1-1	0-1	10	Porter [88]	1851
11	Oct 1	A	Carlisle U	L 0-2	0-0	11		4516
12	8	H	Newport Co	D 0-0	0-0	11		3088
13	15	A	Doncaster R	L 0-1	0-1	13		5007
14	22	H	Morecambe	D 2-2	2-1	15	Porter 2 (1 pen) [4, 39 (p)]	2815
15	29	A	Plymouth Arg	L 1-2	1-1	18	Slater [31]	8650
16	Nov 12	H	Leyton Orient	L 0-3	0-1	21		7003
17	19	A	Yeovil T	L 1-2	0-0	23	Guthrie [49]	2985
18	22	A	Cheltenham T	W 3-0	0-0	17	Slater [48], Dickenson [65], Eastman [68]	2276
19	26	H	Crewe Alex	W 4-0	1-0	15	Guthrie [20], Garvan [72], Drey Wright [76], Dickenson [90]	2931
20	Dec 10	A	Mansfield T	D 0-0	0-0	16		3398
21	17	H	Notts Co	W 2-1	1-1	13	Guthrie [24], Duffy (og) [77]	3385
22	26	A	Luton T	W 1-0	0-0	10	Slater [83]	9164
23	31	A	Stevenage	W 4-2	2-1	9	Dickenson [15], Guthrie (pen) [19], Porter [81], Fosu [90]	3076
24	Jan 2	H	Cheltenham T	W 2-0	1-0	8	Eastman [10], Dickenson [84]	3840
25	7	H	Carlisle U	W 4-1	2-1	6	Porter [11], Guthrie 3 [33, 50, 90]	3525
26	14	A	Newport Co	D 1-1	1-1	7	Porter (pen) [35]	2397
27	21	A	Exeter C	L 0-3	0-1	7		4114
28	Feb 4	A	Blackpool	D 1-1	1-1	9	Guthrie [18]	2772
29	11	H	Barnet	W 2-1	2-0	9	Guthrie [18], Dickenson [42]	3606
30	14	H	Crawley T	L 2-3	1-2	10	Johnstone [18], Dickenson [90]	2675
31	18	A	Accrington S	L 1-2	0-2	11	Porter (pen) [76]	1310
32	21	H	Wycombe W	W 1-0	1-0	7	Elokobi [13]	3031
33	25	H	Hartlepool U	W 2-1	0-0	7	Guthrie [63], Porter (pen) [78]	3357
34	28	A	Grimsby T	L 0-1	0-1	9		4186
35	Mar 4	A	Cambridge U	D 1-1	0-1	9	Szmodics [84]	5708
36	11	H	Portsmouth	L 0-4	0-1	10		6504
37	14	H	Mansfield T	W 2-0	2-0	9	Dickenson [20], Szmodics [28]	2526
38	18	A	Crewe Alex	L 0-2	0-1	11		3407
39	25	H	Luton T	W 2-1	2-0	10	Porter 2 [4, 31]	5445
40	Apr 1	A	Notts Co	L 1-3	1-2	12	Porter [21]	6104
41	8	H	Stevenage	W 4-0	4-0	10	Dickenson [12], Porter [30], McQuoid (og) [34], Lee (og) [39]	3583
42	14	H	Doncaster R	D 1-1	1-1	9	Dickenson [16]	4720
43	17	A	Morecambe	D 1-1	1-0	10	Brindley [22]	1447
44	22	H	Plymouth Arg	D 0-0	0-0	12		5432
45	29	A	Leyton Orient	W 3-1	1-0	10	Fosu [26], Porter [78], Bonne [80]	6854
46	May 6	H	Yeovil T	W 2-0	1-0	8	Fosu 2 [36, 77]	6565

Final League Position: 8

GOALSCORERS

League (67): Porter 16 (4 pens), Dickenson 12, Guthrie 12 (1 pen), Fosu 5, Szmodics 5, Eastman 3, Slater 3, Johnstone 2, Drey Wright 2, Bonne 1, Brindley 1, Elokobi 1, Garvan 1, own goals 3.
FA Cup (1): Fosu 1.
EFL Cup (0).
EFL Checkatrade Trophy (2): Bonne 1, Sembie-Ferris 1.

Walker S 46	Brindley R 40 + 1	Prosser L 14	Eastman T 35	Kinsella L 11 + 2	Wright Drey 31 + 11	Slater C 23 + 5	Lapslie T 37	Guthrie K 32 + 1	Porter C 32 + 6	Szmodics S 16 + 3	Johnstone D 15 + 13	Sembie-Ferris D — + 7	Bonne M 1 + 17	Dickenson B 35 + 1	Loft D 2 + 6	Wynter A 10 + 5	Fosu T 14 + 19	Kamara G 1 + 3	Vincent-Young K 6 + 12	Akinwande F — + 1	James C 13 + 1	Doyley L 2 + 1	Kent F 13	Elokobi G 29	Garvan O 18	Briggs M 11 + 4	Murray S 15 + 1	Pyke R 4 + 8	Edge C — + 1	O'Sullivan T — + 3	Match No.
1	2	3	4	5	6^{3}	7	8	9	10^{1}	11^{2}	12	13	14																		1
1	2	4	3	5	6	14	7	8^{2}	11^{3}	10^{1}	13			9	12																2
1	2	4	3	5	6	13	7	8^{2}	11^{1}	10^{3}	14			9	12																3
1	2	4	3	5	12	6^{3}	8	9^{2}	13		11^{1}		14	10	7																4
1	2	3	4	5	7	14	6^{3}	8	11^{1}	9^{2}	12			10		13															5
1	2	4	3	5^{3}	6^{1}		7	8	11^{2}	10	13	14		9			12														6
1	2	4	3	5^{2}	6	14	7^{1}	8^{3}	11	10				9			12	13													7
1	2	3	4	13	8^{3}	6		7	11	9^{1}				5			10^{2}	12	14												8
1	2	4	3	5	6	7		8^{1}	11^{3}	10	12			14			9^{2}			13											9
1	2^{2}	4	3	5	8	6		7	14	9	11^{1}	13					10^{3}		12												10
1	2	4	3	5	6^{3}	7		8	13	10^{2}	11	12					9^{1}	14													11
1	2		4	5^{1}	6	7		8	11^{3}	10	14	13				3	9^{2}				12										12
1	2	4	3		10	7		8^{3}	9^{1}	6	13	12	14			5			11^{2}												13
1	2	4	3		9	6		12	10	8^{2}	11^{1}		13			5	14		7^{3}												14
1	2	4			9	6^{3}		8	10	13	11^{1}		12			5	14		7^{2}			3									15
1	2^{3}		3		8	12	6	9			13		11^{2}	10		5	14	7^{1}					4								16
1	5		3		8^{3}	7	6^{2}	9			11^{1}	12	13	10		4	14		2												17
1	2^{2}		3		12	6	7	10			11^{1}			9			14		13				4	5	8^{3}						18
1	5^{2}		2		12	7	6	10			11^{3}		14	9					13				3	4	8^{1}						19
1	2		3		13	6^{1}	7	10		12	11^{2}			9									4	5	8						20
1	5^{1}		2		12	7^{3}	6	10			11^{2}		13	9					14				3	4	8						21
1	5^{2}		3		13	7^{3}	6	10	12		11^{1}			9					14				2	4	8						22
1	9^{3}		4		8^{2}		7	11	12		10^{1}			5			13					14	3	2	6						23
1	5^{2}		2		12	9^{3}	6	11	10^{1}				14	8			13						3	4	7						24
1	5^{3}		2		13	7^{2}	6	11	10^{1}		12			9			14						3	4	8						25
1	5		2			9^{1}	6	10^{2}	11		12			8			13						3	4	7						26
1	5^{1}		2		9^{2}	6	7^{3}	10	11		13			8			12		14				3	4							27
1	5^{3}		2			6^{2}	7	11^{1}	10		14								13				3	4	8	9	12■				28
1						8	7	10			11^{3}			6		12	14		2			3^{2}	4^{1}	5	9	13					29
1	5^{3}						6	10			11			9		2	7^{1}		12					3	8^{2}	4		13	14		30
1	2^{3}				13	6	8^{2}	9	12		10^{1}			11		3			5					4	7	14					31
1	5				12		6	11	10^{2}					9			13				2			3	8	4	7^{1}				32
1	5^{2}				12		6	10^{3}	11^{1}					8			13				2			3	7	4	9	14			33
1					8^{2}		7^{1}		10					5			11		13		4			3	6	2	9	12			34
1					5		7		10^{2}	13			14	9			11^{3}				3			2	8	4	6^{1}	12			35
1					5^{3}		6		11	10^{1}			14	9			12		13		2			4	8^{2}	3	7				36
1					5		6		10	7^{3}			13	9		12			14		2^{2}			3		4	8	11^{1}			37
1	14				6^{1}		7		10	9^{2}			13	5			12				3			4		2	8	11^{3}			38
1	5		4		8^{3}		6		10^{1}				14	9		12	13				2^{2}			3			7	11			39
1	5		4		8		6^{2}		10				13	9			14				2^{1}			3		12	7	11^{3}			40
1	5		3	14	7^{2}		6		10^{3}					9^{1}			11				2			4			8	13		12	41
1	5		2		11^{1}		6^{2}		10					8	14		9				3			4^{3}		13	7	12			42
1	5		2		9^{2}				11					8	6^{1}	12	10^{3}				3			4			7	14		13	43
1	5		2		10		6^{1}		11					8	13		9^{2}				3			4			7	12			44
1	5		2		10		6		11				12		13	3	8							4		9^{2}	7^{1}				45
1	5		2		10^{3}		6^{2}		11^{1}				13		12	3	9							4		8	7			14	46

FA Cup
First Round Chesterfield (h) 1-2

EFL Cup
First Round Brighton & HA (a) 0-4

EFL Checkatrade Trophy
Southern Group E Crawley T (a) 0-1
Southern Group E Southampton U21 (h) 1-2
Southern Group E Charlton Ath (h) 1-1
(*Colchester U won 4-3 on penalties*)

COVENTRY CITY

FOUNDATION

Workers at Singers' cycle factory formed a club in 1883. The first success of Singers' FC was to win the Birmingham Junior Cup in 1891 and this led in 1894 to their election to the Birmingham & District League. Four years later they changed their name to Coventry City and joined the Southern League in 1908 at which time they were playing in blue and white quarters.

Ricoh Arena, Phoenix Way, Coventry CV6 6GE.

Telephone: (02476) 991 987.

Fax: (02476) 303 872.

Ticket Office: (02476) 991 987.

Website: www.ccfc.co.uk

Email: info@ccfc.co.uk

Ground Capacity: 32,609.

Record Attendance: 51,455 v Wolverhampton W, Division 2, 29 April 1967 (at Highfield Road); 31,407 v Chelsea, FA Cup 6th rd, 7 March 2009 (at Ricoh Arena).

Pitch Measurements: 100m × 68m (109.5yd × 74.5yd).

Chairman: Tim Fisher.

Chief Operating Officer: Vicki Gough.

Manager: Mark Robins.

Assistant Manager: Steve Taylor.

Colours: Sky blue and white striped shirts, sky blue shorts, sky blue socks.

Year Formed: 1883.

Turned Professional: 1893.

Previous Name: 1883, Singers' FC; 1898, Coventry City.

Club Nickname: 'Sky Blues'.

Grounds: 1883, Binley Road; 1887, Stoke Road; 1899, Highfield Road; 2005, Ricoh Arena; 2013, Sixfields Stadium (groundshare with Northampton T); 2014, Ricoh Arena.

First Football League Game: 30 August 1919, Division 2, v Tottenham H (h) L 0–5 – Lindon; Roberts, Chaplin, Allan, Hawley, Clarke, Sheldon, Mercer, Sambrooke, Lowes, Gibson.

Record League Victory: 9–0 v Bristol C, Division 3 (S), 28 April 1934 – Pearson; Brown, Bisby; Perry, Davidson, Frith; White (2), Lauderdale, Bourton (5), Jones (2), Lake.

Record Cup Victory: 8–0 v Rushden & D, League Cup 2nd rd, 2 October 2002 – Debec; Caldwell, Quinn, Betts (1p), Konjic (Shaw), Davenport, Pipe, Safri (Stanford), Mills (2) (Bothroyd (2)), McSheffery (3), Partridge.

Record Defeat: 2–10 v Norwich C, Division 3 (S), 15 March 1930.

Most League Points (2 for a win): 60, Division 4, 1958–59 and Division 3, 1963–64.

HONOURS

League Champions: Division 2 – 1966–67; Division 3 – 1963–64; Division 3S – 1935–36.
Runners-up: Division 3S – 1933–34; Division 4 – 1958–59.

FA Cup Winners: 1987.

League Cup: semi-final – 1981, 1990.

League Trophy Winners: 2017.

European Competitions
Fairs Cup: 1970–71.

sky SPORTS FACT FILE

Coventry City's only venture into European football came in the 1970–71 season when they qualified for the Fairs Cup. They easily defeated Bulgarian club Trakia Plovdiv in the first round but were then drawn to play Bayern Munich. The Sky Blues lost the first leg 6-1 but gained some consolation with a 2-1 victory at Highfield Road in the second leg.

Most League Points (3 for a win): 69, FL 1, 2015–16.

Most League Goals: 108, Division 3 (S), 1931–32.

Highest League Scorer in Season: Clarrie Bourton, 49, Division 3 (S), 1931–32.

Most League Goals in Total Aggregate: Clarrie Bourton, 173, 1931–37.

Most League Goals in One Match: 5, Clarrie Bourton v Bournemouth, Division 3 (S), 17 October 1931; 5, Arthur Bacon v Gillingham, Division 3 (S), 30 December 1933.

Most Capped Player: Magnus Hedman, 44 (58), Sweden.

Most League Appearances: Steve Ogrizovic, 507, 1984–2000.

Youngest League Player: Ben Mackey, 16 years 167 days v Ipswich T, 12 April 2003.

Record Transfer Fee Received: £13,000,000 from Internazionale for Robbie Keane, July 2000.

Record Transfer Fee Paid: £6,500,000 to Norwich C for Craig Bellamy, August 2000.

Football League Record: 1919 Elected to Division 2; 1925–26 Division 3 (N); 1926–36 Division 3 (S); 1936–52 Division 2; 1952–58 Division 3 (S); 1958–59 Division 4; 1959–64 Division 3; 1964–67 Division 2; 1967–92 Division 1; 1992–2001 FA Premier League; 2001–04 Division 1; 2004–12 FL C; 2012–17 FL 1; 2017– FL 2.

LATEST SEQUENCES

Longest Sequence of League Wins: 6, 25.4.1964 – 5.9.1964.

Longest Sequence of League Defeats: 9, 30.8.1919 – 11.10.1919.

Longest Sequence of League Draws: 6, 1.11.2003 – 29.11.2003.

Longest Sequence of Unbeaten League Matches: 25, 26.11.1966 – 13.5.1967.

Longest Sequence Without a League Win: 19, 30.8.1919 – 20.12.1919.

Successive Scoring Runs: 25 from 10.9.1966.

Successive Non-scoring Runs: 11 from 11.10.1919.

MANAGERS

H. R. Buckle 1909–10
Robert Wallace 1910–13 (*Secretary-Manager*)
Frank Scott-Walford 1913–15
William Clayton 1917–19
H. Pollitt 1919–20
Albert Evans 1920–24
Jimmy Kerr 1924–28
James McIntyre 1928–31
Harry Storer 1931–45
Dick Bayliss 1945–47
Billy Frith 1947–48
Harry Storer 1948–53
Jack Fairbrother 1953–54
Charlie Elliott 1954–55
Jesse Carver 1955–56
George Raynor 1956
Harry Warren 1956–57
Billy Frith 1957–61
Jimmy Hill 1961–67
Noel Cantwell 1967–72
Bob Dennison 1972
Joe Mercer 1972–75
Gordon Milne 1972–81
Dave Sexton 1981–83
Bobby Gould 1983–84
Don Mackay 1985–86
George Curtis 1986–87 (*became Managing Director*)
John Sillett 1987–90
Terry Butcher 1990–92
Don Howe 1992
Bobby Gould 1992–93 (*with Don Howe, June 1992*)
Phil Neal 1993–95
Ron Atkinson 1995–96 (*became Director of Football*)
Gordon Strachan 1996–2001
Roland Nilsson 2001–02
Gary McAllister 2002–04
Eric Black 2004
Peter Reid 2004–05
Micky Adams 2005–07
Iain Dowie 2007–08
Chris Coleman 2008–10
Aidy Boothroyd 2010–11
Andy Thorn 2011–12
Mark Robins 2012–13
Steven Pressley 2013–15
Tony Mowbray 2015–16
Mark Robins March 2017–

TEN YEAR LEAGUE RECORD

		P	W	D	L	F	A	Pts	Pos
2007-08	FL C	46	14	11	21	52	64	53	21
2008-09	FL C	46	13	15	18	47	58	54	17
2009-10	FL C	46	13	15	18	47	64	54	19
2010-11	FL C	46	14	13	19	54	58	55	18
2011-12	FL C	46	9	13	24	41	65	40	23
2012-13	FL 1	46	18	11	17	66	59	55*	15
2013-14	FL 1	46	16	13	17	74	77	51*	18
2014-15	FL 1	46	13	16	17	49	60	55	17
2015-16	FL 1	46	19	12	15	67	49	69	8
2016-17	FL 1	46	9	12	25	37	68	39	23

** 10 pts deducted.*

DID YOU KNOW ?

Coventry City's 5-5 draw at Southampton in May 1982 was the first time a top flight game had produced a score draw of 10 goals since December 1966. Mark Hateley scored a hat-trick for the Sky Blues including a vital last-minute equaliser.

COVENTRY CITY – SKY BET LEAGUE ONE 2016–17 LEAGUE RECORD

Match No.	Date	Venue	Opponents	Result		H/T Score	Lg Pos.	Goalscorers	Attendance
1	Aug 6	A	Swindon T	L	0-1	0-0	17		9023
2	13	H	Shrewsbury T	D	0-0	0-0	18		10,296
3	16	H	Bury	D	0-0	0-0	18		9098
4	20	A	Bradford C	L	1-3	1-0	21	Agyei 13	17,595
5	27	H	Northampton T	D	1-1	0-1	22	Tudgay 63	10,022
6	Sept 3	A	Fleetwood T	L	0-2	0-0	23		3557
7	10	A	Millwall	D	1-1	1-0	23	Sordell 23	8755
8	17	H	Oldham Ath	D	0-0	0-0	24		8813
9	24	A	Gillingham	L	1-2	1-1	24	Reid 21	7664
10	28	H	AFC Wimbledon	D	2-2	1-1	24	Sordell 2, Wright 90	8030
11	Oct 1	A	Port Vale	W	2-0	1-0	23	Sordell 36, McCann 72	5605
12	15	A	Charlton Ath	L	0-3	0-1	24		11,406
13	18	H	Oxford U	W	2-1	2-0	23	Stevenson 28, Sordell 43	9912
14	22	H	Rochdale	W	2-0	1-0	21	Agyei 28, Wright 84	8133
15	29	A	Walsall	D	1-1	1-0	19	Rose 36	6719
16	Nov 1	H	Chesterfield	W	2-0	0-0	18	Willis 69, Rose 81	7941
17	12	H	Scunthorpe U	L	0-1	0-0	18		9737
18	19	A	Oxford U	L	1-4	0-3	19	Tudgay (pen) 90	9199
19	22	A	Bolton W	L	0-1	0-1	19		12,290
20	26	H	Milton Keynes D	L	1-2	1-1	21	Stevenson 38	9640
21	Dec 10	A	Southend U	L	1-3	0-1	21	Agyei 89	6430
22	15	H	Sheffield U	L	1-2	0-1	21	Agyei 51	8801
23	26	A	Bristol R	L	1-4	0-1	23	Willis 57	11,200
24	31	A	Peterborough U	D	1-1	1-0	23	Willis 19	5866
25	Jan 2	H	Bolton W	D	2-2	1-0	22	Tudgay 37, Beavon 69	8397
26	14	A	Chesterfield	L	0-1	0-0	24		5896
27	21	H	Fleetwood T	L	0-1	0-0	24		8129
28	28	A	Northampton T	L	0-3	0-0	24		7543
29	Feb 4	H	Millwall	L	0-2	0-1	24		8764
30	11	A	Oldham Ath	L	2-3	1-1	24	Tudgay 9, Thomas, K 76	3766
31	14	A	AFC Wimbledon	D	1-1	0-0	24	Jones 71	4022
32	18	H	Gillingham	W	2-1	2-0	24	Thomas, K 16, Thomas, G 21	8718
33	25	H	Swindon T	L	1-3	0-2	24	Thomas, G 90	9543
34	28	A	Bury	L	1-2	0-2	24	Beavon 65	2611
35	Mar 4	A	Shrewsbury T	D	0-0	0-0	24		6205
36	11	H	Bradford C	L	0-2	0-0	24		9150
37	14	H	Southend U	L	0-2	0-2	24		7646
38	18	A	Milton Keynes D	L	0-1	0-0	24		9060
39	21	H	Port Vale	W	2-1	2-0	24	Reid 37, Thomas, K 41	7695
40	25	H	Bristol R	W	1-0	0-0	24	Thomas, G 80	11,946
41	Apr 5	A	Sheffield U	L	0-2	0-0	24		24,334
42	8	H	Peterborough U	W	1-0	0-0	24	Lameiras 51	10,551
43	14	H	Charlton Ath	D	1-1	1-0	24	Thomas, G 28	9479
44	17	A	Rochdale	L	0-2	0-1	24		3202
45	22	H	Walsall	W	1-0	1-0	23	Thomas, G 39	9284
46	30	A	Scunthorpe U	L	1-3	1-0	23	Gadzhev 36	5796

Final League Position: 23

GOALSCORERS

League (37): Thomas, G 5, Agyei 4, Sordell 4, Tudgay 4 (1 pen), Thomas, K 3, Willis 3, Beavon 2, Reid 2, Rose 2, Stevenson 2, Wright 2, Gadzhev 1, Jones 1, Lameiras 1, McCann 1.
FA Cup (3): Sordell 2, Sterry 1.
EFL Cup (4): Gadzhev 1, Haynes 1, Lameiras 1 (1 pen), Rose 1.
EFL Checkatrade Trophy (20): Thomas, G 4, Haynes 3, Lameiras 3, Bigirimana 2, Turnbull 2, Willis 2, Agyei 1, Beavon 1, Jones 1, Sordell 1.

Charles-Cook R 13+2	Willis J 36	Ricketts S 6+1	Harries C 6+2	Kelly-Evans Dion 13+12	Rose A 19+2	Gadzhev V 13+1	Haynes R 17+2	Jones J 11+23	Sordell M 18+2	Thomas G 23+5	Reid K 19+10	Lameiras R 14+13	Thomas K 8+6	Stevenson B 22+6	Page L 22	Tudgay M 21+7	Spence K —+1	McCann C 13	Turnbull J 36	Agyei D 12+4	Bigirimana G 28+2	Sterry J 16	Wright A 7+4	Burge L 33	Maycock C —+3	McBean J —+2	Clarke N 18	Reilly C 17+1	Beavon S 13+1	Foley K 11+1	Rawson F 12+2	Vernam C 3+1	Yakubu A —+3	Stokes C 5+2	Shipley J —+1	Camwell C 1	Folivi M —+1	Match No.
1	2	3	4	5	6	7	8	9[1]	10[3]	11[2]	12	13	14																									1
1	2	3	4		5	7		9[2]			10[3]	11[1]	14	6	8	12	13																					2
1	2	3	4	12	5[3]	6	8	13		11[2]	14	9[1]				10		7																				3
1	2	3[2]	13	5		7				14	11[1]			6	9	12		8	4■	10[3]																		4
1	2		4[1]	5		6		12	9[3]		13				8	11		7	3	10[2]	14																	5
1	2		4			7[2]			11					13	9	12		8[3]	3	10[1]	6	5	14															6
1	4	2		12		7		13	11		9[2]	10[3]			5[1]				3	14	8	6																7
1	3			13		7[3]		8	11		9[2]	12		14	5	10			4		6	2[1]																8
1	2	4		5[2]		7[1]		12	10		9			13	8				3	14	6		11[3]															9
1	3							12	11		8[3]			6[1]	5	10[2]		9	4	13	7	2	14															10
	3								9[2]			12		6	5	13		8	4	11[1]	7	2	10	1														11
	3[3]	12						14	11		13	8		7	5[2]			9	4		6	2	10[1]	1														12
	3								10		13	9[2]		6	5	12		8	4	11[1]	7	2		1														13
	3							14	11[1]		12	9		6	5			8[2]	4	10[3]	7	2	13	1														14
	3				7[2]			12	11		14	9[3]		8	5				4	10[1]	6	2	13	1														15
	3				12			8[1]	14		10	13		7	5■	11[3]			4	9[2]	6	2		1														16
	3				6[1]			13	10		14	12		8	5				4	11[2]	7	2	9[3]	1														17
	3		12			8[2]			10			11[3]		6[1]	5	14			4		7	2	9	1	13													18
	3		7[3]					12	10		9[2]	13		6	5				4	11[1]	8	2		1		14												19
	3			2	6[1]			9[3]			11	14		8■	5	10[2]			4		7			1	12	13												20
12	3			2	6			13	11[1]						5			8[3]	4	10	7		9	1[2]	14													21
1	3			2	6				10	12		13			5			8	4	9[1]	7		11[2]															22
	3				6				11	12	9				5	10[1]		7	4	13	8[2]	2		1														23
	2			12	7			13	14	11[2]	9			6	4[1]	10[3]		8	3			5		1														24
					7		5			6	9[1]	12				11			4		13	2		1			3	8	10[2]									25
	3			13	7		5			6	9			12		11								1			4	8[1]	10	2[2]								26
	5				6[1]		9	12		10		13		7					4					1			3	8	11[2]		2							27
	2■			12	13		8	14		5[1]				6[3]		10[2]								1			4	7	11		3	9						28
					7[2]	13	5	12		6	9					11[1]								1			4	8	10	2	3							29
1					8	11[3]	5	13		6[2]	9[1]	14	12			10											4	7		2	3							30
				2	9			13		7[1]			10			11[2]			5					1			4	8		6	3		12					31
12				2	8		5	13		7[2]			10[1]			11			4					1[3]			3	9		6			14					32
				2	8[2]		5			7	14		10[3]			11[1]			4					1			3	9	12	6			13					33
	2			12			13	14		6[3]			10						5					1			3	7	11	8	4[1]	9[2]						34
				2	7[2]		5	13		11			9[1]	12					3		6			1			4	8	10									35
				12				13		6			9	7					4					1			3	8	11	2[3]	14	10[2]		5[1]				36
				5			9			13			12	7		11			4[1]		6[2]			1			3	8	10		2							37
	2[1]			13			14	10		6		8		7		11[3]								1			4	9			3	12		5[2]				38
	2						5	12		6	9[1]		10								7			1			3	8	11[2]		4			13				39
	2[3]			12			5	6[2]		10	9[1]	13									7			1			3	8	11		4			14				40
	2[2]						9[1]	8		13		10		12		11			4		7			1			3			6				5				41
							5	12		6	9[2]	10		8[1]					4		7			1			3	13	11	2								42
	2[3]						5	9[1]		6	14	10	12	7					3		8			1					11[2]	13	4							43
	2[1]			14						9	10[3]	12	11[2]	6		13			3		7			1				8			4			5				44
1	3			14		7[1]		10		8		9				11			4		6									2[3]	12			5[2]	13			45
	2			4		8		9[1]		11[2]		6	12			10			3		7			1												5	13	46

FA Cup

First Round	Morecambe	(a)	1-1
Replay	Morecambe	(h)	2-1
Second Round	Cambridge U	(a)	0-4

EFL Cup

First Round (*aet*)	Portsmouth	(h)	3-2
Second Round	Norwich C	(a)	1-6

EFL Checkatrade Trophy

Southern Group D	West Ham U U21	(h)	4-2
Southern Group D	Northampton T	(h)	3-1
Southern Group D	Wycombe W	(a)	4-2
Second Round South	Crawley T	(h)	1-0
Third Round	Brighton & HA U21	(h)	3-0
Quarter-Final	Swansea C U21	(a)	1-1
(*Coventry C won 4-2 on penalties*)			
Semi-Final	Wycombe W	(h)	2-1
Final	Oxford U	(Wembley)	2-1

CRAWLEY TOWN

FOUNDATION

Formed in 1896, Crawley Town initially entered the West Sussex League before switching to the mid-Sussex League in 1901, winning the Second Division in its second season. The club remained at such level until 1951 when it became members of the Sussex County League and five years later moved to the Metropolitan League while remaining as an amateur club. It was not until 1962 that the club turned semi-professional and a year later, joined the Southern League. Many honours came the club's way, but the most successful run was achieved in 2010–11 when they reached the fifith round of the FA Cup and played before a crowd of 74,778 spectators at Old Trafford against Manchester United. Crawley Town spent 48 years at the Town Mead ground before a new site was occupied at Broadfield in 1997, ideally suited to access from the neighbouring motorway. History was also made on 9 April when the team won promotion to the Football League after beating Tamworth 3-0 to stretch their unbeaten League record to 26 games. They finished the season with a Conference record points total of 105 and at the same time, established another milestone for the longest unbeaten run, having extended it to 30 matches by the end of the season.

Checkatrade.com Stadium, Winfield Way, Crawley, West Sussex RH11 9RX.

Telephone: (01293) 410 000.

Fax: (01293) 410 002.

Ticket Office: (01293) 410 005.

Website: www.crawleytownfc.com

Email: feedback@crawleytownfc.com

Ground Capacity: 5,748.

Record Attendance: 5,880 v Reading, FA Cup 3rd rd, 5 January 2013.

Pitch Measurements: 103.5m × 66m (113yd × 72yd).

Chairman: Ziya Eren.

Operations Director: Kelly Derham.

Manager: Harry Kewell.

Assistant Manager: Warren Feeney.

Colours: Red shirts with black trim, red shorts with black trim, red socks with black trim.

Year Formed: 1896. ***Turned Professional:*** 1962.

Club Nickname: 'The Red Devils'.

Grounds: Up to 1997, Town Mead; 1997 Broadfield Stadium (renamed Checkatrade.com Stadium 2013).

First Football League Game: 6 August 2011, FL 2 v Port Vale (a) D 2-2 – Shearer; Hunt, Howell, Bulman, McFadzean (1), Dempster (Thomas), Simpson, Torres, Tubbs (Neilson), Barnett (1) (Wassmer), Smith.

HONOURS

League Champions: Conference – 2010–11.
FL 2 – (3rd) 2011–12 *(promoted).*

FA Cup: 5th rd – 2011, 2012.

League Cup: 3rd rd – 2013.

sky SPORTS FACT FILE

Barry Hines, author of *A Kestrel for a Knave* which was turned into the award-winning film *Kes*, turned out for Crawley Town in the closing stages of the 1961–62 season. An amateur, he made 11 first team appearances in Metropolitan League and League Cup games.

Record League Victory: 5–1 v Barnsley, FL 1, 14 February 2015 – Price; Dickson, Bradley (1), Ward, Fowler (Smith); Young, Elliott (1), Edwards, Wordsworth (Morgan), Pogba (Tomlin); McLeod (3).

Record League Defeat: 6-0 v Morecambe, FL 2, 10 September 2011.

Most League Points (3 for a win): 84, FL 2, 2011–12.

Most League Goals: 76, FL 2, 2011–12.

Highest League Scorer in Season: James Collins, 20, FL 2, 2016–17.

Most League Goals in Total Aggregate: Billy Clarke, 20, 2011–14; Matt Tubbs, 20, 2011–12, 2013–14.

Most League Goals in One Match: 3, Izale McLeod v Barnsley, FL 1, 14 February 2015; 3, Jimmy Smith v Colchester U, FL 2, 14 February 2017.

Most Capped Player: Dean Morgan, 1 (3), Montserrat.

Most League Appearances: Josh Simpson, 122, 2011–15.

Youngest League Player: Hiram Boateng, 18 years 55 days v Stevenage, 4 March 2014.

Record Transfer Fee Received: £1,100,000 from Peterborough U for Tyrone Barnett, July 2012.

Record Transfer Fee Paid: £220,000 to York C for Richard Brodie, August 2010.

Football League Record: 2011 Promoted from Conference Premier; 2011–12 FL 2; 2012–15 FL 1; 2015– FL 2.

MANAGERS

John Maggs 1978–90
Brian Sparrow 1990–92
Steve Wicks 1992–93
Ted Shepherd 1993–95
Colin Pates 1995–96
Billy Smith 1997–99
Cliff Cant 1999–2000
Billy Smith 2000–03
Francis Vines 2003–05
John Hollins 2005–06
David Woozley, Ben Judge and John Yems 2006–07
Steve Evans 2007–12
Sean O'Driscoll 2012
Richie Barker 2012–13
John Gregory 2013–14
Dean Saunders 2014–15
Mark Yates 2015–16
Dermot Drummy 2016–17
Harry Kewell May 2017–

LATEST SEQUENCES

Longest Sequence of League Wins: 7, 17.9.2011 – 25.10.2011.

Longest Sequence of League Defeats: 8, 28.3.2016 – 7.5.2016.

Longest Sequence of League Draws: 5, 25.10.2014 – 29.11.2014.

Longest Sequence of Unbeaten League Matches: 13, 17.9.2011 – 17.12.2011.

Longest Sequence Without a League Win: 13, 25.10.2014 – 27.1.2015.

Successive Scoring Runs: 16 from 17.9.2011.

Successive Non-scoring Runs: 4 from 22.10.2013.

TEN YEAR LEAGUE RECORD

		P	*W*	*D*	*L*	*F*	*A*	*Pts*	*Pos*
2007-08	Conf P	46	19	9	18	73	67	60	15
2008-09	Conf P	46	19	14	13	77	55	70	9
2009-10	Conf P	44	19	9	16	50	57	66	7
2010-11	Conf P	46	31	12	3	93	50	105	1
2011-12	FL 2	46	23	15	8	76	54	84	3
2012-13	FL 1	46	18	14	14	59	58	68	10
2013-14	FL 1	46	14	15	17	48	54	57	14
2014-15	FL 1	46	13	11	22	53	79	50	22
2015-16	FL 2	46	13	8	25	45	78	47	20
2016-17	FL 2	46	13	12	21	53	71	51	19

DID YOU KNOW?

Crawley Town were elected to the Southern League for the 1963–64 season, initially playing in Division One (the second tier). Their first game in the competition took place on 24 August 1963 when they won 3-2 at Dover.

CRAWLEY TOWN – SKY BET LEAGUE TWO 2016–17 LEAGUE RECORD

Match No.	Date	Venue	Opponents	Result		H/T Score	Lg Pos.	Goalscorers	Attendance
1	Aug 6	H	Wycombe W	W	1-0	0-0	8	Smith[59]	2471
2	13	A	Doncaster R	D	1-1	1-0	8	Collins[26]	4327
3	16	A	Exeter C	W	1-0	0-0	4	Yorwerth[83]	2660
4	20	H	Barnet	D	1-1	0-1	2	McNerney[67]	1929
5	27	H	Notts Co	L	1-3	0-0	9	Boldewijn[47]	2087
6	Sept 3	A	Portsmouth	L	0-3	0-3	13		16,347
7	10	A	Stevenage	L	1-2	0-1	18	Collins[86]	2157
8	17	H	Luton T	W	2-0	1-0	13	Collins[43], Boldewijn[90]	2904
9	24	A	Morecambe	W	3-2	0-0	11	Yussuf[72], Collins[83], Smith[90]	1304
10	27	H	Colchester U	D	1-1	1-0	12	Yussuf[18]	1851
11	Oct 1	H	Blackpool	W	1-0	0-0	5	Connolly[69]	2300
12	8	A	Hartlepool U	D	1-1	0-1	6	Collins (pen)[74]	3693
13	15	A	Cheltenham T	L	1-2	0-1	9	Djalo[78]	2678
14	22	H	Accrington S	D	0-0	0-0	9		2092
15	29	A	Carlisle U	L	1-3	0-3	10	Connolly[90]	5619
16	Nov 12	H	Cambridge U	L	1-3	1-2	12	Collins[8]	2408
17	19	A	Mansfield T	L	1-3	0-0	16	Bennett (og)[82]	2984
18	26	H	Grimsby T	W	3-2	1-1	16	Collins[31], Roberts 2[56, 79]	2315
19	Dec 3	A	Yeovil T	L	0-5	0-3	16		2817
20	10	A	Crewe Alex	W	2-0	1-0	15	Collins 2[21, 75]	3392
21	17	H	Newport Co	W	3-1	1-1	11	Collins[3], Yorwerth[48], Smith[52]	2022
22	26	A	Leyton Orient	L	2-3	0-3	12	Mezague (og)[54], Boldewijn[78]	4486
23	31	A	Plymouth Arg	L	0-2	0-0	15		9039
24	Jan 2	H	Yeovil T	W	2-0	2-0	13	Yorwerth[29], Collins (pen)[38]	2304
25	14	H	Hartlepool U	W	1-0	0-0	13	Collins[63]	4266
26	28	A	Notts Co	L	1-2	0-0	15	Collins[86]	5023
27	Feb 4	H	Stevenage	L	1-2	1-0	16	Collins (pen)[28]	2124
28	7	A	Blackpool	D	0-0	0-0	16		2080
29	11	A	Luton T	L	1-2	0-0	17	Collins[60]	7316
30	14	A	Colchester U	W	3-2	2-1	15	Smith 3[23, 34, 51]	2675
31	18	H	Morecambe	L	1-3	0-3	16	Collins (pen)[77]	2091
32	25	A	Wycombe W	W	2-1	1-1	16	McNerney[43], Payne[84]	3206
33	28	H	Exeter C	L	1-2	0-0	16	Connolly[90]	1826
34	Mar 4	H	Doncaster R	D	0-0	0-0	16		2417
35	7	H	Portsmouth	L	0-2	0-0	16		5350
36	11	A	Barnet	D	2-2	1-1	16	Murphy[31], Boldewijn[54]	1701
37	14	H	Crewe Alex	L	0-3	0-1	17		1566
38	18	A	Grimsby T	D	1-1	1-1	19	Collins[45]	4263
39	25	H	Leyton Orient	W	3-0	3-0	17	Collins[23], McNerney[29], Boldewijn[32]	2918
40	Apr 1	A	Newport Co	L	0-1	0-1	18		2946
41	8	H	Plymouth Arg	L	1-2	1-0	18	Cox[28]	3432
42	14	H	Cheltenham T	D	0-0	0-0	18		2008
43	17	A	Accrington S	L	0-1	0-0	19		1652
44	22	H	Carlisle U	D	3-3	2-2	19	Collins 2 (1 pen)[12, 25 (p)], Smith[90]	2003
45	29	A	Cambridge U	L	0-2	0-1	21		5675
46	May 6	H	Mansfield T	D	2-2	1-2	19	Cox[34], Roberts[55]	2635

Final League Position: 19

GOALSCORERS

League (53): Collins 20 (5 pens), Smith 7, Boldewijn 5, Connolly 3, McNerney 3, Roberts 3, Yorwerth 3, Cox 2, Yussuf 2, Djalo 1, Murphy 1, Payne 1, own goals 2.
FA Cup (3): Clifford 1, Harrold 1, Roberts 1.
EFL Cup (1): Boldewijn 1.
EFL Checkatrade Trophy (3): Collins 2, Yussuf 1.

Mersin Y 6 + 2	Young L 42 + 1	Connolly M 40 + 1	McNerney J 33 + 1	Blackman A 31 + 1	Smith J 46	Banton J 11 + 3	Payne J 23 + 9	Roberts J 14 + 9	Collins J 45	Boldewijn E 43 + 3	Clifford B 26 + 10	Harrold M 1 + 10	Yussuf A 6 + 10	Davey A 8 + 6	Bawling B 2 + 27	Yorwerth J 14 + 7	Arthur C 3 + 3	Beeney M 1	Morris G 39	Djalo K 24 + 4	Tajbakhsh A 2 + 2	Garnett A 1 + 1	Henderson C 8 + 4	Watt S — + 2	Cox D 20 + 2	Lelan J 10 + 3	Murphy R 7 + 8	*Match No.*
1	2	3	4	5■	6	7[1]	8	9	10[2]	11[3]	12	13	14															1
1	2		3	5	7	10[1]	8		11[2]	6	9[3]	14		4	12	13												2
1	2	4		5	8	9[2]	7[3]		11	6	10[1]	12		3	14	13												3
1	2		4	5	7	11	6[2]		10	9[1]	8[3]	14	12	3		13												4
1	2	12	4	5	8	11[1]			10	9	7[2]		13	3	14	6[3]												5
1	2	3		5[1]	8	6	12		10	9			11[2]	4	14	7[3]	13											6
	2	4	3	12	8	9[2]	7		10.	6[1]	11		13		14		5[3]	1										7
	2	3	4	5[3]	6	11[1]		13	10	9	7[2]			14			12		1	8								8
	5	3	4	2	7	9[1]			11	6[3]	10[2]		12	13	14				1	8								9
	2	3	4	5	6	13			11	8[3]	9[1]		10[2]	12	14				1	7								10
	2	3	4	5	6	12			11	10[1]	9[3]		8[2]	14	13				1	7								11
	2	3	4	5[2]	7	10[1]			11	6	8				12		13		1	9								12
	2	3	4		6[3]	11[2]			10	8	9[1]		14		12		5		1	7	13							13
	2	3[2]	4	5	7				11	8[1]	9		12	13	10[3]				1	6	14							14
	2	4		5	7	14			10	6	12		11[2]	3	13				1	8[1]	9[3]							15
	2	3[3]			6			14	11	10[1]	9		13	4	8[2]		5		1	7		12						16
	2	3[2]		5	7			9	10	6[1]	8	11		12[3]	13				1	14		4						17
	2	3		5	6		7	10[3]	11	12	9[2]	14	8[1]			4			1	13								18
		4		5[3]	7		6	10[2]	11	13	9		8	3	12				1		2[1]		14					19
	2	3		5	7		6	10[2]	11	8[1]	9		13		12	4			1									20
	2	3		5	6		7	10[2]	11	8[3]	9[1]		13		12	4			1	14								21
	2	3	12	5[1]	6		7	10[2]	11	8	9				13	4			1									22
	5	3[2]	2		7		8[3]	9	11	10	6[1]				13	4			1	12				14				23
	5	2	3		6		8	12	11	10[3]	7[1]				14	4			1					13	9[2]			24
	5	2	3		6		8	12	10	11[1]	7[2]				13	4			1				14		9[3]			25
	2	5	4		8		7	12	11	9[1]	10[2]				13	3			1						6			26
		2	3		6		8[1]	9[2]	11	10[3]	13				14	4			1						7	5	12	27
		2	3	8[1]	6			9	11[3]	12					13				1	10			4		7[2]	5	14	28
	2	4			7		14	5	11	6[1]					13				1	9[2]			8[3]		10	3	12	29
	2	4			7[2]		13	5	11	6					12				1	8			9		10[1]	3		30
	2	3			8			5	11	7	13				14				1	9[3]			6		10[2]	4[1]	12	31
	12	3	4	5[3]	6		14		11	8						13			1	7[2]			9		10	2[1]		32
	2	3	4	5	8[1]		14		11	7	13								1	9[2]			6		10[3]		12	33
	5	3	4		7		6		11	8	9[1]								1						10	2	12	34
	5	3	4		7		8[1]		11	6[3]	12				14				1				13		9[2]	2	10	35
	5	4	3		8		13		11	6[2]					12				1				7		9	2	10[1]	36
	5	3[3]	4		7[2]		14		10	6	13					12			1				8		9[1]	2	11	37
	2		3	5[2]	6		7		11	8		13				4			1	9[1]						12	10	38
	2		4	5[1]	7		8		11	6[2]	12					3			1	9[3]					14	13	10	39
	2		3	5	6		7[3]		11	9		13				4■			1	8[1]			14		12		10[2]	40
	2	3	4	5	6		13		10■	9	7[3]	12							1	8[1]					11[2]		14	41
	2	3[3]	4	5	6		13	12		8	9								1	7[2]					11	14	10[1]	42
	2	4	3	5	9[2]		7	12	11	8	13								1	6[3]					10[1]		14	43
13	2	3[1]	4	5	6		7	14	10	9						12			1[3]	8[2]					11			44
12	2	3	4	5	9		6■	14	11	8[2]		13							1[1]	7[3]					10			45
	2	3[2]	4	5	6			10	11	8	13	14				12			1	7[3]					9[1]			46

FA Cup

First Round	Bristol R	(h)	1-1
Replay	Bristol R	(a)	2-4
(*aet*)			

EFL Cup

First Round	Wolverhampton W	(a)	1-2

EFL Checkatrade Trophy

Southern Group E	Colchester U	(h)	1-0
Southern Group E	Charlton Ath	(a)	2-0
Southern Group E	Southampton U21	(a)	0-4
Second Round South	Coventry C	(a)	0-1

CREWE ALEXANDRA

FOUNDATION

The first match played at Crewe was on 1 December 1877 against Basford, the leading North Staffordshire team of that time. During the club's history they have also played in a number of other leagues including the Football Alliance, Football Combination, Lancashire League, Manchester League, Central League and Lancashire Combination. Two former players, Aaron Scragg in 1899 and Jackie Pearson in 1911, had the distinction of refereeing FA Cup finals. Pearson was also capped for England against Ireland in 1892.

The Alexandra Stadium, Gresty Road, Crewe, Cheshire CW2 6EB.

Telephone: (01270) 213 014.

Fax: (01270) 216 320.

Ticket Office: (01270) 252 610.

Website: www.crewealex.net

Email: info@crewealex.net

Ground Capacity: 10,109.

Record Attendance: 20,000 v Tottenham H, FA Cup 4th rd, 30 January 1960.

Pitch Measurements: 100.5m × 67m (110yd × 73yd).

Chairman: John Bowler MBE.

Vice-chairman: David Rowlinson.

Manager: David Artell.

Assistant Manager: Kenny Lunt.

Colours: Red and white hooped shirts with black trim, white shorts with red trim, red socks with white trim.

Year Formed: 1877. ***Turned Professional:*** 1893. ***Club Nickname:*** 'The Railwaymen'.

Ground: 1898, Gresty Road.

First Football League Game: 3 September 1892, Division 2, v Burton Swifts (a) L 1–7 – Hickton; Moore, Cope; Linnell, Johnson, Osborne; Bennett, Pearson (1), Bailey, Barnett, Roberts.

Record League Victory: 8–0 v Rotherham U, Division 3 (N), 1 October 1932 – Foster; Pringle, Dawson; Ward, Keenor (1), Turner (1); Gillespie, Swindells (1), McConnell (2), Deacon (2), Weale (1).

Record Cup Victory: 8–0 v Hartlepool U, Auto Windscreens Shield 1st rd, 17 October 1995 – Gayle; Collins (1), Booty, Westwood (Unsworth), Macauley (1), Whalley (1), Garvey (1), Murphy (1), Savage (1) (Rivers (1p)), Lennon, Edwards, (1 og). 8–0 v Doncaster R, LDV Vans Trophy 3rd rd, 10 November 2002 – Bankole; Wright, Walker, Foster, Tierney; Lunt (1), Brammer, Sorvel, Vaughan (1) (Bell); Ashton (3) (Miles), Jack (2) (Jones (1)).

Record Defeat: 2–13 v Tottenham H, FA Cup 4th rd replay, 3 February 1960.

HONOURS

League: *Runners-up:* Second Division – 2002–03.

FA Cup: semi-final – 1888.

League Cup: never past 3rd rd.

League Trophy Winners: 2013.

Welsh Cup Winners: 1936, 1937.

sky SPORTS FACT FILE

Crewe Alexandra topped the Fourth Division table after a 1-1 draw with Barnsley on 25 September 1974. They then went into a run which saw them gain just a single victory in the following 17 games by which time they had slipped into the bottom four of the table.

Most League Points (2 for a win): 59, Division 4, 1962–63.

Most League Points (3 for a win): 86, Division 2, 2002–03.

Most League Goals: 95, Division 3 (N), 1931–32.

Highest League Scorer in Season: Terry Harkin, 35, Division 4, 1964–65.

Most League Goals in Total Aggregate: Bert Swindells, 126, 1928–37.

Most League Goals in One Match: 5, Tony Naylor v Colchester U, Division 3, 24 April 1993.

Most Capped Player: Clayton Ince, 38 (79), Trinidad & Tobago.

Most League Appearances: Tommy Lowry, 436, 1966–78.

Youngest League Player: Steve Walters, 16 years 119 days v Peterborough U, 6 May 1988.

Record Transfer Fee Received: £3,000,000 (rising to £6,000,000) from Manchester U for Nick Powell, June 2012.

Record Transfer Fee Paid: £650,000 to Torquay U for Rodney Jack, June 1998.

Football League Record: 1892 Original Member of Division 2; 1896 Failed re-election; 1921 Re-entered Division (N); 1958–63 Division 4; 1963–64 Division 3; 1964–68 Division 4; 1968–69 Division 3; 1969–89 Division 4; 1989–91 Division 3; 1991–92 Division 4; 1992–94 Division 3; 1994–97 Division 2; 1997–2002 Division 1; 2002–03 Division 2; 2003–04 Division 1; 2004–06 FL C; 2006–09 FL 1; 2009–12 FL 2; 2012–16 FL 1; 2016– FL 2.

LATEST SEQUENCES

Longest Sequence of League Wins: 7, 30.4.1994 – 3.9.1994.

Longest Sequence of League Defeats: 10, 16.4.1979 – 22.8.1979.

Longest Sequence of League Draws: 5, 18.9.2010 – 9.10.2010.

Longest Sequence of Unbeaten League Matches: 17, 25.3.1995 – 16.9.1995.

Longest Sequence Without a League Win: 30, 22.9.1956 – 6.4.1957.

Successive Scoring Runs: 26 from 7.4.1934.

Successive Non-scoring Runs: 9 from 6.11.1974.

MANAGERS

W. C. McNeill 1892–94 (*Secretary-Manager*)
J. G. Hall 1895–96 (*Secretary-Manager*)
R. Roberts (*1st team Secretary-Manager*) 1897
J. B. Blomerley 1898–1911 (*Secretary-Manager, continued as Hon. Secretary to 1925*)
Tom Bailey (*Secretary only*) 1925–38
George Lillycrop (*Trainer*) 1938–44
Frank Hill 1944–48
Arthur Turner 1948–51
Harry Catterick 1951–53
Ralph Ward 1953–55
Maurice Lindley 1956–57
Willie Cook 1957–58
Harry Ware 1958–60
Jimmy McGuigan 1960–64
Ernie Tagg 1964–71 (*continued as Secretary to 1972*)
Dennis Viollet 1971
Jimmy Melia 1972–74
Ernie Tagg 1974
Harry Gregg 1975–78
Warwick Rimmer 1978–79
Tony Waddington 1979–81
Arfon Griffiths 1981–82
Peter Morris 1982–83
Dario Gradi 1983–2007
Steve Holland 2007–08
Gudjon Thordarson 2008–09
Dario Gradi 2009–11
Steve Davis 2011–17
David Artell January 2017–

TEN YEAR LEAGUE RECORD

		P	W	D	L	F	A	Pts	Pos
2007-08	FL 1	46	12	14	20	47	65	50	20
2008-09	FL 1	46	12	10	24	59	82	46	22
2009-10	FL 2	46	15	10	21	68	73	55	18
2010-11	FL 2	46	18	11	17	87	65	65	10
2011-12	FL 2	46	20	12	14	67	59	72	7
2012-13	FL 1	46	18	10	18	54	62	64	13
2013-14	FL 1	46	13	12	21	54	80	51	19
2014-15	FL 1	46	14	10	22	43	75	52	20
2015-16	FL 1	46	7	13	26	46	83	34	24
2016-17	FL 2	46	14	13	19	58	67	55	17

DID YOU KNOW ?

Crewe Alexandra were one of a number of English clubs that entered the Welsh Cup in the 1930s. They won the trophy twice, in 1936 and 1937, on the latter occasion recording a 9-2 victory over Llay Welfare en route to victory over Rhyl in the final.

CREWE ALEXANDRA – SKY BET LEAGUE TWO 2016–17 LEAGUE RECORD

Match No.	*Date*	*Venue*	*Opponents*	*Result*		*H/T Score*	*Lg Pos.*	*Goalscorers*	*Attendance*
1	Aug 6	A	Stevenage	W	2-1	0-0	7	Lowe [64], Kiwomya [80]	2544
2	13	H	Portsmouth	D	0-0	0-0	9		4742
3	16	H	Hartlepool U	D	3-3	2-1	8	Dagnall [31], Kiwomya [45], Cooper [56]	3482
4	20	A	Newport Co	D	1-1	1-0	9	Kiwomya [16]	2268
5	27	A	Cheltenham T	L	0-2	0-2	16		2623
6	Sept 3	H	Doncaster R	W	2-1	1-0	10	Lowe [14], Jones [87]	3830
7	10	H	Exeter C	W	2-0	1-0	6	Kiwomya [23], Hollands [87]	3896
8	17	A	Grimsby T	W	2-0	1-0	3	Cooper [45], Jones [85]	5289
9	24	H	Blackpool	D	1-1	0-1	4	Lowe [71]	4185
10	27	A	Wycombe W	L	1-5	0-3	8	Cooper [71]	2572
11	Oct 1	H	Mansfield T	D	1-1	0-0	8	Dagnall [56]	3831
12	8	A	Luton T	D	1-1	0-1	7	Lowe [64]	7716
13	15	A	Notts Co	D	1-1	0-0	8	Kiwomya [81]	8012
14	22	H	Yeovil T	L	0-1	0-0	12		3659
15	29	A	Leyton Orient	W	2-0	2-0	7	Cooper [34], Davis [42]	4366
16	Nov 12	H	Plymouth Arg	L	1-2	1-1	7	Kiwomya [16]	4573
17	19	A	Barnet	D	0-0	0-0	9		1603
18	22	H	Morecambe	W	2-1	2-1	7	Kiwomya [19], Jones [42]	2844
19	26	A	Colchester U	L	0-4	0-1	10		2931
20	Dec 10	H	Crawley T	L	0-2	0-1	14		3392
21	17	A	Cambridge U	L	1-2	0-0	16	Jones [68]	4167
22	26	H	Carlisle U	D	1-1	1-1	15	Cooper [45]	4962
23	31	H	Accrington S	L	0-1	0-1	16		3471
24	Jan 2	A	Morecambe	D	0-0	0-0	17		1722
25	7	A	Mansfield T	L	0-3	0-1	18		3040
26	14	H	Luton T	L	1-2	1-1	18	Lowe [28]	4368
27	21	A	Doncaster R	L	1-3	1-1	19	Jones [32]	5737
28	28	H	Cheltenham T	D	0-0	0-0	19		3373
29	Feb 4	A	Exeter C	L	0-4	0-1	21		4534
30	11	H	Grimsby T	W	5-0	4-0	18	Cooper 2 [2, 25], Dagnall 2 [16, 29], Cooke [87]	4003
31	14	H	Wycombe W	W	2-1	1-0	18	Dagnall [11], Jones (pen) [87]	2896
32	18	A	Blackpool	D	2-2	0-2	18	Dagnall [62], Turton [88]	3389
33	25	H	Stevenage	L	1-2	0-2	18	Jones (pen) [71]	3547
34	28	A	Hartlepool U	L	0-4	0-1	20		3043
35	Mar 4	A	Portsmouth	W	1-0	0-0	19	Ray [77]	16,810
36	11	H	Newport Co	L	1-2	1-0	21	Cooke [22]	3725
37	14	A	Crawley T	W	3-0	1-0	19	Jones (pen) [37], Bowery [50], Dagnall [52]	1566
38	18	H	Colchester U	W	2-0	1-0	18	Dagnall 2 [26, 84]	3407
39	25	A	Carlisle U	W	2-0	1-0	16	Cooke [34], Bowery [60]	4695
40	Apr 1	H	Cambridge U	L	1-2	0-1	16	Legge (og) [58]	3759
41	8	A	Accrington S	L	2-3	2-0	17	Cooke [15], Dagnall [41]	1720
42	14	H	Notts Co	D	2-2	1-1	17	Dagnall [38], Jones [66]	5016
43	17	A	Yeovil T	L	0-3	0-2	19		3167
44	22	H	Leyton Orient	W	3-0	3-0	17	Ainley [26], Wintle [30], Cooper [45]	3745
45	29	A	Plymouth Arg	L	1-2	1-0	17	Jones [6]	13,313
46	May 6	H	Barnet	W	4-1	2-0	17	Dagnall 3 [8, 25, 67], Cooper [76]	4587

Final League Position: 17

GOALSCORERS

League (58): Dagnall 14, Jones 10 (3 pens), Cooper 9, Kiwomya 7, Lowe 5, Cooke 4, Bowery 2, Ainley 1, Davis 1, Hollands 1, Ray 1, Turton 1, Wintle 1, own goal 1.
FA Cup (2): Jones 1, Lowe 1.
EFL Cup (5): Dagnall 2, Lowe 2, Bingham 1.
EFL Checkatrade Trophy (5): Ainley 1, Cooper 1, Dagnall 1, Lowe 1, Udoh 1.

Garratt B 46	Turton O 45	Guthrie J 33	Davis H 25	Bakayogo Z 36 + 4	Cooper G 43 + 3	Jones J 42 + 3	Bingham B 25 + 5	Kirk C 11 + 11	Lowe R 21 + 1	Dagnall C 39 + 2	Ainley C 6 + 21	Kiwomya A 22 + 12	Ray G 18 + 5	Hollands D 23 + 1	Udoh D 1 + 8	Wintle R 7 + 10	Lowery T 2 + 5	Ng P 9 + 7	Nugent B 15 + 5	Saunders C 1 + 4	Bowery J 18 + 1	Cooke C 18	Pickering H — + 1	Finney O — + 1	Match No.
1	2	3	4	5	6^{2}	7	8	9^{1}	10^{3}	11	12	13	14												1
1	2	4	3	5	6^{1}	7	8	9^{2}	10	11	13	12													2
1	2	4	3	5	6^{1}	7	8	12	10	11		9													3
1	2	4	3	5	6^{1}	7	8^{3}		11	10^{2}	14	9	13	12											4
1	2	3	4	5	6^{1}	12	8		11	10	13	9		7^{2}											5
1	2	3	4	5	6^{2}	8	12		11	10		9^{1}	13	7											6
1	2	3	4^{2}	5	6^{3}	8		14	10^{1}	11	12	9	13	7											7
1	2	3	4	5	6^{1}	8	13	12	11	10		9^{2}		7											8
1	2	3	8	5	6	4	13	9^{1}	10	11	12			7^{2}											9
1	2	3	4	5	9	7		12	10^{2}	11^{3}	6^{1}			8	13	14									10
1	2	4	3^{2}	5	6	7			11	10	9^{1}		13	8	12										11
1	2	4	3	5	9		7	6^{1}	11	10				8			12								12
1	2	3	4	5	9	13	7^{1}		10	11		12		8			6^{2}								13
1	2	4	3	5	6	12	8^{1}		11	10	13	9		7^{2}											14
1	2	4	3	5	6^{1}	7	12		10^{2}	11		9^{3}		8			13	14							15
1		4	3	5^{3}	7	8					9^{2}	10		6	11^{1}		13	2	12	14					16
1	2	4	3		6	7			11^{3}		12			8	13		9^{1}	5	14	10^{2}					17
1	2	4	3		6^{2}	7			11	10^{3}		9^{1}		8		14	12	5		13					18
1	2	4	3		9	8^{2}			11	10^{1}	14	6		7	13			5^{3}	12						19
1	2	4	3		6	7^{2}		13	11	10	12	9^{3}		8^{1}				5	14						20
1	2	4	3	5	9	8	12	13	11^{3}	10^{1}		6		7^{2}	14										21
1	2	3	4	5	9	7	8	11		10		6													22
1	2	4	3	5	6	7	8	10^{2}		11	12	9^{1}			13										23
1	2	4	3	5	9	7	8	11^{1}		10	12	6													24
1	2	4	3	5	9^{1}	7	8	10	12	11	13	6^{2}													25
1	2	4		5^{3}	6	7		11^{2}	10	12		9	3	8^{1}		14				13					26
1	2	4		5^{3}	9^{1}	7		6^{2}		11		12	3	8		14			13		10				27
1	5	4			8	6		9^{1}		10^{2}		12	2	7	13				3		11				28
1	2	5		12	9	8		14■		13		11^{2}	3^{3}	7^{1}					4		10	6			29
1	2	5^{2}		12	9^{3}	6				10^{1}	14	13	3	7					4		11	8			30
1	2	5			9^{1}	6				10^{3}		13	3	7^{2}		12		14	4		11	8			31
1	2	5^{1}		13	9	8				10^{3}	12	14	3			7^{2}			4		11	6			32
1	2	5^{2}		13	11	7				10■		12	3			8^{1}			4		9	6			33
1	2			5^{3}	9^{2}	7	8	13			12	11^{1}	3					14	4		10	6			34
1	2			5	12	8	6				13	9^{1}	3			11			4		10	7^{2}			35
1	2^{2}			5	12	7	8	14			13	11^{3}	3			9			4		10	6^{1}			36
1	2			5	11^{2}	6	7			9^{1}	14	13	3^{3}					12	4		10	8			37
1	2			5^{1}	9^{2}	7	8			10			3			13		12	4		11	6			38
1	2			5	9	7	8			10^{1}	13		3			12			4		11^{2}	6			39
1	2			5^{1}	8	6	9			11		12	3					13	4		10	7^{2}			40
1	2			5	8	6^{1}	9			11			4			12			3	13	10^{2}	7			41
1	2			5	11^{2}	7	6			9			3			12		13	4^{1}		10	8			42
1	2			5	14	6	9			11	10^{1}	13	3^{2}			12		4			8	7^{3}			43
1	2			5	11^{1}	7	3	14		10	6^{2}				13	8		4				9^{3}	12		44
1	2			5	11^{2}	7	3			10	6^{1}					8	13	4			12	9			45
1	2			5	11^{2}	6^{3}	3	14		9	12					7		4			10	8^{1}		13	46

FA Cup

First Round	Cheltenham T	(a)	1-1
Replay	Cheltenham T	(h)	1-4

EFL Cup

First Round (*aet*)	Sheffield U	(a)	2-1
Second Round (*aet*)	Blackburn R	(a)	3-4

EFL Checkatrade Trophy

Northern Group B	Accrington S	(a)	3-0
Northern Group B	Wolverhampton W U21	(h)	2-3
Northern Group B	Chesterfield	(h)	0-2

CRYSTAL PALACE

FOUNDATION

There was a Crystal Palace club as early as 1861 but the present organisation was born in 1905 after the formation of a club by the company that controlled the Crystal Palace (building) had been rejected by the FA, who did not like the idea of the Cup Final hosts running their own club. A separate company had to be formed and they had their home on the old Cup Final ground until 1915.

Selhurst Park Stadium, Whitehorse Lane, London SE25 6PU.

Telephone: (020) 8768 6000.

Fax: (020) 8771 5311.

Ticket Office: (0871) 200 0071.

Website: www.cpfc.co.uk

Email: info@cpfc.co.uk

Ground Capacity: 26,309.

Record Attendance: 51,482 v Burnley, Division 2, 11 May 1979 (at Selhurst Park).

Pitch Measurements: 101m × 68m (109yd × 75yd).

Chairman: Steve Parish.

Chief Executive: Phil Alexander.

Manager: Frank de Boer.

Assistant Manager: Sammy Lee.

Physio: Alex Manos.

Colours: Blue with red sleeves and side panel, blue shorts with red side panel, blue socks with red trim.

Year Formed: 1905.

Turned Professional: 1905.

Club Nickname: 'The Eagles'.

Grounds: 1905, Crystal Palace; 1915, Herne Hill; 1918, The Nest; 1924, Selhurst Park.

First Football League Game: 28 August 1920, Division 3, v Merthyr T (a) L 1–2 – Alderson; Little, Rhodes; McCracken, Jones, Feebury; Bateman, Conner, Smith, Milligan (1), Whibley.

Record League Victory: 9–0 v Barrow, Division 4, 10 October 1959 – Rouse; Long, Noakes; Truett, Evans, McNichol; Gavin (1), Summersby (4 incl. 1p), Sexton, Byrne (2), Colfar (2).

Record Cup Victory: 8–0 v Southend U, Rumbelows League Cup 2nd rd (1st leg), 25 September 1990 – Martyn; Humphrey (Thompson (1)), Shaw, Pardew, Young, Thorn, McGoldrick, Thomas, Bright (3), Wright (3), Barber (Hodges (1)).

Record Defeat: 0–9 v Burnley, FA Cup 2nd rd replay, 10 February 1909; 0–9 v Liverpool, Division 1, 12 September 1990.

HONOURS

League Champions: First Division – 1993–94; Division 2 – 1978–79; Division 3S – 1920–21.
Runners-up: Division 2 – 1968–69; Division 3 – 1963–64; Division 3S – 1928–29, 1930–31, 1938–39; Division 4 – 1960–61.

FA Cup: *Runners-up:* 1990, 2016.

League Cup: semi-final – 1993, 1995, 2001, 2012.

Full Members' Cup Winners: 1991.

European Competition
Intertoto Cup: 1998.

sky SPORTS FACT FILE

Crystal Palace once scored six goals in a cup tie but still lost! Playing at Exeter in a Division Three South Cup fixture in January 1934, Palace went down to an 11-6 defeat. They had fielded a weakened team as they were due to play Arsenal in an FA Cup tie the following Saturday, which they also lost, 7-0.

Most League Points (2 for a win): 64, Division 4, 1960–61.

Most League Points (3 for a win): 90, Division 1, 1993–94.

Most League Goals: 110, Division 4, 1960–61.

Highest League Scorer in Season: Peter Simpson, 46, Division 3 (S), 1930–31.

Most League Goals in Total Aggregate: Peter Simpson, 153, 1930–36.

Most League Goals in One Match: 6, Peter Simpson v Exeter C, Division 3 (S), 4 October 1930.

Most Capped Player: Mile Jedinak, 37 (71), Australia.

Most League Appearances: Jim Cannon, 571, 1973–88.

Youngest League Player: John Bostock, 15 years 287 days v Watford, 29 October 2007.

Record Transfer Fee Received: £25,000,000 from Everton for Yannick Bolasie, August 2016.

Record Transfer Fee Paid: £27,000,000 to Liverpool for Christian Benteke, August 2016.

Football League Record: 1920 Original Members of Division 3; 1921–25 Division 2; 1925–58 Division 3 (S); 1958–61 Division 4; 1961–64 Division 3; 1964–69 Division 2; 1969–73 Division 1; 1973–74 Division 2; 1974–77 Division 3; 1977–79 Division 2; 1979–81 Division 1; 1981–89 Division 2; 1989–92 Division 1; 1992–93 FA Premier League; 1993–94 Division 1; 1994–95 FA Premier League; 1995–97 Division 1; 1997–98 FA Premier League; 1998–2004 Division 1; 2004–05 FA Premier League; 2005–13 FL C; 2013– FA Premier League.

LATEST SEQUENCES

Longest Sequence of League Wins: 8, 9.2.1921 – 26.3.1921.

Longest Sequence of League Defeats: 8, 10.1.1998 – 14.3.1998.

Longest Sequence of League Draws: 5, 21.9.2002 – 19.10.2002.

Longest Sequence of Unbeaten League Matches: 18, 22.2.1969 – 13.8.1969.

Longest Sequence Without a League Win: 20, 3.3.1962 – 8.9.1962.

Successive Scoring Runs: 24 from 27.4.1929.

Successive Non-scoring Runs: 9 from 19.11.1994.

MANAGERS

John T. Robson 1905–07
Edmund Goodman 1907–25 (*Secretary 1905–33*)
Alex Maley 1925–27
Fred Mavin 1927–30
Jack Tresadern 1930–35
Tom Bromilow 1935–36
R. S. Moyes 1936
Tom Bromilow 1936–39
George Irwin 1939–47
Jack Butler 1947–49
Ronnie Rooke 1949–50
Charlie Slade and Fred Dawes (*Joint Managers*) 1950–51
Laurie Scott 1951–54
Cyril Spiers 1954–58
George Smith 1958–60
Arthur Rowe 1960–62
Dick Graham 1962–66
Bert Head 1966–72 (*continued as General Manager to 1973*)
Malcolm Allison 1973–76
Terry Venables 1976–80
Ernie Walley 1980
Malcolm Allison 1980–81
Dario Gradi 1981
Steve Kember 1981–82
Alan Mullery 1982–84
Steve Coppell 1984–93
Alan Smith 1993–95
Steve Coppell (*Technical Director*) 1995–96
Dave Bassett 1996–97
Steve Coppell 1997–98
Attilio Lombardo 1998
Terry Venables (*Head Coach*) 1998–99
Steve Coppell 1999–2000
Alan Smith 2000–01
Steve Bruce 2001
Trevor Francis 2001–03
Steve Kember 2003
Iain Dowie 2003–06
Peter Taylor 2006–07
Neil Warnock 2007–10
Paul Hart 2010
George Burley 2010–11
Dougie Freedman 2011–12
Ian Holloway 2012–13
Tony Pulis 2013–14
Neil Warnock 2014
Alan Pardew 2015–16
Sam Allardyce 2016–17
Frank de Boer June 2017–

TEN YEAR LEAGUE RECORD

		P	W	D	L	F	A	Pts	Pos
2007-08	FL C	46	18	17	11	58	42	71	5
2008-09	FL C	46	15	12	19	52	55	57	15
2009-10	FL C	46	14	17	15	50	53	49*	21
2010-11	FL C	46	12	12	22	44	69	48	20
2011-12	FL C	46	13	17	16	46	51	56	17
2012-13	FL C	46	19	15	12	73	62	72	5
2013-14	PR Lge	38	13	6	19	33	48	45	11
2014-15	PR Lge	38	13	9	16	47	51	48	10
2015-16	PR Lge	38	11	9	18	39	51	42	15
2016-17	PR Lge	38	12	5	21	50	63	41	14

** 10 pts deducted.*

DID YOU KNOW ?

Crystal Palace were forced to play their home FA Cup tie with Rotherham County in December 1906 at Stamford Bridge as their own ground was in use for the rugby union international between England and South Africa. Only around 1,000 turned out to watch Palace record a comfortable 4-0 victory.

CRYSTAL PALACE – PREMIER LEAGUE 2016–17 LEAGUE RECORD

Match No.	Date	Venue	Opponents	Result	H/T Score	Lg Pos.	Goalscorers	Attendance
1	Aug 13	H	WBA	L 0-1	0-0	20		24,490
2	20	A	Tottenham H	L 0-1	0-0	20		31,447
3	27	H	Bournemouth	D 1-1	0-1	16	Dann 90	23,503
4	Sept 10	A	Middlesbrough	W 2-1	1-1	11	Benteke, C 16, Zaha 47	30,551
5	18	H	Stoke C	W 4-1	2-0	8	Tomkins 9, Dann 11, McArthur 71, Townsend 75	23,781
6	24	A	Sunderland	W 3-2	0-1	7	Ledley 61, McArthur 76, Benteke, C 90	38,941
7	30	A	Everton	D 1-1	0-1	7	Benteke, C 50	38,758
8	Oct 15	H	West Ham U	L 0-1	0-1	8		25,643
9	22	A	Leicester C	L 1-3	0-1	11	Cabaye 85	31,969
10	29	H	Liverpool	L 2-4	2-3	11	McArthur 2 18, 33	25,628
11	Nov 5	A	Burnley	L 2-3	0-2	14	Wickham 60, Benteke, C (pen) 81	19,196
12	19	H	Manchester C	L 1-2	0-1	16	Wickham 66	25,529
13	26	A	Swansea C	L 4-5	1-1	16	Zaha 19, Tomkins 75, Cork (og) 82, Benteke, C 84	20,276
14	Dec 3	H	Southampton	W 3-0	2-0	13	Benteke, C 2 33, 85, Tomkins 36	25,393
15	10	A	Hull C	D 3-3	0-1	14	Benteke, C (pen) 52, Zaha 70, Campbell 89	17,403
16	14	H	Manchester U	L 1-2	0-1	15	McArthur 66	25,547
17	17	H	Chelsea	L 0-1	0-1	16		25,259
18	26	A	Watford	D 1-1	1-0	17	Cabaye 26	20,304
19	Jan 1	A	Arsenal	L 0-2	0-1	17		59,975
20	3	H	Swansea C	L 1-2	0-1	17	Zaha 83	24,913
21	14	A	West Ham U	L 0-3	0-0	17		56,984
22	21	H	Everton	L 0-1	0-0	17		25,594
23	31	A	Bournemouth	W 2-0	0-0	17	Dann 46, Benteke, C 90	11,286
24	Feb 4	H	Sunderland	L 0-4	0-4	19		25,310
25	11	A	Stoke C	L 0-1	0-0	19		27,007
26	25	H	Middlesbrough	W 1-0	1-0	17	Van Aanholt 34	25,416
27	Mar 4	A	WBA	W 2-0	0-0	17	Zaha 55, Townsend 84	24,051
28	18	H	Watford	W 1-0	0-0	15	Deeney (og) 68	25,109
29	Apr 1	A	Chelsea	W 2-1	2-1	15	Zaha 9, Benteke, C 11	41,489
30	5	A	Southampton	L 1-3	1-1	16	Benteke, C 31	29,968
31	10	H	Arsenal	W 3-0	1-0	16	Townsend 17, Cabaye 63, Milivojevic (pen) 68	25,648
32	15	H	Leicester C	D 2-2	0-1	15	Cabaye 54, Benteke, C 70	25,504
33	23	A	Liverpool	W 2-1	1-1	12	Benteke, C 2 42, 74	53,086
34	26	H	Tottenham H	L 0-1	0-0	12		25,596
35	29	H	Burnley	L 0-2	0-1	13		25,013
36	May 6	A	Manchester C	L 0-5	0-1	16		54,119
37	14	H	Hull C	W 4-0	2-0	13	Zaha 3, Benteke, C 34, Milivojevic (pen) 85, Van Aanholt 90	25,176
38	21	A	Manchester U	L 0-2	0-2	14		75,254

Final League Position: 14

GOALSCORERS

League (50): Benteke, C 15 (2 pens), Zaha 7, McArthur 5, Cabaye 4, Dann 3, Tomkins 3, Townsend 3, Milivojevic 2 (2 pens), Van Aanholt 2, Wickham 2, Campbell 1, Ledley 1, own goals 2.
FA Cup (2): Benteke, C 2.
EFL Cup (2): Dann 1, Wickham 1.

Hennessey W 29	Ward J 38	Dann S 19 + 4	Delaney D 21 + 9	Souare P 3	Jedinak M 1	Puncheon J 35 + 1	Townsend A 30 + 6	Lee C 4 + 11	Zaha W 34 + 1	Wickham C 4 + 4	Bolasie Y — + 1	Cabaye Y 25 + 7	Kelly M 25 + 4	Ledley J 13 + 5	Mutch J — + 4	Tomkins J 23 + 1	Mandanda S 9	McArthur J 24 + 5	Benteke C 36	Benteke J — + 1	Flamini M 3 + 7	Fryers Z — + 8	Campbell F — + 12	Sako B — + 7	Remy L 1 + 4	Schlupp J 11 + 4	Van Aanholt P 8 + 3	Milivojevic L 14	Sakho M 8	KaiKai S — + 1	*Match No.*
1	2	3	4	5^{3}	6	7^{2}	8	9^{1}	10	11	12	13	14																		1
1	2	3	4^{2}	5		7	8	9^{3}	10	11		12		6^{1}	13	14															2
	2^{1}	3	4	5		6	9	12	13	10^{2}		7	14				1	8^{3}	11												3
	2	3	4			9	10^{3}	12	8				5	7^{2}			1	6	11^{1}	13	14										4
	2	3	12			9	10^{1}	14	8				5	6^{3}		4^{2}	1	7	11		13										5
	2		4			8^{3}	10	14		12		9^{1}	5^{2}	7		3	1	6	11			13									6
	2		4			9	8^{1}	13	10			12	5	7		3	1	6^{2}	11												7
	2		4			9	8		10	14		13	5^{1}	7^{3}		3	1	6^{2}	11			12									8
	2		4				8^{2}	12	10			9	5^{3}	7^{1}		3	1	6	11			14	13								9
	2	3				13	12	10^{2}	8			6	5	7^{1}		4	1	9^{3}	11				14								10
	2	3	4			9^{3}	8		10	12		7	5^{2}	14			1	6^{1}	11			13									11
1	2	3				9	10^{2}	13	8	12		6	5^{3}			4		7	11^{1}					14							12
1	2	3				9	12		6	11^{1}		7	5^{2}			4		8^{3}	10			13		14							13
1	5	3	4			9	8^{2}		10				13	7		2^{3}		6^{1}	11		14			12							14
1	5	3	4			9	10^{3}		8			13	2^{2}	7				6^{1}	11			12	14								15
1	5	3	4					9^{1}	10			7	2	12				6^{3}	11		8^{2}	13	14								16
1	5	3	4			10^{1}	12		8			9^{2}	2^{3}	7				6	11			14	13								17
1	5	3	4			9	8^{2}		10			7	2		12				11		6^{1}		13								18
1	5	3				6	8^{2}	13	10			9^{1}	2		12	4			11^{3}		7		14								19
1	5		4			7	8^{2}		10			9	2^{1}	6	14	3			11^{3}				12	13							20
1	5	3	4			10	8^{3}	13				9		7^{2}		2		6^{1}	11						12	14					21
1	5	3	4			7	14	12				6^{3}		13		2		9	11						10^{2}	8^{1}					22
1	5	3	4			7^{1}	12		9			6^{3}		13		2		11^{2}	10		14						8				23
1	5	3	4^{2}			6	13		9			7^{3}		12		2		11^{1}	10						14		8				24
1	2		4			9^{3}	10		8^{2}			13				3		7^{1}	11						14	12	5	6			25
1	2	14				9	7		10^{2}			8^{3}				3		12	11							13	5^{1}	6	4		26
1	2	13				9	10		8^{3}			6^{2}				3		14	11							12	5^{1}	7	4		27
1	2	12	14			9	10^{2}		8			6^{1}				3^{3}			11					13		5		7	4		28
1	2	12^{3}	14			9	10^{1}		8			7	13			3^{2}			11							5		6	4		29
1	2		13			9	8		10			6^{1}	3						11		14			12		5^{3}		7^{2}	4		30
1	2		14			9	10		8^{1}			7^{3}	3					12	11		13					5		6^{2}	4		31
1	2					9	8		10^{1}			7	3					13	11							5^{2}	12	6	4		32
1	2		13			9	10		7^{2}			8^{1}	3			4			11^{3}				14			5	12	6			33
1	2		12			9	10		7			13	3					8^{2}	11^{1}				14			5		6	4^{3}		34
1	2		4			8	11		9				3					6^{1}	10^{2}				13		12		5	7			35
1	2		14			8	11^{1}	12	9				3^{2}					6	10		13					4	5	7^{3}			36
1	2		14			6	10^{3}		8			9^{2}	3			4^{1}		12	11							5	13	7			37
1	2					8			9^{2}				3			4		6^{1}	10				14	12		5	11^{3}	7		13	38

FA Cup

Third Round	Bolton W	(a)	0-0
Replay	Bolton W	(h)	2-1
Fourth Round	Manchester C	(h)	0-3

EFL Cup

Second Round	Blackpool	(h)	2-0
Third Round	Southampton	(a)	0-2

DERBY COUNTY

FOUNDATION

Derby County was formed by members of the Derbyshire County Cricket Club in 1884, when football was booming in the area and the cricketers thought that a football club would help boost finances for the summer game. To begin with, they sported the cricket club's colours of amber, chocolate and pale blue, and went into the game at the top immediately entering the FA Cup.

The iPro Stadium, Pride Park, Derby DE21 4TB.

Telephone: (0871) 472 1884.

Fax: (01332) 671 137.

Ticket Office: (0871) 472 1884 (option 1).

Website: www.dcfc.co.uk

Email: derby.county@dcfc.co.uk

Ground Capacity: 33,055.

Record Attendance: 41,826 v Tottenham H, Division 1, 20 September 1969 (at Baseball Ground); 33,378 v Liverpool, FA Premier League, 18 March 2000 (at Pride Park).

Stadium Record Attendance: 33,597, England v Mexico, 25 May 2001 (at Pride Park).

Pitch Measurements: 105m × 68m (115yd × 74yd).

Chairman: Mel Morris.

Chief Operating Officer: John Vicars.

Manager: Gary Rowett.

Assistant Manager: Kevin Summerfield.

Colours: White shirts with black trim, black shorts with white trim, white socks with black trim.

Year Formed: 1884.

Turned Professional: 1884.

Club Nickname: 'The Rams'.

Grounds: 1884, Racecourse Ground; 1895, Baseball Ground; 1997, Pride Park (renamed The iPro Stadium 2013).

First Football League Game: 8 September 1888, Football League, v Bolton W (a) W 6–3 – Marshall; Latham, Ferguson, Williamson; Monks, Walter Roulstone; Bakewell (2), Cooper (2), Higgins, Harry Plackett, Lol Plackett (2).

Record League Victory: 9–0 v Wolverhampton W, Division 1, 10 January 1891 – Bunyan; Archie Goodall, Roberts; Walker, Chalmers, Walter Roulstone (1); Bakewell, McLachlan, Johnny Goodall (1), Holmes (2), McMillan (5). 9–0 v Sheffield W, Division 1, 21 January 1899 – Fryer; Methven, Staley; Cox, Archie Goodall, May; Oakden (1), Bloomer (6), Boag, McDonald (1), Allen, (1 og).

HONOURS

League Champions: Division 1 – 1971–72, 1974–75; Division 2 – 1911–12, 1914–15, 1968–69, 1986–87; Division 3N – 1956–57.
Runners-up: Division 1 – 1895–96, 1929–30, 1935–36; First Division – 1995–96; Division 2 – 1925–26; Division 3N – 1955–56.

FA Cup Winners: 1946.
Runners-up: 1898, 1899, 1903.

League Cup: semi-final – 1968, 2009.

Texaco Cup Winners: 1972.

Anglo-Italian Cup: *Runners-up:* 1993–94, 1994–95.

European Competitions
European Cup: 1972–73 (*sf*), 1975–76.
UEFA Cup: 1974–75, 1976–77.

SKY SPORTS FACT FILE

Tommy Powell and his son Steve both made over 400 appearances for Derby County, their only senior club. Both played in the first team at 16 and both were members of teams that won divisional titles with the Rams, Tommy winning Division Three North in 1956–57 and Steve featuring in the 1971–72 and 1974–75 Division One successes.

Record Cup Victory: 12–0 v Finn Harps, UEFA Cup 1st rd 1st leg, 15 September 1976 – Moseley; Thomas, Nish, Rioch (1), McFarland, Todd (King), Macken, Gemmill, Hector (5), George (3), James (3).

Record Defeat: 2–11 v Everton, FA Cup 1st rd, 1889–90.

Most League Points (2 for a win): 63, Division 2, 1968–69 and Division 3 (N), 1955–56 and 1956–57.

Most League Points (3 for a win): 85, FL C, 2013–14.

Most League Goals: 111, Division 3 (N), 1956–57.

Highest League Scorer in Season: Jack Bowers, 37, Division 1, 1930–31; Ray Straw, 37 Division 3 (N), 1956–57.

Most League Goals in Total Aggregate: Steve Bloomer, 292, 1892–1906 and 1910–14.

Most League Goals in One Match: 6, Steve Bloomer v Sheffield W, Division 1, 2 January 1899.

Most Capped Player: Deon Burton, 42 (59), Jamaica.

Most League Appearances: Kevin Hector, 486, 1966–78 and 1980–82.

Youngest League Player: Mason Bennett, 15 years 99 days v Middlesbrough 22 October 2011.

Record Transfer Fee Received: £10,500,000 from Burnley for Jeff Hendrick, August 2016.

Record Transfer Fee Paid: £8,000,000 to Watford for Matej Vydra, August 2016.

Football League Record: 1888 Founder Member of the Football League; 1907–12 Division 2; 1912–14 Division 1; 1914–15 Division 2; 1915–21 Division 1; 1921–26 Division 2; 1926–53 Division 1; 1953–55 Division 2; 1955–57 Division 3 (N); 1957–69 Division 2; 1969–80 Division 1; 1980–84 Division 2; 1984–86 Division 3; 1986–87 Division 2; 1987–91 Division 1; 1991–92 Division 2; 1992–96 Division 1; 1996–2002 FA Premier League; 2002–04 Division 1; 2004–07 FL C; 2007–08 FA Premier League; 2008– FL C.

MANAGERS

W. D. Clark 1896–1900
Harry Newbould 1900–06
Jimmy Methven 1906–22
Cecil Potter 1922–25
George Jobey 1925–41
Ted Magner 1944–46
Stuart McMillan 1946–53
Jack Barker 1953–55
Harry Storer 1955–62
Tim Ward 1962–67
Brian Clough 1967–73
Dave Mackay 1973–76
Colin Murphy 1977
Tommy Docherty 1977–79
Colin Addison 1979–82
Johnny Newman 1982
Peter Taylor 1982–84
Roy McFarland 1984
Arthur Cox 1984–93
Roy McFarland 1993–95
Jim Smith 1995–2001
Colin Todd 2001–02
John Gregory 2002–03
George Burley 2003–05
Phil Brown 2005–06
Billy Davies 2006–07
Paul Jewell 2007–08
Nigel Clough 2009–13
Steve McClaren 2013–15
Paul Clement 2015–16
Darren Wassall 2016
Nigel Pearson 2016
Steve McClaren 2016–17
Gary Rowett March 2017–

LATEST SEQUENCES

Longest Sequence of League Wins: 9, 15.3.1969 – 19.4.1969.

Longest Sequence of League Defeats: 8, 12.12.1987 – 10.2.1988.

Longest Sequence of League Draws: 6, 26.3.1927 – 18.4.1927.

Longest Sequence of Unbeaten League Matches: 22, 8.3.1969 – 20.9.1969.

Longest Sequence Without a League Win: 36, 22.9.2007 – 30.8.2008.

Successive Scoring Runs: 29 from 3.12.1960.

Successive Non-scoring Runs: 8 from 30.10.1920.

TEN YEAR LEAGUE RECORD

		P	W	D	L	F	A	Pts	Pos
2007-08	PR Lge	38	1	8	29	20	89	11	20
2008-09	FL C	46	14	12	20	55	67	54	18
2009-10	FL C	46	15	11	20	53	63	56	14
2010-11	FL C	46	13	10	23	58	71	49	19
2011-12	FL C	46	18	10	18	50	58	64	12
2012-13	FL C	46	16	13	17	65	62	61	10
2013-14	FL C	46	25	10	11	84	52	85	3
2014-15	FL C	46	21	14	11	85	56	77	8
2015-16	FL C	46	21	15	10	66	43	78	5
2016-17	FL C	46	18	13	15	54	50	67	9

DID YOU KNOW

Derby County flew to Germany in August 1945 to play two games against British Forces teams to entertain the troops stationed there. They won both games, defeating an RAF XI 10-4 at Neuberg and then the 8th Corps Army XI 1-0 at Kiel.

DERBY COUNTY – SKY BET CHAMPIONSHIP 2016–17 LEAGUE RECORD

Match No.	Date	Venue	Opponents	Result	H/T Score	Lg Pos.	Goalscorers	Attendance
1	Aug 6	H	Brighton & HA	D 0-0	0-0	13		28,749
2	13	A	Barnsley	L 0-2	0-1	17		15,049
3	16	A	Preston NE	W 1-0	0-0	14	Forsyth [87]	10,628
4	20	H	Aston Villa	D 0-0	0-0	13		31,205
5	26	A	Burton Alb	L 0-1	0-1	17		6746
6	Sept 10	H	Newcastle U	L 0-2	0-1	19		30,405
7	13	H	Ipswich T	L 0-1	0-0	20		26,425
8	17	A	Bristol C	D 1-1	1-0	20	Anya [44]	19,451
9	24	H	Blackburn R	L 1-2	0-0	22	Vydra [69]	26,602
10	27	A	Cardiff C	W 2-0	0-0	20	Ince [55], Blackman (pen) [80]	14,131
11	Oct 1	A	Reading	D 1-1	0-0	20	Vydra [62]	17,002
12	15	H	Leeds U	W 1-0	0-0	19	Russell [56]	31,170
13	18	H	Brentford	D 0-0	0-0	19		26,707
14	22	A	Huddersfield T	L 0-1	0-0	20		19,749
15	29	H	Sheffield W	W 2-0	1-0	19	Christie [17], Pearce [67]	30,064
16	Nov 5	A	Wolverhampton W	W 3-2	2-0	16	Ince 2 (1 pen) [6, 77 (p)], Bent [15]	19,858
17	19	H	Rotherham U	W 3-0	2-0	12	Ince 2 [15, 63], Bent [19]	28,191
18	26	H	Norwich C	W 1-0	0-0	7	Johnson [65]	29,311
19	Dec 3	A	Wigan Ath	W 1-0	1-0	9	Johnson [16]	12,526
20	11	H	Nottingham F	W 3-0	1-0	5	Bendtner (og) [33], Ince [55], Hughes [64]	32,600
21	14	A	QPR	W 1-0	0-0	5	Ince [86]	12,371
22	17	A	Fulham	D 2-2	1-1	7	Ince [34], Pearce [75]	18,748
23	27	H	Birmingham C	W 1-0	0-0	7	Bent (pen) [64]	32,616
24	31	H	Wigan Ath	D 0-0	0-0	6		29,289
25	Jan 2	A	Norwich C	L 0-3	0-1	7		26,422
26	13	A	Leeds U	L 0-1	0-1	7		25,546
27	21	H	Reading	W 3-2	1-1	7	Bent [36], Ince [63], Hughes [74]	28,393
28	31	A	Ipswich T	W 3-0	3-0	6	Bryson [9], Ince [12], Bent [45]	14,719
29	Feb 4	A	Newcastle U	L 0-1	0-1	8		52,231
30	11	H	Bristol C	D 3-3	0-3	8	Bent 2 (1 pen) [57, 81 (p)], Ince [76]	28,043
31	14	H	Cardiff C	L 3-4	2-1	11	De Sart [7], Bent 2 [17, 74]	26,541
32	21	H	Burton Alb	D 0-0	0-0	11		31,081
33	25	A	Aston Villa	L 0-1	0-1	11		30,935
34	28	A	Blackburn R	L 0-1	0-0	11		10,536
35	Mar 4	H	Barnsley	W 2-1	0-0	10	Ince [54], Nugent [76]	30,280
36	7	H	Preston NE	D 1-1	0-0	10	Vydra [50]	26,301
37	10	A	Brighton & HA	L 0-3	0-2	10		27,552
38	18	A	Nottingham F	D 2-2	0-1	10	Vydra [47], Nugent [53]	26,665
39	31	H	QPR	W 1-0	0-0	10	Vydra [70]	27,690
40	Apr 4	H	Fulham	W 4-2	2-1	9	Nugent 3 [8, 42, 59], Russell [67]	27,221
41	8	A	Birmingham C	W 2-1	1-0	8	Kuszczak (og) [3], Ince [90]	19,381
42	14	A	Brentford	L 0-4	0-1	8		11,133
43	17	H	Huddersfield T	D 1-1	0-1	8	Butterfield [88]	29,031
44	22	A	Sheffield W	L 1-2	0-0	10	Bent [48]	28,889
45	29	H	Wolverhampton W	W 3-1	2-1	9	Nugent [12], Johnson [29], Bryson [57]	31,051
46	May 7	A	Rotherham U	D 1-1	0-0	9	Ince (pen) [84]	10,763

Final League Position: 9

GOALSCORERS

League (54): Ince 14 (2 pens), Bent 10 (2 pens), Nugent 6, Vydra 5, Johnson 3, Bryson 2, Hughes 2, Pearce 2, Russell 2, Anya 1, Blackman 1 (1 pen), Butterfield 1, Christie 1, De Sart 1, Forsyth 1, own goals 2.
FA Cup (5): Bent 2, Bryson 1, Camara 1, Ince 1.
EFL Cup (2): Bent 1, Keogh 1.
EFL Checkatrade Trophy (4): Weimann 2, Hanson 1, Wilson 1.

Carson S 46	Christie C 24 + 3	Keogh R 42	Shackell J 7 + 1	Baird C 28 + 5	Blackman N 2 + 7	Bryson C 23 + 11	Hendrick J 2	Johnson B 33	Ince T 41 + 4	Bent D 22 + 15	Hughes W 28 + 10	Martin C 3 + 2	Butterfield J 34 + 6	Forsyth C 3	Russell J 29 + 7	Camara A 3 + 12	Pearce A 39 + 1	Olsson M 30	Wilson J 3 + 1	Anya I 14 + 12	Vydra M 20 + 13	Weimann A 1 + 10	Lowe M 8 + 1	Hanson J 2 + 3	De Sart J 8 + 1	Nugent D 11 + 6	Bennett M — + 2	Match No.
1	2	3	4	5	6^{3}	7	8	9^{2}	10^{1}	11	12	13	14															1
1	2	3	4		6	7	8^{2}		10	11^{1}	12	13	9^{3}	5	14													2
1	2	3	4			9			7^{1}	14	6	11^{2}	8^{3}	5	10	12	13											3
1	2	3	4	13		9			7^{2}	14	6	11	8^{3}	5^{1}	10	12												4
1	2	3	4			8			6^{1}	13	7	11^{3}	10^{2}		9	12		5	14									5
1	2	3	4^{2}		12	8			13	14	7				6			5	11^{1}	9^{3}	10							6
1	2	3			13	7				12	8		6				4	5^{1}	11^{2}	9	10							7
1	2	3				8			14	13	7		6^{1}				4	5	11^{3}	9^{2}	10	12						8
1	2	3			12	7^{3}			14	10^{3}	8		6				4	5^{2}		9	11	13						9
1	2	3			12			7	9^{1}		6		8		13		4			11^{3}	10^{2}	14	5					10
1	2	3		12	14			7	9		6^{1}		8		13		4	5^{2}		11	10^{3}							11
1	2	3		14		13		7	9		6^{3}		8^{2}		12		4			11^{1}	10		5					12
1	2	3		5^{2}		12		7	9	14	6^{3}		8		13		4			11	10^{1}							13
1	2	3						7	9^{1}	13	6		8		11^{2}		4	5		12	10^{3}	14						14
1	2	3						8	9^{2}	10^{3}			6		11^{1}		4	5		13	12		14	7				15
1	2^{2}	3				14		8	9	10^{3}	7^{1}		6		11		4				13		5	12				16
1		3		2		14		7^{3}	9	10^{1}	6		8		11^{2}		4				13	12	5					17
1		3		2		12		7	9	10^{1}	6^{3}		8		11^{2}		4				14	13	5					18
1		3		2		13		7	9		6^{3}		8^{2}		11^{1}		4	5			10	12		14				19
1		3		2		13		7	9^{2}	10^{1}	6^{3}		8		11		4	5			12	14						20
1		3		2		14		7	9	10^{2}	6^{1}		8			13	4	5			12	11^{3}						21
1		3		2		8		7	9^{2}	12			6		11^{1}	13	4	5			10^{3}	14						22
1		3		2				7	9	10^{2}	6		8		11^{1}	14	4	5^{3}		12	13							23
1		3		2		13		7	9	10^{3}	6		8^{2}		11^{1}	12	4			5	14							24
1		3		2		8		7	9^{3}	14			6▪		11^{1}		4			5^{2}	10	12		13				25
1		3	4	2		6		8▪	9	10^{2}	13					11^{1}					12			5	7^{3}	14		26
1	13	3	14	2		8^{2}			9	10^{1}	6				11^{3}		4	5			12				7			27
1	14	3		2^{3}		8		7	9	10^{1}			6			11^{2}	4	5		12	13							28
1		3		2		8^{3}		7^{2}	9	10			6		11^{1}	13	4	5		14					12			29
1		3		2^{2}		8^{3}		7^{1}	9	10	6		12			11	4	5		13						14		30
1		3		2^{1}	14				9	10	6^{2}		8^{3}		12		4	5		11					7	13		31
1	2	3							9	10	6^{2}		8			12	4			11^{1}			5		7	13		32
1	2	3^{1}		12					9	10	6		8^{3}		11^{2}		4						5		7	13	14	33
1	2			3				8	9		6^{3}				11^{1}	13	4			14	12		5^{2}		7	10		34
1	2			3				8	10		13		12		6^{2}		4	5		14	9^{3}				7^{1}	11		35
1	2			3		14		8	10	13			7		6^{3}	12	4	5			9^{1}					11^{2}		36
1	2			3		13			6	11	12		8				4	5			9				7^{2}	10^{1}		37
1		3		2		6		7	8				12		9		4	5			10^{1}					11^{2}	13	38
1		3		2		8		7	6^{2}	14	13				9		4	5		12	10^{3}					11^{1}		39
1		3		2		8^{2}		7	6		14		12		9		4	5		13	10^{3}					11^{1}		40
1		3		2		8^{3}		7	9	14	12		6^{2}		11^{1}		4	5		13						10		41
1		3		2		8^{3}		7^{2}	9	13	12		6		11		4	5			14					10^{1}		42
1	2	3						8^{3}	6^{2}	11	7		13		14	12	4	5		9	10^{1}							43
1	2	3		12				8	14	11^{2}	7^{3}				6		4	5^{1}		9	10					13		44
1	12	3		2		6		8	9				7		11		4^{1}	5^{2}		13						10		45
1		3		2	14	8^{2}		9	7	13	12		6		10^{1}		4	5								11^{3}		46

FA Cup
Third Round WBA (a) 2-1
Fourth Round Leicester C (h) 2-2
Replay Leicester C (a) 1-3
(*aet*)

EFL Cup
First Round Grimsby T (h) 1-0
Second Round Carlisle U (h) 1-1
(*aet; Derby Co won 14-13 on penalties*)
Third Round Liverpool (h) 0-3

EFL Checkatrade Trophy (Derby Co U21)
Northern Group E Port Vale (a) 0-1
Northern Group E Doncaster R (a) 2-2
(*Doncaster R won 4-3 on penalties*)
Northern Group E Mansfield T (h) 2-3

DONCASTER ROVERS

FOUNDATION

In 1879, Mr Albert Jenkins assembled a team to play a match against the Yorkshire Institution for the Deaf. The players remained together as Doncaster Rovers, joining the Midland Alliance in 1889 and the Midland Counties League in 1891.

Keepmoat Stadium, Stadium Way, Lakeside, Doncaster, South Yorkshire DN4 5JW.

Telephone: (01302) 764 664.

Fax: (01302) 363 525.

Ticket Office: (01302) 762 576.

Website: www.doncasterroversfc.co.uk

Email: info@clubdoncaster.co.uk

Ground Capacity: 15,123.

Record Attendance: 37,149 v Hull C, Division 3 (N), 2 October 1948 (at Belle Vue); 15,001 v Leeds U, FL 1, 1 April 2008 (at Keepmoat Stadium).

Pitch Measurements: 100m × 66m (109.5yd × 72yd).

Chairman: David Blunt.

Chief Executive: Gavin Baldwin.

Manager: Darren Ferguson.

Assistant Manager: Gavin Strachan.

Colours: Red and white hooped shirts with black trim, white shorts with red and black trim, white socks with red trim.

Year Formed: 1879.

Turned Professional: 1885.

Club Nickname: 'Rovers', 'Donny'.

Grounds: 1880–1916, Intake Ground; 1920, Benetthorpe Ground; 1922, Low Pasture, Belle Vue; 2007, Keepmoat Stadium.

First Football League Game: 7 September 1901, Division 2, v Burslem Port Vale (h) D 3–3 – Eggett; Simpson, Layton; Longden, Jones, Wright, Langham, Murphy, Price, Goodson (2), Bailey (1).

Record League Victory: 10–0 v Darlington, Division 4, 25 January 1964 – Potter; Raine, Meadows, Windross (1), White, Ripley (2), Robinson, Book (2), Hale (4), Jeffrey, Broadbent (1).

Record Cup Victory: 7–0 v Blyth Spartans, FA Cup 1st rd, 27 November 1937 – Imrie; Shaw, Rodgers, McFarlane, Bycroft, Cyril Smith, Burton (1), Killourhy (4), Morgan (2), Malam, Dutton.

Record Defeat: 0–12 v Small Heath, Division 2, 11 April 1903.

Most League Points (2 for a win): 72, Division 3 (N), 1946–47.

HONOURS

League Champions: FL 1 – 2012–13; Division 3N – 1934–35, 1946–47, 1949–50; Third Division – 2003–04; Division 4 – 1965–66, 1968–69.
Runners-up: Division 3N – 1937–38, 1938–39; Division 4 – 1983–84; Conference – (3rd) 2002–03 *(promoted via play-offs (and golden goal)).*

FA Cup: 5th rd – 1952, 1954, 1955, 1956.

League Cup: 5th rd – 1976, 2006.

League Trophy Winners: 2007.

sky SPORTS FACT FILE

Doncaster Rovers' centre-half John Nicholson was driving on the A630 road near Warmsworth on 1 September 1966 when his car was in a collision with a lorry. Nicholson was badly injured in the crash and never regained consciousness. He died early the following Sunday morning from his injuries.

Most League Points (3 for a win): 92, Division 3, 2003–04.

Most League Goals: 123, Division 3 (N), 1946–47.

Highest League Scorer in Season: Clarrie Jordan, 42, Division 3 (N), 1946–47.

Most League Goals in Total Aggregate: Tom Keetley, 180, 1923–29.

Most League Goals in One Match: 6, Tom Keetley v Ashington, Division 3 (N), 16 February 1929.

Most Capped Player: Len Graham, 14, Northern Ireland.

Most League Appearances: James Coppinger, 472, 2004–17.

Youngest League Player: Alick Jeffrey, 15 years 229 days v Fulham, 15 September 1954.

Record Transfer Fee Received: £2,000,000 from Reading for Matthew Mills, July 2009.

Record Transfer Fee Paid: £1,150,000 to Sheffield U for Billy Sharp, August 2010.

Football League Record: 1901 Elected to Division 2; 1903 Failed re-election; 1904 Re-elected; 1905 Failed re-election; 1923 Re-elected to Division 3 (N); 1935–37 Division 2; 1937–47 Division 3 (N); 1947–48 Division 2; 1948–50 Division 3 (N); 1950–58 Division 2; 1958–59 Division 3; 1959–66 Division 4; 1966–67 Division 3; 1967–69 Division 4; 1969–71 Division 3; 1971–81 Division 4; 1981–83 Division 3; 1983–84 Division 4; 1984–88 Division 3; 1988–92 Division 4; 1992–98 Division 3; 1998–2003 Conference; 2003–04 Division 3; 2004–08 FL 1; 2008–12 FL C; 2012–13 FL 1; 2013–14 FL C; 2014–16 FL 1; 2016–17 FL 2; 2017– FL 1.

LATEST SEQUENCES

Longest Sequence of League Wins: 10, 22.1.1947 – 4.4.1947.

Longest Sequence of League Defeats: 9, 14.1.1905 – 1.4.1905.

Longest Sequence of League Draws: 4, 19.9.2009 – 3.10.2009.

Longest Sequence of Unbeaten League Matches: 20, 26.12.1968 – 12.4.1969.

Longest Sequence Without a League Win: 20, 9.8.1997 – 29.11.1997.

Successive Scoring Runs: 27 from 10.11.1934.

Successive Non-scoring Runs: 7 from 27.9.1947.

MANAGERS

Arthur Porter 1920–21
Harry Tufnell 1921–22
Arthur Porter 1922–23
Dick Ray 1923–27
David Menzies 1928–36
Fred Emery 1936–40
Bill Marsden 1944–46
Jackie Bestall 1946–49
Peter Doherty 1949–58
Jack Hodgson and Sid Bycroft (*Joint Managers*) 1958
Jack Crayston 1958–59 (*continued as Secretary-Manager to 1961*)
Jackie Bestall 1959–60
Norman Curtis 1960–61
Danny Malloy 1961–62
Oscar Hold 1962–64
Bill Leivers 1964–66
Keith Kettleborough 1966–67
George Raynor 1967–68
Lawrie McMenemy 1968–71
Maurice Setters 1971–74
Stan Anderson 1975–78
Billy Bremner 1978–85
Dave Cusack 1985–87
Dave Mackay 1987–89
Billy Bremner 1989–91
Steve Beaglehole 1991–93
Ian Atkins 1994
Sammy Chung 1994–96
Kerry Dixon (*Player-Manager*) 1996–97
Dave Cowling 1997
Mark Weaver 1997–98
Ian Snodin 1998–99
Steve Wignall 1999–2001
Dave Penney 2002–06
Sean O'Driscoll 2006–11
Dean Saunders 2011–13
Brian Flynn 2013
Paul Dickov 2013–15
Darren Ferguson October 2015–

TEN YEAR LEAGUE RECORD

		P	*W*	*D*	*L*	*F*	*A*	*Pts*	*Pos*
2007-08	FL 1	46	23	11	12	65	41	80	3
2008-09	FL C	46	17	7	22	42	53	58	14
2009-10	FL C	46	15	15	16	59	58	60	12
2010-11	FL C	46	11	15	20	55	81	48	21
2011-12	FL C	46	8	12	26	43	80	36	24
2012-13	FL 1	46	25	9	12	62	44	84	1
2013-14	FL C	46	11	11	24	39	70	44	22
2014-15	FL 1	46	16	13	17	58	62	61	13
2015-16	FL 1	46	11	13	22	48	64	46	21
2016-17	FL 2	46	25	10	11	85	55	85	3

DID YOU KNOW

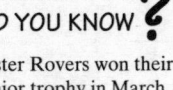

Doncaster Rovers won their first major trophy in March 1991 when they defeated Sheffield United 2-1 at Bramall Lane to win the Sheffield Challenge Cup. Rovers fought back with goals from George James and Tom Kisbey after falling behind in the opening minutes.

DONCASTER ROVERS – SKY BET LEAGUE TWO 2016–17 LEAGUE RECORD

Match No.	Date	Venue	Opponents	Result		H/T Score	Lg Pos.	Goalscorers	Attendance
1	Aug 6	A	Accrington S	L	2-3	1-2	17	Rowe 12, Williams 82	2647
2	13	H	Crawley T	D	1-1	0-1	18	Coppinger 49	4327
3	16	H	Cambridge U	W	1-0	0-0	13	Marquis 74	4768
4	20	A	Cheltenham T	W	1-0	0-0	6	Marquis 53	2923
5	27	H	Yeovil T	W	4-1	1-0	3	Williams 3 1, 82, 90, Coppinger 54	4686
6	Sept 3	A	Crewe Alex	L	1-2	0-1	6	Rowe (pen) 82	3830
7	10	A	Morecambe	W	5-1	2-1	4	Butler 4, Marquis 2 17, 66, Blair 74, Coppinger 80	1791
8	17	H	Newport Co	W	2-0	1-0	1	Coppinger 17, Williams 59	5254
9	24	A	Luton T	L	1-3	1-2	3	Coppinger 21	7917
10	27	H	Carlisle U	D	2-2	2-1	3	Rowe 18, Marquis 44	4773
11	Oct 1	A	Portsmouth	W	2-1	2-1	2	Marquis 7, Williams 34	16,950
12	8	H	Barnet	W	3-2	2-0	2	Coppinger 15, Blair 32, Williams 90	4861
13	15	H	Colchester U	W	1-0	1-0	2	Rowe 45	5007
14	22	A	Blackpool	L	2-4	1-2	3	Taylor (og) 1, Rowe (pen) 66	3623
15	29	H	Wycombe W	D	2-2	2-1	3	Rowe 29, Marquis 40	5287
16	Nov 12	A	Exeter C	W	3-1	0-0	3	Mandeville 72, Marquis 2 77, 90	3540
17	19	H	Hartlepool U	W	2-1	1-1	3	Marquis 23, Mandeville 90	5009
18	26	H	Leyton Orient	W	3-1	1-1	3	Houghton 45, Mandeville 2 (2 pens) 59, 66	5135
19	Dec 3	A	Stevenage	W	4-3	3-0	1	Butler 28, Mandeville 35, Blair 39, Marquis 73	2705
20	10	A	Plymouth Arg	L	0-2	0-1	3		8575
21	17	H	Grimsby T	W	1-0	1-0	3	Mandeville 3	10,084
22	26	A	Notts Co	W	1-0	0-0	1	Williams 60	5828
23	31	A	Mansfield T	D	1-1	0-0	1	Mandeville (pen) 77	5042
24	Jan 2	H	Stevenage	W	1-0	0-0	1	Franks (og) 85	5604
25	5	H	Portsmouth	W	3-1	1-1	1	Marquis 2 5, 71, Rowe 58	5568
26	14	A	Barnet	W	3-1	3-1	1	Coppinger 2 18, 31, Marquis 28	2582
27	21	H	Crewe Alex	W	3-1	1-1	1	Grant 22, Marquis 56, Rowe 68	5737
28	28	A	Yeovil T	W	3-0	2-0	1	Baudry 31, Marquis 2 35, 79	3627
29	Feb 4	H	Morecambe	D	1-1	0-1	1	Marquis 56	6096
30	10	A	Newport Co	D	0-0	0-0	1		2653
31	14	A	Carlisle U	L	1-2	0-1	1	Rowe 90	4527
32	18	H	Luton T	D	1-1	0-0	1	May 80	7506
33	25	H	Accrington S	D	2-2	1-1	1	Rowe 20, Marquis 58	5272
34	28	A	Cambridge U	W	3-2	2-0	1	Rowe 18, Baudry 23, Marquis (pen) 71	4236
35	Mar 4	A	Crawley T	D	0-0	0-0	1		2417
36	11	H	Cheltenham T	W	2-0	1-0	1	Butler 23, Marquis 81	5737
37	14	H	Notts Co	W	3-1	1-1	1	Coppinger 43, Baudry 47, Williams 90	5760
38	18	A	Leyton Orient	W	4-1	1-1	1	Rowe 36, Marquis 2 55, 82, Baudry 86	4791
39	26	H	Plymouth Arg	L	0-1	0-0	1		7414
40	Apr 1	A	Grimsby T	W	5-1	2-1	1	Marquis 3 37, 43, 61, Williams 78, May 88	6821
41	8	H	Mansfield T	W	1-0	0-0	1	Rowe 74	9903
42	14	A	Colchester U	D	1-1	1-1	1	Baudry 45	4720
43	17	H	Blackpool	L	0-1	0-0	1		6914
44	22	A	Wycombe W	L	1-2	1-2	1	May 18	4587
45	29	H	Exeter C	L	1-3	1-1	2	Coppinger 26	7790
46	May 6	A	Hartlepool U	L	1-2	1-0	3	Williams 31	6799

Final League Position: 3

GOALSCORERS

League (85): Marquis 26 (1 pen), Rowe 13 (2 pens), Williams 11, Coppinger 10, Mandeville 7 (3 pens), Baudry 5, Blair 3, Butler 3, May 3, Grant 1, Houghton 1, own goals 2.
FA Cup (1): Mandeville 1 (1 pen).
EFL Cup (1): Mandeville 1.
EFL Checkatrade Trophy (5): Beestin 1, Calder 1, Longbottom 1, Mandeville 1, Williams 1.

Etheridge R 3 + 3	Lund M 4 + 2	Butler A 44	Mason N 37 + 1	Blair M 45	Rowe T 46	Coppinger J 38 + 1	Houghton J 32	Calder R 5 + 10	Marquis J 45	Williams A 25 + 12	Evina C 13 + 3	Middleton H 6 + 19	Mandeville L 9 + 12	Wright J 18 + 4	Garrett T 1 + 1	Marosi M 24 + 1	Richardson F 3 + 1	Beestin A — + 3	Longbottom W — + 3	Baudry M 26 + 5	Alcock C 24 + 3	Keegan P — + 6	Grant C 20 + 1	Lawlor I 19	May A 9 + 7	McSheffrey G 3 + 9	McCullough L 6 + 1	Taylor-Sinclair A 1 + 3	*Match No.*
1	2	3	4	5	6	7^1	8^3	9^2	10	11	12	13	14																1
1	13	3	4^1	5	6	7	8	9^3	10	11			14	2^2	12														2
	2	4		7	8	9	6		11	10	12			3	5^1	1													3
	2	4		6^1	9	7^2	8		10	11	5	13	12	3		1													4
	2^1	4		7	8	9^2	6		10	11	5	12	13	3		1													5
		4		7	8	9	6	12	10	11	5	13		3^1		1	2^2												6
		3		5	9	8^2	7	12	11	10^3	4	6^1	13	2		1		14											7
		4		2	9	8^3	7	12	10^1	11	5	6^2	13	3		1			14										8
		4		7	8^1	9	6	13	10	11	5^2	14		3		1	2^3			12									9
		4		2	8	9^3	6	7^2	10	11^1	5	13	14	3		1	12												10
		4	13	6	8	9^2	7	12^3	10	11	5	14		3		1	2^1												11
		4	2^2	5	7	8^1	6^3	13		11	9	14	10	3		1				12									12
		4	2	7	8^3	9	6	12	10		5	14	11^2	3^1		1				13									13
13		4	2	8	10	9^3	7	14	11		5	6^1	12			1^2				3									14
1		4	2	7	8^1	11	6	9	10		5							12		3									15
		4^1	2^2	7	9	10	6	8	11		5		14	3^3		1				12	13								16
12		4	5	7	8	9^2	6		10				11			1^1				3	2	13							17
		4	5	7	8	9^2	6		10				11^1			1		13	12	3	2								18
		3	5	6	10	8^2	7		11	13			9^1			1				4	2	12							19
		4^2	5^1	6	9	8■	7	13	10	12			11			1				3	2								20
		3	5	2	8		6	12	10	11^1		7^2	9	13		1				4									21
		4	5	6	9^1		7		10	11		13	8	12		1				3^2	2								22
		3	5	7	9		6		10	11		12	8^1			1				4	2^2	13							23
		4	5	2	6	9^1	7		10	12		8^2				1				3		13	11						24
14		3	2	9^1	6	10^2	7		11	12		13				1^3				4	5		8						25
		4	5	2	9	6^1	7		10	11^3				12						3^2		13	8	1	14				26
		4	5	2^1	9	8	7		10	11										3	12		6	1					27
		4	5	2^2	8	9^1	6		10	11		13								3	12		7	1					28
		4	5	2	8	7	6^2		10	11^1		13	12							3			9	1					29
		4	5	6	9		7		11	10				3							2		8	1					30
			5	2	9	7	6		11	10^1				3							4		8	1	12				31
		4	5^2	2	8	9	6^1		10	11^3		12									3		7	1	13	14			32
		3	4	5	9	7^2			11	13		6								12	2		8	1	10^1				33
		4	5	2	8	9^1			10	12		13								6	3	14	7^2	1	11^3				34
		3	6	2	8	9^2			10	12										4	5		7	1	11^1	13			35
		4	6	2	8	9^1			11	14		12								3	5		7^2	1	10^3	13			36
	12	4	6	2^2	7	9^3			11	14										3	5		8	1	10^1	13			37
		3	7	2	6	8^3			10	13						12				4	5		9	1^1	11^2	14			38
		4	6^1	2	9	7			11	13										3	5^3		8	1	10^2	14	12		39
		4	9^3	5	8				10^1	11	13	12								3	2			1	14	6^2	7		40
		4	5^1	7	8	13			11	10^3				14						3	2			1	12	9^2	6		41
		3	8	5	9				11							1				2^1	4		7		13	10^2	6	12	42
			6	7■	9				11			12		4		1			14	3	2		8^2		10^1	13		5^3	43
		4	5		8	9^2			10				14							3	2^1		7	1	11^3	12	6	13	44
		4	9	5	8	11^2			10	13			12	3^1							2		6^3	1	14		7		45
		3	9	8	7	6^2			10	11				4							5^1		12	1		14	2^3	13	46

FA Cup
First Round Oldham Ath (a) 1-2

EFL Cup
First Round Nottingham F (h) 1-2

EFL Checkatrade Trophy

Northern Group E	Mansfield T	(a)	2-0
Northern Group E	Derby Co U21	(h)	2-2
(Doncaster R won 4-2 on penalties)			
Northern Group E	Port Vale	(h)	0-0
(Port Vale won 4-3 on penalties)			
Second Round North	Blackpool	(h)	1-1
(Blackpool won 8-7 on penalties)			

EVERTON

FOUNDATION

St Domingo Church Sunday School formed a football club in 1878 which played at Stanley Park. Enthusiasm was so great that in November 1879 they decided to expand membership and changed the name to Everton, playing in black shirts with a scarlet sash and nicknamed the 'Black Watch'. After wearing several other colours, royal blue was adopted in 1901.

Goodison Park, Goodison Road, Liverpool L4 4EL.

Telephone: (0151) 556 1878.

Fax: (0151) 281 1046.

Ticket Office: (0151) 556 1878.

Website: www.evertonfc.com

Email: everton@evertonfc.com

Ground Capacity: 40,157.

Record Attendance: 78,299 v Liverpool, Division 1, 18 September 1948.

Pitch Measurements: 100.48m × 68m (109yd × 74yd).

Chairman: Bill Kenwright CBE.

Chief Executive: Robert Elstone.

Manager: Ronald Koeman.

Assistant Manager: Erwin Koeman.

Physio: Matt Connery.

Colours: Blue shirts with white and yellow trim, white shorts with blue and yellow trim, white socks with blue and yellow band.

Year Formed: 1878.

Turned Professional: 1885.

Previous Name: 1878, St Domingo FC; 1879, Everton.

Club Nickname: 'The Toffees'.

Grounds: 1878, Stanley Park; 1882, Priory Road; 1884, Anfield Road; 1892, Goodison Park.

First Football League Game: 8 September 1888, Football League, v Accrington (h) W 2–1 – Smalley; Dick, Ross; Holt, Jones, Dobson; Fleming (2), Waugh, Lewis, Edgar Chadwick, Farmer.

Record League Victory: 9–1 v Manchester C, Division 1, 3 September 1906 – Scott; Balmer, Crelley; Booth, Taylor (1), Abbott (1); Sharp, Bolton (1), Young (4), Settle (2), George Wilson. 9–1 v Plymouth Arg, Division 2, 27 December 1930 – Coggins; Williams, Cresswell; McPherson, Griffiths, Thomson; Critchley, Dunn, Dean (4), Johnson (1), Stein (4).

HONOURS

League Champions: Division 1 – 1914–15, 1927–28, 1931–32, 1938–39, 1962–63, 1969–70, 1984–85, 1986–87; Football League 1890–91; Division 2 – 1930–31.
Runners-up: Division 1 – 1894–95, 1901–02, 1904–05, 1908–09, 1911–12, 1985–86; Football League 1889–90; Division 2 – 1953–54.

FA Cup Winners: 1906, 1933, 1966, 1984, 1995.
Runners-up: 1893, 1897, 1907, 1968, 1985, 1986, 1989, 2009.

League Cup: *Runners-up:* 1977, 1984.

League Super Cup: *Runners-up:* 1986.

Full Members' Cup: *Runners-up:* 1989, 1991.

European Competitions
European Cup: 1963–64, 1970–71 *(qf)*.
Champions League: 2005–06.
Fairs Cup: 1962–63, 1964–65, 1965–66.
UEFA Cup: 1975–76, 1978–79, 1979–80, 2005–06, 2007–08, 2008–09.
Europa League: 2009–10, 2014–15.
European Cup-Winners' Cup: 1966–67, 1984–85 *(winners)*, 1995–96.

sky SPORTS FACT FILE

Bob Latchford became Britain's most expensive footballer when he joined Everton from Birmingham City in February 1974. The deal, which saw Toffees players Howard Kendall and Archie Styles move in the opposite direction, was valued at £300,000. Latchford went on to score over a century of goals during his stay with the club, finishing top scorer four seasons in a row.

Record Cup Victory: 11–2 v Derby Co, FA Cup 1st rd, 18 January 1890 – Smalley; Hannah, Doyle (1); Kirkwood, Holt (1), Parry; Latta, Brady (3), Geary (3), Edgar Chadwick, Millward (3).

Record Defeat: 4–10 v Tottenham H, Division 1, 11 October 1958.

Most League Points (2 for a win): 66, Division 1, 1969–70.

Most League Points (3 for a win): 90, Division 1, 1984–85.

Most League Goals: 121, Division 2, 1930–31.

Highest League Scorer in Season: William Ralph 'Dixie' Dean, 60, Division 1, 1927–28 (All-time League record).

Most League Goals in Total Aggregate: William Ralph 'Dixie' Dean, 349, 1925–37.

Most League Goals in One Match: 6, Jack Southworth v WBA, Division 1, 30 December 1893.

Most Capped Player: Tim Howard, 93 (115), USA.

Most League Appearances: Neville Southall, 578, 1981–98.

Youngest League Player: Jose Baxter, 16 years 191 days v Blackburn R, 16 August 2008.

Record Transfer Fee Received: £75,000,000 from Manchester U for Romelu Lukaku, July 2017.

Record Transfer Fee Paid: £25,000,000 (rising to £30,000,000) to Sunderland for Jordan Pickford, June 2017; £25,000,000 (rising to £30,000,000) to Burnley for Michael Keane, July 2017.

Football League Record: 1888 Founder Member of the Football League; 1930–31 Division 2; 1931–51 Division 1; 1951–54 Division 2; 1954–92 Division 1; 1992– FA Premier League.

MANAGERS

W. E. Barclay 1888–89
(Secretary-Manager)
Dick Molyneux 1889–1901
(Secretary-Manager)
William C. Cuff 1901–18
(Secretary-Manager)
W. J. Sawyer 1918–19
(Secretary-Manager)
Thomas H. McIntosh 1919–35
(Secretary-Manager)
Theo Kelly 1936–48
Cliff Britton 1948–56
Ian Buchan 1956–58
Johnny Carey 1958–61
Harry Catterick 1961–73
Billy Bingham 1973–77
Gordon Lee 1977–81
Howard Kendall 1981–87
Colin Harvey 1987–90
Howard Kendall 1990–93
Mike Walker 1994
Joe Royle 1994–97
Howard Kendall 1997–98
Walter Smith 1998–2002
David Moyes 2002–13
Roberto Martinez 2013–16
Ronald Koeman June 2016–

LATEST SEQUENCES

Longest Sequence of League Wins: 12, 24.3.1894 – 13.10.1894.

Longest Sequence of League Defeats: 6, 27.8.2005– 15.10.2005.

Longest Sequence of League Draws: 5, 4.5.1977 – 16.5.1977.

Longest Sequence of Unbeaten League Matches: 20, 29.4.1978 – 16.12.1978.

Longest Sequence Without a League Win: 14, 6.3.1937 – 4.9.1937.

Successive Scoring Runs: 40 from 15.3.1930.

Successive Non-scoring Runs: 6 from 27.8.2005.

TEN YEAR LEAGUE RECORD

		P	W	D	L	F	A	Pts	Pos
2007-08	PR Lge	38	19	8	11	55	33	65	5
2008-09	PR Lge	38	17	12	9	55	37	63	5
2009-10	PR Lge	38	16	13	9	60	49	61	8
2010-11	PR Lge	38	13	15	10	51	45	54	7
2011-12	PR Lge	38	15	11	12	50	40	56	7
2012-13	PR Lge	38	16	15	7	55	40	63	6
2013-14	PR Lge	38	21	9	8	61	39	72	5
2014-15	PR Lge	38	12	11	15	48	50	47	11
2015-16	PR Lge	38	11	14	13	59	55	47	11
2016-17	PR Lge	38	17	10	11	62	44	61	7

DID YOU KNOW 

Everton have been the best-supported club in English football on three occasions: 1955–56, 1962–63 and 1963–64. The highest average attendance at Goodison Park was 51,603 in 1962–63 when the Toffees won the Football League title.

EVERTON – PREMIER LEAGUE 2016–17 LEAGUE RECORD

Match No.	Date	Venue	Opponents	Result		H/T Score	Lg Pos.	Goalscorers	Attendance
1	Aug 13	H	Tottenham H	D	1-1	1-0	3	Barkley [5]	39,494
2	20	A	WBA	W	2-1	1-1	5	Mirallas [45], Barry [60]	23,654
3	27	H	Stoke C	W	1-0	0-0	2	Given (og) [51]	39,581
4	Sept 12	A	Sunderland	W	3-0	0-0	3	Lukaku 3 [60, 68, 71]	42,406
5	17	H	Middlesbrough	W	3-1	3-1	1	Barry [24], Coleman [42], Lukaku [45]	39,074
6	24	A	Bournemouth	L	0-1	0-1	2		11,291
7	30	H	Crystal Palace	D	1-1	1-0	3	Lukaku [35]	38,758
8	Oct 15	A	Manchester C	D	1-1	0-0	6	Lukaku [64]	54,512
9	22	A	Burnley	L	1-2	0-1	6	Bolasie [58]	21,416
10	30	H	West Ham U	W	2-0	0-0	6	Lukaku [50], Barkley [76]	39,574
11	Nov 5	A	Chelsea	L	0-5	0-3	6		41,429
12	19	H	Swansea C	D	1-1	0-1	6	Coleman [89]	38,773
13	27	A	Southampton	L	0-1	0-1	7		31,132
14	Dec 4	H	Manchester U	D	1-1	0-1	8	Baines (pen) [89]	39,550
15	10	A	Watford	L	2-3	1-1	9	Lukaku 2 [17, 86]	20,769
16	13	H	Arsenal	W	2-1	1-1	7	Coleman [44], Williams, A [86]	39,510
17	19	H	Liverpool	L	0-1	0-0	9		39,590
18	26	A	Leicester C	W	2-0	0-0	7	Mirallas [51], Lukaku [90]	31,985
19	30	A	Hull C	D	2-2	1-1	7	Marshall (og) [45], Barkley [84]	20,111
20	Jan 2	H	Southampton	W	3-0	0-0	7	Valencia [73], Baines (pen) [81], Lukaku [89]	38,891
21	15	H	Manchester C	W	4-0	1-0	7	Lukaku [34], Mirallas [47], Davies [79], Lookman [90]	39,588
22	21	A	Crystal Palace	W	1-0	0-0	7	Coleman [87]	25,594
23	Feb 1	A	Stoke C	D	1-1	1-1	7	Shawcross (og) [39]	27,612
24	4	H	Bournemouth	W	6-3	3-0	7	Lukaku 4 [1, 29, 83, 84], McCarthy [23], Barkley [90]	39,026
25	11	A	Middlesbrough	D	0-0	0-0	7		31,496
26	25	H	Sunderland	W	2-0	1-0	7	Gana [40], Lukaku [80]	39,595
27	Mar 5	A	Tottenham H	L	2-3	0-1	7	Lukaku [81], Valencia [90]	31,962
28	11	H	WBA	W	3-0	2-0	7	Mirallas [39], Schneiderlin [45], Lukaku [82]	39,592
29	18	H	Hull C	W	4-0	1-0	6	Calvert-Lewin [9], Valencia [78], Lukaku 2 [90, 90]	39,248
30	Apr 1	A	Liverpool	L	1-3	1-2	7	Pennington [28]	52,920
31	4	A	Manchester U	D	1-1	1-0	7	Jagielka [22]	75,272
32	9	H	Leicester C	W	4-2	3-2	6	Davies [1], Lukaku 2 [23, 57], Jagielka [41]	39,573
33	15	H	Burnley	W	3-1	0-0	5	Jagielka [49], Mee (og) [71], Lukaku [74]	39,328
34	22	A	West Ham U	D	0-0	0-0	6		56,971
35	30	H	Chelsea	L	0-3	0-0	7		39,595
36	May 6	A	Swansea C	L	0-1	0-1	7		20,827
37	12	H	Watford	W	1-0	0-0	7	Barkley [56]	38,550
38	21	A	Arsenal	L	1-3	0-2	7	Lukaku (pen) [58]	59,976

Final League Position: 7

GOALSCORERS

League (62): Lukaku 25 (1 pen), Barkley 5, Coleman 4, Mirallas 4, Jagielka 3, Valencia 3, Baines 2 (2 pens), Barry 2, Davies 2, Bolasie 1, Calvert-Lewin 1, Gana 1, Lookman 1, McCarthy 1, Pennington 1, Schneiderlin 1, Williams, A 1, own goals 4.
FA Cup (1): Lukaku 1.
EFL Cup (4): Kone 2, Barkley 1, Lennon 1.
EFL Checkatrade Trophy (4): Charsley 1, Dyson 1, McAleny 1, own goal 1.

Stekelenburg M 19	Holgate M 16 + 2	Jagielka P 25 + 2	Funes Mori R 16 + 7	McCarthy J 7 + 5	Gana I 32 + 1	Barry G 23 + 10	Baines L 32	Barkley R 32 + 4	Deulofeu G 4 + 7	Mirallas K 23 + 12	Kone A — + 6	Lennon A 6 + 5	Cleverley T 4 + 6	Lukaku R 36 + 1	Bolasie Y 12 + 1	Williams A 35 + 1	Davies T 18 + 6	Coleman S 26	Valencia E 5 + 16	Oviedo B 6	Robles J 19 + 1	Calvert-Lewin D 5 + 6	Schneiderlin M 12 + 2	Lookman A 3 + 5	Pennington M 2 + 1	Kenny J — + 1	Match No.
1	2	3	4	5	6	7²	8	9	10¹	11³	12	13	14														1
1	2	3	4	5¹	6	7	8	10	11²	9³				12	13	14											2
1	2	3	13		6	7	5	9²		10¹	12			11	8³	4	14										3
1		3			6	7	5	9¹	12	8	14			11²	10³	4	13	2									4
1		3			6	7³	5	9	13	8¹			14	11²	10	4		2	12								5
1		3			6²	7¹		9	13	10³			12	11	8	4		2	14	5							6
1		3	13		6	7		9²		12			8	10	11	4		2		5¹							7
1		3	14	12	8	7			11³	13			6¹	10	9²	4		2		5							8
1		3³			6²	7		8	12	11¹			13	10	9	4		2	14	5							9
		13	4		6	7		9²		10³		14	12	11	8¹	3		2		5	1						10
1		4	5			8²		9		12		13	7	10	11¹	3	14	2		6³							11
1		3¹		6³	7		5	9	12	13		8²		11	10	4		2	14								12
1		3			6	7	5²	9³	12	13		8¹		11	10	4		2	14								13
1	13		4		7	8	5		12	11			9³	10	6¹	3		2²	14								14
1			4	9	6¹	7	5²	12	8	10³		14		11		3		2	13								15
1		3■	14	6²	7		5	8		12		11³		10		4		2	9¹			13					16
1³			4	6²	7	12	5	9				10		11		3		2	8¹		13	14					17
	2		4		6	7¹	8	13		10²		9³	14	11		3	12	5			1						18
		3	14		6	7¹	5	9		10³				11		4	12	2	8²		1	13					19
			4		6	14	5	10³		12		8¹		11		3	7	2	13		1	9²					20
	2		4	13		7²	9	8³		10¹				11		3	6	5			1		12	14			21
	2	14	4			7³	9	8¹		11²				10		3	6	5			1		12	13			22
	2¹		4	12			9	8		11²				10		3	6	5			1		7	13			23
	14		4	6¹		7²	5	9		13				10		3	12	2			1		8	11³			24
			4		8³	14	5	9¹				13		10		3	6	2	12		1		7	11²			25
			4	14	8		5	9²		12				10		3	6¹	2	13		1		7	11³			26
			4	13	6³	8²	5	10		12				11		3	9¹	2	14		1		7				27
		3	12		13	7²	5³	8		10¹				11		4	9	2			1	14	6				28
		3	13		9	12	5	7						11		4	8²	2	14		1	10¹	6³				29
	5	4			7	13	8	9		14				10		3	6¹		12		1	11³			2²		30
	2	3			6	7	5	9²		11¹				10		4■	8				1	13			12		31
	2	4			6	12	5	9		11				10			8				1		7¹		3		32
	2	3			6¹	13	5	9²		11³				10		4	8		12		1		7	14			33
1	2	3			6³	13	5	9		11¹				10		4	8²					14	7	12			34
1	2	3			6		5	9		12	13			11		4	7		8¹			10²					35
1	2²	3			6	7¹	5	12		9				10		4	8		13			11³				14	36
	2²	3			6	13	5	9³		11¹	14			10		4	8		12		1		7				37
	2	3			6¹	13	5	12		11	14			10		4	8²		9³		1		7				38

FA Cup

Third Round	Leicester C	(h)	1-2

EFL Cup

Second Round	Yeovil T	(h)	4-0
Third Round	Norwich C	(h)	0-2

EFL Checkatrade Trophy (Everton U21)

Northern Group A	Bolton W	(a)	2-0
Northern Group A	Cheltenham T	(a)	1-2
Northern Group A	Blackpool	(h)	1-1

(*Blackpool won 5-4 on penalties*)

EXETER CITY

FOUNDATION

Exeter City was formed in 1904 by the amalgamation of St Sidwell's United and Exeter United. The club first played in the East Devon League and then the Plymouth & District League. After an exhibition match between West Bromwich Albion and Woolwich Arsenal, which was held to test interest as Exeter was then a rugby stronghold, it was decided to form Exeter City. At a meeting at the Red Lion Hotel in 1908, the club turned professional.

St James Park, Stadium Way, Exeter, Devon EX4 6PX.

Telephone: (01392) 411 243.

Fax: (01392) 413 959.

Ticket Office: (01392) 411 243.

Website: www.exetercityfc.co.uk

Email: reception@exetercityfc.co.uk

Ground Capacity: 8,714.

Record Attendance: 20,984 v Sunderland, FA Cup 6th rd (replay), 4 March 1931.

Pitch Measurements: 104m × 64m (113.5yd × 70yd).

Trust Board Chairman: Martin Weiler.

Manager: Paul Tisdale.

Director of Football: Steve Perryman.

Colours: Red and white striped shirts with red sleeves, black shorts with red trim, white socks with black hoops.

Year Formed: 1904.

Turned Professional: 1908.

Club Nickname: 'The Grecians'.

Ground: 1904, St James Park.

First Football League Game: 28 August 1920, Division 3, v Brentford (h) W 3–0 – Pym; Coleburne, Feebury (1p); Crawshaw, Carrick, Mitton; Appleton, Makin, Wright (1), Vowles (1), Dockray.

Record League Victory: 8–1 v Coventry C, Division 3 (S), 4 December 1926 – Bailey; Pollard, Charlton; Pullen, Pool, Garrett; Purcell (2), McDevitt, Blackmore (2), Dent (2), Compton (2). 8–1 v Aldershot, Division 3 (S), 4 May 1935 – Chesters; Gray, Miller; Risdon, Webb, Angus; Jack Scott (1), Wrightson (1), Poulter (3), McArthur (1), Dryden (1), (1 og).

Record Cup Victory: 14–0 v Weymouth, FA Cup 1st qual rd, 3 October 1908 – Fletcher; Craig, Bulcock; Ambler, Chadwick, Wake; Parnell (1), Watson (1), McGuigan (4), Bell (6), Copestake (2).

Record Defeat: 0–9 v Notts Co, Division 3 (S), 16 October 1948. 0–9 v Northampton T, Division 3 (S), 12 April 1958.

Most League Points (2 for a win): 62, Division 4, 1976–77.

HONOURS

League Champions: Division 4 – 1989–90.
Runners-up: Division 3S – 1932–33; FL 2 – 2008–09; Division 4 – 1976–77; Conference – (4th) 2007–08 *(promoted via play-offs)*.

FA Cup: 6th rd replay – 1931; 6th rd – 1981.

League Cup: never past 4th rd.

sky SPORTS FACT FILE

Exeter City played in the Plymouth and District League before turning professional in the summer of 1908 when they joined the Southern League. They played their first match in the new competition on 2 September 1908 when they drew 2-2 away to Millwall; James Bell scored both City's goals.

Most League Points (3 for a win): 89, Division 4, 1989–90.

Most League Goals: 88, Division 3 (S), 1932–33.

Highest League Scorer in Season: Fred Whitlow, 33, Division 3 (S), 1932–33.

Most League Goals in Total Aggregate: Tony Kellow, 129, 1976–78, 1980–83, 1985–88.

Most League Goals in One Match: 4, Harold 'Jazzo' Kirk v Portsmouth, Division 3 (S), 3 March 1923; 4, Fred Dent v Bristol R, Division 3 (S), 5 November 1927; 4, Fred Whitlow v Watford, Division 3 (S), 29 October 1932.

Most Capped Player: Joel Grant, 2 (14), Jamaica.

Most League Appearances: Arnold Mitchell, 495, 1952–66.

Youngest League Player: Ethan Ampadu, 15 years 337 days v Crawley T, 16 August 2016.

Record Transfer Fee Received: £1,750,000 from Swansea C for Matt Grimes, January 2015.

Record Transfer Fee Paid: £65,000 to Blackpool for Tony Kellow, March 1980.

Football League Record: 1920 Elected to Division 3; 1921–58 Division 3 (S); 1958–64 Division 4; 1964–66 Division 3; 1966–77 Division 4; 1977–84 Division 3; 1984–90 Division 4; 1990–92 Division 3; 1992–94 Division 2; 1994–2003 Division 3; 2003–08 Conference; 2008–09 FL 2; 2009–12 FL 1; 2012– FL 2.

MANAGERS

Arthur Chadwick 1910–22
Fred Mavin 1923–27
Dave Wilson 1928–29
Billy McDevitt 1929–35
Jack English 1935–39
George Roughton 1945–52
Norman Kirkman 1952–53
Norman Dodgin 1953–57
Bill Thompson 1957–58
Frank Broome 1958–60
Glen Wilson 1960–62
Cyril Spiers 1962–63
Jack Edwards 1963–65
Ellis Stuttard 1965–66
Jock Basford 1966–67
Frank Broome 1967–69
Johnny Newman 1969–76
Bobby Saxton 1977–79
Brian Godfrey 1979–83
Gerry Francis 1983–84
Jim Iley 1984–85
Colin Appleton 1985–87
Terry Cooper 1988–91
Alan Ball 1991–94
Terry Cooper 1994–95
Peter Fox 1995–2000
Noel Blake 2000–01
John Cornforth 2001–02
Neil McNab 2002–03
Gary Peters 2003
Eamonn Dolan 2003–04
Alex Inglethorpe 2004–06
Paul Tisdale June 2006–

LATEST SEQUENCES

Longest Sequence of League Wins: 7, 31.12.2016 – 4.2.2017.

Longest Sequence of League Defeats: 7, 14.1.1984 – 25.2.1984.

Longest Sequence of League Draws: 6, 13.9.1986 – 4.10.1986.

Longest Sequence of Unbeaten League Matches: 13, 23.8.1986 – 25.10.1986.

Longest Sequence Without a League Win: 18, 21.2.1995 – 19.8.1995.

Successive Scoring Runs: 22 from 15.9.1958.

Successive Non-scoring Runs: 6 from 17.1.1986.

TEN YEAR LEAGUE RECORD

		P	W	D	L	F	A	Pts	Pos
2007-08	Conf P	46	22	17	7	83	58	83	4
2008-09	FL 2	46	22	13	11	65	50	79	2
2009-10	FL 1	46	11	18	17	48	60	51	18
2010-11	FL 1	46	20	10	16	66	73	70	8
2011-12	FL 1	46	10	12	24	46	75	42	23
2012-13	FL 2	46	18	10	18	63	62	64	10
2013-14	FL 2	46	14	13	19	54	57	55	16
2014-15	FL 2	46	17	13	16	61	65	64	10
2015-16	FL 2	46	17	13	16	63	65	64	14
2016-17	FL 2	46	21	8	17	75	56	71	5

DID YOU KNOW ?

Exeter City forward Harold Houghton was included in the FA party that toured Canada in the summer of 1931, winning all 17 fixtures. He played in 8 of the games scoring 9 goals, including hat-tricks against New Ontario and Saskatoon.

EXETER CITY – SKY BET LEAGUE TWO 2016–17 LEAGUE RECORD

Match No.	Date	Venue	Opponents	Result		H/T Score	Lg Pos.	Goalscorers	Attendance
1	Aug 6	A	Blackpool	L	0-2	0-1	21		3754
2	13	H	Hartlepool U	L	1-2	1-0	23	McAlinden [31]	3322
3	16	H	Crawley T	L	0-1	0-0	24		2660
4	20	A	Accrington S	W	2-1	0-0	23	Harley [66], Taylor [72]	1300
5	27	H	Portsmouth	L	0-1	0-0	23		4512
6	Sept 3	A	Colchester U	W	3-2	1-2	18	Simpson [8], Watkins [51], Grant [67]	3364
7	10	A	Crewe Alex	L	0-2	0-1	21		3896
8	17	H	Plymouth Arg	L	0-2	0-2	21		6612
9	24	A	Stevenage	W	2-0	0-0	20	Holmes [70], Watkins [71]	2244
10	27	H	Notts Co	L	0-2	0-2	22		3081
11	Oct 1	A	Wycombe W	L	0-1	0-0	23		3297
12	8	H	Grimsby T	D	0-0	0-0	23		3557
13	15	A	Barnet	W	4-1	1-1	20	Taylor [43], Holmes [50], Wheeler [56], Reid (pen) [81]	1640
14	22	H	Cambridge U	L	1-2	0-2	23	Grant [73]	3485
15	29	A	Morecambe	W	3-0	3-0	19	Wheeler [4], Grant [16], Holmes [35]	1302
16	Nov 12	H	Doncaster R	L	1-3	0-0	22	Reid (pen) [51]	3540
17	19	A	Carlisle U	L	2-3	1-1	24	Reid [1], Holmes [54]	5058
18	22	A	Leyton Orient	W	1-0	1-0	21	Watkins [26]	2926
19	26	H	Luton T	D	0-0	0-0	21		3823
20	Dec 10	A	Cheltenham T	W	3-1	0-0	17	Holmes [55], Wheeler 2 [81, 85]	3113
21	17	H	Mansfield T	W	2-0	1-0	15	Watkins 2 [19, 90]	3626
22	26	A	Yeovil T	D	0-0	0-0	15		6086
23	31	A	Newport Co	W	4-1	1-0	11	Watkins 3 [45, 47, 90], Wheeler [53]	2663
24	Jan 2	H	Leyton Orient	W	4-0	1-0	11	Wheeler [4], Harley 2 (1 pen) [50, 65 (p)], McAlinden [82]	4537
25	14	A	Grimsby T	W	3-0	1-0	10	Reid [41], Wheeler [59], Watkins [80]	5009
26	21	H	Colchester U	W	3-0	1-0	9	Reid [20], Wheeler [77], McAlinden [89]	4114
27	28	A	Portsmouth	W	1-0	0-0	7	Wheeler [57]	17,195
28	31	H	Wycombe W	W	4-2	1-1	4	Wheeler [19], Brown [65], Grant [67], Watkins [90]	3656
29	Feb 4	H	Crewe Alex	W	4-0	1-0	4	Moore-Taylor [8], Wheeler 2 [58, 68], James [85]	4534
30	11	A	Plymouth Arg	L	0-3	0-2	5		14,671
31	14	A	Notts Co	D	2-2	1-0	6	Wheeler [33], Harley [88]	4047
32	18	H	Stevenage	D	1-1	0-1	6	Reid [52]	4125
33	25	H	Blackpool	D	2-2	1-2	6	Watkins [45], Reid [90]	4125
34	28	A	Crawley T	W	2-1	0-0	6	Watkins [50], Moore-Taylor [68]	1826
35	Mar 4	A	Hartlepool U	L	1-3	1-0	7	Watkins [14]	3775
36	11	H	Accrington S	L	0-2	0-1	7		3897
37	14	H	Cheltenham T	W	3-0	1-0	7	Reid 2 (1 pen) [43 (p), 51], Taylor [57]	3539
38	18	A	Luton T	D	1-1	0-0	7	Taylor [59]	7657
39	25	H	Yeovil T	D	3-3	0-0	7	Wheeler [88], Brown [90], Reid [90]	5492
40	Apr 1	A	Mansfield T	W	2-1	0-1	6	Harley [84], Reid (pen) [90]	3878
41	8	H	Newport Co	L	0-1	0-0	6		4040
42	14	H	Barnet	W	2-1	2-0	5	Moore-Taylor [4], Wheeler [6]	4780
43	17	A	Cambridge U	L	0-1	0-1	6		6130
44	22	H	Morecambe	W	3-1	0-0	5	Wheeler [47], Reid (pen) [90], McAlinden [90]	3991
45	29	A	Doncaster R	W	3-1	1-1	5	Moore-Taylor [16], Wheeler [61], McAlinden [86]	7790
46	May 6	H	Carlisle U	L	2-3	2-1	5	Reid [9], Moore-Taylor [45]	6774

Final League Position: 5

GOALSCORERS

League (75): Wheeler 17, Reid 13 (5 pens), Watkins 13, Harley 5 (1 pen), Holmes 5, McAlinden 5, Moore-Taylor 5, Grant 4, Taylor 4, Brown 2, James 1, Simpson 1.
FA Cup (1): Reid 1.
EFL Cup (2): Harley 1, Taylor 1.
EFL Checkatrade Trophy (6): McAlinden 2, Wheeler 2, Jay 1, Watkins 1.
League Two Play-Offs (7): Watkins 2, Wheeler 2, Grant 1, Harley 1, Stacey 1.

Olejnik R 17 + 1	Woodman C 33	Sweeney P 27 + 2	Brown T 28 + 2	Moore-Taylor J 42	Taylor J 43	James L 42 + 1	Harley R 28 + 3	Holmes L 12 + 4	Simpson R 14 + 12	Watkins O 40 + 5	Oakley M 5 + 14	McAlinden L 9 + 23	Wheeler D 33 + 5	McCready T 1 + 1	Tillson J 9 + 11	Riley-Lowe C 4 + 2	Jay M — + 2	Egan K — + 1	Ampadu E 6 + 2	Grant J 9 + 11	Croll L 16 + 3	Stacey J 27 + 7	Reid R 31 + 5	Pym C 28	Hamon J 1	Archibald-Henville T 1 + 2	*Match No.*
1	2^{1}	3	4^{2}	5	6	7	8	9	10^{3}	11	12	13	14														1
1	5^{3}	3		4	6	7			11	9		10^{1}		2^{2}	8	12	13	14									2
1		2		5	6^{2}	7	8		10	9	4	11^{1}		13		12			3								3
1	2	4	3	5	6	7	8		10	11					12	9^{1}											4
1		2	3		8	7	9		13	10	14	11^{3}			6^{1}	5			4^{2}	12							5
1		2	13	5	8	7	6		10^{2}	11	14								3^{1}	12	4^{3}	9					6
1		4		3	2	7	9		10	8	12					5				6^{1}		11					7
1		3		5	6	7	8^{2}	12	10	9										11^{1}	4	2	13				8
1	5	2		4■	8^{1}	7		12	11	9	13										3	6	10^{2}				9
1	5	3			8	7		9	11^{3}	6		14	13						12		4^{2}	2^{1}	10				10
1	5	12		4	8	7		9^{2}	11^{3}	6		14	13								3	2^{1}	10				11
	5	2		4	8	7		9	11^{2}	12		13	6								3		10^{1}	1			12
	5	2		4	7	8		9^{1}		11		14	6^{2}							13	3	12	10^{3}	1			13
	5	2		4		13		9	10	11	8^{2}		6							12	3^{1}	7		1			14
12	5	2		4	8	7		9	13				6							10	3^{1}	14	11^{2}	1^{3}			15
	5	3			8	7		9	12	10	4		6^{1}				13					2	11^{2}		1		16
	5	4	14	3	8			9^{2}	13	10	7	12	6^{3}								2		11^{1}	1			17
	5	2		4	8	6			14	9^{1}	12	10^{2}	7^{3}								3	13	11	1			18
	5	2^{2}	3	4	8	7			14	11	12	9^{3}	6^{1}						13				10	1			19
	5		3		7	8		9		10	4^{1}	13	6		12							2	11^{2}	1			20
	5		3	4	7	8^{3}		9^{1}		11	13	14	6		12							2	10^{2}	1			21
	5^{2}		3	4	8	7	12	9^{3}		10		13	6							14		2	11^{1}	1			22
			3	4	7	8	12		14	9		11^{3}	6^{1}		13	5				10^{2}		2		1			23
	5^{2}		3	4		7	9^{3}		13	11		12	6		8							2	10^{1}	1		14	24
	5		3	4	8	7^{1}	9^{2}		14	10		12	6		13							2	11^{3}	1			25
	5		3	4	8	7	9^{2}		13	11^{1}		12	6		14							2	10^{3}	1			26
	5		3	4	8	7	9			10		12	6									2	11^{1}	1			27
	5		3	4	8	7			11^{3}	12		13	6		14					9^{2}		2	10^{1}	1			28
	5		3	4^{1}	8	7	9^{3}		12	10^{2}		11	6							14	13	2		1			29
	5		3	4	8	7	9		12	10		13	6^{1}									2	11^{2}	1			30
	5		4	3	7■	8	6			11		12	9									2	10^{1}	1			31
1	5		3	4		7	9			10		12	6		8^{1}					13		2	11^{2}				32
	5		3	4	8	7^{3}	9		10^{2}	12		11^{1}	6							14		2	13	1			33
1	5		3	4	8	7^{1}	9			11	13	12	6^{2}		14							2	10^{3}				34
1	5^{3}	14	3	4	8^{1}	7	9			11		12	6							13		2	10^{2}				35
1	5^{2}	2		4	8	7^{1}	12			10		14	6							9	3^{3}	13	11				36
1	5		3	4	9^{3}	8	6			12	14	13	11^{1}		7							2	10^{2}				37
1	5		3	4^{3}	8^{1}	7	9			10	14		6		13						12	2	11^{2}				38
	5^{3}	2	3	4	6^{2}	7	9			10		11^{1}	12		8							13	14	1			39
		2	3	4	8	7^{2}	9			10	13		11							14	5^{3}	6^{1}	12	1			40
		2	3	4^{2}	6	7^{1}	9			13	14		11		8^{3}						5	12	10	1			41
		2		4	8		9			11	12		6		7				3^{1}		5		10^{2}	1		13	42
		2		4	8^{2}	7	9	14		11			12							6	5	13	10^{3}	1		3^{1}	43
		2	3	5	8		9	13		10^{3}		14	11		4				7^{2}	6^{1}			12	1			44
		3	4	2	7	6	8			10		13	5		12					9^{2}			11^{1}	1			45
		2	3	4	6^{3}	8^{2}	9^{1}			11			5		13				7	14	12		10	1			46

FA Cup

First Round	Luton T	(h)	1-3

EFL Cup

First Round (*aet*)	Brentford	(h)	1-0
Second Round	Hull C	(h)	1-3

EFL Checkatrade Trophy

Southern Group C	Oxford U	(a)	2-4
Southern Group C	Chelsea U21	(h)	3-2
Southern Group C	Swindon T	(h)	1-1

(*Swindon T won 4-2 on penalties*)

League Two Play-Offs

Semi-Final 1st leg	Carlisle U	(a)	3-3
Semi-Final 2nd leg	Carlisle U	(h)	3-2
Final	Blackpool	(Wembley)	1-2

FLEETWOOD TOWN

FOUNDATION

Originally formed in 1908 as Fleetwood FC, it was liquidated in 1976. Re-formed as Fleetwood Town in 1977, it folded again in 1996. Once again, it was re-formed a year later as Fleetwood Wanderers, but a sponsorship deal saw the club's name immediately changed to Fleetwood Freeport through the local retail outlet centre. This sponsorship ended in 2002, but since then local energy businessman Andy Pilley took charge and the club has risen through the non-league pyramid until finally achieving Football League status in 2012 as Fleetwood Town.

Highbury Stadium, Park Avenue, Fleetwood, Lancashire FY7 6TX.

Telephone: (01253) 775 080.

Fax: (01253) 775 081.

Ticket Office: (01253) 775 080

Website: www.fleetwoodtownfc.com

Email: info@fleetwoodtownfc.com

Ground Capacity: 5,133.

Record Attendance: (Before 1997) 6,150 v Rochdale, FA Cup 1st rd, 13 November 1965; (Since 1997) 5,194 v York C, FL 2 Play-Off semi-final 2nd leg, 16 May 2014.

Pitch Measurements: 100.5m × 65m (110yd × 71yd).

Chairman: Andy Pilley.

Chief Executive: Steve Curwood.

Head Coach: Uwe Rosler.

Assistant Head Coach: Rob Kelly.

Colours: Red shirts with white sleeves and red trim, white shorts with red trim, red socks with white trim.

Year Formed: 1908 (re-formed 1997).

Previous Names: 1908, Fleetwood FC; 1977, Fleetwood Town; 1997, Fleetwood Wanderers; 2002 Fleetwood Town.

Club Nicknames: 'The Trawlermen', 'The Cod Army'.

Grounds: 1908, North Euston Hotel; 1934, Memorial Park (now Highbury Stadium).

HONOURS

League Champions: Conference – 2011–12.

FA Cup: 3rd rd – 2012, 2017.

League Cup: never past 1st rd.

sky SPORTS FACT FILE

Fleetwood Town have met local rivals Blackpool at senior level on four occasions and have yet to record a win. The teams met twice in FA Cup action when Fleetwood were non-league, resulting in losses of 4-0 and 5-1 for Fleetwood, while the two clashes in League One in 2015–16 resulted in a 1-0 win for Blackpool and a goalless draw.

MANAGER

Alan Tinsley 1997
Mark Hughes 1998
Brian Wilson 1998–99
Mick Hoyle 1999–2001
Les Attwood 2001
Mark Hughes 2001
Alan Tinsley 2001–02
Mick Hoyle 2002–03
Tony Greenwood 2003–08
Micky Mellon 2008–12
Graham Alexander 2012–15
Steven Pressley 2015–16
Uwe Rosler July 2016–

First Football League Game: 18 August 2012, FL 2, v Torquay U (h) D 0–0 – Davies; Beeley, Mawene, McNulty, Howell, Nicolson, Johnson, McGuire, Ball, Parkin, Mangan.

Record League Victory: 13–0 v Oldham T, North West Counties Div 2, 5 December 1998.

Record Defeat: 0–7 v Billingham T, FA Cup 1st qual rd, 15 September 2001.

Most League Points (3 for a win): 82, FL 1, 2016–17.

Most League Goals: 66, FL 2, 2013–14.

Highest League Scorer in Season: David Ball, 14, FL 1, 2016–17.

Most League Goals in Total Aggregate: David Ball, 41, 2012–17.

Most League Goals in One Match: 3, Steven Schumacher v Newport Co, FL 2, 2 November 2013.

Most Capped Player: Conor McLaughlin, 26, Northern Ireland.

Most League Appearances: David Ball, 179, 2012–17.

Youngest League Player: Jamie Allen, 17 years 227 days v Northampton T, 5 January 2013.

Record Transfer Fee Received: £1,000,000 from Leicester C for Jamie Vardy, May 2012.

Record Transfer Fee Paid: £300,000 to Kidderminster H for Jamille Matt, January 2013.

Football League Record: 2012 Promoted from Conference Premier; 2012–14 FL 2; 2014– FL 1.

LATEST SEQUENCES

Longest Sequence of League Wins: 5, 31.12.2016 – 24.1.2017.

Longest Sequence of League Defeats: 5, 19.9.2015 – 10.10.2015.

Longest Sequence of League Draws: 3, 28.1.2017 – 11.2.2017

Longest Sequence of Unbeaten League Matches: 18, 19.11.2016 – 4.3.2017.

Longest Sequence Without a League Win: 8, 29.8.2015 – 10.10.2015.

Successive Scoring Runs: 24 from 2.5.2016.

Successive Non-scoring Runs: 4 from 22.2.2014.

TEN YEAR LEAGUE RECORD

		P	*W*	*D*	*L*	*F*	*A*	*Pts*	*Pos*
2007-08	Uni Pr	40	28	7	5	81	39	91	1
2008-09	Conf N	42	17	11	14	70	66	62	8
2009-10	Conf N	42	26	7	7	86	44	85	2
2010-11	Conf P	46	22	12	12	68	42	78	5
2011-12	Conf P	46	31	10	5	102	48	103	1
2012-13	FL 2	46	15	15	16	55	57	60	13
2013-14	FL 2	46	22	10	14	66	52	76	4
2014-15	FL 1	46	17	12	17	49	52	63	10
2015-16	FL 1	46	12	15	19	52	56	51	19
2016-17	FL 1	46	23	13	10	64	43	82	4

DID YOU KNOW ?

Centre-forward Bob Morris joined Fleetwood from West Ham United in the summer of 1920. He was a huge success, scoring 23 goals from just 11 Lancashire Combination fixtures and in October 1920 he returned to the Football League, signing for Barnsley.

FLEETWOOD TOWN – SKY BET LEAGUE ONE 2016–17 LEAGUE RECORD

Match No.	Date	Venue	Opponents	Result		H/T Score	Lg Pos.	Goalscorers	Attendance
1	Aug 6	A	Northampton T	D	1-1	0-1	11	Nirennold 52	5157
2	13	H	Scunthorpe U	D	2-2	1-0	13	Jonsson 37, Ball 51	2509
3	17	H	Oxford U	W	2-0	0-0	8	Ball 50, Hunter 70	2614
4	20	A	Bolton W	L	1-2	1-0	12	Ball 34	13,524
5	27	A	Southend U	W	2-0	1-0	8	Long 18, Hunter 77	5507
6	Sept 3	H	Coventry C	W	2-0	0-0	3	Long 58, Woolford 71	3557
7	10	H	Charlton Ath	D	2-2	2-1	4	Long 5, Ball 44	3371
8	17	A	Rochdale	L	1-2	1-1	7	Grant (pen) 23	2499
9	24	H	Milton Keynes D	L	1-4	0-1	11	Grant 70	2518
10	27	A	Bradford C	L	1-2	1-1	13	Grant 33	16,759
11	Oct 1	H	Sheffield U	D	1-1	1-0	14	Ball 13	4004
12	15	H	Peterborough U	W	2-0	1-0	13	Sowerby 3, Baldwin (og) 65	2711
13	18	A	Chesterfield	W	1-0	1-0	11	McLaughlin 41	4598
14	22	A	Millwall	L	1-2	0-1	13	Hunter 65	8085
15	29	H	Gillingham	W	2-1	1-0	9	Ball 19, Hunter 82	2600
16	Nov 1	A	Bristol R	L	1-2	1-0	10	Hunter 4	10,088
17	12	A	Port Vale	L	1-2	0-0	13	Long 52	3890
18	19	H	Chesterfield	W	2-1	1-0	10	Bell 27, Nirennold 62	2901
19	22	H	Shrewsbury T	W	3-0	1-0	8	McLaughlin 38, Ball 2 53, 73	2111
20	26	A	AFC Wimbledon	D	2-2	1-0	8	Bolger 12, McLaughlin 90	4023
21	Dec 10	H	Walsall	W	2-1	1-0	5	Hunter 42, Grant 67	2708
22	17	A	Swindon T	D	1-1	1-1	8	Ball 22	6143
23	26	H	Bury	D	0-0	0-0	7		4017
24	31	H	Oldham Ath	W	1-0	0-0	7	Law (og) 90	3189
25	Jan 2	A	Shrewsbury T	W	1-0	1-0	6	Cole 9	5080
26	14	H	Bristol R	W	3-1	2-0	6	Hunter 13, Bolger 23, Ball 82	3728
27	21	A	Coventry C	W	1-0	0-0	4	Bolger 90	8129
28	24	A	Sheffield U	W	2-0	1-0	4	McLaughlin 20, Cole 66	19,012
29	28	H	Southend U	D	1-1	0-1	4	Ball 90	2675
30	Feb 4	A	Charlton Ath	D	1-1	0-1	4	Bell 90	9916
31	11	H	Rochdale	D	0-0	0-0	4		3186
32	14	H	Bradford C	W	2-1	0-1	4	Cole 68, Law (og) 81	3418
33	18	A	Milton Keynes D	W	1-0	0-0	4	Bolger 61	8278
34	25	H	Northampton T	W	3-0	1-0	3	Cole 42, Grant 56, Ball 60	3361
35	Mar 4	A	Scunthorpe U	W	2-0	1-0	2	Cole 41, Grant 90	5541
36	11	H	Bolton W	L	2-4	1-2	2	Dempsey 22, Grant 87	5123
37	14	A	Walsall	W	1-0	1-0	2	Bolger 22	3890
38	18	H	AFC Wimbledon	D	0-0	0-0	3		2802
39	25	A	Bury	D	0-0	0-0	3		4174
40	Apr 1	H	Swindon T	L	0-1	0-0	3		3128
41	5	A	Oxford U	W	3-1	1-1	3	Grant (pen) 6, Eastham 76, Ball 87	6728
42	8	A	Oldham Ath	L	0-2	0-1	3		3933
43	14	A	Peterborough U	W	2-1	2-0	3	Grant 25, Eastham 42	5629
44	17	H	Millwall	W	1-0	1-0	3	Davies 45	3665
45	22	A	Gillingham	W	3-2	0-1	3	Hunter 54, Ball 80, Dempsey 90	8760
46	30	H	Port Vale	D	0-0	0-0	4		4733

Final League Position: 4

GOALSCORERS

League (64): Ball 14, Grant 9 (2 pens), Hunter 8, Bolger 5, Cole 5, Long 4, McLaughlin 4, Bell 2, Dempsey 2, Eastham 2, Nirennold 2, Davies 1, Jonsson 1, Sowerby 1, Woolford 1, own goals 3.
FA Cup (7): Cole 2, Hunter 2, Bell 1, Bolger 1, Holloway 1.
EFL Cup (2): Holloway 1, Hunter 1.
EFL Checkatrade Trophy (3): Cole 1, Jakubiak 1, Sowerby 1.
League One Play-Offs (0).

Neal C 17	McLaughlin C 42	Pond N 30 + 2	Eastham A 34 + 1	Bell A 44	Hunter A 24 + 20	Jonsson E 8 + 4	Ryan J 16	Nirennold V 6 + 20	Ball D 39 + 7	Grant R 44 + 2	Cole D 18 + 17	Amadi-Holloway A 1 + 5	Duckworth M 2 + 2	Kip R — + 1	Long C 15 + 3	Woolford M 3 + 7	Dempsey K 35 + 3	Jakubiak A — + 3	Bolger C 29 + 3	Sowerby J 5 + 3	Cairns A 29 + 1	Ekpolo G 4 + 2	Glendon G 19 + 7	Davis J 3 + 1	Davies B 22	Schwabl M 8 + 5	Burns W 3 + 7	Brannagan C 5 + 8	Maguire J 1 + 2	Match No.
1	2	3	4	5	6³	7	8	9	10¹	11²	12	13	14																	1
1	2	3	4	5	12	7	6	8³	11	9¹	10²	13		14																2
1	2	3	4	5	13	7²	8	12	9	6	10³	14			11¹															3
1	2	3	4	5	9¹	8²	7	10	6³	12	14	13			11															4
1	2	3	4	5	13	7	6	14	10²	9¹	8				11³	12														5
1		3	4	5	14	7¹	6		9	8	10²		2		11³	13	12													6
1	2	4	3	5	13	12	7³		9	8²	10¹				11	14	6													7
1	2²	3	4	5		12		6¹	10	7	11³		13		9	14	8													8
1	2	3	4	5	9²		7		10	8	13				11¹	14	6³	12												9
1	2	3	4	5	13	11²	7		10	8	9³					6¹		12	14											10
1	7	3	4	5	13	14	8²		10¹	9			2		11³	12	6													11
1	2	3	4	5	11¹		8	13	10	9²	12					14	7			6³										12
1²	2	4	3	5	11³		7	14	10	6	13						8			9¹	12									13
1	5	4	3¹	2	12		8		10	6	13				11²	9³	7		14											14
1	2	3		5	13		8	12	11²	9	14				10³		7		4	6¹										15
1	2	4		5	11	7¹	8²	12	13	9³	14				10		6		3											16
1		3		5	9		7¹	13	14	6	11²				10▮		8		4			2³	12							17
	5	3	4	9	11³			12	10²	8	13	14					6		2¹		1		7							18
	5	3	4	9	12			13	10	8	11¹						6³		2	14	1		7²							19
	5	3		9	10¹			13	11	8	12						6		2	14	1		7²	4³						20
	5	3		9	11¹			14	10³	8	13				12		6²		2		1		7	4						21
	2	3		5	9¹	14		12	6	8	11				10²			13	4		1		7³							22
	5	4		8	13			12	11	6	14	9²			10¹				2		1		7	3³						23
	2	3		9	10²			13	11	8	12				14		6¹		4	5³	1		7							24
	9	3		5	12			6	14	8	11³				10¹		7²		2		1		13		4					25
	5	3³	12	9	10²			13	11	8	14						6		2		1		7¹		4					26
	5		2	9	11¹				10²	8					12		6		3		1		7³		4	13	14			27
	5		2	9	12				13	8	11²						6		3		1		14		4	7¹	10³			28
	5		2	9²	11				10	8¹	14						6		3		1		7³		4	13	12			29
	5¹		2	9	13				12	8	11						6		3		1				4	7³	10²	14		30
			2	9	10¹			12	11	8							6		3	5²	1		7³		4	13	14			31
	5		2	9²	13				11	12	10						6		3		1	14			4	7¹		8³		32
	5³		2	9	14				12	11	10²						8		3		1	13	7		4			6¹		33
	5		2	9	13			12	10	8	11²						6¹		3		1		7³		4			14		34
	5		2		14			12	10	8	11²						6³		3		1				4	7		13	9¹	35
	7		2	9³	12			5²	10	8	11¹						6		3		1		13		4			14		36
	5			9	11				12	10							6¹		3		1	2	13		4	7		8²		37
	5		2	9	10¹			13	11	8							6²		3		1				4	7		12		38
			5	6	13				11	10							9		4		1	8	14	12	7¹	3²		2³		39
	5		2	9¹	10²				11³	8							6		3		1		7		4		12	14	13	40
	6	13	4	9	7²				10	11							8³		3	14	1	2¹	12		5					41
	2	3			9				10	8						11²	14		4		1		6³		5	7¹	13		12	42
	5	3	2	9	11³				10	6							8²				1		7¹		4	14	12	13		43
	5	3	2	9²				12	10	8							13				1		7		4	14	11¹	6³		44
	5	3³	2²	9	11				10	8	13						6		12		1		7¹		4		14			45
	5²	12	2	9	10				11	8	13						6		3¹		1		7³		4			14		46

FA Cup

First Round	Southport	(a)	0-0
Replay	Southport	(h)	4-1
(*aet*)			
Second Round	Shrewsbury T	(a)	0-0
Replay	Shrewsbury T	(h)	3-2
Third Round	Bristol C	(a)	0-0
Replay	Bristol C	(h)	0-1

EFL Checkatrade Trophy

Northern Group D	Blackburn R U21	(h)	1-0
Northern Group D	Oldham Ath	(h)	0-2
Northern Group D	Carlisle U	(a)	2-4

EFL Cup

First Round	Leeds U	(h)	2-2

(*aet; Leeds U won 5-4 on penalties*)

League One Play-Offs

Semi-Final 1st leg	Bradford C	(a)	0-1
Semi-Final 2nd leg	Bradford C	(h)	0-0

FOREST GREEN ROVERS

FOUNDATION

A football club was recorded at Forest Green as early as October 1889, established by Rev Edward Peach, a local Congregationalist minister. This club joined the Mid-Gloucestershire League for 1894–95 but disappeared around 1896 and was reformed as Forest Green Rovers in 1898. Rovers affiliated to the Gloucestershire county FA from 1899–1900 and competed in local leagues, mostly the Stroud & District and Dursley & District Leagues before joining the Gloucestershire Senior League North in 1937, where they remained until 1968. They became founder members of the Gloucestershire County League in 1968 and progressed to the Hellenic League in 1975. Success over Rainworth MW in the 1982 FA Vase final at Wembley was the start of the club's rise up the pyramid, firstly to the Southern League for the 1982–83 season and then the Football Conference from 1998–99. Rovers reached the play-offs in 2014–15 and 2015–16, losing to Bristol Rovers and Grimsby Town respectively, before finally achieving their goal of a place in the Football League with their 3-1 Play-Off victory over Tranmere Rovers on 14 May 2017.

The New Lawn Stadium, Another Way, Nailsworth, GL6 0ET.

Telephone: (01453) 834 860.

Fax: (01453) 835 291.

Ticket Office: (01453) 834 860.

Website: forestgreenroversfc.com

Email: reception@forestgreenroversfc.com

Ground Capacity: 5,141.

Record Attendance: 4,836 v Derby Co, FA Cup 3rd rd, 3 January 2009.

Pitch Measurements: 100.5m × 64m (110yd × 70yd).

Chairman: Dale Vince.

Club Secretary: Philip Catherall.

Manager: Mark Cooper.

Assistant Manager: Scott Lindsey.

HONOURS

League Champions: Southern League – 1997–98.

FA Cup: 3rd rd – 2008–09, 2009–10.

FA Trophy: *Runners-up:* 1998–99, 2000–01.

FA Vase: *Winners:* 1981–82.

sky SPORTS FACT FILE

The first player who transferred from Forest Green Rovers to a Football League club is believed to have been goalkeeper Jack Brock. Brock signed amateur forms for Swindon Town in September 1936 and went on to make five Football League appearances for the Robins during the 1936–37 season.

Colours: Green and black hooped shirts, green shorts with black trim, green and black hooped socks.

Year Formed: 1889.

Previous Names: 1889, Forest Green; 1898, Forest Green Rovers; 1911, Nailsworth & Forest Green United; 1919 Forest Green Rovers; 1989, Stroud; 1992, Forest Green Rovers.

Club Nicknames: Rovers, The Green, FGR, The Little Club on the Hill, Green Army, The Green Devils.

Grounds: 1890, The Lawn Ground; 2006– The New Lawn.

Record Victory: 8–0 v Fareham T, Southern League Southern Division, 1996–97; 8–0 v Hyde U, Football Conference, 10 August 2013.

Record Defeat: 0–10 v Gloucester, Mid-Gloucestershire League, 13 January 1900.

Record Transfer Fee Received: £35,000 from Oxford U for Wayne Hatswell, 1 December 2000.

Record Transfer Fee Paid: £25,000 to Bury for Adrian Randall, August 1999.

Football League Record: 2017 Promoted from National League; 2017– FL 2.

MANAGERS

Bill Thomas 1955–56
Eddie Cowley 1957–58
Don Cowley 1958–60
Jimmy Sewell 1966–67
Alan Morris 1967–68
Peter Goring 1968–79
Tony Morris 1979–80
Bob Mursell 1980–82
Roy Hillman 1982
Steve Millard 1983–87
John Evans 1987–90
Jeff Evans 1990
Bobby Jones 1990–91
Tim Harris 1991–92
Pat Casey 1992–94
Frank Gregan 1994–2000
Nigel Spink and David Norton 2000–01
Nigel Spink 2001–02
Colin Addison 2002–03
Tim Harris 2003–04
Alan Lewer 2004–05
Gary Owers 2005–06
Jim Harvey 2006–09
Dave Hockaday 2009–13
Adrian Pennock 2013–16
Mark Cooper May 2016–

TEN YEAR LEAGUE RECORD

		P	W	D	L	F	A	Pts	Pos
2007-08	Conf	46	19	14	13	76	59	71	8
2008-09	Conf	46	12	16	18	70	76	52	18
2009-10	Conf	46	12	9	23	50	76	45	21
2010-11	Conf	46	10	16	20	53	72	46	20
2011-12	Conf	46	19	13	14	66	45	70	10
2012-13	Conf	46	18	11	17	63	49	65	10
2013-14	Conf	46	19	10	17	80	66	67	10
2014-15	Conf	46	22	16	8	80	54	79*	5
2015-16	NL	46	26	11	9	69	42	89	2
2016-17	NL	46	25	11	10	88	56	86	3

**3 pts deducted.*

DID YOU KNOW ?

Forest Green Rovers' National League play-off against Tranmere Rovers in May 2017 was the club's third visit to Wembley Stadium. In 1982 they defeated Rainworth Miners Welfare to win the FA Vase, while in 1999 they lost to Kingstonian in the FA Trophy final.

FULHAM

FOUNDATION

Churchgoers were responsible for the foundation of Fulham, which first saw the light of day as Fulham St Andrew's Church Sunday School FC in 1879. They won the West London Amateur Cup in 1887 and the championship of the West London League in its initial season of 1892–93. The name Fulham had been adopted in 1888.

Craven Cottage, Stevenage Road, London SW6 6HH.

Telephone: (0843) 208 1222.

Fax: (020) 8336 7526.

Ticket Line: (0843) 208 1234 (option 2).

Website: www.fulhamfc.com

Email: enquiries@fulhamfc.com

Ground Capacity: 25,700.

Record Attendance: 49,335 v Millwall, Division 2, 8 October 1938.

Pitch Measurements: 100m × 65m (109.5yd × 71yd).

Chairman: Shadid Khan.

Chief Executive: Alistair Mackintosh.

Head Coach: Slavisa Jokanovic.

Assistant Head Coach: Javier Pereira.

Colours: White shirts with black trim, black shorts with white trim, white socks with red trim.

Year Formed: 1879.

Turned Professional: 1898.

Reformed: 1987.

Previous Name: 1879, Fulham St Andrew's; 1888, Fulham.

Club Nickname: 'The Cottagers'.

Grounds: 1879, Star Road, Fulham; c.1883, Eel Brook Common, 1884, Lillie Road; 1885, Putney Lower Common; 1886, Ranelagh House, Fulham; 1888, Barn Elms, Castelnau; 1889, Purser's Cross (Roskell's Field), Parsons Green Lane; 1891, Eel Brook Common; 1891, Half Moon, Putney; 1895, Captain James Field, West Brompton; 1896, Craven Cottage.

First Football League Game: 3 September 1907, Division 2, v Hull C (h) L 0–1 – Skene; Ross, Lindsay; Collins, Morrison, Goldie; Dalrymple, Freeman, Bevan, Hubbard, Threlfall.

Record League Victory: 10–1 v Ipswich T, Division 1, 26 December 1963 – Macedo; Cohen, Langley; Mullery (1), Keetch, Robson (1); Key, Cook (1), Leggat (4), Haynes, Howfield (3).

Record Cup Victory: 7–0 v Swansea C, FA Cup 1st rd, 11 November 1995 – Lange; Jupp (1), Herrera, Barkus (Brooker (1)), Moore, Angus, Thomas (1), Morgan, Brazil (Hamill), Conroy (3) (Bolt), Cusack (1).

Record Defeat: 0–10 v Liverpool, League Cup 2nd rd 1st leg, 23 September 1986.

Most League Points (2 for a win): 60, Division 2, 1958–59 and Division 3, 1970–71.

HONOURS

League Champions: First Division – 2000–01; Division 2 – 1948–49; Second Division – 1998–99; Division 3S – 1931–32.
Runners-up: Division 2 – 1958–59; Division 3 – 1970–71; Third Division – 1996–97.

FA Cup: *Runners-up:* 1975.

League Cup: quarter-final – 1968, 1971, 2000, 2005.

European Competitions
UEFA Cup: 2002–03.
Europa League: 2009–10 *(runners-up)*, 2011–12.
Intertoto Cup: 2002 *(winners)*.

sky SPORTS FACT FILE

Fulham are unique in having two father and son combinations among their former managers. Harry Bradshaw (1904–09) was followed by his son Joe (1926–29) while Bill Dodgin snr (1949–53) and his son Bill jnr (1968–92) repeated this in the post-war period.

Most League Points (3 for a win): 101, Division 2, 1998–99. 101, Division 1, 2000–01.

Most League Goals: 111, Division 3 (S), 1931–32.

Highest League Scorer in Season: Frank Newton, 43, Division 3 (S), 1931–32.

Most League Goals in Total Aggregate: Gordon Davies, 159, 1978–84, 1986–91.

Most League Goals in One Match: 5, Fred Harrison v Stockport Co, Division 2, 5 September 1908; 5, Bedford Jezzard v Hull C, Division 2, 8 October 1955; 5, Jimmy Hill v Doncaster R, Division 2, 15 March 1958; 5, Steve Earle v Halifax T, Division 3, 16 September 1969.

Most Capped Player: Johnny Haynes, 56, England.

Most League Appearances: Johnny Haynes, 594, 1952–70.

Youngest League Player: Matthew Briggs, 16 years 65 days v Middlesbrough, 13 May 2007.

Record Transfer Fee Received: £15,000,000 from Tottenham H for Moussa Dembele, August 2012.

Record Transfer Fee Paid: £12,400,00 to Olympiacos for Konstantinos Mitroglou, January 2014.

Football League Record: 1907 Elected to Division 2; 1928–32 Division 3 (S); 1932–49 Division 2; 1949–52 Division 1; 1952–59 Division 2; 1959–68 Division 1; 1968–69 Division 2; 1969–71 Division 3; 1971–80 Division 2; 1980–82 Division 3; 1982–86 Division 2; 1986–92 Division 3; 1992–94 Division 2; 1994–97 Division 3; 1997–99 Division 2; 1999–2001 Division 1; 2001–14 FA Premier League; 2014– FL C.

LATEST SEQUENCES

Longest Sequence of League Wins: 12, 7.5.2000 – 18.10.2000.

Longest Sequence of League Defeats: 11, 2.12.1961 – 24.2.1962.

Longest Sequence of League Draws: 6, 23.12.2006 – 20.1.2007.

Longest Sequence of Unbeaten League Matches: 15, 26.1.1999 – 13.4.1999.

Longest Sequence Without a League Win: 15, 25.2.1950 – 23.8.1950.

Successive Scoring Runs: 26 from 28.3.1931.

Successive Non-scoring Runs: 6 from 21.8.1971.

MANAGERS

Harry Bradshaw 1904–09
Phil Kelso 1909–24
Andy Ducat 1924–26
Joe Bradshaw 1926–29
Ned Liddell 1929–31
Jim McIntyre 1931–34
Jimmy Hogan 1934–35
Jack Peart 1935–48
Frank Osborne 1948–64
(was Secretary-Manager or General Manager for most of this period and Team Manager 1953–56)
Bill Dodgin Snr 1949–53
Duggie Livingstone 1956–58
Bedford Jezzard 1958–64
(General Manager for last two months)
Vic Buckingham 1965–68
Bobby Robson 1968
Bill Dodgin Jnr 1968–72
Alec Stock 1972–76
Bobby Campbell 1976–80
Malcolm Macdonald 1980–84
Ray Harford 1984–96
Ray Lewington 1986–90
Alan Dicks 1990–91
Don Mackay 1991–94
Ian Branfoot 1994–96
(continued as General Manager)
Micky Adams 1996–97
Ray Wilkins 1997–98
Kevin Keegan 1998–99
(Chief Operating Officer)
Paul Bracewell 1999–2000
Jean Tigana 2000–03
Chris Coleman 2003–07
Lawrie Sanchez 2007
Roy Hodgson 2007–10
Mark Hughes 2010–11
Martin Jol 2011–13
Rene Muelenstein 2013–14
Felix Magath 2014
Kit Symons 2014–15
Slavisa Jokanovic December 2015–

TEN YEAR LEAGUE RECORD

		P	W	D	L	F	A	Pts	Pos
2007-08	PR Lge	38	8	12	18	38	60	36	17
2008-09	PR Lge	38	14	11	13	39	34	53	7
2009-10	PR Lge	38	12	10	16	39	46	46	12
2010-11	PR Lge	38	11	16	11	49	43	49	8
2011-12	PR Lge	38	14	10	14	48	51	52	9
2012-13	PR Lge	38	11	10	17	50	60	43	12
2013-14	PR Lge	38	9	5	24	40	85	32	19
2014-15	FL C	46	14	10	22	62	83	52	17
2015-16	FL C	46	12	15	19	66	79	51	20
2016-17	FL C	46	22	14	10	85	57	80	6

DID YOU KNOW

Fulham were the last top-flight club in England to install floodlights. The new lights were inaugurated for the visit of Sheffield Wednesday on 18 September 1962, Fulham winning 4-1 including a hat-trick from Maurice Cook.

FULHAM – SKY BET CHAMPIONSHIP 2016–17 LEAGUE RECORD

Match No.	*Date*	*Venue*	*Opponents*	*Result*		*H/T Score*	*Lg Pos.*	*Goalscorers*	*Attendance*
1	Aug 5	H	Newcastle U	W	1-0	1-0	1	Smith [45]	23,922
2	13	A	Preston NE	W	2-1	1-0	3	Aluko [33], Smith [67]	10,809
3	16	A	Leeds U	D	1-1	0-0	4	Cairney [77]	21,204
4	20	H	Cardiff C	D	2-2	1-0	4	Sessegnon [44], McDonald [86]	15,401
5	27	A	Blackburn R	W	1-0	0-0	2	Cairney [90]	10,464
6	Sept 10	H	Birmingham C	L	0-1	0-0	6		17,603
7	13	H	Burton Alb	D	1-1	0-0	5	Sessegnon [90]	15,288
8	17	A	Wigan Ath	D	0-0	0-0	9		10,582
9	24	H	Bristol C	L	0-4	0-1	13		20,585
10	27	A	Nottingham F	D	1-1	0-0	12	Cairney [72]	17,388
11	Oct 1	H	QPR	L	1-2	0-1	13	Ream [47]	19,609
12	15	A	Barnsley	W	4-2	2-2	9	Piazon [37], Aluko [42], Malone [46], Martin [65]	11,974
13	18	H	Norwich C	D	2-2	0-2	11	Johansen [55], Martin [66]	17,082
14	22	A	Aston Villa	L	0-1	0-0	13		32,201
15	29	H	Huddersfield T	W	5-0	3-0	11	Martin 2 (1 pen) [8, 63 (p)], Kalas [34], Piazon [42], McDonald [66]	19,858
16	Nov 4	A	Brentford	W	2-0	1-0	7	Aluko [36], Cairney [90]	12,052
17	19	H	Sheffield W	D	1-1	0-1	8	Malone [90]	20,255
18	26	A	Brighton & HA	L	1-2	1-0	9	McDonald [18]	29,445
19	Dec 3	H	Reading	W	5-0	1-0	7	Gunter (og) [15], Martin 2 [49, 90], Aluko [68], Johansen [71]	18,217
20	10	A	Wolverhampton W	D	4-4	3-1	9	Johansen [32], Ayite 2 [39, 90], Cairney [42]	19,020
21	13	H	Rotherham U	W	2-1	1-1	9	Johansen [32], Ayite [54]	13,735
22	17	H	Derby Co	D	2-2	1-1	9	Ayite [45], Johansen [61]	18,748
23	26	A	Ipswich T	W	2-0	1-0	7	Martin [36], Sigurdsson [78]	19,723
24	Jan 2	H	Brighton & HA	L	1-2	0-0	10	Piazon [55]	24,300
25	14	H	Barnsley	W	2-0	1-0	8	Martin (pen) [45], Malone [55]	18,010
26	21	A	QPR	D	1-1	0-1	9	Martin [75]	17,025
27	24	A	Reading	L	0-1	0-0	9		16,012
28	Feb 1	A	Burton Alb	W	2-0	0-0	9	Johansen [48], Malone [71]	3725
29	4	A	Birmingham C	L	0-1	0-0	10		17,426
30	11	H	Wigan Ath	W	3-2	1-2	9	Ayite [25], Odoi [71], Kebano [90]	15,552
31	14	H	Nottingham F	W	3-2	2-1	8	Cairney [30], Piazon [33], Hobbs (og) [72]	15,365
32	22	A	Bristol C	W	2-0	1-0	7	Piazon [17], Cairney [54]	17,272
33	25	A	Cardiff C	D	2-2	1-1	7	Johansen [17], Kebano [68]	15,656
34	Mar 4	H	Preston NE	W	3-1	1-0	7	Aluko [22], Martin [60], Kebano [77]	20,205
35	7	H	Leeds U	D	1-1	0-1	7	Cairney [90]	22,239
36	11	A	Newcastle U	W	3-1	1-0	7	Cairney [15], Sessegnon 2 [51, 59]	51,903
37	14	H	Blackburn R	D	2-2	1-0	7	Aluko [45], Cyriac [86]	15,487
38	18	H	Wolverhampton W	L	1-3	0-1	7	Odoi [54]	20,668
39	Apr 1	A	Rotherham U	W	1-0	0-0	6	Aluko [66]	9004
40	4	A	Derby Co	L	2-4	1-2	6	Ayite 2 [35, 79]	27,221
41	8	H	Ipswich T	W	3-1	2-0	6	Ayite [17], Malone [30], Johansen [61]	20,959
42	14	A	Norwich C	W	3-1	1-0	7	Johansen [5], Cairney (pen) [48], Ayite [89]	27,023
43	17	H	Aston Villa	W	3-1	1-0	5	Sessegnon [17], Aluko [56], Kebano [79]	23,891
44	22	A	Huddersfield T	W	4-1	4-1	6	Malone [16], Cairney (pen) [20], Johansen 2 [36, 45]	21,023
45	29	H	Brentford	D	1-1	1-1	6	Cairney [8]	24,594
46	May 7	A	Sheffield W	W	2-1	1-1	6	Kebano 2 [25, 79]	33,681

Final League Position: 6

GOALSCORERS

League (85): Cairney 12 (2 pens), Johansen 11, Martin 10 (2 pens), Ayite 9, Aluko 8, Kebano 6, Malone 6, Piazon 5, Sessegnon 5, McDonald 3, Odoi 2, Smith 2, Cyriac 1, Kalas 1, Ream 1, Sigurdsson 1, own goals 2.
FA Cup (6): Johansen 2, Sessegnon 2, Aluko 1, Martin 1.
EFL Cup (6): Woodrow 2, Adeniran 1, Christensen 1, Piazon 1, own goal 1.
Championship Play-Offs (1): Cairney 1.

Button D 40	Odoi D 21 + 9	Kalas T 36	Madl M 14 + 2	Malone S 34 + 2	McDonald K 43	Tunnicliffe R 3 + 4	Cairney T 44 + 1	Aluko S 44 + 1	Ayite F 22 + 9	Smith M 7 + 9	Christensen L — + 4	Parker S 12 + 17	Ream T 28 + 6	Woodrow C 1 + 4	Sessegnon R 17 + 8	Jozabed S 1 + 6	Kebano N 12 + 16	Johansen S 35 + 1	Martin C 27 + 4	Sigurdsson R 15 + 2	Piazon L 19 + 10	Adeniran D — + 1	Fredericks R 25 + 5	Humphrys S — + 2	Cyriac G — + 9	Bettinelli M 6	*Match No.*
1	2	3	4	5^{2}	6	7^{1}	8	9	10	11^{3}	12	13	14														1
1	2	3	4	5^{1}	7		8	9	10^{2}	11^{3}	13	6	14	12													2
1	2	3	4		7	13	8	9	10^{2}	11^{3}		6^{1}		12	5	14											3
1	2	3	4	5^{2}	7		8	9	10^{1}	13	14	6		11^{3}	12												4
1	2	3	4		7		8	9		11^{3}	14	6^{2}		12	5	13	10^{1}										5
1	2	3	4▪	5	6		8	9	10^{3}	11^{2}						12	13	7^{1}	14								6
1	2	3			7^{1}		8	9	13	12		6			5	14	10^{3}		11^{2}	4							7
1	2	3			7	14	8^{3}			13		6		12	5	9^{2}	10		11^{1}	4							8
1	2		3^{3}		7▪		8	9		13		6^{2}			5	14	10^{1}	12	11	4							9
1	2			5^{1}		7	9^{2}	10		11		6	4		13				12	3	8^{3}	14					10
1	2			5		7	8^{2}	9		12		6^{1}	4			14	13		11^{3}	3	10						11
1	2			5		12	9^{2}	10		14		6	4				13	7^{3}	11^{1}	3	8						12
1	2^{2}			5	6^{1}	13		10		14		7	4					9	11	3	8^{3}		12				13
1	2		4		7		12	10^{2}	14	13		6			5			9^{3}	11	3	8^{1}						14
1		3^{1}		5	7^{2}		8	9^{3}	12			14	13					6	11	4	10		2				15
1		3		5^{1}	7		6	8^{3}	12			13	14					9	11	4	10^{2}		2				16
1	14	3		5	7^{3}		6	8	12			13						10	11	4	9^{2}		2^{1}				17
1	2^{3}	3		5	7		6	8^{1}	10^{2}								14	9	11	4	12		13				18
1		3		5	7		9	8^{3}	10^{1}			13	4				14	6^{2}	11		12		2				19
1		3		5	6		9	8^{1}	10			12	4^{2}				13	7	11				2				20
1		3	4		7^{1}		9	8^{2}	10			13			5			6	11		12		2				21
1		3^{3}	12	5	6		9	8^{1}	11			13						7		4^{2}	10		2	14			22
1	2		3	5	6		9	8^{3}	10^{1}			14	4					7^{2}	11	12	13						23
1	13			5	7^{2}		9	8		11^{1}			4				14	6		3	10^{3}		2	12			24
1	14	3		5	7		9	8^{2}				12	4		13			6^{1}	11		10^{3}		2				25
1	12	3		5	6		9	8^{2}		14			4		13			7	11		10^{3}		2^{1}				26
1		3	2^{3}	8^{1}	6^{2}		9	10				14	4		13			7	11		12		5				27
1	13	3		5	6		9	8^{2}	12				4					7	11		10		2^{1}				28
1		3		12	6		9	8^{2}	13				4		5^{3}			7	11		10^{1}		2▪		14		29
1	2		3	5	6^{2}		9	8^{3}	10			14	4				13	7	11^{1}						12		30
1	2		12		6		9	8^{1}	11^{3}			14	4		5		13	7		3^{2}	10						31
1	2	3			6		9	14	11^{3}				4		5		8^{2}	7	12		10^{1}		13				32
1		3		5	6		9	8	11^{1}				4				12	7			10^{2}		2		13		33
1	14	3			7		6	9^{2}				12	4		5		11	8^{1}	10^{3}				2		13		34
1		3		5^{3}	7^{2}		9	8				13	4		12		10	6	11^{1}				2		14		35
1	2	3		5	6		9	11^{2}				14	4		10		8^{1}	7^{3}					12		13		36
1	14	3		5^{2}	7		6	10					4		11		9^{3}	8^{1}	12				2		13		37
1	13	3		14	7^{3}		6	10	11				4		5^{1}		9	8					2^{2}		12		38
1		3	4	5^{3}	6		9	8^{1}	12				13		14		10^{2}	7	11				2				39
1		3		5^{3}	6		9	11	10				4		14		12	7^{1}			8^{2}		2		13		40
		3	4^{1}	5	6		9	8	10^{2}				12				14	7^{3}	11		13		2			1	41
		3		5	7		9	8^{3}	10^{1}				4				14	6^{2}	11▪	13	12		2			1	42
		3		5^{1}	7		6	9^{2}	10				4		11		12	8			13		2			1	43
	12	3		5	7		6	10^{2}	9				4		11		14	8^{1}			13		2^{3}			1	44
		3		5	7		9	8	11^{1}				4		10^{2}		13	6			12		2			1	45
	2	3^{3}		5	6		7^{2}	8^{1}	12			14	4				10		11		9		13			1	46

FA Cup

Third Round	Cardiff C	(a)	2-1
Fourth Round	Hull C	(h)	4-1
Fifth Round	Tottenham H	(h)	0-3

Championship Play-Offs

Semi-Final 1st leg	Reading	(h)	1-1
Semi-Final 2nd leg	Reading	(a)	0-1

EFL Cup

First Round	Leyton Orient	(a)	3-2
Second Round (*aet*)	Middlesbrough	(h)	2-1
Third Round	Bristol C	(h)	1-2

GILLINGHAM

FOUNDATION

The success of the pioneering Royal Engineers of Chatham excited the interest of the residents of the Medway Towns and led to the formation of many clubs including Excelsior. After winning the Kent Junior Cup and the Chatham District League in 1893, Excelsior decided to go for bigger things and it was at a meeting in the Napier Arms, Brompton, in 1893 that New Brompton FC came into being, buying and developing the ground which is now Priestfield Stadium. They changed their name to Gillingham in 1913, when they also changed their strip from black and white stripes to predominantly blue.

MEMS Priestfield Stadium, Redfern Avenue, Gillingham, Kent ME7 4DD.

Telephone: (01634) 300 000.

Fax: (01634) 850 986.

Ticket Office: (01634) 300 000 (option 1).

Website: www.gillinghamfootballclub.com

Email: info@priestfield.com

Ground Capacity: 11,440.

Record Attendance: 23,002 v QPR, FA Cup 3rd rd, 10 January 1948.

Pitch Measurements: 100.5m × 64m (110yd × 70yd).

Chairman: Paul D. P. Scally.

Vice-chairman: Michael Anderson.

Manager: Adrian Pennock.

First-Team Coaches: Steve Lovell, Jamie Day.

Colours: Blue shirts with white trim, blue shorts with white trim, white socks with blue trim.

Year Formed: 1893.

Turned Professional: 1894.

Previous Name: 1893, New Brompton; 1913, Gillingham.

Club Nickname: 'The Gills'.

Ground: 1893, Priestfield Stadium (renamed KRBS Priestfield Stadium 2009, MEMS Priestfield Stadium 2011).

First Football League Game: 28 August 1920, Division 3, v Southampton (h) D 1–1 – Branfield; Robertson, Sissons; Battiste, Baxter, Wigmore; Holt, Hall, Gilbey (1), Roe, Gore.

Record League Victory: 10–0 v Chesterfield, Division 3, 5 September 1987 – Kite; Haylock, Pearce, Shipley (2) (Lillis), West, Greenall (1), Pritchard (2), Shearer (2), Lovell, Elsey (2), David Smith (1).

Record Cup Victory: 10–1 v Gorleston, FA Cup 1st rd, 16 November 1957 – Brodie; Parry, Hannaway; Riggs, Boswell, Laing; Payne, Fletcher (2), Saunders (5), Morgan (1), Clark (2).

Record Defeat: 2–9 v Nottingham F, Division 3 (S), 18 November 1950.

HONOURS

League Champions: FL 2 – 2012–13; Division 4 – 1963–64.
Runners-up: Third Division – 1995–96; Division 4 – 1973–74.

FA Cup: 6th rd – 2000.

League Cup: 4th rd – 1964, 1997.

sky SPORTS FACT FILE

Gillingham, playing under their original name of New Brompton, were winners of the inaugural Southern League Second Division in 1894–95. This wasn't enough to guarantee promotion, which was achieved by defeating Swindon Town, the bottom club in the First Division, by a 5-1 margin in the end-of-season 'Test Match'.

Most League Points (2 for a win): 62, Division 4, 1973–74.

Most League Points (3 for a win): 85, Division 2, 1999–2000.

Most League Goals: 90, Division 4, 1973–74.

Highest League Scorer in Season: Ernie Morgan, 31, Division 3 (S), 1954–55; Brian Yeo, 31, Division 4, 1973–74.

Most League Goals in Total Aggregate: Brian Yeo, 135, 1963–75.

Most League Goals in One Match: 6, Fred Cheesmur v Merthyr T, Division 3 (S), 26 April 1930.

Most Capped Player: Andrew Crofts, 13 (includes 1 on loan from Brighton & HA) (28), Wales.

Most League Appearances: John Simpson, 571, 1957–72.

Youngest League Player: Luke Freeman, 15 years 247 days v Hartlepool U, 24 November 2007.

Record Transfer Fee Received: £1,500,000 from Manchester C for Robert Taylor, November 1999.

Record Transfer Fee Paid: £600,000 to Reading for Carl Asaba, August 1998.

Football League Record: 1920 Original Member of Division 3; 1921 Division 3 (S); 1938 Failed re-election; Southern League 1938–44; Kent League 1944–46; Southern League 1946–50; 1950 Re-elected to Division 3 (S); 1958–64 Division 4; 1964–71 Division 3; 1971–74 Division 4; 1974–89 Division 3; 1989–92 Division 4; 1992–96; Division 3; 1996–2000 Division 2; 2000–04 Division 1; 2004–05 FL C; 2005–08 FL 1; 2008–09 FL 2; 2009–10 FL 1; 2010–13 FL 2; 2013– FL 1.

LATEST SEQUENCES

Longest Sequence of League Wins: 7, 18.12.1954 – 29.1.1955.

Longest Sequence of League Defeats: 10, 20.9.1988 – 5.11.1988.

Longest Sequence of League Draws: 5, 21.1.2017 – 14.2.2017.

Longest Sequence of Unbeaten League Matches: 20, 13.10.1973 – 10.2.1974.

Longest Sequence Without a League Win: 15, 1.4.1972 – 2.9.1972.

Successive Scoring Runs: 20 from 31.10.1959.

Successive Non-scoring Runs: 6 from 11.2.1961.

MANAGERS

W. Ironside Groombridge 1896–1906 *(Secretary-Manager)* *(previously Financial Secretary)*
Steve Smith 1906–08
W. I. Groombridge 1908–19 *(Secretary-Manager)*
George Collins 1919–20
John McMillan 1920–23
Harry Curtis 1923–26
Albert Hoskins 1926–29
Dick Hendrie 1929–31
Fred Mavin 1932–37
Alan Ure 1937–38
Bill Harvey 1938–39
Archie Clark 1939–58
Harry Barratt 1958–62
Freddie Cox 1962–65
Basil Hayward 1966–71
Andy Nelson 1971–74
Len Ashurst 1974–75
Gerry Summers 1975–81
Keith Peacock 1981–87
Paul Taylor 1988
Keith Burkinshaw 1988–89
Damien Richardson 1989–92
Glenn Roeder 1992–93
Mike Flanagan 1993–95
Neil Smillie 1995
Tony Pulis 1995–99
Peter Taylor 1999–2000
Andy Hessenthaler 2000–04
Stan Ternent 2004–05
Neale Cooper 2005
Ronnie Jepson 2005–07
Mark Stimson 2007–10
Andy Hessenthaler 2010–12
Martin Allen 2012–13
Peter Taylor 2013–14
Justin Edinburgh 2015–17
Adrian Pennock January 2017–

TEN YEAR LEAGUE RECORD

		P	W	D	L	F	A	Pts	Pos
2007-08	FL 1	46	11	13	22	44	73	46	22
2008-09	FL 2	46	21	12	13	58	55	75	5
2009-10	FL 1	46	12	14	20	48	64	50	21
2010-11	FL 2	46	17	17	12	67	57	68	8
2011-12	FL 2	46	20	10	16	79	62	70	8
2012-13	FL 2	46	23	14	9	66	39	83	1
2013-14	FL 1	46	15	8	23	60	79	53	17
2014-15	FL 1	46	16	14	16	65	66	62	12
2015-16	FL 1	46	19	12	15	71	56	69	9
2016-17	FL 1	46	12	14	20	59	79	50	20

DID YOU KNOW?

Simeon Raleigh topped the Gillingham scoring charts with 18 goals in 1933–34. In December 1934 he was injured early on in the Gills' home fixture with Brighton but carried on playing until collapsing in the second half. He was rushed to hospital but died from a brain haemorrhage later the same day. He was 25 years old.

GILLINGHAM – SKY BET LEAGUE ONE 2016–17 LEAGUE RECORD

Match No.	Date	Venue	Opponents	Result	H/T Score	Lg Pos.	Goalscorers	Attendance
1	Aug 6	A	Southend U	W 3-1	1-1	2	Emmanuel-Thomas [38], Ehmer [47], Osaoabe [79]	8141
2	13	H	Bury	W 2-1	1-0	1	Jackson [6], Kay (og) [57]	5324
3	16	H	Swindon T	D 1-1	0-0	3	Donnelly [71]	5512
4	20	A	Scunthorpe U	L 0-5	0-3	10		3718
5	27	A	Shrewsbury T	W 3-2	0-2	6	Emmanuel-Thomas 2 [59, 73], Ehmer [90]	4611
6	Sept 4	H	Sheffield U	L 1-2	1-0	8	Dack [34]	5598
7	10	H	Bradford C	D 1-1	1-1	10	McDonald [12]	5079
8	17	A	Port Vale	L 1-2	1-0	13	Wright [25]	4719
9	24	H	Coventry C	W 2-1	1-1	8	Ehmer [26], Knott [72]	7664
10	27	A	Chesterfield	D 3-3	0-1	8	Emmanuel-Thomas 2 (2 pens) [65, 76], Wagstaff [90]	4714
11	Oct 1	A	AFC Wimbledon	L 0-2	0-2	12		4653
12	8	H	Oldham Ath	L 1-2	1-0	12	McDonald [10]	6435
13	15	A	Bristol R	L 1-2	0-0	18	Wright [62]	9489
14	18	H	Walsall	D 1-1	1-0	18	McDonald [25]	5542
15	22	H	Charlton Ath	D 1-1	1-0	18	Dack [41]	8670
16	29	A	Fleetwood T	L 1-2	0-1	18	Hessenthaler [52]	2600
17	Nov 12	H	Northampton T	W 2-1	0-1	17	Ehmer [48], Emmanuel-Thomas [90]	5790
18	19	A	Walsall	W 2-1	1-1	15	McDonald [2], Emmanuel-Thomas [84]	5420
19	22	A	Oxford U	L 0-1	0-1	16		6848
20	26	H	Rochdale	W 3-0	0-0	15	Nouble [53], Emmanuel-Thomas [89], Byrne [90]	5409
21	Dec 12	A	Bolton W	L 0-4	0-2	17		13,861
22	17	H	Milton Keynes D	W 1-0	0-0	12	McDonald [72]	5681
23	26	A	Peterborough U	D 1-1	0-0	16	Cargill [90]	6239
24	30	A	Millwall	L 1-2	0-1	16	Dack [76]	10,821
25	Jan 2	H	Oxford U	L 0-1	0-0	17		6414
26	14	A	Oldham Ath	L 0-1	0-1	17		3475
27	21	A	Sheffield U	D 2-2	0-1	17	Wright 2 [51, 58]	20,649
28	28	H	Shrewsbury T	D 1-1	1-0	17	Oshilaja [45]	5316
29	Feb 4	A	Bradford C	D 2-2	1-2	17	Wright [14], Oshilaja [49]	18,840
30	11	H	Port Vale	D 1-1	0-0	18	Parker [90]	4942
31	14	H	Chesterfield	D 1-1	0-0	17	Ehmer [67]	4595
32	18	A	Coventry C	L 1-2	0-2	18	Ehmer [55]	8718
33	21	H	AFC Wimbledon	D 2-2	2-1	18	Dack [19], Wright [36]	4956
34	25	H	Southend U	W 2-1	2-0	17	Wright 2 (1 pen) [41 (p), 45]	6542
35	28	A	Swindon T	L 1-3	1-0	19	McDonald [10]	6133
36	Mar 4	A	Bury	W 2-1	1-0	17	Dack [14], McDonald [47]	3203
37	11	H	Scunthorpe U	W 3-2	0-1	16	Wright 3 (3 pens) [77, 82, 86]	6851
38	14	H	Bolton W	L 0-4	0-3	16		5199
39	18	A	Rochdale	L 1-4	1-2	18	Parker [17]	2582
40	25	H	Peterborough U	L 0-1	0-0	19		7561
41	Apr 1	A	Milton Keynes D	L 2-3	0-2	20	McDonald [56], Wright [90]	8807
42	8	H	Millwall	D 1-1	0-0	20	Quigley [67]	7221
43	14	H	Bristol R	W 3-1	0-0	17	Wright [64], McDonald 2 [90, 90]	5916
44	17	A	Charlton Ath	L 0-3	0-2	18		12,449
45	22	H	Fleetwood T	L 2-3	1-0	20	Cairns (og) [38], Donnelly [65]	8760
46	30	A	Northampton T	D 0-0	0-0	20		7034

Final League Position: 20

GOALSCORERS

League (59): Wright 13 (4 pens), McDonald 10, Emmanuel-Thomas 8 (2 pens), Ehmer 6, Dack 5, Donnelly 2, Oshilaja 2, Parker 2, Byrne 1, Cargill 1, Hessenthaler 1, Jackson 1, Knott 1, Nouble 1, Osaoabe 1, Quigley 1, Wagstaff 1, own goals 2.
FA Cup (5): Nouble 2, Hessenthaler 1, McDonald 1, Wagstaff 1.
EFL Cup (5): Emmanuel-Thomas 2, Byrne 1, Dack 1, McDonald 1.
EFL Checkatrade Trophy (4): Oldaker 2, Emmanuel-Thomas 1 (1 pen), Wright 1.

Nelson S 33 + 1	Jackson R 30 + 4	Ehmer M 45	Oshilaja A 31 + 2	Konchesky P 25	Wright J 41	Byrne M 22 + 9	Osaoabe E 12 + 12	Dack B 32 + 2	McDonald C 40 + 4	Emmanuel-Thomas J 23 + 5	Donnelly R 11 + 17	Quigley J 8 + 2	Knott B 15 + 2	Pask J 7 + 3	Hessenthaler J 24 + 4	O'Hara J — + 2	List E 3 + 12	Oldaker D 2 + 3	Bond J 7	Wagstaff S 23 + 3	Herd C 12	Nouble F 7 + 5	Cargill B 9	Garmston B 1 + 4	Martin L 14 + 3	Parker J 5 + 11	Rehman Z 10	Muldoon O 3 + 1	Dickenson M 1 + 1	Cundle G — + 2	Holy T 6	Cornick H 4 + 2	Match No.
1	2	3	4	5	6	7	8^{1}	9	10^{2}	11^{3}	12	13	14																				1
1	2		3	5	7	8	6		10^{2}	11^{1}	13	14	9^{3}	4	12																		2
1	2	4	14	5	7	8	6		10^{3}	11	13		9^{1}	3^{2}		12																	3
1		3	4	5	6	7	8^{1}		12	11	10^{3}		9^{2}	2			13	14															4
		2	3	4	5	9	8	12	10^{3}	11	13		7^{1}	6^{2}				14	1														5
	2	3	4	5	6	7		9^{3}	10	11^{1}	14		8^{2}	12		13			1														6
	2▪	3	4	5	6	8	7		10^{2}	11^{3}	9^{1}			14			13		1	12													7
		3	4^{1}	5	7	8	6	9^{2}	11	13				2			12		1	10													8
1	2^{2}	3	4	5	6^{3}	12	13	9	11	14	10^{1}		8							7													9
1		2	3			6	5	10		11			8^{1}	4			12	7		9													10
1		2	4	5		7	6	10^{2}		11^{1}	12▪		9	3			13	8															11
1	13	3	4	5	6	14	12	9^{3}	10						8					7^{1}	2^{2}	11											12
	2	3	4	5	6	13		9^{2}	11^{3}						10		14		1	8^{1}	7	12											13
	2	3	4	5	7	12		9	11				13		10				1	8^{2}	6^{1}												14
12	2^{1}	4		5			13	6	10	11			8		7				1^{2}		3	9											15
1		4	2	5	7				10^{3}	11	14		8	12	6		13				3^{1}	9^{2}											16
1	2	3		5	7			12	10	9			8		6							11^{1}	4										17
1		3		5	7	12	13	9^{2}	10	11			6^{1}		8					2			4										18
1		3		5	8			9	10	11			7^{1}		6					2		12	4										19
1		3		5	6	13		9^{2}	10^{1}	11	14		8^{3}		7					2		12	4										20
1	12	3		5	7	14		9^{2}	11	6^{1}	13				8					2		10^{3}	4										21
1	12	3		5	7			8	10	9					6					2		11^{1}	4										22
1	2	3		5	6			8	10^{2}	9	13				7^{1}					11		12	4										23
1	2^{1}	3	13	5▪	6			9▪	10^{2}	11	14				8^{3}					7		12	4										24
1	2	3	4▪		7^{1}	8			12	11	13				6			14		9^{2}		10^{3}	5										25
1	5	4		2	7		14	10	12	11^{1}	13		8				6^{3}			9	3^{2}												26
1	2	3	5		8	14	12	10	11		13				7^{2}		6^{1}			9	4^{3}												27
1	2	3	4	5	8			10^{3}	11^{1}	13	14				7		9^{2}			6				12									28
1	2	4	5^{1}		8			10^{2}	11^{3}	14	9				7		13			6	3			12									29
1	2	3	5		8			10	11^{3}	14	9				7^{2}					6^{1}	4				12	13							30
1	2	3	4		7	13		8^{2}	11^{1}	10^{3}	9									6				5	14	12							31
1	2	4	5		7	6		8	10^{2}	11^{3}	9										3^{1}			14	12	13							32
1	2	3	5^{1}		8	7		10	13		9^{2}									14	4			12^{3}	6	11							33
1	2	3			6		7		10		8^{1}	11								5					9	12	4						34
1	2	3			6		7^{1}		10			11^{3}			14		12			5					9^{2}	8	4	13					35
1	2^{2}	3			7	5	8	6	10			11^{1}													9	13	4		12				36
1		2	8		7	6	12	9	10			11^{1}			14						4^{3}				5^{2}	13	3						37
1		2	4			8	13	7	10^{1}			11^{3}			6		14								9^{2}	12	3	5					38
1		2				6		7	11^{2}						8^{1}		13			12					9	10^{3}	3▪	5	4	14			39
	12	3	4		6	8		9	11^{2}		10^{3}									2^{1}					5	14		7			1	13	40
	5^{2}	2	3		8	7		9▪	11								13								6	12	4				1	10^{1}	41
	5	2	4		7	6^{2}	13		10			11			12										8		3				1	9^{1}	42
	2	3	4		7	6^{1}	14		11		12	10^{2}			9										8	13					1	5^{3}	43
	2	3	4		7		14	9	10		13	11^{2}			6										8^{1}	12					1	5^{3}	44
	5	2	3		7		13		10^{2}		11^{1}				6										8^{3}	9	4			14	1	12	45
1	5	2	3		9	7			10						6										8	11	4						46

FA Cup

First Round	Brackley T	(h)	2-2
Replay	Brackley T	(a)	3-4
(aet)			

EFL Checkatrade Trophy

Southern Group H	Luton T	(h)	1-2
Southern Group H	Millwall	(a)	1-2
Southern Group H	WBA U21	(a)	2-0

EFL Cup

First Round	Southend U	(a)	3-1
Second Round	Watford	(a)	2-1
(aet)			
Third Round	Tottenham H	(a)	0-5

GRIMSBY TOWN

FOUNDATION

Grimsby Pelham FC, as they were first known, came into being at a meeting held at the Wellington Arms in September 1878. Pelham is the family name of big landowners in the area, the Earls of Yarborough. The receipts for their first game amounted to 6s. 9d. (approx. 39p). After a year, the club name was changed to Grimsby Town.

Blundell Park, Cleethorpes, North East Lincolnshire DN35 7PY.

Telephone: (01472) 605 050.

Fax: (01472) 693 665.

Ticket Office: (01472) 605 050 (option 4).

Website: www.grimsby-townfc.co.uk

Email: webmaster@gtfc.co.uk

Ground Capacity: 9,052.

Record Attendance: 31,657 v Wolverhampton W, FA Cup 5th rd, 20 February 1937.

Pitch Measurements: 101m × 68m (110yd × 74yd).

Chairman: John Fenty.

Chief Executive: Ian Fleming.

Manager: Russell Slade.

Assistant Manager: Paul Wilkinson.

Colours: Black and white striped shirts with red trim, black shorts with red and white trim, red socks with white trim.

Year Formed. 1878. ***Turned Professional:*** 1890. ***Ltd Co.:*** 1890.

Previous Name: 1878, Grimsby Pelham; 1879, Grimsby Town.

Club Nickname: 'The Mariners'.

Grounds: 1880, Clee Park; 1889, Abbey Park; 1899, Blundell Park.

First Football League Game: 3 September 1892, Division 2, v Northwich Victoria (h) W 2–1 – Whitehouse; Lundie, T. Frith; C. Frith, Walker, Murrell; Higgins, Henderson, Brayshaw, Riddoch (2), Ackroyd.

Record League Victory: 9–2 v Darwen, Division 2, 15 April 1899 – Bagshaw; Lockie, Nidd; Griffiths, Bell (1), Nelmes; Jenkinson (3), Richards (1), Cockshutt (3), Robinson, Chadburn (1).

Record Cup Victory: 8–0 v Darlington, FA Cup 2nd rd, 21 November 1885 – G. Atkinson; J. H. Taylor, H. Taylor; Hall, Kimpson, Hopewell; H. Atkinson (1), Garnham, Seal (3), Sharman, Monument (4).

Record Defeat: 1–9 v Arsenal, Division 1, 28 January 1931.

Most League Points (2 for a win): 68, Division 3 (N), 1955–56.

Most League Points (3 for a win): 83, Division 3, 1990–91.

HONOURS

League Champions: Division 2 – 1900–01, 1933–34; Division 3 – 1979–80; Division 3N – 1925–26, 1955–56; Division 4 – 1971–72.
Runners-up: Division 2 – 1928–29; Division 3 – 1961–62; Division 3N – 1951–52; Division 4 – 1978–79, 1989–90. Conference – (4th) 2015–16 *(promoted via play-offs)*.

FA Cup: semi-final – 1936, 1939.

League Cup: 5th rd – 1980, 1985.

League Trophy Winners: 1998.
Runners-up: 2008.

sky SPORTS FACT FILE

Goalkeeper Harry Wainman was Grimsby Town's first-ever Player of the Season in 1971–72 when the Mariners won the Fourth Division title. He went on to make 472 first-team appearances for the club and also won Player of the Season in 1975–76.

Most League Goals: 103, Division 2, 1933–34.

Highest League Scorer in Season: Pat Glover, 42, Division 2, 1933–34.

Most League Goals in Total Aggregate: Pat Glover, 180, 1930–39.

Most League Goals in One Match: 6, Tommy McCairns v Leicester Fosse, Division 2, 11 April 1896.

Most Capped Player: Pat Glover, 7, Wales.

Most League Appearances: John McDermott, 647, 1987–2007.

Youngest League Player: Tony Ford, 16 years 143 days v Walsall, 4 October 1975.

Record Transfer Fee Received: £1,500,000 from Everton for John Oster, July 1997.

Record Transfer Fee Paid: £500,000 to Preston NE for Lee Ashcroft, August 1998.

Football League Record: 1892 Original Member of Division 2; 1901–03 Division 1; 1903 Division 2; 1910 Failed re-election; 1911 re-elected Division 2; 1920–21 Division 3; 1921–26 Division 3 (N); 1926–29 Division 2; 1929–32 Division 1; 1932–34 Division 2; 1934–48 Division 1; 1948–51 Division 2; 1951–56 Division 3 (N); 1956–59 Division 2; 1959–62 Division 3; 1962–64 Division 2; 1964–68 Division 3; 1968–72 Division 4; 1972–77 Division 3; 1977–79 Division 4; 1979–80 Division 3; 1980–87 Division 2; 1987–88 Division 3; 1988–90 Division 4; 1990–91 Division 3; 1991–92 Division 2; 1992–97 Division 1; 1997–98 Division 2; 1998–2003 Division 1; 2003–04 Division 2; 2004–10 FL 2; 2010–16 Conference/National League; 2016– FL 2.

LATEST SEQUENCES

Longest Sequence of League Wins: 11, 19.1.1952 – 29.3.1952.

Longest Sequence of League Defeats: 9, 30.11.1907 – 18.1.1908.

Longest Sequence of League Draws: 5, 6.2.1965 – 6.3.1965.

Longest Sequence of Unbeaten League Matches: 19, 16.2.1980 – 30.8.1980.

Longest Sequence Without a League Win: 22, 24.3.2008 – 1.11.2008.

Successive Scoring Runs: 33 from 6.10.1928.

Successive Non-scoring Runs: 6 from 11.3.2000.

MANAGERS

H. N. Hickson 1902–20
(Secretary-Manager)
Haydn Price 1920
George Fraser 1921–24
Wilf Gillow 1924–32
Frank Womack 1932–36
Charles Spencer 1937–51
Bill Shankly 1951–53
Billy Walsh 1954–55
Allenby Chilton 1955–59
Tim Ward 1960–62
Tom Johnston 1962–64
Jimmy McGuigan 1964–67
Don McEvoy 1967–68
Bill Harvey 1968–69
Bobby Kennedy 1969–71
Lawrie McMenemy 1971–73
Ron Ashman 1973–75
Tom Casey 1975–76
Johnny Newman 1976–79
George Kerr 1979–82
David Booth 1982–85
Mike Lyons 1985–87
Bobby Roberts 1987–88
Alan Buckley 1988–94
Brian Laws 1994–96
Kenny Swain 1997
Alan Buckley 1997–2000
Lennie Lawrence 2000–01
Paul Groves 2001–04
Nicky Law 2004
Russell Slade 2004–06
Graham Rodger 2006
Alan Buckley 2006–08
Mike Newell 2008–09
Neil Woods 2009–11
Rob Scott and Paul Hurst 2011–13
Paul Hurst 2013–16
Marcus Bignot 2016–17
Russell Slade April 2017–

TEN YEAR LEAGUE RECORD

		P	W	D	L	F	A	Pts	Pos
2007-08	FL 2	46	15	10	21	55	66	55	16
2008-09	FL 2	46	9	14	23	51	69	41	22
2009-10	FL 2	46	9	17	20	45	71	44	23
2010-11	Conf	46	15	17	14	72	62	62	11
2011-12	Conf	46	19	13	14	79	60	70	11
2012-13	Conf	46	23	14	9	70	38	83	4
2013-14	Conf	46	22	12	12	65	46	78	4
2014-15	Conf	46	25	11	10	74	40	86	3
2015-16	NL	46	22	14	10	82	45	80	4
2016-17	FL 2	46	17	11	18	59	63	62	14

DID YOU KNOW?

In the 1930–31 season Grimsby Town's average gate of 13,082 was the second lowest of any First Division club. That was 1,500 more than the team with the lowest top flight gates that season: Manchester United attracted just 11,685 on average.

GRIMSBY TOWN – SKY BET LEAGUE TWO 2016–17 LEAGUE RECORD

Match No.	Date	Venue	Opponents	Result		H/T Score	Lg Pos.	Goalscorers	Attendance
1	Aug 6	H	Morecambe	W	2-0	1-0	3	Jackson [6], Davies [63]	6004
2	13	A	Wycombe W	L	1-2	0-0	11	Boyce [79]	3686
3	16	A	Colchester U	L	2-3	0-3	16	Disley [48], Bogle [90]	3287
4	20	H	Leyton Orient	L	1-2	0-0	21	Vose [90]	4991
5	27	H	Stevenage	W	5-2	2-1	12	Bogle 3 [15, 50, 90], Summerfield [40], Vose [49]	4425
6	Sept 3	A	Notts Co	D	2-2	1-0	14	Pearson [34], Bogle [56]	6861
7	10	A	Luton T	W	2-1	1-0	11	Bogle 2 [29, 82]	8005
8	17	H	Crewe Alex	L	0-2	0-1	15		5289
9	24	A	Mansfield T	W	1-0	1-0	10	Bogle (pen) [17]	4401
10	27	H	Newport Co	W	1-0	0-0	6	Bogle (pen) [88]	4296
11	Oct 1	H	Hartlepool U	L	0-3	0-2	9		5713
12	8	A	Exeter C	D	0-0	0-0	9		3557
13	15	A	Cambridge U	W	1-0	1-0	6	Berrett [26]	5121
14	22	H	Cheltenham T	L	0-1	0-1	8		4809
15	29	A	Yeovil T	D	0-0	0-0	8		3733
16	Nov 12	H	Barnet	D	2-2	2-0	6	Bogle 2 [22, 35]	5519
17	19	A	Plymouth Arg	W	3-0	1-0	6	Collins [44], Bogle 2 [62, 86]	10,241
18	22	H	Carlisle U	D	2-2	0-1	6	Bogle (pen) [50], Bolarinwa [78]	4818
19	26	A	Crawley T	L	2-3	1-1	9	Bogle 2 [45, 90]	2315
20	Dec 10	H	Portsmouth	L	0-1	0-0	12		6560
21	17	A	Doncaster R	L	0-1	0-1	14		10,084
22	26	H	Accrington S	W	2-0	1-0	11	Bolarinwa [32], Chambers [88]	5782
23	31	H	Blackpool	D	0-0	0-0	11		5637
24	Jan 2	A	Carlisle U	W	3-1	0-1	12	Bogle 2 [48, 74], Yussuf [78]	6865
25	7	A	Hartlepool U	W	1-0	1-0	10	Yussuf [34]	4388
26	14	H	Exeter C	L	0-3	0-1	11		5009
27	21	H	Notts Co	W	2-0	1-0	11	Bogle [27], Vernon [82]	5421
28	28	A	Stevenage	L	0-2	0-1	12		3394
29	Feb 4	H	Luton T	D	1-1	0-0	11	Clements [56]	5114
30	11	A	Crewe Alex	L	0-5	0-4	13		4003
31	14	A	Newport Co	D	0-0	0-0	13		1868
32	18	H	Mansfield T	W	3-0	1-0	12	Clements [40], Dyson 2 (1 pen) [61, 73 (p)]	5550
33	25	A	Morecambe	L	0-1	0-1	14		1824
34	28	H	Colchester U	W	1-0	1-0	10	Jones, S [42]	4186
35	Mar 4	H	Wycombe W	L	1-2	1-0	13	Dyson (pen) [17]	4668
36	11	A	Leyton Orient	W	3-0	1-0	13	Jones, S [7], Kennedy (og) [71], Vernon [87]	5288
37	14	A	Portsmouth	L	0-4	0-3	13		16,492
38	18	H	Crawley T	D	1-1	1-1	13	Jones, S [22]	4263
39	25	A	Accrington S	D	1-1	0-0	13	Asante [70]	2312
40	Apr 1	H	Doncaster R	L	1-5	1-2	14	Jones, S [34]	6821
41	8	A	Blackpool	W	3-1	2-1	14	Collins [17], Jones, S 2 [45, 70]	4668
42	14	H	Cambridge U	W	2-1	0-0	14	Dyson (pen) [57], Clements [84]	5166
43	17	A	Cheltenham T	L	1-2	0-2	14	Berrett [72]	3550
44	22	H	Yeovil T	W	4-2	2-0	14	Jones, S (pen) [6], Clements [36], Vernon [59], Osborne [62]	4061
45	29	A	Barnet	L	1-3	0-2	14	Disley [74]	3247
46	May 6	H	Plymouth Arg	D	1-1	1-0	14	Pearson [1]	6866

Final League Position: 14

GOALSCORERS

League (59): Bogle 19 (3 pens), Jones, S 7 (1 pen), Clements 4, Dyson 4 (3 pens), Vernon 3, Berrett 2, Bolarinwa 2, Collins 2, Disley 2, Pearson 2, Vose 2, Yussuf 2, Asante 1, Boyce 1, Chambers 1, Davies 1, Jackson 1, Osborne 1, Summerfield 1, own goal 1.
FA Cup (0).
EFL Cup (0).
EFL Checkatrade Trophy (4): Boyce 1, Disley 1, Jackson 1, Summerfield 1.

McKeown J 39	Davies B 22 + 3	Gowling J 17 + 1	Boyce A 12 + 5	Andrew D 46	Berrett J 15 + 4	Summerfield L 22 + 1	McAllister S 3	Bolarinwa T 16 + 18	Vernon S 12 + 16	Jackson K 15 + 5	Pearson S 30 + 4	Bogle O 25 + 2	Chambers A 14 + 2	Browne R — + 5	Disley C 15 + 13	Vose D 15 + 8	Comley B 26 + 7	Tuton S 5 + 5	Collins D 36	Mills Z 30	Jones D 2 + 1	Henderson D 7	Yussuf A 4 + 7	Gunning G 12 + 2	Clements C 16	Osborne J 17 + 2	Asante A 2 + 7	Dyson C 14 + 2	Catic D — + 2	Jones S 16	Maxwell L 1 + 3	*Match No.*
1	2	3▮	4	5	6	7	8	9^2	10^3	11^1	12	13	14																			1
1	2	4	3	5	9	8	7^3	6^2	10^1	11		12	13	14																		2
1	2	4	3^2	5	7	8		9^1		11	12	10	6^3	14	13																	3
1	2	4		5	6^2	8			13	11^1	3	10	9		7	12																4
1	2	3	14	5		9		13	12	11^2	4	10^1	6		7	8^3																5
1	2	4		5	12	7			13		3	10	6^2		14	9^3	8	11^1														6
1	2	4		5	13	7				12	3	11	6			9^1	8	10^2														7
1	2	4		5		7		13		12	3	10	6			9^1	8	11^2														8
1	2			5		7			13	11^1	4	10^2	6			9	8	12	3													9
1	2		14	5		7		12		11^2	4	10	6^1			9^3	8	13	3													10
1	2			5	13	7		12	14		4	10	9^3			6^1	8	11^2	3													11
1	6	3		5	7	12		14	13			10				9^2	8^1	11^3	4	2												12
1		4		5	8	6		12		10^2		9			13	11^3	7^1	14	3	2												13
1		3		5	8^3	9^1		12		6		11			7	10^2	13	14	4	2												14
1		4		5	8	7		11^3	9^1	14		10		13	6^2		12		3	2												15
1		3		5	6^2	7		12	14	11^3		10	9^1		13		8		4	2												16
1		3		5	9	7		12	14	11		10^1	6^2		13		8^3		4	2												17
1		3		5	9^1	7		6		11^2		10		14	12	13	8^3		4	2												18
1		3		5		7^2		6	14	10^3		11		12	8^1	9	13		4	2												19
1		3		5	4	8		12	13	10		11	6^2				9^1		7	2												20
1				5	6	7		11	10	9^2	3^1						8	12	4	2	13											21
	2^1		14	5		8		7^2	11	13	3	10	6		12		9^3		4			1										22
				5		8^1		7		12	3	10	6^2		13	11	9		4	2		1										23
	6	13	4^1	5					11^2		3	10			8		7		9	2		1	12									24
	5		2	9							3	10			8	12	7		4	6		1	11^1									25
	5		2	9				13			3^1	11			8	14	7^3		4	6		1	10^2	12								26
	13		4	5					10^2		3	11			12		7		2	9		1		14	6^1	8^3						27
	13		3^3	6					11		5	10					8		4	2^1		1	12		9^2	7	14					28
1	2			5					14		3						6		4				7^3	8	10^1	11	13	9^2	12			29
1	2			6^2				13			3						8		5				10^1	4	7	9	14	11^3	12			30
1				8				9	13		2				7				4	5			12	3			10^1	11^2		6		31
1				6				11^1			3						12		5	2			14	4^2	9	8^3		10		7	13	32
1	13			5				7^3			3								4	2			14	6^1	8	9^2	12	10		11		33
1				5				6	13		4						12		3	2				7	9	8^3		10^2		11^1	14	34
1				5				9			3					12			4^1	2			14	6^3	8	7^2		11		10	13	35
1				5				6^2	14		3				8	9	7		4	2						12	13	11^3		10^1		36
1	2			5					10		4				13		12		3	8			14			7^2	11^3			9^1	6	37
1				5				12	14		3				6^2	9	7^1		4▮	2						10	13	8^3		11		38
1			3	5				13	11^3		14				6	10				2				4^1	7	8^2	12			9		39
1			7	5				13								12	3^2			2	6^1			8	9	4		10		11		40
1			3	5							13				14	12			4^2	2	6^3			7^1	10	8		11		9		41
1			3	5	6^2			12							13				4	2				7	10	8		11		9^1		42
1	6			5	12				13		4				14				3	2				8▮	7^1	9^2		10		11^3		43
1				5	7^2			14	11^3		3				6	13			4	2					10	8^1		12		9		44
1	2		13	5				14	11^1		3^2				7		6		4						8	9^3		12		10		45
1	2^1		12	5			7	9^3			4				6^2		14		3						8	13		11		10		46

FA Cup
First Round | Bolton W | (a) | 0-1

EFL Cup
First Round | Derby Co | (a) | 0-1

EFL Checkatrade Trophy
Northern Group H | Walsall | (a) | 2-5
Northern Group H | Leicester C U21 | (h) | 0-1
Northern Group H | Sheffield U | (h) | 2-4

HARTLEPOOL UNITED

FOUNDATION

The inspiration for the launching of Hartlepool United was the West Hartlepool club which won the FA Amateur Cup in 1904–05. They had been in existence since 1881 and their cup success led in 1908 to the formation of the new professional concern which first joined the North-Eastern League. In those days they were Hartlepools United and won the Durham Senior Cup in their first two seasons.

The Northern Gas & Power Stadium, Clarence Road, Hartlepool TS24 8BZ.

Telephone: (01429) 272 584.

Fax: (01429) 863 007.

Ticket Office: (01429) 272 584 (option 2).

Website: www.hartlepoolunited.co.uk

Email: enquires@hartlepoolunited.co.uk

Ground Capacity: 7,856.

Record Attendance: 17,426 v Manchester U, FA Cup 3rd rd, 5 January 1957.

Pitch Measurements: 100.5m × 67.5m (110yd × 74yd).

Chief Executive: Pam Duxbury.

Manager: Craig Harrison.

Assistant Manager: Paul Jenkins.

Colours: Blue shirts with white stripes, blue shorts with white trim, white socks.

Year Formed: 1908.

Turned Professional: 1908.

Previous Names: 1908, Hartlepools United; 1968, Hartlepool; 1977, Hartlepool United.

Club Nickname: 'The Pool', 'Monkey Hangers'.

Ground: 1908, Victoria Park; 2016, renamed The Northern Gas & Power Stadium.

First Football League Game: 27 August 1921, Division 3 (N), v Wrexham (a) W 2–0 – Gill; Thomas, Crilly; Dougherty, Hopkins, Short; Kessler, Mulholland (1), Lister (1), Robertson, Donald.

Record League Victory: 10–1 v Barrow, Division 4, 4 April 1959 – Oakley; Cameron, Waugh; Johnson, Moore, Anderson; Scott (1), Langland (1), Smith (3), Clark (2), Luke (2), (1 og).

Record Cup Victory: 6–0 v North Shields, FA Cup 1st rd, 30 November 1946 – Heywood; Brown, Gregory; Spelman, Lambert, Jones; Price, Scott (2), Sloan (4), Moses, McMahon; 6–0 v Gainsborough Trinity (a), FA Cup 1st rd, 10 November 2007 – Budtz; McCunnie, Humphreys, Liddle (1) (Antwi), Nelson, Clark, Moore (1), Sweeney, Barker (2) (Monkhouse), Mackay (Porter 1), Brown (1).

Record Defeat: 1–10 v Wrexham, Division 4, 3 March 1962.

Most League Points (2 for a win): 60, Division 4, 1967–68.

Most League Points (3 for a win): 88, FL 2, 2006–07.

HONOURS

League: *Runners-up:* Division 3N – 1956–57; FL 2 – 2006–07; Third Division – 2002–03.

FA Cup: 4th rd – 1955, 1978, 1989, 1993, 2005, 2009.

League Cup: 4th rd – 1975.

sky SPORTS FACT FILE

Tom Burlison who made over 150 appearances for the then-named Hartlepools United between 1957 and 1964 was later a senior trades union and Labour Party official. In October 1997 he was created a life peer and he sat in the House of Lords with the title Baron Burlison of Rowlands Gill.

Most League Goals: 90, Division 3 (N), 1956–57.

Highest League Scorer in Season: William Robinson, 28, Division 3 (N), 1927–28; Joe Allon, 28, Division 4, 1990–91.

Most League Goals in Total Aggregate: Ken Johnson, 98, 1949–64.

Most League Goals in One Match: 5, Harry Simmons v Wigan Borough, Division 3 (N), 1 January 1931; 5, Bobby Folland v Oldham Ath, Division 3 (N), 15 April 1961.

Most Capped Player: Ambrose Fogarty, 1 (11), Republic of Ireland.

Most League Appearances: Richie Humphreys, 481, 2001–13.

Youngest League Player: David Foley, 16 years 105 days v Port Vale, 25 August 2003.

Record Transfer Fee Received: £750,000 from Ipswich T for Tommy Miller, July 2001.

Record Transfer Fee Paid: £80,000 to Mansfield T for Darrell Clarke, July 2001.

Football League Record: 1921 Original Member of Division 3 (N); 1958–68 Division 4; 1968–69 Division 3; 1969–91 Division 4; 1991–92 Division 3; 1992–94 Division 2; 1994–2003 Division 3; 2003–04 Division 2; 2004–06 FL 1; 2006–07 FL 2; 2007–13 FL 1; 2013–17 FL 2; 2017– National League.

LATEST SEQUENCES

Longest Sequence of League Wins: 9, 18.11.2006 – 1.1.2007.

Longest Sequence of League Defeats: 8, 27.1.1993 – 27.2.1993.

Longest Sequence of League Draws: 6, 30.4.2011 – 20.8.2011.

Longest Sequence of Unbeaten League Matches: 23, 18.11.2006 – 30.3.2007.

Longest Sequence Without a League Win: 20, 8.9.2012 – 26.12.2012.

Successive Scoring Runs: 27 from 18.11.2006.

Successive Non-scoring Runs: 11 from 9.1.1993.

MANAGERS

Alfred Priest 1908–12
Percy Humphreys 1912–13
Jack Manners 1913–20
Cecil Potter 1920–22
David Gordon 1922–24
Jack Manners 1924–27
Bill Norman 1927–31
Jack Carr 1932–35
(had been Player-Coach from 1931)
Jimmy Hamilton 1935–43
Fred Westgarth 1943–57
Ray Middleton 1957–59
Bill Robinson 1959–62
Allenby Chilton 1962–63
Bob Gurney 1963–64
Alvan Williams 1964–65
Geoff Twentyman 1965
Brian Clough 1965–67
Angus McLean 1967–70
John Simpson 1970–71
Len Ashurst 1971–74
Ken Hale 1974–76
Billy Horner 1976–83
Johnny Duncan 1983
Mike Docherty 1983
Billy Horner 1984–86
John Bird 1986–88
Bobby Moncur 1988–89
Cyril Knowles 1989–91
Alan Murray 1991–93
Viv Busby 1993
John MacPhail 1993–94
David McCreery 1994–95
Keith Houchen 1995–96
Mick Tait 1996–99
Chris Turner 1999–2002
Mike Newell 2002–03
Neale Cooper 2003–05
Martin Scott 2005–06
Danny Wilson 2006–08
Chris Turner 2008–10
Mick Wadsworth 2010–11
Neale Cooper 2011–12
John Hughes 2012–13
Colin Cooper 2013–14
Paul Murray 2014
Ronnie Moore 2014–16
Craig Hignett 2016–17
Dave Jones 2017
Craig Harrison May 2017–

TEN YEAR LEAGUE RECORD

		P	W	D	L	F	A	Pts	Pos
2007-08	FL 1	46	15	9	22	63	66	54	15
2008-09	FL 1	46	13	11	22	66	79	50	19
2009-10	FL 1	46	14	11	21	59	67	50*	20
2010-11	FL 1	46	15	12	19	47	65	57	16
2011-12	FL 1	46	14	14	18	50	55	56	13
2012-13	FL 1	46	9	14	23	39	67	41	23
2013-14	FL 2	46	14	11	21	50	56	53	19
2014-15	FL 2	46	12	9	25	39	70	45	22
2015-16	FL 2	46	15	6	25	49	72	51	16
2016-17	FL 2	46	11	13	22	54	75	46	23

**3 pts deducted.*

DID YOU KNOW ?

Hartlepool United won their first trophy in March 1909, less than 12 months after being formed. Pools defeated Seaham White Star 3-2 at Stockton to win the Durham Senior Cup in front of a 10,000 crowd with Tommy Brown netting two and Frank Edgley adding a third.

HARTLEPOOL UNITED – SKY BET LEAGUE TWO 2016–17 LEAGUE RECORD

Match No.	Date	Venue	Opponents	Result		H/T Score	Lg Pos.	Goalscorers	Attendance
1	Aug 6	H	Colchester U	D	1-1	1-1	14	Paynter (pen) [27]	4055
2	13	A	Exeter C	W	2-1	0-1	6	Woods [74], Paynter [75]	3322
3	16	A	Crewe Alex	D	3-3	1-2	7	Magnay 2 [42, 76], Amond [72]	3482
4	20	H	Notts Co	L	1-2	1-0	13	Nsiala [8]	3708
5	27	H	Newport Co	D	2-2	2-2	15	Featherstone [2], Amond [38]	3261
6	Sept 3	A	Stevenage	L	1-6	1-2	19	Thomas [4]	2401
7	10	A	Yeovil T	W	2-1	0-0	14	Thomas 2 [67, 90]	2749
8	17	H	Mansfield T	D	0-0	0-0	17		3775
9	24	A	Plymouth Arg	D	1-1	1-0	15	Thomas [21]	7591
10	27	H	Luton T	D	1-1	1-0	15	Thomas [45]	3533
11	Oct 1	A	Grimsby T	W	3-0	2-0	13	Amond 2 [25, 36], Thomas [60]	5713
12	8	H	Crawley T	D	1-1	1-0	12	Alessandra [12]	3693
13	15	A	Carlisle U	L	2-3	0-1	14	Alessandra [66], Amond [75]	7333
14	22	H	Leyton Orient	L	1-3	1-0	17	Laurent [45]	3700
15	29	A	Barnet	L	2-3	1-0	20	Thomas [31], Amond [53]	1690
16	Nov 12	H	Cheltenham T	W	2-0	1-0	16	Alessandra [45], Bates [79]	3316
17	19	A	Doncaster R	L	1-2	1-1	18	Amond (pen) [42]	5009
18	22	H	Accrington S	W	2-0	0-0	13	Deverdics [62], Alessandra [90]	2514
19	26	A	Wycombe W	L	0-2	0-1	18		3288
20	Dec 10	H	Cambridge U	L	0-5	0-0	19		3261
21	17	A	Portsmouth	D	0-0	0-0	18		17,081
22	26	H	Blackpool	L	0-1	0-0	18		3767
23	30	H	Morecambe	W	3-2	3-0	18	Amond [10], Paynter (pen) [14], Featherstone [24]	2996
24	Jan 2	A	Accrington S	D	2-2	0-0	18	Amond [60], Harrison [86]	1590
25	7	H	Grimsby T	L	0-1	0-1	19		4388
26	14	A	Crawley T	L	0-1	0-0	19		4266
27	21	H	Stevenage	W	2-0	2-0	18	Featherstone [41], Walker [45]	3363
28	28	A	Newport Co	L	1-3	0-1	18	Amond [90]	2271
29	Feb 4	H	Yeovil T	D	1-1	0-0	18	Amond [64]	3410
30	11	A	Mansfield T	L	0-4	0-2	19		4309
31	14	A	Luton T	L	0-3	0-2	19		6965
32	18	H	Plymouth Arg	D	1-1	1-0	22	Oates [27]	3684
33	25	A	Colchester U	L	1-2	0-0	22	Thomas [82]	3357
34	28	H	Crewe Alex	W	4-0	1-0	22	Alessandra 2 [45, 85], Amond [71], Thomas [90]	3043
35	Mar 4	H	Exeter C	W	3-1	0-1	21	Alessandra 2 [66, 90], Amond [69]	3775
36	11	A	Notts Co	L	1-2	0-0	22	Hollis (og) [78]	8653
37	14	A	Cambridge U	W	1-0	0-0	20	Woods [63]	3824
38	18	H	Wycombe W	L	0-2	0-1	20		3356
39	25	A	Blackpool	L	1-2	1-1	21	Alessandra [18]	5374
40	Apr 1	H	Portsmouth	L	0-2	0-1	22		4500
41	8	A	Morecambe	D	1-1	1-0	22	Amond [39]	1548
42	14	H	Carlisle U	D	1-1	0-1	22	Oates [64]	5011
43	17	A	Leyton Orient	L	1-2	1-2	22	Oates [8]	5411
44	22	H	Barnet	L	0-2	0-0	23		4208
45	29	A	Cheltenham T	L	0-1	0-1	23		5606
46	May 6	H	Doncaster R	W	2-1	0-1	23	Rodney 2 [74, 83]	6799

Final League Position: 23

GOALSCORERS

League (54): Amond 14 (1 pen), Alessandra 9, Thomas 9, Featherstone 3, Oates 3, Paynter 3 (2 pens), Magnay 2, Rodney 2, Woods 2, Bates 1, Deverdics 1, Harrison 1, Laurent 1, Nsiala 1, Walker 1, own goal 1.
FA Cup (3): Deverdics 1, Paynter 1, own goal 1.
EFL Cup (0).
EFL Checkatrade Trophy (2): Oates 2.

Carson T 23	Magnay C 11 + 2	Nsiala A 20 + 1	Jones R 3 + 1	Carroll J 19 + 2	Featherstone N 43	Hawkins L 27 + 7	Alessandra L 39 + 7	Amond P 37 + 9	Thomas N 31 + 2	Paynter B 12 + 9	Woods M 25 + 11	Deverdics N 15 + 13	Laurent J 18 + 7	Bates M 19 + 1	Oates R 17 + 9	Richards J 12 + 3	Harrison S 35 + 3	Donnelly L 31 + 1	Bartlett A 9 + 1	Fewster B — + 4	Heardman T — + 2	Green K — + 1	Martin J 3	Kavanagh S 9	Walker B 19 + 1	Smith C — + 1	Nelson A 3 + 1	Rooney L 3 + 4	Richardson K 9 + 2	Fryer J 14	Hawkes J — + 2	Rodney D — + 4	Blackford J — + 1	Simpson C — + 2	*Match No.*
1	2	3	4	5	6[1]	7	8	9[2]	10	11[3]	12	13	14																						1
1	2	3	4[1]	5	8	7[3]	9	13	11	10[2]	6			12	14																				2
1	2	3		5	7[2]		6	10	9	11	12	8[1]	13	4																					3
1	2[1]	3		5	7	13	6	10	9	11[3]	8[2]		14	4		12																			4
1		3■		5	8	14	6	10[3]	9	11[1]	7			4[2]		2	12	13																	5
	3			5	7		9	10[1]	11	12	6[2]	8[3]	14			2	4		1	13															6
1	5	3	2[1]		6	7[3]	12	11[2]	10			14	8				4	9		13															7
1	2[3]	3		12	7	8[2]	11	13	9	10[1]		14	6				4	5																	8
1		3		5	7	6[2]	9	10[3]	11[1]	13		12	8			14	4■	2																	9
1		3		5	7■	8	9[2]	10[3]	11[1]			12	6			2		4		14	13														10
1		3		5		8	9	10[1]	11[2]	13		7[3]	6			2	14	4		12															11
		3		5		8	9	10[2]	11	13		7[1]	6			2	4		1		14	12[3]													12
1		4		5[2]		6	9	10	11	12	13		7			2[1]	3	8																	13
1		3		5	7	8[2]	9	10[3]	11	12	13	14	6			2[1]		4																	14
1		3		5	7	6[1]	10	11	9[2]			13	8			12	4	2■																	15
1[2]		3		5	7	8	9	10			13	11[3]	6	4			14	2[1]	12																16
1		4	14	5	6	8[2]	11[3]	10		13	12	9[1]	7	3		2																			17
1		2		12	7	6	11	10			13	8[2]	5	3			4						9[1]												18
1		2			6	5[1]	9[2]	10		13	12	11[3]	7	3	14		4						8												19
1		3[2]			7[3]	6	12	9		10	14	11[1]	8	4	13			2					5												20
1		14		5	6	8	11[2]	13		10[1]		12	7	3	9[3]		4	2																	21
1				5	7	6	11[3]	12		10[2]	13	14	8[1]	4	9		3	2																	22
1		3		9	7	5	12	10		11[2]	6[3]	8[1]	14		13		4	2																	23
				6[3]	7	12	14	10		11[2]	8		9[1]	3	13	5	4	2	1																24
					7	6	12	10		11[1]	8			3	13	5[2]	4	2	1					9											25
					7		11	10[3]		12	8[2]		6	2	13	5[1]	3	4	1					9	14										26
					7	9	11[3]	12	14		8		13	3	10[1]		4	2	1					5	6[2]										27
					7	9[2]	11	13			8[1]		14	3	10[3]		4	2	1					5	6	12									28
					7		10[1]	9	12					3			4	2	1					5	6		8	11							29
					7		13	9[1]	10[2]					4	14		3	2[3]	1					5	6		8	11	12						30
					6		12	13	11		7			4[1]	10		3							5	8		9[2]		2	1					31
					7	13	8	10	9[1]		6				11		4							5	3		12[2]		2	1					32
					8	13	9[2]	11	6		7				10[1]		4	5							3			12	2	1					33
					7	13	8	12	11		6[1]				9[2]		4	5							3			10[3]	2	1	14				34
					7	13	8	10	11		6[2]				9[1]		4	2						5[3]	3				12	1	14				35
					3	7[1]	8	10	11		6	12			9		4	5											2	1					36
					3		8	10	9		6	12			11[1]		4	5							7				2	1					37
					7	8[1]	11	10	9		6	5					4								3			12	2	1					38
					7	8	11	10	9		6[1]	5					4	2							3			12		1					39
	13				7		8	10	11		6	5			9[2]		4	2[1]							3					1		12			40
					8		6[2]	11	9		7	13			10[1]		3	5							4				2	1		12			41
	12				7		8	10	11		6				9		4	5							3				2[1]	1					42
	2				7[3]		6	10[1]	11		12	8[2]			9		4	5■							3			14		1		13			43
	2				7[1]		9[2]	12	11		6	5		3	10		4								8					1			13		44
1	5				6	8[2]	10	11	7[1]		9				12	2	3								4									13	45
1	5				7[1]	8	9	10			6[2]	12			11[3]		4	2							3							13		14	46

FA Cup

First Round	Stamford	(h)	3-0
Second Round	Port Vale	(a)	0-4

EFL Cup

First Round	Preston NE	(a)	0-1

EFL Checkatrade Trophy

Northern Group F	Notts Co	(a)	1-2
Northern Group F	Sunderland U21	(h)	0-1
Northern Group F	Rochdale	(h)	1-2

HUDDERSFIELD TOWN

FOUNDATION

A meeting, attended largely by members of the Huddersfield & District FA, was held at the Imperial Hotel in 1906 to discuss the feasibility of establishing a football club in this rugby stronghold. However, it was not until a man with both the enthusiasm and the money to back the scheme came on the scene that real progress was made. This benefactor was Mr Hilton Crowther and it was at a meeting at the Albert Hotel in 1908 that the club formally came into existence with an investment of £2,000 and joined the North-Eastern League.

John Smith's Stadium, Stadium Way, Leeds Road, Huddersfield, West Yorkshire HD1 6PX.

Telephone: (01484) 484 112.

Fax: (01484) 484 101.

Ticket Office: (01484) 484 123.

Website: www.htafc.com

Email: info@htafc.com

Ground Capacity: 24,590.

Record Attendance: 67,037 v Arsenal, FA Cup 6th rd, 27 February 1932 (at Leeds Road); 24,129 v Manchester C, FA Cup 5th rd, 18 February 2017 (at John Smith's Stadium).

Pitch Measurements: 105m × 69.5m (115yd × 76yd).

Chairman: Dean Hoyle.

Chief Executive: Julian Winter.

Head Coach: David Wagner.

Assistant Head Coach: Christoph Buehler.

Colours: Blue and white striped shirts, white shorts with blue trim, white socks with blue trim.

Year Formed: 1908.

Turned Professional: 1908.

Club Nickname: 'The Terriers'.

Grounds: 1908, Leeds Road; 1994, The Alfred McAlpine Stadium (renamed the Galpharm Stadium 2004, John Smith's Stadium 2012).

First Football League Game: 3 September 1910, Division 2, v Bradford PA (a) W 1–0 – Mutch; Taylor, Morris; Beaton, Hall, Bartlett; Blackburn, Wood, Hamilton (1), McCubbin, Jee.

Record League Victory: 10–1 v Blackpool, Division 1, 13 December 1930 – Turner; Goodall, Spencer; Redfern, Wilson, Campbell; Bob Kelly (1), McLean (4), Robson (3), Davies (1), Smailes (1).

Record Cup Victory: 7–0 v Lincoln U, FA Cup 1st rd, 16 November 1991 – Clarke; Trevitt, Charlton, Donovan (2), Mitchell, Doherty, O'Regan (1), Stapleton (1) (Wright), Roberts (2), Onuora (1), Barnett (Ireland). *N.B.* 11–0 v Heckmondwike (a), FA Cup pr rd, 18 September 1909 – Doggart; Roberts, Ewing; Hooton, Stevenson, Randall; Kenworthy (2), McCreadie (1), Foster (4), Stacey (4), Jee.

Record Defeat: 1–10 v Manchester C, Division 2, 7 November 1987.

Most League Points (2 for a win): 66, Division 4, 1979–80.

HONOURS

League Champions: Division 1 – 1923–24, 1924–25, 1925–26; Division 2 – 1969–70; Division 4 – 1979–80.
Runners-up: Division 1 – 1926–27, 1927–28, 1933–34; Division 2 – 1919–20, 1952–53.

FA Cup Winners: 1922.
Runners-up: 1920, 1928, 1930, 1938.

League Cup: semi-final – 1968.

League Trophy: *Runners-up:* 1994.

sky SPORTS FACT FILE

Huddersfield Town's first-ever game took place at Leeds Road on 2 September 1908 when a crowd of around 1,000 saw the Terriers beat Bradford Park Avenue 2-1 in a friendly match. Their first competitive match took place three days later and resulted in a 2-0 away loss to South Shields Adelaide in a North Eastern League fixture.

Most League Points (3 for a win): 87, FL 1, 2010–11.

Most League Goals: 101, Division 4, 1979–80.

Highest League Scorer in Season: Sam Taylor, 35, Division 2, 1919–20; George Brown, 35, Division 1, 1925–26; Jordan Rhodes, 35, 2011–12.

Most League Goals in Total Aggregate: George Brown, 142, 1921–29; Jimmy Glazzard, 142, 1946–56.

Most League Goals in One Match: 5, Dave Mangnall v Derby Co, Division 1, 21 November 1931; 5, Alf Lythgoe v Blackburn R, Division 1, 13 April 1935; 5, Jordan Rhodes v Wycombe W, FL 1, 6 January 2012.

Most Capped Player: Jimmy Nicholson, 31 (41), Northern Ireland.

Most League Appearances: Billy Smith, 521, 1914–34.

Youngest League Player: Denis Law, 16 years 303 days v Notts Co, 24 December 1956.

Record Transfer Fee Received: £8,000,000 from Blackburn R for Jordan Rhodes, August 2012.

Record Transfer Fee Paid: £11,500,000 to Montpellier for Steve Mounie, July 2017.

Football League Record: 1910 Elected to Division 2; 1920–52 Division 1; 1952–53 Division 2; 1953–56 Division 1; 1956–70 Division 2; 1970–72 Division 1; 1972–73 Division 2; 1973–75 Division 3; 1975–80 Division 4; 1980–83 Division 3; 1983–88 Division 2; 1988–92 Division 3; 1992–95 Division 2; 1995–2001 Division 1; 2001–03 Division 2; 2003–04 Division 3; 2004–12 FL 1; 2012–17 FL C; 2017– FA Premier League.

LATEST SEQUENCES

Longest Sequence of League Wins: 11, 5.4.1920 – 4.9.1920.

Longest Sequence of League Defeats: 7, 8.10.1955 – 19.11.1955.

Longest Sequence of League Draws: 6, 3.3.1987 – 3.4.1987.

Longest Sequence of Unbeaten League Matches: 43, 1.1.2011 – 19.11.2011.

Longest Sequence Without a League Win: 22, 4.12.1971 – 29.4.1972.

Successive Scoring Runs: 27 from 12.3.2005.

Successive Non-scoring Runs: 7 from 14.10.2000.

MANAGERS

Fred Walker 1908–10
Richard Pudan 1910–12
Arthur Fairclough 1912–19
Ambrose Langley 1919–21
Herbert Chapman 1921–25
Cecil Potter 1925–26
Jack Chaplin 1926–29
Clem Stephenson 1929–42
Ted Magner 1942–43
David Steele 1943–47
George Stephenson 1947–52
Andy Beattie 1952–56
Bill Shankly 1956–59
Eddie Boot 1960–64
Tom Johnston 1964–68
Ian Greaves 1968–74
Bobby Collins 1974
Tom Johnston 1975–78
(had been General Manager since 1975)
Mike Buxton 1978–86
Steve Smith 1986–87
Malcolm Macdonald 1987–88
Eoin Hand 1988–92
Ian Ross 1992–93
Neil Warnock 1993–95
Brian Horton 1995–97
Peter Jackson 1997–99
Steve Bruce 1999–2000
Lou Macari 2000–02
Mick Wadsworth 2002–03
Peter Jackson 2003–07
Andy Ritchie 2007–08
Stan Ternent 2008
Lee Clark 2008–12
Simon Grayson 2012–13
Mark Robins 2013–14
Chris Powell 2014–15
David Wagner November 2015–

TEN YEAR LEAGUE RECORD

		P	*W*	*D*	*L*	*F*	*A*	*Pts*	*Pos*
2007-08	FL 1	46	20	6	20	50	62	66	10
2008-09	FL 1	46	18	14	14	62	65	68	9
2009-10	FL 1	46	23	11	12	82	56	80	6
2010-11	FL 1	46	25	12	9	77	48	87	3
2011-12	FL 1	46	21	18	7	79	47	81	4
2012-13	FL C	46	15	13	18	53	73	58	19
2013-14	FL C	46	14	11	21	58	65	53	17
2014-15	FL C	46	13	16	17	58	75	55	16
2015-16	FL C	46	13	12	21	59	70	51	19
2016-17	FL C	46	25	6	15	56	58	81	5

DID YOU KNOW ?

After beating Derby County 2-1 at Leeds Road on 27 November, Huddersfield Town did not win a single home game for the rest of the 1971–72 season. Of the remaining 11 games 5 were drawn and 6 were lost, with the team scoring just twice in over 16 hours of play.

HUDDERSFIELD TOWN – SKY BET CHAMPIONSHIP 2016–17 LEAGUE RECORD

Match No.	Date	Venue	Opponents	Result	H/T Score	Lg Pos.	Goalscorers	Attendance
1	Aug 6	H	Brentford	W 2-1	0-0	5	Kachunga 50, Palmer 79	18,479
2	13	A	Newcastle U	W 2-1	1-0	2	Wells 45, Payne 82	52,079
3	16	A	Aston Villa	D 1-1	0-1	3	Hefele 86	34,924
4	20	H	Barnsley	W 2-1	1-0	1	Lowe 27, Hogg 90	20,001
5	27	H	Wolverhampton W	W 1-0	1-0	1	van La Parra 6	19,972
6	Sept 10	A	Leeds U	W 1-0	0-0	1	Mooy 55	28,514
7	13	A	Brighton & HA	L 0-1	0-0	1		24,166
8	17	H	QPR	W 2-1	1-0	1	Palmer 14, Kachunga 62	20,595
9	24	A	Reading	L 0-1	0-1	2		17,030
10	27	H	Rotherham U	W 2-1	2-1	1	Kachunga 2, Wells 38	18,808
11	Oct 1	A	Ipswich T	W 1-0	0-0	1	Schindler 58	16,146
12	16	H	Sheffield W	L 0-1	0-0	3		22,368
13	19	A	Preston NE	L 1-3	0-2	4	Wells 81	12,862
14	22	H	Derby Co	W 1-0	0-0	2	Kachunga 90	19,749
15	29	A	Fulham	L 0-5	0-3	3		19,858
16	Nov 5	H	Birmingham C	D 1-1	0-0	3	Kachunga 69	20,200
17	19	A	Cardiff C	L 2-3	1-3	3	Smith 28, Billing 70	15,930
18	28	H	Wigan Ath	L 1-2	0-1	6	Mooy 50	18,943
19	Dec 3	A	Blackburn R	D 1-1	1-1	5	Palmer 6	12,034
20	10	H	Bristol C	W 2-1	1-1	4	Kachunga 10, Wells 58	18,333
21	13	A	Burton Alb	W 1-0	0-0	4	Wells 85	4564
22	16	A	Norwich C	W 2-1	2-1	3	Kachunga 2 5, 40	25,275
23	26	H	Nottingham F	W 2-1	0-1	3	Palmer 53, Mancienne (og) 59	22,100
24	31	H	Blackburn R	D 1-1	0-0	4	Wells 90	21,311
25	Jan 2	A	Wigan Ath	W 1-0	0-0	4	Wells 80	13,480
26	14	A	Sheffield W	L 0-2	0-0	5		28,173
27	21	H	Ipswich T	W 2-0	1-0	3	Brown 41, Schindler 57	19,113
28	Feb 2	H	Brighton & HA	W 3-1	3-1	5	Smith 9, Wells 36, Kachunga 45	20,104
29	5	H	Leeds U	W 2-1	1-1	4	Brown 27, Hefele 89	22,400
30	11	A	QPR	W 2-1	2-0	3	Brown 26, Wells 36	14,044
31	14	A	Rotherham U	W 3-2	1-1	3	Lolley 19, Kachunga 75, Smith 90	10,114
32	21	H	Reading	W 1-0	0-0	3	Billing 82	19,894
33	25	A	Barnsley	D 1-1	1-0	3	Hefele 18	18,075
34	Mar 4	H	Newcastle U	L 1-3	0-2	3	Mooy (pen) 72	23,213
35	7	H	Aston Villa	W 1-0	0-0	3	Smith 69	20,584
36	11	A	Brentford	W 1-0	1-0	3	van La Parra 28	11,278
37	17	A	Bristol C	L 0-4	0-2	3		16,984
38	Apr 1	H	Burton Alb	L 0-1	0-0	3		20,154
39	5	H	Norwich C	W 3-0	0-0	3	Kachunga 66, Mooy 70, Wells 73	18,706
40	8	A	Nottingham F	L 0-2	0-1	3		20,411
41	14	H	Preston NE	W 3-2	1-1	3	Kachunga 43, Payne 70, Quaner 90	21,254
42	17	A	Derby Co	D 1-1	1-0	3	Quaner 9	29,031
43	22	H	Fulham	L 1-4	1-4	5	Lowe (pen) 4	21,023
44	25	A	Wolverhampton W	W 1-0	1-0	3	Brown 31	17,505
45	29	A	Birmingham C	L 0-2	0-1	3		26,914
46	May 7	H	Cardiff C	L 0-3	0-2	5		20,583

Final League Position: 5

GOALSCORERS

League (56): Kachunga 12, Wells 10, Brown 4, Mooy 4 (1 pen), Palmer 4, Smith 4, Hefele 3, Billing 2, Lowe 2 (1 pen), Payne 2, Quaner 2, Schindler 2, van La Parra 2, Hogg 1, Lolley 1, own goal 1.
FA Cup (9): Bunn 2, Hefele 2, Payne 2, Brown 1 (1 pen), Palmer 1, Quaner 1.
EFL Cup (1): Kachunga 1.
Championship Play-Offs (1): own goal 1.

Ward D 43	Smith T 40 + 2	Hudson M 17 + 5	Schindler C 43 + 1	Lowe C 39 + 2	Hogg J 33 + 4	Mooy A 42 + 3	Lolley J 8 + 11	Payne J 10 + 13	van La Parra R 36 + 4	Kachunga E 41 + 1	Scannell S 8 + 7	Palmer K 16 + 8	Paurevic I — + 1	Wells N 31 + 12	Hefele M 28 + 9	Whitehead D 10 + 6	Bunn H 6 + 10	Cranie M 7 + 7	Holmes-Dennis T 7 + 2	Stankovic J 4 + 3	Billing P 13 + 11	Coleman J 3 + 2	Brown I 12 + 3	Quaner C 9 + 7	*Match No.*
1	2	3	4	5	6	7	8^{3}	9^{1}	10	11^{2}	12	13	14												1
1	2	3	4	5	8	7	6^{1}	14	9^{3}	10	13	12		11^{2}											2
1	2	3	4	5^{3}	6	7	8^{2}	9^{1}	10	11	12			13	14										3
1	2	3	4	5	12	7^{3}			10	9	8^{2}	13		11^{1}		6	14								4
1	2	3	4	5	6	7		12	10^{2}	8	14	9^{3}		11^{1}			13								5
1	2	3	4	5	6	7		9^{1}	10	11^{3}		13		12	14		8^{2}								6
1	2	3	4	5^{2}	6	7		9^{1}	10	11		14		12	13		8^{3}								7
1	2	3	4	5	6	7			10^{3}	8		9^{2}		11^{1}	14	13	12								8
1	2	3	4	5^{2}	6	7			10■	8		9^{1}		11	14		12^{3}	13							9
1	2		4		13	7		12		10	8^{1}	9^{3}		11	3	6^{2}			5	14					10
1	2	3	4^{1}	5	7	9			12	10	8^{3}			11	13	6^{2}		14							11
1	2	3	4	5^{1}	6	7		12	10	8		9^{2}		11	13										12
1	2	3	4	5	6	7		9	10^{3}	11^{1}	8^{2}	14		12			13								13
1	2		4	5	7	12		14	10^{1}	8		9		11^{2}	3	6^{3}	13								14
1	2^{2}	3	4	5^{3}		7		12		8		9		11		6^{1}	10	14	13						15
1	2		4	5	6	7		13	12	10	8^{2}	9^{1}		11	3										16
1	5		4^{2}	8	6^{1}	7				9	13	10		11	2					3	12				17
1	2	3^{2}	12	5	6^{1}	7			10	11	8^{3}	9		13						4	14				18
1			4	5	6^{2}	7			10	8		9		11^{1}	3		13	2^{3}		14	12				19
1	2		4	5	6	7		14	10^{2}	8		9^{1}		11^{3}	3			13			12				20
1			4	14	6	7			13	8		12		11	3		10^{2}	2	5^{3}		9^{1}				21
1	2		4	5	6^{3}	7			10^{2}	8		9		11^{1}	14		12			3	13				22
	2		4	13	6	7		12	10^{3}	8		9^{1}		11	3			14	5^{2}			1			23
1	2	14	4	5		7		12	10^{2}	8		9^{3}		11	3	6^{1}	13								24
1		3				7	12	9^{3}		8				11	14	13	10^{2}	2	5	4	6^{1}				25
1	2	14	4	5		7	12	9■		8				11	3	13^{3}					6^{1}		10^{2}		26
1	2	14	4	5	6^{3}		12		10	8				11^{1}	3	13					7		9^{2}		27
1	2		4	5	6	7	13		10^{3}	8		12		11^{1}	3								9^{2}	14	28
1	2		4	5	6	7	13		10^{3}	8		9^{2}		14	3								12	11^{1}	29
1	14		4	5	6^{2}	7	13		10^{3}	8				11	3			2^{1}			12		9		30
1	2		4			7	8^{2}	14	12	10				13	3				5		6		9^{3}	11^{1}	31
1	2		4	5		7	13	12	10^{1}	8				11^{3}	3						6		9^{2}	14	32
1	2		4^{3}	5		7	14		10^{2}	8					3	6^{1}				12	13		9	11	33
1^{2}	2		4	5^{1}	13	7			10	8				11	3						6^{3}	12	9	14	34
	2		4	5	6	7			10^{2}	8				12	3			13			14	1	9^{3}	11^{1}	35
1	2		4	5	6	13		9^{2}	10^{1}	8				11	3			14			7^{3}		12		36
1	2	3	4	5	6^{1}	7	13		10	8^{2}				11							12		9^{3}	14	37
1	2		4	5		7	8^{1}	9^{2}	10	12				13	3	6■					14			11^{3}	38
1	2	14	4	5^{3}	6^{2}	9	12		10	8				11	3^{1}				13		7				39
1	2		4		6^{1}	9	12		10^{2}	8				11	3	13			5^{3}		7			14	40
1	2	14	4	5	6	9		12^{3}	10	8				11^{2}	3						7^{1}			13	41
1	12		4	5	14	7	8^{3}		10^{2}	9				13	3	6		2^{1}						11	42
1	2		4	5	6	9	8^{2}		10		13				3						7^{1}		12	11	43
1			4	5	6	7			10		8^{2}			11^{1}	3		13	2			14		9^{3}	12	44
	2	3^{3}				13	8	9			14			12		6	10^{2}	4	5^{1}		7	1		11	45
1■	2		4	5	6^{3}	7			10		8^{2}			13	3	14						12	9^{1}	11	46

FA Cup

Third Round	Port Vale	(h)	4-0
Fourth Round	Rochdale	(a)	4-0
Fifth Round	Manchester C	(h)	0-0
Replay	Manchester C	(a)	1-5

EFL Cup

First Round	Shrewsbury T	(a)	1-2

Championship Play-Offs

Semi-Final 1st leg	Sheffield W	(h)	0-0
Semi-Final 2nd leg	Sheffield W	(a)	1-1

(*aet; Huddersfield T won 4-3 on penalties*)

Final	Reading	(Wembley)	0-0

(*aet; Huddersfield T won 4-3 on penalties*)

HULL CITY

FOUNDATION

The enthusiasts who formed Hull City in 1904 were brave men indeed. More than that, they were audacious for they immediately put the club on the map in this Rugby League fortress by obtaining a three-year agreement with the Hull Rugby League club to rent their ground! They had obtained quite a number of conversions to the dribbling code, before the Rugby League forbade the use of any of their club grounds by Association Football clubs. By that time, Hull City were well away, having entered the FA Cup in their initial season and the Football League, Second Division after only a year.

The KCOM Stadium, West Park, Hull, East Yorkshire HU3 6HU.

Telephone: (01482) 504 600.

Fax: (01482) 636 301.

Ticket Office: (01482) 505 600.

Website: www.hullcitytigers.com

Email: info@hulltigers.com

Ground Capacity: 24,983.

Record Attendance: 55,019 v Manchester U, FA Cup 6th rd, 26 February 1949 (at Boothferry Park); 25,512 v Sunderland, FL C, 28 October 2007 (at KC Stadium).

Pitch Measurements: 105m × 68m (115yd × 74.5yd).

Chairman: Dr Assem Allam.

Vice-chairman: Ehab Allam.

Head Coach: Leonid Slutsky.

First-Team Coach: Tony Pennock.

Colours: Amber shirts with black stripes and white trim, black shorts, amber socks with black trim.

Year Formed: 1904.

Turned Professional: 1905.

Club Nickname: 'The Tigers'.

Grounds: 1904, Boulevard Ground (Hull RFC); 1905, Anlaby Road (Hull CC); 1944, Boulevard Ground; 1946, Boothferry Park; 2002, Kingston Communications Stadium; 2016, renamed KCOM stadium.

First Football League Game: 2 September 1905, Division 2, v Barnsley (h) W 4–1 – Spendiff; Langley, Jones; Martin, Robinson, Gordon (2); Rushton, Spence (1), Wilson (1), Howe, Raisbeck.

Record League Victory: 11–1 v Carlisle U, Division 3 (N), 14 January 1939 – Ellis; Woodhead, Dowen; Robinson (1), Blyth, Hardy; Hubbard (2), Richardson (2), Dickinson (2), Davies (2), Cunliffe (2).

Record Cup Victory: 8–2 v Stalybridge Celtic (a), FA Cup 1st rd, 26 November 1932 – Maddison; Goldsmith, Woodhead; Gardner, Hill (1), Denby; Forward (1), Duncan, McNaughton (1), Wainscoat (4), Sargeant (1).

HONOURS

League Champions: Division 3 – 1965–66; Division 3N – 1932–33, 1948–49.
Runners-up: FL C – 2012–13; FL 1 – 2004–05; Division 3 – 1958–59; Third Division – 2003–04; Division 4 – 1982–83.

FA Cup: *Runners-up:* 2014.

League Cup: quarter-final – 2016.

League Trophy: *Runners-up:* 1984.

European Competitions
Europa League: 2014–15.

sky SPORTS FACT FILE

Hull City have twice lost to Wrexham on penalties in cup competitions. In 1995–96 they lost 3-1 on penalties in the FA Cup first round replay, while in 2004–05 the first round Carling Cup tie between the two clubs was again decided by spot kicks, with the Tigers once more losing out 3-1.

Record Defeat: 0–8 v Wolverhampton W, Division 2, 4 November 1911.

Most League Points (2 for a win): 69, Division 3, 1965–66.

Most League Points (3 for a win): 90, Division 4, 1982–83.

Most League Goals: 109, Division 3, 1965–66.

Highest League Scorer in Season: Bill McNaughton, 39, Division 3 (N), 1932–33.

Most League Goals in Total Aggregate: Chris Chilton, 193, 1960–71.

Most League Goals in One Match: 5, Ken McDonald v Bristol C, Division 2, 17 November 1928; 5, Simon 'Slim' Raleigh v Halifax T, Division 3 (N), 26 December 1930.

Most Capped Player: Theo Whitmore, 28 (105), Jamaica.

Most League Appearances: Andy Davidson, 520, 1952–67.

Youngest League Player: Matthew Edeson, 16 years 63 days v Fulham, 10 October 1992.

Record Transfer Fee Received: £12,000,000 from Leicester C for Harry Maguire, June 2017.

Record Transfer Fee Paid: £13,000,000 to Tottenham H for Ryan Mason, August 2016.

Football League Record: 1905 Elected to Division 2; 1930–33 Division 3 (N); 1933–36 Division 2; 1936–49 Division 3 (N); 1949–56 Division 2; 1956–58 Division 3 (N); 1958–59 Division 3; 1959–60 Division 2; 1960–66 Division 3; 1966–78 Division 2; 1978–81 Division 3; 1981–83 Division 4; 1983–85 Division 3; 1985–91 Division 2; 1991–92 Division 3; 1992–96 Division 2; 1996–2004 Division 3; 2004–05 FL 1; 2005–08 FL C; 2008–10 FA Premier League; 2010–13 FL C; 2013–15 FA Premier League; 2015–16 FL C; 2016–17 FA Premier League; 2017– FL C.

LATEST SEQUENCES

Longest Sequence of League Wins: 10, 23.2.1966 – 20.4.1966.

Longest Sequence of League Defeats: 8, 7.4.1934 – 8.9.1934.

Longest Sequence of League Draws: 5, 14.2.2012 – 10.3.2012.

Longest Sequence of Unbeaten League Matches: 19, 13.3.2001 – 22.9.2001.

Longest Sequence Without a League Win: 27, 27.3.1989 – 4.11.1989.

Successive Scoring Runs: 26 from 10.4.1990.

Successive Non-scoring Runs: 6 from 13.11.1920.

MANAGERS

James Ramster 1904–05 *(Secretary-Manager)*
Ambrose Langley 1905–13
Harry Chapman 1913–14
Fred Stringer 1914–16
David Menzies 1916–21
Percy Lewis 1921–23
Bill McCracken 1923–31
Haydn Green 1931–34
John Hill 1934–36
David Menzies 1936
Ernest Blackburn 1936–46
Major Frank Buckley 1946–48
Raich Carter 1948–51
Bob Jackson 1952–55
Bob Brocklebank 1955–61
Cliff Britton 1961–70 *(continued as General Manager to 1971)*
Terry Neill 1970–74
John Kaye 1974–77
Bobby Collins 1977–78
Ken Houghton 1978–79
Mike Smith 1979–82
Bobby Brown 1982
Colin Appleton 1982–84
Brian Horton 1984–88
Eddie Gray 1988–89
Colin Appleton 1989
Stan Ternent 1989–91
Terry Dolan 1991–97
Mark Hateley 1997–98
Warren Joyce 1998–2000
Brian Little 2000–02
Jan Molby 2002
Peter Taylor 2002–06
Phil Parkinson 2006
Phil Brown *(after caretaker role December 2006)* 2007–10
Ian Dowie *(consultant)* 2010
Nigel Pearson 2010–11
Nick Barmby 2011–12
Steve Bruce 2012–16
Mike Phelan 2016–17
Marco Silva 2017
Leonid Slutsky June 2017–

TEN YEAR LEAGUE RECORD

		P	W	D	L	F	A	Pts	Pos
2007-08	FL C	46	21	12	13	65	47	75	3
2008-09	PR Lge	38	8	11	19	39	64	35	17
2009-10	PR Lge	38	6	12	20	34	75	30	19
2010-11	FL C	46	16	17	13	52	51	65	11
2011-12	FL C	46	19	11	16	47	44	68	8
2012-13	FL C	46	24	7	15	61	52	79	2
2013-14	PR Lge	38	10	7	21	38	53	37	16
2014-15	PR Lge	38	8	11	19	33	51	35	18
2015-16	FL C	46	24	11	11	69	35	83	4
2016-17	PR Lge	38	9	7	22	37	80	34	18

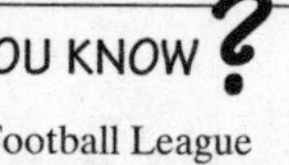

When the Football League expanded the old First Division to 22 clubs for the 1920–21 season, Hull City were one of eight clubs to apply for the vacant two positions. However, the Tigers managed only one vote in the poll and thus remained as members of the Second Division.

HULL CITY – PREMIER LEAGUE 2016–17 LEAGUE RECORD

Match No.	Date	Venue	Opponents	Result	H/T Score	Lg Pos.	Goalscorers	Attendance
1	Aug 13	H	Leicester C	W 2-1	1-0	1	Diomande 45, Snodgrass 57	21,037
2	20	A	Swansea C	W 2-0	0-0	3	Maloney 79, Hernandez 90	20,024
3	27	H	Manchester U	L 0-1	0-0	5		24,560
4	Sept 10	A	Burnley	D 1-1	0-0	5	Snodgrass 90	18,803
5	17	H	Arsenal	L 1-4	0-1	10	Snodgrass (pen) 79	22,536
6	24	A	Liverpool	L 1-5	0-3	12	Meyler 51	53,109
7	Oct 1	H	Chelsea	L 0-2	0-0	15		21,257
8	15	A	Bournemouth	L 1-6	1-3	15	Mason 34	11,029
9	22	H	Stoke C	L 0-2	0-1	18		18,522
10	29	A	Watford	L 0-1	0-0	18		20,022
11	Nov 6	H	Southampton	W 2-1	0-1	18	Snodgrass 61, Dawson 63	17,768
12	19	A	Sunderland	L 0-3	0-1	18		41,271
13	26	H	WBA	D 1-1	0-1	18	Dawson 72	18,086
14	Dec 5	A	Middlesbrough	L 0-1	0-0	19		27,395
15	10	H	Crystal Palace	D 3-3	1-0	18	Snodgrass (pen) 27, Diomande 72, Livermore 78	17,403
16	14	A	Tottenham H	L 0-3	0-1	19		31,347
17	17	A	West Ham U	L 0-1	0-0	20		56,952
18	26	H	Manchester C	L 0-3	0-0	20		23,134
19	30	H	Everton	D 2-2	1-1	19	Dawson 6, Snodgrass 65	20,111
20	Jan 2	A	WBA	L 1-3	1-0	19	Snodgrass 21	23,402
21	14	H	Bournemouth	W 3-1	1-1	18	Hernandez 2 32, 50, Mings (og) 62	17,963
22	22	A	Chelsea	L 0-2	0-1	19		41,605
23	Feb 1	A	Manchester U	D 0-0	0-0	19		75,297
24	4	H	Liverpool	W 2-0	1-0	18	N'Diaye 44, Niasse 84	24,822
25	11	A	Arsenal	L 0-2	0-1	18		59,962
26	25	H	Burnley	D 1-1	0-0	19	Huddlestone (pen) 72	20,156
27	Mar 4	A	Leicester C	L 1-3	1-1	19	Clucas 14	31,971
28	11	H	Swansea C	W 2-1	0-0	18	Niasse 2 69, 78	19,195
29	18	A	Everton	L 0-4	0-1	18		39,248
30	Apr 1	H	West Ham U	W 2-1	0-1	18	Robertson 53, Ranocchia 85	20,820
31	5	H	Middlesbrough	W 4-2	3-2	17	Markovic 13, Niasse 27, Hernandez 33, Maguire 70	20,380
32	8	A	Manchester C	L 1-3	0-1	17	Ranocchia 85	54,393
33	15	A	Stoke C	L 1-3	0-1	17	Maguire 51	27,505
34	22	H	Watford	W 2-0	0-0	17	Markovic 62, Clucas 71	20,432
35	29	A	Southampton	D 0-0	0-0	17		31,120
36	May 6	H	Sunderland	L 0-2	0-0	17		22,480
37	14	A	Crystal Palace	L 0-4	0-2	18		25,176
38	21	H	Tottenham H	L 1-7	0-3	18	Clucas 66	23,804

Final League Position: 18

GOALSCORERS

League (37): Snodgrass 7 (2 pens), Hernandez 4, Niasse 4, Clucas 3, Dawson 3, Diomande 2, Maguire 2, Markovic 2, Ranocchia 2, Huddlestone 1 (1 pen), Livermore 1, Maloney 1, Mason 1, Meyler 1, N'Diaye 1, Robertson 1, own goal 1.
FA Cup (3): Evandro 1, Hernandez 1, Tymon 1.
EFL Cup (10): Diomande 2, Snodgrass 2, Dawson 1, Henriksen 1, Huddlestone 1 (1 pen), Maguire 1, Mason 1, Niasse 1.

Jakupovic E 22	Elmohamady A 28 + 5	Livermore J 20 + 1	Davies C 25 + 1	Robertson A 31 + 2	Meyler D 9 + 11	Huddlestone T 23 + 8	Clucas S 36 + 1	Snodgrass R 19 + 1	Hernandez A 16 + 8	Diomande A 13 + 9	Maloney S 2 + 7	Maguire H 25 + 4	Keane W 4 + 1	Mason R 11 + 5	Mbokani D 8 + 4	Marshall D 16	Henriksen M 6 + 9	Dawson M 19 + 3	Bowen J 1 + 6	Tymon J 4 + 1	Evandro G 7 + 4	Niasse O 12 + 5	Elabdellaoui O 7 + 1	Markovic L 12	Ranocchia A 15 + 1	N'Diaye A 15	Grosicki K 12 + 3	*Match No.*
1	2	3	4	5	6	7	8	9	10	11																		1
1	2	3	4	5	6	7	8	9	10	11^{1}	12																	2
1	2	3	4	5	8	6	7	9^{1}	10^{2}	11	12	13																3
1	2	3	4	5	9^{1}	8	6^{2}	7	11	10^{3}	14		12	13														4
1	2	3▮	4	5	8	6^{1}	7	9	10^{3}	11^{2}		12		13	14													5
	2▮	3	4	5	12	7^{2}	8	6	11	10^{3}		13		9^{1}		1	14											6
		3	4	5	2	14	8^{1}	6	13	10^{2}	12			9	11	1	7^{3}											7
	2	6	4	5^{2}	14	12	7	9		13	10^{3}	3	11	8^{1}		1												8
	2	8	4		7^{2}	6^{1}	5	10	12	14		13	11^{3}	9		1		3										9
	5	7	4		12		9		10			2	11^{2}	8		1	6^{1}	3	13									10
	5	7	4			14	9	13	10^{2}			2^{1}	11^{3}	8	12	1	6	3										11
	2	7	4		13		8	6						9^{1}	11	1	10	3	12	5^{2}								12
	2	7	4	14	13		9	6		12				8^{3}	11	1	10^{1}	3		5^{2}								13
	2	7^{3}	4	5	14	13	8	6		11				9^{1}		1	10^{2}	3	12									14
	5	6	4	9		7	8^{1}	10		11		2				1	12	3										15
	5	6^{1}	4	9	13	7	8^{2}	10^{3}		11		2		12		1		3	14									16
	5	6^{1}	4	9		7^{2}	8	10		13		2			11^{3}	1	12	3	14									17
	5	6^{2}	4	9		7^{3}	8^{1}	10		14		2		12	11	1	13	3										18
	5	8	4	9	7^{2}	13	12	6		10^{1}		2			11	1		3										19
	5	6	4^{2}			7	8	9		11		2		12	10^{1}	1	13	3										20
1		14	4	9		7	8	10^{2}	11^{3}	5		2		6^{1}				3			12	13						21
1			4^{1}	8	12	6	10		11^{2}	14		2		7^{3}				3			9	13	5					22
1				5	2	6	9		13			4						3		10^{3}	8^{1}	11^{2}	14	7	12			23
1				5	14	6	10		11^{3}			4								12	9^{1}	13	2		3	7	8^{2}	24
1	13			5		6^{2}	9▮			14		4									12	11	2^{1}	7	3	8	10^{3}	25
1	8			5	13	7			14		9^{3}	4			11^{1}							12	2^{2}		3	6	10	26
1	2			5		6	9		12	13		4										11		7^{1}	3	8^{2}	10	27
1	13			5	14	6	9		11^{1}			4										12	2	7^{2}	3	8^{3}	10	28
1	14		5^{2}	6		8▮	10		11^{3}	13		4											2	7^{1}	3	9	12	29
1	5		4^{2}	8			7		11^{1}		13	2					14					10		9	3	6^{3}	12	30
1	2			5			8		11^{2}			4^{3}					14	13			12	10		6	3	7	9^{1}	31
1	2			5			8^{3}		12		14						13	3			10^{2}	11^{1}		6	4	7	9	32
1	13			5		8^{1}	10		12			2			14			3				11^{2}		6^{3}	4	7	9	33
1	2			5		13	7		12			4						14			9^{2}	11▮		8^{3}	3	6	10^{1}	34
1	2			5		13	7					4					12	14			9^{3}	11		8^{1}	3	6	10^{2}	35
1	2^{2}			5		12	8		10			4			13						14	11		6^{1}	3	7^{3}	9	36
1	6		14	5^{2}			8				13	2^{1}						3	12		10	11			4^{3}	7	9	37
	13		4^{2}	14		6	10									1		3	9^{1}	8^{3}		11	5		2	7	12	38

FA Cup

Third Round	Swansea C	(h)	2-0
Fourth Round	Fulham	(a)	1-4

EFL Cup

Second Round	Exeter C	(a)	3-1
Third Round	Stoke C	(a)	2-1
Fourth Round	Bristol C	(a)	2-1
Quarter-Final	Newcastle U	(h)	1-1
(*aet; Hull C won 3-1 on penalties*)			
Semi-Final 1st leg	Manchester U	(a)	0-2
Semi-Final 2nd leg	Manchester U	(h)	2-1

IPSWICH TOWN

FOUNDATION

Considering that Ipswich Town only reached the Football League in 1938, many people outside of East Anglia may be surprised to learn that this club was formed at a meeting held in the Town Hall as far back as 1878 when Mr T. C. Cobbold, MP, was voted president. Originally it was the Ipswich Association FC to distinguish it from the older Ipswich Football Club which played rugby. These two amalgamated in 1888 and the handling game was dropped in 1893.

Portman Road, Ipswich, Suffolk IP1 2DA.

Telephone: (01473) 400 500.

Fax: (01473) 400 040.

Ticket Office: (03330) 050 503

Website: www.itfc.co.uk

Email: customerservices@itfc.co.uk

Ground Capacity: 30,311.

Record Attendance: 38,010 v Leeds U, FA Cup 6th rd, 8 March 1975.

Pitch Measurements: 102.5m × 66m (112yd × 72.5yd).

Managing Directors: Ian Milne, Jonathan Symonds.

Manager: Mick McCarthy.

Assistant Manager: Terry Connor.

Colours: Blue shirts with white sleeves, blue shorts with white trim, blue socks with white trim.

Year Formed: 1878.

Turned Professional: 1936.

Previous Name: 1878, Ipswich Association FC; 1888, Ipswich Town.

Club Nicknames: 'The Blues', 'Town', 'The Tractor Boys'.

Grounds: 1878, Broom Hill and Brook's Hall; 1884, Portman Road.

First Football League Game: 27 August 1938, Division 3 (S), v Southend U (h) W 4–2 – Burns; Dale, Parry; Perrett, Fillingham, McLuckie; Williams, Davies (1), Jones (2), Alsop (1), Little.

Record League Victory: 7–0 v Portsmouth, Division 2, 7 November 1964 – Thorburn; Smith, McNeil; Baxter, Bolton, Thompson; Broadfoot (1), Hegan (2), Baker (1), Leadbetter, Brogan (3). 7–0 v Southampton, Division 1, 2 February 1974 – Sivell; Burley, Mills (1), Morris, Hunter, Beattie (1), Hamilton (2), Viljoen, Johnson, Whymark (2), Lambert (1) (Woods). 7–0 v WBA, Division 1, 6 November 1976 – Sivell; Burley, Mills, Talbot, Hunter, Beattie (1), Osborne, Wark (1), Mariner (1) (Bertschin), Whymark (4), Woods.

HONOURS

League Champions: Division 1 – 1961–62; Division 2 – 1960–61, 1967–68, 1991–92; Division 3S – 1953–54, 1956–57.
Runners-up: Division 1 – 1980–81, 1981–82.

FA Cup Winners: 1978.

League Cup: semi-final – 1982, 1985, 2001, 2011.

Texaco Cup Winners: 1973.

European Competitions
European Cup: 1962–63.
UEFA Cup: 1973–74, 1974–75, 1975–76, 1977–78, 1979–80, 1980–81 *(winners)*, 1981–82, 1982–83, 2001–02, 2002–03.
European Cup-Winners' Cup: 1978–79 *(qf)*.

sky SPORTS FACT FILE

Ipswich Town's defeat by Lincoln City in the 2016–17 FA Cup was not the first time they have lost to non-league opposition in the competition. In January 1955 they went down to a 3-0 defeat away to Bishop Auckland in the replayed third-round tie. They also lost out to then Midland League club Peterborough United in both 1955–56 and 1959–60.

Record Cup Victory: 10–0 v Floriana, European Cup prel. rd, 25 September 1962 – Bailey; Malcolm, Compton; Baxter, Laurel, Elsworthy (1); Stephenson, Moran (2), Crawford (5), Phillips (2), Blackwood.

Record Defeat: 1–10 v Fulham, Division 1, 26 December 1963.

Most League Points (2 for a win): 64, Division 3 (S), 1953–54 and 1955–56.

Most League Points (3 for a win): 87, Division 1, 1999–2000.

Most League Goals: 106, Division 3 (S), 1955–56.

Highest League Scorer in Season: Ted Phillips, 41, Division 3 (S), 1956–57.

Most League Goals in Total Aggregate: Ray Crawford, 204, 1958–63 and 1966–69.

Most League Goals in One Match: 5, Alan Brazil v Southampton, Division 1, 16 February 1981.

Most Capped Player: Allan Hunter, 47 (53), Northern Ireland.

Most League Appearances: Mick Mills, 591, 1966–82.

Youngest League Player: Conor Wickham, 16 years 11 days, v Doncaster R, 11 April 2009.

Record Transfer Fee Received: £8,000,000 from Sunderland for Connor Wickham, June 2011; £8,000,000 from AFC Bournemouth for Tyrone Mings, June 2015.

Record Transfer Fee Paid: £5,000,000 to Sampdoria for Matteo Sereni, August 2001.

Football League Record: 1938 Elected to Division 3 (S); 1954–55 Division 2; 1955–57 Division 3 (S); 1957–61 Division 2; 1961–64 Division 1; 1964–68 Division 2; 1968–86 Division 1; 1986–92 Division 2; 1992–95 FA Premier League; 1995–2000 Division 1; 2000–02 FA Premier League; 2002–04 Division 1; 2004– FL C.

MANAGERS

Mick O'Brien 1936–37
Scott Duncan 1937–55
(continued as Secretary)
Alf Ramsey 1955–63
Jackie Milburn 1963–64
Bill McGarry 1964–68
Bobby Robson 1969–82
Bobby Ferguson 1982–87
Johnny Duncan 1987–90
John Lyall 1990–94
George Burley 1994–2002
Joe Royle 2002–06
Jim Magilton 2006–09
Roy Keane 2009–11
Paul Jewell 2011–12
Mick McCarthy November 2012–

LATEST SEQUENCES

Longest Sequence of League Wins: 8, 23.9.1953 – 31.10.1953.

Longest Sequence of League Defeats: 10, 4.9.1954 – 16.10.1954.

Longest Sequence of League Draws: 7, 10.11.1990 – 21.12.1990.

Longest Sequence of Unbeaten League Matches: 23, 8.12.1979 – 26.4.1980.

Longest Sequence Without a League Win: 21, 28.8.1963 – 14.12.1963.

Successive Scoring Runs: 31 from 7.3.2004.

Successive Non-scoring Runs: 7 from 28.2.1995.

TEN YEAR LEAGUE RECORD

		P	W	D	L	F	A	Pts	Pos
2007-08	FL C	46	18	15	13	65	56	69	8
2008-09	FL C	46	17	15	14	62	53	66	9
2009-10	FL C	46	12	20	14	50	61	56	15
2010-11	FL C	46	18	8	20	62	68	62	13
2011-12	FL C	46	17	10	19	69	77	61	15
2012-13	FL C	46	16	12	18	48	61	60	14
2013-14	FL C	46	18	14	14	60	54	68	9
2014-15	FL C	46	22	12	12	72	54	78	6
2015-16	FL C	46	18	15	13	53	51	69	7
2016-17	FL C	46	13	16	17	48	58	55	16

DID YOU KNOW ?

Vernon Lewis, Ipswich Town's captain for the period 1903–07, was awarded a gold medal in December 1909. Attending the Bostock & Wombwell menagerie on their visit to the town he entered the lion's cage on both nights, remaining for a few minutes on each occasion. He emerged unscathed and was awarded the gold medal for his courage.

IPSWICH TOWN – SKY BET CHAMPIONSHIP 2016–17 LEAGUE RECORD

Match No.	*Date*		*Venue*	*Opponents*	*Result*		*H/T Score*	*Lg Pos.*	*Goalscorers*	*Attendance*
1	Aug	6	H	Barnsley	W	4-2	0-0	2	Ward 3 [46, 61, 84], McGoldrick (pen) [63]	17,370
2		13	A	Brentford	L	0-2	0-0	13		10,089
3		16	A	Wolverhampton W	D	0-0	0-0	12		19,991
4		21	H	Norwich C	D	1-1	1-1	13	Knudsen [45]	23,350
5		27	H	Preston NE	W	1-0	1-0	8	Ward [15]	15,296
6	Sept	9	A	Reading	L	1-2	0-1	13	Pitman (pen) [50]	15,146
7		13	A	Derby Co	W	1-0	0-0	8	Varney [53]	26,425
8		17	H	Aston Villa	D	0-0	0-0	11		19,249
9		24	A	Leeds U	L	0-1	0-1	14		22,554
10		27	H	Brighton & HA	D	0-0	0-0	13		15,228
11	Oct	1	H	Huddersfield T	L	0-1	0-0	16		16,146
12		15	A	Blackburn R	D	0-0	0-0	17		10,820
13		18	H	Burton Alb	W	2-0	1-0	12	Chambers [15], Sears [88]	15,816
14		22	A	Newcastle U	L	0-3	0-1	17		51,963
15		29	H	Rotherham U	D	2-2	1-1	15	Sears [3], McGoldrick [90]	15,247
16	Nov	5	A	Sheffield W	W	2-1	1-1	15	Lawrence [32], Chambers [87]	25,851
17		19	H	Nottingham F	L	0-2	0-2	16		15,417
18		26	H	QPR	W	3-0	1-0	14	Ward [13], Varney [54], Lawrence [61]	16,510
19	Dec	3	A	Bristol C	L	0-2	0-1	16		18,309
20		10	H	Cardiff C	D	1-1	0-1	17	Varney [52]	15,042
21		13	A	Birmingham C	L	1-2	0-1	17	Webster [69]	15,212
22		17	A	Wigan Ath	W	3-2	1-1	15	Pitman 2 (1 pen) [7 (p), 68], McGoldrick [88]	10,071
23		26	H	Fulham	L	0-2	0-1	15		19,723
24		30	H	Bristol C	W	2-1	1-0	14	Bru [39], Pitman [86]	15,640
25	Jan	2	A	QPR	L	1-2	0-1	15	Lawrence [48]	15,136
26		14	H	Blackburn R	W	3-2	1-1	14	Lawrence 2 [38, 57], Berra [53]	15,009
27		21	A	Huddersfield T	L	0-2	0-1	14		19,113
28		28	A	Preston NE	D	1-1	1-0	14	Lawrence [16]	10,656
29		31	H	Derby Co	L	0-3	0-3	17		14,719
30	Feb	4	H	Reading	D	2-2	1-0	15	Lawrence 2 [43, 61]	15,091
31		11	A	Aston Villa	W	1-0	0-0	13	Huws [83]	30,796
32		14	A	Brighton & HA	D	1-1	1-1	13	Chambers [9]	26,360
33		18	H	Leeds U	D	1-1	1-1	13	Sears [9]	18,748
34		26	A	Norwich C	D	1-1	0-0	15	Knudsen [63]	27,107
35	Mar	4	H	Brentford	D	1-1	1-1	15	Huws [26]	15,863
36		7	H	Wolverhampton W	D	0-0	0-0	16		15,076
37		11	A	Barnsley	D	1-1	0-0	16	Lawrence [90]	11,836
38		18	A	Cardiff C	L	1-3	1-1	17	Chambers [23]	15,182
39	Apr	1	H	Birmingham C	D	1-1	0-0	16	Ward [72]	16,667
40		4	H	Wigan Ath	W	3-0	2-0	16	McGoldrick [22], Sears 2 [30, 85]	14,661
41		8	A	Fulham	L	1-3	0-2	17	Berra [90]	20,959
42		14	A	Burton Alb	W	2-1	0-0	15	Varney (og) [52], Sears [79]	5236
43		17	H	Newcastle U	W	3-1	1-0	15	Sears [42], McGoldrick [69], Huws [90]	25,684
44		22	A	Rotherham U	L	0-1	0-0	16		8266
45		29	H	Sheffield W	L	0-1	0-0	16		19,000
46	May	7	A	Nottingham F	L	0-3	0-1	16		28,249

Final League Position: 16

GOALSCORERS

League (48): Lawrence 9, Sears 7, Ward 6, McGoldrick 5 (1 pen), Chambers 4, Pitman 4 (2 pens), Huws 3, Varney 3, Berra 2, Knudsen 2, Bru 1, Webster 1, own goal 1.
FA Cup (2): Lawrence 2.
EFL Cup (0).

Bialkowski B 44	Chambers L 46	Webster A 21 + 2	Berra C 44	Knudsen J 35 + 1	Skuse C 40	Bru K 14 + 12	Bishop T 7 + 12	Sears F 29 + 11	McGoldrick D 25 + 5	Murphy D 4	Grant C 3 + 3	Ward G 35 + 8	Pitman B 13 + 9	Douglas J 17 + 4	Varney L 4 + 11	Smith T 6 + 4	Lawrence T 32 + 2	Best L 5 + 6	Emmanuel J 11 + 4	Williams J 1 + 7	Digby P 2 + 2	Kenlock M 16 + 2	Dozzell A 5 + 1	Gerken D 2	Spence J 15 + 2	Moore K — + 11	Diagouraga T 10 + 2	Taylor S 3	Huws E 13	Rowe D 2 + 2	Samuel D 2 + 4	*Match No.*
1	2	3	4	5	6	7^{3}	8^{2}	9	10^{1}	11	12	13	14																			1
1	2	3	4	5	7	6^{2}	12	11		10	9^{1}	8		13																		2
1	2	3	4	5	7	12	6^{1}	11^{2}		10		9		8	13																	3
1	2	3	4	5	7	6^{2}	12	11^{1}		10		9		8	13																	4
1	2	14	4	5	7	6^{3}	12	11				9^{2}	10^{1}	8	13	3																5
1	2		4	5	7	9^{2}	12	10				8^{1}	11	6	13	3																6
1	2	3	4	5	7^{2}	9^{1}	14				10^{3}	8	11	6	13		12															7
1	2	3	4	5	6		12^{3}	9				8	11^{1}	7	13		10^{2}	14														8
1	2	3^{1}	4	5	7	14		11				6^{2}	10^{3}	8			9	12	13													9
1	3		4	5	7	9^{2}	14	12			13	8^{3}		6			10	11^{1}	2													10
1	3		4	5	7	9^{1}	13	12				8^{3}		6	14		10^{2}	11	2													11
1	2	3	4	5	7		12	10				6^{2}		8			9^{1}	11		13												12
1	2	3	4	5	7^{3}	6	8^{1}	11			12	13					9	10^{2}			14											13
1	2	3	4	5^{2}				10^{3}	12		7	9		6			8	11^{1}	13	14												14
1	2	3	4		6		7^{3}	11	9			8^{2}			14		10	13		12		5^{1}										15
1	2	3	4	5	8	13	7^{2}	11	10			6^{1}			14		9^{3}			12												16
1	3		4	5	7	12	6^{2}	10	11			8^{3}			14		9		2^{1}	13												17
1	2	3	4	5	7			12	11			6		8	10^{2}		9^{1}	13														18
1	2	3	4	5	7			12	10			6^{2}		8	11^{1}		9^{3}	13		14												19
1	2	3	4	5	7		14	12	10			6^{2}	13	8^{1}	11^{3}		9															20
1	2	3	4		8			14	10^{2}			6^{1}	12	7	11^{3}		9			13		5										21
1	2	3	4	5	7	13		6^{1}	12			14	11				10			8^{2}			9^{3}									22
1	2	3	4	5	8			6	12				11^{1}	7			10	13					9^{2}									23
1	2	3	4		7	8^{2}		13	10^{3}			6^{1}	11		14		9					5	12									24
1	2	3	4	14	8	7^{2}			11			12	10	13			9		6^{3}			5^{1}										25
1	3	4	5	6	8	9^{1}		11				12					10		2		13		7^{2}									26
	3		4	9	6	7^{2}		11					14	12			10				2		8^{3}	1	5^{1}	13						27
1	3		4	5	8	12		10^{1}	13			6	11^{2}				9		2							14	7^{3}					28
1	4		5	6	8	7		10	12			13	11^{2}				9^{1}				3^{3}				2	14						29
1	3		5	6	8^{2}		14		10			12					11		2						13		7^{3}	4	9^{1}			30
1	3		5^{3}	6		14			11			7					10		2			12			13		8	4^{2}	9^{1}			31
1	3			4				14	10^{1}			6		12			11^{3}		5			9			2	13	7^{2}		8			32
1	3		4	5	8^{1}	12	13	11	10^{2}			7										6			2	14			9^{3}			33
1	3		4	5	8			11^{3}	10			7				12						6^{2}			2	13	14		9^{1}			34
1	2		3	4	7	13			11			6^{1}					10^{2}					9			5	14	12		8^{3}			35
1	3		4	6	8				11			7				5^{1}	10		2^{2}			12				13	9					36
1	2		3	4	7			13	10			12	14				11					9^{2}			5		6^{3}		8^{1}			37
1	3		4	6	8			13	10^{2}			7	12			5^{3}	11								2		9^{1}			14		38
1	3		4	5	7^{2}	12		9	11			6	10^{1}	8											2						13	39
1	3		4			13		11	10^{3}			7				12						6			2		8	5^{1}	9^{2}		14	40
1	3		5					10	11^{3}			7	14			4^{2}	12					6			2		9		8^{1}		13	41
1	3		4		7			11	10^{2}			6	12			13	9^{1}					5			2				8			42
1	3		4		7			9	10^{3}			6	14			13	11^{1}		12			5^{2}			2				8			43
	3					13	7^{3}	14					11			4			2			5	9	1		12	8^{2}			6^{1}	10	44
1	3		4		6			9^{2}	11			8^{1}					10^{3}					5			2	14			7	12	13	45
1	3	14	4^{3}		7			10^{1}				9							12			5^{2}			2	13			6	8	11	46

FA Cup

Third Round	Lincoln C	(h)	2-2
Replay	Lincoln C	(a)	0-1

EFL Cup

First Round	Stevenage	(h)	0-1

LEEDS UNITED

FOUNDATION

Immediately the Leeds City club (founded in 1904) was wound up by the FA in October 1919, following allegations of illegal payments to players, a meeting was called by a Leeds solicitor, Mr Alf Masser, at which Leeds United was formed. They joined the Midland League, playing their first game in that competition in November 1919. It was in this same month that the new club had discussions with the directors of a virtually bankrupt Huddersfield Town who wanted to move to Leeds in an amalgamation. But Huddersfield survived even that crisis.

Elland Road Stadium, Elland Road, Leeds, West Yorkshire LS11 0ES.

Telephone: (0871) 334 1919.

Fax: (0113) 367 6450.

Ticket Office: (0871) 334 1992.

Website: www.leedsunited.com

Email: reception@leedsunited.com

Ground Capacity: 37,890.

Record Attendance: 57,892 v Sunderland, FA Cup 5th rd (replay), 15 March 1967.

Pitch Measurements: 105m × 68m (115yd × 74yd).

Chairman: Andrea Radrizzani.

Chief Executive: Angus Kinnear.

Head Coach: Thomas Christiansen.

Assistant Head Coach: Julio Banuelos.

Colours: White shirts with blue trim, white shorts, white socks with blue trim.

Year Formed: 1919, as Leeds United after disbandment (by FA order) of Leeds City (formed in 1904).

Turned Professional: 1920.

Club Nickname: 'The Whites'.

Ground: 1919, Elland Road.

First Football League Game: 28 August 1920, Division 2, v Port Vale (a) L 0–2 – Down; Duffield, Tillotson; Musgrove, Baker, Walton; Mason, Goldthorpe, Thompson, Lyon, Best.

Record League Victory: 8–0 v Leicester C, Division 1, 7 April 1934 – Moore; George Milburn, Jack Milburn; Edwards, Hart, Copping; Mahon (2), Firth (2), Duggan (2), Furness (2), Cochrane.

HONOURS

League Champions: Division 1 – 1968–69, 1973–74, 1991–92; Division 2 – 1923–24, 1963–64, 1989–90.
Runners-up: Division 1 – 1964–65, 1965–66, 1969–70, 1970–71, 1971–72; Division 2 – 1927–28, 1931–32, 1955–56; FL 1 – 2009–10.

FA Cup Winners: 1972.
Runners-up: 1965, 1970, 1973.

League Cup Winners: 1968.
Runners-up: 1996.

European Competitions
European Cup: 1969–70 *(sf)*, 1974–75 *(runners-up)*.
Champions League: 1992–93, 2000–01 *(sf)*.
Fairs Cup: 1965–66 *(sf)*, 1966–67 *(runners-up)*, 1967–68 *(winners)*, 1968–69 *(qf)*, 1970–71 *(winners)*.
UEFA Cup: 1971–72, 1973–74, 1979–80, 1995–96, 1998–99, 1999–2000 *(sf)*, 2001–02, 2002–03.
European Cup-Winners' Cup: 1972–73 *(runners-up)*.

sky SPORTS FACT FILE

Leeds United's Elland Road game was closed for the opening weeks of the 1971–72 season and the club were forced to play their first four home matches at other venues. Two were played at Huddersfield Town's Leeds Road ground, one at Boothferry Park, Hull, and one at Hillsborough. United won two and drew two of the fixtures played.

Record Cup Victory: 10–0 v Lyn (Oslo), European Cup 1st rd 1st leg, 17 September 1969 – Sprake; Reaney, Cooper, Bremner (2), Charlton, Hunter, Madeley, Clarke (2), Jones (3), Giles (2) (Bates), O'Grady (1).

Record Defeat: 1–8 v Stoke C, Division 1, 27 August 1934.

Most League Points (2 for a win): 67, Division 1, 1968–69.

Most League Points (3 for a win): 86, FL 1, 2009–10.

Most League Goals: 98, Division 2, 1927–28.

Highest League Scorer in Season: John Charles, 42, Division 2, 1953–54.

Most League Goals in Total Aggregate: Peter Lorimer, 168, 1965–79 and 1983–86.

Most League Goals in One Match: 5, Gordon Hodgson v Leicester C, Division 1, 1 October 1938.

Most Capped Player: Lucas Radebe, 58 (70), South Africa.

Most League Appearances: Jack Charlton, 629, 1953–73.

Youngest League Player: Peter Lorimer, 15 years 289 days v Southampton, 29 September 1962.

Record Transfer Fee Received: £30,800,000 from Manchester U for Rio Ferdinand, July 2002.

Record Transfer Fee Paid: £18,000,000 to West Ham U for Rio Ferdinand, November 2000.

Football League Record: 1920 Elected to Division 2; 1924–27 Division 1; 1927–28 Division 2; 1928–31 Division 1; 1931–32 Division 2; 1932–47 Division 1; 1947–56 Division 2; 1956–60 Division 1; 1960–64 Division 2; 1964–82 Division 1; 1982–90 Division 2; 1990–92 Division 1; 1992–2004 FA Premier League; 2004–07 FL C; 2007–10 FL 1; 2010– FL C.

MANAGERS

Dick Ray 1919–20
Arthur Fairclough 1920–27
Dick Ray 1927–35
Bill Hampson 1935–47
Willis Edwards 1947–48
Major Frank Buckley 1948–53
Raich Carter 1953–58
Bill Lambton 1958–59
Jack Taylor 1959–61
Don Revie OBE 1961–74
Brian Clough 1974
Jimmy Armfield 1974–78
Jock Stein CBE 1978
Jimmy Adamson 1978–80
Allan Clarke 1980–82
Eddie Gray MBE 1982–85
Billy Bremner 1985–88
Howard Wilkinson 1988–96
George Graham 1996–98
David O'Leary 1998–2002
Terry Venables 2002–03
Peter Reid 2003
Eddie Gray *(Caretaker)* 2003–04
Kevin Blackwell 2004–06
Dennis Wise 2006–08
Gary McAllister 2008
Simon Grayson 2008–12
Neil Warnock 2012–13
Brian McDermott 2013–14
Dave Hockaday 2014
Darko Milanic 2014
Neil Redfearn 2014–15
Uwe Rosler 2015
Steve Evans 2015–16
Garry Monk 2016–17
Thomas Christiansen June 2017–

LATEST SEQUENCES

Longest Sequence of League Wins: 9, 18.4.2009 – 5.9.2009.

Longest Sequence of League Defeats: 6, 28.12.2003 – 7.2.2004.

Longest Sequence of League Draws: 5, 2.5.2015 – 22.8.2015.

Longest Sequence of Unbeaten League Matches: 34, 26.10.1968 – 26.8.1969.

Longest Sequence Without a League Win: 17, 1.2.1947 – 26.5.1947.

Successive Scoring Runs: 30 from 27.8.1927.

Successive Non-scoring Runs: 6 from 30.1.1982.

TEN YEAR LEAGUE RECORD

		P	*W*	*D*	*L*	*F*	*A*	*Pts*	*Pos*
2007-08	FL 1	46	27	10	9	72	38	76*	5
2008-09	FL 1	46	26	6	14	77	49	84	4
2009-10	FL 1	46	25	11	10	77	44	86	2
2010-11	FL C	46	19	15	12	81	70	72	7
2011-12	FL C	46	17	10	19	65	68	61	14
2012-13	FL C	46	17	10	19	57	66	61	13
2013-14	FL C	46	16	9	21	59	67	57	15
2014-15	FL C	46	15	11	20	50	61	56	15
2015-16	FL C	46	14	17	15	50	58	59	13
2016-17	FL C	46	22	9	15	61	47	75	7

**15 pts deducted.*

DID YOU KNOW ?

Centre-forward John Charles scored hat-tricks for Leeds United in the opening two games of the 1953–54 season, netting four times in a 6-0 win over Notts County and three in the 4-2 win over Rotherham. He finished the season as the Football League's leading scorer with a total of 42 goals.

LEEDS UNITED – SKY BET CHAMPIONSHIP 2016–17 LEAGUE RECORD

Match No.	Date	Venue	Opponents	Result	H/T Score	Lg Pos.	Goalscorers	Attendance
1	Aug 7	A	QPR	L 0-3	0-1	24		16,764
2	13	H	Birmingham C	L 1-2	1-1	24	Sacko [27]	27,392
3	16	H	Fulham	D 1-1	0-0	20	Wood [90]	21,204
4	20	A	Sheffield W	W 2-0	0-0	19	Antonsson [63], Wood [85]	29,075
5	27	A	Nottingham F	L 1-3	0-1	21	Philips [83]	20,995
6	Sept 10	H	Huddersfield T	L 0-1	0-0	22		28,514
7	13	H	Blackburn R	W 2-1	0-0	17	Wood [65], Bartley [86]	19,009
8	17	A	Cardiff C	W 2-0	0-0	14	Wood (pen) [62], Hernandez [82]	16,608
9	24	H	Ipswich T	W 1-0	1-0	12	Wood [35]	22,554
10	27	A	Bristol C	L 0-1	0-0	14		19,699
11	Oct 1	H	Barnsley	W 2-1	1-0	11	Bartley [36], Hernandez [54]	27,350
12	15	A	Derby Co	L 0-1	0-0	13		31,170
13	18	H	Wigan Ath	D 1-1	1-0	13	Wood [29]	19,861
14	22	A	Wolverhampton W	W 1-0	0-0	10	Silvio (og) [70]	23,607
15	29	H	Burton Alb	W 2-0	0-0	9	Wood (pen) [83], Doukara [90]	24,220
16	Nov 5	A	Norwich C	W 3-2	0-1	6	Jansson [57], Wood [74], Vieira [90]	26,903
17	20	H	Newcastle U	L 0-2	0-1	7		36,002
18	26	A	Rotherham U	W 2-1	2-0	5	Wood [14], Doukara [45]	10,513
19	Dec 3	H	Aston Villa	W 2-0	0-0	4	Roofe [68], Wood [90]	32,648
20	9	A	Brighton & HA	L 0-2	0-1	4		28,206
21	13	H	Reading	W 2-0	1-0	5	Wood [19], Doukara (pen) [90]	21,242
22	17	H	Brentford	W 1-0	0-0	5	Bartley [89]	25,134
23	26	A	Preston NE	W 4-1	3-1	5	Roofe [17], Sacko [23], Doukara [31], Hernandez [88]	21,255
24	29	A	Aston Villa	D 1-1	0-0	4	Jansson [54]	37,078
25	Jan 2	H	Rotherham U	W 3-0	0-0	5	Bartley [47], Wood 2 [66, 79]	33,397
26	13	H	Derby Co	W 1-0	1-0	3	Wood [45]	25,546
27	21	A	Barnsley	L 2-3	1-1	3	Wood 2 (1 pen) [18, 68 (p)]	17,817
28	25	H	Nottingham F	W 2-0	0-0	3	Wood [55], Doukara [74]	24,838
29	Feb 1	A	Blackburn R	W 2-1	0-0	4	Dallas [74], Jansson [89]	17,026
30	5	A	Huddersfield T	L 1-2	1-1	5	Wood [35]	22,400
31	11	H	Cardiff C	L 0-2	0-0	5		31,516
32	14	H	Bristol C	W 2-1	1-0	4	Wood [27], Hernandez [47]	22,402
33	18	A	Ipswich T	D 1-1	1-1	5	Dallas [42]	18,748
34	25	H	Sheffield W	W 1-0	1-0	4	Wood [24]	35,093
35	Mar 3	A	Birmingham C	W 3-1	1-0	4	Wood 2 [14, 67], Pedraza [81]	20,321
36	7	A	Fulham	D 1-1	1-0	4	Ream (og) [5]	22,239
37	11	H	QPR	D 0-0	0-0	4		30,870
38	18	H	Brighton & HA	W 2-0	0-0	4	Wood 2 (1 pen) [63, 85 (p)]	29,767
39	Apr 1	A	Reading	L 0-1	0-1	5		23,055
40	4	A	Brentford	L 0-2	0-2	5		10,759
41	8	H	Preston NE	W 3-0	2-0	5	Roofe [18], Hernandez [45], Doukara [90]	31,851
42	14	A	Newcastle U	D 1-1	0-0	4	Wood [90]	52,301
43	17	H	Wolverhampton W	L 0-1	0-1	7		32,351
44	22	A	Burton Alb	L 1-2	0-0	7	Bartley [80]	6073
45	29	H	Norwich C	D 3-3	1-3	7	Wood [45], Bartley [49], Hernandez [78]	34,292
46	May 7	A	Wigan Ath	D 1-1	0-1	7	Wood (pen) [50]	15,280

Final League Position: 7

GOALSCORERS

League (61): Wood 27 (5 pens), Bartley 6, Doukara 6 (1 pen), Hernandez 6, Jansson 3, Roofe 3, Dallas 2, Sacko 2, Antonsson 1, Pedraza 1, Philips 1, Vieira 1, own goals 2.
FA Cup (2): Dallas 1, Mowatt 1.
EFL Cup (6): Wood 3 (1 pen), Antonsson 2, Denton 1.

Green R 46	Berardi G 24 + 2	Bartley K 45	Bamba S 2	Taylor C 26 + 3	Vieira R 24 + 10	Diagouraga T 1	Dallas S 20 + 11	Grimes M 1 + 6	Roofe K 28 + 14	Wood C 41 + 3	Coyle L 3 + 1	Antonsson M 6 + 10	Sacko H 28 + 10	Ayling L 42	Hernandez P 32 + 3	Mowatt A 4 + 11	Philips K 23 + 10	Cooper L 8 + 3	Bridcutt L 22 + 3	Doukara S 17 + 17	Jansson P 34	O'Kane E 20 + 4	Barrow M 1 + 4	Pedraza A 8 + 6	Match No.
1	2[2]	3	4	5	6	7	8	9[3]	10[1]	11	12	13	14												1
1		4	3	5	7		14		12	10[3]		11	6	2	8[1]	9[2]	13								2
1		3		5	12		8[3]		9[2]	11		10	14	2	6[1]	13	7	4							3
1		3		5	8				13	11		10[1]	6[3]	2		9[2]	14	4	7	12					4
1		3		5	8[2]				13	10		11	6[1]	2	9[3]	14	12	4	7						5
1		3		5					13	10		11[1]	6[2]	2		9	8		7	12	4				6
1		3		5			10			13		11[3]	8	2	9	14	12		6[2]		4	7[1]			7
1		3		5	6		10[1]		12	11[2]		14	8	2	9[3]		13				4	7			8
1		3		5			10[2]	14	12	11			8[1]	2	9[3]	13	6				4	7			9
1		3		5			10[2]		13	11			8	2	9		6	12			4[1]	7			10
1		3		5	14		10[1]		13	11		12	8[3]	2	9[2]		7				4	6			11
1		3		5				13	12	11[3]		14	8[2]	2	9	10[1]	6				4	7			12
1		3		5				12	10	11[2]		14	8[1]	2	9[3]	13	7				4	6			13
1		3		5	8[1]				10	11[3]			7[2]	2		12	9	13		14	4	6			14
1		3		5	13				10[2]	11			8[1]	2	9[3]	14	7			12	4	6			15
1		3		5	13			14	8[3]	11			12	2	9[1]		6			10[2]	4	7			16
1		3		5	7[2]				8	11		13	12	2			9			10[1]	4	6			17
1	14	3		5			12		9[3]	11		13	8[2]	2			6	4		10[1]		7			18
1		3		5	7		12		9[1]	11			8	2		13	6			10[2]	4				19
1		3		5	7		13	12	9	11			8[2]	2			6■	14		10[1]	4[3]				20
1		3		5	6		10[1]	14	8[3]	11[2]			7	2		13			12	9	4				21
1	12	3		5[3]	6		10		9			14	8	2			7[2]		13	11[1]	4				22
1	5	3					10		9[1]	13		14	8[3]	2	12		7		6	11[2]	4				23
1	5				14		10[1]		9[3]	13			8	2	12		7	4	6[2]	11	3				24
1	5	3			12		13		11	10[2]		14	7[1]	2	8				6	9[3]	4				25
1	5	3			7		12		8[2]	11	2			4	9[1]	13			6	10					26
1	5	3			7[1]		13		8	11	2			4	9				6[2]	10		12			27
1	5	3			13		10[3]		8	11				2	9[2]	14			7	12	4	6[1]			28
1	5	3			14		10		9[2]	11			8[3]	2	12				7	13	4	6[1]			29
1	5	3			7		10[2]			11				2	9[1]				6	8[3]	4	14	13	12	30
1	5	3			7[1]		8[2]		13	11			12	2	9			4	6■	14				10[3]	31
1	5	3			6				10[2]	11			8	2	9[3]		13			14	4	7[1]	12		32
1	5	3			6[2]		10			11[1]			8[3]	2	9				12	14	4	7	13		33
1	5	3			13		14		12	11			8[3]	2	9[2]				6	10	4	7[1]			34
1	5	3					8[1]		14	11				2	9[2]		12		6	10	4	7[3]		13	35
1	2	3		5	14		13		9[2]				8[1]				7■		6	11	4		12	10[3]	36
1	5	3			7[2]				8[3]	11			12	2	9				6	13	4	14		10[1]	37
1	2	3		5	7		13			11			8[3]		9[1]			4	6	12		14		10[2]	38
1	2	3		5	7[1]				14	11			8[3]		9		13	4	6	12				10[2]	39
1	5	3					10[3]		13	11				2	9		7		6[1]	14	4		8[2]	12	40
1	5	3		14	6		12		8[2]	11[1]				2	9[3]		7			13	4			10	41
1	5[2]	3		14					8	11			12	2	9		7		6[1]	13	4			10[3]	42
1	5[3]	3		13					8	11			12	2	9		7		6[1]	14	4			10[2]	43
1		3		5	7				8	11			12	2	9		6[1]			10[2]	4			13	44
1	5	3			6		10[1]		8	11				2[2]	9		14			12	4	7[3]		13	45
1	5	3			6[3]		8[1]		10	11	2		13	4	9[2]		14					7		12	46

FA Cup

Third Round	Cambridge U	(a)	2-1
Fourth Round	Sutton U	(a)	0-1

EFL Cup

First Round	Fleetwood T	(a)	2-2
(aet; Leeds U won 5-4 on penalties)			
Second Round	Luton T	(a)	1-0
Third Round	Blackburn R	(h)	1-0
Fourth Round	Norwich C	(h)	2-2
(aet; Leeds U won 3-2 on penalties)			
Quarter-Final	Liverpool	(a)	0-2

LEICESTER CITY

FOUNDATION

In 1884 a number of young footballers, who were mostly old boys of Wyggeston School, held a meeting at a house on the Roman Fosse Way and formed Leicester Fosse FC. They collected 9d (less than 4p) towards the cost of a ball, plus the same amount for membership. Their first professional, Harry Webb from Stafford Rangers, was signed in 1888 for 2s 6d (12p) per week, plus travelling expenses.

King Power Stadium, Filbert Way, Leicester LE2 7FL.
Telephone: (0344) 815 5000.
Fax: (0116) 291 5278.
Ticket Office: (0344) 815 5000 (option 1).
Website: www.lcfc.com
Email: sales@lcfc.co.uk
Ground Capacity: 32,273.
Record Attendance: 47,298 v Tottenham H, FA Cup 5th rd, 18 February 1928 (at Filbert Street); 32,242 v Sunderland, FA Premier League, 8 August 2016 (at King Power Stadium).
Pitch Measurements: 105m × 68m (115yd × 75yd).
Chairman: Khun Vichai Srivaddhanaprabha.
Chief Executive: Susan Whelan.
Manager: Craig Shakespeare.
Assistant Manager: Michael Appleton.
Physio: Dave Rennie.
Colours: Surf the web blue shirts, surf the web blue shorts, surf the web blue socks.
Year Formed: 1884.
Turned Professional: 1888.
Previous Name: 1884, Leicester Fosse; 1919, Leicester City.
Club Nickname: 'The Foxes'.
Grounds: 1884, Victoria Park; 1887, Belgrave Road; 1888, Victoria Park; 1891, Filbert Street; 2002, Walkers Stadium (now known as King Power Stadium from 2011).
First Football League Game: 1 September 1894, Division 2, v Grimsby T (a) L 3–4 – Thraves; Smith, Bailey; Seymour, Brown, Henrys; Hill, Hughes, McArthur (1), Skea (2), Priestman.
Record League Victory: 10–0 v Portsmouth, Division 1, 20 October 1928 – McLaren; Black, Brown; Findlay, Carr, Watson; Adcock, Hine (3), Chandler (6), Lochhead, Barry (1).
Record Cup Victory: 8–1 v Coventry C (a), League Cup 5th rd, 1 December 1964 – Banks; Sjoberg, Norman (2); Roberts, King, McDerment; Hodgson (2), Cross, Goodfellow, Gibson (1), Stringfellow (2), (1 og).
Record Defeat: 0–12 (as Leicester Fosse) v Nottingham F, Division 1, 21 April 1909.

HONOURS

League Champions: FA Premier League – 2015–16; FL C – 2013–14; Division 2 – 1924–25, 1936–37, 1953–54, 1956–57, 1970–71, 1979–80; FL 1 – 2008–09.
Runners-up: Division 1 – 1928–29; First Division – 2002–03; Division 2 – 1907–08.
FA Cup: ***Runners-up:*** 1949, 1961, 1963, 1969.
League Cup Winners: 1964, 1997, 2000.
Runners-up: 1965, 1999.
European Competitions
UEFA Champions League: 2016–17 (*qf*).
UEFA Cup: 1997–98, 2000–01.
European Cup-Winners' Cup: 1961–62.

sky SPORTS FACT FILE

Leicester City's Filbert Street ground hosted the first amateur international match to be televised. The BBC showed the second half of the game between England and Wales on 20 January 1951. Viewers saw England score three times over the 45 minutes' play to win 4-1.

Most League Points (2 for a win): 61, Division 2, 1956–57.

Most League Points (3 for a win): 102, FL C, 2013–14.

Most League Goals: 109, Division 2, 1956–57.

Highest League Scorer in Season: Arthur Rowley, 44, Division 2, 1956–57.

Most League Goals in Total Aggregate: Arthur Chandler, 259, 1923–35.

Most League Goals in One Match: 6, John Duncan v Port Vale, Division 2, 25 December 1924; 6, Arthur Chandler v Portsmouth, Division 1, 20 October 1928.

Most Capped Player: John O'Neill, 39, Northern Ireland; Andy King, 39, Wales.

Most League Appearances: Adam Black, 528, 1920–35.

Youngest League Player: Dave Buchanan, 16 years 192 days v Oldham Ath, 1 January 1979.

Record Transfer Fee Received: £30,000,000 from Chelsea for N'Golo Kanté, July 2016.

Record Transfer Fee Paid: £29,700,000 to Sporting Lisbon for Islam Slimani, August 2016.

Football League Record: 1894 Elected to Division 2; 1908–09 Division 1; 1909–25 Division 2; 1925–35 Division 1; 1935–37 Division 2; 1937–39 Division 1; 1946–54 Division 2; 1954–55 Division 1; 1955–57 Division 2; 1957–69 Division 1; 1969–71 Division 2; 1971–78 Division 1; 1978–80 Division 2; 1980–81 Division 1; 1981–83 Division 2; 1983–87 Division 1; 1987–92 Division 2; 1992–94 Division 1; 1994–95 FA Premier League; 1995–96 Division 1; 1996–2002 FA Premier League; 2002–03 Division 1; 2003–04 FA Premier League; 2004–08 FL C; 2008–09 FL 1; 2009–14 FL C; 2014– FA Premier League.

LATEST SEQUENCES

Longest Sequence of League Wins: 9, 21.12.2013 – 1.2.2014.

Longest Sequence of League Defeats: 8, 17.3.2001 – 28.4.2001.

Longest Sequence of League Draws: 6, 2.10.2004 – 2.11.2004.

Longest Sequence of Unbeaten League Matches: 23, 1.11.2008 – 7.3.2009.

Longest Sequence Without a League Win: 18, 12.4.1975 – 1.11.1975.

Successive Scoring Runs: 32 from 23.11.2013.

Successive Non-scoring Runs: 7 from 21.11.1987.

MANAGERS

Frank Gardner 1884–92
Ernest Marson 1892–94
J. Lee 1894–95
Henry Jackson 1895–97
William Clark 1897–98
George Johnson 1898–1912
Jack Bartlett 1912–14
Louis Ford 1914–15
Harry Linney 1915–19
Peter Hodge 1919–26
Willie Orr 1926–32
Peter Hodge 1932–34
Arthur Lochhead 1934–36
Frank Womack 1936–39
Tom Bromilow 1939–45
Tom Mather 1945–46
John Duncan 1946–49
Norman Bullock 1949–55
David Halliday 1955–58
Matt Gillies 1958–68
Frank O'Farrell 1968–71
Jimmy Bloomfield 1971–77
Frank McLintock 1977–78
Jock Wallace 1978–82
Gordon Milne 1982–86
Bryan Hamilton 1986–87
David Pleat 1987–91
Gordon Lee 1991
Brian Little 1991–94
Mark McGhee 1994–95
Martin O'Neill 1995–2000
Peter Taylor 2000–01
Dave Bassett 2001–02
Micky Adams 2002–04
Craig Levein 2004–06
Robert Kelly 2006–07
Martin Allen 2007
Gary Megson 2007
Ian Holloway 2007–08
Nigel Pearson 2008–10
Paulo Sousa 2010
Sven-Göran Eriksson 2010–11
Nigel Pearson 2011–15
Claudio Ranieri 2015–17
Craig Shakespeare March 2017–

TEN YEAR LEAGUE RECORD

		P	W	D	L	F	A	Pts	Pos
2007-08	FL C	46	12	16	18	42	45	52	22
2008-09	FL 1	46	27	15	4	84	39	96	1
2009-10	FL C	46	21	13	12	61	45	76	5
2010-11	FL C	46	19	10	17	76	71	67	10
2011-12	FL C	46	18	12	16	66	55	66	9
2012-13	FL C	46	19	11	16	71	48	68	6
2013-14	FL C	46	31	9	6	83	43	102	1
2014-15	PR Lge	38	11	8	19	46	55	41	14
2015-16	PR Lge	38	23	12	3	68	36	81	1
2016-17	PR Lge	38	12	8	18	48	63	44	12

DID YOU KNOW?

Leicester City officially inaugurated their floodlighting system with a game against Borussia Dortmund in October 1957. The Foxes won 1-0 with a goal from Willie Gardiner in front of a crowd of 18,398.

LEICESTER CITY – PREMIER LEAGUE 2016–17 LEAGUE RECORD

Match No.	Date	Venue	Opponents	Result		H/T Score	Lg Pos.	Goalscorers	Atten-dance
1	Aug 13	A	Hull C	L	1-2	0-1	18	Mahrez (pen) [47]	21,037
2	20	H	Arsenal	D	0-0	0-0	15		32,008
3	27	H	Swansea C	W	2-1	1-0	8	Vardy [32], Morgan [52]	31,727
4	Sept 10	A	Liverpool	L	1-4	1-2	13	Vardy [38]	51,232
5	17	H	Burnley	W	3-0	1-0	9	Slimani 2 [45, 48], Mee (og) [78]	31,916
6	24	A	Manchester U	L	1-4	0-4	11	Gray [59]	75,256
7	Oct 2	H	Southampton	D	0-0	0-0	12		31,563
8	15	A	Chelsea	L	0-3	0-2	13		41,547
9	22	H	Crystal Palace	W	3-1	1-0	12	Musa [42], Okazaki [63], Fuchs [80]	31,969
10	29	A	Tottenham H	D	1-1	0-1	11	Musa [48]	31,868
11	Nov 6	H	WBA	L	1-2	0-0	14	Slimani [55]	31,879
12	19	A	Watford	L	1-2	1-2	14	Mahrez (pen) [15]	20,640
13	26	H	Middlesbrough	D	2-2	1-1	13	Mahrez (pen) [34], Slimani (pen) [90]	32,058
14	Dec 3	A	Sunderland	L	1-2	0-0	15	Okazaki [80]	39,725
15	10	H	Manchester C	W	4-2	3-0	14	Vardy 3 [3, 20, 78], King [5]	31,966
16	13	A	Bournemouth	L	0-1	0-1	14		11,068
17	17	A	Stoke C	D	2-2	0-2	14	Ulloa [74], Amartey [88]	27,663
18	26	H	Everton	L	0-2	0-0	16		31,985
19	31	H	West Ham U	W	1-0	1-0	15	Slimani [20]	32,060
20	Jan 2	A	Middlesbrough	D	0-0	0-0	14		32,437
21	14	H	Chelsea	L	0-3	0-1	15		32,066
22	22	A	Southampton	L	0-3	0-2	15		30,548
23	31	A	Burnley	L	0-1	0-0	15		19,202
24	Feb 5	H	Manchester U	L	0-3	0-2	16		32,072
25	12	A	Swansea C	L	0-2	0-2	17		20,391
26	27	H	Liverpool	W	3-1	2-0	15	Vardy 2 [28, 60], Drinkwater [39]	32,034
27	Mar 4	H	Hull C	W	3-1	1-1	14	Fuchs [27], Mahrez [59], Huddlestone (og) [90]	31,971
28	18	A	West Ham U	W	3-2	3-1	15	Mahrez [5], Huth [7], Vardy [38]	56,979
29	Apr 1	H	Stoke C	W	2-0	1-0	12	Ndidi [25], Vardy [47]	31,958
30	4	H	Sunderland	W	2-0	0-0	9	Slimani [69], Vardy [78]	31,757
31	9	A	Everton	L	2-4	2-3	11	Slimani [4], Albrighton [10]	39,573
32	15	A	Crystal Palace	D	2-2	1-0	10	Huth [6], Vardy [52]	25,504
33	26	A	Arsenal	L	0-1	0-0	15		59,829
34	29	A	WBA	W	1-0	1-0	11	Vardy [43]	24,611
35	May 6	H	Watford	W	3-0	1-0	9	Ndidi [38], Mahrez [58], Albrighton [90]	31,628
36	13	A	Manchester C	L	1-2	1-2	10	Okazaki [42]	54,407
37	18	H	Tottenham H	L	1-6	0-2	11	Chilwell [59]	31,351
38	21	H	Bournemouth	D	1-1	0-1	12	Vardy [51]	32,000

Final League Position: 12

GOALSCORERS

League (48): Vardy 13, Slimani 7 (1 pen), Mahrez 6 (3 pens), Okazaki 3, Albrighton 2, Fuchs 2, Huth 2, Musa 2, Ndidi 2, Amartey 1, Chilwell 1, Drinkwater 1, Gray 1, King 1, Morgan 1, Ulloa 1, own goals 2.
FA Cup (7): Musa 2, Gray 1, King 1, Morgan 1, Ndidi 1, own goal 1.
EFL Cup (2): Okazaki 2.
EFL Checkatrade Trophy (2): Kapustka 1, Mitchell 1.
Community Shield (1): Vardy 1.
UEFA Champions League (11): Mahrez 4 (1 pen), Vardy 3, Albrighton 2, Morgan 1, Okazaki 1.

Schmeichel K 30	Simpson D 34 + 1	Hernandez L 3 + 1	Morgan W 27	Fuchs C 35 + 1	Mahrez R 33 + 3	King A 15 + 8	Drinkwater D 27 + 2	Gray D 9 + 21	Musa A 7 + 14	Vardy J 33 + 2	Amartey D 17 + 7	Okazaki S 21 + 9	Ulloa J 3 + 13	Huth R 33	Mendy N 4	Albrighton M 29 + 4	Zieler R 8 + 1	Slimani I 13 + 10	Schlupp J 1 + 3	James M — + 1	Wasilewski M 1	Chilwell B 7 + 5	Ndidi O 17	Benalouane Y 11	*Match No.*
1	2^3	3	4	5	6	7^1	8	9^2	10	11	12	13	14												1
1	2		3	5	6	12	7		14	11		10^2	13	4	8^1	9^3									2
1^3	2		3	5	6		8		13	11	7	10^2	14	4		9^1	12								3
1	2^2	12	3	5	6		8		13	11	7	10^1	14	4		9^3									4
	2		3	5	6^2	12	8^1	13		10	7			4		9	1	11							5
	2		3	5	6^2	12	8	13		11^3	7			4		9^1	1	10	14						6
1	2		3	5	6		7	13		11^1	8	12	14	4		9^2		10^3							7
1		2	3	5	13	14	7		10^2	11	8			4		9^1		12	6^3						8
1	2		3	5	6	8^1	7	13	9^2	12	14	10		4				11^3							9
1	2		3	5	6^3	8	7		9^2	11		10^1	14	4		13			12						10
	2		3	5	6	7	8	13	9^3	12		11^2	14	4^1			1	10							11
	2		3	5^2	6		7	13	14	11	8	10^1		4		9^3	1		12						12
	2		3	5	6^3	8		14	13	11^1	7	10^2		4		9	1	12							13
	2		3	5	6^1	8		14	13	10	7	12		4		9^3	1	11^2							14
	2		3	5	6^3	7		13		10^1	8	12		4		9	1	11^2		14					15
		2	3	5	6	7			13	11	8	12	14	4^1		9^2	1	10^3							16
1	2		3	5	6^1	7		13	14	11	8		12	4		9^2		10^3							17
1	2		4		13	7^3	12	6^1			8	10^2	14			9		11			3	5			18
1	2		3	12	9^1		7	10^2			6	13	14	4		8		11^3				5			19
1	2		3	5	10^2	8		13	12		7	9^1	11	4	6^3	14									20
1	14		2	4			6	13	11^1	10		12		3^3	8	5^2						9	7		21
1	2		3	5			7	10	13	11		9^2		4	8^1	12							6		22
1	2		3	5	6		7	11^1	12	10		13		4		9^2							8		23
1	2		3	5	8	12	6	13	10^1	11		9^2		4									7		24
1	2^2		3	5^3	6		7	10		11	14			4		9^1		13				12	8		25
1	2		3	5	6^1		7	13		11	12	10^3		4		9^2						14	8		26
1	2		3	5	8^1		6	12		11		9^2		4		10		13					7		27
1	2			5	6^2		7		12	11^3		10^1		4		9		13				14	8	3	28
1	2			5	6		7	9^1		11^3	12	10^2		4				13				14	8	3	29
1	2			5	6	14	8	9^2		10		11^3		4		13		12					7^1	3	30
1					13	7	8	9^2	12	11^3	2		14	4		6^1		10				5		3	31
1	2			5	6^1	8^3	12	13		11			10	4		9						14	7	3^2	32
1	2			5	6		7	13		10		12	11^1	4		9							8	3^2	33
1	2			5	6^2	13	7			11		10^1	12	4		9							8	3	34
1	2			5	6^3	13	7^1	14		11		10^2		4		9		12					8	3	35
1	2			4	6	8^3		14		11	12	10^2				9^1		13				5	7	3	36
1	2			4	6			13	14	11^2	7	10^1				9		12				5	8	3^3	37
1	2			4	6	7		13		10	12					9^2		11				5	8	3^1	38

FA Cup

Third Round	Everton	(a)	2-1
Fourth Round	Derby Co	(a)	2-2
Replay	Derby Co	(h)	3-1
(*aet*)			
Fifth Round	Millwall	(a)	0-1

EFL Cup

Third Round	Chelsea	(h)	2-4
(*aet*)			

EFL Checkatrade Trophy (Leicester C U21)

Northern Group H	Sheffield U	(a)	0-0
(*Leicester C won 5-4 on penalties*)			
Northern Group H	Grimsby T	(a)	1-0
Northern Group H	Walsall	(h)	0-1
Second Round North	Cheltenham T	(a)	1-6

Community Shield

	Manchester U	(Wembley)	1-2

UEFA Champions League

Group G	Club Brugge	(a)	3-0
Group G	Porto	(h)	1-0
Group G	FC Copenhagen	(h)	1-0
Group G	FC Copenhagen	(a)	0-0
Group G	Club Brugge	(h)	2-1
Group G	Porto	(a)	0-5
Round of 16 1st leg	Sevilla	(a)	1-2
Round of 16 2nd leg	Sevilla	(h)	2-0
Leicester C won 3-2 on aggregate.			
Quarter-Finals 1st leg	Atletico Madrid	(a)	0-1
Quarter-Finals 2nd leg	Atletico Madrid	(h)	1-1
Atletico Madrid won 2-1 on aggregate.			

LEYTON ORIENT

FOUNDATION

There is some doubt about the foundation of Leyton Orient, and, indeed, some confusion with clubs like Leyton and Clapton over their early history. As regards the foundation, the most favoured version is that Leyton Orient was formed originally by members of Homerton Theological College who established Glyn Cricket Club in 1881 and then carried on through the following winter playing football. Eventually many employees of the Orient Shipping Line became involved and so the name Orient was chosen in 1888.

Matchroom Stadium, Brisbane Road, Leyton, London E10 5NF.

Telephone: (0871) 310 1881.

Fax: (0871) 310 1882.

Ticket Office: (0871) 310 1883.

Website: www.leytonorient.com

Email: info@leytonorient.net

Ground Capacity: 9,136.

Record Attendance: 34,345 v West Ham U, FA Cup 4th rd, 25 January 1964.

Pitch Measurements: 100.5m × 65m (110yd × 71yd).

Chairman: Nigel Travis.

Interim Chief Executive: Marshall Taylor.

Director of Football: Martin Ling.

First-Team Coach: Steve Davis.

Colours: Red shirts with black trim, red shorts with black trim, red socks.

Year Formed: 1881.

Turned Professional: 1903.

Previous Names: 1881, Glyn Cricket and Football Club; 1886, Eagle Football Club; 1888, Orient Football Club; 1898, Clapton Orient; 1946, Leyton Orient; 1966, Orient; 1987, Leyton Orient.

Club Nickname: 'The O's'.

Grounds: 1884, Glyn Road; 1896, Whittles Athletic Ground; 1900, Millfields Road; 1930, Lea Bridge Road; 1937, Brisbane Road (renamed Matchroom Stadium).

First Football League Game: 2 September 1905, Division 2, v Leicester Fosse (a) L 1–2 – Butler; Holmes, Codling; Lamberton, Boden, Boyle; Kingaby (1), Wootten, Leigh, Evenson, Bourne.

Record League Victory: 8–0 v Crystal Palace, Division 3 (S), 12 November 1955 – Welton; Lee, Earl; Blizzard, Aldous, McKnight; White (1), Facey (3), Burgess (2), Heckman, Hartburn (2). 8–0 v Rochdale, Division 4, 20 October 1987 – Wells; Howard, Dickenson (1), Smalley (1), Day, Hull, Hales (2), Castle (Sussex), Shinners (2), Godfrey (Harvey), Comfort (2). 8–0 v Colchester U, Division 4, 15 October 1988 – Wells; Howard, Dickenson, Hales (1p), Day (1), Sitton (1), Baker (1), Ward, Hull (3), Juryeff, Comfort (1). 8–0 v Doncaster R, Division 3, 28 December 1997 – Hyde; Channing, Naylor, Smith (1p), Hicks, Clark, Ling, Roger Joseph, Griffiths (3) (Harris), Richards (2) (Baker (1)), Inglethorpe (1) (Simpson).

HONOURS

League Champions: Division 3 – 1969–70; Division 3S – 1955–56.
Runners-up: Division 2 – 1961–62; Division 3S – 1954–55.

FA Cup: semi-final – 1978.

League Cup: 5th rd – 1963.

sky SPORTS FACT FILE

Leyton Orient, who were at the time still known as Clapton Orient, moved to their Brisbane Road ground in 1937 after rejecting switching headquarters to Mitcham Stadium. The O's drew 1-1 with Cardiff City in the opening match at the new ground on 28 August 1937. The attendance was 14,598.

Record Cup Victory: 9–2 v Chester, League Cup 3rd rd, 15 October 1962 – Robertson; Charlton, Taylor; Gibbs, Bishop, Lea; Deeley (1), Waites (3), Dunmore (2), Graham (3), Wedge.

Record Defeat: 0–8 v Aston Villa, FA Cup 4th rd, 30 January 1929.

Most League Points (2 for a win): 66, Division 3 (S), 1955–56.

Most League Points (3 for a win): 86, FL 1, 2013–14.

Most League Goals: 106, Division 3 (S), 1955–56.

Highest League Scorer in Season: Tom Johnston, 35, Division 2, 1957–58.

Most League Goals in Total Aggregate: Tom Johnston, 121, 1956–58, 1959–61.

Most League Goals in One Match: 4, Wally Leigh v Bradford C, Division 2, 13 April 1906; 4, Albert Pape v Oldham Ath, Division 2, 1 September 1924; 4, Peter Kitchen v Millwall, Division 3, 21 April 1984.

Most Capped Player: Jobi McAnuff, 23 (32), Jamaica.

Most League Appearances: Peter Allen, 432, 1965–78.

Youngest League Player: Paul Went, 15 years 327 days v Preston NE, 4 September 1965.

Record Transfer Fee Received: £1,000,000 (rising to £1,500,000) from Fulham for Gabriel Zakuani, July 2006.

Record Transfer Fee Paid: £200,000 to Oldham Ath for Liam Kelly, July 2016.

Football League Record: 1905 Elected to Division 2; 1929–56 Division 3 (S); 1956–62 Division 2; 1962–63 Division 1; 1963–66 Division 2; 1966–70 Division 3; 1970–82 Division 2; 1982–85 Division 3; 1985–89 Division 4; 1989–92 Division 3; 1992–95 Division 2; 1995–2004 Division 3; 2004–06 FL 2; 2006–15 FL 1; 2015–17 FL 2; 2017– National League.

LATEST SEQUENCES

Longest Sequence of League Wins: 10, 21.1.1956 – 30.3.1956.

Longest Sequence of League Defeats: 9, 1.4.1995 – 6.5.1995.

Longest Sequence of League Draws: 6, 30.11.1974 – 28.12.1974.

Longest Sequence of Unbeaten League Matches: 15, 13.4.2013 – 19.10.2013.

Longest Sequence Without a League Win: 23, 6.10.1962 – 13.4.1963.

Successive Scoring Runs: 22 from 12.3.1927.

Successive Non-scoring Runs: 8 from 19.11.1994.

MANAGERS

Sam Omerod 1905–06
Ike Ivenson 1906
Billy Holmes 1907–22
Peter Proudfoot 1922–29
Arthur Grimsdell 1929–30
Peter Proudfoot 1930–31
Jimmy Seed 1931–33
David Pratt 1933–34
Peter Proudfoot 1935–39
Tom Halsey 1939
Bill Wright 1939–45
Willie Hall 1945
Bill Wright 1945–46
Charlie Hewitt 1946–48
Neil McBain 1948–49
Alec Stock 1949–59
Les Gore 1959–61
Johnny Carey 1961–63
Benny Fenton 1963–64
Dave Sexton 1965
Dick Graham 1966–68
Jimmy Bloomfield 1968–71
George Petchey 1971–77
Jimmy Bloomfield 1977–81
Paul Went 1981
Ken Knighton 1981–83
Frank Clark 1983–91 *(Managing Director)*
Peter Eustace 1991–94
Chris Turner and John Sitton 1994–95
Pat Holland 1995–96
Tommy Taylor 1996–2001
Paul Brush 2001–03
Martin Ling 2003–09
Geraint Williams 2009–10
Russell Slade 2010–14
Kevin Nugent 2014
Mauro Milanese 2014
Fabio Liverani 2014–15
Ian Hendon 2015–16
Kevin Nolan 2016
Andy Hessenthaler 2016
Alberto Cavasin 2016
Andy Edwards 2016–17
Danny Webb 2017
Martin Ling June 2017–

TEN YEAR LEAGUE RECORD

		P	W	D	L	F	A	Pts	Pos
2007-08	FL 1	46	16	12	18	49	63	60	14
2008-09	FL 1	46	15	11	20	45	57	56	14
2009-10	FL 1	46	13	12	21	53	63	51	17
2010-11	FL 1	46	19	13	14	71	62	70	7
2011-12	FL 1	46	13	11	22	48	75	50	20
2012-13	FL 1	46	21	8	17	55	48	71	7
2013-14	FL 1	46	25	11	10	85	45	86	3
2014-15	FL 1	46	12	13	21	59	69	49	23
2015-16	FL 2	46	19	12	15	60	61	69	8
2016-17	FL 2	46	10	6	30	47	87	36	24

DID YOU KNOW ?

Leyton Orient did not finish their regular League fixtures in the 1946–47 season until June. Adverse winter weather led to the season being extended and the O's played their final game at home against Cardiff City on 7 June.

LEYTON ORIENT – SKY BET LEAGUE TWO 2016–17 LEAGUE RECORD

Match No.	Date	Venue	Opponents	Result	H/T Score	Lg Pos.	Goalscorers	Attendance
1	Aug 6	A	Cheltenham T	D 1-1	1-0	15	Massey 3	3912
2	13	H	Newport Co	L 0-1	0-1	20		4184
3	16	H	Stevenage	W 3-0	2-0	10	Massey 2 20, 75, Cox 37	3779
4	20	A	Grimsby T	W 2-1	0-0	4	Kelly 58, Palmer 77	4991
5	27	H	Mansfield T	L 1-2	0-0	10	Kelly 73	3996
6	Sept 3	A	Morecambe	W 2-1	1-0	7	Kelly 27, Bowery 55	1665
7	10	A	Carlisle U	D 2-2	1-0	8	McCallum 44, Cornick 64	4465
8	17	H	Yeovil T	L 0-1	0-0	10		4557
9	24	A	Notts Co	L 1-3	0-0	14	McCallum 86	4289
10	27	H	Plymouth Arg	L 0-2	0-1	16		4366
11	Oct 1	A	Barnet	D 0-0	0-0	17		2682
12	8	H	Portsmouth	L 0-1	0-0	18		6078
13	15	H	Luton T	L 1-2	0-1	22	Palmer 79	5471
14	22	A	Hartlepool U	W 3-1	0-1	19	Semedo 55, Palmer 2 62, 71	3700
15	29	H	Crewe Alex	L 0-2	0-2	23		4366
16	Nov 12	A	Colchester U	W 3-0	1-0	18	Simpson 2 11, 66, Hunt 46	7003
17	19	H	Blackpool	L 1-2	0-1	20	McCallum 89	4376
18	22	H	Exeter C	L 0-1	0-1	22		2926
19	26	A	Doncaster R	L 1-3	1-1	22	Kennedy 19	5135
20	Dec 10	H	Accrington S	W 1-0	0-0	21	Simpson 65	3964
21	17	A	Wycombe W	L 0-1	0-0	21		4517
22	26	H	Crawley T	W 3-2	3-0	18	Dalby 4, McCallum 2 (1 pen) 11, 45 (p)	4486
23	31	H	Cambridge U	D 1-1	0-1	20	Palmer 90	5897
24	Jan 2	A	Exeter C	L 0-4	0-1	20		4537
25	7	H	Barnet	L 1-3	0-0	21	McCallum 79	4642
26	14	A	Portsmouth	L 1-2	1-1	20	Massey 37	16,564
27	28	A	Mansfield T	L 0-2	0-0	23		3925
28	Feb 4	H	Carlisle U	L 1-2	1-1	23	Massey 25	4306
29	7	H	Morecambe	L 0-1	0-0	23		2660
30	11	A	Yeovil T	D 1-1	0-1	23	Massey 88	3120
31	14	A	Plymouth Arg	W 3-2	1-1	23	Massey 2 43, 88, Semedo 90	8054
32	18	H	Notts Co	L 2-3	0-1	23	McCallum 49, Mezague 81	5585
33	25	H	Cheltenham T	L 0-1	0-1	23		4747
34	28	A	Stevenage	L 1-4	1-2	23	McCallum 24	2908
35	Mar 4	A	Newport Co	W 4-0	3-0	23	Alzate 8, Koroma 3 (1 pen) 13, 45, 64 (p)	3378
36	11	H	Grimsby T	L 0-3	0-1	23		5288
37	14	A	Accrington S	L 0-5	0-1	24		1306
38	18	H	Doncaster R	L 1-4	1-1	24	Parkes 44	4791
39	25	A	Crawley T	L 0-3	0-3	24		2918
40	Apr 1	H	Wycombe W	L 0-2	0-2	24		4526
41	8	A	Cambridge U	L 0-3	0-2	24		4681
42	14	A	Luton T	D 2-2	0-1	24	Kelly (pen) 54, Abrahams 61	8601
43	17	H	Hartlepool U	W 2-1	2-1	24	Adeboyejo 18, Abrahams 34	5411
44	22	A	Crewe Alex	L 0-3	0-3	24		3745
45	29	H	Colchester U	L 1-3	0-1	24	Semedo 52	6854
46	May 6	A	Blackpool	L 1-3	0-2	24	Janse 50	3602

Final League Position: 24

GOALSCORERS

League (47): Massey 8, McCallum 8 (1 pen), Palmer 5, Kelly 4 (1 pen), Koroma 3 (1 pen), Semedo 3, Simpson 3, Abrahams 2, Adeboyejo 1, Alzate 1, Bowery 1, Cornick 1, Cox 1, Dalby 1, Hunt 1, Janse 1, Kennedy 1, Mezague 1, Parkes 1.
FA Cup (0).
EFL Cup (2): McCallum 2.
EFL Checkatrade Trophy (3): McCallum 2, Semedo 1.

Cisak A 28	Clohessy S 2	Erichot Y 18 + 1	Parkes T 41	Semedo S 35 + 7	Massey G 36	Atangana N 25 + 4	Weir R 15 + 2	Cornick H 9 + 2 / Happe D 1 + 1	Palmer O 10 + 10	Bowery J 9 + 8	Kelly L 19 + 2	Hunt N 34 + 1	Gnanduillet A — + 1	Cox D 4	McCallum P 20 + 9	Simpson J 12 + 2	Kennedy C 31 + 1	Pollock A 8 + 1	N'Nomo U 1 + 5	Janse J 8	Dunne A — + 5	Benedicic Z — + 1	Collins M 28 + 2	Adeboyejo V 4 + 9	Judd M 20	Koroma J 12 + 10	Mezague T 11 + 6	Dalby S 10 + 6	Moore S 3 + 1	Sargeant S 15	Liburd R 4 + 4	Clark M 8 + 1	Moncur F 5 + 4	Alzate S 9 + 3	Grainger C 3	Abrahams T 4 + 5	Ochieng H 4 + 2	*Match No.*
1	2	3	4²	5	6	7	8³	9	10	11¹	12	13	14																									1
1	2	3	4	5	6	14	7¹	13	11	12	8			9³	10²																							2
1		3	4	5	7	9²	12	8	14	13	6	2		10¹		11³																						3
1		3	4	5	9	8		6	12	11	7	2		10¹																								4
1		3	4	5	10	7		8²	11¹	13	6	2		9	12																							5
1		3	4		9		7	6		10	8	2			11		5																					6
1		3	4	13	9		8	6	12	10¹	7	2			11²		5																					7
1		3	4		9	14	8¹	6		10²	7	2³			11	13	5	12																				8
1		3	4	13	6¹		8	9²		14	7	2			11	10³	5		12																			9
1			4	9	6	12³	7■	13		14	8²	3			11¹	10	5			2■																		10
1		3	4	9³	6			7²	14	12	8	2			10	11¹	5		13																			11
1		3	4	12	9				14		8²	2			10¹	11	5		6³	7	13																	12
1		3	4	9	6	7²			10			2			12	11¹	5			8	13																	13
1			4	2¹	6	7	8³		11	10²		3					5		13	9	12	14																14
1			4	9	6¹	7³	8		11	10²		3				14	5		13	2			12															15
1		3	4	12	7³	8	6		10¹			2			13	11²	5						9	14														16
1		3³	4	13	7	8	6		10¹			2			14	11	5				12		9²															17
1			4	12	7	8	6²		14			3			10¹	11	5³				13		9		2													18
1			4	7²		8	6		10¹						13	11	5	3					9		2	12												19
1			3	9²	6	7	8			10³		5			12	11	2						14		4¹		13											20
1			4	13	6	8	7²			9³		3			10	11	5¹								2		12	14										21
1			4	9	6	8				12		5			10								7		2		3	11¹										22
1		12	4	9³	6	8			13			5			10								7		2	14	3²	11¹										23
1		3	4		6	8	13³		10²			5			11		9¹						7	14	2	12												24
1		3	4		8	7			12			2			11		5		13				9			10²	6¹											25
1			3	10¹	8	6			13	12		2			11								9		5		4		7²									26
1			4	9	6				12			2			10²		5						8	13			3	11¹	7									27
			4	9	6	7						3					5³						8	13	2		14	11¹	12	1	10²							28
		3	4	9	6	8					13	5											7¹	11³	2	14		10²		1	12							29
		3¹	4	10	7	9²					6	5			13		12						8		2	14				1	11³							30
			4	9	10						8	3					5						7		2	6		11		1								31
			4¹	9	10	7									11		5						8		2	6	3	12		1								32
			4²	9	10	7									11³		5						8		2	6¹	3	13		1	14	12						33
				9²	10							3			11³		5						8	14	2	6			7¹	1		4	12	13				34
			4	9								3					5						7	13	2	6³	14	10¹					8²	11	1	12		35
			4	9								3					5						7		2	6		10¹					8	11	1	12		36
			4	10	8	13						3²					5						7		2	9	12	11¹			14		6³		1			37
1			4	6	11	7¹					8							2					9		5	10²		12				3		13				38
			3¹	10	11	7³					6	4					5								2	8²	12			1	13			9			14	39
			4■	9							7	2					5			6¹			8			11²	3	13		1	10³			14		12		40
				8				4³			6							3					7	13		11²				1	10¹	2	5	9		12	14	41
				5							7							3					6	11		13	4	10²		1		2	14	8¹		12	9³	42
				8							6				12			2					7	10³		13	3			1		4	14	11²		9¹	5	43
			4	5											12			3					6³	10²		13	8¹	14		1		2		9		11	7	44
			4	11											10³		8	3		5²			7¹	12		13				1		2	14	6		9		45
				11				14									9	3³		4			8	12		13				1		2	5¹	7		10²	6	46

FA Cup

First Round	Sheffield U	(a)	0-6

EFL Cup

First Round	Fulham	(h)	2-3

EFL Checkatrade Trophy

Southern Group G	Stevenage	(h)	3-1
Southern Group G	Southend U	(a)	0-1
Southern Group G	Brighton & HA U21	(a)	0-1

LINCOLN CITY

FOUNDATION

The original Lincoln Football Club was established in the early 1860s and was one of the first provisional clubs to affiliate to the Football Association. In their early years, they regularly played matches against the famous Sheffield Football Club and later became known as Lincoln Lindum. The present organisation was formed at a public meeting held in the Monson Arms Hotel in June 1884 and won the Lincolnshire Cup in only their third season. They were founder members of the Midland League in 1889 and that competition's first champions.

Sincil Bank Stadium, Sincil Bank, Lincoln LN5 8LD.

Telephone: (01522) 880 011.

Fax: (01522) 880 020.

Ticket Office: (01522) 880 011.

Website: www.redimps.com

Email: info@lincolncityfc.co.uk

Ground Capacity: 10,120.

Record Attendance: 23,196 v Derby Co, League Cup 4th rd, 15 November 1967.

Pitch Measurements: 100m × 65m.

Chairman: Bob Dorrian.

Managing Director: Kevin Cooke.

Manager: Danny Cowley.

Assistant Manager: Nicky Cowley.

Colours: Red and white striped shirts with black trim, black shorts with white trim, red socks.

Year Formed: 1884.

Turned Professional: 1892.

Ltd Co.: 1895.

Club Nickname: 'The Red Imps'.

Grounds: 1883, John O'Gaunt's; 1894, Sincil Bank.

First Football League Game: 3 September 1892, Division 2, v Sheffield U (a) L 2–4 – William Gresham; Coulton, Neill; Shaw, Mettam, Moore; Smallman, Irving (1), Cameron (1), Kelly, James Gresham.

Record League Victory: 11–1 v Crewe Alex, Division 3 (N), 29 September 1951 – Jones; Green (1p), Varney; Wright, Emery, Grummett (1); Troops (1), Garvey, Graver (6), Whittle (1), Johnson (1).

Record Cup Victory: 8–1 v Bromley, FA Cup 2nd rd, 10 December 1938 – McPhail; Hartshorne, Corbett; Bean, Leach, Whyte (1); Hancock, Wilson (1), Ponting (3), Deacon (1), Clare (2).

Record Defeat: 3–11 v Manchester C, Division 2, 23 March 1895.

Most League Points (2 for a win): 74, Division 4, 1975–76.

Most League Points (3 for a win): 77, Division 3, 1981–82.

HONOURS

League Champions: Division 3 (N) – 1931–32, 1947–48, 1951–52; Division 4 – 1975–76; National League – 1987–88, 2016–17.
Runners-up: Division 3 (N) – 1927–28, 1930–31, 1936–37; Division 4 – 1980–81.

FA Cup: quarter-final – 2017.

League Cup: 4th rd – 1968.

sky SPORTS FACT FILE

Lincoln City hold the record for the number of times a club has entered the Football League. They have done this six times: as founder members of Division 2 and Division 3 North (1892, 1921), on election to Division 2 (1909, 1912) and through automatic promotion (1988, 2017).

Most League Goals: 121, Division 3 (N), 1951–52.

Highest League Scorer in Season: Allan Hall, 41, Division 3 (N), 1931–32.

Most League Goals in Total Aggregate: Andy Graver, 143, 1950–55 and 1958–61.

Most League Goals in One Match: 6, Frank Keetley v Halifax T, Division 3 (N), 16 January 1932; 6, Andy Graver v Crewe Alex, Division 3 (N), 29 September 1951.

Most Capped Player: Gareth McAuley, 5 (30), Northern Ireland.

Most League Appearances: Grant Brown, 407, 1989–2002.

Youngest League Player: Shane Nicholson, 16 years 172 days v Burnley, 22 November 1986.

Record Transfer Fee Received: £750,000 from Liverpool for Jack Hobbs, August 2005.

Record Transfer Fee Paid: £75,000 to Carlisle U for Dean Walling, October 1997 and £75,000 to Bury for Tony Battersby, August 1998.

Football League Record: 1892 Founder member of Division 2. Remained in Division 2 until 1920 when they failed re-election but also missed seasons 1908–09 and 1911–12 when not re-elected. 1921–32 Division 3 (N); 1932–34 Division 2; 1934–48 Division 3 (N); 1948–49 Division 2; 1949–52 Division 3 (N); 1952–61 Division 2; 1961–62 Division 3; 1962–76 Division 4; 1976–79 Division 3; 1979–81 Division 4; 1981–86 Division 3; 1986–87 Division 4; 1987–88 GM Vauxhall Conference; 1988–92 Division 4; 1992–98 Division 3; 1998–99 Division 2; 1999–2004 Division 3; 2004–11 FL 2; 2011–17 Conference National League; 2017– FL 2.

LATEST SEQUENCES

Longest Sequence of League Wins: 10, 1.9.1930 – 18.10.1930.

Longest Sequence of League Defeats: 12, 21.9.1896 – 9.1.1897.

Longest Sequence of League Draws: 5, 21.2.1981 – 7.3.1981.

Longest Sequence of Unbeaten League Matches: 18, 11.3.1980 – 13.9.1980.

Longest Sequence Without a League Win: 19, 22.8.1978 – 23.12.1978.

Successive Scoring Runs: 37 from 1.3.1930.

Successive Non-scoring Runs: 5 from 15.11.1913.

MANAGERS

Alf Martin 1896–97
(Secretary/Manager)
David Calderhead 1900–07
John Henry Strawson 1907–14
(had been Secretary)
George Fraser 1919–21
David Calderhead Jnr. 1921–24
Horace Henshall 1924–27
Harry Parkes 1927–36
Joe McClelland 1936–46
Bill Anderson 1946–65
(General Manager to 1966)
Roy Chapman 1965–66
Ron Gray 1966–70
Bert Loxley 1970–71
David Herd 1971–72
Graham Taylor 1972–77
George Kerr 1977–78
Willie Bell 1977–78
Colin Murphy 1978–85
John Pickering 1985
George Kerr 1985–87
Peter Daniel 1987
Colin Murphy 1987–90
Allan Clarke 1990
Steve Thompson 1990–93
Keith Alexander 1993–94
Sam Ellis 1994–95
Steve Wicks *(Head Coach)* 1995
John Beck 1995–98
Shane Westley 1998
John Reames 1998–2000
Phil Stant 2000–01
Alan Buckley 2001–02
Keith Alexander 2002–06
John Schofield 2006–07
Peter Jackson 2007–09
Chris Sutton 2009–10
Steve Tilson 2010–11
David Holdsworth 2011–13
Gary Simpson 2013–14
Chris Moyses 2014–16
Danny Cowley May 2016–

TEN YEAR LEAGUE RECORD

		P	W	D	L	F	A	Pts	Pos
2007-08	FL 2	46	18	4	24	61	77	58	15
2008-09	FL 2	46	14	17	15	53	52	59	13
2009-10	FL 2	46	13	11	22	42	65	50	20
2010-11	FL 2	46	13	8	25	45	81	47	23
2011-12	Conf	46	13	10	23	56	66	49	17
2012-13	Conf	46	15	11	20	72	86	54	16
2013-14	Conf	46	17	14	15	60	59	65	14
2014-15	Conf	46	16	10	20	62	71	58	15
2015-16	NL	46	16	13	17	69	68	61	13
2016-17	NL	46	30	9	7	83	40	99	1

DID YOU KNOW ?

Winger John Walker who played for Lincoln City in the 1899–1900 season is believed to have been the first black outfield player to appear in the Football League. Walker, whose father came from Trinidad, made six appearances for the Imps having previously played in Scotland with Leith Athletic and Hearts.

LIVERPOOL

FOUNDATION

But for a dispute between Everton FC and their landlord at Anfield in 1892, there may never have been a Liverpool club. This dispute persuaded the majority of Evertonians to quit Anfield for Goodison Park, leaving the landlord, Mr John Houlding, to form a new club. He originally tried to retain the name 'Everton' but when this failed, he founded Liverpool Association FC on 15 March 1892.

Anfield Stadium, Anfield Road, Anfield, Liverpool L4 0TH.

Telephone: (0151) 263 2361.

Fax: (0151) 260 8813.

Ticket Office: (0843) 170 5555.

Website: www.liverpoolfc.com

Email: customerservices@liverpoolfc.com

Ground Capacity: 54,074.

Record Attendance: 61,905 v Wolverhampton W, FA Cup 4th rd, 2 February 1952.

Pitch Measurements: 101m × 68m (110yd × 74yd).

Chairman: Tom Werner.

Chief Executive: Peter Moore.

Manager: Jürgen Klopp.

Assistant Coach: Zeljko Buvac.

Colours: Red shirts, red shorts, red socks.

Year Formed: 1892.

Turned Professional: 1892.

Club Nicknames: 'The Reds', 'Pool'.

Ground: 1892, Anfield.

First Football League Game: 2 September 1893, Division 2, v Middlesbrough Ironopolis (a) W 2–0 – McOwen; Hannah, McLean; Henderson, McQue (1), McBride; Gordon, McVean (1), Matt McQueen, Stott, Hugh McQueen.

HONOURS

League Champions: Division 1 – 1900–01, 1905–06, 1921–22, 1922–23, 1946–47, 1963–64, 1965–66, 1972–73, 1975–76, 1976–77, 1978–79, 1979–80, 1981–82, 1982–83, 1983–84, 1985–86, 1987–88, 1989–90; Division 2 – 1893–94, 1895–96, 1904–05, 1961–62.
Runners-up: FA Premier League – 2001–02, 2008–09, 2013–14; Division 1 – 1898–99, 1909–10, 1968–69, 1973–74, 1974–75, 1977–78, 1984–85, 1986–87, 1988–89, 1990–91.

FA Cup Winners: 1965, 1974, 1986, 1989, 1992, 2001, 2006.
Runners-up: 1914, 1950, 1971, 1977, 1988, 1996, 2012.

League Cup Winners: 1981, 1982, 1983, 1984, 1995, 2001, 2003, 2012.
Runners-up: 1978, 1987, 2005, 2016.

League Super Cup Winners: 1986.

European Competitions

European Cup: 1964–65 *(sf)*, 1966–67, 1973–74, 1976–77 *(winners)*, 1977–78 *(winners)*, 1978–79, 1979–80, 1980–81 *(winners)*, 1981–82 *(qf)*, 1982–83 *(qf)*, 1983–84 *(winners)*, 1984–85 *(runners-up)*.
Champions League: 2001–02 *(qf)*, 2002–03, 2004–05 *(winners)*, 2005–06, 2006–07 *(runners-up)*, 2007–08 *(sf)*, 2008–09 *(qf)*, 2009–10, 2014–15.
Fairs Cup: 1967–68, 1968–69, 1969–70, 1970–71 *(sf)*.
UEFA Cup: 1972–73 *(winners)*, 1975–76 *(winners)*, 1991–92 *(qf)*, 1995–96, 1997–98, 1998–99, 2000–01 *(winners)*, 2002–03 *(qf)*, 2003–04.
Europa League: 2009–10 *(sf)*, 2010–11, 2012–13, 2014–15, 2015–16 *(runners-up)*.
European Cup-Winners' Cup: 1965–66 *(runners-up)*, 1971–72, 1974–75, 1992–93, 1996–97 *(sf)*.
Super Cup: 1977 *(winners)*, 1978, 1984, 2001 *(winners)*, 2005 *(winners)*.
World Club Championship: 1981, 1984.
FIFA Club World Cup: 2005.

sky SPORTS FACT FILE

Jack Balmer scored the quickest goal in Liverpool's history in February 1938 when he netted after just 10 seconds of the derby clash with Everton at Goodison Park. Although Everton equalised the Reds won the game with two goals in the last 10 minutes from teenager John Shafto.

Record League Victory: 10–1 v Rotherham T, Division 2, 18 February 1896 – Storer; Goldie, Wilkie; McCartney, McQue, Holmes; McVean (3), Ross (2), Allan (4), Becton (1), Bradshaw.

Record Cup Victory: 11–0 v Stromsgodset Drammen, ECWC 1st rd 1st leg, 17 September 1974 – Clemence; Smith (1), Lindsay (1p), Thompson (2), Cormack (1), Hughes (1), Boersma (2), Hall, Heighway (1), Kennedy (1), Callaghan (1).

Record Defeat: 1–9 v Birmingham C, Division 2, 11 December 1954.

Most League Points (2 for a win): 68, Division 1, 1978–79.

Most League Points (3 for a win): 90, Division 1, 1987–88.

Most League Goals: 106, Division 2, 1895–96.

Highest League Scorer in Season: Roger Hunt, 41, Division 2, 1961–62.

Most League Goals in Total Aggregate: Roger Hunt, 245, 1959–69.

Most League Goals in One Match: 5, Andy McGuigan v Stoke C, Division 1, 4 January 1902; 5, John Evans v Bristol R, Division 2, 15 September 1954; 5, Ian Rush v Luton T, Division 1, 29 October 1983.

Most Capped Player: Steven Gerrard, 114, England.

Most League Appearances: Ian Callaghan, 640, 1960–78.

Youngest League Player: Jack Robinson, 16 years 250 days v Hull C, 9 May 2010.

Record Transfer Fee Received: £75,000,000 from Barcelona for Luis Suarez, July 2014.

Record Transfer Fee Paid: £36,900,000 (rising to £43,000,000) to Roma for Mohamed Salah, June 2017.

Football League Record: 1893 Elected to Division 2; 1894–95 Division 1; 1895–96 Division 2; 1896–1904 Division 1; 1904–05 Division 2; 1905–54 Division 1; 1954–62 Division 2; 1962–92 Division 1; 1992– FA Premier League.

MANAGERS

W. E. Barclay 1892–96
Tom Watson 1896–1915
David Ashworth 1920–23
Matt McQueen 1923–28
George Patterson 1928–36
(continued as Secretary)
George Kay 1936–51
Don Welsh 1951–56
Phil Taylor 1956–59
Bill Shankly 1959–74
Bob Paisley 1974–83
Joe Fagan 1983–85
Kenny Dalglish 1985–91
Graeme Souness 1991–94
Roy Evans 1994–98
(then Joint Manager)
Gerard Houllier 1998–2004
Rafael Benitez 2004–10
Roy Hodgson 2010–11
Kenny Dalglish 2011–12
Brendan Rodgers 2012–15
Jürgen Klopp October 2015–

LATEST SEQUENCES

Longest Sequence of League Wins: 12, 21.4.1990 – 6.10.1990.

Longest Sequence of League Defeats: 9, 29.4.1899 – 14.10.1899.

Longest Sequence of League Draws: 6, 19.2.1975 – 19.3.1975.

Longest Sequence of Unbeaten League Matches: 31, 4.5.1987 – 16.3.1988.

Longest Sequence Without a League Win: 14, 12.12.1953 – 20.3.1954.

Successive Scoring Runs: 29 from 27.4.1957.

Successive Non-scoring Runs: 5 from 21.4.2000.

TEN YEAR LEAGUE RECORD

		P	*W*	*D*	*L*	*F*	*A*	*Pts*	*Pos*
2007-08	PR Lge	38	21	13	4	67	28	76	4
2008-09	PR Lge	38	25	11	2	77	27	86	2
2009-10	PR Lge	38	18	9	11	61	35	63	7
2010-11	PR Lge	38	17	7	14	59	44	58	6
2011-12	PR Lge	38	14	10	14	47	40	52	8
2012-13	PR Lge	38	16	13	9	71	43	61	7
2013-14	PR Lge	38	26	6	6	101	50	84	2
2014-15	PR Lge	38	18	8	12	52	48	62	6
2015-16	PR Lge	38	16	12	10	63	50	60	8
2016-17	PR Lge	38	22	10	6	78	42	76	4

DID YOU KNOW ?

Mark Walters scored Liverpool's first Premier League goal when he netted the equaliser against Sheffield United at Anfield in August 1992. Later the same season he became the first player to score a Premier League hat-trick for the club with his goals helping defeat Coventry City 4-0.

LIVERPOOL – PREMIER LEAGUE 2016–17 LEAGUE RECORD

Match No.	Date	Venue	Opponents	Result	H/T Score	Lg Pos.	Goalscorers	Atten-dance
1	Aug 14	A	Arsenal	W 4-3	1-1	2	Coutinho 2 [45, 56], Lallana [49], Mane [63]	60,033
2	20	A	Burnley	L 0-2	0-2	8		21,313
3	27	A	Tottenham H	D 1-1	1-0	9	Milner (pen) [43]	31,211
4	Sept 10	H	Leicester C	W 4-1	2-1	4	Firmino 2 [13, 89], Mane [31], Lallana [56]	51,232
5	16	A	Chelsea	W 2-1	2-0	4	Lovren [17], Henderson [36]	41,514
6	24	H	Hull C	W 5-1	3-0	3	Lallana [17], Milner 2 (2 pens) [30, 71], Mane [36], Coutinho [52]	53,109
7	Oct 1	A	Swansea C	W 2-1	0-1	2	Firmino [54], Milner (pen) [84]	20,862
8	17	H	Manchester U	D 0-0	0-0	4		52,769
9	22	H	WBA	W 2-1	2-0	2	Mane [20], Coutinho [35]	53,218
10	29	A	Crystal Palace	W 4-2	3-2	1	Can [16], Lovren [21], Matip [44], Firmino [71]	25,628
11	Nov 6	H	Watford	W 6-1	3-0	1	Mane 2 [27, 60], Coutinho [30], Can [43], Firmino [57], Wijnaldum [90]	53,163
12	19	A	Southampton	D 0-0	0-0	1		31,848
13	26	H	Sunderland	W 2-0	0-0	2	Origi [75], Milner (pen) [90]	53,114
14	Dec 4	A	Bournemouth	L 3-4	2-0	3	Mane [20], Origi [22], Can [64]	11,183
15	11	H	West Ham U	D 2-2	1-2	3	Lallana [5], Origi [48]	53,068
16	14	A	Middlesbrough	W 3-0	1-0	2	Lallana 2 [29, 68], Origi [60]	32,704
17	19	A	Everton	W 1-0	0-0	2	Mane [90]	39,590
18	27	H	Stoke C	W 4-1	2-1	2	Lallana [34], Firmino [44], Imbula (og) [59], Sturridge [70]	53,094
19	31	H	Manchester C	W 1-0	1-0	2	Wijnaldum [8]	53,120
20	Jan 2	A	Sunderland	D 2-2	1-1	2	Sturridge [19], Mane [72]	46,494
21	15	A	Manchester U	D 1-1	1-0	3	Milner (pen) [27]	75,276
22	21	H	Swansea C	L 2-3	0-0	3	Firmino 2 [55, 69]	53,169
23	31	H	Chelsea	D 1-1	0-1	4	Wijnaldum [57]	53,157
24	Feb 4	A	Hull C	L 0-2	0-1	4		24,822
25	11	H	Tottenham H	W 2-0	2-0	4	Mane 2 [16, 18]	53,159
26	27	A	Leicester C	L 1-3	0-2	5	Coutinho [68]	32,034
27	Mar 4	H	Arsenal	W 3-1	2-0	3	Firmino [9], Mane [40], Wijnaldum [90]	53,146
28	12	H	Burnley	W 2-1	1-1	4	Wijnaldum [45], Can [61]	53,145
29	19	A	Manchester C	D 1-1	0-0	4	Milner (pen) [51]	54,449
30	Apr 1	H	Everton	W 3-1	2-1	3	Mane [8], Coutinho [31], Origi [60]	52,920
31	5	H	Bournemouth	D 2-2	1-1	3	Coutinho [40], Origi [59]	53,292
32	8	A	Stoke C	W 2-1	0-1	3	Coutinho [70], Firmino [72]	27,568
33	16	A	WBA	W 1-0	1-0	3	Firmino [45]	25,669
34	23	H	Crystal Palace	L 1-2	1-1	3	Coutinho [24]	53,086
35	May 1	A	Watford	W 1-0	1-0	3	Can [45]	20,959
36	7	H	Southampton	D 0-0	0-0	3		53,159
37	14	A	West Ham U	W 4-0	1-0	3	Sturridge [35], Coutinho 2 [57, 61], Origi [76]	56,985
38	21	H	Middlesbrough	W 3-0	1-0	4	Wijnaldum [45], Coutinho [51], Lallana [56]	53,191

Final League Position: 4

GOALSCORERS

League (78): Coutinho 13, Mane 13, Firmino 11, Lallana 8, Milner 7 (7 pens), Origi 7, Wijnaldum 6, Can 5, Sturridge 3, Lovren 2, Henderson 1, Matip 1, own goal 1.
FA Cup (2): Lucas 1, Origi 1.
EFL Cup (12): Sturridge 4, Origi 3, Coutinho 1, Firmino 1, Klavan 1, Woodburn 1, own goal 1.

Mignolet S 28	Clyne N 37	Lovren D 29	Klavan R 15 + 5	Moreno A 2 + 10	Lallana A 27 + 4	Henderson J 24	Wijnaldum G 33 + 3	Mane S 26 + 1	Firmino R 34 + 1	Coutinho P 28 + 3	Can E 26 + 6	Origi D 14 + 20	Stewart K — + 4	Milner J 36	Sturridge D 7 + 13	Grujic M — + 5	Matip J 27 + 2	Lucas 12 + 12	Karius L 10	Ejaria O — + 2	Woodburn B 1 + 4	Alexander-Arnold T 2 + 5	Match No.
1	2	3	4	5	6^{2}	7	8^{3}	9	10	11^{1}	12	13	14										1
1	2	3	4	13	6^{1}	7	8		10	11		12		5^{3}	9^{2}	14							2
1	2	4			6^{2}	7	8	9^{1}	10	11^{3}		12	14	5	13		3						3
1	2			14	6	7	8^{3}	9^{1}	11	12			13	5	10^{2}		3	4					4
1	2	4			6	7	8^{2}	9		11^{1}		12	14	5	10^{3}		3	13					5
	2		4		6^{3}	7^{1}	8	9	10	11^{2}	13			5	12	14	3		1				6
	2	4			6^{2}	7	8^{3}	9	10^{1}	11	13	14		5	12		3		1				7
	2	4		14	12	7		9	11^{2}	8	6	13		5^{3}	10^{1}		3		1				8
	2	4			6^{1}	7	12	9^{3}	10	11^{2}	8	14		5			3	13	1				9
	2	4	14	5	6^{3}	7	12	9^{2}	10	11^{1}	8	13					3		1				10
	2				6^{2}	7	12	9^{1}	10	11^{3}	8			5	13		3	4	1	14			11
	2	4				7	6	9^{2}	10	11	8^{1}	13		5	12		3		1				12
	2	4				7	6^{1}	9	10^{2}	11^{3}	8	12		5			3	13	1		14		13
	2	4			12	7	6	9^{1}	11		8	10		5				3	1				14
	2	4^{1}	12		6	7	8	9	11			10		5			3		1				15
1	2	3	4		6^{1}	7	8^{2}	9	11			10^{3}		5				12		13		14	16
1	2	3	4		6^{1}	7	8	9^{3}	11		12	10^{2}		5	13			14					17
1	2	3	4	14	6^{1}	7	8	9	11^{2}		12	10^{3}		5	13								18
1	2	3	4		11	7^{2}	6	9^{1}	10		8	12		5				13					19
1	2	3	4	12	6		8^{2}	9	11		7	13		5^{1}	10^{3}			14					20
1		3	4		11	7	6		9	12	8	10^{1}		5								2	21
1	2	3	4		9	7	6^{1}		10	11^{2}	8^{3}	13		5	12		14						22
1	2	4			9^{1}	7	6	12	10	11^{2}	8	13		5			3						23
1	2			14	6^{1}	7		9	10	11	8^{2}	13		5^{2}	12		3	4					24
1	2		13		6	7	8	9^{1}	10	11^{3}	12			5			3	4^{2}				14	25
1	2			13	6^{3}		8	9^{2}	10	11	7	12		5			3	4^{1}			14		26
1	2		4		8^{3}		6	9^{1}	10	11^{2}	7	12		5			3	13				14	27
1	2		4		8		6	9		11^{1}	7	10^{2}		5			3	13			12		28
1	2		4		6		8	9	10^{1}	11^{2}	7	12		5			3	13					29
1	2	4	14				8	9^{3}	10^{1}	11^{2}	6	12		5			3	7				13	30
1	2	3	4				8		9	11^{1}	6	10		5			12	7					31
1	9	2	4				6		12	13	7	11^{2}		8	14		3				10^{3}	5^{1}	32
1	2	4		13			6		9	11^{1}	8	10^{2}		5	12		3	7					33
1	2^{3}	4^{1}		13			8		9	11	6	10		5^{2}		14	3	7				12	34
1	2	4	14		12^{3}		7		9	11^{2}	8	10^{1}		5	13		3	6					35
1	2	4			12		8^{2}		9	11	6	10^{3}		5	13	14	3	7^{1}					36
1	2	4			9^{2}		7			8^{3}	6	10		5	11^{1}	13	3	12			14		37
1	2	4		14	9		7		11^{2}	8	6	13		5^{1}	10^{3}		3	12					38

FA Cup

Third Round	Plymouth Arg	(h)	0-0
Replay	Plymouth Arg	(a)	1-0
Fourth Round	Wolverhampton W	(h)	1-2

EFL Cup

Second Round	Burton Alb	(a)	5-0
Third Round	Derby Co	(a)	3-0
Fourth Round	Tottenham H	(h)	2-1
Quarter-Final	Leeds U	(h)	2-0
Semi-Final 1st leg	Southampton	(a)	0-1
Semi-Final 2nd leg	Southampton	(h)	0-1

LUTON TOWN

FOUNDATION

Formed by an amalgamation of two leading local clubs, Wanderers and Excelsior a works team, at a meeting in Luton Town Hall in April 1885. The Wanderers had three months earlier changed their name to Luton Town Wanderers and did not take too kindly to the formation of another Town club but were talked around at this meeting. Wanderers had already appeared in the FA Cup and the new club entered in its inaugural season.

Kenilworth Road Stadium, 1 Maple Road, Luton, Bedfordshire LU4 8AW.

Telephone: (01582) 411 622.

Fax: (01582) 405 070.

Ticket Office: (01582) 416 976.

Website: www.lutontown.co.uk

Email: info@lutontown.co.uk

Ground Capacity: 10,413.

Record Attendance: 30,069 v Blackpool, FA Cup 6th rd replay, 4 March 1959.

Pitch Measurements: 101m × 66m (110yd × 72yd).

Chairman: Nick Owen.

Chief Executive: Gary Sweet.

Manager: Nathan Jones.

Assistant Manager: Paul Hart.

Colours: Orange shirts with white trim, navy blue shorts with orange trim, orange socks with navy blue trim.

Year Formed: 1885.

Turned Professional: 1890.

Ltd Co.: 1897.

Club Nickname: 'The Hatters'.

Grounds: 1885, Excelsior, Dallow Lane; 1897, Dunstable Road; 1905, Kenilworth Road.

First Football League Game: 4 September 1897, Division 2, v Leicester Fosse (a) D 1–1 – Williams; McCartney, McEwen; Davies, Stewart, Docherty; Gallacher, Coupar, Birch, McInnes, Ekins (1).

Record League Victory: 12–0 v Bristol R, Division 3 (S), 13 April 1936 – Dolman; Mackey, Smith; Finlayson, Nelson, Godfrey; Rich, Martin (1), Payne (10), Roberts (1), Stephenson.

Record Cup Victory: 9–0 v Clapton, FA Cup 1st rd (replay after abandoned game), 30 November 1927 – Abbott; Kingham, Graham; Black, Rennie, Fraser; Pointon, Yardley (4), Reid (2), Woods (1), Dennis (2).

Record Defeat: 0–9 v Small Heath, Division 2, 12 November 1898.

HONOURS

League Champions: Division 2 – 1981–82; FL 1 – 2004–05; Division 3S – 1936–37; Division 4 – 1967–68; Conference – 2013–14.
Runners-up: Division 2 – 1954–55, 1973–74; Division 3 – 1969–70; Division 3S – 1935–36; Third Division – 2001–02.

FA Cup: *Runners-up:* 1959.

League Cup Winners: 1988.
Runners-up: 1989.

League Trophy Winners: 2009.

Full Members' Cup: *Runners-up:* 1988.

sky SPORTS FACT FILE

Like many clubs, Luton Town's nickname derives from the town's main industrial role in the nineteenth century. Luton were originally known as 'The Straw Plaiters' and then 'The Straw Hatters' before the use of 'The Hatters' came into vogue shortly before the First World War.

Most League Points (2 for a win): 66, Division 4, 1967–68.

Most League Points (3 for a win): 98, FL 1 2004–05.

Most League Goals: 103, Division 3 (S), 1936–37.

Highest League Scorer in Season: Joe Payne, 55, Division 3 (S), 1936–37.

Most League Goals in Total Aggregate: Gordon Turner, 243, 1949–64.

Most League Goals in One Match: 10, Joe Payne v Bristol R, Division 3 (S), 13 April 1936.

Most Capped Player: Mal Donaghy, 58 (91), Northern Ireland.

Most League Appearances: Bob Morton, 495, 1948–64.

Youngest League Player: Mike O'Hara, 16 years 32 days v Stoke C, 1 October 1960.

Record Transfer Fee Received: £3,000,000 from WBA for Curtis Davies, August 2005; £3,000,000 from Birmingham C for Rowan Vine, January 2007.

Record Transfer Fee Paid: £850,000 to Odense for Lars Elstrup, August 1989.

Football League Record: 1897 Elected to Division 2; 1900 Failed re-election; 1920 Division 3; 1921–37 Division 3 (S); 1937–55 Division 2; 1955–60 Division 1; 1960–63 Division 2; 1963–65 Division 3; 1965–68 Division 4; 1968–70 Division 3; 1970–74 Division 2; 1974–75 Division 1; 1975–82 Division 2; 1982–96 Division 1; 1996–2001 Division 2; 2001–02 Division 3; 2002–04 Division 2; 2004–05 FL 1; 2005–07 FL C; 2007–08 FL 1; 2008–09 FL 2; 2009–14 Conference Premier; 2014– FL 2.

MANAGERS

Charlie Green 1901–28 (Secretary-Manager)
George Thomson 1925
John McCartney 1927–29
George Kay 1929–31
Harold Wightman 1931–35
Ted Liddell 1936–38
Neil McBain 1938–39
George Martin 1939–47
Dally Duncan 1947–58
Syd Owen 1959–60
Sam Bartram 1960–62
Bill Harvey 1962–64
George Martin 1965–66
Allan Brown 1966–68
Alec Stock 1968–72
Harry Haslam 1972–78
David Pleat 1978–86
John Moore 1986–87
Ray Harford 1987–89
Jim Ryan 1990–91
David Pleat 1991–95
Terry Westley 1995
Lennie Lawrence 1995–2000
Ricky Hill 2000
Lil Fuccillo 2000
Joe Kinnear 2001–03
Mike Newell 2003–07
Kevin Blackwell 2007–08
Mick Harford 2008–09
Richard Money 2009–11
Gary Brabin 2011–12
Paul Buckle 2012–13
John Still 2013–15
Nathan Jones January 2016–

LATEST SEQUENCES

Longest Sequence of League Wins: 12, 19.2.2002 – 6.4.2002.

Longest Sequence of League Defeats: 8, 11.11.1899 – 6.1.1900.

Longest Sequence of League Draws: 5, 28.8.1971 – 18.9.1971.

Longest Sequence of Unbeaten League Matches: 19, 8.4.1969 – 7.10.1969.

Longest Sequence Without a League Win: 16, 9.9.1964 – 6.11.1964.

Successive Scoring Runs: 25 from 24.10.1931.

Successive Non-scoring Runs: 5 from 10.4.1973.

TEN YEAR LEAGUE RECORD

		P	W	D	L	F	A	Pts	Pos
2007-08	FL 1	46	11	10	25	43	63	33*	24
2008-09	FL 2	46	13	17	16	58	65	26†	24
2009-10	Conf P	44	26	10	8	84	40	88	2
2010-11	Conf P	46	23	15	8	85	37	84	3
2011-12	Conf P	46	22	15	9	78	42	81	5
2012-13	Conf P	46	18	13	15	70	62	67	7
2013-14	Conf P	46	30	11	5	102	35	101	1
2014-15	FL 2	46	19	11	16	54	44	68	8
2015-16	FL 2	46	19	9	18	63	61	66	11
2016-17	FL 2	46	20	17	9	70	43	77	4

**10 pts deducted; †30 points deducted.*

DID YOU KNOW?

Luton Town's visit to Newcastle's St James' Park on 3 January 1948 attracted a crowd of 64,931. This is the highest attendance for any Football League match which the Hatters have played in, either home or away.

LUTON TOWN – SKY BET LEAGUE TWO 2016–17 LEAGUE RECORD

Match No.	*Date*	*Venue*	*Opponents*	*Result*		*H/T Score*	*Lg Pos.*	*Goalscorers*	*Attendance*
1	Aug 6	A	Plymouth Arg	W	3-0	0-0	1	Hylton [50], Marriott [69], Smith [90]	9761
2	13	H	Yeovil T	D	1-1	1-0	1	O'Donnell [26]	7800
3	16	H	Newport Co	W	2-1	0-0	1	McGeehan 2 (2 pens) [62, 90]	7058
4	20	A	Stevenage	L	1-2	1-0	3	McGeehan [15]	3517
5	27	A	Cambridge U	W	3-0	0-0	2	Coulson (og) [62], Marriott [63], Hylton [90]	5606
6	Sept 3	H	Wycombe W	W	4-1	1-0	1	Hylton 3 (1 pen) [10, 56, 88 (p)], Cook [90]	8097
7	10	H	Grimsby T	L	1-2	0-1	3	Rea [59]	8005
8	17	A	Crawley T	L	0-2	0-1	6		2904
9	24	H	Doncaster R	W	3-1	2-1	2	McGeehan 2 (1 pen) [36, 81 (p)], Marriott [41]	7917
10	27	A	Hartlepool U	D	1-1	0-1	2	Sheehan [78]	3533
11	Oct 1	A	Cheltenham T	D	1-1	0-0	4	Hylton [52]	3660
12	8	H	Crewe Alex	D	1-1	1-0	4	Hylton [44]	7716
13	15	A	Leyton Orient	W	2-1	1-0	4	McGeehan [30], Hylton [74]	5471
14	22	H	Mansfield T	D	1-1	0-1	4	McGeehan [77]	7787
15	29	A	Notts Co	D	0-0	0-0	4		6313
16	Nov 12	H	Accrington S	W	1-0	0-0	4	McGeehan [75]	8008
17	19	A	Morecambe	W	2-0	1-0	4	Hylton [26], Vassell [60]	1507
18	22	H	Portsmouth	L	1-3	1-2	5	Hylton [7]	8805
19	26	A	Exeter C	D	0-0	0-0	5		3823
20	Dec 10	H	Carlisle U	D	1-1	1-1	5	Hylton [10]	7953
21	17	A	Blackpool	W	2-0	1-0	4	Marriott [31], McGeehan [48]	3992
22	26	H	Colchester U	L	0-1	0-0	5		9164
23	31	H	Barnet	W	3-1	1-1	5	Sheehan [31], McGeehan [49], Gilliead [56]	8262
24	Jan 2	A	Portsmouth	L	0-1	0-1	6		17,402
25	14	A	Crewe Alex	W	2-1	1-1	5	Marriott [45], Gray [69]	4368
26	21	A	Wycombe W	D	1-1	0-0	6	Cuthbert [56]	5387
27	28	H	Cambridge U	W	2-0	1-0	4	Vassell [33], Cook (pen) [82]	8917
28	31	H	Cheltenham T	L	2-3	1-2	5	Vassell [41], Davis (og) [72]	6708
29	Feb 4	A	Grimsby T	D	1-1	0-0	5	Vassell [77]	5114
30	11	H	Crawley T	W	2-1	0-0	4	Hylton 2 [70, 76]	7316
31	14	H	Hartlepool U	W	3-0	2-0	4	Hylton [5], Gambin [13], Palmer [81]	6965
32	18	A	Doncaster R	D	1-1	0-0	4	Cook [54]	7506
33	25	H	Plymouth Arg	D	1-1	1-1	5	Hylton [8]	9124
34	Mar 4	A	Yeovil T	W	4-0	2-0	4	Hylton 2 (1 pen) [7 (p), 31], Rea [55], Ruddock [85]	4194
35	11	H	Stevenage	L	0-2	0-1	6		9045
36	14	A	Carlisle U	D	0-0	0-0	5		4052
37	18	H	Exeter C	D	1-1	0-0	5	Hylton [68]	7657
38	21	A	Newport Co	D	1-1	1-1	5	Hylton (pen) [5]	2304
39	25	A	Colchester U	L	1-2	0-2	6	Vassell [90]	5445
40	Apr 1	H	Blackpool	W	1-0	0-0	5	Palmer [90]	7968
41	8	A	Barnet	W	1-0	0-0	4	Lee [67]	3313
42	14	H	Leyton Orient	D	2-2	1-0	4	Hylton [33], Vassell [73]	8601
43	17	A	Mansfield T	D	1-1	0-1	4	Hylton (pen) [51]	4632
44	22	H	Notts Co	W	2-1	2-1	4	Palmer [16], Ruddock [45]	7719
45	29	A	Accrington S	W	4-1	1-1	4	Justin [28], Beckles (og) [49], Vassell [54], Marriott [90]	2150
46	May 6	H	Morecambe	W	3-1	1-0	4	Vassell [28], Marriott 2 [74, 86]	8399

Final League Position: 4

GOALSCORERS

League (70): Hylton 21 (4 pens), McGeehan 10 (3 pens), Marriott 8, Vassell 8, Cook 3 (1 pen), Palmer 3, Rea 2, Ruddock 2, Sheehan 2, Cuthbert 1, Gambin 1, Gilliead 1, Gray 1, Justin 1, Lee 1, O'Donnell 1, Smith 1, own goals 3.
FA Cup (10): Hylton 3 (2 pens), Marriott 2, O'Donnell 2, Gray 1, Mullins 1, Rea 1.
EFL Cup (3): Gray 1, McGeehan 1, own goal 1.
EFL Checkatrade Trophy (19): Vassell 5, Hylton 2, Marriott 2, McQuoid 2, Cook 1, Gilliead 1, Gray 1, Mackail-Smith 1 (1 pen), Musonda 1, Sheehan 1, Smith 1, own goal 1.
League Two Play-Offs (5): Cuthbert 1, Hylton 1 (1 pen), Potts 1, Vassell 1, own goal 1.

Walton C 27	O'Donnell S 27 + 3	Mullins J 21 + 2	Cuthbert S 37 + 1	Potts D 22 + 1	Ruddock P 34 + 8	Rea G 36 + 3	Cook J 31 + 4	McGeehan C 24	Hylton D 38 + 1	Marriott J 25 + 14	Smith J 12 + 13	Gray J 11 + 8	Lee O 24 + 9	Vassell I 22 + 18	Famewo A 1 + 2	McQuoid J 1 + 2	Sheehan A 31 + 3	Gilliead A 10 + 8	Justin J 24 + 5	Mackail-Smith C — + 2	D'Ath L 8 + 3	Senior J 9 + 1	Gambin L 8 + 8	Moore S 8	Palmer O 4 + 13	Macey M 11	*Match No.*
1	2	3	4	5■	6^{3}	7	8^{1}	9	10	11^{2}	12	13	14														1
1	2	3	4	5	6^{1}	8	9	7^{2}	10	11^{3}	13	12		14													2
1	2	3■	4	5	7		8^{2}	9	11	10^{1}			6	13	12												3
1	2		4	5	12	3	9	8^{1}	11	10^{3}		7^{2}	6	13		14											4
1	2	4	12	5	8^{3}	3	7	9	11	10^{2}	13		6^{1}	14													5
1	2	4	3	5	7^{3}		11	6	10^{2}	8^{1}	12		9	13	14												6
1	2	4		5	8^{1}	13	7	9	10^{3}	11			6^{2}	12			3	14									7
1	2	3		5			8	9	13	12	7^{2}		6	10^{1}		11^{3}	4	14									8
1		4	3^{1}	5	8		9^{2}	7^{3}	10■	11		13	6				12	14	2								9
1				5	9		13	7		10		6^{1}	8	12	3		4	11^{2}	2								10
1			4	5	9^{2}		8	6	11	10^{1}	12		7				3	13	2								11
1			3	5	7^{3}	13		9	10	11^{1}		8	6^{2}			14	4	12	2								12
1	2	14	3	5		6	8^{3}	7^{1}	10	11	12	13					4	9^{2}									13
1	2		3	5^{2}	12	6	11^{1}	7		10		8^{3}	14	13			4	9									14
1	11	4	3		13	7	8	6^{1}	10	2^{2}			12	14			5	9^{3}									15
1		14	4			3	8■	7	10	11^{2}	13		6^{1}	12			5	9^{3}	2								16
1		3			7^{2}	4		9	10	12	13	14	6	11^{1}			5	8^{3}	2								17
1		4			7	3	12	8	10	13			6	11^{2}			5	9^{1}	2^{3}	14							18
1		4	3		12	6	10^{2}	9	11	14			7^{3}	8^{1}			5	13	2								19
1	5	2	3	8	13	7	14	6	10	9^{2}				11^{3}			4^{1}	12									20
1	5	3	4		12	6		8^{3}	11	10^{1}	14		9	13				7^{2}	2								21
1	5	4	3		13	2	14	6	11	10^{1}			7^{2}	12				9^{3}	8								22
1	5	2	3	8^{1}		6	10	9^{2}	11		7		14				4^{3}	12	13								23
1	6	4	5		12	3	10^{3}	9^{2}	11		8		14	13				7^{1}	2								24
1		3	4		6		9^{3}		10	11^{2}	13	8		14			5■		2		7^{1}	12					25
1	14	4■	3		6	13			11^{3}	10^{2}	7	9^{1}		12					2			5	8				26
1			3		6	4	8			10^{3}	7			11			13		2	14	12	5^{1}	9^{2}				27
			3		6	4	9			10^{3}	7^{2}	14	12	11					2		13	5	8^{1}	1			28
			3		6	4	9		10	14		8^{1}		11^{3}			12		2			5	7^{2}	1	13		29
	2		3		7	6	9^{1}		10^{3}	14	8			11^{2}			4					5	13		12	1	30
	2	3			7	6			10^{2}	13	12			11^{3}			4				8^{1}	5	9		14	1	31
	2		3		7	6	9^{1}		11		8			10^{2}			4					5	13		12	1	32
			3		6	7	10		11	14	8^{3}			9^{1}			4		2			5^{2}	12		13	1	33
	2		3	12	6	4	9		10^{2}	14	8	7^{1}		11^{3}			5								13	1	34
	2		3^{2}	5^{3}	7	6	10^{1}		11		8			9			4		13				12		14	1	35
	3			2^{2}	7	8	10		11	12			4	9^{3}			5		13				6^{1}		14	1	36
	2				7	3	9^{2}		11	10^{1}	8		14	12			4					5	6^{3}		13	1	37
	2	3^{2}	4		8	5	7^{3}		10^{1}	14			13	9			6		12						11	1	38
	2		3		6	4	9^{2}			10^{1}		7^{3}	14	11			5		12		8				13	1	39
	2^{3}		4		8	3			10^{1}	13			9	11^{2}			5		6		7		14		12	1	40
	2^{2}		3		7	4			10		14		8	11^{3}			5		6		9^{1}		12	1	13		41
			3		9^{2}	4	8^{3}		10	11^{1}		14	7	13			5		2		6		12	1			42
	13		2	9^{1}	7	4			11				6	10^{2}			3		5		8			1	12		43
			4	6	7	5			11■			12	9	13			3		2		8^{1}			1	10^{2}		44
			3	9	7^{2}	2				12	13	6^{3}	8	10^{1}			4		5				14	1	11		45
	12		3	5	9	7				13		6	8	10^{3}					2^{1}		14		11^{2}	1	4		46

FA Cup

First Round	Exeter C	(a)	3-1
Second Round	Solihull Moors	(h)	6-2
Third Round	Accrington S	(a)	1-2

EFL Cup

First Round	Aston Villa	(h)	3-1
Second Round	Leeds U	(h)	0-1

EFL Checkatrade Trophy

Southern Group H	Gillingham	(a)	2-1
Southern Group H	WBA U21	(h)	2-0
Southern Group H	Millwall	(h)	1-3
Second Round South	Swindon T	(a)	3-2
Third Round	Chesterfield	(h)	4-0
Quarter-Final	Yeovil T	(h)	5-2
Semi-Final	Oxford U	(h)	2-3

League Two Play-Offs

Semi-Final 1st leg	Blackpool	(a)	2-3
Semi-Final 2nd leg	Blackpool	(h)	3-3

MANCHESTER CITY

FOUNDATION

Manchester City was formed as a limited company in 1894 after their predecessors Ardwick had been forced into bankruptcy. However, many historians like to trace the club's lineage as far back as 1880 when St Mark's Church, West Gorton added a football section to their cricket club. They amalgamated with Belle Vue for one season before splitting again under the name Gorton Association FC in 1884–85. In 1887 Gorton AFC turned professional and moved ground to Hyde Road under the new name Ardwick AFC.

Etihad Stadium, Etihad Campus, Manchester M11 3FF.

Telephone: (0161) 444 1894.

Fax: (0161) 438 7999.

Ticket Office: (0161) 444 1894.

Website: www.mancity.com

Email: mancity@mancity.com

Ground Capacity: 55,097.

Record Attendance: 84,569 v Stoke C, FA Cup 6th rd, 3 March 1934 (at Maine Road; British record for any game outside London or Glasgow); 54,693 v Leicester C, FA Premier League, 6 February 2016 (at Etihad Stadium).

Pitch Measurements: 105m × 68m (114yd × 74yd).

Chairman: Khaldoon Al Mubarak.

Chief Executive: Ferran Soriano.

Manager: Pep Guardiola

Assistant Managers: Domene Torrent, Brian Kidd.

Colours: Field blue shirts with dark blue trim, field blue shorts with dark blue trim, white socks.

Year Formed: 1887 as Ardwick FC; 1894 as Manchester City.

Turned Professional: 1887 as Ardwick FC.

Previous Names: 1880, St Mark's Church, West Gorton; 1884, Gorton; 1887, Ardwick; 1894, Manchester City.

Club Nicknames: 'The Blues', 'The Citizens'.

Grounds: 1880, Clowes Street; 1881, Kirkmanshulme Cricket Ground; 1882, Queens Road; 1884, Pink Bank Lane; 1887, Hyde Road (1894–1923 as City); 1923, Maine Road; 2003, City of Manchester Stadium (renamed Etihad Stadium 2011).

First Football League Game: 3 September 1892, Division 2, v Bootle (h) W 7–0 – Douglas; McVickers, Robson; Middleton, Russell, Hopkins; Davies (3), Morris (2), Angus (1), Weir (1), Milarvie.

Record League Victory: 10–1 v Huddersfield T, Division 2, 7 November 1987 – Nixon; Gidman, Hinchcliffe, Clements, Lake, Redmond, White (3), Stewart (3), Adcock (3), McNab (1), Simpson.

Record Cup Victory: 10–1 v Swindon T, FA Cup 4th rd, 29 January 1930 – Barber; Felton, McCloy; Barrass, Cowan, Heinemann; Toseland, Marshall (5), Tait (3), Johnson (1), Brook (1).

HONOURS

League Champions: FA Premier League – 2011–12, 2013–14; Division 1 – 1936–37, 1967–68; First Division – 2001–02; Division 2 – 1898–99, 1902–03, 1909–10, 1927–28, 1946–47, 1965–66.
Runners-up: FA Premier League – 2012–13, 2014–15; Division 1 – 1903–04, 1920–21, 1976–77; First Division – 1999–2000; Division 2 – 1895–96, 1950–51, 1988–89.

FA Cup Winners: 1904, 1934, 1956, 1969, 2011.
Runners-up: 1926, 1933, 1955, 1981, 2013.

League Cup Winners: 1970, 1976, 2014, 2016.
Runners-up: 1974.

Full Members Cup: *Runners-up:* 1986.

European Competitions
European Cup: 1968–69.
Champions League: 2011–12, 2012–13, 2013–14, 2014–15, 2015–16 *(sf)*, 2016–17.
UEFA Cup: 1972–73, 1976–77, 1977–78, 1978–79 *(qf)*, 2003–04, 2008–09 *(qf)*.
Europa League: 2010–11, 2011–12.
European Cup-Winners' Cup: 1969–70 *(winners)*, 1970–71 *(sf)*.

sky SPORTS FACT FILE

Manchester City attracted a new record attendance of 41,709 to Hyde Road for the FA Cup tie with Sunderland on 1 February 1913. However, the ground was so overcrowded the match started 20 minutes late and play was interrupted before the game was eventually abandoned after an hour with the visitors leading 2-0. City were subsequently fined £500 by the FA.

Record Defeat: 1–9 v Everton, Division 1, 3 September 1906.

Most League Points (2 for a win): 62, Division 2, 1946–47.

Most League Points (3 for a win): 99, Division 1, 2001–02.

Most League Goals: 108, Division 2, 1926–27, 108, Division 1, 2001–02.

Highest League Scorer in Season: Tommy Johnson, 38, Division 1, 1928–29.

Most League Goals in Total Aggregate: Tommy Johnson, 158, 1919–30.

Most League Goals in One Match: 5, Fred Williams v Darwen, Division 2, 18 February 1899; 5, Tom Browell v Burnley, Division 2, 24 October 1925; 5, Tom Johnson v Everton, Division 1, 15 September 1928; 5, George Smith v Newport Co, Division 2, 14 June 1947; 5, Sergio Aguero v Newcastle U, FA Premier League, 3 October 2015.

Most Capped Player: David Silva, 75 (113), Spain.

Most League Appearances: Alan Oakes, 564, 1959–76.

Youngest League Player: Glyn Pardoe, 15 years 314 days v Birmingham C, 11 April 1962.

Record Transfer Fee Received: £22,000,000 from Valencia for Álvaro Negredo, July 2015.

Record Transfer Fee Paid: £55,000,000 to Wolfsburg for Kevin De Bruyne, August 2015.

Football League Record: 1892 Ardwick elected founder member of Division 2; 1894 Newly-formed Manchester C elected to Division 2; Division 1 1899–1902, 1903–09, 1910–26, 1928–38, 1947–50, 1951–63, 1966–83, 1985–87, 1989–92; Division 2 1902–03, 1909–10, 1926–28, 1938–47, 1950–51, 1963–66, 1983–85, 1987–89; 1992–96 FA Premier League; 1996–98 Division 1; 1998–99 Division 2; 1999–2000 Division 1; 2000–01 FA Premier League; 2001–02 Division 1; 2002– FA Premier League.

LATEST SEQUENCES

Longest Sequence of League Wins: 11, 19.4.2015 – 12.9.2015.

Longest Sequence of League Defeats: 8, 23.8.1995 – 14.10.1995.

Longest Sequence of League Draws: 7, 5.10.2009 – 28.11.2009.

Longest Sequence of Unbeaten League Matches: 22, 16.11.1946 – 19.4.1947.

Longest Sequence Without a League Win: 17, 26.12.1979 – 7.4.1980.

Successive Scoring Runs: 44 from 3.10.1936.

Successive Non-scoring Runs: 6 from 30.1.1971.

MANAGERS

Joshua Parlby 1893–95 *(Secretary-Manager)*
Sam Omerod 1895–1902
Tom Maley 1902–06
Harry Newbould 1906–12
Ernest Magnall 1912–24
David Ashworth 1924–25
Peter Hodge 1926–32
Wilf Wild 1932–46 *(continued as Secretary to 1950)*
Sam Cowan 1946–47
John 'Jock' Thomson 1947–50
Leslie McDowall 1950–63
George Poyser 1963–65
Joe Mercer 1965–71 *(continued as General Manager to 1972)*
Malcolm Allison 1972–73
Johnny Hart 1973
Ron Saunders 1973–74
Tony Book 1974–79
Malcolm Allison 1979–80
John Bond 1980–83
John Benson 1983
Billy McNeill 1983–86
Jimmy Frizzell 1986–87 *(continued as General Manager)*
Mel Machin 1987–89
Howard Kendall 1989–90
Peter Reid 1990–93
Brian Horton 1993–95
Alan Ball 1995–96
Steve Coppell 1996
Frank Clark 1996–98
Joe Royle 1998–2001
Kevin Keegan 2001–05
Stuart Pearce 2005–07
Sven-Göran Eriksson 2007–08
Mark Hughes 2008–09
Roberto Mancini 2009–13
Manuel Pellegrini 2013–16
Pep Guardiola June 2016–

TEN YEAR LEAGUE RECORD

		P	W	D	L	F	A	Pts	Pos
2007-08	PR Lge	38	15	10	13	45	53	55	9
2008-09	PR Lge	38	15	5	18	58	50	50	10
2009-10	PR Lge	38	18	13	7	73	45	67	5
2010-11	PR Lge	38	21	8	9	60	33	71	3
2011-12	PR Lge	38	28	5	5	93	29	89	1
2012-13	PR Lge	38	23	9	6	66	34	78	2
2013-14	PR Lge	38	27	5	6	102	37	86	1
2014-15	PR Lge	38	24	7	7	83	38	79	2
2015-16	PR Lge	38	19	9	10	71	41	66	4
2016-17	PR Lge	38	23	9	6	80	39	78	3

DID YOU KNOW?

Going into the final game of the 1997–98 season, Manchester City's fate was still not decided. Despite winning 5-2 against Stoke both teams were relegated to the third level of English football as both Portsmouth and Port Vale gained away victories.

MANCHESTER CITY – PREMIER LEAGUE 2016–17 LEAGUE RECORD

Match No.	*Date*	*Venue*	*Opponents*	*Result*	*H/T Score*	*Lg Pos.*	*Goalscorers*	*Attendance*
1	Aug 13	H	Sunderland	W 2-1	1-0	2	Aguero (pen) [4], McNair (og) [87]	54,362
2	20	A	Stoke C	W 4-1	2-0	1	Aguero 2 (1 pen) [27 (p), 36], Nolito 2 [86, 90]	27,455
3	28	H	West Ham U	W 3-1	2-0	1	Sterling 2 [7, 90], Fernandinho [18]	54,008
4	Sept 10	A	Manchester U	W 2-1	2-1	1	De Bruyne [15], Iheanacho [36]	75,272
5	17	H	Bournemouth	W 4-0	2-0	1	De Bruyne [15], Iheanacho [25], Sterling [48], Gundogan [66]	54,335
6	24	A	Swansea C	W 3-1	1-1	1	Aguero 2 (1 pen) [9, 65 (p)], Sterling [77]	20,786
7	Oct 2	A	Tottenham H	L 0-2	0-2	1		31,793
8	15	H	Everton	D 1-1	0-0	1	Nolito [72]	54,512
9	23	H	Southampton	D 1-1	0-1	1	Iheanacho [55]	53,731
10	29	A	WBA	W 4-0	2-0	1	Aguero 2 [19, 28], Gundogan 2 [79, 90]	22,470
11	Nov 5	H	Middlesbrough	D 1-1	1-0	2	Aguero [43]	54,294
12	19	A	Crystal Palace	W 2-1	1-0	1	Toure 2 [39, 83]	25,529
13	26	A	Burnley	W 2-1	1-1	1	Aguero 2 [37, 60]	21,794
14	Dec 3	H	Chelsea	L 1-3	1-0	3	Cahill (og) [45]	54,457
15	10	A	Leicester C	L 2-4	0-3	4	Kolarov [82], Nolito [90]	31,966
16	14	H	Watford	W 2-0	1-0	3	Zabaleta [33], Silva [86]	51,527
17	18	H	Arsenal	W 2-1	0-1	2	Sane [47], Sterling [71]	54,409
18	26	A	Hull C	W 3-0	0-0	2	Toure (pen) [72], Iheanacho [78], Davies (og) [90]	23,134
19	31	A	Liverpool	L 0-1	0-1	3		53,120
20	Jan 2	H	Burnley	W 2-1	0-0	3	Clichy [58], Aguero [62]	54,463
21	15	A	Everton	L 0-4	0-1	5		39,588
22	21	H	Tottenham H	D 2-2	0-0	5	Sane [49], De Bruyne [54]	54,402
23	Feb 1	A	West Ham U	W 4-0	3-0	5	De Bruyne [17], Silva [21], Gabriel Jesus [39], Toure (pen) [67]	56,980
24	5	H	Swansea C	W 2-1	1-0	3	Gabriel Jesus 2 [11, 90]	54,065
25	13	A	Bournemouth	W 2-0	1-0	2	Sterling [29], Mings (og) [69]	11,129
26	Mar 5	A	Sunderland	W 2-0	1-0	2	Aguero [42], Sane [59]	41,107
27	8	H	Stoke C	D 0-0	0-0	3		52,625
28	19	H	Liverpool	D 1-1	0-0	2	Aguero [69]	54,449
29	Apr 2	A	Arsenal	D 2-2	2-1	4	Sane [5], Aguero [42]	60,001
30	5	A	Chelsea	L 1-2	1-2	4	Aguero [26]	41,528
31	8	H	Hull C	W 3-1	1-0	4	Elmohamady (og) [31], Aguero [48], Delph [64]	54,393
32	15	A	Southampton	W 3-0	0-0	3	Kompany [55], Sane [77], Aguero [80]	31,850
33	27	H	Manchester U	D 0-0	0-0	4		54,176
34	30	A	Middlesbrough	D 2-2	0-1	4	Aguero (pen) [69], Gabriel Jesus [85]	29,763
35	May 6	H	Crystal Palace	W 5-0	1-0	3	Silva [2], Kompany [49], De Bruyne [59], Sterling [82], Otamendi [90]	54,119
36	13	H	Leicester C	W 2-1	2-1	3	Silva [29], Gabriel Jesus (pen) [36]	54,407
37	16	H	WBA	W 3-1	2-0	3	Gabriel Jesus [27], De Bruyne [29], Toure [57]	53,624
38	21	A	Watford	W 5-0	4-0	3	Kompany [5], Aguero 2 [23, 36], Fernandinho [41], Gabriel Jesus [58]	20,829

Final League Position: 3

GOALSCORERS

League (80): Aguero 20 (4 pens), Gabriel Jesus 7 (1 pen), Sterling 7, De Bruyne 6, Sane 5, Toure 5 (2 pens), Iheanacho 4, Nolito 4, Silva 4, Gundogan 3, Kompany 3, Fernandinho 2, Clichy 1, Delph 1, Kolarov 1, Otamendi 1, Zabaleta 1, own goals 5.
FA Cup (16): Aguero 5 (1 pen), Sane 2, Silva 2, Toure 2 (1 pen), Iheanacho 1, Sterling 1, Stones 1, Zabaleta 1, own goal 1.
EFL Cup (2): Clichy 1, Garcia 1.
UEFA Champions League (24): Aguero 8, Gundogan 2, Iheanacho 2, Nolito 2, Sane 2, Silva 2, Sterling 2, De Bruyne 1, Delph 1, Fernandinho 1, Stones 1.

Caballero W 16 + 1	Sagna B 14 + 3	Stones J 23 + 4	Kolarov A 27 + 2	Clichy G 24 + 1	Fernandinho L 31 + 1	Silva D 31 + 3	Sterling R 29 + 4	De Bruyne K 33 + 3	Nolito M 9 + 10	Aguero S 25 + 6	Jesus Navas G 12 + 12	Delph F 2 + 5	Iheanacho K 5 + 15	Zabaleta P 11 + 9	Otamendi N 29 + 1	Nasri S — + 1	Fernando F 5 + 10	Bravo C 22	Sane L 20 + 6	Gundogan I 9 + 1	Garcia A 1 + 3	Kompany V 10 + 1	Toure Y 22 + 3	Gabriel Jesus F 8 + 2	*Match No.*
1	2	3	4	5[3]	6	7[2]	8	9	10[1]	11	12	13	14												1
1		4	5		7	8	11	6[1]	12	10[2]	9[3]	14	13	2	3										2
1		3[2]	12	5	7	8	9	6	11[3]	10[1]				2	4	13	14								3
	2	3	5		7	8	9[2]	6[3]	11				10[1]	14	4		12	1	13						4
	2	12	4	5	6		8	9[3]	10■				11		3[2]			1	13	7[1]	14				5
	2[1]	4	5		6	9	7	10[2]		11	14			13	3		12	1		8[3]					6
		4	5		7	9	10[3]			11	8[1]		13	2	3		6[2]	1	14	12					7
		3		4	6	8	11	9	13	12			10[3]		2			1	5[2]	7[1]		14			8
		2	4		6	10	8	9[1]	14	11	13		12					1	5[3]	7		3[2]			9
		3	5		7	9[1]	8[3]	12	10[2]	11	13				4		2	1		6	14				10
		3	4	5	6	10		8	12	11[1]	7[2]		14	2				1		9[3]	13				11
	2		5		6	13	8	9	10[2]	11[3]				12	4		14	1				3[1]	7		12
	2		4	5	6		8[1]	13	10[3]	11[2]	14				3		7	1	12				9		13
		3[3]	4	12	6■	10		9		11■	5		14		2			1	8[2]	7[1]			13		14
	2	3	4			7	12	11	14		9[2]		10[3]	5			6	1		8[1]			13		15
			4	5		10	8	9[1]	11[3]		13			2	3		12	1	14	7[2]			6		16
	12		4	5		9	11	10[1]			13		14	2[2]	3		6	1	7[3]				8		17
	2	4[3]	12	5	6	9[1]	8	11	10[2]				13		3		14	1					7		18
		3	5		7	10	8	9		11	12		13	2[2]	4			1					6[1]		19
	2	14	4	5	7■	13	10[2]	9		12	8[1]		11[3]		3			1					6		20
	2	4		5		9	8	10		11			12	6[1]	3			1					7		21
		13	4	5[1]		9[3]	7[2]	8		11		14		2	3			1	10				6	12	22
1	2	3	5		12	9[2]	7[3]	8[1]		13		14			4				10				6	11	23
1		3	4	5	2	8[1]	9[2]	6[3]		13				12			14		11				7	10	24
1	2	3	4		5	8	9[2]	6	14	12					13				11				7[1]	10[3]	25
1	2	3	4	5	6	8	9[1]	12	13	10		14							11[2]				7[3]		26
1	2		4	5	6	12		9		11	7[2]		13		3				10				8[1]		27
1	12	3		5	2	9	7	8		11					4		13		10[2]				6[1]		28
1		3		5	6	9[1]	8[2]	7		11	2			13	4				10				12		29
1		3		5	6	9	12	8[2]	13	11	2	7							10[1]			4			30
		3	4	5		9[2]	8		12	11	2	7	13				14	1	10[3]				6[1]		31
				5	6	9[2]	13	8		11[3]	2		14	12	4			1	10[1]			3	7		32
12			5		7		8[3]	9		11	13			2	4			1[1]	10[2]			3	6	14	33
1			4	8[2]	6		13	9	14	10[3]	5				2				12		7[1]	3		11	34
1				5	2	9[2]	10	8			14		13	12	4				7[3]			3	6	11[1]	35
1				5	2	9	7[2]	8[3]		12	14			13	4				10			3	6	11[1]	36
1		13	5		2	9[1]		8		11				12	4		14		10			3[3]	6[2]	7	37
1	13			5	2	7		9		11[2]	12		14		4				10[3]			3	6[1]	8	38

FA Cup

Third Round	West Ham U	(a)	5-0
Fourth Round	Crystal Palace	(a)	3-0
Fifth Round	Huddersfield T	(a)	0-0
Replay	Huddersfield T	(h)	5-1
Sixth Round	Middlesbrough	(a)	2-0
Semi-Final	Arsenal	(a)	1-2
(*aet*)			

EFL Cup

Third Round	Swansea C	(a)	2-1
Fourth Round	Manchester U	(a)	0-1

UEFA Champions League

Play-off Round 1st leg	Steau Bucharest	(a)	5-0
Play-off Round 2nd leg	Steau Bucharest	(h)	1-0
Manchester C won 6-0 on aggregate.			
Group C	Borussia M'gladbach	(h)	4-0
Group C	Celtic	(a)	3-3
Group C	Barcelona	(a)	0-4
Group C	Barcelona	(h)	3-1
Group C	Borussia M'gladbach	(a)	1-1
Group C	Celtic	(h)	1-1
Round of 16 1st leg	Monaco	(h)	5-3
Round of 16 2nd leg	Monaco	(a)	1-3

Monaco won on away goals (6-6 on aggregate).

MANCHESTER UNITED

FOUNDATION

Manchester United was formed as comparatively recently as 1902 after their predecessors, Newton Heath, went bankrupt. However, it is usual to give the date of the club's foundation as 1878 when the dining room committee of the carriage and waggon works of the Lancashire and Yorkshire Railway Company formed Newton Heath L and YR Cricket and Football Club. They won the Manchester Cup in 1886 and as Newton Heath FC were admitted to the Second Division in 1892.

Old Trafford, Sir Matt Busby Way, Manchester M16 0RA.

Telephone: (0161) 868 8000.

Fax: (0161) 868 8804.

Ticket Office: (0161) 868 8000 (option 1).

Website: www.manutd.co.uk

Email: enquiries@manutd.co.uk

Ground Capacity: 75,643.

Record Attendance: 76,098 v Blackburn R, FA Premier League, 31 March 2007.

Ground Record Attendance: 76,962 Wolverhampton W v Grimsby T, FA Cup semi-final, 25 March 1939.

Pitch Measurements: 105m × 68m (114yd × 74yd).

Co-Chairmen: Joel and Avram Glazer.

Chief Executive: Edward Woodward.

Manager: Jose Mourinho.

Assistant Manager: Rui Faria.

Colours: Red shirts with white trim, white shorts with red trim, black socks with red trim.

Year Formed: 1878 as Newton Heath LYR; 1902, Manchester United.

Turned Professional: 1885.

Previous Name: 1880, Newton Heath; 1902, Manchester United.

Club Nickname: 'Red Devils'.

Grounds: 1880, North Road, Monsall Road; 1893, Bank Street; 1910, Old Trafford (played at Maine Road 1941–49).

HONOURS

League Champions: FA Premier League – 1992–93, 1993–94, 1995–96, 1996–97, 1998–99, 1999–2000, 2000–01, 2002–03, 2006–07, 2007–08, 2008–09, 2010–11, 2012–13; Division 1 – 1907–08, 1910–11, 1951–52, 1955–56, 1956–57, 1964–65, 1966–67; Division 2 – 1935–36, 1974–75.
Runners-up: FA Premier League – 1994–95, 1997–98, 2005–06, 2009–10, 2011–12; Division 1 – 1946–47, 1947–48, 1948–49, 1950–51, 1958–59, 1963–64, 1967–68, 1979–80, 1987–88, 1991–92; Division 2 – 1896–97, 1905–06, 1924–25, 1937–38.

FA Cup Winners: 1909, 1948, 1963, 1977, 1983, 1985, 1990, 1994, 1996, 1999, 2004, 2016.
Runners-up: 1957, 1958, 1976, 1979, 1995, 2005, 2007.

League Cup Winners: 1992, 2006, 2009, 2010, 2017.
Runners-up: 1983, 1991, 1994, 2003.

European Competitions
European Cup: 1956–57 *(sf)*, 1957–58 *(sf)*, 1965–66 *(sf)*, 1967–68 *(winners)*, 1968–69 *(sf)*.
Champions League: 1993–94, 1994–95, 1996–97 *(sf)*, 1997–98 *(qf)*, 1998–99 *(winners)*, 1999–2000 *(qf)*, 2000–01 *(qf)*, 2001–02 *(sf)*, 2002–03 *(qf)*, 2003–04, 2004–05, 2005–06, 2006–07 *(sf)*, 2007–08 *(winners)*, 2008–09 *(runners-up)*, 2009–10 *(qf)*, 2010–11 *(runners-up)*, 2011–12, 2012–13, 2013–14 *(qf)*, 2015–16.
Fairs Cup: 1964–65.
UEFA Cup: 1976–77, 1980–81, 1982–83, 1984–85 *(qf)*, 1992–93, 1995–96.
Europa League: 2011–12, 2015–16, 2016–17 *(winners)*.
European Cup-Winners' Cup: 1963–64 *(qf)*, 1977–78, 1983–84 *(sf)*, 1990–91 *(winners)*, 1991–92.
Super Cup: 1991 *(winners)*, 1999, 2008.
World Club Championship: 1968, 1999 *(winners)*, 2000.
FIFA Club World Cup: 2008 *(winners)*.
NB: In 1958–59 FA refused permission to compete in European Cup.

sky SPORTS FACT FILE

Sandy Turnbull had the distinction of scoring the first goal at the newly opened Old Trafford on 19 February 1910 when he netted against Liverpool. The stadium, which replaced United's old ground at Clayton, was originally due to open in October the previous year but the work was delayed. The first game attracted an attendance estimated at 50,000.

MANAGERS

J. Ernest Mangnall 1903–12
John Bentley 1912–14
John Robson 1914–21
(Secretary-Manager from 1916)
John Chapman 1921–26
Clarence Hilditch 1926–27
Herbert Bamlett 1927–31
Walter Crickmer 1931–32
Scott Duncan 1932–37
Walter Crickmer 1937–45
(Secretary-Manager)
Matt Busby 1945–69
(continued as General Manager then Director)
Wilf McGuinness 1969–70
Sir Matt Busby 1970–71
Frank O'Farrell 1971–72
Tommy Docherty 1972–77
Dave Sexton 1977–81
Ron Atkinson 1981–86
Sir Alex Ferguson 1986–2013
David Moyes 2013–14
Louis van Gaal 2014–16
Jose Mourinho June 2016–

First Football League Game: 3 September 1892, Division 1, v Blackburn R (a) L 3–4 – Warner; Clements, Brown; Perrins, Stewart, Erentz; Farman (1), Coupar (1), Donaldson (1), Carson, Mathieson.

Record League Victory (as Newton Heath): 10–1 v Wolverhampton W, Division 1, 15 October 1892 – Warner; Mitchell, Clements; Perrins, Stewart (3), Erentz; Farman (1), Hood (1), Donaldson (3), Carson (1), Hendry (1).

Record League Victory (as Manchester U): 9–0 v Ipswich T, FA Premier League, 4 March 1995 – Schmeichel; Keane (1) (Sharpe), Irwin, Bruce (Butt), Kanchelskis, Pallister, Cole (5), Ince (1), McClair, Hughes (2), Giggs.

Record Cup Victory: 10–0 v RSC Anderlecht, European Cup prel. rd 2nd leg, 26 September 1956 – Wood; Foulkes, Byrne; Colman, Jones, Edwards; Berry (1), Whelan (2), Taylor (3), Viollet (4), Pegg.

Record Defeat: 0–7 v Blackburn R, Division 1, 10 April 1926; 0–7 v Aston Villa, Division 1, 27 December 1930; 0–7 v Wolverhampton W, Division 2, 26 December 1931.

Most League Points (2 for a win): 64, Division 1, 1956–57.

Most League Points (3 for a win): 92, FA Premier League, 1993–94.

Most League Goals: 103, Division 1, 1956–57 and 1958–59.

Highest League Scorer in Season: Dennis Viollet, 32, 1959–60.

Most League Goals in Total Aggregate: Bobby Charlton, 199, 1956–73.

Most League Goals in One Match: 5, Andy Cole v Ipswich T, FA Premier League, 3 March 1995; 5, Dimitar Berbatov v Blackburn R, FA Premier League, 27 November 2010.

Most Capped Player: Bobby Charlton, 106, England.

Most League Appearances: Ryan Giggs, 672, 1991–2014.

Youngest League Player: Jeff Whitefoot, 16 years 105 days v Portsmouth, 15 April 1950.

Record Transfer Fee Received: £80,000,000 from Real Madrid for Cristiano Ronaldo, July 2009.

Record Transfer Fee Paid: £89,300,000 to Juventus for Paul Pogba, August 2016.

Football League Record: 1892 Newton Heath elected to Division 1; 1894–1906 Division 2; 1906–22 Division 1; 1922–25 Division 2; 1925–31 Division 1; 1931–36 Division 2; 1936–37 Division 1; 1937–38 Division 2; 1938–74 Division 1; 1974–75 Division 2; 1975–92 Division 1; 1992– FA Premier League.

LATEST SEQUENCES

Longest Sequence of League Wins: 14, 15.10.1904 – 3.1.1905.

Longest Sequence of League Defeats: 14, 26.4.1930 – 25.10.1930.

Longest Sequence of League Draws: 6, 30.10.1988 – 27.11.1988.

Longest Sequence of Unbeaten League Matches: 29, 11.4.2010 – 1.2.2011.

Longest Sequence Without a League Win: 16, 19.4.1930 – 25.10.1930.

Successive Scoring Runs: 36 from 3.12.2007.

Successive Non-scoring Runs: 5 from 7.2.1981.

TEN YEAR LEAGUE RECORD

		P	W	D	L	F	A	Pts	Pos
2007-08	PR Lge	38	27	6	5	80	22	87	1
2008-09	PR Lge	38	28	6	4	68	24	90	1
2009-10	PR Lge	38	27	4	7	86	28	85	2
2010-11	PR Lge	38	23	11	4	78	37	80	1
2011-12	PR Lge	38	28	5	5	89	33	89	2
2012-13	PR Lge	38	28	5	5	86	43	89	1
2013-14	PR Lge	38	19	7	12	64	43	64	7
2014-15	PR Lge	38	20	10	8	62	37	70	4
2015-16	PR Lge	38	19	9	10	49	35	66	5
2016-17	PR Lge	38	18	15	5	54	29	69	6

DID YOU KNOW ?

In October 1977 United were forced to play their Cup Winners' Cup 1st rd 2nd leg tie against Saint-Etienne at Plymouth's ground. United were initially thrown out of the competition following crowd trouble at the 1st leg but were reinstated on condition the home leg was played at least 200km from home. United won the tie 2-0 going through 3-1 on aggregate.

MANCHESTER UNITED – PREMIER LEAGUE 2016–17 LEAGUE RECORD

Match No.	*Date*	*Venue*	*Opponents*	*Result*		*H/T Score*	*Lg Pos.*	*Goalscorers*	*Attendance*
1	Aug 14	A	Bournemouth	W	3-1	1-0	1	Mata [40], Rooney [59], Ibrahimovic [64]	11,355
2	19	H	Southampton	W	2-0	1-0	1	Ibrahimovic 2 (1 pen) [36, 52 (p)]	75,326
3	27	A	Hull C	W	1-0	0-0	2	Rashford [90]	24,560
4	Sept 10	H	Manchester C	L	1-2	1-2	3	Ibrahimovic [42]	75,272
5	18	A	Watford	L	1-3	0-1	7	Rashford [62]	21,118
6	24	H	Leicester C	W	4-1	4-0	5	Smalling [22], Mata [37], Rashford [40], Pogba [42]	75,256
7	Oct 2	H	Stoke C	D	1-1	0-0	6	Martial [69]	75,251
8	17	A	Liverpool	D	0-0	0-0	7		52,769
9	23	A	Chelsea	L	0-4	0-2	7		41,424
10	29	H	Burnley	D	0-0	0-0	7		75,325
11	Nov 6	A	Swansea C	W	3-1	3-0	6	Pogba [15], Ibrahimovic 2 [21, 33]	20,938
12	19	H	Arsenal	D	1-1	0-0	6	Mata [68]	75,264
13	27	H	West Ham U	D	1-1	1-1	6	Ibrahimovic [21]	75,313
14	Dec 4	A	Everton	D	1-1	1-0	6	Ibrahimovic [42]	39,550
15	11	H	Tottenham H	W	1-0	1-0	6	Mkhitaryan [29]	75,271
16	14	A	Crystal Palace	W	2-1	1-0	6	Pogba [45], Ibrahimovic [88]	25,547
17	17	A	WBA	W	2-0	1-0	6	Ibrahimovic 2 [5, 56]	26,308
18	26	H	Sunderland	W	3-1	1-0	6	Blind [39], Ibrahimovic [82], Mkhitaryan [86]	75,325
19	31	H	Middlesbrough	W	2-1	0-0	6	Martial [85], Pogba [86]	75,314
20	Jan 2	A	West Ham U	W	2-0	0-0	6	Mata [63], Ibrahimovic [78]	56,996
21	15	H	Liverpool	D	1-1	0-1	6	Ibrahimovic [84]	75,276
22	21	A	Stoke C	D	1-1	0-1	6	Rooney [90]	27,423
23	Feb 1	H	Hull C	D	0-0	0-0	6		75,297
24	5	A	Leicester C	W	3-0	2-0	6	Mkhitaryan [42], Ibrahimovic [44], Mata [49]	32,072
25	11	H	Watford	W	2-0	1-0	6	Mata [32], Martial [60]	75,301
26	Mar 4	H	Bournemouth	D	1-1	1-1	6	Rojo [23]	75,245
27	19	A	Middlesbrough	W	3-1	1-0	5	Fellaini [30], Lingard [62], Valencia [90]	32,689
28	Apr 1	H	WBA	D	0-0	0-0	5		75,397
29	4	H	Everton	D	1-1	0-1	5	Ibrahimovic (pen) [90]	75,272
30	9	A	Sunderland	W	3-0	1-0	5	Ibrahimovic [30], Mkhitaryan [46], Rashford [89]	43,779
31	16	H	Chelsea	W	2-0	1-0	5	Rashford [7], Ander Herrera [49]	75,272
32	23	A	Burnley	W	2-0	2-0	5	Martial [21], Rooney [39]	21,870
33	27	A	Manchester C	D	0-0	0-0	5		54,176
34	30	H	Swansea C	D	1-1	1-0	5	Rooney (pen) [45]	75,271
35	May 7	A	Arsenal	L	0-2	0-0	5		60,055
36	14	A	Tottenham H	L	1-2	0-1	6	Rooney [71]	31,848
37	17	A	Southampton	D	0-0	0-0	6		31,425
38	21	H	Crystal Palace	W	2-0	2-0	6	Harrop [15], Pogba [19]	75,254

Final League Position: 6

GOALSCORERS

League (54): Ibrahimovic 17 (2 pens), Mata 6, Pogba 5, Rashford 5, Rooney 5 (1 pen), Martial 4, Mkhitaryan 4, Ander Herrera 1, Blind 1, Fellaini 1, Harrop 1, Lingard 1, Rojo 1, Smalling 1, Valencia 1.
FA Cup (10): Rashford 3, Fellaini 1, Ibrahimovic 1, Martial 1, Mkhitaryan 1, Rooney 1, Schweinsteiger 1, Smalling 1.
EFL Cup (14): Ibrahimovic 4, Martial 2, Mata 2, Ander Herrera 1, Carrick 1, Fellaini 1, Lingard 1, Pogba 1, Rashford 1.
Community Shield (2): Ibrahimovic 1, Lingard 1.
UEFA Europa League (25): Mkhitaryan 6, Ibrahimovic 5 (1 pen), Pogba 3 (1 pen), Lingard 2, Mata 2, Rashford 2, Rooney 2, Fellani 1, Martial 1 (1 pen), own goal 1.

De Gea D 35	Valencia A 27 + 1	Bailly E 24 + 1	Blind D 20 + 3	Shaw L 9 + 2	Fellaini M 18 + 10	Ander Herrera A 27 + 4	Mata J 19 + 6	Rooney W 15 + 10	Martial A 18 + 7	Ibrahimovic Z 27 + 1	Mkhitaryan H 15 + 9	Schneiderlin M — + 3	Depay M — + 4	Pogba P 29 + 1	Smalling C 13 + 5	Rashford M 16 + 16	Lingard J 18 + 7	Young A 8 + 4	Carrick M 18 + 5	Rojo M 18 + 3	Darmian M 15 + 3	Jones P 18	Fosu-Mensah T 1 + 3	Romero S 2	Tuanzebe A 4	McTominay S 1 + 1	Castro J 1	Mitchell D 1	Harrop J 1	Gomes A — + 1	*Match No.*
1	2	3	4	5	6	7	8^1	9^2	10^3	11	12	13	14																		1
1	2	3	4	5	6	13	8^1	9^3	10^2	11	12			7	14																2
1	2	3	4	5	6		8^3	9^2	10^1	11	12			7	14	13															3
1	2	3	4	5^3	6	13		9	14	11	8^1			7		12	10^2														4
1	2^3	3		5^1	6		13	9	8^2	11			14	7	4	10		12													5
1	2	3	5			6	9^1	13		11				7	4	10^3	8^2	14	12												6
1	2	3	5			6^2	9^3	12	13	11			14	7	4	10	8^1														7
1	2	3	5	13	7	6		12		11				9	4	8^2		10^1													8
1	2	3^1	5		6^3	7	12		14	11				9	4	8	10^2			13											9
1			3	5	13	6■	9^1	12		11			14	7		10^3	8^2			4	2										10
1					7		8^3	10^1		11		13		9^2			12	2	6	4	5	3	14								11
1	2		13			6	9^1	12	11^2			14		8		10			7	4	5^3	3									12
1	2				14	6	9^2	12		11	13			7		10^3	8^1			4	5	3									13
1	2				13	6			11^2	10	9^1			8		12			7	4	5	3									14
1	2	13			14	6^1			11^3	10	9^2			8		12			7	4	5	3									15
1		2^1	5			6	9^2	11^3		10				8		14	13		7	4	12	3									16
1	2				13	6^3		11^2		10				8	14	12	9^1		7	4	5	3									17
1	2		5		14	6^1	9^2		13	10	12			8			11^3		7	4		3									18
1	2	3	5^2		6^1	7	12		11	10	9			8	4^3	14				13											19
1	2					6	12			10	11^2			8	14	13	9^3		7	4	5^1	3									20
1	2				14	6	13	12	11^3	10	9			8					7^2	4	5^1	3									21
1	2		5		6^1	7	9^3	13		10	11^2			8	3	12	14					4									22
1	2		5			6	14	12		10	9^2			8	13	11			7^3	4		3^1									23
1	2	3	12		13	7	6^2			11	9			8	4	10^1		14		5^3											24
1	2	3	5		12	6	8^1		10^3	11	9^2			7	4	13	14														25
1	2			5^3	14		8	9^1	10	11				7		12	13		6^2	4		3									26
1	8	2			7		9^2		13						3	11^3	10^1	5	6	12	14	4									27
1	2	3			7			12	10		9^1					11	8	5	6	4											28
1		3	5^3	14	8	6				10	13			12		11	9	2^2	7^1	4											29
		3	12	5^2	6	7			14	10	9^3			8		13	11^1			4	2			1							30
1	5	2			7	6				13				8		10^3	11^2	9^1	12	3	4		14								31
1		3	4		7	6		11	10^2		13			8^1		12	9^3	2	14		5										32
1	2	3	4		8■	6			11^1		10^3					9^2	12	14	7		5		13								33
1	12	3^2	4	5^3		6		9^1	10		14					11	8	2	7		13										34
1						6^2	9^3	8	10		11^1				3	13	12		7		5	4			2	14					35
1		2	5			13	9^1	10	11		12				3	14	8^3		6			4			7^2						36
		2			6^1	14	8^3	11	10		9				3	13			12		5	4		1	7^2						37
		3						10^1	13					8^2			9^3		12			4	2		7	6	1	5	11	14	38

FA Cup

Third Round	Reading	(h)	4-0
Fourth Round	Wigan Ath	(h)	4-0
Fifth Round	Blackburn R	(a)	2-1
Sixth Round	Chelsea	(a)	0-1

EFL Cup

Third Round	Northampton T	(a)	3-1
Fourth Round	Manchester C	(h)	1-0
Quarter-Final	West Ham U	(h)	4-1
Semi-Final 1st leg	Hull C	(h)	2-0
Semi-Final 2nd leg	Hull C	(a)	1-2
Final	Southampton	(h)	3-2

Community Shield

	Leicester C	Wembley	2-1

UEFA Europa League

Group A	Feyenoord	(a)	0-1
Group A	Zorya Luhansk	(h)	1-0
Group A	Fenerbache	(h)	4-1
Group A	Fenerbache	(a)	1-2
Group A	Feyenoord	(h)	4-0
Group A	Zorya Luhansk	(a)	2-0
Round of 32 1st leg	Saint Etienne	(h)	3-0
Round of 32 2nd leg	Saint Etienne	(a)	1-0
Manchester U won 4-0 on aggregate.			
Round of 16 1st leg	Rostov	(a)	1-1
Round of 16 2nd leg	Rostov	(h)	1-0
Manchester U won 2-1 on aggregate.			
Quarter-Finals 1st leg	Anderlecht	(a)	1-1
Quarter-Finals 2nd leg	Anderlecht	(h)	2-1
aet; Manchester U won 3-2 on aggregate.			
Semi-Finals 1st leg	Celta Vigo	(a)	1-0
Semi-Finals 2nd leg	Celta Vigo	(h)	1-1
Manchester U won 2-1 on aggregate.			
Final	Ajax	(Stockholm)	2-0

MANSFIELD TOWN

FOUNDATION

The club was formed as Mansfield Wesleyans in 1897, and changed their name to Mansfield Wesley in 1906 and Mansfield Town in 1910. This was after the Mansfield Wesleyan Chapel trustees had requested that the club change its name as 'it has no longer had any connection with either the chapel or school'. The new club participated in the Notts and Derby District League, but in the following season 1911–12 joined the Central Alliance.

One Call Stadium, Quarry Lane, Mansfield, Nottinghamshire NG18 5DA.

Telephone: (01623) 482 482.

Fax: (01623) 482 495.

Ticket Office: (01623) 482 482.

Website: www.mansfieldtown.net

Email: info@mansfieldtown.net

Ground Capacity: 9,186.

Record Attendance: 24,467 v Nottingham F, FA Cup 3rd rd, 10 January 1953.

Pitch Measurements: 100.5m × 64m (110yd × 70yd).

Chairman: John Radford.

Chief Executive: Carolyn Radford.

Manager: Steve Evans.

Assistant Manager: Paul Raynor.

Colours: Yellow shirts with blue stripe and trim, blue shorts, yellow socks with blue trim.

Year Formed: 1897.

Turned Professional: 1906.

Ltd Co.: 1922.

Previous Name: 1897, Mansfield Wesleyans; 1906, Mansfield Wesley; 1910, Mansfield Town.

Grounds: 1897–99, Westfield Lane; 1899–1901, Ratcliffe Gate; 1901–12, Newgate Lane; 1912–16, Ratcliffe Gate; 1916, Field Mill (renamed One Call Stadium 2012).

Club Nickname: 'The Stags'.

First Football League Game: 29 August 1931, Division 3 (S), v Swindon T (h) W 3–2 – Wilson; Clifford, England; Wake, Davis, Blackburn; Gilhespy, Readman (1), Johnson, Broom (2), Baxter.

Record League Victory: 9–2 v Rotherham U, Division 3 (N), 27 December 1932 – Wilson; Anthony, England; Davies, S. Robinson, Slack; Prior, Broom, Readman (3), Hoyland (3), Bowater (3).

Record Cup Victory: 8–0 v Scarborough (a), FA Cup 1st rd, 22 November 1952 – Bramley; Chessell, Bradley; Field, Plummer, Lewis; Scott, Fox (3), Marron (2), Sid Watson (1), Adam (2).

Record Defeat: 1–8 v Walsall, Division 3 (N), 19 January 1933.

Most League Points (2 for a win): 68, Division 4, 1974–75.

HONOURS

League Champions: Division 3 – 1976–77; Division 4 – 1974–75; Conference – 2012–13.
Runners-up: Division 3N – 1950–51, Third Division – (3rd) 2001–02 *(promoted to Second Division)*.

FA Cup: 6th rd – 1969.

League Cup: 5th rd – 1976.

League Trophy Winners: 1987.

sky SPORTS FACT FILE

Mansfield Town's Field Mill ground hosted two of the earliest games played in England under modern electrical floodlighting systems. In February 1930 around 6,000 attended the North Notts League Senior Cup final between Ollerton Forest and Welbeck Athletic and the following Wednesday Mansfield Town, then members of the Midland League, drew 2-2 with Shirebrook in a friendly game under the lights.

Most League Points (3 for a win): 81, Division 4, 1985–86.

Most League Goals: 108, Division 4, 1962–63.

Highest League Scorer in Season: Ted Harston, 55, Division 3 (N), 1936–37.

Most League Goals in Total Aggregate: Harry Johnson, 104, 1931–36.

Most League Goals in One Match: 7, Ted Harston v Hartlepools U, Division 3N, 23 January 1937.

Most Capped Player: John McClelland, 6 (53), Northern Ireland; Reggie Lambe, 6 (26), Bermuda.

Most League Appearances: Rod Arnold, 440, 1970–83.

Youngest League Player: Cyril Poole, 15 years 351 days v New Brighton, 27 February 1937.

Record Transfer Fee Received: £500,000 from Manchester C for Lee Peacock, October 1999.

Record Transfer Fee Paid: £125,000 to Wolverhampton W for Colin Larkin, July 2002.

Football League Record: 1931 Elected to Division 3 (S); 1932–37 Division 3 (N); 1937–47 Division 3 (S); 1947–58 Division 3 (N); 1958–60 Division 3; 1960–63 Division 4; 1963–72 Division 3; 1972–75 Division 4; 1975–77 Division 3; 1977–78 Division 2; 1978–80 Division 3; 1980–86 Division 4; 1986–91 Division 3; 1991–92 Division 4; 1992–93 Division 2; 1993–2002 Division 3; 2002–03 Division 2; 2003–04 Division 3; 2004–08 FL 2; 2008–13 Conference Premier; 2013– FL 2.

LATEST SEQUENCES

Longest Sequence of League Wins: 7, 13.9.1991 – 26.10.1991.

Longest Sequence of League Defeats: 7, 18.1.1947 – 15.3.1947.

Longest Sequence of League Draws: 5, 18.10.1986 – 22.11.1986.

Longest Sequence of Unbeaten League Matches: 20, 14.2.1976 – 21.8.1976.

Longest Sequence Without a League Win: 14, 25.3.2000 – 2.9.2000.

Successive Scoring Runs: 27 from 1.10.1962.

Successive Non-scoring Runs: 8 from 25.3.2000.

MANAGERS

John Baynes 1922–25
Ted Davison 1926–28
Jack Hickling 1928–33
Henry Martin 1933–35
Charlie Bell 1935
Harold Wightman 1936
Harold Parkes 1936–38
Jack Poole 1938–44
Lloyd Barke 1944–45
Roy Goodall 1945–49
Freddie Steele 1949–51
George Jobey 1952–53
Stan Mercer 1953–55
Charlie Mitten 1956–58
Sam Weaver 1958–60
Raich Carter 1960–63
Tommy Cummings 1963–67
Tommy Eggleston 1967–70
Jock Basford 1970–71
Danny Williams 1971–74
Dave Smith 1974–76
Peter Morris 1976–78
Billy Bingham 1978–79
Mick Jones 1979–81
Stuart Boam 1981–83
Ian Greaves 1983–89
George Foster 1989–93
Andy King 1993–96
Steve Parkin 1996–99
Billy Dearden 1999–2002
Stuart Watkiss 2002
Keith Curle 2002–04
Carlton Palmer 2004–05
Peter Shirtliff 2005–06
Billy Dearden 2006–08
Paul Holland 2008
Billy McEwan 2008
David Holdsworth 2008–10
Duncan Russell 2010–11
Paul Cox 2011–14
Adam Murray 2014–16
Steve Evans November 2016–

TEN YEAR LEAGUE RECORD

		P	*W*	*D*	*L*	*F*	*A*	*Pts*	*Pos*
2007-08	FL 2	46	11	9	26	48	68	42	23
2008-09	Conf P	46	19	9	18	57	55	62	12
2009-10	Conf P	44	17	11	16	69	60	62	9
2010-11	Conf P	46	17	10	19	73	75	61	13
2011-12	Conf P	46	25	14	7	87	48	89	3
2012-13	Conf P	46	30	5	11	92	52	95	1
2013-14	FL 2	46	15	15	16	49	58	60	11
2014-15	FL 2	46	13	9	24	38	62	48	21
2015-16	FL 2	46	17	13	16	61	53	64	12
2016-17	FL 2	46	17	15	14	54	50	66	12

DID YOU KNOW ?

The only occasion that Mansfield Town needed to seek re-election to the Football League was after the 1946–47 season when they were unanimously re-elected at the AGM. The Stags still changed divisions for the following season as they were switched to Division Three North to accommodate the two southern-based clubs relegated from Division Two.

MANSFIELD TOWN – SKY BET LEAGUE TWO 2016–17 LEAGUE RECORD

Match No.	Date	Venue	Opponents	Result		H/T Score	Lg Pos.	Goalscorers	Attendance
1	Aug 6	A	Newport Co	W	3-2	1-1	6	Green [12], Rose, D [66], Hurst [90]	2790
2	13	H	Cheltenham T	D	1-1	0-0	5	Rose, M [49]	2884
3	16	H	Yeovil T	W	1-0	0-0	3	Green (pen) [64]	2503
4	20	A	Plymouth Arg	L	0-2	0-2	7		6935
5	27	A	Leyton Orient	W	2-1	0-0	5	Rose, M [68], Green [89]	3996
6	Sept 3	H	Cambridge U	D	0-0	0-0	5		2981
7	10	H	Barnet	L	0-1	0-0	10		2523
8	17	A	Hartlepool U	D	0-0	0-0	9		3775
9	24	H	Grimsby T	L	0-1	0-1	11		4401
10	27	A	Accrington S	D	1-1	1-0	13	Clements [31]	1134
11	Oct 1	A	Crewe Alex	D	1-1	0-0	14	Hoban [51]	3831
12	8	H	Notts Co	W	3-1	0-0	9	Green 2 (1 pen) [54, 90 (p)], Henderson [90]	5763
13	15	H	Wycombe W	D	1-1	0-1	11	Green [81]	2898
14	22	A	Luton T	D	1-1	1-0	11	Green [9]	7787
15	29	H	Stevenage	L	1-2	0-1	13	Hoban [54]	2716
16	Nov 12	A	Portsmouth	L	0-4	0-1	18		16,393
17	19	H	Crawley T	W	3-1	0-0	11	Clements 2 [50, 60], Hoban [54]	2984
18	22	H	Blackpool	W	1-0	0-0	9	Rose, D [90]	2801
19	26	A	Carlisle U	L	2-5	1-1	12	Hoban [6], Rose, D [85]	4822
20	Dec 10	H	Colchester U	D	0-0	0-0	13		3398
21	17	A	Exeter C	L	0-2	0-1	17		3626
22	26	H	Morecambe	L	0-1	0-1	17		3237
23	31	H	Doncaster R	D	1-1	0-0	17	Green [59]	5042
24	Jan 2	A	Blackpool	W	1-0	1-0	16	Green [29]	2948
25	7	H	Crewe Alex	W	3-0	1-0	14	Arquin [5], Whiteman [48], Bennett [83]	3040
26	14	A	Notts Co	D	0-0	0-0	14		11,328
27	21	A	Cambridge U	W	3-1	1-1	12	Legge (og) [43], Pearce [58], Coulthirst [73]	4211
28	28	H	Leyton Orient	W	2-0	0-0	10	Whiteman [48], Rose, D [56]	3925
29	Feb 4	A	Barnet	W	2-0	1-0	8	Whiteman [37], Coulthirst (pen) [60]	1859
30	11	H	Hartlepool U	W	4-0	2-0	7	Whiteman 2 [19, 76], Rose, D [26], MacDonald [71]	4309
31	14	H	Accrington S	D	4-4	2-3	7	Bennett [33], White [45], Coulthirst (pen) [63], Arquin [89]	3226
32	18	A	Grimsby T	L	0-3	0-1	7		5550
33	25	H	Newport Co	W	2-1	1-1	8	Pearce [17], Coulthirst (pen) [75]	3824
34	28	A	Yeovil T	D	0-0	0-0	8		2766
35	Mar 4	A	Cheltenham T	D	0-0	0-0	8		2941
36	11	H	Plymouth Arg	L	0-2	0-0	8		4546
37	14	A	Colchester U	L	0-2	0-2	10		2526
38	18	H	Carlisle U	W	2-0	0-0	9	Green [63], Coulthirst [76]	4463
39	25	A	Morecambe	W	3-1	3-1	9	Rose, D 2 [4, 33], Whiteman [39]	1497
40	Apr 1	H	Exeter C	L	1-2	1-0	9	Benning [38]	3878
41	8	A	Doncaster R	L	0-1	0-0	12		9903
42	14	A	Wycombe W	W	1-0	1-0	10	Pearce [13]	4218
43	17	H	Luton T	D	1-1	1-0	12	Potter [23]	4632
44	22	A	Stevenage	W	1-0	1-0	8	Rose, D [44]	2765
45	29	H	Portsmouth	L	0-1	0-0	12		6819
46	May 6	A	Crawley T	D	2-2	2-1	12	Rose, D [12], Whiteman [23]	2635

Final League Position: 12

GOALSCORERS

League (54): Green 10 (2 pens), Rose, D 9, Whiteman 7, Coulthirst 5 (3 pens), Hoban 4, Clements 3, Pearce 3, Arquin 2, Bennett 2, Rose, M 2, Benning 1, Henderson 1, Hurst 1, MacDonald 1, Potter 1, White 1, own goal 1.
FA Cup (1): Hemmings 1.
EFL Cup (1): Rose, M 1.
EFL Checkatrade Trophy (10): Green 3 (1 pen), Hoban 2, Clements 1, Hemmings 1, Henderson 1, Pearce 1, Rose, D 1.

Shearer S 24 + 1	Bennett R 46	Collins Lee 35 + 2	Taft G 9 + 4	Benning M 45	Rose M 17 + 1	Hurst K 12 + 2	Clements C 18 + 2	Chapman A 5	Rose D 25 + 12	Green M 31 + 11	Hemmings A 10 + 6	Hoban P 13 + 8	Howkins K 13 + 2	Henderson D 3 + 10	Jensen B 3	Hamilton C 13 + 16	Pearce K 41	Baxendale J 3 + 9	McGuire J 13 + 4	Iacovitti A 4 + 4	Gobern O 6 + 3	Thomas J — + 6	Kean J 19	Whiteman B 23	Byrom J 21 + 1	Arquin Y 3 + 9	White H 18	Coulthirst S 15 + 5	Potter A 5 + 7	MacDonald A 13 + 5	Match No.
1	2	3	4	5	6	7	8	9	10^{1}	11^{2}	12	13																			1
1	2	3	4	5	6	9^{2}	8		11^{1}	10	12		7	13																	2
	2	3	13	5	8		7	6	11■	10^{1}	9^{2}		4	14	1	12^{3}															3
	2	4	14	5	8^{2}	7^{1}	9	6		11	10^{3}		3	12	1	13															4
	2	7		5	6	9^{2}		8^{1}		11			3	10^{3}	1	12	4	13	14												5
1	2	6	3	5	9^{2}	8^{3}		7		10	13	14		11^{1}		12	4														6
1	2	8	5^{3}	6	7^{1}	13			10	11	9^{2}			14		12	3			4											7
1	5	3		9	6				11^{2}	10	13					7^{1}	4		8	2	12										8
1	2	7		5	9	6	14		11^{3}	10		13				12	3			4^{1}	8^{2}										9
1	2	4		5	7	9^{3}	8		11^{2}	14	12	10^{1}					3		6	13											10
1	2	3		5	7^{1}	9	8		11^{3}	14		10^{2}					4		6	13	12										11
1	2	3		5	9	6^{3}	7		11^{1}	12		10^{2}		14			4		8		13										12
1	2	6		5	7		8		11^{2}	12		10^{3}	4	14			3				9^{1}	13									13
1	2	8		5	6^{3}	9^{1}	7			11		10^{2}	3			14	4			13		12									14
1	2	6		9		7^{1}	8		14	11		10^{2}	4	13			3			5^{3}		12									15
1	2			5^{2}			9		14	10^{1}	11		4■	12			3	8^{3}	6	13■	7										16
1	2			5	9		7		13	10^{1}	6^{3}	11^{2}		14			3	12	8		4										17
1	3			5	2		7		12	11	9^{1}	10					4		6		8										18
1	2	3		5	9^{1}		7		13	11	12	10^{2}					4	14	6		8^{3}										19
1	2	3		5			7		12	11	8					10	4	9^{1}	6												20
1	4	2		5■		8^{2}	6			11	9	10^{1}		12		13	3		7^{3}			14									21
1	2	5					7		13	6	9	11^{3}	4	10^{1}		12	3		8^{2}			14									22
1	2	6		5	13	14	8^{2}		11^{3}	10		12	4			9	3	7^{1}													23
	2	6		5					12	11^{3}			3			8	4	14	13				1	7	9^{2}	10^{1}					24
	2	6		5			14		12	11^{3}			3			9	4	13					1	8^{2}	7	10^{1}					25
	3	6		5					13	10^{1}		12				9	4	14					1	8	7^{2}	11^{3}	2				26
	4	8		5					10^{1}			13				9	3	14				12	1	6^{3}	7		2	11^{2}			27
	4	6		5					11^{3}	12						9	3	13					1	7^{2}	8	14	2	10^{1}			28
	4	6		5					11^{3}	12						9	3						1	7	8^{2}		2	10^{1}	13	14	29
	4	7		5					10^{2}	13							3						1	6	8	14	2	11^{1}	9^{3}	12	30
	2	7		5					11^{3}	13						12	3						1	9	8^{1}	14	4	10		6^{2}	31
	4	7		5						8^{3}						14	3						1	6	13	12	2■	11	9^{2}	10^{1}	32
12	3	2		5								11^{1}				7	4		6^{2}				1^{3}	9	8	14		10		13	33
1	4	6		5								13				10	3		12					9	8		2^{3}	11^{2}	14	7^{1}	34
1	3	6		5								11^{1}				10	4		7^{2}					8		13	2	12	14	9^{3}	35
1	3	7^{3}		5					13	11^{2}						10	4							8	6		2	12	14	9^{1}	36
1	4	6^{1}		5					13	11	10^{2}					12	3							8	7		2	14		9^{3}	37
	3			5					10^{3}	9			12			13	4^{2}						1	8	7	14	2	11		6^{1}	38
	3			5					11^{3}	9^{1}			4					13					1	8	7	12	2	10	14	6^{2}	39
	2	13	3^{2}	5					10^{1}	9			12				4						1	8	7			11	14	6^{3}	40
	2		4	5					10^{1}	9						12	3						1	7	8			11	13	6^{2}	41
	3		5	6					10^{3}	11^{1}							4						1	7	8	14	2	12	9^{2}	13	42
	2		4	9					11^{2}	14						13	3						1	7	6		5^{1}	10	8^{3}	12	43
	2	13	4^{1}	9					11^{3}	12							3		14				1	7	6		5	10		8^{2}	44
	3	6^{1}	13	5					11^{2}	12		14					4						1	7	8		2	10		9^{3}	45
	3		13	5					11^{3}	10						14	4						1	6	8		2^{1}	12	7^{2}	9	46

FA Cup

First Round	Plymouth Arg	(h)	1-2

EFL Cup

First Round	Blackburn R	(h)	1-3

EFL Checkatrade Trophy

Northern Group E	Doncaster R	(h)	0-2
Northern Group E	Port Vale	(a)	1-0
Northern Group E	Derby Co U21	(a)	3-2
Second Round North	Carlisle U	(a)	3-2
Third Round	Oldham Ath	(h)	2-0
Quarter-Final	Wycombe W	(h)	1-2

MIDDLESBROUGH

FOUNDATION

A previous belief that Middlesbrough Football Club was founded at a tripe supper at the Corporation Hotel has proved to be erroneous. In fact, members of Middlesbrough Cricket Club were responsible for forming it at a meeting in the gymnasium of the Albert Park Hotel in 1875.

Riverside Stadium, Middlesbrough TS3 6RS.

Telephone: (0844) 499 6789.

Fax: (01642) 757 697.

Ticket Office: (0844) 499 1234.

Website: www.mfc.co.uk

Email: enquiries@mfc.co.uk

Ground Capacity: 33,746.

Record Attendance: 53,536 v Newcastle U, Division 1, 27 December 1949 (at Ayresome Park); 34,814 v Newcastle U, FA Premier League, 5 March 2003 (at Riverside Stadium); 35,000, England v Slovakia, Euro 2004 qualifier, 11 June 2003.

Pitch Measurements: 105m × 68m (115yd × 74.5yd).

Chairman: Steve Gibson.

Chief Executive: Neil Bausor.

Head Coach: Garry Monk.

Assistant Head Coach: Joe Jordan.

Colours: Power red shirts with bold blue and white trim, white shorts with power red trim, power red socks with white trim.

Year Formed: 1876; re-formed 1986.

Turned Professional: 1889; became amateur 1892, and professional again, 1899.

Club Nickname: 'Boro'.

Grounds: 1877, Old Archery Ground, Albert Park; 1879, Breckon Hill; 1882, Linthorpe Road Ground; 1903, Ayresome Park; 1995, Riverside Stadium.

First Football League Game: 2 September 1899, Division 2, v Lincoln C (a) L 0–3 – Smith; Shaw, Ramsey; Allport, McNally, McCracken; Wanless, Longstaffe, Gettins, Page, Pugh.

Record League Victory: 9–0 v Brighton & HA, Division 2, 23 August 1958 – Taylor; Bilcliff, Robinson; Harris (2p), Phillips, Walley; Day, McLean, Clough (5), Peacock (2), Holliday.

Record Cup Victory: 7–0 v Hereford U, Coca-Cola Cup 2nd rd, 1st leg, 18 September 1996 – Miller; Fleming (1), Branco (1), Whyte, Vickers, Whelan, Emerson (1), Mustoe, Stamp, Juninho, Ravanelli (4).

Record Defeat: 0–9 v Blackburn R, Division 2, 6 November 1954.

HONOURS

League Champions: First Division – 1994–95; Division 2 – 1926–27, 1928–29, 1973–74.
Runners-up: FL C – 2015–16; First Division – 1997–98; Division 2 – 1901–02, 1991–92; Division 3 – 1966–67, 1986–87.

FA Cup: *Runners-up:* 1997.

League Cup Winners: 2004.
Runners-up: 1997, 1998.

Amateur Cup Winners: 1895, 1898.

Anglo-Scottish Cup Winners: 1976.

Full Members' Cup: *Runners-up:* 1990.

European Competitions
UEFA Cup: 2004–05, 2005–06 *(runners-up)*.

sky SPORTS FACT FILE

Middlesbrough created a new British transfer record in February 1905 paying out the first £1,000 fee for a player when they bought forward Alf Common from Sunderland. Boro, who were under threat of relegation, were rewarded when Common netted the winner at Bramall Lane on his debut and they narrowly avoided the drop.

Most League Points (2 for a win): 65, Division 2, 1973–74.

Most League Points (3 for a win): 94, Division 3, 1986–87.

Most League Goals: 122, Division 2, 1926–27.

Highest League Scorer in Season: George Camsell, 59, Division 2, 1926–27 (Second Division record).

Most League Goals in Total Aggregate: George Camsell, 325, 1925–39.

Most League Goals in One Match: 5, John Wilkie v Gainsborough T, Division 2, 2 March 1901; 5, Andy Wilson v Nottingham F, Division 1, 6 October 1923; 5, George Camsell v Manchester C, Division 2, 25 December 1926; 5, George Camsell v Aston Villa, Division 1, 9 September 1935; 5, Brian Clough v Brighton & HA, Division 2, 22 August 1958.

Most Capped Player: Mark Schwarzer, 52, Australia.

Most League Appearances: Tim Williamson, 563, 1902–23.

Youngest League Player: Luke Williams, 16 years 200 days v Barnsley, 18 December 2009.

Record Transfer Fee Received: £12,000,000 from Atletico Madrid for Juninho, July 1997; £12,000,000 from Aston Villa for Stewart Downing, July 2009.

Record Transfer Fee Paid: £14,000,000 to Nottingham F for Britt Assombalonga, July 2017.

Football League Record: 1899 Elected to Division 2; 1902–24 Division 1; 1924–27 Division 2; 1927–28 Division 1; 1928–29 Division 2; 1929–54 Division 1; 1954–66 Division 2; 1966–67 Division 3; 1967–74 Division 2; 1974–82 Division 1; 1982–86 Division 2; 1986–87 Division 3; 1987–88 Division 2; 1988–89 Division 1; 1989–92 Division 2; 1992–93 FA Premier League; 1993–95 Division 1; 1995–97 FA Premier League; 1997–98 Division 1; 1998–2009 FA Premier League; 2009–16 FL C; 2016–17 FA Premier League; 2017– FL C.

MANAGERS

John Robson 1899–1905
Alex Mackie 1905–06
Andy Aitken 1906–09
J. Gunter 1908–10
(Secretary-Manager)
Andy Walker 1910–11
Tom McIntosh 1911–19
Jimmy Howie 1920–23
Herbert Bamlett 1923–26
Peter McWilliam 1927–34
Wilf Gillow 1934–44
David Jack 1944–52
Walter Rowley 1952–54
Bob Dennison 1954–63
Raich Carter 1963–66
Stan Anderson 1966–73
Jack Charlton 1973–77
John Neal 1977–81
Bobby Murdoch 1981–82
Malcolm Allison 1982–84
Willie Maddren 1984–86
Bruce Rioch 1986–90
Colin Todd 1990–91
Lennie Lawrence 1991–94
Bryan Robson 1994–2001
Steve McClaren 2001–06
Gareth Southgate 2006–09
Gordon Strachan 2009–10
Tony Mowbray 2010–13
Aitor Karanka 2013–17
Garry Monk June 2017–

LATEST SEQUENCES

Longest Sequence of League Wins: 9, 16.2.1974 – 6.4.1974.

Longest Sequence of League Defeats: 8, 26.12.1995 – 17.2.1996.

Longest Sequence of League Draws: 8, 3.4.1971 – 1.5.1971.

Longest Sequence of Unbeaten League Matches: 24, 8.9.1973 – 19.1.1974.

Longest Sequence Without a League Win: 19, 3.10.1981 – 6.3.1982.

Successive Scoring Runs: 26 from 21.9.1946.

Successive Non-scoring Runs: 7, 25.1.2014 – 1.3.2014.

TEN YEAR LEAGUE RECORD

		P	*W*	*D*	*L*	*F*	*A*	*Pts*	*Pos*
2007-08	PR Lge	38	10	12	16	43	53	42	13
2008-09	PR Lge	38	7	11	20	28	57	32	19
2009-10	FL C	46	16	14	16	58	50	62	11
2010-11	FL C	46	17	11	18	68	68	62	12
2011-12	FL C	46	18	16	12	52	51	70	7
2012-13	FL C	46	18	5	23	61	70	59	16
2013-14	FL C	46	16	16	14	62	50	64	12
2014-15	FL C	46	25	10	11	68	37	85	4
2015-16	FL C	46	26	11	9	63	31	89	2
2016-17	PR Lge	38	5	13	20	27	53	28	19

DID YOU KNOW ?

Wing-half Harry Bell made over 300 appearances for Middlesbrough in the 1950s. He was also a talented cricketer and played exactly 100 games for Durham between 1944 and 1962, scoring four centuries.

MIDDLESBROUGH – PREMIER LEAGUE 2016–17 LEAGUE RECORD

Match No.	*Date*	*Venue*	*Opponents*	*Result*	*H/T Score*	*Lg Pos.*	*Goalscorers*	*Attendance*
1	Aug 13	H	Stoke C	D 1-1	1-0	6	Negredo [11]	32,110
2	21	A	Sunderland	W 2-1	2-0	6	Stuani 2 [13, 45]	43,515
3	28	A	WBA	D 0-0	0-0	6		23,690
4	Sept 10	H	Crystal Palace	L 1-2	1-1	9	Ayala [38]	30,551
5	17	A	Everton	L 1-3	1-3	9	Stekelenburg (og) [21]	39,074
6	24	H	Tottenham H	L 1-2	0-2	15	Gibson [65]	32,703
7	Oct 1	A	West Ham U	D 1-1	0-0	16	Stuani [51]	56,945
8	16	H	Watford	L 0-1	0-0	17		28,131
9	22	A	Arsenal	D 0-0	0-0	16		59,982
10	29	H	Bournemouth	W 2-0	1-0	15	Ramirez [39], Downing [56]	29,600
11	Nov 5	A	Manchester C	D 1-1	0-1	14	de Roon [90]	54,294
12	20	H	Chelsea	L 0-1	0-1	15		32,704
13	26	A	Leicester C	D 2-2	1-1	15	Negredo 2 [13, 71]	32,058
14	Dec 5	H	Hull C	W 1-0	0-0	13	Ramirez [60]	27,395
15	11	A	Southampton	L 0-1	0-0	16		28,976
16	14	H	Liverpool	L 0-3	0-1	16		32,704
17	17	H	Swansea C	W 3-0	2-0	13	Negredo 2 (1 pen) [18, 29 (p)], de Roon [58]	28,302
18	26	A	Burnley	L 0-1	0-0	15		21,562
19	31	A	Manchester U	L 1-2	0-0	16	Leadbitter [67]	75,314
20	Jan 2	H	Leicester C	D 0-0	0-0	16		32,437
21	14	A	Watford	D 0-0	0-0	16		20,659
22	21	H	West Ham U	L 1-3	1-2	16	Stuani [27]	30,848
23	31	H	WBA	D 1-1	1-1	15	Negredo (pen) [17]	27,316
24	Feb 4	A	Tottenham H	L 0-1	0-0	15		31,949
25	11	H	Everton	D 0-0	0-0	15		31,496
26	25	A	Crystal Palace	L 0-1	0-1	16		25,416
27	Mar 4	A	Stoke C	L 0-2	0-2	18		27,644
28	19	H	Manchester U	L 1-3	0-1	19	Gestede [77]	32,689
29	Apr 2	A	Swansea C	D 0-0	0-0	19		20,354
30	5	A	Hull C	L 2-4	2-3	19	Negredo [5], de Roon [45]	20,380
31	8	H	Burnley	D 0-0	0-0	19		29,547
32	17	H	Arsenal	L 1-2	0-1	19	Negredo [50]	31,298
33	22	A	Bournemouth	L 0-4	0-2	19		10,890
34	26	H	Sunderland	W 1-0	1-0	19	de Roon [8]	30,742
35	30	H	Manchester C	D 2-2	1-0	19	Negredo [38], Chambers [77]	29,763
36	May 8	A	Chelsea	L 0-3	0-2	19		41,500
37	13	H	Southampton	L 1-2	0-1	19	Bamford [72]	28,203
38	21	A	Liverpool	L 0-3	0-1	19		53,191

Final League Position: 19

GOALSCORERS

League (27): Negredo 9 (2 pens), de Roon 4, Stuani 4, Ramirez 2, Ayala 1, Bamford 1, Chambers 1, Downing 1, Gestede 1, Gibson 1, Leadbitter 1, own goal 1.
FA Cup (7): Leadbitter 2 (1 pen), de Roon 1, Downing 1, Gestede 1, Negredo 1, Stuani 1.
EFL Cup (1): Nugent 1.
EFL Checkatrade Trophy (2): Cooke 1, Tavernier 1.

Valdes V 28	Nsue E 4	Barragan A 26	Gibson B 38	Friend G 20 + 4	Clayton A 32 + 2	de Roon M 32 + 1	Adomah A 1 + 1	Ramirez G 20 + 4	Downing S 24 + 6	Negredo A 33 + 3	Forshaw A 30 + 4	Nugent D — + 4	Guzan B 10	Stuani C 16 + 7	Ayala D 11 + 3	Fischer V 6 + 7	Traore A 16 + 11	Chambers C 24	Rhodes J 2 + 4	Leadbitter G 7 + 6	Da Silva F 21 + 3	Bernardo E 10 + 1	Gestede R 4 + 12	Bamford P 2 + 6	Guedioura A — + 5	Husband J 1	*Match No.*
1	2	3	4	5	6	7^{1}	8	9^{2}	10	11	12	13															1
	2^{2}	3	4	5	7		12	9^{3}	10	11^{1}	6	14	1	8	13												2
	2	5	4		7			9^{2}	10	11	6	12	1	8^{1}	3	13											3
1		2	4	5	6^{1}	12		13	10	11	7			8^{3}	3	9^{2}	14										4
1	8^{2}	2	4	5	14	6		9^{3}	10	11	7^{1}	12			3	13											5
1		2	4	5	7^{3}	6		9^{1}	10	11^{2}	14			8			13	3	12								6
1		2	4	5		6		12	9	13	7			8		10^{2}		3	11^{1}								7
1		2^{1}	4	5		6^{3}		9	10	11	7			8^{2}	13		12	3	14								8
1		2	4	5	8	7		10^{1}	12	11^{2}	9			13	3		6										9
1		2	4	5	7			9^{1}	10	11^{2}	6					14	8^{3}	3	13	12							10
1		2	4	5	8	9			10^{2}	11	7			13		12	6^{1}	3									11
1		2	4		8^{3}	7		10	12	11	9^{1}					13	6	3		14	5^{2}						12
1		2	4		8	7		10^{2}		11	9			12		13	6^{1}	3			5						13
1		2	4		7	6		9^{2}	13	10	8			12		11^{1}		3			5						14
1		2	4		7	8					6			9^{1}		11	12	3	10		5						15
1		2	4		7^{2}	8			13	10^{1}	6					11^{3}	9	3	14	12	5						16
1		2	4	13	7	6		9^{2}	12	10	8					11^{1}	14	3			5^{3}						17
1		2	4	13	7	8^{2}		11		10	6			9^{1}			12	3			5						18
1			4	5	13	6		12	10^{1}	11	8						7^{3}	2		9^{2}	14	3					19
		2^{2}	4	12	7	6		11	13	10	8^{3}		1				9^{1}	3		14	5						20
1			4	9		5				10	8			11^{1}				3		7	6	2	12				21
1			4	5	6	7				10	8^{2}			11^{1}			9	2				3	13	12			22
1		2	4		7	6				10^{2}	8			11^{1}			9				5	3	13	12			23
1			4		7	6			11^{1}	10	8^{3}			13			9^{2}	2			5	3		14	12		24
1			4		7	6		13		10^{2}	8^{1}			11^{3}			9	2			5	3	14		12		25
1			5			7		8	6	10^{3}	9^{1}			11^{2}	3		14				2	4	12		13		26
1			4	5	8	7		9^{3}						13	3^{1}		11			6^{2}	2	12	10		14		27
1		2	4		7	6		11^{2}	9	10							13			8^{1}	5	3	12				28
1		2	4		6	7		10^{1}	9	11	13						8				5^{2}	3	12				29
1		2	4		7	8			9	10^{2}				14	3		6						11^{3}	13	12	5^{1}	30
1		5	4		6				9	12	8			10^{2}	2		13			7		3^{3}	11^{1}	14			31
		2	4	12	6	7^{3}		11^{2}	9	10			1		3		13			8	5^{1}		14				32
		2^{2}	5	6	9	8^{3}		7■	10	11^{1}	12		1		4			3			13		14				33
			4	5	7	6			11	10^{2}	8		1	9	3^{1}			2			12		13				34
			4	5	7	6			11	10^{2}	8		1	9^{1}			12	3			2		13				35
			4	5	7	6			11	10^{1}	8^{2}		1				9^{3}	3		12	2		14	13			36
			4	5	7	6			11^{2}	10	8^{1}		1			12		3		13	2			9			37
			4	5	7				11	12	8		1		13			3		6	2^{1}		10^{2}	9			38

FA Cup

Third Round	Sheffield W	(h)	3-0
Fourth Round	Accrington S	(h)	1-0
Fifth Round	Oxford U	(h)	3-2
Sixth Round	Manchester C	(h)	0-2

EFL Cup

Second Round (*aet*)	Fulham	(a)	1-2

EFL Checkatrade Trophy (Middlesbrough U21)

Northern Group G	Scunthorpe U	(a)	1-2
Northern Group G	Cambridge U	(a)	1-2
Northern Group G	Shrewsbury T	(h)	0-3

MILLWALL

FOUNDATION

Formed in 1885 as Millwall Rovers by employees of Morton & Co, a jam and marmalade factory in West Ferry Road. The founders were predominantly Scotsmen. Their first headquarters was The Islanders pub in Tooke Street, Millwall. Their first trophy was the East End Cup in 1887.

The Den, Zampa Road, London SE16 3LN.

Telephone: (020) 7232 1222. ***Fax:*** (020) 7231 3663.

Ticket Office: (0844) 826 2004.

Website: www.millwallfc.co.uk

Email: questions@millwallplc.com

Ground Capacity: 19,734.

Record Attendance: 48,672 v Derby Co, FA Cup 5th rd, 20 February 1937 (at The Den, Cold Blow Lane); 20,093 v Arsenal, FA Cup 3rd rd, 10 January 1994 (at The Den, Bermondsey).

Pitch Measurements: 106m × 68m (116yd × 74.5yd).

Chairman: John G. Berylson.

Chief Executive: Steve Kavanagh.

Manager: Neil Harris.

Assistant Manager: Dave Livermore.

Colours: Blue and white striped shirts, blue shorts, blue socks with white trim.

Year Formed: 1885.

Turned Professional: 1893.

Previous Names: 1885, Millwall Rovers; 1889, Millwall Athletic; 1899, Millwall; 1985, Millwall Football & Athletic Company.

Club Nickname: 'The Lions'.

Grounds: 1885, Glengall Road, Millwall; 1886, Back of 'Lord Nelson'; 1890, East Ferry Road; 1901, North Greenwich; 1910, The Den, Cold Blow Lane; 1993, The Den, Bermondsey.

First Football League Game: 28 August 1920, Division 3, v Bristol R (h) W 2–0 – Lansdale; Fort, Hodge; Voisey (1), Riddell, McAlpine; Waterall, Travers, Broad (1), Sutherland, Dempsey.

Record League Victory: 9–1 v Torquay U, Division 3 (S), 29 August 1927 – Lansdale, Tilling, Hill, Amos, Bryant (3), Graham, Chance, Hawkins (3), Landells (1), Phillips (2), Black. 9–1 v Coventry C, Division 3 (S), 19 November 1927 – Lansdale, Fort, Hill, Amos, Collins (1), Graham, Chance, Landells (4), Cock (2), Phillips (2), Black.

Record Cup Victory: 7–0 v Gateshead, FA Cup 2nd rd, 12 December 1936 – Yuill; Ted Smith, Inns; Brolly, Hancock, Forsyth; Thomas (1), Mangnall (1), Ken Burditt (2), McCartney (2), Thorogood (1).

Record Defeat: 1–9 v Aston Villa, FA Cup 4th rd, 28 January 1946.

Most League Points (2 for a win): 65, Division 3 (S), 1927–28 and Division 3, 1965–66.

Most League Points (3 for a win): 93, Division 2, 2000–01.

HONOURS

League Champions: Division 2 – 1987–88; Second Division – 2000–01; Division 3S – 1927–28, 1937–38; Division 4 – 1961–62.
Runners-up: Division 3 – 1965–66, 1984–85; Division 3S – 1952–53; Division 4 – 1964–65.

FA Cup: *Runners-up:* 2004.

League Cup: 5th rd – 1974, 1977, 1995.

League Trophy: *Runners-up:* 1999.

European Competitions
UEFA Cup: 2004–05.

sky SPORTS FACT FILE

Millwall have had to apply for re-election to the Football League on two separate occasions. In 1950 they were re-elected unanimously after it was agreed to expand membership from 88 to 92 clubs, while in 1958 they topped the poll with 46 votes to comfortably retain membership of the competition.

Most League Goals: 127, Division 3 (S), 1927–28.

Highest League Scorer in Season: Richard Parker, 37, Division 3 (S), 1926–27.

Most League Goals in Total Aggregate: Neil Harris, 124, 1995–2004; 2006–11.

Most League Goals in One Match: 5, Richard Parker v Norwich C, Division 3 (S), 28 August 1926.

Most Capped Player: David Forde, 24, Republic of Ireland.

Most League Appearances: Barry Kitchener, 523, 1967–82.

Youngest League Player: Moses Ashikodi, 15 years 240 days v Brighton & HA, 22 February 2003.

Record Transfer Fee Received: £2,800,000 from Norwich C for Steve Morison, June 2011.

Record Transfer Fee Paid: £800,000 to Derby Co for Paul Goddard, December 1989.

Football League Record: 1920 Original Members of Division 3; 1921 Division 3 (S); 1928–34 Division 2; 1934–38 Division 3 (S); 1938–48 Division 2; 1948–58 Division 3 (S); 1958–62 Division 4; 1962–64 Division 3; 1964–65 Division 4; 1965–66 Division 3; 1966–75 Division 2; 1975–76 Division 3; 1976–79 Division 2; 1979–85 Division 3; 1985–88 Division 2; 1988–90 Division 1; 1990–92 Division 2; 1992–96 Division 1; 1996–2001 Division 2; 2001–04 Division 1; 2004–06 FL C; 2006–10 FL 1; 2010–15 FL C; 2015–17 FL 1; 2017– FL C.

LATEST SEQUENCES

Longest Sequence of League Wins: 10, 10.3.1928 – 25.4.1928.

Longest Sequence of League Defeats: 11, 10.4.1929 – 16.9.1929.

Longest Sequence of League Draws: 5, 22.12.1973 – 12.1.1974.

Longest Sequence of Unbeaten League Matches: 19, 22.8.1959 – 31.10.1959.

Longest Sequence Without a League Win: 20, 26.12.1989 – 5.5.1990.

Successive Scoring Runs: 22 from 27.11.1954.

Successive Non-scoring Runs: 6 from 27.4.2013.

MANAGERS

F. B. Kidd 1894–99
(Hon. Treasurer/Manager)
E. R. Stopher 1899–1900
(Hon. Treasurer/Manager)
George Saunders 1900–11
(Hon. Treasurer/Manager)
Herbert Lipsham 1911–19
Robert Hunter 1919–33
Bill McCracken 1933–36
Charlie Hewitt 1936–40
Bill Voisey 1940–44
Jack Cock 1944–48
Charlie Hewitt 1948–56
Ron Gray 1956–57
Jimmy Seed 1958–59
Reg Smith 1959–61
Ron Gray 1961–63
Billy Gray 1963–66
Benny Fenton 1966–74
Gordon Jago 1974–77
George Petchey 1978–80
Peter Anderson 1980–82
George Graham 1982–86
John Docherty 1986–90
Bob Pearson 1990
Bruce Rioch 1990–92
Mick McCarthy 1992–96
Jimmy Nicholl 1996–97
John Docherty 1997
Billy Bonds 1997–98
Keith Stevens 1998–2000
(then Joint Manager)
(*plus* **Alan McLeary** 1999–2000)
Mark McGhee 2000–03
Dennis Wise 2003–05
Steve Claridge 2005
Colin Lee 2005
David Tuttle 2005–06
Nigel Spackman 2006
Willie Donachie 2006–07
Kenny Jackett 2007–13
Steve Lomas 2013
Ian Holloway 2014–15
Neil Harris March 2015–

TEN YEAR LEAGUE RECORD

		P	W	D	L	F	A	Pts	Pos
2007-08	FL 1	46	14	10	22	45	60	52	17
2008-09	FL 1	46	25	7	14	63	53	82	5
2009-10	FL 1	46	24	13	9	76	44	85	3
2010-11	FL C	46	18	13	15	62	48	67	9
2011-12	FL C	46	15	12	19	55	57	57	16
2012-13	FL C	46	15	11	20	51	62	56	20
2013-14	FL C	46	11	15	20	46	74	48	19
2014-15	FL C	46	9	14	23	42	76	41	22
2015-16	FL 1	46	24	9	13	73	49	81	4
2016-17	FL 1	46	20	13	13	66	57	73	6

DID YOU KNOW ?

The Den was closed by the FA for a seven-day period in December 1947 and Millwall switched their home game with Newcastle United to Selhurst Park. A crowd of 33,356 turned out to watch the Lions win 2-1. The attendance was nearly 10,000 higher than any Crystal Palace home game that season.

MILLWALL – SKY BET LEAGUE ONE 2016–17 LEAGUE RECORD

Match No.	*Date*	*Venue*	*Opponents*	*Result*		*H/T Score*	*Lg Pos.*	*Goalscorers*	*Attendance*
1	Aug 6	H	Oldham Ath	W	3-0	2-0	1	Gregory (pen) [13], O'Brien [45], Webster [46]	9787
2	13	A	Milton Keynes D	D	2-2	2-2	3	Downing (og) [24], Worrall [27]	10,232
3	16	A	Peterborough U	L	1-5	0-3	12	Morison [79]	5007
4	20	H	Sheffield U	W	2-1	1-1	8	Williams [14], Morison (pen) [89]	9058
5	27	A	Chesterfield	W	3-1	3-0	5	Ferguson [13], Morison 2 [38, 41]	5630
6	Sept 3	H	Bradford C	D	1-1	0-1	4	Martin [49]	9067
7	10	H	Coventry C	D	1-1	0-1	5	O'Brien [71]	8755
8	17	A	Southend U	L	1-3	1-1	8	O'Brien [33]	7752
9	24	H	Rochdale	L	2-3	2-1	14	O'Brien [11], Gregory (pen) [18]	8143
10	27	A	Port Vale	L	1-3	0-1	17	Gregory (pen) [84]	3934
11	Oct 1	A	Walsall	L	1-2	1-1	19	Onyedinma [22]	4474
12	15	A	Northampton T	W	3-1	1-0	17	Gregory [32], Butcher [60], Morison [89]	6908
13	18	H	Bolton W	L	0-2	0-1	20		7898
14	22	H	Fleetwood T	W	2-1	1-0	16	Gregory 2 (2 pens) [31, 48]	8085
15	29	A	Oxford U	W	2-1	1-1	12	Morison [36], O'Brien [50]	7944
16	Nov 12	H	Bristol R	W	4-0	1-0	8	O'Brien [22], Williams [64], Gregory [68], Smith [88]	9645
17	19	A	Bolton W	L	0-2	0-1	13		13,110
18	22	H	AFC Wimbledon	D	0-0	0-0	13		8614
19	26	A	Bury	W	3-2	0-0	9	Williams (pen) [70], Butcher [86], O'Brien [90]	3028
20	Dec 10	H	Shrewsbury T	L	0-1	0-1	11		8354
21	17	A	Scunthorpe U	L	0-3	0-2	14		4355
22	21	H	Charlton Ath	W	3-1	2-0	10	O'Brien [40], Morison 2 [42, 60]	14,395
23	26	H	Swindon T	W	2-0	1-0	9	Gregory 2 [10, 65]	8515
24	30	H	Gillingham	W	2-1	1-0	7	Gregory [13], Onyedinma [63]	10,821
25	Jan 2	A	AFC Wimbledon	D	2-2	2-1	7	O'Brien [5], Morison [40]	4742
26	14	A	Charlton Ath	D	0-0	0-0	8		15,315
27	21	A	Bradford C	D	1-1	0-0	9	Gregory [50]	17,712
28	Feb 1	H	Walsall	D	0-0	0-0	10		7392
29	4	A	Coventry C	W	2-0	1-0	9	Cooper [33], Morison [79]	8764
30	11	H	Southend U	W	1-0	0-0	6	Onyedinma [62]	10,323
31	14	H	Port Vale	W	2-0	1-0	6	O'Brien [26], Cooper [52]	7032
32	21	H	Chesterfield	D	0-0	0-0	7		9005
33	25	A	Oldham Ath	D	0-0	0-0	7		3856
34	28	H	Peterborough U	W	1-0	0-0	6	Gregory (pen) [54]	8032
35	Mar 4	H	Milton Keynes D	W	2-1	1-1	6	Gregory 2 (1 pen) [24, 90 (p)]	9636
36	18	H	Bury	D	0-0	0-0	7		9049
37	21	A	Rochdale	D	3-3	2-2	7	Gregory (pen) [14], O'Brien [25], Wallace [77]	2334
38	25	A	Swindon T	L	0-1	0-0	7		7038
39	28	A	Sheffield U	L	0-2	0-1	7		20,832
40	Apr 1	H	Scunthorpe U	W	3-1	1-0	7	Williams (pen) [3], Ferguson [57], O'Brien [68]	9789
41	4	A	Shrewsbury T	W	2-1	1-0	7	Webster [35], Hutchinson [77]	4712
42	8	A	Gillingham	D	1-1	0-0	6	Morison [72]	7221
43	14	H	Northampton T	W	3-0	3-0	6	O'Brien [27], Wallace 2 [38, 45]	10,886
44	17	A	Fleetwood T	L	0-1	0-1	6		3665
45	22	H	Oxford U	L	0-3	0-2	6		12,533
46	30	A	Bristol R	W	4-3	3-2	6	Gregory 2 [5, 35], Craig [25], Hutchinson [85]	11,750

Final League Position: 6

GOALSCORERS

League (66): Gregory 17 (8 pens), O'Brien 13, Morison 11 (1 pen), Williams 4 (2 pens), Onyedinma 3, Wallace 3, Butcher 2, Cooper 2, Ferguson 2, Hutchinson 2, Webster 2, Craig 1, Martin 1, Smith 1, Worrall 1, own goal 1.
FA Cup (11): Smith 3, Cummings 2, Ferguson 2, Morison 2, O'Brien 1, Romeo 1.
EFL Cup (5): Morison 1, O'Brien 1, Onyedinma 1 (1 pen), Williams 1, own goal 1.
EFL Checkatrade Trophy (8): Morison 2 (1 pen), Onyedinma 2, Smith 2, Abdou 1, Worrall 1.
League One Play-Offs (4): Morison 3, Gregory 1.

Archer J 36	Romeo M 31 + 1	Craig T 43	Webster B 44	Ferguson S 22 + 18	Worrall D 14 + 19	Thompson B 36 + 2	Williams S 43 + 1	O'Brien A 35 + 8	Morison S 35 + 3	Gregory L 35 + 2	Martin J 19 + 4	Onyedinma F 23 + 19	Wylde G 1 + 4	Abdou N 6 + 6	Hutchinson S 13 + 3	Nelson S 2 + 1	Butcher C 9 + 21	Philpot J — + 2	Smith H 7 + 2	Cummings S 15 + 1	Pavey A — + 1	Cooper J 13 + 2	Wallace J 14 + 2	King T 10 + 1	Match No.
1	2	3	4	5[1]	6	7	8	9[2]	10	11[3]	12	13	14												1
1	5	4	3	2[2]	9[1]	8	7[3]	6	11	10	13	14		12											2
1	2	4	3	6[2]		8		9[1]	11	10	5[3]	13	12	7	14										3
1	2	4	3	12	6	7	8	9[1]	11	10[2]	5	13													4
1	2	3	4	9[2]	6	7	8	11	10		5[1]	12[3]				13	14								5
1	2	3	4		6	7	8	11	10		5	12	9[1]												6
1	4	3	5	12	7	8[3]	6	11[1]	10		2	9[2]					13	14							7
1	2	4	3	9	6	13	8	11	10	12	5[2]						7[1]								8
1	2	5	4	9[1]	12	7[1]	8	6[2]	10	11[3]		14		13		3									9
1	2	4	3	9	6[2]		12		10	11	5[3]	14	13	8			7[1]								10
1	2	3	4	9		12	7		11	10	5[3]	6[2]	13	8[1]				14							11
1	2	4	3	12	13	9[1]	8		11	10[3]	5	6[2]		14			7								12
1	2	4	3	13	14	9[3]	8	12	11	10	5[1]	6[2]					7								13
1	2	3	4	5[3]		8	7	9[2]	11	10[1]	13	6		12	14										14
1	2	3	4	5		8[3]	7	9[2]	10	11[1]	12	6		14			13								15
1	2	4	3		12	7[1]	8[2]	9[3]		10	5	6					13		11	14					16
1	2	4	3	13	12	8[1]	7	6		11[2]	5[3]	9					14		10						17
1	2	4	3	9	6	8[1]	7	11[2]			5	12					13		10						18
1	2	3	4	9	6[1]		7	12			5[2]	11		8[3]			13		10		14				19
1	2	4		9	14	7	8	12		11	5[1]	6[2]				3[3]	13		10						20
1	2[2]	4		9	13	8	7	11	12	10	5[3]	6[1]			3		14								21
1		5	3	12	13	6	8	11[3]	10	9[1]		7[2]			4		14			2					22
1		2	3	12	13	7	8	9[1]	10[2]	11[3]		6			4		14			5					23
1		5	3	12	13	7	8	9[3]	10	11[1]		6[2]			4		14			2					24
1		5	3		12	7[2]	8	9[1]	11	10		6			4		13			2					25
1		5	3	12	13	8	7	9[2]	11	10		6[1]			4					2					26
1		5	3	13		7	8	9[2]	11	10		6[1]								2		4	12		27
1		5	3	6[2]		8	7	12	11	10		13								2		4	9[1]		28
1	2	5	3	14		7[2]	8	9	11	10[3]		13		12								4	6[1]		29
1		5	3	12	13			9[2]	11			10		7			8			2		4	6[1]		30
1		5	3	13	14		7	11[1]	10[3]			9[2]					8		12	2		4	6		31
	2	5	4	12	6[1]	8[2]	7	10[3]		11		9			3		13		14					1	32
		5	3	13	6[1]		8	9[2]		10		12					7		11	2		4		1	33
		5	3	9		7[3]	8	12		10[1]		6			14		13		11[2]	2		4		1	34
		5	4	9[2]		7[1]	8	6	12	10		11[3]					14			2		3	13	1	35
		5	3	9[3]	14	7[2]	8	12	11	10							13			2[1]		4	6	1	36
1	12	5	3				8	9[2]	10	11		13					7			2[1]		4	6		37
1	2	5	3	13			8	9[2]	10[1]	11		12					7					4	6		38
1[3]	2	5[1]	3	9		7	8	14	13	11		10[2]										4	6	12	39
	2	5	4	9[2]	12	8	7	11[1]	10			13			3		14						6[3]	1	40
	2	5	4	10[3]	13	7	8	9[1]	11			12			3		14						6[2]	1	41
	2		4		6[2]	7	8	11[1]	10	12	5	13			3								9	1	42
	2		4		12	7	8	9	11[1]	10[2]	5	13			3		14						6[3]	1	43
	2		4	13		8[1]	7	9	10	11	5[2]				3[3]		14					12	6	1	44
1	2	5[1]	3	12	13	8	7	9[2]	11	10												4	6		45
1		5	3	9[2]	6[3]		8	13	11	10[1]		12		7	4					2		14			46

FA Cup

First Round	Southend U	(h)	1-0
Second Round	Braintree T	(h)	5-2
Third Round	Bournemouth	(h)	3-0
Fourth Round	Watford	(h)	1-0
Fifth Round	Leicester C	(h)	1-0
Sixth Round	Tottenham H	(a)	0-6

EFL Cup

First Round	Barnet	(a)	4-0
Second Round	Nottingham F	(h)	1-2

EFL Checkatrade Trophy

Southern Group H	WBA U21	(h)	2-0
Southern Group H	Gillingham	(h)	2-1
Southern Group H	Luton T	(a)	3-1
Second Round South	Wycombe W	(h)	1-3

League One Play-Offs

Semi-Final 1st leg	Scunthorpe U	(h)	0-0
Semi-Final 2nd leg	Scunthorpe U	(a)	3-2
Final	Bradford C	(Wembley)	1-0

MILTON KEYNES DONS

FOUNDATION

In July 2004 Wimbledon became MK Dons and relocated to Milton Keynes. In 2007 it recognised itself as a new club with no connection to the old Wimbledon FC. In August of that year the replica trophies and other Wimbledon FC memorabilia were returned to the London Borough of Merton.

Stadiummk, Stadium Way West, Milton Keynes, Buckinghamshire MK1 1ST.

Telephone: (01908)) 622 922.

Fax: (01908) 622 933.

Ticket Office: (0333) 200 5343.

Website: www.mkdons.com

Email: info@mkdons.com

Ground Capacity: 30,690.

Record Attendance: 28,127 v Chelsea, FA Cup 4th rd, 31 January 2016.

Pitch Measurements: 104m × 67.5m (114yd × 74yd).

Chairman: Pete Winkelman.

Executive Director: Andrew Cullen.

Manager: Robbie Neilson.

Assistant Manager: Neil McFarlane.

Colours: White shirts , white shorts, white socks.

Year Formed: 2004.

Turned Professional: 2004.

Club Nickname: 'The Dons'.

Grounds: 2004, The National Hockey Stadium; 2007, Stadiummk.

First Football League Game: 7 August 2004, FL 1, v Barnsley (h) D 1–1 – Rachubka; Palmer, Lewington, Harding, Williams, Oyedele, Kamara, Smith, Smart (Herve), McLeod (1) (Hornuss), Small.

Record League Victory: 7–0 v Oldham Ath, FL 1, 20 December 2014 – Martin; Spence, McFadzean, Kay (Baldock), Lewington; Potter (1), Alli (1); Baker C (1), Carruthers (Green), Bowditch (1) (Afobe (1)); Grigg (2).

HONOURS

League Champions: FL 2 – 2007–08.
Runners-up: FL 1 – 2014–15.

FA Cup: 5th rd – 2013.

League Cup: 4th rd – 2015.

League Trophy Winners: 2008.

sky SPORTS FACT FILE

Milton Keynes Dons' first FA Cup match saw them face Lancaster City of the Conference North in a first-round tie in November 2004 with Wade Small scoring the only goal of the game. The Dons defeated Cambridge City in the second round before going out of the competition to Peterborough United.

Record Cup Victory: 6–0 v Nantwich T, FA Cup 1st rd, 12 November 2011 – Martin; Chicksen, Baldock G, Doumbe (1), Flanagan, Williams S, Powell (1) (O'Shea (1), Chadwick (Galloway), Bowditch (2), MacDonald (Williams G (1)), Balanta.

Record Defeat: 0–6 v Southampton, Capital One Cup 3rd rd, 23 September 2015.

Most League Points (3 for a win): 97, FL 2, 2007–08.

Most League Goals: 101, FL 1, 2014–15.

Highest League Scorer in Season: Izale McLeod, 21, 2006–07.

MANAGERS

Stuart Murdock 2004
Danny Wilson 2004–06
Martin Allen 2006–07
Paul Ince 2007–08
Roberto Di Matteo 2008–09
Paul Ince 2009–10
Karl Robinson 2010–16
Robbie Neilson December 2016–

Most League Goals in Total Aggregate: Izale McLeod, 62, 2004–07; 2012–14.

Most Capped Player: Lee Hodson, 7 (20), Northern Ireland.

Most League Goals in One Match: 3, Clive Platt v Barnet, FL 2, 20 January 2007; 3, Mark Wright v Bury, FL 2, 2 February 2008; 3, Aaron Wilbraham v Cheltenham T, FL 1, 31 January 2009; 3, Sam Baldock v Colchester U, FL 1, 12 March 2011; 3, Sam Baldock v Chesterfield, FL 1, 20 August 2012; 3, Dean Bowditch v Bury, FL 1, 22 September 2012; 3, Dele Alli v Notts Co, FL 1, 11 March 2014; 3, Dele Alli v Crewe Alex, FL 1, 20 September 2014; 3, Benik Afobe v Colchester U, FL 1, 29 November 2014; 3, Robert Hall v Leyton Orient, FL 1, 18 April 2015; 3, Ryan Colclough v Fleetwood T, FL 1, 9 September 2016.

Most League Appearances: Dean Lewington, 551, 2004–17.

Youngest League Player: Brendon Galloway, 16 years 42 days v Rochdale, 28 April 2012.

Record Transfer Fee Received: £5,000,000 from Tottenham H for Dele Alli, February 2015.

Record Transfer Fee Paid: £400,000 to Bristol C for Kieran Agard, August 2016.

Football League Record: 2004–06 FL 1; 2006–08 FL 2; 2008–15 FL 1; 2015–16 FL C; 2016– FL 1.

LATEST SEQUENCES

Longest Sequence of League Wins: 8, 7.9.2007 – 20.10.2007.

Longest Sequence of League Defeats: 4, 29.8.2015 – 26.9.2015.

Longest Sequence of League Draws: 4, 12.2.2013 – 2.3.2013.

Longest Sequence of Unbeaten League Matches: 18, 29.1.2008 – 3.5.2008.

Longest Sequence Without a League Win: 11, 8.3.2016 – 7.5.2016.

Successive Scoring Runs: 18 from 7.4.2007.

Successive Non-scoring Runs: 4, 17.12.2005.

TEN YEAR LEAGUE RECORD

		P	*W*	*D*	*L*	*F*	*A*	*Pts*	*Pos*
2007-08	FL 2	46	29	10	7	82	37	97	1
2008-09	FL 1	46	26	9	11	83	47	87	3
2009-10	FL 1	46	17	9	20	60	68	60	12
2010-11	FL 1	46	23	8	15	67	60	77	5
2011-12	FL 1	46	22	14	10	84	47	80	5
2012-13	FL 1	46	19	13	14	62	45	70	8
2013-14	FL 1	46	17	9	20	63	65	60	10
2014-15	FL 1	46	27	10	9	101	44	91	2
2015-16	FL C	46	9	12	25	39	69	39	23
2016-17	FL 1	46	16	13	17	60	58	61	12

DID YOU KNOW ?

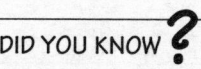

In 2007–08 Milton Keynes Dons had four players selected in the PFA League Two Team of the Year. Danny Swailes, Dean Lewington, Keith Andrews and Lloyd Dyer were all honoured at the end of a season in which the Dons won the title, finishing five points clear of their nearest rivals Peterborough United.

MILTON KEYNES DONS FC – SKY BET LEAGUE ONE 2016–17 LEAGUE RECORD

Match No.	Date	Venue	Opponents	Result	H/T Score	Lg Pos.	Goalscorers	Attendance
1	Aug 6	A	Shrewsbury T	W 1-0	0-0	8	Powell [73]	5452
2	13	H	Millwall	D 2-2	2-2	8	Agard 2 [28, 33]	10,232
3	16	H	Bradford C	L 1-2	0-2	10	Upson [90]	8166
4	20	A	Rochdale	W 1-0	0-0	7	Wootton [90]	2176
5	27	H	Peterborough U	L 0-2	0-1	12		10,621
6	Sept 4	A	Northampton T	L 2-3	1-3	14	Bowditch [38], Carruthers [90]	6618
7	10	A	Bolton W	D 1-1	0-1	15	Colclough [54]	12,727
8	17	H	Oxford U	D 0-0	0-0	16		12,340
9	24	A	Fleetwood T	W 4-1	1-0	12	Colclough 3 (1 pen) [9, 68, 90 (p)], Bowditch (pen) [61]	2518
10	27	H	Bury	L 1-3	0-1	14	Reeves [63]	7652
11	Oct 1	A	Oldham Ath	W 2-0	1-0	9	Reeves [36], Agard [55]	3273
12	9	H	Port Vale	L 0-1	0-1	12		8259
13	15	A	Scunthorpe U	L 1-2	1-0	16	Agard [37]	4238
14	18	H	Bristol R	D 3-3	2-0	16	Bowditch [16], George B Williams [24], Reeves [66]	8366
15	22	H	Southend U	L 0-3	0-2	19		11,039
16	29	A	Sheffield U	L 1-2	0-1	20	Potter [49]	20,495
17	Nov 12	H	Walsall	D 1-1	0-1	20	Bowditch [90]	8188
18	19	A	Bristol R	D 0-0	0-0	21		9031
19	22	H	Chesterfield	L 2-3	0-1	21	Powell [67], Colclough [73]	7429
20	26	A	Coventry C	W 2-1	1-1	19	Upson 2 [35, 80]	9640
21	Dec 10	H	AFC Wimbledon	W 1-0	0-0	18	Bowditch (pen) [63]	11,185
22	17	A	Gillingham	L 0-1	0-0	18		5681
23	26	H	Charlton Ath	L 0-1	0-1	18		10,257
24	30	H	Swindon T	W 3-2	2-1	18	Agard 2 [9, 26], Maynard [54]	9385
25	Jan 2	A	Chesterfield	D 0-0	0-0	18		5554
26	21	H	Northampton T	W 5-3	2-0	16	Agard [38], Aneke 2 (1 pen) [43 (p), 56], Nyatanga (og) [63], Barnes [79]	12,300
27	28	A	Peterborough U	W 4-0	0-0	15	Barnes [59], Agard [71], Aneke 2 [74, 83]	6617
28	Feb 4	H	Bolton W	D 1-1	0-1	15	Agard [59]	21,545
29	7	H	Oldham Ath	W 1-0	0-0	14	Maynard [90]	7598
30	11	A	Oxford U	L 0-1	0-0	14		9179
31	14	A	Bury	D 0-0	0-0	14		2005
32	18	H	Fleetwood T	L 0-1	0-0	16		8278
33	25	H	Shrewsbury T	W 2-1	2-0	15	Agard [5], Barnes [11]	8322
34	28	A	Bradford C	D 2-2	2-2	14	O'Keefe [4], George B Williams [35]	16,725
35	Mar 4	A	Millwall	L 1-2	1-1	14	Reeves [30]	9636
36	11	H	Rochdale	D 2-2	0-1	17	Agard [70], Reeves [90]	10,569
37	14	A	AFC Wimbledon	L 0-2	0-0	17		4112
38	18	H	Coventry C	W 1-0	0-0	16	O'Keefe [51]	9060
39	25	A	Port Vale	D 0-0	0-0	15		3887
40	Apr 1	H	Gillingham	W 3-2	2-0	14	Muirhead [5], Barnes [10], Lewington [90]	8807
41	4	A	Charlton Ath	W 2-0	1-0	12	O'Keefe [7], Barnes [57]	10,943
42	8	A	Swindon T	D 1-1	1-0	12	Agard (pen) [43]	7946
43	14	H	Scunthorpe U	L 0-1	0-1	12		9274
44	17	A	Southend U	W 2-1	0-0	12	Walsh [53], Reeves [62]	9009
45	22	H	Sheffield U	L 0-3	0-1	12		18,180
46	30	A	Walsall	W 4-1	2-0	12	Muirhead [11], Reeves [32], O'Keefe [71], Barnes [85]	5004

Final League Position: 12

GOALSCORERS

League (60): Agard 12 (1 pen), Reeves 7, Barnes 6, Bowditch 5 (2 pens), Colclough 5 (1 pen), Aneke 4 (1 pen), O'Keefe 4, Upson 3, Maynard 2, Muirhead 2, Powell 2, George B Williams 2, Carruthers 1, Lewington 1, Potter 1, Walsh 1, Wootton 1, own goal 1.
FA Cup (6): Reeves 2, Agard 1, Bowditch 1, Powell 1, Thomas-Asante 1.
EFL Cup (5): Bowditch 3 (2 pens), Tilney 1, Tshimanga 1.
EFL Checkatrade Trophy (5): Agard 1, Reeves 1, Tapp 1, Walsh 1, own goal 1.

Martin D 39 + 1	Baldock G 36 + 1	Walsh J 39	Downing P 34 + 3	Lewington D 36	Potter D 32 + 5	Upson E 40 + 2	Powell D 8 + 12	Carruthers S 18 + 5	Williams George C 5 + 6	Maynard N 20 + 11	Rasulo G 1 + 2	Thomas-Asante B — + 6	Williams George B 29 + 4	Agard K 33 + 9	Bowditch D 20 + 8	Wootton S 1	Reeves B 26 + 8	Tshimanga K — + 6	Colclough R 12 + 6	Hendry J 6 + 1	Aneke C 9 + 6	Nicholls L 7 + 1	Muirhead R 12 + 7	Barnes H 18 + 3	Brittain C 2 + 4	O'Keefe S 17 + 1	Ngombo M 1 + 8	Tilney B 5 + 1	Match No.
1	2	3	4	5	6	7	8	9^{1}	10^{2}	11^{3}	12	13	14																1
1	5	4	3	2	7	8	9		6^{2}	11		13		10^{1}	12														2
1	2	3	4	5	10^{1}	9	7	12	6^{2}	11				8	13														3
1	2	3		5		6	10	7	8	11^{1}					9^{2}	4	12	13											4
1	2	3	4	5	7	6^{3}	10	9	8^{2}	11^{1}					13		12	14											5
1	5	3	4	2	8	7^{3}	14	6		11^{1}				13	10		12		9^{2}										6
1	2	3	4	5	8	7^{2}	13	12		14				11	10		6^{1}		9^{3}										7
1	2	4	3	5	6	7		12	13					11	10		9^{1}		8^{2}										8
1	2	4	3	5	7	8		12	13	11				10	9^{1}				6^{2}										9
1	2	3	4	5	7	6^{1}		12		11^{2}				8			9	13	10										10
1	2^{2}	4	3	5	6	14		7		11			12	8	13		9^{3}		10^{1}										11
1		4	3^{1}	5	6	7^{2}		9		13		14	2	11	8		12		10^{3}										12
1		3	4^{2}	2	8		13	6		9			5	10	11^{3}		7^{1}	14	12										13
1			3	5		6	12	7		13			2	8	11^{2}		9		10^{1}	4									14
1		5	4		7	12	8^{1}	6				13	2		11		9		10	3^{2}									15
1	2	4		5	7	8	14	6^{3}		13				12	10^{1}		9		11^{2}	3									16
1	2		4^{1}	5		6		7^{2}		12			13	8	11		9	14	10^{3}	3									17
1	2	4		5		7	13	6	12				14	8	11^{2}		9^{3}		10^{1}	3									18
1	2	4		5		6	10	7^{3}	14					8^{1}	11		9^{2}		12	3	13								19
1	2	4	3	5	9	6	10^{3}	7^{2}						8^{1}	11		13		12		14								20
1	2		3	4	7	6	13	8^{3}					5	11^{1}	9^{2}		10		14		12								21
1	2^{1}		3	4	7	6		8		13			5	11^{3}	9^{2}		10		14	12									22
1		4	3	2		6	13	9^{2}	12	11			5	10^{3}	8^{1}		7				14								23
1		4	3	5		6	12	9		11^{3}			2	10^{1}			7	14	13		8^{2}								24
1		4	3	5	6	7	13		12	11			2	10^{2}			8				9^{1}								25
1^{1}	5	3	2	4	7	6				10			8	9^{2}							11^{3}	12	13	14					26
1	2	3	5		6	7	13			10			4	9^{1}							11^{2}		12	8^{3}	14				27
1	2	4	3		7	6				11^{3}			5	10^{2}	13						8^{1}			9		12	14		28
1	2	4	3		6					14			5	8	10^{2}						13		9^{1}	12		7	11^{3}		29
1	2	3	4		7■	6				11^{2}			5	12							9^{3}		13	10^{1}		8	14		30
1	2		3			7	13						5	11^{1}	10						8^{2}			9		6	12	4	31
1	2		3		6					11^{1}			4	13	8^{2}						9		14	10		7^{3}	12	5	32
1	2	4	3		6					12			5	11^{1}			9^{2}				10^{3}		14	8		7	13		33
1	5	2	3	4	14	6				11^{2}			9	13							12^{3}		10^{1}	7		8			34
1	5	2	3	4	7	6				13			9	10^{2}	14		8^{3}						11^{1}	12					35
1		3	4^{3}		14	8				10^{1}			2	12			9						11^{2}	6		7	13	5	36
1		2	10		4	3^{2}				13			6	11			12						8^{1}	9		7		5	37
1	2^{1}	3	14	4	13	6							5	11^{2}			8						9^{3}	10		7	12		38
1	2	3		5	13	8^{2}				14			4	10^{3}			7						11^{1}	6		9	12		39
	2	4	14	5	12	6^{1}							3■	11^{2}	13		8^{3}					1	10	9		7			40
	2	3	4	5	8	6								12	14		10^{1}					1	11^{2}	7	13	9^{3}			41
	2	4	12	5	8	6							3	11^{1}			10^{2}					1	13	7^{3}	14	9			42
	2	4		5		7					8^{2}	14	3	13			12					1	10^{3}	11	9^{1}	6			43
	13	4		5	8	6							3	10^{3}			9^{1}					1	12	11	2^{2}	7		14	44
14	2	4		5	7^{2}	6						12	3	10			13					1^{1}	9^{3}	11		8			45
	2			3	7^{2}	6					12		4	14			11^{3}					1	10^{1}	9	13	8		5	46

FA Cup
First Round Spennymoor T (h) 3-2
Second Round Charlton Ath (a) 0-0
Replay Charlton Ath (h) 3-1
(aet)
Third Round Brighton & HA (a) 0-2

EFL Cup
First Round Newport Co (a) 3-2
Second Round Reading (a) 2-2
(*aet; Reading won 4-2 on penalties*)

EFL Checkatrade Trophy
Southern Group F Barnet (h) 2-2
(*Milton Keynes D won 5-3 on penalties*)
Southern Group F Peterborough U (a) 1-0
Southern Group F Norwich C U21 (a) 1-4
Second Round South Yeovil T (a) 1-4

MORECAMBE

FOUNDATION

Several attempts to start a senior football club in a rugby stronghold finally succeeded on 7 May 1920 at the West View Hotel, Morecambe and a team competed in the Lancashire Combination for 1920–21. The club shared with a local cricket club at Woodhill Lane for the first season and a crowd of 3,000 watched the first game. The club moved to Roseberry Park, the name of which was changed to Christie Park after J.B. Christie who as President had purchased the ground.

Globe Arena, Christie Way, Westgate, Morecambe, Lancashire LA4 4TB.

Telephone: (01524) 411 797.

Fax: (01524) 832 230.

Ticket Office: (01524) 411 797.

Website: www.morecambefc.com

Email: office@morecambefc.com

Ground Capacity: 6,241.

Record Attendance: 9,383 v Weymouth, FA Cup 3rd rd, 6 January 1962 (at Christie Park); 5,375 v Newcastle U, League Cup, 28 August 2013 (at Globe Arena).

Pitch Measurements: 103m × 71m (113yd × 78yd).

Chairman: Peter McGuigan.

Co-Chairman: Diego Lemos.

Manager: Jim Bentley.

Assistant Manager: Ken McKenna.

Colours: Red shirts with thin black stripes and black sleeves, black shorts with white trim, red socks with black trim.

Year Formed: 1920.

Turned Professional: 1920.

Club Nickname: 'The Shrimps'.

Grounds: 1920, Woodhill Lane; 1921, Christie Park; 2010, Globe Arena.

First Football League game: 11 August 2007, FL 2, v Barnet (h) D 0–0 – Lewis; Yates, Adams, Artell, Bentley, Stanley, Baker (Burns), Sorvel, Twiss (Newby), Curtis, Hunter (Thompson).

HONOURS

League: *Runners-up:* Conference – (3rd) 2006–07 *(promoted via play-offs)*.

FA Cup: 3rd rd – 1962, 2001, 2003.

League Cup: 3rd rd – 2008.

sky SPORTS FACT FILE

Morecambe reached the FA Cup rounds proper for the first time in the 1936–37 season. They were drawn away to South Liverpool, who also played in the Lancashire Combination, and went down to a 1-0 defeat in front of a crowd of around 6,000.

Record League Victory: 6–0 v Crawley T, FL 2, 10 September 2011 – Roche; Reid, Wilson (pen), McCready, Haining (Parrish), Fenton (1), Drummond, McDonald, Price (Jevons), Carlton (3) (Alessandra), Ellison (1).

Record Cup Victory: 6–2 v Nelson (a), Lancashire Trophy, 27 January 2004.

Record Defeat: 0–7 v Cambridge U, FL 2, 19 April 2016.

Most League Points (3 for a win): 73, FL 2, 2009–10.

Most League Goals: 73, FL 2, 2009–10.

Highest League Scorer in Season: Phil Jevons, 18, 2009–10.

Most League Goals in Total Aggregate: Kevin Ellison, 64, 2011–17.

Most League Goals in One Match: 3, Jon Newby v Rotherham U, FL 2, 29 March 2008.

Most League Appearances: Barry Roche, 358, 2008–17.

Youngest League Player: Aaron McGowan, 16 years 263 days, 20 April 2013.

Record Transfer Fee Received: £225,000 from Stockport Co for Carl Baker, July 2008.

Record Transfer Fee Paid: £50,000 to Southport for Carl Baker, July 2007.

Football League Record: 2006–07 Promoted from Conference; 2007– FL 2.

MANAGERS

Jimmy Milne 1947–48
Albert Dainty 1955–56
Ken Horton 1956–61
Joe Dunn 1961–64
Geoff Twentyman 1964–65
Ken Waterhouse 1965–69
Ronnie Clayton 1969–70
Gerry Irving and Ronnie Mitchell 1970
Ken Waterhouse 1970–72
Dave Roberts 1972–75
Alan Spavin 1975–76
Johnny Johnson 1976–77
Tommy Ferber 1977–78
Mick Hogarth 1978–79
Don Curbage 1979–81
Jim Thompson 1981
Les Rigby 1981–84
Sean Gallagher 1984–85
Joe Wojciechowicz 1985–88
Eric Whalley 1988
Billy Wright 1988–89
Lawrie Milligan 1989
Bryan Griffiths 1989–93
Leighton James 1994
Jim Harvey 1994–2006
Sammy McIlroy 2006–11
Jim Bentley May 2011–

LATEST SEQUENCES

Longest Sequence of League Wins: 7, 31.10.2009 – 12.12.2009.

Longest Sequence of League Defeats: 7, 4.3.2017 – 1.4.2017.

Longest Sequence of League Draws: 5, 3.1.2015 – 31.1.2015.

Longest Sequence of Unbeaten League Matches: 12, 31.1.2009 – 21.3.2009.

Longest Sequence Without a League Win: 10, 29.12.2013 – 1.3.2014.

Successive Scoring Runs: 17 from 13.8.2011.

Successive Non-scoring Runs: 3 from 29.10.2016.

TEN YEAR LEAGUE RECORD

		P	*W*	*D*	*L*	*F*	*A*	*Pts*	*Pos*
2007-08	FL 2	46	16	12	18	59	63	60	11
2008-09	FL 2	46	15	18	13	53	56	63	11
2009-10	FL 2	46	20	13	13	73	64	73	4
2010-11	FL 2	46	13	12	21	54	73	51	20
2011-12	FL 2	46	14	14	18	63	57	56	15
2012-13	FL 2	46	15	13	18	55	61	58	16
2013-14	FL 2	46	13	15	18	52	64	54	18
2014-15	FL 2	46	17	12	17	53	52	63	11
2015-16	FL 2	46	12	10	24	69	91	46	21
2016-17	FL 2	46	14	10	22	53	73	52	18

DID YOU KNOW ?

Morecambe played their first-ever competitive game at home to Fleetwood on 28 August 1920. The Shrimps went down to a 4-1 defeat in the Lancashire Combination fixture with their goal coming from Lewis.

MORECAMBE – SKY BET LEAGUE TWO 2016–17 LEAGUE RECORD

Match No.	Date	Venue	Opponents	Result	H/T Score	Lg Pos.	Goalscorers	Attendance
1	Aug 6	A	Grimsby T	L 0-2	0-1	22		6004
2	13	H	Blackpool	W 2-1	1-1	15	Dunn (pen) [45], Rose [76]	3676
3	16	H	Portsmouth	W 2-0	2-0	5	Edwards [10], Barkhuizen [21]	1838
4	20	A	Yeovil T	W 1-0	0-0	1	Ellison [55]	2937
5	27	A	Accrington S	W 3-2	1-2	1	Stockton 2 [45, 57], Ellison [46]	1763
6	Sept 3	H	Leyton Orient	L 1-2	0-1	2	Ellison [49]	1665
7	10	H	Doncaster R	L 1-5	1-2	7	Stockton [45]	1791
8	17	A	Cambridge U	W 2-1	0-1	3	Dunn (pen) [62], Mullin [64]	4110
9	24	H	Crawley T	L 2-3	0-0	7	Rose [89], Stockton [90]	1304
10	27	A	Barnet	D 2-2	1-2	6	Barkhuizen [9], Stockton [81]	1164
11	Oct 8	H	Carlisle U	L 0-3	0-1	14		3773
12	11	A	Notts Co	W 2-1	1-0	7	Barkhuizen 2 (1 pen) [16, 55 (p)]	3507
13	15	H	Stevenage	L 0-2	0-1	10		1212
14	22	A	Colchester U	D 2-2	1-2	10	Barkhuizen [27], Molyneux [77]	2815
15	29	H	Exeter C	L 0-3	0-3	12		1302
16	Nov 12	A	Wycombe W	L 0-2	0-0	14		3019
17	19	H	Luton T	L 0-2	0-1	17		1507
18	22	A	Crewe Alex	L 1-2	1-2	20	Turner [8]	2844
19	26	H	Plymouth Arg	W 2-1	1-1	17	Rose (pen) [20], Murphy [63]	1435
20	Dec 17	H	Cheltenham T	L 1-2	1-0	19	Murphy [6]	1297
21	26	A	Mansfield T	W 1-0	1-0	18	Fleming [13]	3237
22	30	A	Hartlepool U	L 2-3	0-3	19	Fleming [52], Mullin [90]	2996
23	Jan 2	H	Crewe Alex	D 0-0	0-0	19		1722
24	7	H	Notts Co	W 4-1	3-0	17	Molyneux [2], Mullin [27], Rose (pen) [31], Ellison [90]	1315
25	14	A	Carlisle U	D 1-1	1-0	16	Wildig [7]	5524
26	Feb 4	A	Doncaster R	D 1-1	1-0	17	Murphy [24]	6096
27	7	A	Leyton Orient	W 1-0	0-0	17	Mullin [72]	2660
28	11	H	Cambridge U	W 2-0	0-0	15	Ellison 2 [50, 55]	2162
29	14	H	Barnet	L 0-1	0-0	17		1100
30	18	A	Crawley T	W 3-1	3-0	15	Turner [3], Mullin 2 [7, 40]	2091
31	21	A	Newport Co	D 1-1	0-1	15	Rose [64]	1988
32	25	H	Grimsby T	W 1-0	1-0	13	Molyneux [2]	1824
33	28	A	Portsmouth	D 1-1	0-0	14	Molyneux [83]	15,592
34	Mar 4	A	Blackpool	L 1-3	0-1	15	Evans [83]	3453
35	11	H	Yeovil T	L 1-3	0-1	15	Evans [53]	1433
36	14	H	Newport Co	L 0-1	0-0	15		1080
37	18	A	Plymouth Arg	L 0-1	0-1	15		8785
38	21	H	Accrington S	L 1-2	0-1	16	Wildig [82]	1506
39	25	H	Mansfield T	L 1-3	1-3	19	Mullin [6]	1497
40	Apr 1	A	Cheltenham T	L 1-3	0-1	19	Boyle (og) [78]	2751
41	8	H	Hartlepool U	D 1-1	0-1	19	Mullin [59]	1548
42	14	A	Stevenage	W 1-0	0-0	17	Molyneux [68]	3117
43	17	H	Colchester U	D 1-1	0-1	17	Rose (pen) [88]	1447
44	22	A	Exeter C	L 1-3	0-0	18	Ellison [61]	3991
45	29	H	Wycombe W	D 1-1	0-0	18	Ellison [81]	1742
46	May 6	A	Luton T	L 1-3	0-1	18	Rose (pen) [58]	8399

Final League Position: 18

GOALSCORERS

League (53): Ellison 8, Mullin 8, Rose 7 (4 pens), Barkhuizen 5 (1 pen), Molyneux 5, Stockton 5, Murphy 3, Dunn 2 (2 pens), Evans 2, Fleming 2, Turner 2, Wildig 2, Edwards 1, own goal 1.
FA Cup (2): Winnard 2.
EFL Cup (6): Dunn 3 (1 pen), Stockton 2, Ellison 1.
EFL Checkatrade Trophy (8): Stockton 3, Mullin 2, Dunn 1, Edwards 1, Murphy 1.

Roche B 41	Wakefield L 22 + 3	Edwards R 43	Whitmore A 35	McGowan A 22 + 8	Fleming A 25 + 5	Rose M 43	Barkhuizen T 14	Wildig A 23 + 5	Ellison K 39 + 6	Dunn J 9 + 4	Stockton C 17 + 2	Turner R 13 + 17	Molyneux L 22 + 18	Conlan L 16 + 5	Kenyon A 14 + 5	Mullin P 28 + 12	Jennings J 12 + 1	Massanka N — + 10	Winnard D 23	Murphy P 22 + 10	Jordan L — + 6	Evans A 7 + 7	Duckworth M 11 + 3	Hawley K — + 1	Nizic D 5	Yawson S — + 1	Hedley B — + 1	Match No.
1	2^1	3	4	5	6	7	8	9^2	10	11^3	12	13	14															1
1	2	3	4		14	7	8^1		12	9^2	11		10	5^3	6	13												2
1	2	3	4		6	7	8^1		10	9^3	11^2		12	5	14	13												3
1	2		3	14	6	7	8^2		10	9^3	11^1	13	12	5	4													4
1	2	3	4		6^1	7	8		10	9^2	11^3	14	12	5	13													5
1	2	3	4	5	6^2	7	8		10	9^1	11^3	12			13	14												6
1	2^2	3	4■			7	8		10	9^1	11		13	5^3	6		12	14										7
1	2	3		14	6^2	7			10	9	11^3			5		8^1		13	4	12								8
1	2	3				7	8		10	9^1	12			5		11^2		13	4	6								9
1	5	4				7	9^1		8	12	11		13		6^2	10^3	2		3	14								10
1		4	3	5	6		8^1		10	12	11		13			9^2	2	14		7^3								11
1	2	3	4		6	7	5		11^3		10^1	13	9^2			14	8			12								12
1	2	3	4		7	6^3	5		11		10		9^1	13		12	8^2			14								13
1		3	4	2	6^2	7	8		10^1		11		12				5	13		9								14
1		3	4	2		7	8		9^1	12	11		10^2				5	13		6								15
1		3	5	2		9		10^3	12	14	11		13			7^1	6^2		4	8								16
1		2	4■	5		7			10^1		11^2	13	9			12	8	14	3	6^3								17
1	2	3		5		8		7^2	13		11	10^3	12	9^1		14	4			6								18
1	2	4		14		7		9^2	10^1		11	8^3				12	5	13	3	6								19
1	4^1	3		5	12	6						10^3	14	9	8■	11		13	2	7^2								20
1		3		5	8	6		13	11^1			10^2		9		12	4		2	7								21
1		2		4	10	9		14	8			11^1	13	5^3		12	6^2		3	7								22
1		3	4	5^1	10	8		6^2	11				13	9		12		14	2	7^3								23
1	2	4			6■	7		9^2	11				8	5^1	12	10^3			3	14	13							24
1	14	4		2		5		7^2	11			12	10^1	13	9	6^3			3■	8								25
1		2	4	5^3		8		7^2	10			13	9		3	11^1				6		12	14					26
1		3	2	14		5^2		10	9			12	6^3		13	11^1			4	7			8					27
1		3	2			6		7^1	10^2			12	5		4	11^3				8	14	13	9					28
1	13	3	4			6		7	10			12	5^3		2^2	11^1				8■	14		9					29
1	5	3	2	14	7	8		13	12			10^2	9			11^3			4			6^1						30
1	2	3	4	12	6	7		9^1	10			8	13	5^3		11^2						14						31
1	2	3	4	5	6	7		12	10			13	8			11^2						9^1						32
1	2^2	3	4	13	6^1	7		8	9			11^3	5	12		10				14								33
1	2^1	3	4	13	6^2			8^3	10			12	9			11				7		14	5					34
1		2	4					9	11^1			12	8			10			3	7	13	6^2	5					35
1	5^1	3	2		6	7			8^2			11	13			10			4	14		9^3	12					36
1		4	3			7		9^1	12			8^2	10	5		11				6	13		2					37
1		3	4		13	7		9	10			11	8^1	14		12			5^2	6^3			2					38
1			4		7^1	6		9	10			8^3	14	5^2		11			3		12	13	2					39
1		3	4	5^3		6		9^2	10				8^1		7■	11			2	12		13		14				40
		3	4	2	6	7		12	10			8^2	13			11						9^1	5		1			41
		3	4	5	6	7		9^1	11			13	8^3	14		10^2			2	12					1			42
			2	8	6	7		10^3	11^2			13			3^1	9			4	14		12	5		1			43
		3		8	6	7		9	12			14	13		4^3	10^1			2			11^2	5		1			44
	14	3	2	5^2	12	8			11				9		7	10^1			4	6^3					1	13		45
1		3	2	7^1	12	8		6^2	10				9		4	11						5^3	14				13	46

FA Cup
First Round | Coventry C | (h) | 1-1
Replay | Coventry C | (a) | 1-2

EFL Cup
First Round (*aet*) | Rotherham U | (a) | 5-4
Second Round | Bournemouth | (h) | 1-2

EFL Checkatrade Trophy
Northern Group C | Bury | (a) | 1-4
Northern Group C | Stoke C U21 | (h) | 3-1
Northern Group C | Bradford C | (h) | 3-2
Second Round North | Scunthorpe U | (a) | 1-1
(*Scunthorpe U won 5-3 on penalties*)

NEWCASTLE UNITED

FOUNDATION

In October 1882 a club called Stanley, which had been formed in 1881, changed its name to Newcastle East End to avoid confusion with two other local clubs, Stanley Nops and Stanley Albion. Shortly afterwards another club, Rosewood, merged with them. Newcastle West End had been formed in August 1882 and they played on a pitch which was part of the Town Moor. They moved to Brandling Park in 1885 and St James' Park 1886 (home of Newcastle Rangers). West End went out of existence after a bad run and the remaining committee men invited East End to move to St James' Park. They accepted and, at a meeting in Bath Lane Hall in 1892, changed their name to Newcastle United.

St James' Park, Newcastle-upon-Tyne NE1 4ST.
Telephone: (0844) 372 1892.
Fax: (0191) 201 8600.
Ticket Office: (0844) 372 1892 (option 1).
Website: www.nufc.co.uk
Email: see website
Ground Capacity: 52,354.
Record Attendance: 68,386 v Chelsea, Division 1, 3 September 1930.
Pitch Measurements: 105m × 68m (114yd × 74yd).
Managing Director: Lee Charnley.
Manager: Rafael Benitez.
First-Team Coaches: Mikel Antia, Antonio Gomez Perez, Francisco Moreno.
Colours: Black and white striped shirts, black shorts with white trim, black and white hooped socks.
Year Formed: 1881.
Turned Professional: 1889.
Previous Names: 1881, Stanley; 1882, Newcastle East End; 1892, Newcastle United.
Club Nickname: 'The Magpies', 'The Toon'.
Grounds: 1881, South Byker; 1886, Chillingham Road, Heaton; 1892, St James' Park.
First Football League Game: 2 September 1893, Division 2, v Royal Arsenal (a) D 2–2 – Ramsay; Jeffery, Miller; Crielly, Graham, McKane; Bowman, Crate (1), Thompson, Sorley (1), Wallace. Graham not Crate scored according to some reports.
Record League Victory: 13–0 v Newport Co, Division 2, 5 October 1946 – Garbutt; Cowell, Graham; Harvey, Brennan, Wright; Milburn (2), Bentley (1), Wayman (4), Shackleton (6), Pearson.

HONOURS

League Champions: Division 1 – 1904–05, 1906–07, 1908–09, 1926–27; FL C – 2009–10, 2016–17; First Division – 1992–93; Division 2 – 1964–65.
Runners-up: FA Premier League – 1995–96, 1996–97; Division 2 – 1897–98, 1947–48.

FA Cup Winners: 1910, 1924, 1932, 1951, 1952, 1955.
Runners-up: 1905, 1906, 1908, 1911, 1974, 1998, 1999.

League Cup: *Runners-up:* 1976.

Texaco Cup Winners: 1974, 1975.
Anglo-Italian Cup Winners: 1972–73.

European Competitions
Champions League: 1997–98, 2002–03, 2003–04.
Fairs Cup: 1968–69 *(winners)*, 1969–70 *(qf)*, 1970–71.
UEFA Cup: 1977–78, 1994–95, 1996–97 *(qf)*, 1999–2000, 2003–04 *(sf)*, 2004–05 *(qf)*, 2006–07.
Europa League: 2012–13 *(qf)*.
European Cup Winners' Cup: 1998–99.
Intertoto Cup: 2001 *(runners-up)*, 2005, 2006 *(winners)*.

sky SPORTS FACT FILE

Newcastle United reached three FA Cup finals in the 1950s but struggled to win a game in the competition in the 1960s. In the 12 seasons from 1961–62 they went out in the third round on eight occasions and never progressed beyond the fourth round. Most disappointing of all for Magpies fans was the home defeat to Southern League Bedford Town in January 1964.

Record Cup Victory: 9–0 v Southport (at Hillsborough), FA Cup 4th rd, 1 February 1932 – McInroy; Nelson, Fairhurst; McKenzie, Davidson, Weaver (1); Boyd (1), Jimmy Richardson (3), Cape (2), McMenemy (1), Lang (1).

Record Defeat: 0–9 v Burton Wanderers, Division 2, 15 April 1895.

Most League Points (2 for a win): 57, Division 2, 1964–65.

Most League Points (3 for a win): 102, FL C, 2009–10.

Most League Goals: 98, Division 1, 1951–52.

Highest League Scorer in Season: Hughie Gallacher, 36, Division 1, 1926–27.

Most League Goals in Total Aggregate: Jackie Milburn, 177, 1946–57.

Most League Goals in One Match: 6, Len Shackleton v Newport Co, Division 2, 5 October 1946.

Most Capped Player: Shay Given, 82 (134), Republic of Ireland.

Most League Appearances: Jim Lawrence, 432, 1904–22.

Youngest League Player: Steve Watson, 16 years 223 days v Wolverhampton W, 10 November 1990.

Record Transfer Fee Received: £35,000,000 from Liverpool for Andy Carroll, January 2011.

Record Transfer Fee Paid: £16,000,000 to Real Madrid for Michael Owen, September 2005.

Football League Record: 1893 Elected to Division 2; 1898–1934 Division 1; 1934–48 Division 2; 1948–61 Division 1; 1961–65 Division 2; 1965–78 Division 1; 1978–84 Division 2; 1984–89 Division 1; 1989–92 Division 2; 1992–93 Division 1; 1993–2009 FA Premier League; 2009–10 FL C; 2010–16 FA Premier League; 2016–17 FL C; 2017– FA Premier League.

MANAGERS

Frank Watt 1895–32
(Secretary-Manager)
Andy Cunningham 1930–35
Tom Mather 1935–39
Stan Seymour 1939–47
(Hon. Manager)
George Martin 1947–50
Stan Seymour 1950–54
(Hon. Manager)
Duggie Livingstone 1954–56
Stan Seymour 1956–58
(Hon. Manager)
Charlie Mitten 1958–61
Norman Smith 1961–62
Joe Harvey 1962–75
Gordon Lee 1975–77
Richard Dinnis 1977
Bill McGarry 1977–80
Arthur Cox 1980–84
Jack Charlton 1984
Willie McFaul 1985–88
Jim Smith 1988–91
Ossie Ardiles 1991–92
Kevin Keegan 1992–97
Kenny Dalglish 1997–98
Ruud Gullit 1998–99
Sir Bobby Robson 1999–2004
Graeme Souness 2004–06
Glenn Roeder 2006–07
Sam Allardyce 2007–08
Kevin Keegan 2008
Joe Kinnear 2008–09
Alan Shearer 2009
Chris Hughton 2009–10
Alan Pardew 2010–15
John Carver 2015
Steve McClaren 2015–16
Rafael Benitez March 2016–

LATEST SEQUENCES

Longest Sequence of League Wins: 13, 25.4.1992 – 18.10.1992.

Longest Sequence of League Defeats: 10, 23.8.1977 – 15.10.1977.

Longest Sequence of League Draws: 4, 15.11.2008 – 6.12.2008.

Longest Sequence of Unbeaten League Matches: 17, 13.2.2010 – 2.5.2010.

Longest Sequence Without a League Win: 21, 14.1.1978 – 23.8.1978.

Successive Scoring Runs: 25 from 15.4.1939.

Successive Non-scoring Runs: 6 from 29.10.1988.

TEN YEAR LEAGUE RECORD

		P	W	D	L	F	A	Pts	Pos
2007-08	PR Lge	38	11	10	17	45	65	43	12
2008-09	PR Lge	38	7	13	18	40	59	34	18
2009-10	FL C	46	30	12	4	90	35	102	1
2010-11	PR Lge	38	11	13	14	56	57	46	12
2011-12	PR Lge	38	19	8	11	56	51	65	5
2012-13	PR Lge	38	11	8	19	45	68	41	16
2013-14	PR Lge	38	15	4	19	43	59	49	10
2014-15	PR Lge	38	10	9	19	40	63	39	15
2015-16	PR Lge	38	9	10	19	44	65	37	18
2016-17	FL C	46	29	7	10	85	40	94	1

DID YOU KNOW 

Newcastle United were one of four teams that took part in the final series of Test Matches that decided promotion and relegation in the Football League up to 1898. The Magpies initially seemed to have missed out on promotion, but it was then decided to expand the First Division by two clubs and they were elected to a place in the top flight along with Blackburn Rovers.

NEWCASTLE UNITED – SKY BET CHAMPIONSHIP 2016–17 LEAGUE RECORD

Match No.	Date	Venue	Opponents	Result	H/T Score	Lg Pos.	Goalscorers	Attendance
1	Aug 5	A	Fulham	L 0-1	0-1	24		23,922
2	13	H	Huddersfield T	L 1-2	0-1	22	Gayle [60]	52,079
3	17	H	Reading	W 4-1	1-1	17	Hayden [20], Ritchie (pen) [50], Gayle 2 [69, 89]	48,209
4	20	A	Bristol C	W 1-0	1-0	7	Gayle [19]	22,512
5	27	H	Brighton & HA	W 2-0	1-0	4	Lascelles [15], Shelvey [63]	49,196
6	Sept 10	A	Derby Co	W 2-0	1-0	2	Gouffran [20], Yedlin [90]	30,405
7	13	A	QPR	W 6-0	2-0	2	Shelvey 2 [12, 48], Perez [30], Clark [56], Mitrovic [63], Hanley [79]	17,404
8	17	H	Wolverhampton W	L 0-2	0-1	3		52,117
9	24	A	Aston Villa	D 1-1	1-0	3	Elphick (og) [28]	32,062
10	28	H	Norwich C	W 4-3	1-1	3	Gayle 3 [24, 71, 90], Gouffran [90]	48,236
11	Oct 1	A	Rotherham U	W 1-0	1-0	2	Atsu [41]	11,653
12	15	H	Brentford	W 3-1	2-0	2	Clark [11], Gayle 2 [16, 49]	51,885
13	18	A	Barnsley	W 2-0	0-0	1	Gayle 2 [49, 68]	18,597
14	22	H	Ipswich T	W 3-0	1-0	1	Perez 2 [1, 73], Ritchie [78]	51,963
15	29	A	Preston NE	W 2-1	0-0	1	Mitrovic 2 [59, 71]	20,724
16	Nov 5	H	Cardiff C	W 2-1	2-0	1	Atsu [3], Gouffran [45]	51,257
17	20	A	Leeds U	W 2-0	1-0	1	Gayle 2 [23, 54]	36,002
18	26	H	Blackburn R	L 0-1	0-0	1		52,092
19	Dec 2	A	Nottingham F	L 1-2	1-0	1	Ritchie [45]	21,317
20	10	H	Birmingham C	W 4-0	2-0	1	Gayle 3 [18, 24, 77], Gouffran [47]	52,145
21	14	A	Wigan Ath	W 2-0	1-0	1	Diame [26], Atsu [78]	14,562
22	17	A	Burton Alb	W 2-1	2-1	1	Gayle [15], Diame [34]	6665
23	26	H	Sheffield W	L 0-1	0-0	1		52,179
24	30	H	Nottingham F	W 3-1	1-1	1	Ritchie [4], Gayle 2 [63, 80]	52,228
25	Jan 2	A	Blackburn R	L 0-1	0-0	2		18,524
26	14	A	Brentford	W 2-1	1-0	1	Gayle [20], Murphy [79]	11,435
27	21	H	Rotherham U	W 4-0	1-0	1	Murphy [45], Ritchie 2 [49, 77], Perez [59]	52,208
28	Feb 1	H	QPR	D 2-2	1-1	2	Shelvey [1], Ritchie [54]	47,907
29	4	H	Derby Co	W 1-0	1-0	1	Ritchie [27]	52,231
30	11	A	Wolverhampton W	W 1-0	1-0	1	Mitrovic [44]	24,876
31	14	A	Norwich C	D 2-2	1-2	1	Perez [1], Lascelles [81]	26,841
32	20	H	Aston Villa	W 2-0	1-0	1	Gouffran [42], Lansbury (og) [59]	50,024
33	25	H	Bristol C	D 2-2	0-2	2	Smith (og) [59], Clark [82]	52,131
34	28	A	Brighton & HA	W 2-1	0-1	1	Diame [81], Perez [89]	30,230
35	Mar 4	A	Huddersfield T	W 3-1	2-0	1	Ritchie (pen) [10], Murphy [32], Gayle [90]	23,213
36	7	A	Reading	D 0-0	0-0	1		23,121
37	11	H	Fulham	L 1-3	0-1	1	Murphy [76]	51,903
38	18	A	Birmingham C	D 0-0	0-0	1		19,796
39	Apr 1	H	Wigan Ath	W 2-1	1-0	1	Gayle [36], Ritchie [57]	51,849
40	5	H	Burton Alb	W 1-0	0-0	1	Ritchie [68]	48,814
41	8	A	Sheffield W	L 1-2	0-0	2	Shelvey [88]	28,883
42	14	H	Leeds U	D 1-1	0-0	2	Lascelles [67]	52,301
43	17	A	Ipswich T	L 1-3	0-1	2	Murphy [62]	25,684
44	24	H	Preston NE	W 4-1	2-1	2	Perez 2 [7, 67], Atsu [45], Ritchie (pen) [65]	50,212
45	28	A	Cardiff C	W 2-0	0-0	2	Atsu [55], Hayden [65]	23,153
46	May 7	H	Barnsley	W 3-0	1-0	1	Perez [23], Mbemba [59], Gayle [90]	52,276

Final League Position: 1

GOALSCORERS

League (85): Gayle 23, Ritchie 12 (3 pens), Perez 9, Atsu 5, Gouffran 5, Murphy 5, Shelvey 5, Mitrovic 4, Clark 3, Diame 3, Lascelles 3, Hayden 2, Hanley 1, Mbemba 1, Yedlin 1, own goals 3.
FA Cup (4): Ritchie 2 (1 pen), Gouffran 1, Murphy 1.
EFL Cup (11): Diame 3, Perez 3, Mitrovic 2, Ritchie 2 (1 pen), Gouffran 1.

Sels M 9	Janmaat D 2	Lascelles J 41 + 2	Hanley G 5 + 5	Dummett P 44 + 1	Anita V 24 + 3	Hayden I 28 + 5	Colback J 24 + 5	Ritchie M 40 + 2	Perez A 25 + 11	Gayle D 26 + 6	Aarons R 1 + 3	Armstrong A — + 2	Shelvey J 38 + 4	Mbemba C 12	Diame M 27 + 10	Clark C 34	Gouffran Y 33 + 6	Jesus Gamez D 2 + 3	Yedlin D 21 + 6	Mitrovic A 11 + 14	Atsu C 15 + 17	Tiote C — + 1	Darlow K 34	Lazaar A — + 4	Murphy D 7 + 8	Ameobi S — + 4	Sterry J — + 2	Elliot R 3	Haidara M — + 1	Match No.
1	2	3	4	5	6	7^{1}	8^{3}	9	10^{2}	11	12	13	14																	1
1	2^{3}	4		5	6	7		12	13	11	9^{1}	14	8	3	10^{2}															2
1		12		5	2	6	13	8^{2}	9^{3}	11	14		7	3		4	10^{1}													3
1		4			2	7^{1}	8	6	12	11^{2}	14		13	3	10^{3}	5	9													4
1		4		5	2^{2}	7	13	6	11				8	3	10^{1}		9^{3}	12	14											5
1		4		5	2	14	8	6	13	11^{2}			7	3	10^{3}		9^{1}		12											6
1		3	13	5^{2}	2	7		9	10				8			4	6^{1}		14	11^{3}	12									7
1		4		5	2■	8^{1}		6^{2}	9	11			7	3	10					13	12									8
1		3		5		7		6		11^{2}			8		10	4	9		2^{1}	13		12								9
		3		5^{3}		12	8^{1}	6		11			7		10^{2}	4	9		2	13	14		1							10
		3	14	5	2		8	12		11^{1}			7		10^{2}	4	9			13	6^{3}		1							11
		3^{2}	12	5	2		8		10	11			7			4	9^{1}		13		6^{3}		1	14						12
		3		5	2	7	13	8^{2}		11			6		9^{1}	4	10				12		1							13
		3		5		14	7	6	10	11^{1}			8^{2}			4	9^{3}		2	13	12		1							14
		3	14	5		7		6^{2}	12				8		10	4	9		2^{3}	11^{1}	13		1							15
		3		5	12	8			10				7		13	4	9^{1}		2	11	6^{2}		1							16
		3		5	2	14	7^{1}	6	10	11^{2}			8		12	4	9^{3}			13			1							17
				12		7		6	10	13			8	3^{2}		4		5^{1}	2	11	9		1							18
		3		5■	12	6		8	9^{2}	11^{1}			7■		13	4	10^{3}		2	14			1							19
		3		5	2	8^{3}		6		11^{2}			7		10	4	9^{1}			13	12		1	14						20
		3		5	2	8		6^{1}	13	11^{2}			7		10	4	9				12		1							21
		3		5		8		9^{1}		11			7		10	4	12		2		6		1							22
		3		5	2	7	8^{2}	6	13	11					10^{1}	4	9^{3}			14	12		1							23
		3		5		8	7^{3}	6^{1}	10	11^{2}					12	4			2	14	9		1	13						24
		3		5	2^{3}	7	8^{1}	6	12	11					10	4	9^{2}				13		1		14					25
		3	14	5	13^{3}	7^{2}	8	6	10	11^{1}						4	9		2				1		12					26
		3		5		7		6	10				8			4	9^{1}		2^{2}				1	13	11^{3}	12	14			27
		3		5		8		6	10^{1}				7		13	4	9		2				1		11^{2}	12				28
		14	3	5		8^{1}		6	12				7		10	4	9^{3}		2	11^{2}			1			13				29
		3		5			7	6^{3}	14				8		10^{1}	4	9		2	11^{2}	12		1		13					30
		3		5			8^{2}	6^{1}	10	14			7		12	4	9		2	11^{3}	13		1							31
		3		5			8	6		11^{2}			7		10	4	9^{1}		2	12	13		1							32
		3		5			7^{1}	8	9^{2}				6		12	4	13		2	11	10		1							33
		3		5			8^{1}	9	13				7		10	4	11^{2}		2		6		1		12					34
		3		5	2		8^{2}	9		12			7		10	4	13		14		6^{3}		1		11^{1}					35
		3		5			8^{2}	6	10	13			7		14	4	9^{1}	2			12		1		11^{3}					36
		3		5	2		7	9		11^{2}			8		10^{3}	4^{1}	14	13			6		1		12					37
		3	4	5	2		8	6	10^{3}	12			13		7		9^{2}				14		1		11^{1}					38
		3	4	5	2	13	8	6	14	11^{3}			7		10^{1}		9^{2}				12		1							39
		3		5	2			6	10	11^{2}			7	4	8						9^{1}		1		13	12				40
		3		5	2			6^{3}	10	11^{2}			7	4	8^{1}		9			14	13		1		12					41
		3		5	2	8^{1}	12	6^{2}	10^{3}				7	4	14		9		13	11			1							42
		3	4	5		8^{2}		9^{3}					7		10		12	13	2^{1}	14	6		1		11					43
		3		5	2	7	13	6	10^{2}				8^{3}			4	12			11	9^{1}				14			1		44
				5		7	8^{3}		6^{1}				13	3	10	4			2	12	9				11^{2}		14	1		45
				5		3^{3}	8		10^{1}	14			7^{2}	4	13		9		2	11	6							1	12	46

FA Cup			
Third Round	Birmingham C	(a)	1-1
Replay	Birmingham C	(h)	3-1
Fourth Round	Oxford U	(a)	0-3

EFL Cup			
Second Round	Cheltenham T	(h)	2-0
Third Round	Wolverhampton W	(h)	2-0
Fourth Round	Preston NE	(h)	6-0
Quarter-Final	Hull C	(a)	1-1

(*aet; Hull C won 3-1 on penalties*)

NEWPORT COUNTY

FOUNDATION

In 1912 Newport County were formed following a meeting at The Tredegar Arms Hotel. A professional football club had existed in the town called Newport FC, but they ceased to exist in 1907. The first season as Newport County was in the second division of the Southern League. They started life playing at Somerton Park where they remained through their League years. They were elected to the Football League for the beginning of the 1920–21 season as founder members of Division 3. At the end of the 1987–88 season, they were relegated from the Football League and replaced by Lincoln City. On February 27 1989, Newport County went out of business and from the ashes Newport AFC was born. Starting down the pyramid in the Hellenic League, they eventally gained promotion to the Conference in 2011 and were promoted to the Football League after a play-off with Wrexham in 2013.

Rodney Parade, Rodney Road, Newport, South Wales NP19 0UU.

Telephone: (01633) 481 896.

Ticket Office: (01633) 481 896.

Website: www.newport-county.co.uk

Email: office@newport-county.co.uk

Ground Capacity: 7,850.

Record Attendance: 24,268 v Cardiff C, Division 3 (S), 16 October 1937 (Somerton Park); 4,660 v Swansea C, FA Cup 1st rd, 11 November 2006 (Newport Stadium); 7,326 v Notts Co, FL 2, 6 May 2017 (Rodney Parade).

Pitch Measurements: 100.5m × 64m (110yd × 70yd).

Chairman: Malcolm Temple.

Manager: Michael Flynn.

Assistant Manager: Wayne Hatswell.

Colours: Amber shirts with black trim, amber shorts with black trim, amber socks with black hoops.

Year Formed: 1912.

Turned Professional: 1912.

Previous Names: Newport County, 1912; Newport AFC, 1989; Newport County, 1999.

Club Nicknames: 'The Exiles', 'The Ironsides', 'The Port', 'The County'.

Grounds: 1912–89, 1990–92, Somerton Park; 1992–94, Meadow Park Stadium; 1994, Newport Stadium; 2012, Rodney Parade.

First Football League Game: 28 August 1920, Division 3, v Reading (h) L 0–1.

HONOURS

League Champions: Division 3S – 1938–39.
Runners-up: Conference – (3rd) 2012–13 *(promoted via play-offs)*.

FA Cup: 5th rd – 1949.

League Cup: never past 3rd rd.

Welsh Cup Winners: 1980.
Runners-up: 1963, 1987.

European Competitions
European Cup Winners' Cup: 1980–81 *(qf)*.

sky SPORTS FACT FILE

Newport County won their last five games of the 1976–77 season and so avoided having to seek re-election. The final game at home to Workington attracted a season-high attendance of 8,313 to Somerton Park for what proved to be the Cumbrian club's last-ever Football League game.

Record League Victory: 10-0 v Merthyr T, Division 3(S), 10 April 1930 – Martin (5), Gittins (2), Thomas (1), Bagley (1), Lawson (1).

Record Cup Victory: 7-0 v Working, FA Cup 1st rd, 24 November 1928 – Young (3), Pugh (2) Gittins (1), Reid (1).

Record Defeat: 0–13 v Newcastle U, Division 2, 5 October 1946.

Most League Points (2 for a win): 61, Division 4, 1979–80.

Most League Points (3 for a win): 78, Division 3, 1982–83.

Most League Goals: 85, Division 4, 1964–65.

Highest League Scorer in Season: Tudor Martin, 34, Division 3 (S), 1929–30.

Most League Goals in Total Aggregate: Reg Parker, 99, 1948–54.

Most League Goals in One Match: 5, Tudor Martin v Merthyr T, Dvision 3 (S), 10 April 1930.

Most Capped Player: Nigel Vaughan, 3 (10), Wales.

Most League Appearances: Len Weare, 527, 1955–70.

Youngest League Player: Regan Poole, 16 years 94 days v Shrewsbury T, 20 September 2014.

Record Transfer Fee Received: £500,000 (rising to £1,000,000) from Peterborough U for Conor Washington, January 2014.

Record Transfer Fee Paid: £80,000 to Swansea C for Alan Waddle, January 1981.

Football League Record: 1920 Original member of Division 3; 1921–31 Divsion 3 (S) – dropped out of Football League; 1932 Re-elected to Division 3 (S); 1932–39 Division 3 (S); 1946–47 Division 2; 1947–58 Division 3 (S); 1958–62 Division 3; 1962–80 Division 4; 1980–87 Division 3; 1987–88 Division 4 (relegated from Football League); 2011 Promoted to Conference; 2011–13 Conference Premier; 2013– FL 2.

LATEST SEQUENCES

Longest Sequence of League Wins: 4, 26.12.2014 – 10.1.2015.

Longest Sequence of League Defeats: 8, 22.11.2016 – 7.1.2017.

Longest Sequence of League Draws: 4, 31.10.2015 – 24.11.2015.

Longest Sequence of Unbeaten League Matches: 9, 10.11.2014 – 13.12.2014

Longest Sequence Without a League Win: 12, 15.3.2016 – 6.8.2017.

Successive Scoring Runs: 12 from 11.3.2017.

Successive Non-scoring Runs: 4 from 17.1.2015.

MANAGERS

Davy McDougle 1912–13 *(Player-Manager)*
Sam Hollis 1913–17
Harry Parkes 1919–22
Jimmy Hindmarsh 1922–35
Louis Page 1935–36
Tom Bromilow 1936–37
Billy McCandless 1937–45
Tom Bromilow 1945–50
Fred Stansfield 1950–53
Billy Lucas 1953–61
Bobby Evans 1961–62
Billy Lucas 1962–67
Leslie Graham 1967–69
Bobby Ferguson 1969–70 *(Player-Manager)*
Billy Lucas 1970–74
Brian Harris 1974–75
Dave Elliott 1975–76 *(Player-Manager)*
Jimmy Scoular 1976–77
Colin Addison 1977–78
Len Ashurst 1978–82
Colin Addison 1982–85
Bobby Smith 1985–86
John Relish 1986
Jimmy Mullen 1986–87
John Lewis 1987
Brian Eastick 1987–88
David Williams 1988
Eddie May 1988
John Mahoney 1988–89
John Relish 1989–93
Graham Rogers 1993–96
Chris Price 1997
Tim Harris 1997–2002
Peter Nicholas 2002–04
John Cornforth 2004–05
Peter Beadle 2005–08
Dean Holdsworth 2008–11
Anthony Hudson 2011
Justin Edinburgh 2011–15
Jimmy Dack 2015
Terry Butcher 2015
John Sheridan 2015–16
Warren Feeney 2016
Graham Westley 2016–17
Michael Flynn May 2017–

TEN YEAR LEAGUE RECORD

		P	W	D	L	F	A	Pts	Pos
2007-08	Conf S	42	18	12	12	64	49	66	9
2008-09	Conf S	42	16	11	15	50	51	59	10
2009-10	Conf S	42	32	7	3	93	26	103	1
2010-11	Conf P	46	18	15	13	78	60	69	9
2011-12	Conf P	46	11	14	21	53	65	47	19
2012-13	Conf P	46	25	10	11	85	60	85	3
2013-14	FL 2	46	14	16	16	56	59	58	14
2014-15	FL 2	46	18	11	17	51	54	65	9
2015-16	FL 2	46	10	13	23	43	64	43	22
2016-17	FL 2	46	12	12	22	51	73	48	22

DID YOU KNOW 

When the original Newport County folded in February 1989 they continued to sign players right up until the end. Goalkeeper Kenny Allen and defender Derek Dawkins arrived at Somerton Park so late that the club closed down before they had time to make an appearance.

NEWPORT COUNTY – SKY BET LEAGUE TWO 2016–17 LEAGUE RECORD

Match No.	Date	Venue	Opponents	Result		H/T Score	Lg Pos.	Goalscorers	Atten-dance
1	Aug 6	H	Mansfield T	L	2-3	1-1	18	Compton 18, Labadie 78	2790
2	13	A	Leyton Orient	W	1-0	1-0	12	Turley 34	4184
3	16	A	Luton T	L	1-2	0-0	18	Myrie-Williams 70	7058
4	20	H	Crewe Alex	D	1-1	0-1	17	Rigg 81	2268
5	27	A	Hartlepool U	D	2-2	2-2	18	Rigg 4, Parkin 27	3261
6	Sept 10	H	Cheltenham T	D	2-2	2-2	20	Parkin 2 18, 37	2656
7	17	A	Doncaster R	L	0-2	0-1	20		5254
8	24	H	Cambridge U	L	1-2	1-0	23	Healey 10	2225
9	27	A	Grimsby T	L	0-1	0-0	24		4296
10	Oct 8	A	Colchester U	D	0-0	0-0	24		3088
11	15	A	Yeovil T	L	0-1	0-0	24		3353
12	22	H	Plymouth Arg	L	1-3	0-1	24	Parkin 50	3460
13	25	H	Barnet	D	2-2	1-0	24	Tozer 33, Rigg (pen) 89	2381
14	29	A	Accrington S	W	3-1	0-0	24	Healey 47, Barnum-Bobb 62, Sheehan 90	1251
15	Nov 12	H	Carlisle U	W	2-0	1-0	24	Sheehan 2, Healey 72	2521
16	19	A	Notts Co	W	3-0	2-0	22	Rigg 34, Healey 38, Sheehan 62	3883
17	22	H	Wycombe W	L	0-1	0-0	24		2010
18	26	A	Blackpool	L	1-4	1-1	24	Healey 21	3062
19	Dec 6	H	Stevenage	L	0-2	0-2	24		1877
20	17	A	Crawley T	L	1-3	1-1	24	Labadie 33	2022
21	26	H	Portsmouth	L	2-3	1-0	24	Sheehan 25, Healey 51	3714
22	31	H	Exeter C	L	1-4	0-1	24	Rigg 81	2663
23	Jan 2	A	Wycombe W	L	1-2	0-0	24	Randall 60	4288
24	7	A	Stevenage	L	1-3	0-2	24	Butler 89	2185
25	14	H	Colchester U	D	1-1	1-1	24	Sheehan 23	2397
26	21	A	Barnet	D	0-0	0-0	24		2623
27	28	H	Hartlepool U	W	3-1	1-0	24	Bird 15, Williams 56, Butler 71	2271
28	Feb 4	A	Cheltenham T	D	1-1	0-0	24	Gordon 90	3763
29	10	H	Doncaster R	D	0-0	0-0	24		2653
30	14	H	Grimsby T	D	0-0	0-0	24		1868
31	18	A	Cambridge U	L	2-3	1-0	24	Bird 2 43, 57	4175
32	21	H	Morecambe	D	1-1	1-0	24	Williams 18	1988
33	25	A	Mansfield T	L	1-2	1-1	24	Bird 5	3824
34	Mar 4	H	Leyton Orient	L	0-4	0-3	24		3378
35	11	A	Crewe Alex	W	2-1	0-1	24	Butler 53, Labadie 89	3725
36	14	A	Morecambe	W	1-0	0-0	23	Bird (pen) 67	1080
37	18	H	Blackpool	L	1-3	0-1	23	Samuel 74	2427
38	21	H	Luton T	D	1-1	1-1	23	Rigg 28	2304
39	25	A	Portsmouth	L	1-2	0-1	23	Samuel 77	17,364
40	Apr 1	H	Crawley T	W	1-0	1-0	23	Demetriou 18	2946
41	8	A	Exeter C	W	1-0	0-0	23	Owen-Evans 53	4040
42	14	H	Yeovil T	W	1-0	0-0	23	Demetriou 57	3789
43	17	A	Plymouth Arg	L	1-6	0-2	23	Williams 90	13,971
44	22	H	Accrington S	W	1-0	0-0	22	Bird 60	3719
45	29	A	Carlisle U	L	1-2	1-0	22	Demetriou 12	5402
46	May 6	H	Notts Co	W	2-1	1-0	22	Demetriou (pen) 32, O'Brien 89	7326

Final League Position: 22

GOALSCORERS

League (51): Bird 6 (1 pen), Healey 6, Rigg 6 (1 pen), Sheehan 5, Demetriou 4 (1 pen), Parkin 4, Butler 3, Labadie 3, Williams 3, Samuel 2, Barnum-Bobb 1, Compton 1, Gordon 1, Myrie-Williams 1, O'Brien 1, Owen-Evans 1, Randall 1, Tozer 1, Turley 1.
FA Cup (5): Sheehan 2, Barnum-Bobb 1, Green 1, Healey 1.
EFL Cup (2): Jackson 1, Randall 1 (1 pen).
EFL Checkatrade Trophy (4): Barnum-Bobb 1, Bennett 1, Green 1, Myrie-Williams 1.

Day J 45	Barnum-Bobb J 15+11	Bennett S 38+1	Turley J 6	Butler D 38+2	Compton J 2+6	Labadie J 17+2	Randall M 22+3	Myrie-Williams J 14+9	Rigg S 29+5	Jackson M 9+13	Tozer B 17+6	Jones Darren 29+2	Green J 4+6	Owen-Evans T 12+12	Parkin J 8+2	Bignot P 9+1	Grego-Cox R 7	Healey R 13+4	Blanchard M 1	Cameron K 6	Sheehan J 17+3	Wood F —+3	Bittner J 1+1	John-Lewis L 1+1	O'Hanlon J 5+2	Jebb J 4+1	Meite A 3+1	Williams A 8+9	O'Brien M 20	Nelson S 12+2	Pipe D 21	Gordon J 2+8	Reid C 9+1	Bajaj F —+1	Samuel A 15+3	Demetriou M 12+5	Rose M 12	Bird R 19	Flynn M 4+1	Match No.
1	2	3	4	5	6	7	8	9^{1}	10	11	12																													1
1	12	4	2	5		8	7^{3}	9^{1}	10	11	13	3	6^{2}	14																										2
1	12	4	2	5		8	7^{3}	9	11	10^{1}	14	3	6^{2}		13																									3
1	12	3	2^{2}	5		7^{1}	8	9	10	11	14	4	6^{3}		13																									4
1	14	3		5	12	7^{1}	6	8^{2}	11	9^{3}	13	4			10	2																								5
1		4	3	5	9^{1}	8	7^{2}		11	12	14				10^{3}	2	6	13																						6
1		4	2	5	12	7^{2}	8		9^{1}	14	10	3			11^{3}		6	13																						7
1		4		5			8^{2}		9	12	7				11^{1}	2	6	10		3	13																			8
1		4		5			7	13	9	12	8				10	2	6^{2}	11^{1}		3																				9
1	5	4		9				8^{1}	12	13	7	3	14		11	2	6^{3}	10^{2}																						10
1	2	3		5	13			9^{3}	6	11^{2}	8	4	12		10						7^{1}	14																		11
1■	2	3			14				11		7	4	9^{2}		10^{1}		6	13		5	8^{3}		12																	12
	14	3					8^{3}	13	10		7	4	12			2^{2}	6^{1}	11		5	9		1																	13
1	6	4		12				11^{1}	9		8	3				2		10		5	7																			14
1	2	3		6				13	8		9	5		12				11		4^{1}	7^{3}	14			10^{2}															15
1	2	4		5				13	6		7	3		12				10^{1}			8				11	9^{2}														16
1	2	3		5^{2}			14	13	9		8	4		12				10			7				11^{1}	6^{3}														17
1	2^{3}			5	14		3^{1}	13	9		8	4						10			7				11^{2}	6	12													18
1	9	3		2^{1}		14		6		13	7^{3}	4		12		5		11			10					8^{2}														19
1	2	4				9^{2}		5		10^{3}	6^{1}	3	13	7				12			8	14			11															20
1	5	3					13	9	11	12	6^{3}	2	14	8^{1}				10			7						4^{2}													21
1	2	4^{1}			12		6	5	11	9^{2}	7^{3}		13					10			8				14		3													22
1	2						8	6	9^{2}			3		12		5^{1}		10			7^{3}				14	13	4	11												23
1	2^{2}	4		12			8	10^{3}		13	9																	11	3	5	6	7^{1}	14							24
1		8		6			9^{2}					5		12							7							11	4	3	2		10^{1}	13						25
1		8		4			7^{1}					2		13							9							11	3	5	6^{2}		10^{3}		12	14				26
1		7		6								3^{1}																9^{3}	4	5	2		11		14	13	8^{2}	10	12	27
1		7^{2}		8					12			4									14							11^{1}	3	2	5	13	9^{3}				6	10		28
1				9								3							7									11^{1}	4	2	5	12	8				6	10		29
1				8								3									9^{3}							14	4	2^{2}	5	13	11^{1}		12		6	10	7	30
1	13			6										12							9^{1}								4		2	14	11^{3}		8^{2}	5	7■	10	3	31
1				5						14				12														10^{3}	3^{1}		2	13	7^{2}		6	9	8	11	4	32
1		2		5						14		3				12^{3}					13											11■	7^{1}		6	4	9	10	8^{2}	33
1		2		5		12			13	11^{1}		4^{3}																14	7	8^{2}					6	3	9	10		34
1	13	7		5		8			10^{2}					9															4	3	2^{3}	14			6^{1}	12		11		35
1	13	7		5		8			9^{1}					6														14	4^{3}	3	2				10^{2}	12		11		36
1	13	4		9		6^{2}			8					7^{1}															2	3^{3}	5	14			10	12		11		37
1		6		8		7			9	13		3		12															4■	2^{2}	5				11			10^{1}		38
1		5		6		7	14	12	9	13		3^{2}		8^{1}																	2				11	4		10^{3}		39
1		3		8		7■		13	9					12															2	14	5				10^{3}	4	6^{2}	11^{1}		40
1		3		6			8^{2}	14				13		7														12	5		2				10^{1}	4	9	11^{3}		41
1		4		6			7^{2}		12			13		9														14	3^{1}		2				10^{3}	5	8	11		42
1	12	3^{2}		9			6^{3}		11			2		8														13		14	5^{1}				10	4	7			43
1	13			5		7	8^{1}		9					6														12	4		2	14			10^{2}	3		11^{3}		44
1		13		5		7	8^{3}		10					6										14				12	4		2				9^{2}	3		11^{1}		45
1		2		9		6	7^{3}		12	13				8^{1}										11^{2}				14	3		5					4		10		46

FA Cup

First Round	Alfreton T	(a)	1-1
Replay	Alfreton T	(h)	4-1
(aet)			
Second Round	Plymouth Arg	(a)	0-0
Replay	Plymouth Arg	(h)	0-1
(aet)			

EFL Cup

First Round	Milton Keynes D	(h)	2-3

EFL Checkatrade Trophy

Southern Group B	Plymouth Arg	(a)	1-4
Southern Group B	Swansea C U21	(h)	1-2
Southern Group B	AFC Wimbledon	(h)	2-0

NORTHAMPTON TOWN

FOUNDATION

Formed in 1897 by schoolteachers connected with the Northampton & District Elementary Schools' Association, they survived a financial crisis at the end of their first year when they were £675 in the red and became members of the Midland League – a fast move indeed for a new club. They achieved Southern League membership in 1901.

Sixfields Stadium, Upton Way, Northampton NN5 5QA.

Telephone: (01604) 683 700.

Fax: (01604) 751 613.

Ticket Office: (01604) 683 777.

Website: www.ntfc.co.uk

Email: wendy.lambell@ntfc.co.uk

Ground Capacity: 7,798.

Record Attendance: 24,523 v Fulham, Division 1, 23 April 1966 (at County Ground); 7,798 v Manchester U, EFL Cup 3rd rd, 21 September 2016 (at Sixfields Stadium).

Pitch Measurements: 106m × 66m (116yd × 72yd).

Chairman: Kelvin Thomas.

Chief Executive: James Whiting.

Manager: Justin Edinburgh.

Assistant Manager: David Kerslake.

Colours: Claret shirts with white trim, white shorts with claret trim, claret socks with white trim.

Year Formed: 1897.

Turned Professional: 1901.

Grounds: 1897, County Ground; 1994, Sixfields Stadium.

Club Nickname: 'The Cobblers'.

First Football League Game: 28 August 1920, Division 3, v Grimsby T (a) L 0–2 – Thorpe; Sproston, Hewison; Jobey, Tomkins, Pease; Whitworth, Lockett, Thomas, Freeman, MacKechnie.

Record League Victory: 10–0 v Walsall, Division 3 (S), 5 November 1927 – Hammond; Watson, Jeffs; Allen, Brett, Odell; Daley, Smith (3), Loasby (3), Hoten (1), Wells (3).

Record Cup Victory: 10–0 v Sutton T, FA Cup prel rd, 7 December 1907 – Cooch; Drennan, Lloyd Davies, Tirrell (1), McCartney, Hickleton, Badenock (3), Platt (3), Lowe (1), Chapman (2), McDiarmid.

Record Defeat: 0–11 v Southampton, Southern League, 28 December 1901.

HONOURS

League Champions: Division 3 – 1962–63; FL 2 – 2015–16; Division 4 – 1986–87.
Runners-up: Division 2 – 1964–65; Division 3S – 1927–28, 1949–50; FL 2 – 2005–06; Division 4 – 1975–76.

FA Cup: 5th rd – 1934, 1950, 1970.

League Cup: 5th rd – 1965, 1967.

sky SPORTS FACT FILE

Bill Gormlie, who made almost 150 appearances for Northampton Town in the 1930s, was appointed as coach of the Belgium national team in April 1947. He remained in post until the summer of 1953, taking charge of the team for a total of 44 matches. He also served RSC Anderlecht as manager from 1950 to 1959.

Most League Points (2 for a win): 68, Division 4, 1975–76.

Most League Points (3 for a win): 99, Division 4, 1986–87; FL 2, 2015–16.

Most League Goals: 109, Division 3, 1962–63 and Division 3 (S), 1952–53.

Highest League Scorer in Season: Cliff Holton, 36, Division 3, 1961–62.

Most League Goals in Total Aggregate: Jack English, 135, 1947–60.

Most League Goals in One Match: 5, Ralph Hoten v Crystal Palace, Division 3 (S), 27 October 1928.

Most Capped Player: Edwin Lloyd Davies, 12 (16), Wales.

Most League Appearances: Tommy Fowler, 521, 1946–61.

Youngest League Player: Adrian Mann, 16 years 297 days v Bury, 5 May 1984.

Record Transfer Fee Received: £470,000 from Blackburn R for Mark Bunn, September 2008.

Record Transfer Fee Paid: £165,000 to Oldham Ath for Josh Low, July 2003.

Football League Record: 1920 Original Member of Division 3; 1921 Division 3 (S); 1958–61 Division 4; 1961–63 Division 3; 1963–65 Division 2; 1965–66 Division 1; 1966–67 Division 2; 1967–69 Division 3; 1969–76 Division 4; 1976–77 Division 3; 1977–87 Division 4; 1987–90 Division 3; 1990–92 Division 4; 1992–97 Division 3; 1997–99 Division 2; 1999–2000 Division 3; 2000–03 Division 2; 2003–04 Division 3; 2004–06 FL 2; 2006–09 FL 1; 2009–16 FL 2; 2016– FL 1.

LATEST SEQUENCES

Longest Sequence of League Wins: 10, 28.12.2015 – 23.2.2016.

Longest Sequence of League Defeats: 8, 26.10.1935 – 21.12.1935.

Longest Sequence of League Draws: 6, 5.2.2011 – 26.2.2011.

Longest Sequence of Unbeaten League Matches: 31, 28.12.2015 – 10.9.2016.

Longest Sequence Without a League Win: 18, 5.2.2011 – 25.4.2011.

Successive Scoring Runs: 28 from 29.8.2015.

Successive Non-scoring Runs: 7 from 7.4.1939.

MANAGERS

Arthur Jones 1897–1907
(Secretary-Manager)
Herbert Chapman 1907–12
Walter Bull 1912–13
Fred Lessons 1913–19
Bob Hewison 1920–25
Jack Tresadern 1925–30
Jack English 1931–35
Syd Puddefoot 1935–37
Warney Cresswell 1937–39
Tom Smith 1939–49
Bob Dennison 1949–54
Dave Smith 1954–59
David Bowen 1959–67
Tony Marchi 1967–68
Ron Flowers 1968–69
Dave Bowen 1969–72
(continued as General Manager and Secretary 1972–85 when joined the board)
Billy Baxter 1972–73
Bill Dodgin Jnr 1973–76
Pat Crerand 1976–77
By committee 1977
Bill Dodgin Jnr 1977
John Petts 1977–78
Mike Keen 1978–79
Clive Walker 1979–80
Bill Dodgin Jnr 1980–82
Clive Walker 1982–84
Tony Barton 1984–85
Graham Carr 1985–90
Theo Foley 1990–92
Phil Chard 1992–93
John Barnwell 1993–94
Ian Atkins 1995–99
Kevin Wilson 1999–2001
Kevan Broadhurst 2001–03
Terry Fenwick 2003
Martin Wilkinson 2003
Colin Calderwood 2003–06
John Gorman 2006
Stuart Gray 2007–09
Ian Sampson 2009–11
Gary Johnson 2011
Aidy Boothroyd 2011–13
Chris Wilder 2014–16
Rob Page 2016–17
Justin Edinburgh January 2017–

TEN YEAR LEAGUE RECORD

		P	W	D	L	F	A	Pts	Pos
2007-08	FL 1	46	17	15	14	60	55	66	9
2008-09	FL 1	46	12	13	21	61	65	49	21
2009-10	FL 2	46	18	13	15	62	53	67	11
2010-11	FL 2	46	11	19	16	63	71	52	16
2011-12	FL 2	46	12	12	22	56	79	48	20
2012-13	FL 2	46	21	10	15	64	55	73	6
2013-14	FL 2	46	13	14	19	42	57	53	21
2014-15	FL 2	46	18	7	21	67	62	61	12
2015-16	FL 2	46	29	12	5	82	46	99	1
2016-17	FL 1	46	14	11	21	60	73	53	16

DID YOU KNOW 

Northampton Town replaced their original floodlighting system in the summer of 1980. The new lights were due to be used for the first time in the home fixture with Southend United on Friday 29 August 1980, but failed to work and the match was abandoned at half-time with the match goalless.

NORTHAMPTON TOWN – SKY BET LEAGUE ONE 2016–17 LEAGUE RECORD

Match No.	*Date*	*Venue*	*Opponents*	*Result*	*H/T Score*	*Lg Pos.*	*Goalscorers*	*Attendance*
1	Aug 6	H	Fleetwood T	D 1-1	1-0	12	Neal (og) [9]	5157
2	13	A	Charlton Ath	D 1-1	1-0	14	Revell [16]	11,567
3	16	A	Oldham Ath	D 0-0	0-0	14		3327
4	20	H	AFC Wimbledon	D 0-0	0-0	15		5185
5	27	A	Coventry C	D 1-1	1-0	15	Beautyman [30]	10,022
6	Sept 4	H	Milton Keynes D	W 3-2	3-1	11	Beautyman [8], Revell [13], Taylor, M [28]	6618
7	10	H	Walsall	W 2-0	1-0	8	Taylor, M [23], Revell (pen) [78]	5538
8	17	A	Chesterfield	L 1-3	0-1	11	Anderson, P [62]	5910
9	24	H	Southend U	W 4-0	0-0	5	O'Toole [46], Revell (pen) [51], Taylor, M [59], Anderson, P [78]	6138
10	27	A	Swindon T	W 3-1	1-0	4	Beautyman [7], O'Toole [76], Gorre [82]	6590
11	Oct 1	H	Bristol R	L 2-3	1-0	5	Revell 2 [9, 76]	6642
12	8	A	Scunthorpe U	D 1-1	0-1	4	McCourt [74]	4714
13	15	H	Millwall	L 1-3	0-1	9	Richards [80]	6908
14	18	A	Peterborough U	L 0-3	0-2	12		9157
15	22	A	Shrewsbury T	W 4-2	2-1	8	Zakuani [22], Anderson, P 2 [31, 89], Hoskins [65]	5023
16	29	H	Bury	W 3-2	1-0	5	Richards 2 (1 pen) [36, 64 (p)], Taylor, M [71]	5739
17	Nov 12	A	Gillingham	L 1-2	1-0	7	O'Toole [36]	5790
18	19	H	Peterborough U	L 0-1	0-0	12		7675
19	22	A	Bradford C	L 0-1	0-0	15		15,935
20	26	H	Bolton W	L 0-1	0-1	16		7018
21	Dec 10	A	Port Vale	W 3-2	1-0	13	Zakuani [22], Hoskins [78], Anderson, P [90]	4739
22	17	H	Rochdale	L 2-3	1-1	15	Taylor, M [16], Hoskins [57]	5247
23	26	A	Oxford U	W 1-0	0-0	13	Richards [90]	11,790
24	31	A	Sheffield U	L 0-1	0-0	15		24,194
25	Jan 2	H	Bradford C	L 1-2	1-0	16	Revell [39]	6931
26	7	A	Bristol R	L 0-5	0-4	16		8424
27	14	H	Scunthorpe U	L 1-2	1-1	16	Revell [42]	5649
28	21	A	Milton Keynes D	L 3-5	0-2	18	Wylde [61], Richards 2 (1 pen) [71, 84 (p)]	12,300
29	28	H	Coventry C	W 3-0	0-0	16	Anderson, K 3 [53, 64, 76]	7543
30	Feb 4	A	Walsall	L 1-2	1-0	16	O'Toole [23]	4954
31	11	H	Chesterfield	W 3-1	2-0	16	O'Toole 2 [12, 42], Richards [48]	5824
32	14	H	Swindon T	W 2-1	0-0	16	Jones (og) [64], O'Toole [82]	5094
33	18	A	Southend U	D 2-2	2-2	14	Richards [29], O'Toole [44]	8425
34	25	A	Fleetwood T	L 0-3	0-1	16		3361
35	28	H	Oldham Ath	L 1-2	0-1	17	O'Toole [84]	4686
36	Mar 4	H	Charlton Ath	W 2-1	1-1	15	Smith, M [32], O'Toole [62]	7118
37	11	A	AFC Wimbledon	W 1-0	0-0	15	Taylor, M (pen) [86]	4512
38	14	H	Port Vale	W 2-1	0-0	14	Phillips [63], Taylor, M [88]	4812
39	18	A	Bolton W	L 1-2	0-0	14	Smith, M [57]	14,255
40	25	H	Oxford U	D 0-0	0-0	14		7434
41	Apr 1	A	Rochdale	D 1-1	0-0	15	Anderson, P [90]	2939
42	8	H	Sheffield U	L 1-2	1-0	15	Richards [45]	7425
43	14	A	Millwall	L 0-3	0-3	16		10,886
44	17	H	Shrewsbury T	D 1-1	1-0	16	Richards [21]	6211
45	22	A	Bury	L 0-3	0-1	16		5190
46	30	H	Gillingham	D 0-0	0-0	16		7034

Final League Position: 16

GOALSCORERS

League (60): O'Toole 10, Richards 10 (2 pens), Revell 8 (2 pens), Taylor, M 7 (1 pen), Anderson, P 6, Anderson, K 3, Beautyman 3, Hoskins 3, Smith, M 2, Zakuani 2, Gorre 1, McCourt 1, Phillips 1, Wylde 1, own goals 2.
FA Cup (6): Richards 2, Anderson, P 1, Hooper 1, O'Toole 1, Taylor, M 1.
EFL Cup (5): Revell 2 (1 pen), Diamond 1, O'Toole 1, own goal 1.
EFL Checkatrade Trophy (2): Beautyman 1, Richards 1.

Smith A 40	Phillips A 18 + 2	Zakuani G 20 + 1	Diamond Z 37 + 2	Buchanan D 45	Gorre K 9 + 4	Beautyman H 11 + 10	O'Toole J 34 + 6	Taylor M 43	Richards M 28 + 14	Revell A 29 + 3	Potter A 3 + 8	Hoskins S 18 + 7	Byrom J 1 + 1	Sonupe E — + 1	McCourt J 17 + 9	Moloney B 19 + 4	D'Ath L — + 1	Hooper J 5 + 5	Nyatanga L 34 + 3	Anderson P 28 + 8	Cornell D 6	McDonald R 2 + 5	Hanley R — + 1	Iaciofano J — + 1	Wylde G 6 + 6	Boateng H 11 + 5	Eardley N 10	Anderson K 9 + 5	Williams L 8	Smith M 13 + 1	McWilliams S 2 + 3	Match No.
1	2	3	4	5	6^{1}	7^{2}	8	9	10	11	12	13																				1
1	2	3	4	5	6^{2}	7^{1}	9	10	13	11	8	12																				2
1	2	3	4	5	10	12	7^{3}	8	14	11^{1}	6^{2}	9	13																			3
1	2	3	4	5	9^{2}	12	7	8	10^{1}	11		6^{3}		13	14																	4
1	14	3	4	5	10	8^{1}	9^{2}	7		11					6	2^{3}	12	13														5
1			4	2	11^{1}	8		7	14	10^{2}	12	13			6	5			3	9^{3}												6
1			3	5	8^{1}	7^{3}	14	10		11	12	13			9	2			4	6^{2}												7
1			3	5	11^{1}	6^{2}	14	8	13	10		12			7^{3}	2			4	9												8
1		4	3	5		12	6	8	13	10^{1}		9^{3}			7^{2}	2		14		11												9
1		5	3	6	12	8^{3}	7	9		10		11^{2}				2		13	14	4^{1}												10
1		4■	3	5	13	9^{3}	6	7	12	11		10^{2}			14	2				8^{1}												11
1			3	5			6	7■	13	11		12			9	2		10^{2}	4	8^{1}												12
1			3	5	14	8^{3}	7		13	11		12			9■	2		10^{2}	4	6^{1}												13
1		3	2	9			12		11	10		8	7^{1}			5		13	4^{2}	6												14
1		4^{2}	3	5			6^{1}		13	11		9			7	2		10	12	8												15
1		4	3	5			13	7	11^{3}		12	9			6^{1}	2		10	14	8^{2}												16
1			3	5	13		6	7	11^{1}	12		9				2		10^{2}	4	8												17
1		12	3^{1}	5		13	6	7		11		10			9^{2}	2			4	8												18
		3		5			6	8	13	10	14	9^{3}			7^{2}	2				11^{1}	1	4	12									19
	2	4		5	10^{2}		13	7	12	11	14	9			6^{1}				3	8^{3}	1											20
	2	3		5				8	11	10		9			7				4	6	1											21
	5	4		2			6	8	12	11	13	9			7^{1}				3	10^{2}	1											22
1	2	3		5		12	7	8	10	11	6^{1}								4	9												23
1	2	3		5		13	7	8	10^{2}	11	12	6^{1}							4	9^{3}				14								24
1	2^{2}	4	12	5			7^{1}	8	11	10		6			14				3	9^{3}					13							25
1			4	2		7^{1}	13	8	12	10		11						14		5^{2}		3			9^{3}	6						26
1			2	5			7	8	11	10		6			12				4							9^{1}	3					27
1			3	5		6^{2}	8	9	11	10^{1}									4						13	7	2	12				28
1			3	5		14	6	8	10										4	13					12	7^{3}	2	11^{1}	9^{2}			29
1			4^{1}	5		14	6	10	11										3			12				7^{3}	2	8^{2}	9	13		30
1			4	5			6	10	11										3	13					12	7^{1}	2	8^{2}		9		31
1			3	5			7	8^{1}	11						12				4						13	9	2	6^{2}		10		32
1			3	5			8	7	11						13				4	12					6^{1}	9^{2}	2			10		33
1			3	5			6	8^{3}	11^{2}						14				4	13					7^{1}	12	2	9		10		34
1		3		2		14	7	8	12						13				4						6^{2}	9^{3}	5	11		10^{1}		35
1	6	3^{2}	12	5			7	8	11						14				4	13					9^{3}				2^{1}	10		36
1	2		4^{1}	5			7	8	11										3	14		13			9^{3}			12	6^{2}	10		37
1	2		3	5			7	8	11										4	13						12		6^{2}	9^{1}	10		38
1	2^{3}		3	5			8	7	10						9^{1}	13			4	12								14	6	11^{2}		39
1	2^{2}		3	5				8	10						6^{3}	14			4	9					13	12		7^{1}		11		40
1	2^{1}		3	5			7^{3}	8	10						6^{2}	14			4	9						12				11	13	41
1			3	5			7	8	11	13						2			4	6^{1}		14							9^{2}	10^{3}	12	42
1	2		3	5				6	10	13						14			4	7						12		8^{3}	9^{2}	11^{1}		43
1	12		3	5■			7■	8^{1}	11	10^{2}						2			4	9		14				6^{3}					13	44
	5		3			14		9	10	11^{1}						2^{2}			4	8	1	12					6^{3}	13			7	45
			3	5				8	11	10						2			4	9	1					6^{1}		12			7	46

FA Cup

First Round	Harrow Bor	(h)	6-0
Second Round	Stourbridge	(a)	0-1

EFL Checkatrade Trophy

Southern Group D	Wycombe W	(h)	0-3
Southern Group D	Coventry C	(a)	1-3
Southern Group D	West Ham U U21	(h)	1-1

(*West Ham U U21 won 3-2 on penalties*)

EFL Cup

First Round	Barnsley	(a)	2-1

(*aet*)

Second Round	WBA	(h)	2-2

(*aet; Northampton T won 4-3 on penalties*)

Third Round	Manchester U	(h)	1-3

NORWICH CITY

FOUNDATION

Formed in 1902, largely through the initiative of two local schoolmasters who called a meeting at the Criterion Cafe, they were shocked by an FA Commission which in 1904 declared the club professional and ejected them from the FA Amateur Cup. However, this only served to strengthen their determination. New officials were appointed and a professional club established at a meeting in the Agricultural Hall in March 1905.

Carrow Road, Norwich, Norfolk NR1 1JE.

Telephone: (01603) 760 760.

Fax: (01603) 613 886.

Ticket Office: (0870) 444 1902.

Website: www.canaries.co.uk

Email: reception@ncfc-canaries.co.uk

Ground Capacity: 27,359.

Record Attendance: 25,037 v Sheffield W, FA Cup 5th rd, 16 February 1935 (at The Nest); 43,984 v Leicester C, FA Cup 6th rd, 30 March 1963 (at Carrow Road).

Pitch Measurements: 105m × 68m (114yd × 74yd).

Chairman: Ed Balls.

Joint Majority Shareholders: Delia Smith and Michael Wynn-Jones.

Managing Director: Steve Stone.

Manager: Daniel Farke.

Assistant Manager: Edmund Riemer.

HONOURS

League Champions: First Division – 2003–04; Division 2 – 1971–72, 1985–86; FL 1 – 2009–10; Division 3S – 1933–34.
Runners-up: FL C – 2010–11; Division 3 – 1959–60; Division 3S – 1950–51.

FA Cup: semi-final – 1959, 1989, 1992.

League Cup Winners: 1962, 1985.
Runners-up: 1973, 1975.

European Competitions
UEFA Cup: 1993–94.

Colours: Yellow shirts with green trim, green shorts with yellow trim, yellow socks with green trim.

Year Formed: 1902.

Turned Professional: 1905.

Club Nickname: 'The Canaries'.

Grounds: 1902, Newmarket Road; 1908, The Nest, Rosary Road; 1935, Carrow Road.

First Football League Game: 28 August 1920, Division 3, v Plymouth Arg (a) D 1–1 – Skermer; Gray, Gadsden; Wilkinson, Addy, Martin; Laxton, Kidger, Parker, Whitham (1), Dobson.

Record League Victory: 10–2 v Coventry C, Division 3 (S), 15 March 1930 – Jarvie; Hannah, Graham; Brown, O'Brien, Lochhead (1); Porter (1), Anderson, Hunt (5), Scott (2), Slicer (1).

Record Cup Victory: 8–0 v Sutton U, FA Cup 4th rd, 28 January 1989 – Gunn; Culverhouse, Bowen, Butterworth, Linighan, Townsend (Crook), Gordon, Fleck (3), Allen (4), Phelan, Putney (1).

Record Defeat: 2–10 v Swindon T, Southern League, 5 September 1908.

Most League Points (2 for a win): 64, Division 3 (S), 1950–51.

Most League Points (3 for a win): 95, FL 1, 2009–10.

sky SPORTS FACT FILE

Norwich City led the Division Three South attendance charts on three occasions in the 1950s. In the period from 1946 through until the change in divisions in 1958 the Canaries' attendances were in the top four for the division on every occasion, yet the team had to seek re-election to the Football League three times during that period.

Most League Goals: 99, Division 3 (S), 1952–53.

Highest League Scorer in Season: Ralph Hunt, 31, Division 3 (S), 1955–56.

Most League Goals in Total Aggregate: Johnny Gavin, 122, 1945–54, 1955–58.

Most League Goals in One Match: 5, Tommy Hunt v Coventry C, Division 3 (S), 15 March 1930; 5, Roy Hollis v Walsall, Division 3 (S), 29 December 1951.

Most Capped Player: Wes Hoolahan, 39 (40).

Most League Appearances: Ron Ashman, 592, 1947–64.

Youngest League Player: Ryan Jarvis, 16 years 282 days v Walsall, 19 April 2003.

Record Transfer Fee Received: £13,000,000 from Burnley for Robbie Brady, January 2017.

Record Transfer Fee Paid: £8,500,000 to Sporting Lisbon for Ricky van Wolfswinkel, July 2013; £8,500,000 to Everton for Steven Naismith, January 2016.

Football League Record: 1920 Original Member of Division 3; 1921 Division 3 (S): 1934–39 Division 2; 1946–58 Division 3 (S); 1958–60 Division 3; 1960–72 Division 2; 1972–74 Division 1; 1974–75 Division 2; 1975–81 Division 1; 1981–82 Division 2; 1982–85 Division 1; 1985–86 Division 2; 1986–92 Division 1; 1992–95 FA Premier League; 1995–2004 Division 1; 2004–05 FA Premier League; 2005–09 FL C; 2009–10 FL 1; 2010–11 FL C; 2011–14 FA Premier League; 2014–15 FL C; 2015–16 FA Premier League; 2016– FL C.

LATEST SEQUENCES

Longest Sequence of League Wins: 10, 23.11.1985 – 25.1.1986.

Longest Sequence of League Defeats: 7, 1.4.1995 – 6.5.1995.

Longest Sequence of League Draws: 7, 15.1.1994 – 26.2.1994.

Longest Sequence of Unbeaten League Matches: 20, 31.8.1950 – 30.12.1950.

Longest Sequence Without a League Win: 25, 22.9.1956 – 23.2.1957.

Successive Scoring Runs: 25 from 14.9.2009.

Successive Non-scoring Runs: 5 from 18.9.2007.

MANAGERS

John Bowman 1905–07
James McEwen 1907–08
Arthur Turner 1909–10
Bert Stansfield 1910–15
Major Frank Buckley 1919–20
Charles O'Hagan 1920–21
Albert Gosnell 1921–26
Bert Stansfield 1926
Cecil Potter 1926–29
James Kerr 1929–33
Tom Parker 1933–37
Bob Young 1937–39
Jimmy Jewell 1939
Bob Young 1939–45
Duggie Lochhead 1945–46
Cyril Spiers 1946–47
Duggie Lochhead 1947–50
Norman Low 1950–55
Tom Parker 1955–57
Archie Macaulay 1957–61
Willie Reid 1961–62
George Swindin 1962
Ron Ashman 1962–66
Lol Morgan 1966–69
Ron Saunders 1969–73
John Bond 1973–80
Ken Brown 1980–87
Dave Stringer 1987–92
Mike Walker 1992–94
John Deehan 1994–95
Martin O'Neill 1995
Gary Megson 1995–96
Mike Walker 1996–98
Bruce Rioch 1998–2000
Bryan Hamilton 2000
Nigel Worthington 2000–06
Peter Grant 2006–07
Glenn Roeder 2007–09
Bryan Gunn 2009
Paul Lambert 2009–12
Chris Hughton 2012–14
Neil Adams 2014–15
Alex Neil 2015–17
Daniel Farke May 2017–

TEN YEAR LEAGUE RECORD

		P	W	D	L	F	A	Pts	Pos
2007-08	FL C	46	15	10	21	49	59	55	17
2008-09	FL C	46	12	10	24	57	70	46	22
2009-10	FL 1	46	29	8	9	89	47	95	1
2010-11	FL C	46	23	15	8	83	58	84	2
2011-12	PR Lge	38	12	11	15	52	66	47	12
2012-13	PR Lge	38	10	14	14	41	58	44	11
2013-14	PR Lge	38	8	9	21	28	62	33	18
2014-15	FL C	46	25	11	10	88	48	86	3
2015-16	PR Lge	38	9	7	22	39	67	34	19
2016-17	FL C	46	20	10	16	85	69	70	8

DID YOU KNOW ?

Norwich City were the first English side to win a competitive European tie away to Bayern Munich at the Olympic Stadium. The Canaries won the 1993–94 UEFA Cup tie 2-1 with goals from Mark Bowen and Jeremy Goss and followed up with a 1-1 draw at Carrow Road to win the tie 3-2 on aggregate.

NORWICH CITY – SKY BET CHAMPIONSHIP 2016–17 LEAGUE RECORD

Match No.	Date	Venue	Opponents	Result		H/T Score	Lg Pos.	Goalscorers	Attendance
1	Aug 6	A	Blackburn R	W	4-1	3-0	1	Murphy, Jacob [12], Hoolahan [17], Jerome [25], Naismith [58]	12,641
2	13	H	Sheffield W	D	0-0	0-0	3		26,236
3	16	H	Bristol C	W	1-0	1-0	2	Howson [38]	26,297
4	21	A	Ipswich T	D	1-1	1-1	4	Jerome [26]	23,350
5	27	A	Birmingham C	L	0-3	0-1	9		16,295
6	Sept 10	H	Cardiff C	W	3-2	1-0	5	Jerome [16], Howson [59], Murphy, Josh [90]	25,519
7	13	H	Wigan Ath	W	2-1	2-0	3	Murphy, Jacob 2 [3, 11]	25,992
8	17	A	Nottingham F	W	2-1	0-1	2	Howson [52], Dorrans [66]	20,323
9	24	H	Burton Alb	W	3-1	1-0	1	Olsson [29], Murphy, Jacob [47], Ivo Pinto [89]	26,104
10	28	A	Newcastle U	L	3-4	1-1	2	Dorrans (pen) [44], Jerome [52], Murphy, Jacob [69]	48,236
11	Oct 1	A	Wolverhampton W	W	2-1	1-0	2	Jerome [2], Brady [73]	18,793
12	15	H	Rotherham U	W	3-1	1-0	1	Hoolahan [17], Jerome [65], Naismith [89]	26,813
13	18	A	Fulham	D	2-2	2-0	2	Dorrans 2 (2 pens) [17, 41]	17,082
14	22	H	Preston NE	L	0-1	0-0	3		26,239
15	29	A	Brighton & HA	L	0-5	0-1	4		29,469
16	Nov 5	H	Leeds U	L	2-3	1-0	5	Brady [24], Lafferty [88]	26,903
17	19	A	QPR	L	1-2	0-2	6	Naismith [78]	17,187
18	26	A	Derby Co	L	0-1	0-0	6		29,311
19	Dec 3	H	Brentford	W	5-0	2-0	7	Murphy, Jacob [6], Dorrans [16], Brady [59], Nelson Oliveira [79], Pritchard [88]	26,076
20	10	A	Barnsley	L	1-2	0-2	8	Nelson Oliveira [52]	12,306
21	13	H	Aston Villa	W	1-0	0-0	8	Nelson Oliveira [62]	26,044
22	16	H	Huddersfield T	L	1-2	1-2	9	Howson [6]	25,275
23	26	A	Reading	L	1-3	0-1	12	Nelson Oliveira [60]	21,180
24	31	A	Brentford	D	0-0	0-0	12		9377
25	Jan 2	H	Derby Co	W	3-0	1-0	9	Nelson Oliveira 3 [15, 78, 80]	26,422
26	14	A	Rotherham U	L	1-2	0-1	11	Jerome [51]	10,000
27	21	H	Wolverhampton W	W	3-1	1-0	9	Naismith [13], Brady (pen) [75], Howson [90]	26,303
28	28	H	Birmingham C	W	2-0	2-0	8	Jerome [15], Klose [43]	25,678
29	Feb 4	A	Cardiff C	W	1-0	1-0	7	Jerome [40]	15,901
30	7	A	Wigan Ath	D	2-2	1-0	7	Nelson Oliveira [40], Dijks [73]	10,193
31	11	H	Nottingham F	W	5-1	3-0	7	Howson [10], Murphy, Josh [16], Hoolahan [18], Pritchard 2 [61, 89]	26,831
32	14	H	Newcastle U	D	2-2	2-1	7	Murphy, Jacob [12], Jerome [17]	26,841
33	18	A	Burton Alb	L	1-2	0-1	7	Jerome [52]	5263
34	26	H	Ipswich T	D	1-1	0-0	8	Murphy, Jacob [69]	27,107
35	Mar 4	A	Sheffield W	L	1-5	1-3	8	Jerome [38]	28,178
36	7	A	Bristol C	D	1-1	1-0	8	Wildschut [39]	17,035
37	11	H	Blackburn R	D	2-2	1-0	9	Jerome 2 [19, 81]	26,224
38	18	H	Barnsley	W	2-0	1-0	8	Murphy, Jacob [44], MacDonald (og) [71]	26,105
39	Apr 1	A	Aston Villa	L	0-2	0-1	8		32,605
40	5	A	Huddersfield T	L	0-3	0-0	10		18,706
41	8	H	Reading	W	7-1	6-1	10	Nelson Oliveira (pen) [3], Hoolahan 2 [15, 41], Pritchard 2 [26, 35], Martin [31], Jerome [89]	26,163
42	14	H	Fulham	L	1-3	0-1	10	Jerome [76]	27,023
43	17	A	Preston NE	W	3-1	2-0	8	Dorrans [28], Murphy, Josh [40], Maddison [90]	11,373
44	21	H	Brighton & HA	W	2-0	2-0	8	Stockdale (2 ogs) [18, 39]	26,932
45	29	A	Leeds U	D	3-3	3-1	8	Naismith [28], Nelson Oliveira 2 [34, 45]	34,292
46	May 7	H	QPR	W	4-0	1-0	8	Hoolahan 2 [22, 90], Pritchard [60], Murphy, Josh [85]	27,005

Final League Position: 8

GOALSCORERS

League (85): Jerome 16, Nelson Oliveira 11 (1 pen), Jacob Murphy 9, Hoolahan 7, Dorrans 6 (3 pens), Howson 6, Pritchard 6, Naismith 5, Brady 4 (1 pen), Josh Murphy 4, Dijks 1, Ivo Pinto 1, Klose 1, Lafferty 1, Maddison 1, Martin 1, Olsson 1, Wildschut 1, own goals 3.
FA Cup (2): Naismith 1, Whittaker 1 (1 pen).
EFL Cup (10): Canos 2, Godfrey 1, Lafferty 1, Martin 1, Josh Murphy 1, Jacob Murphy 1, Naismith 1, Oliveira 1, Pritchard 1.
EFL Checkatrade Trophy (15): Josh Murphy 5, Andreu 3, Oliveira 3 (1 pen), Adams 1, Canos 1, Maddison 1, Morris 1.

Ruddy J 27	Ivo Pinto D 37	Bennett R 24 + 9	Klose T 31 + 1	Olsson M 16 + 3	Tettey A 33 + 2	Howson J 37 + 1	Murphy Jacob 32 + 5	Naismith S 20 + 9	Hoolahan W 30 + 3	Jerome C 31 + 9	Whittaker S 7 + 5	Mulumbu Y 7 + 6	Pritchard A 19 + 11	Brady R 22 + 1	Murphy Josh 9 + 18	McGovern M 19 + 1	Canos S 1 + 2	Lafferty K — + 12	Martin R 36 + 1	Dorrans G 22 + 1	Thompson L 1 + 2	Nelson Oliveira M 16 + 12	Bassong S 8 + 1	Godfrey B — + 2	Dijks M 15	Wildschut Y 6 + 3	Maddison J — + 3	*Match No.*
1	2	3	4	5^{1}	6	7^{2}	8	9	10^{3}	11	12	13	14															1
1^{3}	2	3	4	5^{2}	7	6		9	8	11^{1}		14		10	12	13												2
	2	3	4		7	6		9	10^{1}	11^{2}		13		5	8^{3}	1	12	14										3
	2^{2}	3	4		6	9	13	8^{3}	10	11	12	7^{1}		5		1	14											4
		3	4		6	9	10	11^{2}	8		2			5	13	1	7^{1}	12										5
	2	12	4		7	8	10^{2}		9^{1}	11			13	5^{3}	14	1			3	6								6
	2^{1}	12	4	5	7^{3}	8	10		9^{2}	11		14	13			1			3	6								7
	2	13	4	5		6	8^{3}		9^{1}	11^{2}				10		1		14	3	7	12							8
	2		4	5		6	8^{3}		9^{1}	11^{2}				10	13	1			3	7	12	14						9
	2	12		5	6	9	8^{1}			11^{2}				10		1			3	7		13	4					10
	2	14	4	5	6	12	8^{3}		9^{2}	11^{1}				10		1			3	7		13						11
	2		4	5	6		8^{1}	13	9^{2}	11			10^{3}		12	1			3	7		14						12
	2		4	5	7		8	12	9^{1}	11				10^{2}		1			3	6		13						13
		3	4	5	6		8^{1}		9	11			13	10^{2}		1			2	7		12						14
		3	4	5	7		8^{1}	13	9^{3}	11			10^{2}	14		1			2	6		12						15
		3	4	5			12		9	11			10^{2}	8^{1}		1		13	2	6	7							16
1		3		5■	6		8	9^{2}		12				10	13				2	7		11^{1}	4					17
1		3			6^{3}		8	10	9^{2}	11^{3}	14	7	13	5				12	2				4					18
1	2^{2}	3				6^{1}	8	10^{3}				14	9	5	13				12	7		11	4					19
1	2	3		13		6	8					12	9^{3}	5^{1}	10^{2}			14		7		11	4					20
1	2	3		5	12	9	8^{3}	13				6^{2}		10				14		7		11^{1}	4					21
1	2	3		5	12	9	8	13		14		6^{1}		10						7^{2}		11^{3}	4					22
1	2	3		12	6	8■	10	9^{1}	13	14				5						7^{2}		11^{3}	4					23
1	5^{3}	2	4	13	6		12	14		10^{1}		8	7^{2}	9■					3			11						24
1	2		4	5	6	7	8	9^{2}	10	13			12						3			11^{1}						25
1	2		4		6^{1}	7^{2}	8^{3}	9	10	12	5		13					14	3			11■						26
1	2		4		6	7	8^{2}	10	9^{1}	11^{3}			12	5	13			14	3									27
1	2		4		7^{2}	6	8^{1}	10	9^{3}	11				5	12			14	3					13				28
1	2	14	4		6	7	8^{3}		9^{1}	11					12				3			13			5	10^{2}		29
1	2		4			8	13			11		7	6^{1}		12				3			10			5	9^{2}		30
1	2^{2}	13	4			6			10^{1}		12	7	9		8				3			11			5^{3}	14		31
1			4		6	7	8		9^{3}	11^{1}	2		12		14			13	3						5	10^{2}		32
1			4		6	7	8^{2}		12	11	2		9^{1}		13			14	3						5	10^{3}		33
1	2		4		7	6	8	10^{1}	9^{2}	11			13		12				3						5			34
1	2	12	4		6	7	8^{1}	10^{2}	9^{3}	11			13		14				3						5			35
	2	3			7	6		9		11					8^{1}	1			4				12		5	10		36
	2	3			6	7	14		10^{2}	11	12		9^{3}		8^{1}	1			4						5■	13		37
	2	3			7	6	8^{2}	12	10^{3}	11^{1}	5		9			1			4	14		13						38
	2■	3			6^{1}	9	8^{2}	12		11	5		10			1			4	7^{3}		14				13		39
		3	4		6^{2}	7		10		11	5		9^{1}		13	1			2			12				8		40
1	2		4		6	7	8	13	10^{3}	14			9^{2}		12				3			11^{1}			5			41
1	2	12	4^{2}		6	7	8^{1}		10^{3}	13			9		14				3			11			5			42
1	2	4				6		8		11^{2}			9^{1}		10				3	7		12			5		13	43
1	2	4				6		8	12				9^{2}		10^{1}				3	7		11			5		13	44
1	2	3	13			7		8■		12			9		10^{1}				4	6		11^{2}			5			45
1	2^{3}		4			6			8	12			9^{2}		10				3	7		11^{1}		14	5		13	46

FA Cup

Third Round	Southampton	(h)	2-2
Replay	Southampton	(a)	0-1

EFL Cup

Second Round	Coventry C	(h)	6-1
Third Round	Everton	(a)	2-0
Fourth Round	Leeds U	(a)	2-2

(*aet; Leeds U won 3-2 on penalties*)

EFL Checkatrade Trophy (Norwich C U21)

Southern Group F	Peterborough U	(a)	6-1
Southern Group F	Barnet	(a)	5-0
Southern Group F	Milton Keynes D	(h)	4-1
Second Round South	Swansea C U21	(h)	0-1

NOTTINGHAM FOREST

FOUNDATION

One of the oldest football clubs in the world, Nottingham Forest was formed at a meeting in the Clinton Arms in 1865. Known originally as the Forest Football Club, the game which first drew the founders together was 'shinney', a form of hockey. When they determined to change to football in 1865, one of their first moves was to buy a set of red caps to wear on the field.

The City Ground, Pavilion Road, Nottingham NG2 5FJ.
Telephone: (0115) 982 4444.
Fax: (0115) 982 4455.
Ticket Office: (0115) 982 4388
Website: www.nottinghamforest.co.uk
Email: info@nottinghamforest.co.uk
Ground Capacity: 30,445.
Record Attendance: 49,946 v Manchester U, Division 1, 28 October 1967.
Pitch Measurements: 102.5m × 67.5m (112yd × 74yd).
Chairman: Nicholas Randall QC.
Manager: Mark Warburton.
Assistant Manager: David Weir.
Colours: Red shirt with white trim, white shorts with red trim, red socks with white trim.
Year Formed: 1865.
Turned Professional: 1889.
Previous Name: Forest Football Club.
Club Nickname: 'The Reds'.
Grounds: 1865, Forest Racecourse; 1879, The Meadows; 1880, Trent Bridge Cricket Ground; 1882, Parkside, Lenton; 1885, Gregory, Lenton; 1890, Town Ground; 1898, City Ground.
First Football League Game: 3 September 1892, Division 1, v Everton (a) D 2–2 – Brown; Earp, Scott; Hamilton, Albert Smith, McCracken; McCallum, 'Tich' Smith, Higgins (2), Pike, McInnes.
Record League Victory: 12–0 v Leicester Fosse, Division 1, 12 April 1909 – Iremonger; Dudley, Maltby; Hughes (1), Needham, Armstrong; Hooper (3), Marrison, West (3), Morris (2), Spouncer (3 incl. 1p).
Record Cup Victory: 14–0 v Clapton (away), FA Cup 1st rd, 17 January 1891 – Brown; Earp, Scott; Albert Smith, Russell, Jeacock; McCallum (2), 'Tich' Smith (1), Higgins (5), Lindley (4), Shaw (2).
Record Defeat: 1–9 v Blackburn R, Division 2, 10 April 1937.
Most League Points (2 for a win): 70, Division 3 (S), 1950–51.
Most League Points (3 for a win): 94, Division 1, 1997–98.
Most League Goals: 110, Division 3 (S), 1950–51.
Highest League Scorer in Season: Wally Ardron, 36, Division 3 (S), 1950–51.

HONOURS

League Champions: Division 1 – 1977–78; First Division – 1997–98; Division 2 – 1906–07, 1921–22; Division 3S – 1950–51.
Runners-up: Division 1 – 1966–67, 1978–79; First Division – 1993–94; Division 2 – 1956–57; FL 1 – 2007–08.

FA Cup Winners: 1898, 1959.
Runners-up: 1991.

League Cup Winners: 1978, 1979, 1989, 1990.
Runners-up: 1980, 1992.
Anglo-Scottish Cup Winners: 1977.
Full Members' Cup Winners: 1989, 1992.

European Competitions
European Cup: 1978–79 *(winners)*, 1979–80 *(winners)*, 1980–81.
Fairs Cup: 1961–62, 1967–68.
UEFA Cup: 1983–84 *(sf)*, 1984–85, 1995–96 *(qf)*.
Super Cup: 1979 *(winners)*, 1980.
World Club Championship: 1980.

sky SPORTS FACT FILE

A total of 37 Nottingham Forest players have been capped for England in the period to the end of the 2016–17 season. The first player to be honoured was Arthur Goodyer, who played against Scotland in April 1879, and the most recent was Stuart Pearce who won the 76th of his total 78 caps against Italy in June 1997.

Most League Goals in Total Aggregate: Grenville Morris, 199, 1898–1913.

Most League Goals in One Match: 4, Enoch West v Sunderland, Division 1, 9 November 1907; 4, Tommy Gibson v Burnley, Division 2, 25 January 1913; 4, Tom Peacock v Port Vale, Division 2, 23 December 1933; 4, Tom Peacock v Barnsley, Division 2, 9 November 1935; 4, Tom Peacock v Port Vale, Division 2, 23 November 1935; 4, Tom Peacock v Doncaster R, Division 2, 26 December 1935; 4, Tommy Capel v Gillingham, Division 3 (S), 18 November 1950; 4, Wally Ardron v Hull C, Division 2, 26 December 1952; 4, Tommy Wilson v Barnsley, Division 2, 9 February 1957; 4, Peter Withe v Ipswich T, Division 1, 4 October 1977; 4, Marlon Harewood v Stoke C, Division 1, 22 February 2003; Gareth McCleary v Leeds U, FL C, 20 March 2012.

Most Capped Player: Stuart Pearce, 76 (78), England.

Most League Appearances: Bob McKinlay, 614, 1951–70.

Youngest League Player: Craig Westcarr, 16 years 257 days v Burnley, 13 October 2001.

Record Transfer Fee Received: £14,000,000 from Middlesbrough for Britt Assombalonga, July 2017.

Record Transfer Fee Paid: £5,500,000 to Peterborough U for Britt Assombalonga, August 2014.

Football League Record: 1892 Elected to Division 1; 1906–07 Division 2; 1907–11 Division 1; 1911–22 Division 2; 1922–25 Division 1; 1925–49 Division 2; 1949–51 Division 3 (S); 1951–57 Division 2; 1957–72 Division 1; 1972–77 Division 2; 1977–92 Division 1; 1992–93 FA Premier League; 1993–94 Division 1; 1994–97 FA Premier League; 1997–98 Division 1; 1998–99 FA Premier League; 1999–2004 Division 1; 2004–05 FL C; 2005–08 FL 1; 2008– FL C.

MANAGERS

Harry Radford 1889–97
(Secretary-Manager)
Harry Haslam 1897–1909
(Secretary-Manager)
Fred Earp 1909–12
Bob Masters 1912–25
John Baynes 1925–29
Stan Hardy 1930–31
Noel Watson 1931–36
Harold Wightman 1936–39
Billy Walker 1939–60
Andy Beattie 1960–63
Johnny Carey 1963–68
Matt Gillies 1969–72
Dave Mackay 1972
Allan Brown 1973–75
Brian Clough 1975–93
Frank Clark 1993–96
Stuart Pearce 1996–97
Dave Bassett 1997–99
(previously General Manager)
Ron Atkinson 1999
David Platt 1999–2001
Paul Hart 2001–04
Joe Kinnear 2004
Gary Megson 2005–06
Colin Calderwood 2006–08
Billy Davies 2009–11
Steve McClaren 2011
Steve Cotterill 2011–12
Sean O'Driscoll 2012
Alex McLeish 2012–13
Billy Davies 2013–14
Stuart Pearce 2014–15
Dougie Freedman 2015–16
Philippe Montanier 2016–17
Mark Warburton March 2017–

LATEST SEQUENCES

Longest Sequence of League Wins: 7, 9.5.1979 – 1.9.1979.

Longest Sequence of League Defeats: 14, 21.3.1913 – 27.9.1913.

Longest Sequence of League Draws: 7, 29.4.1978 – 2.9.1978.

Longest Sequence of Unbeaten League Matches: 42, 26.11.1977 – 25.11.1978.

Longest Sequence Without a League Win: 19, 8.9.1998 – 16.1.1999.

Successive Scoring Runs: 22 from 28.3.1931.

Successive Non-scoring Runs: 7 from 26.11.2011.

TEN YEAR LEAGUE RECORD

		P	W	D	L	F	A	Pts	Pos
2007-08	FL 1	46	22	16	8	64	32	82	2
2008-09	FL C	46	13	14	19	50	65	53	19
2009-10	FL C	46	22	13	11	65	40	79	3
2010-11	FL C	46	20	15	11	69	50	75	6
2011-12	FL C	46	14	8	24	48	63	50	19
2012-13	FL C	46	17	16	13	63	59	67	8
2013-14	FL C	46	16	17	13	67	64	65	11
2014-15	FL C	46	15	14	17	71	69	59	14
2015-16	FL C	46	13	16	17	43	47	55	16
2016-17	FL C	46	14	9	23	62	72	51	21

DID YOU KNOW ?

Nottingham Forest's home game with Leeds United on 26 August 1968 was abandoned at half-time after fire destroyed the centre stand at the City Ground. Forest played their next five home fixtures at Meadow Lane, but failed to record a single victory, drawing three and losing two of the games.

NOTTINGHAM FOREST – SKY BET CHAMPIONSHIP 2016–17 LEAGUE RECORD

Match No.	*Date*	*Venue*	*Opponents*	*Result*		*H/T Score*	*Lg Pos.*	*Goalscorers*	*Attendance*
1	Aug 6	H	Burton Alb	W	4-3	2-2	3	Assombalonga 2 [23, 77], Lam [45], Burke [49]	23,012
2	12	A	Brighton & HA	L	0-3	0-1	10		25,748
3	16	A	Brentford	L	0-1	0-1	18		10,004
4	20	H	Wigan Ath	W	4-3	1-1	11	Assombalonga [6], Burke 2 [53, 78], Lam [90]	17,750
5	27	H	Leeds U	W	3-1	1-0	7	Kasami [16], Perquis [71], Burke [90]	20,995
6	Sept 11	A	Aston Villa	D	2-2	0-0	10	Vellios [57], Lansbury [87]	30,619
7	14	A	Rotherham U	D	2-2	0-1	10	Mills [76], Vellios [85]	10,243
8	17	H	Norwich C	L	1-2	1-0	13	Vellios [40]	20,323
9	24	A	Sheffield W	L	1-2	1-0	15	Lansbury [35]	27,350
10	27	H	Fulham	D	1-1	0-0	15	Bendtner [60]	17,388
11	Oct 1	A	Bristol C	L	1-2	1-0	16	Vellios [33]	18,922
12	14	H	Birmingham C	W	3-1	1-0	13	Lichaj [33], Vellios [63], Pereira [83]	19,208
13	18	A	Blackburn R	L	1-2	0-2	16	Perquis [90]	10,462
14	22	H	Cardiff C	L	1-2	0-2	19	Lansbury (pen) [90]	16,539
15	29	A	Reading	L	0-2	0-1	20		17,093
16	Nov 5	H	QPR	D	1-1	1-0	20	Assombalonga [38]	20,043
17	19	A	Ipswich T	W	2-0	2-0	18	Assombalonga 2 [1, 45]	15,417
18	25	A	Barnsley	W	5-2	3-2	16	Lansbury 3 (1 pen) [13, 45, 82 (p)], Vellios [24], Osborn [63]	13,180
19	Dec 2	H	Newcastle U	W	2-1	0-1	13	Bendtner [52], Lascelles (og) [86]	21,317
20	11	A	Derby Co	L	0-3	0-1	16		32,600
21	14	H	Preston NE	D	1-1	0-1	16	Maxwell (og) [68]	15,864
22	17	H	Wolverhampton W	L	0-2	0-1	17		19,037
23	26	A	Huddersfield T	L	1-2	1-0	17	Pereira [25]	22,100
24	30	A	Newcastle U	L	1-3	1-1	18	Dumitru [29]	52,228
25	Jan 2	H	Barnsley	L	0-1	0-0	20		22,105
26	14	A	Birmingham C	D	0-0	0-0	19		18,041
27	21	H	Bristol C	W	1-0	0-0	19	Osborn [67]	17,418
28	25	A	Leeds U	L	0-2	0-0	19		24,838
29	31	H	Rotherham U	W	2-0	0-0	18	Assombalonga 2 (1 pen) [50 (p), 71]	15,770
30	Feb 4	H	Aston Villa	W	2-1	1-1	15	Assombalonga [42], Brereton [90]	19,866
31	11	A	Norwich C	L	1-5	0-3	17	McCormack [75]	26,831
32	14	A	Fulham	L	2-3	1-2	17	Kasami [2], Brereton [47]	15,365
33	18	H	Sheffield W	L	1-2	0-1	18	Osborn [60]	20,164
34	25	A	Wigan Ath	D	0-0	0-0	18		11,254
35	Mar 4	H	Brighton & HA	W	3-0	0-0	18	Clough 2 (1 pen) [60, 90 (p)], Osborn [89]	22,020
36	7	H	Brentford	L	2-3	0-1	18	Brereton [82], Clough [90]	16,903
37	11	A	Burton Alb	L	0-1	0-1	19		6115
38	18	H	Derby Co	D	2-2	1-0	20	Clough [5], Pinillos [90]	26,665
39	Apr 1	A	Preston NE	D	1-1	1-0	20	Assombalonga [22]	12,459
40	4	A	Wolverhampton W	L	0-1	0-0	20		21,408
41	8	H	Huddersfield T	W	2-0	1-0	19	Lichaj [32], Ward [57]	20,411
42	14	H	Blackburn R	L	0-1	0-0	20		26,279
43	17	A	Cardiff C	L	0-1	0-0	21		16,413
44	22	H	Reading	W	3-2	1-0	20	Assombalonga 2 [31, 47], Carayol [54]	20,323
45	29	A	QPR	L	0-2	0-0	21		16,474
46	May 7	H	Ipswich T	W	3-0	1-0	21	Assombalonga 2 (1 pen) [43 (p), 69], Cohen [57]	28,249

Final League Position: 21

GOALSCORERS

League (62): Assombalonga 14 (2 pens), Lansbury 6 (2 pens), Vellios 6, Burke 4, Clough 4 (1 pen), Osborn 4, Brereton 3, Bendtner 2, Kasami 2, Lam 2, Lichaj 2, Pereira 2, Perquis 2, Carayol 1, Cohen 1, Dumitru 1, McCormack 1, Mills 1, Pinillos 1, Ward 1, own goals 2.
FA Cup (0).
EFL Cup (4): Paterson 1, Vaughan 1, Veldwijk 1, Ward 1.

De Vries D 1	Pereira H 16 + 6	Mills M 24 + 3	Lam T 11 + 8	Iacovitti A 2	Lansbury H 16 + 1	Burke O 4 + 1	Grant J 4 + 2	Cash M 18 + 10	Osborn B 45 + 1	Assombalonga B 20 + 12	Henderson S 11 + 1	Kasami P 19 + 6	Lichaj E 39 + 2	Mancienne M 24 + 4	Perquis D 17	Veldwijk L 1	Ward J 13 + 5	Traore A 9 + 3	Paterson J — + 1	Vellios A 12 + 16	Fox D 22 + 1	Vaughan D 25 + 6	Cohen C 20	Stojkovic V 20	Carayol M 13 + 6	Dumitru N 6 + 4	Bendtner N 7 + 8	Lica P 2 + 3	Worrall J 21	Pinillos D 14 + 2	Hobbs J 9	Ahmedhodzic A — + 1	Brereton B 13 + 5	Clough Z 9 + 5	Tshibola A 2 + 2	Smith J 14 + 1	McCormack R 3 + 4	*Match No.*
1^{2}	2^{3}	3	4	5	6	7	8^{1}	9	10	11	12	13	14																									1
	5			4^{2}	6	9^{1}			8		1	7		2	3	10	11^{3}	12	13	14																		2
	9	3			8	12			11	13	1	6	2		4■					10	5^{1}	7^{2}																3
	2	14	4			9		8	11	10^{2}	1	6^{1}	13	3						12	5^{3}		7															4
	2	12			8	9		13	11		1	6	5	3	4^{1}					10^{2}			7															5
	13■		12^{3}		7			8^{2}	9			6	2	3	4					10	5			1	11^{1}	14												6
		3			7		6^{2}		9			8	2	12	4^{3}			5		10				1		11^{1}	13	14										7
	6	3			13				14			8	2	4						10^{3}	5		7^{1}	1	9	11^{2}	12											8
	2	3			8		6^{1}		11			12	5	4						10^{3}			7	1	9^{2}	14	13											9
	13								9			7	2	3	4					14	5	6		1	8^{1}	10^{2}	11^{3}	12										10
		3	12		8				11^{1}			6	2		4^{2}			14		10	5		7	1			13	9^{3}										11
	13	3	14		9				10				2		4			5^{2}		12		6	7	1	8^{3}		11^{1}											12
	2■	3			9				10^{1}	14		12	5		4					11		6^{2}	7	1	8^{3}	13												13
			4■		9		13		10	12		6	2		3			5^{2}		11			7	1		8^{1}												14
		2			8				10	12		6	5		3			9^{1}		11^{2}	13		7^{3}	1		14			4									15
	5■	2	12		8				10	11^{1}		6	9		3					13			7^{2}	1					4									16
		2	8^{1}		7		14		10	11^{2}		6	5	13	3					12				1					4	9^{3}								17
		2	7		8			13	10			6		5^{2}	3					11^{3}	9^{1}	14		1			12		4									18
		2	8^{3}		6			5	10	12		7	9	4^{2}	3					14				1	13		11^{1}											19
	13	2	7^{2}					5^{1}	8			6	9	4	3					12		14		1	10^{3}		11											20
	5	2	8^{3}					6	10			14	9		3^{2}			12		13		7		1			11^{1}		4									21
	13	3					7^{3}	9	10			6^{2}	5	2						11		12		1	8^{1}			14	4									22
	10^{3}	2	13					5	6^{1}	12			9	7■								8		1	14		11		4^{2}		3							23
	9	3■	7^{2}					2	10	12		6	5									13		1		8^{3}	11^{1}				4	14						24
	9		7^{1}					2	10	11^{3}	1	12	5	3						13		6				8^{2}	14				4							25
	8^{2}	3	6					7	9	11	1		5	2								13						10^{1}		12	4							26
		3^{1}						8	9	11	1		2	6			10					7					12			5	4							27
			12					8	9	11^{1}	1		2	6			10^{2}				4	7					13			5	3^{3}		14					28
								13	9	11^{3}	1		2	7			6^{1}			14	4	8			12					5	3		10^{2}					29
			13					8^{2}	7	11	1		2	3			10^{3}				4	6			14					5			12	9^{1}				30
			14						10	11^{3}	1^{1}		2■				8^{2}				4	7								5	3			9	6	12	13	31
								5	8	14		6^{2}									4	13		1					2	9^{1}	3		10	12	7^{3}		11	32
								6^{3}	8	13		14	2				9^{2}				4	7			12				3	5			10			1	11^{1}	33
									8	11			2				12				4	7			9				3	5			10^{1}	6^{2}		1	13	34
	8^{3}							6	9	11^{1}			2				10^{2}	5			4		7						3				13	12	14	1		35
	8^{3}							6	9	11^{2}			2				10^{1}				4	7							3	5			12	13		1	14	36
	13							12	8				2^{3}	6^{1}				5		14	4	7							3				11^{2}	10		1	9	37
								13	10	11^{2}				2						14	4	6	7^{1}						3	5			8	9^{3}		1	12	38
								13	10	11^{2}			2				12			14	4	6	9						3	5			7^{1}	8^{3}		1		39
		3							10^{2}	11^{3}				2			12	5		14	4■	6	9		13								7^{1}	8		1		40
		3							8	14			5	13			11^{1}	4^{3}				6	7						2				10	9^{2}	12	1		41
		3^{2}						13	8	14			5	12			9^{1}	4				7^{3}	6						2				11	10		1		42
									11	12			2				10^{1}			14	4	8	7		9				3	5^{3}			6^{2}	13		1		43
								14	9	11			2	4			12				5^{2}	6	8		10^{3}				3	13			7^{1}			1		44
		14						13	9	11			2	4			12					6	8		10^{1}				3	5^{2}			7^{3}			1		45
		3						14	8	11			5	4			9^{3}					7	6^{1}		10^{2}				2				13	12		1		46

FA Cup

Third Round	Wigan Ath	(a)	0-2

EFL Cup

First Round	Doncaster R	(a)	2-1
Second Round	Millwall	(a)	2-1
Third Round	Arsenal	(h)	0-4

NOTTS COUNTY

FOUNDATION

According to the official history of Notts County 'the true date of Notts' foundation has to be the meeting at the George Hotel on 7 December 1864'. However, there is documented evidence of continuous play from 1862, when club members played organised matches amongst themselves in The Park in Nottingham. They are the world's oldest professional football club.

Meadow Lane Stadium, Meadow Lane, Nottingham NG2 3HJ.

Telephone: (0115) 952 9000.

Fax: (0115) 955 3994.

Ticket Office: (0115) 955 7210.

Website: www.nottscountyfc.co.uk

Email: office@nottscountyfc.co.uk

Ground Capacity: 19,841.

Record Attendance: 47,310 v York C, FA Cup 6th rd, 12 March 1955.

Pitch Measurements: 103.5m × 64m (113yd × 70yd).

Chairman: Alan Hardy.

Chief Executive: Jason Turner.

Manager: Kevin Nolan.

Assistant Manager: Richard Thomas.

HONOURS

League Champions: Division 2 – 1896–97, 1913–14, 1922–23; Division 3S – 1930–31, 1949–50; FL 2 – 2009–10; Third Division – 1997–98; Division 4 – 1970–71.
Runners-up: Division 2 – 1894–95, 1980–81; Division 3 – 1972–73; Division 3S – 1936–37; Division 4 – 1959–60.

FA Cup Winners: 1894.
Runners-up: 1891.

League Cup: 5th rd – 1964, 1973, 1976.

Anglo-Italian Cup Winners: 1995.
Runners-up: 1994.

Colours: Black and white striped shirts, black shorts with yellow trim, white socks with black hoops.

Year Formed: 1862* (*see Foundation*). ***Turned Professional:*** 1885.

Club Nickname: 'The Magpies'.

Grounds: 1862, The Park; 1864, The Meadows; 1877, Beeston Cricket Ground; 1880, Castle Ground; 1883, Trent Bridge; 1910, Meadow Lane.

First Football League Game: 15 September 1888, Football League, v Everton (a) L 1–2 – Holland; Guttridge, McLean; Brown, Warburton, Shelton; Hodder, Harker, Jardine, Albert Moore (1), Wardle.

Record League Victory: 11–1 v Newport Co, Division 3 (S), 15 January 1949 – Smith; Southwell, Purvis; Gannon, Baxter, Adamson; Houghton (1), Sewell (4), Lawton (4), Pimbley, Johnston (2).

Record Cup Victory: 15–0 v Rotherham T (at Trent Bridge), FA Cup 1st rd, 24 October 1885 – Sherwin; Snook, Henry Thomas Moore; Dobson (1), Emmett (1), Chapman; Gunn (1), Albert Moore (2), Jackson (3), Daft (2), Cursham (4), (1 og).

Record Defeat: 1–9 v Blackburn R, Division 1, 16 November 1889. 1–9 v Aston Villa, Division 1, 29 September 1888. 1–9 v Portsmouth, Division 2, 9 April 1927.

Most League Points (2 for a win): 69, Division 4, 1970–71.

Most League Points (3 for a win): 99, Division 3, 1997–98.

Most League Goals: 107, Division 4, 1959–60.

sky SPORTS FACT FILE

Notts County changed their shirt colours from black and white stripes to chocolate and blue halves for the 1934–35 season, hoping that a change in colours would produce a change in the team's fortunes. Unfortunately 'The Chocolate and Blues' had a dreadful season, finishing bottom of the Second Division, and there was a quick return to black and white stripes for 1935–36.

Highest League Scorer in Season: Tom Keetley, 39, Division 3 (S), 1930–31.

Most League Goals in Total Aggregate: Les Bradd, 125, 1967–78.

Most League Goals in One Match: 5, Robert Jardine v Burnley, Division 1, 27 October 1888; 5, Daniel Bruce v Port Vale, Division 2, 26 February 1895; 5, Bertie Mills v Barnsley, Division 2, 19 November 1927.

Most Capped Player: Kevin Wilson, 15 (42), Northern Ireland.

Most League Appearances: Albert Iremonger, 564, 1904–26.

Youngest League Player: Tony Bircumshaw, 16 years 54 days v Brentford, 3 April 1961.

Record Transfer Fee Received: £2,500,000 from Derby Co for Craig Short, September 1992.

Record Transfer Fee Paid: £800,000 to Manchester C for Kasper Schmeichel, July 2009.

Football League Record: 1888 Founder Member of the Football League; 1893–97 Division 2; 1897–1913 Division 1; 1913–14 Division 2; 1914–20 Division 1; 1920–23 Division 2; 1923–26 Division 1; 1926–30 Division 2; 1930–31 Division 3 (S); 1931–35 Division 2; 1935–50 Division 3 (S); 1950–58 Division 2; 1958–59 Division 3; 1959–60 Division 4; 1960–64 Division 3; 1964–71 Division 4; 1971–73 Division 3; 1973–81 Division 2; 1981–84 Division 1; 1984–85 Division 2; 1985–90 Division 3; 1990–91 Division 2; 1991–95 Division 1; 1995–97 Division 2; 1997–98 Division 3; 1998–2004 Division 2; 2004–10 FL 2; 2010–15 FL 1; 2015– FL 2.

LATEST SEQUENCES

Longest Sequence of League Wins: 10, 3.12.1997 – 31.1.1998.

Longest Sequence of League Defeats: 10, 12.11.2016 – 7.1.2017.

Longest Sequence of League Draws: 6, 16.8.2008 – 20.9.2008.

Longest Sequence of Unbeaten League Matches: 19, 26.4.1930 – 6.12.1930.

Longest Sequence Without a League Win: 20, 3.12.1996 – 31.3.1997.

Successive Scoring Runs: 35 from 10.10.1959.

Successive Non-scoring Runs: 5 from 15.3.2011.

MANAGERS

Edwin Browne 1883–93; **Tom Featherstone** 1893; **Tom Harris** 1893–1913; **Albert Fisher** 1913–27; **Horace Henshall** 1927–34; **Charlie Jones** 1934; **David Pratt** 1935; **Percy Smith** 1935–36; **Jimmy McMullan** 1936–37; **Harry Parkes** 1938–39; **Tony Towers** 1939–42; **Frank Womack** 1942–43; **Major Frank Buckley** 1944–46; **Arthur Stollery** 1946–49; **Eric Houghton** 1949–53; **George Poyser** 1953–57; **Tommy Lawton** 1957–58; **Frank Hill** 1958–61; **Tim Coleman** 1961–63; **Eddie Lowe** 1963–65; **Tim Coleman** 1965–66; **Jack Burkitt** 1966–67; **Andy Beattie** *(General Manager)* 1967; **Billy Gray** 1967–68; **Jack Wheeler** (*Caretaker Manager*) 1968–69; **Jimmy Sirrel** 1969–75; **Ron Fenton** 1975–77; **Jimmy Sirrel** 1978–82 *(continued as General Manager to 1984)*; **Howard Wilkinson** 1982–83; **Larry Lloyd** 1983–84; **Richie Barker** 1984–85; **Jimmy Sirrel** 1985–87; **John Barnwell** 1987–88; **Neil Warnock** 1989–93; **Mick Walker** 1993–94; **Russell Slade** 1994–95; **Howard Kendall** 1995; **Colin Murphy** 1995–96 *(General Manager)*; **Steve Thompson** 1995–96; **Sam Allardyce** 1997–99; **Gary Brazil** 1999–2000; **Jocky Scott** 2000–01; **Gary Brazil** 2001–02; **Billy Dearden** 2002–04; **Gary Mills** 2004; **Ian Richardson** 2004–05; **Gudjon Thordarson** 2005–06; **Steve Thompson** 2006–07; **Ian McParland** 2007–09; **Hans Backe** 2009; **Sven-Göran Eriksson** 2009–10 *(Director of Football)*; **Steve Cotterill** 2010; **Craig Short** 2010; **Paul Ince** 2010–11; **Martin Allen** 2011–12; **Keith Curle** 2012–13; **Chris Kiwomya** 2013; **Shaun Derry** 2013–15; **Ricardo Moniz** 2015; **Jamie Fullarton** 2016; **Mark Cooper** 2016; **John Sheridan** 2016–17; **Kevin Nolan** January 2017–

TEN YEAR LEAGUE RECORD

		P	W	D	L	F	A	Pts	Pos
2007-08	FL 2	46	10	18	18	37	53	48	21
2008-09	FL 2	46	11	14	21	49	69	47	19
2009-10	FL 2	46	27	12	7	96	31	93	1
2010-11	FL 1	46	14	8	24	46	60	50	19
2011-12	FL 1	46	21	10	15	75	63	73	7
2012-13	FL 1	46	16	17	13	61	49	65	12
2013-14	FL 1	46	15	5	26	64	77	50	20
2014-15	FL 1	46	12	14	20	45	63	50	21
2015-16	FL 2	46	14	9	23	54	83	51	17
2016-17	FL 2	46	16	8	22	54	76	56	16

DID YOU KNOW ?

The presence of England international centre-forward Tommy Lawton in their line-up attracted huge crowds to watch Notts County in the late 1940s. When the Magpies won the Division Three South title in 1949–50 their average attendance of 35,176 was a club record and higher than nine First Division clubs.

NOTTS COUNTY – SKY BET LEAGUE TWO 2016–17 LEAGUE RECORD

Match No.	Date	Venue	Opponents	Result		H/T Score	Lg Pos.	Goalscorers	Attendance
1	Aug 6	A	Yeovil T	L	0-2	0-2	23		3715
2	13	H	Stevenage	D	1-1	1-1	22	Stead [18]	3987
3	16	H	Plymouth Arg	L	1-2	1-2	21	Stead [17]	3718
4	20	A	Hartlepool U	W	2-1	0-1	19	Laing [65], Stead [76]	3708
5	27	A	Crawley T	W	3-1	0-0	11	Collins (og) [54], Campbell, A [61], Stead (pen) [87]	2087
6	Sept 3	H	Grimsby T	D	2-2	0-1	12	Forte [77], Collins [89]	6861
7	10	H	Accrington S	L	0-2	0-1	17		3988
8	17	A	Cheltenham T	W	3-2	2-1	12	Forte [4], Stead 2 [41, 56]	3067
9	24	H	Leyton Orient	W	3-1	0-0	9	Forte [53], Stead [55], Collins [90]	4289
10	27	A	Exeter C	W	2-0	2-0	5	Stead 2 [3, 34]	3081
11	Oct 8	A	Mansfield T	L	1-3	0-0	8	Rodman [82]	5763
12	11	H	Morecambe	L	1-2	0-1	10	Oliver [90]	3507
13	15	H	Crewe Alex	D	1-1	0-0	12	Forte [80]	8012
14	22	A	Portsmouth	W	2-1	1-1	6	Campbell, A 2 [21, 71]	17,269
15	29	H	Luton T	D	0-0	0-0	6		6313
16	Nov 12	A	Blackpool	L	0-4	0-1	8		3443
17	19	H	Newport Co	L	0-3	0-2	12		3883
18	22	H	Cambridge U	L	0-1	0-1	15		2736
19	26	A	Barnet	L	2-3	1-1	19	O'Connor [15], Forte [77]	1958
20	Dec 10	H	Wycombe W	L	0-2	0-1	20		3680
21	17	A	Colchester U	L	1-2	1-1	20	Hewitt [17]	3385
22	26	H	Doncaster R	L	0-1	0-0	21		5828
23	31	H	Carlisle U	L	2-3	2-2	22	Stead [30], Forte [39]	3825
24	Jan 2	A	Cambridge U	L	0-4	0-1	22		4981
25	7	A	Morecambe	L	1-4	0-3	22	Forte [80]	1315
26	14	H	Mansfield T	D	0-0	0-0	23		11,328
27	21	A	Grimsby T	L	0-2	0-1	23		5421
28	28	H	Crawley T	W	2-1	0-0	21	Audel [75], Forte [90]	5023
29	Feb 4	A	Accrington S	L	0-2	0-1	22		1731
30	11	H	Cheltenham T	W	2-1	2-0	22	Stead [24], Duffy [33]	7910
31	14	H	Exeter C	D	2-2	0-1	21	Duffy [90], Grant [90]	4047
32	18	A	Leyton Orient	W	3-2	1-0	20	Grant [35], Stead 2 [48, 84]	5585
33	25	H	Yeovil T	D	0-0	0-0	21		7141
34	28	A	Plymouth Arg	W	1-0	1-0	19	Grant [21]	7566
35	Mar 4	A	Stevenage	L	0-3	0-1	22		3248
36	11	H	Hartlepool U	W	2-1	0-0	19	Ameobi [47], Grant [70]	8653
37	14	A	Doncaster R	L	1-3	1-1	21	Duffy [20]	5760
38	19	H	Barnet	W	1-0	0-0	20	Tootle [49]	7178
39	25	A	Wycombe W	W	1-0	1-0	20	Ameobi [27]	4362
40	Apr 1	H	Colchester U	W	3-1	2-1	16	Hollis [8], Ameobi 2 [34, 73]	6104
41	8	A	Carlisle U	W	2-1	0-0	15	Stead [85], Tootle [89]	4361
42	14	A	Crewe Alex	D	2-2	1-1	15	Campbell, A [9], O'Connor [51]	5016
43	17	H	Portsmouth	L	1-3	0-1	15	Grant [51]	12,184
44	22	A	Luton T	L	1-2	1-2	16	Hewitt [6]	7719
45	29	H	Blackpool	W	1-0	1-0	16	Duffy [34]	7108
46	May 6	A	Newport Co	L	1-2	0-1	16	Grant [61]	7326

Final League Position: 16

GOALSCORERS

League (54): Stead 14 (1 pen), Forte 8, Grant 6, Ameobi 4, Campbell, A 4, Duffy 4, Collins 2, Hewitt 2, O'Connor 2, Tootle 2, Audel 1, Hollis 1, Laing 1, Oliver 1, Rodman 1, own goal 1.
FA Cup (6): Campbell, A 3, Collins 1, Forte 1, Laing 1.
EFL Cup (0).
EFL Checkatrade Trophy (4): Burke 1 (1 pen), Campbell, A 1, Forte 1, Snijders 1.

Collin A 43	Duffy R 42	Hollis H 30 + 1	Audel T 12 + 4	Hewitt E 23 + 6	Tootle M 32 + 1	Rodman A 15 + 1	Dickinson C 33 + 1	Aborah S 6 + 2	Forte J 28 + 7	Stead J 37 + 1	Oliver V 2 + 17	Burke G 2 + 3	Smith A 7 + 12	O'Connor M 30 + 2	Laing L 19 + 2	Campbell A 21 + 8	Milsom R 36 + 2	Snijders G 3 + 2	Collins A 3 + 15	Richards J 7 + 5	Edwards M 2	Thompson C 11 + 2	Loach S 3	Osborne S 1 + 2	Gibson M — + 1	Yeates M 11 + 3	Bola M 10 + 3	Campbell T 1 + 10	Ameobi S 13 + 4	Grant J 15 + 2	Clackstone J 7 + 1	Howes A 1 + 1	*Match No.*
1	2	3	4	5[1]	6	7	8	9[2]	10	11[3]	12	13	14																				1
1	3	4	2	14	6	8	5	9[2]	10[3]	11	12	13		7[1]																			2
1	3		2		6[1]	8	5	9	10	11[2]	13			7	4	12																	3
1	3		14		2	9	5	8[2]	6[1]	11[3]	12		13	7	4	10																	4
1	3		12		2	6	5			11[2]	13		7[3]	8	4	10	9[1]	14															5
1	4		12		2	6	5	8[3]	9	10[1]	14			7	3	11[2]			13														6
1	4		2		7[3]	6	5		9	11[1]	10[2]			8	3	14	13		12														7
1	3	4			2	6[2]	5		9[1]	11[3]	14			8	7		10		13	12													8
1	3	4			5	6	9		11[2]	10[1]	13			7[3]	2■		8		12	14													9
1	3	2		4	5	6[3]	9		11[2]	10[1]	12			7			8		13	14													10
1	3	4[2]			2	8	6	7[3]	10	11[1]	14				5		9		13	12													11
1	3	4[1]	12		5	6	9		10	11[2]	14	8[3]			2				13	7													12
1	4		2[3]	14	8	6[1]			10	11[2]					3	9	5	13	12	7													13
1	3	4			5	12	9		10[1]				13		2	6[2]	8		11■	7													14
1	3	4				5	8		11		12			13	2	9[2]	6		10[1]	7													15
1	2	4		6	5		9[2]		8		12■		11[1]	7	3	10[3]	13		14														16
1	3	4[2]		12			5					9	13		2	10	8	6	11[1]	7													17
1	3			2[2]	12		6		10				11[1]	8	5	14	9	7	13		4[3]												18
1	4				2		3		8		10	13		6	7	11[2]		5[1]	12		9												19
1	3	4			6		5		11[1]	10[3]	12			7■	2	9[2]	8		14	13													20
1	3		2	4	5		9		11[3]	10	12				13	14	6			8[1]		7[2]											21
	3	4			2[1]		5		11	10[2]	13				12	6	9		14	7		8[3]	1										22
	4[2]	12		2		6	5		11	10[1]	14			8	3	13	9					7[3]	1										23
1		3		4			2		11[1]	10[2]			7	8	5	13	6		12			9											24
	4			3	2[3]		5	12	13	11				8		10	9		14			7[1]	1	6[2]									25
1	4		3		2		5		11	10			12	7		6[1]	9					8											26
1	4		3		5		2	14	6[1]	11				8		10[2]	7[3]					9		12	13								27
1	2	4	3	13	5				11	10[1]			12	7[2]		9[3]	8					6■		14									28
1	4	5	3[2]		2				10[1]	11				8		6	9									7[3]	12	13	14				29
1	3		4	2					13	11				7			8					9[3]				6[2]	5	12	10[1]	14			30
1	3		4[1]	2						10			11[3]	8			7					6				9[2]	5		14	13	12		31
1	4			3						10[1]			13	7			8					12				6[2]	5		11	9	2		32
1		4		3						11				7			8									9[1]	5	12	10	6	2		33
1		4		3					11[1]	12			10[2]	7			8					14				9[3]	5		13	6	2		34
1		4		3			13		12	11[2]							8					6				9[1]	5[3]	14	10	7	2		35
1	3	4		7	2				11[3]				13			14	8									6[1]	5	12	10	9[2]			36
1	4	3		12	2				14				10[3]	7			8[2]									9[1]	5	11	13	6			37
1	3	4		12	2					10[1]				7			8									9■	5		11	6			38
1	3	4		6	2		5			10			12	7			8												11[1]	9			39
1	3	4		7[1]	2		5			11[2]			14			6[3]	8											12	10	9		13	40
1	3	4		9	2		5[3]			11				12		6[1]	7[2]										13	14	10	8			41
1	3	4		8	2		5		14	11[2]				7		9[1]										12		13	10[3]	6			42
1	3	4		8	2					11				7[1]		6[2]	9									12	5	13		10			43
1	3	4		8			2		12	11[1]						10[2]	6[3]									13		14	5	7	9		44
1	3	4		7			5		14	11[2]			13			12	8									6[1]			10	9[3]	2		45
1	4	3		8			5[2]			10			13				7										12		11	9	2	6[1]	46

FA Cup

First Round	Boreham Wood	(a)	2-2
Replay	Boreham Wood	(h)	2-0
Second Round	Peterborough U	(h)	2-2
Replay	Peterborough U	(a)	0-2

EFL Cup

First Round (*aet*)	Scunthorpe U	(a)	0-2

EFL Checkatrade Trophy

Northern Group F	Hartlepool U	(h)	2-1
Northern Group F	Rochdale	(a)	1-2
Northern Group F	Sunderland U21	(a)	1-2

OLDHAM ATHLETIC

FOUNDATION

It was in 1895 that John Garland, the landlord of the Featherstall and Junction Hotel, decided to form a football club. As Pine Villa they played in the Oldham Junior League. In 1899 the local professional club, Oldham County, went out of existence and one of the liquidators persuaded Pine Villa to take over their ground at Sheepfoot Lane and change their name to Oldham Athletic.

SportsDirect.com Park, Furtherwood Road, Oldham, Lancashire OL1 2PB.

Telephone: (0161) 624 4972.

Fax: (0161) 627 5915.

Ticket Office: (0161) 785 5150.

Website: www.oldhamathletic.co.uk

Email: enquiries@oldhamathletic.co.uk

Ground Capacity: 13,488.

Record Attendance: 46,471 v Sheffield W, FA Cup 4th rd, 25 January 1930.

Pitch Measurements: 100m × 68m (109yd × 74yd).

Chairman: Simon Corney.

Chief Executive: Mark Moisley.

Manager: John Sheridan.

Assistant Manager: Tommy Wright.

Colours: Blue shirts with white trim, blue shorts with white trim, blue socks with white trim.

Year Formed: 1895.

Turned Professional: 1899.

Previous Name: 1895, Pine Villa; 1899, Oldham Athletic.

Club Nickname: 'The Latics'.

Grounds: 1895, Sheepfoot Lane; 1900, Hudson Field; 1906, Sheepfoot Lane; 1907, Boundary Park (renamed SportsDirect.com Park 2014).

First Football League Game: 9 September 1907, Division 2, v Stoke (a) W 3–1 – Hewitson; Hodson, Hamilton; Fay, Walders, Wilson; Ward, Billy Dodds (1), Newton (1), Hancock, Swarbrick (1).

Record League Victory: 11–0 v Southport, Division 4, 26 December 1962 – Bollands; Branagan, Marshall; McCall, Williams, Scott; Ledger (1), Johnstone, Lister (6), Colquhoun (1), Whitaker (3).

Record Cup Victory: 10–1 v Lytham, FA Cup 1st rd, 28 November 1925 – Gray; Wynne, Grundy; Adlam, Heaton, Naylor (1), Douglas, Pynegar (2), Ormston (2), Barnes (3), Watson (2).

Record Defeat: 4–13 v Tranmere R, Division 3 (N), 26 December 1935.

HONOURS

League Champions: Division 2 – 1990–91; Division 3 – 1973–74; Division 3N – 1952–53;.

Runners-up: Division 1 – 1914–15; Division 2 – 1909–10; Division 4 – 1962–63.

FA Cup: semi-final – 1913, 1990, 1994.

League Cup: *Runners-up:* 1990.

sky SPORTS FACT FILE

Oldham Athletic played home matches at Boundary Park on an artificial surface for five seasons between 1986 and 1991. The club enjoyed one of their best-ever seasons in 1989–90, reaching the final of the League Cup and the FA Cup semi-finals, while the following season they won promotion to the First Division. The grass surface was restored for top flight football.

Most League Points (2 for a win): 62, Division 3, 1973–74.

Most League Points (3 for a win): 88, Division 2, 1990–91.

Most League Goals: 95, Division 4, 1962–63.

Highest League Scorer in Season: Tom Davis, 33, Division 3 (N), 1936–37.

Most League Goals in Total Aggregate: Roger Palmer, 141, 1980–94.

Most League Goals in One Match: 7, Eric Gemmell v Chester, Division 3 (N), 19 January 1952.

Most Capped Player: Gunnar Halle, 24 (64), Norway.

Most League Appearances: Ian Wood, 525, 1966–80.

Youngest League Player: Wayne Harrison, 16 years 347 days v Notts Co, 27 October 1984.

Record Transfer Fee Received: £1,700,000 from Aston Villa for Earl Barrett, February 1992.

Record Transfer Fee Paid: £750,000 to Aston Villa for Ian Olney, June 1992.

Football League Record: 1907 Elected to Division 2; 1910–23 Division 1; 1923–35 Division 2; 1935–53 Division 3 (N); 1953–54 Division 2; 1954–58 Division 3 (N); 1958–63 Division 4; 1963–69 Division 3; 1969–71 Division 4; 1971–74 Division 3; 1974–91 Division 2; 1991–92 Division 1; 1992–94 FA Premier League; 1994–97 Division 1; 1997–2004 Division 2; 2004– FL 1.

LATEST SEQUENCES

Longest Sequence of League Wins: 10, 12.1.1974 – 12.3.1974.

Longest Sequence of League Defeats: 8, 15.12.1934 – 2.2.1935.

Longest Sequence of League Draws: 5, 26.12.1982 – 15.1.1983.

Longest Sequence of Unbeaten League Matches: 20, 1.5.1990 – 10.11.1990.

Longest Sequence Without a League Win: 17, 4.9.1920 – 18.12.1920.

Successive Scoring Runs: 25 from 25.8.1962.

Successive Non-scoring Runs: 6 from 12.2.2011.

MANAGERS

David Ashworth 1906–14
Herbert Bamlett 1914–21
Charlie Roberts 1921–22
David Ashworth 1923–24
Bob Mellor 1924–27
Andy Wilson 1927–32
Bob Mellor 1932–33
Jimmy McMullan 1933–34
Bob Mellor 1934–45
(continued as Secretary to 1953)
Frank Womack 1945–47
Billy Wootton 1947–50
George Hardwick 1950–56
Ted Goodier 1956–58
Norman Dodgin 1958–60
Danny McLennan 1960
Jack Rowley 1960–63
Les McDowall 1963–65
Gordon Hurst 1965–66
Jimmy McIlroy 1966–68
Jack Rowley 1968–69
Jimmy Frizzell 1970–82
Joe Royle 1982–94
Graeme Sharp 1994–97
Neil Warnock 1997–98
Andy Ritchie 1998–2001
Mick Wadsworth 2001–02
Iain Dowie 2002–03
Brian Talbot 2004–05
Ronnie Moore 2005–06
John Sheridan 2006–09
Joe Royle 2009
Dave Penney 2009–10
Paul Dickov 2010–13
Lee Johnson 2013–15
Dean Holden 2015
Darren Kelly 2015
David Dunn 2015–16
John Sheridan 2016
Stephen Robinson 2016–17
John Sheridan January 2017–

TEN YEAR LEAGUE RECORD

		P	W	D	L	F	A	Pts	Pos
2007-08	FL 1	46	18	13	15	58	46	67	8
2008-09	FL 1	46	16	17	13	66	65	65	10
2009-10	FL 1	46	13	13	20	39	57	52	16
2010-11	FL 1	46	13	17	16	53	60	56	17
2011-12	FL 1	46	14	12	20	50	66	54	16
2012-13	FL 1	46	14	9	23	46	59	51	19
2013-14	FL 1	46	14	14	18	50	59	56	15
2014-15	FL 1	46	14	15	17	54	67	57	15
2015-16	FL 1	46	12	18	16	44	58	54	17
2016-17	FL 1	46	12	17	17	31	44	53	17

DID YOU KNOW ?

Oldham Athletic hold a unique record as the only winners of the Ford Sporting League. The competition, which took into account each club's disciplinary records and goals scored, ran for the 1970–71 season only. The Latics won a total of £70,000 and spent the money on building a new stand.

OLDHAM ATHLETIC – SKY BET LEAGUE ONE 2016–17 LEAGUE RECORD

Match No.	*Date*		*Venue*	*Opponents*	*Result*		*H/T Score*	*Lg Pos.*	*Goalscorers*	*Attendance*
1	Aug	6	A	Millwall	L	0-3	0-2	24		9787
2		13	H	Walsall	D	0-0	0-0	21		3914
3		16	H	Northampton T	D	0-0	0-0	19		3327
4		20	A	Bury	W	1-0	1-0	13	Barnett (og) [10]	4479
5		27	A	Bradford C	D	1-1	1-0	13	Clarke [5]	17,793
6	Sept	3	H	Shrewsbury T	L	2-3	1-1	16	Law [24], Erwin [82]	3697
7		10	H	Chesterfield	D	0-0	0-0	17		3457
8		17	A	Coventry C	D	0-0	0-0	19		8813
9		24	H	Swindon T	L	0-2	0-1	22		3403
10		27	A	Charlton Ath	D	1-1	0-1	23	Clarke [83]	8745
11	Oct	1	H	Milton Keynes D	L	0-2	0-1	24		3273
12		8	A	Gillingham	W	2-1	0-1	21	Ladapo [65], Flynn [89]	6435
13		15	A	Bolton W	L	0-2	0-1	22		14,891
14		18	H	Scunthorpe U	W	2-0	2-0	21	Ladapo [42], Erwin [45]	2911
15		22	H	Bristol R	L	0-2	0-1	22		4394
16		29	A	Rochdale	L	0-1	0-1	22		5204
17	Nov	12	H	AFC Wimbledon	D	0-0	0-0	22		3856
18		19	A	Scunthorpe U	L	0-1	0-0	22		4323
19		22	A	Port Vale	D	2-2	0-0	22	Banks [48], Winchester [90]	3152
20	Dec	10	A	Oxford U	D	1-1	1-0	22	Burgess [10]	7430
21		17	H	Southend U	L	0-2	0-1	24		3414
22		26	A	Sheffield U	L	0-2	0-0	24		25,821
23		31	A	Fleetwood T	L	0-1	0-0	24		3189
24	Jan	2	H	Port Vale	D	0-0	0-0	24		3451
25		14	H	Gillingham	W	1-0	1-0	23	Law [39]	3475
26		21	A	Shrewsbury T	L	0-1	0-0	23		5537
27		24	H	Peterborough U	W	2-0	0-0	23	Green (pen) [69], McLaughlin [82]	7224
28		28	H	Bradford C	L	1-2	1-1	23	Wilson [44]	6516
29	Feb	4	A	Chesterfield	W	1-0	0-0	21	Clarke [90]	6375
30		7	A	Milton Keynes D	L	0-1	0-0	21		7598
31		11	H	Coventry C	W	3-2	1-1	20	Foley (og) [8], Clarke [66], McLaughlin [70]	3766
32		14	H	Charlton Ath	W	1-0	1-0	19	Banks [4]	2946
33		18	A	Swindon T	D	0-0	0-0	19		6773
34		25	H	Millwall	D	0-0	0-0	20		3856
35		28	A	Northampton T	W	2-1	1-0	20	Obadeyi [23], Erwin [90]	4686
36	Mar	4	A	Walsall	L	0-2	0-0	20		6003
37		11	H	Bury	D	0-0	0-0	20		5776
38		14	H	Oxford U	W	2-1	1-0	20	Erwin 2 [36, 70]	3124
39		18	A	Peterborough U	D	1-1	1-0	19	Erwin [11]	4222
40		25	H	Sheffield U	D	1-1	1-0	18	Obadeyi [44]	8448
41	Apr	1	A	Southend U	L	0-3	0-0	19		7617
42		8	H	Fleetwood T	W	2-0	1-0	17	Pond (og) [25], Erwin [55]	3933
43		15	H	Bolton W	W	1-0	0-0	17	Erwin [76]	8788
44		17	A	Bristol R	L	0-1	0-0	17		9083
45		22	H	Rochdale	D	1-1	0-1	17	Clarke [67]	6865
46		30	A	AFC Wimbledon	D	0-0	0-0	17		4867

Final League Position: 17

GOALSCORERS

League (31): Erwin 8, Clarke 5, Banks 2, Ladapo 2, Law 2, McLaughlin 2, Obadeyi 2, Burgess 1, Flynn 1, Green 1 (1 pen), Wilson 1, Winchester 1, own goals 3.
FA Cup (4): McKay 2, Clarke 1, Flynn 1.
EFL Cup (2): Flynn 1, Law 1.
EFL Checkatrade Trophy (11): Erwin 2, McKay 2, Osei 2, Banks 1, Burgess 1, Croft 1, Ladapo 1, Wilson 1.

Ripley C 46	Wilson B 25 + 1	Clarke P 46	Burgess C 23	Reckord J 12 + 1	Green P 36 + 5	Banks O 24 + 9	Flynn R 31 + 6	Fane O 31 + 8	Erwin L 25 + 9	McKay B 20 + 6	Law J 19 + 3	Osei D 4 + 15	Klok M 6 + 4	McLaughlin R 31 + 5	Dunne C 13 + 1	Croft L 5 + 15	Jahraldo-Martin C — + 4	Woodland L — + 1	Ladapo F 12 + 5	Dummigan C 11 + 1	Winchester C 4 + 5	Edmundson S 2 + 1	Glackin B — + 1	Gerrard A 14	Ngoo M 3 + 10	Amadi-Holloway A 14 + 1	Hunt R 9 + 1	O'Neill A 12 + 3	Taylor C 14 + 2	Obadeyi T 10 + 5	Stott J 4	*Match No.*
1	2	3	4	5^{1}	6	7^{2}	8	9	10^{3}	11	12	13	14																			1
1		3	4	5	6	13	9	8^{3}	10^{1}	11	2	14	7^{2}	12																		2
1		3	4		9		8^{1}	7	10	11^{2}	2	13	14		5	6^{3}	12															3
1		4	3		7		9^{2}	8	11	10^{1}	2	13	6^{3}		5	12		14														4
1		4	3		8	12	9	7^{2}	10^{3}	11^{1}	2	14	6	13	5																	5
1		3	4		7	14	6^{3}	8■	9	11^{1}	2	12			5^{2}	13			10													6
1		3	4		8	14	6^{1}		9	11^{3}	2	10	7^{2}	13	5	12																7
1	4	3	5		9	8	14		11		2^{3}	13	7^{1}		6	12			10^{2}													8
1		3	4		7	8		12	11^{2}	14	2	13	6^{3}		5	9^{3}			10													9
1		3	4	5	8		6^{3}	9	12	11		13	14	7^{1}					10^{2}	2												10
1		3	4	5^{1}	7		9	8^{2}	13	10		14		6	12				11^{3}	2												11
1	2	3	4	5	9	14	6	8	11^{3}	10^{2}						12			13		7^{1}											12
1	2^{2}	3	4	5	9		6	8^{3}	11	10^{1}							13		12	14	7											13
1		3	4	5	8		6	7	9^{1}	14		13	12						11^{3}	2	10^{2}											14
1		3	4	5	7^{3}		9	8	11			13		12			14		10^{1}	2	6^{2}											15
1		3	4	5	9^{1}		8	6^{2}	11	12				7			14		10^{3}	2	13											16
1		3	4			8	9	7	11^{2}	10^{1}				6	5	12			13	2												17
1		3	4		8■	7	6	12	14	10^{3}				9^{1}	2	13			11	5^{2}												18
1		3	4			7	6^{1}	8^{3}	13	10	5			9^{2}	2	14			11		12											19
1	14	5	3		7	9	10^{1}	8■	12	11^{2}	2			6^{3}	4	13																20
1		3	4		7^{2}	8	9^{1}		14	11	2			6^{3}	5	12			10		13											21
1	7	4			8^{1}		6			10	2	11^{3}		9	5^{2}	13			12	3	14											22
1	4	3	2		7^{2}	14	8^{1}			11	6	10^{3}		9		12			13	5												23
1	2	3	4		14	8^{3}	7^{2}	6		12		10		5		9			11^{1}		13											24
1	3	4			13		7	6	10^{1}	11^{2}	8	12^{3}		5						9		2	14									25
1	5	4				13	9	8	14	10^{1}	7			6						2^{3}				3	11^{2}	12						26
1	2	3		5	7	8	9	6		12				10^{2}										4	13	11^{1}						27
1	2	3		5	7	8^{1}	9^{2}	6		12				10^{3}										4	14	11	13					28
1	2	4			12		6^{1}	8				14		11										3■		10^{3}	5	7	9^{2}	13		29
1	2	4			3^{1}		13	7				12		11		14										10	5	8	6^{2}	9^{3}		30
1	2	3			12	13	8^{2}	6^{1}						9										4	14	10^{3}	5	7	11			31
1	2	4			6	7^{1}		13	10^{2}					11										3	12		5	8	9			32
1	3	4				8		7			2			6^{1}		12									13	11^{2}	5	10	9			33
1	3	4			7	6	12	13						2											14	9^{3}	5	8^{1}	11	10^{2}		34
1		3			7	6	11^{2}	14	13					2										4		9	5	8^{1}	12	10^{3}		35
1	4■	8			10^{2}			12	13					2		6■								3		9	5	7		11^{1}		36
1		3		5	6	8	12							2										4		9		7^{1}	11	10		37
1	2	3			8	7		14	11^{2}		12			6										4		10	5^{3}		9^{1}	13		38
1	6	5		13	8	7			11^{1}					2										3^{2}	14	10^{3}		4	9	12		39
1	2^{3}	3			6	8	14	7^{1}	11^{2}		5											12		4	13				9	10		40
1		3			6^{2}	7	13	8^{1}	10		5^{3}			2										4	12			14	9	11		41
1	2	3			6	8^{1}		7	11^{2}					5										4	12	10^{3}		13	9	14		42
1	2	3			6	8		7	11					5											10■					9	4	43
1	2	4			12	6^{3}	8	13	10					5		14												7^{1}	9	11^{2}	3	44
1	2	3			6	8^{1}		7	11^{3}		13			5												10		14	9^{2}	12	4	45
1		4				14	7	6^{1}			2			13		9^{2}						3			11^{3}			8	12	10	5	46

FA Cup

First Round	Doncaster R	(h)	2-1
Second Round	Lincoln C	(a)	2-3

EFL Cup

First Round	Wigan Ath	(h)	2-1
Second Round	Preston NE	(a)	0-2

EFL Checkatrade Trophy

Northern Group D	Carlisle U	(h)	4-5
Northern Group D	Fleetwood T	(a)	2-0
Northern Group D	Blackburn R U21	(a)	2-2
(*Oldham Ath won 5-4 on penalties*)			
Second Round North	Walsall	(a)	3-1
Third Round	Mansfield T	(a)	0-2

OXFORD UNITED

FOUNDATION

There had been an Oxford United club around the time of World War I but only in the Oxfordshire Thursday League and there is no connection with the modern club which began as Headington in 1893, adding 'United' a year later. Playing first on Quarry Fields and subsequently Wootten's Fields, they owe much to a Dr Hitchings for their early development.

The Kassam Stadium, Grenoble Road, Oxford OX4 4XP.

Telephone: (01865) 337 500.

Fax: (01865) 337 501.

Ticket Office: (01865) 337 533.

Website: www.oufc.co.uk

Email: admin@oufc.co.uk

Ground Capacity: 12,573.

Record Attendance: 22,730 v Preston NE, FA Cup 6th rd, 29 February 1964 (at Manor Ground); 12,243 v Leyton Orient, FL 2, 6 May 2006 (at The Kassam Stadium).

Pitch Measurements: 100.5m × 64m (110yd × 70yd).

Executive Chairman: Darryl Eales.

Head Coach: Pep Clotet.

Assistant Head Coaches: Derek Fazackerley and Chris Allen.

Colours: Yellow shirts with thin blue stripes, blue shorts with yellow trim, blue socks with yellow trim.

Year Formed: 1893.

Turned Professional: 1949.

Previous Names: 1893, Headington; 1894, Headington United; 1960, Oxford United.

Club Nickname: 'The U's'.

Grounds: 1893, Headington Quarry; 1894, Wootten's Fields; 1898, Sandy Lane Ground; 1902, Britannia Field; 1909, Sandy Lane; 1910, Quarry Recreation Ground; 1914, Sandy Lane; 1922, The Paddock Manor Road; 1925, Manor Ground; 2001, The Kassam Stadium.

First Football League Game: 18 August 1962, Division 4, v Barrow (a) L 2–3 – Medlock; Beavon, Quartermain; Ron Atkinson, Kyle, Jones; Knight, Graham Atkinson (1), Houghton (1), Cornwell, Colfar.

Record League Victory: 7–0 v Barrow, Division 4, 19 December 1964 – Fearnley; Beavon, Quartermain; Ron Atkinson (1), Kyle, Jones; Morris, Booth (3), Willey (1), Graham Atkinson (1), Harrington (1).

Record Cup Victory: 9–1 v Dorchester T, FA Cup 1st rd, 11 November 1995 – Whitehead; Wood (2), Mike Ford (1), Smith, Elliott, Gilchrist, Rush (1), Massey (Murphy), Moody (3), Bobby Ford (1), Angel (Beauchamp (1)).

Record Defeat: 0–7 v Sunderland, Division 1, 19 September 1998.

Most League Points (2 for a win): 61, Division 4, 1964–65.

HONOURS

League Champions: Division 2 – 1984–85; Division 3 – 1967–68, 1983–84.

Runners-up: Second Division – 1995–96; FL 2 – 2015–16; Conference – (3rd) 2009–10 *(promoted via play-offs)*.

FA Cup: 6th rd – 1964.

League Cup Winners: 1986.

League Trophy: *Runners-up:* 2016, 2017.

sky SPORTS FACT FILE

Tony Jones became the first Oxford United player to net a hat-trick in the Football League when he scored four goals in a 5-1 home victory over Newport County in September 1962. Jones had been playing at left-half but was switched to inside-left for the game. The result ended the U's run of seven Division Four games without a win.

Most League Points (3 for a win): 95, Division 3, 1983–84.

Most League Goals: 91, Division 3, 1983–84.

Highest League Scorer in Season: John Aldridge, 30, Division 2, 1984–85.

Most League Goals in Total Aggregate: Graham Atkinson, 77, 1962–73.

Most League Goals in One Match: 4, Tony Jones v Newport Co, Division 4, 22 September 1962; 4, Arthur Longbottom v Darlington, Division 4, 26 October 1963; 4, Richard Hill v Walsall, Division 2, 26 December 1988; 4, John Durnin v Luton T, 14 November 1992; 4, Tom Craddock v Accrington S, FL 2, 20 October 2011.

Most Capped Player: Jim Magilton, 18 (52), Northern Ireland.

Most League Appearances: John Shuker, 478, 1962–77.

Youngest League Player: Jason Seacole, 16 years 149 days v Mansfield T, 7 September 1976.

Record Transfer Fee Received: £3,000,000 from Leeds U for Kemar Roofe, July 2016.

Record Transfer Fee Paid: £475,000 to Aberdeen for Dean Windass, August 1998.

Football League Record: 1962 Elected to Division 4; 1965–68 Division 3; 1968–76 Division 2; 1976–84 Division 3; 1984–85 Division 2; 1985–88 Division 1; 1988–92 Division 2; 1992–94 Division 1; 1994–96 Division 2; 1996–99 Division 1; 1999–2001 Division 2; 2001–04 Division 3; 2004–06 FL 2; 2006–10 Conference; 2010–16 FL 2; 2016– FL 1.

MANAGERS

Harry Thompson 1949–58
(Player-Manager) 1949–51
Arthur Turner 1959–69
(continued as General Manager to 1972)
Ron Saunders 1969
Gerry Summers 1969–75
Mick Brown 1975–79
Bill Asprey 1979–80
Ian Greaves 1980–82
Jim Smith 1982–85
Maurice Evans 1985–88
Mark Lawrenson 1988
Brian Horton 1988–93
Denis Smith 1993–97
Malcolm Crosby 1997–98
Malcolm Shotton 1998–99
Micky Lewis 1999–2000
Denis Smith 2000
David Kemp 2000–01
Mark Wright 2001
Ian Atkins 2001–04
Graham Rix 2004
Ramon Diaz 2004–05
Brian Talbot 2005–06
Darren Patterson 2006
Jim Smith 2006–07
Darren Patterson 2007–08
Chris Wilder 2008–14
Gary Waddock 2014
Michael Appleton 2014–17
Pep Clotet June 2017–

LATEST SEQUENCES

Longest Sequence of League Wins: 6, 13.4.2013 – 17.8.2013.

Longest Sequence of League Defeats: 8, 18.4.2014 – 23.8.2014.

Longest Sequence of League Draws: 5, 7.10.1978 – 28.10.1978.

Longest Sequence of Unbeaten League Matches: 20, 17.3.1984 – 29.9.1984.

Longest Sequence Without a League Win: 27, 14.11.1987 – 27.8.1988.

Successive Scoring Runs: 17 from 22.4.2006.

Successive Non-scoring Runs: 6 from 26.3.1988.

TEN YEAR LEAGUE RECORD

		P	W	D	L	F	A	Pts	Pos
2007-08	Conf P	46	20	11	15	56	48	71	9
2008-09	Conf P	46	24	10	12	72	51	77*	7
2009-10	Conf P	44	25	11	8	64	31	86	3
2010-11	FL 2	46	17	12	17	58	60	63	12
2011-12	FL 2	46	17	17	12	59	48	68	9
2012-13	FL 2	46	19	8	19	60	61	65	9
2013-14	FL 2	46	16	14	16	53	50	62	8
2014-15	FL 2	46	15	16	15	50	49	61	13
2015-16	FL 2	46	24	14	8	84	41	86	2
2016-17	FL 1	46	20	9	17	65	52	69	8

**5 pts deducted.*

DID YOU KNOW ?

Oxford United's final competitive game at the Manor Ground resulted in a 1-1 draw against Port Vale on 1 May 2001. The Division Two fixture attracted United's second-best home gate of the season with an attendance of 7,080. Andy Scott gave United the lead only for Vale to level in the final minute.

OXFORD UNITED – SKY BET LEAGUE ONE 2016–17 LEAGUE RECORD

Match No.	Date	Venue	Opponents	Result	H/T Score	Lg Pos.	Goalscorers	Attendance
1	Aug 6	H	Chesterfield	D 1-1	1-0	13	Thomas [31]	8679
2	14	A	Bristol R	L 1-2	1-1	17	Hemmings [42]	10,053
3	17	A	Fleetwood T	L 0-2	0-0	21		2614
4	20	H	Peterborough U	W 2-1	0-0	19	Thomas [46], Maguire (pen) [90]	7500
5	27	A	Sheffield U	L 1-2	1-0	18	Hemmings [16]	19,313
6	Sept 3	H	Rochdale	W 1-0	0-0	14	Sercombe [88]	6939
7	10	H	Swindon T	W 2-0	1-0	11	Maguire 2 (1 pen) [44 (p), 61]	11,042
8	17	A	Milton Keynes D	D 0-0	0-0	12		12,340
9	24	H	Charlton Ath	D 1-1	0-0	13	Maguire [67]	8847
10	27	A	Southend U	L 1-2	1-1	16	Hemmings [45]	5593
11	Oct 1	A	Bolton W	W 2-0	0-0	10	Thomas [81], Maguire [90]	14,207
12	9	H	AFC Wimbledon	L 1-3	0-3	13	Charles (og) [49]	7742
13	15	H	Bradford C	W 1-0	0-0	10	Maguire [90]	8245
14	18	A	Coventry C	L 1-2	0-2	13	Crowley [90]	9912
15	22	A	Port Vale	D 2-2	2-0	14	Dunkley [11], Crowley [19]	4837
16	29	H	Millwall	L 1-2	1-1	16	Sercombe [31]	7944
17	Nov 12	A	Shrewsbury T	L 0-2	0-1	19		5491
18	19	H	Coventry C	W 4-1	3-0	16	Hemmings [7], Sterry (og) [30], Maguire (pen) [36], MacDonald [60]	9199
19	22	H	Gillingham	W 1-0	1-0	14	Johnson [32]	6848
20	26	A	Scunthorpe U	D 1-1	0-1	14	Edwards [47]	4338
21	Dec 10	H	Oldham Ath	D 1-1	0-1	14	Hall [54]	7430
22	17	A	Bury	W 3-2	2-2	10	Maguire 2 [14, 43], Leigh (og) [70]	2986
23	26	H	Northampton T	L 0-1	0-0	14		11,790
24	31	H	Walsall	D 0-0	0-0	13		8340
25	Jan 2	A	Gillingham	W 1-0	0-0	12	Dunkley [66]	6414
26	14	A	AFC Wimbledon	L 1-2	1-2	13	Hall [6]	4808
27	21	A	Rochdale	W 4-0	2-0	12	Johnson [18], Hall [29], Taylor [53], Ledson [73]	3246
28	Feb 5	A	Swindon T	W 2-1	0-1	13	Sercombe [70], Hall [73]	10,658
29	11	H	Milton Keynes D	W 1-0	0-0	11	Hemmings [88]	9179
30	14	H	Southend U	L 0-2	0-0	11		7277
31	21	A	Charlton Ath	W 1-0	1-0	10	McAleny [12]	9109
32	25	A	Chesterfield	W 4-0	2-0	9	Hall [17], McAleny 3 [35, 60, 69]	5901
33	Mar 4	H	Bristol R	L 0-2	0-2	10		9862
34	7	H	Sheffield U	L 2-3	1-0	11	Dunkley [22], Martinez [90]	8965
35	11	A	Peterborough U	W 2-1	1-0	10	Edwards [23], McAleny [71]	5469
36	14	A	Oldham Ath	L 1-2	0-1	10	Maguire (pen) [60]	3124
37	18	H	Scunthorpe U	W 2-1	0-1	9	Lundstram [52], Edwards [90]	7652
38	21	H	Bolton W	L 2-4	1-2	9	Hemmings [42], Maguire [75]	7146
39	25	A	Northampton T	D 0-0	0-0	10		7434
40	28	H	Bury	W 5-1	3-0	8	Johnson [11], Rothwell [35], McAleny 3 [39, 49, 90]	6552
41	Apr 5	H	Fleetwood T	L 1-3	1-1	10	Nelson [8]	6728
42	8	A	Walsall	D 1-1	0-0	10	Maguire [74]	5417
43	14	A	Bradford C	L 0-1	0-0	10		19,346
44	17	H	Port Vale	W 2-0	1-0	10	Ruffels [14], Maguire [82]	7646
45	22	A	Millwall	W 3-0	2-0	9	McAleny 2 [6, 9], Ruffels [71]	12,533
46	30	H	Shrewsbury T	W 2-0	2-0	8	Nelson [16], Hall [17]	9287

Final League Position: 8

GOALSCORERS

League (65): Maguire 13 (4 pens), McAleny 10, Hall 6, Hemmings 6, Dunkley 3, Edwards 3, Johnson 3, Sercombe 3, Thomas 3, Crowley 2, Nelson 2, Ruffels 2, Ledson 1, Lundstram 1, MacDonald 1, Martinez 1, Rothwell 1, Taylor 1, own goals 3.
FA Cup (16): Hemmings 5, Martinez 2, Taylor 2, Edwards 1, MacDonald 1, Maguire 1, Nelson 1, Roberts, T 1, Rothwell 1, Ruffels 1.
EFL Cup (3): Crowley 1, Sercombe 1, Thomas 1.
EFL Checkatrade Trophy (16): Hemmings 4 (1 pen), Johnson 3, Maguire 3 (2 pens), Edwards 1, MacDonald 1, Roberts, T 1, Sercombe 1, Taylor 1, own goal 1.

Eastwood S 46	Long S 2 + 1	Nelson C 33	Dunkley C 40	Skarz J 28 + 2	MacDonald A 17 + 5	Sercombe L 24 + 6	Lundstram J 44 + 1	Maguire C 40 + 2	Taylor R 9 + 12	Thomas W 8 + 5	Ruffels J 14 + 6	Roberts T — + 14	Hemmings K 22 + 18	Martin A 2 + 2	Crowley D 2 + 4	Rothwell J 19 + 14	Welch-Hayes M 1	Edwards P 37 + 1	Raglan C 16	Johnson M 33 + 6	Ledson R 20 + 2	Hall R 21 + 5	Martinez A 8 + 7	McAleny C 14 + 4	Carroll C 3 + 1	Ribeiro C 3	*Match No.*
1	2	3	4^{3}	5	6	7	8	9^{2}	10	11^{1}	12	13	14														1
1	5■	3		2	9^{1}	8	7	6^{3}	10			14	11^{2}	4	12	13											2
1			3	5	6^{3}	7	8	9^{1}	10^{2}	12		13	11	4		14	2										3
1			3	4	6^{3}	8	7	9	13	11^{2}	5	12	10^{1}		14			2									4
1			3	2^{3}	9^{1}	7	8	6	13	10	4		11^{2}	12		14		5									5
1			3	5	14	7	8	9	13	11^{1}			10^{3}			6^{2}		2	4	12							6
1			4	2	13	9^{2}	8	10	12	11^{1}						7^{3}		5	3	6	14						7
1			3	5	14	9	7^{3}	8	12	11^{1}						6		2	4	10^{2}	13						8
1			3	2^{2}	13	9	8	10	11^{1}		14		12			7^{3}		5	4	6							9
1			4	5^{2}		9	7	6	13	12			11^{1}			8		2	3	10							10
1			3	5	12	8	9	10		13			11			7^{1}		2	4	6^{2}							11
1			3	5^{1}	6	7^{2}	8	9		11^{3}			10		12	14		2	4	13							12
1			3		6^{2}		8	9	11	10^{1}	5		13			7		2	4	12							13
1			3		6^{2}		8	10	11^{1}		5	14	9^{3}		13	7		2	4	12							14
1		3	4	2		9	7	11				12			10	6		5		8^{1}							15
1		5	3	2^{1}		9	10	11				12	13		7	6		4^{2}		8							16
1		3	4	5^{1}		6^{2}	14	11		13			10			8			2	9	7^{3}	12					17
1		4	3	2^{1}	9		7	6		12^{3}	14	13	11					5			8	10^{2}					18
1		3	4^{2}		6		8	10	14		12		11^{1}	13				2		5	7	9^{3}					19
1		3	4	5	6^{3}		8	10	14			13	11^{2}					2		12	7	9^{1}					20
1		4	3		9^{2}		8	10	14		12	13	11^{1}					2		5	7	6^{3}					21
1		3	4		9		7	10	13			12	11^{2}					2		5	8	6^{1}					22
1		3	4		6		7	10	12			13	11^{1}					2		5	8	9^{2}					23
1		3	4		6^{1}		7	10	12			13	11^{3}			14		2		5	8	9^{2}					24
1		3	4		9		7	10	11			12						2		5	8	6^{1}					25
1		4	3		6^{1}	13	7	10	11^{3}				12			14		2		5	8^{2}	9					26
1		4	3	5		12	8^{2}	10	11^{3}				13			14		2		9	7	6^{1}					27
1		3	4			6	7	9					12					2		5	8	11^{1}	10^{2}	13			28
1		4	3			6^{1}	7	9					12					2		5	8	10	11^{2}	13			29
1		4	3			6^{2}	7	9^{1}					12					2		5	8	10	11	13			30
1		7	9	2		4^{1}	5	14					12					8		10	11	13	3^{3}	6^{2}			31
1		4	3	5		7		6			8					12		2				9^{1}	11	10			32
1			4	5^{1}		6	8									12		2	3	9	7		10	11			33
1		4	3			13	7	6					11^{3}			12		2		5	8^{1}	9^{2}	14	10			34
1		4	3			13	7	6					11^{2}			12		2		5	8	9^{3}	14	10^{1}			35
1		3	4			12	8	6					11^{2}			14		2		5	7^{1}	9^{3}	13	10			36
1		4	3	5		6	7				8		13			9^{1}		2		12			11^{2}	10			37
1		4	3	5^{3}			7^{1}	10			8		11			14		2		9		6^{2}	13	12			38
1		4	3	14		6	7				8^{3}		12			9		2		5		13	10^{1}	11^{2}			39
1		3	4	14		12	7				8		11^{2}			9^{1}		2		5^{3}		6	13	10			40
1		3	4			6	7	10^{1}			8^{2}		13			9				5			12	11	2		41
1		4		5			7	10			14		13			6^{1}			3	9^{3}	8^{2}		12	11	2		42
1		3		5			7	6^{3}			8		12			9^{2}		14	4	10		13		11		2^{1}	43
1		3		5			7	12			8		13			9^{2}		2	4	11		6^{1}		10			44
1		3		5			7	8^{3}			6		14			12			4	11^{1}		13		10	9^{2}	2	45
1	12	3		5^{3}			7	10^{2}			8		14			9			4	11		6			13	2^{1}	46

FA Cup

First Round	Merstham	(a)	5-0
Second Round	Macclesfield T	(a)	0-0
Replay	Macclesfield T	(h)	3-0
Third Round	Rotherham U	(a)	3-2
Fourth Round	Newcastle U	(h)	3-0
Fifth Round	Middlesbrough	(a)	2-3

EFL Cup

First Round	Birmingham C	(a)	1-0
(*aet*)			
Second Round	Brighton & HA	(h)	2-4

EFL Checkatrade Trophy

Southern Group C	Exeter C	(h)	4-2
Southern Group C	Swindon T	(a)	0-0
(*Swindon T won 3-1 on penalties*)			
Southern Group C	Chelsea U21	(a)	1-1
(*Chelsea U21 won 13-12 on penalties*)			
Second Round South	Southend U	(a)	1-1
(*Oxford U won 4-3 on penalties*)			
Third Round	Scunthorpe U	(h)	4-1
Quarter-Final	Bradford C	(h)	2-1
Semi-Final	Luton T	(a)	3-2
Final	Coventry C	(Wembley)	1-2

PETERBOROUGH UNITED

FOUNDATION

The old Peterborough & Fletton club, founded in 1923, was suspended by the FA during season 1932–33 and disbanded. Local enthusiasts determined to carry on and in 1934 a new professional club, Peterborough United, was formed and entered the Midland League the following year. Peterborough's first success came in 1939–40, but from 1955–56 to 1959–60 they won five successive titles. During the 1958–59 season they were undefeated in the Midland League. They reached the third round of the FA Cup, won the Northamptonshire Senior Cup, the Maunsell Cup and were runners-up in the East Anglian Cup.

ABAX Stadium, London Road, Peterborough PE2 8AL.

Telephone: (01733) 563 947. ***Fax:*** (01733) 344 140.

Ticket Office: (0844) 847 1934.

Website: www.theposh.com

Email: info@theposh.com

Ground Capacity: 14,084.

Record Attendance: 30,096 v Swansea T, FA Cup 5th rd, 20 February 1965.

Pitch Measurements: 102.5m × 64m (112yd × 70yd).

Chairman: Darragh MacAnthony.

Chief Executive: Bob Symns.

Manager: Grant McCann.

Assistant Manager: David Oldfield.

Colours: Blue shirts with white trim, white shorts, blue socks.

Year Formed: 1934.

Turned Professional: 1934.

Club Nickname: 'The Posh'.

Ground: 1934, London Road Stadium (renamed ABAX Stadium 2014).

First Football League Game: 20 August 1960, Division 4, v Wrexham (h) W 3–0 – Walls; Stafford, Walker; Rayner, Rigby, Norris; Hails, Emery (1), Bly (1), Smith, McNamee (1).

Record League Victory: 9–1 v Barnet (a) Division 3, 5 September 1998 – Griemink; Hooper (1), Drury (Farell), Gill, Bodley, Edwards, Davies, Payne, Grazioli (5), Quinn (2) (Rowe), Houghton (Etherington) (1).

Record Cup Victory: 9–1 v Rushden T, FA Cup 1st qual rd, 6 October 1945 – Hilliard; Bryan, Parrott, Warner, Hobbs, Woods, Polhill (1), Fairchild, Laxton (6), Tasker (1), Rodgers (1); 9–1 v Kingstonian, FA Cup 1st rd, 25 November 1992. Match ordered to be replayed by FA. Peterborough won replay 1–0.

Record Defeat: 1–8 v Northampton T, FA Cup 2nd rd (2nd replay), 18 December 1946.

Most League Points (2 for a win): 66, Division 4, 1960–61.

HONOURS

League Champions: Division 4 – 1960–61, 1973–74.
Runners-up: FL 1 – 2008–09; FL 2 – 2007–08.

FA Cup: 6th rd – 1965.

League Cup: semi-final – 1966.

League Trophy Winners: 2014.

sky SPORTS FACT FILE

Peterborough United won the Midland League five seasons in a row before gaining election to the Football League for the 1960–61 season. They scored more than 100 goals each season in league competition and continued this run for their first two seasons in the Football League. In the seven-year period they netted 931 goals in just 298 league games.

Most League Points (3 for a win): 92, FL 2, 2007–08.

Most League Goals: 134, Division 4, 1960–61.

Highest League Scorer in Season: Terry Bly, 52, Division 4, 1960–61.

Most League Goals in Total Aggregate: Jim Hall, 122, 1967–75.

Most League Goals in One Match: 5, Guiliano Grazioli v Barnet, Division 3, 5 September 1998.

Most Capped Player: Gabriel Zakuani, 17 (28), DR Congo.

Most League Appearances: Tommy Robson, 482, 1968–81.

Youngest League Player: Matthew Etherington, 15 years 262 days v Brentford, 3 May 1997.

Record Transfer Fee Received: £5,500,000 from Nottingham F for Britt Assombalonga, August 2014.

Record Transfer Fee Paid: £1,250,000 to Watford for Britt Assombalonga, July 2013.

Football League Record: 1960 Elected to Division 4; 1961–68 Division 3, when they were demoted for financial irregularities; 1968–74 Division 4; 1974–79 Division 3; 1979–91 Division 4; 1991–92 Division 3; 1992–94 Division 1; 1994–97 Division 2; 1997–2000 Division 3; 2000–04 Division 2; 2004–05 FL 1; 2005–08 FL 2; 2008–09 FL 1; 2009–10 FL C; 2010–11 FL 1; 2011–13 FL C; 2013– FL 1.

LATEST SEQUENCES

Longest Sequence of League Wins: 9, 1.2.1992 – 14.3.1992.

Longest Sequence of League Defeats: 8, 16.12.2006 – 27.1.2007.

Longest Sequence of League Draws: 8, 18.12.1971 – 12.2.1972.

Longest Sequence of Unbeaten League Matches: 17, 15.1.2008 – 5.4.2008.

Longest Sequence Without a League Win: 17, 23.9.1978 – 30.12.1978.

Successive Scoring Runs: 33 from 20.9.1960.

Successive Non-scoring Runs: 6 from 13.8.2002.

MANAGERS

Jock Porter 1934–36
Fred Taylor 1936–37
Vic Poulter 1937–38
Sam Haden 1938–48
Jack Blood 1948–50
Bob Gurney 1950–52
Jack Fairbrother 1952–54
George Swindin 1954–58
Jimmy Hagan 1958–62
Jack Fairbrother 1962–64
Gordon Clark 1964–67
Norman Rigby 1967–69
Jim Iley 1969–72
Noel Cantwell 1972–77
John Barnwell 1977–78
Billy Hails 1978–79
Peter Morris 1979–82
Martin Wilkinson 1982–83
John Wile 1983–86
Noel Cantwell 1986–88 *(continued as General Manager)*
Mick Jones 1988–89
Mark Lawrenson 1989–90
Dave Booth 1990–91
Chris Turner 1991–92
Lil Fuccillo 1992–93
Chris Turner 1993–94
John Still 1994–95
Mick Halsall 1995–96
Barry Fry 1996–2005
Mark Wright 2005–06
Steve Bleasdale 2006
Keith Alexander 2006–07
Darren Ferguson 2007–09
Mark Cooper 2009–10
Jim Gannon 2010
Gary Johnson 2010–11
Darren Ferguson 2011–15
Dave Robertson 2015
Graham Westley 2015–16
Grant McCann April 2016–

TEN YEAR LEAGUE RECORD

		P	W	D	L	F	A	Pts	Pos
2007-08	FL 2	46	28	8	10	84	43	92	2
2008-09	FL 1	46	26	11	9	78	54	89	2
2009-10	FL C	46	8	10	28	46	80	34	24
2010-11	FL 1	46	23	10	13	106	75	79	4
2011-12	FL C	46	13	11	22	67	77	50	18
2012-13	FL C	46	15	9	22	66	75	54	22
2013-14	FL 1	46	23	5	18	72	58	74	6
2014-15	FL 1	46	18	9	19	53	56	63	9
2015-16	FL 1	46	19	6	21	82	73	63	13
2016-17	FL 1	46	17	11	18	62	62	62	11

DID YOU KNOW ?

The largest pre-war attendance at Peterborough United's London Road ground was for boxing rather than football. Well over 10,000 turned out in June 1938 to watch British Lightweight title holder Eric Boon controversially knock out Glasgow's Johnny McGrory in the ninth round of their bout.

PETERBOROUGH UNITED – SKY BET LEAGUE ONE 2016–17 LEAGUE RECORD

Match No.	Date	Venue	Opponents	Result		H/T Score	Lg Pos.	Goalscorers	Attendance
1	Aug 6	A	Rochdale	W	3-2	2-2	6	Maddison[21], Forrester[37], Edwards, G[89]	3243
2	13	H	Bradford C	L	0-1	0-1	11		5906
3	16	H	Millwall	W	5-1	3-0	6	Maddison[6], Taylor, P[7], Edwards, G 2[20, 52], Nichols[67]	5007
4	20	A	Oxford U	L	1-2	0-0	11	Nichols[62]	7500
5	27	A	Milton Keynes D	W	2-0	1-0	7	Hughes[2], Bostwick[71]	10,621
6	Sept 3	H	Swindon T	D	2-2	1-0	6	Edwards, G[36], Maddison (pen)[63]	4501
7	10	H	Port Vale	D	2-2	1-1	6	Moncur 2[8, 84]	4711
8	17	A	Sheffield U	L	0-1	0-1	9		19,555
9	24	H	Walsall	D	1-1	1-1	10	Maddison[27]	4906
10	27	A	Shrewsbury T	D	1-1	1-0	9	Edwards, G[32]	4314
11	Oct 1	A	Southend U	D	1-1	0-0	13	Maddison[90]	6417
12	8	H	Bury	W	3-1	1-1	5	Forrester[38], Maddison[48], Kay (og)[52]	3964
13	15	A	Fleetwood T	L	0-2	0-1	11		2711
14	18	H	Northampton T	W	3-0	2-0	7	Coulthirst[14], Tafazolli[36], Nichols[82]	9157
15	22	H	AFC Wimbledon	L	0-1	0-1	10		6642
16	29	A	Bristol R	W	2-1	0-0	6	Coulthirst[62], Nichols[90]	9839
17	Nov 13	H	Bolton W	W	1-0	1-0	5	Smith[27]	4780
18	19	A	Northampton T	W	1-0	0-0	5	Forrester[90]	7675
19	22	H	Scunthorpe U	L	0-2	0-1	6		5222
20	Dec 10	H	Chesterfield	W	5-2	2-2	6	Nichols 2[1, 65], Edwards, G[45], Taylor, P[55], Bostwick[82]	5120
21	17	A	Charlton Ath	W	2-0	1-0	6	Tafazolli[21], Edwards, G[66]	10,193
22	26	H	Gillingham	D	1-1	0-0	6	Angol[78]	6239
23	31	H	Coventry C	D	1-1	0-1	6	Bostwick[90]	5866
24	Jan 2	A	Scunthorpe U	D	1-1	0-1	8	Goode (og)[83]	4855
25	14	A	Bury	L	1-5	1-4	10	Nichols[4]	2820
26	21	A	Swindon T	W	1-0	0-0	8	Forrester[46]	6514
27	24	A	Oldham Ath	L	0-2	0-0	8		7224
28	28	H	Milton Keynes D	L	0-4	0-0	9		6617
29	Feb 4	A	Port Vale	W	3-0	1-0	8	Maddison[20], Morias 2[90, 90]	4259
30	11	H	Sheffield U	L	0-1	0-0	9		10,258
31	14	H	Shrewsbury T	W	2-1	0-1	8	Tafazolli[71], Ball[78]	4116
32	18	A	Walsall	L	0-2	0-0	9		4759
33	21	H	Southend U	L	1-4	0-1	9	Nichols[80]	4597
34	25	H	Rochdale	W	3-1	2-1	8	Baldwin[36], Nichols[38], Taylor, P[84]	4457
35	28	A	Millwall	L	0-1	0-0	8		8032
36	Mar 4	A	Bradford C	L	0-1	0-1	9		17,220
37	11	H	Oxford U	L	1-2	0-1	12	Mackail-Smith[90]	5469
38	14	A	Chesterfield	D	3-3	3-2	11	Mackail-Smith 2[7, 30], Nichols[17]	5048
39	18	H	Oldham Ath	D	1-1	0-1	12	Morias[73]	4222
40	25	A	Gillingham	W	1-0	0-0	11	Morias[90]	7561
41	Apr 1	H	Charlton Ath	W	2-0	0-0	11	Samuelsen[74], Maddison[83]	5482
42	8	A	Coventry C	L	0-1	0-0	11		10,551
43	14	H	Fleetwood T	L	1-2	0-2	11	Mackail-Smith[68]	5629
44	17	A	AFC Wimbledon	D	0-0	0-0	11		4294
45	22	H	Bristol R	W	4-2	2-0	11	Da Silva Lopes 2[13, 56], Maddison[30], Mackail-Smith[64]	5498
46	30	A	Bolton W	L	0-3	0-1	11		22,590

Final League Position: 11

GOALSCORERS

League (62): Nichols 10, Maddison 9 (1 pen), Edwards, G 7, Mackail-Smith 5, Forrester 4, Morias 4, Bostwick 3, Tafazolli 3, Taylor, P 3, Coulthirst 2, Da Silva Lopes 2, Moncur 2, Angol 1, Baldwin 1, Ball 1, Hughes 1, Samuelsen 1, Smith 1, own goals 2.
FA Cup (7): Coulthirst 2, Edwards, G 2, Da Silva Lopes 1, Nichols 1, Taylor, P 1.
EFL Cup (4): Nichols 2, Da Silva Lopes 1, Taylor, P 1.
EFL Checkatrade Trophy (3): Anderson 1, Moncur 1, Taylor, P 1.

Alnwick B 4	White H 4 + 2	Tafazolli R 30 + 1	Baldwin J 27	Hughes A 37 + 2	Forrester C 39 + 4	Anderson J 5 + 2	Da Silva Lopes L 32 + 6	Maddison M 37 + 4	Coulthirst S 11 + 5	Taylor P 25 + 14	Bostwick M 38 + 1	Edwards G 23 + 10	Nichols T 37 + 6	Williams J 9 + 1	Chettle C 5 + 6	Smith M 39	Nabi A — + 2	Gormley J — + 1	Tyler M 3	Moncur G 5 + 8	Oduwa N — + 6	McGee L 39	Moore D — + 4	Stevens M — + 1	Angol L 5 + 8	Inman B 5 + 6	Santos R — + 1	Samuelsen M 4 + 7	Morias J 7 + 13	Ball D 6	Grant A 11	Mackail-Smith C 14 + 4	Anderson H — + 1	Freestone L 4	Borg A 1 + 2	Match No.
1	2	3[1]	4	5	6	7[2]	8	9	10[3]	11	12	13	14																							1
1	2		3		8[1]	14	7[2]	6	13	11	4	9[3]	10	5	12																					2
1			3	5	7	8		6	12	10[2]	4	9[3]	11[1]			2	13	14																		3
1			3■	5	8[2]	7	12	6[3]	14	10[1]	4	9	11			2	13																			4
			3	5	8	14	7	6	13	11[2]	4	9[3]	10[1]		12	2			1																	5
			3	7	6	5	8	9		10	4	2[2]	11[1]						1	12	13															6
	14		4	5■	7	8[3]	12	6[1]		13	3	9	10			2[2]				11		1														7
			4		8		7[2]	6		9[3]	3	14	11[1]	5	13	2				10		1	12													8
		4		5	7			6		8[2]	3	9	10			2				11[1]	13	1	12													9
	12	4■		5	6			9		10	3	7	11[2]			2				8[1]		1	13													10
			4	5	6		7[2]	8		9	3	10	11[1]			2[3]				12	14	1	13													11
	2	3	4	5	8[1]		7	6[2]	11	14		9	10[3]		13					12		1														12
	2[1]	4	3	5	6		8		10	12		7	11[3]							9[2]	13	1		14												13
		3	4	5	7		8[3]	9	10[2]	11[1]	6	13	12		14	2						1														14
		3	4	5	6[1]		8	9		11		12	10		7[2]	2				13		1														15
		3	4	5	7		8[1]	9	10[2]	12	6	13	11			2						1														16
		4	3	5	8[3]		7	9	10[1]	12	6	14	11[2]			2						1			13											17
		4	3	5	8		7[3]	9	10[2]	12	6	14	11[1]			2						1			13											18
		4	3	5	7		8[2]	9	10[1]		6[3]	13	11			2				14		1			12											19
		3		5	6		9[3]		10[1]	8	4	7[2]	11			2				12	14	1				13										20
		4		5	7		9		10[3]	6[1]	3	8[2]	11			2				12		1				13	14									21
		3		5	8		10	6[1]	9[2]		4	7	11[3]			2				13	14	1			12											22
		4		5	6		8[3]	12	14	9[1]	3	7	10[2]		13	2						1			11											23
		4		5	7		12	9		11[1]	3	6[3]	14			2						1			13			8	10[2]							24
		4[3]		5	8		7[1]	13		10[2]	3	6	11			2						1			14			12	9							25
		4		5	7		13	9[3]		12	3	6[1]	10[2]			2						1			11			14		8						26
		3		5	7		13	9		12	6	8[3]	11[2]			2						1			10[1]				14	4						27
		4			7[3]		8	6		11	3	13	12	5[2]		2						1			10[1]			9	14							28
		4					6[2]	7				9[3]	11	5		2						1				12		14	13	3	8	10[1]				29
		3			12			6				9[1]	11[3]	5		2						1				7[2]		14	13	4	8	10				30
		4			7		14	6[1]		12		9[3]		5[2]		2						1			10				11	3	8	13				31
		4		5	7■			12		11[3]		6[2]				2[1]						1			13			14	9	3	8	10				32
		4	3	5			8	6		13	7		12			2						1						9[2]	11[1]			10				33
		4	3■	5			6[1]	9		11	8		10[2]			2						1				7			13			12				34
		3		5	13		8[2]	9		11	4		10			2[1]						1			14	7					6[3]	12				35
		3		5	7			6		9[1]	4		11[3]			2						1				12		13	14		8[2]	10				36
		4	3[3]	5	7		8■			9	6		11[2]			2[1]						1				13			14			10	12			37
		3	4	5	7					9	6		11[1]			2						1				8			12			10				38
			3	5[3]	7			12		9[1]	4		11[2]	14		2			1							6			13		8	10				39
			4	14	7		8[2]	9		13	3		11[1]	5		2						1							12		6	10[3]				40
			4	14	8[2]		7	9			3		11[3]	5[1]		2						1						13	10		6	12				41
			4		12		7	6		14	3		13	5[3]		2						1						9	11		8[1]	10[2]				42
				4	13		8[3]	9		14	3				7[2]	2						1							12		6	10		5	11[1]	43
				4	6		8	9		13	3		10		7[1]	2						1							12			11[2]		5		44
			4	2	8[3]		7	9[1]			3		11		6							1				14			13			10[2]		5	12	45
		13	3	4[2]	6		5[3]	9			2	12	10[1]		7							1										11		8	14	46

FA Cup

First Round	Chesham U	(h)	2-1
Second Round	Notts Co	(a)	2-2
Replay	Notts Co	(h)	2-0
Third Round	Chelsea	(a)	1-4

EFL Cup

First Round	AFC Wimbledon	(h)	3-2
Second Round	Swansea C	(h)	1-3

EFL Checkatrade Trophy

Southern Group F	Norwich C U21	(h)	1-6
Southern Group F	Milton Keynes D	(h)	0-1
Southern Group F	Barnet	(a)	2-1

PLYMOUTH ARGYLE

FOUNDATION

The club was formed in September 1886 as the Argyle Athletic Club by former public and private school pupils who wanted to continue playing the game. The meeting was held in a room above the Borough Arms (a coffee house), Bedford Street, Plymouth. It was common then to choose a local street/terrace as a club name and Argyle or Argyll was a fashionable name throughout the land due to Queen Victoria's great interest in Scotland.

Home Park, Plymouth, Devon PL2 3DQ.

Telephone: (01752) 562 561.

Fax: (01752) 606 167.

Ticket Office: (01752) 907 700.

Website: www.pafc.co.uk

Email: argyle@pafc.co.uk

Ground Capacity: 16,388.

Record Attendance: 43,596 v Aston Villa, Division 2, 10 October 1936.

Pitch Measurements: 105m × 68.5m (115yd × 75yd).

Chairman: James Brent.

Chief Executive: Martyn Starnes.

Manager: Derek Adams.

Assistant Manager: Craig Brewster.

Colours: Dark green shirts with thin white stripes and black trim, dark green shorts with black trim, dark green socks with black trim.

Year Formed: 1886.

Turned Professional: 1903.

Previous Name: 1886, Argyle Athletic Club; 1903, Plymouth Argyle.

Club Nickname: 'The Pilgrims'.

Ground: 1886, Home Park.

First Football League Game: 28 August 1920, Division 3, v Norwich C (h) D 1–1 – Craig; Russell, Atterbury; Logan, Dickinson, Forbes; Kirkpatrick, Jack, Bowler, Heeps (1), Dixon.

Record League Victory: 8–1 v Millwall, Division 2, 16 January 1932 – Harper; Roberts, Titmuss; Mackay, Pullan, Reed; Grozier, Bowden (2), Vidler (3), Leslie (1), Black (1), (1 og). 8–1 v Hartlepool U (a), Division 2, 7 May 1994 – Nicholls; Patterson (Naylor), Hill, Burrows, Comyn, McCall (1), Barlow, Castle (1), Landon (3), Marshall (1), Dalton (2).

Record Cup Victory: 6–0 v Corby T, FA Cup 3rd rd, 22 January 1966 – Leiper; Book, Baird; Williams, Nelson, Newman; Jones (1), Jackson (1), Bickle (3), Piper (1), Jennings.

HONOURS

League Champions: Second Division – 2003–04; Division 3 – 1958–59; Division 3S – 1929–30, 1951–52; Third Division – 2001–02.
Runners-up: FL 2 – 2016–17; Division 3 – 1974–75, 1985–86; Division 3S – 1921–22, 1922–23, 1923–24, 1924–25, 1925–26, 1926–27.

FA Cup: semi-final – 1984.

League Cup: semi-final – 1965, 1974.

sky SPORTS FACT FILE

Plymouth Argyle's Home Park stadium hosted the Football League representative team's 12-0 victory over the Irish League on 21 September 1966 with Johnny Byrne netting four of the goals. The Football League team included six of the England team which won the FIFA World Cup just two months earlier.

Record Defeat: 0–9 v Stoke C, Division 2, 17 December 1960.

Most League Points (2 for a win): 68, Division 3 (S), 1929–30.

Most League Points (3 for a win): 102, Division 3, 2001–02.

Most League Goals: 107, Division 3 (S), 1925–26 and 1951–52.

Highest League Scorer in Season: Jack Cock, 32, Division 3 (S), 1926–27.

Most League Goals in Total Aggregate: Sammy Black, 174, 1924–38.

Most League Goals in One Match: 5, Wilf Carter v Charlton Ath, Division 2, 27 December 1960.

Most Capped Player: Moses Russell, 20 (23), Wales.

Most League Appearances: Kevin Hodges, 530, 1978–92.

Youngest League Player: Lee Phillips, 16 years 43 days v Gillingham, 29 October 1996.

Record Transfer Fee Received: £2,000,000 from Hull C for Peter Halmosi, July 2008.

Record Transfer Fee Paid: £500,000 to Cardiff C for Steve MacLean, January 2008.

Football League Record: 1920 Original Member of Division 3; 1921–30 Division 3 (S); 1930–50 Division 2; 1950–52 Division 3 (S); 1952–56 Division 2; 1956–58 Division 3 (S); 1958–59 Division 3; 1959–68 Division 2; 1968–75 Division 3; 1975–77 Division 2; 1977–86 Division 3; 1986–95 Division 2; 1995–96 Division 3; 1996–98 Division 2; 1998–2002 Division 3; 2002–04 Division 2; 2004–10 FL C; 2010–11 FL 1; 2011–17 FL 2; 2017– FL 1.

LATEST SEQUENCES

Longest Sequence of League Wins: 9, 8.3.1986 – 12.4.1986.

Longest Sequence of League Defeats: 9, 12.10.1963 – 7.12.1963.

Longest Sequence of League Draws: 5, 26.2.2000 – 14.3.2000.

Longest Sequence of Unbeaten League Matches: 22, 20.4.1929 – 21.12.1929.

Longest Sequence Without a League Win: 13, 13.4.2009 – 27.9.2009.

Successive Scoring Runs: 39 from 15.4.1939.

Successive Non-scoring Runs: 5 from 21.11.2009.

MANAGERS

Frank Brettell 1903–05
Bob Jack 1905–06
Bill Fullerton 1906–07
Bob Jack 1910–38
Jack Tresadern 1938–47
Jimmy Rae 1948–55
Jack Rowley 1955–60
Neil Dougall 1961
Ellis Stuttard 1961–63
Andy Beattie 1963–64
Malcolm Allison 1964–65
Derek Ufton 1965–68
Billy Bingham 1968–70
Ellis Stuttard 1970–72
Tony Waiters 1972–77
Mike Kelly 1977–78
Malcolm Allison 1978–79
Bobby Saxton 1979–81
Bobby Moncur 1981–83
Johnny Hore 1983–84
Dave Smith 1984–88
Ken Brown 1988–90
David Kemp 1990–92
Peter Shilton 1992–95
Steve McCall 1995
Neil Warnock 1995–97
Mick Jones 1997–98
Kevin Hodges 1998–2000
Paul Sturrock 2000–04
Bobby Williamson 2004–05
Tony Pulis 2005–06
Ian Holloway 2006–07
Paul Sturrock 2007–09
Paul Mariner 2009–10
Peter Reid 2010–11
Carl Fletcher 2011–13
John Sheridan 2013–15
Derek Adams June 2015–

TEN YEAR LEAGUE RECORD

		P	W	D	L	F	A	Pts	Pos
2007-08	FL C	46	17	13	16	60	50	64	10
2008-09	FL C	46	13	12	21	44	57	51	21
2009-10	FL C	46	11	8	27	43	68	41	23
2010-11	FL 1	46	15	7	24	51	74	42*	23
2011-12	FL 2	46	10	16	20	47	64	46	21
2012-13	FL 2	46	13	13	20	46	55	52	21
2013-14	FL 2	46	16	12	18	51	58	60	10
2014-15	FL 2	46	20	11	15	55	37	71	7
2015-16	FL 2	46	24	9	13	72	46	81	5
2016-17	FL 2	46	26	9	11	71	46	87	2

** 10 pts deducted.*

DID YOU KNOW ?

Plymouth Argyle won promotion from Division Three in the 1985–86 season by winning 13 and drawing one of their final 15 fixtures. They secured their place as runners-up in the division with a 4-0 home win over Bristol City watched by an attendance of 24,888.

PLYMOUTH ARGYLE – SKY BET LEAGUE TWO 2016–17 LEAGUE RECORD

Match No.	Date	Venue	Opponents	Result		H/T Score	Lg Pos.	Goalscorers	Attendance
1	Aug 6	H	Luton T	L	0-3	0-0	24		9761
2	13	A	Carlisle U	L	0-1	0-1	24		5129
3	16	A	Notts Co	W	2-1	2-1	19	Jervis [14], Bulvitis [34]	3718
4	20	H	Mansfield T	W	2-0	2-0	11	Carey 2 [19, 24]	6935
5	27	A	Blackpool	W	1-0	0-0	7	Bulvitis [50]	3085
6	Sept 3	H	Cheltenham T	W	1-0	0-0	3	Bradley [90]	7552
7	10	H	Cambridge U	W	2-1	1-0	1	Carey [9], Slew [59]	7068
8	17	A	Exeter C	W	2-0	2-0	1	Carey [6], Garita [26]	6612
9	24	H	Hartlepool U	D	1-1	0-1	1	Jervis (pen) [84]	7591
10	27	A	Leyton Orient	W	2-0	1-0	1	Spencer [11], Donaldson [84]	4366
11	Oct 1	H	Yeovil T	W	4-1	2-1	1	Spencer [39], Jervis 2 [43, 86], Carey [71]	8529
12	8	A	Stevenage	W	2-1	0-0	1	Bradley 2 [47, 58]	2881
13	15	H	Portsmouth	D	2-2	1-1	1	Songo'o [21], Smith [89]	13,508
14	22	A	Newport Co	W	3-1	1-0	1	Carey 2 (2 pens) [38, 55], Slew [78]	3460
15	29	H	Colchester U	W	2-1	1-1	1	Tanner [16], Donaldson [87]	8650
16	Nov 12	A	Crewe Alex	W	2-1	1-1	1	Tanner [41], Carey [74]	4573
17	19	H	Grimsby T	L	0-3	0-1	1		10,241
18	22	H	Barnet	L	0-2	0-2	1		7188
19	26	A	Morecambe	L	1-2	1-1	2	Threlkeld [44]	1435
20	Dec 10	H	Doncaster R	W	2-0	1-0	1	Carey [33], Jervis (pen) [63]	8575
21	17	A	Accrington S	W	1-0	0-0	1	Tanner [76]	1573
22	26	H	Wycombe W	D	3-3	2-1	2	Slew [18], Jervis [40], Songo'o [56]	12,210
23	31	H	Crawley T	W	2-0	0-0	1	Threlkeld [69], Tanner [90]	9039
24	Jan 2	A	Barnet	L	0-1	0-1	2		3045
25	14	H	Stevenage	W	4-2	2-2	2	Slew [35], Jervis [42], Garita [54], Goodwillie [90]	8137
26	21	A	Cheltenham T	W	2-1	1-0	2	Bradley 2 [26, 90]	4729
27	31	A	Yeovil T	L	1-2	0-0	2	Sokolik [77]	4788
28	Feb 4	A	Cambridge U	W	1-0	1-0	2	Sarcevic [41]	5084
29	11	H	Exeter C	W	3-0	2-0	2	Kennedy [14], Taylor [45], Jervis (pen) [90]	14,671
30	14	H	Leyton Orient	L	2-3	1-1	2	Sarcevic [10], Kennedy [54]	8054
31	18	A	Hartlepool U	D	1-1	0-1	2	Kennedy [76]	3684
32	25	A	Luton T	D	1-1	1-1	2	Tanner [25]	9124
33	28	H	Notts Co	L	0-1	0-1	2		7566
34	Mar 4	H	Carlisle U	W	2-0	2-0	2	Carey [21], Jervis (pen) [45]	10,381
35	7	H	Blackpool	L	0-3	0-2	2		10,568
36	11	A	Mansfield T	W	2-0	0-0	2	Bradley [69], Carey [74]	4546
37	14	A	Wycombe W	D	1-1	0-1	2	Blissett [72]	3638
38	18	H	Morecambe	W	1-0	1-0	2	Carey [17]	8785
39	26	A	Doncaster R	W	1-0	0-0	2	Bradley [50]	7414
40	Apr 1	H	Accrington S	L	0-1	0-1	2		9708
41	8	A	Crawley T	W	2-1	0-1	2	Carey (pen) [63], Taylor [90]	3432
42	14	A	Portsmouth	D	1-1	1-0	2	Jervis [12]	18,625
43	17	H	Newport Co	W	6-1	2-0	2	Kennedy 2 [39, 65], Jervis 2 [42, 73], Carey [52], Taylor [58]	13,971
44	22	A	Colchester U	D	0-0	0-0	2		5432
45	29	H	Crewe Alex	W	2-1	0-1	1	Taylor [74], Blissett [79]	13,313
46	May 6	A	Grimsby T	D	1-1	0-1	2	Spencer [61]	6866

Final League Position: 2

GOALSCORERS

League (71): Carey 14 (3 pens), Jervis 12 (4 pens), Bradley 7, Kennedy 5, Tanner 5, Slew 4, Taylor 4, Spencer 3, Blissett 2, Bulvitis 2, Donaldson 2, Garita 2, Sarcevic 2, Songo'o 2, Threlkeld 2, Goodwillie 1, Smith 1, Sokolik 1.
FA Cup (3): Carey 1 (1 pen), Fox 1, Slew 1.
EFL Cup (0).
EFL Checkatrade Trophy (5): Bulvitis 1, Jervis 1, Slew 1, Smith 1, Tanner 1.

McCormick L 46	Miller G 27 + 4	Songo'o Y 41 + 5	Bradley S 43 + 1	Sawyer G 21	Ijaha D 2 + 1	Threlkeld O 33 + 3	Donaldson R 14 + 12	Carey G 46	Spencer J 17 + 8	Goodwillie D 5 + 11	Jervis J 28 + 14	Fox D 37 + 3	Slew J 19 + 13	Bulvitis N 16 + 2	Smith C 12 + 13	Purrington B 16 + 3	Tanner C 11 + 15	Garita P 8 + 6	Rooney L — + 1	Osborne K — + 1	Blissett N 1 + 8	Sokolik J 15 + 3	Sarcevic A 16 + 1	Kennedy M 17	Taylor R 15 + 3	*Match No.*
1	2	3	4	5	6²	7	8¹	9	10	11³	12	13	14													1
1	5	2	4	9	6²	7¹	14	8	10	11³	13			3	12											2
1	5	3	4	9		6	13	7¹	10³		11²		12	2	8	14										3
1		7	4	5		2	8	11	10²	12	9³		13	3	6¹	14										4
1	13	7	4	5²		2	8¹	10³	11		9			3	6	12	14									5
1		6	4			2	10³	9	11¹	12	8²	14		3	7	5		13								6
1	2²	7	4			12		9		14		6³	10¹	3	13	5	8	11								7
1	2	7	3			14		8¹		13	12	6	9³	4		5	10	11²								8
1	2	6²	4					10	14	11	12	7	8³	3	13	5	9¹									9
1	2	6²	4				14	7	10	9	11¹	12		3	8³	5	13									10
1	2	6	4			12	10¹	9³	11	14	8	7²		3		5	13									11
1	2	6	4		13			9¹	11	14	8	7³	10²	3	12	5										12
1	2	6	4				13	9	11¹		8²	7	10³	3	12	5	14									13
1	2	7	4				14	9	11³		12	6¹	10	3	13	5	8²									14
1	2	6	4				13	8	11²		12	7	10³	3	14	5	9¹									15
1	2	3	4				7	6	10³	14	12	8	11²		13	5	9¹									16
1	2	3	4				6	8		13	12	7	10³			5	9²	11¹	14							17
1	2	6²	4			5³		10		11	8	7	14	3¹	9		13	12								18
1	2	6	4			5	10	8¹			7²		11■	3³	9		14	12		13						19
1	2	3	4			5	10	9			8	6	11		7											20
1	2	3	4			5	10²	9		14	8³	7	11¹		6		12	13								21
1	2	3	4			5		9			8	7	10		6			11								22
1	2²	3	4			6		9			8	7	10¹	13	14	5	12	11³								23
1	12	3	4			2		6		14	8³	7	10		13	5²	9	11¹								24
1		3	4			2		9		12	8²	7	10³		6	5	13	11¹			14					25
1		4	3			2	7	9			8³	6	10²			5	14	11¹			13	12				26
1		6	3	5		2	8³	9			12	7²	13				10				11¹	4	14			27
1		6	4	5		2	12	8				7	13									3	9	10²	11¹	28
1		6	4	5		2	12	8²			13	7¹	14									3	9	10³	11	29
1		6	4¹	5		2	13	8²			14	7		12								3	9³	10	11	30
1		6²	4	5		2	13	7³	12		9¹	8									14	3		11	10	31
1		3	4	5		2	14	8	13			7¹					9²					12	6	11³	10	32
1		6	4	5		2		9	12		13		14				7²					3¹	8	10³	11	33
1		12	4	5		2	14	9	13		7¹	6										3³	8	10	11²	34
1		3²	4	5		2	6	9	13		8³	7	14				12							10¹	11	35
1	14	6	4	5		2	8	9	12		13	7²	10¹									3			11³	36
1	2	13	4			5		8	10³		9	7	14								12	3	6¹	11²		37
1	2	14	4			5		9	11³		8	6	13									3	7²	10¹	12	38
1	2	12	3			5		8²	11³		6	9									14	4	7	10¹	13	39
1	2	12	4			5		9	11²		8³	7									13	3	6	10¹	14	40
1	2²	3	4	5		6		9			14	8					12³	13					7	11¹	10	41
1		3	4¹	5		2		9			8³	6			13		14					12	7	10²	11	42
1	13	3		5		2²		9³			8	6¹			12		14					4	7	10	11	43
1		3		5		2		10			8¹	6³	13		9²		14	12				4	7		11	44
1	2	3³	13	5				9			8²	7	14								12	4	6	10¹	11	45
1	2	3	4	5				8	13			7³	9¹		14						12		6	11²	10	46

FA Cup

First Round	Mansfield T	(a)	2-1
Second Round	Newport Co	(h)	0-0
Replay	Newport Co	(a)	1-0
(aet)			
Third Round	Liverpool	(a)	0-0
Replay	Liverpool	(h)	0-1

EFL Cup

First Round	Reading	(a)	0-2

EFL Checkatrade Trophy

Southern Group B	Newport Co	(h)	4-1
Southern Group B	AFC Wimbledon	(a)	1-2
Southern Group B	Swansea C U21	(a)	0-2

PORT VALE

FOUNDATION

Port Vale Football Club was formed in 1876 and took its name from the venue of the inaugural meeting at 'Port Vale House' situated in a suburb of Stoke-on-Trent. Upon moving to Burslem in 1884 the club changed its name to 'Burslem Port Vale' and after several seasons in the Midland League became founder members of the Football League Division Two in 1892. The prefix 'Burslem' was dropped from the name as a new ground several miles away was acquired.

Vale Park, Hamil Road, Burslem, Stoke-on-Trent, Staffordshire ST6 1AW.

Telephone: (01782) 655 800.

Fax: (01782) 655 816.

Ticket Office: (01782) 655 800 (option 1).

Website: www.port-vale.co.uk

Email: enquiries@port-vale.co.uk

Ground Capacity: 19,148.

Record Attendance: 22,993 v Stoke C, Division 2, 6 March 1920 (at Recreation Ground); 49,768 v Aston Villa, FA Cup 5th rd, 20 February 1960 (at Vale Park).

Pitch Measurements: 104m × 69.5m (114yd × 76yd).

Chairman: Norman Smurthwaite.

Chief Executive: Colin Garlick.

Manager: Michael Brown.

Assistant Manager: David Kelly.

Colours: White shirts with yellow and black trim, black shorts with white trim, black socks with white trim.

Year Formed: 1876.

Turned Professional: 1885.

Previous Names: 1876, Port Vale; 1884, Burslem Port Vale; 1909, Port Vale.

Club Nickname: 'Valiants'.

Grounds: 1876, Limekin Lane, Longport; 1881, Westport; 1884, Moorland Road, Burslem; 1886, Athletic Ground, Cobridge; 1913, Recreation Ground, Hanley; 1950, Vale Park.

First Football League Game: 3 September 1892, Division 2, v Small Heath (a) L 1–5 – Frail; Clutton, Elson; Farrington, McCrindle, Delves; Walker, Scarratt, Bliss (1), Jones. (Only 10 men).

Record League Victory: 9–1 v Chesterfield, Division 2, 24 September 1932 – Leckie; Shenton, Poyser; Sherlock, Round, Jones; McGrath, Mills, Littlewood (6), Kirkham (2), Morton (1).

Record Cup Victory: 7–1 v Irthlingborough, FA Cup 1st rd, 12 January 1907 – Matthews; Dunn, Hamilton; Eardley, Baddeley, Holyhead; Carter, Dodds (2), Beats, Mountford (2), Coxon (3).

HONOURS

League Champions: Division 3N – 1929–30, 1953–54; Division 4 – 1958–59.
Runners-up: Second Division – 1993–94; Division 3N – 1952–53.

FA Cup: semi-final – 1954.

League Cup: 4th rd – 2007.

League Trophy Winners: 1993, 2001.

Anglo-Italian Cup: *Runners-up:* 1996.

sky SPORTS FACT FILE

One of the earliest legal cases involving footballers' contracts came in November 1886. Burslem Port Vale won damages from goalkeeper William Rowley who had played for neighbours Stoke in breach of his contract. Shortly after the case Rowley signed for Stoke on a permanent basis.

Record Defeat: 0–10 v Sheffield U, Division 2, 10 December 1892. 0–10 v Notts Co, Division 2, 26 February 1895.

Most League Points (2 for a win): 69, Division 3 (N), 1953–54.

Most League Points (3 for a win): 89, Division 2, 1992–93.

Most League Goals: 110, Division 4, 1958–59.

Highest League Scorer in Season: Wilf Kirkham 38, Division 2, 1926–27.

Most League Goals in Total Aggregate: Wilf Kirkham, 153, 1923–29, 1931–33.

Most League Goals in One Match: 6, Stewart Littlewood v Chesterfield, Division 2, 24 September 1922.

Most Capped Player: Chris Birchall, 24 (43), Trinidad & Tobago.

Most League Appearances: Roy Sproson, 760, 1950–72.

Youngest League Player: Malcolm McKenzie, 15 years 347 days v Newport Co, 12 April 1966.

Record Transfer Fee Received: £2,000,000 from Wimbledon for Gareth Ainsworth, October 1998.

Record Transfer Fee Paid: £500,000 to Lincoln C for Gareth Ainsworth, September 1997.

Football League Record: 1892 Original Member of Division 2. Failed re-election in 1896; Re-elected 1898; Resigned 1907; Returned in Oct, 1919, when they took over the fixtures of Leeds City; 1929–30 Division 3 (N); 1930–36 Division 2; 1936–38 Division 3 (N); 1938–52 Division 3 (S); 1952–54 Division 3 (N); 1954–57 Division 2; 1957–58 Division 3 (S); 1958–59 Division 4; 1959–65 Division 3; 1965–70 Division 4; 1970–78 Division 3; 1978–83 Division 4; 1983–84 Division 3; 1984–86 Division 4; 1986–89 Division 3; 1989–94 Division 2; 1994–2000 Division 1; 2000–04 Division 2; 2004–08 FL 1; 2008–13 FL 2; 2013–17 FL 1; 2017– FL 2.

MANAGERS

Sam Gleaves 1896–1905 *(Secretary-Manager)*
Tom Clare 1905–11
A. S. Walker 1911–12
H. Myatt 1912–14
Tom Holford 1919–24 *(continued as Trainer)*
Joe Schofield 1924–30
Tom Morgan 1930–32
Tom Holford 1932–35
Warney Cresswell 1936–37
Tom Morgan 1937–38
Billy Frith 1945–46
Gordon Hodgson 1946–51
Ivor Powell 1951
Freddie Steele 1951–57
Norman Low 1957–62
Freddie Steele 1962–65
Jackie Mudie 1965–67
Sir Stanley Matthews *(General Manager)* 1965–68
Gordon Lee 1968–74
Roy Sproson 1974–77
Colin Harper 1977
Bobby Smith 1977–78
Dennis Butler 1978–79
Alan Bloor 1979
John McGrath 1980–83
John Rudge 1983–99
Brian Horton 1999–2004
Martin Foyle 2004–07
Lee Sinnott 2007–08
Dean Glover 2008–09
Micky Adams 2009–10
Jim Gannon 2011
Micky Adams 2011–14
Robert Page 2014–16
Bruno Ribeiro 2016
Michael Brown May 2017–

LATEST SEQUENCES

Longest Sequence of League Wins: 8, 8.4.1893 – 30.9.1893.

Longest Sequence of League Defeats: 9, 9.3.1957 – 20.4.1957.

Longest Sequence of League Draws: 6, 26.4.1981 – 12.9.1981.

Longest Sequence of Unbeaten League Matches: 19, 5.5.1969 – 8.11.1969.

Longest Sequence Without a League Win: 17, 7.12.1991 – 21.3.1992.

Successive Scoring Runs: 22 from 12.9.1992.

Successive Non-scoring Runs: 5 from 4.4.2017.

TEN YEAR LEAGUE RECORD

		P	*W*	*D*	*L*	*F*	*A*	*Pts*	*Pos*
2007-08	FL 1	46	9	11	26	47	81	38	23
2008-09	FL 2	46	13	9	24	44	66	48	18
2009-10	FL 2	46	17	17	12	61	50	68	10
2010-11	FL 2	46	17	14	15	54	49	65	11
2011-12	FL 2	46	20	9	17	68	60	59*	12
2012-13	FL 2	46	21	15	10	87	52	78	3
2013-14	FL 1	46	18	7	21	59	73	61	9
2014-15	FL 1	46	15	9	22	55	65	54	18
2015-16	FL 1	46	18	11	17	56	58	65	12
2016-17	FL 1	46	12	13	21	45	70	49	21

**10 pts deducted.*

DID YOU KNOW ?

Port Vale inside-left Tom Butler suffered a compound fracture of the left arm playing against Clapton Orient on 3 November 1923. The wound became infected with tetanus and he died in a Hackney hospital eight days later leaving a wife and three young children.

PORT VALE – SKY BET LEAGUE ONE 2016–17 LEAGUE RECORD

Match No.	Date	Venue	Opponents	Result		H/T Score	Lg Pos.	Goalscorers	Attendance
1	Aug 6	A	Bradford C	D	0-0	0-0	15		18,558
2	13	H	Southend U	W	2-0	1-0	7	Forrester 40, Streete 75	4727
3	16	H	Rochdale	W	1-0	0-0	4	Smith 52	3941
4	20	A	Swindon T	L	0-1	0-0	6		6182
5	27	H	Scunthorpe U	W	3-1	1-1	4	Forrester 33, Jones 2 49, 84	4557
6	Sept 3	A	Bury	L	1-4	0-3	6	Smith 58	4042
7	10	A	Peterborough U	D	2-2	1-1	9	Jones 2 (1 pen) 6, 90 (p)	4711
8	17	H	Gillingham	W	2-1	0-1	5	Streete 76, Jones 84	4719
9	24	A	Bristol R	L	1-2	1-1	6	Paterson 23	9088
10	27	H	Millwall	W	3-1	1-0	5	Jones 4, Paterson 59, Streete 71	3934
11	Oct 1	H	Coventry C	L	0-2	0-1	6		5605
12	9	A	Milton Keynes D	W	1-0	1-0	4	Jones 35	8259
13	15	A	Sheffield U	L	0-4	0-2	7		19,699
14	18	H	Charlton Ath	D	1-1	0-1	6	Jones (pen) 85	3494
15	22	H	Oxford U	D	2-2	0-2	7	Cicilia 54, Taylor (pen) 59	4837
16	29	A	Bolton W	L	1-3	0-3	10	Hart 75	13,937
17	Nov 12	H	Fleetwood T	W	2-1	0-0	6	Cicilia 75, Jones 86	3890
18	19	A	Charlton Ath	L	0-2	0-2	11		8992
19	22	H	Oldham Ath	D	2-2	0-0	12	Streete 51, Cicilia 78	3152
20	26	A	Shrewsbury T	D	0-0	0-0	12		5429
21	Dec 10	H	Northampton T	L	2-3	0-1	15	Taylor 52, Cicilia 90	4739
22	17	A	AFC Wimbledon	L	0-4	0-0	17		4291
23	26	H	Walsall	L	0-1	0-1	17		5854
24	30	H	Chesterfield	W	1-0	0-0	17	Thomas 61	4027
25	Jan 2	A	Oldham Ath	D	0-0	0-0	15		3451
26	20	H	Bury	D	2-2	2-1	15	Walker 20, Taylor (pen) 45	4338
27	28	A	Scunthorpe U	L	2-3	1-0	18	Walker 38, Hooper 59	4442
28	Feb 4	H	Peterborough U	L	0-3	0-1	19		4259
29	11	A	Gillingham	D	1-1	0-0	19	Streete 49	4942
30	14	A	Millwall	L	0-2	0-1	20		7032
31	18	H	Bristol R	D	1-1	0-0	21	Harris (og) 54	4460
32	25	H	Bradford C	L	1-2	0-1	21	Hooper 58	4953
33	Mar 4	A	Southend U	D	1-1	0-0	22	Eagles 78	7545
34	11	H	Swindon T	W	3-2	1-1	21	Eagles 36, Hooper 2 50, 87	4510
35	14	A	Northampton T	L	1-2	0-0	21	Hooper 73	4812
36	17	H	Shrewsbury T	W	2-1	0-0	21	Foley 66, Taylor 69	4626
37	21	A	Coventry C	L	1-2	0-2	21	Smith 74	7695
38	25	H	Milton Keynes D	D	0-0	0-0	21		3887
39	Apr 1	H	AFC Wimbledon	W	2-0	1-0	18	Smith 21, Eagles 69	4308
40	4	A	Rochdale	L	0-3	0-3	20		4387
41	8	A	Chesterfield	L	0-1	0-0	21		5527
42	14	H	Sheffield U	L	0-3	0-2	21		8999
43	17	A	Oxford U	L	0-2	0-1	21		7646
44	22	H	Bolton W	L	0-2	0-0	21		8890
45	25	A	Walsall	W	1-0	0-0	21	Eagles 85	4266
46	30	A	Fleetwood T	D	0-0	0-0	21		4733

Final League Position: 21

GOALSCORERS

League (45): Jones 9 (2 pens), Hooper 5, Streete 5, Cicilia 4, Eagles 4, Smith 4, Taylor 4 (2 pens), Forrester 2, Paterson 2, Walker 2, Foley 1, Hart 1, Thomas 1, own goal 1.
FA Cup (5): Cicilia 1, Jones 1, Streete 1, Taylor 1 (1 pen), own goal 1.
EFL Cup (1): Grant 1.
EFL Checkatrade Trophy (1): Smith 1.

Alnwick J 26	Knops K 28 + 1	Smith N 46	Streete R 36 + 1	Purkiss B 32	Foley S 32	Tavares P 19 + 3	Grant A 20	Thomas J 23	Cicilia R 16 + 13	de Freitas A 16 + 8	Mbamba C — + 6	Forrester A 12 + 9	Pereira Q 2 + 12	MacIntosh C 3	Hooper J 21 + 2	Jones A 17 + 2	Amoros S 7 + 3	Paterson M 10 + 6	Hart S 9 + 2	Shalaj G — + 7	Brown M 1 + 2	Kiko F 11 + 10	Turner D 3 + 13	Kelly S 9 + 12	Taylor R 22	Boot R 1	Guy C 10 + 1	Walker T 5 + 1	Eagles C 16 + 4	Tanser S 8 + 3	Fasan L 10	Shodipo O 4 + 2	Pugh D 13 + 1	Reeves W 4 + 8	Mehmet D 9	Bikey A 5 + 2	*Match No.*
1	2	3	4	5	6	7	8	9^3	10^2	11^1	12	13	14																								1
1	5	4	3		7	6^2	8	9^1	11^3	13		12	14	2	10																						2
1	5^2	4	3	2	10	7	8	9^3		12	13	11^1			6	14																					3
1	5	4	3	2	10	7^1	8		14	9^3	13	11^2			6	12																					4
1	5	4	3	2	6	8^3	7	9^1				11^2				10	12	13	14																		5
1	5	4	3	2	6			11	14	8^2		10^1				9^3	7	12		13																	6
1	5	4	3	2	6^3	7^1	8	9	12				13			10	14	11^2																			7
1	5	4	3	2	10	8^3	7	9^1	13							6		11^2		12	14																8
1	5	3	4	2		8^3	7	11^1	13				6^2			9		10		12	14																9
1	5	4	3	2	10^2	8	7		12				14			6		11^3	9^1			13															10
1		4	3	2	10	8		9^2				13^3	12			6		11	5	14	7^1																11
1	5	3	4	2	8		6						14			9^3	7	11^2	10^1			12	13														12
1	5	4	3	2	10^2		8						12			6	7^3	11^1	9			14	13														13
1	5^2	4	3			7	8		13				10^1	2		6		11^3	9				14	12													14
1		3	4		10^1	7	8	6	11	14	12		13	5^3					2						9^2												15
1	5	4	3			7	8	6^3	11^2	12	14							13	2					10^1	9												16
1		4	3			7	8▪	10	12				14			6		11^1	5^3			13		9^2	2												17
1	5	4	3			7		6^2		9		14	13			11	8^1	12						10^3	2												18
1	2	3	4			7^2			14	8		10^1	13			9		11^3				12		6	5												19
1	5	4	3			13			12	7						11	6		8^2			10^1	14	9^3	2												20
1		4	3			7^1			11	9						6	8	13		12		5		10^2	2												21
1		4	3			8^1			11	7			12			10	6^2		13			5		9	2												22
1	5^2	4	3			8^3	7	9	11	10^1						6		14				13		12	2												23
1	5	4	3	2			8	11^2	10	7^3							14					13	12	6^1	9												24
1	5	4	3	2			7	10	11	6^2	13											12		8^1	9												25
	5	4	3	2			8	9^2	14			13			11^3										6	1	7	10^1	12								26
1	12	4^2	3	2			8	9		6		14			10^3												7^1	11	13	5							27
		4	3	2	7					8^1		14			10												6^3	11	13	5	1	9^2	12				28
	5	4	3	2	8					6		12			11^1												7	10^2	13		1		9				29
	5	4	3^1	2	6					8^2		14			9												7	10^3		12	1	13	11				30
	4	3		2	7			9				11			10^2							5		12			14	13^3	6^1		1		8				31
		3		2	8			9^1				10^3			11					14		5	13				7		6^2		1	12	4				32
		4		3	8			9^1				11			10								14	12			2		6^3	5	1		7^2	13			33
	4	3		2	7^2	14						11			10							5		12			8		6^3		1	9^1		13			34
	3^1	4	14	2	9							8			11							12		13			10		6	5^3	1	7^2					35
		4	3	2	8							10^1			11							5	13	14	9		7^3		6^2					12	1		36
		4	3	2^2	7	14			11													5	13	12	6				10^3			9		8^1	1		37
		4	3^1	2	7				14			11^2			6							5^3			9				10	13			8		1	12	38
	5	4		2	8^3				11^1	12					9								14		6				10^2				7	13	1	3	39
	5^2	4		2	8^3				11^1	13					9							12			6				10				7▪	14	1	3	40
		4		2	7				10	9^1					11							5^2	13		8				6	14				12	1	3^3	41
		4		2^2	8				11						9^3							5	13	14	6				10^1				7	12	1	3	42
		3	4		9				10	14					11^3								12	13	5				6	2^2			8	7^1	1		43
		4			7			9^2	11▪						12					13			10^3		2				6^1	5			8	14	1	3	44
		4	3		8			9^3							12								11^2	13	2				7^1	5	1		6	10		14	45
		4	3	2	7				14	13					11^3								10	12					9	5^2	1		6^1	8			46

FA Cup

First Round	Stevenage	(h)	1-0
Second Round	Hartlepool U	(h)	4-0
Third Round	Huddersfield T	(a)	0-4

EFL Cup

First Round	Carlisle U	(a)	1-2

EFL Checkatrade Trophy

Northern Group E	Derby Co U21	(h)	1-0
Northern Group E	Mansfield T	(h)	0-1
Northern Group E	Doncaster R	(a)	0-0

(*Port Vale won 4-3 on penalties*)

PORTSMOUTH

FOUNDATION

At a meeting held in his High Street, Portsmouth offices in 1898, solicitor Alderman J. E. Pink and five other business and professional men agreed to buy some ground close to Goldsmith Avenue for £4,950 which they developed into Fratton Park in record breaking time. A team of professionals was signed up by manager Frank Brettell and entry to the Southern League obtained for the new club's September 1899 kick-off.

Fratton Park, Frogmore Road, Portsmouth, Hampshire PO4 8RA.

Telephone: (02392) 731 204.

Fax: (02392) 734 129.

Ticket Office: (0345) 646 1898.

Website: www.portsmouthfc.co.uk

Email: info@pompeyfc.co.uk

Ground Capacity: 18,931.

Record Attendance: 51,385 v Derby Co, FA Cup 6th rd, 26 February 1949.

Pitch Measurements: 100m × 66m (109.5yd × 72yd).

Chairman: Iain McInnes.

Chief Executive: Mark Catlin.

Manager: Kenny Jackett.

Assistant Manager: Joe Gallen.

Colours: Blue shirts with white trim, white shorts with blue trim, red socks.

Year Formed: 1898.

Turned Professional: 1898.

Club Nickname: 'Pompey'.

Ground: 1898, Fratton Park.

First Football League Game: 28 August 1920, Division 3, v Swansea T (h) W 3–0 – Robson; Probert, Potts; Abbott, Harwood, Turner; Thompson, Stringfellow (1), Reid (1), James (1), Beedie.

Record League Victory: 9–1 v Notts Co, Division 2, 9 April 1927 – McPhail; Clifford, Ted Smith; Reg Davies (1), Foxall, Moffat; Forward (1), Mackie (2), Haines (3), Watson, Cook (2).

Record Cup Victory: 7–0 v Stockport Co, FA Cup 3rd rd, 8 January 1949 – Butler; Rookes, Ferrier; Scoular, Flewin, Dickinson; Harris (3), Barlow, Clarke (2), Phillips (2), Froggatt.

Record Defeat: 0–10 v Leicester C, Division 1, 20 October 1928.

Most League Points (2 for a win): 65, Division 3, 1961–62.

HONOURS

League Champions: Division 1 – 1948–49, 1949–50; First Division – 2002–03; Division 3 – 1961–62, 1982–83; Division 3S – 1923–24; FL 2 – 2016–17.
Runners-up: Division 2 – 1926–27, 1986–87.

FA Cup Winners: 1939, 2008.
Runners-up: 1929, 1934, 2010.

League Cup: 5th rd – 1961, 1986, 1994, 2010.

European Competitions
UEFA Cup: 2008–09.

sky SPORTS FACT FILE

In their early days Portsmouth wore salmon pink shirts with cerise collars and cuffs and white shorts. This was changed to white shirts and navy blue shorts for the 1909–10 season, and then to the now traditional navy blue shirts with white shorts in May 1912. Navy blue was chosen due to the town's close association with the Royal Navy.

Most League Points (3 for a win): 98, Division 1, 2002–03.

Most League Goals: 97, Division 1, 2002–03.

Highest League Scorer in Season: Guy Whittingham, 42, Division 1, 1992–93.

Most League Goals in Total Aggregate: Peter Harris, 194, 1946–60.

Most League Goals in One Match: 5, Alf Strange v Gillingham, Division 3, 27 January 1923; 5, Peter Harris v Aston Villa, Division 1, 3 September 1958.

Most Capped Player: Jimmy Dickinson, 48, England.

Most League Appearances: Jimmy Dickinson, 764, 1946–65.

Youngest League Player: Clive Green, 16 years 259 days v Wrexham, 21 August 1976.

Record Transfer Fee Received: £20,000,000 from Real Madrid for Lassana Diarra, January 2009.

Record Transfer Fee Paid: £9,000,000 (rising to £11,000,000) to Liverpool for Peter Crouch, July 2008.

Football League Record: 1920 Original Member of Division 3; 1921 Division 3 (S); 1924–27 Division 2; 1927–59 Division 1; 1959–61 Division 2; 1961–62 Division 3; 1962–76 Division 2; 1976–78 Division 3; 1978–80 Division 4; 1980–83 Division 3; 1983–87 Division 2; 1987–88 Division 1; 1988–92 Division 2; 1992–2003 Division 1; 2003–10 FA Premier League; 2010–12 FL C; 2012–13 FL 1; 2013–17 FL 2; 2017– FL 1.

LATEST SEQUENCES

Longest Sequence of League Wins: 7, 17.8.2002 – 17.9.2002.

Longest Sequence of League Defeats: 9, 26.12.2012 – 9.2.2013.

Longest Sequence of League Draws: 5, 16.12.2000 – 13.1.2001.

Longest Sequence of Unbeaten League Matches: 15, 18.4.1924 – 18.10.1924.

Longest Sequence Without a League Win: 25, 29.11.1958 – 22.8.1959.

Successive Scoring Runs: 23 from 30.8.1930.

Successive Non-scoring Runs: 6 from 27.12.1993.

MANAGERS

Frank Brettell 1898–1901
Bob Blyth 1901–04
Richard Bonney 1905–08
Bob Brown 1911–20
John McCartney 1920–27
Jack Tinn 1927–47
Bob Jackson 1947–52
Eddie Lever 1952–58
Freddie Cox 1958–61
George Smith 1961–70
Ron Tindall 1970–73
(General Manager to 1974)
John Mortimore 1973–74
Ian St John 1974–77
Jimmy Dickinson 1977–79
Frank Burrows 1979–82
Bobby Campbell 1982–84
Alan Ball 1984–89
John Gregory 1989–90
Frank Burrows 1990–91
Jim Smith 1991–95
Terry Fenwick 1995–98
Alan Ball 1998–99
Tony Pulis 2000
Steve Claridge 2000–01
Graham Rix 2001–02
Harry Redknapp 2002–04
Velimir Zajec 2004–05
Alain Perrin 2005
Harry Redknapp 2005–08
Tony Adams 2008–09
Paul Hart 2009
Avram Grant 2009–10
Steve Cotterill 2010–11
Michael Appleton 2011–12
Guy Whittingham 2012–13
Richie Barker 2013–14
Andy Awford 2014–15
Paul Cook 2015–17
Kenny Jackett June 2017–

TEN YEAR LEAGUE RECORD

		P	W	D	L	F	A	Pts	Pos
2007-08	PR Lge	38	16	9	13	48	40	57	8
2008-09	PR Lge	38	10	11	17	38	57	41	14
2009-10	PR Lge	38	7	7	24	34	66	19*	20
2010-11	FL C	46	15	13	18	53	60	58	16
2011-12	FL C	46	13	11	22	50	59	40†	22
2012-13	FL 1	46	10	12	24	51	69	32‡	24
2013-14	FL 2	46	14	17	15	56	66	59	13
2014-15	FL 2	46	14	15	17	52	54	57	16
2015-16	FL 2	46	21	15	10	75	44	78	6
2016-17	FL 2	46	26	9	11	79	40	87	1

**9 pts deducted; †10 pts deducted; ‡10 pts deducted.*

DID YOU KNOW ?

Portsmouth played their first game at Fratton Park under floodlights on 2 March 1953. A crowd of more than 22,000 saw Pompey draw 1-1 with local rivals Southampton. Extra transport was laid on to maximise attendance, including a special late-night ferry service to the Isle of Wight.

PORTSMOUTH – SKY BET LEAGUE TWO 2016–17 LEAGUE RECORD

Match No.	Date	Venue	Opponents	Result	H/T Score	Lg Pos.	Goalscorers	Attendance
1	Aug 6	H	Carlisle U	D 1-1	1-1	16	Baker [42]	17,570
2	13	A	Crewe Alex	D 0-0	0-0	17		4742
3	16	A	Morecambe	L 0-2	0-2	20		1838
4	20	H	Colchester U	W 2-0	0-0	14	Roberts 2 (1 pen) [79 (p), 84]	15,967
5	27	A	Exeter C	W 1-0	0-0	8	Roberts (pen) [85]	4512
6	Sept 3	H	Crawley T	W 3-0	3-0	4	Main 2 [9, 37], Roberts [12]	16,347
7	10	H	Wycombe W	W 4-2	3-2	2	Burgess [34], Roberts (pen) [45], Chaplin [45], Baker [53]	16,262
8	17	A	Accrington S	L 0-1	0-0	4		2461
9	24	H	Barnet	W 5-1	1-1	2	Chaplin [34], Roberts [50], Baker [56], Lalkovic [78], Rose [90]	16,280
10	27	A	Blackpool	L 1-3	1-1	4	Chaplin [34]	3055
11	Oct 1	H	Doncaster R	L 1-2	1-2	6	Baker [41]	16,950
12	8	A	Leyton Orient	W 1-0	0-0	3	Burgess [57]	6078
13	15	A	Plymouth Arg	D 2-2	1-1	5	Bennett [40], Rose [86]	13,508
14	22	H	Notts Co	L 1-2	1-1	5	Chaplin [27]	17,269
15	29	A	Cambridge U	W 1-0	1-0	5	Chaplin [24]	6397
16	Nov 12	H	Mansfield T	W 4-0	1-0	4	Roberts (pen) [11], Hunt [84], Baker 2 [88, 90]	16,393
17	19	A	Cheltenham T	D 1-1	0-0	5	Smith [82]	4702
18	22	A	Luton T	W 3-1	2-1	4	Smith [11], Evans [45], Naismith [85]	8805
19	26	H	Stevenage	L 1-2	0-0	4	Smith [80]	15,987
20	Dec 10	A	Grimsby T	W 1-0	0-0	4	Naismith [86]	6560
21	17	H	Hartlepool U	D 0-0	0-0	4		17,081
22	26	A	Newport Co	W 3-2	0-1	4	Rose [56], Stevens [80], Naismith [87]	3714
23	30	A	Yeovil T	D 0-0	0-0	4		6306
24	Jan 2	H	Luton T	W 1-0	1-0	4	Burgess [31]	17,402
25	5	A	Doncaster R	L 1-3	1-1	4	Naismith [41]	5568
26	14	H	Leyton Orient	W 2-1	1-1	4	Chaplin 2 [22, 47]	16,564
27	28	H	Exeter C	L 0-1	0-0	5		17,195
28	Feb 4	A	Wycombe W	L 0-1	0-0	7		6028
29	11	H	Accrington S	W 2-0	1-0	6	Clarke [2], Naismith [90]	15,955
30	14	H	Blackpool	W 2-0	1-0	5	Evans [27], Doyle, E [90]	15,132
31	18	A	Barnet	D 1-1	0-0	5	Chaplin [89]	4571
32	25	A	Carlisle U	W 3-0	0-0	4	Roberts [73], Linganzi [86], Whatmough [90]	7197
33	28	H	Morecambe	D 1-1	0-0	4	Naismith [64]	15,592
34	Mar 4	H	Crewe Alex	L 0-1	0-0	5		16,810
35	7	A	Crawley T	W 2-0	0-0	3	Burgess [54], Bennett [71]	5350
36	11	A	Colchester U	W 4-0	1-0	3	Doyle, E [22], Bennett [46], Rose [61], Doyle, M [74]	6504
37	14	H	Grimsby T	W 4-0	3-0	3	Bennett [12], Rose [35], Baker [45], Naismith [47]	16,492
38	18	A	Stevenage	L 0-3	0-2	3		4185
39	25	H	Newport Co	W 2-1	1-0	3	Bennett [42], Naismith [59]	17,364
40	Apr 1	A	Hartlepool U	W 2-0	1-0	3	Naismith [17], Roberts [60]	4500
41	8	H	Yeovil T	W 3-1	1-0	3	Evans (pen) [15], Naismith [68], Lowe [78]	17,564
42	14	H	Plymouth Arg	D 1-1	0-1	3	Roberts [57]	18,625
43	17	A	Notts Co	W 3-1	1-0	3	Evans (pen) [14], Lowe 2 [77, 90]	12,184
44	22	H	Cambridge U	W 2-1	1-0	3	Baker [20], Naismith [51]	18,165
45	29	A	Mansfield T	W 1-0	0-0	3	Baker [56]	6819
46	May 6	H	Cheltenham T	W 6-1	1-0	1	O'Shaughnessy (og) [13], Bennett [62], Naismith 2 [66, 84], Lowe [72], Evans (pen) [75]	17,956

Final League Position: 1

GOALSCORERS

League (79): Naismith 13, Roberts 10 (4 pens), Baker 9, Chaplin 8, Bennett 6, Evans 5 (3 pens), Rose 5, Burgess 4, Lowe 4, Smith 3, Doyle, E 2, Main 2, Clarke 1, Doyle, M 1, Hunt 1, Lalkovic 1, Linganzi 1, Stevens 1, Whatmough 1, own goal 1.
FA Cup (1): Evans 1.
EFL Cup (2): Main 1 (1 pen), Naismith 1.
EFL Checkatrade Trophy (6): Smith 3, Main 2, Naismith 1.

Forde D 46	Talbot D 5	Burgess C 44	Whatmough J 4 + 6	Stevens E 45	Doyle M 46	Rose D 33 + 5	Baker C 40 + 5	Roberts G 31 + 10	Lalkovic M 5 + 8	Smith M 14 + 4	Bennett K 33 + 6	Chaplin C 13 + 26	Hunt N 4 + 16	Naismith K 22 + 15	Main C 4 + 8	Barton A 2 + 1	Linganzi A 12 + 7	Davies T 10 + 2	Evans G 41	Clarke M 33	Lowe J 5 + 9	Doyle E 12	Kabamba N 1 + 3	Aborah S 1 + 3	Match No.
1	2	3	4	5	6	7^{3}	8	9	10^{2}	11^{1}	12	13	14												1
1	2	3	4^{1}		6	7	8	9	10^{2}	11^{3}	13			5	12	14									2
1	2	4		5	7	6^{1}	9	8	12	11^{2}	10^{3}		14		13	3									3
1	2	4		5	8	7^{2}	6	10			9^{3}	13	12		11^{1}	3	14								4
1	2	3		5	6	7	8^{2}	9	10^{3}			12	14	13	11^{1}			4							5
1		4		5	6	7	8	9^{2}	10^{1}	14		12		13	11^{3}			3	2						6
1		3		5	7	6	8	9^{3}	10^{2}			12	14	13	11^{1}			4	2						7
1		3		5	7	6^{2}	8^{1}	9^{3}	14	11	10	12		13				4	2						8
1		4		5	7	6	8^{2}	9	12		14	11^{3}		10^{1}	13			3	2						9
1		4		5^{3}	8	7	6^{1}	10		13	12	11^{2}		9	14			3	2						10
1		4		5	7	8^{3}	6	10	12			11^{2}		9^{1}	14		13		2	3					11
1		3		5	7	13	8	9	14		10^{2}	11^{3}			12		6^{1}		2	4					12
1		3		5	7	12	8	9	14		10^{3}	11^{2}			13		6^{1}	4	2						13
1		3		5^{2}	6		8	9	14		7^{1}	11^{2}		12	13		10	4	2						14
1		3		5	6	13	8	9^{2}			10^{1}	11^{3}	12				7■	14	2	4					15
1		4		5	7	6	10	9^{1}		14	8^{2}	11^{3}	12	13					2	3					16
1		4		5	6	7	8	9^{3}		12	10^{1}	11^{2}	13	14					2	3					17
1		3	13	5	6	7	10	9^{2}		11^{1}	8^{3}		14	12					2	4					18
1		3^{2}	13	5	6^{3}	7	8	9		11	10^{1}	14					12		2	4					19
1		3		4	7	6	5	9^{1}		10^{2}	11^{3}	13	14	12					8	2					20
1		3		5	6	7^{1}	8	9^{2}		11	10^{3}	13	14	12					2	4					21
1		3		5	8	7	6^{2}			10		12	11^{1}	9			13		2	4					22
1		4		5	8^{2}	7	6^{3}			11	12	13	10^{1}	9			14		2	3					23
1		4		2	6	7^{1}	10^{2}	12		11	9^{3}		13	8			14		5	3					24
1		4		2	6	7	10^{3}	13	12	11	8^{1}	14		9^{2}					5	3					25
1		4		5	7	8	6			10	14	11^{2}		9^{3}			13		2^{1}	3	12				26
1		4		5	8	7	6^{1}	13		10^{2}		11		9					2	3	12				27
1		3		5	7		13	9^{3}			10^{2}	14		12			6		2	4	8^{1}	11			28
1		4		5	7		12	9^{3}			10^{1}		14	13			6		2	3	8^{2}	11			29
1		4	14	5	7		12	9			10^{3}			13			6		2^{2}	3	8^{1}	11			30
1		4		5	7	12	14	9^{1}			10^{2}	13					6		2	3	8^{3}	11			31
1		3	12	4	7		8^{2}	11^{1}			5^{3}	13		14			6		9	2		10			32
1		4		5	7	14	8^{2}	9			10^{3}	12		13			6^{1}		2	3		11			33
1		4		5	6		13	9^{3}			10^{1}	12	14	8			7^{2}		2	3		11			34
1		4		5^{1}	6	7	9				10^{2}		12	8				13	2	3		11			35
1		3		5	7	6	10	13			9^{1}	14	12	8^{2}					2	4		11^{3}			36
1		4		5	6	7	8	12			10^{1}	14		9^{3}					2	3	13	11^{2}			37
1		3■		7	4	8	6^{1}	12				14	10^{3}					9	5	2		11^{2}	13		38
1			14	5	7	6	8				10^{1}	12		9^{3}				3	2	4	13	11^{2}			39
1		3		5	7	6		12			8	13	11^{3}	10^{2}					2	4	9^{1}		14		40
1		3		5	7	6	8^{3}	9^{1}			10	12		11^{2}					2	4	13		14		41
1		3		5	7	6	10^{1}	9^{2}			8	12		11					2	4	13				42
1		3	4	5	7		10^{1}	9^{3}			8^{2}	12		11			6		2		13			14	43
1			3	5	7		8^{1}	14			10^{2}	12		9					2	4	13		11^{3}	6	44
1		3	12	5	7	6	8^{1}	13			10^{2}	11^{3}		9					2	4				14	45
1		3		5	7	6^{3}	8^{1}	13			10	11^{2}		9					2	4	12			14	46

FA Cup

First Round	Wycombe W	(h)	1-2

EFL Cup

First Round (*aet*)	Coventry C	(a)	2-3

EFL Checkatrade Trophy

Southern Group A	Yeovil T	(a)	3-4
Southern Group A	Reading U21	(h)	2-2
(*Reading U21 won 4-3 on penalties*)			
Southern Group A	Bristol R	(h)	1-0

PRESTON NORTH END

FOUNDATION

North End Cricket and Rugby Club, which was formed in 1863, indulged in most sports before taking up soccer in about 1879. In 1881 they decided to stick to football to the exclusion of other sports and even a 16–0 drubbing by Blackburn Rovers in an invitation game at Deepdale, a few weeks after taking this decision, did not deter them for they immediately became affiliated to the Lancashire FA.

Deepdale Stadium, Sir Tom Finney Way, Deepdale, Preston, Lancashire PR1 6RU.

Telephone: (0344) 856 1964.

Fax: (01772) 693 366.

Ticket Office: (0344) 856 1966.

Website: www.pnefc.net

Email: enquiries@pne.co.uk

Ground Capacity: 23,404.

Record Attendance: 42,684 v Arsenal, Division 1, 23 April 1938.

Pitch Measurements: 100m × 67m (109.5yd × 73.5yd).

Chief Executive: John Kay.

Manager: Alex Neil.

First-Team Coach: Steve Thompson.

Colours: White shirts with blue trim, blue shorts, blue socks with white hoops.

Year Formed: 1880.

Turned Professional: 1885.

Club Nicknames: 'The Lilywhites', 'North End'.

Ground: 1881, Deepdale.

First Football League Game: 8 September 1888, Football League, v Burnley (h) W 5–2 – Trainer; Howarth, Holmes; Robertson, William Graham, Johnny Graham; Gordon (1), Jimmy Ross (2), Goodall, Dewhurst (2), Drummond.

Record League Victory: 10–0 v Stoke, Division 1, 14 September 1889 – Trainer; Howarth, Holmes; Kelso, Russell (1), Johnny Graham; Gordon, Jimmy Ross (2), Nick Ross (3), Thomson (2), Drummond (2).

Record Cup Victory: 26–0 v Hyde, FA Cup 1st rd, 15 October 1887 – Addision; Howarth, Nick Ross; Russell (1), Thomson (5), Johnny Graham (1); Gordon (5), Jimmy Ross (8), John Goodall (1), Dewhurst (3), Drummond (2).

Record Defeat: 0–7 v Nottingham F, Division 2, 9 April 1927; 0–7 v Blackpool, Division 1, 1 May 1948.

Most League Points (2 for a win): 61, Division 3, 1970–71.

Most League Points (3 for a win): 95, Division 2, 1999–2000.

Most League Goals: 100, Division 2, 1927–28 and Division 1, 1957–58.

Highest League Scorer in Season: Ted Harper, 37, Division 2, 1932–33.

HONOURS

League Champions: Football League 1888–89, 1889–90; Division 2 – 1903–04, 1912–13, 1950–51; Second Division – 1999–2000; Division 3 – 1970–71; Third Division – 1995–96.
Runners-up: Football League 1890–91, 1891–92; Division 1 – 1892–93, 1905–06, 1952–53, 1957–58; Division 2 – 1914–15, 1933–34; Division 4 – 1986–87.

FA Cup Winners: 1889, 1938.
Runners-up: 1888, 1922, 1937, 1954, 1964.

League Cup: 4th rd – 1963, 1966, 1972, 1981, 2003, 2017.

Double Performed: 1888–89.

sky SPORTS FACT FILE

Inside-forward Jimmy Wilson made over 150 first-team appearances for Preston North End in the seasons leading up to the First World War. He then emigrated to the Netherlands where he established a very successful sportswear firm, NV Wilson and Frankenberg. He returned to England when war broke out in 1939 and took on a senior position with Slazenger.

Most League Goals in Total Aggregate: Tom Finney, 187, 1946–60.

Most League Goals in One Match: 4, Jimmy Ross v Stoke, Division 1, 6 October 1888; 4, Nick Ross v Derby Co, Division 1, 11 January 1890; 4, George Drummond v Notts Co, Division 1, 12 December 1891; 4, Frank Becton v Notts Co, Division 1, 31 March 1893; 4, George Harrison v Grimsby T, Division 2, 3 November 1928; 4, Alex Reid v Port Vale, Division 2, 23 February 1929; 4, James McClelland v Reading, Division 2, 6 September 1930; 4, Dick Rowley v Notts Co, Division 2, 16 April 1932; 4, Ted Harper v Burnley, Division 2, 29 August 1932; 4, Ted Harper v Lincoln C, Division 2, 11 March 1933; 4, Charlie Wayman v QPR, Division 2, 25 December 1950; 4, Alex Bruce v Colchester U, Division 3, 28 February 1978; 4, Joe Garner v Crewe Alex, FL 1, 14 March 2015.

Most Capped Player: Tom Finney, 76, England.

Most League Appearances: Alan Kelly, 447, 1961–75.

Youngest League Player: Steve Doyle, 16 years 166 days v Tranmere R, 15 November 1974.

Record Transfer Fee Received: £6,000,000 from Portsmouth for David Nugent, August 2007.

Record Transfer Fee Paid: £1,500,000 to Manchester U for David Healy, December 2000.

Football League Record: 1888 Founder Member of League; 1901–04 Division 2; 1904–12 Division 1; 1912–13 Division 2; 1913–14 Division 1; 1914–15 Division 2; 1919–25 Division 1; 1925–34 Division 2; 1934–49 Division 1; 1949–51 Division 2; 1951–61 Division 1; 1961–70 Division 2; 1970–71 Division 3; 1971–74 Division 2; 1974–78 Division 3; 1978–81 Division 2; 1981–85 Division 3; 1985–87 Division 4; 1987–92 Division 3; 1992–93 Division 2; 1993–96 Division 3; 1996–2000 Division 2; 2000–04 Division 1; 2004–11 FL C; 2011–15 FL 1; 2015– FL C.

LATEST SEQUENCES

Longest Sequence of League Wins: 14, 25.12.1950 – 27.3.1951.

Longest Sequence of League Defeats: 8, 22.9.1984 – 27.10.1984.

Longest Sequence of League Draws: 6, 24.2.1979 – 20.3.1979.

Longest Sequence of Unbeaten League Matches: 23, 8.9.1888 – 14.9.1889.

Longest Sequence Without a League Win: 15, 14.4.1923 – 20.10.1923.

Successive Scoring Runs: 30 from 15.11.1952.

Successive Non-scoring Runs: 6 from 19.11.1960.

MANAGERS

Charlie Parker 1906–15
Vincent Hayes 1919–23
Jim Lawrence 1923–25
Frank Richards 1925–27
Alex Gibson 1927–31
Lincoln Hayes 1931–32
Run by committee 1932–36
Tommy Muirhead 1936–37
Run by committee 1937–49
Will Scott 1949–53
Scot Symon 1953–54
Frank Hill 1954–56
Cliff Britton 1956–61
Jimmy Milne 1961–68
Bobby Seith 1968–70
Alan Ball Snr 1970–73
Bobby Charlton 1973–75
Harry Catterick 1975–77
Nobby Stiles 1977–81
Tommy Docherty 1981
Gordon Lee 1981–83
Alan Kelly 1983–85
Tommy Booth 1985–86
Brian Kidd 1986
John McGrath 1986–90
Les Chapman 1990–92
Sam Allardyce 1992 (*Caretaker*)
John Beck 1992–94
Gary Peters 1994–98
David Moyes 1998–2002
Kelham O'Hanlon 2002 (*Caretaker*)
Craig Brown 2002–04
Billy Davies 2004–06
Paul Simpson 2006–07
Alan Irvine 2007–09
Darren Ferguson 2010
Phil Brown 2011
Graham Westley 2012–13
Simon Grayson 2013–17
Alex Neil July 2017–

TEN YEAR LEAGUE RECORD

		P	W	D	L	F	A	Pts	Pos
2007-08	FL C	46	15	11	20	50	56	56	15
2008-09	FL C	46	21	11	14	66	54	74	6
2009-10	FL C	46	13	15	18	58	73	54	17
2010-11	FL C	46	10	12	24	54	79	42	22
2011-12	FL 1	46	13	15	18	54	68	54	15
2012-13	FL 1	46	14	17	15	54	49	59	14
2013-14	FL 1	46	23	16	7	72	46	85	5
2014-15	FL 1	46	25	14	7	79	40	89	3
2015-16	FL C	46	15	17	14	45	45	62	11
2016-17	FL C	46	16	14	16	64	63	62	11

DID YOU KNOW ?

Preston North End installed an artificial surface at Deepdale in 1986 and home games were played on this until it was restored to grass for the 1994–95 season. North End's play-off second leg game against Torquay United on 18 May 1994 was the last-ever Football League game to be played on an artificial surface.

PRESTON NORTH END – SKY BET CHAMPIONSHIP 2016–17 LEAGUE RECORD

Match No.	Date	Venue	Opponents	Result		H/T Score	Lg Pos.	Goalscorers	Attendance
1	Aug 6	A	Reading	L	0-1	0-1	22		15,764
2	13	H	Fulham	L	1-2	0-1	22	Robinson [71]	10,809
3	16	H	Derby Co	L	0-1	0-0	23		10,628
4	20	A	QPR	W	2-0	1-0	22	Beckford [21], Onuoha (og) [52]	13,307
5	27	A	Ipswich T	L	0-1	0-1	23		15,296
6	Sept 10	H	Barnsley	L	1-2	0-1	23	McGeady [64]	11,852
7	13	H	Cardiff C	W	3-0	2-0	18	Clarke [36], Robinson [41], Hugill [88]	9216
8	17	A	Brentford	L	0-5	0-1	19		9920
9	23	H	Wigan Ath	W	1-0	1-0	18	Hugill [7]	13,077
10	27	A	Birmingham C	D	2-2	2-1	19	Baptiste [19], Johnson [35]	15,779
11	Oct 1	H	Aston Villa	W	2-0	2-0	17	Pearson [5], Hugill [39]	17,696
12	15	A	Brighton & HA	D	2-2	1-0	18	Hugill [10], Makienok Christoffersen [90]	27,606
13	19	H	Huddersfield T	W	3-1	2-0	13	Clarke [6], Baptiste [42], Gallagher [53]	12,862
14	22	A	Norwich C	W	1-0	0-0	8	Baptiste [75]	26,239
15	29	H	Newcastle U	L	1-2	0-0	13	Lascelles (og) [90]	20,724
16	Nov 5	A	Rotherham U	W	3-1	2-0	11	Hugill [22], Robinson [27], Vermijl [81]	10,013
17	19	H	Wolverhampton W	D	0-0	0-0	11		12,683
18	26	H	Burton Alb	D	1-1	1-1	11	Robinson [45]	10,696
19	Dec 3	A	Sheffield W	L	1-2	0-1	14	Doyle [82]	24,843
20	10	H	Blackburn R	W	3-2	2-1	12	Johnson 2 (1 pen) [18, 31 (p)], Robinson [80]	14,527
21	14	A	Nottingham F	D	1-1	1-0	11	Makienok Christoffersen [45]	15,864
22	17	A	Bristol C	W	2-1	1-0	11	Makienok Christoffersen [21], Johnson [85]	18,619
23	26	H	Leeds U	L	1-4	1-3	13	Vermijl [27]	21,255
24	31	H	Sheffield W	D	1-1	0-0	13	Cunningham [77]	14,802
25	Jan 2	A	Burton Alb	W	1-0	1-0	11	Clarke [45]	5144
26	14	H	Brighton & HA	W	2-0	1-0	9	Huntington [13], Robinson [53]	11,391
27	21	A	Aston Villa	D	2-2	0-2	8	Hugill 2 [64, 76]	32,415
28	28	H	Ipswich T	D	1-1	0-1	10	Hugill [89]	10,656
29	31	A	Cardiff C	L	0-2	0-2	10		13,894
30	Feb 4	A	Barnsley	D	0-0	0-0	11		12,590
31	11	H	Brentford	W	4-2	1-1	11	McGeady 2 [18, 75], Robinson [52], Horgan [77]	10,130
32	14	H	Birmingham C	W	2-1	1-0	10	Robinson [8], Hugill [78]	10,233
33	18	A	Wigan Ath	D	0-0	0-0	10		15,117
34	25	H	QPR	W	2-1	1-1	8	McGeady [45], Hugill [71]	10,848
35	Mar 4	A	Fulham	L	1-3	0-1	9	Barkhuizen [68]	20,205
36	7	A	Derby Co	D	1-1	0-0	9	Barkhuizen [90]	26,301
37	11	H	Reading	W	3-0	2-0	8	Barkhuizen 2 [31, 49], Horgan [40]	10,787
38	18	A	Blackburn R	D	2-2	1-1	8	Barkhuizen [13], McGeady [90]	18,435
39	Apr 1	H	Nottingham F	D	1-1	0-1	8	McGeady [52]	12,459
40	4	H	Bristol C	W	5-0	1-0	8	Barkhuizen [25], McGeady (pen) [47], Clarke [53], Robinson 2 [64, 68]	10,224
41	8	A	Leeds U	L	0-3	0-2	9		31,851
42	14	A	Huddersfield T	L	2-3	1-1	9	McGeady [23], Hugill [79]	21,254
43	17	H	Norwich C	L	1-3	0-2	10	Spurr [67]	11,373
44	24	A	Newcastle U	L	1-4	1-2	11	Hugill [14]	50,212
45	29	H	Rotherham U	D	1-1	1-1	11	May [41]	11,032
46	May 7	A	Wolverhampton W	L	0-1	0-1	11		20,163

Final League Position: 11

GOALSCORERS

League (64): Hugill 12, Robinson 10, McGeady 8 (1 pen), Barkhuizen 6, Clarke 4, Johnson 4 (1 pen), Baptiste 3, Makienok Christoffersen 3, Horgan 2, Vermijl 2, Beckford 1, Cunningham 1, Doyle 1, Gallagher 1, Huntington 1, May 1, Pearson 1, Spurr 1, own goals 2.
FA Cup (1): Robinson 1.
EFL Cup (6): Makienok 3, Doyle 2, Hugill 1.

Lindegaard A 8	Grimshaw L 3 + 2	Clarke T 42	Huntington P 26 + 7	Wright B 18	Cunningham G 40	Gallagher P 28 + 3	Pringle B 7 + 3	Johnson D 30 + 10	Beckford J 4 + 14	Garner J 2	Browne A 21 + 10	Humphrey C 4 + 6	Hugill J 35 + 9	Doyle E 6 + 5	Robinson C 34 + 8	Makienok Christoffersen S 7 + 18	Spurr T 11 + 6	Welsh J 6	Vermijl M 13 + 5	Baptiste A 23 + 1	McGeady A 32 + 2	Maxwell C 38	Pearson B 29 + 2	Horgan D 10 + 9	Barkhuizen T 12 + 5	Browning T 8	May S 2 + 2	Boyle A 7	*Match No.*
1	2^{1}	3^{3}	4	5	6	7	8	9	10	11^{2}	12	13	14																1
1	2^{1}	3		4	5	9	6^{3}	8	12	11	7	14		10^{2}	13														2
1	2^{2}	3		4	5	8	6		11^{1}		7	14	12	10^{3}	9	13													3
1		3	14	4	5	7^{1}		9	11^{2}		13	2^{3}	12		10		6	8											4
1	14	3		4	5	7		9^{3}	10^{2}			2	12	13	11		6^{1}	8											5
1		3			5	9^{1}		13					12	11^{2}	10	14	6^{3}	8	2	4	7								6
1		3			5	7		14			8	12	10^{1}	11^{2}	6^{3}	13			2	4	9								7
1		3			5	7		12			8^{3}	14	11^{2}	10^{1}	9	13			2	4	6								8
		3		4	5	7^{2}		12			8		11		9	10^{1}				2	6	1	13						9
		4	13	5	6			7			12	2^{3}	10		11			8^{2}		3	14	1	9^{1}						10
		3	12	4	5			9			13		11		10			8		2	6^{1}	1	7^{2}						11
		2	3			13	12	7^{2}				5^{3}	10		11^{1}	14	9	8		4		1	6						12
		3		4	5	6^{2}	9^{1}	8				12	10^{3}	13	11	14				2		1	7						13
		3	14	4	5	9^{2}	10^{3}	8			12		11		7^{1}		13			2		1	6						14
		3		4	5	9	6^{1}	8	12				11^{2}		10^{3}	13			14	2		1	7						15
		3		4	5	7	9^{1}	8	14				11^{3}		10	12			13	2	6^{2}	1							16
		3		4	5	6^{1}		7					11		10^{2}	12			13	2	8	1	9						17
		3		4	5			8					11^{1}	13	10	12			6^{2}	2	9	1	7						18
		3		4	5			6	13■		8^{2}		10	14■	11				12	2^{1}	9^{3}	1	7						19
		3	14	4	5		12	7					10^{3}		9^{1}	11	13		6^{2}	2		1	8						20
		4	14	5	6		12	9			7		13		10^{1}	11			2^{3}	3		1	8^{2}						21
		3	4		5			8			9		13		7^{1}	11			12	2	10^{2}	1	6						22
		3	4		5			7^{3}	13■		8		12	14	9^{2}	11^{1}			6	2		1	10						23
		3	4		5	6		8			14		12		10^{2}	11^{3}	13			2	9^{1}	1	7						24
		2	4	3	5	13		8			6		10^{3}	9^{2}	11^{1}	14					12	1	7						25
	14	3	4		5	7					8		11		10^{3}		13		2		9^{1}	1		6^{2}	12				26
		3	4			6		8	13		7		11^{1}		10^{2}		5		2		9	1		12					27
		3	4			6^{1}		8	13				10		11^{3}	14	5		2^{2}		9	1	7	12					28
		3	4		5	6		8^{2}	12		14		11		13						10	1	7^{1}	9^{3}		2			29
		3	4		5	9^{1}			13		7		10		12	11^{2}					6	1	8			2			30
		3	4		5			13			8		11		10^{1}						9^{3}	1	7	6^{2}	12	2	14		31
		3	4		5			13			7		11^{1}		10^{3}	14					9^{2}	1	8	6	12	2			32
		3	4		5				12		7		11^{1}		10^{3}	13					9	1	8	6^{2}	14	2			33
		2	3		8			7			6		10		11		4				9	1		5^{1}	12				34
		3	4		2			8			7^{3}		11^{2}		12		5				10	1	13	9^{1}	6		14		35
		2	4		5	8^{2}		13					11^{1}		10^{3}	14					9	1	7	12	6			3	36
		2	4		5			7	14		12		11^{1}		13						9	1	8	6^{2}	10^{3}			3	37
		2	4		5	13		7^{1}					11^{2}		12	14					9	1	8	6^{3}	10			3	38
		2	4		5	7^{3}					14		11		12					13	9	1	8	6^{2}	10			3^{1}	39
		2	4		5	7		12	14				11		10					3	9^{3}	1	8^{2}	13	6^{1}				40
		2	3		8	6^{3}		12	13						11^{2}	14			5^{1}	4■	9	1	7		10				41
		3^{3}	4		5	8^{1}		9			14		11				12		2^{2}		6	1	7	13	10				42
			4		5^{1}	7		14			8		11		10^{2}		12		2^{3}		9	1		13	6			3	43
			4			7■		8			6		10				5				9^{1}	1		12	11	2		3	44
			4					7			8		10^{1}		12	14	5			3	9	1		13	6^{2}	2	11^{3}		45
			12			6			13				10^{3}				8			4	9	1	7	14	5^{2}	2^{1}	11	3	46

FA Cup

Third Round	Arsenal	(h)	1-2

EFL Cup

First Round	Hartlepool U	(h)	1-0
Second Round	Oldham Ath	(h)	2-0
Third Round (*aet*)	Bournemouth	(a)	3-2
Fourth Round	Newcastle U	(a)	0-6

QUEENS PARK RANGERS

FOUNDATION

There is an element of doubt about the date of the foundation of this club, but it is believed that in either 1885 or 1886 it was formed through the amalgamation of Christchurch Rangers and St Jude's Institute FC. The leading light was George Wodehouse, whose family maintained a connection with the club until comparatively recent times. Most of the players came from the Queen's Park district so this name was adopted after a year as St Jude's Institute.

Loftus Road Stadium, South Africa Road, Shepherds Bush, London W12 7PJ.

Telephone: (020) 8743 0262.

Fax: (020) 8749 0994.

Ticket Office: (08444) 777 007.

Website: www.qpr.co.uk

Email: customerservices@qpr.co.uk

Ground Capacity: 18,238.

Record Attendance: 41,097 v Leeds U, FA Cup 3rd rd, 9 January 1932 (at White City); 35,353 v Leeds U, Division 1, 27 April 1974 (at Loftus Road).

Pitch Measurements: 100m × 66m (109yd × 72yd).

Co-Chairmen: Tony Fernandes and Ruben Gnanalingham.

Chief Executive: Lee Hoos.

Manager: Ian Holloway.

Assistant Manager: Marc Bircham.

Colours: Blue and white hooped shirts with red trim, white shorts with blue trim, white socks with red and blue trim.

Year Formed: 1885* (*see Foundation*).

Turned Professional: 1898.

Previous Name: 1885, St Jude's; 1887, Queens Park Rangers. ***Club Nicknames:*** 'Rangers', 'The Hoops', 'R's'.

Grounds: 1885* (*see Foundation*), Welford's Fields; 1888–99, London Scottish Ground, Brondesbury, Home Farm, Kensal Rise Green, Gun Club Wormwood Scrubs, Kilburn Cricket Ground; 1899, Kensal Rise Athletic Ground; 1901, Latimer Road, Notting Hill; 1904, Agricultural Society, Park Royal; 1907, Park Royal Ground; 1917, Loftus Road; 1931, White City; 1933, Loftus Road; 1962, White City; 1963, Loftus Road.

First Football League Game: 28 August 1920, Division 3, v Watford (h) L 1–2 – Price; Blackman, Wingrove; McGovern, Grant, O'Brien; Faulkner, Birch (1), Smith, Gregory, Middlemiss.

Record League Victory: 9–2 v Tranmere R, Division 3, 3 December 1960 – Drinkwater; Woods, Ingham; Keen, Rutter, Angell; Lazarus (2), Bedford (2), Evans (2), Andrews (1), Clark (2).

Record Cup Victory: 8–1 v Bristol R (a), FA Cup 1st rd, 27 November 1937 – Gilfillan; Smith, Jefferson; Lowe, James, March; Cape, Mallett, Cheetham (3), Fitzgerald (3) Bott (2). 8–1 v Crewe Alex, Milk Cup 1st rd, 3 October 1983 – Hucker; Neill, Dawes, Waddock (1), McDonald (1), Fenwick, Micklewhite (1), Stewart (1), Allen (1), Stainrod (3), Gregory.

HONOURS

League Champions: FL C – 2010–11; Division 2 – 1982–83; Division 3 – 1966–67; Division 3S – 1947–48.
Runners-up: Division 1 – 1975–76; Division 2 – 1967–68, 1972–73; Second Division – 2003–04; Division 3S – 1946–47.

FA Cup: *Runners-up:* 1982.

League Cup Winners: 1967.
Runners-up: 1986.

European Competitions
UEFA Cup: 1976–77 (*qf*), 1984–85.

sky SPORTS FACT FILE

Brian Bedford was leading scorer for Queens Park Rangers in each of the six seasons he played for the club after signing in July 1959. He scored over 20 goals each season and netted a total of 180 goals in 284 appearances. His tally included 14 hat-tricks. In the 1980s he returned to Loftus Road as stadium manager serving the club for a further five years.

Record Defeat: 1–8 v Mansfield T, Division 3, 15 March 1965. 1–8 v Manchester U, Division 1, 19 March 1969.

Most League Points (2 for a win): 67, Division 3, 1966–67.

Most League Points (3 for a win): 88, FL C, 2010–11.

Most League Goals: 111, Division 3, 1961–62.

Highest League Scorer in Season: George Goddard, 37, Division 3 (S), 1929–30.

Most League Goals in Total Aggregate: George Goddard, 174, 1926–34.

Most League Goals in One Match: 4, George Goddard v Merthyr T, Division 3 (S), 9 March 1929; 4, George Goddard v Swindon T, Division 3 (S), 12 April 1930; 4, George Goddard v Exeter C, Division 3 (S), 20 December 1930; 4, George Goddard v Watford, Division 3 (S), 19 September 1931; 4, Tom Cheetham v Aldershot, Division 3 (S), 14 September 1935; 4, Tom Cheetham v Aldershot, Division 3 (S), 12 November 1938.

Most Capped Player: Alan McDonald, 52, Northern Ireland.

Most League Appearances: Tony Ingham, 514, 1950–63.

Youngest League Player: Frank Sibley, 16 years 97 days v Bristol C, 10 March 1964.

Record Transfer Fee Received: £12,000,000 from Anzhi Makhachkala for Chris Samba, July 2013.

Record Transfer Fee Paid: £12,500,000 to Anzhi Makhachkala for Chris Samba, January 2013.

Football League Record: 1920 Original Members of Division 3; 1921–48 Division 3 (S); 1948–52 Division 2; 1952–58 Division 3 (S); 1958–67 Division 3; 1967–68 Division 2; 1968–69 Division 1; 1969–73 Division 2; 1973–79 Division 1; 1979–83 Division 2; 1983–92 Division 1; 1992–96 FA Premier League; 1996–2001 Division 1; 2001–04 Division 2; 2004–11 FL C; 2011–13 FA Premier League; 2013–14 FL C; 2014–15 FA Premier League; 2015– FL C.

LATEST SEQUENCES

Longest Sequence of League Wins: 8, 7.11.1931 – 28.12.1931.

Longest Sequence of League Defeats: 9, 25.2.1969 – 5.4.1969.

Longest Sequence of League Draws: 6, 29.1.2000 – 5.3.2000.

Longest Sequence of Unbeaten League Matches: 20, 11.3.1972 – 23.9.1972.

Longest Sequence Without a League Win: 20, 7.12.1968 – 7.4.1969.

Successive Scoring Runs: 33 from 9.12.1961.

Successive Non-scoring Runs: 6 from 18.3.1939.

MANAGERS

James Cowan 1906–13
Jimmy Howie 1913–20
Ned Liddell 1920–24
Will Wood 1924–25
(had been Secretary since 1903)
Bob Hewison 1925–31
John Bowman 1931
Archie Mitchell 1931–33
Mick O'Brien 1933–35
Billy Birrell 1935–39
Ted Vizard 1939–44
Dave Mangnall 1944–52
Jack Taylor 1952–59
Alec Stock 1959–65
(General Manager to 1968)
Bill Dodgin Jnr 1968
Tommy Docherty 1968
Les Allen 1968–71
Gordon Jago 1971–74
Dave Sexton 1974–77
Frank Sibley 1977–78
Steve Burtenshaw 1978–79
Tommy Docherty 1979–80
Terry Venables 1980–84
Gordon Jago 1984
Alan Mullery 1984
Frank Sibley 1984–85
Jim Smith 1985–88
Trevor Francis 1988–89
Don Howe 1989–91
Gerry Francis 1991–94
Ray Wilkins 1994–96
Stewart Houston 1996–97
Ray Harford 1997–98
Gerry Francis 1998–2001
Ian Holloway 2001–06
Gary Waddock 2006
John Gregory 2006–07
Luigi Di Canio 2007–08
Iain Dowie 2008
Paulo Sousa 2008–09
Jim Magilton 2009
Paul Hart 2009–10
Neil Warnock 2010–12
Mark Hughes 2012
Harry Redknapp 2012–15
Chris Ramsey 2015
Jimmy Floyd Hasselbaink 2015–16
Ian Holloway November 2016–

TEN YEAR LEAGUE RECORD

		P	W	D	L	F	A	Pts	Pos
2007-08	FL C	46	14	16	16	60	66	58	14
2008-09	FL C	46	15	16	15	42	44	61	11
2009-10	FL C	46	14	15	17	58	65	57	13
2010-11	FL C	46	24	16	6	71	32	88	1
2011-12	PR Lge	38	10	7	21	43	66	37	17
2012-13	PR Lge	38	4	13	21	30	60	25	20
2013-14	FL C	46	23	11	12	60	44	80	4
2014-15	PR Lge	38	8	6	24	42	73	30	20
2015-16	FL C	46	14	18	14	54	54	60	12
2016-17	FL C	46	15	8	23	52	66	53	18

DID YOU KNOW ?

Shortly after winning promotion to the Second Division in 1948 Queens Park Rangers purchased the freehold of their Loftus Road ground plus 39 houses in adjoining streets for the total sum of £26,250. The club funded the deal through a share issue.

QUEENS PARK RANGERS – SKY BET CHAMPIONSHIP 2016–17 LEAGUE RECORD

Match No.	Date	Venue	Opponents	Result	H/T Score	Lg Pos.	Goalscorers	Attendance
1	Aug 7	H	Leeds U	W 3-0	1-0	2	Onuoha 4, Chery (pen) 73, Polter 90	16,764
2	14	A	Cardiff C	W 2-0	0-0	1	Caulker 76, Chery (pen) 85	15,869
3	17	A	Barnsley	L 2-3	0-1	5	Chery (pen) 47, Polter (pen) 74	11,613
4	20	H	Preston NE	L 0-2	0-1	6		13,307
5	27	A	Wigan Ath	W 1-0	0-0	5	Onuoha 48	10,606
6	Sept 10	H	Blackburn R	D 1-1	0-0	7	Chery 65	13,210
7	13	H	Newcastle U	L 0-6	0-2	13		17,404
8	17	A	Huddersfield T	L 1-2	0-1	16	Sylla 76	20,595
9	24	H	Birmingham C	D 1-1	1-1	16	Caulker 39	13,693
10	27	A	Burton Alb	D 1-1	0-0	16	Polter 70	3725
11	Oct 1	A	Fulham	W 2-1	1-0	12	Washington 20, Sylla 87	19,609
12	15	H	Reading	D 1-1	1-1	14	Wszolek 14	15,048
13	18	H	Bristol C	W 1-0	0-0	9	Sylla 75	12,552
14	22	A	Sheffield W	L 0-1	0-1	13		25,903
15	28	H	Brentford	L 0-2	0-1	13		16,888
16	Nov 5	A	Nottingham F	D 1-1	0-1	16	Sylla 85	20,043
17	19	H	Norwich C	W 2-1	2-0	13	Washington 21, Polter 27	17,187
18	26	A	Ipswich T	L 0-3	0-1	15		16,510
19	Dec 1	H	Wolverhampton W	L 1-2	0-0	15	Lynch 90	12,222
20	10	A	Rotherham U	L 0-1	0-1	18		8704
21	14	H	Derby Co	L 0-1	0-0	18		12,371
22	18	H	Aston Villa	L 0-1	0-0	19		16,285
23	27	A	Brighton & HA	L 0-3	0-1	20		30,176
24	31	A	Wolverhampton W	W 2-1	0-0	19	Sylla 53, Wszolek 87	21,132
25	Jan 2	H	Ipswich T	W 2-1	1-0	17	Sylla 30, Wszolek 83	15,136
26	12	A	Reading	W 1-0	1-0	15	Mackie 28	12,655
27	21	H	Fulham	D 1-1	1-0	17	Manning 25	17,025
28	28	H	Burton Alb	L 1-2	0-1	17	Washington 63	12,116
29	Feb 1	A	Newcastle U	D 2-2	1-1	18	Washington 44, Clark (og) 90	47,907
30	4	A	Blackburn R	L 0-1	0-0	18		10,846
31	11	H	Huddersfield T	L 1-2	0-2	19	Freeman 60	14,044
32	18	A	Birmingham C	W 4-1	1-0	16	Smith 18, Washington 47, Sylla 84, Ngbakoto 88	20,265
33	21	H	Wigan Ath	W 2-1	1-1	15	Smith 4, Washington 60	12,101
34	25	A	Preston NE	L 1-2	1-1	16	LuaLua 36	10,848
35	Mar 4	H	Cardiff C	W 2-1	0-1	16	Ngbakoto 62, Richards (og) 83	15,103
36	7	H	Barnsley	W 2-1	1-0	14	Sylla 7, MacDonald (og) 66	11,635
37	11	A	Leeds U	D 0-0	0-0	15		30,870
38	18	H	Rotherham U	W 5-1	2-1	15	Smith 5, Freeman 15, Ngbakoto (pen) 49, Luongo 57, Onuoha 90	13,383
39	31	A	Derby Co	L 0-1	0-0	15		27,690
40	Apr 4	A	Aston Villa	L 0-1	0-1	15		27,154
41	7	H	Brighton & HA	L 1-2	0-0	16	Smith 74	16,503
42	14	A	Bristol C	L 1-2	0-2	16	Sylla 90	20,404
43	17	H	Sheffield W	L 1-2	1-2	17	Sylla 20	15,708
44	22	A	Brentford	L 1-3	0-1	19	Lynch 62	11,888
45	29	H	Nottingham F	W 2-0	0-0	18	Washington 49, Lynch 60	16,474
46	May 7	A	Norwich C	L 0-4	0-1	18		27,005

Final League Position: 18

GOALSCORERS

League (52): Sylla 10, Washington 7, Chery 4 (3 pens), Polter 4 (1 pen), Smith 4, Lynch 3, Ngbakoto 3 (1 pen), Onuoha 3, Wszolek 3, Caulker 2, Freeman 2, LuaLua 1, Luongo 1, Mackie 1, Manning 1, own goals 3.
FA Cup (1): Bidwell 1 (1 pen).
EFL Cup (5): Sandro 3, Ngbakoto 1, Washington 1.

Smithies A 46	Onuoha N 43 + 1	Hall G 34	Caulker S 12 + 1	Bidwell J 36	Henry K 13 + 1	Luongo M 35	Gladwin B 3 + 4	Chery T 22	Shodipo O 5 + 6	Potter S 12 + 8	Cousins J 17 + 1	El Khayati A 1 + 5	Perch J 29 + 3	Ngbakoto Y 13 + 13	Washington C 26 + 14	Borysiuk A 8 + 3	Sylla I 14 + 18	Wszolek P 23 + 6	Lynch J 28 + 2	Hamalainen N 1 + 2	Robinson J 7	Sandro 3 + 3	Mackie J 11 + 7	Kakay O — + 1	Manning R 17 + 1	Furlong D 13 + 1	LuaLua K 2 + 9	Doughty M 2 + 2	Comley B — + 1	Freeman L 12 + 4	Goss S 3 + 3	Smith M 13 + 3	Morrison R 1 + 4	Petrasso M 1 + 1	Bowler J — + 1	Grego-Cox R — + 1	Match No.
1	2	3	4	5	6	7	8^{1}	9^{3}	10^{2}	11	12	13	14																								1
1	2	4	3	5	6	7	10^{2}	9^{1}		11^{3}	8		14	12	13																						2
1	2	4▪	3	5	6	7		9		11	8^{1}	12		10^{2}	13																						3
1	3		4	5	6^{2}	7		9		11	8	13	2	10^{1}	12																						4
1	3	4		5	6	7		9^{1}		11	8		2	10		12																					5
1	3	4		5	7			9	8	11^{1}	6	10^{2}	2		12		13																				6
1	2	4	3^{2}	5	8			10			7		6^{1}	9^{3}	11		13	12	14																		7
1	2	4	3	5	6^{1}	7		9	10^{3}	13	8				11^{2}	12	14																				8
1	2	4	3	5		7		9	10^{2}	13	8^{1}					6	11	12																			9
1	2	4	3	5^{1}	6	7		9		12					11	8^{2}		10	13																		10
1	2	4	3		6	7		9	13	11^{3}					10		12	8^{2}	5^{1}	14																	11
1	3	4^{1}	12		7			9	10^{2}	11			2		13	6	14	8^{3}	5																		12
1	3		4			7	13	9		14	8^{1}		2		10	6	11^{2}		5^{3}	12																	13
1	3		4			7	9^{2}	8	14	12			2		10	6^{3}	11^{1}	13		5																	14
1	3		4			7	14	9		13	8		2		10^{1}	6^{2}	11	12			5^{3}																15
1	3	4			7▪			9	12	11	6	14	2		10^{1}		13	8^{2}			5^{3}																16
1	3	6				7^{2}		8	13	11^{3}	9		2		10		14		4		5^{1}	12															17
1	2	3		9	8			6		11^{1}	7^{2}		5^{3}	14	10		12		4			13															18
1	3	7			13	9		8		10^{3}			2▪	12	11^{1}		14		4		5	6^{2}															19
1	2	3		5		7	13	8^{1}		12	9			10^{2}	11			14	4			6^{3}															20
1	3	8		5		7	12	10^{2}	14	13	6^{1}		2	9	11^{3}				4																		21
1	3	8		5		7		10^{3}	13				2	9	11^{2}		12	6^{1}	4				14														22
1	3▪	4		5		7					6^{3}		2	11^{1}		8^{2}	10	9				13	12	14													23
1		3		5									2	9^{2}	13	12	11	8	4			6^{1}	10		7												24
1	13	3		5							9	14	2		12	6^{1}	11^{3}	8	4				10		7^{2}												25
1	3	7		5		6											10^{3}	9	4				11^{2}		8^{1}	2	12	13	14								26
1	3	7^{2}		5		6							14		12		10^{3}	9	4				11^{1}		8	2	13										27
1	3	7^{2}		5^{3}		6									12		10	9	4				14		13	2	11	8^{1}									28
1	2			9		7							3		10			6	4				11^{1}		8^{2}	5^{3}	13			12	14						29
1	2			9		6^{3}							3		10			7	4				11^{2}		8	5^{1}	14					12	13				30
1	2	3		8^{2}		6							4	14	11			5^{3}					9^{1}		7		12			13		10					31
1	2	3		8										13	11^{3}		12	9^{2}	4						6	5	14			7		10^{1}					32
1	2	3^{1}		8										13	10^{3}		14	9	4						6	5	12			7		11^{2}					33
1	2			8									3	13			12	9	4				14		6	5^{2}	10^{3}			7▪		11^{1}					34
1	2	3		8		6^{2}							5	12	10			14	4				9^{1}								7^{3}	11	13				35
1	3	2		8		6							5^{3}	10^{1}	13		11	9^{2}							4	12				7			14				36
1	2	3		8		6								13	10^{2}		12	9^{1}	4				14			5				7		11^{3}					37
1	2	3		8		6^{2}								10	12		9		4							5				7^{3}	14	11^{1}	13				38
1	2	3		8									4	13	10^{1}		14	9^{2}							6	5^{3}				7	12	11					39
1	3	4		5		6								9	13		10^{3}						11			2^{1}				7	8^{2}	12		14			40
1	2	3				6							5	13	10		14		4^{2}		8^{3}				7					12		11	9^{1}				41
1	3			5		6								11^{3}	12		13	9	4				14		7	2^{1}				8		10^{2}					42
1				4		7							2		13		11		3		9^{2}		10		8^{1}		12			6		14		5^{3}			43
1	3			5		6							2	14	11^{2}		13		4				9^{3}				12			8	7^{1}	10					44
1	3			5		6							2	13	11^{2}			9	4				12		7			14		8^{1}		10^{3}					45
1	3					7							2		10^{1}			6	4		5^{2}				9			8		12		11^{3}			13	14	46

FA Cup

Third Round	Blackburn R	(h)	1-2

EFL Cup

First Round	Swindon T	(h)	2-2
(aet; QPR won 4-2 on penalties)			
Second Round	Rochdale	(h)	2-1
Third Round	Sunderland	(h)	1-2

READING

FOUNDATION

Reading was formed as far back as 1871 at a public meeting held at the Bridge Street Rooms. They first entered the FA Cup as early as 1877 when they amalgamated with the Reading Hornets. The club was further strengthened in 1889 when Earley FC joined them. They were the first winners of the Berks & Bucks Cup in 1878–79.

Madejski Stadium, Junction 11, M4, Reading, Berkshire RG2 0FL.

Telephone: (0118) 968 1100.

Fax: (0118) 968 1101.

Ticket Office: (0118) 968 1313.

Website: www.readingfc.co.uk

Email: customerservice@readingfc.co.uk

Ground Capacity: 24,162.

Record Attendance: 33,042 v Brentford, FA Cup 5th rd, 19 February 1927 (at Elm Park); 24,184 v Everton, FA Premier League, 17 November 2012 (at Madejski Stadium).

Pitch Measurements: 105m × 68m (115yd × 74.5yd).

Co-Chairman: Sir John Madejski.

Co-Chairwoman: Khunying Sasima Srivikorn.

Chief Executive: Nigel Howe.

Manager: Jaap Stam.

Assistant Managers: Andries Ulderink and Said Bakkati.

Colours: Blue and white hooped shirts, blue shorts with white trim, white socks with blue hoops.

Year Formed: 1871.

Turned Professional: 1895.

Club Nickname: 'The Royals'.

Grounds: 1871, Reading Recreation; Reading Cricket Ground; 1882, Coley Park; 1889, Caversham Cricket Ground; 1896, Elm Park; 1998, Madejski Stadium.

First Football League Game: 28 August 1920, Division 3, v Newport Co (a) W 1–0 – Crawford; Smith, Horler; Christie, Mavin, Getgood; Spence, Weston, Yarnell, Bailey (1), Andrews.

Record League Victory: 10–2 v Crystal Palace, Division 3 (S), 4 September 1946 – Groves; Glidden, Gulliver; McKenna, Ratcliffe, Young; Chitty, Maurice Edelston (3), McPhee (4), Barney (1), Deverell (2).

Record Cup Victory: 6–0 v Leyton, FA Cup 2nd rd, 12 December 1925 – Duckworth; Eggo, McConnell; Wilson, Messer, Evans; Smith (2), Braithwaite (1), Davey (1), Tinsley, Robson (2).

Record Defeat: 0–18 v Preston NE, FA Cup 1st rd, 1893–94.

HONOURS

League Champions: FL C – 2005–06, 2011–12; Second Division – 1993–94; Division 3 – 1985–86; Division 3S – 1925–26; Division 4 – 1978–79.
Runners-up: First Division – 1994–95; Second Division – 2001–02; Division 3S – 1931–32, 1934–35, 1948–49, 1951–52.

FA Cup: semi-final – 1927, 2015.

League Cup: 5th rd – 1996, 1998.

Full Members' Cup Winners: 1988.

sky SPORTS FACT FILE

The floodlights at Elm Park were officially opened for the visit of Racing Club de Paris on 6 October 1954. The Royals won 3-0 in front of a crowd of 12,789. The second half of the game was shown live on BBC television, for which the club were paid the sum of £175.

Most League Points (2 for a win): 65, Division 4, 1978–79.

Most League Points (3 for a win): 106, Championship, 2005–06 (Football League Record).

Most League Goals: 112, Division 3 (S), 1951–52.

Highest League Scorer in Season: Ronnie Blackman, 39, Division 3 (S), 1951–52.

Most League Goals in Total Aggregate: Ronnie Blackman, 158, 1947–54.

Most League Goals in One Match: 6, Arthur Bacon v Stoke C, Division 2, 3 April 1931.

Most Capped Player: Chris Gunter, 42 (79) Wales.

Most League Appearances: Martin Hicks, 500, 1978–91.

Youngest League Player: Peter Castle, 16 years 49 days v Watford, 30 April 2003.

Record Transfer Fee Received: £7,000,000 from TSG 1899 Hoffenheim for Gylfi Sigurdsson, August 2010.

Record Transfer Fee Paid: £2,500,000 to Nantes for Emerse Fae, August 2007.

Football League Record: 1920 Original Member of Division 3; 1921–26 Division 3 (S); 1926–31 Division 2; 1931–58 Division 3 (S); 1958–71 Division 3; 1971–76 Division 4; 1976–77 Division 3; 1977–79 Division 4; 1979–83 Division 3; 1983–84 Division 4; 1984–86 Division 3; 1986–88 Division 2; 1988–92 Division 3; 1992–94 Division 2; 1994–98 Division 1; 1998–2002 Division 2; 2002–04 Division 1; 2004–06 FL C; 2006–08 FA Premier League; 2008–12 FL C; 2012–13 FA Premier League; 2013– FL C.

MANAGERS

Thomas Sefton 1897–1901
(Secretary-Manager)
James Sharp 1901–02
Harry Matthews 1902–20
Harry Marshall 1920–22
Arthur Chadwick 1923–25
H. S. Bray 1925–26
(Secretary only since 1922 and 1926–35)
Andrew Wylie 1926–31
Joe Smith 1931–35
Billy Butler 1935–39
John Cochrane 1939
Joe Edelston 1939–47
Ted Drake 1947–52
Jack Smith 1952–55
Harry Johnston 1955–63
Roy Bentley 1963–69
Jack Mansell 1969–71
Charlie Hurley 1972–77
Maurice Evans 1977–84
Ian Branfoot 1984–89
Ian Porterfield 1989–91
Mark McGhee 1991–94
Jimmy Quinn and Mick Gooding 1994–97
Terry Bullivant 1997–98
Tommy Burns 1998–99
Alan Pardew 1999–2003
Steve Coppell 2003–09
Brendan Rodgers 2009
Brian McDermott 2009–13
Nigel Adkins 2013–14
Steve Clarke 2014–15
Brian McDermott 2015–16
Jaap Stam June 2016–

LATEST SEQUENCES

Longest Sequence of League Wins: 13, 17.8.1985 – 19.10.1985.

Longest Sequence of League Defeats: 8, 29.12.2007 – 24.2.2008.

Longest Sequence of League Draws: 6, 23.3.2002 – 20.4.2002.

Longest Sequence of Unbeaten League Matches: 33, 9.8.2005 – 14.2.2006.

Longest Sequence Without a League Win: 14, 30.4.1927 – 29.10.1927.

Successive Scoring Runs: 32 from 1.10.1932.

Successive Non-scoring Runs: 6 from 29.3.2008.

TEN YEAR LEAGUE RECORD

		P	W	D	L	F	A	Pts	Pos
2007-08	PR Lge	38	10	6	22	41	66	36	18
2008-09	FL C	46	21	14	11	72	40	77	4
2009-10	FL C	46	17	12	17	68	63	63	9
2010-11	FL C	46	20	17	9	77	51	77	5
2011-12	FL C	46	27	8	11	69	41	89	1
2012-13	PR Lge	38	6	10	22	43	73	28	19
2013-14	FL C	46	19	14	13	70	56	71	7
2014-15	FL C	46	13	11	22	48	69	50	19
2015-16	FL C	46	13	13	20	52	59	52	17
2016-17	FL C	46	26	7	13	68	64	85	3

DID YOU KNOW ?

Reading moved to Elm Park in 1896, taking the ground on a ten-year lease with an option to buy when this ended. The Royals subsequently purchased the ground in the summer of 1906 for the agreed sum of £3,200 and stayed there until 1998.

READING – SKY BET CHAMPIONSHIP 2016–17 LEAGUE RECORD

Match No.	Date	Venue	Opponents	Result		H/T Score	Lg Pos.	Goalscorers	Attendance
1	Aug 6	H	Preston NE	W	1-0	1-0	7	Swift ^{35}	15,764
2	13	A	Wolverhampton W	L	0-2	0-1	15		20,425
3	17	A	Newcastle U	L	1-4	1-1	20	McCleary (pen) ^{45}	48,209
4	20	H	Brighton & HA	D	2-2	1-1	20	Swift ^{2}, McShane ^{59}	16,781
5	27	A	Cardiff C	W	1-0	0-0	12	Kermorgant ^{89}	15,013
6	Sept 9	H	Ipswich T	W	2-1	1-0	3	McCleary (pen) ^{45}, Williams (pen) ^{90}	15,146
7	13	H	Birmingham C	D	0-0	0-0	9		14,602
8	17	A	Barnsley	W	2-1	2-0	5	McCleary ^{9}, Swift ^{27}	12,675
9	24	H	Huddersfield T	W	1-0	1-0	4	Beerens ^{41}	17,030
10	27	A	Brentford	L	1-4	0-2	8	Kermorgant (pen) ^{64}	9679
11	Oct 1	H	Derby Co	D	1-1	0-0	8	Evans ^{90}	17,002
12	15	A	QPR	D	1-1	1-1	7	Williams ^{21}	15,048
13	18	H	Aston Villa	L	1-2	0-1	10	Kermorgant ^{54}	20,331
14	22	A	Rotherham U	W	1-0	0-0	8	McShane ^{86}	8800
15	29	H	Nottingham F	W	2-0	1-0	5	McCleary ^{10}, Gunter ^{62}	17,093
16	Nov 5	A	Wigan Ath	W	3-0	2-0	4	McCleary 2 $^{1, 5}$, Kermorgant (pen) ^{63}	10,277
17	19	H	Burton Alb	W	3-0	2-0	3	Samuel ^{22}, Williams ^{29}, Brayford (og) ^{77}	15,545
18	26	H	Bristol C	W	2-1	2-0	3	McCleary ^{13}, Beerens ^{19}	18,778
19	Dec 3	A	Fulham	L	0-5	0-1	3		18,217
20	10	H	Sheffield W	W	2-1	0-0	3	Beerens 2 $^{57, 76}$	18,153
21	13	A	Leeds U	L	0-2	0-1	3		21,242
22	17	A	Blackburn R	W	3-2	1-1	3	Samuel ^{32}, Moore ^{60}, Evans ^{90}	10,982
23	26	H	Norwich C	W	3-1	1-0	3	Kermorgant ^{37}, McCleary ^{68}, Harriott ^{90}	21,180
24	Jan 2	A	Bristol C	W	3-2	0-1	3	Kelly ^{72}, Kermorgant 2 $^{86, 90}$	20,074
25	12	H	QPR	L	0-1	0-1	3		12,655
26	21	A	Derby Co	L	2-3	1-1	5	Swift ^{16}, Meite ^{80}	28,393
27	24	H	Fulham	W	1-0	0-0	3	Beerens ^{49}	16,012
28	28	H	Cardiff C	W	2-1	1-1	3	Swift ^{42}, Kermorgant ^{60}	18,558
29	31	A	Birmingham C	W	1-0	0-0	3	Swift ^{77}	16,672
30	Feb 4	A	Ipswich T	D	2-2	0-1	3	Mutch ^{52}, Obita ^{78}	15,091
31	11	H	Barnsley	D	0-0	0-0	4		16,222
32	14	H	Brentford	W	3-2	1-0	3	Swift ^{22}, Williams ^{77}, Beerens ^{81}	15,710
33	21	A	Huddersfield T	L	0-1	0-0	4		19,894
34	25	A	Brighton & HA	L	0-3	0-1	4		29,613
35	Mar 4	H	Wolverhampton W	W	2-1	0-0	5	Kermorgant ^{48}, McShane ^{78}	18,629
36	7	H	Newcastle U	D	0-0	0-0	5		23,121
37	11	A	Preston NE	L	0-3	0-2	5		10,787
38	17	A	Sheffield W	W	2-0	1-0	4	Kermorgant ^{13}, Popa ^{90}	26,072
39	Apr 1	H	Leeds U	W	1-0	1-0	4	Kermorgant ^{21}	23,055
40	4	H	Blackburn R	W	3-1	2-0	3	Kermorgant 2 $^{14, 29}$, McCleary ^{78}	15,353
41	8	A	Norwich C	L	1-7	1-6	4	Kermorgant ^{39}	26,163
42	15	A	Aston Villa	W	3-1	1-1	4	Mendes 2 $^{6, 46}$, Grabban (pen) ^{79}	30,742
43	17	H	Rotherham U	W	2-1	0-1	3	Grabban ^{66}, Swift ^{79}	16,711
44	22	A	Nottingham F	L	2-3	0-1	3	Kermorgant 2 $^{58, 74}$	20,323
45	29	H	Wigan Ath	W	1-0	1-0	3	Kermorgant ^{6}	19,177
46	May 7	A	Burton Alb	W	4-2	2-0	3	Mendes ^{3}, Obita ^{21}, Kermorgant ^{64}, Grabban ^{84}	6264

Final League Position: 3

GOALSCORERS

League (68): Kermorgant 18 (2 pens), McCleary 9 (2 pens), Swift 8, Beerens 6, Williams 4 (1 pen), Grabban 3 (1 pen), McShane 3, Mendes 3, Evans 2, Obita 2, Samuel 2, Gunter 1, Harriott 1, Kelly 1, Meite 1, Moore 1, Mutch 1, Popa 1, own goal 1.
FA Cup (0).
EFL Cup (6): Harriott 2, Beerens 1, Quinn 1, Swift 1, van den Berg 1.
EFL Checkatrade Trophy (8): Mendes 2 (2 pens), Novakovich 2, Barrett 1 (1 pen), Keown 1, Sheppard 1, Stacey 1.
Championship Play-Offs (2): Kermorgant 1 (1 pen), Obita 1.

Al Habsi A 46	Gunter C 46	McShane P 29 + 1	van den Berg J 25 + 2	Obita J 28 + 9	Williams D 36 + 5	Swift J 31 + 5	Evans G 24 + 11	McCleary G 39 + 2	Rakels D 1 + 1	Beerens R 37 + 3	Watson T — + 3	Harriott C 3 + 9	Kermorgant Y 34 + 8	Meite Y 1 + 13	Mendes J 2 + 10	Quinn S 1 + 6	Cooper J — + 3	Moore L 40	Blackett T 33 + 1	Samuel D 6 + 3	Gravenberch D — + 2	Kelly L 21 + 7	Tiago Ilori A 2 + 3	Mutch J 8 + 1	Grabban L 7 + 9	Popa A 4 + 4	Oxford R 2 + 3	*Match No.*
1	2	3	4	5^{1}	6	7	8	9^{2}	10^{3}	11	12	13	14															1
1	2	3	4	5	7	9^{3}	6	8^{1}	14	10^{2}		13	11	12														2
1	2	3	4	5	7	9	6^{2}	8		10^{1}			11	12	13													3
1	2	4	3■	5	7	9^{2}	6	8^{3}		10^{1}			11		13	12	14											4
1	2	3	6	13	9		7^{2}	8		10			11			12		4	5^{1}									5
1	2	3	7	14	6	13	8^{2}	9^{1}		11			10			12		4	5^{3}									6
1	2	3		5	8	12	7	9^{3}		11^{2}		13	10		14	6^{1}		4										7
1	2	3		12	6	9^{2}	7	8■		10^{3}			11^{1}		14	13		4	5									8
1	2	3	7^{2}	5^{1}	8	6^{3}	13			11	12	9	10			14		4										9
1	2	3	6^{2}	5		9	7			8^{1}		10^{3}	11		14	12		4		13								10
1	2^{2}	3		5	6	9	7	8^{1}		10		12	11		13			4										11
1	2		4	12	7	9	6	8^{1}		10		13	11					3	5^{2}									12
1	2		4		7	9	6^{1}	8		10			11					3	5		12							13
1	2	12	4	5	7	9^{1}	13	8		10			11					3				6^{2}						14
1	2	3	6^{1}	14	7	9	12	8^{3}		10^{2}		13	11					4	5									15
1	2	3	12		7	9^{3}	6	8^{2}				10^{1}	11	14				4	5	13								16
1	2	4		9	8		7	10^{2}		6^{3}				12	13			3	5	11^{1}		14						17
1	2	3		10	7		6	9^{2}		8^{3}		13		12				4	5	11^{1}		14						18
1	2	3	8	5	7■		6	9^{1}		11^{3}		14		13					4	10^{2}		12						19
1	2	3	6^{1}	10			7	9^{3}		8			12		14			4	5	11^{2}		13						20
1	2	3	7				6^{1}	9		10			12	13			14	4	5	11^{3}		8^{2}						21
1	2	3	6				7	8		10			12				13	4	5	11^{1}		9^{2}						22
1	2	3	6^{1}		7	13	12	10		8^{3}		14	11					4	5			9^{2}						23
1	2	3	6	12	7	9^{2}		8^{1}		10			11	14				4	5^{3}			13						24
1	2		4	5	6	8^{1}		9		10			11	12				3				7						25
1	2	4		6■	7	9^{2}		10					11	13				5^{1}		12		8	3					26
1	2	3	5		7	9	13	11		10^{2}			14					4	6^{1}			8^{3}	12					27
1	9	2	4^{1}	14	6	8^{3}	13	5		11^{2}			10					3	12			7						28
1	2			8	5	9	7	10^{1}		11^{2}				12	13			3	4			6						29
1	2			8	5	9^{1}	13	10					11					3	4			6^{2}		7	12			30
1	2			5	7		6	8^{2}		10^{3}			11	14				3	4			9^{1}			12	13		31
1	2			8	5	7^{3}	13	9		12			14					3	4			10^{1}		6	11^{2}			32
1	2			5	6	14		9^{2}		11			13					3	4			7		8^{3}	10^{1}	12		33
1	2	3			7	12	6^{1}	9^{2}		11			10					4	5			13		8^{3}	14			34
1	2	3	6^{1}		7	9	14			10^{3}			11	13				4	5						12	8^{2}		35
1	2	3	7	13	12			10					11					4^{2}	5			6^{1}		9	8			36
1	2	3^{3}	7	5	12	6		11		14			10						4					8^{2}	9^{1}		13	37
1	2		7	5	6	9^{2}		10^{3}		8^{1}			11					3	4						12	13	14	38
1	2			5^{2}	7	9		8		10^{1}			11					3	4			6^{3}		13	12		14	39
1	2				13	9		12		10			11					3	5			6^{2}	14	7		8^{3}	4^{1}	40
1	2			12		9^{2}		8			13		11					4	5^{1}		14	7		6^{3}	10		3	41
1	2			9	8	6	14	12					13		11^{1}			3	4			7^{2}			10	5^{3}		42
1	2			5	7	6		10^{3}		9^{2}			11	8^{1}				3	4			12			13	14		43
1	2			8	7^{2}	9^{1}	13			12			10		14			3	4			6			11	5^{3}		44
1	2			5	13	9^{3}	7^{2}	8^{1}		10			11					3	4			6	14		12			45
1	2	3^{2}	12	6	14		7			8^{1}			11		10^{3}			4				9	5		13			46

FA Cup

Third Round	Manchester U	(a)	0-4

EFL Cup

First Round	Plymouth Arg	(h)	2-0
Second Round	Milton Keynes D	(h)	2-2
(*aet; Reading won 4-2 on penalties*)			
Third Round	Brighton & HA	(a)	2-1
Fourth Round	Arsenal	(a)	0-2

EFL Checkatrade Trophy (Reading U21)

Southern Group A	Bristol R	(a)	3-2
Southern Group A	Portsmouth	(a)	2-2
(*Reading U21 won 4-3 on penalties*)			
Southern Group A	Yeovil T	(h)	0-2
Second Round South	Southampton U21	(a)	1-1
(*Reading U21 won 4-3 on penalties*)			
Third Round	Yeovil T	(a)	2-4

Championship Play-Offs

Semi-Final 1st leg	Fulham	(a)	1-1
Semi-Final 2nd leg	Fulham	(h)	1-0
Final	Huddersfield T	(Wembley)	0-0
(*aet; Huddersfield T won 4-3 on penalties*)			

ROCHDALE

FOUNDATION

Considering the love of rugby in their area, it is not surprising that Rochdale had difficulty in establishing an Association Football club. The earlier Rochdale Town club formed in 1900 went out of existence in 1907 when the present club was immediately established and joined the Manchester League, before graduating to the Lancashire Combination in 1908.

The Crown Oil Arena, Willbutts Lane, Rochdale, Lancashire OL11 5DS.

Telephone: (0844) 826 1907.

Fax: (01706) 648 466.

Ticket Office: (0844) 826 1907 (option 8).

Website: www.rochdaleafc.co.uk

Email: admin@rochdaleafc.co.uk

Ground Capacity: 10,037.

Record Attendance: 24,231 v Notts Co, FA Cup 2nd rd, 10 December 1949.

Pitch Measurements: 104m × 69.5m (114yd × 76yd).

Chairman: Chris Dunphy.

Chief Executive: Russ Green.

Manager: Keith Hill.

Assistant Manager: Chris Beech.

Colours: Blue shirts with white and black trim, white shorts with blue and black trim, blue socks with white and black trim.

Year Formed: 1907.

Turned Professional: 1907.

Club Nickname: 'The Dale'.

Ground: 1907, St Clements Playing Fields (renamed Spotland) (renamed The Crown Oil Arena, 2016).

First Football League Game: 27 August 1921, Division 3 (N), v Accrington Stanley (h) W 6–3 – Crabtree; Nuttall, Sheehan; Hill, Farrer, Yarwood; Hoad, Sandiford, Dennison (2), Owens (3), Carney (1).

Record League Victory: 8–1 v Chesterfield, Division 3 (N), 18 December 1926 – Hill; Brown, Ward; Hillhouse, Parkes, Braidwood; Hughes, Bertram, Whitehurst (5), Schofield (2), Martin (1).

Record Cup Victory: 8–2 v Crook T, FA Cup 1st rd, 26 November 1927 – Moody; Hopkins, Ward; Braidwood, Parkes, Barker; Tompkinson, Clennell (3) Whitehurst (4), Hall, Martin (1).

Record Defeat: 1–9 v Tranmere R, Division 3 (N), 25 December 1931.

Most League Points (2 for a win): 62, Division 3 (N), 1923–24.

HONOURS

League: *Runners-up:* Division 3N – 1923–24, 1926–27.

FA Cup: 5th rd – 1990, 2003.

League Cup: *Runners-up:* 1962.

sky SPORTS FACT FILE

In January 1920 Rochdale, then members of the Central League, were drawn at home to Arsenal in the FA Cup. Dale were persuaded to switch the tie to Highbury and were rewarded with an attendance of 26,596. At half-time they held a shock 2-1 lead but eventually went down to a 4-2 defeat.

Most League Points (3 for a win): 82, FL 2, 2009–10.

Most League Goals: 105, Division 3 (N), 1926–27.

Highest League Scorer in Season: Albert Whitehurst, 44, Division 3 (N), 1926–27.

Most League Goals in Total Aggregate: Reg Jenkins, 119, 1964–73.

Most League Goals in One Match: 6, Tommy Tippett v Hartlepools U, Division 3 (N), 21 April 1930.

Most Capped Player: Leo Bertos, 6 (56), New Zealand.

Most League Appearances: Gary Jones, 470, 1998–2001; 2003–12.

Youngest League Player: Zac Hughes, 16 years 105 days v Exeter C, 19 September 1987.

Record Transfer Fee Received: £750,000 from Brentford for Scott Hogan, July 2014.

Record Transfer Fee Paid: £150,000 to Stoke C for Paul Connor, March 2001.

Football League Record: 1921 Elected to Division 3 (N); 1958–59 Division 3; 1959–69 Division 4; 1969–74 Division 3; 1974–92 Division 4; 1992–2004 Division 3; 2004–10 FL 2; 2010–12 FL 1; 2012–14 FL 2; 2014– FL 1.

LATEST SEQUENCES

Longest Sequence of League Wins: 8, 29.9.1969 – 3.11.1969.

Longest Sequence of League Defeats: 17, 14.11.1931 – 12.3.1932.

Longest Sequence of League Draws: 6, 17.8.1968 – 14.9.1968.

Longest Sequence of Unbeaten League Matches: 20, 15.9.1923 – 19.1.1924.

Longest Sequence Without a League Win: 28, 14.11.1931 – 29.8.1932.

Successive Scoring Runs: 29 from 10.10.2008.

Successive Non-scoring Runs: 9 from 14.3.1980.

MANAGERS

Billy Bradshaw 1920
Run by committee 1920–22
Tom Wilson 1922–23
Jack Peart 1923–30
Will Cameron 1930–31
Herbert Hopkinson 1932–34
Billy Smith 1934–35
Ernest Nixon 1935–37
Sam Jennings 1937–38
Ted Goodier 1938–52
Jack Warner 1952–53
Harry Catterick 1953–58
Jack Marshall 1958–60
Tony Collins 1960–68
Bob Stokoe 1967–68
Len Richley 1968–70
Dick Conner 1970–73
Walter Joyce 1973–76
Brian Green 1976–77
Mike Ferguson 1977–78
Doug Collins 1979
Bob Stokoe 1979–80
Peter Madden 1980–83
Jimmy Greenhoff 1983–84
Vic Halom 1984–86
Eddie Gray 1986–88
Danny Bergara 1988–89
Terry Dolan 1989–91
Dave Sutton 1991–94
Mick Docherty 1994–96
Graham Barrow 1996–99
Steve Parkin 1999–2001
John Hollins 2001–02
Paul Simpson 2002–03
Alan Buckley 2003
Steve Parkin 2003–06
Keith Hill 2007–11
(Caretaker from December 2006)
Steve Eyre 2011
John Coleman 2012–13
Keith Hill January 2013–

TEN YEAR LEAGUE RECORD

		P	*W*	*D*	*L*	*F*	*A*	*Pts*	*Pos*
2007-08	FL 2	46	23	11	12	77	54	80	5
2008-09	FL 2	46	19	13	14	70	59	70	6
2009-10	FL 2	46	25	7	14	82	48	82	3
2010-11	FL 1	46	18	14	14	63	55	68	9
2011-12	FL 1	46	8	14	24	47	81	38	24
2012-13	FL 2	46	16	13	17	68	70	61	12
2013-14	FL 2	46	24	9	13	69	48	81	3
2014-15	FL 1	46	19	6	21	72	66	63	8
2015-16	FL 1	46	19	12	15	68	61	69	10
2016-17	FL 1	46	19	12	15	71	62	69	9

DID YOU KNOW ?

Rochdale have always struggled to attract supporters due to their geographical proximity to so many other senior clubs. They have been the worst supported Football League club on six occasions: 1951–52, 1966–67, 1977–78, 1978–79, 1979–80 and 1996–97.

ROCHDALE – SKY BET LEAGUE ONE 2016–17 LEAGUE RECORD

Match No.	Date	Venue	Opponents	Result	H/T Score	Lg Pos.	Goalscorers	Attendance
1	Aug 6	H	Peterborough U	L 2-3	2-2	16	Cannon [8], Henderson (pen) [32]	3243
2	13	A	Sheffield U	D 1-1	1-0	16	Cannon [43]	19,399
3	16	A	Port Vale	L 0-1	0-0	21		3941
4	20	H	Milton Keynes D	L 0-1	0-0	22		2176
5	27	H	AFC Wimbledon	D 1-1	0-1	23	Allen [90]	2274
6	Sept 3	A	Oxford U	L 0-1	0-0	24		6939
7	10	A	Bristol R	D 2-2	2-1	24	Camps [17], Henderson [22]	8057
8	17	H	Fleetwood T	W 2-1	1-1	23	Lund [10], Davies [85]	2499
9	24	A	Millwall	W 3-2	1-2	19	Camps [9], Andrew [67], Henderson (pen) [90]	8143
10	27	H	Bolton W	W 1-0	0-0	15	Davies [52]	6011
11	Oct 1	A	Charlton Ath	W 1-0	1-0	11	Andrew [25]	14,460
12	8	H	Southend U	W 3-0	2-0	5	Canavan [18], Andrew [27], Mendez-Laing [83]	2600
13	15	H	Bury	W 2-0	1-0	4	Henderson (pen) [38], Mendez-Laing [74]	5344
14	18	A	Swindon T	L 0-3	0-2	5		6048
15	22	A	Coventry C	L 0-2	0-1	9		8133
16	29	H	Oldham Ath	W 1-0	1-0	6	Lund [40]	5204
17	Nov 12	A	Bradford C	L 0-4	0-2	10		18,205
18	19	H	Swindon T	W 4-0	1-0	7	Bunney [29], Lund [55], Davies 2 (1 pen) [57, 66 (p)]	2196
19	22	H	Walsall	W 4-0	2-0	5	Rathbone [32], Noble-Lazarus [41], Davies 2 (1 pen) [76 (p), 90]	1907
20	26	A	Gillingham	L 0-3	0-0	5		5409
21	Dec 10	H	Scunthorpe U	W 3-2	1-0	5	Thompson [41], Rathbone [53], Andrew [75]	3445
22	17	A	Northampton T	W 3-2	1-1	5	Lund 3 [19, 63, 67]	5247
23	26	H	Chesterfield	W 3-0	1-0	4	Henderson 2 [44, 84], Andrew [59]	3863
24	30	H	Shrewsbury T	W 2-1	2-0	4	Henderson [4], Davies [28]	3235
25	Jan 2	A	Walsall	W 2-0	1-0	4	Henderson [23], Thompson [74]	4667
26	14	A	Southend U	L 1-2	0-1	5	Andrew [66]	6570
27	21	H	Oxford U	L 0-4	0-2	6		3246
28	Feb 4	H	Bristol R	D 0-0	0-0	7		3168
29	11	A	Fleetwood T	D 0-0	0-0	7		3186
30	14	A	Bolton W	L 0-1	0-0	7		13,313
31	18	H	Charlton Ath	D 3-3	1-1	8	Canavan [4], Andrew [70], Mendez-Laing [84]	2842
32	25	A	Peterborough U	L 1-3	1-2	10	Thompson [40]	4457
33	Mar 4	H	Sheffield U	D 3-3	1-2	11	Davies [20], Lund [46], Mendez-Laing [78]	6214
34	11	A	Milton Keynes D	D 2-2	1-0	11	Davies [17], Mendez-Laing [84]	10,569
35	14	A	Scunthorpe U	L 1-2	1-0	13	Henderson [41]	3225
36	18	H	Gillingham	W 4-1	2-1	10	Mendez-Laing [10], Henderson [33], Camps [49], Vincenti [90]	2582
37	21	H	Millwall	D 3-3	2-2	10	Mendez-Laing [33], Henderson [44], Camps [54]	2334
38	25	A	Chesterfield	W 3-1	3-0	8	Henderson [16], Camps [40], Allen [42]	5927
39	28	A	AFC Wimbledon	L 1-3	0-0	9	Camps [65]	3812
40	Apr 1	H	Northampton T	D 1-1	0-0	10	Mendez-Laing [58]	2939
41	4	H	Port Vale	W 3-0	3-0	8	Lund [34], McDermott [43], Henderson (pen) [45]	4387
42	8	A	Shrewsbury T	L 0-1	0-1	9		5002
43	13	A	Bury	W 1-0	1-0	8	Camps [45]	4850
44	17	H	Coventry C	W 2-0	1-0	8	Henderson 2 [18, 52]	3202
45	22	A	Oldham Ath	D 1-1	1-0	8	Camps [13]	6865
46	30	H	Bradford C	D 1-1	0-1	9	Lund [66]	6876

Final League Position: 9

GOALSCORERS

League (71): Henderson 15 (4 pens), Davies 9 (2 pens), Lund 9, Camps 8, Mendez-Laing 8, Andrew 7, Thompson 3, Allen 2, Canavan 2, Cannon 2, Rathbone 2, Bunney 1, McDermott 1, Noble-Lazarus 1, Vincenti 1.
FA Cup (7): Davies 3 (1 pen), Henderson 2, Camps 1, Mendez-Laing 1.
EFL Cup (4): Cannon 1, Henderson 1, Lund 1, Mendez-Laing 1.
EFL Checkatrade Trophy (5): Davies 1, Gillam 1, Henderson 1, Noble-Lazarus 1, Odelusi 1.

Lillis J 14	Rafferty J 36 + 4	Canavan N 23 + 2	McGahey H 30 + 6	McNulty J 33 + 2	Cannon A 14 + 11	Allen J 26 + 5	Bunney J 28 + 1	Camps C 37 + 7	Mendez-Laing N 30 + 9	Henderson I 39 + 3	Andrew C 31 + 8	McDermott D 9 + 8	Odelusi S 1 + 14	Tanser S 5	Thompson J 17 + 4	Logan C 24	Lund M 27 + 2	Davies S 16 + 13	Vincenti P 3 + 11	Keane K 27 + 2	Morley A 2	Rathbone O 18 + 9	Noble-Lazarus R 3 + 7	Owuso D — + 1	Wilson B 8	Taylor J 1	Kitching M 4 + 1	Redshaw J — + 1	Match No.
1	2	3	4	5	6	7	8^3	9^2	10^1	11	12	13	14																1
1	2	4	3	5	8^1	6		13	9^2	7	10	11	12																2
1		3	4	5	8^3	6		12	9	7	10	11^2	13	2^1	14														3
		3	4	5	2	7	9^2		11^1	10	12	13			8^3	1	6	14											4
		3	4	5	2	9		12■	10	11	13	7^3	14			1	6^1	8^2											5
	2	3	4	5	9^3	8	13		10	7		12	6^2			1		11^1	14										6
1	2	3■	4	12		7	11	8^1		10	13			5^2			6		9^3	14									7
1			3	4			11	7		10^2	14	6^1	13		2^3		8	12	9	5									8
1	12	3	4^3				5	6		10	9	11^1	14		2^2		8	13		7									9
1	2	3				7	5	8		9^2	11		13		10^1		6	12		4									10
1	2	3	14			8^3	5	6			10	12	13		9^1		7	11^2		4									11
1	2	3			8		5	7	12		9		14		11^3			10^1		4	6^2	13							12
1	2	3			12		5	6	10^1	11	8		13				7	9^2		4									13
1	2	3			12		5■	8	11^3	10	9		14				6^1	7^2		4		13							14
1	2^2	3			11		5	8^1	12	10	9^3	14					6	13		4		7							15
1	2	3			6^1		5	7	11^2		9		14		12		8	10^3		4		13							16
1	2^3	4■	14	13	7		5^2	8	11						9			10		3	6^1		12						17
	2		12	4			5	9	6	14					10	1	8	13		3^1		7^3	11^2						18
	2		3	4				7	10^3	13			14	5	11	1	6	12				8^2	9^1						19
	2		4	3			11^2	8	6^3	12			14	5	10	1	7	13				9^1							20
	2		3	4	13		5	7	14	10^1	12				11	1	6	9^3				8^2							21
	5^1		14	3			2	6	13	7	12				10	1	9	11^2		4		8^3							22
	2			4	12	13	5	9		11^1	8					1	6	10		3		7^2							23
	2			4		13	5	9^3	14	11	8				12	1	6	10^2		3		7^1							24
	2		12	3			5^2	6	14	11	10				9^1	1	7	13		4		8^3							25
	2		4	3		14		6	13	11	9					1	5^1	10^3		7■		8^2	12						26
	2	14	3	4^3	7^2	6		9	10	11	8^1			5		1			12					13					27
	6		2	3		14		7		10		13							12	4		9^3	11^2		1	5^1	8		28
	7	3			2	6		13	9^2	11	12				10^1					4		8^3			1		5	14	29
	2^2	3	6			8		14	13	11	10				9^1				12	4		7^3			1		5		30
	2	4				7		6	14	11	10	8^2			9^3					3		13	12		1		5^1		31
	5■		12	4	14	8		6	10^3	9	11	7■			2^2					3^1					1		13		32
			4	2	9	7		14	5	10							6	11^1	13	3^3		8^2	12		1				33
	2	14	3	4	8^2	7		13	9	11	5				12			10^3				6^1			1				34
	2^1	3	4	5	12	6		7	9	11	10								13			8^2			1				35
		3	2	4		8	5	6	11^1	9	10^3	14				1	7^2		13			12							36
	12	3	2	4		8	5	7^1	9	11	10					1			6^2			13							37
	12	2	5	3		7	8^1	6	11^3	10	9^2					1		14	13	4									38
	12		2	5	13	6	4^3	8	11^1	10	9					1	7^2			3■		14							39
	2		3	4		8		6^3	11	9	5					1	7	10^2	12			13							40
	2		3	4		12		6	9	10^1	5	11^3				1	7	14				8^2	13						41
	2		4	3				6	9	11	5	10^1				1	7^3	14		13		8^2	12						42
	2^2		4	3	12	6^3	5	8	10	9	11					1		14		7^1		13							43
	2		3	4	12	6	5^2	8	9^1	11	10^3					1	13		14	7									44
	2		3	4	12	6	5^3	8	9	10	11^1					1	13		14	7^2									45
	2		3	4	13	8	5	6	9	10^1	11	12^3				1	7^2						14						46

FA Cup

First Round	Maidstone U	(a)	1-1
Replay	Maidstone U	(h)	2-0
Second Round	Carlisle U	(a)	2-0
Third Round	Barrow	(a)	2-0
Fourth Round	Huddersfield T	(h)	0-4

EFL Cup

First Round	Chesterfield	(h)	3-1
Second Round	QPR	(a)	1-2

EFL Checkatrade Trophy

Northern Group F	Sunderland U21	(h)	1-1
(*Rochdale won 4-2 on penalties*)			
Northern Group F	Notts Co	(h)	2-1
Northern Group F	Hartlepool U	(a)	2-1
Second Round North	Chesterfield	(h)	0-2

ROTHERHAM UNITED

FOUNDATION

Rotherham were formed in 1870 before becoming Town in the late 1880s. Thornhill United were founded in 1877 and changed their name to Rotherham County in 1905. The Town amalgamated with Rotherham County to form Rotherham United in 1925.

The AESSEAL New York Stadium, New York Way, Rotherham, South Yorkshire S60 1AH.

Telephone: (0844) 4140 733.

Fax: (0844) 4140 744.

Ticket Office: (0844) 4140 754.

Website: www.themillers.co.uk

Email: office@rotherhamunited.net

Ground Capacity: 12,053.

Record Attendance: 25,170 v Sheffield U, Division 2, 13 December 1952 (at Millmoor); 7,082 v Aldershot T, FL 2 Play-offs semi-final 2nd leg, 19 May 2010 (at Don Valley); 11,758 v Sheffield U, FL 1, 7 September 2013 (at New York Stadium).

Pitch Measurements: 102m × 66m (111.5yd × 72yd).

Chairman: Tony Stewart.

Chief Operating Officer: Paul Douglas.

Manager: Paul Warne.

Assistant Manager: Richie Barker.

HONOURS

League Champions: Division 3 – 1980–81; Division 3N – 1950–51; Division 4 – 1988–89.

Runners-up: Second Division – 2000–01; Division 3N – 1946–47, 1947–48, 1948–49; FL 2 – 2012–13; Third Division – 1999–2000; Division 4 – 1991–92.

FA Cup: 5th rd – 1953, 1968.

League Cup: *Runners-up:* 1961.

League Trophy Winners: 1996.

Colours: Red shirts with white and yellow trim, white shorts with red trim, red socks with white and yellow trim.

Year Formed: 1870. ***Turned Professional:*** 1905. ***Club Nickname:*** 'The Millers'.

Previous Names: 1877, Thornhill United; 1905, Rotherham County; 1925, amalgamated with Rotherham Town under Rotherham United.

Grounds: 1870, Red House Ground; 1907, Millmoor; 2008, Don Valley Stadium; 2012, New York Stadium (renamed The AESSEAL New York Stadium, 2014).

First Football League Game: 2 September 1893, Division 2, Rotherham T v Lincoln C (a) D 1–1 – McKay; Thickett, Watson; Barr, Brown, Broadhead; Longden, Cutts, Leatherbarrow, McCormick, Pickering, (1 og). 30 August 1919, Division 2, Rotherham Co v Nottingham F (h) W 2–0 – Branston; Alton, Baines; Bailey, Coe, Stanton; Lee (1), Cawley (1), Glennon, Lees, Lamb.

Record League Victory: 8–0 v Oldham Ath, Division 3 (N), 26 May 1947 – Warnes; Selkirk, Ibbotson; Edwards, Horace Williams, Danny Williams; Wilson (2), Shaw (1), Ardron (3), Guest (1), Hainsworth (1).

Record Cup Victory: 6–0 v Spennymoor U, FA Cup 2nd rd, 17 December 1977 – McAlister; Forrest, Breckin, Womble, Stancliffe, Green, Finney, Phillips (3), Gwyther (2) (Smith), Goodfellow, Crawford (1). 6–0 v Wolverhampton W, FA Cup 1st rd, 16 November 1985 – O'Hanlon; Forrest, Dungworth, Gooding (1), Smith (1), Pickering, Birch (2), Emerson, Tynan (1), Simmons (1), Pugh. 6–0 v King's Lynn, FA Cup 2nd rd, 6 December 1997 – Mimms; Clark, Hurst (Goodwin), Garner (1) (Hudson) (1), Warner (Bass), Richardson (1), Berry (1), Thompson, Druce (1), Glover (1), Roscoe.

Record Defeat: 1–11 v Bradford C, Division 3 (N), 25 August 1928.

sky SPORTS FACT FILE

In their 1959–60 FA Cup campaign Rotherham United faced second replays in consecutive rounds. The Millers drew home and away with Arsenal before winning the second replay 2-0 in a game staged at Sheffield Wednesday's Hillsborough Stadium. The Millers drew twice with Brighton & Hove Albion in the fourth round and found themselves at Highbury for the second replay which Brighton won 6-0.

Most League Points (2 for a win): 71, Division 3 (N), 1950–51.

Most League Points (3 for a win): 91, Division 2, 2000–01.

Most League Goals: 114, Division 3 (N), 1946–47.

Highest League Scorer in Season: Wally Ardron, 38, Division 3 (N), 1946–47.

Most League Goals in Total Aggregate: Gladstone Guest, 130, 1946–56.

Most League Goals in One Match: 4, Roland Bastow v York C, Division 3 (N), 9 November 1935; 4, Roland Bastow v Rochdale, Division 3 (N), 7 March 1936; 4, Wally Ardron v Crewe Alex, Division 3 (N), 5 October 1946; 4, Wally Ardron v Carlisle U, Division 3 (N), 13 September 1947; 4, Wally Ardron v Hartlepools U, Division 3 (N), 13 October 1948; 4, Ian Wilson v Liverpool, Division 2, 2 May 1955; 4, Carl Gilbert v Swansea C, Division 3, 28 September 1971; 4, Carl Airey v Chester, Division 3, 31 August 1987; 4, Shaun Goater v Hartlepool U, Division 3, 9 April 1994; 4, Lee Glover v Hull C, Division 3, 28 December 1997; 4, Darren Byfield v Millwall, Division 1, 10 August 2002; 4, Adam Le Fondre v Cheltenham T, FL 2, 21 August 2010.

Most Capped Player: Kari Arnason, 20 (60), Iceland.

Most League Appearances: Danny Williams, 461, 1946–62.

Youngest League Player: Kevin Eley, 16 years 72 days v Scunthorpe U, 15 May 1984.

Record Transfer Fee Received: £900,000 from Bristol C for Kieran Agard, August 2014.

Record Transfer Fee Paid: £500,000 to Peterborough U for Jon Taylor, August 2016.

Football League Record: 1893 Rotherham Town elected to Division 2; 1896 Failed re-election; 1919 Rotherham County elected to Division 2; 1923–51 Division 3 (N); 1951–68 Division 2; 1968–73 Division 3; 1973–75 Division 4; 1975–81 Division 3; 1981–83 Division 2; 1983–88 Division 3; 1988–89 Division 4; 1989–91 Division 3; 1991–92 Division 4; 1992–97 Division 2; 1997–2000 Division 3; 2000–01 Division 2; 2001–04 Division 1; 2004–05 FL C; 2005–07 FL 1; 2007–13 FL 2; 2013–14 FL 1; 2014–17 FL C; 2017– FL 1.

MANAGERS

Billy Heald 1925–29 *(Secretary only for several years)*
Stanley Davies 1929–30
Billy Heald 1930–33
Reg Freeman 1934–52
Andy Smailes 1952–58
Tom Johnston 1958–62
Danny Williams 1962–65
Jack Mansell 1965–67
Tommy Docherty 1967–68
Jimmy McAnearney 1968–73
Jimmy McGuigan 1973–79
Ian Porterfield 1979–81
Emlyn Hughes 1981–83
George Kerr 1983–85
Norman Hunter 1985–87
Dave Cusack 1987–88
Billy McEwan 1988–91
Phil Henson 1991–94
Archie Gemmill and John McGovern 1994–96
Danny Bergara 1996–97
Ronnie Moore 1997–2005
Mick Harford 2005
Alan Knill 2005–07
Mark Robins 2007–09
Ronnie Moore 2009–11
Andy Scott 2011–12
Steve Evans 2012–15
Neil Redfearn 2015–16
Neil Warnock 2016
Alan Stubbs 2016
Kenny Jackett 2016
Paul Warne January 2017–

LATEST SEQUENCES

Longest Sequence of League Wins: 9, 2.2.1982 – 6.3.1982.

Longest Sequence of League Defeats: 10, 14.2.2017 – 8.4.2017.

Longest Sequence of League Draws: 6, 13.10.1969 – 22.11.1969.

Longest Sequence of Unbeaten League Matches: 18, 13.10.1969 – 7.2.1970.

Longest Sequence Without a League Win: 21, 9.5.2004 – 20.11.2004.

Successive Scoring Runs: 30 from 3.4.1954.

Successive Non-scoring Runs: 6 from 21.8.2004.

TEN YEAR LEAGUE RECORD

		P	*W*	*D*	*L*	*F*	*A*	*Pts*	*Pos*
2007-08	FL 2	46	21	11	14	62	58	64*	9
2008-09	FL 2	46	21	12	13	60	46	58†	14
2009-10	FL 2	46	21	10	15	55	52	73	5
2010-11	FL 2	46	17	15	14	75	60	66	9
2011-12	FL 2	46	18	13	15	67	63	67	10
2012-13	FL 2	46	24	7	15	74	59	79	2
2013-14	FL 1	46	24	14	8	86	58	86	4
2014-15	FL C	46	11	16	19	46	67	46‡	21
2015-16	FL C	46	13	10	23	53	71	49	21
2016-17	FL C	46	5	8	33	40	98	23	24

**10 pts deducted; †17 pts deducted; ‡3 pts deducted.*

DID YOU KNOW ?

Rotherham United's first visit to Wembley came in April 1996 when they faced Shrewsbury Town in the final of the Auto Windscreens Shield. The Millers won 2-1 in front of an attendance of 35,235 with Nigel Jemson netting both goals.

ROTHERHAM UNITED – SKY BET CHAMPIONSHIP 2016–17 LEAGUE RECORD

Match No.	Date	Venue	Opponents	Result	H/T Score	Lg Pos.	Goalscorers	Attendance
1	Aug 6	H	Wolverhampton W	D 2-2	2-1	8	Ward, D 9, Vaulks 20	11,291
2	13	A	Aston Villa	L 0-3	0-2	18		33,286
3	16	A	Brighton & HA	L 0-3	0-2	21		25,128
4	20	H	Brentford	W 1-0	1-0	21	Ward, D 32	8367
5	27	A	Barnsley	L 0-4	0-0	22		15,283
6	Sept 10	H	Bristol C	D 2-2	1-0	20	Brown 6, Flint (og) 58	8559
7	14	H	Nottingham F	D 2-2	1-0	20	Taylor 2 30, 87	10,243
8	17	A	Blackburn R	L 2-4	1-2	21	Ward, D 2 12, 83	10,699
9	24	H	Cardiff C	L 1-2	0-0	23	Brown 60	8348
10	27	A	Huddersfield T	L 1-2	1-2	24	Ward, D 34	18,808
11	Oct 1	H	Newcastle U	L 0-1	0-1	24		11,653
12	15	A	Norwich C	L 1-3	0-1	24	Blackstock 74	26,813
13	18	A	Birmingham C	L 2-4	1-3	24	Ward, D 31, Taylor 56	16,404
14	22	H	Reading	L 0-1	0-0	24		8800
15	29	A	Ipswich T	D 2-2	1-1	24	Ward, D 2 7, 48	15,247
16	Nov 5	H	Preston NE	L 1-3	0-2	24	Wood 71	10,013
17	19	A	Derby Co	L 0-3	0-2	24		28,191
18	26	H	Leeds U	L 1-2	0-2	24	Wood 86	10,513
19	Dec 3	A	Burton Alb	L 1-2	0-1	24	Adeyemi 90	4446
20	10	H	QPR	W 1-0	1-0	24	Brown 24	8704
21	13	A	Fulham	L 1-2	1-1	24	Newell 19	13,735
22	17	A	Sheffield W	L 0-1	0-0	24		27,242
23	26	H	Wigan Ath	W 3-2	3-0	24	Belaid 8, Wood 32, Burn (og) 45	10,158
24	29	H	Burton Alb	L 1-2	1-2	24	Adeyemi 45	9806
25	Jan 2	A	Leeds U	L 0-3	0-0	24		33,397
26	14	H	Norwich C	W 2-1	1-0	24	Yates 7, Adeyemi 55	10,000
27	21	A	Newcastle U	L 0-4	0-1	24		52,208
28	28	H	Barnsley	L 0-1	0-0	24		11,050
29	31	A	Nottingham F	L 0-2	0-0	24		15,770
30	Feb 4	A	Bristol C	L 0-1	0-0	24		18,737
31	11	H	Blackburn R	D 1-1	0-0	24	Taylor 47	9438
32	14	H	Huddersfield T	L 2-3	1-1	24	Ajayi 11, Adeyemi 71	10,114
33	18	A	Cardiff C	L 0-5	0-2	24		15,650
34	25	A	Brentford	L 2-4	0-1	24	Belaid 67, Forde 87	9918
35	Mar 4	H	Aston Villa	L 0-2	0-0	24		10,720
36	7	H	Brighton & HA	L 0-2	0-0	24		8366
37	11	A	Wolverhampton W	L 0-1	0-1	24		20,077
38	18	A	QPR	L 1-5	1-2	24	Newell 13	13,383
39	Apr 1	H	Fulham	L 0-1	0-0	24		9004
40	4	H	Sheffield W	L 0-2	0-2	24		10,669
41	8	A	Wigan Ath	L 2-3	1-1	24	Ward, D 29, Forde 61	10,085
42	14	H	Birmingham C	D 1-1	0-0	24	Ward, D 85	10,160
43	17	A	Reading	L 1-2	1-0	24	Adeyemi 19	16,711
44	22	H	Ipswich T	W 1-0	0-0	24	Adeyemi 79	8266
45	29	A	Preston NE	D 1-1	1-1	24	Smallwood 9	11,032
46	May 7	H	Derby Co	D 1-1	0-0	24	Frecklington 66	10,763

Final League Position: 24

GOALSCORERS

League (40): Ward, D 10, Adeyemi 6, Taylor 4, Brown 3, Wood 3, Belaid 2, Forde 2, Newell 2, Ajayi 1, Blackstock 1, Frecklington 1, Smallwood 1, Vaulks 1, Yates 1, own goals 2.
FA Cup (2): Adeyemi 1, Ward, D 1.
EFL Cup (4): Yates 2, Forde 1, Halford 1 (1 pen).

Camp L 18	Kelly S 16 + 4	Broadfoot K 3	Wood R 28 + 1	Mattock J 33 + 3	Frecklington L 18 + 4	Vaulks W 31 + 9	Forster-Caskey J 5 + 1	Forde A 20 + 12	Ward D 40 + 1	Taylor J 35 + 7	Smallwood R 20 + 5	Thorpe T — + 2	Allan S 4 + 6	Ball D 12 + 1	Yates J 7 + 14	Fisher D 33 + 1	Wilson K 8	Adeyemi T 28 + 1	Brown I 17 + 3	Newell J 28 + 6	Fry D 10	Halford G 10 + 4	Blackstock D 4 + 12	Odemwingie P 3 + 4	Price L 16 + 1	Belaid A 14 + 3	O'Donnell R 12	Bray A — + 5	Ajayi S 17	Purrington B 7 + 3	Ekstrand J 1	Morris C 6 + 2	Clarke-Harris J 2 + 5	Bailey-King D — + 1	*Match No.*
1	2	3	4	5^{2}	6^{3}	7	8^{1}	9	10	11	12	13	14																						1
1	2		4	5^{2}		7	6^{1}	9	10	11	8			3	12	13																			2
1	3			6		8		7^{1}	11	10	9	13	12	5		2^{2}	4																		3
1	5			14		7		13	11	6	12		10^{1}	3		2	4	8^{3}	9^{2}																4
1	5					6	7^{2}	14	11	8^{3}			9	3	12	2	4		10^{1}	13															5
1	5					13		12	11	8^{2}			14	6		2	4		9^{3}	10^{1}	3	7													6
1	14			5	13				11^{2}	6			9		12^{3}	2■	4	8^{1}	10		3	7													7
1	2			5	12	14			11	6			9^{3}		13		4	8^{2}	10		3	7^{1}													8
1				5	7				11	6						2	4		10	9^{1}	3	8	12												9
1				5	8			13	11	6				4		2		7^{3}	10^{1}	9^{2}	3	14	12												10
1					8	12			11	6				4		5		7^{1}	10	9^{2}	3	2	13												11
1					7	8^{2}	14		11	6			13	4		5			10^{3}	9^{1}	3	2	12												12
1	2				8	6^{1}	9		11	7				4		5	3^{2}		10			12	13												13
1			4	5	8			13	10	6						2			12	9^{1}	3	7	11^{2}												14
1			4	5		8			10	6^{2}				12		2				9	3	7^{1}	11	13											15
1			4	5		8			11	6^{2}				7^{3}		2			14	9	3	12	10^{1}	13											16
1			4	5		12	7^{1}		11	8^{2}						2		6	13	9		3		10											17
1^{2}	2		4			12		14	10					3		5		6	9	8^{1}		7^{3}		11■	13										18
			4	5		8		9^{1}	11	6^{2}				3	13	2		7	10	12					1										19
	14		3	5	8	12		6	11	13						2		7^{2}	10^{1}	9^{3}					1	4									20
			3	5	14	8		6	11^{3}	12						2		7^{1}	10^{2}	9			13		1	4									21
			3■	5	8			6	11							2		7		9			12	10^{1}	1	4									22
			3	5	8	13		6	11							2		7	10^{2}	9^{1}				12	1	4									23
			3	5^{1}	8			6^{3}	11							2		7^{2}	10	9		13	14	12	1	4									24
		3^{1}	14	5	8	13		6^{3}	11	12						2		7	10	9^{2}					1	4									25
		3	4	5		6		8		12	7				11	2		9		10^{1}					1										26
	14		3	5		8		7^{1}	12	10^{3}	6		13		11^{2}	2		9								4	1								27
	12		3	5		7		6^{2}	11	9	8		13		10	2^{3}										4^{1}	1	14							28
	2		4	5		9		7^{2}	11	10	6^{1}				12			8^{3}		13			14				1		3						29
	2^{3}		4	10^{2}		8		7^{1}	11	13	6				12					9			14				1		3	5					30
	2		4			13		10^{1}	11	7	6				12			8^{2}		9							1		3	5					31
	2		4	14		8			11^{1}	6^{2}	12				10^{3}			7		9			13				1		3	5					32
	2		4	10^{1}		8		12		7	6				13					9			11^{3}			14	1			5	3^{2}				33
	2			13		8		12	11	6	7^{2}							10		9^{3}			14		1	4^{1}			3	5					34
	2^{2}				13	8		6	11^{1}	9^{3}	12				10			7		14					1	4			3	5					35
				5^{2}	8	2		6^{1}		9	7^{3}				11			10		12					1	4		13	3	14					36
				5	8	2		6^{2}	11	12	7^{1}				13			10		9^{3}					1	4		14	3						37
					8	2		12	10^{1}	6^{2}	14				11^{3}			7		9					1	4			3	5		13			38
					8^{3}	2		14	10	6	7				12	5^{2}				9					1	4			3	13		11^{1}			39
			4	5		8		13	10	6^{3}	7^{2}					2				9					1			14	3			11^{1}	12		40
			4^{3}	5		8		6^{2}	11	13	7					2				9^{1}					1	12			3			10	14		41
			4	5		7			11	6	8				13	2^{3}		12		9^{1}							1		3			10^{2}	14		42
			4	5		9			10	7	6				14	2^{1}		8^{3}		12							1		3			11^{2}	13		43
			4	5		6		13	11^{1}	9	7					2		8									1	12	3^{3}			10^{2}	14		44
			4^{1}	5	6^{3}	8				9	7				13	2		10								14	1		3			12	11^{2}		45
			4	5	6	8				9^{1}	7					2		10									1		3	12^{2}			11	13	46

FA Cup
Third Round Oxford U (h) 2-3

EFL Cup
First Round Morecambe (h) 4-5
(*aet*)

SCUNTHORPE UNITED

FOUNDATION

The year of foundation for Scunthorpe United has often been quoted as 1910, but the club can trace its history back to 1899 when Brumby Hall FC, who played on the Old Showground, consolidated their position by amalgamating with some other clubs and changing their name to Scunthorpe United. The year 1910 was when that club amalgamated with North Lindsey United as Scunthorpe and Lindsey United. The link is Mr W. T. Lockwood whose chairmanship covers both years.

Glanford Park, Jack Brownsword Way, Scunthorpe, North Lincolnshire DN15 8TD.

Telephone: (01724) 840 139.

Fax: (01724) 857 986.

Ticket Office: (01724) 747 670.

Website: www.scunthorpe-united.co.uk

Email: receptionist@scunthorpe-united.co.uk

Ground Capacity: 9,144.

Record Attendance: 23,935 v Portsmouth, FA Cup 4th rd, 30 January 1954 (at Old Showground); 9,077 v Manchester U, League Cup 3rd rd, 22 September 2010 (at Glanford Park).

Pitch Measurements: 102.5m × 66m (112yd × 72yd).

Chairman: Peter Swann.

Chief Executive: James Rodwell.

Manager: Graham Alexander.

Assistant Manager: Chris Lucketti.

Colours: Claret and light blue striped shirts, claret shorts with light blue trim, light blue socks with claret trim.

Year Formed: 1899.

Turned Professional: 1912.

Previous Names: Amalgamated first with Brumby Hall then North Lindsey United to become Scunthorpe and Lindsey United, 1910; 1958, Scunthorpe United.

Club Nickname: 'The Iron'.

Grounds: 1899, Old Showground; 1988, Glanford Park.

First Football League Game: 19 August 1950, Division 3 (N), v Shrewsbury T (h) D 0–0 – Thompson; Barker, Brownsword; Allen, Taylor, McCormick; Mosby, Payne, Gorin, Rees, Boyes.

Record League Victory: 8–1 v Luton T, Division 3, 24 April 1965 – Sidebottom; Horstead, Hemstead; Smith, Neale, Lindsey; Bramley (1), Scott, Thomas (5), Mahy (1), Wilson (1). 8–1 v Torquay U (a), Division 3, 28 October 1995 – Samways; Housham, Wilson, Ford (1), Knill (1), Hope (Nicholson), Thornber, Bullimore (Walsh), McFarlane (4) (Young), Eyre (2), Paterson.

HONOURS

League Champions: FL 1 – 2006–07; Division 3N – 1957–58.
Runners-up: FL 2 – 2004–05, 2013–14.

FA Cup: 5th rd – 1958, 1970.

League Cup: 4th rd – 2010.

League Trophy: *Runners-up:* 2009.

sky SPORTS FACT FILE

Scunthorpe United were originally nicknamed 'The Nuts' but after winning a place in the Football League for the 1950–51 season this was changed to 'The Iron' and they have been known as this ever since. The cumbersome official title of Scunthorpe & Lindsey United was only shortened following promotion to Division Two in 1958.

Record Cup Victory: 9–0 v Boston U, FA Cup 1st rd, 21 November 1953 – Malan; Hubbard, Brownsword; Sharpe, White, Bushby; Mosby (1), Haigh (3), Whitfield (2), Gregory (1), Mervyn Jones (2).

Record Defeat: 0–8 v Carlisle U, Division 3 (N), 25 December 1952.

Most League Points (2 for a win): 66, Division 3 (N), 1956–57, 1957–58.

Most League Points (3 for a win): 91, FL 1, 2006–07.

Most League Goals: 88, Division 3 (N), 1957–58.

Highest League Scorer in Season: Barrie Thomas, 31, Division 2, 1961–62.

Most League Goals in Total Aggregate: Steve Cammack, 110, 1979–81, 1981–86.

Most League Goals in One Match: 5, Barrie Thomas v Luton T, Division 3, 24 April 1965.

Most Capped Player: Grant McCann, 12 (40), Northern Ireland.

Most League Appearances: Jack Brownsword, 597, 1950–65.

Youngest League Player: Hakeeb Adelakun, 16 years 201 days v Tranmere R, 29 December 2012.

Record Transfer Fee Received: £2,500,000 from Celtic for Gary Hooper, August 2010.

Record Transfer Fee Paid: £700,000 to Hibernian for Rob Jones, July 2009.

Football League Record: 1950 Elected to Division 3 (N); 1958–64 Division 2; 1964–68 Division 3; 1968–72 Division 4; 1972–73 Division 3; 1973–83 Division 4; 1983–84 Division 3; 1984–92 Division 4; 1992–99 Division 3; 1999–2000 Division 2; 2000–04 Division 3; 2004–05 FL 2; 2005–07 FL 1; 2007–08 FL C; 2008–09 FL 1; 2009–11 FL C; 2011–13 FL 1; 2013–14 FL 2; 2014– FL 1.

MANAGERS

Harry Allcock 1915–53 *(Secretary-Manager)*
Tom Crilly 1936–37
Bernard Harper 1946–48
Leslie Jones 1950–51
Bill Corkhill 1952–56
Ron Suart 1956–58
Tony McShane 1959
Bill Lambton 1959
Frank Soo 1959–60
Dick Duckworth 1960–64
Fred Goodwin 1964–66
Ron Ashman 1967–73
Ron Bradley 1973–74
Dick Rooks 1974–76
Ron Ashman 1976–81
John Duncan 1981–83
Allan Clarke 1983–84
Frank Barlow 1984–87
Mick Buxton 1987–91
Bill Green 1991–93
Richard Money 1993–94
David Moore 1994–96
Mick Buxton 1996–97
Brian Laws 1997–2004; 2004–06
Nigel Adkins 2006–10
Ian Baraclough 2010–11
Alan Knill 2011–12
Brian Laws 2012–13
Russ Wilcox 2013–14
Mark Robins 2014–16
Nick Daws 2016
Graham Alexander March 2016–

LATEST SEQUENCES

Longest Sequence of League Wins: 7, 9.4.2016 – 6.8.2017.

Longest Sequence of League Defeats: 8, 29.11.1997 – 20.1.1998.

Longest Sequence of League Draws: 6, 2.1.1984 – 25.2.1984.

Longest Sequence of Unbeaten League Matches: 28, 23.11.2013 – 21.4.2014.

Longest Sequence Without a League Win: 14, 22.3.1975 – 6.9.1975.

Successive Scoring Runs: 24 from 13.1.2007.

Successive Non-scoring Runs: 7 from 19.4.1975.

TEN YEAR LEAGUE RECORD

		P	W	D	L	F	A	Pts	Pos
2007-08	FL C	46	11	13	22	46	69	46	23
2008-09	FL 1	46	22	10	14	82	63	76	6
2009-10	FL C	46	14	10	22	62	84	52	20
2010-11	FL C	46	12	6	28	43	87	42	24
2011-12	FL 1	46	10	22	14	55	59	52	18
2012-13	FL 1	46	13	9	24	49	73	48	21
2013-14	FL 2	46	20	21	5	68	44	81	2
2014-15	FL 1	46	14	14	18	62	75	56	16
2015-16	FL 1	46	21	11	14	60	47	74	7
2016-17	FL 1	46	24	10	12	80	54	82	3

DID YOU KNOW

Scunthorpe & Lindsey United, as they were then known, were drawn to play a Football League club for the very first time in round one proper of 1923–24. United drew 1-1 at home to Rotherham County in front of a record crowd of 5,000 at The Old Showground, but lost the replay 2-0.

SCUNTHORPE UNITED – SKY BET LEAGUE ONE 2016–17 LEAGUE RECORD

Match No.	Date	Venue	Opponents	Result		H/T Score	Lg Pos.	Goalscorers	Attendance
1	Aug 6	H	Bristol R	W	3-1	0-1	3	van Veen 66, Morris 81, Wootton 90	4636
2	13	A	Fleetwood T	D	2-2	0-1	4	Hopper 63, van Veen 67	2509
3	16	A	AFC Wimbledon	W	2-1	2-0	2	Hopper 23, Morris (pen) 41	4163
4	20	H	Gillingham	W	5-0	3-0	2	van Veen 5, Morris 2 (1 pen) 20 (p), 59, Clarke 45, Hopper 82	3718
5	27	A	Port Vale	L	1-3	1-1	3	Morris 45	4557
6	Sept 10	H	Southend U	W	4-0	2-0	2	Madden 36, van Veen 41, Morris 57, Smallwood 87	3723
7	17	A	Shrewsbury T	W	1-0	1-0	1	Mirfin 45	4878
8	20	H	Charlton Ath	D	0-0	0-0	1		3801
9	24	H	Sheffield U	D	2-2	0-1	1	Morris 55, Holmes 82	6243
10	27	A	Walsall	W	4-1	2-1	1	Morris 3 (1 pen) 11 (p), 13, 82, Bishop 47	3970
11	Oct 1	A	Bury	W	2-1	1-0	1	Wiseman 42, Morris 65	5355
12	8	H	Northampton T	D	1-1	1-0	1	Morris 44	4714
13	15	H	Milton Keynes D	W	2-1	0-1	1	Madden 2 65, 81	4238
14	18	A	Oldham Ath	L	0-2	0-2	1		2911
15	22	A	Chesterfield	W	3-0	0-0	1	Morris 49, van Veen 60, Mantom 85	6328
16	29	H	Swindon T	W	4-1	4-0	1	Madden 2 15, 45, Holmes 21, van Veen 43	4262
17	Nov 12	A	Coventry C	W	1-0	0-0	1	Morris 55	9737
18	19	H	Oldham Ath	W	1-0	0-0	1	Wiseman 80	4323
19	22	A	Peterborough U	W	2-0	1-0	1	van Veen 21, Bishop 83	5222
20	26	H	Oxford U	D	1-1	1-0	1	Holmes 35	4338
21	Dec 10	A	Rochdale	L	2-3	0-1	1	Hopper 80, Bishop 84	3445
22	17	H	Millwall	W	3-0	2-0	1	Madden 2 36, 67, Adelakun 45	4355
23	26	A	Bradford C	D	0-0	0-0	1		21,874
24	31	A	Bolton W	L	1-2	0-1	2	Bishop 62	17,062
25	Jan 2	H	Peterborough U	D	1-1	1-0	3	Morris 45	4855
26	7	H	Bury	W	3-2	3-1	2	Toffolo 8, Dawson 19, Morris 44	5173
27	14	A	Northampton T	W	2-1	1-1	2	van Veen 21, Morris 83	5649
28	28	H	Port Vale	W	3-2	0-1	1	Morris (pen) 49, Toney 62, Hopper 71	4442
29	Feb 4	A	Southend U	L	1-3	1-1	2	Wallace 5	7346
30	11	H	Shrewsbury T	L	0-1	0-0	2		4367
31	14	H	Walsall	D	0-0	0-0	2		3168
32	18	A	Sheffield U	D	1-1	0-0	2	Madden 47	27,980
33	25	A	Bristol R	D	1-1	0-1	2	Lockyer (og) 73	8784
34	28	H	AFC Wimbledon	L	1-2	0-0	2	Morris 74	3368
35	Mar 4	H	Fleetwood T	L	0-2	0-1	3		5541
36	7	A	Charlton Ath	L	1-2	0-1	3	van Veen 75	9088
37	11	A	Gillingham	L	2-3	1-0	5	Madden 4, Toffolo 73	6851
38	14	H	Rochdale	W	2-1	0-1	4	Madden 54, Crooks 90	3225
39	18	A	Oxford U	L	1-2	1-0	5	Madden 12	7652
40	26	H	Bradford C	W	3-2	1-2	4	Toney 2 3, 47, Crooks 82	5247
41	Apr 1	A	Millwall	L	1-3	0-1	5	Crooks 90	9789
42	8	H	Bolton W	W	1-0	1-0	5	Mirfin 11	6149
43	14	A	Milton Keynes D	W	1-0	1-0	5	Toney 29	9274
44	17	H	Chesterfield	W	3-1	2-0	4	McGinn (og) 21, Toney 2 37, 73	4636
45	22	A	Swindon T	W	2-1	1-0	4	Wallace 5, Mantom 71	7579
46	30	H	Coventry C	W	3-1	0-1	3	van Veen 52, Bishop 84, Adelakun 89	5796

Final League Position: 3

GOALSCORERS

League (80): Morris 19 (4 pens), Madden 11, van Veen 10, Toney 6, Bishop 5, Hopper 5, Crooks 3, Holmes 3, Adelakun 2, Mantom 2, Mirfin 2, Toffolo 2, Wallace 2, Wiseman 2, Clarke 1, Dawson 1, Smallwood 1, Wootton 1, own goals 2.
FA Cup (1): Hopper 1.
EFL Cup (3): van Veen 2, Morris 1 (1 pen).
EFL Checkatrade Trophy (8): Adelakun 2, Williams 2 (1 pen), Mantom 1, Margetts 1, Wallace 1, own goal 1.
League One Play-Offs (2): Dawson 1, Toney 1.

Daniels L 39	Townsend C 24	Wallace M 46	Mirfin D 33 + 1	Clarke J 23	Bishop N 36 + 6	Dawson S 41 + 2	Adelakun H 7 + 10	Morris J 44	van Veen K 25 + 8	Hopper T 22 + 9	Ness J 9 + 3	Wootton K — + 2	Wiseman S 17 + 7	Mantom S 10 + 16	Holmes D 28 + 4	Williams L 1 + 6	Goode C 13 + 7	Laird S — + 1	Madden P 28 + 6	Smallwood R 6 + 10	Toffolo H 21 + 1	Anyon J 7 + 1	Sutton L 6 + 2	Margetts J — + 2	Davies C 3 + 16	Toney I 9 + 6	Crooks M 8 + 4	*Match No.*
1	2	3	4	5	6^{1}	7	8	9	10^{3}	11^{2}	12	13	14															1
1	5	4	3	2	14	7^{1}	6^{3}	9	10	12				8	11^{2}	13												2
1	5	3	4	2	6	7	12^{3}	9	10^{1}	11				13		8^{2}	14											3
1	5	3	4	2	8	7	12	9^{3}	10^{1}	11		13			6^{2}			14										4
1	5	4	3	2■	8	6^{3}		9	10	11^{2}			12	13	7^{1}				14									5
1	2	4	3		8	7		6^{2}	10				5	13	9^{1}				11^{3}	12	14							6
1		4	3^{2}	2	8	7		9	11				14		6^{1}		12		10^{3}	13	5							7
1		4	3	2	8	7^{2}	13	9	11					14	6^{1}				10^{3}	12	5							8
1		4	3	2	8	7^{2}		9	11^{1}	12					6				13	10	5							9
1		4	3	2^{1}	7	13		11	14	10^{3}			12	8	9^{2}					6	5							10
1		3	4		7	6		11^{3}	12	10			2	13	9^{1}		14			8^{2}	5							11
1		4	3		8	11^{1}	14	9		10			2	12	6^{3}				13	7^{2}	5							12
1^{1}		4	3		6	8		10	13	11			5		7^{2}				12	9^{3}	2	14						13
	5	3	4		6^{2}	8		10	12	7^{1}	14		2	9^{3}	13				11			1						14
1	5	4	3		8	7^{1}		9^{2}	11					12	6^{3}		14		10	13			2					15
1	2	4	3		7^{1}	8		9	11^{3}	14			5^{2}		6				10	12			13					16
1	5	4	3^{1}		7	8		6		11			2		9^{2}	14	12		10^{3}	13								17
1	2	3			8	7		6	10^{1}	11^{2}			5		9^{3}	12	4			14				13				18
1	5	3			8	7^{2}		9	10^{1}	11^{3}			2	13	6	14	4			12								19
1	5	4			7		14	9	11	10^{1}	13		2		6^{3}		3		12	8^{2}								20
1	5^{1}	3			7	8		9	11^{3}	14			2	13	6^{2}	12	4		10									21
1		4		2	8	7	6	9		10^{1}				12			3		11		5							22
1		3		2	7	8	9^{1}	6^{3}		10				12	14		4		11^{2}	13	5							23
1		4		2	8	9	6^{2}	10	12	13				7			3		11^{1}		5							24
1		3		2	8	13	6^{3}	9	11^{1}					7	5^{2}	12	4		10					14				25
1		4		2	7	8		9	10^{1}	11^{2}				6^{3}	14		3			13	5				12			26
1		4		2		8		9	11^{1}	10^{2}				7	6^{3}		3				5				12	13	14	27
1		4			13	7		9		12			2	8	6^{1}		3				5				11^{3}	10^{2}	14	28
1		3			8■	7^{1}	14	9		13			2		6^{3}		4				5				11^{2}	10	12	29
1		3	4		8	7		9	11^{2}	10^{1}					6				12		5		2^{3}		14	13		30
1		3	4		14	7		9	13		8^{1}				6^{3}				11		5		2		12	10^{2}		31
1		3	4		8	7		11	9^{2}	12				13					10^{3}		5■		2		14		6^{1}	32
1	5	3	4^{2}		8			9		11^{1}				7	6		12		10				2		13			33
1	5	4	3	2^{3}	7^{2}	8		6	13				14		9				10						11^{1}		12	34
1	4	3	5^{1}	2	8^{3}	7^{2}		9	11				13		12				10							14	6	35
1		3	4^{1}	2	12	7		9^{2}	11	13					6^{3}				10		5				14		8	36
1		3	4^{3}	2	12	6			10	11^{2}	7^{1}								9		5				14	13	8	37
1		4	3	2		7	12		10^{3}	11^{1}	6						14		9^{2}		5					13	8	38
1		3	4^{2}	2	9	8^{1}	13	7		11^{3}	6								10		5				14	12		39
1	5	4	12	2		7	6^{1}	9					13				3^{3}		11						14	10^{2}	8	40
	4	2	3			5	13	9			6								10^{1}			1	8		12	11^{2}	7	41
	5	3	4		12	7^{2}		9			8		2	13					10^{1}			1			14	11	6^{3}	42
	5	4	3		8	7		9			6		2	13					11^{1}			1			12	10^{2}		43
	5	3	4		6	7		9	12		8^{1}		2	13					10^{2}			1			14	11^{3}		44
	5	4	3		8	6		9			7		2	12					11^{2}			1			13	10^{1}		45
	5	4	3	2^{1}	8		12	9^{2}	10^{3}					7	6				11			1	14		13			46

FA Cup
First Round | Charlton Ath | (a) | 1-3

EFL Cup
First Round (*aet*) | Notts Co | (h) | 2-0
Second Round (*aet*) | Bristol C | (h) | 1-2

EFL Checkatrade Trophy
Northern Group G | Middlesbrough U21 | (h) | 2-1
Northern Group G | Shrewsbury T | (h) | 2-0
Northern Group G | Cambridge U | (a) | 2-0
Second Round North | Morecambe | (h) | 1-1
(*Scunthorpe U won 5-3 on penalties*)
Third Round | Oxford U | (a) | 1-4

League One Play-Offs
Semi-Final 1st leg | Millwall | (a) | 0-0
Semi-Final 2nd leg | Millwall | (h) | 2-3

SHEFFIELD UNITED

FOUNDATION

In March 1889, Yorkshire County Cricket Club formed Sheffield United six days after an FA Cup semi-final between Preston North End and West Bromwich Albion had finally convinced Charles Stokes, a member of the cricket club, that the formation of a professional football club would prove successful at Bramall Lane. The United's first secretary, Mr J. B. Wostinholm, was also secretary of the cricket club.

Bramall Lane Ground, Cherry Street, Bramall Lane, Sheffield, South Yorkshire S2 4SU.

Telephone: (01142) 537 200.

Fax: (0871) 663 2430.

Ticket Office: (0871) 995 1889.

Website: www.sufc.co.uk

Email: info@sufc.co.uk

Ground Capacity: 32,275.

Record Attendance: 68,287 v Leeds U, FA Cup 5th rd, 15 February 1936.

Pitch Measurements: 100.5m × 67m (110yd × 73yd).

Co-Chairmen: Kevin McCabe, James Phipps.

Manager: Chris Wilder.

Assistant Manager: Alan Knill.

Colours: Red and white striped shirts with black trim, black shorts with red trim, black socks with white trim.

Year Formed: 1889.

Turned Professional: 1889.

Club Nickname: 'The Blades'.

Ground: 1889, Bramall Lane.

First Football League Game: 3 September 1892, Division 2, v Lincoln C (h) W 4–2 – Lilley; Witham, Cain; Howell, Hendry, Needham (1); Wallace, Dobson, Hammond (3), Davies, Drummond.

Record League Victory: 10–0 v Burslem Port Vale (a), Division 2, 10 December 1892 – Howlett; Witham, Lilley; Howell, Hendry, Needham; Drummond (1), Wallace (1), Hammond (4), Davies (2), Watson (2). 10-0 v Burnley, Division 1 (h), 19 January 1929.

Record Cup Victory: 6–0 v Leyton Orient (h), FA Cup 1st rd, 6 November 2016 – Ramsdale; Basham (1), O'Connell, Wright, Freeman (1), Coutts (Whiteman), Duffy (Brooks), Fleck, Lafferty, Scougall (1) (Lavery), Chapman (3).

Record Defeat: 0–13 v Bolton W, FA Cup 2nd rd, 1 February 1890.

Most League Points (2 for a win): 60, Division 2, 1952–53.

HONOURS

League Champions: Division 1 – 1897–98; Division 2 – 1952–53; FL 1 – 2016–17; Division 4 – 1981–82.
Runners-up: Division 1 – 1896–97, 1899–1900; FL C – 2005–06; Division 2 – 1892–93, 1938–39, 1960–61, 1970–71, 1989–90; Division 3 – 1988–89.

FA Cup Winners: 1899, 1902, 1915, 1925.
Runners-up: 1901, 1936.

League Cup: semi-final – 2003, 2015.

sky SPORTS FACT FILE

Sheffield United's home game with West Bromwich Albion in March 2012 was abandoned after 82 minutes with the Blades reduced to six men. Three players were sent off and when another two men went off injured the game was stopped. Albion were leading 3-0 at the time and the Football League awarded them a 3-0 victory and the points.

Most League Points (3 for a win): 100, FL 1, 2016–17.

Most League Goals: 102, Division 1, 1925–26.

Highest League Scorer in Season: Jimmy Dunne, 41, Division 1, 1930–31.

Most League Goals in Total Aggregate: Harry Johnson, 201, 1919–30.

Most League Goals in One Match: 5, Harry Hammond v Bootle, Division 2, 26 November 1892; 5, Harry Johnson v West Ham U, Division 1, 26 December 1927.

Most Capped Player: Billy Gillespie, 25, Northern Ireland.

Most League Appearances: Joe Shaw, 632, 1948–66.

Youngest League Player: Louis Reed, 16 years 257 days v Rotherham U, 8 April 2014.

Record Transfer Fee Received: £4,000,000 from Everton for Phil Jagielka, July 2007; £4,000,000 from Tottenham H for Kyle Naughton, July 2009; £4,000,000 from Tottenham H for Kyle Walker, July 2009.

Record Transfer Fee Paid: £4,000,000 to Everton for James Beattie, August 2007.

Football League Record: 1892 Elected to Division 2; 1893–1934 Division 1; 1934–39 Division 2; 1946–49 Division 1; 1949–53 Division 2; 1953–56 Division 1; 1956–61 Division 2; 1961–68 Division 1; 1968–71 Division 2; 1971–76 Division 1; 1976–79 Division 2; 1979–81 Division 3; 1981–82 Division 4; 1982–84 Division 3; 1984–88 Division 2; 1988–89 Division 3; 1989–90 Division 2; 1990–92 Division 1; 1992–94 FA Premier League; 1994–2004 Division 1; 2004–06 FL C; 2006–07 FA Premier League; 2007–11 FL C; 2011–17 FL 1; 2017– FL C.

MANAGERS

J. B. Wostinholm 1889–99 *(Secretary-Manager)*
John Nicholson 1899–1932
Ted Davison 1932–52
Reg Freeman 1952–55
Joe Mercer 1955–58
Johnny Harris 1959–68 *(continued as General Manager to 1970)*
Arthur Rowley 1968–69
Johnny Harris *(General Manager resumed Team Manager duties)* 1969–73
Ken Furphy 1973–75
Jimmy Sirrel 1975–77
Harry Haslam 1978–81
Martin Peters 1981
Ian Porterfield 1981–86
Billy McEwan 1986–88
Dave Bassett 1988–95
Howard Kendall 1995–97
Nigel Spackman 1997–98
Steve Bruce 1998–99
Adrian Heath 1999
Neil Warnock 1999–2007
Bryan Robson 2007–08
Kevin Blackwell 2008–10
Gary Speed 2010
Micky Adams 2010–11
Danny Wilson 2011–13
David Weir 2013
Nigel Clough 2013–15
Nigel Adkins 2015–16
Chris Wilder May 2016–

LATEST SEQUENCES

Longest Sequence of League Wins: 8, 20.8.2005 – 27.9.2005.

Longest Sequence of League Defeats: 7, 19.8.1975 – 20.9.1975.

Longest Sequence of League Draws: 6, 6.5.2001 – 8.9.2001.

Longest Sequence of Unbeaten League Matches: 22, 2.9.1899 – 13.1.1900.

Longest Sequence Without a League Win: 19, 27.9.1975 – 7.2.1976.

Successive Scoring Runs: 34 from 30.3.1956.

Successive Non-scoring Runs: 6 from 4.12.1993.

TEN YEAR LEAGUE RECORD

		P	W	D	L	F	A	Pts	Pos
2007-08	FL C	46	17	15	14	56	51	66	9
2008-09	FL C	46	22	14	10	64	39	80	3
2009-10	FL C	46	17	14	15	62	55	65	8
2010-11	FL C	46	11	9	26	44	79	42	23
2011-12	FL 1	46	27	9	10	92	51	90	3
2012-13	FL 1	46	19	18	9	56	42	75	5
2013-14	FL 1	46	18	13	15	48	46	67	7
2014-15	FL 1	46	19	14	13	66	53	71	5
2015-16	FL 1	46	18	12	16	64	59	66	11
2016-17	FL 1	46	30	10	6	92	47	100	1

DID YOU KNOW

Sheffield United played a friendly match with Bolton Wanderers under artificial light in November 1889. The Bramall Lane ground was illuminated by 17 Wells' Lights (similar to a giant flare) and 3,000 turned out to watch Wanderers defeat the newly formed club 2-0.

SHEFFIELD UNITED – SKY BET LEAGUE ONE 2016–17 LEAGUE RECORD

Match No.	*Date*		*Venue*	*Opponents*	*Result*		*H/T Score*	*Lg Pos.*	*Goalscorers*	*Attendance*
1	Aug	6	A	Bolton W	L	0-1	0-1	18		17,050
2		13	H	Rochdale	D	1-1	0-1	17	Sharp [81]	19,399
3		16	H	Southend U	L	0-3	0-3	22		17,410
4		20	A	Millwall	L	1-2	1-1	24	Scougall [21]	9058
5		27	H	Oxford U	W	2-1	0-1	20	Sharp [65], Wilson [73]	19,313
6	Sept	4	A	Gillingham	W	2-1	0-1	16	Freeman [65], Sharp (pen) [90]	5598
7		10	A	AFC Wimbledon	W	3-2	2-1	12	Duffy [20], Sharp [26], Done [60]	4810
8		17	H	Peterborough U	W	1-0	1-0	6	Done [13]	19,555
9		24	A	Scunthorpe U	D	2-2	1-0	7	Basham [34], Sharp (pen) [85]	6243
10		27	H	Bristol R	W	1-0	0-0	6	Chapman [65]	19,196
11	Oct	1	A	Fleetwood T	D	1-1	0-1	4	Ebanks-Landell [90]	4004
12		15	H	Port Vale	W	4-0	2-0	5	Ebanks-Landell 2 [23, 45], Duffy [62], Scougall [83]	19,699
13		18	A	Shrewsbury T	W	3-0	0-0	4	Sharp 2 [46, 66], Lafferty [63]	5460
14		22	A	Bradford C	D	3-3	1-1	3	Sharp 2 [18, 51], Basham [72]	20,972
15		29	H	Milton Keynes D	W	2-1	1-0	4	Scougall [5], Sharp [63]	20,495
16	Nov	13	A	Chesterfield	W	4-1	0-1	3	Freeman [54], Fleck [72], Sharp [73], Clarke [81]	8451
17		19	H	Shrewsbury T	W	2-1	2-0	2	Sharp [8], Scougall [24]	20,195
18		22	H	Bury	W	1-0	0-0	2	Ebanks-Landell [90]	19,022
19		26	A	Charlton Ath	D	1-1	1-0	3	Duffy [32]	12,580
20		29	H	Walsall	L	0-1	0-1	3		18,343
21	Dec	10	H	Swindon T	W	4-0	0-0	2	Duffy 2 [52, 60], Coutts [54], Lavery [77]	19,196
22		15	A	Coventry C	W	2-1	1-0	2	Sharp 2 [23, 87]	8801
23		26	H	Oldham Ath	W	2-0	0-0	2	Sharp 2 [72, 88]	25,821
24		31	H	Northampton T	W	1-0	0-0	1	Freeman [89]	24,194
25	Jan	2	A	Bury	W	3-1	1-1	1	Sharp [21], Etuhu (og) [72], Freeman [81]	6123
26		7	A	Southend U	W	4-2	2-1	1	Ebanks-Landell [3], O'Connell [42], Lavery [72], Freeman [76]	7702
27		14	A	Walsall	L	1-4	1-1	1	O'Connell [10]	6899
28		21	H	Gillingham	D	2-2	1-0	1	Sharp [32], Freeman [61]	20,649
29		24	H	Fleetwood T	L	0-2	0-1	1		19,012
30	Feb	4	H	AFC Wimbledon	W	4-0	2-0	1	Sharp [2], Hanson [37], Fleck [79], Lavery [90]	20,549
31		11	A	Peterborough U	W	1-0	0-0	1	Sharp [87]	10,258
32		14	A	Bristol R	D	0-0	0-0	1		9175
33		18	H	Scunthorpe U	D	1-1	0-0	1	Sharp [49]	27,980
34		25	H	Bolton W	W	2-0	1-0	1	Sharp 2 (1 pen) [12, 70 (p)]	27,165
35	Mar	4	A	Rochdale	D	3-3	2-1	1	Duffy [5], Lafferty [11], Sharp [68]	6214
36		7	A	Oxford U	W	3-2	0-1	1	Sharp 2 (1 pen) [55, 76 (p)], Freeman [72]	8965
37		14	A	Swindon T	W	4-2	2-0	1	Lavery [29], Freeman [35], O'Shea [58], Coutts (pen) [90]	7012
38		18	H	Charlton Ath	W	2-1	1-1	1	O'Connell [14], Lafferty [48]	23,308
39		25	A	Oldham Ath	D	1-1	0-1	1	O'Shea [50]	8448
40		28	H	Millwall	W	2-0	1-0	1	O'Connell [16], Freeman [55]	20,832
41	Apr	5	H	Coventry C	W	2-0	0-0	1	Clarke [70], Fleck [75]	24,334
42		8	A	Northampton T	W	2-1	0-1	1	Clarke [61], Fleck [88]	7425
43		14	A	Port Vale	W	3-0	2-0	1	O'Shea [2], Clarke [30], Done [90]	8999
44		17	H	Bradford C	W	3-0	3-0	1	Clarke 2 [13, 42], Sharp [20]	26,838
45		22	A	Milton Keynes D	W	3-0	1-0	1	Clarke [45], Sharp 2 [67, 81]	18,180
46		30	H	Chesterfield	W	3-2	1-1	1	Freeman [18], Sharp [59], Lafferty [82]	31,003

Final League Position: 1

GOALSCORERS

League (92): Sharp 30 (4 pens), Freeman 10, Clarke 7, Duffy 6, Ebanks-Landell 5, Fleck 4, Lafferty 4, Lavery 4, O'Connell 4, Scougall 4, Done 3, O'Shea 3, Basham 2, Coutts 2 (1 pen), Chapman 1, Hanson 1, Wilson 1, own goal 1.
FA Cup (8): Chapman 3, Basham 1, Coutts 1, Freeman 1, O'Connell 1, Scougall 1.
EFL Cup (1): Clarke 1.
EFL Checkatrade Trophy (5): Clarke 1, Coutts 1, O'Connell 1, Slater 1, own goal 1.

Long G 3	Brayford J 3	O'Connell J 40 + 4	Wilson J 7	Hussey C 5 + 2	Duffy M 38 + 1	Fleck J 41 + 3	Basham C 42 + 1	Done M 24 + 7	Clarke L 12 + 11	Sharp B 44 + 2	Adams C — + 1	Scougall S 6 + 19	Chapman H — + 12	Coutts P 40 + 3	Moore S 43	Freeman K 39 + 2	McNulty M 1 + 3	Wright Jake 28 + 2	Lafferty D 37	Ebanks-Landell E 29 + 5	Lavery C 6 + 21	Brown R — + 2	Whiteman B — + 2	Carruthers S 2 + 12	Hanson J 10 + 3	O'Shea J 5 + 5	Riley J 1 + 1	Match No.
1	2	3	4	5	6^{1}	7	8	9^{2}	10	11	12	13																1
1	2	4	3	5	6^{1}	8	7	9^{2}	10	11		13	12															2
1	2	4	3	5	6^{1}	8^{3}	7	9^{2}	11	10		14	12	13														3
		4	3	5	9		8	12	11	10^{1}		6^{2}	13	7	1	2^{3}	14											4
		12	4	2^{3}	6	13	8	10	14	11^{1}		9^{2}		7	1	5		3										5
		3	4^{2}		6^{3}		8	11^{1}	13	10		14		7	1	5		2	9	12								6
		3			6	12	8^{3}	11^{1}	13	10^{2}		14		7	1	5		2	9	4								7
		4			8^{3}	13	6	10		11^{2}		12		7	1	5		2	9^{1}	3	14							8
		4			9^{1}	7	2■	11		10^{2}		12		6	1	5			8	3	13							9
		4			7^{1}	6		10		11^{2}		8^{3}	12	2	1	5			9	3	13	14						10
		4		12	7^{2}	6		10		11		13	14	8	1	5		2^{3}	9^{1}	3								11
		4		12	7^{2}	8		10^{3}		11		14	13	6	1	5		2	9^{1}	3								12
					7^{1}	6	3	11		10				8	1	5^{2}		4	9	2		13	12					13
					7	8	2	11^{2}		10		13		6^{1}	1	5		4	9	3	12							14
		13			7^{2}	8	2			11		10^{1}		6	1	5		4	9	3	12							15
		13			9	7	3	11^{1}	12	10^{3}				6	1	5		4^{2}	8	2	14							16
		13			7^{1}	8	2	10		11		12	14	6^{2}	1	5^{3}		4	9	3								17
		2				8	7	11^{1}	12	10		5^{3}	13	6	1			4^{2}	9	3	14							18
		2			5^{1}	8	7		11^{2}	10		14		6	1	12		4^{3}	9	3	13							19
		4			7	8	2^{1}		11	10			12	6	1	5			9^{2}	3	13							20
		3			9^{1}	7	4	11^{3}	13	10^{2}		14		8	1	2			6	5	12							21
		2			6^{2}	8	3	11^{3}	13	10				7^{1}	1	5			9	4	12		14					22
		2			7^{1}	6	3	11^{3}	12	10		14		8^{2}	1	5		13	9	4								23
		2			7	6	3^{3}	14	11^{2}	10		13		8	1	5			9^{1}	4	12							24
		4			12	7	8	14		11^{1}		6^{2}		13	1	5		3	9^{3}	2	10							25
		3			7^{2}	8	4	12		10		14		6	1	5			9^{1}	2	11			13^{3}				26
		4			7	8	2^{2}	9	12	11		13		6	1	5				3	10^{1}							27
		2			7	6	4	9^{2}		10		13		8	1	5	12			3	11^{1}							28
		4			7	6	2^{3}	14		11		13		8	1	5	10^{1}		9^{2}	3	12							29
		4			7^{3}	8	12			11^{2}				6	1	5		2	9	3^{1}	13			14	10			30
		3			6^{2}	7	4			10					1	2		9	5^{1}		13			8^{3}	11	12	14	31
		3				8	4	10^{2}		12				6	1			2	9	13	11					7^{1}	5	32
		4^{2}			6	8	2	14		10				7	1	5		3	9^{1}		12				11^{3}	13		33
		4			6^{3}	8	2			10^{1}				7	1	5		3	9	14	13			12	11^{2}			34
		4^{1}			6^{2}	8	2			10				7	1	5		3	9	13	14			12	11^{3}			35
		4				8	2			10				7	1	5		3^{2}	9	6	13			12	11^{1}			36
		4				6	3			11^{2}				7	1	5		14	8	2	10^{1}			12	13	9^{3}		37
		2			9^{3}	6	4			11				7^{1}	1	5			8	3	13			12	10^{2}	14		38
		4				7	6	8^{1}	14	11				12	1	5		3		2	13^{3}				10	9^{2}		39
		4			7^{1}	8	2			11^{2}				6	1	5		3	9					12	10	13		40
		4			7^{1}	8	2		12	10^{2}				6	1	5		3^{3}	9					13	11	14		41
		4				8	3		10^{2}	12				7	1	2		5	6	14				9^{3}	13	11^{1}		42
		3				6	4	8	11^{2}	10^{1}			13	7	1	12	14	2		5						9^{3}		43
		4			6^{1}	8	2		10	11				7	1	5		3	9					12				44
		4	3^{1}		9^{2}	8	2	13	10	11			14	7	1	5^{3}			6					12				45
		4			7^{3}	8	2		11^{2}	10			14	6	1	5		3^{1}	9					13	12			46

FA Cup

First Round	Leyton Orient	(h)	6-0
Second Round	Bolton W	(a)	2-3

EFL Cup

First Round	Crewe Alex	(h)	1-2

(*aet*)

EFL Checkatrade Trophy

Northern Group H	Leicester C U21	(h)	0-0
(*Leicester C U21 won 5-4 on penalties*)			
Northern Group H	Walsall	(h)	1-2
Northern Group H	Grimsby T	(a)	4-2

SHEFFIELD WEDNESDAY

FOUNDATION

Sheffield being one of the principal centres of early Association Football, this club was formed as long ago as 1867 by the Sheffield Wednesday Cricket Club (formed 1825) and their colours from the start were blue and white. The inaugural meeting was held at the Adelphi Hotel and the original committee included Charles Stokes who was subsequently a founder member of Sheffield United.

Hillsborough Stadium, Sheffield, South Yorkshire S6 1SW.

Telephone: (0370) 020 1867.

Fax: (0114) 221 2122.

Ticket Office: (0370) 020 1867 (option 1).

Website: www.swfc.co.uk

Email: footballenquiries@swfc.co.uk

Ground Capacity: 38,385.

Record Attendance: 72,841 v Manchester C, FA Cup 5th rd, 17 February 1934.

Pitch Measurements: 105m × 68m (115yd × 74yd).

Chairman: Dejphon Chansiri.

Chief Operating Officer: Joe Palmer.

Head Coach: Carlos Carvalhal.

Coaches: Lee Bullen, Joao Mario Oliveria, Bruno Lage, Jhony Conceicao.

Colours: Blue shirts with thin white stripes and white trim, blue shorts with white trim, blue socks with white hoops.

Year Formed: 1867 (fifth oldest League club).

Turned Professional: 1887.

Previous Name: The Wednesday until 1929.

Club Nickname: 'The Owls'.

Grounds: 1867, Highfield; 1869, Myrtle Road; 1877, Sheaf House; 1887, Olive Grove; 1899, Owlerton (since 1912 known as Hillsborough). Some games were played at Endcliffe in the 1880s. Until 1895 Bramall Lane was used for some games.

First Football League Game: 3 September 1892, Division 1, v Notts Co (a) W 1–0 – Allan; Tom Brandon (1), Mumford; Hall, Betts, Harry Brandon; Spiksley, Brady, Davis, Bob Brown, Dunlop.

Record League Victory: 9–1 v Birmingham, Division 1, 13 December 1930 – Brown; Walker, Blenkinsop; Strange, Leach, Wilson; Hooper (3), Seed (2), Ball (2), Burgess (1), Rimmer (1).

Record Cup Victory: 12–0 v Halliwell, FA Cup 1st rd, 17 January 1891 – Smith; Thompson, Brayshaw; Harry Brandon (1), Betts, Cawley (2); Winterbottom, Mumford (2), Bob Brandon (1), Woolhouse (5), Ingram (1).

HONOURS

League Champions: Division 1 – 1902–03, 1903–04, 1928–29, 1929–30; Division 2 – 1899–1900, 1925–26, 1951–52, 1955–56, 1958–59.
Runners-up: Division 1 – 1960–61; Division 2 – 1949–50, 1983–84; FL 1 – 2011–12.

FA Cup Winners: 1896, 1907, 1935.
Runners-up: 1890, 1966, 1993.

League Cup Winners: 1991.
Runners-up: 1993.

European Competitions
Fairs Cup: 1961–62 *(qf)*, 1963–64.
UEFA Cup: 1992–93.
Intertoto Cup: 1995.

sky SPORTS FACT FILE

Sheffield Wednesday's home match with Aston Villa in the 1888–89 season took over three months to complete. The game on 25 November was abandoned with Wednesday 3-1 up. The Football League instructed the clubs to play out the remaining minutes on 25 March when both teams played different line-ups. Wednesday added another goal to finish up 4-1 winners.

Record Defeat: 0–10 v Aston Villa, Division 1, 5 October 1912.

Most League Points (2 for a win): 62, Division 2, 1958–59.

Most League Points (3 for a win): 93, FL 1, 2011–12.

Most League Goals: 106, Division 2, 1958–59.

Highest League Scorer in Season: Derek Dooley, 46, Division 2, 1951–52.

Most League Goals in Total Aggregate: Andrew Wilson, 199, 1900–20.

Most League Goals in One Match: 6, Doug Hunt v Norwich C, Division 2, 19 November 1938.

Most Capped Player: Nigel Worthington, 50 (66), Northern Ireland.

Most League Appearances: Andrew Wilson, 501, 1900–20.

Youngest League Player: Peter Fox, 15 years 269 days v Orient, 31 March 1973.

Record Transfer Fee Received: £3,000,000 from WBA for Chris Brunt, August 2007.

Record Transfer Fee Paid: £5,000,000 (rising to £7,000,000) to Middlesborough for Adam Reach, September 2016.

Football League Record: 1892 Elected to Division 1; 1899–1900 Division 2; 1900–20 Division 1; 1920–26 Division 2; 1926–37 Division 1; 1937–50 Division 2; 1950–51 Division 1; 1951–52 Division 2; 1952–55 Division 1; 1955–56 Division 2; 1956–58 Division 1; 1958–59 Division 2; 1959–70 Division 1; 1970–75 Division 2; 1975–80 Division 3; 1980–84 Division 2; 1984–90 Division 1; 1990–91 Division 2; 1991–92 Division 1; 1992–2000 FA Premier League; 2000–03 Division 1; 2003–04 Division 2; 2004–05 FL 1; 2005–10 FL C; 2010–12 FL 1; 2012– FL C.

MANAGERS

Arthur Dickinson 1891–1920 *(Secretary-Manager)*
Robert Brown 1920–33
Billy Walker 1933–37
Jimmy McMullan 1937–42
Eric Taylor 1942–58 *(continued as General Manager to 1974)*
Harry Catterick 1958–61
Vic Buckingham 1961–64
Alan Brown 1964–68
Jack Marshall 1968–69
Danny Williams 1969–71
Derek Dooley 1971–73
Steve Burtenshaw 1974–75
Len Ashurst 1975–77
Jackie Charlton 1977–83
Howard Wilkinson 1983–88
Peter Eustace 1988–89
Ron Atkinson 1989–91
Trevor Francis 1991–95
David Pleat 1995–97
Ron Atkinson 1997–98
Danny Wilson 1998–2000
Peter Shreeves *(Acting)* 2000
Paul Jewell 2000–01
Peter Shreeves 2001
Terry Yorath 2001–02
Chris Turner 2002–04
Paul Sturrock 2004–06
Brian Laws 2006–09
Alan Irvine 2010–11
Gary Megson 2011–12
Dave Jones 2012–13
Stuart Gray 2013–15
Carlos Carvalhal June 2015–

LATEST SEQUENCES

Longest Sequence of League Wins: 9, 23.4.1904 – 15.10.1904.

Longest Sequence of League Defeats: 8, 9.9.2000 – 17.10.2000.

Longest Sequence of League Draws: 7, 15.3.2008 – 14.4.2008.

Longest Sequence of Unbeaten League Matches: 19, 10.12.1960 – 8.4.1961.

Longest Sequence Without a League Win: 20, 11.1.1975 – 30.8.1975.

Successive Scoring Runs: 40 from 14.11.1959.

Successive Non-scoring Runs: 8 from 8.3.1975.

TEN YEAR LEAGUE RECORD

		P	W	D	L	F	A	Pts	Pos
2007-08	FL C	46	14	13	19	54	55	55	16
2008-09	FL C	46	16	13	17	51	58	61	12
2009-10	FL C	46	11	14	21	49	69	47	22
2010-11	FL 1	46	16	10	20	67	67	58	15
2011-12	FL 1	46	28	9	9	81	48	93	2
2012-13	FL C	46	16	10	20	53	61	58	18
2013-14	FL C	46	13	14	19	63	65	53	16
2014-15	FL C	46	14	18	14	43	49	60	13
2015-16	FL C	46	19	17	10	66	45	74	6
2016-17	FL C	46	24	9	13	60	45	81	4

DID YOU KNOW ?

Sheffield Wednesday were one of the first English clubs to make use of a mascot figure in their marketing of goods. Ozzie Owl was created by the same company that produced World Cup Willie and was launched in January 1967.

SHEFFIELD WEDNESDAY – SKY BET CHAMPIONSHIP 2016–17 LEAGUE RECORD

Match No.	Date	Venue	Opponents	Result		H/T Score	Lg Pos.	Goalscorers	Attendance
1	Aug 7	H	Aston Villa	W	1-0	0-0	9	Forestieri [85]	30,060
2	13	A	Norwich C	D	0-0	0-0	6		26,236
3	16	A	Burton Alb	L	1-3	1-2	13	Hooper (pen) [12]	4997
4	20	H	Leeds U	L	0-2	0-0	20		29,075
5	27	A	Brentford	D	1-1	0-0	19	Hutchinson [90]	9677
6	Sept 10	H	Wigan Ath	W	2-1	1-1	16	Fletcher [29], Forestieri [62]	24,860
7	13	H	Bristol C	W	3-2	0-2	9	Fletcher [52], Bannan [75], Lee [90]	24,151
8	17	A	Birmingham C	L	1-2	0-0	12	Hooper [76]	16,786
9	24	H	Nottingham F	W	2-1	0-1	11	Lee 2 [68, 90]	27,350
10	27	A	Blackburn R	W	1-0	1-0	7	Fletcher [22]	12,844
11	Oct 1	H	Brighton & HA	L	1-2	0-1	9	Hooper [90]	25,605
12	16	A	Huddersfield T	W	1-0	0-0	7	Forestieri (pen) [68]	22,368
13	19	A	Cardiff C	D	1-1	0-1	6	Pudil [55]	15,887
14	22	H	QPR	W	1-0	1-0	5	Hooper [40]	25,903
15	29	A	Derby Co	L	0-2	0-1	7		30,064
16	Nov 5	H	Ipswich T	L	1-2	1-1	10	Hooper [36]	25,851
17	19	A	Fulham	D	1-1	1-0	9	Forestieri [10]	20,255
18	26	A	Wolverhampton W	W	2-0	2-0	7	Forestieri (pen) [15], Lee [29]	27,293
19	Dec 3	H	Preston NE	W	2-1	1-0	6	Forestieri [9], Fletcher (pen) [79]	24,843
20	10	A	Reading	L	1-2	0-0	6	Fletcher [90]	18,153
21	13	H	Barnsley	W	2-0	1-0	6	MacDonald (og) [37], Hutchinson [80]	27,248
22	17	H	Rotherham U	W	1-0	0-0	6	Fletcher (pen) [90]	27,242
23	26	A	Newcastle U	W	1-0	0-0	4	Loovens [53]	52,179
24	31	A	Preston NE	D	1-1	0-0	6	Reach [90]	14,802
25	Jan 2	H	Wolverhampton W	D	0-0	0-0	6		30,549
26	14	H	Huddersfield T	W	2-0	0-0	6	Wallace [54], Forestieri [90]	28,173
27	20	A	Brighton & HA	L	1-2	1-1	6	Dunk (og) [45]	27,162
28	31	A	Bristol C	D	2-2	1-1	7	Forestieri [17], Wallace [51]	17,438
29	Feb 3	A	Wigan Ath	W	1-0	1-0	6	Wallace [43]	13,037
30	10	H	Birmingham C	W	3-0	1-0	6	Rhodes [9], Winnall [80], Reach [86]	24,805
31	14	H	Blackburn R	W	2-1	2-1	6	Sasso 2 [18, 44]	24,603
32	18	A	Nottingham F	W	2-1	1-0	6	Abdi [28], Forestieri [52]	20,164
33	21	H	Brentford	L	1-2	0-2	6	Forestieri [90]	25,014
34	25	A	Leeds U	L	0-1	0-1	6		35,093
35	Mar 4	H	Norwich C	W	5-1	3-1	6	Wallace [15], Rhodes 2 [22, 54], Fox [41], Forestieri [66]	28,178
36	7	H	Burton Alb	D	1-1	1-1	6	Wallace [16]	24,929
37	11	A	Aston Villa	L	0-2	0-1	6		31,143
38	17	H	Reading	L	0-2	0-1	6		26,072
39	Apr 1	A	Barnsley	D	1-1	0-0	6	Winnall [50]	18,003
40	4	A	Rotherham U	W	2-0	2-0	6	Fletcher 2 [19, 44]	10,669
41	8	H	Newcastle U	W	2-1	0-0	6	Lees [59], Fletcher [68]	28,883
42	14	H	Cardiff C	W	1-0	0-0	6	Forestieri [84]	28,007
43	17	A	QPR	W	2-1	2-1	5	Reach [12], Pudil [31]	15,708
44	22	H	Derby Co	W	2-1	0-0	4	Fletcher [58], Hooper [64]	28,889
45	29	A	Ipswich T	W	1-0	0-0	4	Lee [77]	19,000
46	May 7	H	Fulham	L	1-2	1-1	4	Winnall [9]	33,681

Final League Position: 4

GOALSCORERS

League (60): Forestieri 12 (2 pens), Fletcher 10 (2 pens), Hooper 6 (1 pen), Lee 5, Wallace 5, Reach 3, Rhodes 3, Winnall 3, Hutchinson 2, Pudil 2, Sasso 2, Abdi 1, Bannan 1, Fox 1, Lees 1, Loovens 1, own goals 2.
FA Cup (0).
EFL Cup (1): Lucas Joao 1.
Championship Play-Offs (1): Fletcher 1.

Westwood K 43	Hunt J 31 + 1	Lees T 35	Hutchinson S 33	Pudil D 26	Wallace R 32 + 9	Lee K 26	Bannan B 42 + 1	Abdi A 11 + 5	Forestieri F 25 + 10	Fletcher S 22 + 16	Hooper G 17 + 6	Nuhiu A 2 + 18	Palmer L 15 + 6	Lucas Joao E 7 + 3	Buckley W 2 + 9	Semedo J 2 + 8	Jones D 18 + 11	Reach A 36 + 3	Sasso V 12 + 2	Loovens G 29 + 3	Dawson C 2 + 2	Hirst G — + 1	McManaman C 2 + 9	Winnall S 10 + 4	Fox M 10	Rhodes J 14 + 4	Marco Matias A 1 + 1	Wildsmith J 1	Emanuelson U — + 1	Match No.
1	2^{2}	3	4	5	6^{3}	7	8	9	10	11^{1}	12	13	14																	1
1	2	3	4	5	6^{1}	7	8	9		12	10^{3}	14		11^{2}	13															2
1	2		4	5	6	7	8	9^{3}	13	10	11^{1}	14	12			3^{2}														3
1	2^{3}	3	4	5	6^{1}	8	7	9^{2}	10	11	12				14		13													4
1		3	4	5		7	6	14	9	11^{3}	12	13	2^{2}	10^{1}			8■													5
1		3	4	5^{1}	6	7	8^{2}	10^{3}	9	11	12		2		14			13												6
1	2	3	4■	5^{3}	13	8	6		12	11	10^{1}						7^{2}	9	14											7
1		3			6^{3}	7	8	9^{2}	10	11^{1}	12	13	2		14			5		4										8
1	2	3^{1}	4		6	7	8^{3}	13	9	11	10^{2}	14						5		12										9
1		3	4^{1}			7	9		13	11^{2}	10^{3}	14	2		6		8	5		12										10
1^{2}	2	3		5^{1}	6	7	8		10	11	13							9		4	12									11
1		3	4	5	12	7	6^{3}		10^{2}		11^{1}	13	2				8	9		14										12
1^{1}		3	4	5	6^{3}	9		7^{2}	13		10		2		14		8	11			12									13
	2^{1}	3	4	5	14	7^{2}	6		10	13	11^{3}		12				8	9			1									14
		3	4	5^{2}	13	7	6		10	12^{3}	11	14	2				8^{1}	9			1									15
1	2	3	4	5	13	7	6	14	12	10	11^{3}						8^{2}	9^{1}												16
1	2	3	8^{1}		6	7	9		11	13	10^{2}						12	5		4										17
1	2^{3}	3	8		6	7	9^{1}		11	13			12	10^{2}	14			5		4										18
1	2	3	7		9^{2}	8	6		10■	14				11^{1}	12		13	5		4^{3}										19
1	2	3	8^{2}		6	7	9			12		11^{1}		10				5		4		13								20
1		3	7	5	12	6	8^{3}			10^{1}		14	2	9^{2}			13	11		4										21
1		3	7	5^{3}	12	6^{2}		8^{1}		10		14	2	9			13	11		4										22
1		3	7	5	6^{2}		8^{3}		11^{1}	10		14	2	12			13	9		4										23
1	13	3	7	5	6^{2}		8			10		11^{1}	2^{3}	14			12	9		4										24
1	2	3	8		12	7^{1}	9		11	10^{2}				13			14	5	4				6^{3}							25
1	2^{1}	3	7	5	6^{2}		8		11	10^{3}			13					9		4			14	12						26
1	2^{3}	3	7■	5^{1}	6		8		10	13■			12					9		4			14	11^{2}						27
1		3			6		7		11			12	2				8	9		4			13	10^{1}	5^{2}					28
1	2			5^{2}	6^{1}		7	13	11^{3}							14	8	9	3	4			12			10				29
1	2		7		6^{3}		8^{1}	13	9^{2}									12	3	4			14	10	5	11				30
1	2		7^{1}		6		8		12	13							14	9	3	4				10^{3}	5^{2}	11				31
1	2		8	5	12		9	7^{3}	11^{1}	13								6	3	4				14		10^{2}				32
1			7		6		9^{1}	8^{2}	11	14			2					5	3	4^{3}			13	12		10				33
1	2		7		6		14	8^{2}	11	13								9	3	4			12		5^{3}	10^{1}				34
1	2		7^{2}		6^{3}		8^{1}		9							13	12		3	4			14	11	5	10				35
1	2				6^{1}		8		9	13					14		7	12	3	4				11^{3}	5^{2}	10				36
1	2				6		8			12						13	7	9	3■	4^{1}				11^{2}	5	10				37
1	2	3					8			13		14			6		7^{3}	9		4^{1}			12	11^{2}	5	10				38
1	2	3	7^{1}				8			13							12	9		4			6^{2}	11	5	10^{3}	14			39
1	2	3			7		8			11^{3}	9^{2}	13				12	6	5		4				14		10^{1}				40
1	2	3		5	6^{1}		8			11	10^{2}					14	7	9	12	4^{3}						13				41
1	2	3		5	6		8		13	11^{3}	10^{1}	14					7^{2}	9	4							12				42
1		3		5	6^{1}		8		12		11^{3}	14	2			13	7	9		4						10^{2}				43
1	2	3		5	6	7^{1}	8		14	10^{3}	11^{2}					13		9		4						12				44
1	2	3		5	6^{1}	7	8		12	10^{3}	11^{2}					14		9		4						13				45
			7^{3}			9^{2}						14	2		12	4	8		3					10	5	11^{1}	6■	1	13	46

FA Cup
Third Round | Middlesbrough | (a) | 0-3

EFL Cup
First Round | Cambridge U | (a) | 1-2
(*aet*)

Championship Play-Offs
Semi-Final 1st leg | Huddersfield T | (a) | 0-0
Semi-Final 2nd leg | Huddersfield T | (h) | 1-1
(*aet; Huddersfield T won 4-3 on penalties*)

SHREWSBURY TOWN

FOUNDATION

Shrewsbury School having provided a number of the early England and Wales international players it is not surprising that there was a Town club as early as 1876 which won the Birmingham Senior Cup in 1879. However, the present Shrewsbury Town club was formed in 1886 and won the Welsh FA Cup as early as 1891.

Greenhous Meadow, Oteley Road, Shrewsbury, Shropshire SY2 6ST.

Telephone: (01743) 289 177.

Fax: (01743) 246 957.

Ticket Office: (01743) 273 943.

Website: www.shrewsburytown.com

Email: info@shrewsburytown.co.uk

Ground Capacity: 9,875.

Record Attendance: 18,917 v Walsall, Division 3, 26 April 1961 (at Gay Meadow); 10,210 v Chelsea, League Cup 4th rd, 28 October 2014 (at Greenhous Meadow).

Pitch Measurements: 101m × 66m (110yd × 72yd).

Chairman: Roland Wycherley.

Chief Executive: Brian Caldwell.

Manager: Paul Hurst.

Assistant Manager: Chris Doig.

HONOURS

League Champions: Division 3 – 1978–79; Third Division – 1993–94. *Runners-up:* FL 2 – 2011–12, 2014–15; Division 4 – 1974–75; Conference – (3rd) 2003–04 *(promoted via play-offs).*

FA Cup: 6th rd – 1979, 1982.

League Cup: semi-final – 1961.

League Trophy: *Runners-up:* 1996.

Welsh Cup Winners: 1891, 1938, 1977, 1979, 1984, 1985.
Runners-up: 1931, 1948, 1980.

Colours: Blue and yellow striped shirts, blue shorts with yellow trim, blue socks with yellow trim.

Year Formed: 1886.

Turned Professional: 1896.

Club Nicknames: 'Town', 'Blues', 'Salop'. The name 'Salop' is a colloquialism for the county of Shropshire. Since Shrewsbury is the only club in Shropshire, cries of 'Come on Salop' are frequently used!

Grounds: 1886, Old Racecourse Ground; 1889, Ambler's Field; 1893, Sutton Lane; 1895, Barracks Ground; 1910, Gay Meadow; 2007, New Meadow (re-named ProStar Stadium 2008; Greenhous Meadow 2010).

First Football League Game: 19 August 1950, Division 3 (N), v Scunthorpe U (a) D 0–0 – Egglestone; Fisher, Lewis; Wheatley, Depear, Robinson; Griffin, Hope, Jackson, Brown, Barker.

Record League Victory: 7–0 v Swindon T, Division 3 (S), 6 May 1955 – McBride; Bannister, Skeech; Wallace, Maloney, Candlin; Price, O'Donnell (1), Weigh (4), Russell, McCue (2); 7-0 v Gillingham, FL 2, 13 September 2008 – Daniels; Herd, Tierney, Davies (2), Jackson (1) (Langmead), Coughlan (1), Cansdell-Sherriff (1), Thornton, Hibbert (1) (Hindmarch), Holt (pen), McIntyre (Ashton).

Record Cup Victory: 11–2 v Marine, FA Cup 1st rd, 11 November 1995 – Edwards; Seabury (Dempsey (1)), Withe (1), Evans (1), Whiston (2), Scott (1), Woods, Stevens (1), Spink (3) (Anthrobus), Walton, Berkley, (1 og).

sky SPORTS FACT FILE

The attendance for Shrewsbury Town's Checkatrade Trophy game away to Middlesbrough U21s in November 2016 was just 308, the lowest the club have played against in any Football League competition. The Shrews have played before a smaller crowd on only four occasions: a Welsh Cup tie at Portmadoc in November 1973, and three games in the Shropshire Senior Cup.

Record Defeat: 1–8 v Norwich C, Division 3 (S), 13 September 1952; 1–8 v Coventry C, Division 3, 22 October 1963.

Most League Points (2 for a win): 62, Division 4, 1974–75.

Most League Points (3 for a win): 89, FL 2, 2014–15.

Most League Goals: 101, Division 4, 1958–59.

Highest League Scorer in Season: Arthur Rowley, 38, Division 4, 1958–59.

Most League Goals in Total Aggregate: Arthur Rowley, 152, 1958–65 (thus completing his League record of 434 goals).

Most League Goals in One Match: 5, Alf Wood v Blackburn R, Division 3, 2 October 1971.

Most Capped Player: Jimmy McLaughlin, 5 (12), Northern Ireland; Bernard McNally, 5, Northern Ireland.

Most League Appearances: Mickey Brown, 418, 1986–91; 1992–94; 1996–2001.

Youngest League Player: Graham French, 16 years 177 days v Reading, 30 September 1961.

Record Transfer Fee Received: £600,000 (rising to £1,500,000) from Manchester C for Joe Hart, May 2006.

Record Transfer Fee Paid: £170,000 to Nottingham F for Grant Holt, June 2008.

Football League Record: 1950 Elected to Division 3 (N); 1951–58 Division 3 (S); 1958–59 Division 4; 1959–74 Division 3; 1974–75 Division 4; 1975–79 Division 3; 1979–89 Division 2; 1989–94 Division 3; 1994–97 Division 2; 1997–2003 Division 3; 2003–04 Conference; 2004–12 FL 2; 2012–14 FL 1; 2014–15 FL 2; 2015– FL 1.

MANAGERS

W. Adams 1905–12
(Secretary-Manager)
A. Weston 1912–34
(Secretary-Manager)
Jack Roscamp 1934–35
Sam Ramsey 1935–36
Ted Bousted 1936–40
Leslie Knighton 1945–49
Harry Chapman 1949–50
Sammy Crooks 1950–54
Walter Rowley 1955–57
Harry Potts 1957–58
Johnny Spuhler 1958
Arthur Rowley 1958–68
Harry Gregg 1968–72
Maurice Evans 1972–73
Alan Durban 1974–78
Richie Barker 1978
Graham Turner 1978–84
Chic Bates 1984–87
Ian McNeill 1987–90
Asa Hartford 1990–91
John Bond 1991–93
Fred Davies 1994–97
(previously Caretaker-Manager 1993–94)
Jake King 1997–99
Kevin Ratcliffe 1999–2003
Jimmy Quinn 2003–04
Gary Peters 2004–08
Paul Simpson 2008–10
Graham Turner 2010–14
Mike Jackson 2014
Micky Mellon 2014–16
Paul Hurst October 2016–

LATEST SEQUENCES

Longest Sequence of League Wins: 7, 28.10.1995 – 16.12.1995.

Longest Sequence of League Defeats: 11, 9.4.2003 – 14.8.2004. (Spread over 2 periods in Football League. 2003–04 season in Conference.)

Longest Sequence of League Draws: 6, 30.10.1963 – 14.12.1963.

Longest Sequence of Unbeaten League Matches: 16, 30.10.1993 – 26.2.1994.

Longest Sequence Without a League Win: 18, 8.3.2003 – 14.8.2004.

Successive Scoring Runs: 28 from 7.9.1960.

Successive Non-scoring Runs: 6 from 1.1.1991.

TEN YEAR LEAGUE RECORD

		P	*W*	*D*	*L*	*F*	*A*	*Pts*	*Pos*
2007-08	FL 2	46	12	14	20	56	65	50	18
2008-09	FL 2	46	17	18	11	61	44	69	7
2009-10	FL 2	46	17	12	17	55	54	63	12
2010-11	FL 2	46	22	13	11	72	49	79	4
2011-12	FL 2	46	26	10	10	66	41	88	2
2012-13	FL 1	46	13	16	17	54	60	55	16
2013-14	FL 1	46	9	15	22	44	65	42	23
2014-15	FL 2	46	27	8	11	67	31	89	2
2015-16	FL 1	46	13	11	22	58	79	50	20
2016-17	FL 1	46	13	12	21	46	63	51	18

DID YOU KNOW ?

Despite losing their manager Richie Barker in mid season, Shrewsbury Town went on to win their first-ever Football League divisional title when they headed the old Division Three in 1978–79. New boss Graham Turner provided a steadying influence and a great run-in of four wins from the last five games saw the title secured.

SHREWSBURY TOWN – SKY BET LEAGUE ONE 2016–17 LEAGUE RECORD

Match No.	Date	Venue	Opponents	Result		H/T Score	Lg Pos.	Goalscorers	Atten-dance
1	Aug 6	H	Milton Keynes D	L	0-1	0-0	19		5452
2	13	A	Coventry C	D	0-0	0-0	19		10,296
3	16	A	Charlton Ath	L	0-3	0-3	23		9174
4	20	H	Chesterfield	W	2-1	1-1	20	Brown ^{24}, El-Abd ^{84}	4936
5	27	H	Gillingham	L	2-3	2-0	21	Dodds 2 $^{17, 30}$	4611
6	Sept 3	A	Oldham Ath	W	3-2	1-1	15	Brown ^{43}, Toney (pen) ^{50}, Riley ^{62}	3697
7	10	A	Bury	L	1-2	0-0	18	Toney ^{76}	2990
8	17	H	Scunthorpe U	L	0-1	0-1	22		4878
9	24	A	AFC Wimbledon	D	1-1	0-1	21	Black ^{46}	4318
10	27	H	Peterborough U	D	1-1	0-1	22	Black ^{56}	4314
11	Oct 1	H	Swindon T	D	1-1	1-1	22	Toney ^{44}	5103
12	8	A	Bradford C	L	0-2	0-1	23		17,703
13	15	A	Walsall	L	2-3	1-2	23	Lancashire ^{30}, Brown ^{58}	4759
14	18	H	Sheffield U	L	0-3	0-0	24		5460
15	22	H	Northampton T	L	2-4	1-2	24	Toney 2 (2 pens) $^{36, 90}$	5023
16	29	A	Southend U	D	1-1	1-1	24	El-Abd ^{26}	7321
17	Nov 12	H	Oxford U	W	2-0	1-0	23	Leitch-Smith ^{19}, Whalley ^{90}	5491
18	19	A	Sheffield U	L	1-2	0-2	23	Dodds ^{72}	20,195
19	22	A	Fleetwood T	L	0-3	0-1	24		2111
20	26	H	Port Vale	D	0-0	0-0	24		5429
21	Dec 10	A	Millwall	W	1-0	1-0	23	Dodds ^{17}	8354
22	17	H	Bristol R	W	2-0	1-0	21	Dodds ^{16}, Black (pen) ^{73}	6139
23	26	A	Bolton W	L	1-2	0-2	21	Brown ^{84}	16,238
24	30	A	Rochdale	L	1-2	0-2	21	Toney ^{86}	3235
25	Jan 2	H	Fleetwood T	L	0-1	0-1	23		5080
26	7	A	Swindon T	D	1-1	0-0	20	Sadler ^{80}	6137
27	14	H	Bradford C	W	1-0	1-0	21	Ladapo ^{41}	5590
28	21	H	Oldham Ath	W	1-0	0-0	20	Ladapo ^{68}	5537
29	28	A	Gillingham	D	1-1	0-1	19	Rodman ^{63}	5316
30	Feb 4	H	Bury	W	2-1	0-0	18	Roberts, T ^{47}, Ladapo ^{77}	5368
31	11	A	Scunthorpe U	W	1-0	0-0	17	Ladapo ^{69}	4367
32	14	A	Peterborough U	L	1-2	1-0	18	Humphrys (pen) ^{31}	4116
33	18	H	AFC Wimbledon	W	2-1	0-0	17	Roberts, T ^{65}, Nsiala ^{90}	5751
34	25	A	Milton Keynes D	L	1-2	0-2	18	Humphrys ^{90}	8322
35	28	H	Charlton Ath	W	4-3	1-2	16	Dodds 2 $^{11, 75}$, Roberts, T ^{51}, Whalley ^{52}	4913
36	Mar 4	H	Coventry C	D	0-0	0-0	18		6205
37	11	A	Chesterfield	D	1-1	1-1	18	Roberts, T ^{3}	6317
38	17	A	Port Vale	L	1-2	0-0	19	Dodds ^{74}	4626
39	25	H	Bolton W	L	0-2	0-0	20		7532
40	Apr 1	A	Bristol R	L	0-2	0-0	21		9498
41	4	H	Millwall	L	1-2	0-1	21	Whalley ^{90}	4712
42	8	H	Rochdale	W	1-0	1-0	19	Payne ^{16}	5002
43	14	H	Walsall	D	1-1	0-1	19	Payne ^{70}	6801
44	17	A	Northampton T	D	1-1	0-1	19	Sadler ^{66}	6211
45	22	H	Southend U	W	1-0	0-0	18	Brown ^{64}	7341
46	30	A	Oxford U	L	0-2	0-2	18		9287

Final League Position: 18

GOALSCORERS

League (46): Dodds 8, Toney 6 (3 pens), Brown 5, Ladapo 4, Roberts, T 4, Black 3 (1 pen), Whalley 3, El-Abd 2, Humphrys 2 (1 pen), Payne 2, Sadler 2, Lancashire 1, Leitch-Smith 1, Nsiala 1, Riley 1, Rodman 1.
FA Cup (5): Dodds 1, Grimmer 1, Leitch-Smith 1, O'Brien 1, Sadler 1.
EFL Cup (2): Dodds 1, Leitch-Smith 1.
EFL Checkatrade Trophy (3): Leitch-Smith 2, Toney 1.

Leutwiler J 43	Riley J 28 + 4	El-Abd A 24 + 4	McGivern R 14 + 1	Brown J 43	Deegan G 36 + 4	Sarcevic A 7 + 5	Whalley S 23 + 9	Dodds L 29 + 9	O'Brien J 14 + 4	Leitch-Smith A 8 + 8	Ogogo A 25 + 1	Mangan A 2 + 8	Jones E 1 + 3	Toney I 19	Lancashire O 13 + 3	Black I 15 + 4	Waring G 4 + 9	El Ouriachi M 1 + 3	Grimmer J 22 + 2	Ebanks-Blake S 5 + 2	Sadler M 33 + 1	Smith D 5 + 5	Halstead M 3	Nsiala A 21	Rodman A 18 + 2	Ladapo F 10 + 5	Roberts T 11 + 2	Morris B 8 + 5	Humphrys S 3 + 11	Payne S 9 + 3	Yates R 9 + 3	Mcatee J — + 1	*Match No.*
1	2	3	4	5	6	7[3]	8[1]	9	10	11[2]	12	13	14																				1
1	2	3	4	5	6	7[2]		9	10				8[1]	11	12	13																	2
1	5	3	4	8	6		13	9[3]	11[2]					10	2[1]	7	12	14															3
1	2	3	4	5	8			13	9	10[3]			12	11[2]		7	14	6[1]															4
1	2	3	4	5	6	13		9		12	8	10[2]		11		7[1]																	5
1	5	3		9	6			7[1]			8	12		10[3]	4	13	14		2	11[2]													6
1	5	4▮	2		7		12	8[2]			6	14		10				13	3	11[1]	9[3]												7
1			3	10	5		6[2]	9	8[1]	13	7	12			4		14		2	11[3]													8
1	5[2]	4	2	9		6	12	13	8[3]	11[1]				10▮	14	7			3														9
1	5	3	4	9	6	8[1]	10[2]	12		11[3]		13				7		14	2														10
1		3	4	5	8▮	13		10[1]	7	12[2]				11	2	6			9														11
1	5	3		8[2]		12			9[3]		6	14		10	4	7[1]	11		2		13												12
1	5	3[1]	4▮	9		7			13		6	10[2]			12	8	11[3]		2	14													13
1	5			8	6	9[1]		12			7	13		11	3		10[2]		2		4												14
1	5		3	9	12	13		7		14	8			11	2[2]	6[1]	10[3]				4												15
1		3		9	7	8[1]		11	13		5	12		10		6[2]					4	2											16
		3			6		13	9[2]	8[1]	10[3]	7			11	4	12			2		5	14	1										17
		4		5	6			9	8▮	10[1]	7▮			11[2]	3	12			2	13			1										18
		3		5	6	13		9	8[1]	10				11		7[2]	12		2		4		1										19
1		3	4	9	7			6		10[1]			12	11		8			2[2]		5	13											20
1	13	4	2[2]	8	7			10[1]	9		6			11					12		3	5											21
1	14			9			13	11[1]	6[3]		7				3	8	12		5	10[2]	2	4											22
1				9			13	10	6[2]		7				3	8	12		5	11[1]	2	4											23
1		4		9[1]	12		6	10			7			11	3	8[2]	13		2		5												24
1	12	4		9	7		6[2]	11	13		8			10	3[1]		14				5	2[3]											25
1	2	3		9	8		12	10			7										5			4▮	6[1]	11							26
1	2	4[3]		9	8		13	11[2]	12		7										5	14		3	6[1]	10							27
1	2	12		9	8		3[1]				7										5			4	6	10	11[2]	13					28
1	2			5	7		6	13			8[3]										4			3	9	10[2]	11[1]	14	12				29
1	2			5	8		6				7										3			4	9[1]	12	10[3]	14	13	11[2]			30
1	2	13		5	8		6	12		14	7										3			4	9[1]	10[3]	11[2]						31
1	2		14	5	7		6[1]	9[2]													3			4	11		13	8[3]	10▮		12		32
1	2[2]	14		5	8		6														3	12		4	9	10[3]	11[1]			13	7		33
1				5	8		6	14		13									2		4			3	9[3]	10[2]			12	11[1]	7		34
1		13		5	8		6	9[1]											2		3			4	14	12	11[3]		10[2]		7		35
1	14			5	7		6[3]	10[2]											2		4			3	12	13	11		9[1]		8		36
1	2	4			8		6	13													5			3	9	10[2]	11[1]	7	12				37
1	2[1]			3	6		8[2]	12		14											5			4	9		10	7	13	11[3]			38
1	2	3		9	8[1]		12	6													5			4		11[2]	10	14		13	7[3]		39
1	2			5	8		6[2]	10[3]													4			3	9		11[1]	13	12	14	7▮		40
1	2[1]			5	8		6												12		4			3	9	11[2]	13[3]	7	14	10			41
1				5	8		6[1]	11											2		3			4	9	13		7[2]	12	10[3]	14		42
1				5	7		6	10[3]											2		3			4	9[1]	13		8	12	11[2]	14		43
1				5			6	10		13	7								2		4			3	9[2]				12	11[1]	8		44
1	2			5	13		6				7										3			4	9[2]			11	12	10	8[1]		45
1	2[1]			5	13		6				8										4	12		3	9			10[3]		11	7[2]	14	46

FA Cup

First Round	Barnet	(h)	3-0
Second Round	Fleetwood T	(h)	0-0
Replay	Fleetwood T	(a)	2-3

EFL Cup

First Round	Huddersfield T	(h)	2-1
Second Round	Sunderland	(a)	0-1

EFL Checkatrade Trophy

Northern Group G	Cambridge U	(h)	0-1
Northern Group G	Scunthorpe U	(a)	0-2
Northern Group G	Middlesbrough U21	(a)	3-0

SOUTHAMPTON

FOUNDATION

The club was formed by members of the St Mary's Church of England Young Men's Association at a meeting of the Y.M.A. in November 1885 and it was named as such. For the sake of brevity this was usually shortened to St Mary's Y.M.A. The rector Canon Albert Basil Orme Wilberforce was elected president. The name was changed to plain St Mary's during 1887–88 and did not become Southampton St Mary's until 1894, the inaugural season in the Southern League.

St Mary's Stadium, Britannia Road, Southampton, Hampshire SO14 5FP.

Telephone: (0845) 688 9448.

Fax: (02380) 727 727.

Ticket Office: (0845) 688 9288.

Website: www.southamptonfc.com

Email: see website.

Ground Capacity: 32,384.

Record Attendance: 31,044 v Manchester U, Division 1, 8 October 1969 (at The Dell); 32,363 v Coventry C, FL C, 28 April 2012 (at St Mary's).

Pitch Measurements: 105m × 68m (114yd × 74yd).

Chairman: Ralph Krueger.

Chief Executive: Gareth Rogers.

Manager: Mauricio Pellegrino.

Assistant Manager: Eric Black.

Colours: Red and white striped shirts, black shorts, black socks with white hoops.

Year Formed: 1885.

Turned Professional: 1894.

Previous Names: 1885, St Mary's Young Men's Association; 1887–88, St Mary's; 1894–95 Southampton St Mary's; 1897, Southampton.

Club Nickname: 'Saints'.

Grounds: 1885, 'The Common' (from 1887 also used the County Cricket Ground and Antelope Cricket Ground); 1889, Antelope Cricket Ground; 1896 The County Cricket Ground; 1898, The Dell; 2001, St Mary's.

First Football League Game: 28 August 1920, Division 3, v Gillingham (a) D 1–1 – Allen; Parker, Titmuss; Shelley, Campbell, Turner; Barratt, Dominy (1), Rawlings, Moore, Foxall.

Record League Victory: 8–0 v Sunderland, FA Premier League, 18 October 2014 – Forster; Clyne, Fonte, Alderweireld, Bertrand; Davis S (Mané), Schneiderlin, Cork (1); Long (Wanyama (1)), Pelle (2) (Mayuka), Tadic (1) (plus 3 Sunderland own goals).

Record Cup Victory: 7–1 v Ipswich T, FA Cup 3rd rd, 7 January 1961 – Reynolds; Davies, Traynor, Conner, Page, Huxford, Paine (1), O'Brien (3 incl. 1p), Reeves, Mulgrew (2), Penk (1).

HONOURS

League Champions: Division 3 – 1959–60; Division 3S – 1921–22.
Runners-up: Division 1 – 1983–84; FL C – 2011–12; Division 2 – 1965–66, 1977–78; FL 1 – 2010–11; Division 3 – 1920–21.

FA Cup Winners: 1976.
Runners-up: 1900, 1902, 2003.

League Cup: *Runners-up:* 1979, 2017.

League Trophy Winners: 2010.

Full Members' Cup: *Runners-up:* 1992.

European Competitions
Fairs Cup: 1969–70.
UEFA Cup: 1971–72, 1981–82, 1982–83, 1984–85, 2003–04.
Europa League: 2015–16, 2016–17.
European Cup-Winners' Cup: 1976–77 *(qf)*.

sky SPORTS FACT FILE

After their 1-1 draw at Swansea on Boxing Day 1962, Southampton did not complete another League fixture for almost two months. Because of postponements during the Big Freeze of early 1963 it was not until 23 February that Saints played their next game, a 1-0 defeat at Preston North End.

Record Defeat: 0–8 v Tottenham H, Division 2, 28 March 1936; 0–8 v Everton, Division 1, 20 November 1971.

Most League Points (2 for a win): 61, Division 3 (S), 1921–22 and Division 3, 1959–60.

Most League Points (3 for a win): 92, FL 1, 2010–11.

Most League Goals: 112, Division 3 (S), 1957–58.

Highest League Scorer in Season: Derek Reeves, 39, Division 3, 1959–60.

Most League Goals in Total Aggregate: Mike Channon, 185, 1966–77, 1979–82.

Most League Goals in One Match: 5, Charlie Wayman v Leicester C, Division 2, 23 October 1948.

Most Capped Player: Maya Yoshida, 58 (75).

Most League Appearances: Terry Paine, 713, 1956–74.

Youngest League Player: Theo Walcott, 16 years 143 days v Wolverhampton W, 6 August 2005.

Record Transfer Fee Received: £34,000,000 (rising to £36,000,000) from Liverpool for Sadio Mané, June 2016.

Record Transfer Fee Paid: £16,000,000 to Lille for Sofiane Boufal, August 2016.

Football League Record: 1920 Original Member of Division 3; 1921–22 Division 3 (S); 1922–53 Division 2; 1953–58 Division 3 (S); 1958–60 Division 3; 1960–66 Division 2; 1966–74 Division 1; 1974–78 Division 2; 1978–92 Division 1; 1992–2005 FA Premier League; 2005–09 FL C; 2009–11 FL 1; 2011–12 FL C; 2012– FA Premier League.

LATEST SEQUENCES

Longest Sequence of League Wins: 10, 16.4.2011 – 20.8.2011.

Longest Sequence of League Defeats: 5, 16.8.1998 – 12.9.1998.

Longest Sequence of League Draws: 8, 29.8.2005 – 15.10.2005.

Longest Sequence of Unbeaten League Matches: 19, 5.9.1921 – 31.12.1921.

Longest Sequence Without a League Win: 20, 30.8.1969 – 27.12.1969.

Successive Scoring Runs: 28 from 10.2.2008.

Successive Non-scoring Runs: 5 from 2.4.2001.

MANAGERS

Cecil Knight 1894–95 *(Secretary-Manager)*
Charles Robson 1895–97
Er Arnfield 1897–1911 *(Secretary-Manager) (continued as Secretary)*
George Swift 1911–12
Er Arnfield 1912–19
Jimmy McIntyre 1919–24
Arthur Chadwick 1925–31
George Kay 1931–36
George Gross 1936–37
Tom Parker 1937–43
J. R. Sarjantson stepped down from the board to act as Secretary-Manager 1943–47 with the next two listed being Team Managers during this period
Arthur Dominy 1943–46
Bill Dodgin Snr 1946–49
Sid Cann 1949–51
George Roughton 1952–55
Ted Bates 1955–73
Lawrie McMenemy 1973–85
Chris Nicholl 1985–91
Ian Branfoot 1991–94
Alan Ball 1994–95
Dave Merrington 1995–96
Graeme Souness 1996–97
Dave Jones 1997–2000
Glenn Hoddle 2000–01
Stuart Gray 2001
Gordon Strachan 2001–04
Paul Sturrock 2004
Steve Wigley 2004
Harry Redknapp 2004–05
George Burley 2005–08
Nigel Pearson 2008
Jan Poortvliet 2008–09
Mark Wotte 2009
Alan Pardew 2009–10
Nigel Adkins 2010–13
Mauricio Pochettino 2013–14
Ronald Koeman 2014–16
Claude Puel 2016–17
Mauricio Pellegrino June 2017–

TEN YEAR LEAGUE RECORD

		P	W	D	L	F	A	Pts	Pos
2007-08	FL C	46	13	15	18	56	72	54	20
2008-09	FL C	46	10	15	21	46	69	45	23
2009-10	FL 1	46	23	14	9	85	47	73*	7
2010-11	FL 1	46	28	8	10	86	38	92	2
2011-12	FL C	46	26	10	10	85	46	88	2
2012-13	PR Lge	38	9	14	15	49	60	41	14
2013-14	PR Lge	38	15	11	12	54	46	56	8
2014-15	PR Lge	38	18	6	14	54	33	60	7
2015-16	PR Lge	38	18	9	11	59	41	63	6
2016-17	PR Lge	38	12	10	16	41	48	46	8

**10 pts deducted.*

DID YOU KNOW ?

Inside-forward Rigger Coates was the first Royal Navy player to be capped for England Amateurs. Coates, who served on the Royal Yacht, turned out for Southampton as an amateur when his service duties permitted and made over 100 first-team appearances for the Saints between 1928 and 1933.

SOUTHAMPTON – PREMIER LEAGUE 2016–17 LEAGUE RECORD

Match No.	Date	Venue	Opponents	Result		H/T Score	Lg Pos.	Goalscorers	Attendance
1	Aug 13	H	Watford	D	1-1	0-1	7	Redmond [58]	31,488
2	19	A	Manchester U	L	0-2	0-1	13		75,326
3	27	H	Sunderland	D	1-1	0-0	14	Rodriguez [85]	30,152
4	Sept 10	A	Arsenal	L	1-2	1-1	16	Cech (og) [18]	59,962
5	18	H	Swansea C	W	1-0	0-0	13	Austin [64]	29,087
6	25	A	West Ham U	W	3-0	1-0	9	Austin [40], Tadic [62], Ward-Prowse [90]	56,864
7	Oct 2	A	Leicester C	D	0-0	0-0	10		31,563
8	16	H	Burnley	W	3-1	0-0	8	Austin 2 (1 pen) [52, 66 (p)], Redmond [60]	29,040
9	23	A	Manchester C	D	1-1	1-0	8	Redmond [27]	53,731
10	30	H	Chelsea	L	0-2	0-1	9		31,827
11	Nov 6	A	Hull C	L	1-2	1-0	10	Austin (pen) [6]	17,768
12	19	H	Liverpool	D	0-0	0-0	10		31,848
13	27	H	Everton	W	1-0	1-0	10	Austin [1]	31,132
14	Dec 3	A	Crystal Palace	L	0-3	0-2	10		25,393
15	11	H	Middlesbrough	W	1-0	0-0	10	Boufal [53]	28,976
16	14	A	Stoke C	D	0-0	0-0	8		27,002
17	18	A	Bournemouth	W	3-1	1-1	7	Bertrand [14], Rodriguez 2 [48, 85]	11,113
18	28	H	Tottenham H	L	1-4	1-1	8	van Dijk [2]	31,853
19	31	H	WBA	L	1-2	1-1	9	Long [41]	30,975
20	Jan 2	A	Everton	L	0-3	0-0	10		38,891
21	14	A	Burnley	L	0-1	0-0	11		20,254
22	22	H	Leicester C	W	3-0	2-0	11	Ward-Prowse [26], Rodriguez [39], Tadic (pen) [86]	30,548
23	31	A	Swansea C	L	1-2	0-1	12	Long [57]	20,359
24	Feb 4	H	West Ham U	L	1-3	1-2	12	Gabbiadini [12]	31,891
25	11	A	Sunderland	W	4-0	2-0	11	Gabbiadini 2 [30, 45], Denayer (og) [88], Long [90]	39,931
26	Mar 4	A	Watford	W	4-3	2-1	10	Tadic [28], Redmond 2 [45, 86], Gabbiadini [83]	20,670
27	19	A	Tottenham H	L	1-2	0-2	10	Ward-Prowse [52]	31,697
28	Apr 1	H	Bournemouth	D	0-0	0-0	10		31,847
29	5	H	Crystal Palace	W	3-1	1-1	9	Redmond [45], Yoshida [83], Ward-Prowse [85]	29,968
30	8	A	WBA	W	1-0	1-0	9	Clasie [25]	24,697
31	15	H	Manchester C	L	0-3	0-0	9		31,850
32	25	A	Chelsea	L	2-4	1-2	9	Romeu [24], Bertrand [90]	41,168
33	29	H	Hull C	D	0-0	0-0	9		31,120
34	May 7	A	Liverpool	D	0-0	0-0	10		53,159
35	10	H	Arsenal	L	0-2	0-0	10		31,474
36	13	A	Middlesbrough	W	2-1	1-0	9	Rodriguez [42], Redmond [57]	28,203
37	17	H	Manchester U	D	0-0	0-0	8		31,425
38	21	H	Stoke C	L	0-1	0-0	8		31,286

Final League Position: 8

GOALSCORERS

League (41): Redmond 7, Austin 6 (2 pens), Rodriguez 5, Gabbiadini 4, Ward-Prowse 4, Long 3, Tadic 3 (1 pen), Bertrand 2, Boufal 1, Clasie 1, Romeu 1, van Dijk 1, Yoshida 1, own goals 2.
FA Cup (3): Long 1, van Dijk 1, Yoshida 1.
EFL Cup (9): Gabbiadini 2, Austin 1 (1 pen), Bertrand 1, Boufal 1, Clasie 1, Hesketh 1, Long 1, Redmond 1.
EFL Checkatrade Trophy (7): Olomola 2, Isgrove 1, McQueen 1, Mdlalose 1, Slattery 1, own goal 1.
UEFA Europa League (6): Austin 2 (1 pen), van Dijk 2, Rodriguez 1, own goal 1.

Forster F 38	Cedric Soares R 30	Yoshida M 23	van Dijk V 21	Targett M 5	Romeu O 35	Davis S 29 + 3	Ward-Prowse J 22 + 8	Tadic D 30 + 3	Long S 10 + 22	Redmond N 32 + 5	Hojbjerg P 14 + 8	Pied J 1 + 3	Austin C 11 + 4	Fonte J 17	Clasie J 12 + 4	Rodriguez J 9 + 15	Bertrand R 28	Martina C 6 + 3	McQueen S 5 + 8	Boufal S 12 + 12	Reed H 1 + 2	Sims J 1 + 6	Stephens J 15 + 2	Gabbiadini M 10 + 1	Caceres M 1	*Match No.*
1	2^2	3	4	5	6	7	8^1	9	10^3	11	12	13	14													1
1	2		3	5	6^2	8^1		9	10^3	11	7		13	4	12	14										2
1	2		4	5	6	8	14	9^2	12	10	7^1		11^3	3		13										3
1	2		4		7	8	14	9^1	12	11	13			3	6^3	10^2	5									4
1	2		4		6	8		9^3	10^2	11	13		12	3	7^1		5	14								5
1	2^1		4		6	8	13	9^2	12	11	7		10^3	3			5	14								6
1	2^3		4		6	8	14	9^1	13	11	7		10^2	3			5	12								7
1			4	5^1	6	8	14	9		10^2			11^3	3	7	13		2	12							8
1			4		7	8	14	9^2		10	12		11^3	3	6^1			2	5	13						9
1			4		6	7		9^1		11	14		10	3	8^2		5^3	2	13	12						10
1		2	4		7	8	13	9^3		11^1			10	3	6^2	14	5			12						11
1	2		4		7	8			12	9	6^2		10^3	3		13	5			11^1	14					12
1	2		4		7		8		14	9^1	6		10^3	3	12		5		13			11^2				13
1	2		4		7		8		14	9	6^3		10^1	3			5		13	11^2		12				14
1			4		7	13	8	9^2	14	12				3	6^3	10		2	5	11^1						15
1			4		6	7	8	12	11^2	10^3				3		13	5	2^1	14	9						16
1	2	3	4			12		13	14	9	6				8	10^1	5			11^3	7^2					17
1	2		4		7	8^3	6	12	14	9■	13			3		10^2	5			11^1						18
1		3	4■		7	8	14	9^3	10		6^2					12		2^1	5	11		13				19
1	2^3	4			7		8	9^2	14	11				3	6^1	10			5	13			12			20
1	2	3	4		7		8	11^2	10	9^1	6					12	5					13				21
1	2	3	4^3		7		8	11	14	9	6^2				13	10^1	5						12			22
1	2	4			7	6		9^1	10	11^3					8^2		5		13	12		14	3			23
1	2	4			7	6	8		13	12						11^2	5			9^1			3	10		24
1	2	4			7	6	8	9^1	12	10	13						5						3	11^2		25
1	2	4			7	6	8^1	9^2	13	10					14		5			12			3	11^3		26
1	2	4			7	6	8	9^2	12	10^1						14	5			13			3	11^3		27
1	2	4			7	6	8^3	9^1	12	10						11^2	5		14	13			3			28
1	2	4			7	6^2	8	9	11	10^1	12					13			5				3			29
1	2	4					8^3	9	11	10^1	7				6^2		5		12		14	13	3			30
1	2	4				6	8^2	9	12^3	10	7					14	5			13			3	11^1		31
1	2	4			6	8	9^2	7	13	12						14	5			10^1			3	11^3		32
1	2	4			7	6		9	13	10^2						14	5			8^3		12	3	11^1		33
1	2	4			8	7	9	6	13	12							5			10^2			3	11^1		34
1	2	4			7	6	8^3	9^2	12	10^1						14	5			13			3	11		35
1		4			7	13			9^1	12	8^2	2	14		6	10	5			11^3					3	36
1	2^1	4		5	7	6	8^3	9		11		13				12				14			3	10^2		37
1	2	4			7	6	8^1	9^3		10		14	11^2				5			13			3	12		38

FA Cup

Third Round	Norwich C	(a)	2-2
Replay	Norwich C	(h)	1-0
Fourth Round	Arsenal	(h)	0-5

EFL Cup

Third Round	Crystal Palace	(h)	2-0
Fourth Round	Sunderland	(h)	1-0
Quarter-Final	Arsenal	(a)	2-0
Semi-Final 1st leg	Liverpool	(h)	1-0
Semi-Final 2nd leg	Liverpool	(a)	1-0
Final	Manchester U	(Wembley)	2-3

EFL Checkatrade Trophy (Southampton U21)

Southern Group E	Charlton Ath	(a)	0-0
(*Charlton Ath won 5-4 on penalties*)			
Southern Group E	Colchester U	(a)	2-1
Southern Group E	Crawley T	(h)	4-0
Second Round South	Reading U21	(h)	1-1
(*Reading U21 won 4-3 on penalties*)			

UEFA Europa League

Group K	Sparta Prague	(h)	3-0
Group K	Hapoel Beer Sheva	(a)	0-0
Group K	Inter Milan	(a)	0-1
Group K	Inter Milan	(h)	2-1
Group K	Sparta Prague	(a)	0-1
Group K	Hapoel Beer Sheva	(h)	1-1

SOUTHEND UNITED

FOUNDATION

The leading club in Southend around the turn of the 20th century was Southend Athletic, but they were an amateur concern. Southend United was a more ambitious professional club when they were founded in 1906, employing Bob Jack as secretary-manager and immediately joining the Second Division of the Southern League.

Roots Hall Stadium, Victoria Avenue, Southend-on-Sea, Essex SS2 6NQ.

Telephone: (01702) 304 050.

Fax: (01702) 304 124.

Ticket Office: (08444) 770 077.

Website: www.southendunited.co.uk

Email: info@southend-united.co.uk

Ground Capacity: 12,086.

Record Attendance: 22,862 v Tottenham H, FA Cup 3rd rd replay, 11 January 1936 (at Southend Stadium); 31,090 v Liverpool, FA Cup 3rd rd, 10 January 1979 (at Roots Hall).

Pitch Measurements: 100.5m × 67.5m (110yd × 74yd).

Chairman: Ronald Martin.

Manager: Phil Brown.

Assistant Manager: Graham Coughlan.

Colours: Navy blue shirts with white trim, navy blue shorts with white trim, white socks.

Year Formed: 1906.

Turned Professional: 1906.

Club Nicknames: 'The Blues', 'The Shrimpers'.

Grounds: 1906, Roots Hall, Prittlewell; 1920, Kursaal; 1934, Southend Stadium; 1955, Roots Hall Football Ground.

First Football League Game: 28 August 1920, Division 3, v Brighton & HA (a) W 2–0 – Capper; Reid, Newton; Wileman, Henderson, Martin; Nicholls, Nuttall, Fairclough (2), Myers, Dorsett.

Record League Victory: 9–2 v Newport Co, Division 3 (S), 5 September 1936 – McKenzie; Nelson, Everest (1); Deacon, Turner, Carr; Bolan, Lane (1), Goddard (4), Dickinson (2), Oswald (1).

Record Cup Victory: 10–1 v Golders Green, FA Cup 1st rd, 24 November 1934 – Moore; Morfitt, Kelly; Mackay, Joe Wilson, Carr (1); Lane (1), Johnson (5), Cheesmuir (2), Deacon (1), Oswald. 10–1 v Brentwood, FA Cup 2nd rd, 7 December 1968 – Roberts; Bentley, Birks; McMillan (1) Beesley, Kurila; Clayton, Chisnall, Moore (4), Best (5), Hamilton. 10–1 v Aldershot, Leyland DAF Cup Prel rd, 6 November 1990 – Sansome; Austin, Powell, Cornwell, Prior (1), Tilson (3), Cawley, Butler, Ansah (1), Benjamin (1), Angell (4).

Record Defeat: 1–9 v Brighton & HA, Division 3, 27 November 1965; 0–8 v Crystal Palace, League Cup 2nd rd (1st leg), 25 September 1990.

HONOURS

League Champions: FL 1 – 2005–06; Division 4 – 1980–81.
Runners-up: Division 3 – 1990–91; Division 4 – 1971–72, 1977–78.

FA Cup: 3rd rd – 1921; 5th rd – 1926, 1952, 1976, 1993.

League Cup: quarter-final – 2007.

League Trophy: *Runners-up:* 2004, 2005, 2013.

sky SPORTS FACT FILE

Southend United achieved their best-ever attendances during the 1949–50 season. An average of 12,089 watched Division Three South games at Southend Stadium that season, with the team finishing in third place in the table.

Most League Points (2 for a win): 67, Division 4, 1980–81.

Most League Points (3 for a win): 85, Division 3, 1990–91.

Most League Goals: 92, Division 3 (S), 1950–51.

Highest League Scorer in Season: Jim Shankly, 31, 1928–29; Sammy McCrory, 1957–58, both in Division 3 (S).

Most League Goals in Total Aggregate: Roy Hollis, 122, 1953–60.

Most League Goals in One Match: 5, Jim Shankly v Merthyr T, Division 3 (S), 1 March 1930.

Most Capped Player: George McKenzie, 9, Republic of Ireland.

Most League Appearances: Sandy Anderson, 452, 1950–63.

Youngest League Player: Phil O'Connor, 16 years 76 days v Lincoln C, 26 December 1969.

Record Transfer Fee Received: £2,000,000 (rising to £2,750,000) from Nottingham F for Stan Collymore, June 1993.

Record Transfer Fee Paid: £500,000 to Galatasaray for Mike Marsh, September 1995.

Football League Record: 1920 Original Member of Division 3; 1921–58 Division 3 (S); 1958–66 Division 3; 1966–72 Division 4; 1972–76 Division 3; 1976–78 Division 4; 1978–80 Division 3; 1980–81 Division 4; 1981–84 Division 3; 1984–87 Division 4; 1987–89 Division 3; 1989–90 Division 4; 1990–91 Division 3; 1991–92 Division 2; 1992–97 Division 1; 1997–98 Division 2; 1998–2004 Division 3; 2004–05 FL 2; 2005–06 FL 1; 2006–07 FL C; 2007–10 FL 1; 2010–15 FL 2; 2015– FL 1.

LATEST SEQUENCES

Longest Sequence of League Wins: 8, 29.8.2005 – 9.10.2005.

Longest Sequence of League Defeats: 7, 16.4.2016 – 13.8.2016.

Longest Sequence of League Draws: 6, 30.1.1982 – 19.2.1982.

Longest Sequence of Unbeaten League Matches: 16, 20.2.1932 – 29.8.1932.

Longest Sequence Without a League Win: 17, 26.8.2006 – 2.12.2006.

Successive Scoring Runs: 24 from 23.3.1929.

Successive Non-scoring Runs: 6 from 6.4.1979.

MANAGERS

Bob Jack 1906–10
George Molyneux 1910–11
O. M. Howard 1911–12
Joe Bradshaw 1912–19
Ned Liddell 1919–20
Tom Mather 1920–21
Ted Birnie 1921–34
David Jack 1934–40
Harry Warren 1946–56
Eddie Perry 1956–60
Frank Broome 1960
Ted Fenton 1961–65
Alvan Williams 1965–67
Ernie Shepherd 1967–69
Geoff Hudson 1969–70
Arthur Rowley 1970–76
Dave Smith 1976–83
Peter Morris 1983–84
Bobby Moore 1984–86
Dave Webb 1986–87
Dick Bate 1987
Paul Clark 1987–88
Dave Webb *(General Manager)* 1988–92
Colin Murphy 1992–93
Barry Fry 1993
Peter Taylor 1993–95
Steve Thompson 1995
Ronnie Whelan 1995–97
Alvin Martin 1997–99
Alan Little 1999–2000
David Webb 2000–01
Rob Newman 2001–03
Steve Wignall 2003
Steve Tilson 2003–10
Paul Sturrock 2010–13
Phil Brown March 2013–

TEN YEAR LEAGUE RECORD

		P	*W*	*D*	*L*	*F*	*A*	*Pts*	*Pos*
2007-08	FL 1	46	22	10	14	70	55	76	6
2008-09	FL 1	46	21	8	17	58	61	71	8
2009-10	FL 1	46	10	13	23	51	72	43	23
2010-11	FL 2	46	16	13	17	62	56	61	13
2011-12	FL 2	46	25	8	13	77	48	83	4
2012-13	FL 2	46	16	13	17	61	55	61	11
2013-14	FL 2	46	19	15	12	56	39	72	5
2014-15	FL 2	46	24	12	10	54	38	84	5
2015-16	FL 1	46	16	11	19	58	64	59	14
2016-17	FL 1	46	20	12	14	70	53	72	7

DID YOU KNOW?

Southend United played their first-ever fixture on 1 September 1906. Swindon Town reserves were the visitors to Roots Hall for a Southern League Second Division match and came away with a 1-0 victory.

SOUTHEND UNITED – SKY BET LEAGUE ONE 2016–17 LEAGUE RECORD

Match No.	*Date*	*Venue*	*Opponents*	*Result*	*H/T Score*	*Lg Pos.*	*Goalscorers*	*Attendance*
1	Aug 6	H	Gillingham	L 1-3	1-1	22	McLaughlin [23]	8141
2	13	A	Port Vale	L 0-2	0-1	24		4727
3	16	A	Sheffield U	W 3-0	3-0	15	O'Connell (og) [5], McLaughlin [13], Cox [15]	17,410
4	20	H	Bristol R	D 1-1	0-0	16	Cox (pen) [81]	6084
5	27	H	Fleetwood T	L 0-2	0-1	19		5507
6	Sept 3	A	Bolton W	D 1-1	1-0	20	Kyprianou [3]	13,519
7	10	A	Scunthorpe U	L 0-4	0-2	22		3723
8	17	H	Millwall	W 3-1	1-1	20	Mooney [6], McLaughlin [50], O'Neill [87]	7752
9	24	A	Northampton T	L 0-4	0-0	23		6138
10	27	H	Oxford U	W 2-1	1-1	19	Leonard [13], Wordsworth (pen) [74]	5593
11	Oct 1	H	Peterborough U	D 1-1	0-0	21	Wordsworth [78]	6417
12	8	A	Rochdale	L 0-3	0-2	22		2600
13	15	H	Chesterfield	W 1-0	1-0	19	Thompson [29]	6004
14	18	A	Bradford C	D 1-1	0-1	19	Wordsworth [54]	16,112
15	22	A	Milton Keynes D	W 3-0	2-0	15	Cox [2], Wordsworth 2 [24, 90]	11,039
16	29	H	Shrewsbury T	D 1-1	1-1	16	McLaughlin [39]	7321
17	Nov 12	A	Bury	W 4-1	2-1	12	Ranger 2 [9, 61], Cox [12], McLaughlin [76]	3033
18	19	H	Bradford C	W 3-0	1-0	9	Atkinson 2 [14, 72], Vincelot (og) [86]	7005
19	22	H	Swindon T	D 1-1	1-0	9	Atkinson [12]	5715
20	26	A	Walsall	D 0-0	0-0	10		4342
21	Dec 10	H	Coventry C	W 3-1	1-0	8	Wordsworth [6], Ferdinand [64], McLaughlin [69]	6430
22	17	A	Oldham Ath	W 2-0	1-0	7	Ranger [18], McGlashan [76]	3414
23	26	H	AFC Wimbledon	W 3-0	2-0	6	Cox 2 [10, 84], Atkinson [41]	8493
24	31	H	Charlton Ath	D 1-1	1-0	6	Cox [24]	10,329
25	Jan 2	A	Swindon T	D 0-0	0-0	7		7102
26	7	H	Sheffield U	L 2-4	1-2	7	Cox [19], McGlashan [88]	7702
27	14	H	Rochdale	W 2-1	1-0	7	Fortune [15], Cox [90]	6570
28	28	A	Fleetwood T	D 1-1	1-0	7	Wordsworth [37]	2675
29	Feb 4	H	Scunthorpe U	W 3-1	1-1	6	Fortune [39], Cox [76], Leonard [81]	7346
30	11	A	Millwall	L 0-1	0-0	8		10,323
31	14	A	Oxford U	W 2-0	0-0	7	Fortune [62], Robinson [88]	7277
32	18	H	Northampton T	D 2-2	2-2	6	McGlashan [20], Cox [31]	8425
33	21	A	Peterborough U	W 4-1	1-0	5	Demetriou [45], Fortune [60], Wordsworth [64], Timlin [90]	4597
34	25	A	Gillingham	L 1-2	0-2	6	Ranger [83]	6542
35	Mar 4	H	Port Vale	D 1-1	0-0	7	Wordsworth [83]	7545
36	11	A	Bristol R	L 0-2	0-2	7		9274
37	14	A	Coventry C	W 2-0	2-0	7	Ranger [2], Leonard [23]	7646
38	18	H	Walsall	W 3-2	0-2	6	Ranger [63], Ferdinand [76], Cox [83]	6756
39	25	A	AFC Wimbledon	W 2-0	1-0	6	Ranger [35], Cox [64]	4803
40	Apr 1	H	Oldham Ath	W 3-0	0-0	6	Ranger [75], Robinson [78], Wordsworth (pen) [90]	7617
41	4	H	Bolton W	L 0-1	0-0	6		9340
42	8	A	Charlton Ath	L 1-2	1-1	7	White [11]	11,730
43	14	A	Chesterfield	W 4-0	1-0	7	Cox 2 (1 pen) [15 (p), 67], Wordsworth [57], Fortune [71]	5529
44	17	H	Milton Keynes D	L 1-2	0-0	7	Cox (pen) [90]	9009
45	22	A	Shrewsbury T	L 0-1	0-0	7		7341
46	30	H	Bury	W 1-0	1-0	7	McLaughlin [22]	9245

Final League Position: 7

GOALSCORERS

League (70): Cox 16 (3 pens), Wordsworth 11 (2 pens), Ranger 8, McLaughlin 7, Fortune 5, Atkinson 4, Leonard 3, McGlashan 3, Ferdinand 2, Robinson 2, Demetriou 1, Kyprianou 1, Mooney 1, O'Neill 1, Thompson 1, Timlin 1, White 1, own goals 2.
FA Cup (0).
EFL Cup (1): McLaughlin 1.
EFL Checkatrade Trophy (4): Fortune 1, Kyprianou 1, Mooney 1, Wordsworth 1.

Oxley M 20	Demetriou J 40 + 1	Barrett A 12	Thompson A 40	Coker B 29 + 2	McGlashan J 13 + 22	Leonard R 43	Atkinson W 35 + 2	McLaughlin S 32 + 2	Cox S 39 + 5	Mooney D 10 + 3	Williams J — + 7	King A 5 + 2	O'Neill L 6 + 11	Sokolik J 2 + 3	Bridge J 1 + 3	Ranger N 19 + 8	Smith T 19	White J 11 + 2	Ferdinand A 34	Kyprianou H 2 + 1	Wordsworth A 33 + 1	Inniss R 8 + 2	Fortune M 16 + 16	Timlin M 25 + 2	Hines Z — + 5	Nouble F — + 5	Robinson T 3 + 15	Amos L 2 + 1	Walton C 7	Match No.
1	2^{1}	3	4	5	6	7	8	9^{3}	10	11^{2}	12	13	14																	1
1	2	3		5	6^{3}	7	8^{1}	9	11^{2}	10	14	12		4	13															2
1	2	4	3	5		8	13	9	10^{2}	12^{3}	14	7	6			11^{1}														3
1	2^{3}	4	3	5	12	7		9	11	10^{2}	14	8	6^{1}		13															4
1	2	4	3	5	12	7		9	10^{2}	13	14	8^{1}	6		11^{3}															5
		5	3		14	7	9		11^{2}	10^{1}	13	8		12			1	2	4^{3}	6										6
		3	4	14	12	8	6	13	11	10		7^{1}		2^{2}			1	9		5^{3}										7
1	7	4	3	5	6^{2}	8	9	10^{1}	14	11^{3}			12					2		13										8
1	5■	3^{2}	4	8	9	6	7	11^{3}	14	10^{1}								2			12	13								9
1	5	4		8	9^{1}	6	13	11		10			12						3		7^{2}	2								10
1	5	4		8	9^{1}	6		11^{2}	12	10^{3}			14						3		7	2	13							11
1		4		8	9^{1}	6		11^{2}	14	10^{3}			5			13			2		7	3	12							12
1	2		3	5	12	7	9	6^{2}	10							11^{1}			4		8		13							13
1	2		4	5	12	7	6	9^{3}	10^{1}	13						11^{2}			3		8		14							14
1	2		4	5	13	7	6	9	10^{2}							11^{1}			3		8		12							15
1	2		3	5	12	7	9^{2}	6^{1}	10		14		13						4		8		11^{3}							16
1			4	2		8	9	6	10				12	13		11^{2}		5^{3}	3^{1}				14	7						17
1	2		3	5^{3}		7	9	6^{2}	10^{1}				14			11			4		8		13	12						18
1	2		3			7	9	6	10							11^{1}			4		8		12	5						19
1	2		3		13	7	6	9	10^{2}							11			4		8^{1}		12	5						20
1	2		3			7		9	10				6	13		11^{2}			4^{1}		8		12	5						21
1	2		3		13	8	6	9	10^{1}							11^{2}			4		7		12	5						22
	2		3		12	7	6	9	10								1		4		8		11^{1}	5						23
	2		3		13	7	6	9^{2}	10^{1}							12	1		4		8		11	5						24
	2		3		9^{1}	7	6		10						14	12	1		4		8^{3}		11^{2}	5	13					25
	2		3		12	7	6^{1}		9							10	1		4		8		11^{2}	5	13					26
	2		3	12	6■	7	9		10								1		4		8^{2}		11^{1}	5	13					27
	2		3	5		7	6		10^{1}				14				1	4			8		11^{3}	9^{2}	12	13				28
	2		3	5	13	7	6		10								1		4		8		11^{2}	9^{1}			12			29
	2		4	5	13	7	6■		10^{1}								1		3		8		11^{3}	9^{2}		14	12			30
	2		3	5	6^{3}	7			10^{2}				14			13	1		4		8		11^{1}	9			12			31
	2		3	5	11^{2}	7			6							13	1		4^{3}		8	14	10^{1}	9			12			32
	2		4	5	9^{2}	7			10^{1}				14			13	1				8	3	11^{3}	6			12			33
	2		3	5	6^{1}	7			10							12	1	13			8^{3}	4■	11^{2}	9			14			34
	2		3	5	13	7	6		10^{2}								1		4		8		11^{1}	9^{3}		14	12			35
	2		3	5		9	6^{1}	13	10							12	1		4		8		11^{2}	7^{3}			14			36
				5	13	7	6	9^{3}								11^{1}	1	2	4		8	3	12			14	10^{2}			37
	12			5		6	8^{1}	10	14							11	1	2	4		9	3^{2}					13	7^{3}		38
	2		4	5		8	6	9	11^{1}							10	1		3		7						12			39
	2		3	5	12	7■	6^{2}	9^{1}	11^{3}							10			4		8			14			13		1	40
	2		3		13		7	9^{3}	10^{1}							11		12			8	4^{2}	14	5			6		1	41
	5		4		12		6	9	10				13					2^{2}	3					8		14	11^{3}	7^{1}	1	42
	5		4				6^{3}	9	10^{1}							11^{2}		2	3		7		13	8	12		14		1	43
	2		3		13	7	6^{3}	9^{1}	10							11^{2}			4		8		14	5			12		1	44
	2		3		12	8	6	9^{2}	10							11^{3}		5	4				14	7^{1}			13		1	45
	2		3			7	8	9	10				6^{1}						4				11^{2}	5			13	12	1	46

FA Cup
First Round Millwall (a) 0-1

EFL Cup
First Round Gillingham (h) 1-3

EFL Checkatrade Trophy
Southern Group G Brighton & HA U21 (h) 2-0
Southern Group G Leyton Orient (h) 1-0
Southern Group G Stevenage (a) 0-4
Second Round South Oxford U (h) 1-1
(*Oxford U won 4-3 on penalties*)

STEVENAGE

FOUNDATION

There have been several clubs associated with the town of Stevenage. Stevenage Town was formed in 1884. They absorbed Stevenage Rangers in 1955 and later played at Broadhall Way. The club went into liquidation in 1968 and Stevenage Athletic was formed, but they, too, followed a similar path in 1976. Then Stevenage Borough was founded. The Broadhall Way pitch was dug up and remained unused for three years. Thus the new club started its life in the modest surrounds of the King George V playing fields with a roped-off ground in the Chiltern League. A change of competition followed to the Wallspan Southern Combination and by 1980 the club returned to the council-owned Broadhall Way when "Borough" was added to the name. Entry into the United Counties League was so successful the league and cup were won in the first season. On to the Isthmian League Division Two and the climb up the pyramid continued. In 1995–96 Stevenage Borough won the Conference but was denied a place in the Football League as the ground did not measure up to the competition's standards. Subsequent improvements changed this and the 7,100 capacity venue became one of the best appointed grounds in non-league football. After winning elevation to the Football League the club dropped Borough from its title.

Lamex Stadium, Broadhall Way, Stevenage, Hertfordshire SG2 8RH.

Telephone: (01438) 223 223.

Fax: (01438) 743 666.

Ticket Office: (01438) 223 223.

Website: stevenagefc.com

Email: info@stevenagefc.com

Ground Capacity: 6,772.

Record Attendance: 8,040 v Newcastle U, FA Cup 4th rd, 25 January 1998.

Pitch Measurements: 104m × 64m (114yd × 70yd).

Chairman: Phil Wallace.

Manager: Darren Sarll.

Managerial Advisor: Glenn Roeder.

Colours: White shirts with red diagonal stripes, red shorts with white trim, white socks with red trim.

Nickname: 'The Boro'.

Previous Name: 1976, Stevenage Borough; 2010, Stevenage.

Grounds: 1976, King George V playing fields; 1980, Broadhall Way (renamed Lamex Stadium 2009).

HONOURS

League Champions: Conference – 1995–96, 2009–10.

FA Cup: 5th rd – 2012.

League Cup: 2nd rd – 2012, 2017.

sky SPORTS FACT FILE

Stevenage spent the first four seasons of their existence in junior competitions. They played their first-ever game as a senior club on 16 August 1980. Facing ON Chenecks at home in a United Counties League Division One fixture, Boro ran out 3-1 winners.

First Football League Game: 7 August 2010, FL 2, v Macclesfield T (h) D 2–2 – Day; Henry, Laird, Bostwick, Roberts, Foster, Wilson (Sinclair), Byrom, Griffin (1), Winn (Odubade), Vincenti (1) (Beardsley).

Year Formed: 1976.

Turned Professional: 1976.

Record League Victory: 6–0 v Yeovil T, FL 2, 14 April 2012 – Day; Lascelles (1), Laird, Roberts (1), Ashton (1), Shroot (Mousinho), Wilson (Myrie-Williams), Long, Agyemang (1), Reid (Slew), Freeman (2).

Record Victory: 11–1 v British Timken Ath 1980–81.

Record Defeat: 0–7 v Southwick 1987–88.

Most League Points (3 for a win): 73, FL 1, 2011–12.

Most League Goals: 69, FL 1, 2011–12.

Highest League Scorer in Season: Matthew Godden, 20, FL 2, 2016–17.

Most League Goals in Total Aggregate: Matthew Godden, 20, 2016–17.

MANAGERS

Derek Montgomery 1976–83
Frank Cornwell 1983–87
John Bailey 1987–88
Brian Wilcox 1988–90
Paul Fairclough 1990–98
Richard Hill 1998–2000
Steve Wignall 2000
Paul Fairclough 2000–02
Wayne Turner 2002–03
Graham Westley 2003–06
Mark Stimson 2006–07
Peter Taylor 2007–08
Graham Westley 2008–12
Gary Smith 2012–13
Graham Westley 2013–15
Teddy Sheringham 2015–16
Darren Sarll February 2016–

Most League Goals in One Match: 3, Chris Holroyd v Hereford U, FL 2, 28 September 2010; 3, Dani Lopez v Sheffield U, FL 1, 16 March 2013; 3, Chris Whelpdale v Morecambe, FL 2, 28 November 2015; 3, Matthew Godden v Newport Co, FL 2, 7 January 2017.

Most Capped Player: Marcus Haber, 5 (including 3 on loan at Notts Co) (27), Canada.

Most League Appearances: Chris Day, 219, 2010–17.

Youngest League Player: Ryan Johnson, 17 years 213 days v Brentford, 3 May 2014.

Record Transfer Fee Received: £260,000 from Peterborough U for George Boyd, January 2007.

Record Transfer Fee Paid: £75,000 (rising to £150,000) to Exeter C for James Dunne, May 2012.

Football League Record: 2011 Promoted from Conference Premier; 2010–11 FL 2; 2011–14 FL 1; 2014– FL 2.

LATEST SEQUENCES

Longest Sequence of League Wins: 6, 12.3.2011 – 2.4.2011.

Longest Sequence of League Defeats: 6, 13.4.2013 – 17.8.2013.

Longest Sequence of League Draws: 5, 17.3.2012 – 31.3.2012.

Longest Sequence of Unbeaten League Matches: 17, 9.4.2012 – 6.10.2012.

Longest Sequence Without a League Win: 10, 11.3.2014 – 21.4.2014.

Successive Scoring Runs: 17 from 9.4.2012.

Successive Non-scoring Runs: 4 from 20.2.2016.

TEN YEAR LEAGUE RECORD

		P	*W*	*D*	*L*	*F*	*A*	*Pts*	*Pos*
2007-08	Conf P	46	24	7	15	82	55	79	6
2008-09	Conf P	46	23	12	11	73	54	81	5
2009-10	Conf P	44	30	9	5	79	24	99	1
2010-11	FL 2	46	18	15	13	62	45	69	6
2011-12	FL 1	46	18	19	9	69	44	73	6
2012-13	FL 1	46	15	9	22	47	64	54	18
2013-14	FL 1	46	11	9	26	46	72	42	24
2014-15	FL 2	46	20	12	14	62	54	72	6
2015-16	FL 2	46	11	15	20	52	67	48	18
2016-17	FL 2	46	20	7	19	67	63	67	10

DID YOU KNOW ?

Jack King's header to open the scoring in Stevenage's home game with Portsmouth on 18 March 2017 was the club's 400th goal in the Football League. A total of 227 of these were scored at home and 173 away.

STEVENAGE – SKY BET LEAGUE TWO 2016–17 LEAGUE RECORD

Match No.	*Date*	*Venue*	*Opponents*	*Result*	*H/T Score*	*Lg Pos.*	*Goalscorers*	*Attendance*
1	Aug 6	H	Crewe Alex	L 1-2	0-0	19	Lee [90]	2544
2	13	A	Notts Co	D 1-1	1-1	19	Kennedy [9]	3987
3	16	A	Leyton Orient	L 0-3	0-2	23		3779
4	20	H	Luton T	W 2-1	0-1	20	Hunte [53], Godden [90]	3517
5	27	A	Grimsby T	L 2-5	1-2	22	Franks [45], McAnuff [66]	4425
6	Sept 3	H	Hartlepool U	W 6-1	2-1	15	Pett [27], Walker 2 [44, 57], Wells [53], Tonge (pen) [69], Godden [78]	2401
7	10	H	Crawley T	W 2-1	1-0	12	Walker [44], King [55]	2157
8	17	A	Wycombe W	L 0-1	0-1	16		3181
9	24	H	Exeter C	L 0-2	0-0	18		2244
10	27	A	Cheltenham T	D 0-0	0-0	18		2238
11	Oct 8	H	Plymouth Arg	L 1-2	0-0	21	Bradley (og) [54]	2881
12	15	A	Morecambe	W 2-0	1-0	18	Godden [36], Kennedy [57]	1212
13	22	H	Carlisle U	L 1-2	1-1	22	Godden (pen) [44]	2720
14	29	A	Mansfield T	W 2-1	1-0	17	Lee [32], McKirdy [57]	2716
15	Nov 12	H	Yeovil T	D 2-2	0-0	20	Kennedy 2 [68, 86]	2457
16	19	A	Accrington S	W 1-0	0-0	13	Godden [71]	1283
17	26	A	Portsmouth	W 2-1	0-0	14	Schumacher [71], Godden [75]	15,987
18	Dec 3	H	Doncaster R	L 3-4	0-3	14	Pett [61], Franks [72], Liburd [90]	2705
19	6	A	Newport Co	W 2-0	2-0	9	Jones, Darren (og) [9], Pett [39]	1877
20	10	H	Blackpool	L 0-2	0-0	11		2513
21	17	A	Barnet	W 2-1	1-0	9	Gorman [38], Wilkinson [61]	3228
22	26	H	Cambridge U	L 1-2	0-1	11	Kennedy [46]	3957
23	31	H	Colchester U	L 2-4	1-2	14	Kennedy [40], Godden [51]	3076
24	Jan 2	A	Doncaster R	L 0-1	0-0	15		5604
25	7	H	Newport Co	W 3-1	2-0	13	Godden 3 (1 pen) [9, 42, 62 (p)]	2185
26	14	A	Plymouth Arg	L 2-4	2-2	15	Godden [2], Schumacher [45]	8137
27	21	A	Hartlepool U	L 0-2	0-2	15		3363
28	28	H	Grimsby T	W 2-0	1-0	14	Schumacher [4], McAnuff [61]	3394
29	Feb 4	A	Crawley T	W 2-1	0-1	13	Godden 2 [76, 90]	2124
30	11	H	Wycombe W	W 3-0	2-0	10	Schumacher [25], Godden (pen) [45], Pett [49]	2602
31	14	H	Cheltenham T	W 2-1	1-0	9	Godden (pen) [18], Wilkinson [50]	1930
32	18	A	Exeter C	D 1-1	1-0	8	McAnuff [31]	4125
33	25	A	Crewe Alex	W 2-1	2-0	9	Godden [7], Franks [36]	3547
34	28	H	Leyton Orient	W 4-1	2-1	7	Kennedy [18], Godden (pen) [22], Wilkinson [48], Pett [62]	2908
35	Mar 4	H	Notts Co	W 3-0	1-0	6	Godden 2 [3, 62], King [60]	3248
36	11	A	Luton T	W 2-0	1-0	4	Wilkinson [3], Kennedy [85]	9045
37	14	A	Blackpool	L 0-1	0-1	6		2456
38	18	H	Portsmouth	W 3-0	2-0	4	King [16], Godden [28], McAnuff [46]	4185
39	25	A	Cambridge U	D 0-0	0-0	4		5520
40	Apr 1	H	Barnet	W 1-0	1-0	4	Pett [12]	3657
41	8	A	Colchester U	L 0-4	0-4	5		3583
42	14	H	Morecambe	L 0-1	0-0	6		3117
43	17	A	Carlisle U	D 1-1	0-0	5	Schumacher (pen) [50]	4572
44	22	H	Mansfield T	L 0-1	0-1	7		2765
45	29	A	Yeovil T	D 1-1	0-1	8	McQuoid [53]	3716
46	May 6	H	Accrington S	L 0-3	0-0	10		3517

Final League Position: 10

GOALSCORERS

League (67): Godden 20 (5 pens), Kennedy 8, Pett 6, Schumacher 5 (1 pen), McAnuff 4, Wilkinson 4, Franks 3, King 3, Walker 3, Lee 2, Gorman 1, Hunte 1, Liburd 1, McKirdy 1, McQuoid 1, Tonge 1 (1 pen), Wells 1, own goals 2.
FA Cup (0).
EFL Cup (1): Kennedy 1.
EFL Checkatrade Trophy (7): Liburd 2, Franks 1, Godden 1, McKirdy 1, Schumacher 1, Walker 1.

Jones J 36	Henry R 32 + 1	Wells D 10 + 4	Wilkinson L 38 + 2	Franks F 40 + 1	Lee C 35 + 9	Tonge M 13 + 14	Conlon T 3 + 1	McAnuff J 22 + 9	Godden M 37 + 1	Hyde J 2 + 4	Liburd R 2 + 11	Kennedy B 26 + 10	Fox A 7 + 2	Gorman D 15 + 10	Hunte C 2 + 1	Pett T 35 + 5	Ntlhe K 20 + 2	King J 36	Walker T 7 + 1	Cowans H 12 + 6	Kerr N — + 1	McKirdy H 6 + 5	Schumacher S 27 + 1	Day C 10 + 1	Loft R — + 9	McQuoid J 10 + 6	Ogilvie C 18	Hinds K 4 + 9	Mckee M 1 + 1	Gray J — + 3	*Match No.*
1	2	3	4	5^{2}	6	7	8^{3}	9	10	11^{1}	12	13	14																		1
1	2		4	3	7	8	6	9	11	12		10^{1}	5																		2
1	2		4	3	7^{1}	8	6^{2}	9	10		12	11^{3}	5	13	14																3
1	2	3	4	5	7	8	14	9^{1}	11	10^{2}		13			6^{3}	12															4
1	2	3	5^{2}	4	8	7^{3}		12	10			6	13	14	11^{1}	9															5
1	2^{3}	3^{2}		4	13	8			10				9			6	5	7	11^{1}	12	14										6
1			3	4	2	6			8^{1}		12		10			9	5	7	11^{2}	13											7
1			3	4	2	8^{2}		13	10		14	12	9^{3}			6^{1}	5	7	11												8
1	14		4	3	2	8		6				12	9^{3}			10^{1}	5	7	11^{2}			13									9
1	2			4	6	12				13		11		8^{2}		9	5	3	10^{1}	7											10
1	2	4		3	7	14			10	13			11^{2}			9^{3}	5	6		8^{1}		12									11
1	2		4	3	8				10^{1}	12	13	9^{2}		7			5	6		11											12
1	2		3	4	6	14			10^{3}			9^{1}		7^{2}		12	5	8		11		13									13
1	2	14	3	4	7^{1}						13	9		8^{2}		12	5	6		11		10^{3}									14
1	2		3^{2}	4	7				8		13	9				12	5	6		11^{3}		10^{1}	14								15
1	2	13	3	4	12			14	10^{3}			6		9^{1}			5	8				11^{2}	7								16
1	2	12	4^{3}	3	14				11			10		9^{1}			5	8		6		13	7^{2}								17
1	2	5		4	8^{2}	13					14	11		6^{1}		12		3		9		10	7^{3}								18
1	2	3	4	5	12			14			13	11				6^{2}		8		9^{3}		10^{1}	7								19
	2	4	3	5	10^{3}			14	12		13					6		7		9^{1}		11^{2}	8	1							20
1	2		3	4	14	12		13	10^{3}		11			6^{2}		9	5	7					8^{1}								21
1	2		3	4		13		12	10			11		9^{1}		6	5	7^{2}				14	8^{3}								22
1	2		9^{3}	4	14			12	11			10				6	5	3	13	7^{2}			8^{1}								23
1	2			4	12	8		13	11^{1}		14	9^{2}		7		6	5	3	10^{3}												24
1	2			3	12				11^{1}			10		8		6	5	4	9^{2}	14			7^{3}		13						25
1	2		4	3	14	13			11		10^{2}	9^{3}		8		6	5^{1}						7		12						26
1	4		3	2	6	13			11			10^{2}		5^{1}		9				8^{3}			7		14	12					27
1	2		3	4	8	14		6^{2}	11			10^{1}		13		9^{3}							7			12	5				28
1			4	3	2			8^{3}	11^{1}			10^{2}				9		6					7		14	12	5	13			29
1	2		4		8			6	11^{3}					14		9^{2}		3					7		13	10^{1}	5	12			30
1	2		4	3	8▪	13		6	11^{1}			12				9							7			10^{2}	5				31
1	2		4	3		7		11	10^{2}			12				8				13			6^{3}			9^{1}	5	14			32
1▪			3	2	7	8^{1}		9	10^{3}			13		14		6		4						12		11^{2}	5				33
			4	2	8	7		9^{1}	11^{2}			10				6^{3}		3		12				1	14		5	13			34
			4	2	8			6	11^{1}			10^{2}				9	14	3					7	1		13	5^{3}	12			35
	4^{1}		3		9	13		6^{3}	7			11		12		10		2		14			8^{2}	1			5				36
			4	2	7			11^{2}	10			9^{1}				6		3					8	1		13	5	12			37
			4	2	8			6^{1}	11					13		9	5^{2}	3					7	1	14	10^{3}		12			38
			3	2	8	12			11			13				6^{1}		4					7	1		10^{2}	5	9			39
			4	2	8				11			10^{3}		14		6^{2}	13	3					7	1		12	5	9^{1}			40
			4	2	7			9^{1}	10					14		8		3					6^{2}	1		11^{3}	5	12	13		41
			4	2	8			6^{3}	11					12		9		3					7^{1}	1	14	10^{2}	5	13			42
1		14	4	12	7			11						3^{2}		9^{1}	2	8					6		13		5	10^{3}			43
1	2^{2}		4		8	14		6				12		7		9		3									5	10^{1}	11^{3}	13	44
1	2	3	14		6^{1}	12		10				11^{2}				9		4					8			7^{3}	5			13	45
1	2	4^{1}	12		8			6	11			13				9		3^{2}					7			10^{3}	5			14	46

FA Cup

First Round	Port Vale	(a)	0-1

EFL Cup

First Round	Ipswich T	(a)	1-0
Second Round	Stoke C	(h)	0-4

EFL Checkatrade Trophy

Southern Group G	Leyton Orient	(a)	1-3
Southern Group G	Brighton & HA U21	(h)	2-2
(Brighton & HA U21 won 4-3 on penalties)			
Southern Group G	Southend U	(h)	4-0

STOKE CITY

FOUNDATION

The date of the formation of this club has long been in doubt. The year 1863 was claimed, but more recent research by local club historian Wade Martin has uncovered nothing earlier than 1868, when a couple of Old Carthusians, who were apprentices at the local works of the old North Staffordshire Railway Company, met with some others from that works, to form Stoke Ramblers. It should also be noted that the old Stoke club went bankrupt in 1908 when a new club was formed.

bet365 Stadium, Stanley Matthews Way, Stoke-on-Trent, Staffordshire ST4 4EG.

Telephone: (01782) 367 598.

Fax: (01782) 646 988.

Ticket Office: (01782) 367 599.

Website: www.stokecityfc.com

Email: info@stokecityfc.com

Ground Capacity: 27,902.

Record Attendance: 51,380 v Arsenal, Division 1, 29 March 1937 (at Victoria Ground); 28,218 v Everton, FA Cup 3rd rd, 5 January 2002 (at Britannia Stadium).

Pitch Measurements: 105m × 68m (115yd × 75yd).

Chairman: Peter Coates.

Chief Executive: Tony Scholes.

Manager: Mark Hughes.

Assistant Manager: Mark Bowen.

Colours: Red and white striped shirts, white shorts with red trim, white socks with red trim.

Year Formed: 1863* (*see Foundation*).

Turned Professional: 1885.

Previous Names: 1868, Stoke Ramblers; 1870, Stoke; 1925, Stoke City.

Club Nickname: 'The Potters'.

Grounds: 1875, Sweeting's Field; 1878, Victoria Ground (previously known as the Athletic Club Ground); 1997, Britannia Stadium (renamed bet365 Stadium, 2016).

First Football League Game: 8 September 1888, Football League, v WBA (h) L 0–2 – Rowley; Clare, Underwood; Ramsey, Shutt, Smith; Sayer, McSkimming, Staton, Edge, Tunnicliffe.

Record League Victory: 10–3 v WBA, Division 1, 4 February 1937 – Doug Westland; Brigham, Harbot; Tutin, Turner (1p), Kirton; Matthews, Antonio (2), Freddie Steele (5), Jimmy Westland, Johnson (2).

Record Cup Victory: 7–1 v Burnley, FA Cup 2nd rd (replay), 20 February 1896 – Clawley; Clare, Eccles; Turner, Grewe, Robertson; Willie Maxwell, Dickson, Alan Maxwell (3), Hyslop (4), Schofield.

Record Defeat: 0–10 v Preston NE, Division 1, 14 September 1889.

Most League Points (2 for a win): 63, Division 3 (N), 1926–27.

HONOURS

League Champions: Division 2 – 1932–33, 1962–63; Second Division – 1992–93; Division 3N – 1926–27.
Runners-up: FL C – 2007–08; Division 2 – 1921–22.

FA Cup: *Runners-up:* 2011.

League Cup Winners: 1972.
Runners-up: 1964.

League Trophy Winners: 1992, 2000.

European Competitions
UEFA Cup: 1972–73, 1974–75.
Europa League: 2011–12.

sky SPORTS FACT FILE

Centre-forward Tommy Sale rejoined Stoke City from Blackburn Rovers in March 1938 and netted 18 times in 1938–39 to finish as the club's second-top scorer. He came into his own during the war years when he scored 200 goals in just 265 appearances. His tally of 56 goals in 1941–42 included ten hat-tricks.

Most League Points (3 for a win): 93, Division 2, 1992–93.

Most League Goals: 92, Division 3 (N), 1926–27.

Highest League Scorer in Season: Freddie Steele, 33, Division 1, 1936–37.

Most League Goals in Total Aggregate: Freddie Steele, 142, 1934–49.

Most League Goals in One Match: 7, Neville Coleman v Lincoln C, Division 2, 23 February 1957.

Most Capped Player: Glenn Whelan, 81, Republic of Ireland.

Most League Appearances: Eric Skeels, 507, 1958–76.

Youngest League Player: Peter Bullock, 16 years 163 days v Swansea C, 19 April 1958.

Record Transfer Fee Received: £8,000,000 from Chelsea for Asmir Begovic, July 2015.

Record Transfer Fee Paid: £18,300,000 to Porto for Gianelli Imbula, February 2016.

Football League Record: 1888 Founder Member of Football League; 1890 Not re-elected; 1891 Re-elected; relegated in 1907, and after one year in Division 2, resigned for financial reasons; 1919 re-elected to Division 2; 1922–23 Division 1; 1923–26 Division 2; 1926–27 Division 3 (N); 1927–33 Division 2; 1933–53 Division 1; 1953–63 Division 2; 1963–77 Division 1; 1977–79 Division 2; 1979–85 Division 1; 1985–90 Division 2; 1990–92 Division 3; 1992–93 Division 2; 1993–98 Division 1; 1998–2002 Division 2; 2002–04 Division 1; 2004–08 FL C; 2008– FA Premier League.

LATEST SEQUENCES

Longest Sequence of League Wins: 8, 30.3.1895 – 21.9.1895.

Longest Sequence of League Defeats: 11, 6.4.1985 – 17.8.1985.

Longest Sequence of League Draws: 5, 13.5.2012 – 15.9.2012.

Longest Sequence of Unbeaten League Matches: 25, 5.9.1992 – 20.2.1993.

Longest Sequence Without a League Win: 17, 22.4.1989 – 14.10.1989.

Successive Scoring Runs: 21 from 24.12.1921.

Successive Non-scoring Runs: 8 from 29.12.1984.

MANAGERS

Tom Slaney 1874–83
(Secretary-Manager)
Walter Cox 1883–84
(Secretary-Manager)
Harry Lockett 1884–90
Joseph Bradshaw 1890–92
Arthur Reeves 1892–95
William Rowley 1895–97
H. D. Austerberry 1897–1908
A. J. Barker 1908–14
Peter Hodge 1914–15
Joe Schofield 1915–19
Arthur Shallcross 1919–23
John 'Jock' Rutherford 1923
Tom Mather 1923–35
Bob McGrory 1935–52
Frank Taylor 1952–60
Tony Waddington 1960–77
George Eastham 1977–78
Alan A'Court 1978
Alan Durban 1978–81
Richie Barker 1981–83
Bill Asprey 1984–85
Mick Mills 1985–89
Alan Ball 1989–91
Lou Macari 1991–93
Joe Jordan 1993–94
Lou Macari 1994–97
Chic Bates 1997–98
Chris Kamara 1998
Brian Little 1998–99
Gary Megson 1999
Gudjon Thordarson 1999–2002
Steve Cotterill 2002
Tony Pulis 2002–05
Johan Boskamp 2005–06
Tony Pulis 2006–13
Mark Hughes May 2013–

TEN YEAR LEAGUE RECORD

		P	W	D	L	F	A	Pts	Pos
2007-08	FL C	46	21	16	9	69	55	79	2
2008-09	PR Lge	38	12	9	17	38	55	45	12
2009-10	PR Lge	38	11	14	13	34	48	47	11
2010-11	PR Lge	38	13	7	18	46	48	46	13
2011-12	PR Lge	38	11	12	15	36	53	45	14
2012-13	PR Lge	38	9	15	14	34	45	42	13
2013-14	PR Lge	38	13	11	14	45	52	50	9
2014-15	PR Lge	38	15	9	14	48	45	54	9
2015-16	PR Lge	38	14	9	15	41	55	51	9
2016-17	PR Lge	38	11	11	16	41	56	44	13

DID YOU KNOW ?

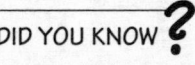

Stoke City took part in the first FA Cup tie to be decided on penalties. The occasion was the match for third place in the 1971–72 competition against Birmingham City at St Andrew's. The match finished goalless but Stoke lost 4-3 on penalties.

STOKE CITY – PREMIER LEAGUE 2016–17 LEAGUE RECORD

Match No.	*Date*	*Venue*	*Opponents*	*Result*	*H/T Score*	*Lg Pos.*	*Goalscorers*	*Attendance*
1	Aug 13	A	Middlesbrough	D 1-1	0-1	8	Shaqiri [67]	32,110
2	20	H	Manchester C	L 1-4	0-2	16	Bojan (pen) [49]	27,455
3	27	A	Everton	L 0-1	0-0	19		39,581
4	Sept 10	H	Tottenham H	L 0-4	0-1	20		27,385
5	18	A	Crystal Palace	L 1-4	0-2	20	Arnautovic [90]	23,781
6	24	H	WBA	D 1-1	0-0	19	Allen [73]	27,645
7	Oct 2	A	Manchester U	D 1-1	0-0	19	Allen [82]	75,251
8	15	H	Sunderland	W 2-0	2-0	18	Allen 2 [8, 45]	27,701
9	22	A	Hull C	W 2-0	1-0	15	Shaqiri 2 [26, 50]	18,522
10	31	H	Swansea C	W 3-1	1-1	12	Bony 2 [3, 73], Mawson (og) [55]	26,602
11	Nov 5	A	West Ham U	D 1-1	0-0	11	Bojan [75]	56,970
12	19	H	Bournemouth	L 0-1	0-1	13		27,815
13	27	A	Watford	W 1-0	1-0	11	Gomes (og) [29]	20,058
14	Dec 3	H	Burnley	W 2-0	2-0	9	Walters [20], Muniesa [35]	27,306
15	10	A	Arsenal	L 1-3	1-1	9	Adam (pen) [29]	59,964
16	14	H	Southampton	D 0-0	0-0	12		27,002
17	17	H	Leicester C	D 2-2	2-0	11	Bojan (pen) [39], Allen [45]	27,663
18	27	A	Liverpool	L 1-4	1-2	13	Walters [12]	53,094
19	31	A	Chelsea	L 2-4	0-1	14	Martins Indi [46], Crouch [64]	41,601
20	Jan 3	H	Watford	W 2-0	1-0	11	Shawcross [45], Crouch [49]	27,010
21	14	A	Sunderland	W 3-1	3-1	9	Arnautovic 2 [15, 22], Crouch [34]	42,722
22	21	H	Manchester U	D 1-1	1-0	9	Mata (og) [19]	27,423
23	Feb 1	H	Everton	D 1-1	1-1	9	Crouch [7]	27,612
24	4	A	WBA	L 0-1	0-1	11		23,921
25	11	H	Crystal Palace	W 1-0	0-0	9	Allen [67]	27,007
26	26	A	Tottenham H	L 0-4	0-4	10		31,864
27	Mar 4	H	Middlesbrough	W 2-0	2-0	9	Arnautovic 2 [29, 42]	27,644
28	8	A	Manchester C	D 0-0	0-0	9		52,625
29	18	H	Chelsea	L 1-2	1-1	9	Walters (pen) [38]	27,724
30	Apr 1	A	Leicester C	L 0-2	0-1	9		31,958
31	4	A	Burnley	L 0-1	0-0	10		19,881
32	8	H	Liverpool	L 1-2	1-0	13	Walters [44]	27,568
33	15	H	Hull C	W 3-1	1-0	10	Arnautovic [6], Crouch [66], Shaqiri [80]	27,505
34	22	A	Swansea C	L 0-2	0-1	11		20,566
35	29	H	West Ham U	D 0-0	0-0	12		27,628
36	May 6	A	Bournemouth	D 2-2	1-0	13	Mousset (og) [33], Diouf [73]	11,046
37	13	H	Arsenal	L 1-4	0-1	13	Crouch [67]	27,535
38	21	A	Southampton	W 1-0	0-0	13	Crouch [60]	31,286

Final League Position: 13

GOALSCORERS

League (41): Crouch 7, Allen 6, Arnautovic 6, Shaqiri 4, Walters 4 (1 pen), Bojan 3 (2 pens), Bony 2, Adam 1 (1 pen), Diouf 1, Martins Indi 1, Muniesa 1, Shawcross 1, own goals 4.
FA Cup (0).
EFL Cup (5): Crouch 3, Arnautovic 1, Bardsley 1.
EFL Checkatrade Trophy (2): Adam 1, Krkic 1.

Given S 5	Bardsley P 14 + 1	Shawcross R 35	Wollscheid P 2	Pieters E 35 + 1	Imbula G 9 + 3	Whelan G 26 + 4	Shaqiri X 21	Bojan K 5 + 4	Arnautovic M 32	Diouf M 15 + 12	Walters J 13 + 10	Allen J 34 + 2	Sobhi R 8 + 9	Cameron G 18 + 1	Crouch P 13 + 14	Martins Indi B 35	Bony W 9 + 1	Adam C 17 + 7	Johnson G 21 + 2	Grant L 28	Muniesa M 7 + 3	Ngoy J — + 5	Afellay I 3 + 9	Berahino S 8 + 5	Butland J 5	Match No.
1	2	3	4	5	6	7	8	9[2]	10	11[1]	12	13														1
1	2	3	4	5	8[2]	7		9	11[1]	10	12	6	13													2
1	2	3		5	7[1]	8		14	11	9[3]	12	6	13	4	10[2]											3
1		3		5	7[2]	6[1]		12	10		8	9		2		4	11	13								4
1		3				6		9[1]	10	12	8	7		4		5	11		2							5
		3		5		7	9[3]		11	14		8[1]		6	12	4	10[2]	13	2	1						6
	14	3		5		7	8[3]		10[2]		13	9		6	12	4	11[1]		2	1						7
	2[1]	3		5		6	8		10		14	9[3]		7		4	11[2]	12		1	13					8
	2	3		5		6	8		10	12		9		7		4	11[1]			1						9
	2	3		5		6	8[1]		10[3]		13	9	12		14	4	11[2]	7		1						10
	2	3		5		6[1]		13		14	8	9	10[2]		12	4	11[3]	7		1						11
	2[3]	3		5			8	9[2]	10		14	7			13	4	11[1]	6	12	1						12
				5	7		9		10[1]	8	11				12	3		6	2	1	4					13
				5	7	14	9[2]		10[3]	8	11	12			13	3		6[1]	2	1	4					14
				8	6		9[2]		11	5[3]		10	13		12	3		7[1]	2	1	4	14				15
		3		5		6	8[2]		10■	12	11	9				4		7[1]	2	1	13					16
		3		5	6	7[1]		10[2]		8	11	9	13			4		12	2	1						17
		3		9	7	6[2]				5[1]	11	8	12		10[3]	4	14		2	1			13			18
		3		8	13		9[1]	12		5		6			11	4		7	2	1			10[2]			19
		3		8		13			11	5[2]	9	6			10	4		7[1]	2	1			12			20
		3		5		6	8[2]		10			9			11	4		7[1]	2	1		13	12			21
		3		5	14	6	8[2]		10[3]			9			11	4		7[1]	2	1		13	12			22
	2	3		5		6			10[1]			9[2]			11	4		7		1		13	8	12		23
	2	3		5		6			10	12		9			11[1]	4		7[2]		1		14	8[3]	13		24
	2[1]	3		5		6			8	14		9	10[3]		11	4		7[2]	12	1			13			25
	2	3		5		6[3]			10			9	8	14	11[1]	4		7[2]		1			13	12		26
		3		5		7			8[1]	12		9	10	6	11[3]	4[2]			2	1			14	13		27
	2	3		5	14	13				6[1]	10	8[3]	9	7		4				1			12	11[2]		28
	2■	3		5					6	12	10	8	9[1]	7	13	4				1				11[2]		29
		3		5		8[3]			6	13	10[2]	7	9		12	4		14	2	1				11[1]		30
		2		8					10	5		9[1]		6	12	3		7		1	4		13	11[2]		31
		3		5		13	6		9		10[1]	8[2]	14	7		4		12[3]	2	1				11		32
		2		8			9[3]		10	14	13			6	12	3		7[2]	5	1	4			11[1]		33
		3		5			6		9[2]	13		8	12	7	10	4			2					11[1]	1	34
		3				7[1]	8		10			9[2]		6	12	4		13	2		5			11	1	35
		3		13		7	8		10[1]	11[2]	12	9		6		4			2		5				1	36
		3		5		7	8		10[1]	11[2]		9[3]	14	6	12	4			2					13	1	37
		3		8		6	9[1]			5[2]	12	7	10	2	11	4					13				1	38

FA Cup

Third Round	Wolverhampton W	(h)	0-2

EFL Cup

Second Round	Stevenage	(a)	4-0
Third Round	Hull C	(h)	1-2

EFL Checkatrade Trophy (Stoke C U21)

Northern Group C	Bradford C	(a)	0-1
Northern Group C	Morecambe	(a)	1-3
Northern Group C	Bury	(h)	1-1

(Stoke C U21 won 4-3 on penalties)

SUNDERLAND

FOUNDATION

A Scottish schoolmaster named James Allan, working at Hendon Board School, took the initiative in the foundation of Sunderland in 1879 when they were formed as The Sunderland and District Teachers' Association FC at a meeting in the Adults School, Norfolk Street. Due to financial difficulties, they quickly allowed members from outside the teaching profession and so became Sunderland AFC in October 1880.

Stadium of Light, Sunderland, Tyne and Wear SR5 1SU.

Telephone: (0871) 911 1200.

Fax: (0191) 551 5123.

Ticket Office: (0871) 911 1973.

Website: www.safc.com

Email: enquiries@safc.com

Ground Capacity: 48,707.

Record Attendance: 75,118 v Derby Co, FA Cup 6th rd replay, 8 March 1933 (at Roker Park); 48,353 v Liverpool, FA Premier League, 13 April 2002 (at Stadium of Light) (FA Premier League figure 46,062).

Pitch Measurements: 105m × 68m (114yd × 74yd).

Chairman: Ellis Short.

Chief Executive: Martin Bain.

Manager: Simon Grayson.

Assistant Manager: Glynn Snodin.

Physio: Peter Brand.

Colours: Red and white striped shirts, black shorts with red trim, black socks with red trim.

Year Formed: 1879.

Turned Professional: 1886.

Previous Names: 1879, Sunderland and District Teachers AFC; 1880, Sunderland.

Club Nickname: 'The Black Cats'.

Grounds: 1879, Blue House Field, Hendon; 1882, Groves Field, Ashbrooke; 1883, Horatio Street; 1884, Abbs Field, Fulwell; 1886, Newcastle Road; 1898, Roker Park; 1997, Stadium of Light.

First Football League Game: 13 September 1890, Football League, v Burnley (h) L 2–3 – Kirtley; Porteous, Oliver; Wilson, Auld, Gibson; Spence (1), Miller, Campbell (1), Scott, Davy Hannah.

Record League Victory: 9–1 v Newcastle U (a), Division 1, 5 December 1908 – Roose; Forster, Melton; Daykin, Thomson, Low; Mordue (1), Hogg (3), Brown, Holley (3), Bridgett (2).

Record Cup Victory: 11–1 v Fairfield, FA Cup 1st rd, 2 February 1895 – Doig; McNeill, Johnston; Dunlop, McCreadie (1), Wilson; Gillespie (1), Millar (5), Campbell, Jimmy Hannah (3), Scott (1).

HONOURS

League Champions: Division 1 – 1892–93, 1894–95, 1901–02, 1912–13, 1935–36; Football League 1891–92; FL C – 2004–05, 2006–07; First Division – 1995–96, 1998–99; Division 2 – 1975–76; Division 3 – 1987–88.
Runners-up: Division 1 – 1893–94, 1897–98, 1900–01, 1922–23, 1934–35; Division 2 – 1963–64, 1979–80.

FA Cup Winners: 1937, 1973.
Runners-up: 1913, 1992.

League Cup: *Runners-up:* 1985, 2014.

European Competitions
European Cup-Winners' Cup: 1973–74.

SKY SPORTS FACT FILE

On the only occasion Sunderland competed for the Sheriff of London Charity Shield they defeated Corinthians 3-0 with club captain Jimmy Miller netting a hat-trick. The match, played at Tottenham Hotspur in February 1903, attracted an estimated attendance of 4,000. The Shield was competed for between the best professional team and the best amateur team of the day with the proceeds going to hospitals and charities.

Record Defeat: 0–8 v Sheff Wed, Division 1, 26 December 1911; 0–8 v West Ham U, Division 1, 19 October 1968; 0–8 v Watford, Division 1, 25 September 1982; 0–8 v Southampton, FA Premier League, 18 October 2014.

Most League Points (2 for a win): 61, Division 2, 1963–64.

Most League Points (3 for a win): 105, Division 1, 1998–99.

Most League Goals: 109, Division 1, 1935–36.

Highest League Scorer in Season: Dave Halliday, 43, Division 1, 1928–29.

Most League Goals in Total Aggregate: Charlie Buchan, 209, 1911–25.

Most League Goals in One Match: 5, Charlie Buchan v Liverpool, Division 1, 7 December 1919; 5, Bobby Gurney v Bolton W, Division 1, 7 December 1935; 5, Dominic Sharkey v Norwich C, Division 2, 20 February 1962.

Most Capped Player: Seb Larsson, 59 (90), Sweden.

Most League Appearances: Jim Montgomery, 537, 1962–77.

Youngest League Player: Derek Forster, 15 years 184 days v Leicester C, 22 August 1964.

Record Transfer Fee Received: £25,000,000 (rising to £30,000,000) from Everton for Jordan Pickford, June 2017.

Record Transfer Fee Paid: £10,000,000 (rising to £16,500,000) to Tottenham H for Darren Bent, August 2009.

Football League Record: 1890 Elected to Division 1; 1958–64 Division 2; 1964–70 Division 1; 1970–76 Division 2; 1976–77 Division 1; 1977–80 Division 2; 1980–85 Division 1; 1985–87 Division 2; 1987–88 Division 3; 1988–90 Division 2; 1990–91 Division 1; 1991–92 Division 2; 1992–96 Division 1; 1996–97 FA Premier League; 1997–99 Division 1; 1999–2003 FA Premier League; 2003–04 Division 1; 2004–05 FL C; 2005–06 FA Premier League; 2006–07 FL C; 2007–17 FA Premier League; 2017– FL C.

MANAGERS

Tom Watson 1888–96
Bob Campbell 1896–99
Alex Mackie 1899–1905
Bob Kyle 1905–28
Johnny Cochrane 1928–39
Bill Murray 1939–57
Alan Brown 1957–64
George Hardwick 1964–65
Ian McColl 1965–68
Alan Brown 1968–72
Bob Stokoe 1972–76
Jimmy Adamson 1976–78
Ken Knighton 1979–81
Alan Durban 1981–84
Len Ashurst 1984–85
Lawrie McMenemy 1985–87
Denis Smith 1987–91
Malcolm Crosby 1991–93
Terry Butcher 1993
Mick Buxton 1993–95
Peter Reid 1995–2002
Howard Wilkinson 2002–03
Mick McCarthy 2003–06
Niall Quinn 2006
Roy Keane 2006–08
Ricky Sbragia 2008–09
Steve Bruce 2009–11
Martin O'Neill 2011–13
Paolo Di Canio 2013
Gus Poyet 2013–15
Dick Advocaat 2015
Sam Allardyce 2015–16
David Moyes 2016–17
Simon Grayson June 2017–

LATEST SEQUENCES

Longest Sequence of League Wins: 13, 14.11.1891 – 2.4.1892.

Longest Sequence of League Defeats: 17, 18.1.2003 – 16.8.2003.

Longest Sequence of League Draws: 6, 26.3.1949 – 19.4.1949.

Longest Sequence of Unbeaten League Matches: 19, 3.5.1998 – 14.11.1998.

Longest Sequence Without a League Win: 22, 21.12.2002 – 16.8.2003.

Successive Scoring Runs: 29 from 8.11.1997.

Successive Non-scoring Runs: 10 from 27.11.1976.

TEN YEAR LEAGUE RECORD

		P	W	D	L	F	A	Pts	Pos
2007-08	PR Lge	38	11	6	21	36	59	39	15
2008-09	PR Lge	38	9	9	20	34	54	36	16
2009-10	PR Lge	38	11	11	16	48	56	44	13
2010-11	PR Lge	38	12	11	15	45	56	47	10
2011-12	PR Lge	38	11	12	15	45	46	45	13
2012-13	PR Lge	38	9	12	17	41	54	39	17
2013-14	PR Lge	38	10	8	20	41	60	38	14
2014-15	PR Lge	38	7	17	14	31	53	38	16
2015-16	PR Lge	38	9	12	17	48	62	39	17
2016-17	PR Lge	38	6	6	26	29	69	24	20

DID YOU KNOW ?

In 1977 full-back Joe Bolton was the inaugural winner of Sunderland's Player of the Year award. Joe was a product of the Black Cats' youth team and went on to make over 300 first-team appearances for the club before he was transferred to rivals Middlesbrough in July 1981.

SUNDERLAND – PREMIER LEAGUE 2016–17 LEAGUE RECORD

Match No.	Date	Venue	Opponents	Result	H/T Score	Lg Pos.	Goalscorers	Attendance
1	Aug 13	A	Manchester C	L 1-2	0-1	18	Defoe [71]	54,362
2	21	H	Middlesbrough	L 1-2	0-2	18	Van Aanholt [71]	43,515
3	27	A	Southampton	D 1-1	0-0	17	Defoe (pen) [80]	30,152
4	Sept 12	H	Everton	L 0-3	0-0	19		42,406
5	18	A	Tottenham H	L 0-1	0-0	19		31,251
6	24	H	Crystal Palace	L 2-3	1-0	20	Defoe 2 [39, 60]	38,941
7	Oct 1	H	WBA	D 1-1	0-1	19	Van Aanholt [83]	40,043
8	15	A	Stoke C	L 0-2	0-2	20		27,701
9	22	A	West Ham U	L 0-1	0-0	20		56,985
10	29	H	Arsenal	L 1-4	0-1	20	Defoe (pen) [65]	44,322
11	Nov 5	A	Bournemouth	W 2-1	1-1	20	Anichebe [33], Defoe (pen) [74]	11,084
12	19	H	Hull C	W 3-0	1-0	19	Defoe [34], Anichebe 2 [62, 84]	41,271
13	26	A	Liverpool	L 0-2	0-0	20		53,114
14	Dec 3	H	Leicester C	W 2-1	0-0	18	Huth (og) [64], Defoe [77]	39,725
15	10	A	Swansea C	L 0-3	0-0	20		20,453
16	14	H	Chelsea	L 0-1	0-1	20		41,008
17	17	H	Watford	W 1-0	0-0	18	Van Aanholt [49]	40,267
18	26	A	Manchester U	L 1-3	0-1	18	Borini [90]	75,325
19	31	A	Burnley	L 1-4	0-1	18	Defoe [71]	21,124
20	Jan 2	H	Liverpool	D 2-2	1-1	18	Defoe 2 (2 pens) [25, 84]	46,494
21	14	H	Stoke C	L 1-3	1-3	19	Defoe [40]	42,722
22	21	A	WBA	L 0-2	0-2	20		24,380
23	31	H	Tottenham H	D 0-0	0-0	19		40,058
24	Feb 4	A	Crystal Palace	W 4-0	4-0	20	Kone [9], Ndong [43], Defoe 2 [45, 45]	25,310
25	11	H	Southampton	L 0-4	0-2	20		39,931
26	25	A	Everton	L 0-2	0-1	20		39,595
27	Mar 5	H	Manchester C	L 0-2	0-1	20		41,107
28	18	H	Burnley	D 0-0	0-0	20		41,518
29	Apr 1	A	Watford	L 0-1	0-0	20		20,805
30	4	A	Leicester C	L 0-2	0-0	20		31,757
31	9	H	Manchester U	L 0-3	0-1	20		43,779
32	15	H	West Ham U	D 2-2	1-1	20	Khazri [26], Borini [90]	40,168
33	26	A	Middlesbrough	L 0-1	0-1	20		30,742
34	29	H	Bournemouth	L 0-1	0-0	20		38,394
35	May 6	A	Hull C	W 2-0	0-0	20	Jones [69], Defoe [90]	22,480
36	13	H	Swansea C	L 0-2	0-2	20		38,781
37	16	A	Arsenal	L 0-2	0-0	20		59,510
38	21	A	Chelsea	L 1-5	1-1	20	Manquillo [3]	41,618

Final League Position: 20

GOALSCORERS

League (29): Defoe 15 (5 pens), Anichebe 3, Van Aanholt 3, Borini 2, Jones 1, Khazri 1, Kone 1, Manquillo 1, Ndong 1, own goal 1.
FA Cup (0).
EFL Cup (3): McNair 2, Januzaj 1.
EFL Checkatrade Trophy (5): Beadling 1, Embleton 1, Love 1, Maja 1, own goal 1.

Mannone V 9	Love D 6 + 6	Kone L 29 + 1	Kaboul Y 1	Van Aanholt P 20 + 1	Rodwell J 17 + 3	O'Shea J 26 + 2	Watmore D 11 + 3	Borini F 19 + 5	Gooch L 4 + 7	Defoe J 37	Januzaj A 18 + 7	Khazri W 7 + 14	McNair P 5 + 4	Djilobodji P 17 + 1	Pienaar S 10 + 5	Lens J — + 2	Asoro J — + 1	Pickford J 29	Manquillo J 15 + 5	Kirchhoff J 5 + 2	Ndong D 27 + 4	Denayer J 22 + 2	Cattermole L 8	Anichebe V 14 + 4	Jones B 25 + 2	Larsson S 17 + 4	Honeyman G 2 + 3	Oviedo B 10	Gibson D 7 + 5	Lescott J 1 + 1	Match No.
1	2	3	4	5	6	7	8^1	9	10^2	11^3	12	13	14																		1
1	2			5	6	3^3	10^2		9	11	8		7^1	4	12	13	14														2
	14	3		5	6		12	10^2	7^3	11	9			4	8^1	13		1	2												3
		3		5	7		6^1		9^2	11	10	12		4				1	2	8^3	13	14									4
		3					12			10	9■	13	14	4	11^1			1	5	7^2	6	2^3	8								5
		3		5			12			10	9^3		14	4	11^2			1	2	7	6		8^1	13							6
		3		12	13	4	7		14	11		10^2	9^1					1	2	6^3	8	5									7
				5^2	7^3	3	6			11		10	9^1	4	13			1	2		8			14	12						8
		3		5	7	4	6^3		12	11		10^2	13		9^1			1	2		8				14						9
		3		5	8	4^2	10^3		14	11	13	6		12	9^1			1			7				2						10
	13	3		5			6^1		14	11^3			9^2	4	7■			1			8	12		10	2						11
	13	3		5		12	8			11			6^2	4■				1			9	7^1		10	2						12
		3		5		4	9^2		12	10	13				8^1			1			7	6		11	2						13
		3		5			9^3			10				4	6^2			1	14	13	7	8^1		11	2	12					14
		3		5						11	12			4	9^1			1	14	13	7^2	8		10	2	6^3					15
	13	2		8		3		11^3		10	9	14		4				1		7^1		6			5^2	12					16
	2^1	3		5		12		8^2		11	9^3	14		4				1			6	7		10		13					17
	13	3		5				11		10		12		4				1			8^2	7		9	2	6^1					18
1	14	3^2		5		7^1		11		10	8			4	13						12			9^3	2	6					19
1	2			5	8^2	3		6		11	10^1	13		4					12		7					9					20
1	2			5	6	3		8		11	9			4								7				10					21
1				8	7	3		13		11	9^1			4								2^2		12	5	6	10				22
1		2			7	3		10^1		11									9		6	4			5	8	12				23
1		2			7^3	3^1				11	10^2				14						6	4			5	8		9	12	13	24
1		2				3^3		13		11	10	14			12						6	4			5	8^2		9	7^1		25
		3				4		10^3		11	6	13						1	14		9				2^2	8	12	5	7^1		26
		4			12	3		10		11	6^2	13						1			7				2	9		5	8^1		27
					7	4		11		10	9	13						1			12	3			2	8^2		5	6^1		28
		3			9	4		8		11	10^2	13						1			12	6			2			5	7^1		29
		3			8^3			11		10		13						1			7	4	6^1	12	2	9^2		5	14		30
		3			8			13		10								1	12		7	4	6^1	11	2	9■		5^2			31
		14				3		13		10	12	9						1	5^1		6	4	7^2	11	2^3				8		32
					14	3		12		10	13	9^2						1	5		6	4	7^3	11	2				8^1		33
	2	3				4		7		11		9			8^1			1	5		6			10			12				34
		3				4		9		10								1	5		6	7		11	2	12	8^1				35
		3				4		9		10		13						1	5		8	7^2		11^1	2	6			12		36
		4				3		10	12	11	13							1	5^3		6^2		7^1		2	8		9	14		37
					8	3		11	12		10^2							1	5				7^1		2	6		9	13	4	38

FA Cup

Third Round	Burnley	(h)	0-0
Replay	Burnley	(a)	0-2

EFL Cup

Second Round	Shrewsbury T	(h)	1-0
Third Round	QPR	(a)	2-1
Fourth Round	Southampton	(a)	0-1

EFL Checkatrade Trophy (Sunderland U21)

Northern Group F	Rochdale	(a)	1-1
(Rochdale won 4-2 on penalties)			
Northern Group F	Hartlepool U	(a)	1-0
Northern Group F	Notts Co	(h)	2-1
Second Round North	Wolverhampton W U21	(a)	1-1
(Wolverhampton W U21 won 4-3 on penalties)			

SWANSEA CITY

FOUNDATION

The earliest Association Football in Wales was played in the northern part of the country and no international took place in the south until 1894, when a local paper still thought it necessary to publish an outline of the rules and an illustration of the pitch markings. There had been an earlier Swansea club, but this has no connection with Swansea Town (now City) formed at a public meeting in June 1912.

Liberty Stadium, Morfa, Landore, Swansea SA1 2FA.

Telephone: (01792) 616 600.

Fax: (01792) 616 606.

Ticket Office: (0844) 815 6665.

Website: www.swanseacity.net

Email: info@swanseacityfc.co.uk

Ground Capacity: 21,088.

Record Attendance: 32,796 v Arsenal, FA Cup 4th rd, 17 February 1968 (at Vetch Field); 20,972 v Liverpool, FA Premier League, 1 May 2016 (at Liberty Stadium).

Pitch Measurements: 105m × 68m (114yd × 74yd).

Chairman: Huw Jenkins.

Chief Operating Officer: Chris Pearlman.

Head Coach: Paul Clement.

Assistant Coach: Nigel Gibbs.

Colours: White shirts, white shorts, white socks.

Year Formed: 1912.

Turned Professional: 1912.

Previous Name: 1912, Swansea Town; 1970, Swansea City.

Club Nicknames: 'The Swans', 'The Jacks'.

Grounds: 1912, Vetch Field; 2005, Liberty Stadium.

First Football League Game: 28 August 1920, Division 3, v Portsmouth (a) L 0–3 – Crumley; Robson, Evans; Smith, Holdsworth, Williams; Hole, Ivor Jones, Edmundson, Rigsby, Spottiswood.

Record League Victory: 8–0 v Hartlepool U, Division 4, 1 April 1978 – Barber; Evans, Bartley, Lally (1) (Morris), May, Bruton, Kevin Moore, Robbie James (3 incl. 1p), Curtis (3), Toshack (1), Chappell.

Record Cup Victory: 12–0 v Sliema W (Malta), ECWC 1st rd 1st leg, 15 September 1982 – Davies; Marustik, Hadziabdic (1), Irwin (1), Kennedy, Rajkovic (1), Loveridge (2) (Leighton James), Robbie James, Charles (2), Stevenson (1), Latchford (1) (Walsh (3)).

Record Defeat: 0–8 v Liverpool, FA Cup 3rd rd, 9 January 1990; 0–8 v Monaco, ECWC, 1st rd 2nd leg, 1 October 1991.

Most League Points (2 for a win): 62, Division 3 (S), 1948–49.

Most League Points (3 for a win): 92, FL 1, 2007–08.

HONOURS

League Champions: FL 1 – 2007–08; Division 3S – 1924–25, 1948–49; Third Division – 1999–2000.

FA Cup: semi-final – 1926, 1964.

League Cup Winners: 2013.

League Trophy Winners: 1994, 2006.

Welsh Cup Winners: 11 times; *Runners-up:* 8 times.

European Competitions
Europa League: 2013–14.
European Cup-Winners' Cup: 1961–62, 1966–67, 1981–82, 1982–83, 1983–84, 1989–90, 1991–92.

sky SPORTS FACT FILE

In 2007–08 Swansea City had five players included in the PFA League One Team of the Year after winning the division by ten points ahead of their nearest challengers Nottingham Forest. The players voted into the team by their fellow professionals were Angel Rangel, Garry Monk, Andy Robinson, Ferrie Bodde and Jason Scotland.

Most League Goals: 90, Division 2, 1956–57.

Highest League Scorer in Season: Cyril Pearce, 35, Division 2, 1931–32.

Most League Goals in Total Aggregate: Ivor Allchurch, 166, 1949–58, 1965–68.

Most League Goals in One Match: 5, Jack Fowler v Charlton Ath, Division 3S, 27 December 1924.

Most Capped Player: Ashley Williams, 64 (71), Wales.

Most League Appearances: Wilfred Milne, 587, 1919–37.

Youngest League Player: Nigel Dalling, 15 years 289 days v Southport, 6 December 1974.

Record Transfer Fee Received: £25,000,000 (rising to £28,000,000) from Manchester C for Wilfried Bony, January 2015.

Record Transfer Fee Paid: £15,500,000 to Atletico Madrid for Borja Bastón, August 2016.

Football League Record: 1920 Original Member of Division 3; 1921–25 Division 3 (S); 1925–47 Division 2; 1947–49 Division 3 (S); 1949–65 Division 2; 1965–67 Division 3; 1967–70 Division 4; 1970–73 Division 3; 1973–78 Division 4; 1978–79 Division 3; 1979–81 Division 2; 1981–83 Division 1; 1983–84 Division 2; 1984–86 Division 3; 1986–88 Division 4; 1988–92 Division 3; 1992–96 Division 2; 1996–2000 Division 3; 2000–01 Division 2; 2001–04 Division 3; 2004–05 FL 2; 2005–08 FL 1; 2008–11 FL C; 2011– FA Premier League.

LATEST SEQUENCES

Longest Sequence of League Wins: 9, 27.11.1999 – 22.01.2000.

Longest Sequence of League Defeats: 9, 26.1.1991 – 19.3.1991.

Longest Sequence of League Draws: 8, 25.11.2008 – 28.12.2008.

Longest Sequence of Unbeaten League Matches: 19, 19.10.1970 – 9.3.1971.

Longest Sequence Without a League Win: 15, 25.3.1989 – 2.9.1989.

Successive Scoring Runs: 27 from 28.8.1947.

Successive Non-scoring Runs: 6 from 6.2.1996.

MANAGERS

Walter Whittaker 1912–14
William Bartlett 1914–15
Joe Bradshaw 1919–26
Jimmy Thomson 1927–31
Neil Harris 1934–39
Haydn Green 1939–47
Bill McCandless 1947–55
Ron Burgess 1955–58
Trevor Morris 1958–65
Glyn Davies 1965–66
Billy Lucas 1967–69
Roy Bentley 1969–72
Harry Gregg 1972–75
Harry Griffiths 1975–77
John Toshack 1978–83 *(resigned October re-appointed in December)* 1983–84
Colin Appleton 1984
John Bond 1984–85
Tommy Hutchison 1985–86
Terry Yorath 1986–89
Ian Evans 1989–90
Terry Yorath 1990–91
Frank Burrows 1991–95
Bobby Smith 1995
Kevin Cullis 1996
Jan Molby 1996–97
Micky Adams 1997
Alan Cork 1997–98
John Hollins 1998–2001
Colin Addison 2001–02
Nick Cusack 2002
Brian Flynn 2002–04
Kenny Jackett 2004–07
Roberto Martinez 2007–09
Paulo Sousa 2009–10
Brendan Rodgers 2010–12
Michael Laudrup 2012–14
Garry Monk 2014–15
Francesco Guidolin 2016
Bob Bradley 2016
Paul Clement January 2017–

TEN YEAR LEAGUE RECORD

		P	W	D	L	F	A	Pts	Pos
2007-08	FL 1	46	27	11	8	82	42	92	1
2008-09	FL C	46	16	20	10	63	50	68	8
2009-10	FL C	46	17	18	11	40	37	69	7
2010-11	FL C	46	24	8	14	69	42	80	3
2011-12	PR Lge	38	12	11	15	44	51	47	11
2012-13	PR Lge	38	11	13	14	47	51	46	9
2013-14	PR Lge	38	11	9	18	54	54	42	12
2014-15	PR Lge	38	16	8	14	46	49	56	8
2015-16	PR Lge	38	12	11	15	42	52	47	12
2016-17	PR Lge	38	12	5	21	45	70	41	15

DID YOU KNOW ?

Harry Griffiths gave over 25 years' service to Swansea after joining the club as a groundstaff boy in 1949. He made almost 450 appearances in 15 seasons as a player and returned to the club in 1967 as a member of the backroom staff. At the time of his death in 1978 he was assistant manager to John Toshack.

SWANSEA CITY – PREMIER LEAGUE 2016–17 LEAGUE RECORD

Match No.	Date	Venue	Opponents	Result	H/T Score	Lg Pos.	Goalscorers	Attendance
1	Aug 13	A	Burnley	W 1-0	0-0	1	Fer [82]	19,126
2	20	H	Hull C	L 0-2	0-0	10		20,024
3	27	A	Leicester C	L 1-2	0-1	13	Fer [80]	31,727
4	Sept 11	H	Chelsea	D 2-2	0-1	13	Sigurdsson (pen) [59], Fer [62]	20,865
5	18	A	Southampton	L 0-1	0-0	15		29,087
6	24	H	Manchester C	L 1-3	1-1	16	Llorente [13]	20,786
7	Oct 1	H	Liverpool	L 1-2	1-0	17	Fer [8]	20,862
8	15	A	Arsenal	L 2-3	1-2	17	Sigurdsson [38], Borja Baston [66]	60,007
9	22	H	Watford	D 0-0	0-0	19		20,694
10	31	A	Stoke C	L 1-3	1-1	19	Routledge [8]	26,602
11	Nov 6	H	Manchester U	L 1-3	0-3	19	van der Hoorn [69]	20,938
12	19	A	Everton	D 1-1	1-0	19	Sigurdsson (pen) [41]	38,773
13	26	H	Crystal Palace	W 5-4	1-1	19	Sigurdsson [36], Fer 2 [66, 68], Llorente 2 [90, 90]	20,276
14	Dec 3	A	Tottenham H	L 0-5	0-2	20		31,663
15	10	H	Sunderland	W 3-0	0-0	17	Sigurdsson (pen) [51], Llorente 2 [54, 80]	20,453
16	14	A	WBA	L 1-3	0-0	18	Routledge [78]	21,467
17	17	A	Middlesbrough	L 0-3	0-2	19		28,302
18	26	H	West Ham U	L 1-4	0-1	19	Llorente [89]	20,757
19	31	H	Bournemouth	L 0-3	0-2	20		20,316
20	Jan 3	A	Crystal Palace	W 2-1	1-0	19	Mawson [42], Rangel [88]	24,913
21	14	H	Arsenal	L 0-4	0-1	20		20,875
22	21	A	Liverpool	W 3-2	0-0	17	Llorente 2 [48, 52], Sigurdsson [74]	53,169
23	31	H	Southampton	W 2-1	1-0	17	Mawson [38], Sigurdsson [70]	20,359
24	Feb 5	A	Manchester C	L 1-2	0-1	17	Sigurdsson [81]	54,065
25	12	H	Leicester C	W 2-0	2-0	15	Mawson [36], Olsson [45]	20,391
26	25	A	Chelsea	L 1-3	1-1	15	Llorente [45]	41,612
27	Mar 4	H	Burnley	W 3-2	1-1	16	Llorente 2 [12, 90], Olsson [69]	20,679
28	11	A	Hull C	L 1-2	0-0	16	Mawson [90]	19,195
29	18	A	Bournemouth	L 0-2	0-1	16		11,240
30	Apr 2	H	Middlesbrough	D 0-0	0-0	17		20,354
31	5	H	Tottenham H	L 1-3	1-0	18	Routledge [11]	20,855
32	8	A	West Ham U	L 0-1	0-1	18		56,973
33	15	A	Watford	L 0-1	0-1	18		20,272
34	22	H	Stoke C	W 2-0	1-0	18	Llorente [10], Carroll [70]	20,566
35	30	A	Manchester U	D 1-1	0-1	18	Sigurdsson [79]	75,271
36	May 6	H	Everton	W 1-0	1-0	17	Llorente [29]	20,827
37	13	A	Sunderland	W 2-0	2-0	17	Llorente [9], Naughton [45]	38,781
38	21	H	WBA	W 2-1	0-1	15	Ayew, J [72], Llorente [86]	20,889

Final League Position: 15

GOALSCORERS

League (45): Llorente 15, Sigurdsson 9 (3 pens), Fer 6, Mawson 4, Routledge 3, Olsson 2, Ayew, J 1, Borja Baston 1, Carroll 1, Naughton 1, Rangel 1, van der Hoorn 1.
FA Cup (0).
EFL Cup (4): McBurnie 2, Fulton 1, Sigurdsson 1.
EFL Checkatrade Trophy (8): McBurnie 5 (1 pen), Bia Bi 1, James 1, Samuel 1.

Fabianski L 37	Naughton K 31	Fernandez F 27	Amat J 15 + 2	Kingsley S 12 + 1	Cork J 25 + 5	Britton L 16	Fer L 27 + 7	Barrow M 12 + 6	Llorente F 28 + 5	Routledge W 24 + 3	Sigurdsson G 37 + 1	Montero J 2 + 11	Rangel A 8 + 10	Ki S 13 + 10	Dyer N 3 + 5	McBurnie O — + 5	Taylor N 11	Borja Baston G 4 + 14	van der Hoorn M 7 + 1	Fulton J 9 + 2	Mawson A 27	Olsson M 14 + 1	Carroll T 16 + 1	Narsingh L 3 + 10	Ayew J 9 + 5	Nordfeldt K 1	*Match No.*
1	2	3	4	5	6	7^2	8	9^3	10	11^1	12	13	14														1
1	2	3	4	5	6		7^2	8^1	11	10^3	9	12		13	14												2
1	2	3	4	5	7^1		6	8	11	10^2	9^3	13		12		14											3
1	5	2	3	4	7		6	12	11		10^2		13	8			9^1										4
1	2	3	4	5^3	7^1		8	9	10		11	13	12	6^2				14									5
1	5		4		7^2	6^1	9	12	11	10^3	8		2	13				14	3								6
1	5		4		8	7^2	6^3	12		9^1	11		2	13				10	3	14							7
1	2	3	4		8^2	7^1	10	6^2		9	11		14	13			5	12									8
1	2			5		6		8	12	10^1	9			7				11	3		4						9
1	2^1				14		6	8^2	11	10	9		12	7^3			5	13	3		4						10
1				5		7^1	14	12	11^2	6^3	9	13	2	8				10	3		4						11
1	2	3	4		6		8	9^1		11	10			13	12		5			7^2							12
1	2^3	3	4		6		8	9^1	12	11^2	10	14	13				5			7							13
1	2		4		6		8	9^2	12	14	10	11^3					5	13	3	7^1							14
1			4			6		10^1	11^2	8	9	12	2			13	5			7	3						15
1			4		14	7^1		12	11^3	8	9	10^2	2				5	13		6	3						16
1			4			6^3	13	8^1	11	10^2	9	14	2				5	12		7	3						17
1				5	6	7			12	9	11	13^3	2		14			10^2	3	8^1	4						18
1	2		3		14	7^3	9^2	12	11^1		10			6	8	13	5				4						19
1	2	3			8		12		10	9^3	11		13	7	14		5^1			6^2	4						20
1	2	3		5	7^1		12		11^2	10	9			6	8^3	14		13			4						21
1	2	3			7		6^2		10^3	9	11		12					13		14	4	5^1	8				22
1	2	3			7		6^3		10	9^2	11		14	13							4	5^1	8	12			23
1	2	3			7		6		10^2	9^1	11				13			14			4	5	8^3	12			24
1	2	3			7		6		10^2	12^3	11				9^1						4	5	8	14	13		25
1	2	3			7		6		10	9^1	11										4	5	8^2	13	12		26
1	2^1	3	14		7		6		10		11		13								4	5	8^2	9^3	12		27
1		3	12		7		6		10^3	9^2	11		2^1								4	5	8	14	13		28
1		3		5	6		2		11^3	13	10			8^2				14			4		9	12	7^1		29
1	2	3			7		6				11										4	5	8	9	10		30
1	2^1	3			7		6			9^3	11			12		13					4	5	8	14	10^2		31
1	2	3			7^3		6		13	9^2	11	14									4	5	8^1	12	10		32
1	2	3					6		10^2		11			8				12		7^3	4	5	13	9^1	14		33
1	2	3		5		7^2	6^3		10^1		11			12				14	13		4		8		9		34
1	2	3		5		7^2	12		11		9	13^3		6^1							4	14	8		10		35
1	2	3			12	7^2	13		11^1		9			6^3				14			4	5	8		10		36
1	2	3			13	7^1	12		11^2		9			6^3							4	5	8	14	10		37
	2	3		14		7^2	6^1		10		11			13							4	5	8	12	9^3	1	38

FA Cup

Third Round	Hull C	(a)	0-2

EFL Cup

Second Round	Peterborough U	(a)	3-1
Third Round	Manchester C	(h)	1-2

EFL Checkatrade Trophy (Swansea C U21)

Southern Group B	AFC Wimbledon	(a)	0-3
Southern Group B	Newport Co	(a)	2-1
Southern Group B	Plymouth Arg	(h)	2-0
Second Round South	Norwich C U21	(a)	1-0
Third Round	Wolverhampton W U21	(h)	2-1
Quarter-Final	Coventry C	(h)	1-1

(*Coventry C won 4-2 on penalties*)

SWINDON TOWN

FOUNDATION

It is generally accepted that Swindon Town came into being in 1881, although there is no firm evidence that the club's founder, Rev. William Pitt, captain of the Spartans (an offshoot of a cricket club), changed his club's name to Swindon Town before 1883, when the Spartans amalgamated with St Mark's Young Men's Friendly Society.

The County Ground, County Road, Swindon, Wiltshire SN1 2ED.

Telephone: (0871) 876 1879.

Fax: (0844) 880 1112.

Ticket Office: (0871) 876 1993.

Website: www.swindontownfc.co.uk

Email: enquiries@swindontownfc.co.uk

Ground Capacity: 15,547.

Record Attendance: 32,000 v Arsenal, FA Cup 3rd rd, 15 January 1972.

Pitch Measurements: 100.5m × 68m (110yd × 74.5yd).

Chairman: Lee Power.

General Manager: Steve Anderson.

Manager: David Flitcroft.

Assistant Manager: Ben Futcher.

Colours: Red shirts with white trim, white shorts with red trim, red socks with white trim.

Year Formed: 1881* (*see Foundation*).

Turned Professional: 1894.

Club Nickname: 'The Robins'.

Grounds: 1881, The Croft; 1896, County Ground.

First Football League Game: 28 August 1920, Division 3, v Luton T (h) W 9–1 – Nash; Kay, Macconachie; Langford, Hawley, Wareing; Jefferson (1), Fleming (4), Rogers, Batty (2), Davies (1), (1 og).

Record League Victory: 9–1 v Luton T, Division 3 (S), 28 August 1920 – Nash; Kay, Macconachie; Langford, Hawley, Wareing; Jefferson (1), Fleming (4), Rogers, Batty (2), Davies (1), (1 og).

Record Cup Victory: 10–1 v Farnham U Breweries (away), FA Cup 1st rd (replay), 28 November 1925 – Nash; Dickenson, Weston, Archer, Bew, Adey; Denyer (2), Wall (1), Richardson (4), Johnson (3), Davies.

Record Defeat: 1–10 v Manchester C, FA Cup 4th rd (replay), 25 January 1930.

HONOURS

League Champions: Second Division – 1995–96; FL 2 – 2011–12; Division 4 – 1985–86.

Runners-up: Division 3 – 1962–63, 1968–69.

FA Cup: semi-final – 1910, 1912.

League Cup Winners: 1969.

League Trophy: *Runners-up:* 2012.

Anglo-Italian Cup Winners: 1970.

sky SPORTS FACT FILE

Swindon Town created a string of club records in the 1985–86 season when they won the Division Four title. As well as most points (102) the Robins recorded their best-ever totals for most wins, fewest defeats, fewest away goals conceded and their largest goal difference in a Football League season.

Most League Points (2 for a win): 64, Division 3, 1968–69.

Most League Points (3 for a win): 102, Division 4, 1985–86.

Most League Goals: 100, Division 3 (S), 1926–27.

Highest League Scorer in Season: Harry Morris, 47, Division 3 (S), 1926–27.

Most League Goals in Total Aggregate: Harry Morris, 216, 1926–33.

Most League Goals in One Match: 5, Harry Morris v QPR, Division 3 (S), 18 December 1926; 5, Harry Morris v Norwich C, Division 3 (S), 26 April 1930; 5, Keith East v Mansfield T, Division 3, 20 November 1965.

Most Capped Player: Rod Thomas, 30 (50), Wales.

Most League Appearances: John Trollope, 770, 1960–80.

Youngest League Player: Paul Rideout, 16 years 107 days v Hull C, 29 November 1980.

Record Transfer Fee Received: A combined £4,000,000 from QPR for Ben Gladwin and Massimo Luongo, May 2015.

Record Transfer Fee Paid: £800,000 to West Ham U for Joey Beauchamp, August 1994.

Football League Record: 1920 Original Member of Division 3; 1921–58 Division 3 (S); 1958–63 Division 3; 1963–65 Division 2; 1965–69 Division 3; 1969–74 Division 2; 1974–82 Division 3; 1982–86 Division 4; 1986–87 Division 3; 1987–92 Division 2; 1992–93 Division 1; 1993–94 FA Premier League; 1994–95 Division 1; 1995–96 Division 2; 1996–2000 Division 1; 2000–04 Division 2; 2004–06 FL 1; 2006–07 FL 2; 2007–11 FL 1; 2011–12 FL 2; 2012–17 FL 1; 2017– FL 2.

MANAGERS

Sam Allen 1902–33
Ted Vizard 1933–39
Neil Harris 1939–41
Louis Page 1945–53
Maurice Lindley 1953–55
Bert Head 1956–65
Danny Williams 1965–69
Fred Ford 1969–71
Dave Mackay 1971–72
Les Allen 1972–74
Danny Williams 1974–78
Bobby Smith 1978–80
John Trollope 1980–83
Ken Beamish 1983–84
Lou Macari 1984–89
Ossie Ardiles 1989–91
Glenn Hoddle 1991–93
John Gorman 1993–94
Steve McMahon 1994–98
Jimmy Quinn 1998–2000
Colin Todd 2000
Andy King 2000–01
Roy Evans 2001
Andy King 2001–05
Iffy Onuora 2005–06
Dennis Wise 2006
Paul Sturrock 2006–07
Maurice Malpas 2008
Danny Wilson 2008–11
Paul Hart 2011
Paolo Di Canio 2011–13
Kevin MacDonald 2013
Mark Cooper 2013–15
Martin Ling 2015
Luke Williams 2015–17
David Flitcroft June 2017–

LATEST SEQUENCES

Longest Sequence of League Wins: 10, 31.12.2011 – 28.2.2012

Longest Sequence of League Defeats: 8, 29.8.2005 – 8.10.2005.

Longest Sequence of League Draws: 6, 22.11.1991 – 28.12.1991.

Longest Sequence of Unbeaten League Matches: 22, 12.1.1986 – 23.8.1986.

Longest Sequence Without a League Win: 19, 30.10.1999 – 4.3.2000.

Successive Scoring Runs: 31 from 17.4.1926.

Successive Non-scoring Runs: 5 from 5.4.1997.

TEN YEAR LEAGUE RECORD

		P	W	D	L	F	A	Pts	Pos
2007-08	FL 1	46	16	13	17	63	56	61	13
2008-09	FL 1	46	12	17	17	68	71	53	15
2009-10	FL 1	46	22	16	8	73	57	82	5
2010-11	FL 1	46	9	14	23	50	72	41	24
2011-12	FL 2	46	29	6	11	75	32	93	1
2012-13	FL 1	46	20	14	12	72	39	74	6
2013-14	FL 1	46	19	9	18	63	59	66	8
2014-15	FL 1	46	23	10	13	76	57	79	4
2015-16	FL 1	46	16	11	19	64	71	59	15
2016-17	FL 1	46	11	11	24	44	66	44	22

DID YOU KNOW ?

Swindon Town reached the final of the FA Youth Cup in the 1963–64 season when they played Manchester United in the final over two legs. The teams drew 1-1 at The County Ground, with United winning the second leg at Old Trafford 4-1 to take the trophy.

SWINDON TOWN – SKY BET LEAGUE ONE 2016–17 LEAGUE RECORD

Match No.	*Date*	*Venue*	*Opponents*	*Result*	*H/T Score*	*Lg Pos.*	*Goalscorers*	*Attendance*
1	Aug 6	H	Coventry C	W 1-0	0-0	9	Kasim 86	9023
2	13	A	Chesterfield	L 1-3	0-2	12	Furlong 88	5378
3	16	A	Gillingham	D 1-1	0-0	13	Doughty (pen) 55	5512
4	20	H	Port Vale	W 1-0	0-0	9	Barry 47	6182
5	Sept 3	A	Peterborough U	D 2-2	0-1	11	Doughty (pen) 51, Baldwin (og) 76	4501
6	10	A	Oxford U	L 0-2	0-1	16		11,042
7	17	H	Bury	L 1-2	0-2	18	Obika 64	6931
8	20	H	Bristol R	L 1-2	1-0	20	Jones 6	6760
9	24	A	Oldham Ath	W 2-0	1-0	17	Obika 18, Ormonde-Ottewill 55	3403
10	27	H	Northampton T	L 1-3	0-1	18	Murray 67	6590
11	Oct 1	A	Shrewsbury T	D 1-1	1-1	20	Goddard 9	5103
12	8	H	Bolton W	L 0-1	0-0	20		7023
13	15	A	AFC Wimbledon	D 0-0	0-0	20		4800
14	18	H	Rochdale	W 3-0	2-0	17	Furlong 24, Delfouneso 32, Thompson, N 80	6048
15	22	H	Walsall	L 0-2	0-1	20		6655
16	29	A	Scunthorpe U	L 1-4	0-4	21	Thompson, N 52	4262
17	Nov 12	H	Charlton Ath	W 3-0	1-0	19	Fox (og) 43, Jones 50, Goddard 86	6599
18	19	A	Rochdale	L 0-4	0-1	20		2196
19	22	A	Southend U	D 1-1	0-1	18	Obika 73	5715
20	26	H	Bradford C	W 1-0	1-0	18	Rodgers 19	6344
21	Dec 10	A	Sheffield U	L 0-4	0-0	19		19,196
22	17	H	Fleetwood T	D 1-1	1-1	19	Norris 12	6143
23	26	A	Millwall	L 0-2	0-1	19		8515
24	30	A	Milton Keynes D	L 2-3	1-2	19	Norris 35, Branco 66	9385
25	Jan 2	H	Southend U	D 0-0	0-0	19		7102
26	7	H	Shrewsbury T	D 1-1	0-0	19	Goddard (pen) 55	6137
27	14	A	Bolton W	W 2-1	0-0	18	Gladwin 65, Kasim 89	13,955
28	21	H	Peterborough U	L 0-1	0-0	19		6514
29	28	A	Bristol R	L 0-1	0-1	19		10,557
30	Feb 5	H	Oxford U	L 1-2	1-0	20	Dabo 19	10,658
31	11	A	Bury	L 0-1	0-1	22		2713
32	14	A	Northampton T	L 1-2	0-0	22	Norris 81	5094
33	18	H	Oldham Ath	D 0-0	0-0	22		6773
34	25	A	Coventry C	W 3-1	2-0	22	Ajose 2 32, 71, Obika 38	9543
35	28	H	Gillingham	W 3-1	0-1	21	Ince 56, Obika 61, Branco 75	6133
36	Mar 4	H	Chesterfield	L 0-1	0-0	21		6691
37	11	A	Port Vale	L 2-3	1-1	22	Ajose 35, Norris 90	4510
38	14	H	Sheffield U	L 2-4	0-2	22	Colkett 46, Gladwin 53	7012
39	18	A	Bradford C	L 1-2	0-0	22	Ajose 75	17,916
40	25	H	Millwall	W 1-0	0-0	22	Thomas 90	7038
41	Apr 1	A	Fleetwood T	W 1-0	0-0	22	Ajose 81	3128
42	8	H	Milton Keynes D	D 1-1	0-1	22	Obika 90	7946
43	14	H	AFC Wimbledon	D 0-0	0-0	22		7716
44	17	A	Walsall	L 0-1	0-0	22		5196
45	22	H	Scunthorpe U	L 1-2	0-1	22	Ince 85	7579
46	30	A	Charlton Ath	L 0-3	0-2	22		11,932

Final League Position: 22

GOALSCORERS

League (44): Obika 6, Ajose 5, Norris 4, Goddard 3 (1 pen), Branco 2, Doughty 2 (2 pens), Furlong 2, Gladwin 2, Ince 2, Jones 2, Kasim 2, Thompson, N 2, Barry 1, Colkett 1, Dabo 1, Delfouneso 1, Murray 1, Ormonde-Ottewill 1, Rodgers 1, Thomas 1, own goals 2.
FA Cup (2): Delfouneso 1, Doughty 1 (1 pen).
EFL Cup (2): Brophy 1, Stewart 1.
EFL Checkatrade Trophy (5): Norris 2, Branco 1, Delfouneso 1, Iandolo 1.

Vigouroux L 43	Thompson N 34	Sendles-White J 5	Thomas C 29 + 4	Barry B 17 + 6	Kasim Y 18 + 2	Rodgers A 19 + 3	Doughty M 13 + 1	Brophy J 22 + 8	Goddard J 28 + 14	Obika J 27 + 3	Young J 1 + 1	Ormonde-Ottewill B 18 + 3	Norris L 18 + 21	Hylton J 4 + 8	Furlong D 21 + 3	Stewart J — + 7	Iandolo E 5 + 5	Jones L 23 + 1	Delfouneso N 13 + 5	Murray S 13 + 5	Henry W 3	Branco R 34	Smith T 4 + 4	Evans J — + 1	Dabo F 15	Colkett C 19	Gladwin B 15 + 3	Feruz I 4	Conroy D 11 + 3	Ajose N 15	Ince R 14	Starkey J 1	Twine S — + 1	*Match No.*
1	2	3	4	5	6	7	8	9	10^1	11	12																							1
1	3	4	2	5^3	7	6	8				10^1	9	11^2	12	13	14																		2
1	3	4	2	5^2		7	8	10	11^1			9■			6	12	13																	3
1	3	4	12	5	7	6^3	8	9^2					11		13	14		2	10^1															4
1	3		8	2		7^3	6	10^2	9^1			14	13		5			4	11	12														5
1■	3		2^3	6	13	7^1	8		10^2	12		9	11		5			4■	14															6
	3	4^3	8	9	7			5	13	11			14		12				10^1	6^2	1	2												7
1	3		9		8			7^3	13	10		12	14		5			4	11^1	6^2		2												8
1	2		7^3		8	13			6^2	11		9	12		5		14	4	10^1			3												9
1	3		6		7				8	10		9	11^1		5			4^2	13	12		2												10
1	3		2		8			13	7	11		9^2	12		5				10^1	6		4												11
1	3		4^1		8			12	6			9	11		5				10	7		2■												12
1	4		3	13	6	7		5	9				12		2		8^1		11^2	10														13
1	4		3	13		6		5	8^1				12		2		10^2		11	9^3			7	14										14
1	4		3	12	7	6		5^1	8				13		2		10^2		11	9														15
1	5		4		7	6	13		8^1						2	14	10^3	12	11^2	9		3												16
1			7^2		6	12	8^1		9			5	11^3		2		14	4	13	10		3												17
1				10^2		6^3	8		9	11^1		5	12		2		14	4	13			3	7											18
1			6			7			10^2	11		5	12		2			4	8	9^1		3	13											19
1						7	8	9^1	6	10		5^2	14		2		12	4	11^3			3	13											20
1			3			4	2^2		7^1	11^3		5	10	12	9			8	13			6	14											21
1	3				9	8^2	7					10^1	11	6	2			5		12		4	13											22
1	5				8		9		12				10	11	2			4		6		3	7^1											23
1	5^2		7^1					12	13	10			9	11	4			3		6		2	8											24
1			8^2			7	9	5	6^1	10			11	13	2			4		12		3												25
1			6	2	12	7^1		5■	9	10			11	13				4		8^2		3												26
1			7		2				6				11	12				3		13		4			5	8^1	9	10^2						27
1	2^2				6			14	9^3				10	12		13		4				3			5	7	8	11^1						28
1	2							8	9				11^2	12		13		4^3				3			5	7	6	10^1	14					29
1■	6		12		8^3			5	13				10	14				4				3			2	7^1	9^2			11				30
1	3							6		12				11^1								5			2	8	7		4	10	9			31
1	3							9	14	10^1		12	13					4				7			2^2	6	8		5^3	11				32
1	3			2				9^1	12	10^3		5	13					4								6	7		14	11	8^2			33
1	3		14	2^1				9^2	13	10		5						4^3								7	8		12	11	6			34
1	3			2		14		8^1	12	11^3		5	13									4				7^2	9			10	6			35
1	3		14	2		7^2		9	12	10		5	11^1			13						4					6^3				8			36
1	2			4■				6	12	9		5	13									3				8	10^1			11^2	7			37
	2								9	10			12								1	4			5	8	7^1		3	11	6			38
1	2			12					9	10			13									4			5^1	8	7^2		3	11	6			39
1	2^1		7	14				12	9^2	10			13									3			5^3	8			4	11	6			40
1	2		7						9^1	11			13									4			5	8	12		3	10^2	6			41
1	2		7	14				13	9^2	11												3			5^1	8	12		4^3	10	6			42
1			7	2					9^1	10			13									3			5	8^2	12		4	11	6			43
1			7^2	2				13	12	11												3			5^1	8	9		4	10	6			44
1			7	2^3				12	13	10			14									3			5^1	8^2	9		4	11	6			45
			3			8		5	12	13			10				7^3				1				2	9		11^1	4			6^2	14	46

FA Cup

First Round	Eastleigh	(a)	1-1
Replay	Eastleigh	(h)	1-3

EFL Cup

First Round	QPR	(a)	2-2

(*aet; QPR won 4-2 on penalties*)

EFL Checkatrade Trophy

Southern Group C	Chelsea U21	(h)	2-1
Southern Group C	Oxford U	(h)	0-0
(*Swindon T won 3-1 on penalties*)			
Southern Group C	Exeter C	(a)	1-1
(*Swindon T won 4-2 on penalties*)			
Second Round South	Luton T	(h)	2-3

TOTTENHAM HOTSPUR

FOUNDATION

The Hotspur Football Club was formed from an older cricket club in 1882. Most of the founders were old boys of St John's Presbyterian School and Tottenham Grammar School. The Casey brothers were well to the fore as the family provided the club's first goalposts (painted blue and white) and their first ball. They soon adopted the local YMCA as their meeting place, but after a couple of moves settled at the Red House, which is still their headquarters, although now known simply as 748 High Road.

White Hart Lane, Bill Nicholson Way, 748 High Road, Tottenham, London N17 0AP. (Playing at Wembley from start of 2017–18 season whilst White Hart Lane rebuilt.)

Telephone: (0844) 499 5000.

Fax: (020) 3544 8563.

Ticket Office: (0844) 499 5000.

Website: www.tottenhamhotspur.com

Email: email@tottenhamhotspur.com

Ground Capacity: 36,284.

Record Attendance: 75,038 v Sunderland, FA Cup 6th rd, 5 March 1938; 85,512 v Bayer Leverkusen (h), UEFA Champions League Group E, 2 November 2016 (at Wembley).

Pitch Measurements: 100m × 67m (109yd × 73yd).

Chairman: Daniel Levy.

Head Coach: Mauricio Pochettino.

Assistant Head Coach: Jesus Perez.

Colours: White shirts with navy blue trim, navy blue shorts, navy blue socks.

Year Formed: 1882. ***Turned Professional:*** 1895.

Previous Name: 1882, Hotspur Football Club; 1884, Tottenham Hotspur.

Club Nickname: 'Spurs'.

Grounds: 1882, Tottenham Marshes; 1888, Northumberland Park; 1899, White Hart Lane.

First Football League Game: 1 September 1908, Division 2, v Wolverhampton W (h) W 3–0 – Hewitson; Coquet, Burton; Morris (1), Danny Steel, Darnell; Walton, Woodward (2), Macfarlane, Bobby Steel, Middlemiss.

Record League Victory: 9–0 v Bristol R, Division 2, 22 October 1977 – Daines; Naylor, Holmes, Hoddle (1), McAllister, Perryman, Pratt, McNab, Moores (3), Lee (4), Taylor (1).

HONOURS

League Champions: Division 1 – 1950–51, 1960–61; Division 2 – 1919–20, 1949–50.
Runners-up: FA Premier League – 2016–17; Division 1 – 1921–22, 1951–52, 1956–57, 1962–63; Division 2 – 1908–09, 1932–33.

FA Cup Winners: 1901 (as non-league club), 1921, 1961, 1962, 1967, 1981, 1982, 1991.
Runners-up: 1987.

League Cup Winners: 1971, 1973, 1999, 2008.
Runners-up: 1982, 2002, 2009, 2015.

European Competitions
European Cup: 1961–62 *(sf)*.
Champions League: 2010–11 *(qf)*, 2016–17. ***UEFA Cup:*** 1971–72 *(winners)*, 1972–73 *(sf)*, 1973–74 *(runners-up)*, 1983–84 *(winners)*, 1984–85 *(qf)*, 1999–2000, 2006–07 *(qf)*, 2007–08, 2008–09.
Europa League: 2011–12, 2012–13 *(qf)*, 2013–14, 2014–15, 2015–16, 2016–17. ***European Cup-Winners' Cup:*** 1962–63 *(winners)*, 1963–64, 1967–68, 1981–82 *(sf)*, 1982–83, 1991–92 *(qf)*.
Intertoto Cup: 1995.

sky SPORTS FACT FILE

Tottenham Hotspur's FA Cup tie against Aston Villa at White Hart Lane on 20 February 1904 attracted a huge crowd of around 30,000 with some 10,000 locked out. The start was delayed and after several incursions of fans onto the pitch the referee abandoned the match with Villa leading 1-0. Tottenham won the replay at Villa Park 1-0.

Record Cup Victory: 13–2 v Crewe Alex, FA Cup 4th rd (replay), 3 February 1960 – Brown; Hills, Henry; Blanchflower, Norman, Mackay; White, Harmer (1), Smith (4), Allen (5), Jones (3 incl. 1p).

Record Defeat: 0–8 v Cologne, UEFA Intertoto Cup, 22 July 1995.

Most League Points (2 for a win): 70, Division 2, 1919–20.

Most League Points (3 for a win): 86, FA Premier League, 2016–17.

Most League Goals: 115, Division 1, 1960–61.

Highest League Scorer in Season: Jimmy Greaves, 37, Division 1, 1962–63.

Most League Goals in Total Aggregate: Jimmy Greaves, 220, 1961–70.

Most League Goals in One Match: 5, Ted Harper v Reading, Division 2, 30 August 1930; 5, Alf Stokes v Birmingham C, Division 1, 18 September 1957; 5, Bobby Smith v Aston Villa, Division 1, 29 March 1958; 5, Jermain Defoe v Wigan Ath, FA Premier League, 22 November 2009.

Most Capped Player: Pat Jennings, 74 (119), Northern Ireland.

Most League Appearances: Steve Perryman, 655, 1969–86.

Youngest League Player: Ally Dick, 16 years 301 days v Manchester C, 20 February 1982.

Record Transfer Fee Received: £85,300,000 from Real Madrid for Gareth Bale, September 2013.

Record Transfer Fee Paid: £30,000,000 to AS Roma for Erik Lamela, August 2013; £30,000,000 to Newcastle U for Moussa Sissoko, August 2016.

Football League Record: 1908 Elected to Division 2; 1909–15 Division 1; 1919–20 Division 2; 1920–28 Division 1; 1928–33 Division 2; 1933–35 Division 1; 1935–50 Division 2; 1950–77 Division 1; 1977–78 Division 2; 1978–92 Division 1; 1992– FA Premier League.

MANAGERS

Frank Brettell 1898–99
John Cameron 1899–1906
Fred Kirkham 1907–08
Peter McWilliam 1912–27
Billy Minter 1927–29
Percy Smith 1930–35
Jack Tresadern 1935–38
Peter McWilliam 1938–42
Arthur Turner 1942–46
Joe Hulme 1946–49
Arthur Rowe 1949–55
Jimmy Anderson 1955–58
Bill Nicholson 1958–74
Terry Neill 1974–76
Keith Burkinshaw 1976–84
Peter Shreeves 1984–86
David Pleat 1986–87
Terry Venables 1987–91
Peter Shreeves 1991–92
Doug Livermore 1992–93
Ossie Ardiles 1993–94
Gerry Francis 1994–97
Christian Gross *(Head Coach)* 1997–98
George Graham 1998–2001
Glenn Hoddle 2001–03
David Pleat (*Caretaker*) 2003–04
Jacques Santini 2004
Martin Jol 2004–07
Juande Ramos 2007–08
Harry Redknapp 2008–12
Andre Villas-Boas 2012–13
Tim Sherwood 2013–14
Mauricio Pochettino May 2014–

LATEST SEQUENCES

Longest Sequence of League Wins: 13, 23.4.1960 – 1.10.1960.

Longest Sequence of League Defeats: 7, 1.1.1994 – 27.2.1994.

Longest Sequence of League Draws: 6, 9.1.1999 – 27.2.1999.

Longest Sequence of Unbeaten League Matches: 22, 31.8.1949 – 31.12.1949.

Longest Sequence Without a League Win: 16, 29.12.1934 – 13.4.1935.

Successive Scoring Runs: 32 from 24.2.1962.

Successive Non-scoring Runs: 6 from 28.12.1985.

TEN YEAR LEAGUE RECORD

		P	*W*	*D*	*L*	*F*	*A*	*Pts*	*Pos*
2007-08	PR Lge	38	11	13	14	66	61	46	11
2008-09	PR Lge	38	14	9	15	45	45	51	8
2009-10	PR Lge	38	21	7	10	67	41	70	4
2010-11	PR Lge	38	16	14	8	55	46	62	5
2011-12	PR Lge	38	20	9	9	66	41	69	4
2012-13	PR Lge	38	21	9	8	66	46	72	5
2013-14	PR Lge	38	21	6	11	55	51	69	6
2014-15	PR Lge	38	19	7	12	58	53	64	5
2015-16	PR Lge	38	19	13	6	69	35	70	3
2016-17	PR Lge	38	26	8	4	86	26	86	2

DID YOU KNOW ?

Tottenham Hotspur created a new British record for a transfer fee when they signed Martin Peters from West Ham United in March 1970 with the first £200,000 deal. Jimmy Greaves, who moved in the opposite direction, was valued at £50,000 with the balance of £150,000 being paid.

TOTTENHAM HOTSPUR – PREMIER LEAGUE 2016–17 LEAGUE RECORD

Match No.	*Date*	*Venue*	*Opponents*	*Result*		*H/T Score*	*Lg Pos.*	*Goalscorers*	*Attendance*
1	Aug 13	A	Everton	D	1-1	0-1	4	Lamela [59]	39,494
2	20	H	Crystal Palace	W	1-0	0-0	6	Wanyama [82]	31,447
3	27	H	Liverpool	D	1-1	0-1	6	Rose [72]	31,211
4	Sept 10	A	Stoke C	W	4-0	1-0	4	Son 2 [41, 56], Alli [59], Kane [70]	27,385
5	18	H	Sunderland	W	1-0	0-0	3	Kane [59] .	31,251
6	24	A	Middlesbrough	W	2-1	2-0	2	Son 2 [7, 23]	32,703
7	Oct 2	H	Manchester C	W	2-0	2-0	2	Kolarov (og) [9], Alli [37]	31,793
8	15	A	WBA	D	1-1	0-0	3	Alli [89]	24,263
9	22	A	Bournemouth	D	0-0	0-0	3		11,201
10	29	H	Leicester C	D	1-1	1-0	4	Janssen (pen) [44]	31,868
11	Nov 6	A	Arsenal	D	1-1	0-1	5	Kane (pen) [51]	60,039
12	19	H	West Ham U	W	3-2	0-1	5	Winks [51], Kane 2 (1 pen) [89, 90 (p)]	31,212
13	26	A	Chelsea	L	1-2	1-1	5	Eriksen [11]	41,513
14	Dec 3	H	Swansea C	W	5-0	2-0	5	Kane 2 (1 pen) [39 (p), 49], Son [45], Eriksen 2 [70, 90]	31,663
15	11	A	Manchester U	L	0-1	0-1	5		75,271
16	14	H	Hull C	W	3-0	1-0	5	Eriksen 2 [14, 63], Wanyama [73]	31,347
17	18	H	Burnley	W	2-1	1-1	5	Alli [27], Rose [71]	31,467
18	28	A	Southampton	W	4-1	1-1	5	Alli 2 [19, 87], Kane [52], Son [85]	31,853
19	Jan 1	A	Watford	W	4-1	3-0	4	Kane 2 [27, 33], Alli 2 [41, 46]	20,882
20	4	H	Chelsea	W	2-0	1-0	3	Alli 2 [45, 54]	31,491
21	14	H	WBA	W	4-0	2-0	2	Kane 3 [12, 77, 82], McAuley (og) [26]	31,613
22	21	A	Manchester C	D	2-2	0-0	2	Alli [58], Son [77]	54,402
23	31	A	Sunderland	D	0-0	0-0	2		40,058
24	Feb 4	H	Middlesbrough	W	1-0	0-0	2	Kane (pen) [58]	31,949
25	11	A	Liverpool	L	0-2	0-2	2		53,159
26	26	H	Stoke C	W	4-0	4-0	2	Kane 3 [14, 32, 37], Alli [45]	31,864
27	Mar 5	H	Everton	W	3-2	1-0	2	Kane 2 [20, 56], Alli [90]	31,962
28	19	H	Southampton	W	2-1	2-0	2	Eriksen [14], Alli (pen) [33]	31,697
29	Apr 1	A	Burnley	W	2-0	0-0	2	Dier [66], Son [77]	21,684
30	5	A	Swansea C	W	3-1	0-1	2	Alli [88], Eriksen [90], Son [90]	20,855
31	8	H	Watford	W	4-0	3-0	2	Alli [33], Dier [39], Son 2 [44, 54]	31,706
32	15	H	Bournemouth	W	4-0	2-0	2	Dembele [16], Son [19], Kane [48], Janssen [90]	31,943
33	26	A	Crystal Palace	W	1-0	0-0	2	Eriksen [78]	25,596
34	30	H	Arsenal	W	2-0	0-0	2	Alli [55], Kane (pen) [58]	31,811
35	May 5	A	West Ham U	L	0-1	0-0	2		56,992
36	14	H	Manchester U	W	2-1	1-0	2	Wanyama [6], Kane [48]	31,848
37	18	A	Leicester C	W	6-1	2-0	2	Kane 4 [25, 63, 88, 90], Son 2 [36, 71]	31,351
38	21	A	Hull C	W	7-1	3-0	2	Kane 3 [11, 13, 72], Alli [45], Wanyama [69], Davies [84], Alderweireld [87]	23,804

Final League Position: 2

GOALSCORERS

League (86): Kane 29 (5 pens), Alli 18 (1 pen), Son 14, Eriksen 8, Wanyama 4, Dier 2, Janssen 2 (1 pen), Rose 2, Alderweireld 1, Davies 1, Dembele 1, Lamela 1, Winks 1, own goals 2.
FA Cup (17): Son 6, Kane 4, Alli 3, Janssen 2 (1 pen), Davies 1, Eriksen 1.
EFL Cup (6): Eriksen 2, Janssen 2 (2 pens), Lamela 1, Onomah 1.
UEFA Champions League (6): Kane 2 (1 pen), Alderweireld 1, Alli 1, Son 1, own goal 1.
UEFA Europa League (2): Eriksen 1, Wanyama 1.

Lloris H 34	Walker K 31 + 2	Alderweireld T 30	Vertonghen J 33	Rose D 18	Dier E 34 + 2	Wanyama V 35 + 1	Lamela E 6 + 3	Alli B 35 + 2	Eriksen C 36	Kane H 29 + 1	Vorm M 4 + 1	Janssen V 7 + 20	Carroll T — + 1	Onomah J — + 5	Winks H 3 + 18	Davies B 18 + 5	Son H 23 + 11	Sissoko M 8 + 17	Dembele M 24 + 6	Nkoudou G — + 8	Wimmer K 4 + 1	Trippier K 6 + 6	Lesniak F — + 1	*Match No.*
1^{2}	2	3	4	5	6^{1}	7	8	9	10	11	12	13												1
	2	3	4	5	6	7	10^{1}	12	8^{3}	9^{2}	1	11	13	14										2
	2^{2}	3	4	5	6	7	8	9	10^{3}	11^{1}	1	12		13	14									3
1	2	3	4		6	7^{2}	12	9	8^{3}	11^{1}		13				5	10	14						4
1	2	4	5		3^{3}	6	12	9		11^{2}		14				13	10	8	7^{1}					5
1	2	3	4			7	12	8	6^{3}			10^{1}			13	5	11	9^{2}		14				6
1	2	3	4	5	12	6	10	9^{3}	8			14					11^{2}	7^{1}		13				7
1	2	3^{2}	4		12	6	10^{1}	9	8			11				5	14	7^{3}	13					8
1	2		4	5	3	6	10	9^{2}	8			12					11^{1}	13	7					9
1	2		4	5	3	6^{2}		9^{1}	8			11			13		10		7	12				10
1	5^{2}		4	8	2	6			9	11^{1}		12			14		10^{3}		7		3	13		11
1	2^{2}		4	5	3	7		12	9	10		11^{3}			8		13		6^{1}			14		12
1	2		4		3	6		9^{3}	8	11		14			12		10^{2}		7^{1}	13	5			13
1	2		4	5	3	6		9	8	11^{1}				14	13		10^{3}	12	7^{2}					14
1	2	3	4	5		6		9	8^{2}	11					13		10^{3}	12	7^{1}	14				15
1	5	3	4	8	2	6		11^{3}	7	10^{2}				14	12		13	9^{1}						16
1	2		4	5^{2}	3	7		10^{1}	8	11					6	14	13	12	9^{3}					17
1	2		4	5	3	7		9	10	11^{2}		14			13		12	8^{1}	6^{3}					18
1		3		9^{2}	2	5		8^{1}	7	10^{3}		14			12	13	11				4	6		19
1	5	3	4	8	2	7		10^{3}	9	11^{2}					12		14	13	6^{1}					20
1	5	3	4^{3}	8	2	6		10	9	11^{1}					13	12	14		7^{2}					21
1	5	3^{2}		8	2	6		10	9	11					13		12	14	7^{3}		4^{1}			22
	2	4		5^{3}	3	7		10	9	11	1	14				12	8^{2}	13	6^{1}					23
1	2	4			3	7		9^{2}	8	11^{3}		14			13	5	10^{1}	12	6					24
1	2	3			4	7		9	8^{2}	11		14			12	5	10^{1}	13	6^{3}					25
1	5	3^{3}	4^{2}		2	6		10	9	11^{1}					13	8	14		7		12			26
1	5	3	4		2	6		10	9^{1}	11^{3}		14			12	8		13	7^{2}					27
1	5^{1}	3	4		2	6		10	9^{2}			14			12	8	11^{3}		7			13		28
1		3	4		2	6^{1}		10	9			11^{3}			7^{2}	8	14	13	12			5		29
	2	3	4		6			9	10		1	12				5^{1}	11^{2}	8^{3}	7	13		14		30
1		3	4		6			9	8	12		11^{2}		14		5	10^{1}	13	7^{3}			2		31
1	2	3	4		6	12		9^{3}	8^{1}	11^{2}		14				5	10	13	7					32
1	5	3	4		2	6^{1}		10^{3}	9	11						8	12	13	7^{2}			14		33
1	13	3	4		6	7		9^{3}	8	11						5	10^{1}	14	12			2^{2}		34
1	2^{2}	3	4^{3}		6	7^{1}		9	8	11		13				5	10		12			14		35
1	13	3	4		6	7		9	8^{1}	11						5	10^{2}		12	14		2^{3}		36
1		2	4		3	6		9		11		12				8	10^{2}	5^{3}	7^{1}	14			13	37
1		3	4		6^{1}	7		9^{3}	8	11^{2}		14				5	10	13	12			2		38

FA Cup

Third Round	Aston Villa	(h)	2-0
Fourth Round	Wycombe W	(h)	4-3
Fifth Round	Fulham	(a)	3-0
Sixth Round	Millwall	(h)	6-0
Semi-Final	Chelsea	(a)	2-4

EFL Cup

Third Round	Gillingham	(h)	5-0
Fourth Round	Liverpool	(a)	1-2

UEFA Champions League

Tottenham H home games at Wembley

Group E	Monaco	(h)	1-2
Group E	CSKA Moscow	(a)	1-0
Group E	Bayer Leverkusen	(a)	0-0
Group E	Bayer Leverkusen	(h)	0-1
Group E	Monaco	(a)	1-2
Group E	CSKA Moscow	(h)	3-1

UEFA Europa League

Tottenham H home games at Wembley

Round of 32 1st leg	AA Gent	(a)	0-1
Round of 32 2nd leg	AA Gent	(h)	2-2

WALSALL

FOUNDATION

Two of the leading clubs around Walsall in the 1880s were Walsall Swifts (formed 1877) and Walsall Town (formed 1879). The Swifts were winners of the Birmingham Senior Cup in 1881, while the Town reached the 4th round (5th round modern equivalent) of the FA Cup in 1883. These clubs amalgamated as Walsall Town Swifts in 1888, becoming simply Walsall in 1895.

Banks's Stadium, Bescot Crescent, Walsall WS1 4SA.
Telephone: (01922) 622 791. ***Fax:*** (01922) 639 100.
Ticket Office: (01922) 651 414/416.
Website: www.saddlers.co.uk
Email: info@walsallfc.co.uk
Ground Capacity: 10,910.
Record Attendance: 25,453 v Newcastle U, Division 2, 29 August 1961 (at Fellows Park); 11,049 v Rotherham U, Division 1, 9 May 2004 (at Bescot Stadium).
Pitch Measurements: 100.5m × 67m (110yd × 73yd).
Chairman: Jeff Bonser.
Chief Executive: Stefan Gamble.
Manager: Jon Whitney.
First-Team Coach: Ian Sharps.
Colours: Red shirts with black squares, red shorts with black trim, red socks with black hoops.
Year Formed: 1888.
Turned Professional: 1888.
Previous Names: Walsall Swifts (founded 1877) and Walsall Town (founded 1879) amalgamated in 1888 as Walsall Town Swifts; 1895, Walsall.
Club Nickname: 'The Saddlers'.
Grounds: 1888, Fellows Park; 1990, Bescot Stadium (renamed Banks's Stadium 2007).
First Football League Game: 3 September 1892, Division 2, v Darwen (h) L 1–2 – Hawkins; Withington, Pinches; Robinson, Whitrick, Forsyth; Marshall, Holmes, Turner, Gray (1), Pangbourn.
Record League Victory: 10–0 v Darwen, Division 2, 4 March 1899 – Tennent; Ted Peers (1), Davies; Hickinbotham, Jenkyns, Taggart; Dean (3), Vail (2), Aston (4), Martin, Griffin.
Record Cup Victory: 7–0 v Macclesfield T (a), FA Cup 2nd rd, 6 December 1997 – Walker; Evans, Marsh, Viveash (1), Ryder, Peron, Boli (2 incl. 1p) (Ricketts), Porter (2), Keates, Watson (Platt), Hodge (2 incl. 1p).
Record Defeat: 0–12 v Small Heath, 17 December 1892; 0–12 v Darwen, 26 December 1896, both Division 2.
Most League Points (2 for a win): 65, Division 4, 1959–60.
Most League Points (3 for a win): 89, FL 2, 2006–07.
Most League Goals: 102, Division 4, 1959–60.
Highest League Scorer in Season: Gilbert Alsop, 40, Division 3 (N), 1933–34 and 1934–35.

HONOURS

League Champions: FL 2 – 2006–07; Division 4 – 1959–60.
Runners-up: Second Division – 1998–99; Division 3 – 1960–61; Third Division – 1994–95; Division 4 – 1979–80.

FA Cup: last 16 – 1889; 5th rd – 1939, 1975, 1978, 1987, 2002, 2003.

League Cup: semi-final – 1984.

League Trophy: *Runners-up:* 2015.

sky SPORTS FACT FILE

Walsall's Fellows Park ground was badly affected by waterlogging in the 1969–70 season and no home games took place for a two-month period from 27 January. The 'home' fixture with Brighton & Hove Albion on 25 February was switched to The Hawthorns and attracted a crowd of 7,535, the Saddlers' second-highest home gate of the season.

Most League Goals in Total Aggregate: Tony Richards, 184, 1954–63; Colin Taylor, 184, 1958–63, 1964–68, 1969–73.

Most League Goals in One Match: 5, Gilbert Alsop v Carlisle U, Division 3 (N), 2 February 1935; 5, Bill Evans v Mansfield T, Division 3 (N), 5 October 1935; 5, Johnny Devlin v Torquay U, Division 3 (S), 1 September 1949.

Most Capped Player: Mick Kearns, 15 (18), Republic of Ireland.

Most League Appearances: Colin Harrison, 473, 1964–82.

Youngest League Player: Geoff Morris, 16 years 218 days v Scunthorpe U, 14 September 1965.

Record Transfer Fee Received: £1,000,000 from Coventry C for Scott Dann, January 2008; £1,000,000 from Brentford for Rico Henry, August 2016.

Record Transfer Fee Paid: £300,000 to Anorthosis Famagusta for Andreas Makris, August 2016.

Football League Record: 1892 Elected to Division 2; 1895 Failed re-election; 1896–1901 Division 2; 1901 Failed re-election; 1921 Original Member of Division 3 (N); 1927–31 Division 3 (S); 1931–36 Division 3 (N); 1936–58 Division 3 (S); 1958–60 Division 4; 1960–61 Division 3; 1961–63 Division 2; 1963–79 Division 3; 1979–80 Division 4; 1980–88 Division 3; 1988–89 Division 2; 1989–90 Division 3; 1990–92 Division 4; 1992–95 Division 3; 1995–99 Division 2; 1999–2000 Division 1; 2000–01 Division 2; 2001–04 Division 1; 2004–06 FL 1; 2006–07 FL 2; 2007– FL 1.

LATEST SEQUENCES

Longest Sequence of League Wins: 7, 9.4.2005 – 9.8.2005.

Longest Sequence of League Defeats: 15, 29.10.1988 – 4.2.1989.

Longest Sequence of League Draws: 5, 7.5.1988 – 17.9.1988.

Longest Sequence of Unbeaten League Matches: 21, 6.11.1979 – 22.3.1980.

Longest Sequence Without a League Win: 18, 15.10.1988 – 4.2.1989.

Successive Scoring Runs: 27 from 6.11.1979.

Successive Non-scoring Runs: 5 from 10.4.2004.

MANAGERS

H. Smallwood 1888–91 *(Secretary-Manager)*
A. G. Burton 1891–93
J. H. Robinson 1893–95
C. H. Ailso 1895–96 *(Secretary-Manager)*
A. E. Parsloe 1896–97 *(Secretary-Manager)*
L. Ford 1897–98 *(Secretary-Manager)*
G. Hughes 1898–99 *(Secretary-Manager)*
L. Ford 1899–1901 *(Secretary-Manager)*
J. E. Shutt 1908–13 *(Secretary-Manager)*
Haydn Price 1914–20
Joe Burchell 1920–26
David Ashworth 1926–27
Jack Torrance 1927–28
James Kerr 1928–29
Sid Scholey 1929–30
Peter O'Rourke 1930–32
Bill Slade 1932–34
Andy Wilson 1934–37
Tommy Lowes 1937–44
Harry Hibbs 1944–51
Tony McPhee 1951
Brough Fletcher 1952–53
Major Frank Buckley 1953–55
John Love 1955–57
Billy Moore 1957–64
Alf Wood 1964
Reg Shaw 1964–68
Dick Graham 1968
Ron Lewin 1968–69
Billy Moore 1969–72
John Smith 1972–73
Ronnie Allen 1973
Doug Fraser 1973–77
Dave Mackay 1977–78
Alan Ashman 1978
Frank Sibley 1979
Alan Buckley 1979–86
Neil Martin *(Joint Manager with Buckley)* 1981–82
Tommy Coakley 1986–88
John Barnwell 1989–90
Kenny Hibbitt 1990–94
Chris Nicholl 1994–97
Jan Sorensen 1997–98
Ray Graydon 1998–2002
Colin Lee 2002–04
Paul Merson 2004–06
Kevin Broadhurst 2006
Richard Money 2006–08
Jimmy Mullen 2008–09
Chris Hutchings 2009–11
Dean Smith 2011–15
Sean O'Driscoll 2015–16
Jon Whitney March 2016–

TEN YEAR LEAGUE RECORD

		P	W	D	L	F	A	Pts	Pos
2007-08	FL 1	46	16	16	14	52	46	64	12
2008-09	FL 1	46	17	10	19	61	66	61	13
2009-10	FL 1	46	16	14	16	60	63	62	10
2010-11	FL 1	46	12	12	22	56	75	48	20
2011-12	FL 1	46	10	20	16	51	57	50	19
2012-13	FL 1	46	17	17	12	65	58	68	9
2013-14	FL 1	46	14	16	16	49	49	58	13
2014-15	FL 1	46	14	17	15	50	54	59	14
2015-16	FL 1	46	24	12	10	71	49	84	3
2016-17	FL 1	46	14	16	16	51	58	58	14

DID YOU KNOW ?

Walsall played their first-ever Football League Cup tie away to Everton on 31 October 1961. The Saddlers lost 3-1 in front of an attendance of 14,137. The goalscorer was John Davies who, along with Grenville Palin, was one of two reserves in the line-up.

WALSALL – SKY BET LEAGUE ONE 2016–17 LEAGUE RECORD

Match No.	*Date*	*Venue*	*Opponents*	*Result*	*H/T Score*	*Lg Pos.*	*Goalscorers*	*Attendance*
1	Aug 6	H	AFC Wimbledon	W 3-1	2-0	4	Oztumer ^{7}, Jackson 2 $^{38, 72}$	5845
2	13	A	Oldham Ath	D 0-0	0-0	6		3914
3	16	A	Chesterfield	L 0-2	0-0	11		5406
4	20	H	Charlton Ath	L 1-2	0-1	17	Morris ^{72}	4586
5	27	H	Bury	D 3-3	3-0	16	Morris ^{6}, Oztumer ^{14}, Jackson ^{32}	4393
6	Sept 10	A	Northampton T	L 0-2	0-1	20		5538
7	13	A	Bristol R	D 1-1	1-1	20	Oztumer ^{16}	7805
8	17	H	Bolton W	W 1-0	1-0	15	McCarthy ^{25}	5962
9	24	A	Peterborough U	D 1-1	1-1	18	Jackson ^{17}	4906
10	27	H	Scunthorpe U	L 1-4	1-2	20	Oztumer ^{45}	3970
11	Oct 1	H	Millwall	W 2-1	1-1	16	Jackson ^{17}, Moussa ^{49}	4474
12	15	H	Shrewsbury T	W 3-2	2-1	14	Bakayoko ^{23}, Morris ^{42}, Oztumer ^{88}	4759
13	18	A	Gillingham	D 1-1	0-1	14	Moussa ^{59}	5542
14	22	A	Swindon T	W 2-0	1-0	12	Oztumer 2 $^{17, 51}$	6655
15	29	H	Coventry C	D 1-1	0-1	12	Oztumer ^{76}	6719
16	Nov 12	A	Milton Keynes D	D 1-1	1-0	14	Laird ^{28}	8188
17	19	H	Gillingham	L 1-2	1-1	17	McCarthy ^{9}	5420
18	22	A	Rochdale	L 0-4	0-2	17		1907
19	26	H	Southend U	D 0-0	0-0	17		4342
20	29	A	Sheffield U	W 1-0	1-0	16	Bakayoko ^{42}	18,343
21	Dec 10	A	Fleetwood T	L 1-2	0-1	16	Dobson ^{76}	2708
22	17	H	Bradford C	D 1-1	0-0	16	Osbourne ^{49}	5148
23	26	A	Port Vale	W 1-0	1-0	15	Laird ^{27}	5854
24	31	A	Oxford U	D 0-0	0-0	14		8340
25	Jan 2	H	Rochdale	L 0-2	0-1	14		4667
26	14	H	Sheffield U	W 4-1	1-1	14	Bakayoko ^{5}, McCarthy ^{58}, Edwards ^{67}, Oztumer (pen) ^{76}	6899
27	21	H	Bristol R	W 3-1	1-0	13	O'Connell ^{45}, Jackson ^{68}, Edwards ^{73}	6029
28	28	A	Bury	D 3-3	0-2	12	Oztumer ^{71}, McCarthy 2 $^{76, 79}$	3280
29	Feb 1	A	Millwall	D 0-0	0-0	12		7392
30	4	H	Northampton T	W 2-1	0-1	11	Preston ^{64}, Oztumer ^{69}	4954
31	11	A	Bolton W	L 1-4	1-3	12	Oztumer ^{4}	13,610
32	14	A	Scunthorpe U	D 0-0	0-0	12		3168
33	18	H	Peterborough U	W 2-0	0-0	11	Morris ^{90}, Oztumer ^{90}	4759
34	25	A	AFC Wimbledon	L 0-1	0-0	12		4586
35	Mar 4	H	Oldham Ath	W 2-0	0-0	12	Oztumer (pen) ^{79}, Bakayoko ^{90}	6003
36	7	H	Chesterfield	W 1-0	0-0	8	Laird ^{53}	3963
37	11	A	Charlton Ath	D 1-1	1-0	9	Jackson ^{44}	9900
38	14	H	Fleetwood T	L 0-1	0-1	9		3890
39	18	A	Southend U	L 2-3	2-0	11	Moussa 2 $^{18, 25}$	6756
40	Apr 1	A	Bradford C	L 0-1	0-0	13		17,880
41	8	H	Oxford U	D 1-1	0-0	14	Makris ^{48}	5417
42	14	A	Shrewsbury T	D 1-1	1-0	14	Morris ^{35}	6801
43	17	H	Swindon T	W 1-0	0-0	13	Edwards ^{85}	5196
44	22	A	Coventry C	L 0-1	0-1	13		9284
45	25	H	Port Vale	L 0-1	0-0	13		4266
46	30	H	Milton Keynes D	L 1-4	0-2	14	Oztumer ^{84}	5004

Final League Position: 14

GOALSCORERS

League (51): Oztumer 15 (2 pens), Jackson 7, McCarthy 5, Morris 5, Bakayoko 4, Moussa 4, Edwards 3, Laird 3, Dobson 1, Makris 1, O'Connell 1, Osbourne 1, Preston 1.
FA Cup (0).
EFL Cup (0).
EFL Checkatrade Trophy (9): Bakayoko 6, Kouhyar 1, Laird 1, Morris 1.

Etheridge N 41	Edwards J 43	O'Connor J 40	McCarthy J 46	Henry R 2	Chambers A 43	Osbourne I 27 + 3	Oztumer E 34 + 7	Cuvelier F 15 + 7	Morris K 28 + 7	Jackson S 24 + 14	Preston M 25 + 5	Bakayoko A 18 + 21	Moussa F 14 + 8	Kinsella L 5 + 3	Makris A 17 + 15	Dobson G 9 + 12	Kouhyar M 2 + 4	Toner K 16	Laird S 26 + 2	Ginnelly J 4 + 5	Roberts K 4	O'Connell E 17	Randall W — + 2	Candlin M 1 + 4	MacGillivray C 5	Hayles-Docherty T — + 1	*Match No.*
1	2	3^{1}	4	5	6	7	8^{2}	9^{3}	10	11	12	13	14														1
1	2	4	3	5^{1}		6	9^{3}	10^{2}		11	12	14	8	7	13												2
1	2	3	5					12	8^{1}	11	4	13	9^{2}	6	10	7^{3}	14										3
1	2	4	5			7	14	13	10	11	3	12	9^{3}		8^{1}	6^{2}											4
1	5		3		7	6^{1}	9^{2}		10	11		13		2	8^{3}	12	14	4									5
1	6		3		7		8		10^{2}	13		11	12	4^{1}	14		2^{3}	5	9								6
1	2		4		8		10		7	11		13	9^{2}		6^{1}		12	3	5								7
1	6▮	3	2		7		9^{1}		10	11		12		13	8^{2}			4	5								8
1		4	2		6	13	9	8^{1}	7	11			12		10^{2}			3	5								9
1		3	5		6	7^{3}	9	10^{1}	8^{2}	11		13	12	2	14			4									10
1		4	2		6		9		8	11^{3}			10^{1}	13	14	7^{2}	12	3	5								11
1	6	3	2		7		9^{2}		10^{3}		13	11▮	8^{1}		14			4	5	12							12
1	7	3	2		6		9		8				10^{1}		11			4	5	12							13
1	7	3	2		6		9		8^{2}			12	11		10^{1}			4	5	13							14
1	6	3	2		7		9		10^{1}	12			8^{3}	14	11^{2}			4	5	13							15
1	7		2		6	13	9			11^{1}	4	12	10					3	5	8^{2}							16
1	2^{2}		3		9		7	12		11	5	13	8^{1}					4	6	10							17
1	7		2		6		9^{2}	13		11^{1}	3	12	10		14			4	5	8^{3}							18
1	7	3	2		6		9^{2}		8	14	12	13			11^{1}			4^{3}	5	10							19
1	6	3	2		10	13	9^{3}		8	14	4	11^{2}				7^{1}			5	12							20
1	6^{1}	3	5		7		10			12	2	11			13	8		4^{2}	9								21
1	8	3	2		7	6	14	9^{3}		11^{1}	4	10^{2}	12		13				5								22
1	6	4	2		8	7	12	9^{3}	14	11^{2}	3	10^{1}			13				5								23
1	6	4	2		8	7	12	9^{2}	13	10^{1}		11^{3}			14				5		3						24
1	6	3	2		7		12	8	9^{1}	10^{2}		11	13						5		4						25
1	5	2	9		6	7	10^{1}	8^{3}	14	13	3	11^{2}				12						4					26
1	6	3	2		7	9	10^{1}	8^{3}		12	4	11^{2}			13	14						5					27
1	9	2	5		6	8	10^{2}	7^{3}		12	3	11^{1}			14	13						4					28
1	2	4	6		8	9	11^{1}	7^{2}	13	12	5	10^{3}										3	14				29
1	6	3	2		7	9^{2}	10	8^{1}		12	4	11^{3}				13			14			5					30
1	9^{1}	3	5		7	8	10	6		13	2	11^{2}										4	12				31
1	9	3	5		7	8	11^{1}	6^{3}	12	10^{2}	2	13				14						4					32
1	9	3	5		7	6^{1}	10^{3}		8	11^{2}	2	13	14			12						4					33
1	9^{1}	3	5		7	6	10		8	11	4^{2}	12							13			2					34
1	2^{2}	4	5		6	10	8		9	7^{1}		12			13				3			11					35
1	9	3	5		7	8	10^{2}		6^{3}	11^{1}		12			14	13			4			2					36
1	9	3	2		6	7	10		8^{2}	11^{3}		12				13			5			4					37
1	9	3	5		7	8	10			11^{2}	12	13			14	6^{3}			4			2^{1}					38
1	9	3	5		7	6	11^{1}		14		2	13	12^{3}		10^{2}	8			4								39
1	8	2	5		7^{1}	6			10	12	3		9		11^{2}				4					13			40
1	9	3	5		7	6		14	8^{2}	12	2		10^{3}		11^{1}	13			4								41
	9	2	5		7	6		13	8^{3}	12	3	10^{2}			11^{1}							4		14	1		42
	9	3	5		7	6^{1}	12		8		2	10			11^{2}	13						4			1		43
	9	2	5		7	6^{1}	12		8^{3}		3	10			11^{2}	13						4▮		14	1		44
	8	3	5		6				9		2	10^{2}				7	11^{1}				4			13	1	12	45
	8	3	5		6		9	12	13						10	7					2^{2}	4		11^{1}	1		46

FA Cup

First Round	Macclesfield T	(h)	0-1

EFL Cup

First Round (*aet*)	Yeovil T	(h)	0-2

EFL Checkatrade Trophy

Northern Group H	Grimsby T	(h)	5-2
Northern Group H	Sheffield U	(a)	2-1
Northern Group H	Leicester C U21	(a)	1-0
Second Round North	Oldham Ath	(h)	1-3

WATFORD

FOUNDATION

The club was formed as Watford Rovers in 1881. The name was changed to West Herts in 1893 and then the name Watford was adopted after rival club Watford St Mary's was absorbed in 1898.

Vicarage Road Stadium, Vicarage Road, Watford, Hertfordshire WD18 0ER.

Telephone: (01923) 496 000.

Fax: (01923) 496 001.

Ticket Office: (01923) 223 023.

Website: www.watfordfc.com

Email: yourvoice@watfordfc.com

Ground Capacity: 21,438.

Record Attendance: 34,099 v Manchester U, FA Cup 4th rd (replay), 3 February 1969.

Pitch Measurements: 105m × 68m (115yd × 74.5yd).

Executive Chairman: Raffaele Riva.

Chief Executive: Scott Duxbury.

Head Coach: Marco Silva.

Colours: Yellow shirts with black and red trim, black shorts with yellow trim, black socks with yellow trim.

Year Formed: 1881.

Turned Professional: 1897.

Previous Names: 1881, Watford Rovers; 1893, West Herts; 1898, Watford.

Club Nickname: 'The Hornets'.

Grounds: 1883, Vicarage Meadow, Rose and Crown Meadow; 1889, Colney Butts; 1890, Cassio Road; 1922, Vicarage Road.

First Football League Game: 28 August 1920, Division 3, v QPR (a) W 2–1 – Williams; Horseman, Fred Gregory; Bacon, Toone, Wilkinson; Bassett, Ronald (1), Hoddinott, White (1), Waterall.

Record League Victory: 8–0 v Sunderland, Division 1, 25 September 1982 – Sherwood; Rice, Rostron, Taylor, Terry, Bolton, Callaghan (2), Blissett (4), Jenkins (2), Jackett, Barnes.

Record Cup Victory: 10–1 v Lowestoft T, FA Cup 1st rd, 27 November 1926 – Yates; Prior, Fletcher (1); Frank Smith, Bert Smith, Strain; Stephenson, Warner (3), Edmonds (3), Swan (1), Daniels (1), (1 og).

Record Defeat: 0–10 v Wolverhampton W, FA Cup 1st rd (replay), 24 January 1912.

Most League Points (2 for a win): 71, Division 4, 1977–78.

HONOURS

League Champions: Second Division – 1997–98; Division 3 – 1968–69; Division 4 – 1977–78.
Runners-up: Division 1 – 1982–83; FL C – 2014–15; Division 2 – 1981–82; Division 3 – 1978–79.

FA Cup: *Runners-up:* 1984.

League Cup: semi-final – 1979, 2005.

European Competitions
UEFA Cup: 1983–84.

sky SPORTS FACT FILE

Brothers Fred and Les Le May both joined Watford from Thames and after spending the 1931–32 season at Vicarage Road moved on to Clapton Orient. Winger Fred, 5 foot tall and weighing just 7 stone 10 pounds, is believed to be the smallest and lightest player to feature in the Football League.

Most League Points (3 for a win): 89, FL C, 2014–15

Most League Goals: 92, Division 4, 1959–60.

Highest League Scorer in Season: Cliff Holton, 42, Division 4, 1959–60.

Most League Goals in Total Aggregate: Luther Blissett, 148, 1976–83, 1984–88, 1991–92.

Most League Goals in One Match: 5, Eddie Mummery v Newport Co, Division 3 (S), 5 January 1924.

Most Capped Players: John Barnes, 31 (79), England; Kenny Jackett, 31, Wales.

Most League Appearances: Luther Blissett, 415, 1976–83, 1984–88, 1991–92.

Youngest League Player: Keith Mercer, 16 years 125 days v Tranmere R, 16 February 1973.

Record Transfer Fee Received: £20,000,000 from Changchun Yatai for Odion Ighalo, January 2017.

Record Transfer Fee Paid: £13,000,000 to Juventus for Roberto Pereyra, August 2016.

Football League Record: 1920 Original Member of Division 3; 1921–58 Division 3 (S); 1958–60 Division 4; 1960–69 Division 3; 1969–72 Division 2; 1972–75 Division 3; 1975–78 Division 4; 1978–79 Division 3; 1979–82 Division 2; 1982–88 Division 1; 1988–92 Division 2; 1992–96 Division 1; 1996–98 Division 2; 1998–99 Division 1; 1999–2000 FA Premier League; 2000–04 Division 1; 2004–06 FL C; 2006–07 FA Premier League; 2007–15 FL C; 2015– FA Premier League.

LATEST SEQUENCES

Longest Sequence of League Wins: 7, 28.8.2000 – 14.10.2000.

Longest Sequence of League Defeats: 9, 26.12.1972 – 27.2.1973.

Longest Sequence of League Draws: 7, 16.2.2008 – 22.3.2008.

Longest Sequence of Unbeaten League Matches: 22, 1.10.1996 – 1.3.1997.

Longest Sequence Without a League Win: 19, 27.11.1971 – 8.4.1972.

Successive Scoring Runs: 22 from 20.8.1985.

Successive Non-scoring Runs: 7 from 18.12.1971.

MANAGERS

John Goodall 1903–10
Harry Kent 1910–26
Fred Pagnam 1926–29
Neil McBain 1929–37
Bill Findlay 1938–47
Jack Bray 1947–48
Eddie Hapgood 1948–50
Ron Gray 1950–51
Haydn Green 1951–52
Len Goulden 1952–55
(General Manager to 1956)
Johnny Paton 1955–56
Neil McBain 1956–59
Ron Burgess 1959–63
Bill McGarry 1963–64
Ken Furphy 1964–71
George Kirby 1971–73
Mike Keen 1973–77
Graham Taylor 1977–87
Dave Bassett 1987–88
Steve Harrison 1988–90
Colin Lee 1990
Steve Perryman 1990–93
Glenn Roeder 1993–96
Graham Taylor 1996
Kenny Jackett 1996–97
Graham Taylor 1997–2001
Gianluca Vialli 2001–02
Ray Lewington 2002–05
Adrian Boothroyd 2005–08
Brendan Rodgers 2008–09
Malky Mackay 2009–11
Sean Dyche 2011–12
Gianfranco Zola 2012–13
Beppe Sannino 2013–14
Oscar Garcia 2014
Billy McKinlay 2014
Slavisa Jokanovic 2014–15
Quique Flores 2015–16
Walter Mazzarri 2016–17
Marco Silva May 2017–

TEN YEAR LEAGUE RECORD

		P	*W*	*D*	*L*	*F*	*A*	*Pts*	*Pos*
2007-08	FL C	46	18	16	12	62	56	70	6
2008-09	FL C	46	16	10	20	68	72	58	13
2009-10	FL C	46	14	12	20	61	68	54	16
2010-11	FL C	46	16	13	17	77	71	61	14
2011-12	FL C	46	16	16	14	56	64	64	11
2012-13	FL C	46	23	8	15	85	58	77	3
2013-14	FL C	46	15	15	16	74	64	60	13
2014-15	FL C	46	27	8	11	91	50	89	2
2015-16	PR Lge	38	12	9	17	40	50	45	13
2016-17	PR Lge	38	11	7	20	40	68	40	17

DID YOU KNOW ?

The first substitute used by Watford in a Football League game was Roger Hugo who came off the bench to replace Billy Houghton at Peterborough United on 4 September 1965. Hugo, signed during the close season from West Ham United, scored for the Hornets in the 2-2 draw.

WATFORD – PREMIER LEAGUE 2016–17 LEAGUE RECORD

Match No.	Date	Venue	Opponents	Result	H/T Score	Lg Pos.	Goalscorers	Attendance
1	Aug 13	A	Southampton	D 1-1	1-0	10	Capoue ^{9}	31,488
2	20	H	Chelsea	L 1-2	0-0	13	Capoue ^{55}	20,772
3	27	H	Arsenal	L 1-3	0-3	18	Pereyra ^{57}	20,545
4	Sept 10	A	West Ham U	W 4-2	2-2	10	Ighalo ^{41}, Deeney ^{45}, Capoue ^{53}, Holebas ^{63}	56,974
5	18	H	Manchester U	W 3-1	1-0	9	Capoue ^{34}, Zuniga ^{83}, Deeney (pen) ^{90}	21,118
6	26	A	Burnley	L 0-2	0-1	11		18,519
7	Oct 1	H	Bournemouth	D 2-2	0-1	11	Deeney ^{50}, Success ^{65}	20,575
8	16	A	Middlesbrough	W 1-0	0-0	9	Holebas ^{54}	28,131
9	22	A	Swansea C	D 0-0	0-0	9		20,694
10	29	H	Hull C	W 1-0	0-0	7	Dawson (og) ^{82}	20,022
11	Nov 6	A	Liverpool	L 1-6	0-3	8	Janmaat ^{75}	53,163
12	19	H	Leicester C	W 2-1	2-1	8	Capoue ^{1}, Pereyra ^{12}	20,640
13	27	H	Stoke C	L 0-1	0-1	8		20,058
14	Dec 3	A	WBA	L 1-3	0-2	10	Kabasele ^{60}	22,244
15	10	H	Everton	W 3-2	1-1	7	Okaka 2 $^{36, 64}$, Prodl ^{59}	20,769
16	14	A	Manchester C	L 0-2	0-1	9		51,527
17	17	A	Sunderland	L 0-1	0-0	12		40,267
18	26	H	Crystal Palace	D 1-1	0-1	10	Deeney (pen) ^{71}	20,304
19	Jan 1	H	Tottenham H	L 1-4	0-3	13	Kaboul ^{90}	20,882
20	3	A	Stoke C	L 0-2	0-1	14		27,010
21	14	H	Middlesbrough	D 0-0	0-0	14		20,659
22	21	A	Bournemouth	D 2-2	1-0	14	Kabasele ^{24}, Deeney ^{64}	11,123
23	31	A	Arsenal	W 2-1	2-0	13	Kaboul ^{10}, Deeney ^{13}	60,035
24	Feb 4	H	Burnley	W 2-1	2-0	10	Deeney ^{10}, Niang ^{45}	20,178
25	11	A	Manchester U	L 0-2	0-1	12		75,301
26	25	H	West Ham U	D 1-1	1-0	12	Deeney (pen) ^{3}	20,702
27	Mar 4	H	Southampton	L 3-4	1-2	13	Deeney ^{4}, Okaka ^{79}, Doucoure ^{90}	20,670
28	18	A	Crystal Palace	L 0-1	0-0	14		25,109
29	Apr 1	H	Sunderland	W 1-0	0-0	12	Britos ^{59}	20,805
30	4	H	WBA	W 2-0	1-0	9	Niang ^{13}, Deeney ^{49}	20,090
31	8	A	Tottenham H	L 0-4	0-3	10		31,706
32	15	H	Swansea C	W 1-0	1-0	10	Capoue ^{42}	20,272
33	22	A	Hull C	L 0-2	0-0	10		20,432
34	May 1	H	Liverpool	L 0-1	0-1	13		20,959
35	6	A	Leicester C	L 0-3	0-1	15		31,628
36	12	A	Everton	L 0-1	0-0	15		38,550
37	15	A	Chelsea	L 3-4	1-2	16	Capoue ^{24}, Janmaat ^{51}, Okaka ^{74}	41,473
38	21	H	Manchester C	L 0-5	0-4	17		20,829

Final League Position: 17

GOALSCORERS

League (40): Deeney 10 (3 pens), Capoue 7, Okaka 4, Holebas 2, Janmaat 2, Kabasele 2, Kaboul 2, Niang 2, Pereyra 2, Britos 1, Doucoure 1, Ighalo 1, Prodl 1, Success 1, Zuniga 1, own goal 1.
FA Cup (2): Kabasele 1, Sinclair 1.
EFL Cup (1): Ighalo 1.

Gomes H 38	Cathcart C 13 + 2	Prodl S 32 + 1	Britos M 27	Amrabat N 25 + 4	Capoue E 37	Behrami V 26 + 1	Guedioura A 9 + 3	Holebas J 33	Deeney T 31 + 6	Ighalo O 14 + 4	Watson B — + 4	Zuniga J 6 + 15	Anya I — + 1	Doucoure A 14 + 6	Vydra M — + 1	Kaboul Y 22	Kabasele C 7 + 9	Pereyra R 12 + 1	Janmaat D 18 + 9	Success I 2 + 17	Okaka S 10 + 9	Kenedy R — + 1	Pantilimon C — + 2	Sinclair J 1 + 4	Mason B 1 + 1	Folivi M — + 1	Cleverley T 16 + 1	Niang M 15 + 1	Zarate M 3	Mariappa A 6 + 1	Pereira D — + 2	Eleftheriou A — + 1	*Match No.*
1	2	3	4	5	6	7^{2}	8^{3}	9	10	11^{1}	12▮	13	14																				1
1	2	3	4	6	8^{3}	5	7^{1}	9^{2}	10	11		14		12	13																		2
1		3		5^{1}	8	7	6^{2}	9	11	10						2	4^{3}	12	13	14													3
1	3	14	5		9	8		6	10^{2}	11^{1}						4^{3}		7	2	12	13												4
1	2	3	4	12	7^{1}	6		8	10	11^{3}		13						9	5^{2}	14													5
1	3^{3}	4	5	2^{2}	9	8		6	11	10		12						7^{1}		13		14											6
1		3		9	8^{2}	7	13	5	10	11^{1}		2				4		6		12													7
1		4	5^{3}	2^{2}	8	9		6	11		14	12				3	13	7		10^{1}													8
1		3	5	12	9^{1}	8	13	6	10	11		2^{2}				4		7															9
1		2^{2}	4	5^{3}	8	7		9	11	10		13				3^{1}	14	6	12														10
1^{1}			4	6	8	7^{2}		5	11	10	13	14				3		9^{3}	2				12										11
1		2	4	9^{2}	7	6	12		10^{1}			8				3		11	5		13												12
1		3	4▮	9^{3}	7	6		8^{1}	10	13						2^{2}	12	11	5		14												13
1		4		9	8		7	5	11	12		2^{2}					3	6▮			10^{1}			13									14
1		3	4	9	8	7	6^{1}	5	10		13	2^{2}					14		12		11^{3}												15
1		3	4	6	7		8	5	14	11		12						9^{3}	2^{1}	13				10^{2}									16
1		3^{1}	4	6	8	7		5	11	10		9^{3}				2^{2}	12		14	13													17
1		3	4	10	9	7^{2}	6	8	13	11		12^{3}				2			5^{1}					14									18
1	2	3		5^{3}	6^{1}		7	8^{2}	11	10				9		4	14							13	12								19
1		3^{3}	4		8	7^{1}	6^{2}	9	11	12				10		2	5							13		14							20
1^{1}		3	4		6	7^{3}		8^{2}	10			14		9		2	5				11		12				13						21
1	13	3	4		6			8	11	14				7^{3}		2	5^{2}		12		10^{1}						9						22
1	2	4	5		7	8^{1}			11^{2}					12		3			6	13	14						9	10^{3}					23
1	2	4			6	7^{1}		5	10					12		3			14	13							8	9^{3}	11^{2}				24
1	2^{2}	4	5^{1}		8			10	11							3			12	14	13						6	9	7^{3}				25
1	13		4		6	7		5	10					12		3			2^{2}	14							8	9^{3}	11^{1}				26
1		3	4		6^{2}	7		5	10					13		2				12	11^{1}						8	9					27
1	2	3	5	13	9	8^{3}			11					12		4			6^{1}	14							7^{2}	10					28
1	2		4	6^{2}	9			5				14		8		3^{1}			12	13	11						7	10^{3}					29
1	2	3^{3}	4▮	6^{1}	7			5	11					8					12	14							9	10^{2}		13			30
1	4			6^{2}				5	13			12		8^{1}			14		2	7	11^{3}						9	10		3			31
1		3		9^{1}	6	14		5	10					7			12		2		13						8^{2}	11^{3}		4			32
1		3	4	8^{2}	9			5^{3}	11			14		7^{1}					2	12	13						6	10					33
1		3	4^{1}	5^{3}	6^{2}				10					7			12		9	13	14						8	11		2			34
1		3		5	8^{3}				12			13		7			2^{1}		9		10						6	11^{2}		4	14		35
1		3		13	8^{1}	6^{2}		9	11			12		7			4^{3}		5		10							14		2			36
1		3▮		5	10^{2}	7		4	13					8					9		12						6	11^{1}		2			37
1				8^{3}	9	3		4	13					7					2^{2}		11				5		6	10^{1}			14	12	38

FA Cup

Third Round	Burton Alb	(h)	2-0
Fourth Round	Millwall	(a)	0-1

EFL Cup

Second Round	Gillingham	(h)	1-2
(*aet*)			

WEST BROMWICH ALBION

FOUNDATION

There is a well known story that when employees of Salter's Spring Works in West Bromwich decided to form a football club, they had to send someone to the nearby Association Football stronghold of Wednesbury to purchase a football. A weekly subscription of 2d (less than 1p) was imposed and the name of the new club was West Bromwich Strollers.

The Hawthorns, West Bromwich, West Midlands B71 4LF.

Telephone: (0871) 271 1100.

Fax: (0871) 271 9851.

Ticket Office: (0121) 227 2227.

Website: www.wba.co.uk

Email: enquiries@wbafc.co.uk

Ground Capacity: 26,850.

Record Attendance: 64,815 v Arsenal, FA Cup 6th rd, 6 March 1937.

Pitch Measurements: 105m × 68m (114yd × 74yd).

Chairman: Jeremy Peace.

Chief Executive: Mark Jenkins.

Head Coach: Tony Pulis.

Assistant Head Coaches: David Kemp, Mark O'Connor and Ben Garner.

Colours: Navy blue and white striped shirts, white shorts with navy blue trim, white socks with navy blue hoops.

Year Formed: 1878.

Turned Professional: 1885.

Previous Name: 1878, West Bromwich Strollers; 1881, West Bromwich Albion.

Club Nicknames: 'The Throstles', 'The Baggies', 'Albion'.

Grounds: 1878, Coopers Hill; 1879, Dartmouth Park; 1881, Bunns Field, Walsall Street; 1882, Four Acres (Dartmouth Cricket Club); 1885, Stoney Lane; 1900, The Hawthorns.

First Football League Game: 8 September 1888, Football League, v Stoke (a) W 2–0 – Roberts; Jack Horton, Green; Ezra Horton, Perry, Bayliss; Bassett, Woodhall (1), Hendry, Pearson, Wilson (1).

Record League Victory: 12–0 v Darwen, Division 1, 4 April 1892 – Reader; Jack Horton, McCulloch; Reynolds (2), Perry, Groves; Bassett (3), McLeod, Nicholls (1), Pearson (4), Geddes (1), (1 og).

Record Cup Victory: 10–1 v Chatham (away), FA Cup 3rd rd, 2 March 1889 – Roberts; Jack Horton, Green; Timmins (1), Charles Perry, Ezra Horton; Bassett (2), Walter Perry (1), Bayliss (2), Pearson, Wilson (3), (1 og).

League Champions: Division 1 – 1919–20; FL C – 2007–08; Division 2 – 1901–02, 1910–11.
Runners-up: Division 1 – 1924–25, 1953–54; FL C – 2009–10; First Division – 2001–02, 2003–04; Division 2 – 1930–31, 1948–49.

FA Cup Winners: 1888, 1892, 1931, 1954, 1968.
Runners-up: 1886, 1887, 1895, 1912, 1935.

League Cup Winners: 1966.
Runners-up: 1967, 1970.

European Competitions
Fairs Cup: 1966–67.
UEFA Cup: 1978–79 *(qf)*, 1979–80, 1981–82.
European Cup-Winners' Cup: 1968–69 *(qf)*.

sky SPORTS FACT FILE

Goalkeeper Tony Godden played in every West Bromwich Albion League and Cup match from the start of the 1977–78 season through until the end of October 1981. The run extended to 228 games of which 180 were Football League fixtures.

Record Defeat: 3–10 v Stoke C, Division 1, 4 February 1937.

Most League Points (2 for a win): 60, Division 1, 1919–20.

Most League Points (3 for a win): 91, FL C, 2009–10.

Most League Goals: 105, Division 2, 1929–30.

Highest League Scorer in Season: William 'Ginger' Richardson, 39, Division 1, 1935–36.

Most League Goals in Total Aggregate: Tony Brown, 218, 1963–79.

Most League Goals in One Match: 6, Jimmy Cookson v Blackpool, Division 2, 17 September 1927.

Most Capped Player: James Morrison, 44, Scotland.

Most League Appearances: Tony Brown, 574, 1963–80.

Youngest League Player: Charlie Wilson, 16 years 73 days v Oldham Ath, 1 October 1921.

Record Transfer Fee Received: £12,000,000 from Stoke C for Saido Berahino, January 2017.

Record Transfer Fee Paid: £13,000,000 to Tottenham H for Nacer Chadli, August 2016.

Football League Record: 1888 Founder Member of Football League; 1901–02 Division 2; 1902–04 Division 1; 1904–11 Division 2; 1911–27 Division 1; 1927–31 Division 2; 1931–38 Division 1; 1938–49 Division 2; 1949–73 Division 1; 1973–76 Division 2; 1976–86 Division 1; 1986–91 Division 2; 1991–92 Division 3; 1992–93 Division 2; 1993–2002 Division 1; 2002–03 FA Premier League; 2003–04 Division 1; 2004–06 FA Premier League; 2006–08 FL C; 2008–09 FA Premier League; 2009–10 FL C; 2010– FA Premier League.

LATEST SEQUENCES

Longest Sequence of League Wins: 11, 5.4.1930 – 8.9.1930.

Longest Sequence of League Defeats: 11, 28.10.1995 – 26.12.1995.

Longest Sequence of League Draws: 5, 30.8.1999 – 3.10.1999.

Longest Sequence of Unbeaten League Matches: 17, 7.9.1957 – 7.12.1957.

Longest Sequence Without a League Win: 15, 16.10.2004 – 16.1.2005.

Successive Scoring Runs: 36 from 26.4.1958.

Successive Non-scoring Runs: 5 from 1.4.2017.

MANAGERS

Louis Ford 1890–92
(Secretary-Manager)
Henry Jackson 1892–94
(Secretary-Manager)
Edward Stephenson 1894–95
(Secretary-Manager)
Clement Keys 1895–96
(Secretary-Manager)
Frank Heaven 1896–1902
(Secretary-Manager)
Fred Everiss 1902–48
Jack Smith 1948–52
Jesse Carver 1952
Vic Buckingham 1953–59
Gordon Clark 1959–61
Archie Macaulay 1961–63
Jimmy Hagan 1963–67
Alan Ashman 1967–71
Don Howe 1971–75
Johnny Giles 1975–77
Ronnie Allen 1977
Ron Atkinson 1978–81
Ronnie Allen 1981–82
Ron Wylie 1982–84
Johnny Giles 1984–85
Nobby Stiles 1985–86
Ron Saunders 1986–87
Ron Atkinson 1987–88
Brian Talbot 1988–91
Bobby Gould 1991–92
Ossie Ardiles 1992–93
Keith Burkinshaw 1993–94
Alan Buckley 1994–97
Ray Harford 1997
Denis Smith 1997–1999
Brian Little 1999–2000
Gary Megson 2000–04
Bryan Robson 2004–06
Tony Mowbray 2006–09
Roberto Di Matteo 2009–11
Roy Hodgson 2011–12
Steve Clarke 2012–13
Pepe Mel 2014
Alan Irvine 2014
Tony Pulis January 2015–

TEN YEAR LEAGUE RECORD

		P	W	D	L	F	A	Pts	Pos
2007-08	FL C	46	23	12	11	88	55	81	1
2008-09	PR Lge	38	8	8	22	36	67	32	20
2009-10	FL C	46	26	13	7	89	48	91	2
2010-11	PR Lge	38	12	11	15	56	71	47	11
2011-12	PR Lge	38	13	8	17	45	52	47	10
2012-13	PR Lge	38	14	7	17	53	57	49	8
2013-14	PR Lge	38	7	15	16	43	59	36	17
2014-15	PR Lge	38	11	11	16	38	51	44	13
2015-16	PR Lge	38	10	13	15	34	48	43	14
2016-17	PR Lge	38	12	9	17	43	51	45	10

DID YOU KNOW ?

West Bromwich Albion were visitors to Stoke's Victoria Ground for both the first and the last Football League games played there. Albion won 2-0 on 8 September 1888 in the first game played at the venue, but lost 2-1 on 4 May 1997.

WEST BROMWICH ALBION – PREMIER LEAGUE 2016–17 LEAGUE RECORD

Match No.	*Date*	*Venue*	*Opponents*	*Result*		*H/T Score*	*Lg Pos.*	*Goalscorers*	*Attendance*
1	Aug 13	A	Crystal Palace	W	1-0	0-0	2	Rondon [74]	24,490
2	20	H	Everton	L	1-2	1-1	8	McAuley [9]	23,654
3	28	H	Middlesbrough	D	0-0	0-0	10		23,690
4	Sept 10	A	Bournemouth	L	0-1	0-0	11		11,184
5	17	H	West Ham U	W	4-2	3-0	8	Chadli 2 (1 pen) [8 (p), 56], Rondon [37], McClean [44]	22,209
6	24	A	Stoke C	D	1-1	0-0	9	Rondon [90]	27,645
7	Oct 1	A	Sunderland	D	1-1	1-0	9	Chadli [35]	40,043
8	15	H	Tottenham H	D	1-1	0-0	10	Chadli [82]	24,263
9	22	A	Liverpool	L	1-2	0-2	13	McAuley [81]	53,218
10	29	H	Manchester C	L	0-4	0-2	15		22,470
11	Nov 6	A	Leicester C	W	2-1	0-0	11	Morrison [52], Phillips [72]	31,879
12	21	H	Burnley	W	4-0	3-0	9	Phillips [4], Morrison [16], Fletcher [37], Rondon [64]	23,016
13	26	A	Hull C	D	1-1	1-0	9	McAuley [34]	18,086
14	Dec 3	H	Watford	W	3-1	2-0	6	Evans [16], Brunt [34], Phillips [90]	22,244
15	11	A	Chelsea	L	0-1	0-0	8		41,622
16	14	H	Swansea C	W	3-1	0-0	7	Rondon 3 [50, 61, 63]	21,467
17	17	H	Manchester U	L	0-2	0-1	7		26,308
18	26	A	Arsenal	L	0-1	0-0	8		59,925
19	31	A	Southampton	W	2-1	1-1	8	Phillips [43], Robson-Kanu [50]	30,975
20	Jan 2	H	Hull C	W	3-1	0-1	8	Brunt [49], McAuley [62], Morrison [73]	23,402
21	14	A	Tottenham H	L	0-4	0-2	8		31,613
22	21	H	Sunderland	W	2-0	2-0	8	Fletcher [30], Brunt [36]	24,380
23	31	A	Middlesbrough	D	1-1	1-1	8	Morrison [6]	27,316
24	Feb 4	H	Stoke C	W	1-0	1-0	8	Morrison [6]	23,921
25	11	A	West Ham U	D	2-2	1-0	8	Chadli [6], McAuley [90]	56,983
26	25	H	Bournemouth	W	2-1	2-1	8	Dawson [10], McAuley [21]	24,162
27	Mar 4	H	Crystal Palace	L	0-2	0-0	8		24,051
28	11	A	Everton	L	0-3	0-2	8		39,592
29	18	H	Arsenal	W	3-1	1-1	8	Dawson 2 [12, 75], Robson-Kanu [55]	24,065
30	Apr 1	A	Manchester U	D	0-0	0-0	8		75,397
31	4	A	Watford	L	0-2	0-1	8		20,090
32	8	H	Southampton	L	0-1	0-1	8		24,697
33	16	H	Liverpool	L	0-1	0-1	8		25,669
34	29	H	Leicester C	L	0-1	0-1	8		24,611
35	May 6	A	Burnley	D	2-2	0-0	8	Rondon [66], Dawson [78]	20,825
36	12	H	Chelsea	L	0-1	0-0	8		25,367
37	16	A	Manchester C	L	1-3	0-2	9	Robson-Kanu [87]	53,624
38	21	A	Swansea C	L	1-2	1-0	10	Evans [33]	20,889

Final League Position: 10

GOALSCORERS

League (43): Rondon 8, McAuley 6, Chadli 5 (1 pen), Morrison 5, Dawson 4, Phillips 4, Brunt 3, Robson-Kanu 3, Evans 2, Fletcher 2, McClean 1.
FA Cup (1): Phillips 1.
EFL Cup (2): McAuley 1, McClean 1.
EFL Checkatrade Trophy (0).

Foster B 38	Dawson C 37	McAuley G 36	Olsson J 7	Evans J 30 + 1	Phillips M 26 + 1	Fletcher D 37 + 1	Yacob C 27 + 6	Gardner C 2 + 7	Rondon J 32 + 6	Berahino S 3 + 1	McClean J 13 + 21	Morrison J 17 + 14	Leko J — + 9	Lambert R — + 1	Galloway B 3	Field S 4 + 4	Chadli N 27 + 4	Nyom A 29 + 3	Robson-Kanu H 5 + 24	Brunt C 27 + 4	Livermore J 15 + 1	Wilson M 3 + 1	*Match No.*
1	2	3	4	5	6	7	8	9^2	10	11^1	12	13											1
1	2	3	4	5	6^3	7	8	9^2	11	10^1	12		13	14									2
1	2	3		4	8	6	7	14	11	13	10^1		12^3		5	9^2							3
1	2	3		4	8	6^2	7^3	13	12	11^1			14		5	9	10						4
1	2	3		4	8	6	7		11^3		10	13			5^2		9^1	12	14				5
1	2	3		4	7^2	8	6^3		11		10^1	13	14				9	5	12				6
1	2	3		4	6	7	8	12	11^2		9^3	13					10^1	5	14				7
1	2	3		4	8^1	6	7	13	11		10						9^2	5		12			8
1	2	3	4		7^2	8	6^3		11		10^1	13					9	5	14	12			9
1	2	3	4^3	6		8^2			11		10	12	13				7^1	5	14	9			10
1	2	3		4	10^2	6	7	12	11			9^1						5	13	8			11
1	2	3		4	10^1	6	7	14	11^2		12	9^3						5	13	8			12
1	2	3		4	10^1	6^2	7		11		12	9^3					13	5	14	8			13
1	2	3		4	10	6	7		11^2		13	9^1					12	5	14	8^3			14
1	2	3		4	10^2	6	7		11		13	9^1					12	5	14	8^3			15
1		3	4		10	6	7	13	11^1		12	9^3					8^2	2	14	5			16
1	2^2	3	4		10^1	6	7		11			12	14				9^3	5	13	8			17
1	2	3		4	10	7	6		11^2		12						9^1	5	13	8			18
1	2	3		4	8	7	6		14		12	13					9^3	5^2	11^1	10			19
1	2	3		4^3	10	6	7		11^1		14	9					8^2	12	13	5			20
1	2	3	4		10^1	6	7		11		12	9				14	8^3		13	5^2			21
1	3	4			8	6	7		11^1		13	9^2					10^3	2	14	5	12		22
1	3	4			10	6	7		11^2		12	9					8^1	2	13	5			23
1	3	4			8^2	6			11		12	9^3				14	10^1	2	13	5	7		24
1	3	4		12	8^1	6	14		11			9^2					10^3	2	13	5	7		25
1	2^3	3		4		8	13		11		12	9^1				14	10^2	5		7	6		26
1	2	3		4		8^3			11		12	9	14				10^2	5^1	13	7	6		27
1	2	3		4		8	7^1		13		11^2	14					9	5	10^3	12	6		28
1	2	3		4		7	13		11^1		10					14	6^2	5	12	9^3	8		29
1	2	3		4		7	13		14		10^1	12					6^2	5	11^3	9	8		30
1	2	3^3		4	12	6			14		11^2	13					9	5	10	8	7^1		31
1	2	3^3		4	10^2	7^1			11		13	9					8	5	14	12	6		32
1	2	3		4	9	8	7^2		13		14	12					11^1		10^3	5	6		33
1	2	3		4		13	7^3		11		12	9^1	14				10	5^2		8	6		34
1	2	3		4^1		6	14		11		10	13				9^2		12		7	8	5^3	35
1	2	3^3		4		6	12		11		10^1					9^2	13	5		7	8	14	36
1	3			4		8	6		11^2		12	13					7	2	14	10	9^1	5^3	37
1	2			3		6	7		11		12	10^1	14					5	13	9	8^2	4^3	38

FA Cup
Third Round Derby Co (h) 1-2

EFL Cup
Second Round Northampton T (a) 2-2
(*aet; Northampton T won 4-3 on penalties*)

EFL Checkatrade Trophy (WBA U21)
Southern Group H Millwall (a) 0-2
Southern Group H Luton T (a) 0-2
Southern Group H Gillingham (h) 0-2

WEST HAM UNITED

FOUNDATION

Thames Ironworks FC was formed by employees of this famous shipbuilding company in 1895 and entered the FA Cup in their initial season at Chatham and the London League in their second. The committee wanted to introduce professional players, so Thames Ironworks was wound up in June 1900 and relaunched a month later as West Ham United.

London Stadium, Queen Elizabeth Olympic Park, London E20 2ST

Telephone: (020) 8548 2748.

Fax: (020) 8548 2758.

Ticket Office: (0871) 529 1966.

Website: www.whufc.com

Email: supporterservices@westhamunited.co.uk

Ground Capacity: 60,000.

Record Attendance: 42,322 v Tottenham H, Division 1, 17 October 1970 (at Boleyn Ground); 56,996 v Manchester U, FA Premier League, 2 January 2017 (at London Stadium).

Pitch Measurements: 105m × 68m (114yd × 74yd).

Joint Chairmen: David Sullivan and David Gold.

Vice-chairman: Baroness Karren Brady CBE.

Chief Operating Officer: Ben Illingworth.

Manager: Slaven Bilic.

Assistant Manager: Nikola Jurcevic.

Colours: Claret shirts with sky blue trim, white shorts with sky blue trim, claret socks with sky blue trim.

Year Formed: 1895.

Turned Professional: 1900.

Previous Name: 1895, Thames Ironworks FC; 1900, West Ham United.

Club Nicknames: 'The Hammers', 'The Irons'.

Grounds: 1895, Memorial Recreation Ground, Canning Town; 1904, Boleyn Ground; 2016, London Stadium.

First Football League Game: 30 August 1919, Division 2, v Lincoln C (h) D 1–1 – Hufton; Cope, Lee; Lane, Fenwick, McCrae; David Smith, Moyes (1), Puddefoot, Morris, Bradshaw.

Record League Victory: 8–0 v Rotherham U, Division 2, 8 March 1958 – Gregory; Bond, Wright; Malcolm, Brown, Lansdowne; Grice, Smith (2), Keeble (2), Dick (4), Musgrove. 8–0 v Sunderland, Division 1, 19 October 1968 – Ferguson; Bonds, Charles; Peters, Stephenson, Moore (1); Redknapp, Boyce, Brooking (1), Hurst (6), Sissons.

HONOURS

League Champions: Division 2 – 1957–58, 1980–81.
Runners-up: First Division – 1992–93; Division 2 – 1922–23, 1990–91.

FA Cup Winners: 1964, 1975, 1980.
Runners-up: 1923, 2006.

League Cup: *Runners-up:* 1966, 1981.

European Competitions
UEFA Cup: 1999–2000; 2006–07.
Europa League: 2015–16, 2016–17.
European Cup-Winners' Cup: 1964–65 *(winners)*, 1965–66 *(sf)*, 1975–76 *(runners-up)*, 1980–81 *(qf)*.
Intertoto Cup: 1999 *(winners)*.

sky SPORTS FACT FILE

West Ham United won the BBC Sports Personality Team of the Year award in 1965 after their success in that year's European Cup Winners' Cup tournament. The following year Hammers captain Bobby Moore became the first footballer to win the BBC Sports Personality of the Year award after leading England to victory in the World Cup. Hat-trick hero Geoff Hurst finished in third place.

Record Cup Victory: 10–0 v Bury, League Cup 2nd rd (2nd leg), 25 October 1983 – Parkes; Stewart (1), Walford, Bonds (Orr), Martin (1), Devonshire (2), Allen, Cottee (4), Swindlehurst, Brooking (2), Pike.

Record Defeat: 2–8 v Blackburn R, Division 1, 26 December 1963; 0–6 v Oldham Ath, League Cup semi-final (1st leg), 14 February 1990.

Most League Points (2 for a win): 66, Division 2, 1980–81.

Most League Points (3 for a win): 88, Division 1, 1992–93.

Most League Goals: 101, Division 2, 1957–58.

Highest League Scorer in Season: Vic Watson, 42, Division 1, 1929–30.

Most League Goals in Total Aggregate: Vic Watson, 298, 1920–35.

Most League Goals in One Match: 6, Vic Watson v Leeds U, Division 1, 9 February 1929; 6, Geoff Hurst v Sunderland, Division 1, 19 October 1968.

Most Capped Player: Bobby Moore, 108, England.

Most League Appearances: Billy Bonds, 663, 1967–88.

Youngest League Player: Billy Williams, 16 years 221 days v Blackpool, 6 May 1922.

Record Transfer Fee Received: £25,000,000 from Marseille for Dmitri Payet, January 2017.

Record Transfer Fee Paid: £20,500,000 to Swansea C for Andre Ayew, August 2016.

Football League Record: 1919 Elected to Division 2; 1923–32 Division 1; 1932–58 Division 2; 1958–78 Division 1; 1978–81 Division 2; 1981–89 Division 1; 1989–91 Division 2; 1991–93 Division 1; 1993–2003 FA Premier League; 2003–04 Division 1; 2004–05 FL C; 2005–11 FA Premier League; 2011–12 FL C; 2012– FA Premier League.

MANAGERS

Syd King 1902–32
Charlie Paynter 1932–50
Ted Fenton 1950–61
Ron Greenwood 1961–74
(continued as General Manager to 1977)
John Lyall 1974–89
Lou Macari 1989–90
Billy Bonds 1990–94
Harry Redknapp 1994–2001
Glenn Roeder 2001–03
Alan Pardew 2003–06
Alan Curbishley 2006–08
Gianfranco Zola 2008–10
Avram Grant 2010–11
Sam Allardyce 2011–15
Slaven Bilic June 2015–

LATEST SEQUENCES

Longest Sequence of League Wins: 9, 19.10.1985 – 14.12.1985.

Longest Sequence of League Defeats: 9, 28.3.1932 – 29.8.1932.

Longest Sequence of League Draws: 5, 29.11.2015 – 26.12.2015.

Longest Sequence of Unbeaten League Matches: 27, 27.12.1980 – 10.10.1981.

Longest Sequence Without a League Win: 17, 31.1.1976 – 21.8.1976.

Successive Scoring Runs: 27 from 5.10.1957.

Successive Non-scoring Runs: 5 from 17.9.2006.

TEN YEAR LEAGUE RECORD

		P	W	D	L	F	A	Pts	Pos
2007-08	PR Lge	38	13	10	15	42	50	49	10
2008-09	PR Lge	38	14	9	15	42	45	51	9
2009-10	PR Lge	38	8	11	19	47	66	35	17
2010-11	PR Lge	38	7	12	19	43	70	33	20
2011-12	FL C	46	24	14	8	81	48	86	3
2012-13	PR Lge	38	12	10	16	45	53	46	10
2013-14	PR Lge	38	11	7	20	40	51	40	13
2014-15	PR Lge	38	12	11	15	44	47	47	12
2015-16	PR Lge	38	16	14	8	65	51	62	7
2016-17	PR Lge	38	12	9	17	47	64	45	11

DID YOU KNOW ?

After three games of the 1980–81 season West Ham United had acquired just two points, and were lying in the lower reaches of the Second Division table. A run of seven wins from the next eight pushed them to top position and they led the table from November onwards, finishing the season as champions.

WEST HAM UNITED – PREMIER LEAGUE 2016–17 LEAGUE RECORD

Match No.	Date	Venue	Opponents	Result	H/T Score	Lg Pos.	Goalscorers	Attendance
1	Aug 15	A	Chelsea	L 1-2	0-0	17	Collins [77]	41,521
2	21	H	Bournemouth	W 1-0	0-0	10	Antonio [85]	56,977
3	28	A	Manchester C	L 1-3	0-2	12	Antonio [58]	54,008
4	Sept 10	H	Watford	L 2-4	2-2	17	Antonio 2 [5, 33]	56,974
5	17	A	WBA	L 2-4	0-3	17	Antonio [61], Lanzini (pen) [65]	22,209
6	25	H	Southampton	L 0-3	0-1	18		56,864
7	Oct 1	H	Middlesbrough	D 1-1	0-0	18	Payet [57]	56,945
8	15	A	Crystal Palace	W 1-0	1-0	15	Lanzini [19]	25,643
9	22	H	Sunderland	W 1-0	0-0	15	Reid [90]	56,985
10	30	A	Everton	L 0-2	0-0	16		39,574
11	Nov 5	H	Stoke C	D 1-1	0-0	16	Whelan (og) [65]	56,970
12	19	A	Tottenham H	L 2-3	1-0	17	Antonio [24], Lanzini (pen) [68]	31,212
13	27	A	Manchester U	D 1-1	1-1	16	Sakho [2]	75,313
14	Dec 3	H	Arsenal	L 1-5	0-1	17	Carroll [83]	56,980
15	11	A	Liverpool	D 2-2	2-1	17	Payet [27], Antonio [39]	53,068
16	14	H	Burnley	W 1-0	1-0	15	Noble [45]	56,990
17	17	H	Hull C	W 1-0	0-0	13	Noble (pen) [76]	56,952
18	26	A	Swansea C	W 4-1	1-0	10	Ayew [13], Reid [50], Antonio [78], Carroll [90]	20,757
19	31	A	Leicester C	L 0-1	0-1	12		32,060
20	Jan 2	H	Manchester U	L 0-2	0-0	13		56,996
21	14	H	Crystal Palace	W 3-0	0-0	12	Feghouli [68], Carroll [79], Lanzini [86]	56,984
22	21	A	Middlesbrough	W 3-1	2-1	10	Carroll 2 [9, 43], Calleri [90]	30,848
23	Feb 1	H	Manchester C	L 0-4	0-3	11		56,980
24	4	A	Southampton	W 3-1	2-1	9	Carroll [14], Obiang [44], Noble [52]	31,891
25	11	H	WBA	D 2-2	0-1	10	Feghouli [63], Lanzini [86]	56,983
26	25	A	Watford	D 1-1	0-1	9	Ayew [73]	20,702
27	Mar 6	H	Chelsea	L 1-2	0-1	11	Lanzini [90]	56,984
28	11	A	Bournemouth	L 2-3	1-1	11	Antonio [10], Ayew [83]	11,369
29	18	H	Leicester C	L 2-3	1-3	12	Lanzini [20], Ayew [63]	56,979
30	Apr 1	A	Hull C	L 1-2	1-0	13	Carroll [18]	20,820
31	5	A	Arsenal	L 0-3	0-0	15		59,961
32	8	H	Swansea C	W 1-0	1-0	14	Kouyate [44]	56,973
33	15	A	Sunderland	D 2-2	1-1	12	Ayew [5], Collins [47]	40,168
34	22	H	Everton	D 0-0	0-0	13		56,971
35	29	A	Stoke C	D 0-0	0-0	15		27,628
36	May 5	H	Tottenham H	W 1-0	0-0	9	Lanzini [65]	56,992
37	14	H	Liverpool	L 0-4	0-1	12		56,985
38	21	A	Burnley	W 2-1	1-1	11	Feghouli [27], Ayew [72]	21,634

Final League Position: 11

GOALSCORERS

League (47): Antonio 9, Lanzini 8 (2 pens), Carroll 7, Ayew 6, Feghouli 3, Noble 3 (1 pen), Collins 2, Payet 2, Reid 2, Calleri 1, Kouyate 1, Obiang 1, Sakho 1, own goal 1.
FA Cup (0).
EFL Cup (4): Fernandes 1, Fletcher 1, Kouyate 1, Payet 1.
EFL Checkatrade Trophy (3): Martinez 2, Parfitt-Williams 1.
UEFA Europa League (5): Noble 2 (2 pens), Kouyate 2, Feghouli 1.

Adrian 16	Antonio M 29	Collins J 19 + 3	Reid W 30	Masuaku A 11 + 2	Kouyate C 31	Nordtveit H 11 + 5	Noble M 29 + 1	Ayew A 16 + 9	Carroll A 15 + 3	Valencia E 3	Tore G 3 + 2	Byram S 13 + 5	Payet D 17 + 1	Calleri J 4 + 12	Fletcher A 2 + 14	Obiang P 21 + 1	Ogbonna A 20	Lanzini M 31 + 4	Zaza S 5 + 3	Feghouli S 11 + 10	Arbeloa A 1 + 2	Fernandes E 8 + 20	Cresswell A 24 + 2	Randolph D 22	Sakho D 2 + 2	Fonte J 16	Snodgrass R 8 + 7	Rice D — + 1	*Match No.*
1	2^{2}	3	4	5	6	7^{3}	8	9^{1}	10	11	12	13	14																1
1	10	3	4	5	6	7^{2}	9			11^{1}	8^{3}	2		12	13	14													2
1	5	2	3^{3}	9	8		7			11^{2}	6^{1}	12		14	10		4	13											3
1	8	4	3	5	6		7^{1}				14	2^{3}	10	12	13			9	11^{2}										4
1	8	3		5^{1}	7	2	6^{2}						10	12	14		4	9	11^{3}	13									5
1	8		3		7	2^{1}	6^{3}						10		13		4	9^{2}	11	12	5	14							6
1	10	3	4		8		6^{2}				9^{1}	2^{3}	11			7	5	14	13		12								7
1	5		2		3	14	6						10^{1}	13		7	4	9^{3}	11^{2}			12	8■						8
1	5^{3}		3		2		6						11	13	14	7	4	9^{1}	10^{2}	12		8							9
1	11		3		2		6	12					10			7^{3}	4	9^{1}	13	14		5^{2}	8						10
1	5	3			2		6	10^{2}					11		13	7^{1}	4	9^{3}		14		12	8						11
	5		3■		2	14		9^{2}					10^{3}			7	4	6	13			12	8	1	11^{1}				12
	5	3			2		7	13					10^{3}		12	6	4	9^{1}		14			8	1	11^{2}				13
		2^{2}	3	8			6^{1}	13	14				10		11	7	4	9			12	5^{3}		1					14
	11		3			2	8	7^{2}	12				10			6	4	9^{1}				13	5	1					15
	5		3		2	14	6^{3}	12	11^{1}				10		13	7	4	9^{2}					8	1					16
	5		3		2	14	7	13	11				10^{1}			6^{3}	4	9^{2}				12	8	1					17
	8^{1}		3		7	2	6	9^{3}	11^{2}				10		14		4			13		12	5	1					18
	8		3		7^{3}	2	6^{1}	9^{2}	11				10				4	12		13		14	5	1					19
	10		3		6^{3}	2		14	12				11^{1}			7	4	8^{2}		9■		13	5	1					20
	5^{3}	2	3				6		11			12			14	7	4^{1}	9^{2}		10		13	8	1					21
	10	14	3				6^{2}		11^{3}			2		13		7	4	9		8^{1}		12	5	1					22
	9		4				7		11^{1}			2			14	6^{2}		10		8^{3}		12	5	1		3	13		23
	10	13	4		2^{2}		7		11^{3}					14		8		12		6^{1}			5	1		3	9		24
	11	14	4		2		6							12		7		10		8^{1}		13	5^{3}	1		3	9^{2}		25
	11■		4		2		6	12								7		10^{2}		8		13	5	1		3	9^{1}		26
			4^{1}		2		6^{2}	13	10			12				7		8		9^{3}		14	5	1		3	11		27
	10		4		2^{1}		7^{3}	13	11			14				8		9		6^{2}			5	1		3	12		28
	10		4^{2}	14	6			8	11			2				7^{3}		9				13	5^{1}	1		3	12		29
		4		13	6^{3}			9	11			2		14				7		8		12	5^{1}	1		3	10^{2}		30
	10^{1}	4		5	6		8^{2}	7	11^{3}			2						9				14		1	13	3	12		31
	10^{1}	4		5	8		7	11^{2}				2		12				9		13		14		1		3	6^{3}		32
		4		5	7	12		9^{2}	11			2■		13				10				6		1		3	8^{1}		33
1		4	3	8	6^{1}	7		10						11^{2}				9				5	13		12	2			34
1		4	3	8^{1}	6	7	13	10^{2}						11^{3}				9				5	12			2	14		35
1		4	3		7		6	9^{3}				5		11^{2}	13			10^{1}				14	8			2	12		36
1		4	3			7		9^{2}				5		11^{1}	12			10		13		6	8			2^{3}	14		37
1		3						11				5			12		4	6		10		7^{2}	8			2	9^{1}	13	38

FA Cup

Third Round	Manchester C	(h)	0-5

EFL Cup

Third Round	Accrington S	(h)	1-0
Fourth Round	Chelsea	(h)	2-1
Quarter-Final	Manchester U	(a)	1-4

EFL Checkatrade Trophy (West Ham U U21)

Southern Group D	Coventry C	(a)	2-4
Southern Group D	Wycombe W	(a)	0-3
Southern Group D	Northampton T	(a)	1-1

(*West Ham U U21 won 3-2 on penalties*)

UEFA Europa League

Third Qualifying Round 1st leg	Domzale	(a)	1-2
Third Qualifying Round 2nd leg	Domzale	(h)	3-0

West Ham U won 4-2 on aggregate.

Play-off Round 1st leg	Astra Giurgiu	(a)	1-1
Play-off Round 2nd leg	Astra Giurgiu	(h)	0-1

Astra Giurgiu won 2-1 on aggregate.

WIGAN ATHLETIC

FOUNDATION

Following the demise of Wigan Borough and their resignation from the Football League in 1931, a public meeting was called in Wigan at the Queen's Hall in May 1932 at which a new club, Wigan Athletic, was founded in the hope of carrying on in the Football League. With this in mind, they bought Springfield Park for £2,250, but failed to gain admission to the Football League until 46 years later.

The DW Stadium, Loire Drive, Newtown, Wigan, Lancashire WN5 0UZ.

Telephone: (01942) 774 000.

Fax: (01942) 770 477.

Ticket Office: (0871) 663 3552.

Website: www.wiganlatics.co.uk

Email: feedback@wiganathletic.com

Ground Capacity: 25,133.

Record Attendance: 27,526 v Hereford U, 12 December 1953 (at Springfield Park); 25,133 v Manchester U, FA Premier League, 11 May 2008 (at DW Stadium).

Pitch Measurements: 105m × 68m (115yd × 74.5yd).

Chairman: David Sharpe.

Chief Executive: Jonathan Jackson.

Manager: Paul Cook.

Assistant Manager: Leam Richardson.

Colours: Blue and white striped shirts with red trim, blue shorts with red trim, white socks with blue trim.

Year Formed: 1932.

Turned Professional: 1932.

Club Nickname: 'The Latics'.

Grounds: 1932, Springfield Park; 1999, JJB Stadium (renamed the DW Stadium, 2009).

First Football League Game: 19 August 1978, Division 4, v Hereford U (a) D 0–0 – Brown; Hinnigan, Gore, Gillibrand, Ward, Davids, Corrigan, Purdie, Houghton, Wilkie, Wright.

Record League Victory: 7–1 v Scarborough, Division 3, 11 March 1997 – Lee Butler; John Butler, Sharp (Morgan), Greenall, McGibbon (Biggins (1)), Martinez (1), Diaz (2), Jones (Lancashire (1)), Lowe (2), Rogers, Kilford.

Record Cup Victory: 6–0 v Carlisle U (a), FA Cup 1st rd, 24 November 1934 – Caunce; Robinson, Talbot; Paterson, Watson, Tufnell; Armes (2), Robson (1), Roberts (2), Felton, Scott (1).

Record Defeat: 1–9 v Tottenham H, FA Premier League, 22 November 2009; 0–8 v Chelsea, FA Premier League, 9 May 2010.

HONOURS

League Champions: FL 1 – 2015–16; Second Division – 2002–03; Third Division – 1996–97.
Runners-up: FL C – 2004–05.

FA Cup Winners: 2013.

League Cup: *Runners-up:* 2006.

League Trophy Winners: 1985, 1999.

European Competitions
Europa League: 2013–14.

sky SPORTS FACT FILE

Wigan Athletic have played at Wembley Stadium in five different competitions: FA Trophy (1973), FA Cup (2013, 2014), FA Community Shield (2013), Associate Members Cup (1985, 1999) and Football League play-offs (2000). They missed out on a sixth because the 2006 Football League Cup final was played at Cardiff's Millennium Stadium.

Most League Points (2 for a win): 55, Division 4, 1978–79 and 1979–80.

Most League Points (3 for a win): 100, Division 2, 2002–03.

Most League Goals: 84, Division 3, 1996–97.

Highest League Scorer in Season: Graeme Jones, 31, Division 3, 1996–97.

Most League Goals in Total Aggregate: Andy Liddell, 70, 1998–2004.

Most League Goals in One Match: Not more than three goals by one player.

Most Capped Players: Kevin Kilbane, 22 (110), Republic of Ireland; Henri Camara, 22 (99), Senegal.

Most League Appearances: Kevin Langley, 317, 1981–86, 1990–94.

Youngest League Player: Steve Nugent, 16 years 132 days v Leyton Orient, 16 September 1989.

Record Transfer Fee Received: £15,250,000 from Manchester U for Antonio Valencia, June 2009.

Record Transfer Fee Paid: £6,500,000 to Estudiantes for Mauro Boselli, August 2010.

Football League Record: 1978 Elected to Division 4; 1982–92 Division 3; 1992–93 Division 2; 1993–97 Division 3; 1997–2003 Division 2; 2003–04 Division 1; 2004–05 FL C; 2005–13 FA Premier League; 2013–15 FL C; 2015–16 FL 1; 2016–17 FL C; 2017– FL 1.

LATEST SEQUENCES

Longest Sequence of League Wins: 11, 2.11.2002 – 18.1.2003.

Longest Sequence of League Defeats: 8, 10.9.2011 – 6.11.2011.

Longest Sequence of League Draws: 6, 11.12.2001 – 5.1.2002.

Longest Sequence of Unbeaten League Matches: 25, 8.5.1999 – 3.1.2000.

Longest Sequence Without a League Win: 14, 9.5.1989 – 17.10.1989.

Successive Scoring Runs: 24 from 27.4.1996.

Successive Non-scoring Runs: 4 from 25.4.2015.

MANAGERS

Charlie Spencer 1932–37
Jimmy Milne 1946–47
Bob Pryde 1949–52
Ted Goodier 1952–54
Walter Crook 1954–55
Ron Suart 1955–56
Billy Cooke 1956
Sam Barkas 1957
Trevor Hitchen 1957–58
Malcolm Barrass 1958–59
Jimmy Shirley 1959
Pat Murphy 1959–60
Allenby Chilton 1960
Johnny Ball 1961–63
Allan Brown 1963–66
Alf Craig 1966–67
Harry Leyland 1967–68
Alan Saunders 1968
Ian McNeill 1968–70
Gordon Milne 1970–72
Les Rigby 1972–74
Brian Tiler 1974–76
Ian McNeill 1976–81
Larry Lloyd 1981–83
Harry McNally 1983–85
Bryan Hamilton 1985–86
Ray Mathias 1986–89
Bryan Hamilton 1989–93
Dave Philpotts 1993
Kenny Swain 1993–94
Graham Barrow 1994–95
John Deehan 1995–98
Ray Mathias 1998–99
John Benson 1999–2000
Bruce Rioch 2000–01
Steve Bruce 2001
Paul Jewell 2001–07
Chris Hutchings 2007
Steve Bruce 2007–09
Roberto Martinez 2009–13
Owen Coyle 2013
Uwe Rosler 2013–14
Malky Mackay 2014–15
Gary Caldwell 2015–16
Warren Joyce 2016–17
Paul Cook May 2017–

TEN YEAR LEAGUE RECORD

		P	W	D	L	F	A	Pts	Pos
2007-08	PR Lge	38	10	10	18	34	51	40	14
2008-09	PR Lge	38	12	9	17	34	45	45	11
2009-10	PR Lge	38	9	9	20	37	79	36	16
2010-11	PR Lge	38	9	15	14	40	61	42	16
2011-12	PR Lge	38	11	10	17	42	62	43	15
2012-13	PR Lge	38	9	9	20	47	73	36	18
2013-14	FL C	46	21	10	15	61	48	73	5
2014-15	FL C	46	9	12	25	39	64	39	23
2015-16	FL 1	46	24	15	7	82	45	87	1
2016-17	FL C	46	10	12	24	40	57	42	23

DID YOU KNOW ?

Wigan Athletic wore red and white halved shirts in the early years of their existence, similar to a former kit of their predecessors Wigan Borough The switch to blue and white was made for the 1947–48 season, coinciding with a move from the Cheshire League to the Lancashire Combination.

WIGAN ATHLETIC – SKY BET CHAMPIONSHIP 2016–17 LEAGUE RECORD

Match No.	Date		Venue	Opponents	Result		H/T Score	Lg Pos.	Goalscorers	Attendance
1	Aug	6	A	Bristol C	L	1-2	1-0	20	Gilbey ^{32}	17,635
2		13	H	Blackburn R	W	3-0	2-0	10	Grigg ^{14}, Powell ^{33}, Duffy (og) ^{63}	12,216
3		16	H	Birmingham C	D	1-1	0-1	10	Davies ^{90}	11,182
4		20	A	Nottingham F	L	3-4	1-1	16	Jacobs ^{11}, Grigg 2 $^{65, 86}$	17,750
5		27	H	QPR	L	0-1	0-0	20		10,606
6	Sept	10	A	Sheffield W	L	1-2	1-1	21	Grigg ^{5}	24,860
7		13	A	Norwich C	L	1-2	0-2	23	Gomez ^{72}	25,992
8		17	H	Fulham	D	0-0	0-0	22		10,582
9		23	A	Preston NE	L	0-1	0-1	22		13,077
10		27	H	Wolverhampton W	W	2-1	1-1	21	Le Fondre ^{5}, Grigg ^{88}	10,723
11	Oct	1	A	Brentford	D	0-0	0-0	20		9547
12		15	H	Burton Alb	D	0-0	0-0	22		10,430
13		18	A	Leeds U	D	1-1	0-1	21	MacDonald ^{90}	19,861
14		22	H	Brighton & HA	L	0-1	0-0	23		10,430
15		29	A	Cardiff C	W	1-0	0-0	22	Gomez ^{86}	15,969
16	Nov	5	H	Reading	L	0-3	0-2	22		10,277
17		19	A	Barnsley	D	0-0	0-0	23		12,181
18		28	A	Huddersfield T	W	2-1	1-0	22	Burke, R ^{40}, Wildschut ^{60}	18,943
19	Dec	3	H	Derby Co	L	0-1	0-1	23		12,526
20		10	A	Aston Villa	L	0-1	0-0	23		29,392
21		14	H	Newcastle U	L	0-2	0-1	23		14,562
22		17	H	Ipswich T	L	2-3	1-1	23	Wildschut 2 $^{35, 62}$	10,071
23		26	A	Rotherham U	L	2-3	0-3	23	Wildschut ^{51}, Gomez ^{79}	10,158
24		31	A	Derby Co	D	0-0	0-0	23		29,289
25	Jan	2	H	Huddersfield T	L	0-1	0-0	23		13,480
26		14	A	Burton Alb	W	2-0	1-0	23	Connolly 2 $^{45, 64}$	4411
27		21	H	Brentford	W	2-1	2-0	21	Morsy ^{28}, Dean (og) ^{32}	10,244
28	Feb	3	H	Sheffield W	L	0-1	0-1	22		13,037
29		7	H	Norwich C	D	2-2	0-1	23	Bogle 2 $^{62, 68}$	10,193
30		11	A	Fulham	L	2-3	2-1	23	Malone (og) ^{32}, Jacobs ^{45}	15,552
31		14	A	Wolverhampton W	W	1-0	0-0	22	Buxton ^{88}	17,156
32		18	H	Preston NE	D	0-0	0-0	22		15,117
33		21	A	QPR	L	1-2	1-1	22	Bogle (pen) ^{17}	12,101
34		25	H	Nottingham F	D	0-0	0-0	22		11,254
35	Mar	4	A	Blackburn R	L	0-1	0-0	23		13,165
36		7	A	Birmingham C	W	1-0	1-0	23	Burn ^{19}	15,596
37		11	H	Bristol C	L	0-1	0-0	23		10,787
38		18	H	Aston Villa	L	0-2	0-0	23		14,811
39	Apr	1	A	Newcastle U	L	1-2	0-1	23	Jacobs ^{50}	51,849
40		4	A	Ipswich T	L	0-3	0-2	23		14,661
41		8	H	Rotherham U	W	3-2	1-1	23	Obertan ^{34}, Gilbey ^{65}, Powell ^{90}	10,085
42		13	H	Barnsley	W	3-2	0-1	22	Powell 3 (1 pen) $^{71, 72, 82 (p)}$	10,838
43		17	A	Brighton & HA	L	1-2	0-1	23	Powell ^{85}	29,940
44		22	H	Cardiff C	D	0-0	0-0	23		10,875
45		29	A	Reading	L	0-1	0-1	23		19,177
46	May	7	H	Leeds U	D	1-1	1-0	23	Tunnicliffe ^{6}	15,280

Final League Position: 23

GOALSCORERS

League (40): Powell 6 (1 pen), Grigg 5, Wildschut 4, Bogle 3 (1 pen), Gomez 3, Jacobs 3, Connolly 2, Gilbey 2, Burke, R 1, Burn 1, Buxton 1, Davies 1, Le Fondre 1, MacDonald 1, Morsy 1, Obertan 1, Tunnicliffe 1, own goals 3.
FA Cup (2): Grigg 1, Wildschut 1.
EFL Cup (1): Grigg 1.

Bogdan A 17	Buxton J 39	Morgan C 15 + 5	Burn D 39 + 3	Burke L 4 + 1 / Laurent J — + 1	Gilbey A 11 + 4	Perkins D 24 + 3	Power M 40 + 2	Warnock S 45	Grigg W 24 + 9	Wildschut Y 19 + 6	Jacobs M 39 + 4	Daniels D — + 1	Colclough R 2 + 8	Powell N 10 + 11	Chow T — + 1	Davies C 1 + 13 / Byrne J — + 2	MacDonald S 36 + 3	Garbutt L 7 + 1	Gomez J 12 + 3	Burke R 10	Le Fondre A 3 + 9	Byrne N 6 + 8 / Bruce A — + 2	Knoyle K — + 1	Jaaskelainen J 8 + 1	Woolery K — + 1	Kellett A 4 + 1	Flores J — + 2	Haugaard J 8	Connolly C 14 + 3	Morsy S 13 + 2	Tunnicliffe R 8 + 1	Weir J 1 + 3	Bogle O 12 + 2	Gilks M 13 + 1	Hanson J 14 + 3	Obertan G 7 + 5	Mandron M 1 + 2	*Match No.*
1	2	3	4	5^{3}	6	7	8	9	10^{2}	11^{1}	12	13	14																									1
1		3	4	2^{3}	7	6	9	5	11^{1}	10	12			8^{2}	13	14																						2
1		3	4	2^{3}	7	6^{2}	8^{1}	5	11	10	12			9		14	13																					3
1		2	3	12	9^{1}		7	4	10	5^{2}	11			13		14	6^{3}	8																				4
1	4	3			7^{1}		2	5	11	12	10			9		14	8^{2}	6^{3}	13																			5
1	3			5^{3}	9		6	4	11	14	10			7^{2}			12	8^{1}		2	13																	6
1	3		4		6^{2}		9	5	11	12	10					14	7^{1}		8	2^{3}		13																7
1	3		4		2^{1}		9	5	11^{2}	10	6			14			8		7^{3}		13	12																8
1	3		4			13	8	5	11	10	7^{3}			12		14	6^{1}		9			2^{2}																9
1	3		4			2	8	5	12	10	14			13			6		9^{3}		11^{1}	7^{2}																10
1	3		4			7	8	5	11^{2}	12	10			13			6		9^{1}		14	2^{3}																11
1	3	12	4				7	5	13	10^{2}	8			9		14	6				11^{1}	2^{3}																12
1	3^{2}	13	4			9	8	5	11	12	10^{3}			7			6		14			2^{1}																13
1	3		4			9^{1}	8	5	11^{2}		7			10^{3}		14	6			2	13	12																14
1	3		4			7		5	11^{1}	10^{3}	8^{2}					13	6		9	2		12	14															15
1	3^{2}		4			7	8	5	14	12	10						6		9^{3}	2	11^{1}	13																16
1^{3}	4	3				9	7	5		11^{1}	10			8^{2}		14	6	12		2				13														17
	3		12			9	8	4		11^{3}	10			13		14	7	5		2^{1}		6^{2}		1														18
	4	3				9^{3}	7^{2}	5	12	11	10						6	2	8^{1}		13			1	14													19
	4	3	14			9^{2}	8	5	13	11	10^{3}						6	7	12	2^{1}				1														20
	4	3^{1}	13			9	8	5	11	7	10					14	6^{3}	2^{2}						1		12												21
	3		4			7^{1}	8	2	11	9	6								10			12		1		5												22
	3		4				7	5	9	11	6					10^{2}			8		12	13		1		2^{1}												23
	3		4				7	5	11^{3}	10^{2}	6						8		9		13	12		1		2^{1}	14											24
	4^{2}		3				2	5	9	11	8		12	10^{1}		14	6^{3}		7		13			1														25
	3	13	4				8^{2}	5	11	10^{1}	7						6										12	1	2	9								26
	3	14	4			9^{1}	7^{3}	5	11^{2}		10						6				13							1	2	8	12							27
	3		4			8^{1}	6	5	11^{2}		10						7											1	2	9		12	13					28
	3		4				8	5	12		7						6											1	2	9		10^{1}	11					29
	3		4			10^{2}	9	5	14		7						6											1^{3}	2	8			11^{1}	12	13			30
	3		4				6	5	10		9^{2}						7												2	8			11^{1}	1	12	13		31
	3		4			13	6^{1}	5	9								7^{2}												2	8	10		11	1	12			32
	3		4				6	5	10^{2}																				2	8	9		11	1	7^{1}	12	13	33
	3		4		13		6^{2}	5	14								7													8	9		10^{1}	1	2	12	11^{3}	34
	3		4				12	5	14		10^{2}						6^{3}												7^{1}	9	8		11	1	2	13		35
	3		4	13	9^{3}	12	7^{1}	8			5																		2			14	11	1	6	10^{2}		36
	3		4		9^{2}	7		5^{1}			8						14												2			12	11	1	6	10^{3}	13	37
	3	2	4		14						8		13				7									5^{3}			12	9^{2}			11	1	6	10^{1}		38
	3	14	4		12		6	8			9		13				7^{1}												2	10^{2}			11^{3}	1	5			39
	3	2	4		12	6^{2}	9	8^{3}			11		10				7^{1}												13					1	5	14		40
		3	4		6^{2}		8^{1}	5			9		11	13		14	7											1		12					2	10^{3}		41
	3		4				8	5			10		12	14		13	6											1	2^{1}	9^{2}					7	11^{3}		42
	3		4			10	8	5			7		13	12			6^{3}											1		14	9^{2}				2	11^{1}		43
		3	4			9^{1}		5			7		13	12			6			2		14									10			1	8^{3}	11^{2}		44
		4	5			9	12	6			7			11^{1}			8^{2}			3^{3}									13		10		14	1	2			45
		3^{1}	4			6^{2}	7	8			9^{3}		14	13								12							2		10		11	1	5			46

FA Cup

Third Round	Nottingham F	(h)	2-0
Fourth Round	Manchester U	(a)	0-4

EFL Cup

First Round	Oldham Ath	(a)	1-2

WOLVERHAMPTON WANDERERS

FOUNDATION

Enthusiasts of the game at St Luke's School, Blakenhall formed a club in 1877. In the same neighbourhood a cricket club called Blakenhall Wanderers had a football section. Several St Luke's footballers played cricket for them and shortly before the start of the 1879–80 season the two amalgamated and Wolverhampton Wanderers FC was brought into being.

Molineux Stadium, Waterloo Road, Wolverhampton WV1 4QR.

Telephone: (0871) 222 2220.

Fax: (01902) 687 006.

Ticket Office: (0871) 222 1877.

Website: wolves.co.uk

Email: info@wolves.co.uk

Ground Capacity: 30,852.

Record Attendance: 61,315 v Liverpool, FA Cup 5th rd, 11 February 1939.

Pitch Measurements: 102m × 64m (112yd × 70yd).

Managing Director: Laurie Dalrymple.

Head Coach: Nuno Espirito Santo

Assistant Head Coach: Rui Pedro Silva.

Colours: Gold shirts with thin black stripes and black trim, black shorts with gold trim, gold socks with black trim.

Year Formed: 1877* (*see Foundation*).

Turned Professional: 1888.

Previous Names: 1879, St Luke's combined with Wanderers Cricket Club to become Wolverhampton Wanderers (1923) Ltd. New limited companies followed in 1982 and 1986 (current).

Club Nickname: 'Wolves'.

Grounds: 1877, Windmill Field; 1879, John Harper's Field; 1881, Dudley Road; 1889, Molineux.

First Football League Game: 8 September 1888, Football League, v Aston Villa (h) D 1–1 – Baynton; Baugh, Mason; Fletcher, Allen, Lowder; Hunter, Cooper, Anderson, White, Cannon, (1 og).

Record League Victory: 10–1 v Leicester C, Division 1, 15 April 1938 – Sidlow; Morris, Dowen; Galley, Cullis, Gardiner; Maguire (1), Horace Wright, Westcott (4), Jones (1), Dorsett (4).

Record Cup Victory: 14–0 v Crosswell's Brewery, FA Cup 2nd rd, 13 November 1886 – Ike Griffiths; Baugh, Mason; Pearson, Allen (1), Lowder; Hunter (4), Knight (2), Brodie (4), Bernie Griffiths (2), Wood. Plus one goal 'scrambled through'.

Record Defeat: 1–10 v Newton Heath, Division 1, 15 October 1892.

HONOURS

League Champions: Division 1 – 1953–54, 1957–58, 1958–59; FL C – 2008–09; Division 2 – 1931–32, 1976–77; FL 1 – 2013–14; Division 3 – 1988–89; Division 3N – 1923–24; Division 4 – 1987–88.
Runners-up: Division 1 – 1937–38, 1938–39, 1949–50, 1954–55, 1959–60; Division 2 – 1966–67, 1982–83.

FA Cup Winners: 1893, 1908, 1949, 1960.
Runners-up: 1889, 1896, 1921, 1939.

League Cup Winners: 1974, 1980.

League Trophy Winners: 1988.

Texaco Cup Winners: 1971.

European Competitions
European Cup: 1958–59, 1959–60 *(qf)*.
UEFA Cup: 1971–72 (*runners-up*), 1973–74, 1974–75, 1980–81.
European Cup-Winners' Cup: 1960–61 *(sf)*.

sky SPORTS FACT FILE

Wolverhampton Wanderers are one of only five clubs who can claim to have finished third in the FA Cup. Having been beaten semi-finalists in 1972–73 they travelled to Highbury to take part in the play-off match against Arsenal and finished 3-1 winners with two goals from Derek Dougan and one from Jim McCalliog.

Most League Points (2 for a win): 64, Division 1, 1957–58.

Most League Points (3 for a win): 103, FL 1, 2013–14.

Most League Goals: 115, Division 2, 1931–32.

Highest League Scorer in Season: Dennis Westcott, 38, Division 1, 1946–47.

Most League Goals in Total Aggregate: Steve Bull, 250, 1986–99.

Most League Goals in One Match: 5, Joe Butcher v Accrington, Division 1, 19 November 1892; 5, Tom Phillipson v Barnsley, Division 2, 26 April 1926; 5, Tom Phillipson v Bradford C, Division 2, 25 December 1926; 5, Billy Hartill v Notts Co, Division 2, 12 October 1929; 5, Billy Hartill v Aston Villa, Division 1, 3 September 1934.

Most Capped Player: Billy Wright, 105, England (70 consecutive).

Most League Appearances: Derek Parkin, 501, 1967–82.

Youngest League Player: Jimmy Mullen, 16 years 43 days v Leeds U, 18 February 1939.

Record Transfer Fee Received: £12,000,000 (rising to £14,000,000) from Sunderland for Steven Fletcher, August 2012.

Record Transfer Fee Paid: £15,800,000 to Porto for Ruben Neves, July 2017.

Football League Record: 1888 Founder Member of Football League: 1906–23 Division 2; 1923–24 Division 3 (N); 1924–32 Division 2; 1932–65 Division 1; 1965–67 Division 2; 1967–76 Division 1; 1976–77 Division 2; 1977–82 Division 1; 1982–83 Division 2; 1983–84 Division 1; 1984–85 Division 2; 1985–86 Division 3; 1986–88 Division 4; 1988–89 Division 3; 1989–92 Division 2; 1992–2003 Division 1; 2003–04 FA Premier League; 2004–09 FL C; 2009–12 FA Premier League; 2012–13 FL C; 2013–14 FL 1; 2014– FL C.

MANAGERS

George Worrall 1877–85 *(Secretary-Manager)*
John Addenbrooke 1885–1922
George Jobey 1922–24
Albert Hoskins 1924–26 *(had been Secretary since 1922)*
Fred Scotchbrook 1926–27
Major Frank Buckley 1927–44
Ted Vizard 1944–48
Stan Cullis 1948–64
Andy Beattie 1964–65
Ronnie Allen 1966–68
Bill McGarry 1968–76
Sammy Chung 1976–78
John Barnwell 1978–81
Ian Greaves 1982
Graham Hawkins 1982–84
Tommy Docherty 1984–85
Bill McGarry 1985
Sammy Chapman 1985–86
Brian Little 1986
Graham Turner 1986–94
Graham Taylor 1994–95
Mark McGhee 1995–98
Colin Lee 1998–2000
Dave Jones 2001–04
Glenn Hoddle 2004–06
Mick McCarthy 2006–12
Stale Solbakken 2012–13
Dean Saunders 2013
Kenny Jackett 2013–16
Walter Zenga 2016
Paul Lambert 2016–17
Nuno Espirito Santo May 2017–

LATEST SEQUENCES

Longest Sequence of League Wins: 9, 11.1.2014 – 11.3.2014.

Longest Sequence of League Defeats: 8, 5.12.1981 – 13.2.1982.

Longest Sequence of League Draws: 6, 22.4.1995 – 20.8.1995.

Longest Sequence of Unbeaten League Matches: 21, 15.1.2005 – 13.8.2005.

Longest Sequence Without a League Win: 19, 1.12.1984 – 6.4.1985.

Successive Scoring Runs: 41 from 20.12.1958.

Successive Non-scoring Runs: 7 from 2.2.1985.

TEN YEAR LEAGUE RECORD

		P	W	D	L	F	A	Pts	Pos
2007-08	FL C	46	18	16	12	53	48	70	7
2008-09	FL C	46	27	9	10	80	52	90	1
2009-10	PR Lge	38	9	11	18	32	56	38	15
2010-11	PR Lge	38	11	7	20	46	66	40	17
2011-12	PR Lge	38	5	10	23	40	82	25	20
2012-13	FL C	46	14	9	23	55	69	51	23
2013-14	FL 1	46	31	10	5	89	31	103	1
2014-15	FL C	46	22	12	12	70	56	78	7
2015-16	FL C	46	14	16	16	53	58	58	14
2016-17	FL C	46	16	10	20	54	58	58	15

DID YOU KNOW ?

Wolverhampton Wanderers won the Daily Express National Five-a-side Championship on two occasions. In November 1975 they took the title by beating Tottenham Hotspur 3-1, while 12 months later they won again, beating Stoke City 2-1 in the final.

WOLVERHAMPTON WANDERERS – SKY BET CHAMPIONSHIP 2016–17 LEAGUE RECORD

Match No.	*Date*	*Venue*	*Opponents*	*Result*		*H/T Score*	*Lg Pos.*	*Goalscorers*	*Attendance*
1	Aug 6	A	Rotherham U	D	2-2	1-2	9	Saville [39], Bodvarsson [65]	11,291
2	13	H	Reading	W	2-0	1-0	6	Doherty [42], Mason [47]	20,425
3	16	H	Ipswich T	D	0-0	0-0	8		19,991
4	20	A	Birmingham C	W	3-1	0-1	1	Mason [47], Batth [61], Bodvarsson [89]	18,569
5	27	A	Huddersfield T	L	0-1	0-1	6		19,972
6	Sept 10	H	Burton Alb	D	1-1	0-0	11	Oniangue [77]	22,049
7	13	H	Barnsley	L	0-4	0-0	16		18,668
8	17	A	Newcastle U	W	2-0	1-0	10	Mbemba (og) [29], Helder Costa [62]	52,117
9	24	H	Brentford	W	3-1	0-0	8	Joao Teixeira 2 [47, 57], Ivan Cavaleiro [90]	20,637
10	27	A	Wigan Ath	L	1-2	1-1	11	Oniangue [34]	10,723
11	Oct 1	H	Norwich C	L	1-2	0-1	12	Edwards [80]	18,793
12	15	A	Aston Villa	D	1-1	1-1	11	Helder Costa (pen) [34]	32,533
13	18	A	Brighton & HA	L	0-1	0-1	15		25,231
14	22	H	Leeds U	L	0-1	0-0	18		23,607
15	29	A	Blackburn R	D	1-1	0-1	17	Edwards [78]	10,652
16	Nov 5	H	Derby Co	L	2-3	0-2	19	Helder Costa [61], Edwards [82]	19,858
17	19	A	Preston NE	D	0-0	0-0	19		12,683
18	26	H	Sheffield W	L	0-2	0-2	21		27,293
19	Dec 1	A	QPR	W	2-1	0-0	19	Edwards [60], Helder Costa [67]	12,222
20	10	H	Fulham	D	4-4	1-3	19	Hause [22], Doherty [65], Ivan Cavaleiro [74], Edwards [90]	19,020
21	13	A	Cardiff C	L	1-2	1-0	20	Doherty [2]	14,853
22	17	A	Nottingham F	W	2-0	1-0	18	Helder Costa [40], Ivan Cavaleiro [79]	19,037
23	26	H	Bristol C	W	3-2	1-2	15	Edwards [3], Helder Costa [57], Ivan Cavaleiro (pen) [84]	24,669
24	31	H	QPR	L	1-2	0-0	16	Edwards [61]	21,132
25	Jan 2	A	Sheffield W	D	0-0	0-0	16		30,549
26	14	H	Aston Villa	W	1-0	1-0	16	Mason [15]	27,255
27	21	A	Norwich C	L	1-3	0-1	17	Helder Costa (pen) [57]	26,303
28	31	A	Barnsley	W	3-1	2-0	16	Hause [5], Edwards 2 [36, 77]	11,808
29	Feb 4	A	Burton Alb	L	1-2	1-0	17	Helder Costa (pen) [40]	5608
30	11	H	Newcastle U	L	0-1	0-1	18		24,876
31	14	H	Wigan Ath	L	0-1	0-0	18		17,156
32	24	H	Birmingham C	L	1-2	0-2	20	Dicko [73]	27,541
33	Mar 4	A	Reading	L	1-2	0-0	21	Marshall [50]	18,629
34	7	A	Ipswich T	D	0-0	0-0	21		15,076
35	11	H	Rotherham U	W	1-0	1-0	20	Weimann [45]	20,077
36	14	A	Brentford	W	2-1	0-1	18	Doherty [86], Helder Costa [89]	8732
37	18	A	Fulham	W	3-1	1-0	16	Ivan Cavaleiro [34], Weimann [47], Edwards [72]	20,668
38	Apr 1	H	Cardiff C	W	3-1	2-1	16	Batth 2 [9, 41], Helder Costa [82]	20,519
39	4	H	Nottingham F	W	1-0	0-0	15	Dicko [62]	21,408
40	8	A	Bristol C	L	1-3	0-2	15	Bodvarsson [78]	20,323
41	14	H	Brighton & HA	L	0-2	0-1	16		23,221
42	17	A	Leeds U	W	1-0	1-0	16	Dicko [38]	32,351
43	22	H	Blackburn R	D	0-0	0-0	15		20,249
44	25	H	Huddersfield T	L	0-1	0-1	15		17,505
45	29	A	Derby Co	L	1-3	1-2	15	Marshall [45]	31,051
46	May 7	H	Preston NE	W	1-0	1-0	15	Batth [1]	20,163

Final League Position: 15

GOALSCORERS

League (54): Edwards 10, Helder Costa 10 (3 pens), Ivan Cavaleiro 5 (1 pen), Batth 4, Doherty 4, Bodvarsson 3, Dicko 3, Mason 3, Hause 2, Joao Teixeira 2, Marshall 2, Oniangue 2, Weimann 2, Saville 1, own goal 1.
FA Cup (4): Doherty 1, Helder Costa 1, Stearman 1, Weimann 1.
EFL Cup (4): Coady 1, Helder Costa 1, Mason 1, Wallace 1.
EFL Checkatrade Trophy (10): Enobakhare 3, Herc 3, Dicko 2, Ronan 1 (1 pen), Wilson 1.

Ikeme C 31	Iorfa D 21 + 1	Batth D 39	Hause K 23 + 1	Doherty M 41 + 1	Edwards D 42 + 2	Evans L 12 + 3	Saville G 15 + 9	Wallace J 5 + 4	Bodvarsson J 22 + 20	Henry J 1 + 1	Mason J 9 + 10	Joao Teixeira B 9 + 8	Helder Costa W 30 + 5	Coady C 35 + 5	Price J 17 + 2	Oniangue P 8 + 2	Stearman R 18	Borthwick-Jackson C 6	Gladon P 1 + 1	Ivan Cavaleiro R 17 + 14	Saiss R 19 + 5	Silvio S 4	John O — + 2	Dicko N 19 + 11	Lonergan A 9 + 2	Enobakhare B 8 + 5	Burgoyne H 6	Ronan C 3 + 1	Weimann A 15 + 4	Marshall B 13 + 3	White M 2 + 5	Williamson M 5	Wilson D — + 1	Graham J 1 + 1	Match No.
1	2■	3	4	5	6	7	8	9^{1}	10^{2}	11^{3}	12	13	14																						1
1	3	4		5	6	7	8^{3}	12	10	14	9^{1}	11^{2}		2	13																				2
1	2	3	4	5	8^{1}	7	12	14	10^{3}		9	11^{2}	13	6																					3
1	2	3	4	5	12	7^{3}	14	9	10^{1}		11			6	8^{2}	13																			4
1	3	4		5	6^{1}		8^{2}	11^{3}	10		9	12	13	2	7	14																			5
1		3		2	14				13		12	8^{2}	9	7		6	4	5	10^{3}	11^{1}															6
1	2^{1}	3		5				9^{2}	10		11	13	12	7	6^{3}	8	4			14															7
1	3	4		2	6				10^{2}		13	11^{3}	9^{1}	14		8		5		12	7														8
1	3	4		2	8				11		13	10^{3}	7^{1}	14		9^{2}		5		12	6														9
1	3	4		2	6		13					11^{2}	9			8^{1}			12	10^{3}	7	5	14												10
1	3	4		2	6						14	11^{2}	9	12		8^{3}		5^{1}		10	7			13											11
1	2	3	4	5	9				11^{1}		14		7^{2}	8		10^{3}				13	6			12											12
1	2	3	4	5	9				13			14	6	7^{1}		10^{2}				12	8			11^{3}											13
1		3	4	5^{2}	7				10			9^{3}	6	13						12	8	2	14	11^{1}											14
1^{1}		3	4	2	8			11^{3}	10			13	9	6				5		14	7^{2}				12										15
	3	4		2	8		12	14	10^{2}			6^{1}	9	7^{3}				5		11				13	1										16
	2	3	4	5			10	12	11				8^{2}	6	7^{3}					14				13	1	9^{1}									17
	2		4	5	9		10^{2}		11^{1}			13	8^{3}	6	7		3			14				12	1										18
1^{2}	2	3		5	6		12		13				9	8			4			11^{1}	7			10^{3}	14										19
	2	3	4	5	9				12			13	8^{1}	6^{3}	14					10	7^{2}			11			1								20
	2	3		5	6		8		14			12	9^{3}				4			11^{1}	7			10^{2}		13	1								21
1		3		5	6				14				8^{2}	2	7		4			10	12			11^{3}		9^{1}		13							22
1		3		5	7				13		12		8	2	6		4			10				11^{2}		9^{1}									23
1		3		5	6				13		12		8	2	7		4			10				11^{2}		9^{1}									24
1		3		5	6				11		9		8^{1}	2	7		4			12				13				10^{2}							25
1		3		5	6^{1}		13		14		9		8	2	7		4			10^{2}				11^{3}		12									26
1■	2	3		5	6				11^{2}		9^{3}		8		7		4			10^{1}				14		13			12						27
		3	4	5	6	14	13		11		8			2^{1}	7											9^{3}	1	10^{2}	12						28
1			4	5	10	7	8^{2}		14				6^{3}	2			3							11		12			9^{1}	13					29
1		3		5	6	12			13				10	2	7^{2}		4							11		9^{3}			8^{1}	14					30
1		3		5	6	7^{1}			11				8	13			4									9^{3}		10	14	2^{2}	12				31
1		3		5	9		7^{1}		11				8	2	6		4							12					10						32
1	2		4	14	8		5^{3}		13				9	6^{1}							7			10^{2}					12	11		3■			33
1		3	4	2	9		5		11				12		6						7								8^{1}	10					34
1			4		9		5		12				8^{2}	2	6^{3}					14	7								11	10^{1}	13	3			35
1		3	4	5	9	6	7^{2}						10	2						12				11^{1}					8^{3}	13	14				36
1		3	4	5	7	6	14						8^{2}	2						9^{3}	13			12					11	10^{1}					37
		3	4	5	6	7	14		13				8	2						9^{2}	12				1				11^{3}	10^{1}					38
		3	4	5	7	6			14					2						9^{3}	13			8^{1}	1				11	10^{2}	12				39
		3	4	5	6	7^{2}			13					2						12	14			11^{3}	1				8	10	9^{1}				40
		3	4	5	7				11^{1}					2						9	6			12	1				8	10^{2}			13		41
			14	5	7	12	10^{2}		13					2			4				6			11^{1}	1				9	8^{3}		3			42
				5^{3}	7		10		13					2			4			12	6			11^{1}	1				9	8^{2}	14	3			43
	2	3			7				11^{1}		12				6		4					5^{2}		14			1		8	10	9^{3}			13	44
			4		8	6	5		13					2						11■	7			10^{1}		12	1			9^{2}		3			45
	14	3	4		6				13		12			2							7	5		11^{1}		9	1		8^{3}					10^{2}	46

FA Cup

Third Round	Stoke C	(a)	2-0
Fourth Round	Liverpool	(a)	2-1
Fifth Round	Chelsea	(h)	0-2

EFL Cup

First Round	Crawley T	(h)	2-1
Second Round	Cambridge U	(h)	2-1
Third Round	Newcastle U	(a)	0-2

EFL Checkatrade Trophy (Wolverhampton W U21)

Northern Group B	Chesterfield	(a)	1-2
Northern Group B	Crewe Alex	(a)	3-2
Northern Group B	Accrington S	(h)	4-0
Second Round North	Sunderland U21	(h)	1-1
(*Wolverhampton W U21 won 4-3 on penalties*)			
Third Round	Swansea C U21	(a)	1-2

WYCOMBE WANDERERS

FOUNDATION

In 1887 a group of young furniture trade workers called a meeting at the Steam Engine public house with the aim of forming a football club and entering junior football. It is thought that they were named after the famous FA Cup winners, The Wanderers, who had visited the town in 1877 for a tie with the original High Wycombe club. It is also possible that they played informally before their formation, although there is no proof of this.

Adams Park, Hillbottom Road, High Wycombe, Buckinghamshire HP12 4HJ.

Telephone: (01494) 472 100. ***Fax:*** (01494) 441 589.

Ticket Office: (01494) 441 118.

Website: www.wycombewanderers.co.uk.com

Email: wwfc@wwfc.com

Ground Capacity: 9,552.

Record Attendance: 15,850 v St Albans C, FA Amateur Cup 4th rd, 25 February 1950 (at Loakes Park); 9,921 v Fulham, FA Cup 3rd rd, 9 January 2002 (at Adams Park).

Pitch Measurements: 100.5m × 64m (110yd × 70yd).

Chairman: Andrew Woodward.

Manager: Gareth Ainsworth.

Assistant Manager: Richard Dobson.

Colours: Light blue and dark blue quartered shirts, dark blue shorts with light blue trim, dark blue socks with light blue hoops.

Year Formed: 1887. ***Turned Professional:*** 1974.

Club Nicknames: 'The Chairboys' (after High Wycombe's tradition of furniture making), 'The Blues'.

Grounds: 1887, The Rye; 1893, Spring Meadow; 1895, Loakes Park; 1899, Daws Hill Park; 1901, Loakes Park; 1990, Adams Park.

First Football League Game: 14 August 1993, Division 3 v Carlisle U (a) D 2–2: Hyde; Cousins, Horton (Langford), Kerr, Crossley, Ryan, Carroll, Stapleton, Thompson, Scott, Guppy (1) (Hutchinson), (1 og).

Record League Victory: 5–0 v Burnley, Division 2, 15 April 1997 – Parkin; Cousins, Bell, Kavanagh, McCarthy, Forsyth, Carroll (2p) (Simpson), Scott (Farrell), Stallard (1), McGavin (1) (Read (1)), Brown.
5–0 v Northampton T, Division 2, 4 January 2003 – Talia; Senda, Ryan, Thomson, McCarthy, Johnson, Bulman, Simpson (1), Faulconbridge (Harris), Dixon (1) (Roberts 3), Brown (Currie).
5–0 v Hartlepool U, FL 1, 25 February 2012 – Bull; McCoy, Basey, Eastmond (Bloomfield), Laing, Doherty (1), Hackett, Lewis, Bevon (2) (Strevons), Hayes (2) (McClure), McNamee.

Record Cup Victory: 5–0 v Hitchin T (a), FA Cup 2nd rd, 3 December 1994 – Hyde; Cousins, Brown, Crossley, Evans, Ryan (1), Carroll, Bell (1), Thompson, Garner (3) (Hemmings), Stapleton (Langford).
5–0 v Chesterfield (a), FA Cup 2nd rd, 3 December 2017 – Blackman; Harriman, Stewart (1), Pierre, Jacobson, Bloomfield (Wood), O'Nien, Gape (Bean), Kashket (3) (Cowan-Hall), Hayes (1), Akinfenwa.

HONOURS

League Champions: Conference – 1992–93.
Runners-up: FL 2 – (3rd) 2008–09, 2010–11 *(promoted to FL 1)*; Conference – 1991–92.

FA Cup: semi-final – 2001.

League Cup: semi-final – 2007.

FA Amateur Cup Winners: 1931.

sky SPORTS FACT FILE

Wycombe Wanderers gained their first significant prize on Easter Monday 1902 when they defeated Slough 3-0 at Maidenhead to win the Berks & Bucks Senior Cup. This was the fourth occasion Wanderers had made it to the final and each time previously they had lost out to Marlow for the trophy.

Record Defeat: 0–7 v Shrewsbury T, Johnstone's Paint Trophy, 7 October 2008.

Most League Points (3 for a win): 84, FL 2, 2014–15.

Most League Goals: 72, FL 2, 2005–06.

Highest League Scorer in Season: Scott McGleish, 25, 2007–08.

Most League Goals in Total Aggregate: Nathan Tyson, 42, 2004–06.

Most League Goals in One Match: 3, Miquel Desouza v Bradford C, Division 2, 2 September 1995; 3, John Williams v Stockport Co, Division 2, 24 February 1996; 3, Mark Stallard v Walsall, Division 2, 21 October 1997; 3, Sean Devine v Reading, Division 2, 2 October 1999; 3, Sean Divine v Bury, Division 2, 26 February 2000; 3, Stuart Roberts v Northampton T, Division 2, 4 January 2003; 3, Nathan Tyson v Lincoln C, FL 2, 5 March 2005; 3, Nathan Tyson v Kidderminster H, FL 2, 2 April 2005; 3, Nathan Tyson v Stockport Co, FL 2, 10 September 2005; 3, Kevin Betsy v Mansfield T, FL 2, 24 September 2005; 3, Scott McGleish v Mansfield T, FL 2, 8 January 2008; 3, Stuart Beavon v Bury, FL 1, 17 March 2012.

Most Capped Player: Mark Rogers, 7, Canada; Marvin McCoy, 7 (8), Antigua and Barbuda.

Most League Appearances: Matt Bloomfield, 379, 2003–17.

Youngest League Player: Jordon Ibe, 15 years 311 days v Hartlepool U, 15 October 2011.

Record Transfer Fee Received: £675,000 from Nottingham F for Nathan Tyson, January 2006.

Record Transfer Fee Paid: £200,000 to Barnet for Sean Devine, April 1999; £200,000 to Barnet for Darren Currie, July 2001.

Football League Record: 1993 Promoted to Division 3 from Conference; 1993–94 Division 3; 1994–2004 Division 2; 2004–09 FL 2; 2009–10 FL 1; 2010–11 FL 2; 2011–12 FL 1; 2012– FL 2.

MANAGERS

First coach appointed 1951.
Prior to Brian Lee's appointment in 1969 the team was selected by a Match Committee which met every Monday evening.

James McCormack 1951–52
Sid Cann 1952–61
Graham Adams 1961–62
Don Welsh 1962–64
Barry Darvill 1964–68
Brian Lee 1969–76
Ted Powell 1976–77
John Reardon 1977–78
Andy Williams 1978–80
Mike Keen 1980–84
Paul Bence 1984–86
Alan Gane 1986–87
Peter Suddaby 1987–88
Jim Kelman 1988–90
Martin O'Neill 1990–95
Alan Smith 1995–96
John Gregory 1996–98
Neil Smillie 1998–99
Lawrie Sanchez 1999–2003
Tony Adams 2003–04
John Gorman 2004–06
Paul Lambert 2006–08
Peter Taylor 2008–09
Gary Waddock 2009–12
Gareth Ainsworth November 2012–

LATEST SEQUENCES

Longest Sequence of League Wins: 6, 12.11.2016 – 17.12.2016.

Longest Sequence of League Defeats: 6, 18.3.2006 – 17.4.2006.

Longest Sequence of League Draws: 5, 24.1.2004 – 21.2.2004.

Longest Sequence of Unbeaten League Matches: 21, 6.8.2005 – 10.12.2005.

Longest Sequence Without a League Win: 13, 10.1.2004 – 20.3.2004.

Successive Scoring Runs: 16 from 13.9.2014.

Successive Non-scoring Runs: 5 from 15.10.1996.

TEN YEAR LEAGUE RECORD

		P	*W*	*D*	*L*	*F*	*A*	*Pts*	*Pos*
2007-08	FL 2	46	22	12	12	56	42	78	7
2008-09	FL 2	46	20	18	8	54	33	78	3
2009-10	FL 1	46	10	15	21	56	76	45	22
2010-11	FL 2	46	22	14	10	69	50	80	3
2011-12	FL 1	46	11	10	25	65	88	43	21
2012-13	FL 2	46	17	9	20	50	60	60	15
2013-14	FL 2	46	12	14	20	46	54	50	22
2014-15	FL 2	46	23	15	8	67	45	84	4
2015-16	FL 2	46	17	13	16	45	44	64	13
2016-17	FL 2	46	19	12	15	58	53	69	9

DID YOU KNOW?

Wycombe Wanderers played their 1,000th Football League game away to Luton on 24 March 2015 and came away with a 3-2 win. The final game of the 2016–17 season at home to Cambridge United was their 1,100th League fixture and was also won, 1-0.

WYCOMBE WANDERERS – SKY BET LEAGUE TWO 2016–17 LEAGUE RECORD

Match No.	*Date*	*Venue*	*Opponents*	*Result*	*H/T Score*	*Lg Pos.*	*Goalscorers*	*Attendance*
1	Aug 6	A	Crawley T	L 0-1	0-0	20		2471
2	13	H	Grimsby T	W 2-1	0-0	13	Jombati [55], Stewart [90]	3686
3	16	H	Accrington S	D 1-1	1-0	14	Akinfenwa [5]	2747
4	20	A	Blackpool	D 0-0	0-0	15		3144
5	27	H	Colchester U	L 0-2	0-0	19		3439
6	Sept 3	A	Luton T	L 1-4	0-1	22	Bloomfield [63]	8097
7	10	A	Portsmouth	L 2-4	2-3	22	Hayes 2 [10, 45]	16,262
8	17	H	Stevenage	W 1-0	1-0	19	Southwell [45]	3181
9	24	A	Carlisle U	L 0-1	0-0	19		4354
10	27	H	Crewe Alex	W 5-1	3-0	19	Wood [19], Cowan-Hall [39], Gape [43], Kashket 2 [63, 69]	2572
11	Oct 1	H	Exeter C	W 1-0	0-0	15	Akinfenwa [85]	3297
12	8	A	Yeovil T	L 0-1	0-1	16		3187
13	15	A	Mansfield T	D 1-1	1-0	16	Bloomfield [23]	2898
14	22	H	Barnet	L 0-2	0-0	21		3596
15	29	A	Doncaster R	D 2-2	1-2	21	Bloomfield 2 [19, 78]	5287
16	Nov 12	H	Morecambe	W 2-0	0-0	16	Pierre [47], O'Nien [81]	3019
17	19	A	Cambridge U	W 2-1	1-0	10	Hayes (pen) [6], Pierre [90]	4139
18	22	A	Newport Co	W 1-0	0-0	8	Jombati [88]	2010
19	26	H	Hartlepool U	W 2-0	1-0	6	Kashket 2 [23, 80]	3288
20	Dec 10	A	Notts Co	W 2-0	1-0	6	Akinfenwa [37], Kashket [55]	3680
21	17	H	Leyton Orient	W 1-0	0-0	6	Kashket [50]	4517
22	26	A	Plymouth Arg	D 3-3	1-2	6	Kashket [8], Akinfenwa [59], Weston [89]	12,210
23	30	A	Cheltenham T	W 1-0	1-0	5	Kashket [9]	3761
24	Jan 2	H	Newport Co	W 2-1	0-0	5	Wood [70], Cowan-Hall [80]	4288
25	14	H	Yeovil T	D 1-1	1-1	5	Jacobson (pen) [26]	3493
26	21	H	Luton T	D 1-1	0-0	5	Akinfenwa [82]	5387
27	31	A	Exeter C	L 2-4	1-1	7	Thompson [38], Jakubiak [89]	3656
28	Feb 4	H	Portsmouth	W 1-0	0-0	6	Kashket [48]	6028
29	11	A	Stevenage	L 0-3	0-2	8		2602
30	14	A	Crewe Alex	L 1-2	0-1	8	Akinfenwa [75]	2896
31	18	H	Carlisle U	L 1-2	1-2	9	Akinfenwa [2]	3858
32	21	A	Colchester U	L 0-1	0-1	10		3031
33	25	H	Crawley T	L 1-2	1-1	11	Akinfenwa [15]	3206
34	28	A	Accrington S	D 2-2	0-1	11	Akinfenwa 2 [56, 58]	1045
35	Mar 4	A	Grimsby T	W 2-1	0-1	10	Collins (og) [67], Cowan-Hall [71]	4668
36	11	H	Blackpool	D 0-0	0-0	11		3774
37	14	H	Plymouth Arg	D 1-1	1-0	11	Weston [18]	3638
38	18	A	Hartlepool U	W 2-0	1-0	10	Akinfenwa [24], Cowan-Hall [90]	3356
39	25	H	Notts Co	L 0-1	0-1	11		4362
40	Apr 1	A	Leyton Orient	W 2-0	2-0	10	Bloomfield [37], Weston [38]	4526
41	8	H	Cheltenham T	D 3-3	2-2	11	Thompson 2 [21, 43], Jacobson (pen) [81]	3596
42	14	H	Mansfield T	L 0-1	0-1	13		4218
43	17	A	Barnet	W 2-0	1-0	10	Saunders [21], Jacobson (pen) [90]	2507
44	22	H	Doncaster R	W 2-1	2-1	9	O'Nien 2 [9, 32]	4587
45	29	A	Morecambe	D 1-1	0-0	11	Akinfenwa [89]	1742
46	May 6	H	Cambridge U	W 1-0	0-0	9	Kashket [65]	6313

Final League Position: 9

GOALSCORERS

League (58): Akinfenwa 12, Kashket 10, Bloomfield 5, Cowan-Hall 4, Hayes 3 (1 pen), Jacobson 3 (3 pens), O'Nien 3, Thompson 3, Weston 3, Jombati 2, Pierre 2, Wood 2, Gape 1, Jakubiak 1, Saunders 1, Southwell 1, Stewart 1, own goal 1.
FA Cup (12): Hayes 3 (1 pen), Kashket 3, Akinfenwa 2, Cowan-Hall 1, Stewart 1, Thompson 1, Wood 1.
EFL Cup (0).
EFL Checkatrade Trophy (15): Akinfenwa 4 (1 pen), Kashket 3, Thompson 3, Freeman 1, Hayes 1, McGinn 1, Rowe 1, Stewart 1.

Brown S 3	Harriman M 38	Stewart A 30 + 1	Pierre A 38 + 1	Jacobson J 39	Wood S 21 + 11	Bean M 15 + 4	O'Nien L 28 + 3	Thompson G 21 + 21	Southwell D 11 + 2	Weston M 9 + 10	Bloomfield M 24 + 9	Akinfenwa A 32 + 10	Jombati S 23 + 2	Dawson C 1	McGinn S 3 + 2	Rowe D 10 + 2	Freeman N 4 + 10	Blackman J 42	Hayes P 18 + 5	De Havilland W 12 + 4	Gape D 29 + 3	Cowan-Hall P 20 + 8	Kashket S 13 + 8	Saunders S 11 + 6	Muller M 7 + 2	Jakubiak A 4 + 6	*Match No.*
1	2¹	3	4	5	6	7	8²	9	10	11³	12	13	14														1
	6	3	4	5	9			10	11²		7¹	12	2	1	8³	13	14										2
	9	4	3	2²	6³	14		13	11		7	10¹	5		8		12	1									3
	6	3	4	5		7		11²	12		13	10¹	2			8³	9	1	14								4
	2	3	4		9³	7		6²	11		14	10	5			8¹	13	1	12								5
	3	4						13	11²		8	14	2		9³	6	7¹	1	10	5	12						6
	2	4	3		11			9	12		8	13	5¹		14	6³		1	10²		7						7
	5	3	4		9¹			6	11²		7		2			13		1	10		8	12					8
	5	3	4		9			6			8¹	10²	2		12			1	11²		7	13	14				9
	2	3	4	5	9			6³			14					7	13	1	10¹		8	11²	12				10
	2	3	4	5	9¹			6			14	12				7		1	10²		8	11³	13				11
	2	3	4³	5	9			6¹			13	12				7	14	1	10		8²	11					12
	2	3	4	5	13			12			6¹	11				8		1	10²		7	9					13
	2	3	4	5				6¹		12■	14	10				7	9²	1			8³	11	13				14
	2		4	5	13		8³	14			9²	12				6¹		1	11	3	7	10					15
	2	3	4	5		12	8	13			6	10						1	11¹		7²	9					16
	2	3	4	5	12		8	13			6	10						1	9¹		7	11²					17
		3	4	5	12	7¹	8	9			6	13	2					1	10³			11²	14				18
	2	3	4	5	12	14	7	13			6³	10¹						1	11²		8		9				19
	2	3	4	5	13	14	7	12			6²	10■						1			8	11³	9¹				20
	2	3	4	5	12		6	9		13	8							1			7	11²	10¹				21
	2²	3	4	5			6³	14		13	8	10	12					1			7	11	9¹				22
1		3	4	2	14		7	12		13	6²	10	5								8	9³	11¹				23
1		3	4	5	9		8	6¹		10²		12	2						11³		7	13	14				24
		3³	4	5	8²		6	14		11¹		10	2					1	13	12	7	9					25
		3	4	5	8		6					10	2					1	9¹		7	11²	13	12			26
	2		13			6		10²		11¹			5				14	1		4	7		9³	8	3	12	27
		3	4²	5	8		6	14				10	2					1	9¹	13	7		11³	12			28
		3	4	5	8		7²	14		13³		10	2					1			6		11¹	9		12	29
		3	4²	5	8¹		6	13				10	2					1		12	7		11³	14		9	30
	2	4		5	14		8	13			12	10						1		3	7²	9¹		6³		11	31
	2	4		5■	14	7¹	8	13				10						1		3²		9		6	12	11³	32
	5				11		8³			14	6¹	10	2					1		3	7	9²		12	4	13	33
	2			5	8	6	13	11			7²	10						1		4		9¹			3	12	34
	2			5	9¹	8	12	6²	11³	14	7	10						1		3		13			4		35
	2		4	5	7³	6	9		10¹	12		11						1				8²		14	3	13	36
	2		4	5		8	6		11²	9³		10						1		13	7	12		14	3¹		37
	2		3³	5			6	14	11¹	9		10²						1		4	7	13■		8	12		38
	2			5			6	12		9³		10					14	1	13	4	7²			8	3	11¹	39
	2		3	5	13		8³	9		11¹	7	10					12	1		4	14			6²			40
	2		4	5	8			9	10¹		6	12					11	1	14	3²	7³		13				41
	2		3	5		6	7	9³		13	8²	10	4				12	1					11¹			14	42
	2		3	5		6	7²	13			14	10	4				12	1	9¹				11³	8			43
	2		4	5		6	7	12			8	10	3					1			13		11¹	9²			44
	2	13	4	5²		6	7	9¹		14		10	3					1	11³			12		8			45
	2		4	5		7	12	14		11¹	6²	10	3					1				13	9³	8			46

FA Cup

First Round	Portsmouth	(a)	2-1
Second Round	Chesterfield	(a)	5-0
Third Round	Stourbridge	(h)	2-1
Fourth Round	Tottenham H	(a)	3-4

EFL Cup

First Round	Bristol C	(h)	0-1

EFL Checkatrade Trophy

Southern Group D	Northampton T	(a)	3-0
Southern Group D	West Ham U U21	(h)	3-0
Southern Group D	Coventry C	(h)	2-4
Second Round South	Millwall	(a)	3-1
Third Round	Blackpool	(a)	1-1
(*Wycombe W won 5-4 on penalties*)			
Quarter-Final	Mansfield T	(a)	2-1
Semi-Final	Coventry C	(a)	1-2

YEOVIL TOWN

FOUNDATION

One of the prime movers of Yeovil football was Ernest J. Sercombe. His association with the club began in 1895 as a playing member of Yeovil Casuals, of which team he became vice-captain and in his last season 1899–1900, he was chosen to play for Somerset against Devon. Upon the reorganisation of the club, he became secretary of the old Yeovil Town FC and with the amalgamation with Petters United in 1914, he continued to serve until his resignation in 1930.

Huish Park, Lufton Way, Yeovil, Somerset BA22 8YF.

Telephone: (01935) 423 662.

Fax: (01935) 473 956.

Ticket Office: (01935) 847 888.

Website: www.ytfc.net

Email: info@ytfc.net

Ground Capacity: 9,565.

HONOURS

League Champions: FL 2 – 2004–05; Conference – 2002–03.
Runners-up: Conference – 2000–01.

FA Cup: 5th rd – 1949.

League Cup: never past 2nd rd.

Record Attendance: 16,318 v Sunderland, FA Cup 4th rd, 29 January 1949 (at Huish); 9,527 v Leeds U, FL 1, 25 April 2008 (at Huish Park).

Pitch Measurements: 108m × 67m (118yd × 73yd).

Chairman: John R. Fry.

Manager: Darren Way.

Assistant Manager: Terry Skiverton.

Colours: Green and white hooped shirts with black sleeves, green shorts, white socks with green trim.

Year Formed: 1895.

Turned Professional: 1921.

Previous Names: 1895, Yeovil Casuals; 1907, Yeovil Town; 1915, Yeovil & Petters United; 1946, Yeovil Town.

Club Nickname: 'The Glovers'.

Grounds: 1895, Pen Mill Ground; 1921, Huish; 1990, Huish Park.

First Football League Game: 9 August 2003, Division 3 v Rochdale (a) W 3-1: Weale; Williams (Lindegaard), Crittenden, Lockwood, O'Brien, Pluck (Rodrigues), Gosling (El Kholti), Way, Jackson, Gall (2), Johnson (1).

Record League Victory: 6–1 v Oxford U, FL 2, 18 September 2004 – Weale; Rose, O'Brien, Way, Skiverton, Fontaine, Caceres (Tarachulski), Johnson, Jevons (3), Stoicers (2) (Mirza), Terry (Gall 1).

Record Cup Victory: 12–1 v Westbury United, FA Cup 1st qual rd, 1923–24.

Record Defeat: 0–8 v Manchester United, FA Cup 5th rd, 12 February 1949.

Most League Points (3 for a win): 83, FL 2, 2004–05.

Most League Goals: 90, FL 2, 2004–05.

sky SPORTS FACT FILE

Yeovil Town, then known as Yeovil & Petters United, reorganised as a limited company in the summer of 1923. The board appointed the former Queens Park Rangers winger Jack Gregory as player-manager and he achieved instant success, with the Glovers winning the Western Section of the Southern League by a six-point margin in 1923–24.

Highest League Scorer in Season: Phil Jevons, 27, 2004–05.

Most League Goals in Total Aggregate: Phil Jevons, 42, 2004–06.

Most League Goals in One Match: 3, Phil Jevons v Oxford U, FL 2, 18 September 2004; 3, Phil Jevons v Chester C, FL 2, 30 October 2004; 3, Phil Jevons v Bristol R, FL 2, 12 February 2005; 3, Arron Davies v Chesterfield, FL 1, 4 March 2006; 3, Jack Compton v AFC Wimbledon, FL 2, 30 January 2016.

Most Capped Players: Joel Grant, 12 (14), Jamaica.

Most League Appearances: Nathan Smith, 229, 2008–11 and 2014–17.

Youngest League Player: Ollie Bassett, 17 years 197 days v Crawley T, 19 September 2015.

Record Transfer Fee Received: A combined £1,000,000 from Nottingham F for Arron Davies and Chris Cohen, July 2007.

Record Transfer Fee Paid: £250,000 to Quilmes for Pablo Bastianini, August 2005.

Football League Record: 2003 Promoted to Division 3 from Conference; 2003–04 Division 3; 2004–05 FL 2; 2005–13 FL 1; 2013–14 FL C; 2014–15 FL 1; 2015– FL 2.

LATEST SEQUENCES

Longest Sequence of League Wins: 8, 29.12.2012 – 16.2.2013.

Longest Sequence of League Defeats: 6, 10.3.2015 – 6.4.2015.

Longest Sequence of League Draws: 3, 15.3.2017 – 25.3.2017.

Longest Sequence of Unbeaten League Matches: 9, 29.12.2012 – 23.2.2013.

Longest Sequence Without a League Win: 16, 26.9.2015 – 28.12.2015.

Successive Scoring Runs: 22 from 30.10.2004.

Successive Non-scoring Runs: 4 from 18.2.2017.

MANAGERS

Jack Gregory 1922–28
Tommy Lawes 1928–29
Dave Pratt 1929–33
Louis Page 1933–35
Dave Halliday 1935–38
Billy Kingdon 1938–46
Alec Stock 1946–49
George Patterson 1949–51
Harry Lowe 1951–53
Ike Clarke 1953–57
Norman Dodgin 1957
Jimmy Baldwin 1957–60
Basil Hayward 1960–64
Glyn Davies 1964–65
Joe McDonald 1965–67
Ron Saunders 1967–69
Mike Hughes 1969–72
Cecil Irwin 1972–75
Stan Harland 1975–81
Barry Lloyd 1978–81
Malcolm Allison 1981
Jimmy Giles 1981–83
Trevor Finnigan and Mike Hughes 1983
Steve Coles 1983–84
Ian McFarlane 1984
Gerry Gow 1984–87
Brian Hall 1987–90
Clive Whitehead 1990–91
Steve Rutter 1991–93
Brian Hall 1994–95
Graham Roberts 1995–98
Colin Lippiatt 1998–99
Steve Thompson 1999–2000
Dave Webb 2000
Gary Johnson 2001–05
Steve Thompson 2005–06
Russell Slade 2006–09
Terry Skiverton 2009–12
Gary Johnson 2012–15
Terry Skiverton 2015
Paul Sturrock 2015
Darren Way December 2015–

TEN YEAR LEAGUE RECORD

		P	W	D	L	F	A	Pts	Pos
2007-08	FL 1	46	14	10	22	38	59	52	18
2008-09	FL 1	46	12	15	19	41	66	51	17
2009-10	FL 1	46	13	14	19	55	59	53	15
2010-11	FL 1	46	16	11	19	56	66	59	14
2011-12	FL 1	46	14	12	20	59	80	54	17
2012-13	FL 1	46	23	8	15	71	56	77	4
2013-14	FL C	46	8	13	25	44	75	37	24
2014-15	FL 1	46	10	10	26	36	75	40	24
2015-16	FL 2	46	11	15	20	43	59	48	19
2016-17	FL 2	46	11	17	18	49	64	50	20

DID YOU KNOW ?

Before entering the Football League Yeovil Town were renowned for their FA Cup giant-killing feats, but since their promotion for the 1993–94 season they have often been victims themselves. Five non-league teams have eliminated them in this time: Rushden & D, Torquay U, Oxford U, Fleetwood T and Solihull Moors.

YEOVIL TOWN – SKY BET LEAGUE TWO 2016–17 LEAGUE RECORD

Match No.	*Date*	*Venue*	*Opponents*	*Result*	*H/T Score*	*Lg Pos.*	*Goalscorers*	*Attendance*
1	Aug 6	H	Notts Co	W 2-0	2-0	4	Dawson ^{16}, Khan ^{23}	3715
2	13	A	Luton T	D 1-1	0-1	4	Eaves ^{78}	7800
3	16	A	Mansfield T	L 0-1	0-0	12		2503
4	20	H	Morecambe	L 0-1	0-0	16		2937
5	27	A	Doncaster R	L 1-4	0-1	21	Hedges ^{55}	4686
6	Sept 3	H	Blackpool	L 0-3	0-0	23		3108
7	10	H	Hartlepool U	L 1-2	0-0	23	Butcher ^{56}	2749
8	17	A	Leyton Orient	W 1-0	0-0	21	Eaves ^{76}	4557
9	24	H	Cheltenham T	W 4-2	3-1	19	Khan ^{6}, Ward ^{16}, Dolan ^{45}, Eaves ^{90}	3448
10	27	A	Cambridge U	L 0-1	0-0	20		3556
11	Oct 1	A	Plymouth Arg	L 1-4	1-2	21	Ward ^{45}	8529
12	8	H	Wycombe W	W 1-0	1-0	18	Hedges ^{36}	3187
13	15	H	Newport Co	W 1-0	0-0	15	Butler (og) ^{81}	3353
14	22	A	Crewe Alex	W 1-0	0-0	13	Dolan ^{62}	3659
15	29	H	Grimsby T	D 0-0	0-0	11		3733
16	Nov 12	A	Stevenage	D 2-2	0-0	10	Hedges ^{48}, Whitfield ^{90}	2457
17	19	H	Colchester U	W 2-1	0-0	8	Zoko ^{86}, Campbell ^{90}	2985
18	26	A	Accrington S	D 1-1	0-0	13	Khan ^{51}	1263
19	Dec 3	H	Crawley T	W 5-0	3-0	6	Eaves ^{16}, Hedges ^{28}, Khan 2 $^{42, 51}$, Zoko ^{73}	2817
20	10	H	Barnet	L 0-1	0-0	10		3254
21	17	A	Carlisle U	L 1-2	0-2	12	Smith ^{48}	4646
22	26	H	Exeter C	D 0-0	0-0	13		6086
23	30	H	Portsmouth	D 0-0	0-0	12		6306
24	Jan 2	A	Crawley T	L 0-2	0-2	14		2304
25	14	A	Wycombe W	D 1-1	1-1	16	Dawson (pen) ^{20}	3493
26	21	A	Blackpool	D 2-2	1-0	16	Zoko ^{34}, Ward ^{80}	2885
27	28	H	Doncaster R	L 0-3	0-2	16		3627
28	31	H	Plymouth Arg	W 2-1	0-0	15	Smith ^{62}, Lacey ^{64}	4788
29	Feb 4	A	Hartlepool U	D 1-1	0-0	15	Dolan (pen) ^{69}	3410
30	11	H	Leyton Orient	D 1-1	1-0	16	Zoko ^{45}	3120
31	14	H	Cambridge U	D 1-1	0-0	16	Zoko ^{78}	2847
32	18	A	Cheltenham T	L 0-2	0-0	17		3347
33	25	A	Notts Co	D 0-0	0-0	17		7141
34	28	H	Mansfield T	D 0-0	0-0	17		2766
35	Mar 4	H	Luton T	L 0-4	0-2	17		4194
36	11	A	Morecambe	W 3-1	1-0	17	Butcher ^{45}, Lacey ^{65}, Mugabi ^{71}	1433
37	15	A	Barnet	D 2-2	1-1	17	Whitfield ^{14}, Shephard ^{90}	1525
38	18	H	Accrington S	D 1-1	0-0	17	Zoko ^{74}	2991
39	25	A	Exeter C	D 3-3	0-0	18	Zoko ^{62}, Harrison ^{70}, Lacey ^{78}	5492
40	Apr 1	H	Carlisle U	L 0-2	0-1	19		3145
41	8	A	Portsmouth	L 1-3	0-1	20	Stevens (og) ^{51}	17,564
42	14	A	Newport Co	L 0-1	0-0	20		3789
43	17	H	Crewe Alex	W 3-0	2-0	18	Dolan ^{29}, Akpa Akpro ^{45}, Khan ^{70}	3167
44	22	A	Grimsby T	L 2-4	0-2	20	Lawless ^{47}, Zoko ^{75}	4061
45	29	H	Stevenage	D 1-1	1-0	19	Akpa Akpro ^{44}	3716
46	May 6	A	Colchester U	L 0-2	0-1	20		6565

Final League Position: 20

GOALSCORERS

League (49): Zoko 8, Khan 6, Dolan 4 (1 pen), Eaves 4, Hedges 4, Lacey 3, Ward 3, Akpa Akpro 2, Butcher 2, Dawson 2 (1 pen), Smith 2, Whitfield 2, Campbell 1, Harrison 1, Lawless 1, Mugabi 1, Shephard 1, own goals 2.
FA Cup (3): Hedges 1, Khan 1, Zoko 1.
EFL Cup (2): Dolan 1, own goal 1.
EFL Checkatrade Trophy (16): Zoko 4 (1 pen), Eaves 3, Sowunmi 2, Dawson 1 (1 pen), Khan 1, Lacey 1, McLeod 1, Mugabi 1, Whitfield 1, own goal 1.

Krysiak A 41	Shephard L 38	Smith N 33 + 1	Lacey A 38 + 2	Dickson R 34	Dolan M 38	Dawson K 39	Lawless A 30 + 3	Eaves T 30 + 10	Khan O 27 + 2	Hedges R 20 + 1	Ward D 14 + 2	Campbell T 6 + 13	Butcher M 27 + 7	Mugabi B 20 + 11	Sowunmi O 4 + 7	Zoko F 22 + 13	McLeod I 2 + 2	Whitfield B 22 + 12	Storer J 1	Goodship B 1 + 7	Harrison S 4 + 10	Akpa Akpro J 9 + 4	Jones O — + 2	James T 1 + 1	Maddison J 5	*Match No.*
1	2	3²	4	5	6	7¹	8	9	10³	11	12	13	14													1
1			4²	5	6	7	8	10¹	9	11		12	3	2	13											2
1		4¹	12	5²	8	6	7	11	9³	10		13	3	2		14										3
1		4		5²	8	6	7	10	11¹	9³		12	3	2	14	13										4
1	2	3			6	7	8	10¹	9³	11²		13	4	5■			12	14								5
1	2	3		5	8	6²	7	10	11¹			12	4				9	13								6
1	2	3	4		6	7	8³	9²	10¹	11		12	5				13	14								7
1	2	5	3		8	6		10	9¹	11	4		7	12												8
1	2	5	3		6		12	10	9	11	4¹		7	13				8²								9
1	2¹	5	3		6	8	13	10	11³	9	4²		7	12				14								10
1	2¹	11	4	5³	8	9	6			12	3	14	7	13			10²									11
1		5	4		6	7	8		9¹	11	3	10		2				12								12
1		5	4		6	8	7	12	11³	10¹	3	9²		2		13		14								13
1		5	3		8	6	7	12	9¹	11	4	10²		2		13										14
1		5	3		6	7	8	12	9¹	11	4	10²		2		13										15
1	2²	5	3		8			10	11¹	9	4		6	7		12		13								16
1	2		4	5	8¹	6²		10	11³	9	3	14	7			13		12								17
1	2	4	3	5		6	7	10²	11³	9		14		13		12		8¹								18
1	2²	4	3	5		6	7	10³	9	11		14		12		13		8¹								19
1	2	3	4	5		8	7	10¹	11	9		13				12		6²								20
1	2	3	4	5		8	7	13	12	6		11²	9¹			10³		14								21
1	2	3	4	5		6	7	10	11	9¹			12			13		8²								22
1	2³	3	4	5		6	7	10	9			11²	14	12		13		8¹								23
1		3	4	5		9	6	8	10¹			14	12	2		13		7³	11²							24
1	2	4	3	5	6	8		12					7	14	10²	11¹		9³		13						25
1	2	4		5¹	6	8		9			3		7	14	10²	11³		12			13					26
1	2	5	3		8	6		11			4		7¹		10²	9		12			13					27
1	2	3	4	5	8	7		11¹					6		13	10²		9³		12	14					28
1	2	3	4¹	5	7			10²			12		8		13	11		6				9³	14			29
1	2	3		5²	6		7	9			4			13	14	10¹		8			12	11³				30
1	2			5	6	8	7	10¹					4	3	12	9		11²					13			31
1	2		12	5²	8	6	7¹	10³			3		4		14	11		13				9				32
1	5		3	9	8	6	7	12					4	2		11²					13	10¹				33
1	2		4	5	6	8	7	12						3		9		10²		13	11¹					34
1	2		4	5	6²	8	7	13						3		10		9³		14	12	11¹				35
1	2		4	5	6	8	7¹	10					12	3		11		9								36
1	2		4	5	6	8		10¹					7	3		11		9			12					37
1	2		4	5	8²	9		10¹					7	3		11		6			13	12				38
1	2		4	5	8	6		13					7	3		10¹		9²		14	11³	12				39
1	2		4	5		6		10¹					7	3		11		8■		13	9²			12		40
1	2	13	4		6	7		10¹	14				8	3³		11				9²		12		5		41
	2	3	4	5	7	8	14		6¹				9³		10²	11					13	12			1	42
	2	3	4	5	7	6	8		9							10						11			1	43
	2¹	3	4	5	7		8		6					12		10		9²			13	11			1	44
	2	3	4	5	8		7		9				12			10		6¹				11			1	45
	2	4	3	5	8		7³	12	9				13					6¹		14	10²	11			1	46

FA Cup

First Round	Solihull Moors	(h)	2-2
Replay	Solihull Moors	(a)	1-1

(*aet; Solihull Moors won 4-2 on penalties*)

EFL Cup

First Round	Walsall	(a)	2-0

(*aet*)

Second Round	Everton	(a)	0-4

EFL Checkatrade Trophy

Southern Group A	Portsmouth	(h)	4-3
Southern Group A	Bristol R	(a)	0-0

(*Bristol R won 5-3 on penalties*)

Southern Group A	Reading U21	(a)	2-0
Second Round South	Milton Keynes D	(h)	4-1
Third Round	Reading U21	(h)	4-2
Quarter-Final	Luton T	(a)	2-5

ENGLISH LEAGUE PLAYERS DIRECTORY

Players listed represent those with their clubs during the 2016–17 season.

Players are listed alphabetically on pages 539–545.

The number alongside each player corresponds to the team number heading. (Aarons, Rolando 56 = team 56 (Newcastle U)). Club names in italic indicate loans.

ACCRINGTON S (1)

BECKLES, Omar (D) **41 2**
H: 6 2 W: 12 04 b.Kettering 25-10-91
From Aldershot T.

2016–17	Accrington S	41	2	**41**	**2**

BOCO, Romuald (F) **197 23**
H: 5 10 W: 10 13 b.Bernay 8-7-85
Internationals: Benin Full caps.

2006–07	Accrington S	32	3		
2007–08	Accrington S	11	0		
2008–09	Accrington S	0	0		
2009–10	Burton Alb	8	0	**8**	**0**
From Sligo					
2012–13	Accrington S	42	10		
2013–14	Plymouth Arg	27	1	**27**	**1**
2014–15	Chesterfield	13	1	**13**	**1**
2014–15	Bharat FC	20	0	**20**	**0**
2015–16	Portsmouth	4	0	**4**	**0**
2015–16	Accrington S	11	2		
2016–17	Accrington S	29	6	**125**	**21**

BROWN, Scott (M) **179 12**
H: 5 9 W: 10 02 b.Runcorn 8-5-85
Internationals: England U17, U18, U19.

2001–02	Everton	0	0		
2002–03	Everton	0	0		
2003–04	Everton	0	0		
2004–05	Bristol C	19	0		
2005–06	Bristol C	29	1		
2006–07	Bristol C	15	4	**63**	**5**
2006–07	Cheltenham T	4	0		
2007–08	Cheltenham T	20	0		
2008–09	Port Vale	18	1	**18**	**1**
2009–10	Cheltenham T	1	0	**25**	**0**
2010–11	Morecambe	32	3	**32**	**3**
From Fleetwood T, York C, Macclesfield T, Chester FC, Southport, Grimsby T.					
2015–16	Accrington S	13	3		
2016–17	Accrington S	28	0	**41**	**3**

CHAPMAN, Aaron (G) **23 0**
H: 6 8 W: 14 07 b.Rotherham 29-5-90

2013–14	Chesterfield	0	0		
2014–15	Chesterfield	0	0		
2014–15	*Accrington S*	3	0		
2015–16	Chesterfield	0	0		
2015–16	*Bristol R*	5	0	**5**	**0**
2016–17	Accrington S	15	0	**18**	**0**

CLARK, Jordan (F) **98 6**
H: 6 0 W: 11 07 b.Barnsley 22-9-93

2010–11	Barnsley	4	0		
2011–12	Barnsley	2	0		
2012–13	Barnsley	0	0		
2012–13	*Chesterfield*	2	0	**2**	**0**
2013–14	Barnsley	0	0	**6**	**0**
2013–14	*Scunthorpe U*	1	0	**1**	**0**
2014–15	Shrewsbury T	27	3		
2015–16	Shrewsbury T	20	2	**47**	**5**
2016–17	Accrington S	42	1	**42**	**1**

CONNEELY, Seamus (D) **186 9**
H: 5 9 W: 10 10 b.Galway 9-7-88
Internationals: Republic of Ireland U21, U23.

2008	Galway U	20	0		
2009	Galway U	34	2		
2010	Galway U	32	0	**86**	**2**
2010–11	Sheffield U	0	0		
2011–12	Sheffield U	0	0		
2014–15	Accrington S	16	3		
2015–16	Accrington S	46	3		
2016–17	Accrington S	38	1	**100**	**7**

DAVIES, Arron (M) **331 39**
H: 5 9 W: 11 00 b.Cardiff 22-6-84
Internationals: Wales U19, U21, Full caps.

2002–03	Southampton	0	0		
2003–04	Southampton	0	0		
2003–04	*Barnsley*	4	0	**4**	**0**
2004–05	Southampton	0	0		
2004–05	Yeovil T	23	8		
2005–06	Yeovil T	39	8		
2006–07	Yeovil T	39	6		
2007–08	Nottingham F	19	1		
2008–09	Nottingham F	13	0		
2009–10	Nottingham F	0	0	**32**	**1**
2009–10	*Brighton & HA*	7	0	**7**	**0**
2009–10	Yeovil T	10	0	**111**	**22**
2010–11	Peterborough U	22	1	**22**	**1**
2011–12	Northampton T	15	4	**15**	**4**
2012–13	Exeter C	37	3		
2013–14	Exeter C	32	2		
2014–15	Exeter C	39	4		
2015–16	Exeter C	28	1	**136**	**10**
2016–17	Accrington S	4	1	**4**	**1**

DONACIEN, Janoi (D) **97 1**
H: 6 0 W: 11 11 b.St Lucia 3-11-93
Internationals: St Lucia Full caps.

2011–12	Aston Villa	0	0		
2012–13	Aston Villa	0	0		
2013–14	Aston Villa	0	0		
2014–15	Aston Villa	0	0		
2014–15	*Tranmere R*	31	0	**31**	**0**
2015–16	Aston Villa	0	0		
2015–16	*Wycombe W*	2	0	**2**	**0**
2015–16	*Newport Co*	29	0	**29**	**0**
2016–17	Accrington S	35	1	**35**	**1**

GORNELL, Terry (F) **276 49**
H: 5 11 W: 12 04 b.Liverpool 16-12-89

2008–09	Tranmere R	10	1		
2008–09	*Accrington S*	11	4		
2009–10	Tranmere R	27	2		
2010–11	Tranmere R	3	0	**40**	**3**
2010–11	Accrington S	40	13		
2011–12	Shrewsbury T	41	9		
2012–13	Shrewsbury T	12	0	**53**	**9**
2012–13	*Rochdale*	19	5	**19**	**5**
2013–14	Cheltenham T	34	3		
2014–15	Cheltenham T	25	3	**59**	**6**
2014–15	Accrington S	15	4		
2015–16	Accrington S	20	3		
2016–17	Accrington S	19	2	**105**	**26**

HERY, Bastien (M) **54 2**
H: 5 9 W: 10 03 b.Brou sur Chantereine 23-3-92
Internationals: France U18.

2012–13	Sheffield W	0	0		
2013–14	Rochdale	12	1		
2014–15	Rochdale	21	1	**33**	**2**
2015–16	Carlisle U	20	0	**20**	**0**
2016–17	Accrington S	1	0	**1**	**0**

HEWITT, Steven (M) **11 0**
H: 5 7 W: 11 00 b.Manchester 5-12-93

2011–12	Burnley	1	0		
2012–13	Burnley	0	0		
2013–14	Burnley	1	0		
2014–15	Burnley	0	0		
2015–16	Burnley	0	0	**2**	**0**
2016–17	Accrington S	9	0	**9**	**0**

HUGHES, Mark (D) **365 22**
H: 6 1 W: 13 03 b.Liverpool 9-12-86

2004–05	Everton	0	0		
2005–06	Everton	0	0		
2005–06	*Stockport Co*	3	1	**3**	**1**
2006–07	Everton	1	0	**1**	**0**
2006–07	Northampton T	17	2		
2007–08	Northampton T	35	1		
2008–09	Northampton T	41	1	**93**	**4**
2009–10	Walsall	26	1	**26**	**1**
2010–11	N Queensland F	30	4	**30**	**4**
2011–12	Bury	25	0		
2012–13	Bury	27	0	**52**	**0**
2012–13	*Accrington S*	5	0		
2013–14	Morecambe	44	5		
2014–15	Morecambe	40	3	**84**	**8**
2015–16	Stevenage	20	1	**20**	**1**
2015–16	Accrington S	15	1		
2016–17	Accrington S	36	2	**56**	**3**

KEE, Billy (F) **289 89**
H: 5 9 W: 11 04 b.Loughborough 1-12-90
Internationals: Northern Ireland U19, U21.

2009–10	Leicester C	0	0		
2009–10	*Accrington S*	37	9		
2010–11	Torquay U	40	9		
2011–12	Torquay U	4	0	**44**	**9**
2011–12	Burton Alb	20	12		
2012–13	Burton Alb	40	13		
2013–14	Burton Alb	37	12		
2014–15	Burton Alb	2	2	**99**	**39**
2014–15	Scunthorpe U	12	0	**12**	**0**
2014–15	*Mansfield T*	13	2	**13**	**2**
2015–16	Accrington S	45	17		
2016–17	Accrington S	39	13	**121**	**39**

LACEY, Patrick (M) **11 1**
H: 6 0 W: 12 04 b.Liverpool 16-3-93

2011–12	Bradford C	0	0		
From Southport, Vauxhall Motors, Droylsden, Altrincham, Barrow.					
2016–17	Accrington S	11	1	**11**	**1**

LITTLE, Jack (G) **0 0**

2016–17	Accrington S	0	0		

McCARTAN, Shay (M) **111 25**
H: 5 10 W: 11 09 b.Newry 18-5-94
Internationals: Northern Ireland U17, U19, U21, Full caps.

2011–12	Burnley	1	0		
2012–13	Burnley	0	0	**1**	**0**
2013–14	Accrington S	18	1		
2014–15	Accrington S	31	6		
2015–16	Accrington S	27	7		
2016–17	Accrington S	34	11	**110**	**25**

McCONVILLE, Sean (M) **163 24**
H: 5 8 W: 11 07 b.Liverpool 6-3-89

2008–09	Accrington S	5	0		
2009–10	Accrington S	28	1		
2010–11	Accrington S	43	13		
2011–12	Rochdale	4	0	**4**	**0**
From Barrow, Stalybridge Celtic, Chester.					
2015–16	Accrington S	42	5		
2016–17	Accrington S	41	5	**159**	**24**

McKEOWN, Rory (D) **127 4**
H: 5 11 W: 12 08 b.Belfast 8-4-93
Internationals: Northern Ireland U16, U17, U19, U21.

2011–12	Kilmarnock	18	1		
2012–13	Kilmarnock	16	0		
2013–14	Kilmarnock	9	0	**43**	**1**
2013–14	*Cowdenbeath*	12	2	**12**	**2**
2014–15	Raith R	36	0		
2015–16	Raith R	36	1	**72**	**1**
2016–17	Accrington S	0	0		

OGLE, Reagan (D) **1 0**
H: 5 8 W: 10 06 b. 29-3-99

2016–17	Accrington S	1	0	**1**	**0**

PARISH, Elliot (G) **86 0**
H: 6 2 W: 13 00 b.Towcester 20-5-90
Internationals: England U20.

2008–09	Aston Villa	0	0		
2009–10	Aston Villa	0	0		
2010–11	Aston Villa	0	0		
2010–11	*Lincoln C*	9	0	**9**	**0**
2011–12	Aston Villa	0	0		
2011–12	Cardiff C	0	0		
2012–13	Wycombe W	2	0	**2**	**0**
2012–13	Cardiff C	0	0		
2013–14	Bristol C	19	0	**19**	**0**
2013–14	*Newport Co*	7	0	**7**	**0**
2014–15	Blackpool	13	0	**13**	**0**
2015–16	Colchester U	25	0	**25**	**0**
2016–17	Accrington S	11	0	**11**	**0**

PEARSON, Matthew (D) **98 11**
H: 6 3 W: 11 05 b.Keighley 3-8-93
Internationals: England C, U18.

2012–13	Rochdale	9	0		
2013–14	Rochdale	0	0	**9**	**0**
2015–16	Accrington S	46	3		
2016–17	Accrington S	43	8	**89**	**11**

SHAW, Brayden (F) **6 0**
H: 5 10 W: 10 01 b.Blackburn 25-2-97

2014–15	Bury	0	0		
2015–16	Bury	0	0		
2015–16	Accrington S	4	0		
2016–17	Accrington S	2	0	**6**	**0**

SYKES, Ross (D) 0 0
H: 6 5 W: 11 07 b.Burnley 26-3-99
2016–17 Accrington S 0 0

TAYLOR-FLETCHER, Gary (F) 443 88
H: 6 0 W: 11 00 b.Widnes 4-6-81
2000–01 Hull C 5 0 5 0
2001–02 Leyton Orient 9 0
2002–03 Leyton Orient 12 1 21 1
2003–04 Lincoln C 42 16
2004–05 Lincoln C 38 11 80 27
2005–06 Huddersfield T 43 10
2006–07 Huddersfield T 39 11 82 21
2007–08 Blackpool 42 6
2008–09 Blackpool 38 5
2009–10 Blackpool 32 6
2010–11 Blackpool 31 6
2011–12 Blackpool 37 8
2012–13 Blackpool 35 5 215 36
2013–14 Leicester C 21 3
2014–15 Leicester C 1 0 22 3
2014–15 *Sheffield W* 4 0 4 0
2014–15 *Millwall* 10 0 10 0
2016–17 Accrington S 4 0 4 0

WALL, Luke (M) 0 0
H: 5 11 W: 10 08 b.Liverpool 11-11-96
From Blackburn R.
2016–17 Accrington S 0 0

WEBB, Nathan (F) 0 0
H: 5 6 W: 9 13 b. 9-9-98
2016–17 Accrington S 0 0

WHITE, Paul (G) 0 0
H: 6 4 W: 12 00 b. 11-10-94
2016–17 Accrington S 0 0

Scholars
Blackburn, Harry; Burgess, Jack David; Cooper, Adam James Alfred; Hmami, Joshua Majid; Jones, Isaac Samuel; Little, Jack David; Mills, Joel William; Mohammed, Zehn Mekhal; Moran, Luke; Ogle, Reagan; Randell, Jack Andrew; Rathbone, Joseph Arnold; Reilly, Thomas Stephen; Waterhouse, Harry; Watson, Niall Robert; Wolland, Nathan David.

AFC WIMBLEDON (2)

ANTWI, Jayden (F) 1 0
b.Lambeth
2016–17 AFC Wimbledon 1 0 1 0

BARCHAM, Andy (F) 314 43
H: 5 8 W: 11 10 b.Basildon 16-12-86
Internationals: England U16.
2005–06 Tottenham H 0 0
2006–07 Tottenham H 0 0
2007–08 Tottenham H 0 0
2007–08 *Leyton Orient* 25 1 25 1
2008–09 Tottenham H 0 0
2008–09 Gillingham 33 6
2009–10 Gillingham 42 7
2010–11 Gillingham 24 6 99 19
2011–12 Scunthorpe U 41 9
2012–13 Scunthorpe U 34 0 75 9
2013–14 Portsmouth 26 3
2014–15 Portsmouth 19 1 45 4
2015–16 AFC Wimbledon 33 5
2016–17 AFC Wimbledon 37 5 70 10

BARNETT, Tyrone (F) 254 58
H: 6 3 W: 13 05 b.Stevenage 28-10-85
2010–11 Macclesfield T 45 13 45 13
2011–12 Crawley T 26 14 26 14
2011–12 Peterborough U 13 4
2012–13 Peterborough U 18 1
2012–13 *Ipswich T* 3 0 3 0
2013–14 Peterborough U 21 6
2013–14 *Bristol C* 17 1 17 1
2014–15 Peterborough U 4 0 56 11
2014–15 *Oxford U* 12 4 12 4
2014–15 Shrewsbury T 18 4
2015–16 Shrewsbury T 21 4 39 8
2015–16 *Southend U* 20 5 20 5
2016–17 AFC Wimbledon 36 2 36 2

BEERE, Tom (F) 28 0
H: 5 11 W: 11 09 b.Southwark 27-1-95
2012–13 AFC Wimbledon 0 0
2013–14 AFC Wimbledon 0 0
2014–15 AFC Wimbledon 18 0
2015–16 AFC Wimbledon 2 0
2016–17 AFC Wimbledon 8 0 28 0

BULMAN, Dannie (M) 444 22
H: 5 9 W: 11 12 b.Ashford 24-1-79
1998–99 Wycombe W 11 1
1999–2000 Wycombe W 29 1
2000–01 Wycombe W 36 4
2001–02 Wycombe W 46 5
2002–03 Wycombe W 42 3
2003–04 Wycombe W 38 0 202 14
From Stevenage, Crawley T.
2010–11 Oxford U 5 0 5 0
2011–12 Crawley T 41 3
2012–13 Crawley T 36 1
2013–14 Crawley T 39 0 116 4
2014–15 AFC Wimbledon 41 1
2015–16 AFC Wimbledon 42 3
2016–17 AFC Wimbledon 38 0 121 4

BURSIK, Josef (G) 0 0
Internationals: England U17.
2016–17 AFC Wimbledon 0 0

CHARLES, Darius (M) 224 16
H: 6 1 W: 13 05 b.Ealing 10-12-87
Internationals: England C.
2004–05 Brentford 1 0
2005–06 Brentford 2 0
2006–07 Brentford 17 1
2007–08 Brentford 17 0 37 1
From Ebbsfleet U.
2010–11 Stevenage 28 2
2011–12 Stevenage 28 4
2012–13 Stevenage 37 1
2013–14 Stevenage 22 4
2014–15 Stevenage 29 2 144 13
2015–16 Burton Alb 0 0
2015–16 *AFC Wimbledon* 9 0
2016–17 AFC Wimbledon 34 2 43 2

CLARKE, Ryan (G) 226 0
H: 6 3 W: 13 00 b.Bristol 30-4-82
2001–02 Bristol R 1 0
2002–03 Bristol R 2 0
2003–04 Bristol R 2 0
2004–05 Bristol R 18 0 23 0
2004–05 *Southend U* 1 0 1 0
2004–05 *Kidderminster H* 6 0 6 0
From Salisbury C.
2010–11 Oxford U 46 0
2011–12 Oxford U 42 0
2012–13 Oxford U 24 0
2013–14 Oxford U 46 0
2014–15 Oxford U 31 0 189 0
2015–16 Northampton T 0 0
2016–17 AFC Wimbledon 7 0 7 0

EGAN, Alfie (M) 9 0
b. 3-9-97
2016–17 AFC Wimbledon 9 0 9 0

ELLIOTT, Tom (F) 188 31
H: 6 3 W: 12 00 b.Hunslet 9-11-90
Internationals: England U16, U18.
2006–07 Leeds U 3 0
2007–08 Leeds U 0 0
2008–09 Leeds U 0 0
2008–09 *Macclesfield T* 6 0 6 0
2009–10 Leeds U 0 0
2009–10 *Bury* 16 1 16 1
2010–11 Leeds U 0 0 3 0
2010–11 *Rotherham U* 6 0 6 0
2011–12 Hamilton A 7 0 7 0
2011–12 Stockport Co 42 7 42 7
2014–15 Cambridge U 30 8 30 8
2015–16 AFC Wimbledon 39 6
2016–17 AFC Wimbledon 39 9 78 15

FITZPATRICK, David (M) 13 1
H: 5 10 W: 12 02 b.Surbiton 10-2-95
2011–12 QPR 0 0
2012–13 QPR 0 0
2013–14 QPR 0 0
2014–15 AFC Wimbledon 3 0
2015–16 AFC Wimbledon 4 1
2016–17 AFC Wimbledon 6 0 13 1

FRANCOMB, George (D) 188 11
H: 5 11 W: 11 07 b.Hackney 8-9-91
2009–10 Norwich C 2 0
2010–11 Norwich C 0 0
2010–11 *Barnet* 13 0 13 0
2011–12 Norwich C 0 0
2011–12 *Hibernian* 14 0 14 0
2012–13 Norwich C 0 0 2 0
2012–13 *AFC Wimbledon* 15 0
2013–14 AFC Wimbledon 33 3
2014–15 AFC Wimbledon 37 3
2015–16 AFC Wimbledon 40 3
2016–17 AFC Wimbledon 34 2 159 11

FULLER, Barry (D) 351 2
H: 5 10 W: 11 10 b.Ashford 25-9-84
Internationals: England C.
2004–05 Charlton Ath 0 0
2005–06 Charlton Ath 0 0
2005–06 *Barnet* 15 1
From Stevenage B.
2007–08 Gillingham 10 0
2008–09 Gillingham 37 0
2009–10 Gillingham 36 0
2010–11 Gillingham 42 0
2011–12 Gillingham 9 0
2012–13 Gillingham 0 0 134 0
2012–13 Barnet 39 0 54 1
2013–14 AFC Wimbledon 45 0
2014–15 AFC Wimbledon 45 1
2015–16 AFC Wimbledon 45 0
2016–17 AFC Wimbledon 28 0 163 1

GALLAGHER, Dan (M) 1 0
H: 6 0 W: 12 02 b.Epsom 20-6-97
2014–15 AFC Wimbledon 1 0
2015–16 AFC Wimbledon 0 0
2016–17 AFC Wimbledon 0 0 1 0

KAJA, Egli (M) 3 0
H: 5 10 W: 12 04 b. 26-7-97
Internationals: Albania U21.
2015–16 AFC Wimbledon 2 0
2016–17 AFC Wimbledon 1 0 3 0

KALAMBAYI, Paul (D) 0 0
2015–16 AFC Wimbledon 0 0
2016–17 AFC Wimbledon 0 0

KELLY, Sean (D) 118 8
H: 6 3 W: 12 00 b.Glasgow 1-11-93
Internationals: Scotland U21.
2012–13 St Mirren 0 0
2012–13 *East Stirlingshire* 9 0 9 0
2013–14 St Mirren 26 1
2014–15 St Mirren 31 3
2015–16 St Mirren 26 2 83 6
2016–17 AFC Wimbledon 26 2 26 2

McDONNELL, Joe (G) 7 0
H: 5 10 W: 9 13 b.Basingstoke 19-5-94
2014–15 AFC Wimbledon 4 0
2015–16 AFC Wimbledon 0 0
2016–17 AFC Wimbledon 3 0 7 0

MEADES, Jonathan (M) 98 6
H: 6 1 W: 13 00 b.Cardiff 2-3-92
Internationals: Wales U17, U21.
2010–11 Cardiff C 0 0
2011–12 Cardiff C 0 0
2012–13 Bournemouth 0 0
2012–13 *AFC Wimbledon* 26 1
2013–14 Oxford U 0 0
2014–15 Oxford U 7 0 7 0
2015–16 AFC Wimbledon 41 3
2016–17 AFC Wimbledon 24 2 91 6

NIGHTINGALE, Will (M) 20 0
H: 6 1 W: 13 03 b.Wandsworth 2-7-95
2013–14 AFC Wimbledon 0 0
2014–15 AFC Wimbledon 4 0
2015–16 AFC Wimbledon 4 0
2016–17 AFC Wimbledon 12 0 20 0

OAKLEY, George (F) 9 0
H: 6 2 W: 13 08 b.Wandsworth 18-11-95
2013–14 AFC Wimbledon 0 0
2014–15 AFC Wimbledon 6 0
2015–16 AFC Wimbledon 1 0
2016–17 AFC Wimbledon 2 0 9 0

OLUSANYA, Toyosi (M) 1 1
H: 5 9 W: 10 10 b. 1-2-98
2015–16 AFC Wimbledon 1 1
2016–17 AFC Wimbledon 0 0 1 1

OWENS, Seth (D) 3 0
H: 5 10 W: 10 01 b.Hackney 6-11-98
2015–16 Brentford 0 0
2016–17 AFC Wimbledon 3 0 3 0

PARRETT, Dean (M) 135 16
H: 5 10 W: 11 04 b.Hampstead 16-11-91
Internationals: England U16, U17, U19, U20.
2008–09 Tottenham H 0 0
2009–10 Tottenham H 0 0
2009–10 *Aldershot T* 4 0 4 0
2010–11 Tottenham H 0 0
2010–11 *Plymouth Arg* 8 1 8 1
2010–11 *Charlton Ath* 9 1 9 1
2011–12 Tottenham H 0 0
2011–12 *Yeovil T* 10 1 10 1
2012–13 Tottenham H 0 0
2012–13 *Swindon T* 3 0 3 0
2013–14 Stevenage 12 1

2014–15 Stevenage 30 4
2015–16 Stevenage 27 3 **69 8**
2016–17 AFC Wimbledon 32 5 **32 5**

POLEON, Dominic (F) 144 21
H: 6 3 W: 12 13 b.Newham 7-9-93
2012–13 Leeds U 6 2
2012–13 *Bury* 7 2 **7 2**
2012–13 *Sheffield U* 7 0 **7 0**
2013–14 Leeds U 19 1
2014–15 Leeds U 4 0 **29 3**
2014–15 Oldham Ath 35 4
2015–16 Oldham Ath 25 4 **60 8**
2016–17 AFC Wimbledon 41 8 **41 8**

REEVES, Jake (M) 159 5
H: 5 8 W: 11 11 b.Lewisham 30-6-93
2010–11 Brentford 1 0
2011–12 Brentford 8 0
2012–13 Brentford 6 0
2012–13 *AFC Wimbledon* 5 0
2013–14 Brentford 20 0 **35 0**
2014–15 Swindon T 10 1 **10 1**
2014–15 AFC Wimbledon 23 2
2015–16 AFC Wimbledon 40 1
2016–17 AFC Wimbledon 46 1 **114 4**

ROBERTSON, Chris (D) 259 11
H: 6 3 W: 11 08 b.Dundee 11-10-85
2005–06 Sheffield U 0 0
2005–06 *Chester C* 1 0 **1 0**
2006–07 Sheffield U 0 0
2006–07 Torquay U 9 1
2009–10 Torquay U 45 2
2010–11 Torquay U 43 2
2011–12 Torquay U 25 1 **122 6**
2011–12 Preston NE 18 1
2012–13 Preston NE 21 0 **39 1**
2013–14 Port Vale 37 3
2014–15 Port Vale 24 0 **61 3**
2015–16 Ross Co 23 0 **23 0**
2016–17 AFC Wimbledon 13 1 **13 1**

ROBINSON, Paul (D) 436 23
H: 6 1 W: 11 09 b.Barnet 7-1-82
2000–01 Millwall 0 0
2001–02 Millwall 0 0
2002–03 Millwall 14 0
2003–04 Millwall 9 0
2004–05 Millwall 0 0
2004–05 *Torquay U* 12 0 **12 0**
2005–06 Millwall 32 0
2006–07 Millwall 38 3
2007–08 Millwall 45 3
2008–09 Millwall 26 2
2009–10 Millwall 34 4
2010–11 Millwall 37 3
2011–12 Millwall 41 1
2012–13 Millwall 3 0
2013–14 Millwall 25 0 **304 16**
2014–15 Portsmouth 33 2 **33 2**
2015–16 AFC Wimbledon 44 3
2016–17 AFC Wimbledon 43 2 **87 5**

SHEA, James (G) 96 0
H: 5 11 W: 12 00 b.Islington 16-6-91
2009–10 Arsenal 0 0
2010–11 Arsenal 0 0
2011–12 Arsenal 0 0
2011–12 *Dagenham & R* 1 0 **1 0**
2012–13 Arsenal 0 0
2013–14 Arsenal 0 0
2014–15 AFC Wimbledon 38 0
2015–16 AFC Wimbledon 21 0
2016–17 AFC Wimbledon 36 0 **95 0**

SIBBICK, Toby (D) 2 0
H: 6 0 W: 10 12 b.Isleworth 23-5-99
2016–17 AFC Wimbledon 2 0 **2 0**

SOARES, Tom (M) 381 38
H: 6 0 W: 11 04 b.Reading 10-7-86
Internationals: England U20, U21.
2003–04 Crystal Palace 3 0
2004–05 Crystal Palace 22 0
2005–06 Crystal Palace 44 1
2006–07 Crystal Palace 37 3
2007–08 Crystal Palace 39 6
2008–09 Crystal Palace 4 1 **149 11**
2008–09 Stoke C 7 0
2008–09 *Charlton Ath* 11 1 **11 1**
2009–10 Stoke C 0 0
2009–10 *Sheffield W* 25 2 **25 2**
2010–11 Stoke C 0 0
2011–12 Stoke C 0 0 **7 0**
2011–12 *Hibernian* 10 2 **10 2**
2012–13 Bury 23 2
2013–14 Bury 30 6
2014–15 Bury 43 8
2015–16 Bury 42 4
2016–17 Bury 26 2 **164 22**
2016–17 AFC Wimbledon 15 0 **15 0**

TAYLOR, Lyle (F) 195 47
H: 6 2 W: 12 00 b.Greenwich 29-3-90
Internationals: Montserrat Full caps.
2007–08 Millwall 0 0
2008–09 Millwall 0 0
From Concord R
2010–11 Bournemouth 11 0
2011–12 Bournemouth 18 0 **29 0**
2011–12 *Hereford U* 8 2 **8 2**
2013–14 Sheffield U 20 2 **20 2**
2013–14 *Partick Thistle* 20 7
2014–15 Scunthorpe U 18 3 **18 3**
2014–15 *Partick Thistle* 15 3 **35 10**
2015–16 AFC Wimbledon 42 20
2016–17 AFC Wimbledon 43 10 **85 30**

TZANEV, Nikola (G) 0 0
Internationals: New Zealand U20.
From Brentford.
2016–17 AFC Wimbledon 0 0

WHELPDALE, Chris (M) 310 51
H: 6 0 W: 12 08 b.Harold Wood 27-1-87
2007–08 Peterborough U 35 3
2008–09 Peterborough U 39 7
2009–10 Peterborough U 29 1
2010–11 Peterborough U 22 1 **125 12**
2010–11 *Gillingham* 4 3
2011–12 Gillingham 39 12
2012–13 Gillingham 41 7
2013–14 Gillingham 24 1 **108 23**
2014–15 Stevenage 39 7
2015–16 Stevenage 21 8 **60 15**
2016–17 AFC Wimbledon 17 1 **17 1**

Players retained or with offer of contract
Bellikli, Neset Can; Hartigan, Anthony Rhys; Mbiya-Kalambayi, Paul Mbwebwe.

Scholars
Bursik, Josef John; Carpene, Valentino Enrique Garcia; Chapman, Judah David; Evans, Great Nil-Okai; Marchant, George Robert; Nelson-Roberts, Ethan Cameron O'Neil; Perana, Dean; Scott, Thomas Norman; Urhoghide, Osaze; Walker, Barth Antonio; Williams-Bowers, Reece Ian Seton; Wingate, Jack Steven; Wood, Nathan Laurence.

ARSENAL (3)

AKPOM, Chuba (F) 66 3
H: 6 0 W: 12 02 b.London 9-10-95
Internationals: England U16, U17, U19, U20, U21.
2012–13 Arsenal 0 0
2013–14 Arsenal 1 0
2013–14 *Brentford* 4 0 **4 0**
2013–14 *Coventry C* 6 0 **6 0**
2014–15 Arsenal 3 0
2014–15 *Nottingham F* 7 0 **7 0**
2015–16 Arsenal 0 0
2015–16 *Hull C* 35 3 **35 3**
2016–17 Arsenal 0 0 **4 0**
2016–17 *Brighton & HA* 10 0 **10 0**

BELLERIN, Hector (D) 97 4
H: 5 10 W: 11 09 b.Barcelona 19-3-95
Internationals: Spain U16, U17, U19, U21, Full caps.
2012–13 Arsenal 0 0
2013–14 Arsenal 0 0
2013–14 *Watford* 8 0 **8 0**
2014–15 Arsenal 20 2
2015–16 Arsenal 36 1
2016–17 Arsenal 33 1 **89 4**

BENNACER, Ismael (M) 22 1
H: 5 9 W: 11 00 b.Arles 1-12-97
Internationals: France U18, U19. Algeria Full caps.
2014–15 Arles 6 0 **6 0**
2015–16 Arsenal 0 0
2016–17 Arsenal 0 0
2016–17 *Tours* 16 1 **16 1**

BIELIK, Krystian (M) 15 0
H: 5 10 W: 11 00 b.Vrinnevi 4-1-98
Internationals: Poland U16, U17, U18, U19.
2014–15 Legia Warsaw 5 0 **5 0**
2014–15 Arsenal 0 0
2015–16 Arsenal 0 0
2016–17 Arsenal 0 0
2016–17 *Birmingham C* 10 0 **10 0**

BOLA, Marc (D) 13 0
H: 6 1 W: 12 04 b.Greenwich 9-12-97
2016–17 Arsenal 0 0
2016–17 *Notts Co* 13 0 **13 0**

CAZORLA, Santi (M) 381 64
H: 5 5 W: 10 07 b.Lugo De Llanera 13-12-84
Internationals: Spain U21, Full caps.
2003–04 Villarreal 2 0
2004–05 Villarreal 28 2
2005–06 Villarreal 23 0
2006–07 *Recreativo Huelva* 34 5 **34 5**
2007–08 Villarreal 36 5
2008–09 Villarreal 30 8
2009–10 Villarreal 24 5
2010–11 Villarreal 37 5 **180 25**
2011–12 Malaga 38 9
2012–13 Malaga 0 0 **38 9**
2012–13 Arsenal 38 12
2013–14 Arsenal 31 4
2014–15 Arsenal 37 7
2015–16 Arsenal 15 0
2016–17 Arsenal 8 2 **129 25**

CECH, Petr (G) 530 0
H: 6 5 W: 14 07 b.Plzen 20-5-82
Internationals: Czech Republic U15, U16, U17, U18, U20, U21, Full caps.
1998–99 Viktoria Plzen 0 0
1999–2000 Chmel 1 0
2000–01 Chmel 26 0 **27 0**
2001–02 Sparta Prague 26 0 **26 0**
2002–03 Rennes 37 0
2003–04 Rennes 38 0 **75 0**
2004–05 Chelsea 35 0
2005–06 Chelsea 34 0
2006–07 Chelsea 20 0
2007–08 Chelsea 26 0
2008–09 Chelsea 35 0
2009–10 Chelsea 34 0
2010–11 Chelsea 38 0
2011–12 Chelsea 34 0
2012–13 Chelsea 36 0
2013–14 Chelsea 34 0
2014–15 Chelsea 7 0 **333 0**
2015–16 Arsenal 34 0
2016–17 Arsenal 35 0 **69 0**

CHAMBERS, Calum (M) 82 3
H: 6 0 W: 10 05 b.Petersfield 20-1-95
Internationals: England U17, U19, U21, Full caps.
2011–12 Southampton 0 0
2012–13 Southampton 0 0
2013–14 Southampton 22 0 **22 0**
2014–15 Arsenal 23 1
2015–16 Arsenal 12 0
2016–17 Arsenal 1 1 **36 2**
2016–17 *Middlesbrough* 24 1 **24 1**

COQUELIN, Francis (M) 143 1
H: 5 10 W: 11 08 b.Laval 13-5-91
Internationals: France U17, U18, U19, U20, U21.
2008–09 Arsenal 0 0
2009–10 Arsenal 0 0
2010–11 Arsenal 0 0
2010–11 *Lorient* 24 1 **24 1**
2011–12 Arsenal 10 0
2012–13 Arsenal 11 0
2013–14 Arsenal 0 0
2013–14 *SC Freiburg* 16 0 **16 0**
2014–15 Arsenal 22 0
2014–15 *Charlton Ath* 5 0 **5 0**
2015–16 Arsenal 26 0
2016–17 Arsenal 29 0 **98 0**

CROWLEY, Daniel (M) 33 4
H: 5 9 W: 10 10 b.Coventry 3-8-97
Internationals: Republic of Ireland U16, U17. England U16, U17, U19.
2015–16 Arsenal 0 0
2015–16 *Barnsley* 11 0 **11 0**
2016–17 Arsenal 0 0
2016–17 *Oxford U* 6 2 **6 2**
2016–17 *Go Ahead Eagles* 16 2 **16 2**

DA SILVA, Josh (M) 0 0
b. 23-10-98
Internationals: England U19.
2016–17 Arsenal 0 0

DEBUCHY, Mathieu (D) 294 18
H: 5 10 W: 12 02 b.Fretin 28-7-85
Internationals: France U21, Full caps.
2003–04 Lille 6 0
2004–05 Lille 16 3
2005–06 Lille 26 4

2006–07	Lille	22	1		
2007–08	Lille	16	0		
2008–09	Lille	30	0		
2009–10	Lille	31	1		
2010–11	Lille	35	2		
2011–12	Lille	32	5		
2012–13	Lille	15	0	**229**	**16**
2012–13	Newcastle U	14	0		
2013–14	Newcastle U	29	1	**43**	**1**
2014–15	Arsenal	10	1		
2015–16	Arsenal	2	0		
2015–16	*Bordeaux*	9	0	**9**	**0**
2016–17	Arsenal	1	0	**13**	**1**

EL-NENNY, Mohamed (M) 151 7
H: 5 11 W: 11 00 b.Al-Mahalla Al-Kubra 11-7-92
Internationals: Egypt U20, U23, Full caps.

2010–11	El Mokawloon	21	2		
2011–12	El Mokawloon	14	0	**35**	**2**
2012–13	Basel	15	0		
2013–14	Basel	32	1		
2014–15	Basel	28	2	**75**	**3**
2015–16	Basle	16	2	**16**	**2**
2015–16	Arsenal	11	0		
2016–17	Arsenal	14	0	**25**	**0**

GABRIEL, Armando (D) 160 2
H: 6 2 W: 13 05 b.Sao Paulo 26-11-90

2010	Vitoria	11	0		
2011	Vitoria	17	0		
2012	Vitoria	35	0		
2013	Vitoria	14	1	**77**	**1**
2013–14	Villareal	18	0	**18**	**0**
2014–15	Villarreal	19	0	**19**	**0**
2014–15	Arsenal	6	0		
2015–16	Arsenal	21	1		
2016–17	Arsenal	19	0	**46**	**1**

GIBBS, Kieran (M) 144 2
H: 5 10 W: 10 02 b.Lambeth 26-9-89
Internationals: England U19, U20, U21, Full caps

2007–08	Arsenal	0	0		
2007–08	*Norwich C*	7	0	**7**	**0**
2008–09	Arsenal	8	0		
2009–10	Arsenal	3	0		
2010–11	Arsenal	7	0		
2011–12	Arsenal	16	1		
2012–13	Arsenal	27	0		
2013–14	Arsenal	28	0		
2014–15	Arsenal	22	0		
2015–16	Arsenal	15	1		
2016–17	Arsenal	11	0	**137**	**2**

GIROUD, Olivier (F) 316 133
H: 6 3 W: 13 11 b.Chambery 30-9-86
Internationals: France Full caps.

2005–06	Grenoble	3	0		
2006–07	Grenoble	15	2	**18**	**2**
2008–09	Tours	23	8		
2009–10	Tours	38	21	**61**	**29**
2010–11	Montpellier	37	12		
2011–12	Montpellier	36	21	**73**	**33**
2012–13	Arsenal	34	11		
2013–14	Arsenal	36	16		
2014–15	Arsenal	27	14		
2015–16	Arsenal	38	16		
2016–17	Arsenal	29	12	**164**	**69**

HINDS, Kaylen (F) 13 0
b.Brent 28-1-98
Internationals: England U16, U17, U18.

2016–17	Arsenal	0	0		
2016–17	*Stevenage*	13	0	**13**	**0**

HOLDING, Rob (D) 36 1
b.Tameside 20-9-95
Internationals: England U21.

2014–15	Bolton W	0	0		
2014–15	*Bury*	1	0	**1**	**0**
2015–16	Bolton W	26	1	**26**	**1**
2016–17	Arsenal	9	0	**9**	**0**

IWOBI, Alex (M) 39 5
H: 5 11 W: 11 11 b.Lagos 3-5-96
Internationals: England U16, U17, U18. Nigeria Full caps.

2012–13	Arsenal	0	0		
2013–14	Arsenal	0	0		
2014–15	Arsenal	0	0		
2015–16	Arsenal	13	2		
2016–17	Arsenal	26	3	**39**	**5**

JENKINSON, Carl (D) 98 3
H: 6 1 W: 12 02 b.Harlow 8-2-92
Internationals: Finland U19, U21. England U17, U21, Full caps.

2010–11	Charlton Ath	8	0	**8**	**0**
2010–11	Arsenal	0	0		
2011–12	Arsenal	9	0		
2012–13	Arsenal	14	0		
2013–14	Arsenal	14	1		
2014–15	Arsenal	0	0		
2014–15	*West Ham U*	32	0		
2015–16	Arsenal	0	0		
2015–16	*West Ham U*	20	2	**52**	**2**
2016–17	Arsenal	1	0	**38**	**1**

KAMARA, Glen (F) 10 0
H: 5 10 W: 13 00 b.Tampere 28-10-95
Internationals: Finland U19, U20, U21.

2012–13	Arsenal	0	0		
2014–15	Arsenal	0	0		
2015–16	Arsenal	0	0		
2015–16	*Southend U*	6	0	**6**	**0**
2016–17	Arsenal	0	0		
2016–17	*Colchester U*	4	0	**4**	**0**

KOSCIELNY, Laurent (D) 356 26
H: 6 1 W: 11 11 b.Tulle 10-9-85
Internationals: France Full caps.

2004–05	Guingamp	11	0		
2005–06	Guingamp	9	0		
2006–07	Guingamp	21	0	**41**	**0**
2007–08	Tours	33	1		
2008–09	Tours	34	5	**67**	**6**
2009–10	Lorient	35	3	**35**	**3**
2010–11	Arsenal	30	2		
2011–12	Arsenal	33	2		
2012–13	Arsenal	25	2		
2013–14	Arsenal	32	2		
2014–15	Arsenal	27	3		
2015–16	Arsenal	33	4		
2016–17	Arsenal	33	2	**213**	**17**

LUCAS PEREZ, Martinez (F) 159 49
H: 5 11 W: 11 07 b.A Coruna 10-9-88

2009–10	Rayo Vallecano	2	0		
2010–11	Rayo Vallecano	5	1	**7**	**1**
2010–11	Karpaty Lviv	8	0		
2011–12	Karpaty Lviv	26	6		
2012–13	Karpaty Lviv	17	8	**51**	**14**
2012–13	*Dynamo Kyiv*	0	0		
2013–14	PAOK	32	9	**32**	**9**
2014–15	*Deportivo La Coruna*	21	6		
2015–16	Deportivo La Coruna	36	17		
2016–17	Deportivo La Coruna	1	1	**58**	**24**
2016–17	Arsenal	11	1	**11**	**1**

MACEY, Matt (G) 15 0
H: 6 6 W: 14 05 b.Bristol 9-9-94

2011–12	Bristol R	0	0		
2012–13	Bristol R	0	0		
2013–14	Arsenal	0	0		
2014–15	Arsenal	0	0		
2014–15	*Accrington S*	4	0	**4**	**0**
2015–16	Arsenal	0	0		
2016–17	Arsenal	0	0		
2016–17	*Luton T*	11	0	**11**	**0**

MAITLAND-NILES, Ainsley (F) 32 1
H: 5 10 W: 11 05 b.Goodmayes 29-8-97
Internationals: England U17, U18, U19 U20.

2014–15	Arsenal	1	0		
2015–16	Arsenal	0	0		
2015–16	*Ipswich T*	30	1	**30**	**1**
2016–17	Arsenal	1	0	**2**	**0**

MARTINEZ, Damian (G) 39 0
H: 6 3 W: 13 05 b.Mar del Plata 2-9-92
Internationals: Argentina U17, U20.

2010–11	Arsenal	0	0		
2011–12	Arsenal	0	0		
2011–12	*Oxford U*	1	0	**1**	**0**
2012–13	Arsenal	0	0		
2013–14	Arsenal	0	0		
2013–14	*Sheffield W*	11	0	**11**	**0**
2014–15	Arsenal	4	0		
2014–15	*Rotherham U*	8	0	**8**	**0**
2015–16	Arsenal	0	0		
2015–16	*Wolverhampton W*	13	0	**13**	**0**
2016–17	Arsenal	2	0	**6**	**0**

MAVIDIDI, Stephy (F) 5 0
b.Derby 31-5-98
Internationals: England U17, U18, U19.

2016–17	Arsenal	0	0		
2016–17	*Charlton Ath*	5	0	**5**	**0**

MERTESACKER, Per (D) 370 24
H: 6 6 W: 14 -02 b.Hannover 29-9-84
Internationals: Germany U20, U21, Full caps.

2003–04	Hannover	13	0		
2004–05	Hannover	31	2		
2005–06	Hannover	30	5	**74**	**7**
2006–07	Werder Bremen	25	2		
2007–08	Werder Bremen	32	1		
2008–09	Werder Bremen	23	2		
2009–10	Werder Bremen	33	5		
2010–11	Werder Bremen	29	2		
2011–12	Werder Bremen	4	0	**146**	**12**
2011–12	Arsenal	21	0		
2012–13	Arsenal	34	3		
2013–14	Arsenal	35	2		
2014–15	Arsenal	35	0		
2015–16	Arsenal	24	0		
2016–17	Arsenal	1	0	**150**	**5**

MONREAL, Nacho (D) 307 4
H: 5 10 W: 11 04 b.Pamplona 26-2-86
Internationals: Spain U19, U21, Full caps.

2006–07	Osasuna	11	0		
2007–08	Osasuna	27	0		
2008–09	Osasuna	28	0		
2009–10	Osasuna	31	1		
2010–11	Osasuna	31	1	**128**	**2**
2011–12	Malaga	31	0		
2012–13	Malaga	14	1	**45**	**1**
2012–13	Arsenal	10	1		
2013–14	Arsenal	23	0		
2014–15	Arsenal	28	0		
2015–16	Arsenal	37	0		
2016–17	Arsenal	36	0	**134**	**1**

MUSTAFI, Shkodran (D) 140 9
H: 6 0 W: 11 07 b.Bad Hersfeld 17-4-92
Internationals: Germany U16, U17, U18, U19, U20, U21, Full caps.

2009–10	Everton	0	0		
2010–11	Everton	0	0		
2011–12	Everton	0	0		
2011–12	Sampdoria	1	0		
2012–13	Sampdoria	17	0		
2013–14	Sampdoria	33	1	**51**	**1**
2014–15	Valencia	33	4		
2015–16	Valencia	30	2	**63**	**6**
2016–17	Arsenal	26	2	**26**	**2**

OSPINA, David (G) 310 0
H: 6 0 W: 12 00 b.Medellin 31-8-88
Internationals: Colombia U20, Full caps.

2006	Atletico Nacional	34	0		
2007	Atletico Nacional	47	0		
2008	Atletico Nacional	16	0	**97**	**0**
2008–09	Nice	25	0		
2009–10	Nice	37	0		
2010–11	Nice	35	0		
2011–12	Nice	37	0		
2012–13	Nice	26	0		
2013–14	Nice	29	0	**189**	**0**
2014–15	Arsenal	18	0		
2015–16	Arsenal	4	0		
2016–17	Arsenal	2	0	**24**	**0**

OXLADE-CHAMBERLAIN, Alex (M) 165 18
H: 5 11 W: 11 00 b.Portsmouth 15-8-93
Internationals: England U18, U19, U21, Full caps.

2009–10	Southampton	2	0		
2010–11	Southampton	34	9	**36**	**9**
2011–12	Arsenal	16	2		
2012–13	Arsenal	25	1		
2013–14	Arsenal	14	2		
2014–15	Arsenal	23	1		
2015–16	Arsenal	22	1		
2016–17	Arsenal	29	2	**129**	**9**

OZIL, Mesut (M) 321 55
H: 5 11 W: 11 06 b.Gelsenkirchen 15-10-88
Internationals: Germany U19, U21, Full caps.

2005–06	Schalke 04	0	0		
2006–07	Schalke 04	19	0		
2007–08	Schalke 04	11	0	**30**	**0**
2007–08	Werder Bremen	12	1		
2008–09	Werder Bremen	27	3		
2009–10	Werder Bremen	31	9		
2010–11	Werder Bremen	0	0	**70**	**13**
2010–11	Real Madrid	36	6		
2011–12	Real Madrid	35	4		
2012–13	Real Madrid	32	9		
2013–14	Real Madrid	2	0	**105**	**19**
2013–14	Arsenal	26	5		
2014–15	Arsenal	22	4		
2015–16	Arsenal	35	6		
2016–17	Arsenal	33	8	**116**	**23**

RAMSEY, Aaron (M) 237 31
H: 5 9 W: 10 07 b.Caerphilly 26-12-90
Internationals: Wales U17, U21, Full caps. Great Britain.

2006–07	Cardiff C	1	0		
2007–08	Cardiff C	15	1		
2008–09	Arsenal	9	0		
2009–10	Arsenal	18	3		
2010–11	Arsenal	7	1		
2010–11	*Nottingham F*	5	0	**5**	**0**
2010–11	*Cardiff C*	6	1	**22**	**2**

2011–12	Arsenal	34	2		
2012–13	Arsenal	36	1		
2013–14	Arsenal	23	10		
2014–15	Arsenal	29	6		
2015–16	Arsenal	31	5		
2016–17	Arsenal	23	1	**210**	**29**

REINE-ADELAIDE, Jeff (M) 0 0
H: 6 0 W: 11 11 b.Champigny-sur-Marne 17-1-98
Internationals: France U16, U17, U18, U19.

2014–15	Lens	0	0
2015–16	Arsenal	0	0
2016–17	Arsenal	0	0

SANCHEZ, Alexis (F) 388 129
H: 5 6 W: 11 09 b.Tocopilla 19-12-88
Internationals: Chile U20, Full caps.

2005	Cobreloa	35	3		
2006	Cobreloa	12	6	**47**	**9**
2006–07	Udinese	0	0		
2006–07	*Colo Colo*	32	5	**32**	**5**
2007–08	*River Plate*	23	4	**23**	**4**
2008–09	Udinese	32	3		
2009–10	Udinese	32	5		
2010–11	Udinese	31	12	**95**	**20**
2011–12	Barcelona	25	11		
2012–13	Barcelona	29	8		
2013–14	Barcelona	34	19	**88**	**38**
2014–15	Arsenal	35	16		
2015–16	Arsenal	30	13		
2016–17	Arsenal	38	24	**103**	**53**

SHEAF, Ben (M) 0 0
H: 5 10 W: 10 01 b.Dartford 5-2-98
Internationals: England U18.

2015–16	Arsenal	0	0
2016–17	Arsenal	0	0

SZCZESNY, Wojciech (G) 232 0
H: 5 10 W: 11 11 b.Warsaw 18-4-90
Internationals: Poland U20, U21, Full caps.

2007–08	Arsenal	0	0		
2008–09	Arsenal	0	0		
2009–10	Arsenal	0	0		
2009–10	*Brentford*	28	0	**28**	**0**
2010–11	Arsenal	15	0		
2011–12	Arsenal	38	0		
2012–13	Arsenal	25	0		
2013–14	Arsenal	37	0		
2014–15	Arsenal	17	0		
2015–16	Arsenal	0	0		
2015–16	*Roma*	34	0		
2016–17	Arsenal	0	0	**132**	**0**
2016–17	*Roma*	38	0	**72**	**0**

TORAL, Jon (M) 82 16
H: 6 0 W: 12 07 b.Reus 5-2-95

2013–14	Arsenal	0	0		
2014–15	Arsenal	0	0		
2014–15	*Brentford*	34	6	**34**	**6**
2015–16	Arsenal	0	0		
2015–16	*Birmingham C*	36	8	**36**	**8**
2016–17	Arsenal	0	0		
2016–17	*Rangers*	12	2	**12**	**2**

WALCOTT, Theo (F) 285 69
H: 5 9 W: 11 01 b.Stanmore 16-3-89
Internationals: England U16, U17, U19, U21, Full caps.

2005–06	Southampton	21	4	**21**	**4**
2005–06	Arsenal	0	0		
2006–07	Arsenal	16	0		
2007–08	Arsenal	25	4		
2008–09	Arsenal	22	2		
2009–10	Arsenal	23	3		
2010–11	Arsenal	28	9		
2011–12	Arsenal	35	8		
2012–13	Arsenal	32	14		
2013–14	Arsenal	13	5		
2014–15	Arsenal	14	5		
2015–16	Arsenal	28	5		
2016–17	Arsenal	28	10	**264**	**65**

WELBECK, Danny (F) 178 38
H: 6 1 W: 11 07 b.Manchester 26-11-90
Internationals: England U17, U18, U19, U21, Full caps.

2007–08	Manchester U	0	0		
2008–09	Manchester U	3	1		
2009–10	Manchester U	5	0		
2009–10	*Preston NE*	8	2	**8**	**2**
2010–11	Manchester U	0	0		
2010–11	*Sunderland*	26	6	**26**	**6**
2011–12	Manchester U	30	9		
2012–13	Manchester U	27	1		
2013–14	Manchester U	25	9		
2014–15	Manchester U	2	0	**92**	**20**
2014–15	Arsenal	25	4		
2015–16	Arsenal	11	4		
2016–17	Arsenal	16	2	**52**	**10**

WILLOCK, Chris (M) 0 0
H: 5 10 W: 10 08 b.London 31-1-98
Internationals: England U16, U17, U18, U19.

2015–16	Arsenal	0	0
2016–17	Arsenal	0	0

WILSHERE, Jack (M) 146 7
H: 5 7 W: 11 03 b.Stevenage 1-1-92
Internationals: England U16, U17, U19, U21, Full caps.

2008–09	Arsenal	1	0		
2009–10	Arsenal	1	0		
2009–10	*Bolton W*	14	1	**14**	**1**
2010–11	Arsenal	35	1		
2011–12	Arsenal	0	0		
2012–13	Arsenal	25	0		
2013–14	Arsenal	24	3		
2014–15	Arsenal	14	2		
2015–16	Arsenal	3	0		
2016–17	Arsenal	2	0	**105**	**6**
2016–17	*Bournemouth*	27	0	**27**	**0**

XHAKA, Granit (M) 182 9
H: 6 0 W: 11 00 b.Gnjilane 27-9-92
Internationals: Switzerland U17, U18, U19, U21, Full caps.

2010–11	Basel	19	1		
2011–12	Basel	23	0	**42**	**1**
2012–13	Borussia M'gladbach	22	1		
2013–14	Borussia M'gladbach	28	0		
2014–15	Borussia M'gladbach	30	2		
2015–16	Borussia M'gladbach	28	3	**108**	**6**
2016–17	Arsenal	32	2	**32**	**2**

ZELALEM, Gedion (M) 30 1
H: 5 10 W: 11 00 b.Berlin 26-1-97
Internationals: Germany U16, U17. USA U20, U23.

2013–14	Arsenal	0	0		
2014–15	Arsenal	0	0		
2015–16	Arsenal	0	0		
2015–16	*Rangers*	21	0	**21**	**0**
2016–17	Arsenal	0	0		
2016–17	*VVV Venlo*	9	1	**9**	**1**

Players retained or with offer of contract
Armando, De Abreu Gabriel; Asano, Takuma; Bola, Tolaji; Bramall, Cohen; Crean, Alexander Felix; Dragomir, Vlad-Mihai; Eyoma, Aaron Jordan; Fortune, Yassin Enzo; Gilmour, Charlie Ian; Huddart, Ryan David; Iliev, Deyan; Johnson, Chiori; Keto, Hugo Oliver; Malen, Donyell; McGuane, Marcus; Moore, Tafari Lalibela; Mourgos, Savvas; Nelson, Reiss; Nketiah, Edward; Nwakali, Kelechi; Osei-Tutu, Jordi; Pleguezuelo, Julio Jose; Virginia, Joao.

Scholars
Ballard, Daniel George; Beckford, Jay Lloyd; Benson, Josh; Burton, Robert; Medley, Zechariah Joshua Henry; Olowu, Joseph Olugbenga; Omole, Tobi; Smith, Rowe Emile; Thompson, Dominic; Tormey, Nathan Alexander; Willock, Joseph George.

ASTON VILLA (4)

ADOMAH, Albert (F) 411 62
H: 6 1 W: 11 08 b.Lambeth 13-12-87
Internationals: Ghana Full caps.

2007–08	Barnet	22	5		
2008–09	Barnet	45	9		
2009–10	Barnet	45	5	**112**	**19**
2010–11	Bristol C	46	5		
2011–12	Bristol C	45	5		
2012–13	Bristol C	40	7	**131**	**17**
2013–14	Middlesbrough	42	12		
2014–15	Middlesbrough	43	5		
2015–16	Middlesbrough	43	6		
2016–17	Middlesbrough	2	0	**130**	**23**
2016–17	Aston Villa	38	3	**38**	**3**

AGBONLAHOR, Gabriel (F) 345 74
H: 5 11 W: 12 05 b.Birmingham 13-10-86
Internationals: England U21, Full caps.

2005–06	Aston Villa	9	1		
2005–06	*Watford*	2	0	**2**	**0**
2005–06	*Sheffield W*	8	0	**8**	**0**
2006–07	Aston Villa	38	9		
2007–08	Aston Villa	37	11		
2008–09	Aston Villa	36	11		
2009–10	Aston Villa	36	13		
2010–11	Aston Villa	26	3		
2011–12	Aston Villa	33	5		
2012–13	Aston Villa	28	9		
2013–14	Aston Villa	30	4		
2014–15	Aston Villa	34	6		
2015–16	Aston Villa	15	1		
2016–17	Aston Villa	13	1	**335**	**74**

AMAVI, Jordan (D) 99 4
H: 5 9 W: 11 00 b.Toulon 9-3-94
Internationals: France U18, U20, U21.

2013–14	Nice	19	0		
2014–15	Nice	36	4	**55**	**4**
2015–16	Aston Villa	10	0		
2016–17	Aston Villa	34	0	**44**	**0**

BACUNA, Leandro (M) 168 14
H: 6 2 W: 12 00 b.Groningen 21-8-91
Internationals: Netherlands U19, U21. Curacao Full caps.

2009–10	FC Groningen	20	2		
2012–13	FC Groningen	33	5	**53**	**7**
2013–14	Aston Villa	35	5		
2014–15	Aston Villa	19	0		
2015–16	Aston Villa	31	1		
2016–17	Aston Villa	30	1	**115**	**7**

BAKER, Nathan (D) 171 2
H: 6 2 W: 11 11 b.Worcester 23-4-91
Internationals: England U19, U20, U21.

2008–09	Aston Villa	0	0		
2009–10	Aston Villa	0	0		
2009–10	*Lincoln C*	18	0	**18**	**0**
2010–11	Aston Villa	4	0		
2011–12	Aston Villa	8	0		
2011–12	*Millwall*	6	0	**6**	**0**
2012–13	Aston Villa	26	0		
2013–14	Aston Villa	30	0		
2014–15	Aston Villa	11	0		
2015–16	Aston Villa	0	0		
2015–16	*Bristol C*	36	1	**36**	**1**
2016–17	Aston Villa	32	1	**111**	**1**

BJARNASON, Birkir (M) 251 43
H: 6 0 W: 11 07 b.Akureyri 27-5-88
Internationals: Iceland U17, U19, U21, Full caps.

2004	Por Akureyri	0	0		
2005	KA Akureyri	0	0		
2006	Viking Stavanger	16	1		
2007	Viking Stavanger	6	0		
2008	Viking Stavanger	0	0		
2008	*FK Bodo/Glimt*	22	5	**22**	**5**
2009	Viking Stavanger	30	7		
2010	Viking Stavanger	25	8		
2011	Viking Stavanger	25	0	**102**	**16**
2011–12	Standard Liege	16	0		
2012–13	Standard Liege	0	0	**16**	**0**
2012–13	*Pescara Calcio*	24	2		
2013–14	Pescara Calcio	1	0		
2013–14	Sampdoria	14	0	**14**	**0**
2014–15	Pescara Calcio	35	10	**60**	**12**
2015–16	Basle	29	10		
2016–17	Basle	0	0	**29**	**10**
2016–17	Aston Villa	8	0	**8**	**0**

BREE, James (D) 57 0
H: 5 10 W: 11 09 b.Wakefield 11-10-97

2013–14	Barnsley	1	0		
2014–15	Barnsley	11	0		
2015–16	Barnsley	19	0		
2016–17	Barnsley	19	0	**50**	**0**
2016–17	Aston Villa	7	0	**7**	**0**

BUNN, Mark (G) 170 0
H: 6 0 W: 12 02 b.Southgate 16-11-84

2004–05	Northampton T	0	0		
2005–06	Northampton T	0	0		
2006–07	Northampton T	42	0		
2007–08	Northampton T	45	0		
2008–09	Northampton T	3	0	**90**	**0**
2008–09	Blackburn R	0	0		
2008–09	*Leicester C*	3	0	**3**	**0**
2009–10	Blackburn R	0	0		
2009–10	*Sheffield U*	32	0	**32**	**0**
2010–11	Blackburn R	3	0		
2011–12	Blackburn R	3	0		
2012–13	Blackburn R	0	0	**6**	**0**
2012–13	Norwich C	23	0		
2013–14	Norwich C	0	0		
2014–15	Norwich C	0	0	**23**	**0**
2015–16	Aston Villa	10	0		
2016–17	Aston Villa	6	0	**16**	**0**

CALDER, Ricardo (M) 38 0
H: 6 0 W: 12 06 b.Birmingham 26-1-96
Internationals: England U17.

2013–14	Aston Villa	0	0		
2014–15	Aston Villa	0	0		
2015–16	Aston Villa	0	0		
2015–16	*Dundee*	11	0	**11**	**0**
2015–16	*Doncaster R*	12	0		

2016–17 Aston Villa 0 0
2016–17 *Doncaster R* 15 0 **27 0**

CHESTER, James (D) 240 12
H: 5 11 W: 11 04 b.Warrington 23-1-89
Internationals: Wales Full caps.
2007–08 Manchester U 0 0
2008–09 Manchester U 0 0
2008–09 *Peterborough U* 5 0 **5 0**
2009–10 Manchester U 0 0
2009–10 *Plymouth Arg* 3 0 **3 0**
2010–11 Manchester U 0 0
2010–11 *Carlisle U* 18 2 **18 2**
2010–11 Hull C 21 1
2011–12 Hull C 44 2
2012–13 Hull C 44 1
2013–14 Hull C 24 1
2014–15 Hull C 23 2 **156 7**
2015–16 WBA 13 0 **13 0**
2016–17 Aston Villa 45 3 **45 3**

CISSOKHO, Aly (D) 242 3
H: 5 11 W: 11 10 b.Blois 15-9-87
Internationals: France Full caps.
2006–07 Gueugnon 1 0
2007–08 Gueugnon 21 0 **22 0**
2008–09 Vitoria Setubal 13 0 **13 0**
2008–09 Porto 15 0 **15 0**
2009–10 Lyon 30 0
2010–11 Lyon 29 1
2011–12 Lyon 31 0
2012–13 Lyon 2 0 **92 1**
2012–13 Valencia 25 2
2013–14 Valencia 0 0 **25 2**
2013–14 *Liverpool* 15 0 **15 0**
2014–15 Aston Villa 25 0
2015–16 Aston Villa 18 0
2015–16 *FC Porto* 2 0 **2 0**
2016–17 Aston Villa 12 0 **55 0**
2016–17 *Olympiacos* 3 0 **3 0**

COWANS, Henry (M) 18 0
H: 5 9 W: 11 05 b.Birmingham 2-10-96
2016–17 Aston Villa 0 0
2016–17 *Stevenage* 18 0 **18 0**

DAVIS, Keinan (M) 6 0
H: 5 6 W: 10 10 b.Stevenage 13-2-98
2015–16 Aston Villa 0 0
2016–17 Aston Villa 6 0 **6 0**

DE LAET, Ritchie (D) 170 5
H: 6 1 W: 12 02 b.Antwerp 28-11-88
Internationals: Belgium U21, Full caps.
2007–08 Stoke C 0 0
2008–09 Stoke C 0 0
2008–09 Manchester U 1 0
2009–10 Manchester U 2 0
2010–11 Manchester U 0 0
2010–11 *Sheffield U* 6 0 **6 0**
2010–11 *Preston NE* 5 0 **5 0**
2010–11 *Portsmouth* 22 0 **22 0**
2011–12 Manchester U 0 0 **3 0**
2011–12 *Norwich C* 6 1 **6 1**
2012–13 Leicester C 41 1
2013–14 Leicester C 36 2
2014–15 Leicester C 26 0
2015–16 Leicester C 12 1 **115 4**
2015–16 *Middlesbrough* 10 0 **10 0**
2016–17 Aston Villa 3 0 **3 0**

ELPHICK, Tommy (M) 309 12
H: 5 11 W: 11 07 b.Brighton 7-9-87
2005–06 Brighton & HA 1 0
2006–07 Brighton & HA 3 0
2007–08 Brighton & HA 39 2
2008–09 Brighton & HA 39 1
2009–10 Brighton & HA 44 3
2010–11 Brighton & HA 27 1
2011–12 Brighton & HA 0 0
2012–13 Brighton & HA 0 0 **153 7**
2012–13 Bournemouth 34 2
2013–14 Bournemouth 38 1
2014–15 Bournemouth 46 1
2015–16 Bournemouth 12 1 **130 5**
2016–17 Aston Villa 26 0 **26 0**

GARDNER, Gary (M) 104 10
H: 6 2 W: 12 13 b.Solihull 29-6-92
Internationals: England U17, U19, U20, U21.
2009–10 Aston Villa 0 0
2010–11 Aston Villa 0 0
2011–12 Aston Villa 14 0
2011–12 *Coventry C* 4 1 **4 1**
2012–13 Aston Villa 2 0
2013–14 Aston Villa 0 0
2013–14 *Sheffield W* 3 0 **3 0**
2014–15 Aston Villa 0 0
2014–15 *Brighton & HA* 17 2 **17 2**
2014–15 Nottingham F 18 4
2015–16 Aston Villa 0 0
2015–16 *Nottingham F* 20 2 **38 6**
2016–17 Aston Villa 26 1 **42 1**

GIL, Carles (M) 123 9
H: 5 7 W: 10 03 b.Valencia 2-11-92
Internationals: Spain U21.
2012–13 Elche 31 4
2013–14 Elche 33 1 **64 5**
2014–15 Valencia 8 1 **8 1**
2014–15 Aston Villa 5 0
2015–16 Aston Villa 23 2
2016–17 Aston Villa 0 0 **28 2**
2016–17 *Deportivo La Coruna* 23 1 **23 1**

GOLLINI, Pierluigi (G) 53 0
H: 6 2 W: 12 13 b.Bologna 18-3-95
Internationals: Italy U18, U19, U20, U21.
2013–14 Manchester U 0 0
2014–15 Verona 3 0
2015–16 Verona 26 0 **29 0**
2016–17 Aston Villa 20 0 **20 0**
2016–17 *Atalanta* 4 0 **4 0**

GREALISH, Jack (M) 102 11
H: 5 9 W: 10 10 b.Birmingham 10-9-95
Internationals: Republic of Ireland U17, U18, U21. England U21.
2012–13 Aston Villa 0 0
2013–14 Aston Villa 1 0
2013–14 *Notts Co* 37 5 **37 5**
2014–15 Aston Villa 17 0
2015–16 Aston Villa 16 1
2016–17 Aston Villa 31 5 **65 6**

GREEN, Andre (F) 17 0
H: 5 11 W: 11 03 b.Solihull 2-5-98
Internationals: England U16, U17, U18, U19.
2014–15 Aston Villa 0 0
2015–16 Aston Villa 2 0
2016–17 Aston Villa 15 0 **17 0**

HEPBURN-MURPHY, Rushian (F) 5 0
H: 5 8 W: 9 04 b.Birmingham 19-9-98
Internationals: England U16, U17, U18, U19.
2014–15 Aston Villa 1 0
2015–16 Aston Villa 1 0
2016–17 Aston Villa 3 0 **5 0**

HOGAN, Scott (F) 79 39
H: 5 11 W: 10 01 b.Salford 13-4-92
2009–10 Rochdale 0 0
2013–14 Rochdale 33 17 **33 17**
2014–15 Brentford 1 0
2015–16 Brentford 7 7
2016–17 Brentford 25 14 **33 21**
2016–17 Aston Villa 13 1 **13 1**

HOURIHANE, Conor (M) 254 45
H: 5 11 W: 9 11 b.Cork 2-2-91
Internationals: Republic of Ireland U19, U21, Full caps.
2008–09 Sunderland 0 0
2009–10 Sunderland 0 0
2010–11 Ipswich T 0 0
2011–12 Plymouth Arg 38 2
2012–13 Plymouth Arg 42 5
2013–14 Plymouth Arg 45 8 **125 15**
2014–15 Barnsley 46 13
2015–16 Barnsley 41 10
2016–17 Barnsley 25 6 **112 29**
2016–17 Aston Villa 17 1 **17 1**

HUTTON, Alan (D) 300 4
H: 6 1 W: 11 05 b.Glasgow 30-11-84
Internationals: Scotland U21, Full caps.
2004–05 Rangers 10 0
2005–06 Rangers 19 0
2006–07 Rangers 33 1
2007–08 Rangers 20 0 **82 1**
2007–08 Tottenham H 14 0
2008–09 Tottenham H 8 0
2009–10 Tottenham H 8 0
2009–10 *Sunderland* 11 0 **11 0**
2010–11 Tottenham H 21 2
2011–12 Tottenham H 0 0 **51 2**
2011–12 Aston Villa 31 0
2012–13 Aston Villa 0 0
2012–13 *Nottingham F* 7 0 **7 0**
2012–13 *Mallorca* 17 0 **17 0**
2013–14 Aston Villa 0 0
2013–14 *Bolton W* 9 0 **9 0**
2014–15 Aston Villa 30 1
2015–16 Aston Villa 28 0
2016–17 Aston Villa 34 0 **123 1**

JEDINAK, Mile (M) 388 39
H: 6 2 W: 13 12 b.Sydney 3-8-84
Internationals: Australia U20, Full caps.
2000–01 Sydney U 3 0
2001–02 Sydney U 7 1
2002–03 Sydney U 18 2
2003–04 Varteks 0 0
2004–05 Sydney U 24 3
2005–06 Sydney U 30 6 **82 12**
2006–07 Central Coast M 8 0
2007–08 Central Coast M 22 2
2008–09 Central Coast M 15 6 **45 8**
2008–09 Genclerbirligi 15 1
2009–10 Genclerbirligi 2 0
2009–10 Antalya 28 5 **28 5**
2010–11 Genclerbirligi 21 3 **38 4**
2011–12 Crystal Palace 31 1
2012–13 Crystal Palace 41 3
2013–14 Crystal Palace 38 1
2014–15 Crystal Palace 24 5
2015–16 Crystal Palace 27 0
2016–17 Crystal Palace 1 0 **162 10**
2016–17 Aston Villa 33 0 **33 0**

KODJIA, Jonathan (F) 199 71
H: 6 2 W: 12 02 b.Saint-Denis 22-10-89
Internationals: Ivory Coast Full caps.
2008–09 Reims 2 0
2009–10 Reims 0 0
2010–11 Reims 5 0
2011–12 Reims 2 0
2011–12 *Cherbourg* 16 4 **16 4**
2012–13 Reims 0 0
2012–13 *Amiens SC* 34 9 **34 9**
2013–14 Reims 0 0 **9 0**
2013–14 *Caen* 27 5 **27 5**
2014–15 Angers SCO 28 15 **28 15**
2015–16 Bristol C 45 19
2016–17 Bristol C 4 0 **49 19**
2016–17 Aston Villa 36 19 **36 19**

KOZAK, Libor (F) 102 18
H: 6 4 W: 12 11 b.Brumov-Bylnice 30-5-89
Internationals: Czech Republic U19, U21, Full caps.
2008–09 Lazio 3 0
2009–10 *Brescia* 25 4 **25 4**
2010–11 Lazio 19 6
2011–12 Lazio 16 4
2012–13 Lazio 19 0 **57 10**
2013–14 Aston Villa 14 4
2014–15 Aston Villa 0 0
2015–16 Aston Villa 4 0
2016–17 Aston Villa 2 0 **20 4**

LANSBURY, Henri (M) 264 46
H: 6 0 W: 13 06 b.Enfield 12-10-90
Internationals: England U16, U17, U19, U21.
2007–08 Arsenal 0 0
2008–09 Arsenal 0 0
2008–09 *Scunthorpe U* 16 4 **16 4**
2009–10 Arsenal 1 0
2009–10 *Watford* 37 5 **37 5**
2010–11 Arsenal 0 0
2010–11 *Norwich C* 23 4 **23 4**
2011–12 Arsenal 2 0
2011–12 *West Ham U* 22 1 **22 1**
2012–13 Arsenal 0 0 **3 0**
2012–13 Nottingham F 32 5
2013–14 Nottingham F 29 7
2014–15 Nottingham F 39 10
2015–16 Nottingham F 28 4
2016–17 Nottingham F 17 6 **145 32**
2016–17 Aston Villa 18 0 **18 0**

LYDEN, Jordan (M) 4 0
H: 5 10 W: 11 00 b.Perth 30-1-96
Internationals: Australia U20.
2015–16 Aston Villa 4 0
2016–17 Aston Villa 0 0 **4 0**

MASON, Niall (M) 38 0
b. 10-1-97
2015–16 Aston Villa 0 0
2016–17 Aston Villa 0 0
2016–17 *Doncaster R* 38 0 **38 0**

McCORMACK, Ross (F) 412 137
H: 5 9 W: 11 00 b.Glasgow 18-8-86
Internationals: Scotland U21, B, Full caps.
2003–04 Rangers 2 1
2004–05 Rangers 1 0
2005–06 Rangers 8 1 **11 2**
2005–06 Doncaster R 19 4 **19 4**
2006–07 Motherwell 12 2
2007–08 Motherwell 36 9 **48 11**
2008–09 Cardiff C 38 21
2009–10 Cardiff C 34 4
2010–11 Cardiff C 2 0 **74 25**
2010–11 Leeds U 21 2
2011–12 Leeds U 45 18
2012–13 Leeds U 32 5
2013–14 Leeds U 46 28 **144 53**
2014–15 Fulham 44 17

2015–16	Fulham	45	21	**89**	**38**
2016–17	Aston Villa	20	3	**20**	**3**
2016–17	*Nottingham F*	7	1	**7**	**1**

McKIRDY, Harry (M) **11 1**
H: 5 9 W: 11 00 b.Stoke-on-Trent 29-3-97
From Stoke C.

2016–17	Aston Villa	0	0		
2016–17	*Stevenage*	11	1	**11**	**1**

O'HARE, Callum (F) **0 0**
b.Solihull 1-5-98

2016–17	Aston Villa	0	0		

RICHARDS, Micah (D) **215 8**
H: 5 11 W: 13 00 b.Birmingham 24-6-88
Internationals: England U16, U19, U21, Full caps. Great Britain.

2005–06	Manchester C	13	0		
2006–07	Manchester C	28	1		
2007–08	Manchester C	25	0		
2008–09	Manchester C	34	1		
2009–10	Manchester C	23	3		
2010–11	Manchester C	18	1		
2011–12	Manchester C	29	1		
2012–13	Manchester C	7	0		
2013–14	Manchester C	2	0		
2014–15	Manchester C	0	0	**179**	**7**
2014–15	*Fiorentina*	10	0	**10**	**0**
2015–16	Aston Villa	24	1		
2016–17	Aston Villa	2	0	**26**	**1**

SANCHEZ, Carlos (M) **324 14**
H: 6 0 W: 12 08 b.Quidbo 6-2-86
Internationals: Colombia Full caps.

2005–06	River Plate	14	0		
2006–07	River Plate	26	1	**40**	**1**
2007–08	Valenciennes	34	0		
2008–09	Valenciennes	37	1		
2009–10	Valenciennes	28	5		
2010–11	Valenciennes	28	2		
2011–12	Valenciennes	21	1		
2012–13	Valenciennes	27	2	**175**	**11**
2013–14	Elche	30	0	**30**	**0**
2014–15	Aston Villa	28	1		
2015–16	Aston Villa	20	0		
2016–17	Aston Villa	0	0	**48**	**1**
2016–17	*Fiorentina*	31	1	**31**	**1**

SARKIC, Matija (G) **0 0**
H: 6 4 W: 11 07 b.Podgorica 23-6-97
Internationals: Montenegro U19.

2014–15	Anderlecht	0	0		
2015–16	Aston Villa	0	0		
2016–17	Aston Villa	0	0		

STEER, Jed (G) **76 0**
H: 6 2 W: 14 00 b.Norwich 23-9-92
Internationals: England U16, U17, U19.

2009–10	Norwich C	0	0		
2010–11	Norwich C	0	0		
2011–12	Norwich C	0	0		
2011–12	*Yeovil T*	12	0		
2012–13	Cambridge U	0	0		
2012–13	Norwich C	0	0		
2013–14	Aston Villa	0	0		
2014–15	Aston Villa	1	0		
2014–15	*Doncaster R*	13	0	**13**	**0**
2014–15	*Yeovil T*	12	0	**24**	**0**
2015–16	Aston Villa	0	0		
2015–16	*Huddersfield T*	38	0	**38**	**0**
2016–17	Aston Villa	0	0	**1**	**0**

SULIMAN, Easah (D) **9 0**
H: 6 2 W: 12 08 b. 26-1-98
Internationals: England U16, U17, U18, U19.

2015–16	Aston Villa	0	0		
2016–17	Aston Villa	0	0		
2016–17	*Cheltenham T*	9	0	**9**	**0**

TAYLOR, Corey (F) **1 0**
b.Erdington 23-9-97
Internationals: England U17.

2015–16	Aston Villa	0	0		
2016–17	Aston Villa	1	0	**1**	**0**

TAYLOR, Neil (D) **200 0**
H: 5 9 W: 10 02 b.Ruthin 7-2-89
Internationals: Wales U17, U19, U21, Full caps. Great Britain.

2007–08	Wrexham	26	0	**26**	**0**
2010–11	Swansea C	29	0		
2011–12	Swansea C	36	0		
2012–13	Swansea C	6	0		
2013–14	Swansea C	10	0		
2014–15	Swansea C	34	0		
2015–16	Swansea C	34	0		
2016–17	Swansea C	11	0	**160**	**0**
2016–17	Aston Villa	14	0	**14**	**0**

TONER, Kevin (D) **22 1**
b. 18-7-96
Internationals: Republic of Ireland U19.

2015–16	Aston Villa	4	0		
2016–17	Aston Villa	0	0	**4**	**0**
2016–17	*Walsall*	16	0	**16**	**0**
2016–17	*Bradford C*	2	1	**2**	**1**

TSHIBOLA, Aaron (M) **48 1**
H: 6 3 W: 11 01 b.Newham 2-1-95
Internationals: England U18.

2011–12	Reading	0	0		
2012–13	Reading	0	0		
2013–14	Reading	0	0		
2014–15	Reading	1	0		
2014–15	*Hartlepool U*	23	0	**23**	**0**
2015–16	Reading	12	0	**13**	**0**
2016–17	Aston Villa	8	1	**8**	**1**
2016–17	*Nottingham F*	4	0	**4**	**0**

VERETOUT, Jordan (M) **190 17**
H: 5 9 W: 10 06 b.Ancenis 1-3-93
Internationals: France U18, U19, U20, U21.

2010–11	Nantes	1	0		
2011–12	Nantes	35	6		
2012–13	Nantes	31	0		
2013–14	Nantes	27	1		
2014–15	Nantes	36	7	**130**	**14**
2015–16	Aston Villa	25	0		
2016–17	Aston Villa	0	0	**25**	**0**
2016–17	*St Etienne*	35	3	**35**	**3**

Players retained or with offer of contract
Abdo, Khalid; Bedeau, Jacob Mitchell; Borg, Oscar Francis; Clark, Mitchell; Clarke, Jack Aidan; Cox, Jordan Raymond; Doyle, Hayes Jake Billy; Finnerty, James John; Idem, Emmanuel Okokon; Johansson, Viktor Tobias; Mooney, Kelsey; Pastorek, Jozef; Prosser, Alexander; Watkins, Bradley.

Scholars
Bazeley, Isaiah Robert Graham; Birch, Mason Lewis; Boucher, Kieran David; Coates, Jack Lewis; Hall, Louis Aiden; Knibbs, Harvey; Rowe, Callum Miles; Stretch, Callum Blu; Williams, Joshua Arthur.

BARNET (5)

AKINDE, John (F) **194 61**
H: 6 2 W: 10 01 b.Camberwell 8-7-89

2008–09	Bristol C	7	1		
2008–09	*Wycombe W*	11	7		
2009–10	Bristol C	7	0		
2009–10	*Wycombe W*	6	1	**17**	**8**
2009–10	*Brentford*	2	0	**2**	**0**
2010–11	Bristol C	2	0	**16**	**1**
2010–11	*Bristol R*	14	0	**14**	**0**
2010–11	*Dagenham & R*	9	2		
2011–12	Crawley T	25	1		
2011–12	*Dagenham & R*	5	0	**14**	**2**
2012–13	Crawley T	6	0	**31**	**1**
2012–13	Portsmouth	11	0		
2013–14	Portsmouth	0	0	**11**	**0**
2015–16	Barnet	43	23		
2016–17	Barnet	46	26	**89**	**49**

AKINDE, Sam (F) **1 0**
b. 14-4-93
From Kettering T, Ebbsfleet U, Alfreton T, Dover Ath, Kingstonian, Hereford U, Welling U, Basingstoke T, St Albans C.

2016–17	Barnet	1	0	**1**	**0**

AKINOLA, Simeon (F) **19 2**
H: 5 10 W: 12 00 b. 6-8-92
From Boreham Wood, Harrow Bor, Braintree T.

2016–17	Barnet	19	2	**19**	**2**

AKPA AKPRO, Jean-Louis (F) **356 52**
H: 6 0 W: 10 12 b.Toulouse 4-1-85

2004–05	Toulouse	13	0		
2005–06	Toulouse	14	3	**27**	**3**
2006–07	*Brest*	15	2	**15**	**2**
2007–08	FC Brussels	3	0	**3**	**0**
2008–09	Grimsby T	20	3		
2009–10	Grimsby T	36	5	**56**	**8**
2010–11	Rochdale	32	4		
2011–12	Rochdale	41	7	**73**	**11**
2012–13	Tranmere R	28	8		
2013–14	Tranmere R	25	2	**53**	**10**
2013–14	*Bury*	10	0	**10**	**0**
2014–15	Shrewsbury T	45	9		
2015–16	Shrewsbury T	38	6	**83**	**15**
2016–17	Barnet	23	1	**23**	**1**
2016–17	*Yeovil T*	13	2	**13**	**2**

AMALUZOR, Justin (F) **11 0**
H: 6 0 W: 12 00 b. 17-10-96
From Dartford.

2016–17	Barnet	11	0	**11**	**0**

BATT, Shaun (M) **180 16**
H: 6 3 W: 12 08 b.Harlow 22-2-87

2008–09	Peterborough U	30	2		
2009–10	Peterborough U	20	2	**50**	**4**
2009–10	*Millwall*	16	3		
2010–11	Millwall	0	0		
2011–12	Millwall	4	0		
2011–12	*Crawley T*	5	0	**5**	**0**
2012–13	Millwall	16	1		
2012–13	*Leyton Orient*	11	2		
2013–14	Millwall	0	0	**36**	**4**
2013–14	Leyton Orient	35	4		
2014–15	Leyton Orient	16	1	**62**	**7**
2015–16	Barnet	16	0		
2016–17	Barnet	11	1	**27**	**1**

BROWN, Tyler (D) **0 0**

2016–17	Barnet	0	0		

CAMPBELL-RYCE, Jamal (M) **446 37**
H: 5 7 W: 12 03 b.Lambeth 6-4-83
Internationals: Jamaica Full caps.

2002–03	Charlton Ath	1	0		
2002–03	*Leyton Orient*	17	2		
2003–04	Charlton Ath	2	0		
2003–04	*Wimbledon*	4	0	**4**	**0**
2004–05	Charlton Ath	0	0	**3**	**0**
2004–05	*Chesterfield*	14	0		
2004–05	Rotherham U	24	0		
2005–06	Rotherham U	7	0	**31**	**0**
2005–06	*Southend U*	13	0		
2005–06	*Colchester U*	4	0	**4**	**0**
2006–07	Southend U	43	2		
2007–08	Southend U	2	0	**58**	**2**
2007–08	Barnsley	37	3		
2008–09	Barnsley	40	9		
2009–10	Barnsley	13	0	**90**	**12**
2009–10	Bristol C	14	0		
2010–11	Bristol C	31	2		
2011–12	Bristol C	17	0	**62**	**2**
2011–12	*Leyton Orient*	8	1	**25**	**3**
2012–13	Notts Co	37	8		
2013–14	Notts Co	36	3		
2014–15	Sheffield U	19	4		
2014–15	*Notts Co*	4	0	**77**	**11**
2015–16	Sheffield U	18	0	**37**	**4**
2015–16	*Chesterfield*	9	2	**23**	**2**
2016–17	Barnet	32	1	**32**	**1**

CHAMPION, Tom (M) **90 1**
H: 6 3 W: 12 04 b.London 15-5-86

2014–15	Cambridge U	38	0	**38**	**0**
2015–16	Barnet	26	0		
2016–17	Barnet	26	1	**52**	**1**

CLOUGH, Charlie (D) **20 1**
H: 6 0 W: 12 04 b.Somerset 3-9-90

2007–08	Bristol R	0	0		
2008–09	Bristol R	0	0		
2009–10	Bristol R	0	0		
2010–11	Bristol R	2	0		
2011–12	Bristol R	0	0	**2**	**0**

From Dorchester, Sutton U, Forest Green R.

2016–17	Barnet	18	1	**18**	**1**

COJOCAREL, Shane (M) **3 0**
H: 5 7 W: 10 03 b.Bucharest 20-3-97
Internationals: Romania U16.

2015–16	Barnet	0	0		
2016–17	Barnet	3	0	**3**	**0**

COKER, Tobi (D) **0 0**

2016–17	Barnet	0	0		

CONNELL, Rio (F) **0 0**

2016–17	Barnet	0	0		

COULSON, Luke (D) **11 0**
H: 5 10 W: 11 01 b.St Helens 6-3-94

2012–13	Cardiff C	0	0		
2013–14	Cardiff C	0	0		
2016–17	Barnet	11	0	**11**	**0**

DEMBELE, Bira (D) **131 11**
H: 6 2 W: 11 10 b. 22-3-88
Internationals: France U21.

2007–08	Rennes	7	0		
2008–09	Rennes	2	0		
2009–10	Rennes	0	0		
2009–10	*Boulogne*	23	1	**23**	**1**
2010–11	Rennes	0	0	**9**	**0**
2011–12	Sedan	1	0		
2011–12	*Red Star 93*	9	0	**9**	**0**
2012–13	Sedan	0	0	**1**	**0**
2013–14	Stevenage	13	1		
2014–15	Stevenage	27	2	**40**	**3**

2015–16	Barnet	26	3		
2016–17	Barnet	23	4	**49**	**7**

FONGUCK, Wesley (M)				**4**	**0**
H: 6 1 b. 16-7-97					
2015–16	Barnet	1	0		
2016–17	Barnet	3	0	**4**	**0**

GASH, Michael (F)				**36**	**9**
H: 5 10 W: 12 02 b.Cambridge 3-9-86					
Internationals: England C.					
From Cambridge C, Cambridge U, Ebbsfleet U, York C, Kidderminster H.					
2015–16	Barnet	34	9		
2016–17	Barnet	2	0	**36**	**9**

HOYTE, Gavin (D)				**160**	**1**
H: 5 11 W: 11 00 b.Waltham Forest 6-6-90					
Internationals: England U17, U18, U19, U20. Trinidad & Tobago Full caps.					
2007–08	Arsenal	0	0		
2008–09	Arsenal	1	0		
2008–09	*Watford*	7	0	**7**	**0**
2009–10	Arsenal	0	0		
2009–10	*Brighton & HA*	18	0	**18**	**0**
2010–11	Arsenal	0	0		
2010–11	*Lincoln C*	12	0	**12**	**0**
2011–12	Arsenal	0	0	**1**	**0**
2011–12	*AFC Wimbledon*	3	0	**3**	**0**
2012–13	Dagenham & R	26	0		
2013–14	Dagenham & R	42	0	**68**	**0**
2014–15	Gillingham	30	0	**30**	**0**
2015–16	Barnet	19	1		
2016–17	Barnet	2	0	**21**	**1**

JOHNSON, Elliot (D)				**103**	**2**
H: 5 10 W: 12 02 b.Edgeware 17-8-94					
2012–13	Barnet	26	1		
2015–16	Barnet	41	1		
2016–17	Barnet	36	0	**103**	**2**

KYEI, Nana (M)				**13**	**0**
H: 5 11 W: 11 00 b. 10-1-98					
2015–16	Barnet	1	0		
2016–17	Barnet	12	0	**13**	**0**

MASON-CLARK, Ephron (M)				**6**	**0**
H: 5 10 W: 12 00 b.Lambeth 25-8-99					
2016–17	Barnet	6	0	**6**	**0**

McKENZIE-LYLE, Kai (G)				**1**	**0**
H: 6 5 W: 13 08 b. 30-11-97					
Internationals: Guyana Full caps.					
2015–16	Barnet	1	0		
2016–17	Barnet	0	0	**1**	**0**

MUGGLETON, Sam (D)				**38**	**0**
H: 5 11 W: 11 03 b.Melton Mowbray 17-11-95					
2012–13	Gillingham	1	0		
2013–14	Gillingham	1	0	**2**	**0**
2015–16	Barnet	23	0		
2016–17	Barnet	13	0	**36**	**0**

N'GALA, Bondz (D)				**181**	**7**
H: 6 0 W: 12 03 b.Forest Gate 13-9-89					
2007–08	West Ham U	0	0		
2008–09	West Ham U	0	0		
2008–09	*Milton Keynes D*	3	0	**3**	**0**
2009–10	West Ham U	0	0		
2009–10	*Scunthorpe U*	2	0	**2**	**0**
2009–10	*Plymouth Arg*	9	0		
2010–11	Plymouth Arg	26	1	**35**	**1**
2011–12	Yeovil T	31	2	**31**	**2**
2012–13	Stevenage	25	0	**25**	**0**
2012–13	*Barnet*	6	0		
2013–14	Portsmouth	27	3	**27**	**3**
2015–16	Barnet	42	1		
2016–17	Barnet	10	0	**58**	**1**

NELSON, Michael (D)				**588**	**37**
H: 6 2 W: 13 03 b.Gateshead 15-3-82					
2000–01	Bury	2	1		
2001–02	Bury	31	2		
2002–03	Bury	39	5	**72**	**8**
2003–04	Hartlepool U	40	3		
2004–05	Hartlepool U	43	1		
2005–06	Hartlepool U	43	2		
2006–07	Hartlepool U	42	1		
2007–08	Hartlepool U	45	2		
2008–09	Hartlepool U	46	5	**259**	**14**
2009–10	Norwich C	31	3		
2010–11	Norwich C	8	2	**39**	**5**
2010–11	Scunthorpe U	20	0		
2011–12	Scunthorpe U	10	1	**30**	**1**
2011–12	Kilmarnock	15	1		
2012–13	Kilmarnock	21	1	**36**	**2**
2012–13	Bradford C	13	0	**13**	**0**
2013–14	Hibernian	34	2		
2014–15	Hibernian	2	0	**36**	**2**
2014–15	Cambridge U	33	3	**33**	**3**
2015–16	Barnet	27	1		
2016–17	Barnet	43	1	**70**	**2**

NICHOLLS, Alex (M)				**305**	**44**
H: 5 10 W: 11 00 b.Stourbridge 9-12-87					
2005–06	Walsall	8	0		
2006–07	Walsall	0	0		
2007–08	Walsall	19	2		
2008–09	Walsall	45	6		
2009–10	Walsall	37	4		
2010–11	Walsall	37	5		
2011–12	Walsall	45	7	**191**	**24**
2012–13	Northampton T	15	7		
2013–14	Northampton T	0	0		
2014–15	Northampton T	6	1	**21**	**8**
2014–15	*Exeter C*	32	5		
2015–16	Exeter C	35	5	**67**	**10**
2016–17	Barnet	17	2	**17**	**2**
2016–17	*Dundee U*	9	0	**9**	**0**

PASCAL, Dwight (M)				**0**	**0**
b.Hackney					
2016–17	Barnet	0	0		

PAYNE, Joe (D)				**0**	**0**
2016–17	Barnet	0	0		

RUBEN BOVER, Izquierdo (M)				**14**	**0**
H: 5 7 W: 10 04 b.Majorca 24-6-92					
2012–13	Charlton Ath	0	0		
2012–13	New York RB	0	0		
2016–17	Barnet	14	0	**14**	**0**

SANTOS, Ricardo (D)				**78**	**3**
H: 6 5 W: 12 02 b.Almada 18-6-95					
2012–13	Dagenham & R	0	0		
2013–14	Dagenham & R	0	0		
2013–14	Peterborough U	1	0		
2014–15	Peterborough U	24	0		
2015–16	Peterborough U	37	1		
2016–17	Peterborough U	1	0	**63**	**1**
2016–17	Barnet	15	2	**15**	**2**

SESAY, Alie (D)				**26**	**0**
b. 25-7-93					
Internationals: Sierra Leone Full caps.					
2013–14	Leicester C	0	0		
2013–14	*Colchester U*	3	0		
2014–15	*Colchester U*	0	0	**3**	**0**
2015–16	Leicester C	0	0		
2015–16	*Cambridge U*	5	0	**5**	**0**
2015–16	Barnet	13	0		
2016–17	Barnet	5	0	**18**	**0**
Transferred to IK Frej, January 2017.					

SHOMOTUN, Fumnaya (M)				**14**	**1**
H: 5 8 W: 10 08 b. 29-5-97					
2015–16	Barnet	10	1		
2016–17	Barnet	4	0	**14**	**1**

SMITH, Darnell (D)				**0**	**0**
2016–17	Barnet	0	0		

STEPHENS, Jamie (G)				**69**	**0**
H: 6 1 W: 12 04 b.Wotton 24-8-93					
2012–13	Liverpool	0	0		
2012–13	*Airbus UK*	13	0	**13**	**0**
2013–14	Newport Co	2	0		
2014–15	Newport Co	7	0	**9**	**0**
2015–16	Barnet	29	0		
2016–17	Barnet	18	0	**47**	**0**

SWEENEY, Dan (M)				**4**	**0**
H: 6 3 W: 11 11 b.Kingston upon Thames 25-4-94					
Internationals: England C.					
From AFC Wimbledon, Kingstonian, Dulwich Hamlet, Maidstone U.					
2016–17	Barnet	4	0	**4**	**0**

TAYLOR, Harry (D)				**33**	**0**
H: 6 2 b. 4-5-97					
2015–16	Barnet	8	0		
2016–17	Barnet	25	0	**33**	**0**

TAYLOR, Jack (D)				**14**	**0**
H: 6 1 W: 11 00 b. 23-6-98					
2016–17	Barnet	14	0	**14**	**0**

TOGWELL, Sam (M)				**372**	**13**
H: 5 11 W: 12 04 b.Beaconsfield 14-10-84					
2002–03	Crystal Palace	1	0		
2003–04	Crystal Palace	0	0		
2004–05	Crystal Palace	0	0		
2004–05	*Oxford U*	4	0	**4**	**0**
2004–05	*Northampton T*	8	0	**8**	**0**
2005–06	Crystal Palace	0	0	**1**	**0**
2005–06	*Port Vale*	27	2	**27**	**2**
2006–07	Barnsley	44	1		
2007–08	Barnsley	22	1	**66**	**2**
2008–09	Scunthorpe U	40	2		
2009–10	Scunthorpe U	41	2		
2010–11	Scunthorpe U	36	0		
2011–12	Scunthorpe U	39	1	**156**	**5**
2012–13	Chesterfield	45	3		
2013–14	Chesterfield	10	0	**55**	**3**
2013–14	*Wycombe W*	4	0	**4**	**0**
2015–16	Barnet	39	1		
2016–17	Barnet	12	0	**51**	**1**

TUTONDA, David (D)				**31**	**3**
H: 5 11 W: 11 00 b.Kinshasa 11-10-95					
2014–15	Cardiff C	0	0		
2014–15	*Newport Co*	12	2	**12**	**2**
2015–16	Cardiff C	0	0		
2015–16	*York C*	12	0	**12**	**0**
2016–17	Cardiff C	0	0		
2016–17	Barnet	7	1	**7**	**1**

VILHETE, Mauro (M)				**85**	**3**
H: 5 8 W: 11 09 b.Sintra 10-5-93					
2009–10	Barnet	2	0		
2010–11	Barnet	20	0		
2011–12	Barnet	3	0		
2012–13	Barnet	5	0		
2015–16	Barnet	15	0		
2016–17	Barnet	40	3	**85**	**3**

WATSON, Ryan (M)				**35**	**1**
H: 6 1 W: 11 07 b.Crewe 7-7-93					
2011–12	Wigan Ath	0	0		
2012–13	Wigan Ath	0	0		
2012–13	*Accrington S*	0	0		
2013–14	Leicester C	0	0		
2014–15	Leicester C	0	0		
2014–15	*Northampton T*	5	0		
2015–16	Leicester C	0	0		
2015–16	*Northampton T*	11	0	**16**	**0**
2016–17	Barnet	19	1	**19**	**1**

WESTON, Curtis (M)				**298**	**26**
H: 5 11 W: 11 09 b.Greenwich 24-1-87					
2003–04	Millwall	1	0		
2004–05	Millwall	3	0		
2005–06	Millwall	0	0	**4**	**0**
2006–07	Swindon T	27	1	**27**	**1**
2007–08	Leeds U	7	1		
2007–08	*Scunthorpe U*	7	0	**7**	**0**
2008–09	Leeds U	0	0	**7**	**1**
2008–09	Gillingham	45	5		
2009–10	Gillingham	39	6		
2010–11	Gillingham	33	4		
2011–12	Gillingham	30	0	**147**	**15**
2012–13	Barnet	29	0		
2015–16	Barnet	37	3		
2016–17	Barnet	40	6	**106**	**9**

Players retained or with offer of contract
Bover, Izquierdo Ruben; Day, Thomas Steven.

Scholars
Abbey, Darren; Adinna, Greg; Busby, Charlie James; Cheema, Daniel Singh; Hernandez, Loic; Loughney, Kieron; Mohamed, Arale Mohamoud; Syla, Roy.

BARNSLEY (6)

BIRD, Jared (M)				**0**	**0**
H: 5 9 W: 9 11 b.Nottingham 21-8-97					
From Derby Co.					
2016–17	Barnsley	0	0		

BRADSHAW, Tom (F)				**201**	**59**
H: 5 5 W: 11 02 b.Shrewsbury 27-7-92					
Internationals: Wales U19, U21, Full caps.					
2009–10	Shrewsbury T	6	3		
2010–11	Shrewsbury T	26	6		
2011–12	Shrewsbury T	8	1		
2012–13	Shrewsbury T	21	0		
2013–14	Shrewsbury T	28	7	**89**	**17**
2014–15	Walsall	29	17		
2015–16	Walsall	41	17	**70**	**34**
2016–17	Barnsley	42	8	**42**	**8**

BROWN, Jacob (M)				**2**	**0**
H: 5 10 W: 9 11 b. 10-4-98					
2014–15	Barnsley	0	0		
2015–16	Barnsley	0	0		
2016–17	Barnsley	2	0	**2**	**0**

D'ALMEIDA, Sessi (M)				**5**	**0**
H: 5 9 W: 11 09 b.Bordeaux 22-11-95					
Internationals: Benin Full caps.					
2013–14	Bordeaux	0	0		
2014–15	Bordeaux	2	0	**2**	**0**
2015–16	Paris Saint-Germain	0	0		
2016–17	Barnsley	3	0	**3**	**0**

DAVIES, Adam (G) 107 0
H: 6 1 W: 11 11 b.Rinteln 17-7-92
2009–10 Everton 0 0
2010–11 Everton 0 0
2011–12 Everton 0 0
2013–14 Sheffield W 0 0
2014–15 Barnsley 23 0
2015–16 Barnsley 38 0
2016–17 Barnsley 46 0 **107 0**

EVANS, Callum (D) 3 0
H: 5 10 W: 11 05 b.Bristol 11-10-95
From Manchester U.
2015–16 Barnsley 0 0
2016–17 Barnsley 3 0 **3 0**

HAMMILL, Adam (M) 313 28
H: 5 11 W: 11 07 b.Liverpool 25-1-88
Internationals: England U19, U21.
2005–06 Liverpool 0 0
2006–07 Liverpool 0 0
2006–07 *Dunfermline Ath* 13 1 **13 1**
2007–08 Liverpool 0 0
2007–08 *Southampton* 25 0 **25 0**
2008–09 Liverpool 0 0
2008–09 *Blackpool* 22 1 **22 1**
2008–09 *Barnsley* 14 1
2009–10 Barnsley 39 4
2010–11 Barnsley 25 8
2010–11 Wolverhampton W 10 0
2011–12 Wolverhampton W 9 0
2011–12 *Middlesbrough* 10 0 **10 0**
2012–13 Wolverhampton W 4 0 **23 0**
2012–13 *Huddersfield T* 16 2
2013–14 Huddersfield T 44 4
2014–15 Huddersfield T 5 0
2014–15 *Rotherham U* 14 0 **14 0**
2015–16 Huddersfield T 1 0 **66 6**
2015–16 Barnsley 25 4
2016–17 Barnsley 37 3 **140 20**

HEDGES, Ryan (M) 52 6
H: 6 1 W: 10 03 b.Swansea 7-9-95
Internationals: Wales U19, U21.
2013–14 Swansea C 0 0
2014–15 Swansea C 0 0
2014–15 *Leyton Orient* 17 2 **17 2**
2015–16 Swansea C 0 0
2015–16 *Stevenage* 6 0 **6 0**
2016–17 Swansea C 0 0
2016–17 *Yeovil T* 21 4 **21 4**
2016–17 Barnsley 8 0 **8 0**

JACKSON, Adam (D) 39 3
H: 6 2 W: 12 04 b.Darlington 18-5-94
Internationals: England U16, U17, U18, U19.
2011–12 Middlesbrough 0 0
2012–13 Middlesbrough 0 0
2013–14 Middlesbrough 0 0
2014–15 Middlesbrough 0 0
2015–16 Middlesbrough 0 0
2015–16 *Coventry C* 0 0
2015–16 *Hartlepool U* 29 3 **29 3**
2016–17 Barnsley 10 0 **10 0**

JACKSON, Kayden (F) 20 1
H: 5 11 W: 11 07 b.Bradford 22-2-94
Internationals: England C.
2013–14 Swindon T 0 0
2014–15 Swindon T 0 0
2014–15 Tamworth 0 0
2016–17 Barnsley 0 0
2016–17 *Grimsby T* 20 1 **20 1**

JANKO, Saidy (D) 36 2
H: 5 10 W: 11 00 b.Zurich 22-10-95
Internationals: Switzerland U18, U19, U20, U21.
2014–15 Manchester U 0 0
2014–15 *Bolton W* 10 1 **10 1**
2015–16 Celtic 10 0
2016–17 Celtic 2 0 **12 0**
On loan from Celtic.
2016–17 Barnsley 14 1 **14 1**

KAY, Josh (M) 1 0
H: 5 5 W: 10 01 b.Blackpool 28-10-96
From AFC Fylde.
2015–16 Barnsley 0 0
2016–17 Barnsley 1 0 **1 0**

KPEKAWA, Cole (D) 28 0
H: 6 3 W: 12 08 b.Blackpool 20-5-96
Internationals: England U20.
2014–15 QPR 1 0
2014–15 *Colchester U* 4 0 **4 0**
2014–15 *Portsmouth* 2 0 **2 0**
2015–16 QPR 5 0
2015–16 *Leyton Orient* 9 0 **9 0**
2016–17 QPR 0 0 **6 0**
2016–17 Barnsley 7 0 **7 0**

LEE, Elliot (F) 42 6
H: 5 11 W: 11 05 b.Co. Durham 16-12-94
2011–12 West Ham U 0 0
2012–13 West Ham U 0 0
2013–14 West Ham U 1 0
2013–14 *Colchester U* 4 1
2014–15 West Ham U 1 0
2014–15 *Southend U* 0 0
2014–15 *Luton T* 11 3 **11 3**
2015–16 West Ham U 0 0 **2 0**
2015–16 *Blackpool* 4 0 **4 0**
2015–16 *Colchester U* 15 2 **19 3**
2016–17 Barnsley 6 0 **6 0**

MACDONALD, Angus (D) 59 1
H: 6 0 W: 11 00 b.Winchester 15-10-92
Internationals: England C, U16, U19.
2011–12 Reading 0 0
2011–12 *Torquay U* 2 0
2012–13 Reading 0 0
2012–13 *AFC Wimbledon* 4 0 **4 0**
2012–13 *Torquay U* 14 0 **16 0**
From Salisbury C, Torquay U.
2016–17 Barnsley 39 1 **39 1**

MONCUR, George (M) 133 27
H: 5 9 W: 10 00 b.Swindon 18-8-93
Internationals: England U18.
2010–11 West Ham U 0 0
2011–12 West Ham U 0 0
2011–12 *AFC Wimbledon* 20 2 **20 2**
2012–13 West Ham U 0 0
2013–14 West Ham U 0 0
2013–14 *Partick Thistle* 2 1 **2 1**
2014–15 Colchester U 41 8
2015–16 Colchester U 45 12 **86 20**
2016–17 Peterborough U 13 2 **13 2**
2016–17 Barnsley 12 2 **12 2**

MOWATT, Alex (D) 127 13
H: 5 10 W: 11 03 b.Doncaster 13-2-95
Internationals: England U19, U20.
2013–14 Leeds U 29 1
2014–15 Leeds U 38 9
2015–16 Leeds U 34 2
2016–17 Leeds U 15 0 **116 12**
2016–17 Barnsley 11 1 **11 1**

NYATANGA, Lewin (D) 348 17
H: 6 2 W: 12 08 b.Burton 18-8-88
Internationals: Wales U17, U21, Full caps.
2005–06 Derby Co 24 1
2006–07 Derby Co 7 1
2006–07 *Sunderland* 11 0 **11 0**
2006–07 *Barnsley* 10 1
2007–08 Derby Co 2 1
2007–08 *Barnsley* 41 1
2008–09 Derby Co 30 1 **63 4**
2009–10 Bristol C 37 1
2010–11 Bristol C 20 1
2010–11 *Peterborough U* 3 0 **3 0**
2011–12 Bristol C 29 0
2012–13 Bristol C 19 2 **105 4**
2013–14 Barnsley 12 0
2014–15 Barnsley 45 5
2015–16 Barnsley 21 2
2016–17 Barnsley 0 0 **129 9**
2016–17 *Northampton T* 37 0 **37 0**

PAYNE, Stefan (F) 48 3
H: 5 10 W: 11 07 b.Lambeth 10-8-91
Internationals: England C.
2009–10 Fulham 0 0
2010–11 Gillingham 16 0
2011–12 Gillingham 12 1 **28 1**
2011–12 *Aldershot T* 1 0 **1 0**
From Sutton U, Macclesfield T, Ebbsfleet U, AFC Hornchurch, Dover Ath.
2015–16 Barnsley 0 0
2016–17 Barnsley 7 0 **7 0**
2016–17 *Shrewsbury T* 12 2 **12 2**

ROBERTS, Marc (D) 72 5
H: 6 0 W: 12 11 b.Wakefield 26-7-90
Internationals: England C.
2014–15 Barnsley 0 0
2015–16 Barnsley 32 1
2016–17 Barnsley 40 4 **72 5**

SCOWEN, Josh (M) 187 13
H: 5 10 W: 11 09 b.Cheshunt 28-3-93
2010–11 Wycombe W 2 0
2011–12 Wycombe W 0 0
2012–13 Wycombe W 34 1
2013–14 Wycombe W 37 1
2014–15 Wycombe W 18 1 **91 3**
2014–15 Barnsley 21 4
2015–16 Barnsley 34 4
2016–17 Barnsley 41 2 **96 10**

SMITH, Will (D) 0 0
2016–17 Barnsley 0 0

TOWNSEND, Nick (G) 8 0
H: 5 11 W: 13 11 b.Solihull 1-11-94
2012–13 Birmingham C 0 0
2013–14 Birmingham C 0 0
2014–15 Birmingham C 0 0
2015–16 Barnsley 8 0
2016–17 Barnsley 0 0 **8 0**

TUTON, Shaun (F) 17 0
b.Sheffield 3-12-91
From Belper T, Matlock T, Buxton, FC Halifax T.
2015–16 Barnsley 7 0
2016–17 Barnsley 0 0 **7 0**
2016–17 *Grimsby T* 10 0 **10 0**

WARDLE, Louis (D) 0 0
b.Barnsley 29-3-99
2016–17 Barnsley 0 0

WATKINS, Marley (M) 161 24
H: 5 10 W: 10 03 b.London 17-10-90
2008–09 Cheltenham T 12 0
2009–10 Cheltenham T 13 1
2010–11 Cheltenham T 1 0 **26 1**
From Bath C, Hereford U
2013–14 Inverness CT 26 1
2014–15 Inverness CT 33 7 **59 8**
2015–16 Barnsley 34 5
2016–17 Barnsley 42 10 **76 15**

WHITE, Aidan (D) 149 5
H: 5 7 W: 10 00 b.Otley 10-10-91
Internationals: England U19. Republic of Ireland U21.
2008–09 Leeds U 5 0
2009–10 Leeds U 8 0
2010–11 Leeds U 2 0
2010–11 *Oldham Ath* 24 4 **24 4**
2011–12 Leeds U 36 0
2012–13 Leeds U 24 1
2013–14 Leeds U 9 0
2013–14 *Sheffield U* 8 0 **8 0**
2014–15 Leeds U 1 0 **85 1**
2015–16 Rotherham U 8 0 **8 0**
2015–16 Barnsley 14 0
2016–17 Barnsley 10 0 **24 0**

WILLIAMS, Ryan (F) 68 8
H: 5 11 W: 12 00 b.Perth 28-10-93
Internationals: Australia U20, U23.
2011–12 Portsmouth 4 0 **4 0**
2011–12 Fulham 0 0
2012–13 Fulham 0 0
2013–14 Fulham 0 0
2013–14 *Oxford U* 36 7 **36 7**
2014–15 Fulham 2 0 **2 0**
2014–15 *Barnsley* 5 0
2015–16 Barnsley 5 0
2016–17 Barnsley 16 1 **26 1**

YIADOM, Andy (M) 118 10
H: 5 11 W: 11 11 b.Camden 9-12-91
Internationals: England C. Ghana Full caps.
2011–12 Barnet 7 1
2012–13 Barnet 39 3
2015–16 Barnet 40 6 **86 10**
2016–17 Barnsley 32 0 **32 0**

Players retained or with offer of contract
Ash, Bradley Luke; Dolan, Rhys Darby; Mottley-Henry, Dylan; Palmer, Romal Jordan; Walton, Jack James.

Scholars
Alderton, William Jack; Bertie, Shamaul Daris Theo; Clare, Thomas Patrick; Greatorex, Jake Roy Vincent; Lund, Adam John; McGowan, Jeffrey James; Miller, Robbie; Murphy, Arron James; Ocran, Wilberforce Paa Kwesi; Ottley, Samuel David; Peters, Philroy Clifton; Rowe, Louis Kofi; Saeed, Mohamed Stephen Tahar; Simpson, Cameron Morgan; Smith, William Owen; Swinburn, Kane; Tingle, Samuel James; Wardle, Louis Aaron; Wolfe, Matthew Ryan.

BIRMINGHAM C (7)

ADAMS, Charlee (M) **11 0**
H: 5 11 W: 12 01 b.Redbridge 16-2-95
2013–14 Birmingham C 0 0
2014–15 Birmingham C 0 0
2015–16 Birmingham C 2 0
2016–17 Birmingham C 0 0 **2 0**
2016–17 *Kilmarnock* 9 0 **9 0**

ADAMS, Che (F) **87 18**
H: 5 10 W: 10 06 b.Leicester 13-7-96
Internationals: England C, U20.
2014–15 Sheffield U 10 0
2015–16 Sheffield U 36 11
2016–17 Sheffield U 1 0 **47 11**
2016–17 Birmingham C 40 7 **40 7**

ARTHUR, Koby (M) **24 3**
H: 5 6 W: 10 09 b.Kumasi 3-1-96
2012–13 Birmingham C 2 0
2013–14 Birmingham C 1 0
2014–15 Birmingham C 9 0
2014–15 *Cheltenham T* 7 3
2015–16 Birmingham C 0 0
2016–17 Birmingham C 0 0 **12 0**
2016–17 *Cheltenham T* 5 0 **12 3**

BROCK-MADSEN, Nicolai (F) **119 23**
H: 6 4 W: 13 12 b. 9-1-93
Internationals: Denmark U18, U19, U20, U21, Olympic.
2010–11 Randers 0 0
2011–12 Randers 14 2
2012–13 Randers 28 5
2013–14 Randers 27 4
2014–15 Randers 17 4
2015–16 Randers 4 1 **90 16**
2015–16 Birmingham C 6 0
2016–17 Birmingham C 0 0 **6 0**
2016–17 *PEC Zwolle* 23 7 **23 7**

BROWN, Reece (M) **21 0**
H: 5 9 W: 12 04 b.Dudley 3-3-96
Internationals: England U16, U17, U18, U20.
2013–14 Birmingham C 6 0
2014–15 Birmingham C 1 0
2014–15 *Notts Co* 3 0 **3 0**
2015–16 Birmingham C 1 0
2016–17 Birmingham C 8 0 **16 0**
2016–17 *Chesterfield* 2 0 **2 0**

COTTERILL, David (F) **388 51**
H: 5 9 W: 11 02 b.Cardiff 4-12-87
Internationals: Wales U19, U21, Full caps.
2004–05 Bristol C 12 0
2005–06 Bristol C 45 7
2006–07 Bristol C 5 1
2006–07 Wigan Ath 16 1
2007–08 Wigan Ath 2 0 **18 1**
2007–08 *Sheffield U* 16 0
2008–09 Sheffield U 24 4
2009–10 Sheffield U 14 2 **54 6**
2009–10 Swansea C 21 3
2010–11 Swansea C 14 1
2010–11 *Portsmouth* 15 1 **15 1**
2011–12 Swansea C 0 0 **35 4**
2011–12 Barnsley 11 1 **11 1**
2012–13 Doncaster R 44 10
2013–14 Doncaster R 40 4 **84 14**
2014–15 Birmingham C 42 9
2015–16 Birmingham C 29 4
2016–17 Birmingham C 25 1 **96 14**
2016–17 *Bristol C* 13 2 **75 10**

DACRES-COGLEY, Josh (D) **14 0**
H: 5 9 W: 10 10 b.Coventry 12-3-96
2016–17 Birmingham C 14 0 **14 0**

DAVIS, David (M) **211 10**
H: 5 8 W: 12 03 b.Smethwick 20-2-91
2009–10 Wolverhampton W 0 0
2009–10 *Darlington* 5 0 **5 0**
2010–11 Wolverhampton W 0 0
2010–11 *Walsall* 7 0 **7 0**
2010–11 *Shrewsbury T* 19 2 **19 2**
2011–12 Wolverhampton W 7 0
2011–12 *Chesterfield* 9 0 **9 0**
2012–13 Wolverhampton W 28 0
2013–14 Wolverhampton W 18 0 **53 0**
2014–15 Birmingham C 42 3
2015–16 Birmingham C 35 1
2016–17 Birmingham C 41 4 **118 8**

DONALDSON, Clayton (F) **381 130**
H: 6 1 W: 11 07 b.Bradford 7-2-84
Internationals: England C. Jamaica Full caps.
2002–03 Hull C 2 0
2003–04 Hull C 0 0
2004–05 Hull C 0 0 **2 0**
From York C
2007–08 Hibernian 17 5 **17 5**
2008–09 Crewe Alex 37 6
2009–10 Crewe Alex 37 13
2010–11 Crewe Alex 43 28 **117 47**
2011–12 Brentford 46 11
2012–13 Brentford 44 18
2013–14 Brentford 46 17 **136 46**
2014–15 Birmingham C 46 15
2015–16 Birmingham C 40 11
2016–17 Birmingham C 23 6 **109 32**

FABBRINI, Diego (F) **194 14**
H: 5 11 W: 11 12 b.San Giuliano Terme 31-7-90
Internationals: Italy U21, Full caps.
2009–10 Empoli 29 1
2010–11 Empoli 26 2 **55 3**
2011–12 Udinese 14 2
2012–13 Udinese 6 0 **20 2**
2012–13 *Palermo* 8 1 **8 1**
2013–14 Watford 21 1
2013–14 *Siena* 10 1 **10 1**
2014–15 Watford 2 0
2014–15 *Millwall* 12 1 **12 1**
2014–15 *Birmingham C* 5 0
2015–16 Watford 0 0 **23 1**
2015–16 *Middlesbrough* 22 4 **22 4**
2015–16 Birmingham C 14 0
2016–17 Birmingham C 7 0 **26 0**
2016–17 *Spezia* 18 1 **18 1**

FREI, Kerim (M) **48 1**
H: 5 7 W: 10 05 b.Feldkirch 19-11-93
Internationals: Switzerland Youth, U21. Turkey Youth, Full caps.
2010–11 Fulham 0 0
2011–12 Fulham 16 0
2012–13 Fulham 7 0
2012–13 *Cardiff C* 3 0 **3 0**
2013–14 Fulham 0 0 **23 0**
2013–14 Besiktas 9 0
2016–17 Besiktas 0 0 **9 0**
2016–17 Birmingham C 13 1 **13 1**

GLEESON, Stephen (M) **334 26**
H: 6 2 W: 11 00 b.Dublin 3-8-88
Internationals: Republic of Ireland U21, Full caps.
2006–07 Wolverhampton W 3 0
2006–07 *Stockport Co* 14 2
2007–08 Wolverhampton W 0 0
2007–08 *Hereford U* 4 0 **4 0**
2007–08 *Stockport Co* 6 0
2008–09 Wolverhampton W 0 0 **3 0**
2008–09 *Stockport Co* 21 2 **41 4**
2008–09 *Milton Keynes D* 5 0
2009–10 Milton Keynes D 29 0
2010–11 Milton Keynes D 36 2
2011–12 Milton Keynes D 39 5
2012–13 Milton Keynes D 30 6
2013–14 Milton Keynes D 35 3 **174 16**
2014–15 Birmingham C 39 0
2015–16 Birmingham C 44 5
2016–17 Birmingham C 29 1 **112 6**

GROUNDS, Jonathan (D) **297 11**
H: 6 1 W: 13 10 b.Thornaby 2-2-88
2007–08 Middlesbrough 5 0
2008–09 Middlesbrough 2 0
2008–09 *Norwich C* 16 3 **16 3**
2009–10 Middlesbrough 20 0
2010–11 Middlesbrough 6 1
2011–12 Middlesbrough 0 0 **33 1**
2011–12 *Chesterfield* 13 0 **13 0**
2011–12 *Yeovil T* 14 0 **14 0**
2012–13 Oldham Ath 44 1
2013–14 Oldham Ath 45 2 **89 3**
2014–15 Birmingham C 45 1
2015–16 Birmingham C 45 1
2016–17 Birmingham C 42 2 **132 4**

JUTKIEWICZ, Lucas (F) **304 64**
H: 6 1 W: 12 11 b.Southampton 20-3-89
2005–06 Swindon T 5 0
2006–07 Swindon T 33 5 **38 5**
2006–07 Everton 0 0
2007–08 Everton 0 0
2007–08 *Plymouth Arg* 3 0 **3 0**
2008–09 Everton 1 0
2008–09 *Huddersfield T* 7 0 **7 0**
2009–10 Everton 0 0 **1 0**
2009–10 *Motherwell* 33 12 **33 12**
2010–11 Coventry C 42 9
2011–12 Coventry C 25 9 **67 18**
2011–12 Middlesbrough 19 2
2012–13 Middlesbrough 24 8
2013–14 Middlesbrough 22 1 **65 11**
2013–14 *Bolton W* 20 7 **20 7**
2014–15 Burnley 25 0
2015–16 Burnley 5 0
2016–17 Burnley 2 0 **32 0**
2016–17 Birmingham C 38 11 **38 11**

KEITA, Cheick (D) **55 0**
H: 5 7 W: 12 00 b.Paris 16-7-96
From Monaco.
2014–15 Virtus Entella 0 0
2015–16 Virtus Entella 31 0
2016–17 Virtus Entella 14 0 **45 0**
2016–17 Birmingham C 10 0 **10 0**

KIEFTENBELD, Maikel (M) **296 9**
H: 5 10 W: 11 11 b.Lemelerveld 26-6-90
Internationals: Netherlands U21.
2008–09 Go Ahead Eagles 30 1
2009–10 Go Ahead Eagles 33 2 **63 3**
2010–11 Groningen 33 0
2011–12 Groningen 26 1
2012–13 Groningen 29 1
2013–14 Groningen 31 0
2014–15 Groningen 33 0 **152 2**
2015–16 Birmingham C 42 3
2016–17 Birmingham C 39 1 **81 4**

KUSZCZAK, Tomasz (G) **252 0**
H: 6 3 W: 13 03 b.Krosno Odrzansia 20-3-82
Internationals: Poland U16, U18, U21, Full caps.
2001–02 Hertha Berlin 0 0
2002–03 Hertha Berlin 0 0
2003–04 Hertha Berlin 0 0
2004–05 WBA 3 0
2005–06 WBA 28 0
2006–07 WBA 0 0 **31 0**
2006–07 *Manchester U* 6 0
2007–08 Manchester U 9 0
2008–09 Manchester U 4 0
2009–10 Manchester U 8 0
2010–11 Manchester U 5 0
2011–12 Manchester U 0 0 **32 0**
2011–12 *Watford* 13 0 **13 0**
2012–13 Brighton & HA 43 0
2013–14 Brighton & HA 41 0 **84 0**
2014–15 Wolverhampton W 13 0 **13 0**
2015–16 Birmingham C 41 0
2016–17 Birmingham C 38 0 **79 0**

LEGZDINS, Adam (G) **114 0**
H: 6 1 W: 14 02 b.Penkridge 28-11-86
2006–07 Birmingham C 0 0
2007–08 Birmingham C 0 0
2008–09 Crewe Alex 0 0
2009–10 Crewe Alex 6 0 **6 0**
2010–11 Burton Alb 46 0
2011–12 Derby Co 4 0
2011–12 *Burton Alb* 1 0 **47 0**
2012–13 Derby Co 31 0
2013–14 Derby Co 0 0 **35 0**
2014–15 Leyton Orient 11 0 **11 0**
2015–16 Birmingham C 5 0
2016–17 Birmingham C 10 0 **15 0**

MAGHOMA, Jacques (M) **279 36**
H: 5 9 W: 11 06 b.Lubumbashi 23-10-87
Internationals: DR Congo Full caps.
2005–06 Tottenham H 0 0
2006–07 Tottenham H 0 0
2007–08 Tottenham H 0 0
2008–09 Tottenham H 0 0
2009–10 Burton Alb 35 3
2010–11 Burton Alb 41 4
2011–12 Burton Alb 36 4
2012–13 Burton Alb 43 15 **155 26**
2013–14 Sheffield W 25 2
2014–15 Sheffield W 32 0 **57 2**
2015–16 Birmingham C 40 5
2016–17 Birmingham C 27 3 **67 8**

MAXWELL, Luke (M) **4 0**
b. 6-7-97
2015–16 Birmingham C 0 0
2016–17 Birmingham C 0 0
2016–17 *Grimsby T* 4 0 **4 0**

MORRISON, Michael (D) **323 17**
H: 6 0 W: 12 00 b.Bury St Edmunds 3-3-88
Internationals: England C.
2008–09 Leicester C 35 3
2009–10 Leicester C 31 2
2010–11 Leicester C 11 0 **77 5**
2010–11 Sheffield W 12 0 **12 0**
2011–12 Charlton Ath 45 4
2012–13 Charlton Ath 44 1
2013–14 Charlton Ath 45 1
2014–15 Charlton Ath 2 0 **136 6**
2014–15 Birmingham C 21 0

2015–16	Birmingham C	46	3		
2016–17	Birmingham C	31	3	**98**	**6**

NSUE, Emilio (F) **301 29**
H: 5 10 W: 11 11 b.Palma 30-9-89
Internationals: Spain U16, U17, U19, U20, U21. Equatorial Guinea Full caps.

2007–08	Mallorca	2	0		
2008–09	Mallorca	0	0		
2008–09	*Castellon*	37	7	**37**	**7**
2009–10	Mallorca	0	0		
2009–10	*Real Sociedad*	34	5	**34**	**5**
2010–11	Mallorca	38	4		
2011–12	Mallorca	30	3		
2012–13	Mallorca	32	2		
2013–14	Mallorca	40	4	**142**	**13**
2014–15	Middlesbrough	26	0		
2015–16	Middlesbrough	40	3		
2016–17	Middlesbrough	4	0	**70**	**3**
2016–17	Birmingham C	18	1	**18**	**1**

O'KEEFFE, Corey (M) **1 0**
H: 6 1 W: 11 00 b.Birmingham 5-6-88
Internationals: Republic of Ireland U17, U18, U19.

2016–17	Birmingham C	1	0	**1**	**0**

ROBINSON, Paul (D) **676 15**
H: 5 9 W: 11 12 b.Watford 14-12-78
Internationals: England U21.

1996–97	Watford	12	0		
1997–98	Watford	22	2		
1998–99	Watford	29	0		
1999–2000	Watford	32	0		
2000–01	Watford	39	0		
2001–02	Watford	38	3		
2002–03	Watford	37	3		
2003–04	Watford	10	0	**219**	**8**
2003–04	WBA	31	0		
2004–05	WBA	30	1		
2005–06	WBA	33	0		
2006–07	WBA	42	2		
2007–08	WBA	43	1		
2008–09	WBA	35	0		
2009–10	WBA	0	0	**214**	**4**
2009–10	*Bolton W*	25	0		
2010–11	Bolton W	35	0		
2011–12	Bolton W	17	0	**77**	**0**
2011–12	*Leeds U*	10	0	**10**	**0**
2012–13	Birmingham C	35	0		
2013–14	Birmingham C	40	0		
2014–15	Birmingham C	34	0		
2015–16	Birmingham C	25	3		
2016–17	Birmingham C	22	0	**156**	**3**

SHINNIE, Andrew (M) **156 24**
H: 5 11 W: 10 13 b.Aberdeen 17-7-89
Internationals: Scotland U19, U21, Full caps.

2005–06	Rangers	0	0		
2006–07	Rangers	2	0		
2007–08	Rangers	0	0		
2008–09	Rangers	0	0		
2009–10	Rangers	0	0		
2010–11	Rangers	0	0	**2**	**0**
2011–12	Inverness CT	19	7		
2012–13	Inverness CT	38	12	**57**	**19**
2013–14	Birmingham C	26	2		
2014–15	Birmingham C	27	2		
2015–16	Birmingham C	14	0		
2015–16	*Rotherham U*	3	0	**3**	**0**
2016–17	Birmingham C	0	0	**67**	**4**
2016–17	*Hibernian*	27	1	**27**	**1**

SHOTTON, Ryan (D) **203 12**
H: 6 3 W: 13 05 b.Stoke 30-9-88

2006–07	Stoke C	0	0		
2007–08	Stoke C	0	0		
2008–09	Stoke C	0	0		
2008–09	*Tranmere R*	33	5	**33**	**5**
2009–10	Stoke C	0	0		
2009–10	*Barnsley*	30	0	**30**	**0**
2010–11	Stoke C	2	0		
2011–12	Stoke C	23	1		
2012–13	Stoke C	23	0		
2013–14	Stoke C	0	0	**48**	**1**
2013–14	*Wigan Ath*	9	1	**9**	**1**
2014–15	Derby Co	25	2		
2015–16	Derby Co	6	0	**31**	**2**
2015–16	*Birmingham C*	9	1		
2016–17	Birmingham C	43	2	**52**	**3**

SOLOMON-OTABOR, Viv (M) **29 1**
H: 5 9 W: 12 02 b.London 2-1-96
From Crystal Palace.

2015–16	Birmingham C	22	1		
2016–17	Birmingham C	3	0	**25**	**1**
2016–17	*Bolton W*	4	0	**4**	**0**

SPECTOR, Jonathan (D) **277 1**
H: 6 0 W: 12 08 b.Chicago 1-3-86
Internationals: USA U17, U20, Full caps.

2003–04	Manchester U	0	0		
2004–05	Manchester U	3	0		
2005–06	Manchester U	0	0	**3**	**0**
2005–06	*Charlton Ath*	20	0	**20**	**0**
2006–07	West Ham U	25	0		
2007–08	West Ham U	26	0		
2008–09	West Ham U	9	0		
2009–10	West Ham U	27	0		
2010–11	West Ham U	14	1	**101**	**1**
2011–12	Birmingham C	31	0		
2012–13	Birmingham C	29	0		
2013–14	Birmingham C	22	0		
2014–15	Birmingham C	24	0		
2015–16	Birmingham C	25	0		
2016–17	Birmingham C	22	0	**153**	**0**

Transferred to Orlando C, January 2017.

STEWART, Greg (F) **211 53**
H: 5 11 W: 11 07 b.Stirling 17-3-90

2010–11	Cowdenbeath	32	9		
2011–12	Cowdenbeath	29	6		
2012–13	Cowdenbeath	25	5		
2013–14	Cowdenbeath	33	11	**119**	**31**
2014–15	Dundee	34	13		
2015–16	Dundee	37	9	**71**	**22**
2016–17	Birmingham C	21	0	**21**	**0**

STORER, Jack (F) **6 0**
H: 6 1 W: 11 00 b.Birmingham 2-1-98

2014–15	Stevenage	0	0		
2015–16	Stevenage	1	0	**1**	**0**
2016–17	Birmingham C	4	0	**4**	**0**
2016–17	*Yeovil T*	1	0	**1**	**0**

TESCHE, Robert (M) **207 12**
H: 5 11 W: 11 03 b.Wismar 27-5-87

2006–07	Arminia Bielefeld	7	0		
2007–08	Arminia Bielefeld	15	1	**22**	**1**
2008–09	Arminia Bielefeld	26	2	**26**	**2**
2009–10	Hamburg	16	2		
2010–11	Hamburg	11	0		
2011–12	Hamburg	23	2		
2012–13	Hamburg	4	0		
2012–13	*Fortuna Dusseldorf*	14	0	**14**	**0**
2013–14	Hamburg	9	0	**63**	**4**
2014–15	Nottingham F	22	2		
2014–15	*Birmingham C*	12	2		
2015–16	Nottingham F	24	1	**46**	**3**
2016–17	Birmingham C	24	0	**36**	**2**

TRUEMAN, Connal (G) **0 0**
H: 6 1 W: 11 10 b.Birmingham 26-3-96

2014–15	Birmingham C	0	0		
2014–15	*Oldham Ath*	0	0		
2015–16	Birmingham C	0	0		
2016–17	Birmingham C	0	0		

Players retained or with offer of contract
Bailey, Odin Ohray; Bernard, Dominic Archie; Chapman, Hale Ronan Aiden Connolly Shea; Cleary, Daniel; Harding, Wesley Nathan Hylton; Lubala, Beryly Logos; McDonald, Wesley Nurettin; McFarlane, Raewkon Kyle; Popa, David; Scarr, Daniel George; Seddon, Steven Jeffrey; Weaver, Jacob William Robert.

Scholars
Anderson, Tom; Bajrami, Geraldo; Beardmore, Max; Boyd, Munce Caolan Stephen; Brown, Leo Calvin; Chisholm, Tai-Reece D'Mel Amari; Clarke, Jordan Alexander Joseph; Concannon, Jack Paul; Dawes, Kieron Michael; Ebbutt, Cameron; Hamilton, Tyrell Anthony; Iyamu, Noskhare Michael; Lakin, Charlie; McLean, Ben Neil; Mulders, Oliver; Redmond, Joseph; Siviter, Adam; Tibbetts, Joshua Joseph; Timms, Matthew; Yuill, Louis George William.

BLACKBURN R (8)

AKPAN, Hope (M) **167 10**
H: 6 0 W: 10 08 b.Liverpool 14-8-91
Internationals: Nigeria Full caps.

2007–08	Everton	0	0		
2008–09	Everton	0	0		
2009–10	Everton	0	0		
2010–11	Everton	0	0		
2010–11	*Hull C*	2	0	**2**	**0**
2011–12	Crawley T	26	1		
2012–13	Crawley T	21	4	**47**	**5**
2012–13	Reading	9	0		
2013–14	Reading	29	1		
2014–15	Reading	20	0	**58**	**1**
2015–16	Blackburn R	35	3		
2016–17	Blackburn R	25	1	**60**	**4**

BENNETT, Elliott (M) **299 25**
H: 5 9 W: 10 11 b.Telford 18-12-88

2006–07	Wolverhampton W	0	0		
2007–08	Wolverhampton W	0	0		
2007–08	*Crewe Alex*	9	1	**9**	**1**
2007–08	*Bury*	19	1		
2008–09	Wolverhampton W	0	0		
2008–09	*Bury*	46	3	**65**	**4**
2009–10	Wolverhampton W	0	0		
2009–10	*Brighton & HA*	43	7		
2010–11	Brighton & HA	46	6		
2011–12	Norwich C	33	1		
2012–13	Norwich C	24	1		
2013–14	Norwich C	2	0		
2014–15	Norwich C	9	0		
2014–15	*Brighton & HA*	7	0	**96**	**13**
2015–16	Norwich C	0	0	**68**	**2**
2015–16	*Bristol C*	15	0	**15**	**0**
2015–16	Blackburn R	21	2		
2016–17	Blackburn R	25	3	**46**	**5**

BROWN, Wes (D) **313 5**
H: 6 1 W: 13 08 b.Manchester 13-10-79
Internationals: England U21, Full caps.

1996–97	Manchester U	0	0		
1997–98	Manchester U	2	0		
1998–99	Manchester U	14	0		
1999–2000	Manchester U	0	0		
2000–01	Manchester U	28	0		
2001–02	Manchester U	17	0		
2002–03	Manchester U	22	0		
2003–04	Manchester U	17	0		
2004–05	Manchester U	21	1		
2005–06	Manchester U	19	0		
2006–07	Manchester U	22	0		
2007–08	Manchester U	36	1		
2008–09	Manchester U	8	1		
2009–10	Manchester U	19	0		
2010–11	Manchester U	7	0	**232**	**3**
2011–12	Sunderland	20	1		
2012–13	Sunderland	0	0		
2013–14	Sunderland	25	0		
2014–15	Sunderland	25	0		
2015–16	Sunderland	6	0	**76**	**1**
2016–17	Blackburn R	5	1	**5**	**1**

CONWAY, Craig (M) **401 42**
H: 5 7 W: 10 07 b.Irvine 2-5-85
Internationals: Scotland Full caps.

2002–03	Ayr U	1	0		
2003–04	Ayr U	6	0		
2004–05	Ayr U	23	3		
2005–06	Ayr U	31	4	**61**	**7**
2006–07	Dundee U	30	0		
2007–08	Dundee U	15	1		
2008–09	Dundee U	36	5		
2009–10	Dundee U	33	4		
2010–11	Dundee U	22	3	**136**	**13**
2011–12	Cardiff C	31	3		
2012–13	Cardiff C	27	2		
2013–14	Cardiff C	0	0	**58**	**5**
2013–14	*Brighton & HA*	13	1	**13**	**1**
2013–14	Blackburn R	18	4		
2014–15	Blackburn R	38	3		
2015–16	Blackburn R	35	3		
2016–17	Blackburn R	42	6	**133**	**16**

DOYLE, Jack (D) **0 0**
H: 5 10 W: 10 01 b. 2-2-97

2015–16	Blackburn R	0	0		
2016–17	Blackburn R	0	0		

EVANS, Corry (M) **202 9**
H: 5 8 W: 10 12 b.Belfast 30-7-90
Internationals: Northern Ireland U16, U17, U19, U21, B, Full caps.

2007–08	Manchester U	0	0		
2008–09	Manchester U	0	0		
2009–10	Manchester U	0	0		
2010–11	Manchester U	0	0		
2010–11	*Carlisle U*	1	0	**1**	**0**
2010–11	*Hull C*	18	3		
2011–12	Hull C	43	2		
2012–13	Hull C	32	1		
2013–14	Hull C	0	0	**93**	**6**
2013–14	Blackburn R	21	1		
2014–15	Blackburn R	38	1		
2015–16	Blackburn R	30	1		
2016–17	Blackburn R	19	0	**108**	**3**

FEENEY, Liam (M) **314 26**
H: 5 10 W: 12 02 b.Hammersmith 21-1-87

2008–09	Southend U	1	0	**1**	**0**
2008–09	Bournemouth	14	3		
2009–10	Bournemouth	44	5		
2010–11	Bournemouth	46	4		

2011–12 Bournemouth 5 0 **109 12**
2011–12 Millwall 34 4
2012–13 Millwall 22 1
2013–14 Millwall 17 0 **73 5**
2013–14 *Bolton W* 4 0
2013–14 *Blackburn R* 6 0
2014–15 Bolton W 41 3
2015–16 Bolton W 37 5 **82 8**
2015–16 *Ipswich T* 9 1 **9 1**
2016–17 Blackburn R 34 0 **40 0**

FISHER, Andy (G) 0 0
b. 12-2-98
2016–17 Blackburn R 0 0

GRAHAM, Danny (F) 421 120
H: 5 11 W: 12 05 b.Gateshead 12-8-85
Internationals: England U20.
2003–04 Middlesbrough 0 0
2003–04 *Darlington* 9 2 **9 2**
2004–05 Middlesbrough 11 1
2005–06 Middlesbrough 3 0
2005–06 *Derby Co* 14 0 **14 0**
2005–06 *Leeds U* 3 0 **3 0**
2006–07 Middlesbrough 1 0
2006–07 *Blackpool* 4 1 **4 1**
2006–07 *Carlisle U* 11 7
2007–08 Carlisle U 45 14
2008–09 Carlisle U 44 15 **100 36**
2009–10 Watford 46 14
2010–11 Watford 45 23 **91 37**
2011–12 Swansea C 36 12
2012–13 Swansea C 18 3 **54 15**
2012–13 Sunderland 13 0
2013–14 Sunderland 0 0
2013–14 *Hull C* 18 1 **18 1**
2013–14 *Middlesbrough* 18 6 **33 7**
2014–15 Sunderland 14 1
2014–15 *Wolverhampton W* 5 1 **5 1**
2015–16 Sunderland 10 0 **37 1**
2015–16 *Blackburn R* 18 7
2016–17 Blackburn R 35 12 **53 19**

GREER, Gordon (D) 447 12
H: 6 2 W: 12 05 b.Glasgow 14-12-80
Internationals: Scotland B, Full caps.
2000–01 Clyde 30 0 **30 0**
2000–01 Blackburn R 0 0
2001–02 Blackburn R 0 0
2002–03 Blackburn R 0 0
2002–03 *Stockport Co* 5 1 **5 1**
2003–04 Kilmarnock 25 0
2004–05 Kilmarnock 22 1
2005–06 Kilmarnock 27 2
2006–07 Kilmarnock 33 0 **107 3**
2007–08 Doncaster R 11 1
2008–09 Doncaster R 1 0 **12 1**
2008–09 *Swindon T* 19 1
2009–10 Swindon T 44 1 **63 2**
2010–11 Brighton & HA 32 0
2011–12 Brighton & HA 42 1
2012–13 Brighton & HA 38 1
2013–14 Brighton & HA 40 1
2014–15 Brighton & HA 37 2
2015–16 Brighton & HA 20 0 **209 5**
2016–17 Blackburn R 21 0 **21 0**

GUTHRIE, Danny (M) 238 13
H: 5 9 W: 11 06 b.Shrewsbury 18-4-87
Internationals: England U16.
2004–05 Liverpool 0 0
2005–06 Liverpool 0 0
2006–07 Liverpool 3 0
2006–07 *Southampton* 10 0 **10 0**
2007–08 Liverpool 0 0 **3 0**
2007–08 *Bolton W* 25 0 **25 0**
2008–09 Newcastle U 24 2
2009–10 Newcastle U 38 4
2010–11 Newcastle U 14 0
2011–12 Newcastle U 16 1 **92 7**
2012–13 Reading 21 1
2013–14 Reading 32 4
2014–15 Reading 9 0 **62 5**
2014–15 *Fulham* 6 0 **6 0**
2015–16 Blackburn R 16 0
2016–17 Blackburn R 24 1 **40 1**

HENLEY, Adam (D) 80 1
H: 5 10 W: 12 02 b.Knoxville 14-6-94
Internationals: Wales U19, U21, Full caps.
2011–12 Blackburn R 7 0
2012–13 Blackburn R 15 0
2013–14 Blackburn R 14 0
2014–15 Blackburn R 18 1
2015–16 Blackburn R 24 0
2016–17 Blackburn R 2 0 **80 1**

LENIHAN, Darragh (M) 83 1
H: 5 10 W: 12 00 b.Dublin 16-3-94
Internationals: Republic of Ireland U17, U19, U21.
2011–12 Blackburn R 0 0
2012–13 Blackburn R 0 0
2013–14 Blackburn R 0 0
2014–15 Blackburn R 3 0
2014–15 *Burton Alb* 17 1 **17 1**
2015–16 Blackburn R 23 0
2016–17 Blackburn R 40 0 **66 0**

LOWE, Jason (M) 180 3
H: 6 0 W: 12 08 b.Wigan 2-9-91
Internationals: England U20, U21.
2009–10 Blackburn R 0 0
2010–11 Blackburn R 1 0
2010–11 *Oldham Ath* 7 2 **7 2**
2011–12 Blackburn R 32 0
2012–13 Blackburn R 36 0
2013–14 Blackburn R 39 1
2014–15 Blackburn R 12 0
2015–16 Blackburn R 10 0
2016–17 Blackburn R 43 0 **173 1**

MAHONEY, Connor (M) 20 0
H: 5 9 W: 10 08 b.Blackburn 12-2-97
Internationals: England U17, U18.
2013–14 Accrington S 4 0 **4 0**
2013–14 Blackburn R 0 0
2014–15 Blackburn R 0 0
2015–16 Blackburn R 2 0
2016–17 Blackburn R 14 0 **16 0**

MULGREW, Charlie (D) 269 35
H: 6 3 W: 13 01 b.Glasgow 6-3-86
Internationals: Scotland U21, Full caps.
2002–03 Celtic 0 0
2003–04 Celtic 0 0
2004–05 Celtic 0 0
2005–06 Celtic 0 0
2005–06 *Dundee U* 13 2 **13 2**
2006–07 Wolverhampton W 6 0
2007–08 *Southend U* 18 1 **18 1**
2007–08 Wolverhampton W 0 0 **6 0**
2008–09 Aberdeen 35 5
2009–10 Aberdeen 37 4 **72 9**
2010–11 Celtic 23 0
2011–12 Celtic 30 8
2012–13 Celtic 30 5
2013–14 Celtic 28 6
2014–15 Celtic 10 0
2015–16 Celtic 11 1 **132 20**
2016–17 Blackburn R 28 3 **28 3**

NYAMBE, Ryan (D) 25 0
H: 6 0 W: 12 00 b.Katima Mulilo 4-12-97
2014–15 Blackburn R 0 0
2015–16 Blackburn R 0 0
2016–17 Blackburn R 25 0 **25 0**

RAYA, David (G) 12 0
H: 6 0 W: 12 08 b.Barcelona 15-9-95
2013–14 Blackburn R 0 0
2014–15 Blackburn R 2 0
2015–16 Blackburn R 5 0
2016–17 Blackburn R 5 0 **12 0**

RITTENBERG, Dean (F) 0 0
b. 13-5-96
Internationals: England U18.
2013–14 Blackburn R 0 0
2014–15 Blackburn R 0 0
2015–16 Blackburn R 0 0
2016–17 Blackburn R 0 0

STEELE, Jason (G) 257 0
H: 6 2 W: 12 07 b.Newton Aycliffe 18-8-90
Internationals: England U16, U17, U19, U21. Great Britain.
2007–08 Middlesbrough 0 0
2008–09 Middlesbrough 0 0
2009–10 Middlesbrough 0 0
2009–10 *Northampton T* 13 0 **13 0**
2010–11 Middlesbrough 35 0
2011–12 Middlesbrough 34 0
2012–13 Middlesbrough 46 0
2013–14 Middlesbrough 16 0
2014–15 Middlesbrough 0 0 **131 0**
2014–15 *Blackburn R* 31 0
2015–16 Blackburn R 41 0
2016–17 Blackburn R 41 0 **113 0**

STOKES, Anthony (F) 274 104
H: 5 11 W: 11 00 b.Dublin 25-7-88
Internationals: Republic of Ireland U21, B, Full caps.
2005–06 Arsenal 0 0
2006–07 Arsenal 0 0
2006–07 *Falkirk* 16 14 **16 14**
2006–07 Sunderland 14 2
2007–08 Sunderland 20 1
2008–09 Sunderland 2 0 **36 3**
2008–09 *Sheffield U* 12 0 **12 0**
2008–09 *Crystal Palace* 13 1 **13 1**
2009–10 Hibernian 37 21
2010–11 Hibernian 3 1
2010–11 Celtic 29 14
2011–12 Celtic 34 12
2012–13 Celtic 17 5
2013–14 Celtic 33 20
2014–15 Celtic 21 7
2015–16 Celtic 1 0 **135 58**
2015–16 *Hibernian* 14 5 **54 27**
2016–17 Blackburn R 8 1 **8 1**

THOMSON, Connor (D) 0 0
H: 6 3 b. 14-2-96
2013–14 Carlisle U 0 0
2014–15 Carlisle U 0 0
2014–15 Blackburn R 0 0
2015–16 Blackburn R 0 0
2016–17 Blackburn R 0 0

TOMLINSON, Willem (M) 1 0
H: 5 10 W: 10 03 b.Burnley 27-1-98
2015–16 Blackburn R 0 0
2016–17 Blackburn R 1 0 **1 0**

TRAVIS, Lewis (D) 0 0
b. 16-10-97
2016–17 Blackburn R 0 0

WARD, Elliot (D) 286 21
H: 6 2 W: 13 00 b.Harrow 19-1-85
2001–02 West Ham U 0 0
2002–03 West Ham U 0 0
2003–04 West Ham U 0 0
2004–05 West Ham U 11 0
2004–05 *Bristol R* 3 0 **3 0**
2005–06 West Ham U 4 0 **15 0**
2005–06 *Plymouth Arg* 16 1 **16 1**
2006–07 Coventry C 39 3
2007–08 Coventry C 37 6
2008–09 Coventry C 33 5
2009–10 Coventry C 8 0 **117 14**
2009–10 *Doncaster R* 6 1 **6 1**
2009–10 *Preston NE* 4 0 **4 0**
2010–11 Norwich C 39 1
2011–12 Norwich C 12 0
2012–13 Norwich C 0 0 **51 1**
2012–13 *Nottingham F* 31 3 **31 3**
2013–14 Bournemouth 23 0
2014–15 Bournemouth 2 0
2015–16 Bournemouth 0 0 **25 0**
2015–16 *Huddersfield T* 5 0 **5 0**
2015–16 Blackburn R 7 1
2016–17 Blackburn R 6 0 **13 1**

WHARTON, Scott (D) 11 1
b.Blackburn 3-10-97
2015–16 Blackburn R 0 0
2016–17 Blackburn R 2 0 **2 0**
2016–17 *Cambridge U* 9 1 **9 1**

WILLIAMS, Derrick (D) 151 5
H: 5 11 W: 11 11 b.Waterford 17-1-93
Internationals: Republic of Ireland U19, U21.
2009–10 Aston Villa 0 0
2010–11 Aston Villa 0 0
2011–12 Aston Villa 0 0
2012–13 Aston Villa 1 0 **1 0**
2013–14 Bristol C 43 1
2014–15 Bristol C 44 2
2015–16 Bristol C 24 1 **111 4**
2016–17 Blackburn R 39 1 **39 1**

Players retained or with offer of contract
Hardcastle, Lewis James; Mansell, Lewis David; Platt, Matthew James; Powell, Joshua Henry Alexander; Rankin-Costello, Joseph Scott.

Scholars
Ascroft, Ben Paul; Buckley, John Keaton; Butterworth, Daniel James; Campbell, Matthew Scott; Carter, Hayden James; Curran, Alex Samuel; Donnelly-Blackburn, Ben Thomas George; Doyle, Charley Ian; Evans, Jack Lucas James; Fawns, Mason Matthew; Grayson, Joseph Nicholas; Hendry, Callum David; Jackson, Andrew Ellis; Jones, Frank Peter; Lynch, Bradley James; Magloire, Tyler Jordan; Makinson, Matthew Harry; Mols, Stefan Edouard; Paton, Benjamin Alan; Pemberton, Tre Kingsley; Steer, Joel Samuel Anthony; Thompson, Lewis; Williams, Benjamin Joseph; Wright, Callum.

Non-Contract
Powell, Joshua Henry Alexander.

BLACKPOOL (9)

AIMSON, Will (D) **35 0**
H: 5 10 W: 11 00 b.Christchurch 1-1-94
2013–14 Hull C 0 0
2014–15 Hull C 0 0
2014–15 *Tranmere R* 2 0 **2 0**
2015–16 Hull C 0 0
2015–16 Blackpool 15 0
2016–17 Blackpool 18 0 **33 0**

ALDRED, Tom (D) **188 10**
H: 6 2 W: 13 02 b.Bolton 11-9-90
Internationals: Scotland U19.
2008–09 Carlisle U 0 0
2009–10 Carlisle U 5 0 **5 0**
2010–11 Watford 0 0
2010–11 *Stockport Co* 7 0 **7 0**
2011–12 Watford 0 0
2011–12 Colchester U 0 0
2011–12 *Torquay U* 0 0
2012–13 Colchester U 0 0
2012–13 Accrington S 13 0
2013–14 Accrington S 46 2
2014–15 Accrington S 25 1 **84 3**
2014–15 *Blackpool* 6 0
2015–16 Blackpool 42 5
2016–17 Blackpool 44 2 **92 7**

BLACK, Ian (M) **361 22**
H: 5 8 W: 9 13 b.Edinburgh 14-3-85
Internationals: Scotland B, Full caps.
2002–03 Blackburn R 0 0
2003–04 Blackburn R 0 0
2004–05 Inverness CT 13 0
2005–06 Inverness CT 26 1
2006–07 Inverness CT 26 0
2007–08 Inverness CT 33 3
2008–09 Inverness CT 34 4 **132 8**
2009–10 Hearts 26 1
2010–11 Hearts 32 1
2011–12 Hearts 29 2 **87 4**
2012–13 Rangers 29 2
2013–14 Rangers 32 3
2014–15 Rangers 22 1 **83 6**
2015–16 Shrewsbury T 30 1
2016–17 Shrewsbury T 19 3 **49 4**
2016–17 Blackpool 10 0 **10 0**

BONEY, Miles (G) **1 0**
H: 5 11 W: 11 09 b.Blackpool 1-2-98
2014–15 Blackpool 0 0
2015–16 Blackpool 0 0
2016–17 Blackpool 1 0 **1 0**

CAMERON, Henry (M) **25 1**
H: 5 10 W: 11 00 b.Lytham St Annes 28-6-97
Internationals: New Zealand Full caps.
2013–14 Blackpool 0 0
2014–15 Blackpool 11 1
2015–16 Blackpool 14 0
2016–17 Blackpool 0 0 **25 1**

CORREIA, Raul (F) **0 0**
From Radcliffe Bor.
2016–17 Blackpool 0 0

CULLEN, Mark (F) **152 33**
H: 5 9 W: 11 11 b.Ashington 21-4-92
2009–10 Hull C 3 1
2010–11 Hull C 17 0
2010–11 *Bradford C* 4 0 **4 0**
2011–12 Hull C 4 0
2011–12 *Bury* 4 0
2012–13 Hull C 0 0
2012–13 Hull C 0 0 **24 1**
2012–13 *Bury* 10 1 **14 1**
2014–15 Luton T 42 13 **42 13**
2015–16 Blackpool 41 9
2016–17 Blackpool 27 9 **68 18**

DANIEL, Colin (M) **258 28**
H: 5 11 W: 11 06 b.Eastwood 15-2-88
2006–07 Crewe Alex 0 0
2007–08 Crewe Alex 1 0
2008–09 Crewe Alex 13 1 **14 1**
2008–09 *Macclesfield T* 8 0
2009–10 Macclesfield T 38 3
2010–11 Macclesfield T 43 8
2011–12 Macclesfield T 36 2 **125 13**
2013–14 Mansfield T 28 2
2014–15 Port Vale 28 4
2015–16 Port Vale 20 2 **48 6**
2015–16 *Mansfield T* 9 2 **37 4**
2016–17 Blackpool 34 4 **34 4**

DELFOUNESO, Nathan (F) **204 22**
H: 6 1 W: 12 04 b.Birmingham 2-2-91
Internationals: England U16, U17, U19, U21.
2007–08 Aston Villa 0 0
2008–09 Aston Villa 4 0
2009–10 Aston Villa 9 1
2010–11 Aston Villa 11 1
2010–11 *Burnley* 11 1 **11 1**
2011–12 Aston Villa 6 0
2011–12 *Leicester C* 4 0 **4 0**
2012–13 Aston Villa 1 0
2012–13 *Blackpool* 40 6
2013–14 Aston Villa 0 0 **31 2**
2013–14 *Blackpool* 11 0
2013–14 *Coventry C* 14 3 **14 3**
2014–15 Blackpool 38 3
2015–16 Blackburn R 15 1 **15 1**
2015–16 *Bury* 4 0 **4 0**
2016–17 Swindon T 18 1 **18 1**
2016–17 Blackpool 18 5 **107 14**

GNANDUILLET, Armand (F) **141 24**
H: 6 4 W: 13 12 b.Angers 13-2-92
Internationals: Ivory Coast U20.
2012–13 Chesterfield 13 3
2013–14 Chesterfield 34 5
2014–15 Chesterfield 26 2
2014–15 *Tranmere R* 4 2 **4 2**
2014–15 *Oxford U* 4 0 **4 0**
2015–16 Chesterfield 9 0 **82 10**
2015–16 *Stevenage* 14 5 **14 5**
2015–16 Leyton Orient 17 4
2016–17 Leyton Orient 1 0 **18 4**
2016–17 Blackpool 19 3 **19 3**

HERRON, John (M) **42 1**
H: 6 0 W: 11 07 b.Coatbridge 1-2-94
Internationals: Scotland U16, U17, U18, U19, U20, U21.
2012–13 Celtic 1 0
2013–14 Celtic 1 0
2014–15 Celtic 0 0 **2 0**
2014–15 *Cowdenbeath* 5 0 **5 0**
2015–16 Blackpool 15 0
2016–17 Blackpool 0 0 **15 0**
2016–17 *Dunfermline Ath* 20 1 **20 1**

HIGHAM, Luke (M) **11 0**
H: 6 1 W: 12 02 b.Blackpool 21-10-96
2014–15 Blackpool 0 0
2015–16 Blackpool 11 0
2016–17 Blackpool 0 0 **11 0**

LETHEREN, Kyle (G) **66 0**
H: 6 2 W: 13 00 b.Swansea 26-12-87
Internationals: Wales U21.
2010–11 Kilmarnock 0 0
2011–12 Kilmarnock 2 0
2012–13 Kilmarnock 9 0 **11 0**
2013–14 Dundee 35 0
2014–15 Dundee 15 0 **50 0**
2015–16 Blackpool 5 0
2016–17 Blackpool 0 0 **5 0**

LYNESS, Dean (G) **59 0**
H: 6 3 W: 11 12 b.Birmingham 20-7-91
Internationals: England U17.
2012–13 Burton Alb 15 0
2013–14 Burton Alb 21 0
2014–15 Burton Alb 1 0
2015–16 Burton Alb 0 0 **37 0**
2015–16 *Blackpool* 9 0
2016–17 Blackpool 13 0 **22 0**

MATT, Jamille (F) **107 23**
H: 6 1 W: 11 11 b.Walsall 20-10-89
2012–13 Fleetwood T 14 3
2013–14 Fleetwood T 25 8
2014–15 Fleetwood T 0 0
2015–16 Fleetwood T 17 3 **56 14**
2015–16 *Stevenage* 8 1 **8 1**
2015–16 *Plymouth Arg* 11 5 **11 5**
2016–17 Blackpool 32 3 **32 3**

McALISTER, Jim (M) **262 11**
H: 5 10 W: 13 00 b.Rothesay 2-11-85
2009–10 Greenock Morton 30 1 **30 1**
2010–11 Hamilton A 19 0
2011–12 Hamilton A 36 1 **55 1**
2012–13 Dundee 38 3
2013–14 Dundee 36 4
2014–15 Dundee 37 2 **111 9**
2015–16 Blackpool 44 0
2016–17 Blackpool 22 0 **66 0**

MELLOR, Kelvin (D) **198 8**
H: 5 10 W: 11 09 b.Copenhagen 25-1-91
2007–08 Crewe Alex 0 0
2008–09 Crewe Alex 0 0
2009–10 Crewe Alex 0 0
2010–11 Crewe Alex 1 0
2011–12 Crewe Alex 12 1
2012–13 Crewe Alex 35 0
2013–14 Crewe Alex 28 1 **76 2**
2014–15 Plymouth Arg 37 1
2015–16 Plymouth Arg 41 1 **78 2**
2016–17 Blackpool 44 4 **44 4**

N'GUESSAN, Christian (M) **0 0**
2016–17 Blackpool 0 0

NOLAN, Eddie (D) **209 3**
H: 6 0 W: 13 05 b.Waterford 5-8-88
Internationals: Republic of Ireland U21, B, Full caps.
2005–06 Blackburn R 0 0
2006–07 Blackburn R 0 0
2006–07 *Stockport Co* 4 0 **4 0**
2007–08 Blackburn R 0 0
2007–08 *Hartlepool U* 11 0 **11 0**
2008–09 Blackburn R 0 0
2008–09 Preston NE 21 0
2009–10 Preston NE 19 0
2009–10 *Sheffield W* 14 1 **14 1**
2010–11 Preston NE 0 0 **40 0**
2010–11 Scunthorpe U 35 0
2011–12 Scunthorpe U 30 1
2012–13 Scunthorpe U 12 0
2013–14 Scunthorpe U 39 0
2014–15 Scunthorpe U 6 0 **122 1**
2015–16 York C 15 1 **15 1**
2016–17 Blackpool 3 0 **3 0**

PAYNE, Jack (M) **254 12**
H: 5 9 W: 9 02 b.Gravesend 5-12-91
2008–09 Gillingham 2 0
2009–10 Gillingham 19 0
2010–11 Gillingham 31 1
2011–12 Gillingham 30 2
2012–13 Gillingham 19 2 **101 5**
2012–13 *Peterborough U* 14 0
2013–14 Peterborough U 32 2
2014–15 Peterborough U 41 3
2015–16 Peterborough U 2 0 **89 5**
2015–16 *Leyton Orient* 29 1 **29 1**
2016–17 Blackpool 35 1 **35 1**

PHILLISKIRK, Daniel (M) **154 18**
H: 5 10 W: 11 05 b.Oldham 10-4-91
Internationals: England U17.
2008–09 Chelsea 0 0
2009–10 Chelsea 0 0
2010–11 Chelsea 0 0
2010–11 *Oxford U* 1 0
2010–11 *Sheffield U* 3 0
2011–12 Sheffield U 0 0
2011–12 *Oxford U* 4 0 **5 0**
2012–13 Sheffield U 1 0 **4 0**
2012–13 Coventry C 1 0
2013–14 Coventry C 0 0 **1 0**
2013–14 Oldham Ath 38 4
2014–15 Oldham Ath 43 4
2015–16 Oldham Ath 23 5 **104 13**
2015–16 Blackpool 22 5
2016–17 Blackpool 18 0 **40 5**

POTTS, Brad (M) **190 25**
H: 6 2 W: 12 09 b.Carlisle 3-7-94
Internationals: England U19.
2012–13 Carlisle U 27 0
2013–14 Carlisle U 37 2
2014–15 Carlisle U 39 7 **103 9**
2015–16 Blackpool 45 6
2016–17 Blackpool 42 10 **87 16**

REDSHAW, Jack (F) **159 43**
H: 5 6 W: 10 00 b.Salford 20-11-90
2009–10 Manchester C 0 0
2010–11 Rochdale 2 0
From Salford C, Altrincham
2011–12 Morecambe 11 2
2012–13 Morecambe 40 15
2013–14 Morecambe 29 8
2014–15 Morecambe 40 11 **120 36**
2015–16 Blackpool 36 7
2016–17 Blackpool 0 0 **36 7**
2016–17 *Rochdale* 1 0 **3 0**

ROACHE, Rowan (F) **0 0**
Internationals: Republic of Ireland U16.
2016–17 Blackpool 0 0

ROBERTSON, Clark (D) **139 1**
H: 6 2 W: 12 00 b.Aberdeen 5-9-93
Internationals: Scotland U19, U21.
2009–10 Aberdeen 3 0
2010–11 Aberdeen 13 0
2011–12 Aberdeen 9 0
2012–13 Aberdeen 23 0
2013–14 Aberdeen 8 0

2014–15 Aberdeen 1 0 **57 0**
2015–16 Blackpool 38 1
2016–17 Blackpool 44 0 **82 1**

SAMUEL, Bright (F) 60 4
H: 5 9 W: 11 05 b. 1-2-97
2014–15 Blackpool 6 0
2015–16 Blackpool 23 0
2016–17 Blackpool 31 4 **60 4**

SLOCOMBE, Sam (G) 172 0
H: 6 0 W: 11 11 b.Scunthorpe 5-6-88
2008–09 Scunthorpe U 0 0
2009–10 Scunthorpe U 1 0
2010–11 Scunthorpe U 2 0
2011–12 Scunthorpe U 28 0
2012–13 Scunthorpe U 29 0
2013–14 Scunthorpe U 46 0
2014–15 Scunthorpe U 9 0 **115 0**
2015–16 Oxford U 23 0 **23 0**
2016–17 Blackpool 34 0 **34 0**

TAYLOR, Andy (D) 304 9
H: 5 11 W: 11 07 b.Blackburn 14-3-86
Internationals: England U16, U17, U18, U19, U20.
2004–05 Blackburn R 0 0
2005–06 Blackburn R 0 0
2005–06 *QPR* 3 0 **3 0**
2005–06 *Blackpool* 3 0
2006–07 Blackburn R 0 0
2006–07 *Crewe Alex* 4 0 **4 0**
2006–07 *Huddersfield T* 8 0 **8 0**
2007–08 Blackburn R 0 0
2007–08 Tranmere R 30 2
2008–09 Tranmere R 39 1 **69 3**
2009–10 Sheffield U 26 0
2010–11 Sheffield U 9 0
2011–12 Sheffield U 4 0
2012–13 Sheffield U 0 0 **39 0**
2012–13 Nottingham F 0 0
2012–13 Walsall 34 0
2013–14 Walsall 33 1
2014–15 Walsall 39 1
2015–16 Walsall 34 2 **140 4**
2016–17 Blackpool 38 2 **41 2**

TURENNE DES PRES, Sebastien (M) 0 0
2016–17 Blackpool 0 0

VASSELL, Kyle (F) 89 17
H: 6 0 W: 12 04 b.Milton Keynes 7-2-93
2013–14 Peterborough U 6 0
2014–15 Peterborough U 17 5
2014–15 *Oxford U* 6 1 **6 1**
2015–16 Peterborough U 5 0 **28 5**
2015–16 *Dagenham & R* 8 0 **8 0**
2015–16 *Shrewsbury T* 13 0 **13 0**
2016–17 Blackpool 34 11 **34 11**

WILSON, Macauley (M) 0 0
H: 5 9 W: 11 00 b. 2-9-97
2015–16 Blackpool 0 0
2016–17 Blackpool 0 0

Players retained or with offer of contract
Brito, Rodrigues Correia Raul Edvanio; Osayi, Samuel Bright; Richards, Caleb Joel; Sims, Jack Stephen John; Williams, Denzel Owusu; King, Jeff Francis.

Scholars
Agyeman-Badu, Benjamin; Chea, Raph; Dunne, William Joseph; Flynn, Alwyn Michael John; Jacobson, Ben Aron; N'Guessan, Christian Dashiell; Newton, Jack Philip; Roache, Rowan Gerald; Robinson, Liam Anthony; Rufus, Tyler Olushola; Sinclair-Smith, Finlay; Steele, Jack; Sumner, Dylan Jack; Thordarson, Craig Raymond; Wainwright, Lewis.

BOLTON W (10)

ALNWICK, Ben (G) 173 0
H: 6 2 W: 13 12 b.Prudhoe 1-1-87
Internationals: England U16, U17, U18, U19, U21.
2003–04 Sunderland 0 0
2004–05 Sunderland 3 0
2005–06 Sunderland 5 0
2006–07 Sunderland 11 0 **19 0**
2006–07 Tottenham H 0 0
2007–08 Tottenham H 0 0
2007–08 *Luton T* 4 0 **4 0**
2007–08 *Leicester C* 8 0 **8 0**
2008–09 Tottenham H 0 0
2008–09 *Carlisle U* 6 0 **6 0**
2009–10 Tottenham H 1 0
2009–10 *Norwich C* 3 0 **3 0**
2010–11 Tottenham H 0 0
2010–11 *Leeds U* 0 0
2010–11 *Doncaster R* 0 0
2011–12 Tottenham H 0 0
2011–12 *Leyton Orient* 6 0
2012–13 Tottenham H 0 0 **1 0**
2012–13 Barnsley 10 0
2013–14 Barnsley 0 0 **10 0**
2013–14 Charlton Ath 10 0 **10 0**
2013–14 Leyton Orient 1 0 **7 0**
2014–15 Peterborough U 41 0
2015–16 Peterborough U 39 0
2016–17 Peterborough U 4 0 **84 0**
2016–17 Bolton W 21 0 **21 0**

AMOS, Ben (G) 109 0
H: 6 1 W: 13 00 b.Macclesfield 10-4-90
Internationals: England U16, U17, U18, U19, U20, U21.
2007–08 Manchester U 0 0
2008–09 Manchester U 0 0
2009–10 Manchester U 0 0
2009–10 *Peterborough U* 1 0 **1 0**
2010–11 Manchester U 0 0
2010–11 *Oldham Ath* 16 0 **16 0**
2011–12 Manchester U 1 0
2012–13 Manchester U 0 0
2012–13 *Hull C* 17 0 **17 0**
2013–14 Manchester U 0 0
2013–14 *Carlisle U* 9 0 **9 0**
2014–15 Manchester U 0 0 **1 0**
2014–15 *Bolton W* 9 0
2015–16 Bolton W 40 0
2016–17 Bolton W 0 0 **49 0**
2016–17 *Cardiff C* 16 0 **16 0**

BEEVERS, Mark (D) 329 17
H: 6 4 W: 13 00 b.Barnsley 21-11-89
Internationals: England U19.
2006–07 Sheffield W 2 0
2007–08 Sheffield W 28 0
2008–09 Sheffield W 34 0
2009–10 Sheffield W 35 0
2010–11 Sheffield W 28 2
2011–12 Sheffield W 7 0
2011–12 *Milton Keynes D* 14 1 **14 1**
2012–13 Sheffield W 6 0 **140 2**
2012–13 Millwall 35 1
2013–14 Millwall 28 0
2014–15 Millwall 25 2
2015–16 Millwall 42 4 **130 7**
2016–17 Bolton W 45 7 **45 7**

BUXTON, Lewis (D) 355 7
H: 6 1 W: 13 11 b.Newport (IW) 10-12-83
2000–01 Portsmouth 0 0
2001–02 Portsmouth 29 0
2002–03 Portsmouth 1 0
2002–03 *Exeter C* 4 0 **4 0**
2002–03 *Bournemouth* 17 0
2003–04 Portsmouth 0 0
2003–04 *Bournemouth* 26 0 **43 0**
2004–05 Portsmouth 0 0 **30 0**
2004–05 Stoke C 16 0
2005–06 Stoke C 32 1
2006–07 Stoke C 1 0
2007–08 Stoke C 4 0
2008–09 Stoke C 0 0 **53 1**
2008–09 Sheffield W 32 1
2009–10 Sheffield W 28 0
2010–11 Sheffield W 30 1
2011–12 Sheffield W 37 1
2012–13 Sheffield W 40 0
2013–14 Sheffield W 20 3
2014–15 Sheffield W 9 0 **196 6**
2015–16 Rotherham U 20 0 **20 0**
2016–17 Bolton W 9 0 **9 0**

CLAYTON, Max (F) 101 11
H: 5 9 W: 11 00 b.Crewe 9-8-94
Internationals: England U16, U17, U18, U19.
2010–11 Crewe Alex 2 0
2011–12 Crewe Alex 24 3
2012–13 Crewe Alex 35 4
2013–14 Crewe Alex 13 2 **74 9**
2014–15 Bolton W 9 1
2015–16 Bolton W 8 0
2016–17 Bolton W 10 1 **27 2**

DAVIES, Mark (M) 218 16
H: 5 11 W: 11 08 b.Willenhall 18-2-88
Internationals: England U16, U17, U19.
2004–05 Wolverhampton W 0 0
2005–06 Wolverhampton W 20 1
2006–07 Wolverhampton W 7 0
2007–08 Wolverhampton W 0 0
2008–09 Wolverhampton W 0 0 **27 1**
2008–09 *Leicester C* 7 1 **7 1**
2008–09 Bolton W 10 0
2009–10 Bolton W 17 0
2010–11 Bolton W 24 1
2011–12 Bolton W 35 4
2012–13 Bolton W 24 6
2013–14 Bolton W 18 1
2014–15 Bolton W 15 2
2015–16 Bolton W 36 0
2016–17 Bolton W 5 0 **184 14**

DERVITE, Dorian (D) 172 6
H: 6 3 W: 13 06 b.Lille 25-7-88
Internationals: France U16, U17, U18, U19, U21.
2008–09 Southend U 18 0 **18 0**
2010–11 Villarreal B 9 0
2011–12 Villarreal B 2 0 **11 0**
2012–13 Villarreal 0 0
2012–13 Charlton Ath 30 3
2013–14 Charlton Ath 40 2 **70 5**
2014–15 Bolton W 37 0
2015–16 Bolton W 22 1
2016–17 Bolton W 14 0 **73 1**

EARING, Jack (M) 0 0
b.Bury 21-1-99
2016–17 Bolton W 0 0

FINNEY, Alex (D) 2 0
H: 6 1 W: 11 00 b.Huddersfield 6-6-96
2013–14 Leyton Orient 0 0
2014–15 Leyton Orient 0 0
2015–16 Bolton W 2 0
2016–17 Bolton W 0 0 **2 0**

HOWARD, Mark (G) 173 0
H: 6 0 W: 11 13 b.Southwark 21-9-86
2005–06 Falkirk 8 0 **8 0**
2006–07 Cardiff C 0 0
2006–07 Swansea C 0 0
2007–08 St Mirren 10 0
2008–09 St Mirren 33 0
2009–10 St Mirren 2 0 **45 0**
2010–11 Aberdeen 9 0 **9 0**
2011–12 Blackpool 4 0 **4 0**
2011–12 Sheffield U 0 0
2012–13 Sheffield U 11 0
2013–14 Sheffield U 19 0
2014–15 Sheffield U 35 0
2015–16 Sheffield U 15 0 **80 0**
2016–17 Bolton W 27 0 **27 0**

KARACAN, Jem (M) 180 13
H: 5 10 W: 11 13 b.Lewisham 21-2-89
Internationals: Turkey U17, U18, U19, U21.
2007–08 Reading 0 0
2007–08 *Bournemouth* 13 1 **13 1**
2007–08 *Millwall* 7 0 **7 0**
2008–09 Reading 15 1
2009–10 Reading 27 0
2010–11 Reading 40 3
2011–12 Reading 37 3
2012–13 Reading 21 1
2013–14 Reading 7 2
2014–15 Reading 8 1
2015–16 Reading 0 0 **155 11**
2015–16 Galatasaray 0 0
2016–17 Galatasaray 0 0
2016–17 Bolton W 5 1 **5 1**

MADINE, Gary (F) 282 61
H: 6 1 W: 12 00 b.Gateshead 24-8-90
2007–08 Carlisle U 11 0
2008–09 Carlisle U 14 1
2008–09 *Rochdale* 3 0 **3 0**
2009–10 Carlisle U 20 4
2009–10 *Coventry C* 9 0
2009–10 *Chesterfield* 4 0 **4 0**
2010–11 Carlisle U 21 8
2010–11 Sheffield W 22 5
2011–12 Sheffield W 38 18
2012–13 Sheffield W 30 3
2013–14 Sheffield W 1 0
2013–14 *Carlisle U* 5 2 **71 15**
2014–15 Sheffield W 10 0 **101 26**
2014–15 *Coventry C* 11 3 **20 3**
2014–15 *Blackpool* 15 3 **15 3**
2015–16 Bolton W 32 5
2016–17 Bolton W 36 9 **68 14**

MORAIS, Filipe (M) 297 30
H: 5 9 W: 11 10 b.Lisbon 21-11-85
Internationals: Portugal U21.
2003–04 Chelsea 0 0
2004–05 Chelsea 0 0
2005–06 Chelsea 0 0
2005–06 *Milton Keynes D* 13 0 **13 0**
2006–07 Millwall 12 1 **12 1**
2006–07 *St Johnstone* 13 1
2007–08 Hibernian 28 1

2008–09 Hibernian 2 0 **30 1**
2008–09 Inverness CT 12 3 **12 3**
2009–10 St Johnstone 30 2 **43 3**
2010–11 Oldham Ath 23 3
2011–12 Oldham Ath 36 5
2012–13 Oldham Ath 0 0 **59 8**
2012–13 Stevenage 28 3
2013–14 Stevenage 27 4 **55 7**
2014–15 Bradford C 30 3
2015–16 Bradford C 7 1
2016–17 Bradford C 17 1 **54 5**
2016–17 Bolton W 19 2 **19 2**

MOXEY, Dean (D) 258 8
H: 6 2 W: 11 00 b.Exeter 14-1-86
Internationals: England C.
2008–09 Exeter C 43 4 **43 4**
2009–10 Derby Co 30 0
2010–11 Derby Co 22 2 **52 2**
2010–11 Crystal Palace 17 1
2011–12 Crystal Palace 24 0
2012–13 Crystal Palace 30 0
2013–14 Crystal Palace 20 0 **91 1**
2014–15 Bolton W 20 1
2015–16 Bolton W 33 0
2016–17 Bolton W 19 0 **72 1**

OSEDE, Derik (D) 48 0
H: 5 11 W: 11 09 b.Madrid 21-2-93
Internationals: Spain U16, U17, U18, U19, U20, U21.
2014–15 Real Madrid 0 0
2015–16 Bolton W 23 0
2016–17 Bolton W 25 0 **48 0**

PERRY, Alex (M) 0 0
b.Liverpool 4-3-98
2016–17 Bolton W 0 0

PRATLEY, Darren (M) 370 41
H: 6 1 W: 10 12 b.Barking 22-4-85
2001–02 Fulham 0 0
2002–03 Fulham 0 0
2003–04 Fulham 1 0
2004–05 Fulham 0 0
2004–05 *Brentford* 14 1
2005–06 Fulham 0 0 **1 0**
2005–06 *Brentford* 32 4 **46 5**
2006–07 Swansea C 28 1
2007–08 Swansea C 42 5
2008–09 Swansea C 37 4
2009–10 Swansea C 36 7
2010–11 Swansea C 34 9 **177 26**
2011–12 Bolton W 25 1
2012–13 Bolton W 31 2
2013–14 Bolton W 20 2
2014–15 Bolton W 22 4
2015–16 Bolton W 36 1
2016–17 Bolton W 12 0 **146 10**

PROCTOR, Jamie (F) 228 38
H: 6 2 W: 12 03 b.Preston 25-3-92
2009–10 Preston NE 1 0
2010–11 Preston NE 5 1
2010–11 *Stockport Co* 7 0 **7 0**
2011–12 Preston NE 31 3 **37 4**
2012–13 Swansea C 0 0
2012–13 *Shrewsbury T* 2 0 **2 0**
2012–13 Crawley T 18 7
2013–14 Crawley T 44 6 **62 13**
2014–15 Fleetwood T 41 8
2015–16 Fleetwood T 23 4 **64 12**
2015–16 Bradford C 18 5 **18 5**
2016–17 Bolton W 21 0 **21 0**
2016–17 *Carlisle U* 17 4 **17 4**

SAMIZADEH, Alex (F) 1 0
b. 10-11-98
2015–16 Bolton W 1 0
2016–17 Bolton W 0 0 **1 0**

SPEARING, Jay (M) 214 12
H: 5 6 W: 11 01 b.Wallasey 25-11-88
2006–07 Liverpool 0 0
2007–08 Liverpool 0 0
2008–09 Liverpool 0 0
2009–10 Liverpool 3 0
2009–10 *Leicester C* 7 1 **7 1**
2010–11 Liverpool 11 0
2011–12 Liverpool 16 0
2012–13 Liverpool 0 0
2012–13 *Bolton W* 37 2
2013–14 Liverpool 0 0 **30 0**
2013–14 Bolton W 45 2
2014–15 Bolton W 21 1
2014–15 *Blackburn R* 15 1 **15 1**
2015–16 Bolton W 22 2
2016–17 Bolton W 37 3 **162 10**

TAYLOR, Chris (M) 380 40
H: 5 11 W: 11 00 b.Oldham 20-12-86
2005–06 Oldham Ath 14 0
2006–07 Oldham Ath 44 4
2007–08 Oldham Ath 42 5
2008–09 Oldham Ath 42 10
2009–10 Oldham Ath 32 1
2010–11 Oldham Ath 42 11
2011–12 Oldham Ath 38 2
2012–13 Millwall 22 3
2013–14 Blackburn R 34 0
2014–15 Blackburn R 16 1
2015–16 Blackburn R 12 0 **62 1**
2015–16 *Millwall* 10 3 **32 6**
2016–17 Bolton W 16 0 **16 0**
2016–17 *Oldham Ath* 16 0 **270 33**

TROTTER, Liam (M) 269 35
H: 6 2 W: 12 02 b.Ipswich 24-8-88
2005–06 Ipswich T 1 0
2006–07 Ipswich T 0 0
2006–07 *Millwall* 2 0
2007–08 Ipswich T 7 1
2008–09 Ipswich T 3 1
2008–09 *Grimsby T* 15 2 **15 2**
2008–09 *Scunthorpe U* 12 1 **12 1**
2009–10 Ipswich T 12 0 **23 2**
2009–10 *Millwall* 20 1
2010–11 Millwall 35 7
2011–12 Millwall 35 7
2012–13 Millwall 36 6
2013–14 Millwall 19 3 **147 24**
2013–14 *Bolton W* 16 1
2014–15 Bolton W 14 1
2015–16 Bolton W 13 1
2015–16 *Nottingham F* 9 1 **9 1**
2016–17 Bolton W 20 2 **63 5**

TURNER, Jake (G) 0 0
b.Wilmslow 25-2-99
Internationals: England U18.
2016–17 Bolton W 0 0

VELA, Joshua (M) 120 11
H: 5 11 W: 11 07 b.Salford 14-12-93
2010–11 Bolton W 0 0
2011–12 Bolton W 3 0
2012–13 Bolton W 4 0
2013–14 Bolton W 0 0
2013–14 *Notts Co* 7 0 **7 0**
2014–15 Bolton W 29 0
2015–16 Bolton W 31 2
2016–17 Bolton W 46 9 **113 11**

WABARA, Reece (D) 128 3
H: 6 0 W: 12 06 b.Birmingham 28-12-91
Internationals: England U19, U20.
2008–09 Manchester C 0 0
2009–10 Manchester C 0 0
2010–11 Manchester C 1 0
2011–12 Manchester C 0 0
2011–12 *Ipswich T* 6 0 **6 0**
2012–13 Manchester C 0 0
2012–13 *Oldham Ath* 25 0 **25 0**
2012–13 *Blackpool* 1 0 **1 0**
2013–14 Manchester C 0 0 **1 0**
2013–14 *Doncaster R* 13 0
2014–15 Doncaster R 43 1 **56 1**
2015–16 Barnsley 19 1 **19 1**
2015–16 Wigan Ath 19 1
2016–17 Wigan Ath 0 0 **19 1**
2016–17 Bolton W 1 0 **1 0**

WALKER, Tom (M) 29 1
H: 6 0 b.Salford 12-12-95
2014–15 Bolton W 11 1
2015–16 Bolton W 7 0
2016–17 Bolton W 0 0 **18 1**
2016–17 *Bury* 11 0 **11 0**

WHEATER, David (D) 309 26
H: 6 5 W: 12 12 b.Redcar 14-2-87
Internationals: England U16, U17, U18, U19, U21.
2004–05 Middlesbrough 0 0
2005–06 Middlesbrough 6 0
2005–06 *Doncaster R* 7 1 **7 1**
2006–07 Middlesbrough 2 1
2006–07 *Wolverhampton W* 1 0 **1 0**
2006–07 *Darlington* 15 2 **15 2**
2007–08 Middlesbrough 34 3
2008–09 Middlesbrough 32 1
2009–10 Middlesbrough 42 1
2010–11 Middlesbrough 24 3 **140 9**
2010–11 Bolton W 7 0
2011–12 Bolton W 24 2
2012–13 Bolton W 4 0
2013–14 Bolton W 23 1
2014–15 Bolton W 17 1
2015–16 Bolton W 28 1
2016–17 Bolton W 43 9 **146 14**

WILKINSON, Conor (F) 66 9
H: 6 1 W: 12 02 b.Croydon 23-1-95
Internationals: Republic of Ireland U17, U19, U21.
2012–13 Millwall 0 0
2013–14 Bolton W 0 0
2013–14 *Torquay U* 3 0 **3 0**
2014–15 Bolton W 4 0
2014–15 *Oldham Ath* 17 3 **17 3**
2015–16 Bolton W 0 0
2015–16 *Barnsley* 8 1 **8 1**
2015–16 *Newport Co* 12 1 **12 1**
2015–16 *Portsmouth* 1 0 **1 0**
2016–17 Bolton W 9 0 **13 0**
2016–17 *Chesterfield* 12 4 **12 4**

WILSON, Lawrie (D) 219 16
H: 5 11 W: 11 06 b.London 11-9-87
2006–07 Colchester U 0 0
2010–11 Stevenage 42 5
2011–12 Stevenage 46 5 **88 10**
2012–13 Charlton Ath 30 2
2013–14 Charlton Ath 42 2
2014–15 Charlton Ath 24 0 **96 4**
2014–15 *Rotherham U* 3 0 **3 0**
2015–16 Bolton W 12 1
2015–16 *Peterborough U* 2 0 **2 0**
2016–17 Bolton W 18 1 **30 2**

Scholars
Abdo, Anas; Aspinall, James Alexander; Brockbank, Harry William; Earing, Jack James; Everest, Jack William; Fearnley, Matthew Neil; Grant, Jordan Lee; Grivosti, Tom; Hartshorne, William Lancaster; Honeyball, Alexander Robert; Jones-Griffiths, Shakeel Tyrik Zane; Lonsdale, Cole Stephen; Marsh, Matthew Calum; Moore, Cameron James; Navarro, Luca; Pearson, Ronaldo Steve; Perry, Alexander Anthony; Politic, Dennis-Dorian; Samizadeh, Alexander; Spooner, Callum Michael; Turner, Jake Edward; White, Ryan.

BOURNEMOUTH (11)

AFOBE, Benik (F) 182 51
H: 5 10 W: 11 00 b.Leyton 12-2-93
Internationals: England U16, U17, U19, U21.
2009–10 Arsenal 0 0
2010–11 Arsenal 0 0
2010–11 *Huddersfield T* 28 5 **28 5**
2011–12 Arsenal 0 0
2011–12 *Reading* 3 0 **3 0**
2012–13 Arsenal 0 0
2012–13 *Bolton W* 20 2 **20 2**
2012–13 *Millwall* 5 0 **5 0**
2013–14 Arsenal 0 0
2013–14 *Sheffield W* 12 2 **12 2**
2014–15 Arsenal 0 0
2014–15 *Milton Keynes D* 22 10 **22 10**
2014–15 Wolverhampton W 21 13
2015–16 Wolverhampton W 25 9 **46 22**
2015–16 Bournemouth 15 4
2016–17 Bournemouth 31 6 **46 10**

ALLSOP, Ryan (G) 86 0
H: 6 2 W: 12 06 b.Birmingham 17-6-92
Internationals: England U17.
2012–13 Leyton Orient 20 0 **20 0**
2012–13 Bournemouth 10 0
2013–14 Bournemouth 12 0
2014–15 Bournemouth 0 0
2014–15 *Coventry C* 24 0 **24 0**
2015–16 Bournemouth 1 0
2015–16 *Wycombe W* 18 0 **18 0**
2015–16 Portsmouth 0 0
2016–17 Bournemouth 1 0 **24 0**

ARTER, Harry (M) 224 28
H: 5 9 W: 11 07 b.Sidcup 28-12-89
Internationals: Republic of Ireland U17, U19, Full caps.
2007–08 Charlton Ath 0 0
2008–09 Charlton Ath 0 0
From Woking.
2010–11 Bournemouth 18 0
2010–11 *Carlisle U* 5 1 **5 1**
2011–12 Bournemouth 34 5
2012–13 Bournemouth 37 8
2013–14 Bournemouth 31 3
2014–15 Bournemouth 43 9
2015–16 Bournemouth 21 1
2016–17 Bournemouth 35 1 **219 27**

BORUC, Artur (G) **377** **0**
H: 6 4 W: 13 08 b.Siedlce 20-2-80
Internationals: Poland Full caps.
2005–06 Celtic 34 0
2006–07 Celtic 36 0
2007–08 Celtic 30 0
2008–09 Celtic 34 0
2009–10 Celtic 28 0 **162** **0**
2010–11 Fiorentina 26 0
2011–12 Fiorentina 36 0 **62** **0**
2012–13 Southampton 20 0
2013–14 Southampton 29 0
2014–15 Southampton 0 0 **49** **0**
2014–15 *Bournemouth* 37 0
2015–16 Bournemouth 32 0
2016–17 Bournemouth 35 0 **104** **0**

BUCKLEY, Callum (D) **0** **0**
H: 5 11 W: 11 11 b.Basingstoke 12-1-96
2014–15 Bournemouth 0 0
2015–16 Bournemouth 0 0
2016–17 Bournemouth 0 0

BUTCHER, Matt (M) **34** **2**
H: 6 2 W: 12 13 b.Portsmouth 14-5-97
From Poole T.
2015–16 Bournemouth 0 0
2016–17 Bournemouth 0 0
2016–17 *Yeovil T* 34 2 **34** **2**

CARGILL, Baily (D) **20** **2**
H: 6 2 W: 13 10 b.Winchester 13-10-95
Internationals: England U20.
2012–13 Bournemouth 0 0
2013–14 Bournemouth 0 0
2013–14 *Torquay U* 5 0 **5** **0**
2014–15 Bournemouth 0 0
2015–16 Bournemouth 0 0
2015–16 *Coventry C* 5 1 **5** **1**
2016–17 Bournemouth 1 0 **1** **0**
2016–17 *Gillingham* 9 1 **9** **1**

COOK, Lewis (M) **86** **1**
H: 5 9 W: 11 03 b.York 3-2-97
Internationals: England U16, U17, U18, U19, U20.
2014–15 Leeds U 37 0
2015–16 Leeds U 43 1 **80** **1**
2016–17 Bournemouth 6 0 **6** **0**

COOK, Steve (D) **220** **15**
H: 6 1 W: 12 13 b.Hastings 19-4-91
2008–09 Brighton & HA 2 0
2009–10 Brighton & HA 0 0
2010–11 Brighton & HA 0 0
2011–12 Brighton & HA 1 0 **3** **0**
2011–12 Bournemouth 26 0
2012–13 Bournemouth 33 1
2013–14 Bournemouth 38 3
2014–15 Bournemouth 46 5
2015–16 Bournemouth 36 4
2016–17 Bournemouth 38 2 **217** **15**

CORNICK, Harry (F) **53** **8**
H: 5 11 W: 13 03 b.Poole 6-3-95
2013–14 Bournemouth 0 0
2014–15 Bournemouth 0 0
2015–16 Bournemouth 0 0
2015–16 *Yeovil T* 36 7 **36** **7**
2016–17 Bournemouth 0 0
2016–17 *Leyton Orient* 11 1 **11** **1**
2016–17 *Gillingham* 6 0 **6** **0**

DANIELS, Charlie (M) **346** **19**
H: 6 1 W: 12 12 b.Harlow 7-9-86
2005–06 Tottenham H 0 0
2006–07 Tottenham H 0 0
2006–07 *Chesterfield* 2 0 **2** **0**
2007–08 Tottenham H 0 0
2007–08 *Leyton Orient* 31 2
2008–09 Tottenham H 0 0
2008–09 *Gillingham* 5 1 **5** **1**
2008–09 Leyton Orient 21 2
2009–10 Leyton Orient 41 0
2010–11 Leyton Orient 42 0
2011–12 Leyton Orient 13 0 **148** **4**
2011–12 Bournemouth 21 2
2012–13 Bournemouth 34 4
2013–14 Bournemouth 23 0
2014–15 Bournemouth 42 1
2015–16 Bournemouth 37 3
2016–17 Bournemouth 34 4 **191** **14**

FEDERICI, Adam (G) **227** **1**
H: 6 2 W: 14 02 b.Nowra 31-1-85
Internationals: Australia U20, U23, Full caps.
2005–06 Reading 0 0
2006–07 Reading 2 0
2007–08 Reading 0 0
2008–09 Reading 15 1
2008–09 *Southend U* 10 0 **10** **0**
2009–10 Reading 46 0
2010–11 Reading 34 0
2011–12 Reading 46 0
2012–13 Reading 21 0
2013–14 Reading 2 0
2014–15 Reading 43 0 **209** **1**
2015–16 Bournemouth 6 0
2016–17 Bournemouth 2 0 **8** **0**

FRANCIS, Simon (D) **511** **9**
H: 6 0 W: 12 06 b.Nottingham 16-2-85
2002–03 Bradford C 25 1
2003–04 Bradford C 30 0 **55** **1**
2003–04 Sheffield U 5 0
2004–05 Sheffield U 6 0
2005–06 Sheffield U 1 0 **12** **0**
2005–06 *Grimsby T* 5 0 **5** **0**
2005–06 *Tranmere R* 17 1 **17** **1**
2006–07 Southend U 40 1
2007–08 Southend U 27 2
2008–09 Southend U 45 0
2009–10 Southend U 45 1 **157** **4**
2010–11 Charlton Ath 34 0
2011–12 Charlton Ath 0 0 **34** **0**
2011–12 Bournemouth 29 0
2012–13 Bournemouth 42 1
2013–14 Bournemouth 46 1
2014–15 Bournemouth 42 1
2015–16 Bournemouth 38 0
2016–17 Bournemouth 34 0 **231** **3**

FRASER, Ryan (M) **130** **11**
H: 5 4 W: 10 13 b.Aberdeen 24-2-94
Internationals: Scotland U19, U21, Full caps.
2010–11 Aberdeen 2 0
2011–12 Aberdeen 3 0
2012–13 Aberdeen 16 0 **21** **0**
2012–13 Bournemouth 5 0
2013–14 Bournemouth 37 3
2014–15 Bournemouth 21 1
2015–16 Bournemouth 0 0
2015–16 *Ipswich T* 18 4 **18** **4**
2016–17 Bournemouth 28 3 **91** **7**

GOSLING, Dan (M) **161** **14**
H: 6 0 W: 11 00 b.Brixham 2-2-90
Internationals: England U17, U18, U19, U21.
2006–07 Plymouth Arg 12 2
2007–08 Plymouth Arg 10 0 **22** **2**
2007–08 Everton 0 0
2008–09 Everton 11 2
2009–10 Everton 11 2 **22** **4**
2010–11 Newcastle U 1 0
2011–12 Newcastle U 12 1
2012–13 Newcastle U 3 0
2013–14 Newcastle U 8 0 **24** **1**
2013–14 *Blackpool* 14 2 **14** **2**
2014–15 Bournemouth 18 0
2015–16 Bournemouth 34 3
2016–17 Bournemouth 27 2 **79** **5**

GRABBAN, Lewis (F) **314** **86**
H: 6 0 W: 11 03 b.Croydon 12-1-88
2005–06 Crystal Palace 0 0
2006–07 Crystal Palace 8 1
2006–07 *Oldham Ath* 9 0 **9** **0**
2007–08 Crystal Palace 2 0 **10** **1**
2007–08 *Motherwell* 6 0 **6** **0**
2007–08 Millwall 13 3
2008–09 Millwall 31 6
2009–10 Millwall 11 0
2009–10 *Brentford* 7 2
2010–11 Millwall 1 0 **56** **9**
2010–11 Brentford 22 5 **29** **7**
2011–12 Rotherham U 43 18 **43** **18**
2012–13 Bournemouth 42 13
2013–14 Bournemouth 44 22
2014–15 Norwich C 35 12
2015–16 Norwich C 6 1 **41** **13**
2015–16 Bournemouth 15 0
2016–17 Bournemouth 3 0 **104** **35**
2016–17 *Reading* 16 3 **16** **3**

GRADEL, Max (M) **264** **67**
H: 5 10 W: 11 00 b.Abidjan 30-11-87
Internationals: Ivory Coast Full caps.
2005–06 Leicester C 0 0
2006–07 Leicester C 0 0
2007–08 Leicester C 0 0
2007–08 *Bournemouth* 34 9
2008–09 Leicester C 27 1
2009–10 Leicester C 0 0 **27** **1**
2009–10 Leeds U 32 6
2010–11 Leeds U 41 18
2011–12 Leeds U 4 1 **77** **25**
2011–12 St Etienne 29 6
2012–13 St Etienne 23 3
2013–14 St Etienne 18 5
2014–15 St Etienne 31 17 **101** **31**
2015–16 Bournemouth 14 1
2016–17 Bournemouth 11 0 **59** **10**

GREEN, Jordan (F) **10** **0**
H: 5 6 W: 10 03 b.London 22-2-95
2015–16 Bournemouth 0 0
2016–17 Bournemouth 0 0
2016–17 *Newport Co* 10 0 **10** **0**

HARFIELD, Ollie (D) **0** **0**
2016–17 Bournemouth 0 0

HOLMES, Jordan (G) **0** **0**
b.Nowra 8-5-97
2015–16 Bournemouth 0 0
2016–17 Bournemouth 0 0

HYNDMAN, Emerson (M) **38** **5**
H: 5 7 W: 9 08 b.Dallas 9-4-96
Internationals: USA U17, U20, U23, Full caps.
2013–14 Fulham 0 0
2014–15 Fulham 9 0
2015–16 Fulham 16 1 **25** **1**
2016–17 Bournemouth 0 0
2016–17 *Rangers* 13 4 **13** **4**

IBE, Jordan (F) **104** **8**
H: 5 9 W: 11 00 b.Southwark 8-12-95
Internationals: England U18, U19, U20, U21.
2011–12 Wycombe W 7 1 **7** **1**
2011–12 Liverpool 0 0
2012–13 Liverpool 1 0
2013–14 Liverpool 1 0
2013–14 *Birmingham C* 11 1 **11** **1**
2014–15 Liverpool 12 0
2014–15 *Derby Co* 20 5 **20** **5**
2015–16 Liverpool 27 1 **41** **1**
2016–17 Bournemouth 25 0 **25** **0**

JORDAN, Corey (D) **0** **0**
H: 6 1 W: 11 11 b.Bournemouth 4-3-99
2015–16 Bournemouth 0 0
2016–17 Bournemouth 0 0

KING, Josh (F) **159** **28**
H: 5 11 W: 11 09 b.Oslo 15-1-92
Internationals: Norway U15, U16, U18, U19, U21, Full caps.
2008–09 Manchester U 0 0
2009–10 Manchester U 0 0
2010–11 Manchester U 0 0
2010–11 *Preston NE* 8 0 **8** **0**
2011–12 Manchester U 0 0
2011–12 *Moenchengladbach* 2 0 **2** **0**
2011–12 *Hull C* 18 1 **18** **1**
2012–13 Manchester U 0 0
2012–13 Blackburn R 16 2
2013–14 Blackburn R 32 2
2014–15 Blackburn R 16 1 **64** **5**
2015–16 Bournemouth 31 6
2016–17 Bournemouth 36 16 **67** **22**

LEE, Jordan (D) **0** **0**
H: 5 10 W: 12 08 b. 31-12-96
2015–16 Bournemouth 0 0
2016–17 Bournemouth 0 0

MATTHEWS, Sam (M) **0** **0**
b. 1-3-97
2013–14 Bournemouth 0 0
2014–15 Bournemouth 0 0
2015–16 Bournemouth 0 0
2016–17 Bournemouth 0 0

MINGS, Tyrone (D) **65** **1**
H: 6 3 W: 12 00 b.Bath 19-3-93
2012–13 Ipswich T 1 0
2013–14 Ipswich T 16 0
2014–15 Ipswich T 40 1 **57** **1**
2015–16 Bournemouth 1 0
2016–17 Bournemouth 7 0 **8** **0**

MOUSSET, Lys (M) **45** **14**
H: 6 0 W: 12 08 b.Montvilliers 8-2-96
Internationals: France U20, U21.
2013–14 Le Havre 5 0
2014–15 Le Havre 1 0
2015–16 Le Havre 28 14 **34** **14**
2016–17 Bournemouth 11 0 **11** **0**

O'CONNELL, Keelan (M) **0** **0**
2016–17 Bournemouth 0 0

PUGH, Marc (M) **392** **67**
H: 5 11 W: 11 04 b.Bacup 2-4-87
2005–06 Burnley 0 0
2005–06 Bury 6 1
2006–07 Bury 35 3 **41** **4**
2007–08 Shrewsbury T 37 4
2008–09 Shrewsbury T 7 0 **44** **4**

2008–09 *Luton T* 4 0 **4 0**
2008–09 *Hereford U* 9 1
2009–10 Hereford U 40 13 **49 14**
2010–11 Bournemouth 41 12
2011–12 Bournemouth 42 8
2012–13 Bournemouth 40 6
2013–14 Bournemouth 42 5
2014–15 Bournemouth 42 9
2015–16 Bournemouth 26 3
2016–17 Bournemouth 21 2 **254 45**

QUIGLEY, Joe (F) **10 1**
H: 6 4 W: 13 01 b.Hayes 10-12-96
2016–17 Bournemouth 0 0
2016–17 *Gillingham* 10 1 **10 1**

RAMSDALE, Aaron (G) **0 0**
b. 14-5-98
Internationals: England U18, U19.
2015–16 Sheffield U 0 0
2016–17 Sheffield U 0 0
2016–17 Bournemouth 0 0

SIMPSON, Jack (D) **0 0**
H: 5 10 W: 13 01 b. 8-1-97
2015–16 Bournemouth 0 0
2016–17 Bournemouth 0 0

SMITH, Adam (D) **212 7**
H: 5 8 W: 10 07 b.Leytonstone 29-4-91
Internationals: England U16, U17, U19, U20, U21.
2007–08 Tottenham H 0 0
2008–09 Tottenham H 0 0
2009–10 Tottenham H 0 0
2009–10 *Wycombe W* 3 0 **3 0**
2009–10 *Torquay U* 16 0 **16 0**
2010–11 Tottenham H 0 0
2010–11 *Bournemouth* 38 1
2011–12 Tottenham H 1 0
2011–12 *Milton Keynes D* 17 2 **17 2**
2011–12 *Leeds U* 3 0 **3 0**
2012–13 Tottenham H 0 0
2012–13 *Millwall* 25 1 **25 1**
2013–14 Tottenham H 0 0 **1 0**
2013–14 *Derby Co* 8 0 **8 0**
2013–14 Bournemouth 5 0
2014–15 Bournemouth 29 0
2015–16 Bournemouth 31 2
2016–17 Bournemouth 36 1 **139 4**

SMITH, Bradley (D) **17 0**
H: 5 10 W: 11 00 b.New South Wales 9-4-94
Internationals: England U17, U19, U20. Australia U23, Full caps.
2011–12 Liverpool 0 0
2012–13 Liverpool 0 0
2013–14 Liverpool 1 0
2014–15 Liverpool 0 0
2014–15 *Swindon T* 7 0 **7 0**
2015–16 Liverpool 4 0 **5 0**
2016–17 Bournemouth 5 0 **5 0**

STANISLAS, Junior (M) **196 25**
H: 6 0 W: 12 00 b.Kidbrooke 26-11-89
Internationals: England U20, U21.
2007–08 West Ham U 0 0
2008–09 West Ham U 9 2
2008–09 *Southend U* 6 1 **6 1**
2009–10 West Ham U 26 3
2010–11 West Ham U 6 1
2011–12 West Ham U 1 0 **42 6**
2011–12 Burnley 31 0
2012–13 Burnley 35 5
2013–14 Burnley 27 2 **93 7**
2014–15 Bournemouth 13 1
2015–16 Bournemouth 21 3
2016–17 Bournemouth 21 7 **55 11**

SURMAN, Andrew (M) **366 33**
H: 5 10 W: 11 06 b.Johannesburg 20-8-86
Internationals: England U21.
2003–04 Southampton 0 0
2004–05 Southampton 0 0
2004–05 *Walsall* 14 2 **14 2**
2005–06 Southampton 12 2
2005–06 *Bournemouth* 24 6
2006–07 Southampton 37 4
2007–08 Southampton 40 2
2008–09 Southampton 44 7
2009–10 Southampton 0 0 **133 15**
2009–10 Wolverhampton W 7 0 **7 0**
2010–11 Norwich C 22 3
2011–12 Norwich C 25 4
2012–13 Norwich C 4 0
2013–14 Norwich C 0 0
2013–14 *Bournemouth* 35 0
2014–15 Norwich C 1 0 **52 7**
2014–15 Bournemouth 41 3
2015–16 Bournemouth 38 0
2016–17 Bournemouth 22 0 **160 9**

SURRIDGE, Sam (F) **0 0**
b.Wimborne 28-7-98
2015–16 Bournemouth 0 0
2016–17 Bournemouth 0 0

WHITFIELD, Ben (M) **34 2**
H: 5 5 W: 9 11 b. 28-2-96
2013–14 Bournemouth 0 0
2014–15 Bournemouth 0 0
2015–16 Bournemouth 0 0
2016–17 Bournemouth 0 0
2016–17 *Yeovil T* 34 2 **34 2**

WIGGINS, Rhoys (D) **200 3**
H: 5 8 W: 11 05 b.Uxbridge 4-11-87
Internationals: Wales U17, U19, U21.
2006–07 Crystal Palace 0 0
2007–08 Crystal Palace 0 0
2008–09 Crystal Palace 1 0 **1 0**
2008–09 *Bournemouth* 13 0
2009–10 Norwich C 0 0
2009–10 *Bournemouth* 19 0
2010–11 Bournemouth 35 2
2011–12 Charlton Ath 45 1
2012–13 Charlton Ath 20 0
2013–14 Charlton Ath 38 0
2014–15 Charlton Ath 21 0 **124 1**
2015–16 Sheffield W 6 0 **6 0**
2015–16 Bournemouth 0 0
2016–17 Birmingham C 2 0 **2 0**
2016–17 Bournemouth 0 0 **67 2**

WILSON, Callum (M) **127 53**
H: 5 11 W: 10 06 b.Coventry 27-2-92
Internationals: England U21.
2009–10 Coventry C 0 0
2010–11 Coventry C 1 0
2011–12 Coventry C 0 0
2012–13 Coventry C 11 1
2013–14 Coventry C 37 21 **49 22**
2014–15 Bournemouth 45 20
2015–16 Bournemouth 13 5
2016–17 Bournemouth 20 6 **78 31**

WILSON, Marc (M) **217 4**
H: 6 2 W: 12 07 b.Lisburn 17-8-87
Internationals: Republic of Ireland U18, U19, U21, Full caps.
2005–06 Portsmouth 0 0
2005–06 *Yeovil T* 2 0 **2 0**
2006–07 Portsmouth 0 0
2006–07 *Bournemouth* 19 3
2007–08 Portsmouth 0 0
2007–08 *Bournemouth* 7 0
2007–08 *Luton T* 4 0 **4 0**
2008–09 Portsmouth 3 0
2009–10 Portsmouth 28 0
2010–11 Portsmouth 4 0 **35 0**
2010–11 Stoke C 28 1
2011–12 Stoke C 35 0
2012–13 Stoke C 19 0
2013–14 Stoke C 33 0
2014–15 Stoke C 27 0
2015–16 Stoke C 4 0 **146 1**
2016–17 Bournemouth 0 0 **26 3**
2016–17 *WBA* 4 0 **4 0**

WORTHINGTON, Matt (M) **1 0**
b.Southampton 18-12-97
2016–17 Bournemouth 1 0 **1 0**

Players retained or with offer of contract
Dobre, Mihai-Alexandru; Hobson, Shaun Jermaine; Ndjoli, Mikael Bongili; O'Flaherty, Patrick; Stanton, Callum James Frank; Travers, Mark.

Scholars
Anthony, Jaidon; Boote, James Peter; Cordner, Tyler Jack; Dennis, William Jonathon; Diaz, Antonio Javier; Gillela, Dinesh; Kilkenny, Gavin; Morrison, Connal John; Ofoborh, Nathan Nnamdi Ugochukwu; Pope, Ashley; Seaman, Charlie; Sherring, Sam; Taylor, Kyle Frazer.

BRADFORD C (12)

BOATENG, Kwame (D) **0 0**
2016–17 Bradford C 0 0

CLARKE, Billy (F) **308 67**
H: 5 7 W: 10 01 b.Cork 13-12-87
Internationals: Republic of Ireland U17, U19, U21.
2004–05 Ipswich T 0 0
2005–06 Ipswich T 2 0
2005–06 *Colchester U* 6 0 **6 0**
2006–07 Ipswich T 27 3
2007–08 Ipswich T 20 0
2007–08 *Falkirk* 8 1 **8 1**
2008–09 Ipswich T 0 0 **49 3**
2008–09 *Darlington* 20 8 **20 8**
2008–09 *Northampton T* 5 3 **5 3**
2008–09 *Brentford* 8 6 **8 6**
2009–10 Blackpool 18 1
2010–11 Blackpool 0 0
2011–12 Blackpool 9 0 **27 1**
2011–12 *Sheffield U* 5 1 **5 1**
2011–12 Crawley T 17 3
2012–13 Crawley T 36 10
2013–14 Crawley T 29 7 **82 20**
2014–15 Bradford C 36 13
2015–16 Bradford C 29 4
2016–17 Bradford C 33 7 **98 24**

CRACKNELL, Joe (G) **0 0**
H: 6 0 W: 11 02 b.Hull 5-6-94
2012–13 Hull C 0 0
2013–14 Hull C 0 0
2015–16 Bradford C 0 0
2016–17 Bradford C 0 0

DARBY, Stephen (D) **265 0**
H: 5 9 W: 10 00 b.Liverpool 6-10-88
Internationals: England U19.
2006–07 Liverpool 0 0
2007–08 Liverpool 0 0
2008–09 Liverpool 0 0
2009–10 Liverpool 1 0
2009–10 *Swindon T* 12 0 **12 0**
2010–11 Liverpool 0 0
2010–11 *Notts Co* 23 0 **23 0**
2011–12 Liverpool 0 0 **1 0**
2011–12 *Rochdale* 35 0 **35 0**
2012–13 Bradford C 35 0
2013–14 Bradford C 46 0
2014–15 Bradford C 45 0
2015–16 Bradford C 46 0
2016–17 Bradford C 22 0 **194 0**

DEVINE, Daniel (M) **11 0**
H: 5 11 W: 12 00 b.Bradford 4-9-97
Internationals: Northern Ireland U21.
2015–16 Bradford C 0 0
2016–17 Bradford C 11 0 **11 0**

DIENG, Timothee (M) **105 4**
H: 5 11 W: 12 00 b.Grenoble 9-4-92
2011–12 Brest 0 0
2012–13 Brest 2 0
2013–14 Brest 4 0 **6 0**
2014–15 Oldham Ath 22 0
2015–16 Oldham Ath 38 1 **60 1**
2016–17 Bradford C 39 3 **39 3**

DOYLE, Colin (G) **125 0**
H: 6 5 W: 14 05 b.Cork 12-8-85
Internationals: Republic of Ireland U21, B, Full caps.
2004–05 Birmingham C 0 0
2004–05 *Chester C* 0 0
2004–05 *Nottingham F* 3 0 **3 0**
2005–06 Birmingham C 0 0
2005–06 *Millwall* 14 0 **14 0**
2006–07 Birmingham C 19 0
2007–08 Birmingham C 3 0
2008–09 Birmingham C 2 0
2009–10 Birmingham C 0 0
2010–11 Birmingham C 1 0
2011–12 Birmingham C 5 0
2012–13 Birmingham C 0 0
2013–14 Birmingham C 0 0
2014–15 Birmingham C 1 0 **31 0**
2015–16 Blackpool 33 0 **33 0**
2016–17 Bradford C 44 0 **44 0**

HANSON, Jacob (D) **0 0**
b. 30-11-97
2015–16 Huddersfield T 0 0
2016–17 Bradford C 0 0

HUDSON, Ellis (M) **1 0**
b.Bradford 14-2-99
2016–17 Bradford C 1 0 **1 0**

JONES, Alex (F) **34 14**
b. 28-9-94
From WBA.
2015–16 Birmingham C 0 0
2016–17 Port Vale 19 9 **19 9**
2016–17 Bradford C 15 5 **15 5**

KILGALLON, Matthew (D) **291 9**
H: 6 1 W: 12 10 b.York 8-1-84
Internationals: England U20, U21.
2000–01 Leeds U 0 0
2001–02 Leeds U 0 0

2002–03	Leeds U	2	0		
2003–04	Leeds U	8	2		
2003–04	*West Ham U*	3	0	**3**	**0**
2004–05	Leeds U	26	0		
2005–06	Leeds U	25	1		
2006–07	Leeds U	19	0	**80**	**3**
2006–07	Sheffield U	6	0		
2007–08	Sheffield U	40	2		
2008–09	Sheffield U	40	1		
2009–10	Sheffield U	21	1	**107**	**4**
2009–10	Sunderland	7	0		
2010–11	Sunderland	0	0		
2010–11	*Middlesbrough*	2	0	**2**	**0**
2010–11	*Doncaster R*	12	0	**12**	**0**
2011–12	Sunderland	10	0		
2012–13	Sunderland	6	0	**23**	**0**
2013–14	Blackburn R	25	1		
2014–15	Blackburn R	22	1		
2015–16	Blackburn R	10	0	**57**	**2**
2016–17	Bradford C	7	0	**7**	**0**

KING, James (D) **0** **0**
H: 5 10 W: 11 07 b. 27-12-96

2014–15	Bradford C	0	0
2015–16	Bradford C	0	0
2016–17	Bradford C	0	0

KNIGHT-PERCIVAL, Nathaniel (M) **151** **7**
H: 6 0 W: 11 06 b.Cambridge 31-3-87

2012–13	Peterborough U	31	0		
2013–14	Peterborough U	15	1	**46**	**1**
2014–15	Shrewsbury T	28	1		
2015–16	Shrewsbury T	35	5	**63**	**6**
2016–17	Bradford C	42	0	**42**	**0**

LAW, Nicky (M) **342** **44**
H: 5 10 W: 11 07 b.Nottingham 29-3-88

2005–06	Sheffield U	0	0		
2006–07	Sheffield U	4	0		
2006–07	*Yeovil T*	6	0	**6**	**0**
2007–08	Sheffield U	1	0		
2007–08	*Bradford C*	10	2		
2008–09	Sheffield U	0	0	**5**	**0**
2008–09	*Bradford C*	33	0		
2009–10	Rotherham U	42	4		
2010–11	Rotherham U	44	4	**86**	**8**
2011–12	Motherwell	38	4		
2012–13	Motherwell	38	6	**76**	**10**
2013–14	Rangers	32	9		
2014–15	Rangers	36	10		
2015–16	Rangers	18	1	**86**	**20**
2016–17	Bradford C	40	4	**83**	**6**

MARSHALL, Mark (M) **231** **20**
H: 5 7 W: 10 07 b.Jamaica 9-5-86

2008–09	Swindon T	12	0		
2009–10	Swindon T	7	0	**19**	**0**
2009–10	*Hereford U*	8	0	**8**	**0**
2010–11	Barnet	46	6		
2011–12	Barnet	25	1	**71**	**7**
2013–14	Coventry C	14	0	**14**	**0**
2014–15	Port Vale	46	7	**46**	**7**
2015–16	Bradford C	31	0		
2016–17	Bradford C	42	6	**73**	**6**

McARDLE, Rory (D) **385** **20**
H: 6 1 W: 11 04 b.Doncaster 1-5-87
Internationals: Northern Ireland U21, Full caps.

2005–06	Sheffield W	0	0		
2005–06	*Rochdale*	19	1		
2006–07	Sheffield W	1	0	**1**	**0**
2006–07	Rochdale	25	0		
2007–08	Rochdale	43	3		
2008–09	Rochdale	41	2		
2009–10	Rochdale	20	0	**148**	**6**
2010–11	Aberdeen	28	2		
2011–12	Aberdeen	25	0	**53**	**2**
2012–13	Bradford C	40	2		
2013–14	Bradford C	41	3		
2014–15	Bradford C	43	3		
2015–16	Bradford C	35	3		
2016–17	Bradford C	24	1	**183**	**12**

McMAHON, Tony (D) **320** **18**
H: 5 10 W: 11 04 b.Bishop Auckland 24-3-86
Internationals: England U16, U17, U19.

2003–04	Middlesbrough	0	0		
2004–05	Middlesbrough	13	0		
2005–06	Middlesbrough	3	0		
2006–07	Middlesbrough	0	0		
2007–08	Middlesbrough	1	0		
2007–08	*Blackpool*	2	0		
2008–09	Middlesbrough	13	0		
2008–09	*Sheffield W*	15	1	**15**	**1**
2009–10	Middlesbrough	21	0		
2010–11	Middlesbrough	34	2		
2011–12	Middlesbrough	34	1	**119**	**3**
2012–13	Sheffield U	38	2		
2013–14	Sheffield U	23	0	**61**	**2**
2013–14	Blackpool	18	0		
2014–15	Blackpool	32	1	**52**	**1**
2014–15	*Bradford C*	8	1		
2015–16	Bradford C	40	4		
2016–17	Bradford C	25	6	**73**	**11**

MEREDITH, James (D) **185** **4**
H: 6 1 W: 11 06 b.Albury, Australia 4-4-88
Internationals: Australia Full caps.

2006–07	Derby Co	0	0		
2006–07	*Chesterfield*	1	0	**1**	**0**
2007–08	Shrewsbury T	3	0	**3**	**0**
From York C					
2012–13	Bradford C	32	1		
2013–14	Bradford C	26	0		
2014–15	Bradford C	40	0		
2015–16	Bradford C	42	1		
2016–17	Bradford C	41	2	**181**	**4**

PAYNE, Niah (M) **0** **0**
b. 25-9-98

2016–17	Bradford C	0	0

PETERS, Curtis (M) **0** **0**

2016–17	Bradford C	0	0

PYBUS, Daniel (M) **1** **0**
b.South Shields 12-12-97
From Sunderland.

2016–17	Bradford C	1	0	**1**	**0**

RABIEGA, Vincent (F) **1** **0**
W: 12 00 b.Berlin 14-6-95
Internationals: Poland U17, U19, U20.
From RB Leipzig.

2016–17	Bradford C	1	0	**1**	**0**

SATTELMAIER, Rouven (G) **101** **0**
H: 6 1 W: 13 05 b.Ludvigsburg 7-8-87

2007–08	Jahn Regensburg	1	0		
2008–09	Jahn Regensburg	27	0		
2009–10	Jahn Regensburg	37	0	**65**	**0**
2010–11	Bayern Munich	0	0		
2011–12	Bayern Munich	0	0		
2012–13	Heidenheim	2	0		
2013–14	Heidenheim	6	0		
2014–15	Heidenheim	5	0	**13**	**0**
2015–16	Stuttgart Kickers	21	0	**21**	**0**
2016–17	Bradford C	2	0	**2**	**0**

VINCELOT, Romain (M) **316** **25**
H: 5 9 W: 11 02 b.Poitiers 29-10-85

2004–05	Chamois Niortais	3	0	**3**	**0**
2005–06	Chemois Niortais	28	1		
2006–07	Chemois Niortais	9	0		
2007–08	Chemois Niortais	6	0	**43**	**1**
2008–09	Gueugnon	20	0	**20**	**0**
2009–10	Dagenham & R	9	1		
2010–11	Dagenham & R	46	12	**55**	**13**
2011–12	Brighton & HA	15	1		
2012–13	Brighton & HA	0	0	**15**	**1**
2012–13	*Gillingham*	9	1	**9**	**1**
2012–13	Leyton Orient	15	1		
2013–14	Leyton Orient	39	0		
2014–15	Leyton Orient	27	2	**81**	**3**
2015–16	Coventry C	45	4	**45**	**4**
2016–17	Bradford C	45	2	**45**	**2**

WEBB-FOSTER, Reece (F) **2** **0**
b. 7-3-97

2014–15	Bradford C	1	0		
2015–16	Bradford C	0	0		
2016–17	Bradford C	1	0	**2**	**0**

WINDLE, Tom (D) **0** **0**

2016–17	Bradford C	0	0

WRIGHT, Sam (M) **0** **0**
H: 5 9 W: 10 12 b.Bradford 28-9-97

2013–14	Bradford C	0	0
2014–15	Bradford C	0	0
2015–16	Bradford C	0	0
2016–17	Bradford C	0	0

WYKE, Charlie (F) **148** **47**
b.Middlesbrough 6-12-92

2011–12	Middlesbrough	0	0		
2012–13	Middlesbrough	0	0		
2012–13	*Hartlepool U*	25	2		
2013–14	Middlesbrough	0	0		
2013–14	*AFC Wimbledon*	17	2	**17**	**2**
2014–15	Middlesbrough	0	0		
2014–15	*Hartlepool U*	13	4	**38**	**6**
2014–15	Carlisle U	17	6		
2015–16	Carlisle U	34	12		
2016–17	Carlisle U	26	14	**77**	**32**
2016–17	Bradford C	16	7	**16**	**7**

Scholars
Boateng, Kwame Owusu; Gardezi, Omed; Mullett, Ross Peter; Patience, Neil William; Payne, Niah Ashante Lewis; Peters, Curtis Andrew; Powell, Reece; Sykes-Kenworthy, George William; Taglione, Casey Joe; Warren, Harry Jack; Windle, Thomas Jack; Wright, Sam.

BRENTFORD (13)

BALCOMBE, Ellery (G) **0** **0**
b. 15-10-99
Internationals: England U18, U20.

2016–17	Brentford	0	0

BARBET, Yoann (D) **74** **4**
H: 6 2 W: 12 11 b.Talence 10-5-93
Internationals: France U18.

2014–15	Chamois Niortais	33	2	**33**	**2**
2015–16	Brentford	18	1		
2016–17	Brentford	23	1	**41**	**2**

BENTLEY, Daniel (G) **186** **0**
H: 6 2 W: 11 05 b.Wickford 13-7-93

2011–12	Southend U	1	0		
2012–13	Southend U	9	0		
2013–14	Southend U	46	0		
2014–15	Southend U	42	0		
2015–16	Southend U	43	0	**141**	**0**
2016–17	Brentford	45	0	**45**	**0**

BJELLAND, Andreas (D) **206** **7**
H: 6 2 W: 13 05 b.Fredensborg 11-7-88
Internationals: Denmark U16, U18, U19, U21, Full caps.

2007–08	Lyngby	11	0		
2008–09	Lyngby	22	1		
2009–10	Lyngby	4	0	**37**	**1**
2009–10	Nordsjaelland	22	1		
2010–11	Nordsjaelland	24	1		
2011–12	Nordsjaelland	26	1	**72**	**3**
2012–13	FC Twente	10	0		
2013–14	FC Twente	33	0		
2014–15	FC Twente	26	3	**69**	**3**
2015–16	Brentford	0	0		
2016–17	Brentford	28	0	**28**	**0**

BONHAM, Jack (G) **3** **0**
H: 6 4 W: 14 13 b.Stevenage 14-9-93
Internationals: Republic of Ireland U17.

2010–11	Watford	0	0		
2011–12	Watford	0	0		
2012–13	Watford	1	0	**1**	**0**
2013–14	Brentford	1	0		
2014–15	Brentford	0	0		
2015–16	Brentford	0	0		
2016–17	Brentford	1	0	**2**	**0**

CANOS, Sergi (M) **60** **11**
H: 5 8 W: 11 11 b.Nules 2-2-97
Internationals: Spain U16, U17, U19.

2015–16	Liverpool	1	0	**1**	**0**
2015–16	*Brentford*	38	7		
2016–17	Norwich C	3	0	**3**	**0**
2016–17	Brentford	18	4	**56**	**11**

CHATZITHEODORIDIS, Ilias (D) **0** **0**
b.Katerini 5-11-97
From Arsenal.

2016–17	Brentford	0	0

CLARKE, Josh (M) **53** **5**
H: 5 8 W: 11 00 b.Waltham Forest 5-7-95

2012–13	Brentford	0	0		
2013–14	Brentford	1	0		
2014–15	Brentford	0	0		
2014–15	*Dagenham & R*	0	0		
2014–15	*Stevenage*	1	0	**1**	**0**
2015–16	Brentford	11	0		
2015–16	*Barnet*	10	3	**10**	**3**
2016–17	Brentford	30	2	**42**	**2**

COLE, Reece (M) **1** **0**
b. 17-2-98

2015–16	Brentford	0	0		
2016–17	Brentford	1	0	**1**	**0**

COLIN, Maxime (D) **185** **5**
H: 5 11 W: 12 00 b.Arras 15-11-91
Internationals: France U20.

2010–11	Boulogne	26	0		
2011–12	Boulogne	23	0		
2012–13	Boulogne	4	0	**53**	**0**
2012–13	Troyes	18	0		
2013–14	Troyes	35	0		
2014–15	Troyes	2	0	**55**	**0**
2014–15	Anderlecht	17	1		
2015–16	Anderlecht	1	0	**18**	**1**
2015–16	Brentford	21	0		
2016–17	Brentford	38	4	**59**	**4**

DANIELS, Luke (G)				**198**	**0**
H: 6 1 W: 12 10 b.Bolton 5-1-88					
Internationals: England U18, U19.					
2006–07	WBA	0	0		
2007–08	*Motherwell*	2	0	**2**	**0**
2007–08	WBA	0	0		
2008–09	WBA	0	0		
2008–09	*Shrewsbury T*	38	0	**38**	**0**
2009–10	WBA	0	0		
2009–10	*Tranmere R*	37	0	**37**	**0**
2010–11	WBA	0	0		
2010–11	*Charlton Ath*	0	0		
2010–11	*Rochdale*	1	0	**1**	**0**
2010–11	*Bristol R*	9	0	**9**	**0**
2011–12	WBA	0	0		
2011–12	*Southend U*	9	0	**9**	**0**
2012–13	WBA	0	0		
2013–14	WBA	1	0		
2014–15	WBA	0	0	**1**	**0**
2014–15	Scunthorpe U	23	0		
2015–16	Scunthorpe U	39	0		
2016–17	Scunthorpe U	39	0	**101**	**0**
2016–17	Brentford	0	0		

DEAN, Harlee (M)				**222**	**8**
H: 6 0 W: 11 10 b.Basingstoke 26-7-91					
2008–09	Dagenham & R	0	0		
2009–10	Dagenham & R	1	0	**1**	**0**
2010–11	Southampton	0	0		
2011–12	Southampton	0	0		
2011–12	*Brentford*	26	1		
2012–13	Brentford	44	3		
2013–14	Brentford	32	0		
2014–15	Brentford	35	1		
2015–16	Brentford	42	0		
2016–17	Brentford	42	3	**221**	**8**

EGAN, John (D)				**134**	**15**
H: 6 1 W: 11 11 b.Cork 20-10-92					
Internationals: Republic of Ireland U17, U19, U21, Full caps.					
2009–10	Sunderland	0	0		
2010–11	Sunderland	0	0		
2011–12	Sunderland	0	0		
2011–12	*Crystal Palace*	1	0	**1**	**0**
2011–12	*Sheffield U*	1	0	**1**	**0**
2012–13	Sunderland	0	0		
2012–13	*Bradford C*	4	0	**4**	**0**
2013–14	Sunderland	0	0		
2013–14	*Southend U*	13	1	**13**	**1**
2014–15	Gillingham	45	4		
2015–16	Gillingham	36	6	**81**	**10**
2016–17	Brentford	34	4	**34**	**4**

FIELD, Tom (D)				**16**	**1**
H: 5 10 W: 10 13 b.Kingston upon Thames 2-8-85					
Internationals: Republic of Ireland U16.					
2013–14	Brentford	0	0		
2014–15	Brentford	0	0		
2015–16	Brentford	1	0		
2016–17	Brentford	15	1	**16**	**1**

HENRY, Rico (D)				**58**	**2**
H: 5 7 W: 10 06 b.Birmingham 8-7-97					
Internationals: England U19, U20.					
2014–15	Walsall	9	0		
2015–16	Walsall	35	2		
2016–17	Walsall	2	0	**46**	**2**
2016–17	Brentford	12	0	**12**	**0**

HOFMANN, Philipp (F)				**123**	**25**
H: 6 4 W: 13 10 b.Arnsberg 30-3-93					
Internationals: Germany U18, U19, U20, U21.					
2012–13	Schalke 04	0	0		
2012–13	*Paderborn*	31	7	**31**	**7**
2013–14	Schalke 04	0	0		
2013–14	*Ingolstadt 04*	31	8	**31**	**8**
2014–15	Kaiserslautern	30	6	**30**	**6**
2015–16	Brentford	21	4		
2016–17	Brentford	10	0	**31**	**4**

HOLLDACK, Jan (D)				**0**	**0**
H: 5 11 W: 11 11 b.Nuenkirchen 11-5-96					
Internationals: Germany U18.					
From FC Koln.					
2016–17	Brentford	0	0		

JOTA, Ramallo (M)				**125**	**34**
H: 5 11 W: 10 08 b.A Coruna 16-6-91					
2010–11	Celta Vigo	4	0		
2011–12	Celta Vigo	0	0		
2012–13	Celta Vigo	0	0		
2013–14	Celta Vigo	0	0	**4**	**0**
2013–14	*Eibar*	35	11		
2014–15	Brentford	42	11		
2015–16	Brentford	5	0		
2015–16	*Eibar*	13	0		
2016–17	Brentford	21	12	**68**	**23**
2016–17	*Eibar*	5	0	**53**	**11**

JOZEFZOON, Florian (F)				**118**	**13**
H: 5 8 W: 11 00 b.Amsterdam 9-2-91					
Internationals: Netherlands U19, U21.					
2010–11	Ajax	4	0		
2011–12	Ajax	0	0	**4**	**0**
2011–12	*NAC Breda*	16	0	**16**	**0**
2012–13	RKC Waalwijk	34	7	**34**	**7**
2013–14	PSV Eindhoven	16	2		
2014–15	PSV Eindhoven	15	2		
2015–16	PSV Eindhoven	9	1		
2016–17	PSV Eindhoven	5	0	**45**	**5**
2016–17	Brentford	19	1	**19**	**1**

KERSCHBAUMER, Konstantin (M)				**184**	**22**
H: 5 10 W: 11 05 b.Tulin 1-7-92					
Internationals: Austria, U16, U17, U18, U19.					
2011–12	Vienna	32	5	**32**	**5**
2012–13	St Polten	33	6		
2013–14	St Polten	33	7		
2014–15	St Polten	20	2	**86**	**15**
2014–15	Admira Wacker	16	1	**16**	**1**
2015–16	Brentford	30	0		
2016–17	Brentford	20	1	**50**	**1**

KURASIK, Domanic (G)				**0**	**0**
H: 6 2 W: 13 01 b.Melbourne 4-11-96					
From Stoke C.					
2016–17	Brentford	0	0		

LEDESMA, Emmanuel (M)				**137**	**17**
H: 5 11 W: 12 02 b.Quilmes 24-5-88					
2007–08	Genoa	1	0		
2008–09	*QPR*	17	1	**17**	**1**
2008–09	*Salernitana*	8	1	**8**	**1**
2009–10	Genoa	0	0		
2009–10	*Novara*	8	1	**8**	**1**
2010–11	Genoa	0	0	**1**	**0**
2010–11	*Crotone*	10	0	**10**	**0**
2010–11	Walsall	10	1		
2011–12	Walsall	10	4	**20**	**5**
2012–13	Middlesbrough	28	2		
2013–14	Middlesbrough	27	6		
2014–15	Middlesbrough	1	0	**56**	**8**
2014–15	*Rotherham U*	7	1		
2014–15	*Brighton & HA*	4	0	**4**	**0**
2015–16	Rotherham U	5	0	**12**	**1**
2016–17	Brentford	1	0	**1**	**0**
Transferred to Panetolikos, December 2016.					

MACLEOD, Lewis (M)				**66**	**11**
H: 5 9 W: 11 05 b.Law 16-6-94					
Internationals: Scotland U16, U17, U18, U19, U21.					
2012–13	Rangers	21	3		
2013–14	Rangers	18	5		
2014–15	Rangers	13	3	**52**	**11**
2014–15	Brentford	0	0		
2015–16	Brentford	1	0		
2016–17	Brentford	13	0	**14**	**0**

McCORMACK, Alan (M)				**394**	**25**
H: 5 8 W: 11 00 b.Dublin 10-1-84					
Internationals: Republic of Ireland U19.					
2002–03	Preston NE	0	0		
2003–04	Preston NE	5	0		
2003–04	*Leyton Orient*	10	0	**10**	**0**
2004–05	Preston NE	3	0		
2004–05	*Southend U*	7	2		
2005–06	Preston NE	0	0		
2005–06	*Motherwell*	24	2	**24**	**2**
2006–07	Preston NE	3	0	**11**	**0**
2006–07	Southend U	22	3		
2007–08	Southend U	42	8		
2008–09	Southend U	34	2		
2009–10	Southend U	41	3	**146**	**18**
2010–11	Charlton Ath	24	1	**24**	**1**
2011–12	Swindon T	40	2		
2012–13	Swindon T	40	0	**80**	**2**
2013–14	Brentford	43	1		
2014–15	Brentford	18	1		
2015–16	Brentford	27	0		
2016–17	Brentford	11	0	**99**	**2**

McEACHRAN, Josh (D)				**128**	**0**
H: 5 10 W: 10 03 b.Oxford 1-3-93					
Internationals: England U16, U17, U19, U20, U21.					
2010–11	Chelsea	9	0		
2011–12	Chelsea	2	0		
2011–12	*Swansea C*	4	0	**4**	**0**
2012–13	Chelsea	0	0		
2012–13	*Middlesbrough*	38	0	**38**	**0**
2013–14	Chelsea	0	0		
2013–14	*Watford*	7	0	**7**	**0**
2013–14	*Wigan Ath*	8	0	**8**	**0**
2014–15	Chelsea	0	0	**11**	**0**
2014–15	*Vitesse*	19	0	**19**	**0**
2015–16	Brentford	14	0		
2016–17	Brentford	27	0	**41**	**0**

MEPHAM, Chris (D)				**0**	**0**
2016–17	Brentford	0	0		

ONARIASE, Manny (D)				**22**	**1**
H: 6 1 b. 29-1-95					
2014–15	West Ham U	0	0		
2015–16	West Ham U	0	0		
2016–17	Brentford	0	0		
2016–17	*Cheltenham T*	22	1	**22**	**1**

SAWYERS, Romaine (M)				**187**	**18**
H: 5 9 W: 11 00 b.Birmingham 2-11-91					
Internationals: St Kitts and Nevis U23, Full caps.					
2009–10	WBA	0	0		
2010–11	WBA	0	0		
2010–11	*Port Vale*	1	0	**1**	**0**
2011–12	WBA	0	0		
2011–12	*Shrewsbury T*	7	0	**7**	**0**
2012–13	WBA	0	0		
2012–13	Walsall	4	0		
2013–14	Walsall	44	6		
2014–15	Walsall	42	4		
2015–16	Walsall	46	6	**136**	**16**
2016–17	Brentford	43	2	**43**	**2**

SHAIBU, Justin (F)				**24**	**0**
H: 5 11 b. 28-10-97					
Internationals: Denmark U17, U18.					
2014–15	HB Koge	8	0		
2015–16	HB Koge	12	0	**20**	**0**
2016–17	Brentford	4	0	**4**	**0**

VIBE, Lasse (F)				**265**	**111**
H: 5 11 W: 11 07 b.Tranjberg 22-2-87					
Internationals: Denmark Full caps.					
2006–07	AGF	1	0		
2007–08	AGF	0	0	**1**	**0**
2008–09	Fyn	13	7		
2009–10	Fyn	30	7	**43**	**14**
2010–11	Vestsjaelland	29	12		
2011–12	Vestsjaelland	14	6	**43**	**18**
2011–12	SonderjyskE	14	6		
2012–13	SonderjyskE	33	13	**47**	**19**
2013	Gothenburg	14	2		
2014	Gothenburg	26	23		
2015	Gothenburg	16	6	**56**	**31**
2015–16	Brentford	41	14		
2016–17	Brentford	34	15	**75**	**29**

WESTBROOKE, Zain (M)				**1**	**0**
b. 28-10-96					
From Chelsea.					
2016–17	Brentford	1	0	**1**	**0**

WOODS, Ryan (M)				**174**	**3**
H: 5 8 W: 13 01 b.Norton Canes 13-12-93					
2012–13	Shrewsbury T	2	0		
2013–14	Shrewsbury T	41	1		
2014–15	Shrewsbury T	43	0		
2015–16	Shrewsbury T	5	0	**91**	**1**
2015–16	Brentford	41	2		
2016–17	Brentford	42	0	**83**	**2**

YENNARIS, Nico (D)				**103**	**9**
H: 5 7 W: 10 03 b.Leytonstone 23-5-93					
Internationals: England U17, U18, U19.					
2010–11	Arsenal	0	0		
2011–12	Arsenal	1	0		
2011–12	*Notts Co*	2	0	**2**	**0**
2012–13	Arsenal	0	0		
2013–14	Arsenal	0	0	**1**	**0**
2013–14	*Bournemouth*	0	0		
2013–14	Brentford	8	0		
2014–15	Brentford	1	0		
2014–15	Wycombe W	14	1	**14**	**1**
2015–16	Brentford	31	2		
2016–17	Brentford	46	6	**86**	**8**

Players retained or with offer of contract
Assibey-Mensah, Raphael; Clayton, Bradley Luca Brand; Edobor, Jarvis Daniel Osagie Osahon; Gogia, Akaki; Hardy, Joseph Keith; Johansson, Henrik; Judge, Alan; Novak, Jan; Ramallo, Jose Ignacio Peleteiro; Rodrigues, Alves Herson Domingos; Talbro, Lukas.

Scholars
Dunn, Luke Christopher Arthur; Fenn-Evans, Julius Louis; Greaves, Cameron Edward; Harmes, George Thomas.

BRIGHTON & HA (14)

ADEKUGBE, Sam (D) 17 0
H: 5 9 W: 11 11 b.London 16-1-95
Internationals: Canada U18, U20, Full caps.
2013 Vancouver Whitecaps 1 0
2014 Vancouver Whitecaps 4 0
2015 Vancouver Whitecaps 9 0
2016 Vancouver Whitecaps 2 0 **16 0**
On loan from Vancouver Whitecaps.
2016–17 Brighton & HA 1 0 **1 0**

ANKERGREN, Casper (G) 273 0
H: 6 3 W: 14 07 b.Koge 9-11-79
Internationals: Denmark U17, U21.
2001–02 Brondby 1 0
2002–03 Brondby 16 0
2003–04 Brondby 1 0
2004–05 Brondby 32 0
2005–06 Brondby 18 0
2006–07 Brondby 18 0 **86 0**
2006–07 Leeds U 14 0
2007–08 Leeds U 43 0
2008–09 Leeds U 33 0
2009–10 Leeds U 29 0 **119 0**
2010–11 Brighton & HA 45 0
2011–12 Brighton & HA 19 0
2012–13 Brighton & HA 3 0
2013–14 Brighton & HA 1 0
2014–15 Brighton & HA 0 0
2015–16 Brighton & HA 0 0
2016–17 Brighton & HA 0 0 **68 0**

BALDOCK, Sam (F) 285 90
H: 5 7 W: 10 07 b.Buckingham 15-3-89
Internationals: England U20.
2005–06 Milton Keynes D 0 0
2006–07 Milton Keynes D 1 0
2007–08 Milton Keynes D 5 0
2008–09 Milton Keynes D 40 12
2009–10 Milton Keynes D 20 5
2010–11 Milton Keynes D 30 12
2011–12 Milton Keynes D 4 4 **100 33**
2011–12 West Ham U 23 5
2012–13 West Ham U 0 0 **23 5**
2012–13 Bristol C 34 10
2013–14 Bristol C 45 24
2014–15 Bristol C 4 0 **83 34**
2014–15 Brighton & HA 20 3
2015–16 Brighton & HA 28 4
2016–17 Brighton & HA 31 11 **79 18**

BJORDAL, Henrik Rorvik (M) 54 1
H: 5 9 W: 12 08 b. 4-2-97
Internationals: Norway U17, U19, U21.
2013 Aalesund 2 0
2014 Aalesund 22 0
2015 Aalesund 30 1 **54 1**
2015–16 Brighton & HA 0 0
2016–17 Brighton & HA 0 0

BONG, Gaetan (D) 232 3
H: 6 0 W: 11 09 b.Sakbayeme 25-4-88
Internationals: France U21. Cameroon Full caps.
2005–06 Metz 3 0
2006–07 Metz 2 0
2007–08 Metz 11 0
2008–09 Metz 0 0 **16 0**
2008–09 *Tours* 34 0 **34 0**
2009–10 Valenciennes 29 2
2010–11 Valenciennes 22 1
2011–12 Valenciennes 28 0
2012–13 Valenciennes 29 0
2013–14 Valenciennes 1 0 **109 3**
2013–14 Olympiacos 19 0 **19 0**
2014–15 Wigan Ath 14 0 **14 0**
2015–16 Brighton & HA 16 0
2016–17 Brighton & HA 24 0 **40 0**

CADMAN, Tom (D) 0 0
b. 4-5-98
Internationals: Republic of Ireland U18, U19.
2016–17 Brighton & HA 0 0

DALLISON, Tom (M) 6 0
H: 5 10 W: 14 01 b. 2-2-96
2012–13 Arsenal 0 0
2013–14 Brighton & HA 0 0
2014–15 Brighton & HA 0 0
2015–16 Brighton & HA 0 0
2015–16 *Crawley T* 1 0 **1 0**
2016–17 Brighton & HA 0 0
2016–17 *Cambridge U* 5 0 **5 0**

DUFFY, Shane (D) 155 10
H: 6 4 W: 12 00 b.Derry 1-1-92
Internationals: Northern Ireland U16, U17, U19, U21, B. Republic of Ireland U19, U21, Full caps.
2008–09 Everton 0 0
2009–10 Everton 0 0
2010–11 Everton 0 0
2010–11 *Burnley* 1 0 **1 0**
2011–12 Everton 4 0
2011–12 *Scunthorpe U* 18 2 **18 2**
2012–13 Everton 1 0
2013–14 Everton 0 0
2013–14 *Yeovil T* 37 1 **37 1**
2014–15 Everton 0 0 **5 0**
2014–15 Blackburn R 19 1
2015–16 Blackburn R 41 4
2016–17 Blackburn R 3 0 **63 5**
2016–17 Brighton & HA 31 2 **31 2**

DUNK, Lewis (D) 172 10
H: 6 3 W: 12 02 b.Brighton 1-12-91
2009–10 Brighton & HA 1 0
2010–11 Brighton & HA 5 0
2011–12 Brighton & HA 31 0
2012–13 Brighton & HA 8 0
2013–14 Brighton & HA 6 0
2013–14 *Bristol C* 2 0 **2 0**
2014–15 Brighton & HA 38 5
2015–16 Brighton & HA 38 3
2016–17 Brighton & HA 43 2 **170 10**

FORREN, Vegard (D) 125 4
H: 6 1 W: 13 04 b.Trondheim 16-2-88
Internationals: Norway U21, U23, Full caps.
2007–08 Molde 12 0
2008–09 Molde 28 1
2009–10 Molde 25 2
2010–11 Molde 26 0
2011–12 Molde 34 1
2012–13 Southampton 0 0
2016–17 Molde 0 0 **125 4**
2016–17 Brighton & HA 0 0

GOLDSON, Connor (D) 139 10
H: 6 3 W: 13 05 b.York 18-12-92
2010–11 Shrewsbury T 3 0
2011–12 Shrewsbury T 4 0
2012–13 Shrewsbury T 17 1
2013–14 Shrewsbury T 36 0
2013–14 *Cheltenham T* 4 0 **4 0**
2014–15 Shrewsbury T 44 7
2015–16 Shrewsbury T 2 0 **106 8**
2015–16 Brighton & HA 24 2
2016–17 Brighton & HA 5 0 **29 2**

HARPER, Jack (F) 0 0
b.Malaga 28-2-96
Internationals: Scotland U17, U19.
2014–15 Real Madrid 0 0
2015–16 Brighton & HA 0 0
2016–17 Brighton & HA 0 0

HEMED, Tomer (F) 333 85
H: 6 0 W: 12 04 b.Haifa 2-5-87
Internationals: Israel U17, U18, U19, U21, Full caps.
2005–06 Maccabi Haifa 3 1
2006–07 Maccabi Haifa 8 2
2007–08 Maccabi Haifa 7 0
2007–08 *Maccabi Herzliya* 17 3 **17 3**
2008–09 Maccabi Haifa 0 0
2008–09 *Bnei Yehuda* 28 1 **28 1**
2009–10 Maccabi Haifa 0 0
2009–10 *Maccabi Ahi Nazareth* 33 9 **33 9**
2010–11 Maccabi Haifa 31 13 **49 16**
2011–12 Mallorca 29 7
2012–13 Mallorca 37 11
2013–14 Mallorca 24 2 **90 20**
2014–15 Almeria 35 8 **35 8**
2015–16 Brighton & HA 44 17
2016–17 Brighton & HA 37 11 **81 28**

HOLLA, Danny (M) 221 35
H: 5 10 W: 11 09 b.Almere 31-12-87
2006–07 Groningen 6 0
2007–08 *Zwolle* 23 8 **23 8**
2007–08 Groningen 6 0
2008–09 Groningen 34 6
2009–10 Groningen 22 2
2010–11 Groningen 22 2
2011–12 Groningen 13 0 **103 10**
2011–12 *VVV* 16 2 **16 2**
2012–13 Den Haag 28 11
2013–14 Den Haag 26 3 **54 14**
2014–15 Brighton & HA 24 1
2015–16 Brighton & HA 1 0
2016–17 Brighton & HA 0 0 **25 1**
Transferred to PEC Zwolle, September 2016.

HORNBY-FORBES, Tyler (M) 33 2
b. 8-3-96
2014–15 Fleetwood T 17 0
2015–16 Fleetwood T 16 2 **33 2**
2016–17 Brighton & HA 0 0

HUNEMEIER, Uwe (D) 172 14
H: 6 1 W: 12 06 b.Rietberg 9-1-86
Internationals: Germany U17.
2005–06 Borussia Dortmund 2 0
2006–07 Borussia Dortmund 0 0
2007–08 Borussia Dortmund 0 0
2008–09 Borussia Dortmund 1 0
2009–10 Borussia Dortmund 0 0 **3 0**
2010–11 Energie Cottbus 30 9
2011–12 Energie Cottbus 23 0
2012–13 Energie Cottbus 23 0 **76 9**
2013–14 Paderborn 33 2
2014–15 Paderborn 32 2
2015–16 Paderborn 2 0 **67 4**
2015–16 Brighton & HA 15 0
2016–17 Brighton & HA 11 1 **26 1**

HUNT, Robert (M) 11 0
H: 5 7 W: 10 08 b.Dagenham 7-7-95
2013–14 Brighton & HA 0 0
2014–15 Brighton & HA 0 0
2015–16 Brighton & HA 0 0
2016–17 Brighton & HA 1 0 **1 0**
2016–17 *Oldham Ath* 10 0 **10 0**

INCE, Rohan (D) 98 4
H: 6 3 W: 12 08 b.Whitechapel 8-11-92
2010–11 Chelsea 0 0
2011–12 Chelsea 0 0
2012–13 Chelsea 0 0
2012–13 *Yeovil T* 2 0 **2 0**
2013–14 Brighton & HA 28 0
2014–15 Brighton & HA 32 1
2015–16 Brighton & HA 12 0
2015–16 *Fulham* 10 1 **10 1**
2016–17 Brighton & HA 0 0 **72 1**
2016–17 *Swindon T* 14 2 **14 2**

KAYAL, Beram (M) 224 7
H: 5 10 W: 11 09 b.Jadeidi 2-5-88
Internationals: Israel U17, U18, U19, U21, Full caps.
2008–09 Maccabi Haifa 30 1
2009–10 Maccabi Haifa 27 1 **57 2**
2010–11 Celtic 21 2
2011–12 Celtic 19 0
2012–13 Celtic 27 0
2013–14 Celtic 13 0
2014–15 Celtic 6 0 **86 2**
2014–15 Brighton & HA 18 1
2015–16 Brighton & HA 43 2
2016–17 Brighton & HA 20 0 **81 3**

KNOCKAERT, Anthony (M) 211 48
H: 5 8 W: 10 11 b.Lille 20-11-91
Internationals: France U20, U21.
2011–12 Guingamp 34 10 **34 10**
2012–13 Leicester C 42 8
2013–14 Leicester C 42 5
2014–15 Leicester C 9 0 **93 13**
2015–16 Standard Liege 20 5 **20 5**
2015–16 Brighton & HA 19 5
2016–17 Brighton & HA 45 15 **64 20**

LUALUA, Kazenga (F) 181 18
H: 5 11 W: 12 00 b.Kinshasa 10-12-90
2007–08 Newcastle U 2 0
2008–09 Newcastle U 3 0
2008–09 *Doncaster R* 4 0 **4 0**
2009–10 Newcastle U 1 0
2009–10 *Brighton & HA* 11 0
2010–11 Newcastle U 2 0
2010–11 *Brighton & HA* 11 4
2011–12 Newcastle U 0 0 **8 0**
2011–12 Brighton & HA 27 1
2012–13 Brighton & HA 22 5
2013–14 Brighton & HA 32 1
2014–15 Brighton & HA 34 3
2015–16 Brighton & HA 18 3
2016–17 Brighton & HA 3 0 **158 17**
2016–17 *QPR* 11 1 **11 1**

MAENPAA, Niki (G) 187 0
H: 6 3 W: 13 05 b.Espoo 23-1-85
Internationals: Finland U18, U19, U21, Full caps.
2006–07 Den Bosch 27 0
2007–08 Den Bosch 33 0
2008–09 Den Bosch 7 0 **67 0**
2009–10 Willem II 6 0
2010–11 Willem II 12 0 **18 0**
2011–12 AZ Alkmaar 0 0
2012–13 VVV-Venlo 33 0

2013–14 VVV-Venlo 33 0
2014–15 VVV-Venlo 35 0 **101 0**
2015–16 Brighton & HA 0 0
2016–17 Brighton & HA 1 0 **1 0**

MANU, Elvis (F) 97 23
H: 5 8 W: 10 01 b.Rotterdam 13-8-93
Internationals: Netherlands U16, U17, U19, U20, U21.
2010–11 Feyenoord 0 0
2011–12 Feyenoord 4 1
2012–13 Feyenoord 0 0
2012–13 *Excelsior* 20 8 **20 8**
2013–14 Feyenoord 1 0
2013–14 *Cambuur* 15 5 **15 5**
2014–15 Feyenoord 27 7
2015–16 Feyenoord 1 0 **33 8**
2015–16 Brighton & HA 8 0
2015–16 *Huddersfield T* 5 0 **5 0**
2016–17 Brighton & HA 2 0 **10 0**
2016–17 *Go Ahead Eagles* 14 2 **14 2**

MARCH, Solly (M) 75 7
H: 6 1 W: 12 02 b.Lewes 26-7-94
Internationals: England U20, U21.
2012–13 Brighton & HA 0 0
2013–14 Brighton & HA 23 0
2014–15 Brighton & HA 11 1
2015–16 Brighton & HA 16 3
2016–17 Brighton & HA 25 3 **75 7**

MURPHY, Jamie (F) 343 59
H: 6 0 W: 12 00 b.Glasgow 28-8-89
Internationals: Scotland U19, U21.
2006–07 Motherwell 2 0
2007–08 Motherwell 16 1
2008–09 Motherwell 30 2
2009–10 Motherwell 35 6
2010–11 Motherwell 35 6
2011–12 Motherwell 36 9
2012–13 Motherwell 22 10 **176 34**
2012–13 Sheffield U 17 2
2013–14 Sheffield U 34 4
2014–15 Sheffield U 43 11
2015–16 Sheffield U 1 0 **95 17**
2015–16 Brighton & HA 37 6
2016–17 Brighton & HA 35 2 **72 8**

MURRAY, Glenn (F) 405 163
H: 6 1 W: 12 12 b.Maryport 25-9-83
2005–06 Carlisle U 26 3
2006–07 Carlisle U 1 0 **27 3**
2006–07 *Stockport Co* 11 3 **11 3**
2006–07 Rochdale 31 16
2007–08 Rochdale 23 9 **54 25**
2007–08 Brighton & HA 21 9
2008–09 Brighton & HA 23 11
2009–10 Brighton & HA 32 12
2010–11 Brighton & HA 42 22
2011–12 Crystal Palace 38 6
2012–13 Crystal Palace 42 30
2013–14 Crystal Palace 14 1
2014–15 Crystal Palace 17 7
2014–15 *Reading* 18 8 **18 8**
2015–16 Crystal Palace 2 0 **113 44**
2015–16 Bournemouth 19 3 **19 3**
2016–17 Brighton & HA 45 23 **163 77**

NORWOOD, Oliver (M) 233 15
H: 5 11 W: 11 13 b.Burnley 12-4-91
Internationals: England U16, U17. Northern Ireland U19, U21, B, Full caps.
2009–10 Manchester U 0 0
2010–11 Manchester U 0 0
2010–11 *Carlisle U* 6 0 **6 0**
2011–12 Manchester U 0 0
2011–12 *Scunthorpe U* 15 1 **15 1**
2011–12 *Coventry C* 18 2 **18 2**
2012–13 Huddersfield T 39 3
2013–14 Huddersfield T 40 5
2014–15 Huddersfield T 1 0 **80 8**
2014–15 Reading 38 1
2015–16 Reading 43 3 **81 4**
2016–17 Brighton & HA 33 0 **33 0**

O'GRADY, Chris (F) 426 85
H: 6 3 W: 12 04 b.Nottingham 25-1-86
2002–03 Leicester C 1 0
2003–04 Leicester C 0 0
2004–05 Leicester C 0 0
2004–05 *Notts Co* 9 0 **9 0**
2005–06 Leicester C 13 1
2005–06 *Rushden & D* 22 4 **22 4**
2006–07 Leicester C 10 0 **24 1**
2006–07 Rotherham U 13 4
2007–08 Rotherham U 38 9 **51 13**
2008–09 Oldham Ath 13 0 **13 0**
2008–09 *Bury* 6 0 **6 0**
2008–09 *Bradford C* 2 0 **2 0**
2008–09 *Stockport Co* 18 2 **18 2**
2009–10 Rochdale 43 22
2010–11 Rochdale 46 9
2011–12 Rochdale 1 0 **90 31**
2011–12 Sheffield W 32 5
2012–13 Sheffield W 21 4 **53 9**
2012–13 *Barnsley* 16 5
2013–14 Barnsley 40 15 **56 20**
2014–15 Brighton & HA 28 1
2014–15 *Sheffield U* 4 1 **4 1**
2015–16 Brighton & HA 3 0
2015–16 *Nottingham F* 21 2 **21 2**
2016–17 Brighton & HA 0 0 **31 1**
2016–17 *Burton Alb* 26 1 **26 1**

ROSENIOR, Liam (D) 389 4
H: 5 10 W: 11 05 b.Wandsworth 9-7-84
Internationals: England U20, U21.
2001–02 Bristol C 1 0
2002–03 Bristol C 21 2
2003–04 Bristol C 0 0 **22 2**
2003–04 Fulham 0 0
2003–04 *Torquay U* 10 0 **10 0**
2004–05 Fulham 17 0
2005–06 Fulham 24 0
2006–07 Fulham 38 0
2007–08 Fulham 0 0 **79 0**
2007–08 Reading 17 0
2008–09 Reading 42 0
2009–10 Reading 5 0
2009–10 *Ipswich T* 29 1 **29 1**
2010–11 Reading 0 0 **64 0**
2010–11 Hull C 26 0
2011–12 Hull C 44 0
2012–13 Hull C 32 0
2013–14 Hull C 29 1
2014–15 Hull C 13 0 **144 1**
2015–16 Brighton & HA 31 0
2016–17 Brighton & HA 10 0 **41 0**

SALTOR, Bruno (D) 388 7
H: 5 10 W: 11 10 b.Masnou (Barca) 1-10-80
2001–02 Espanyol 1 0 **1 0**
2001–02 *Gimnastic* 12 0 **12 0**
2004–05 Lleida 1 1
2005–06 Lleida 38 0 **39 1**
2006–07 Almeria 23 0
2007–08 Almeria 34 0
2008–09 Almeria 34 0 **91 0**
2009–10 Valencia 26 0
2010–11 Valencia 19 0
2011–12 Valencia 14 0 **59 0**
2012–13 Brighton & HA 30 1
2013–14 Brighton & HA 33 1
2014–15 Brighton & HA 35 3
2015–16 Brighton & HA 46 1
2016–17 Brighton & HA 42 0 **186 6**

SIDWELL, Steve (M) 425 57
H: 5 10 W: 11 00 b.Wandsworth 14-12-82
Internationals: England U20, U21.
2001–02 Arsenal 0 0
2001–02 *Brentford* 30 4 **30 4**
2002–03 Arsenal 0 0
2002–03 *Brighton & HA* 12 5
2002–03 Reading 13 2
2003–04 Reading 43 8
2004–05 Reading 44 5
2005–06 Reading 33 10
2006–07 Reading 35 4 **168 29**
2007–08 Chelsea 15 0 **15 0**
2008–09 Aston Villa 16 3
2009–10 Aston Villa 25 0
2010–11 Aston Villa 4 0 **45 3**
2010–11 Fulham 12 2
2011–12 Fulham 14 1
2012–13 Fulham 28 4
2013–14 Fulham 38 7 **92 14**
2014–15 Stoke C 12 0
2015–16 Stoke C 1 0 **13 0**
2015–16 *Brighton & HA* 16 1
2016–17 Brighton & HA 34 1 **62 7**

SKALAK, Jiri (F) 153 20
H: 5 9 W: 10 10 b.Pardubice 12-3-92
Internationals: Czech Republic U16, U17, U18, U19, U20, U21, Full caps.
2010–11 Sparta Prague 0 0
2011–12 Sparta Prague 0 0
2011–12 *MFA Ruzomberok* 27 3 **27 3**
2012–13 Sparta Prague 7 0
2012–13 *1.FC Slovacko* 9 0 **9 0**
2013–14 Sparta Prague 3 0
2013–14 *Zbrojovka Brno* 24 3 **24 3**
2014–15 Sparta Prague 0 0 **10 0**
2014–15 *Mlada Boleslav* 24 6
2015–16 Mlada Boleslav 16 6 **40 12**
2015–16 Brighton & HA 12 2
2016–17 Brighton & HA 31 0 **43 2**

STEPHENS, Dale (M) 279 36
H: 5 7 W: 11 04 b.Bolton 12-6-89
2006–07 Bury 3 0
2007–08 Bury 6 1 **9 1**
2008–09 Oldham Ath 0 0
2009–10 Oldham Ath 26 2
2009–10 *Rochdale* 6 1 **6 1**
2010–11 Oldham Ath 34 9 **60 11**
2010–11 *Southampton* 6 0 **6 0**
2011–12 Charlton Ath 30 5
2012–13 Charlton Ath 28 2
2013–14 Charlton Ath 26 3 **84 10**
2013–14 Brighton & HA 14 2
2014–15 Brighton & HA 16 2
2015–16 Brighton & HA 45 7
2016–17 Brighton & HA 39 2 **114 13**

STOCKDALE, David (G) 299 0
H: 6 3 W: 13 04 b.Leeds 20-9-85
Internationals: England C.
2002–03 York C 1 0
2003–04 York C 0 0 **1 0**
2006–07 Darlington 6 0
2007–08 Darlington 41 0 **47 0**
2008–09 Fulham 0 0
2008–09 *Rotherham U* 8 0 **8 0**
2008–09 *Leicester C* 8 0 **8 0**
2009–10 Fulham 1 0
2009–10 *Plymouth Arg* 21 0 **21 0**
2010–11 Fulham 7 0
2011–12 Fulham 8 0
2011–12 *Ipswich T* 18 0 **18 0**
2012–13 Fulham 2 0
2012–13 *Hull C* 24 0 **24 0**
2013–14 Fulham 21 0 **39 0**
2014–15 Brighton & HA 42 0
2015–16 Brighton & HA 46 0
2016–17 Brighton & HA 45 0 **133 0**

TILLEY, James (F) 1 0
H: 5 6 W: 9 04 b.Billingshurt 13-6-98
2014–15 Brighton & HA 1 0
2015–16 Brighton & HA 0 0
2016–17 Brighton & HA 0 0 **1 0**

TOWELL, Richie (D) 128 44
H: 5 8 W: 10 06 b.Dublin 17-7-91
Internationals: Republic of Ireland U17, U19, U21.
2010–11 Celtic 1 0
2011–12 Celtic 0 0
2011–12 *Hibernian* 16 0
2012–13 Celtic 0 0 **1 0**
2012–13 *Hibernian* 14 1 **30 1**
2013 Dundalk 31 7
2014 Dundalk 33 11
2015 Dundalk 32 25 **96 43**
2015–16 Brighton & HA 0 0
2016–17 Brighton & HA 1 0 **1 0**

WALTON, Christian (G) 45 0
H: 6 0 W: 11 11 b.Wadebridge 9-11-95
Internationals: England U19, U20, U21.
2011–12 Plymouth Arg 0 0
2012–13 Plymouth Arg 0 0
2013–14 Brighton & HA 0 0
2014–15 Brighton & HA 3 0
2015–16 Brighton & HA 0 0
2015–16 *Bury* 4 0 **4 0**
2015–16 *Plymouth Arg* 4 0 **4 0**
2016–17 Brighton & HA 0 0 **3 0**
2016–17 *Luton T* 27 0 **27 0**
2016–17 *Southend U* 7 0 **7 0**

WARD, Joe (M) 0 0
b. 9-4-95
2015–16 Brighton & HA 0 0
2016–17 Brighton & HA 0 0

WHITE, Ben (D) 0 0
b.Poole 8-11-97
2016–17 Brighton & HA 0 0

Players retained or with offer of contract
Ajiboye, David Ibukun; Ayunga, Jonah Ananias Paul; Barclay, Benjamin Philip; Collar, William Guy; Collings, Billy Paul; Cox, George Frederick; Davies, Jordan Andrew; Garcia, Martinez Luis; Hall, Ben; Hutchinson, Desmond John; Lynch, Sanchez Robert; Maguire-Drew, Jordan Luke; Mandroiu, Daniel Jordan; Molumby, Jayson Patrick; Moore, Owen James; O'Sullivan, Rian Michael; Sanders, Max Harrison; Vose, Bailey Jack.

Scholars
Barker, Danny Ryan; Cochrane, Alexander William; Connolly, Aaron Anthony; Davies, Archie Daniel; Ferguson, Charles Christopher; Fornah, Tyrese Momodu; Hobbs, George Charles; Hutchinson, Isaac; Ljubicic, Stefan Alexander; McGill, Thomas Peter Wayne; Morrison, Hamish John; Myles, Meekums Reece Christopher; Rolph, Samuel Luca-Ray.

BRISTOL C (15)

BROWNHILL, Josh (M) 94 8
H: 5 10 W: 10 12 b.Warrington 19-12-95
2013–14 Preston NE 24 3
2014–15 Preston NE 18 2
2015–16 Preston NE 3 0 **45 5**
2015–16 *Barnsley* 22 2 **22 2**
2016–17 Bristol C 27 1 **27 1**

BRYAN, Joe (D) 169 12
H: 5 7 W: 11 05 b.Bristol 17-9-93
2011–12 Bristol C 1 0
2012–13 Bristol C 13 0
2012–13 *Plymouth Arg* 10 1 **10 1**
2013–14 Bristol C 21 2
2014–15 Bristol C 41 6
2015–16 Bristol C 39 2
2016–17 Bristol C 44 1 **159 11**

DE GIROLAMO, Diago (F) 25 5
H: 5 10 W: 11 00 b.Chesterfield 5-10-95
Internationals: Italy U18, U19, U20.
2012–13 Sheffield U 2 0
2013–14 Sheffield U 0 0
2014–15 Sheffield U 0 0
2014–15 *York C* 12 4 **12 4**
2014–15 *Northampton T* 6 0 **6 0**
2015–16 Sheffield U 0 0 **2 0**
2016–17 Bristol C 0 0
2016–17 *Cheltenham T* 5 1 **5 1**

DJURIC, Milan (F) 267 43
H: 6 3 W: 13 05 b. 22-5-90
Internationals: Bosnia-Herzegovina U21, Full caps
2007–08 Cesena 24 2
2008–09 Cesena 21 3
2009–10 Cesena 28 3
2010–11 Parma 0 0
2010–11 *Ascoli* 17 2 **17 2**
2010–11 *Crotone* 16 5
2011–12 Parma 0 0
2011–12 *Crotone* 29 2 **45 7**
2012–13 Parma 0 0
2012–13 *Cremonese* 20 3 **20 3**
2013–14 Cesena 0 0
2013–14 *Trapani* 13 3 **13 3**
2013–14 *Cittadella* 15 4 **15 4**
2014–15 Cesena 28 2
2015–16 Cesena 26 7
2016–17 Cesena 19 6 **146 23**
2016–17 Bristol C 11 1 **11 1**

EKSTRAND, Joel (D) 178 3
H: 6 2 W: 12 00 b.Lund 4-2-89
Internationals: Sweden U17, U19, U21, Full caps.
2007–08 Helsingborgs IF 12 0
2008–09 Helsingborgs IF 24 0
2009–10 Helsingborgs IF 25 1
2010–11 Helsingborgs IF 12 0 **73 1**
2010–11 Udinese 1 0
2011–12 Udinese 12 0 **13 0**
2012–13 *Watford* 32 1
2013–14 Watford 33 0
2014–15 Watford 24 1
2015–16 Watford 0 0 **89 2**
2016–17 Bristol C 2 0 **2 0**
2016–17 *Rotherham U* 1 0 **1 0**

ENGVALL, Gustav (F) 79 23
H: 6 0 W: 12 11 b.Kalmar 29-4-96
Internationals: Sweden U17, U19, U21, Full caps.
2013 Gothenburg 3 0
2014 Gothenburg 20 8
2015 Gothenburg 25 5
2016 Gothenburg 16 3 **64 16**
2016–17 Bristol C 2 0 **2 0**
2016–17 *Djurgarden* 13 7 **13 7**

FIELDING, Frank (G) 275 0
H: 5 11 W: 12 00 b.Blackburn 4-4-88
Internationals: England U19, U21.
2006–07 Blackburn R 0 0
2007–08 Blackburn R 0 0
2007–08 *Wycombe W* 36 0 **36 0**
2008–09 Blackburn R 0 0
2008–09 *Northampton T* 12 0 **12 0**
2008–09 *Rochdale* 23 0
2009–10 Blackburn R 0 0
2009–10 *Rochdale* 18 0 **41 0**
2010–11 Blackburn R 0 0
2010–11 Derby Co 16 0
2011–12 Derby Co 44 0
2012–13 Derby Co 16 0 **76 0**
2013–14 Bristol C 16 0
2014–15 Bristol C 46 0
2015–16 Bristol C 21 0
2016–17 Bristol C 27 0 **110 0**

FLINT, Aiden (D) 234 32
H: 6 2 W: 12 00 b.Pinxton 11-7-89
Internationals: England C.
2010–11 Swindon T 3 0
2011–12 Swindon T 32 2
2012–13 Swindon T 29 2 **64 4**
2013–14 Bristol C 34 3
2014–15 Bristol C 46 14
2015–16 Bristol C 44 6
2016–17 Bristol C 46 5 **170 28**

GARITA, Paul Arnold (M) 43 7
H: 5 10 W: 12 02 b.Douala 18-6-95
2012–13 Chateauroux 3 0
2013–14 Chateauroux 8 3
2014–15 Chateauroux 13 1
2015–16 Chateauroux 5 1 **29 5**
2015–16 Bristol C 0 0
2016–17 Bristol C 0 0
2016–17 *Plymouth Arg* 14 2 **14 2**

GIEFER, Fabian (G) 82 0
H: 6 5 W: 13 08 b.Adenau 17-5-90
Internationals: Germany U16, U17, U18, U20.
2007–08 Bayer Leverkusen 0 0
2008–09 Bayer Leverkusen 0 0
2009–10 Bayer Leverkusen 3 0
2010–11 Bayer Leverkusen 2 0
2011–12 Bayer Leverkusen 1 0 **6 0**
2012–13 Fortuna Dusseldorf 34 0
2013–14 Fortuna Dusseldorf 30 0 **64 0**
2014–15 Schalke 04 2 0
2015–16 Schalke 04 0 0
2016–17 Schalke 04 0 0 **2 0**
On loan from Schalke 04.
2016–17 Bristol C 10 0 **10 0**

GOLBOURNE, Scott (M) 336 6
H: 5 8 W: 11 08 b.Bristol 29-2-88
Internationals: England U17, U19.
2004–05 Bristol C 9 0
2005–06 Bristol C 5 0
2005–06 Reading 1 0
2006–07 Reading 0 0
2006–07 *Wycombe W* 34 1 **34 1**
2007–08 Reading 1 0
2007–08 *Bournemouth* 5 0 **5 0**
2008–09 Reading 0 0 **2 0**
2008–09 *Oldham Ath* 8 0 **8 0**
2009–10 Exeter C 34 0
2010–11 Exeter C 44 2
2011–12 Exeter C 26 0 **104 2**
2011–12 Barnsley 12 1
2012–13 Barnsley 31 1
2013–14 Barnsley 4 0 **47 2**
2013–14 Wolverhampton W 40 1
2014–15 Wolverhampton W 27 0
2015–16 Wolverhampton W 20 0 **87 1**
2015–16 Bristol C 16 0
2016–17 Bristol C 19 0 **49 0**

HEGELER, Jens (M) 188 12
H: 6 4 W: 12 08 b.Cologne 22-1-88
Internationals: Germany U21.
2007–08 Bayer Leverkusen 1 0
2008–09 Bayer Leverkusen 6 2
2008–09 *Augsburg* 11 0
2009–10 Bayer Leverkusen 0 0
2009–10 *Augsburg* 2 2 **13 2**
2010–11 Bayer Leverkusen 0 0
2010–11 *Nurembourg* 34 3
2011–12 Bayer Leverkusen 0 0
2011–12 *Nurembourg* 31 1 **65 4**
2012–13 Bayer Leverkusen 27 3
2013–14 Bayer Leverkusen 18 0 **52 5**
2014–15 Hertha Berlin 24 1
2015–16 Hertha Berlin 16 0
2016–17 Hertha Berlin 6 0 **46 1**
2016–17 Bristol C 12 0 **12 0**

KELLY, Lloyd (D) 0 0
H: 5 10 W: 11 00 b. 1-10-98
2016–17 Bristol C 0 0

LITTLE, Mark (D) 310 4
H: 6 1 W: 12 10 b.Worcester 20-8-88
Internationals: England U19.
2005–06 Wolverhampton W 0 0
2006–07 Wolverhampton W 26 0
2007–08 Wolverhampton W 1 0
2007–08 *Northampton T* 17 0
2008–09 Wolverhampton W 0 0
2008–09 *Northampton T* 9 0 **26 0**
2009–10 Wolverhampton W 0 0 **27 0**
2009–10 *Chesterfield* 12 0 **12 0**
2009–10 *Peterborough U* 9 0
2010–11 Peterborough U 35 0
2011–12 Peterborough U 35 1
2012–13 Peterborough U 40 1
2013–14 Peterborough U 38 1 **157 3**
2014–15 Bristol C 37 1
2015–16 Bristol C 23 0
2016–17 Bristol C 28 0 **88 1**

LUCIC, Ivan (G) 3 0
H: 6 4 W: 14 07 b.Brcko 23-3-95
Internationals: Austria U16, U17, U18, U19.
2012–13 Ried 0 0
2013–14 Ried 1 0 **1 0**
2014–15 Bayern Munich 0 0
2015–16 Bayern Munich 0 0
2016–17 Bristol C 2 0 **2 0**
2016–17 *Aalborg* 0 0

MAGNUSSON, Hordur (D) 93 2
H: 6 0 W: 12 02 b.Reykjavik 28-3-86
Internationals: Iceland U17, U19, U21, Full caps.
2009 Fram 3 0
2010 Fram 3 0 **6 0**
2011–12 Juventus 0 0
2012–13 Juventus 0 0
2013–14 Juventus 0 0
2013–14 *Spezia* 20 0 **20 0**
2014–15 Juventus 0 0
2014–15 *Cesena* 12 0
2015–16 Juventus 0 0
2015–16 *Cesena* 27 1 **39 1**
2016–17 Bristol C 28 1 **28 1**

McCLOUSKY, Shawn (F) 0 0
b.London 6-1-97
2016–17 Bristol C 0 0

MOORE, Taylor (D) 33 0
H: 6 0 W: 12 08 b.Walthamstow 12-5-97
Internationals: England U17, U18, U19, U20.
From West Ham U.
2014–15 Lens 4 0
2015–16 Lens 5 0 **9 0**
2016–17 Bristol C 5 0 **5 0**
2016–17 *Bury* 19 0 **19 0**

O'DOWDA, Callum (M) 121 12
H: 5 11 W: 11 11 b.Oxford 23-4-95
Internationals: Republic of Ireland U21, Full caps.
2012–13 Oxford U 0 0
2013–14 Oxford U 10 0
2014–15 Oxford U 39 4
2015–16 Oxford U 38 8 **87 12**
2016–17 Bristol C 34 0 **34 0**

O'LEARY, Max (G) 0 0
H: 6 1 W: 12 03 b.Bath 10-10-96
2013–14 Bristol C 0 0
2014–15 Bristol C 0 0
2015–16 Bristol C 0 0
2016–17 Bristol C 0 0

O'NEIL, Gary (M) 454 30
H: 5 10 W: 11 00 b.Beckenham 18-5-83
Internationals: England U19, U20, U21.
1999–2000 Portsmouth 1 0
2000–01 Portsmouth 10 1
2001–02 Portsmouth 33 1
2002–03 Portsmouth 31 3
2003–04 Portsmouth 3 2
2003–04 *Walsall* 7 0 **7 0**
2004–05 Portsmouth 24 2
2004–05 *Cardiff C* 9 1 **9 1**
2005–06 Portsmouth 36 6
2006–07 Portsmouth 35 1
2007–08 Portsmouth 2 0 **175 16**
2007–08 Middlesbrough 26 0
2008–09 Middlesbrough 29 4
2009–10 Middlesbrough 36 4
2010–11 Middlesbrough 18 0 **109 8**
2010–11 West Ham U 8 0
2011–12 West Ham U 16 2
2012–13 West Ham U 24 1 **48 3**
2013–14 QPR 29 1 **29 1**
2014–15 Norwich C 21 0

2015–16	Norwich C	27	0	**48**	**0**
2016–17	Bristol C	29	1	**29**	**1**

PACK, Marlon (M) **305 21**
H: 6 2 W: 11 09 b.Portsmouth 25-3-91

2008–09	Portsmouth	0	0		
2009–10	Portsmouth	0	0		
2009–10	*Wycombe W*	8	0	**8**	**0**
2009–10	*Dagenham & R*	17	1	**17**	**1**
2010–11	Portsmouth	1	0	**1**	**0**
2010–11	*Cheltenham T*	38	2		
2011–12	Cheltenham T	43	5		
2012–13	Cheltenham T	43	7		
2013–14	Cheltenham T	0	0	**124**	**14**
2013–14	Bristol C	43	0		
2014–15	Bristol C	34	3		
2015–16	Bristol C	45	1		
2016–17	Bristol C	33	2	**155**	**6**

PATERSON, Jamie (F) **204 34**
H: 5 9 W: 10 07 b.Coventry 20-12-91

2010–11	Walsall	14	0		
2011–12	Walsall	34	3		
2012–13	Walsall	46	12	**94**	**15**
2013–14	Nottingham F	32	8		
2014–15	Nottingham F	21	1		
2015–16	Nottingham F	1	0	**54**	**9**
2015–16	*Huddersfield T*	34	6	**34**	**6**
2016–17	Bristol C	22	4	**22**	**4**

PLAVOTIC, Tin (D) **11 1**
H: 6 6 W: 15 02 b.Vienna 30-6-97

2014–15	Admira	0	0		
2015–16	Schalke 04	0	0		
2016–17	Schalke 04	0	0		
2016–17	Bristol C	0	0		
2016–17	*Cheltenham T*	11	1	**11**	**1**

REID, Bobby (M) **130 10**
H: 5 7 W: 10 10 b.Bristol 1-3-93

2010–11	Bristol C	1	0		
2011–12	Bristol C	0	0		
2011–12	*Cheltenham T*	1	0	**1**	**0**
2012–13	Bristol C	4	1		
2012–13	*Oldham Ath*	7	0	**7**	**0**
2013–14	Bristol C	24	1		
2014–15	Bristol C	2	0		
2014–15	*Plymouth Arg*	33	3	**33**	**3**
2015–16	Bristol C	28	2		
2016–17	Bristol C	30	3	**89**	**7**

SMITH, Jon (M) **5 0**
H: 5 10 W: 10 01 b.Liverpool 27-7-97

2016–17	Bristol C	0	0		
2016–17	*Cheltenham T*	5	0	**5**	**0**

SMITH, Korey (M) **251 5**
H: 5 9 W: 11 01 b.Hatfield 31-1-91

2008–09	Norwich C	2	0		
2009–10	Norwich C	37	4		
2010–11	Norwich C	28	0		
2011–12	Norwich C	0	0		
2011–12	*Barnsley*	12	0	**12**	**0**
2012–13	Norwich C	0	0	**67**	**4**
2012–13	*Yeovil T*	17	0	**17**	**0**
2012–13	*Oldham Ath*	10	0		
2013–14	Oldham Ath	42	1	**52**	**1**
2014–15	Bristol C	44	0		
2015–16	Bristol C	36	0		
2016–17	Bristol C	23	0	**103**	**0**

TAYLOR, Matty (F) **88 45**
H: 5 9 W: 11 05 b. 30-3-90
Internationals: England C.
From Oxford U, North Leigh, Forest Green R.

2015–16	Bristol R	46	27		
2016–17	Bristol R	27	16	**73**	**43**
2016–17	Bristol C	15	2	**15**	**2**

TOMLIN, Lee (F) **253 55**
H: 5 11 W: 11 09 b.Leicester 12-1-89
Internationals: England C.

2010–11	Peterborough U	37	8		
2011–12	Peterborough U	37	8		
2012–13	Peterborough U	42	11		
2013–14	Peterborough U	19	5	**135**	**32**
2013–14	Middlesbrough	14	4		
2014–15	Middlesbrough	42	7	**56**	**11**
2015–16	Bournemouth	6	0	**6**	**0**
2015–16	*Bristol C*	18	6		
2016–17	Bristol C	38	6	**56**	**12**

VYNER, Zak (D) **23 0**
H: 5 10 W: 10 10 b.Bath 14-5-97

2015–16	Bristol C	4	0		
2016–17	Bristol C	3	0	**7**	**0**
2016–17	*Accrington S*	16	0	**16**	**0**

WILBRAHAM, Aaron (F) **535 121**
H: 6 3 W: 12 04 b.Knutsford 21-10-79

1997–98	Stockport Co	7	1		
1998–99	Stockport Co	26	0		
1999–2000	Stockport Co	26	4		
2000–01	Stockport Co	36	12		
2001–02	Stockport Co	21	3		
2002–03	Stockport Co	15	7		
2003–04	Stockport Co	41	8	**172**	**35**
2004–05	Hull C	19	2	**19**	**2**
2004–05	*Oldham Ath*	4	2	**4**	**2**
2005–06	Milton Keynes D	31	4		
2005–06	*Bradford C*	5	1	**5**	**1**
2006–07	Milton Keynes D	32	7		
2007–08	Milton Keynes D	35	10		
2008–09	Milton Keynes D	33	16		
2009–10	Milton Keynes D	35	10		
2010–11	Milton Keynes D	10	2	**176**	**49**
2010–11	Norwich C	12	1		
2011–12	Norwich C	11	1	**23**	**2**
2012–13	Crystal Palace	21	0		
2013–14	Crystal Palace	4	0	**25**	**0**
2014–15	Bristol C	37	18		
2015–16	Bristol C	43	8		
2016–17	Bristol C	31	4	**111**	**30**

WRIGHT, Bailey (D) **200 9**
H: 5 9 W: 13 05 b.Melbourne 28-7-92
Internationals: Australia U17, Full caps.

2010–11	Preston NE	2	0		
2011–12	Preston NE	13	1		
2012–13	Preston NE	38	2		
2013–14	Preston NE	43	4		
2014–15	Preston NE	27	1		
2015–16	Preston NE	38	0		
2016–17	Preston NE	18	0	**179**	**8**
2016–17	Bristol C	21	1	**21**	**1**

Players retained or with offer of contract
Andrews, Jake; Baldwin, Aden; Dowling, George Philip Denzil; Harper, Ashley Stephen; Harris, Charlie; Lemonheigh, Evans Connor; Moir-Pring, Cameron Lewis; Morrell, Joseff John; Sesay, Alhaji; Wollacott, Joseph Luke.

Scholars
Akpobire, God'S Will Kelechi Onome; Ali, Jayden Rehman Robert; Allen, Cameron Shaun; Barry, Owen William; Begovic, Denis; Carey, James Dean; Edwards, Opanin Osafo-Adjei; Mortimore, Joshua Stephen; Morton, James Samuel; Nurse, George Damien; Parsons, Aaron Mathew; Rees, Ricardo Estaban; Reeves, Harrison Jack; Richards, Tom James; Smith, Harry Myles; Smith, Harvey George Charles; Turner, Jack William Peter; Turner, Williams Christian Michael.

BRISTOL R (16)

BODIN, Billy (M) **189 40**
H: 5 11 W: 11 00 b.Swindon 24-3-92
Internationals: Wales U17, U19, U21.

2009–10	Swindon T	0	0		
2010–11	Swindon T	5	0		
2011–12	Swindon T	11	3	**16**	**3**
2011–12	*Torquay U*	17	5		
2011–12	*Crewe Alex*	8	0	**8**	**0**
2012–13	Torquay U	43	5		
2013–14	Torquay U	27	1	**87**	**11**
2014–15	Northampton T	4	0	**4**	**0**
2015–16	Bristol R	38	13		
2016–17	Bristol R	36	13	**74**	**26**

BROOM, Ryan (M) **6 0**
H: 5 10 W: 12 08 b.Newport 4-9-96

2015–16	Bristol R	1	0		
2016–17	Bristol R	5	0	**6**	**0**

BROWN, Lee (M) **210 18**
H: 6 0 W: 12 06 b.Bromley 10-8-90
Internationals: England C.

2008–09	QPR	0	0		
2009–10	QPR	1	0		
2010–11	QPR	0	0	**1**	**0**
2011–12	Bristol R	42	7		
2012–13	Bristol R	39	3		
2013–14	Bristol R	41	2		
2015–16	Bristol R	46	6		
2016–17	Bristol R	41	0	**209**	**18**

BURN, Jonathan (D) **22 1**
b. 1-8-95

2014–15	Middlesbrough	0	0		
2015–16	Middlesbrough	0	0		
2015–16	*Oldham Ath*	12	1	**12**	**1**
2016–17	Middlesbrough	0	0		
2016–17	*Kilmarnock*	8	0	**8**	**0**
2016–17	Bristol R	2	0	**2**	**0**

CLARKE, James (D) **59 0**
H: 6 0 W: 13 03 b.Aylesbury 17-11-89
From Watford, Oxford U, Oxford C, Salisbury C, Woking.

2015–16	Bristol R	37	0		
2016–17	Bristol R	22	0	**59**	**0**

CLARKE, Ollie (M) **101 8**
H: 5 11 W: 11 11 b.Bristol 29-6-92

2009–10	Bristol R	0	0		
2010–11	Bristol R	1	0		
2011–12	Bristol R	0	0		
2012–13	Bristol R	5	0		
2013–14	Bristol R	32	2		
2015–16	Bristol R	33	2		
2016–17	Bristol R	30	4	**101**	**8**

EASTER, Jermaine (F) **412 89**
H: 5 9 W: 12 02 b.Cardiff 15-1-82
Internationals: Wales Full caps.

2000–01	Wolverhampton W	0	0		
2000–01	Hartlepool U	4	0		
2001–02	Hartlepool U	12	2		
2002–03	Hartlepool U	8	0		
2003–04	Hartlepool U	3	0	**27**	**2**
2003–04	*Cambridge U*	15	2		
2004–05	Cambridge U	24	6	**39**	**8**
2004–05	Boston U	9	3	**9**	**3**
2005–06	Stockport Co	19	8	**19**	**8**
2005–06	Wycombe W	15	2		
2006–07	Wycombe W	38	17		
2007–08	Wycombe W	6	2	**59**	**21**
2007–08	Plymouth Arg	32	6		
2008–09	Plymouth Arg	4	0	**36**	**6**
2008–09	*Millwall*	5	1		
2008–09	*Colchester U*	5	2	**5**	**2**
2009–10	Milton Keynes D	36	14		
2010–11	Milton Keynes D	14	0	**50**	**14**
2010–11	*Swansea C*	6	1	**6**	**1**
2010–11	Crystal Palace	14	1		
2011–12	Crystal Palace	33	5		
2012–13	Crystal Palace	8	1	**55**	**7**
2012–13	*Millwall*	9	1		
2013–14	Millwall	20	3		
2014–15	Millwall	9	1	**43**	**6**
2015–16	Bristol R	43	7		
2016–17	Bristol R	21	4	**64**	**11**

GAFFNEY, Rory (M) **64 16**
H: 6 0 W: 12 04 b.Tuam 23-10-89

2014–15	Cambridge U	0	0		
2015–16	Cambridge U	6	2	**6**	**2**
2015–16	*Bristol R*	24	8		
2016–17	Bristol R	34	6	**58**	**14**

GOSLING, Jake (M) **43 1**
H: 5 9 W: 10 10 b.Newquay 11-8-93
Internationals: Gibraltar Full caps.

2011–12	Exeter C	0	0		
2012–13	Exeter C	12	1		
2013–14	Exeter C	3	0	**15**	**1**
2014–15	Bristol R	0	0		
2015–16	Bristol R	18	0		
2015–16	*Newport Co*	6	0	**6**	**0**
2016–17	Bristol R	0	0	**18**	**0**
2016–17	*Cambridge U*	4	0	**4**	**0**

HARRIS, Robert (D) **235 14**
H: 5 8 W: 10 00 b.Glasgow 28-8-87

2004–05	Clyde	1	0		
2005–06	Clyde	20	0		
2006–07	Clyde	24	0	**45**	**0**
2007–08	Queen of the South	26	2		
2008–09	Queen of the South	21	2		
2009–10	Queen of the South	32	4		
2010–11	Queen of the South	31	2	**110**	**10**
2011–12	Blackpool	5	0		
2012–13	Blackpool	4	0		
2012–13	*Rotherham U*	5	1	**5**	**1**
2013–14	Blackpool	4	0	**13**	**0**
2013–14	Sheffield U	11	0		
2014–15	Sheffield U	40	3		
2015–16	Sheffield U	5	0	**56**	**3**
2015–16	*Fleetwood T*	1	0	**1**	**0**
2016–17	Bristol R	5	0	**5**	**0**

HARRISON, Ellis (F) **108 19**
H: 5 11 W: 12 06 b.Newport 1-2-94
Internationals: Wales U21.

2010–11	Bristol R	1	0		
2011–12	Bristol R	0	0		
2012–13	Bristol R	13	3		
2013–14	Bristol R	25	1		
2015–16	Bristol R	30	7		
2015–16	*Hartlepool U*	2	0	**2**	**0**
2016–17	Bristol R	37	8	**106**	**19**

HARTLEY, Peter (D) **309 23**
H: 6 0 W: 12 06 b.Hartlepool 3-4-88

Season	Club	Apps	Gls	Total	Gls
2006–07	Sunderland	1	0		
2007–08	Sunderland	0	0		
2007–08	*Chesterfield*	12	0	**12**	**0**
2008–09	Sunderland	0	0	**1**	**0**
2009–10	Hartlepool U	38	2		
2010–11	Hartlepool U	40	2		
2011–12	Hartlepool U	44	4		
2012–13	Hartlepool U	43	2		
2013–14	Hartlepool U	1	0	**166**	**10**
2013–14	Stevenage	31	2	**31**	**2**
2014–15	Plymouth Arg	39	4		
2015–16	Plymouth Arg	42	2	**81**	**6**
2016–17	Bristol R	18	5	**18**	**5**

HODGES, Kieran (G) **0 0**
b.Somerset 14-9-98

Season	Club	Apps	Gls	Total	Gls
2016–17	Bristol R	0	0		

LAWRENCE, Liam (M) **494 85**
H: 5 11 W: 12 06 b.Retford 14-12-81
Internationals: Republic of Ireland Full caps.

Season	Club	Apps	Gls	Total	Gls
1999–2000	Mansfield T	2	0		
2000–01	Mansfield T	18	4		
2001–02	Mansfield T	32	2		
2002–03	Mansfield T	43	10		
2003–04	Mansfield T	41	18	**136**	**34**
2004–05	Sunderland	32	7		
2005–06	Sunderland	29	3		
2006–07	Sunderland	12	0	**73**	**10**
2006–07	Stoke C	27	5		
2007–08	Stoke C	41	14		
2008–09	Stoke C	20	3		
2009–10	Stoke C	25	1		
2010–11	Stoke C	0	0	**113**	**23**
2010–11	Portsmouth	31	7		
2011–12	Portsmouth	23	0	**54**	**7**
2011–12	*Cardiff C*	13	1	**13**	**1**
2012–13	PAOK Salonika	22	3		
2013–14	PAOK Salonika	2	0	**24**	**3**
2013–14	Barnsley	14	1	**14**	**1**
2014–15	Shrewsbury T	33	5		
2015–16	Shrewsbury T	18	0	**51**	**5**
2015–16	Bristol R	12	1		
2016–17	Bristol R	4	0	**16**	**1**

LEADBITTER, Daniel (D) **78 0**
H: 6 0 W: 11 00 b.Newcastle upon Tyne 17-10-90

Season	Club	Apps	Gls	Total	Gls
2011–12	Torquay U	2	0		
2012–13	Torquay U	13	0	**15**	**0**
2015–16	Bristol R	33	0		
2016–17	Bristol R	30	0	**63**	**0**

LINES, Chris (M) **369 29**
H: 6 2 W: 12 00 b.Bristol 30-11-88

Season	Club	Apps	Gls	Total	Gls
2005–06	Bristol R	4	0		
2006–07	Bristol R	7	0		
2007–08	Bristol R	27	3		
2008–09	Bristol R	45	4		
2009–10	Bristol R	42	10		
2010–11	Bristol R	42	3		
2011–12	Bristol R	1	0		
2011–12	Sheffield W	41	3		
2012–13	Sheffield W	6	0	**47**	**3**
2012–13	*Milton Keynes D*	16	0	**16**	**0**
2013–14	Port Vale	34	1		
2014–15	Port Vale	27	2	**61**	**3**
2015–16	Bristol R	33	0		
2016–17	Bristol R	44	3	**245**	**23**

LOCKYER, Tom (D) **134 1**
H: 6 0 W: 11 05 b.Bristol 30-12-94
Internationals: Wales U21.

Season	Club	Apps	Gls	Total	Gls
2012–13	Bristol R	4	0		
2013–14	Bristol R	41	1		
2015–16	Bristol R	43	0		
2016–17	Bristol R	46	0	**134**	**1**

LUCAS, Jamie (F) **3 0**
H: 6 2 W: 13 01 b.Pontypridd 6-12-95

Season	Club	Apps	Gls	Total	Gls
2013–14	Bristol R	1	0		
2015–16	Bristol R	1	0		
2016–17	Bristol R	1	0	**3**	**0**

LUMLEY, Joe (G) **25 0**
H: 6 3 W: 11 07 b.Harlow 15-2-95

Season	Club	Apps	Gls	Total	Gls
2013–14	QPR	0	0		
2014–15	QPR	0	0		
2014–15	*Accrington S*	5	0	**5**	**0**
2014–15	*Morecambe*	0	0		
2015–16	QPR	1	0		
2015–16	*Stevenage*	0	0		
2016–17	QPR	0	0	**1**	**0**
2016–17	Bristol R	19	0	**19**	**0**

MANSELL, Lee (D) **387 33**
H: 5 10 W: 11 10 b.Gloucester 28-10-82

Season	Club	Apps	Gls	Total	Gls
2000–01	Luton T	18	5		
2001–02	Luton T	11	1		
2002–03	Luton T	1	0		
2003–04	Luton T	16	2		
2004–05	Luton T	1	0	**47**	**8**
2005–06	Oxford U	44	1	**44**	**1**
2006–07	Torquay U	45	4		
2009–10	Torquay U	39	2		
2010–11	Torquay U	45	0		
2011–12	Torquay U	45	12		
2012–13	Torquay U	42	2		
2013–14	Torquay U	43	2	**259**	**22**
2015–16	Bristol R	28	2		
2016–17	Bristol R	9	0	**37**	**2**

McCHRYSTAL, Mark (D) **199 3**
H: 6 1 W: 13 07 b.Derry 26-6-84
Internationals: Northern Ireland U18, U21.

Season	Club	Apps	Gls	Total	Gls
2001–02	Wolverhampton W	0	0		
2003	Derry C	5	0		
2003	*Institute*	6	0	**6**	**0**
2004	Derry C	9	1		
2005	Derry C	9	0		
2006–07	Partick Thistle	15	1	**15**	**1**
2007	Derry C	3	0		
2008	Derry C	11	0		
2009	Derry C	13	0	**50**	**1**
2009–10	Lisburn Distillery	3	0	**3**	**0**
2010–11	Tranmere R	23	0		
2011–12	Tranmere R	18	1		
2012–13	Tranmere R	0	0	**41**	**1**
2012–13	*Scunthorpe U*	3	0	**3**	**0**
2012–13	Bristol R	21	0		
2013–14	Bristol R	35	0		
2015–16	Bristol R	21	0		
2016–17	Bristol R	4	0	**81**	**0**

MILDENHALL, Steve (G) **431 1**
H: 6 4 W: 14 01 b.Swindon 13-5-78

Season	Club	Apps	Gls	Total	Gls
1996–97	Swindon T	1	0		
1997–98	Swindon T	4	0		
1998–99	Swindon T	0	0		
1999–2000	Swindon T	5	0		
2000–01	Swindon T	23	0	**33**	**0**
2001–02	Notts Co	26	0		
2002–03	Notts Co	21	0		
2003–04	Notts Co	28	0		
2004–05	Notts Co	1	0	**76**	**0**
2004–05	Oldham Ath	6	0	**6**	**0**
2005–06	Grimsby T	46	1	**46**	**1**
2006–07	Yeovil T	46	0		
2007–08	Yeovil T	29	0	**75**	**0**
2008–09	Southend U	34	0		
2009–10	Southend U	44	0		
2010–11	Southend U	0	0	**78**	**0**
2010–11	Millwall	0	0		
2011–12	Millwall	10	0		
2012–13	Millwall	0	0	**10**	**0**
2012–13	*Scunthorpe U*	9	0	**9**	**0**
2012–13	Bristol R	22	0		
2013–14	Bristol R	46	0		
2015–16	Bristol R	26	0		
2016–17	Bristol R	4	0	**98**	**0**

MONTANO, Cristian (F) **130 16**
H: 5 11 W: 12 00 b.Cali 11-12-91

Season	Club	Apps	Gls	Total	Gls
2010–11	West Ham U	0	0		
2011–12	West Ham U	0	0		
2011–12	*Notts Co*	15	4	**15**	**4**
2011–12	*Swindon T*	4	1	**4**	**1**
2011–12	*Dagenham & R*	10	3	**10**	**3**
2011–12	*Oxford U*	9	2	**9**	**2**
2012–13	Oldham Ath	30	1		
2013–14	Oldham Ath	10	2	**40**	**3**
2015–16	Bristol R	27	2		
2016–17	Bristol R	25	1	**52**	**3**

MOORE, Byron (M) **340 36**
H: 6 0 W: 10 06 b.Stoke 24-8-88

Season	Club	Apps	Gls	Total	Gls
2006–07	Crewe Alex	0	0		
2007–08	Crewe Alex	33	3		
2008–09	Crewe Alex	36	3		
2009–10	Crewe Alex	32	3		
2010–11	Crewe Alex	38	6		
2011–12	Crewe Alex	42	8		
2012–13	Crewe Alex	41	4		
2013–14	Crewe Alex	40	3	**262**	**30**
2014–15	Port Vale	15	1		
2015–16	Port Vale	36	3	**51**	**4**
2016–17	Bristol R	27	2	**27**	**2**

PARTINGTON, Joe (M) **59 2**
H: 5 11 W: 11 13 b.Portsmouth 1-4-90
Internationals: Wales U17, U19, U21.

Season	Club	Apps	Gls	Total	Gls
2007–08	Bournemouth	6	1		
2008–09	Bournemouth	11	1		
2009–10	Bournemouth	11	0		
2010–11	Bournemouth	5	0		
2011–12	Bournemouth	5	0		
2012–13	Bournemouth	14	0		
2013–14	Bournemouth	0	0		
2014–15	Bournemouth	0	0	**52**	**2**
2016–17	Bristol R	7	0	**7**	**0**

PUDDY, Will (G) **9 0**
H: 6 1 W: 13 00 b.Salisbury 4-10-87

Season	Club	Apps	Gls	Total	Gls
2005–06	Cheltenham T	0	0		
2006–07	Cheltenham T	0	0		
2007–08	Cheltenham T	0	0		
2008–09	Cheltenham T	1	0		
2009–10	Cheltenham T	0	0	**1**	**0**

From Swindon Supermarine, Chippenham T, Salisbury C.

Season	Club	Apps	Gls	Total	Gls
2015–16	Bristol R	1	0		
2016–17	Bristol R	7	0	**8**	**0**

SINCLAIR, Stuart (M) **68 3**
H: 5 7 W: 10 08 b.Houghton Conquest 9-11-87
From Luton T, Cambridge C, Bedford T, Dunstable T, Arlesey T, Salisbury C.

Season	Club	Apps	Gls	Total	Gls
2015–16	Bristol R	30	2		
2016–17	Bristol R	38	1	**68**	**3**

Players retained or with offer of contract
Kilgour, Alfie George Alexander; Thomas, Dominic William.

Scholars
Blake, Samuel Joseph; Brace, Joshua Sebastian; Carey, Jordan; Chamberlain, Harrison David; Clarke, Alfie Jack; Ellington, Lewis Owen; Hedges, Sam William; Hodges, Kieran Michael; Iles, Samuel John; Jones, Connor Stephen Malcom; Lammiman, Daniel; Leigh-Gilchrist, Lewis Gordon; Rennie, Toby James; Russe, Luke Cameron; Spruce, James Alexander; Swan, Matthew James; Tucker-Dixon, Tyrone Devante Junior.

Non-Contract
Thomas, Dominic William.

BURNLEY (17)

AGYEI, Daniel (F) **19 4**
H: 6 0 W: 12 02 b.Dansoman 1-6-97

Season	Club	Apps	Gls	Total	Gls
2014–15	AFC Wimbledon	0	0		
2015–16	Burnley	0	0		
2016–17	Burnley	3	0	**3**	**0**
2016–17	*Coventry C*	16	4	**16**	**4**

ANDERSON, Thomas (M) **61 2**
H: 6 4 W: 13 01 b.Burnley 2-9-93

Season	Club	Apps	Gls	Total	Gls
2012–13	Burnley	0	0		
2013–14	Burnley	0	0		
2014–15	Burnley	0	0		
2014–15	*Carlisle U*	8	0	**8**	**0**
2015–16	Burnley	0	0		
2015–16	*Chesterfield*	18	0		
2016–17	Burnley	0	0		
2016–17	*Chesterfield*	35	2	**53**	**2**

ARFIELD, Scott (M) **363 39**
H: 5 10 W: 10 01 b.Livingston 1-11-88
Internationals: Scotland U19, U21, B. Canada Full caps.

Season	Club	Apps	Gls	Total	Gls
2007–08	Falkirk	35	3		
2008–09	Falkirk	37	7		
2009–10	Falkirk	36	3	**108**	**13**
2010–11	Huddersfield T	40	4		
2011–12	Huddersfield T	35	2		
2012–13	Huddersfield T	21	1	**96**	**7**
2013–14	Burnley	45	8		
2014–15	Burnley	37	2		
2015–16	Burnley	46	8		
2016–17	Burnley	31	1	**159**	**19**

BARNES, Ashley (F) **269 62**
H: 6 0 W: 12 00 b.Bath 30-10-89
Internationals: Austria U20.

Season	Club	Apps	Gls	Total	Gls
2006–07	Plymouth Arg	0	0		
2007–08	Plymouth Arg	0	0		
2008–09	Plymouth Arg	15	1		
2009–10	Plymouth Arg	7	1	**22**	**2**
2009–10	*Torquay U*	6	0	**6**	**0**
2009–10	*Brighton & HA*	8	4		
2010–11	Brighton & HA	42	18		
2011–12	Brighton & HA	43	11		
2012–13	Brighton & HA	34	8		
2013–14	Brighton & HA	22	5	**149**	**46**
2013–14	Burnley	21	3		
2014–15	Burnley	35	5		
2015–16	Burnley	8	0		
2016–17	Burnley	28	6	**92**	**14**

BARTON, Joey (M) **386 33**
H: 5 11 W: 12 05 b.Huyton 2-9-82
Internationals: England U21, Full caps.

Season	Club	Apps	Gls	Total	Gls
2001–02	Manchester C	0	0		
2002–03	Manchester C	7	1		
2003–04	Manchester C	28	1		
2004–05	Manchester C	31	1		
2005–06	Manchester C	31	6		
2006–07	Manchester C	33	6	**130**	**15**
2007–08	Newcastle U	23	1		
2008–09	Newcastle U	9	1		
2009–10	Newcastle U	15	1		
2010–11	Newcastle U	32	4		
2011–12	Newcastle U	2	0	**81**	**7**
2011–12	QPR	31	3		
2012–13	QPR	0	0		
2012–13	*Marseille*	25	0	**25**	**0**
2013–14	QPR	34	3		
2014–15	QPR	28	1	**93**	**7**
2015–16	Burnley	38	3		
2016–17	Rangers	5	0	**5**	**0**
2016–17	Burnley	14	1	**52**	**4**

BIRCH, Arlen (D) **0 0**
b. 12-9-96
Internationals: England U16, U18.

Season	Club	Apps	Gls	Total	Gls
2014–15	Everton	0	0		
2015–16	Burnley	0	0		
2016–17	Burnley	0	0		

BOYD, George (M) **427 83**
H: 5 10 W: 11 07 b.Chatham 2-10-85
Internationals: Scotland B, Full caps.

Season	Club	Apps	Gls	Total	Gls
2006–07	Peterborough U	20	6		
2007–08	Peterborough U	46	12		
2008–09	Peterborough U	46	9		
2009–10	Peterborough U	32	9		
2009–10	*Nottingham F*	6	1	**6**	**1**
2010–11	Peterborough U	43	15		
2011–12	Peterborough U	45	7		
2012–13	Peterborough U	31	6	**263**	**64**
2012–13	*Hull C*	13	4		
2013–14	Hull C	29	2		
2014–15	Hull C	1	0	**43**	**6**
2014–15	Burnley	35	5		
2015–16	Burnley	44	5		
2016–17	Burnley	36	2	**115**	**12**

BRADY, Robert (F) **187 18**
H: 5 9 W: 10 12 b.Belfast 14-1-92
Internationals: Republic of Ireland Youth, U21, Full caps.

Season	Club	Apps	Gls	Total	Gls
2008–09	Manchester U	0	0		
2009–10	Manchester U	0	0		
2010–11	Manchester U	0	0		
2011–12	Manchester U	0	0		
2011–12	*Hull C*	39	3		
2012–13	Manchester U	0	0		
2012–13	Hull C	32	4		
2013–14	Hull C	16	3		
2014–15	Hull C	27	0	**114**	**10**
2015–16	Norwich C	36	3		
2016–17	Norwich C	23	4	**59**	**7**
2016–17	Burnley	14	1	**14**	**1**

DARIKWA, Tendayi (M) **146 10**
H: 6 2 W: 12 02 b.Nottingham 13-12-91

Season	Club	Apps	Gls	Total	Gls
2010–11	Chesterfield	0	0		
2011–12	Chesterfield	2	0		
2012–13	Chesterfield	36	5		
2013–14	Chesterfield	41	3		
2014–15	Chesterfield	46	1	**125**	**9**
2015–16	Burnley	21	1		
2016–17	Burnley	0	0	**21**	**1**

DEFOUR, Steven (M) **306 27**
H: 5 8 W: 10 03 b.Mechelen 15-4-88
Internationals: Belgium U16, U17, U18, Full caps.

Season	Club	Apps	Gls	Total	Gls
2004–05	Genk	4	0		
2005–06	Genk	26	1	**30**	**1**
2006–07	Standard Liege	29	4		
2007–08	Standard Liege	24	1		
2008–09	Standard Liege	33	4		
2009–10	Standard Liege	13	1		
2010–11	Standard Liege	27	3		
2011–12	Standard Liege	1	0	**127**	**13**
2011–12	Porto	24	1		
2012–13	Porto	25	2		
2013–14	Porto	16	0	**65**	**3**
2014–15	Anderlecht	29	6		
2015–16	Anderlecht	32	2		
2016–17	Anderlecht	2	1	**63**	**9**
2016–17	Burnley	21	1	**21**	**1**

GINNELLY, Josh (M) **12 0**
b.Coventry 24-3-97

Season	Club	Apps	Gls	Total	Gls
2013–14	Shrewsbury T	0	0		
2014–15	Shrewsbury T	3	0	**3**	**0**
2015–16	Burnley	0	0		
2016–17	Burnley	0	0		
2016–17	*Walsall*	9	0	**9**	**0**

GRAY, Andre (F) **124 50**
H: 5 10 W: 12 06 b.Shrewsbury 26-6-91
Internationals: England C.

Season	Club	Apps	Gls	Total	Gls
2009–10	Shrewsbury T	4	0	**4**	**0**
From Hinckley U, Luton T.					
2014–15	Brentford	45	16		
2015–16	Brentford	2	2	**47**	**18**
2015–16	Burnley	41	23		
2016–17	Burnley	32	9	**73**	**32**

GREEN, George (M) **13 1**
b.Dewsbury 2-1-96
Internationals: England U16, U17, U18.

Season	Club	Apps	Gls	Total	Gls
2013–14	Everton	0	0		
2014–15	Everton	0	0		
2014–15	*Tranmere R*	6	1	**6**	**1**
2015–16	Oldham Ath	3	0	**3**	**0**
2015–16	Burnley	0	0		
2016–17	Burnley	0	0		
2016–17	*Kilmarnock*	4	0	**4**	**0**

GUDMUNDSSON, Johann Berg (M) **220 26**
H: 6 1 W: 12 06 b.Reykjavik 27-10-90
Internationals: Iceland U19, U21, Full caps.

Season	Club	Apps	Gls	Total	Gls
2009–10	AZ	0	0		
2010–11	AZ	23	1		
2011–12	AZ	30	3		
2012–13	AZ	31	2		
2013–14	AZ	35	3	**119**	**9**
2014–15	Charlton Ath	41	10		
2015–16	Charlton Ath	40	6	**81**	**16**
2016–17	Burnley	20	1	**20**	**1**

HEATON, Tom (G) **300 0**
H: 6 1 W: 13 12 b.Chester 15-4-86
Internationals: England 16, U17, U18, U19, U21, Full caps.

Season	Club	Apps	Gls	Total	Gls
2003–04	Manchester U	0	0		
2004–05	Manchester U	0	0		
2005–06	Manchester U	0	0		
2005–06	*Swindon T*	14	0	**14**	**0**
2006–07	Manchester U	0	0		
2007–08	Manchester U	0	0		
2008–09	Manchester U	0	0		
2008–09	*Cardiff C*	21	0		
2009–10	Manchester U	0	0		
2009–10	*Rochdale*	12	0	**12**	**0**
2009–10	*Wycombe W*	16	0	**16**	**0**
2010–11	Cardiff C	27	0		
2011–12	Cardiff C	2	0	**50**	**0**
2012–13	Bristol C	43	0	**43**	**0**
2013–14	Burnley	46	0		
2014–15	Burnley	38	0		
2015–16	Burnley	46	0		
2016–17	Burnley	35	0	**165**	**0**

HENDRICK, Jeff (M) **228 24**
H: 6 1 W: 11 11 b.Dublin 31-1-92
Internationals: Republic of Ireland U17, U19, U21, Full caps.

Season	Club	Apps	Gls	Total	Gls
2010–11	Derby Co	4	0		
2011–12	Derby Co	42	3		
2012–13	Derby Co	45	6		
2013–14	Derby Co	30	4		
2014–15	Derby Co	41	7		
2015–16	Derby Co	32	2		
2016–17	Derby Co	2	0	**196**	**22**
2016–17	Burnley	32	2	**32**	**2**

HENDRIE, Luke (M) **53 0**
b. 27-8-94
Internationals: England U16, U17.

Season	Club	Apps	Gls	Total	Gls
2013–14	Derby Co	0	0		
2014–15	Derby Co	0	0		
2015–16	Burnley	0	0		
2015–16	*Hartlepool U*	3	0	**3**	**0**
2015–16	*York C*	18	0	**18**	**0**
2016–17	Burnley	0	0		
2016–17	*Kilmarnock*	32	0	**32**	**0**

JACKSON, Brad (M) **0 0**
H: 5 9 W: 11 00 b.Manchester 20-10-96

Season	Club	Apps	Gls	Total	Gls
2015–16	Burnley	0	0		
2016–17	Burnley	0	0		

KEANE, Michael (D) **143 12**
H: 5 7 W: 12 13 b.Stockport 11-1-93
Internationals: Republic of Ireland U17, U19. England U19, U20, U21, Full caps.

Season	Club	Apps	Gls	Total	Gls
2011–12	Manchester U	0	0		
2012–13	Manchester U	0	0		
2012–13	*Leicester C*	22	2	**22**	**2**
2013–14	Manchester U	0	0		
2013–14	*Derby Co*	7	0	**7**	**0**
2013–14	*Blackburn R*	13	3	**13**	**3**
2014–15	Manchester U	1	0	**1**	**0**
2014–15	Burnley	21	0		
2015–16	Burnley	44	5		
2016–17	Burnley	35	2	**100**	**7**

KIGHTLY, Michael (F) **249 39**
H: 5 10 W: 10 10 b.Basildon 24-1-86
Internationals: England U21.

Season	Club	Apps	Gls	Total	Gls
2002–03	Southend U	1	0		
2003–04	Southend U	11	0		
2004–05	Southend U	1	0	**13**	**0**
From Grays Ath.					
2006–07	Wolverhampton W	24	8		
2007–08	Wolverhampton W	21	4		
2008–09	Wolverhampton W	38	8		
2009–10	Wolverhampton W	9	0		
2010–11	Wolverhampton W	4	0		
2011–12	Wolverhampton W	18	3		
2011–12	*Watford*	12	3	**12**	**3**
2012–13	Wolverhampton W	0	0	**114**	**23**
2012–13	Stoke C	22	3		
2013–14	Stoke C	0	0	**22**	**3**
2013–14	*Burnley*	36	5		
2014–15	Burnley	17	1		
2015–16	Burnley	18	0		
2016–17	Burnley	5	0	**76**	**6**
2016–17	*Burton Alb*	12	4	**12**	**4**

LONG, Chris (F) **52 10**
H: 5 7 W: 12 02 b.Huyton 25-2-95
Internationals: England U16, U17, U18, U19, U20.

Season	Club	Apps	Gls	Total	Gls
2013–14	Everton	0	0		
2013–14	*Milton Keynes D*	4	1	**4**	**1**
2014–15	Everton	0	0		
2014–15	*Brentford*	10	4	**10**	**4**
2015–16	Burnley	10	0		
2016–17	Burnley	0	0	**10**	**0**
2016–17	*Fleetwood T*	18	4	**18**	**4**
2016–17	*Bolton W*	10	1	**10**	**1**

LONG, Kevin (D) **114 6**
H: 6 3 W: 13 01 b.Cork 18-8-90
Internationals: Republic of Ireland Full caps.

Season	Club	Apps	Gls	Total	Gls
2009	Cork C	16	0	**16**	**0**
2009–10	Burnley	0	0		
2010–11	Burnley	0	0		
2010–11	*Accrington S*	15	0		
2011–12	Burnley	0	0		
2011–12	*Accrington S*	24	4	**39**	**4**
2011–12	*Rochdale*	16	0	**16**	**0**
2012–13	Burnley	14	0		
2012–13	*Portsmouth*	5	0	**5**	**0**
2013–14	Burnley	7	0		
2014–15	Burnley	1	0		
2015–16	Burnley	0	0		
2015–16	*Barnsley*	11	2	**11**	**2**
2015–16	*Milton Keynes D*	2	0	**2**	**0**
2016–17	Burnley	3	0	**25**	**0**

LOWTON, Matt (M) **218 13**
H: 5 11 W: 12 04 b.Chesterfield 9-6-89

Season	Club	Apps	Gls	Total	Gls
2008–09	Sheffield U	0	0		
2009–10	Sheffield U	2	0		
2009–10	*Ferencvaros*	5	0	**5**	**0**
2010–11	Sheffield U	32	4		
2011–12	Sheffield U	44	6	**78**	**10**
2012–13	Aston Villa	37	2		
2013–14	Aston Villa	23	0		
2014–15	Aston Villa	12	0	**72**	**2**
2015–16	Burnley	27	1		
2016–17	Burnley	36	0	**63**	**1**

MARNEY, Dean (M) **362 20**
H: 5 10 W: 11 09 b.Barking 31-1-84
Internationals: England U21.

Season	Club	Apps	Gls	Total	Gls
2002–03	Tottenham H	0	0		
2002–03	*Swindon T*	9	0	**9**	**0**
2003–04	Tottenham H	3	0		
2003–04	*QPR*	2	0	**2**	**0**
2004–05	Tottenham H	5	2		
2004–05	*Gillingham*	3	0	**3**	**0**
2005–06	Tottenham H	0	0	**8**	**2**
2005–06	*Norwich C*	13	0	**13**	**0**
2006–07	Hull C	37	2		
2007–08	Hull C	41	6		
2008–09	Hull C	31	0		
2009–10	Hull C	16	1	**125**	**9**
2009–10	Burnley	0	0		
2010–11	Burnley	36	3		
2011–12	Burnley	37	0		
2012–13	Burnley	38	2		
2013–14	Burnley	38	3		
2014–15	Burnley	20	0		
2015–16	Burnley	12	0		
2016–17	Burnley	21	1	**202**	**9**

MASSANKA, Ntumba (F)				**13**	**0**
H: 6 3 W: 12 08 b.Tottenham 30-11-96					
2015–16	Burnley	0	0		
2015–16	*York C*	3	0	**3**	**0**
2016–17	Burnley	0	0		
2016–17	*Morecambe*	10	0	**10**	**0**

MEE, Ben (D)				**216**	**6**
H: 5 11 W: 11 09 b.Sale 21-9-89					
Internationals: England U19, U20, U21.					
2007–08	Manchester C	0	0		
2008–09	Manchester C	0	0		
2009–10	Manchester C	0	0		
2010–11	Manchester C	0	0		
2010–11	*Leicester C*	15	0	**15**	**0**
2011–12	Manchester C	0	0		
2011–12	Burnley	31	0		
2012–13	Burnley	19	1		
2013–14	Burnley	38	0		
2014–15	Burnley	33	2		
2015–16	Burnley	46	2		
2016–17	Burnley	34	1	**201**	**6**

MITCHELL, Conor (G)				**0**	**0**
b. 9-5-96					
Internationals: Northern Ireland U17, U19, U21.					
2015–16	Burnley	0	0		
2016–17	Burnley	0	0		

O'NEILL, Aiden (M)				**18**	**0**
H: 5 10 W: 11 00 b.Brisbane 4-7-98					
From Brisbane Ath.					
2016–17	Burnley	3	0	**3**	**0**
2016–17	*Oldham Ath*	15	0	**15**	**0**

POPE, Nick (G)				**77**	**0**
H: 6 3 W: 11 13 b.Cambridge 19-4-92					
2011–12	Charlton Ath	0	0		
2012–13	Charlton Ath	1	0		
2013–14	Charlton Ath	0	0		
2013–14	*York C*	22	0	**22**	**0**
2014–15	Charlton Ath	8	0		
2014–15	*Bury*	22	0	**22**	**0**
2015–16	Charlton Ath	24	0	**33**	**0**
2016–17	Burnley	0	0		

ROBINSON, Paul (G)				**424**	**1**
H: 6 1 W: 14 07 b.Beverley 15-10-79					
Internationals: England U21, Full caps					
1996–97	Leeds U	0	0		
1997–98	Leeds U	0	0		
1998–99	Leeds U	5	0		
1999–2000	Leeds U	0	0		
2000–01	Leeds U	16	0		
2001–02	Leeds U	0	0		
2002–03	Leeds U	38	0		
2003–04	Leeds U	36	0	**95**	**0**
2003–04	Tottenham H	0	0		
2004–05	Tottenham H	36	0		
2005–06	Tottenham H	38	0		
2006–07	Tottenham H	38	1		
2007–08	Tottenham H	25	0	**137**	**1**
2008–09	Blackburn R	35	0		
2009–10	Blackburn R	35	0		
2010–11	Blackburn R	36	0		
2011–12	Blackburn R	34	0		
2012–13	Blackburn R	21	0		
2013–14	Blackburn R	21	0		
2014–15	Blackburn R	7	0	**189**	**0**
2015–16	Burnley	0	0		
2016–17	Burnley	3	0	**3**	**0**

TARKOWSKI, James (D)				**165**	**9**
H: 6 1 W: 12 10 b.Manchester 19-11-92					
2010–11	Oldham Ath	9	0		
2011–12	Oldham Ath	16	1		
2012–13	Oldham Ath	21	2		
2013–14	Oldham Ath	26	2	**72**	**5**
2013–14	Brentford	13	2		
2014–15	Brentford	34	1		
2015–16	Brentford	23	1	**70**	**4**
2015–16	Burnley	4	0		
2016–17	Burnley	19	0	**23**	**0**

THOMAS, Jamie (F)				**0**	**0**
b. 10-1-97					
Internationals: Wales U19.					
2015–16	Bolton W	0	0		
2016–17	Burnley	0	0		

ULVESTAD, Fredrik (M)				**140**	**15**
H: 6 0 W: 12 06 b.Alesund 19-5-92					
Internationals: Norway U20, U21, U23, Full caps.					
2010	Aalesund	1	0		
2011	Aalesund	24	2		
2012	Aalesund	25	2		
2013	Aalesund	27	7		
2014	Aalesund	29	3	**106**	**14**
2014–15	Burnley	2	0		
2015–16	Burnley	5	0		
2016–17	Burnley	0	0	**7**	**0**
2016–17	*Charlton Ath*	27	1	**27**	**1**

VOKES, Sam (F)				**323**	**79**
H: 6 1 W: 13 10 b.Lymington 21-10-89					
Internationals: Wales U21, Full caps.					
2006–07	Bournemouth	13	4		
2007–08	Bournemouth	41	12	**54**	**16**
2008–09	Wolverhampton W	36	6		
2009–10	Wolverhampton W	5	0		
2009–10	*Leeds U*	8	1	**8**	**1**
2010–11	Wolverhampton W	2	0		
2010–11	*Bristol C*	1	0	**1**	**0**
2010–11	*Sheffield U*	6	1	**6**	**1**
2010–11	*Norwich C*	4	1	**4**	**1**
2011–12	Wolverhampton W	4	0		
2011–12	*Burnley*	9	2		
2011–12	*Brighton & HA*	14	3	**14**	**3**
2012–13	Wolverhampton W	0	0	**47**	**6**
2012–13	Burnley	46	4		
2013–14	Burnley	39	20		
2014–15	Burnley	15	0		
2015–16	Burnley	43	15		
2016–17	Burnley	37	10	**189**	**51**

WARD, Stephen (D)				**408**	**26**
H: 5 11 W: 12 02 b.Dublin 20-8-85					
Internationals: Republic of Ireland U20, U21, B, Full caps.					
2003	Bohemians	6	0		
2004	Bohemians	16	2		
2005	Bohemians	29	7		
2006	Bohemians	21	2	**72**	**11**
2006–07	Wolverhampton W	18	3		
2007–08	Wolverhampton W	29	0		
2008–09	Wolverhampton W	42	0		
2009–10	Wolverhampton W	22	0		
2010–11	Wolverhampton W	34	1		
2011–12	Wolverhampton W	38	3		
2012–13	Wolverhampton W	39	2		
2013–14	Wolverhampton W	0	0	**222**	**9**
2013–14	*Brighton & HA*	44	4	**44**	**4**
2014–15	Burnley	9	0		
2015–16	Burnley	24	1		
2016–17	Burnley	37	1	**70**	**2**

WESTWOOD, Ashley (M)				**284**	**19**
H: 5 10 W: 11 00 b.Nantwich 1-4-90					
2008–09	Crewe Alex	2	0		
2009–10	Crewe Alex	36	6		
2010–11	Crewe Alex	46	5		
2011–12	Crewe Alex	41	3		
2012–13	Crewe Alex	3	0	**128**	**14**
2012–13	Aston Villa	30	0		
2013–14	Aston Villa	35	3		
2014–15	Aston Villa	27	0		
2015–16	Aston Villa	32	2		
2016–17	Aston Villa	23	0	**147**	**5**
2016–17	Burnley	9	0	**9**	**0**

WHITMORE, Alex (D)				**35**	**0**
H: 5 11 W: 10 10 b.Newcastle upon Tyne 7-9-95					
2016–17	Burnley	0	0		
2016–17	*Morecambe*	35	0	**35**	**0**

Players retained or with offer of contract

Dunne, James Gerard; Flowers, Harry Edward; Koiki, Abd-Al-Ali Morakinyo; Leitch, Robbie; Limb, Harry; Yao, Abodje Freddy Bruce.

Scholars

Bayode, Olatunde Tobias; Bruce, Adam David; Chakwana, Tinashe; Clarke, James Michael Neil; Cropper, Jordan; Egan, Leighton Michael Paul; Fenton, Miles Andrew; Howarth, Mark David; Jumeau, Tristan Samuel; King, Connor Lewis; Layton, Samuel Jay Dixon; McNeil, Dwight James Matthew; Metz, Khius; Mpofu, Kwazinkosi; Wilson, Scott John; Wood, Tommy Paul; Wusiewicz, Marcel; Younger, Oliver.

BURTON ALB (18)

AKINS, Lucas (F)				**296**	**47**
H: 5 10 W: 11 07 b.Huddersfield 25-2-89					
2006–07	Huddersfield T	2	0		
2007–08	Huddersfield T	3	0	**5**	**0**
2008–09	Hamilton A	11	0		
2008–09	*Partick Thistle*	9	1	**9**	**1**
2009–10	Hamilton A	0	0	**11**	**0**
2010–11	Tranmere R	33	2		
2011–12	Tranmere R	44	5	**77**	**7**
2012–13	Stevenage	46	10		
2013–14	Stevenage	31	3	**77**	**13**
2014–15	Burton Alb	35	9		
2015–16	Burton Alb	44	12		
2016–17	Burton Alb	38	5	**117**	**26**

BARKER, Shaun (D)				**360**	**18**
H: 6 2 W: 12 08 b.Nottingham 19-9-82					
2002–03	Rotherham U	11	0		
2003–04	Rotherham U	36	2		
2004–05	Rotherham U	33	2		
2005–06	Rotherham U	43	3	**123**	**7**
2006–07	Blackpool	45	3		
2007–08	Blackpool	46	2		
2008–09	Blackpool	43	0	**134**	**5**
2009–10	Derby Co	35	5		
2010–11	Derby Co	43	1		
2011–12	Derby Co	20	0		
2012–13	Derby Co	0	0		
2013–14	Derby Co	0	0		
2014–15	Derby Co	0	0	**98**	**6**
2016–17	Burton Alb	5	0	**5**	**0**

BYWATER, Steve (G)				**332**	**0**
H: 6 2 W: 12 10 b.Manchester 7-6-81					
Internationals: England U20, U21.					
1997–98	Rochdale	0	0		
1998–99	West Ham U	0	0		
1999–2000	West Ham U	4	0		
1999–2000	*Wycombe W*	2	0	**2**	**0**
1999–2000	*Hull C*	4	0	**4**	**0**
2000–01	West Ham U	1	0		
2001–02	West Ham U	0	0		
2001–02	*Wolverhampton W*	0	0		
2001–02	*Cardiff C*	0	0		
2002–03	West Ham U	0	0		
2003–04	West Ham U	17	0		
2004–05	West Ham U	36	0		
2005–06	West Ham U	1	0	**59**	**0**
2005–06	*Coventry C*	14	0	**14**	**0**
2006–07	Derby Co	37	0		
2007–08	Derby Co	18	0		
2007–08	*Ipswich T*	17	0	**17**	**0**
2008–09	Derby Co	31	0		
2009–10	Derby Co	42	0		
2010–11	Derby Co	22	0	**150**	**0**
2010–11	*Cardiff C*	8	0	**8**	**0**
2011–12	Sheffield W	32	0		
2012–13	Sheffield W	0	0	**32**	**0**
2013–14	Millwall	7	0		
2014–15	Millwall	0	0	**7**	**0**
2014–15	*Gillingham*	13	0	**13**	**0**
2014–15	Doncaster R	21	0	**21**	**0**
2015–16	Burton Alb	0	0		
2016–17	Burton Alb	5	0	**5**	**0**

CAMPBELL, Harry (G)				**0**	**0**
H: 6 1 W: 12 02 b.Blackburn 16-11-95					
2015–16	Bolton W	0	0		
2016–17	Burton Alb	0	0		

DELANEY, Ryan (D)				**0**	**0**
H: 6 0 W: 11 05 b.Wexford 6-9-96					
From Wexford.					
2016–17	Burton Alb	0	0		

DYER, Lloyd (M)				**448**	**58**
H: 5 8 W: 10 03 b.Birmingham 13-9-82					
2001–02	WBA	0	0		
2002–03	WBA	0	0		
2003–04	WBA	17	2		
2003–04	*Kidderminster H*	7	1	**7**	**1**
2004–05	WBA	4	0		
2004–05	*Coventry C*	6	0	**6**	**0**
2005–06	WBA	0	0	**21**	**2**
2005–06	*QPR*	15	0	**15**	**0**
2005–06	Millwall	6	0	**6**	**0**
2006–07	Milton Keynes D	41	5		
2007–08	Milton Keynes D	45	11	**86**	**16**
2008–09	Leicester C	44	10		
2009–10	Leicester C	33	3		
2010–11	Leicester C	35	3		
2011–12	Leicester C	36	4		
2012–13	Leicester C	42	3		
2013–14	Leicester C	40	7	**230**	**30**
2014–15	Watford	14	1		
2014–15	*Birmingham C*	18	1	**18**	**1**
2015–16	Watford	0	0	**14**	**1**
2015–16	Burnley	3	0	**3**	**0**
2016–17	Burton Alb	42	7	**42**	**7**

EDWARDS, Phil (D)				**439**	**34**
H: 5 8 W: 11 03 b.Bootle 8-11-85					
2005–06	Wigan Ath	0	0		
2006–07	Accrington S	33	1		
2007–08	Accrington S	31	1		
2008–09	Accrington S	46	0		
2009–10	Accrington S	46	8		
2010–11	Accrington S	44	13	**200**	**23**
2011–12	Stevenage	22	0	**22**	**0**

2011–12 *Rochdale* 3 0
2012–13 Rochdale 44 0 **47 0**
2013–14 Burton Alb 41 2
2014–15 Burton Alb 45 6
2015–16 Burton Alb 46 0
2016–17 Burton Alb 0 0 **132 8**
2016–17 *Oxford U* 38 3 **38 3**

FLANAGAN, Tom (D) 113 4
H: 6 2 W: 11 05 b.Hammersmith 21-10-91
Internationals: Northern Ireland U21, Full caps.
2009–10 Milton Keynes D 1 0
2010–11 Milton Keynes D 2 0
2011–12 Milton Keynes D 21 3
2012–13 Milton Keynes D 0 0
2012–13 *Gillingham* 13 1 **13 1**
2012–13 *Barnet* 9 0 **9 0**
2013–14 Milton Keynes D 7 0
2013–14 *Stevenage* 2 0 **2 0**
2014–15 Milton Keynes D 6 0 **37 3**
2014–15 *Plymouth Arg* 4 0 **4 0**
2015–16 Burton Alb 18 0
2016–17 Burton Alb 30 0 **48 0**

FOX, Ben (M) 1 0
H: 5 11 W: 12 00 b.Burton upon Trent 1-2-98
2016–17 Burton Alb 1 0 **1 0**

HARNESS, Marcus (M) 36 0
H: 6 0 W: 11 00 b.Coventry 1-8-94
2013–14 Burton Alb 3 0
2014–15 Burton Alb 18 0
2015–16 Burton Alb 5 0
2016–17 Burton Alb 10 0 **36 0**

IRVINE, Jackson (M) 134 15
H: 5 10 W: 11 00 b.Melbourne 7-3-93
Internationals: Scotland U19. Australia U20, U23, Full caps.
2012–13 Celtic 1 0
2013–14 Celtic 0 0
2013–14 *Kilmarnock* 27 1 **27 1**
2014–15 Celtic 0 0 **1 0**
2014–15 *Ross Co* 28 2
2015–16 Ross Co 36 2 **64 4**
2016–17 Burton Alb 42 10 **42 10**

LUND, Matthew (M) 160 25
H: 6 0 W: 11 13 b.Manchester 21-11-90
Internationals: Northern Ireland U21, Full caps.
2009–10 Stoke C 0 0
2010–11 Stoke C 0 0
2010–11 *Hereford U* 2 0 **2 0**
2011–12 Stoke C 0 0
2011–12 *Oldham Ath* 3 0 **3 0**
2011–12 *Bristol R* 13 2
2012–13 Stoke C 0 0
2012–13 *Bristol R* 18 2 **31 4**
2012–13 Southend U 12 1 **12 1**
2013–14 Rochdale 40 8
2014–15 Rochdale 14 2
2015–16 Rochdale 29 1
2016–17 Rochdale 29 9 **112 20**
2016–17 Burton Alb 0 0

McCRORY, Damien (M) 273 11
H: 6 2 W: 12 10 b.Limerick 22-2-90
Internationals: Republic of Ireland U18, U19.
2008–09 Plymouth Arg 0 0
2008–09 *Port Vale* 12 0
2009–10 Plymouth Arg 0 0
2009–10 *Port Vale* 5 0 **17 0**
2009–10 *Grimsby T* 10 0 **10 0**
2009–10 Dagenham & R 20 0
2010–11 Dagenham & R 23 0
2011–12 Dagenham & R 33 1 **76 1**
2012–13 Burton Alb 42 1
2013–14 Burton Alb 40 1
2014–15 Burton Alb 34 5
2015–16 Burton Alb 38 3
2016–17 Burton Alb 16 0 **170 10**

McFADZEAN, Kyle (D) 207 10
H: 6 1 W: 13 04 b.Sheffield 20-2-87
Internationals: England C.
2004–05 Sheffield U 0 0
2005–06 Sheffield U 0 0
2006–07 Sheffield U 0 0
From Alfreton T
2011–12 Crawley T 37 2
2012–13 Crawley T 17 3
2013–14 Crawley T 42 1 **96 6**
2014–15 Milton Keynes D 41 3
2015–16 Milton Keynes D 39 0 **80 3**
2016–17 Burton Alb 31 1 **31 1**

McLAUGHLIN, Jon (G) 258 0
H: 6 2 W: 13 00 b.Edinburgh 9-9-87
2008–09 Bradford C 1 0
2009–10 Bradford C 7 0
2010–11 Bradford C 25 0
2011–12 Bradford C 23 0
2012–13 Bradford C 23 0
2013–14 Bradford C 46 0 **125 0**
2014–15 Burton Alb 45 0
2015–16 Burton Alb 45 0
2016–17 Burton Alb 43 0 **133 0**

MOUSINHO, John (M) 360 20
H: 6 1 W: 12 07 b.Hounslow 30-4-86
2005–06 Brentford 7 0
2006–07 Brentford 34 0
2007–08 Brentford 23 2 **64 2**
2008–09 Wycombe W 34 2
2009–10 Wycombe W 39 1 **73 3**
2010–11 Stevenage 38 7
2011–12 Stevenage 19 3
2012–13 Preston NE 24 1
2013–14 Preston NE 2 0 **26 1**
2013–14 *Gillingham* 4 1 **4 1**
2013–14 *Stevenage* 16 1 **73 11**
2014–15 Burton Alb 42 2
2015–16 Burton Alb 46 0
2016–17 Burton Alb 32 0 **120 2**

NAYLOR, Tom (D) 145 10
H: 5 11 W: 11 05 b.Sutton-in-Ashfield 28-6-91
2011–12 Derby Co 8 0
2012–13 Derby Co 0 0
2012–13 *Bradford C* 5 0 **5 0**
2013–14 Derby Co 0 0
2013–14 *Newport Co* 33 1 **33 1**
2014–15 Derby Co 0 0 **8 0**
2014–15 *Cambridge U* 8 0 **8 0**
2014–15 *Burton Alb* 17 0
2015–16 Burton Alb 41 6
2016–17 Burton Alb 33 3 **91 9**

PALMER, Matthew (M) 139 6
H: 5 10 W: 12 06 b.Derby 1-8-93
2012–13 Burton Alb 2 0
2013–14 Burton Alb 40 0
2014–15 Burton Alb 33 4
2015–16 Burton Alb 14 0
2015–16 *Oldham Ath* 14 1 **14 1**
2016–17 Burton Alb 36 1 **125 5**

REILLY, Callum (M) 94 2
H: 6 1 W: 12 03 b.Warrington 3-10-93
Internationals: Republic of Ireland U21.
2012–13 Birmingham C 18 1
2013–14 Birmingham C 25 0
2014–15 Birmingham C 17 1 **60 2**
2014–15 *Burton Alb* 2 0
2015–16 Burton Alb 14 0
2016–17 Burton Alb 0 0 **16 0**
2016–17 *Coventry C* 18 0 **18 0**

SBARRA, Joe (M) 1 0
H: 5 10 W: 11 00 b.Lichfield 21-12-98
2016–17 Burton Alb 1 0 **1 0**

SORDELL, Marvin (F) 218 45
H: 5 9 W: 12 06 b.Pinner 17-2-91
Internationals: England U20, U21. Great Britain.
2009–10 Watford 6 1
2009–10 *Tranmere R* 8 1 **8 1**
2010–11 Watford 43 12
2011–12 Watford 26 8 **75 21**
2011–12 Bolton W 3 0
2012–13 Bolton W 22 4
2013–14 Bolton W 0 0 **25 4**
2013–14 *Charlton Ath* 31 7 **31 7**
2014–15 Burnley 14 0
2015–16 Burnley 3 0 **17 0**
2015–16 Colchester U 21 4 **21 4**
2016–17 Coventry C 20 4 **20 4**
2016–17 Burton Alb 21 4 **21 4**

TURNER, Ben (D) 236 9
H: 6 4 W: 14 04 b.Birmingham 21-1-88
Internationals: England U19.
2005–06 Coventry C 1 0
2006–07 Coventry C 1 0
2006–07 *Peterborough U* 8 0 **8 0**
2006–07 *Oldham Ath* 1 0 **1 0**
2007–08 Coventry C 19 0
2008–09 Coventry C 24 0
2009–10 Coventry C 13 0
2010–11 Coventry C 14 4
2011–12 Cardiff C 37 2
2012–13 Cardiff C 31 1
2013–14 Cardiff C 31 0
2014–15 Cardiff C 11 0
2015–16 Cardiff C 1 0 **111 3**
2015–16 *Coventry C* 5 1 **77 5**
2016–17 Burton Alb 39 1 **39 1**

VARNEY, Luke (F) 393 72
H: 5 11 W: 11 00 b.Leicester 28-9-82
2002–03 Crewe Alex 0 0
2003–04 Crewe Alex 8 1
2004–05 Crewe Alex 26 4
2005–06 Crewe Alex 27 5
2006–07 Crewe Alex 34 17 **95 27**
2007–08 Charlton Ath 39 8
2008–09 Charlton Ath 18 2 **57 10**
2008–09 *Sheffield W* 4 2
2008–09 Derby Co 10 1
2009–10 Derby Co 1 0
2009–10 *Sheffield W* 39 9 **43 11**
2010–11 Derby Co 1 0 **12 1**
2010–11 *Blackpool* 30 5 **30 5**
2011–12 Portsmouth 30 6 **30 6**
2012–13 Leeds U 34 4
2013–14 Leeds U 11 2 **45 6**
2013–14 *Blackburn R* 12 0
2014–15 Blackburn R 11 0 **23 0**
2014–15 *Ipswich T* 10 1
2015–16 Ipswich T 18 1
2016–17 Ipswich T 15 3 **43 5**
2016–17 Burton Alb 15 1 **15 1**

WILLIAMSON, Lee (M) 504 36
H: 5 10 W: 10 04 b.Derby 7-6-82
Internationals: Jamaica Full caps.
1999–2000 Mansfield T 4 0
2000–01 Mansfield T 15 0
2001–02 Mansfield T 46 3
2002–03 Mansfield T 40 0
2003–04 Mansfield T 35 0
2004–05 Mansfield T 4 0 **144 3**
2004–05 Northampton T 37 0 **37 0**
2005–06 Rotherham U 37 4
2006–07 Rotherham U 19 5 **56 9**
2006–07 Watford 5 0
2007–08 Watford 32 2
2008–09 Watford 34 2 **71 4**
2008–09 *Preston NE* 5 1 **5 1**
2009–10 Sheffield U 20 3
2010–11 Sheffield U 16 3
2011–12 Sheffield U 40 13
2012–13 Sheffield U 0 0 **76 19**
2012–13 Portsmouth 22 0 **22 0**
2012–13 Blackburn R 9 0
2013–14 Blackburn R 32 0
2014–15 Blackburn R 28 0
2015–16 Blackburn R 10 0 **79 0**
2016–17 Burton Alb 14 0 **14 0**

Players retained or with offer of contract
Dinanga, Nyambu Marcus; Hornby, Samuel Connor; McCrory, Damien Paul; Myers-Harness, Marcus Anthony.

Scholars
Brown, Joseph Malcolm Alan; Cotterill, Jayden Michael; Davies, Jake Michael; Dowd, Charlie George; Garnett, Dylan Gabriel; Hallahan, Jack Patrick Daniel; Hammerton, Thomas James; Harrison, James Finley; Hawkins, Callum David; Hunt, Joseph James; Hutchinson, Reece Christopher; Saville, Jacob Malcolm; Shaw, Cameron George; Smith, Max; Thompson-Matthews, Tristan Luke; Walker, Lewis Joseph Paul.

BURY (19)

BARNETT, Leon (D) 287 14
H: 6 0 W: 12 04 b.Stevenage 30-11-85
2003–04 Luton T 0 0
2004–05 Luton T 0 0
2005–06 Luton T 20 0
2006–07 Luton T 39 3 **59 3**
2007–08 WBA 32 3
2008–09 WBA 11 0
2009–10 WBA 2 0
2009–10 *Coventry C* 20 0 **20 0**
2010–11 WBA 0 0 **45 3**
2010–11 Norwich C 25 1
2011–12 Norwich C 17 1
2012–13 Norwich C 8 0
2012–13 *Cardiff C* 8 0 **8 0**
2013–14 Norwich C 0 0 **50 2**
2013–14 Wigan Ath 41 4
2014–15 Wigan Ath 20 0
2015–16 Wigan Ath 20 1 **81 5**
2016–17 Bury 24 1 **24 1**

BEDEAU, Jordan (D) 7 0
b.Waltham Forest 24-12-99

2016–17	Bury	7	0	**7**	**0**

BROWN, Chris (F) 349 58
H: 6 3 W: 13 01 b.Doncaster 11-12-84

2002–03	Sunderland	0	0		
2003–04	Sunderland	0	0		
2003–04	*Doncaster R*	22	10		
2004–05	Sunderland	37	5		
2005–06	Sunderland	13	1		
2005–06	*Hull C*	13	1	**13**	**1**
2006–07	Sunderland	16	3	**66**	**9**
2006–07	Norwich C	4	0		
2007–08	Norwich C	14	1	**18**	**1**
2007–08	Preston NE	17	5		
2008–09	Preston NE	30	6		
2009–10	Preston NE	43	6		
2010–11	Preston NE	16	1	**106**	**18**
2011–12	Doncaster R	11	2		
2012–13	Doncaster R	36	8		
2013–14	Doncaster R	40	9	**109**	**29**
2014–15	Blackburn R	20	0		
2015–16	Blackburn R	17	0	**37**	**0**
2016–17	Bury	0	0		

BROWN, Reece (D) 91 1
H: 6 2 W: 13 02 b.Manchester 1-11-91
Internationals: England U19, U20.

2010–11	Manchester U	0	0		
2010–11	*Bradford C*	3	0	**3**	**0**
2011–12	Manchester U	0	0		
2011–12	*Doncaster R*	3	0	**3**	**0**
2011–12	*Oldham Ath*	15	0	**15**	**0**
2012–13	Manchester U	0	0		
2012–13	*Coventry C*	6	0	**6**	**0**
2012–13	*Ipswich T*	1	0	**1**	**0**
2013–14	Watford	1	0	**1**	**0**
2013–14	*Carlisle U*	12	0	**12**	**0**
2014–15	Barnsley	13	0	**13**	**0**
2015–16	Bury	28	0		
2016–17	Sheffield U	2	0	**2**	**0**
2016–17	Bury	7	1	**35**	**1**

BURGESS, Scott (M) 20 2
H: 5 10 W: 11 00 b.Warrington 27-6-96

2013–14	Bury	1	0		
2014–15	Bury	0	0		
2015–16	Bury	3	0		
2016–17	Bury	16	2	**20**	**2**

CADDIS, Paul (D) 267 20
H: 5 7 W: 10 07 b.Irvine 19-4-88
Internationals: Scotland U19, U21, Full caps.

2007–08	Celtic	2	0		
2008–09	Celtic	5	0		
2008–09	*Dundee U*	11	0	**11**	**0**
2009–10	Celtic	10	0	**17**	**0**
2010–11	Swindon T	38	1		
2011–12	Swindon T	39	4		
2012–13	Swindon T	0	0		
2012–13	*Birmingham C*	27	0		
2013–14	Swindon T	0	0	**77**	**5**
2013–14	Birmingham C	38	5		
2014–15	Birmingham C	45	6		
2015–16	Birmingham C	39	4		
2016–17	Birmingham C	0	0	**149**	**15**
2016–17	Bury	13	0	**13**	**0**

CAMERON, Nathan (D) 156 9
H: 6 2 W: 12 04 b.Birmingham 21-11-91
Internationals: England U20.

2009–10	Coventry C	0	0		
2010–11	Coventry C	25	0		
2011–12	Coventry C	14	0		
2012–13	Coventry C	9	0	**48**	**0**
2012–13	*Northampton T*	3	0	**3**	**0**
2013–14	Bury	27	4		
2014–15	Bury	46	2		
2015–16	Bury	28	3		
2016–17	Bury	4	0	**105**	**9**

CLARK, Nicky (F) 194 59
H: 5 8 W: 10 06 b.Bellshill 3-6-91

2009–10	Aberdeen	0	0		
2009–10	*Peterhead*	23	4		
2010–11	Peterhead	24	4	**47**	**8**
2011–12	Queen of the South	30	0		
2012–13	Queen of the South	36	32	**66**	**32**
2013–14	Rangers	23	9		
2014–15	Rangers	33	8		
2015–16	Rangers	22	2	**78**	**19**
2016–17	Bury	3	0	**3**	**0**

Transferred to Dunfermline Ath, August 2016.

COONEY, Ryan (M) 0 0
b. 26-2-00

2016–17	Bury	0	0		

DANNS, Neil (M) 424 65
H: 5 10 W: 10 12 b.Liverpool 23-11-82
Internationals: Guyana Full caps.

2000–01	Blackburn R	0	0		
2001–02	Blackburn R	0	0		
2002–03	Blackburn R	2	0		
2003–04	Blackpool	12	2		
2003–04	Blackburn R	1	0		
2003–04	*Hartlepool U*	9	1	**9**	**1**
2004–05	Blackburn R	0	0	**3**	**0**
2004–05	Colchester U	32	11		
2005–06	Colchester U	41	8	**73**	**19**
2006–07	Birmingham C	29	3		
2007–08	Birmingham C	2	0	**31**	**3**
2007–08	Crystal Palace	4	0		
2008–09	Crystal Palace	20	2		
2009–10	Crystal Palace	42	8		
2010–11	Crystal Palace	37	8	**103**	**18**
2011–12	Leicester C	29	5		
2012–13	Leicester C	1	0		
2012–13	*Bristol C*	9	2	**9**	**2**
2012–13	*Huddersfield T*	17	2	**17**	**2**
2013–14	Leicester C	0	0	**30**	**5**
2013–14	Bolton W	33	6		
2014–15	Bolton W	41	1		
2015–16	Bolton W	32	2	**106**	**9**
2016–17	Bury	18	2	**18**	**2**
2016–17	*Blackpool*	13	2	**25**	**4**

DAWSON, Stephen (M) 442 19
H: 5 9 W: 11 09 b.Dublin 4-12-85
Internationals: Republic of Ireland U21.

2003–04	Leicester C	0	0		
2004–05	Leicester C	0	0		
2005–06	Mansfield T	40	1		
2006–07	Mansfield T	34	1		
2007–08	Mansfield T	43	2	**117**	**4**
2008–09	Bury	43	2		
2009–10	Bury	45	4		
2010–11	Leyton Orient	40	2		
2011–12	Leyton Orient	20	1	**60**	**3**
2011–12	Barnsley	12	0		
2012–13	Barnsley	32	4		
2013–14	Barnsley	37	1	**81**	**5**
2014–15	Rochdale	30	0	**30**	**0**
2015–16	Scunthorpe U	23	0		
2016–17	Scunthorpe U	43	1	**66**	**1**
2016–17	Bury	0	0	**88**	**6**

DUDLEY, Anthony (F) 9 0
H: 5 10 W: 11 00 b.Manchester 3-1-96

2013–14	Bury	2	0		
2014–15	Bury	1	0		
2015–16	Bury	3	0		
2016–17	Bury	3	0	**9**	**0**

ETUHU, Kelvin (F) 174 8
H: 5 11 W: 11 02 b.Kano 30-5-88

2005–06	Manchester C	0	0		
2006–07	Manchester C	0	0		
2006–07	*Rochdale*	4	2	**4**	**2**
2007–08	Manchester C	6	1		
2007–08	*Leicester C*	4	0	**4**	**0**
2008–09	Manchester C	4	0		
2009–10	Manchester C	0	0		
2009–10	*Cardiff C*	16	0	**16**	**0**
2010–11	Manchester C	0	0	**10**	**1**
2011–12	Kavala	0	0		
2011–12	Portsmouth	13	1		
2012–13	Portsmouth	0	0	**13**	**1**
2012–13	Barnsley	26	0		
2013–14	Barnsley	20	0	**46**	**0**
2014–15	Bury	43	2		
2015–16	Bury	18	0		
2016–17	Bury	20	2	**81**	**4**

FERRY, Will (M) 0 0

2016–17	Bury	0	0		

HARKER, Rob (M) 0 0
b. 6-3-00

2015–16	Bury	0	0		
2016–17	Bury	0	0		

HOPE, Hallam (F) 94 13
H: 5 10 W: 12 00 b.Manchester 17-3-94
Internationals: England U16, U17, U18, U19.

2010–11	Everton	0	0		
2011–12	Everton	0	0		
2012–13	Everton	0	0		
2013–14	*Northampton T*	3	1	**3**	**1**
2013–14	*Bury*	8	5		
2014–15	Everton	0	0		
2014–15	*Sheffield W*	4	0	**4**	**0**
2014–15	Bury	19	0		
2015–16	Bury	6	0		
2015–16	*Carlisle U*	21	4	**21**	**4**
2016–17	Bury	33	3	**66**	**8**

HULME, Callum (M) 0 0
From Manchester C.

2016–17	Bury	0	0		

ISMAIL, Zeli (M) 80 11
H: 5 8 W: 11 12 b.Kukes 12-12-93
Internationals: England U16, U17.

2010–11	Wolverhampton W	0	0		
2011–12	Wolverhampton W	0	0		
2012–13	Wolverhampton W	0	0		
2012–13	*Milton Keynes D*	7	0	**7**	**0**
2013–14	Wolverhampton W	9	0		
2013–14	*Burton Alb*	15	3		
2014–15	Wolverhampton W	0	0		
2014–15	*Notts Co*	14	4	**14**	**4**
2015–16	Wolverhampton W	0	0	**9**	**0**
2015–16	*Burton Alb*	3	0	**18**	**3**
2015–16	*Oxford U*	5	0	**5**	**0**
2015–16	*Cambridge U*	11	1	**11**	**1**
2016–17	Bury	16	3	**16**	**3**

JONES, Craig (M) 260 34
H: 5 7 W: 10 13 b.Chester 20-3-87

2004–05	Airbus UK	2	2		
2005–06	Airbus UK	7	6	**9**	**8**
2007–08	Rhyl	27	8		
2008–09	Rhyl	14	2	**41**	**10**
2008–09	Connah's Quay	12	0	**12**	**0**
2009–10	New Saints FC	26	7	**26**	**7**
2010–11	Port Talbot	14	1		
2011–12	Port Talbot	7	0	**21**	**1**
2012–13	Bury	25	1		
2013–14	Bury	37	1		
2014–15	Bury	40	3		
2015–16	Bury	36	3		
2016–17	Bury	13	0	**151**	**8**

KAY, Antony (D) 535 44
H: 5 11 W: 11 08 b.Barnsley 21-10-82

1999–2000	Barnsley	0	0		
2000–01	Barnsley	7	0		
2001–02	Barnsley	1	0		
2002–03	Barnsley	16	0		
2003–04	Barnsley	43	3		
2004–05	Barnsley	39	6		
2005–06	Barnsley	36	1		
2006–07	Barnsley	32	1	**174**	**11**
2007–08	Tranmere R	38	6		
2008–09	Tranmere R	44	11	**82**	**17**
2009–10	Huddersfield T	40	6		
2010–11	Huddersfield T	27	3		
2011–12	Huddersfield T	28	1		
2012–13	Huddersfield T	0	0	**95**	**10**
2012–13	Milton Keynes D	33	1		
2013–14	Milton Keynes D	30	2		
2014–15	Milton Keynes D	45	1		
2015–16	Milton Keynes D	34	2	**142**	**6**
2016–17	Bury	42	0	**42**	**0**

LAINTON, Robert (G) 53 0
H: 6 2 W: 12 06 b.Ashton-under-Lyne 12-10-89

2009–10	Bolton W	0	0		
2010–11	Bolton W	0	0		
2011–12	Bolton W	0	0		
2012–13	Bolton W	0	0		
2013–14	Bury	4	0		
2013–14	*Burton Alb*	14	0	**14**	**0**
2014–15	Bury	17	0		
2015–16	Bury	10	0		
2016–17	Bury	7	0	**38**	**0**
2016–17	*Cheltenham T*	1	0	**1**	**0**

LEIGH, Greg (D) 89 3
H: 5 11 b.Manchester 30-9-94
Internationals: England U19.

2013–14	Manchester C	0	0		
2014–15	Manchester C	0	0		
2014–15	*Crewe Alex*	38	1	**38**	**1**
2015–16	Bradford C	6	1	**6**	**1**
2016–17	Bury	45	1	**45**	**1**

LOWE, Ryan (F) 586 175
H: 5 10 W: 12 08 b.Liverpool 18-9-78

2000–01	Shrewsbury T	30	4		
2001–02	Shrewsbury T	38	7		
2002–03	Shrewsbury T	39	9		
2003–04	Shrewsbury T	0	0		
2004–05	Shrewsbury T	30	3	**137**	**23**
2004–05	Chester C	8	4		
2005–06	Chester C	32	10		
2005–06	Crewe Alex	0	0		
2006–07	Crewe Alex	37	8		
2007–08	Crewe Alex	27	4		
2007–08	*Stockport Co*	4	0	**4**	**0**
2008–09	Chester C	45	16	**85**	**30**
2009–10	Bury	39	18		
2010–11	Bury	46	27		
2011–12	Bury	5	4		

2011–12 Sheffield W 26 8
2012–13 Sheffield W 0 0 **26 8**
2012–13 Milton Keynes D 42 11 **42 11**
2013–14 Tranmere R 45 19 **45 19**
2013–14 Bury 0 0
2014–15 Bury 34 9
2015–16 Bury 19 6
2015–16 *Crewe Alex* 6 2
2016–17 Crewe Alex 22 5 **92 19**
2016–17 Bury 12 1 **155 65**

MACKRETH, Jack (M) **3 0**
H: 5 11 W: 10 10 b.Liverpool 13-4-92
From Tranmere R, Barrow, Macclesfield T, Grimsby T.
2016–17 Bury 3 0 **3 0**

MAHER, Niall (D) **32 0**
b.Manchester 31-7-95
2014–15 Bolton W 0 0
2014–15 *Blackpool* 10 0 **10 0**
2015–16 Bolton W 5 0 **5 0**
2016–17 Bury 17 0 **17 0**

MAYOR, Danny (M) **228 23**
H: 6 0 W: 11 12 b.Leyland 18-10-90
2008–09 Preston NE 0 0
2008–09 *Tranmere R* 3 0 **3 0**
2009–10 Preston NE 7 0
2010–11 Preston NE 21 0
2011–12 Preston NE 36 2
2012–13 Preston NE 0 0 **64 2**
2012–13 Sheffield W 8 0
2012–13 *Southend U* 5 0 **5 0**
2013–14 Sheffield W 0 0 **8 0**
2013–14 Bury 39 5
2014–15 Bury 44 8
2015–16 Bury 44 5
2016–17 Bury 21 3 **148 21**

MELLIS, Jacob (M) **171 13**
H: 5 11 W: 10 11 b.Nottingham 8-1-91
Internationals: England U16, U17, U19.
2009–10 Chelsea 0 0
2009–10 *Southampton* 12 0 **12 0**
2010–11 Chelsea 0 0
2010–11 *Barnsley* 15 2
2012–13 Barnsley 36 6
2013–14 Barnsley 30 2 **81 10**
2014–15 Blackpool 13 0 **13 0**
2014–15 *Oldham Ath* 7 0 **7 0**
2015–16 Bury 23 0
2016–17 Bury 35 3 **58 3**

MILLER, George (F) **29 7**
H: 5 10 W: 10 01 b.Bolton 11-8-98
2015–16 Bury 1 0
2016–17 Bury 28 7 **29 7**

MILLER, Ishmael (F) **227 39**
H: 6 3 W: 14 00 b.Manchester 5-3-87
2005–06 Manchester C 1 0
2006–07 Manchester C 16 0
2007–08 Manchester C 0 0 **17 0**
2007–08 WBA 34 9
2008–09 WBA 15 3
2009–10 WBA 15 2
2010–11 WBA 6 0 **70 14**
2010–11 *QPR* 12 1 **12 1**
2011–12 Nottingham F 21 3
2012–13 Nottingham F 0 0
2012–13 *Middlesbrough* 25 5 **25 5**
2013–14 Nottingham F 4 0 **25 3**
2013–14 *Yeovil T* 19 10 **19 10**
2014–15 Blackpool 22 2 **22 2**
2014–15 Huddersfield T 16 3
2015–16 Huddersfield T 18 1 **34 4**
2016–17 Bury 3 0 **3 0**

OBI, Chuckwuemeka (D) **0 0**
b. 6-6-01
2016–17 Bury 0 0

PENNANT, Jermaine (M) **340 24**
H: 5 9 W: 10 06 b.Nottingham 15-1-83
Internationals: England U21.
1998–99 Notts Co 0 0
1998–99 Arsenal 0 0
1999–2000 Arsenal 0 0
2000–01 Arsenal 0 0
2001–02 Arsenal 0 0
2001–02 *Watford* 9 2
2002–03 Arsenal 5 3
2002–03 *Watford* 12 0 **21 2**
2003–04 Arsenal 0 0
2003–04 *Leeds U* 36 2 **36 2**
2004–05 Arsenal 7 0 **12 3**
2004–05 Birmingham C 12 0
2005–06 Birmingham C 38 2 **50 2**
2006–07 Liverpool 34 1
2007–08 Liverpool 18 2
2008–09 Liverpool 3 0 **55 3**
2008–09 *Portsmouth* 13 0 **13 0**
2009–10 Zaragoza 25 0 **25 0**
2010–11 Stoke C 29 3
2011–12 Stoke C 27 0
2012–13 Stoke C 1 0
2012–13 *Wolverhampton W* 15 0 **15 0**
2013–14 Stoke C 8 1 **65 4**
2014 Pune C 7 0 **7 0**
2014–15 Wigan Ath 13 3 **13 3**
2016 Tampines R 21 5 **21 5**
2016–17 Bury 7 0 **7 0**

RACHUBKA, Paul (G) **329 0**
H: 6 1 W: 13 05 b.San Luis Opispo 21-5-81
Internationals: England U16, U18, U20.
1999–2000 Manchester U 0 0
2000–01 Manchester U 1 0
2001–02 Manchester U 0 0 **1 0**
2001–02 *Oldham Ath* 16 0
2001–02 Charlton Ath 0 0
2002–03 Charlton Ath 0 0
2003–04 Charlton Ath 0 0
2003–04 *Huddersfield T* 13 0
2004–05 Charlton Ath 0 0
2004–05 *Milton Keynes D* 4 0 **4 0**
2004–05 *Northampton T* 10 0 **10 0**
2004–05 Huddersfield T 29 0
2005–06 Huddersfield T 34 0
2006–07 Huddersfield T 0 0 **76 0**
2006–07 *Peterborough U* 4 0 **4 0**
2006–07 *Blackpool* 8 0
2007–08 Blackpool 46 0
2008–09 Blackpool 42 0
2009–10 Blackpool 20 0
2010–11 Blackpool 2 0 **118 0**
2011–12 Leeds U 6 0
2011–12 *Tranmere R* 10 0 **10 0**
2011–12 *Leyton Orient* 8 0 **8 0**
2012–13 Leeds U 0 0 **6 0**
2012–13 *Accrington S* 21 0 **21 0**
2013–14 Oldham Ath 10 0
2014–15 Oldham Ath 22 0 **48 0**
2014–15 Crewe Alex 15 0 **15 0**
2015–16 Bolton W 7 0 **7 0**
2016–17 Bury 1 0 **1 0**

STYLES, Callum (F) **14 0**
b. 28-3-00
2015–16 Bury 1 0
2016–17 Bury 13 0 **14 0**

TUTTE, Andrew (M) **212 21**
H: 5 9 W: 10 10 b.Huyton 21-9-90
Internationals: England U19, U20.
2007–08 Manchester C 0 0
2008–09 Manchester C 0 0
2009–10 Manchester C 0 0
2010–11 Manchester C 0 0
2010–11 *Rochdale* 7 0
2010–11 *Shrewsbury T* 2 0 **2 0**
2010–11 *Yeovil T* 15 2 **15 2**
2011–12 Rochdale 40 1
2012–13 Rochdale 37 7
2013–14 Rochdale 11 2 **95 10**
2013–14 Bury 19 1
2014–15 Bury 42 3
2015–16 Bury 22 4
2016–17 Bury 17 1 **100 9**

VAUGHAN, James (F) **222 71**
H: 5 11 W: 13 00 b.Birmingham 14-7-88
Internationals: England U17, U19, U21.
2004–05 Everton 2 1
2005–06 Everton 1 0
2006–07 Everton 14 4
2007–08 Everton 8 1
2008–09 Everton 13 0
2009–10 Everton 8 1
2009–10 *Derby Co* 2 0 **2 0**
2010–11 Everton 1 0 **47 7**
2010–11 *Crystal Palace* 30 9 **30 9**
2011–12 Norwich C 5 0
2012–13 Norwich C 0 0 **5 0**
2012–13 *Huddersfield T* 33 14
2013–14 Huddersfield T 23 10
2014–15 Huddersfield T 26 7
2015–16 Huddersfield T 4 0 **86 31**
2015–16 *Birmingham C* 15 0 **15 0**
2016–17 Bury 37 24 **37 24**

WILLIAMS, Ben (G) **374 0**
H: 6 0 W: 13 01 b.Manchester 27-8-82
2001–02 Manchester U 0 0
2002–03 Manchester U 0 0
2002–03 *Coventry C* 0 0
2002–03 *Chesterfield* 14 0 **14 0**
2003–04 Manchester U 0 0
2003–04 *Crewe Alex* 10 0
2004–05 Crewe Alex 23 0
2005–06 Crewe Alex 17 0
2006–07 Crewe Alex 39 0
2007–08 Crewe Alex 46 0 **135 0**
2008–09 Carlisle U 31 0 **31 0**
2009–10 Colchester U 46 0
2010–11 Colchester U 33 0
2011–12 Colchester U 36 0 **115 0**
2014–15 Bradford C 14 0
2015–16 Bradford C 43 0 **57 0**
2016–17 Bury 22 0 **22 0**

Players retained or with offer of contract
Pope, Thomas John.

Scholars
Alli, Millenic Oluwole Sulaiman; Arizie, Jesse Kerem; Best, Ciaran; Cooney, Ryan Thomas; Dasilva-Olajide, Wealth Abraham; Harker, Robert William; Mulgrew, Charlie Dean; Nyaupembe, Douglas Nqobile; Osgathorpe, William Alex; Styles, Callum John; Turner, Nathan Les.

CAMBRIDGE U (20)

ADAMS, Blair (D) **149 1**
H: 5 11 W: 11 05 b.South Shields 8-9-91
Internationals: England U20.
2010–11 Sunderland 0 0
2011–12 Sunderland 0 0
2011–12 *Brentford* 7 0 **7 0**
2011–12 *Northampton T* 22 0 **22 0**
2012–13 Sunderland 0 0
2012–13 Coventry C 16 0
2013–14 Coventry C 36 0 **52 0**
2014–15 Notts Co 34 1
2015–16 Notts Co 15 0 **49 1**
2015–16 *Mansfield T* 13 0 **13 0**
2016–17 Cambridge U 6 0 **6 0**
Transferred to Hamilton A, January 2017.

BERRY, Luke (D) **122 30**
H: 5 10 W: 11 05 b.Bassingbourn 12-7-92
2014–15 Barnsley 31 1 **31 1**
2015–16 Cambridge U 46 12
2016–17 Cambridge U 45 17 **91 29**

CARROLL, Jake (D) **137 3**
H: 6 0 W: 12 03 b.Dublin 11-1-91
Internationals: Republic of Ireland U18.
2011 St Patricks 7 0
2012 St Patricks 19 1
2013 St Patricks 7 0 **33 1**
2013–14 Huddersfield T 4 0
2013–14 *Bury* 6 1 **6 1**
2014–15 Huddersfield T 2 0 **6 0**
2014–15 *Partick Thistle* 10 0 **10 0**
2015–16 Hartlepool U 41 1
2016–17 Hartlepool U 21 0 **62 1**
2016–17 Cambridge U 20 0 **20 0**

CORR, Barry (F) **274 77**
H: 6 3 W: 12 07 b.Co. Wicklow 2-4-85
2001–02 Leeds U 0 0
2002–03 Leeds U 0 0
2003–04 Leeds U 0 0
2004–05 Leeds U 0 0
2005–06 Sheffield W 16 0
2006–07 Sheffield W 1 0 **17 0**
2006–07 *Bristol C* 3 0 **3 0**
2006–07 *Swindon T* 8 3
2007–08 Swindon T 17 5
2008–09 Swindon T 11 2 **36 10**
2009–10 Exeter C 34 3 **34 3**
2010–11 Southend U 41 18
2011–12 Southend U 0 0
2012–13 Southend U 32 6
2013–14 Southend U 43 12
2014–15 Southend U 39 14 **155 50**
2015–16 Cambridge U 22 12
2016–17 Cambridge U 7 2 **29 14**

COULSON, Josh (D) **76 2**
H: 6 3 W: 11 11 b.Cambridge 28-1-89
2014–15 Cambridge U 46 1
2015–16 Cambridge U 23 1
2016–17 Cambridge U 7 0 **76 2**

DARLING, Harry (D) **0 0**
2016–17 Cambridge U 0 0

DAVIES, Leon (D) **5 0**
b. 21-11-99
2015–16 Cambridge U 0 0
2016–17 Cambridge U 5 0 **5 0**

DUNK, Harrison (M) **115 8**
H: 6 0 W: 11 07 b. 25-10-90
2014–15 Cambridge U 32 2
2015–16 Cambridge U 45 4
2016–17 Cambridge U 38 2 **115 8**

DUNNE, James (M) **275 14**
H: 5 11 W: 10 12 b.Bromley 18-9-89
2007–08 Arsenal 0 0
2008–09 Arsenal 0 0
2008–09 *Nottingham F* 0 0
2009–10 Exeter C 23 3
2010–11 Exeter C 42 1
2011–12 Exeter C 45 2 **110 6**
2012–13 Stevenage 42 4
2013–14 Stevenage 13 1 **55 5**
2013–14 *St Johnstone* 13 0 **13 0**
2014–15 Portsmouth 36 1
2015–16 Portsmouth 0 0 **36 1**
2015–16 *Dagenham & R* 9 0 **9 0**
2015–16 Cambridge U 19 1
2016–17 Cambridge U 33 1 **52 2**

ELITO, Medy (M) **219 29**
H: 6 2 W: 13 00 b.Kinshasa 20-3-90
Internationals: England U17, U18, U19.
2007–08 Colchester U 11 1
2008–09 Colchester U 5 0
2009–10 Colchester U 3 0
2009–10 *Cheltenham T* 12 3
2010–11 Colchester U 0 0 **19 1**
2010–11 *Dagenham & R* 10 2
2010–11 *Cheltenham T* 2 0 **14 3**
2011–12 Dagenham & R 24 4
2012–13 Dagenham & R 46 6
2013–14 Dagenham & R 45 7 **125 19**
2015–16 Newport Co 38 1 **38 1**
2016–17 Cambridge U 23 5 **23 5**

FOY, Matt (F) **0 0**
2014–15 Cambridge U 0 0
2015–16 Cambridge U 0 0
2016–17 Cambridge U 0 0

GREGORY, David (G) **1 0**
H: 6 1 W: 11 00 b.Croydon 1-10-94
2016–17 Cambridge U 1 0 **1 0**

HALLIDAY, Bradley (M) **92 2**
H: 5 11 W: 10 10 b.Redcar 10-7-95
2013–14 Middlesbrough 0 0
2014–15 Middlesbrough 0 0
2014–15 *York C* 24 1 **24 1**
2015–16 Middlesbrough 0 0
2015–16 *Hartlepool U* 6 0 **6 0**
2015–16 *Accrington S* 32 0 **32 0**
2016–17 Middlesbrough 0 0
2016–17 Cambridge U 30 1 **30 1**

IKPEAZU, Uche (F) **101 17**
H: 6 3 W: 12 04 b.London 28-2-95
2013–14 Watford 0 0
2013–14 *Crewe Alex* 15 4
2014–15 Watford 0 0
2014–15 *Crewe Alex* 17 2 **32 6**
2014–15 *Doncaster R* 7 0 **7 0**
2015–16 Watford 0 0
2015–16 *Port Vale* 21 5 **21 5**
2015–16 *Blackpool* 12 0 **12 0**
2016–17 Cambridge U 29 6 **29 6**

IRON, Finley (G) **0 0**
2016–17 Cambridge U 0 0

KEANE, Keith (M) **252 8**
H: 5 9 W: 11 01 b.Luton 20-11-86
Internationals: Republic of Ireland U19, U21.
2003–04 Luton T 15 1
2004–05 Luton T 17 0
2005–06 Luton T 10 1
2006–07 Luton T 19 1
2007–08 Luton T 28 1
2008–09 Luton T 40 0 **129 4**
2012–13 Preston NE 26 1
2013–14 Preston NE 38 2
2014–15 Preston NE 0 0 **64 3**
2014–15 *Crawley T* 12 0 **12 0**
2014–15 *Stevenage* 7 0
2015–16 Cambridge U 4 0
2015–16 *Stevenage* 6 1 **13 1**
2016–17 Cambridge U 1 0 **5 0**
2016–17 *Rochdale* 29 0 **29 0**

LEGGE, Leon (D) **258 26**
H: 6 1 W: 11 02 b.Bexhill 1-7-85
2009–10 Brentford 29 2
2010–11 Brentford 30 3
2011–12 Brentford 28 4
2012–13 Brentford 7 0 **94 9**
2012–13 Gillingham 22 2
2013–14 Gillingham 37 2
2014–15 Gillingham 22 4 **81 8**
2015–16 Cambridge U 39 3
2016–17 Cambridge U 44 6 **83 9**

LEWIS, Paul (M) **13 0**
H: 6 1 W: 11 00 b. 17-12-94
Internationals: England C.
From Macclesfield T.
2016–17 Cambridge U 13 0 **13 0**

MARIS, George (F) **26 4**
b.Sheffield 6-3-96
2014–15 Barnsley 2 0
2015–16 Barnsley 1 0 **3 0**
2016–17 Cambridge U 23 4 **23 4**

McGURK, Adam (F) **192 27**
H: 5 9 W: 12 13 b.Larne 24-1-89
Internationals: Northern Ireland U21.
2005–06 Aston Villa 0 0
2006–07 Aston Villa 0 0
2007–08 Aston Villa 0 0
2008–09 Aston Villa 0 0
2009–10 Aston Villa 0 0
From Hednesford T.
2010–11 Tranmere R 21 3
2011–12 Tranmere R 31 4
2012–13 Tranmere R 27 3 **79 10**
2013–14 Burton Alb 34 9
2014–15 Burton Alb 37 6 **71 15**
2015–16 Portsmouth 27 2 **27 2**
2016–17 Cambridge U 15 0 **15 0**

MINGOIA, Piero (M) **171 18**
H: 5 6 W: 10 12 b.Enfield 20-10-91
2010–11 Watford 5 0
2011–12 Watford 0 0
2011–12 *Brentford* 0 0
2012–13 Watford 0 0
2012–13 *Accrington S* 7 1
2013–14 Watford 0 0 **5 0**
2013–14 Accrington S 37 1
2014–15 Accrington S 36 8
2015–16 Accrington S 46 3 **126 13**
2016–17 Cambridge U 40 5 **40 5**

NEWTON, Conor (M) **78 3**
H: 5 11 W: 11 00 b.Whickham 17-10-91
2010–11 Newcastle U 0 0
2011–12 Newcastle U 0 0
2012–13 Newcastle U 0 0
2012–13 *St Mirren* 16 2 **16 2**
2014–15 Rotherham U 13 0 **13 0**
2015–16 Cambridge U 22 0
2016–17 Cambridge U 27 1 **49 1**

NORRIS, Will (G) **69 0**
H: 6 5 W: 11 09 b.Royston 12-7-93
2014–15 Cambridge U 3 0
2015–16 Cambridge U 21 0
2016–17 Cambridge U 45 0 **69 0**

O'NEIL, Liam (D) **95 5**
H: 6 0 W: 12 06 b.Cambridge 31-7-93
2011–12 WBA 0 0
2011–12 *VPS* 14 0 **14 0**
2012–13 WBA 0 0
2013–14 WBA 3 0
2014–15 WBA 0 0 **3 0**
2014–15 *Scunthorpe U* 22 2 **22 2**
2015–16 Chesterfield 26 0
2016–17 Chesterfield 17 2 **43 2**
2016–17 Cambridge U 13 1 **13 1**

PIGOTT, Joe (F) **97 17**
H: 6 0 W: 9 05 b.London 24-11-93
2012–13 Charlton Ath 0 0
2013–14 Charlton Ath 11 0
2013–14 *Gillingham* 7 1 **7 1**
2014–15 Charlton Ath 1 0
2014–15 *Newport Co* 10 3 **10 3**
2014–15 *Southend U* 20 6
2015–16 Charlton Ath 0 0 **12 0**
2015–16 *Southend U* 23 3 **43 9**
2015–16 *Luton T* 15 4 **15 4**
2016–17 Cambridge U 10 0 **10 0**

ROBERTS, Mark (D) **290 24**
H: 6 1 W: 12 00 b.Northwich 16-10-83
2002–03 Crewe Alex 0 0
2003–04 Crewe Alex 0 0
2004–05 Crewe Alex 6 0
2005–06 Crewe Alex 0 0
2005–06 *Chester C* 1 0 **1 0**
2006–07 Crewe Alex 0 0 **6 0**
2007–08 Accrington S 34 0 **34 0**
From Northwich Vic.
2010–11 Stevenage 42 6
2011–12 Stevenage 46 6
2012–13 Stevenage 44 2 **132 14**
2013–14 Fleetwood T 33 3
2014–15 Fleetwood T 27 3 **60 6**
2015–16 Cambridge U 30 2
2016–17 Cambridge U 27 2 **57 4**

TAYLOR, Greg (D) **95 2**
H: 6 1 W: 12 02 b.Bedford 15-1-90
Internationals: England C.
2008–09 Northampton T 0 0
2014–15 Cambridge U 43 0
2015–16 Cambridge U 16 0
2016–17 Cambridge U 36 2 **95 2**

WILLIAMSON, Ben (F) **235 41**
H: 5 11 W: 11 13 b.Lambeth 25-12-88
2010–11 Jerez Industrial 12 8 **12 8**
2010–11 Bournemouth 4 0
2011–12 Bournemouth 0 0 **4 0**
2011–12 Port Vale 35 3
2012–13 Port Vale 33 8
2013–14 Port Vale 38 4
2014–15 Port Vale 43 6 **149 21**
2015–16 Gillingham 9 0 **9 0**
2015–16 *Cambridge U* 28 12
2016–17 Cambridge U 33 0 **61 12**

Scholars
Bell-Toxtle, Fernando Luis; Emmins, Joshua Matthew; Iron, Finley Robert; Lea, Harry James; Mutswunguma, Prince Karikoga; Norville-Williams, Jordan Zion Wilford Jr; Shaw, Stevan; Squire, Samuel Joseph; Watkins, Lee Jacob; Williams, Jordan.

CARDIFF C (21)

ADEYEMI, Tom (M) **218 19**
H: 6 1 W: 12 04 b.Milton Keynes 24-10-91
2008–09 Norwich C 0 0
2009–10 Norwich C 11 0
2010–11 Norwich C 0 0
2010–11 *Bradford C* 34 5 **34 5**
2011–12 Norwich C 0 0
2011–12 *Oldham Ath* 36 2 **36 2**
2012–13 Norwich C 0 0 **11 0**
2012–13 *Brentford* 30 2 **30 2**
2013–14 Birmingham C 35 1 **35 1**
2014–15 Cardiff C 20 1
2015–16 Cardiff C 0 0
2015–16 *Leeds U* 23 2 **23 2**
2016–17 Cardiff C 0 0 **20 1**
2016–17 *Rotherham U* 29 6 **29 6**

AJAYI, Semi (D) **35 1**
H: 6 4 W: 13 00 b.Croydon 9-11-93
Internationals: Nigeria U20.
2012–13 Charlton Ath 0 0
2013–14 Charlton Ath 0 0
2014–15 Arsenal 0 0
2014–15 *Cardiff C* 0 0
2015–16 Cardiff C 0 0
2015–16 *AFC Wimbledon* 5 0 **5 0**
2015–16 *Crewe Alex* 13 0 **13 0**
2016–17 Cardiff C 0 0
2016–17 *Rotherham U* 17 1 **17 1**

BAMBA, Souleymane (D) **272 14**
H: 6 3 W: 14 02 b.Ivry-sur-Seine 13-1-85
Internationals: Ivory Coast Full caps.
2004–05 Paris Saint-Germain 1 0
2005–06 Paris Saint-Germain 0 0 **1 0**
2006–07 Dunfermline Ath 23 0
2007–08 Dunfermline Ath 15 0
2008–09 Dunfermline Ath 1 0 **39 0**
2008–09 Hibernian 29 0
2009–10 Hibernian 30 2
2010–11 Hibernian 16 2 **75 4**
2010–11 Leicester C 16 2
2011–12 Leicester C 36 1 **52 3**
2012–13 Trabzonspor 18 0
2013–14 Trabzonspor 9 0 **27 0**
2014–15 Palermo 1 0 **1 0**
2014–15 *Leeds U* 19 1
2015–16 Leeds U 30 4
2016–17 Leeds U 2 0 **51 5**
2016–17 Cardiff C 26 2 **26 2**

BENNETT, Joe (D) **183 5**
H: 5 10 W: 10 04 b.Rochdale 28-3-90
Internationals: England U19, U20, U21.
2008–09 Middlesbrough 1 0
2009–10 Middlesbrough 12 0
2010–11 Middlesbrough 31 0
2011–12 Middlesbrough 41 1
2012–13 Middlesbrough 0 0 **85 1**
2012–13 Aston Villa 25 0
2013–14 Aston Villa 5 0
2014–15 Brighton & HA 41 1 **41 1**

2015–16	Aston Villa	0	0		
2015–16	*Bournemouth*	0	0		
2015–16	*Sheffield W*	3	0	**3**	**0**
2016–17	Aston Villa	0	0	**30**	**0**
2016–17	Cardiff C	24	3	**24**	**3**

CHAMAKH, Marouane (F) **335** **71**
H: 6 1 W: 11 00 b.Tonnens 10-1-84
Internationals: France U19. Morocco Full caps.

2002–03	Bordeaux	10	1		
2003–04	Bordeaux	25	6		
2004–05	Bordeaux	33	10		
2005–06	Bordeaux	29	7		
2006–07	Bordeaux	29	5		
2007–08	Bordeaux	32	4		
2008–09	Bordeaux	34	13		
2009–10	Bordeaux	38	10	**230**	**56**
2010–11	Arsenal	29	7		
2011–12	Arsenal	11	1		
2012–13	Arsenal	0	0		
2012–13	*West Ham U*	3	0	**3**	**0**
2013–14	Arsenal	0	0	**40**	**8**
2013–14	Crystal Palace	32	5		
2014–15	Crystal Palace	18	2		
2015–16	Crystal Palace	10	0	**60**	**7**
2016–17	Cardiff C	2	0	**2**	**0**

CONNOLLY, Matthew (D) **282** **13**
H: 6 1 W: 11 03 b.Barnet 24-9-87

2005–06	Arsenal	0	0		
2006–07	Arsenal	0	0		
2006–07	*Bournemouth*	5	1	**5**	**1**
2007–08	Arsenal	0	0		
2007–08	*Colchester U*	16	2	**16**	**2**
2007–08	QPR	20	0		
2008–09	QPR	35	0		
2009–10	QPR	19	2		
2010–11	QPR	36	0		
2011–12	QPR	6	0		
2011–12	*Reading*	6	0	**6**	**0**
2012–13	QPR	0	0	**116**	**2**
2012–13	Cardiff C	36	5		
2013–14	Cardiff C	3	0		
2014–15	Cardiff C	23	0		
2014–15	*Watford*	6	1	**6**	**1**
2015–16	Cardiff C	43	1		
2016–17	Cardiff C	28	1	**133**	**7**

ECUELE MANGA, Bruno (D) **249** **13**
H: 6 2 W: 11 11 b.Libreville 16-7-88
Internationals: Gabon Full caps.

2008–09	Angers	29	1		
2009–10	Angers	28	3	**57**	**4**
2010–11	Lorient	31	1		
2011–12	Lorient	32	2		
2012–13	Lorient	17	0		
2013–14	Lorient	35	1		
2014–15	Lorient	3	0	**118**	**4**
2014–15	Cardiff C	29	3		
2015–16	Cardiff C	24	2		
2016–17	Cardiff C	21	0	**74**	**5**

GOUNONGBE, Frederic (F) **173** **77**
H: 6 3 W: 13 05 b.Brussels 1-5-88
Internationals: Benin Full caps.

2009–10	Woluwe-Aventem	23	10		
2010–11	Woluwe-Aventem	15	6		
2011–12	Woluwe-Aventem	33	19	**71**	**35**
2012–13	Zulte-Waregem	0	0		
2012–13	*RWDM Brussels*	28	9		
2013–14	RWDM Brussels	18	11	**46**	**20**
2014–15	Westerlo	17	9		
2015–16	Westerlo	28	13	**45**	**22**
2016–17	Cardiff C	11	0	**11**	**0**

GUNNARSSON, Aron (M) **346** **29**
H: 5 9 W: 11 00 b.Akureyri 22-9-89
Internationals: Iceland U17, U19, U21, Full caps.

2007–08	AZ	1	0	**1**	**0**
2008–09	Coventry C	40	1		
2009–10	Coventry C	40	1		
2010–11	Coventry C	42	4	**122**	**6**
2011–12	Cardiff C	42	5		
2012–13	Cardiff C	45	8		
2013–14	Cardiff C	23	1		
2014–15	Cardiff C	45	4		
2015–16	Cardiff C	28	2		
2016–17	Cardiff C	40	3	**223**	**23**

HALFORD, Greg (D) **442** **45**
H: 6 4 W: 12 10 b.Chelmsford 8-12-84
Internationals: England U20.

2002–03	Colchester U	1	0		
2003–04	Colchester U	18	4		
2004–05	Colchester U	44	4		
2005–06	Colchester U	45	7		
2006–07	Colchester U	28	3	**136**	**18**
2006–07	Reading	3	0	**3**	**0**
2007–08	Sunderland	8	0		
2007–08	*Charlton Ath*	16	2	**16**	**2**
2008–09	Sunderland	0	0		
2008–09	*Sheffield U*	41	4	**41**	**4**
2009–10	Sunderland	0	0	**8**	**0**
2009–10	Wolverhampton W	15	0		
2010–11	Wolverhampton W	2	0	**17**	**0**
2010–11	*Portsmouth*	33	5		
2011–12	Portsmouth	42	7	**75**	**12**
2012–13	Nottingham F	37	3		
2013–14	Nottingham F	36	4		
2014–15	Nottingham F	0	0	**73**	**7**
2014–15	*Brighton & HA*	19	0	**19**	**0**
2015–16	Rotherham U	21	2		
2015–16	*Birmingham C*	3	0	**3**	**0**
2016–17	Rotherham U	14	0	**35**	**2**
2016–17	Cardiff C	16	0	**16**	**0**

HARRIS, Kedeem (M) **94** **6**
H: 5 9 W: 10 08 b.Westminster 8-6-93

2009–10	Wycombe W	2	0		
2010–11	Wycombe W	0	0		
2011–12	Wycombe W	17	0	**19**	**0**
2011–12	Cardiff C	0	0		
2012–13	Cardiff C	0	0		
2013–14	Cardiff C	0	0		
2013–14	*Brentford*	10	1	**10**	**1**
2014–15	Cardiff C	14	1		
2015–16	Cardiff C	3	0		
2015–16	*Barnsley*	11	0	**11**	**0**
2016–17	Cardiff C	37	4	**54**	**5**

HARRIS, Mark (M) **2** **0**
b. 29-12-98
Internationals: Wales U17, U19, U20.

2016–17	Cardiff C	2	0	**2**	**0**

HEALEY, Rhys (M) **53** **12**
H: 5 8 W: 10 10 b.Manchester 6-12-94

2012–13	Cardiff C	0	0		
2013–14	Cardiff C	1	0		
2014–15	Cardiff C	0	0		
2014–15	*Colchester U*	21	4	**21**	**4**
2015–16	Cardiff C	0	0		
2015–16	*Dundee*	7	1	**7**	**1**
2016–17	Newport Co	17	6	**17**	**6**
2016–17	Cardiff C	7	1	**8**	**1**

HOILETT, Junior (M) **259** **32**
H: 5 8 W: 11 00 b.Ottawa 5-6-90
Internationals: Canada Full caps.

2007–08	Blackburn R	0	0		
2007–08	*Paderborn*	12	1	**12**	**1**
2008–09	Blackburn R	0	0		
2008–09	*St Pauli*	21	6	**21**	**6**
2009–10	Blackburn R	23	0		
2010–11	Blackburn R	24	5		
2011–12	Blackburn R	34	7	**81**	**12**
2012–13	QPR	26	1		
2013–14	QPR	35	4		
2014–15	QPR	22	0		
2015–16	QPR	29	6		
2016–17	QPR	0	0	**112**	**11**
2016–17	Cardiff C	33	2	**33**	**2**

HUWS, Emyr (M) **89** **10**
H: 5 10 W: 11 07 b.Llanelli 30-9-93
Internationals: Wales U17, U19, U21, Full caps.

2010–11	Manchester C	0	0		
2011–12	Manchester C	0	0		
2012–13	Manchester C	0	0		
2012–13	*Northampton T*	10	0	**10**	**0**
2013–14	Manchester C	0	0		
2013–14	*Birmingham C*	17	2	**17**	**2**
2014–15	Wigan Ath	16	0		
2015–16	Wigan Ath	0	0	**16**	**0**
2015–16	*Huddersfield T*	30	5	**30**	**5**
2016–17	Cardiff C	3	0	**3**	**0**
2016–17	*Ipswich T*	13	3	**13**	**3**

IMMERS, Lex (M) **274** **61**
H: 6 2 W: 12 04 b.Den Haag 8-6-86

2007–08	Den Haag	31	6		
2008–09	Den Haag	27	3		
2009–10	Den Haag	26	1		
2010–11	Den Haag	30	7		
2011–12	Den Haag	31	8	**145**	**25**
2012–13	Feyenoord	32	12		
2013–14	Feyenoord	33	12		
2014–15	Feyenoord	30	7		
2015–16	Feyenoord	6	0	**101**	**31**
2015–16	*Cardiff C*	15	5		
2016–17	Cardiff C	13	0	**28**	**5**

Transferred to Club Brugge, January 2017.

JOHN, Declan (M) **63** **0**
H: 5 10 W: 11 10 b.Merthyr Tydfil 30-6-95
Internationals: Wales U17, U19, Full caps.

2010–11	Llanelli	1	0	**1**	**0**
2011–12	Afan Lido	5	0	**5**	**0**
2012–13	Cardiff C	0	0		
2013–14	Cardiff C	20	0		
2014–15	Cardiff C	6	0		
2014–15	*Barnsley*	9	0	**9**	**0**
2015–16	Cardiff C	1	0		
2015–16	*Chesterfield*	6	0	**6**	**0**
2016–17	Cardiff C	15	0	**42**	**0**

KENNEDY, Matthew (M) **88** **6**
H: 5 9 W: 10 02 b.Irvine 1-11-94
Internationals: Scotland U16, U17, U18, U19, U21.

2011–12	Kilmarnock	11	0		
2012–13	Kilmarnock	3	0	**14**	**0**
2012–13	Everton	0	0		
2013–14	Everton	0	0		
2013–14	*Tranmere R*	8	0	**8**	**0**
2013–14	*Milton Keynes D*	7	1	**7**	**1**
2014–15	Everton	0	0		
2014–15	*Hibernian*	13	0	**13**	**0**
2014–15	Cardiff C	14	0		
2015–16	Cardiff C	1	0		
2015–16	*Port Vale*	12	0	**12**	**0**
2016–17	Cardiff C	2	0	**17**	**0**
2016–17	*Plymouth Arg*	17	5	**17**	**5**

LAMBERT, Ricky (F) **607** **219**
H: 6 2 W: 14 08 b.Liverpool 16-2-82
Internationals: England Full caps.

1999–2000	Blackpool	3	0		
2000–01	Blackpool	0	0	**3**	**0**
2000–01	Macclesfield T	9	0		
2001–02	Macclesfield T	35	8	**44**	**8**
2001–02	Stockport Co	0	0		
2002–03	Stockport Co	29	2		
2003–04	Stockport Co	40	12		
2004–05	Stockport Co	29	4	**98**	**18**
2004–05	Rochdale	15	6		
2005–06	Rochdale	46	22		
2006–07	Rochdale	3	0	**64**	**28**
2006–07	Bristol R	36	8		
2007–08	Bristol R	46	14		
2008–09	Bristol R	45	29		
2009–10	Bristol R	1	1	**128**	**52**
2009–10	Southampton	45	30		
2010–11	Southampton	45	21		
2011–12	Southampton	42	27		
2012–13	Southampton	38	15		
2013–14	Southampton	37	13	**207**	**106**
2014–15	Liverpool	25	2	**25**	**2**
2015–16	WBA	19	1		
2016–17	WBA	1	0	**20**	**1**
2016–17	Cardiff C	18	4	**18**	**4**

LE FONDRE, Adam (F) **455** **167**
H: 5 9 W: 11 04 b.Stockport 2-12-86

2004–05	Stockport Co	20	4		
2005–06	Stockport Co	22	6		
2006–07	Stockport Co	21	7	**63**	**17**
2006–07	*Rochdale*	7	4		
2007–08	Rochdale	46	16		
2008–09	Rochdale	44	18		
2009–10	Rochdale	1	0	**98**	**38**
2009–10	Rotherham U	44	25		
2010–11	Rotherham U	45	23		
2011–12	Rotherham U	4	4	**93**	**52**
2011–12	Reading	32	12		
2012–13	Reading	34	12		
2013–14	Reading	38	15	**104**	**39**
2014–15	Cardiff C	23	3		
2014–15	*Bolton W*	17	8		
2015–16	Cardiff C	0	0		
2015–16	*Wolverhampton W*	26	3	**26**	**3**
2016–17	Cardiff C	0	0	**23**	**3**
2016–17	*Wigan Ath*	12	1	**12**	**1**
2016–17	*Bolton W*	19	6	**36**	**14**

MEITE, Ibrahim (F) **1** **0**
H: 6 1 W: 11 05 b.Wandsworth 1-6-96

2016–17	Cardiff C	1	0	**1**	**0**

MORRISON, Sean (D) **230** **24**
H: 6 4 W: 14 00 b.Plymouth 8-1-91

2007–08	Swindon T	2	0		
2008–09	Swindon T	20	1		
2009–10	Swindon T	9	1		
2009–10	*Southend U*	8	0	**8**	**0**
2010–11	Swindon T	19	4	**50**	**6**
2010–11	Reading	0	0		
2010–11	*Huddersfield T*	0	0		
2011–12	Reading	0	0		
2011–12	*Huddersfield T*	19	1	**19**	**1**
2012–13	Reading	16	2		
2013–14	Reading	21	1		

2014–15	*Reading*	1	1	**38**	**4**
2014–15	Cardiff C	41	6		
2015–16	Cardiff C	30	3		
2016–17	Cardiff C	44	4	**115**	**13**

MURPHY, Brian (G) **159** **0**
H: 6 0 W: 13 00 b.Waterford 7-5-83
Internationals: Republic of Ireland U16.

2000–01	Manchester C	0	0		
2001–02	Manchester C	0	0		
2002–03	Manchester C	0	0		
2002–03	*Oldham Ath*	0	0		
2002–03	*Peterborough U*	1	0	**1**	**0**
From Waterford					
2003–04	Swansea C	11	0		
2004–05	Swansea C	2	0		
2005–06	Swansea C	0	0		
2006–07	Swansea C	0	0	**13**	**0**
2007	Bohemians	29	0		
2008	Bohemians	33	0		
2009	Bohemians	35	0	**97**	**0**
2009–10	Ipswich T	16	0		
2010–11	Ipswich T	4	0		
2011–12	Ipswich T	0	0	**20**	**0**
2011–12	QPR	0	0		
2012–13	QPR	0	0		
2013–14	QPR	2	0		
2014–15	QPR	0	0	**2**	**0**
2015–16	Portsmouth	21	0		
2016–17	Portsmouth	0	0	**21**	**0**
2016–17	Cardiff C	5	0	**5**	**0**

NOONE, Craig (M) **279** **27**
H: 6 3 W: 12 07 b.Kirkby 17-11-87

2008–09	Plymouth Arg	21	1		
2009–10	Plymouth Arg	17	1		
2009–10	*Exeter C*	7	2	**7**	**2**
2010–11	Plymouth Arg	17	3	**55**	**5**
2010–11	Brighton & HA	23	2		
2011–12	Brighton & HA	33	2		
2012–13	Brighton & HA	3	0	**59**	**4**
2012–13	Cardiff C	32	7		
2013–14	Cardiff C	17	1		
2014–15	Cardiff C	37	1		
2015–16	Cardiff C	38	5		
2016–17	Cardiff C	34	2	**158**	**16**

O'KEEFE, Stuart (M) **106** **7**
H: 5 8 W: 10 00 b.Eye 4-3-91

2008–09	Southend U	3	0		
2009–10	Southend U	7	0		
2010–11	Southend U	0	0	**10**	**0**
2010–11	Crystal Palace	4	0		
2011–12	Crystal Palace	13	0		
2012–13	Crystal Palace	5	0		
2013–14	Crystal Palace	12	1		
2014–15	Crystal Palace	2	0	**36**	**1**
2014–15	*Blackpool*	4	0	**4**	**0**
2014–15	Cardiff C	6	0		
2015–16	Cardiff C	24	2		
2016–17	Cardiff C	8	0	**38**	**2**
2016–17	*Milton Keynes D*	18	4	**18**	**4**

OSHILAJA, Adedeji (D) **88** **6**
H: 5 11 W: 11 10 b.Bermondsey 16-7-93

2012–13	Cardiff C	0	0		
2013–14	Cardiff C	0	0		
2013–14	*Newport Co*	8	0	**8**	**0**
2013–14	*Sheffield W*	2	0	**2**	**0**
2014–15	Cardiff C	0	0		
2014–15	*AFC Wimbledon*	23	1	**23**	**1**
2015–16	Cardiff C	0	0		
2015–16	*Gillingham*	22	3		
2016–17	Cardiff C	0	0		
2016–17	*Gillingham*	33	2	**55**	**5**

PELTIER, Lee (D) **364** **5**
H: 5 10 W: 12 00 b.Liverpool 11-12-86
Internationals: England U18.

2004–05	Liverpool	0	0		
2005–06	Liverpool	0	0		
2006–07	Liverpool	0	0		
2006–07	*Hull C*	7	0	**7**	**0**
2007–08	Liverpool	0	0		
2007–08	Yeovil T	34	0		
2008–09	Yeovil T	35	1	**69**	**1**
2009–10	Huddersfield T	42	0		
2010–11	Huddersfield T	38	1		
2011–12	Leicester C	40	2		
2012–13	Leicester C	0	0	**40**	**2**
2012–13	Leeds U	41	0		
2013–14	Leeds U	25	1	**66**	**1**
2013–14	*Nottingham F*	7	0	**7**	**0**
2014–15	Huddersfield T	11	0	**91**	**1**
2014–15	Cardiff C	15	0		
2015–16	Cardiff C	41	0		
2016–17	Cardiff C	28	0	**84**	**0**

PILKINGTON, Anthony (M) **337** **66**
H: 5 11 W: 12 00 b.Blackburn 3-11-87
Internationals: Republic of Ireland U21, Full caps.

2006–07	Stockport Co	24	5		
2007–08	Stockport Co	29	6		
2008–09	Stockport Co	24	5	**77**	**16**
2008–09	Huddersfield T	16	2		
2009–10	Huddersfield T	43	7		
2010–11	Huddersfield T	31	10	**90**	**19**
2011–12	Norwich C	30	8		
2012–13	Norwich C	30	5		
2013–14	Norwich C	15	1	**75**	**14**
2014–15	Cardiff C	20	1		
2015–16	Cardiff C	41	9		
2016–17	Cardiff C	34	7	**95**	**17**

RALLS, Joe (M) **164** **13**
H: 5 10 W: 11 00 b.Farnborough 13-10-93
Internationals: England U19.

2011–12	Cardiff C	10	1		
2012–13	Cardiff C	4	0		
2013–14	Cardiff C	0	0		
2013–14	*Yeovil T*	37	3	**37**	**3**
2014–15	Cardiff C	28	2		
2015–16	Cardiff C	43	1		
2016–17	Cardiff C	42	6	**127**	**10**

RICHARDS, Ashley (M) **121** **0**
H: 6 1 W: 12 04 b.Swansea 12-4-91
Internationals: Wales U17, U19, U21, Full caps.

2009–10	Swansea C	15	0		
2010–11	Swansea C	6	0		
2011–12	Swansea C	8	0		
2012–13	Swansea C	0	0		
2012–13	*Crystal Palace*	11	0	**11**	**0**
2013–14	Swansea C	0	0		
2013–14	*Huddersfield T*	9	0	**9**	**0**
2014–15	Swansea C	10	0	**39**	**0**
2014–15	*Fulham*	14	0		
2015–16	Fulham	22	0	**36**	**0**
2016–17	Cardiff C	26	0	**26**	**0**

RICHARDSON, Kieran (M) **271** **24**
H: 5 9 W: 11 13 b.Greenwich 21-10-84
Internationals: England U18, U21, Full caps.

2002–03	Manchester U	2	0		
2003–04	Manchester U	0	0		
2004–05	Manchester U	2	0		
2004–05	*WBA*	12	3	**12**	**3**
2005–06	Manchester U	22	1		
2006–07	Manchester U	15	1	**41**	**2**
2007–08	Sunderland	17	3		
2008–09	Sunderland	32	4		
2009–10	Sunderland	29	1		
2010–11	Sunderland	26	4		
2011–12	Sunderland	29	2		
2012–13	Sunderland	1	0	**134**	**14**
2012–13	Fulham	14	1		
2013–14	Fulham	31	4	**45**	**5**
2014–15	Aston Villa	22	0		
2015–16	Aston Villa	11	0		
2016–17	Aston Villa	0	0	**33**	**0**
2016–17	Cardiff C	6	0	**6**	**0**

WHITTINGHAM, Peter (M) **487** **86**
H: 5 10 W: 9 13 b.Nuneaton 8-9-84
Internationals: England U19, U20, U21.

2002–03	Aston Villa	4	0		
2003–04	Aston Villa	32	0		
2004–05	Aston Villa	13	1		
2004–05	*Burnley*	7	0	**7**	**0**
2005–06	Aston Villa	4	0		
2005–06	*Derby Co*	11	0	**11**	**0**
2006–07	Aston Villa	3	0	**56**	**1**
2006–07	Cardiff C	19	4		
2007–08	Cardiff C	41	5		
2008–09	Cardiff C	33	3		
2009–10	Cardiff C	41	20		
2010–11	Cardiff C	45	11		
2011–12	Cardiff C	46	12		
2012–13	Cardiff C	40	8		
2013–14	Cardiff C	32	3		
2014–15	Cardiff C	43	6		
2015–16	Cardiff C	36	6		
2016–17	Cardiff C	37	7	**413**	**85**

WILSON, Ben (G) **19** **0**
H: 6 1 W: 11 09 b.Stanley 9-8-92

2010–11	Sunderland	0	0		
2011–12	Sunderland	0	0		
2013–14	Accrington S	0	0		
2013–14	Cardiff C	0	0		
2014–15	Cardiff C	0	0		
2015–16	Cardiff C	0	0		
2015–16	*AFC Wimbledon*	8	0	**8**	**0**
2016–17	Cardiff C	3	0	**3**	**0**
2016–17	*Rochdale*	8	0	**8**	**0**

ZOHORE, Kenneth (F) **109** **29**
H: 6 4 W: 12 06 b.Copenhagen 31-1-94
Internationals: Denmark U17, U18, U19, U21.

2009–10	Copenhagen	1	0		
2010–11	Copenhagen	15	1		
2011–12	Copenhagen	0	0	**16**	**1**
2011–12	Fiorentina	0	0		
2012–13	Fiorentina	0	0		
2013–14	Fiorentina	0	0		
2013–14	*Brondby*	25	5	**25**	**5**
2014–15	Fiorentina	0	0		
2014–15	*Gothenburg*	11	2	**11**	**2**
2015–16	Odense BK	16	7	**16**	**7**
2015–16	KV Kortrijk	0	0		
2015–16	*Cardiff C*	12	2		
2016–17	Cardiff C	29	12	**41**	**14**

Players retained or with offer of contract
Abbruzzese, Rhys; Byrne, Oliver Joseph; Coxe, Cameron Terry; Evitt-Healey, Rhys; Humphries, Lloyd; Saadi, Idriss; Veale, Jamie Lawrence; Waite, James Tyler; Weymans, Marco; Young, Connor.

Scholars
Baldwin, Lewis Elland; Bodenham, Jack Tomas; Burwood, Warren Robert John; Coughlan, Scott James; Kelly, Isaac Benjamin; Madden, Alfie William; Proctor, Keiron; So, Sani Ibraim; Welch, Jarrad Neil; Williams, Cai; Wootton, Laurence Thomas.

CARLISLE U (22)

ADAMS, Nicky (F) **409** **36**
H: 5 10 W: 11 00 b.Bolton 16-10-86
Internationals: Wales U21.

2005–06	Bury	15	1		
2006–07	Bury	19	1		
2007–08	Bury	43	12		
2008–09	Leicester C	12	0		
2008–09	*Rochdale*	14	1		
2009–10	Leicester C	18	0	**30**	**0**
2009–10	*Leyton Orient*	6	0	**6**	**0**
2010–11	Brentford	7	0	**7**	**0**
2010–11	Rochdale	30	0		
2011–12	Rochdale	41	4	**85**	**5**
2012–13	Crawley T	46	8		
2013–14	Crawley T	24	1	**70**	**9**
2013–14	Rotherham U	15	1	**15**	**1**
2013–14	Bury	0	0		
2014–15	Bury	38	1	**115**	**15**
2015–16	Northampton T	39	3	**39**	**3**
2016–17	Carlisle U	42	3	**42**	**3**

ASAMOAH, Derek (F) **441** **75**
H: 5 6 W: 10 04 b.Ghana 1-5-81
Internationals: Ghana Full caps.

2001–02	Northampton T	40	3		
2002–03	Northampton T	42	4		
2003–04	Northampton T	31	3	**113**	**10**
2004–05	Mansfield T	30	5	**30**	**5**
2004–05	Lincoln C	10	0		
2005–06	Lincoln C	25	2	**35**	**2**
2005–06	*Chester C*	17	8	**17**	**8**
2006–07	Shrewsbury T	39	10	**39**	**10**
2007–08	Nice	0	0		
2008–09	Hamilton A	3	0	**3**	**0**
2009–10	Lokomotiv Sofia	22	6		
2010–11	Lokomotiv Sofia	14	7	**36**	**13**
2011	Pohang Steelers	27	7		
2012	Pohang Steelers	30	6		
2013	Pohang Steelers	0	0	**57**	**13**
2013	Daegu	33	4	**33**	**4**
2014–15	Carlisle U	27	4		
2015–16	Carlisle U	43	6		
2016–17	Carlisle U	8	0	**78**	**10**

ATKINSON, David (D) **32** **0**
b.Shildon 27-4-93

2010–11	Middlesbrough	0	0		
2011–12	Middlesbrough	0	0		
2012–13	Middlesbrough	0	0		
2013–14	Middlesbrough	0	0		
2014–15	Middlesbrough	0	0		
2014–15	*Hartlepool U*	0	0		
2014–15	*Carlisle U*	7	0		
2015–16	Carlisle U	24	0		
2016–17	Carlisle U	1	0	**32**	**0**

BACON, Morgan (G) **0** **0**
H: 6 2 W: 12 13 b. 1-6-98

2015–16	Carlisle U	0	0		
2016–17	Carlisle U	0	0		

BAILEY, James (M)				**209**	**4**
H: 6 0 W: 12 05 b.Bollington 18-9-88					
2006–07	Crewe Alex	0	0		
2007–08	Crewe Alex	1	0		
2008–09	Crewe Alex	24	0		
2009–10	Crewe Alex	21	0	**46**	**0**
2010–11	Derby Co	36	1		
2011–12	Derby Co	22	0		
2012–13	Derby Co	0	0		
2012–13	*Coventry C*	30	2	**30**	**2**
2013–14	Derby Co	1	0	**59**	**1**
2014–15	Barnsley	25	0	**25**	**0**
2015	Pune C	8	1	**8**	**1**
2016	Ottawa Fury	29	0	**29**	**0**
2016–17	Carlisle U	12	0	**12**	**0**

BRISLEY, Shaun (M)				**262**	**11**
H: 6 2 W: 12 02 b.Macclesfield 6-5-90					
2007–08	Macclesfield T	10	2		
2008–09	Macclesfield T	38	0		
2009–10	Macclesfield T	33	1		
2010–11	Macclesfield T	14	0		
2011–12	Macclesfield T	29	3	**124**	**6**
2011–12	Peterborough U	11	0		
2012–13	Peterborough U	28	0		
2013–14	Peterborough U	22	0		
2014–15	Peterborough U	15	1		
2014–15	*Scunthorpe U*	7	0	**7**	**0**
2015–16	Peterborough U	2	0	**78**	**1**
2015–16	*Northampton T*	9	1	**9**	**1**
2015–16	*Leyton Orient*	16	1	**16**	**1**
2016–17	Carlisle U	28	2	**28**	**2**

BROUGH, Patrick (M)				**40**	**0**
H: 5 8 b.Carlisle 20-2-96					
2013–14	Carlisle U	3	0		
2014–15	Carlisle U	29	0		
2015–16	Carlisle U	7	0		
2016–17	Carlisle U	1	0	**40**	**0**

CROCOMBE, Max (G)				**9**	**0**
H: 6 4 b.Auckland 12-8-93					
Internationals: New Zealand U20, U23, Full caps.					
2012–13	Oxford U	4	0		
2013–14	Oxford U	0	0		
2014–15	Oxford U	0	0		
2015–16	Oxford U	0	0	**4**	**0**
2015–16	*Barnet*	5	0	**5**	**0**
2016–17	Carlisle U	0	0		

DEVITT, Jamie (F)				**201**	**22**
H: 5 10 W: 10 05 b.Dublin 6-7-90					
Internationals: Republic of Ireland U21.					
2007–08	Hull C	0	0		
2008–09	Hull C	0	0		
2009–10	Hull C	0	0		
2009–10	*Darlington*	6	1	**6**	**1**
2009–10	*Shrewsbury T*	9	2	**9**	**2**
2009–10	*Grimsby T*	15	5	**15**	**5**
2010–11	Hull C	16	0		
2011–12	Hull C	0	0		
2011–12	*Bradford C*	7	1	**7**	**1**
2011–12	*Accrington S*	16	2	**16**	**2**
2012–13	Hull C	0	0	**16**	**0**
2012–13	*Rotherham U*	1	0	**1**	**0**
2013–14	Chesterfield	7	0	**7**	**0**
2013–14	*Morecambe*	14	2		
2014–15	Morecambe	36	3		
2015–16	Morecambe	39	6	**89**	**11**
2016–17	Carlisle U	35	0	**35**	**0**

ELLIS, Mark (D)				**248**	**17**
H: 6 2 W: 12 04 b.Kingsbridge 30-9-88					
2007–08	Bolton W	0	0		
2009–10	Torquay U	27	3		
2010–11	Torquay U	27	2		
2011–12	Torquay U	35	3	**89**	**8**
2012–13	Crewe Alex	44	5		
2013–14	Crewe Alex	37	1	**81**	**6**
2014–15	Shrewsbury T	32	2		
2015–16	Shrewsbury T	9	1	**41**	**3**
2015–16	Carlisle U	30	0		
2016–17	Carlisle U	7	0	**37**	**0**

GILLESPIE, Mark (G)				**161**	**0**
H: 6 3 W: 13 07 b.Newcastle upon Tyne 27-3-92					
2009–10	Carlisle U	1	0		
2010–11	Carlisle U	0	0		
2011–12	Carlisle U	0	0		
2012–13	Carlisle U	35	0		
2013–14	Carlisle U	15	0		
2014–15	Carlisle U	19	0		
2015–16	Carlisle U	45	0		
2016–17	Carlisle U	46	0	**161**	**0**

GRAINGER, Danny (D)				**250**	**21**
H: 5 10 W: 10 10 b.Kettering 28-7-86					
2008–09	Dundee U	9	0	**9**	**0**
2009–10	St Johnstone	36	1		
2010–11	St Johnstone	33	2	**69**	**3**
2011–12	Hearts	27	0		
2012–13	Hearts	13	2	**40**	**2**
2013–14	St Mirren	13	0	**13**	**0**
2013–14	Dunfermline Ath	11	2	**11**	**2**
2014–15	Carlisle U	41	3		
2015–16	Carlisle U	36	5		
2016–17	Carlisle U	31	6	**108**	**14**

HOLT, Jordan (M)				**0**	**0**
H: 5 9 W: 11 00 b.Carlisle 4-5-94					
2016–17	Carlisle U	0	0		

HOOPER, James (D)				**3**	**0**
H: 5 10 W: 11 09 b. 10-2-97					
2014–15	Rochdale	0	0		
2015–16	Rochdale	2	0	**2**	**0**
From FC United of Manchester, Stockport.					
2016–17	Carlisle U	1	0	**1**	**0**

IBEHRE, Jabo (F)				**532**	**110**
H: 6 2 W: 13 13 b.Islington 28-1-83					
1999–2000	Leyton Orient	3	0		
2000–01	Leyton Orient	5	2		
2001–02	Leyton Orient	28	4		
2002–03	Leyton Orient	25	5		
2003–04	Leyton Orient	35	4		
2004–05	Leyton Orient	19	2		
2005–06	Leyton Orient	33	8		
2006–07	Leyton Orient	30	4		
2007–08	Leyton Orient	31	7	**209**	**36**
2008–09	Walsall	39	10	**39**	**10**
2009–10	Milton Keynes D	10	1		
2009–10	*Southend U*	4	0	**4**	**0**
2009–10	*Stockport Co*	20	5	**20**	**5**
2010–11	Milton Keynes D	42	3		
2011–12	Milton Keynes D	39	8		
2012–13	Milton Keynes D	3	0	**94**	**12**
2012–13	Colchester U	30	8		
2013–14	Colchester U	37	8		
2014–15	Colchester U	5	0	**72**	**16**
2014–15	*Oldham Ath*	11	2	**11**	**2**
2014–15	*Barnsley*	9	2	**9**	**2**
2015–16	Carlisle U	36	15		
2016–17	Carlisle U	38	12	**74**	**27**

JOACHIM, Junior (F)				**20**	**5**
H: 5 10 W: 12 00 b.Ulis 13-5-82					
2011–12	Nancy	0	0		
2012–13	Nancy	2	0		
2012–13	*Bologne*	6	2	**6**	**2**
2013–14	Nancy	0	0		
2014–15	Nancy	0	0	**2**	**0**
2015–16	Wiltz	10	3	**10**	**3**
2016–17	Carlisle U	2	0	**2**	**0**

JONES, Mike (M)				**376**	**35**
H: 5 11 W: 12 04 b.Birkenhead 15-8-87					
2005–06	Tranmere R	1	0		
2006–07	Tranmere R	0	0		
2006–07	*Shrewsbury T*	13	1	**13**	**1**
2007–08	Tranmere R	9	1	**10**	**1**
2008–09	Bury	46	4		
2009–10	Bury	41	5		
2010–11	Bury	42	8		
2011–12	Bury	24	3	**153**	**20**
2011–12	Sheffield W	10	0		
2012–13	Sheffield W	0	0	**10**	**0**
2012–13	Crawley T	40	1		
2013–14	Crawley T	42	3	**82**	**4**
2014–15	Oldham Ath	45	6		
2015–16	Oldham Ath	35	3	**80**	**9**
2016–17	Carlisle U	28	0	**28**	**0**

JOYCE, Luke (M)				**354**	**11**
H: 5 11 W: 12 03 b.Bolton 9-7-87					
2005–06	Wigan Ath	0	0		
2005–06	Carlisle U	0	0		
2006–07	Carlisle U	16	1		
2007–08	Carlisle U	3	1		
2008–09	Carlisle U	7	0		
2009–10	Accrington S	41	1		
2010–11	Accrington S	27	1		
2011–12	Accrington S	43	2		
2012–13	Accrington S	44	0		
2013–14	Accrington S	46	1		
2014–15	Accrington S	45	3	**246**	**8**
2015–16	Carlisle U	37	0		
2016–17	Carlisle U	45	1	**108**	**3**

KENNEDY, Jason (M)				**400**	**39**
H: 6 1 W: 13 02 b.Stockton 11-9-86					
2004–05	Middlesbrough	1	0		
2005–06	Middlesbrough	3	0		
2006–07	Middlesbrough	0	0		
2006–07	*Boston U*	13	1	**13**	**1**
2006–07	*Bury*	12	0	**12**	**0**
2007–08	Middlesbrough	0	0	**4**	**0**
2007–08	*Livingston*	18	2	**18**	**2**
2007–08	*Darlington*	13	2		
2008–09	Darlington	46	5	**59**	**7**
2009–10	Rochdale	42	0		
2010–11	Rochdale	45	4		
2011–12	Rochdale	44	4		
2012–13	Rochdale	46	4		
2013–14	Bradford C	8	1		
2013–14	*Rochdale*	7	0	**184**	**12**
2014–15	Bradford C	20	2	**28**	**3**
2014–15	*Carlisle U*	11	3		
2015–16	Carlisle U	44	2		
2016–17	Carlisle U	27	9	**82**	**14**

LAMBE, Reggie (M)				**179**	**19**
H: 5 7 W: 10 09 b.Bermuda 4-2-91					
Internationals: Bermuda Full caps.					
2009–10	Ipswich T	0	0		
2010–11	Ipswich T	2	0	**2**	**0**
2010–11	*Bristol R*	7	0	**7**	**0**
2012	Toronto	27	2		
2013	Toronto	27	0	**54**	**2**
2014	Nykoping	11	1	**11**	**1**
2014–15	Mansfield T	30	5		
2015–16	Mansfield T	37	5	**67**	**10**
2016–17	Carlisle U	38	6	**38**	**6**

LIDDLE, Gary (D)				**448**	**27**
H: 6 1 W: 12 06 b.Middlesbrough 15-6-86					
2003–04	Middlesbrough	0	0		
2004–05	Middlesbrough	0	0		
2005–06	Middlesbrough	0	0		
2006–07	Hartlepool U	42	3		
2007–08	Hartlepool U	41	2		
2008–09	Hartlepool U	43	0		
2009–10	Hartlepool U	40	3		
2010–11	Hartlepool U	42	6		
2011–12	Hartlepool U	39	4	**247**	**18**
2012–13	Notts Co	46	0		
2013–14	Notts Co	32	4	**78**	**4**
2014–15	Bradford C	41	1		
2015–16	Bradford C	20	2	**61**	**3**
2015–16	Chesterfield	15	0		
2016–17	Chesterfield	26	1	**41**	**1**
2016–17	Carlisle U	21	1	**21**	**1**

McKEE, Joe (M)				**7**	**0**
H: 5 11 W: 10 05 b.Linlithgow 30-10-92					
Internationals: Scotland U19.					
2009–10	Livingston	1	0	**1**	**0**
2009–10	Burnley	0	0		
2010–11	Burnley	0	0		
2011–12	Burnley	0	0		
2011–12	*St Mirren*	2	0	**2**	**0**
2012–13	Bolton W	0	0		
2013–14	Bolton W	0	0		
2016–17	Carlisle U	4	0	**4**	**0**
Transferred to Falkirk, January 2017.					

McQUEEN, Alexander (D)				**25**	**0**
H: 6 2 W: 11 00 b. 24-3-95					
From Tottenham H.					
2015–16	Carlisle U	21	0		
2016–17	Carlisle U	4	0	**25**	**0**

MILLER, Shaun (F)				**289**	**65**
H: 5 10 W: 11 08 b.Alsager 25-9-87					
2006–07	Crewe Alex	7	3		
2007–08	Crewe Alex	15	1		
2008–09	Crewe Alex	33	4		
2009–10	Crewe Alex	33	7		
2010–11	Crewe Alex	42	18		
2011–12	Crewe Alex	33	5	**163**	**38**
2012–13	Sheffield U	15	4		
2013–14	Sheffield U	13	0	**28**	**4**
2013–14	*Shrewsbury T*	8	3	**8**	**3**
2014–15	Coventry C	12	1	**12**	**1**
2014–15	*Crawley T*	5	0	**5**	**0**
2014–15	*York C*	6	0	**6**	**0**
2015–16	Morecambe	37	15	**37**	**15**
2016–17	Carlisle U	30	4	**30**	**4**

MILLER, Tom (D)				**70**	**5**
H: 5 11 W: 11 07 b.Ely 29-6-90					
From Rangers, Dundalk, Newport Co, Lincoln C.					
2015–16	Carlisle U	29	5		
2016–17	Carlisle U	41	0	**70**	**5**

NABI, Samir (M)				**2**	**0**
H: 5 11 W: 12 00 b.Birmingham 16-12-96					
2016	Delhi Dynamos	1	0	**1**	**0**
2016–17	Carlisle U	1	0	**1**	**0**

O'SULLIVAN, John (M) **83 6**
H: 5 11 W: 13 01 b.Birmingham 18-9-93
Internationals: Republic of Ireland U19, U21.
2011–12 Blackburn R 0 0
2012–13 Blackburn R 1 0
2013–14 Blackburn R 0 0
2014–15 Blackburn R 2 0
2014–15 *Accrington S* 13 4
2014–15 *Barnsley* 8 0 **8 0**
2015–16 Blackburn R 2 0
2015–16 *Rochdale* 2 0 **2 0**
2015–16 *Bury* 19 0 **19 0**
2016–17 Blackburn R 0 0 **5 0**
2016–17 *Accrington S* 19 1 **32 5**
2016–17 Carlisle U 17 1 **17 1**

PENN, Russ (M) **287 14**
H: 5 11 W: 12 13 b.Dudley 8-11-85
Internationals: England C.
2009–10 Burton Alb 40 4
2010–11 Burton Alb 41 3 **81 7**
2011–12 Cheltenham T 43 1
2012–13 Cheltenham T 43 1
2013–14 Cheltenham T 19 0 **105 2**
2013–14 York C 21 0
2014–15 York C 45 2
2015–16 York C 34 3 **100 5**
2016–17 Carlisle U 1 0 **1 0**

RAYNES, Michael (D) **367 11**
H: 6 4 W: 12 00 b.Wythenshawe 15-10-87
2004–05 Stockport Co 19 0
2005–06 Stockport Co 25 1
2006–07 Stockport Co 9 0
2007–08 Stockport Co 27 0
2008–09 Stockport Co 35 3
2009–10 Stockport Co 25 1 **140 5**
2009–10 Scunthorpe U 12 0
2010–11 Scunthorpe U 22 0 **34 0**
2011–12 Rotherham U 33 0 **33 0**
2012–13 Oxford U 38 1
2013–14 Oxford U 27 0
2014–15 Oxford U 4 0 **69 1**
2014–15 Mansfield T 10 0 **10 0**
2015–16 Carlisle U 40 3
2016–17 Carlisle U 41 2 **81 5**

SALKELD, Cameron (M) **0 0**
H: 6 0 W: 10 03 b. 1-12-98
2016–17 Carlisle U 0 0

TOMLINSON, Ben (F) **33 6**
H: 5 8 W: 11 11 b.Dinnington 11-9-90
From Worksop T.
2011–12 Macclesfield T 25 6 **25 6**
From Alfreton T, Lincoln C.
2015–16 Barnet 3 0
2016–17 Barnet 3 0 **6 0**
2016–17 Carlisle U 2 0 **2 0**

WARD, Joe (M) **0 0**
H: 6 0 W: 12 02 b. 27-9-96
2015–16 WBA 0 0
2016–17 WBA 0 0
2016–17 Carlisle U 0 0

WRIGHT, Kevin (D) **2 0**
H: 5 9 W: 10 08 b.Waltham Forest 28-12-95
From Chelsea.
2016–17 Carlisle U 2 0 **2 0**
Transferred to Fredrikstad, January 2017.

Players retained or with offer of contract
Adewusi, Samuel Adebola Ife Oluwa; Thompson-Lambe, Reginald Everard Vibart.

Scholars
Ashton, Lee Andrew John; Bacon, Morgan Jonathan Anthony; Breen, Joe; Brown, Max William; Cowburn, Max David; Egan, Jack James; Goldthorpe, Alexis Ewart; Groves, Rhys Alexander; Hall, Kieran James Robert; Holt, Jordan; Hutchinson, Aidan John; Lloyd, Luke Martin; Miller, Jaic Lee; Olsen, Keiron; Salkeld, Cameron John; Taylor, Luke William; Watson, Dean Allan.

CHARLTON ATH (23)

AHEARNE-GRANT, Karlan (F) **33 1**
H: 6 0 b.London 19-12-97
Internationals: England U17, U18, U19.
2014–15 Charlton Ath 5 0
2015–16 Charlton Ath 17 1
2015–16 *Cambridge U* 3 0 **3 0**
2016–17 Charlton Ath 8 0 **30 1**

AJOSE, Nicholas (F) **229 76**
H: 5 8 W: 11 00 b.Bury 7-10-91
Internationals: England U16, U17. Nigeria U20.
2009–10 Manchester U 0 0
2010–11 Manchester U 0 0
2010–11 *Bury* 28 13
2011–12 Peterborough U 2 0
2011–12 *Scunthorpe U* 7 0 **7 0**
2011–12 *Chesterfield* 12 1 **12 1**
2012–13 *Crawley T* 19 2 **19 2**
2012–13 Peterborough U 0 0
2012–13 *Bury* 19 4 **47 17**
2013–14 Peterborough U 22 7 **24 7**
2013–14 *Swindon T* 16 6
2014–15 Leeds U 3 0
2014–15 *Crewe Alex* 27 8 **27 8**
2015–16 Leeds U 0 0 **3 0**
2015–16 Swindon T 38 24
2016–17 Charlton Ath 21 6 **21 6**
2016–17 *Swindon T* 15 5 **69 35**

ARIBO, Joe (M) **19 0**
b.Camberwell 21-7-96
From Staines T.
2015–16 Charlton Ath 0 0
2016–17 Charlton Ath 19 0 **19 0**

BARNES, Aaron (D) **1 0**
b. 14-10-96
2016–17 Charlton Ath 1 0 **1 0**

BAUER, Patrick (D) **100 7**
H: 6 4 W: 13 08 b.Backnang 28-10-92
Internationals: Germany U17, U18, U20.
2010–11 Stuttgart 0 0
2011–12 Stuttgart 0 0
2012–13 Stuttgart 0 0
2013–14 Maritimo 16 0
2014–15 Maritimo 29 2 **45 2**
2015–16 Charlton Ath 19 1
2016–17 Charlton Ath 36 4 **55 5**

BEENEY, Jordan (G) **0 0**
b. 12-5-98
2014–15 Charlton Ath 0 0
2015–16 Charlton Ath 0 0
2016–17 Charlton Ath 0 0

CHARLES, Regan (M) **1 0**
H: 5 9 W: 10 12 b.London 1-3-97
From Arsenal.
2015–16 Charlton Ath 1 0
2016–17 Charlton Ath 0 0 **1 0**

CHICKSEN, Adam (D) **132 3**
H: 5 8 W: 11 09 b.Milton Keynes 27-9-91
2008–09 Milton Keynes D 1 0
2009–10 Milton Keynes D 6 0
2010–11 Milton Keynes D 14 0
2011–12 Milton Keynes D 20 0
2011–12 *Leyton Orient* 3 0
2012–13 Milton Keynes D 32 2
2013–14 Milton Keynes D 0 0 **73 2**
2013–14 Brighton & HA 1 0
2014–15 Brighton & HA 5 0
2014–15 *Gillingham* 3 0
2014–15 *Fleetwood T* 13 0 **13 0**
2015–16 Brighton & HA 1 0 **7 0**
2015–16 *Leyton Orient* 6 0 **9 0**
2015–16 *Gillingham* 6 0 **9 0**
2016–17 Charlton Ath 21 1 **21 1**

CROFTS, Andrew (D) **417 36**
H: 5 10 W: 12 09 b.Chatham 29-5-84
Internationals: Wales U19, U21, Full caps.
2000–01 Gillingham 1 0
2001–02 Gillingham 0 0
2002–03 Gillingham 0 0
2003–04 Gillingham 8 0
2004–05 Gillingham 27 2
2005–06 Gillingham 45 2
2006–07 Gillingham 43 8
2007–08 Gillingham 41 5
2008–09 Gillingham 9 0
2008–09 *Peterborough U* 9 0 **9 0**
2009–10 Brighton & HA 44 5
2010–11 Norwich C 44 8
2011–12 Norwich C 24 0
2012–13 Norwich C 0 0 **68 8**
2012–13 Brighton & HA 24 0
2013–14 Brighton & HA 23 5
2014–15 Brighton & HA 7 0
2015–16 Brighton & HA 17 0 **115 10**
2015–16 *Gillingham* 6 0 **180 17**
2016–17 Charlton Ath 45 1 **45 1**

DIJKSTEEL, Anfernee (M) **0 0**
b. 27-10-96
Internationals: Netherlands U20.
2016–17 Charlton Ath 0 0

FORSTER-CASKEY, Jake (M) **124 11**
H: 5 10 W: 10 00 b.Southend 25-4-94
Internationals: England U16, U17, U18, U20, U21.
2009–10 Brighton & HA 1 0
2010–11 Brighton & HA 0 0
2011–12 Brighton & HA 4 1
2012–13 Brighton & HA 3 0
2012–13 *Oxford U* 16 3 **16 3**
2013–14 Brighton & HA 28 3
2014–15 Brighton & HA 29 1
2015–16 Brighton & HA 2 0 **67 5**
2015–16 *Milton Keynes D* 20 1 **20 1**
2016–17 Charlton Ath 15 2 **15 2**
2016–17 *Rotherham U* 6 0 **6 0**

HANLAN, Brandon (F) **9 0**
H: 6 0 W: 11 07 b.Chelsea 31-5-97
2016–17 Charlton Ath 9 0 **9 0**

HOLMES, Ricky (M) **228 44**
H: 6 2 W: 11 11 b.Southend 19-6-87
Internationals: England C.
2010–11 Barnet 25 2
2011–12 Barnet 41 8
2012–13 Barnet 25 5 **91 15**
2013–14 Portsmouth 40 2
2014–15 Portsmouth 13 0 **53 2**
2014–15 Northampton T 21 5
2015–16 Northampton T 28 9 **49 14**
2016–17 Charlton Ath 35 13 **35 13**

JACKSON, Johnnie (M) **434 70**
H: 6 1 W: 12 00 b.Camden 15-8-82
Internationals: England U17, U18, U20.
1999–2000 Tottenham H 0 0
2000–01 Tottenham H 0 0
2001–02 Tottenham H 0 0
2002–03 Tottenham H 0 0
2002–03 *Swindon T* 13 1 **13 1**
2002–03 *Colchester U* 8 0
2003–04 Tottenham H 11 1
2003–04 *Coventry C* 5 2 **5 2**
2004–05 Tottenham H 8 0
2004–05 *Watford* 15 0 **15 0**
2005–06 Tottenham H 1 0 **20 1**
2005–06 *Derby Co* 6 0 **6 0**
2006–07 Colchester U 32 2
2007–08 Colchester U 46 7
2008–09 Colchester U 29 4
2009–10 Colchester U 0 0 **115 13**
2009–10 Notts Co 24 2 **24 2**
2009–10 *Charlton Ath* 4 0
2010–11 Charlton Ath 30 13
2011–12 Charlton Ath 36 12
2012–13 Charlton Ath 43 12
2013–14 Charlton Ath 38 5
2014–15 Charlton Ath 26 2
2015–16 Charlton Ath 29 3
2016–17 Charlton Ath 30 4 **236 51**

JOHNSON, Roger (D) **473 35**
H: 6 3 W: 11 00 b.Ashford (Middlesex) 28-4-83
1999–2000 Wycombe W 1 0
2000–01 Wycombe W 1 0
2001–02 Wycombe W 7 1
2002–03 Wycombe W 33 3
2003–04 Wycombe W 28 2
2004–05 Wycombe W 42 6
2005–06 Wycombe W 45 7 **157 19**
2006–07 Cardiff C 32 2
2007–08 Cardiff C 42 5
2008–09 Cardiff C 45 5 **119 12**
2009–10 Birmingham C 38 0
2010–11 Birmingham C 38 2 **76 2**
2011–12 Wolverhampton W 27 0
2012–13 Wolverhampton W 42 2
2013–14 Wolverhampton W 0 0
2013–14 *Sheffield W* 17 0 **17 0**
2013–14 *West Ham U* 4 0 **4 0**
2014–15 Wolverhampton W 0 0 **69 2**
2014–15 Charlton Ath 14 0
2015 Pune C 11 0 **11 0**
2015–16 Charlton Ath 4 0
2016–17 Charlton Ath 2 0 **20 0**

KONSA, Ezri (D) **32 0**
H: 6 0 W: 12 02 b. 23-10-97
2015–16 Charlton Ath 0 0
2016–17 Charlton Ath 32 0 **32 0**

LAPSLIE, George (M) **0 0**
b. 5-9-97
2016–17 Charlton Ath 0 0

LENNON, Harry (M) **33 4**
H: 6 3 W: 11 11 b.Barking 16-12-94
2012–13 Charlton Ath 0 0
2013–14 Charlton Ath 2 0
2014–15 Charlton Ath 0 0
2014–15 *Cambridge U* 2 0 **2 0**
2014–15 *Gillingham* 2 0
2015–16 Charlton Ath 19 2
2015–16 *Gillingham* 6 2 **8 2**
2016–17 Charlton Ath 2 0 **23 2**

MAGENNIS, Josh (F) **240 38**
H: 6 2 W: 14 07 b.Bangor 15-8-90
Internationals: Northern Ireland U17, U19, U21, Full caps.
2009–10 Cardiff C 9 0 **9 0**
2009–10 *Grimsby T* 2 0 **2 0**
2010–11 Aberdeen 29 3
2011–12 Aberdeen 23 1
2012–13 Aberdeen 35 5
2013–14 Aberdeen 18 1 **105 10**
2013–14 *St Mirren* 13 0 **13 0**
2014–15 Kilmarnock 38 8
2015–16 Kilmarnock 34 10 **72 18**
2016–17 Charlton Ath 39 10 **39 10**

MITOV, Dimitar (G) **0 0**
H: 6 2 W: 12 00 b. 22-1-97
Internationals: Bulgaria U17, U19.
2014–15 Charlton Ath 0 0
2015–16 Charlton Ath 0 0
2016–17 Charlton Ath 0 0

NOVAK, Lee (F) **267 60**
H: 6 0 W: 12 04 b.Newcastle upon Tyne 28-9-88
2008–09 Huddersfield T 0 0
2009–10 Huddersfield T 37 12
2010–11 Huddersfield T 31 5
2011–12 Huddersfield T 41 13
2012–13 Huddersfield T 35 4 **144 34**
2013–14 Birmingham C 38 9
2014–15 Birmingham C 21 1
2015–16 Birmingham C 0 0 **59 10**
2015–16 *Chesterfield* 35 14 **35 14**
2016–17 Charlton Ath 29 2 **29 2**

PAGE, Lewis (D) **36 0**
b.London 20-5-96
2014–15 West Ham U 0 0
2015–16 West Ham U 0 0
2015–16 *Cambridge U* 6 0 **6 0**
2016–17 West Ham U 0 0
2016–17 *Coventry C* 22 0 **22 0**
2016–17 Charlton Ath 8 0 **8 0**

PEARCE, Jason (D) **374 16**
H: 5 11 W: 12 00 b.Hillingdon 6-12-87
2006–07 Portsmouth 0 0
2007–08 Bournemouth 33 1
2008–09 Bournemouth 44 2
2009–10 Bournemouth 39 1
2010–11 Bournemouth 46 3 **162 7**
2011–12 Portsmouth 43 2 **43 2**
2011–12 Leeds U 0 0
2012–13 Leeds U 33 0
2013–14 Leeds U 45 2
2014–15 Leeds U 21 0 **99 2**
2014–15 Wigan Ath 16 2
2015–16 Wigan Ath 31 2 **47 4**
2016–17 Charlton Ath 23 1 **23 1**

PHILLIPS, Dillon (M) **8 0**
H: 6 2 W: 11 11 b. 11-6-95
2012–13 Charlton Ath 0 0
2013–14 Charlton Ath 0 0
2014–15 Charlton Ath 0 0
2015–16 Charlton Ath 0 0
2016–17 Charlton Ath 8 0 **8 0**

SOLLY, Chris (D) **224 2**
H: 5 8 W: 10 07 b.Rochester 20-1-91
Internationals: England U16, U17.
2008–09 Charlton Ath 1 0
2009–10 Charlton Ath 9 0
2010–11 Charlton Ath 14 1
2011–12 Charlton Ath 44 0
2012–13 Charlton Ath 45 1
2013–14 Charlton Ath 12 0
2014–15 Charlton Ath 38 0
2015–16 Charlton Ath 34 0
2016–17 Charlton Ath 27 0 **224 2**

TEIXEIRA, Jorge (D) **192 17**
H: 6 2 b.Lisbon 27-8-86
2009–10 Maccabi Haifa 24 0 **24 0**
2010–11 Zurich 26 4
2011–12 Zurich 29 0
2012–13 Zurich 12 2
2012–13 *Siena* 9 0 **9 0**
2013–14 Zurich 25 2 **92 8**
2014–15 Standard Liege 12 2
2015–16 Standard Liege 16 1 **28 3**
2015–16 Charlton Ath 19 2
2016–17 Charlton Ath 20 4 **39 6**

THOMAS, Terell (D) **0 0**
H: 6 0 b. 13-10-97
2014–15 Charlton Ath 0 0
2015–16 Charlton Ath 0 0
2016–17 Charlton Ath 0 0

UMERAH, Josh (F) **6 0**
b.Catford 1-4-98
2015–16 Charlton Ath 1 0
2016–17 Charlton Ath 1 0 **2 0**
2016–17 *Kilmarnock* 4 0 **4 0**

VETOKELE, Igor (F) **171 45**
H: 5 8 W: 11 00 b.Ostend 23-3-92
Internationals: Belgium U17, U18, U19, U20, U21. Angola Full caps.
2010–11 Gent 0 0
2011–12 Cercle Brugge 34 8
2012–13 Cercle Brugge 4 1 **38 9**
2012–13 Copenhagen 15 3
2013–14 Copenhagen 29 13 **44 16**
2014–15 Charlton Ath 41 11
2015–16 Charlton Ath 16 1
2016–17 Charlton Ath 0 0 **57 12**
2016–17 *Zulte Waregem* 15 0 **15 0**
2016–17 *Sint-Truidense* 17 8 **17 8**

WATT, Tony (F) **157 33**
H: 5 8 W: 12 00 b.Bellshill 29-3-93
Internationals: Scotland U19, U20, U21, Full caps.
2009–10 Airdrieonians 1 0
2010–11 Airdrieonians 15 3 **16 3**
2011–12 Celtic 3 2
2012–13 Celtic 20 5
2013–14 Celtic 2 0 **25 7**
2013–14 *Lierse* 17 8 **17 8**
2014–15 Standard Liege 13 2 **13 2**
2014–15 Charlton Ath 22 5
2015–16 Charlton Ath 14 2
2015–16 *Cardiff C* 9 2 **9 2**
2015–16 *Blackburn R* 9 1 **9 1**
2016–17 Charlton Ath 16 2 **52 9**
2016–17 *Hearts* 16 1 **16 1**

Players retained or with offer of contract
Avelino, Teixeira Jorge Filipe; Bowry, Daniel Robert; Carter, Matthew James; Ceballos, Prieto Cristian; Edwards, Archie David; Hackett-Fairchild, Reeco Lee; Jordan, Bekithemba; Kashi, Ahmed; Kennedy, Mikhail Caolan Patrick; Maynard-Brewer, Ashley; Sarr, Mouhamadou-Naby; Stow, Harry John; Yamfam, Louis-Michel; Yao, Kenneth William.

Scholars
Bangura-Williams, Mustapha Mohamed; Birch, Daniel George; Carey, Luke Anthony; Dempsey, Ben Michael; Doughty, Alfie Henry; Hall-Anderson, Terrique Dominic; Harvey, Edward James; Maloney, Taylor Peter; Morgan, Albie Robert; Nwosu, Samuel Chibuike; Pollard, Harry Shaw; Prall, Aiden Noyes; Sarpong, Wiredu Brendan Nana Akwasi; Simpson, Romarno Arnelle; Willis, Alexander William; Zemura, Jordan Bekithemba.

Non-Contract
Stow, Harry John.

CHELSEA (24)

ABRAHAM, Tammy (F) **43 23**
H: 6 3 W: 12 13 b.London 2-10-97
Internationals: England U18, U19, U21.
2015–16 Chelsea 2 0
2016–17 Chelsea 0 0 **2 0**
2016–17 *Bristol C* 41 23 **41 23**

AINA, Ola (D) **3 0**
H: 5 9 W: 10 03 b.London 8-10-96
Internationals: England U16, U17, U18, U19, U20.
2015–16 Chelsea 0 0
2016–17 Chelsea 3 0 **3 0**

AKE, Nathan (M) **46 4**
H: 5 11 W: 11 01 b.Den Haag 18-2-95
Internationals: Netherlands U15, U16, U17, U19, U21, Full caps.
2012–13 Chelsea 3 0
2013–14 Chelsea 1 0
2014–15 Chelsea 1 0
2014–15 *Reading* 5 0 **5 0**
2015–16 Chelsea 0 0
2015–16 *Watford* 24 1 **24 1**
2016–17 Chelsea 2 0 **7 0**
2016–17 *Bournemouth* 10 3 **10 3**

ALONSO, Marcus (D) **180 18**
H: 6 2 W: 13 05 b.Madrid 28-12-90
Internationals: Spain U19.
2008–09 RM Castilla 11 0
2009–10 RM Castilla 28 3 **39 3**
2009–10 Real Madrid 1 0 **1 0**
2010–11 Bolton W 4 0
2011–12 Bolton W 5 1
2012–13 Bolton W 26 4 **35 5**
2013–14 Fiorentina 3 0
2013–14 *Sunderland* 16 0 **16 0**
2014–15 Fiorentina 22 1
2015–16 Fiorentina 31 3 **31 3**
2016–17 Fiorentina 2 0 **27 1**
2016–17 Chelsea 31 6 **31 6**

ATSU, Christian (F) **119 19**
H: 5 8 W: 10 09 b.Ada Foah 10-1-92
Internationals: Ghana Full caps.
2010–11 Porto 0 0
2011–12 Porto 0 0
2011–12 *Rio Ave* 27 6 **27 6**
2012–13 Porto 17 1 **17 1**
2013–14 Chelsea 0 0
2013–14 *Vitesse* 26 5 **26 5**
2014–15 Chelsea 0 0
2014–15 *Everton* 5 0 **5 0**
2015–16 Chelsea 0 0
2015–16 *Bournemouth* 0 0
2015–16 *Malaga* 12 2 **12 2**
2016–17 Chelsea 0 0
2016–17 *Newcastle U* 32 5 **32 5**

AZPILICUETA, Cesar (D) **306 4**
H: 5 10 W: 10 13 b.Pamplona 28-8-89
Internationals: Spain U16, U17, U19, U20, U21, U23, Full caps.
2006–07 Osasuna 1 0
2007–08 Osasuna 29 0
2008–09 Osasuna 36 0
2009–10 Osasuna 33 0 **99 0**
2010–11 Marseille 15 0
2011–12 Marseille 30 1
2012–13 Marseille 2 0 **47 1**
2012–13 Chelsea 27 0
2013–14 Chelsea 29 0
2014–15 Chelsea 29 0
2015–16 Chelsea 37 2
2016–17 Chelsea 38 1 **160 3**

BABA, Abdul Rahman (D) **128 2**
H: 5 10 W: 12 00 b.Tamale 2-7-94
Internationals: Ghana U20, Full caps.
2011–12 Asante Kotoko 25 0 **25 0**
2012–13 Greuther Furth 20 0
2013–14 Greuther Furth 22 0
2014–15 Greuther Furth 2 2 **44 2**
2014–15 Augsburg 31 0 **31 0**
2015–16 Chelsea 15 0
2016–17 Chelsea 0 0 **15 0**
2016–17 *Schalke 04* 13 0 **13 0**

BAKER, Lewis (M) **80 18**
b.Luton 25-4-95
Internationals: England U17, U19, U20, U21.
2012–13 Chelsea 0 0
2013–14 Chelsea 0 0
2014–15 Chelsea 0 0
2014–15 *Sheffield W* 4 0 **4 0**
2014–15 *Milton Keynes D* 12 3 **12 3**
2015–16 Chelsea 0 0
2015–16 *Vitesse* 31 5
2016–17 Chelsea 0 0
2016–17 *Vitesse* 33 10 **64 15**

BAMFORD, Patrick (F) **125 44**
H: 6 1 W: 11 02 b.Newark 5-9-93
Internationals: Republic of Ireland U18. England U18, U19, U21.
2010–11 Nottingham F 0 0
2011–12 Nottingham F 2 0 **2 0**
2011–12 Chelsea 0 0
2012–13 Chelsea 0 0
2012–13 *Milton Keynes D* 14 4
2013–14 Chelsea 0 0
2013–14 *Milton Keynes D* 23 14 **37 18**

2013–14	*Derby Co*	21	8	**21**	**8**
2014–15	Chelsea	0	0		
2014–15	*Middlesbrough*	38	17		
2015–16	Chelsea	0	0		
2015–16	*Crystal Palace*	6	0	**6**	**0**
2015–16	*Norwich C*	7	0	**7**	**0**
2016–17	Chelsea	0	0		
2016–17	*Burnley*	6	0	**6**	**0**
2016–17	*Middlesbrough*	8	1	**46**	**18**

BATSHUAYI, Michy (F) **179** **70**
H: 5 11 W: 12 04 b.Brussels 2-10-93
Internationals: Belgium U21, Full caps.

2010–11	Standard Liege	2	0		
2011–12	Standard Liege	23	6		
2012–13	Standard Liege	34	12		
2013–14	Standard Liege	38	21	**97**	**39**
2014–15	Marseille	26	9		
2015–16	Marseille	36	17	**62**	**26**
2016–17	Chelsea	20	5	**20**	**5**

BEENEY, Mitchell (G) **5** **0**
H: 6 0 W: 12 04 b.Leeds 3-10-95
Internationals: England U19.

2014–15	Chelsea	0	0		
2015–16	Chelsea	0	0		
2015–16	*Newport Co*	4	0	**4**	**0**
2016–17	Chelsea	0	0		
2016–17	*Crawley T*	1	0	**1**	**0**

BEGOVIC, Asmir (G) **223** **1**
H: 6 5 W: 13 01 b.Trebinje 20-6-87
Internationals: Canada U20. Bosnia & Herzogovina Full caps.

2006–07	Portsmouth	0	0		
2006–07	*Macclesfield T*	3	0	**3**	**0**
2007–08	Portsmouth	0	0		
2007–08	*Bournemouth*	8	0	**8**	**0**
2007–08	*Yeovil T*	2	0		
2008–09	Portsmouth	2	0		
2008–09	*Yeovil T*	14	0	**16**	**0**
2009–10	Portsmouth	9	0	**11**	**0**
2009–10	*Ipswich T*	6	0	**6**	**0**
2009–10	Stoke C	4	0		
2010–11	Stoke C	28	0		
2011–12	Stoke C	23	0		
2012–13	Stoke C	38	0		
2013–14	Stoke C	32	1		
2014–15	Stoke C	35	0	**160**	**1**
2015–16	Chelsea	17	0		
2016–17	Chelsea	2	0	**19**	**0**

BLACKMAN, Jamal (G) **54** **0**
H: 6 6 W: 14 09 b.Croydon 27-10-93
Internationals: England U16, U17, U18, U19.

2011–12	Chelsea	0	0		
2012–13	Chelsea	0	0		
2013–14	Chelsea	0	0		
2014–15	Chelsea	0	0		
2014–15	*Middlesbrough*	0	0		
2015–16	Chelsea	0	0		
2015–16	*Ostersunds FK*	12	0	**12**	**0**
2016–17	Chelsea	0	0		
2016–17	*Wycombe W*	42	0	**42**	**0**

BOGA, Jeremie (F) **53** **4**
H: 5 8 W: 10 10 b.Marseille 3-1-97
Internationals: France U16, U19, Ivory Coast Full caps.

2014–15	Chelsea	0	0		
2015–16	Chelsea	0	0		
2015–16	*Rennes*	27	2	**27**	**2**
2016–17	Chelsea	0	0		
2016–17	*Granada*	26	2	**26**	**2**

BROWN, Isaiah (M) **59** **8**
H: 6 0 W: 10 13 b.Peterborough 7-1-97
Internationals: England U16, U17, U19, U20.

2012–13	WBA	1	0	**1**	**0**
2013–14	Chelsea	0	0		
2014–15	Chelsea	1	0		
2015–16	Chelsea	0	0		
2015–16	*Vitesse*	22	1	**22**	**1**
2016–17	Chelsea	0	0	**1**	**0**
2016–17	*Rotherham U*	20	3	**20**	**3**
2016–17	*Huddersfield T*	15	4	**15**	**4**

CAHILL, Gary (D) **363** **30**
H: 6 2 W: 12 06 b.Dronfield 19-12-85
Internationals: England U20, U21, Full caps.

2003–04	Aston Villa	0	0		
2004–05	Aston Villa	0	0		
2004–05	*Burnley*	27	1	**27**	**1**
2005–06	Aston Villa	7	1		
2006–07	Aston Villa	20	0		
2007–08	Aston Villa	1	0	**28**	**1**
2007–08	*Sheffield U*	16	2	**16**	**2**
2007–08	Bolton W	13	0		
2008–09	Bolton W	33	3		
2009–10	Bolton W	29	5		
2010–11	Bolton W	36	3		
2011–12	Bolton W	19	2	**130**	**13**
2011–12	Chelsea	10	1		
2012–13	Chelsea	26	2		
2013–14	Chelsea	30	1		
2014–15	Chelsea	36	1		
2015–16	Chelsea	23	2		
2016–17	Chelsea	37	6	**162**	**13**

CHALOBAH, Nathaniel (D) **103** **9**
H: 6 1 W: 11 11 b.Sierra Leone 12-12-94
Internationals: England U16, U17, U19, U20, U21.

2010–11	Chelsea	0	0		
2011–12	Chelsea	0	0		
2012–13	Chelsea	0	0		
2012–13	*Watford*	38	5	**38**	**5**
2013–14	Chelsea	0	0		
2013–14	*Nottingham F*	12	2	**12**	**2**
2013–14	*Middlesbrough*	19	1	**19**	**1**
2014–15	Chelsea	0	0		
2014–15	*Burnley*	4	0	**4**	**0**
2014–15	*Reading*	15	1	**15**	**1**
2015–16	Chelsea	0	0		
2015–16	*Napoli*	5	0	**5**	**0**
2016–17	Chelsea	10	0	**10**	**0**

CHRISTENSEN, Andreas (D) **63** **5**
H: 6 2 W: 11 09 b.Allerod 10-4-96
Internationals: Denmark U16, U17, U19, U21, Full caps.

2012–13	Chelsea	0	0		
2013–14	Chelsea	0	0		
2014–15	Chelsea	1	0		
2015–16	Chelsea	0	0		
2015–16	*Borussia M'gladbach*	31	3		
2016–17	Chelsea	0	0	**1**	**0**
2016–17	Borussia M'gladbach	31	2	**62**	**5**

CLARKE-SALTER, Jake (D) **13** **1**
H: 6 2 W: 11 00 b.Carshalton 22-9-97
Internationals: England U18, U19, U20.

2015–16	Chelsea	1	0		
2016–17	Chelsea	0	0	**1**	**0**
2016–17	*Bristol R*	12	1	**12**	**1**

COLKETT, Charlie (M) **34** **4**
H: 5 9 W: 10 03 b.London 4-9-96
Internationals: England U16, U17, U18, U19, U20.

2015–16	Chelsea	0	0		
2016–17	Chelsea	0	0		
2016–17	*Bristol R*	15	3	**15**	**3**
2016–17	*Swindon T*	19	1	**19**	**1**

COSTA, Diego (F) **318** **133**
H: 6 1 W: 12 04 b.Lagarto 7-10-88
Internationals: Brazil Full caps. Spain Full caps.

2006–07	Penafiel	13	5	**13**	**5**
2006–07	Sporting Braga	7	0	**7**	**0**
2007–08	Celta Vigo	30	6	**30**	**6**
2008–09	Albacete	35	9	**35**	**9**
2009–10	Valladolid	34	8	**34**	**8**
2010–11	Atletico Madrid	28	6		
2011–12	Atletico Madrid	0	0		
2011–12	*Rayo Vallecano*	16	10	**16**	**10**
2012–13	Atletico Madrid	31	10		
2013–14	Atletico Madrid	35	27	**94**	**43**
2014–15	Chelsea	26	20		
2015–16	Chelsea	28	12		
2016–17	Chelsea	35	20	**89**	**52**

COURTOIS, Thibaut (G) **243** **0**
H: 6 6 W: 14 02 b.Bree 11-5-92
Internationals: Belgium U18, Full caps.

2008–09	Genk	1	0		
2009–10	Genk	0	0		
2010–11	Genk	40	0	**41**	**0**
2011–12	Chelsea	0	0		
2011–12	*Atletico Madrid*	37	0		
2012–13	Chelsea	0	0		
2012–13	*Atletico Madrid*	37	0		
2013–14	Chelsea	0	0		
2013–14	*Atletico Madrid*	37	0	**111**	**0**
2014–15	Chelsea	32	0		
2015–16	Chelsea	23	0		
2016–17	Chelsea	36	0	**91**	**0**

CUADRADO, Juan Guillermo (M) **239** **31**
H: 5 10 W: 10 06 b.Necodi 26-5-88
Internationals: Colombia Full caps.

2008	Medellin	21	2		
2009	Medellin	9	0	**30**	**2**
2009–10	Udinese	11	0		
2010–11	Udinese	9	0		
2011–12	Udinese	0	0	**20**	**0**
2011–12	*Lecce*	33	3	**33**	**3**
2012–13	Fiorentina	36	5		
2013–14	Fiorentina	32	11		
2014–15	Fiorentina	17	4	**85**	**20**
2014–15	Chelsea	12	0		
2015–16	Chelsea	1	0		
2015–16	*Juventus*	28	4		
2016–17	Chelsea	0	0	**13**	**0**
2016–17	*Juventus*	30	2	**58**	**6**

CUEVAS, Cristian (M) **63** **2**
H: 5 8 b. 2-4-95
Internationals: Chile U20.

2013–14	Chelsea	0	0		
2013–14	*Vitesse*	0	0		
2013–14	*PSV Eindhoven*	13	1	**13**	**1**
2014–15	Chelsea	0	0		
2014–15	*Universidad de Chile*	4	0	**4**	**0**
2015–16	Chelsea	0	0		
2015–16	*Sint-Truiden*	28	1		
2016–17	Chelsea	0	0		
2016–17	*Sint-Truiden*	18	0	**46**	**1**

DABO, Fankaty (D) **15** **1**
H: 5 11 W: 12 02 b.Southwark 11-10-95
Internationals: England U16, U17, U10.

2016–17	Chelsea	0	0		
2016–17	*Swindon T*	15	1	**15**	**1**

DASILVA, Jay (D) **10** **0**
b. 22-4-98
Internationals: England U16, U17, U18, U19.

2016–17	Chelsea	0	0		
2016–17	*Charlton Ath*	10	0	**10**	**0**

DAVEY, Alex (D) **39** **0**
H: 6 3 W: 13 03 b.Luton 24-11-94
Internationals: Scotland U19.

2012–13	Chelsea	0	0		
2013–14	Chelsea	0	0		
2014–15	Chelsea	0	0		
2014–15	*Scunthorpe U*	13	0	**13**	**0**
2015–16	Chelsea	0	0		
2015–16	*Peterborough U*	7	0	**7**	**0**
2016	*Stabaek*	5	0	**5**	**0**
2016–17	Chelsea	0	0		
2016–17	*Crawley T*	14	0	**14**	**0**

EDUARDO, Carvalho (G) **275** **0**
H: 6 2 W: 13 03 b.Mirandela 19-9-82
Internationals: Portugal U21, Full caps.

2005–06	Braga	0	0		
2006–07	Braga	0	0		
2006–07	*Beira-Mar Aveiro*	15	0	**15**	**0**
2007–08	Braga	0	0		
2007–08	*Victoria Setubal*	30	0	**30**	**0**
2008–09	Braga	30	0		
2009–10	Braga	30	0		
2010–11	Genoa	37	0		
2011–12	Genoa	0	0		
2011–12	*Benfica*	1	0	**1**	**0**
2012–13	Genoa	0	0		
2012–13	*Istanbul BB*	33	0	**33**	**0**
2013–14	Genoa	0	0	**37**	**0**
2013–14	*Braga*	29	0	**89**	**0**
2014–15	Dinamo Zagreb	34	0		
2015–16	Dinamo Zagreb	32	0		
2016–17	Dinamo Zagreb	4	0	**70**	**0**
2016–17	Chelsea	0	0		

FABREGAS, Francesc (M) **408** **76**
H: 5 11 W: 11 01 b.Arenys de Mar 4-5-87
Internationals: Spain Youth, U21, Full caps.

2003–04	Arsenal	0	0		
2004–05	Arsenal	33	2		
2005–06	Arsenal	35	3		
2006–07	Arsenal	38	2		
2007–08	Arsenal	32	7		
2008–09	Arsenal	22	3		
2009–10	Arsenal	27	15		
2010–11	Arsenal	25	3	**212**	**35**
2011–12	Barcelona	28	9		
2012–13	Barcelona	32	11		
2013–14	Barcelona	36	8	**96**	**28**
2014–15	Chelsea	34	3		
2015–16	Chelsea	37	5		
2016–17	Chelsea	29	5	**100**	**13**

FERUZ, Islam (F) **20** **0**
H: 5 4 W: 8 07 b.Somalia 10-9-95
Internationals: Scotland U16, U17, U19, U20, U21.

2011–12	Chelsea	0	0		
2013–14	Chelsea	0	0		
2014–15	Chelsea	0	0		
2014–15	*OFI Crete*	1	0	**1**	**0**
2014–15	*Blackpool*	2	0	**2**	**0**
2015–16	Chelsea	0	0		
2015–16	*Hibernian*	6	0	**6**	**0**
2016–17	Chelsea	0	0		
2016–17	*Mouscron*	7	0	**7**	**0**
2016–17	*Swindon T*	4	0	**4**	**0**

HAZARD, Eden (M) 320 93
H: 5 7 W: 8 11 b.La Louviere 7-1-91
Internationals: Belgium U15, U16, U17, U19, Full caps.

2007–08	Lille	3	0		
2008–09	Lille	30	4		
2009–10	Lille	37	5		
2010–11	Lille	38	7		
2011–12	Lille	38	20	**146**	**36**
2012–13	Chelsea	34	9		
2013–14	Chelsea	35	14		
2014–15	Chelsea	38	14		
2015–16	Chelsea	31	4		
2016–17	Chelsea	36	16	**174**	**57**

HECTOR, Michael (D) 194 12
H: 6 4 W: 12 13 b.Newham 19-7-92
Internationals: Jamaica Full caps.

2009–10	Reading	0	0		
2010–11	Reading	0	0		
2011	*Dundalk*	11	2	**11**	**2**
2011–12	Reading	0	0		
2011–12	*Barnet*	27	2	**27**	**2**
2012–13	Reading	0	0		
2012–13	*Shrewsbury T*	8	0	**8**	**0**
2012–13	*Aldershot T*	8	1	**8**	**1**
2012–13	Cheltenham T	18	1	**18**	**1**
2013–14	Reading	9	0		
2013–14	*Aberdeen*	20	1	**20**	**1**
2014–15	Reading	41	3		
2015–16	Chelsea	0	0		
2015–16	*Reading*	30	1	**80**	**4**
2016–17	Chelsea	0	0		
2016–17	*Ein Frankfurt*	22	1	**22**	**1**

HOUGHTON, Jordan (M) 53 3
H: 6 2 W: 12 13 b.Chertsey 9-11-95
Internationals: England U16, U17, U20.

2015–16	Chelsea	0	0		
2015–16	*Gillingham*	11	1	**11**	**1**
2015–16	*Plymouth Arg*	10	1	**10**	**1**
2016–17	Chelsea	0	0		
2016–17	*Doncaster R*	32	1	**32**	**1**

IVANOVIC, Branislav (M) 389 34
H: 6 0 W: 12 04 b.Sremska Mitreovica 22-2-84
Internationals: Serbia U21, Full caps.

2002–03	Sremska	19	2	**19**	**2**
2003–04	OFK Belgrade	13	0		
2004–05	OFK Belgrade	27	2		
2005–06	OFK Belgrade	15	3	**55**	**5**
2006	Loko Moscow	28	2		
2007	Loko Moscow	26	3	**54**	**5**
2007–08	Chelsea	0	0		
2008–09	Chelsea	16	0		
2009–10	Chelsea	28	1		
2010–11	Chelsea	34	4		
2011–12	Chelsea	29	3		
2012–13	Chelsea	34	5		
2013–14	Chelsea	36	3		
2014–15	Chelsea	38	4		
2015–16	Chelsea	33	2		
2016–17	Chelsea	13	0	**261**	**22**

Transferred to Zenit St Petersburg, February 2017.

KALAS, Tomas (D) 120 2
H: 6 0 W: 12 00 b.Olomouc 15-5-93
Internationals: Czech Republic U17, U18, U19, U21, Full caps.

2009–10	Sigma Olomouc	1	0		
2010–11	Chelsea	0	0		
2010–11	*Sigma Olomouc*	4	0	**5**	**0**
2011–12	Chelsea	0	0		
2012–13	Chelsea	0	0		
2012–13	*Vitesse*	34	1	**34**	**1**
2013–14	Chelsea	2	0		
2014–15	Chelsea	0	0		
2014–15	*Cologne*	0	0		
2014–15	*Middlesbrough*	17	0		
2015–16	Chelsea	0	0		
2015–16	*Middlesbrough*	26	0	**43**	**0**
2016–17	Chelsea	0	0	**2**	**0**
2016–17	*Fulham*	36	1	**36**	**1**

KANE, Todd (D) 88 4
H: 5 11 W: 11 00 b.Huntingdon 17-9-93
Internationals: England U19.

2011–12	Chelsea	0	0		
2012–13	Chelsea	0	0		
2012–13	*Preston NE*	3	0	**3**	**0**
2012–13	*Blackburn R*	14	0		
2013–14	Chelsea	0	0		
2013–14	*Blackburn R*	27	2	**41**	**2**
2014–15	Chelsea	0	0		
2014–15	*Bristol C*	5	0	**5**	**0**
2014–15	*Nottingham F*	8	1	**8**	**1**
2015–16	Chelsea	0	0		
2015–16	*NEC*	31	1	**31**	**1**
2016–17	Chelsea	0	0		

KANTE, Ngolo (M) 185 9
H: 5 7 W: 11 00 b.Paris 29-3-91
Internationals: France Full caps.

2011–12	Boulogne	1	0		
2012–13	Boulogne	37	3	**38**	**3**
2013–14	Caen	38	2		
2014–15	Caen	37	2	**75**	**4**
2015–16	Leicester C	37	1	**37**	**1**
2016–17	Chelsea	35	1	**35**	**1**

KENEDY, Robert (F) 46 3
H: 6 0 W: 12 08 b.Santa Rita do Sapucai 8-2-96
Internationals: Brazil U17, U20.

2013	Fluminense	9	0		
2014	Fluminense	20	2		
2015	Fluminense	1	0	**30**	**2**
2015–16	Chelsea	14	1		
2016–17	Chelsea	1	0	**15**	**1**
2016–17	*Watford*	1	0	**1**	**0**

KIWOMYA, Alex (M) 43 7
H: 5 10 W: 10 08 b.Sheffield 20-5-96
Internationals: England U16, U17, U18, U19.

2014–15	Chelsea	0	0		
2014–15	*Barnsley*	5	0	**5**	**0**
2015–16	Chelsea	0	0		
2015–16	*Fleetwood T*	4	0	**4**	**0**
2016–17	Chelsea	0	0		
2016–17	*Crewe Alex*	34	7	**34**	**7**

LOFTUS-CHEEK, Ruben (M) 22 1
H: 6 4 W: 11 03 b.Lewisham 23-1-96
Internationals: England U16, U17, U19, U21.

2012–13	Chelsea	0	0		
2013–14	Chelsea	0	0		
2014–15	Chelsea	3	0		
2015–16	Chelsea	13	1		
2016–17	Chelsea	6	0	**22**	**1**

LUIZ, David (D) 222 12
H: 6 2 W: 13 03 b.Sao Paulo 22-4-87
Internationals: Brazil U20, Full caps.

2005	Vitoria	0	0		
2006	Vitoria	26	1	**26**	**1**
2006–07	Benfica	10	0		
2007–08	Benfica	8	0		
2008–09	Benfica	19	2		
2009–10	Benfica	29	2		
2010–11	Benfica	16	0	**82**	**4**
2010–11	Chelsea	12	2		
2011–12	Chelsea	20	2		
2012–13	Chelsea	30	2		
2013–14	Chelsea	19	0		
2014–15	Paris Saint-Germain	0	0		
2016–17	PSG	0	0		
2016–17	Chelsea	33	1	**114**	**7**

MATIC, Nemanja (M) 289 16
H: 6 4 W: 13 02 b.Sabac 1-8-88
Internationals: Serbia U21, Full caps.

2005–06	Jedinstvo	7	0		
2006–07	Jedinstvo	9	0	**16**	**0**
2006–07	Kosice	13	1		
2007–08	Kosice	25	1		
2008–09	Kosice	29	2	**67**	**4**
2009–10	Chelsea	2	0		
2010–11	Chelsea	0	0		
2010–11	*Vitesse*	27	2	**27**	**2**
2011–12	Benfica	16	1		
2012–13	Benfica	26	3		
2013–14	Benfica	14	2	**56**	**6**
2013–14	Chelsea	17	0		
2014–15	Chelsea	36	1		
2015–16	Chelsea	33	2		
2016–17	Chelsea	35	1	**123**	**4**

MIAZGA, Matt (D) 59 1
H: 6 4 W: 12 08 b.Clifton, NJ 19-7-95
Internationals: Poland U18. USA U18, U20, U23, Full caps.

2013	New York Red Bulls	1	0		
2014	New York Red Bulls	7	0		
2015	New York Red Bulls	26	1	**34**	**1**
2015–16	Chelsea	2	0		
2016–17	Chelsea	0	0	**2**	**0**
2016–17	*Vitesse*	23	0	**23**	**0**

MOSES, Victor (M) 248 28
H: 5 10 W: 11 07 b.Lagos 12-12-90
Internationals: England U16, U17, U19, U21. Nigeria Full caps.

2007–08	Crystal Palace	13	3		
2008–09	Crystal Palace	27	2		
2009–10	Crystal Palace	18	6	**58**	**11**
2009–10	Wigan Ath	14	1		
2010–11	Wigan Ath	21	1		
2011–12	Wigan Ath	38	6		
2012–13	Wigan Ath	1	0	**74**	**8**
2012–13	Chelsea	23	1		
2013–14	Chelsea	0	0		
2013–14	*Liverpool*	19	1	**19**	**1**
2014–15	Chelsea	0	0		
2014–15	*Stoke C*	19	3	**19**	**3**
2015–16	Chelsea	0	0		
2015–16	*West Ham U*	21	1	**21**	**1**
2016–17	Chelsea	34	3	**57**	**4**

OMERUO, Kenneth (D) 111 1
H: 6 1 W: 12 00 b.Nigeria 17-10-93
Internationals: Nigeria U17, U20, Full caps

2011–12	Chelsea	0	0		
2012–13	Chelsea	0	0		
2012–13	*Den Haag*	27	0	**27**	**0**
2013–14	Chelsea	0	0		
2013–14	*Middlesbrough*	14	0		
2014–15	Chelsea	0	0		
2014–15	*Middlesbrough*	19	0	**33**	**0**
2015–16	Chelsea	0	0		
2015–16	*Kasimpasa*	25	0	**25**	**0**
2016–17	Chelsea	0	0		
2016–17	*Alanyaspor*	26	1	**26**	**1**

OSCAR, Emboaba (M) 169 31
H: 5 11 W: 10 04 b.Americana 9-9-91
Internationals: Brazil U20, U23, Full caps.

2008–09	Sao Paulo	1	0		
2009–10	Sao Paulo	3	0	**4**	**0**
2010–11	Internacional	7	2		
2011–12	Internacional	27	8	**34**	**10**
2012–13	Chelsea	34	4		
2013–14	Chelsea	33	8		
2014–15	Chelsea	28	6		
2015–16	Chelsea	27	3		
2016–17	Chelsea	9	0	**131**	**21**

Transferred to Shanghai SIPG, December 2016.

PALMER, Kasey (M) 24 4
H: 5 11 W: 10 10 b.London 9-11-96
Internationals: England U17, U18, U20, U21.

2015–16	Chelsea	0	0		
2016–17	Chelsea	0	0		
2016–17	*Huddersfield T*	24	4	**24**	**4**

PASALIC, Mario (M) 103 22
H: 6 1 W: 12 04 b.Mainz 9-2-95
Internationals: Croatia U16, U17, U19, U21, Full caps.

2012–13	Hajduk Split	2	0		
2013–14	Hajduk Split	30	11	**32**	**11**
2014–15	Chelsea	0	0		
2014–15	*Elche*	31	3	**31**	**3**
2015–16	Chelsea	0	0		
2015–16	*Monaco*	16	3	**16**	**3**
2016–17	Chelsea	0	0		
2016–17	*AC Milan*	24	5	**24**	**5**

PEDRO, Rodriguez (F) 268 74
H: 5 7 W: 10 01 b.Santa Cruz de Tenerife 28-7-87
Internationals: Spain U21, Full caps.

2007–08	Barcelona	2	0		
2008–09	Barcelona	6	0		
2009–10	Barcelona	34	12		
2010–11	Barcelona	33	13		
2011–12	Barcelona	29	5		
2012–13	Barcelona	28	7		
2013–14	Barcelona	37	15		
2014–15	Barcelona	35	6	**204**	**58**
2015–16	Chelsea	29	7		
2016–17	Chelsea	35	9	**64**	**16**

PIAZON, Lucas (M) 93 19
H: 6 0 W: 11 11 b.Curitiba 20-1-94
Internationals: Brazil U15, U17, U20, U23.

2011–12	Chelsea	0	0		
2012–13	Chelsea	1	0		
2012–13	*Malaga*	11	0	**11**	**0**
2013–14	Chelsea	0	0		
2013–14	*Vitesse*	29	11		
2014–15	Chelsea	0	0		
2014–15	Vitesse	0	0	**29**	**11**
2014–15	*Eintracht Frankfurt*	0	0		
2015–16	Chelsea	0	0		
2015–16	*Reading*	23	3	**23**	**3**
2016–17	Chelsea	0	0	**1**	**0**
2016–17	*Fulham*	29	5	**29**	**5**

REMY, Loic (F) 243 83
H: 6 0 W: 10 04 b.Lyon 2-1-87
Internationals: France U20, U21, Full caps.

2006–07	Lyon	6	0		
2007–08	Lyon	6	0	**12**	**0**
2007–08	*Lens*	10	3	**10**	**3**
2008–09	Nice	32	10		
2009–10	Nice	34	14		

2010–11 Nice 2 1 **68 25**
2010–11 Marseille 31 15
2011–12 Marseille 29 11
2012–13 Marseille 14 1 **74 27**
2012–13 QPR 14 6
2013–14 QPR 0 0
2013–14 *Newcastle U* 26 14 **26 14**
2014–15 QPR 2 0 **16 6**
2014–15 Chelsea 19 7
2015–16 Chelsea 13 1
2016–17 Chelsea 0 0 **32 8**
2016–17 *Crystal Palace* 5 0 **5 0**

RODRIGUEZ, Joao (F) 14 0
b.Cali 12-5-96
Internationals: Colombia U17, U20.
2014–15 Univ Autonoma 0 0
2014–15 Bastia 0 0
2014–15 Chelsea 0 0
2015–16 Chelsea 0 0
2015–16 *St. Truidense* 10 0 **10 0**
2016–17 Chelsea 0 0
2016–17 *Cortulua* 4 0 **4 0**

SOLANKE, Dominic (F) 25 7
H: 6 1 W: 11 11 b.Reading 14-9-97
Internationals: England U16, U17, U18, U19, U21.
2014–15 Chelsea 0 0
2015–16 Chelsea 0 0
2015–16 *Vitesse* 25 7 **25 7**
2016–17 Chelsea 0 0

TERRY, John (D) 498 41
H: 6 1 W: 14 02 b.Barking 7-12-80
Internationals: England U21, Full caps.
1997–98 Chelsea 0 0
1998–99 Chelsea 2 0
1999–2000 Chelsea 4 0
1999–2000 *Nottingham F* 6 0 **6 0**
2000–01 Chelsea 22 1
2001–02 Chelsea 33 1
2002–03 Chelsea 20 3
2003–04 Chelsea 33 2
2004–05 Chelsea 36 3
2005–06 Chelsea 36 4
2006–07 Chelsea 28 1
2007–08 Chelsea 23 1
2008–09 Chelsea 35 1
2009–10 Chelsea 37 2
2010–11 Chelsea 33 3
2011–12 Chelsea 31 6
2012–13 Chelsea 14 4
2013–14 Chelsea 34 2
2014–15 Chelsea 38 5
2015–16 Chelsea 24 1
2016–17 Chelsea 9 1 **492 41**

TOMORI, Fikayo (D) 10 0
H: 6 0 W: 11 11 b.Calgary 19-12-97
Internationals: England U19, U20. Canada U20.
2015–16 Chelsea 1 0
2016–17 Chelsea 0 0 **1 0**
2016–17 *Brighton & HA* 9 0 **9 0**

TRAORE, Bertrand (M) 82 28
H: 5 10 W: 12 00 b.Bob-Dioulasso 6-9-95
Internationals: Burkina Faso U17, Full caps
2013–14 Chelsea 0 0
2013–14 *Vitesse* 15 3
2014–15 Chelsea 0 0
2014–15 *Vitesse* 33 14 **48 17**
2015–16 Chelsea 10 2
2016–17 Chelsea 0 0 **10 2**
2016–17 *Ajax* 24 9 **24 9**

VAN GINKEL, Marco (M) 160 34
H: 6 1 W: 12 11 b.Amersfoort 1-12-92
Internationals: Netherlands U15, U19, U21, Full caps
2009–10 Vitesse 3 0
2010–11 Vitesse 26 5
2011–12 Vitesse 34 5
2012–13 Vitesse 33 8 **96 18**
2013–14 Chelsea 2 0
2014–15 Chelsea 0 0
2014–15 *AC Milan* 17 1 **17 1**
2015–16 Chelsea 0 0
2015–16 *Stoke C* 17 0 **17 0**
2015–16 *PSV Eindhoven* 13 8
2016–17 Chelsea 0 0 **2 0**
2016–17 *PSV Eindhoven* 15 7 **28 15**

WILLIAN, da Silva (M) 266 40
H: 5 9 W: 11 10 b.Ribeirao 9-8-88
Internationals: Brazil U20, Full caps.
2006 Corinthians 5 0
2007 Corinthians 0 0 **5 0**
2008–09 Shakhtar Donetsk 29 5
2009–10 Shakhtar Donetsk 22 5
2010–11 Shakhtar Donetsk 28 3
2011–12 Shakhtar Donetsk 27 5
2012–13 Shakhtar Donetsk 14 2 **120 20**
2012–13 Anzhi Makhachkala 7 1
2013–14 Anzhi Makhachkala 4 0 **11 1**
2013–14 Chelsea 25 4
2014–15 Chelsea 36 2
2015–16 Chelsea 35 5
2016–17 Chelsea 34 8 **130 19**

ZOUMA, Kurt (D) 108 4
H: 6 2 W: 13 04 b.Lyon 27-10-94
Internationals: France U16, U17, U19, U20, U21, Full caps.
2011–12 St Etienne 20 1
2012–13 St Etienne 18 2
2013–14 Chelsea 0 0
2013–14 *St Etienne* 23 0 **61 3**
2014–15 Chelsea 15 0
2015–16 Chelsea 23 1
2016–17 Chelsea 9 0 **47 1**

Players retained or with offer of contract
Ali, Mukhtar Abdullahi; Angban, Bekanty Victorien; Baxter, Nathan; Brown, Charlie; Bulka, Marcin; Chalobah, Trevoh Tom; Christie-Davies, Isaac David; Colley, Joseph; Collins, Bradley Ray; Cumming, James Andrew; Dasilva, Cole Perry; De Souza, Nathan Allan; Delac, Matej; Familia-Castillo, Juan Carlos; Gallagher, Conor; Grant, Joshua; Hinckson-Mars, Malakai Daylan; James, Reece; Jameson, Kyle Alexander; Maddox, Jacob; McCormick, Luke; Mount, Mason; Muheim, Miro Max Maria; Musonda, Charles; Nartey, Richard Nicos Tettey; Oliveira, Dos Santos Wallace; Pantic, Danilo; Quintero, Quintero Josimar Aldair; Sammut, Ruben; Scott, Kyle; St Clair, Harvey; Sterling, Dujon; Suljic, Ali; Taylor-Crossdale, Martell; Thompson, Jared; Ugbo, Ike; Uwakwe, Tariq; Wakefield, Charlie Mark.

Scholars
Guehi, Addji Keaninkin Marc-Israel; McEachran, George James.

CHELTENHAM T (25)

BARTHRAM, Jack (D) 45 1
H: 5 8 W: 11 09 b.Newham 13-10-93
2012–13 Tottenham H 0 0
2013–14 Swindon T 11 0
2014–15 Swindon T 5 0 **16 0**
2016–17 Cheltenham T 29 1 **29 1**

BOWER, Matthew (D) 0 0
H: 6 6 W: 11 05 b. 11-12-98
2016–17 Cheltenham T 0 0

BOYLE, William (D) 46 2
H: 6 2 W: 11 00 b.Garforth 1-9-95
2014–15 Huddersfield T 1 0
2015–16 Huddersfield T 1 0
2015–16 *York C* 12 0 **12 0**
2016–17 Huddersfield T 0 0 **2 0**
2016–17 *Kilmarnock* 11 0 **11 0**
2016–17 Cheltenham T 21 2 **21 2**

CLAYTON, Lewis (G) 0 0
2016–17 Cheltenham T 0 0

COOPER, Alex (M) 77 5
H: 5 11 W: 11 00 b.Inverness 4-11-91
Internationals: Scotland U17.
From Liverpool.
2011–12 Ross Co 0 0
2011–12 *Elgin C* 8 0 **8 0**
2012–13 Ross Co 15 0
2013–14 Ross Co 17 1 **32 1**
2014–15 Falkirk 24 3
2015–16 Falkirk 0 0 **24 3**
2015–16 St Mirren 12 1 **12 1**
2016–17 Cheltenham T 1 0 **1 0**
Transferred to East Fife, March 2017.

CRANSTON, Jordan (D) 47 0
H: 5 11 W: 13 01 b.Wednesfield 11-3-93
Internationals: Wales U19.
2012–13 Wolverhampton W 0 0
2013–14 Wolverhampton W 0 0
2014–15 Notts Co 9 0 **9 0**
2015–16 Cheltenham T 0 0
2016–17 Cheltenham T 38 0 **38 0**

DAVIS, Liam (M) 233 14
H: 5 9 W: 11 07 b.Wandsworth 23-11-86
2005–06 Coventry C 2 0
2006–07 Coventry C 3 0
2006–07 *Peterborough U* 7 0 **7 0**
2007–08 Coventry C 6 0 **11 0**
2008–09 Northampton T 29 4
2009–10 Northampton T 17 2
2010–11 Northampton T 33 2 **79 8**
2011–12 Oxford U 44 2
2012–13 Oxford U 23 1 **67 3**
2013–14 Yeovil T 27 1
2014–15 Yeovil T 8 0 **35 1**
2016 GAIS 18 2 **18 2**
2016–17 Cheltenham T 16 0 **16 0**

DAWSON, Kevin (M) 172 10
H: 5 10 W: 12 08 b.Dublin 30-6-90
Internationals: Republic of Ireland U18.
2011 Shelbourne 26 2
2012 Shelbourne 25 2 **51 4**
2012–13 Yeovil T 20 2
2013–14 Yeovil T 35 1
2014–15 Yeovil T 17 1
2015–16 Yeovil T 10 0
2016–17 Yeovil T 39 2 **121 6**
2016–17 Cheltenham T 0 0

DAYTON, James (M) 160 14
H: 5 8 W: 10 00 b.Enfield 12-12-88
2007–08 Crystal Palace 0 0
2008–09 Crystal Palace 0 0
2008–09 *Yeovil T* 2 0 **2 0**
From Bishop's Stortford, Bromley
2010–11 Kilmarnock 10 2
2011–12 Kilmarnock 29 3
2012–13 Kilmarnock 27 1 **66 6**
2013–14 Oldham Ath 34 3
2014–15 Oldham Ath 17 1 **51 4**
2014–15 *St Mirren* 13 1 **13 1**
2016–17 Cheltenham T 28 3 **28 3**

DOWNES, Aaron (D) 272 20
H: 6 2 W: 13 02 b.Mudgee 15-5-85
Internationals: Australia Youth, U20, U21, U23.
2004–05 Chesterfield 9 2
2005–06 Chesterfield 22 0
2006–07 Chesterfield 45 3
2007–08 Chesterfield 40 2
2008–09 Chesterfield 42 2
2009–10 Chesterfield 7 1
2010–11 Chesterfield 0 0
2011–12 Chesterfield 9 0 **174 10**
2011–12 *Bristol R* 8 0 **8 0**
2012–13 Torquay U 38 5
2013–14 Torquay U 32 4 **70 9**
2016–17 Cheltenham T 20 1 **20 1**

HALL, Asa (M) 222 30
H: 6 2 W: 11 09 b.Sandwell 29-11-86
Internationals: England U19, U20.
2004–05 Birmingham C 0 0
2005–06 Birmingham C 0 0
2005–06 *Boston U* 12 0 **12 0**
2006–07 Birmingham C 0 0
2007–08 Birmingham C 0 0
2007–08 *Shrewsbury T* 15 3
2008–09 Luton T 42 10
2009–10 Luton T 0 0 **42 10**
2010–11 Oxford U 41 4
2011–12 Oxford U 34 7
2012–13 Shrewsbury T 15 2
2012–13 *Aldershot T* 16 0 **16 0**
2013–14 Shrewsbury T 17 0 **47 5**
2013–14 *Oxford U* 19 3 **94 14**
2014–15 Cheltenham T 1 0
2016–17 Cheltenham T 10 1 **11 1**

HOLMAN, Dan (F) 28 1
H: 5 11 W: 11 03 b.Northampton 5-6-90
2014–15 Colchester U 4 0
2015–16 Colchester U 0 0 **4 0**
2015–16 *Woking* 0 0
2015–16 Cheltenham T 0 0
2016–17 Cheltenham T 24 1 **24 1**

JENNINGS, James (D) 87 4
H: 5 10 W: 12 00 b.Manchester 2-9-87
2006–07 Macclesfield T 9 0
2007–08 Macclesfield T 11 0
2008–09 Macclesfield T 18 0 **38 0**
From Kettering T, Cambridge U
2013–14 Mansfield T 33 4 **33 4**
From Forest Green R.
2016–17 Cheltenham T 3 0 **3 0**
2016–17 *Morecambe* 13 0 **13 0**

KITSCHA, Calum (G) 0 0
H: 6 2 W: 12 13 b. 6-4-93
Internationals: England C.
From Histon, Hayes & Yeading.
2016–17 Cheltenham T 0 0

LOVETT, Rhys (G) 0 0
b. 15-5-97
From Rochdale.
2016–17 Cheltenham T 0 0

LYMN, Jordan (D) 0 0
H: 5 10 W: 10 03 b. 21-12-97
2016–17 Cheltenham T 0 0

MORGAN-SMITH, Amari (M) 31 2
H: 6 0 W: 13 06 b.Wolverhampton 3-4-89
Internationals: England C.
2007–08 Stockport Co 1 0 **1 0**
From Ilkeston T, Luton T, Macclesfield T, Kidderminster H.
2014–15 Oldham Ath 13 2 **13 2**
2016–17 Cheltenham T 17 0 **17 0**

MUNNS, Jack (M) 18 1
H: 5 5 W: 10 01 b.Dagenham 18-11-93
2012–13 *Aldershot T* 0 0
2013–14 Charlton Ath 0 0
2014–15 Charlton Ath 0 0
2016–17 Cheltenham T 18 1 **18 1**

O'SHAUGHNESSY, Daniel (D) 28 3
H: 6 1 W: 12 00 b.Riihimaki 14-9-94
Internationals: Finland U16, U17, U18, U20, U21, Full caps.
2014–15 Brentford 0 0
2015–16 Brentford 0 0
2015–16 *FC Midtjylland* 1 0 **1 0**
2016–17 Cheltenham T 27 3 **27 3**

PARSLOW, Daniel (D) 79 1
H: 5 11 W: 12 05 b.Cardiff 11-9-85
Internationals: Wales U17, U19, U21.
2012–13 York C 45 1
2013–14 York C 13 0
2014–15 York C 0 0 **58 1**
2016–17 Cheltenham T 21 0 **21 0**

PELL, Harry (M) 148 16
H: 6 4 W: 13 05 b.Tilbury 21-10-91
2010–11 Bristol R 10 0 **10 0**
2010–11 *Hereford U* 7 0
2011–12 Hereford U 30 3 **37 3**
2012–13 AFC Wimbledon 17 2
2013–14 AFC Wimbledon 33 4
2014–15 AFC Wimbledon 9 0 **59 6**
2016–17 Cheltenham T 42 7 **42 7**

ROWE, James (M) 58 3
H: 5 11 W: 10 02 b.Oxford 21-10-91
2010–11 Reading 0 0
2011–12 Reading 0 0
From Forest Green R
2013–14 Tranmere R 19 1
2014–15 Tranmere R 7 2 **26 3**
2016–17 Cheltenham T 32 0 **32 0**

STORER, Kyle (M) 23 0
H: 5 11 W: 11 11 b.Nuneaton 30-4-87
2014–15 Cheltenham T 0 0
2016–17 Cheltenham T 23 0 **23 0**

THOMAS, Josh (M) 0 0
H: 5 8 W: 9 13 b. 17-4-99
2016–17 Cheltenham T 0 0

WATERS, Billy (M) 71 14
H: 5 9 W: 11 07 b.Epsom 15-10-94
2012–13 Crewe Alex 0 0
2013–14 Crewe Alex 9 0
2014–15 Crewe Alex 16 2 **25 2**
2016–17 Cheltenham T 46 12 **46 12**

WINCHESTER, Carl (D) 140 9
H: 5 10 W: 11 08 b.Belfast 12-4-93
Internationals: Northern Ireland U16, U17, U18, U19, U21, Full caps.
2010–11 Oldham Ath 6 1
2011–12 Oldham Ath 12 0
2012–13 Oldham Ath 9 0
2013–14 Oldham Ath 12 1
2014–15 Oldham Ath 41 4
2015–16 Oldham Ath 31 1
2016–17 Oldham Ath 9 1 **120 8**
2016–17 Cheltenham T 20 1 **20 1**

WRIGHT, Danny (F) 41 9
H: 6 2 W: 13 08 b.Doncaster 10-9-84
From Histon, Cambridge U, Forest Green R, Gateshead, Kidderminster H.
2016–17 Cheltenham T 41 9 **41 9**

Players retained or with offer of contract
Page, Adam Richard.

Scholars
Clayton, Lewis Scott; Cordell, Taylor; Davis, Ryan Alan James; Grimshaw, Ross Nathaniel; Hailwood, Ben Andrew; Hance, Joe Alexander; Hancocks, James Oliver; Kilkenny, Jamie; Llewelyn, Lee Lance; Lloyd, George Robert Lawrence; Nutting, Jacob Wiiliam; Thomas, Joshua James.

Non-Contract
Downes, Aaron Terry.

CHESTERFIELD (26)

ALLINSON, Lloyd (G) 6 0
H: 6 2 W: 13 00 b.Rothwell 7-9-93
2010–11 Huddersfield T 0 0
2011–12 Huddersfield T 0 0
2012–13 Huddersfield T 0 0
2013–14 Huddersfield T 0 0
2014–15 Huddersfield T 0 0
2015–16 Huddersfield T 1 0 **1 0**
2016–17 Chesterfield 5 0 **5 0**

ANYON, Joe (G) 27 0
H: 6 4 W: 14 01 b.Blackpool 29-12-86
Internationals: England U16.
2006–07 Port Vale 0 0
2010–11 Lincoln C 0 0
2010–11 *Morecambe* 0 0
2012–13 Shrewsbury T 0 0
2013–14 Shrewsbury T 11 0
2014–15 Shrewsbury T 0 0 **11 0**
2014–15 Scunthorpe U 0 0
2015–16 Scunthorpe U 8 0
2016–17 Scunthorpe U 8 0 **16 0**
2016–17 Chesterfield 0 0

BARRY, Bradley (D) 58 1
H: 6 0 W: 12 00 b.Hastings 13-12-95
2013–14 Brighton & HA 0 0
2014–15 Brighton & HA 0 0
2015–16 Swindon T 35 0
2016–17 Swindon T 23 1 **58 1**
2016–17 Chesterfield 0 0

BEESLEY, Jake (F) 7 0
H: 6 1 W: 10 08 b.Sheffield 2-12-96
2013–14 Chesterfield 0 0
2014–15 Chesterfield 0 0
2015–16 Chesterfield 0 0
2016–17 Chesterfield 7 0 **7 0**

BROWNELL, Jack (M) 1 0
b.Sheffield
2016–17 Chesterfield 1 0 **1 0**

DALEY, Derek (M) 2 0
b.Limerick 25-8-97
2015–16 Chesterfield 1 0
2016–17 Chesterfield 1 0 **2 0**

DENNIS, Kristian (F) 39 9
H: 5 11 W: 11 00 b.Macclesfield 12-3-90
2007–08 Macclesfield T 1 0
2008–09 Macclesfield T 3 1
2009–10 Macclesfield T 0 0 **4 1**
From Woodley Sports, Mossley, Curzon Ashton, Stockport Co.
2015–16 Chesterfield 0 0
2016–17 Chesterfield 35 8 **35 8**

DIMAIO, Connor (D) 37 1
H: 5 10 W: 11 05 b.Chesterfield 28-1-96
Internationals: Republic of Ireland U16, U17, U19, U21.
2013–14 Sheffield U 3 0
2014–15 Sheffield U 0 0
2015–16 Sheffield U 0 0 **3 0**
2015–16 Chesterfield 11 1
2016–17 Chesterfield 23 0 **34 1**

DONOHUE, Dion (M) 54 1
H: 5 11 W: 10 06 b.Bodedern 26-8-93
2015–16 Chesterfield 17 0
2016–17 Chesterfield 37 1 **54 1**

DUKE, Matt (G) 185 0
H: 6 5 W: 13 04 b.Sheffield 16-7-77
1999–2000 Sheffield U 0 0
2000–01 Sheffield U 0 0
2001–02 Sheffield U 0 0
2004–05 Hull C 2 0
2005–06 Hull C 2 0
2005–06 *Stockport Co* 3 0 **3 0**
2005–06 *Wycombe W* 5 0 **5 0**
2006–07 Hull C 1 0
2007–08 Hull C 3 0
2008–09 Hull C 10 0
2009–10 Hull C 11 0
2010–11 Hull C 21 0 **50 0**
2011–12 Bradford C 18 0
2011–12 *Northampton T* 9 0
2012–13 Bradford C 24 0 **42 0**
2013–14 Northampton T 46 0
2014–15 Northampton T 30 0 **85 0**
From Alfreton T.
2016–17 Chesterfield 0 0

EBANKS-BLAKE, Sylvan (F) 314 95
H: 5 10 W: 13 04 b.Cambridge 29-3-86
Internationals: England U21.
2004–05 Manchester U 0 0
2005–06 Manchester U 0 0
2006–07 Plymouth Arg 41 10
2007–08 Plymouth Arg 25 11 **66 21**
2007–08 Wolverhampton W 20 12
2008–09 Wolverhampton W 41 25
2009–10 Wolverhampton W 23 2
2010–11 Wolverhampton W 30 7
2011–12 Wolverhampton W 23 1
2012–13 Wolverhampton W 40 14 **177 61**
2013–14 Ipswich T 9 0 **9 0**
2014–15 Preston NE 9 1 **9 1**
2015–16 Chesterfield 33 10
2016–17 Shrewsbury T 7 0 **7 0**
2016–17 Chesterfield 13 2 **46 12**

EL FITOURI, Sadiq (D) 2 0
H: 5 11 W: 10 10 b.Benghazi 10-10-94
Internationals: Libya Full caps.
From Salford C, Manchester U.
2016–17 Chesterfield 2 0 **2 0**

EL-FITOUR, Sadiq (D) 0 0
From Manchester U.
2016–17 Chesterfield 0 0

EVANS, Ched (F) 172 58
H: 6 0 W: 12 00 b.Rhyl 28-12-88
Internationals: Wales U21, Full caps.
2006–07 Manchester C 0 0
2007–08 Manchester C 0 0
2007–08 *Norwich C* 28 10 **28 10**
2008–09 Manchester C 16 1 **16 1**
2009–10 Sheffield U 33 4
2010–11 Sheffield U 34 9
2011–12 Sheffield U 36 29 **103 42**
2016–17 Chesterfield 25 5 **25 5**

EVATT, Ian (D) 513 23
H: 6 3 W: 13 12 b.Coventry 19-11-81
1998–99 Derby Co 0 0
1999–2000 Derby Co 0 0
2000–01 Derby Co 1 0
2001–02 *Northampton T* 11 0 **11 0**
2001–02 Derby Co 3 0
2002–03 Derby Co 30 0 **34 0**
2003–04 Chesterfield 43 5
2004–05 Chesterfield 41 4
2005–06 QPR 27 0
2006–07 QPR 0 0 **27 0**
2006–07 Blackpool 44 0
2007–08 Blackpool 29 0
2008–09 Blackpool 33 1
2009–10 Blackpool 36 4
2010–11 Blackpool 38 1
2011–12 Blackpool 39 3
2012–13 Blackpool 11 0 **230 9**
2013–14 Chesterfield 35 1
2014–15 Chesterfield 39 1
2015–16 Chesterfield 23 1
2016–17 Chesterfield 30 2 **211 14**

GARDNER, Dan (M) 109 12
H: 6 1 W: 12 05 b.Manchester 5-4-90
2009–10 Crewe Alex 2 0 **2 0**
From Droylsden, FC Halifax T
2013–14 Chesterfield 16 3
2014–15 Chesterfield 17 1
2014–15 *Tranmere R* 4 2 **4 2**
2015–16 Chesterfield 30 4
2015–16 *Bury* 6 0 **6 0**
2016–17 Chesterfield 34 2 **97 10**

GERMAN, Ricky (F) 7 0
H: 6 2 W: 12 08 b.Brent 13-1-99
2016–17 Chesterfield 7 0 **7 0**

GRAHAM, Liam (D) 10 0
H: 5 11 b.Melbourne 14-8-92
Internationals: New Zealand U20, Full caps.
2012–13 Vicenza 0 0
2012–13 *Ascoli* 1 0 **1 0**
2014–15 Monza 0 0
2014–15 *Pro Patria* 5 0 **5 0**
2015–16 Chesterfield 0 0
2016–17 Chesterfield 4 0 **4 0**

HIRD, Samuel (D) 341 11
H: 5 7 W: 10 12 b.Askern 7-9-87
2005–06 Leeds U 0 0
2006–07 Leeds U 0 0
2006–07 *Doncaster R* 5 0

2007–08	Doncaster R	4	0		
2007–08	*Grimsby T*	17	0	**17**	**0**
2008–09	Doncaster R	37	1		
2009–10	Doncaster R	36	0		
2010–11	Doncaster R	32	0		
2011–12	Doncaster R	31	0	**145**	**1**
2012–13	Chesterfield	41	2		
2013–14	Chesterfield	35	2		
2014–15	Chesterfield	28	3		
2015–16	Chesterfield	40	2		
2016–17	Chesterfield	35	1	**179**	**10**

HUMPHREYS, Richie (M) 643 47
H: 5 11 W: 12 07 b.Sheffield 30-11-77
Internationals: England U20, U21.

1995–96	Sheffield W	5	0		
1996–97	Sheffield W	29	3		
1997–98	Sheffield W	7	0		
1998–99	Sheffield W	19	1		
1999–2000	Sheffield W	0	0		
1999–2000	*Scunthorpe U*	6	2	**6**	**2**
1999–2000	*Cardiff C*	9	2	**9**	**2**
2000–01	Sheffield W	7	0	**67**	**4**
2000–01	Cambridge U	7	3	**7**	**3**
2001–02	Hartlepool U	46	5		
2002–03	Hartlepool U	46	11		
2003–04	Hartlepool U	46	3		
2004–05	Hartlepool U	46	3		
2005–06	Hartlepool U	46	2		
2006–07	Hartlepool U	38	3		
2006–07	*Port Vale*	7	0	**7**	**0**
2007–08	Hartlepool U	45	3		
2008–09	Hartlepool U	45	0		
2009–10	Hartlepool U	38	0		
2010–11	Hartlepool U	25	2		
2011–12	Hartlepool U	29	1		
2012–13	Hartlepool U	31	1	**481**	**34**
2013–14	Chesterfield	42	2		
2014–15	Chesterfield	19	0		
2015–16	Chesterfield	3	0		
2016–17	Chesterfield	2	0	**66**	**2**

JONES, Daniel (D) 229 6
H: 6 2 W: 13 00 b.Rowley Regis 14-7-86

2005–06	Wolverhampton W	1	0		
2006–07	Wolverhampton W	8	0		
2007–08	Wolverhampton W	1	0		
2007–08	*Northampton T*	33	3	**33**	**3**
2008–09	Wolverhampton W	0	0		
2008–09	*Oldham Ath*	23	1	**23**	**1**
2009–10	Wolverhampton W	0	0	**10**	**0**
2009–10	*Notts Co*	7	0	**7**	**0**
2009–10	*Bristol R*	17	0	**17**	**0**
2010–11	Sheffield W	25	0		
2011–12	Sheffield W	3	0		
2012–13	Sheffield W	9	0	**37**	**0**
2012–13	Port Vale	16	1		
2013–14	Port Vale	20	0	**36**	**1**
2014–15	Chesterfield	33	0		
2015–16	Chesterfield	19	1		
2016–17	Chesterfield	14	0	**66**	**1**

KAKAY, Osman (D) 19 0
b.Westminster 25-8-97

2015–16	QPR	0	0		
2015–16	*Livingston*	10	0	**10**	**0**
2016–17	QPR	1	0	**1**	**0**
2016–17	Chesterfield	8	0	**8**	**0**

MAGUIRE, Laurence (D) 11 0
H: 5 10 W: 11 00 b.Sheffield 8-2-97

2013–14	Chesterfield	0	0		
2014–15	Chesterfield	0	0		
2015–16	Chesterfield	0	0		
2016–17	Chesterfield	11	0	**11**	**0**

MARTINEZ, Angel (M) 218 10
H: 5 9 W: 11 13 b.Girona 31-1-86
Internationals: Spain U19, U21.

2006–07	Espanyol B	27	5	**27**	**5**
2006–07	Espanyol	7	0		
2007–08	Espanyol	28	2		
2008–09	Espanyol	15	0	**50**	**2**
2009–10	Rayo Vallecano	27	2	**27**	**2**
2010–11	Girona	36	0	**36**	**0**
2011–12	Blackpool	15	1		
2012–13	Blackpool	21	0		
2013–14	Blackpool	26	0	**62**	**1**
2014–15	Millwall	4	0	**4**	**0**
2015–16	Chesterfield	3	0		
2016–17	Chesterfield	9	0	**12**	**0**

McGINN, Paul (D) 210 5
H: 5 9 W: 10 05 b.Glasgow 22-10-90

2008–09	Queen's Park	1	0		
2009–10	Queen's Park	6	0		
2010–11	Queen's Park	26	1		
2011–12	Queen's Park	34	0		
2012–13	St Mirren	0	0		
2012–13	*Queen's Park*	8	1	**75**	**2**
2012–13	*Dumbarton*	14	1		
2013–14	Dumbarton	35	0	**49**	**1**
2014–15	Dundee	34	1		
2015–16	Dundee	34	0	**68**	**1**
2016–17	Chesterfield	18	1	**18**	**1**

MITCHELL, Reece (M) 28 2
b.London 19-7-95
Internationals: England U16.
From Chelsea.

2016–17	Chesterfield	28	2	**28**	**2**

MORRISON, Curtis (F) 1 0
H: 5 10 W: 12 13 b.Sheffield 2-10-97

2016–17	Chesterfield	1	0	**1**	**0**

NOLAN, Jon (M) 30 1
H: 5 11 W: 11 05 b.Huyton 22-4-92
Internationals: England C.
From Everton, Stockport Co, Lindoln C, Grimsby T.

2016–17	Chesterfield	30	1	**30**	**1**

O'SHEA, Jay (M) 317 63
H: 5 9 W: 12 00 b.Dun Laoghaire 10-8-88
Internationals: Republic of Ireland U19, U21, U23.

2007	Bray Wanderers	27	4	**27**	**4**
2008	Galway U	29	8		
2009	Galway U	19	3	**48**	**11**
2009–10	Birmingham C	1	0		
2009–10	*Middlesbrough*	2	0	**2**	**0**
2010–11	Birmingham C	0	0	**1**	**0**
2010–11	*Stevenage*	5	0	**5**	**0**
2010–11	*Port Vale*	5	1	**5**	**1**
2011–12	Milton Keynes D	28	5		
2012–13	Milton Keynes D	11	1	**39**	**6**
2012–13	*Chesterfield*	26	7		
2013–14	Chesterfield	40	9		
2014–15	Chesterfield	41	7		
2015–16	Chesterfield	46	9		
2016–17	Chesterfield	27	6	**180**	**38**
2016–17	*Sheffield U*	10	3	**10**	**3**

OFOEGBU, Ify (D) 0 0

2016–17	Chesterfield	0	0		

PARKIN, Dylan (G) 0 0
b. 11-11-99

2016–17	Chesterfield	0	0		

ROWLEY, Joe (M) 7 1

2016–17	Chesterfield	7	1	**7**	**1**

SIMONS, Rai (F) 39 4
H: 6 0 W: 11 05 b.Hamilton 11-1-96
Internationals: Bermuda U17, U20, Full caps.
From Newcastle T, Ilkeston.

2015–16	Chesterfield	20	4		
2016–17	Chesterfield	19	0	**39**	**4**

STUCKMANN, Thorsten (G) 394 0
H: 6 6 W: 14 11 b.Gutersloh 17-3-81
Internationals: Germany U20, U21.

2000–01	Pr Munster	25	0		
2001–02	Pr Munster	19	0		
2002–03	Pr Munster	30	0	**74**	**0**
2003–04	E Braunschweig	21	0		
2004–05	E Braunschweig	36	0		
2005–06	E Braunschweig	34	0		
2006–07	E Braunschweig	34	0	**125**	**0**
2007–08	A Aachen	16	0		
2008–09	A Aachen	34	0		
2009–10	A Aachen	31	0		
2010–11	A Aachen	1	0	**82**	**0**
2011–12	Preston NE	28	0		
2012–13	Preston NE	22	0		
2013–14	Preston NE	0	0		
2014–15	Preston NE	7	0	**57**	**0**
2015–16	Doncaster R	36	0	**36**	**0**
2016–17	Partick Thistle	5	0	**5**	**0**
2016–17	Chesterfield	15	0	**15**	**0**

WAKEFIELD, Charlie (M) 1 0
b.Derby 5-7-99
From Chelsea.

2016–17	Chesterfield	1	0	**1**	**0**

WISEMAN, Scott (D) 345 7
H: 6 0 W: 11 06 b.Hull 9-10-85
Internationals: England U20. Gilbraltar Full caps.

2003–04	Hull C	2	0		
2004–05	Hull C	3	0		
2004–05	*Boston U*	2	0	**2**	**0**
2005–06	Hull C	11	0		
2006–07	Hull C	0	0	**16**	**0**
2006–07	*Rotherham U*	18	1	**18**	**1**
2006–07	*Darlington*	10	0		
2007–08	Darlington	7	0	**17**	**0**
2008–09	Rochdale	32	0		
2009–10	Rochdale	36	1		
2010–11	Rochdale	37	0	**105**	**1**
2011–12	Barnsley	43	1		
2012–13	Barnsley	36	0		
2013–14	Barnsley	23	0	**102**	**1**
2013–14	Preston NE	15	0		
2014–15	Preston NE	22	2	**37**	**2**
2015–16	Scunthorpe U	24	0		
2016–17	Scunthorpe U	24	2	**48**	**2**
2016–17	Chesterfield	0	0		

Players retained or with offer of contract
Lee, Thomas Edward.

Scholars
Brownell, Jack Thomas; Darwent, Owen; Fowler, Conor David; Hand, Dylan Patrick; Jones, Bradley James Roger; Lynam, George David; McKenna, Marc Patrick; Ofoegbu, Ifeanyi Convenant; Parkin, Dylan Thomas; Phillips, Joel; Sennett-Neilson, Aaron; Smith, Jay Alexander; Taylor, Harry; Thistlethwaite, Daniel; Tipping, Josh; Wakefield, Charlie George.

Non-Contract
Duke, Matthew.

COLCHESTER U (27)

AKINWANDE, Femi (F) 3 0
b. 1-5-96

2015–16	Colchester U	2	0		
2016–17	Colchester U	1	0	**3**	**0**

BARNES, Dillon (G) 0 0
H: 6 4 W: 11 11 b. 8-4-96
From Bedford T.

2015–16	Colchester U	0	0		
2016–17	Colchester U	0	0		

BONNE, Macauley (F) 75 7
H: 5 11 W: 12 00 b.Ipswich 26-10-95
Internationals: Zimbabwe U23.

2013–14	Colchester U	14	2		
2014–15	Colchester U	10	1		
2015–16	Colchester U	33	3		
2016–17	Colchester U	18	1	**75**	**7**

BRANSGROVE, James (G) 1 0
H: 6 4 W: 12 04 b. 12-5-95

2013–14	Colchester U	0	0		
2014–15	Colchester U	0	0		
2015–16	Colchester U	1	0		
2016–17	Colchester U	0	0	**1**	**0**

BRIGGS, Matthew (D) 97 1
H: 6 1 W: 11 12 b.Wandsworth 6-3-91
Internationals: England U16, U17, U19, U20, U21. Guyana Full caps.

2006–07	Fulham	1	0		
2007–08	Fulham	0	0		
2008–09	Fulham	0	0		
2009–10	Fulham	0	0		
2009–10	*Leyton Orient*	1	0	**1**	**0**
2010–11	Fulham	3	0		
2011–12	Fulham	2	0		
2011–12	*Peterborough U*	5	0	**5**	**0**
2012–13	Fulham	5	0		
2012–13	*Bristol C*	4	0	**4**	**0**
2012–13	*Watford*	7	1	**7**	**1**
2013–14	Fulham	2	0	**13**	**0**
2014–15	Millwall	8	0	**8**	**0**
2014–15	*Colchester U*	18	0		
2015–16	Colchester U	26	0		
2016–17	Colchester U	15	0	**59**	**0**

BRILL, Dean (G) 219 0
H: 6 2 W: 14 05 b.Luton 2-12-85

2003–04	Luton T	5	0		
2004–05	Luton T	0	0		
2005–06	Luton T	5	0		
2006–07	Luton T	11	0		
2006–07	*Gillingham*	8	0	**8**	**0**
2007–08	Luton T	37	0		
2008–09	Luton T	23	0	**81**	**0**
2009–10	Oldham Ath	28	0		
2010–11	Oldham Ath	30	0	**58**	**0**
2011–12	Barnet	36	0	**36**	**0**

From Luton T.

2013–14	Inverness CT	12	0		
2014–15	Inverness CT	24	0		
2015–16	Inverness CT	0	0	**36**	**0**
2016–17	Motherwell	0	0		
2016–17	Colchester U	0	0		

BRINDLEY, Richard (D) **106 2**

H: 5 10 W: 11 09 b.Coventry 30-11-87

2012–13	Chesterfield	12	0	**12**	**0**
2013–14	Rotherham U	16	0		
2014–15	Rotherham U	2	0	**18**	**0**
2014–15	*Scunthorpe U*	3	0	**3**	**0**
2014–15	*Oxford U*	3	0	**3**	**0**
2014–15	*Colchester U*	8	0		
2015–16	Colchester U	21	1		
2016–17	Colchester U	41	1	**70**	**2**

DICKENSON, Brennan (F) **134 18**

H: 6 0 W: 12 07 b.Ferndown 26-2-93

2012–13	Brighton & HA	0	0		
2012–13	*Chesterfield*	11	1	**11**	**1**
2012–13	*AFC Wimbledon*	7	2	**7**	**2**
2013–14	Brighton & HA	0	0		
2013–14	*Northampton T*	13	1	**13**	**1**
2014–15	Gillingham	34	1		
2015–16	Gillingham	33	1	**67**	**2**
2016–17	Colchester U	36	12	**36**	**12**

DOYLEY, Lloyd (D) **401 2**

H: 5 10 W: 12 13 b.Whitechapel 1-12-82

Internationals: Jamaica Full caps.

2000–01	Watford	0	0		
2001–02	Watford	20	0		
2002–03	Watford	22	0		
2003–04	Watford	9	0		
2004–05	Watford	29	0		
2005–06	Watford	44	0		
2006–07	Watford	21	0		
2007–08	Watford	36	0		
2008–09	Watford	37	0		
2009–10	Watford	44	1		
2010–11	Watford	36	0		
2011–12	Watford	33	0		
2012–13	Watford	34	1		
2013–14	Watford	24	0		
2014–15	Watford	6	0		
2015–16	Watford	0	0	**395**	**2**
2015–16	Rotherham U	3	0		
2016–17	Rotherham U	0	0	**3**	**0**
2016–17	Colchester U	3	0	**3**	**0**

DUNNE, Louis (M) **2 0**

b.Waltham Forest 7-9-98

Internationals: Republic of Ireland U17, U18.

2015–16	Colchester U	2	0		
2016–17	Colchester U	0	0	**2**	**0**

EASTMAN, Tom (D) **230 11**

H: 6 3 W: 13 12 b.Clacton 21-10-91

2009–10	Ipswich T	1	0		
2010–11	Ipswich T	9	0	**10**	**0**
2011–12	Colchester U	25	3		
2011–12	*Crawley T*	6	0	**6**	**0**
2012–13	Colchester U	29	2		
2013–14	Colchester U	36	0		
2014–15	Colchester U	46	1		
2015–16	Colchester U	43	2		
2016–17	Colchester U	35	3	**214**	**11**

EDGE, Charley (F) **1 0**

b.Aberystwyth 14-5-97

Internationals: Wales U17.

From Everton.

2016–17	Colchester U	1	0	**1**	**0**

ELOKOBI, George (D) **212 10**

H: 5 10 W: 13 02 b.Cameroon 31-1-86

2004–05	Colchester U	0	0		
2004–05	*Chester C*	5	0	**5**	**0**
2005–06	Colchester U	12	1		
2006–07	Colchester U	10	0		
2007–08	Colchester U	17	1		
2007–08	Wolverhampton W	15	0		
2008–09	Wolverhampton W	4	0		
2009–10	Wolverhampton W	22	0		
2010–11	Wolverhampton W	27	2		
2011–12	Wolverhampton W	9	0		
2011–12	*Nottingham F*	12	0	**12**	**0**
2012–13	Wolverhampton W	2	0		
2012–13	*Bristol C*	1	0	**1**	**0**
2013–14	Wolverhampton W	6	0	**85**	**2**
2014–15	Oldham Ath	24	3	**24**	**3**
2015–16	Colchester U	17	2		
2016–17	Colchester U	29	1	**85**	**5**

GARVAN, Owen (M) **306 25**

H: 6 0 W: 10 07 b.Dublin 29-1-88

Internationals: Republic of Ireland U21.

2005–06	Ipswich T	31	3		
2006–07	Ipswich T	27	1		
2007–08	Ipswich T	43	2		
2008–09	Ipswich T	37	7		
2009–10	Ipswich T	25	0	**163**	**13**
2010–11	Crystal Palace	26	3		
2011–12	Crystal Palace	22	3		
2012–13	Crystal Palace	27	4		
2013–14	Crystal Palace	2	0		
2013–14	*Millwall*	13	0	**13**	**0**
2014–15	Crystal Palace	0	0	**77**	**10**
2014–15	*Bolton W*	3	0	**3**	**0**
2015–16	Colchester U	32	1		
2016–17	Colchester U	18	1	**50**	**2**

GUTHRIE, Kurtis (F) **46 12**

H: 5 11 W: 11 00 b.Jersey 21-4-93

Internationals: England C.

2011–12	Accrington S	13	0		
2012–13	Accrington S	0	0	**13**	**0**
2012–13	Bath City	0	0		
2012–13	Welling	0	0		
2016–17	Colchester U	33	12	**33**	**12**

ISSA, Tariq (M) **0 0**

H: 5 7 W: 10 08 b. 2-9-97

2016–17	Colchester U	0	0		

JAMES, Cameron (D) **15 0**

H: 6 0 W: 12 00 b.Chelmsford 11-2-98

2015–16	Colchester U	1	0		
2016–17	Colchester U	14	0	**15**	**0**

JOHNSTONE, Denny (F) **40 4**

H: 6 2 W: 13 01 b.Dumfries 9-1-95

Internationals: Scotland U16, U17, U18, U19.

2013–14	Celtic	0	0		
2014–15	Birmingham C	2	0		
2014–15	*Cheltenham T*	5	1	**5**	**1**
2014–15	*Burton Alb*	5	1	**5**	**1**
2015–16	Birmingham C	0	0	**2**	**0**
2016–17	Colchester U	28	2	**28**	**2**

KENT, Frankie (D) **50 0**

H: 6 2 W: 12 00 b.Romford 21-11-95

2013–14	Colchester U	1	0		
2014–15	Colchester U	10	0		
2015–16	Colchester U	26	0		
2016–17	Colchester U	13	0	**50**	**0**

KINSELLA, Lewis (D) **16 0**

H: 5 9 W: 11 05 b.Watford 2-9-94

2013–14	Aston Villa	0	0		
2014–15	Aston Villa	0	0		
2014–15	*Luton T*	3	0	**3**	**0**
2015–16	Aston Villa	0	0		
2016–17	Colchester U	13	0	**13**	**0**

LAPSLIE, Tom (M) **58 2**

H: 5 6 W: 10 12 b.Waltham Forest 5-5-95

2013–14	Colchester U	0	0		
2014–15	Colchester U	11	1		
2015–16	Colchester U	10	1		
2016–17	Colchester U	37	0	**58**	**2**

LOFT, Doug (M) **294 25**

H: 6 0 W: 12 01 b.Maidstone 25-12-86

2005–06	Brighton & HA	3	1		
2006–07	Brighton & HA	11	1		
2007–08	Brighton & HA	13	0		
2008–09	Brighton & HA	12	0	**39**	**2**
2008–09	*Dagenham & R*	11	0	**11**	**0**
2009–10	Port Vale	32	3		
2010–11	Port Vale	29	1		
2011–12	Port Vale	44	4		
2012–13	Port Vale	32	1		
2013–14	Port Vale	37	9	**174**	**18**
2014–15	Gillingham	36	1		
2015–16	Gillingham	26	4	**62**	**5**
2016–17	Colchester U	8	0	**8**	**0**

MURRAY, Sean (M) **116 12**

H: 5 9 W: 10 10 b.Abbots Langley 11-10-93

Internationals: Republic of Ireland U17, U19, U21.

2010–11	Watford	2	0		
2011–12	Watford	18	7		
2012–13	Watford	15	1		
2013–14	Watford	34	3		
2014–15	Watford	6	0		
2015–16	Watford	0	0		
2015–16	*Wigan Ath*	7	0	**7**	**0**
2016–17	Watford	0	0	**75**	**11**
2016–17	Swindon T	18	1	**18**	**1**
2016–17	Colchester U	16	0	**16**	**0**

O'DONOGHUE, Michael (D) **1 0**

H: 5 11 W: 11 00 b.Islington 18-1-96

2013–14	Colchester U	0	0		
2014–15	Colchester U	1	0		
2015–16	Colchester U	0	0		
2016–17	Colchester U	0	0	**1**	**0**

O'SULLIVAN, Tommy (M) **28 1**

H: 5 9 W: 11 04 b.Mountain Ash 18-1-95

Internationals: Wales U17, U19, U21.

2012–13	Cardiff C	0	0		
2013–14	Cardiff C	0	0		
2014–15	Cardiff C	0	0		
2014–15	*Port Vale*	5	0	**5**	**0**
2015–16	Cardiff C	0	0		
2015–16	*Newport Co*	20	1	**20**	**1**
2016–17	Colchester U	3	0	**3**	**0**

PETER, Dexter (D) **0 0**

2016–17	Colchester U	0	0		

PORTER, Chris (F) **427 124**

H: 6 1 W: 12 09 b.Wigan 12-12-83

2002–03	Bury	2	0		
2003–04	Bury	37	9		
2004–05	Bury	32	9	**71**	**18**
2005–06	Oldham Ath	31	7		
2006–07	Oldham Ath	35	21	**66**	**28**
2007–08	Motherwell	37	14		
2008–09	Motherwell	22	9	**59**	**23**
2008–09	Derby Co	5	3		
2009–10	Derby Co	21	4		
2010–11	Derby Co	18	2	**44**	**9**
2011–12	Sheffield U	34	5		
2012–13	Sheffield U	21	3		
2012–13	*Shrewsbury T*	5	1	**5**	**1**
2013–14	Sheffield U	32	7		
2013–14	*Chesterfield*	3	0	**3**	**0**
2014–15	Sheffield U	1	0	**88**	**15**
2014–15	Colchester U	21	7		
2015–16	Colchester U	32	7		
2016–17	Colchester U	38	16	**91**	**30**

PROSSER, Luke (D) **186 9**

H: 6 2 W: 12 04 b.Waltham Cross 28-5-88

2005–06	Port Vale	0	0		
2006–07	Port Vale	0	0		
2007–08	Port Vale	5	0		
2008–09	Port Vale	26	1		
2009–10	Port Vale	2	1	**33**	**2**
2010–11	Southend U	17	1		
2011–12	Southend U	21	1		
2012–13	Southend U	25	0		
2013–14	Southend U	25	3		
2014–15	Southend U	30	0		
2015–16	Southend U	13	2	**131**	**7**
2015–16	*Northampton T*	8	0	**8**	**0**
2016–17	Colchester U	14	0	**14**	**0**

REGIS, Chris (M) **0 0**

b. 11-11-96

Internationals: England U17.

From Southampton.

2016–17	Colchester U	0	0		

SEMBIE-FERRIS, Dion (F) **25 0**

H: 5 8 W: 11 00 b.Peterborough 23-5-96

2013–14	Colchester U	0	0		
2014–15	Colchester U	10	0		
2015–16	Colchester U	8	0		
2016–17	Colchester U	7	0	**25**	**0**

SLATER, Craig (M) **104 10**

H: 5 10 W: 11 09 b.Glasgow 26-4-94

Internationals: Scotland U16, U17, U19, U21.

From St Mirren.

2012–13	Kilmarnock	2	0		
2013–14	Kilmarnock	22	1		
2014–15	Kilmarnock	26	4		
2015–16	Kilmarnock	26	2	**76**	**7**
2016–17	Colchester U	28	3	**28**	**3**

SZMIDICS, Sammie (M) **62 9**

H: 5 6 W: 10 01 b.Colchester 24-9-95

2013–14	Colchester U	7	0		
2014–15	Colchester U	31	4		
2015–16	Colchester U	5	0		
2016–17	Colchester U	19	5	**62**	**9**

VINCENT-YOUNG, Kane (D) **32 0**

H: 5 11 W: 11 00 b.Camden Town 15-3-96

2014–15	Colchester U	0	0		
2015–16	Colchester U	14	0		
2016–17	Colchester U	18	0	**32**	**0**

WALKER, Sam (G) **215 0**

H: 6 5 W: 14 00 b.Gravesend 2-10-91

2009–10	Chelsea	0	0		
2010–11	Chelsea	0	0		
2010–11	*Barnet*	7	0	**7**	**0**
2011–12	Chelsea	0	0		
2011–12	*Northampton T*	21	0	**21**	**0**
2011–12	*Yeovil T*	20	0	**20**	**0**
2012–13	Chelsea	0	0		
2012–13	*Bristol R*	11	0	**11**	**0**
2012–13	*Colchester U*	19	0		
2013–14	Colchester U	46	0		
2014–15	Colchester U	45	0		
2015–16	Colchester U	0	0		
2016–17	Colchester U	46	0	**156**	**0**

WRIGHT, Diaz (M)				**0**	**0**
2016–17	Colchester U	0	0		

WRIGHT, Drey (M)				**90**	**5**
H: 5 9 W: 10 11 b.Greenwich 30-4-94					
2012–13	Colchester U	21	3		
2013–14	Colchester U	11	0		
2014–15	Colchester U	5	0		
2015–16	Colchester U	11	0		
2016–17	Colchester U	42	2	**90**	**5**

WYNTER, Alex (M)				**61**	**1**
H: 6 0 W: 13 04 b.Camberwell 15-9-93					
2009–10	Crystal Palace	0	0		
2010–11	Crystal Palace	0	0		
2011–12	Crystal Palace	0	0		
2012–13	Crystal Palace	0	0		
2013–14	Crystal Palace	0	0		
2013–14	*Colchester U*	6	1		
2014–15	Crystal Palace	0	0		
2014–15	*Portsmouth*	10	0	**10**	**0**
2014–15	*Colchester U*	18	0		
2015–16	Colchester U	12	0		
2016–17	Colchester U	15	0	**51**	**1**

Players retained or with offer of contract
Ogbodu-Wilson, Osase Junior John; Phipps, Elijah Paul; Senior, Courtney Fitzroy; Sheriff, De-Carrey Deavon.

Scholars
Ager, Dean Fred; Clampin, Ryan; Debrick, Ross Richard; Ferlisi, Shakeem Devante; Howard, Robert William; Jones, Callum Wiiliam Adam; Kensdale, Oliver James; Keys, George Harvey; McKeown, Eoin Francis Okorie; Moore, Joshua Alexander; Mulryne, Jake; Phillips, George William Joseph; Pollard, Joshua Kelly; Syrett, Josce

COVENTRY C (28)

ADDAI, Corey (G)				**0**	**0**
b. 10-10-97					
2015–16	Coventry C	0	0		
2016–17	Coventry C	0	0		

BEAVON, Stuart (F)				**284**	**52**
H: 5 7 W: 10 10 b.Reading 5-5-84					
2008–09	Wycombe W	8	0		
2009–10	Wycombe W	25	3		
2010–11	Wycombe W	37	3		
2011–12	Wycombe W	43	21		
2012–13	Wycombe W	2	1	**115**	**28**
2012–13	Preston NE	31	6		
2013–14	Preston NE	27	3	**58**	**9**
2014–15	Burton Alb	44	6		
2015–16	Burton Alb	43	7		
2016–17	Burton Alb	10	0	**97**	**13**
2016–17	Coventry C	14	2	**14**	**2**

BIGIRIMANA, Gael (M)				**82**	**1**
H: 5 9 W: 11 09 b.Burundi 22-10-93					
Internationals: England U20.					
2011–12	Coventry C	26	0		
2012–13	Newcastle U	13	1		
2013–14	Newcastle U	0	0		
2014–15	Newcastle U	0	0		
2014–15	*Rangers*	0	0		
2015–16	Newcastle U	0	0	**13**	**1**
2015–16	*Coventry C*	13	0		
2016–17	Coventry C	30	0	**69**	**0**

BURGE, Lee (G)				**60**	**0**
H: 5 11 W: 11 00 b.Hereford 9-1-93					
2011–12	Coventry C	0	0		
2012–13	Coventry C	0	0		
2013–14	Coventry C	0	0		
2014–15	Coventry C	18	0		
2015–16	Coventry C	9	0		
2016–17	Coventry C	33	0	**60**	**0**

CAMWELL, Chris (D)				**1**	**0**
b. 27-10-98					
2016–17	Coventry C	1	0	**1**	**0**

CHARLES-COOK, Reice (G)				**54**	**0**
H: 6 1 W: 12 08 b.London 8-4-94					
2013–14	Bury	2	0	**2**	**0**
2014–15	Coventry C	0	0		
2015–16	Coventry C	37	0		
2016–17	Coventry C	15	0	**52**	**0**

CLARKE, Nathan (D)				**465**	**11**
H: 6 2 W: 12 00 b.Halifax 30-11-83					
2001–02	Huddersfield T	36	1		
2002–03	Huddersfield T	3	0		
2003–04	Huddersfield T	26	1		
2004–05	Huddersfield T	37	0		
2005–06	Huddersfield T	46	0		
2006–07	Huddersfield T	16	0		
2007–08	Huddersfield T	44	2		
2008–09	Huddersfield T	38	3		
2009–10	Huddersfield T	17	1		
2010–11	Huddersfield T	1	0		
2010–11	*Colchester U*	18	0	**18**	**0**
2011–12	Huddersfield T	0	0	**264**	**8**
2011–12	*Oldham Ath*	16	1	**16**	**1**
2011–12	*Bury*	11	0	**11**	**0**
2012–13	Leyton Orient	34	0		
2013–14	Leyton Orient	46	2		
2014–15	Leyton Orient	33	0	**113**	**2**
2015–16	Bradford C	25	0		
2016–17	Bradford C	0	0	**25**	**0**
2016–17	Coventry C	18	0	**18**	**0**

FINCH, Jack (M)				**16**	**0**
H: 6 1 W: 12 02 b.Southam 6-8-96					
2013–14	Coventry C	0	0		
2014–15	Coventry C	16	0		
2015–16	Coventry C	0	0		
2016–17	Coventry C	0	0	**16**	**0**

FOLEY, Kevin (D)				**393**	**8**
H: 5 9 W: 11 11 b.Luton 1-11-84					
Internationals: Republic of Ireland U21, B, Full caps.					
2002–03	Luton T	2	0		
2003–04	Luton T	33	1		
2004–05	Luton T	39	2		
2005–06	Luton T	38	0		
2006–07	Luton T	39	0	**151**	**3**
2007–08	Wolverhampton W	44	1		
2008–09	Wolverhampton W	45	1		
2009–10	Wolverhampton W	25	0		
2010–11	Wolverhampton W	33	2		
2011–12	Wolverhampton W	16	0		
2012–13	Wolverhampton W	26	0		
2013–14	Wolverhampton W	5	1		
2013–14	*Blackpool*	5	0		
2014–15	Wolverhampton W	0	0	**194**	**5**
2014–15	*Blackpool*	4	0	**9**	**0**
2014–15	FC Copenhagen	4	0	**4**	**0**
2015–16	Ipswich T	8	0	**8**	**0**
2016–17	Charlton Ath	15	0	**15**	**0**
2016–17	Coventry C	12	0	**12**	**0**

GADZHEV, Vladimir (M)				**227**	**28**
H: 5 10 W: 12 00 b.Pazardzhik 18-7-87					
Internationals: Bulgaria U21, Full caps.					
2005–06	Panathinaikos	0	0		
2006–07	Panathinaikos	0	0		
2006–07	*Levadiakos*	26	5	**26**	**5**
2007–08	Panathinaikos	0	0		
2007–08	*OFI Crete*	19	0	**19**	**0**
2008–09	Panathinaikos	0	0		
2008–09	*Levski Sofia*	23	1		
2009–10	Levski Sofia	10	1		
2010–11	Levski Sofia	23	2		
2011–12	Levski Sofia	27	6		
2012–13	Levski Sofia	22	1		
2013–14	Levski Sofia	32	5		
2014–15	Levski Sofia	22	5		
2015–16	Levski Sofia	7	1	**166**	**22**
2015–16	Coventry C	2	0		
2016–17	Coventry C	14	1	**16**	**1**

HARRIES, Cian (D)				**9**	**0**
H: 6 1 W: 12 02 b. 1-4-97					
Internationals: Wales U17, U19, U20.					
2015–16	Coventry C	1	0		
2016–17	Coventry C	8	0	**9**	**0**

HAYNES, Ryan (D)				**67**	**1**
H: 5 7 W: 10 10 b.Northampton 27-9-95					
2012–13	Coventry C	1	0		
2013–14	Coventry C	2	0		
2014–15	Coventry C	26	1		
2015–16	Coventry C	9	0		
2015–16	*Cambridge U*	10	0	**10**	**0**
2016–17	Coventry C	19	0	**57**	**1**

JONES, Jodi (F)				**75**	**5**
b.London 22-10-97					
2014–15	Dagenham & R	8	1		
2015–16	Dagenham & R	27	3	**35**	**4**
2015–16	Coventry C	6	0		
2016–17	Coventry C	34	1	**40**	**1**

KELLY-EVANS, Devon (M)				**0**	**0**
H: 5 10 W: 12 06 b.Coventry 21-9-96					
2016–17	Coventry C	0	0		

KELLY-EVANS, Dion (D)				**26**	**0**
H: 5 10 W: 12 06 b.Coventry 21-9-96					
2014–15	Coventry C	0	0		
2015–16	Coventry C	1	0		
2016–17	Coventry C	25	0	**26**	**0**

LAMEIRAS, Ruben (M)				**67**	**3**
H: 5 9 W: 11 00 b.Lisbon 22-12-94					
2014–15	Tottenham H	0	0		
2015	*Atvidabergs*	11	0	**11**	**0**
2015–16	Coventry C	29	2		
2016–17	Coventry C	27	1	**56**	**3**

MAYCOCK, Callum (D)				**3**	**0**
b. 23-12-97					
2016–17	Coventry C	3	0	**3**	**0**

McBEAN, Jack (F)				**21**	**2**
H: 6 0 W: 12 06 b.Newport Beach 15-12-94					
Internationals: USA U17, U18.					
2011	LA Galaxy	1	1		
2012	LA Galaxy	1	0		
2013	LA Galaxy	15	1		
2014	LA Galaxy	0	0		
2015	LA Galaxy	0	0		
2016	LA Galaxy	2	0	**19**	**2**
On loan from LA Galaxy.					
2016–17	Coventry C	2	0	**2**	**0**

McCANN, Chris (M)				**343**	**36**
H: 6 1 W: 11 11 b.Dublin 21-7-87					
Internationals: Republic of Ireland U19.					
2005–06	Burnley	23	2		
2006–07	Burnley	38	5		
2007–08	Burnley	35	5		
2008–09	Burnley	44	6		
2009–10	Burnley	7	0		
2010–11	Burnley	4	1		
2011–12	Burnley	46	4		
2012–13	Burnley	41	4	**238**	**27**
2013–14	Wigan Ath	27	2		
2014–15	Wigan Ath	17	2		
2015–16	Wigan Ath	38	4	**82**	**8**
2016	Atlanta U	10	0	**10**	**0**
On loan from Altanta U.					
2016–17	Coventry C	13	1	**13**	**1**

McDONALD, Rod (D)				**30**	**3**
H: 6 3 W: 12 13 b.Crewe 11-4-92					
2010–11	Oldham Ath	0	0		
From Colwyn Bay, Nantwich T, Hereford U, AFC Telford U.					
2015–16	Northampton T	23	3		
2016–17	Northampton T	7	0	**30**	**3**
2016–17	Coventry C	0	0		

McNULTY, Marc (M)				**187**	**58**
H: 5 10 W: 11 00 b.Edinburgh 14-9-92					
2009–10	Livingston	9	1		
2010–11	Livingston	5	1		
2011–12	Livingston	30	11		
2012–13	Livingston	26	7		
2013–14	Livingston	35	17	**105**	**37**
2014–15	Sheffield U	31	9		
2015–16	Sheffield U	5	1		
2015–16	*Portsmouth*	27	10	**27**	**10**
2016–17	Sheffield U	4	0	**40**	**10**
2016–17	*Bradford C*	15	1	**15**	**1**
2016–17	Coventry C	0	0		

REID, Kyel (M)				**276**	**23**
H: 5 10 W: 12 05 b.Deptford 26-11-87					
Internationals: England U17, U18, U19.					
2004–05	West Ham U	0	0		
2005–06	West Ham U	2	0		
2006–07	West Ham U	0	0		
2006–07	*Barnsley*	26	2	**26**	**2**
2007–08	West Ham U	1	0		
2007–08	*Crystal Palace*	2	0	**2**	**0**
2008–09	West Ham U	0	0	**3**	**0**
2008–09	*Blackpool*	7	0	**7**	**0**
2008–09	*Wolverhampton W*	8	1	**8**	**1**
2009–10	Sheffield U	7	0	**7**	**0**
2009–10	*Charlton Ath*	17	4		
2010–11	Charlton Ath	32	1	**49**	**5**
2011–12	Bradford C	37	4		
2012–13	Bradford C	33	2		
2013–14	Bradford C	26	4		
2014–15	Preston NE	14	0		
2015–16	Preston NE	1	0	**15**	**0**
2015–16	*Bradford C*	34	3	**130**	**13**
2016–17	Coventry C	29	2	**29**	**2**

RICKETTS, Sam (D)				**447**	**7**
H: 6 1 W: 12 01 b.Aylesbury 11-10-81					
Internationals: England C. Wales Full caps.					
1999–2000	Oxford U	0	0		
2000–01	Oxford U	14	0		
2001–02	Oxford U	29	1		
2002–03	Oxford U	2	0	**45**	**1**
From Telford U					
2004–05	Swansea C	42	0		
2005–06	Swansea C	44	1	**86**	**1**
2006–07	Hull C	40	1		
2007–08	Hull C	44	0		

2008–09 Hull C 29 0
2009–10 Hull C 0 0 **113 1**
2009–10 Bolton W 27 0
2010–11 Bolton W 17 0
2011–12 Bolton W 20 1
2012–13 Bolton W 32 0 **96 1**
2013–14 Wolverhampton W 44 2
2014–15 Wolverhampton W 4 0 **48 2**
2014–15 *Swindon T* 9 0 **9 0**
2015–16 Coventry C 43 1
2016–17 Coventry C 7 0 **50 1**

ROSE, Andy (M) 124 9
H: 6 2 W: 12 02 b.Melbourne 13-2-90
2012 Seattle Sounders 25 1
2013 Seattle Sounders 19 1
2014 Seattle Sounders 18 3
2015 Seattle Sounders 29 0 **91 5**
2015–16 Coventry C 12 2
2016–17 Coventry C 21 2 **33 4**

SHIPLEY, Jordan (M) 1 0
b. 26-6-97
2016–17 Coventry C 1 0 **1 0**

SPENCE, Kyle (F) 1 0
H: 5 5 W: 11 03 b.Croydon 14-1-97
Internationals: Scotland U16.
2014–15 Coventry C 0 0
2015–16 Coventry C 0 0
2016–17 Coventry C 1 0 **1 0**

STEVENSON, Ben (M) 28 2
H: 6 0 W: 10 08 b.Leicester 23-3-97
2015–16 Coventry C 0 0
2016–17 Coventry C 28 2 **28 2**

STOKES, Chris (M) 61 3
H: 5 7 W: 10 04 b.Trowbridge 8-3-91
Internationals: England C, U17.
2009–10 Crewe Alex 2 0 **2 0**
From Forest Green R.
2014–15 Coventry C 16 1
2015–16 Coventry C 36 2
2016–17 Coventry C 7 0 **59 3**

THOMAS, George (M) 47 5
H: 5 8 W: 12 00 b.Leicester 24-3-97
Internationals: Wales U17, U19, U21.
2013–14 Coventry C 1 0
2014–15 Coventry C 6 0
2015–16 Coventry C 7 0
2015–16 *Yeovil T* 5 0 **5 0**
2016–17 Coventry C 28 5 **42 5**

THOMAS, Kwame (F) 41 3
H: 5 10 W: 12 00 b.Nottingham 28-9-95
Internationals: England U16, U17, U20.
2011–12 Derby Co 0 0
2012–13 Derby Co 0 0
2013–14 Derby Co 0 0
2014–15 Derby Co 4 0
2014–15 *Notts Co* 5 0 **5 0**
2015–16 Derby Co 0 0 **4 0**
2015–16 *Blackpool* 18 0 **18 0**
2016–17 Coventry C 14 3 **14 3**

THOMPSON, Jordan (D) 0 0
2016–17 Coventry C 0 0

TUDGAY, Marcus (F) 439 95
H: 5 10 W: 12 04 b.Shoreham 3-2-83
2002–03 Derby Co 8 0
2003–04 Derby Co 29 6
2004–05 Derby Co 34 9
2005–06 Derby Co 21 2 **92 17**
2005–06 Sheffield W 18 5
2006–07 Sheffield W 40 11
2007–08 Sheffield W 35 7
2008–09 Sheffield W 42 14
2009–10 Sheffield W 43 10
2010–11 Sheffield W 17 2 **195 49**
2010–11 Nottingham F 22 7
2011–12 Nottingham F 34 5
2012–13 Nottingham F 3 0
2012–13 *Barnsley* 9 3
2013–14 Nottingham F 2 1 **61 13**
2013–14 *Barnsley* 5 1 **14 4**
2013–14 *Charlton Ath* 2 0 **2 0**
2014–15 Coventry C 22 4
2015–16 Coventry C 25 4
2016–17 Coventry C 28 4 **75 12**

TURNBULL, Jordan (D) 122 1
H: 6 1 W: 11 05 b.Trowbridge 30-10-94
Internationals: England U19, U20.
2014–15 Southampton 0 0
2014–15 *Swindon T* 44 1
2015–16 Southampton 0 0
2015–16 *Swindon T* 42 0 **86 1**
2016–17 Coventry C 36 0 **36 0**

WILLIS, Jordan (D) 106 3
H: 5 11 W: 11 00 b.Coventry 24-8-94
Internationals: England U18, U19.
2011–12 Coventry C 3 0
2012–13 Coventry C 1 0
2013–14 Coventry C 28 0
2014–15 Coventry C 34 0
2015–16 Coventry C 4 0
2016–17 Coventry C 36 3 **106 3**

YAKUBU, Ayegbeni (F) 406 162
H: 6 0 W: 14 07 b.Benin City 22-11-82
Internationals: Nigeria U21, U23, Full caps.
1999–2000 Gil Vicente 0 0
1999–2000 Hapoel Kfar-Sava 23 6 **23 6**
2000–01 Maccabi Haifa 14 3
2001–02 Maccabi Haifa 22 13 **36 16**
2002–03 Portsmouth 14 7
2003–04 Portsmouth 37 16
2004–05 Portsmouth 30 12 **81 35**
2005–06 Middlesbrough 34 13
2006–07 Middlesbrough 37 12
2007–08 Middlesbrough 2 0 **73 25**
2007–08 Everton 29 15
2008–09 Everton 14 4
2009–10 Everton 25 5
2010–11 Everton 14 1
2010–11 *Leicester C* 20 11 **20 11**
2011–12 Everton 0 0 **82 25**
2011–12 Blackburn R 30 17 **30 17**
2012–13 Guangzhou R&F 43 24 **43 24**
2013–14 Al Rayyan 8 3 **8 3**
2014–15 Reading 7 0 **7 0**
2016–17 Coventry C 3 0 **3 0**

Players retained or with offer of contract
Leahy, Darragh John; Sayoud, Bilal Mohamed.

Scholars
Bayliss, Thomas David; Camwell, Christopher Paul; Doyle, Liam Thomas; Eccles, Joshua Elliot; Finn, Kyle Patrick; Ford, Reece Colin; Green, Lewis Craig; Green, Sion Nathan; Hendricks, Ronee Deshaun Anthony; Hickman, Jak Anthony; Johnson, Tyler Marc; Mantsounga, Dagry Joph Paul; McMahon, Ross Joseph; Naylor, Samuel Thomas; Ponticelli, Jordan; Skuza, Konrad Michal; Smith, Daniel Rhys; Stedman, Billy Jay; Thompson, Jordon.

CRAWLEY T (29)

ARTHUR, Chris (M) 39 1
H: 5 10 W: 12 02 b.Enfield 25-1-90
2011–12 Northampton T 7 0 **7 0**
2013–14 AFC Wimbledon 26 1
2014–15 AFC Wimbledon 0 0 **26 1**
2016–17 Crawley T 6 0 **6 0**

BANTON, Jason (F) 96 10
H: 5 10 W: 11 05 b.Tottenham 15-12-92
Internationals: England U17.
2009–10 Blackburn R 0 0
2010–11 Blackburn R 0 0
2010–11 Liverpool 0 0
2011–12 Liverpool 0 0
2011–12 *Burton Alb* 1 0 **1 0**
2012–13 Crystal Palace 0 0
2012–13 *Plymouth Arg* 14 6
2013–14 Crystal Palace 0 0
2013–14 *Milton Keynes D* 11 2 **11 2**
2013–14 Plymouth Arg 13 1
2014–15 Plymouth Arg 25 0 **52 7**
2015–16 Wycombe W 5 1 **5 1**
2015–16 *Hartlepool U* 4 0 **4 0**
2015–16 Notts Co 9 0 **9 0**
2016–17 Crawley T 14 0 **14 0**
2016–17 *Partick Thistle* 0 0

BAWLING, Bobson (M) 72 0
H: 5 10 W: 11 00 b.London 21-9-95
2013–14 Watford 0 0
2014–15 Crawley T 28 0
2015–16 Crawley T 15 0
2016–17 Crawley T 29 0 **72 0**

BLACKMAN, Andre (D) 46 0
H: 5 11 W: 11 05 b.Lambeth 10-11-90
2009–10 Bristol C 0 0
2011–12 Celtic 3 0
2012–13 Celtic 0 0 **3 0**
2012–13 *Inverness CT* 2 0 **2 0**
2013–14 Plymouth Arg 6 0 **6 0**
2014–15 Blackpool 3 0 **3 0**
2016–17 Crawley T 32 0 **32 0**

BOLDEWIJN, Enzio (F) 181 22
H: 6 1 W: 12 06 b.Almere 17-11-92
2010–11 Utrecht 0 0
2011–12 Utrecht 11 0 **11 0**
2012–13 Den Bosch 31 1 **31 1**
2013–14 Almere City 27 2
2014–15 Almere City 31 7
2015–16 Almere City 35 7 **93 16**
2015–16 Crawley T 0 0
2016–17 Crawley T 46 5 **46 5**

CLIFFORD, Billy (M) 67 1
H: 5 7 W: 10 03 b.Slough 18-10-92
2010–11 Chelsea 0 0
2011–12 Chelsea 0 0
2012–13 Chelsea 0 0
2012–13 *Colchester U* 18 1 **18 1**
2013–14 Chelsea 0 0
2013–14 *Yeovil T* 0 0
2014–15 Walsall 13 0 **13 0**
2016–17 Crawley T 36 0 **36 0**

COLLINS, James S (F) 298 97
H: 6 2 W: 13 08 b.Coventry 1-12-90
Internationals: Republic of Ireland U19, U21.
2008–09 Aston Villa 0 0
2009–10 Aston Villa 0 0
2009–10 *Darlington* 7 2 **7 2**
2010–11 Aston Villa 0 0
2010–11 *Burton Alb* 10 4 **10 4**
2010–11 Shrewsbury T 24 8
2011–12 Shrewsbury T 42 14
2012–13 Swindon T 45 15 **45 15**
2013–14 Hibernian 36 6 **36 6**
2014–15 Shrewsbury T 45 15
2015–16 Shrewsbury T 23 5 **134 42**
2015–16 *Northampton T* 21 8 **21 8**
2016–17 Crawley T 45 20 **45 20**

CONNOLLY, Mark (D) 144 8
H: 6 1 W: 12 01 b.Monaghan 16-12-91
Internationals: Republic of Ireland U17, U19, U21.
2009–10 Bolton W 0 0
2009–10 *St Johnstone* 1 0 **1 0**
2010–11 Bolton W 0 0
2011–12 Bolton W 0 0
2011–12 *Macclesfield T* 7 0 **7 0**
2012–13 Crawley T 33 2
2013–14 Crawley T 36 1
2014–15 Kilmarnock 26 2 **26 2**
2016–17 Crawley T 41 3 **110 6**

COX, Dean (M) 395 62
H: 5 4 W: 9 08 b.Cuckfield 12-8-87
2005–06 Brighton & HA 1 0
2006–07 Brighton & HA 42 6
2007–08 Brighton & HA 42 6
2008–09 Brighton & HA 40 4
2009–10 Brighton & HA 21 0 **146 16**
2010–11 Leyton Orient 45 11
2011–12 Leyton Orient 38 7
2012–13 Leyton Orient 44 4
2013–14 Leyton Orient 45 12
2014–15 Leyton Orient 37 6
2015–16 Leyton Orient 14 3
2016–17 Leyton Orient 4 1 **227 44**
2016–17 Crawley T 22 2 **22 2**

DJALO, Kaby (M) 87 5
H: 5 7 W: 10 03 b.Bissau 5-2-92
Internationals: Portugal U17, U18, U21. Guinea-Bissau Full caps.
From Chelsea.
2011–12 AEL Limassol 4 0
2012–13 AEL Limassol 0 0 **4 0**
2013–14 Gaz Metan Mediaz 3 0
2014–15 Gaz Metan Mediaz 0 0 **3 0**
2014–15 *Pogon Siedlce* 12 0 **12 0**
2015 *PS Kemi* 23 3
2016 PS Kemi 17 1 **40 4**
2016–17 Crawley T 28 1 **28 1**

GARNETT, Addison (D) 2 0
H: 6 4 W: 14 02 b.London 13-9-96
2016–17 Crawley T 2 0 **2 0**

HARROLD, Matt (F) 402 75
H: 6 1 W: 11 10 b.Leyton 25-7-84
2003–04 Brentford 13 2
2004–05 Brentford 19 0 **32 2**
2004–05 *Grimsby T* 6 2 **6 2**
2005–06 Yeovil T 42 9
2006–07 Yeovil T 5 0 **47 9**
2006–07 Southend U 36 3
2007–08 Southend U 16 0
2008–09 Southend U 0 0 **52 3**
2008–09 Wycombe W 37 9
2009–10 Wycombe W 36 8 **73 17**

2010–11	Shrewsbury T	41	8	**41**	**8**
2011–12	Bristol R	40	16		
2012–13	Bristol R	6	2		
2013–14	Bristol R	30	6	**76**	**24**
2014–15	Crawley T	20	1		
2014–15	*Cambridge U*	7	1	**7**	**1**
2015–16	Crawley T	37	8		
2016–17	Crawley T	11	0	**68**	**9**

HENDERSON, Conor (M) **37** **2**
H: 6 1 W: 11 13 b.Sidcup 8-9-91
Internationals: England U17. Republic of Ireland U19, U21.

2008–09	Arsenal	0	0		
2009–10	Arsenal	0	0		
2010–11	Arsenal	0	0		
2011–12	Arsenal	0	0		
2012–13	Arsenal	0	0		
2012–13	*Coventry C*	2	0	**2**	**0**
2013–14	Hull C	0	0		
2013–14	*Stevenage*	3	0	**3**	**0**
2014–15	Crawley T	17	2		
2015–16	Crawley T	3	0		
2016–17	Crawley T	12	0	**32**	**2**

LELAN, Josh (D) **29** **0**
H: 6 1 W: 11 00 b.Derby 21-12-94
Internationals: Kenya Full caps.

2012–13	Derby Co	0	0		
2013–14	Derby Co	0	0		
2014–15	Derby Co	0	0		
2014–15	*Swindon T*	5	0	**5**	**0**
2015–16	Northampton T	11	0		
2016–17	Northampton T	0	0	**11**	**0**
2016–17	Crawley T	13	0	**13**	**0**

McNERNEY, Joe (D) **45** **4**
H: 6 4 W: 13 03 b. 24-1-89
From Woking.

2015–16	Crawley T	11	1		
2016–17	Crawley T	34	3	**45**	**4**

MERSIN, Yusuf (G) **8** **0**
H: 6 5 W: 13 05 b.Greenwich 23-9-94
Internationals: Turkey U17, U18.
From Liverpool, Kasimpasa.

2016–17	Crawley T	8	0	**8**	**0**

MORRIS, Glenn (G) **232** **0**
H: 6 0 W: 12 03 b.Woolwich 20-12-83

2001–02	Leyton Orient	2	0		
2002–03	Leyton Orient	23	0		
2003–04	Leyton Orient	27	0		
2004–05	Leyton Orient	12	0		
2005–06	Leyton Orient	4	0		
2006–07	Leyton Orient	3	0		
2007–08	Leyton Orient	16	0		
2008–09	Leyton Orient	26	0		
2009–10	Leyton Orient	11	0	**124**	**0**
2010–11	Southend U	33	0		
2011–12	Southend U	24	0		
2012–13	Southend U	0	0	**57**	**0**
2012–13	Aldershot T	2	0	**2**	**0**
2014–15	Gillingham	10	0		
2015–16	Gillingham	0	0	**10**	**0**
2016–17	Crawley T	39	0	**39**	**0**

MURPHY, Rhys (F) **138** **36**
H: 6 1 W: 11 13 b.Shoreham 6-11-90
Internationals: England U16, U17, U19. Republic of Ireland U21.

2007–08	Arsenal	0	0		
2008–09	Arsenal	0	0		
2009–10	Arsenal	0	0		
2009–10	*Brentford*	5	0	**5**	**0**
2010–11	Arsenal	0	0		
2011–12	Arsenal	0	0		
2011–12	*Preston NE*	5	0	**5**	**0**
2012–13	Arsenal	0	0		
2012–13	Stormvogels Telstar	26	8	**26**	**8**
2013–14	Dagenham & R	32	13		
2014–15	Dagenham & R	9	1	**41**	**14**
2014–15	Oldham Ath	11	0		
2015–16	Oldham Ath	13	3	**24**	**3**
2015–16	*Crawley T*	15	9		
2015–16	*AFC Wimbledon*	7	1	**7**	**1**

On loan from Forest Green R.

2016–17	Crawley T	15	1	**30**	**10**

PAPPOE, Daniel (D) **2** **0**
H: 6 3 W: 14 09 b.Accra 30-12-93
Internationals: Ghana U20.

2011–12	Chelsea	0	0		
2012–13	Chelsea	0	0		
2013–14	Chelsea	0	0		
2013–14	*Colchester U*	2	0	**2**	**0**

From Hemel Hempstead, Berlin AK.

2016–17	Crawley T	0	0		

PAYNE, Josh (M) **117** **7**
H: 6 0 W: 11 09 b.Basingstoke 25-11-90
Internationals: England C.

2008–09	West Ham U	2	0		
2008–09	*Cheltenham T*	11	1	**11**	**1**
2009–10	West Ham U	0	0		
2009–10	*Colchester U*	3	0	**3**	**0**
2009–10	*Wycombe W*	3	1	**3**	**1**
2010–11	West Ham U	0	0	**2**	**0**
2010–11	Doncaster R	0	0		
2010–11	Oxford U	28	1		
2011–12	Oxford U	6	0	**34**	**1**
2011–12	Aldershot T	17	2		
2012–13	Aldershot T	15	1	**32**	**3**
2016–17	Crawley T	32	1	**32**	**1**

ROBERTS, Jordan (M) **41** **5**
H: 5 11 W: 12 13 b.Watford 5-1-94
Internationals: England C.

2011–12	Aldershot T	4	0		
2012–13	Aldershot T	5	0	**9**	**0**

From Havant & Waterlooville, Bishops Stortford, Aldershot T.

2015–16	Inverness CT	9	2	**9**	**2**
2016–17	Crawley T	23	3	**23**	**3**

SMITH, Jimmy (M) **366** **36**
H: 6 0 W: 10 03 b.Newham 7-1-87
Internationals: England U16, U17, U19.

2004–05	Chelsea	0	0		
2005–06	Chelsea	1	0		
2006–07	Chelsea	0	0		
2006–07	*QPR*	29	6	**29**	**6**
2007–08	Chelsea	0	0		
2007–08	*Norwich C*	9	0	**9**	**0**
2008–09	Chelsea	0	0	**1**	**0**
2008–09	*Sheffield W*	12	0	**12**	**0**
2008–09	*Leyton Orient*	16	0		
2009–10	Leyton Orient	40	2		
2010–11	Leyton Orient	31	7		
2011–12	Leyton Orient	38	6		
2012–13	Leyton Orient	35	3		
2013–14	Leyton Orient	0	0	**160**	**18**
2013–14	Stevenage	42	3	**42**	**3**
2014–15	Crawley T	36	1		
2015–16	Crawley T	31	1		
2016–17	Crawley T	46	7	**113**	**9**

TAJBAKHSH, Aryan (M) **4** **0**
H: 6 1 W: 11 06 b.Istanbul 20-10-90
From Cray W.

2016–17	Crawley T	4	0	**4**	**0**

WATT, Sanchez (M) **101** **11**
H: 5 11 W: 12 00 b.Hackney 14-2-91
Internationals: England U16, U17, U19.

2008–09	Arsenal	0	0		
2009–10	Arsenal	0	0		
2009–10	*Southend U*	4	0	**4**	**0**
2009–10	*Leeds U*	6	0		
2010–11	Arsenal	0	0		
2010–11	*Leeds U*	22	1	**28**	**1**
2011–12	Arsenal	0	0		
2011–12	*Sheffield W*	4	0	**4**	**0**
2011–12	*Crawley T*	14	2		
2012–13	Arsenal	0	0		
2012–13	*Colchester U*	6	2		
2013–14	Colchester U	22	3		
2014–15	Colchester U	21	3	**49**	**8**
2016–17	Kerala Blasters	0	0		
2016–17	Crawley T	2	0	**16**	**2**

YORWERTH, Josh (D) **45** **3**
H: 6 1 W: 11 09 b.Bridgend 1-1-95
Internationals: Wales U17, U19, U21.

2014–15	Cardiff C	0	0		
2015–16	Ipswich T	0	0		
2015–16	*Crawley T*	24	0		
2016–17	Crawley T	21	3	**45**	**3**

YOUNG, Lewis (M) **194** **0**
H: 5 10 W: 11 02 b.Stevenage 27-9-89

2008–09	Watford	1	0		
2009–10	Watford	0	0	**1**	**0**
2009–10	*Hereford U*	6	0	**6**	**0**
2010–11	Burton Alb	19	0	**19**	**0**
2011–12	Northampton T	30	0	**30**	**0**
2012–13	Yeovil T	15	0		
2013–14	Yeovil T	0	0	**15**	**0**
2013–14	Bury	4	0	**4**	**0**
2014–15	Crawley T	38	0		
2015–16	Crawley T	38	0		
2016–17	Crawley T	43	0	**119**	**0**

CREWE ALEX (30)

AINLEY, Callum (M) **43** **2**
H: 5 8 W: 10 01 b.Middlewich 2-11-97

2015–16	Crewe Alex	16	1		
2016–17	Crewe Alex	27	1	**43**	**2**

BAKAYOGO, Zaoumana (D) **206** **6**
H: 5 9 W: 10 08 b.Paris 11-8-86
Internationals: Ivory Coast U23.

2006–07	Millwall	5	0		
2007–08	Millwall	10	0	**15**	**0**

From Alfortville.

2009–10	Tranmere R	29	0		
2010–11	Tranmere R	27	1		
2011–12	Tranmere R	26	0		
2012–13	Tranmere R	46	4	**128**	**5**
2013–14	Leicester C	0	0		
2013–14	*Yeovil T*	1	0	**1**	**0**
2015–16	Crewe Alex	22	1		
2016–17	Crewe Alex	40	0	**62**	**1**

BINGHAM, Billy (D) **168** **8**
H: 5 11 W: 11 02 b.Welling 15-7-90

2008–09	Dagenham & R	0	0		
2009–10	Dagenham & R	2	0		
2010–11	Dagenham & R	6	0		
2011–12	Dagenham & R	27	2		
2012–13	Dagenham & R	18	2		
2013–14	Dagenham & R	30	0		
2014–15	Dagenham & R	34	4	**117**	**8**
2015–16	Crewe Alex	21	0		
2016–17	Crewe Alex	30	0	**51**	**0**

COOPER, George (M) **95** **13**
H: 5 9 W: 11 05 b.Warrington 2-11-96

2014–15	Crewe Alex	22	3		
2015–16	Crewe Alex	27	1		
2016–17	Crewe Alex	46	9	**95**	**13**

DAGNALL, Chris (F) **421** **109**
H: 5 8 W: 12 03 b.Liverpool 15-4-86

2003–04	Tranmere R	10	1		
2004–05	Tranmere R	23	6		
2005–06	Tranmere R	6	0	**39**	**7**
2005–06	Rochdale	21	3		
2006–07	Rochdale	37	17		
2007–08	Rochdale	14	7		
2008–09	Rochdale	40	7		
2009–10	Rochdale	45	20	**157**	**54**
2010–11	Scunthorpe U	37	5		
2011–12	Scunthorpe U	23	4	**60**	**9**
2011–12	Barnsley	9	0		
2011–12	*Bradford C*	7	1	**7**	**1**
2012–13	Barnsley	36	5		
2013–14	Barnsley	8	1	**53**	**6**
2013–14	*Coventry C*	6	1	**6**	**1**
2013–14	Leyton Orient	20	6		
2014–15	Leyton Orient	38	11	**58**	**17**
2015–16	Kerala Blasters	0	0		
2015–16	Hibernian	0	0		
2016–17	Crewe Alex	41	14	**41**	**14**

DALE, Owen (F) **0** **0**
H: 5 9 W: 10 03 b.Warrington 1-11-98

2016–17	Crewe Alex	0	0		

DAVIS, Harry (D) **190** **14**
H: 6 2 W: 12 04 b.Burnley 24-9-91

2009–10	Crewe Alex	1	0		
2010–11	Crewe Alex	1	0		
2011–12	Crewe Alex	41	5		
2012–13	Crewe Alex	42	1		
2013–14	Crewe Alex	32	3		
2014–15	Crewe Alex	31	1		
2015–16	Crewe Alex	11	1		
2016–17	Crewe Alex	25	1	**184**	**12**
2016–17	*St Mirren*	6	2	**6**	**2**

DAWBER, Andrew (G) **5** **0**
H: 6 0 W: 12 04 b.Wigan 20-11-94

2012–13	Accrington S	2	0		
2013–14	Accrington S	3	0		
2014–15	Accrington S	0	0	**5**	**0**
2015–16	Fulham	0	0		
2016–17	Crewe Alex	0	0		

FINNEY, Oliver (M) **1** **0**
b.Stoke-on-Trent 15-12-97

2015–16	Crewe Alex	0	0		
2016–17	Crewe Alex	1	0	**1**	**0**

GARRATT, Ben (G) **149** **0**
H: 6 1 W: 10 06 b.Market Drayton 25-4-94
Internationals: England U17, U18, U19.

2011–12	Crewe Alex	0	0		
2012–13	Crewe Alex	1	0		
2013–14	Crewe Alex	26	0		
2014–15	Crewe Alex	30	0		

2015–16 Crewe Alex 46 0
2016–17 Crewe Alex 46 0 **149 0**

GUTHRIE, Jon (D) 122 1
H: 5 10 W: 11 00 b.Devizes 1-2-93
2011–12 Crewe Alex 0 0
2012–13 Crewe Alex 2 0
2013–14 Crewe Alex 23 0
2014–15 Crewe Alex 25 0
2015–16 Crewe Alex 39 1
2016–17 Crewe Alex 33 0 **122 1**

HOLLANDS, Danny (M) 394 42
H: 6 0 W: 11 11 b.Ashford (Middlesex) 6-11-85
2003–04 Chelsea 0 0
2004–05 Chelsea 0 0
2005–06 Chelsea 0 0
2005–06 *Torquay U* 10 1 **10 1**
2006–07 Bournemouth 33 1
2007–08 Bournemouth 37 4
2008–09 Bournemouth 42 6
2009–10 Bournemouth 39 6
2010–11 Bournemouth 42 7 **193 24**
2011–12 Charlton Ath 43 7
2012–13 Charlton Ath 14 0
2012–13 *Swindon T* 10 2 **10 2**
2013–14 Charlton Ath 0 0 **57 7**
2013–14 *Gillingham* 17 1 **17 1**
2013–14 *Portsmouth* 7 5
2014–15 Portsmouth 44 1
2015–16 Portsmouth 32 0 **83 6**
2016–17 Crewe Alex 24 1 **24 1**

JONES, James (M) 100 11
H: 5 9 W: 10 10 b.Winsford 1-2-96
Internationals: Scotland U19, U21.
2014–15 Crewe Alex 24 1
2015–16 Crewe Alex 31 0
2016–17 Crewe Alex 45 10 **100 11**

KIRK, Charlie (M) 36 0
H: 5 7 W: 11 00 b.Winsford 24-12-97
2015–16 Crewe Alex 14 0
2016–17 Crewe Alex 22 0 **36 0**

LOWERY, Tom (M) 7 0
b.Holmes Chapel 31-12-97
2016–17 Crewe Alex 7 0 **7 0**

NG, Perry (D) 22 0
H: 5 11 W: 12 02 b.Liverpool 24-6-94
2014–15 Crewe Alex 0 0
2015–16 Crewe Alex 6 0
2016–17 Crewe Alex 16 0 **22 0**

NUGENT, Ben (D) 105 3
H: 6 1 W: 13 00 b.Street 28-11-93
2012–13 Cardiff C 12 1
2013–14 Cardiff C 0 0
2013–14 *Brentford* 0 0
2013–14 *Peterborough U* 11 0 **11 0**
2014–15 Cardiff C 0 0 **12 1**
2014–15 *Yeovil T* 23 1 **23 1**
2015–16 Crewe Alex 39 1
2016–17 Crewe Alex 20 0 **59 1**

PICKERING, Harry (D) 1 0
b.Chester 29-12-98
2016–17 Port Vale 0 0
2016–17 Crewe Alex 1 0 **1 0**

RAY, George (D) 93 3
H: 5 10 W: 11 03 b.Warrington 13-10-93
Internationals: Wales U21.
2011–12 Crewe Alex 0 0
2012–13 Crewe Alex 4 0
2013–14 Crewe Alex 9 0
2014–15 Crewe Alex 35 2
2015–16 Crewe Alex 22 0
2016–17 Crewe Alex 23 1 **93 3**

RICHARDS, Dave (G) 0 0
H: 5 11 W: 11 11 b.Abergavenny 31-12-93
2013–14 Cardiff C 0 0
2013–14 Bristol C 0 0
2014–15 Bristol C 0 0
2015–16 Crewe Alex 0 0
2016–17 Crewe Alex 0 0

SAUNDERS, Callum (F) 27 2
H: 5 10 W: 11 11 b.Istanbul 26-9-95
Internationals: Wales U19, U21.
2014–15 Crewe Alex 4 0
2015–16 Crewe Alex 18 2
2016–17 Crewe Alex 5 0 **27 2**

TURTON, Oliver (D) 170 4
H: 5 11 W: 11 11 b.Manchester 6-12-92
2010–11 Crewe Alex 1 0
2011–12 Crewe Alex 2 0
2012–13 Crewe Alex 20 0
2013–14 Crewe Alex 12 1
2014–15 Crewe Alex 44 1
2015–16 Crewe Alex 46 1
2016–17 Crewe Alex 45 1 **170 4**

UDOH, Daniel (F) 15 0
H: 6 0 W: 13 01 b. 30-8-96
Internationals: Nigeria U17.
2015–16 Crewe Alex 6 0
2016–17 Crewe Alex 9 0 **15 0**

WINTLE, Ryan (M) 20 1
H: 5 5 W: 10 01 b.Newcastle-under-Lyme 13-6-97
2015–16 Crewe Alex 3 0
2016–17 Crewe Alex 17 1 **20 1**

Players retained or with offer of contract
Poscha, Marcus Anthony.

Scholars
Appleyard, William Hugh; Barlow, Luke James; Culpeper, Arturo; Griffiths, Regan Jon; Harrison, Oliver Charlie; Hilton, Jake; Hurst, Alexander Charles; Johnson, Travis Joel Gary; Jones, Morgan Wyn; Lundstram, Joshua; Lynch, Joseph Steven; Manuel, Adao Luis; Offord, Luke William; Reilly, Lewis Colin; Sass-Davies, William John; Thompson, Joseph Jordan Cosgrove; Walley, Luke Antony; Walsh, Luke Albert; Wardley, Scott Graham; Wilkinson, Jamie Paul; Woodcock, Ross Callum.

CRYSTAL PALACE (31)

ANDERSON, Keshi (F) 29 7
H: 5 9 W: 10 10 b.Luton 15-11-95
2014–15 Crystal Palace 0 0
2015–16 Crystal Palace 0 0
2015–16 *Doncaster R* 7 3 **7 3**
2016–17 Crystal Palace 0 0
2016–17 *Bolton W* 8 1 **8 1**
2016–17 *Northampton T* 14 3 **14 3**

BENTEKE, Christian (F) 258 102
H: 6 3 W: 13 00 b.Kinshasa 3-12-90
Internationals: Belgium U17, U18, U19, U21, Full caps.
2007–08 Genk 7 0
2008–09 Genk 3 0
2008–09 Standard Liege 9 3
2009–10 *KV Kortrijk* 24 9 **24 9**
2010–11 Standard Liege 5 0
2010–11 *KV Mechelen* 15 5 **15 5**
2011–12 Standard Liege 4 0 **18 3**
2011–12 Genk 32 16
2012–13 Genk 5 3 **47 19**
2012–13 Aston Villa 34 19
2013–14 Aston Villa 26 10
2014–15 Aston Villa 29 13 **89 42**
2015–16 Liverpool 29 9 **29 9**
2016–17 Crystal Palace 36 15 **36 15**

BENTEKE, Jonathan (F) 42 4
b. 28-4-95
From Standard Liege.
2013–14 Vise 20 2 **20 2**
2014–15 Zulte-Waregem 6 2
2015–16 Zulte-Waregem 15 0
2016–17 Zulte-Waregem 0 0 **21 2**
2016–17 Crystal Palace 1 0 **1 0**

BOATENG, Hiram (M) 51 1
H: 5 7 W: 11 00 b.Wandsworth 8-1-96
2012–13 Crystal Palace 0 0
2013–14 Crystal Palace 0 0
2013–14 *Crawley T* 1 0 **1 0**
2014–15 Crystal Palace 0 0
2015–16 Crystal Palace 1 0
2015–16 *Plymouth Arg* 24 1 **24 1**
2016–17 Crystal Palace 0 0 **1 0**
2016–17 *Bristol R* 9 0 **9 0**
2016–17 *Northampton T* 16 0 **16 0**

CABAYE, Yohan (M) 335 57
H: 5 9 W: 11 05 b.Tourcoing 14-1-86
Internationals: France U16, U18, U19, U20, U21, Full caps.
2004–05 Lille 6 0
2005–06 Lille 27 1
2006–07 Lille 22 3
2007–08 Lille 36 7
2008–09 Lille 32 5
2009–10 Lille 32 13
2010–11 Lille 36 2 **191 31**
2011–12 Newcastle U 34 4
2012–13 Newcastle U 26 6
2013–14 Newcastle U 19 7 **79 17**
2015–16 Crystal Palace 33 5
2016–17 Crystal Palace 32 4 **65 9**

CAMPBELL, Frazier (F) 196 40
H: 5 11 W: 12 04 b.Huddersfield 13-9-87
Internationals: England U16, U17, U18, U21, Full caps.
2005–06 Manchester U 0 0
2006–07 Manchester U 0 0
2007–08 Manchester U 1 0
2007–08 *Hull C* 34 15 **34 15**
2008–09 Manchester U 1 0
2008–09 *Tottenham H* 10 1 **10 1**
2009–10 Manchester U 0 0 **2 0**
2009–10 Sunderland 31 4
2010–11 Sunderland 3 0
2011–12 Sunderland 12 1
2012–13 Sunderland 12 1 **58 6**
2012–13 Cardiff C 12 7
2013–14 Cardiff C 37 6 **49 13**
2014–15 Crystal Palace 20 4
2015–16 Crystal Palace 11 0
2016–17 Crystal Palace 12 1 **43 5**

CROLL, Luke (D) 22 0
H: 6 1 W: 12 08 b.Lambeth 10-1-95
2014–15 Crystal Palace 0 0
2015–16 Crystal Palace 0 0
2015–16 *Plymouth Arg* 3 0 **3 0**
2016–17 Crystal Palace 0 0
2016–17 *Exeter C* 19 0 **19 0**

DANN, Scott (D) 360 28
H: 6 2 W: 12 00 b.Liverpool 14-2-87
Internationals: England U21.
2004–05 Walsall 1 0
2005–06 Walsall 0 0
2006–07 Walsall 30 4
2007–08 Walsall 28 3 **59 7**
2007–08 Coventry C 16 0
2008–09 Coventry C 31 3 **47 3**
2009–10 Birmingham C 30 0
2010–11 Birmingham C 20 2
2011–12 Birmingham C 0 0 **50 2**
2011–12 Blackburn R 27 1
2012–13 Blackburn R 46 4
2013–14 Blackburn R 25 0 **98 5**
2013–14 Crystal Palace 14 1
2014–15 Crystal Palace 34 2
2015–16 Crystal Palace 35 5
2016–17 Crystal Palace 23 3 **106 11**

DELANEY, Damien (D) 573 16
H: 6 3 W: 14 00 b.Cork 20-7-81
Internationals: Republic of Ireland Full caps.
2000–01 Leicester C 5 0
2001–02 Leicester C 3 0
2001–02 *Stockport Co* 12 1 **12 1**
2001–02 *Huddersfield T* 2 0 **2 0**
2002–03 Leicester C 0 0 **8 0**
2002–03 *Mansfield T* 7 0 **7 0**
2002–03 Hull C 30 1
2003–04 Hull C 46 2
2004–05 Hull C 43 1
2005–06 Hull C 46 0
2006–07 Hull C 37 1
2007–08 Hull C 22 0 **224 5**
2007–08 QPR 17 1
2008–09 QPR 37 1
2009–10 QPR 0 0 **54 2**
2009–10 Ipswich T 36 0
2010–11 Ipswich T 32 2
2011–12 Ipswich T 29 0
2012–13 Ipswich T 1 0 **98 2**
2012–13 Crystal Palace 40 3
2013–14 Crystal Palace 37 1
2014–15 Crystal Palace 29 0
2015–16 Crystal Palace 32 2
2016–17 Crystal Palace 30 0 **168 6**

DREHER, Luke (M) 0 0
H: 6 1 W: 12 00 b.Epsom 27-11-98
2015–16 Crystal Palace 0 0
2016–17 Crystal Palace 0 0

FLAMINI, Mathieu (M) 284 17
H: 5 10 W: 10 07 b.Marseille 7-3-84
Internationals: France U21, Full caps.
2003–04 Marseille 14 0 **14 0**
2004–05 Arsenal 21 1
2005–06 Arsenal 31 0
2006–07 Arsenal 20 3
2007–08 Arsenal 30 3
2008–09 AC Milan 28 0
2009–10 AC Milan 23 0
2010–11 AC Milan 22 2
2011–12 AC Milan 2 1
2012–13 AC Milan 17 4 **92 7**
2013–14 Arsenal 27 2

2014–15	Arsenal	23	1		
2015–16	Arsenal	16	0	**168**	**10**
2016–17	Crystal Palace	10	0	**10**	**0**

FRYERS, Zeki (D) 38 0
H: 6 0 W: 12 00 b.Manchester 9-9-92
Internationals: England U16, U17, U19.

2011–12	Manchester U	2	0	**2**	**0**
2012–13	Standard Liege	7	0	**7**	**0**
2012–13	Tottenham H	0	0		
2013–14	Tottenham H	7	0	**7**	**0**
2014–15	Crystal Palace	1	0		
2014–15	*Rotherham U*	10	0	**10**	**0**
2014–15	*Ipswich T*	3	0	**3**	**0**
2015–16	Crystal Palace	0	0		
2016–17	Crystal Palace	8	0	**9**	**0**

HENNESSEY, Wayne (G) 241 0
H: 6 0 W: 11 06 b.Anglesey 24-1-87
Internationals: Wales U17, U19, U21, Full caps.

2004–05	Wolverhampton W	0	0		
2005–06	Wolverhampton W	0	0		
2006–07	Wolverhampton W	0	0		
2006–07	*Bristol C*	0	0		
2006–07	*Stockport Co*	15	0	**15**	**0**
2007–08	Wolverhampton W	46	0		
2008–09	Wolverhampton W	35	0		
2009–10	Wolverhampton W	13	0		
2010–11	Wolverhampton W	24	0		
2011–12	Wolverhampton W	34	0		
2012–13	Wolverhampton W	0	0		
2013–14	Wolverhampton W	0	0	**152**	**0**
2013–14	*Yeovil T*	12	0	**12**	**0**
2013–14	Crystal Palace	1	0		
2014–15	Crystal Palace	3	0		
2015–16	Crystal Palace	29	0		
2016–17	Crystal Palace	29	0	**62**	**0**

HUSIN, Noor (M) 11 1
H: 5 10 W: 10 03 b.Mazar-i-Sharif 3-3-97

2015–16	Reading	0	0		
2016–17	Crystal Palace	0	0		
2016–17	*Accrington S*	11	1	**11**	**1**

INNISS, Ryan (D) 41 0
H: 6 5 W: 13 02 b.Kent 5-6-95
Internationals: England U16, U17.

2012–13	Crystal Palace	0	0		
2013–14	Crystal Palace	0	0		
2013–14	*Cheltenham T*	2	0	**2**	**0**
2013–14	*Gillingham*	3	0	**3**	**0**
2014–15	Crystal Palace	0	0		
2014–15	*Yeovil T*	6	0	**6**	**0**
2014–15	*Port Vale*	5	0		
2015–16	Crystal Palace	0	0		
2015–16	*Port Vale*	15	0	**20**	**0**
2016–17	Crystal Palace	0	0		
2016–17	*Southend U*	10	0	**10**	**0**

KAIKAI, Sullay (F) 76 20
H: 6 0 W: 11 07 b.London 26-8-95

2013–14	Crystal Palace	0	0		
2013–14	*Crawley T*	5	0	**5**	**0**
2014–15	Crystal Palace	0	0		
2014–15	*Cambridge U*	25	5	**25**	**5**
2015–16	Crystal Palace	1	0		
2015–16	*Shrewsbury T*	26	12	**26**	**12**
2016–17	Brentford	18	3	**18**	**3**
2016–17	Crystal Palace	1	0	**2**	**0**

KELLY, Martin (D) 113 1
H: 6 3 W: 12 02 b.Bolton 27-4-90
Internationals: England U19, U20, U21, Full caps.

2007–08	Liverpool	0	0		
2008–09	Liverpool	0	0		
2008–09	*Huddersfield T*	7	1	**7**	**1**
2009–10	Liverpool	1	0		
2010–11	Liverpool	11	0		
2011–12	Liverpool	12	0		
2012–13	Liverpool	4	0		
2013–14	Liverpool	5	0	**33**	**0**
2014–15	Crystal Palace	31	0		
2015–16	Crystal Palace	13	0		
2016–17	Crystal Palace	29	0	**73**	**0**

LADAPO, Freddie (F) 38 6
H: 6 0 W: 12 06 b.Romford 1-2-93

2011–12	Colchester U	0	0		
2012–13	Colchester U	4	0		
2013–14	Colchester U	2	0	**6**	**0**
2015–16	Crystal Palace	0	0		
2016–17	Crystal Palace	0	0		
2016–17	*Oldham Ath*	17	2	**17**	**2**
2016–17	*Shrewsbury T*	15	4	**15**	**4**

LEDLEY, Joe (M) 415 51
H: 6 0 W: 11 06 b.Cardiff 23-1-87
Internationals: Wales U17, U19, U21, Full caps.

2004–05	Cardiff C	28	3		
2005–06	Cardiff C	42	3		
2006–07	Cardiff C	46	2		
2007–08	Cardiff C	41	10		
2008–09	Cardiff C	40	4		
2009–10	Cardiff C	29	3	**226**	**25**
2010–11	Celtic	29	2		
2011–12	Celtic	32	7		
2012–13	Celtic	25	7		
2013–14	Celtic	20	4	**106**	**20**
2013–14	Crystal Palace	14	2		
2014–15	Crystal Palace	32	2		
2015–16	Crystal Palace	19	1		
2016–17	Crystal Palace	18	1	**83**	**6**

LEE, Chung Yong (M) 258 28
H: 5 11 W: 10 09 b.Seoul 2-7-88
Internationals: South Korea U19, U20, Full caps.

2006	FC Seoul	2	0		
2007	FC Seoul	15	3		
2008	FC Seoul	20	5		
2009	FC Seoul	14	2	**51**	**10**
2009–10	Bolton W	34	4		
2010–11	Bolton W	31	3		
2011–12	Bolton W	2	0		
2012–13	Bolton W	41	4		
2013–14	Bolton W	45	3		
2014–15	Bolton W	23	3	**176**	**17**
2014–15	Crystal Palace	3	0		
2015–16	Crystal Palace	13	1		
2016–17	Crystal Palace	15	0	**31**	**1**

MANDANDA, Steve (G) 410 0
H: 6 1 W: 12 13 b.Kinshasa 28-3-85
Internationals: France U21, B, Full caps.

2005–06	Le Havre	30	0		
2006–07	Le Havre	37	0	**67**	**0**
2007–08	Marseille	34	0		
2008–09	Marseille	38	0		
2009–10	Marseille	36	0		
2010–11	Marseille	38	0		
2011–12	Marseille	38	0		
2012–13	Marseille	38	0		
2013–14	Marseille	38	0		
2014–15	Marseille	38	0		
2015–16	Marseille	36	0	**334**	**0**
2016–17	Crystal Palace	9	0	**9**	**0**

McARTHUR, James (M) 386 29
H: 5 6 W: 9 13 b.Glasgow 7-10-87
Internationals: Scotland U21, Full caps.

2004–05	Hamilton A	6	0		
2005–06	Hamilton A	20	1		
2006–07	Hamilton A	36	1		
2007–08	Hamilton A	34	4		
2008–09	Hamilton A	37	2		
2009–10	Hamilton A	35	1	**168**	**9**
2010–11	Wigan Ath	18	0		
2011–12	Wigan Ath	31	3		
2012–13	Wigan Ath	34	3		
2013–14	Wigan Ath	41	4		
2014–15	Wigan Ath	5	1	**129**	**11**
2014–15	Crystal Palace	32	2		
2015–16	Crystal Palace	28	2		
2016–17	Crystal Palace	29	5	**89**	**9**

MILIVOJEVIC, Luka (M) 185 24
H: 6 0 b.Kragujevac 7-4-91
Internationals: Serbia U21, Full caps.

2007–08	Radnicki Kraguejevac	5	1	**5**	**1**
2008–09	Rad Belgrade	1	0		
2009–10	Rad Belgrade	9	0		
2010–11	Rad Belgrade	26	0		
2011–12	Rad Belgrade	13	3	**49**	**3**
2011–12	Red Star Belgrade	11	1		
2012–13	Red Star Belgrade	25	6	**36**	**7**
2013–14	Anderlecht	16	0		
2014–15	Anderlecht	3	0	**19**	**0**
2014–15	Olympiacos	23	2		
2015–16	Olympiacos	22	3		
2016–17	Olympiacos	17	6	**62**	**11**
2016–17	Crystal Palace	14	2	**14**	**2**

MUTCH, Jordon (M) 173 17
H: 5 9 W: 10 03 b.Derby 2-12-91
Internationals: England U17, U19, U20, U21.

2007–08	Birmingham C	0	0		
2008–09	Birmingham C	0	0		
2009–10	Birmingham C	0	0		
2009–10	*Hereford U*	3	0	**3**	**0**
2009–10	*Doncaster R*	17	2	**17**	**2**
2010–11	Birmingham C	3	0		
2010–11	*Watford*	23	5	**23**	**5**
2011–12	Birmingham C	21	2	**24**	**2**
2012–13	Cardiff C	22	0		
2013–14	Cardiff C	35	7	**57**	**7**
2014–15	QPR	9	0	**9**	**0**
2014–15	Crystal Palace	7	0		
2015–16	Crystal Palace	20	0		
2016–17	Crystal Palace	4	0	**31**	**0**
2016–17	*Reading*	9	1	**9**	**1**

PERNTREOU, Kleiton (M) 0 0
H: 5 8 b. 8-1-95

2012–13	Bristol C	0	0		
2013–14	Bristol C	0	0		
2013–14	Hibernian	0	0		
2016–17	Crystal Palace	0	0		

PHILLIPS, Michael (M) 0 0

2016–17	Crystal Palace	0	0		

PUNCHEON, Jason (M) 401 59
H: 5 9 W: 12 05 b.Croydon 26-6-86

2003–04	Wimbledon	8	0	**8**	**0**
2004–05	Milton Keynes D	25	1		
2005–06	Milton Keynes D	1	0		
2006–07	Barnet	37	5		
2007–08	Barnet	41	10	**78**	**15**
2008–09	Plymouth Arg	6	0		
2008–09	*Milton Keynes D*	27	4		
2009–10	Plymouth Arg	0	0	**6**	**0**
2009–10	*Milton Keynes D*	24	7	**77**	**12**
2009–10	Southampton	19	3		
2010–11	Southampton	15	0		
2010–11	*Millwall*	7	5	**7**	**5**
2010–11	*Blackpool*	11	3	**11**	**3**
2011–12	Southampton	8	0		
2011–12	*QPR*	2	0	**2**	**0**
2012–13	Southampton	32	6		
2013–14	Southampton	0	0	**74**	**9**
2013–14	Crystal Palace	34	7		
2014–15	Crystal Palace	37	6		
2015–16	Crystal Palace	31	2		
2016–17	Crystal Palace	36	0	**138**	**15**

SAKO, Bakary (M) 315 61
H: 5 11 W: 11 12 b.Ivry Sur Seine 26-4-88
Internationals: France U21. Mali U17, Full caps.

2006–07	Chateauroux	17	0		
2007–08	Chateauroux	12	1		
2008–09	Chateauroux	35	9	**64**	**10**
2009–10	St Etienne	30	1		
2010–11	St Etienne	38	7		
2011–12	St Etienne	36	5		
2012–13	St Etienne	2	0	**106**	**13**
2012–13	Wolverhampton W	37	9		
2013–14	Wolverhampton W	40	12		
2014–15	Wolverhampton W	41	15	**118**	**36**
2015–16	Crystal Palace	20	2		
2016–17	Crystal Palace	7	0	**27**	**2**

SCHLUPP, Jeffrey (M) 150 16
H: 5 8 W: 11 00 b.Hamburg 23-12-92
Internationals: Ghana Full caps.

2010–11	Leicester C	0	0		
2010–11	*Brentford*	9	6	**9**	**6**
2011–12	Leicester C	21	2		
2012–13	Leicester C	19	3		
2013–14	Leicester C	26	1		
2014–15	Leicester C	32	3		
2015–16	Leicester C	24	1		
2016–17	Leicester C	4	0	**126**	**10**
2016–17	Crystal Palace	15	0	**15**	**0**

SOUARE, Pape (D) 125 3
H: 5 10 W: 10 10 b.Mbao 6-6-90
Internationals: Senegal U23, Full caps.

2010–11	Lille	4	0		
2011–12	Lille	7	0		
2012–13	Lille	0	0		
2012–13	*Reims*	23	0	**23**	**0**
2013–14	Lille	33	3		
2014–15	Lille	12	0	**56**	**3**
2014–15	Crystal Palace	9	0		
2015–16	Crystal Palace	34	0		
2016–17	Crystal Palace	3	0	**46**	**0**

SPERONI, Julian (G) 453 0
H: 6 0 W: 11 00 b.Buenos Aires 18-5-79
Internationals: Argentina U20, U21.

1999–2000	Platense	2	0		
2000–01	Platense	0	0	**2**	**0**
2001–02	Dundee	17	0		
2002–03	Dundee	38	0		
2003–04	Dundee	37	0	**92**	**0**
2004–05	Crystal Palace	6	0		
2005–06	Crystal Palace	4	0		
2006–07	Crystal Palace	5	0		
2007–08	Crystal Palace	46	0		
2008–09	Crystal Palace	45	0		
2009–10	Crystal Palace	45	0		
2010–11	Crystal Palace	45	0		

2011–12 Crystal Palace 42 0
2012–13 Crystal Palace 46 0
2013–14 Crystal Palace 37 0
2014–15 Crystal Palace 36 0
2015–16 Crystal Palace 2 0
2016–17 Crystal Palace 0 0 **359 0**

TOMKINS, James (D) 239 11
H: 6 3 W: 11 10 b.Basildon 29-3-89
Internationals: England U16, U17, U18, U19, U20, U21. Great Britain.
2005–06 West Ham U 0 0
2006–07 West Ham U 0 0
2007–08 West Ham U 6 0
2008–09 West Ham U 12 1
2008–09 *Derby Co* 7 0 **7 0**
2009–10 West Ham U 23 0
2010–11 West Ham U 19 1
2011–12 West Ham U 44 4
2012–13 West Ham U 26 1
2013–14 West Ham U 31 0
2014–15 West Ham U 22 1
2015–16 West Ham U 25 0 **208 8**
2016–17 Crystal Palace 24 3 **24 3**

TOWNSEND, Andros (M) 200 21
H: 6 0 W: 12 00 b.Chingford 16-7-91
Internationals: England U16, U17, U19, U21, Full caps.
2008–09 Tottenham H 0 0
2008–09 *Yeovil T* 10 1 **10 1**
2009–10 Tottenham H 0 0
2009–10 *Leyton Orient* 22 2 **22 2**
2009–10 *Milton Keynes D* 9 2 **9 2**
2010–11 Tottenham H 0 0
2010–11 *Ipswich T* 13 1 **13 1**
2010–11 *Watford* 3 0 **3 0**
2010–11 *Millwall* 11 2 **11 2**
2011–12 Tottenham H 0 0
2011–12 *Leeds U* 6 1 **6 1**
2011–12 *Birmingham C* 15 0 **15 0**
2012–13 Tottenham H 5 0
2012–13 *QPR* 12 2 **12 2**
2013–14 Tottenham H 25 1
2014–15 Tottenham H 17 2
2015–16 Tottenham H 3 0 **50 3**
2015–16 Newcastle U 13 4 **13 4**
2016–17 Crystal Palace 36 3 **36 3**

VAN AANHOLT, Patrick (D) 204 15
H: 5 9 W: 10 08 b.Den Bosch 3-7-88
Internationals: Netherlands U16, U17, U18, U19, U20, U21, Full caps.
2007–08 Chelsea 0 0
2008–09 Chelsea 0 0
2009–10 Chelsea 2 0
2009–10 *Coventry C* 20 0 **20 0**
2009–10 *Newcastle U* 7 0 **7 0**
2010–11 Chelsea 0 0
2010–11 *Leicester C* 12 1 **12 1**
2011–12 Chelsea 0 0
2011–12 *Wigan Ath* 3 0 **3 0**
2011–12 *Vitesse* 9 0
2012–13 Chelsea 0 0
2012–13 *Vitesse* 31 1
2013–14 Chelsea 0 0 **2 0**
2013–14 *Vitesse* 27 4 **67 5**
2014–15 Sunderland 28 0
2015–16 Sunderland 33 4
2016–17 Sunderland 21 3 **82 7**
2016–17 Crystal Palace 11 2 **11 2**

WAN BISSAKA, Aaron (M) 0 0
b. 26-11-97
2016–17 Crystal Palace 0 0

WARD, Joel (D) 276 10
H: 6 2 W: 11 13 b.Emsworth 29-10-89
2008–09 Portsmouth 0 0
2008–09 *Bournemouth* 21 1 **21 1**
2009–10 Portsmouth 3 0
2010–11 Portsmouth 42 3
2011–12 Portsmouth 44 3 **89 6**
2012–13 Crystal Palace 25 0
2013–14 Crystal Palace 36 0
2014–15 Crystal Palace 37 1
2015–16 Crystal Palace 30 2
2016–17 Crystal Palace 38 0 **166 3**

WICKHAM, Connor (F) 195 40
H: 6 0 W: 14 01 b.Hereford 31-3-93
Internationals: England U16, U17, U19, U21.
2008–09 Ipswich T 2 0
2009–10 Ipswich T 26 4
2010–11 Ipswich T 37 9 **65 13**
2011–12 Sunderland 16 1
2012–13 Sunderland 12 0
2012–13 *Sheffield W* 6 1
2013–14 Sunderland 15 5
2013–14 *Sheffield W* 11 8 **17 9**
2013–14 *Leeds U* 5 0 **5 0**
2014–15 Sunderland 36 5 **79 11**
2015–16 Crystal Palace 21 5
2016–17 Crystal Palace 8 2 **29 7**

WILLIAMS, Jon (M) 106 2
H: 5 6 W: 10 00 b.Tunbridge Wells 9-10-93
Internationals: Wales U17, U19, U21, Full caps.
2010–11 Crystal Palace 0 0
2011–12 Crystal Palace 14 0
2012–13 Crystal Palace 29 0
2013–14 Crystal Palace 9 0
2013–14 *Ipswich T* 13 1
2014–15 Crystal Palace 2 0
2014–15 *Ipswich T* 7 1
2015–16 Crystal Palace 1 0
2015–16 *Nottingham F* 10 0 **10 0**
2015–16 *Milton Keynes D* 13 0 **13 0**
2016–17 Crystal Palace 0 0 **55 0**
2016–17 *Ipswich T* 8 0 **28 2**

WYNTER, Ben (D) 0 0
2016–17 Crystal Palace 0 0

ZAHA, Wilfried (F) 240 26
H: 5 11 W: 10 05 b.Ivory Coast 10-11-92
Internationals: England U19, U21, Full caps.
2009–10 Crystal Palace 1 0
2010–11 Crystal Palace 41 1
2011–12 Crystal Palace 41 6
2012–13 Crystal Palace 43 6
2012–13 Manchester U 0 0
2013–14 Manchester U 2 0 **2 0**
2013–14 *Cardiff C* 12 0 **12 0**
2014–15 Crystal Palace 31 4
2015–16 Crystal Palace 34 2
2016–17 Crystal Palace 35 7 **226 26**

Players retained or with offer of contract
Berkeley-Agyepong, Jacob Kwame; Coker, Andre Jordan Coleridge; Eyenga, Lokilo Jason; Flanagan, Kian; Fundi, Victor; Jno, Baptiste Francis; Kirby, Nya Jerome; Lumeka, Levi Jeremiah; McGregor, Giovanni Donald; Mitchell, Tyrick; O'Dwyer, Oliver; Tavares, Nikola; Wan-Bissaka, Aaron.

Scholars
Bryon, Lewis; Coates, Liam; Daly, James Stanley; Demby, Andrew; Funnell, Matthew Ross; Hungbo, Joseph Oluwagbemiga; Lynch, Kyle Jordan Victor; Ossai, Tariq Eddie; Ozono, Will; Peynado-Peart, Malachi Darnell; Serrato, Jordan; Webber, Oliver Henry; Woods, Samuel John.

DERBY CO (32)

ANYA, Ikechi (M) 183 12
H: 5 5 W: 11 04 b.Glasgow 3-1-88
Internationals: Scotland Full caps.
2004–05 Wycombe W 3 0
2005–06 Wycombe W 2 0
2006–07 Wycombe W 13 0
2007–08 Wycombe W 0 0 **18 0**
2008–09 Northampton T 14 3 **14 3**
2010–11 Celta Vigo 1 0 **1 0**
From Cadiz
2012–13 Watford 25 3
2013–14 Watford 35 5
2014–15 Watford 35 0
2015–16 Watford 28 0
2016–17 Watford 1 0 **124 8**
2016–17 Derby Co 26 1 **26 1**

BAIRD, Chris (D) 302 7
H: 5 10 W: 11 11 b.Ballymoney 25-2-82
Internationals: Northern Ireland U18, U21, Full caps.
2000–01 Southampton 0 0
2001–02 Southampton 0 0
2002–03 Southampton 3 0
2003–04 Southampton 4 0
2003–04 *Walsall* 10 0 **10 0**
2003–04 *Watford* 8 0 **8 0**
2004–05 Southampton 0 0
2005–06 Southampton 17 0
2006–07 Southampton 44 3 **68 3**
2007–08 Fulham 18 0
2008–09 Fulham 10 0
2009–10 Fulham 32 0
2010–11 Fulham 29 2
2011–12 Fulham 19 0
2012–13 Fulham 19 2
2013–14 Reading 9 0 **9 0**
2013–14 Burnley 7 0 **7 0**
2014–15 WBA 19 0 **19 0**
2015–16 Derby Co 14 0
2015–16 *Fulham* 7 0 **134 4**
2016–17 Derby Co 33 0 **47 0**

BENNETT, Mason (F) 64 3
H: 5 10 W: 10 02 b.Shirebrook 15-7-96
Internationals: England U16, U17, U19.
2011–12 Derby Co 9 0
2012–13 Derby Co 6 0
2013–14 Derby Co 13 1
2013–14 *Chesterfield* 5 0 **5 0**
2014–15 Derby Co 2 0
2014–15 *Bradford C* 11 1 **11 1**
2015–16 Derby Co 0 0
2015–16 *Burton Alb* 16 1 **16 1**
2016–17 Derby Co 2 0 **32 1**

BENT, Darren (F) 471 178
H: 5 11 W: 12 07 b.Wandsworth 6-2-84
Internationals: England U15, U16, U17, U19, U21, Full caps.
2001–02 Ipswich T 5 1
2002–03 Ipswich T 35 12
2003–04 Ipswich T 37 16
2004–05 Ipswich T 45 20 **122 49**
2005–06 Charlton Ath 36 18
2006–07 Charlton Ath 32 13 **68 31**
2007–08 Tottenham H 27 6
2008–09 Tottenham H 33 12
2009–10 Tottenham H 0 0 **60 18**
2009–10 Sunderland 38 24
2010–11 Sunderland 20 8 **58 32**
2010–11 Aston Villa 16 9
2011–12 Aston Villa 22 9
2012–13 Aston Villa 16 3
2013–14 Aston Villa 0 0
2013–14 *Fulham* 24 3 **24 3**
2014–15 Aston Villa 7 0 **61 21**
2014–15 *Brighton & HA* 5 2 **5 2**
2014–15 Derby Co 15 10
2015–16 Derby Co 21 2
2016–17 Derby Co 37 10 **73 22**

BLACKMAN, Nick (F) 217 45
H: 6 2 W: 11 08 b.Whitefield 11-11-89
2006–07 Macclesfield T 1 0
2007–08 Macclesfield T 11 1
2008–09 Macclesfield T 0 0 **12 1**
2008–09 Blackburn R 0 0
2008–09 *Blackpool* 5 1 **5 1**
2009–10 Blackburn R 0 0
2009–10 *Oldham Ath* 12 1 **12 1**
2010–11 Blackburn R 0 0
2010–11 *Motherwell* 18 10 **18 10**
2010–11 *Aberdeen* 15 2 **15 2**
2011–12 Blackburn R 1 0
2012–13 Blackburn R 0 0 **1 0**
2012–13 Sheffield U 28 11 **28 11**
2012–13 Reading 11 0
2013–14 Reading 30 4
2014–15 Reading 37 3
2015–16 Reading 25 11 **103 18**
2015–16 Derby Co 14 0
2016–17 Derby Co 9 1 **23 1**

BRYSON, Craig (M) 432 56
H: 5 7 W: 10 00 b.Rutherglen 6-11-86
Internationals: Scotland U21, Full caps.
2003–04 Clyde 0 0
2004–05 Clyde 28 3
2005–06 Clyde 33 2
2006–07 Clyde 34 3 **95 8**
2007–08 Kilmarnock 19 4
2008–09 Kilmarnock 33 2
2009–10 Kilmarnock 33 4
2010–11 Kilmarnock 33 2 **118 12**
2011–12 Derby Co 44 6
2012–13 Derby Co 37 5
2013–14 Derby Co 45 16
2014–15 Derby Co 38 4
2015–16 Derby Co 21 3
2016–17 Derby Co 34 2 **219 36**

BUTTERFIELD, Jacob (D) 265 26
H: 5 10 W: 11 00 b.Bradford 10-6-90
Internationals: England U21.
2007–08 Barnsley 3 0
2008–09 Barnsley 3 0
2009–10 Barnsley 20 1
2010–11 Barnsley 40 2
2011–12 Barnsley 24 5 **90 8**
2012–13 Norwich C 0 0
2012–13 *Bolton W* 8 0 **8 0**
2012–13 *Crystal Palace* 9 0 **9 0**
2013–14 Norwich C 0 0
2013–14 Middlesbrough 31 3 **31 3**
2014–15 Huddersfield T 45 6
2015–16 Huddersfield T 5 1 **50 7**

2015–16 Derby Co 37 7
2016–17 Derby Co 40 1 **77 8**

CAMARA, Abdoul (F) 193 15
H: 5 9 W: 10 12 b.Mamar 20-2-90
Internationals: France U17, U18, U21. Ghana Full caps.
2008–09 Rennes 1 0
2009–10 Rennes 0 0
2009–10 *Vannes* 37 4 **37 4**
2010–11 Rennes 24 0
2011–12 Rennes 2 0 **27 0**
2011–12 Sochaux 21 1
2012–13 Sochaux 15 0
2012–13 *PAOK* 13 2 **13 2**
2013–14 Sochaux 11 0 **47 1**
2013–14 *Mallorca* 6 0 **6 0**
2014–15 Angers 27 6
2015–16 Angers 17 2 **44 8**
2015–16 Derby Co 4 0
2016–17 Derby Co 15 0 **19 0**

CARSON, Scott (G) 392 0
H: 6 0 W: 13 06 b.Whitehaven 3-9-85
Internationals: England U18, U21, B, Full caps.
2002–03 Leeds U 0 0
2003–04 Leeds U 3 0
2004–05 Leeds U 0 0 **3 0**
2004–05 Liverpool 4 0
2005–06 Liverpool 0 0
2005–06 *Sheffield W* 9 0 **9 0**
2006–07 Liverpool 0 0
2006–07 *Charlton Ath* 36 0 **36 0**
2007–08 Liverpool 0 0 **4 0**
2007–08 *Aston Villa* 35 0 **35 0**
2008–09 WBA 35 0
2009–10 WBA 43 0
2010–11 WBA 32 0 **110 0**
2011–12 Bursaspor 34 0
2012–13 Bursaspor 29 0 **63 0**
2013–14 Wigan Ath 16 0
2014–15 Wigan Ath 34 0 **50 0**
2015–16 Derby Co 36 0
2016–17 Derby Co 46 0 **82 0**

CHRISTIE, Cyrus (D) 209 4
H: 6 2 W: 12 03 b.Coventry 30-9-92
Internationals: Republic of Ireland Full caps.
2011–12 Coventry C 37 0
2012–13 Coventry C 31 2
2013–14 Coventry C 34 0 **102 2**
2014–15 Derby Co 38 0
2015–16 Derby Co 42 1
2016–17 Derby Co 27 1 **107 2**

ELSNIK, Timi (M) 0 0
H: 5 10 W: 10 03 b.Kidricevo 29-4-98
Internationals: Slovenia U16, U17, U19.
2015–16 Derby Co 0 0
2016–17 Derby Co 0 0

FORSYTH, Craig (M) 238 19
H: 6 0 W: 12 00 b.Carnoustie 24-2-89
Internationals: Scotland Full caps.
2006–07 Dundee 1 0
2007–08 Dundee 0 0
2007–08 *Montrose* 9 0 **9 0**
2008–09 Dundee 1 0
2008–09 *Arbroath* 26 2 **26 2**
2009–10 Dundee 24 2
2010–11 Dundee 33 8 **59 10**
2011–12 Watford 20 3
2012–13 Watford 2 0 **22 3**
2012–13 *Bradford C* 7 0 **7 0**
2012–13 *Derby Co* 10 0
2013–14 Derby Co 46 2
2014–15 Derby Co 44 1
2015–16 Derby Co 12 0
2016–17 Derby Co 3 1 **115 4**

GRANT, Lee (G) 465 0
H: 6 3 W: 13 01 b.Hemel Hempstead 27-1-83
Internationals: England U16, U17, U18, U19, U21.
2000–01 Derby Co 0 0
2001–02 Derby Co 0 0
2002–03 Derby Co 29 0
2003–04 Derby Co 36 0
2004–05 Derby Co 2 0
2005–06 Derby Co 0 0
2005–06 *Burnley* 1 0
2005–06 *Oldham Ath* 16 0 **16 0**
2006–07 Derby Co 7 0
2007–08 Sheffield W 44 0
2008–09 Sheffield W 46 0
2009–10 Sheffield W 46 0 **136 0**
2010–11 Burnley 25 0
2011–12 Burnley 43 0
2012–13 Burnley 46 0 **115 0**
2013–14 Derby Co 46 0
2014–15 Derby Co 40 0
2015–16 Derby Co 10 0
2016–17 Derby Co 0 0 **170 0**
2016–17 *Stoke C* 28 0 **28 0**

GUY, Callum (M) 11 0
b. 25-11-96
2015–16 Derby Co 0 0
2016–17 Derby Co 0 0
2016–17 *Port Vale* 11 0 **11 0**

HANSON, Jamie (F) 42 1
H: 6 3 W: 12 06 b.Burton-upon-Trent 10-11-95
Internationals: England U20.
2012–13 Derby Co 0 0
2013–14 Derby Co 0 0
2014–15 Derby Co 2 1
2015–16 Derby Co 18 0
2016–17 Derby Co 5 0 **25 1**
2016–17 *Wigan Ath* 17 0 **17 0**

HUGHES, Will (M) 165 9
H: 6 1 W: 11 08 b.Weybridge 7-4-95
Internationals: England U17, U21.
2011–12 Derby Co 3 0
2012–13 Derby Co 35 2
2013–14 Derby Co 41 3
2014–15 Derby Co 42 2
2015–16 Derby Co 6 0
2016–17 Derby Co 38 2 **165 9**

INCE, Tom (M) 193 63
H: 5 10 W: 10 06 b.Stockport 30-1-92
Internationals: England U17, U19, U21.
2011–12 Blackpool 0 0
2012–13 Blackpool 44 18
2013–14 Blackpool 23 7 **67 25**
2013–14 *Crystal Palace* 8 1 **8 1**
2014–15 Hull C 7 0 **7 0**
2014–15 *Nottingham F* 6 0 **6 0**
2014–15 *Derby Co* 18 11
2015–16 Derby Co 42 12
2016–17 Derby Co 45 14 **105 37**

JOHNSON, Brad (M) 387 56
H: 6 0 W: 12 10 b.Hackney 28-4-87
2004–05 Cambridge U 1 0 **1 0**
2005–06 Northampton T 3 0
2006–07 Northampton T 27 5
2007–08 Northampton T 23 2 **53 7**
2007–08 Leeds U 21 3
2008–09 Leeds U 15 1
2008–09 *Brighton & HA* 10 4 **10 4**
2009–10 Leeds U 36 7
2010–11 Leeds U 45 5 **117 16**
2011–12 Norwich C 28 2
2012–13 Norwich C 37 1
2013–14 Norwich C 32 3
2014–15 Norwich C 41 15
2015–16 Norwich C 4 0 **142 21**
2015–16 Derby Co 31 5
2016–17 Derby Co 33 3 **64 8**

KEOGH, Richard (D) 453 15
H: 6 0 W: 11 02 b.Harlow 11-8-86
Internationals: Republic of Ireland U21, Full caps.
2004–05 Stoke C 0 0
2005–06 Bristol C 9 1
2005–06 *Wycombe W* 3 0 **3 0**
2006–07 Bristol C 31 2
2007–08 Bristol C 0 0 **40 3**
2007–08 *Huddersfield T* 9 1 **9 1**
2007–08 *Carlisle U* 7 0
2007–08 *Cheltenham T* 10 0 **10 0**
2008–09 Carlisle U 32 1
2009–10 Carlisle U 41 3 **80 4**
2010–11 Coventry C 46 1
2011–12 Coventry C 45 0 **91 1**
2012–13 Derby Co 46 4
2013–14 Derby Co 41 1
2014–15 Derby Co 45 0
2015–16 Derby Co 46 1
2016–17 Derby Co 42 0 **220 6**

LOWE, Max (D) 9 0
H: 5 9 W: 11 09 b.Birmingham 11-5-97
Internationals: England U16, U17, U18, U20.
2013–14 Derby Co 0 0
2014–15 Derby Co 0 0
2015–16 Derby Co 0 0
2016–17 Derby Co 9 0 **9 0**

MACDONALD, Calum (D) 0 0
Internationals: Scotland U21.
2016–17 Derby Co 0 0

MARTIN, Chris (F) 353 109
H: 6 2 W: 12 06 b.Beccles 4-11-88
Internationals: England U19. Scotland Full caps.
2006–07 Norwich C 18 4
2007–08 Norwich C 7 0
2008–09 Norwich C 0 0
2008–09 *Luton T* 40 11 **40 11**
2009–10 Norwich C 42 17
2010–11 Norwich C 30 4
2011–12 Norwich C 4 0
2011–12 *Crystal Palace* 26 7 **26 7**
2012–13 Norwich C 1 0 **102 25**
2012–13 *Swindon T* 12 1 **12 1**
2012–13 *Derby Co* 13 2
2013–14 Derby Co 44 20
2014–15 Derby Co 35 18
2015–16 Derby Co 45 15
2016–17 Derby Co 5 0 **142 55**
2016–17 *Fulham* 31 10 **31 10**

MITCHELL, Jonathan (G) 5 0
H: 5 11 W: 13 08 b.Hartlepool 24-11-94
Internationals: England U21.
2014–15 Derby Co 0 0
2015–16 Derby Co 0 0
2015–16 *Luton T* 5 0 **5 0**
2016–17 Derby Co 0 0

NUGENT, Dave (F) 508 141
H: 5 11 W: 12 13 b.Liverpool 2-5-85
Internationals: England U20, U21, Full caps.
2001–02 Bury 5 0
2002–03 Bury 31 4
2003–04 Bury 26 3
2004–05 Bury 26 11 **88 18**
2004–05 Preston NE 18 8
2005–06 Preston NE 32 10
2006–07 Preston NE 44 15 **94 33**
2007–08 Portsmouth 15 0
2008–09 Portsmouth 16 3
2009–10 Portsmouth 3 0
2009–10 *Burnley* 30 6 **30 6**
2010–11 Portsmouth 44 13 **78 16**
2011–12 Leicester C 42 15
2012–13 Leicester C 42 14
2013–14 Leicester C 46 20
2014–15 Leicester C 29 5 **159 54**
2015–16 Middlesbrough 38 8
2016–17 Middlesbrough 4 0 **42 8**
2016–17 Derby Co 17 6 **17 6**

OLSSON, Marcus (M) 250 14
H: 5 11 W: 10 10 b.Gavle 17-5-88
Internationals: Sweden U21, Full caps.
2008 Halmstad 21 2
2009 Halmstad 20 4
2010 Halmstad 30 4
2011 Halmstad 29 2 **100 12**
2011–12 Blackburn R 12 0
2012–13 Blackburn R 23 1
2013–14 Blackburn R 8 0
2014–15 Blackburn R 41 0
2015–16 Blackburn R 20 0 **104 1**
2015–16 Derby Co 16 1
2016–17 Derby Co 30 0 **46 1**

PEARCE, Alex (D) 305 19
H: 6 0 W: 11 10 b.Wallingford 9-11-88
Internationals: Scotland U19, U21, Full caps.
2006–07 Reading 0 0
2006–07 *Northampton T* 15 1 **15 1**
2007–08 Reading 0 0
2007–08 *Bournemouth* 11 0 **11 0**
2007–08 *Norwich C* 11 0 **11 0**
2008–09 Reading 16 1
2008–09 *Southampton* 9 2 **9 2**
2009–10 Reading 25 4
2010–11 Reading 21 1
2011–12 Reading 46 5
2012–13 Reading 19 0
2013–14 Reading 45 3
2014–15 Reading 40 0 **212 14**
2015–16 Derby Co 0 0
2015–16 *Bristol C* 7 0 **7 0**
2016–17 Derby Co 40 2 **40 2**

RAWSON, Farrend (D) 34 2
H: 6 1 W: 11 07 b.Nottingham 11-7-96
2014–15 Derby Co 0 0
2014–15 *Rotherham U* 4 0
2015–16 Derby Co 0 0
2015–16 *Rotherham U* 16 2 **20 2**
2016–17 Derby Co 0 0
2016–17 *Coventry C* 14 0 **14 0**

ROOS, Kelle (G) **37** **0**
H: 6 4 W: 14 02 b.Rijkevoort 31-5-92

2013–14	Derby Co	0	0		
2014–15	Derby Co	0	0		
2015–16	Derby Co	0	0		
2015–16	*Rotherham U*	4	0	**4**	**0**
2015–16	*AFC Wimbledon*	17	0	**17**	**0**
2016–17	Derby Co	0	0		
2016–17	*Bristol R*	16	0	**16**	**0**

RUSSELL, Johnny (F) **261** **57**
H: 5 10 W: 12 03 b.Glasgow 8-4-90
Internationals: Scotland U19, U21, Full caps.

2006–07	Dundee U	1	0		
2007–08	Dundee U	2	0		
2008–09	Dundee U	0	0		
2009–10	Dundee U	0	0		
2010–11	Dundee U	30	9		
2011–12	Dundee U	37	9		
2012–13	Dundee U	32	13	**102**	**31**
2013–14	Derby Co	39	9		
2014–15	Derby Co	39	6		
2015–16	Derby Co	45	9		
2016–17	Derby Co	36	2	**159**	**26**

SANTOS, Alefe (M) **27** **1**
H: 5 10 W: 10 06 b.Sao Paulo 28-1-95

2012–13	Bristol R	1	0		
2013	Ponte Preta	0	0		
2013–14	Bristol R	23	1	**24**	**1**
2014–15	Derby Co	0	0		
2014–15	*Notts Co*	3	0	**3**	**0**
2015–16	Derby Co	0	0		
2016–17	Derby Co	0	0		

SHACKELL, Jason (D) **438** **13**
H: 6 4 W: 13 06 b.Stevenage 27-9-83

2002–03	Norwich C	2	0		
2003–04	Norwich C	6	0		
2004–05	Norwich C	11	0		
2005–06	Norwich C	17	0		
2006–07	Norwich C	43	3		
2007–08	Norwich C	39	0		
2008–09	Norwich C	15	0	**133**	**3**
2008–09	Wolverhampton W	12	0		
2009–10	Wolverhampton W	0	0	**12**	**0**
2009–10	*Doncaster R*	21	1	**21**	**1**
2010–11	Barnsley	44	3		
2011–12	Barnsley	0	0	**44**	**3**
2011–12	Derby Co	46	1		
2012–13	Burnley	44	2		
2013–14	Burnley	46	2		
2014–15	Burnley	38	0	**128**	**4**
2015–16	Derby Co	46	1		
2016–17	Derby Co	8	0	**100**	**2**

VERNAM, Charles (F) **13** **1**
b. 8-10-96

2013–14	Derby Co	0	0		
2014–15	Derby Co	0	0		
2015–16	Derby Co	0	0		
2016	*Vestmannaeyjar*	9	1	**9**	**1**
2016–17	Derby Co	0	0		
2016–17	*Coventry C*	4	0	**4**	**0**

VYDRA, Matej (F) **187** **51**
H: 5 10 W: 11 09 b.Chotebor 1-5-92
Internationals: Czech Republic U16, U17, U18, U19, U21, Full caps.

2009–10	Banik Ostrava	13	4	**13**	**4**
2010–11	Udinese	2	0		
2011–12	Udinese	0	0		
2011–12	*Club Brugge*	1	0	**1**	**0**
2012–13	Udinese	0	0		
2012–13	*Watford*	41	20		
2013–14	Udinese	0	0		
2013–14	*WBA*	23	3	**23**	**3**
2014–15	Udinese	0	0	**2**	**0**
2014–15	*Watford*	42	16		
2015–16	Watford	0	0		
2015–16	*Reading*	31	3	**31**	**3**
2016–17	Watford	1	0	**84**	**36**
2016–17	Derby Co	33	5	**33**	**5**

WALKER, Lewis (F) **0** **0**

2015–16	Derby Co	0	0		
2016–17	Derby Co	0	0		

WEALE, Chris (G) **295** **1**
H: 6 2 W: 13 03 b.Chard 9-2-82
Internationals: England C.

2003–04	Yeovil T	35	0		
2004–05	Yeovil T	38	0		
2005–06	Yeovil T	25	0		
2006–07	Bristol C	1	0		
2007–08	Hereford U	1	0		
2007–08	Bristol C	3	0		
2008–09	Bristol C	5	0	**9**	**0**
2008–09	*Hereford U*	1	0	**2**	**0**
2008–09	*Yeovil T*	10	1		
2009–10	Leicester C	45	0		
2010–11	Leicester C	29	0		
2011–12	Leicester C	1	0	**75**	**0**
2011–12	*Northampton T*	3	0	**3**	**0**
2012–13	Shrewsbury T	46	0		
2013–14	Shrewsbury T	35	0	**81**	**0**
2014–15	Yeovil T	8	0		
2014–15	*Burton Alb*	0	0		
2015–16	Yeovil T	9	0		
2016–17	Yeovil T	0	0	**125**	**1**
2016–17	Derby Co	0	0		

WEIMANN, Andreas (F) **194** **27**
H: 5 9 W: 11 09 b.Vienna 5-8-91
Internationals: Austria U17, U19, U20, U21, Full caps.

2008–09	Aston Villa	0	0		
2009–10	Aston Villa	0	0		
2010–11	Aston Villa	1	0		
2010–11	*Watford*	18	4		
2011–12	Aston Villa	14	2		
2011–12	*Watford*	3	0	**21**	**4**
2012–13	Aston Villa	30	7		
2013–14	Aston Villa	37	5		
2014–15	Aston Villa	31	3	**113**	**17**
2015–16	Derby Co	30	4		
2016–17	Derby Co	11	0	**41**	**4**
2016–17	*Wolverhampton W*	19	2	**19**	**2**

Players retained or with offer of contract
Babos, Alexander Jon; Barnes, Joshua Edwin; Cover, Alexander Robert; Cresswell, Cameron Ian; Gordon, Kellan Sheene; Jakobsen, Emil Riis; McAllister, Kyle; Mitchell-Lawson, Jayden; Ravas, Henrich; Sostaric, Karic Sven; Stabana, Kyron Thomas; Thomas, Luke; Thorne, George Louis Elliot; Wassall, Ethan Luca; Zanzala, Offrande.

Scholars
Bateman, Joseph Joshua; Bogle, Jayden Ian; Carter-Thompson, Russell L-Jay; Davidson-Miller, Jahvan O'Mahr; Davie, Adam Edward; Edwards, Micah Elijah; Fryatt, Joseph Eric; Haywood, Jack; Hitchman, Brandon Samuel; Jibodu, Ayomide Opeyemi; Mabondo, Mbuti Michel; Magno, Giann Michael; Mills, Jordan Matthew; Rashid, Fuseine; Thomas, Cain; Thorne, Jaydan William; Wise, Henry Dennis Paul; Yates, Matthew Dean.

DONCASTER R (33)

ALCOCK, Craig (D) **284** **3**
H: 5 8 W: 11 00 b.Cornwall 8-12-87

2006–07	Yeovil T	1	0		
2007–08	Yeovil T	8	0		
2008–09	Yeovil T	30	1		
2009–10	Yeovil T	42	1		
2010–11	Yeovil T	26	1	**107**	**3**
2011–12	Peterborough U	41	0		
2012–13	Peterborough U	27	0		
2013–14	Peterborough U	28	0	**96**	**0**
2014–15	Sheffield U	24	0		
2015–16	Sheffield U	3	0	**27**	**0**
2015–16	Doncaster R	27	0		
2016–17	Doncaster R	27	0	**54**	**0**

AMOS, Danny (D) **0** **0**
b.Sheffield

2016–17	Doncaster R	0	0		

BAUDRY, Mathieu (D) **206** **15**
H: 6 2 W: 12 08 b.Le Havre 24-2-88

2007–08	Troyes	2	1		
2008–09	Troyes	17	0		
2009–10	Troyes	7	0	**26**	**1**
2010–11	Bournemouth	3	1		
2011–12	Bournemouth	7	0	**10**	**1**
2011–12	*Dagenham & R*	11	0	**11**	**0**
2012–13	Leyton Orient	24	3		
2013–14	Leyton Orient	39	2		
2014–15	Leyton Orient	31	1		
2015–16	Leyton Orient	34	2	**128**	**8**
2016–17	Doncaster R	31	5	**31**	**5**

BEESTIN, Alfie (F) **3** **0**
H: 5 10 W: 11 11 b.Leeds 1-10-97

2016–17	Doncaster R	3	0	**3**	**0**

BLAIR, Matty (M) **161** **15**
H: 5 10 W: 11 09 b.Coventry 30-11-87
Internationals: England C.

2012–13	York C	44	6	**44**	**6**
2013–14	Fleetwood T	24	3		
2013–14	*Northampton T*	3	1	**3**	**1**
2014–15	Fleetwood T	8	0	**32**	**3**
2014–15	*Cambridge U*	2	0	**2**	**0**
2014–15	Mansfield T	3	0		
2015–16	Mansfield T	32	2	**35**	**2**
2016–17	Doncaster R	45	3	**45**	**3**

BUTLER, Andy (D) **482** **44**
H: 6 0 W: 13 00 b.Doncaster 4-11-83

2003–04	Scunthorpe U	35	2		
2004–05	Scunthorpe U	37	10		
2005–06	Scunthorpe U	16	1		
2006–07	Scunthorpe U	11	1		
2006–07	*Grimsby T*	4	0	**4**	**0**
2007–08	Scunthorpe U	36	2	**135**	**16**
2008–09	Huddersfield T	42	4		
2009–10	Huddersfield T	11	0	**53**	**4**
2009–10	*Blackpool*	7	0	**7**	**0**
2010–11	Walsall	31	4		
2011–12	Walsall	42	5		
2012–13	Walsall	41	3		
2013–14	Walsall	45	2		
2014–15	Sheffield U	0	0		
2014–15	*Walsall*	7	0	**166**	**14**
2014–15	Doncaster R	33	3		
2015–16	Doncaster R	40	4		
2016–17	Doncaster R	44	3	**117**	**10**

COPPINGER, James (F) **546** **63**
H: 5 7 W: 10 03 b.Middlesbrough 10-1-81
Internationals: England U16.

1997–98	Newcastle U	0	0		
1998–99	Newcastle U	0	0		
1999–2000	Newcastle U	0	0		
1999–2000	*Hartlepool U*	10	3		
2000–01	Newcastle U	1	0		
2001–02	Newcastle U	0	0	**1**	**0**
2001–02	*Hartlepool U*	14	2	**24**	**5**
2002–03	Exeter C	43	5	**43**	**5**
2004–05	Doncaster R	31	0		
2005–06	Doncaster R	36	5		
2006–07	Doncaster R	39	4		
2007–08	Doncaster R	39	3		
2008–09	Doncaster R	32	5		
2009–10	Doncaster R	39	4		
2010–11	Doncaster R	40	7		
2011–12	Doncaster R	38	2		
2012–13	Doncaster R	25	2		
2012–13	*Nottingham F*	6	0	**6**	**0**
2013–14	Doncaster R	41	4		
2014–15	Doncaster R	34	4		
2015–16	Doncaster R	39	3		
2016–17	Doncaster R	39	10	**472**	**53**

ETHERIDGE, Ross (G) **27** **0**
H: 6 2 W: 11 00 b. 4-9-94

2013–14	Derby Co	0	0		
2014–15	Derby Co	0	0		
2014–15	*Crewe Alex*	0	0		
2015–16	Accrington S	21	0	**21**	**0**
2016–17	Doncaster R	6	0	**6**	**0**

EVINA, Cedric (D) **127** **3**
H: 5 11 W: 12 08 b,Cameroon 16-11-91

2009–10	Arsenal	0	0		
2010–11	Arsenal	0	0		
2010–11	Oldham Ath	27	2	**27**	**2**
2011–12	Charlton Ath	3	0		
2012–13	Charlton Ath	12	0		
2013–14	Charlton Ath	8	0	**23**	**0**
2014–15	Doncaster R	19	0		
2015–16	Doncaster R	42	1		
2016–17	Doncaster R	16	0	**77**	**1**

FIELDING, Reece (M) **0** **0**
H: 6 2 W: 12 00 b.Doncaster 23-10-98

2016–17	Doncaster R	0	0		

FLETCHER, Jacob (F) **0** **0**

2016–17	Doncaster R	0	0		

GARRETT, Tyler (D) **5** **0**
b. 26-10-96

2015–16	Bolton W	3	0	**3**	**0**
2016–17	Doncaster R	2	0	**2**	**0**

JAMES, Morgan (D) **0** **0**

2016–17	Doncaster R	0	0		

JONES, Louis (G) **0** **0**

2016–17	Doncaster R	0	0		

KEEGAN, Paul (M) **285** **14**
H: 5 11 W: 11 05 b.Dublin 5-7-84
Internationals: Republic of Ireland U16, U21, U23.

2000–01	Leeds U	0	0		
2001–02	Leeds U	0	0		
2002–03	Leeds U	0	0		
2003–04	Leeds U	0	0		
2003–04	*Scunthorpe U*	2	0	**2**	**0**
2004–05	Leeds U	0	0		
2005	Drogheda	11	0		

2006	Drogheda	25	4		
2007	Drogheda	30	1		
2008	Drogheda	27	1	**93**	**6**
2009	Bohemians	34	2		
2010	Bohemians	32	4	**66**	**6**
2010–11	Doncaster R	10	0		
2011–12	Doncaster R	2	0		
2012–13	Doncaster R	25	1		
2013–14	Doncaster R	34	0		
2014–15	Doncaster R	32	0		
2015–16	Doncaster R	15	1		
2016–17	Doncaster R	6	0	**124**	**2**

LAWLOR, Ian (G) 36 0
H: 6 4 W: 12 08 b.Dublin 27-10-94
Internationals: Republic of Ireland U17, U19, U21.

2011–12	Manchester C	0	0		
2012–13	Manchester C	0	0		
2013–14	Manchester C	0	0		
2014–15	Manchester C	0	0		
2015–16	Manchester C	0	0		
2015–16	*Barnet*	5	0	**5**	**0**
2015–16	*Bury*	12	0	**12**	**0**
2016–17	Doncaster R	19	0	**19**	**0**

LONGBOTTOM, William (F) 4 0
H: 5 9 W: 9 11 b.Leeds 12-12-98

2015–16	Doncaster R	1	0		
2016–17	Doncaster R	3	0	**4**	**0**

LUND, Mitchell (D) 40 1
H: 6 1 W: 11 11 b.Leeds 27-8-96

2014–15	Doncaster R	4	0		
2015–16	Doncaster R	30	1		
2016–17	Doncaster R	6	0	**40**	**1**

MANDEVILLE, Liam (F) 32 8
H: 5 11 W: 12 02 b.Lincoln 17-2-97

2014–15	Doncaster R	3	0		
2015–16	Doncaster R	8	1		
2016–17	Doncaster R	21	7	**32**	**8**

MAROSI, Marko (G) 29 0
H: 6 3 W: 12 08 b. 23-10-93
Internationals: Slovakia U21.

2013–14	Wigan Ath	0	0		
2014–15	Doncaster R	3	0		
2015–16	Doncaster R	1	0		
2016–17	Doncaster R	25	0	**29**	**0**

MARQUIS, John (F) 183 52
H: 6 1 W: 11 03 b.Lewisham 16-5-92

2009–10	Millwall	1	0		
2010–11	Millwall	11	4		
2011–12	Millwall	17	1		
2012–13	Millwall	10	0		
2013–14	Millwall	2	0		
2013–14	*Portsmouth*	5	1	**5**	**1**
2013–14	*Torquay U*	5	3	**5**	**3**
2013–14	*Northampton T*	14	2		
2014–15	Millwall	1	0		
2014–15	*Cheltenham T*	13	1	**13**	**1**
2014–15	*Gillingham*	21	8	**21**	**8**
2015–16	Millwall	10	0	**52**	**5**
2015–16	*Leyton Orient*	13	0	**13**	**0**
2015–16	*Northampton T*	15	6	**29**	**8**
2016–17	Doncaster R	45	26	**45**	**26**

MAY, Alfie (F) 16 3
From Hythe T.

2016–17	Doncaster R	16	3	**16**	**3**

McCULLOUGH, Luke (D) 87 0
H: 6 2 W: 12 11 b.Portadown 15-2-94
Internationals: Northern Ireland U16, U17, U19, U20, U21, Full caps.

2012–13	Manchester U	0	0		
2012–13	*Cheltenham T*	1	0	**1**	**0**
2013–14	Doncaster R	14	0		
2014–15	Doncaster R	33	0		
2015–16	Doncaster R	32	0		
2016–17	Doncaster R	7	0	**86**	**0**

McSHEFFREY, Gary (F) 480 103
H: 5 8 W: 10 06 b.Coventry 13-8-82
Internationals: England U18, U20.

1998–99	Coventry C	1	0		
1999–2000	Coventry C	3	0		
2000–01	Coventry C	0	0		
2001–02	*Stockport Co*	5	1	**5**	**1**
2001–02	Coventry C	8	1		
2002–03	Coventry C	29	4		
2003–04	Coventry C	19	11		
2003–04	*Luton T*	18	9		
2004–05	Coventry C	37	12		
2004–05	*Luton T*	5	1	**23**	**10**
2005–06	Coventry C	43	15		
2006–07	Coventry C	3	1		
2006–07	Birmingham C	40	13		
2007–08	Birmingham C	32	3		
2008–09	Birmingham C	6	0		
2008–09	*Nottingham F*	4	0	**4**	**0**
2009–10	Birmingham C	5	0	**83**	**16**
2009–10	*Leeds U*	10	1	**10**	**1**
2010–11	Coventry C	33	8		
2011–12	Coventry C	39	8		
2012–13	Coventry C	32	1		
2013–14	Coventry C	0	0	**247**	**61**
2013–14	Chesterfield	9	1	**9**	**1**
2013–14	Scunthorpe U	13	0		
2014–15	Scunthorpe U	41	7		
2015–16	Scunthorpe U	26	5	**80**	**12**
2015–16	*Doncaster R*	7	1		
2016–17	Doncaster R	12	0	**19**	**1**

MIDDLETON, Harry (M) 63 0
H: 5 11 W: 11 00 b.Doncaster 12-4-95

2012–13	Doncaster R	0	0		
2013–14	Doncaster R	0	0		
2014–15	Doncaster R	4	0		
2015–16	Doncaster R	34	0		
2016–17	Doncaster R	25	0	**63**	**0**

PUGH, Joseph (F) 0 0
b. 10-10-97

2015–16	Doncaster R	0	0		
2016–17	Doncaster R	0	0		

RICHARDSON, Frazer (D) 322 5
H: 5 11 W: 11 12 b.Rotherham 29-10-82

1999–2000	Leeds U	0	0		
2000–01	Leeds U	0	0		
2001–02	Leeds U	0	0		
2002–03	Leeds U	0	0		
2002–03	*Stoke C*	7	0		
2003–04	Leeds U	4	0		
2003–04	*Stoke C*	6	1	**13**	**1**
2004–05	Leeds U	38	1		
2005–06	Leeds U	23	1		
2006–07	Leeds U	22	0		
2007–08	Leeds U	39	1		
2008–09	Leeds U	23	0	**149**	**3**
2009–10	Charlton Ath	38	1	**38**	**1**
2010–11	Southampton	21	0		
2011–12	Southampton	34	0		
2012–13	Southampton	5	0	**60**	**0**
2013–14	Middlesbrough	11	0	**11**	**0**
2013–14	*Ipswich T*	7	0	**7**	**0**
2014–15	Rotherham U	23	0		
2015–16	Rotherham U	17	0		
2016–17	Rotherham U	0	0	**40**	**0**
2016–17	Doncaster R	4	0	**4**	**0**

ROWE, Tommy (M) 334 53
H: 5 11 W: 12 11 b.Manchester 1-5-89

2006–07	Stockport Co	4	0		
2007–08	Stockport Co	24	6		
2008–09	Stockport Co	44	7	**72**	**13**
2008–09	Peterborough U	0	0		
2009–10	Peterborough U	32	2		
2010–11	Peterborough U	35	5		
2011–12	Peterborough U	43	4		
2012–13	Peterborough U	31	5		
2013–14	Peterborough U	34	7	**175**	**23**
2014–15	Wolverhampton W	14	0		
2015–16	Wolverhampton W	3	0	**17**	**0**
2015–16	*Scunthorpe U*	14	1	**14**	**1**
2015–16	*Doncaster R*	10	3		
2016–17	Doncaster R	46	13	**56**	**16**

SCATTERGOOD, Lewis (F) 0 0

2016–17	Doncaster R	0	0		

TAYLOR-SINCLAIR, Aaron (D) 207 11
H: 6 1 W: 11 07 b.Aberdeen 8-4-91

2008–09	Montrose	1	0		
2009–10	Montrose	30	2		
2010–11	Montrose	35	3	**66**	**5**
2011–12	Partick Thistle	30	1		
2012–13	Partick Thistle	28	1		
2013–14	Partick Thistle	36	2	**94**	**4**
2014–15	Wigan Ath	0	0		
2015–16	Doncaster R	43	2		
2016–17	Doncaster R	4	0	**47**	**2**

WALKER, Tyler (F) 0 0

2016–17	Doncaster R	0	0		

WILLIAMS, Andy (F) 408 95
H: 5 11 W: 11 09 b.Hereford 14-8-86

2006–07	Hereford U	41	8		
2007–08	Bristol R	41	4		
2008–09	Bristol R	4	1		
2008–09	*Hereford U*	26	2	**67**	**10**
2009–10	Bristol R	43	3	**88**	**8**
2010–11	Yeovil T	37	6		
2011–12	Yeovil T	35	16		
2012–13	Swindon T	40	11		
2013–14	Swindon T	3	0		
2013–14	*Yeovil T*	9	0	**81**	**22**
2014–15	Swindon T	46	21	**89**	**32**
2015–16	Doncaster R	46	12		
2016–17	Doncaster R	37	11	**83**	**23**

WRIGHT, Joe (D) 42 0
H: 6 4 W: 12 06 b. 26-2-95
Internationals: Wales U21.

2013–14	Huddersfield T	0	0		
2014–15	Huddersfield T	0	0		
2015–16	Huddersfield T	0	0		
2015–16	*Accrington S*	20	0	**20**	**0**
2016–17	Doncaster R	22	0	**22**	**0**

Players retained or with offer of contract
Donaldson, Anthony Kevin.

Scholars
Amos, Daniel; Barker, Joshua Ryan; Bingley, Kane Joseph; Fletcher, Jacob Frederick; Gains, Matthew Anthony George; Henderson, Lloyd John; James, Morgan Daniel; Leverton, James Leslie; Morris, James; Overton, Matthew James; Prior, Cody Patrick James; Scattergood, Lewis Matthew; Townrow, Keegan Terry; Walker, Tyler.

EVERTON (34)

BAINES, Leighton (D) 457 31
H: 5 8 W: 11 00 b.Liverpool 11-12-84
Internationals: England U21, Full caps.

2002–03	Wigan Ath	6	0		
2003–04	Wigan Ath	26	0		
2004–05	Wigan Ath	41	1		
2005–06	Wigan Ath	37	0		
2006–07	Wigan Ath	35	3		
2007–08	Wigan Ath	0	0	**145**	**4**
2007–08	Everton	22	0		
2008–09	Everton	31	1		
2009–10	Everton	37	1		
2010–11	Everton	38	5		
2011–12	Everton	33	4		
2012–13	Everton	38	5		
2013–14	Everton	32	5		
2014–15	Everton	31	2		
2015–16	Everton	18	2		
2016–17	Everton	32	2	**312**	**27**

BARKLEY, Ross (M) 167 25
H: 6 2 W: 12 00 b.Liverpool 5-12-93
Internationals: England U16, U17, U19, U20, U21, Full caps.

2010–11	Everton	0	0		
2011–12	Everton	6	0		
2012–13	Everton	7	0		
2012–13	*Sheffield W*	13	4	**13**	**4**
2012–13	*Leeds U*	4	0	**4**	**0**
2013–14	Everton	34	6		
2014–15	Everton	29	2		
2015–16	Everton	38	8		
2016–17	Everton	36	5	**150**	**21**

BARRY, Gareth (M) 628 52
H: 5 11 W: 12 06 b.Hastings 23-2-81
Internationals: England B, U21, Full caps.

1997–98	Aston Villa	2	0		
1998–99	Aston Villa	32	2		
1999–2000	Aston Villa	30	1		
2000–01	Aston Villa	30	0		
2001–02	Aston Villa	20	0		
2002–03	Aston Villa	35	3		
2003–04	Aston Villa	36	3		
2004–05	Aston Villa	34	7		
2005–06	Aston Villa	36	3		
2006–07	Aston Villa	35	8		
2007–08	Aston Villa	37	9		
2008–09	Aston Villa	38	5	**365**	**41**
2009–10	Manchester C	34	2		
2010–11	Manchester C	33	2		
2011–12	Manchester C	34	1		
2012–13	Manchester C	31	1		
2013–14	Manchester C	0	0	**132**	**6**
2013–14	*Everton*	32	3		
2014–15	Everton	33	0		
2015–16	Everton	33	0		
2016–17	Everton	33	2	**131**	**5**

BESIC, Muhamed (M) 85 1
H: 5 10 W: 11 11 b.Berlin 10-9-92
Internationals: Bosnia-Herzegovina U21, Full caps.

2010–11	Hamburg	3	0		
2011–12	Hamburg	0	0		
2012–13	Hamburg	0	0	**3**	**0**
2012–13	Ferencvaros	22	1		
2013–14	Ferencvaros	25	0	**47**	**1**

2014–15	Everton	23	0		
2015–16	Everton	12	0		
2016–17	Everton	0	0	**35**	**0**

BOLASIE, Yannick (M) 262 27
H: 6 2 W: 13 02 b.DR Congo 24-5-89
Internationals: DR Congo Full caps.

2008–09	Plymouth Arg	0	0		
2008–09	*Barnet*	20	3		
2009–10	Plymouth Arg	16	1		
2009–10	*Barnet*	22	2	**42**	**5**
2010–11	Plymouth Arg	35	7	**51**	**8**
2011–12	Bristol C	23	1		
2012–13	Bristol C	0	0	**23**	**1**
2012–13	Crystal Palace	43	3		
2013–14	Crystal Palace	29	0		
2014–15	Crystal Palace	34	4		
2015–16	Crystal Palace	26	5		
2016–17	Crystal Palace	1	0	**133**	**12**
2016–17	Everton	13	1	**13**	**1**

BROWNING, Tyias (D) 17 0
H: 5 11 W: 12 00 b.Liverpool 27-5-94
Internationals: England U17, U19, U20.

2011–12	Everton	0	0		
2012–13	Everton	0	0		
2013–14	Everton	0	0		
2013–14	*Wigan Ath*	2	0	**2**	**0**
2014–15	Everton	2	0		
2015–16	Everton	5	0		
2016–17	Everton	0	0	**7**	**0**
2016–17	*Preston NE*	8	0	**8**	**0**

CALVERT-LEWIN, Dominic (M) 42 6
b. 16-3-97
Internationals: England U20.

2013–14	Sheffield U	0	0		
2014–15	Sheffield U	2	0		
2015–16	Sheffield U	9	0		
2015–16	*Northampton T*	20	5	**20**	**5**
2016–17	Sheffield U	0	0	**11**	**0**
2016–17	Everton	11	1	**11**	**1**

CLEVERLEY, Tom (M) 208 24
H: 5 9 W: 10 07 b.Basingstoke 12-8-89
Internationals: England U20, U21, Full caps. Great Britain.

2007–08	Manchester U	0	0		
2008–09	Manchester U	0	0		
2008–09	*Leicester C*	15	2	**15**	**2**
2009–10	Manchester U	0	0		
2009–10	*Watford*	33	11		
2010–11	Manchester U	0	0		
2010–11	*Wigan Ath*	25	3	**25**	**3**
2011–12	Manchester U	10	0		
2012–13	Manchester U	22	2		
2013–14	Manchester U	22	1		
2014–15	Manchester U	1	0	**55**	**3**
2014–15	*Aston Villa*	31	3	**31**	**3**
2015–16	Everton	22	2		
2016–17	Everton	10	0	**32**	**2**
2016–17	*Watford*	17	0	**50**	**11**

COLEMAN, Seamus (D) 215 19
H: 6 4 W: 10 07 b.Donegal 11-10-88
Internationals: Republic of Ireland U21, U23, Full caps.

2008–09	Everton	0	0		
2009–10	Everton	3	0		
2009–10	*Blackpool*	9	1	**9**	**1**
2010–11	Everton	34	4		
2011–12	Everton	18	0		
2012–13	Everton	26	0		
2013–14	Everton	36	6		
2014–15	Everton	35	3		
2015–16	Everton	28	1		
2016–17	Everton	26	4	**206**	**18**

CONNOLLY, Callum (D) 21 2
b.Liverpool 23-9-97
Internationals: England U17, U18, U19, U20.

2015–16	Everton	1	0		
2015–16	*Barnsley*	3	0	**3**	**0**
2016–17	Everton	0	0	**1**	**0**
2016–17	*Wigan Ath*	17	2	**17**	**2**

DAVIES, Tom (M) 26 2
b.Liverpool 30-6-98
Internationals: England U16, U17, U18, U19.

2015–16	Everton	2	0		
2016–17	Everton	24	2	**26**	**2**

DEULOFEU, Gerard (F) 81 9
H: 5 10 W: 11 01 b.Riudarenes 13-3-94
Internationals: Spain U16, U17, U19, U20, U21, Full caps.

2010–11	Barcelona	0	0		
2011–12	Barcelona	1	0		
2012–13	Barcelona	1	0		
2013–14	Barcelona	0	0	**2**	**0**
2013–14	*Everton*	25	3		
2015–16	Everton	26	2		
2016–17	Everton	11	0	**62**	**5**
2016–17	*AC Milan*	17	4	**17**	**4**

DUFFUS, Courtney (F) 3 0
H: 5 7 W: 12 00 b.Cheltenham 24-10-95
Internationals: Republic of Ireland U21.

2013–14	Everton	0	0		
2014–15	Everton	0	0		
2014–15	*Bury*	3	0	**3**	**0**
2015–16	Everton	0	0		
2016–17	Everton	0	0		

DYSON, Calum (F) 16 4
b. 19-9-96

2015–16	Everton	0	0		
2016–17	Everton	0	0		
2016–17	*Grimsby T*	16	4	**16**	**4**

EVANS, Antony (M) 14 2
b.Fazakerley 23-9-98

2016–17	Everton	0	0		
2016–17	*Morecambe*	14	2	**14**	**2**

FOULDS, Matthew (D) 0 0
b.Bradford 1-2-98

2015–16	Bury	0	0		
2015–16	Everton	0	0		
2016–17	Everton	0	0		

FUNES MORI, Ramiro (D) 127 11
H: 6 3 W: 13 12 b.Mendoza 5-3-91
Internationals: Argentina Full caps.

2010–11	River Plate	0	0		
2011–12	River Plate	19	2		
2012–13	River Plate	10	0		
2013–14	River Plate	19	1		
2014	River Plate	17	2		
2015	River Plate	11	2	**76**	**7**
2015–16	Everton	28	4		
2016–17	Everton	23	0	**51**	**4**

GALLOWAY, Brendon (M) 30 0
H: 6 2 W: 13 10 b.Zimbabwe 17-3-96
Internationals: England U17, U18, U19, U21.

2011–12	Milton Keynes D	1	0		
2012–13	Milton Keynes D	1	0		
2013–14	Milton Keynes D	8	0	**10**	**0**
2014–15	Everton	2	0		
2015–16	Everton	15	0		
2016–17	Everton	0	0	**17**	**0**
2016–17	*WBA*	3	0	**3**	**0**

GANA, Idrissa (M) 202 6
H: 5 9 W: 11 05 b.Dakar 26-9-89
Internationals: Senegal Full caps.

2010–11	Lille	11	0		
2011–12	Lille	25	0		
2012–13	Lille	29	0		
2013–14	Lille	37	1		
2014–15	Lille	32	4	**134**	**5**
2015–16	Aston Villa	35	0	**35**	**0**
2016–17	Everton	33	1	**33**	**1**

GARBUTT, Luke (D) 91 5
H: 5 10 W: 11 07 b.Harrogate 21-5-93
Internationals: England U16, U17, U18, U19, U20, U21.

2010–11	Everton	0	0		
2011–12	Everton	0	0		
2011–12	*Cheltenham T*	34	2	**34**	**2**
2012–13	Everton	0	0		
2013–14	Everton	1	0		
2013–14	*Colchester U*	19	2	**19**	**2**
2014–15	Everton	4	0		
2015–16	Everton	0	0		
2015–16	*Fulham*	25	1	**25**	**1**
2016–17	Everton	0	0	**5**	**0**
2016–17	*Wigan Ath*	8	0	**8**	**0**

GRANT, Conor (M) 57 4
H: 5 9 W: 12 08 b.Fazakerley 18-4-95
Internationals: England U18.

2013–14	Everton	0	0		
2014–15	Everton	0	0		
2014–15	*Motherwell*	11	1	**11**	**1**
2015–16	Everton	0	0		
2015–16	*Doncaster R*	19	2		
2016–17	Everton	0	0		
2016–17	*Ipswich T*	6	0	**6**	**0**
2016–17	*Doncaster R*	21	1	**40**	**3**

GRIFFITHS, Russell (G) 28 0
b.Gravesend 13-4-96
Internationals: England U19, U20.

2014–15	Everton	0	0		
2015–16	Everton	0	0		
2016–17	Everton	0	0		
2016–17	*Cheltenham T*	24	0	**24**	**0**
2016–17	*Motherwell*	4	0	**4**	**0**

HENEN, David (F) 11 1
b. 19-4-96
Internationals: Belgium U16, U17, U18, U19.

2013–14	Anderlecht	0	0		
2014–15	Olympiacos	0	0		
2014–15	*Everton*	0	0		
2015–16	Everton	0	0		
2015–16	*Fleetwood T*	11	1	**11**	**1**
2016–17	Everton	0	0		

HEWELT, Mateusz (G) 0 0
b. 23-9-96

2016–17	Everton	0	0		

HOLGATE, Mason (D) 38 1
H: 5 11 W: 11 11 b.Doncaster 22-10-96
Internationals: England U20, U21.

2014–15	Barnsley	20	1	**20**	**1**
2015–16	Everton	0	0		
2016–17	Everton	18	0	**18**	**0**

JAGIELKA, Phil (D) 544 31
H: 6 0 W: 13 01 b.Manchester 17-8-82
Internationals: England U20, U21, B, Full caps.

1999–2000	Sheffield U	1	0		
2000–01	Sheffield U	15	0		
2001–02	Sheffield U	23	3		
2002–03	Sheffield U	42	0		
2003–04	Sheffield U	43	3		
2004–05	Sheffield U	46	0		
2005–06	Sheffield U	46	8		
2006–07	Sheffield U	38	4	**254**	**18**
2007–08	Everton	34	1		
2008–09	Everton	34	0		
2009–10	Everton	12	0		
2010–11	Everton	33	1		
2011–12	Everton	30	2		
2012–13	Everton	36	2		
2013–14	Everton	26	0		
2014–15	Everton	37	4		
2015–16	Everton	21	0		
2016–17	Everton	27	3	**290**	**13**

JONES, Gethin (D) 23 0
H: 5 10 W: 11 09 b.Perth 13-10-95
Internationals: Wales U17, U19, U21.

2014–15	Everton	0	0		
2014–15	*Plymouth Arg*	6	0	**6**	**0**
2015–16	Everton	0	0		
2016–17	Everton	0	0		
2016–17	*Barnsley*	17	0	**17**	**0**

KENNY, Jonjoe (D) 26 0
H: 5 9 W: 10 08 b.Kirkdale 15-3-97
Internationals: England U16, U17, U18, U19, U20.

2014–15	Everton	0	0		
2015–16	Everton	1	0		
2015–16	*Wigan Ath*	7	0	**7**	**0**
2015–16	*Oxford U*	17	0	**17**	**0**
2016–17	Everton	1	0	**2**	**0**

KONE, Arouna (F) 299 93
H: 6 0 W: 11 08 b.Anyama 11-11-83
Internationals: Ivory Coast Full caps.

2002–03	Lierse	21	11	**21**	**11**
2003–04	Roda JC	28	11		
2004–05	Roda JC	32	14		
2005–06	Roda JC	1	1	**61**	**26**
2005–06	PSV Eindhoven	21	11		
2006–07	PSV Eindhoven	31	10		
2007–08	PSV Eindhoven	1	0	**53**	**21**
2007–08	Sevilla	21	1		
2008–09	Sevilla	6	0		
2009–10	Sevilla	12	0		
2009–10	*Hannover 96*	8	2	**8**	**2**
2010–11	Sevilla	1	0	**40**	**1**
2011–12	Levante	34	15	**34**	**15**
2012–13	Wigan Ath	34	11	**34**	**11**
2013–14	Everton	5	0		
2014–15	Everton	12	1		
2015–16	Everton	25	5		
2016–17	Everton	6	0	**48**	**6**

LENNON, Aaron (M) 354 34
H: 5 6 W: 10 03 b.Leeds 16-4-87
Internationals: England U17, U19, U21, B, Full caps.

2003–04	Leeds U	11	0		
2004–05	Leeds U	27	1	**38**	**1**
2005–06	Tottenham H	27	2		
2006–07	Tottenham H	26	3		
2007–08	Tottenham H	29	2		
2008–09	Tottenham H	35	5		
2009–10	Tottenham H	22	3		
2010–11	Tottenham H	34	3		
2011–12	Tottenham H	23	3		
2012–13	Tottenham H	34	4		

2013–14 Tottenham H 27 1
2014–15 Tottenham H 9 0
2014–15 *Everton* 14 2
2015–16 Tottenham H 0 0 **266 26**
2015–16 Everton 25 5
2016–17 Everton 11 0 **50 7**

LOOKMAN, Ademola (F) 53 11
H: 5 9 b.Wandsworth 18-7-98
Internationals: England U19, U20.
2015–16 Charlton Ath 24 5
2016–17 Charlton Ath 21 5 **45 10**
2016–17 Everton 8 1 **8 1**

LUKAKU, Romelu (F) 259 118
H: 6 3 W: 13 00 b.Antwerp 13-5-93
Internationals: Belgium U15, U18, U21, Full caps.
2008–09 Anderlecht 1 0
2009–10 Anderlecht 33 15
2010–11 Anderlecht 37 16
2011–12 Anderlecht 2 2 **73 33**
2011–12 Chelsea 8 0
2012–13 Chelsea 0 0
2012–13 *WBA* 35 17 **35 17**
2013–14 Chelsea 2 0 **10 0**
2013–14 *Everton* 31 15
2014–15 Everton 36 10
2015–16 Everton 37 18
2016–17 Everton 37 25 **141 68**

McALENY, Conor (F) 56 16
H: 5 10 W: 12 05 b.Liverpool 12-8-92
2009–10 Everton 0 0
2010–11 Everton 0 0
2011–12 Everton 2 0
2011–12 *Scunthorpe U* 3 0 **3 0**
2012–13 Everton 0 0
2013–14 Everton 0 0
2013–14 *Brentford* 4 0 **4 0**
2014–15 Everton 0 0
2014–15 *Cardiff C* 8 2 **8 2**
2015–16 Everton 0 0
2015–16 *Charlton Ath* 8 0 **8 0**
2015–16 *Wigan Ath* 13 4 **13 4**
2016–17 Everton 0 0 **2 0**
2016–17 *Oxford U* 18 10 **18 10**

McCARTHY, James (M) 318 27
H: 5 11 W: 11 05 b.Glasgow 12-11-90
Internationals: Republic of Ireland U17, U18, U19, U21, Full caps.
2006–07 Hamilton A 23 1
2007–08 Hamilton A 35 7
2008–09 Hamilton A 37 6 **95 14**
2009–10 Wigan Ath 20 1
2010–11 Wigan Ath 24 3
2011–12 Wigan Ath 33 0
2012–13 Wigan Ath 38 3
2013–14 Wigan Ath 5 0 **120 7**
2013–14 Everton 34 1
2014–15 Everton 28 2
2015–16 Everton 29 2
2016–17 Everton 12 1 **103 6**

McGEADY, Aiden (M) 336 52
H: 5 10 W: 11 03 b.Glasgow 4-4-86
Internationals: Republic of Ireland Full caps.
2003–04 Celtic 4 1
2004–05 Celtic 27 4
2005–06 Celtic 20 4
2006–07 Celtic 34 5
2007–08 Celtic 36 7
2008–09 Celtic 29 3
2009–10 Celtic 35 7 **185 31**
2010–11 Spartak Moscow 11 2
2011–12 Spartak Moscow 31 3
2012–13 Spartak Moscow 17 5
2013–14 Spartak Moscow 13 1 **72 11**
2013–14 Everton 16 0
2014–15 Everton 16 1
2015–16 Everton 0 0
2015–16 *Sheffield W* 13 1 **13 1**
2016–17 Everton 0 0 **32 1**
2016–17 *Preston NE* 34 8 **34 8**

MIRALLAS, Kevin (F) 323 76
H: 6 0 W: 11 10 b.Leige 5-10-87
Internationals: Belgium U16, U17, U18, U19, U21, Full caps.
2004–05 Lille 1 1
2005–06 Lille 15 1
2006–07 Lille 23 2
2007–08 Lille 35 6 **74 10**
2008–09 St Etienne 30 3
2009–10 St Etienne 23 0 **53 3**
2010–11 *Olympiacos* 26 14
2011–12 *Olympiacos* 24 20
2012–13 *Olympiacos* 0 0 **50 34**
2012–13 Everton 27 6
2013–14 Everton 32 8
2014–15 Everton 29 7
2015–16 Everton 23 4
2016–17 Everton 35 4 **146 29**

NIASSE, Oumar (F) 84 28
H: 6 0 b.Ouakam 18-4-90
Internationals: Senegal U23, Full caps.
2013–14 Akhisar Belediyespor 34 12 **34 12**
2014–15 Lokomotiv Moscow 13 4
2015–16 Lokomotiv Moscow 15 8 **28 12**
2015–16 Everton 5 0
2016–17 Everton 0 0 **5 0**
2016–17 *Hull C* 17 4 **17 4**

PENNINGTON, Matthew (D) 53 3
H: 6 1 W: 12 02 b.Warrington 6-10-94
Internationals: England U19.
2013–14 Everton 0 0
2013–14 *Tranmere R* 17 2 **17 2**
2014–15 Everton 0 0
2014–15 *Coventry C* 24 0 **24 0**
2015–16 Everton 4 0
2015–16 *Walsall* 5 0 **5 0**
2016–17 Everton 3 1 **7 1**

ROBINSON, Antonee (D) 0 0
H: 6 0 W: 11 07 b.Milton Keynes 8-8-97
Internationals: USA U18.
2015–16 Everton 0 0
2016–17 Everton 0 0

ROBLES, Joel (G) 66 0
H: 6 5 W: 13 04 b.Leganes 17-6-90
Internationals: Spain U16, U17, U21, U23.
2009–10 Atletico Madrid 2 0
2011–12 *Rayo Vallecano* 13 0 **13 0**
2012–13 Atletico Madrid 0 0 **2 0**
2012–13 *Wigan Ath* 9 0 **9 0**
2013–14 Everton 2 0
2014–15 Everton 7 0
2015–16 Everton 13 0
2016–17 Everton 20 0 **42 0**

SAMBOU, Bassala (F) 0 0
H: 6 1 W: 11 11 b. 15-10-97
2015–16 Coventry C 0 0
2016–17 Everton 0 0

SCHNEIDERLIN, Morgan (M) 282 16
H: 5 11 W: 11 11 b.Obernai 8-11-89
Internationals: France U16, U17, U18, U19, U20, U21, Full caps.
2007–08 Strasbourg 5 0 **5 0**
2008–09 Southampton 30 0
2009–10 Southampton 37 1
2010–11 Southampton 27 0
2011–12 Southampton 42 2
2012–13 Southampton 36 5
2013–14 Southampton 33 2
2014–15 Southampton 26 4 **231 14**
2015–16 Manchester U 29 1
2016–17 Manchester U 3 0 **32 1**
2016–17 Everton 14 1 **14 1**

STEKELENBURG, Maarten (G) 293 0
H: 6 6 W: 14 05 b.Haarlem 22-9-82
Internationals: Netherlands U21, Full caps.
2001–02 Ajax 0 0
2002–03 Ajax 9 0
2003–04 Ajax 10 0
2004–05 Ajax 11 0
2005–06 Ajax 27 0
2006–07 Ajax 32 0
2007–08 Ajax 31 0
2008–09 Ajax 12 0
2009–10 Ajax 33 0
2010–11 Ajax 26 0 **191 0**
2011–12 Roma 29 0
2012–13 Roma 18 0 **47 0**
2013–14 Fulham 19 0
2014–15 Fulham 0 0
2014–15 Monaco 0 0
2015–16 Fulham 0 0 **19 0**
2015–16 *Southampton* 17 0 **17 0**
2016–17 Everton 19 0 **19 0**

TARASHAJ, Shani (F) 65 13
b. 7-2-95
Internationals: Switzerland U17, U18, U19, U21, Full caps.
2014–15 Grasshoppers 19 1
2015–16 Grasshoppers 18 8 **52 12**
2015–16 Everton 0 0
2015–16 *Grasshoppers* 15 3
2016–17 Everton 0 0
2016–17 *Eintracht Frankfurt* 13 1 **13 1**

WALSH, Liam (M) 15 1
b. 15-9-97
Internationals: England U16, U18.
2015–16 Everton 0 0
2015–16 *Yeovil T* 15 1 **15 1**
2016–17 Everton 0 0

WILLIAMS, Ashley (D) 520 18
H: 6 0 W: 11 02 b.Wolverhampton 23-8-84
Internationals: Wales Full caps.
2003–04 Stockport Co 10 0
2004–05 Stockport Co 44 1
2005–06 Stockport Co 36 1
2006–07 Stockport Co 46 1
2007–08 Stockport Co 26 0 **162 3**
2007–08 *Swansea C* 3 0
2008–09 Swansea C 46 2
2009–10 Swansea C 46 5
2010–11 Swansea C 46 3
2011–12 Swansea C 37 1
2012–13 Swansea C 37 0
2013–14 Swansea C 34 1
2014–15 Swansea C 37 0
2015–16 Swansea C 36 2 **322 14**
2016–17 Everton 36 1 **36 1**

WILLIAMS, Joe (M) 0 0
H: 5 10 W: 10 06 b.Liverpool 8-12-96
Internationals: England U20.
2014–15 Everton 0 0
2015–16 Everton 0 0
2016–17 Everton 0 0

Players retained or with offer of contract
Baningime, Beni; Broadhead, Nathan Paul; Byrne, Sam John; Charsley, Henry William James; Dowell, Kieran O'Neil; Feeney, Morgan; Gray, Louis; Gueye, Idrissa Gana; Kinsella, Steven; Renshaw, Christopher Thomas; Rodriguez, Leandro Joaquin.

Scholars
Ball, Charles Thomas; Baxter, Nathan; Bramall, Daniel Luke; Corke, Jordan Robert; Denny, Alexander; Duke-McKenna, Stephen Winston; Hilton, Joseph Robert; Hornby, Fraser; Johnson, Matthew; Kerr, Sidney David Junior; Kiersey, Jack Alexander; Lavery, Shayne Francis; Mampala, Manasse; Moore, Nathan; Murphy, Tomas Bernard; Ouzounidis, Con; Phillips, Kieran James; Scully, Thomas.

EXETER C (35)

AMPADU, Ethan (M) 8 0
b.Exeter 14-9-00
Internationals: England U16, Wales U17, U19.
2016–17 Exeter C 8 0 **8 0**

ARCHIBALD-HENVILLE, Troy (D) 177 6
H: 6 2 W: 13 03 b.Newham 4-11-88
2007–08 Tottenham H 0 0
2008–09 Tottenham H 0 0
2008–09 *Norwich C* 0 0
2008–09 *Exeter C* 19 0
2009–10 Tottenham H 0 0
2009–10 Exeter C 15 0
2010–11 Exeter C 36 1
2011–12 Exeter C 45 2
2012–13 Swindon T 5 0
2013–14 Carlisle U 4 0
2013–14 Swindon T 14 0 **19 0**
2014–15 Carlisle U 24 1
2015–16 Carlisle U 12 2 **40 3**
2016–17 Exeter C 3 0 **118 3**

BROWN, Troy (D) 222 14
H: 6 1 W: 12 01 b.Croydon 17-9-90
Internationals: Wales U17, U19, U21.
2009–10 Ipswich T 1 0
2010–11 Ipswich T 12 0 **13 0**
2011–12 Rotherham U 6 1 **6 1**
2011–12 *Aldershot T* 17 2
2012–13 Aldershot T 34 3 **51 5**
2013–14 Cheltenham T 39 4
2014–15 Cheltenham T 43 1 **82 5**
2015–16 Exeter C 40 1
2016–17 Exeter C 30 2 **70 3**

BUTTERFIELD, Danny (D) 488 9
H: 5 10 W: 11 06 b.Boston 21-11-79
1997–98 Grimsby T 7 0
1998–99 Grimsby T 12 0
1999–2000 Grimsby T 29 0
2000–01 Grimsby T 30 1
2001–02 Grimsby T 46 2 **124 3**
2002–03 Crystal Palace 46 1

2003–04	Crystal Palace	45	4		
2004–05	Crystal Palace	7	0		
2005–06	Crystal Palace	13	0		
2006–07	Crystal Palace	28	0		
2007–08	Crystal Palace	30	0		
2008–09	Crystal Palace	26	1		
2008–09	*Charlton Ath*	12	0	**12**	**0**
2009–10	Crystal Palace	37	0	**232**	**6**
2010–11	Southampton	34	0		
2011–12	Southampton	10	0		
2012–13	Southampton	0	0		
2012–13	*Bolton W*	6	0	**6**	**0**
2013–14	Southampton	0	0	**44**	**0**
2013–14	Carlisle U	1	0	**1**	**0**
2013–14	Exeter C	29	0		
2014–15	Exeter C	30	0		
2015–16	Exeter C	10	0		
2016–17	Exeter C	0	0	**69**	**0**

BYRNE, Alex (M) **0 0**
H: 5 9 W: 11 07 b.Barnstaple 15-6-96

2014–15	Exeter C	0	0
2015–16	Exeter C	0	0
2016–17	Exeter C	0	0

COLLINS, Archie (M) **0 0**

2016–17	Exeter C	0	0

DOWN, Toby (D) **0 0**

2016–17	Exeter C	0	0

EGAN, Kyle (D) **1 0**
b. 15-12-98

2015–16	Exeter C	0	0		
2016–17	Exeter C	1	0	**1**	**0**

GRANT, Joel (F) **275 44**
H: 6 0 W: 12 01 b.Acton 26-8-87
Internationals: Jamaica U20, Full caps.

2005–06	Watford	7	0		
2006–07	Watford	0	0	**7**	**0**
From Aldershot T.					
2008–09	Crewe Alex	28	2		
2009–10	Crewe Alex	43	9		
2010–11	Crewe Alex	25	5	**96**	**16**
2011–12	Wycombe W	30	4		
2012–13	Wycombe W	41	10	**71**	**14**
2013–14	Yeovil T	34	3		
2014–15	Yeovil T	21	3	**55**	**6**
2015–16	Exeter C	26	4		
2016–17	Exeter C	20	4	**46**	**8**

HAMON, James (G) **23 0**
H: 6 1 W: 11 00 b. 1-7-95

2013–14	Exeter C	0	0		
2014–15	Exeter C	21	0		
2015–16	Exeter C	1	0		
2016–17	Exeter C	1	0	**23**	**0**

HARLEY, Ryan (M) **250 40**
H: 5 11 W: 11 00 b.Bristol 22-1-85

2004–05	Bristol C	2	0		
2005–06	Bristol C	0	0	**2**	**0**
2008–09	Exeter C	31	4		
2009–10	Exeter C	44	10		
2010–11	Exeter C	21	6		
2010–11	Swansea C	0	0		
2010–11	*Exeter C*	21	4		
2011–12	Swansea C	0	0		
2011–12	Brighton & HA	16	2		
2012–13	Brighton & HA	2	0	**18**	**2**
2012–13	*Milton Keynes D*	8	0	**8**	**0**
2013–14	Swindon T	21	1		
2014–15	Swindon T	0	0	**21**	**1**
2014–15	Exeter C	25	4		
2015–16	Exeter C	28	4		
2016–17	Exeter C	31	5	**201**	**37**

HOLMES, Lee (M) **268 24**
H: 5 8 W: 10 06 b.Mansfield 2-4-87
Internationals: England U16, U17, U19.

2002–03	Derby Co	2	0		
2003–04	Derby Co	23	2		
2004–05	Derby Co	3	0		
2004–05	*Swindon T*	15	1		
2005–06	Derby Co	18	0		
2006–07	Derby Co	0	0		
2006–07	*Bradford C*	16	0	**16**	**0**
2007–08	Derby Co	0	0	**46**	**2**
2007–08	*Walsall*	19	4	**19**	**4**
2008–09	Southampton	11	0		
2009–10	Southampton	5	0		
2010–11	Southampton	7	0		
2011–12	Southampton	6	1	**29**	**1**
2011–12	*Oxford U*	7	2	**7**	**2**
2011–12	*Swindon T*	10	1	**25**	**2**
2012–13	Preston NE	28	3		
2013–14	Preston NE	32	3		
2014–15	Preston NE	0	0	**60**	**6**
2014–15	*Portsmouth*	5	0	**5**	**0**
2014–15	*Exeter C*	8	0		
2015–16	Exeter C	37	2		
2016–17	Exeter C	16	5	**61**	**7**

JAMES, Lloyd (M) **279 12**
H: 5 11 W: 11 01 b.Bristol 16-2-88
Internationals: Wales U17, U19, U21.

2005–06	Southampton	0	0		
2006–07	Southampton	0	0		
2007–08	Southampton	0	0		
2008–09	Southampton	41	0		
2009–10	Southampton	30	2	**71**	**2**
2010–11	Colchester U	28	0		
2011–12	Colchester U	23	1	**51**	**1**
2011–12	*Crawley T*	6	0	**6**	**0**
2012–13	Leyton Orient	28	0		
2013–14	Leyton Orient	42	3		
2014–15	Leyton Orient	13	1		
2015–16	Leyton Orient	25	4	**108**	**8**
2016–17	Exeter C	43	1	**43**	**1**

JAY, Matt (D) **7 0**
H: 5 10 W: 10 12 b.Torbay 27-2-96

2013–14	Exeter C	2	0		
2014–15	Exeter C	3	0		
2015–16	Exeter C	0	0		
2016–17	Exeter C	2	0	**7**	**0**

McALINDEN, Liam (F) **88 14**
H: 6 1 W: 11 10 b.Cannock 26-9-93
Internationals: Northern Ireland U21. Republic of Ireland U21.

2010–11	Wolverhampton W	0	0		
2011–12	Wolverhampton W	0	0		
2012–13	Wolverhampton W	1	0		
2013–14	Wolverhampton W	7	1		
2013–14	*Shrewsbury T*	9	3		
2014–15	Wolverhampton W	6	0		
2014–15	*Fleetwood T*	19	4	**19**	**4**
2015–16	Wolverhampton W	0	0	**14**	**1**
2015–16	*Shrewsbury T*	8	0	**17**	**3**
2015–16	*Crawley T*	6	1	**6**	**1**
2016–17	Exeter C	32	5	**32**	**5**

McCREADY, Tom (M) **22 0**
H: 6 0 W: 11 11 b.Chester 7-6-91

2014–15	Morecambe	7	0	**7**	**0**
2014–15	Exeter C	3	0		
2015–16	Exeter C	10	0		
2016–17	Exeter C	2	0	**15**	**0**

MOORE-TAYLOR, Jordan (D) **136 8**
H: 5 10 W: 13 01 b.Exeter 21-1-94

2012–13	Exeter C	7	0		
2013–14	Exeter C	29	1		
2014–15	Exeter C	26	2		
2015–16	Exeter C	32	0		
2016–17	Exeter C	42	5	**136**	**8**

OAKLEY, Matthew (M) **614 33**
H: 5 10 W: 12 06 b.Peterborough 17-8-77
Internationals: England U21.

1994–95	Southampton	1	0		
1995–96	Southampton	10	0		
1996–97	Southampton	28	3		
1997–98	Southampton	33	1		
1998–99	Southampton	22	2		
1999–2000	Southampton	31	3		
2000–01	Southampton	35	1		
2001–02	Southampton	27	1		
2002–03	Southampton	31	0		
2003–04	Southampton	7	0		
2004–05	Southampton	7	1		
2005–06	Southampton	29	2	**261**	**14**
2006–07	Derby Co	37	6		
2007–08	Derby Co	19	3	**56**	**9**
2007–08	Leicester C	20	0		
2008–09	Leicester C	45	8		
2009–10	Leicester C	38	0		
2010–11	Leicester C	34	2		
2011–12	Leicester C	0	0	**137**	**10**
2011–12	*Exeter C*	7	0		
2012–13	Exeter C	36	0		
2013–14	Exeter C	24	0		
2014–15	Exeter C	45	0		
2015–16	Exeter C	29	0		
2016–17	Exeter C	19	0	**160**	**0**

OLEJNIK, Robert (G) **328 0**
H: 6 0 W: 15 06 b.Vienna 26-11-86
Internationals: Austria U21.

2004–05	Aston Villa	0	0		
2005–06	Aston Villa	0	0		
2006–07	Aston Villa	0	0		
2006–07	*Lincoln C*	0	0		
2007–08	Falkirk	13	0		
2008–09	Falkirk	15	0		
2009–10	Falkirk	38	0		
2010–11	Falkirk	36	0	**102**	**0**
2011–12	Torquay U	46	0	**46**	**0**
2012–13	Peterborough U	46	0		
2013–14	Peterborough U	42	0		
2014–15	Peterborough U	0	0	**88**	**0**
2014–15	*Scunthorpe U*	13	0	**13**	**0**
2014–15	*York C*	16	0	**16**	**0**
2015–16	Exeter C	45	0		
2016–17	Exeter C	18	0	**63**	**0**

PYM, Christy (G) **62 0**
H: 6 0 W: 11 09 b.Exeter 24-4-95
Internationals: England U20.

2012–13	Exeter C	0	0		
2013–14	Exeter C	9	0		
2014–15	Exeter C	25	0		
2015–16	Exeter C	0	0		
2016–17	Exeter C	28	0	**62**	**0**

REID, Reuben (F) **342 93**
H: 6 0 W: 12 02 b.Bristol 26-7-88

2005–06	Plymouth Arg	1	0		
2006–07	Plymouth Arg	6	0		
2006–07	*Rochdale*	2	0	**2**	**0**
2006–07	*Torquay U*	7	2	**7**	**2**
2007–08	Plymouth Arg	0	0		
2007–08	*Wycombe W*	11	1	**11**	**1**
2007–08	Brentford	10	1	**10**	**1**
2008–09	Rotherham U	41	18	**41**	**18**
2009–10	WBA	4	0		
2009–10	*Peterborough U*	13	0	**13**	**0**
2010–11	WBA	0	0	**4**	**0**
2010–11	*Walsall*	18	3	**18**	**3**
2010–11	Oldham Ath	19	2		
2011–12	Oldham Ath	20	5	**39**	**7**
2012–13	Yeovil T	19	4	**19**	**4**
2012–13	*Plymouth Arg*	18	2		
2013–14	Plymouth Arg	46	17		
2014–15	Plymouth Arg	42	18		
2015–16	Plymouth Arg	29	7		
2016–17	Plymouth Arg	0	0	**142**	**44**
2016–17	Exeter C	36	13	**36**	**13**

RILEY-LOWE, Conor (D) **9 0**
H: 5 10 W: 10 10 b. 10-1-96

2014–15	Exeter C	3	0		
2015–16	Exeter C	0	0		
2016–17	Exeter C	6	0	**9**	**0**

SIMPSON, Robbie (F) **274 29**
H: 6 1 W: 11 11 b.Poole 15-3-85

2007–08	Coventry C	28	1		
2008–09	Coventry C	33	3	**61**	**4**
2009–10	Huddersfield T	13	0		
2010–11	Huddersfield T	0	0		
2010–11	*Brentford*	27	4	**27**	**4**
2011–12	Huddersfield T	0	0	**13**	**0**
2011–12	Oldham Ath	29	6		
2012–13	Oldham Ath	37	2		
2013–14	*Oldham Ath*	0	0	**66**	**8**
2013–14	Leyton Orient	14	0	**14**	**0**
2014–15	Cambridge U	35	8		
2015–16	Cambridge U	32	4	**67**	**12**
2016–17	Exeter C	26	1	**26**	**1**

SMALLCOMBE, Max (M) **0 0**
b. 27-3-99

2016–17	Exeter C	0	0

STOREY, Jordan (D) **0 0**
H: 6 2 W: 12 00 b. 2-9-97

2016–17	Exeter C	0	0

SWEENEY, Pierce (D) **29 0**
H: 5 10 W: 12 07 b.Dublin 11-9-94
Internationals: Republic of Ireland U17, U19, U21.

2012–13	Reading	0	0		
2013–14	Reading	0	0		
2014–15	Reading	0	0		
2015–16	Reading	0	0		
2016–17	Exeter C	29	0	**29**	**0**

TAYLOR, Jake (M) **145 14**
H: 5 10 W: 12 01 b.Ascot 1-12-91
Internationals: Wales U17, U19, U21, Full caps.

2010–11	Reading	1	0		
2011–12	Reading	0	0		
2011–12	*Aldershot T*	3	0	**3**	**0**
2011–12	*Exeter C*	30	3		
2012–13	Reading	0	0		
2012–13	*Cheltenham T*	8	1	**8**	**1**
2012–13	*Crawley T*	4	0	**4**	**0**
2013–14	Reading	8	0		
2014–15	Reading	22	2		
2014–15	*Leyton Orient*	3	0	**3**	**0**
2015–16	Reading	0	0	**31**	**2**
2015–16	*Motherwell*	7	0	**7**	**0**
2015–16	Exeter C	16	4		
2016–17	Exeter C	43	4	**89**	**11**

TILLSON, Jordan (D) **50 1**
H: 6 0 W: 11 09 b.Bath 5-3-93

2012–13	Exeter C	0	0		
2013–14	Exeter C	1	0		
2014–15	Exeter C	3	0		
2015–16	Exeter C	26	1		
2016–17	Exeter C	20	0	**50**	**1**

WATKINS, Ollie (F) **68 21**
H: 5 10 W: 11 00 b.Torbay 30-12-95

2013–14	Exeter C	1	0		
2014–15	Exeter C	2	0		
2015–16	Exeter C	20	8		
2016–17	Exeter C	45	13	**68**	**21**

WHEELER, David (M) **149 33**
H: 5 11 W: 12 00 b.Brighton 4-10-90
Internationals: England U18.

2013–14	Exeter C	35	3		
2014–15	Exeter C	45	7		
2015–16	Exeter C	31	6		
2016–17	Exeter C	38	17	**149**	**33**

WOODMAN, Craig (D) **475 7**
H: 5 9 W: 10 11 b.Tiverton 22-12-82

1999–2000	Bristol C	0	0		
2000–01	Bristol C	2	0		
2001–02	Bristol C	6	0		
2002–03	Bristol C	10	0		
2003–04	Bristol C	21	0		
2004–05	Bristol C	3	0		
2004–05	*Mansfield T*	8	1	**8**	**1**
2004–05	*Torquay U*	22	1		
2005–06	Bristol C	37	1		
2005–06	*Torquay U*	2	0	**24**	**1**
2006–07	Bristol C	11	0	**90**	**1**
2007–08	Wycombe W	29	0		
2008–09	Wycombe W	46	1		
2009–10	Wycombe W	44	1	**119**	**2**
2010–11	Brentford	41	1		
2011–12	Brentford	18	0	**59**	**1**
2012–13	Exeter C	44	0		
2013–14	Exeter C	41	1		
2014–15	Exeter C	32	0		
2015–16	Exeter C	25	0		
2016–17	Exeter C	33	0	**175**	**1**

Players retained or with offer of contract
Gillard, Max Christian James; Green, Daniel; Hancock, Joshua Matthew; Hargreaves, Cameron; Haynes, Samuel Lee; Key, Joshua Myles Abraham; Kite, Harry; O'Loughlin, Joseph Samuel; Parsons, Brandon Jack; Randall, Joel John; Reid, James Tyrrell; Rogers, Steven Christopher John; Seymour, Benjamin Mark; Thomas, Mitchell; White, Lucas Graham; Williams, Lewis Benjamin.

Scholars
Collins, Archie Finn; Gillard, Max Christian James; Hancock, Joshua Matthew; Hargreaves, Cameron; Haynes, Samuel Lee; Key, Joshua Myles Abraham; Kite, Harry; O'Loughlin, Joseph Samuel; Parsons, Brandon Jack; Randall, Joel John; Rogers, Steven Christopher John; Seymour, Benjamin Mark; Smallcombe, Max Frederick; Thomas, Mitchell; White, Lucas Graham; Williams, Lewis Benjamin.

Non-Contract
Green, Daniel; Tisdale, Paul Robert.

FLEETWOOD T (36)

BALL, David (F) **252 55**
H: 6 0 W: 11 08 b.Whitefield 14-12-89

2007–08	Manchester C	0	0		
2008–09	Manchester C	0	0		
2009–10	Manchester C	0	0		
2010–11	Manchester C	0	0		
2010–11	*Swindon T*	18	2	**18**	**2**
2010–11	Peterborough U	19	5		
2011–12	Peterborough U	22	4		
2011–12	*Rochdale*	14	3	**14**	**3**
2012–13	Peterborough U	0	0	**41**	**9**
2012–13	Fleetwood T	34	7		
2013–14	Fleetwood T	30	8		
2014–15	Fleetwood T	32	8		
2015–16	Fleetwood T	37	4		
2016–17	Fleetwood T	46	14	**179**	**41**

BELL, Amari (D) **106 2**
H: 5 11 W: 12 00 b.Burton-upon-Trent 5-5-94

2012–13	Birmingham C	0	0		
2013–14	Birmingham C	1	0		
2014–15	Birmingham C	0	0	**1**	**0**
2014–15	*Swindon T*	10	0	**10**	**0**
2014–15	*Gillingham*	7	0	**7**	**0**
2015–16	Fleetwood T	44	0		
2016–17	Fleetwood T	44	2	**88**	**2**

BOLGER, Cian (D) **139 8**
H: 6 4 W: 12 05 b.Co. Kildare 12-3-92
Internationals: Republic of Ireland U19, U21.

2009–10	Leicester C	0	0		
2010–11	Leicester C	0	0		
2010–11	*Bristol R*	6	0		
2011–12	Leicester C	0	0		
2011–12	*Bristol R*	39	2		
2012–13	Leicester C	0	0		
2012–13	*Bristol R*	3	0	**48**	**2**
2012–13	Bolton W	0	0		
2013–14	Bolton W	0	0		
2013–14	*Colchester U*	4	0	**4**	**0**
2013–14	*Southend U*	1	0		
2014–15	Southend U	23	1		
2015–16	Southend U	22	0	**46**	**1**
2015–16	*Bury*	9	0	**9**	**0**
2016–17	Fleetwood T	32	5	**32**	**5**

BURNS, Wes (F) **103 13**
H: 5 8 W: 10 10 b.Cardiff 28-12-95
Internationals: Wales U21.

2012–13	Bristol C	6	0		
2013–14	Bristol C	20	1		
2014–15	Bristol C	3	1		
2014–15	*Oxford U*	9	1	**9**	**1**
2014–15	*Cheltenham T*	14	4	**14**	**4**
2015–16	Bristol C	14	1	**43**	**3**
2015–16	*Fleetwood T*	14	5		
2016–17	Fleetwood T	10	0	**24**	**5**
2016–17	*Aberdeen*	13	0	**13**	**0**

CAIRNS, Alex (G) **31 0**
H: 6 0 W: 11 05 b.Doncaster 4-1-93

2011–12	Leeds U	1	0		
2012–13	Leeds U	0	0		
2013–14	Leeds U	0	0		
2014–15	Leeds U	0	0	**1**	**0**
2015–16	Chesterfield	0	0		
2015–16	Rotherham U	0	0		
2016–17	Fleetwood T	30	0	**30**	**0**

CHARLES, Dion (M) **0 0**
H: 5 10 W: 10 08 b.Preston 7-10-95
Internationals: Northern Ireland U21.

2013–14	Blackpool	0	0		

From AFC Fylde.

2016–17	Fleetwood T	0	0		

COLE, Devante (F) **102 20**
H: 6 1 W: 11 06 b.Alderley Edge 10-5-95
Internationals: England U16, U17, U18, U19.

2013–14	Manchester C	0	0		
2014–15	Manchester C	0	0		
2014–15	*Barnsley*	19	5	**19**	**5**
2014–15	*Milton Keynes D*	15	3	**15**	**3**
2015–16	Bradford C	19	5	**19**	**5**
2015–16	Fleetwood T	14	2		
2016–17	Fleetwood T	35	5	**49**	**7**

DAVIS, Joe (D) **50 0**
H: 6 0 W: 11 07 b.Burnley 10-11-93

2010–11	Port Vale	1	0		
2011–12	Port Vale	8	0		
2012–13	Port Vale	7	0		
2013–14	Port Vale	11	0	**27**	**0**
2014–15	Leicester C	0	0		
2015–16	Leicester C	0	0		
2015–16	Fleetwood T	19	0		
2016–17	Fleetwood T	4	0	**23**	**0**

DEACON, Keano (M) **1 0**
H: 5 7 W: 10 08 b. 4-4-96

2013–14	Fleetwood T	0	0		
2014–15	Fleetwood T	0	0		
2015–16	Fleetwood T	1	0		
2016–17	Fleetwood T	0	0	**1**	**0**

DUCKWORTH, Michael (M) **98 3**
H: 5 11 W: 11 11 b. 28-6-92

2013–14	Hartlepool U	30	0		
2014–15	Hartlepool U	37	3		
2015–16	Hartlepool U	13	0	**80**	**3**
2016–17	Fleetwood T	4	0	**4**	**0**
2016–17	*Morecambe*	14	0	**14**	**0**

DUNBAR, Kieran (M) **0 0**
H: 6 0 W: 11 07 b. 14-9-96

2015–16	Fleetwood T	0	0		
2016–17	Fleetwood T	0	0		

EASTHAM, Ashley (D) **190 8**
H: 6 3 W: 12 06 b.Preston 22-3-91

2009–10	Blackpool	1	0		
2009–10	*Cheltenham T*	20	0		
2010–11	Blackpool	0	0		
2010–11	*Cheltenham T*	9	0	**29**	**0**
2010–11	*Carlisle U*	0	0		
2011–12	Blackpool	0	0		
2011–12	*Bury*	25	2		
2012–13	Blackpool	0	0	**1**	**0**
2012–13	*Fleetwood T*	1	0		
2012–13	*Notts Co*	4	0	**4**	**0**
2012–13	*Bury*	19	0	**44**	**2**
2013–14	Rochdale	15	0		
2014–15	Rochdale	41	2		
2015–16	Rochdale	20	2	**76**	**4**
2016–17	Fleetwood T	35	2	**36**	**2**

EKPOLO, Godswill (D) **6 0**
H: 5 11 W: 11 07 b.Benin City 14-5-95
Internationals: Nigeria U17.
From Barcelona.

2016–17	Fleetwood T	6	0	**6**	**0**

GLENDON, George (M) **26 0**
H: 5 10 W: 11 00 b.Manchester 3-5-95
Internationals: England U16, U17.

2013–14	Manchester C	0	0		
2014–15	Manchester C	0	0		
2015–16	Manchester C	0	0		
2016–17	Fleetwood T	26	0	**26**	**0**

GRANT, Robert (M) **298 67**
H: 5 11 W: 12 00 b.Liverpool 1-7-90

2006–07	Accrington S	1	0		
2007–08	Accrington S	7	0		
2008–09	Accrington S	15	1		
2009–10	Accrington S	42	14		
2010–11	Scunthorpe U	27	0		
2010–11	*Rochdale*	6	2		
2011–12	Scunthorpe U	29	7		
2011–12	*Accrington S*	8	3	**73**	**18**
2012–13	Scunthorpe U	3	0	**59**	**7**
2012–13	Rochdale	36	15	**42**	**17**
2013–14	Blackpool	6	0		
2013–14	*Fleetwood T*	1	0		
2014–15	Blackpool	0	0	**6**	**0**
2014–15	*Shrewsbury T*	33	6	**33**	**6**
2015–16	Fleetwood T	38	10		
2016–17	Fleetwood T	46	9	**85**	**19**

HAUGHTON, Nick (M) **40 1**
b.Manchester 20-9-94

2013–14	Fleetwood T	0	0		
2014–15	Fleetwood T	22	1		
2015–16	Fleetwood T	18	0		
2016–17	Fleetwood T	0	0	**40**	**1**

HUNTER, Ashley (F) **80 14**
H: 5 10 W: 10 08 b.Derby 29-9-93

2014–15	Fleetwood T	12	1		
2015–16	Fleetwood T	24	5		
2016–17	Fleetwood T	44	8	**80**	**14**

JONSSON, Eggert (D) **213 17**
H: 6 2 W: 11 05 b.Reykjavik 18-8-88
Internationals: Iceland Youth, U21, Full caps.

2005	Fjaroabyggo	22	5	**22**	**5**
2005–06	Hearts	0	0		
2006–07	Hearts	3	0		
2007–08	Hearts	28	1		
2008–09	Hearts	30	3		
2009–10	Hearts	28	3		
2010–11	Hearts	29	0		
2011–12	Hearts	16	1	**134**	**8**
2011–12	Wolverhampton W	3	0		
2012–13	Wolverhampton W	1	0	**4**	**0**
2012–13	*Charlton Ath*	2	0	**2**	**0**
2013–14	Belenenses	0	0		
2015–16	Fleetwood T	39	3		
2016–17	Fleetwood T	12	1	**51**	**4**

Transferred to SonderjskE, January 2017.

KIP, Ricardo (M) **130 26**
H: 5 7 W: 10 12 b. 15-3-92

2012–13	Almere C	17	0		
2013–14	Almere C	30	4		
2014–15	Almere C	37	5		
2015–16	Almere C	33	15	**117**	**24**
2016–17	Fleetwood T	1	0	**1**	**0**
2016–17	*SC Cambuur*	12	2	**12**	**2**

MAGUIRE, Joe (D) **3 0**
H: 5 10 W: 11 00 b.Manchester 18-1-96

2015–16	Liverpool	0	0		
2015–16	*Leyton Orient*	0	0		
2016–17	Liverpool	0	0		
2016–17	Fleetwood T	3	0	**3**	**0**

McLAUGHLIN, Conor (D) **200 7**
H: 6 0 W: 11 02 b.Belfast 26-7-91
Internationals: Northern Ireland U21, Full caps.

2009–10	Preston NE	0	0		
2010–11	Preston NE	7	0		
2011–12	Preston NE	17	0	**24**	**0**
2011–12	*Shrewsbury T*	4	0	**4**	**0**

2012–13 Fleetwood T 19 0
2013–14 Fleetwood T 35 0
2014–15 Fleetwood T 39 1
2015–16 Fleetwood T 37 2
2016–17 Fleetwood T 42 4 **172 7**

NADESAN, Ashley (F) 0 0
2015–16 Fleetwood T 0 0
2016–17 Fleetwood T 0 0

NEAL, Chris (G) 217 0
H: 6 2 W: 12 04 b.St Albans 23-10-85
2004–05 Preston NE 1 0
2005–06 Preston NE 0 0
2006–07 Preston NE 0 0
2006–07 *Shrewsbury T* 0 0
2007–08 *Morecambe* 0 0
2007–08 Preston NE 0 0
2008–09 Preston NE 0 0 **1 0**
2009–10 Shrewsbury T 7 0
2010–11 Shrewsbury T 22 0
2011–12 Shrewsbury T 35 0 **64 0**
2012–13 Port Vale 46 0
2013–14 Port Vale 31 0
2014–15 Port Vale 40 0
2015–16 Port Vale 6 0 **123 0**
2015–16 *Doncaster R* 2 0 **2 0**
2015–16 *Bury* 10 0 **10 0**
2016–17 Fleetwood T 17 0 **17 0**

NIRENNOLD, Victor (D) 43 2
H: 6 4 W: 12 13 b.Rennes 5-4-91
From Miami City.
2015–16 Fleetwood T 17 0
2016–17 Fleetwood T 26 2 **43 2**

OSBORNE, Elliot (M) 0 0
b. 12-5-96
2016–17 Fleetwood T 0 0

POND, Nathan (M) 133 2
H: 6 3 W: 11 00 b.Preston 5-1-85
2012–13 Fleetwood T 12 0
2013–14 Fleetwood T 41 1
2014–15 Fleetwood T 27 1
2015–16 Fleetwood T 21 0
2016–17 Fleetwood T 32 0 **133 2**

REID, Alex (F) 0 0
2016–17 Fleetwood T 0 0

ROBERTS, Oliver (M) 0 0
b.Ashton-under-Lyne 23-9-96
From Stoke C.
2016–17 Fleetwood T 0 0

RYAN, James (M) 344 34
H: 5 8 W: 11 08 b.Maghull 6-9-88
Internationals: Republic of Ireland U21.
2006–07 Liverpool 0 0
2007–08 Liverpool 0 0
2007–08 *Shrewsbury T* 4 0 **4 0**
2008–09 Accrington S 44 10
2009–10 Accrington S 39 3
2010–11 Accrington S 46 9 **129 22**
2011–12 Scunthorpe U 24 2
2012–13 Scunthorpe U 45 2 **69 4**
2013–14 Chesterfield 39 2
2014–15 Chesterfield 44 4 **83 6**
2015–16 Fleetwood T 43 2
2016–17 Fleetwood T 16 0 **59 2**

SCHWABL, Markus (D) 190 1
H: 6 0 W: 11 09 b. 26-8-90
2008–09 Unterhaching 0 0
2009–10 Unterhaching 17 0
2010–11 Unterhaching 5 1
2011–12 Unterhaching 32 0
2012–13 Unterhaching 36 0
2013–14 1860 Munich 4 0 **4 0**
2014–15 Unterhaching 28 0 **118 1**
2015–16 Aalen 37 0
2016–17 Aalen 18 0 **55 0**
2016–17 Fleetwood T 13 0 **13 0**

SOWERBY, Jack (F) 16 1
b. 23-3-95
2014–15 Fleetwood T 0 0
2015–16 Fleetwood T 8 0
2016–17 Fleetwood T 8 1 **16 1**

URWIN, Matthew (G) 0 0
H: 6 1 W: 12 00 b. 28-11-93
2012–13 Blackburn R 0 0
2013–14 Blackburn R 0 0
2014–15 Bradford C 0 0
2016–17 Fleetwood T 0 0

WOOLFORD, Martyn (M) 289 32
H: 6 0 W: 11 09 b.Castleford 13-10-85
Internationals: England C.
2008–09 Scunthorpe U 39 4
2009–10 Scunthorpe U 40 5
2010–11 Scunthorpe U 24 6 **103 15**
2010–11 Bristol C 15 0
2011–12 Bristol C 25 1
2012–13 Bristol C 15 3 **55 4**
2012–13 Millwall 15 1
2013–14 Millwall 40 7
2014–15 Millwall 38 3 **93 11**
2015–16 Sheffield U 28 1 **28 1**
2016–17 Fleetwood T 10 1 **10 1**

Players retained or with offer of contract
Djabi, Mamadou; Sheron, Nathan; Wright, Akil Valentine.

Scholars
Abubakar, Malki Soloman; Baines, Lewis Robert George; Bishop, Jack Matthew; Bridge, Owen James; Collings, Liam; Crellin, William Francis; Dodd, Alexander Paul; Finlayson, Connor James; Garner, Gerard; Holgate, Harrison James; Kerrigan, Dominic James; Mooney, Daniel John; Shorrock, Lewis Allan James; Turner, Henry; Unsworth, Benjamin John.

FULHAM (37)

ADENIRAN, Dennis (M) 1 0
H: 5 11 b.London 2-1-99
Internationals: England U17, U18.
2016–17 Fulham 1 0 **1 0**

ALUKO, Sone (M) 259 43
H: 5 8 W: 9 10 b.Birmingham 19-2-89
Internationals: England U16, U17, U18, U19. Nigeria U20, Full caps.
2005–06 Birmingham C 0 0
2006–07 Birmingham C 0 0
2007–08 Birmingham C 0 0
2007–08 *Aberdeen* 20 3
2008–09 Birmingham C 0 0
2008–09 *Blackpool* 1 0 **1 0**
2008–09 Aberdeen 32 2
2009–10 Aberdeen 22 3
2010–11 Aberdeen 28 2 **102 10**
2011–12 Rangers 21 12 **21 12**
2012–13 Hull C 23 8
2013–14 Hull C 17 1
2014–15 Hull C 25 1
2015–16 Hull C 25 3 **90 13**
2016–17 Fulham 45 8 **45 8**

AYITE, Floyd (M) 212 36
H: 5 9 W: 10 10 b.Bordeaux 15-12-88
Internationals: Togo Full caps.
2008–09 Bordeaux 0 0
2008–09 *Angers* 33 3 **33 3**
2009–10 Bordeaux 0 0
2009–10 *Nancy* 6 0 **6 0**
2010–11 Bordeaux 7 0
2011–12 Bordeaux 0 0 **7 0**
2011–12 Reims 18 3
2012–13 Reims 23 2
2013–14 Reims 32 5 **73 10**
2014–15 Bastia 30 6
2015–16 Bastia 32 8 **62 14**
2016–17 Fulham 31 9 **31 9**

BETTINELLI, Marcus (G) 95 0
H: 6 4 W: 12 13 b.Camberwell 24-5-92
Internationals: England U21.
2010–11 Fulham 0 0
2011–12 Fulham 0 0
2012–13 Fulham 0 0
2013–14 Fulham 0 0
2013–14 *Accrington S* 39 0 **39 0**
2014–15 Fulham 39 0
2015–16 Fulham 11 0
2016–17 Fulham 6 0 **56 0**

BURGESS, Cameron (D) 45 1
H: 6 4 W: 12 11 b.Aberdeen 21-10-95
Internationals: Scotland U19. Australia U20, U23.
2014–15 Fulham 4 0
2014–15 *Ross Co* 0 0
2015–16 Fulham 0 0
2016–17 Fulham 0 0 **4 0**
2016–17 *Oldham Ath* 23 1 **23 1**
2016–17 *Bury* 18 0 **18 0**

BUTTON, David (G) 269 0
H: 6 3 W: 13 00 b.Stevenage 27-2-89
Internationals: England U16, U17, U19, U20.
2005–06 Tottenham H 0 0
2006–07 Tottenham H 0 0
2007–08 *Rochdale* 0 0
2007–08 Tottenham H 0 0
2008–09 Tottenham H 0 0
2008–09 *Bournemouth* 4 0 **4 0**
2008–09 *Luton T* 0 0
2008–09 *Dagenham & R* 3 0 **3 0**
2009–10 Tottenham H 0 0
2009–10 *Crewe Alex* 10 0 **10 0**
2009–10 *Shrewsbury T* 26 0 **26 0**
2010–11 Tottenham H 0 0
2010–11 *Plymouth Arg* 30 0 **30 0**
2011–12 Tottenham H 0 0
2011–12 *Leyton Orient* 1 0 **1 0**
2011–12 *Doncaster R* 7 0 **7 0**
2011–12 *Barnsley* 9 0 **9 0**
2012–13 Tottenham H 0 0
2012–13 Charlton Ath 5 0 **5 0**
2013–14 Brentford 42 0
2014–15 Brentford 46 0
2015–16 Brentford 46 0 **134 0**
2016–17 Fulham 40 0 **40 0**

CAIRNEY, Tom (M) 230 30
H: 6 0 W: 11 05 b.Nottingham 20-1-91
Internationals: Scotland U19, U21, Full caps.
2009–10 Hull C 11 1
2010–11 Hull C 22 1
2011–12 Hull C 27 0
2012–13 Hull C 10 0
2013–14 Hull C 0 0 **70 2**
2013–14 Blackburn R 37 5
2014–15 Blackburn R 39 3 **76 8**
2015–16 Fulham 39 8
2016–17 Fulham 45 12 **84 20**

CHRISTENSEN, Lasse Vigen (M) 72 6
H: 5 10 W: 10 04 b.Esbjerg 15-8-94
Internationals: Denmark U16, U17, U18, U19, U21.
2012–13 Fulham 0 0
2013–14 Fulham 0 0
2014–15 Fulham 25 5
2015–16 Fulham 27 1
2016–17 Fulham 4 0 **56 6**
2016–17 *Burton Alb* 16 0 **16 0**

COLE, Larnell (M) 54 4
H: 5 4 W: 12 04 b.Manchester 9-3-93
Internationals: England U19, U20.
2011–12 Manchester U 0 0
2012–13 Manchester U 0 0
2013–14 Manchester U 0 0
2013–14 Fulham 1 0
2013–14 *Milton Keynes D* 3 0 **3 0**
2014–15 Fulham 0 0
2015–16 Fulham 0 0
2015–16 *Shrewsbury T* 29 3 **29 3**
2016–17 Fulham 0 0 **1 0**
2016–17 *Inverness CT* 21 1 **21 1**

CYRIAC, Gohi (F) 198 65
H: 5 9 W: 10 06 b.Daloa 15-8-90
Internationals: Ivory Coast Full caps.
2007 Mimosas Abidjan 0 0
2008 Mimosas Abidjan 29 22 **29 22**
2008–09 Standard Liege 1 0
2009–10 Standard Liege 7 2
2010–11 Standard Liege 18 8
2011–12 Standard Liege 22 6 **48 16**
2012–13 Anderlecht 2 0
2013–14 Anderlecht 27 4
2014–15 Anderlecht 29 4 **58 8**
2015–16 KV Ostend 33 14
2016–17 KV Ostend 21 4 **54 18**
On loan from KV Ostend.
2016–17 Fulham 9 1 **9 1**

DE LA TORRE, Luca (M) 0 0
H: 5 9 W: 9 13 b.San Diego 23-5-98
Internationals: USA U17, U20.
2016–17 Fulham 0 0

EDUN, Tayo (D) 0 0
H: 5 9 b.London 14-5-98
Internationals: England U17, U18, U19.
2016–17 Fulham 0 0

FREDERICKS, Ryan (M) 101 1
H: 5 8 W: 11 10 b.Potters Bar 10-10-92
Internationals: England U19.
2010–11 Tottenham H 0 0
2011–12 Tottenham H 0 0
2012–13 Tottenham H 0 0
2012–13 *Brentford* 4 0 **4 0**

2013–14 Tottenham H 0 0
2013–14 *Millwall* 14 1 **14 1**
2014–15 Tottenham H 0 0
2014–15 *Middlesbrough* 17 0 **17 0**
2015–16 Bristol C 4 0 **4 0**
2015–16 Fulham 32 0
2016–17 Fulham 30 0 **62 0**

GRIMMER, Jack (M) 81 2
H: 6 0 W: 12 06 b.Aberdeen 25-1-94
Internationals: Scotland U16, U17, U18, U19, U21.
2009–10 Aberdeen 2 0
2010–11 Aberdeen 2 0
2011–12 Aberdeen 0 0 **4 0**
2011–12 Fulham 0 0
2012–13 Fulham 0 0
2013–14 Fulham 0 0
2013–14 *Port Vale* 13 1 **13 1**
2014–15 Fulham 13 0
2014–15 *Shrewsbury T* 6 0
2015–16 Fulham 0 0
2015–16 *Shrewsbury T* 21 1
2016–17 Fulham 0 0 **13 0**
2016–17 *Shrewsbury T* 24 0 **51 1**

HUMPHRYS, Stephen (F) 16 2
b.Oldham 15-9-97
2016–17 Fulham 2 0 **2 0**
2016–17 *Shrewsbury T* 14 2 **14 2**

JOHANSEN, Stefan (F) 205 31
H: 6 0 W: 12 04 b.Vardo 8-1-91
Internationals: Norway U16, U17, U18, U19, U21, U23, Full caps.
2007 Bodo/Glimt 4 0
2008 Bodo/Glimt 1 0
2009 Bodo/Glimt 4 0
2010 Bodo/Glimt 20 0 **29 0**
2011 Stromsgodset 13 1
2012 Stromsgodset 27 3
2013 Stromsgodset 27 4 **67 8**
2013–14 Celtic 16 2
2014–15 Celtic 34 9
2015–16 Celtic 23 1 **73 12**
2016–17 Fulham 36 11 **36 11**

JORONEN, Jesse (G) 36 1
H: 6 6 W: 14 00 b.Rautjarvi 21-3-93
Internationals: Finland U17, U19, U21, Full caps.
2013–14 Fulham 0 0
2013–14 *FC Lahti* 18 0 **18 0**
2014–15 Fulham 4 0
2014–15 *Accrington S* 4 0 **4 0**
2015–16 Fulham 0 0
2015–16 *Stevenage* 10 1 **10 1**
2016–17 Fulham 0 0 **4 0**

JOZABED, Sanchez Ruiz (M) 115 16
H: 5 11 W: 11 00 b.Mairena del Alcor 8-3-91
2011–12 Sevilla 0 0
2012–13 Ponferradina 3 0 **3 0**
2013–14 Real Jaen 36 4 **36 4**
2014–15 Rayo Vallecano 23 1
2015–16 Rayo Vallecano 27 9 **50 10**
2016–17 Fulham 7 0 **7 0**
2016–17 *Celta Vigo* 19 2 **19 2**

KAVANAGH, Sean (D) 37 1
H: 5 8 W: 9 11 b.Dublin 24-1-94
Internationals: Republic of Ireland U21.
2014–15 Fulham 19 1
2015–16 Fulham 2 0
2015–16 *Mansfield T* 7 0 **7 0**
2016–17 Fulham 0 0 **21 1**
2016–17 *Hartlepool U* 9 0 **9 0**

KEBANO, Neeskens (M) 110 25
H: 5 11 W: 11 11 b.Montereau 10-3-92
Internationals: France U17, U18, U19, U20. DR Congo Full caps.
2010–11 Paris Saint-Germain 3 0
2011–12 Paris Saint-Germain 0 0
2012–13 Paris Saint-Germain 0 0 **3 0**
2012–13 *Caen* 12 1 **12 1**
2013–14 Charleroi 26 5
2014–15 Charleroi 33 12
2015–16 Charleroi 5 1 **64 18**
2016–17 Genk 3 0 **3 0**
2016–17 Fulham 28 6 **28 6**

MADL, Michael (D) 238 10
b. 21-3-88
Internationals: Austria U21.
2006–07 Austria Vienna 5 0
2007–08 Austria Vienna 0 0
2007–08 *Wacker Innsbruck* 21 2 **21 2**
2008–09 Austria Vienna 17 0
2009–10 Austria Vienna 1 0 **23 0**
2010–11 Wiener Neustadt 23 0
2011–12 Wiener Neustadt 31 3 **54 3**
2012–13 Sturm Graz 33 1
2013–14 Sturm Graz 28 1
2014–15 Sturm Graz 32 1
2015–16 Sturm Graz 18 1 **111 4**
On loan from Sturm Graz.
2015–16 Fulham 13 1
2016–17 Fulham 16 0 **29 1**

MALONE, Scott (D) 236 20
H: 6 2 W: 11 11 b.Rowley Regis 25-3-91
Internationals: England U19.
2008–09 Wolverhampton W 0 0
2008–09 *Ujpest* 7 1 **7 1**
2009–10 Wolverhampton W 0 0
2009–10 *Southend U* 17 0 **17 0**
2010–11 Wolverhampton W 0 0
2010–11 *Burton Alb* 22 1 **22 1**
2011–12 Wolverhampton W 0 0
2011–12 Bournemouth 32 5 **32 5**
2012–13 Millwall 15 1
2013–14 Millwall 33 3
2014–15 Millwall 20 1 **68 5**
2014–15 Cardiff C 13 0
2015–16 Cardiff C 41 2 **54 2**
2016–17 Fulham 36 6 **36 6**

McDONALD, Kevin (M) 398 33
H: 6 2 W: 13 03 b.Carnoustie 4-11-88
Internationals: Scotland U19, U21.
2005–06 Dundee 26 3
2006–07 Dundee 31 2
2007–08 Dundee 34 9 **91 14**
2008–09 Burnley 25 1
2009–10 Burnley 26 1
2010–11 Burnley 0 0 **51 2**
2010–11 *Scunthorpe U* 5 1 **5 1**
2010–11 *Notts Co* 11 0 **11 0**
2011–12 Sheffield U 31 3
2012–13 Sheffield U 45 1
2013–14 Sheffield U 1 1 **77 5**
2013–14 Wolverhampton W 41 5
2014–15 Wolverhampton W 46 0
2015–16 Wolverhampton W 33 3 **120 8**
2016–17 Fulham 43 3 **43 3**

ODOI, Dennis (D) 286 10
H: 5 10 W: 11 09 b.Leuven 27-5-88
Internationals: Belgium U20, U21, Full caps.
2006–07 Oud-Heverlee Leuven 3 0
2007–08 Oud-Heverlee Leuven 21 0
2008–09 Oud-Heverlee Leuven 33 3 **57 3**
2009–10 Sint-Truiden 26 1
2010–11 Sint-Truiden 33 2 **59 3**
2011–12 Anderlecht 19 0
2012–13 Anderlecht 14 0 **33 0**
2013–14 Lokeren 37 1
2014–15 Lokeren 35 0
2015–16 Lokeren 35 1 **107 2**
2016–17 Fulham 30 2 **30 2**

PARKER, Scott (M) 486 31
H: 5 9 W: 11 10 b.Lambeth 13-10-80
Internationals: England U16, U18, U21, Full caps.
1997–98 Charlton Ath 3 0
1998–99 Charlton Ath 4 0
1999–2000 Charlton Ath 15 1
2000–01 Charlton Ath 20 1
2000–01 *Norwich C* 6 1 **6 1**
2001–02 Charlton Ath 38 1
2002–03 Charlton Ath 28 4
2003–04 Charlton Ath 20 2 **128 9**
2003–04 Chelsea 11 1
2004–05 Chelsea 4 0 **15 1**
2005–06 Newcastle U 26 1
2006–07 Newcastle U 29 3 **55 4**
2007–08 West Ham U 18 1
2008–09 West Ham U 28 1
2009–10 West Ham U 31 2
2010–11 West Ham U 32 5
2011–12 West Ham U 4 1 **113 10**
2011–12 Tottenham H 29 0
2012–13 Tottenham H 21 0
2013–14 Tottenham H 0 0 **50 0**
2013–14 Fulham 29 2
2014–15 Fulham 37 3
2015–16 Fulham 24 1
2016–17 Fulham 29 0 **119 6**

PETSOS, Thanos (M) 131 6
H: 6 0 W: 12 08 b.Dusseldorf 5-6-91
Internationals: Greece U17, U19, U21, Full caps.
2009–10 Bayer Leverkusen 1 0 **1 0**
2010–11 Kaiserslautern 20 0
2011–12 Kaiserslautern 19 0 **39 0**
2012–13 Greuther Furth 14 1 **14 1**
2013–14 Rapid Vienna 27 3
2014–15 Rapid Vienna 27 1
2015–16 Rapid Vienna 20 1 **74 5**
2016–17 Werder Bremen 3 0 **3 0**
On loan from Werder Bremen.
2016–17 Fulham 0 0

REAM, Tim (D) 336 8
H: 6 1 W: 11 05 b.St Louis 5-10-87
Internationals: USA Full caps.
2006 St Louis Billikens 19 0
2007 St Louis Billikens 19 0
2008 St Louis Billikens 22 0
2008 Chicago Fire 12 0
2009 Chicago Fire 7 0 **19 0**
2009 St Louis Billikens 22 6 **82 6**
2010 New York RB 30 1
2011 New York RB 28 0 **58 1**
2011–12 Bolton W 13 0
2012–13 Bolton W 15 0
2013–14 Bolton W 42 0
2014–15 Bolton W 44 0 **114 0**
2015–16 Fulham 29 0
2016–17 Fulham 34 1 **63 1**

RODAK, Marek (G) 20 0
H: 6 2 W: 10 12 b. 13-12-96
Internationals: Slovakia U17, U19, U21.
2014–15 Fulham 0 0
2015–16 Fulham 0 0
2016–17 Fulham 0 0
2016–17 *Accrington S* 20 0 **20 0**

SESSEGNON, Ryan (D) 25 5
H: 5 10 W: 11 02 b.London 18-5-00
Internationals: England U16, U17, U19.
2016–17 Fulham 25 5 **25 5**

SIGURDSSON, Ragnar (D) 284 20
H: 6 2 W: 13 03 b.Reykjavik 19-6-86
Internationals: Iceland U17, U19, U21, Full caps.
2004 Fylkir 3 0
2005 Fylkir 17 1
2006 Fylkir 18 1 **38 2**
2007 Gothenburg 26 0
2008 Gothenburg 29 4
2009 Gothenburg 29 4
2010 Gothenburg 28 1
2011 Gothenburg 13 3 **125 12**
2011–12 Copenhagen 24 1
2012–13 Copenhagen 31 3
2013–14 Copenhagen 14 0 **69 4**
2014–15 Krasnodar 6 0
2015–16 Krasnodar 26 1
2016–17 Krasnodar 3 0 **35 1**
2016–17 Fulham 17 1 **17 1**

STEARMAN, Richard (D) 390 12
H: 6 2 W: 10 08 b.Wolverhampton 19-8-87
Internationals: England U16, U17, U19, U21.
2004–05 Leicester C 8 1
2005–06 Leicester C 34 3
2006–07 Leicester C 35 1
2007–08 Leicester C 39 2 **116 7**
2008–09 Wolverhampton W 37 1
2009–10 Wolverhampton W 16 1
2010–11 Wolverhampton W 31 0
2011–12 Wolverhampton W 30 0
2012–13 Wolverhampton W 12 1
2012–13 *Ipswich T* 15 0 **15 0**
2013–14 Wolverhampton W 40 2
2014–15 Wolverhampton W 42 0
2015–16 Wolverhampton W 4 0
2015–16 Fulham 29 0
2016–17 Fulham 0 0 **29 0**
2016–17 *Wolverhampton W* 18 0 **230 5**

TUNNICLIFFE, Ryan (M) 146 4
H: 6 0 W: 14 02 b.Bury 30-12-92
Internationals: England U16, U17.
2009–10 Manchester U 0 0
2010–11 Manchester U 0 0
2011–12 Manchester U 0 0
2011–12 *Peterborough U* 27 0 **27 0**
2012–13 Manchester U 0 0
2012–13 *Barnsley* 2 0 **2 0**
2013–14 Manchester U 0 0
2013–14 *Ipswich T* 27 0 **27 0**
2013–14 Fulham 3 0
2013–14 *Wigan Ath* 5 0
2014–15 Fulham 22 0
2014–15 *Blackburn R* 17 1 **17 1**
2015–16 Fulham 27 2
2016–17 Fulham 7 0 **59 2**
2016–17 *Wigan Ath* 9 1 **14 1**

WILLIAMS, George C (F) **40 0**
H: 5 10 W: 12 04 b.Milton Keynes 7-9-95
Internationals: Wales U17, U19, U21, Full caps.
2012–13 Fulham 0 0
2013–14 Fulham 0 0
2014–15 Fulham 14 0
2014–15 *Milton Keynes D* 4 0
2015–16 Fulham 1 0
2015–16 *Gillingham* 10 0 **10 0**
2016–17 Fulham 0 0 **15 0**
2016–17 *Milton Keynes D* 11 0 **15 0**

WOODROW, Cauley (F) **87 15**
H: 6 0 W: 12 04 b.Hemel Hempstead 2-12-94
Internationals: England U17, U20, U21.
2011–12 Fulham 0 0
2012–13 Fulham 0 0
2013–14 Fulham 6 1
2013–14 *Southend U* 19 2 **19 2**
2014–15 Fulham 29 3
2015–16 Fulham 14 4
2016–17 Fulham 5 0 **54 8**
2016–17 *Burton Alb* 14 5 **14 5**

Players retained or with offer of contract
Adebayo, Elijah Anuoluwapo; Andrason, Atli Hrafn; Davies, Aron Paul; Fossey, Marlon Joseph; Jenz, Moritz; Kait, Mattias; Kwietniewski, Mikolaj; Nabay, Foday; Norman, Magnus; Opoku, Jerome; Pearce, Isaac Richard Kai; Sanchez, Ruiz Jozabed; Thorsteinsson, Jon Dagur.

Scholars
Ashby-Hammond, Taye; Elstone, Michael Colin; Felix, Joseph Rabole; Garrido, Rodriguez Jose; Harris, Jayden John-Lloyd; Kelly, Vishna Christopher; Lukwata, Joshua Benon; Martin, Daniel John; Mundle-Smith, Jaydn Josiah; Norman, Felix; Santos, Clase Nicolas; Schwarzer, Julian; Sessegnon, Kouassi Ryan; Sessegnon, Zeze Steven; Spence, Diop Tehuti Djed-Hotep; Thomas, Cassian Diogo David; York, Reece Cable.

GILLINGHAM (38)

BYRNE, Mark (M) **232 21**
H: 5 9 W: 11 00 b.Dublin 9-11-88
2006–07 Nottingham F 0 0
2007–08 Nottingham F 1 0
2008–09 Nottingham F 1 0
2009–10 Nottingham F 0 0
2010–11 Nottingham F 0 0 **2 0**
2010–11 *Barnet* 28 6
2011–12 Barnet 43 5
2012–13 Barnet 40 3 **111 14**
2014–15 Newport Co 42 4
2015–16 Newport Co 46 2 **88 6**
2016–17 Gillingham 31 1 **31 1**

CHAPMAN, Ben (M) **0 0**
2016–17 Gillingham 0 0

CUNDLE, Gregory (F) **2 0**
b. 20-3-97
2015–16 Gillingham 0 0
2016–17 Gillingham 2 0 **2 0**

DACK, Bradley (M) **160 31**
H: 5 9 b.Greenwich 31-12-93
2012–13 Gillingham 16 1
2013–14 Gillingham 28 3
2014–15 Gillingham 42 9
2015–16 Gillingham 40 13
2016–17 Gillingham 34 5 **160 31**

DICKENSON, Mitchell (D) **2 0**
b. 14-9-96
2015–16 Gillingham 0 0
2016–17 Gillingham 2 0 **2 0**

DONNELLY, Rory (F) **135 37**
H: 6 2 W: 12 10 b.Belfast 18-2-92
Internationals: Northern Ireland U21.
2010–11 Cliftonville 31 7
2011–12 Cliftonville 18 13 **49 20**
2011–12 Swansea C 0 0
2012–13 Swansea C 0 0
2013–14 Swansea C 0 0
2013–14 *Coventry C* 0 0
2014–15 Swansea C 0 0
2014–15 *Tranmere R* 20 5 **20 5**
2015–16 Gillingham 38 10
2016–17 Gillingham 28 2 **66 12**

EHMER, Max (M) **181 9**
H: 6 2 W: 11 00 b.Frankfurt 3-2-92
2009–10 QPR 0 0
2010–11 QPR 0 0
2010–11 *Yeovil T* 27 0
2011–12 QPR 0 0
2011–12 *Yeovil T* 24 0 **51 0**
2011–12 *Preston NE* 9 0 **9 0**
2012–13 QPR 0 0
2012–13 *Stevenage* 6 1 **6 1**
2013–14 QPR 1 0
2013–14 *Carlisle U* 12 1 **12 1**
2014–15 QPR 0 0 **1 0**
2014–15 *Gillingham* 27 1
2015–16 Gillingham 30 0
2016–17 Gillingham 45 6 **102 7**

GARMSTON, Bradley (D) **59 1**
H: 5 9 W: 10 12 b.Greenwich 18-1-94
Internationals: Republic of Ireland U17, U9, U21.
2012–13 WBA 0 0
2012–13 *Colchester U* 13 0 **13 0**
2013–14 WBA 0 0
2014–15 WBA 0 0
2014–15 *Gillingham* 8 1
2015–16 Gillingham 33 0
2016–17 Gillingham 5 0 **46 1**

HADDLER, Tom (G) **0 0**
b. 30-7-96
2014–15 Gillingham 0 0
2015–16 Gillingham 0 0
2016–17 Gillingham 0 0

HERD, Chris (M) **111 7**
H: 5 9 W: 11 04 b.Perth 4-4-89
Internationals: Australia U20, Full caps.
2007–08 Aston Villa 0 0
2007–08 *Port Vale* 11 2 **11 2**
2007–08 *Wycombe W* 4 0 **4 0**
2008–09 Aston Villa 0 0
2009–10 Aston Villa 0 0
2009–10 *Lincoln C* 20 4 **20 4**
2010–11 Aston Villa 6 0
2011–12 Aston Villa 19 1
2012–13 Aston Villa 9 0
2013–14 Aston Villa 2 0
2014–15 Aston Villa 0 0 **36 1**
2014–15 *Bolton W* 2 0 **2 0**
2014–15 *Wigan Ath* 3 0 **3 0**
2015–16 Chesterfield 23 0
2016–17 Chesterfield 0 0 **23 0**
2016–17 Gillingham 12 0 **12 0**

HESSENTHALER, Jake (M) **122 7**
b.Gravesend 20-4-94
2012–13 Gillingham 0 0
2013–14 Gillingham 19 1
2014–15 Gillingham 37 1
2015–16 Gillingham 38 4
2016–17 Gillingham 28 1 **122 7**

HOLY, Tomas (G) **76 0**
H: 6 9 W: 16 05 b.Rychnov nad Kneznou 10-12-91
Internationals: Czech Republic U16, U17, U18.
2010–11 Sparta Prague 0 0
2011–12 Sparta Prague 0 0
2012–13 Sparta Prague 0 0
2013–14 Sparta Prague 0 0
2013–14 *Vlasim* 9 0 **9 0**
2013–14 *Viktoria Zizkov* 14 0
2014–15 Sparta Prague 0 0
2014–15 *Viktoria Zizkov* 27 0 **41 0**
2015–16 Sparta Prague 0 0
2015–16 *Zlin* 20 0 **20 0**
2016–17 Fastav Zlin 0 0
2016–17 Gillingham 6 0 **6 0**

JACKSON, Ryan (M) **141 3**
H: 5 9 W: 10 03 b.Streatham 31-7-90
Internationals: England C.
2011–12 AFC Wimbledon 7 0 **7 0**
2013–14 Newport Co 29 0
2014–15 Newport Co 34 0 **63 0**
2015–16 Gillingham 37 2
2016–17 Gillingham 34 1 **71 3**

KNOTT, Billy (M) **137 10**
H: 5 8 W: 11 02 b.Canvey Island 28-11-92
Internationals: England U16, U17, U20.
2010–11 Sunderland 0 0
2011–12 Sunderland 0 0
2011–12 *AFC Wimbledon* 20 3 **20 3**
2012–13 Sunderland 1 0
2013–14 Sunderland 0 0 **1 0**
2013–14 *Wycombe W* 17 1 **17 1**
2013–14 *Port Vale* 18 2 **18 2**
2014–15 Bradford C 40 3
2015–16 Bradford C 24 0 **64 3**
2016–17 Gillingham 17 1 **17 1**

KONCHESKY, Paul (D) **544 14**
H: 5 10 W: 11 07 b.Barking 15-5-81
Internationals: England U18, U20, U21, Full caps.
1997–98 Charlton Ath 3 0
1998–99 Charlton Ath 2 0
1999–2000 Charlton Ath 8 0
2000–01 Charlton Ath 23 0
2001–02 Charlton Ath 34 1
2002–03 Charlton Ath 30 3
2003–04 Charlton Ath 21 0
2003–04 *Tottenham H* 12 0 **12 0**
2004–05 Charlton Ath 28 1 **149 5**
2005–06 West Ham U 37 1
2006–07 West Ham U 22 0 **59 1**
2007–08 Fulham 33 0
2008–09 Fulham 36 1
2009–10 Fulham 27 1
2010–11 Fulham 1 0 **97 2**
2010–11 Liverpool 15 0 **15 0**
2010–11 *Nottingham F* 15 1 **15 1**
2011–12 Leicester C 42 2
2012–13 Leicester C 39 1
2013–14 Leicester C 31 1
2014–15 Leicester C 26 1
2015–16 Leicester C 0 0 **138 5**
2015–16 *QPR* 34 0 **34 0**
2016–17 Gillingham 25 0 **25 0**

LACEY, Alex (D) **78 3**
b.Milton Keynes 31-5-93
2014–15 Luton T 18 0 **18 0**
2015–16 Yeovil T 20 0
2016–17 Yeovil T 40 3 **60 3**
2016–17 Gillingham 0 0

LIST, Elliott (M) **21 0**
b.Camberwell 12-5-97
From Crystal Palace.
2015–16 Gillingham 6 0
2016–17 Gillingham 15 0 **21 0**

M'BO, Noel (F) **0 0**
2015–16 Gillingham 0 0
2016–17 Gillingham 0 0

MARTIN, Lee (M) **260 14**
H: 5 10 W: 10 03 b.Taunton 9-2-87
2004–05 Manchester U 0 0
2005–06 Manchester U 0 0
2006–07 Manchester U 0 0
2006–07 *Rangers* 7 0 **7 0**
2006–07 *Stoke C* 13 1 **13 1**
2007–08 Manchester U 0 0
2007–08 *Plymouth Arg* 12 2 **12 2**
2007–08 *Sheffield U* 6 0 **6 0**
2008–09 Manchester U 1 0
2008–09 *Nottingham F* 13 1 **13 1**
2009–10 Manchester U 0 0 **1 0**
2009–10 Ipswich T 16 1
2010–11 Ipswich T 16 0
2010–11 *Charlton Ath* 20 2 **20 2**
2011–12 Ipswich T 34 5
2012–13 Ipswich T 34 0
2013–14 Ipswich T 0 0 **100 6**
2013–14 Millwall 26 1
2014–15 Millwall 27 1
2015–16 Millwall 8 0 **61 2**
2015–16 *Northampton T* 10 0 **10 0**
2016–17 Gillingham 17 0 **17 0**

McDONALD, Cody (F) **268 88**
H: 5 10 W: 11 03 b.Witham 30-5-86
2008–09 Norwich C 7 1
2009–10 Norwich C 17 3
2010–11 Norwich C 0 0
2010–11 *Gillingham* 41 25
2011–12 Norwich C 0 0 **24 4**
2011–12 Coventry C 23 4
2012–13 Coventry C 20 3 **43 7**
2012–13 *Gillingham* 7 4
2013–14 Gillingham 44 17
2014–15 Gillingham 43 16
2015–16 Gillingham 22 5
2016–17 Gillingham 44 10 **201 77**

MULDOON, Oliver (M) **25 0**
b.Hornchurch 3-9-94
2014–15 Charlton Ath 0 0
2014–15 *Gillingham* 3 0
2015–16 Charlton Ath 0 0
2015–16 *Dagenham & R* 18 0 **18 0**
2016–17 Charlton Ath 0 0
2016–17 Gillingham 4 0 **7 0**

NELSON, Stuart (G) **420** **0**
H: 6 1 W: 12 12 b.Stroud 17-9-81

2003–04	Brentford	9	0		
2004–05	Brentford	43	0		
2005–06	Brentford	45	0		
2006–07	Brentford	19	0	**116**	**0**
2007–08	Leyton Orient	30	0	**30**	**0**
2008–09	Norwich C	0	0		
2010–11	Notts Co	33	0		
2011–12	Notts Co	46	0	**79**	**0**
2012–13	Gillingham	45	0		
2013–14	Gillingham	46	0		
2014–15	Gillingham	24	0		
2015–16	Gillingham	46	0		
2016–17	Gillingham	34	0	**195**	**0**

O'HARA, Jamie (M) **214** **19**
H: 5 11 W: 12 04 b.Dartford 25-9-86
Internationals: England U21.

2004–05	Tottenham H	0	0		
2005–06	Tottenham H	0	0		
2005–06	*Chesterfield*	19	5	**19**	**5**
2006–07	Tottenham H	0	0		
2007–08	Tottenham H	17	1		
2007–08	*Millwall*	14	2	**14**	**2**
2008–09	Tottenham H	15	1		
2009–10	Tottenham H	2	0		
2009–10	*Portsmouth*	26	2	**26**	**2**
2010–11	Tottenham H	0	0	**34**	**2**
2010–11	*Wolverhampton W*	14	3		
2011–12	Wolverhampton W	19	2		
2012–13	Wolverhampton W	20	0		
2013–14	Wolverhampton W	2	0		
2014–15	Wolverhampton W	0	0	**55**	**5**
2014–15	Blackpool	27	2	**27**	**2**
2015–16	Fulham	37	1	**37**	**1**
2016–17	Gillingham	2	0	**2**	**0**

O'MARA, Finn (D) **0** **0**

2016–17	Gillingham	0	0

OLDAKER, Darren (M) **5** **0**
b.London 4-1-99

2015–16	Gillingham	0	0		
2016–17	Gillingham	5	0	**5**	**0**

OSAOABE, Emmanuel (M) **42** **3**
b.Dundalk 1-10-96

2015–16	Gillingham	18	2		
2016–17	Gillingham	24	1	**42**	**3**

PARKER, Josh (F) **105** **17**
H: 5 11 W: 12 00 b.Slough 1-12-90
Internationals: Antigua and Barbuda Full caps.

2009–10	QPR	4	0		
2010–11	QPR	1	0	**5**	**0**
2010–11	*Northampton T*	3	0	**3**	**0**
2010–11	*Wycombe W*	1	0	**1**	**0**
2011–12	Oldham Ath	13	0	**13**	**0**
2011–12	*Dagenham & R*	8	0	**8**	**0**
2012–13	Oxford U	15	0	**15**	**0**
2013–14	Domzale	25	11	**25**	**11**
2014–15	Red Star Belgrade	9	2		
2015–16	Red Star Belgrade	3	2	**12**	**4**
2015–16	*Aberdeen*	7	0	**7**	**0**
2016–17	Gillingham	16	2	**16**	**2**

REHMAN, Zesh (D) **279** **12**
H: 6 2 W: 12 13 b.Birmingham 14-10-83
Internationals: England U18, U19, U29. Pakistan Full caps.

2001–02	Fulham	0	0		
2002–03	Fulham	0	0		
2003–04	Fulham	1	0		
2003–04	*Brighton & HA*	11	2	**11**	**2**
2004–05	Fulham	17	0		
2005–06	Fulham	3	0	**21**	**0**
2005–06	*Norwich C*	5	0	**5**	**0**
2006–07	QPR	25	0		
2006–07	*Brighton*	8	0	**8**	**0**
2007–08	QPR	21	0		
2008–09	QPR	0	0	**46**	**0**
2008–09	*Blackpool*	3	0	**3**	**0**
2008–09	*Bradford C*	17	0		
2009–10	Bradford C	38	2		
2010–11	Bradford C	8	0	**63**	**2**
2011–12	Muathong U	30	1	**30**	**1**
2011–12	Kitchee	9	0		
2012–13	Kitchee	15	0		
2013–14	Kitchee	6	0	**30**	**0**
2014	Panhang	21	1		
2015	Panhang	21	6		
2016	Panhang	10	0	**52**	**7**
2016–17	Gillingham	10	0	**10**	**0**

SIMPSON, Aaron (M) **0** **0**

2016–17	Gillingham	0	0

STEVENSON, Bradley (M) **0** **0**

2016–17	Gillingham	0	0

WAGSTAFF, Scott (M) **227** **26**
H: 5 10 W: 10 03 b.Maidstone 31-3-90

2007–08	Charlton Ath	2	0		
2008–09	Charlton Ath	2	0		
2008–09	*Bournemouth*	5	0	**5**	**0**
2009–10	Charlton Ath	30	4		
2010–11	Charlton Ath	40	8		
2011–12	Charlton Ath	34	4		
2012–13	Charlton Ath	9	1	**117**	**17**
2012–13	*Leyton Orient*	7	0	**7**	**0**
2013–14	Bristol C	37	5		
2014–15	Bristol C	26	2		
2015–16	Bristol C	9	1	**72**	**8**
2016–17	Gillingham	26	1	**26**	**1**

WRIGHT, Josh (M) **278** **18**
H: 6 1 W: 11 07 b.Bethnal Green 6-11-89
Internationals: England U16, U17, U18, U19.

2007–08	Charlton Ath	0	0		
2007–08	*Barnet*	32	1	**32**	**1**
2008–09	Charlton Ath	2	0	**2**	**0**
2008–09	*Brentford*	5	0	**5**	**0**
2008–09	*Gillingham*	5	0		
2009–10	Scunthorpe U	35	0		
2010–11	Scunthorpe U	36	0	**71**	**0**
2011–12	Millwall	18	1		
2012–13	Millwall	24	0		
2013–14	Millwall	3	0		
2013–14	*Leyton Orient*	2	0		
2014–15	Millwall	1	0	**46**	**1**
2014–15	*Crawley T*	4	0	**4**	**0**
2014–15	Leyton Orient	29	2	**31**	**2**
2015–16	Gillingham	41	1		
2016–17	Gillingham	41	13	**87**	**14**

Players retained or with offer of contract
Morris, Aaron John; Wignal-List, Elliott Ricardo.

Scholars
Arnold, Henry George; Catherall, Louie Sydney; Chapman, Benjamin Scott; Conway, Jack William James; Divine, Danny Paul; Gildea, Jaydn; Hlabi, Leroy; Huckle, Ryan Cockburn; Lawford, Samuel Dean; Mbo, Noel; O'Mara, Finn George; Simpson, Aaron Michael; Stevenson, Bradley; Sykes, William Peter Barry; Tucker, Jack Robert; White, Theodore Stephen; Woods, Henry.

GRIMSBY T (39)

ANDREW, Danny (D) **128** **4**
H: 5 11 W: 11 06 b.Holbeach 23-12-90

2009–10	Peterborough U	2	0	**2**	**0**
2009–10	*Cheltenham T*	10	0		
2010–11	Cheltenham T	43	4		
2011–12	Cheltenham T	10	0		
2012–13	Cheltenham T	1	0	**64**	**4**

From Gloucester C, Macclesfield T.

2014–15	Fleetwood T	7	0		
2015–16	Fleetwood T	9	0	**16**	**0**
2016–17	Grimsby T	46	0	**46**	**0**

ASANTE, Akwasi (F) **21** **3**
H: 5 7 W: 10 00 b.Amsterdam 22-9-92

2010–11	Birmingham C	0	0		
2011–12	Birmingham C	0	0		
2011–12	*Northampton T*	4	1	**4**	**1**
2012–13	Birmingham C	0	0		
2012–13	*Shrewsbury T*	7	1		
2013–14	Birmingham C	0	0		
2013–14	*Shrewsbury T*	1	0	**8**	**1**

From Kidderminster H, Solihull Moors.

2016–17	Grimsby T	9	1	**9**	**1**

BERRETT, James (M) **288** **32**
H: 5 10 W: 10 13 b.Halifax 13-1-89
Internationals: Republic of Ireland U18, U19, U21.

2006–07	Huddersfield T	2	0		
2007–08	Huddersfield T	15	1		
2008–09	Huddersfield T	9	1		
2009–10	Huddersfield T	9	0	**35**	**2**
2010–11	Carlisle U	46	10		
2011–12	Carlisle U	42	9		
2012–13	Carlisle U	42	2		
2013–14	Carlisle U	40	2	**170**	**23**
2014–15	Yeovil T	28	1	**28**	**1**
2015–16	York C	36	4	**36**	**4**
2016–17	Grimsby T	19	2	**19**	**2**

BOLARINWA, Tom (M) **34** **2**
H: 5 11 W: 11 11 b.Greenwich 21-1-90
From Sutton U.

2016–17	Grimsby T	34	2	**34**	**2**

BOYCE, Andrew (D) **59** **2**
H: 6 3 W: 12 08 b.Doncaster 5-11-89

2013–14	Scunthorpe U	2	0		
2014–15	Scunthorpe U	29	1		
2015–16	Scunthorpe U	0	0	**31**	**1**
2015–16	*Hartlepool U*	8	0	**8**	**0**
2015–16	*Notts Co*	3	0	**3**	**0**
2016–17	Grimsby T	17	1	**17**	**1**

BROWNE, Rhys (M) **5** **0**
H: 5 10 W: 12 08 b.Romford 16-11-95
Internationals: Antigua and Barbuda Full caps.
From Norwich C, Charlton Ath, Aldershot T.

2016–17	Grimsby T	5	0	**5**	**0**

CATIC, Dzenan (F) **2** **0**
b.Jablanica 26-5-92

2016–17	Grimsby T	2	0	**2**	**0**

CHAMBERS, Ashley (F) **144** **17**
H: 5 10 W: 11 06 b.Leicester 1-3-90
Internationals: England C, U16, U17, U18, U19.

2005–06	Leicester C	0	0		
2006–07	Leicester C	0	0		
2007–08	Leicester C	5	0		
2008–09	Leicester C	1	0		
2009–10	Leicester C	0	0	**6**	**0**
2009–10	*Wycombe W*	0	0		
2009–10	*Grimsby T*	0	0		
2012–13	York C	38	10		
2013–14	York C	15	0	**53**	**10**
2013–14	*Dagenham & R*	6	0		
2014–15	Dagenham & R	32	2		
2015–16	Dagenham & R	31	4	**69**	**6**
2016–17	Grimsby T	16	1	**16**	**1**

CLEMENTS, Chris (M) **146** **15**
H: 5 9 W: 10 04 b.Birmingham 6-2-90

2008–09	Crewe Alex	0	0		
2009	*IBV*	15	1	**15**	**1**
2009–10	Crewe Alex	0	0		
2010–11	Crewe Alex	0	0		
2013–14	Mansfield T	23	1		
2014–15	Mansfield T	34	1		
2015–16	Mansfield T	38	5		
2016–17	Mansfield T	20	3	**115**	**10**
2016–17	Grimsby T	16	4	**16**	**4**

CLIFTON, Harry (M) **0** **0**

2016–17	Grimsby T	0	0

COLLINS, Danny (D) **369** **14**
H: 6 2 W: 11 13 b.Buckley 6-8-80
Internationals: England C. Wales Full caps.

2004–05	Chester C	12	1	**12**	**1**
2004–05	Sunderland	14	0		
2005–06	Sunderland	23	1		
2006–07	Sunderland	38	0		
2007–08	Sunderland	36	1		
2008–09	Sunderland	35	1		
2009–10	Sunderland	3	0	**149**	**3**
2009–10	Stoke C	25	0		
2010–11	Stoke C	25	0		
2011–12	Stoke C	0	0	**50**	**0**
2011–12	*Ipswich T*	16	3	**16**	**3**
2011–12	*West Ham U*	11	1	**11**	**1**
2012–13	Nottingham F	40	0		
2013–14	Nottingham F	23	1		
2014–15	Nottingham F	8	1	**71**	**2**
2015–16	Rotherham U	24	2		
2016–17	Rotherham U	0	0	**24**	**2**
2016–17	Grimsby T	36	2	**36**	**2**

DAVIES, Ben (M) **455** **75**
H: 5 7 W: 12 03 b.Birmingham 27-5-81

2000–01	Kidderminster H	3	0		
2001–02	Kidderminster H	9	0	**12**	**0**
2004–05	Chester C	44	2		
2005–06	Chester C	45	7	**89**	**9**
2006–07	Shrewsbury T	43	12		
2007–08	Shrewsbury T	27	6		
2008–09	Shrewsbury T	42	12	**112**	**30**
2009–10	Notts Co	45	15		
2010–11	Notts Co	22	5	**67**	**20**
2010–11	Derby Co	13	1		
2011–12	Derby Co	35	2		
2012–13	Derby Co	23	4		
2013–14	Derby Co	4	0	**75**	**7**
2013–14	*Sheffield U*	18	3		
2014–15	Sheffield U	14	4	**32**	**7**
2015–16	Portsmouth	43	1	**43**	**1**
2016–17	Grimsby T	25	1	**25**	**1**

DISLEY, Craig (M) **414** **46**
H: 5 11 W: 11 00 b.Worksop 24-8-81

1999–2000	Mansfield T	5	0
2000–01	Mansfield T	24	0
2001–02	Mansfield T	36	7

2002–03	Mansfield T	42	4		
2003–04	Mansfield T	34	5	**141**	**16**
2004–05	Bristol R	28	4		
2005–06	Bristol R	42	8		
2006–07	Bristol R	45	4		
2007–08	Bristol R	44	6		
2008–09	Bristol R	44	3	**203**	**25**
2009–10	Shrewsbury T	18	1		
2010–11	Shrewsbury T	24	2	**42**	**3**
2016–17	Grimsby T	28	2	**28**	**2**

GOWLING, Josh (D) **183** **5**
H: 6 3 W: 12 08 b.Coventry 29-11-83

2004–05	Herfolge	13	0	**13**	**0**
2005–06	Bournemouth	13	0		
2006–07	Bournemouth	33	1		
2007–08	Bournemouth	37	0	**83**	**1**
2008–09	Carlisle U	4	0		
2008–09	*Hereford U*	13	0	**13**	**0**
2009–10	Carlisle U	0	0	**4**	**0**
2009–10	Gillingham	30	2		
2010–11	Gillingham	22	2	**52**	**4**

From Lincoln C, Kidderminster H.

2016–17	Grimsby T	18	0	**18**	**0**

GUNNING, Gavin (D) **169** **8**
H: 5 11 W: 13 08 b.Dublin 26-1-91
Internationals: Republic of Ireland U17, U19, U21.

2007–08	Blackburn R	0	0		
2008–09	Blackburn R	0	0		
2009–10	Blackburn R	0	0		
2009–10	*Tranmere R*	6	0	**6**	**0**
2009–10	*Rotherham U*	21	0	**21**	**0**
2010–11	Blackburn R	0	0		
2010–11	*Bury*	2	0	**2**	**0**
2010–11	*Motherwell*	14	0	**14**	**0**
2011–12	Dundee U	31	2		
2012–13	Dundee U	25	3		
2013–14	Dundee U	27	3		
2014–15	Birmingham C	0	0		
2015–16	Oldham Ath	0	0		
2015–16	Dundee U	19	0	**102**	**8**
2016–17	Greenock Morton	10	0	**10**	**0**
2016–17	Grimsby T	14	0	**14**	**0**

JONES, Dan (D) **40** **0**
H: 6 0 W: 12 05 b.Bishop Auckland 14-12-94

2013–14	Hartlepool U	1	0		
2014–15	Hartlepool U	25	0		
2015–16	Hartlepool U	11	0	**37**	**0**
2016–17	Grimsby T	3	0	**3**	**0**

JONES, Sam (M) **16** **7**
H: 6 2 W: 12 08 b.Doncaster 18-9-91
Internationals: Wales U19.
From Alfreton T, Gateshead.

2016–17	Grimsby T	16	7	**16**	**7**

McALLISTER, Sean (M) **188** **5**
H: 5 8 W: 10 07 b.Bolton 15-8-87

2005–06	Sheffield W	2	0		
2006–07	Sheffield W	6	1		
2007–08	Sheffield W	8	0		
2007–08	*Mansfield T*	7	0	**7**	**0**
2007–08	*Bury*	0	0		
2008–09	Sheffield W	40	3		
2009–10	Sheffield W	12	0	**68**	**4**
2010–11	Shrewsbury T	18	0		
2011–12	Shrewsbury T	17	1	**35**	**1**
2012–13	Port Vale	2	0	**2**	**0**
2013–14	Scunthorpe U	39	0		
2014–15	Scunthorpe U	23	0		
2015–16	Scunthorpe U	11	0	**73**	**0**
2016–17	Grimsby T	3	0	**3**	**0**

McKEOWN, James (G) **45** **0**
H: 6 1 W: 14 00 b.Birmingham 24-7-89
Internationals: Republic of Ireland U19.

2005–06	Walsall	0	0		
2006–07	Walsall	0	0		
2007–08	Peterborough U	1	0		
2008–09	Peterborough U	1	0		
2009–10	Peterborough U	4	0	**6**	**0**
2016–17	Grimsby T	39	0	**39**	**0**

MILLS, Zak (D) **30** **0**
b. 28-5-92
From Histon, Boston U.

2016–17	Grimsby T	30	0	**30**	**0**

OSBORNE, Jamey (M) **19** **1**
H: 6 1 W: 12 04 b.Solihull 7-6-92
From Hednesford T, Redditch U, Solihull Moors.

2016–17	Grimsby T	19	1	**19**	**1**

PEARSON, Shaun (D) **34** **2**
H: 6 0 W: 12 04 b.York 28-4-89
Internationals: England C.
From Spalding U, Stamford, Boston U.

2016–17	Grimsby T	34	2	**34**	**2**

ROSE, Mitchell (M) **70** **4**
H: 5 9 W: 12 03 b.Doncaster 4-7-94

2012–13	Rotherham U	5	0		
2013–14	Rotherham U	0	0		
2014–15	Rotherham U	0	0	**5**	**0**
2014–15	*Crawley T*	1	0	**1**	**0**
2015–16	Mansfield T	34	2		
2016–17	Mansfield T	18	2	**52**	**4**
2016–17	Newport Co	12	0	**12**	**0**
2016–17	Grimsby T	0	0		

SUMMERFIELD, Luke (M) **294** **24**
H: 6 0 W: 11 00 b.Ivybridge 6-12-87

2004–05	Plymouth Arg	1	0		
2005–06	Plymouth Arg	0	0		
2006–07	Plymouth Arg	23	1		
2006–07	*Bournemouth*	8	1	**8**	**1**
2007–08	Plymouth Arg	7	0		
2008–09	Plymouth Arg	29	2		
2009–10	Plymouth Arg	12	0		
2009–10	*Leyton Orient*	14	0	**14**	**0**
2010–11	Plymouth Arg	7	1	**79**	**4**
2011–12	Cheltenham T	41	4	**41**	**4**
2012–13	Shrewsbury T	36	2		
2013–14	Shrewsbury T	28	1	**64**	**3**
2014–15	York C	31	4		
2015–16	York C	34	7	**65**	**11**
2016–17	Grimsby T	23	1	**23**	**1**

VENNEY, Josh (M) **0** **0**
H: 5 5 W: 9 06 b.Grimsby 9-2-97

2016–17	Grimsby T	0	0		

VERNON, Scott (F) **428** **92**
H: 6 1 W: 11 06 b.Manchester 13-12-83

2002–03	Oldham Ath	8	1		
2003–04	Oldham Ath	45	12		
2004–05	Oldham Ath	22	7	**75**	**20**
2004–05	*Blackpool*	4	3		
2005–06	Blackpool	17	1		
2005–06	*Colchester U*	7	1		
2006–07	Blackpool	38	11		
2007–08	Blackpool	15	4	**74**	**19**
2007–08	Colchester U	17	5		
2008–09	Colchester U	33	4		
2008–09	*Northampton T*	6	1	**6**	**1**
2009–10	Colchester U	7	3	**64**	**13**
2009–10	*Gillingham*	1	0	**1**	**0**
2009–10	*Southend U*	17	4	**17**	**4**
2010–11	Aberdeen	33	10		
2011–12	Aberdeen	35	11		
2012–13	Aberdeen	35	3		
2013–14	Aberdeen	25	6	**128**	**30**
2014–15	Shrewsbury T	22	1		
2015–16	Shrewsbury T	13	1	**35**	**2**
2016–17	Grimsby T	28	3	**28**	**3**

WARRINGTON, Andy (G) **372** **0**
H: 6 3 W: 12 13 b.Sheffield 10-6-76

1994–95	York C	0	0		
1995–96	York C	6	0		
1996–97	York C	27	0		
1997–98	York C	17	0		
1998–99	York C	11	0	**61**	**0**
2003–04	Doncaster R	46	0		
2004–05	Doncaster R	34	0		
2005–06	Doncaster R	9	0		
2006–07	Doncaster R	0	0	**89**	**0**
2006–07	Bury	20	0	**20**	**0**
2007–08	Rotherham U	46	0		
2008–09	Rotherham U	38	0		
2009–10	Rotherham U	46	0		
2010–11	Rotherham U	38	0		
2011–12	Rotherham U	7	0		
2012–13	Rotherham U	27	0		
2013–14	Rotherham U	0	0	**202**	**0**
2016–17	Grimsby T	0	0		

WRIGHT, Max (M) **0** **0**
b.Grimsby 6-4-98

2016–17	Grimsby T	0	0		

YUSSUF, Abdi (F) **78** **10**
H: 6 1 W: 11 13 b.Zanzibar 3-10-92

2010–11	Leicester C	0	0		
2011–12	Burton Alb	17	1		
2012–13	Burton Alb	8	0	**25**	**1**

From Lincoln C, Oxford C.

2015–16	Mansfield T	26	5	**26**	**5**
2016–17	Crawley T	16	2	**16**	**2**
2016–17	Grimsby T	11	2	**11**	**2**

Scholars
Briggs, Corey Jack; Burchell, Lawrence; Davis, Michael John; Evans, Ryan Lewis Lee; Flowerdew, Benjamen John; Goddard, Jamie Alexander; Heath-Drury, Oakley; Hough, Cameron Kane; Keeble, Jack Edward; Lawis, Adam Daniel; Lawman, Myles Luke; Lofts, Charlie Brian; McMillan, Alexander James; Paul-Jones, Ty-Rhys Jaden; Sawyer, Thomas James; Sesay, Bilal Abdulai; Slater, Declan John.

Non-Contract
Warrington, Andrew Clifford.

HARTLEPOOL U (40)

ALESSANDRA, Lewis (F) **300** **45**
H: 5 9 W: 11 07 b.Heywood 8-2-89

2007–08	Oldham Ath	15	2		
2008–09	Oldham Ath	32	5		
2009–10	Oldham Ath	1	0		
2010–11	Oldham Ath	19	1	**67**	**8**
2011–12	Morecambe	42	4		
2012–13	Morecambe	40	3	**82**	**7**
2013–14	Plymouth Arg	42	7		
2014–15	Plymouth Arg	44	11	**86**	**18**
2015–16	Rochdale	8	1	**8**	**1**
2015–16	*York C*	11	2	**11**	**2**
2016–17	Hartlepool U	46	9	**46**	**9**

AMOND, Padraig (F) **325** **86**
H: 5 11 W: 12 05 b.Carlow 15-4-88
Internationals: Republic of Ireland U21.

2006	Shamrock R	10	1		
2007	Shamrock R	6	1		
2007	*Kildare Co*	13	5	**13**	**5**
2008	Shamrock R	26	9		
2009	Shamrock R	20	4	**62**	**15**
2010	Sligo R	27	17	**27**	**17**
2010–11	Pacos	17	0	**17**	**0**
2011–12	Accrington S	42	7		
2012–13	Accrington S	36	9		
2013–14	Accrington S	0	0	**78**	**16**
2013–14	Morecambe	45	11		
2014–15	Morecambe	37	8	**82**	**19**
2016–17	Hartlepool U	46	14	**46**	**14**

BARTLETT, Adam (G) **22** **0**
H: 6 0 W: 11 11 b.Newcastle upon Tyne 27-2-86
Internationals: England C.
From Blyth Spartans, Kidderminster H, Hereford U, Gateshead.

2015–16	Hartlepool U	12	0		
2016–17	Hartlepool U	10	0	**22**	**0**

BATES, Matthew (D) **225** **8**
H: 5 10 W: 12 03 b.Stockton 10-12-86
Internationals: England U18, U19.

2003–04	Middlesbrough	0	0		
2004–05	Middlesbrough	2	0		
2004–05	*Darlington*	4	0	**4**	**0**
2005–06	Middlesbrough	16	0		
2006–07	Middlesbrough	1	0		
2006–07	*Ipswich T*	2	0	**2**	**0**
2007–08	Middlesbrough	0	0		
2007–08	*Norwich C*	3	0	**3**	**0**
2008–09	Middlesbrough	17	1		
2009–10	Middlesbrough	0	0		
2010–11	Middlesbrough	31	3		
2011–12	Middlesbrough	37	2	**104**	**6**
2012–13	Bristol C	13	0		
2013–14	Bristol C	0	0	**13**	**0**
2013–14	Bradford C	22	0	**22**	**0**
2014–15	Hartlepool U	25	1		
2015–16	Hartlepool U	32	0		
2016–17	Hartlepool U	20	1	**77**	**2**

BLACKFORD, Jack (M) **2** **0**
b. 13-5-98

2015–16	Hartlepool U	1	0		
2016–17	Hartlepool U	1	0	**2**	**0**

CARSON, Trevor (G) **235** **0**
H: 6 0 W: 14 11 b.Downpatrick 5-3-88
Internationals: Northern Ireland U17, U18, U19, U20, U21, B.

2004–05	Sunderland	0	0		
2005–06	Sunderland	0	0		
2006–07	Sunderland	0	0		
2007–08	Sunderland	0	0		
2008–09	Sunderland	0	0		
2008–09	*Chesterfield*	18	0	**18**	**0**
2009–10	Sunderland	0	0		
2010–11	Sunderland	0	0		
2010–11	*Lincoln C*	16	0	**16**	**0**
2010–11	*Brentford*	1	0	**1**	**0**

2011–12 Sunderland 0 0
2011–12 *Hull C* 0 0
2011–12 Bury 17 0
2012–13 Bury 39 0
2013–14 Bury 5 0 **61 0**
2013–14 *Portsmouth* 36 0 **36 0**
2014–15 Cheltenham T 46 0 **46 0**
2015–16 Hartlepool U 34 0
2016–17 Hartlepool U 23 0 **57 0**

CATTERICK, Ryan (G) 0 0
2016–17 Hartlepool U 0 0

DEVERDICS, Nicky (M) 28 1
H: 5 11 W: 12 04 b.Gateshead 24-11-87
From Dover Ath.
2016–17 Hartlepool U 28 1 **28 1**

DONNELLY, Liam (D) 42 0
H: 5 11 W: 11 03 b.Dungannon 7-3-96
Internationals: Northern Ireland U16, U17, U21, Full caps
2013–14 Fulham 0 0
2014–15 Fulham 0 0
2015–16 Fulham 0 0
2015–16 *Crawley T* 10 0 **10 0**
2016–17 Hartlepool U 32 0 **32 0**

DUDZINSKI, Ben (G) 0 0
H: 6 2 W: 12 04 b.Kingston upon Thames 12-5-96
2016–17 Hartlepool U 0 0

FEATHERSTONE, Nicky (M) 249 4
H: 5 7 W: 11 02 b.Ferriby 22-9-88
2006–07 Hull C 2 0
2007–08 Hull C 6 0
2008–09 Hull C 0 0
2009–10 Hull C 0 0 **8 0**
2009–10 *Grimsby T* 8 0 **8 0**
2010–11 Hereford U 27 1
2011–12 Hereford U 38 0 **65 1**
2012–13 Walsall 31 0
2013–14 Walsall 25 0 **56 0**
2014–15 Scunthorpe U 0 0
2014–15 Hartlepool U 25 0
2015–16 Hartlepool U 44 0
2016–17 Hartlepool U 43 3 **112 3**

GREEN, Kieran (M) 2 0
H: 5 9 W: 12 08 b.Stockton-on-Tees 30-6-97
2014–15 Hartlepool U 1 0
2015–16 Hartlepool U 0 0
2016–17 Hartlepool U 1 0 **2 0**

HARRISON, Scott (D) 103 3
b.Middlesbrough 3-9-93
2012–13 Sunderland 0 0
2013–14 Sunderland 0 0
2013–14 *Bury* 1 0 **1 0**
2013–14 *Hartlepool U* 6 0
2014–15 Sunderland 0 0
2014–15 *Hartlepool U* 36 1
2015–16 Hartlepool U 22 1
2016–17 Hartlepool U 38 1 **102 3**

HAWKES, Josh (M) 2 0
b.Stockton-on-Tees 28-1-99
2016–17 Hartlepool U 2 0 **2 0**

HAWKINS, Lewis (M) 76 2
H: 5 10 W: 12 04 b.Middlesbrough 15-6-93
2011–12 Hartlepool U 1 0
2012–13 Hartlepool U 1 0
2013–14 Hartlepool U 5 0
2014–15 Hartlepool U 12 0
2015–16 Hartlepool U 23 2
2016–17 Hartlepool U 34 0 **76 2**

JONES, Rob (D) 335 32
H: 6 7 W: 12 02 b.Stockton 30-11-79
2002–03 Stockport Co 0 0
2003–04 Stockport Co 16 2 **16 2**
2003–04 *Macclesfield T* 1 0 **1 0**
2004–05 Grimsby T 20 1
2005–06 Grimsby T 40 4 **60 5**
2006–07 Hibernian 34 4
2007–08 Hibernian 30 0
2008–09 Hibernian 32 4 **96 8**
2009–10 Scunthorpe U 28 1
2010–11 Scunthorpe U 14 1 **42 2**
2010–11 *Sheffield W* 8 1
2011–12 Sheffield W 33 4 **41 5**
2012–13 Doncaster R 44 7
2013–14 Doncaster R 12 1
2014–15 Doncaster R 10 2
2015–16 Doncaster R 2 0 **68 10**
2015–16 Hartlepool U 7 0
2016–17 Hartlepool U 4 0 **11 0**

MAGNAY, Carl (D) 50 3
H: 6 0 W: 12 00 b.Gateshead 20-1-89
Internationals: Northern Ireland U21.
2006–07 Chelsea 0 0
2007–08 Chelsea 0 0
2008–09 Chelsea 0 0
2008–09 *Milton Keynes D* 2 0 **2 0**
2008–09 *Northampton T* 2 0 **2 0**
2009–10 Chelsea 0 0
2010–11 Chelsea 0 0
From Gateshead, Grimsby T.
2015–16 Hartlepool U 33 1
2016–17 Hartlepool U 13 2 **46 3**

MARTIN, James (D) 3 0
H: 5 7 W: 10 08 b.Newcastle upon Tyne 23-6-98
From Queen of the South.
2016–17 Hartlepool U 3 0 **3 0**

OATES, Rhys (D) 73 5
H: 6 0 W: 11 09 b.Pontefract 4-12-94
2012–13 Barnsley 0 0
2013–14 Barnsley 0 0
2014–15 Barnsley 9 0 **9 0**
2015–16 Hartlepool U 38 2
2016–17 Hartlepool U 26 3 **64 5**

ORRELL, Jake (F) 2 0
H: 5 4 W: 9 00 b.Sunderland 17-7-97
From Gateshead.
2015–16 Chesterfield 2 0 **2 0**
2016–17 Hartlepool U 0 0

PAYNTER, Billy (F) 477 116
H: 6 1 W: 14 01 b.Liverpool 13-7-84
2000–01 Port Vale 1 0
2001–02 Port Vale 7 0
2002–03 Port Vale 31 5
2003–04 Port Vale 44 13
2004–05 Port Vale 45 10
2005–06 Port Vale 16 2 **144 30**
2005–06 Hull C 22 3 **22 3**
2006–07 Southend U 9 0
2006–07 *Bradford C* 15 4 **15 4**
2007–08 Southend U 0 0 **9 0**
2007–08 Swindon T 36 8
2008–09 Swindon T 42 11
2009–10 Swindon T 42 26 **120 45**
2010–11 Leeds U 22 1
2011–12 Leeds U 5 2
2011–12 *Brighton & HA* 10 0 **10 0**
2012–13 Leeds U 0 0 **27 3**
2012–13 Doncaster R 37 13
2013–14 Doncaster R 9 0 **46 13**
2013–14 *Sheffield U* 13 0 **13 0**
2014–15 Carlisle U 18 1 **18 1**
2015–16 Hartlepool U 32 14
2016–17 Hartlepool U 21 3 **53 17**

POLLOCK, Ben (D) 0 0
H: 6 1 W: 13 08 b.Bolton 6-1-98
From Newcastle U.
2016–17 Hartlepool U 0 0

RICHARDS, Jordan (M) 67 0
H: 5 9 W: 11 05 b.Sunderland 25-4-93
2011–12 Hartlepool U 2 0
2012–13 Hartlepool U 11 0
2013–14 Hartlepool U 19 0
2014–15 Hartlepool U 9 0
2015–16 Hartlepool U 11 0
2016–17 Hartlepool U 15 0 **67 0**

RICHARDSON, Kenton (M) 11 0
b.Durham 22-1-98
2016–17 Hartlepool U 11 0 **11 0**

RODNEY, Devante (F) 4 2
b.Manchester 19-5-98
From Sheffield W.
2016–17 Hartlepool U 4 2 **4 2**

SIMPSON, Connor (F) 2 0
b.Guisborough 24-1-00
2016–17 Hartlepool U 2 0 **2 0**

SMITH, Connor (M) 15 0
b. 14-10-96
2013–14 Hartlepool U 1 0
2014–15 Hartlepool U 8 0
2015–16 Hartlepool U 5 0
2016–17 Hartlepool U 1 0 **15 0**

THOMAS, Nathan (F) 93 16
H: 5 10 W: 12 08 b.Barwick 27-9-94
2013–14 Plymouth Arg 10 0
2014–15 Plymouth Arg 9 1 **19 1**
2014–15 Motherwell 2 0 **2 0**
2015–16 Mansfield T 17 1 **17 1**
2015–16 Hartlepool U 22 5
2016–17 Hartlepool U 33 9 **55 14**

WALKER, Brad (M) 107 10
H: 6 1 W: 12 08 b. 25-4-95
2012–13 Hartlepool U 0 0
2013–14 Hartlepool U 36 3
2014–15 Hartlepool U 28 5
2015–16 Hartlepool U 23 1
2016–17 Hartlepool U 20 1 **107 10**

WISE, Harly (D) 0 0
H: 6 1 W: 12 06 b.London 7-6-96
2015–16 QPR 0 0
2016–17 Hartlepool U 0 0

WOODS, Michael (M) 97 7
H: 6 0 W: 12 07 b.Pocklington 6-4-90
Internationals: England U16, U17, U19.
2006–07 Chelsea 0 0
2007–08 Chelsea 0 0
2008–09 Chelsea 0 0
2009–10 Chelsea 0 0
2010–11 Chelsea 0 0
2010–11 *Notts Co* 0 0
2011–12 Chelsea 0 0
2011–12 Yeovil T 5 1 **5 1**
2012–13 Doncaster R 0 0
2014–15 Hartlepool U 23 1
2015–16 Hartlepool U 33 3
2016–17 Hartlepool U 36 2 **92 6**

Players retained or with offer of contract
Cunningham, Aaron Ross; Nearney, Joshua William.

Scholars
Catterick, Ryan James; Cooper, Jack Robert; Elliott, Dylan Michael; Fielding, Jordan; Holliday, Cameron Lee Dale; Moloney, Scott Gavin; Orrell, Lewis Lee; Owen, Jacob Peter; Robinson, Ryan Paul; Short, Niall Alex; Simpson, Connor Mark; Skidmore, Nathaniel; Travers, Liam William Edward; Turnbull, Jack Thomas; Weirs, Jon James; Wood, Ethan.

HUDDERSFIELD T (41)

BILLING, Phillip (M) 38 3
H: 6 4 W: 12 08 b. 11-6-96
Internationals: Denmark U19.
2013–14 Huddersfield T 1 0
2014–15 Huddersfield T 0 0
2015–16 Huddersfield T 13 1
2016–17 Huddersfield T 24 2 **38 3**

BOJAJ, Florent (M) 11 1
b. 13-4-96
Internationals: Albania U17.
2013–14 Huddersfield T 0 0
2014–15 Huddersfield T 0 0
2015–16 Huddersfield T 8 1
2016–17 Huddersfield T 0 0 **8 1**
2016–17 *Newport Co* 1 0 **1 0**
2016–17 *Kilmarnock* 2 0 **2 0**

BOOTY, Regan (M) 0 0
b. 3-4-98
2015–16 Huddersfield T 0 0
2016–17 Huddersfield T 0 0

BUNN, Harry (F) 115 16
H: 5 9 W: 11 10 b.Oldham 25-11-92
2010–11 Manchester C 0 0
2011–12 Manchester C 0 0
2011–12 *Rochdale* 6 0 **6 0**
2011–12 *Preston NE* 1 1 **1 1**
2011–12 *Oldham Ath* 11 0 **11 0**
2012–13 Manchester C 0 0
2012–13 *Crewe Alex* 4 0 **4 0**
2013–14 Manchester C 0 0
2013–14 *Sheffield U* 2 0 **2 0**
2013–14 *Huddersfield T* 3 0
2014–15 Manchester C 0 0
2014–15 *Huddersfield T* 30 9
2015–16 Huddersfield T 42 6
2016–17 Huddersfield T 16 0 **91 15**

CODDINGTON, Luke (G) 0 0
b.Middlesbrough 6-6-95
Internationals: England U17, U18, U19.
2013–14 Middlesbrough 0 0
2014–15 Middlesbrough 0 0
2015–16 Middlesbrough 0 0
2016–17 Huddersfield T 0 0

COLEMAN, Joel (G) 48 0
H: 6 6 W: 12 13 b.Bolton 26-9-95
2013–14 Oldham Ath 0 0
2014–15 Oldham Ath 11 0
2015–16 Oldham Ath 32 0 **43 0**
2016–17 Huddersfield T 5 0 **5 0**

CRANIE, Martin (D) 333 2
H: 6 1 W: 12 09 b.Yeovil 23-9-86
Internationals: England U17, U18, U19, U20, U21.
2003–04 Southampton 1 0
2004–05 Southampton 3 0
2004–05 *Bournemouth* 3 0 **3 0**
2005–06 Southampton 11 0
2006–07 Southampton 1 0 **16 0**
2006–07 *Yeovil T* 12 0 **12 0**
2007–08 Portsmouth 2 0
2007–08 *QPR* 6 0 **6 0**
2008–09 Portsmouth 0 0
2008–09 *Charlton Ath* 19 0 **19 0**
2009–10 Portsmouth 0 0 **2 0**
2009–10 Coventry C 40 1
2010–11 Coventry C 36 0
2011–12 Coventry C 38 0 **114 1**
2012–13 Barnsley 36 0
2013–14 Barnsley 35 0
2014–15 Barnsley 39 1 **110 1**
2015–16 Huddersfield T 37 0
2016–17 Huddersfield T 14 0 **51 0**

DAVIDSON, Jason (D) 132 5
H: 5 11 W: 11 05 b.Melbourne 29-6-91
Internationals: Australia U20, Full caps.
2009 Hume City 16 2 **16 2**
2009–10 Pacos de Ferreira 5 0
2010–11 Pacos de Ferreira 0 0 **5 0**
2010–11 *Sporting Covilha* 14 0 **14 0**
2011–12 Heracles 6 0
2012–13 Heracles 10 0
2013–14 Heracles 32 2 **48 2**
2014–15 WBA 2 0 **2 0**
2015–16 Huddersfield T 27 1
2016–17 Huddersfield T 0 0 **27 1**
2016–17 *Groningen* 20 0 **20 0**

DEMPSEY, Kyle (M) 106 13
b.Whitehaven 17-9-95
2013–14 Carlisle U 4 0
2014–15 Carlisle U 43 10 **47 10**
2015–16 Huddersfield T 21 1
2016–17 Huddersfield T 0 0 **21 1**
2016–17 *Fleetwood T* 38 2 **38 2**

HEFELE, Michael (D) 157 14
H: 6 4 W: 13 10 b.Pfaffenhofen 1-9-90
2010–11 Unterhaching 27 0
2011–12 Unterhaching 6 1 **33 1**
2012–13 Greuther Furth 1 0
2013–14 Greuther Furth 2 0 **3 0**
2013–14 *Wacker Burghausen* 15 0 **15 0**
2014–15 Dynamo Dresden 31 3
2015–16 Dynamo Dresden 38 7 **69 10**
2016–17 Huddersfield T 37 3 **37 3**

HIWULA, Jordy (F) 95 23
H: 5 10 W: 11 12 b.Manchester 24-9-94
Internationals: England U18, U19.
2013–14 Manchester C 0 0
2014–15 Manchester C 0 0
2014–15 *Yeovil T* 8 0 **8 0**
2014–15 *Walsall* 19 9
2015–16 Huddersfield T 0 0
2015–16 *Wigan Ath* 14 2 **14 2**
2015–16 *Walsall* 13 3 **32 12**
2016–17 Huddersfield T 0 0
2016–17 *Bradford C* 41 9 **41 9**

HOGG, Jonathan (M) 226 2
H: 5 7 W: 10 05 b.Middlesbrough 6-12-88
2007–08 Aston Villa 0 0
2008–09 Aston Villa 0 0
2009–10 Aston Villa 0 0
2009–10 *Darlington* 5 1 **5 1**
2010–11 Aston Villa 5 0
2010–11 *Portsmouth* 19 0 **19 0**
2011–12 Aston Villa 0 0 **5 0**
2011–12 Watford 40 0
2012–13 Watford 38 0 **78 0**
2013–14 Huddersfield T 34 0
2014–15 Huddersfield T 26 0
2015–16 Huddersfield T 22 0
2016–17 Huddersfield T 37 1 **119 1**

HOLMES-DENNIS, Tareiq (M) 62 1
H: 5 9 W: 11 11 b.Farnborough 31-10-95
Internationals: England U18.
2012–13 Charlton Ath 0 0
2013–14 Charlton Ath 0 0
2014–15 Charlton Ath 0 0
2014–15 *Oxford U* 14 0 **14 0**
2014–15 *Plymouth Arg* 17 1 **17 1**
2015–16 Charlton Ath 11 0
2015–16 *Oldham Ath* 10 0 **10 0**
2016–17 Charlton Ath 1 0 **12 0**
2016–17 Huddersfield T 9 0 **9 0**

HUDSON, Mark (D) 424 26
H: 6 1 W: 12 01 b.Guildford 30-3-82
1998–99 Fulham 0 0
1999–2000 Fulham 0 0
2000–01 Fulham 0 0
2001–02 Fulham 0 0
2002–03 Fulham 0 0
2003–04 Fulham 0 0
2003–04 *Oldham Ath* 15 0 **15 0**
2003–04 *Crystal Palace* 14 0
2004–05 Crystal Palace 7 1
2005–06 Crystal Palace 15 0
2006–07 Crystal Palace 39 4
2007–08 Crystal Palace 45 2 **120 7**
2008–09 Charlton Ath 43 3 **43 3**
2009–10 Cardiff C 27 2
2010–11 Cardiff C 40 0
2011–12 Cardiff C 39 5
2012–13 Cardiff C 33 4
2013–14 Cardiff C 2 0
2014–15 Cardiff C 3 0 **144 11**
2014–15 Huddersfield T 41 2
2015–16 Huddersfield T 39 3
2016–17 Huddersfield T 22 0 **102 5**

KACHUNGA, Elias (F) 151 37
H: 5 9 W: 10 01 b.Cologne 22-4-92
Internationals: Germany U19, U21, DR Congo Full caps.
2009–10 Borussia M'gladbach 0 0
2010–11 Borussia M'gladbach 2 0
2011–12 Borussia M'gladbach 0 0
2011–12 *Osnabruck* 17 10 **17 10**
2012–13 Borussia M'gladbach 0 0 **2 0**
2012–13 *Hertha Berlin* 2 0 **2 0**
2012–13 *Paderborn* 13 3
2013–14 Paderborn 33 6
2014–15 Paderborn 32 6 **78 15**
2015–16 Ingolstadt 10 0
2016–17 Ingolstadt 0 0 **10 0**
On loan from Ingolstadt.
2016–17 Huddersfield T 42 12 **42 12**

LOLLEY, Joe (F) 80 8
H: 5 10 W: 11 05 b.Redditch 25-8-92
Internationals: England C.
2013–14 Huddersfield T 6 1
2014–15 Huddersfield T 17 2
2015–16 Huddersfield T 32 4
2015–16 *Scunthorpe U* 6 0 **6 0**
2016–17 Huddersfield T 19 1 **74 8**

LOWE, Chris (D) 231 15
H: 5 7 W: 10 10 b.Plauen 16-4-89
2008–09 Chemnitzer 17 1
2009–10 Chemnitzer 34 4
2010–11 Chemnitzer 33 4 **84 9**
2011–12 Borussia Dortmund 7 0
2012–13 Borussia Dortmund 0 0 **7 0**
2012–13 Kaiserslauten 14 0
2013–14 Kaiserslauten 29 1
2014–15 Kaiserslauten 33 2
2015–16 Kaiserslauten 23 1 **99 4**
2016–17 Huddersfield T 41 2 **41 2**

MURPHY, Joe (G) 470 0
H: 6 2 W: 13 06 b.Dublin 21-8-81
Internationals: Republic of Ireland Youth, U21, Full caps.
1999–2000 Tranmere R 21 0
2000–01 Tranmere R 20 0
2001–02 Tranmere R 22 0 **63 0**
2002–03 WBA 2 0
2003–04 WBA 3 0
2004–05 WBA 0 0 **5 0**
2004–05 *Walsall* 25 0
2005–06 Sunderland 0 0
2005–06 *Walsall* 14 0 **39 0**
2006–07 Scunthorpe U 45 0
2007–08 Scunthorpe U 45 0
2008–09 Scunthorpe U 42 0
2009–10 Scunthorpe U 40 0
2010–11 Scunthorpe U 29 0 **201 0**
2011–12 Coventry C 46 0
2012–13 Coventry C 45 0
2013–14 Coventry C 46 0 **137 0**
2014–15 Huddersfield T 2 0
2014–15 *Chesterfield* 0 0
2015–16 Huddersfield T 7 0
2016–17 Huddersfield T 0 0 **9 0**
2016–17 *Bury* 16 0 **16 0**

PAUREVIC, Ivan (D) 80 5
H: 6 4 W: 13 08 b.Essen 1-7-91
Internationals: Croatia U19, U21.
2012–13 Fortuna Dusseldorf 4 0
2013–14 Fortuna Dusseldorf 18 0 **22 0**
2014–15 Ufa 29 2
2015–16 Ufa 28 3 **57 5**
2016–17 Huddersfield T 1 0 **1 0**
Transferred to Ufa, January 2017.

PAYNE, Jack (M) 100 17
H: 5 5 W: 9 06 b.Tower Hamlets 25-10-94
2013–14 Southend U 11 0
2014–15 Southend U 34 6
2015–16 Southend U 32 9 **77 15**
2016–17 Huddersfield T 23 2 **23 2**

PYKE, Rekeil (F) 12 0
H: 5 10 W: 10 03 b. 1-9-97
2016–17 Huddersfield T 0 0
2016–17 *Colchester U* 12 0 **12 0**

QUANER, Collin (F) 123 19
H: 6 3 W: 12 11 b.Dusseldorf 18-6-91
From Fortuna Dusseldorf.
2010–11 Armenia Bielefeld 17 1 **17 1**
2011–12 Ingolstadt 04 15 1
2012–13 Ingolstadt 04 1 0
2013–14 Ingolstadt 04 11 1 **27 2**
2013–14 *Rostock* 7 0 **7 0**
2014–15 Aalen 27 6 **27 6**
2015–16 Union Berlin 15 1
2016–17 Union Berlin 14 7 **29 8**
2016–17 Huddersfield T 16 2 **16 2**

SCANNELL, Sean (F) 288 20
H: 5 9 W: 11 07 b.Croydon 19-9-90
Internationals: Republic of Ireland U17, U18, U19, U21, B.
2007–08 Crystal Palace 23 2
2008–09 Crystal Palace 25 2
2009–10 Crystal Palace 26 2
2010–11 Crystal Palace 19 2
2011–12 Crystal Palace 37 4 **130 12**
2012–13 Huddersfield T 34 2
2013–14 Huddersfield T 38 1
2014–15 Huddersfield T 42 4
2015–16 Huddersfield T 29 1
2016–17 Huddersfield T 15 0 **158 8**

SCHINDLER, Christopher (D) 196 6
H: 6 2 W: 12 02 b.Munich 29-4-90
Internationals: Germany U21.
2009–10 1860 Munich 0 0
2010–11 1860 Munich 16 1
2011–12 1860 Munich 30 1
2012–13 1860 Munich 18 0
2013–14 1860 Munich 26 0
2014–15 1860 Munich 29 1
2015–16 1860 Munich 33 1 **152 4**
2016–17 Huddersfield T 44 2 **44 2**

SMITH, Tommy (D) 143 4
H: 6 1 W: 13 02 b.Warrington 14-4-92
2012–13 Huddersfield T 0 0
2013–14 Huddersfield T 24 0
2014–15 Huddersfield T 41 0
2015–16 Huddersfield T 36 0
2016–17 Huddersfield T 42 4 **143 4**

STANKOVIC, Jon (M) 25 0
H: 6 3 W: 12 04 b.Ljubijana 14-1-96
Internationals: Slovenia U16, U17, U18, U19, U21.
2012–13 Domzale 6 0
2013–14 Domzale 12 0
2014–15 Domzale 0 0
2015–16 Domzale 0 0 **18 0**
2016–17 Huddersfield T 7 0 **7 0**

VAN LA PARRA, Rajiv (M) 209 20
H: 5 11 W: 11 05 b.Rotterdam 4-6-91
Internationals: Netherlands, U17, U19, U21.
2008–09 Caan 2 0
2009–10 Caan 8 1
2010–11 Caan 6 0 **16 1**
2011–12 Heerenveen 23 4
2012–13 Heerenveen 31 5
2013–14 Heerenveen 32 5 **86 14**
2014–15 Wolverhampton W 40 1
2015–16 Wolverhampton W 13 0 **53 1**
2015–16 *Brighton & HA* 6 2 **6 2**
2015–16 Huddersfield T 8 0
2016–17 Huddersfield T 40 2 **48 2**

WELLS, Nahki (F) 238 87
H: 5 7 W: 11 00 b.Bermuda 1-6-90
Internationals: Bermuda Full caps.
2010–11 Carlisle U 3 0 **3 0**
2011–12 Bradford C 33 10

2012–13	Bradford C	39	18		
2013–14	Bradford C	19	14	**91**	**42**
2013–14	Huddersfield T	22	7		
2014–15	Huddersfield T	35	11		
2015–16	Huddersfield T	44	17		
2016–17	Huddersfield T	43	10	**144**	**45**

WHITEHEAD, Dean (M) **544** **26**
H: 5 11 W: 12 06 b.Abingdon 12-1-82

1999–2000	Oxford U	0	0		
2000–01	Oxford U	20	0		
2001–02	Oxford U	40	1		
2002–03	Oxford U	18	1		
2003–04	Oxford U	44	7	**122**	**9**
2004–05	Sunderland	42	5		
2005–06	Sunderland	37	3		
2006–07	Sunderland	45	4		
2007–08	Sunderland	27	1		
2008–09	Sunderland	34	0		
2009–10	Sunderland	0	0	**185**	**13**
2009–10	Stoke C	36	0		
2010–11	Stoke C	37	2		
2011–12	Stoke C	33	0		
2012–13	Stoke C	26	1	**132**	**3**
2013–14	Middlesbrough	37	1		
2014–15	Middlesbrough	18	0	**55**	**1**
2015–16	Huddersfield T	34	0		
2016–17	Huddersfield T	16	0	**50**	**0**

Players retained or with offer of contract
Cogill, Dylan Joseph; Dalling, Deshane; Dorrington, George Edward; Edmonds-Green, Rarmani River Miguel Joseph; Gorenc, Stankovic Jon; Horsfall, Fraser Matthew; Kane, Danny; O'Brien, Lewis John; Ryan, Tadhg Ryan; Schofield, Ryan James; Williams, Jordan Lee.

Scholars
Brooke, Owen Harvey; Carvalho, Denilson Almeida Leonel; Clibbens, Harry; Colville, Luca Robert; Danaher, George Charles; Dyson, Oliver Jason Lee; Elliott, Callum Keith; Gibson, Samuel Joseph; Marriott, Isaac William; Raw, Alfie; Scott, Cedwyn; Taylor, Cameron Gerrard; Tear, Darren Dominic; Thompson, Oran James.

HULL C (42)

BATTY, Daniel (D) **0** **0**
b.Featherstone 10-12-97

2016–17	Hull C	0	0		

BOWEN, Jarrod (F) **7** **0**
b.Leominster 1-1-96

2014–15	Hull C	0	0		
2015–16	Hull C	0	0		
2016–17	Hull C	7	0	**7**	**0**

BRUCE, Alex (D) **272** **4**
H: 6 0 W: 11 06 b.Norwich 28-9-84
Internationals: Republic of Ireland B, U21, Full caps. Northern Ireland Full caps.

2002–03	Blackburn R	0	0		
2003–04	Blackburn R	0	0		
2004–05	Blackburn R	0	0		
2004–05	*Oldham Ath*	12	0	**12**	**0**
2004–05	Birmingham C	0	0		
2004–05	*Sheffield W*	6	0	**6**	**0**
2005–06	Birmingham C	6	0	**6**	**0**
2005–06	*Tranmere R*	11	0	**11**	**0**
2006–07	Ipswich T	41	0		
2007–08	Ipswich T	36	0		
2008–09	Ipswich T	25	1		
2009–10	Ipswich T	13	1		
2009–10	*Leicester C*	3	0	**3**	**0**
2010–11	Ipswich T	0	0	**115**	**2**
2010–11	Leeds U	21	1		
2011–12	Leeds U	8	0	**29**	**1**
2011–12	*Huddersfield T*	3	0	**3**	**0**
2012–13	Hull C	32	0		
2013–14	Hull C	20	0		
2014–15	Hull C	22	0		
2015–16	Hull C	11	1		
2016–17	Hull C	0	0	**85**	**1**
2016–17	*Wigan Ath*	2	0	**2**	**0**

CLACKSTONE, Josh (D) **8** **0**
b. 18-9-96

2016–17	Hull C	0	0		
2016–17	*Notts Co*	8	0	**8**	**0**

CLARK, Max (D) **36** **1**
H: 5 11 W: 11 07 b.Hull 19-1-96
Internationals: England U16, U17.

2015–16	Hull C	0	0		
2015–16	*Cambridge U*	9	0		
2016–17	Hull C	0	0		
2016–17	*Cambridge U*	27	1	**36**	**1**

CLUCAS, Sam (M) **182** **26**
H: 5 10 W: 11 08 b.Lincoln 25-9-90
Internationals: England C

2009–10	Lincoln C	0	0		
2011–12	Hereford U	17	0	**17**	**0**
2013–14	Mansfield T	38	8		
2014–15	Mansfield T	5	0	**43**	**8**
2014–15	Chesterfield	41	9	**41**	**9**
2015–16	Hull C	44	6		
2016–17	Hull C	37	3	**81**	**9**

DAVIES, Curtis (D) **394** **22**
H: 6 2 W: 11 13 b.Waltham Forest 15-3-85
Internationals: England U21.

2003–04	Luton T	6	0		
2004–05	Luton T	44	1		
2005–06	Luton T	6	1	**56**	**2**
2005–06	WBA	33	2		
2006–07	WBA	32	0		
2007–08	WBA	0	0	**65**	**2**
2007–08	*Aston Villa*	12	1		
2008–09	Aston Villa	35	1		
2009–10	Aston Villa	2	1		
2010–11	Aston Villa	0	0	**49**	**3**
2010–11	*Leicester C*	12	0	**12**	**0**
2010–11	Birmingham C	6	0		
2011–12	Birmingham C	42	5		
2012–13	Birmingham C	41	6	**89**	**11**
2013–14	Hull C	37	2		
2014–15	Hull C	21	0		
2015–16	Hull C	39	2		
2016–17	Hull C	26	0	**123**	**4**

DAWSON, Michael (D) **401** **19**
H: 6 2 W: 12 02 b.Leyburn 18-11-83
Internationals: England U21, B, Full caps.

2000–01	Nottingham F	0	0		
2001–02	Nottingham F	1	0		
2002–03	Nottingham F	38	5		
2003–04	Nottingham F	30	1		
2004–05	Nottingham F	14	1	**83**	**7**
2004–05	Tottenham H	5	0		
2005–06	Tottenham H	32	0		
2006–07	Tottenham H	37	1		
2007–08	Tottenham H	27	1		
2008–09	Tottenham H	16	1		
2009–10	Tottenham H	29	2		
2010–11	Tottenham H	24	1		
2011–12	Tottenham H	7	0		
2012–13	Tottenham H	27	1		
2013–14	Tottenham H	32	0	**236**	**7**
2014–15	Hull C	28	1		
2015–16	Hull C	32	1		
2016–17	Hull C	22	3	**82**	**5**

DIOMANDE, Adama (F) **176** **66**
H: 5 11 W: 11 11 b.Oslo 14-2-90
Internationals: Norway U23, Full caps.

2008	Lyn	2	0		
2009	Lyn	1	0	**3**	**0**
2010	Skeid	12	8	**12**	**8**
2010	Hodd	10	4		
2011	Hodd	28	14	**38**	**18**
2012	Stromsgodset	21	7		
2013	Stromsgodset	25	8	**46**	**15**
2014–15	Dynamo Minsk	23	3	**23**	**3**
2015	Stabaek	21	17	**21**	**17**
2015–16	Hull C	11	3		
2016–17	Hull C	22	2	**33**	**5**

EDWARDS, Jonathan (M) **13** **1**
H: 5 11 W: 10 01 b.Luton 24-11-96

2014–15	Peterborough U	3	0		
2015–16	Peterborough U	0	0	**3**	**0**
2016–17	Hull C	0	0		
2016–17	*Accrington S*	10	1	**10**	**1**

ELABDELLAOUI, Omar (M) **99** **4**
H: 5 10 W: 11 05 b.Norway 5-12-91
Internationals: Norway U17, U19, U21, U23, Full caps.

2009–10	Manchester C	0	0		
2010–11	Manchester C	0	0		
2011	*Stromsgodset*	10	0	**10**	**0**
2011–12	Manchester C	0	0		
2012–13	Manchester C	0	0		
2012–13	*Feyenoord*	5	0	**5**	**0**
2013–14	Eintracht Braunschweig	29	1	**29**	**1**
2014–15	Olympiacos	24	1		
2015–16	Olympiacos	21	2		
2016–17	Olympiacos	2	0	**47**	**3**

On loan from Olympiacos.

2016–17	Hull C	8	0	**8**	**0**

ELMOHAMADY, Ahmed (M) **322** **25**
H: 5 11 W: 12 10 b.El Mahalla El-Kubra 9-9-87
Internationals: Egypt Full caps.

2003–04	Ghazi Al-Mehalla	0	0		
2004–05	Ghazi Al-Mehalla	14	4		
2005–06	Ghazi Al-Mehalla	3	0	**17**	**4**
2006–07	ENPPI	12	2		
2007–08	ENPPI	6	1		
2008–09	ENPPI	28	6		
2009–10	ENPPI	12	1	**58**	**10**
2010–11	Sunderland	36	0		
2011–12	Sunderland	18	1		
2012–13	Sunderland	2	0	**56**	**1**
2012–13	*Hull C*	41	3		
2013–14	Hull C	38	2		
2014–15	Hull C	38	2		
2015–16	Hull C	41	3		
2016–17	Hull C	33	0	**191**	**10**

EVANDRO, Goebel (M) **271** **43**
H: 5 10 W: 9 11 b.Blumenau 23-8-86
Internationals: Brazil U20.

2005	Atletico Paranaense	28	4		
2006	Atletico Paranaense	16	2		
2007	Atletico Paranaense	15	1		
2008	Atletico Paranaense	0	0		
2008	*Goias*	3	0	**3**	**0**
2008	*Palmeiras*	26	0		
2009	Atletico Paranaense	0	0		
2009	*Palmeiras*	8	2	**34**	**2**
2009	*Atletico Mineiro*	28	3		
2010	Atletico Paranaense	0	0	**59**	**7**
2010	*Atletico Mineiro*	2	0	**30**	**3**
2010	*Vitoria*	7	2	**7**	**2**
2010–11	Red Star Belgrade	9	5		
2011–12	Red Star Belgrade	25	8		
2012–13	Red Star Belgrade	1	0	**35**	**13**
2012–13	Estoril	25	3		
2013–14	Estoril	28	11	**53**	**14**
2014–15	Porto	21	1		
2015–16	Porto	11	1		
2016–17	Porto	7	0	**39**	**2**
2016–17	Hull C	11	0	**11**	**0**

GROSICKI, Kamil (M) **286** **47**
H: 5 11 W: 12 04 b.Szczecin 8-6-88
Internationals: Poland U19, U21, Full caps.

2005–06	Pognon Szczecin	2	0		
2006–07	Pognon Szczecin	21	2	**23**	**2**
2007–08	Legia Warsaw	11	1		
2007–08	Sion	8	2	**8**	**2**
2008–09	Legia Warsaw	0	0	**11**	**1**
2008–09	Jagiellonia	13	4		
2009–10	Jagiellonia	30	4		
2010–11	Jagiellonia	15	6	**58**	**14**
2010–11	Sivasspor	17	6		
2011–12	Sivasspor	40	7		
2012–13	Sivasspor	28	2		
2013–14	Sivasspor	5	0	**90**	**15**
2013–14	Rennes	13	0		
2014–15	Rennes	19	0		
2015–16	Rennes	33	9		
2016–17	Rennes	16	4	**81**	**13**
2016–17	Hull C	15	0	**15**	**0**

HENRIKSEN, Markus (M) **201** **37**
H: 6 2 W: 13 05 b.Trondheim 25-7-92
Internationals: Norway U16, U17, U18, U19, U21, U23, Full caps.

2009	Rosenborg	3	0		
2010	Rosenborg	28	7		
2011	Rosenborg	29	3		
2012	Rosenborg	18	1	**78**	**11**
2012–13	AZ Alkmaar	29	3		
2013–14	AZ Alkmaar	26	2		
2014–15	AZ Alkmaar	22	7		
2015–16	AZ Alkmaar	28	12		
2016–17	AZ Alkmaar	3	2	**108**	**26**
2016–17	Hull C	15	0	**15**	**0**

HERNANDEZ, Abel (F) **237** **71**
H: 6 1 W: 11 00 b.Pando Canelones 8-8-90
Internationals: Uruguay U20, U23, Full caps.

2006–07	Central Espanol	6	0		
2007–08	Central Espanol	24	9	**30**	**9**
2008–09	Penarol	8	3	**8**	**3**
2008–09	Palermo	6	0		
2009–10	Palermo	21	7		
2010–11	Palermo	22	3		
2011–12	Palermo	20	6		
2012–13	Palermo	14	1		
2013–14	Palermo	28	14	**111**	**31**
2014–15	Hull C	25	4		
2015–16	Hull C	39	20		
2016–17	Hull C	24	4	**88**	**28**

HINCHLIFFE, Ben (M) **0** **0**

2016–17	Hull C	0	0		

HUDDLESTONE, Tom (M) 380 15
H: 6 2 W: 11 02 b.Nottingham 28-12-86
Internationals: England U16, U17, U19, U20, U21, Full caps.
2003–04 Derby Co 43 0
2004–05 Derby Co 45 0 **88 0**
2005–06 Tottenham H 4 0
2005–06 *Wolverhampton W* 13 1 **13 1**
2006–07 Tottenham H 21 1
2007–08 Tottenham H 28 3
2008–09 Tottenham H 22 0
2009–10 Tottenham H 33 2
2010–11 Tottenham H 14 2
2011–12 Tottenham H 2 0
2012–13 Tottenham H 20 0
2013–14 Tottenham H 0 0 **144 8**
2013–14 Hull C 36 3
2014–15 Hull C 31 0
2015–16 Hull C 37 2
2016–17 Hull C 31 1 **135 6**

JAKUPOVIC, Eldin (G) 159 1
H: 6 3 W: 13 00 b.Kozarac 2-10-84
Internationals: Bosnia & Herzegovina U21, Switzerland U21, Full caps.
2004–05 Grasshoppers 8 0
2005–06 FC Thun 23 0 **23 0**
2007–08 Grasshoppers 23 1
2008–09 Grasshoppers 32 0 **63 1**
2010–11 Olympiacos Volou 26 0 **26 0**
2011–12 Aris Salonika 1 0 **1 0**
2012–13 Hull C 5 0
2013–14 Hull C 1 0
2013–14 *Leyton Orient* 13 0 **13 0**
2014–15 Hull C 3 0
2015–16 Hull C 2 0
2016–17 Hull C 22 0 **33 0**
Transferred to Empoli, January 2017.

KEANE, Will (F) 54 4
H: 6 2 W: 11 05 b.Stockport 11-1-93
Internationals: England U16, U17, U19, U20, U21.
2009–10 Manchester U 0 0
2010–11 Manchester U 0 0
2011–12 Manchester U 1 0
2012–13 Manchester U 0 0
2013–14 Manchester U 0 0
2013–14 *Wigan Ath* 4 0 **4 0**
2013–14 *QPR* 10 0 **10 0**
2014–15 Manchester U 0 0
2014–15 *Sheffield W* 13 3 **13 3**
2015–16 Manchester U 1 0
2015–16 *Preston NE* 20 1 **20 1**
2016–17 Manchester U 0 0 **2 0**
2016–17 Hull C 5 0 **5 0**

KUCIAK, Dusan (G) 308 0
H: 6 2 W: 12 06 b.Zilina 21-5-85
Internationals: Slovakia Full caps.
2001–02 Trencin 1 0 **1 0**
2002–03 MSK Zilina 0 0
2003–04 MSK Zilina 0 0
2004–05 MSK Zilina 0 0
2004–05 *West Ham U* 0 0
2005–06 MSK Zilina 21 0
2006–07 MSK Zilina 35 0
2007–08 MSK Zilina 33 0 **89 0**
2008–09 Vaslui 34 0
2009–10 Vaslui 23 0
2010–11 Vaslui 30 0 **87 0**
2011–12 Legia Warsaw 27 0
2012–13 Legia Warsaw 30 0
2013–14 Legia Warsaw 25 0
2014–15 Legia Warsaw 31 0
2015–16 Legia Warsaw 18 0 **131 0**
2015–16 Hull C 0 0
2016–17 Hull C 0 0

LUER, Greg (F) 18 0
H: 5 11 W: 11 07 b.Brighton 6-12-94
2014–15 Hull C 0 0
2014–15 *Port Vale* 2 0 **2 0**
2015–16 Hull C 2 0
2015–16 *Scunthorpe U* 4 0 **4 0**
2015–16 *Stevenage* 10 0 **10 0**
2016–17 Hull C 0 0 **2 0**

MAGUIRE, Harry (D) 204 12
H: 6 2 W: 12 06 b.Mosborough 5-3-93
Internationals: England U21.
2010–11 Sheffield U 5 0
2011–12 Sheffield U 44 1
2012–13 Sheffield U 44 3
2013–14 Sheffield U 41 5 **134 9**
2014–15 Hull C 3 0
2014–15 *Wigan Ath* 16 1 **16 1**
2015–16 Hull C 22 0
2016–17 Hull C 29 2 **54 2**

MALONEY, Shaun (M) 311 63
H: 5 7 W: 10 01 b.Miri 24-1-83
Internationals: Scotland U20, U21, B, Full caps.
1999–2000 Celtic 0 0
2000–01 Celtic 4 0
2001–02 Celtic 16 5
2002–03 Celtic 20 3
2003–04 Celtic 17 5
2004–05 Celtic 2 0
2005–06 Celtic 36 13
2006–07 Celtic 9 0
2006–07 Aston Villa 8 1
2007–08 Aston Villa 22 4 **30 5**
2008–09 Celtic 21 4
2009–10 Celtic 10 4
2010–11 Celtic 21 5
2011–12 Celtic 3 0 **159 39**
2011–12 Wigan Ath 13 3
2012–13 Wigan Ath 36 6
2013–14 Wigan Ath 10 3
2014–15 Wigan Ath 20 2 **79 14**
2015 Chicago Fire 14 3 **14 3**
2015–16 Hull C 20 1
2016–17 Hull C 9 1 **29 2**

MANNION, Will (G) 0 0
b. 1-4-98
Internationals: England U19.
From AFC Wimbledon.
2016–17 Hull C 0 0

MARSHALL, David (G) 409 0
H: 6 3 W: 13 04 b.Glasgow 5-3-85
Internationals: Scotland Youth, U21, B, Full caps.
2003–04 Celtic 11 0
2004–05 Celtic 18 0
2005–06 Celtic 4 0
2006–07 Celtic 2 0 **35 0**
2006–07 Norwich C 2 0
2007–08 Norwich C 46 0
2008–09 Norwich C 46 0 **94 0**
2008–09 Cardiff C 0 0
2009–10 Cardiff C 43 0
2010–11 Cardiff C 11 0
2011–12 Cardiff C 45 0
2012–13 Cardiff C 46 0
2013–14 Cardiff C 37 0
2014–15 Cardiff C 38 0
2015–16 Cardiff C 40 0
2016–17 Cardiff C 4 0 **264 0**
2016–17 Hull C 16 0 **16 0**

MASON, Ryan (F) 139 14
H: 5 9 W: 10 00 b.Enfield 13-6-91
Internationals: England U19, U20, Full caps.
2007–08 Tottenham H 0 0
2008–09 Tottenham H 0 0
2009–10 Tottenham H 0 0
2009–10 *Yeovil T* 28 6 **28 6**
2010–11 Tottenham H 0 0
2010–11 *Doncaster R* 15 0
2011–12 Tottenham H 0 0
2011–12 *Doncaster R* 4 0 **19 0**
2011–12 *Millwall* 5 0 **5 0**
2012–13 Tottenham H 0 0
2012–13 *Lorient* 0 0
2013–14 Tottenham H 0 0
2013–14 *Swindon T* 18 5 **18 5**
2014–15 Tottenham H 31 1
2015–16 Tottenham H 22 1
2016–17 Tottenham H 0 0 **53 2**
2016–17 Hull C 16 1 **16 1**

MBOKANI, Dieumerci (F) 337 188
H: 6 1 W: 11 11 b.Kinshasa 22-11-85
Internationals: DR Congo Full caps.
2004 Bel'Or 27 21 **27 21**
2005 Mazembe 40 40
2006 Mazembe 32 27 **72 67**
2006–07 *Anderlecht* 9 4
2007–08 Standard Liege 32 15
2008–09 Standard Liege 29 16
2009–10 Standard Liege 24 7 **85 38**
2010–11 Monaco 10 1 **10 1**
2010–11 *Wolfsburg* 7 0 **7 0**
2011–12 Anderlecht 26 15
2012–13 Anderlecht 27 19 **62 38**
2013–14 Dynamo Kiev 25 13
2014–15 Dynamo Kiev 8 3
2015–16 Dynamo Kiev 0 0
2015–16 *Norwich C* 29 7 **29 7**
2016–17 Dynamo Kiev 0 0 **33 16**
On loan from Dynamo Kiev.
2016–17 Hull C 12 0 **12 0**

McGREGOR, Allan (G) 373 0
H: 6 0 W: 11 08 b.Edinburgh 31-1-82
Internationals: Scotland U21, B, Full caps.
1998–99 Rangers 0 0
1999–2000 Rangers 0 0
2000–01 Rangers 0 0
2001–02 Rangers 2 0
2002–03 Rangers 0 0
2003–04 Rangers 4 0
2004–05 Rangers 2 0
2005–06 Rangers 0 0
2005–06 *Dunfermline Ath* 26 0 **26 0**
2006–07 Rangers 31 0
2007–08 Rangers 31 0
2008–09 Rangers 27 0
2009–10 Rangers 34 0
2010–11 Rangers 37 0
2011–12 Rangers 37 0 **205 0**
2012–13 Besiktas 27 0 **27 0**
2013–14 Hull C 26 0
2014–15 Hull C 26 0
2015–16 Hull C 44 0
2016–17 Hull C 0 0 **96 0**
2016–17 *Cardiff C* 19 0 **19 0**

MEYLER, David (M) 159 11
H: 6 3 W: 11 09 b.Cork 29-5-89
Internationals: Republic of Ireland U21, Full caps.
2008 Cork C 2 0 **2 0**
2008–09 Sunderland 0 0
2009–10 Sunderland 10 0
2010–11 Sunderland 5 0
2011–12 Sunderland 7 0
2012–13 Sunderland 3 0 **25 0**
2012–13 Hull C 28 5
2013–14 Hull C 30 2
2014–15 Hull C 28 1
2015–16 Hull C 26 2
2016–17 Hull C 20 1 **132 11**

N'DIAYE, Alfred (M) 175 8
H: 6 2 W: 13 08 b.Paris 6-3-90
Internationals: France U17, U19, U20, U21. Senegal Full caps.
2008–09 AS Nancy 24 0
2009–10 AS Nancy 23 0
2010–11 AS Nancy 13 0 **60 0**
2011–12 Bursaspor 32 3
2012–13 Bursaspor 13 1 **45 4**
2012–13 Sunderland 16 0
2013–14 Sunderland 0 0 **16 0**
2013–14 *Eskisehirspor* 16 3 **16 3**
2013–14 *Real Betis* 16 0 **16 0**
2016–17 Villarreal 7 0 **7 0**
On loan from Villarreal.
2016–17 Hull C 15 1 **15 1**

OLLEY, Greg (M) 0 0
b. 2-2-96
From Newcastle U.
2016–17 Hull C 0 0

RANOCCHIA, Andrea (D) 266 15
H: 6 3 W: 12 04 b.Assissi 16-2-88
From Perugia.
2006–07 Arezzo 24 1
2007–08 Arezzo 32 0 **56 1**
2008–09 Genoa 0 0
2008–09 *Bari* 17 1
2009–10 Genoa 0 0
2009–10 *Bari* 17 2 **34 3**
2010–11 Inter Milan 18 1
2010–11 *Genoa* 16 2 **16 2**
2011–12 Inter Milan 12 1
2012–13 Inter Milan 32 2
2013–14 Inter Milan 24 1
2014–15 Inter Milan 33 2
2015–16 Inter Milan 10 0
2015–16 *Sampdoria* 10 0 **10 0**
2016–17 Inter Milan 5 0 **134 7**
On loan from Inter Milan.
2016–17 Hull C 16 2 **16 2**

ROBERTSON, Andrew (D) 169 8
H: 5 10 W: 10 00 b.Glasgow 11-3-94
Internationals: Scotland U21, Full caps.
2012–13 Queen's Park 34 2 **34 2**
2013–14 Dundee U 36 3 **36 3**
2014–15 Hull C 24 0
2015–16 Hull C 42 2
2016–17 Hull C 33 1 **99 3**

RODGERS, Harvey (M) 19 1
H: 5 10 W: 12 06 b.York 20-10-96
2016–17 Hull C 0 0
2016–17 *Accrington S* 19 1 **19 1**

TYMON, Josh (D) **5 0**
b. 22-5-99
Internationals: England U17, U18.

2015–16	Hull C	0	0		
2016–17	Hull C	5	0	**5**	**0**

WEIR, James (M) **5 0**
H: 5 10 W: 11 03 b.Preston 4-8-95
Internationals: England U18, U19.

2014–15	Manchester U	0	0		
2015–16	Manchester U	1	0		
2016–17	Manchester U	0	0	**1**	**0**
2016–17	Hull C	0	0		
2016–17	*Wigan Ath*	4	0	**4**	**0**

Players retained or with offer of contract
Annan, William John; Barkworth, Ellis; Curry, Adam; Eissa, Ahmed Elmehamady; Fleming, Brandon James; Hamilton, Tyler Lee; Lenihan, Brian Patrick; McKenzie, Robbie; Odubajo, Moses Adeshina Ayoola; Ritson, Lewis Barry Ryan.

Scholars
Andrew, Charlie Alfred; Chadwick, William Anthony; Dunkerley, Charlie; Holmes, Elliot Charles; Kelledy, Marc Thomas Michael; Salam, Ahmed Mamdoh Abdel; Saltmer, Jonathan David; Sheaf, Max; Thacker, Joshua; Tymon, Joshua Lewis; Wilson-Rhiney, Mason Alexander.

IPSWICH T (43)

BERRA, Christophe (D) **438 18**
H: 6 1 W: 12 10 b.Edinburgh 31-1-85
Internationals: Scotland U21, B, Full caps.

2003–04	Hearts	6	0		
2004–05	Hearts	12	0		
2005–06	Hearts	12	1		
2006–07	Hearts	35	1		
2007–08	Hearts	35	2		
2008–09	Hearts	23	0	**123**	**4**
2008–09	Wolverhampton W	15	0		
2009–10	Wolverhampton W	32	0		
2010–11	Wolverhampton W	32	0		
2011–12	Wolverhampton W	32	0		
2012–13	Wolverhampton W	30	0	**141**	**0**
2013–14	Ipswich T	42	5		
2014–15	Ipswich T	45	6		
2015–16	Ipswich T	43	1		
2016–17	Ipswich T	44	2	**174**	**14**

BEST, Leon (F) **281 58**
H: 6 1 W: 13 03 b.Nottingham 19-9-86
Internationals: Republic of Ireland U21, Full caps.

2004–05	Southampton	3	0		
2004–05	*QPR*	5	0	**5**	**0**
2005–06	Southampton	3	0		
2005–06	*Sheffield W*	13	2		
2006–07	Southampton	9	4	**15**	**4**
2006–07	*Bournemouth*	15	3	**15**	**3**
2006–07	*Yeovil T*	15	10	**15**	**10**
2007–08	Coventry C	34	8		
2008–09	Coventry C	31	2		
2009–10	Coventry C	27	9	**92**	**19**
2009–10	Newcastle U	13	0		
2010–11	Newcastle U	11	6		
2011–12	Newcastle U	18	4	**42**	**10**
2012–13	Blackburn R	6	0		
2013–14	Blackburn R	8	2		
2013–14	*Sheffield W*	15	4	**28**	**6**
2014–15	Blackburn R	0	0		
2014–15	*Derby Co*	15	0	**15**	**0**
2014–15	*Brighton & HA*	13	0	**13**	**0**
2015–16	Blackburn R	0	0	**14**	**2**
2015–16	Rotherham U	16	4		
2016–17	Rotherham U	0	0	**16**	**4**
2016–17	Ipswich T	11	0	**11**	**0**

BIALKOWSKI, Bartosz (G) **210 0**
H: 6 3 W: 12 10 b.Braniewo 6-7-87
Internationals: Poland U20, U21.

2004–05	Gornik Zabrze	7	0	**7**	**0**
2005–06	Southampton	5	0		
2006–07	Southampton	8	0		
2007–08	Southampton	1	0		
2008–09	Southampton	0	0		
2009–10	Southampton	7	0		
2009–10	*Barnsley*	2	0	**2**	**0**
2010–11	Southampton	0	0		
2011–12	Southampton	1	0	**22**	**0**
2012–13	Notts Co	40	0		
2013–14	Notts Co	44	0	**84**	**0**
2014–15	Ipswich T	31	0		
2015–16	Ipswich T	20	0		
2016–17	Ipswich T	44	0	**95**	**0**

BISHOP, Teddy (M) **56 1**
H: 5 11 W: 10 03 b.Cambridge 15-7-96

2013–14	Ipswich T	0	0		
2014–15	Ipswich T	33	1		
2015–16	Ipswich T	4	0		
2016–17	Ipswich T	19	0	**56**	**1**

BRU, Kevin (M) **226 13**
H: 6 0 W: 11 05 b.Paris 12-12-88
Internationals: France U19. Mauritius Full caps.

2006–07	Rennes	2	0	**2**	**0**
2007–08	Chateauroux	10	0	**10**	**0**
2008–09	Clermont Foot Avergne	25	2	**25**	**2**
2009–10	Dijon	14	2		
2010–11	Dijon	11	0	**25**	**2**
2010–11	Bologne	9	0		
2011–12	Bologne	19	2	**28**	**2**
2012–13	Istres	31	2	**31**	**2**
2013–14	Levski Sofia	20	1	**20**	**1**
2014–15	Ipswich T	31	1		
2015–16	Ipswich T	28	2		
2016–17	Ipswich T	26	1	**85**	**4**

CHAMBERS, Luke (D) **555 32**
H: 6 1 W: 11 13 b.Kettering 29-8-85

2002–03	Northampton T	1	0		
2003–04	Northampton T	24	0		
2004–05	Northampton T	27	0		
2005–06	Northampton T	43	0		
2006–07	Northampton T	29	1	**124**	**1**
2006–07	Nottingham F	14	0		
2007–08	Nottingham F	42	6		
2008–09	Nottingham F	39	2		
2009–10	Nottingham F	23	3		
2010–11	Nottingham F	44	6		
2011–12	Nottingham F	43	0	**205**	**17**
2012–13	Ipswich T	44	3		
2013–14	Ipswich T	46	3		
2014–15	Ipswich T	45	1		
2015–16	Ipswich T	45	3		
2016–17	Ipswich T	46	4	**226**	**14**

CROWE, Michael (G) **0 0**
H: 6 2 W: 11 11 b.London 13-11-95
Internationals: Wales U19, U21.

2013–14	Ipswich T	0	0		
2014–15	Ipswich T	0	0		
2014–15	Woking	0	0		
2015–16	Ipswich T	0	0		
2015–16	*Stevenage*	0	0		
2016–17	Ipswich T	0	0		

DOUGLAS, Jonathan (M) **501 36**
H: 5 11 W: 11 11 b.Monaghan 22-11-81
Internationals: Republic of Ireland Full caps.

1999–2000	Blackburn R	0	0		
2000–01	Blackburn R	0	0		
2001–02	Blackburn R	0	0		
2002–03	Blackburn R	1	0		
2002–03	*Chesterfield*	7	1	**7**	**1**
2003–04	Blackpool	16	3	**16**	**3**
2003–04	Blackburn R	14	1		
2004–05	Blackburn R	1	0		
2004–05	*Gillingham*	10	0	**10**	**0**
2005–06	Blackburn R	0	0		
2005–06	*Leeds U*	40	5		
2006–07	Blackburn R	0	0	**16**	**1**
2006–07	Leeds U	35	1		
2007–08	Leeds U	24	3		
2008–09	Leeds U	43	1	**142**	**10**
2009–10	Swindon T	43	0		
2010–11	Swindon T	39	1	**82**	**1**
2011–12	Brentford	46	2		
2012–13	Brentford	44	4		
2013–14	Brentford	35	3		
2014–15	Brentford	44	8	**169**	**17**
2015–16	Ipswich T	38	3		
2016–17	Ipswich T	21	0	**59**	**3**

DOWNES, Flynn (M) **0 0**

2016–17	Ipswich T	0	0		

DOZZELL, Andre (M) **8 1**
b.Ipswich 2-5-99
Internationals: England U16, U17, U18, U19.

2015–16	Ipswich T	2	1		
2016–17	Ipswich T	6	0	**8**	**1**

EMMANUEL, Josh (D) **21 0**
H: 5 11 W: 11 00 b.London 18-8-97

2015–16	Ipswich T	4	0		
2015–16	*Crawley T*	2	0	**2**	**0**
2016–17	Ipswich T	15	0	**19**	**0**

FOWLER, George (D) **0 0**

2016–17	Ipswich T	0	0		

GERKEN, Dean (G) **254 0**
H: 6 3 W: 12 08 b.Southend 22-5-85

2003–04	Colchester U	1	0		
2004–05	Colchester U	13	0		
2005–06	Colchester U	7	0		
2006–07	Colchester U	27	0		
2007–08	Colchester U	40	0		
2008–09	Colchester U	21	0	**109**	**0**
2008–09	*Darlington*	7	0	**7**	**0**
2009–10	Bristol C	39	0		
2010–11	Bristol C	1	0		
2011–12	Bristol C	10	0		
2012–13	Bristol C	3	0	**53**	**0**
2013–14	Ipswich T	41	0		
2014–15	Ipswich T	16	0		
2015–16	Ipswich T	26	0		
2016–17	Ipswich T	2	0	**85**	**0**

KENLOCK, Myles (D) **20 0**
H: 6 1 W: 10 08 b.Croydon 29-11-96

2015–16	Ipswich T	2	0		
2016–17	Ipswich T	18	0	**20**	**0**

KNUDSEN, Jonas (D) **183 7**
H: 6 1 W: 11 05 b.Esbjerg 16-9-92
Internationals: Denmark U18, U19, U20, U21, Full caps.

2009–10	Esbjerg	7	0		
2010–11	Esbjerg	5	0	**5**	**0**
2011–12	Esbjerg	0	0		
2012–13	Esbjerg	32	1		
2013–14	Esbjerg	31	1		
2014–15	Esbjerg	28	2		
2015–16	Esbjerg	2	0	**100**	**4**
2015–16	Ipswich T	42	1		
2016–17	Ipswich T	36	2	**78**	**3**

McDONNELL, Adam (M) **1 0**
H: 5 9 W: 11 05 b.Dublin 14-5-97
Internationals: Republic of Ireland U16, U17, U18, U19.
From Shelbourne.

2014–15	Ipswich T	0	0		
2015–16	Ipswich T	1	0		
2016–17	Ipswich T	0	0	**1**	**0**

McGOLDRICK, David (F) **316 79**
H: 6 1 W: 11 10 b.Nottingham 29-11-87
Internationals: Republic of Ireland Full caps.

2003–04	Notts Co	4	0		
2004–05	Notts Co	0	0		
2005–06	Southampton	1	0		
2005–06	*Notts Co*	6	0	**10**	**0**
2006–07	Southampton	9	0		
2006–07	*Bournemouth*	12	6	**12**	**6**
2007–08	Southampton	8	0		
2007–08	*Port Vale*	17	2	**17**	**2**
2008–09	Southampton	46	12	**64**	**12**
2009–10	Nottingham F	33	3		
2010–11	Nottingham F	21	5		
2011–12	Nottingham F	9	0		
2011–12	*Sheffield W*	4	1	**4**	**1**
2012–13	Nottingham F	0	0	**63**	**8**
2012–13	*Coventry C*	22	16	**22**	**16**
2012–13	*Ipswich T*	13	4		
2013–14	Ipswich T	31	14		
2014–15	Ipswich T	26	7		
2015–16	Ipswich T	24	4		
2016–17	Ipswich T	30	5	**124**	**34**

McLOUGHLIN, Shane (D) **0 0**
b.Castleisland 1-3-97
Internationals: Republic of Ireland U18.

2014–15	Ipswich T	0	0		
2015–16	Ipswich T	0	0		
2016–17	Ipswich T	0	0		

MOORE, Kieffer (F) **70 7**
H: 6 5 W: 13 01 b.Torquay 8-8-92
Internationals: England C.
From Truro C, Dorchester T.

2013–14	Yeovil T	20	4		
2014–15	Yeovil T	30	3	**50**	**7**
2015	Viking	9	0	**9**	**0**

From Forest Green R, Torquay U.

2016–17	Ipswich T	11	0	**11**	**0**

MORRIS, Ben (F) **0 0**
b. 6-6-99
Internationals: England U17, U18.

2016–17	Ipswich T	0	0		

NYDAM, Tristan (M) **0 0**
Internationals: England U18.

2016–17	Ipswich T	0	0		

PITMAN, Brett (F) **409 129**
H: 6 0 W: 11 00 b.Jersey 31-1-88

2005–06	Bournemouth	19	1		
2006–07	Bournemouth	29	5		

2007–08 Bournemouth 39 6
2008–09 Bournemouth 39 17
2009–10 Bournemouth 46 26
2010–11 Bournemouth 2 3
2010–11 Bristol C 39 13
2011–12 Bristol C 35 7
2012–13 Bristol C 3 0 **77 20**
2012–13 Bournemouth 26 19
2013–14 Bournemouth 34 5
2014–15 Bournemouth 34 13 **268 95**
2015–16 Ipswich T 42 10
2016–17 Ipswich T 22 4 **64 14**

ROWE, Danny (M) 4 0
H: 6 0 b.Wythenshawe 9-3-92
2016–17 Ipswich T 4 0 **4 0**

SEARS, Freddie (F) 291 55
H: 5 8 W: 10 01 b.Hornchurch 27-11-89
Internationals: England U19, U20, U21.
2007–08 West Ham U 7 1
2008–09 West Ham U 17 0
2009–10 West Ham U 1 0
2009–10 *Crystal Palace* 18 0 **18 0**
2009–10 *Coventry C* 10 0 **10 0**
2010–11 West Ham U 11 1
2010–11 *Scunthorpe U* 9 0 **9 0**
2011–12 West Ham U 10 0 **46 2**
2011–12 *Colchester U* 11 2
2012–13 Colchester U 35 7
2013–14 Colchester U 32 12
2014–15 Colchester U 24 10 **102 31**
2014–15 Ipswich T 21 9
2015–16 Ipswich T 45 6
2016–17 Ipswich T 40 7 **106 22**

SKUSE, Cole (M) 441 10
H: 6 1 W: 11 05 b.Bristol 29-3-86
2004–05 Bristol C 7 0
2005–06 Bristol C 38 2
2006–07 Bristol C 42 0
2007–08 Bristol C 25 0
2008–09 Bristol C 33 2
2009–10 Bristol C 43 2
2010–11 Bristol C 30 1
2011–12 Bristol C 36 2
2012–13 Bristol C 25 0 **279 9**
2013–14 Ipswich T 43 0
2014–15 Ipswich T 40 1
2015–16 Ipswich T 39 0
2016–17 Ipswich T 40 0 **162 1**

SMITH, Tommy (D) 258 21
H: 6 2 W: 12 02 b.Macclesfield 31-3-90
Internationals: England U17, U18. New Zealand Full caps.
2007–08 Ipswich T 0 0
2008–09 Ipswich T 2 0
2009–10 Ipswich T 14 0
2009–10 *Brentford* 8 0 **8 0**
2010–11 Ipswich T 22 3
2010–11 *Colchester U* 6 0 **6 0**
2011–12 Ipswich T 26 3
2012–13 Ipswich T 38 3
2013–14 Ipswich T 45 6
2014–15 Ipswich T 42 4
2015–16 Ipswich T 45 2
2016–17 Ipswich T 10 0 **244 21**

SPENCE, Jordan (D) 178 2
H: 6 2 W: 12 07 b.Woodford 24-5-90
Internationals: England U16, U17, U18, U19, U21.
2007–08 West Ham U 0 0
2008–09 West Ham U 0 0
2008–09 *Leyton Orient* 20 0 **20 0**
2009–10 West Ham U 1 0
2009–10 *Scunthorpe U* 9 0 **9 0**
2010–11 West Ham U 2 0
2010–11 *Bristol C* 11 0
2011–12 West Ham U 0 0
2011–12 *Bristol C* 10 0 **21 0**
2012–13 West Ham U 4 0
2013–14 West Ham U 0 0 **7 0**
2013–14 *Sheffield W* 4 0 **4 0**
2013–14 *Milton Keynes D* 29 2
2014–15 Milton Keynes D 38 0
2015–16 Milton Keynes D 33 0
2016–17 Milton Keynes D 0 0 **100 2**
2016–17 Ipswich T 17 0 **17 0**

TAYLOR, Steven (D) 235 15
H: 6 2 W: 13 01 b.Greenwich 23-1-86
Internationals: England U16, U17, U20, U21, B.
2002–03 Newcastle U 0 0
2003–04 Newcastle U 1 0
2003–04 *Wycombe W* 6 0 **6 0**
2004–05 Newcastle U 13 0
2005–06 Newcastle U 12 0
2006–07 Newcastle U 27 2
2007–08 Newcastle U 31 1
2008–09 Newcastle U 27 4
2009–10 Newcastle U 21 1
2010–11 Newcastle U 14 3
2011–12 Newcastle U 14 0
2012–13 Newcastle U 25 0
2013–14 Newcastle U 10 1
2014–15 Newcastle U 10 1
2015–16 Newcastle U 10 0 **215 13**
2016 Portland Timbers 11 2 **11 2**
2016–17 Ipswich T 3 0 **3 0**

WARD, Grant (M) 117 9
H: 5 10 W: 11 07 b.Lewisham 5-12-94
2013–14 Tottenham H 0 0
2014 *Chicago Fire* 23 1 **23 1**
2014–15 Tottenham H 0 0
2014–15 *Coventry C* 11 0 **11 0**
2015–16 Tottenham H 0 0
2015–16 *Rotherham U* 40 2 **40 2**
2016–17 Ipswich T 43 6 **43 6**

WEBBER, Patrick (D) 0 0
2016–17 Ipswich T 0 0

WEBSTER, Adam (D) 90 6
H: 6 1 W: 11 11 b.West Wittering 4-1-95
Internationals: England U18, U19.
2011–12 Portsmouth 3 0
2012–13 Portsmouth 18 0
2013–14 Portsmouth 4 2
2014–15 Portsmouth 15 1
2015–16 Portsmouth 27 2 **67 5**
2016–17 Ipswich T 23 1 **23 1**

Players retained or with offer of contract
Benyu, Kundai Leroy Jeremiah; Blanchfield, James Elliott; George-Kenlock, Myles Lewis; Hayes, Nicholas Michael; Hyam, Luke Thomas; Patterson, Monty Mark; Smith, Chris; Wright, Harry Edward.

Scholars
Cahill, Steven John; Cathline, Kieron Raymond Kobina; Daniels, Declan Anthony; Downes, Flynn; Folami, Gbenga Tai; Fullwood, Callum Leigh; Lankester, Jack Richard; Marshall, Ross Steven; McGavin, Brett; McKendry, Conor; Meldrum, Ross Alexander; Muamba, Daniel; Murrell, Ellis Andrew John; Ndaba, Corrie Richard; Salaudeen, Kolade Abdulahi Olamide; Ware, Mitchell Vincent; Webber, Patrick Damian; Wilton, Albert; Woolfenden, Luke Matthew.

LEEDS U (44)

ANTONSSON, Marcus (F) 128 34
H: 5 11 W: 12 08 b.Unnaryds 8-5-91
2010 Halmstad 1 0
2011 Halmstad 6 0
2012 Halmstad 18 1
2013 Halmstad 20 4
2014 Halmstad 26 6 **71 11**
2015 Kalmar 29 12
2016 Kalmar 12 10 **41 22**
2016–17 Leeds U 16 1 **16 1**

AYLING, Luke (D) 288 6
H: 5 11 W: 10 08 b.Lambeth 25-8-91
2009–10 Arsenal 0 0
2009–10 *Yeovil T* 4 0
2010–11 Yeovil T 37 0
2011–12 Yeovil T 44 0
2012–13 Yeovil T 39 0
2013–14 Yeovil T 42 2 **166 2**
2014–15 Bristol C 46 4
2015–16 Bristol C 33 0
2016–17 Bristol C 1 0 **80 4**
2016–17 Leeds U 42 0 **42 0**

BELLUSCI, Giuseppe (D) 224 4
H: 6 1 W: 11 07 b.Trebisacce 21-8-89
Internationals: Italy U21.
2006–07 Ascoli 3 0
2007–08 Ascoli 2 0
2008–09 Ascoli 30 1 **35 1**
2009–10 Catania 12 0
2010–11 Catania 9 0
2011–12 Catania 32 0
2012–13 Catania 26 0
2013–14 Catania 20 0 **99 0**
2014–15 Leeds U 30 2
2015–16 Leeds U 27 0
2016–17 Leeds U 0 0 **57 2**
2016–17 *Empoli* 33 1 **33 1**

BERARDI, Gaetano (D) 216 0
H: 5 10 W: 11 00 b.Sorengo 21-8-88
Internationals: Switzerland U20, U21, Full caps.
2006–07 Brescia 1 0
2007–08 Brescia 9 0
2008–09 Brescia 26 0
2009–10 Brescia 29 0
2010–11 Brescia 27 0
2011–12 Brescia 13 0 **105 0**
2011–12 Sampdoria 9 0
2012–13 Sampdoria 21 0
2013–14 Sampdoria 5 0 **35 0**
2014–15 Leeds U 22 0
2015–16 Leeds U 28 0
2016–17 Leeds U 26 0 **76 0**

BOTAKA, Jordan (M) 113 13
H: 6 0 W: 11 07 b.Kinshasa 24-6-93
Internationals: Netherlands U19. DR Congo Full caps.
2012–13 Club Brugge 0 0
2012–13 *Belenenses* 1 0 **1 0**
2013–14 Excelsior 36 10
2014–15 Excelsior 33 1
2015–16 Excelsior 4 0 **73 11**
2015–16 Leeds U 13 0
2016–17 Leeds U 0 0 **13 0**
2016–17 *Charlton Ath* 26 2 **26 2**

BRIDCUTT, Liam (M) 241 2
H: 5 9 W: 11 07 b.Reading 8-5-89
Internationals: Scotland Full caps.
2007–08 Chelsea 0 0
2007–08 *Yeovil T* 9 0 **9 0**
2008–09 Chelsea 0 0
2008–09 *Watford* 6 0 **6 0**
2009–10 Chelsea 0 0
2009–10 *Stockport Co* 15 0 **15 0**
2010–11 Chelsea 0 0
2010–11 Brighton & HA 37 2
2011–12 Brighton & HA 43 0
2012–13 Brighton & HA 41 0
2013–14 Brighton & HA 11 0 **132 2**
2013–14 Sunderland 12 0
2014–15 Sunderland 18 0
2015–16 Sunderland 0 0 **30 0**
2015–16 *Leeds U* 24 0
2016–17 Leeds U 25 0 **49 0**

COOPER, Liam (D) 171 8
H: 6 2 W: 13 07 b.Hull 30-8-91
Internationals: Scotland U17, U19.
2008–09 Hull C 0 0
2009–10 Hull C 2 0
2010–11 Hull C 2 0
2010–11 *Carlisle U* 6 1 **6 1**
2011–12 Hull C 7 0
2011–12 *Huddersfield T* 4 0 **4 0**
2012–13 Hull C 0 0 **11 0**
2012–13 Chesterfield 29 2
2013–14 Chesterfield 41 3
2014–15 Chesterfield 1 0 **71 5**
2014–15 Leeds U 29 1
2015–16 Leeds U 39 1
2016–17 Leeds U 11 0 **79 2**

COYLE, Lewie (M) 15 0
H: 5 8 W: 10 08 b.Hull 15-10-95
2015–16 Leeds U 11 0
2016–17 Leeds U 4 0 **15 0**

DALLAS, Stuart (M) 172 42
H: 6 0 W: 12 09 b.Cookstown 19-4-91
Internationals: Northern Ireland U21, U23, Full caps.
2010–11 Crusaders 13 16
2011–12 Crusaders 8 8 **21 24**
2012–13 Brentford 7 0
2013–14 Brentford 18 2
2013–14 *Northampton T* 12 3 **12 3**
2014–15 Brentford 38 6 **63 8**
2015–16 Leeds U 45 5
2016–17 Leeds U 31 2 **76 7**

DENTON, Tyler (D) 0 0
H: 5 8 W: 10 06 b.Dewsbury 6-9-95
Internationals: England U17.
2016–17 Leeds U 0 0

DIAGOURAGA, Toumani (M) 369 12
H: 6 2 W: 11 05 b.Paris 10-6-87
2004–05 Watford 0 0
2005–06 Watford 1 0
2005–06 *Swindon T* 8 0 **8 0**
2006–07 Watford 0 0
2006–07 *Rotherham U* 7 0 **7 0**
2007–08 Watford 0 0 **1 0**
2007–08 *Hereford U* 41 2

2008–09	Hereford U	45	2	**86**	**4**
2009–10	Peterborough U	19	0	**19**	**0**
2009–10	*Brentford*	20	0		
2010–11	Brentford	32	1		
2011–12	Brentford	35	4		
2012–13	Brentford	39	1		
2013–14	Brentford	19	0		
2013–14	*Portsmouth*	8	0	**8**	**0**
2014–15	Brentford	38	0		
2015–16	Brentford	27	0	**210**	**6**
2015–16	Leeds U	17	2		
2016–17	Leeds U	1	0	**18**	**2**
2016–17	*Ipswich T*	12	0	**12**	**0**

DOUKARA, Souleymane (F)				**116**	**20**
H: 6 4 W: 13 08 b.Meudon 29-9-91					
2012–13	Catania	12	0		
2013–14	Catania	1	0	**13**	**0**
2013–14	*Juve Stabia*	21	6	**21**	**6**
2014–15	Leeds U	25	5		
2015–16	Leeds U	23	3		
2016–17	Leeds U	34	6	**82**	**14**

ERWIN, Lee (F)				**93**	**21**
H: 6 2 W: 12 07 b.Bellshill 19-3-94					
Internationals: Scotland U17, U18, U19.					
2012–13	Motherwell	0	0		
2013–14	Motherwell	0	0		
2013–14	*Arbroath*	11	8	**11**	**8**
2014–15	Motherwell	34	5	**34**	**5**
2015–16	Leeds U	11	0		
2015–16	*Bury*	3	0	**3**	**0**
2016–17	Leeds U	0	0	**11**	**0**
2016–17	*Oldham Ath*	34	8	**34**	**8**

GREEN, Rob (G)				**609**	**0**
H: 6 3 W: 14 09 b.Chertsey 18-1-80					
Internationals: England U16, U18, B, Full caps.					
1997–98	Norwich C	0	0		
1998–99	Norwich C	2	0		
1999–2000	Norwich C	3	0		
2000–01	Norwich C	5	0		
2001–02	Norwich C	41	0		
2002–03	Norwich C	46	0		
2003–04	Norwich C	46	0		
2004–05	Norwich C	38	0		
2005–06	Norwich C	42	0	**223**	**0**
2006–07	West Ham U	26	0		
2007–08	West Ham U	38	0		
2008–09	West Ham U	38	0		
2009–10	West Ham U	38	0		
2010–11	West Ham U	37	0		
2011–12	West Ham U	42	0	**219**	**0**
2012–13	QPR	16	0		
2013–14	QPR	45	0		
2014–15	QPR	36	0		
2015–16	QPR	24	0	**121**	**0**
2016–17	Leeds U	46	0	**46**	**0**

HERNANDEZ, Pablo (M)				**297**	**47**
H: 5 8 W: 10 00 b.Castellon 11-4-85					
Internationals: Spain Full caps.					
2005–06	Valencia	1	0		
2006–07	*Cadiz*	14	4	**14**	**4**
2007–08	Getafe	28	3	**28**	**3**
2008–09	Valencia	21	4		
2009–10	Valencia	33	5		
2010–11	Valencia	26	5		
2011–12	Valencia	30	3	**111**	**17**
2012–13	Swansea C	30	3		
2013–14	Swansea C	27	2	**57**	**5**
2014–15	Al Arabi	13	6		
2014–15	*Al-Nasr*	12	3	**12**	**3**
2015–16	Al Arabi	0	0	**13**	**6**
2015–16	*Rayo Vallecano*	27	3	**27**	**3**
2016–17	Leeds U	35	6	**35**	**6**

JANSSON, Pontus (D)				**157**	**14**
H: 6 3 W: 13 08 b.Arlov 13-2-91					
Internationals: Sweden U17, U19, U21, Full caps.					
2009	Malmo	2	0		
2009	*IFK Malmo*	9	4	**9**	**4**
2010	Malmo	18	1		
2011	Malmo	15	2		
2012	Malmo	30	1		
2013	Malmo	24	1		
2014	Malmo	9	1	**98**	**6**
2014–15	Torino	9	0		
2015–16	Torino	7	1	**16**	**1**
On loan from Torino.					
2016–17	Leeds U	34	3	**34**	**3**

McKAY, Paul (M)				**0**	**0**
H: 6 3 W: 12 13 b.Glasgow 19-11-96					
2014–15	Doncaster R	0	0		
2015–16	Doncaster R	0	0		
2015–16	Leeds U	0	0		
2016–17	Leeds U	0	0		

MURPHY, Luke (M)				**283**	**29**
H: 6 1 W: 11 05 b.Alsager 21-10-89					
2008–09	Crewe Alex	9	1		
2009–10	Crewe Alex	32	3		
2010–11	Crewe Alex	39	3		
2011–12	Crewe Alex	42	8		
2012–13	Crewe Alex	39	6	**161**	**21**
2013–14	Leeds U	37	3		
2014–15	Leeds U	30	3		
2015–16	Leeds U	36	1		
2016–17	Leeds U	0	0	**103**	**7**
2016–17	*Burton Alb*	19	1	**19**	**1**

O'KANE, Eunan (M)				**244**	**18**
H: 5 8 W: 13 04 b.Derry 10-7-90					
Internationals: Northern Ireland U16, U17, U19, U20, U21. Republic of Ireland U21, Full caps.					
2007–08	Everton	0	0		
2008–09	Everton	0	0		
2009–10	Coleraine	13	4	**13**	**4**
2009–10	Torquay U	16	1		
2010–11	Torquay U	45	6		
2011–12	Torquay U	45	5		
2012–13	Torquay U	0	0	**106**	**12**
2012–13	Bournemouth	37	1		
2013–14	Bournemouth	37	1		
2014–15	Bournemouth	11	0		
2015–16	Bournemouth	16	0	**101**	**2**
2016–17	Leeds U	24	0	**24**	**0**

PEACOCK-FARRELL, Bailey (G)				**1**	**0**
H: 6 2 W: 11 07 b.Darlington 29-10-96					
2015–16	Leeds U	1	0		
2016–17	Leeds U	0	0	**1**	**0**

PEDRAZA, Alfonso (M)				**63**	**13**
b. 9-4-96					
Internationals: Spain U19, U21.					
2011–12	Real Vallodolid	1	0	**1**	**0**
2012–13	Villarreal	0	0		
2013–14	Villarreal	0	0		
2014–15	Villarreal	2	0		
2015–16	Villarreal	2	0		
2015–16	Villarreal	22	6		
2016–17	Villarreal	0	0	**26**	**6**
2016–17	*Lugo*	22	6	**22**	**6**
On loan from Villareal.					
2016–17	Leeds U	14	1	**14**	**1**

PHILIPS, Kalvin (M)				**45**	**2**
H: 5 10 W: 11 05 b.Leeds 2-12-95					
2014–15	Leeds U	2	1		
2015–16	Leeds U	10	0		
2016–17	Leeds U	33	1	**45**	**2**

ROOFE, Kemar (M)				**115**	**28**
H: 5 10 W: 11 03 b.Walsall 6-1-93					
2011–12	WBA	0	0		
2012–13	WBA	0	0		
2012–13	*Northampton T*	6	0	**6**	**0**
2013–14	WBA	0	0		
2013–14	*Cheltenham T*	9	1	**9**	**1**
2014–15	WBA	0	0		
2014–15	*Colchester U*	2	0	**2**	**0**
2014–15	*Oxford U*	16	6		
2015–16	Oxford U	40	18	**56**	**24**
2016–17	Leeds U	42	3	**42**	**3**

SACKO, Hadi (F)				**79**	**7**
H: 6 0 W: 12 06 b.Corbeil-Essonnes 24-3-94					
Internationals: France U16, U18, U19, U20.					
2012–13	Bordeaux	4	0		
2013–14	Bordeaux	5	0		
2013–14	*Le Havre*	18	4	**18**	**4**
2014–15	Bordeaux	2	0	**11**	**0**
2014–15	Sporting Lisbon	0	0		
2015–16	Sporting Lisbon	0	0		
2015–16	*Sochaux*	12	1	**12**	**1**
2016–17	Sporting Lisbon	0	0		
On loan from Sporting Lisbon.					
2016–17	Leeds U	38	2	**38**	**2**

SILVESTRI, Marco (G)				**143**	**0**
H: 6 3 W: 12 08 b.Castelnuovo ne Monti 2-3-91					
Internationals: Italy U20, U21.					
2011–12	Chievo	0	0		
2011–12	*Reggiana*	27	0	**27**	**0**
2012–13	Chievo	0	0		
2012–13	*Padova*	25	0	**25**	**0**
2013–14	Chievo	0	0		
2013–14	*Cagliari*	3	0	**3**	**0**
2014–15	Leeds U	43	0		
2015–16	Leeds U	45	0		
2016–17	Leeds U	0	0	**88**	**0**

TAYLOR, Charlie (D)				**139**	**3**
H: 5 9 W: 11 00 b.York 18-9-93					
Internationals: England U19.					
2011–12	Leeds U	2	0		
2011–12	*Bradford C*	3	0	**3**	**0**
2012–13	Leeds U	0	0		
2012–13	*York C*	4	0	**4**	**0**
2012–13	*Inverness CT*	7	0	**7**	**0**
2013–14	Leeds U	0	0		
2013–14	*Fleetwood T*	32	0	**32**	**0**
2014–15	Leeds U	23	2		
2015–16	Leeds U	39	1		
2016–17	Leeds U	29	0	**93**	**3**

TURNBULL, Ross (G)				**148**	**0**
H: 6 4 W: 15 00 b.Bishop Auckland 4-1-85					
Internationals: England U16, U17, U18, U19.					
2002–03	Middlesbrough	0	0		
2003–04	Middlesbrough	0	0		
2003–04	*Darlington*	1	0	**1**	**0**
2003–04	*Barnsley*	3	0		
2004–05	Middlesbrough	0	0		
2004–05	*Bradford C*	2	0	**2**	**0**
2004–05	*Barnsley*	23	0		
2005–06	Middlesbrough	2	0		
2005–06	*Crewe Alex*	29	0	**29**	**0**
2006–07	Middlesbrough	0	0		
2007–08	Middlesbrough	3	0		
2007–08	*Cardiff C*	6	0	**6**	**0**
2008–09	Middlesbrough	22	0		
2009–10	Middlesbrough	0	0	**27**	**0**
2009–10	Chelsea	2	0		
2010–11	Chelsea	0	0		
2011–12	Chelsea	2	0		
2012–13	Chelsea	3	0	**7**	**0**
2013–14	Doncaster R	28	0	**28**	**0**
2014–15	Barnsley	22	0	**48**	**0**
2015–16	Leeds U	0	0		
2016–17	Leeds U	0	0		

VANN, Jack (D)				**0**	**0**
b. 12-6-98					
Internationals: England U16.					
2016–17	Leeds U	0	0		

VIEIRA, Ronaldo (M)				**35**	**1**
H: 5 11 W: 12 04 b.Bissau 10-8-98					
Internationals: England U20.					
2015–16	Leeds U	1	0		
2016–17	Leeds U	34	1	**35**	**1**

WHITEHOUSE, Billy (M)				**6**	**0**
H: 5 11 W: 11 05 b.Rotherham 13-6-96					
2014–15	Doncaster R	4	0		
2015–16	Doncaster R	2	0	**6**	**0**
2016–17	Leeds U	0	0		

WILKS, Mallik (F)				**0**	**0**
b.Leeds 15-12-98					
2016–17	Leeds U	0	0		

WOOD, Chris (F)				**259**	**86**
H: 6 3 W: 12 10 b.Auckland 7-12-91					
Internationals: New Zealand U17, U23, Full caps.					
2008–09	WBA	2	0		
2009–10	WBA	18	1		
2010–11	WBA	1	0		
2010–11	*Barnsley*	7	0	**7**	**0**
2010–11	*Brighton & HA*	29	8	**29**	**8**
2011–12	WBA	0	0		
2011–12	*Birmingham C*	23	9	**23**	**9**
2011–12	*Bristol C*	19	3	**19**	**3**
2012–13	WBA	0	0	**21**	**1**
2012–13	*Millwall*	19	11	**19**	**11**
2012–13	Leicester C	20	9		
2013–14	Leicester C	26	4		
2014–15	Leicester C	7	1	**53**	**14**
2014–15	*Ipswich T*	8	0	**8**	**0**
2015–16	Leeds U	36	13		
2016–17	Leeds U	44	27	**80**	**40**

Players retained or with offer of contract

Haidara, Amadou; McKay, Jack; O'Connor, Padhraic John; Oduor, Clarke Sydney Omondi; Pearce, Tom Mark; Shaughnessy, Conor Glynn; Stokes, Eoghan.

Scholars

Abioye, Moses Falola; Amissah, Samuel; Croft, Jake Spencer; Downing, Matthew Christopher; Ferguson, Ryan Alexander; Godden, Thomas MacKenzie; Gotts, Robbie; Hill, Maxwell Connor; Huffer, William Matthew Scobie; Kamwa, Bobby-Emmanuel; Keogh, Matthew Liam; Kitching, Liam James; Knight, Lewis Andrew; Kroma, Moise; McCalmont, Alfie John; Nicell, Callum Luke; Richardson, Theo Huw; Rollinson, Henry James; Shackleton, Jamie Stuart; Wollerton, Alexander.

LEICESTER C (45)

ALBRIGHTON, Marc (M) **179 13**
H: 6 2 W: 12 06 b.Tamworth 18-11-89
Internationals: England U20, U21.

2008–09	Aston Villa	0	0		
2009–10	Aston Villa	3	0		
2010–11	Aston Villa	29	5		
2011–12	Aston Villa	26	2		
2012–13	Aston Villa	9	0		
2013–14	Aston Villa	19	0	**86**	**7**
2013–14	*Wigan Ath*	4	0	**4**	**0**
2014–15	Leicester C	18	2		
2015–16	Leicester C	38	2		
2016–17	Leicester C	33	2	**89**	**6**

AMARTEY, Daniel (M) **107 4**
H: 6 0 W: 12 04 b.Accra 1-12-94
Internationals: Ghana U20, Full caps.

2013	Djurgardens	23	0		
2014	Djurgardens	11	0	**34**	**0**
2014–15	Copenhagen	29	3		
2015–16	Copenhagen	15	0	**44**	**3**
2015–16	Leicester C	5	0		
2016–17	Leicester C	24	1	**29**	**1**

BARNES, Harvey (M) **21 6**
b. 8-12-97
Internationals: England U18.

2016–17	Leicester C	0	0		
2016–17	*Milton Keynes D*	21	6	**21**	**6**

BENALOUANE, Yohan (D) **175 5**
H: 6 1 W: 12 06 b.Bagnois-sur-Ceze 28-3-87
Internationals: France U21.

2007–08	St Etienne	6	1		
2008–09	St Etienne	29	1		
2009–10	St Etienne	29	1		
2010–11	St Etienne	1	0	**65**	**3**
2010–11	Cesena	15	0		
2011–12	Cesena	11	0		
2012–13	Cesena	0	0	**26**	**0**
2012–13	*Parma*	21	1		
2013–14	Parma	4	0	**25**	**1**
2013–14	*Atalanta*	17	0		
2014–15	Atalanta	27	1	**44**	**1**
2015–16	Leicester C	4	0		
2015–16	*Fiorentina*	0	0		
2016–17	Leicester C	11	0	**15**	**0**

CAIN, Michael (M) **40 3**
H: 6 0 W: 10 08 b.Luton 18-2-94

2011–12	Leicester C	0	0		
2012–13	Leicester C	0	0		
2013–14	Leicester C	0	0		
2013–14	*Mansfield T*	2	0	**2**	**0**
2014–15	Leicester C	0	0		
2014–15	*Walsall*	32	2	**32**	**2**
2015–16	Leicester C	0	0		
2016–17	Leicester C	0	0		
2016–17	*Blackpool*	6	1	**6**	**1**

CHILWELL, Ben (D) **20 1**
H: 5 10 W: 11 03 b.Milton Keynes 21-12-96
Internationals: England U18, U19, U20, U21.

2015–16	Leicester C	0	0		
2015–16	*Huddersfield T*	8	0	**8**	**0**
2016–17	Leicester C	12	1	**12**	**1**

CHOUDHURY, Hamza (M) **26 0**
H: 5 10 W: 10 01 b.Loughborough 1-10-97

2015–16	Leicester C	0	0		
2015–16	*Burton Alb*	13	0		
2016–17	Leicester C	0	0		
2016–17	*Burton Alb*	13	0	**26**	**0**

DEBAYO, Josh (D) **0 0**
H: 6 0 W: 10 10 b.London 17-10-96

2015–16	Southampton	0	0		
2016–17	Leicester C	0	0		

DRINKWATER, Daniel (M) **264 16**
H: 5 10 W: 11 00 b.Manchester 5-3-90
Internationals: England U18, U19, Full caps.

2008–09	Manchester U	0	0		
2009–10	Manchester U	0	0		
2009–10	*Huddersfield T*	33	2	**33**	**2**
2010–11	Manchester U	0	0		
2010–11	*Cardiff C*	9	0	**9**	**0**
2010–11	*Watford*	12	0	**12**	**0**
2011–12	Manchester U	0	0		
2011–12	*Barnsley*	17	1	**17**	**1**
2011–12	Leicester C	19	2		
2012–13	Leicester C	42	1		
2013–14	Leicester C	45	7		
2014–15	Leicester C	23	0		
2015–16	Leicester C	35	2		
2016–17	Leicester C	29	1	**193**	**13**

ELDER, Callum (D) **50 1**
H: 5 11 W: 10 08 b.Sydney 27-1-95
Internationals: Australia U20.

2013–14	Leicester C	0	0		
2014–15	Leicester C	0	0		
2014–15	*Mansfield T*	21	0	**21**	**0**
2015–16	Leicester C	0	0		
2015–16	*Peterborough U*	18	1	**18**	**1**
2016–17	Leicester C	0	0		
2016–17	*Brentford*	6	0	**6**	**0**
2016–17	*Barnsley*	5	0	**5**	**0**

FUCHS, Christian (D) **403 24**
H: 6 1 W: 12 08 b.Pitten 7-4-86
Internationals: Austria U17, U19, U21, Full caps.

2002–03	Wiener Neustadt	12	0	**12**	**0**
2003–04	Mattersburg	13	0		
2004–05	Mattersburg	24	2		
2005–06	Mattersburg	35	1		
2006–07	Mattersburg	35	6		
2007–08	Mattersburg	33	3	**140**	**12**
2008–09	Bochum	22	2		
2009–10	Bochum	31	4		
2010–11	Bochum	0	0	**53**	**6**
2010–11	*Mainz 05*	31	0	**31**	**0**
2011–12	Schalke	29	2		
2012–13	Schalke	29	0		
2013–14	Schalke	16	0		
2014–15	Schalke	25	2	**99**	**4**
2015–16	Leicester C	32	0		
2016–17	Leicester C	36	2	**68**	**2**

GRAY, Demarai (M) **114 9**
H: 5 10 W: 10 04 b.Birmingham 28-6-96
Internationals: England U18, U19, U20, U21.

2013–14	Birmingham C	7	1		
2014–15	Birmingham C	41	6		
2015–16	Birmingham C	24	1	**72**	**8**
2015–16	Leicester C	12	0		
2016–17	Leicester C	30	1	**42**	**1**

HAMER, Ben (G) **219 0**
H: 5 11 W: 12 04 b.Chard 20-11-87

2006–07	Reading	0	0		
2007–08	Reading	0	0		
2007–08	*Brentford*	20	0		
2008–09	Reading	0	0		
2008–09	*Brentford*	45	0		
2009–10	Reading	0	0		
2010–11	Reading	0	0		
2010–11	*Brentford*	10	0	**75**	**0**
2010–11	*Exeter C*	18	0	**18**	**0**
2011–12	Charlton Ath	41	0		
2012–13	Charlton Ath	41	0		
2013–14	Charlton Ath	32	0	**114**	**0**
2014–15	Leicester C	8	0		
2015–16	Leicester C	0	0		
2015–16	*Bristol C*	4	0	**4**	**0**
2016–17	Leicester C	0	0	**8**	**0**

HERNANDEZ, Luis (D) **140 1**
b.Madrid 14-8-89

2010–11	Real Madrid	0	0		
2011–12	Sporting Gijon	0	0		
2012–13	Sporting Gijon	21	0		
2013–14	Sporting Gijon	38	1		
2014–15	Sporting Gijon	41	0		
2015–16	Sporting Gijon	36	0	**136**	**1**
2016–17	Leicester C	4	0	**4**	**0**

Transferred to Malaga, January 2017.

HUTH, Robert (D) **326 21**
H: 6 3 W: 14 07 b.Berlin 18-8-84
Internationals: Germany U21, Full caps.

2001–02	Chelsea	1	0		
2002–03	Chelsea	2	0		
2003–04	Chelsea	16	0		
2004–05	Chelsea	10	0		
2005–06	Chelsea	13	0	**42**	**0**
2006–07	Middlesbrough	12	1		
2007–08	Middlesbrough	13	1		
2008–09	Middlesbrough	24	0		
2009–10	Middlesbrough	4	0	**53**	**2**
2009–10	Stoke C	32	3		
2010–11	Stoke C	35	6		
2011–12	Stoke C	34	3		
2012–13	Stoke C	35	1		
2013–14	Stoke C	12	0		
2014–15	Stoke C	1	0	**149**	**13**
2014–15	Leicester C	14	1		
2015–16	Leicester C	35	3		
2016–17	Leicester C	33	2	**82**	**6**

JAMES, Matthew (M) **133 7**
H: 6 0 W: 11 12 b.Bacup 22-7-91
Internationals: England U16, U17, U19, U20.

2007–08	Manchester U	0	0		
2008–09	Manchester U	0	0		
2009–10	Manchester U	0	0		
2009–10	*Preston NE*	18	2		
2010–11	Manchester U	0	0		
2010–11	*Preston NE*	10	0	**28**	**2**
2011–12	Manchester U	0	0		
2012–13	Leicester C	24	3		
2013–14	Leicester C	35	1		
2014–15	Leicester C	27	0		
2015–16	Leicester C	0	0		
2016–17	Leicester C	1	0	**87**	**4**
2016–17	*Barnsley*	18	1	**18**	**1**

KAPUSTKA, Bartosz (M) **60 6**
b.Tarnow 23-12-96
Internationals: Poland U17, U18, U19, U20, Full caps.

2013–14	Cracovia Krakow	2	0		
2014–15	Cracovia Krakow	23	2		
2015–16	Cracovia Krakow	33	4		
2016–17	Cracovia Krakow	2	0	**60**	**6**
2016–17	Leicester C	0	0		

KING, Andy (M) **318 54**
H: 6 0 W: 11 10 b.Barnstaple 29-10-88
Internationals: Wales U19, U21, Full caps.

2007–08	Leicester C	11	1		
2008–09	Leicester C	45	9		
2009–10	Leicester C	43	9		
2010–11	Leicester C	45	15		
2011–12	Leicester C	30	4		
2012–13	Leicester C	42	7		
2013–14	Leicester C	30	4		
2014–15	Leicester C	24	2		
2015–16	Leicester C	25	2		
2016–17	Leicester C	23	1	**318**	**54**

LAWRENCE, Tom (F) **107 17**
H: 5 9 W: 11 11 b.Wrexham 13-1-94
Internationals: Wales U17, U19, U21, Full caps.

2012–13	Manchester U	0	0		
2013–14	Manchester U	1	0	**1**	**0**
2013–14	*Carlisle U*	9	3	**9**	**3**
2013–14	*Yeovil T*	19	2	**19**	**2**
2014–15	Leicester C	3	0		
2014–15	*Rotherham U*	6	1	**6**	**1**
2015–16	Leicester C	0	0		
2015–16	*Blackburn R*	21	2	**21**	**2**
2015–16	*Cardiff C*	14	0	**14**	**0**
2016–17	Leicester C	0	0	**3**	**0**
2016–17	*Ipswich T*	34	9	**34**	**9**

MAHREZ, Riyad (M) **180 36**
H: 5 10 W: 9 10 b.Sarcelles 21-2-91
Internationals: Algeria Full caps.

2011–12	Le Havre	9	0		
2012–13	Le Havre	32	4		
2013–14	Le Havre	17	2	**58**	**6**
2013–14	Leicester C	19	3		
2014–15	Leicester C	30	4		
2015–16	Leicester C	37	17		
2016–17	Leicester C	36	6	**122**	**30**

MENDY, Nampalys (D) **188 1**
H: 5 6 W: 10 10 b.La Seyne-sur-Mer 9-6-92
Internationals: France U18, U19, U20, U21.

2010–11	Monaco	14	0		
2011–12	Monaco	28	0		
2012–13	Monaco	32	0	**74**	**0**
2013–14	Nice	36	0		
2014–15	Nice	36	0		
2015–16	Nice	38	1	**110**	**1**
2016–17	Leicester C	4	0	**4**	**0**

MOORE, Elliott (D) **0 0**
b. 16-3-97
Internationals: England U18, U20.

2016–17	Leicester C	0	0		

MORGAN, Wes (D) **566 21**
H: 6 2 W: 14 00 b.Nottingham 21-1-84
Internationals: Jamaica Full caps.

2002–03	Nottingham F	0	0		
2002–03	*Kidderminster H*	5	1	**5**	**1**
2003–04	Nottingham F	32	2		
2004–05	Nottingham F	43	1		
2005–06	Nottingham F	43	2		
2006–07	Nottingham F	38	0		
2007–08	Nottingham F	42	1		
2008–09	Nottingham F	42	1		
2009–10	Nottingham F	44	3		
2010–11	Nottingham F	46	1		
2011–12	Nottingham F	22	1	**352**	**12**
2011–12	Leicester C	17	0		
2012–13	Leicester C	45	1		
2013–14	Leicester C	45	2		
2014–15	Leicester C	37	2		
2015–16	Leicester C	38	2		
2016–17	Leicester C	27	1	**209**	**8**

MUSA, Ahmed (F)				**226**	**74**
H: 5 9 W: 10 03 b.Jos 14-10-92					
Internationals: Nigeria U20, U23, Full caps.					
2008–09	GBS Football Academy	0	0		
2008–09	*Josh UTH*	18	4	**18**	**4**
2009–10	GBS Football Academy	0	0		
2009–10	*Kano Pillars*	25	18	**25**	**18**
2010–11	VVV Venlo	23	5		
2011–12	VVV Venlo	14	3	**37**	**8**
2011–12	CSKA Moscow	11	1		
2012–13	CSKA Moscow	28	11		
2013–14	CSKA Moscow	26	7		
2014–15	CSKA Moscow	30	10		
2015–16	CSKA Moscow	30	13	**125**	**42**
2016–17	Leicester C	21	2	**21**	**2**

NDIDI, Onyinye (D)				**78**	**6**
b. 16-12-96					
Internationals: Nigeria U20, Full caps.					
2014–15	Genk	6	0		
2015–16	Genk	36	4		
2016–17	Genk	19	0	**61**	**4**
2016–17	Leicester C	17	2	**17**	**2**

OKAZAKI, Shinji (F)				**315**	**87**
H: 5 9 W: 11 00 b.Hyogo 16-4-86					
Internationals: Japan U23, Full caps.					
2005	Shimizu S-Pulse	1	0		
2006	Shimizu S-Pulse	7	0		
2007	Shimizu S-Pulse	21	5		
2008	Shimizu S-Pulse	27	10		
2009	Shimizu S-Pulse	34	14		
2010	Shimizu S-Pulse	31	13	**121**	**42**
2010–11	Stuttgart	12	2		
2011–12	Stuttgart	26	7		
2012–13	Stuttgart	25	1	**63**	**10**
2013–14	Mainz 05	33	15		
2014–15	Mainz 05	32	12	**65**	**27**
2015–16	Leicester C	36	5		
2016–17	Leicester C	30	3	**66**	**8**

SCHMEICHEL, Kasper (G)				**389**	**0**
H: 6 1 W: 13 00 b.Copenhagen 5-11-86					
Internationals: Denmark U19, U20, U21, Full caps.					
2003–04	Manchester C	0	0		
2004–05	Manchester C	0	0		
2005–06	Manchester C	0	0		
2005–06	*Darlington*	4	0	**4**	**0**
2005–06	*Bury*	15	0		
2006–07	Manchester C	0	0		
2006–07	*Falkirk*	15	0	**15**	**0**
2006–07	*Bury*	14	0	**29**	**0**
2007–08	Manchester C	7	0		
2007–08	*Cardiff C*	14	0	**14**	**0**
2007–08	*Coventry C*	9	0	**9**	**0**
2008–09	Manchester C	1	0		
2009–10	Manchester C	0	0	**8**	**0**
2009–10	Notts Co	43	0	**43**	**0**
2010–11	Leeds U	37	0	**37**	**0**
2011–12	Leicester C	46	0		
2012–13	Leicester C	46	0		
2013–14	Leicester C	46	0		
2014–15	Leicester C	24	0		
2015–16	Leicester C	38	0		
2016–17	Leicester C	30	0	**230**	**0**

SIMPSON, Danny (D)				**273**	**1**
H: 5 9 W: 11 05 b.Eccles 4-1-87					
2005–06	Manchester U	0	0		
2006–07	Manchester U	0	0		
2006–07	*Sunderland*	14	0	**14**	**0**
2007–08	Manchester U	3	0		
2007–08	*Ipswich T*	8	0	**8**	**0**
2008–09	Manchester U	0	0		
2008–09	*Blackburn R*	12	0	**12**	**0**
2009–10	Manchester U	0	0	**3**	**0**
2009–10	Newcastle U	39	1		
2010–11	Newcastle U	30	0		
2011–12	Newcastle U	35	0		
2012–13	Newcastle U	19	0	**123**	**1**
2013–14	QPR	33	0		
2014–15	QPR	1	0	**34**	**0**
2014–15	Leicester C	14	0		
2015–16	Leicester C	30	0		
2016–17	Leicester C	35	0	**79**	**0**

SLIMANI, Islam (F)				**223**	**105**
H: 6 2 W: 12 06 b.Algiers 18-6-88					
Internationals: Algeria Full caps.					
2008–09	JSM Cheraga	20	18	**20**	**18**
2009–10	CR Belouizdad	30	8		
2010–11	CR Belouizdad	27	10		
2011–12	CR Belouizdad	26	10		
2012–13	CR Belouizdad	15	4	**98**	**32**
2013–14	Sporting Lisbon	26	8		
2014–15	Sporting Lisbon	21	12		
2015–16	Sporting Lisbon	33	27		
2016–17	Sporting Lisbon	2	1	**82**	**48**
2016–17	Leicester C	23	7	**23**	**7**

ULLOA, Jose (F)				**309**	**116**
H: 6 1 W: 11 10 b.General Roca 26-7-86					
2004–05	San Lorenzo	0	0		
2005–06	San Lorenzo	22	3		
2006–07	San Lorenzo	6	0	**25**	**3**
2007–08	Arsenal Sarandi	6	1	**6**	**1**
2007–08	Olimpo	8	1	**8**	**1**
2008–09	Castellon	33	17		
2009–10	Castellon	32	14		
2010–11	Castellon	1	0	**66**	**31**
2010–11	Almeria	34	7		
2011–12	Almeria	28	29		
2012–13	Almeria	10	3	**72**	**39**
2012–13	Brighton & HA	17	9		
2013–14	Brighton & HA	33	14	**50**	**23**
2014–15	Leicester C	37	11		
2015–16	Leicester C	29	6		
2016–17	Leicester C	16	1	**82**	**18**

VARDY, Jamie (F)				**168**	**62**
H: 5 10 W: 11 12 b.Sheffield 11-1-87					
Internationals: England Full caps.					
2012–13	Leicester C	26	4		
2013–14	Leicester C	37	16		
2014–15	Leicester C	34	5		
2015–16	Leicester C	36	24		
2016–17	Leicester C	35	13	**168**	**62**

WAGUE, Molla (D)				**86**	**6**
H: 6 3 W: 13 10 b.Verdon 21-2-91					
Internationals: France U19. Mali Full caps.					
2011–12	Caen	5	1		
2012–13	Caen	20	2		
2013–14	Caen	24	1	**49**	**4**
2014–15	Granada	0	0		
2014–15	*Udinese*	10	2		
2015–16	Granada	0	0		
2015–16	*Udinese*	21	0		
2016–17	Granada	0	0		
2016–17	*Udinese*	6	0	**37**	**2**
On loan from Granada.					
2016–17	Leicester C	0	0		

WASILEWSKI, Marcin (D)				**302**	**33**
H: 6 1 W: 13 11 b.Krakow 9-6-80					
Internationals: Poland Full caps.					
2002–03	Wisla Plock	24	1		
2003–04	Wisla Plock	21	1		
2004–05	Wisla Plock	15	1	**60**	**3**
2005–06	Amica Wronki	24	4	**24**	**4**
2006–07	Lech Poznan	14	5	**14**	**5**
2006–07	Anderlecht	14	2		
2007–08	Anderlecht	26	3		
2008–09	Anderlecht	30	8		
2009–10	Anderlecht	6	1		
2010–11	Anderlecht	17	3		
2011–12	Anderlecht	30	3		
2012–13	Anderlecht	20	0	**143**	**20**
2013–14	Leicester C	31	0		
2014–15	Leicester C	25	1		
2015–16	Leicester C	4	0		
2016–17	Leicester C	1	0	**61**	**1**

ZIELER, Ron-Robert (G)				**196**	**0**
H: 6 2 W: 11 07 b.Cologne 12-2-89					
Internationals: Germany U16, U17, U18, U19, U20, Full caps.					
2008–09	Manchester U	0	0		
2008–09	*Northampton T*	2	0	**2**	**0**
2009–10	Manchester U	0	0		
2010–11	Hannover 96	15	0		
2011–12	Hannover 96	34	0		
2012–13	Hannover 96	34	0		
2013–14	Hannover 96	34	0		
2014–15	Hannover 96	34	0		
2015–16	Hannover 96	34	0	**185**	**0**
2016–17	Leicester C	9	0	**9**	**0**

Players retained or with offer of contract
Bolkiah, Faiq Jefri; Bramley, Max; Felix-Eppiah, Joshua; Gordon, Joshua Luke; Iversen, Daniel; Johnson, Darnell Tobias Jack; Knight, Joshua Michael; Martis, Liandro Rudwendry Felipe; Muskwe, Admiral Dalindlela; Ndukwu, Layton Julius; Uche, Rubio Raul; Watts, Dylan Billy; Wood, Connor.

Scholars
Brown, Morgan Lea; Dewsbury-Hall, Kiernan; Edwards-John, Kairo; Fielding, Thomas Christian; Gill, Rubyn; Heaven, George William; Keaveny, Jozsef Phelim; Leshabela, Thakgalo Khanya; Pascanu, Alexandru Stefan; Sherif, Lamine Kaba; Tee, Conor; Thandi, Simranjit Singh; Ughelumba, Calvin; Williams, Kian; Yates, Cameron James.

LEYTON ORIENT (46)

ABRAHAMS, Tristan (F)				**9**	**2**
H: 5 9 W: 10 08 b.Lewisham 29-12-98					
2016–17	Leyton Orient	9	2	**9**	**2**

ADEBOYEJO, Victor (F)				**15**	**1**
b. 12-1-98					
2014–15	Leyton Orient	1	0		
2015–16	Leyton Orient	1	0		
2016–17	Leyton Orient	13	1	**15**	**1**

ALDERSON, Sam (M)				**0**	**0**
2016–17	Leyton Orient	0	0		

ALZATE, Steve (M)				**12**	**1**
H: 5 10 W: 10 03 b.Camden Town 1-9-98					
2016–17	Leyton Orient	12	1	**12**	**1**

ATANGANA, Nigel (M)				**88**	**1**
H: 6 2 W: 11 05 b.Corbeil-Essonnes 9-9-89					
2014–15	Portsmouth	30	1		
2015–16	Portsmouth	13	0	**43**	**1**
2015–16	Leyton Orient	16	0		
2016–17	Leyton Orient	29	0	**45**	**0**

BARKER, Charley (M)				**0**	**0**
2016–17	Leyton Orient	0	0		

BENEDICIC, Zan (M)				**2**	**0**
H: 5 10 W: 11 00 b.Krani 3-10-95					
Internationals: Slovenia U17, U18, U21.					
2014–15	AC Milan	0	0		
2014–15	*Leeds U*	1	0	**1**	**0**
2016–17	Ascoli	0	0		
2016–17	Leyton Orient	1	0	**1**	**0**

BOWERY, Jordan (F)				**201**	**25**
H: 6 1 W: 12 00 b.Nottingham 2-7-91					
2008–09	Chesterfield	3	0		
2009–10	Chesterfield	10	0		
2010–11	Chesterfield	27	1		
2011–12	Chesterfield	40	8		
2012–13	Chesterfield	3	1	**83**	**10**
2012–13	Aston Villa	10	0		
2013–14	Aston Villa	9	0	**19**	**0**
2013–14	*Doncaster R*	3	0	**3**	**0**
2014–15	Rotherham U	33	5		
2015–16	Rotherham U	7	0	**40**	**5**
2015–16	*Bradford C*	3	0	**3**	**0**
2015–16	Oxford U	17	7	**17**	**7**
2016–17	Leyton Orient	17	1	**17**	**1**
2016–17	*Crewe Alex*	19	2	**19**	**2**

CISAK, Aleksander (G)				**171**	**0**
H: 6 3 W: 14 11 b.Krakow 19-5-89					
Internationals: Australia U20.					
2006–07	Leicester C	0	0		
2007–08	Leicester C	0	0		
2008–09	Leicester C	0	0		
2009–10	Leicester C	0	0		
2010–11	Accrington S	21	0	**21**	**0**
2011–12	Oldham Ath	38	0		
2012–13	Oldham Ath	10	0	**48**	**0**
2012–13	*Portsmouth*	1	0	**1**	**0**
2013–14	Burnley	1	0		
2014–15	Burnley	0	0	**1**	**0**
2014–15	*York C*	10	0	**10**	**0**
2014–15	*Leyton Orient*	19	0		
2015–16	Leyton Orient	43	0		
2016–17	Leyton Orient	28	0	**90**	**0**

CLARK, Michael (D)				**9**	**0**
2016–17	Leyton Orient	9	0	**9**	**0**

CLOHESSY, Sean (D)				**280**	**7**
H: 5 11 W: 12 07 b.Croydon 12-12-86					
2005–06	Gillingham	20	1		
2006–07	Gillingham	6	0		
2007–08	Gillingham	17	0	**43**	**1**
From Salisbury C.					
2010–11	Southend U	46	1		
2011–12	Southend U	45	0		
2012–13	Southend U	46	3	**137**	**4**
2013–14	Kilmarnock	24	2	**24**	**2**
2014–15	Colchester U	32	0	**32**	**0**
2015–16	Leyton Orient	42	0		
2016–17	Leyton Orient	2	0	**44**	**0**

COLLINS, Michael (M)				**337**	**23**
H: 6 0 W: 11 00 b.Halifax 30-4-86					
Internationals: Republic of Ireland U18, U19, U21.					
2004–05	Huddersfield T	8	0		
2005–06	Huddersfield T	17	1		
2006–07	Huddersfield T	43	4		
2007–08	Huddersfield T	41	2		
2008–09	Huddersfield T	36	9		
2009–10	Huddersfield T	28	3	**173**	**19**
2010–11	Scunthorpe U	32	1		

2011–12 Scunthorpe U 1 0

2012–13 Scunthorpe U 29 1

2013–14 Scunthorpe U 17 0 **79 2**

2013–14 *AFC Wimbledon* 9 0 **9 0**

2014–15 Oxford U 39 2

2015–16 Oxford U 0 0 **39 2**

2015–16 *York C* 7 0 **7 0**

2016–17 Leyton Orient 30 0 **30 0**

DALBY, Sam (F) 16 1

b.Leytonstone 17-1-00

2016–17 Leyton Orient 16 1 **16 1**

DUNNE, Alan (D) 354 17

H: 5 10 W: 10 13 b.Dublin 23-8-82

1999–2000 Millwall 0 0

2000–01 Millwall 0 0

2001–02 Millwall 1 0

2002–03 Millwall 4 0

2003–04 Millwall 8 0

2004–05 Millwall 19 3

2005–06 Millwall 40 0

2006–07 Millwall 32 6

2007–08 Millwall 19 3

2008–09 Millwall 24 0

2009–10 Millwall 32 2

2010–11 Millwall 39 0

2011–12 Millwall 30 0

2012–13 Millwall 25 1

2013–14 Millwall 29 0

2014–15 Millwall 39 2 **341 17**

2015–16 Leyton Orient 8 0

2016–17 Leyton Orient 5 0 **13 0**

ERICHOT, Yvan (D) 119 4

H: 6 2 b.Chambray-les-Tours 25-3-90

Internationals: France U17.

2010–11 Monaco 0 0

2010–11 *Clermont* 9 0 **9 0**

2011–12 Monaco 0 0

2011–12 *Uniao Leiria* 1 0 **1 0**

2012–13 Monaco 0 0

2012–13 Sint-Truiden 7 0

2013–14 Sint-Truiden 25 1

2014–15 Sint-Truiden 28 3

2015–16 Sint-Truiden 30 0 **90 4**

2016–17 Leyton Orient 19 0 **19 0**

GRAINGER, Charlie (G) 5 0

b. 31-7-96

Internationals: England U18.

2012–13 Leyton Orient 0 0

2013–14 Leyton Orient 0 0

2014–15 Leyton Orient 0 0

2015–16 Leyton Orient 2 0

2016–17 Leyton Orient 3 0 **5 0**

HAPPE, Daniel (D) 2 0

b.Tower Hamlets 28-9-98

2016–17 Leyton Orient 2 0 **2 0**

HUNT, Nicky (D) 340 3

H: 6 1 W: 13 07 b.Westhoughton 3-9-83

Internationals: England U21.

2000–01 Bolton W 1 0

2001–02 Bolton W 0 0

2002–03 Bolton W 0 0

2003–04 Bolton W 31 1

2004–05 Bolton W 29 0

2005–06 Bolton W 20 0

2006–07 Bolton W 33 0

2007–08 Bolton W 14 0

2008–09 Bolton W 0 0

2008–09 *Birmingham C* 11 0 **11 0**

2009–10 Bolton W 0 0 **128 1**

2009–10 *Derby Co* 21 0 **21 0**

2010–11 Bristol C 7 0

2011–12 Bristol C 0 0 **7 0**

2011–12 Preston NE 17 1 **17 1**

2012–13 Rotherham U 9 0 **9 0**

2012–13 Accrington S 11 0

2013–14 Accrington S 37 0

2014–15 Accrington S 29 0 **77 0**

2015–16 Mansfield T 19 0 **19 0**

2015–16 Leyton Orient 16 0

2016–17 Leyton Orient 35 1 **51 1**

JANATA, Arthur (G) 0 0

2016–17 Leyton Orient 0 0

JANSE, Jens (M) 223 3

H: 6 0 W: 11 11 b.Venlo 1-7-86

Internationals: Netherlands U19, U21.

2005–06 Willem II 9 0

2006–07 Willem II 16 0

2007–08 Willem II 32 0

2008–09 Willem II 27 1

2009–10 Willem II 18 0 **102 1**

2010–11 NAC Breda 18 0

2011–12 NAC Breda 16 0

2012–13 NAC Breda 24 0 **58 0**

2013–14 Cordoba 11 0 **11 0**

2013–14 Dinamo Tbilisi 3 0 **3 0**

2014–15 Ternana 20 0

2015–16 Ternana 21 1

2016–17 Ternana 0 0 **41 1**

2016–17 Leyton Orient 8 1 **8 1**

JUDD, Myles (D) 20 0

H: 5 10 W: 10 08 b.Redbridge 26-8-99

2015–16 Leyton Orient 0 0

2016–17 Leyton Orient 20 0 **20 0**

KELLY, Liam (M) 220 26

H: 6 2 W: 13 11 b.Milton Keynes 10-2-90

Internationals: Scotland U18, U21, Full caps.

2009–10 Kilmarnock 15 1

2010–11 Kilmarnock 32 7

2011–12 Kilmarnock 34 1

2012–13 Kilmarnock 19 6 **100 15**

2012–13 Bristol C 19 0

2013–14 Bristol C 2 0 **21 0**

2014–15 Oldham Ath 37 1

2015–16 Oldham Ath 41 6 **78 7**

2016–17 Leyton Orient 21 4 **21 4**

KENNEDY, Callum (D) 157 3

H: 6 1 W: 12 10 b.Chertsey 9-11-89

2007–08 Swindon T 0 0

2008–09 Swindon T 4 0

2009–10 Swindon T 8 0

2010–11 Swindon T 3 0

2010–11 *Gillingham* 3 0 **3 0**

2010–11 *Rotherham U* 5 0 **5 0**

2011–12 Swindon T 18 1 **33 1**

2012–13 Scunthorpe U 17 0 **17 0**

2013–14 AFC Wimbledon 22 0

2014–15 AFC Wimbledon 26 0

2015–16 AFC Wimbledon 19 1 **67 1**

2016–17 Leyton Orient 32 1 **32 1**

KOROMA, Josh (F) 25 3

H: 5 10 W: 10 06 b. 8-11-98

2015–16 Leyton Orient 3 0

2016–17 Leyton Orient 22 3 **25 3**

MASSEY, Gavin (F) 225 31

H: 5 11 W: 11 06 b.Watford 14-10-92

2009–10 Watford 1 0

2010–11 Watford 3 0

2011–12 Watford 3 0

2011–12 *Yeovil T* 16 3 **16 3**

2011–12 *Colchester U* 8 0

2012–13 Watford 0 0 **7 0**

2012–13 Colchester U 40 6

2013–14 Colchester U 30 3

2014–15 Colchester U 46 7

2015–16 Colchester U 42 4 **166 20**

2016–17 Leyton Orient 36 8 **36 8**

McCALLUM, Paul (F) 75 21

H: 6 3 W: 12 00 b.Streatham 28-7-93

2010–11 West Ham U 0 0

2011–12 West Ham U 0 0

2011–12 *Rochdale* 0 0

2012–13 West Ham U 0 0

2012–13 *AFC Wimbledon* 9 4 **9 4**

2012–13 *Aldershot T* 9 3 **9 3**

2013–14 West Ham U 0 0

2013–14 *Torquay U* 5 3 **5 3**

2013–14 *Hearts* 6 0 **6 0**

2014–15 West Ham U 0 0

2014–15 *Portsmouth* 7 0 **7 0**

2015–16 Leyton Orient 10 3

2016–17 Leyton Orient 29 8 **39 11**

McLEAN, Rian (D) 0 0

2016–17 Leyton Orient 0 0

MEZAGUE, Teddy (D) 118 5

H: 6 1 W: 13 01 b.Marseille 27-5-90

2011–12 Montpellier 0 0

2011–12 *Martigues* 28 3 **28 3**

2012–13 Montpellier 5 0

2013–14 Montpellier 9 0 **14 0**

2014–15 Mouscron 25 0

2015–16 Mouscron 34 1 **59 1**

2016–17 Leyton Orient 17 1 **17 1**

MONCUR, Freddy (M) 9 0

b. 8-9-96

2015–16 Leyton Orient 0 0

2016–17 Leyton Orient 9 0 **9 0**

MOORE, Sammy (M) 194 16

H: 5 8 W: 9 00 b.Dover 7-9-87

2006–07 Ipswich T 1 0

2007–08 Ipswich T 0 0

2007–08 *Brentford* 20 2 **20 2**

2008–09 Ipswich T 0 0 **1 0**

2011–12 AFC Wimbledon 41 6

2012–13 AFC Wimbledon 28 2

2013–14 AFC Wimbledon 40 4

2014–15 AFC Wimbledon 30 0 **139 12**

2015–16 Leyton Orient 30 2

2016–17 Leyton Orient 4 0 **34 2**

N'NOMO, Ulrich (F) 46 7

H: 5 11 W: 11 09 b.Yaounde 28-2-96

Internationals: France U16, U17, U19, U20.

2014–15 Chateauroux 19 3

2015–16 Chateauroux 21 4 **40 7**

2016–17 Leyton Orient 6 0 **6 0**

OCHIENG, Henry (M) 6 0

H: 5 10 W: 10 08 b.Redbridge 11-11-98

2016–17 Leyton Orient 6 0 **6 0**

PALMER, Oliver (F) 136 20

b.London 21-1-92

2013–14 Mansfield T 38 4

2014–15 Mansfield T 16 1 **54 5**

2015–16 Leyton Orient 45 7

2016–17 Leyton Orient 20 5 **65 12**

2016–17 *Luton T* 17 3 **17 3**

PARKES, Tom (D) 202 4

H: 6 3 W: 12 05 b.Sutton-in-Ashfield 15-1-92

Internationals: England U17. England C.

2008–09 Leicester C 0 0

2009–10 Leicester C 0 0

2009–10 *Burton Alb* 22 1

2010–11 Leicester C 0 0

2010–11 *Yeovil T* 1 0 **1 0**

2010–11 *Burton Alb* 5 0

2011–12 Leicester C 0 0

2011–12 *Burton Alb* 4 0 **31 1**

2011–12 *Bristol R* 14 0

2012–13 Leicester C 0 0

2012–13 Bristol R 40 1

2013–14 Bristol R 44 1

2015–16 Bristol R 31 0 **129 2**

2016–17 Leyton Orient 41 1 **41 1**

PERKINS, Teddy (D) 0 0

2016–17 Leyton Orient 0 0

POLLOCK, Aron (D) 11 0

H: 6 0 W: 11 09 b.Basildon 23-3-98

2015–16 Leyton Orient 2 0

2016–17 Leyton Orient 9 0 **11 0**

SARGEANT, Sam (G) 16 0

H: 6 0 W: 10 08 b. 23-9-97

2014–15 Leyton Orient 0 0

2015–16 Leyton Orient 1 0

2016–17 Leyton Orient 15 0 **16 0**

SEMEDO, Sandro (F) 45 3

H: 5 9 W: 9 11 b. 3-12-96

2015–16 Leyton Orient 3 0

2016–17 Leyton Orient 42 3 **45 3**

SIMPSON, Jay (F) 295 69

H: 5 11 W: 13 04 b.Enfield 1-12-88

Internationals: England U17.

2007–08 Arsenal 0 0

2007–08 *Millwall* 41 6

2008–09 Arsenal 0 0

2008–09 *WBA* 13 1 **13 1**

2009–10 Arsenal 0 0

2009–10 *QPR* 39 12 **39 12**

2010–11 Hull C 32 6

2011–12 Hull C 3 0

2011–12 *Millwall* 16 4 **57 10**

2012–13 Hull C 43 6

2013–14 Hull C 0 0 **78 12**

2014–15 Buriram United 21 1 **21 1**

2014–15 Leyton Orient 28 5

2015–16 Leyton Orient 45 25

2016–17 Leyton Orient 14 3 **87 33**

Transferred to Philadelphia Union, January 2017.

WEIR, Robbie (M) 234 10

H: 5 9 W: 11 07 b.Belfast 9-12-88

Internationals: Northern Ireland U18, U19, U21, B.

2007–08 Sunderland 0 0

2008–09 Sunderland 0 0

2009–10 Sunderland 0 0

2010–11 Sunderland 0 0

2010–11 *Tranmere R* 18 0

2011–12 Tranmere R 39 3 **57 3**

2012–13 Burton Alb 42 5

2013–14 Burton Alb 41 2

2014–15 Burton Alb 41 0

2015–16 Burton Alb 36 0 **160 7**

2016–17 Leyton Orient 17 0 **17 0**

Scholars
Adamson, Patrick James; Adeboyejo, Ayomide Victor; Alderson, Sam Edmund; Balogun, Daniel Olalekan Oladeji; Barker, Charley Samuel; Camilo, Tayaca Andrew; Happe, Daniel Keith; Janata, Arthur Sidney; McLean, Rian Tyrone; Perkins, Teddy Arthur; Roach, Sam David; Sotiriou, Ruel Demetrios; Stevenson, Toby James.

LIVERPOOL (47)

ALEXANDER-ARNOLD, Trent (M) 7 0
b. 7-10-98
Internationals: England U16, U17, U18, U19.

2016–17	Liverpool	7	0	**7**	**0**

BOGDAN, Adam (G) 124 0
H: 6 4 W: 14 02 b.Budapest 27-9-87
Internationals: Hungary U21, Full caps.

2007–08	Bolton W	0	0		
2008–09	Bolton W	0	0		
2009–10	Bolton W	0	0		
2009–10	*Crewe Alex*	1	0	**1**	**0**
2010–11	Bolton W	4	0		
2011–12	Bolton W	20	0		
2012–13	Bolton W	41	0		
2013–14	Bolton W	29	0		
2014–15	Bolton W	10	0	**104**	**0**
2015–16	Liverpool	2	0		
2016–17	Wigan Ath	17	0	**17**	**0**
2016–17	Liverpool	0	0	**2**	**0**

BRANNAGAN, Cameron (M) 16 0
H: 5 11 W: 11 03 b.Manchester 9-5-96
Internationals: England U18, U20.

2013–14	Liverpool	0	0		
2014–15	Liverpool	0	0		
2015–16	Liverpool	3	0		
2016–17	Liverpool	0	0	**3**	**0**
2016–17	*Fleetwood T*	13	0	**13**	**0**

BREWSTER, Rhian (F) 0 0
Internationals: England U17.
From Chelsea.

2016–17	Liverpool	0	0		

CAN, Emre (M) 122 11
H: 6 1 W: 11 09 b.Frankfurt 12-1-94
Internationals: Germany U16, U17, U19, U21, Full caps.

2011–12	Bayern Munich	0	0		
2012–13	Bayern Munich	4	1	**4**	**1**
2013–14	Bayer Leverkusen	29	3	**29**	**3**
2014–15	Liverpool	27	1		
2015–16	Liverpool	30	1		
2016–17	Liverpool	32	5	**89**	**7**

CHIRIVELLA, Pedro (M) 18 2
b. 23-5-97
Internationals: Spain U17.

2014–15	Valencia	0	0		
2015–16	Liverpool	1	0		
2016–17	Liverpool	0	0	**1**	**0**
2016–17	*Go Ahead Eagles*	17	2	**17**	**2**

CLYNE, Nathaniel (D) 286 5
H: 5 9 W: 10 07 b.Stockwell 5-4-91
Internationals: England U19, U21, Full caps.

2008–09	Crystal Palace	26	0		
2009–10	Crystal Palace	22	1		
2010–11	Crystal Palace	46	0		
2011–12	Crystal Palace	28	0	**122**	**1**
2012–13	Southampton	34	1		
2013–14	Southampton	25	0		
2014–15	Southampton	35	2	**94**	**3**
2015–16	Liverpool	33	1		
2016–17	Liverpool	37	0	**70**	**1**

COUTINHO, Philippe (M) 188 43
H: 5 7 W: 10 09 b.Rio de Janeiro 12-6-92
Internationals: Brazil U17, U20, Full caps.

2009–10	Vasco da Gama	7	1	**7**	**1**
2010–11	Inter Milan	12	1		
2011–12	Inter Milan	5	1		
2011–12	*Espanyol*	16	5	**16**	**5**
2012–13	Inter Milan	10	1	**27**	**3**
2012–13	Liverpool	13	3		
2013–14	Liverpool	33	5		
2014–15	Liverpool	35	5		
2015–16	Liverpool	26	8		
2016–17	Liverpool	31	13	**138**	**34**

DUNN, Jack (F) 19 5
H: 5 8 W: 10 08 b.Liverpool 19-11-94
Internationals: England U17, U18, U19.

2011–12	Liverpool	0	0		
2012–13	Liverpool	0	0		
2013–14	Liverpool	0	0		
2014–15	Liverpool	0	0		
2014–15	*Cheltenham T*	5	3	**5**	**3**
2014–15	*Burton Alb*	1	0	**1**	**0**
2015–16	Liverpool	0	0		
2016–17	Liverpool	0	0		
2016–17	*Morecambe*	13	2	**13**	**2**

EJARIA, Oviemuno (M) 2 0
H: 6 0 W: 11 11 b.Southwark 18-11-97
Internationals: England U20.
From Arsenal.

2016–17	Liverpool	2	0	**2**	**0**

FIRMINO, Roberto (M) 244 67
H: 5 11 W: 12 00 b.Maceio 2-10-91
Internationals: Brazil Full caps.

2009	Figueirense	2	0		
2010	Figueirense	36	8	**38**	**8**
2010–11	Hoffenheim	11	3		
2011–12	Hoffenheim	30	7		
2012–13	Hoffenheim	33	5		
2013–14	Hoffenheim	33	16		
2014–15	Hoffenheim	33	7	**140**	**38**
2015–16	Liverpool	31	10		
2016–17	Liverpool	35	11	**66**	**21**

FLANAGAN, John (D) 46 1
H: 5 11 W: 12 06 b.Liverpool 1-1-93
Internationals: England U19, U20, U21, Full caps.

2010–11	Liverpool	7	0		
2011–12	Liverpool	5	0		
2012–13	Liverpool	0	0		
2013–14	Liverpool	23	1		
2014–15	Liverpool	0	0		
2015–16	Liverpool	5	0		
2016–17	Liverpool	0	0	**40**	**1**
2016–17	*Burnley*	6	0	**6**	**0**

FULTON, Ryan (G) 38 0
H: 6 0 W: 12 00 b.Burnley 23-5-96
Internationals: Scotland U16, U19, U21.

2015–16	Liverpool	0	0		
2015–16	*Portsmouth*	12	0	**12**	**0**
2016–17	Liverpool	0	0		
2016–17	*Chesterfield*	26	0	**26**	**0**

GOMEZ, Joseph (D) 26 0
H: 6 2 W: 14 00 b.Catford 23-5-97
Internationals: England U16, U17, U19, U21.

2014–15	Charlton Ath	21	0	**21**	**0**
2015–16	Liverpool	5	0		
2016–17	Liverpool	0	0	**5**	**0**

GRUJIC, Marko (M) 49 8
b. 13-4-96
Internationals: Serbia U16, U17, U19, U20, U21, Full caps.

2012–13	Red Star Belgrade	1	0		
2013–14	Red Star Belgrade	0	0		
2014–15	Red Star Belgrade	9	0		
2014–15	*Kolubara*	5	2	**5**	**2**
2015–16	Red Star Belgrade	29	6	**39**	**6**
2016–17	Liverpool	5	0	**5**	**0**

HART, Sam (D) 11 1
b. 10-9-96

2016–17	Liverpool	0	0		
2016–17	*Port Vale*	11	1	**11**	**1**

HENDERSON, Jordan (M) 261 25
H: 6 0 W: 10 07 b.Sunderland 17-6-90
Internationals: England U19, U20, U21, Full caps.

2008–09	Sunderland	1	0		
2008–09	*Coventry C*	10	1	**10**	**1**
2009–10	Sunderland	33	1		
2010–11	Sunderland	37	3	**71**	**4**
2011–12	Liverpool	37	2		
2012–13	Liverpool	30	5		
2013–14	Liverpool	35	4		
2014–15	Liverpool	37	6		
2015–16	Liverpool	17	2		
2016–17	Liverpool	24	1	**180**	**20**

INGS, Danny (F) 155 47
H: 5 10 W: 11 07 b.Winchester 16-3-92
Internationals: England U21, Full caps.

2009–10	Bournemouth	0	0		
2010–11	Bournemouth	26	7		
2011–12	Bournemouth	1	0	**27**	**7**
2011–12	Burnley	15	3		
2012–13	Burnley	32	3		
2013–14	Burnley	40	21		
2014–15	Burnley	35	11	**122**	**38**
2015–16	Liverpool	6	2		
2016–17	Liverpool	0	0	**6**	**2**

JONES, Lloyd (D) 51 3
H: 6 3 W: 11 11 b.Plymouth 7-10-95
Internationals: Wales U17, U18. England U19, U20.

2012–13	Liverpool	0	0		
2013–14	Liverpool	0	0		
2014–15	Liverpool	0	0		
2014–15	*Cheltenham T*	6	0	**6**	**0**
2014–15	*Accrington S*	11	1	**11**	**1**
2015–16	Liverpool	0	0		
2015–16	*Blackpool*	10	0	**10**	**0**
2016–17	Liverpool	0	0		
2016–17	*Swindon T*	24	2	**24**	**2**

KARIUS, Loris (G) 101 0
H: 6 2 W: 11 11 b.Biberach 22-6-93

2009–10	Manchester C	0	0		
2010–11	Manchester C	0	0		
2011–12	Manchester C	0	0		
2012–13	Manchester C	0	0		
2012–13	Mainz 05	1	0		
2013–14	Mainz 05	23	0		
2014–15	Mainz 05	33	0		
2015–16	Mainz 05	34	0	**91**	**0**
2016–17	Liverpool	10	0	**10**	**0**

KENT, Ryan (M) 61 4
H: 5 8 W: 10 03 b.Oldham 11-11-96
Internationals: England U18, U20.

2015–16	Liverpool	0	0		
2015–16	*Coventry C*	17	1	**17**	**1**
2016–17	Liverpool	0	0		
2016–17	*Barnsley*	44	3	**44**	**3**

KLAVAN, Ragnar (D) 401 17
H: 6 1 W: 12 02 b.Viljandi 31-10-85

2001	Elva	25	5	**25**	**5**
2002	Tulevik	18	0		
2003	Tulevik	10	2	**28**	**2**
2003	Flora	12	1		
2004	Flora	16	1		
2004	*Valerenga*	2	0		
2005	Flora	0	0	**28**	**2**
2005	*Valerenga*	0	0	**2**	**0**
2005–06	Heracles	15	0		
2006–07	Heracles	32	1		
2007–08	Heracles	29	2		
2008–09	Heracles	19	1	**95**	**4**
2008–09	*AZ Alkmaar*	12	0		
2009–10	AZ Alkmaar	11	0		
2010–11	AZ Alkmaar	28	0		
2011–12	AZ Alkmaar	27	0	**78**	**0**
2012–13	Augsburg	30	0		
2013–14	Augsburg	30	2		
2014–15	Augsburg	34	2		
2015–16	Augsburg	31	0	**125**	**4**
2016–17	Liverpool	20	0	**20**	**0**

LALLANA, Adam (M) 326 65
H: 5 8 W: 11 06 b.St Albans 10-5-88
Internationals: England U18, U19, U21, Full caps.

2005–06	Southampton	0	0		
2006–07	Southampton	1	0		
2007–08	Southampton	5	1		
2007–08	*Bournemouth*	3	0	**3**	**0**
2008–09	Southampton	40	1		
2009–10	Southampton	44	15		
2010–11	Southampton	36	8		
2011–12	Southampton	41	11		
2012–13	Southampton	30	3		
2013–14	Southampton	38	9	**235**	**48**
2014–15	Liverpool	27	5		
2015–16	Liverpool	30	4		
2016–17	Liverpool	31	8	**88**	**17**

LOVREN, Dejan (D) 269 8
H: 6 2 W: 13 02 b.Karlovac 5-7-89
Internationals: Croatia U17, U18, U19, U20, U21, Full caps.

2005–06	Dinamo Zagreb	1	0		
2006–07	Dinamo Zagreb	0	0		
2006–07	*Inter Zapresic*	21	0		
2007–08	Dinamo Zagreb	0	0		
2007–08	*Inter Zapresic*	29	1	**50**	**1**
2008–09	Dinamo Zagreb	22	1		
2009–10	Dinamo Zagreb	14	0	**37**	**1**
2009–10	Lyon	8	0		
2010–11	Lyon	28	0		
2011–12	Lyon	18	1		
2012–13	Lyon	18	1	**72**	**2**
2013–14	Southampton	31	2	**31**	**2**
2014–15	Liverpool	26	0		
2015–16	Liverpool	24	0		
2016–17	Liverpool	29	2	**79**	**2**

LUCAS (M) **280** **5**
H: 5 10 W: 11 09 b.Dourados 9-1-87
Internationals: Brazil U20, U23, Full caps.

2005	Gremio	3	0		
2006	Gremio	30	4	**33**	**4**
2007–08	Liverpool	18	0		
2008–09	Liverpool	25	1		
2009–10	Liverpool	35	0		
2010–11	Liverpool	33	0		
2011–12	Liverpool	12	0		
2012–13	Liverpool	26	0		
2013–14	Liverpool	27	0		
2014–15	Liverpool	20	0		
2015–16	Liverpool	27	0		
2016–17	Liverpool	24	0	**247**	**1**

MANE, Sadio (F) **179** **67**
H: 5 9 W: 12 00 b.Sedhiou 10-4-92
Internationals: Senegal U23, Full caps.

2011–12	Metz	19	1		
2012–13	Metz	3	1	**22**	**2**
2012–13	Red Bull Salzburg	26	16		
2013–14	Red Bull Salzburg	33	13		
2014–15	Red Bull Salzburg	4	2	**63**	**31**
2014–15	Southampton	30	10		
2015–16	Southampton	37	11	**67**	**21**
2016–17	Liverpool	27	13	**27**	**13**

MANNINGER, Alex (G) **256** **0**
H: 6 2 W: 13 03 b.Salzburg 4-6-77
Internationals: Austria Full caps.

1995–96	Salzburg	1	0	**1**	**0**
1995–96	*Vorwaerts Steyr*	5	0	**5**	**0**
1996–97	Graz	23	0	**23**	**0**
1997–98	Arsenal	7	0		
1998–99	Arsenal	6	0		
1999–2000	Arsenal	15	0		
2000–01	Arsenal	11	0		
2001–02	Arsenal	0	0	**39**	**0**
2001–02	*Fiorentina*	24	0	**24**	**0**
2002–03	Espanyol	0	0		
2002–03	Torino	3	0	**3**	**0**
2003–04	Bologna	0	0		
2004–05	Bologna	0	0		
2004–05	*Siena*	18	0		
2005–06	Red Bull Salzburg	16	0	**16**	**0**
2006–07	Siena	38	0		
2007–08	Siena	26	0	**82**	**0**
2008–09	Udinese	0	0		
2008–09	Juventus	16	0		
2009–10	Juventus	11	0		
2010–11	Juventus	0	0		
2011–12	Juventus	0	0	**27**	**0**
2012–13	Augsburg	12	0		
2013–14	Augsburg	13	0		
2014–15	Augsburg	9	0		
2015–16	Augsburg	2	0	**36**	**0**
2016–17	Liverpool	0	0		

MARKOVIC, Lazar (F) **123** **23**
H: 5 9 W: 10 03 b.Cacak 2-3-94
Internationals: Serbia U17, U21, Full caps.

2010–11	Partizan Belgrade	1	0		
2011–12	Partizan Belgrade	26	6		
2012–13	Partizan Belgrade	19	7	**46**	**13**
2013–14	Benfica	26	5	**26**	**5**
2014–15	Liverpool	19	2		
2015–16	Liverpool	0	0		
2015–16	*Fenerbahce*	14	0	**14**	**0**
2016–17	Liverpool	0	0	**19**	**2**
2016–17	*Sporting Lisbon*	6	1	**6**	**1**
2016–17	*Hull C*	12	2	**12**	**2**

MATIP, Joel (M) **223** **15**
H: 6 4 W: 13 01 b.Bochum 8-8-91
Internationals: Cameroon Full caps.

2009–10	Schalke 04	20	3		
2010–11	Schalke 04	26	0		
2011–12	Schalke 04	30	3		
2012–13	Schalke 04	32	0		
2013–14	Schalke 04	31	3		
2014–15	Schalke 04	21	2		
2015–16	Schalke 04	34	3	**194**	**14**
2016–17	Liverpool	29	1	**29**	**1**

MIGNOLET, Simon (G) **348** **1**
H: 6 4 W: 13 10 b.St Truiden 6-3-88
Internationals: Belgium U16, U17, U18, U19, U20, U21, Full caps.

2006–07	St Truiden	2	0		
2007–08	St Truiden	25	0		
2008–09	St Truiden	35	1		
2009–10	St Truiden	37	0		
2010–11	St Truiden	23	0	**122**	**1**
2010–11	Sunderland	23	0		
2011–12	Sunderland	29	0		
2012–13	Sunderland	38	0	**90**	**0**
2013–14	Liverpool	38	0		
2014–15	Liverpool	36	0		
2015–16	Liverpool	34	0		
2016–17	Liverpool	28	0	**136**	**0**

MILNER, James (M) **459** **50**
H: 5 9 W: 11 00 b.Leeds 4-1-86
Internationals: England U16, U17, U19, U20, U21, Full caps.

2002–03	Leeds U	18	2		
2003–04	Leeds U	30	3	**48**	**5**
2003–04	*Swindon T*	6	2	**6**	**2**
2004–05	Newcastle U	25	1		
2005–06	Newcastle U	3	0		
2005–06	*Aston Villa*	27	1		
2006–07	Newcastle U	35	3		
2007–08	Newcastle U	29	2		
2008–09	Newcastle U	2	0	**94**	**6**
2008–09	Aston Villa	36	3		
2009–10	Aston Villa	36	7		
2010–11	Aston Villa	1	1	**100**	**12**
2010–11	Manchester C	32	0		
2011–12	Manchester C	26	3		
2012–13	Manchester C	26	4		
2013–14	Manchester C	31	1		
2014–15	Manchester C	32	5	**147**	**13**
2015–16	Liverpool	28	5		
2016–17	Liverpool	36	7	**64**	**12**

MORENO, Alberto (D) **127** **6**
H: 5 7 W: 10 01 b.Seville 5-7-92
Internationals: Spain U21, Full caps.

2011–12	Sevilla	11	0		
2012–13	Sevilla	15	0		
2013–14	Sevilla	29	3	**55**	**3**
2014–15	Liverpool	28	2		
2015–16	Liverpool	32	1		
2016–17	Liverpool	12	0	**72**	**3**

OJO, Sheyi (M) **36** **2**
H: 5 10 W: 10 01 b.Hemel Hempstead 19-6-97
Internationals: England U16, U17, U18, U19, U20.

2014–15	Liverpool	0	0		
2014–15	*Wigan Ath*	11	0	**11**	**0**
2015–16	Liverpool	8	0		
2015–16	*Wolverhampton W*	17	2	**17**	**2**
2016–17	Liverpool	0	0	**8**	**0**

ORIGI, Divock (F) **123** **26**
H: 6 1 W: 11 11 b.Oostende 18-4-95
Internationals: Belgium U16, U17, U19, U21, Full caps.

2012–13	Lille	10	1		
2013–14	Lille	30	5		
2014–15	Lille	33	8	**73**	**14**
2015–16	Liverpool	16	5		
2016–17	Liverpool	34	7	**50**	**12**

PAULINHO, Paulo (M) **0** **0**
From Porto.

2016–17	Liverpool	0	0		

RANDALL, Connor (D) **4** **0**
H: 5 11 W: 12 00 b.Liverpool 21-10-95
Internationals: England U17.

2014–15	Liverpool	0	0		
2014–15	*Shrewsbury T*	1	0	**1**	**0**
2015–16	Liverpool	3	0		
2016–17	Liverpool	0	0	**3**	**0**

SAKHO, Mamadou (D) **215** **9**
H: 6 2 W: 12 07 b.Paris 13-2-90
Internationals: France U16, U17, U18, U19, U21, Full caps.

2006–07	Paris Saint-Germain	0	0		
2007–08	Paris Saint-Germain	12	0		
2008–09	Paris Saint-Germain	23	1		
2009–10	Paris Saint-Germain	32	0		
2010–11	Paris Saint-Germain	35	4		
2011–12	Paris Saint-Germain	22	0		
2012–13	Paris Saint-Germain	27	2	**151**	**7**
2013–14	Liverpool	18	1		
2014–15	Liverpool	16	0		
2015–16	Liverpool	22	1		
2016–17	Liverpool	0	0	**56**	**2**
2016–17	*Crystal Palace*	8	0	**8**	**0**

STEWART, Kevin (D) **31** **3**
H: 5 7 W: 11 06 b.Enfield 7-9-93

2012–13	Tottenham H	0	0		
2012–13	*Crewe Alex*	4	0		
2013–14	Crewe Alex	0	0	**4**	**0**
2014–15	Liverpool	0	0		
2014–15	*Cheltenham T*	4	1	**4**	**1**
2014–15	*Burton Alb*	7	2	**7**	**2**
2015–16	Liverpool	7	0		
2015–16	*Swindon T*	5	0	**5**	**0**
2016–17	Liverpool	4	0	**11**	**0**

STURRIDGE, Daniel (F) **185** **72**
H: 6 2 W: 12 00 b.Birmingham 1-9-89
Internationals: England U16, U17, U18, U19, U20, U21, Full caps. Great Britain.

2006–07	Manchester C	2	0		
2007–08	Manchester C	3	1		
2008–09	Manchester C	16	4		
2009–10	Manchester C	0	0	**21**	**5**
2009–10	Chelsea	13	1		
2010–11	Chelsea	13	0		
2010–11	*Bolton W*	12	8	**12**	**8**
2011–12	Chelsea	30	11		
2012–13	Chelsea	7	1	**63**	**13**
2012–13	Liverpool	14	10		
2013–14	Liverpool	29	21		
2014–15	Liverpool	12	4		
2015–16	Liverpool	14	8		
2016–17	Liverpool	20	3	**89**	**46**

WARD, Danny (G) **71** **0**
H: 5 11 W: 13 12 b.Wrexham 22-6-93
Internationals: Wales U17, U19, U21, Full caps.

2011–12	Liverpool	0	0		
2012–13	Liverpool	0	0		
2013–14	Liverpool	0	0		
2014–15	Liverpool	0	0		
2014–15	*Morecambe*	5	0	**5**	**0**
2015–16	Liverpool	2	0		
2015–16	*Aberdeen*	21	0	**21**	**0**
2016–17	Liverpool	0	0	**2**	**0**
2016–17	*Huddersfield T*	43	0	**43**	**0**

WIJNALDUM, Georginio (M) **294** **81**
H: 5 8 W: 10 10 b.Rotterdam 11-11-90
Internationals: Netherlands U17, U19, U21, Full caps.

2006–07	Feyenoord	3	0		
2007–08	Feyenoord	10	1		
2008–09	Feyenoord	33	4		
2009–10	Feyenoord	31	4		
2010–11	Feyenoord	34	14	**111**	**23**
2011–12	PSV Eindhoven	32	9		
2012–13	PSV Eindhoven	33	14		
2013–14	PSV Eindhoven	11	4		
2014–15	PSV Eindhoven	33	14	**109**	**41**
2015–16	Newcastle U	38	11	**38**	**11**
2016–17	Liverpool	36	6	**36**	**6**

WILLIAMS, Jordan (M) **17** **0**
H: 6 0 W: 12 02 b.Bangor 6-11-95
Internationals: Wales U17, U21.

2014–15	Liverpool	0	0		
2014–15	*Notts Co*	8	0	**8**	**0**
2015–16	Liverpool	0	0		
2015–16	*Swindon T*	9	0		
2016–17	Liverpool	0	0		
2016–17	*Swindon T*	0	0	**9**	**0**

WILSON, Harry (M) **7** **0**
H: 5 8 W: 11 00 b.Wrexham 22-3-97
Internationals: Wales U17, U19, U21, Full caps.

2015–16	Liverpool	0	0		
2015–16	*Crewe Alex*	7	0	**7**	**0**
2016–17	Liverpool	0	0		

WISDOM, Andre (D) **98** **0**
H: 6 1 W: 12 04 b.Leeds 9-5-93
Internationals: England U16, U17, U19, U21.

2009–10	Liverpool	0	0		
2010–11	Liverpool	0	0		
2011–12	Liverpool	0	0		
2012–13	Liverpool	12	0		
2013–14	Liverpool	2	0		
2013–14	*Derby Co*	34	0	**34**	**0**
2014–15	Liverpool	0	0		
2014–15	*WBA*	24	0	**24**	**0**
2015–16	Liverpool	0	0		
2015–16	*Norwich C*	10	0	**10**	**0**
2016–17	Liverpool	0	0	**14**	**0**
2016–17	*Red Bull Salzburg*	16	0	**16**	**0**

WOODBURN, Ben (F) **5** **0**
H: 5 9 W: 11 05 b.Chester 16-11-99
Internationals: Wales U16, U17, U19.

2016–17	Liverpool	5	0	**5**	**0**

Players retained or with offer of contract
Adekanye, Omobolaji Habeeb; Awoniyi, Taiwo; Correia, Gomes Toni; Coyle, Liam; Dhanda, Yan; Firth, Andrew; Garcia, Rey Juan Manuel; George, Shamal; Grabara, Kamil; Johnston, George; Jones, Lloyd Richard; Kane, Herbie; Kelleher, Caoimhin; Lennon, Brooks; Masterson, Conor; McAuley, Glen; Millar, Liam; Neves, Alves Paulo Manuel; Phillips, Nathaniel Harry;

Rodrigues, De Souza Allan; Virtue, Thick Matthew Joseph; Whelan, Corey.

Scholars
Atherton, Daniel; Brewster, Rhian; Camacho, Rafael Euclides Soares; Driscoll-Glennon, Anthony; Hunter, Jordan; Lattie, Diego Omar; Lewis, Adam; Parker, Mich'El; Simmonds, Okera; Whyte, Harvey; Williams, Ben.

LUTON T (48)

ATKINSON, Alex (M) 0 0
2016–17 Luton T 0 0

BAKINSON, Tyreeq (M) 1 0
H: 6 1 W: 11 00 b.Camden 8-1-98
2015–16 Luton T 1 0
2016–17 Luton T 0 0 **1 0**

BANTON, Zane (F) 4 0
H: 5 8 W: 11 07 b. 6-6-96
2014–15 Luton T 0 0
2015–16 Luton T 4 0
2016–17 Luton T 0 0 **4 0**

BEAN, Harry (D) 0 0
2016–17 Luton T 0 0

COOK, Jordan (F) 142 16
H: 5 10 W: 10 10 b.Hetton-le-Hole 20-3-90
2007–08 Sunderland 0 0
2008–09 Sunderland 0 0
2009–10 Sunderland 0 0
2009–10 *Darlington* 5 0 **5 0**
2010–11 Sunderland 3 0
2010–11 *Walsall* 8 1
2011–12 Sunderland 0 0 **3 0**
2011–12 *Carlisle U* 14 4 **14 4**
2012–13 Charlton Ath 7 0
2012–13 *Yeovil T* 1 0 **1 0**
2013–14 Charlton Ath 3 0 **10 0**
2014–15 Walsall 32 5
2015–16 Walsall 34 3 **74 9**
2016–17 Luton T 35 3 **35 3**

COTTER, Kavan (M) 0 0
b.Harrow
2016–17 Luton T 0 0

CUTHBERT, Scott (D) 320 14
H: 6 2 W: 14 00 b.Alexandria 15-6-87
Internationals: Scotland U19, U20, U21, B.
2004–05 Celtic 0 0
2005–06 Celtic 0 0
2006–07 Celtic 0 0
2006–07 *Livingston* 4 1 **4 1**
2007–08 Celtic 0 0
2008–09 Celtic 0 0
2008–09 *St Mirren* 29 0 **29 0**
2009–10 Swindon T 39 3
2010–11 Swindon T 41 2 **80 5**
2011–12 Leyton Orient 33 1
2012–13 Leyton Orient 18 0
2013–14 Leyton Orient 44 4
2014–15 Leyton Orient 38 2 **133 7**
2015–16 Luton T 36 0
2016–17 Luton T 38 1 **74 1**

D'ATH, Lawson (M) 137 15
H: 5 9 W: 12 02 b.Witney 24-12-92
2010–11 Reading 0 0
2011–12 Reading 0 0
2011–12 *Yeovil T* 14 1 **14 1**
2012–13 Reading 0 0
2012–13 *Cheltenham T* 2 1 **2 1**
2012–13 *Exeter C* 8 1 **8 1**
2013–14 Reading 0 0
2013–14 *Dagenham & R* 21 1 **21 1**
2014–15 Northampton T 41 7
2015–16 Northampton T 39 4
2016–17 Northampton T 1 0 **81 11**
2016–17 Luton T 11 0 **11 0**

FAMEWO, Akin (D) 3 0
H: 5 11 W: 10 06 b.Lewisham 9-11-98
2016–17 Luton T 3 0 **3 0**

GAMBIN, Luke (M) 90 11
H: 5 6 W: 11 00 b.Surrey 16-3-93
Internationals: Malta Full caps.
2011–12 Barnet 1 0
2012–13 Barnet 10 2
2015–16 Barnet 44 4
2016–17 Barnet 19 4 **74 10**
2016–17 Luton T 16 1 **16 1**

GOOCH, Liam (G) 0 0
b.Borehamwood 25-11-97
2014–15 Luton T 0 0
2015–16 Luton T 0 0
2016–17 Luton T 0 0

GRAY, Jake (F) 52 6
H: 5 11 W: 11 00 b.Aylesbury 25-12-95
2014–15 Crystal Palace 0 0
2014–15 *Cheltenham T* 4 0 **4 0**
2015–16 Crystal Palace 0 0
2015–16 *Hartlepool U* 29 5 **29 5**
2016–17 Luton T 19 1 **19 1**

HINDS, Freddy (F) 0 0
b.Potton
2016–17 Luton T 0 0

HYLTON, Danny (F) 303 82
H: 6 0 W: 11 13 b.Camden 25-2-89
2008–09 Aldershot T 29 5
2009–10 Aldershot T 21 3
2010–11 Aldershot T 33 5
2011–12 Aldershot T 44 13
2012–13 Aldershot T 27 4 **154 30**
2013–14 Rotherham U 1 0 **1 0**
2013–14 *Bury* 7 2 **7 2**
2013–14 *AFC Wimbledon* 17 3 **17 3**
2014–15 Oxford U 44 14
2015–16 Oxford U 41 12 **85 26**
2016–17 Luton T 39 21 **39 21**

JUSTIN, James (F) 30 1
H: 6 0 W: 11 03 b.Luton 11-7-97
2015–16 Luton T 1 0
2016–17 Luton T 29 1 **30 1**

KING, Craig (G) 0 0
H: 6 0 W: 10 06 b. 1-7-97
2014–15 Luton T 0 0
2015–16 Luton T 0 0
2016–17 Luton T 0 0

LEE, Oliver (M) 138 10
H: 5 11 W: 12 07 b.Hornchurch 11-7-91
2009–10 West Ham U 0 0
2010–11 West Ham U 0 0
2010–11 *Dagenham & R* 5 0
2011–12 West Ham U 0 0
2011–12 *Dagenham & R* 16 3 **21 3**
2011–12 *Gillingham* 8 0 **8 0**
2012–13 Barnet 11 0 **11 0**
2012–13 Birmingham C 0 0
2013–14 Birmingham C 16 1
2014–15 Birmingham C 0 0 **16 1**
2014–15 *Plymouth Arg* 15 2 **15 2**
2015–16 Luton T 34 3
2016–17 Luton T 33 1 **67 4**

MACKAIL-SMITH, Craig (F) 350 110
H: 6 3 W: 12 04 b.Watford 25-2-84
Internationals: England C. Scotland Full caps.
2006–07 Peterborough U 15 8
2007–08 Peterborough U 36 12
2008–09 Peterborough U 46 23
2009–10 Peterborough U 43 10
2010–11 Peterborough U 45 27
2011–12 Brighton & HA 45 9
2012–13 Brighton & HA 29 11
2013–14 Brighton & HA 5 0
2014–15 Brighton & HA 30 1 **109 21**
2014–15 *Peterborough U* 3 0
2015–16 Luton T 33 4
2016–17 Luton T 2 0 **35 4**
2016–17 *Peterborough U* 18 5 **206 85**

MARRIOTT, Jack (F) 91 23
H: 5 8 W: 11 03 b.Beverley 9-9-94
2012–13 Ipswich T 1 0
2013–14 Ipswich T 1 0
2013–14 *Gillingham* 1 0 **1 0**
2014–15 Ipswich T 0 0 **2 0**
2014–15 *Carlisle U* 4 0 **4 0**
2014–15 *Colchester U* 5 1 **5 1**
2015–16 Luton T 40 14
2016–17 Luton T 39 8 **79 22**

McGEEHAN, Cameron (M) 84 28
H: 5 11 W: 11 03 b.Kingston upon Thames 6-4-95
Internationals: Northern Ireland U17, U19, U21.
2013–14 Norwich C 0 0
2014–15 Norwich C 0 0
2014–15 *Luton T* 15 3
2014–15 *Cambridge U* 4 3 **4 3**
2015–16 Luton T 41 12
2016–17 Luton T 24 10 **80 25**

McQUOID, Josh (F) 213 23
H: 5 9 W: 10 10 b.Southampton 15-12-89
Internationals: Northern Ireland U19, U21, B, Full caps.
2006–07 Bournemouth 2 0
2007–08 Bournemouth 5 0
2008–09 Bournemouth 16 0
2009–10 Bournemouth 29 1
2010–11 Bournemouth 17 9
2010–11 Millwall 11 1
2011–12 Millwall 5 0 **16 1**
2011–12 *Burnley* 17 1 **17 1**
2012–13 Bournemouth 34 3
2013–14 Bournemouth 1 0
2013–14 *Peterborough U* 14 1 **14 1**
2014–15 Bournemouth 0 0 **104 13**
2014–15 *Coventry C* 14 3 **14 3**
2015–16 Luton T 29 3
2016–17 Luton T 3 0 **32 3**
2016–17 *Stevenage* 16 1 **16 1**

MULLINS, John (D) 425 24
H: 5 11 W: 12 07 b.Hampstead 6-11-85
2004–05 Reading 0 0
2004–05 *Kidderminster H* 21 2 **21 2**
2005–06 Reading 0 0
2006–07 Mansfield T 43 2
2007–08 Mansfield T 43 2 **86 4**
2008–09 Stockport Co 33 3
2009–10 Stockport Co 36 1 **69 4**
2010–11 Rotherham U 35 1
2011–12 Rotherham U 35 2
2012–13 Rotherham U 29 4 **99 7**
2012–13 *Oxford U* 8 2
2013–14 Oxford U 35 3
2014–15 Oxford U 44 2
2015–16 Oxford U 40 0 **127 7**
2016–17 Luton T 23 0 **23 0**

MUSONDA, Frankie (D) 3 0
H: 6 0 W: 11 03 b.Bedford 12-12-97
2015–16 Luton T 3 0
2016–17 Luton T 0 0 **3 0**

O'DONNELL, Stephen (D) 181 10
H: 6 0 W: 11 10 b.Bellshill 11-5-92
Internationals: Scotland U21.
2011–12 Partick Thistle 31 2
2012–13 Partick Thistle 29 2
2013–14 Partick Thistle 27 0
2014–15 Partick Thistle 34 5 **121 9**
2015–16 Luton T 30 0
2016–17 Luton T 30 1 **60 1**

POTTS, Danny (D) 52 0
H: 5 8 W: 11 00 b.Barking 13-4-94
Internationals: USA U20. England U18, U19, U20.
2011–12 West Ham U 3 0
2012–13 West Ham U 2 0
2012–13 *Colchester U* 5 0 **5 0**
2013–14 West Ham U 0 0
2013–14 *Portsmouth* 5 0 **5 0**
2014–15 West Ham U 0 0 **5 0**
2015–16 Luton T 14 0
2016–17 Luton T 23 0 **37 0**

REA, Glen (D) 63 2
H: 6 0 W: 11 07 b.Brighton 3-9-94
Internationals: Republic of Ireland U21.
2013–14 Brighton & HA 0 0
2014–15 Brighton & HA 0 0
2015–16 Brighton & HA 0 0
2015–16 *Southend U* 14 0 **14 0**
2015–16 *Luton T* 10 0
2016–17 Luton T 39 2 **49 2**

RUDDOCK, Pelly (M) 79 5
H: 5 9 W: 9 13 b.Hendon 17-7-93
2011–12 West Ham U 0 0
2013–14 West Ham U 0 0
2014–15 Luton T 16 1
2015–16 Luton T 21 2
2016–17 Luton T 42 2 **79 5**

SENIOR, Jack (D) 10 0
H: 5 8 W: 9 13 b.Halifax 13-1-97
2015–16 Huddersfield T 0 0
2016–17 Luton T 10 0 **10 0**

SHEEHAN, Alan (D) 317 21
H: 5 11 W: 11 02 b.Athlone 14-9-86
Internationals: Republic of Ireland U21.
2004–05 Leicester C 1 0
2005–06 Leicester C 2 0
2006–07 Leicester C 0 0
2006–07 *Mansfield T* 10 0 **10 0**
2007–08 Leicester C 20 1 **23 1**
2007–08 *Leeds U* 10 1
2008–09 Leeds U 11 1

2008–09	*Crewe Alex*	3	0	**3**	**0**
2009–10	Leeds U	0	0	**21**	**2**
2009–10	*Oldham Ath*	8	1	**8**	**1**
2009–10	*Swindon T*	22	1		
2010–11	Swindon T	21	1	**43**	**2**
2011–12	Notts Co	39	2		
2012–13	Notts Co	33	0		
2013–14	Notts Co	42	7		
2014–15	Bradford C	23	1		
2014–15	*Peterborough U*	2	0	**2**	**0**
2015–16	Bradford C	2	0	**25**	**1**
2015–16	*Notts Co*	14	2	**128**	**11**
2015–16	*Luton T*	20	1		
2016–17	Luton T	34	2	**54**	**3**

SMITH, Jonathan (M) **147 10**
H: 6 3 W: 11 02 b.Preston 17-10-86

2011–12	Swindon T	38	3	**38**	**3**
2012–13	York C	12	0	**12**	**0**
2014–15	Luton T	35	2		
2015–16	Luton T	37	4		
2016–17	Luton T	25	1	**97**	**7**

TOMLINSON, Connor (F) **0 0**
b. 12-2-01

2016–17	Luton T	0	0		

VASSELL, Isaac (F) **46 8**
H: 5 7 W: 11 02 b.Newquay 9-9-93

2011–12	Plymouth Arg	6	0		
2012–13	Plymouth Arg	0	0		
2013–14	Plymouth Arg	0	0	**6**	**0**

From Truro C.

2016–17	Luton T	40	8	**40**	**8**

Players retained or with offer of contract
Mpanzu, Pelly Ruddock; Read, Arthur James.

Scholars
Bean, Harry George; Belgrove, Scott; Cotter, Kavan John; Craig, Geo Luca; Gordon-Stearn, Ciaran Gabriel Cornelius; James, Jack Alexander; Jones, Ciaren Alexander; Mead, Joe Thomas; Murray, George William; Shamalo, Michel Oladie Ndjova; Snelus, Jack Simon Bez; Sorunke, Olaoluwakitan Jonathan; Verney, James Albert.

MANCHESTER C (49)

ADARABIOYO, Tosin (D) **0 0**
H: 6 3 b. 24-9-97
Internationals: England U16, U17, U18, U19.

2014–15	Manchester C	0	0		
2015–16	Manchester C	0	0		
2016–17	Manchester C	0	0		

AGUERO, Sergio (F) **410 219**
H: 5 8 W: 11 09 b.Buenos Aires 2-6-88
Internationals: Argentina U17, U20, U23, Full caps.

2002–03	Independiente	1	0		
2003–04	Independiente	5	0		
2004–05	Independiente	12	5		
2005–06	Independiente	36	18	**54**	**23**
2006–07	Atletico Madrid	38	6		
2007–08	Atletico Madrid	37	19		
2008–09	Atletico Madrid	37	17		
2009–10	Atletico Madrid	31	12		
2010–11	Atletico Madrid	32	20	**175**	**74**
2011–12	Manchester C	34	23		
2012–13	Manchester C	30	12		
2013–14	Manchester C	23	17		
2014–15	Manchester C	33	26		
2015–16	Manchester C	30	24		
2016–17	Manchester C	31	20	**181**	**122**

BONY, Wilfried (F) **223 101**
H: 6 0 W: 13 11 b.Bingerville 10-12-88
Internationals: Ivory Coast Full caps.

2008–09	Sparta Prague	16	3		
2009–10	Sparta Prague	29	9		
2010–11	Sparta Prague	13	10	**58**	**22**
2010–11	Vitesse	7	3		
2011–12	Vitesse	28	12		
2012–13	Vitesse	30	31	**65**	**46**
2013–14	Swansea C	34	16		
2014–15	Swansea C	20	9	**54**	**25**
2014–15	Manchester C	10	2		
2015–16	Manchester C	26	4		
2016–17	Manchester C	0	0	**36**	**6**
2016–17	*Stoke C*	10	2	**10**	**2**

BRAVO, Claudio (G) **414 2**
H: 6 0 W: 11 00 b.Viluco 13-4-83
Internationals: Chile U23, Full caps.

2003	Colo Colo	25	1		
2004	Colo Colo	18	0		
2005	Colo Colo	36	0		
2006	Colo Colo	14	0	**93**	**1**
2006–07	Real Sociedad	29	0		
2007–08	Real Sociedad	0	0		
2008–09	Real Sociedad	32	0		
2009–10	Real Sociedad	25	1		
2010–11	Real Sociedad	38	0		
2011–12	Real Sociedad	37	0		
2012–13	Real Sociedad	31	0		
2013–14	Real Sociedad	37	0	**229**	**1**
2014–15	Barcelona	37	0		
2015–16	Barcelona	32	0		
2016–17	Barcelona	1	0	**70**	**0**
2016–17	Manchester C	22	0	**22**	**0**

BRYAN, Kean (M) **12 0**
H: 6 1 b.Manchester 1-11-96
Internationals: England U16, U17, U19, U20.

2016–17	Manchester C	0	0		
2016–17	*Bury*	12	0	**12**	**0**

CABALLERO, Willy (G) **321 0**
H: 6 1 W: 12 08 b.Santa Elena 28-9-81
Internationals: Argentina U21.

2001–04	Boca Juniors	15	0	**15**	**0**
2004–08	Elche	67	0		
2008–09	Elche	38	0		
2009–10	Elche	39	0		
2010–11	Elche	22	0	**166**	**0**
2010–11	Malaga	15	0		
2011–12	Malaga	28	0		
2012–13	Malaga	36	0		
2013–14	Malaga	38	0	**117**	**0**
2014–15	Manchester C	2	0		
2015–16	Manchester C	4	0		
2016–17	Manchester C	17	0	**23**	**0**

CLICHY, Gael (D) **325 3**
H: 5 9 W: 10 04 b.Toulouse 26-7-85
Internationals: France U15, U17, U18, U19, 21, B, Full caps.

2003–04	Arsenal	12	0		
2004–05	Arsenal	15	0		
2005–06	Arsenal	7	0		
2006–07	Arsenal	27	0		
2007–08	Arsenal	38	0		
2008–09	Arsenal	31	1		
2009–10	Arsenal	24	0		
2010–11	Arsenal	33	0	**187**	**1**
2011–12	Manchester C	28	0		
2012–13	Manchester C	28	0		
2013–14	Manchester C	20	0		
2014–15	Manchester C	23	1		
2015–16	Manchester C	14	0		
2016–17	Manchester C	25	1	**138**	**2**

DE BRUYNE, Kevin (M) **212 47**
H: 5 11 W: 12 00 b.Ghent 28-6-91
Internationals: Belgium U18, U19, U21, Full caps.

2008–09	Genk	2	0		
2009–10	Genk	30	3		
2010–11	Genk	32	5		
2011–12	Genk	15	6	**79**	**14**
2011–12	Chelsea	0	0		
2012–13	Chelsea	0	0		
2012–13	*Werder Bremen*	33	10	**33**	**10**
2013–14	Chelsea	3	0	**3**	**0**
2014–15	Wolfsburg	34	10		
2015–16	Wolfsburg	2	0	**36**	**10**
2015–16	Manchester C	25	7		
2016–17	Manchester C	36	6	**61**	**13**

DELPH, Fabian (D) **185 12**
H: 5 8 W: 11 00 b.Bradford 21-11-89
Internationals: England U19, U21, Full caps.

2006–07	Leeds U	1	0		
2007–08	Leeds U	1	0		
2008–09	Leeds U	42	6		
2009–10	Aston Villa	8	0		
2010–11	Aston Villa	7	0		
2011–12	Aston Villa	11	0		
2011–12	*Leeds U*	5	0	**49**	**6**
2012–13	Aston Villa	24	0		
2013–14	Aston Villa	34	3		
2014–15	Aston Villa	28	0	**112**	**3**
2015–16	Manchester C	17	2		
2016–17	Manchester C	7	1	**24**	**3**

DENAYER, Jason (D) **70 5**
H: 6 0 W: 12 13 b.Brussels 28-6-95
Internationals: Belgium U19, U21, Full caps.

2013–14	Manchester C	0	0		
2014–15	Manchester C	0	0		
2014–15	*Celtic*	29	5	**29**	**5**
2015–16	Manchester C	0	0		
2015–16	*Galatasaray*	17	0	**17**	**0**
2016–17	Manchester C	0	0		
2016–17	*Sunderland*	24	0	**24**	**0**

DIAZ, Brahim (M) **0 0**
Internationals: Spain U17, U19.
From Malaga.

2016–17	Manchester C	0	0		

FACEY, Shay (D) **30 0**
H: 5 10 W: 10 00 b.Manchester 7-1-95
Internationals: England U16, U17, U19, U20.

2013–14	Manchester C	0	0		
2014–15	Manchester C	0	0		
2014–15	New York City	0	0		
2015–16	Manchester C	0	0		
2015–16	*New York City*	22	0	**22**	**0**
2015–16	*Rotherham U*	5	0	**5**	**0**
2016–17	Manchester C	0	0		
2016–17	*Heerenveen*	3	0	**3**	**0**

FAUPALA, David (F) **17 2**
H: 6 1 b.Bully les Mines 11-2-97
Internationals: France U16, U17, U18.

2014–15	Lens	0	0		
2015–16	Manchester C	0	0		
2016–17	Manchester C	0	0		
2016–17	*NAC*	3	1	**3**	**1**
2016–17	*Chesterfield*	14	1	**14**	**1**

FERNANDINHO, Luis (M) **357 46**
H: 5 10 W: 10 09 b.Londrina 4-5-85
Internationals: Brazil Full caps.

2003	Paranaense	29	5		
2004	Paranaense	41	9		
2005	Paranaense	2	0	**72**	**14**
2005–06	Shakhtar Donetsk	22	1		
2006–07	Shakhtar Donetsk	25	1		
2008–09	Shakhtar Donetsk	21	5		
2009–10	Shakhtar Donetsk	24	4		
2010–11	Shakhtar Donetsk	15	3		
2011–12	Shakhtar Donetsk	24	4		
2012–13	Shakhtar Donetsk	23	2	**154**	**20**
2013–14	Manchester C	33	5		
2014–15	Manchester C	33	3		
2015–16	Manchester C	33	2		
2016–17	Manchester C	32	2	**131**	**12**

FERNANDO, Francisco (M) **232 7**
H: 6 1 W: 11 00 b.Brasilia 25-7-87
Internationals: Brazil U20.

2007–08	Porto	0	0		
2007–08	*Estrella Amadora*	26	1	**26**	**1**
2008–09	Porto	25	0		
2009–10	Porto	25	0		
2010–11	Porto	21	0		
2011–12	Porto	22	1		
2012–13	Porto	24	1		
2013–14	Porto	25	0	**142**	**2**
2014–15	Manchester C	25	2		
2015–16	Manchester C	24	2		
2016–17	Manchester C	15	0	**64**	**4**

FODEN, Phil (M) **0 0**
Internationals: England U16, U17.

2016–17	Manchester C	0	0		

GABRIEL JESUS, Fernando (F) **57 23**
b. 3-4-97
Internationals: Brazil U20, U23, Full caps.

2015	Palmeiras	20	4		
2016	Palmeiras	27	12		
2016–17	Palmeiras	0	0	**47**	**16**
2016–17	Manchester C	10	7	**10**	**7**

GARCIA, Aleix (D) **5 0**
H: 5 8 W: 9 08 b.Ulldecona 28-6-97
Internationals: Spain U16, U17, U18, U19.

2014–15	Villareal	1	0	**1**	**0**
2015–16	Manchester C	0	0		
2016–17	Manchester C	4	0	**4**	**0**

GUNDOGAN, Ilkay (M) **163 19**
H: 5 11 W: 11 00 b.Gelsenkirchen 24-10-90
Internationals: Germany U18, U19, U20, U21, Full caps.

2008–09	Bochum	0	0		
2008–09	Nuremburg	1	0		
2009–10	Nuremburg	22	1		
2010–11	Nuremburg	25	5	**48**	**6**
2011–12	Borussia Dortmund	28	3		
2012–13	Borussia Dortmund	28	3		
2013–14	Borussia Dortmund	1	0		
2014–15	Borussia Dortmund	23	3		
2015–16	Borussia Dortmund	25	1	**105**	**10**
2016–17	Manchester C	10	3	**10**	**3**

GUNN, Angus (G) **0 0**
H: 6 0 W: 12 02 b.Norwich 22-1-96
Internationals: England U16, U17, U18, U19, U21.

2013–14	Manchester C	0	0		
2014–15	Manchester C	0	0		

2015–16 Manchester C 0 0
2016–17 Manchester C 0 0

HART, Joe (G) 401 0
H: 6 3 W: 13 03 b.Shrewsbury 19-4-87
Internationals: England U19, U21, Full caps.
2004–05 Shrewsbury T 6 0
2005–06 Shrewsbury T 46 0 **52 0**
2006–07 Manchester C 1 0
2006–07 *Tranmere R* 6 0 **6 0**
2006–07 *Blackpool* 5 0 **5 0**
2007–08 Manchester C 26 0
2008–09 Manchester C 23 0
2009–10 Manchester C 0 0
2009–10 *Birmingham C* 36 0 **36 0**
2010–11 Manchester C 38 0
2011–12 Manchester C 38 0
2012–13 Manchester C 38 0
2013–14 Manchester C 31 0
2014–15 Manchester C 36 0
2015–16 Manchester C 35 0
2016–17 Manchester C 0 0 **266 0**
2016–17 *Torino* 36 0 **36 0**

IHEANACHO, Kelechi (M) 46 12
H: 6 2 W: 13 08 b.Imo 3-10-96
Internationals: Nigeria U17, U20, Full caps.
2014–15 Manchester C 0 0
2015–16 Manchester C 26 8
2016–17 Manchester C 20 4 **46 12**

JESUS NAVAS, Gonzalez (M) 408 27
H: 5 7 W: 9 05 b.Los Palacios 21-11-85
Internationals: Spain U21, Full caps.
2003–04 Sevilla 5 0
2004–05 Sevilla 23 2
2005–06 Sevilla 34 2
2006–07 Sevilla 29 1
2007–08 Sevilla 36 4
2008–09 Sevilla 35 4
2009–10 Sevilla 34 4
2010–11 Sevilla 15 1
2011–12 Sevilla 37 5
2012–13 Sevilla 37 0 **285 23**
2013–14 Manchester C 30 4
2014–15 Manchester C 35 0
2015–16 Manchester C 34 0
2016–17 Manchester C 24 0 **123 4**

KOLAROV, Aleksandar (D) 329 24
H: 6 2 W: 13 05 b.Belgrade 10-11-85
Internationals: Serbia U21, Full caps.
2004–05 Cukaricki 27 2
2005–06 Cukaricki 17 0 **44 2**
2005–06 OFK Belgrade 11 1
2006–07 OFK Belgrade 27 4 **38 5**
2007–08 Lazio 24 1
2008–09 Lazio 25 2
2009–10 Lazio 33 3 **82 6**
2010–11 Manchester C 24 1
2011–12 Manchester C 12 2
2012–13 Manchester C 20 1
2013–14 Manchester C 30 1
2014–15 Manchester C 21 2
2015–16 Manchester C 29 3
2016–17 Manchester C 29 1 **165 11**

KOMPANY, Vincent (D) 321 21
H: 6 3 W: 13 05 b.Brussels 10-4-86
Internationals: Belgium U16, U17, Full caps.
2004–05 Anderlecht 29 2
2005–06 Anderlecht 32 2 **61 4**
2006–07 Hamburg 6 0
2007–08 Hamburg 22 1
2008–09 Hamburg 1 0 **29 1**
2008–09 Manchester C 34 1
2009–10 Manchester C 25 2
2010–11 Manchester C 37 0
2011–12 Manchester C 31 3
2012–13 Manchester C 26 1
2013–14 Manchester C 28 4
2014–15 Manchester C 25 0
2015–16 Manchester C 14 2
2016–17 Manchester C 11 3 **231 16**

MAFFEO, Pablo (D) 16 1
b. 12-6-97
Internationals: Spain U16, U17, U19.
From Espanyol.
2015–16 Manchester C 0 0
2015–16 *Girona* 2 0
2016–17 Manchester C 0 0
2016–17 *Girona* 14 1 **16 1**

MANGALA, Eliaquim (D) 206 10
H: 6 2 W: 11 09 b.Colombes 13-2-91
Internationals: France U21, Full caps.
2008–09 Standard Liege 11 0
2009–10 Standard Liege 31 1
2010–11 Standard Liege 35 1 **77 2**
2011–12 Porto 7 0
2012–13 Porto 23 4
2013–14 Porto 21 2 **51 6**
2014–15 Manchester C 25 0
2015–16 Manchester C 23 0
2016–17 Manchester C 0 0 **48 0**
2016–17 *Valencia* 30 2 **30 2**

MOOY, Aaron (M) 168 27
H: 5 9 W: 10 10 b.Sydney 15-9-90
Internationals: Australia U20, U23, Full caps.
2009–10 Bolton W 0 0
2010–11 St Mirren 13 0
2011–12 St Mirren 8 1 **21 1**
2012–13 Western Sydney W 23 1
2013–14 Western Sydney W 26 3 **49 4**
2014–15 Melbourne C 27 7
2015–16 Melbourne C 26 11 **53 18**
2016–17 Manchester C 0 0
2016–17 *Huddersfield T* 45 4 **45 4**

NASRI, Samir (M) 359 49
H: 5 9 W: 11 11 b.Marseille 26-6-87
Internationals: France U16, U17, U18, U19, U21, Full caps.
2004–05 Marseille 24 1
2005–06 Marseille 30 1
2006–07 Marseille 37 3
2007–08 Marseille 30 6 **121 11**
2008–09 Arsenal 29 6
2009–10 Arsenal 26 2
2010–11 Arsenal 30 10
2011–12 Arsenal 1 0 **86 18**
2011–12 Manchester C 30 5
2012–13 Manchester C 28 2
2013–14 Manchester C 34 7
2014–15 Manchester C 24 2
2015–16 Manchester C 12 2
2016–17 Manchester C 1 0 **129 18**
2016–17 *Sevilla* 23 2 **23 2**

NOLITO, Manuel Agudo (F) 272 96
H: 5 9 W: 11 07 b.Sanlucar de Barrmeda 15-10-86
Internationals: Spain Full caps.
2005–06 Atletico Sanluqueno 32 24 **32 24**
2006–07 Ecija 31 2
2007–08 Ecija 36 12 **67 14**
2008–09 Barcelona 0 0
2009–10 Barcelona 0 0
2010–11 Barcelona 2 0 **2 0**
2011–12 Benfica 29 11
2012–13 Benfica 6 1 **35 12**
2012–13 *Granada* 17 3 **17 3**
2013–14 Celta Vigo 35 14
2014–15 Celta Vigo 36 13
2015–16 Celta Vigo 29 12 **100 39**
2016–17 Manchester C 19 4 **19 4**

OTAMENDI, Nicolas (D) 217 16
H: 5 10 W: 11 09 b.Buenos Aires 12-2-88
Internationals: Argentina Full caps.
2007–08 Velez Sarsfield 1 0
2008–09 Velez Sarsfield 18 0
2009–10 Velez Sarsfield 19 1
2010–11 Velez Sarsfield 2 0 **40 1**
2010–11 Porto 15 5
2011–12 Porto 20 1
2012–13 Porto 29 1
2013–14 Porto 13 0 **77 7**
2013–14 *Atletico Mineiro* 5 0 **5 0**
2014–15 Valencia 35 6 **35 6**
2015–16 Manchester C 30 1
2016–17 Manchester C 30 1 **60 2**

SAGNA, Bakari (D) 354 4
H: 5 10 W: 11 05 b.Sens 14-2-83
Internationals: France U21, Full caps.
2003–04 Auxerre 0 0
2004–05 Auxerre 26 0
2005–06 Auxerre 23 0
2006–07 Auxerre 38 0 **87 0**
2007–08 Arsenal 29 1
2008–09 Arsenal 35 0
2009–10 Arsenal 35 0
2010–11 Arsenal 33 1
2011–12 Arsenal 21 1
2012–13 Arsenal 25 0
2013–14 Arsenal 35 1 **213 4**
2014–15 Manchester C 9 0
2015–16 Manchester C 28 0
2016–17 Manchester C 17 0 **54 0**

SANE, Leroy (M) 73 16
H: 5 8 W: 9 13 b.Essen 11-1-96
Internationals: Germany U19, U21, Full caps.
2013–14 Schalke 04 1 0
2014–15 Schalke 04 13 3
2015–16 Schalke 04 33 8 **47 11**
2016–17 Manchester C 26 5 **26 5**

SILVA, David (F) 422 69
H: 5 7 W: 10 07 b.Arguineguin 8-1-86
Internationals: Spain U16, U17, U19, U20, U21, Full caps.
2003–04 Mestalla 14 1 **14 1**
2004–05 Eibar 35 5 **35 5**
2005–06 Celta Vigo 34 3 **34 3**
2006–07 Valencia 36 5
2007–08 Valencia 34 4
2008–09 Valencia 19 4
2009–10 Valencia 30 8 **119 21**
2010–11 Manchester C 35 4
2011–12 Manchester C 36 6
2012–13 Manchester C 32 4
2013–14 Manchester C 27 7
2014–15 Manchester C 32 12
2015–16 Manchester C 24 2
2016–17 Manchester C 34 4 **220 39**

STERLING, Raheem (F) 159 31
H: 5 7 W: 10 00 b.Kingston 8-12-94
Internationals: England U16, U17, U19, U21, Full caps.
2011–12 Liverpool 3 0
2012–13 Liverpool 24 2
2013–14 Liverpool 33 9
2014–15 Liverpool 35 7 **95 18**
2015–16 Manchester C 31 6
2016–17 Manchester C 33 7 **64 13**

STONES, John (D) 128 1
H: 6 2 W: 11 00 b.Barnsley 28-5-94
Internationals: England U19, U20, U21, Full caps
2011–12 Barnsley 2 0
2012–13 Barnsley 22 0 **24 0**
2012–13 Everton 0 0
2013–14 Everton 21 0
2014–15 Everton 23 1
2015–16 Everton 33 0 **77 1**
2016–17 Manchester C 27 0 **27 0**

TASENDE, Jose (D) 31 0
H: 5 7 W: 10 10 b.Coristanco 4-1-97
Internationals: Spain U17.
2014–15 Manchester C 0 0
2015 *New York C* 14 0 **14 0**
2015–16 Manchester C 0 0
2016–17 Manchester C 0 0
2016–17 *Mallorca* 17 0 **17 0**

TOURE, Yaya (M) 444 80
H: 6 3 W: 14 02 b.Sokoura Bouake 13-5-83
Internationals: Ivory Coast Full caps.
2001–02 Beveren 28 0
2002–03 Beveren 30 3
2003–04 Beveren 12 0 **70 3**
2003–04 Metalurgs Donetsk 11 1
2004–05 Metalurgs Donetsk 22 2 **33 3**
2005–06 Olympiacos 20 3 **20 3**
2006–07 Monaco 27 5 **27 5**
2007–08 Barcelona 26 1
2008–09 Barcelona 25 2
2009–10 Barcelona 23 1 **74 4**
2010–11 Manchester C 35 8
2011–12 Manchester C 32 6
2012–13 Manchester C 32 7
2013–14 Manchester C 35 20
2014–15 Manchester C 29 10
2015–16 Manchester C 32 6
2016–17 Manchester C 25 5 **220 62**

ZABALETA, Pablo (D) 376 20
H: 5 8 W: 10 12 b.Buenos Aires 16-1-85
Internationals: Argentina U20, U23, Full caps.
2002–03 San Lorenzo 11 0
2003–04 San Lorenzo 27 3
2004–05 San Lorenzo 28 5 **66 8**
2005–06 Espanyol 27 2
2006–07 Espanyol 21 0
2007–08 Espanyol 32 1 **80 3**
2008–09 Manchester C 29 1
2009–10 Manchester C 27 0
2010–11 Manchester C 26 2
2011–12 Manchester C 21 1
2012–13 Manchester C 30 2
2013–14 Manchester C 35 1
2014–15 Manchester C 29 1
2015–16 Manchester C 13 0
2016–17 Manchester C 20 1 **230 9**

Players retained or with offer of contract
Agyepong, Thomas; Agyiri, Ernest; Ambrose, Thierry; Barker, Brandon Lee; Boadu-Adjei, Denzeil; Brattan, Nathan Luke; Buckley-Ricketts, Isaac; Bytyqi, Sinan; Caceres, Anthony; Celina, Bersant; Davenport, Jacob

Alexander; Dele-Bashiru, Ayotomiwa Sherif; Diallo, Sadou; Dilrosun, Javairo Joreno Faustino; Duhaney, Demeaco; Duran, Manuel Agudo; Esmoris, Tasende Jose Angel; Faour, Zackarias; Garcia, Alonso Manuel; Grimshaw, Daniel James; Haug, Christian Kjetil; Herrera, Ravelo Yangel Clemente; Horsfield, James; Humphreys-Grant, Cameron; Kigbu, Ahogrenashinme; Kongolo, Rodney; Luiz, Roza Fernando; Mari, Villar Pablo; Moreno, Duran Marlos; Muric, Arijanet Anan; Naah, Divine Yelsarmba; Nemane, Aaron Evans; Nmecha, Lukas; Ntcham, Jules Olivier; Nwakali, Chidiebere Chikioke; Oliver, Charles William Corrigan; Patching, William Luke; Reges, Fernando Francisco; Roberts, Patrick John Joseph; Sarmiento, Martinez Erik; Smith-Brown, Ashley; Sobrino, Pozuelo Ruben; Tanor, Collins; Unal, Enes; Wood, Marcus James; Yeboah, Yaw; Zinchenko, Oleksandr; Zuculini, Bruno.

Scholars
Blackshaw, Lewis Robert; Bolton, Luke Phillip; Coveney, Joseph Charles; Foden, Philip Walter; Francis, Edward Albert; Garre, Benjamin Antonio; Gonzalez, Lorenzo Jose; Latibeaudiere, Joel Owen; Poveda-Ocampo, Ian Carlo; Pozo, La Rosa Iker; Rosler, Colin; Sancho, Jadon Malik; Smith, Matthew; Sokol, Pawel Kazimierz; Wilson, Tyreke.

MANCHESTER U (50)

ANDER HERRERA, Aguera (M) **244 22**
H: 6 0 W: 10 10 b.Bilbao 14-8-89
Internationals: Spain U20, U21, U23, Full caps.

2008–09	Real Zaragoza	17	2		
2009–10	Real Zaragoza	30	2		
2010–11	Real Zaragoza	19	1	**66**	**5**
2011–12	Athletic Bilbao	32	1		
2012–13	Althetic Bilbao	29	1	**29**	**1**
2013–14	Athletic Bilbao	33	5	**65**	**6**
2014–15	Manchester U	26	6		
2015–16	Manchester U	27	3		
2016–17	Manchester U	31	1	**84**	**10**

BAILLY, Eric (D) **65 0**
H: 6 2 W: 12 02 b.Bingerville 12-4-94
Internationals: Ivory Coast Full caps.

2014–15	Espanyol	5	0	**5**	**0**
2014–15	Villareal	10	0		
2015–16	Villareal	25	0	**35**	**0**
2016–17	Manchester U	25	0	**25**	**0**

BLIND, Daley (M) **202 7**
H: 5 11 W: 10 10 b.Amsterdam 9-3-90
Internationals: Netherlands U16, U17, U19, U21, Full caps.

2008–09	Ajax	5	0		
2009–10	Ajax	0	0		
2009–10	*Groningen*	17	0	**17**	**0**
2010–11	Ajax	10	0		
2011–12	Ajax	21	0		
2012–13	Ajax	34	2		
2013–14	Ajax	29	1		
2014–15	Ajax	3	0	**102**	**3**
2014–15	Manchester U	25	2		
2015–16	Manchester U	35	1		
2016–17	Manchester U	23	1	**83**	**4**

BORTHWICK-JACKSON, Cameron (D) **16 0**
H: 6 3 W: 13 10 b.Manchester 2-2-97
Internationals: England U16, U17, U19, U20.

2015–16	Manchester U	10	0		
2016–17	Manchester U	0	0	**10**	**0**
2016–17	*Wolverhampton W*	6	0	**6**	**0**

CARRICK, Michael (M) **522 27**
H: 6 1 W: 11 10 b.Wallsend 28-7-81
Internationals: England U18, U21, B, Full caps.

1998–99	West Ham U	0	0		
1999–2000	West Ham U	8	1		
1999–2000	*Swindon T*	6	2	**6**	**2**
1999–2000	*Birmingham C*	2	0	**2**	**0**
2000–01	West Ham U	33	1		
2001–02	West Ham U	30	2		
2002–03	West Ham U	30	1		
2003–04	West Ham U	35	1		
2004–05	West Ham U	0	0	**136**	**6**
2004–05	Tottenham H	29	0		
2005–06	Tottenham H	35	2	**64**	**2**
2006–07	Manchester U	33	3		
2007–08	Manchester U	31	2		
2008–09	Manchester U	28	4		
2009–10	Manchester U	30	3		
2010–11	Manchester U	28	0		
2011–12	Manchester U	30	2		
2012–13	Manchester U	36	1		
2013–14	Manchester U	29	1		
2014–15	Manchester U	18	1		
2015–16	Manchester U	28	0		
2016–17	Manchester U	23	0	**314**	**17**

CASTRO, Joel (G) **7 0**
H: 6 2 W: 12 13 b. 28-6-96
Internationals: Switzerland U16, U17. Portugal U17, U18, U19, U20, U21.

2015–16	Manchester U	0	0		
2015–16	*Rochdale*	6	0	**6**	**0**
2016–17	Belenenses	0	0		
2016–17	Manchester U	1	0	**1**	**0**

DARMIAN, Matteo (D) **216 5**
H: 6 0 W: 11 00 b.Legnano 2-12-89
Internationals: Italy U17, U18, U19, U20, U21, Full caps.

2006–07	AC Milan	1	0		
2007–08	AC Milan	0	0		
2008–09	AC Milan	3	0		
2009–10	AC Milan	0	0	**4**	**0**
2009–10	*Padova*	22	1	**22**	**1**
2010–11	Palermo	11	0	**11**	**0**
2011–12	Torino	33	1		
2012–13	Torino	30	0		
2013–14	Torino	37	0		
2014–15	Torino	33	2	**133**	**3**
2015–16	Manchester U	28	1		
2016–17	Manchester U	18	0	**46**	**1**

DE GEA, David (G) **257 0**
H: 6 3 W: 12 13 b.Madrid 7-11-90
Internationals: Spain U15, U17, U19, U20, U21, U23, Full caps.

2009–10	Atletico Madrid	19	0		
2010–11	Atletico Madrid	38	0	**57**	**0**
2011–12	Manchester U	29	0		
2012–13	Manchester U	28	0		
2013–14	Manchester U	37	0		
2014–15	Manchester U	37	0		
2015–16	Manchester U	34	0		
2016–17	Manchester U	35	0	**200**	**0**

DEARNLEY, Zachary (M) **0 0**

2016–17	Manchester U	0	0		

DEPAY, Memphis (F) **123 41**
H: 5 10 W: 12 04 b.Moordrecht 13-2-94
Internationals: Netherlands U16, U17, U19, U21, Full caps.

2011–12	PSV Eindhoven	8	3		
2012–13	PSV Eindhoven	20	2		
2013–14	PSV Eindhoven	32	12		
2014–15	PSV Eindhoven	30	22	**90**	**39**
2015–16	Manchester U	29	2		
2016–17	Manchester U	4	0	**33**	**2**

Transferred to Lyon, January 2017.

FELLAINI, Marouane (M) **292 39**
H: 6 4 W: 13 05 b.Brussels 22-11-87
Internationals: Belgium U18, U19, U21, Full caps.

2006–07	Standard Liege	29	0		
2007–08	Standard Liege	30	6		
2008–09	Standard Liege	3	0	**62**	**6**
2008–09	Everton	30	8		
2009–10	Everton	23	2		
2010–11	Everton	20	1		
2011–12	Everton	34	3		
2012–13	Everton	31	11		
2013–14	Everton	3	0	**141**	**25**
2013–14	Manchester U	16	0		
2014–15	Manchester U	27	6		
2015–16	Manchester U	18	1		
2016–17	Manchester U	28	1	**89**	**8**

FOSU-MENSAH, Timothy (D) **12 0**
H: 5 10 W: 10 10 b.Amsterdam 3-1-98
Internationals: Netherlands U16, U17, U19, U21.

2015–16	Manchester U	8	0		
2016–17	Manchester U	4	0	**12**	**0**

GOMES, Angel (M) **1 0**
b.Enfield 31-8-00
Internationals: England U16, U17.

2016–17	Manchester U	1	0	**1**	**0**

HARROP, Josh (M) **1 1**
H: 5 9 W: 11 00 b.Stockport 15-12-95
Internationals: England U20.

2016–17	Manchester U	1	1	**1**	**1**

HENDERSON, Dean (G) **7 0**
H: 6 3 W: 12 13 b.Whitehaven 12-3-97
Internationals: England U16, U17, U20.

2015–16	Manchester U	0	0		
2016–17	Manchester U	0	0		
2016–17	*Grimsby T*	7	0	**7**	**0**

IBRAHIMOVIC, Zlatan (F) **512 319**
H: 6 4 W: 13 03 b.Malmo 3-10-81
Internationals: Sweden U18, U21, Full caps.

1999	Malmo	6	1		
2000	Malmo	26	12		
2001	Malmo	8	3	**40**	**16**
2001–02	Ajax	24	6		
2002–03	Ajax	25	13		
2003–04	Ajax	22	13		
2004–05	Ajax	3	3	**74**	**35**
2004–05	Juventus	35	16		
2005–06	Juventus	35	7	**70**	**23**
2006–07	Inter Milan	27	15		
2007–08	Inter Milan	26	17		
2008–09	Inter Milan	35	25	**88**	**57**
2009–10	Barcelona	29	16		
2010–11	Barcelona	0	0	**29**	**16**
2010–11	*AC Milan*	29	14		
2011–12	AC Milan	32	28	**61**	**42**
2012–13	Paris Saint-Germain	34	30		
2013–14	Paris Saint-Germain	33	26		
2014–15	Paris Saint-Germain	24	19		
2015–16	Paris Saint-Germain	31	38	**122**	**113**
2016–17	Manchester U	28	17	**28**	**17**

JANUZAJ, Adrian (M) **81 5**
H: 5 11 W: 11 11 b.Brussels 5-2-95
Internationals: Belgium Full caps.

2011–12	Manchester U	0	0		
2012–13	Manchester U	0	0		
2013–14	Manchester U	27	4		
2014–15	Manchester U	18	0		
2015–16	Manchester U	5	1		
2015–16	*Borussia Dortmund*	6	0	**6**	**0**
2016–17	Manchester U	0	0	**50**	**5**
2016–17	*Sunderland*	25	0	**25**	**0**

JOHNSTONE, Samuel (G) **95 0**
H: 6 0 W: 12 10 b.Preston 25-3-93
Internationals: England U16, U17, U19, U20.

2009–10	Manchester U	0	0		
2010–11	Manchester U	0	0		
2011–12	Manchester U	0	0		
2011–12	*Scunthorpe U*	12	0	**12**	**0**
2012–13	Manchester U	0	0		
2012–13	*Walsall*	7	0	**7**	**0**
2013–14	Manchester U	0	0		
2013–14	*Yeovil T*	1	0	**1**	**0**
2013–14	*Doncaster R*	18	0		
2014–15	Manchester U	0	0		
2014–15	*Doncaster R*	10	0	**28**	**0**
2014–15	*Preston NE*	22	0		
2015–16	Manchester U	0	0		
2015–16	*Preston NE*	4	0	**26**	**0**
2016–17	Manchester U	0	0		
2016–17	*Aston Villa*	21	0	**21**	**0**

JONES, Phil (D) **157 2**
H: 5 11 W: 11 02 b.Preston 21-2-92
Internationals: England U19, U21, Full caps.

2009–10	Blackburn R	9	0		
2010–11	Blackburn R	26	0	**35**	**0**
2011–12	Manchester U	29	1		
2012–13	Manchester U	17	0		
2013–14	Manchester U	26	1		
2014–15	Manchester U	22	0		
2015–16	Manchester U	10	0		
2016–17	Manchester U	18	0	**122**	**2**

LINGARD, Jesse (M) **98 16**
H: 5 3 W: 11 11 b.Warrington 15-12-92
Internationals: England U17, U21, Full caps.

2011–12	Manchester U	0	0		
2012–13	Manchester U	0	0		
2012–13	*Leicester C*	5	0	**5**	**0**
2013–14	Manchester U	0	0		
2013–14	*Birmingham C*	13	6	**13**	**6**
2013–14	*Brighton & HA*	15	3	**15**	**3**
2014–15	Manchester U	1	0		
2014–15	*Derby Co*	14	2	**14**	**2**
2015–16	Manchester U	25	4		
2016–17	Manchester U	25	1	**51**	**5**

MARTIAL, Anthony (F) 108 26
H: 5 11 W: 12 08 b.Massy 5-12-95
Internationals: France U16, U17, U18, U19, U21, Full caps.
2012–13 Lyon 3 0 **3 0**
2013–14 Monaco 11 2
2014–15 Monaco 35 9
2015–16 Monaco 3 0 **49 11**
2015–16 Manchester U 31 11
2016–17 Manchester U 25 4 **56 15**

MATA, Juan (M) 361 88
H: 5 7 W: 11 00 b.Ocon de Villafranca 28-4-88
Internationals: Spain U16, U17, U19, U20, U21, U23, Full caps.
2006–07 Real Madrid B 39 10 **39 10**
2007–08 Valencia 24 5
2008–09 Valencia 37 11
2009–10 Valencia 35 9
2010–11 Valencia 33 8 **129 33**
2011–12 Chelsea 34 6
2012–13 Chelsea 35 12
2013–14 Chelsea 13 0 **82 18**
2013–14 Manchester U 15 6
2014–15 Manchester U 33 9
2015–16 Manchester U 38 6
2016–17 Manchester U 25 6 **111 27**

McTOMINAY, Scott (M) 2 0
H: 5 10 W: 10 03 b.Lancaster 8-12-96
2016–17 Manchester U 2 0 **2 0**

MITCHELL, Demetri (D) 1 0
H: 5 9 W: 11 11 b.Manchester 11-1-97
Internationals: England U16, U17, U18, U20.
2016–17 Manchester U 1 0 **1 0**

MKHITARYAN, Henrikh (M) 293 107
H: 5 10 W: 12 00 b.Yerevan 21-1-89
Internationals: Armenia U17, U19, U21, Full caps.
2006 Pyunik 12 1
2007 Pyunik 24 12
2008 Pyunik 24 6
2009 Pyunik 10 11 **70 30**
2009–10 Metalurg Donetsk 29 9
2010–11 Metalurg Donetsk 8 3 **37 12**
2010–11 Shakhtar Donetsk 17 3
2011–12 Shakhtar Donetsk 26 10
2012–13 Shakhtar Donetsk 29 25 **72 38**
2013–14 Borussia Dortmund 31 9
2014–15 Borussia Dortmund 28 3
2015–16 Borussia Dortmund 31 11 **90 23**
2016–17 Manchester U 24 4 **24 4**

O'HARA, Kieran (G) 5 0
b. 22-4-96
Internationals: Republic of Ireland U21.
2015–16 Manchester U 0 0
2015–16 *Morecambe* 5 0
2016–17 Morecambe 0 0 **5 0**
2016–17 Manchester U 0 0

POGBA, Paul (M) 157 33
H: 6 1 W: 12 08 b.Lagny-sur-Marne 15-3-93
Internationals: France U16, U17, U18, U19, U20, Full caps.
2009–10 Manchester U 0 0
2010–11 Manchester U 0 0
2011–12 Manchester U 3 0
2012–13 Juventus 27 5
2013–14 Juventus 36 7
2014–15 Juventus 26 8
2015–16 Juventus 35 8 **124 28**
2016–17 Manchester U 30 5 **33 5**

RASHFORD, Marcus (F) 43 10
H: 5 11 W: 11 00 b.Manchester 31-10-97
Internationals: England U16, U18, U20, U21, Full caps.
2015–16 Manchester U 11 5
2016–17 Manchester U 32 5 **43 10**

RILEY, Joe (D) 2 0
H: 6 0 W: 11 03 b.Blackpool 6-12-96
2016–17 Manchester U 0 0
2016–17 *Sheffield U* 2 0 **2 0**

ROJO, Marcos (D) 159 9
H: 6 2 W: 12 06 b.La Plata 20-3-90
Internationals: Argentina Full caps.
2008–09 Estudiantes 6 1
2009–10 Estudiantes 18 0
2010–11 Estudiantes 19 2 **43 3**
2011–12 Spartak Moscow 8 0 **8 0**
2012–13 Sporting Lisbon 24 1
2013–14 Sporting Lisbon 25 4 **49 5**
2014–15 Manchester U 22 0
2015–16 Manchester U 16 0
2016–17 Manchester U 21 1 **59 1**

ROMERO, Sergio (G) 175 0
H: 6 4 W: 13 01 b.Yrigoyen 22-2-87
Internationals: Argentina U20, Full caps.
2006–07 Racing Club 5 0 **5 0**
2007–08 AZ Alkmaar 12 0
2008–09 AZ Alkmaar 28 0
2009–10 AZ Alkmaar 27 0
2010–11 AZ Alkmaar 23 0
2011–12 AZ Alkmaar 0 0 **90 0**
2011–12 Sampdoria 29 0
2012–13 Sampdoria 32 0
2013–14 Sampdoria 0 0
2013–14 *Monaco* 3 0 **3 0**
2014–15 Sampdoria 10 0 **71 0**
2015–16 Manchester U 4 0
2016–17 Manchester U 2 0 **6 0**

ROONEY, Wayne (F) 460 198
H: 5 10 W: 12 13 b.Liverpool 24-10-85
Internationals: England U15, U16, U19, Full caps.
2002–03 Everton 33 6
2003–04 Everton 34 9 **67 15**
2004–05 Manchester U 29 11
2005–06 Manchester U 36 16
2006–07 Manchester U 35 14
2007–08 Manchester U 27 12
2008–09 Manchester U 30 12
2009–10 Manchester U 32 26
2010–11 Manchester U 28 11
2011–12 Manchester U 34 27
2012–13 Manchester U 27 12
2013–14 Manchester U 29 17
2014–15 Manchester U 33 12
2015–16 Manchester U 28 8
2016–17 Manchester U 25 5 **393 183**

SCHWEINSTEIGER, Bastian (M) 360 46
H: 6 0 W: 12 06 b.Kolbermoor 1-8-84
Internationals: Germany U16, U18, U19, U21, Full caps.
2002–03 Bayern Munich 14 0
2003–04 Bayern Munich 26 4
2004–05 Bayern Munich 26 3
2005–06 Bayern Munich 30 3
2006–07 Bayern Munich 27 4
2007–08 Bayern Munich 30 1
2008–09 Bayern Munich 31 5
2009–10 Bayern Munich 33 2
2010–11 Bayern Munich 32 4
2011–12 Bayern Munich 22 3
2012–13 Bayern Munich 28 7
2013–14 Bayern Munich 23 4
2014–15 Bayern Munich 20 5 **342 45**
2015–16 Manchester U 18 1
2016–17 Manchester U 0 0 **18 1**
Transferred to Chicago Fire, March 2017.

SHAW, Luke (D) 92 0
H: 6 1 W: 11 11 b.Kingston 12-7-95
Internationals: England U16, U17, U21, Full caps.
2011–12 Southampton 0 0
2012–13 Southampton 25 0
2013–14 Southampton 35 0 **60 0**
2014–15 Manchester U 16 0
2015–16 Manchester U 5 0
2016–17 Manchester U 11 0 **32 0**

SMALLING, Chris (D) 166 7
H: 6 4 W: 14 02 b.Greenwich 22-11-89
Internationals: England U18, U20, U21, Full caps.
2008–09 Fulham 1 0
2009–10 Fulham 12 0 **13 0**
2010–11 Manchester U 16 0
2011–12 Manchester U 19 1
2012–13 Manchester U 15 0
2013–14 Manchester U 25 1
2014–15 Manchester U 25 4
2015–16 Manchester U 35 0
2016–17 Manchester U 18 1 **153 7**

TUANZEBE, Axel (D) 4 0
H: 6 0 W: 11 11 b.Bunia 14-11-97
Internationals: England U19, U20.
2015–16 Manchester U 0 0
2016–17 Manchester U 4 0 **4 0**

VALENCIA, Antonio (M) 377 32
H: 5 10 W: 12 04 b.Lago Agrio 5-8-85
Internationals: Ecuador U20, 21, U23, Full caps.
2002 El Nacional 1 0
2003 El Nacional 26 2
2004 El Nacional 42 5
2005 El Nacional 14 4 **83 11**
2005–06 Villarreal 2 0 **2 0**
2005–06 *Recreativo* 4 0 **4 0**
2006–07 Wigan Ath 22 1
2007–08 Wigan Ath 31 3
2008–09 Wigan Ath 31 3 **84 7**
2009–10 Manchester U 34 5
2010–11 Manchester U 10 1
2011–12 Manchester U 27 4
2012–13 Manchester U 30 1
2013–14 Manchester U 29 2
2014–15 Manchester U 32 0
2015–16 Manchester U 14 0
2016–17 Manchester U 28 1 **204 14**

VARELA, Guillermo (D) 11 0
H: 5 7 W: 10 11 b.Montevideo 24-3-93
Internationals: Uruguay U17, U20.
2013–14 Manchester U 0 0
2014–15 Manchester U 0 0
2015–16 Manchester U 4 0
2016–17 Manchester U 0 0 **4 0**
2016–17 *Eintracht Frankfurt* 7 0 **7 0**

WILLOCK, Matthew (M) 0 0
b. 20-8-96
2016–17 Manchester U 0 0

WILSON, James (F) 44 8
H: 6 0 W: 12 04 b.Biddulph 1-12-95
Internationals: England U16, U19, U20, U21.
2013–14 Manchester U 1 2
2014–15 Manchester U 13 1
2015–16 Manchester U 1 0
2015–16 *Brighton & HA* 25 5 **25 5**
2016–17 Derby Co 4 0 **4 0**
2016–17 Manchester U 0 0 **15 3**

YOUNG, Ashley (M) 375 60
H: 5 10 W: 10 03 b.Stevenage 9-7-85
Internationals: England U21, Full caps.
2002–03 Watford 0 0
2003–04 Watford 5 3
2004–05 Watford 34 0
2005–06 Watford 39 13
2006–07 Watford 20 3 **98 19**
2006–07 Aston Villa 13 2
2007–08 Aston Villa 37 9
2008–09 Aston Villa 36 7
2009–10 Aston Villa 37 5
2010–11 Aston Villa 34 7 **157 30**
2011–12 Manchester U 25 6
2012–13 Manchester U 19 0
2013–14 Manchester U 20 2
2014–15 Manchester U 26 2
2015–16 Manchester U 18 1
2016–17 Manchester U 12 0 **120 11**

Players retained or with offer of contract
Bohui, Joshua Raymond; Boonen, Indy Zeb Pepe; Chong, Tahith; Ercolani, Luca; Gribbin, Callum Anthony; Hamilton, Ethan Billy; Herrera, Aguera Ander; Hoelgebaum, Pereira Andreas Hugo; Johnstone, Max Oliver; Kehinde, Tosin Samuel; Kenyon, Jake Barry; McIntosh-Buffonge, Darren Raekwon; Moutha-Sebtaoui, Ilias; Olosunde, Matthew Olawale; Poole, Regan Leslie; Redmond, Devonte Vincent; Scott, Charlie Thomas; Warren, Tyrell Nathaniel; Whelan, Callum Tyler; Williams, Ro-Shaun Oman.

Scholars
Barlow, Aidan Will; Barrett, Jake George; Burkart, Nishan Connell; Dunne, Max Edward; Fojticek, Alex; Gomes, Adilson Angel Abreu de; O'Connor, Lee Patrick; Spratt, Harry; Tanner, George.

MANSFIELD T (51)

ANDERSON, Paul (M) 292 31
H: 5 9 W: 10 04 b.Leicester 23-7-88
Internationals: England U19.
2005–06 Hull C 0 0
2005–06 Liverpool 0 0
2006–07 Liverpool 0 0
2007–08 Liverpool 0 0
2007–08 *Swansea C* 31 7 **31 7**
2008–09 Liverpool 0 0
2008–09 *Nottingham F* 26 2
2009–10 Nottingham F 37 4
2010–11 Nottingham F 36 3
2011–12 Nottingham F 17 0
2012–13 Nottingham F 0 0 **116 9**
2012–13 Bristol C 29 3 **29 3**
2013–14 Ipswich T 31 5
2014–15 Ipswich T 35 1 **66 6**
2015–16 Bradford C 11 0

2016–17	Bradford C	3	0	**14**	**0**
2016–17	Northampton T	36	6	**36**	**6**
2016–17	Mansfield T	0	0		

ARQUIN, Yoann (F) 150 35
H: 6 2 W: 13 04 b.Le Havre 15-4-88
Internationals: Martinique Full caps.

2008–09	Quimper	24	9	**24**	**9**
2010–11	Red Star 93	11	2	**11**	**2**
2011–12	Hereford U	34	8	**34**	**8**
2012–13	Notts Co	41	7		
2013–14	Notts Co	12	3	**53**	**10**
2013–14	Ross Co	16	4	**16**	**4**
2016–17	Mansfield T	12	2	**12**	**2**

BAXENDALE, James (M) 133 8
H: 5 8 W: 10 03 b.Thorne 16-9-92

2011–12	Doncaster R	2	0		
2011–12	*Hereford U*	1	0	**1**	**0**
2012–13	Doncaster R	0	0	**2**	**0**
2012–13	Walsall	32	4		
2013–14	Walsall	40	2		
2014–15	Walsall	28	1		
2015–16	Walsall	3	0	**103**	**7**
2015–16	Mansfield T	15	1		
2016–17	Mansfield T	12	0	**27**	**1**

BENNETT, Rhys (D) 142 6
H: 6 3 W: 12 00 b.Manchester 1-9-91

2011–12	Bolton W	0	0		
2011–12	*Falkirk*	19	0	**19**	**0**
2013–14	Rochdale	22	0		
2014–15	Rochdale	39	2		
2015–16	Rochdale	16	2	**77**	**4**
2016–17	Mansfield T	46	2	**46**	**2**

BENNING, Malvind (D) 131 7
H: 5 10 W: 12 00 b.Sandwell 2-11-93

2012–13	Walsall	10	0		
2013–14	Walsall	16	2		
2014–15	Walsall	20	0	**46**	**2**
2014–15	*York C*	9	0	**9**	**0**
2015–16	Mansfield T	31	4		
2016–17	Mansfield T	45	1	**76**	**5**

BYROM, Joel (M) 175 13
H: 6 0 W: 12 04 b.Accrington 14-9-86
Internationals: England C.

2004–05	Blackburn R	0	0		
2005–06	Blackburn R	0	0		
2006–07	Accrington S	1	0	**1**	**0**

From Clitheroe, Southport, Clitheroe, Northwich Vic.

2010–11	Stevenage	7	0		
2011–12	Stevenage	32	4	**39**	**4**
2012–13	Preston NE	22	2		
2013–14	Preston NE	11	2	**33**	**4**
2013–14	*Oldham Ath*	4	0	**4**	**0**
2014–15	Northampton T	39	3		
2015–16	Northampton T	35	2		
2016–17	Northampton T	2	0	**76**	**5**
2016–17	Mansfield T	22	0	**22**	**0**

CHAPMAN, Adam (M) 157 8
H: 5 10 W: 11 00 b.Doncaster 29-11-89
Internationals: Northern Ireland U21.

2008–09	Sheffield U	0	0		
2009–10	Sheffield U	0	0		
2010–11	Oxford U	0	0		
2011–12	Oxford U	14	1		
2012–13	Oxford U	26	1	**40**	**2**
2013–14	*Mansfield T*	0	0		
2013–14	Newport Co	39	1		
2014–15	Newport Co	36	3	**75**	**4**
2015–16	Mansfield T	37	2		
2016–17	Mansfield T	5	0	**42**	**2**

COLLINS, Lee (D) 319 5
H: 6 1 W: 11 10 b.Telford 23-9-83

2006–07	Wolverhampton W	0	0		
2007–08	Wolverhampton W	0	0		
2007–08	*Hereford U*	16	0	**16**	**0**
2008–09	Wolverhampton W	0	0		
2008–09	Port Vale	39	1		
2009–10	Port Vale	45	1		
2010–11	Port Vale	42	2		
2011–12	Port Vale	16	0	**142**	**4**
2011–12	Barnsley	7	0		
2012–13	Barnsley	0	0	**7**	**0**
2012–13	Shrewsbury T	8	0	**8**	**0**
2012–13	Northampton T	15	0		
2013–14	Northampton T	22	1		
2014–15	Northampton T	37	0	**74**	**1**
2015–16	Mansfield T	35	0		
2016–17	Mansfield T	37	0	**72**	**0**

COLLINS, Lewis (M) 0 0
b. 16-10-96
Internationals: Northern Ireland U19.
From Reading.

2016–17	Mansfield T	0	0		

DIAMOND, Zander (D) 387 26
H: 6 2 W: 11 07 b.Alexandria 3-12-85
Internationals: Scotland U21, B.

2003–04	Aberdeen	19	2		
2004–05	Aberdeen	29	3		
2005–06	Aberdeen	33	0		
2006–07	Aberdeen	21	0		
2007–08	Aberdeen	26	3		
2008–09	Aberdeen	28	4		
2009–10	Aberdeen	16	3		
2010–11	Aberdeen	32	1	**204**	**16**
2011–12	Oldham Ath	23	2	**23**	**2**
2012–13	Burton Alb	37	4		
2013–14	Burton Alb	10	1	**47**	**5**
2013–14	*Northampton T*	14	1		
2014–15	Northampton T	21	1		
2015–16	Northampton T	39	1		
2016–17	Northampton T	39	0	**113**	**3**
2016–17	Mansfield T	0	0		

DIGBY, Paul (M) 29 0
H: 5 9 W: 10 00 b.Sheffield 2-2-95
Internationals: England U19, U20.

2011–12	Barnsley	4	0		
2012–13	Barnsley	0	0		
2013–14	Barnsley	5	0		
2014–15	Barnsley	11	0		
2015–16	Barnsley	1	0	**21**	**0**
2015–16	*Ipswich T*	4	0		
2016–17	Ipswich T	4	0	**8**	**0**
2016–17	Mansfield T	0	0		

GOBERN, Oscar (M) 111 4
H: 5 11 W: 10 10 b.Birmingham 26-1-91
Internationals: England U19.

2008–09	Southampton	6	0		
2009–10	Southampton	4	0		
2009–10	*Milton Keynes D*	2	0	**2**	**0**
2010–11	Southampton	11	1	**21**	**1**
2011–12	Huddersfield T	21	2		
2012–13	Huddersfield T	15	0		
2013–14	Huddersfield T	23	0		
2014–15	Huddersfield T	12	1	**71**	**3**
2014–15	*Chesterfield*	3	0	**3**	**0**
2015–16	QPR	0	0		
2015–16	*Doncaster R*	5	0	**5**	**0**
2016–17	Mansfield T	9	0	**9**	**0**

Transferred to Ross Co, January 2017.

GREEN, Matt (F) 142 27
H: 6 0 W: 12 09 b.Bath 2-1-87
Internationals: England C.

2006–07	Cardiff C	6	0		
2007–08	Cardiff C	0	0	**6**	**0**
2007–08	*Darlington*	4	0	**4**	**0**

From Torquay U

2010–11	Oxford U	17	0	**17**	**0**
2010–11	*Cheltenham T*	19	0	**19**	**0**

From Mansfield T

2013–14	Birmingham C	10	1		
2014–15	Birmingham C	0	0	**10**	**1**
2015–16	Mansfield T	44	16		
2016–17	Mansfield T	42	10	**86**	**26**

HAKEEM, Zayn (M) 1 0
b. 15-2-99
Internationals: Antigua and Barbuda U20.

2015–16	Mansfield T	1	0		
2016–17	Mansfield T	0	0	**1**	**0**

HAMILTON, CJ (M) 29 0
H: 5 7 W: 11 09 b.Harrow 23-3-95

2015–16	Sheffield U	0	0		
2016–17	Mansfield T	29	0	**29**	**0**

HARRISON, Kieran (M) 0 0

2016–17	Mansfield T	0	0		

HEALEY, Cameron (M) 0 0
From Walsall.

2016–17	Mansfield T	0	0		

HEMMINGS, Ashley (M) 191 14
H: 5 8 W: 11 06 b.Lewisham 3-3-91
Internationals: England U17.

2008–09	Wolverhampton W	2	0		
2008–09	*Cheltenham T*	1	0	**1**	**0**
2009–10	Wolverhampton W	0	0		
2010–11	Wolverhampton W	0	0		
2010–11	*Torquay U*	9	0	**9**	**0**
2011–12	Wolverhampton W	0	0	**2**	**0**
2011–12	*Plymouth Arg*	23	2	**23**	**2**
2012–13	Walsall	28	1		
2013–14	Walsall	27	2	**55**	**3**
2013–14	*Burton Alb*	5	0	**5**	**0**
2014–15	Dagenham & R	41	5		
2015–16	Dagenham & R	39	4	**80**	**9**
2016–17	Mansfield T	16	0	**16**	**0**

HENDERSON, Darius (F) 450 117
H: 6 3 W: 14 03 b.Sutton 7-9-81

1999–2000	Reading	6	0		
2000–01	Reading	4	0		
2001–02	Reading	38	7		
2002–03	Reading	22	4		
2003–04	Reading	1	0	**71**	**11**
2003–04	*Brighton & HA*	10	2	**10**	**2**
2003–04	Gillingham	4	0		
2004–05	Gillingham	32	9	**36**	**9**
2004–05	*Swindon T*	6	5	**6**	**5**
2005–06	Watford	30	14		
2006–07	Watford	35	3		
2007–08	Watford	40	12	**105**	**29**
2008–09	Sheffield U	32	6		
2009–10	Sheffield U	32	12		
2010–11	Sheffield U	8	2	**72**	**20**
2011–12	Millwall	31	15		
2012–13	Millwall	20	7	**51**	**22**
2012–13	Nottingham F	11	2		
2013–14	Nottingham F	34	8	**45**	**10**
2014–15	Leyton Orient	23	8	**23**	**8**
2015–16	Scunthorpe U	13	0	**13**	**0**
2015–16	Coventry C	5	0	**5**	**0**
2016–17	Mansfield T	13	1	**13**	**1**

HOBAN, Patrick (F) 65 7
b.Galway 28-7-91

2014–15	Oxford U	20	1		
2015–16	Oxford U	23	2	**43**	**3**
2015–16	*Stevenage*	1	0	**1**	**0**
2016–17	Mansfield T	21	4	**21**	**4**

HURST, Kevan (M) 382 36
H: 5 10 W: 11 07 b.Chesterfield 27-8-85

2003–04	*Boston U*	7	1	**7**	**1**
2004–05	Sheffield U	1	0		
2004–05	*Stockport Co*	14	1	**14**	**1**
2005–06	Sheffield U	0	0		
2005–06	*Chesterfield*	37	4		
2006–07	Sheffield U	0	0	**1**	**0**
2006–07	*Chesterfield*	25	3	**62**	**7**
2006–07	*Scunthorpe U*	13	0		
2007–08	Scunthorpe U	33	1		
2008–09	Scunthorpe U	20	2	**66**	**3**
2009–10	Carlisle U	33	2		
2010–11	Carlisle U	2	0	**35**	**2**
2010–11	*Morecambe*	21	2	**21**	**2**
2011–12	Walsall	34	2	**34**	**2**
2012–13	Southend U	44	5		
2013–14	Southend U	42	11		
2014–15	Southend U	28	1		
2015–16	Southend U	14	0	**128**	**17**
2016–17	Mansfield T	14	1	**14**	**1**

JENSEN, Brian (G) 402 0
H: 6 1 W: 12 04 b.Copenhagen 8-6-75

1997–98	AZ	0	0		
1998–99	AZ	1	0	**1**	**0**
1999–2000	WBA	12	0		
2000–01	WBA	33	0		
2001–02	WBA	1	0		
2002–03	WBA	0	0	**46**	**0**
2003–04	Burnley	46	0		
2004–05	Burnley	27	0		
2005–06	Burnley	39	0		
2006–07	Burnley	31	0		
2007–08	Burnley	19	0		
2008–09	Burnley	45	0		
2009–10	Burnley	38	0		
2010–11	Burnley	21	0		
2011–12	Burnley	4	0		
2012–13	Burnley	1	0	**271**	**0**
2013–14	Bury	36	0	**36**	**0**
2014–15	Crawley T	20	0	**20**	**0**
2015–16	Mansfield T	25	0		
2016–17	Mansfield T	3	0	**28**	**0**

LAW, Jason (F) 0 0

2015–16	Mansfield T	0	0		
2016–17	Mansfield T	0	0		

LOGAN, Conrad (G) 177 0
H: 6 2 W: 14 00 b.Letterkenny 18-4-86

2003–04	Leicester C	0	0		
2004–05	Leicester C	0	0		
2005–06	Leicester C	0	0		
2005–06	*Boston U*	13	0	**13**	**0**
2006–07	Leicester C	18	0		
2007–08	Leicester C	0	0		
2007–08	*Stockport Co*	34	0		
2008–09	Leicester C	0	0		
2008–09	*Luton T*	22	0	**22**	**0**
2008–09	*Stockport Co*	7	0	**41**	**0**

2009–10	Leicester C	2	0		
2010–11	Leicester C	3	0		
2010–11	*Bristol R*	16	0	**16**	**0**
2011–12	Leicester C	0	0		
2011–12	*Rotherham U*	19	0	**19**	**0**
2012–13	Leicester C	0	0		
2013–14	Leicester C	0	0		
2014–15	Leicester C	0	0	**23**	**0**
2014–15	*Rochdale*	19	0		
2016–17	Rochdale	24	0	**43**	**0**
2016–17	Mansfield T	0	0		

MACDONALD, Alex (F) **232** **24**
H: 5 7 W: 11 04 b.Warrington 14-4-90
Internationals: Scotland U19, U21.

2007–08	Burnley	2	0		
2008–09	Burnley	3	0		
2009–10	Burnley	0	0		
2009–10	*Falkirk*	11	1	**11**	**1**
2010–11	Burnley	0	0		
2010–11	*Inverness CT*	10	1	**10**	**1**
2011–12	Burnley	5	0		
2011–12	*Plymouth Arg*	18	4		
2012–13	Burnley	1	0	**11**	**0**
2012–13	*Plymouth Arg*	16	1	**34**	**5**
2012–13	*Burton Alb*	15	1		
2013–14	Burton Alb	35	0		
2014–15	Burton Alb	21	6	**71**	**7**
2014–15	Oxford U	15	3		
2015–16	Oxford U	40	5		
2016–17	Oxford U	22	1	**77**	**9**
2016–17	Mansfield T	18	1	**18**	**1**

MARRIOTT, Tom (M) **0** **0**
From Derby Co.

2016–17	Mansfield T	0	0		

McGUIRE, Jamie (M) **130** **4**
H: 5 7 W: 10 13 b.Birkenhead 13-11-83

2001–02	Tranmere R	0	0		
2002–03	Tranmere R	0	0		
2003–04	Tranmere R	0	0		
From Northwich Vic, Droylsden					
2012–13	Fleetwood T	37	1	**37**	**1**
2013–14	Mansfield T	27	2		
2014–15	Mansfield T	29	1		
2015–16	Mansfield T	20	0		
2016–17	Mansfield T	17	0	**93**	**3**

MIRFIN, David (D) **436** **20**
H: 6 3 W: 13 00 b.Sheffield 18-4-85

2002–03	Huddersfield T	1	0		
2003–04	Huddersfield T	21	2		
2004–05	Huddersfield T	41	4		
2005–06	Huddersfield T	31	1		
2006–07	Huddersfield T	38	1		
2007–08	Huddersfield T	29	1	**161**	**9**
2008–09	Scunthorpe U	33	0		
2009–10	Scunthorpe U	37	1		
2010–11	Scunthorpe U	23	3		
2011–12	Watford	4	0	**4**	**0**
2011–12	*Scunthorpe U*	19	1		
2012–13	Scunthorpe U	30	0		
2013–14	Scunthorpe U	45	2		
2014–15	Scunthorpe U	0	0		
2014–15	*Hartlepool U*	15	0	**15**	**0**
2015–16	Scunthorpe U	35	2		
2016–17	Scunthorpe U	34	2	**256**	**11**
2016–17	Mansfield T	0	0		

PEARCE, Krystian (D) **249** **17**
H: 6 1 W: 13 05 b.Birmingham 5-1-90
Internationals: England U17, U19.

2006–07	Birmingham C	0	0		
2007–08	Birmingham C	0	0		
2007–08	*Port Vale*	12	0	**12**	**0**
2007–08	*Notts Co*	8	1		
2008–09	Birmingham C	0	0		
2008–09	*Scunthorpe U*	39	0	**39**	**0**
2009–10	Birmingham C	0	0		
2009–10	*Peterborough U*	2	0	**2**	**0**
2009–10	Huddersfield T	1	0	**1**	**0**
2010–11	Notts Co	27	1		
2011–12	Notts Co	27	3		
2012–13	Notts Co	2	1	**64**	**6**
2012–13	*Barnet*	17	1	**17**	**1**
2013–14	Torquay U	35	4	**35**	**4**
2015–16	Mansfield T	38	3		
2016–17	Mansfield T	41	3	**79**	**6**

POTTER, Alfie (M) **206** **23**
H: 5 7 W: 9 06 b.Islington 9-1-89

2007–08	Peterborough U	2	0	**2**	**0**
From Kettering T.					
2010–11	Oxford U	38	2		
From Kettering T.					
2011–12	Oxford U	25	2		
2012–13	Oxford U	43	10		
2013–14	Oxford U	24	4		
2014–15	Oxford U	15	2	**145**	**20**
2014–15	AFC Wimbledon	15	1	**15**	**1**
2014–15	Northampton T	0	0		
2015–16	Northampton T	21	1		
2016–17	Northampton T	11	0	**32**	**1**
2016–17	Mansfield T	12	1	**12**	**1**

ROSE, Danny (F) **123** **28**
H: 5 8 W: 9 00 b.Barnsley 10-12-93

2010–11	Barnsley	1	0		
2011–12	Barnsley	4	0		
2012–13	Barnsley	8	1		
2013–14	Barnsley	3	0		
2013–14	*Bury*	6	3		
2014–15	Barnsley	1	0	**17**	**1**
2014–15	*Bury*	35	10		
2015–16	Bury	28	5	**69**	**18**
2016–17	Mansfield T	37	9	**37**	**9**

SHIRES, Corbin (D) **1** **0**
H: 6 4 W: 10 10 b.Sheffield 31-12-97

2014–15	Mansfield T	1	0		
2015–16	Mansfield T	0	0		
2016–17	Mansfield T	0	0	**1**	**0**

SPENCER, James (F) **161** **34**
H: 6 1 W: 13 00 b.Leeds 13-12-91

2008–09	Huddersfield T	0	0		
2009–10	Huddersfield T	0	0		
2010–11	Huddersfield T	0	0		
2010–11	*Morecambe*	32	8	**32**	**8**
2011–12	Huddersfield T	0	0		
2011–12	*Cheltenham T*	41	10	**41**	**10**
2012–13	Huddersfield T	1	0		
2012–13	*Brentford*	2	0	**2**	**0**
2013–14	Huddersfield T	0	0	**1**	**0**
2013–14	*Scunthorpe U*	13	1	**13**	**1**
2013–14	Notts Co	13	5		
2014–15	Notts Co	9	1		
2015–16	Notts Co	7	0	**29**	**6**
2015–16	Cambridge U	18	6	**18**	**6**
2016–17	Plymouth Arg	25	3	**25**	**3**
2016–17	Mansfield T	0	0		

TAFT, George (D) **57** **2**
H: 5 9 W: 11 09 b.Leicester 29-7-93
Internationals: England U18, U19.

2010–11	Leicester C	0	0		
2011–12	Leicester C	0	0		
2012–13	Leicester C	0	0		
2013–14	Leicester C	0	0		
2013–14	*York C*	3	0	**3**	**0**
2014–15	Burton Alb	30	1		
2015–16	Burton Alb	0	0	**30**	**1**
2015–16	*Cambridge U*	11	1	**11**	**1**
2016–17	Mansfield T	13	0	**13**	**0**

THOMAS, Jack (M) **52** **3**
H: 5 9 W: 10 10 b.Sutton-in-Ashfield 3-6-96

2013–14	Mansfield T	1	0		
2014–15	Mansfield T	12	1		
2015–16	Mansfield T	33	2		
2016–17	Mansfield T	6	0	**52**	**3**

Players retained or with offer of contract
Blake, Tyler Steffen; Danquah, Louis Kofi.

Scholars
Bircumshaw, Harry; Blake, Nyle Hedley; Bloor, Teddy John; Fikula, Steven Johnson; Holmes, Harrison Kieran; Marriott, Tom William; Morgan, Luke James; Reittie, Devante Paul; Smith, Cain; Sundby, Xavier Le Flock; Walker, Aiden; Ward, Keaton Brodie; Wilder, Henri Liam; Wilson, Samuel John.

MIDDLESBROUGH (52)

AYALA, Daniel (M) **151** **13**
H: 6 3 W: 13 03 b.Sevilla 7-11-90
Internationals: Spain U21.

2007–08	Liverpool	0	0		
2008–09	Liverpool	0	0		
2009–10	Liverpool	5	0		
2010–11	Liverpool	0	0	**5**	**0**
2010–11	*Hull C*	12	1	**12**	**1**
2010–11	*Derby Co*	17	0	**17**	**0**
2011–12	Norwich C	7	0		
2012–13	Norwich C	0	0		
2012–13	*Nottingham F*	12	1	**12**	**1**
2013–14	Norwich C	0	0	**7**	**0**
2013–14	Middlesbrough	19	3		
2014–15	Middlesbrough	30	4		
2015–16	Middlesbrough	35	3		
2016–17	Middlesbrough	14	1	**98**	**11**

BAPTISTE, Alex (D) **450** **24**
H: 6 0 W: 11 11 b.Sutton-in-Ashfield 31-1-86

2002–03	Mansfield T	4	0		
2003–04	Mansfield T	17	0		
2004–05	Mansfield T	41	1		
2005–06	Mansfield T	41	1		
2006–07	Mansfield T	46	3		
2007–08	Mansfield T	25	0	**174**	**5**
2008–09	Blackpool	21	1		
2009–10	Blackpool	42	3		
2010–11	Blackpool	21	2		
2011–12	Blackpool	43	1		
2012–13	Blackpool	43	1	**170**	**8**
2013–14	Bolton W	39	4		
2014–15	Bolton W	0	0	**39**	**4**
2014–15	*Blackburn R*	32	3	**32**	**3**
2015–16	Middlesbrough	0	0		
2015–16	*Sheffield U*	11	1	**11**	**1**
2016–17	Middlesbrough	0	0		
2016–17	*Preston NE*	24	3	**24**	**3**

BARRAGAN, Antonio (D) **203** **3**
H: 6 0 W: 12 00 b.Seville 12-6-87
Internationals: Spain U17, U19, U20, U21.

2005–06	Liverpool	0	0		
2006–07	Deportivo La Coruna	16	2		
2007–08	Deportivo La Coruna	10	0		
2008–09	Deportivo La Coruna	0	0	**26**	**2**
2009–10	Real Vallodolid	17	0		
2010–11	Real Vallodolid	23	0		
2011–12	Real Vallodolid	1	0	**41**	**0**
2011–12	Valencia	18	0		
2012–13	Valencia	14	0		
2013–14	Valencia	20	0		
2014–15	Valencia	34	1		
2015–16	Valencia	24	0	**110**	**1**
2016–17	Middlesbrough	26	0	**26**	**0**

BERNARDO, Espinosa (D) **154** **10**
H: 6 4 W: 13 03 b.Cali 11-7-89

2010–11	Sevilla	1	0		
2011–12	Sevilla	0	0	**1**	**0**
2011–12	*Racing Santander*	25	2	**25**	**2**
2012–13	Sporting Gijon	22	2		
2013–14	Sporting Gijon	38	2		
2014–15	Sporting Gijon	41	3		
2015–16	Sporting Gijon	16	1	**117**	**8**
2016–17	Middlesbrough	11	0	**11**	**0**

CHAPMAN, Harry (M) **23** **2**
H: 5 10 W: 11 00 b.Hartlepool 5-11-97
Internationals: England U18, U20.

2015–16	Middlesbrough	0	0		
2015–16	*Barnsley*	11	1	**11**	**1**
2016–17	Middlesbrough	0	0		
2016–17	*Sheffield U*	12	1	**12**	**1**

CLAYTON, Adam (M) **291** **20**
H: 5 9 W: 11 11 b.Manchester 14-1-89
Internationals: England U20.

2007–08	Manchester C	0	0		
2008–09	Manchester C	0	0		
2009–10	Manchester C	0	0		
2009–10	*Carlisle U*	28	1	**28**	**1**
2010–11	Leeds U	4	0		
2010–11	*Peterborough U*	7	0	**7**	**0**
2010–11	*Milton Keynes D*	6	1	**6**	**1**
2011–12	Leeds U	43	6	**47**	**6**
2012–13	Huddersfield T	43	4		
2013–14	Huddersfield T	42	7	**85**	**11**
2014–15	Middlesbrough	41	0		
2015–16	Middlesbrough	43	1		
2016–17	Middlesbrough	34	0	**118**	**1**

COOKE, Callum (F) **18** **4**
H: 5 8 W: 11 05 b.Peterlee 21-2-97
Internationals: England U16, U17, U18.

2016–17	Middlesbrough	0	0		
2016–17	*Crewe Alex*	18	4	**18**	**4**

DA SILVA, Fabio (M) **131** **2**
H: 5 8 W: 10 03 b.Rio de Janeiro 9-7-90
Internationals: Brazil U17, Full caps.

2008–09	Manchester U	0	0		
2009–10	Manchester U	5	0		
2010–11	Manchester U	11	1		
2011–12	Manchester U	5	0		
2012–13	Manchester U	0	0		
2012–13	*QPR*	21	0	**21**	**0**
2013–14	Manchester U	1	0	**22**	**1**
2013–14	Cardiff C	13	0		
2014–15	Cardiff C	28	0		
2015–16	Cardiff C	23	1	**64**	**1**
2016–17	Middlesbrough	24	0	**24**	**0**

DE PENA, Carlos (M) **64 15**
b. 11-3-92
2012–13 Nacional 6 1
2013–14 Nacional 24 3
2014–15 Nacional 26 9
2015–16 Nacional 2 2 **58 15**
2015–16 Middlesbrough 6 0
2016–17 Middlesbrough 0 0 **6 0**

DE ROON, Marten (M) **214 12**
H: 6 1 W: 12 00 b. 29-3-91
Internationals: Netherlands U19, Full caps.
2009–10 Sparta Rotterdam 3 0
2010–11 Sparta Rotterdam 27 0
2011–12 Sparta Rotterdam 28 2 **58 2**
2012–13 Heerenveen 24 1
2013–14 Heerenveen 31 3
2014–15 Heerenveen 32 1 **87 5**
2015–16 Atalanta 36 1 **36 1**
2016–17 Middlesbrough 33 4 **33 4**

DE SART, Julien (M) **73 4**
H: 6 0 W: 10 10 b.Waremme 23-12-94
Internationals: Belgium U16, U17, U18, U19, U21.
2013–14 Standard Liege 24 2
2014–15 Standard Liege 26 1
2015–16 Standard Liege 12 0 **62 3**
2015–16 Middlesbrough 2 0
2016–17 Middlesbrough 0 0 **2 0**
2016–17 *Derby Co* 9 1 **9 1**

DOWNING, Stewart (M) **460 43**
H: 5 11 W: 10 04 b.Middlesbrough 22-7-84
Internationals: England U21, B, Full caps.
2001–02 Middlesbrough 3 0
2002–03 Middlesbrough 2 0
2003–04 Middlesbrough 20 0
2003–04 *Sunderland* 7 3 **7 3**
2004–05 Middlesbrough 35 5
2005–06 Middlesbrough 12 1
2006–07 Middlesbrough 34 2
2007–08 Middlesbrough 38 9
2008–09 Middlesbrough 37 0
2009–10 Aston Villa 25 2
2010–11 Aston Villa 38 7 **63 9**
2011–12 Liverpool 36 0
2012–13 Liverpool 29 3
2013–14 Liverpool 0 0 **65 3**
2013–14 West Ham U 32 1
2014–15 West Ham U 37 6 **69 7**
2015–16 Middlesbrough 45 3
2016–17 Middlesbrough 30 1 **256 21**

FEWSTER, Bradley (F) **28 8**
H: 5 10 W: 11 00 b.Middlesbrough 27-1-96
Internationals: England U16, U17, U18, U19.
2013–14 Middlesbrough 0 0
2014–15 Middlesbrough 0 0
2014–15 *Preston NE* 0 0
2015–16 Middlesbrough 0 0
2015–16 *York C* 24 8 **24 8**
2016–17 Middlesbrough 0 0
2016–17 *Hartlepool U* 4 0 **4 0**

FISCHER, Viktor (F) **92 24**
H: 5 11 W: 11 03 b.Aarhus 9-6-94
Internationals: Denmark U16, U17, U19, U21, Full caps.
2012–13 Ajax 23 10
2013–14 Ajax 24 3
2014–15 Ajax 4 3
2015–16 Ajax 28 8 **79 24**
2016–17 Middlesbrough 13 0 **13 0**

FORSHAW, Adam (M) **187 14**
H: 6 1 W: 11 02 b.Liverpool 8-10-91
2009–10 Everton 0 0
2010–11 Everton 1 0
2011–12 Everton 0 0 **1 0**
2011–12 *Brentford* 7 0
2012–13 Brentford 43 3
2013–14 Brentford 39 8 **89 11**
2014–15 Wigan Ath 16 1 **16 1**
2014–15 Middlesbrough 18 0
2015–16 Middlesbrough 29 2
2016–17 Middlesbrough 34 0 **81 2**

FRIEND, George (D) **280 8**
H: 6 2 W: 13 01 b.Barnstaple 19-10-87
2008–09 Exeter C 4 0
2008–09 Wolverhampton W 6 0
2009–10 Wolverhampton W 1 0 **7 0**
2009–10 *Millwall* 6 0 **6 0**
2009–10 *Southend U* 6 1 **6 1**
2009–10 *Scunthorpe U* 4 0 **4 0**
2009–10 *Exeter C* 13 1 **17 1**
2010–11 Doncaster R 32 1
2011–12 Doncaster R 27 0
2012–13 Doncaster R 0 0 **59 1**
2012–13 Middlesbrough 34 0
2013–14 Middlesbrough 41 3
2014–15 Middlesbrough 42 1
2015–16 Middlesbrough 40 1
2016–17 Middlesbrough 24 0 **181 5**

FRY, Dael (D) **17 0**
H: 6 1 W: 11 05 b.Middlesbrough 30-8-97
Internationals: England U17, U18, U19, U20.
2015–16 Middlesbrough 7 0
2016–17 Middlesbrough 0 0 **7 0**
2016–17 *Rotherham U* 10 0 **10 0**

FRYER, Joe (G) **14 0**
b.Chester-le-Street 14-11-95
2016–17 Middlesbrough 0 0
2016–17 *Hartlepool U* 14 0 **14 0**

GESTEDE, Rudy (F) **228 58**
H: 6 4 W: 13 07 b.Nancy 10-10-88
Internationals: France U19. Benin Full caps.
2008–09 Metz 5 0
2009–10 *Cannes* 22 4 **22 4**
2010–11 Metz 11 3 **16 3**
2010–11 Metz B 3 1 **3 1**
2011–12 Cardiff C 25 2
2012–13 Cardiff C 27 5
2013–14 Cardiff C 3 0 **55 7**
2013–14 Blackburn R 27 13
2014–15 Blackburn R 39 20 **66 33**
2015–16 Aston Villa 32 5
2016–17 Aston Villa 18 4 **50 9**
2016–17 Middlesbrough 16 1 **16 1**

GIBSON, Ben (D) **181 4**
H: 6 1 W: 12 04 b.Nunthorpe 15-1-93
Internationals: England U17, U18, U20, U21.
2010–11 Middlesbrough 1 0
2011–12 Middlesbrough 0 0
2011–12 *Plymouth Arg* 13 0 **13 0**
2012–13 Middlesbrough 1 0
2012–13 *Tranmere R* 28 1 **28 1**
2013–14 Middlesbrough 31 1
2014–15 Middlesbrough 36 0
2015–16 Middlesbrough 33 1
2016–17 Middlesbrough 38 1 **140 3**

GUEDIOURA, Adiene (M) **255 20**
H: 6 1 W: 12 08 b.La Roche-sur-Yon 12-11-85
Internationals: Algeria Full caps.
2004–05 Sedan 0 0
2005–06 Noisy-Le-Sec 15 1 **15 1**
2006–07 L'Entente 21 3 **21 3**
2007–08 Creteil 24 6 **24 6**
2008–09 Kortrijk 10 0 **10 0**
2008–09 Charleroi 12 0
2009–10 Charleroi 13 1 **25 1**
2009–10 Wolverhampton W 14 1
2010–11 Wolverhampton W 10 1
2011–12 Wolverhampton W 10 0 **34 2**
2011–12 *Nottingham F* 19 1
2012–13 Nottingham F 35 3
2013–14 Nottingham F 5 0 **59 4**
2013–14 Crystal Palace 8 0
2014–15 Crystal Palace 7 0
2014–15 *Watford* 17 3
2015–16 Crystal Palace 0 0 **15 0**
2015–16 Watford 18 0
2016–17 Watford 12 0 **47 3**
2016–17 Middlesbrough 5 0 **5 0**

GUZAN, Brad (G) **249 0**
H: 6 4 W: 14 11 b.Chicago 9-9-84
Internationals: USA U23, Full caps.
2005 Chivas USA 24 0
2006 Chivas USA 13 0
2007 Chivas USA 27 0
2008 Chivas USA 15 0 **79 0**
2008–09 Aston Villa 1 0
2009–10 Aston Villa 0 0
2010–11 Aston Villa 0 0
2010–11 *Hull C* 16 0 **16 0**
2011–12 Aston Villa 7 0
2012–13 Aston Villa 36 0
2013–14 Aston Villa 38 0
2014–15 Aston Villa 34 0
2015–16 Aston Villa 28 0 **144 0**
2016–17 Middlesbrough 10 0 **10 0**

HUSBAND, James (D) **96 4**
H: 5 10 W: 10 00 b.Leeds 3-1-94
2011–12 Doncaster R 3 0
2012–13 Doncaster R 33 3
2013–14 Doncaster R 28 1 **64 4**
2014–15 Middlesbrough 3 0
2014–15 *Fulham* 5 0
2015–16 Middlesbrough 0 0
2015–16 *Fulham* 12 0 **17 0**
2015–16 *Huddersfield T* 11 0 **11 0**
2016–17 Middlesbrough 1 0 **4 0**

KITCHING, Mark (D) **6 0**
b.Guisborough 4-9-95
2013–14 Middlesbrough 0 0
2014–15 Middlesbrough 0 0
2015–16 Middlesbrough 0 0
2015–16 *York C* 1 0 **1 0**
2016–17 Middlesbrough 0 0
2016–17 *Rochdale* 5 0 **5 0**

KONSTANTOPOULOS, Dimitrios (G) **312 0**
H: 6 4 W: 14 02 b.Kalamata 29-11-78
Internationals: Greece U21, Full caps.
2003–04 Hartlepool U 0 0
2004–05 Hartlepool U 25 0
2005–06 Hartlepool U 46 0
2006–07 Hartlepool U 46 0 **117 0**
2007–08 Coventry C 21 0
2008–09 Coventry C 0 0
2008–09 *Swansea C* 4 0 **4 0**
2008–09 *Cardiff C* 6 0 **6 0**
2009–10 Coventry C 3 0 **24 0**
2010–11 Kerkyra 30 0 **30 0**
2011–12 AEK Athens 9 0
2012–13 AEK Athens 24 0 **33 0**
2013–14 Middlesbrough 12 0
2014–15 Middlesbrough 40 0
2015–16 Middlesbrough 46 0
2016–17 Middlesbrough 0 0 **98 0**

LEADBITTER, Grant (M) **410 50**
H: 5 9 W: 11 06 b.Chester-le-Street 7-1-86
Internationals: England U16, U17, U19, U20, U21.
2002–03 Sunderland 0 0
2003–04 Sunderland 0 0
2004–05 Sunderland 0 0
2005–06 Sunderland 12 0
2005–06 *Rotherham U* 5 1 **5 1**
2006–07 Sunderland 44 7
2007–08 Sunderland 31 2
2008–09 Sunderland 23 2
2009–10 Sunderland 1 0 **111 11**
2009–10 Ipswich T 38 3
2010–11 Ipswich T 44 5
2011–12 Ipswich T 34 5
2012–13 Ipswich T 0 0 **116 13**
2012–13 Middlesbrough 42 3
2013–14 Middlesbrough 39 6
2014–15 Middlesbrough 43 11
2015–16 Middlesbrough 41 4
2016–17 Middlesbrough 13 1 **178 25**

MALONEY, Lewis (D) **0 0**
b. 5-5-95
Internationals: Northern Ireland U21.
2015–16 Middlesbrough 0 0
2016–17 Middlesbrough 0 0

MEJIAS, Tomas (G) **11 0**
H: 6 5 W: 13 02 b.Madrid 30-1-89
Internationals: Spain U19, U20.
2010–11 Real Madrid 1 0
2011–12 Real Madrid 0 0
2012–13 Real Madrid 0 0
2013–14 Real Madrid 0 0 **1 0**
2013–14 *Middlesbrough* 1 0
2014–15 Middlesbrough 7 0
2015–16 Middlesbrough 0 0
2016–17 Middlesbrough 0 0 **8 0**
2016–17 *Rayo Vallecano* 2 0 **2 0**

MORRIS, Bryn (M) **30 0**
H: 6 0 W: 11 01 b.Hartlepool 25-4-96
Internationals: England U16, U17, U18, U19, U20.
2012–13 Middlesbrough 1 0
2013–14 Middlesbrough 1 0
2014–15 Middlesbrough 0 0
2014–15 *Burton Alb* 5 0 **5 0**
2015–16 Middlesbrough 0 0
2015–16 *Coventry C* 6 0 **6 0**
2015–16 *York C* 3 0 **3 0**
2015–16 *Walsall* 1 0 **1 0**
2016–17 Middlesbrough 0 0 **2 0**
2016–17 *Shrewsbury T* 13 0 **13 0**

NEGREDO, Alvaro (F) **332 129**
H: 6 1 W: 12 11 b.Madrid 20-8-85
Internationals: Spain U21, Full caps.
2007–08 Almeria 36 13
2008–09 Almeria 34 18 **70 31**
2009–10 Sevilla 35 11
2010–11 Sevilla 38 20
2011–12 Sevilla 30 14
2012–13 Sevilla 36 25 **139 70**
2013–14 Manchester C 32 9

2014–15	Manchester C	0	0	**32**	**9**
2014–15	*Valencia*	30	5		
2015–16	Valencia	25	5		
2016–17	Valencia	0	0	**55**	**10**

On loan from Valencia.

2016–17	Middlesbrough	36	9	**36**	**9**

RAMIREZ, Gaston (M) 169 28
H: 6 0 W: 12 00 b.Montevideo 2-12-90
Internationals: Uruguay U20, U23, Full caps.

2010–11	Bologna	24	4		
2011–12	Bologna	33	8	**57**	**12**
2012–13	Southampton	26	5		
2013–14	Southampton	18	1		
2014–15	Southampton	1	0		
2014–15	*Hull C*	22	1	**22**	**1**
2015–16	Southampton	3	0	**48**	**6**
2015–16	*Middlesbrough*	18	7		
2016–17	Middlesbrough	24	2	**42**	**9**

RHODES, Jordan (F) 354 174
H: 6 1 W: 11 03 b.Oldham 5-2-90
Internationals: Scotland U21, Full caps.

2007–08	Ipswich T	8	1		
2008–09	Ipswich T	2	0	**10**	**1**
2008–09	*Rochdale*	5	2	**5**	**2**
2008–09	*Brentford*	14	7	**14**	**7**
2009–10	Huddersfield T	45	19		
2010–11	Huddersfield T	37	16		
2011–12	Huddersfield T	40	35		
2012–13	Huddersfield T	2	2	**124**	**72**
2012–13	Blackburn R	43	27		
2013–14	Blackburn R	46	25		
2014–15	Blackburn R	45	21		
2015–16	Blackburn R	25	10	**159**	**83**
2015–16	Middlesbrough	18	6		
2016–17	Middlesbrough	6	0	**24**	**6**
2016–17	*Sheffield W*	18	3	**18**	**3**

RIPLEY, Connor (G) 99 0
H: 5 11 W: 11 13 b.Middlesbrough 13-2-93
Internationals: England U19, U20.

2010–11	Middlesbrough	1	0		
2011–12	Middlesbrough	1	0		
2011–12	*Oxford U*	1	0	**1**	**0**
2012–13	Middlesbrough	0	0		
2013–14	Middlesbrough	0	0		
2013–14	*Bradford C*	0	0		
2014	*Ostersunds*	14	0	**14**	**0**
2014–15	Middlesbrough	0	0		
2015–16	Middlesbrough	0	0		
2015–16	*Motherwell*	36	0	**36**	**0**
2016–17	Middlesbrough	0	0	**2**	**0**
2016–17	*Oldham Ath*	46	0	**46**	**0**

STUANI, Christian (F) 331 112
H: 6 0 W: 11 05 b.Tala 12-10-86
Internationals: Uruguay Full caps.

2003–04	Danubio	2	0		
2004–05	Danubio	5	0		
2005–06	Danubio	15	4		
2006–07	Danubio	0	0		
2006–07	*Bella Vista*	14	12	**14**	**12**
2007–08	Danubio	14	19	**36**	**23**
2007–08	Reggina	12	0		
2008–09	Reggina	6	1		
2009–10	Reggina	0	0		
2009–10	*Albacete*	39	23	**39**	**23**
2010–11	Reggina	0	0		
2010–11	*Levante*	30	8	**30**	**8**
2011–12	Reggina	0	0		
2011–12	*Racing Santander*	32	9	**32**	**9**
2012–13	Reggina	0	0	**18**	**1**
2012–13	*Espanyol*	32	7		
2013–14	Espanyol	34	6		
2014–15	Espanyol	37	12	**103**	**25**
2015–16	Middlesbrough	36	7		
2016–17	Middlesbrough	23	4	**59**	**11**

TRAORE, Adama (F) 39 0
H: 5 10 W: 12 00 b.L'Hospitalet de Llobregat 25-1-96
Internationals: Spain U16, U17, U19.

2013–14	Barcelona	1	0		
2014–15	Barcelona	0	0	**1**	**0**
2015–16	Aston Villa	10	0		
2016–17	Aston Villa	1	0	**11**	**0**
2016–17	Middlesbrough	27	0	**27**	**0**

VALDES, Victor (G) 422 0
H: 6 2 W: 12 04 b.L'Hospitalet de Llobregat 14-1-82
Internationals: Spain U18, U19, U20, U21, Full caps.

2002–03	Barcelona	14	0		
2003–04	Barcelona	33	0		
2004–05	Barcelona	35	0		
2005–06	Barcelona	35	0		
2006–07	Barcelona	38	0		
2007–08	Barcelona	35	0		
2008–09	Barcelona	35	0		
2009–10	Barcelona	38	0		
2010–11	Barcelona	32	0		
2011–12	Barcelona	35	0		
2012–13	Barcelona	31	0		
2013–14	Barcelona	26	0	**387**	**0**
2014–15	Manchester U	2	0		
2015–16	Manchester U	0	0	**2**	**0**
2015–16	*Standard Liege*	5	0	**5**	**0**
2016–17	Middlesbrough	28	0	**28**	**0**

Players retained or with offer of contract
Asiedu, William Opoku; Bamford, Patrick James; Cook, James Michael; Coulson, Hayden Ross; Curry, Mitchell; Elsdon, Matthew; Espinosa, Zuniga Bernardo Jose; Hegarty, Liam Michael; John-Baptiste, Alex; Johnson, Callum Charles; Liddle, Ben George; McGinley, Nathan; Morelli, Joao Neto; Osorio, Tomas Mejias; Pattison, Alexander Antony; Pears, Aynsley Alan William; Sanchez, Ayala Daniel; Soisalo, Mikael; Tavernier, Marcus Joseph; Tinkler, Robbie.

Scholars
Cooke, Liam; Dale, Nathan; Guru, Nathan; Hemming, Zachary; James, Bradley David; Lambert, Jack; Malley, Connor; O'Neill, Tyrone; Reading, Patrick James; Renton, Anthony Peter; Storey, Keiran; Wilson, Jay Harry.

MILLWALL (53)

ABDOU, Nadjim (M) 427 11
H: 5 10 W: 11 02 b.Martigues 13-7-84
Internationals: Comoros Full caps.

2002–03	Martigues	26	1	**26**	**1**
2003–04	Sedan	17	0		
2004–05	Sedan	32	2		
2005–06	Sedan	14	0		
2006–07	Sedan	17	0	**80**	**2**
2007–08	Plymouth Arg	31	1	**31**	**1**
2008–09	Millwall	36	3		
2009–10	Millwall	43	1		
2010–11	Millwall	34	0		
2011–12	Millwall	40	0		
2012–13	Millwall	39	1		
2013–14	Millwall	24	0		
2014–15	Millwall	33	1		
2015–16	Millwall	29	1		
2016–17	Millwall	12	0	**290**	**7**

ARCHER, Jordan (G) 115 0
H: 6 1 W: 12 08 b.Walthamstow 12-4-93
Internationals: Scotland U19, U20, U21.

2011–12	Tottenham H	0	0		
2012–13	Tottenham H	0	0		
2012–13	*Wycombe W*	27	0	**27**	**0**
2013–14	Tottenham H	0	0		
2014–15	Tottenham H	0	0		
2014–15	*Northampton T*	13	0	**13**	**0**
2014–15	*Millwall*	0	0		
2015–16	Millwall	39	0		
2016–17	Millwall	36	0	**75**	**0**

BROWN, James (D) 0 0

2016–17	Millwall	0	0		

BUTCHER, Calum (D) 94 8
H: 6 1 W: 13 01 b.Rochford 26-2-91

2007–08	Tottenham H	0	0		
2008–09	Tottenham H	0	0		
2009–10	Tottenham H	0	0		
2009–10	*Barnet*	3	0	**3**	**0**

From Hayes & Yeading.

2013–14	Dundee U	6	0		
2014–15	Dundee U	15	1	**21**	**1**
2015–16	Burton Alb	39	5		
2016–17	Burton Alb	1	0	**40**	**5**
2016–17	Millwall	30	2	**30**	**2**

CHESMAIN, Noah (F) 1 0
b. 16-12-97

2015–16	Millwall	1	0		
2016–17	Millwall	0	0	**1**	**0**

CRAIG, Tony (D) 408 9
H: 6 0 W: 10 03 b.Greenwich 20-4-85

2002–03	Millwall	2	1		
2003–04	Millwall	9	0		
2004–05	Millwall	10	0		
2004–05	*Wycombe W*	14	0	**14**	**0**
2005–06	Millwall	28	0		
2006–07	Millwall	30	1		
2007–08	Crystal Palace	13	0	**13**	**0**
2007–08	*Millwall*	5	1		
2008–09	Millwall	44	2		
2009–10	Millwall	30	2		
2010–11	Millwall	24	0		
2011–12	Millwall	23	0		
2011–12	*Leyton Orient*	4	0	**4**	**0**
2012–13	Brentford	44	0		
2013–14	Brentford	44	0		
2014–15	Brentford	23	0	**111**	**0**
2015–16	Millwall	18	1		
2016–17	Millwall	43	1	**266**	**9**

CUMMINGS, Shaun (D) 156 2
H: 6 0 W: 11 10 b.Hammersmith 25-2-89
Internationals: Jamaica Full caps.

2007–08	Chelsea	0	0		
2008–09	Chelsea	0	0		
2008–09	*Milton Keynes D*	32	0	**32**	**0**
2009–10	Chelsea	0	0		
2009–10	*WBA*	3	0	**3**	**0**
2009–10	Reading	8	0		
2010–11	Reading	10	0		
2011–12	Reading	34	0		
2012–13	Reading	9	0		
2013–14	Reading	11	0		
2014–15	Reading	5	1	**77**	**1**
2014–15	Millwall	12	0		
2015–16	Millwall	16	1		
2016–17	Millwall	16	0	**44**	**1**

DONOVAN, Harry (M) 0 0
From Arsenal.

2016–17	Millwall	0	0		

FARRELL, Kyron (M) 0 0
b. 17-8-97
Internationals: Republic of Ireland U17, U18, U19.

2015–16	Millwall	0	0		
2016–17	Millwall	0	0		

FERGUSON, Shane (D) 131 6
H: 5 9 W: 10 01 b.Limavady 12-7-91
Internationals: Northern Ireland U17, U19, U21, B, Full caps.

2008–09	Newcastle U	0	0		
2009–10	Newcastle U	0	0		
2010–11	Newcastle U	7	0		
2011–12	Newcastle U	7	0		
2012–13	Newcastle U	9	0		
2012–13	*Birmingham C*	11	1		
2013–14	Newcastle U	0	0		
2013–14	*Birmingham C*	18	0	**29**	**1**
2014–15	Newcastle U	0	0		
2014–15	*Rangers*	0	0		
2015–16	Newcastle U	0	0	**23**	**0**
2015–16	Millwall	39	3		
2016–17	Millwall	40	2	**79**	**5**

FORDE, David (G) 441 0
H: 6 3 W: 13 06 b.Galway 20-12-79
Internationals: Republic of Ireland Full caps.

2001–02	West Ham U	0	0		
2002–03	West Ham U	0	0		
2003–04	West Ham U	0	0		
2004	Derry C	11	0		
2005	Derry C	33	0		
2006	Derry C	29	0	**73**	**0**
2006–07	Cardiff C	7	0		
2007–08	Cardiff C	0	0	**7**	**0**
2007–08	*Luton T*	5	0	**5**	**0**
2007–08	*Bournemouth*	11	0	**11**	**0**
2008–09	Millwall	46	0		
2009–10	Millwall	46	0		
2010–11	Millwall	46	0		
2011–12	Millwall	27	0		
2012–13	Millwall	40	0		
2013–14	Millwall	40	0		
2014–15	Millwall	46	0		
2015–16	Millwall	8	0		
2016–17	Millwall	0	0	**299**	**0**
2016–17	*Portsmouth*	46	0	**46**	**0**

GIRLING, Harry (G) 0 0
b. 15-1-98

2015–16	Millwall	0	0		
2016–17	Millwall	0	0		

GREGORY, Lee (F) 117 44
H: 6 2 b.Sheffield 26-8-88

2014–15	Millwall	39	9		
2015–16	Millwall	41	18		
2016–17	Millwall	37	17	**117**	**44**

HUTCHINSON, Shaun (D) 171 11
H: 6 1 W: 12 04 b.Newcastle upon Tyne 23-11-90

2008–09	Motherwell	1	0		
2009–10	Motherwell	5	3		
2010–11	Motherwell	19	1		
2011–12	Motherwell	30	1		

Season	Club	Apps	Gls	Total Apps	Total Gls
2012–13	Motherwell	31	1		
2013–14	Motherwell	35	1	**121**	**7**
2014–15	Fulham	25	2		
2015–16	Fulham	9	0	**34**	**2**
2016–17	Millwall	16	2	**16**	**2**

KING, Tom (G) **11 0**
H: 6 1 b.Plymouth 9-3-95
Internationals: England U17.

Season	Club	Apps	Gls	Total Apps	Total Gls
2011–12	Crystal Palace	0	0		
2012–13	Crystal Palace	0	0		
2014–15	Millwall	0	0		
2015–16	Millwall	0	0		
2016–17	Millwall	11	0	**11**	**0**

MARTIN, Joe (M) **235 11**
H: 6 0 W: 12 13 b.Dagenham 29-11-88
Internationals: England U16, U17.

Season	Club	Apps	Gls	Total Apps	Total Gls
2005–06	Tottenham H	0	0		
2006–07	Tottenham H	0	0		
2007–08	Tottenham H	0	0		
2007–08	*Blackpool*	1	0		
2008–09	Blackpool	15	0		
2009–10	Blackpool	6	0	**22**	**0**
2010–11	Gillingham	17	1		
2011–12	Gillingham	35	1		
2012–13	Gillingham	38	2		
2013–14	Gillingham	46	2		
2014–15	Gillingham	25	2	**161**	**8**
2015–16	Millwall	29	2		
2016–17	Millwall	23	1	**52**	**3**

MBULU, Christian (D) **0 0**
b. 6-8-96

Season	Club	Apps	Gls	Total Apps	Total Gls
2015–16	Millwall	0	0		
2016–17	Millwall	0	0		

MORISON, Steven (F) **325 87**
H: 6 2 W: 13 07 b.Enfield 29-8-83
Internationals: England C. Wales Full caps.

Season	Club	Apps	Gls	Total Apps	Total Gls
2001–02	Northampton T	1	0		
2002–03	Northampton T	13	1		
2003–04	Northampton T	5	1		
2004–05	Northampton T	4	1	**23**	**3**
From Stevenage B.					
2008–09	Millwall	0	0		
2009–10	Millwall	43	20		
2010–11	Millwall	40	15		
2011–12	Norwich C	34	9		
2012–13	Norwich C	19	1	**53**	**10**
2012–13	Leeds U	15	3		
2013–14	Leeds U	0	0		
2013–14	*Millwall*	41	8		
2014–15	Leeds U	26	2	**41**	**5**
2015–16	Millwall	46	15		
2016–17	Millwall	38	11	**208**	**69**

NELSON, Sid (D) **40 0**
H: 6 1 b.London 1-1-96

Season	Club	Apps	Gls	Total Apps	Total Gls
2013–14	Millwall	0	0		
2014–15	Millwall	14	0		
2015–16	Millwall	9	0		
2016–17	Millwall	3	0	**26**	**0**
2016–17	*Newport Co*	14	0	**14**	**0**

O'BRIEN, Aiden (F) **117 25**
H: 5 8 W: 10 12 b.Islington 4-10-93
Internationals: Republic of Ireland U17, U19, U21.

Season	Club	Apps	Gls	Total Apps	Total Gls
2010–11	Millwall	0	0		
2011–12	Millwall	0	0		
2012–13	Millwall	0	0		
2012–13	*Crawley T*	9	0	**9**	**0**
2013–14	Millwall	0	0		
2013–14	*Torquay U*	3	0	**3**	**0**
2014–15	Millwall	19	2		
2015–16	Millwall	43	10		
2016–17	Millwall	43	13	**105**	**25**

ONYEDINMA, Fred (M) **107 15**
H: 6 1 b.London 24-11-96

Season	Club	Apps	Gls	Total Apps	Total Gls
2013–14	Millwall	4	0		
2014–15	Millwall	2	0		
2014–15	*Wycombe W*	25	8	**25**	**8**
2015–16	Millwall	34	4		
2016–17	Millwall	42	3	**82**	**7**

PAVEY, Alfie (F) **6 0**
b. 2-10-95

Season	Club	Apps	Gls	Total Apps	Total Gls
2013–14	Millwall	0	0		
2014–15	Millwall	1	0		
2015–16	Millwall	4	0		
2016–17	Millwall	1	0	**6**	**0**

PHILPOT, Jamie (F) **9 1**
b. 2-10-96

Season	Club	Apps	Gls	Total Apps	Total Gls
2014–15	Millwall	1	1		
2015–16	Millwall	6	0		
2016–17	Millwall	2	0	**9**	**1**

ROMEO, Mahlon (M) **51 1**
H: 5 10 W: 11 05 b.Westminster 19-9-95
Internationals: Antigua and Barbuda Full caps.

Season	Club	Apps	Gls	Total Apps	Total Gls
2012–13	Gillingham	1	0		
2013–14	Gillingham	0	0		
2014–15	Gillingham	0	0	**1**	**0**
2015–16	Millwall	18	1		
2016–17	Millwall	32	0	**50**	**1**

ROONEY, Paul (D) **0 0**
b.Dublin 22-3-97
From St Patricks Ath, Bohemians.

Season	Club	Apps	Gls	Total Apps	Total Gls
2016–17	Millwall	0	0		

SMITH, Harry (F) **9 1**
H: 6 5 b. 18-5-95
From Sittingbourne, Folkestone Invicta.

Season	Club	Apps	Gls	Total Apps	Total Gls
2016–17	Millwall	9	1	**9**	**1**

THOMPSON, Ben (M) **66 1**
H: 5 11 W: 12 04 b. 3-10-95

Season	Club	Apps	Gls	Total Apps	Total Gls
2014–15	Millwall	0	0		
2015–16	Millwall	28	1		
2016–17	Millwall	38	0	**66**	**1**

TWARDEK, Kris (M) **0 0**
b.Toronto 8-3-97
Internationals: Czech Republic U17, U18, U19. Canada Full caps.

Season	Club	Apps	Gls	Total Apps	Total Gls
2015–16	Millwall	0	0		
2016–17	Millwall	0	0		

WEBSTER, Byron (D) **252 20**
H: 6 5 W: 12 07 b.Sherburn-in-Elmet 31-3-87

Season	Club	Apps	Gls	Total Apps	Total Gls
2007–08	Siad Most	23	4		
2008–09	Siad Most	0	0	**23**	**4**
2009–10	Doncaster R	5	0		
2010–11	Doncaster R	7	0	**12**	**0**
2010–11	*Hereford U*	2	0	**2**	**0**
2010–11	*Northampton T*	8	0		
2011–12	Northampton T	13	0	**21**	**0**
2012–13	Yeovil T	44	5		
2013–14	Yeovil T	41	3		
2014–15	Millwall	11	0		
2014–15	*Yeovil T*	14	0	**99**	**8**
2015–16	Millwall	40	6		
2016–17	Millwall	44	2	**95**	**8**

WILLIAMS, Shaun (M) **323 51**
H: 5 9 W: 11 11 b.Dublin 19-10-86
Internationals: Republic of Ireland U21, U23.

Season	Club	Apps	Gls	Total Apps	Total Gls
2007	Drogheda U	0	0		
2007	*Dundalk*	19	9	**19**	**9**
2008	Drogheda U	4	0		
2008	*Finn Harps*	14	2	**14**	**2**
2009	Drogheda U	1	0	**5**	**0**
2009	Sporting Fingal	13	7		
2010	Sporting Fingal	32	5	**45**	**12**
2011–12	Milton Keynes D	39	8		
2012–13	Milton Keynes D	44	3		
2013–14	Milton Keynes D	25	8	**108**	**19**
2013–14	Millwall	17	1		
2014–15	Millwall	38	2		
2015–16	Millwall	33	2		
2016–17	Millwall	44	4	**132**	**9**

WORRALL, David (M) **303 23**
H: 6 0 W: 11 03 b.Manchester 12-6-90

Season	Club	Apps	Gls	Total Apps	Total Gls
2006–07	Bury	1	0		
2007–08	Bury	0	0		
2007–08	WBA	0	0		
2008–09	*Accrington S*	4	0	**4**	**0**
2008–09	*Shrewsbury T*	9	0	**9**	**0**
2009–10	WBA	0	0		
2009–10	Bury	40	4		
2010–11	Bury	40	2		
2011–12	Bury	41	3		
2012–13	Bury	41	2	**163**	**11**
2013–14	Rotherham U	3	1	**3**	**1**
2013–14	*Oldham Ath*	18	1	**18**	**1**
2014–15	Southend U	38	6		
2015–16	Southend U	35	3	**73**	**9**
2016–17	Millwall	33	1	**33**	**1**

WYLDE, Gregg (M) **165 15**
H: 5 9 W: 11 04 b.Kirkintilloch 23-3-91
Internationals: Scotland U17, U19, U21.

Season	Club	Apps	Gls	Total Apps	Total Gls
2009–10	Rangers	4	0		
2010–11	Rangers	30	0		
2011–12	Rangers	42	4	**76**	**4**
2012–13	Bolton W	0	0		
2012–13	*Bury*	4	0	**4**	**0**
2013–14	Aberdeen	8	1	**8**	**1**
2013–14	St Mirren	17	2	**17**	**2**
2015–16	Plymouth Arg	43	7	**43**	**7**
2016–17	Millwall	5	0	**5**	**0**
2016–17	*Northampton T*	12	1	**12**	**1**

Players retained or with offer of contract
Sandford, Ryan David Luca.

Scholars
Campbell-Mhlope, Matthew Blair; Day, Matthew George; Debrah, Jesse John Kodjo; Ebuzoeme, Ii Ezechukwu Aniere Uzoma; Green, Ryan Aaron; Hanson, Jethro Kirk; Jackson, Samuel John; Leighton, Noel Stuart; McNamara, Danny John; Mundle-Smith, Kyren Cassius; Neary, Matthew Kieron; Olaofe, Isaac Tanitoluwaloba; Queeley, Kristopher Reuben; Saunders-Henry, Mason Bradley; White, James Alan; White, Lewis Antonio; Wicks, Joseph Ryan.

MILTON KEYNES D (54)

AGARD, Kieran (F) **222 61**
H: 5 10 W: 10 10 b.Newham 10-10-89

Season	Club	Apps	Gls	Total Apps	Total Gls
2006–07	Everton	0	0		
2007–08	Everton	0	0		
2008–09	Everton	0	0		
2009–10	Everton	1	0		
2010–11	Everton	0	0	**1**	**0**
2010–11	*Kilmarnock*	8	1	**8**	**1**
2010–11	*Peterborough U*	0	0		
2011–12	Yeovil T	29	6	**29**	**6**
2012–13	Rotherham U	30	6		
2013–14	Rotherham U	46	21		
2014–15	Rotherham U	2	0	**78**	**27**
2014–15	Bristol C	39	13		
2015–16	Bristol C	25	2	**64**	**15**
2016–17	Milton Keynes D	42	12	**42**	**12**

ANEKE, Chuks (M) **98 26**
H: 6 3 W: 13 01 b.Newham 3-7-93
Internationals: England U16, U17, U18, U19.

Season	Club	Apps	Gls	Total Apps	Total Gls
2010–11	Arsenal	0	0		
2011–12	Arsenal	0	0		
2011–12	*Stevenage*	6	0	**6**	**0**
2011–12	*Preston NE*	7	1	**7**	**1**
2012–13	Arsenal	0	0		
2012–13	*Crewe Alex*	30	6		
2013–14	Arsenal	0	0		
2013–14	*Crewe Alex*	40	15	**70**	**21**
2014–15	Arsenal	0	0		
2014–15	Zulte-Waregem	0	0		
2016–17	Milton Keynes D	15	4	**15**	**4**

BALDOCK, George (M) **148 5**
H: 5 9 W: 10 07 b.Buckingham 26-1-93

Season	Club	Apps	Gls	Total Apps	Total Gls
2009–10	Milton Keynes D	1	0		
2010–11	Milton Keynes D	2	0		
2011–12	Milton Keynes D	0	0		
2011–12	*Northampton T*	5	0	**5**	**0**
2012–13	Milton Keynes D	2	0		
2013–14	Milton Keynes D	38	2		
2014–15	Milton Keynes D	9	0		
2014–15	*Oxford U*	12	1		
2015–16	Milton Keynes D	15	0		
2015–16	*Oxford U*	27	2	**39**	**3**
2016–17	Milton Keynes D	37	0	**104**	**2**

BOWDITCH, Dean (F) **384 77**
H: 5 11 W: 11 05 b.Bishops Stortford 15-6-86
Internationals: England U16, U17, U19.

Season	Club	Apps	Gls	Total Apps	Total Gls
2002–03	Ipswich T	5	0		
2003–04	Ipswich T	16	4		
2004–05	Ipswich T	21	3		
2004–05	*Burnley*	10	1	**10**	**1**
2005–06	Ipswich T	21	0		
2005–06	*Wycombe W*	11	1	**11**	**1**
2006–07	Ipswich T	9	1		
2006–07	*Brighton & HA*	3	1		
2007–08	Ipswich T	0	0		
2007–08	*Northampton T*	10	2	**10**	**2**
2007–08	*Brighton & HA*	5	0	**8**	**1**
2008–09	Ipswich T	1	0	**73**	**8**
2008–09	*Brentford*	9	2	**9**	**2**
2009–10	Yeovil T	30	10		
2010–11	Yeovil T	41	15	**71**	**25**
2011–12	Milton Keynes D	41	12		
2012–13	Milton Keynes D	39	8		
2013–14	Milton Keynes D	12	1		
2014–15	Milton Keynes D	35	7		
2015–16	Milton Keynes D	37	4		
2016–17	Milton Keynes D	28	5	**192**	**37**

BRITTAIN, Callum (F) **6 0**
H: 5 10 W: 10 10 b.Bedford 12-3-98

Season	Club	Apps	Gls	Total Apps	Total Gls
2015–16	Milton Keynes D	0	0		
2016–17	Milton Keynes D	6	0	**6**	**0**

BURNS, Charlie (G) **5 0**
H: 6 2 b.Croydon 27-5-95

Season	Club	Apps	Gls	Total Apps	Total Gls
2012–13	Milton Keynes D	0	0		

2013–14 Milton Keynes D 1 0
2014–15 Milton Keynes D 0 0
2015–16 Milton Keynes D 4 0
2016–17 Milton Keynes D 0 0 **5 0**

DOWNING, Paul (D) 225 6
H: 6 1 W: 12 06 b.Taunton 26-10-91
2009–10 WBA 0 0
2009–10 *Hereford U* 6 0
2010–11 WBA 0 0
2010–11 *Hereford U* 0 0 **6 0**
2010–11 *Swansea C* 0 0
2011–12 WBA 0 0
2011–12 *Barnet* 26 0 **26 0**
2012–13 Walsall 31 1
2013–14 Walsall 44 1
2014–15 Walsall 35 1
2015–16 Walsall 46 3 **156 6**
2016–17 Milton Keynes D 37 0 **37 0**

FURLONG, Connor (M) 1 0
b. 7-2-98
Internationals: Scotland U16.
2015–16 Milton Keynes D 1 0
2016–17 Milton Keynes D 0 0 **1 0**

JACKSON, Oran (D) 1 0
b. 16-10-98
2015–16 Milton Keynes D 1 0
2016–17 Milton Keynes D 0 0 **1 0**

KASUMU, David (M) 0 0
b. 5-10-99
2015–16 Milton Keynes D 0 0
2016–17 Milton Keynes D 0 0

LEWINGTON, Dean (D) 580 21
H: 5 11 W: 11 07 b.Kingston 18-5-84
2002–03 Wimbledon 1 0
2003–04 Wimbledon 28 1 **29 1**
2004–05 Milton Keynes D 43 2
2005–06 Milton Keynes D 44 1
2006–07 Milton Keynes D 45 1
2007–08 Milton Keynes D 45 0
2008–09 Milton Keynes D 40 2
2009–10 Milton Keynes D 42 1
2010–11 Milton Keynes D 42 3
2011–12 Milton Keynes D 46 3
2012–13 Milton Keynes D 38 1
2013–14 Milton Keynes D 43 1
2014–15 Milton Keynes D 41 3
2015–16 Milton Keynes D 46 1
2016–17 Milton Keynes D 36 1 **551 20**

LOGAN, Hugo (F) 0 0
b. 21-9-98
Internationals: England U17.
2016–17 Milton Keynes D 0 0

MARTIN, David E (G) 331 0
H: 6 1 W: 13 04 b.Romford 22-1-86
Internationals: England U16, U17, U18, U19.
2003–04 Wimbledon 2 0 **2 0**
2004–05 Milton Keynes D 15 0
2005–06 Milton Keynes D 0 0
2005–06 Liverpool 0 0
2006–07 Liverpool 0 0
2006–07 *Accrington S* 10 0 **10 0**
2007–08 Liverpool 0 0
2008–09 Liverpool 0 0
2008–09 *Leicester C* 25 0 **25 0**
2009–10 Liverpool 0 0
2009–10 *Tranmere R* 3 0 **3 0**
2009–10 *Leeds U* 0 0
2009–10 *Derby Co* 2 0 **2 0**
2010–11 Milton Keynes D 43 0
2011–12 Milton Keynes D 46 0
2012–13 Milton Keynes D 31 0
2013–14 Milton Keynes D 40 0
2014–15 Milton Keynes D 39 0
2015–16 Milton Keynes D 35 0
2016–17 Milton Keynes D 40 0 **289 0**

MAYNARD, Nicky (F) 302 93
H: 5 11 W: 11 00 b.Winsford 11-12-86
2005–06 Crewe Alex 1 1
2006–07 Crewe Alex 31 16
2007–08 Crewe Alex 27 14 **59 31**
2008–09 Bristol C 43 11
2009–10 Bristol C 42 20
2010–11 Bristol C 13 6
2011–12 Bristol C 27 8 **125 45**
2011–12 West Ham U 14 2
2012–13 West Ham U 0 0 **14 2**
2012–13 Cardiff C 4 1
2013–14 Cardiff C 8 0
2013–14 *Wigan Ath* 16 4 **16 4**
2014–15 Cardiff C 10 1 **22 2**
2015–16 Milton Keynes D 35 7
2016–17 Milton Keynes D 31 2 **66 9**

MUIRHEAD, Robbie (F) 99 11
b. 8-3-96
Internationals: Scotland U16, U17, U18, U19.
2012–13 Kilmarnock 1 0
2013–14 Kilmarnock 21 2 **22 2**
2014–15 Kilmarknock 20 2 **20 2**
2014–15 Dundee U 13 2
2015–16 Dundee U 0 0 **13 2**
2015–16 *Partick Thistle* 8 2 **8 2**
2016–17 Hearts 17 1 **17 1**
2016–17 Milton Keynes D 19 2 **19 2**

NGOMBO, Maecky (F) 32 4
b. 31-3-95
Internationals: Belgium U21.
2015–16 Roda 17 4 **17 4**
2016–17 Fortuna Dusseldorf 6 0 **6 0**
On loan from Fortuna Dusseldorf.
2016–17 Milton Keynes D 9 0 **9 0**

NICHOLLS, Lee (G) 87 0
H: 6 3 W: 13 05 b.Huyton 5-10-92
Internationals: England U19.
2009–10 Wigan Ath 0 0
2010–11 Wigan Ath 0 0
2010–11 *Hartlepool U* 0 0
2010–11 *Shrewsbury T* 0 0
2010–11 *Sheffield W* 0 0
2011–12 Wigan Ath 0 0
2011–12 *Accrington S* 9 0 **9 0**
2012–13 Wigan Ath 0 0
2012–13 *Northampton T* 46 0 **46 0**
2013–14 Wigan Ath 6 0
2014–15 Wigan Ath 1 0
2015–16 Wigan Ath 2 0 **9 0**
2015–16 *Bristol R* 15 0 **15 0**
2016–17 Milton Keynes D 8 0 **8 0**

NOMBE, Sam (F) 0 0
2016–17 Milton Keynes D 0 0

OSEI- BONSU, Andrew (M) 0 0
2016–17 Milton Keynes D 0 0

POTTER, Darren (M) 393 17
H: 6 0 W: 10 08 b.Liverpool 21-12-84
Internationals: Republic of Ireland Full caps.
2001–02 Liverpool 0 0
2002–03 Liverpool 0 0
2003–04 Liverpool 0 0
2004–05 Liverpool 2 0
2005–06 Liverpool 0 0
2005–06 *Southampton* 10 0 **10 0**
2006–07 Liverpool 0 0 **2 0**
2006–07 Wolverhampton W 38 0
2007–08 Wolverhampton W 18 0
2008–09 Wolverhampton W 0 0 **56 0**
2008–09 *Sheffield W* 17 2
2009–10 Sheffield W 46 3
2010–11 Sheffield W 33 3 **96 8**
2011–12 Milton Keynes D 40 2
2012–13 Milton Keynes D 46 4
2013–14 Milton Keynes D 29 0
2014–15 Milton Keynes D 40 2
2015–16 Milton Keynes D 37 0
2016–17 Milton Keynes D 37 1 **229 9**

POWELL, Daniel (F) 231 37
H: 5 11 W: 13 03 b.Luton 12-3-91
2008–09 Milton Keynes D 7 1
2009–10 Milton Keynes D 2 1
2010–11 Milton Keynes D 29 9
2011–12 Milton Keynes D 43 6
2012–13 Milton Keynes D 34 7
2013–14 Milton Keynes D 32 1
2014–15 Milton Keynes D 42 8
2015–16 Milton Keynes D 22 2
2016–17 Milton Keynes D 20 2 **231 37**

RASULO, Georgio (M) 16 0
b.Banbury 23-1-97
Internationals: England U16, U17.
2012–13 Milton Keynes D 1 0
2013–14 Milton Keynes D 7 0
2014–15 Milton Keynes D 0 0
2014–15 *Oxford U* 1 0 **1 0**
2015–16 Milton Keynes D 1 0
2015–16 *Oldham Ath* 3 0 **3 0**
2016–17 Milton Keynes D 3 0 **12 0**

REEVES, Ben (D) 130 25
H: 5 10 W: 10 07 b.Verwood 19-11-91
Internationals: Northern Ireland Full caps.
2008–09 Southampton 0 0
2009–10 Southampton 0 0
2010–11 Southampton 0 0
2011–12 Southampton 2 0
2011–12 *Dagenham & R* 5 0 **5 0**
2012–13 Southampton 3 0 **5 0**
2012–13 *Southend U* 10 1 **10 1**
2013–14 Milton Keynes D 28 7
2014–15 Milton Keynes D 30 7
2015–16 Milton Keynes D 18 3
2016–17 Milton Keynes D 34 7 **110 24**

TAPP, Finn (D) 0 0
2016–17 Milton Keynes D 0 0

THOMAS-ASANTE, Brandon (F) 6 0
H: 5 11 W: 12 08 b. 29-12-98
2016–17 Milton Keynes D 6 0 **6 0**

TILNEY, Ben (M) 6 0
H: 5 9 W: 10 01 b.Luton 28-2-97
2014–15 Milton Keynes D 0 0
2015–16 Milton Keynes D 0 0
2016–17 Milton Keynes D 6 0 **6 0**

TSHIMANGA, Kabongo (F) 6 0
b. 31-5-96
2014–15 Milton Keynes D 0 0
2015–16 Milton Keynes D 0 0
2016–17 Milton Keynes D 6 0 **6 0**
2016–17 *Yeovil T* 0 0

UPSON, Edward (M) 248 15
H: 5 10 W: 11 07 b.Bury St Edmunds 21-11-89
Internationals: England U17, U19.
2006–07 Ipswich T 0 0
2007–08 Ipswich T 0 0
2008–09 Ipswich T 0 0
2009–10 Ipswich T 0 0
2009–10 *Barnet* 9 1 **9 1**
2010–11 Yeovil T 23 0
2011–12 Yeovil T 41 3
2012–13 Yeovil T 41 2
2013–14 Yeovil T 24 4 **129 9**
2013–14 Millwall 10 0
2014–15 Millwall 26 2
2015–16 Millwall 32 0 **68 2**
2016–17 Milton Keynes D 42 3 **42 3**

WALSH, Joe (D) 156 10
H: 5 11 W: 11 00 b.Cardiff 15-5-92
Internationals: Wales U17, U19, U21.
2010–11 Swansea C 0 0
2011–12 Swansea C 0 0
2012–13 Crawley T 30 2
2013–14 Crawley T 39 5
2014–15 Crawley T 28 1 **97 8**
2014–15 *Milton Keynes D* 2 0
2015–16 Milton Keynes D 18 1
2016–17 Milton Keynes D 39 1 **59 2**

WILLIAMS, George B (D) 58 3
H: 5 9 W: 11 00 b.Hillingdon 14-4-93
2011–12 Milton Keynes D 2 0
From Worcester C.
2014–15 Barnsley 4 0
2015–16 Barnsley 19 1 **23 1**
2016–17 Milton Keynes D 33 2 **35 2**

WOOTTON, Scott (D) 107 3
H: 6 2 W: 13 00 b.Birkenhead 12-9-91
Internationals: England U17.
2009–10 Manchester U 0 0
2010–11 Manchester U 0 0
2010–11 *Tranmere R* 7 1 **7 1**
2011–12 Manchester U 0 0
2011–12 *Peterborough U* 11 0
2011–12 *Nottingham F* 13 0 **13 0**
2012–13 Manchester U 0 0
2012–13 *Peterborough U* 2 1 **13 1**
2013–14 Manchester U 0 0
2013–14 Leeds U 20 0
2014–15 Leeds U 23 0
2014–15 *Rotherham U* 7 0 **7 0**
2015–16 Leeds U 23 0 **66 0**
2016–17 Milton Keynes D 1 1 **1 1**

Players retained or with offer of contract
Sole, Liam Anthony.

Scholars
Bell, Bradley Steven; Evans, Joseph William; Hope, Tommy William; Kasumu, David Ayomide; Kioso, Peter Katako; Logan, Hugo James; Nombe, Samuel Tshiayima; Omar, Juma Abdulla; Osei-Bonsu, Andrew Kwadjo; Pickworth, Nathan Michael; Stratton, Harry; Tapp, Finley.

Non-Contract
Sole, Liam Anthony.

MORECAMBE (55)

CONLAN, Luke (D)				**40**	**0**
H: 5 11 W: 11 05 b.Portaferry 31-10-94					
Internationals: Northern Ireland U16, U17, U19, U21.					
2011–12	Burnley	0	0		
2012–13	Burnley	0	0		
2013–14	Burnley	0	0		
2014–15	Burnley	0	0		
2015–16	Burnley	0	0		
2015–16	*St Mirren*	3	0	**3**	**0**
2015–16	*Morecambe*	16	0		
2016–17	Morecambe	21	0	**37**	**0**

EDWARDS, Ryan (D)				**160**	**1**
b.Liverpool 7-10-93					
2011–12	Blackburn R	0	0		
2012–13	Rochdale	26	0	**26**	**0**
2012–13	Blackburn R	0	0		
2012–13	*Fleetwood T*	9	0	**9**	**0**
2013–14	Blackburn R	0	0		
2013–14	*Chesterfield*	5	0	**5**	**0**
2013–14	*Tranmere R*	0	0		
2013–14	*Morecambe*	9	0		
2014–15	Morecambe	31	0		
2015–16	Morecambe	37	0		
2016–17	Morecambe	43	1	**120**	**1**

ELLISON, Kevin (M)				**549**	**112**
H: 6 0 W: 12 00 b.Liverpool 23-2-79					
2000–01	Leicester C	1	0		
2001–02	Leicester C	0	0	**1**	**0**
2001–02	Stockport Co	11	0		
2002–03	Stockport Co	23	1		
2003–04	Stockport Co	14	1	**48**	**2**
2003–04	*Lincoln C*	11	0	**11**	**0**
2004–05	Chester C	24	9		
2004–05	Hull C	16	1		
2005–06	Hull C	23	1	**39**	**2**
2006–07	Tranmere R	34	4	**34**	**4**
2007–08	Chester C	36	11		
2008–09	Chester C	39	8	**99**	**28**
2008–09	Rotherham U	0	0		
2009–10	Rotherham U	39	8		
2010–11	Rotherham U	23	3	**62**	**11**
2010–11	*Bradford C*	7	1	**7**	**1**
2011–12	Morecambe	34	15		
2012–13	Morecambe	40	11		
2013–14	Morecambe	42	10		
2014–15	Morecambe	43	11		
2015–16	Morecambe	44	9		
2016–17	Morecambe	45	8	**248**	**64**

FLEMING, Andy (M)				**218**	**18**
H: 6 1 W: 12 00 b.Liverpool 18-2-89					
Internationals: England C.					
2006–07	Wrexham	2	0		
2007–08	Wrexham	4	0	**6**	**0**
2010–11	Morecambe	30	2		
2011–12	Morecambe	17	2		
2012–13	Morecambe	32	5		
2013–14	Morecambe	35	2		
2014–15	Morecambe	35	2		
2015–16	Morecambe	33	3		
2016–17	Morecambe	30	2	**212**	**18**

HAWLEY, Kyle (F)				**1**	**0**
2016–17	Morecambe	1	0	**1**	**0**

HEDLEY, Ben (M)				**1**	**0**
2015–16	Morecambe	0	0		
2016–17	Morecambe	1	0	**1**	**0**

JORDAN, Luke (M)				**6**	**0**
2016–17	Morecambe	6	0	**6**	**0**

KENYON, Alex (M)				**124**	**6**
H: 5 11 W: 11 12 b.Preston 17-7-92					
2013–14	Morecambe	39	0		
2014–15	Morecambe	37	3		
2015–16	Morecambe	29	3		
2016–17	Morecambe	19	0	**124**	**6**

MAHER, Niall (G)				**0**	**0**
2015–16	Morecambe	0	0		
2016–17	Morecambe	0	0		

McGOWAN, Aaron (D)				**62**	**1**
b.Maghull 20-9-95					
2012–13	Morecambe	1	0		
2013–14	Morecambe	2	0		
2014–15	Morecambe	8	1		
2015–16	Morecambe	21	0		
2016–17	Morecambe	30	0	**62**	**1**

MOLYNEUX, Lee (D)				**177**	**23**
H: 6 1 W: 12 09 b.Liverpool 24-2-89					
Internationals: England U16, U17, U18.					
2005–06	Everton	0	0		
2006–07	Everton	0	0		
2007–08	Everton	0	0		
2008–09	Southampton	4	0		
2009–10	Southampton	0	0	**4**	**0**
2010–11	Plymouth Arg	9	0	**9**	**0**
2012–13	Accrington S	39	8		
2013–14	Crewe Alex	7	0		
2013–14	*Rochdale*	3	0	**3**	**0**
2013–14	*Accrington S*	17	6		
2014–15	Crewe Alex	3	0	**10**	**0**
2014–15	*Accrington S*	10	1	**66**	**15**
2014–15	Tranmere R	11	0	**11**	**0**
2015–16	Morecambe	34	3		
2016–17	Morecambe	40	5	**74**	**8**

MULLIN, Paul (F)				**122**	**25**
H: 5 10 W: 11 01 b. 6-11-94					
2013–14	Huddersfield T	0	0		
2014–15	Morecambe	42	8		
2015–16	Morecambe	40	9		
2016–17	Morecambe	40	8	**122**	**25**

MURPHY, Peter (D)				**236**	**29**
H: 6 0 W: 11 10 b.Liverpool 13-2-90					
2007–08	Accrington S	2	0		
2008–09	Accrington S	3	0		
2009–10	Accrington S	10	0		
2010–11	Accrington S	13	0		
2011–12	Accrington S	38	4		
2012–13	Accrington S	45	5		
2013–14	Accrington S	44	9	**155**	**18**
2014–15	Wycombe W	42	7	**42**	**7**
2015–16	Morecambe	7	1		
2016–17	Morecambe	32	3	**39**	**4**

NIZIC, Daniel (G)				**5**	**0**
H: 6 2 W: 12 02 b.Sydney 15-3-95					
Internationals: Australia U20.					
2015–16	Burnley	0	0		
2015–16	*Crewe Alex*	0	0		
2016–17	Morecambe	5	0	**5**	**0**

ROCHE, Barry (G)				**497**	**1**
H: 6 5 W: 14 08 b.Dublin 6-4-82					
Internationals: Republic of Ireland U17.					
1999–2000	Nottingham F	0	0		
2000–01	Nottingham F	2	0		
2001–02	Nottingham F	0	0		
2002–03	Nottingham F	1	0		
2003–04	Nottingham F	8	0		
2004–05	Nottingham F	2	0	**13**	**0**
2005–06	Chesterfield	41	0		
2006–07	Chesterfield	40	0		
2007–08	Chesterfield	45	0	**126**	**0**
2008–09	Morecambe	46	0		
2009–10	Morecambe	42	0		
2010–11	Morecambe	42	0		
2011–12	Morecambe	44	0		
2012–13	Morecambe	42	0		
2013–14	Morecambe	45	0		
2014–15	Morecambe	14	0		
2015–16	Morecambe	42	1		
2016–17	Morecambe	41	0	**358**	**1**

ROSE, Michael (D)				**407**	**30**
H: 5 11 W: 12 04 b.Salford 28-7-82					
Internationals: England C.					
1999–2000	Manchester U	0	0		
2000–01	Manchester U	0	0		
2001–02	Manchester U	0	0		
From Hereford U					
2004–05	Yeovil T	40	1		
2005–06	Yeovil T	1	0	**41**	**1**
2005–06	*Cheltenham T*	3	0	**3**	**0**
2005–06	*Scunthorpe U*	15	0	**15**	**0**
2006–07	Stockport Co	25	3		
2007–08	Stockport Co	28	3		
2008–09	Stockport Co	27	0		
2009–10	Stockport Co	24	2	**104**	**8**
2009–10	*Norwich C*	12	1	**12**	**1**
2010–11	Swindon T	35	3	**35**	**3**
2010–11	Colchester U	0	0		
2011–12	Colchester U	14	0		
2012–13	Colchester U	22	2	**36**	**2**
2012–13	Rochdale	14	2		
2013–14	Rochdale	42	4		
2014–15	Rochdale	32	1		
2015–16	Rochdale	30	1	**118**	**8**
2016–17	Morecambe	43	7	**43**	**7**

STOCKTON, Cole (F)				**101**	**16**
H: 6 1 W: 11 11 b.Huyton 13-3-94					
2011–12	Tranmere R	1	0		
2012–13	Tranmere R	31	3		
2013–14	Tranmere R	21	2		
2014–15	Tranmere R	22	4		
2015–16	Tranmere R	0	0	**75**	**9**
2015–16	*Morecambe*	7	2		
On loan from Tranmere R.					
2016–17	Morecambe	19	5	**26**	**7**

TURNER, Rhys (F)				**61**	**6**
b.Preston 22-7-95					
2013–14	Oldham Ath	2	0		
2014–15	Oldham Ath	14	3		
2015–16	Oldham Ath	6	0	**22**	**3**
2015–16	*York C*	9	1	**9**	**1**
2016–17	Morecambe	30	2	**30**	**2**

WAKEFIELD, Liam (D)				**46**	**0**
H: 6 0 W: 11 00 b.Doncaster 9-4-94					
2012–13	Doncaster R	0	0		
2013–14	Doncaster R	4	0		
2014–15	Doncaster R	5	0	**9**	**0**
2015–16	Accrington S	12	0	**12**	**0**
2016–17	Morecambe	25	0	**25**	**0**

WILDIG, Aaron (M)				**149**	**11**
H: 5 9 W: 11 02 b.Hereford 15-4-92					
Internationals: Wales U16.					
2009–10	Cardiff C	11	1		
2010–11	Cardiff C	2	0		
2010–11	*Hamilton A*	3	0	**3**	**0**
2011–12	Cardiff C	0	0	**13**	**1**
2011–12	*Shrewsbury T*	12	2		
2012–13	Shrewsbury T	21	1		
2013–14	Shrewsbury T	30	2		
2014–15	Shrewsbury T	1	0	**64**	**5**
2014–15	*Morecambe*	9	1		
2015–16	Morecambe	32	2		
2016–17	Morecambe	28	2	**69**	**5**

WINNARD, Dean (D)				**273**	**5**
H: 5 9 W: 10 04 b.Wigan 20-8-89					
2006–07	Blackburn R	0	0		
2007–08	Blackburn R	0	0		
2008–09	Blackburn R	0	0		
2009–10	Accrington S	44	0		
2010–11	Accrington S	45	1		
2011–12	Accrington S	30	1		
2012–13	Accrington S	40	1		
2013–14	Accrington S	39	2		
2014–15	Accrington S	37	0		
2015–16	Accrington S	15	0	**250**	**5**
2016–17	Morecambe	23	0	**23**	**0**

YAWSON, Steven (M)				**1**	**0**
2016–17	Morecambe	1	0	**1**	**0**

Players retained or with offer of contract

Brownsword, Tyler Shawn.

Scholars

Armstrong, Cameron James; Box, Oliver Tyler; Davis, Leif; Dawson, Paul; Dutton-Kay, Nathan Ryan; Fairclough, Luke James; Fletcher, Benjamin James; Hawley, Kyle; Hedley, Ben; Ingham, Benjamin Marc; Jenkinson, Robbie Jake; Maher, Niall Michael; Nelligan, Joe; Taylor, Jack Charles; Webb, Alexander Lawrence; Yawson, Steven.

NEWCASTLE U (56)

AARONS, Rolando (M)				**18**	**2**
H: 5 9 W: 10 08 b.Kingston 16-11-95					
Internationals: England U20.					
2014–15	Newcastle U	4	1		
2015–16	Newcastle U	10	1		
2016–17	Newcastle U	4	0	**18**	**2**

AMEOBI, Sam (F)				**123**	**6**
H: 6 3 W: 10 04 b.Newcastle upon Tyne 1-5-92					
Internationals: Nigeria U20. England U21.					
2010–11	Newcastle U	1	0		
2011–12	Newcastle U	10	0		
2012–13	Newcastle U	8	0		
2012–13	*Middlesbrough*	9	1	**9**	**1**
2013–14	Newcastle U	10	0		
2014–15	Newcastle U	25	2		
2015–16	Newcastle U	0	0		
2015–16	*Cardiff C*	36	1	**36**	**1**
2016–17	Newcastle U	4	0	**58**	**2**
2016–17	*Bolton W*	20	2	**20**	**2**

ANITA, Vurnon (M)				**242**	**7**
H: 5 5 W: 10 04 b.Willemstad 4-4-89					
Internationals: Netherlands U15, U17, U19, U20, U21, Full caps.					
2005–06	Ajax	1	0		
2006–07	Ajax	1	0		
2008–09	Ajax	16	0		
2009–10	Ajax	26	0		
2010–11	Ajax	31	3		
2011–12	Ajax	33	2		
2012–13	Ajax	1	0	**109**	**5**
2012–13	Newcastle U	25	0		
2013–14	Newcastle U	34	1		
2014–15	Newcastle U	19	0		

2015–16	Newcastle U	28	1		
2016–17	Newcastle U	27	0	**133**	**2**

ARMSTRONG, Adam (F) **91 26**
H: 5 8 W: 10 12 b.Newcastle upon Tyne 10-2-97
Internationals: England U16, U17, U18, U19, U20.

2013–14	Newcastle U	4	0		
2014–15	Newcastle U	11	0		
2015–16	Newcastle U	0	0		
2015–16	*Coventry C*	40	20	**40**	**20**
2016–17	Newcastle U	2	0	**17**	**0**
2016–17	*Barnsley*	34	6	**34**	**6**

BARLASER, Daniel (M) **0 0**
H: 6 0 W: 9 11 b.Gateshead 18-1-97
Internationals: Turkey U16, U17. England U18.

2015–16	Newcastle U	0	0		
2016–17	Newcastle U	0	0		

CAMERON, Kyle (D) **24 1**
H: 6 3 W: 12 00 b.Hexham 15-1-97
Internationals: England U16, U17. Scotland U17, U19, U21.

2015–16	Newcastle U	0	0		
2015–16	*York C*	18	1	**18**	**1**
2016–17	Newcastle U	0	0		
2016–17	*Newport Co*	6	0	**6**	**0**

CLARK, Ciaran (D) **168 10**
H: 6 2 W: 12 00 b.Harrow 26-9-89
Internationals: England U17, U18, U19, U20. Republic of Ireland Full caps.

2008–09	Aston Villa	0	0		
2009–10	Aston Villa	1	0		
2010–11	Aston Villa	19	3		
2011–12	Aston Villa	15	1		
2012–13	Aston Villa	29	1		
2013–14	Aston Villa	27	0		
2014–15	Aston Villa	25	1		
2015–16	Aston Villa	18	1	**134**	**7**
2016–17	Newcastle U	34	3	**34**	**3**

COLBACK, Jack (M) **258 13**
H: 5 9 W: 11 05 b.Killingworth 24-10-89
Internationals: England U20.

2007–08	Sunderland	0	0		
2008–09	Sunderland	0	0		
2009–10	Sunderland	1	0		
2009–10	*Ipswich T*	37	4		
2010–11	Sunderland	11	0		
2010–11	*Ipswich T*	13	0	**50**	**4**
2011–12	Sunderland	35	1		
2012–13	Sunderland	35	0		
2013–14	Sunderland	33	3	**115**	**4**
2014–15	Newcastle U	35	4		
2015–16	Newcastle U	29	1		
2016–17	Newcastle U	29	0	**93**	**5**

DARLOW, Karl (G) **158 0**
H: 6 1 W: 12 05 b.Northampton 8-10-90

2009–10	Nottingham F	0	0		
2010–11	Nottingham F	1	0		
2011–12	Nottingham F	0	0		
2012–13	Nottingham F	20	0		
2012–13	*Walsall*	9	0	**9**	**0**
2013–14	Nottingham F	43	0		
2014–15	Newcastle U	0	0		
2014–15	*Nottingham F*	42	0	**106**	**0**
2015–16	Newcastle U	9	0		
2016–17	Newcastle U	34	0	**43**	**0**

DE JONG, Siem (M) **207 64**
H: 6 1 W: 12 00 b.Aigle 28-1-89
Internationals: Netherlands U17, U19, U21, B, Full caps.

2007–08	Ajax	22	2		
2008–09	Ajax	10	1		
2009–10	Ajax	22	10		
2010–11	Ajax	32	12		
2011–12	Ajax	29	13		
2012–13	Ajax	33	12		
2013–14	Ajax	18	7	**166**	**57**
2014–15	Newcastle U	4	1		
2015–16	Newcastle U	18	0		
2016–17	Newcastle U	0	0	**22**	**1**
2016–17	*PSV Einhoven*	19	6	**19**	**6**

DIAME, Mohamed (M) **320 31**
H: 6 1 W: 11 02 b.Creteil 14-6-87
Internationals: Senegal U23, Full caps.

2006–07	Lens	0	0		
2007–08	Linares	31	1	**31**	**1**
2008–09	Rayo Vallecano	35	2	**35**	**2**
2009–10	Wigan Ath	34	1		
2010–11	Wigan Ath	36	1		
2011–12	Wigan Ath	26	3	**96**	**5**
2012–13	West Ham U	33	3		
2013–14	West Ham U	35	4		
2014–15	West Ham U	3	0	**71**	**7**
2014–15	Hull C	12	4		
2015–16	Hull C	38	9	**50**	**13**
2016–17	Newcastle U	37	3	**37**	**3**

DUMMETT, Paul (D) **141 4**
H: 5 10 W: 10 02 b.Newcastle upon Tyne 26-9-91
Internationals: Wales U21, Full caps.

2010–11	Newcastle U	0	0		
2011–12	Newcastle U	0	0		
2012–13	Newcastle U	0	0		
2012–13	*St Mirren*	30	2	**30**	**2**
2013–14	Newcastle U	18	1		
2014–15	Newcastle U	25	0		
2015–16	Newcastle U	23	1		
2016–17	Newcastle U	45	0	**111**	**2**

EL-MHANNI, Yasin (M) **0 0**
From Farnborough, Lewes.

2016–17	Newcastle U	0	0		

ELLIOT, Rob (G) **146 0**
H: 6 3 W: 14 10 b.Chatham 30-4-86
Internationals: Republic of Ireland U19, Full caps.

2004–05	Charlton Ath	0	0		
2004–05	*Notts Co*	4	0	**4**	**0**
2005–06	Charlton Ath	0	0		
2006–07	Charlton Ath	0	0		
2006–07	*Accrington S*	7	0	**7**	**0**
2007–08	Charlton Ath	1	0		
2008–09	Charlton Ath	23	0		
2009–10	Charlton Ath	33	0		
2010–11	Charlton Ath	35	0		
2011–12	Charlton Ath	4	0	**96**	**0**
2011–12	Newcastle U	0	0		
2012–13	Newcastle U	10	0		
2013–14	Newcastle U	2	0		
2014–15	Newcastle U	3	0		
2015–16	Newcastle U	21	0		
2016–17	Newcastle U	3	0	**39**	**0**

FINDLAY, Stuart (D) **51 0**
H: 6 4 W: 13 08 b.Glasgow 14-9-95
Internationals: Scotland U16, U17, U19, U21.

2013–14	Celtic	0	0		
2013–14	*Greenock Morton*	14	0	**14**	**0**
2014–15	Celtic	0	0		
2014–15	*Dumbarton*	15	0	**15**	**0**
2015–16	Celtic	0	0		
2015–16	*Kilmarnock*	22	0	**22**	**0**
2016–17	Newcastle U	0	0		

GAYLE, Dwight (F) **143 58**
H: 5 10 W: 11 07 b.Walthamstow 20-10-89

2011–12	Dagenham & R	0	0		
2012–13	Dagenham & R	18	7	**18**	**7**
2012–13	Peterborough U	29	13	**29**	**13**
2013–14	Crystal Palace	23	7		
2014–15	Crystal Palace	25	5		
2015–16	Crystal Palace	16	3	**64**	**15**
2016–17	Newcastle U	32	23	**32**	**23**

GILLESPHEY, Macaulay (D) **55 2**
H: 5 11 W: 11 00 b. 24-11-95

2015–16	Newcastle U	0	0		
2015–16	*Carlisle U*	23	2		
2016–17	Newcastle U	0	0		
2016–17	*Carlisle U*	32	0	**55**	**2**

GILLIEAD, Alex (F) **62 6**
H: 6 0 W: 11 00 b.Shotley Bridge 11-2-96
Internationals: England U16, U17, U18, U20.

2014–15	Newcastle U	0	0		
2015–16	Newcastle U	0	0		
2015–16	*Carlisle U*	35	5	**35**	**5**
2016–17	Newcastle U	0	0		
2016–17	*Luton T*	18	1	**18**	**1**
2016–17	*Bradford C*	9	0	**9**	**0**

GOOD, Curtis (D) **31 2**
H: 6 2 W: 13 05 b.Melbourne 23-3-93
Internationals: Australia U20, U23, Full caps.

2011–12	Melbourne Heart	24	1	**24**	**1**
2012–13	Newcastle U	0	0		
2012–13	*Bradford C*	3	0	**3**	**0**
2013–14	Newcastle U	0	0		
2013–14	*Dundee U*	4	1	**4**	**1**
2014–15	Newcastle U	0	0		
2015–16	Newcastle U	0	0		
2016–17	Newcastle U	0	0		

GOUFFRAN, Yoan (F) **377 81**
H: 5 9 W: 11 11
b.Villeneuve-Saint-Georges 25-5-86
Internationals: France U21.

2004–05	Caen	8	0		
2005–06	Caen	29	8		
2006–07	Caen	37	15		
2007–08	Caen	36	10	**110**	**33**
2008–09	Bordeaux	32	3		
2009–10	Bordeaux	32	5		
2010–11	Bordeaux	21	2		
2011–12	Bordeaux	34	14		
2012–13	Bordeaux	20	8	**139**	**32**
2012–13	Newcastle U	15	3		
2013–14	Newcastle U	35	6		
2014–15	Newcastle U	31	2		
2015–16	Newcastle U	8	0		
2016–17	Newcastle U	39	5	**128**	**16**

HAIDARA, Massadio (D) **82 0**
H: 5 11 W: 11 10 b.Trappes 2-12-92
Internationals: France U19, U20, U21.

2010–11	AS Nancy	8	0		
2011–12	AS Nancy	19	0		
2012–13	AS Nancy	17	0	**44**	**0**
2012–13	Newcastle U	4	0		
2013–14	Newcastle U	11	0		
2014–15	Newcastle U	15	0		
2015–16	Newcastle U	7	0		
2016–17	Newcastle U	1	0	**38**	**0**

HANLEY, Grant (D) **193 8**
H: 6 2 W: 12 00 b.Dumfries 20-11-91
Internationals: Scotland U19, U21, Full caps.

2008–09	Blackburn R	0	0		
2009–10	Blackburn R	1	0		
2010–11	Blackburn R	7	0		
2011–12	Blackburn R	23	1		
2012–13	Blackburn R	39	2		
2013–14	Blackburn R	38	1		
2014–15	Blackburn R	31	1		
2015–16	Blackburn R	44	2	**183**	**7**
2016–17	Newcastle U	10	1	**10**	**1**

HAYDEN, Isaac (D) **51 3**
H: 6 2 W: 12 06 b.Chelmsford 22-3-95
Internationals: England U16, U17, U18, U19, U20, U21.

2011–12	Arsenal	0	0		
2012–13	Arsenal	0	0		
2013–14	Arsenal	0	0		
2014–15	Arsenal	0	0		
2015–16	Arsenal	0	0		
2015–16	*Hull C*	18	1	**18**	**1**
2016–17	Newcastle U	33	2	**33**	**2**

HEARDMAN, Tom (F) **2 0**
H: 6 2 W: 12 08 b.Gosforth 12-9-95

2015–16	Newcastle U	0	0		
2016–17	Newcastle U	0	0		
2016–17	*Hartlepool U*	2	0	**2**	**0**

JESUS GAMEZ, Duarte (D) **259 1**
H: 6 0 W: 11 00 b.Malaga 10-4-85
Internationals: Spain U23.

2005–06	Malaga	15	0		
2006–07	Malaga	1	0		
2007–08	Malaga	35	1		
2008–09	Malaga	35	0		
2009–10	Malaga	32	0		
2010–11	Malaga	30	0		
2011–12	Malaga	26	0		
2012–13	Malaga	28	0		
2013–14	Malaga	28	0	**230**	**1**
2014–15	Atletico Madrid	14	0		
2015–16	Atletico Madrid	10	0	**24**	**0**
2016–17	Newcastle U	5	0	**5**	**0**

KRUL, Tim (G) **209 0**
H: 6 2 W: 11 08 b.Den Haag 3-4-88
Internationals: Netherlands U15, U16, U17, U19, U20, U21, Full caps.

2005–06	Newcastle U	0	0		
2006–07	Newcastle U	0	0		
2007–08	*Falkirk*	22	0	**22**	**0**
2007–08	Newcastle U	0	0		
2008–09	Newcastle U	0	0		
2008–09	*Carlisle U*	9	0	**9**	**0**
2009–10	Newcastle U	3	0		
2010–11	Newcastle U	21	0		
2011–12	Newcastle U	38	0		
2012–13	Newcastle U	24	0		
2013–14	Newcastle U	36	0		
2014–15	Newcastle U	30	0		
2015–16	Newcastle U	8	0		
2016–17	Newcastle U	0	0	**160**	**0**
2016–17	*Ajax*	0	0		
2016–17	*AZ Alkmaar*	18	0	**18**	**0**

LASCELLES, Jamaal (D) **126 9**
H: 6 2 W: 13 01 b.Derby 11-11-93
Internationals: England U18, U19, U20, U21.

2010–11	Nottingham F	0	0		
2011–12	Nottingham F	1	0		
2011–12	*Stevenage*	7	1	**7**	**1**
2012–13	Nottingham F	2	0		
2013–14	Nottingham F	29	2		

2014–15	Newcastle U	0	0		
2014–15	*Nottingham F*	26	1	**58**	**3**
2015–16	Newcastle U	18	2		
2016–17	Newcastle U	43	3	**61**	**5**

LAZAAR, Achraf (D) **115** **3**
H: 5 8 W: 10 08 b.Casablanca 22-1-92
Internationals: Morocco Full caps.

2011–12	Varese	0	0		
2012–13	Varese	21	0		
2013–14	Varese	17	0	**38**	**0**
2013–14	Palermo	14	0		
2014–15	Palermo	29	2		
2015–16	Palermo	30	1		
2016–17	Palermo	0	0	**73**	**3**
2016–17	Newcastle U	4	0	**4**	**0**

MBABU, Kevin (D) **19** **1**
H: 6 0 W: 12 03 b.Zurich 19-4-95
Internationals: Switzerland U16, U17, U18, U19.

2012–13	Servette	1	0	**1**	**0**
2012–13	Newcastle U	0	0		
2013–14	Newcastle U	0	0		
2014–15	Newcastle U	0	0		
2014–15	*Rangers*	0	0		
2015–16	Newcastle U	3	0		
2016–17	Newcastle U	0	0	**3**	**0**
2016–17	*Young Boys*	15	1	**15**	**1**

MBEMBA, Chancel (D) **108** **7**
H: 6 0 W: 12 00 b.Kinshasa 8-8-94
Internationals: DR Congo Full caps.

2011–12	Anderlecht	0	0		
2012–13	Anderlecht	0	0		
2013–14	Anderlecht	35	5		
2014–15	Anderlecht	28	1	**63**	**6**
2015–16	Newcastle U	33	0		
2016–17	Newcastle U	12	1	**45**	**1**

MITROVIC, Aleksandar (F) **181** **69**
H: 6 2 W: 13 10 b.Smederevo 16-9-94
Internationals: Serbia U19, U21, Full caps.

2011–12	Teleoptik	25	7	**25**	**7**
2012–13	Partizan Belgrade	25	10		
2013–14	Partizan Belgrade	3	3	**28**	**13**
2013–14	Anderlecht	32	16		
2014–15	Anderlecht	37	20	**69**	**36**
2015–16	Newcastle U	34	9		
2016–17	Newcastle U	25	4	**59**	**13**

MURPHY, Daryl (F) **365** **89**
H: 6 2 W: 13 12 b.Waterford 15-3-83
Internationals: Republic of Ireland U21, Full caps.

2000–01	Luton T	0	0		
2001–02	Luton T	0	0		
2005–06	Sunderland	18	1		
2005–06	*Sheffield W*	4	0	**4**	**0**
2006–07	Sunderland	38	10		
2007–08	Sunderland	28	3		
2008–09	Sunderland	23	0		
2009–10	Sunderland	3	0	**110**	**14**
2009–10	*Ipswich T*	18	6		
2010–11	Celtic	18	3		
2011–12	Ipswich T	33	4		
2012–13	Celtic	1	0	**19**	**3**
2012–13	*Ipswich T*	39	7		
2013–14	Ipswich T	45	13		
2014–15	Ipswich T	44	27		
2015–16	Ipswich T	34	10		
2016–17	Ipswich T	4	0	**217**	**67**
2016–17	Newcastle U	15	5	**15**	**5**

PEREZ, Ayoze (F) **152** **39**
H: 5 10 W: 10 06 b.Santa Cruz de Tenerife 23-7-93
Internationals: Spain U21.

2012–13	Tenerife	16	1		
2013–14	Tenerife	30	16	**46**	**17**
2014–15	Newcastle U	36	7		
2015–16	Newcastle U	34	6		
2016–17	Newcastle U	36	9	**106**	**22**

RITCHIE, Matt (M) **339** **83**
H: 5 8 W: 11 00 b.Gosport 10-9-89
Internationals: Scotland Full caps.

2008–09	Portsmouth	0	0		
2008–09	*Dagenham & R*	37	11	**37**	**11**
2009–10	Portsmouth	2	0		
2009–10	*Notts Co*	16	3	**16**	**3**
2009–10	*Swindon T*	4	0		
2010–11	Portsmouth	5	0	**7**	**0**
2010–11	Swindon T	36	7		
2011–12	Swindon T	40	10		
2012–13	Swindon T	27	9	**107**	**26**
2012–13	Bournemouth	17	3		
2013–14	Bournemouth	30	9		
2014–15	Bournemouth	46	15		
2015–16	Bournemouth	37	4	**130**	**31**
2016–17	Newcastle U	42	12	**42**	**12**

RIVIERE, Emmanuel (F) **202** **41**
H: 6 0 W: 12 00 b.Lamentin 3-3-90
Internationals: France U16, U17, U18, U19, U21.

2008–09	St Etienne	8	1		
2009–10	St Etienne	30	8		
2010–11	St Etienne	35	8	**73**	**17**
2011–12	Toulouse	26	5		
2012–13	Toulouse	18	4	**44**	**9**
2012–13	Monaco	14	4		
2013–14	Monaco	30	10	**44**	**14**
2014–15	Newcastle U	23	1		
2015–16	Newcastle U	3	0		
2016–17	Newcastle U	0	0	**26**	**1**
2016–17	*Osasuna*	15	0	**15**	**0**

ROBERTS, Callum (M) **10** **0**
b. 1-4-97
Internationals: England U20.

2014–15	Newcastle U	0	0		
2015–16	Newcastle U	0	0		
2016–17	Newcastle U	0	0		
2016–17	*Kilmarnock*	10	0	**10**	**0**

SAIVET, Henri (M) **183** **21**
H: 5 9 W: 10 08 b.Dakar 26-10-90
Internationals: France U16, U17, U18, U21. Senegal Full caps.

2007–08	Bordeaux	1	0		
2008–09	Bordeaux	1	0		
2009–10	Bordeaux	3	0		
2010–11	Bordeaux	6	0		
2010–11	*Angers*	18	3	**18**	**3**
2011–12	Bordeaux	24	1		
2012–13	Bordeaux	34	8		
2013–14	Bordeaux	33	6		
2014–15	Bordeaux	14	0		
2015–16	Bordeaux	18	2	**134**	**17**
2015–16	Newcastle U	4	0		
2016–17	Newcastle U	0	0	**4**	**0**
2016–17	*St Etienne*	27	1	**27**	**1**

SELS, Matz (G) **109** **0**
H: 6 2 W: 11 11 b.Lint 26-2-92
Internationals: Belgium U17, U18, U19, U21.

2010–11	Lierse	1	0		
2011–12	Lierse	0	0		
2012–13	Lierse	30	0		
2013–14	Lierse	0	0	**31**	**0**
2013–14	Gent	9	0		
2014–15	Gent	30	0		
2015–16	Gent	30	0	**69**	**0**
2016–17	Newcastle U	9	0	**9**	**0**

SHELVEY, Jonjo (M) **235** **30**
H: 6 1 W: 11 02 b.Romford 27-2-92
Internationals: England U16, U17, U19, U21, Full caps.

2007–08	Charlton Ath	2	0		
2008–09	Charlton Ath	16	3		
2009–10	Charlton Ath	24	4	**42**	**7**
2010–11	Liverpool	15	0		
2011–12	Liverpool	13	1		
2011–12	*Blackpool*	10	6	**10**	**6**
2012–13	Liverpool	19	1	**47**	**2**
2013–14	Swansea C	32	6		
2014–15	Swansea C	31	3		
2015–16	Swansea C	16	1	**79**	**10**
2015–16	Newcastle U	15	0		
2016–17	Newcastle U	42	5	**57**	**5**

STERRY, Jamie (D) **19** **0**
H: 5 11 W: 11 00 b.Newcastle upon Tyne 21-11-95

2014–15	Newcastle U	0	0		
2015–16	Newcastle U	1	0		
2016–17	Newcastle U	2	0	**3**	**0**
2016–17	*Coventry C*	16	0	**16**	**0**

TIOTE, Cheik (M) **227** **4**
H: 5 11 W: 12 06 b.Yamoussoukro 21-6-86
Internationals: Ivory Coast Full caps.

2005–06	Anderlecht	2	0		
2006–07	Anderlecht	2	0	**4**	**0**
2007–08	Roda JC	26	2	**26**	**2**
2008–09	Twente	28	0		
2009–10	Twente	28	1		
2010–11	Twente	2	0	**58**	**1**
2010–11	Newcastle U	26	1		
2011–12	Newcastle U	24	0		
2012–13	Newcastle U	24	0		
2013–14	Newcastle U	33	0		
2014–15	Newcastle U	11	0		
2015–16	Newcastle U	20	0		
2016–17	Newcastle U	1	0	**139**	**1**

Transferred to Beijing Enterprises Group, February 2017.

TONEY, Ivan (F) **104** **24**
H: 5 10 W: 12 00 b.Northampton 16-3-96

2012–13	Northampton T	0	0		
2013–14	Northampton T	13	3		
2014–15	Northampton T	40	8	**53**	**11**
2015–16	Newcastle U	2	0		
2015–16	*Barnsley*	15	1	**15**	**1**
2016–17	Newcastle U	0	0	**2**	**0**
2016–17	*Shrewsbury T*	19	6	**19**	**6**
2016–17	*Scunthorpe U*	15	6	**15**	**6**

VUCKIC, Haris (F) **81** **16**
H: 6 2 W: 12 02 b.Ljubljana 21-8-92
Internationals: Slovenia U17, U19, U21, Full caps.

2007–08	Domzale	1	0		
2008–09	Domzale	4	0	**5**	**0**
2009–10	Newcastle U	2	0		
2010–11	Newcastle U	0	0		
2011–12	Newcastle U	4	0		
2011–12	*Cardiff C*	5	1	**5**	**1**
2012–13	Newcastle U	0	0		
2013–14	Newcastle U	0	0		
2013–14	*Rotherham U*	22	4	**22**	**4**
2014–15	Newcastle U	1	0		
2014–15	*Rangers*	17	8	**17**	**8**
2015–16	Newcastle U	0	0		
2015–16	*Wigan Ath*	15	2	**15**	**2**
2016–17	Newcastle U	0	0	**7**	**0**
2016–17	*Bradford C*	10	1	**10**	**1**

WOODMAN, Freddie (G) **25** **0**
H: 6 1 W: 10 12 b.London 4-3-97
Internationals: England U16, U17, U18, U19, U20, U21.

2014–15	Newcastle U	0	0		
2014–15	*Hartlepool U*	0	0		
2015–16	Newcastle U	0	0		
2015–16	*Crawley T*	11	0	**11**	**0**
2016–17	Newcastle U	0	0		
2016–17	*Kilmarnock*	14	0	**14**	**0**

YEDLIN, DeAndre (D) **113** **3**
H: 5 9 W: 11 07 b.Seattle 9-7-93
Internationals: USA U20, Full caps.

2013	Seattle Sounders	33	2		
2014	Seattle Sounders	29	0	**62**	**2**
2014–15	Tottenham H	1	0		
2015–16	Tottenham H	0	0	**1**	**0**
2015–16	*Sunderland*	23	0	**23**	**0**
2016–17	Newcastle U	27	1	**27**	**1**

Players retained or with offer of contract
Cabella, Remy; Fernandez, Satue Victor; Gibson, Liam Steven; Longstaff, Sean David; Pearson, Brendan Conor; Sangare, Mohammed; Smith, Liam Phillip; Sorensen, Elias Fritjof Graenge; Thauvin, Florian; Williams, Callum Dylan.

Scholars
Adu-Peprah, Gideon; Allan, Thomas David; Aplin, Kieren Glen; Aziakonou, Yannick; Bailey, Owen John Edward; Cass, Lewis Graham; Charman, Luke; Gallacher, Owen John; Gamblin, Isaac William; Gibson, Lewis Jack; Goodridge, Mace Lewin; Harker, Nathan; Heaney, Mackenzie; Holmes, Jamie Jason; Hunter, Jack David; Huuhtanen, Otto Eemeli; Kitchen, Benjamin; Long, Oliver James; Longstaff, Matthew Ben; Lowther, Daniel Robert; McNall, Lewis; Newberry, Michael; Robson, Jack; Russell, Kurtis; Smith, Ben Joseph; Smith, Callum; Spooner, Craig; Walters, Oliver Reece; Ward, Daniel John; Watts, Kelland John William James; Wilson, Adam Ayiro; Woolston, Paul Hudson.

NEWPORT CO (57)

ANGEL, Liam (M) **0** **0**
b. 17-3-99
Internationals: Wales U16, U17.

2015–16	Newport Co	0	0		
2016–17	Newport Co	0	0		

BARNUM-BOBB, Jazzi (D) **38** **1**
b.Enfield 15-9-95

2014–15	Cardiff C	0	0		
2015–16	Cardiff C	0	0		
2015–16	*Newport Co*	12	0		
2016–17	Newport Co	26	1	**38**	**1**

BEAUCHAMP, Marcus (G) **0** **0**
From Norwich C.

2016–17	Newport Co	0	0		

BENNETT, Scott (D) **200** **18**
H: 5 10 W: 12 10 b.Newquay 30-11-90

2008–09	Exeter C	0	0		
2009–10	Exeter C	0	0		
2010–11	Exeter C	1	0		
2011–12	Exeter C	15	3		
2012–13	Exeter C	43	6		
2013–14	Exeter C	45	6		
2014–15	Exeter C	28	3	**132**	**18**
2015–16	Notts Co	6	0	**6**	**0**
2015–16	*Newport Co*	12	0		
2015–16	*York C*	11	0	**11**	**0**
2016–17	Newport Co	39	0	**51**	**0**

BIGNOT, Paul (D) **54** **0**
H: 6 1 W: 12 03 b.Birmingham 14-2-86
Internationals: England C.

2004–05	Crewe Alex	5	0		
2005–06	Crewe Alex	5	0		
2006–07	Crewe Alex	11	0	**21**	**0**

From Kidderminster H.

2011–12	Blackpool	0	0		
2011–12	*Plymouth Arg*	14	0	**14**	**0**
2012–13	Blackpool	0	0		

From Grimsby T.

2015	Keflavik	9	0	**9**	**0**

From Solihull Moors.

2016–17	Newport Co	10	0	**10**	**0**

BIRD, Ryan (F) **105** **25**
H: 6 4 W: 12 06 b.Slough 15-11-87

2013–14	Portsmouth	18	3		
2014–15	Portsmouth	2	0	**20**	**3**
2014–15	Cambridge U	24	6	**24**	**6**
2014–15	*Hartlepool U*	6	2	**6**	**2**
2015–16	Yeovil T	36	8	**36**	**8**
2016–17	Newport Co	19	6	**19**	**6**

BITTNER, James (G) **4** **0**
H: 6 2 W: 12 09 b.Devizes 2-2-82
Internationals: England C.

2001–02	Bournemouth	0	0		

From Exeter C.

2005–06	Torquay U	0	0		

From Woking, Salisbury C, Chippenham T, Forest Green R, Hereford U.

2013–14	Newport Co	0	0		

From Salisbury C.

2014–15	Plymouth Arg	1	0		
2015–16	Plymouth Arg	1	0	**2**	**0**
2016–17	Newport Co	2	0	**2**	**0**

BLANCHARD, Maximo (D) **247** **10**
H: 5 11 W: 11 13 b.Alencon 27-9-86

2006–07	Laval	4	0		
2007–08	Laval	22	0	**26**	**0**
2008–09	Entente	35	1	**35**	**1**
2009–10	Moulins	35	1	**35**	**1**
2010–11	Tranmere R	20	0	**20**	**0**
2011–12	Plymouth Arg	28	2		
2012–13	Plymouth Arg	40	1		
2013–14	Plymouth Arg	36	1	**104**	**4**
2015	Shamrock R	17	4		
2016	Shamrock R	9	0	**26**	**4**
2016–17	Newport Co	1	0	**1**	**0**

BUTLER, Dan (D) **88** **3**
b.Cowes 26-8-94

2012–13	Portsmouth	17	0		
2013–14	Portsmouth	1	0		
2014–15	Portsmouth	30	0	**48**	**0**
2016–17	Newport Co	40	3	**40**	**3**

COMPTON, Jack (M) **153** **12**
H: 5 8 W: 10 07 b.Torquay 2-9-88

2008–09	Brighton & HA	0	0		

From Havant & Waterloovlle, Weston-Super-Mare.

2010–11	Falkirk	24	3		
2011–12	Falkirk	13	0	**37**	**3**
2011–12	*Bradford C*	14	0	**14**	**0**
2011–12	*St Johnstone*	0	0		
2012–13	Portsmouth	12	0	**12**	**0**
2012–13	*Colchester U*	7	0	**7**	**0**
2013–14	Hartlepool U	34	4		
2014–15	Hartlepool U	21	0	**55**	**4**
2015–16	Yeovil T	20	4	**20**	**4**
2016–17	Newport Co	8	1	**8**	**1**

DAY, Joe (G) **126** **0**
H: 6 1 W: 12 00 b.Brighton 13-8-90

2011–12	Peterborough U	0	0		
2012–13	Peterborough U	0	0		
2013–14	Peterborough U	4	0		
2014–15	Peterborough U	0	0	**4**	**0**
2014–15	*Newport Co*	36	0		
2015–16	Newport Co	41	0		
2016–17	Newport Co	45	0	**122**	**0**

DEMETRIOU, Mickey (D) **75** **7**
b.Durrington 12-3-90
Internationals: England C.

2014–15	Shrewsbury T	42	3		
2015–16	Shrewsbury T	1	0		
2015–16	*Cambridge U*	15	0	**15**	**0**
2016–17	Shrewsbury T	0	0	**43**	**3**
2016–17	Newport Co	17	4	**17**	**4**

FLYNN, Michael (M) **333** **42**
H: 5 10 W: 13 04 b.Newport 17-10-80

2002–03	Wigan Ath	17	1		
2003–04	Wigan Ath	8	0		
2004–05	Wigan Ath	13	1	**38**	**2**
2004–05	*Blackpool*	6	0		
2004–05	Gillingham	16	3		
2005–06	Gillingham	36	6		
2006–07	Gillingham	45	10	**97**	**19**
2007–08	Blackpool	28	3	**34**	**3**
2008–09	*Darlington*	0	0		
2008–09	Huddersfield T	25	4	**25**	**4**
2009–10	Bradford C	42	6		
2010–11	Bradford C	19	0		
2011–12	Bradford C	30	4	**91**	**10**
2013–14	Newport Co	32	4		
2014–15	Newport Co	11	0		
2016–17	Newport Co	5	0	**48**	**4**

JACKSON, Marlon (F) **77** **3**
H: 5 11 W: 11 12 b.Bristol 6-12-90
Internationals: England C.

2009–10	Bristol C	0	0		
2009–10	*Hereford U*	5	0	**5**	**0**
2009–10	*Aldershot T*	22	1		
2010–11	Bristol C	4	0		
2010–11	*Aldershot T*	9	0	**31**	**1**
2011–12	Bristol C	0	0	**4**	**0**
2011–12	*Northampton T*	6	1	**6**	**1**
2011–12	*Cheltenham T*	1	0	**1**	**0**
2013–14	Bury	8	1	**8**	**1**

From Lincoln C, Halifax T, Oxford C, Tranmere R.

2016–17	Newport Co	22	0	**22**	**0**

JEBB, Jack (M) **19** **0**
H: 6 0 W: 11 09 b.London 11-9-95
Internationals: England U16, U17.

2012–13	Arsenal	0	0		
2013–14	Arsenal	0	0		
2014–15	Arsenal	0	0		
2014–15	*Stevenage*	9	0		
2015–16	Arsenal	0	0		
2015–16	*Stevenage*	5	0	**14**	**0**
2016–17	Newport Co	5	0	**5**	**0**

JOHN-LEWIS, Lemell (M) **185** **20**
H: 5 10 W: 11 10 b.Hammersmith 17-5-89

2006–07	Lincoln C	0	0		
2007–08	Lincoln C	21	3		
2008–09	Lincoln C	27	4		
2009–10	Lincoln C	24	1	**72**	**8**
2010–11	Bury	39	2		
2011–12	Bury	28	5		
2012–13	Bury	16	2	**83**	**9**
2015–16	Newport Co	28	3		
2016–17	Newport Co	2	0	**30**	**3**

JONES, Dafydd (F) **0** **0**
H: 5 9 W: 11 05 b.Abergavenny 5-6-98

2015–16	Newport Co	0	0		
2016–17	Newport Co	0	0		

JONES, Darren (D) **304** **12**
H: 6 0 W: 14 12 b.Newport 28-8-83

2000–01	Bristol C	0	0		
2001–02	Bristol C	2	0		
2002–03	Bristol C	0	0		
2003–04	Bristol C	0	0	**2**	**0**
2003–04	*Cheltenham T*	14	1	**14**	**1**

From Forest Green R.

2009–10	Hereford U	41	3	**41**	**3**
2010–11	Aldershot T	43	1		
2011–12	Aldershot T	42	0	**85**	**1**
2012–13	Shrewsbury T	38	1		
2013–14	Shrewsbury T	15	0	**53**	**1**
2013–14	AFC Wimbledon	18	1	**18**	**1**
2014–15	Newport Co	43	4		

From Forest Green R.

2015–16	Newport Co	17	1		
2016–17	Newport Co	31	0	**91**	**5**

LABADIE, Joss (M) **222** **32**
H: 5 7 W: 11 02 b.Croydon 31-8-90

2008–09	WBA	0	0		
2008–09	*Shrewsbury T*	1	0		
2009–10	WBA	0	0		
2009–10	*Shrewsbury T*	13	5	**14**	**5**
2009–10	*Cheltenham T*	11	0	**11**	**0**
2009–10	*Tranmere R*	9	3		
2010–11	Tranmere R	34	2		
2011–12	Tranmere R	27	5	**70**	**10**
2012–13	Notts Co	24	2		
2012–13	*Torquay U*	7	4		
2013–14	Notts Co	15	1	**39**	**3**
2013–14	*Torquay U*	10	1	**17**	**5**
2014–15	Dagenham & R	24	2		
2015–16	Dagenham & R	28	4	**52**	**6**
2016–17	Newport Co	19	3	**19**	**3**

MEITE, Abdoulaye (D) **309** **4**
H: 6 1 W: 12 11 b.Paris 6-10-80
Internationals: Ivory Coast Full caps.

1998–99	Red Star 93	4	1		
1999–2000	Red Star 93	0	0	**4**	**1**
2000–01	Marseille	1	0		
2001–02	Marseille	10	0		
2002–03	Marseille	28	0		
2003–04	Marseille	30	0		
2004–05	Marseille	34	1		
2005–06	Marseille	13	0	**116**	**1**
2006–07	Bolton W	35	0		
2007–08	Bolton W	21	0	**56**	**0**
2008–09	WBA	18	0		
2009–10	WBA	20	0		
2010–11	WBA	10	0	**48**	**0**
2011–12	Dijon	25	1	**25**	**1**
2013	FC Honka	26	0	**26**	**0**
2013–14	Doncaster R	21	1	**21**	**1**
2014–15	OFI Crete	9	0	**9**	**0**
2014–15	Ross Co	0	0		
2016–17	SJK	0	0		
2016–17	Newport Co	4	0	**4**	**0**

MOLYNEUX, Dion (D) **0** **0**

2016–17	Newport Co	0	0		

MYRIE-WILLIAMS, Jennison (F) **282** **30**
H: 5 11 W: 12 08 b.Lambeth 17-5-88
Internationals: England U18.

2005–06	Bristol C	1	0		
2006–07	Bristol C	25	2		
2007–08	Bristol C	0	0		
2007–08	*Cheltenham T*	12	0		
2007–08	*Tranmere R*	25	3		
2008–09	Bristol C	0	0		
2008–09	*Cheltenham T*	5	1	**17**	**1**
2008–09	*Carlisle U*	8	0	**8**	**0**
2008–09	*Hereford U*	15	2	**15**	**2**
2009–10	Bristol C	0	0	**26**	**2**
2009–10	Dundee U	24	1	**24**	**1**
2010–11	St Johnstone	6	0	**6**	**0**
2011–12	Stevenage	17	0	**17**	**0**
2011–12	*Port Vale*	6	1		
2012–13	Port Vale	44	9		
2013–14	Port Vale	38	7	**88**	**17**
2014–15	Scunthorpe U	15	0		
2014–15	*Tranmere R*	18	3	**43**	**6**
2015–16	Scunthorpe U	0	0	**15**	**0**
2015–16	Sligo	0	0		
2016–17	Newport Co	23	1	**23**	**1**

O'BRIEN, Mark (D) **77** **1**
H: 5 11 W: 12 02 b.Dublin 20-11-92
Internationals: Republic of Ireland U17, U19, U21.

2008–09	Derby Co	1	0		
2009–10	Derby Co	0	0		
2010–11	Derby Co	2	0		
2011–12	Derby Co	20	0		
2012–13	Derby Co	9	0		
2013–14	Derby Co	0	0	**32**	**0**
2014–15	Motherwell	19	0	**19**	**0**
2015–16	Luton T	6	0	**6**	**0**

From Southport.

2016–17	Newport Co	20	1	**20**	**1**

O'HANLON, Josh (F) **32** **7**
H: 6 0 W: 12 00 b.Dublin 25-9-95

2013	Longford T	22	7	**22**	**7**
2013–14	Bournemouth	0	0		
2014–15	Bournemouth	0	0		
2014–15	*York C*	3	0	**3**	**0**
2015–16	Bournemouth	0	0		
2016–17	Bournemouth	0	0		
2016–17	Newport Co	7	0	**7**	**0**

OWEN-EVANS, Tom (F) **40** **1**
H: 5 11 W: 10 06 b.Bristol 18-3-97

2014–15	Newport Co	1	0		
2015–16	Newport Co	15	0		
2016–17	Newport Co	24	1	**40**	**1**

PARKIN, Jon (F) **429** **116**
H: 6 4 W: 13 07 b.Barnsley 30-12-81

1998–99	Barnsley	2	0		
1999–2000	Barnsley	0	0		
2000–01	Barnsley	4	0		
2001–02	Barnsley	4	0	**10**	**0**
2001–02	*Hartlepool U*	1	0	**1**	**0**

2001–02 York C 18 2
2002–03 York C 41 10
2003–04 York C 15 2 **74 14**
2003–04 Macclesfield T 12 1
2004–05 Macclesfield T 42 22
2005–06 Macclesfield T 11 7 **65 30**
2005–06 Hull C 18 5
2006–07 Hull C 29 6 **47 11**
2006–07 *Stoke C* 6 3
2007–08 Stoke C 29 2 **35 5**
2008–09 Preston NE 39 11
2009–10 Preston NE 43 10
2010–11 Preston NE 19 7 **101 28**
2010–11 Cardiff C 11 1
2011–12 Cardiff C 0 0 **11 1**
2011–12 *Doncaster R* 5 0 **5 0**
2011–12 *Huddersfield T* 3 0 **3 0**
2011–12 *Scunthorpe U* 14 6 **14 6**
2012–13 Fleetwood T 22 10
2013–14 Fleetwood T 31 7 **53 17**
2016–17 Newport Co 10 4 **10 4**

PARSELLE, Kieran (D) 7 0
b. 30-11-96
2014–15 Newport Co 0 0
2015–16 Newport Co 7 0
2016–17 Newport Co 0 0 **7 0**

PIPE, David (M) 302 8
H: 5 9 W: 12 01 b.Caerphilly 5-11-83
Internationals: Wales U21, Full caps.
2002–03 Coventry C 21 1
2003–04 Coventry C 0 0 **21 1**
2003–04 Notts Co 18 0
2004–05 Notts Co 41 2
2005–06 Notts Co 43 2
2006–07 Notts Co 39 0 **141 4**
2007–08 Bristol R 40 2
2008–09 Bristol R 39 1
2009–10 Bristol R 7 0 **86 3**
2009–10 *Cheltenham T* 8 0 **8 0**
2013–14 Newport Co 25 0
From Forest Green R, Eastleigh.
2016–17 Newport Co 21 0 **46 0**

RANDALL, Mark (M) 133 6
H: 6 0 W: 12 12 b.Milton Keynes 28-9-89
Internationals: England U17, U18.
2006–07 Arsenal 0 0
2007–08 Arsenal 1 0
2007–08 *Burnley* 10 0 **10 0**
2008–09 Arsenal 1 0
2009–10 Arsenal 0 0
2009–10 *Milton Keynes D* 16 0
2010–11 Arsenal 0 0 **2 0**
2010–11 *Rotherham U* 10 1 **10 1**
2011–12 Chesterfield 16 1
2012–13 Chesterfield 29 1
2013–14 Chesterfield 0 0 **45 2**
2013–14 Milton Keynes D 4 0
2014–15 Milton Keynes D 9 0
2015–16 Milton Keynes D 0 0 **29 0**
2015–16 Barnet 12 2 **12 2**
2016–17 Newport Co 25 1 **25 1**

REID, Craig (F) 122 19
H: 5 10 W: 11 10 b.Coventry 17-12-85
2004–05 Coventry C 0 0
2005–06 Coventry C 0 0
2006–07 Cheltenham T 6 0
2007–08 Cheltenham T 8 0 **14 0**
From Grays Ath, Newport Co.
2010–11 Stevenage 20 2
2011–12 Stevenage 29 6
2012–13 Stevenage 0 0
2012–13 Aldershot T 39 11 **39 11**
2013–14 Southend U 6 0 **6 0**
2013–14 Stevenage 4 0 **53 8**
2014–15 Kidderminster H 0 0
2016–17 Newport Co 10 0 **10 0**

RIGG, Sean (F) 339 38
H: 5 9 W: 12 01 b.Bristol 1-10-88
2006–07 Bristol R 18 1
2007–08 Bristol R 31 1
2008–09 Bristol R 8 0
2009–10 Bristol R 0 0 **57 2**
2009–10 *Port Vale* 26 3
2010–11 Port Vale 25 3
2011–12 Port Vale 42 10 **93 16**
2012–13 Oxford U 44 5
2013–14 Oxford U 28 2 **72 7**
2014–15 AFC Wimbledon 44 5
2015–16 AFC Wimbledon 39 2 **83 7**
2016–17 Newport Co 34 6 **34 6**

TOURAY, Momodou (F) 0 0
Internationals: Wales U18.
2016–17 Newport Co 0 0

TOZER, Ben (D) 226 7
H: 6 1 W: 12 11 b.Plymouth 1-3-90
2007–08 Swindon T 2 0 **2 0**
2007–08 Newcastle U 0 0
2008–09 Newcastle U 0 0
2009–10 Newcastle U 1 0
2010–11 Newcastle U 0 0 **1 0**
2010–11 *Northampton T* 31 3
2011–12 Northampton T 45 3
2012–13 Northampton T 46 0
2013–14 Northampton T 29 0
2013–14 *Colchester U* 1 0 **1 0**
2014–15 Northampton T 22 0 **173 6**
2015–16 Yeovil T 26 0 **26 0**
2016–17 Newport Co 23 1 **23 1**

TURLEY, Jamie (D) 6 1
H: 6 1 W: 12 13 b.Reading 7-4-90
Internationals: England C.
2014–15 Swindon T 0 0
2015–16 Newport Co 0 0
2016–17 Newport Co 6 1 **6 1**

WILLIAMS, Aaron (F) 33 5
H: 5 11 W: 12 05 b. 21-10-93
Internationals: England C.
2012–13 Walsall 6 0
2013–14 Walsall 0 0 **6 0**
From Worcester C, Rushall Olympic, Nuneaton T.
2015–16 Peterborough U 10 2
2016–17 Peterborough U 0 0 **10 2**
2016–17 Newport Co 17 3 **17 3**

WOOD, Finley (D) 3 0
b.Newport
2016–17 Newport Co 3 0 **3 0**

Scholars
Cook, Michael John; Davies, Rhys Paul Richard; Evans, Andrew James; Hunt, Joe Lewis; Kavanagh, Rhys Michael; Molyneux, Dion Richard; Press, Evan Lewis; Savigar, Thomas Anthony; Smith, Cairan; Tolland, Kyron; Touray, Momodou; Warman, Liam; Williams, Jay Andrew; Williams, Joshua Lee; Wood, Finlay.

Non-Contract
Demetriou, Michael; Flynn, Michael John Samuel; O'Brien, Mark Leo.

NORTHAMPTON T (58)

BEAUTYMAN, Harry (M) 61 8
H: 5 10 W: 11 09 b.Newham 1-4-92
Internationals: England C.
2010–11 Leyton Orient 0 0
From Sutton U, Welling U.
2014–15 Peterborough U 18 2
2015–16 Peterborough U 22 3 **40 5**
2016–17 Northampton T 21 3 **21 3**

BUCHANAN, David (M) 415 2
H: 5 7 W: 11 03 b.Rochdale 6-5-86
Internationals: Northern Ireland U19, U21.
2004–05 Bury 3 0
2005–06 Bury 23 0
2006–07 Bury 41 0
2007–08 Bury 35 0
2008–09 Bury 46 0
2009–10 Bury 38 0 **186 0**
2010–11 Hamilton A 28 1 **28 1**
2011–12 Tranmere R 41 1 **41 1**
2012–13 Preston NE 33 0
2013–14 Preston NE 19 0
2014–15 Preston NE 17 0 **69 0**
2015–16 Northampton T 46 0
2016–17 Northampton T 45 0 **91 0**

CORNELL, David (G) 50 0
H: 5 11 W: 11 07 b.Gorseinon 28-3-91
Internationals: Wales U17, U19, U21.
2009–10 Swansea C 0 0
2010–11 Swansea C 0 0
2011–12 Swansea C 0 0
2011–12 *Hereford U* 25 0 **25 0**
2012–13 Swansea C 0 0
2013–14 Swansea C 0 0
2013–14 *St Mirren* 5 0 **5 0**
2014–15 Swansea C 0 0
2014–15 *Portsmouth* 0 0
2015–16 Oldham Ath 14 0 **14 0**
2016–17 Northampton T 6 0 **6 0**

EARDLEY, Neal (M) 244 12
H: 5 11 W: 11 10 b.Llandudno 6-11-88
Internationals: Wales U17, U19, U21, Full caps.
2005–06 Oldham Ath 1 0
2006–07 Oldham Ath 36 2
2007–08 Oldham Ath 42 6
2008–09 Oldham Ath 34 2
2009–10 Oldham Ath 0 0 **113 10**
2009–10 Blackpool 24 0
2010–11 Blackpool 31 1
2011–12 Blackpool 26 1
2012–13 Blackpool 23 0 **104 2**
2013–14 Birmingham C 5 0
2014–15 Birmingham C 4 0
2014–15 *Leyton Orient* 1 0 **1 0**
2015–16 Birmingham C 5 0 **14 0**
2016–17 Hibernian 2 0 **2 0**
2016–17 Northampton T 10 0 **10 0**

FOLEY, Sam (M) 174 14
H: 6 0 W: 11 08 b.St Albans 17-10-86
2012–13 Yeovil T 41 5
2013–14 Yeovil T 7 0
2013–14 *Shrewsbury T* 9 0 **9 0**
2014–15 Yeovil T 40 2 **88 7**
2015–16 Port Vale 45 6
2016–17 Port Vale 32 1 **77 7**
2016–17 Northampton T 0 0

HANLEY, Raheem (D) 1 0
H: 5 8 W: 11 00 b.Blackburn 24-3-94
Internationals: England U19.
2011–12 Blackburn R 0 0
2012–13 Blackburn R 0 0
2013–14 Blackburn R 0 0
2013–14 Swansea C 0 0
2014–15 Swansea C 0 0
2015–16 Swansea C 0 0
2016–17 Northampton T 1 0 **1 0**

HOSKINS, Sam (F) 112 13
H: 5 8 W: 10 07 b.Dorchester 4-2-93
2011–12 Southampton 0 0
2011–12 *Preston NE* 0 0
2011–12 *Rotherham U* 8 2 **8 2**
2012–13 Southampton 0 0
2012–13 *Stevenage* 14 1 **14 1**
2013–14 Yeovil T 19 0
2014–15 Yeovil T 12 1 **31 1**
2015–16 Northampton T 34 6
2016–17 Northampton T 25 3 **59 9**

IACIOFANO, Joe (F) 1 0
b.Northampton 9-9-98
2016–17 Northampton T 1 0 **1 0**

McCOURT, Jak (M) 40 1
H: 5 10 W: 10 10 b.Leicester 6-7-95
2013–14 Leicester C 0 0
2013–14 *Torquay U* 11 0 **11 0**
2014–15 Leicester C 0 0
2015–16 Leicester C 0 0
2015–16 *Port Vale* 2 0 **2 0**
2015–16 Barnsley 1 0 **1 0**
2016–17 Northampton T 26 1 **26 1**

McWILLIAMS, Shaun (M) 5 0
b.Northampton 14-8-98
2014–15 Northampton T 0 0
2015–16 Northampton T 0 0
2016–17 Northampton T 5 0 **5 0**

MOLONEY, Brendan (M) 196 4
H: 6 1 W: 11 12 b.Killarney 18-1-89
Internationals: Republic of Ireland U21.
2005–06 Nottingham F 0 0
2006–07 Nottingham F 1 0
2007–08 Nottingham F 2 0
2007–08 *Chesterfield* 9 1 **9 1**
2008–09 Nottingham F 12 0
2009–10 Nottingham F 0 0
2009–10 *Notts Co* 18 1 **18 1**
2009–10 *Scunthorpe U* 3 0 **3 0**
2010–11 Nottingham F 6 0
2011–12 Nottingham F 8 0
2012–13 Nottingham F 13 0 **42 0**
2012–13 Bristol C 17 0
2013–14 Bristol C 32 0 **49 0**
2014–15 Yeovil T 5 0 **5 0**
2014–15 *Northampton T* 22 1
2015–16 Northampton T 25 1
2016–17 Northampton T 23 0 **70 2**

O'TOOLE, John (M) 312 53
H: 6 2 W: 13 07 b.Harrow 30-9-88
Internationals: Republic of Ireland U21.
2007–08 Watford 35 3
2008–09 Watford 22 7
2008–09 *Sheffield U* 9 1 **9 1**

2009–10 Watford 0 0 **57 10**
2009–10 Colchester U 31 2
2010–11 Colchester U 11 0
2011–12 Colchester U 15 0
2012–13 Colchester U 15 0 **72 2**
2012–13 *Bristol R* 18 3
2013–14 Bristol R 41 13 **59 16**
2014–15 Northampton T 35 2
2014–15 *Southend U* 2 0 **2 0**
2015–16 Northampton T 38 12
2016–17 Northampton T 40 10 **113 24**

PHILLIPS, Aaron (D) 73 2
H: 5 7 W: 11 00 b.Warwick 20-11-93
2012–13 Coventry C 0 0
2013–14 Coventry C 11 1
2014–15 Coventry C 19 0
2015–16 Coventry C 23 0 **53 1**
2016–17 Northampton T 20 1 **20 1**

REVELL, Alex (F) 450 86
H: 6 3 W: 13 00 b.Cambridge 7-7-83
2000–01 Cambridge U 4 0
2001–02 Cambridge U 24 2
2002–03 Cambridge U 9 0
2003–04 Cambridge U 20 3 **57 5**
From Braintree T.
2006–07 Brighton & HA 38 7
2007–08 Brighton & HA 21 6 **59 13**
2007–08 Southend U 8 0
2008–09 Southend U 23 4
2009–10 Southend U 3 0 **34 4**
2009–10 *Swindon T* 10 2 **10 2**
2009–10 Wycombe W 15 6 **15 6**
2010–11 Leyton Orient 39 13
2011–12 Leyton Orient 5 0 **44 13**
2011–12 Rotherham U 40 10
2012–13 Rotherham U 41 6
2013–14 Rotherham U 45 8
2014–15 Rotherham U 24 4 **150 28**
2014–15 Cardiff C 16 2
2015–16 Cardiff C 10 0 **26 2**
2015–16 *Wigan Ath* 6 1 **6 1**
2015–16 Milton Keynes D 17 4 **17 4**
2016–17 Northampton T 32 8 **32 8**

RICHARDS, Marc (F) 515 168
H: 6 2 W: 12 06 b.Wolverhampton 8-7-82
Internationals: England U18, U20.
1999–2000 Blackburn R 0 0
2000–01 Blackburn R 0 0
2001–02 Blackburn R 0 0
2001–02 *Crewe Alex* 4 0 **4 0**
2001–02 *Oldham Ath* 5 0 **5 0**
2001–02 *Halifax T* 5 0 **5 0**
2002–03 Blackburn R 0 0
2002–03 *Swansea C* 17 7 **17 7**
2003–04 Northampton T 41 8
2004–05 Northampton T 12 2
2004–05 *Rochdale* 5 2 **5 2**
2005–06 Northampton T 0 0
2005–06 Barnsley 38 12
2006–07 Barnsley 31 6 **69 18**
2007–08 Port Vale 29 5
2008–09 Port Vale 30 10
2009–10 Port Vale 46 20
2010–11 Port Vale 40 16
2011–12 Port Vale 36 17 **181 68**
2012–13 Chesterfield 34 12
2013–14 Chesterfield 38 8 **72 20**
2013–14 Northampton T 0 0
2014–15 Northampton T 31 18
2015–16 Northampton T 31 15
2016–17 Northampton T 42 10 **157 53**

SMITH, Adam (G) 90 0
H: 5 11 W: 11 00 b.Sunderland 23-11-92
2010–11 Leicester C 0 0
2011–12 Leicester C 0 0
2011–12 *Chesterfield* 0 0
2011–12 *Bristol R* 0 0
2012–13 Leicester C 0 0
2013–14 Leicester C 0 0
2013–14 *Stevenage* 0 0
2014–15 Leicester C 0 0
2014–15 *Mansfield T* 4 0 **4 0**
2015–16 Northampton T 46 0
2016–17 Northampton T 40 0 **86 0**

SONUPE, Emmanuel (M) 5 0
b.London 21-3-96
Internationals: England U16, U18.
2014–15 Tottenham H 0 0
2014–15 *St Mirren* 4 0 **4 0**
2015–16 Tottenham H 0 0
2016–17 Northampton T 1 0 **1 0**

TAYLOR, Matthew (D) 587 75
H: 5 11 W: 12 03 b.Oxford 27-11-81
Internationals: England U21, B.
1998–99 Luton T 0 0
1999–2000 Luton T 41 4
2000–01 Luton T 45 1
2001–02 Luton T 43 11 **129 16**
2002–03 Portsmouth 35 7
2003–04 Portsmouth 30 0
2004–05 Portsmouth 32 1
2005–06 Portsmouth 34 6
2006–07 Portsmouth 35 8
2007–08 Portsmouth 13 1 **179 23**
2007–08 Bolton W 16 3
2008–09 Bolton W 34 10
2009–10 Bolton W 37 8
2010–11 Bolton W 36 2 **123 23**
2011–12 West Ham U 28 1
2012–13 West Ham U 28 1
2013–14 West Ham U 20 0 **76 2**
2014–15 Burnley 10 0
2015–16 Burnley 27 4 **37 4**
2016–17 Northampton T 43 7 **43 7**

ZAKUANI, Gaby (D) 377 15
H: 6 1 W: 12 13 b.DR Congo 31-5-86
Internationals: DR Congo Full caps.
2002–03 Leyton Orient 1 0
2003–04 Leyton Orient 10 2
2004–05 Leyton Orient 33 0
2005–06 Leyton Orient 43 1 **87 3**
2006–07 Fulham 0 0
2006–07 *Stoke C* 9 0
2007–08 Fulham 0 0
2007–08 *Stoke C* 19 0 **28 0**
2008–09 Fulham 0 0
2008–09 Peterborough U 32 1
2009–10 Peterborough U 29 0
2010–11 Peterborough U 30 2
2011–12 Peterborough U 41 1
2012–13 Peterborough U 33 1
2013–14 Peterborough U 15 0
2013–14 *Kalloni* 15 1 **15 1**
2014–15 Peterborough U 22 1
2015–16 Peterborough U 24 3 **226 9**
2016–17 Northampton T 21 2 **21 2**

Players retained or with offer of contract
Goff, James William; McDonald, Rodney Troy.

Scholars
Anaele, Prudence Chukwudike; Andrews-Lamptey, Ethan Jack Nii-Odartei; Bako, Shama; Gillard, James William; Hall, Jamie Luke; Hammond, James; Irwin, Lewis Cameron Leigh; Marett, Vaughn Andrew Ronnie; McCammon, Joshua Lewis; North, Adam Peter; Patrick, Seth; Toseland, Ben; Whaler, Sean Andrew; Wilson, Jarvis Zachary.

NORWICH C (59)

ANDREU, Tony (M) 216 57
H: 5 10 W: 11 05 b.Cagnes-Sur-Mer 22-5-88
2009–10 Nyon 29 2
2010–11 Nyon 21 2
2011–12 Nyon 27 6 **77 10**
2012–13 Livingston 33 7 **33 7**
2013–14 Hamilton A 35 13
2014–15 Hamilton A 23 12 **58 25**
2014–15 Norwich C 6 0
2015–16 Norwich C 0 0
2015–16 *Rotherham U* 11 2 **11 2**
2016–17 Norwich C 0 0 **6 0**
2016–17 *Dundee U* 31 13 **31 13**

BASSONG, Sebastien (D) 294 7
H: 6 2 W: 11 07 b.Paris 9-7-86
Internationals: France U21. Cameroon Full caps.
2005–06 Metz 23 0
2006–07 Metz 37 1
2007–08 Metz 19 0 **79 1**
2008–09 Newcastle U 30 0
2009–10 Newcastle U 0 0 **30 0**
2009–10 Tottenham H 28 1
2010–11 Tottenham H 12 1
2011–12 Tottenham H 5 0
2011–12 *Wolverhampton W* 9 0 **9 0**
2012–13 Tottenham H 0 0 **45 2**
2012–13 Norwich C 34 3
2013–14 Norwich C 27 0
2014–15 Norwich C 18 0
2014–15 *Watford* 11 0 **11 0**
2015–16 Norwich C 32 1
2016–17 Norwich C 9 0 **120 4**

BENNETT, Ryan (M) 292 14
H: 6 2 W: 11 00 b.Thurrock 6-3-90
Internationals: England U18, U21.
2006–07 Grimsby T 5 0
2007–08 Grimsby T 40 1
2008–09 Grimsby T 45 5
2009–10 Grimsby T 13 0 **103 6**
2009–10 Peterborough U 22 1
2010–11 Peterborough U 34 4
2011–12 Peterborough U 32 1 **88 6**
2011–12 Norwich C 8 0
2012–13 Norwich C 15 1
2013–14 Norwich C 16 1
2014–15 Norwich C 7 0
2015–16 Norwich C 22 0
2016–17 Norwich C 33 0 **101 2**

DIJKS, Mitchell (D) 114 1
H: 6 4 W: 14 02 b.Purmerend 9-2-93
Internationals: Netherlands U16, U18, U19, U21.
2012–13 Ajax 6 0
2013–14 Ajax 0 0
2013–14 *Heerenveen* 24 0 **24 0**
2014–15 Willem II 28 0 **28 0**
2015–16 Ajax 29 0
2016–17 Ajax 12 0 **47 0**
On loan from Ajax.
2016–17 Norwich C 15 1 **15 1**

DORRANS, Graham (F) 316 51
H: 5 9 W: 11 07 b.Glasgow 5-5-87
Internationals: Scotland U20, U21, Full caps.
2006–07 Livingston 8 0
2006–07 *Partick Thistle* 15 5 **15 5**
2006–07 Livingston 34 5
2007–08 Livingston 34 11 **76 16**
2008–09 WBA 8 0
2009–10 WBA 45 13
2010–11 WBA 21 1
2011–12 WBA 31 3
2012–13 WBA 26 1
2013–14 WBA 14 2
2014–15 WBA 21 1 **166 21**
2014–15 *Norwich C* 15 3
2015–16 Norwich C 21 0
2016–17 Norwich C 23 6 **59 9**

GODFREY, Ben (M) 14 1
H: 6 0 W: 11 09 b.York 15-1-98
2014–15 York C 0 0
2015–16 York C 12 1 **12 1**
2015–16 Norwich C 0 0
2016–17 Norwich C 2 0 **2 0**

GRANT, Ray (M) 0 0
b.Morningthorpe 1-11-96
Internationals: Scotland U19.
2016–17 Norwich C 0 0

HOOLAHAN, Wes (M) 497 68
H: 5 6 W: 10 03 b.Dublin 10-8-83
Internationals: Republic of Ireland U21, B, Full caps.
2001–02 Shelbourne 20 3
2002–03 Shelbourne 23 0
2004 Shelbourne 31 2
2005 Shelbourne 29 4 **103 9**
2005–06 Livingston 16 0 **16 0**
2006–07 Blackpool 42 8
2007–08 Blackpool 45 5 **87 13**
2008–09 Norwich C 32 2
2009–10 Norwich C 37 11
2010–11 Norwich C 41 10
2011–12 Norwich C 33 4
2012–13 Norwich C 33 3
2013–14 Norwich C 16 1
2014–15 Norwich C 36 4
2015–16 Norwich C 30 4
2016–17 Norwich C 33 7 **291 46**

HOWSON, Jonathan (M) 361 45
H: 5 11 W: 12 01 b.Morley 21-5-88
Internationals: England U21.
2006–07 Leeds U 9 1
2007–08 Leeds U 26 3
2008–09 Leeds U 40 4
2009–10 Leeds U 45 4
2010–11 Leeds U 46 10
2011–12 Leeds U 19 1 **185 23**
2011–12 Norwich C 11 1
2012–13 Norwich C 30 2
2013–14 Norwich C 27 2
2014–15 Norwich C 34 8
2015–16 Norwich C 36 3
2016–17 Norwich C 38 6 **176 22**

IVO PINTO, Daniel (D) 194 1
H: 6 0 W: 11 07 b.Lourosa 7-1-90
Internationals: Portugal U16, U17, U18, U19, U21.

2008–09	Porto	0	0		
2009–10	Porto	0	0		
2009–10	*Vicente*	1	0	**1**	**0**
2009–10	*Vitoria Setubal*	2	0	**2**	**0**
2010–11	Porto	0	0		
2010–11	*Covilha*	22	0	**22**	**0**
2011–12	Rio Ave	0	0		
2011–12	*Uniao Leiria*	25	0	**25**	**0**
2012–13	Cluj	27	0	**27**	**0**
2013–14	Dinamo Zagreb	28	0		
2014–15	Dinamo Zagreb	29	0		
2015–16	Dinamo Zagreb	13	0	**70**	**0**
2015–16	Norwich C	10	0		
2016–17	Norwich C	37	1	**47**	**1**

JARVIS, Matthew (M) 371 36
H: 5 8 W: 11 10 b.Middlesbrough 22-5-86
Internationals: England Full caps.

2003–04	Gillingham	10	0		
2004–05	Gillingham	30	3		
2005–06	Gillingham	35	3		
2006–07	Gillingham	35	6	**110**	**12**
2007–08	Wolverhampton W	26	1		
2008–09	Wolverhampton W	28	3		
2009–10	Wolverhampton W	34	3		
2010–11	Wolverhampton W	37	4		
2011–12	Wolverhampton W	37	8		
2012–13	Wolverhampton W	2	0	**164**	**19**
2012–13	West Ham U	32	2		
2013–14	West Ham U	32	2		
2014–15	West Ham U	11	0		
2015–16	West Ham U	3	0	**78**	**4**
2015–16	Norwich C	19	1		
2016–17	Norwich C	0	0	**19**	**1**

JEROME, Cameron (F) 447 107
H: 6 1 W: 13 06 b.Huddersfield 14-8-86
Internationals: England U21.

2004–05	Cardiff C	29	6		
2005–06	Cardiff C	44	18	**73**	**24**
2005–06	Birmingham C	0	0		
2006–07	Birmingham C	38	7		
2007–08	Birmingham C	33	7		
2008–09	Birmingham C	43	9		
2009–10	Birmingham C	32	11		
2010–11	Birmingham C	34	3		
2011–12	Birmingham C	1	0	**181**	**37**
2011–12	Stoke C	23	4		
2012–13	Stoke C	26	3		
2013–14	Stoke C	1	0	**50**	**7**
2013–14	*Crystal Palace*	28	2	**28**	**2**
2014–15	Norwich C	41	18		
2015–16	Norwich C	34	3		
2016–17	Norwich C	40	16	**115**	**37**

JONES, Paul (G) 281 0
H: 6 3 W: 13 00 b.Maidstone 28-6-86

2008–09	Exeter C	46	0		
2009–10	Exeter C	26	0		
2010–11	Exeter C	18	0	**90**	**0**
2010–11	*Peterborough U*	1	0		
2011–12	Peterborough U	35	0	**36**	**0**
2012–13	Crawley T	46	0		
2013–14	Crawley T	46	0		
2014–15	Portsmouth	46	0		
2015–16	Portsmouth	9	0	**55**	**0**
2015–16	*Crawley T*	8	0	**100**	**0**
2016–17	Norwich C	0	0		

KLOSE, Timm (D) 176 11
H: 6 5 W: 13 10 b.Frankfurt am Main 9-5-88
Internationals: Switzerland U21, U23, Full caps.

2009–10	Thun	29	2		
2010–11	Thun	30	3	**59**	**5**
2011–12	Nuremburg	13	0		
2012–13	Nuremburg	32	2	**45**	**2**
2013–14	Wolfsburg	10	0		
2014–15	Wolfsburg	12	1		
2015–16	Wolfsburg	8	1	**30**	**2**
2015–16	Norwich C	10	1		
2016–17	Norwich C	32	1	**42**	**2**

LAFFERTY, Kyle (F) 306 65
H: 6 4 W: 11 00 b.Northern Ireland 16-9-87
Internationals: Northern Ireland U17, U19, U21, Full caps.

2005–06	Burnley	11	1		
2005–06	*Darlington*	9	3	**9**	**3**
2006–07	Burnley	35	4		
2007–08	Burnley	37	5	**83**	**10**
2008–09	Rangers	25	6		
2009–10	Rangers	28	7		
2010–11	Rangers	31	11		
2011–12	Rangers	20	7	**104**	**31**
2012–13	Sion	25	5	**25**	**5**
2013–14	Palermo	34	11	**34**	**11**
2014–15	Norwich C	18	1		
2014–15	*Caykur Rizespor*	14	2	**14**	**2**
2015–16	Norwich C	1	0		
2015–16	*Birmingham C*	6	1	**6**	**1**
2016–17	Norwich C	12	1	**31**	**2**

MADDISON, James (M) 52 8
H: 5 10 W: 11 07 b.Coventry 23-11-96

2013–14	Coventry C	0	0		
2014–15	Coventry C	12	2		
2015–16	Norwich C	0	0		
2015–16	*Coventry C*	23	3	**35**	**5**
2016–17	Norwich C	3	1	**3**	**1**
2016–17	*Aberdeen*	14	2	**14**	**2**

MARTIN, Russell (M) 451 22
H: 6 0 W: 11 08 b.Brighton 4-1-86
Internationals: Scotland Full caps.

2004–05	Wycombe W	7	0		
2005–06	Wycombe W	23	3		
2006–07	Wycombe W	42	2		
2007–08	Wycombe W	44	0	**116**	**5**
2008–09	Peterborough U	46	1		
2009–10	Peterborough U	10	0	**56**	**1**
2009–10	Norwich C	26	0		
2010–11	Norwich C	46	5		
2011–12	Norwich C	33	2		
2012–13	Norwich C	31	3		
2013–14	Norwich C	31	0		
2014–15	Norwich C	45	2		
2015–16	Norwich C	30	3		
2016–17	Norwich C	37	1	**279**	**16**

MATTHEWS, Remi (G) 28 0
H: 6 0 W: 12 04 b.Gorleston 10-2-94

2014–15	Norwich C	0	0		
2014–15	*Burton Alb*	0	0		
2015–16	Norwich C	0	0		
2015–16	*Burton Alb*	2	0	**2**	**0**
2015–16	*Doncaster R*	9	0	**9**	**0**
2016–17	Norwich C	0	0		
2016–17	*Hamilton A*	17	0	**17**	**0**

McGOVERN, Michael (G) 290 0
H: 6 2 W: 13 07 b.Enniskillen 12-7-84
Internationals: Northern Ireland U19, U21, Full caps.

2004–05	Celtic	0	0		
2004–05	*Stranraer*	19	0	**19**	**0**
2005–06	Celtic	0	0		
2006–07	Celtic	0	0		
2006–07	*St Johnstone*	1	0	**1**	**0**
2007–08	Celtic	0	0		
2008–09	Dundee U	0	0		
2009–10	Ross Co	35	0		
2010–11	Ross Co	36	0	**71**	**0**
2011–12	Falkirk	35	0		
2012–13	Falkirk	35	0		
2013–14	Falkirk	34	0	**104**	**0**
2014–15	Hamilton A	38	0		
2015–16	Hamilton A	37	0	**75**	**0**
2016–17	Norwich C	20	0	**20**	**0**

MIDDLETON, Glenn (M) 0 0
Internationals: Scotland U16, U17.

2016–17	Norwich C	0	0

MORRIS, Carlton (F) 56 8
H: 6 1 W: 13 05 b.Cambridge 16-12-95
Internationals: England U19.

2014–15	Norwich C	1	0		
2014–15	*Oxford U*	7	0	**7**	**0**
2014–15	*York C*	8	0	**8**	**0**
2015–16	Norwich C	0	0		
2015–16	*Hamilton A*	32	8	**32**	**8**
2016–17	Norwich C	0	0	**1**	**0**
2016–17	*Rotherham U*	8	0	**8**	**0**

MULUMBU, Youssef (M) 253 16
H: 5 9 W: 10 03 b.Kinshasa 25-1-87
Internationals: France U20, U21. DR Congo Full caps.

2006–07	Paris Saint-Germain	12	0		
2007–08	Paris Saint-Germain	1	0		
2007–08	*Amiens*	23	1	**23**	**1**
2008–09	Paris Saint-Germain	0	0	**13**	**0**
2008–09	WBA	6	0		
2009–10	WBA	40	3		
2010–11	WBA	34	7		
2011–12	WBA	35	1		
2012–13	WBA	28	2		
2013–14	WBA	37	2		
2014–15	WBA	17	0	**197**	**15**
2015–16	Norwich C	7	0		
2016–17	Norwich C	13	0	**20**	**0**

MURPHY, Jacob (M) 113 25
H: 5 9 W: 11 03 b.Wembley 24-2-95
Internationals: England U18, U19, U20, U21.

2013–14	Norwich C	0	0		
2013–14	*Swindon T*	6	0	**6**	**0**
2013–14	*Southend U*	7	1	**7**	**1**
2014–15	Norwich C	0	0		
2014–15	*Blackpool*	9	2	**9**	**2**
2014–15	*Scunthorpe U*	3	0	**3**	**0**
2014–15	*Colchester U*	11	4	**11**	**4**
2015–16	Norwich C	0	0		
2015–16	*Coventry C*	40	9	**40**	**9**
2016–17	Norwich C	37	9	**37**	**9**

MURPHY, Josh (F) 96 10
H: 5 8 W: 10 07 b.Wembley 24-2-95
Internationals: England U18, U19, U20.

2012–13	Norwich C	0	0		
2013–14	Norwich C	9	0		
2014–15	Norwich C	13	1		
2014–15	*Wigan Ath*	5	0	**5**	**0**
2015–16	Norwich C	0	0		
2015–16	*Milton Keynes D*	42	5	**42**	**5**
2016–17	Norwich C	27	4	**49**	**5**

NAISMITH, Steven (F) 345 81
H: 5 10 W: 11 04 b.Irvine 14-9-86
Internationals: Scotland U21, B, Full caps.

2003–04	Kilmarnock	1	0		
2004–05	Kilmarnock	24	1		
2005–06	Kilmarnock	36	13		
2006–07	Kilmarnock	37	15		
2007–08	Kilmarnock	4	0	**102**	**29**
2007–08	Rangers	21	5		
2008–09	Rangers	7	0		
2009–10	Rangers	28	3		
2010–11	Rangers	31	11		
2011–12	Rangers	11	9	**98**	**28**
2012–13	Everton	31	4		
2013–14	Everton	31	5		
2014–15	Everton	31	6		
2015–16	Everton	10	3	**103**	**18**
2015–16	Norwich C	13	1		
2016–17	Norwich C	29	5	**42**	**6**

NELSON OLIVEIRA, Miguel (F) 171 37
H: 6 1 W: 12 13 b.Barcelos 8-8-91
Internationals: Portugal U16, U17, U19, U20, U21, Full caps.

2009–10	Benfica	0	0		
2009–10	*Rio Ave*	10	0	**10**	**0**
2010–11	Benfica	0	0		
2010–11	*Pacos Ferreira*	23	4	**23**	**4**
2011–12	Benfica	12	0		
2012–13	Benfica	0	0		
2012–13	*La Coruna*	30	4	**30**	**4**
2013–14	Benfica	0	0		
2013–14	*Rennes*	30	8	**30**	**8**
2014–15	Benfica	0	0		
2014–15	*Swansea C*	10	1	**10**	**1**
2015–16	Benfica	0	0	**12**	**0**
2015–16	*Nottingham F*	28	9	**28**	**9**
2016–17	Norwich C	28	11	**28**	**11**

PRITCHARD, Alex (M) 121 24
H: 5 7 W: 9 11 b.Grays 3-5-93
Internationals: England U20, U21.

2011–12	Tottenham H	0	0		
2012–13	Tottenham H	0	0		
2012–13	*Peterborough U*	6	0	**6**	**0**
2013–14	Tottenham H	1	0		
2013–14	*Swindon T*	36	6	**36**	**6**
2014–15	Tottenham H	0	0		
2014–15	*Brentford*	45	12	**45**	**12**
2015–16	Tottenham H	1	0	**2**	**0**
2015–16	*WBA*	2	0	**2**	**0**
2016–17	Norwich C	30	6	**30**	**6**

RAMSEY, Louis (D) 0 0
b. 23-9-97

2016–17	Norwich C	0	0

RUDD, Declan (G) 119 0
H: 6 3 W: 12 06 b.Diss 16-1-91
Internationals: England U16, U17, U19, U20, U21, Full caps.

2008–09	Norwich C	0	0		
2009–10	Norwich C	7	0		
2010–11	Norwich C	1	0		
2011–12	Norwich C	2	0		
2012–13	Norwich C	0	0		
2012–13	*Preston NE*	14	0		
2013–14	Norwich C	0	0		
2013–14	*Preston NE*	46	0	**60**	**0**
2014–15	Norwich C	0	0		
2015–16	Norwich C	11	0		
2016–17	Norwich C	0	0	**21**	**0**
2016–17	*Charlton Ath*	38	0	**38**	**0**

RUDDY, John (G) **369** **0**
H: 6 3 W: 12 07 b.St Ives 24-10-86
Internationals: England Full caps.

2003–04	Cambridge U	1	0		
2004–05	Cambridge U	38	0	**39**	**0**
2005–06	Everton	1	0		
2005–06	*Walsall*	5	0	**5**	**0**
2005–06	*Rushden & D*	3	0	**3**	**0**
2005–06	*Chester C*	4	0	**4**	**0**
2006–07	Everton	0	0		
2006–07	*Stockport Co*	11	0		
2006–07	*Wrexham*	5	0	**5**	**0**
2006–07	*Bristol C*	1	0	**1**	**0**
2007–08	Everton	0	0		
2007–08	*Stockport Co*	12	0	**23**	**0**
2008–09	Everton	0	0		
2008–09	*Crewe Alex*	19	0	**19**	**0**
2009–10	Everton	0	0	**1**	**0**
2009–10	*Motherwell*	34	0	**34**	**0**
2010–11	Norwich C	45	0		
2011–12	Norwich C	37	0		
2012–13	Norwich C	15	0		
2013–14	Norwich C	38	0		
2014–15	Norwich C	46	0		
2015–16	Norwich C	27	0		
2016–17	Norwich C	27	0	**235**	**0**

TETTEY, Alexander (M) **287** **19**
H: 5 11 W: 10 09 b.Accra 4-4-86
Internationals: Norway U18, U19, U21, Full caps.

2004–05	Rosenborg	0	0		
2005–06	Rosenborg	10	1		
2006–07	Rosenborg	21	1		
2007–08	Rosenborg	25	4		
2008–09	Rosenborg	28	6		
2009–10	Rosenborg	1	0	**85**	**12**
2009–10	Rennes	24	0		
2010–11	Rennes	17	1		
2011–12	Rennes	19	1	**60**	**2**
2012–13	Norwich C	27	0		
2013–14	Norwich C	21	1		
2014–15	Norwich C	36	2		
2015–16	Norwich C	23	2		
2016–17	Norwich C	35	0	**142**	**5**

THOMPSON, Louis (M) **95** **6**
H: 5 11 W: 11 10 b.Bristol 19-12-94
Internationals: Wales U19, U21.

2012–13	Swindon T	4	0		
2013–14	Swindon T	28	2		
2014–15	Norwich C	0	0		
2014–15	*Swindon T*	32	2		
2015–16	Norwich C	0	0		
2015–16	*Swindon T*	28	2	**92**	**6**
2016–17	Norwich C	3	0	**3**	**0**

TOFFOLO, Harry (D) **64** **3**
H: 6 0 W: 11 03 b. 19-8-95
Internationals: England U18, U19, U20.

2014–15	Norwich C	0	0		
2014–15	*Swindon T*	28	1	**28**	**1**
2015–16	Norwich C	0	0		
2015–16	*Rotherham U*	7	0	**7**	**0**
2015–16	*Peterborough U*	7	0	**7**	**0**
2016–17	Norwich C	0	0		
2016–17	*Scunthorpe U*	22	2	**22**	**2**

TURNER, Michael (D) **386** **24**
H: 6 4 W: 13 05 b.Lewisham 9-11-83

2001–02	Charlton Ath	0	0		
2002–03	Charlton Ath	0	0		
2002–03	*Leyton Orient*	7	1	**7**	**1**
2003–04	Charlton Ath	0	0		
2004–05	Brentford	45	1		
2005–06	Brentford	46	2	**91**	**3**
2006–07	Hull C	43	3		
2007–08	Hull C	44	5		
2008–09	Hull C	38	4		
2009–10	Hull C	4	0	**129**	**12**
2009–10	Sunderland	29	2		
2010–11	Sunderland	15	0		
2011–12	Sunderland	24	0	**68**	**2**
2012–13	Norwich C	26	3		
2013–14	Norwich C	22	0		
2014–15	Norwich C	23	1		
2014–15	*Fulham*	9	1	**9**	**1**
2015–16	Norwich C	0	0		
2015–16	*Sheffield W*	11	1	**11**	**1**
2016–17	Norwich C	0	0	**71**	**4**

WHITTAKER, Steven (D) **381** **28**
H: 6 1 W: 13 07 b.Edinburgh 16-6-84
Internationals: Scotland U21, Full caps.

2001–02	Hibernian	1	0		
2002–03	Hibernian	6	0		
2003–04	Hibernian	28	1		
2004–05	Hibernian	37	1		
2005–06	Hibernian	34	1		
2006–07	Hibernian	35	1	**141**	**4**
2007–08	Rangers	30	4		
2008–09	Rangers	24	2		
2009–10	Rangers	35	7		
2010–11	Rangers	36	4		
2011–12	Rangers	25	2	**150**	**19**
2012–13	Norwich C	13	1		
2013–14	Norwich C	20	1		
2014–15	Norwich C	37	2		
2015–16	Norwich C	8	1		
2016–17	Norwich C	12	0	**90**	**5**

WILDSCHUT, Yanic (F) **203** **27**
H: 6 2 W: 13 08 b.Amsterdam 1-11-91
Internationals: Netherlands U21.

2010–11	Zwolle	33	3	**33**	**3**
2011–12	VVV	29	7		
2012–13	VVV	32	1	**61**	**8**
2013–14	Heerenveen	18	2		
2013–14	*Den Haag*	7	0	**7**	**0**
2014–15	Heerenveen	4	0	**22**	**2**
2014–15	Middlesbrough	11	2		
2015–16	Middlesbrough	1	0	**12**	**2**
2015–16	Wigan Ath	34	7		
2016–17	Wigan Ath	25	4	**59**	**11**
2016–17	Norwich C	9	1	**9**	**1**

Players retained or with offer of contract
Cantwell, Todd Owen; Crowe, Joe; Efete, Michee; Hallett, Jake; Jaiyesimi, Diallang; Lewis, Jamal; Oxborough, Aston Jay; Rana-Jerome, Cameron Zishan.

Scholars
Aarons, Maximillian James; Aransibia, Devonte; Ashley-Seal, Bernard Patrick; Birse, Zachary Robert; Catton, Bradley Matthew John; Da, Costa Rui Giovanni; Ellesley, Callum John; Fleming, Alan Dwyte; Hale-Brown, Fergal Stanley; Higgs, Kieran Suthun; Hlynsson, Agust Edvald; Kamal, Bilal Noradin; McCracken, Jon Douglas; McIntosh, Louis; Mututala, Sambu Emersson; Oddy, Brandon Owen Nicholas; Odusina, Oluwarotimi Mark; Payne, Alfred Edward; Pollock, Henry; Spyrou, Anthony Jeffrey John; Syme, Toby; Wallis, Owen.

NOTTINGHAM F (60)

AHMEDHODZIC, Anel (D) **1** **0**
H: 6 3 W: 12 00 b. 26-3-99
Internationals: Sweden U16, U17, U18, U19.
From Malmo.

2016–17	Nottingham F	1	0	**1**	**0**

ARIYIBI, Gboly (M) **87** **3**
H: 6 0 W: 11 05 b.West Virginia 18-1-95
Internationals: USA U20, U23.

2013–14	Leeds U	2	0	**2**	**0**
2013–14	*Tranmere R*	2	0	**2**	**0**
2014–15	Chesterfield	17	1		
2015–16	Chesterfield	38	2		
2016–17	Chesterfield	28	0	**83**	**3**
2016–17	Nottingham F	0	0		

ASSOMBALONGA, Britt (F) **155** **68**
H: 5 9 W: 11 13 b.Kinshasa 6-12-92

2010–11	Watford	0	0		
2011–12	Watford	4	0		
2012–13	Watford	0	0		
2012–13	*Southend U*	43	15	**43**	**15**
2013–14	Watford	0	0	**4**	**0**
2013–14	Peterborough U	43	23	**43**	**23**
2014–15	Nottingham F	29	15		
2015–16	Nottingham F	4	1		
2016–17	Nottingham F	32	14	**65**	**30**

BENDTNER, Nicklas (F) **202** **45**
H: 6 2 W: 13 00 b.Copenhagen 16-1-88
Internationals: Denmark U16, U17, U19, U21, Full caps.

2005–06	Arsenal	0	0		
2006–07	Arsenal	0	0		
2006–07	*Birmingham C*	42	11	**42**	**11**
2007–08	Arsenal	27	5		
2008–09	Arsenal	31	9		
2009–10	Arsenal	23	6		
2010–11	Arsenal	17	2		
2011–12	Arsenal	1	0		
2011–12	*Sunderland*	28	8	**28**	**8**
2012–13	Arsenal	0	0		
2012–13	*Juventus*	9	0	**9**	**0**
2013–14	Arsenal	9	2	**108**	**24**
2016–17	Nottingham F	15	2	**15**	**2**

Transferred to Rosenborg, March 2017.

BRERETON, Ben (F) **18** **3**
b.Stoke-on-Trent 18-4-99
Internationals: England U19.
From Stoke C.

2016–17	Nottingham F	18	3	**18**	**3**

BURKE, Oliver (M) **27** **6**
H: 5 9 W: 11 11 b.Melton Mowbray 7-4-97
Internationals: Scotland U19, U20, Full caps.

2014–15	Nottingham F	2	0		
2014–15	*Bradford C*	2	0	**2**	**0**
2015–16	Nottingham F	18	2		
2016–17	Nottingham F	5	4	**25**	**6**

Transferred to RB Leipzig, August 2016.

CARAYOL, Mustapha (F) **184** **29**
H: 5 10 W: 11 11 b.Gambia 10-6-89
Internationals: Gambia Full caps.

2007–08	Milton Keynes D	0	0		
2009–10	Torquay U	20	6	**20**	**6**
2010–11	Lincoln C	33	3	**33**	**3**
2011–12	Bristol R	30	4		
2012–13	Bristol R	0	0	**30**	**4**
2012–13	Middlesbrough	18	3		
2013–14	Middlesbrough	32	8		
2014–15	Middlesbrough	0	0		
2014–15	*Brighton & HA*	5	0	**5**	**0**
2015–16	Middlesbrough	0	0	**50**	**11**
2015–16	*Huddersfield T*	15	3	**15**	**3**
2015–16	*Leeds U*	12	1	**12**	**1**
2016–17	Nottingham F	19	1	**19**	**1**

CASH, Matty (M) **40** **3**
H: 6 2 W: 10 01 b.Slough 7-8-97

2015–16	Nottingham F	0	0		
2015–16	*Dagenham & R*	12	3	**12**	**3**
2016–17	Nottingham F	28	0	**28**	**0**

CLOUGH, Zach (F) **73** **25**
H: 5 7 b.Manchester 8-3-95

2013–14	Bolton W	0	0		
2014–15	Bolton W	8	5		
2015–16	Bolton W	28	7		
2016–17	Bolton W	23	9	**59**	**21**
2016–17	Nottingham F	14	4	**14**	**4**

COHEN, Chris (M) **362** **21**
H: 5 11 W: 10 11 b.Norwich 5-3-87

2003–04	West Ham U	7	0		
2004–05	West Ham U	11	0		
2005–06	West Ham U	0	0	**18**	**0**
2005–06	*Yeovil T*	30	1		
2006–07	Yeovil T	44	6	**74**	**7**
2007–08	Nottingham F	41	2		
2008–09	Nottingham F	41	2		
2009–10	Nottingham F	44	3		
2010–11	Nottingham F	42	2		
2011–12	Nottingham F	7	0		
2012–13	Nottingham F	38	2		
2013–14	Nottingham F	16	1		
2014–15	Nottingham F	6	0		
2015–16	Nottingham F	15	1		
2016–17	Nottingham F	20	1	**270**	**14**

DE VRIES, Dorus (G) **403** **0**
H: 6 1 W: 12 08 b.Bewerwijk 29-12-80

1999–2000	Telstar	1	0		
2000–01	Telstar	27	0		
2001–02	Telstar	27	0		
2002–03	Telstar	26	0	**81**	**0**
2003–04	Den Haag	18	0		
2004–05	Den Haag	32	0		
2005–06	Den Haag	0	0	**50**	**0**
2006–07	Dunfermline Ath	27	0	**27**	**0**
2007–08	Swansea C	46	0		
2008–09	Swansea C	40	0		
2009–10	Swansea C	46	0		
2010–11	Swansea C	46	0	**178**	**0**
2011–12	Wolverhampton W	4	0		
2012–13	Wolverhampton W	10	0	**14**	**0**
2013–14	Nottingham F	3	0		
2014–15	Nottingham F	4	0		
2015–16	Nottingham F	45	0		
2016–17	Nottingham F	1	0	**53**	**0**

Transferred to Celtic, August 2016.

DUMITRU, Nicolao (F) **153** **22**
H: 6 0 W: 12 00 b.Nacka 12-10-91
Internationals: Italy U19, U20.

2008–09	Empoli	1	0		
2009–10	Empoli	1	0		
2010–11	Napoli	9	0		
2011–12	Napoli	0	0		
2011–12	*Empoli*	25	4	**27**	**4**
2012–13	Napoli	0	0		
2012–13	*Ternana*	15	1	**15**	**1**
2012–13	*Cittadella*	5	0		
2013–14	Napoli	0	0		

2013–14 Cittadella 13 1 18 1
2013–14 *Reggina* 13 2 13 2
2014–15 Napoli 0 0
2014–15 *Veria* 27 6 27 6
2015–16 Napoli 0 0
2015–16 *Latina* 34 7 34 7
2016–17 Napoli 0 0 9 0
On loan from Napoli.
2016–17 Nottingham F 10 1 10 1

EDSER, Toby (M) 0 0
From Charlton Ath.
2016–17 Nottingham F 0 0

EVTIMOV, Dimitar (G) 22 0
H: 6 3 W: 13 00 b.Plevan 7-9-93
Internationals: Bulgaria U19, U21.
2012–13 Nottingham F 0 0
2013–14 Nottingham F 1 0
2014–15 Nottingham F 0 0
2014–15 *Mansfield T* 10 0 10 0
2015–16 Nottingham F 1 0
2016–17 Nottingham F 0 0 2 0
2016–17 *Olhanense* 10 0 10 0

FOX, Danny (D) 370 15
H: 5 11 W: 12 06 b.Winsford 29-5-86
Internationals: England U21. Scotland Full caps.
2004–05 Everton 0 0
2004–05 *Stranraer* 11 1 11 1
2005–06 Walsall 33 0
2006–07 Walsall 44 3
2007–08 Walsall 22 3 99 6
2007–08 Coventry C 18 1
2008–09 Coventry C 39 5
2009–10 Coventry C 0 0 57 6
2009–10 Celtic 15 0 15 0
2009–10 Burnley 14 1
2010–11 Burnley 35 0
2011–12 Burnley 1 0 50 1
2011–12 Southampton 41 0
2012–13 Southampton 20 1
2013–14 Southampton 3 0 64 1
2013–14 Nottingham F 14 0
2014–15 Nottingham F 27 0
2015–16 Nottingham F 10 0
2016–17 Nottingham F 23 0 74 0

GRANT, Jorge (M) 34 6
H: 5 9 W: 11 07 b.Oxford 26-9-94
2013–14 Nottingham F 0 0
2014–15 Nottingham F 1 0
2015–16 Nottingham F 10 0
2016–17 Nottingham F 6 0 17 0
2016–17 *Notts Co* 17 6 17 6

HENDERSON, Stephen (G) 162 0
H: 6 3 W: 11 00 b.Dublin 2-5-88
Internationals: Republic of Ireland U16, U17, U19, U21.
2005–06 Aston Villa 0 0
2006–07 Aston Villa 0 0
2007–08 Bristol C 1 0
2008–09 Bristol C 1 0
2009–10 Bristol C 3 0
2009–10 *Aldershot T* 8 0 8 0
2010–11 Bristol C 0 0 5 0
2010–11 *Yeovil T* 33 0 33 0
2011–12 Portsmouth 25 0 25 0
2011–12 *West Ham U* 0 0
2012–13 West Ham U 0 0
2012–13 *Ipswich T* 24 0 24 0
2013–14 West Ham U 0 0
2013–14 *Bournemouth* 2 0 2 0
2014–15 Charlton Ath 31 0
2015–16 Charlton Ath 22 0 53 0
2016–17 Nottingham F 12 0 12 0

HOBBS, Jack (D) 274 4
H: 6 3 W: 13 05 b.Portsmouth 18-8-88
Internationals: England U19.
2004–05 Lincoln C 1 0 1 0
2005–06 Liverpool 0 0
2006–07 Liverpool 0 0
2007–08 Liverpool 2 0
2007–08 *Scunthorpe U* 9 1 9 1
2008–09 Liverpool 0 0 2 0
2008–09 Leicester C 44 1
2009–10 Leicester C 44 0
2010–11 Leicester C 26 0 114 1
2010–11 *Hull C* 13 0
2011–12 Hull C 40 1
2012–13 Hull C 22 0 75 1
2013–14 Nottingham F 27 1
2014–15 Nottingham F 17 0
2015–16 Nottingham F 20 0
2016–17 Nottingham F 9 0 73 1

IACOVITTI, Alex (D) 10 0
b. 2-9-97
Internationals: Scotland U17, U19, U21.
2015–16 Nottingham F 0 0
2016–17 Nottingham F 2 0 2 0
2016–17 *Mansfield T* 8 0 8 0

KASAMI, Pajtim (M) 147 14
H: 6 2 W: 11 00 b.Macedonia 2-6-92
Internationals: Switzerland U17, U18, U21, U23, Full caps.
2009–10 Bellinzona 10 2 10 2
2010–11 Palermo 14 0 14 0
2011–12 Fulham 7 0
2012–13 Fulham 2 0
2012–13 *Lucerne* 16 1 16 1
2013–14 Fulham 29 3 38 3
2014–15 Olympiacos 24 4
2015–16 Olympiacos 20 2
2016–17 Olympiacos 0 0 44 6
On loan from Olympiacos.
2016–17 Nottingham F 25 2 25 2

LAM, Thomas (D) 86 6
H: 6 2 W: 11 07 b.Amsterdam 18-12-93
Internationals: Finland U17, U18, U19, U21, Full caps.
2011–12 AZ Alkmaar 0 0
2012–13 AZ Alkmaar 6 0
2013–14 AZ Alkmaar 0 0 6 0
2014–15 PEC Zwolle 28 2
2015–16 PEC Zwolle 33 2 61 4
2016–17 Nottingham F 19 2 19 2

LICA, Pereira (M) 235 43
H: 5 11 W: 11 00 b.Castro Daire 8-9-88
Internationals: Portugal U21, Full caps.
2007–08 Academica Coimbra 0 0
2007–08 *Tourizense* 27 6 27 6
2008–09 Academica Coimbra 9 1
2009–10 Academica Coimbra 7 0
2009–10 *Trofense* 13 4
2010–11 Academica Coimbra 0 0 16 1
2010–11 *Trofense* 27 5 40 9
2011–12 Estoril 29 12
2012–13 Estoril 30 6
2013–14 Porto 25 3
2014–15 Porto 0 0
2014–15 *Rayo Vallecano* 21 0 21 0
2015–16 Porto 0 0 25 3
2015–16 *Vitoria Guimaraes* 29 5 29 5
2016–17 Guimaraes 0 0
2016–17 Nottingham F 5 0 5 0
2016–17 *Estoril* 13 1 72 19

LICHAJ, Eric (D) 213 5
H: 5 11 W: 12 07 b.Chicago 17-11-88
Internationals: USA U17, U20, Full caps.
2007–08 Aston Villa 0 0
2008–09 Aston Villa 0 0
2009–10 Aston Villa 0 0
2009–10 *Lincoln C* 6 0 6 0
2009–10 *Leyton Orient* 9 1 9 1
2010–11 Aston Villa 5 0
2010–11 *Leeds U* 16 0 16 0
2011–12 Aston Villa 10 1
2012–13 Aston Villa 17 0 32 1
2013–14 Nottingham F 24 0
2014–15 Nottingham F 42 0
2015–16 Nottingham F 43 1
2016–17 Nottingham F 41 2 150 3

MANCIENNE, Michael (D) 262 0
H: 6 0 W: 11 09 b.Isleworth 8-1-88
Internationals: England U16, U17, U18, U19, U21.
2005–06 Chelsea 0 0
2006–07 Chelsea 0 0
2006–07 *QPR* 28 0
2007–08 Chelsea 0 0
2007–08 *QPR* 30 0 58 0
2008–09 Chelsea 4 0
2008–09 *Wolverhampton W* 10 0
2009–10 Chelsea 0 0
2009–10 *Wolverhampton W* 30 0
2010–11 Chelsea 0 0 4 0
2010–11 *Wolverhampton W* 16 0 56 0
2011–12 Hamburg 16 0
2012–13 Hamburg 21 0
2013–14 Hamburg 12 0 49 0
2014–15 Nottingham F 36 0
2015–16 Nottingham F 31 0
2016–17 Nottingham F 28 0 95 0

McDONAGH, Gerry (F) 14 1
H: 5 11 W: 11 00 b.Dublin 14-2-98
Internationals: Republic of Ireland U17.
2015–16 Nottingham F 1 0
2016–17 Nottingham F 0 0 1 0
2016–17 *Cambridge U* 13 1 13 1

MILLS, Matthew (D) 348 23
H: 6 3 W: 12 12 b.Swindon 14-7-86
Internationals: England U18, U19.
2004–05 Southampton 0 0
2004–05 *Coventry C* 4 0 4 0
2004–05 *Bournemouth* 12 3 12 3
2005–06 Southampton 4 0 4 0
2005–06 Manchester C 1 0
2006–07 Manchester C 1 0
2006–07 *Colchester U* 9 0 9 0
2007–08 Manchester C 0 0 2 0
2007–08 *Doncaster R* 34 3
2008–09 Doncaster R 41 0
2009–10 Doncaster R 0 0 75 3
2009–10 Reading 23 2
2010–11 Reading 38 2 61 4
2011–12 Leicester C 25 1 25 1
2012–13 Bolton W 18 1
2013–14 Bolton W 32 1
2014–15 Bolton W 37 4 87 6
2015–16 Nottingham F 42 5
2016–17 Nottingham F 27 1 69 6

OSBORN, Ben (D) 127 10
H: 5 9 W: 11 11 b.Derby 5-8-94
Internationals: England U18, U19, U20.
2011–12 Nottingham F 0 0
2012–13 Nottingham F 0 0
2013–14 Nottingham F 8 0
2014–15 Nottingham F 37 3
2015–16 Nottingham F 36 3
2016–17 Nottingham F 46 4 127 10

PEREIRA, Hildeberto (F) 22 2
H: 5 9 W: 11 00 b.Lisbon 2-3-96
Internationals: Portugal U18, U19, U20.
2015–16 Benfica 0 0
2016–17 Benfica 0 0
On loan from Benfica.
2016–17 Nottingham F 22 2 22 2

PERQUIS, Damien (D) 266 16
H: 6 0 W: 12 04 b.Troyes 10-4-84
Internationals: France U21. Poland Full caps.
2005–06 Saint-Etienne 15 0
2006–07 Saint-Etienne 19 1
2007–08 Saint-Etienne 0 0 34 1
2007–08 *Souchaux* 23 1
2008–09 Souchaux 36 2
2009–10 Souchaux 34 3
2010–11 Souchaux 35 5
2011–12 Souchaux 18 0 146 11
2012–13 Real Betis 10 0
2013–14 Real Betis 13 0
2014–15 Real Betis 9 0 32 0
2015 Toronto 25 1
2016 Toronto 12 1 37 2
2016–17 Nottingham F 17 2 17 2

PINILLOS, Daniel (D) 84 2
H: 6 0 W: 11 09 b.Logrono 22-10-92
2013–14 Ourense 21 0 21 0
2013–14 Cordoba 16 1
2014–15 Cordoba 12 0 28 1
2015–16 Nottingham F 19 0
2016–17 Nottingham F 16 1 35 1

SMITH, Jordan (G) 15 0
b.Nottingham 8-8-94
Internationals: Costa Rica U17, U20, Full caps.
2013–14 Nottingham F 0 0
2014–15 Nottingham F 0 0
2015–16 Nottingham F 0 0
2016–17 Nottingham F 15 0 15 0

STOJKOVIC, Vladimir (G) 280 1
H: 6 5 W: 14 07 b.Loznica 28-7-83
Internationals: Serbia Full caps.
2001–02 Red Star Belgrade 1 0
2002–03 Red Star Belgrade 1 0
2003–04 Red Star Belgrade 0 0
2003–04 *Leotar* 4 0 4 0
2003–04 Lemun 5 0
2004–05 Lemun 28 0 33 0
2005–06 Red Star Belgrade 22 0 24 0
2006–07 Nantes 10 0 10 0
2006–07 *Vitesse* 8 0 8 0
2007–08 Sporting Lisbon 9 0
2008–09 Sporting Lisbon 0 0
2008–09 *Getafe* 5 0 5 0
2009–10 Sporting Lisbon 0 0
2009–10 *Wigan Ath* 4 0 4 0
2010–11 Sporting Lisbon 0 0 9 0
2010–11 *Partizan Belgrade* 26 0
2011–12 Partizan Belgrade 25 0
2012–13 Partizan Belgrade 21 1

2013–14 Partizan Belgrade 14 0 **86 1**
2013–14 Ergotelis 11 0 **11 0**
2014–15 Maccabi Haifa 35 0
2015–16 Maccabi Haifa 31 0 **66 0**
2016–17 Nottingham F 20 0 **20 0**

THORNE, James (F) 0 0
b.Manchester 3-1-96
2016–17 Nottingham F 0 0

TRAORE, Armand (D) 141 3
H: 6 1 W: 12 12 b.Paris 8-10-89
Internationals: France U19, U21. Senegal Full caps.
2006–07 Arsenal 0 0
2007–08 Arsenal 3 0
2008–09 Arsenal 0 0
2008–09 *Portsmouth* 19 1 **19 1**
2009–10 Arsenal 9 0
2010–11 Arsenal 0 0
2010–11 *Juventus* 10 0 **10 0**
2011–12 Arsenal 1 0 **13 0**
2011–12 QPR 23 0
2012–13 QPR 26 0
2013–14 QPR 22 2
2014–15 QPR 16 0
2015–16 QPR 0 0 **87 2**
2016–17 Nottingham F 12 0 **12 0**

VAUGHAN, David (M) 438 27
H: 5 7 W: 11 00 b.Abergele 18-2-83
Internationals: Wales U19, U21, Full caps.
2000–01 Crewe Alex 1 0
2001–02 Crewe Alex 13 0
2002–03 Crewe Alex 32 3
2003–04 Crewe Alex 31 0
2004–05 Crewe Alex 44 6
2005–06 Crewe Alex 34 5
2006–07 Crewe Alex 29 4
2007–08 Crewe Alex 1 0 **185 18**
2007–08 Real Sociedad 7 1 **7 1**
2008–09 Blackpool 33 1
2009–10 Blackpool 41 1
2010–11 Blackpool 35 2 **109 4**
2011–12 Sunderland 22 2
2012–13 Sunderland 24 1
2013–14 Sunderland 3 0 **49 3**
2013–14 *Nottingham F* 9 0
2014–15 Nottingham F 13 0
2015–16 Nottingham F 35 1
2016–17 Nottingham F 31 0 **88 1**

VELDWIJK, Lars (F) 123 58
H: 6 5 W: 14 13 b. 21-8-91
Internationals: South Africa Full caps.
2010–11 Voldendam 2 0 **2 0**
2011–12 Utrecht 5 0 **5 0**
2012–13 *Dordrecht* 31 14 **31 14**
2013–14 Excelsior 38 30 **38 30**
2014–15 Nottingham F 11 0
2015–16 Nottingham F 0 0
2015–16 *PEC Zwolle* 35 14 **35 14**
2016–17 Nottingham F 1 0 **12 0**
Transferred to KV Kortrijk, August 2016.

VELLIOS, Apostolos (F) 74 13
H: 6 3 W: 12 06 b.Salonika 8-1-92
Internationals: Greece U17, U19, U21, Full caps.
2008–09 Iraklis 1 0
2009–10 Iraklis 9 2
2010–11 Iraklis 12 2 **22 4**
2010–11 Everton 3 0
2011–12 Everton 13 3
2012–13 Everton 6 0
2013–14 Everton 0 0
2013–14 *Blackpool* 2 0 **2 0**
2014–15 Everton 0 0 **22 3**
2014–15 Lierse 0 0
2014–15 FC Vestsjaelland 0 0
2016–17 Nottingham F 28 6 **28 6**

WALKER, Tyler (F) 41 7
H: 5 10 W: 9 13 b. 17-10-96
Internationals: England U20.
2013–14 Nottingham F 0 0
2014–15 Nottingham F 7 1
2015–16 Nottingham F 14 0
2015–16 *Burton Alb* 6 1 **6 1**
2016–17 Nottingham F 0 0 **21 1**
2016–17 *Stevenage* 8 3 **8 3**
2016–17 *Port Vale* 6 2 **6 2**

WARD, Jamie (M) 369 89
H: 5 5 W: 9 04 b.Birmingham 12-5-86
Internationals: Northern Ireland U18, U21, Full caps.
2003–04 Aston Villa 0 0
2004–05 Aston Villa 0 0
2005–06 Aston Villa 0 0
2005–06 *Stockport Co* 9 1 **9 1**
2006–07 Torquay U 25 9 **25 9**
2006–07 Chesterfield 9 3
2007–08 Chesterfield 35 12
2008–09 Chesterfield 23 14 **67 29**
2008–09 Sheffield U 16 2
2009–10 Sheffield U 28 7
2010–11 Sheffield U 19 0 **63 9**
2010–11 Derby Co 13 5
2011–12 Derby Co 37 4
2012–13 Derby Co 25 12
2013–14 Derby Co 38 7
2014–15 Derby Co 25 6 **138 34**
2015–16 Nottingham F 31 2
2016–17 Nottingham F 18 1 **49 3**
2016–17 *Burton Alb* 18 4 **18 4**

WORRALL, Joe (D) 35 1
H: 6 3 b.Nottingham 10-1-97
Internationals: England U20.
2015–16 Nottingham F 0 0
2015–16 *Dagenham & R* 14 1 **14 1**
2016–17 Nottingham F 21 0 **21 0**

YATES, Ryan (M) 12 0
b.Nottingham 21-11-97
2016–17 Nottingham F 0 0
2016–17 *Shrewsbury T* 12 0 **12 0**

Players retained or with offer of contract
Crookes, Adam Mark; Erlandsson, Tim Anders Junior; Iacovitti, Alexander; Lawrence-Gabriel, Jordan Jay; Otim, Elvis Apota; Smith, Aaron; Walters, Lewis Henrique Paul.

Scholars
Charlesworth, Choz Micheal; En-Neyah, Yassine; Gomis, Virgil Vilela; Hayes, Kieran; Jemson, Charlie; McCormick, Luke; Preston, Daniel James; Re, Giuseppe David; Smith, Connor David; Soloha, Rudolfs Oskars; Stewart, Ethan; Taylor, Jake Jon; Willetts, Jake Anthony; Wright, Anthony Paul; Wright, Jordan Ian.

NOTTS CO (61)

AMEOBI, Shola (F) 357 60
H: 6 3 W: 11 13 b.Zaria 12-10-81
Internationals: England U21. Nigeria Full caps.
1998–99 Newcastle U 0 0
1999–2000 Newcastle U 0 0
2000–01 Newcastle U 20 2
2001–02 Newcastle U 15 0
2002–03 Newcastle U 28 5
2003–04 Newcastle U 26 7
2004–05 Newcastle U 31 2
2005–06 Newcastle U 30 9
2006–07 Newcastle U 12 3
2007–08 Newcastle U 6 0
2007–08 *Stoke C* 6 0 **6 0**
2008–09 Newcastle U 22 4
2009–10 Newcastle U 18 10
2010–11 Newcastle U 28 6
2011–12 Newcastle U 27 2
2012–13 Newcastle U 23 1
2013–14 Newcastle U 26 2 **312 53**
2014–15 Crystal Palace 4 0 **4 0**
2015–16 Bolton W 8 2 **8 2**
2015–16 Fleetwood T 10 1
2016–17 Fleetwood T 0 0 **10 1**
2016–17 Notts Co 17 4 **17 4**

ATKINSON, Wes (M) 19 0
b.West Bromwich 13-10-94
2014–15 WBA 0 0
2014–15 *Cambridge U* 2 0 **2 0**
2015–16 Notts Co 17 0
2016–17 Notts Co 0 0 **17 0**

AUDEL, Thierry (D) 57 4
H: 6 2 W: 12 08 b. 15-1-87
Internationals: France U19.
2007–08 Triestina 2 0
2008–09 Triestina 0 0
2009–10 Triestina 7 1 **9 1**
From Macclesfield T.
2013–14 Crewe Alex 2 0
2014–15 Crewe Alex 2 0 **4 0**
From Macclesfield T.
2015–16 Notts Co 28 2
2016–17 Notts Co 16 1 **44 3**

BURKE, Graham (F) 46 3
H: 5 11 W: 11 11 b.Dublin 21-9-93
Internationals: Republic of Ireland U19, U21.
2010–11 Aston Villa 0 0
2011–12 Aston Villa 0 0
2012–13 Aston Villa 0 0
2013–14 Aston Villa 0 0
2013–14 *Shrewsbury T* 3 0 **3 0**
2014–15 Aston Villa 0 0
2014–15 *Notts Co* 7 1
2015–16 Notts Co 31 2
2016–17 Notts Co 5 0 **43 3**

CAMPBELL, Adam (F) 92 10
H: 5 7 W: 11 07 b.North Shields 1-1-95
Internationals: England U16, U17, U19.
2011–12 Newcastle U 0 0
2012–13 Newcastle U 3 0
2013–14 Newcastle U 0 0
2013–14 *Carlisle U* 1 0 **1 0**
2013–14 *St Mirren* 11 2 **11 2**
2014–15 Newcastle U 0 0 **3 0**
2014–15 *Fleetwood T* 2 0 **2 0**
2014–15 *Hartlepool U* 2 0 **2 0**
2015–16 Notts Co 44 4
2016–17 Notts Co 29 4 **73 8**

COLLIN, Adam (G) 250 0
H: 6 2 W: 12 00 b.Penrith 9-12-84
2003–04 Newcastle U 0 0
2003–04 *Oldham Ath* 0 0
From Workington
2009–10 Carlisle U 29 0
2010–11 Carlisle U 46 0
2011–12 Carlisle U 46 0
2012–13 Carlisle U 12 0 **133 0**
2013–14 Rotherham U 34 0
2014–15 Rotherham U 36 0
2015–16 Rotherham U 1 0 **71 0**
2015–16 *Aberdeen* 3 0 **3 0**
2016–17 Notts Co 43 0 **43 0**

DICKINSON, Carl (D) 345 7
H: 6 1 W: 12 04 b.Swadlincote 31-3-87
2004–05 Stoke C 1 0
2005–06 Stoke C 5 0
2006–07 Stoke C 13 0
2006–07 *Blackpool* 7 0 **7 0**
2007–08 Stoke C 27 0
2008–09 Stoke C 5 0
2008–09 *Leeds U* 7 0 **7 0**
2009–10 Stoke C 0 0
2009–10 *Barnsley* 28 1 **28 1**
2010–11 Stoke C 0 0 **51 0**
2010–11 *Portsmouth* 36 0
2011–12 Watford 39 2
2012–13 Watford 4 0 **43 2**
2012–13 *Portsmouth* 6 0 **42 0**
2012–13 *Coventry C* 6 0 **6 0**
2013–14 Port Vale 40 0
2014–15 Port Vale 43 1
2015–16 Port Vale 44 3 **127 4**
2016–17 Notts Co 34 0 **34 0**

DUFFY, Richard (D) 400 10
H: 5 9 W: 10 03 b.Swansea 30-8-85
Internationals: Wales U17, U19, U21, Full caps.
2002–03 Swansea C 0 0
2003–04 Swansea C 18 1
2003–04 Portsmouth 1 0
2004–05 Portsmouth 0 0
2004–05 *Burnley* 7 1 **7 1**
2004–05 *Coventry C* 14 0
2005–06 Portsmouth 0 0
2005–06 *Coventry C* 32 0
2006–07 Portsmouth 0 0
2006–07 *Coventry C* 13 0
2006–07 *Swansea C* 11 0 **29 1**
2007–08 Portsmouth 0 0
2007–08 *Coventry C* 2 0 **61 0**
2008–09 Portsmouth 0 0 **1 0**
2008–09 Millwall 12 0 **12 0**
2009–10 Exeter C 42 1
2010–11 Exeter C 42 2
2011–12 Exeter C 28 0 **112 3**
2012–13 Port Vale 36 0
2013–14 Port Vale 28 0
2014–15 Port Vale 27 1
2015–16 Port Vale 45 0 **136 1**
2016–17 Notts Co 42 4 **42 4**

EDWARDS, Mike (D) 551 34
H: 6 0 W: 12 10 b.Hessle 25-4-80
1997–98 Hull C 21 0
1998–99 Hull C 30 0
1999–2000 Hull C 40 1
2000–01 Hull C 42 4
2001–02 Hull C 39 1

2002–03 Hull C 6 0 **178 6**
2002–03 Colchester U 5 0 **5 0**
2003–04 Grimsby T 33 1 **33 1**
2004–05 Notts Co 9 0
2005–06 Notts Co 46 7
2006–07 Notts Co 45 3
2007–08 Notts Co 19 1
2008–09 Notts Co 43 2
2009–10 Notts Co 40 5
2010–11 Notts Co 37 1
2011–12 Notts Co 30 1
2012–13 Carlisle U 23 0
2013–14 Carlisle U 1 0 **24 0**
2014–15 Notts Co 18 3
2015–16 Notts Co 22 4
2016–17 Notts Co 2 0 **311 27**

FORTE, Jonathan (M) 354 68
H: 6 0 W: 12 02 b.Sheffield 25-7-86
Internationals: England U16, U17, U18. Barbados Full caps.
2003–04 Sheffield U 7 0
2004–05 Sheffield U 22 1
2005–06 Sheffield U 1 0
2005–06 *Doncaster R* 13 4
2005–06 *Rotherham U* 11 4 **11 4**
2006–07 Sheffield U 0 0
2006–07 *Doncaster R* 41 5 **54 9**
2007–08 Scunthorpe U 38 4
2008–09 Scunthorpe U 8 0
2008–09 *Notts Co* 18 8
2009–10 Scunthorpe U 28 2
2010–11 Scunthorpe U 24 3 **98 9**
2010–11 Southampton 10 2
2011–12 Southampton 1 0
2011–12 *Preston NE* 3 0 **3 0**
2011–12 *Notts Co* 10 5
2012–13 Southampton 0 0
2012–13 *Crawley T* 12 3 **12 3**
2012–13 *Sheffield U* 12 1 **42 2**
2013–14 Southampton 0 0 **11 2**
2014–15 Oldham Ath 34 15
2015–16 Oldham Ath 26 3 **60 18**
2016–17 Notts Co 35 8 **63 21**

GIBSON, Montel (F) 5 0
b.Birmingham 15-12-97
2015–16 Notts Co 4 0
2016–17 Notts Co 1 0 **5 0**

HEWITT, Elliott (D) 144 3
H: 5 11 W: 11 10 b.Rhyl 30-5-94
Internationals: Wales U17, U21.
2010–11 Macclesfield T 1 0
2011–12 Macclesfield T 21 0 **22 0**
2012–13 Ipswich T 7 0
2013–14 Ipswich T 4 0
2013–14 *Gillingham* 20 0 **20 0**
2014–15 Ipswich T 3 0 **14 0**
2014–15 *Colchester U* 21 1 **21 1**
2015–16 Notts Co 38 0
2016–17 Notts Co 29 2 **67 2**

HOLLIS, Haydn (D) 118 7
H: 6 4 W: 13 01 b.Selston 14-10-92
2011–12 Notts Co 1 0
2012–13 Notts Co 6 0
2013–14 Notts Co 10 4
2014–15 Notts Co 41 0
2015–16 Notts Co 29 2
2016–17 Notts Co 31 1 **118 7**

HOWES, Alex (M) 2 0
2016–17 Notts Co 2 0 **2 0**

LAING, Louis (D) 69 3
H: 5 11 W: 12 00 b.Newcastle upon Tyne 6-3-93
Internationals: England U16, U17, U18, U19.
2009–10 Sunderland 0 0
2010–11 Sunderland 1 0
2011–12 Sunderland 0 0
2011–12 *Wycombe W* 11 0 **11 0**
2012–13 Sunderland 0 0 **1 0**
2014–15 Nottingham F 0 0
2014–15 *Notts Co* 10 0
2014–15 *Motherwell* 11 1
2015–16 Motherwell 15 1
2016–17 Motherwell 0 0 **26 2**
On loan from Motherwell.
2016–17 Notts Co 21 1 **31 1**

LOACH, Scott (G) 236 0
H: 6 1 W: 13 01 b.Nottingham 27-5-88
Internationals: England U21.
2006–07 Watford 0 0
2007–08 Watford 0 0
2007–08 *Morecambe* 2 0 **2 0**
2007–08 *Bradford C* 20 0 **20 0**
2008–09 Watford 31 0
2009–10 Watford 46 0
2010–11 Watford 46 0
2011–12 Watford 31 0 **154 0**
2012–13 Ipswich T 22 0
2013–14 Ipswich T 6 0 **28 0**
2014–15 Rotherham U 2 0 **2 0**
2014–15 *Bury* 2 0 **2 0**
2014–15 *Peterborough U* 5 0 **5 0**
2014–15 *Yeovil T* 6 0 **6 0**
2015–16 Notts Co 14 0
2016–17 Notts Co 3 0 **17 0**

MILSOM, Robert (M) 169 3
H: 5 10 W: 11 04 b.Redhill 2-1-87
2005–06 Fulham 0 0
2006–07 Fulham 0 0
2007–08 Fulham 0 0
2007–08 *Brentford* 6 0 **6 0**
2008–09 Fulham 1 0
2008–09 *Southend U* 6 0 **6 0**
2009–10 Fulham 0 0
2010 *TPS Turku* 14 0 **14 0**
2010–11 Fulham 0 0 **1 0**
2010–11 Aberdeen 18 1
2011–12 Aberdeen 22 1
2012–13 Aberdeen 13 0 **53 2**
2013–14 Rotherham U 27 1
2014–15 Rotherham U 8 0 **35 1**
2014–15 *Bury* 2 0 **2 0**
2015–16 Notts Co 14 0
2016–17 Notts Co 38 0 **52 0**

O'CONNOR, Michael (M) 350 35
H: 6 1 W: 11 08 b.Belfast 6-10-87
Internationals: Northern Ireland U21, B, Full caps.
2005–06 Crewe Alex 2 0
2006–07 Crewe Alex 29 0
2007–08 Crewe Alex 23 0
2008–09 Crewe Alex 23 3 **77 3**
2008–09 *Lincoln C* 10 1 **10 1**
2009–10 Scunthorpe U 32 2
2010–11 Scunthorpe U 32 8
2011–12 Scunthorpe U 33 1 **97 11**
2012–13 Rotherham U 35 6
2013–14 Rotherham U 29 2 **64 8**
2014–15 Port Vale 44 6
2015–16 Port Vale 26 4 **70 10**
2016–17 Notts Co 32 2 **32 2**

OLIVER, Vadaine (F) 120 18
H: 6 2 W: 12 04 b.Sheffield 21-10-91
2010–11 Sheffield W 0 0
2011–12 Sheffield W 0 0
2013–14 Crewe Alex 25 2
2014–15 Crewe Alex 9 1 **34 3**
2014–15 *Mansfield T* 30 7 **30 7**
2015–16 York C 37 7 **37 7**
On loan from York C.
2016–17 Notts Co 19 1 **19 1**

OSBORNE, Samuel (F) 3 0
From Dunkirk.
2016–17 Notts Co 3 0 **3 0**

RICHARDS, Jordan (D) 12 0
H: 5 11 W: 11 00 b.Nottingham 6-7-97
2015–16 Notts Co 0 0
2016–17 Notts Co 12 0 **12 0**

SEARSON, Joe (G) 0 0
2016–17 Notts Co 0 0

SMITH, Alan (F) 454 47
H: 5 10 W: 12 04 b.Rothwell 28-10-80
Internationals: England U21, B, Full caps.
1997–98 Leeds U 0 0
1998–99 Leeds U 22 7
1999–2000 Leeds U 26 4
2000–01 Leeds U 33 11
2001–02 Leeds U 23 4
2002–03 Leeds U 33 3
2003–04 Leeds U 35 9 **172 38**
2004–05 Manchester U 31 6
2005–06 Manchester U 21 1
2006–07 Manchester U 9 0 **61 7**
2007–08 Newcastle U 33 0
2008–09 Newcastle U 6 0
2009–10 Newcastle U 32 0
2010–11 Newcastle U 11 0
2011–12 Newcastle U 2 0 **84 0**
2011–12 *Milton Keynes D* 16 1
2012–13 Milton Keynes D 27 1
2013–14 Milton Keynes D 24 0 **67 2**
2014–15 Notts Co 23 0
2015–16 Notts Co 28 0
2016–17 Notts Co 19 0 **70 0**

SNIJDERS, Genaro (F) 113 12
H: 5 11 W: 10 12 b.Amsterdam 29-7-89
2008–09 Vitesse 2 0
2009–10 Vitesse 6 0
2009–10 *Almere C* 11 3 **11 3**
2010–11 Vitesse 15 0
2011–12 Vitesse 0 0 **23 0**
2012–13 Willem II 23 2 **23 2**
2013–14 Dordrecht 10 2 **10 2**
2014–15 Oss 27 3 **27 3**
2015–16 Notts Co 14 2
2016–17 Notts Co 5 0 **19 2**

STEAD, Jon (F) 499 118
H: 6 3 W: 13 03 b.Huddersfield 7-4-83
Internationals: England U21.
2001–02 Huddersfield T 0 0
2002–03 Huddersfield T 42 6
2003–04 Huddersfield T 26 16
2003–04 Blackburn R 13 6
2004–05 Blackburn R 29 2 **42 8**
2005–06 Sunderland 30 1
2006–07 Sunderland 5 1 **35 2**
2006–07 *Derby Co* 17 3 **17 3**
2006–07 Sheffield U 14 5
2007–08 Sheffield U 24 3
2008–09 Sheffield U 1 0 **39 8**
2008–09 Ipswich T 39 12
2009–10 Ipswich T 22 6
2009–10 *Coventry C* 10 2 **10 2**
2010–11 Ipswich T 3 1 **64 19**
2010–11 Bristol C 27 9
2011–12 Bristol C 24 6
2012–13 Bristol C 28 5 **79 20**
2013–14 Huddersfield T 12 1
2013–14 *Oldham Ath* 5 0 **5 0**
2013–14 *Bradford C* 8 1
2014–15 Huddersfield T 7 1 **87 24**
2014–15 *Bradford C* 32 6 **40 7**
2015–16 Notts Co 43 11
2016–17 Notts Co 38 14 **81 25**

THOMPSON, Curtis (M) 83 2
H: 5 10 W: 12 06 b.Nottingham 2-9-93
2011–12 Notts Co 0 0
2012–13 Notts Co 2 0
2013–14 Notts Co 11 0
2014–15 Notts Co 31 0
2015–16 Notts Co 26 2
2016–17 Notts Co 13 0 **83 2**

TOOTLE, Matt (D) 248 4
H: 5 9 W: 11 00 b.Widnes 11-10-90
2009–10 Crewe Alex 28 1
2010–11 Crewe Alex 39 0
2011–12 Crewe Alex 37 0
2012–13 Crewe Alex 37 1
2013–14 Crewe Alex 43 0
2014–15 Crewe Alex 15 0 **199 2**
2015–16 Shrewsbury T 16 0 **16 0**
2016–17 Notts Co 33 2 **33 2**

WILDIN, Luther (M) 0 0
b. 3-12-97
Internationals: Antigua and Barbuda U20.
2015–16 Notts Co 0 0
2016–17 Notts Co 0 0

YEATES, Mark (F) 398 47
H: 5 8 W: 13 03 b.Dublin 11-1-85
Internationals: Republic of Ireland U21, B.
2002–03 Tottenham H 0 0
2003–04 Tottenham H 1 0
2003–04 *Brighton & HA* 9 0 **9 0**
2004–05 Tottenham H 2 0
2004–05 *Swindon T* 4 0 **4 0**
2005–06 Tottenham H 0 0
2005–06 *Colchester U* 44 5
2006–07 Tottenham H 0 0 **3 0**
2006–07 *Hull C* 5 0 **5 0**
2006–07 *Leicester C* 9 1 **9 1**
2007–08 Colchester U 29 8
2008–09 Colchester U 43 12 **116 25**
2009–10 Middlesbrough 19 1 **19 1**
2009–10 Sheffield U 20 2
2010–11 Sheffield U 35 5 **55 7**
2011–12 Watford 33 3
2012–13 Watford 29 4 **62 7**
2013–14 Bradford C 29 2
2014–15 Bradford C 41 3 **70 5**
2015–16 Oldham Ath 16 1 **16 1**
2015–16 Blackpool 11 0
2016–17 Blackpool 5 0 **16 0**
2016–17 Notts Co 14 0 **14 0**

Scholars
Brown-Hill, Dominic; Bugg, Harry Joseph; Campbell, Remaye Orvil Kelvin; Clayton-Naute, Tamar Singh; Cobain, Nathan

Anthony; Collett-McCartney, George Robert; Dearle, Peter James; Dunn, Declan Nicholas; Ebanks, Ryan Jenson; Gibbons, Harry Jacob; Hall, Curtis James; Howes, Alex Jacob; Osborne, Samuel Paul; Richards, Jordon George; Rutty-Smith, Yohan; Searson-Smithard, Joseph Luke; Towers, Edwin James.

Non-Contract
Nolan, Kevin Anthony Jance.

OLDHAM ATH (62)

AMADI-HOLLOWAY, Aaron (D) 87 8
H: 6 2 W: 13 00 b.Newark 21-2-93
Internationals: Wales U17, U19.

2012–13	Bristol C	0	0		
2013–14	Bristol C	0	0		
2013–14	Newport Co	4	0	**4**	**0**
2014–15	Wycombe W	29	3		
2015–16	Wycombe W	23	3	**52**	**6**
2015–16	*Oldham Ath*	10	2		
2016–17	Fleetwood T	6	0	**6**	**0**
2016–17	Oldham Ath	15	0	**25**	**2**

BANKS, Oliver (D) 118 12
H: 6 3 W: 11 11 b.Rotherham 21-9-92

2010–11	Rotherham U	1	1		
2011–12	Rotherham U	0	0	**1**	**1**
2013–14	Chesterfield	25	7		
2014–15	Chesterfield	24	0		
2014–15	*Northampton T*	3	0	**3**	**0**
2015–16	Chesterfield	32	2	**81**	**9**
2016–17	Oldham Ath	33	2	**33**	**2**

CASSIDY, Jake (F) 129 20
H: 5 10 W: 11 02 b.Glan Conwy 9-2-93
Internationals: Wales U19, U21.

2010–11	Wolverhampton W	0	0		
2011–12	Wolverhampton W	0	0		
2011–12	*Tranmere R*	10	5		
2012–13	Wolverhampton W	6	0		
2012–13	*Tranmere R*	26	11		
2013–14	Wolverhampton W	14	0		
2013–14	*Tranmere R*	19	1		
2014–15	Wolverhampton W	0	0	**20**	**0**
2014–15	*Tranmere R*	0	0	**55**	**17**
2014–15	*Notts Co*	16	3	**16**	**3**
2014–15	*Southend U*	17	0	**17**	**0**
2015–16	Oldham Ath	21	0		
2016–17	Oldham Ath	0	0	**21**	**0**

CLARKE, Peter (D) 575 42
H: 6 0 W: 12 00 b.Southport 3-1-82
Internationals: England U21.

1998–99	Everton	0	0		
1999–2000	Everton	0	0		
2000–01	Everton	1	0		
2001–02	Everton	7	0		
2002–03	Everton	0	0		
2002–03	*Blackpool*	16	3		
2002–03	*Port Vale*	13	1	**13**	**1**
2003–04	Everton	1	0		
2003–04	*Coventry C*	5	0	**5**	**0**
2004–05	Everton	0	0	**9**	**0**
2004–05	Blackpool	38	5		
2005–06	Blackpool	46	6		
2006–07	Southend U	38	2		
2007–08	Southend U	45	4		
2008–09	Southend U	43	4	**126**	**10**
2009–10	Huddersfield T	46	5		
2010–11	Huddersfield T	46	4		
2011–12	Huddersfield T	31	0		
2012–13	Huddersfield T	43	0		
2013–14	Huddersfield T	26	0	**192**	**9**
2014–15	Blackpool	39	2	**139**	**16**
2015–16	Bury	45	1	**45**	**1**
2016–17	Oldham Ath	46	5	**46**	**5**

CROFT, Lee (F) 285 15
H: 5 11 W: 13 00 b.Wigan 21-6-85
Internationals: England U20.

2002–03	Manchester C	0	0		
2003–04	Manchester C	0	0		
2004–05	Manchester C	7	0		
2004–05	*Oldham Ath*	12	0		
2005–06	Manchester C	21	1	**28**	**1**
2006–07	Norwich C	36	3		
2007–08	Norwich C	41	1		
2008–09	Norwich C	41	5	**118**	**9**
2009–10	Derby Co	19	1		
2010–11	Derby Co	0	0		
2010–11	*Huddersfield T*	3	0	**3**	**0**
2011–12	Derby Co	8	0		
2011–12	*St Johnstone*	11	3	**11**	**3**
2012–13	Derby Co	0	0	**27**	**1**
2012–13	Oldham Ath	45	0		
2015–16	Oldham Ath	21	1		
2016–17	Oldham Ath	20	0	**98**	**1**

DUMMIGAN, Cameron (D) 38 1
H: 5 11 W: 11 00 b.Lurgan 2-6-96
Internationals: Northern Ireland U17, U19, U21.

2013–14	Burnley	0	0		
2014–15	Burnley	0	0		
2015–16	Burnley	0	0		
2015–16	*Oldham Ath*	26	1		
2016–17	Oldham Ath	12	0	**38**	**1**

DUNNE, Charles (F) 102 0
H: 5 9 W: 11 09 b.Lambeth 13-2-93
Internationals: Republic of Ireland U21.

2011–12	Wycombe W	3	0		
2012–13	Wycombe W	38	0		
2013–14	Blackpool	0	0		
2013–14	*Wycombe W*	9	0	**50**	**0**
2014–15	Blackpool	22	0		
2015–16	Blackpool	4	0	**26**	**0**
2015–16	*Crawley T*	12	0	**12**	**0**
2016–17	Oldham Ath	14	0	**14**	**0**

EDMUNDSON, Sam (D) 5 0
H: 6 1 W: 11 11 b.Timperley 15-8-97

2015–16	Oldham Ath	2	0		
2016–17	Oldham Ath	3	0	**5**	**0**

FANE, Ousmane (M) 39 0
H: 6 4 W: 12 08 b.Paris 13-12-93
From Kidderminster H.

2016–17	Oldham Ath	39	0	**39**	**0**

FLYNN, Ryan (M) 259 24
H: 5 8 W: 10 00 b.Falkirk 4-9-88
Internationals: Scotland U19.

2006–07	Liverpool	0	0		
2007–08	*Hereford U*	0	0		
2007–08	Liverpool	0	0		
2008–09	Liverpool	0	0		
2009–10	Liverpool	0	0		
2009–10	Falkirk	36	5		
2010–11	Falkirk	33	5	**69**	**10**
2011–12	Sheffield U	26	2		
2012–13	Sheffield U	36	3		
2013–14	Sheffield U	32	5		
2014–15	Sheffield U	32	1		
2015–16	Sheffield U	27	2	**153**	**13**
2016–17	Oldham Ath	37	1	**37**	**1**

GERRARD, Anthony (D) 393 17
H: 6 2 W: 13 07 b.Huyton 6-2-86
Internationals: Republic of Ireland U18.

2004–05	Everton	0	0		
2004–05	*Walsall*	8	0		
2005–06	Walsall	34	0		
2006–07	Walsall	35	1		
2007–08	Walsall	44	3		
2008–09	Walsall	42	3	**163**	**7**
2009–10	Cardiff C	39	2		
2010–11	Cardiff C	0	0		
2010–11	*Hull C*	41	5	**41**	**5**
2011–12	Cardiff C	20	1		
2012–13	Cardiff C	0	0	**59**	**3**
2012–13	Huddersfield T	38	1		
2013–14	Huddersfield T	40	1		
2014–15	Huddersfield T	3	0	**81**	**2**
2014–15	*Oldham Ath*	6	0		
2015–16	Shrewsbury T	11	0	**11**	**0**
2015–16	Oldham Ath	18	0		
2016–17	Oldham Ath	14	0	**38**	**0**

GLACKIN, Brendy (F) 1 0
b.Belfast

2016–17	Oldham Ath	1	0	**1**	**0**

GREEN, Paul (M) 480 43
H: 5 9 W: 10 02 b.Pontefract 10-4-83
Internationals: Republic of Ireland Full caps.

2003–04	Doncaster R	43	8		
2004–05	Doncaster R	42	7		
2005–06	Doncaster R	34	3		
2006–07	Doncaster R	41	2		
2007–08	Doncaster R	38	5	**198**	**25**
2008–09	Derby Co	29	3		
2009–10	Derby Co	33	2		
2010–11	Derby Co	36	2		
2011–12	Derby Co	27	1	**125**	**8**
2012–13	Leeds U	32	4		
2013–14	Leeds U	9	0	**41**	**4**
2013–14	*Ipswich T*	14	2	**14**	**2**
2014–15	Rotherham U	37	3		
2015–16	Rotherham U	24	0	**61**	**3**
2016–17	Oldham Ath	41	1	**41**	**1**

JAHRALDO-MARTIN, Calaum (F) 22 1
b.Hemel Hempstead 27-4-93
Internationals: Antigua and Barbuda U20, Full caps.

2013–14	Hull C	0	0		
2014–15	Hull C	0	0		
2014–15	*Tranmere R*	2	0	**2**	**0**
2015–16	Hull C	1	0	**1**	**0**
2015–16	*Leyton Orient*	15	1	**15**	**1**
2016–17	Oldham Ath	4	0	**4**	**0**

KETTINGS, Chris (G) 2 0
H: 6 2 W: 12 04 b.Bolton 25-10-92
Internationals: Scotland U19, U21.

2011–12	Blackpool	0	0		
2011–12	*Birmingham C*	0	0		
2011–12	*Morecambe*	2	0	**2**	**0**
2012–13	Blackpool	0	0		
2013–14	Blackpool	0	0		
2013–14	*York C*	0	0		
2014–15	Crystal Palace	0	0		
2015–16	Crystal Palace	0	0		
2016–17	Oldham Ath	0	0		

KING, Dylan (D) 0 0
Internationals: Northern Ireland U16, U17, U19.
From Institute.

2016–17	Oldham Ath	0	0		

KLOK, Marc (M) 52 0
H: 5 10 b.Hauge 20-4-93

2013–14	Ross Co	6	0	**6**	**0**
2014–15	Cherno More	13	0		
2015–16	Cherno More	23	0	**36**	**0**
2016–17	Oldham Ath	10	0	**10**	**0**

Transferred to Dundee, January 2017.

LAW, Josh (M) 85 2
H: 5 11 W: 11 00 b.Nottingham 19-8-89
From Chesterfield, Alfreton T.

2014–15	Motherwell	34	0		
2015–16	Motherwell	29	0	**63**	**0**
2016–17	Oldham Ath	22	2	**22**	**2**

MANTACK, Kallum (D) 0 0

2016–17	Oldham Ath	0	0		

McLAUGHLIN, Ryan (D) 49 2
H: 5 9 W: 10 12 b.Belfast 30-9-94
Internationals: Northern Ireland U16, U17, U19, U21, Full caps.

2011–12	Liverpool	0	0		
2013–14	Liverpool	0	0		
2013–14	*Barnsley*	9	0	**9**	**0**
2014–15	Liverpool	0	0		
2015–16	Liverpool	0	0		
2015–16	*Aberdeen*	4	0	**4**	**0**
2016–17	Oldham Ath	36	2	**36**	**2**

NGOO, Michael (F) 54 5
b.Walthamstow 23-10-92
Internationals: England U19, U20.

2009–10	Liverpool	0	0		
2010–11	Liverpool	0	0		
2011–12	Liverpool	0	0		
2012–13	Liverpool	0	0		
2012–13	*Hearts*	15	4	**15**	**4**
2013–14	Liverpool	0	0		
2013–14	*Yeovil T*	6	0	**6**	**0**
2013–14	*Walsall*	14	1	**14**	**1**
2014–15	Kilmarnock	6	0	**6**	**0**

From Bromley.

2016–17	Oldham Ath	13	0	**13**	**0**

OBADEYI, Temitope (F) 170 21
H: 5 10 W: 11 09 b.Birmingham 29-10-89
Internationals: England U19, U20.

2006–07	Bolton W	0	0		
2007–08	Bolton W	0	0		
2008–09	Bolton W	3	0		
2009–10	Bolton W	0	0		
2009–10	*Swindon T*	12	2	**12**	**2**
2009–10	*Rochdale*	11	1		
2010–11	Bolton W	0	0		
2010–11	*Shrewsbury T*	9	0	**9**	**0**
2011–12	Bolton W	0	0	**3**	**0**
2011–12	*Chesterfield*	5	0	**5**	**0**
2011–12	*Rochdale*	6	1	**17**	**2**
2012–13	Rio Ave	11	0	**11**	**0**
2013–14	Bury	7	0	**7**	**0**
2013–14	*Plymouth Arg*	14	1	**14**	**1**
2014–15	Kilmarnock	29	9		
2015–16	Kilmarnock	30	3	**59**	**12**
2016–17	Dundee U	18	2	**18**	**2**
2016–17	Oldham Ath	15	2	**15**	**2**

OSEI, Darius (F) 19 0
From Stalybridge Celtic.
2016–17 Oldham Ath 19 0 19 0

RECKORD, Jamie (D) 89 1
H: 5 10 W: 11 11 b.Wolverhampton 9-3-92
Internationals: England U16, U17.
2010–11 Wolverhampton W 0 0
2010–11 *Northampton T* 7 0 **7 0**
2011–12 Wolverhampton W 0 0
2011–12 *Scunthorpe U* 17 0 **17 0**
2012–13 Wolverhampton W 0 0
2012–13 *Coventry C* 9 0 **9 0**
2013–14 Wolverhampton W 0 0
2013–14 *Plymouth Arg* 12 0 **12 0**
2013–14 *Swindon T* 5 0 **5 0**
2014–15 Ross Co 26 1 **26 1**
2016–17 Oldham Ath 13 0 **13 0**

STOTT, Jamie (D) 4 0
b. 22-12-97
2016–17 Curzon Ashton 0 0
2016–17 Oldham Ath 4 0 **4 0**

WILSON, Brian (D) 427 17
H: 5 10 W: 11 00 b.Manchester 9-5-83
2001–02 Stoke C 1 0
2002–03 Stoke C 3 0
2003–04 Stoke C 2 0 **6 0**
2003–04 Cheltenham T 14 0
2004–05 Cheltenham T 43 3
2005–06 Cheltenham T 43 9
2006–07 Cheltenham T 25 2 **125 14**
2006–07 Bristol C 19 0
2007–08 Bristol C 18 1
2008–09 Bristol C 20 0
2009–10 Bristol C 3 0 **60 1**
2010–11 Colchester U 26 1
2011–12 Colchester U 46 0
2012–13 Colchester U 41 0
2013–14 Colchester U 38 0 **151 1**
2014–15 Oldham Ath 33 0
2015–16 Oldham Ath 26 0
2016–17 Oldham Ath 26 1 **85 1**

WOODLAND, Luke (M) 7 0
H: 6 0 b.Abu Dhabi 21-7-97
Internationals: England U16, U17, U18. Philippines Full caps.
2013–14 Bolton W 0 0
2014–15 Bolton W 0 0
2014–15 *Oldham Ath* 6 0
2016–17 Oldham Ath 1 0 **7 0**

Scholars
Antoine, Francois Bernard; Arthur, Festus; Boyling, Joseph Lee; Brown, Ronaldo Mushchario; Dry, Edward MacKenzie; Fallon, Mason Kevin; Glackin, Brendan Paul; Hamer, Thomas Philip; Kay, Bradley Steven; King, Dylan John Frederick; Lent, Tommy; Leonard, Ryan Michael Raymond; Middleton, Rory Michael; O'Neill, Callum Terence; Scullion, Callum Patrick; Sheridan, Jay Anthony; Uche, Chinedu Oyinoluwa Praise; Whalley, Bailey Michael.

OXFORD U (63)

AGBOOLA, Manny (G) 0 0
2016–17 Oxford U 0 0

ASHBY, Josh (M) 5 0
b.Oxford 3-5-96
2013–14 Oxford U 0 0
2014–15 Oxford U 2 0
2015–16 Oxford U 3 0
2016–17 Oxford U 0 0 **5 0**

BROWN, Wayne (G) 286 0
H: 6 0 W: 13 11 b.Southampton 14-1-77
Internationals: England C.
1993–94 Bristol C 1 0
1994–95 Bristol C 0 0
1995–96 Bristol C 0 0 **1 0**
From Weston-Super-Mare
1996–97 Chester C 2 0
1997–98 Chester C 13 0
1998–99 Chester C 23 0
1999–2000 Chester C 46 0
2000–01 Chester C 0 0
2001–02 Chester C 0 0
2004–05 Chester C 23 0
2005–06 Chester C 0 0 **107 0**
2006–07 Hereford U 39 0
2007–08 Hereford U 44 0 **83 0**
2008–09 Bury 35 0
2009–10 Bury 41 0 **76 0**
2010–11 Supersport U 13 0 **13 0**
2011–12 Oxford U 2 0
2012–13 Oxford U 4 0
2013–14 Oxford U 0 0
2016–17 Oxford U 0 0 **6 0**

BUCHEL, Benjamin (G) 27 0
H: 6 2 W: 11 08 b.Ruggel 4-7-89
Internationals: Liechtenstein U17, U19, U21, Full caps.
2012–13 Bournemouth 0 0
2013–14 Bournemouth 0 0
2014–15 Bournemouth 0 0
2015–16 Oxford U 23 0
2016–17 Oxford U 0 0 **23 0**
2016–17 *Barnet* 4 0 **4 0**

CARROLL, Canice (M) 4 0
b. 26-1-99
Internationals: Republic of Ireland U17.
2015–16 Oxford U 0 0
2016–17 Oxford U 4 0 **4 0**

DUNKLEY, Cheyenne (D) 78 7
H: 6 2 W: 13 05 b.Wolverhampton 13-2-92
Internationals: England C.
From Kidderminster H.
2014–15 Oxford U 9 0
2015–16 Oxford U 29 4
2016–17 Oxford U 40 3 **78 7**

EASTWOOD, Simon (G) 109 0
H: 6 2 W: 10 13 b.Huddersfield 26-6-89
Internationals: England U18, U19.
2005–06 Huddersfield T 0 0
2006–07 Huddersfield T 0 0
2007–08 Huddersfield T 0 0
2008–09 Huddersfield T 1 0
2009–10 Huddersfield T 0 0 **1 0**
2009–10 *Bradford C* 22 0 **22 0**
2012–13 Portsmouth 27 0 **27 0**
2013–14 Blackburn R 7 0
2014–15 Blackburn R 6 0
2015–16 Blackburn R 0 0 **13 0**
2016–17 Oxford U 46 0 **46 0**

GILES, Jonny (M) 0 0
H: 5 10 W: 10 12 b. 14-5-94
2015–16 Oxford U 0 0
2016–17 Oxford U 0 0

HALL, Robert (F) 124 17
H: 6 2 W: 10 05 b.Aylesbury 20-10-93
Internationals: England U16, U17, U18, U19.
2010–11 West Ham U 0 0
2011–12 West Ham U 3 0
2011–12 *Oxford U* 13 5
2011–12 *Milton Keynes D* 2 0
2012–13 West Ham U 1 0 **4 0**
2012–13 *Birmingham C* 13 0 **13 0**
2012–13 *Bolton W* 1 0
2013–14 Bolton W 22 1
2014–15 Bolton W 9 0
2014–15 *Milton Keynes D* 7 3
2015–16 Bolton W 0 0 **32 1**
2015–16 *Milton Keynes D* 27 2 **36 5**
2016–17 Oxford U 26 6 **39 11**

HEMMINGS, Kane (F) 104 30
b.Burton 8-4-92
2011–12 Rangers 4 0 **4 0**
From Cowdenbeath.
2014–15 Barnsley 23 3 **23 3**
2015–16 Dundee 37 21 **37 21**
2016–17 Oxford U 40 6 **40 6**

JOHNSON, Marvin (F) 92 9
H: 5 10 W: 11 09 b.Birmingham 1-12-90
From Solihull Moors, Kidderminster H.
2014–15 Motherwell 11 0
2015–16 Motherwell 38 5
2016–17 Motherwell 4 1 **53 6**
2016–17 Oxford U 39 3 **39 3**

LEDSON, Ryan (M) 49 1
H: 5 9 W: 10 12 b.Liverpool 19-8-97
Internationals: England U16, U17, U18, U19, U20.
2013–14 Everton 0 0
2014–15 Everton 0 0
2015–16 Everton 0 0
2015–16 *Cambridge U* 27 0 **27 0**
2016–17 Oxford U 22 1 **22 1**

LONG, Sam (D) 18 1
H: 5 10 W: 11 11 b.Oxford 16-1-95
2012–13 Oxford U 1 0
2013–14 Oxford U 3 0
2014–15 Oxford U 10 1
2015–16 Oxford U 1 0
2016–17 Oxford U 3 0 **18 1**

LUNDSTRAM, John (M) 145 6
H: 5 11 W: 11 09 b.Liverpool 18-2-94
Internationals: England U17, U18, U19, U20.
2011–12 Everton 0 0
2012–13 Everton 0 0
2012–13 *Doncaster R* 14 0 **14 0**
2013–14 Everton 0 0
2013–14 *Yeovil T* 14 2 **14 2**
2013–14 *Leyton Orient* 7 0
2014–15 Everton 0 0
2014–15 *Blackpool* 17 0 **17 0**
2014–15 *Leyton Orient* 4 0 **11 0**
2014–15 *Scunthorpe U* 7 0 **7 0**
2015–16 Oxford U 37 3
2016–17 Oxford U 45 1 **82 4**

MAGUIRE, Chris (F) 322 61
H: 5 7 W: 10 05 b.Bellshill 16-1-89
Internationals: Scotland U16, U19, U21, Full caps.
2005–06 Aberdeen 1 0
2006–07 Aberdeen 19 1
2007–08 Aberdeen 28 4
2008–09 Aberdeen 31 3
2009–10 Aberdeen 17 1
2009–10 *Kilmarnock* 14 4 **14 4**
2010–11 Aberdeen 35 7 **131 16**
2011–12 Derby Co 7 1 **7 1**
2011–12 *Portsmouth* 11 3 **11 3**
2012–13 Sheffield W 10 1
2013–14 Sheffield W 27 9
2013–14 *Coventry C* 3 2 **3 2**
2014–15 Sheffield W 42 8 **79 18**
2015–16 Rotherham U 14 0 **14 0**
2015–16 Oxford U 21 4
2016–17 Oxford U 42 13 **63 17**

MARTIN, Aaron (D) 116 6
H: 6 3 W: 11 13 b.Newport (IW) 29-9-89
2009–10 Southampton 2 0
2010–11 Southampton 8 0
2011–12 Southampton 10 1
2012–13 Southampton 0 0
2012–13 *Crystal Palace* 4 0 **4 0**
2012–13 *Coventry C* 12 0
2013–14 Southampton 0 0 **20 1**
2013–14 Birmingham C 8 0 **8 0**
2014–15 Yeovil T 12 3 **12 3**
2014–15 Coventry C 27 0
2015–16 Coventry C 29 2 **68 2**
2016–17 Oxford U 4 0 **4 0**

NELSON, Curtis (D) 244 10
H: 6 0 W: 11 07 b.Newcastle-under-Lyme 21-5-93
Internationals: England U18.
2010–11 Plymouth Arg 35 0
2011–12 Plymouth Arg 17 0
2012–13 Plymouth Arg 27 3
2013–14 Plymouth Arg 44 1
2014–15 Plymouth Arg 42 1
2015–16 Plymouth Arg 46 3 **211 8**
2016–17 Oxford U 33 2 **33 2**

RAGLAN, Charlie (D) 62 1
H: 6 0 W: 11 13 b.Wythenshawe 28-4-93
2011–12 Port Vale 0 0
2012–13 Port Vale 0 0
2013–14 Port Vale 0 0
2014–15 Chesterfield 18 1
2015–16 Chesterfield 27 0
2016–17 Chesterfield 1 0 **46 1**
2016–17 Oxford U 16 0 **16 0**

RIBEIRO, Christian (D) 162 8
H: 5 11 W: 12 02 b.Neath 14-12-89
Internationals: Wales U17, U19, U21, Full caps.
2006–07 Bristol C 0 0
2007–08 Bristol C 0 0
2008–09 Bristol C 0 0
2009–10 Bristol C 5 0
2009–10 *Stockport Co* 7 0 **7 0**
2009–10 *Colchester U* 2 0 **2 0**
2010–11 Bristol C 9 0
2011–12 Bristol C 0 0 **14 0**
2011–12 *Carlisle U* 5 0 **5 0**
2011–12 *Scunthorpe U* 10 0
2012–13 Scunthorpe U 28 2
2013–14 Scunthorpe U 21 0 **59 2**
2014–15 Exeter C 37 2
2015–16 Exeter C 35 4 **72 6**
2016–17 Oxford U 3 0 **3 0**

ROBERTS, James (F) 31 3
b.Stoke Mandeville 21-6-96
2012–13 Oxford U 0 0
2013–14 Oxford U 0 0

2014–15 Oxford U 25 3
2015–16 Oxford U 4 0
2015–16 *Barnet* 2 0 **2 0**
2016–17 Oxford U 0 0 **29 3**

ROTHWELL, Joe (M) 40 1
H: 6 1 W: 12 02 b.Manchester 11-1-95
Internationals: England U16, U17, U19, U20.
2014–15 Manchester U 0 0
2014–15 *Blackpool* 3 0 **3 0**
2015–16 Manchester U 0 0
2015–16 *Barnsley* 4 0 **4 0**
2016–17 Oxford U 33 1 **33 1**

RUFFELS, Joshua (M) 99 3
H: 5 10 W: 11 11 b.Oxford 23-10-93
2011–12 Coventry C 1 0
2012–13 Coventry C 0 0 **1 0**
2013–14 Oxford U 29 1
2014–15 Oxford U 33 0
2015–16 Oxford U 16 0
2016–17 Oxford U 20 2 **98 3**

SERCOMBE, Liam (M) 311 40
H: 5 10 W: 10 10 b.Exeter 25-4-90
2008–09 Exeter C 29 2
2009–10 Exeter C 28 1
2010–11 Exeter C 42 3
2011–12 Exeter C 33 7
2012–13 Exeter C 20 1
2013–14 Exeter C 44 5
2014–15 Exeter C 40 4 **236 23**
2015–16 Oxford U 45 14
2016–17 Oxford U 30 3 **75 17**

SHEARER, Scott (G) 335 0
H: 6 3 W: 12 00 b.Glasgow 15-2-81
Internationals: Scotland B.
2000–01 Albion R 3 0
2001–02 Albion R 10 0
2002–03 Albion R 36 0 **49 0**
2003–04 Coventry C 30 0
2004–05 Coventry C 8 0 **38 0**
2004–05 *Rushden & D* 13 0 **13 0**
2005–06 Bristol R 45 0
2006–07 Bristol R 2 0 **47 0**
2006–07 *Shrewsbury T* 20 0 **20 0**
2007–08 Wycombe W 5 0
2008–09 Wycombe W 29 0
2009–10 Wycombe W 29 0
2010–11 Wycombe W 0 0 **63 0**
2011–12 Crawley T 25 0 **25 0**
2012–13 Rotherham U 19 0
2013–14 Rotherham U 12 0 **31 0**
2014–15 Crewe Alex 2 0 **2 0**
2014–15 *Burton Alb* 1 0 **1 0**
2015–16 Mansfield T 21 0
2016–17 Mansfield T 25 0 **46 0**
2016–17 Oxford U 0 0

SKARZ, Joe (D) 380 7
H: 5 10 W: 11 04 b.Huddersfield 13-7-89
2006–07 Huddersfield T 17 0
2007–08 Huddersfield T 27 0
2008–09 Huddersfield T 9 1
2008–09 *Hartlepool U* 7 0 **7 0**
2009–10 Huddersfield T 15 0 **68 1**
2009–10 *Shrewsbury T* 20 0 **20 0**
2010–11 Bury 46 1
2011–12 Bury 45 1
2012–13 Bury 39 2 **130 4**
2012–13 Rotherham U 8 0
2013–14 Rotherham U 41 2
2014–15 Rotherham U 17 0 **66 2**
2014–15 Oxford U 18 0
2015–16 Oxford U 41 0
2016–17 Oxford U 30 0 **89 0**

STEPHENS, Jack (G) 0 0
b. 2-8-97
2014–15 Oxford U 0 0
2015–16 Oxford U 0 0
2016–17 Oxford U 0 0

THOMAS, Wesley (F) 228 57
H: 5 10 W: 11 00 b.Barking 23-1-87
2008–09 Dagenham & R 5 0
2009–10 Dagenham & R 23 3 **28 3**
2010–11 Cheltenham T 41 18 **41 18**
2011–12 Crawley T 6 1 **6 1**
2011–12 Bournemouth 36 11
2012–13 Bournemouth 6 0
2012–13 *Portsmouth* 6 3 **6 3**
2012–13 *Blackpool* 9 3 **9 3**
2012–13 *Birmingham C* 11 3
2013–14 Bournemouth 10 0 **52 11**
2013–14 Rotherham U 13 5 **13 5**
2014–15 Birmingham C 33 4
2015–16 Birmingham C 0 0 **44 7**
2015–16 *Swindon T* 6 2 **6 2**
2015–16 *Bradford C* 10 1 **10 1**
2016–17 Oxford U 13 3 **13 3**

WELCH-HAYES, Miles (D) 1 0
b.Oxford 25-10-96
2016–17 Oxford U 1 0 **1 0**

Scholars
Agboola, Emmanuel Ayomikun; Baker, Nathan Luke; Baptiste, Shandon Harkeem; Berry-Hargreaves, Matthew Owen; Bryan, Graham John; Carr, Daniel Joshua; Chilcott, Ben William; Clayton, Niall Liam; Hartley, Joseph; Hawtin, Charles Christopher; Heap, Aaron John Harrison; Hopkins, Albert Oscar; Mannings, Rex Arnold; Napa, Malachi Tyrese Mthokozisi; Noel-Williams, Dejon George Franklin; Tuttle, Charley David.

PETERBOROUGH U (64)

ANDERSON, Harry (F) 16 0
H: 5 6 W: 9 11 b. 9-1-97
2014–15 Peterborough U 10 0
2015–16 Peterborough U 5 0
2016–17 Peterborough U 1 0 **16 0**

ANDERSON, Jermaine (M) 59 5
b. 16-5-96
Internationals: England U18, U20.
2012–13 Peterborough U 1 0
2013–14 Peterborough U 13 0
2014–15 Peterborough U 24 1
2015–16 Peterborough U 14 4
2016–17 Peterborough U 7 0 **59 5**

ANGOL, Lee (M) 49 12
H: 5 10 W: 11 04 b. 4-8-94
2012–13 Wycombe W 3 0
2013–14 Wycombe W 0 0 **3 0**
2014–15 Luton T 0 0
2015–16 Peterborough U 33 11
2016–17 Peterborough U 13 1 **46 12**

BALDWIN, Jack (D) 144 6
H: 6 1 W: 11 00 b.Barking 30-6-93
2011–12 Hartlepool U 17 0
2012–13 Hartlepool U 32 2
2013–14 Hartlepool U 28 2 **77 4**
2013–14 Peterborough U 11 0
2014–15 Peterborough U 11 0
2015–16 Peterborough U 18 1
2016–17 Peterborough U 27 1 **67 2**

BORG, Andrea (M) 3 0
b. 12-11-99
2016–17 Peterborough U 3 0 **3 0**

BOSTWICK, Michael (D) 278 32
H: 6 4 W: 14 00 b.Eltham 17-5-88
Internationals: England C.
2006–07 Millwall 0 0
From Rushden & D, Ebbsfleet U
2010–11 Stevenage 41 2
2011–12 Stevenage 43 7 **84 9**
2012–13 Peterborough U 39 5
2013–14 Peterborough U 42 4
2014–15 Peterborough U 38 7
2015–16 Peterborough U 36 4
2016–17 Peterborough U 39 3 **194 23**

CHETTLE, Callum (M) 16 0
b. 28-8-96
Internationals: England C.
From Ilkeston, Nuneaton T.
2015–16 Peterborough U 5 0
2016–17 Peterborough U 11 0 **16 0**

COULTHIRST, Shaquile (F) 97 18
H: 5 9 W: 12 02 b.Hackney 2-1-94
Internationals: England U19.
2012–13 Tottenham H 0 0
2013–14 Tottenham H 0 0
2013–14 *Leyton Orient* 1 1 **1 1**
2013–14 *Torquay U* 6 2 **6 2**
2014–15 Tottenham H 0 0
2014–15 *Southend U* 22 4 **22 4**
2014–15 *York C* 11 2 **11 2**
2015–16 Tottenham H 0 0
2015–16 *Wigan Ath* 2 0 **2 0**
2015–16 Peterborough U 19 2
2016–17 Peterborough U 16 2 **35 4**
2016–17 *Mansfield T* 20 5 **20 5**

DA SILVA LOPES, Leonardo (M) 48 2
H: 5 6 W: 9 08 b.Lisbon 30-11-98
2014–15 Peterborough U 2 0
2015–16 Peterborough U 8 0
2016–17 Peterborough U 38 2 **48 2**

DOUGLAS, Kasey (F) 0 0
2016–17 Peterborough U 0 0

EDWARDS, Gwion (M) 137 21
H: 5 9 W: 12 00 b.Carmarthen 1-3-93
Internationals: Wales U19, U21
2011–12 Swansea C 0 0
2012–13 Swansea C 0 0
2012–13 *St Johnstone* 6 0
2013–14 Swansea C 0 0
2013–14 *St Johnstone* 13 0 **19 0**
2013–14 *Crawley T* 6 2
2014–15 Crawley T 37 4
2015–16 Crawley T 42 8 **85 14**
2016–17 Peterborough U 33 7 **33 7**

FORRESTER, Chris (M) 78 6
b.Dublin 17-12-92
Internationals: Republic of Ireland U21.
From Bohemians, St Patrick's Ath.
2015–16 Peterborough U 35 2
2016–17 Peterborough U 43 4 **78 6**

FREESTONE, Lewis (D) 4 0
b.King's Lynn 26-10-99
2016–17 Peterborough U 4 0 **4 0**

GOODE, James (D) 0 0
2016–17 Peterborough U 0 0

GORMLEY, Joe (F) 6 0
b. 26-11-89
From Cliftonville.
2015–16 Peterborough U 4 0
2016–17 Peterborough U 1 0 **5 0**
2016–17 *St Johnstone* 1 0 **1 0**

GRANT, Anthony (M) 397 15
H: 5 10 W: 11 01 b.Lambeth 4-6-87
Internationals: England U16, U17, U19.
2004–05 Chelsea 1 0
2005–06 Chelsea 0 0
2005–06 *Oldham Ath* 2 0 **2 0**
2006–07 Chelsea 0 0
2006–07 *Wycombe W* 40 0 **40 0**
2007–08 Chelsea 0 0 **1 0**
2007–08 *Luton T* 4 0 **4 0**
2007–08 *Southend U* 10 0
2008–09 Southend U 35 1
2009–10 Southend U 38 0
2010–11 Southend U 43 8
2011–12 Southend U 33 1 **159 10**
2012–13 Stevenage 41 0 **41 0**
2013–14 Crewe Alex 38 2
2014–15 Crewe Alex 43 2 **81 4**
2015–16 Port Vale 38 1
2016–17 Port Vale 20 0 **58 1**
2016–17 Peterborough U 11 0 **11 0**

HENRY, Dion (G) 1 0
H: 5 11 W: 10 03 b.Ipswich 12-9-97
2014–15 Peterborough U 0 0
2015–16 Peterborough U 1 0
2016–17 Peterborough U 0 0 **1 0**

HUGHES, Andrew (D) 106 4
b.Cardiff 5-6-92
Internationals: Wales U18, U23.
2013–14 Newport Co 26 2
2014–15 Newport Co 16 1
2015–16 Newport Co 25 0 **67 3**
2016–17 Peterborough U 39 1 **39 1**

INMAN, Bradden (M) 128 20
H: 5 9 W: 11 03 b.Adelaide 10-12-91
Internationals: Scotland U19, U21.
2009–10 Newcastle U 0 0
2010–11 Newcastle U 0 0
2011–12 Newcastle U 0 0
2012–13 Newcastle U 0 0
2012–13 *Crewe Alex* 21 5
2013–14 Newcastle U 0 0
2013–14 Crewe Alex 36 4
2014–15 Crewe Alex 21 1
2015–16 Crewe Alex 39 10 **117 20**
2016–17 Peterborough U 11 0 **11 0**

JAMES, Luke (M) 176 21
H: 6 0 W: 12 08 b.Amble 4-11-94
2011–12 Hartlepool U 19 3
2012–13 Hartlepool U 26 3
2013–14 Hartlepool U 42 13
2014–15 Hartlepool U 4 0
2014–15 Peterborough U 32 1
2015–16 Peterborough U 0 0
2015–16 *Bradford C* 9 0 **9 0**
2015–16 *Hartlepool U* 20 1 **111 20**
2016–17 Peterborough U 0 0 **32 1**
2016–17 *Bristol R* 24 0 **24 0**

MADDISON, Marcus (M) 109 27
H: 5 9 W: 11 03 b.Sedgefield 26-9-93
Internationals: England C.
2014–15 Peterborough U 29 7
2015–16 Peterborough U 39 11
2016–17 Peterborough U 41 9 **109 27**

MOORE, Deon (F) 4 0
b.Croydon 14-5-99
From Carshalton Ath.
2016–17 Peterborough U 4 0 **4 0**

MORIAS, Junior (F) 48 4
H: 5 8 W: 10 10 b.Kingston 4-7-95
2012–13 Wycombe W 19 0
2013–14 Wycombe W 9 0
2014–15 Wycombe W 0 0 **28 0**
From Boreham Wood, Whitehawk, St Albans C.
2016–17 Peterborough U 20 4 **20 4**

NABI, Adil (F) 18 3
H: 5 9 W: 10 10 b.Birmingham 28-2-94
Internationals: England U16, U17.
2010–11 WBA 0 0
2011–12 WBA 0 0
2012–13 WBA 0 0
2013–14 WBA 0 0
2014–15 WBA 0 0
2015 *Delhi Dynamos* 10 3 **10 3**
2015–16 WBA 0 0
2015–16 Peterborough U 6 0
2016–17 Peterborough U 2 0 **8 0**

NICHOLS, Tom (F) 148 43
H: 5 10 W: 10 10 b.Wellington 1-9-93
2010–11 Exeter C 1 0
2011–12 Exeter C 7 1
2012–13 Exeter C 3 0
2013–14 Exeter C 28 6
2014–15 Exeter C 36 15
2015–16 Exeter C 23 10 **98 32**
2015–16 Peterborough U 7 1
2016–17 Peterborough U 43 10 **50 11**

PENFOLD, Morgan (F) 0 0
2016–17 Peterborough U 0 0

SMITH, Michael (D) 396 20
H: 5 11 W: 11 02 b.Ballyclare 4-9-88
Internationals: Northern Ireland Full caps.
2005–06 Ballyclare Com 1 0
2006–07 Ballyclare Com 25 2
2007–08 Ballyclare Com 39 1
2008–09 Ballyclare Com 27 7 **92 10**
2008–09 Ballymena U 12 1
2009–10 Ballymena U 37 2
2010–11 Ballymena U 34 3 **83 6**
2011–12 Bristol R 20 0
2012–13 Bristol R 38 1
2013–14 Bristol R 43 0 **101 1**
2014–15 Peterborough U 43 1
2015–16 Peterborough U 38 1
2016–17 Peterborough U 39 1 **120 3**

STEVENS, Mathew (F) 11 1
H: 5 11 W: 11 09 b. 12-2-98
2015–16 Barnet 10 1 **10 1**
2016–17 Peterborough U 1 0 **1 0**

TAFAZOLLI, Ryan (D) 135 11
H: 6 5 W: 12 03 b.Sutton 28-9-91
2010–11 Southampton 0 0
From Salisbury, Cambridge C, Carshalton Ath
2013–14 Mansfield T 24 2
2014–15 Mansfield T 36 1
2015–16 Mansfield T 44 5 **104 8**
2016–17 Peterborough U 31 3 **31 3**

TAYLOR, Paul (F) 149 16
H: 5 11 W: 11 02 b.Liverpool 4-11-87
2008–09 Chester C 9 0 **9 0**
2009–10 Montegnee 1 0 **1 0**
2009–10 *Charleoi* 3 0 **3 0**
2010–11 Anderlecht 0 0
2010–11 Peterborough U 1 0
2011–12 Peterborough U 44 12
2012–13 Peterborough U 3 0
2012–13 Ipswich T 3 0
2013–14 Ipswich T 18 1
2013–14 *Peterborough U* 6 0
2014–15 Ipswich T 0 0 **21 1**
2014–15 *Rotherham U* 17 0 **17 0**
2014–15 *Blackburn R* 5 0 **5 0**
2016–17 Peterborough U 39 3 **93 15**

TYLER, Mark (G) 488 0
H: 6 0 W: 12 09 b.Norwich 2-4-77
Internationals: England U18.
1994–95 Peterborough U 5 0
1995–96 Peterborough U 0 0
1996–97 Peterborough U 3 0
1997–98 Peterborough U 46 0
1998–99 Peterborough U 27 0
1999–2000 Peterborough U 32 0
2000–01 Peterborough U 40 0
2001–02 Peterborough U 44 0
2002–03 Peterborough U 29 0
2003–04 Peterborough U 43 0
2004–05 Peterborough U 46 0
2005–06 Peterborough U 40 0
2006–07 Peterborough U 41 0
2007–08 Peterborough U 17 0
2008–09 Peterborough U 0 0
2008–09 *Bury* 11 0 **11 0**
2014–15 Luton T 31 0
2015–16 Luton T 27 0 **58 0**
2015–16 *Peterborough U* 3 0
2016–17 Peterborough U 3 0 **419 0**

WHITE, Hayden (D) 71 2
H: 6 1 W: 10 10 b.Greenwich 15-4-95
2013–14 Bolton W 2 0
2014–15 Bolton W 3 0
2014–15 *Carlisle U* 8 0 **8 0**
2014–15 *Bury* 2 0 **2 0**
2014–15 *Notts Co* 3 0 **3 0**
2015–16 Bolton W 0 0 **5 0**
2015–16 *Blackpool* 29 1 **29 1**
2016–17 Peterborough U 6 0 **6 0**
2016–17 *Mansfield T* 18 1 **18 1**

WILLIAMS, Jerome (D) 59 1
H: 5 11 W: 12 02 b.Croydon 7-3-95
Internationals: England U18, U19.
2013–14 Crystal Palace 0 0
2014–15 Crystal Palace 0 0
2014–15 *Southend U* 21 0 **21 0**
2015–16 Crystal Palace 0 0
2015–16 *Burton Alb* 15 1 **15 1**
2015–16 *Leyton Orient* 13 0 **13 0**
2016–17 Peterborough U 10 0 **10 0**

Players retained or with offer of contract
Binnom-Williams, Jerome Craig; Lloyd-McGoldrick, Daniel James; Miller, Ricky; Nicholson, Jordan.

Scholars
Alban, Jones Hugh Alexander; Baldry, Harry Max; Cartwright, Samuel Elliott; Douglas, Kasey Jamal; Elsom, Lewis John; Ferrier, Glenn; Fieldhouse, Ewan Jack; Goode, James; Gow, Cameron John; Hart, Aaron Richard; Jarvis, Daniel John; Maddison, Layton Luca Robert; Noble, Luke Melvyn William.

PLYMOUTH ARG (65)

BENTLEY, Jordan (D) 1 0
2015–16 Plymouth Arg 1 0
2016–17 Plymouth Arg 0 0 **1 0**

BLISSETT, Nathan (F) 11 2
H: 6 0 W: 12 04 b.West Bromwich 29-6-90
From Kidderminster H.
2015–16 Bristol R 2 0 **2 0**
2016–17 Plymouth Arg 9 2 **9 2**

BRADLEY, Sonny (D) 207 12
H: 6 0 W: 11 05 b.Hedon 14-6-92
2011–12 Hull C 2 0
2011–12 *Aldershot T* 14 0
2012–13 Hull C 0 0 **2 0**
2012–13 *Aldershot T* 42 1 **56 1**
2013–14 Portsmouth 33 2 **33 2**
2014–15 Crawley T 26 1
2015–16 Crawley T 46 1 **72 2**
2016–17 Plymouth Arg 44 7 **44 7**

BULVITIS, Nauris (D) 222 14
H: 6 2 W: 12 06 b.Riga 15-3-87
Internationals: Latvia U19, U21, Full caps.
2007 Daugava Daugavpils 7 0 **7 0**
2008 Siauliai 21 1 **21 1**
2009 Tranzit 17 1 **17 1**
2009–10 *Inverness CT* 32 2 **32 2**
2010 Blazma Rezekne 10 0 **10 0**
2010–11 Spartak Trnava 0 0
2011 Spartaks Jurmala 0 0
2012 Spartaks Jurmala 32 3
2013 Spartaks Jurmala 11 0
2013 Skonta Riga 15 3 **15 3**
2013–14 Aarau 18 0
2014–15 Aarau 4 0 **22 0**
2015 Spartaks Jurmala 26 2
2016 Spartaks Jurmala 11 0 **80 5**
2016–17 Plymouth Arg 18 2 **18 2**

CAREY, Graham (M) 247 40
H: 6 0 W: 10 03 b.Dublin 20-5-89
Internationals: Republic of Ireland U21.
2008–09 Celtic 0 0
2009 *Bohemians* 15 2 **15 2**
2009–10 Celtic 0 0
2009–10 *St Mirren* 15 3
2010–11 Celtic 0 0
2010–11 *Huddersfield T* 19 2 **19 2**
2011–12 St Mirren 29 2
2012–13 St Mirren 26 1 **70 6**
2013–14 Ross Co 36 3
2014–15 Ross Co 22 2 **58 5**
2015–16 Plymouth Arg 39 11
2016–17 Plymouth Arg 46 14 **85 25**

DONALDSON, Ryan (F) 109 9
H: 5 9 W: 11 00 b.Newcastle upon Tyne 1-5-91
Internationals: England U17, U19.
2008–09 Newcastle U 0 0
2009–10 Newcastle U 2 0
2010–11 Newcastle U 0 0
2010–11 *Hartlepool U* 12 0 **12 0**
2011–12 Newcastle U 0 0 **2 0**
2011–12 *Tranmere R* 1 0 **1 0**
2014–15 Cambridge U 38 5
2015–16 Cambridge U 30 2 **68 7**
2016–17 Plymouth Arg 26 2 **26 2**

DOREL, Vincent (G) 4 0
H: 6 3 W: 12 13 b.Rennes 21-3-92
2014–15 Le Poire SV 3 0 **3 0**
2015–16 Plymouth Arg 1 0
2016–17 Plymouth Arg 0 0 **1 0**

FLETCHER, Alex (F) 0 0
2016–17 Plymouth Arg 0 0

FOX, David (M) 294 15
H: 5 9 W: 11 08 b.Leek 13-12-83
Internationals: England U16, U17, U19, U20.
2000–01 Manchester U 0 0
2001–02 Manchester U 0 0
2002–03 Manchester U 0 0
2003–04 Manchester U 0 0
2004–05 Manchester U 0 0
2004–05 *Shrewsbury T* 4 1 **4 1**
2005–06 Manchester U 0 0
2005–06 Blackpool 7 1
2006–07 Blackpool 37 4
2007–08 Blackpool 28 1
2008–09 Blackpool 22 0 **94 6**
2009–10 Colchester U 18 3
2010–11 Norwich C 32 1
2011–12 Norwich C 28 0
2012–13 Norwich C 2 0
2013–14 Norwich C 0 0 **62 1**
2013–14 *Barnsley* 7 0 **7 0**
2014–15 Colchester U 30 2 **48 5**
2015–16 Crewe Alex 39 2 **39 2**
2016–17 Plymouth Arg 40 0 **40 0**

GOODWILLIE, David (F) 247 52
H: 5 9 W: 11 02 b.Stirling 28-3-89
Internationals: Scotland U16, U17, U19, U21, Full caps.
2005–06 Dundee U 10 1
2006–07 Dundee U 17 0
2007–08 Dundee U 2 0
2007–08 *Raith R* 23 9 **23 9**
2008–09 Dundee U 16 3
2009–10 Dundee U 33 8
2010–11 Dundee U 37 16
2011–12 Dundee U 1 0
2011–12 Blackburn R 20 2
2012–13 Blackburn R 8 0
2012–13 *Crystal Palace* 1 0 **1 0**
2013–14 Blackburn R 0 0 **28 2**
2013–14 *Dundee U* 19 3 **135 31**
2013–14 *Blackpool* 13 3 **13 3**
2014–15 Aberdeen 31 6 **31 6**
2016–17 Plymouth Arg 16 1 **16 1**

IJAHA, David (M) 3 0
H: 6 0 W: 11 09 b.Stocksbridge 17-2-90
2016–17 Plymouth Arg 3 0 **3 0**

JERVIS, Jake (F) 182 44
H: 6 3 W: 12 13 b.Birmingham 17-9-91
2009–10 Birmingham C 0 0
2009–10 *Hereford U* 7 2
2010–11 Birmingham C 0 0
2010–11 *Notts Co* 10 0 **10 0**
2010–11 *Hereford U* 4 0 **11 2**
2011–12 Birmingham C 0 0
2011–12 *Swindon T* 12 3 **12 3**
2011–12 *Preston NE* 5 2 **5 2**
2012–13 Birmingham C 2 0 **2 0**

2012–13	*Carlisle U*	5	3	**5**	**3**
2012–13	*Tranmere R*	4	1	**4**	**1**
2012–13	*Portsmouth*	3	1		
2012–13	Elazigspor	4	1	**4**	**1**
2013–14	Portsmouth	15	4	**18**	**5**
2014–15	Ross Co	27	4	**27**	**4**
2015–16	Plymouth Arg	42	11		
2016–17	Plymouth Arg	42	12	**84**	**23**

McCALLUM, Marc (G) **85 0**
H: 6 3 b.Forfar 27-3-93
Internationals: Scotland U17, U19.

2011–12	Dundee U	0	0		
2011–12	*Forfar Ath*	10	0	**10**	**0**
2012–13	Dundee U	0	0		
2012–13	*Peterhead*	6	0	**6**	**0**
2012–13	*Berwick R*	17	0	**17**	**0**
2013–14	Dundee U	1	0		
2014–15	Dundee U	0	0	**1**	**0**
2014–15	*Arbroath*	25	0	**25**	**0**
2015–16	Livingston	26	0	**26**	**0**
2016–17	Plymouth Arg	0	0		

McCORMICK, Luke (G) **174 0**
H: 6 0 W: 13 12 b.Coventry 15-8-83

2012–13	Oxford U	15	0	**15**	**0**
2013–14	Plymouth Arg	27	0		
2014–15	Plymouth Arg	46	0		
2015–16	Plymouth Arg	40	0		
2016–17	Plymouth Arg	46	0	**159**	**0**

MILLER, Gary (D) **287 4**
H: 6 1 W: 11 03 b.Glasgow 15-4-87

2005–06	Livingston	4	0		
2006–07	Livingston	13	0		
2006–07	*Ayr U*	15	1	**15**	**1**
2007–08	Livingston	0	0		
2007–08	*Ross Co*	20	0		
2008–09	Livingston	23	0	**40**	**0**
2009–10	Ross Co	32	0		
2010–11	Ross Co	31	0		
2011–12	Ross Co	36	1	**119**	**1**
2012–13	St Johnstone	17	0		
2013–14	St Johnstone	25	1		
2014–15	St Johnstone	19	0	**61**	**1**
2015–16	Partick Thistle	21	1	**21**	**1**
2016–17	Plymouth Arg	31	0	**31**	**0**

OSBORNE, Karleigh (D) **231 8**
H: 6 2 W: 12 04 b.Southall 19-3-88

2004–05	Brentford	1	0		
2005–06	Brentford	1	0		
2006–07	Brentford	21	0		
2007–08	Brentford	29	1		
2008–09	Brentford	23	4		
2009–10	Brentford	19	0		
2010–11	Brentford	42	1		
2011–12	Brentford	25	0	**161**	**6**
2012–13	Millwall	13	1		
2013–14	Millwall	1	0	**14**	**1**
2013–14	Bristol C	27	1		
2014–15	Bristol C	1	0		
2014–15	*Colchester U*	4	0	**4**	**0**
2015–16	Bristol C	0	0	**28**	**1**
2015–16	*AFC Wimbledon*	23	0	**23**	**0**
2016–17	Plymouth Arg	1	0	**1**	**0**

Transferred to Kilmarnock, January 2017.

PALFREY, Billy (D) **0 0**

2016–17	Plymouth Arg	0	0		

ROONEY, Louis (F) **9 2**
H: 6 0 W: 11 11 b.Carrickfergus 28-9-96
Internationals: Northern Ireland U19, U21.

2015–16	Plymouth Arg	1	2		
2016–17	Plymouth Arg	1	0	**2**	**2**
2016–17	*Hartlepool U*	7	0	**7**	**0**

ROSE, Callum (D) **0 0**

2016–17	Plymouth Arg	0	0		

SARCEVIC, Antoni (M) **159 21**
H: 5 10 W: 11 00 b.Manchester 13-3-92
Internationals: England C.

2009–10	Crewe Alex	0	0		
2010–11	Crewe Alex	6	1		
2011–12	Crewe Alex	6	0	**12**	**1**
2013–14	Fleetwood T	42	13		
2014–15	Fleetwood T	37	2		
2015–16	Fleetwood T	39	3	**118**	**18**
2016–17	Shrewsbury T	12	0	**12**	**0**
2016–17	Plymouth Arg	17	2	**17**	**2**

SAWYER, Gary (D) **291 6**
H: 6 0 W: 11 08 b.Bideford 5-7-85

2004–05	Plymouth Arg	0	0		
2005–06	Plymouth Arg	0	0		
2006–07	Plymouth Arg	22	0		
2007–08	Plymouth Arg	31	1		
2008–09	Plymouth Arg	13	3		
2009–10	Plymouth Arg	29	1		
2009–10	*Bristol C*	2	0	**2**	**0**
2010–11	Bristol R	37	0		
2011–12	Bristol R	24	0	**61**	**0**
2012–13	Leyton Orient	34	1		
2013–14	Leyton Orient	22	0		
2014–15	Leyton Orient	13	0	**69**	**1**
2015–16	Plymouth Arg	43	0		
2016–17	Plymouth Arg	21	0	**159**	**5**

SLEW, Jordan (F) **122 11**
H: 6 3 W: 12 11 b.Sheffield 7-9-92
Internationals: England U19.

2010–11	Sheffield U	7	2		
2011–12	Sheffield U	4	1	**11**	**3**
2011–12	Blackburn R	1	0		
2011–12	*Stevenage*	9	0	**9**	**0**
2012–13	Blackburn R	0	0		
2012–13	*Oldham Ath*	3	0	**3**	**0**
2012–13	*Rotherham U*	7	0	**7**	**0**
2013–14	Blackburn R	0	0		
2013–14	*Ross Co*	20	1	**20**	**1**
2014–15	Blackburn R	0	0	**1**	**0**
2014–15	*Port Vale*	9	2	**9**	**2**
2014–15	Cambridge U	13	1		
2015–16	Cambridge U	10	0	**23**	**1**
2015–16	Chesterfield	7	0	**7**	**0**
2016–17	Plymouth Arg	32	4	**32**	**4**

SMITH, Connor (M) **57 1**
H: 5 11 W: 11 06 b.London 18-2-93
Internationals: Republic of Ireland U19, U21.

2012–13	Watford	7	0		
2013–14	Watford	1	0		
2013–14	*Gillingham*	10	0	**10**	**0**
2014–15	Watford	0	0		
2015–16	Watford	0	0	**8**	**0**
2015–16	*Stevenage*	4	0	**4**	**0**
2015–16	AFC Wimbledon	10	0	**10**	**0**
2016–17	Plymouth Arg	25	1	**25**	**1**

SOKOLIK, Jakub (D) **79 2**
H: 5 6 W: 12 02 b.Ostrava 28-8-93
Internationals: Czech Republic U16, U17, U18.

2010–11	Liverpool	0	0		
2011–12	Liverpool	0	0		
2012–13	Liverpool	0	0		
2013–14	Liverpool	0	0		
2013–14	*Southend U*	10	0		
2014–15	Yeovil T	11	0		
2014–15	*Southend U*	1	0		
2015–16	Yeovil T	34	1	**45**	**1**
2016–17	Southend U	5	0	**16**	**0**
2016–17	Plymouth Arg	18	1	**18**	**1**

SONGO'O, Yann (D) **81 6**
H: 6 0 W: 12 00 b.Yaounde 17-11-91
Internationals: France U16. Cameroon U20.

2011–12	Sabadell	6	0	**6**	**0**
2013	Sporting Kansas C	0	0		
2013	*Orlando C*	12	1	**12**	**1**
2013–14	Blackburn R	0	0		
2013–14	*Ross Co*	17	3	**17**	**3**
2014–15	Blackburn R	0	0		
2016–17	Plymouth Arg	46	2	**46**	**2**

TAYLOR, Ryan (F) **294 46**
H: 6 2 W: 10 10 b.Rotherham 4-5-88

2005–06	Rotherham U	1	0		
2006–07	Rotherham U	10	0		
2007–08	Rotherham U	35	6		
2008–09	Rotherham U	33	4		
2009–10	Rotherham U	19	0		
2009–10	*Exeter C*	7	0	**7**	**0**
2010–11	Rotherham U	34	11	**132**	**21**
2011–12	Bristol C	7	1		
2012–13	Bristol C	25	1		
2013–14	Bristol C	7	0	**39**	**2**
2013–14	Portsmouth	18	6		
2014–15	Portsmouth	37	9	**55**	**15**
2015–16	Oxford U	22	3		
2016–17	Oxford U	21	1	**43**	**4**
2016–17	Plymouth Arg	18	4	**18**	**4**

THRELKELD, Oscar (D) **70 3**
H: 6 0 W: 12 04 b.Bolton 15-12-94

2013–14	Bolton W	2	0		
2014–15	Bolton W	4	0		
2015–16	Bolton W	3	0	**9**	**0**
2015–16	*Plymouth Arg*	25	1		
2016–17	Plymouth Arg	36	2	**61**	**3**

Scholars
Battle, Alex Martin Jon; Bentley, Jordan David James; Cooper, Michael John; Craske, Billy Frederick; Crawford, Elliott Ian; Downing, Harry Edward; Fletcher, Alex Samuel; Hodges, Harry Kenneth; Jephcott, Luke Owen; Law, Ryan James; McAuley, Connor Michael; Richards, Joshua Samuel; Rooney, Daniel Martyn; Rose, Callum Thomas; Ryan, Sam Michael Ellis; Sangster, Cameron; Taylor, Aaron; Ward, Matthew Lawrence.

PORT VALE (66)

ALNWICK, Jak (G) **74 0**
H: 6 2 W: 12 13 b.Hexham 17-6-93
Internationals: England U17, U18, U19, U20.

2010–11	Newcastle U	0	0		
2011–12	Newcastle U	0	0		
2012–13	Newcastle U	0	0		
2013–14	Newcastle U	0	0		
2014–15	Newcastle U	6	0	**6**	**0**
2014–15	*Bradford C*	1	0	**1**	**0**
2015–16	Port Vale	41	0		
2016–17	Port Vale	26	0	**67**	**0**

Transferred to Rangers, January 2017.

AMOROS, Sebastien (M) **10 0**
H: 5 9 W: 9 13 b.Cannes 2-7-95
From Monaco.

2016–17	Port Vale	10	0	**10**	**0**

BIKEY, Andre (D) **269 15**
H: 6 0 W: 12 08 b.Douala 8-1-85
Internationals: Cameroon Full caps.

2003–04	Pacos de Ferreira	2	0	**2**	**0**
2004–05	Dep Aves	0	0		
2005	Shinnik	11	1	**11**	**1**
2005	Loko Moscow	9	0		
2006	Loko Moscow	5	0	**14**	**0**
2006–07	Reading	15	0		
2007–08	Reading	22	3		
2008–09	Reading	25	3		
2009–10	Reading	0	0	**62**	**6**
2009–10	Burnley	28	1		
2010–11	Burnley	28	2		
2011–12	Burnley	14	0	**70**	**3**
2011–12	*Bristol C*	7	0	**7**	**0**
2012–13	Middlesbrough	33	1	**33**	**1**
2013–14	Panetolikos	23	2	**23**	**2**
2014–15	Charlton Ath	31	1	**31**	**1**
2015	NorthEast U	9	1	**9**	**1**
2016–17	Port Vale	7	0	**7**	**0**

BOOT, Ryan (G) **1 0**
H: 6 1 W: 11 03 b.Rocester 9-11-94

2012–13	Port Vale	0	0		
2013–14	Port Vale	0	0		
2014–15	Port Vale	0	0		
2015–16	Port Vale	0	0		
2016–17	Port Vale	1	0	**1**	**0**

BROWN, Michael (M) **562 42**
H: 5 9 W: 12 04 b.Hartlepool 25-1-77
Internationals: England U21.

1994–95	Manchester C	0	0		
1995–96	Manchester C	21	0		
1996–97	Manchester C	11	0		
1996–97	*Hartlepool U*	6	1	**6**	**1**
1997–98	Manchester C	26	0		
1998–99	Manchester C	31	2		
1999–2000	Manchester C	0	0	**89**	**2**
1999–2000	*Portsmouth*	4	0		
1999–2000	Sheffield U	24	3		
2000–01	Sheffield U	36	1		
2001–02	Sheffield U	36	5		
2002–03	Sheffield U	40	16		
2003–04	Sheffield U	15	2	**151**	**27**
2003–04	Tottenham H	17	1		
2004–05	Tottenham H	24	1		
2005–06	Tottenham H	9	0	**50**	**2**
2005–06	Fulham	7	0		
2006–07	Fulham	34	0	**41**	**0**
2007–08	Wigan Ath	31	0		
2008–09	Wigan Ath	25	0		
2009–10	Wigan Ath	2	0	**58**	**0**
2009–10	Portsmouth	24	2		
2010–11	Portsmouth	21	2	**49**	**4**
2011–12	Leeds U	24	1		
2012–13	Leeds U	24	1		
2013–14	Leeds U	18	0	**66**	**2**
2014–15	Port Vale	36	4		
2015–16	Port Vale	13	0		
2016–17	Port Vale	3	0	**52**	**4**

CARLOS SALEIRO, Miguel (F) **158 27**
H: 6 1 W: 12 00 b.Lisbon 25-2-86
Internationals: Portugal U17, U18, U19, U20, U21, U23.

2005–06	Sporting Lisbon	0	0		
2005–06	*Olivais e Moscavide*	2	0		
2006–07	Sporting Lisbon	0	0		
2006–07	*Olivais e Moscavide*	24	4	**26**	**4**
2007–08	Sporting Lisbon	0	0		
2007–08	*Fatima*	26	9	**26**	**9**

2008–09 Sporting Lisbon 0 0
2008–09 *Vitoria Setubal* 5 0 **5 0**
2008–09 *Academica Coimbra* 13 4
2009–10 Sporting Lisbon 16 2
2010–11 Sporting Lisbon 27 1 **43 3**
2011–12 Servette 7 0 **7 0**
2012–13 Academica Coimbra 7 0 **20 4**
2014–15 Oriental 16 2
2015–16 Oriental 15 5 **31 7**
2016–17 Port Vale 0 0
Released August 2016.

CICILIA, Rigino (F) 74 11
b. 23-9-94
Internationals: Curacao U20.
2013–14 Roda JC 0 0
2014–15 Roda JC 20 1
2015–16 Roda JC 2 0 **22 1**
2015–16 *Waalwijk* 23 6 **23 6**
2016–17 Port Vale 29 4 **29 4**

DE FREITAS, Anthony (M) 24 0
b. 10-5-94
Internationals: France U20.
From Monaco.
2016–17 Port Vale 24 0 **24 0**

DENNIS, Luke (D) 0 0
2016–17 Port Vale 0 0

EAGLES, Chris (M) 341 54
H: 5 10 W: 11 07 b.Hemel Hempstead 19-11-85
Internationals: England Youth.
2003–04 Manchester U 0 0
2004–05 Manchester U 0 0
2004–05 *Watford* 13 1
2005–06 Manchester U 0 0
2005–06 *Sheffield W* 25 3 **25 3**
2005–06 *Watford* 17 3 **30 4**
2006–07 Manchester U 2 1
2006–07 *NEC Nijmegen* 15 1 **15 1**
2007–08 Manchester U 4 0 **6 1**
2008–09 Burnley 43 8
2009–10 Burnley 34 2
2010–11 Burnley 43 11 **120 21**
2011–12 Bolton W 34 4
2012–13 Bolton W 43 12
2013–14 Bolton W 16 1 **93 17**
2014–15 Blackpool 7 1 **7 1**
2014–15 Charlton Ath 15 2 **15 2**
2015–16 Bury 4 0 **4 0**
2016–17 Accrington S 6 0 **6 0**
2016–17 Port Vale 20 4 **20 4**

FASAN, Leonardo (G) 10 0
H: 6 2 W: 12 13 b.San Vito al Tagliamento 4-1-94
2014–15 Celtic 0 0
2015–16 Celtic 0 0
2016–17 Celtic 0 0
On loan from Celtic.
2016–17 Port Vale 10 0 **10 0**

FERGUSON, Nathan (M) 0 0
b. 12-10-95
2014–15 Dagenham & R 0 0
2015–16 Burton Alb 0 0
From Dartford.
2016–17 Port Vale 0 0

FORRESTER, Anton (F) 52 8
H: 6 0 W: 12 00 b.Liverpool 11-2-94
2010–11 Everton 0 0
2011–12 Everton 0 0
2012–13 Blackburn R 0 0
2013–14 Blackburn R 0 0
2013–14 *Bury* 28 6 **28 6**
2014–15 Blackburn R 0 0
2015–16 Blackburn R 0 0
2015–16 *Morecambe* 3 0 **3 0**
2016–17 Port Vale 21 2 **21 2**

GIBBONS, James (D) 0 0
2016–17 Port Vale 0 0

HAUGHTON, Omar (M) 0 0
H: 5 9 W: 10 08 b. 24-3-97
2015–16 Port Vale 0 0
2016–17 Port Vale 0 0

HOOPER, JJ (F) 64 10
H: 6 1 W: 13 01 b.Greenwich 9-10-93
2013–14 Northampton T 3 0
From Havant & Waterlooville.
2015–16 Port Vale 28 5
2016–17 Port Vale 23 5 **51 10**
2016–17 *Northampton T* 10 0 **13 0**

KELLY, Sam (M) 49 3
b. 21-10-93
2014–15 Norwich C 0 0
2015–16 Port Vale 28 3
2016–17 Port Vale 21 0 **49 3**

KIKO, Francisco (D) 64 3
H: 6 0 W: 12 08 b.Alcacer do Sal 20-1-93
Internationals: Portugal U19, U20.
2011–12 Vitoria Setubal 3 0
2012–13 Vitoria Setubal 6 0
2013–14 Vitoria Setubal 1 0
2014–15 Vitoria Setubal 11 0
2015–16 Vitoria Setubal 0 0 **21 0**
2015–16 *Academico Viseu* 22 3 **22 3**
2016–17 Port Vale 21 0 **21 0**

KNOPS, Kjell (D) 208 4
H: 6 0 W: 11 11 b.Wijlre 21-8-87
2008–09 Roda JC 1 0
2009–10 Roda JC 0 0 **1 0**
2010–11 EVV 26 2 **26 2**
2011–12 MVV Maastricht 32 1
2012–13 MVV Maastricht 33 1
2013–14 MVV Maastricht 25 0
2014–15 MVV Maastricht 27 0
2015–16 MVV Maastricht 35 0 **152 2**
2016–17 Port Vale 29 0 **29 0**

MACINTOSH, Calvin (D) 148 8
H: 5 11 W: 12 04 b.Amsterdam 9-8-89
From Ajax.
2009–10 Haarlem 22 1 **22 1**
2009–10 Telstar 13 0
2010–11 Telstar 9 1
2011–12 Telstar 1 0
2012–13 Telstar 30 0
2013–14 Telstar 36 4 **89 5**
2014–15 Cambuur 20 0
2015–16 Cambuur 14 2 **34 2**
2016–17 Port Vale 3 0 **3 0**
Transferred to Almere C, January 2017.

MBAMBA, Chris (M) 85 9
H: 6 0 W: 12 04 b.Harare 30-4-92
Internationals: Sweden U17.
2010 Gothenburg 0 0
2011 Gothenburg 0 0
2012 Qviding 18 1
2013 Qviding 17 2 **35 3**
2014 Medkila 14 2 **14 2**
2014 Alta 10 1 **10 1**
2015 HamKam 13 1
2016 HamKam 7 2 **20 3**
2016–17 Port Vale 6 0 **6 0**

MEHMET, Deniz (M) 11 0
b. 9-12-92
Internationals: Turkey U16, U17, U18, U19.
From Welling U.
2011–12 Kayserispor 0 0
2012–13 Kayserispor 0 0
2013–14 Kayserispor 0 0
2014–15 Kayserispor 0 0
2015–16 Falkirk 1 0
2016–17 Falkirk 1 0 **2 0**
2016–17 Port Vale 9 0 **9 0**

MIGUEL SANTOS, Silva (G) 0 0
From Benfica.
2016–17 Port Vale 0 0
Transferred to Fortuna Sittard, January 2017.

PATERSON, Martin (F) 272 57
H: 5 9 W: 10 11 b.Tunstall 13-5-87
Internationals: Northern Ireland U21, Full caps.
2004–05 Stoke C 3 0
2005–06 Stoke C 3 0
2006–07 Stoke C 9 1 **15 1**
2006–07 *Grimsby T* 15 6 **15 6**
2007–08 Scunthorpe U 40 13 **40 13**
2008–09 Burnley 43 12
2009–10 Burnley 23 4
2010–11 Burnley 11 2
2011–12 Burnley 14 3
2012–13 Burnley 39 8 **130 29**
2013–14 Huddersfield T 22 5
2013–14 *Bristol C* 8 1 **8 1**
2014–15 Huddersfield T 3 0 **25 5**
2014–15 *Fleetwood T* 3 0 **3 0**
2015 *Orlando C* 3 0 **3 0**
2015–16 Blackpool 17 0 **17 0**
2016–17 Port Vale 16 2 **16 2**

PEREIRA, Quentin (M) 26 1
H: 5 9 W: 10 06 b.Reims 21-4-92
2011–12 Stade de Reims 6 0
2012–13 Stade de Reims 0 0
2013–14 Stade de Reims 0 0 **6 0**

2015–16 Epernay Champagne 6 1 **6 1**
2016–17 Port Vale 14 0 **14 0**

POPE, Tom (F) 358 90
H: 6 3 W: 11 03 b.Stoke 27-8-85
2005–06 Crewe Alex 0 0
2006–07 Crewe Alex 4 0
2007–08 Crewe Alex 26 7
2008–09 Crewe Alex 26 10 **56 17**
2009–10 Rotherham U 35 3
2010–11 Rotherham U 18 1 **53 4**
2010–11 *Port Vale* 13 3
2011–12 Port Vale 41 5
2012–13 Port Vale 46 31
2013–14 Port Vale 43 12
2014–15 Port Vale 33 8
2015–16 Bury 36 6
2016–17 Bury 37 4 **73 10**
2016–17 Port Vale 0 0 **176 59**

PUGH, Danny (M) 325 15
H: 6 0 W: 12 10 b.Cheadle Hulme 19-10-82
2000–01 Manchester U 0 0
2001–02 Manchester U 0 0
2002–03 Manchester U 1 0
2003–04 Manchester U 0 0 **1 0**
2004–05 Leeds U 38 5
2005–06 Leeds U 12 0
2006–07 Preston NE 45 4
2007–08 Preston NE 7 0
2007–08 Stoke C 30 0
2008–09 Stoke C 17 0
2009–10 Stoke C 7 1
2010–11 Stoke C 10 0
2010–11 *Preston NE* 5 0 **57 4**
2011–12 Stoke C 3 0 **67 1**
2011–12 Leeds U 34 2
2012–13 Leeds U 4 0
2012–13 *Sheffield W* 16 1 **16 1**
2013–14 Leeds U 20 2 **108 9**
2014–15 Coventry C 5 0 **5 0**
2015–16 Bury 39 0 **39 0**
2016–17 Blackpool 18 0 **18 0**
2016–17 Port Vale 14 0 **14 0**

PURKISS, Ben (D) 182 0
H: 6 2 W: 10 13 b.Sheffield 1-4-84
2001–02 Sheffield U 0 0
2002–03 Sheffield U 0 0
From Gainsborough T, York C
2010–11 Oxford U 23 0 **23 0**
2011–12 Hereford U 15 0 **15 0**
2012–13 Walsall 27 0
2013–14 Walsall 14 0
2014–15 Walsall 32 0 **73 0**
2015–16 Port Vale 39 0
2016–17 Port Vale 32 0 **71 0**

REEVES, William (M) 12 0
b. 18-12-96
2015–16 Port Vale 0 0
2016–17 Port Vale 12 0 **12 0**

SHALAJ, Gezim (M) 156 15
b. 28-7-90
2009–10 Dudingen 14 2 **14 2**
2009–10 Kriens 7 1
2010–11 Kriens 29 0
2011–12 Kriens 13 3 **49 4**
2011–12 Luzern 1 0 **1 0**
2012–13 Lugano 20 4
2013–14 Lugano 26 1 **46 5**
2014–15 Panduri Targu 27 3 **27 3**
2015–16 Dinamo Bucharest 7 0 **7 0**
2015–16 Paralimni 5 1 **5 1**
2016–17 Enosis Neon Paralimniou 0 0
2016–17 Port Vale 7 0 **7 0**

SMITH, Nathan (D) 46 4
H: 6 0 W: 11 05 b.Madeley 3-4-96
2013–14 Port Vale 0 0
2014–15 Port Vale 0 0
2015–16 Port Vale 0 0
2016–17 Port Vale 46 4 **46 4**

STREETE, Remie (D) 52 5
H: 6 2 W: 12 13 b.Boldon 2-11-94
2011–12 Newcastle U 0 0
2012–13 Newcastle U 0 0
2013–14 Newcastle U 0 0
2014–15 Newcastle U 0 0
2014–15 *Port Vale* 2 0
2015–16 Port Vale 13 0
2016–17 Port Vale 37 5 **52 5**

TANSER, Scott (D) 54 1
b.Blackpool 23-10-94
2012–13 Rochdale 1 0
2013–14 Rochdale 0 0
2014–15 Rochdale 30 1

2015–16	Rochdale	7	0		
2016–17	Rochdale	5	0	**43**	**1**
2016–17	Port Vale	11	0	**11**	**0**

TAVARES, Paulo (M) **168 14**
H: 5 10 W: 11 03 b.Massarelos 9-12-85

2003–04	Leixoes	1	0		
2004–05	Leixoes	0	0		
2005–06	Leixoes	0	0		
2006–07	Leixoes	0	0		
2007–08	Leixoes	0	0		
2007–08	*Estoril*	13	2	**13**	**2**
2008–09	Leixoes	4	0		
2009–10	Leixoes	4	0		
2010–11	Leixoes	10	0		
2011–12	Leixoes	27	6	**46**	**6**
2012–13	Vitoria Setubal	26	2		
2013–14	Vitoria Setubal	14	3		
2014–15	Vitoria Setubal	26	1		
2015–16	Vitoria Setubal	21	0	**87**	**6**
2016–17	Port Vale	22	0	**22**	**0**

TAYLOR, Ryan (M) **272 30**
H: 5 8 W: 10 04 b.Liverpool 19-8-84
Internationals: England U21.

2001–02	Tranmere R	0	0		
2002–03	Tranmere R	25	1		
2003–04	Tranmere R	30	5		
2004–05	Tranmere R	43	8	**98**	**14**
2005–06	Wigan Ath	11	0		
2006–07	Wigan Ath	16	1		
2007–08	Wigan Ath	17	3		
2008–09	Wigan Ath	12	2	**56**	**6**
2008–09	Newcastle U	10	0		
2009–10	Newcastle U	31	4		
2010–11	Newcastle U	5	0		
2011–12	Newcastle U	31	2		
2012–13	Newcastle U	1	0		
2013–14	Newcastle U	0	0		
2014–15	Newcastle U	14	0	**92**	**6**
2015–16	Hull C	4	0	**4**	**0**
2016–17	Port Vale	22	4	**22**	**4**

THOMAS, Jerome (M) **260 23**
H: 5 9 W: 11 09 b.Wembley 23-3-83
Internationals: England U17, U19, U20, U21.

2001–02	Arsenal	0	0		
2001–02	*QPR*	4	1		
2002–03	Arsenal	0	0		
2002–03	*QPR*	6	2	**10**	**3**
2003–04	Arsenal	0	0		
2003–04	Charlton Ath	1	0		
2004–05	Charlton Ath	24	3		
2005–06	Charlton Ath	25	1		
2006–07	Charlton Ath	20	3		
2007–08	Charlton Ath	32	0		
2008–09	Charlton Ath	1	0	**103**	**7**
2008–09	Portsmouth	3	0		
2009–10	Portsmouth	0	0	**3**	**0**
2009–10	WBA	27	7		
2010–11	WBA	33	3		
2011–12	WBA	29	1		
2012–13	WBA	10	0	**99**	**11**
2012–13	*Leeds U*	6	1	**6**	**1**
2013–14	Crystal Palace	9	0		
2014–15	Crystal Palace	1	0	**10**	**0**
2015–16	Rotherham U	6	0	**6**	**0**
2016–17	Port Vale	23	1	**23**	**1**

TURNER, Dan (F) **17 0**
b. 23-6-98

2015–16	Port Vale	1	0		
2016–17	Port Vale	16	0	**17**	**0**

Players retained or with offer of contract
Slinn, Joseph Antony.

Scholars
Barton, Brian William Alan James; Benns, Harry Francis; Calveley, Michael Thomas; Conlon, Michael Joseph; Crockwell, Dequan Takai Eugene; Daulby, Thomas William; Dennis, Luke Anthony; Fraser, Benjamin Sean Michael; Grimshaw, Jack Cameron; Hill, Zak Thomas; Mottram, Liam Andrew; Ryder-Ackland, Joshua Jordan; Steele, James David; Thomas, Jake Stephen; Walford, Charlie; Ward, Matthew Joseph.

PORTSMOUTH (67)

ABORAH, Stanley (M) **150 13**
H: 5 7 W: 10 08 b.Kumasi 23-6-87
Internationals: Belgium U19.

2004–05	Ajax	4	0		
2005–06	Ajax	0	0	**4**	**0**
2005–06	*Den Bosch*	21	3		
2006–07	Dender	3	0	**3**	**0**
2007–08	Den Bosch	16	3		
2008–09	Den Bosch	21	3	**58**	**9**
2009–10	Trencin	0	0		
2010–11	Gillingham	1	0	**1**	**0**
2010–11	Capellen	14	0	**14**	**0**
2011–12	Vitesse	13	1	**13**	**1**
2012–13	Mura 05	12	1	**12**	**1**
2012–13	Ferencvaros	7	1	**7**	**1**

Unattached since 2013.

2015–16	Notts Co	26	1		
2016–17	Notts Co	8	0	**34**	**1**
2016–17	Portsmouth	4	0	**4**	**0**

BAKER, Carl (M) **355 64**
H: 6 2 W: 12 06 b.Prescot 26-12-82
Internationals: England C.

2007–08	Morecambe	42	10	**42**	**10**
2008–09	Stockport Co	22	3		
2009–10	Stockport Co	20	9	**42**	**12**
2009–10	Coventry C	22	0		
2010–11	Coventry C	32	1		
2011–12	Coventry C	26	1		
2012–13	Coventry C	43	12		
2013–14	Coventry C	37	7	**160**	**21**
2014–15	Milton Keynes D	32	9		
2015–16	Milton Keynes D	34	3	**66**	**12**
2016–17	Portsmouth	45	9	**45**	**9**

BARTON, Adam (M) **132 4**
H: 5 11 W: 12 01 b.Clitheroe 7-1-91
Internationals: Republic of Ireland U21. Northern Ireland Full caps.

2008–09	Preston NE	0	0		
2009–10	Preston NE	1	0		
2010–11	Preston NE	33	1		
2011–12	Preston NE	16	0		
2012–13	Preston NE	0	0	**50**	**1**
2012–13	Coventry C	22	3		
2013–14	Coventry C	14	0		
2013–14	*Fleetwood T*	0	0		
2014–15	Coventry C	27	0	**63**	**3**
2015–16	Portsmouth	16	0		
2016–17	Portsmouth	3	0	**19**	**0**

Transferred to Partick Thistle, August 2016.

BASS, Alex (G) **0 0**
H: 6 2 W: 11 00 b.Southampton 1-1-97

2014–15	Portsmouth	0	0		
2015–16	Portsmouth	0	0		
2016–17	Portsmouth	0	0		

BENNETT, Kyle (F) **251 30**
H: 5 5 W: 9 08 b.Telford 9-9-90
Internationals: England U18.

2007–08	Wolverhampton W	0	0		
2008–09	Wolverhampton W	0	0		
2009–10	Wolverhampton W	0	0		
2010–11	Bury	32	2	**32**	**2**
2011–12	Doncaster R	36	4		
2012–13	Doncaster R	35	3		
2013–14	Doncaster R	3	0		
2013–14	*Crawley T*	4	0	**4**	**0**
2013–14	*Bradford C*	18	1	**18**	**1**
2014–15	Doncaster R	42	8	**116**	**15**
2015–16	Portsmouth	42	6		
2016–17	Portsmouth	39	6	**81**	**12**

BURGESS, Christian (D) **153 8**
H: 6 5 W: 13 02 b. 7-10-91

2012–13	Middlesbrough	1	0		
2013–14	Middlesbrough	0	0	**1**	**0**
2013–14	*Hartlepool U*	41	0	**41**	**0**
2014–15	Peterborough U	30	2	**30**	**2**
2015–16	Portsmouth	37	2		
2016–17	Portsmouth	44	4	**81**	**6**

BUXTON, Adam (D) **56 2**
H: 6 1 W: 12 10 b.Liverpool 12-5-92

2010–11	Wigan Ath	0	0		
2011–12	Wigan Ath	0	0		
2012–13	Wigan Ath	0	0		
2013–14	Wigan Ath	0	0		
2013–14	*Burton Alb*	0	0		
2013–14	*Accrington S*	11	0		
2014–15	Accrington S	17	1		
2015–16	Accrington S	28	1	**56**	**2**
2016–17	Portsmouth	0	0		

CHAPLIN, Conor (M) **78 17**
H: 5 10 W: 10 12 b.Worthing 16-2-97

2014–15	Portsmouth	9	1		
2015–16	Portsmouth	30	8		
2016–17	Portsmouth	39	8	**78**	**17**

CLARKE, Matthew (M) **66 2**
H: 5 11 W: 11 00 b.Ipswich 22-9-96

2013–14	Ipswich T	0	0		
2014–15	Ipswich T	4	0		
2015–16	Ipswich T	0	0	**4**	**0**
2015–16	*Portsmouth*	29	1		
2016–17	Portsmouth	33	1	**62**	**2**

CLOSE, Ben (M) **13 0**
H: 5 9 W: 11 11 b.Portsmouth 8-8-96

2013–14	Portsmouth	0	0		
2014–15	Portsmouth	6	0		
2015–16	Portsmouth	7	0		
2016–17	Portsmouth	0	0	**13**	**0**

DAVIES, Tom (D) **44 1**
H: 5 11 W: 11 00 b.Warrington 18-4-92

2014–15	Fleetwood T	0	0		
2015–16	Accrington S	32	1	**32**	**1**
2016–17	Portsmouth	12	0	**12**	**0**

DOYLE, Micky (M) **585 32**
H: 5 10 W: 11 00 b.Dublin 8-7-81
Internationals: Republic of Ireland U21, Full caps.

2003–04	Coventry C	40	5		
2004–05	Coventry C	44	2		
2005–06	Coventry C	44	0		
2006–07	Coventry C	40	3		
2007–08	Coventry C	42	7		
2008–09	Coventry C	37	2		
2009–10	Coventry C	0	0		
2009–10	*Leeds U*	42	0	**42**	**0**
2010–11	Coventry C	18	1	**265**	**20**
2010–11	Sheffield U	16	0		
2011–12	Sheffield U	43	3		
2012–13	Sheffield U	43	3		
2013–14	Sheffield U	43	2		
2014–15	Sheffield U	43	1	**188**	**9**
2015–16	Portsmouth	44	2		
2016–17	Portsmouth	46	1	**90**	**3**

EVANS, Gary (F) **380 67**
H: 6 0 W: 12 08 b.Stockport 26-4-88

2007–08	Macclesfield T	42	7		
2008–09	Macclesfield T	40	12	**82**	**19**
2009–10	Bradford C	43	11		
2010–11	Bradford C	36	3	**79**	**14**
2011–12	Rotherham U	32	7		
2012–13	Rotherham U	13	2	**45**	**9**
2012–13	Fleetwood T	16	1		
2013–14	Fleetwood T	34	6		
2014–15	Fleetwood T	43	3	**93**	**10**
2015–16	Portsmouth	40	10		
2016–17	Portsmouth	41	5	**81**	**15**

HALL, Nick (G) **0 0**

2016–17	Portsmouth	0	0		

HAUNSTRUP, Brandon (D) **1 0**
b. 26-10-96

2015–16	Portsmouth	1	0		
2016–17	Portsmouth	0	0	**1**	**0**

HUNT, Noel (F) **361 72**
H: 5 8 W: 11 05 b.Waterford 26-12-82
Internationals: Republic of Ireland U21, B, Full caps.

2002–03	Dunfermline Ath	12	1		
2003–04	Dunfermline Ath	13	2		
2004–05	Dunfermline Ath	23	1		
2005–06	Dunfermline Ath	32	4	**80**	**8**
2006–07	Dundee U	28	10		
2007–08	Dundee U	36	13	**64**	**23**
2008–09	Reading	37	11		
2009–10	Reading	10	2		
2010–11	Reading	33	10		
2011–12	Reading	41	8		
2012–13	Reading	24	2	**145**	**33**
2013–14	Leeds U	19	0		
2014–15	Leeds U	1	0	**20**	**0**
2014–15	*Ipswich T*	11	3	**11**	**3**
2015–16	Southend U	21	4	**21**	**4**
2016–17	Portsmouth	20	1	**20**	**1**

KABAMBA, Nicke (F) **4 0**
H: 6 3 W: 11 11 b.Brent 1-2-93
From Uxbridge, Hayes, Burnham, Hampton & Richmond.

2016–17	Portsmouth	4	0	**4**	**0**

LALKOVIC, Milan (F) **136 14**
H: 5 9 W: 10 01 b.Kosice 9-12-92
Internationals: Slovakia U17, U19, U21.

2010–11	Chelsea	0	0		
2011–12	Chelsea	0	0		
2011–12	*Doncaster R*	6	0	**6**	**0**
2011–12	*Den Haag*	2	0	**2**	**0**
2012–13	Chelsea	0	0		
2012–13	*Vitoria Guimaraes*	8	0	**8**	**0**
2013–14	Chelsea	0	0		
2013–14	*Walsall*	38	6		
2014–15	Mlada Boleslav	6	0	**6**	**0**
2014–15	Barnsley	17	0	**17**	**0**

2015–16	Walsall	40	7	**78**	**13**
2016–17	Portsmouth	13	1	**13**	**1**
2016–17	*Ross Co*	6	0	**6**	**0**

LINGANZI, Amine (M) 68 2
H: 6 1 W: 10 00 b.Algiers 16-11-89
Internationals: DR Congo Full caps.

2008–09	St Etienne	3	0		
2009–10	St Etienne	0	0	**3**	**0**
2009–10	Blackburn R	1	0		
2010–11	Blackburn R	1	0		
2010–11	*Preston NE*	1	0	**1**	**0**
2011–12	Blackburn R	0	0		
2012–13	Blackburn R	0	0	**2**	**0**
2012–13	Accrington S	13	0	**13**	**0**
2013–14	Gillingham	20	1		
2014–15	Gillingham	7	0	**27**	**1**
2015–16	Saint-Raphael	3	0	**3**	**0**
2016–17	Portsmouth	19	1	**19**	**1**

LOWE, Jamal (F) 22 4
H: 6 0 W: 12 06 b.Harrow 21-7-94
Internationals: England C.

2012–13	Barnet	8	0	**8**	**0**

From St Albans C, Hemel Hempstead T, Hampton & Richmond.

2016–17	Portsmouth	14	4	**14**	**4**

MAIN, Curtis (F) 176 26
H: 5 9 W: 12 02 b.South Shields 20-6-92

2007–08	Darlington	1	0		
2008–09	Darlington	18	2		
2009–10	Darlington	26	3		
2010–11	Darlington	0	0	**45**	**5**
2011–12	Middlesbrough	12	2		
2012–13	Middlesbrough	13	3		
2013–14	Middlesbrough	23	1	**48**	**6**
2013–14	*Shrewsbury T*	5	0	**5**	**0**
2014–15	Doncaster R	38	8		
2015–16	Doncaster R	10	1	**48**	**9**
2015–16	*Oldham Ath*	18	4	**18**	**4**
2016–17	Portsmouth	12	2	**12**	**2**

MAY, Adam (M) 2 0
b. 6-12-97

2014–15	Portsmouth	1	0		
2015–16	Portsmouth	1	0		
2016–17	Portsmouth	0	0	**2**	**0**

NAISMITH, Kal (F) 133 30
H: 5 7 W: 13 02 b.Glasgow 18-2-92
Internationals: Scotland U16, U17.

2013–14	Accrington S	38	10		
2014–15	Accrington S	35	4	**73**	**14**
2015–16	Portsmouth	19	3		
2015–16	*Hartlepool U*	4	0	**4**	**0**
2016–17	Portsmouth	37	13	**56**	**16**

O'BRIEN, Liam (G) 55 0
H: 6 1 W: 12 06 b.Ruislip 30-11-91
Internationals: England U19.

2008–09	Portsmouth	0	0		
2009–10	Portsmouth	0	0		
2010–11	Barnet	8	0		
2011–12	Barnet	10	0		
2012–13	Barnet	3	0	**21**	**0**
2013–14	Brentford	0	0		
2014–15	Dagenham & R	10	0		
2015–16	Dagenham & R	24	0	**34**	**0**
2016–17	Portsmouth	0	0		

OXLADE-CHAMBERLAIN, Christian (D) 0 0
b. 24-6-98

2015–16	Portsmouth	0	0		
2016–17	Portsmouth	0	0		

ROBERTS, Gary (F) 421 80
H: 5 10 W: 11 09 b.Chester 18-3-84
Internationals: England C.

2006–07	Accrington S	14	8	**14**	**8**
2006–07	Ipswich T	33	2		
2007–08	Ipswich T	21	1	**54**	**3**
2007–08	*Crewe Alex*	4	0	**4**	**0**
2008–09	Huddersfield T	43	9		
2009–10	Huddersfield T	43	7		
2010–11	Huddersfield T	37	9		
2011–12	Huddersfield T	39	6	**162**	**31**
2012–13	Swindon T	39	4	**39**	**4**
2013–14	Chesterfield	40	11		
2014–15	Chesterfield	34	6	**74**	**17**
2015–16	Portsmouth	33	7		
2016–17	Portsmouth	41	10	**74**	**17**

ROSE, Danny (M) 169 14
H: 5 7 W: 10 04 b.Bristol 21-2-88
Internationals: England C.

2006–07	Manchester U	0	0		
2007–08	Manchester U	0	0		

From Oxford U, Newport Co

2012–13	Fleetwood T	0	0		
2012–13	*Aldershot T*	34	2	**34**	**2**
2013–14	Oxford U	40	4		
2014–15	Oxford U	29	2		
2015–16	Oxford U	13	0	**82**	**6**
2015–16	Northampton T	15	1	**15**	**1**
2016–17	Portsmouth	38	5	**38**	**5**

SMITH, Michael (F) 163 43
H: 6 4 W: 11 02 b.Wallsend 17-10-91

2011–12	Charlton Ath	0	0		
2011–12	*Accrington S*	6	3	**6**	**3**
2012–13	Charlton Ath	0	0		
2012–13	*Colchester U*	8	1	**8**	**1**
2013–14	Charlton Ath	0	0		
2013–14	*AFC Wimbledon*	23	9	**23**	**9**
2013–14	Swindon T	20	8		
2014–15	Swindon T	40	13		
2015–16	Swindon T	5	0	**65**	**21**
2015–16	*Barnsley*	13	0	**13**	**0**
2015–16	*Portsmouth*	16	4		
2016–17	Portsmouth	18	3	**34**	**7**
2016–17	*Northampton T*	14	2	**14**	**2**

TALBOT, Drew (F) 339 23
H: 5 10 W: 11 00 b.Barnsley 19-7-86

2003–04	Sheffield W	0	0		
2004–05	Sheffield W	21	4		
2005–06	Sheffield W	0	0		
2006–07	Sheffield W	8	0	**29**	**4**
2006–07	*Scunthorpe U*	3	1	**3**	**1**
2006–07	Luton T	15	3		
2007–08	Luton T	27	0		
2008–09	Luton T	7	0	**49**	**3**
2008–09	*Chesterfield*	17	2		
2009–10	Chesterfield	30	6		
2010–11	Chesterfield	44	3		
2011–12	Chesterfield	43	2		
2012–13	Chesterfield	42	2		
2013–14	Chesterfield	25	0		
2014–15	Chesterfield	9	0		
2014–15	*Plymouth Arg*	9	0	**9**	**0**
2015–16	Chesterfield	34	0	**244**	**15**
2016–17	Portsmouth	5	0	**5**	**0**

TOLLITT, Ben (M) 12 1
b. 30-11-94

2015–16	Portsmouth	12	1		
2016–17	Portsmouth	0	0	**12**	**1**

WHATMOUGH, Jack (D) 46 1
b.Gosport 19-8-96
Internationals: England U18, U19.

2012–13	Portsmouth	0	0		
2013–14	Portsmouth	12	0		
2014–15	Portsmouth	22	0		
2015–16	Portsmouth	2	0		
2016–17	Portsmouth	10	1	**46**	**1**

Players retained or with offer of contract
Procter, Andrew John.

Scholars
Bedford, Jeremy-Finley Dylan; Bradbury, Harvey Lee; Brooks, Jordan Antony Brian; Casey, Matthew Adam; Chandler, Jack Raymond; Collins, Jack; Hall, Nicholas Adam; Mayes, Matthew James; McDowell, Kyle John; Saidy, Ousman; Scutt, Tommy Joel; Smith, Daniel Lewis; Wakley, Eddie Mitchell; Widdrington, Theo Jack.

PRESTON NE (68)

BARKHUIZEN, Tom (F) 148 34
H: 5 9 W: 11 00 b.Blackpool 4-7-93

2011–12	Blackpool	0	0		
2011–12	*Hereford U*	38	11	**38**	**11**
2012–13	Blackpool	0	0		
2012–13	*Fleetwood T*	13	1	**13**	**1**
2013–14	Blackpool	14	1		
2014–15	Blackpool	7	0	**21**	**1**
2014–15	*Morecambe*	5	0		
2015–16	Morecambe	40	10		
2016–17	Morecambe	14	5	**59**	**15**
2016–17	Preston NE	17	6	**17**	**6**

BECKFORD, Jermaine (F) 343 127
H: 6 2 W: 13 02 b.Ealing 9-12-83
Internationals: Jamaica Full caps.

2005–06	Leeds U	5	0		
2006–07	Leeds U	5	0		
2006–07	*Carlisle U*	4	1	**4**	**1**
2006–07	*Scunthorpe U*	18	8	**18**	**8**
2007–08	Leeds U	40	20		
2008–09	Leeds U	34	26		
2009–10	Leeds U	42	25	**126**	**71**
2010–11	Everton	32	8		
2011–12	Everton	2	0	**34**	**8**
2011–12	Leicester C	39	9		
2012–13	Leicester C	4	0	**43**	**9**
2012–13	*Huddersfield T*	21	8	**21**	**8**
2013–14	Bolton W	33	7		
2014–15	Bolton W	13	0	**46**	**7**
2014–15	*Preston NE*	23	12		
2015–16	Preston NE	10	2		
2016–17	Preston NE	18	1	**51**	**15**

BOYLE, Andrew (D) 7 0
H: 5 10 W: 12 02 b.Dublin 7-3-91
Internationals: Republic of Ireland U18, U19, Full caps.
From Dundalk.

2016–17	Preston NE	7	0	**7**	**0**

BROWNE, Alan (M) 95 7
H: 5 8 W: 11 03 b.Cork 15-4-95
Internationals: Republic of Ireland U19, U21, Full caps.

2013–14	Preston NE	8	1		
2014–15	Preston NE	20	3		
2015–16	Preston NE	36	3		
2016–17	Preston NE	31	0	**95**	**7**

CLARKE, Tom (D) 274 12
H: 6 0 W: 11 02 b.Sowerby Bridge 21-12-87
Internationals: England U18, U19.

2004–05	Huddersfield T	12	0		
2005–06	Huddersfield T	17	1		
2006–07	Huddersfield T	9	0		
2007–08	Huddersfield T	3	0		
2008–09	Huddersfield T	15	1		
2008–09	*Bradford C*	6	0	**6**	**0**
2009–10	Huddersfield T	21	0		
2010–11	Huddersfield T	5	1		
2011–12	Huddersfield T	14	0		
2011–12	*Leyton Orient*	10	0	**10**	**0**
2012–13	Huddersfield T	0	0	**96**	**3**
2013–14	Preston NE	42	4		
2014–15	Preston NE	43	1		
2015–16	Preston NE	35	0		
2016–17	Preston NE	42	4	**162**	**9**

CUNNINGHAM, Greg (D) 216 7
H: 6 0 W: 11 00 b.Galway 31-1-91
Internationals: Republic of Ireland U17, U21, Full caps.

2008–09	Manchester C	0	0		
2009–10	Manchester C	2	0		
2010–11	Manchester C	0	0		
2010–11	*Leicester C*	13	0	**13**	**0**
2011–12	Manchester C	0	0		
2011–12	*Nottingham F*	27	0	**27**	**0**
2012–13	Manchester C	0	0	**2**	**0**
2012–13	Bristol C	30	1		
2013–14	Bristol C	37	1		
2014–15	Bristol C	24	2	**91**	**4**
2015–16	Preston NE	43	2		
2016–17	Preston NE	40	1	**83**	**3**

DAVIES, Ben (D) 95 1
H: 6 1 W: 11 09 b.Barrow 11-8-95

2012–13	Preston NE	3	0		
2013–14	Preston NE	0	0		
2013–14	*York C*	44	0	**44**	**0**
2014–15	Preston NE	4	0		
2014–15	*Tranmere R*	3	0	**3**	**0**
2015–16	Preston NE	0	0		
2015–16	*Newport Co*	19	0	**19**	**0**
2016–17	Preston NE	0	0	**7**	**0**
2016–17	*Fleetwood T*	22	1	**22**	**1**

DOYLE, Eoin (F) 269 84
H: 6 0 W: 11 07 b.Tallaght 12-3-88

2009	Sligo	15	3		
2010	Sligo	35	6		
2011	Sligo	34	20	**84**	**29**
2011–12	Hibernian	13	1		
2012–13	Hibernian	36	10	**49**	**11**
2013–14	Chesterfield	43	11		
2014–15	Chesterfield	26	21	**69**	**32**
2014–15	Cardiff C	16	5		
2015–16	Cardiff C	0	0	**16**	**5**
2015–16	*Preston NE*	28	4		
2016–17	Preston NE	11	1	**39**	**5**
2016–17	*Portsmouth*	12	2	**12**	**2**

GALLAGHER, Paul (F) 434 76
H: 6 1 W: 11 00 b.Glasgow 9-8-84
Internationals: Scotland U21, B, Full caps.

2002–03	Blackburn R	1	0		
2003–04	Blackburn R	26	3		
2004–05	Blackburn R	16	2		
2005–06	Blackburn R	1	0		
2005–06	*Stoke C*	37	11		
2006–07	Blackburn R	16	1		
2007–08	Blackburn R	0	0		
2007–08	*Preston NE*	19	1		

2007–08	*Stoke C*	7	0	**44**	**11**
2008–09	Blackburn R	0	0		
2008–09	*Plymouth Arg*	40	13	**40**	**13**
2009–10	Blackburn R	1	0	**61**	**6**
2009–10	Leicester C	41	7		
2010–11	Leicester C	41	10		
2011–12	Leicester C	28	8		
2012–13	Leicester C	8	0		
2012–13	Sheffield U	6	1	**6**	**1**
2013–14	Leicester C	0	0		
2013–14	*Preston NE*	28	6		
2014–15	Leicester C	0	0	**118**	**25**
2014–15	*Preston NE*	46	7		
2015–16	Preston NE	41	5		
2016–17	Preston NE	31	1	**165**	**20**

GARNER, Joe (F) 300 91
H: 5 10 W: 11 02 b.Blackburn 12-4-88
Internationals: England U16, U17, U19.

2004–05	Blackburn R	0	0		
2005–06	Blackburn R	0	0		
2006–07	Blackburn R	0	0		
2006–07	*Carlisle U*	18	5		
2007–08	Carlisle U	31	14		
2008–09	Nottingham F	28	7		
2009–10	Nottingham F	18	2		
2010–11	Nottingham F	0	0		
2010–11	*Huddersfield T*	16	0	**16**	**0**
2010–11	*Scunthorpe U*	18	6	**18**	**6**
2011–12	Nottingham F	2	0	**48**	**9**
2011–12	Watford	22	1		
2012–13	Watford	2	0	**24**	**1**
2012–13	*Carlisle U*	16	7	**65**	**26**
2012–13	Preston NE	14	0		
2013–14	Preston NE	35	18		
2014–15	Preston NE	37	25		
2015–16	Preston NE	41	6		
2016–17	Preston NE	2	0	**129**	**49**

Transferred to Rangers, August 2016.

GRIMSHAW, Liam (D) 18 0
H: 5 10 W: 11 11 b.Burnley 2-2-95
Internationals: England U18.

2013–14	Manchester U	0	0		
2013–14	*Morecambe*	0	0		
2015–16	Manchester U	0	0		
2015–16	*Motherwell*	0	0		
2015–16	Preston NE	0	0		
2016–17	Preston NE	5	0	**5**	**0**
2016–17	*Chesterfield*	13	0	**13**	**0**

HORGAN, Daryl (M) 19 2
H: 5 7 W: 10 10 b.Galway 10-8-92
Internationals: Republic of Ireland U19, U21, Full caps.
From Dundalk.

2016–17	Preston NE	19	2	**19**	**2**

HUDSON, Matthew (G) 1 0
H: 6 4 b.Southport 29-7-98

2014–15	Preston NE	0	0		
2015–16	Preston NE	1	0		
2016–17	Preston NE	0	0	**1**	**0**

HUGILL, Jordan (F) 110 24
H: 6 0 W: 10 01 b.Middlesbrough 4-6-92

2013–14	Port Vale	20	4	**20**	**4**
2014–15	Preston NE	3	0		
2014–15	*Tranmere R*	6	1	**6**	**1**
2014–15	*Hartlepool U*	8	4	**8**	**4**
2015–16	Preston NE	29	3		
2016–17	Preston NE	44	12	**76**	**15**

HUMPHREY, Chris (M) 312 16
H: 5 11 W: 11 07 b.Walsall 19-9-87
Internationals: Jamaica Full caps.

2006–07	Shrewsbury T	12	0		
2007–08	Shrewsbury T	25	0		
2008–09	Shrewsbury T	37	2	**74**	**2**
2009–10	Motherwell	28	0		
2010–11	Motherwell	36	3		
2011–12	Motherwell	35	2		
2012–13	Motherwell	33	3	**132**	**8**
2013–14	Preston NE	42	2		
2014–15	Preston NE	44	4		
2015–16	Preston NE	10	0		
2016–17	Preston NE	10	0	**106**	**6**

Transferred to Hibernian, December 2016.

HUNTINGTON, Paul (D) 298 21
H: 6 3 W: 12 08 b.Carlisle 17-9-87
Internationals: England U18.

2005–06	Newcastle U	0	0		
2006–07	Newcastle U	11	1		
2007–08	Newcastle U	0	0	**11**	**1**
2007–08	Leeds U	17	2		
2008–09	Leeds U	4	0		
2009–10	Leeds U	0	0	**21**	**2**
2009–10	Stockport Co	26	0	**26**	**0**
2010–11	Yeovil T	40	5		
2011–12	Yeovil T	37	2	**77**	**7**
2012–13	Preston NE	37	3		
2013–14	Preston NE	23	2		
2014–15	Preston NE	32	5		
2015–16	Preston NE	38	0		
2016–17	Preston NE	33	1	**163**	**11**

JOHNSON, Daniel (M) 125 23
H: 5 8 W: 10 07 b.Kingston, Jamaica 8-10-92

2010–11	Aston Villa	0	0		
2011–12	Aston Villa	0	0		
2012–13	Aston Villa	0	0		
2012–13	*Yeovil T*	5	0	**5**	**0**
2013–14	Aston Villa	0	0		
2014–15	Aston Villa	0	0		
2014–15	*Chesterfield*	11	0	**11**	**0**
2014–15	*Oldham Ath*	6	3	**6**	**3**
2014–15	Preston NE	20	8		
2015–16	Preston NE	43	8		
2016–17	Preston NE	40	4	**103**	**20**

LINDEGAARD, Anders (G) 113 0
H: 6 4 W: 12 08 b.Odense 13-4-84
Internationals: Denmark U19, U20, Full caps.

2003–04	Odense	0	0		
2004–05	Odense	0	0		
2005–06	Odense	0	0		
2006–07	Odense	1	0		
2007–08	Odense	1	0		
2008–09	*Kolding*	10	0	**10**	**0**
2009	*Aalesund*	26	0		
2009	Odense	4	0	**6**	**0**
2010	Aalesund	30	0	**56**	**0**
2010–11	Manchester U	0	0		
2011–12	Manchester U	8	0		
2012–13	Manchester U	10	0		
2013–14	Manchester U	1	0		
2014–15	Manchester U	0	0		
2015–16	Manchester U	0	0	**19**	**0**
2015–16	WBA	0	0		
2015–16	*Preston NE*	14	0		
2016–17	Preston NE	8	0	**22**	**0**

MAKIENOK CHRISTOFFERSEN, Simon (F) 199 65
H: 6 7 W: 14 11 b.Naestved 21-11-90
Internationals: Denmark U19, U20, U21, Full caps.

2008–09	Herfolge	4	0	**4**	**0**
2009–10	HB Koge	11	1		
2010–11	HB Koge	28	16		
2011–12	HB Koge	17	5	**56**	**22**
2011–12	Brondby	14	5		
2012–13	Brondby	31	15		
2013–14	Brondby	24	12		
2014–15	Brondby	5	3	**74**	**35**
2014–15	Palermo	4	0		
2015–16	Palermo	0	0		
2015–16	*Charlton Ath*	36	5	**36**	**5**
2016–17	Palermo	0	0	**4**	**0**

On loan from Palermo.

2016–17	Preston NE	25	3	**25**	**3**

MAXWELL, Chris (G) 148 0
H: 6 0 W: 11 07 b.Wrexham 30-7-90
Internationals: Wales U17, U19, U21, U23.

2012–13	Fleetwood T	0	0		
2013–14	Fleetwood T	18	0		
2014–15	Fleetwood T	46	0		
2015–16	Fleetwood T	46	0	**110**	**0**
2016–17	Preston NE	38	0	**38**	**0**

MAY, Stevie (F) 167 75
H: 5 3 W: 9 07 b.Perth 3-11-92
Internationals: Scotland U20, U21, Full caps.

2008–09	St Johnstone	1	1		
2009–10	St Johnstone	0	0		
2010–11	St Johnstone	19	2		
2011–12	St Johnstone	1	0		
2011–12	*Alloa Ath*	22	19	**22**	**19**
2012–13	St Johnstone	3	0		
2012–13	*Hamilton A*	33	25	**33**	**25**
2013–14	St Johnstone	38	20	**62**	**23**
2014–15	Sheffield W	39	7		
2015–16	Sheffield W	0	0	**39**	**7**
2015–16	Preston NE	7	0		
2016–17	Preston NE	4	1	**11**	**1**

PEARSON, Ben (M) 91 3
H: 5 5 W: 11 03 b.Oldham 4-1-95
Internationals: England U16, U17, U18, U19, U21, Full caps.

2013–14	Manchester U	0	0		
2014–15	Manchester U	0	0		
2014–15	*Barnsley*	22	1		
2015–16	Manchester U	0	0		
2015–16	*Barnsley*	23	1	**45**	**2**
2015–16	Preston NE	15	0		
2016–17	Preston NE	31	1	**46**	**1**

PRINGLE, Ben (M) 207 23
H: 5 8 W: 11 10 b.Whitley Bay 25-7-88

2009–10	Derby Co	5	0		
2010–11	Derby Co	15	0	**20**	**0**
2010–11	*Torquay U*	5	0	**5**	**0**
2011–12	Rotherham U	21	4		
2012–13	Rotherham U	41	7		
2013–14	Rotherham U	45	5		
2014–15	Rotherham U	40	3	**147**	**19**
2015–16	Fulham	15	2	**15**	**2**
2015–16	*Ipswich T*	10	2	**10**	**2**
2016–17	Preston NE	10	0	**10**	**0**

ROBINSON, Callum (F) 91 16
H: 5 10 W: 11 11 b.Birmingham 2-2-95
Internationals: England U16, U17, U19, U20.

2013–14	Aston Villa	4	0		
2014–15	Aston Villa	0	0		
2014–15	*Preston NE*	25	4		
2015–16	Aston Villa	0	0	**4**	**0**
2015–16	*Bristol C*	6	0	**6**	**0**
2015–16	*Preston NE*	14	2		
2016–17	Preston NE	42	10	**81**	**16**

SMITH, Clive (D) 3 0
H: 5 10 W: 11 00 b. 12-12-97
Internationals: Wales U17.

2015–16	Preston NE	0	0		
2016–17	Preston NE	0	0		
2016–17	*St Johnstone*	3	0	**3**	**0**

SPURR, Tommy (D) 352 10
H: 6 1 W: 11 05 b.Leeds 13-9-87

2005–06	Sheffield W	2	0		
2006–07	Sheffield W	36	0		
2007–08	Sheffield W	41	2		
2008–09	Sheffield W	41	2		
2009–10	Sheffield W	46	1		
2010–11	Sheffield W	26	0	**192**	**5**
2011–12	Doncaster R	19	0		
2012–13	Doncaster R	46	1		
2013–14	Doncaster R	0	0	**65**	**1**
2013–14	Blackburn R	43	3		
2014–15	Blackburn R	12	0		
2015–16	Blackburn R	23	0	**78**	**3**
2016–17	Preston NE	17	1	**17**	**1**

VERMIJL, Marnick (D) 85 6
H: 5 11 W: 11 12 b.Overpelt 13-1-92
Internationals: Belgium U17, U18, U19, U21.

2010–11	Manchester U	0	0		
2011–12	Manchester U	0	0		
2012–13	Manchester U	0	0		
2013–14	Manchester U	0	0		
2013–14	*NEC*	28	3	**28**	**3**
2014–15	Manchester U	0	0		
2014–15	Sheffield W	11	0		
2015–16	Preston NE	28	1		
2016–17	Sheffield W	0	0	**11**	**0**
2016–17	Preston NE	18	2	**46**	**3**

WELSH, John (M) 333 17
H: 5 7 W: 12 02 b.Liverpool 10-1-84
Internationals: England U20, U21.

2000–01	Liverpool	0	0		
2001–02	Liverpool	0	0		
2002–03	Liverpool	0	0		
2003–04	Liverpool	1	0		
2004–05	Liverpool	3	0		
2005–06	Liverpool	0	0	**4**	**0**
2005–06	Hull C	32	2		
2006–07	Hull C	18	1		
2007–08	Hull C	0	0		
2007–08	*Chester C*	6	0	**6**	**0**
2008–09	Hull C	0	0	**50**	**3**
2008–09	*Carlisle U*	4	0	**4**	**0**
2008–09	*Bury*	5	0	**5**	**0**
2009–10	Tranmere R	45	4		
2010–11	Tranmere R	41	4		
2011–12	Tranmere R	44	3	**130**	**11**
2012–13	Preston NE	36	1		
2013–14	Preston NE	36	2		
2014–15	Preston NE	32	0		
2015–16	Preston NE	24	0		
2016–17	Preston NE	6	0	**134**	**3**

WOODS, Calum (D) 250 11
H: 5 11 W: 11 07 b.Liverpool 5-2-87

2006–07	Dunfermline Ath	12	0		
2007–08	Dunfermline Ath	25	0		
2008–09	Dunfermline Ath	30	5		
2009–10	Dunfermline Ath	29	2		
2010–11	Dunfermline Ath	32	3	**128**	**10**
2011–12	Huddersfield T	26	0		
2012–13	Huddersfield T	27	0		
2013–14	Huddersfield T	19	1	**72**	**1**
2014–15	Preston NE	18	0		
2015–16	Preston NE	32	0		
2016–17	Preston NE	0	0	**50**	**0**

Scholars
Barry, Thomas Michael Robinson; Burgoyne, Jack Geoffrey; Campbell, Kamol Shawn; Davidson, Dylan Gary Iain; Earl, Joshua John Francis; Fensome, Lewis George; Garstang, Harry Charles; Howard, Michael Leslie; Kwateng, Akwasi Oduro; Lyons, Charlie; Mason, Myles Jacob David; Meulensteen, Melle Reinhard Maria; O'Neil, Oscar Brian; Roberts, Lee Callum Thornill; Smart, Kian Michael Allan; Stead, Thomas; Tait, Callum Joseph; Wood, Alexander Stuart.

QPR (69)

BIDWELL, Jake (D) **226 3**
H: 6 0 W: 11 00 b.Southport 21-3-93
Internationals: England U16, U17, U18, U19.

2009–10	Everton	0	0		
2010–11	Everton	0	0		
2011–12	Everton	0	0		
2011–12	*Brentford*	24	0		
2012–13	Everton	0	0		
2012–13	*Brentford*	40	0		
2013–14	Brentford	38	0		
2014–15	Brentford	43	0		
2015–16	Brentford	45	3	**190**	**3**
2016–17	QPR	36	0	**36**	**0**

BORYSIUK, Ariel (M) **230 7**
H: 5 10 W: 11 00 b.Biala Podlaska 29-7-91
Internationals: Poland U17, U19, U20, U21.

2007–08	Legia Warsaw	8	1		
2008–09	Legia Warsaw	18	0		
2009–10	Legia Warsaw	23	0		
2010–11	Legia Warsaw	26	2		
2011–12	Legia Warsaw	15	1		
2011–12	Kaiserslautern	12	0		
2012–13	Kaiserslautern	28	0		
2013–14	Kaiserslautern	4	0		
2013–14	*Volga*	4	0	**4**	**0**
2014–15	Kaiserslautern	0	0	**44**	**0**
2014–15	*Lechia Gdansk*	34	0		
2015–16	Lechia Gdansk	20	2		
2015–16	Legia Warsaw	13	0	**103**	**4**
2016–17	QPR	11	0	**11**	**0**
2016–17	*Lechia Gdansk*	14	1	**68**	**3**

BOWLER, Josh (M) **1 0**
b. 5-3-99

2016–17	QPR	1	0	**1**	**0**

CAULKER, Steven (D) **209 12**
H: 6 3 W: 12 00 b.Feltham 29-12-91
Internationals: England U19 U21, Full caps. Great Britain.

2009–10	Tottenham H	0	0		
2009–10	*Yeovil T*	44	0	**44**	**0**
2010–11	Tottenham H	0	0		
2010–11	*Bristol C*	29	2	**29**	**2**
2011–12	Tottenham H	0	0		
2011–12	*Swansea C*	26	0	**26**	**0**
2012–13	Tottenham H	18	2	**18**	**2**
2013–14	Cardiff C	38	5	**38**	**5**
2014–15	QPR	35	1		
2015–16	QPR	0	0		
2015–16	*Southampton*	3	0	**3**	**0**
2015–16	*Liverpool*	3	0	**3**	**0**
2016–17	QPR	13	2	**48**	**3**

CHERY, Tjaronn (M) **275 59**
H: 5 7 W: 10 10 b.Enschede 4-6-88

2008–09	FC Twente	1	0		
2008–09	*Cambuur*	15	0	**15**	**0**
2009–10	FC Twente	0	0	**1**	**0**
2009–10	*Roosendaal*	30	1	**30**	**1**
2010–11	Emmen	33	9	**33**	**9**
2011–12	Den Haag	34	2		
2012–13	Den Haag	32	8		
2013–14	Den Haag	0	0	**66**	**10**
2013–14	*Groningen*	35	10		
2014–15	Groningen	34	15	**69**	**25**
2015–16	QPR	39	10		
2016–17	QPR	22	4	**61**	**14**

Transferred to Guizhou Hengfeng Zhicheng, January 2017.

COMLEY, Brandon (M) **47 0**
H: 5 11 W: 11 05 b.Islington 18-11-95

2014–15	QPR	1	0		
2015–16	QPR	0	0		
2015–16	*Carlisle U*	12	0	**12**	**0**
2016–17	QPR	1	0	**2**	**0**
2016–17	*Grimsby T*	33	0	**33**	**0**

COUSINS, Jordan (D) **143 7**
H: 5 10 W: 11 05 b.Greenwich 6-3-94
Internationals: England U16, U17, U18, U20.

2011–12	Charlton Ath	0	0		
2012–13	Charlton Ath	0	0		
2013–14	Charlton Ath	42	2		
2014–15	Charlton Ath	44	3		
2015–16	Charlton Ath	39	2	**125**	**7**
2016–17	QPR	18	0	**18**	**0**

DOUGHTY, Michael (M) **117 9**
H: 6 1 W: 12 10 b.Westminster 20-11-92
Internationals: Wales U19, U21.

2010–11	QPR	0	0		
2011–12	QPR	0	0		
2011–12	*Crawley T*	16	0	**16**	**0**
2011–12	*Aldershot T*	5	0	**5**	**0**
2012–13	QPR	0	0		
2012–13	*St Johnstone*	5	0	**5**	**0**
2013–14	QPR	0	0		
2013–14	*Stevenage*	36	2	**36**	**2**
2014–15	QPR	3	0		
2014–15	*Gillingham*	9	0	**9**	**0**
2015–16	QPR	5	0		
2015–16	*Swindon T*	20	5		
2016–17	QPR	4	0	**12**	**0**
2016–17	*Swindon T*	14	2	**34**	**7**

EL KHAYATI, Abdenasser (F) **103 29**
H: 6 1 W: 11 11 b.Rotterdam 7-2-89

2008–09	Den Bosh	8	0	**8**	**0**
2009–10	Dan Bosh	2	0	**2**	**0**
2010–11	Breda	0	0		
2012–13	Olympiacos	0	0		
2014–15	Kozakken Boys	17	12	**17**	**12**
2014–15	Burton Alb	18	3		
2015–16	Burton Alb	24	8	**42**	**11**
2015–16	QPR	16	1		
2016–17	QPR	6	0	**22**	**1**
2016–17	*ADO Den Haag*	12	5	**12**	**5**

EMMANUEL-THOMAS, Jay (M) **237 51**
H: 5 9 W: 11 05 b.Forest Gate 27-12-90
Internationals: England U17, U19.

2008–09	Arsenal	0	0		
2009–10	Arsenal	0	0		
2009–10	*Blackpool*	11	1	**11**	**1**
2009–10	*Doncaster R*	14	5	**14**	**5**
2010–11	Arsenal	1	0	**1**	**0**
2010–11	*Cardiff C*	14	2	**14**	**2**
2011–12	Ipswich T	42	6		
2012–13	Ipswich T	29	2	**71**	**8**
2013–14	Bristol C	46	15		
2014–15	Bristol C	36	9	**82**	**24**
2015–16	QPR	12	3		
2015–16	*Milton Keynes D*	4	0	**4**	**0**
2016–17	QPR	0	0	**12**	**3**
2016–17	*Gillingham*	28	8	**28**	**8**

EZE, Eberechi (M) **0 0**
From Millwall.

2016–17	QPR	0	0		

FREEMAN, Luke (F) **245 29**
H: 6 0 W: 10 00 b.Dartford 22-3-92
Internationals: England U16, U17.

2007–08	Gillingham	1	0	**1**	**0**
2008–09	Arsenal	0	0		
2009–10	Arsenal	0	0		
2010–11	Arsenal	0	0		
2010–11	*Yeovil T*	13	2	**13**	**2**
2011–12	Arsenal	0	0		
2011–12	Stevenage	26	7		
2012–13	Stevenage	39	2		
2013–14	Stevenage	45	6	**110**	**15**
2014–15	Bristol C	46	7		
2015–16	Bristol C	41	1		
2016–17	Bristol C	18	2	**105**	**10**
2016–17	QPR	16	2	**16**	**2**

FURLONG, Darnell (D) **72 2**
b. 31-10-95

2014–15	QPR	3	0		
2015–16	QPR	0	0		
2015–16	*Northampton T*	10	0	**10**	**0**
2015–16	*Cambridge U*	21	0	**21**	**0**
2016–17	QPR	14	0	**17**	**0**
2016–17	*Swindon T*	24	2	**24**	**2**

GLADWIN, Ben (D) **93 12**
H: 6 3 b.Reading 8-6-92

2013–14	Swindon T	13	0		
2014–15	Swindon T	34	8		
2015–16	QPR	7	0		
2015–16	*Swindon T*	13	2		
2015–16	*Bristol C*	1	0	**1**	**0**
2016–17	QPR	7	0	**14**	**0**
2016–17	*Swindon T*	18	2	**78**	**12**

GOSS, Sean (M) **6 0**
H: 5 10 W: 11 03 b.Wegberg 1-10-95

2015–16	Manchester U	0	0		
2016–17	Manchester U	0	0		
2016–17	QPR	6	0	**6**	**0**

GREGO-COX, Reece (F) **12 0**
H: 5 7 W: 10 03 b.Hammersmith 12-11-96
Internationals: Republic of Ireland U17, U19, U21.

2014–15	QPR	4	0		
2015–16	QPR	0	0		
2016–17	Newport Co	7	0	**7**	**0**
2016–17	QPR	1	0	**5**	**0**

HALL, Grant (D) **120 2**
H: 5 9 W: 11 02 b.Brighton 29-10-91

2009–10	Brighton & HA	0	0		
2010–11	Brighton & HA	0	0		
2011–12	Brighton & HA	1	0	**1**	**0**
2012–13	Tottenham H	0	0		
2013–14	Tottenham H	0	0		
2013–14	*Swindon T*	27	0	**27**	**0**
2014–15	Tottenham H	0	0		
2014–15	*Birmingham C*	7	0	**7**	**0**
2014–15	*Blackpool*	12	1	**12**	**1**
2015–16	QPR	39	1		
2016–17	QPR	34	0	**73**	**1**

HAMALAINEN, Niko (M) **4 0**
b.Florida 3-5-97
Internationals: Finland U18, U19, U21.

2014–15	QPR	0	0		
2015–16	QPR	0	0		
2015–16	*Dagenham & R*	1	0	**1**	**0**
2016–17	QPR	3	0	**3**	**0**

HENRY, Karl (M) **491 10**
H: 6 0 W: 12 00 b.Wolverhampton 26-11-82
Internationals: England U20.

1999–2000	Stoke C	0	0		
2000–01	Stoke C	0	0		
2001–02	Stoke C	24	0		
2002–03	Stoke C	18	1		
2003–04	Stoke C	20	0		
2003–04	*Cheltenham T*	9	1	**9**	**1**
2004–05	Stoke C	34	0		
2005–06	Stoke C	24	0	**120**	**1**
2006–07	Wolverhampton W	34	3		
2007–08	Wolverhampton W	40	3		
2008–09	Wolverhampton W	43	0		
2009–10	Wolverhampton W	34	0		
2010–11	Wolverhampton W	29	0		
2011–12	Wolverhampton W	31	0		
2012–13	Wolverhampton W	39	0	**250**	**6**
2013–14	QPR	27	1		
2014–15	QPR	33	0		
2015–16	QPR	38	1		
2016–17	QPR	14	0	**112**	**2**

INGRAM, Matt (G) **128 0**
H: 6 3 W: 12 13 b.Croydon 18-12-93

2011–12	Wycombe W	0	0		
2012–13	Wycombe W	8	0		
2013–14	Wycombe W	46	0		
2014–15	Wycombe W	46	0		
2015–16	Wycombe W	24	0	**124**	**0**
2015–16	QPR	4	0		
2016–17	QPR	0	0	**4**	**0**

LUONGO, Massimo (F) **159 14**
H: 5 8 W: 11 10 b.Sydney 25-9-92
Internationals: Australia U20, Full caps.

2010–11	Tottenham H	0	0		
2011–12	Tottenham H	0	0		
2012–13	Tottenham H	0	0		
2012–13	*Ipswich T*	9	0	**9**	**0**
2012–13	*Swindon T*	7	1		
2013–14	Swindon T	44	6		
2014–15	Swindon T	34	6	**85**	**13**
2015–16	QPR	30	0		
2016–17	QPR	35	1	**65**	**1**

LYNCH, Joel (D) **311 16**
H: 6 1 W: 12 10 b.Eastbourne 3-10-87
Internationals: England Youth. Wales Full caps.

2005–06	Brighton & HA	16	1		
2006–07	Brighton & HA	39	0		
2007–08	Brighton & HA	22	1		
2008–09	Brighton & HA	2	0	**79**	**2**
2008–09	*Nottingham F*	23	0		
2009–10	Nottingham F	10	0		
2010–11	Nottingham F	12	0		
2011–12	Nottingham F	35	3	**80**	**3**
2012–13	Huddersfield T	22	1		
2013–14	Huddersfield T	29	2		
2014–15	Huddersfield T	34	3		

2015–16 Huddersfield T 37 2 **122 8**
2016–17 QPR 30 3 **30 3**

MACKIE, Jamie (F) 309 45
H: 5 8 W: 11 00 b.Dorking 22-9-85
Internationals: Scotland Full caps.
2003–04 Wimbledon 13 0 **13 0**
2004–05 Milton Keynes D 3 0 **3 0**
From Exeter C
2007–08 Plymouth Arg 13 3
2008–09 Plymouth Arg 43 5
2009–10 Plymouth Arg 42 8 **98 16**
2010–11 QPR 25 9
2011–12 QPR 31 7
2012–13 QPR 29 2
2013–14 Nottingham F 45 4 **45 4**
2014–15 Reading 32 5 **32 5**
2015–16 QPR 15 1
2016–17 QPR 18 1 **118 20**

MANNING, Ryan (F) 18 1
H: 5 8 W: 10 06 b.Galway 14-6-96
Internationals: Republic of Ireland U17, U19, U21.
From Galway U.
2016–17 QPR 18 1 **18 1**

MORRISON, Ravel (M) 72 12
H: 5 9 W: 11 02 b.Wythenshawe 2-2-93
Internationals: England U16, U17, U18, U21.
2009–10 Manchester U 0 0
2010–11 Manchester U 0 0
2011–12 Manchester U 0 0
2011–12 West Ham U 1 0
2012–13 West Ham U 0 0
2012–13 *Birmingham C* 27 3 **27 3**
2013–14 West Ham U 16 3
2013–14 *QPR* 15 6
2014–15 West Ham U 1 0 **18 3**
2014–15 *Cardiff C* 7 0 **7 0**
2016–17 Lazio 0 0
On loan from Lazio.
2016–17 QPR 5 0 **20 6**

NGBAKOTO, Yeni (F) 211 47
H: 5 8 W: 11 03 b.Croix 23-1-92
Internationals: France U17, U18. DR Congo Full caps.
2009–10 Metz 0 0
2010–11 Metz 22 2
2011–12 Metz 20 0
2012–13 Metz 38 11
2013–14 Metz 37 14
2014–15 Metz 30 5
2015–16 Metz 38 12 **185 44**
2016–17 QPR 26 3 **26 3**

ONUOHA, Nedum (D) 304 11
H: 6 2 W: 12 04 b.Warri 12-11-86
Internationals: England U20, U21.
2004–05 Manchester C 17 0
2005–06 Manchester C 10 0
2006–07 Manchester C 18 0
2007–08 Manchester C 16 1
2008–09 Manchester C 23 1
2009–10 Manchester C 10 1
2010–11 Manchester C 0 0
2010–11 *Sunderland* 31 1 **31 1**
2011–12 Manchester C 1 0 **95 3**
2011–12 QPR 16 0
2012–13 QPR 23 0
2013–14 QPR 26 2
2014–15 QPR 23 0
2015–16 QPR 46 2
2016–17 QPR 44 3 **178 7**

PAUL, Chris (M) 0 0
b.Enfield 25-9-97
Internationals: Northern Ireland U21.
From Tottenham H.
2016–17 QPR 0 0

PERCH, James (D) 403 16
H: 5 11 W: 11 05 b.Mansfield 29-9-85
2002–03 Nottingham F 0 0
2003–04 Nottingham F 0 0
2004–05 Nottingham F 22 0
2005–06 Nottingham F 38 3
2006–07 Nottingham F 46 5
2007–08 Nottingham F 30 0
2008–09 Nottingham F 37 3
2009–10 Nottingham F 17 1 **190 12**
2010–11 Newcastle U 13 0
2011–12 Newcastle U 25 0
2012–13 Newcastle U 27 1 **65 1**
2013–14 Wigan Ath 40 0
2014–15 Wigan Ath 41 3 **81 3**
2015–16 QPR 35 0
2016–17 QPR 32 0 **67 0**

PETRASSO, Michael (M) 40 5
H: 5 6 W: 10 01 b.Toronto 9-7-95
Internationals: Canada U17, U20, U23, Full caps.
2013–14 QPR 1 0
2013–14 *Oldham Ath* 11 1 **11 1**
2013–14 *Coventry C* 7 1 **7 1**
2014–15 QPR 0 0
2014–15 *Leyton Orient* 3 0 **3 0**
2014–15 *Notts Co* 8 3 **8 3**
2015–16 QPR 8 0
2016–17 QPR 2 0 **11 0**

POLTER, Sebastian (F) 131 31
H: 6 3 W: 13 01 b.Wilhelmshaven 1-4-91
Internationals: Germany U18, U20, U21.
2008–09 Wolfsburg 0 0
2009–10 Wolfsburg 0 0
2010–11 Wolfsburg 0 0
2011–12 Wolfsburg 12 2
2012–13 Wolfsburg 0 0 **12 2**
2012–13 *Nurnberg* 26 5 **26 5**
2013–14 Mainz 05 13 0
2014–15 Mainz 05 0 0 **13 0**
2014–15 *Union Berlin* 29 14 **29 14**
2015–16 QPR 31 6
2016–17 QPR 20 4 **51 10**
Transferred to Union Berlin, January 2017.

PROHOULY, Axel (M) 0 0
H: 5 9 W: 10 12 b.Grasse 30-6-97
Internationals: France U19.
2015–16 QPR 0 0
2016–17 QPR 0 0
2016–17 *Port Vale* 0 0

ROBINSON, Jack (D) 86 0
H: 5 11 W: 10 08 b.Warrington 1-9-93
Internationals: England U16, U17, U18, U19, U21.
2009–10 Liverpool 1 0
2010–11 Liverpool 2 0
2011–12 Liverpool 0 0
2012–13 Liverpool 0 0
2012–13 *Wolverhampton W* 11 0 **11 0**
2013–14 Liverpool 0 0 **3 0**
2013–14 *Blackpool* 34 0 **34 0**
2014–15 QPR 0 0
2014–15 *Huddersfield T* 30 0 **30 0**
2015–16 QPR 1 0
2016–17 QPR 7 0 **8 0**

SANDRO (M) 170 8
H: 6 2 W: 11 11 b.Riachinho 15-3-89
Internationals: Brazil U20, U23, Full caps.
2008 Internacional 7 2
2009 Internacional 27 1
2010 Internacional 9 1 **43 4**
2010–11 Tottenham H 19 1
2011–12 Tottenham H 23 0
2012–13 Tottenham H 22 1
2013–14 Tottenham H 17 1 **81 3**
2014–15 QPR 17 1
2015–16 QPR 11 0
2015–16 *WBA* 12 0 **12 0**
2016–17 QPR 6 0 **34 1**
Transferred to Antalyspor, January 2017.

SHODIPO, Olamide (M) 17 0
b.Dublin 5-7-97
Internationals: Republic of Ireland U19, U21.
2016–17 QPR 11 0 **11 0**
2016–17 *Port Vale* 6 0 **6 0**

SMITH, Matt (F) 193 42
H: 6 6 W: 14 00 b.Birmingham 7-6-89
2011–12 Oldham Ath 28 3
2011–12 *Macclesfield T* 8 1 **8 1**
2012–13 Oldham Ath 34 6 **62 9**
2013–14 Leeds U 39 12
2014–15 Leeds U 3 0 **42 12**
2014–15 Fulham 15 5
2014–15 *Bristol C* 14 7 **14 7**
2015–16 Fulham 20 2
2016–17 Fulham 16 2 **51 9**
2016–17 QPR 16 4 **16 4**

SMITHIES, Alex (G) 311 0
H: 6 1 W: 10 01 b.Huddersfield 25-3-90
Internationals: England U16, U17, U18, U19.
2006–07 Huddersfield T 0 0
2007–08 Huddersfield T 2 0
2008–09 Huddersfield T 27 0
2009–10 Huddersfield T 46 0
2010–11 Huddersfield T 22 0
2011–12 Huddersfield T 13 0
2012–13 Huddersfield T 46 0
2013–14 Huddersfield T 46 0
2014–15 Huddersfield T 44 0
2015–16 Huddersfield T 1 0 **247 0**
2015–16 QPR 18 0
2016–17 QPR 46 0 **64 0**

SYLLA, Idrissa (F) 192 54
H: 6 2 W: 11 11 b.Conakry 3-12-90
Internationals: Guinea Full caps.
2010–11 Le Mans 0 0
2010–11 *Bastia* 27 7 **27 7**
2011–12 Le Mans 25 9
2012–13 Le Mans 27 5 **52 14**
2013–14 Zulte Waregem 27 9
2014–15 Zulte Waregem 20 5 **47 14**
2014–15 Anderlecht 0 0
2015–16 Anderlecht 30 7
2016–17 Anderlecht 4 2 **34 9**
2016–17 QPR 32 10 **32 10**

WASHINGTON, Conor (F) 161 38
H: 5 10 W: 11 09 b.Chatham 18-5-92
Internationals: Northern Ireland Full caps.
2013–14 Newport Co 24 4 **24 4**
2013–14 Peterborough U 17 4
2014–15 Peterborough U 40 13
2015–16 Peterborough U 25 10 **82 27**
2015–16 QPR 15 0
2016–17 QPR 40 7 **55 7**

WSZOLEK, Pawel (M) 142 13
H: 6 1 W: 12 04 b.Tczew 30-4-92
Internationals: Poland U17, U18, U19.
2010–11 Polonia Warsaw 7 0
2011–12 Polonia Warsaw 26 2
2012–13 Polonia Warsaw 27 7 **60 9**
2013–14 Sampdoria 19 1
2014–15 Sampdoria 6 0
2015–16 Sampdoria 2 0 **27 1**
2015–16 *Verona* 26 0
2016–17 Verona 0 0 **26 0**
2016–17 QPR 29 3 **29 3**

Players retained or with offer of contract
Adams, Brandon Lea; Brzozowski, Marcin Maurycy; Chair, Ilias Emilian; Darbyshire, Daniel Richard; Dieng, Seny Timothy; Herdman, Martin John; Hudnott, Conor John James; Kaiser, Ethan Jeremiah Muwanguzi; Kakay, Osman Jovan; Lumley, Joseph Patrick; Oteh, Aramide Jay; Rowe, Daniel Isaiah; Wallen, Joshua Thomas; Williams, Jack Dennis.

Scholars
Akinola, Romoluwa Ayomide; Arthur, Jeremy Bernard; Bansal-McNulty, Amrit Padraig Singh; Barzey, Brandon James; Bettache, Faysal; Bowman, Myles Thomas; Clarke, Ruudi Leon; Crichlow, Gianni Dimitri; Dauti, Mus; Disubi, Daniel; Dos, Santos Cardoso Hugo Alexandre; Eales, Jake Callum; Eshun, Kingsley Lewis; Folkes, Anthony Junior Tyreke; Fox, Charles John; Francis-Adeyinka, Jardel Adeolu Adesola; Genovesi, Caden Seamus; Kifwasima-Mayuma, Samuel; Klass, Michael Anthony; McLeod, Kraig Nathaniel Noel; Mesias, Aiden Justino Araujo; Miller, Gilbert Scott Wallace; Platt, Mickel Anton; Ribeiro, Mateus Leandro Rivaldo; Springer-Downes, Rhys Tre Marlon.

READING (70)

AL HABSI, Ali (G) 287 0
H: 6 4 W: 12 06 b.Oman 30-12-81
Internationals: Oman Full caps.
2003 Lyn 13 0
2004 Lyn 24 0
2005 Lyn 25 0 **62 0**
2005–06 Bolton W 0 0
2006–07 Bolton W 0 0
2007–08 Bolton W 10 0
2008–09 Bolton W 0 0
2009–10 Bolton W 0 0
2010–11 Bolton W 0 0 **10 0**
2010–11 *Wigan Ath* 34 0
2011–12 Wigan Ath 38 0
2012–13 Wigan Ath 29 0
2013–14 Wigan Ath 24 0
2014–15 Wigan Ath 11 0 **136 0**
2014–15 *Brighton & HA* 1 0 **1 0**
2015–16 Reading 32 0
2016–17 Reading 46 0 **78 0**

BEERENS, Roy (F) **299 51**
H: 5 8 W: 9 13 b.Bladel 22-12-87
Internationals: Netherlands U21, B, Full caps.

2005–06	PSV Eindhoven	2	0		
2006–07	PSV Eindhoven	7	1	**9**	**1**
2006–07	*NEC*	14	2	**14**	**2**
2007–08	Heerenveen	28	6		
2008–09	Heerenveen	29	9		
2009–10	Heerenveen	29	4		
2010–11	Heerenveen	28	6	**114**	**25**
2011–12	AZ Alkmaar	26	3		
2012–13	AZ Alkmaar	34	5		
2013–14	AZ Alkmaar	33	5	**93**	**13**
2014–15	Hertha Berlin	27	4		
2015–16	Hertha Berlin	2	0	**29**	**4**
2016–17	Reading	40	6	**40**	**6**

BLACKETT, Tyler (D) **61 0**
H: 6 1 W: 11 12 b.Manchester 2-4-94
Internationals: England U16, U17, U18, U19, U21.

2012–13	Manchester U	0	0		
2013–14	Manchester U	0	0		
2013–14	*Blackpool*	5	0	**5**	**0**
2013–14	*Birmingham C*	8	0	**8**	**0**
2014–15	Manchester U	11	0		
2015–16	Manchester U	0	0	**11**	**0**
2015–16	*Celtic*	3	0	**3**	**0**
2016–17	Reading	34	0	**34**	**0**

BOND, Jonathan (G) **54 0**
H: 6 3 W: 13 03 b.Hemel Hempstead 19-5-93
Internationals: Wales U17, U19. England U20, U21.

2010–11	Watford	0	0		
2011–12	Watford	1	0		
2011–12	*Dagenham & R*	5	0	**5**	**0**
2011–12	*Bury*	6	0	**6**	**0**
2012–13	Watford	8	0		
2013–14	Watford	10	0		
2014–15	Watford	3	0	**22**	**0**
2015–16	Reading	14	0		
2016–17	Reading	0	0	**14**	**0**
2016–17	*Gillingham*	7	0	**7**	**0**

COOPER, Jake (D) **57 6**
H: 6 4 W: 13 05 b.Bracknell 3-2-95
Internationals: England U18, U19, U20.

2013–14	Reading	0	0		
2014–15	Reading	15	2		
2015–16	Reading	24	2		
2016–17	Reading	3	0	**42**	**4**
2016–17	*Millwall*	15	2	**15**	**2**

DICKIE, Rob (D) **21 2**
H: 6 0 W: 11 09 b.Wokingham 3-3-96
Internationals: England U18, U19.

2015–16	Reading	1	0		
2016–17	Reading	0	0	**1**	**0**
2016–17	*Cheltenham T*	20	2	**20**	**2**

EVANS, George (M) **92 7**
H: 6 0 W: 11 12 b.Cheadle 13-1-96
Internationals: England U17, U19, U20.

2012–13	Manchester C	0	0		
2013–14	Manchester C	0	0		
2013–14	*Crewe Alex*	23	1	**23**	**1**
2014–15	Manchester C	0	0		
2014–15	*Scunthorpe U*	16	1	**16**	**1**
2015–16	Manchester C	0	0		
2015–16	*Walsall*	12	3	**12**	**3**
2015–16	Reading	6	0		
2016–17	Reading	35	2	**41**	**2**

FOSU, Tarique (M) **48 9**
H: 5 7 W: 10 08 b. 5-11-95
Internationals: England U18.

2013–14	Reading	0	0		
2014–15	Reading	1	0		
2015–16	Reading	0	0		
2015–16	*Fleetwood T*	6	1	**6**	**1**
2015–16	*Accrington S*	8	3	**8**	**3**
2016–17	Reading	0	0	**1**	**0**
2016–17	*Colchester U*	33	5	**33**	**5**

GRAVENBERCH, Danzell (D) **53 1**
H: 6 1 W: 12 08 b.Amsterdam 13-2-94
Internationals: Netherlands U16, U17, U18, U19.

2013–14	Ajax	0	0		
2013–14	*NEC*	6	0	**6**	**0**
2014–15	Ajax	0	0		
2014–15	Universitatea Cluj	17	1	**17**	**1**
2015–16	Dordrecht	28	0	**28**	**0**
2016–17	Reading	2	0	**2**	**0**

GUNTER, Chris (D) **366 3**
H: 5 11 W: 11 02 b.Newport 21-7-89
Internationals: Wales U17, U19, U21, Full caps.

2006–07	Cardiff C	15	0		
2007–08	Cardiff C	13	0	**28**	**0**
2007–08	Tottenham H	2	0		
2008–09	Tottenham H	3	0	**5**	**0**
2008–09	*Nottingham F*	8	0		
2009–10	Nottingham F	44	1		
2010–11	Nottingham F	43	0		
2011–12	Nottingham F	46	1	**141**	**2**
2012–13	Reading	20	0		
2013–14	Reading	44	0		
2014–15	Reading	38	0		
2015–16	Reading	44	0		
2016–17	Reading	46	1	**192**	**1**

HARRIOTT, Callum (M) **118 17**
H: 5 5 W: 10 05 b.Norbury 4-3-94
Internationals: England U19.

2010–11	Charlton Ath	3	0		
2011–12	Charlton Ath	0	0		
2012–13	Charlton Ath	14	2		
2013–14	Charlton Ath	28	5		
2014–15	Charlton Ath	21	1		
2015–16	Charlton Ath	20	3	**86**	**11**
2015–16	*Colchester U*	20	5	**20**	**5**
2016–17	Reading	12	1	**12**	**1**

HURTADO, Paolo (M) **214 36**
H: 5 10 W: 10 08 b.Callao 27-7-90
Internationals: Peru Full caps.

2008	Alianza Lima	20	2		
2009	Alianza Lima	0	0		
2009	*Juan Aurich*	21	3	**21**	**3**
2010	Alianza Lima	36	8		
2011	Alianza Lima	26	4		
2012	Alianza Lima	1	0	**83**	**14**
2012–13	Pacos de Ferreira	28	8		
2013–14	Pacos de Ferreira	8	0		
2013–14	*Penarol*	10	0	**10**	**0**
2014–15	Pacos de Ferreira	21	4	**57**	**12**
2015–16	Reading	5	0		
2015–16	*Guimaraes*	7	1		
2016–17	Reading	0	0	**5**	**0**
2016–17	*Guimaraes*	31	6	**38**	**7**

HYAM, Dominic (D) **16 0**
H: 6 2 W: 11 00 b.Leuchars 20-12-95
Internationals: Scotland U19, U21.

2014–15	Reading	0	0		
2015–16	Reading	0	0		
2015–16	*Dagenham & R*	16	0	**16**	**0**
2016–17	Reading	0	0		
2016–17	*Portsmouth*	0	0		

JAAKKOLA, Anssi (G) **118 0**
H: 6 4 W: 13 12 b.Kemi 13-3-87
Internationals: Finland U21, Full caps.

2005	TP-47	3	0		
2006	TP-47	14	0	**17**	**0**
2006–07	Siena	0	0		
2007–08	Siena	1	0		
2008–09	Siena	0	0		
2008–09	*Colligiana*	7	0	**7**	**0**
2009–10	Siena	0	0	**1**	**0**
2010–11	Slavia Prague	2	0	**2**	**0**
2010–11	Kilmarnock	8	0		
2011–12	Kilmarnock	5	0		
2012–13	Kilmarnock	0	0	**13**	**0**
2013–14	Ajax Cape Town	24	0		
2014–15	Ajax Cape Town	28	0		
2015–16	Ajax Cape Town	26	0	**78**	**0**
2016–17	Reading	0	0		

JULES, Zak (D) **10 1**
b. 2-7-97
Internationals: Scotland U17, U19, U21.

2016–17	Reading	0	0		
2016–17	*Motherwell*	10	1	**10**	**1**

KELLY, Liam (M) **28 1**
b. 22-11-95
Internationals: Republic of Ireland U19, U21.

2014–15	Reading	0	0		
2015–16	Reading	0	0		
2016–17	Reading	28	1	**28**	**1**

KEOWN, Niall (D) **16 0**
b. 5-4-95
Internationals: Republic of Ireland U21.

2013–14	Reading	0	0		
2014–15	Reading	2	0		
2015–16	Reading	0	0		
2016–17	Reading	0	0	**2**	**0**
2016–17	*Partick Thistle*	14	0	**14**	**0**

KERMORGANT, Yann (F) **409 121**
H: 6 0 W: 13 03 b.Vannes 8-11-81
Internationals: Brittany Full caps.

2004–05	Chatellerault	29	14	**29**	**14**
2005–06	Grenoble	26	6		
2006–07	Grenoble	32	10	**58**	**16**
2007–08	Reims	33	4		
2008–09	Reims	34	9	**67**	**13**
2009–10	Leicester C	20	1		
2010–11	Leicester C	0	0	**20**	**1**
2010–11	*Arles-Avignon*	26	3	**26**	**3**
2011–12	Charlton Ath	36	12		
2012–13	Charlton Ath	32	12		
2013–14	Charlton Ath	21	5	**89**	**29**
2013–14	Bournemouth	16	9		
2014–15	Bournemouth	38	15		
2015–16	Bournemouth	7	0	**61**	**24**
2015–16	Reading	17	3		
2016–17	Reading	42	18	**59**	**21**

LEGG, George (G) **0 0**

2016–17	Reading	0	0		

LONG, Sean (D) **16 0**
H: 5 10 W: 11 00 b.Dublin 2-5-95
Internationals: Republic of Ireland U17, U19, U21.

2013–14	Reading	0	0		
2014–15	Reading	0	0		
2015–16	Reading	0	0		
2015–16	*Luton T*	9	0	**9**	**0**
2016–17	Reading	0	0		
2016–17	*Cambridge U*	7	0	**7**	**0**

McCLEARY, Garath (M) **285 35**
H: 5 10 W: 12 06 b.Oxford 15-5-87
Internationals: Jamaica Full caps.

2007–08	Nottingham F	8	1		
2008–09	Nottingham F	39	1		
2009–10	Nottingham F	24	0		
2010–11	Nottingham F	18	2		
2011–12	Nottingham F	22	9	**111**	**13**
2011–12	Reading	0	0		
2012–13	Reading	31	3		
2013–14	Reading	42	5		
2014–15	Reading	26	1		
2015–16	Reading	34	4		
2016–17	Reading	41	9	**174**	**22**

McSHANE, Paul (D) **303 14**
H: 6 0 W: 11 05 b.Wicklow 6-1-86
Internationals: Republic of Ireland U21, Full caps.

2002–03	Manchester U	0	0		
2003–04	Manchester U	0	0		
2004–05	Manchester U	0	0		
2004–05	*Walsall*	4	1	**4**	**1**
2005–06	Manchester U	0	0		
2005–06	*Brighton & HA*	38	3	**38**	**3**
2006–07	WBA	32	2	**32**	**2**
2007–08	Sunderland	21	0		
2008–09	Sunderland	3	0		
2008–09	*Hull C*	17	1		
2009–10	Sunderland	0	0	**24**	**0**
2009–10	Hull C	27	0		
2010–11	Hull C	19	0		
2010–11	*Barnsley*	10	1	**10**	**1**
2011–12	Hull C	1	0		
2011–12	*Crystal Palace*	11	0	**11**	**0**
2012–13	Hull C	25	2		
2013–14	Hull C	10	0		
2014–15	Hull C	20	1	**119**	**4**
2015–16	Reading	35	0		
2016–17	Reading	30	3	**65**	**3**

MEITE, Yakou (M) **15 1**
H: 6 0 W: 11 05 b.Paris 11-2-96
Internationals: Ivory Coast U17, U20.

2015–16	Paris Saint-Germain	1	0	**1**	**0**
2016–17	Reading	14	1	**14**	**1**

MENDES, Joseph (F) **134 21**
H: 6 1 W: 12 08 b.Evreux 30-3-91

2010–11	Grenoble	14	1	**14**	**1**
2011–12	Epinal	22	3	**22**	**3**
2012–13	Le Mans	20	3	**20**	**3**
2013–14	Lokomotiv Plovdiv	7	0	**7**	**0**
2014–15	Le Havre	22	2		
2015–16	Le Havre	37	9	**59**	**11**
2016–17	Reading	12	3	**12**	**3**

MOORE, Liam (D) **136 2**
H: 6 1 W: 13 08 b.Loughborough 31-1-93
Internationals: England U17, U20, U21.

2011–12	Leicester C	2	0		
2011–12	*Bradford C*	17	0	**17**	**0**
2012–13	Leicester C	16	0		
2012–13	*Brentford*	7	0		
2013–14	Leicester C	30	1		

2014–15	Leicester C	11	0		
2014–15	*Brentford*	3	0	**10**	**0**
2015–16	Leicester C	0	0	**59**	**1**
2015–16	*Bristol C*	10	0	**10**	**0**
2016–17	Reading	40	1	**40**	**1**

MOORE, Stuart (G) 12 0
H: 6 2 W: 11 05 b.Sandown 8-9-94

2013–14	Reading	0	0		
2014–15	Reading	0	0		
2015–16	Reading	0	0		
2015–16	*Peterborough U*	4	0	**4**	**0**
2016–17	Reading	0	0		
2016–17	*Luton T*	8	0	**8**	**0**

OBITA, Jordan (M) 167 7
H: 5 11 W: 11 08 b.Oxford 8-12-93
Internationals: England U18, U19, U21.

2010–11	Reading	0	0		
2011–12	Reading	0	0		
2011–12	*Barnet*	5	0	**5**	**0**
2011–12	*Gillingham*	6	3	**6**	**3**
2012–13	Reading	0	0		
2012–13	*Portsmouth*	8	1	**8**	**1**
2012–13	*Oldham Ath*	8	0	**8**	**0**
2013–14	Reading	34	1		
2014–15	Reading	43	0		
2015–16	Reading	26	0		
2016–17	Reading	37	2	**140**	**3**

POPA, Adrian (F) 279 40
H: 5 7 W: 11 00 b.Horezu 24-7-88
Internationals: Romania Full caps.

2006–07	Stiinta Timisoara	3	2		
2007–08	Stiinta Timisoara	25	2		
2008–09	Stiinta Timisoara	0	0	**28**	**4**
2008–09	*Buftea*	11	2	**11**	**2**
2008–09	*Gloria Buzzau*	11	0	**11**	**0**
2009–10	Universitatea Cluj	23	3	**23**	**3**
2010–11	Concordia Chiajna	27	4		
2011–12	Concordia Chiajna	30	3		
2012–13	Concordia Chiajna	4	3	**61**	**10**
2012–13	Steau Bucharest	30	1		
2013–14	Steau Bucharest	28	7		
2014–15	Steau Bucharest	28	5		
2015–16	Steau Bucharest	32	4		
2016–17	Steau Bucharest	19	3	**137**	**20**
2016–17	Reading	8	1	**8**	**1**

QUINN, Stephen (M) 356 25
H: 5 6 W: 9 08 b.Dublin 4-4-86
Internationals: Republic of Ireland U21, Full caps.

2005–06	Sheffield U	0	0		
2005–06	*Milton Keynes D*	15	0	**15**	**0**
2005–06	*Rotherham U*	16	0	**16**	**0**
2006–07	Sheffield U	15	2		
2007–08	Sheffield U	19	2		
2008–09	Sheffield U	43	7		
2009–10	Sheffield U	44	4		
2010–11	Sheffield U	37	1		
2011–12	Sheffield U	45	4		
2012–13	Sheffield U	3	0	**206**	**20**
2012–13	Hull C	42	3		
2013–14	Hull C	15	0		
2014–15	Hull C	28	1	**85**	**4**
2015–16	Reading	27	1		
2016–17	Reading	7	0	**34**	**1**

RAKELS, Deniss (F) 170 72
b.Jekabpils 20-8-92
Internationals: Latvia U17, U19, U21, Full caps.

2009	Metalurgs	14	9		
2010	Metalurgs	26	18	**40**	**27**
2010–11	Zaglebie Lubin	4	0		
2011–12	Zaglebie Lubin	0	0		
2011–12	*Katowice*	20	5		
2012–13	Zaglebie Lubin	0	0		
2012–13	*Katowice*	27	11	**47**	**16**
2013–14	Zaglebie Lubin	5	0	**9**	**0**
2013–14	Cracovia	7	0		
2014–15	Cracovia	33	11		
2015–16	Cracovia	20	15	**60**	**26**
2015–16	Reading	12	3		
2016–17	Reading	2	0	**14**	**3**

SAMUEL, Dominic (F) 58 15
H: 6 0 W: 14 00 b.Southwark 1-4-94
Internationals: England U19.

2011–12	Reading	0	0		
2012–13	Reading	1	0		
2012–13	*Colchester U*	2	0	**2**	**0**
2013–14	Reading	0	0		
2013–14	*Dagenham & R*	1	0	**1**	**0**
2014–15	Reading	0	0		
2014–15	*Coventry C*	13	6	**13**	**6**
2015–16	Reading	1	0		
2015–16	*Gillingham*	25	7	**25**	**7**
2016–17	Reading	9	2	**11**	**2**
2016–17	*Ipswich T*	6	0	**6**	**0**

STACEY, Jack (M) 51 2
H: 6 4 W: 13 05 b.Bracknell 6-4-96

2014–15	Reading	6	0		
2015–16	Reading	0	0		
2015–16	*Barnet*	2	0	**2**	**0**
2015–16	*Carlisle U*	9	2	**9**	**2**
2016–17	Reading	0	0	**6**	**0**
2016–17	*Exeter C*	34	0	**34**	**0**

SWIFT, John (M) 85 17
H: 6 0 W: 11 07 b.Portsmouth 23-6-95
Internationals: England U16, U17, U18, U19, U20, U21.

2013–14	Chelsea	1	0		
2014–15	Chelsea	0	0		
2014–15	*Rotherham U*	3	0	**3**	**0**
2014–15	*Swindon T*	18	2	**18**	**2**
2015–16	Chelsea	0	0	**1**	**0**
2015–16	*Brentford*	27	7	**27**	**7**
2016–17	Reading	36	8	**36**	**8**

TANNER, Craig (F) 90 9
H: 5 7 W: 11 05 b.Reading 27-10-94
Internationals: England U16.

2011–12	Reading	0	0		
2012–13	Reading	0	0		
2013–14	Reading	0	0		
2014–15	Reading	3	0		
2014–15	*AFC Wimbledon*	19	0	**19**	**0**
2015–16	Reading	0	0		
2015–16	*Plymouth Arg*	42	4		
2016–17	Reading	0	0	**3**	**0**
2016–17	*Plymouth Arg*	26	5	**68**	**9**

TIAGO ILORI, Almeida (D) 26 1
H: 6 3 W: 12 07 b.London 26-2-93
Internationals: Portugal U18, U19, U20, U21, U23.

2011–12	Sporting Lisbon	1	0		
2012–13	Sporting Lisbon	11	1	**12**	**1**
2013–14	Liverpool	0	0		
2013–14	*Granada*	9	0	**9**	**0**
2014–15	Liverpool	0	0		
2014–15	Bordeaux	0	0		
2015–16	Liverpool	0	0		
2015–16	*Aston Villa*	0	0		
2016–17	Liverpool	0	0		
2016–17	Reading	5	0	**5**	**0**

VAN DEN BERG, Joey (M) 229 25
H: 5 10 W: 11 00 b.Nijeveen 13-2-86

2004–05	Heerenveen	1	0		
2005–06	Heerenveen	1	0		
2005–06	Almere C	19	1	**19**	**1**
2007–08	Go Ahead Eagles	11	1	**11**	**1**
2010–11	PEC Zwolle	27	5		
2011–12	PEC Zwolle	30	7		
2012–13	PEC Zwolle	16	3	**73**	**15**
2012–13	Heerenveen	13	0		
2013–14	Heerenveen	29	2		
2014–15	Heerenveen	29	2		
2015–16	Heerenveen	26	4	**99**	**8**
2016–17	Reading	27	0	**27**	**0**

WATSON, Tennai (D) 3 0
b. 4-3-97

2015–16	Reading	0	0		
2016–17	Reading	3	0	**3**	**0**

WIESER, Sandro (M) 50 4
H: 6 1 W: 12 06 b.Vaduz 3-2-93
Internationals: Liechtenstein U21, Full caps.

2010–11	Basel	2	0		
2011–12	Basel	0	0	**2**	**0**
2011–12	1899 Hoffenheim	1	0		
2012–13	1899 Hoffenheim	0	0		
2013–14	1899 Hoffenheim	0	0		
2013–14	*SV Ried*	11	0	**11**	**0**
2014–15	1899 Hoffenheim	0	0	**1**	**0**
2014–15	*Aarau*	14	2	**14**	**2**
2015–16	Thun	22	2	**22**	**2**
2016–17	Reading	0	0		

WILLIAMS, Daniel (M) 193 14
H: 6 0 W: 11 12 b.Karlsruhe 8-3-89
Internationals: USA Full caps.

2009–10	SC Freiburg	5	0		
2010–11	SC Freiburg	7	0		
2011–12	SC Freiburg	1	0	**13**	**0**
2011–12	Hoffenheim	24	0		
2012–13	Hoffenheim	21	1	**45**	**1**
2013–14	Reading	30	3		
2014–15	Reading	25	1		
2015–16	Reading	39	5		
2016–17	Reading	41	4	**135**	**13**

Players retained or with offer of contract
Abiola, Delfim Almeida Tiago; Andresson, Axel Oskar; Barrett, Joshua Lee; Davis, Conor Florin; East, Ryan Henry; Frost, Tyler Jayden; Holsgrove, Jordan William; House, Benjamin; Howe, Teddy William; McIntyre, Thomas Peter; Medford-Smith, Ramarni Nelson; Novakovich, Andrija; Osho, Gabriel Jeremiah Adedayo; Richards, Omar Tyrell Crawford; Rinomhota, Andrew Farai; Sheppard, Jake Edwin; Smith, Samuel Toby; Southwood, Luke Kevin; Ward, Lewis Moore.

Scholars
Balogun, Jamal Clinton; Buchanan, Jack James; Burley, Andre Maurice Keith; Coleman, Ethan Jay; Denton, Jack James; Driscoll, Liam Michael-Owen; Green, Cameron Oliver; Holmes, Thomas Richard; Loader, Daniel Namaso; Odimayo, Akinwale Joseph; Okuboyejo, Leon Sholafunmibabajide; Philby, Henry Thomas; Rollinson, Joel Robert Paul; Shokunbi, Ademola Oluwaseyi Abiodun; Sparta, Konstantinos Sebastiano; Wallace, Jazz Oreet; Wilson, Joseph Robert.

ROCHDALE (71)

ALLEN, Jamie (M) 129 11
H: 5 11 W: 11 05 b.Rochdale 29-1-95

2012–13	Rochdale	0	0		
2013–14	Rochdale	25	6		
2014–15	Rochdale	35	0		
2015–16	Rochdale	38	3		
2016–17	Rochdale	31	2	**129**	**11**

ANDREW, Calvin (F) 297 30
H: 6 0 W: 12 11 b.Luton 19-12-86

2004–05	Luton T	8	0		
2005–06	Luton T	1	1		
2005–06	*Grimsby T*	8	1	**8**	**1**
2005–06	*Bristol C*	3	0	**3**	**0**
2006–07	Luton T	7	1		
2007–08	Luton T	39	2	**55**	**4**
2008–09	Crystal Palace	7	0		
2008–09	*Brighton & HA*	9	2	**9**	**2**
2009–10	Crystal Palace	27	1		
2010–11	Crystal Palace	13	0		
2010–11	*Millwall*	3	0	**3**	**0**
2010–11	*Swindon T*	10	1	**10**	**1**
2011–12	Crystal Palace	6	0	**53**	**1**
2011–12	*Leyton Orient*	10	0	**10**	**0**
2012–13	Port Vale	22	1		
2013–14	Port Vale	0	0	**22**	**1**
2013–14	Mansfield T	15	1	**15**	**1**
2013–14	York C	8	1	**8**	**1**
2014–15	Rochdale	32	5		
2015–16	Rochdale	30	6		
2016–17	Rochdale	39	7	**101**	**18**

BARRY-MURPHY, Brian (M) 458 17
H: 5 10 W: 13 01 b.Cork 27-7-78
Internationals: Republic of Ireland U21.

1995–96	Cork C	13	0		
1996–97	Cork C	25	0		
1997–98	Cork C	15	1		
1998–99	Cork C	27	1	**80**	**2**
1999–2000	Preston NE	1	0		
2000–01	Preston NE	14	0		
2001–02	Preston NE	4	0		
2001–02	*Southend U*	8	1	**8**	**1**
2002–03	Preston NE	2	0	**21**	**0**
2002–03	*Hartlepool U*	7	0	**7**	**0**
2002–03	Sheffield W	17	0		
2003–04	Sheffield W	41	0	**58**	**0**
2004–05	Bury	45	6		
2005–06	Bury	40	3		
2006–07	Bury	14	0		
2007–08	Bury	31	1		
2008–09	Bury	42	2		
2009–10	Bury	46	1	**218**	**13**
2010–11	Rochdale	32	0		
2011–12	Rochdale	22	1		
2012–13	Rochdale	8	0		
2013–14	Rochdale	3	0		
2014–15	Rochdale	0	0		
2015–16	Rochdale	1	0		
2016–17	Rochdale	0	0	**66**	**1**

BUNNEY, Joe (F) 102 16
H: 6 1 W: 11 00 b.Manchester 26-9-93

2012–13	Rochdale	1	1		
2013–14	Rochdale	21	3		
2014–15	Rochdale	19	2		

2015–16 Rochdale 32 9
2016–17 Rochdale 29 1 **102 16**

CAMPS, Callum (M) 90 14
b.Stockport 30-11-95
Internationals: Northern Ireland U18, U21.
2012–13 Rochdale 2 0
2013–14 Rochdale 0 0
2014–15 Rochdale 12 1
2015–16 Rochdale 32 5
2016–17 Rochdale 44 8 **90 14**

CANAVAN, Niall (D) 193 18
H: 6 3 W: 12 00 b.Guiseley 11-4-91
Internationals: Republic of Ireland U21.
2009–10 Scunthorpe U 7 1
2010–11 Scunthorpe U 8 0
2010–11 *Shrewsbury T* 3 0 **3 0**
2011–12 Scunthorpe U 12 1
2012–13 Scunthorpe U 40 6
2013–14 Scunthorpe U 45 4
2014–15 Scunthorpe U 32 3
2015–16 Scunthorpe U 10 0 **154 15**
2015–16 *Rochdale* 11 1
2016–17 Rochdale 25 2 **36 3**

CANNON, Andy (M) 68 2
H: 5 9 W: 11 09 b.Ashton-under-Lyne 14-3-96
2014–15 Rochdale 18 0
2015–16 Rochdale 25 0
2016–17 Rochdale 25 2 **68 2**

DAVIES, Steve (F) 292 62
H: 6 0 W: 12 00 b.Liverpool 29-12-87
2005–06 Tranmere R 22 2
2006–07 Tranmere R 28 1
2007–08 Tranmere R 10 2 **60 5**
2008–09 Derby Co 19 3
2009–10 Derby Co 18 1
2010–11 Derby Co 20 5
2011–12 Derby Co 26 11
2012–13 Derby Co 0 0 **83 20**
2012–13 Bristol C 37 13 **37 13**
2013–14 Blackpool 28 3
2014–15 Blackpool 17 5 **45 8**
2014–15 *Sheffield U* 13 2 **13 2**
2015–16 Bradford C 25 5 **25 5**
2016–17 Rochdale 29 9 **29 9**

DIBA MUSANGU, Jonathan (G) 1 0
H: 6 0 W: 11 09 b.Mbuji-Mayi 12-10-97
2014–15 Rochdale 1 0
2015–16 Rochdale 0 0
2016–17 Rochdale 0 0 **1 0**

GILLAM, Matthew (F) 0 0
2016–17 Rochdale 0 0

HENDERSON, Ian (F) 432 96
H: 5 10 W: 11 06 b.Thetford 25-1-85
Internationals: England U18, U20.
2002–03 Norwich C 20 1
2003–04 Norwich C 19 4
2004–05 Norwich C 3 0
2005–06 Norwich C 24 1
2006–07 Norwich C 2 0 **68 6**
2006–07 *Rotherham U* 18 1 **18 1**
2007–08 Northampton T 23 0
2008–09 Northampton T 3 0 **26 0**
2008–09 Luton T 19 1 **19 1**
2009–10 Colchester U 13 2
2009–10 *Ankaragucu* 2 0 **2 0**
2010–11 Colchester U 36 10
2011–12 Colchester U 46 9
2012–13 Colchester U 22 3 **117 24**
2012–13 Rochdale 12 3
2013–14 Rochdale 45 11
2014–15 Rochdale 44 22
2015–16 Rochdale 39 13
2016–17 Rochdale 42 15 **182 64**

HOLLINS, Andrew (D) 0 0
2016–17 Rochdale 0 0

KENGNI-KUEMO, Neil (F) 0 0
2016–17 Rochdale 0 0

LILLIS, Josh (G) 232 0
H: 6 0 W: 12 08 b.Derby 24-6-87
2006–07 Scunthorpe U 1 0
2007–08 Scunthorpe U 3 0
2008–09 Scunthorpe U 5 0
2008–09 *Notts Co* 5 0 **5 0**
2009–10 Scunthorpe U 8 0
2009–10 *Grimsby T* 4 0 **4 0**
2009–10 *Rochdale* 1 0
2010–11 Scunthorpe U 15 0
2010–11 *Rochdale* 23 0
2011–12 Scunthorpe U 6 0 **38 0**
2012–13 Rochdale 46 0
2013–14 Rochdale 45 0
2014–15 Rochdale 16 0
2015–16 Rochdale 40 0
2016–17 Rochdale 14 0 **185 0**

McDERMOTT, Donal (F) 117 10
H: 6 6 W: 12 00 b.Co. Meath 19-10-89
Internationals: Republic of Ireland U17, U18, U19.
2007–08 Manchester C 0 0
2008–09 Manchester C 0 0
2008–09 *Milton Keynes D* 1 0 **1 0**
2009–10 Manchester C 0 0
2009–10 *Chesterfield* 15 5 **15 5**
2009–10 *Scunthorpe U* 9 0 **9 0**
2010–11 Manchester C 0 0
2010–11 *Bournemouth* 9 1
2011–12 Huddersfield T 9 0 **9 0**
2011–12 Bournemouth 14 1
2012–13 Bournemouth 6 0
2013–14 Bournemouth 0 0 **29 2**
2014–15 Rochdale 0 0
2015–16 Rochdale 37 2
2016–17 Rochdale 17 1 **54 3**

McGAHEY, Harrison (D) 66 0
b.Preston 26-9-95
2013–14 Blackpool 4 0 **4 0**
2014–15 Sheffield U 15 0
2014–15 *Tranmere R* 4 0 **4 0**
2015–16 Sheffield U 7 0 **22 0**
2016–17 Rochdale 36 0 **36 0**

McNULTY, Jim (D) 288 5
H: 6 1 W: 12 00 b.Runcorn 13-2-85
Internationals: Scotland U17, U19.
2006–07 Macclesfield T 15 0
2007–08 Macclesfield T 19 1 **34 1**
2007–08 Stockport Co 11 0
2008–09 Stockport Co 26 1 **37 1**
2008–09 Brighton & HA 5 1
2009–10 Brighton & HA 8 0
2009–10 *Scunthorpe U* 3 0
2010–11 Brighton & HA 0 0 **13 1**
2010–11 *Scunthorpe U* 6 0 **9 0**
2011–12 Barnsley 44 2
2012–13 Barnsley 12 0
2013–14 Barnsley 0 0 **56 2**
2013–14 *Tranmere R* 12 0 **12 0**
2013–14 Bury 21 0
2014–15 Bury 25 0 **46 0**
2015–16 Rochdale 46 0
2016–17 Rochdale 35 0 **81 0**

MENDEZ-LAING, Nathaniel (M) 189 26
H: 5 10 W: 11 12 b.Birmingham 15-4-92
Internationals: England U16, U17.
2009–10 Wolverhampton W 0 0
2010–11 Wolverhampton W 0 0
2010–11 *Peterborough U* 33 5
2011–12 Wolverhampton W 0 0
2011–12 *Sheffield U* 8 1 **8 1**
2012–13 Peterborough U 21 3
2012–13 *Portsmouth* 8 0 **8 0**
2013–14 Peterborough U 16 1
2013–14 *Shrewsbury T* 6 0 **6 0**
2014–15 Peterborough U 14 0 **84 9**
2014–15 *Cambridge U* 11 1 **11 1**
2015–16 Rochdale 33 7
2016–17 Rochdale 39 8 **72 15**

MORLEY, Aaron (M) 2 0
2016–17 Rochdale 2 0 **2 0**

NOBLE-LAZARUS, Reuben (F) 89 6
H: 5 11 W: 13 07 b.Huddersfield 16-8-93
2008–09 Barnsley 2 0
2009–10 Barnsley 2 0
2010–11 Barnsley 7 1
2011–12 Barnsley 8 0
2012–13 Barnsley 14 1
2013–14 Barnsley 12 1
2013–14 *Scunthorpe U* 4 0 **4 0**
2014–15 Barnsley 1 0 **46 3**
2014–15 Rochdale 19 1
2015–16 Rochdale 10 1
2016–17 Rochdale 10 1 **39 3**

OWUSO, Dave (F) 1 0
2016–17 Rochdale 1 0 **1 0**

RAFFERTY, Joe (D) 154 2
H: 6 0 W: 11 11 b.Liverpool 6-10-93
Internationals: Republic of Ireland U18, U19.
2012–13 Rochdale 21 0
2013–14 Rochdale 31 0
2014–15 Rochdale 31 1
2015–16 Rochdale 31 1
2016–17 Rochdale 40 0 **154 2**

RATHBONE, Oliver (M) 27 2
H: 5 7 W: 10 06 b.Blackburn 10-10-96
From Manchester U.
2016–17 Rochdale 27 2 **27 2**

STEWART, Jack (M) 0 0
2016–17 Rochdale 0 0

THOMPSON, Joe (M) 209 22
H: 6 0 W: 9 07 b.Rochdale 5-3-89
2005–06 Rochdale 1 0
2006–07 Rochdale 13 0
2007–08 Rochdale 11 1
2008–09 Rochdale 30 5
2009–10 Rochdale 36 6
2010–11 Rochdale 32 2
2011–12 Rochdale 17 1
2012–13 Tranmere R 19 1
2012–13 *Rochdale* 7 0
2013–14 Tranmere R 6 2 **25 3**
2014–15 Bury 1 0 **1 0**
2015–16 Carlisle U 15 1 **15 1**
2016–17 Rochdale 21 3 **168 18**

VINCENTI, Peter (F) 240 42
H: 6 2 W: 11 13 b.St Peter 7-7-86
2007–08 Millwall 0 0
2010–11 Stevenage 5 1 **5 1**
2010–11 Aldershot T 23 6
2011–12 Aldershot T 42 6
2012–13 Aldershot T 39 2 **104 14**
2013–14 Rochdale 42 5
2014–15 Rochdale 37 13
2015–16 Rochdale 38 8
2016–17 Rochdale 14 1 **131 27**

Players retained or with offer of contract
Collis, Stephen Philip; Keane, Keith Francis; Kitching, Mark Stephen.

Scholars
Appiah, Nathaniel Amoako; Chea, Rapheal; Evans, Declan; Gillam, Matthew Rhys; Hollins, Andrew James; Kearney, Keith Leeroy; Kengni, Kuemo Neil Astrio; Lenehan, Jack Joseph; Muralitharan, Jai Ravin; Murray, Elliott Roy; Piggott, Joe; Prescott, Jordan Paul; Renner, Joseph Edward; Stewart, Jack Mathew; Wade, Bradley Calvin; Ward, Isaac Benjamin.

ROTHERHAM U (72)

ALLAN, Scott (M) 55 3
H: 5 9 W: 11 00 b.Glasgow 28-11-91
Internationals: Scotland U17, U21.
2010–11 Dundee U 0 0
2010–11 *Forfar Ath* 4 1 **4 1**
2011–12 Dundee U 8 0 **8 0**
2011–12 WBA 0 0
2011–12 *Portsmouth* 15 1
2012–13 *Milton Keynes D* 4 0 **4 0**
2012–13 WBA 0 0
2012–13 *Portsmouth* 9 1 **24 2**
2013–14 WBA 0 0
2013–14 *Birmingham C* 5 0 **5 0**
2016–17 Celtic 0 0
On loan from Celtic.
2016–17 Rotherham U 10 0 **10 0**

BAILEY, Fabian (D) 0 0
2016–17 Rotherham U 0 0

BAILEY-KING, Darnell (M) 2 0
b. 17-5-98
2015–16 Rotherham U 1 0
2016–17 Rotherham U 1 0 **2 0**

BALL, Dominic (D) 51 1
H: 6 0 W: 12 06 b.Welwyn Garden City 2-8-95
Internationals: Northern Ireland U16, U17, U19, U21. England U19, U20.
2013–14 Tottenham H 0 0
2014–15 Tottenham H 0 0
2014–15 *Cambridge U* 11 0 **11 0**
2015–16 Tottenham H 0 0
2015–16 *Rangers* 21 0 **21 0**
2016–17 Rotherham U 13 0 **13 0**
2016–17 *Peterborough U* 6 1 **6 1**

BELAID, Aymen (D) 116 6
H: 6 2 W: 11 11 b.Paris 2-1-89
Internationals: Tunisia Full caps.
2010–11 Grenoble 8 0 **8 0**
2011–12 Etoile du Sahel 13 2
2012–13 Etoile du Sahel 7 0 **20 2**
2013–14 Loko Plovdiv 12 1 **12 1**

2013–14 Levski Sofia 9 0
2014–15 Levski Sofia 28 0
2015–16 Levski Sofia 19 1 **56 1**
2015–16 Rotherham U 3 0
2016–17 Rotherham U 17 2 **20 2**

BILBOE, Laurence (G) 0 0
b. 21-2-98
2016–17 Rotherham U 0 0

BLACKSTOCK, Dexter (F) 351 85
H: 6 2 W: 13 00 b.Oxford 20-5-86
Internationals: England U18, U19, U20, U21. Antigua and Barbuda Full caps.
2004–05 Southampton 9 1
2004–05 *Plymouth Arg* 14 4 **14 4**
2005–06 Southampton 19 3 **28 4**
2005–06 *Derby Co* 9 3 **9 3**
2006–07 QPR 39 13
2007–08 QPR 35 6
2008–09 QPR 36 11 **110 30**
2008–09 *Nottingham F* 6 2
2009–10 Nottingham F 39 12
2010–11 Nottingham F 17 5
2011–12 Nottingham F 22 8
2012–13 Nottingham F 37 6
2013–14 Nottingham F 1 0
2013–14 *Leeds U* 4 1 **4 1**
2014–15 Nottingham F 19 5
2015–16 Nottingham F 29 4
2016–17 Nottingham F 0 0 **170 42**
2016–17 Rotherham U 16 1 **16 1**

BROADFOOT, Kirk (D) 357 17
H: 6 3 W: 13 13 b.Irvine 8-8-84
Internationals: Scotland U21, B, Full caps.
2002–03 St Mirren 23 1
2003–04 St Mirren 31 3
2004–05 St Mirren 36 4
2005–06 St Mirren 27 2
2006–07 St Mirren 37 3 **154 13**
2007–08 Rangers 15 1
2008–09 Rangers 27 0
2009–10 Rangers 12 0
2010–11 Rangers 8 0
2011–12 Rangers 16 0 **78 1**
2012–13 Blackpool 32 2
2013–14 Blackpool 33 0 **65 2**
2014–15 Rotherham U 25 0
2015–16 Rotherham U 32 1
2016–17 Rotherham U 3 0 **60 1**

CAMP, Lee (G) 447 0
H: 5 11 W: 11 11 b.Derby 22-8-84
Internationals: England U21. Northern Ireland Full caps.
2002–03 Derby Co 1 0
2003–04 Derby Co 0 0
2003–04 *QPR* 12 0
2004–05 Derby Co 45 0
2005–06 Derby Co 40 0
2006–07 Derby Co 3 0 **89 0**
2006–07 *Norwich C* 3 0
2006–07 *QPR* 11 0
2007–08 QPR 46 0
2008–09 QPR 4 0 **73 0**
2008–09 *Nottingham F* 15 0
2009–10 Nottingham F 45 0
2010–11 Nottingham F 46 0
2011–12 Nottingham F 46 0
2012–13 Nottingham F 26 0 **178 0**
2012–13 Norwich C 3 0 **6 0**
2013–14 WBA 0 0
2013–14 Bournemouth 33 0
2014–15 Bournemouth 9 0
2015–16 Bournemouth 0 0 **42 0**
2015–16 Rotherham U 41 0
2016–17 Rotherham U 18 0 **59 0**

CLARKE-HARRIS, Jonson (F) 131 21
H: 6 0 W: 11 01 b.Leicester 21-7-94
2012–13 Peterborough U 0 0
2012–13 *Southend U* 3 0 **3 0**
2012–13 *Bury* 12 4 **12 4**
2013–14 Oldham Ath 40 6
2014–15 Oldham Ath 5 1 **45 7**
2014–15 Rotherham U 15 3
2014–15 *Milton Keynes D* 5 0 **5 0**
2014–15 *Doncaster R* 9 1 **9 1**
2015–16 Rotherham U 35 6
2016–17 Rotherham U 7 0 **57 9**

DAWSON, Chris (M) 13 0
b.Dewsbury 2-9-94
Internationals: Wales U21.
2012–13 Leeds U 1 0
2013–14 Leeds U 0 0
2014–15 Leeds U 3 0 **4 0**

2015–16 Rotherham U 0 0
2016 *Viking* 9 0 **9 0**
2016–17 Rotherham U 0 0

FISHER, Darnell (M) 74 1
H: 5 9 W: 11 00 b.Reading 1-5-94
2012–13 Celtic 0 0
2013–14 Celtic 12 0
2014–15 Celtic 5 0
2015–16 Celtic 0 0 **17 0**
2015–16 *St Johnstone* 23 1 **23 1**
2016–17 Rotherham U 34 0 **34 0**

FORDE, Anthony (M) 139 9
H: 5 9 W: 10 10 b.Limerick 16-11-93
Internationals: Republic of Ireland U19, U21.
2011–12 Wolverhampton W 6 0
2012–13 Wolverhampton W 12 0
2012–13 *Scunthorpe U* 8 0 **8 0**
2013–14 Wolverhampton W 3 0 **21 0**
2014–15 Walsall 37 3
2015–16 Walsall 41 4 **78 7**
2016–17 Rotherham U 32 2 **32 2**

FRECKLINGTON, Lee (M) 365 53
H: 5 8 W: 11 00 b.Lincoln 8-9-85
Internationals: Republic of Ireland B.
2003–04 Lincoln C 0 0
2004–05 Lincoln C 3 0
2005–06 Lincoln C 18 2
2006–07 Lincoln C 42 8
2007–08 Lincoln C 34 4
2008–09 Lincoln C 27 7 **124 21**
2008–09 Peterborough U 7 0
2009–10 Peterborough U 35 2
2010–11 Peterborough U 9 1
2011–12 Peterborough U 37 5
2012–13 Peterborough U 5 0 **93 8**
2012–13 *Rotherham U* 31 6
2013–14 Rotherham U 39 10
2014–15 Rotherham U 29 2
2015–16 Rotherham U 27 5
2016–17 Rotherham U 22 1 **148 24**

KELLY, Stephen (D) 277 3
H: 6 0 W: 12 04 b.Dublin 6-9-83
Internationals: Republic of Ireland U16, U20, U21, Full caps.
2000–01 Tottenham H 0 0
2001–02 Tottenham H 0 0
2002–03 Tottenham H 0 0
2002–03 *Southend U* 10 0 **10 0**
2002–03 *QPR* 7 0 **7 0**
2003–04 Tottenham H 11 0
2003–04 *Watford* 13 0 **13 0**
2004–05 Tottenham H 17 2
2005–06 Tottenham H 9 0 **37 2**
2006–07 Birmingham C 36 0
2007–08 Birmingham C 38 0
2008–09 Birmingham C 5 0
2008–09 *Stoke C* 6 0 **6 0**
2009–10 Birmingham C 0 0 **79 0**
2009–10 Fulham 8 0
2010–11 Fulham 10 0
2011–12 Fulham 24 0
2012–13 Fulham 2 0 **44 0**
2012–13 Reading 16 0
2013–14 Reading 15 1
2014–15 Reading 15 0 **46 1**
2015–16 Rotherham U 15 0
2016–17 Rotherham U 20 0 **35 0**

MATTOCK, Joe (D) 258 5
H: 5 11 W: 12 05 b.Leicester 15-5-90
Internationals: England U17, U19, U21.
2006–07 Leicester C 4 0
2007–08 Leicester C 31 0
2008–09 Leicester C 31 1
2009–10 Leicester C 0 0 **66 1**
2009–10 WBA 29 0
2010–11 WBA 0 0
2010–11 *Sheffield U* 13 0 **13 0**
2011–12 WBA 0 0 **29 0**
2011–12 *Portsmouth* 7 0 **7 0**
2011–12 *Brighton & HA* 15 1 **15 1**
2012–13 Sheffield W 7 0
2013–14 Sheffield W 23 2
2014–15 Sheffield W 27 0 **57 2**
2015–16 Rotherham U 35 1
2016–17 Rotherham U 36 0 **71 1**

McMAHON, George (G) 0 0
2016–17 Rotherham U 0 0

MUSKWE, Kudo (F) 0 0
b.17-9-98
2016–17 Rotherham U 0 0

NEWELL, Joe (M) 165 10
H: 5 11 W: 11 02 b.Tamworth 15-3-93
2010–11 Peterborough U 2 0
2011–12 Peterborough U 14 1
2012–13 Peterborough U 30 0
2013–14 Peterborough U 11 0
2014–15 Peterborough U 39 2 **96 3**
2015–16 Rotherham U 35 5
2016–17 Rotherham U 34 2 **69 7**

O'DONNELL, Richard (G) 185 0
H: 6 2 W: 13 05 b.Sheffield 12-9-88
2007–08 Sheffield W 0 0
2007–08 *Rotherham U* 0 0
2007–08 *Oldham Ath* 4 0 **4 0**
2008–09 Sheffield W 0 0
2009–10 Sheffield W 0 0
2010–11 Sheffield W 9 0
2011–12 Sheffield W 6 0 **15 0**
2011–12 *Macclesfield T* 11 0 **11 0**
2012–13 Chesterfield 14 0 **14 0**
2013–14 Walsall 46 0
2014–15 Walsall 44 0 **90 0**
2015–16 Wigan Ath 10 0 **10 0**
2015–16 Bristol C 21 0
2016–17 Bristol C 8 0 **29 0**
2016–17 Rotherham U 12 0 **12 0**

ODEMWINGIE, Peter (F) 337 91
H: 6 0 W: 11 09 b.Tashkent 15-7-81
Internationals: Nigeria Full caps.
2002–03 La Louviere 14 2
2003–04 La Louviere 27 5
2004–05 La Louviere 3 2 **44 9**
2004–05 Lille 20 4
2005–06 Lille 26 14
2006–07 Lille 29 5 **75 23**
2007 Loko Moscow 14 4
2008 Loko Moscow 26 10
2009 Loko Moscow 25 7
2010 Loko Moscow 10 0 **75 21**
2010–11 WBA 32 15
2011–12 WBA 30 10
2012–13 WBA 25 5 **87 30**
2013–14 Cardiff C 15 1 **15 1**
2013–14 Stoke C 15 5
2014–15 Stoke C 7 0
2015–16 Stoke C 5 0 **27 5**
2015–16 *Bristol C* 7 2 **7 2**
2016–17 Rotherham U 7 0 **7 0**
Transferred to Madura U, April 2017.

PRICE, Lewis (G) 147 0
H: 6 3 W: 13 05 b.Bournemouth 19-7-84
Internationals: Wales U19, U21, Full caps.
2002–03 Ipswich T 0 0
2003–04 Ipswich T 1 0
2004–05 Ipswich T 8 0
2004–05 *Cambridge U* 6 0 **6 0**
2005–06 Ipswich T 25 0
2006–07 Ipswich T 34 0 **68 0**
2007–08 Derby Co 6 0
2008–09 Derby Co 0 0
2008–09 *Milton Keynes D* 2 0 **2 0**
2008–09 *Luton T* 1 0 **1 0**
2009–10 Derby Co 0 0 **6 0**
2009–10 *Brentford* 13 0 **13 0**
2010–11 Crystal Palace 1 0
2011–12 Crystal Palace 5 0
2012–13 Crystal Palace 0 0
2013–14 Crystal Palace 0 0
2013–14 *Mansfield T* 5 0 **5 0**
2014–15 Crystal Palace 0 0 **6 0**
2014–15 *Crawley T* 18 0 **18 0**
2015–16 Sheffield W 5 0 **5 0**
2016–17 Rotherham U 17 0 **17 0**

PURRINGTON, Ben (D) 62 0
H: 5 9 W: 11 07 b.Exeter 5-5-96
2013–14 Plymouth Arg 12 0
2014–15 Plymouth Arg 8 0
2015–16 Plymouth Arg 13 0
2016–17 Plymouth Arg 19 0 **52 0**
2016–17 Rotherham U 10 0 **10 0**

SMALLWOOD, Richard (M) 204 7
H: 5 11 W: 11 05 b.Redcar 29-12-90
Internationals: England U18.
2008–09 Middlesbrough 0 0
2009–10 Middlesbrough 0 0
2010–11 Middlesbrough 13 1
2011–12 Middlesbrough 13 0
2012–13 Middlesbrough 22 2
2013–14 Middlesbrough 13 0
2013–14 *Rotherham U* 18 0

2014–15 Middlesbrough 0 0 **61 3**
2014–15 *Rotherham U* 41 1
2015–16 Rotherham U 43 1
2016–17 Scunthorpe U 16 1 **16 1**
2016–17 Rotherham U 25 1 **127 3**

TAYLOR, Jon (M) 243 40
H: 5 11 W: 12 04 b.Liverpool 23-12-89
2009–10 Shrewsbury T 2 0
2010–11 Shrewsbury T 20 6
2011–12 Shrewsbury T 33 0
2012–13 Shrewsbury T 37 7
2013–14 Shrewsbury T 41 9 **133 22**
2014–15 Peterborough U 24 3
2015–16 Peterborough U 44 11 **68 14**
2016–17 Rotherham U 42 4 **42 4**

THORPE, Tom (D) 40 3
H: 6 0 W: 14 00 b.Manchester 13-1-93
Internationals: England U16, U17, U18, U19, U20, U21.
2010–11 Manchester U 0 0
2011–12 Manchester U 0 0
2012–13 Manchester U 0 0
2013–14 Manchester U 0 0
2013–14 *Birmingham C* 6 0 **6 0**
2014–15 Manchester U 1 0 **1 0**
2015–16 Rotherham U 7 2
2015–16 *Bradford C* 3 0 **3 0**
2016–17 Rotherham U 2 0 **9 2**
2016–17 *Bolton W* 21 1 **21 1**

VAULKS, Will (D) 148 11
H: 5 11 b.Birkenhead 13-9-93
2012–13 Tranmere R 0 0
2012–13 Falkirk 6 0
2013–14 Falkirk 33 1
2014–15 Falkirk 34 3
2015–16 Falkirk 35 6 **108 10**
2016–17 Rotherham U 40 1 **40 1**

WARD, Danny (M) 250 43
H: 5 11 W: 12 05 b.Bradford 11-12-91
2008–09 Bolton W 0 0
2009–10 Bolton W 2 0
2009–10 *Swindon T* 28 7 **28 7**
2010–11 Bolton W 0 0 **2 0**
2010–11 *Coventry C* 5 0 **5 0**
2010–11 *Huddersfield T* 7 3
2011–12 Huddersfield T 39 4
2012–13 Huddersfield T 28 2
2013–14 Huddersfield T 38 10
2014–15 Huddersfield T 12 0 **124 19**
2014–15 *Rotherham U* 16 3
2015–16 Rotherham U 34 4
2016–17 Rotherham U 41 10 **91 17**

WARREN, Mason (D) 0 0
b.Doncaster 28-3-97
2015–16 Rotherham U 0 0
2016–17 Rotherham U 0 0

WILSON, Kelvin (D) 329 4
H: 6 2 W: 12 01 b.Nottingham 3-9-85
2003–04 Notts Co 3 0
2004–05 Notts Co 41 2
2005–06 Notts Co 34 1 **78 3**
2005–06 *Preston NE* 6 0
2006–07 Preston NE 21 1 **27 1**
2007–08 Nottingham F 42 0
2008–09 Nottingham F 36 0
2009–10 Nottingham F 35 0
2010–11 Nottingham F 10 0
2011–12 Celtic 15 0
2012–13 Celtic 32 0 **47 0**
2013–14 Nottingham F 9 0
2014–15 Nottingham F 23 0
2015–16 Nottingham F 14 0 **169 0**
2016–17 Rotherham U 8 0 **8 0**

WOOD, Richard (D) 378 21
H: 6 3 W: 12 13 b.Ossett 5-7-85
2002–03 Sheffield W 3 1
2003–04 Sheffield W 12 0
2004–05 Sheffield W 34 1
2005–06 Sheffield W 30 1
2006–07 Sheffield W 12 0
2007–08 Sheffield W 27 2
2008–09 Sheffield W 42 0
2009–10 Sheffield W 11 2 **171 7**
2009–10 Coventry C 24 3
2010–11 Coventry C 40 1
2011–12 Coventry C 17 1
2012–13 Coventry C 36 3 **117 8**
2013–14 Charlton Ath 21 0 **21 0**
2014–15 Rotherham U 6 0
2014–15 *Crawley T* 10 3 **10 3**
2015–16 Rotherham U 13 0
2015–16 *Fleetwood T* 6 0 **6 0**
2015–16 *Chesterfield* 5 0 **5 0**
2016–17 Rotherham U 29 3 **48 3**

YATES, Jerry (M) 22 1
H: 5 9 W: 10 10 b.Doncaster 10-11-96
2014–15 Rotherham U 1 0
2015–16 Rotherham U 0 0
2016–17 Rotherham U 21 1 **22 1**

Players retained or with offer of contract
Ajayi, Oluwasemilogo Adesewo; Bray, Alexander George; Francis, Akeel Ishmael.

Scholars
Abraham, J-Cee; Adeyemi, Trae Abdulrasheed; Atherton, Deegan Michael; Fidler, Harry Colin; Hinds, Akeem Antony; James, Revarnelle Viedelle; Maguire, Thomas Raymond; Martin, Samuel Peter; McGinley-McFarlane, Reece Thomas; McMahon, George James; Murr, Lewis Harvey; Mvumbi, Prince Mamboti; Naeem, Suleman Joseph; Ogunfaolu-Kayode, Joshua Akinola; Osborne, Jack Daniel Ian; Saxton, Adam Lewis; Sterling, Jovanni Sherma; Wiles, Benjamin Jack.

SCUNTHORPE U (73)

ADELAKUN, Hakeeb (F) 100 12
H: 6 3 W: 11 11 b.Hackney 11-6-96
2012–13 Scunthorpe U 2 0
2013–14 Scunthorpe U 28 2
2014–15 Scunthorpe U 32 6
2015–16 Scunthorpe U 21 2
2016–17 Scunthorpe U 17 2 **100 12**

BISHOP, Neil (M) 405 25
H: 6 1 W: 12 10 b.Stockton 7-8-81
Internationals: England C.
2007–08 Barnet 39 2
2008–09 Barnet 44 1 **83 3**
2009–10 Notts Co 43 1
2010–11 Notts Co 43 1
2011–12 Notts Co 41 2
2012–13 Notts Co 41 7 **168 11**
2013–14 Blackpool 35 1 **35 1**
2014–15 Scunthorpe U 35 4
2015–16 Scunthorpe U 42 1
2016–17 Scunthorpe U 42 5 **119 10**

BURDETT, Noel (F) 0 0
b. 13-11-97
2013–14 Scunthorpe U 0 0
2014–15 Scunthorpe U 0 0
2015–16 Scunthorpe U 0 0
2016–17 Scunthorpe U 0 0

BUTROID, Lewis (D) 0 0
2016–17 Scunthorpe U 0 0

CLARKE, Jordan (D) 209 9
H: 6 0 W: 11 02 b.Coventry 19-11-91
Internationals: England U19, U20.
2009–10 Coventry C 12 0
2010–11 Coventry C 21 1
2011–12 Coventry C 19 1
2012–13 Coventry C 20 0
2013–14 Coventry C 41 1
2014–15 Coventry C 11 1 **124 4**
2014–15 *Yeovil T* 5 2 **5 2**
2014–15 Scunthorpe U 24 0
2015–16 Scunthorpe U 33 2
2016–17 Scunthorpe U 23 1 **80 3**

CROOKS, Matt (M) 66 9
H: 6 0 W: 11 05 b.Leeds 20-1-94
2011–12 Huddersfield T 0 0
2012–13 Huddersfield T 0 0
2013–14 Huddersfield T 0 0
2014–15 Huddersfield T 1 0 **1 0**
2014–15 *Hartlepool U* 3 0 **3 0**
2014–15 Accrington S 16 0
2015–16 Accrington S 32 6 **48 6**
2016–17 Rangers 2 0 **2 0**
On loan from Rangers.
2016–17 Scunthorpe U 12 3 **12 3**

DAVIES, Craig (F) 401 91
H: 6 2 W: 13 05 b.Burton-on-Trent 9-1-86
Internationals: Wales U17, U19, U21, Full caps.
2004–05 Oxford U 28 6
2005–06 Oxford U 20 2 **48 8**
2005–06 Verona 0 0
2006–07 Wolverhampton W 23 0 **23 0**
2007–08 Oldham Ath 32 10
2008–09 Oldham Ath 12 0 **44 10**
2008–09 *Stockport Co* 9 5 **9 5**
2008–09 Brighton & HA 16 1
2009–10 Brighton & HA 5 0 **21 1**
2009–10 *Yeovil T* 4 0 **4 0**
2009–10 *Port Vale* 24 7 **24 7**
2010–11 Chesterfield 41 23 **41 23**
2011–12 Barnsley 40 11
2012–13 Barnsley 20 8 **60 19**
2012–13 Bolton W 18 4
2013–14 Bolton W 8 0
2013–14 *Preston NE* 15 5 **15 5**
2014–15 Bolton W 27 6 **53 10**
2015–16 Wigan Ath 26 2
2016–17 Wigan Ath 14 1 **40 3**
2016–17 Scunthorpe U 19 0 **19 0**

DYCHE, Jack (D) 0 0
b. 11-10-97
2014–15 Scunthorpe U 0 0
2015–16 Scunthorpe U 0 0
2016–17 Scunthorpe U 0 0

GOODE, Charlie (D) 30 1
b. 3-8-95
Internationals: England C.
2015–16 Scunthorpe U 10 1
2016–17 Scunthorpe U 20 0 **30 1**

HOLMES, Duane (M) 65 4
H: 5 8 W: 10 03 b.Wakefield 6-11-94
2012–13 Huddersfield T 0 0
2013–14 Huddersfield T 16 0
2013–14 *Yeovil T* 5 0 **5 0**
2014–15 Huddersfield T 0 0
2014–15 *Bury* 6 0 **6 0**
2015–16 Huddersfield T 6 1 **22 1**
2016–17 Scunthorpe U 32 3 **32 3**

HOPPER, Tom (F) 99 20
H: 6 1 W: 12 00 b.Boston 14-12-93
Internationals: England U18.
2011–12 Leicester C 0 0
2012–13 Leicester C 0 0
2012–13 *Bury* 22 3 **22 3**
2013–14 Leicester C 0 0
2014–15 Leicester C 0 0
2014–15 *Scunthorpe U* 12 4
2015–16 Scunthorpe U 34 8
2016–17 Scunthorpe U 31 5 **77 17**

KELSEY, Adam (G) 0 0
2016–17 Scunthorpe U 0 0

KING, Jack (M) 150 11
H: 6 0 W: 11 11 b.Oxford 20-8-85
2012–13 Preston NE 36 4
2013–14 Preston NE 24 2
2014–15 Preston NE 18 1 **78 7**
2015–16 Scunthorpe U 36 1
2016–17 Scunthorpe U 0 0 **36 1**
2016–17 *Stevenage* 36 3 **36 3**

LAIRD, Scott (D) 235 22
H: 5 11 W: 11 05 b.Taunton 15-5-88
Internationals: Scotland U16. England C.
2006–07 Plymouth Arg 0 0
2007–08 Plymouth Arg 0 0
2010–11 Stevenage 44 4
2011–12 Stevenage 46 8 **90 12**
2012–13 Preston NE 19 4
2013–14 Preston NE 34 1
2014–15 Preston NE 31 0 **84 5**
2015–16 Scunthorpe U 32 2
2016–17 Scunthorpe U 1 0 **33 2**
2016–17 *Walsall* 28 3 **28 3**

MADDEN, Patrick (F) 290 94
H: 6 0 W: 11 13 b.Dublin 4-3-90
Internationals: Republic of Ireland U19, U21, U23, Full caps.
2008 Bohemians 18 4
2009 Bohemians 2 0
2009 Shelbourne 13 6 **13 6**
2010 Bohemians 34 10 **54 14**
2010–11 Carlisle U 13 0
2011–12 Carlisle U 18 1
2012–13 Carlisle U 1 1 **32 2**
2012–13 *Yeovil T* 35 22
2013–14 Yeovil T 9 0 **44 22**
2013–14 Scunthorpe U 21 5
2014–15 Scunthorpe U 46 14
2015–16 Scunthorpe U 46 20
2016–17 Scunthorpe U 34 11 **147 50**

MANTOM, Sam (M) 166 20
H: 5 9 W: 11 00 b.Stourbridge 20-2-92
Internationals: England U17.
2010–11 WBA 0 0
2010–11 *Tranmere R* 2 0 **2 0**
2010–11 *Oldham Ath* 4 0 **4 0**
2011–12 WBA 0 0
2011–12 *Walsall* 13 3
2012–13 WBA 0 0

2012–13 Walsall 29 2
2013–14 Walsall 43 5
2014–15 Walsall 12 0
2015–16 Walsall 37 8 **134** **18**
2016–17 Scunthorpe U 26 2 **26** **2**

MARGETTS, Jonathon (F) **3** **0**
H: 5 9 b.Edenthorpe 28-9-93
2014–15 Hull C 0 0
2014–15 *Cambridge U* 1 0 **1** **0**
From Lincoln C.
2016–17 Scunthorpe U 2 0 **2** **0**

MORRIS, Josh (M) **152** **30**
H: 5 9 W: 10 00 b.Preston 30-9-91
Internationals: England U20.
2010–11 Blackburn R 4 0
2011–12 Blackburn R 2 0
2011–12 *Yeovil T* 5 0 **5** **0**
2012–13 Blackburn R 10 0
2012–13 *Rotherham U* 5 0 **5** **0**
2013–14 Blackburn R 4 0
2013–14 *Carlisle U* 6 0 **6** **0**
2013–14 *Fleetwood T* 14 2
2014–15 Blackburn R 0 0 **20** **0**
2014–15 *Fleetwood T* 45 8 **59** **10**
2015–16 Bradford C 13 1 **13** **1**
2016–17 Scunthorpe U 44 19 **44** **19**

NESS, Jamie (M) **102** **4**
H: 6 2 W: 10 13 b.Irvine 2-3-91
Internationals: Scotland U17, U19, U21.
2010–11 Rangers 11 0
2011–12 Rangers 5 1 **16** **1**
2012–13 Stoke C 0 0
2013–14 Stoke C 0 0
2013–14 *Leyton Orient* 13 1 **13** **1**
2014–15 Stoke C 0 0
2014–15 *Crewe Alex* 34 2 **34** **2**
2015–16 Scunthorpe U 27 0
2016–17 Scunthorpe U 12 0 **39** **0**

SITHOLE, Fortunate (M) **0** **0**
2016–17 Scunthorpe U 0 0

SUTTON, Levi (M) **9** **0**
b. 24-3-96
2014–15 Scunthorpe U 0 0
2015–16 Scunthorpe U 1 0
2016–17 Scunthorpe U 8 0 **9** **0**

TOWNSEND, Conor (D) **99** **2**
H: 5 4 W: 9 11 b.Hessle 4-3-93
2011–12 Hull C 0 0
2012–13 Hull C 0 0
2012–13 *Chesterfield* 20 1 **20** **1**
2013–14 Hull C 0 0
2013–14 *Carlisle U* 12 0 **12** **0**
2014–15 Hull C 0 0
2014–15 *Dundee U* 17 0 **17** **0**
2014–15 *Scunthorpe U* 6 0
2015–16 Hull C 0 0
2015–16 Scunthorpe U 20 1
2016–17 Scunthorpe U 24 0 **50** **1**

VAN VEEN, Kevin (F) **134** **51**
H: 6 1 W: 11 11 b.Eindhoven 1-6-91
2013–14 JVC Cuyk 29 20 **29** **20**
2014–15 FC Oss 20 16 **20** **16**
2014–15 Scunthorpe U 20 2
2015–16 Scunthorpe U 20 2
2015–16 *Cambuur Leeuwarden* 12 1 **12** **1**
2016–17 Scunthorpe U 33 10 **73** **14**

VOSE, Dominic (M) **61** **2**
H: 5 8 W: 11 03 b.Lambeth 23-11-93
2010–11 West Ham U 0 0
2011–12 West Ham U 0 0
2012–13 Barnet 2 0 **2** **0**
2013–14 Colchester U 27 0
2014–15 Colchester U 7 0 **34** **0**
From Wrexham.
2015–16 Scunthorpe U 2 0
2016–17 Scunthorpe U 0 0 **2** **0**
2016–17 *Grimsby T* 23 2 **23** **2**

WALLACE, Murray (D) **149** **9**
H: 6 2 W: 11 07 b.Glasgow 10-1-93
Internationals: Scotland U20, U21.
2011–12 Falkirk 19 2 **19** **2**
2011–12 Huddersfield T 0 0
2012–13 Huddersfield T 6 1
2013–14 Huddersfield T 17 0
2014–15 Huddersfield T 26 2
2015–16 Huddersfield T 2 0 **51** **3**
2015–16 *Scunthorpe U* 33 2
2016–17 Scunthorpe U 46 2 **79** **4**

WATSON, Rory (G) **0** **0**
b. 5-2-96
2014–15 Hull C 0 0
2015–16 Hull C 0 0
2015–16 *Scunthorpe U* 0 0
2016–17 Scunthorpe U 0 0

WILLIAMS, Luke (F) **97** **11**
H: 6 1 W: 11 08 b.Middlesbrough 11-6-93
Internationals: England U17, U19, U20.
2009–10 Middlesbrough 4 0
2010–11 Middlesbrough 6 0
2011–12 Middlesbrough 0 0
2012–13 Middlesbrough 11 2
2013–14 Middlesbrough 9 0
2013–14 *Hartlepool U* 7 2 **7** **2**
2014–15 Middlesbrough 4 0 **34** **2**
2014–15 *Scunthorpe U* 6 2
2014–15 *Coventry C* 5 0 **5** **0**
2014–15 *Peterborough U* 2 0 **2** **0**
2015–16 Scunthorpe U 28 5
2016–17 Scunthorpe U 7 0 **41** **7**
2016–17 *Northampton T* 8 0 **8** **0**

WOOTTON, Kyle (M) **50** **7**
H: 6 2 W: 12 04 b. 11-10-96
2014–15 Scunthorpe U 12 1
2015–16 Scunthorpe U 20 3
2016–17 Scunthorpe U 2 1 **34** **5**
2016–17 *Cheltenham T* 16 2 **16** **2**

Players retained or with offer of contract
Sackey, Leslie Nii Aflah.

Scholars
Ablett, Harvey; Allasan, David; Appleby, Alexander Benn; Barmby, George; Bartholomew, Kane Rhys; Dean-Atkinson, James Peter; Ebraheem, Sami; Hornshaw, George Matthew; Lilley, Sam Joshua; McMichael, Lewis; Parker, Joe; Porter, Kyle Blue; Sithole, Fortunate Chibuzo; Train, Ewan.

SHEFFIELD U (74)

BASHAM, Chris (M) **241** **11**
H: 5 11 W: 12 08 b.Hebburn 20-7-88
2007–08 Bolton W 0 0
2007–08 *Rochdale* 13 0 **13** **0**
2008–09 Bolton W 11 1
2009–10 Bolton W 8 0 **19** **1**
2010–11 Blackpool 2 0
2011–12 Blackpool 17 2
2012–13 Blackpool 26 1
2013–14 Blackpool 40 2 **85** **5**
2014–15 Sheffield U 37 0
2015–16 Sheffield U 44 3
2016–17 Sheffield U 43 2 **124** **5**

BRAYFORD, John (D) **308** **7**
H: 5 8 W: 11 02 b.Stoke 29-12-87
Internationals: England C.
2008–09 Crewe Alex 36 2
2009–10 Crewe Alex 45 0 **81** **2**
2010–11 Derby Co 46 1
2011–12 Derby Co 23 0
2012–13 Derby Co 40 1 **109** **2**
2013–14 Cardiff C 0 0
2013–14 *Sheffield U* 15 1
2014–15 Cardiff C 26 0 **26** **0**
2014–15 Sheffield U 22 1
2015–16 Sheffield U 19 1
2016–17 Sheffield U 3 0 **59** **3**
2016–17 *Burton Alb* 33 0 **33** **0**

BROOKS, David (M) **0** **0**
b. 8-7-98
Internationals: England U20.
2015–16 Sheffield U 0 0
2016–17 Sheffield U 0 0

CANTRILL, George (D) **0** **0**
2016–17 Sheffield U 0 0

CARRUTHERS, Samir (F) **134** **6**
H: 5 8 W: 11 00 b.Islington 4-4-93
Internationals: Republic of Ireland U19, U21.
2011–12 Aston Villa 3 0
2012–13 Aston Villa 0 0
2013–14 Aston Villa 0 0 **3** **0**
2013–14 *Milton Keynes D* 23 2
2014–15 Milton Keynes D 32 2
2015–16 Milton Keynes D 39 1
2016–17 Milton Keynes D 23 1 **117** **6**
2016–17 Sheffield U 14 0 **14** **0**

CLARKE, Leon (F) **378** **113**
H: 6 2 W: 14 02 b.Birmingham 10-2-85
2003–04 Wolverhampton W 0 0
2003–04 *Kidderminster H* 4 0 **4** **0**
2004–05 Wolverhampton W 28 7
2005–06 Wolverhampton W 24 1
2005–06 *QPR* 1 0
2005–06 *Plymouth Arg* 5 0 **5** **0**
2006–07 Wolverhampton W 22 5
2006–07 Sheffield W 10 1
2006–07 *Oldham Ath* 5 3 **5** **3**
2007–08 Sheffield W 8 3
2007–08 *Southend U* 16 8 **16** **8**
2008–09 Sheffield W 29 8
2009–10 Sheffield W 36 6 **83** **18**
2010–11 QPR 13 0 **14** **0**
2010–11 *Preston NE* 6 1 **6** **1**
2011–12 Swindon T 2 0 **2** **0**
2011–12 *Chesterfield* 14 9 **14** **9**
2011–12 Charlton Ath 7 0
2011–12 *Crawley T* 4 1 **4** **1**
2012–13 Charlton Ath 0 0 **7** **0**
2012–13 *Scunthorpe U* 15 11 **15** **11**
2012–13 Coventry C 12 8
2013–14 Coventry C 23 15 **35** **23**
2013–14 Wolverhampton W 13 1
2014–15 Wolverhampton W 16 2 **103** **16**
2014–15 *Wigan Ath* 10 1 **10** **1**
2015–16 Bury 32 15 **32** **15**
2016–17 Sheffield U 23 7 **23** **7**

COUTTS, Paul (M) **284** **9**
H: 5 9 W: 11 11 b.Aberdeen 22-7-88
Internationals: Scotland U21.
2008–09 Peterborough U 37 0
2009–10 Peterborough U 16 0 **53** **0**
2009–10 Preston NE 13 1
2010–11 Preston NE 23 1
2011–12 Preston NE 41 2 **77** **4**
2012–13 Derby Co 44 3
2013–14 Derby Co 8 0
2014–15 Derby Co 7 0 **59** **3**
2014–15 Sheffield U 20 0
2015–16 Sheffield U 32 0
2016–17 Sheffield U 43 2 **95** **2**

CUMMINGS, Joe (D) **0** **0**
2016–17 Sheffield U 0 0

DONE, Matt (M) **344** **34**
H: 5 10 W: 10 04 b.Oswestry 22-6-88
2005–06 Wrexham 6 0
2006–07 Wrexham 34 1
2007–08 Wrexham 26 0 **66** **1**
2008–09 Hereford U 36 0
2009–10 Hereford U 20 0 **56** **0**
2010–11 Rochdale 33 5
2011–12 Barnsley 31 4
2012–13 Barnsley 13 0 **44** **4**
2012–13 *Hibernian* 7 0 **7** **0**
2013–14 Rochdale 38 0
2014–15 Rochdale 23 10 **94** **15**
2014–15 Sheffield U 15 7
2015–16 Sheffield U 31 4
2016–17 Sheffield U 31 3 **77** **14**

DUFFY, Mark (M) **295** **29**
H: 5 9 W: 11 05 b.Liverpool 7-10-85
2008–09 Morecambe 9 1
2009–10 Morecambe 35 4
2010–11 Morecambe 22 0 **66** **5**
2010–11 Scunthorpe U 22 1
2011–12 Scunthorpe U 37 2
2012–13 Scunthorpe U 43 5 **102** **8**
2013–14 Doncaster R 36 2 **36** **2**
2014–15 Birmingham C 4 0
2014–15 *Chesterfield* 3 0 **3** **0**
2015–16 Birmingham C 0 0 **4** **0**
2015–16 *Burton Alb* 45 8 **45** **8**
2016–17 Sheffield U 39 6 **39** **6**

FLECK, John (M) **254** **14**
H: 5 9 W: 11 05 b.Glasgow 24-8-91
Internationals: Scotland U17, U19, U21.
2007–08 Rangers 1 0
2008–09 Rangers 8 1
2009–10 Rangers 15 1
2010–11 Rangers 13 0
2011–12 Rangers 4 0 **41** **2**
2011–12 *Blackpool* 7 0 **7** **0**
2012–13 Coventry C 35 3
2013–14 Coventry C 43 1
2014–15 Coventry C 44 0
2015–16 Coventry C 40 4 **162** **8**
2016–17 Sheffield U 44 4 **44** **4**

FREEMAN, Kieron (D) 169 12
H: 5 10 W: 12 05 b.Nottingham 21-3-92
Internationals: Wales U17, U19, U21.

2010–11	Nottingham F	0	0		
2011–12	Nottingham F	0	0		
2011–12	*Notts Co*	19	1		
2012–13	Derby Co	19	0		
2013–14	Derby Co	6	0		
2013–14	*Notts Co*	16	0	**35**	**1**
2013–14	*Sheffield U*	12	0		
2014–15	Derby Co	0	0	**25**	**0**
2014–15	*Mansfield T*	11	0	**11**	**0**
2014–15	Sheffield U	19	1		
2015–16	Sheffield U	19	0		
2015–16	*Portsmouth*	7	0	**7**	**0**
2016–17	Sheffield U	41	10	**91**	**11**

GILMOUR, Harvey (M) 0 0

2016–17	Sheffield U	0	0

HALLAM, Jordan (M) 0 0

2016–17	Sheffield U	0	0

HANSON, James (F) 296 78
H: 6 4 W: 12 04 b.Bradford 9-11-87

2009–10	Bradford C	34	12		
2010–11	Bradford C	36	6		
2011–12	Bradford C	39	13		
2012–13	Bradford C	43	10		
2013–14	Bradford C	35	12		
2014–15	Bradford C	38	9		
2015–16	Bradford C	41	11		
2016–17	Bradford C	17	4	**283**	**77**
2016–17	Sheffield U	13	1	**13**	**1**

HUSSEY, Chris (D) 201 4
H: 5 10 W: 10 03 b.Hammersmith 2-1-89

2009–10	Coventry C	8	0		
2010–11	Coventry C	11	0		
2010–11	*Crewe Alex*	0	0		
2011–12	Coventry C	29	0		
2012–13	Coventry C	10	0	**58**	**0**
2012–13	AFC Wimbledon	19	0		
2013–14	AFC Wimbledon	0	0	**19**	**0**
2013–14	Burton Alb	27	1	**27**	**1**
2013–14	*Bury*	11	2		
2014–15	Bury	38	0		
2015–16	Bury	41	1	**90**	**3**
2016–17	Sheffield U	7	0	**7**	**0**

KELLY, Graham (D) 1 0
b. 16-10-97
Internationals: Republic of Ireland U18, U19.

2015–16	Sheffield U	1	0		
2016–17	Sheffield U	0	0	**1**	**0**

LAFFERTY, Danny (D) 163 13
H: 6 0 W: 12 08 b.Derry 1-4-89
Internationals: Northern Ireland U17, U19, U21, B, Full caps.

2009–10	Celtic	0	0		
2009–10	*Ayr U*	14	1	**14**	**1**
2010	Derry C	12	0		
2011	Derry C	34	7	**46**	**7**
2011–12	Burnley	5	0		
2012–13	Burnley	24	0		
2013–14	Burnley	10	0		
2014–15	Burnley	1	0		
2014–15	*Rotherham U*	11	0	**11**	**0**
2015–16	Burnley	0	0		
2015–16	*Oldham Ath*	15	1	**15**	**1**
2016–17	Burnley	0	0	**40**	**0**
2016–17	Sheffield U	37	4	**37**	**4**

LAVERY, Caolan (F) 93 20
H: 5 11 W: 11 12 b.Red Deer 22-10-92
Internationals: Canada U17. Northern Ireland U19, U21.

2012–13	Sheffield W	0	0		
2012–13	*Southend U*	3	0	**3**	**0**
2013–14	Sheffield W	21	4		
2013–14	*Plymouth Arg*	8	3	**8**	**3**
2014–15	Sheffield W	13	2		
2014–15	*Chesterfield*	8	3	**8**	**3**
2015–16	Sheffield W	0	0	**34**	**6**
2015–16	*Portsmouth*	13	4	**13**	**4**
2016–17	Sheffield U	27	4	**27**	**4**

LONG, George (G) 123 0
H: 6 0 W: 12 05 b.Sheffield 5-11-93
Internationals: England U18, U20.

2010–11	Sheffield U	1	0		
2011–12	Sheffield U	2	0		
2012–13	Sheffield U	36	0		
2013–14	Sheffield U	27	0		
2014–15	Sheffield U	0	0		
2014–15	*Oxford U*	10	0	**10**	**0**
2014–15	*Motherwell*	13	0	**13**	**0**
2015–16	Sheffield U	31	0		
2016–17	Sheffield U	3	0	**100**	**0**

MOORE, Simon (G) 135 0
H: 6 3 W: 12 02 b.Sandown 19-5-90
Internationals: Isle of Wight Full caps.

2009–10	Brentford	1	0		
2010–11	Brentford	10	0		
2011–12	Brentford	10	0		
2012–13	Brentford	43	0	**64**	**0**
2013–14	Cardiff C	0	0		
2013–14	*Bristol C*	11	0	**11**	**0**
2014–15	Cardiff C	10	0		
2015–16	Cardiff C	7	0	**17**	**0**
2016–17	Sheffield U	43	0	**43**	**0**

O'CONNELL, Jack (D) 148 10
H: 6 3 W: 13 05 b.Liverpool 29-3-94
Internationals: England U18, U19.

2012–13	Blackburn R	0	0		
2012–13	*Rotherham U*	3	0	**3**	**0**
2012–13	*York C*	18	0	**18**	**0**
2013–14	Blackburn R	0	0		
2013–14	*Rochdale*	38	0		
2014–15	Blackburn R	0	0		
2014–15	*Rochdale*	29	5	**67**	**5**
2014–15	Brentford	0	0		
2015–16	Brentford	16	1	**16**	**1**
2016–17	Sheffield U	44	4	**44**	**4**

PERRYMAN, Josh (G) 0 0

2016–17	Sheffield U	0	0

REED, Louis (M) 39 0
b. 25-7-97
Internationals: England U18, U19, U20.

2013–14	Sheffield U	1	0		
2014–15	Sheffield U	19	0		
2015–16	Sheffield U	19	0		
2016–17	Sheffield U	0	0	**39**	**0**

SCOUGALL, Stefan (M) 86 8
H: 5 7 W: 8 13 b.Edinburgh 7-12-92
Internationals: Scotland U21.

2013–14	Sheffield U	15	2		
2014–15	Sheffield U	25	1		
2015–16	Sheffield U	11	0		
2015–16	*Fleetwood T*	10	1	**10**	**1**
2016–17	Sheffield U	25	4	**76**	**7**

SEMPLE, Callum (D) 0 0

2016–17	Sheffield U	0	0

SHARP, Billy (F) 438 191
H: 5 9 W: 11 00 b.Sheffield 5-2-86

2004–05	Sheffield U	2	0		
2004–05	*Rushden & D*	16	9	**16**	**9**
2005–06	Scunthorpe U	37	23		
2006–07	Scunthorpe U	45	30	**82**	**53**
2007–08	Sheffield U	29	4		
2008–09	Sheffield U	22	4		
2009–10	Sheffield U	0	0		
2009–10	*Doncaster R*	33	15		
2010–11	Doncaster R	29	15		
2011–12	Doncaster R	20	10		
2011–12	Southampton	15	9		
2012–13	Southampton	2	0		
2012–13	*Nottingham F*	39	10	**39**	**10**
2013–14	Southampton	0	0	**17**	**9**
2013–14	*Reading*	10	2	**10**	**2**
2013–14	*Doncaster R*	16	4	**98**	**44**
2014–15	Leeds U	33	5	**33**	**5**
2015–16	Sheffield U	44	21		
2016–17	Sheffield U	46	30	**143**	**59**

SLATER, Regan (M) 0 0

2016–17	Sheffield U	0	0

STEVENS, Enda (D) 221 3
H: 6 0 W: 12 04 b.Dublin 9-7-90
Internationals: Republic of Ireland U21.

2008	UCD	2	0	**2**	**0**
2009	St Patrick's Ath	30	0	**30**	**0**
2010	Shamrock R	18	0		
2011	Shamrock R	27	0	**45**	**0**
2011–12	Aston Villa	0	0		
2012–13	Aston Villa	7	0		
2013–14	Aston Villa	0	0		
2013–14	*Notts Co*	2	0	**2**	**0**
2013–14	*Doncaster R*	13	0		
2014–15	Aston Villa	0	0	**7**	**0**
2014–15	*Northampton T*	4	1	**4**	**1**
2014–15	*Doncaster R*	28	1	**41**	**1**
2015–16	Portsmouth	45	0		
2016–17	Portsmouth	45	1	**90**	**1**
2016–17	Sheffield U	0	0		

WALLACE, Kieran (M) 15 0
H: 6 1 W: 11 11 b.Nottingham 26-1-95
Internationals: England U16, U17.

2014–15	Sheffield U	4	0		
2015–16	Sheffield U	11	0		
2016–17	Sheffield U	0	0	**15**	**0**
2016–17	*Fleetwood T*	0	0		

WHITEMAN, Ben (M) 31 7
b.Rochdale 17-6-96

2014–15	Sheffield U	0	0		
2015–16	Sheffield U	6	0		
2016–17	Sheffield U	2	0	**8**	**0**
2016–17	*Mansfield T*	23	7	**23**	**7**

WILSON, James (D) 169 3
H: 6 2 W: 11 05 b.Chepstow 26-2-89
Internationals: Wales U19. U21, Full caps.

2005–06	Bristol C	0	0		
2006–07	Bristol C	0	0		
2007–08	Bristol C	0	0		
2008–09	Bristol C	2	0		
2008–09	*Brentford*	14	0		
2009–10	Bristol C	0	0		
2009–10	*Brentford*	13	0	**27**	**0**
2010–11	Bristol C	2	0		
2011–12	Bristol C	21	0		
2012–13	Bristol C	6	0		
2013–14	Bristol C	0	0	**31**	**0**
2013–14	*Cheltenham T*	4	0	**4**	**0**
2013–14	Oldham Ath	16	1		
2014–15	Oldham Ath	41	1		
2015–16	Oldham Ath	43	0	**100**	**2**
2016–17	Sheffield U	7	1	**7**	**1**

WRIGHT, Jake (D) 259 0
H: 5 10 W: 11 07 b.Keighley 11-3-86

2005–06	Bradford C	1	0	**1**	**0**
From Halifax T, Crawley T					
2009–10	Brighton & HA	6	0	**6**	**0**
2010–11	Oxford U	35	0		
2011–12	Oxford U	43	0		
2012–13	Oxford U	42	0		
2013–14	Oxford U	31	0		
2014–15	Oxford U	42	0		
2015–16	Oxford U	29	0	**222**	**0**
2016–17	Sheffield U	30	0	**30**	**0**

Players retained or with offer of contract
Bennett, Jake William; Eastwood, Jake; Evans, Chedwyn Michael; Hirst, Horatio Michael James.

Scholars
Brown, Alexander Thomas; Burton, Keegan Jon; Cantrill, George; Charlesworth, Thomas Harry; Cummings, Joseph; Doherty, Jordan; Ford, Jake Christopher; Gilmour, Harvey James; Graham, Samuel; Greaves, Oliver; Hallam, Jordan Paul; Hawkes, Cameron; Mallon, Stephen; Parkhouse, David Cain; Perryman, Joshua; Portman, William Tendai; Semple, Callum Charlie; Slater, Regan; Smith, Tyler Gavin Junior; Warhurst, Hugo John.

SHEFFIELD W (75)

ABDI, Almen (M) 312 57
H: 5 11 W: 12 11 b.Prizren 21-10-86
Internationals: Switzerland, U21, Full caps.

2003–04	FC Zurich	11	0		
2004–05	FC Zurich	5	0		
2005–06	FC Zurich	12	0		
2006–07	FC Zurich	28	5		
2007–08	FC Zurich	31	7		
2008–09	FC Zurich	32	19		
2009–10	FC Zurich	8	0	**127**	**31**
2009–10	Le Mans	13	0	**13**	**0**
2010–11	Udinese	19	0		
2011–12	Udinese	22	0	**41**	**0**
2012–13	*Watford*	38	12		
2013–14	Watford	13	2		
2014–15	Watford	32	9		
2015–16	Watford	32	2	**115**	**25**
2016–17	Sheffield W	16	1	**16**	**1**

BANNAN, Barry (D) 217 7
H: 5 10 W: 10 08 b.Glasgow 1-12-89
Internationals: Scotland U21, Full caps.

2008–09	Aston Villa	0	0		
2008–09	*Derby Co*	10	1	**10**	**1**
2009–10	Aston Villa	0	0		
2009–10	*Blackpool*	20	1	**20**	**1**
2010–11	Aston Villa	12	0		
2010–11	*Leeds U*	7	0	**7**	**0**
2011–12	Aston Villa	28	1		
2012–13	Aston Villa	24	0		
2013–14	Aston Villa	0	0	**64**	**1**
2013–14	Crystal Palace	15	1		
2014–15	Crystal Palace	7	0		
2014–15	*Bolton W*	16	0	**16**	**0**
2015–16	Crystal Palace	0	0	**22**	**1**

2015–16 Sheffield W 35 2
2016–17 Sheffield W 43 1 **78 3**

CLARE, Sean (M) 12 1
H: 6 3 b.Sheffield 18-9-96
2015–16 Sheffield W 0 0
2015–16 *Bury* 4 0 **4 0**
2016–17 Sheffield W 0 0
2016–17 *Accrington S* 8 1 **8 1**

DAWSON, Cameron (G) 5 0
H: 6 0 W: 10 12 b.Sheffield 7-7-95
Internationals: England U18, U19.
2013–14 Sheffield W 0 0
2013–14 *Plymouth Arg* 0 0
2014–15 Sheffield W 0 0
2015–16 Sheffield W 0 0
2016–17 Wycombe W 1 0 **1 0**
2016–17 Sheffield W 4 0 **4 0**

EMANUELSON, Urby (M) 258 21
H: 5 8 W: 10 11 b.Amsterdam 16-6-86
Internationals: Holland Youth, U21, B, Full caps.
2004–05 Ajax 2 0
2005–06 Ajax 25 1
2006–07 Ajax 30 3
2007–08 Ajax 31 3
2008–09 Ajax 32 4
2009–10 Ajax 31 5
2010–11 Ajax 18 1 **169 17**
2010–11 AC Milan 9 0
2011–12 AC Milan 30 2
2012–13 AC Milan 12 1
2012–13 *Fulham* 13 1 **13 1**
2013–14 AC Milan 24 0 **75 3**
2016–17 Verona 0 0
2016–17 Sheffield W 1 0 **1 0**

FLETCHER, Steven (F) 396 108
H: 6 1 W: 12 00 b.Shrewsbury 26-3-87
Internationals: Scotland U20, U21, B, Full caps.
2003–04 Hibernian 5 0
2004–05 Hibernian 20 5
2005–06 Hibernian 34 8
2006–07 Hibernian 31 6
2007–08 Hibernian 32 13
2008–09 Hibernian 34 11 **156 43**
2009–10 Burnley 35 8 **35 8**
2010–11 Wolverhampton W 29 10
2011–12 Wolverhampton W 32 12 **61 22**
2012–13 Sunderland 28 11
2013–14 Sunderland 20 3
2014–15 Sunderland 30 5
2015–16 Sunderland 16 4 **94 23**
2015–16 *Marseille* 12 2 **12 2**
2016–17 Sheffield W 38 10 **38 10**

FORESTIERI, Fernando (F) 247 60
H: 5 8 W: 10 07 b.Rosario 16-1-90
Internationals: Italy U17, U19, U20, U21.
2006–07 Genoa 1 1 **1 1**
2007–08 Siena 17 1
2008–09 Siena 2 0 **19 1**
2008–09 Vicenza 13 5 **13 5**
2009–10 Malaga 19 1 **19 1**
2010–11 Empoli 17 3 **17 3**
2011–12 Bari 27 2 **27 2**
2012–13 Udinese 0 0
2012–13 *Watford* 28 8
2013–14 Watford 28 7
2014–15 Watford 24 5 **80 20**
2015–16 Sheffield W 36 15
2016–17 Sheffield W 35 12 **71 27**

FOX, Morgan (D) 120 3
H: 6 1 W: 12 03 b.Chelmsford 21-9-93
Internationals: Wales U21.
2012–13 Charlton Ath 0 0
2013–14 Charlton Ath 6 0
2013–14 *Notts Co* 7 1 **7 1**
2014–15 Charlton Ath 31 0
2015–16 Charlton Ath 42 1
2016–17 Charlton Ath 24 0 **103 1**
2016–17 Sheffield W 10 1 **10 1**

HELAN, Jeremy (M) 142 4
H: 5 11 W: 12 00 b.Paris 9-5-92
Internationals: France U19.
2009–10 Manchester C 0 0
2010–11 Manchester C 0 0
2011–12 Manchester C 0 0
2011–12 *Carlisle U* 2 0 **2 0**
2012–13 Manchester C 0 0
2012–13 *Shrewsbury T* 3 0 **3 0**
2012–13 *Sheffield W* 28 1
2013–14 Sheffield W 43 2
2014–15 Sheffield W 38 1
2015–16 Sheffield W 20 0
2015–16 *Wolverhampton W* 8 0 **8 0**
2016–17 Sheffield W 0 0 **129 4**

HIRST, George (F) 1 0
b.Sheffield 15-2-99
Internationals: England U17, U18, U20.
2016–17 Sheffield W 1 0 **1 0**

HOOPER, Gary (F) 346 158
H: 5 9 W: 11 02 b.Loughton 26-1-88
2006–07 Southend U 19 0
2006–07 *Leyton Orient* 4 2 **4 2**
2007–08 Southend U 13 2 **32 2**
2007–08 *Hereford U* 19 11 **19 11**
2008–09 Scunthorpe U 45 24
2009–10 Scunthorpe U 35 19 **80 43**
2010–11 Celtic 26 20
2011–12 Celtic 37 24
2012–13 Celtic 32 19 **95 63**
2013–14 Norwich C 32 6
2014–15 Norwich C 30 12
2015–16 Norwich C 2 0 **64 18**
2015–16 Sheffield W 29 13
2016–17 Sheffield W 23 6 **52 19**

HUNT, Jack (D) 234 2
H: 5 9 W: 11 02 b.Rothwell 6-12-90
2009–10 Huddersfield T 0 0
2010–11 Huddersfield T 19 1
2010–11 *Chesterfield* 20 0 **20 0**
2011–12 Huddersfield T 43 1
2012–13 Huddersfield T 40 0
2013–14 Huddersfield T 2 0 **104 2**
2013–14 Crystal Palace 0 0
2013–14 *Barnsley* 11 0 **11 0**
2014–15 Crystal Palace 0 0
2014–15 *Nottingham F* 17 0 **17 0**
2014–15 *Rotherham U* 16 0 **16 0**
2015–16 Sheffield W 34 0
2016–17 Sheffield W 32 0 **66 0**

HUTCHINSON, Sam (M) 103 4
H: 6 0 W: 11 07 b.Windsor 3-8-89
Internationals: England U18, U19.
2006–07 Chelsea 1 0
2007–08 Chelsea 0 0
2008–09 Chelsea 0 0
2009–10 Chelsea 2 0
2010–11 Chelsea 0 0
2011–12 Chelsea 2 0
2012–13 Chelsea 0 0
2012–13 *Nottingham F* 9 1 **9 1**
2013–14 Chelsea 0 0 **5 0**
2013–14 *Vitesse* 1 0 **1 0**
2013–14 *Sheffield W* 10 1
2014–15 Sheffield W 20 0
2015–16 Sheffield W 25 0
2016–17 Sheffield W 33 2 **88 3**

JONES, David (M) 343 26
H: 5 11 W: 10 10 b.Southport 4-11-84
Internationals: England U21.
2003–04 Manchester U 0 0
2004–05 Manchester U 0 0
2005–06 Manchester U 0 0
2005–06 *Preston NE* 24 3 **24 3**
2005–06 NEC Nijmegen 17 6 **17 6**
2006–07 Manchester U 0 0
2006–07 Derby Co 28 6
2007–08 Derby Co 14 1 **42 7**
2008–09 Wolverhampton W 34 4
2009–10 Wolverhampton W 20 1
2010–11 Wolverhampton W 12 1 **66 6**
2011–12 Wigan Ath 16 0
2012–13 Wigan Ath 13 0 **29 0**
2012–13 *Blackburn R* 12 2 **12 2**
2013–14 Burnley 46 1
2014–15 Burnley 36 0
2015–16 Burnley 41 1
2016–17 Burnley 1 0 **124 2**
2016–17 Sheffield W 29 0 **29 0**

KEAN, Jake (G) 111 0
H: 6 4 W: 11 13 b.Derby 4-2-91
Internationals: England U20.
2010–11 Blackburn R 0 0
2010–11 *Hartlepool U* 19 0 **19 0**
2011–12 Blackburn R 1 0
2011–12 *Rochdale* 14 0 **14 0**
2012–13 Blackburn R 18 0
2013–14 Blackburn R 18 0
2014–15 Blackburn R 0 0 **37 0**
2014–15 *Yeovil T* 5 0 **5 0**
2014–15 *Oldham Ath* 11 0 **11 0**
2015–16 Norwich C 0 0
2015–16 *Colchester U* 3 0 **3 0**
2015–16 *Swindon T* 3 0 **3 0**
2016–17 Sheffield W 0 0
2016–17 *Mansfield T* 19 0 **19 0**

LEE, Kieran (D) 276 22
H: 6 1 W: 12 00 b.Stalybridge 22-6-88
2006–07 Manchester U 1 0
2007–08 Manchester U 0 0 **1 0**
2007–08 *QPR* 7 0 **7 0**
2008–09 Oldham Ath 7 0
2009–10 Oldham Ath 24 1
2010–11 Oldham Ath 43 2
2011–12 Oldham Ath 43 2 **117 5**
2012–13 Sheffield W 23 0
2013–14 Sheffield W 26 1
2014–15 Sheffield W 33 6
2015–16 Sheffield W 43 5
2016–17 Sheffield W 26 5 **151 17**

LEES, Tom (D) 320 11
H: 6 1 W: 12 04 b.Warwick 28-11-90
Internationals: England U21.
2008–09 Leeds U 0 0
2009–10 Leeds U 0 0
2009–10 *Accrington S* 39 0 **39 0**
2010–11 Leeds U 0 0
2010–11 *Bury* 45 4 **45 4**
2011–12 Leeds U 42 2
2012–13 Leeds U 40 1
2013–14 Leeds U 41 0 **123 3**
2014–15 Sheffield W 44 0
2015–16 Sheffield W 34 3
2016–17 Sheffield W 35 1 **113 4**

LOOVENS, Glenn (D) 355 14
H: 5 10 W: 11 08 b.Doetrinchem 22-10-83
Internationals: Netherlands U21, Full caps.
2001–02 Feyenoord 8 0
2002–03 Feyenoord 12 0
2003–04 Feyenoord 1 0
2003–04 Excelsior 24 2 **24 2**
2004–05 Feyenoord 6 0 **27 0**
2004–05 De Graafschap 11 0 **11 0**
2005–06 Cardiff C 33 2
2006–07 Cardiff C 30 1
2007–08 Cardiff C 36 0
2008–09 Cardiff C 1 0 **100 3**
2008–09 Celtic 17 3
2009–10 Celtic 20 3
2010–11 Celtic 13 1
2011–12 Celtic 11 1 **61 8**
2012–13 Real Zaragoza 21 0 **21 0**
2013–14 Sheffield W 22 0
2014–15 Sheffield W 26 0
2015–16 Sheffield W 31 0
2016–17 Sheffield W 32 1 **111 1**

LUCAS JOAO, Eduardo (F) 136 27
H: 6 4 W: 12 08 b.Luanda 4-9-93
Internationals: Portugal U20, U21, U23, Full caps.
2012–13 Nacional 0 0
2012–13 *Mirandela* 27 12 **27 12**
2013–14 Nacional 16 0
2014–15 Nacional 30 6 **46 6**
2015–16 Sheffield W 40 6
2016–17 Sheffield W 10 0 **50 6**
2016–17 *Blackburn R* 13 3 **13 3**

MARCO MATIAS, Andre (F) 171 35
H: 5 10 W: 10 08 b.Barreiro 10-5-89
Internationals: Portugal U18, U19, U21.
2008–09 Sporting Lisbon 0 0
2008–09 *Varzim* 12 0 **12 0**
2009–10 Sporting Lisbon 0 0
2009–10 *Fatima* 7 2 **7 2**
2009–10 *Real Massama* 15 0 **15 0**
2010–11 Vit Guimaraes 0 0
2010–11 *Freamunde* 24 5
2011–12 Vit Guimaraes 0 0
2011–12 *Freamunde* 19 2 **43 7**
2012–13 Vit Guimaraes 20 0
2013–14 Vit Guimaraes 22 6 **42 6**
2014–15 Nacional 33 17 **33 17**
2015–16 Sheffield W 17 3
2016–17 Sheffield W 2 0 **19 3**

MURPHY, James (M) 0 0
H: 5 11 W: 11 07 b.Scotch Plains 17-9-97
Internationals: USA U20.
2016–17 Sheffield W 0 0

NUHIU, Atdhe (F) 275 42
H: 6 6 W: 13 05 b.Prishtina 29-7-89
Internationals: Austria U19, U20, U21.
Kosovo Full caps.
2008–09 Austria Karnten 16 2
2009–10 Austria Karnten 3 0 **19 2**
2009–10 SV Ried 27 6 **27 6**
2010–11 Rapid Vienna 28 5
2011–12 Rapid Vienna 31 8 **59 13**
2012–13 Eskisehirspor 28 2 **28 2**
2013–14 Sheffield W 38 8

2014–15 Sheffield W 43 8
2015–16 Sheffield W 41 3
2016–17 Sheffield W 20 0 **142 19**

O'GRADY, Connor (D) 0 0
b.Sheffield 5-12-97
2016–17 Sheffield W 0 0

PALMER, Liam (M) 176 1
H: 6 2 W: 12 10 b.Worksop 19-9-91
Internationals: Scotland U19, U21.
2010–11 Sheffield W 9 0
2011–12 Sheffield W 14 1
2012–13 Sheffield W 0 0
2012–13 *Tranmere R* 43 0
2013–14 *Tranmere R* 0 0 **43 0**
2013–14 Sheffield W 39 0
2014–15 Sheffield W 35 0
2015–16 Sheffield W 15 0
2016–17 Sheffield W 21 0 **133 1**

PENNEY, Matt (D) 1 0
b.Chesterfield 11-2-98
2016–17 Sheffield W 0 0
2016–17 *Bradford C* 1 0 **1 0**

PUDIL, Daniel (D) 296 28
H: 6 1 W: 12 11 b.Prague 27-9-85
Internationals: Czech Republic U19, U21, Full caps.
2003–04 Blsany 2 2 **2 2**
2005–06 Liberec 3 4
2006–07 Liberec 3 3 **6 7**
2007–08 Slavia Prague 16 6 **16 6**
2008–09 Genk 29 4
2009–10 Genk 27 1
2010–11 Genk 32 0
2011–12 Genk 18 0 **106 5**
2011–12 Cesena 7 1 **7 1**
2012–13 Watford 37 1
2013–14 Watford 37 2
2014–15 Watford 23 0
2015–16 Watford 0 0 **97 3**
2015–16 *Sheffield W* 36 2
2016–17 Sheffield W 26 2 **62 4**

REACH, Adam (M) 177 19
H: 6 1 W: 11 07 b.Gateshead 3-2-93
Internationals: England U19, U20.
2010–11 Middlesbrough 1 1
2011–12 Middlesbrough 1 0
2012–13 Middlesbrough 16 2
2013–14 Middlesbrough 2 0
2013–14 *Shrewsbury T* 22 3 **22 3**
2013–14 *Bradford C* 18 3 **18 3**
2014–15 Middlesbrough 39 2
2015–16 Middlesbrough 4 1
2015–16 *Preston NE* 35 4 **35 4**
2016–17 Middlesbrough 0 0 **63 6**
2016–17 Sheffield W 39 3 **39 3**

SASSO, Vincent (D) 84 4
H: 6 3 W: 12 13 b.Saint-Cloud 16-2-91
Internationals: France U16, U17, U18, U19, U20, U21.
2010–11 Nantes 20 0
2011–12 Nantes 4 0 **24 0**
2012–13 Beira-Mar 15 2 **15 2**
2012–13 Braga 5 0
2013–14 Braga 7 0
2014–15 Braga 5 0
2015–16 Braga 0 0 **17 0**
2015–16 *Sheffield W* 14 0
2016–17 Sheffield W 14 2 **28 2**

SEMEDO, Jose (D) 334 5
H: 6 0 W: 12 08 b.Setubal 11-1-85
Internationals: Portugal U17, U18, U19, U20, U21, B.
2004–05 Sporting Lisbon 0 0
2004–05 *Casa Pia* 34 2 **34 2**
2005–06 *Feirense* 18 0 **18 0**
2006–07 *Cagliari* 3 0 **3 0**
2007–08 Charlton Ath 37 0
2008–09 Charlton Ath 18 0
2009–10 Charlton Ath 38 1
2010–11 Charlton Ath 42 1 **135 2**
2011–12 Sheffield W 46 1
2012–13 Sheffield W 26 0
2013–14 Sheffield W 22 0
2014–15 Sheffield W 30 0
2015–16 Sheffield W 10 0
2016–17 Sheffield W 10 0 **144 1**

SOUGOU, Moudou (F) 285 46
H: 5 10 W: 10 10 b.Fissel 18-12-84
Internationals: Senegal Full caps.
2004–05 Uniao Leiria 7 0
2005–06 Victoria Setubal 27 0 **27 0**
2006–07 Uniao Leiria 15 5
2007–08 Uniao Leiria 23 1 **45 6**
2008–09 Academica 23 4
2009–10 Academica 29 9
2010–11 Academica 28 6 **80 19**
2011–12 Cluj 33 10
2012–13 Cluj 11 1 **44 11**
2012–13 Marseille 14 0
2013–14 Marseille 0 0
2013–14 *Evian* 29 4
2014–15 Marseille 0 0 **14 0**
2014–15 *Evian* 24 2 **53 6**
2015–16 Sheffield W 9 2
2016–17 Sheffield W 0 0 **9 2**
2016–17 *Moreirense* 13 2 **13 2**

STOBBS, Jack (M) 2 0
H: 5 11 W: 13 05 b.Leeds 27-2-97
2013–14 Sheffield W 1 0
2014–15 Sheffield W 0 0
2015–16 Sheffield W 1 0
2016–17 Sheffield W 0 0 **2 0**

THORNILEY, Jordan (D) 0 0
b.Warrington 24-11-96
From Everton.
2016–17 Sheffield W 0 0

WALLACE, Ross (M) 400 42
H: 5 6 W: 9 12 b.Dundee 23-5-85
Internationals: Scotland U18, U19, U21, B, Full caps.
2001–02 Celtic 0 0
2002–03 Celtic 0 0
2003–04 Celtic 8 1
2004–05 Celtic 16 0
2005–06 Celtic 11 0
2006–07 Celtic 2 0 **37 1**
2006–07 Sunderland 32 6
2007–08 Sunderland 21 2
2008–09 Sunderland 0 0 **53 8**
2008–09 Preston NE 39 5
2009–10 Preston NE 41 7 **80 12**
2010–11 Burnley 40 3
2011–12 Burnley 44 5
2012–13 Burnley 36 3
2013–14 Burnley 14 0
2014–15 Burnley 15 1 **149 12**
2015–16 Sheffield W 40 4
2016–17 Sheffield W 41 5 **81 9**

WESTWOOD, Keiren (G) 397 0
H: 6 1 W: 13 10 b.Manchester 23-10-84
Internationals: Republic of Ireland Full caps.
2001–02 Manchester C 0 0
2002–03 Manchester C 0 0
2003–04 Manchester C 0 0
2003–04 *Oldham Ath* 0 0
2004–05 Manchester C 0 0
2005–06 Manchester C 0 0
2005–06 Carlisle U 35 0
2006–07 Carlisle U 46 0
2007–08 Carlisle U 46 0 **127 0**
2008–09 Coventry C 46 0
2009–10 Coventry C 44 0
2010–11 Coventry C 41 0 **131 0**
2011–12 Sunderland 9 0
2012–13 Sunderland 0 0
2013–14 Sunderland 10 0 **19 0**
2014–15 Sheffield W 43 0
2015–16 Sheffield W 34 0
2016–17 Sheffield W 43 0 **120 0**

WILDSMITH, Joe (G) 12 0
H: 6 0 W: 10 03 b.Sheffield 28-12-95
Internationals: England U20.
2013–14 Sheffield W 0 0
2014–15 Sheffield W 0 0
2014–15 *Barnsley* 2 0 **2 0**
2015–16 Sheffield W 9 0
2016–17 Sheffield W 1 0 **10 0**

WINNALL, Sam (F) 189 76
H: 5 9 W: 11 04 b.Wolverhampton 19-1-91
2009–10 Wolverhampton W 0 0
2010–11 Wolverhampton W 0 0
2010–11 *Burton Alb* 19 7 **19 7**
2011–12 Wolverhampton W 0 0
2011–12 *Hereford U* 8 2 **8 2**
2011–12 *Inverness CT* 2 0 **2 0**
2012–13 Wolverhampton W 0 0
2012–13 *Shrewsbury T* 4 0 **4 0**
2013–14 Scunthorpe U 45 23 **45 23**
2014–15 Barnsley 32 9
2015–16 Barnsley 43 21
2016–17 Barnsley 22 11 **97 41**
2016–17 Sheffield W 14 3 **14 3**

Players retained or with offer of contract
Baker, Ashley Thomas; Clarke, Warren Eliott; Da, Silva Lopes Matias Marco Andre; Dos, Santos Joao Lucas Eduardo; Kirby, Connor Alexander; Lonchar, Jordan Rhys; McGugan, Lewis Shay; Melo, Da Silva Filipe Joaquim; Preston, Fraser Thomas; Stobbs, Jack Thomas; Williams, Liam Shaun.

Scholars
Borukov, Preslav Nikolaev; Brazinskas, Arijus; Brennan, Ciaran Thomas; Cook, Joseph Oliver; Ferguson, Luke; Gavrilov, Stefan Emilov; Hornsby, Benjamin Jack; Hughes, Ben Anthony; Hunt, Alexander John; Price, Lewis Alan; Reaney, Joshua Craig Kenneth; Swaine, Layton John; Walker, Joseph Alan; Wallis, Daniel Michael; West, Joseph William.

SHREWSBURY T (76)

ANDERSON, Kayman (F) 0 0
2013–14 Shrewsbury T 0 0
2014–15 Shrewsbury T 0 0
2016–17 Shrewsbury T 0 0

BARNETT, Ryan (M) 0 0
2016–17 Shrewsbury T 0 0

BROWN, Junior (D) 183 20
H: 5 9 W: 10 09 b.Crewe 7-5-89
2006–07 Crewe Alex 0 0
2007–08 Crewe Alex 1 0 **1 0**
2012–13 Fleetwood T 43 11
2013–14 Fleetwood T 21 1 **64 12**
2013–14 *Tranmere R* 9 1 **9 1**
2014–15 Oxford U 11 0 **11 0**
2014–15 Mansfield T 24 2 **24 2**
2015–16 Shrewsbury T 31 0
2016–17 Shrewsbury T 43 5 **74 5**

BURTON, Callum (G) 1 0
H: 6 2 W: 12 00 b.Newport, Shropshire 15-8-96
Internationals: England U16, U17, U18.
2013–14 Shrewsbury T 0 0
2014–15 Shrewsbury T 0 0
2015–16 Shrewsbury T 1 0
2016–17 Shrewsbury T 0 0 **1 0**

DEEGAN, Gary (M) 276 18
H: 5 9 W: 11 11 b.Dublin 28-9-87
2005–06 Shelbourne 0 0
2006 *Kilkenny City* 18 4 **18 4**
2007 Longford Town 30 3 **30 3**
2008 Galway U 17 0 **17 0**
2008 Bohemians 12 3 **12 3**
2009 Bohemains 23 2 **23 2**
2009–10 Coventry C 17 2
2010–11 Coventry C 1 0
2011–12 Coventry C 24 3 **42 5**
2012–13 Hibernian 20 0 **20 0**
2013–14 Northampton T 27 1 **27 1**
2014–15 Southend U 22 0
2015–16 Southend U 25 0 **47 0**
2016–17 Shrewsbury T 40 0 **40 0**

DODDS, Louis (M) 380 70
H: 5 10 W: 12 04 b.Sheffield 8-10-86
2005–06 Leicester C 0 0
2006–07 Leicester C 0 0
2006–07 *Rochdale* 12 2 **12 2**
2007–08 Leicester C 0 0
2007–08 *Lincoln C* 41 9 **41 9**
2008–09 Port Vale 44 7
2009–10 Port Vale 44 6
2010–11 Port Vale 33 7
2011–12 Port Vale 35 8
2012–13 Port Vale 30 7
2013–14 Port Vale 29 4
2014–15 Port Vale 37 4
2015–16 Port Vale 37 8 **289 51**
2016–17 Shrewsbury T 38 8 **38 8**

EL-ABD, Adam (D) 389 8
H: 5 10 W: 13 05 b.Brighton 11-9-84
Internationals: Egypt Full caps.
2003–04 Brighton & HA 11 0
2004–05 Brighton & HA 16 0
2005–06 Brighton & HA 29 0
2006–07 Brighton & HA 42 1
2007–08 Brighton & HA 35 1
2008–09 Brighton & HA 31 0
2009–10 Brighton & HA 35 1
2010–11 Brighton & HA 37 1
2011–12 Brighton & HA 23 0
2012–13 Brighton & HA 32 1
2013–14 Brighton & HA 9 0 **300 5**
2013–14 Bristol C 14 0
2014–15 Bristol C 2 0
2014–15 *Bury* 24 1 **24 1**

2015–16 Bristol C 0 0 **16 0**
2015–16 *Swindon T* 13 0 **13 0**
2015–16 *Gillingham* 8 0 **8 0**
2016–17 Shrewsbury T 28 2 **28 2**

GROGAN, Callum (D) 0 0
H: 6 1 W: 12 08 b.Liverpool 12-12-97
2016–17 Shrewsbury T 0 0

HALSTEAD, Mark (G) 23 0
H: 6 3 W: 14 00 b.Blackpool 1-9-90
2009–10 Blackpool 0 0
2010–11 Blackpool 1 0
2011–12 Blackpool 0 0
2012–13 Blackpool 2 0
2013–14 Blackpool 0 0 **3 0**
2014–15 Shrewsbury T 1 0
2015–16 Shrewsbury T 16 0
2016–17 Shrewsbury T 3 0 **20 0**

JONES, Ethan (F) 5 0
b.Dudley 4-4-98
2015–16 Shrewsbury T 1 0
2016–17 Shrewsbury T 4 0 **5 0**

LANCASHIRE, Oliver (D) 208 5
H: 6 1 W: 11 10 b.Basingstoke 13-12-88
2006–07 Southampton 0 0
2007–08 Southampton 0 0
2008–09 Southampton 11 0
2009–10 Southampton 2 0 **13 0**
2009–10 *Grimsby T* 25 1 **25 1**
2010–11 Walsall 29 0
2011–12 Walsall 20 1 **49 1**
2012–13 Aldershot T 12 0 **12 0**
2013–14 Rochdale 38 0
2014–15 Rochdale 21 0
2015–16 Rochdale 34 2 **93 2**
2016–17 Shrewsbury T 16 1 **16 1**

LEITCH-SMITH, AJ (F) 207 37
H: 5 11 W: 12 04 b.Crewe 6-3-90
2008–09 Crewe Alex 0 0
2009 *IBV* 18 5 **18 5**
2009–10 Crewe Alex 1 0
2010–11 Crewe Alex 16 5
2011–12 Crewe Alex 38 8
2012–13 Crewe Alex 28 4
2013–14 Crewe Alex 20 2 **103 19**
2014–15 Yeovil T 33 2 **33 2**
2015–16 Port Vale 37 10 **37 10**
2016–17 Shrewsbury T 16 1 **16 1**

LEUTWILER, Jayson (G) 121 0
H: 6 3 W: 12 07 b.Basel 25-4-89
Internationals: Switzerland U16, U17, U18, U19, U20, U21. Canada Full caps.
2012–13 Middlesbrough 0 0
2013–14 Middlesbrough 3 0 **3 0**
2014–15 Shrewsbury T 46 0
2015–16 Shrewsbury T 29 0
2016–17 Shrewsbury T 43 0 **118 0**

MANGAN, Andy (F) 134 26
H: 6 0 W: 11 09 b.Liverpool 30-8-86
Internationals: England C.
2003–04 Blackpool 2 0
2004–05 Blackpool 0 0 **2 0**
From Hyde
2006–07 Accrington S 34 4
2007–08 Bury 20 4 **20 4**
2007–08 *Accrington S* 7 1 **41 5**
From Forest Green R, Wrexham
2012–13 Fleetwood T 12 4 **12 4**
From Forest Green R.
2014–15 Shrewsbury T 30 8
From Tranmere R.
2015–16 Shrewsbury T 19 5
2016–17 Shrewsbury T 10 0 **59 13**

McATEE, John (F) 1 0
2016–17 Shrewsbury T 1 0 **1 0**

McGIVERN, Ryan (D) 192 2
H: 5 10 W: 11 07 b.Newry 8-1-90
Internationals: Northern Ireland U16, U17, U19, U21, B, Full caps.
2007–08 Manchester C 0 0
2008–09 Manchester C 0 0
2008–09 *Morecambe* 5 1 **5 1**
2009–10 Manchester C 0 0
2009–10 *Leicester C* 12 0 **12 0**
2010–11 Manchester C 1 0
2010–11 *Walsall* 15 0 **15 0**
2011–12 Manchester C 0 0
2011–12 *Crystal Palace* 5 0 **5 0**
2011–12 *Bristol C* 31 0 **31 0**
2012–13 Manchester C 0 0 **1 0**
2012–13 *Hibernian* 27 1
2013–14 Hibernian 33 0 **60 1**
2014–15 Port Vale 20 0

2015–16 Port Vale 28 0 **48 0**
2016–17 Shrewsbury T 15 0 **15 0**

NSIALA, Aristote (D) 88 2
H: 6 4 W: 14 09 b.DR Congo 25-3-92
Internationals: DR Congo Full caps.
2009–10 Everton 0 0
2010–11 Everton 0 0
2010–11 *Macclesfield T* 10 0 **10 0**
2011–12 Everton 0 0
2011–12 *Accrington S* 19 0
2012–13 Accrington S 17 0
2013–14 Accrington S 0 0 **36 0**
2016–17 Hartlepool U 21 1 **21 1**
2016–17 Shrewsbury T 21 1 **21 1**

O'BRIEN, Jim (F) 324 22
H: 6 0 W: 11 11 b.Alexandria 28-9-87
Internationals: Republic of Ireland U19, U21.
2006–07 Celtic 0 0
2006–07 *Dunfermline Ath* 13 1 **13 1**
2007–08 Celtic 1 0 **1 0**
2007–08 *Dundee U* 10 0 **10 0**
2008–09 Motherwell 29 1
2009–10 Motherwell 35 3 **64 4**
2010–11 Barnsley 33 1
2011–12 Barnsley 31 2
2012–13 Barnsley 30 2
2013–14 Barnsley 29 2 **123 7**
2014–15 Coventry C 44 6
2015–16 Coventry C 26 2 **70 8**
2015–16 *Scunthorpe U* 9 1 **9 1**
2016–17 Shrewsbury T 18 0 **18 0**
2016–17 *Ross Co* 16 1 **16 1**

OGOGO, Abu (D) 302 20
H: 5 8 W: 10 02 b.Epsom 3-11-89
2007–08 Arsenal 0 0
2008–09 Arsenal 0 0
2008–09 *Barnet* 9 1 **9 1**
2009–10 Dagenham & R 30 2
2010–11 Dagenham & R 33 1
2011–12 Dagenham & R 40 1
2012–13 Dagenham & R 46 1
2013–14 Dagenham & R 44 8
2014–15 Dagenham & R 32 4 **225 17**
2015–16 Shrewsbury T 42 2
2016–17 Shrewsbury T 26 0 **68 2**

RILEY, Joe (D) 107 3
H: 6 0 W: 11 02 b.Salford 13-10-91
2011–12 Bolton W 3 0
2012–13 Bolton W 0 0
2013–14 Bolton W 0 0
2014–15 Bolton W 0 0 **3 0**
2014–15 *Oxford U* 22 0 **22 0**
2014–15 Bury 17 1
2015–16 Bury 33 1 **50 2**
2016–17 Shrewsbury T 32 1 **32 1**

ROBERTS, Callum (D) 0 0
2016–17 Shrewsbury T 0 0

RODMAN, Alex (F) 126 14
H: 6 2 W: 12 08 b.Sutton Coldfield 15-2-87
Internationals: England C.
2010–11 Aldershot T 14 5
2011–12 Aldershot T 18 1
2012–13 Aldershot T 11 1 **43 7**
2012–13 *York C* 18 1 **18 1**
2015–16 Newport Co 29 4 **29 4**
2016–17 Notts Co 16 1 **16 1**
2016–17 Shrewsbury T 20 1 **20 1**

SADLER, Matthew (D) 368 7
H: 5 11 W: 11 08 b.Birmingham 26-2-85
Internationals: England U17, U18, U19.
2001–02 Birmingham C 0 0
2002–03 Birmingham C 2 0
2003–04 Birmingham C 0 0
2003–04 *Northampton T* 7 0 **7 0**
2004–05 Birmingham C 0 0
2005–06 Birmingham C 8 0
2006–07 Birmingham C 36 0
2007–08 Birmingham C 5 0 **51 0**
2007–08 Watford 15 0
2008–09 Watford 15 0
2009–10 Watford 0 0
2009–10 *Stockport Co* 20 0 **20 0**
2010–11 Watford 0 0 **30 0**
2010–11 *Shrewsbury T* 46 0
2011–12 Walsall 46 1 **46 1**
2012–13 Crawley T 46 1
2013–14 Crawley T 46 1
2014–15 Rotherham U 0 0
2014–15 *Crawley T* 10 0 **102 2**
2014–15 *Oldham Ath* 8 0 **8 0**
2014–15 Shrewsbury T 0 0
2015–16 Shrewsbury T 24 2
2016–17 Shrewsbury T 34 2 **104 4**

SEARS, Ryan (D) 0 0
2016–17 Shrewsbury T 0 0

SMITH, Dominic (D) 31 0
H: 6 0 W: 11 11 b.Shrewsbury 9-2-96
Internationals: Wales U19, U21.
2012–13 Shrewsbury T 0 0
2013–14 Shrewsbury T 0 0
2014–15 Shrewsbury T 0 0
2015–16 Shrewsbury T 21 0
2016–17 Shrewsbury T 10 0 **31 0**

WHALLEY, Shaun (M) 74 12
H: 5 9 W: 10 08 b.Whiston 7-8-87
2014–15 Luton T 18 3 **18 3**
2015–16 Shrewsbury T 24 6
2016–17 Shrewsbury T 32 3 **56 9**

Players retained or with offer of contract
Morris, Bryn Andrew; Rowley, Shaun Keith.

Scholars
Bonner, Joel; Esien, Cameron Eniang; Gallagher, Christopher Paul; Gilpin, Aaron Morgan; Gregory, Cameron Akash James; Hassall, George Alan; Higgs, Charley Robert; Hughes, George William; Jones, Mathew George; Kerins, Jake Lawrence Ryan; Lovett, Harri Tomas; McAtee, John George; Ofori, Tyrone Edwine Kwaku; Rammell, Jacob William; Roberts, Callum James; Sears, Ryan Joseph; Shelis, Christos.

SOUTHAMPTON (77)

AUSTIN, Charlie (F) 240 124
H: 6 2 W: 13 03 b.Hungerford 5-7-89
2009–10 Swindon T 33 19
2010–11 Swindon T 21 12 **54 31**
2010–11 Burnley 4 0
2011–12 Burnley 41 16
2012–13 Burnley 37 25 **82 41**
2013–14 QPR 31 17
2014–15 QPR 35 18
2015–16 QPR 16 10 **82 45**
2015–16 Southampton 7 1
2016–17 Southampton 15 6 **22 7**

BERTRAND, Ryan (D) 283 6
H: 5 10 W: 11 00 b.Southwark 5-8-89
Internationals: England U17, U18, U19, U20, U21, Full caps. Great Britain.
2006–07 Chelsea 0 0
2006–07 *Bournemouth* 5 0 **5 0**
2007–08 Chelsea 0 0
2007–08 *Oldham Ath* 21 0 **21 0**
2007–08 *Norwich C* 18 0
2008–09 Chelsea 0 0
2008–09 *Norwich C* 38 0 **56 0**
2009–10 Chelsea 0 0
2009–10 *Reading* 44 1 **44 1**
2010–11 Chelsea 1 0
2010–11 *Nottingham F* 19 0 **19 0**
2011–12 Chelsea 7 0
2012–13 Chelsea 19 0
2013–14 Chelsea 1 0 **28 0**
2013–14 *Aston Villa* 16 0 **16 0**
2014–15 Southampton 34 2
2015–16 Southampton 32 1
2016–17 Southampton 28 2 **94 5**

BOUFAL, Sofiane (M) 113 19
H: 5 7 W: 11 09 b.Paris 17-9-93
Internationals: Morocco Full caps.
2012–13 Angers 2 0
2013–14 Angers 28 0
2014–15 Angers 16 4 **46 4**
2014–15 Lille 14 3
2015–16 Lille 29 11
2016–17 Lille 0 0 **43 14**
2016–17 Southampton 24 1 **24 1**

CACERES, Martin (D) 190 12
H: 5 10 W: 12 02 b.Montevideo 7-4-87
Internationals: Uruguay U20, Full caps.
2005–06 Defensor 2 0
2006–07 Defensor 24 4 **26 4**
2007–08 Villarreal 0 0
2007–08 *Recreativo* 34 2 **34 2**
2008–09 Barcelona 13 0
2009–10 Barcelona 0 0
2009–10 *Juventus* 15 1
2010–11 Barcelona 0 0 **13 0**
2010–11 *Sevilla* 25 1
2011–12 Sevilla 14 1 **39 2**
2011–12 *Juventus* 11 1
2012–13 Juventus 18 1
2013–14 Juventus 17 0
2014–15 Juventus 10 1

2015–16 Juventus 6 0 **77 4**
2016–17 Southampton 1 0 **1 0**

CEDRIC SOARES, Ricardo (D) 145 2
H: 5 8 W: 10 08 b.Gelsenkirchen, Germany 31-8-91
Internationals: Portugal U16, U17, U18, U19, U20, U21, Full caps.
2010–11 Sporting Lisbon 2 0
2011–12 Sporting Lisbon 0 0
2011–12 *Academica* 24 0 **24 0**
2012–13 Sporting Lisbon 13 1
2013–14 Sporting Lisbon 28 1
2014–15 Sporting Lisbon 24 0 **67 2**
2015–16 Southampton 24 0
2016–17 Southampton 30 0 **54 0**

CLASIE, Jordy (M) 199 11
H: 5 7 W: 10 12 b.Haarlem 27-7-91
Internationals: Netherlands U17, U18, U19, U21, Full caps.
2010–11 Feyenoord 0 0
2010–11 *Excelsior* 32 2 **32 2**
2011–12 Feyenoord 33 3
2012–13 Feyenoord 33 2
2013–14 Feyenoord 32 1
2014–15 Feyenoord 31 2 **129 8**
2015–16 Southampton 22 0
2016–17 Southampton 16 1 **38 1**

DAVIS, Steven (M) 432 32
H: 5 8 W: 11 04 b.Ballymena 1-1-85
Internationals: Northern Ireland U15, U16, U17, U19, U21, U23, Full caps.
2004–05 Aston Villa 28 1
2005–06 Aston Villa 35 4
2006–07 Aston Villa 28 0 **91 5**
2007–08 Fulham 22 0 **22 0**
2007–08 *Rangers* 12 0
2008–09 Rangers 34 6
2009–10 Rangers 36 3
2010–11 Rangers 37 4
2011–12 Rangers 33 5 **152 18**
2012–13 Southampton 32 2
2013–14 Southampton 34 2
2014–15 Southampton 35 0
2015–16 Southampton 34 5
2016–17 Southampton 32 0 **167 9**

FORSTER, Fraser (G) 274 0
H: 6 0 W: 12 00 b.Hexham 17-3-88
Internationals: England Full caps.
2007–08 Newcastle U 0 0
2008–09 Newcastle U 0 0
2008–09 *Stockport Co* 6 0 **6 0**
2009–10 Newcastle U 0 0
2009–10 *Bristol R* 4 0 **4 0**
2009–10 *Norwich C* 38 0 **38 0**
2010–11 Newcastle U 0 0
2010–11 *Celtic* 36 0
2011–12 Newcastle U 0 0
2011–12 *Celtic* 33 0
2012–13 Celtic 34 0
2013–14 Celtic 37 0 **140 0**
2014–15 Southampton 30 0
2015–16 Southampton 18 0
2016–17 Southampton 38 0 **86 0**

GABBIADINI, Manolo (F) 196 47
H: 5 10 W: 11 03 b.Bergamo 26-11-91
Internationals: Italy U20, U21, Full caps.
2009–10 Atalanta 2 0
2010–11 Atalanta 0 0
2010–11 *Cittadella* 27 5 **27 5**
2011–12 Atalanta 23 1
2012–13 Atalanta 0 0 **25 1**
2012–13 *Bologna* 30 6 **30 6**
2013–14 Sampdoria 34 8
2014–15 Sampdoria 13 7 **47 15**
2014–15 Napoli 20 8
2015–16 Napoli 23 5
2016–17 Napoli 13 3 **56 16**
2016–17 Southampton 11 4 **11 4**

GALLAGHER, Sam (F) 74 12
H: 6 4 W: 11 11 b.Crediton 15-9-95
Internationals: Scotland U19, England U19, U20.
2013–14 Southampton 18 1
2014–15 Southampton 0 0
2015–16 Southampton 0 0
2015–16 *Milton Keynes D* 13 0 **13 0**
2016–17 Southampton 0 0 **18 1**
2016–17 *Blackburn R* 43 11 **43 11**

GARDOS, Florin (D) 143 4
H: 6 4 W: 10 10 b.Satu Mare 29-10-88
Internationals: Romania U19, U21, Full caps.
2008–09 Concordia Chiajna 22 0
2009–10 Concordia Chiajna 29 1 **51 1**
2010–11 Steau Bucharest 23 0
2011–12 Steau Bucharest 8 0
2012–13 Steau Bucharest 21 1 **52 1**
2013–14 Steau Bucharest 29 2 **29 2**
2014–15 Southampton 11 0
2015–16 Southampton 0 0
2016–17 Southampton 0 0 **11 0**

HASSEN, Mouez (G) 49 0
H: 6 1 W: 11 09 b.Frejus 5-3-95
Internationals: France U16, U17, U18, U19, U20, U21.
2013–14 Nice 5 0
2014–15 Nice 30 0
2015–16 Nice 14 0
2016–17 Nice 0 0 **49 0**
On loan from Nice.
2016–17 Southampton 0 0

HESKETH, Jake (M) 2 0
H: 5 6 W: 9 13 b. 27-3-96
2014–15 Southampton 2 0
2015–16 Southampton 0 0
2016–17 Southampton 0 0 **2 0**

HOJBJERG, Pierre (M) 78 2
H: 6 1 W: 12 11 b. 5-8-95
Internationals: Denmark U16, U17, U19, U21, Full caps.
2012–13 Bayern Munich 2 0
2013–14 Bayern Munich 7 0
2014–15 Bayern Munich 8 0
2014–15 *Augsburg* 16 2 **16 2**
2015–16 Bayern Munich 0 0 **17 0**
2015–16 *Schalke* 23 0 **23 0**
2016–17 Southampton 22 0 **22 0**

ISGROVE, Lloyd (M) 44 1
H: 5 10 W: 11 05 b.Yeovil 12-1-93
Internationals: Wales U21, Full caps.
2011–12 Southampton 0 0
2012–13 Southampton 0 0
2013–14 Southampton 0 0
2013–14 *Peterborough U* 8 1 **8 1**
2014–15 Southampton 1 0
2014–15 *Sheffield W* 8 0 **8 0**
2015–16 Southampton 0 0
2015–16 *Barnsley* 27 0 **27 0**
2016–17 Southampton 0 0 **1 0**

LEWIS, Harry (G) 0 0
b. 20-12-97
Internationals: England U18.
2015–16 Shrewsbury T 0 0
2016–17 Shrewsbury T 0 0
2016–17 Southampton 0 0

LONG, Shane (F) 363 85
H: 5 10 W: 11 02 b.Co. Tipperary 22-1-87
Internationals: Republic of Ireland B, U21, Full caps.
2005 Cork C 1 0 **1 0**
2005–06 Reading 11 3
2006–07 Reading 21 2
2007–08 Reading 29 3
2008–09 Reading 37 9
2009–10 Reading 31 6
2010–11 Reading 44 21
2011–12 Reading 1 0 **174 44**
2011–12 WBA 32 8
2012–13 WBA 34 8
2013–14 WBA 15 3 **81 19**
2013–14 Hull C 15 4 **15 4**
2014–15 Southampton 32 5
2015–16 Southampton 28 10
2016–17 Southampton 32 3 **92 18**

MARTINA, Cuco (D) 198 5
H: 6 1 W: 11 05 b.Rotterdam 25-9-89
Internationals: Curacao Full caps.
2008–09 Roosendaal 14 0
2009–10 Roosendaal 23 1
2010–11 Roosendaal 32 1 **69 2**
2011–12 Waalwijk 23 0
2012–13 Waalwijk 34 1 **57 1**
2013–14 FC Twente 16 1
2014–15 FC Twente 32 0 **48 1**
2015–16 Southampton 15 1
2016–17 Southampton 9 0 **24 1**

McCARTHY, Alex (G) 147 0
H: 6 4 W: 11 12 b.Guildford 3-12-89
Internationals: England U21.
2008–09 Reading 0 0
2008–09 *Aldershot T* 4 0 **4 0**
2009–10 Reading 0 0
2009–10 *Yeovil T* 44 0 **44 0**
2010–11 Reading 13 0
2010–11 *Brentford* 3 0 **3 0**
2011–12 Reading 0 0
2011–12 *Leeds U* 6 0 **6 0**
2011–12 *Ipswich T* 10 0 **10 0**
2012–13 Reading 13 0
2013–14 Reading 44 0 **70 0**
2014–15 QPR 3 0 **3 0**
2015–16 Crystal Palace 7 0 **7 0**
2016–17 Southampton 0 0

McCARTHY, Jason (D) 82 7
H: 6 1 W: 12 08 b.Southampton 7-11-95
2013–14 Southampton 0 0
2014–15 Southampton 1 0
2015–16 Southampton 0 0
2015–16 *Wycombe W* 35 2 **35 2**
2016–17 Southampton 0 0 **1 0**
2016–17 *Walsall* 46 5 **46 5**

McQUEEN, Sam (M) 31 2
H: 5 9 W: 11 00 b.Southampton 6-2-95
Internationals: England U21.
2011–12 Southampton 0 0
2012–13 Southampton 0 0
2013–14 Southampton 0 0
2014–15 Southampton 0 0
2015–16 Southampton 0 0
2015–16 *Southend U* 18 2 **18 2**
2016–17 Southampton 13 0 **13 0**

OLOMOLA, Olufela (F) 0 0
H: 5 7 b.London 5-9-97
2015–16 Southampton 0 0
2016–17 Southampton 0 0

PIED, Jeremy (F) 191 11
H: 5 8 W: 10 12 b.Grenoble 23-2-89
2009–10 Lyon 0 0
2009–10 *Metz* 37 4 **37 4**
2010–11 Lyon 25 3
2011–12 Lyon 14 1
2012–13 Lyon 1 0 **40 4**
2012–13 Nice 26 0
2013–14 Nice 21 1
2014–15 Nice 2 0
2014–15 *Guiangamp* 28 2 **28 2**
2015–16 Nice 33 0 **82 1**
2016–17 Southampton 4 0 **4 0**

REDMOND, Nathan (M) 211 25
H: 5 8 W: 11 11 b.Birmingham 6-3-94
Internationals: England U16, U17, U18, U19, U20, U21, Full caps.
2011–12 Birmingham C 24 5
2012–13 Birmingham C 38 2 **62 7**
2013–14 Norwich C 34 1
2014–15 Norwich C 43 4
2015–16 Norwich C 35 6 **112 11**
2016–17 Southampton 37 7 **37 7**

REED, Harrison (M) 17 0
H: 5 9 W: 11 09 b.Worthing 27-1-95
Internationals: England U19, U20.
2011–12 Southampton 0 0
2012–13 Southampton 0 0
2013–14 Southampton 4 0
2014–15 Southampton 9 0
2015–16 Southampton 1 0
2016–17 Southampton 3 0 **17 0**

RODRIGUEZ, Jay (F) 226 61
H: 6 0 W: 12 00 b.Burnley 29-7-89
Internationals: England U21, Full caps.
2007–08 Burnley 1 0
2007–08 Stirling Alb 11 3 **11 3**
2008–09 Burnley 25 2
2009–10 Burnley 0 0
2009–10 *Barnsley* 6 1 **6 1**
2010–11 Burnley 42 14
2011–12 Burnley 37 15 **105 31**
2012–13 Southampton 35 6
2013–14 Southampton 33 15
2014–15 Southampton 0 0
2015–16 Southampton 12 0
2016–17 Southampton 24 5 **104 26**

ROMEU, Oriol (M) 176 3
H: 6 0 W: 12 06 b.Ulldecona 24-9-91
Internationals: Spain U17, U19, U20, U21, U23.
2008–09 Barcelona B 5 0
2009–10 Barcelona B 26 0
2010–11 Barcelona B 18 1 **49 1**
2010–11 Barcelona 1 0 **1 0**
2011–12 Chelsea 16 0
2012–13 Chelsea 6 0
2013–14 Chelsea 0 0
2013–14 *Valencia* 13 0 **13 0**
2014–15 Chelsea 0 0 **22 0**
2014–15 *Stuttgart* 27 0 **27 0**
2015–16 Southampton 29 1
2016–17 Southampton 35 1 **64 2**

SIMS, Josh (M) 7 0
b. 28-3-97
Internationals: England U17, U18, U20.
From Portsmouth.

2016–17	Southampton	7	0	**7**	**0**

STEPHENS, Jack (D) 86 1
H: 6 1 W: 13 03 b.Torpoint 27-1-94
Internationals: England U18, U19, U20, U21.

2010–11	Plymouth Arg	5	0	**5**	**0**
2010–11	Southampton	0	0		
2011–12	Southampton	0	0		
2012–13	Southampton	0	0		
2013–14	Southampton	0	0		
2013–14	*Swindon T*	10	0		
2014–15	Southampton	0	0		
2014–15	*Swindon T*	37	1	**47**	**1**
2015–16	Southampton	0	0		
2015–16	*Middlesbrough*	1	0	**1**	**0**
2015–16	*Coventry C*	16	0	**16**	**0**
2016–17	Southampton	17	0	**17**	**0**

TADIC, Dusan (M) 339 85
H: 5 11 W: 12 00 b.Backa Topola 20-11-88
Internationals: Serbia Full caps.

2006–07	Vojvodina	23	3		
2007–08	Vojvodina	28	7		
2008–09	Vojvodina	29	9		
2009–10	Vojvodina	27	10	**107**	**29**
2010–11	Groningen	34	7		
2011–12	Groningen	34	7	**68**	**14**
2012–13	FC Twente	33	12		
2013–14	FC Twente	33	16	**66**	**28**
2014–15	Southampton	31	4		
2015–16	Southampton	34	7		
2016–17	Southampton	33	3	**98**	**14**

TARGETT, Matt (D) 25 0
H: 6 0 W: 12 11 b.Edinburgh 18-9-95
Internationals: Scotland U19, England U19, U20, U21.

2013–14	Southampton	0	0		
2014–15	Southampton	6	0		
2015–16	Southampton	14	0		
2016–17	Southampton	5	0	**25**	**0**

TAYLOR, Stuart (G) 75 0
H: 6 5 W: 13 07 b.Romford 28-11-80
Internationals: FA Schools, England U16, U18, U20, U21.

1998–99	Arsenal	0	0		
1999–2000	Arsenal	0	0		
1999–2000	*Bristol R*	4	0	**4**	**0**
2000–01	Arsenal	0	0		
2000–01	*Crystal Palace*	10	0	**10**	**0**
2000–01	*Peterborough U*	6	0	**6**	**0**
2001–02	Arsenal	10	0		
2002–03	Arsenal	8	0		
2003–04	Arsenal	0	0		
2004–05	Arsenal	0	0	**18**	**0**
2004–05	*Leicester C*	10	0	**10**	**0**
2005–06	Aston Villa	2	0		
2006–07	Aston Villa	6	0		
2007–08	Aston Villa	4	0		
2008–09	Aston Villa	0	0	**12**	**0**
2008–09	*Cardiff C*	8	0	**8**	**0**
2009–10	Manchester C	0	0		
2010–11	Manchester C	0	0		
2011–12	Manchester C	0	0		
2012–13	Manchester C	0	0		
2012–13	Reading	4	0		
2013–14	Reading	0	0	**4**	**0**
2014–15	Leeds U	3	0	**3**	**0**
2016–17	Southampton	0	0		

VAN DIJK, Virgil (D) 193 20
H: 6 4 W: 14 07 b.Breda 8-7-91
Internationals: Netherlands U19, U21, Full caps.

2010–11	Groningen	5	2		
2011–12	Groningen	23	3		
2012–13	Groningen	34	2	**62**	**7**
2013–14	Celtic	36	5		
2014–15	Celtic	35	4		
2015–16	Celtic	5	0	**76**	**9**
2015–16	Southampton	34	3		
2016–17	Southampton	21	1	**55**	**4**

WARD-PROWSE, James (M) 137 7
H: 5 8 W: 10 06 b.Portsmouth 1-11-94
Internationals: England U17, U19, U20, U21, Full caps.

2011–12	Southampton	0	0		
2012–13	Southampton	15	0		
2013–14	Southampton	34	0		
2014–15	Southampton	25	1		
2015–16	Southampton	33	2		
2016–17	Southampton	30	4	**137**	**7**

YOSHIDA, Maya (D) 159 9
H: 6 2 W: 12 03 b.Nagasaki 24-8-88
Internationals: Japan U23, Full caps.

2010–11	VVV	20	0		
2011–12	VVV	32	5		
2012–13	VVV	2	0	**54**	**5**
2012–13	Southampton	32	0		
2013–14	Southampton	8	1		
2014–15	Southampton	22	1		
2015–16	Southampton	20	1		
2016–17	Southampton	23	1	**105**	**4**

Players retained or with offer of contract
Bakary, Mohamed Richard; Barnes, Marcus Thomas; Cook, Oliver David Paul; Flannigan, Jake; Freeman, Kieran; Gazzaniga, Paulo Dino; Johnson, Tyreke Martin; Jones, Alfie; Latham, Kingsley Finn; Little, Armani; O'Connor, Thomas James; O'Driscoll, Aaron; Parkes, Adam Darren; Seager, Ryan Paul; Slattery, Callum; Smallbone, William Anthony Patrick; Valery, Yan; Vidal, Oriol Romeu; Vokins, Jake; Wood, William Nicholas.

Scholars
Afolabi, Jonathan; Bradley, Green Jamie; Cull, Alexander; Cull, Benjamin Simon; Davis, Harrison; Gardner, Oliver; Hale, Harlem; Hamblin, Harry Mark; Klarer, Christoph; Mdlalose, Siphesihle Thembinkosi; Nlundulu, Dan; Obafemi, Michael Oluwadurotimi; Rowthorn, Ben John; Siu, Javen Michael; Tella, Nathan.

SOUTHEND U (78)

ALAWODE-WILLIAMS, Jordan (D) 0 0

2015–16	Southend U	0	0		
2016–17	Southend U	0	0		

ATKINSON, Will (M) 291 23
H: 5 10 W: 10 07 b.Beverley 14-10-88

2006–07	Hull C	0	0		
2007–08	Hull C	0	0		
2007–08	*Port Vale*	4	0	**4**	**0**
2007–08	*Mansfield T*	12	0	**12**	**0**
2008–09	Hull C	0	0		
2009–10	Hull C	2	1		
2009–10	*Rochdale*	15	3		
2010–11	Hull C	4	0		
2010–11	*Rotherham U*	3	1	**3**	**1**
2010–11	*Rochdale*	21	2	**36**	**5**
2011–12	Hull C	0	0	**6**	**1**
2011–12	*Plymouth Arg*	22	4	**22**	**4**
2011–12	*Bradford C*	12	1		
2012–13	Bradford C	42	1	**54**	**2**
2013–14	Southend U	45	2		
2014–15	Southend U	36	2		
2015–16	Southend U	36	2		
2016–17	Southend U	37	4	**154**	**10**

BARRETT, Adam (D) 638 45
H: 5 10 W: 12 00 b.Dagenham 29-11-79

1998–99	Plymouth Arg	1	0		
1999–2000	Plymouth Arg	42	3		
2000–01	Plymouth Arg	9	0	**52**	**3**
2000–01	Mansfield T	8	1		
2001–02	Mansfield T	29	0	**37**	**1**
2002–03	Bristol R	45	1		
2003–04	Bristol R	45	4	**90**	**5**
2004–05	Southend U	43	11		
2005–06	Southend U	45	3		
2006–07	Southend U	28	3		
2007–08	Southend U	45	6		
2008–09	Southend U	45	2		
2009–10	Southend U	41	2		
2010–11	Crystal Palace	7	0	**7**	**0**
2010–11	*Leyton Orient*	14	0	**14**	**0**
2011–12	Bournemouth	21	1	**21**	**1**
2012–13	Gillingham	43	1		
2013–14	Gillingham	45	2		
2014–15	Gillingham	0	0	**88**	**3**
2014–15	*AFC Wimbledon*	23	1	**23**	**1**
2014–15	Southend U	10	0		
2015–16	Southend U	37	4		
2016–17	Southend U	12	0	**306**	**31**

BEXON, Josh (G) 0 0

2016–17	Southend U	0	0		

BISHOP, Nathan (G) 0 0

2016–17	Southend U	0	0		

BRIDGE, Jack (M) 6 0
H: 5 10 W: 11 07 b. 21-9-95

2013–14	Southend U	0	0		
2014–15	Southend U	0	0		
2015–16	Southend U	2	0		
2016–17	Southend U	4	0	**6**	**0**

COKER, Ben (D) 189 4
H: 5 11 W: 11 09 b.Hatfield 17-6-89

2010–11	Colchester U	20	0		
2011–12	Colchester U	20	0		
2012–13	Colchester U	1	0	**41**	**0**
2013–14	Southend U	45	2		
2014–15	Southend U	32	1		
2015–16	Southend U	40	1		
2016–17	Southend U	31	0	**148**	**4**

COX, Simon (F) 340 95
H: 5 10 W: 10 12 b.Reading 28-4-87
Internationals: Republic of Ireland Full caps.

2005–06	Reading	2	0		
2006–07	Reading	0	0		
2006–07	*Brentford*	13	0	**13**	**0**
2006–07	*Northampton T*	8	3	**8**	**3**
2007–08	Reading	0	0		
2007–08	Swindon T	36	15		
2008–09	Swindon T	45	29	**81**	**44**
2009–10	WBA	28	9		
2010–11	WBA	19	1		
2011–12	WBA	18	0		
2012–13	WBA	0	0	**65**	**10**
2012–13	Nottingham F	39	5		
2013–14	Nottingham F	34	8	**73**	**13**
2014–15	Reading	37	8		
2015–16	Reading	13	1	**52**	**9**
2015–16	*Bristol C*	4	0	**4**	**0**
2016–17	Southend U	44	16	**44**	**16**

DEMETRIOU, Jason (D) 328 19
H: 5 11 W: 10 08 b.Newham 18-11-87
Internationals: Cyprus Full caps.

2005–06	Leyton Orient	3	0		
2006–07	Leyton Orient	15	2		
2007–08	Leyton Orient	43	3		
2008–09	Leyton Orient	43	4		
2009–10	Leyton Orient	39	1	**143**	**10**
2010–11	AEK Larnaca	15	0		
2011–12	AEK Larnaca	23	1		
2012–13	AEK Larnaca	19	3	**57**	**4**
2013–14	An Famagusta	19	1		
2014–15	An Famagusta	25	0	**44**	**1**
2015–16	Walsall	43	3	**43**	**3**
2016–17	Southend U	41	1	**41**	**1**

FERDINAND, Anton (D) 332 7
H: 6 2 W: 11 00 b.Peckham 18-2-85
Internationals: England U18, U20, U21.

2002–03	West Ham U	0	0		
2003–04	West Ham U	20	0		
2004–05	West Ham U	29	1		
2005–06	West Ham U	33	2		
2006–07	West Ham U	31	0		
2007–08	West Ham U	25	2		
2008–09	West Ham U	0	0	**138**	**5**
2008–09	Sunderland	31	0		
2009–10	Sunderland	24	0		
2010–11	Sunderland	27	0		
2011–12	Sunderland	3	0	**85**	**0**
2011–12	QPR	31	0		
2012–13	QPR	13	0		
2012–13	*Bursaspor*	7	0	**7**	**0**
2013–14	QPR	0	0	**44**	**0**
2013–14	Antalyaspor	3	0	**3**	**0**
2014–15	Reading	2	0		
2015–16	Reading	19	0	**21**	**0**
2016–17	Southend U	34	2	**34**	**2**

FORTUNE, Marc-Antoine (F) 507 90
H: 6 0 W: 11 13 b.Cayenne 2-7-81

2000–01	Angouleme	18	3		
2001–02	Angouleme	36	12	**54**	**15**
2002–03	Nancy	19	1		
2002–03	Lille	15	0	**15**	**0**
2003–04	Rouen	34	10	**34**	**10**
2004–05	Brest	33	10	**33**	**10**
2005–06	Utrecht	31	6		
2006–07	Utrecht	22	5	**53**	**11**
2006–07	Nancy	15	5		
2007–08	Nancy	37	6		
2008–09	Nancy	19	1	**90**	**13**
2009–10	Celtic	30	10		
2010–11	Celtic	2	0	**32**	**10**
2010–11	WBA	25	2		
2011–12	WBA	17	2		
2011–12	*Doncaster R*	5	1	**5**	**1**
2012–13	WBA	21	2	**63**	**6**
2013–14	Wigan Ath	36	4		
2014–15	Wigan Ath	35	1	**71**	**5**
2015–16	Coventry C	25	4		
2016–17	Coventry C	0	0	**25**	**4**
2016–17	Southend U	32	5	**32**	**5**

HINES, Zavon (F) 120 11
H: 5 10 W: 10 07 b.Jamaica 27-12-88
Internationals: England U21.
2007–08 West Ham U 0 0
2007–08 *Coventry C* 7 1 **7 1**
2008–09 West Ham U 0 0
2009–10 West Ham U 13 1
2010–11 West Ham U 9 0 **22 1**
2011–12 Burnley 13 0 **13 0**
2011–12 *Bournemouth* 8 1 **8 1**
2012–13 Bradford C 32 2
2013–14 Bradford C 0 0 **32 2**
2013–14 Dagenham & R 27 6
2014–15 Dagenham & R 0 0
2015–16 Dagenham & R 6 0 **33 6**
2016–17 Southend U 5 0 **5 0**

KYPRIANOU, Harry (D) 3 1
b. 16-3-97
2013–14 Watford 0 0
2014–15 Watford 0 0
2015–16 Watford 0 0
2015–16 Southend U 0 0
2016–17 Southend U 3 1 **3 1**

LEONARD, Ryan (D) 204 16
H: 6 0 W: 11 01 b.Plympton 24-5-92
2009–10 Plymouth Arg 1 0
2010–11 Plymouth Arg 0 0 **1 0**
2011–12 Southend U 17 1
2012–13 Southend U 22 2
2013–14 Southend U 43 5
2014–15 Southend U 41 3
2015–16 Southend U 37 2
2016–17 Southend U 43 3 **203 16**

MATSUZAKA, Daniel (D) 0 0
H: 6 4 W: 11 11 b.Barnet 1-8-98
Internationals: Japan U19.
2014–15 Southend U 0 0
2015–16 Southend U 0 0
2016–17 Southend U 0 0

McGLASHAN, Jermaine (M) 257 25
H: 5 7 W: 10 00 b.Croydon 14-4-88
2010–11 Aldershot T 38 1
2011–12 Aldershot T 23 4 **61 5**
2011–12 Cheltenham T 16 2
2012–13 Cheltenham T 45 4
2013–14 Cheltenham T 43 6 **104 12**
2014–15 Gillingham 40 5
2015–16 Gillingham 17 0 **57 5**
2016–17 Southend U 35 3 **35 3**

McLAUGHLIN, Stephen (M) 141 22
H: 5 9 W: 11 12 b.Derry 14-6-90
2011 Derry C 33 3
2012 Derry C 24 10 **57 13**
2012–13 Nottingham F 0 0
2013–14 Nottingham F 3 0
2013–14 *Bristol C* 5 0 **5 0**
2014–15 Nottingham F 6 0 **9 0**
2014–15 *Notts Co* 13 0 **13 0**
2014–15 *Southend U* 6 1
2015–16 Southend U 17 1
2016–17 Southend U 34 7 **57 9**

MOONEY, David (F) 366 107
H: 6 2 W: 12 06 b.Dublin 30-10-84
Internationals: Republic of Ireland U23.
2005 Longford T 13 4
2005 Shamrock R 14 2 **14 2**
2006 Longford T 21 3
2007 Longford T 32 19 **66 26**
2008 Cork C 22 15 **22 15**
2008–09 Reading 0 0
2008–09 *Stockport Co* 2 0 **2 0**
2008–09 *Norwich C* 9 3 **9 3**
2009–10 Reading 0 0
2009–10 *Charlton Ath* 28 5 **28 5**
2010–11 Reading 0 0
2010–11 *Colchester U* 39 9 **39 9**
2011–12 Leyton Orient 37 5
2012–13 Leyton Orient 32 5
2013–14 Leyton Orient 38 19
2014–15 Leyton Orient 33 9 **140 38**
2015–16 Southend U 33 8
2016–17 Southend U 13 1 **46 9**

NOUBLE, Frank (F) 168 19
H: 6 3 W: 12 08 b.Lewisham 24-9-91
Internationals: England U17, U19.
2009–10 West Ham U 8 0
2009–10 *WBA* 3 0 **3 0**
2009–10 *Swindon T* 8 0 **8 0**
2010–11 West Ham U 2 0
2010–11 *Swansea C* 6 1 **6 1**
2010–11 *Barnsley* 4 0
2010–11 *Charlton Ath* 9 1 **9 1**
2011–12 West Ham U 3 1 **13 1**
2011–12 *Gillingham* 13 5
2011–12 *Barnsley* 6 0 **10 0**
2012–13 Wolverhampton W 2 0 **2 0**
2012–13 Ipswich T 17 2
2013–14 Ipswich T 38 2
2014–15 Ipswich T 1 0 **56 4**
2014–15 Coventry C 31 6 **31 6**
2016–17 Gillingham 12 1 **25 6**
2016–17 Southend U 5 0 **5 0**

O'NEILL, Luke (D) 74 2
H: 6 0 W: 11 04 b.Slough 20-8-91
Internationals: England U17.
2009–10 Leicester C 1 0 **1 0**
2009–10 *Tranmere R* 4 0 **4 0**
From Kettering T, Mansfield T
2012–13 Burnley 1 0
2013–14 Burnley 0 0
2013–14 *York C* 15 1 **15 1**
2013–14 *Southend U* 1 0
2014–15 Burnley 0 0 **1 0**
2014–15 *Scunthorpe U* 13 0 **13 0**
2014–15 *Leyton Orient* 8 0 **8 0**
2015–16 Southend U 14 0
2016–17 Southend U 17 1 **32 1**

OXLEY, Mark (G) 132 1
H: 5 11 W: 11 05 b.Aston 2-6-90
Internationals: England U18, U20.
2008–09 Hull C 0 0
2009–10 Hull C 0 0
2009–10 *Grimsby T* 3 0 **3 0**
2010–11 Hull C 0 0
2011–12 Hull C 0 0
2012–13 Hull C 1 0
2012–13 *Burton Alb* 3 0 **3 0**
2013–14 Hull C 0 0
2013–14 *Oldham Ath* 36 0 **36 0**
2014–15 Hull C 0 0 **1 0**
2014–15 *Hibernian* 35 1
2015–16 Hibernian 34 0 **69 1**
2016–17 Southend U 20 0 **20 0**

RANGER, Nile (F) 128 22
H: 6 2 W: 13 03 b.Wood Green 11-4-91
Internationals: England U19.
2008–09 Newcastle U 0 0
2009–10 Newcastle U 25 2
2010–11 Newcastle U 24 0
2011–12 Newcastle U 0 0
2011–12 *Barnsley* 5 0 **5 0**
2011–12 *Sheffield W* 8 2 **8 2**
2012–13 Newcastle U 2 0 **51 2**
2013–14 Swindon T 23 8 **23 8**
2014–15 Blackpool 14 2
2015–16 Blackpool 0 0 **14 2**
2016–17 Southend U 27 8 **27 8**

ROBINSON, Theo (F) 317 72
H: 5 9 W: 10 03 b.Birmingham 22-1-89
Internationals: Jamaica Full caps.
2005–06 Watford 1 0
2006–07 Watford 1 0
2007–08 Watford 0 0
2007–08 *Hereford U* 43 13 **43 13**
2008–09 Watford 3 0 **5 0**
2008–09 *Southend U* 21 7
2009–10 Huddersfield T 37 13
2010–11 Huddersfield T 1 0
2010–11 Millwall 11 3
2010–11 *Derby Co* 13 2
2011–12 Derby Co 39 10
2012–13 Derby Co 28 8
2012–13 *Huddersfield T* 6 0 **44 13**
2013–14 Millwall 0 0 **11 3**
2013–14 Derby Co 0 0 **80 20**
2013–14 Doncaster R 31 5
2014–15 Doncaster R 32 4 **63 9**
2014–15 *Scunthorpe U* 8 3 **8 3**
2015–16 Motherwell 10 0 **10 0**
2015–16 Port Vale 14 2 **14 2**
2016–17 Southend U 18 2 **39 9**

SMITH, Ted (G) 26 0
b.Benfleet 18-1-96
Internationals: England U18, U19, U20.
2012–13 Southend U 0 0
2013–14 Southend U 0 0
2014–15 Southend U 4 0
2015–16 Southend U 3 0
2016–17 Southend U 19 0 **26 0**

THOMPSON, Adam (D) 146 4
H: 6 2 W: 12 10 b.Harlow 28-9-92
Internationals: Northern Ireland U17, U19, U21, Full caps.
2010–11 Watford 10 1
2011–12 Watford 0 0
2011–12 *Brentford* 20 0 **20 0**
2012–13 Watford 4 0
2012–13 *Wycombe W* 2 0 **2 0**
2012–13 *Barnet* 1 0 **1 0**
2013–14 Watford 0 0 **14 1**
2013–14 Southend U 16 0
2014–15 Southend U 28 0
2015–16 Southend U 25 2
2016–17 Southend U 40 1 **109 3**

TIMLIN, Michael (M) 311 19
H: 5 8 W: 11 08 b.New Cross 19-3-85
Internationals: Republic of Ireland U17, U21.
2002–03 Fulham 0 0
2003–04 Fulham 0 0
2004–05 Fulham 0 0
2005–06 Fulham 0 0
2005–06 *Scunthorpe U* 1 0 **1 0**
2005–06 *Doncaster R* 3 0 **3 0**
2006–07 Fulham 0 0
2006–07 *Swindon T* 24 1
2007–08 Fulham 0 0
2007–08 *Swindon T* 10 1
2008–09 Swindon T 41 2
2009–10 Swindon T 21 0
2010–11 Swindon T 22 2
2010–11 *Southend U* 8 1
2011–12 Swindon T 1 0 **119 6**
2011–12 Southend U 39 4
2012–13 Southend U 25 0
2013–14 Southend U 36 2
2014–15 Southend U 32 3
2015–16 Southend U 21 2
2016–17 Southend U 27 1 **188 13**

WHITE, John (D) 357 3
H: 6 0 W: 12 01 b.Maldon 26-7-86
2004–05 Colchester U 20 0
2005–06 Colchester U 35 0
2006–07 Colchester U 16 0
2007–08 Colchester U 21 0
2008–09 Colchester U 26 0
2009–10 Colchester U 39 0
2009–10 *Southend U* 5 0
2010–11 Colchester U 22 0
2011–12 Colchester U 26 0
2012–13 Colchester U 22 0 **227 0**
2013–14 Southend U 41 1
2014–15 Southend U 42 0
2015–16 Southend U 29 1
2016–17 Southend U 13 1 **130 3**

WILLIAMS, Jason (F) 13 0
H: 6 0 W: 12 06 b. 1-11-95
2013–14 Southend U 2 0
2014–15 Southend U 2 0
2015–16 Southend U 2 0
2016–17 Southend U 7 0 **13 0**

WORDSWORTH, Anthony (M) 274 57
H: 6 1 W: 12 00 b.Camden 3-1-89
2007–08 Colchester U 3 0
2008–09 Colchester U 30 3
2009–10 Colchester U 41 11
2010–11 Colchester U 35 5
2011–12 Colchester U 44 13
2012–13 Colchester U 24 3 **177 35**
2012–13 Ipswich T 7 1
2013–14 Ipswich T 10 1
2014–15 Ipswich T 1 0 **18 2**
2014–15 *Rotherham U* 6 1 **6 1**
2014–15 *Crawley T* 18 4 **18 4**
2015–16 Southend U 21 4
2016–17 Southend U 34 11 **55 15**

Players retained or with offer of contract
Cotton, Nico Lewis; Akinyemi, Afolabi Oladipo Christopher; Georgiou, Andronicos; King, Jack Andrew.

Scholars
Batlokwa, Wedu Reneilwe; Bedford, Joseph; Bexon, Josh Andrew; Bishop, Nathan James; Bwomono, Elvis Okello; Clark, Alex; Clifford, Thomas; Coutts, Sonny Joseph; Curran, Taylor; Cuthbert, Harry David George; Dias, Damani Joseph; Farah, Yonis Abdirizak; Gard, Lewis Thomas; Kinali, Eren; MacKenzie, Joseph Peter Uduakobong; Marah, Sewa Bockarie; Matthews, Imani Anthony George; Musselwhite, Benjamin George John; Phillips, Harry; Pianim, Zak Michael; Pitoula, Wabo Fotsing Norman Arthur; Salami, Abdus-Salam Efosa; Walker, Daniel Charles; Yearwood, Dru Anthony.

STEVENAGE (79)

CONLON, Tom (M) **50 2**
H: 5 8 W: 9 11 b.Stoke-on-Trent 3-2-96
2013–14 Peterborough U 1 0 **1 0**
2014–15 Stevenage 13 0
2015–16 Stevenage 32 2
2016–17 Stevenage 4 0 **49 2**

DAY, Chris (G) **401 0**
H: 6 2 W: 13 07 b.Whipps Cross 28-7-75
Internationals: England U18, U21.
1992–93 Tottenham H 0 0
1993–94 Tottenham H 0 0
1994–95 Tottenham H 0 0
1995–96 Tottenham H 0 0
1996–97 Crystal Palace 24 0 **24 0**
1997–98 Watford 0 0
1998–99 Watford 0 0
1999–2000 Watford 11 0
2000–01 Watford 0 0 **11 0**
2000–01 *Lincoln C* 14 0 **14 0**
2001–02 QPR 16 0
2002–03 QPR 12 0
2003–04 QPR 29 0
2004–05 QPR 30 0 **87 0**
2004–05 *Preston NE* 6 0 **6 0**
2005–06 Oldham Ath 30 0 **30 0**
2006–07 Millwall 5 0
2007–08 Millwall 5 0 **10 0**
2010–11 Stevenage 46 0
2011–12 Stevenage 44 0
2012–13 Stevenage 17 0
2013–14 Stevenage 44 0
2014–15 Stevenage 38 0
2015–16 Stevenage 19 0
2016–17 Stevenage 11 0 **219 0**

FOX, Andrew (D) **27 1**
b. 15-1-93
2015–16 Peterborough U 18 1 **18 1**
2016–17 Stevenage 9 0 **9 0**

FRANKS, Fraser (D) **96 6**
H: 6 0 W: 10 12 b.Hammersmith 22-11-90
Internationals: England C.
2009–10 Brentford 0 0
2011–12 AFC Wimbledon 4 0 **4 0**
2014–15 Luton T 13 0 **13 0**
2015–16 Stevenage 38 3
2016–17 Stevenage 41 3 **79 6**

GODDEN, Matthew (F) **56 20**
H: 6 1 W: 12 03 b.Canterbury 29-7-91
2009–10 Scunthorpe U 0 0
2010–11 Scunthorpe U 5 0
2011–12 Scunthorpe U 1 0
2012–13 Scunthorpe U 8 0
2013–14 Scunthorpe U 4 0
2014–15 Scunthorpe U 0 0 **18 0**
2016–17 Stevenage 38 20 **38 20**

GORMAN, Dale (D) **38 1**
H: 5 11 W: 11 00 b.Letterkenny 28-6-96
Internationals: Northern Ireland U19, U21.
2014–15 Stevenage 0 0
2015–16 Stevenage 13 0
2016–17 Stevenage 25 1 **38 1**

GRAY, Jamie (F) **3 0**
b. 13-4-98
Internationals: Republic of Ireland U17, U18.
2016–17 Stevenage 3 0 **3 0**

HENRY, Ronnie (D) **187 0**
H: 5 11 W: 11 10 b.Hemel Hempstead 2-1-84
Internationals: England C.
2002–03 Tottenham H 0 0
2002–03 *Southend U* 3 0 **3 0**
2004 Dublin C 12 0 **12 0**
2010–11 Stevenage 42 0
2011–12 Stevenage 32 0
2014–15 Stevenage 34 0
2015–16 Stevenage 31 0
2016–17 Stevenage 33 0 **172 0**

HYDE, Jake (F) **160 38**
H: 6 1 W: 13 02 b.Slough 1-7-90
Internationals: England C.
2009–10 Barnet 34 6
2010–11 Dundee 2 3
2010–11 Dunfermline Ath 2 0 **2 0**
2011–12 Dundee 26 6 **28 9**
2012–13 Barnet 40 14 **74 20**
2014–15 York C 39 9
2015–16 York C 11 0 **50 9**
2016–17 Stevenage 6 0 **6 0**

JOHNSON, Ryan (D) **12 0**
H: 6 2 W: 13 05 b. 2-10-96
Internationals: Northern Ireland U21.
2013–14 Stevenage 1 0
2014–15 Stevenage 4 0
2015–16 Stevenage 7 0
2016–17 Stevenage 0 0 **12 0**

JONES, Jamie (G) **255 0**
H: 6 2 W: 14 05 b.Kirkby 18-2-89
2007–08 Everton 0 0
2008–09 Leyton Orient 20 0
2009–10 Leyton Orient 36 0
2010–11 Leyton Orient 35 0
2011–12 Leyton Orient 6 0
2012–13 Leyton Orient 26 0
2013–14 Leyton Orient 28 0 **151 0**
2014–15 Preston NE 17 0
2014–15 *Coventry C* 4 0 **4 0**
2014–15 *Rochdale* 13 0 **13 0**
2015–16 Preston NE 0 0 **17 0**
2015–16 *Colchester U* 17 0 **17 0**
2015–16 Stevenage 17 0
2016–17 Stevenage 36 0 **53 0**

KENNEDY, Ben (F) **73 14**
H: 5 10 W: 11 00 b. 12-1-97
Internationals: Northern Ireland U17, U19, U21.
2014–15 Stevenage 15 4
2015–16 Stevenage 22 2
2016–17 Stevenage 36 8 **73 14**

KERR, Nathan (D) **1 0**
H: 5 11 W: 12 00 b.Belfast 20-1-98
Internationals: Northern Ireland U16, U17, U19.
2015–16 Stevenage 0 0
2016–17 Stevenage 1 0 **1 0**

LEE, Charlie (M) **375 39**
H: 5 11 W: 11 07 b.Whitechapel 5-1-87
2005–06 Tottenham H 0 0
2006–07 Tottenham H 0 0
2006–07 *Millwall* 5 0 **5 0**
2007–08 Peterborough U 42 6
2008–09 Peterborough U 44 5
2009–10 Peterborough U 33 2
2010–11 Peterborough U 34 1 **153 14**
2010–11 *Gillingham* 4 1
2011–12 Gillingham 33 6
2012–13 Gillingham 31 2
2013–14 Gillingham 31 2 **99 11**
2014–15 Stevenage 44 9
2015–16 Stevenage 30 3
2016–17 Stevenage 44 2 **118 14**

LIBURD, Rowan (F) **34 1**
b. 28-8-92
2015–16 Reading 3 0 **3 0**
2015–16 *Wycombe W* 10 0 **10 0**
2016–17 Stevenage 13 1 **13 1**
2016–17 *Leyton Orient* 8 0 **8 0**

McANUFF, Jobi (M) **580 58**
H: 5 11 W: 11 05 b.Edmonton 9-11-81
Internationals: Jamaica Full caps.
2000–01 Wimbledon 0 0
2001–02 Wimbledon 38 4
2002–03 Wimbledon 31 4
2003–04 Wimbledon 27 5 **96 13**
2003–04 West Ham U 12 1
2004–05 West Ham U 1 0 **13 1**
2004–05 Cardiff C 43 2 **43 2**
2005–06 Crystal Palace 41 8
2006–07 Crystal Palace 34 5 **75 13**
2007–08 Watford 39 2
2008–09 Watford 40 3
2009–10 Watford 3 0 **82 5**
2009–10 Reading 36 3
2010–11 Reading 40 4
2011–12 Reading 40 5
2012–13 Reading 38 0
2013–14 Reading 35 2 **189 14**
2014–15 Leyton Orient 34 3
2015–16 Leyton Orient 17 3 **51 6**
2016–17 Stevenage 31 4 **31 4**

McKEE, Mark (F) **2 0**
b. 1-12-98
Internationals: Northern Ireland U16, U17, U19.
From Cliftonville.
2016–17 Stevenage 2 0 **2 0**

NTLHE, Kgosietsile (D) **98 4**
H: 5 9 W: 10 05 b.Pretoria 21-2-94
Internationals: South Africa U20, Full caps.
2010–11 Peterborough U 0 0
2011–12 Peterborough U 2 0
2012–13 Peterborough U 12 1
2013–14 Peterborough U 27 2
2014–15 Peterborough U 28 1
2015–16 Peterborough U 7 0
2016–17 Peterborough U 0 0 **76 4**
2016–17 Stevenage 22 0 **22 0**

PETT, Tom (M) **114 14**
H: 5 8 W: 11 00 b. 3-12-91
2014–15 Stevenage 34 7
2015–16 Stevenage 40 1
2016–17 Stevenage 40 6 **114 14**

PRESTON, Callum (G) **9 0**
b.Stafford 7-1-95
Internationals: Wales U19.
2014–15 Birmingham C 0 0
2015–16 Crawley T 9 0 **9 0**
2016–17 Stevenage 0 0

SCHUMACHER, Steven (M) **415 55**
H: 5 10 W: 11 00 b.Liverpool 30-4-84
2000–01 Everton 0 0
2001–02 Everton 0 0
2002–03 Everton 0 0
2003–04 Everton 0 0
2003–04 *Carlisle U* 4 0 **4 0**
2004–05 Bradford C 43 6
2005–06 Bradford C 30 1
2006–07 Bradford C 44 6 **117 13**
2007–08 Crewe Alex 26 1
2008–09 Crewe Alex 15 2
2009–10 Crewe Alex 32 4 **73 7**
2010–11 Bury 43 9
2011–12 Bury 32 6
2012–13 Bury 39 8 **114 23**
2013–14 Fleetwood T 32 5
2014–15 Fleetwood T 32 0 **64 5**
2015–16 Stevenage 15 2
2016–17 Stevenage 28 5 **43 7**

SLATER, Luke (D) **0 0**
Internationals: Republic of Ireland U17, U18.
2016–17 Stevenage 0 0

TONGE, Michael (M) **444 31**
H: 6 0 W: 11 10 b.Manchester 7-4-83
Internationals: England U20, U21.
2000–01 Sheffield U 2 0
2001–02 Sheffield U 30 3
2002–03 Sheffield U 44 6
2003–04 Sheffield U 46 4
2004–05 Sheffield U 34 2
2005–06 Sheffield U 30 3
2006–07 Sheffield U 27 2
2007–08 Sheffield U 45 1
2008–09 Sheffield U 4 0 **262 21**
2008–09 Stoke C 10 0
2009–10 Stoke C 0 0
2009–10 *Preston NE* 7 0
2009–10 *Derby Co* 18 2 **18 2**
2010–11 Stoke C 2 0
2010–11 *Preston NE* 5 1 **12 1**
2011–12 Stoke C 0 0
2011–12 *Barnsley* 10 0 **10 0**
2012–13 Stoke C 0 0 **12 0**
2012–13 Leeds U 35 4
2013–14 Leeds U 23 0
2014–15 Leeds U 10 0 **68 4**
2014–15 *Millwall* 6 0 **6 0**
2015–16 Stevenage 29 2
2016–17 Stevenage 27 1 **56 3**

WELLS, Dean (D) **85 7**
H: 6 1 W: 13 03 b.Isleworth 25-5-85
2014–15 Stevenage 43 4
2015–16 Stevenage 28 2
2016–17 Stevenage 14 1 **85 7**

WILKINSON, Luke (D) **186 19**
H: 6 2 W: 11 09 b.Wells 2-12-92
2009–10 Portsmouth 0 0
2010–11 Dagenham & R 0 0
2011–12 Dagenham & R 0 0
2012–13 Dagenham & R 43 6
2013–14 Dagenham & R 22 0 **65 6**
2014–15 Luton T 42 4
2015–16 Luton T 20 3 **62 7**
2015–16 Stevenage 19 2
2016–17 Stevenage 40 4 **59 6**

WILMOT, Ben (M) **0 0**
2016–17 Stevenage 0 0

Scholars
Brady, Liam Aiden; Cregan, Michael James; Croud, Jacob William; Etheridge, David Michael Harry; Fraser, Macsen William George; Guerfi, Zakary Zidane; O'Keefe, Charley Jay; Ofosu, Claudio Tsikata; Omar, Ali Mohammed; Schmid, Ryan Stephen; Wade, Slater Luke Keith.

Non-Contract
Preston, Callum.

STOKE C (80)

ADAM, Charlie (M) **350 71**
H: 6 1 W: 12 00 b.Dundee 10-12-85
Internationals: Scotland U21, B, Full caps.

2004–05	Rangers	1	0		
2004–05	*Ross Co*	10	2	**10**	**2**
2005–06	Rangers	1	0		
2005–06	*St Mirren*	29	5	**29**	**5**
2006–07	Rangers	32	11		
2007–08	Rangers	16	2		
2008–09	Rangers	9	0	**59**	**13**
2008–09	Blackpool	13	2		
2009–10	Blackpool	43	16		
2010–11	Blackpool	35	12	**91**	**30**
2011–12	Liverpool	28	2	**28**	**2**
2012–13	Stoke C	27	3		
2013–14	Stoke C	31	7		
2014–15	Stoke C	29	7		
2015–16	Stoke C	22	1		
2016–17	Stoke C	24	1	**133**	**19**

AFELLAY, Ibrahim (M) **252 44**
H: 5 11 W: 10 10 b.Utrecht 2-4-86
Internationals: Netherlands Full caps.

2003–04	PSV Eindhoven	2	0		
2004–05	PSV Eindhoven	7	2		
2005–06	PSV Eindhoven	23	2		
2006–07	PSV Eindhoven	27	6		
2007–08	PSV Eindhoven	24	2		
2008–09	PSV Eindhoven	28	13		
2009–10	PSV Eindhoven	29	4		
2010–11	PSV Eindhoven	19	6	**159**	**35**
2010–11	Barcelona	16	1		
2011–12	Barcelona	4	0		
2012–13	Barcelona	0	0		
2012–13	*Schalke 04*	10	2	**10**	**2**
2013–14	Barcelona	1	0		
2014–15	Barcelona	0	0	**21**	**1**
2014–15	*Olympiacos*	19	4	**19**	**4**
2015–16	Stoke C	31	2		
2016–17	Stoke C	12	0	**43**	**2**

ALLEN, Joe (M) **254 17**
H: 5 6 W: 9 10 b.Carmarthen 14-3-90
Internationals: Wales U17, U19, U21, Full caps. Great Britain.

2006–07	Swansea C	1	0		
2007–08	Swansea C	6	0		
2008–09	Swansea C	23	1		
2009–10	Swansea C	21	0		
2010–11	Swansea C	40	2		
2011–12	Swansea C	36	4		
2012–13	Swansea C	0	0	**127**	**7**
2012–13	Liverpool	27	0		
2013–14	Liverpool	24	1		
2014–15	Liverpool	21	1		
2015–16	Liverpool	19	2	**91**	**4**
2016–17	Stoke C	36	6	**36**	**6**

ARNAUTOVIC, Marko (F) **244 48**
H: 6 4 W: 13 00 b.Floridsdorf 19-4-89
Internationals: Austria U18, U19, U21, Full caps.

2006–07	FC Twente	2	0		
2007–08	FC Twente	14	0		
2008–09	FC Twente	28	12		
2009–10	FC Twente	0	0	**44**	**12**
2009–10	*Inter Milan*	3	0	**3**	**0**
2010–11	Werder Bremen	25	3		
2011–12	Werder Bremen	19	6		
2012–13	Werder Bremen	26	5		
2013–14	Werder Bremen	2	0	**72**	**14**
2013–14	Stoke C	30	4		
2014–15	Stoke C	29	1		
2015–16	Stoke C	34	11		
2016–17	Stoke C	32	6	**125**	**22**

BACHMANN, Daniel (G) **9 0**
H: 6 3 W: 12 11 b.Vienna 9-7-94
Internationals: Austria U16, U17, U18, U19, U21.

2011–12	Stoke C	0	0		
2012–13	Stoke C	0	0		
2013–14	Stoke C	0	0		
2014–15	Stoke C	0	0		
2015–16	Stoke C	0	0		
2015–16	*Ross Co*	1	0	**1**	**0**
2015–16	*Bury*	8	0	**8**	**0**
2016–17	Stoke C	0	0		

BARDSLEY, Phillip (D) **273 8**
H: 5 11 W: 11 13 b.Salford 28-6-85
Internationals: Scotland Full caps.

2003–04	Manchester U	0	0		
2004–05	Manchester U	0	0		
2005–06	Manchester U	8	0		
2005–06	*Burnley*	6	0	**6**	**0**
2006–07	Manchester U	0	0		
2006–07	*Rangers*	5	1	**5**	**1**
2006–07	*Aston Villa*	13	0	**13**	**0**
2007–08	Manchester U	0	0	**8**	**0**
2007–08	*Sheffield U*	16	0	**16**	**0**
2007–08	Sunderland	11	0		
2008–09	Sunderland	28	0		
2009–10	Sunderland	26	0		
2010–11	Sunderland	34	3		
2011–12	Sunderland	31	1		
2012–13	Sunderland	18	1		
2013–14	Sunderland	26	2	**174**	**7**
2014–15	Stoke C	25	0		
2015–16	Stoke C	11	0		
2016–17	Stoke C	15	0	**51**	**0**

BERAHINO, Saido (F) **150 35**
H: 5 10 W: 11 13 b.Burundi 4-8-93
Internationals: England U16, U17, U18, U19, U20, U21.

2010–11	WBA	0	0		
2011–12	WBA	0	0		
2011–12	*Northampton T*	14	6	**14**	**6**
2011–12	*Brentford*	8	4	**8**	**4**
2012–13	WBA	0	0		
2012–13	*Peterborough U*	10	2	**10**	**2**
2013–14	WBA	32	5		
2014–15	WBA	38	14		
2015–16	WBA	31	4		
2016–17	WBA	4	0	**105**	**23**
2016–17	Stoke C	13	0	**13**	**0**

BOJAN, Krkic (F) **243 54**
H: 5 8 W: 10 03 b.Linyola 28-8-90
Internationals: Spain U17, U21, Full caps.

2007–08	Barcelona	31	10		
2008–09	Barcelona	23	2		
2009–10	Barcelona	23	8		
2010–11	Barcelona	27	6		
2011–12	Roma	33	7		
2012–13	Roma	0	0	**33**	**7**
2012–13	*AC Milan*	19	3	**19**	**3**
2013–14	Barcelona	0	0	**104**	**26**
2013–14	*Ajax*	24	3	**24**	**3**
2014–15	Stoke C	16	4		
2015–16	Stoke C	27	7		
2016–17	Stoke C	9	3	**52**	**14**
2016–17	*Mainz*	11	1	**11**	**1**

BUTLAND, Jack (G) **147 0**
H: 6 4 W: 12 00 b.Clevedon 10-3-93
Internationals: England U16, U17, U19, U20, U21, Full caps.

2009–10	Birmingham C	0	0		
2010–11	Birmingham C	0	0		
2011–12	Birmingham C	0	0		
2011–12	*Cheltenham T*	24	0	**24**	**0**
2012–13	Birmingham C	46	0	**46**	**0**
2012–13	Stoke C	0	0		
2013–14	Stoke C	3	0		
2013–14	*Barnsley*	13	0	**13**	**0**
2013–14	*Leeds U*	16	0	**16**	**0**
2014–15	Stoke C	3	0		
2014–15	*Derby Co*	6	0	**6**	**0**
2015–16	Stoke C	31	0		
2016–17	Stoke C	5	0	**42**	**0**

CAMERON, Geoff (D) **272 13**
H: 6 3 W: 13 02 b.Attleboro 11-7-85
Internationals: USA Full caps.

2008	Houston D	24	1		
2009	Houston D	32	2		
2010	Houston D	16	3		
2011	Houston D	37	5		
2012	Houston D	15	0	**124**	**11**
2012–13	Stoke C	35	0		
2013–14	Stoke C	37	2		
2014–15	Stoke C	27	0		
2015–16	Stoke C	30	0		
2016–17	Stoke C	19	0	**148**	**2**

CROUCH, Peter (F) **525 135**
H: 6 7 W: 13 03 b.Macclesfield 30-1-81
Internationals: England U20, U21, B, Full caps.

1998–99	Tottenham H	0	0		
1999–2000	Tottenham H	0	0		
2000–01	QPR	42	10	**42**	**10**
2001–02	Portsmouth	37	18		
2001–02	Aston Villa	7	2		
2002–03	Aston Villa	14	0		
2003–04	Aston Villa	16	4	**37**	**6**
2003–04	*Norwich C*	15	4	**15**	**4**
2004–05	Southampton	27	12	**27**	**12**
2005–06	Liverpool	32	8		
2006–07	Liverpool	32	9		
2007–08	Liverpool	21	5	**85**	**22**
2008–09	Portsmouth	38	11		
2009–10	Portsmouth	0	0	**75**	**29**
2009–10	Tottenham H	38	8		
2010–11	Tottenham H	34	4		
2011–12	Tottenham H	1	0	**73**	**12**
2011–12	Stoke C	32	10		
2012–13	Stoke C	34	7		
2013–14	Stoke C	34	8		
2014–15	Stoke C	33	8		
2015–16	Stoke C	11	0		
2016–17	Stoke C	27	7	**171**	**40**

DIOUF, Mame (F) **248 79**
H: 6 1 W: 12 00 b.Dakar 16-12-87
Internationals: Senegal Full caps.

2007	Molde	21	9		
2008	Molde	23	7		
2009	Molde	29	16	**73**	**32**
2009–10	Manchester U	5	1		
2010–11	Manchester U	0	0		
2010–11	*Blackburn R*	26	3	**26**	**3**
2011–12	Manchester U	0	0	**5**	**1**
2011–12	Hannover 96	10	6		
2012–13	Hannover 96	28	12		
2013–14	Hannover 96	19	8	**57**	**26**
2014–15	Stoke C	34	11		
2015–16	Stoke C	26	5		
2016–17	Stoke C	27	1	**87**	**17**

EDWARDS, Thomas (D) **0 0**
b. 22-1-99

2016–17	Stoke C	0	0		

EL OURIACHI, Moha (M) **15 0**
H: 5 11 W: 11 07 b.Nador 13-1-96
Internationals: Spain U17. Morocco U23.

2014–15	Barcelona	0	0		
2015–16	Stoke C	0	0		
2016–17	Stoke C	0	0		
2016–17	*Shrewsbury T*	4	0	**4**	**0**
2016–17	*Hearts*	11	0	**11**	**0**

GIVEN, Shay (G) **489 0**
H: 6 0 W: 13 03 b.Lifford 20-4-76
Internationals: Republic of Ireland U21, Full caps.

1994–95	Blackburn R	0	0		
1994–95	*Swindon T*	0	0		
1995–96	Blackburn R	0	0		
1995–96	*Swindon T*	5	0	**5**	**0**
1995–96	*Sunderland*	17	0	**17**	**0**
1996–97	Blackburn R	2	0	**2**	**0**
1997–98	Newcastle U	24	0		
1998–99	Newcastle U	31	0		
1999–2000	Newcastle U	14	0		
2000–01	Newcastle U	34	0		
2001–02	Newcastle U	38	0		
2002–03	Newcastle U	38	0		
2003–04	Newcastle U	38	0		
2004–05	Newcastle U	36	0		
2005–06	Newcastle U	38	0		
2006–07	Newcastle U	22	0		
2007–08	Newcastle U	19	0		
2008–09	Newcastle U	22	0	**354**	**0**
2008–09	Manchester C	15	0		
2009–10	Manchester C	35	0		
2010–11	Manchester C	0	0	**50**	**0**
2011–12	Aston Villa	32	0		
2012–13	Aston Villa	2	0		
2013–14	Aston Villa	0	0		
2013–14	*Middlesbrough*	16	0	**16**	**0**
2014–15	Aston Villa	3	0	**37**	**0**
2015–16	Stoke C	3	0		
2016–17	Stoke C	5	0	**8**	**0**

HAUGAARD, Jakob (G) **57 0**
H: 6 6 W: 13 10 b.Sundby 1-5-92
Internationals: Denmark U18, U20.

2010–11	Akademisk BK	14	0	**14**	**0**
2011–12	Midtjylland	0	0		
2012–13	Midtjylland	6	0		
2013–14	Midtjylland	1	0		
2014–15	Midtjylland	23	0	**30**	**0**
2015–16	Stoke C	5	0		
2016–17	Stoke C	0	0	**5**	**0**
2016–17	*Wigan Ath*	8	0	**8**	**0**

IMBULA, Giannelli (M) 193 9
H: 6 0 W: 12 02 b.Vilvoorde 12-9-92
Internationals: France U20, U21.

2009–10	Guingamp	2	0		
2010–11	Guingamp	28	2		
2011–12	Guingamp	27	0		
2012–13	Guingamp	34	2	**91**	**4**
2013–14	Marseille	29	1		
2014–15	Marseille	37	2	**66**	**3**
2015–16	FC Porto	10	0	**10**	**0**
2015–16	Stoke C	14	2		
2016–17	Stoke C	12	0	**26**	**2**

JOHNSON, Glen (D) 357 15
H: 6 0 W: 13 04 b.Greenwich 23-8-84
Internationals: England U20, U21, Full caps.

2001–02	West Ham U	0	0		
2002–03	West Ham U	15	0	**15**	**0**
2002–03	*Millwall*	8	0	**8**	**0**
2003–04	Chelsea	19	3		
2004–05	Chelsea	17	0		
2005–06	Chelsea	4	0		
2006–07	Chelsea	0	0		
2006–07	*Portsmouth*	26	0		
2007–08	Chelsea	2	0	**42**	**3**
2007–08	Portsmouth	29	1		
2008–09	Portsmouth	29	3		
2009–10	Portsmouth	0	0	**84**	**4**
2009–10	Liverpool	25	3		
2010–11	Liverpool	28	2		
2011–12	Liverpool	23	1		
2012–13	Liverpool	36	1		
2013–14	Liverpool	29	0		
2014–15	Liverpool	19	1	**160**	**8**
2015–16	Stoke C	25	0		
2016–17	Stoke C	23	0	**48**	**0**

JOSELU, Mato (F) 148 36
H: 6 3 W: 12 08 b.Stuttgart, Germany 27-3-90
Internationals: Spain U19, U20, U21.

2008–09	Celta Vigo	2	0		
2009–10	Real Madrid	0	0		
2009–10	*Celta Vigo*	24	4	**26**	**4**
2010–11	Real Madrid	1	1		
2011–12	Real Madrid	0	0	**1**	**1**
2012–13	Hoffenheim	25	5		
2013–14	Hoffenheim	0	0	**25**	**5**
2013–14	*Eintracht Frankfurt*	24	9	**24**	**9**
2014–15	Hannover 96	30	8	**30**	**8**
2015–16	Stoke C	22	4		
2016–17	Stoke C	0	0	**22**	**4**
2016–17	*Deportivo La Coruna*	20	5	**20**	**5**

MARTINS INDI, Bruno (D) 184 8
H: 6 1 W: 11 09 b.Barreiro, Portugal 8-2-92
Internationals: Netherlands U17, U19, U21, Full caps.

2010–11	Feyenoord	15	1		
2011–12	Feyenoord	29	1		
2012–13	Feyenoord	32	1		
2013–14	Feyenoord	26	2	**102**	**5**
2014–15	Porto	24	2		
2015–16	Porto	23	0		
2016–17	Porto	0	0	**47**	**2**

On loan from FC Porto.

2016–17	Stoke C	35	1	**35**	**1**

MUNIESA, Marc (D) 59 1
H: 5 10 W: 11 04 b.Lloret de Mar 27-3-92
Internationals: Spain U16, U17, U19, U21.

2008–09	Barcelona	1	0		
2009–10	Barcelona	0	0		
2010–11	Barcelona	0	0		
2011–12	Barcelona	1	0		
2012–13	Barcelona	0	0	**2**	**0**
2013–14	Stoke C	13	0		
2014–15	Stoke C	19	0		
2015–16	Stoke C	15	0		
2016–17	Stoke C	10	1	**57**	**1**

NGOY, Julien (F) 5 0
H: 6 1 W: 10 01 b.Antwerp 2-11-97
Internationals: Belgium U16, U17, U21.

2016–17	Stoke C	5	0	**5**	**0**

PIETERS, Erik (D) 282 3
H: 6 0 W: 13 00 b.Tiel 7-8-88
Internationals: Netherlands U17, U19, U21, Full caps.

2006–07	FC Utrecht	20	0		
2007–08	FC Utrecht	31	2	**51**	**2**
2008–09	PSV Eindhoven	17	0		
2009–10	PSV Eindhoven	27	0		
2010–11	PSV Eindhoven	31	0		
2011–12	PSV Eindhoven	16	0		
2012–13	PSV Eindhoven	2	0	**93**	**0**
2013–14	Stoke C	36	1		
2014–15	Stoke C	31	0		
2015–16	Stoke C	35	0		
2016–17	Stoke C	36	0	**138**	**1**

SHAQIRI, Xherdan (M) 207 37
H: 5 7 W: 11 05 b.Gnjilane 10-10-91
Internationals: Switzerland U17, U18, U19, U21, Full caps.

2009–10	Basel	32	4		
2010–11	Basel	29	5		
2011–12	Basel	31	9	**92**	**18**
2012–13	Bayern Munich	26	4		
2013–14	Bayern Munich	17	6		
2014–15	Bayern Munich	9	1	**52**	**11**
2014–15	Inter Milan	15	1	**15**	**1**
2015–16	Stoke C	27	3		
2016–17	Stoke C	21	4	**48**	**7**

SHAWCROSS, Ryan (D) 332 20
H: 6 3 W: 13 13 b.Buckley 4-10-87
Internationals: England U21, Full caps.

2006–07	Manchester U	0	0		
2007–08	Manchester U	0	0		
2007–08	Stoke C	41	7		
2008–09	Stoke C	30	3		
2009–10	Stoke C	28	2		
2010–11	Stoke C	36	1		
2011–12	Stoke C	36	2		
2012–13	Stoke C	37	1		
2013–14	Stoke C	37	1		
2014–15	Stoke C	32	2		
2015–16	Stoke C	20	0		
2016–17	Stoke C	35	1	**332**	**20**

SOBHI, Ramadan (F) 72 11
b.Cairo 27-1-97
Internationals: Egypt U17, U20, U23, Full caps.

2013–14	Al Ahly	3	1		
2014–15	Al Ahly	24	5		
2015–16	Al Ahly	28	5	**55**	**11**
2016–17	Stoke C	17	0	**17**	**0**

SWEENEY, Ryan (D) 29 0
b.Kingston upon Thames 15-4-97
Internationals: Republic of Ireland U19, U21.

2014–15	AFC Wimbledon	3	0		
2015–16	AFC Wimbledon	10	0	**13**	**0**
2016–17	Stoke C	0	0		
2016–17	*Bristol R*	16	0	**16**	**0**

TAYLOR, Joel (D) 1 0
H: 5 10 W: 10 08 b.West Bromwich 24-3-96

2016–17	Stoke C	0	0		
2016–17	*Rochdale*	1	0	**1**	**0**

VERLINDEN, Thibaud (M) 0 0
Internationals: Belgium U16, U17, U19.
From Club Bruges.

2016–17	Stoke C	0	0		

WADDINGTON, Mark (M) 4 0
H: 6 0 W: 10 06 b.Wigan 11-10-96

2013–14	Blackpool	0	0		
2014–15	Blackpool	3	0	**3**	**0**
2015–16	Stoke C	0	0		
2016–17	Stoke C	0	0		
2016–17	*Kilmarnock*	1	0	**1**	**0**

WALTERS, Jon (F) 489 94
H: 6 0 W: 12 06 b.Birkenhead 20-9-83
Internationals: Republic of Ireland U21, B, Full caps.

2001–02	Bolton W	0	0		
2002–03	Bolton W	4	0		
2002–03	*Hull C*	11	5		
2003–04	Bolton W	0	0	**4**	**0**
2003–04	Crewe Alex	0	0		
2003–04	*Barnsley*	8	0	**8**	**0**
2003–04	Hull C	16	1		
2004–05	Hull C	21	1	**48**	**7**
2004–05	*Scunthorpe U*	3	0	**3**	**0**
2005–06	Wrexham	38	5	**38**	**5**
2006–07	Chester C	26	9	**26**	**9**
2006–07	Ipswich T	16	4		
2007–08	Ipswich T	40	13		
2008–09	Ipswich T	36	5		
2009–10	Ipswich T	43	8		
2010–11	Ipswich T	1	0	**136**	**30**
2010–11	Stoke C	36	6		
2011–12	Stoke C	38	7		
2012–13	Stoke C	38	8		
2013–14	Stoke C	32	5		
2014–15	Stoke C	32	8		
2015–16	Stoke C	27	5		
2016–17	Stoke C	23	4	**226**	**43**

WARING, George (F) 55 7
b.Chester 2-2-94

2013–14	Stoke C	0	0		
2014–15	Stoke C	0	0		
2014–15	*Barnsley*	19	6	**19**	**6**
2015–16	Stoke C	0	0		
2015–16	*Oxford U*	14	1	**14**	**1**
2016–17	Stoke C	0	0		
2016–17	*Shrewsbury T*	13	0	**13**	**0**
2016–17	*Carlisle U*	9	0	**9**	**0**

WHELAN, Glenn (M) 446 17
H: 5 11 W: 12 07 b.Dublin 13-1-84
Internationals: Republic of Ireland U16, U21, B, Full caps.

2000–01	Manchester C	0	0		
2001–02	Manchester C	0	0		
2002–03	Manchester C	0	0		
2003–04	Manchester C	0	0		
2003–04	*Bury*	13	0	**13**	**0**
2004–05	Sheffield W	36	2		
2005–06	Sheffield W	43	1		
2006–07	Sheffield W	38	7		
2007–08	Sheffield W	25	2	**142**	**12**
2007–08	Stoke C	14	1		
2008–09	Stoke C	26	1		
2009–10	Stoke C	33	2		
2010–11	Stoke C	29	0		
2011–12	Stoke C	30	1		
2012–13	Stoke C	32	0		
2013–14	Stoke C	32	0		
2014–15	Stoke C	28	0		
2015–16	Stoke C	37	0		
2016–17	Stoke C	30	0	**291**	**5**

WOLLSCHEID, Philipp (D) 225 11
H: 6 4 W: 13 03 b.Wadern 6-3-89
Internationals: Germany U20, Full caps.

2006–07	Noswendel-Wadern	8	2	**8**	**2**
2007–08	Hasborn-Dautweiler	18	0	**18**	**0**
2007–08	Saarbrucken	7	1		
2008–09	Saarbrucken	23	2	**30**	**3**
2009–10	Nuremberg II	26	1		
2010–11	Nuremberg II	14	0	**40**	**1**
2010–11	Nuremberg	19	3		
2011–12	Nuremberg	2	0	**21**	**3**
2012–13	Bayer Leverkusen	31	2		
2013–14	Bayer Leverkusen	20	0		
2014–15	Bayer Leverkusen	0	0	**51**	**2**
2014–15	*Mainz*	5	0	**5**	**0**
2014–15	Stoke C	12	0		
2015–16	Stoke C	31	0		
2016–17	Stoke C	2	0	**45**	**0**
2016–17	*Wolfsburg*	7	0	**7**	**0**

Players retained or with offer of contract
Abdallah, Hakim; Balde, Rachid; Banks, Lewis; Campbell, Tyrese Kai; Cherdieu, Andrew; Devlin, Jack; Grant, Lee Anderson; Greenidge, Jordan Neil; Gyollai, Daniel; Hill, Ryan; Ireland, Stephen James; Jarvis, Daniel Adam; Krkic, Perez Bojan; Lecygne, Eddy; Marques, De Almeida Luis; Mato, Sanmartin Jose Luis; McJannet, Cameron Allan; Shenton, Oliver; Sorensen, Lasse; Souttar, Harry; Telford, Dominic.

Scholars
Allen, Mitchell; Ayoola, Olusola Adeola; Butler, James Anthony; Da, Silva Monteiro Venancio; Deczki, Mate; Diallo, Mohamed; Dunwoody, Jake; Edwards, Thomas Adam; Jokelainen, Niklas Antero; Karamoko, Vazoumana; Russo, Connor Mickel; Szereto, Krisztofer; Twyford, Jacob Thomas; Wara, Semi Scott.

SUNDERLAND (81)

ANICHEBE, Victor (F) 204 26
H: 6 1 W: 13 00 b.Nigeria 23-4-88
Internationals: Nigeria U23, Full caps.

2005–06	Everton	2	1		
2006–07	Everton	19	3		
2007–08	Everton	27	1		
2008–09	Everton	17	1		
2009–10	Everton	11	1		
2010–11	Everton	16	0		
2011–12	Everton	12	4		
2012–13	Everton	26	6		
2013–14	Everton	1	0	**131**	**17**
2013–14	WBA	24	3		
2014–15	WBA	21	3		
2015–16	WBA	10	0	**55**	**6**
2016–17	Sunderland	18	3	**18**	**3**

ASORO, Joel (F) 1 0
H: 5 9 W: 11 11 b. 27-4-99
Internationals: Sweden U17, U21.

2016–17	Sunderland	1	0	**1**	**0**

BEADLING, Tom (D) **2 0**
H: 6 1 W: 12 08 b.Barrow-in-Furness 16-1-96

2014–15	Sunderland	0	0		
2015–16	Sunderland	0	0		
2016–17	Sunderland	0	0		
2016–17	*Bury*	2	0	**2**	**0**

BORINI, Fabio (F) **144 31**
H: 5 10 W: 11 08 b.Bentivoglio 23-3-91
Internationals: Italy U17, U19, U21, Full caps.

2008–09	Chelsea	0	0		
2009–10	Chelsea	4	0		
2010–11	Chelsea	0	0	**4**	**0**
2010–11	Swansea C	9	6	**9**	**6**
2011–12	Roma	24	9	**24**	**9**
2012–13	Liverpool	13	1		
2013–14	Liverpool	0	0		
2013–14	*Sunderland*	32	7		
2014–15	Liverpool	12	1		
2015–16	Liverpool	0	0	**25**	**2**
2015–16	Sunderland	26	5		
2016–17	Sunderland	24	2	**82**	**14**

BUCKLEY, Will (F) **241 38**
H: 6 0 W: 13 00 b.Oldham 12-8-88

2007–08	Rochdale	7	0		
2008–09	Rochdale	37	10		
2009–10	Rochdale	15	3	**59**	**13**
2009–10	Watford	6	1		
2010–11	Watford	33	4	**39**	**5**
2011–12	Brighton & HA	29	8		
2012–13	Brighton & HA	36	8		
2013–14	Brighton & HA	30	3		
2014–15	Brighton & HA	1	0	**96**	**19**
2014–15	Sunderland	22	0		
2015–16	Sunderland	0	0		
2015–16	*Leeds U*	4	0	**4**	**0**
2015–16	*Birmingham C*	10	1	**10**	**1**
2016–17	Sunderland	0	0	**22**	**0**
2016–17	*Sheffield W*	11	0	**11**	**0**

CATTERMOLE, Lee (M) **271 6**
H: 5 10 W: 11 13 b.Stockton 21-3-88
Internationals: England U16, U17, U18, U19, U21.

2005–06	Middlesbrough	14	1		
2006–07	Middlesbrough	31	1		
2007–08	Middlesbrough	24	1	**69**	**3**
2008–09	Wigan Ath	33	1		
2009–10	Wigan Ath	0	0	**33**	**1**
2009–10	Sunderland	22	0		
2010–11	Sunderland	23	0		
2011–12	Sunderland	23	0		
2012–13	Sunderland	10	0		
2013–14	Sunderland	24	1		
2014–15	Sunderland	28	1		
2015–16	Sunderland	31	0		
2016–17	Sunderland	8	0	**169**	**2**

DEFOE, Jermain (F) **535 198**
H: 5 7 W: 10 04 b.Beckton 7-10-82
Internationals: England U16, U18, U21, B, Full caps.

1999–2000	West Ham U	0	0		
2000–01	West Ham U	1	0		
2000–01	*Bournemouth*	29	18	**29**	**18**
2001–02	West Ham U	35	10		
2002–03	West Ham U	38	8		
2003–04	West Ham U	19	11	**93**	**29**
2003–04	Tottenham H	15	7		
2004–05	Tottenham H	35	13		
2005–06	Tottenham H	36	9		
2006–07	Tottenham H	34	10		
2007–08	Tottenham H	19	4		
2007–08	Portsmouth	12	8		
2008–09	Portsmouth	19	7	**31**	**15**
2008–09	Tottenham H	8	3		
2009–10	Tottenham H	34	18		
2010–11	Tottenham H	22	4		
2011–12	Tottenham H	25	11		
2012–13	Tottenham H	34	11		
2013–14	Tottenham H	14	1	**276**	**91**
2014	Toronto	19	11	**19**	**11**
2014–15	Sunderland	17	4		
2015–16	Sunderland	33	15		
2016–17	Sunderland	37	15	**87**	**34**

DJILOBODJI, Papy (D) **210 12**
H: 6 4 W: 12 13 b.Kaolack 1-12-88
Internationals: Senegal Full caps.

2009–10	Senart-Moissy	7	1	**7**	**1**
2009–10	Nantes	13	0		
2010–11	Nantes	27	2		
2011–12	Nantes	36	4		
2012–13	Nantes	36	0		
2013–14	Nantes	28	3		
2014–15	Nantes	31	0	**171**	**9**
2015–16	Chelsea	0	0		
2015–16	*Werder Bremen*	14	2	**14**	**2**
2016–17	Sunderland	18	0	**18**	**0**

EMBLETON, Elliot (M) **0 0**
Internationals: England U17, U18, U20.

2016–17	Sunderland	0	0		

GIBSON, Darron (M) **115 6**
H: 6 0 W: 12 04 b.Derry 25-10-87
Internationals: Republic of Ireland U21, B, Full caps.

2005–06	Manchester U	0	0		
2006–07	Manchester U	0	0		
2007–08	Manchester U	0	0		
2007–08	*Wolverhampton W*	21	1	**21**	**1**
2008–09	Manchester U	3	1		
2009–10	Manchester U	15	2		
2010–11	Manchester U	12	0		
2011–12	Manchester U	1	0	**31**	**3**
2011–12	Everton	11	1		
2012–13	Everton	23	1		
2013–14	Everton	1	0		
2014–15	Everton	9	0		
2015–16	Everton	7	0		
2016–17	Everton	0	0	**51**	**2**
2016–17	Sunderland	12	0	**12**	**0**

GOOCH, Lynden (M) **21 0**
H: 5 8 W: 10 12 b.Santa Cruz 24-12-95
Internationals: Republic of Ireland U18. USA U20, Full caps.

2015–16	Sunderland	0	0		
2015–16	*Doncaster R*	10	0	**10**	**0**
2016–17	Sunderland	11	0	**11**	**0**

GREENWOOD, Rees (F) **1 0**
b. 2-1-96
Internationals: England U20.

2015–16	Sunderland	1	0		
2016–17	Sunderland	0	0	**1**	**0**

HONEYMAN, George (M) **6 0**
H: 5 8 W: 11 05 b.Prudhoe 8-9-94

2014–15	Sunderland	0	0		
2015–16	Sunderland	1	0		
2016–17	Sunderland	5	0	**6**	**0**

JONES, Billy (M) **423 24**
H: 5 11 W: 13 00 b.Shrewsbury 24-3-87
Internationals: England U16, U17, U19, U20.

2003–04	Crewe Alex	27	1		
2004–05	Crewe Alex	20	0		
2005–06	Crewe Alex	44	6		
2006–07	Crewe Alex	41	1	**132**	**8**
2007–08	Preston NE	29	0		
2008–09	Preston NE	44	3		
2009–10	Preston NE	44	4		
2010–11	Preston NE	43	6	**160**	**13**
2011–12	WBA	18	0		
2012–13	WBA	27	1		
2013–14	WBA	21	0	**66**	**1**
2014–15	Sunderland	14	0		
2015–16	Sunderland	24	1		
2016–17	Sunderland	27	1	**65**	**2**

KHAZRI, Wahbi (M) **259 48**
H: 6 0 W: 12 04 b.Ajaccio 8-2-91
Internationals: France U21. Tunisia U20, Full caps.

2008–09	Bastia	13	3		
2009–10	Bastia	31	2		
2010–11	Bastia	34	4		
2011–12	Bastia	33	9		
2012–13	Bastia	29	7		
2013–14	Bastia	32	6	**172**	**31**
2014–15	Bordeaux	32	9		
2015–16	Bordeaux	20	5	**52**	**14**
2015–16	Sunderland	14	2		
2016–17	Sunderland	21	1	**35**	**3**

KIRCHHOFF, Jan (D) **102 0**
H: 6 4 W: 12 04 b.Frankfurt am Main 1-10-90
Internationals: Germany U18, U19, U21.

2010–11	Mainz	10	0		
2011–12	Mainz	29	0		
2012–13	Mainz	18	0	**57**	**0**
2013–14	Bayern Munich	7	0		
2013–14	Schalke 04	2	0		
2014–15	Bayern Munich	0	0		
2014–15	*Schalke 04*	14	0	**16**	**0**
2015–16	Bayern Munich	0	0	**7**	**0**
2015–16	Sunderland	15	0		
2016–17	Sunderland	7	0	**22**	**0**

KONE, Lamine (D) **245 14**
H: 6 2 W: 13 01 b.Paris 1-2-89
Internationals: France U17, U18, U19, U20. Ivory Coast Full caps.

2006–07	Chateauroux	5	0		
2007–08	Chateauroux	16	0		
2008–09	Chateauroux	27	1		
2009–10	Chateauroux	26	3	**74**	**4**
2010–11	Lorient	7	1		
2011–12	Lorient	21	1		
2012–13	Lorient	32	3		
2013–14	Lorient	18	1		
2014–15	Lorient	30	1		
2015–16	Lorient	18	0	**126**	**7**
2015–16	Sunderland	15	2		
2016–17	Sunderland	30	1	**45**	**3**

LARSSON, Sebastian (M) **363 31**
H: 5 11 W: 11 02 b.Eskilstuna 6-6-85
Internationals: Sweden U16, U17, U19, U21, Full caps.

2002–03	Arsenal	0	0		
2003–04	Arsenal	0	0		
2004–05	Arsenal	0	0		
2005–06	Arsenal	3	0		
2006–07	Arsenal	0	0	**3**	**0**
2006–07	Birmingham C	43	4		
2007–08	Birmingham C	35	6		
2008–09	Birmingham C	38	1		
2009–10	Birmingham C	33	4		
2010–11	Birmingham C	35	4	**184**	**19**
2011–12	Sunderland	32	7		
2012–13	Sunderland	38	1		
2013–14	Sunderland	31	1		
2014–15	Sunderland	36	3		
2015–16	Sunderland	18	0		
2016–17	Sunderland	21	0	**176**	**12**

LEDGER, Michael (D) **13 0**

2016–17	Sunderland	0	0		
2017	*Viking*	13	0	**13**	**0**

LENS, Jeremain (F) **280 78**
H: 5 10 W: 12 08 b.Amsterdam 24-11-87
Internationals: Netherlands U19, U20, U21, Full caps.

2005–06	AZ Alkmaar	2	0		
2006–07	AZ Alkmaar	14	1		
2007–08	AZ Alkmaar	0	0		
2007–08	*NEC*	31	13	**31**	**13**
2008–09	AZ Alkmaar	8	1		
2009–10	AZ Alkmaar	32	12	**56**	**14**
2010–11	PSV Eindhoven	33	10		
2011–12	PSV Eindhoven	33	9		
2012–13	PSV Eindhoven	30	15	**96**	**34**
2013–14	Dynamo Kiev	28	5		
2014–15	Dynamo Kiev	21	5	**49**	**10**
2015–16	Sunderland	20	3		
2016–17	Sunderland	2	0	**22**	**3**
2016–17	*Fenerbahce*	26	4	**26**	**4**

LESCOTT, Jolean (D) **504 36**
H: 6 2 W: 13 00 b.Birmingham 16-8-82
Internationals: England U17, U18, U20, U21, B, Full caps.

1999–2000	Wolverhampton W	0	0		
2000–01	Wolverhampton W	37	2		
2001–02	Wolverhampton W	44	5		
2002–03	Wolverhampton W	44	1		
2003–04	Wolverhampton W	0	0		
2004–05	Wolverhampton W	41	4		
2005–06	Wolverhampton W	46	1	**212**	**13**
2006–07	Everton	38	2		
2007–08	Everton	38	8		
2008–09	Everton	36	4		
2009–10	Everton	1	0	**113**	**14**
2009–10	Manchester C	18	1		
2010–11	Manchester C	22	3		
2011–12	Manchester C	31	2		
2012–13	Manchester C	26	1		
2013–14	Manchester C	10	0	**107**	**7**
2014–15	WBA	34	1		
2015–16	WBA	2	0	**36**	**1**
2015–16	Aston Villa	30	1	**30**	**1**
2016–17	AEK Athens	4	0	**4**	**0**
2016–17	Sunderland	2	0	**2**	**0**

LOVE, Donald (D) **20 0**
H: 5 10 W: 11 05 b.Rochdale 2-12-94
Internationals: Scotland U17, U19, U21.

2015–16	Manchester U	1	0	**1**	**0**
2015–16	*Wigan Ath*	7	0	**7**	**0**
2016–17	Sunderland	12	0	**12**	**0**

MAJA, Josh (F) **0 0**
From Fulham.

2016–17	Sunderland	0	0		

MANNONE, Vito (G) **115 0**
H: 6 0 W: 11 08 b.Milan 2-3-88
Internationals: Italy U21.

2005–06	Arsenal	0	0		
2006–07	Arsenal	0	0		
2006–07	*Barnsley*	2	0	**2**	**0**
2007–08	Arsenal	0	0		
2008–09	Arsenal	1	0		

2009–10 Arsenal 5 0
2010–11 Arsenal 0 0
2010–11 *Hull C* 10 0
2011–12 Arsenal 0 0
2011–12 *Hull C* 21 0 **31 0**
2012–13 Arsenal 9 0 **15 0**
2013–14 Sunderland 29 0
2014–15 Sunderland 10 0
2015–16 Sunderland 19 0
2016–17 Sunderland 9 0 **67 0**

MANQUILLO, Javier (D) 67 1
H: 5 11 W: 12 04 b.Madrid 5-5-94
Internationals: Spain U16, U17, U18, U19, U20, U21.
2012–13 Atletico Madrid 3 0
2013–14 Atletico Madrid 3 0
2014–15 Atletico Madrid 0 0
2014–15 *Liverpool* 10 0 **10 0**
2015–16 Atletico Madrid 0 0 **6 0**
2015–16 *Marseille* 31 0 **31 0**
On loan from Atletico Madrid.
2016–17 Sunderland 20 1 **20 1**

MATTHEWS, Adam (D) 163 5
H: 5 10 W: 11 02 b.Swansea 13-1-92
Internationals: Wales U17, U19, U21, Full caps.
2008–09 Cardiff C 0 0
2009–10 Cardiff C 32 1
2010–11 Cardiff C 8 0 **40 1**
2011–12 Celtic 27 0
2012–13 Celtic 22 2
2013–14 Celtic 23 1
2014–15 Celtic 29 1 **101 4**
2015–16 Sunderland 1 0
2015–16 *Bristol C* 9 0
2016–17 Sunderland 0 0 **1 0**
2016–17 *Bristol C* 12 0 **21 0**

McNAIR, Paddy (D) 33 0
H: 5 8 W: 11 05 b.Ballyclare 27-4-95
Internationals: Northern Ireland U16, U17, U19, U21, Full caps.
2011–12 Manchester U 0 0
2012–13 Manchester U 0 0
2013–14 Manchester U 0 0
2014–15 Manchester U 16 0
2015–16 Manchester U 8 0 **24 0**
2016–17 Sunderland 9 0 **9 0**

MIKA, Michael (G) 78 0
H: 6 2 W: 13 12 b.Yverdon 8-3-91
Internationals: Portugal U20, U21.
2009–10 Uniao Leiria 1 0
2010–11 Uniao Leiria 3 0 **4 0**
2011–12 Benfica 0 0
2012–13 Benfica 0 0
2013–14 Benfica 0 0
2013–14 Atletico 16 0 **16 0**
2014–15 Boavista 29 0
2015–16 Boavista 26 0
2016–17 Boavista 3 0 **58 0**
2016–17 Sunderland 0 0

NDONG , Didier (M) 119 5
H: 5 10 b.Lambarene 17-6-94
Internationals: Gabon U20, Full caps.
2011–12 Sfaxien 1 0
2012–13 Sfaxien 18 1
2013–14 Sfaxien 16 1
2014–15 Sfaxien 5 0 **40 2**
2014–15 Lorient 12 0
2015–16 Lorient 34 2
2016–17 Lorient 2 0 **48 2**
2016–17 Sunderland 31 1 **31 1**

NELSON, Andrew (F) 4 0
b.Stockton-on-Tees 16-9-97
2016–17 Sunderland 0 0
2016–17 *Hartlepool U* 4 0 **4 0**

O'SHEA, John (D) 455 14
H: 6 3 W: 13 07 b.Waterford 30-4-81
Internationals: Republic of Ireland U21, Full caps.
1998–99 Manchester U 0 0
1999–2000 Manchester U 0 0
1999–2000 *Bournemouth* 10 1 **10 1**
2000–01 Manchester U 0 0
2001–02 Manchester U 9 0
2002–03 Manchester U 32 0
2003–04 Manchester U 33 2
2004–05 Manchester U 23 2
2005–06 Manchester U 34 1
2006–07 Manchester U 32 4
2007–08 Manchester U 28 0
2008–09 Manchester U 30 0
2009–10 Manchester U 15 1
2010–11 Manchester U 20 0 **256 10**
2011–12 Sunderland 29 0
2012–13 Sunderland 34 2
2013–14 Sunderland 33 1
2014–15 Sunderland 37 0
2015–16 Sunderland 28 0
2016–17 Sunderland 28 0 **189 3**

OVIEDO, Bryan (M) 104 4
H: 5 8 W: 10 13 b.Alajuela 18-2-90
Internationals: Costa Rica U20, Full caps.
2009–10 FC Copenhagen 3 0
2010–11 FC Copenhagen 1 0
2010–11 *Nordsjaelland* 14 0 **14 0**
2011–12 FC Copenhagen 22 2
2012–13 FC Copenhagen 4 0 **30 2**
2012–13 Everton 15 0
2013–14 Everton 9 2
2014–15 Everton 6 0
2015–16 Everton 14 0
2016–17 Everton 6 0 **50 2**
2016–17 Sunderland 10 0 **10 0**

PICKFORD, Jordan (G) 118 0
H: 6 1 b.Washington 7-3-94
Internationals: England U16, U17, U18, U19, U20, U21.
2010–11 Sunderland 0 0
2011–12 Sunderland 0 0
2012–13 Sunderland 0 0
2013–14 Sunderland 0 0
2013–14 *Burton Alb* 12 0 **12 0**
2013–14 *Carlisle U* 18 0 **18 0**
2014–15 Sunderland 0 0
2014–15 *Bradford C* 33 0 **33 0**
2015–16 Sunderland 2 0
2015–16 *Preston NE* 24 0 **24 0**
2016–17 Sunderland 29 0 **31 0**

PIENAAR, Steven (M) 333 35
H: 5 10 W: 10 06 b.Westbury 17-3-82
Internationals: South Africa U17, Full caps.
2001–02 Ajax 8 1
2002–03 Ajax 31 5
2003–04 Ajax 16 3
2004–05 Ajax 24 4
2005–06 Ajax 15 2 **94 15**
2006–07 Bor Dortmund 25 0 **25 0**
2007–08 Everton 28 2
2008–09 Everton 28 2
2009–10 Everton 30 4
2010–11 Everton 18 1
2010–11 Tottenham H 8 0
2011–12 Tottenham H 2 0
2011–12 *Everton* 14 4
2012–13 Tottenham H 0 0 **10 0**
2012–13 Everton 35 6
2013–14 Everton 23 1
2014–15 Everton 9 0
2015–16 Everton 4 0 **189 20**
2016–17 Sunderland 15 0 **15 0**

ROBSON, Ethan (M) 0 0
2016–17 Sunderland 0 0

ROBSON, Josh (D) 0 0
H: 5 11 W: 11 07 b.Bedlington 3-2-98
2015–16 Sunderland 0 0
2016–17 Sunderland 0 0

ROBSON, Tom (M) 1 0
H: 5 10 W: 11 11 b.Stanley 9-11-95
2014–15 Sunderland 0 0
2015–16 Sunderland 1 0
2016–17 Sunderland 0 0 **1 0**

RODWELL, Jack (D) 166 10
H: 6 2 W: 12 08 b.Southport 11-3-91
Internationals: England U16, U17, U19, U21, Full caps.
2007–08 Everton 2 0
2008–09 Everton 19 0
2009–10 Everton 26 2
2010–11 Everton 24 0
2011–12 Everton 14 2 **85 4**
2012–13 Manchester C 11 2
2013–14 Manchester C 5 0 **16 2**
2014–15 Sunderland 23 3
2015–16 Sunderland 22 1
2016–17 Sunderland 20 0 **65 4**

STRYJEK, Maksymilian (G) 0 0
H: 6 2 W: 12 11 b.Warsaw 18-7-96
Internationals: Poland U17, U18, U19.
2014–15 Sunderland 0 0
2015–16 Sunderland 0 0
2016–17 Sunderland 0 0

WATMORE, Duncan (F) 46 4
H: 5 9 W: 11 05 b.Cheadle Hulme 8-3-94
Internationals: England U20, U21.
2013–14 Sunderland 0 0
2013–14 *Hibernian* 9 1 **9 1**
2014–15 Sunderland 0 0
2015–16 Sunderland 23 3
2016–17 Sunderland 14 0 **37 3**

Players retained or with offer of contract
Brotherton, Sam; Coates, Nion Sebastian; Gamble, Owen Jay; Hume, Denver Jay; Krusnell, Oscar; Molyneux, Luke; Poame, Jean-Yves; Simoes, Domingues Michael; Storey, Alexander Michael; Talbot, James; Taylor, Brandon Lewis; Woud, Michael Cornelis; Wright, Daniel.

Scholars
Allan, Christopher Mark; Bale, Adam James; Connelly, Lee John; Connolly, Jack; Diamond, Jack Tyler; Hackett, Jake Willis; Hickey, Jordan; McAughtrie, Fergus David; Mgunga-Kimpioka, Benjamin; Patterson, Anthony; Young, Jacob Matthew.

SWANSEA C (82)

AMAT, Jordi (D) 120 1
H: 6 0 W: 12 03 b.Barcelona 21-3-92
Internationals: Spain U16, U17, U18, U19, U20, U21.
2009–10 Espanyol 6 0
2010–11 Espanyol 26 0
2011–12 Espanyol 9 0
2012–13 Espanyol 0 0 **41 0**
2012–13 *Rayo Vallecano* 27 1 **27 1**
2013–14 Swansea C 17 0
2014–15 Swansea C 10 0
2015–16 Swansea C 8 0
2016–17 Swansea C 17 0 **52 0**

AYEW, Jordan (F) 224 41
H: 6 0 W: 12 11 b.Marseille 11-9-91
Internationals: Ghana U20, Full caps.
2009–10 Marseille 4 1
2010–11 Marseille 22 2
2011–12 Marseille 34 3
2012–13 Marseille 35 7
2013–14 Marseille 16 1 **111 14**
2013–14 *Sochaux* 17 5 **17 5**
2014–15 Lorient 31 12 **31 12**
2015–16 Aston Villa 30 7
2016–17 Aston Villa 21 2 **51 9**
2016–17 Swansea C 14 1 **14 1**

BARROW, Modou (F) 152 41
H: 5 9 W: 9 13 b.Banjul 13-10-92
Internationals: Gambia Full caps.
2010 Mjolby Al 15 6 **15 6**
2011 Mjolby Sodra 19 23 **19 23**
2012 Norrkping 7 0 **7 0**
2013 Varbergs 28 2 **28 2**
2014 Ostersunds FK 19 9 **19 9**
2014–15 Swansea C 11 0
2014–15 *Nottingham F* 4 0 **4 0**
2015–16 Swansea C 22 1
2015–16 *Blackburn R* 4 0 **4 0**
2016–17 Swansea C 18 0 **51 1**
2016–17 *Leeds U* 5 0 **5 0**

BARTLEY, Kyle (D) 137 10
H: 5 11 W: 11 00 b.Stockport 22-5-91
Internationals: England U16, U17.
2008–09 Arsenal 0 0
2009–10 Arsenal 0 0
2009–10 *Sheffield U* 14 0
2010–11 Arsenal 0 0
2010–11 *Sheffield U* 21 0 **35 0**
2010–11 *Rangers* 5 1
2011–12 Arsenal 0 0
2011–12 *Rangers* 19 0 **24 1**
2012–13 Arsenal 0 0
2012–13 Swansea C 2 0
2013–14 Swansea C 2 0
2013–14 *Birmingham C* 17 3 **17 3**
2014–15 Swansea C 7 0
2015–16 Swansea C 5 0
2016–17 Swansea C 0 0 **16 0**
2016–17 *Leeds U* 45 6 **45 6**

BORJA BASTON, Gonzalez (F) 177 64
H: 6 3 W: 12 13 b. 25-8-92
Internationals: Spain U16, U17, U19.
2009–10 Atletico Madrid 1 0
2010–11 Atletico Madrid 0 0
2011–12 Atletico Madrid 0 0
2011–12 *Murcia* 20 4 **20 4**
2012–13 Atletico Madrid 0 0
2012–13 *Huesca* 31 9 **31 9**

2013–14 Atletico Madrid 0 0
2013–14 *Deportivo La Coruna* 33 10 **33 10**
2014–15 Atletico Madrid 0 0
2014–15 *Zaragoza* 38 22 **38 22**
2015–16 Atletico Madrid 0 0 **1 0**
2015–16 *Eibar* 36 18 **36 18**
2016–17 Swansea C 18 1 **18 1**

BRAY, Alex (M) 6 0
H: 5 10 W: 10 06 b.Bath 25-7-95
Internationals: Wales U19.
2013–14 Swansea C 0 0
2014–15 Swansea C 0 0
2014–15 *Plymouth Arg* 1 0 **1 0**
2015–16 Swansea C 0 0
2016–17 Swansea C 0 0
2016–17 *Rotherham U* 5 0 **5 0**

BRITTON, Leon (M) 480 11
H: 5 6 W: 10 00 b.Merton 16-9-82
Internationals: England U16.
1999–2000 West Ham U 0 0
2000–01 West Ham U 0 0
2001–02 West Ham U 0 0
2002–03 West Ham U 0 0
2002–03 *Swansea C* 25 0
2003–04 Swansea C 42 3
2004–05 Swansea C 30 1
2005–06 Swansea C 38 4
2006–07 Swansea C 41 2
2007–08 Swansea C 40 0
2008–09 Swansea C 43 0
2009–10 Swansea C 36 0
2010–11 Sheffield U 24 0 **24 0**
2010–11 Swansea C 17 1
2011–12 Swansea C 36 0
2012–13 Swansea C 33 0
2013–14 Swansea C 25 0
2014–15 Swansea C 9 0
2015–16 Swansea C 25 0
2016–17 Swansea C 16 0 **456 11**

CARROLL, Tommy (M) 107 3
H: 5 10 W: 10 00 b.Watford 28-5-92
Internationals: England U19, U21.
2010–11 Tottenham H 0 0
2010–11 *Leyton Orient* 12 0 **12 0**
2011–12 Tottenham H 0 0
2011–12 *Derby Co* 12 1 **12 1**
2012–13 Tottenham H 7 0
2013–14 Tottenham H 0 0
2013–14 *QPR* 26 0 **26 0**
2014–15 Tottenham H 0 0
2014–15 *Swansea C* 13 0
2015–16 Tottenham H 19 1
2016–17 Tottenham H 1 0 **27 1**
2016–17 Swansea C 17 1 **30 1**

CORK, Jack (D) 349 10
H: 6 0 W: 10 12 b.Carshalton 25-6-89
Internationals: England U17, U18, U19, U20, U21. Great Britain.
2006–07 Chelsea 0 0
2006–07 *Bournemouth* 7 0 **7 0**
2007–08 Chelsea 0 0
2007–08 *Scunthorpe U* 34 2 **34 2**
2008–09 Chelsea 0 0
2008–09 *Southampton* 23 0
2008–09 *Watford* 19 0 **19 0**
2009–10 Chelsea 0 0
2009–10 *Coventry C* 21 0 **21 0**
2009–10 *Burnley* 11 1
2010–11 Chelsea 0 0
2010–11 *Burnley* 40 3 **51 4**
2011–12 Southampton 46 0
2012–13 Southampton 28 0
2013–14 Southampton 28 0
2014–15 Southampton 12 2 **137 2**
2014–15 Swansea C 15 1
2015–16 Swansea C 35 1
2016–17 Swansea C 30 0 **80 2**

DYER, Nathan (M) 322 28
H: 5 5 W: 9 00 b.Trowbridge 29-11-87
2005–06 Southampton 17 0
2005–06 *Burnley* 5 2 **5 2**
2006–07 Southampton 18 0
2007–08 Southampton 17 1
2008–09 Southampton 4 0 **56 1**
2008–09 *Sheffield U* 7 1 **7 1**
2008–09 *Swansea C* 17 2
2009–10 Swansea C 40 2
2010–11 Swansea C 46 2
2011–12 Swansea C 34 5
2012–13 Swansea C 37 3
2013–14 Swansea C 27 6
2014–15 Swansea C 32 3
2015–16 Swansea C 1 0
2015–16 *Leicester C* 12 1 **12 1**
2016–17 Swansea C 8 0 **242 23**

EMNES, Marvin (M) 263 40
H: 5 11 W: 10 06 b.Rotterdam 27-5-88
Internationals: Netherlands U16, U17, U19, U20, U21.
2005–06 Sparta Rotterdam 11 1
2006–07 Sparta Rotterdam 16 0
2007–08 Sparta Rotterdam 29 8 **56 9**
2008–09 Middlesbrough 15 0
2009–10 Middlesbrough 16 1
2010–11 Middlesbrough 23 3
2010–11 *Swansea C* 4 2
2011–12 Middlesbrough 42 14
2012–13 Middlesbrough 24 5
2013–14 Middlesbrough 22 1 **142 24**
2013–14 *Swansea C* 7 1
2014–15 Swansea C 17 0
2015–16 Swansea C 2 0
2016–17 Swansea C 0 0 **30 3**
2016–17 *Blackburn R* 35 4 **35 4**

FABIANSKI, Lukasz (G) 196 0
H: 6 3 W: 13 01 b.Costrzyn nad Odra 18-4-85
Internationals: Poland U21, Full caps.
2005–06 Legia 30 0
2006–07 Legia 23 0 **53 0**
2007–08 Arsenal 3 0
2008–09 Arsenal 6 0
2009–10 Arsenal 4 0
2010–11 Arsenal 14 0
2011–12 Arsenal 0 0
2012–13 Arsenal 4 0
2013–14 Arsenal 1 0 **32 0**
2014–15 Swansea C 37 0
2015–16 Swansea C 37 0
2016–17 Swansea C 37 0 **111 0**

FER, Leroy (M) 277 44
H: 6 2 W: 12 05 b.Zortermeer 5-1-90
Internationals: Netherlands U16, U17, U19, U21, Full caps.
2007–08 Feyenoord 13 1
2008–09 Feyenoord 31 6
2009–10 Feyenoord 31 2
2010–11 Feyenoord 23 3
2011–12 Feyenoord 4 2 **102 14**
2011–12 FC Twente 26 8
2012–13 FC Twente 26 5 **52 13**
2013–14 Norwich C 29 3
2014–15 Norwich C 1 0 **30 3**
2014–15 QPR 29 6
2015–16 QPR 19 2 **48 8**
2015–16 *Swansea C* 11 0
2016–17 Swansea C 34 6 **45 6**

FERNANDEZ, Federico (D) 204 5
H: 6 3 W: 13 01 b.Tres Algarrobos 21-2-89
Internationals: Argentina U20, Full caps.
2008–09 Estudiantes 14 2
2009–10 Estudiantes 12 0
2010–11 Estudiantes 33 1 **59 3**
2011–12 Napoli 16 0
2012–13 Napoli 2 0
2012–13 *Getafe* 14 1 **14 1**
2013–14 Napoli 26 0 **44 0**
2014–15 Swansea C 28 0
2015–16 Swansea C 32 1
2016–17 Swansea C 27 0 **87 1**

FULTON, Jay (M) 28 0
H: 5 10 W: 10 08 b.Bolton 4-4-94
Internationals: Scotland U18, U19, U21.
2013–14 Swansea C 2 0
2014–15 Swansea C 2 0
2015–16 Swansea C 2 0
2015–16 *Oldham Ath* 11 0 **11 0**
2016–17 Swansea C 11 0 **17 0**

GOMIS, Bafetimbi (F) 428 143
H: 6 0 W: 12 02 b.Seyne-sur-Mer 6-8-85
Internationals: France U17, Full caps.
2003–04 St Etienne 11 2
2004–05 St Etienne 6 0
2004–05 *Troyes* 13 6 **13 6**
2005–06 St Etienne 24 2
2006–07 St Etienne 30 10
2007–08 St Etienne 35 16
2008–09 St Etienne 36 10 **142 40**
2009–10 Lyon 37 10
2010–11 Lyon 35 10
2011–12 Lyon 36 14
2012–13 Lyon 37 16
2013–14 Lyon 33 14 **178 64**
2014–15 Swansea C 31 7
2015–16 Swansea C 33 6
2016–17 Swansea C 0 0 **64 13**
2016–17 *Marseille* 31 20 **31 20**

GORRE, Kenji (M) 19 1
H: 5 10 W: 11 03 b.Paramaribo 29-9-94
2013–14 Swansea C 0 0
2014–15 Swansea C 1 0
2015–16 Swansea C 0 0
2015–16 *ADO Den Haag* 5 0 **5 0**
2016–17 Swansea C 0 0 **1 0**
2016–17 *Northampton T* 13 1 **13 1**

GRIMES, Matt (M) 82 5
H: 5 10 W: 11 00 b.Exeter 15-7-95
Internationals: England U20, U21.
2013–14 Exeter C 35 1
2014–15 Exeter C 23 4 **58 5**
2014–15 Swansea C 3 0
2015–16 Swansea C 1 0
2015–16 *Blackburn R* 13 0 **13 0**
2016–17 Swansea C 0 0 **4 0**
2016–17 *Leeds U* 7 0 **7 0**

JAMES, Daniel (M) 0 0
b. 10-11-97
Internationals: Wales U17, U19, U20, U21, Full caps.
2015–16 Swansea C 0 0
2016–17 Swansea C 0 0

JONES, Owain (F) 2 0
b. 1-10-96
Internationals: Wales U16, U17, U19, U21.
2016–17 Swansea C 0 0
2016–17 *Yeovil T* 2 0 **2 0**

KI, Sung-Yeung (M) 207 22
H: 6 2 W: 11 10 b.Gwangju 24-1-89
Internationals: South Korea U17, U20, U23, Full caps.
2009–10 Celtic 10 0
2010–11 Celtic 26 3
2011–12 Celtic 30 6 **66 9**
2012–13 Swansea C 29 0
2013–14 Swansea C 1 0
2013–14 *Sunderland* 27 3 **27 3**
2014–15 Swansea C 33 8
2015–16 Swansea C 28 2
2016–17 Swansea C 23 0 **114 10**

KING, Adam (M) 33 4
H: 5 11 W: 11 10 b.Edinburgh 11-10-95
Internationals: Scotland U18, U19, U21.
2012–13 Hearts 0 0
2013–14 Hearts 2 0 **2 0**
2013–14 Swansea C 0 0
2014–15 Swansea C 0 0
2015–16 Swansea C 0 0
2015–16 *Crewe Alex* 24 4 **24 4**
2016–17 Swansea C 0 0
2016–17 *Southend U* 7 0 **7 0**

KINGSLEY, Stephen (D) 129 1
H: 5 10 W: 10 09 b.Stirling 23-7-94
Internationals: Scotland U18, U19, U21, Full caps.
2010–11 Falkirk 3 0
2011–12 Falkirk 15 0
2012–13 Falkirk 35 0
2013–14 Falkirk 35 1 **88 1**
2014–15 Swansea C 0 0
2014–15 *Yeovil T* 12 0 **12 0**
2015–16 Swansea C 4 0
2015–16 *Crewe Alex* 12 0 **12 0**
2016–17 Swansea C 13 0 **17 0**

LLORENTE, Fernando (F) 417 139
H: 6 4 W: 13 12 b.Pamplona 26-2-85
Internationals: Spain U17, U20, U21, Full caps.
2003–04 Basconia 33 12 **33 12**
2004–05 Atletico Bilbao 15 3
2005–06 Atletico Bilbao 22 2
2006–07 Atletico Bilbao 23 2
2007–08 Atletico Bilbao 35 11
2008–09 Atletico Bilbao 34 14
2009–10 Atletico Bilbao 37 14
2010–11 Atletico Bilbao 38 18
2011–12 Atletico Bilbao 32 17
2012–13 Atletico Bilbao 26 4 **262 85**
2013–14 Juventus 34 16
2014–15 Juventus 31 7
2015–16 Juventus 1 0 **66 23**

2015–16 Sevilla 23 4 **23 4**
2016–17 Swansea C 33 15 **33 15**

MAWSON, Alfie (D) 121 18
H: 5 8 W: 12 11 b.Hillingdon 19-1-94
Internationals: England U21.
2012–13 Brentford 0 0
2013–14 Brentford 0 0
2014–15 Brentford 0 0
2014–15 *Wycombe W* 45 6 **45 6**
2015–16 Barnsley 45 6
2016–17 Barnsley 4 2 **49 8**
2016–17 Swansea C 27 4 **27 4**

McBURNIE, Oliver (F) 28 3
H: 6 2 W: 10 04 b.Bradford 6-4-96
Internationals: Scotland U19, U21.
2013–14 Bradford C 8 0
2014–15 Bradford C 7 0 **15 0**
2015–16 Swansea C 0 0
2015–16 *Newport Co* 3 3 **3 3**
2015–16 *Bristol R* 5 0 **5 0**
2016–17 Swansea C 5 0 **5 0**

MONTERO, Jefferson (M) 239 34
H: 5 8 W: 11 00 b.Babahoyo 1-9-89
Internationals: Ecuador Full caps.
2007 Emelec 22 2 **22 2**
2008 Independiente de Valle 25 8
2008–09 *Dorados* 5 1 **5 1**
2009 Independiente de Valle 12 11 **37 19**
2010–11 Villareal 9 1
2010–11 *Levante* 11 0 **11 0**
2011–12 Villareal 0 0 **9 1**
2011–12 *Real Betis* 32 1 **32 1**
2012–13 Morelia 32 4
2013–14 Morelia 25 5 **57 9**
2014–15 Swansea C 30 1
2015–16 Swansea C 23 0
2016–17 Swansea C 13 0 **66 1**

NARSINGH, Luciano (F) 190 34
H: 5 10 W: 10 12 b.Amsterdam 13-9-90
Internationals: Netherlands U18, U19, U20, U21, Full caps.
2008–09 Heerenveen 2 0
2009–10 Heerenveen 2 0
2010–11 Heerenveen 24 5
2011–12 Heerenveen 34 8 **62 13**
2012–13 PSV Eindhoven 18 6
2013–14 PSV Eindhoven 20 0
2014–15 PSV Eindhoven 32 6
2015–16 PSV Eindhoven 30 8 **100 20**
2016–17 PSV 15 1 **15 1**
2016–17 Swansea C 13 0 **13 0**

NAUGHTON, Kyle (M) 249 7
H: 5 11 W: 11 07 b.Sheffield 11-11-88
Internationals: England U21.
2006–07 Sheffield U 0 0
2007–08 *Gretna* 18 0 **18 0**
2007–08 Sheffield U 0 0
2008–09 Sheffield U 40 1
2009–10 Sheffield U 0 0 **40 1**
2009–10 Tottenham H 1 0
2009–10 *Middlesbrough* 15 0 **15 0**
2010–11 Tottenham H 0 0
2010–11 *Leicester C* 34 5 **34 5**
2011–12 Tottenham H 0 0
2011–12 *Norwich C* 32 0 **32 0**
2012–13 Tottenham H 14 0
2013–14 Tottenham H 22 0
2014–15 Tottenham H 5 0 **42 0**
2014–15 Swansea C 10 0
2015–16 Swansea C 27 0
2016–17 Swansea C 31 1 **68 1**

NORDFELDT, Kristoffer (G) 217 0
H: 6 3 W: 13 05 b.Stockholm 23-6-89
Internationals: Sweden U19, U21, Full caps.
2006 Brommapojkarna 0 0
2007 Brommapojkarna 0 0
2008 Brommapojkarna 29 0
2009 Brommapojkarna 21 0
2010 Brommapojkarna 25 0
2011 Brommapojkarna 28 0 **103 0**
2011–12 Heerenveen 6 0
2012–13 Heerenveen 33 0
2013–14 Heerenveen 35 0
2014–15 Heerenveen 38 0 **112 0**
2015–16 Swansea C 1 0
2016–17 Swansea C 1 0 **2 0**

OLSSON, Martin (D) 251 8
H: 5 7 W: 12 12 b.Gavle 17-5-88
Internationals: Sweden U19, U21, Full caps.
2005–06 Blackburn R 0 0
2006–07 Blackburn R 0 0
2007–08 Blackburn R 2 0
2008–09 Blackburn R 9 0
2009–10 Blackburn R 21 1
2010–11 Blackburn R 29 2
2011–12 Blackburn R 27 0
2012–13 Blackburn R 29 0 **117 3**
2013–14 Norwich C 34 0
2014–15 Norwich C 42 1
2015–16 Norwich C 24 1
2016–17 Norwich C 19 1 **119 3**
2016–17 Swansea C 15 2 **15 2**

RANGEL, Angel (D) 358 11
H: 5 11 W: 11 09 b.Barcelona 28-10-82
2006–07 Terrassa 34 2 **34 2**
2007–08 Swansea C 43 2
2008–09 Swansea C 40 1
2009–10 Swansea C 38 0
2010–11 Swansea C 38 2
2011–12 Swansea C 34 0
2012–13 Swansea C 33 3
2013–14 Swansea C 30 0
2014–15 Swansea C 27 0
2015–16 Swansea C 23 0
2016–17 Swansea C 18 1 **324 9**

ROBERTS, Connor (D) 47 0
H: 5 9 W: 11 03 b.Neath 23-9-95
Internationals: Wales U19, U21.
2014–15 Swansea C 0 0
2015–16 Swansea C 0 0
2015–16 *Yeovil T* 45 0 **45 0**
2016–17 Bristol R 2 0 **2 0**
2016–17 Swansea C 0 0

ROUTLEDGE, Wayne (M) 444 39
H: 5 6 W: 11 02 b.Sidcup 7-1-85
Internationals: England U20, U21.
2001–02 Crystal Palace 2 0
2002–03 Crystal Palace 26 4
2003–04 Crystal Palace 44 6
2004–05 Crystal Palace 38 0 **110 10**
2005–06 Tottenham H 3 0
2005–06 *Portsmouth* 13 0 **13 0**
2006–07 Tottenham H 0 0
2006–07 *Fulham* 24 0 **24 0**
2007–08 Tottenham H 2 0 **5 0**
2007–08 Aston Villa 1 0
2008–09 Aston Villa 1 0 **2 0**
2008–09 *Cardiff C* 9 2 **9 2**
2008–09 QPR 19 1
2009–10 QPR 25 2
2009–10 Newcastle U 17 3
2010–11 Newcastle U 17 0 **34 3**
2010–11 *QPR* 20 5 **64 8**
2011–12 Swansea C 28 1
2012–13 Swansea C 36 5
2013–14 Swansea C 35 2
2014–15 Swansea C 29 3
2015–16 Swansea C 28 2
2016–17 Swansea C 27 3 **183 16**

SAMUEL, Alex (F) 44 4
H: 6 0 W: 11 11 b.Neath 20-9-95
From Aberystwyth T.
2014–15 Swansea C 0 0
2015–16 Swansea C 0 0
2015–16 *Greenock Morton* 26 2 **26 2**
2016–17 Swansea C 0 0
2016–17 *Newport Co* 18 2 **18 2**

SHEEHAN, Josh (M) 46 7
H: 6 0 W: 11 11 b.Pembrey 30-3-95
Internationals: Wales U19, U21.
2013–14 Swansea C 0 0
2014–15 Swansea C 0 0
2014–15 *Yeovil T* 13 0
2015–16 Swansea C 0 0
2015–16 *Yeovil T* 13 2 **26 2**
2016–17 Swansea C 0 0
2016–17 *Newport Co* 20 5 **20 5**

SHEPHARD, Liam (D) 64 1
H: 5 10 W: 10 08 b.Rhondda 22-11-94
Internationals: Wales U21.
2013–14 Swansea C 0 0
2014–15 Swansea C 0 0
2014–15 *Yeovil T* 20 0
2015–16 Swansea C 0 0
2015–16 *Yeovil T* 6 0
2016–17 Swansea C 0 0
2016–17 *Yeovil T* 38 1 **64 1**

SIGURDSSON, Gylfi (M) 278 73
H: 6 1 W: 12 02 b.Reykjavik 9-9-89
Internationals: Iceland U17, U18, U19, U21, Full caps.
2007–08 Reading 0 0
2008–09 Reading 0 0
2008–09 *Shrewsbury T* 5 1 **5 1**
2008–09 *Crewe Alex* 15 3 **15 3**
2009–10 Reading 38 16
2010–11 Reading 4 2 **42 18**
2010–11 Hoffenheim 28 9
2011–12 Hoffenheim 6 0 **34 9**
2011–12 *Swansea C* 18 7
2012–13 Tottenham H 33 3
2013–14 Tottenham H 25 5 **58 8**
2014–15 Swansea C 32 7
2015–16 Swansea C 36 11
2016–17 Swansea C 38 9 **124 34**

TREMMEL, Gerhard (G) 122 0
H: 6 3 W: 14 00 b.Munich 16-11-78
2006–07 Energie Cottbus 1 0
2007–08 Energie Cottbus 24 0
2008–09 Energie Cottbus 34 0
2009–10 Energie Cottbus 34 0 **93 0**
2011–12 Swansea C 1 0
2012–13 Swansea C 14 0
2013–14 Swansea C 12 0
2014–15 Swansea C 2 0
2015–16 Swansea C 0 0
2015–16 *Werder Bremen* 0 0
2016–17 Swansea C 0 0 **29 0**

VAN DER HOORN, Mike (D) 85 10
H: 6 3 W: 12 11 b.Almere 15-10-92
Internationals: Netherlands U20, U21.
2010–11 Utrecht 1 0
2011–12 Utrecht 12 2
2012–13 Utrecht 31 4 **44 6**
2013–14 Ajax 3 0
2014–15 Ajax 15 2
2015–16 Ajax 15 1 **33 3**
2016–17 Swansea C 8 1 **8 1**

VICKERS, Josh (G) 23 0
H: 6 0 W: 11 05 b.Billericay 1-12-95
From Arsenal.
2015–16 Swansea C 0 0
2016–17 Swansea C 0 0
2016–17 *Barnet* 23 0 **23 0**

Players retained or with offer of contract
Bia, Bi Botti Boulenin; Birighitti, Mark Romano; Blair, Ryan Dominic; Byers, George William; Cooper, Brandon James; Cullen, Liam Jamie; Davies, Keston Ellis; Dulca, Marco-Alexandru; Evans, Jack; Evans, Keiran; Garrick, Jordon D'Andre; Lewis, Aaron James; Maric, Adnan; Plezier, Tom Pieter; Reid, Tyler; Rodon, Joseph Peter; Tabanou, Franck Pascal Paul; Thomas, Lewis Rhys; Zabret, Gregor; Zaragoza, Angel Rangel.

Scholars
Berry, Cameron; Blake, Matthew; Cabango, Benjamin; Cooper, Oliver Joseph; Darame, Causso; Davies, Mael Daniel; Fox, Jack Robert; Hazell, Finley Morgan; Jones, Jordan Levi; Lang, Alex William; Lewis, Joe Cameron; Price, Thomas Owen; Roberts, Matthew Marcus Josef; Williams, Rhydian Iolo.

SWINDON T (83)

BRANCO, Raphael Rossi (D) 114 6
H: 6 3 W: 13 03 b. 25-7-90
2013–14 Swindon T 15 0
2014–15 Swindon T 29 3
2015–16 Swindon T 36 1
2016–17 Swindon T 34 2 **114 6**

BROPHY, James (D) 58 0
b. 25-7-94
From Harrow Bor, Woodlands U, Broadfields U.
2015–16 Swindon T 28 0
2016–17 Swindon T 30 0 **58 0**

CONROY, Dion (D) 14 0
b.Redhill 11-12-95
From Chelsea.
2016–17 Swindon T 14 0 **14 0**

EVANS, Jake (M) **2 0**

b. 8-4-98

2015–16	Swindon T	1	0		
2016–17	Swindon T	1	0	**2**	**0**

GEORGAKLIS, James (M) **0 0**

From Manly U.

2016–17	Swindon T	0	0		

GODDARD, John (M) **42 3**

H: 5 10 W: 11 09 b.Sandhurst 2-6-93

Internationals: England C.

2011–12	Reading	0	0		
2015–16	Woking	0	0		
2015–16	Swindon T	0	0		
2016–17	Swindon T	42	3	**42**	**3**

GUNNER, Callum (M) **0 0**

2016–17	Swindon T	0	0		

HENRY, Will (G) **5 0**

b. 6-7-98

2015–16	Swindon T	2	0		
2016–17	Swindon T	3	0	**5**	**0**

HYLTON, Jermaine (F) **39 1**

H: 5 10 W: 11 00 b.Birmingham 28-6-93

2014–15	Swindon T	11	1		
2015–16	Swindon T	16	0		
2016–17	Swindon T	12	0	**39**	**1**

IANDOLO, Ellis (M) **22 0**

b. 22-8-97

From Maidstone U.

2015–16	Swindon T	12	0		
2016–17	Swindon T	10	0	**22**	**0**

KASIM, Yaser (M) **120 7**

H: 5 11 W: 11 07 b.Baghdad 10-5-91

Internationals: Iraq U23, Full caps.

2010–11	Brighton & HA	1	0		
2011–12	Brighton & HA	0	0		
2012–13	Brighton & HA	0	0	**1**	**0**
2013–14	Swindon T	37	2		
2014–15	Swindon T	35	2		
2015–16	Swindon T	27	1		
2016–17	Swindon T	20	2	**119**	**7**

NORRIS, Luke (F) **140 26**

H: 6 1 W: 13 05 b.Stevenage 3-6-93

2011–12	Brentford	1	0		
2012–13	Brentford	0	0		
2013–14	Brentford	1	0	**2**	**0**
2013–14	*Northampton T*	10	4	**10**	**4**
2013–14	*Dagenham & R*	19	4	**19**	**4**
2014–15	Gillingham	37	6		
2015–16	Gillingham	33	8	**70**	**14**
2016–17	Swindon T	39	4	**39**	**4**

OBIKA, Jonathan (F) **216 48**

H: 6 0 W: 12 00 b.Enfield 12-9-90

Internationals: England U19, U20.

2008–09	Tottenham H	0	0		
2008–09	*Yeovil T*	10	4		
2009–10	Tottenham H	0	0		
2009–10	*Yeovil T*	22	6		
2009–10	*Millwall*	12	2	**12**	**2**
2010–11	Tottenham H	0	0		
2010–11	*Crystal Palace*	7	0	**7**	**0**
2010–11	*Peterborough U*	1	1	**1**	**1**
2010–11	*Swindon T*	5	0		
2010–11	*Yeovil T*	11	3		
2011–12	Tottenham H	0	0		
2011–12	*Yeovil T*	27	4	**70**	**17**
2012–13	Tottenham H	0	0		
2012–13	*Charlton Ath*	10	3		
2013–14	Tottenham H	0	0		
2013–14	*Brighton & HA*	5	0	**5**	**0**
2013–14	*Charlton Ath*	12	0	**22**	**3**
2014–15	Tottenham H	0	0		
2014–15	Swindon T	32	8		
2015–16	Swindon T	32	11		
2016–17	Swindon T	30	6	**99**	**25**

ORMONDE-OTTEWILL, Brandon (D) **49 2**

b.London 21-12-95

Internationals: England U16, U19.

2012–13	Arsenal	0	0		
2013–14	Arsenal	0	0		
2014–15	Arsenal	0	0		
2015–16	Swindon T	28	1		
2016–17	Swindon T	21	1	**49**	**2**

OULDRIDGE, Tom (M) **0 0**

2014–15	Swindon T	0	0		
2015–16	Swindon T	0	0		
2016–17	Swindon T	0	0		

RODGERS, Anton (M) **77 5**

H: 5 7 W: 10 02 b.Reading 26-1-93

Internationals: Republic of Ireland U17, U19.

2011–12	Brighton & HA	0	0		
2012–13	Exeter C	2	0	**2**	**0**
2013–14	Oldham Ath	7	0	**7**	**0**
2014–15	Swindon T	10	2		
2015–16	Swindon T	36	2		
2016–17	Swindon T	22	1	**68**	**5**

SENDLES-WHITE, Jamie (D) **29 0**

H: 6 2 W: 13 05 b.Kingston 10-4-94

Internationals: Northern Ireland U19, U20, U21.

2011–12	QPR	0	0		
2012–13	QPR	0	0		
2013–14	QPR	0	0		
2013–14	*Colchester U*	0	0		
2014–15	QPR	0	0		
2014–15	*Mansfield T*	7	0	**7**	**0**
2015–16	Hamilton A	7	0	**7**	**0**
2015–16	Swindon T	10	0		
2016–17	Swindon T	5	0	**15**	**0**

SHARPE, Rhys (D) **8 0**

b. 17-10-94

Internationals: Northern Ireland U21.

2013–14	Derby Co	0	0		
2014–15	Derby Co	0	0		
2014–15	*Shrewsbury T*	3	0	**3**	**0**
2015–16	Notts Co	5	0		
2016–17	Notts Co	0	0	**5**	**0**
2016–17	Swindon T	0	0		

SIMPSON, Jordan (M) **0 0**

2016–17	Swindon T	0	0		

SMITH, Tom (M) **10 1**

H: 5 10 W: 11 00 b. 25-1-98

2014–15	Swindon T	1	0		
2015–16	Swindon T	1	1		
2016–17	Swindon T	8	0	**10**	**1**

SPALDING, Louis (D) **0 0**

2016–17	Swindon T	0	0		

STARKEY, Jesse (M) **1 0**

b. 1-9-95

Internationals: England U18.

From Chelsea, Brighton & HA.

2016–17	Swindon T	1	0	**1**	**0**

STEWART, Jordan (F) **8 0**

b. 31-3-95

Internationals: Northern Ireland U19, U21.

From Glentoran.

2015–16	Swindon T	1	0		
2016–17	Swindon T	7	0	**8**	**0**

THOMAS, Conor (M) **133 2**

H: 6 1 W: 11 05 b.Coventry 29-10-93

Internationals: England U17, U18.

2010–11	*Liverpool*	0	0		
2010–11	Coventry C	0	0		
2011–12	Coventry C	27	1		
2012–13	Coventry C	11	0		
2013–14	Coventry C	43	0		
2014–15	Coventry C	16	0		
2015–16	Coventry C	3	0	**100**	**1**
2016–17	Swindon T	33	1	**33**	**1**

THOMPSON, Nathan (D) **167 4**

H: 5 7 W: 11 02 b.Chester 9-11-90

2009–10	Swindon T	0	0		
2010–11	Swindon T	3	0		
2011–12	Swindon T	5	0		
2012–13	Swindon T	26	0		
2013–14	Swindon T	41	1		
2014–15	Swindon T	35	0		
2015–16	Swindon T	23	1		
2016–17	Swindon T	34	2	**167**	**4**

TWINE, Scott (F) **1 0**

b.Swindon

2015–16	Swindon T	0	0		
2016–17	Swindon T	1	0	**1**	**0**

VIGOUROUX, Lawrence (G) **76 0**

b.London 19-11-93

2012–13	Tottenham H	0	0		
2013–14	Tottenham H	0	0		
2015–16	Swindon T	33	0		
2016–17	Swindon T	43	0	**76**	**0**

YOUNG, Jordan (F) **5 1**

b. 31-7-99

2015–16	Swindon T	3	1		
2016–17	Swindon T	2	0	**5**	**1**

Scholars

Christopher, William Ernest Francis; Edwards, Jordan Joseph Terence; Frimpong, Christian Addei; Georgaklis, James; Giamattei, Paolo Bruno; Gunner, Callum Andrew Barry; Hathaway, Mason John; Martinez, Ramon Sebastian; Ouldridge, Thomas Neil; Pryce, Sol Easton; Rejek, Oliver James; Romanski, Joseph Rio; Simpson, Jordan Tyler; Spalding, Louis Andre; Stanley, Jack Peter; Twine, Scott Edward.

TOTTENHAM H (84)

ALDERWEIRELD, Toby (D) **233 14**

H: 6 1 W: 11 11 b.Wilrijk 2-3-89

Internationals: Belgium U26, U17, U18, U19, U21, Full caps.

2008–09	Ajax	5	0		
2009–10	Ajax	31	2		
2010–11	Ajax	26	2		
2011–12	Ajax	29	1		
2012–13	Ajax	32	2		
2013–14	Ajax	4	0	**127**	**7**
2013–14	Atletico Madrid	12	1	**12**	**1**
2014–15	Southampton	26	1	**26**	**1**
2015–16	Tottenham H	38	4		
2016–17	Tottenham H	30	1	**68**	**5**

ALLI, Bamidele (M) **142 50**

H: 6 1 W: 11 12 b.Watford 11-4-96

Internationals: England U17, U18, U19, U21, Full caps.

2012–13	Milton Keynes D	0	0		
2013–14	Milton Keynes D	33	6		
2014–15	Milton Keynes D	39	16	**72**	**22**
2015–16	Tottenham H	33	10		
2016–17	Tottenham H	37	18	**70**	**28**

AMOS, Luke (M) **3 0**

H: 5 10 W: 11 00 b.Hatfield 23-2-97

Internationals: England U18.

2016–17	Tottenham H	0	0		
2016–17	*Southend U*	3	0	**3**	**0**

CARTER-VICKERS, Cameron (D) **0 0**

H: 6 1 W: 13 08 b.Westcliff on Sea 31-12-97

Internationals: USA U18, U20, U23.

2015–16	Tottenham H	0	0		
2016–17	Tottenham H	0	0		

DAVIES, Ben (D) **125 4**

H: 5 7 W: 12 00 b.Neath 24-4-93

Internationals: Wales U19, Full caps.

2011–12	Swansea C	0	0		
2012–13	Swansea C	37	1		
2013–14	Swansea C	34	2	**71**	**3**
2014–15	Tottenham H	14	0		
2015–16	Tottenham H	17	0		
2016–17	Tottenham H	23	1	**54**	**1**

DEMBELE, Mousa (F) **376 46**

H: 5 9 W: 10 01 b.Wilrijk 17-7-87

Internationals: Belgium U16, U17, U18, U19, Full caps.

2003–04	Beerschot	1	0		
2004–05	Beerschot	19	1	**20**	**1**
2005–06	Willem II	33	9	**33**	**9**
2006–07	AZ	33	6		
2007–08	AZ	33	4		
2008–09	AZ	23	10		
2009–10	AZ	29	4	**118**	**24**
2010–11	Fulham	24	3		
2011–12	Fulham	36	2		
2012–13	Fulham	2	0	**62**	**5**
2012–13	Tottenham H	30	1		
2013–14	Tottenham H	28	1		
2014–15	Tottenham H	26	1		
2015–16	Tottenham H	29	3		
2016–17	Tottenham H	30	1	**143**	**7**

DIER, Eric (D) **128 8**

H: 6 3 W: 13 08 b.Cheltenham 15-1-94

Internationals: England U18, U19, U20, U21, Full caps.

2012–13	Sporting Lisbon	14	1		
2013–14	Sporting Lisbon	13	0	**27**	**1**
2014–15	Tottenham H	28	2		
2015–16	Tottenham H	37	3		
2016–17	Tottenham H	36	2	**101**	**7**

EDWARDS, Marcus (M) **0 0**
b.London 3-12-98
Internationals: England U16, U17, U18, U19.
2016–17 Tottenham H 0 0

ERIKSEN, Christian (M) **247 56**
H: 5 9 W: 10 02 b.Middelfart 14-2-92
Internationals: Denmark U17, U18, U19, U21, Full caps.
2009–10 Ajax 15 0
2010–11 Ajax 28 6
2011–12 Ajax 33 7
2012–13 Ajax 33 10
2013–14 Ajax 4 2 **113 25**
2013–14 Tottenham H 25 7
2014–15 Tottenham H 38 10
2015–16 Tottenham H 35 6
2016–17 Tottenham H 36 8 **134 31**

HARRISON, Shayon (F) **14 1**
H: 6 0 W: 10 10 b.Hornsey 13-7-97
2016–17 Tottenham H 0 0
2016–17 *Yeovil T* 14 1 **14 1**

JANSSEN, Vincent (F) **130 58**
H: 5 11 W: 12 06 b.Heesch 15-6-94
Internationals: Netherlands U16, U18, U20, U21, Full caps.
2013–14 Almere C 35 10
2014–15 Almere C 34 19 **69 29**
2015–16 AZ Alkmaar 34 27 **34 27**
2016–17 Tottenham H 27 2 **27 2**

KANE, Harry (F) **169 92**
H: 6 0 W: 10 00 b.Chingford 28-7-93
Internationals: England U17, U19, U20, U21, Full caps.
2010–11 Tottenham H 0 0
2010–11 *Leyton Orient* 18 5 **18 5**
2011–12 Tottenham H 0 0
2011–12 *Millwall* 22 7 **22 7**
2012–13 Tottenham H 1 0
2012–13 *Norwich C* 3 0 **3 0**
2012–13 *Leicester C* 13 2 **13 2**
2013–14 Tottenham H 10 3
2014–15 Tottenham H 34 21
2015–16 Tottenham H 38 25
2016–17 Tottenham H 30 29 **113 78**

LAMELA, Erik (F) **180 31**
H: 6 0 W: 10 13 b.Buenos Aires 4-3-92
Internationals: Argentina U20, Full caps.
2008–09 River Plate 1 0
2009–10 River Plate 1 0
2010–11 River Plate 32 4 **34 4**
2011–12 Roma 29 4
2012–13 Roma 32 15 **61 19**
2013–14 Tottenham H 9 0
2014–15 Tottenham H 33 2
2015–16 Tottenham H 34 5
2016–17 Tottenham H 9 1 **85 8**

LESNIAK, Filip (M) **2 0**
b. 14-5-96
Internationals: Slovakia U17, U19, U21.
2016–17 Tottenham H 1 0 **1 0**
2016–17 *Liberec* 1 0 **1 0**

LLORIS, Hugo (G) **388 0**
H: 6 2 W: 12 03 b.Nice 26-12-86
Internationals: France U18, U19, U20, U21, Full caps.
2005–06 Nice 5 0
2006–07 Nice 37 0
2007–08 Nice 30 0 **72 0**
2008–09 Lyon 35 0
2009–10 Lyon 36 0
2010–11 Lyon 37 0
2011–12 Lyon 36 0
2012–13 Lyon 2 0 **146 0**
2012–13 Tottenham H 27 0
2013–14 Tottenham H 37 0
2014–15 Tottenham H 35 0
2015–16 Tottenham H 37 0
2016–17 Tottenham H 34 0 **170 0**

LOFT, Ryan (F) **9 0**
H: 6 3 W: 11 07 b.Gravesend 14-9-97
2016–17 Tottenham H 0 0
2016–17 *Stevenage* 9 0 **9 0**

McGEE, Luke (G) **39 0**
H: 6 2 W: 12 08 b.Edgware 9-2-95
Internationals: England U17.
2014–15 Tottenham H 0 0
2015–16 Tottenham H 0 0
2016–17 Tottenham H 0 0
2016–17 *Peterborough U* 39 0 **39 0**

MILLER, Will (M) **15 1**
H: 5 6 W: 10 01 b.London 8-6-96
Internationals: England U18.
2016–17 Tottenham H 0 0
2016–17 *Burton Alb* 15 1 **15 1**

N'JIE, Clinton (F) **67 11**
H: 5 9 W: 10 10 b.Douala 15-8-93
Internationals: Cameroon U20, Full caps.
2012–13 Lyon 4 0
2013–14 Lyon 3 0
2014–15 Lyon 30 7 **37 7**
2015–16 Tottenham H 8 0
2016–17 Tottenham H 0 0 **8 0**
2016–17 *Marseille* 22 4 **22 4**

NKOUDOU, Georges (M) **70 39**
b. 13-2-95
Internationals: France U17, U19, U20, U21.
2013–14 Nantes 6 1
2014–15 Nantes 28 16 **34 17**
2015–16 Marseilles 28 22 **28 22**
2016–17 Marseille 0 0
2016–17 Tottenham H 8 0 **8 0**

ODUWA, Nathan (F) **34 1**
H: 6 1 W: 11 11 b.London 5-3-96
Internationals: England U17, U18, U20. Nigeria U23.
2013–14 Tottenham H 0 0
2014–15 Tottenham H 0 0
2014–15 *Luton T* 11 0 **11 0**
2015–16 Tottenham H 0 0
2015–16 *Rangers* 15 1 **15 1**
2015–16 *Colchester U* 2 0 **2 0**
2016–17 Tottenham H 0 0
2016–17 *Peterborough U* 6 0 **6 0**

OGILVIE, Connor (D) **39 1**
H: 6 0 W: 12 08 b.Harlow 14-2-96
Internationals: England U16, U17.
2013–14 Tottenham H 0 0
2014–15 Tottenham H 0 0
2015–16 Stevenage 21 1
2016–17 Tottenham H 0 0
2016–17 *Stevenage* 18 0 **39 1**

ONOMAH, Joshua (M) **13 0**
H: 5 11 W: 10 01 b.Enfield 27-4-97
Internationals: England U16, U17, U18, U19, U20, U21.
2013–14 Tottenham H 0 0
2014–15 Tottenham H 0 0
2015–16 Tottenham H 8 0
2016–17 Tottenham H 5 0 **13 0**

PAU LOPEZ, Sabata (G) **38 0**
H: 6 2 W: 12 02 b.Girona 13-12-94
Internationals: Spain U21.
2014–15 Espanyol 2 0
2015–16 Espanyol 36 0
2016–17 Espanyol 0 0 **38 0**
On loan from Espanyol.
2016–17 Tottenham H 0 0

ROSE, Danny (M) **159 9**
H: 5 8 W: 11 11 b.Doncaster 2-6-90
Internationals: England U17, U19, U21, Full caps. Great Britain.
2007–08 Tottenham H 0 0
2008–09 Tottenham H 0 0
2008–09 *Watford* 7 0 **7 0**
2009–10 Tottenham H 1 1
2010–11 Tottenham H 4 0
2010–11 *Bristol C* 17 0 **17 0**
2011–12 Tottenham H 11 0
2012–13 Tottenham H 0 0
2012–13 *Sunderland* 27 1 **27 1**
2013–14 Tottenham H 22 1
2014–15 Tottenham H 28 3
2015–16 Tottenham H 24 1
2016–17 Tottenham H 18 2 **108 8**

SHASHOUA, Samuel (M) **0 0**
b. 13-5-99
Internationals: England U17, U18.
2016–17 Tottenham H 0 0

SISSOKO, Moussa (M) **333 31**
H: 6 2 W: 13 00 b.Le Blanc Mesnil 16-8-89
Internationals: France U16, U17, U18, U19, U21, Full caps.
2007–08 Toulouse 29 1
2008–09 Toulouse 35 4
2009–10 Toulouse 37 7
2010–11 Toulouse 35 5
2011–12 Toulouse 35 2
2012–13 Toulouse 19 1 **190 20**
2012–13 Newcastle U 12 3
2013–14 Newcastle U 35 3
2014–15 Newcastle U 34 4
2015–16 Newcastle U 37 1 **118 11**
2016–17 Tottenham H 25 0 **25 0**

SON, Heung-Min (M) **197 59**
H: 6 0 W: 12 00 b.Chuncheon 8-7-92
Internationals: South Korea U17, U23, Full caps.
2010–11 Hamburg 13 3
2011–12 Hamburg 27 5
2012–13 Hamburg 33 12 **73 20**
2013–14 Bayer Leverkusen 31 10
2014–15 Bayer Leverkusen 30 11
2015–16 Bayer Leverkusen 1 0 **62 21**
2015–16 Tottenham H 28 4
2016–17 Tottenham H 34 14 **62 18**

TRIPPIER, Keiran (D) **230 7**
H: 5 10 W: 11 00 b.Bury 19-9-90
Internationals: England U18, U19, U20, U21, Full caps.
2007–08 Manchester C 0 0
2008–09 Manchester C 0 0
2009–10 Manchester C 0 0
2009–10 *Barnsley* 3 0
2010–11 Manchester C 0 0
2010–11 *Barnsley* 39 2 **42 2**
2011–12 Manchester C 0 0
2011–12 Burnley 46 3
2012–13 Burnley 45 0
2013–14 Burnley 41 1
2014–15 Burnley 38 0 **170 4**
2015–16 Tottenham H 6 1
2016–17 Tottenham H 12 0 **18 1**

VERTONGHEN, Jan (D) **318 30**
H: 6 2 W: 12 05 b.Sint-Niklaas 24-4-87
Internationals: Belgium U16, U21, Full caps.
2006–07 Ajax 3 0
2006–07 *RKC* 12 3 **12 3**
2007–08 Ajax 31 2
2008–09 Ajax 26 4
2009–10 Ajax 32 3
2010–11 Ajax 32 6
2011–12 Ajax 31 8 **155 23**
2012–13 Tottenham H 34 4
2013–14 Tottenham H 23 0
2014–15 Tottenham H 32 0
2015–16 Tottenham H 29 0
2016–17 Tottenham H 33 0 **151 4**

VORM, Michel (G) **270 0**
H: 6 0 W: 13 03 b.Nieuwegein 20-10-83
Internationals: Netherlands Full caps.
2005–06 Den Bosch 35 0 **35 0**
2006–07 Utrecht 33 0
2007–08 Utrecht 11 0
2008–09 Utrecht 26 0
2009–10 Utrecht 33 0
2010–11 Utrecht 33 0 **136 0**
2011–12 Swansea C 37 0
2012–13 Swansea C 26 0
2013–14 Swansea C 26 0 **89 0**
2014–15 Tottenham H 4 0
2015–16 Tottenham H 1 0
2016–17 Tottenham H 5 0 **10 0**

WALKER, Kyle (D) **255 5**
H: 5 10 W: 11 07 b.Sheffield 28-5-90
Internationals: England U19, U21, Full caps.
2008–09 Sheffield U 2 0
2008–09 *Northampton T* 9 0 **9 0**
2009–10 Tottenham H 2 0
2009–10 *Sheffield U* 26 0 **28 0**
2010–11 Tottenham H 1 0
2010–11 *QPR* 20 0 **20 0**
2010–11 *Aston Villa* 15 1 **15 1**
2011–12 Tottenham H 37 2
2012–13 Tottenham H 36 0
2013–14 Tottenham H 26 1
2014–15 Tottenham H 15 0
2015–16 Tottenham H 33 1
2016–17 Tottenham H 33 0 **183 4**

WALKER-PETERS, Kyle (F) **0 0**
H: 5 8 W: 9 13 b.Edmonton 13-4-97
Internationals: England U18, U19, U20.
2015–16 Tottenham H 0 0
2016–17 Tottenham H 0 0

WALKES, Anton (M) **6 1**
b. 8-2-97
2016–17 Tottenham H 0 0
2016–17 *Atlanta U* 6 1 **6 1**

WANYAMA, Victor (M) 231 20
H: 6 2 W: 11 12 b.Nairobi 25-6-91
Internationals: Kenya Full caps.
2009–10 Beerschot 19 0
2010–11 Beerschot 30 2 **49 2**
2011–12 Celtic 29 4
2012–13 Celtic 32 6 **61 10**
2013–14 Southampton 23 0
2014–15 Southampton 32 3
2015–16 Southampton 30 1 **85 4**
2016–17 Tottenham H 36 4 **36 4**

WHITEMAN, Alfie (G) 0 0
b. 2-10-98
Internationals: England U16, U17, U18, U19.
2016–17 Tottenham H 0 0

WIMMER, Kevin (D) 110 6
H: 6 2 W: 13 05 b.Wels 15-11-92
Internationals: Austria U18, U21, Full caps.
2011–12 LASK Linkz 28 4 **28 4**
2012–13 Cologne 9 0
2013–14 Cologne 26 2
2014–15 Cologne 32 0 **67 2**
2015–16 Tottenham H 10 0
2016–17 Tottenham H 5 0 **15 0**

WINKS, Harry (M) 21 1
H: 5 10 W: 10 03 b.Hemel Hempstead 2-2-96
Internationals: England U17, U18, U19, U20, U21.
2013–14 Tottenham H 0 0
2014–15 Tottenham H 0 0
2015–16 Tottenham H 0 0
2016–17 Tottenham H 21 1 **21 1**

Players retained or with offer of contract
Austin, Brandon Anthony; Bennetts, Keanan Chidozie; Bentaleb, Nabil; Dinzeyi, Jonathan Toko Lema; Duncan, Dylan; Eyoma, Timothy Joel; Fazio, Federico; Georgiou, Anthony Michael; Glover, Thomas William; Goddard, Cy; Maghoma, Christian; Marsh, George Owen; Oakley-Boothe, Tashan; Pritchard, Joe Cameron; Roles, Jack; Sterling, Kazaiah; Tanganga, Japhat Manzambi; Tracey, Shilow; Tsaroulla, Nicholas.

Scholars
Brown, Jaden; De, Bie Jonathan; Freeman, Charlie; Griffiths, Reo Revaldo; Hinds, Tariq Devontae Aaron; Lock, Matthew Joseph; Omolabi, Moroyin; Reynolds, Jamie Joe.

WALSALL (85)

BAKAYOKO, Amadou (F) 52 4
H: 6 4 W: 13 05 b. 1-1-96
2013–14 Walsall 6 0
2014–15 Walsall 7 0
2015–16 Walsall 0 0
2016–17 Walsall 39 4 **52 4**

BUTTERFIELD, Kacy (M) 0 0
2016–17 Walsall 0 0

CANDLIN, Mitchell (F) 5 0
2016–17 Walsall 5 0 **5 0**

CHAMBERS, Adam (D) 487 12
H: 5 10 W: 11 12 b.Sandwell 20-11-80
1998–99 WBA 0 0
1999–2000 WBA 0 0
2000–01 WBA 11 1
2001–02 WBA 32 0
2002–03 WBA 13 0
2003–04 WBA 0 0
2003–04 *Sheffield W* 11 0 **11 0**
2004–05 WBA 0 0 **56 1**
2004–05 Kidderminster H 2 0 **2 0**
2006–07 Leyton Orient 38 4
2007–08 Leyton Orient 45 3
2008–09 Leyton Orient 33 1
2009–10 Leyton Orient 29 1
2010–11 Leyton Orient 29 0 **174 9**
2011–12 Walsall 29 2
2012–13 Walsall 37 0
2013–14 Walsall 45 0
2014–15 Walsall 45 0
2015–16 Walsall 45 0
2016–17 Walsall 43 0 **244 2**

COCKERILL-MOLLETT, Callum (D) 0 0
2016–17 Walsall 0 0

CUVELIER, Florent (M) 81 7
H: 6 0 W: 11 05 b.Brussels 12-9-92
Internationals: Belgium U16, U17, U18, U19, U20, U21.
2009–10 Portsmouth 0 0
2010–11 Stoke C 0 0
2011–12 Stoke C 0 0
2011–12 *Walsall* 18 4
2012–13 Stoke C 0 0
2012–13 *Walsall* 19 2
2012–13 *Peterborough U* 1 0 **1 0**
2013–14 Stoke C 0 0
2013–14 Sheffield U 7 0
2013–14 *Port Vale* 1 0 **1 0**
2014–15 Sheffield U 3 0
2014–15 *Burton Alb* 1 1 **1 1**
2015–16 Sheffield U 9 0 **19 0**
2016–17 Walsall 22 0 **59 6**

EDWARDS, Joe (D) 208 9
H: 5 8 W: 11 07 b.Gloucester 31-10-90
2009–10 Bristol C 0 0
2010–11 Bristol C 2 0
2011–12 Bristol C 2 0
2011–12 *Yeovil T* 4 1
2012–13 Bristol C 0 0 **4 0**
2012–13 Yeovil T 35 2
2013–14 Yeovil T 46 1
2014–15 Yeovil T 34 0 **119 4**
2015–16 Colchester U 42 2 **42 2**
2016–17 Walsall 43 3 **43 3**

ETHERIDGE, Neil (G) 101 0
H: 6 3 W: 14 00 b.Enfield 7-2-90
Internationals: England U16. Philippines Full caps.
2008–09 Fulham 0 0
2009–10 Fulham 0 0
2010–11 Fulham 0 0
2011–12 Fulham 0 0
2012–13 Fulham 0 0
2012–13 *Bristol R* 12 0 **12 0**
2013–14 Fulham 0 0
2013–14 *Crewe Alex* 4 0 **4 0**
2014–15 Oldham Ath 0 0
2014–15 Charlton Ath 4 0 **4 0**
2015–16 Walsall 40 0
2016–17 Walsall 41 0 **81 0**

GANLEY, Brandon (G) 0 0
2016–17 Walsall 0 0

HALLWOOD, Chandler (G) 0 0
b.Huddersfield 18-9-97
2014–15 Bradford C 0 0
2015–16 Bradford C 0 0
2016–17 Walsall 0 0

HAYLES-DOCHERTY, Tobias (F) 1 0
2016–17 Walsall 1 0 **1 0**

JACKSON, Simeon (M) 306 71
H: 5 10 W: 10 12 b.Kingston, Jamaica 28-3-87
Internationals: Canada U20, Full caps.
2004–05 Rushden & D 3 0
2005–06 Rushden & D 14 5
2006–07 Rushden & D 0 0
2007–08 Rushden & D 0 0 **17 5**
2007–08 Gillingham 18 4
2008–09 Gillingham 41 17
2009–10 Gillingham 42 14 **101 35**
2010–11 Norwich C 38 13
2011–12 Norwich C 22 3
2012–13 Norwich C 13 1 **73 17**
2013–14 E Braunschweig 9 0 **9 0**
2013–14 Millwall 14 2 **14 2**
2014–15 Coventry C 28 3 **28 3**
2015–16 Barnsley 9 0 **9 0**
2015–16 Blackburn R 17 2 **17 2**
2016–17 Walsall 38 7 **38 7**

KINSELLA, Liam (M) 19 1
b.Colchester 23-2-96
Internationals: Republic of Ireland U19.
2013–14 Walsall 0 0
2014–15 Walsall 4 0
2015–16 Walsall 7 1
2016–17 Walsall 8 0 **19 1**

KOUHYAR, Maz (D) 6 0
H: 5 11 W: 10 12 b. 30-9-97
2015–16 Walsall 0 0
2016–17 Walsall 6 0 **6 0**

MACGILLIVRAY, Craig (G) 12 0
H: 6 2 W: 12 04 b.Harrogate 12-1-93
2014–15 Walsall 2 0
2015–16 Walsall 5 0
2016–17 Walsall 5 0 **12 0**

MAKRIS, Andreas (F) 128 21
H: 5 7 W: 10 10 b.Paphos 27-11-95
Internationals: Cyprus U17, U19, U21, Full caps.
2012–13 Paphos 14 2 **14 2**
2013–14 Anorthosis Famagusta 25 2
2014–15 Anorthosis Famagusta 30 13
2015–16 Anorthosis Famagusta 27 3 **82 18**
2016–17 Walsall 32 1 **32 1**

MORRIS, Kieron (M) 84 10
H: 5 10 W: 11 01 b.Hereford 3-6-94
2012–13 Walsall 0 0
2013–14 Walsall 2 0
2014–15 Walsall 14 2
2015–16 Walsall 33 3
2016–17 Walsall 35 5 **84 10**

MOUSSA, Franck (M) 251 38
H: 5 8 W: 10 08 b.Brussels 24-7-89
Internationals: Belgium U18, U19.
2005–06 Southend U 1 0
2006–07 Southend U 4 0
2007–08 Southend U 16 0
2008–09 Southend U 26 2
2008–09 *Wycombe W* 9 0 **9 0**
2009–10 Southend U 43 5
2010–11 Leicester C 8 1
2010–11 *Doncaster R* 14 2 **14 2**
2011–12 Leicester C 0 0 **8 1**
2011–12 *Chesterfield* 10 4 **10 4**
2012–13 Nottingham F 0 0
2012–13 Coventry C 38 6
2013–14 Coventry C 39 12 **77 18**
2014–15 Charlton Ath 14 1
2015–16 Charlton Ath 6 0 **20 1**
2015–16 Southend U 1 1 **91 8**
2016–17 Walsall 22 4 **22 4**

O'CONNELL, Eoghan (D) 33 2
H: 6 1 W: 12 08 b.Cork 13-8-95
Internationals: Republic of Ireland U19, U21.
2013–14 Celtic 1 0
2014–15 Celtic 3 0
2015–16 Celtic 1 0
2015–16 *Oldham Ath* 2 0 **2 0**
2016 *Cork C* 7 1 **7 1**
2016–17 Celtic 2 0 **7 0**
On loan from Celtic.
2016–17 Walsall 17 1 **17 1**

O'CONNOR, James (D) 404 8
H: 5 10 W: 12 05 b.Birmingham 20-11-84
2003–04 Aston Villa 0 0
2004–05 Aston Villa 0 0
2004–05 *Port Vale* 13 0 **13 0**
2004–05 Bournemouth 6 0
2005–06 Bournemouth 39 1 **45 1**
2006–07 Doncaster R 40 1
2007–08 Doncaster R 40 0
2008–09 Doncaster R 32 1
2009–10 Doncaster R 38 0
2010–11 Doncaster R 34 2
2011–12 Doncaster R 28 0 **212 4**
2012–13 Derby Co 22 1
2013–14 Derby Co 0 0 **22 1**
2013–14 *Bristol C* 3 0 **3 0**
2014–15 Walsall 32 1
2015–16 Walsall 37 1
2016–17 Walsall 40 0 **109 2**

OSBOURNE, Isaiah (M) 186 4
H: 6 2 W: 12 06 b.Birmingham 5-11-87
Internationals: England U16.
2005–06 Aston Villa 0 0
2006–07 Aston Villa 11 0
2007–08 Aston Villa 8 0
2008–09 Aston Villa 0 0
2008–09 *Nottingham F* 8 0 **8 0**
2009–10 Aston Villa 0 0
2009–10 *Middlesbrough* 9 0 **9 0**
2010–11 Aston Villa 0 0 **19 0**
2010–11 *Sheffield W* 10 0 **10 0**
2011–12 Hibernian 30 1 **30 1**
2012–13 Blackpool 28 1
2013–14 Blackpool 24 1 **52 2**
2014–15 Scunthorpe U 28 0 **28 0**
2015–16 Walsall 0 0
2016–17 Walsall 30 1 **30 1**

OZTUMER, Erhun (M) **91 22**
b.Greenwich 29-5-91

Season	Club	Apps	Gls	Total Apps	Total Gls
2014–15	Peterborough U	20	1		
2015–16	Peterborough U	30	6	**50**	**7**
2016–17	Walsall	41	15	**41**	**15**

PETERS, Cameron (F) **0 0**

Season	Club	Apps	Gls	Total Apps	Total Gls
2016–17	Walsall	0	0		

PRESTON, Matt (D) **41 3**
b. 16-3-95

Season	Club	Apps	Gls	Total Apps	Total Gls
2013–14	Walsall	0	0		
2014–15	Walsall	1	0		
2015–16	Walsall	10	2		
2016–17	Walsall	30	1	**41**	**3**

ROBERTS, Kory (D) **4 0**
H: 6 0 W: 11 07 b.Birmingham 17-12-97

Season	Club	Apps	Gls	Total Apps	Total Gls
2016–17	Walsall	4	0	**4**	**0**

SANGHA, Jordan (M) **0 0**
b. 4-1-98

Season	Club	Apps	Gls	Total Apps	Total Gls
2015–16	Walsall	0	0		
2016–17	Walsall	0	0		

SHORROCK, Will (M) **0 0**

Season	Club	Apps	Gls	Total Apps	Total Gls
2016–17	Walsall	0	0		

TONKS, Sam (D) **0 0**

Season	Club	Apps	Gls	Total Apps	Total Gls
2016–17	Walsall	0	0		

VANN, Daniel (D) **0 0**

Season	Club	Apps	Gls	Total Apps	Total Gls
2016–17	Walsall	0	0		

Players retained or with offer of contract
Flanagan, Reece James; Oliver, Rory Benjamin; Roberts, Liam Joseph.

Scholars
Cairns, Joseph Lawrence; Candlin, Mitchel James; Caswell, Bradley William; Cela, Lezion; Fisher, Cody Lee; Freemantle, Ethan James; Ganley, Brandon Rooney; Kendrick, Ben; Maddocks, Ashley Francis; Mason, Stefan Richard; Massamba, Debert; O'Sullivan, Daniel Joseph; Peters, Cameron James; Shorrock, William John; Tonks, Samuel George.

WATFORD (86)

AMRABAT, Nordin (F) **298 48**
H: 5 10 W: 12 02 b.Naarden 31-3-87
Internationals: Netherlands U21. Morocco Full caps.

Season	Club	Apps	Gls	Total Apps	Total Gls
2006–07	Omniworld	36	14	**36**	**14**
2007–08	VVV-Venio	33	10	**33**	**10**
2008–09	PSV Eindhoven	25	5		
2009–10	PSV Eindhoven	25	3		
2010–11	PSV Eindhoven	6	1	**56**	**9**
2010–11	Kayserispor	14	1		
2011–12	Kayserispor	25	5	**39**	**6**
2012–13	Galatasaray	30	1		
2013–14	Galatasaray	4	0		
2013–14	*Malaga*	15	2		
2014–15	Galatasaray	0	0	**34**	**1**
2014–15	*Malaga*	31	6		
2015–16	Malaga	13	0	**59**	**8**
2015–16	Watford	12	0		
2016–17	Watford	29	0	**41**	**0**

ARLAUSKIS, Giedrius (G) **124 0**
H: 6 0 W: 12 08 b.Telsiai 1-12-87
Internationals: Lithuania Full caps.

Season	Club	Apps	Gls	Total Apps	Total Gls
2006	Siauliai	14	0		
2007	Siauliai	19	0	**33**	**0**
2007–08	Unirea Urziceni	4	0		
2008–09	Unirea Urziceni	30	0		
2009–10	Unirea Urziceni	18	0		
2010–11	Unirea Urziceni	3	0	**55**	**0**
2010–11	Rubin Kazan	2	0		
2011–12	Rubin Kazan	3	0		
2012–13	Rubin Kazan	2	0		
2013–14	Rubin Kazan	0	0	**7**	**0**
2014–15	Steau Bucharest	25	0	**25**	**0**
2015–16	Watford	1	0		
2015–16	*Espanyol*	3	0	**3**	**0**
2016–17	Watford	0	0	**1**	**0**

BEHRAMI, Valon (M) **354 11**
H: 6 1 W: 12 04 b.Titova Mitrovika 19-4-85
Internationals: Switzerland Full caps.

Season	Club	Apps	Gls	Total Apps	Total Gls
2002–03	Lugano	2	0	**2**	**0**
2003–04	Genoa	24	0		
2004–05	Genoa	0	0	**24**	**0**
2004–05	*Verona*	33	3	**33**	**3**
2005–06	Lazio	26	2		
2006–07	Lazio	17	1		
2007–08	Lazio	22	1	**65**	**4**
2008–09	West Ham U	24	1		
2009–10	West Ham U	27	1		
2010–11	West Ham U	7	2	**58**	**4**
2010–11	Fiorentina	17	0		
2011–12	Fiorentina	31	0	**48**	**0**
2012–13	Napoli	33	0		
2013–14	Napoli	21	0	**54**	**0**
2014–15	Hamburg	22	0	**22**	**0**
2015–16	Watford	21	0		
2016–17	Watford	27	0	**48**	**0**

BERGHUIS, Steven (F) **133 29**
H: 5 11 W: 11 11 b.Apeldoorn 19-12-91
Internationals: Netherlands U19, U20, U21, Full caps.

Season	Club	Apps	Gls	Total Apps	Total Gls
2010–11	FC Twente	1	0		
2011–12	FC Twente	7	1	**8**	**1**
2011–12	*VVV Venlo*	16	2	**16**	**2**
2012–13	AZ Alkmaar	23	0		
2013–14	AZ Alkmaar	25	8		
2014–15	AZ Alkmaar	22	11	**70**	**19**
2015–16	Watford	9	0		
2016–17	Watford	0	0	**9**	**0**
2016–17	*Feyenoord*	30	7	**30**	**7**

BRITOS, Miguel (D) **261 12**
H: 6 2 W: 12 13 b.Montevideo 17-7-85

Season	Club	Apps	Gls	Total Apps	Total Gls
2005–06	Fenix	12	0	**12**	**0**
2006–07	Juventud	33	3	**33**	**3**
2007–08	Montevideo W	26	1	**26**	**1**
2008–09	Bologna	14	1		
2009–10	Bologna	23	0		
2010–11	Bologna	34	3	**71**	**4**
2011–12	Napoli	11	1		
2012–13	Napoli	22	0		
2013–14	Napoli	16	1		
2014–15	Napoli	19	1	**68**	**3**
2015–16	Watford	24	0		
2016–17	Watford	27	1	**51**	**1**

CAPOUE, Etienne (M) **268 21**
H: 6 2 W: 11 10 b.Niort 11-7-88
Internationals: France U18, U19, U21, Full caps.

Season	Club	Apps	Gls	Total Apps	Total Gls
2006–07	Toulouse	0	0		
2007–08	Toulouse	5	0		
2008–09	Toulouse	32	1		
2009–10	Toulouse	33	0		
2010–11	Toulouse	37	2		
2011–12	Toulouse	33	3		
2012–13	Toulouse	34	7	**174**	**13**
2013–14	Tottenham H	12	1		
2014–15	Tottenham H	12	0	**24**	**1**
2015–16	Watford	33	0		
2016–17	Watford	37	7	**70**	**7**

CATHCART, Craig (D) **247 10**
H: 6 2 W: 11 06 b.Belfast 6-2-89
Internationals: Northern Ireland U16, U17, U20, U21, Full caps.

Season	Club	Apps	Gls	Total Apps	Total Gls
2005–06	Manchester U	0	0		
2006–07	Manchester U	0	0		
2007–08	Manchester U	0	0		
2007–08	*Antwerp*	13	2	**13**	**2**
2008–09	Manchester U	0	0		
2008–09	*Plymouth Arg*	31	1	**31**	**1**
2009–10	Manchester U	0	0		
2009–10	*Watford*	12	0		
2010–11	Blackpool	30	1		
2011–12	Blackpool	27	0		
2012–13	Blackpool	25	1		
2013–14	Blackpool	30	1	**112**	**3**
2014–15	Watford	29	3		
2015–16	Watford	35	1		
2016–17	Watford	15	0	**91**	**4**

DEENEY, Troy (F) **403 128**
H: 5 11 W: 12 00 b.Solihull 29-6-88

Season	Club	Apps	Gls	Total Apps	Total Gls
2006–07	Walsall	1	0		
2007–08	Walsall	35	1		
2008–09	Walsall	45	12		
2009–10	Walsall	42	14	**123**	**27**
2010–11	Watford	36	3		
2011–12	Watford	43	11		
2012–13	Watford	40	19		
2013–14	Watford	44	24		
2014–15	Watford	42	21		
2015–16	Watford	38	13		
2016–17	Watford	37	10	**280**	**101**

DJA DJEDJE, Brice (D) **156 5**
H: 5 9 W: 11 00 b.Abidjan 23-12-90
Internationals: Ivory Coast Full caps.
From Paris Saint-Germain.

Season	Club	Apps	Gls	Total Apps	Total Gls
2010–11	Evian	18	1		
2011–12	Evian	34	2		
2012–13	Evian	27	1		
2013–14	Evian	14	1	**93**	**5**
2013–14	Marseilles	11	0		
2014–15	Marseilles	33	0		
2015–16	Marseilles	19	0	**63**	**0**
2016–17	Watford	0	0		

DOUCOURE, Abdoulaye (M) **110 13**
b.Meulan-en-Yvelines 1-1-93
Internationals: France U17, U18, U19, U20, U21.

Season	Club	Apps	Gls	Total Apps	Total Gls
2012–13	Rennes	4	1		
2013–14	Rennes	20	6		
2014–15	Rennes	35	3		
2015–16	Rennes	16	2	**75**	**12**
2015–16	Watford	0	0		
2015–16	*Granada*	15	0	**15**	**0**
2016–17	Watford	20	1	**20**	**1**

ELEFTHERIOU, Andrew (D) **1 0**
H: 5 10 W: 11 11 b.Islington 8-11-97

Season	Club	Apps	Gls	Total Apps	Total Gls
2016–17	Watford	1	0	**1**	**0**

FOLIVI, Michael (F) **2 0**
H: 5 11 W: 12 06 b.Brent 25-2-98

Season	Club	Apps	Gls	Total Apps	Total Gls
2016–17	Watford	1	0	**1**	**0**
2016–17	*Coventry C*	1	0	**1**	**0**

GILMARTIN, Rene (G) **64 0**
H: 6 5 W: 13 06 b.Dublin 31-5-87
Internationals: Republic of Ireland U21.

Season	Club	Apps	Gls	Total Apps	Total Gls
2005–06	Walsall	2	0		
2006–07	Walsall	0	0		
2007–08	Walsall	0	0		
2008–09	Walsall	11	0		
2009–10	Walsall	22	0	**35**	**0**
2010–11	Watford	0	0		
2011–12	Watford	2	0		
2011–12	*Yeovil T*	8	0	**8**	**0**
2011–12	*Crawley T*	6	0	**6**	**0**
2012–13	Plymouth Arg	13	0		
2013–14	Plymouth Arg	0	0	**13**	**0**
2014–15	Watford	0	0		
2015–16	Watford	0	0		
2016–17	Watford	0	0	**2**	**0**

GOMES, Heurelho (G) **411 0**
H: 6 3 W: 12 13 b.Minas Gerais 15-2-81
Internationals: Brazil U23, Full caps.

Season	Club	Apps	Gls	Total Apps	Total Gls
2001	Cruzeiro	0	0		
2002	Cruzeiro	14	0		
2003	Cruzeiro	40	0		
2004	Cruzeiro	5	0	**59**	**0**
2004–05	PSV Eindhoven	30	0		
2005–06	PSV Eindhoven	32	0		
2006–07	PSV Eindhoven	32	0		
2007–08	PSV Eindhoven	34	0	**128**	**0**
2008–09	Tottenham H	34	0		
2009–10	Tottenham H	31	0		
2010–11	Tottenham H	30	0		
2011–12	Tottenham H	0	0		
2012–13	Tottenham H	0	0		
2012–13	*Hoffenheim*	9	0	**9**	**0**
2013–14	Tottenham H	0	0	**95**	**0**
2014–15	Watford	44	0		
2015–16	Watford	38	0		
2016–17	Watford	38	0	**120**	**0**

HOBAN, Tommie (D) **70 3**
H: 6 2 W: 11 13 b.Walthamstow 24-1-94
Internationals: Republic of Ireland U17, U19, U21.

Season	Club	Apps	Gls	Total Apps	Total Gls
2010–11	Watford	1	0		
2011–12	Watford	0	0		
2012–13	Watford	19	2		
2013–14	Watford	7	0		
2014–15	Watford	27	0		
2015–16	Watford	0	0		
2016–17	Watford	0	0	**54**	**2**
2016–17	*Blackburn R*	16	1	**16**	**1**

HOLEBAS, Jose (M) **269 34**
H: 6 0 W: 12 06 b.Aschaffenburg 27-6-84
Internationals: Greece Full caps.

Season	Club	Apps	Gls	Total Apps	Total Gls
2005–06	Viktoria Kahl	33	15	**33**	**15**
2006–07	1860 Munich	0	0		
2007–08	1860 Munich	19	2		
2008–09	1860 Munich	24	1		
2009–10	1860 Munich	31	4	**74**	**7**
2010–11	Olympiacos	24	1		
2011–12	Olympiacos	23	2		
2012–13	Olympiacos	28	4		
2013–14	Olympiacos	19	2	**94**	**9**
2014–15	Roma	24	1	**24**	**1**
2015–16	Watford	11	0		
2016–17	Watford	33	2	**44**	**2**

IGHALO, Odion Jude (F) 214 63
H: 6 2 W: 11 00 b.Lagos 16-6-89
Internationals: Nigeria U20, Full caps.
2007 Lyn 7 3
2008 Lyn 13 6 **20 9**
2008–09 Udinese 6 1
2009–10 Udinese 0 0
2010–11 Udinese 0 0
2010–11 *Cesena* 3 0 **3 0**
2010–11 *Granada* 21 4
2011–12 Udinese 0 0
2011–12 *Granada* 30 6
2012–13 Udinese 0 0
2012–13 *Granada* 28 5
2013–14 Udinese 0 0
2013–14 *Granada* 16 2 **95 17**
2014–15 Udinese 0 0 **6 1**
2014–15 *Watford* 35 20
2015–16 Watford 37 15
2016–17 Watford 18 1 **90 36**
Transferred to Changchun Yatai, January 2017.

JAKUBIAK, Alex (F) 46 6
H: 5 10 W: 10 06 b.Westminster 27-8-96
Internationals: Scotland U19.
2013–14 Watford 1 0
2014–15 Watford 0 0
2014–15 *Oxford U* 9 1 **9 1**
2014–15 *Dagenham & R* 23 4 **23 4**
2015–16 Watford 0 0
2016–17 Watford 0 0 **1 0**
2016–17 *Fleetwood T* 3 0 **3 0**
2016–17 *Wycombe W* 10 1 **10 1**

JANMAAT, Daryl (D) 269 17
H: 6 1 W: 12 13 b.Leidschendam 22-7-89
Internationals: Netherlands U20, U21, Full caps.
2007–08 Den Haag 25 2 **25 2**
2008–09 Heerenveen 10 0
2009–10 Heerenveen 28 0
2010–11 Heerenveen 24 3
2011–12 Heerenveen 22 2 **84 5**
2012–13 Feyenoord 32 3
2013–14 Feyenoord 30 2 **62 5**
2014–15 Newcastle U 37 1
2015–16 Newcastle U 32 2
2016–17 Newcastle U 2 0 **71 3**
2016–17 Watford 27 2 **27 2**

KABASELE, Christian (D) 166 18
b.Lubumbashi 24-2-91
Internationals: Belgium U19, U20, Full caps.
2008–09 Eupen 3 0
2009–10 Eupen 1 0
2010–11 Eupen 3 0
2010–11 *Mechelen* 4 1 **4 1**
2011–12 Ludogorets 11 3 **11 3**
2012–13 Eupen 26 4
2013–14 Eupen 26 2 **59 6**
2014–15 Genk 34 2
2015–16 Genk 42 4 **76 6**
2016–17 Watford 16 2 **16 2**

KABOUL, Younes (D) 247 15
H: 6 2 W: 13 07 b.Annemasse 4-1-86
Internationals: France U21, Full caps.
2004–05 Auxerre 12 1
2005–06 Auxerre 9 0
2006–07 Auxerre 31 2 **52 3**
2007–08 Tottenham H 21 3
2008–09 Portsmouth 20 1
2009–10 Portsmouth 19 3 **39 4**
2009–10 Tottenham H 10 0
2010–11 Tottenham H 21 1
2011–12 Tottenham H 33 1
2012–13 Tottenham H 1 0
2013–14 Tottenham H 13 1
2014–15 Tottenham H 11 0 **110 6**
2015–16 Sunderland 23 0
2016–17 Sunderland 1 0 **24 0**
2016–17 Watford 22 2 **22 2**

MARIAPPA, Adrian (D) 291 6
H: 5 10 W: 11 12 b.Harrow 3-10-86
Internationals: Jamaica Full caps.
2005–06 Watford 3 0
2006–07 Watford 19 0
2007–08 Watford 25 0
2008–09 Watford 39 1
2009–10 Watford 46 1
2010–11 Watford 45 1
2011–12 Watford 39 1
2012–13 Reading 29 1
2013–14 Reading 0 0 **29 1**
2013–14 Crystal Palace 24 1
2014–15 Crystal Palace 12 0
2015–16 Crystal Palace 3 0 **39 1**
2016–17 Watford 7 0 **223 4**

MASON, Brandon (M) 2 0
H: 5 9 W: 11 00 b.Westminster 30-9-97
2016–17 Watford 2 0 **2 0**

NIANG, M'Baye (F) 146 24
H: 6 0 W: 11 09 b.Meulan 19-12-94
Internationals: France U16, U17, U21.
2010–11 Caen 7 3
2011–12 Caen 23 2 **30 5**
2012–13 AC Milan 20 0
2013–14 AC Milan 8 0
2013–14 *Montpellier* 19 4 **19 4**
2014–15 AC Milan 5 0
2014–15 *Genoa* 14 5 **14 5**
2015–16 AC Milan 16 5
2016–17 AC Milan 18 3 **67 8**
On loan from AC Milan.
2016–17 Watford 16 2 **16 2**

OKAKA, Stefano (F) 259 52
H: 6 2 W: 12 04 b.Castiglion del Lago 9-8-89
Internationals: Italy U19, U20, U21, Full caps.
2005–06 Roma 9 0
2006–07 Roma 6 1
2007–08 Roma 0 0
2007–08 *Modena* 33 7 **33 7**
2008–09 Roma 8 0
2008–09 *Brescia* 17 2 **17 2**
2009–10 Roma 6 0
2009–10 *Fulham* 11 2 **11 2**
2010–11 Roma 4 0 **33 1**
2010–11 *Bari* 10 2 **10 2**
2011–12 Parma 14 3
2012–13 Parma 0 0
2012–13 *Spezia* 38 7 **38 7**
2013–14 Parma 2 0 **16 3**
2013–14 Sampdoria 13 5
2014–15 Sampdoria 32 4 **45 9**
2015–16 Anderlecht 37 15 **37 15**
2016–17 Watford 19 4 **19 4**

PANTILIMON, Costel (G) 156 0
H: 6 5 W: 15 02 b.Bacau 1-2-87
Internationals: Romania U17, U19, U21, Full caps.
2005–06 Aerostar Bacau 9 0 **9 0**
2006–07 Poli Timisoara 8 0
2007–08 Poli Timisoara 5 0 **13 0**
2008–09 Timisoara 31 0
2009–10 Timisoara 21 0
2010–11 Timisoara 28 0 **80 0**
2011–12 *Manchester C* 0 0
2012–13 Manchester C 0 0
2013–14 Manchester C 7 0 **7 0**
2014–15 Sunderland 28 0
2015–16 Sunderland 17 0 **45 0**
2015–16 Watford 0 0
2016–17 Watford 2 0 **2 0**

PAREDES, Juan Carlos (D) 281 14
H: 5 10 W: 11 05 b.Esmeraldas 8-7-87
Internationals: Ecuador Full caps.
2006–07 Barcelona 5 0
2007–08 Deportivo Cuena 19 1
2007–08 *Rocafuerte* 29 2 **29 2**
2008–09 Deportivo Cuena 32 3 **51 4**
2009–10 Deportivo Quito 38 4
2010–11 Deportivo Quito 36 3
2011–12 Deportivo Quito 19 0 **93 7**
2012–13 Barcelona 35 1
2013–14 Barcelona 8 0 **48 1**
2014–15 Watford 39 0
2015–16 Watford 17 0
2016–17 Watford 0 0 **56 0**
2016–17 *Olympiacos* 4 0 **4 0**

PENARANDA, Adalberto (F) 63 9
b.El Vigia 31-5-97
Internationals: Venezuela U17, U20, Full caps.
2013–14 Dep La Guaira 18 1
2014–15 Dep La Guaira 19 3 **37 4**
2015–16 Udinese 0 0
2015–16 Watford 0 0
2015–16 *Granada* 23 5 **23 5**
2016–17 Watford 0 0
2016–17 *Malaga* 3 0 **3 0**

PEREIRA, Dion (M) 2 0
b.Watford 25-3-99
2016–17 Watford 2 0 **2 0**

PEREYRA, Roberto (M) 188 14
H: 6 2 W: 11 11 b.Argentina 17-1-91
Internationals: Argentina U20, Full caps.
2008–09 River Plate 1 0
2009–10 River Plate 15 0
2010–11 River Plate 27 0 **43 0**
2011–12 Udinese 11 1
2012–13 Udinese 37 5
2013–14 Udinese 36 2
2014–15 Udinese 0 0 **84 8**
2014–15 *Juventus* 35 4
2015–16 Juventus 13 0 **48 4**
2016–17 Watford 13 2 **13 2**

PRODL, Sebastien (D) 246 17
H: 6 4 W: 13 05 b.Graz 21-6-87
Internationals: Austria U19, U20, Full caps.
2006–07 Sturm Graz 16 1
2007–08 Sturm Graz 27 3 **43 4**
2008–09 Werder Bremen 22 0
2009–10 Werder Bremen 9 1
2010–11 Werder Bremen 25 1
2011–12 Werder Bremen 16 2
2012–13 Werder Bremen 28 1
2013–14 Werder Bremen 27 2
2014–15 Werder Bremen 22 3 **149 10**
2015–16 Watford 21 2
2016–17 Watford 33 1 **54 3**

ROWAN, Charlie (D) 0 0
2016–17 Watford 0 0

SINCLAIR, Jerome (F) 13 0
H: 5 8 W: 12 06 b.Birmingham 20-9-96
Internationals: England U16, U17.
2012–13 Liverpool 0 0
2013–14 Liverpool 0 0
2014–15 Liverpool 2 0
2014–15 *Wigan Ath* 1 0 **1 0**
2015–16 Liverpool 0 0 **2 0**
2016–17 Watford 5 0 **5 0**
2016–17 *Birmingham C* 5 0 **5 0**

STEWART, Carl (M) 0 0
2016–17 Watford 0 0

SUCCESS, Isaac (F) 68 8
H: 6 1 W: 11 03 b. 7-1-96
Internationals: Nigeria U17, U20, Full caps.
2014–15 Granada 19 1
2015–16 Granada 30 6 **49 7**
2016–17 Watford 19 1 **19 1**

WATSON, Ben (M) 362 36
H: 5 10 W: 10 11 b.Camberwell 9-7-85
Internationals: England U21.
2002–03 Crystal Palace 5 0
2003–04 Crystal Palace 16 1
2004–05 Crystal Palace 21 0
2005–06 Crystal Palace 42 4
2006–07 Crystal Palace 25 3
2007–08 Crystal Palace 42 5
2008–09 Crystal Palace 18 5 **169 18**
2008–09 Wigan Ath 10 2
2009–10 Wigan Ath 5 1
2009–10 *QPR* 16 2 **16 2**
2009–10 *WBA* 7 1 **7 1**
2010–11 Wigan Ath 29 3
2011–12 Wigan Ath 21 3
2012–13 Wigan Ath 12 1
2013–14 Wigan Ath 25 2
2014–15 Wigan Ath 9 1 **111 13**
2014–15 Watford 20 0
2015–16 Watford 35 2
2016–17 Watford 4 0 **59 2**

ZARATE, Mauro (F) 300 80
H: 5 8 W: 10 10 b.Haedo 18-3-87
Internationals: Argentina U20.
2003–04 Velez Sarsfield 4 1
2004–05 Velez Sarsfield 14 2
2005–06 Velez Sarsfield 33 3
2006–07 Velez Sarsfield 32 16
2007–08 Al-Sadd 6 0 **6 0**
2007–08 *Birmingham C* 14 4 **14 4**
2008–09 Al-Saad 0 0
2008–09 *Lazio* 36 13
2009–10 Lazio 32 3
2010–11 Lazio 35 9
2011–12 Lazio 0 0
2011–12 *Inter Milan* 22 2 **22 2**
2012–13 Lazio 1 0 **104 25**
2013–14 Velez Sarsfield 29 19 **112 41**
2014–15 West Ham U 7 2
2014–15 *QPR* 4 0 **4 0**
2015–16 West Ham U 15 3 **22 5**
2015–16 Fiorentina 13 3

2016–17	Fiorentina	0	0	**13**	**3**
2016–17	Watford	3	0	**3**	**0**

ZUNIGA, Juan (D) **304** **14**
H: 5 7 W: 11 05 b.Chigorodo 14-12-85
Internationals: Colombia U20, Full caps.

2002	Atletico National	4	0		
2003	Atletico National	1	0		
2004	Atletico National	23	0		
2005	Atletico National	23	2		
2006	Atletico National	24	1		
2007	Atletico National	32	4		
2008	Atletico National	14	2	**121**	**9**
2008–09	Siena	28	0	**28**	**0**
2009–10	Napoli	22	0		
2010–11	Napoli	27	2		
2011–12	Napoli	31	2		
2012–13	Napoli	32	0		
2013–14	Napoli	6	0		
2014–15	Napoli	7	0		
2015–16	Napoli	0	0		
2015–16	*Bologna*	9	0	**9**	**0**
2016–17	Napoli	0	0	**125**	**4**

On loan from Napoli.

2016–17	Watford	21	1	**21**	**1**

Players retained or with offer of contract
Agbo, Uche Henry; Becerra, Maya Juan Camillo; Charles, Ashley James; Cholevas, Chose Loint; Estupinan, Tenorio Pervis Josue; Gartside, Nathan James; Lewis, Dennon Elliot; Montenegro, Zuniga Eduardo Antonio; Oulare, Mamadou Obbi; Sesay, David Junior Deen; Stevens, Connor John; Suarez, Mata Mario.

Scholars
Adedeji, Jubril; Cabrera, Jesus Cruz; Empson, Bradley; Forster, Harry James; Huja, Marian; Jones, Ben Anthony; Kaikay, Yazid; Lacy, Jamie Sebastian; Mukena, Joy-Richard; Pereira, Dion Enrico; Rogers, Louis Ronald; Ryan, Maximillian Medwyn Richard; Stray, Reece Daniel.

WBA (87)

BRUNT, Chris (M) **457** **65**
H: 6 1 W: 13 04 b.Belfast 14-12-84
Internationals: Northern Ireland U19, U21, U23, Full caps.

2002–03	Middlesbrough	0	0		
2003–04	Middlesbrough	0	0		
2003–04	Sheffield W	9	2		
2004–05	Sheffield W	42	4		
2005–06	Sheffield W	44	7		
2006–07	Sheffield W	44	11		
2007–08	Sheffield W	1	0	**140**	**24**
2007–08	WBA	34	4		
2008–09	WBA	34	8		
2009–10	WBA	40	13		
2010–11	WBA	34	4		
2011–12	WBA	29	2		
2012–13	WBA	31	2		
2013–14	WBA	28	3		
2014–15	WBA	34	2		
2015–16	WBA	22	0		
2016–17	WBA	31	3	**317**	**41**

CAMPBELL, Tahvon (F) **47** **2**
b. 10-1-97

2015–16	WBA	0	0		
2015–16	*Yeovil T*	17	1		
2016–17	WBA	0	0		
2016–17	*Yeovil T*	19	1	**36**	**2**
2016–17	*Notts Co*	11	0	**11**	**0**

CHADLI, Nacer (M) **295** **73**
H: 6 2 W: 12 07 b.Liege 3-6-88
Internationals: Morocco Full caps. Belgium Full caps.

2007–08	AGOVV	19	2		
2008–09	AGOVV	34	9		
2009–10	AGOVV	39	17	**92**	**28**
2010–11	FC Twente	33	7		
2011–12	FC Twente	25	6		
2012–13	FC Twente	26	12	**84**	**25**
2013–14	Tottenham H	24	1		
2014–15	Tottenham H	35	11		
2015–16	Tottenham H	29	3	**88**	**15**
2016–17	WBA	31	5	**31**	**5**

DAWSON, Craig (D) **228** **33**
H: 6 0 W: 12 04 b.Rochdale 6-5-90
Internationals: England U21. Great Britain.

2008–09	Rochdale	0	0		
2009–10	Rochdale	42	9		
2010–11	WBA	0	0		
2010–11	*Rochdale*	45	10	**87**	**19**
2011–12	WBA	8	0		
2012–13	WBA	1	0		
2012–13	*Bolton W*	16	4	**16**	**4**
2013–14	WBA	12	0		
2014–15	WBA	29	2		
2015–16	WBA	38	4		
2016–17	WBA	37	4	**125**	**10**

DONNELLAN, Shaun (D) **0** **0**
b. 22-5-97
Internationals: Republic of Ireland U19, U21.

2015–16	WBA	0	0		
2016–17	WBA	0	0		
2016–17	*Stevenage*	0	0		

EVANS, Jonny (D) **239** **10**
H: 6 2 W: 12 02 b.Belfast 3-1-88
Internationals: Northern Ireland U16, U17, U21, Full caps.

2004–05	Manchester U	0	0		
2005–06	Manchester U	0	0		
2006–07	Manchester U	0	0		
2006–07	*Antwerp*	14	2	**14**	**2**
2006–07	*Sunderland*	18	1		
2007–08	Manchester U	0	0		
2007–08	*Sunderland*	15	0	**33**	**1**
2008–09	Manchester U	17	0		
2009–10	Manchester U	18	0		
2010–11	Manchester U	13	0		
2011–12	Manchester U	29	1		
2012–13	Manchester U	23	3		
2013–14	Manchester U	17	0		
2014–15	Manchester U	14	0		
2015–16	Manchester U	0	0	**131**	**4**
2015–16	WBA	30	1		
2016–17	WBA	31	2	**61**	**3**

FIELD, Sam (M) **9** **0**
b. 8-5-98
Internationals: England U18, U19.

2015–16	WBA	1	0		
2016–17	WBA	8	0	**9**	**0**

FLETCHER, Darren (M) **314** **22**
H: 6 0 W: 11 09 b.Edinburgh 1-2-84
Internationals: Scotland U20, U21, B, Full caps.

2000–01	Manchester U	0	0		
2001–02	Manchester U	0	0		
2002–03	Manchester U	0	0		
2003–04	Manchester U	22	0		
2004–05	Manchester U	18	3		
2005–06	Manchester U	27	1		
2006–07	Manchester U	24	3		
2007–08	Manchester U	16	0		
2008–09	Manchester U	26	3		
2009–10	Manchester U	30	4		
2010–11	Manchester U	26	2		
2011–12	Manchester U	8	1		
2012–13	Manchester U	3	1		
2013–14	Manchester U	12	0		
2014–15	Manchester U	11	0	**223**	**18**
2014–15	WBA	15	1		
2015–16	WBA	38	1		
2016–17	WBA	38	2	**91**	**4**

FOSTER, Ben (G) **314** **0**
H: 6 2 W: 12 08 b.Leamington Spa 3-4-83
Internationals: England Full caps.

2000–01	Stoke C	0	0		
2001–02	Stoke C	0	0		
2002–03	Stoke C	0	0		
2003–04	Stoke C	0	0		
2004–05	Stoke C	0	0		
2004–05	*Kidderminster H*	2	0	**2**	**0**
2004–05	*Wrexham*	17	0	**17**	**0**
2005–06	Manchester U	0	0		
2005–06	*Watford*	44	0		
2006–07	Manchester U	0	0		
2006–07	*Watford*	29	0	**73**	**0**
2007–08	Manchester U	1	0		
2008–09	Manchester U	2	0		
2009–10	Manchester U	9	0	**12**	**0**
2010–11	Birmingham C	38	0		
2011–12	Birmingham C	0	0	**38**	**0**
2011–12	*WBA*	37	0		
2012–13	WBA	30	0		
2013–14	WBA	24	0		
2014–15	WBA	28	0		
2015–16	WBA	15	0		
2016–17	WBA	38	0	**172**	**0**

GARDNER, Craig (M) **280** **33**
H: 5 10 W: 11 13 b.Solihull 25-11-86
Internationals: England U21.

2004–05	Aston Villa	0	0		
2005–06	Aston Villa	8	0		
2006–07	Aston Villa	13	2		
2007–08	Aston Villa	23	3		
2008–09	Aston Villa	14	0		
2009–10	Aston Villa	1	0	**59**	**5**
2009–10	Birmingham C	13	1		
2010–11	Birmingham C	29	8		
2011–12	Sunderland	30	3		
2012–13	Sunderland	33	6		
2013–14	Sunderland	18	2	**81**	**11**
2014–15	WBA	35	3		
2015–16	WBA	34	3		
2016–17	WBA	9	0	**78**	**6**
2016–17	*Birmingham C*	20	2	**62**	**11**

HARPER, Rekeem (M) **0** **0**

2016–17	WBA	0	0		

HOWKINS, Kyle (D) **15** **0**
H: 6 5 W: 12 11 b.Walsall 4-5-96

2015–16	WBA	0	0		
2016–17	WBA	0	0		
2016–17	*Mansfield T*	15	0	**15**	**0**

JONES, Callum (M) **2** **0**
H: 6 0 W: 11 12 b.London 31-1-96
Internationals: England U16, U17.

2013–14	WBA	0	0		
2014–15	WBA	0	0		
2015–16	WBA	0	0		
2016–17	WBA	0	0		
2016–17	*Accrington S*	2	0	**2**	**0**

LEKO, Jonathan (M) **14** **0**
H: 6 0 W: 11 11 b.Kinshasa 24-4-99
Internationals: England U16, U17, U18.

2015–16	WBA	5	0		
2016–17	WBA	9	0	**14**	**0**

LIVERMORE, Jake (M) **225** **11**
H: 5 9 W: 12 08 b.Enfield 14-11-89
Internationals: England Full caps.

2006–07	Tottenham H	0	0		
2007–08	Tottenham H	0	0		
2007–08	*Milton Keynes D*	5	0	**5**	**0**
2008–09	Tottenham H	0	0		
2008–09	*Crewe Alex*	0	0		
2009–10	Tottenham H	1	0		
2009–10	*Derby Co*	16	1	**16**	**1**
2009–10	*Peterborough U*	9	1	**9**	**1**
2010–11	Tottenham H	0	0		
2010–11	*Ipswich T*	12	0	**12**	**0**
2010–11	*Leeds U*	5	0	**5**	**0**
2011–12	Tottenham H	24	0		
2012–13	Tottenham H	11	0		
2013–14	Tottenham H	0	0	**36**	**0**
2013–14	*Hull C*	36	3		
2014–15	Hull C	35	1		
2015–16	Hull C	34	4		
2016–17	Hull C	21	1	**126**	**9**
2016–17	WBA	16	0	**16**	**0**

McAULEY, Gareth (D) **455** **35**
H: 6 3 W: 13 00 b.Larne 5-12-79
Internationals: Northern Ireland B, Full caps.

2004–05	Lincoln C	37	3		
2005–06	Lincoln C	35	5	**72**	**8**
2006–07	Leicester C	30	3		
2007–08	Leicester C	44	2	**74**	**5**
2008–09	Ipswich T	35	0		
2009–10	Ipswich T	41	5		
2010–11	Ipswich T	39	2	**115**	**7**
2011–12	WBA	32	2		
2012–13	WBA	36	3		
2013–14	WBA	32	2		
2014–15	WBA	24	1		
2015–16	WBA	34	1		
2016–17	WBA	36	6	**194**	**15**

McCLEAN, James (M) **274** **37**
H: 5 11 W: 11 00 b.Derry 22-4-89
Internationals: Northern Ireland U21. Republic of Ireland Full caps.

2009	Derry C	27	1		
2010	Derry C	30	10		
2011	Derry C	16	7	**73**	**18**
2011–12	Sunderland	23	5		
2012–13	Sunderland	36	2		
2013–14	Sunderland	0	0	**59**	**7**
2013–14	Wigan Ath	37	3		
2014–15	Wigan Ath	36	6	**73**	**9**
2015–16	WBA	35	2		
2016–17	WBA	34	1	**69**	**3**

McMANAMAN, Callum (F) **124 12**
H: 5 9 W: 11 03 b.Huyton 25-4-91
Internationals: England U20.

2008–09	Wigan Ath	1	0		
2009–10	Wigan Ath	0	0		
2010–11	Wigan Ath	3	0		
2011–12	Wigan Ath	2	0		
2011–12	*Blackpool*	14	2	**14**	**2**
2012–13	Wigan Ath	20	2		
2013–14	Wigan Ath	30	3		
2014–15	Wigan Ath	23	5	**79**	**10**
2014–15	WBA	8	0		
2015–16	WBA	12	0		
2016–17	WBA	0	0	**20**	**0**
2016–17	*Sheffield W*	11	0	**11**	**0**

MORRISON, James (M) **353 36**
H: 5 10 W: 10 06 b.Darlington 25-5-86
Internationals: England U17, U18, U19, U20. Scotland Full caps.

2003–04	Middlesbrough	1	0		
2004–05	Middlesbrough	14	0		
2005–06	Middlesbrough	24	1		
2006–07	Middlesbrough	28	2	**67**	**3**
2007–08	WBA	35	4		
2008–09	WBA	30	3		
2009–10	WBA	11	1		
2010–11	WBA	31	4		
2011–12	WBA	30	5		
2012–13	WBA	35	5		
2013–14	WBA	32	1		
2014–15	WBA	33	2		
2015–16	WBA	18	3		
2016–17	WBA	31	5	**286**	**33**

MYHILL, Boaz (G) **380 0**
H: 6 3 W: 14 06 b.California 9-11-82
Internationals: England U20. Wales Full caps.

2000–01	Aston Villa	0	0		
2001–02	Aston Villa	0	0		
2001–02	*Stoke C*	0	0		
2002–03	Aston Villa	0	0		
2002–03	*Bristol C*	0	0		
2002–03	*Bradford C*	2	0	**2**	**0**
2003–04	Aston Villa	0	0		
2003–04	*Macclesfield T*	15	0	**15**	**0**
2003–04	*Stockport Co*	2	0	**2**	**0**
2003–04	Hull C	23	0		
2004–05	Hull C	45	0		
2005–06	Hull C	45	0		
2006–07	Hull C	46	0		
2007–08	Hull C	43	0		
2008–09	Hull C	28	0		
2009–10	Hull C	27	0	**257**	**0**
2010–11	WBA	6	0		
2011–12	WBA	0	0		
2011–12	*Birmingham C*	42	0	**42**	**0**
2012–13	WBA	8	0		
2013–14	WBA	14	0		
2014–15	WBA	11	0		
2015–16	WBA	23	0		
2016–17	WBA	0	0	**62**	**0**

NYOM, Allan (D) **279 2**
H: 5 7 W: 12 11 b.Neuilly-sur-Seine 10-5-88
Internationals: Cameroon Full caps.

2008–09	Arles-Avignon	37	0	**37**	**0**
2009–10	Udinese	0	0		
2010–11	Udinese	0	0		
2010–11	*Granada*	43	1		
2011–12	Udinese	0	0		
2011–12	*Granada*	32	0		
2012–13	Udinese	0	0		
2012–13	*Granada*	35	0		
2013–14	Udinese	0	0		
2013–14	*Granada*	34	0		
2014–15	Udinese	0	0		
2014–15	*Granada*	34	1	**178**	**2**
2015–16	Watford	32	0		
2016–17	Watford	0	0	**32**	**0**
2016–17	WBA	32	0	**32**	**0**

OLSSON, Jonas (D) **393 18**
H: 6 4 W: 12 08 b.Landskrona 10-3-83
Internationals: Sweden U21, Full caps.

2002	Landskrona	0	0		
2003	Landskrona	22	0		
2004	Landskrona	22	1		
2005	Landskrona	12	0	**56**	**1**
2005–06	NEC Nijmegen	34	0		
2006–07	NEC Nijmegen	32	2		
2007–08	NEC Nijmegen	27	3	**93**	**5**
2008–09	WBA	28	2		
2009–10	WBA	43	4		
2010–11	WBA	24	1		
2011–12	WBA	33	2		
2012–13	WBA	36	0		
2013–14	WBA	32	1		
2014–15	WBA	13	1		
2015–16	WBA	28	1		
2016–17	WBA	7	0	**244**	**12**

Transferred to Djurgarden, March 2017.

PALMER, Alex (G) **0 0**
b. 10-8-96
Internationals: England U16.

2014–15	WBA	0	0		
2015–16	WBA	0	0		
2016–17	WBA	0	0		

PHILLIPS, Matthew (M) **295 43**
H: 6 0 W: 12 10 b.Aylesbury 13-3-91
Internationals: England U19, U20. Scotland Full caps.

2007–08	Wycombe W	2	0		
2008–09	Wycombe W	37	3		
2009–10	Wycombe W	36	5		
2010–11	Wycombe W	3	0	**78**	**8**
2010–11	Blackpool	27	1		
2011–12	Blackpool	33	7		
2011–12	*Sheffield U*	6	5	**6**	**5**
2012–13	Blackpool	34	4		
2013–14	Blackpool	0	0	**94**	**12**
2013–14	QPR	21	3		
2014–15	QPR	25	3		
2015–16	QPR	44	8	**90**	**14**
2016–17	WBA	27	4	**27**	**4**

POCOGNOLI, Sebastien (D) **261 9**
H: 5 11 W: 11 07 b.Liege 1-8-87
Internationals: Belgium U16, U17, U19, U21, U23, Full caps.

2003–04	Genk	1	0		
2004–05	Genk	0	0		
2005–06	Genk	15	1		
2006–07	Genk	30	0	**46**	**1**
2007–08	AZ Alkmaar	28	2		
2008–09	AZ Alkmaar	25	2		
2009–10	AZ Alkmaar	11	1	**64**	**5**
2009–10	Standard Liege	10	1		
2010–11	Standard Liege	34	1		
2011–12	Standard Liege	32	0		
2012–13	Standard Liege	9	0	**85**	**2**
2012–13	Hannover 96	11	0		
2013–14	Hannover 96	19	0	**30**	**0**
2014–15	WBA	15	0		
2015–16	WBA	1	0		
2016–17	WBA	0	0	**16**	**0**
2016–17	*Brighton & HA*	20	1	**20**	**1**

ROBERTS, Tyler (F) **28 4**
H: 5 11 W: 11 11 b.Gloucester 12-1-98
Internationals: Wales U16, U17, U20.

2014–15	WBA	0	0		
2015–16	WBA	1	0		
2016–17	WBA	0	0	**1**	**0**
2016–17	*Oxford U*	14	0	**14**	**0**
2016–17	*Shrewsbury T*	13	4	**13**	**4**

ROBSON-KANU, Hal (F) **269 36**
H: 5 7 W: 11 08 b.Acton 21-5-89
Internationals: England U19, U20. Wales U21, Full caps.

2007–08	Reading	0	0		
2007–08	*Southend U*	8	3		
2008–09	Reading	0	0		
2008–09	*Southend U*	14	2	**22**	**5**
2008–09	*Swindon T*	20	4	**20**	**4**
2009–10	Reading	17	0		
2010–11	Reading	27	5		
2011–12	Reading	36	4		
2012–13	Reading	25	7		
2013–14	Reading	36	4		
2014–15	Reading	29	1		
2015–16	Reading	28	3		
2016–17	Reading	0	0	**198**	**24**
2016–17	WBA	29	3	**29**	**3**

RONDON, Jose Salomon (F) **307 102**
H: 6 1 W: 13 08 b.Caracas 16-9-89
Internationals: Venezuela U20, Full caps.

2006–07	Aragua	21	7		
2007–08	Aragua	28	8	**49**	**15**
2008–09	Las Palmas	10	0		
2009–10	Las Palmas	36	12	**46**	**12**
2010–11	Malaga	30	14		
2011–12	Malaga	37	11	**67**	**25**
2012–13	Rubin Kazan	25	7		
2013–14	Rubin Kazan	11	6	**36**	**13**
2013–14	Zenit St Petersburg	10	7		
2014–15	Zenit St Petersburg	26	13		
2015–16	Zenit St Petersburg	1	0	**37**	**20**
2015–16	WBA	34	9		
2016–17	WBA	38	8	**72**	**17**

ROSE, Jack (G) **9 0**
H: 6 0 W: 11 11 b.Solihull 31-1-95

2014–15	WBA	0	0		
2014–15	*Accrington S*	4	0	**4**	**0**
2015–16	WBA	0	0		
2015–16	*Crawley T*	5	0	**5**	**0**
2016–17	WBA	0	0		

WILSON, Kane (D) **0 0**
Internationals: England U16, U17.

2016–17	WBA	0	0		

WRIGHT, Andre (F) **11 2**
H: 6 0 W: 11 05 b.Sandwell 7-12-96

2016–17	WBA	0	0		
2016–17	*Coventry C*	11	2	**11**	**2**

YACOB, Claudio (M) **269 5**
H: 5 11 W: 11 06 b.Carcarana 18-7-87
Internationals: Argentina U20, Full caps.

2006–07	Racing Club	12	0		
2007–08	Racing Club	24	0		
2008–09	Racing Club	25	1		
2009–10	Racing Club	26	0		
2010–11	Racing Club	21	2		
2011–12	Racing Club	17	1	**125**	**4**
2012–13	WBA	30	0		
2013–14	WBA	27	1		
2014–15	WBA	20	0		
2015–16	WBA	34	0		
2016–17	WBA	33	0	**144**	**1**

Players retained or with offer of contract
Edwards, Kyle Hakeem; Fitzwater, Jack Joseph; Keranovic, Jasmin; McCourt, Robbie; O'Shea, Dara; Ross, Ethan Walker.

Scholars
Artymatas, Panagiotis; Biddle, Bobbie; Bradley, Alex; Chambers, Maurice Jack; Clayton-Phillips, Nicholas; Hall, Myles; Harper, Rekeem; Healy, Kevin; Holsgrove, Kieran; House, Bradley Roy; McCourt, Jack; Melbourne, Max; Meredith, Daniel William; Morrison, Taylor; Morton, Callum Damian Peter; Pierce, Evan; Przybek, Adam; Soleman, Aram; Wilding, Samuel.

WEST HAM U (88)

ADRIAN (G) **138 0**
H: 6 2 W: 12 00 b.Seville 3-1-87

2008–09	Real Betis	0	0		
2009–10	Real Betis	0	0		
2010–11	Real Betis	0	0		
2011–12	Real Betis	0	0		
2012–13	Real Betis	32	0	**32**	**0**
2013–14	West Ham U	20	0		
2014–15	West Ham U	38	0		
2015–16	West Ham U	32	0		
2016–17	West Ham U	16	0	**106**	**0**

ANTONIO, Michael (M) **263 58**
H: 6 0 W: 11 11 b.Wandsworth 28-3-90

2008–09	Reading	0	0		
2008–09	*Cheltenham T*	9	0	**9**	**0**
2009–10	Reading	1	0		
2009–10	*Southampton*	28	3	**28**	**3**
2010–11	Reading	21	1		
2011–12	Reading	6	0		
2011–12	*Colchester U*	15	4	**15**	**4**
2011–12	*Sheffield W*	14	5		
2012–13	Reading	0	0	**28**	**1**
2012–13	Sheffield W	37	8		
2013–14	Sheffield W	27	4	**78**	**17**
2014–15	Nottingham F	46	14		
2015–16	Nottingham F	4	2	**50**	**16**
2015–16	West Ham U	26	8		
2016–17	West Ham U	29	9	**55**	**17**

ARBELOA, Alvaro (D) **279 5**
H: 6 0 W: 12 00 b.Salamanca 17-1-83
Internationals: Spain U17, U19, U21, Full caps.

2004–05	Real Madrid	2	0		
2005–06	R M Castilla	34	0	**34**	**0**
2006–07	Deportivo La Coruna	21	0	**21**	**0**
2006–07	Liverpool	9	1		
2007–08	Liverpool	28	0		
2008–09	Liverpool	29	1	**66**	**2**
2009–10	Real Madrid	30	2		
2010–11	Real Madrid	26	0		

2011–12	Real Madrid	26	0		
2012–13	Real Madrid	25	0		
2013–14	Real Madrid	18	0		
2014–15	Real Madrid	22	1		
2015–16	Real Madrid	6	0	**155**	**3**
2016–17	West Ham U	3	0	**3**	**0**

AYEW, Andre (F) 59 18

H: 5 9 W: 11 05 b.Seclin 17-12-89

Internationals: Ghana U20, Full caps.

2015–16	Swansea C	34	12	**34**	**12**
2016–17	West Ham U	25	6	**25**	**6**

BROWNE, Marcus (M) 0 0

b. 18-12-97

2015–16	West Ham U	0	0		
2016–17	West Ham U	0	0		
2016–17	*Wigan Ath*	0	0		

BURKE, Reece (D) 49 3

H: 6 2 W: 12 11 b.London 2-9-96

Internationals: England U18, U19, U20.

2013–14	West Ham U	0	0		
2014–15	West Ham U	5	0		
2015–16	West Ham U	0	0		
2015–16	*Bradford C*	34	2	**34**	**2**
2016–17	West Ham U	0	0	**5**	**0**
2016–17	*Wigan Ath*	10	1	**10**	**1**

BYRAM, Samuel (M) 152 9

H: 5 11 W: 11 04 b.Thurrock 16-9-93

2012–13	Leeds U	44	3		
2013–14	Leeds U	25	0		
2014–15	Leeds U	39	3		
2015–16	Leeds U	22	3	**130**	**9**
2015–16	West Ham U	4	0		
2016–17	West Ham U	18	0	**22**	**0**

CALLERI, Jonathan (F) 90 25

b. 23-9-93

Internationals: Argentina U23.

2012–13	All Boys	0	0		
2013–14	All Boys	28	5	**28**	**5**
2014	Boca Juniors	15	6		
2015	Boca Juniors	26	10	**41**	**16**
2016	Deportivo Maldonado	0	0		
2016	*Sao Paulo*	5	3	**5**	**3**

On loan from Deportivo Maldonado.

2016–17	West Ham U	16	1	**16**	**1**

CARROLL, Andy (F) 233 68

H: 6 4 W: 11 00 b.Gateshead 6-1-89

Internationals: England U19, U21, Full caps.

2006–07	Newcastle U	4	0		
2007–08	Newcastle U	4	0		
2007–08	*Preston NE*	11	1	**11**	**1**
2008–09	Newcastle U	14	3		
2009–10	Newcastle U	39	17		
2010–11	Newcastle U	19	11	**80**	**31**
2010–11	Liverpool	7	2		
2011–12	Liverpool	35	4		
2012–13	Liverpool	2	0	**44**	**6**
2012–13	*West Ham U*	24	7		
2013–14	West Ham U	15	2		
2014–15	West Ham U	14	5		
2015–16	West Ham U	27	9		
2016–17	West Ham U	18	7	**98**	**30**

COLLINS, James M (D) 332 13

H: 6 2 W: 14 05 b.Newport 23-8-83

Internationals: Wales U19, U20, U21, Full caps.

2000–01	Cardiff C	3	0		
2001–02	Cardiff C	7	1		
2002–03	Cardiff C	2	0		
2003–04	Cardiff C	20	1		
2004–05	Cardiff C	34	1	**66**	**3**
2005–06	West Ham U	14	2		
2006–07	West Ham U	16	0		
2007–08	West Ham U	3	0		
2008–09	West Ham U	18	0		
2009–10	West Ham U	3	0		
2009–10	Aston Villa	27	1		
2010–11	Aston Villa	32	3		
2011–12	Aston Villa	32	1	**91**	**5**
2012–13	West Ham U	29	0		
2013–14	West Ham U	24	1		
2014–15	West Ham U	27	0		
2015–16	West Ham U	19	0		
2016–17	West Ham U	22	2	**175**	**5**

CRESSWELL, Aaron (D) 303 15

H: 5 7 W: 10 05 b.Liverpool 15-12-89

Internationals: England Full caps.

2008–09	Tranmere R	13	1		
2009–10	Tranmere R	14	0		
2010–11	Tranmere R	43	4	**70**	**5**
2011–12	Ipswich T	44	1		
2012–13	Ipswich T	46	3		
2013–14	Ipswich T	42	2	**132**	**6**
2014–15	West Ham U	38	2		
2015–16	West Ham U	37	2		
2016–17	West Ham U	26	0	**101**	**4**

CULLEN, Josh (M) 56 1

H: 5 8 W: 11 00 b.Southend-on-Sea 4-7-96

Internationals: England U16. Republic of Ireland U19, U21.

2014–15	West Ham U	0	0		
2015–16	West Ham U	1	0		
2015–16	*Bradford C*	15	0		
2016–17	West Ham U	0	0	**1**	**0**
2016–17	*Bradford C*	40	1	**55**	**1**

DIANGANA, Grady (M) 0 0

2016–17	West Ham U	0	0		

DOBSON, George (M) 21 1

H: 6 1 b.Harold Wood 15-11-97

From Arsenal.

2015–16	West Ham U	0	0		
2016–17	West Ham U	0	0		
2016–17	*Walsall*	21	1	**21**	**1**

FEGHOULI, Sofiane (M) 236 28

H: 5 10 W: 11 03 b.Levallois-Perret 26-12-89

Internationals: France U18, U21. Algeria Full caps.

2006–07	Grenoble	3	0		
2007–08	Grenoble	26	3		
2008–09	Grenoble	26	0		
2009–10	Grenoble	5	0	**60**	**3**
2010–11	Valencia	3	0		
2010–11	*Almeria*	9	2	**9**	**2**
2011–12	Valencia	30	6		
2012–13	Valencia	27	3		
2013–14	Valencia	32	4		
2014–15	Valencia	33	6		
2015–16	Valencia	21	1	**146**	**20**
2016–17	West Ham U	21	3	**21**	**3**

FERNANDES, Edimilson (M) 59 1

b. 15-4-96

Internationals: Switzerland U21, Full caps.

2014–15	Sion	26	1		
2015–16	Sion	5	0	**31**	**1**
2016–17	West Ham U	28	0	**28**	**0**

FLETCHER, Ashley (F) 37 5

b.Keighley 12-10-95

Internationals: England U20.

2015–16	Manchester U	0	0		
2015–16	*Barnsley*	21	5	**21**	**5**
2016–17	West Ham U	16	0	**16**	**0**

FONTE, Jose (D) 438 24

H: 6 2 W: 12 08 b.Penafiel 22-12-83

Internationals: Portugal U21, B, Full caps.

2004–05	Felgueiros	28	1	**28**	**1**
2005–06	Setubal	15	0	**15**	**0**
2005–06	Benfica	1	0	**1**	**0**
2005–06	*Pacos*	11	1	**11**	**1**
2006–07	*Amadora*	25	1	**25**	**1**
2007–08	Crystal Palace	22	1		
2008–09	Crystal Palace	38	4		
2009–10	Crystal Palace	22	1	**82**	**6**
2009–10	Southampton	21	0		
2010–11	Southampton	43	7		
2011–12	Southampton	42	1		
2012–13	Southampton	27	2		
2013–14	Southampton	36	3		
2014–15	Southampton	37	0		
2015–16	Southampton	37	2		
2016–17	Southampton	17	0	**260**	**15**
2016–17	West Ham U	16	0	**16**	**0**

GORDON, Jaanai (F) 26 2

H: 5 10 W: 10 02 b.Northampton 7-12-95

2012–13	Peterborough U	3	0		
2013–14	Peterborough U	1	0	**4**	**0**
2013–14	West Ham U	0	0		
2014–15	West Ham U	0	0		
2015–16	West Ham U	0	0		
2016	*Sligo*	12	1	**12**	**1**
2016–17	West Ham U	0	0		
2016–17	*Newport Co*	10	1	**10**	**1**

HENDRIE, Stephen (D) 109 1

H: 5 10 W: 11 00 b.Glasgow 8-1-95

Internationals: Scotland U17, U19, U21.

2010–11	Hamilton A	0	0		
2011–12	Hamilton A	25	0		
2012–13	Hamilton A	23	0		
2013–14	Hamilton A	22	0		
2014–15	Hamilton A	30	0	**100**	**0**
2015–16	West Ham U	0	0		
2015–16	*Southend U*	5	1	**5**	**1**
2016–17	West Ham U	0	0		
2016–17	*Blackburn R*	4	0	**4**	**0**

HENRY, Doneil (D) 78 2

H: 6 2 W: 12 13 b.Brampton 20-4-93

Internationals: Canada U20, U23, Full caps.

2010	Toronto	1	0		
2011	Toronto	10	0		
2012	Toronto	18	1		
2013	Toronto	20	0		
2014	Toronto	21	1	**70**	**2**
2014–15	West Ham U	0	0		
2014–15	*Blackburn R*	3	0		
2015–16	West Ham U	0	0		
2015–16	*Blackburn R*	1	0	**4**	**0**
2016–17	West Ham U	0	0		
2016–17	*AC Horsens*	4	0	**4**	**0**

HOLLAND, Nathan (M) 0 0

b. 19-6-98

Internationals: England U16, U17, U18, U19.

2016–17	West Ham U	0	0		

KEMP, Daniel (M) 0 0

Internationals: England U20.

From Chelsea.

2016–17	West Ham U	0	0		

KNOYLE, Kyle (D) 10 0

H: 5 10 W: 9 13 b.Newham 24-9-96

Internationals: England U18.

2015–16	West Ham U	0	0		
2015–16	*Dundee U*	9	0	**9**	**0**
2016–17	West Ham U	0	0		
2016–17	*Wigan Ath*	1	0	**1**	**0**

KOUYATE, Cheikhou (M) 285 17

H: 6 3 W: 11 11 b.Dakar 21-12-89

Internationals: Senegal U20, Full caps.

2007–08	Brussels	10	0		
2008–09	Brussels	0	0	**10**	**0**
2008–09	*Kortrijk*	26	3	**26**	**3**
2009–10	Anderlecht	21	1		
2010–11	Anderlecht	23	1		
2011–12	Anderlecht	38	0		
2012–13	Anderlecht	33	1		
2013–14	Anderlecht	38	1	**153**	**4**
2014–15	West Ham U	31	4		
2015–16	West Ham U	34	5		
2016–17	West Ham U	31	1	**96**	**10**

LANZINI, Manuel (M) 197 37

H: 5 7 W: 11 00 b.Ituzaingo 15-2-93

Internationals: Argentina U20, Full caps.

2010–11	River Plate	22	0		
2010–11	*Fluminense*	22	2		
2011–12	River Plate	0	0		
2011–12	*Fluminense*	6	1	**28**	**3**
2012–13	River Plate	26	8	**26**	**8**
2013–14	River Plate	36	4	**58**	**4**
2014–15	Al-Jazira	24	8		
2015–16	Al-Jazira	0	0	**24**	**8**
2015–16	*West Ham U*	26	6		
2016–17	West Ham U	35	8	**61**	**14**

MAKASI, Moses (M) 0 0

2016–17	West Ham U	0	0		

MARTINEZ, Antonio (F) 15 1

b.Barrio del Progreso 30-6-97

Internationals: Spain U17, U19.

2015–16	Valencia	0	0		
2016–17	West Ham U	0	0		
2016–17	*Oxford U*	15	1	**15**	**1**

MASUAKU, Arthur (D) 91 2

b. 7-11-93

Internationals: France U18, U19.

2012–13	Valenciennes	0	0		
2013–14	Valenciennes	27	1	**27**	**1**
2014–15	Olympiacos	27	0		
2015–16	Olympiacos	24	1	**51**	**1**
2016–17	West Ham U	13	0	**13**	**0**

NOBLE, Mark (M) 365 42

H: 5 11 W: 12 00 b.West Ham 8-5-87

Internationals: England U16, U17, U18, U19, U21.

2004–05	West Ham U	13	0		
2005–06	West Ham U	5	0		
2005–06	*Hull C*	5	0	**5**	**0**
2006–07	West Ham U	10	2		
2006–07	*Ipswich T*	13	1	**13**	**1**
2007–08	West Ham U	31	3		
2008–09	West Ham U	29	3		

Season	Club	App	Gls	Total App	Total Gls
2009–10	West Ham U	27	2		
2010–11	West Ham U	26	4		
2011–12	West Ham U	45	8		
2012–13	West Ham U	28	4		
2013–14	West Ham U	38	3		
2014–15	West Ham U	28	2		
2015–16	West Ham U	37	7		
2016–17	West Ham U	30	3	**347**	**41**

NORDTVEIT, Havard (D) 217 10
H: 6 2 W: 11 10 b.Vats 21-6-90
Internationals: Norway U16, U17, U18, U19, U21, Full caps.

Season	Club	App	Gls	Total App	Total Gls
2006	Haugesund	1	0		
2007	Haugesund	9	0	**10**	**0**
2007–08	Arsenal	0	0		
2008–09	Arsenal	0	0		
2008–09	*Salamanca*	3	0	**3**	**0**
2009	*Lillestrom*	17	0	**17**	**0**
2009–10	Arsenal	0	0		
2009–10	*Nuremberg*	19	0	**19**	**0**
2010–11	Arsenal	0	0		
2010–11	Borussia M'gladbach	16	1		
2011–12	Borussia M'gladbach	31	1		
2012–13	Borussia M'gladbach	31	1		
2013–14	Borussia M'gladbach	21	1		
2014–15	Borussia M'gladbach	22	2		
2015–16	Borussia M'gladbach	31	4	**152**	**10**
2015–16	West Ham U	0	0		
2016–17	West Ham U	16	0	**16**	**0**

OBIANG, Pedro (M) 178 5
H: 6 1 W: 12 13 b.Alcala de Henares 13-5-90
Internationals: Spain U17, U19, U20, U21.

Season	Club	App	Gls	Total App	Total Gls
2008–09	Sampdoria	0	0		
2009–10	Sampdoria	0	0		
2010–11	Sampdoria	4	0		
2011–12	Sampdoria	33	0		
2012–13	Sampdoria	34	1		
2013–14	Sampdoria	27	0		
2014–15	Sampdoria	34	3	**132**	**4**
2015–16	West Ham U	24	0		
2016–17	West Ham U	22	1	**46**	**1**

OGBONNA, Angelo (D) 258 1
H: 6 2 W: 13 08 b.Cassino 23-5-88
Internationals: Italy U21, Full caps.

Season	Club	App	Gls	Total App	Total Gls
2006–07	Torino	4	0		
2007–08	Torino	0	0		
2007–08	*Crotone*	22	0	**22**	**0**
2008–09	Torino	19	0		
2009–10	Torino	28	1		
2010–11	Torino	35	0		
2011–12	Torino	39	0		
2012–13	Torino	22	0	**147**	**1**
2013–14	Juventus	16	0		
2014–15	Juventus	25	0	**41**	**0**
2015–16	West Ham U	28	0		
2016–17	West Ham U	20	0	**48**	**0**

OXFORD, Reece (D) 12 0
H: 6 3 W: 13 08 b.Edmonton 16-12-98
Internationals: England U16, U17, U18, U19, U20.

Season	Club	App	Gls	Total App	Total Gls
2014–15	West Ham U	0	0		
2015–16	West Ham U	7	0		
2016–17	West Ham U	0	0	**7**	**0**
2016–17	*Reading*	5	0	**5**	**0**

PASK, Josh (D) 15 0
b. 1-11-97

Season	Club	App	Gls	Total App	Total Gls
2015–16	West Ham U	0	0		
2015–16	*Dagenham & R*	5	0	**5**	**0**
2016–17	West Ham U	0	0		
2016–17	*Gillingham*	10	0	**10**	**0**

PAYET, Dimitri (M) 353 68
H: 5 9 W: 11 00 b.Saint-Pierre 29-3-87
Internationals: France U21, Full caps.

Season	Club	App	Gls	Total App	Total Gls
2005–06	Nantes	3	1		
2006–07	Nantes	30	4	**33**	**5**
2007–08	St Etienne	31	0		
2008–09	St Etienne	30	4		
2009–10	St Etienne	35	2		
2010–11	St Etienne	33	13	**129**	**19**
2011–12	Lille	33	6		
2012–13	Lille	38	12	**71**	**18**
2013–14	Marseille	36	8		
2014–15	Marseille	36	7	**72**	**15**
2015–16	West Ham U	30	9		
2016–17	West Ham U	18	2	**48**	**11**

Transferred to Marseille, January 2017.

PIKE, Alex (D) 5 0
b. 8-2-97

Season	Club	App	Gls	Total App	Total Gls
2015–16	West Ham U	0	0		
2016–17	West Ham U	0	0		
2016–17	*Cheltenham T*	5	0	**5**	**0**

QUINA, Domingos (F) 0 0
b. 18-11-99
Internationals: Portugal U17, U18, U19.

Season	Club	App	Gls	Total App	Total Gls
2016–17	West Ham U	0	0		

RANDOLPH, Darren (G) 274 0
H: 6 1 W: 12 02 b.Dublin 12-5-87
Internationals: Republic of Ireland U21, B, Full caps.

Season	Club	App	Gls	Total App	Total Gls
2004–05	Charlton Ath	0	0		
2005–06	Charlton Ath	0	0		
2006–07	Charlton Ath	1	0		
2006–07	*Gillingham*	3	0	**3**	**0**
2007–08	Charlton Ath	1	0		
2007–08	*Bury*	14	0	**14**	**0**
2008–09	Charlton Ath	1	0		
2008–09	*Hereford U*	13	0	**13**	**0**
2009–10	Charlton Ath	11	0	**14**	**0**
2010–11	Motherwell	37	0		
2011–12	Motherwell	38	0		
2012–13	Motherwell	36	0	**111**	**0**
2013–14	Birmingham C	46	0		
2014–15	Birmingham C	45	0	**91**	**0**
2015–16	West Ham U	6	0		
2016–17	West Ham U	22	0	**28**	**0**

REID, Winston (D) 260 11
H: 6 3 W: 13 10 b.North Shore 3-7-88
Internationals: Denmark U19, U20, U21. New Zealand Full caps.

Season	Club	App	Gls	Total App	Total Gls
2005–06	Midtjylland	9	0		
2006–07	Midtjylland	11	0		
2007–08	Midtjylland	9	0		
2008–09	Midtjylland	25	2		
2009–10	Midtjylland	29	0	**83**	**2**
2010–11	West Ham U	7	0		
2011–12	West Ham U	28	3		
2012–13	West Ham U	36	1		
2013–14	West Ham U	22	1		
2014–15	West Ham U	30	1		
2015–16	West Ham U	24	1		
2016–17	West Ham U	30	2	**177**	**9**

RICE, Declan (M) 1 0
b. 14-1-99
Internationals: Republic of Ireland U16, U17, U19.

Season	Club	App	Gls	Total App	Total Gls
2016–17	West Ham U	1	0	**1**	**0**

SAKHO, Diafra (F) 169 60
H: 6 0 W: 12 06 b.Guediawaye 24-12-89
Internationals: Senegal Full caps.

Season	Club	App	Gls	Total App	Total Gls
2009–10	Metz	5	0		
2010–11	Metz	30	5		
2011–12	Metz	9	0		
2011–12	*Boulogne*	7	0	**7**	**0**
2012–13	Metz	33	19		
2013–14	Metz	37	20	**114**	**44**
2014–15	West Ham U	23	10		
2015–16	West Ham U	21	5		
2016–17	West Ham U	4	1	**48**	**16**

SAMUELSEN, Martin (F) 31 2
H: 6 2 W: 11 05 b.Haugesund 17-4-97
Internationals: Norway U16, U17, U18, U21, Full caps.

Season	Club	App	Gls	Total App	Total Gls
2015–16	West Ham U	0	0		
2015–16	*Peterborough U*	17	1		
2016–17	West Ham U	0	0		
2016–17	*Blackburn R*	3	0	**3**	**0**
2016–17	*Peterborough U*	11	1	**28**	**2**

SNODGRASS, Robert (M) 386 78
H: 6 0 W: 12 02 b.Glasgow 7-9-87
Internationals: Scotland U20, U21, Full caps.

Season	Club	App	Gls	Total App	Total Gls
2003–04	Livingston	0	0		
2004–05	Livingston	17	2		
2005–06	Livingston	27	4		
2006–07	Livingston	6	0		
2006–07	*Stirling Alb*	12	5	**12**	**5**
2007–08	Livingston	31	9	**81**	**15**
2008–09	Leeds U	42	9		
2009–10	Leeds U	44	7		
2010–11	Leeds U	37	6		
2011–12	Leeds U	43	13	**166**	**35**
2012–13	Norwich C	37	6		
2013–14	Norwich C	30	6	**67**	**12**
2014–15	Hull C	1	0		
2015–16	Hull C	24	4		
2016–17	Hull C	20	7	**45**	**11**
2016–17	West Ham U	15	0	**15**	**0**

SPIEGEL, Raphael (G) 19 0
H: 6 5 W: 15 00 b.Zurich 19-12-92
Internationals: Switzerland U17, U19, U21.

Season	Club	App	Gls	Total App	Total Gls
2011–12	Grasshoppers	0	0		
2011–12	*Bruhl*	17	0	**17**	**0**
2012–13	Grasshoppers	0	0		
2012–13	West Ham U	0	0		
2013–14	West Ham U	0	0		
2014–15	West Ham U	0	0		
2014–15	*Carlisle U*	2	0	**2**	**0**
2015–16	West Ham U	0	0		
2016–17	West Ham U	0	0		

TORE, Gokhan (M) 114 12
H: 5 7 W: 11 07 b. 20-1-92
Internationals: Turkey U16, U17, U21, Full caps.

Season	Club	App	Gls	Total App	Total Gls
2010–11	Chelsea	0	0		
2011–12	Hamburg	22	0	**22**	**0**
2012–13	Rubin Kazan	5	0	**5**	**0**
2013–14	Besiktas	30	4		
2014–15	Besiktas	28	4		
2015–16	Besiktas	24	4		
2016–17	Besiktas	0	0	**82**	**12**

On loan from Besiktas.

Season	Club	App	Gls	Total App	Total Gls
2016–17	West Ham U	5	0	**5**	**0**

VALENCIA, Enner (F) 228 56
H: 5 10 W: 11 05 b.San Lorenzo 11-4-89
Internationals: Ecuador Full caps.

Season	Club	App	Gls	Total App	Total Gls
2010	Emelec	25	1		
2011	Emelec	30	9		
2012	Emelec	40	13		
2013	Emelec	35	4	**130**	**27**
2013–14	Pachuca	23	18	**23**	**18**
2014–15	West Ham U	32	4		
2015–16	West Ham U	19	4		
2016–17	West Ham U	3	0	**54**	**8**
2016–17	*Everton*	21	3	**21**	**3**

ZAZA, Simone (F) 173 60
H: 5 10 W: 11 09 b.Alzano 25-6-91
Internationals: Italy U16, U17, U19, Full caps.

Season	Club	App	Gls	Total App	Total Gls
2008–09	Atalanta	3	0		
2009–10	Atalanta	0	0	**3**	**0**
2010–11	Sampdoria	2	0		
2011–12	Sampdoria	0	0		
2011–12	*Juve Stabia*	4	0	**4**	**0**
2011–12	*Viareggio*	18	11	**18**	**11**
2012–13	Sampdoria	0	0	**2**	**0**
2012–13	*Ascoli*	35	18	**35**	**18**
2013–14	Sassuolo	33	9		
2014–15	Sassuolo	31	11	**64**	**20**
2015–16	Juventus	19	5		
2016–17	Juventus	0	0	**19**	**5**
2016–17	*Valencia*	20	6	**20**	**6**

On loan from Juventus.

Season	Club	App	Gls	Total App	Total Gls
2016–17	West Ham U	8	0	**8**	**0**

Players retained or with offer of contract
Akinola, Olatunji Oluwasehun; Hector-Ingram, Jahmal Justin; Neufville, Vashon; Powell, Joe; San, Miguel Del Castillo Adrian; Scully, Anthony Richard; Sylvestre, Noha; Trott, Nathan Wallace Newman.

Scholars
Barrett, Mason; Coventry, Conor; Hamilton, Malyk; Henry, Korrey; Johnson, Benjamin; Lewis, Alfie; Longelo-Mbule, Rosaire; Matrevics, Rihards; Wells, Ben.

WIGAN ATH (89)

BARRIGAN, James (F) 0 0
b. 25-1-98

Season	Club	App	Gls	Total App	Total Gls
2016–17	Wigan Ath	0	0		

BOGLE, Omar (F) 41 22
H: 6 3 W: 12 08 b.Birmingham 26-7-92
Internationals: England C
From Hinckley U, Solihull Moors.

Season	Club	App	Gls	Total App	Total Gls
2016–17	Grimsby T	27	19	**27**	**19**
2016–17	Wigan Ath	14	3	**14**	**3**

BURKE, Luke (D) 5 0
b. 22-2-98

Season	Club	App	Gls	Total App	Total Gls
2015–16	Wigan Ath	0	0		
2016–17	Wigan Ath	5	0	**5**	**0**

BURN, Dan (D) 165 4
H: 6 6 W: 13 00 b.Blyth 1-5-92

Season	Club	App	Gls	Total App	Total Gls
2009–10	Darlington	4	0	**4**	**0**
2010–11	Fulham	0	0		
2011–12	Fulham	0	0		
2012–13	Fulham	0	0		
2012–13	*Yeovil T*	34	2	**34**	**2**

2013–14	Fulham	9	0		
2013–14	*Birmingham C*	24	0	**24**	**0**
2014–15	Fulham	20	1		
2015–16	Fulham	32	0	**61**	**1**
2016–17	Wigan Ath	42	1	**42**	**1**

BUXTON, Jake (D)				**329**	**17**
H: 6 1 W: 13 05 b.Sutton-in-Ashfield 4-3-85					
2002–03	Mansfield T	3	0		
2003–04	Mansfield T	9	1		
2004–05	Mansfield T	30	1		
2005–06	Mansfield T	39	0		
2006–07	Mansfield T	30	1		
2007–08	Mansfield T	40	2		
2008–09	Mansfield T	0	0	**151**	**5**
From Burton Alb.					
2008–09	Derby Co	0	0		
2009–10	Derby Co	19	1		
2010–11	Derby Co	1	0		
2011–12	Derby Co	21	2		
2012–13	Derby Co	31	3		
2013–14	Derby Co	45	2		
2014–15	Derby Co	19	3		
2015–16	Derby Co	3	0	**139**	**11**
2016–17	Wigan Ath	39	1	**39**	**1**

BYRNE, Jack (M)				**33**	**4**
H: 5 9 W: 11 07 b.Dublin 24-4-96					
Internationals: Republic of Ireland U16, U17, U18, U19, U21.					
2015–16	Manchester C	0	0		
2015–16	*Cambuur*	27	4	**27**	**4**
2016–17	Manchester C	0	0		
2016–17	*Blackburn R*	4	0	**4**	**0**
2016–17	Wigan Ath	2	0	**2**	**0**

BYRNE, Nathan (D)				**177**	**14**
H: 5 10 W: 10 10 b.St Albans 5-6-92					
2010–11	Tottenham H	0	0		
2010–11	*Brentford*	11	0	**11**	**0**
2011–12	Tottenham H	0	0		
2011–12	*Bournemouth*	9	0	**9**	**0**
2012–13	Tottenham H	0	0		
2012–13	*Crawley T*	12	1	**12**	**1**
2012–13	*Swindon T*	7	0		
2013–14	Swindon T	36	4		
2014–15	Swindon T	42	3		
2015–16	Swindon T	5	3	**90**	**10**
2015–16	Wolverhampton W	24	2		
2016–17	Wolverhampton W	0	0	**24**	**2**
2016–17	Wigan Ath	14	0	**14**	**0**
2016–17	*Charlton Ath*	17	1	**17**	**1**

CHOW, Tim (M)				**16**	**1**
H: 5 11 W: 11 06 b.Wigan 18-1-94					
2011–12	Wigan Ath	0	0		
2012–13	Wigan Ath	0	0		
2013–14	Wigan Ath	0	0		
2014–15	Wigan Ath	4	1		
2015–16	Wigan Ath	11	0		
2016–17	Wigan Ath	1	0	**16**	**1**
Transferred to Ross Co, August 2016.					

COLCLOUGH, Ryan (F)				**98**	**19**
H: 6 3 W: 13 01 b.Budapest 27-12-94					
2012–13	Crewe Alex	18	1		
2013–14	Crewe Alex	8	2		
2014–15	Crewe Alex	7	2		
2015–16	Crewe Alex	27	7	**60**	**12**
2015–16	Wigan Ath	10	2		
2016–17	Milton Keynes D	18	5	**18**	**5**
2016–17	Wigan Ath	10	0	**20**	**2**

COSGROVE, Sam (F)				**0**	**0**
b.Beverley 2-12-96					
2014–15	Wigan Ath	0	0		
2015–16	Wigan Ath	0	0		
2016–17	Wigan Ath	0	0		

DANIELS, Donervorn (D)				**87**	**6**
H: 6 1 W: 14 05 b.Montserrat 24-11-93					
Internationals: England U20.					
2011–12	WBA	0	0		
2012–13	WBA	0	0		
2012–13	*Tranmere R*	13	1	**13**	**1**
2013–14	WBA	0	0		
2013–14	*Gillingham*	3	1	**3**	**1**
2014–15	WBA	0	0		
2014–15	*Blackpool*	19	1	**19**	**1**
2014–15	*Aberdeen*	9	0	**9**	**0**
2015–16	Wigan Ath	42	3		
2016–17	Wigan Ath	1	0	**43**	**3**

EVANS, Owen (G)				**0**	**0**
From Hereford U.					
2016–17	Wigan Ath	0	0		

FLORES, Jordan (F)				**25**	**4**
H: 5 9 W: 10 08 b.Wigan 4-10-95					
2014–15	Wigan Ath	1	0		
2015–16	Wigan Ath	3	1		
2016–17	Wigan Ath	2	0	**6**	**1**
2016–17	*Blackpool*	19	3	**19**	**3**

GILBEY, Alex (M)				**125**	**9**
H: 6 0 W: 11 07 b.Dagenham 9-12-94					
2011–12	Colchester U	0	0		
2012–13	Colchester U	3	0		
2013–14	Colchester U	36	1		
2014–15	Colchester U	34	1		
2015–16	Colchester U	37	5	**110**	**7**
2016–17	Wigan Ath	15	2	**15**	**2**

GILKS, Matthew (G)				**376**	**0**
H: 6 3 W: 13 12 b.Rochdale 4-6-82					
Internationals: Scotland Full caps.					
2000–01	Rochdale	3	0		
2001–02	Rochdale	19	0		
2002–03	Rochdale	20	0		
2003–04	Rochdale	12	0		
2004–05	Rochdale	30	0		
2005–06	Rochdale	46	0		
2006–07	Rochdale	46	0	**176**	**0**
2007–08	Norwich C	0	0		
2008–09	Blackpool	5	0		
2008–09	*Shrewsbury T*	4	0	**4**	**0**
2009–10	Blackpool	26	0		
2010–11	Blackpool	18	0		
2011–12	Blackpool	42	0		
2012–13	Blackpool	45	0		
2013–14	Blackpool	46	0	**182**	**0**
2014–15	Burnley	0	0		
2015–16	Burnley	0	0		
2016–17	Rangers	0	0		
2016–17	Wigan Ath	14	0	**14**	**0**

GOMEZ, Jordi (M)				**263**	**39**
H: 5 10 W: 11 09 b.Barcelona 24-5-85					
Internationals: Spain U17.					
2006–07	Espanyol B	21	0	**21**	**0**
2007–08	Espanyol	2	0	**2**	**0**
2008–09	*Swansea C*	44	12	**44**	**12**
2009–10	Wigan Ath	23	1		
2010–11	Wigan Ath	13	1		
2011–12	Wigan Ath	28	5		
2012–13	Wigan Ath	32	3		
2013–14	Wigan Ath	31	7		
2014–15	Sunderland	29	4		
2015–16	Sunderland	6	0	**35**	**4**
2015–16	*Blackburn R*	19	3	**19**	**3**
2016–17	Wigan Ath	15	3	**142**	**20**
Transferred to Rayo Vallecano, January 2017.					

GREGORY, Joshua (M)				**0**	**0**
b.Wigan 5-6-98					
2016–17	Wigan Ath	0	0		

GRIGG, Will (M)				**250**	**82**
H: 5 11 W: 11 00 b.Solihull 3-7-91					
Internationals: Northern Ireland U19, U21, Full caps.					
2008–09	Walsall	1	0		
2009–10	Walsall	0	0		
2010–11	Walsall	28	4		
2011–12	Walsall	29	4		
2012–13	Walsall	41	19	**99**	**27**
2013–14	Brentford	34	5		
2014–15	Brentford	0	0	**34**	**5**
2014–15	*Milton Keynes D*	44	20	**44**	**20**
2015–16	Wigan Ath	40	25		
2016–17	Wigan Ath	33	5	**73**	**30**

HENDRY, Jack (D)				**17**	**0**
H: 6 2 W: 12 00 b.Glasgow 7-5-95					
2014–15	Partick Thistle	1	0		
2015–16	Partick Thistle	3	0	**4**	**0**
2015–16	Wigan Ath	0	0		
2015–16	*Shrewsbury T*	6	0	**6**	**0**
2016–17	Milton Keynes D	7	0	**7**	**0**
2016–17	Wigan Ath	0	0		

JAASKELAINEN, Jussi (G)				**693**	**0**
H: 6 3 W: 12 10 b.Vaasa 19-4-75					
Internationals: Finland U21, Full caps.					
1992	MP	6	0		
1993	MP	6	0		
1994	MP	26	0		
1995	MP	26	0	**64**	**0**
1996	VPS	27	0		
1997	VPS	27	0	**54**	**0**
1997–98	Bolton W	0	0		
1998–99	Bolton W	34	0		
1999–2000	Bolton W	34	0		
2000–01	Bolton W	27	0		
2001–02	Bolton W	34	0		
2002–03	Bolton W	38	0		
2003–04	Bolton W	38	0		
2004–05	Bolton W	36	0		
2005–06	Bolton W	38	0		
2006–07	Bolton W	38	0		
2007–08	Bolton W	28	0		
2008–09	Bolton W	38	0		
2009–10	Bolton W	38	0		
2010–11	Bolton W	35	0		
2011–12	Bolton W	18	0	**474**	**0**
2012–13	West Ham U	38	0		
2013–14	West Ham U	18	0		
2014–15	West Ham U	1	0	**57**	**0**
2015–16	Wigan Ath	35	0		
2016–17	Wigan Ath	9	0	**44**	**0**

JACOBS, Michael (M)				**253**	**35**
H: 5 9 W: 11 08 b.Rothwell 23-3-92					
2009–10	Northampton T	0	0		
2010–11	Northampton T	41	5		
2011–12	Northampton T	46	6	**87**	**11**
2012–13	Derby Co	38	2		
2013–14	Derby Co	3	0	**41**	**2**
2013–14	Wolverhampton W	30	8		
2014–15	Wolverhampton W	12	0	**42**	**8**
2014–15	*Blackpool*	5	1	**5**	**1**
2015–16	Wigan Ath	35	10		
2016–17	Wigan Ath	43	3	**78**	**13**

JAMES, Reece (D)				**40**	**2**
H: 5 6 W: 11 03 b.Bacup 7-11-93					
2012–13	Manchester U	0	0		
2013–14	Manchester U	0	0		
2013–14	*Carlisle U*	1	0	**1**	**0**
2014–15	Manchester U	0	0		
2014–15	*Rotherham U*	7	0	**7**	**0**
2014–15	*Huddersfield T*	6	1	**6**	**1**
2015–16	Wigan Ath	26	1		
2016–17	Wigan Ath	0	0	**26**	**1**

KELLETT, Andy (D)				**30**	**3**
H: 5 8 W: 12 06 b.Bolton 10-11-93					
2012–13	Bolton W	0	0		
2013–14	Bolton W	3	0		
2014–15	Bolton W	1	0		
2014–15	*Plymouth Arg*	12	1	**12**	**1**
2014–15	*Manchester U*	0	0		
2015–16	Bolton W	0	0	**4**	**0**
2015–16	Wigan Ath	9	2		
2016–17	Wigan Ath	5	0	**14**	**2**

LANG, Callum (F)				**0**	**0**
2016–17	Wigan Ath	0	0		

LAURENT, Josh (M)				**32**	**1**
H: 6 0 W: 11 00 b.Leytonstone 6-5-95					
2013–14	QPR	0	0		
2014–15	QPR	0	0		
2015–16	Brentford	0	0		
2015–16	*Newport Co*	3	0	**3**	**0**
2015–16	Hartlepool U	3	0		
2016–17	Hartlepool U	25	1	**28**	**1**
2016–17	Wigan Ath	1	0	**1**	**0**

LAVERCOMBE, Dan (G)				**0**	**0**
H: 6 3 W: 11 03 b.Torquay 16-5-96					
2013–14	Torquay U	0	0		
2015–16	Wigan Ath	0	0		
2016–17	Wigan Ath	0	0		

MACDONALD, Shaun (M)				**208**	**11**
H: 6 1 W: 11 04 b.Swansea 17-6-88					
Internationals: Wales U19, U21, Full caps.					
2005–06	Swansea C	7	0		
2006–07	Swansea C	8	0		
2007–08	Swansea C	1	0		
2008–09	Swansea C	5	0		
2008–09	*Yeovil T*	4	2		
2009–10	Swansea C	3	0		
2009–10	*Yeovil T*	31	3		
2010–11	Swansea C	0	0		
2010–11	*Yeovil T*	26	4	**61**	**9**
2011–12	Swansea C	0	0	**24**	**0**
2011–12	Bournemouth	25	1		
2012–13	Bournemouth	28	0		
2013–14	Bournemouth	23	0		
2014–15	Bournemouth	5	0		
2015–16	Bournemouth	3	0	**84**	**1**
2016–17	Wigan Ath	39	1	**39**	**1**

MANDRON, Mikael (F)				**25**	**1**
H: 6 3 W: 12 13 b.Boulogne 11-10-94					
2011–12	Sunderland	0	0		
2012–13	Sunderland	2	0		
2013–14	Sunderland	0	0		
2013–14	*Fleetwood T*	11	1	**11**	**1**

2014–15	Sunderland	1	0		
2014–15	*Shrewsbury T*	3	0	**3**	**0**
2015–16	Sunderland	0	0	**3**	**0**
2015–16	*Hartlepool U*	5	0	**5**	**0**
2016–17	Wigan Ath	3	0	**3**	**0**

McKAY, Billy (F) **275 83**
H: 5 7 W: 10 10 b.Corby 22-10-88
Internationals: Northern Ireland U18, U20, U21, Full caps.

2007–08	Leicester C	0	0		
2008–09	Leicester C	0	0		
2009–10	Northampton T	40	8		
2010–11	Northampton T	34	5	**74**	**13**
2011–12	Inverness CT	22	3		
2012–13	Inverness CT	38	23		
2013–14	Inverness CT	38	18		
2014–15	Inverness CT	23	10		
2014–15	Wigan Ath	9	0		
2015–16	Wigan Ath	1	0		
2015–16	*Dundee U*	29	12	**29**	**12**
2016–17	Wigan Ath	0	0	**10**	**0**
2016–17	*Oldham Ath*	26	0	**26**	**0**
2016–17	*Inverness CT*	15	4	**136**	**58**

MORGAN, Craig (D) **418 11**
H: 6 0 W: 11 04 b.Flint 18-6-85
Internationals: Wales U17, U19, U21, Full caps.

2001–02	Wrexham	2	0		
2002–03	Wrexham	6	1		
2003–04	Wrexham	18	0		
2004–05	Wrexham	26	0		
2005–06	Milton Keynes D	40	0		
2006–07	Milton Keynes D	3	0	**43**	**0**
2006–07	*Wrexham*	1	0	**53**	**1**
2006–07	Peterborough U	23	1		
2007–08	Peterborough U	41	2		
2008–09	Peterborough U	27	0		
2009–10	Peterborough U	34	1	**125**	**4**
2010–11	Preston NE	31	2		
2011–12	Preston NE	19	1		
2012–13	Preston NE	0	0	**50**	**3**
2012–13	Rotherham U	21	1		
2013–14	Rotherham U	35	0		
2014–15	Rotherham U	35	0	**91**	**1**
2015–16	Wigan Ath	36	2		
2016–17	Wigan Ath	20	0	**56**	**2**

MORSY, Sam (M) **215 13**
H: 5 9 W: 12 06 b.Wolverhampton 10-9-91
Internationals: Egypt Full caps.

2009–10	Port Vale	1	0		
2010–11	Port Vale	16	1		
2011–12	Port Vale	26	1		
2012–13	Port Vale	28	2	**71**	**4**
2013–14	Chesterfield	34	1		
2014–15	Chesterfield	39	2		
2015–16	Chesterfield	26	4	**99**	**7**
2015–16	Wigan Ath	16	1		
2016–17	Barnsley	14	0	**14**	**0**
2016–17	Wigan Ath	15	1	**31**	**2**

O'BRIEN, Danny (M) **0 0**
H: 5 11 b. 12-4-96
Internationals: England U17.
From Aston Villa.

2016–17	Wigan Ath	0	0		

OBERTAN, Gabriel (F) **153 7**
H: 6 1 W: 12 06 b.Paris 26-2-89
Internationals: France U16, U17, U18, U19, U21.

2006–07	Bordeaux	17	1		
2007–08	Bordeaux	26	2		
2008–09	Bordeaux	11	0	**54**	**3**
2008–09	*Lorient*	15	1	**15**	**1**
2009–10	Manchester U	7	0		
2010–11	Manchester U	7	0	**14**	**0**
2011–12	Newcastle U	23	1		
2012–13	Newcastle U	14	0		
2013–14	Newcastle U	3	0		
2014–15	Newcastle U	13	1		
2015–16	Newcastle U	5	0	**58**	**2**
2016–17	Anzhi Makhachkala	0	0		
2016–17	Wigan Ath	12	1	**12**	**1**

ODELUSI, Sanmi (F) **55 4**
H: 6 0 W: 11 11 b.London 11-6-93

2012–13	Bolton W	1	0		
2013–14	Bolton W	5	0		
2013–14	*Milton Keynes D*	10	0	**10**	**0**
2014–15	Bolton W	0	0	**6**	**0**
2014–15	*Coventry C*	14	3	**14**	**3**
2015–16	Wigan Ath	3	0		
2016–17	Wigan Ath	0	0	**3**	**0**

2016–17	*Rochdale*	15	0	**15**	**0**
2016–17	*Blackpool*	7	1	**7**	**1**

PERKINS, David (D) **400 14**
H: 5 6 W: 11 06 b.Heysham 21-6-82
Internationals: England C.

2006–07	Rochdale	18	0		
2007–08	Rochdale	40	4	**58**	**4**
2008–09	Colchester U	38	5		
2009–10	Colchester U	5	1		
2009–10	*Chesterfield*	13	1	**13**	**1**
2009–10	*Stockport Co*	22	0	**22**	**0**
2010–11	Colchester U	36	1	**79**	**7**
2011–12	Barnsley	33	1		
2012–13	Barnsley	35	1		
2013–14	Barnsley	23	0	**91**	**2**
2013–14	Blackpool	20	0		
2014–15	Blackpool	45	0	**65**	**0**
2015–16	Wigan Ath	45	0		
2016–17	Wigan Ath	27	0	**72**	**0**

POWELL, Nick (F) **116 28**
H: 6 0 W: 10 05 b.Crewe 23-3-94
Internationals: England U16, U17, U18, U19, U21.

2010–11	Crewe Alex	17	0		
2011–12	Crewe Alex	38	14	**55**	**14**
2012–13	Manchester U	2	1		
2013–14	Manchester U	0	0		
2013–14	*Wigan Ath*	31	7		
2014–15	Manchester U	0	0		
2014–15	*Leicester C*	3	0	**3**	**0**
2015–16	Manchester U	1	0	**3**	**1**
2015–16	*Hull C*	3	0	**3**	**0**
2016–17	Wigan Ath	21	6	**52**	**13**

POWER, Max (M) **195 18**
H: 5 11 W: 11 13 b.Bebington 27-7-93

2010–11	Tranmere R	0	0		
2011–12	Tranmere R	4	0		
2012–13	Tranmere R	27	3		
2013–14	Tranmere R	33	2		
2014–15	Tranmere R	45	7	**109**	**12**
2015–16	Wigan Ath	44	6		
2016–17	Wigan Ath	42	0	**86**	**6**

ROBERTS, Theo (G) **0 0**
b. 10-9-98

2016–17	Wigan Ath	0	0		

STUBBS, Sam (D) **0 0**
b. 20-11-98

2016–17	Wigan Ath	0	0		

TAYLOR, Andrew (D) **350 6**
H: 5 10 W: 11 04 b.Hartlepool 1-8-86
Internationals: England U16, U17, U18, U19, U20, U21.

2003–04	Middlesbrough	0	0		
2004–05	Middlesbrough	0	0		
2005–06	Middlesbrough	13	0		
2005–06	*Bradford C*	24	0	**24**	**0**
2006–07	Middlesbrough	34	0		
2007–08	Middlesbrough	19	0		
2008–09	Middlesbrough	26	0		
2009–10	Middlesbrough	12	0		
2010–11	Middlesbrough	21	3	**125**	**3**
2010–11	*Watford*	19	1	**19**	**1**
2011–12	Cardiff C	42	1		
2012–13	Cardiff C	43	0		
2013–14	Cardiff C	18	0	**103**	**1**
2014–15	Wigan Ath	26	1		
2015–16	*Reading*	19	0	**19**	**0**
2016–17	Wigan Ath	0	0	**26**	**1**
2016–17	*Bolton W*	34	0	**34**	**0**

WARNOCK, Stephen (D) **430 15**
H: 5 7 W: 11 09 b.Ormskirk 12-12-81
Internationals: England Full caps.

1998–99	Liverpool	0	0		
1999–2000	Liverpool	0	0		
2000–01	Liverpool	0	0		
2001–02	Liverpool	0	0		
2002–03	Liverpool	0	0		
2002–03	*Bradford C*	12	1	**12**	**1**
2003–04	Liverpool	0	0		
2003–04	*Coventry C*	44	3	**44**	**3**
2004–05	Liverpool	19	0		
2005–06	Liverpool	20	1		
2006–07	Liverpool	1	0	**40**	**1**
2006–07	Blackburn R	13	1		
2007–08	Blackburn R	37	1		
2008–09	Blackburn R	37	3		
2009–10	Blackburn R	1	0	**88**	**5**
2009–10	Aston Villa	30	0		
2010–11	Aston Villa	19	0		
2011–12	Aston Villa	35	2		
2012–13	Aston Villa	0	0	**84**	**2**
2012–13	*Bolton W*	15	0	**15**	**0**
2012–13	Leeds U	16	1		
2013–14	Leeds U	27	1		
2014–15	Leeds U	21	1	**64**	**3**
2014–15	Derby Co	7	0		
2015–16	Derby Co	20	0	**27**	**0**
2015–16	*Wigan Ath*	11	0		
2016–17	Wigan Ath	45	0	**56**	**0**

WHITEHEAD, Danny (M) **8 0**
H: 5 10 W: 10 11 b.Trafford 23-10-93

2013–14	West Ham U	0	0		
2014–15	West Ham U	0	0		
2014–15	Accrington S	2	0	**2**	**0**

From Macclesfield T.

2015–16	Wigan Ath	0	0		
2016–17	Wigan Ath	0	0		
2016–17	*Cheltenham T*	6	0	**6**	**0**

WOOLERY, Kaiyne (F) **25 2**
H: 5 10 W: 11 07 b.Hackney 11-1-95

2014–15	Bolton W	1	0		
2014–15	*Notts Co*	5	0	**5**	**0**
2015–16	Bolton W	17	2		
2016–17	Bolton W	1	0	**19**	**2**
2016–17	Wigan Ath	1	0	**1**	**0**

Scholars
Beaumont, Joshua Jack; Carroll-Burgess, Luke Eugene; Cotter, James; Donaghey, Shane Patrick; Downey, Joseph Paul; Fitton, Remell Scott; Forecast, Charlie Joe; Golden, Tylor Reed; Hilton, Thomas Andrew Fred; Lang, Callum Joseph; Malumo, Mwiya; Merrie, Christopher Francis; Perrin, Jordan-John Richard; Plant, Anthony; Powell, Thomas David; Randell, Nathan; Roberts, Theo Paul; Stubbs, Sam Alan; Taylor, Matthew William; White, Jack Kincaid.

WOLVERHAMPTON W (90)

BATTH, Danny (D) **251 16**
H: 6 3 W: 13 05 b.Brierley Hill 21-9-90

2009–10	Wolverhampton W	0	0		
2009–10	*Colchester U*	17	1	**17**	**1**
2010–11	Wolverhampton W	0	0		
2010–11	*Sheffield U*	1	0	**1**	**0**
2010–11	*Sheffield W*	10	0		
2011–12	Wolverhampton W	0	0		
2011–12	*Sheffield W*	44	2	**54**	**2**
2012–13	Wolverhampton W	12	1		
2013–14	Wolverhampton W	46	2		
2014–15	Wolverhampton W	44	4		
2015–16	Wolverhampton W	38	2		
2016–17	Wolverhampton W	39	4	**179**	**13**

BODVARSSON, Jon Dadi (F) **218 38**
H: 6 3 W: 13 05 b.Selfoss 25-5-92
Internationals: Iceland U19, U21, Full caps.

2008	Selfoss	0	0		
2009	Selfoss	16	1		
2010	Selfoss	21	3		
2011	Selfoss	21	7		
2012	Selfoss	22	7	**80**	**18**
2013	Viking	23	1		
2014	Viking	29	5		
2015	Viking	29	9	**81**	**15**
2015–16	Kaiserslautern	15	2	**15**	**2**
2016–17	Wolverhampton W	42	3	**42**	**3**

BROWN, Rory (G) **0 0**
b. 25-3-00
Internationals: Northern Ireland U16.

2016–17	Wolverhampton W	0	0		

BURGOYNE, Harry (G) **8 0**
H: 6 4 W: 13 05 b.Ludlow 28-12-96

2015–16	Wolverhampton W	0	0		
2016–17	Barnet	2	0	**2**	**0**
2016–17	Wolverhampton W	6	0	**6**	**0**

COADY, Conor (D) **162 8**
H: 6 1 W: 11 05 b.Liverpool 25-2-93
Internationals: England U16, U17, U18, U19, U20.

2010–11	Liverpool	0	0		
2011–12	Liverpool	0	0		
2012–13	Liverpool	1	0		
2013–14	Liverpool	0	0	**1**	**0**
2013–14	*Sheffield U*	39	5	**39**	**5**
2014–15	Huddersfield T	45	3	**45**	**3**
2015–16	Wolverhampton W	37	0		
2016–17	Wolverhampton W	40	0	**77**	**0**

COLLINS, Aaron (F) **38 4**
b. 27-5-97
Internationals: Wales U19.
2014–15 Newport Co 2 0
2015–16 Newport Co 18 2 **20 2**
2015–16 Wolverhampton W 0 0
2016–17 Wolverhampton W 0 0
2016–17 *Notts Co* 18 2 **18 2**

DESLANDES, Sylvain (D) **3 0**
H: 6 1 W: 11 11 b.Kouoptamo 25-4-97
Internationals: France U16, U17, U18, U19, U20.
2014–15 Caen 0 0
2015–16 Wolverhampton W 3 0
2016–17 Wolverhampton W 0 0 **3 0**
2016–17 *Bury* 0 0

DICKO, Nouha (M) **177 56**
H: 5 8 W: 11 00 b.Paris 14-5-92
Internationals: Mali Full caps.
2009–10 Strasbourg B 18 4
2010–11 Strasbourg B 24 8 **42 12**
2010–11 Strasbourg 3 0 **3 0**
2011–12 Wigan Ath 0 0
2011–12 *Blackpool* 10 4
2012–13 Wigan Ath 0 0
2012–13 *Blackpool* 22 5 **32 9**
2012–13 *Wolverhampton W* 4 1
2013–14 Wigan Ath 0 0
2013–14 *Rotherham U* 5 5 **5 5**
2013–14 Wolverhampton W 19 12
2014–15 Wolverhampton W 37 14
2015–16 Wolverhampton W 5 0
2016–17 Wolverhampton W 30 3 **95 30**

DOHERTY, Matthew (M) **171 11**
H: 6 0 W: 12 08 b.Dublin 17-1-92
Internationals: Republic of Ireland U19, U21.
2010–11 Wolverhampton W 0 0
2011–12 Wolverhampton W 1 0
2011–12 *Hibernian* 13 2 **13 2**
2012–13 Wolverhampton W 13 1
2012–13 *Bury* 17 1 **17 1**
2013–14 Wolverhampton W 18 1
2014–15 Wolverhampton W 33 0
2015–16 Wolverhampton W 34 2
2016–17 Wolverhampton W 42 4 **141 8**

EBANKS-LANDELL, Ethan (M) **100 10**
H: 5 6 W: 11 02 b.Oldbury 16-12-92
2009–10 Wolverhampton W 0 0
2010–11 Wolverhampton W 0 0
2011–12 Wolverhampton W 0 0
2012–13 Wolverhampton W 0 0
2012–13 *Bury* 24 0 **24 0**
2013–14 Wolverhampton W 7 2
2014–15 Wolverhampton W 14 2
2015–16 Wolverhampton W 21 1
2016–17 Wolverhampton W 0 0 **42 5**
2016–17 *Sheffield U* 34 5 **34 5**

EDWARDS, Dave (M) **405 57**
H: 5 11 W: 11 04 b.Shrewsbury 3-2-86
Internationals: Wales U21, Full caps.
2002–03 Shrewsbury T 1 0
2003–04 Shrewsbury T 0 0
2004–05 Shrewsbury T 27 5
2005–06 Shrewsbury T 30 2
2006–07 Shrewsbury T 45 5 **103 12**
2007–08 Luton T 19 4 **19 4**
2007–08 Wolverhampton W 10 1
2008–09 Wolverhampton W 44 3
2009–10 Wolverhampton W 20 1
2010–11 Wolverhampton W 15 1
2011–12 Wolverhampton W 26 3
2012–13 Wolverhampton W 24 2
2013–14 Wolverhampton W 30 9
2014–15 Wolverhampton W 41 6
2015–16 Wolverhampton W 29 5
2016–17 Wolverhampton W 44 10 **283 41**

ENOBAKHARE, Bright (F) **20 0**
H: 6 0 W: 12 06 b. 8-2-98
2015–16 Wolverhampton W 7 0
2016–17 Wolverhampton W 13 0 **20 0**

EVANS, Lee (M) **94 7**
H: 6 1 W: 13 12 b.Newport 24-7-94
Internationals: Wales U21.
2012–13 Wolverhampton W 0 0
2013–14 Wolverhampton W 26 2
2014–15 Wolverhampton W 18 1
2015–16 Wolverhampton W 0 0
2015–16 *Bradford C* 35 4 **35 4**
2016–17 Wolverhampton W 15 0 **59 3**

FLATT, Jonathan (G) **0 0**
H: 6 1 W: 13 12 b.Wolverhampton 12-9-94
2013–14 Wolverhampton W 0 0
2014–15 Wolverhampton W 0 0
2014–15 *Chesterfield* 0 0
2015–16 Wolverhampton W 0 0
2015–16 *Cheltenham T* 0 0
2016–17 Wolverhampton W 0 0

GLADON, Paul (F) **113 36**
H: 6 2 W: 13 01 b.Haarlem 18-3-92
2010–11 Sparta Rotterdam 2 0
2011–12 Sparta Rotterdam 1 0
2012–13 Sparta Rotterdam 9 0
2013–14 Sparta Rotterdam 0 0
2013–14 *Dordrecht* 36 17 **36 17**
2014–15 Sparta Rotterdam 36 13 **48 13**
2015–16 Heracles 24 4
2016–17 Heracles 3 2 **27 6**
2016–17 Wolverhampton W 2 0 **2 0**

GRAHAM, Jordan (M) **21 1**
H: 6 0 W: 10 10 b.Coventry 5-3-95
Internationals: England U16, U17.
2011–12 Aston Villa 0 0
2012–13 Aston Villa 0 0
2013–14 Aston Villa 0 0
2013–14 *Ipswich T* 2 0 **2 0**
2013–14 *Bradford C* 1 0 **1 0**
2014–15 Wolverhampton W 0 0
2015–16 Wolverhampton W 11 1
2015–16 *Oxford U* 5 0 **5 0**
2016–17 Wolverhampton W 2 0 **13 1**

HAUSE, Kortney (D) **103 5**
H: 6 2 W: 13 03 b.Goodmayes 16-7-95
Internationals: England U20, U21.
2012–13 Wycombe W 9 1
2013–14 Wycombe W 14 1 **23 2**
2013–14 Wolverhampton W 0 0
2014–15 Wolverhampton W 17 0
2014–15 *Gillingham* 14 1 **14 1**
2015–16 Wolverhampton W 25 0
2016–17 Wolverhampton W 24 2 **66 2**

HELDER COSTA, Wander (M) **66 13**
H: 5 10 W: 11 07 b.Luanda 12-1-94
Internationals: Portugal U16, U17, U18, U19, U20, U21, Full caps.
2013–14 Benfica 0 0
2014–15 Benfica 0 0
2014–15 *Deportivo La Coruna* 6 0 **6 0**
2015–16 Benfica 0 0
2015–16 *Monaco* 25 3 **25 3**
2016–17 Benfica 0 0
On loan from Benfica.
2016–17 Wolverhampton W 35 10 **35 10**

HENRY, James (M) **311 45**
H: 6 1 W: 11 11 b.Reading 10-6-89
Internationals: Scotland U16, U19. England U18, U19.
2006–07 Reading 0 0
2006–07 *Nottingham F* 1 0 **1 0**
2007–08 Reading 0 0
2007–08 *Bournemouth* 11 4 **11 4**
2007–08 *Norwich C* 3 0 **3 0**
2008–09 Reading 7 0
2008–09 *Millwall* 16 3
2009–10 Reading 3 0 **10 0**
2009–10 *Millwall* 9 5
2010–11 Millwall 42 5
2011–12 Millwall 39 0
2012–13 Millwall 35 5
2013–14 Millwall 5 0 **146 18**
2013–14 Wolverhampton W 32 10
2014–15 Wolverhampton W 37 5
2015–16 Wolverhampton W 39 7
2016–17 Wolverhampton W 2 0 **110 22**
2016–17 *Bolton W* 30 1 **30 1**

HUNTE, Connor (M) **5 1**
H: 5 10 W: 10 08 b.London 12-9-96
Internationals: England U16, U17.
2014–15 Wolverhampton W 0 0
2015–16 Wolverhampton W 2 0
2016–17 Wolverhampton W 0 0 **2 0**
2016–17 *Stevenage* 3 1 **3 1**

IKEME, Carl (G) **253 0**
H: 6 2 W: 13 09 b.Sutton Coldfield 8-6-86
Internationals: Nigeria Full caps.
2005–06 Wolverhampton W 0 0
2005–06 *Stockport Co* 9 0 **9 0**
2006–07 Wolverhampton W 1 0
2007–08 Wolverhampton W 0 0
2008–09 Wolverhampton W 12 0
2009–10 Wolverhampton W 0 0
2009–10 *Charlton Ath* 4 0 **4 0**
2009–10 *Sheffield U* 2 0 **2 0**
2009–10 *QPR* 17 0 **17 0**
2010–11 Wolverhampton W 0 0
2010–11 *Leicester C* 5 0 **5 0**
2011–12 Wolverhampton W 1 0
2011–12 *Middlesbrough* 10 0 **10 0**
2011–12 *Doncaster R* 15 0 **15 0**
2012–13 Wolverhampton W 38 0
2013–14 Wolverhampton W 41 0
2014–15 Wolverhampton W 33 0
2015–16 Wolverhampton W 34 0
2016–17 Wolverhampton W 31 0 **191 0**

IORFA, Dominic (D) **91 0**
H: 6 2 W: 12 04 b.Southend-on-Sea 24-6-95
Internationals: England U18, U20, U21.
2013–14 Wolverhampton W 0 0
2013–14 *Shrewsbury T* 7 0 **7 0**
2014–15 Wolverhampton W 20 0
2015–16 Wolverhampton W 42 0
2016–17 Wolverhampton W 22 0 **84 0**

IVAN CAVALEIRO, Ricardo (M) **85 9**
H: 5 9 W: 11 07 b.Vialonga 18-10-93
Internationals: Portugal U17, U18, U19, U20, U21, Full caps.
2012–13 Benfica 0 0
2013–14 Benfica 8 0
2014–15 Benfica 0 0 **8 0**
2014–15 *Deportivo La Coruna* 34 3 **34 3**
2015–16 Monaco 12 1 **12 1**
2016–17 Wolverhampton W 31 5 **31 5**

JOAO TEIXEIRA, Brito (M) **22 3**
H: 5 10 W: 10 10 b.Amora 6-2-94
Internationals: Portugal U16, U17, U18, U19, U20, U21.
2012–13 Benfica 0 0
2013–14 Benfica 0 0
2014–15 Benfica 0 0
2015–16 Benfica 0 0
2015–16 *Vitoria de Guimaraes* 5 1 **5 1**
2016–17 Benfica 0 0
On loan from Benfica.
2016–17 Wolverhampton W 17 2 **17 2**

JOHN, Ola (F) **150 16**
H: 5 11 W: 12 08 b.Zwedru 19-5-92
Internationals: Netherlands U17, U19, U21, Full caps.
2010–11 FC Twente 13 1
2011–12 FC Twente 33 8 **46 9**
2012–13 Benfica 22 0
2013–14 Benfica 5 0
2013–14 *Hamburg* 8 0 **8 0**
2014–15 Benfica 26 3
2015–16 Benfica 2 0
2015–16 *Reading* 28 4 **28 4**
2016–17 Benfica 0 0 **55 3**
On loan from Benfica.
2016–17 Wolverhampton W 2 0 **2 0**
2016–17 *Deportivo La Coruna* 11 0 **11 0**

JOHNSON, Connor (D) **0 0**
b.Kettering 10-3-98
2016–17 Wolverhampton W 0 0

LONERGAN, Andrew (G) **339 1**
H: 6 4 W: 13 02 b.Preston 19-10-83
Internationals: Republic of Ireland U16. England U20.
2000–01 Preston NE 1 0
2001–02 Preston NE 0 0
2002–03 Preston NE 0 0
2002–03 *Darlington* 2 0 **2 0**
2003–04 Preston NE 8 0
2004–05 Preston NE 23 1
2005–06 Preston NE 0 0
2005–06 *Wycombe W* 2 0 **2 0**
2006–07 Preston NE 13 0
2006–07 *Swindon T* 1 0 **1 0**
2007–08 Preston NE 43 0
2008–09 Preston NE 46 0
2009–10 Preston NE 45 0
2010–11 Preston NE 29 0 **208 1**
2011–12 Leeds U 35 0 **35 0**
2012–13 Bolton W 5 0
2013–14 Bolton W 17 0
2014–15 Bolton W 29 0 **51 0**
2015–16 Fulham 29 0 **29 0**
2016–17 Wolverhampton W 11 0 **11 0**

MARSHALL, Ben (F) 294 35
H: 5 11 W: 11 13 b.Salford 29-3-91
Internationals: England U21.

2009–10	Stoke C	0	0		
2009–10	*Northampton T*	15	2	**15**	**2**
2009–10	*Cheltenham T*	6	2	**6**	**2**
2009–10	*Carlisle U*	20	3		
2010–11	Stoke C	0	0		
2010–11	*Carlisle U*	33	3	**53**	**6**
2011–12	Stoke C	0	0		
2011–12	*Sheffield W*	22	5	**22**	**5**
2011–12	Leicester C	16	3		
2012–13	Leicester C	40	4		
2013–14	Leicester C	0	0	**56**	**7**
2013–14	Blackburn R	18	2		
2014–15	Blackburn R	42	6		
2015–16	Blackburn R	44	2		
2016–17	Blackburn R	22	1	**126**	**11**
2016–17	Wolverhampton W	16	2	**16**	**2**

MASON, Joe (F) 213 48
H: 5 9 W: 11 11 b.Plymouth 13-5-91
Internationals: Republic of Ireland U18, U19, U21.

2009–10	Plymouth Arg	19	3		
2010–11	Plymouth Arg	34	7	**53**	**10**
2011–12	Cardiff C	39	9		
2012–13	Cardiff C	28	6		
2013–14	Cardiff C	0	0		
2013–14	*Bolton W*	16	6		
2014–15	Cardiff C	7	1		
2014–15	*Bolton W*	12	4	**28**	**10**
2015–16	Cardiff C	23	6	**97**	**22**
2015–16	Wolverhampton W	16	3		
2016–17	Wolverhampton W	19	3	**35**	**6**

ONIANGUE, Prince (D) 237 36
H: 6 3 W: 12 04 b.Paris 4-11-88
Internationals: Congo Full caps.

2008–09	Rennes	5	0		
2009–10	Rennes	0	0	**5**	**0**
2009–10	*Angers*	30	1	**30**	**1**
2010–11	Tours	37	3		
2011–12	Tours	19	1		
2012–13	Tours	28	9	**84**	**13**
2013–14	Reims	35	10		
2014–15	Reims	32	3		
2015–16	Reims	27	4	**94**	**17**
2016–17	Wolverhampton W	10	2	**10**	**2**
2016–17	*Bastia*	14	3	**14**	**3**

PRICE, Jack (M) 103 2
H: 6 3 W: 13 10 b.Shrewsbury 19-12-92

2011–12	Wolverhampton W	0	0		
2012–13	Wolverhampton W	0	0		
2013–14	Wolverhampton W	26	0		
2014–15	Wolverhampton W	23	1		
2014–15	*Yeovil T*	6	0	**6**	**0**
2014–15	*Leyton Orient*	5	0	**5**	**0**
2015–16	Wolverhampton W	24	1		
2016–17	Wolverhampton W	19	0	**92**	**2**

RANDALL, Will (M) 11 0
H: 5 11 W: 10 03 b.Swindon 2-5-97

2013–14	Swindon T	1	0		
2014–15	Swindon T	4	0		
2015–16	Swindon T	4	0	**9**	**0**
2015–16	Wolverhampton W	0	0		
2016–17	Wolverhampton W	0	0		
2016–17	*Walsall*	2	0	**2**	**0**

RONAN, Connor (M) 4 0
H: 5 8 W: 11 00 b.Rochdale 6-3-98
Internationals: England U17. Republic of Ireland U17, U19.

2015–16	Wolverhampton W	0	0		
2016–17	Wolverhampton W	4	0	**4**	**0**

RUDDY, Jack (G) 1 0
H: 6 1 W: 13 01 b.Glasgow 18-5-97
Internationals: Scotland U21.

2014–15	Bury	0	0		
2015–16	Bury	1	0		
2016–17	Bury	0	0	**1**	**0**
2016–17	Wolverhampton W	0	0		

SAISS, Romain (M) 181 10
H: 6 3 W: 12 00 b.Bourg-de-Peage 26-3-90
Internationals: Morocco Full caps.

2010–11	Valence	13	4	**13**	**4**
2011–12	Clermont	17	1		
2012–13	Clermont	31	0	**48**	**1**
2013–14	Le Havre	27	1		
2014–15	Le Havre	34	2	**61**	**3**
2015–16	Angers	35	2	**35**	**2**
2016–17	Wolverhampton W	24	0	**24**	**0**

SAVILLE, George (M) 112 10
H: 5 9 W: 11 07 b.Camberley 1-6-93

2010–11	Chelsea	0	0		
2011–12	Chelsea	0	0		
2012–13	Chelsea	0	0		
2012–13	*Millwall*	3	0		
2013–14	Chelsea	0	0		
2013–14	*Brentford*	40	3	**40**	**3**
2014–15	Wolverhampton W	7	0		
2014–15	*Bristol C*	7	1	**7**	**1**
2015–16	Wolverhampton W	19	5		
2015–16	*Millwall*	12	0	**15**	**0**
2016–17	Wolverhampton W	24	1	**50**	**6**

SILVIO, Sa Pereira (D) 140 3
H: 5 10 W: 11 05 b.Braganca 29-9-87
Internationals: Portugal U19, U23, Full caps.

2007–08	Odivelas	31	0	**31**	**0**
2008–09	Rio Ave	18	0		
2009–10	Rio Ave	27	0	**45**	**0**
2010–11	Braga	20	1	**20**	**1**
2011–12	Atletico Madrid	9	0		
2012–13	Atletico Madrid	1	0		
2012–13	*Deportivo La Coruna*	17	2	**17**	**2**
2013–14	Atletico Madrid	0	0		
2013–14	*Benfica*	8	0		
2014–15	Atletico Madrid	0	0		
2014–15	*Benfica*	1	0		
2015–16	Atletico Madrid	0	0	**10**	**0**
2015–16	*Benfica*	4	0	**13**	**0**
2016–17	Wolverhampton W	4	0	**4**	**0**

WALLACE, Jed (M) 156 31
H: 5 10 W: 10 12 b.Reading 15-12-93
Internationals: England U19.

2011–12	Portsmouth	0	0		
2012–13	Portsmouth	22	6		
2013–14	Portsmouth	44	7		
2014–15	Portsmouth	44	14	**110**	**27**
2015–16	Wolverhampton W	9	0		
2015–16	*Millwall*	12	1		
2016–17	Wolverhampton W	9	0	**18**	**0**
2016–17	*Millwall*	16	3	**28**	**4**

WHITE, Morgan (M) 7 0
b. 27-1-00
Internationals: England U16, U17.

2016–17	Wolverhampton W	7	0	**7**	**0**

WILLIAMSON, Mike (D) 338 14
H: 6 4 W: 13 03 b.Stoke 8-11-83

2001–02	Torquay U	3	0		
2001–02	Southampton	0	0		
2002–03	Southampton	0	0		
2003–04	Southampton	0	0		
2003–04	*Torquay U*	11	0	**14**	**0**
2003–04	*Doncaster R*	0	0		
2004–05	Southampton	0	0		
2004–05	*Wycombe W*	37	2		
2005–06	Wycombe W	39	5		
2006–07	Wycombe W	33	1		
2007–08	Wycombe W	12	0		
2008–09	Wycombe W	22	3	**143**	**11**
2008–09	Watford	17	1		
2009–10	Watford	4	1	**21**	**2**
2009–10	Portsmouth	0	0		
2009–10	Newcastle U	16	0		
2010–11	Newcastle U	29	0		
2011–12	Newcastle U	22	0		
2012–13	Newcastle U	19	0		
2013–14	Newcastle U	33	0		
2014–15	Newcastle U	31	1		
2015–16	Newcastle U	0	0	**150**	**1**
2015–16	Wolverhampton W	5	0		
2016–17	Wolverhampton W	5	0	**10**	**0**

WILSON, Donovan (F) 1 0
b.Yate 14-3-97

2014–15	Wolverhampton W	0	0		
2015–16	Wolverhampton W	0	0		
2016–17	Wolverhampton W	1	0	**1**	**0**

Players retained or with offer of contract
Allan, Jordan Scott; Armstrong, Daniel Charles; Beasley, Harry Alexander; Breslin, Anthony Patrick; Carnat, Nicolae; Ennis, Niall Nathan Michael; Finnie, Ross Steven; Gibbs-White, Morgan Anthony; Goodliffe, Ben David; Harris-Sealy, Andrew Jay; Hayden, Aaron Edward-George; Herc, Christian; John, Cameron Bradley; Leak, Ryan David; Levingston, Conor Thomas; McKenna, Daniel; Nazon, Duckens; Neves, Abreu Cavaleiro Ivan Ricardo; Odoffin, Hakeem; Rainey, Ryan Gavin; Randall-Hurren, William; Simpson, Aaron; Zyro, Michal.

Scholars
Ball, Brandon Levi; Bexton, Thomas; Brown, Rory Francis; Carr, Bradley Paul; Giles, Ryan John; Hesson, Joshua Scott; Moan, Dominic; Osbourne, Adam; Phillips, Sam; Rehman, Akeal; Sanderson, Dion Dannie Leonard; Sibley, Michael Robert; Sinclair, Nyeko; Watt, Elliot William; Whittingham, Joel Cameron.

WYCOMBE W (91)

AKINFENWA, Adebayo (F) 510 160
H: 5 11 W: 13 07 b.Nigeria 10-5-82

2001	Atlantas	19	4		
2002	Atlantas	4	1	**23**	**5**

From Barry T

2003–04	Boston U	3	0	**3**	**0**
2003–04	Leyton Orient	1	0	**1**	**0**
2003–04	Rushden & D	0	0		
2003–04	Doncaster R	9	4	**9**	**4**
2004–05	Torquay U	37	14	**37**	**14**
2005–06	Swansea C	34	9		
2006–07	Swansea C	25	5		
2007–08	Swansea C	0	0	**59**	**14**
2007–08	Millwall	7	0	**7**	**0**
2007–08	Northampton T	15	7		
2008–09	Northampton T	33	13		
2009–10	Northampton T	40	17		
2010–11	Gillingham	44	11		
2011–12	Northampton T	39	18		
2012–13	Northampton T	41	16	**168**	**71**
2013–14	Gillingham	34	10	**78**	**21**
2014–15	AFC Wimbledon	45	13		
2015–16	AFC Wimbledon	38	6	**83**	**19**
2016–17	Wycombe W	42	12	**42**	**12**

BEAN, Marcus (M) 404 25
H: 5 11 W: 11 06 b.Hammersmith 2-11-84
Internationals: Jamaica Full caps.

2002–03	QPR	7	0		
2003–04	QPR	31	1		
2004–05	QPR	20	1		
2004–05	*Swansea C*	8	0		
2005–06	QPR	9	0	**67**	**2**
2005–06	*Swansea C*	9	1	**17**	**1**
2005–06	Blackpool	17	1		
2006–07	Blackpool	6	0		
2007–08	Blackpool	0	0	**23**	**1**
2007–08	*Rotherham U*	12	1	**12**	**1**
2008–09	Brentford	44	9		
2009–10	Brentford	31	0		
2010–11	Brentford	37	3		
2011–12	Brentford	32	2	**144**	**14**
2012–13	Colchester U	31	0		
2013–14	Colchester U	35	5		
2014–15	Colchester U	3	0	**69**	**5**
2014–15	*Portsmouth*	6	1	**6**	**1**
2014–15	Wycombe W	17	0		
2015–16	Wycombe W	30	0		
2016–17	Wycombe W	19	0	**66**	**0**

BLOOMFIELD, Matt (M) 379 31
H: 5 9 W: 11 00 b.Felixstowe 8-2-84
Internationals: England U19.

2001–02	Ipswich T	0	0		
2002–03	Ipswich T	0	0		
2003–04	Ipswich T	0	0		
2003–04	Wycombe W	12	1		
2004–05	Wycombe W	26	2		
2005–06	Wycombe W	39	5		
2006–07	Wycombe W	41	4		
2007–08	Wycombe W	35	4		
2008–09	Wycombe W	20	0		
2009–10	Wycombe W	14	2		
2010–11	Wycombe W	34	3		
2011–12	Wycombe W	31	2		
2012–13	Wycombe W	2	1		
2013–14	Wycombe W	32	0		
2014–15	Wycombe W	33	1		
2015–16	Wycombe W	27	1		
2016–17	Wycombe W	33	5	**379**	**31**

BROWN, Scott (G) 314 0
H: 6 2 W: 13 01 b.Wolverhampton 26-4-85
From Welshpool T

2003–04	Bristol C	0	0		
2004–05	Cheltenham T	0	0		
2005–06	Cheltenham T	1	0		
2006–07	Cheltenham T	11	0		
2007–08	Cheltenham T	0	0		
2008–09	Cheltenham T	35	0		

2009–10 Cheltenham T 46 0
2010–11 Cheltenham T 46 0
2011–12 Cheltenham T 22 0
2012–13 Cheltenham T 46 0
2013–14 Cheltenham T 45 0
2014–15 Aberdeen 25 0
2015–16 Aberdeen 13 0 **38 0**
2016–17 Wycombe W 3 0 **3 0**
2016–17 *Cheltenham T* 21 0 **273 0**

COWAN-HALL, Paris (F) 133 18
H: 5 8 W: 11 08 b.Portsmouth 5-10-90
2008–09 Portsmouth 0 0
2009–10 Portsmouth 0 0
2009–10 *Grimsby T* 3 0 **3 0**
2010–11 Portsmouth 0 0
2010–11 Scunthorpe U 1 0 **1 0**
2012–13 Plymouth Arg 40 3 **40 3**
2013–14 Wycombe W 25 4
2014–15 Wycombe W 20 6
2014–15 Millwall 5 0
2015–16 Millwall 3 0 **8 0**
2015–16 *Bristol R* 3 0 **3 0**
2015–16 *Wycombe W* 5 1
2016–17 Wycombe W 28 4 **78 15**

DE HAVILLAND, Will (D) 16 0
H: 6 0 W: 11 00 b.Huntingdon 8-11-94
2013–14 Millwall 0 0
2014–15 Sheffield W 0 0
2015–16 Sheffield W 0 0
2016–17 Wycombe W 16 0 **16 0**

FREEMAN, Nick (M) 14 0
b. 7-11-95
From Histon, Hemel Hempstead T, Biggleswade T.
2016–17 Wycombe W 14 0 **14 0**

GAPE, Dominic (M) 33 1
H: 5 11 W: 10 13 b.Southampton 9-9-94
2012–13 Southampton 0 0
2013–14 Southampton 0 0
2014–15 Southampton 1 0
2015–16 Southampton 0 0
2016–17 Southampton 0 0 **1 0**
2016–17 Wycombe W 32 1 **32 1**

HARRIMAN, Michael (D) 174 9
H: 5 6 W: 11 10 b.Chichester 23-10-92
Internationals: Republic of Ireland U18, U19, U21.
2010–11 QPR 0 0
2011–12 QPR 1 0
2012–13 QPR 1 0
2012–13 *Wycombe W* 20 0
2013–14 QPR 0 0
2013–14 *Gillingham* 34 1 **34 1**
2014–15 QPR 0 0 **2 0**
2014–15 *Luton T* 35 1 **35 1**
2015–16 Wycombe W 45 7
2016–17 Wycombe W 38 0 **103 7**

HAYES, Paul (F) 517 114
H: 6 0 W: 12 12 b.Dagenham 20-9-83
2002–03 Scunthorpe U 18 8
2003–04 Scunthorpe U 35 2
2004–05 Scunthorpe U 46 18
2005–06 Barnsley 45 6
2006–07 Barnsley 30 5
2006–07 *Huddersfield T* 4 1 **4 1**
2007–08 Scunthorpe U 40 8
2008–09 Scunthorpe U 44 17
2009–10 Scunthorpe U 45 9
2010–11 Preston NE 23 2 **23 2**
2010–11 *Barnsley* 7 0 **82 11**
2011–12 Charlton Ath 19 3 **19 3**
2011–12 *Wycombe W* 6 6
2012–13 Brentford 23 4
2012–13 *Crawley T* 11 2 **11 2**
2013–14 Brentford 0 0 **23 4**
2013–14 *Plymouth Arg* 6 0 **6 0**
2013–14 Scunthorpe U 16 4 **244 66**
2014–15 Wycombe W 39 12
2015–16 Wycombe W 37 4
2016–17 Wycombe W 23 3 **105 25**

JACOBSON, Joe (D) 347 18
H: 5 11 W: 12 06 b.Cardiff 17-11-86
Internationals: Wales U21.
2005–06 Cardiff C 1 0
2006–07 Cardiff C 0 0 **1 0**
2006–07 *Accrington S* 6 1
2006–07 *Bristol R* 11 0
2007–08 Bristol R 40 1
2008–09 Bristol R 22 0 **73 1**
2009–10 Oldham Ath 15 0
2010–11 Oldham Ath 1 0 **16 0**
2010–11 Accrington S 26 2 **32 3**
2011–12 Shrewsbury T 39 1
2012–13 Shrewsbury T 30 2
2013–14 Shrewsbury T 41 4 **110 7**
2014–15 Wycombe W 42 3
2015–16 Wycombe W 34 1
2016–17 Wycombe W 39 3 **115 7**

JOMBATI, Sido (D) 210 7
H: 6 0 W: 11 11 b.Lisbon 20-8-87
2011–12 Cheltenham T 36 2
2012–13 Cheltenham T 37 1
2013–14 Cheltenham T 43 1 **116 4**
2014–15 Wycombe W 35 0
2015–16 Wycombe W 34 1
2016–17 Wycombe W 25 2 **94 3**

KASHKET, Scott (M) 37 11
H: 5 9 W: 10 06 b.London 6-7-95
2014–15 Leyton Orient 1 0
2015–16 Leyton Orient 15 1
2016–17 Leyton Orient 0 0 **16 1**
2016–17 Wycombe W 21 10 **21 10**

McGINN, Stephen (M) 203 13
H: 5 9 W: 10 01 b.Glasgow 2-12-88
Internationals: Scotland U19, U21.
2006–07 St Mirren 4 1
2007–08 St Mirren 25 2
2008–09 St Mirren 26 1
2009–10 St Mirren 18 3 **73 7**
2009–10 Watford 9 0
2010–11 Watford 29 2
2011–12 Watford 0 0
2012–13 Watford 0 0 **38 2**
2012–13 Shrewsbury T 18 2 **18 2**
2013–14 Sheffield U 30 0
2014–15 Sheffield U 0 0 **30 0**
2014–15 *Dundee* 13 1 **13 1**
2015–16 Wycombe W 26 1
2016–17 Wycombe W 5 0 **31 1**
Transferred to St Mirren, January 2017.

MULLER, Max (D) 29 1
b. 16-5-94
2013–14 SV Sandhausen 0 0
2014–15 SV Sandhausen 0 0
2015–16 Austria Salzburg 20 1 **20 1**
2016–17 Wycombe W 9 0 **9 0**

O'NIEN, Luke (M) 67 8
b. 21-11-94
2013–14 Watford 1 0
2014–15 Watford 0 0 **1 0**
2015–16 Wycombe W 35 5
2016–17 Wycombe W 31 3 **66 8**

PIERRE, Aaron (D) 129 9
H: 6 1 W: 13 12 b.Southall 17-2-93
Internationals: Grenada Full caps.
2011–12 Brentford 0 0
2012–13 Brentford 0 0
2013–14 Brentford 0 0
2013–14 *Wycombe W* 8 1
2014–15 Wycombe W 42 4
2015–16 Wycombe W 40 2
2016–17 Wycombe W 39 2 **129 9**

RICHARDSON, Barry (G) 308 0
H: 6 1 W: 12 01 b.Willington Quay 5-8-69
1987–88 Sunderland 0 0
1988–89 Scunthorpe U 0 0
1989–90 Scarborough 24 0
1990–91 Scarborough 6 0 **30 0**
1991–92 Northampton T 27 0
1992–93 Northampton T 42 0
1993–94 Northampton T 27 0 **96 0**
1994–95 Preston NE 17 0
1995–96 Preston NE 3 0 **20 0**
1995–96 Lincoln C 34 0
1996–97 Lincoln C 36 0
1997–98 Lincoln C 26 0
1998–99 Lincoln C 13 0
1999–2000 Lincoln C 22 0
1999–2000 *Mansfield T* 6 0 **6 0**
1999–2000 *Sheffield W* 0 0
2000–01 Lincoln C 0 0 **131 0**
From Doncaster R.
2001–02 Halifax T 24 0 **24 0**
From Gainsborough T.
2003–04 Doncaster R 0 0
2004–05 Nottingham F 0 0
From Cheltenham T, Peterborough U.
2015–16 Wycombe W 1 0
2016–17 Wycombe W 0 0 **1 0**

ROWE, Daniel (D) 47 1
H: 6 2 W: 12 08 b.Middlesbrough 24-10-95
2012–13 Rotherham U 0 0
2013–14 Rotherham U 0 0
2013–14 *Wycombe W* 7 0
2014–15 Rotherham U 0 0
2014–15 *Wycombe W* 16 0
2015–16 Wycombe W 12 1
2016–17 Wycombe W 12 0 **47 1**

SAUNDERS, Sam (M) 260 43
H: 5 6 W: 11 04 b.Erith 29-8-83
2007–08 Dagenham & R 22 0
2008–09 Dagenham & R 40 14 **62 14**
2009–10 Brentford 26 1
2010–11 Brentford 21 2
2011–12 Brentford 37 10
2012–13 Brentford 31 3
2013–14 Brentford 17 5
2014–15 Brentford 5 2
2014–15 Wycombe W 11 2
2015–16 Brentford 25 3
2016–17 Brentford 8 0 **170 26**
2016–17 Wycombe W 17 1 **28 3**

SOUTHWELL, Dayle (F) 13 1
H: 5 11 W: 12 08 b.Grimsby 20-10-93
Internationals: England C.
From Grimsby T, Boston U.
2016–17 Wycombe W 13 1 **13 1**

STEWART, Anthony (D) 124 6
H: 5 10 W: 12 03 b.Brixton 18-9-92
2011–12 Wycombe W 4 0
2012–13 Wycombe W 19 1
2013–14 Wycombe W 33 3
2014–15 Crewe Alex 10 0 **10 0**
2015–16 Wycombe W 27 1
2016–17 Wycombe W 31 1 **114 6**

THOMPSON, Gary (M) 362 57
H: 6 0 W: 14 02 b.Kendal 24-11-80
2007–08 Morecambe 40 7 **40 7**
2008–09 Scunthorpe U 24 3
2009–10 Scunthorpe U 36 9
2010–11 Scunthorpe U 12 1
2011–12 Scunthorpe U 39 7 **111 20**
2012–13 Bradford C 41 6
2013–14 Bradford C 44 2 **85 8**
2014–15 Notts Co 41 12 **41 12**
2015–16 Wycombe W 43 7
2016–17 Wycombe W 42 3 **85 10**

WESTON, Myles (M) 327 30
H: 5 11 W: 12 05 b.Lewisham 12-3-88
Internationals: England U16, U17, U18, U19. Antigua and Barbuda Full caps.
2006–07 Charlton Ath 0 0
2006–07 *Notts Co* 4 0
2007–08 Notts Co 25 0
2008–09 Notts Co 44 3 **73 3**
2009–10 Brentford 40 8
2010–11 Brentford 42 3
2011–12 Brentford 26 1 **108 12**
2012–13 Gillingham 37 8
2013–14 Gillingham 39 2 **76 10**
2014–15 Southend U 34 2
2015–16 Southend U 17 0 **51 2**
2016–17 Wycombe W 19 3 **19 3**

WOOD, Sam (M) 316 19
H: 6 0 W: 11 05 b.Sidcup 9-8-86
2008–09 Brentford 40 1
2009–10 Brentford 43 2
2010–11 Brentford 20 1
2011–12 Brentford 5 0 **108 4**
2011–12 *Rotherham U* 26 1 **26 1**
2012–13 Wycombe W 35 3
2013–14 Wycombe W 43 2
2014–15 Wycombe W 44 5
2015–16 Wycombe W 28 2
2016–17 Wycombe W 32 2 **182 14**

Non-Contract
Ainsworth, Gareth; Richardson, Barry.

YEOVIL T (92)

BASSETT, Ollie (F) 2 0
b. 6-3-98
Internationals: Northern Ireland U19.
2015–16 Yeovil T 2 0
2016–17 Yeovil T 0 0 **2 0**

DICKSON, Ryan (M) 288 10
H: 5 10 W: 11 05 b.Saltash 14-12-86
2004–05 Plymouth Arg 3 0

2005–06 Plymouth Arg 0 0
2006–07 Plymouth Arg 2 0
2006–07 *Torquay U* 9 1 **9 1**
2007–08 Plymouth Arg 0 0 **5 0**
2007–08 Brentford 31 0
2008–09 Brentford 39 1
2009–10 Brentford 27 2 **97 3**
2010–11 Southampton 23 1
2011–12 Southampton 0 0
2011–12 *Yeovil T* 5 1
2011–12 *Leyton Orient* 9 0 **9 0**
2012–13 Southampton 0 0 **23 1**
2012–13 *Bradford C* 5 1 **5 1**
2013–14 Colchester U 32 0 **32 0**
2014–15 Crawley T 32 1 **32 1**
2015–16 Yeovil T 37 2
2016–17 Yeovil T 34 0 **76 3**

DOLAN, Matthew (M) 131 10
b.Hartlepool 11-2-93
2010–11 Middlesbrough 0 0
2011–12 Middlesbrough 0 0
2012–13 Middlesbrough 0 0
2012–13 *Yeovil T* 8 1
2013–14 Middlesbrough 0 0
2013–14 *Hartlepool U* 20 2
2013–14 *Bradford C* 11 0
2014–15 Bradford C 13 0 **24 0**
2014–15 *Hartlepool U* 2 0 **22 2**
2015–16 Yeovil T 39 3
2016–17 Yeovil T 38 4 **85 8**

EAVES, Tom (M) 132 20
H: 6 3 W: 13 07 b.Liverpool 14-1-92
2009–10 Oldham Ath 15 0
2010–11 Bolton W 0 0
2010–11 *Oldham Ath* 0 0 **15 0**
2011–12 Bolton W 0 0
2012–13 Bolton W 3 0
2012–13 *Bristol R* 16 7 **16 7**
2012–13 *Shrewsbury T* 10 6
2013–14 Bolton W 0 0
2013–14 *Rotherham U* 8 0 **8 0**
2013–14 *Shrewsbury T* 25 2 **35 8**
2014–15 Bolton W 1 0
2014–15 *Yeovil T* 5 0
2014–15 *Bury* 9 1 **9 1**
2015–16 Bolton W 0 0 **4 0**
2016–17 Yeovil T 40 4 **45 4**

EZEWELE, Josh (D) 0 0
From WBA.
2016–17 Yeovil T 0 0

GOODSHIP, Brandon (F) 18 1
b. 1-1-86
2013–14 Bournemouth 0 0
2014–15 Bournemouth 0 0
2015–16 Bournemouth 0 0
2015–16 *Yeovil T* 10 1
2016–17 Yeovil T 8 0 **18 1**

JAMES, Tom (D) 3 0
H: 5 11 W: 11 00 b.Leamington Spa 19-11-88
Internationals: Wales U19.
2013–14 Cardiff C 1 0
2014–15 Cardiff C 0 0
2015–16 Cardiff C 0 0
2016–17 Cardiff C 0 0 **1 0**
2016–17 Yeovil T 2 0 **2 0**

KHAN, Otis (M) 34 6
H: 5 9 W: 11 03 b.Ashton-under-Lyme 5-9-95
2013–14 Sheffield U 2 0
2014–15 Sheffield U 0 0
2015–16 Sheffield U 0 0 **2 0**
2015–16 Barnsley 3 0 **3 0**
2016–17 Yeovil T 29 6 **29 6**

KRYSIAK, Artur (G) 266 0
H: 6 1 W: 12 00 b.Lodz 11-8-89
Internationals: Poland U19.
2006–07 Birmingham C 0 0
2007–08 *Gretna* 4 0 **4 0**
2007–08 Birmingham C 0 0
2008–09 Birmingham C 0 0
2008–09 *Motherwell* 1 0 **1 0**
2008–09 *Swansea C* 2 0 **2 0**
2009–10 Birmingham C 0 0
2009–10 *Burton Alb* 38 0 **38 0**
2010–11 Exeter C 10 0
2011–12 Exeter C 38 0
2012–13 Exeter C 42 0
2013–14 Exeter C 37 0 **127 0**
2014–15 Yeovil T 15 0
2015–16 Yeovil T 38 0
2016–17 Yeovil T 41 0 **94 0**

LAWLESS, Alex (M) 90 5
H: 5 11 W: 10 08 b.Llwynupion 5-2-83
Internationals: Wales U19, U21.
2003–04 Fulham 0 0
2004–05 Fulham 0 0
2005–06 Torquay U 14 0 **14 0**
From Forest Green R, York C.
2014–15 Luton T 15 3
2015–16 Luton T 28 1 **43 4**
2016–17 Yeovil T 33 1 **33 1**

LEA, Joe (M) 0 0
From Southampton.
2016–17 Yeovil T 0 0

MADDISON, Johnny (G) 5 0
H: 6 0 W: 11 12 b.Chester le Street 4-9-94
2012–13 Crawley T 0 0
2013–14 Crawley T 0 0
2014–15 Crawley T 0 0
2015–16 Leicester C 0 0
2016–17 Yeovil T 5 0 **5 0**

McLEOD, Izale (F) 439 142
H: 6 1 W: 11 02 b.Birmingham 15-10-84
Internationals: England U21.
2002–03 Derby Co 29 3
2003–04 Derby Co 10 1 **39 4**
2003–04 *Sheffield U* 7 0 **7 0**
2004–05 Milton Keynes D 43 16
2005–06 Milton Keynes D 39 17
2006–07 Milton Keynes D 34 21
2007–08 Charlton Ath 18 1
2007–08 *Colchester U* 2 0 **2 0**
2008–09 Charlton Ath 2 0
2008–09 *Millwall* 7 2 **7 2**
2009–10 Charlton Ath 11 2
2009–10 *Peterborough U* 4 0 **4 0**
2010–11 Charlton Ath 0 0 **31 3**
2010–11 Barnet 29 14
2011–12 Barnet 44 18 **73 32**
2012–13 Portsmouth 24 10 **24 10**
2012–13 Milton Keynes D 13 1
2013–14 Milton Keynes D 36 7 **165 62**
2013–14 *Northampton T* 4 1 **4 1**
2014–15 Crawley T 42 19 **42 19**
2015–16 Notts Co 37 9 **37 9**
2016–17 Yeovil T 4 0 **4 0**

MUGABI, Bevis (D) 31 1
H: 6 2 W: 11 11 b.Harrow 1-5-95
From Southampton.
2016–17 Yeovil T 31 1 **31 1**

SMITH, Nathan (D) 296 4
H: 5 11 W: 12 00 b.Enfield 11-1-87
Internationals: Jamaica Full caps.
2007–08 Yeovil T 7 0
2008–09 Yeovil T 33 1
2009–10 Yeovil T 34 0
2010–11 Yeovil T 40 0
2011–12 Chesterfield 25 0
2012–13 Chesterfield 29 0
2013–14 Chesterfield 13 0 **67 0**
2014–15 Yeovil T 41 0
2015–16 Yeovil T 40 1
2016–17 Yeovil T 34 2 **229 4**

SOWUNMI, Omar (D) 16 1
H: 6 6 W: 14 09 b.Colchester 7-11-95
2015–16 Yeovil T 5 1
2016–17 Yeovil T 11 0 **16 1**

TOMLINSON, Joseph (D) 0 0
b. 9-6-00
2016–17 Yeovil T 0 0

WARD, Darren (D) 554 21
H: 6 3 W: 11 04 b.Harrow 13-9-78
1995–96 Watford 1 0
1996–97 Watford 7 0
1997–98 Watford 0 0
1998–99 Watford 1 0
1999–2000 Watford 9 1
1999–2000 *QPR* 14 0 **14 0**
2000–01 Watford 40 1
2001–02 Watford 1 0
2001–02 Millwall 14 0
2002–03 Millwall 39 1
2003–04 Millwall 46 3
2004–05 Millwall 43 0
2005–06 Crystal Palace 43 5
2006–07 Crystal Palace 20 0 **63 5**
2007–08 Wolverhampton W 30 0
2008–09 Wolverhampton W 1 0 **31 0**
2008–09 *Watford* 9 1 **68 3**
2008–09 *Charlton Ath* 16 0 **16 0**
2009–10 Millwall 31 1
2010–11 Millwall 31 1
2011–12 Millwall 30 0
2012–13 Millwall 1 0 **235 6**
2012–13 *Swindon T* 39 2
2013–14 Swindon T 36 0
2014–15 Swindon T 0 0 **75 2**
2014–15 *Crawley T* 18 1 **18 1**
2015–16 Yeovil T 18 1
2016–17 Yeovil T 16 3 **34 4**

ZOKO, Francois (F) 475 87
H: 6 0 W: 11 05 b.Daloa 13-9-83
Internationals: Ivory Coast U20, U23.
2001–02 Nancy 24 3
2002–03 Nancy 28 2
2003–04 Nancy 19 3 **71 8**
2004–05 Laval 27 7
2005–06 Laval 33 2 **60 9**
2006–07 Mons 23 4
2007–08 Mons 32 8 **55 12**
2008–09 Hacettepe 27 1 **27 1**
2009–10 Ostend 11 4 **11 4**
2010–11 Carlisle U 44 6
2011–12 Carlisle U 45 13
2012–13 Carlisle U 0 0 **89 19**
2012–13 Notts Co 38 7
2013–14 Notts Co 1 0 **39 7**
2013–14 Stevenage 33 10 **33 10**
2014–15 Blackpool 14 1 **14 1**
2014–15 *Bradford C* 16 1 **16 1**
2015–16 Yeovil T 25 7
2016–17 Yeovil T 35 8 **60 15**

Scholars
Akinuli, Paul Oluwarotimi; Cherrett, Bradley Frederick; Corbridge, Jayden Shaun Alan; Fripp, Charlie John; Gyebi, Jeremiah Boateng; Hilton-Jones, Jack Alexander; Ismail, Samyan Hassan; Iwyeh, Nwabudike Prince; MacFoy, Johnston Dion Thomas Nyake; McCann, Mitchell William; Nyman, Luis James Antonio; Rice-Lethaby, Jack Renauld; Tomlinson, Joseph William George; Warren, Arthur James Reuben Lewis.

ENGLISH LEAGUE PLAYERS – INDEX

NATIONAL LIST OF REFEREES FOR SEASON 2017–18

Adcock, JG (James) – Nottinghamshire
Atkinson, M (Martin) – West Yorkshire
Attwell, SB (Stuart) – Warwickshire
Backhouse, A (Anthony) – Cumbria
Bankes, P (Peter) – Merseyside
Bond, D (Darren) – Lancashire
Boyeson, C (Carl) – East Yorkshire
Breakspear, C (Charles) – Surrey
Brooks, J (John) – Leicestershire
Brown, M (Mark) – East Yorkshire
Busby, J (John) – Oxfordshire
Clark, R (Richard) – Northumberland
Coggins, A (Antony) – Oxfordshire
Collins, LM (Lee) – Surrey
Coote, D (David) – West Yorkshire
Coy, M (Martin) – County Durham
Davies, A (Andy) – Hampshire
Deadman, D (Darren) – Cambridgeshire
Dean, ML (Mike) – Merseyside
Drysdale, D (Darren) – Lincolnshire
Duncan, S (Scott) – Northumberland
East, R (Roger) – Wiltshire
Eltringham, G (Geoff) – Tyne & Wear
England, D (Darren) – South Yorkshire
Friend, KA (Kevin) – Leicestershire
Haines, A (Andy) – Tyne & Wear
Handley, D (Darren) – Lancashire
Harrington, T (Tony) – Cleveland
Haywood, M (Mark) – West Yorkshire
Heywood, M (Mark) – Cheshire
Hicks, C (Craig) – Surrey
Hooper, SA (Simon) – Wiltshire
Horwood, G (Graham) – Bedfordshire
Huxtable, B (Brett) – Devon
Ilderton, EL (Eddie) – Tyne & Wear
Johnson, K (Kevin) – Somerset
Jones, MJ (Michael) – Cheshire
Jones, RJ (Robert) – Merseyside
Joyce, R (Ross) – Cleveland
Kavanagh, C (Chris) – Lancashire
Kettle, TM (Trevor) – Leicestershire
Kinseley, N (Nick) – Essex
Langford, O (Oliver) – West Midlands
Lewis, RL (Rob) – Shropshire
Linington, JJ (James) – Isle of Wight
Madley, AJ (Andy) – West Yorkshire
Madley, RJ (Bobby) – West Yorkshire
Malone, BJ (Brendan) – Wiltshire
Marriner, AM (Andre) – West Midlands
Martin, S (Stephen) – Staffordshire
Mason, LS (Lee) – Lancashire
Miller, NS (Nigel) – County Durham
Moss, J (Jon) – West Yorkshire
Nield, T (Tom) – West Yorkshire
Oldham, S (Scott) – Lancashire
Oliver, M (Michael) – Northumberland
Pawson, CL (Craig) – South Yorkshire
Probert, LW (Lee) – Wiltshire
Robinson, T (Tim) – West Sussex
Salisbury, G (Graham) – Lancashire
Salisbury, M (Michael) – Lancashire
Sarginson, CD (Chris) – Staffordshire
Scott, GD (Graham) – Oxfordshire
Simpson, J (Jeremy) – Lancashire
Stockbridge, S (Seb) – Tyne & Wear
Stroud, KP (Keith) – Hampshire
Swabey, L (Lee) – Devon
Swarbrick, ND (Neil) – Lancashire
Taylor, A (Anthony) – Cheshire
Tierney, P Paul) – Lancashire
Toner, B (Ben) – Lancashire
Ward, GL (Gavin) – Surrey
Webb, D (David) – County Durham
Whitestone, D (Dean) – Northamptonshire
Woolmer, KA (Andy) – Northamptonshire
Yates, O (Ollie) – Staffordshire

ASSISTANT REFEREES

Akers, C (Chris) – South Yorkshire
Amey, JR (Justin) – Dorset
Amphlett, MJ (Marvyn) – Worcestershire
Aspinall, N (Natalie) – Lancashire
Atkin, R (Robert) – Lincolnshire
Avent, D (David) – Northamptonshire
Aylott, A (Andrew) – Bedfordshire
Barnard, N (Nicholas) – Cheshire
Bartlett, R (Richard) – Cheshire
Beck, S (Simon) – Bedfordshire
Bennett, S (Simon) – Staffordshire
Benton, DK (David) – South Yorkshire
Beswick, G (Gary) – County Durham
Betts, L (Lee) – Norfolk
Bickle, O (Oliver) – Derbyshire
Blunden, D (Darren) – Kent
Bristow, M (Matthew) – Manchester
Brown, S (Stephen) – Kent
Bryan, D (Dave) – Lincolnshire
Burt, S (Stuart) – Northamptonshire
Butler, S (Stuart) – Kent
Byrne, H (Helen) – Durham
Cann, D (Darren) – Norfolk
Cheosiaua, D-R (Dumitru-Ravel) – Worcestershire
Child, S (Stephen) – Kent
Clark, J (Joseph) – West Midlands
Clayton, A (Alan) – Cheshire
Clayton, S (Simon) – County Durham
Cobb, B (Ben) – Dorset
Collin, J (Jake) – Merseyside
Cook, D (Dan) – Hampshire
Cook, D (Daniel) – Essex
Cooper, IJ (Ian) – Kent
Cooper, N (Nicholas) – Suffolk
Cropp, B (Barry) – Lancashire
Crowhurst, L (Leigh) – Sussex
Crysell, A (Adam) – Northamptonshire
Cunliffe, Mark – Merseyside
Dabbs, R (Robert) – Dorset
Da Costa, A (Anthony) – Cambridgeshire
D'aguilar, M (Michael) – Staffordshire
Davies, N (Neil) – London
Degnarain, A (Ashvin) – London
Denton, MJ (Michael) – Lancashire
Dermott, P (Philip) – Lancashire
Derrien, M (Mark) – Dorset
Dudley, IA (Ian) – Nottinghamshire
Duncan, M (Mark) – Cheshire
Dwyer, M (Mark) – West Yorkshire
Eaton, D (Derek) – Gloucestershire
Eva, M (Matt) – Surrey
Farries, J (John) – Oxfordshire
Finch, S (Steven) – Suffolk
Fitch-Jackson, C (Carl) – Suffolk
Flynn, J (John) – Oxfordshire
Foley, MJ (Matt) – Hertfordshire
Ford, D (Declan) – Lincolnshire
Fox, A (Andrew) – Warwickshire
Freeman, L (Lee) – Yorkshire
Fyvie, G (Graeme) – Tyne & Wear
Ganfield, R (Ron) – Somerset
Garratt, A (Andy) – West Midlands
George, M (Mike) – Norfolk
Gooch, P (Peter) – Lancashire
Gordon, B (Barry) – County Durham
Graham, P (Paul) – Manchester
Gratton, D (Danny) – Staffordshire
Greenhalgh, N (Nick) – Lancashire

Greenwood, AH (Alf) – North Yorkshire
Griffiths, M (Mark) – West Midlands
Grunnill, W (Wayne) – East Yorkshire
Halliday, A (Andy) – North Yorkshire
Hanley, M (Michael) – Merseyside
Harty, T (Thomas) – West Midlands
Hatzidakis, C (Constantine) – Kent
Haycock, KW (Ken) – South Yorkshire
Hendley, AR (Andy) – West Midlands
Hilton, G (Gary) – Lancashire
Hobday, P (Paul) – West Midlands
Hodskinson, P (Paul) – Lancashire
Holmes, A (Adrian) – West Yorkshire
Hopkins, AJ (Adam) – Devon
Hopton, N (Nicholas) – Derbyshire
Howick, K (Kevin) – Oxfordshire
Howson, A (Akil) – Leicestershire
Hudson, S (Shaun) – Tyne & Wear
Hunt, J (Jonathan) – Merseyside
Husband, C (Christopher) – Worcestershire –
Hussin, I (Ian) – Merseyside
Hyde, RA (Robert) – Essex
Isherwood, C (Chris) – Lancashire
Jones, MT (Mark) – Nottinghamshire
Jones, M (Matthew) – Staffordshire
Kane, G (Graham) – East Sussex
Kelly, P (Paul) – Kent
Kendall, R (Richard) – Bedfordshire
Khan, A (Abbas) – East Midlands
Khatib, B (Billy) – County Durham
Kidd, C (Chris) – Oxfordshire
Kirkup, P (Peter) – Northamptonshire
Knapp, SC (Simon) – Bristol
Laver, AA (Andrew) – Hampshire
Leach, D (Daniel) – Oxfordshire
Ledger, S (Scott) – South Yorkshire
Lee, M (Matthew) – West Sussex
Lennard, H (Harry) – East Sussex
Lewis, S (Sam) – Bedfordshire
Liddle, G (Geoff) – County Durham
Long, S (Simon) – Cornwall
Lugg, N (Nigel) – Surrey
McDonough, M (Mick) – Northumberland
Mcgrath, M (Matt) – East Yorkshire
Mainwaring, J (James) – Lancashire
Marks, L (Louis) – Hampshire
Maskell, G (Garry) – London
Massey-Ellis, S (Sian) – West Midlands
Matthews, A (Adam) – Gloucestershire
Mellor, G (Gareth) – West Yorkshire
Mellor, JM (Mark) – Hertfordshire
Merchant, R (Rob) – Staffordshire
Meredith, S (Steven) – Nottinghamshire
Metcalfe, RL (Lee) – Lancashire
Moore, A (Anthony) – Manchester
Morris, K (Kevin) – Herefordshire
Mulraine, K (Kevin) – Cumbria
Newbold, AM (Andy) – Leicestershire
Newhouse, P (Paul) – County Durham
Nunn, A (Adam) – Wiltshire
Ogles, S (Samuel) – Hampshire
Parry, MJ (Matthew) – Merseyside
Pashley, A (Alix) – Derbyshire
Peart, T (Tony) – North Yorkshire
Perry, M (Marc) – West Midlands
Plane, S (Steven) – Worcestershire
Plowright, DP (David) – Nottinghamshire
Pottage, M (Mark) – Dorset
Powell, CI (Chris) – Dorset
Ramsey, T (Thomas) – Essex
Rashid, L (Lisa) – West Midlands
Rathbone, I (Ian) – Northamptonshire
Read, G (Gregory) – Surrey
Rees, P (Paul) – Somerset
Robathan, DM (Daniel) – Bedfordshire
Rushton, S (Steven) – Staffordshire
Russell, GR (Geoff) – Northamptonshire
Russell, M (Mark) – Somerset
Scholes, M (Mark) – Buckinghamshire
Sharp, N (Neil) – Cleveland
Shaw, S (Simon) – Gloucestershire
Siddall, I (Iain) – Manchester
Simpson, J (Joe) – Manchester
Slaughter, A (Ashley) – West Sussex
Smallwood, W (William) – Cheshire
Smart, E (Eddie) – West Midlands
Smedley, I (Ian) – Derbyshire
Smith, M (Michael) – Essex
Smith, N (Nigel) – Derbyshire
Smith, R (Rob) – Hertfordshire
Smith, W (Wade) – Cheshire
Strain, D (Darren) – Cheshire
Street, DR (Duncan) – West Yorkshire
Taylor, C (Craig) – West Midlands
Taylor, G (Grant) – Warwickshire
Thompson, PI (Paul) – Derbyshire
Tranter, A (Adrian) – Dorset
Treleaven, D (Dean) – West Sussex
Venamore, L (Lee) – Kent
Wade, C (Christopher) – Hampshire
Wade, S (Stephen) – East Yorkshire
Walchester, C (Callum) – Suffolk
Ward, C (Chris) – South Yorkshire
Warren, (George) – London
Waters, A (Adrian) – London
Webb, MP (Michael) – Surrey
West, R (Richard) – East Riding
Wigglesworth, RJ (Richard) – South Yorkshire
Wild, R (Richard) – Lancashire
Wilding, D (Darren) – Worcestershire
Wilkes, M (Matthew) – West Midlands
Williams, A (Andrew) – Middlesex
Wilson, J (James) – Cheshire
Wilson, M (Marc) – Cambridgeshire
Wood, T (Tim) – Gloucestershire
Yates, P (Paul) – Kent

MANAGERS – IN AND OUT 2016–17

JULY 2016

9 Stephen Robinson appointed manager of Oldham Ath.
22 Sam Allardyce leaves as manager of Sunderland to become manager of the England national team.
Steve Bruce resigns as manager of Hull C.
23 David Moyes appointed manager of Sunderland.
26 Steven Pressley resigns as manager of Fleetwood T.
29 Kenny Jackett sacked as manager of Wolverhampton W.
30 Walter Zenga appointed manager of Wolverhampton W.
Uwe Rosler appointed manager of Fleetwood T.

SEPTEMBER 2016

26 Andy Hessenthaler sacked as manager of Leyton Orient. Assistant manager Andy Edwards takes temporary charge.
27 Sam Allardyce leaves his post as manager of the England national team after only one game in charge over newspaper claims of inappropriate conduct. Gareth Southgate appointed interim manager.
Nigel Pearson suspended as manager of Derby Co. Assistant manager Chris Powell takes temporary charge.
28 Warren Feeney sacked as manager of Newport Co. First-team coaches Sean McCarthey and James Bittner take temporary charge.
29 Tony Mowbray resigns as manager of Coventry C. Assistant manager Mark Venus takes temporary charge.

OCTOBER 2016

2 Alberto Cavasin appointed manager of Leyton Orient.
3 Roberto di Matteo sacked as manager of Aston Villa. Assistant Steve Clarke takes temporary charge.
Francesco Guidolin sacked as manager of Swansea C. Bob Bradley appointed new manager.
4 Paul Trollope sacked as manager of Cardiff C.
5 Neil Warnock appointed manager of Cardiff C.
6 Micky Mellon leaves as manager of Shrewsbury T and takes over as manager at Tranmere R. Goalkeeping coach Danny Coyne takes temporary charge.
7 Graham Westley appointed manager of Newport Co.
8 Nigel Pearson leaves his post as manager of Derby Co by mutual consent. Chris Powell remains in temporary charge.
12 Steve McClaren appointed manager of Derby Co.
Steve Bruce appointed manager of Aston Villa.
14 Mike Phelan appointed full-time manager of Hull C after after being in temporary charge.
19 Alan Stubbs sacked as manager of Rotherham U. Fitness coach Paul Warne takes temporary charge.
21 Kenny Jackett appointed manager of Rotherham U.
23 Karl Robinson sacked as manager of Milton Keynes D. Head of coaching Richie Barker takes temporary charge.
24 Paul Hurst appointed manager of Shrewsbury T.
25 Walter Zenga sacked as manager of Wolverhampton W. First-team coach Rob Edwards takes temporary charge.
Gary Caldwell sacked as manager of Wigan Ath. Assistant manager Graham Barrow takes temporary charge.

NOVEMBER 2016

2 Warren Joyce appointed manager of Wigan Ath.
5 Jimmy Floyd Hasselbaink sacked as manager of QPR.
Paul Lambert appointed manager of Wolverhampton W.
11 Ian Holloway appointed manager of QPR.
14 Russell Slade sacked as manager of Charlton Athletic. Assistant manager Kevin Nugent takes temporary charge.
16 David Flitcroft sacked as manager of Bury. Head of football operations Chris Brass takes temporary charge.
23 Alberto Cavasin sacked as manager of Leyton Orient. Assistant manager Andy Edwards takes charge until the end of the season.
24 Karl Robinson appointed manager of Charlton Ath.
28 Kenny Jackett resigns as manager of Rotherham U. Coach Paul Warne takes temporary charge.
30 Gareth Southgate appointed manager of England.

DECEMBER 2016

1 Martin Allen leaves as manager of Barnet to become manager of National League Eastleigh. Development team coach Rossi Eames takes temporary charge.
2 Robbie Neilson leaves Hearts to become manager of Milton Keynes D.
14 Gary Rowett sacked as manager of Birmingham C. Gianfranco Zola appoined manager.
15 Chris Brass appointed manager of Bury.
21 Russell Slade appointed manager of Coventry C.
22 Alan Pardew sacked as manager of Crystal Palace.
23 Sam Allardyce appointed manager of Crystal Palace.
26 Bruno Ribeiro resigns as manager of Port Vale. Assistant manager Michael Brown takes temporary charge.
27 Bob Bradley sacked as manager of Swansea C. First team coaches Alan Curtis and Paul Williams take temporary charge.

JANUARY 2017

2 John Sheridan sacked as manager of Notts Co. Player-coach Alan Smith takes temporary charge.
3 Mike Phelan sacked as manger of Hull C.
Paul Clement appointed manager of Swansea C.
Justin Edinburgh sacked as manager of Gillingham. Ady Pennock appointed new manager.
5 Marco Silva appointed manager of Hull C.
8 Steve Davis sacked as manager of Crewe Alex. David Artell appointed new manager.
Danny Wilson sacked as manager of Chesterfield. Ritchie Humphreys takes temporary charge.
9 Robert Page sacked as manager of Northampton T. Paul Wilkinson takes temporary charge.

12 Stephen Robinson sacked as manager of Oldham Ath. John Sheridan appointed new manager.
Kevin Nolan appointed manager of Notts Co.
13 Justin Edinburgh appointed manager of Northampton T.
14 Philippe Montanier sacked as manager of Nottingham F. Academy manager Gary Brazil takes temporary charge.
15 Craig Hignett leaves as manager of Hartlepool U by mutual consent. Sam Collins takes temporary charge.
17 Gary Caldwell appointed manager of Chesterfield.
18 Dave Jones appointed manager of Hartlepool U.
29 Andy Edwards resigns as manager of Leyton Orient to take up a coaching role with the FA. Danny Webb appointed new manager.

FEBRUARY 2017

15 Lee Clark leaves Kilmarnock and replaces Chris Brass as manager of Bury.
Kevin Nugent appointed manager of Barnet.
21 Owen Coyle sacked as manager of Blackburn R.
22 Tony Mowbray appointed manager of Blackburn R.
23 Claudio Ranieri sacked as manager of Leicester C. Assistant manager Craig Shakespeare takes temporary charge.

MARCH 2017

5 Russell Slade sacked as manager of Coventry C.
6 Mark Robins appointed manager of Coventry C.
9 Graham Westley sacked as manager of Newport Co. First-team coach Mike Flynn takes temporary charge until the end of the season.
10 Alex Neil sacked as manager of Norwich C. First-team coach Alan Irvine takes temporary charge.
12 Craig Shakespeare appointed Leicester C manager until the end of the season.
Steve McClaren sacked as manager of Derby Co.
13 Warren Joyce sacked as manager of Wigan Ath. Assistant manager Graham Barrow takes temporary charge.
14 Gary Rowett appointed manager of Derby Co.
Mark Warburton appointed manager of Nottingham F.
16 Aitor Karanka sacked as manager of Middlesbrough. Assistant manager Steve Agnew takes charge until the end of the season.
30 Danny Webb resigns as manager of Leyton Orient. Assistant manager Omer Riza appointed manager until the end of the season.

APRIL 2017

5 Paul Warne appointed manager of Rotherham U after being in temporary charge.
10 Marcus Bignot sacked as manager of Grimsby T.
12 Russell Slade appointed manager of Grimsby T.
15 Kevin Nugent leaves as manager of Barnet by mutual consent. Development team coach Rossi Eames takes temporary charge.
17 Gianfranco Zola resigns as manager of Birmingham C.
18 Harry Redknapp appointed manager of Birmingham C until the end of the season.
24 Dave Jones leaves Hartlepool U by mutual consent. Matthew Bates takes temporary charge.

MAY 2017

3 Michael Brown appointed manager of Port Vale after being in temporary charge.
4 Dermot Drummy leaves as manager of Crawley T by mutual consent. Matt Harrold takes temporary charge.
5 Luke Williams leaves as manager of Swindon T by mutual consent.
9 Mike Flynn appointed manager of Newport Co after being in temporary charge.
19 Rossi Eames appointed manager of Barnet after being in temporary charge.
21 Walter Mazzarri sacked as manager of Watford.
22 David Moyes resigns as manager of Sunderland.
23 Sam Allardyce resigns as manager of Crystal Palace.
Harry Kewell appointed manager of Crawley T.
25 Marco Silva resigns as manager of Hull C.
Garry Monk resigns as manager of Leeds U.
Daniel Farke appointed manager of Norwich C.
26 Craig Harrison appointed manager of Hartlepool U.
27 Marco Silva appointed manager of Watford.
30 Paul Lambert sacked as manager of Wolverhampton W.
31 Nuno Espirito Santo appointed manager of Wolverhampton W.
Paul Cook leaves as manager of Portsmouth to become manager of Wigan Ath.

JUNE 2017

2 Kenny Jackett appointed manager of Portsmouth.
5 David Flitcroft appointed manager of Swindon T.
9 Leonid Slutsky appointed manager of Hull C.
Garry Monk appointed manager of Middlesbrough.
14 Claude Puel sacked as manager of Southampton.
Thomas Christiansen appointed manager of Leeds U.
20 Michael Appleton leaves as manager of Oxford U to become assistant manager at Leicester C.
23 Mauricio Pellegrino appointed manager of Southampton.
26 Frank de Boer appointed manager of Crystal Palace.
29 Simon Grayson leaves Preston NE to become manager of Sunderland.

JULY 2017

1 Pep Clotet appointed manager of Oxford U.
4 Alex Neil appointed manager of Preston NE.

TRANSFERS 2016–17

JUNE 2016	From	To	Fee in £
27 Ajose, Nicky	Swindon T	Charlton Ath	Undisclosed
29 Alessandra, Lewis	Rochdale	Hartlepool U	Free
20 Amond, Padraig	Grimsby T	Hartlepool U	Free
8 Andrew, Danny	Fleetwood T	Grimsby T	Free
27 Archibald-Henville, Troy	Carlisle U	Exeter C	Free
8 Arthur, Chris	Woking	Crawley T	Free
15 Azeez, Ade	AFC Wimbledon	Partick Thistle	Free
14 Baker, Carl	Milton Keynes D	Portsmouth	Free
23 Barnum-Bobb, Jazzi	Cardiff C	Newport Co	Free
18 Beckles, Omar	Aldershot T	Accrington S	Free
9 Bennett, Rhys	Rochdale	Mansfield T	Free
30 Berrett, James	York C	Grimsby T	Undisclosed
16 Bittner, James	Plymouth Arg	Newport Co	Free
23 Blyth, Jacob	Leicester C	Motherwell	Free
9 Boden, Scott	Newport Co	Inverness CT	Free
30 Bolarinwa, Tom	Sutton T	Grimsby T	Undisclosed
21 Boyce, Andrew	Scunthorpe U	Grimsby T	Free
21 Browne, Rhys	Aldershot T	Grimsby T	Undisclosed
2 Brownhill, Josh	Preston NE	Bristol C	Compensation
23 Burn, Dan	Fulham	Wigan Ath	Free
28 Butler, Dan	Torquay U	Newport Co	Free
15 Byrne, Mark	Newport Co	Gillingham	Free
24 Chambers, Ashley	Dagenham & R	Grimsby T	Free
17 Chapman, Aaron	Chesterfield	Accrington S	Free
25 Clark, Nicky	Rangers	Bury	Free
6 Clarke, Matt	Ipswich T	Portsmouth	Part-exchange
21 Clarke, Ryan	Northampton T	AFC Wimbledon	Free
24 Cobain, Jamie	Newcastle U	Kilmarnock	Free
7 Coleman, Joel	Oldham Ath	Huddersfield T	Undisclosed
15 Collin, Adam	Rotherham U	Notts Co	Free
20 Compton, Jack	Yeovil T	Newport Co	Free
9 Conlan, Luke	Burnley	Morecambe	Free
21 Cornell, David	Oldham Ath	Northampton T	Free
24 Coulibaly, Souleymane	Peterborough U	Kilmarnock	Free
21 Cuvelier, Florent	Sheffield U	Walsall	Free
29 Davies, Ben	Portsmouth	Grimsby T	Free
28 Dembele, Moussa	Fulham	Celtic	Undisclosed
23 Demetriou, Jason	Walsall	Southend U	Free
6 Deverdics, Nicky	Dover Ath	Hartlepool U	Free
6 Devitt, Jamie	Morecambe	Carlisle U	Free
29 Dickenson, Brennan	Gillingham	Colchester U	Free
28 Dickinson, Carl	Port Vale	Notts Co	Free
28 Digby, Paul	Barnsley	Ipswich T	Free
6 Doherty, Josh	Watford	Leyton Orient	Free
16 Donaldson, Ryan	Cambridge U	Plymouth Arg	Free
27 Downing, Paul	Walsall	Milton Keynes D	Free
29 Doyle, Eoin	Cardiff C	Preston NE	Undisclosed
17 Duckworth, Michael	Hartlepool U	Fleetwood T	Undisclosed
1 Duffy, Mark	Birmingham C	Sheffield U	Free
27 Duffy, Richard	Eastleigh	Notts Co	Free
23 Eastwood, Simon	Blackburn R	Oxford U	Free
24 Edwards, Gwion	Crawley T	Peterborough U	Undisclosed
24 Edwards, Joe	Colchester U	Walsall	Free
13 Elito, Medy	Newport Co	Cambridge U	Free
20 Elphick, Tommy	Bournemouth	Aston Villa	Undisclosed
25 Feeney, Liam	Bolton W	Blackburn R	Free
30 Forde, Anthony	Walsall	Rotherham U	Undisclosed
23 Fox, Andrew	Peterborough U	Stevenage	Free
28 Garrett, Tyler	Bolton W	Doncaster R	Free
24 Gilks, Matt	Burnley	Rangers	Free
7 Godden, Matt	Ebbsfleet U	Stevenage	Undisclosed
29 Goodwillie, David	Aberdeen	Plymouth Arg	Free
23 Graham, Danny	Sunderland	Blackburn R	Free
3 Gregory, David	Crystal Palace	Cambridge U	Free
14 Hall, Ben	Motherwell	Brighton & HA	Undisclosed
6 Hamilton, CJ	Sheffield U	Mansfield T	Free
14 Hanley, Raheem	Swansea C	Northampton T	Free
16 Hartley, Peter	Plymouth Arg	Bristol R	Free
3 Hemmings, Ashley	Dagenham & R	Mansfield T	Free
20 Hery, Bastien	Carlisle U	Accrington S	Free
17 Hill, Clint	QPR	Rangers	Free
23 Hoban, Pat	Oxford U	Mansfield T	Free
29 Hodson, Lee	Milton Keynes D	Rangers	Undisclosed
16 Holmes, Ricky	Northampton T	Charlton Ath	Undisclosed
29 Holt, Grant	Wigan Ath	Hibernian	Free
6 Hughes, Andrew	Newport Co	Peterborough U	Free
29 Hurst, Kevan	Southend U	Mansfield T	Free
1 Hussey, Chris	Bury	Sheffield U	Undisclosed
21 Hutchinson, Shaun	Fulham	Millwall	Free
17 Hyndman, Emerson	Fulham	Bournemouth	Compensation
27 Inman, Brad	Crewe Alex	Peterborough U	Free
24 Ismail, Zeli	Wolverhampton W	Bury	Free
28 Johnstone, Denny	Birmingham C	Colchester U	Undisclosed
24 Jones, Dan	Hartlepool U	Grimsby T	Free
14 Jones, Jamie	Preston NE	Stevenage	Free
24 Jones, Jordan	Middlesbrough	Kilmarnock	Free
22 Jones, Mike	Oldham Ath	Carlisle U	Free
19 Kay, Antony	Milton Keynes D	Bury	Free

10	Kennedy, Callum	AFC Wimbledon	Leyton Orient	Free
10	Kenny, Paddy	Rotherham U	Northampton T	Free
27	Kirkland, Chris	Preston NE	Bury	Free
16	Knott, Billy	Bradford C	Gillingham	Free
7	Labadie, Joss	Dagenham & R	Newport Co	Free
28	Lalkovic, Milan	Walsall	Portsmouth	Undisclosed
6	Lambe, Reggie	Mansfield T	Carlisle U	Free
29	Law, Nicky	Rangers	Bradford C	Free
24	Lee, Elliot	West Ham U	Barnsley	Undisclosed
30	Leitch, Robbie	Motherwell	Burnley	Compensation
3	Leitch-Smith, AJ	Port Vale	Shrewsbury T	Free
15	Lewis, Joe	Cardiff C	Aberdeen	Free
8	Lonergan, Andy	Fulham	Wolverhampton W	Undisclosed
29	Lynch, Joel	Huddersfield T	QPR	Undisclosed
24	Maher, Niall	Bolton W	Bury	Free
28	Mane, Sadio	Southampton	Liverpool	£34m
30	Mantom, Sam	Walsall	Scunthorpe U	Free
3	Maris, George	Barnsley	Cambridge U	Free
13	Marquis, John	Millwall	Doncaster R	Free
25	Martin, Aaron	Coventry C	Oxford U	Free
8	Massey, Gavin	Colchester U	Leyton Orient	Undisclosed
14	Matt, Jamille	Fleetwood T	Blackpool	Free
23	McAllister, Sean	Scunthorpe U	Grimsby T	Free
24	McCourt, Jak	Barnsley	Northampton T	Free
24	McEveley, Jay	Sheffield U	Ross Co	Free
24	McFadzean, Callum	Sheffield U	Kilmarnock	Free
16	McGahey, Harrison	Sheffield U	Rochdale	Free
22	McGinn, Paul	Dundee	Chesterfield	Free
3	McGivern, Ryan	Port Vale	Shrewsbury T	Free
23	McGlashan, Jermaine	Gillingham	Southend U	Free
6	McSheffrey, Gary	Scunthorpe U	Doncaster R	Free
23	Miller, Gary	Partick Thistle	Plymouth Arg	Free
17	Miller, Shaun	Morecambe	Carlisle U	Free
15	Mills, Zak	Boston U	Grimsby T	Free
2	Mingoia, Piero	Accrington S	Cambridge U	Free
29	Mitchell, Reece	Chelsea	Chesterfield	Free
21	Moncur, George	Colchester U	Barnsley	£500,000
17	Moore, Byron	Port Vale	Bristol R	Free
15	Morris, Josh	Bradford C	Scunthorpe U	Free
17	Mulraney, Jake	QPR	Inverness	Undisclosed
17	Novak, Lee	Birmingham C	Charlton Ath	Free
16	Nsiala, Aristote	Grimsby T	Hartlepool U	Undisclosed
17	O'Brien, Jim	Coventry C	Shrewsbury T	Free
25	O'Connor, Anthony	Burton Alb	Aberdeen	Free
29	O'Connor, Michael	Port Vale	Notts Co	Free
9	O'Neil, Gary	Norwich C	Bristol C	Free
7	Orrell, Jake	Chesterfield	Hartlepool U	Free
24	Osborne, Karleigh	Bristol C	Plymouth Arg	Free
17	Oztumer, Erhun	Peterborough U	Walsall	Free
17	Paloschi, Alberto	Swansea C	Atalanta	Undisclosed
21	Parish, Elliot	Colchester U	Accrington S	Free
15	Parkes, Tom	Bristol R	Leyton Orient	Free
20	Payne, Jack	Southend U	Huddersfield T	Compensation
3	Phillips, Aaron	Coventry C	Northampton T	Free
21	Prosser, Luke	Southend U	Colchester U	Free
24	Rathbone, Oliver	Manchester U	Rochdale	Free
27	Rea, Glen	Brighton & HA	Luton T	Undisclosed
25	Redmond, Nathan	Norwich C	Southampton	£10m
14	Revell, Alex	Milton Keynes D	Northampton T	Free
28	Ribeiro, Christian	Exeter C	Oxford U	Free
20	Rigg, Sean	AFC Wimbledon	Newport Co	Free
28	Roberts, Jordan	Inverness CT	Crawley T	Free
24	Rodman, Alex	Newport Co	Notts Co	Free
3	Rose, Danny	Northampton T	Portsmouth	Free
14	Sammon, Conor	Derby Co	Hearts	Undisclosed
28	Senior, Courtney	Brentford	Colchester U	Free
23	Shaw, Frazer	Leyton Orient	Accrington S	Free
30	Shotton, Ryan	Derby Co	Birmingham C	Undisclosed
10	Sidwell, Steve	Stoke C	Brighton & HA	Free
30	Sinclair, Jerome	Liverpool	Watford	£4m
25	Slew, Jordan	Chesterfield	Plymouth Arg	Free
21	Smith, Connor	AFC Wimbledon	Plymouth Arg	Undisclosed
24	Smith, Martin	Sunderland	Kilmarnock	Free
23	Smith, Michael	Swindon T	Portsmouth	Undisclosed
19	Songo'o, Yann	Blackburn R	Plymouth Arg	Free
21	Southwell, Dayle	Boston U	Wycombe W	Undisclosed
29	Spencer, Jimmy	Cambridge U	Plymouth Arg	Free
27	Spurr, Tommy	Blackburn R	Preston NE	Free
17	Stokes, Anthony	Celtic	Blackburn R	Free
28	Summerfield, Luke	York C	Grimsby T	Free
6	Tafazolli, Ryan	Mansfield T	Peterborough U	Free
23	Tait, Richard	Grimsby T	Motherwell	Free
22	Talbot, Drew	Chesterfield	Portsmouth	Free
24	Tesche, Robert	Nottingham F	Birmingham C	Free
25	Thomas, Wes	Birmingham C	Oxford U	Free
23	Tootle, Matt	Shrewsbury T	Notts Co	Free
23	Turner, Ben	Cardiff C	Burton Alb	Free
3	Upson, Ed	Millwall	Milton Keynes D	Free
18	Urwin, Matt	AFC Fylde	Fleetwood T	Free
16	Vassell, Kyle	Peterborough U	Blackpool	Free
28	Wakefield, Liam	Accrington S	Morecambe	Free
23	Wanyama, Victor	Southampton	Tottenham H	£11m
24	Webb, Joshua	Aston Villa	Kilmarnock	Free

6 Webster, Adam	Portsmouth	Ipswich T	£750,000
6 Weir, Robbie	Burton Alb	Leyton Orient	Free
30 Weston, Myles	Southend U	Wycombe W	Free
28 Whelpdale, Chris	Stevenage	AFC Wimbledon	Free
24 Williams, Ben	Bradford C	Bury	Free
28 Williams, George	Barnsley	Milton Keynes D	Free
1 Winnard, Dean	Accrington S	Morecambe	Free
15 Worrall, David	Southend U	Millwall	Free
1 Wright, Joe	Huddersfield T	Doncaster R	Free
25 Wylde, Gregg	Plymouth Arg	Millwall	Free
1 Yorwerth, Josh	Ipswich T	Crawley T	Free
24 Zakuani, Gabriel	Peterborough U	Northampton T	Free
JULY 2016			
28 Abdi, Almen	Watford	Sheffield W	Undisclosed
10 Akinfenwa, Adebayo	AFC Wimbledon	Wycombe W	Free
10 Albentosa, Raul	Derby Co	Deportivo La Coruna	Undisclosed
25 Allen, Joe	Liverpool	Stoke C	£13m
8 Aluko, Sone	Hull C	Fulham	Free
1 Angella, Gabriele	Watford	Udinese	Undisclosed
19 Banks, Ollie	Chesterfield	Oldham Ath	Free
19 Barnett, Leon	Wigan Ath	Bury	Free
21 Beautyman, Harry	Peterborough U	Northampton T	Undisclosed
3 Beevers, Mark	Millwall	Bolton W	Free
1 Bentley, Daniel	Southend U	Brentford	Undisclosed
1 Bidwell, Jake	Brentford	QPR	Undisclosed
5 Bowery, Jordan	Oxford U	Leyton Orient	Free
11 Bradley, Sonny	Crawley T	Plymouth Arg	Free
14 Bradshaw, Tom	Walsall	Barnsley	Undisclosed
4 Brisley, Shaun	Peterborough U	Carlisle U	Free
26 Brown, Scott	Aberdeen	Wycombe W	Free
19 Button, David	Brentford	Fulham	Undisclosed
26 Buxton, Jake	Derby Co	Wigan Ath	Undisclosed
11 Byers, George	Watford	Swansea C	Free
13 Canos, Sergi	Liverpool	Norwich C	Undisclosed
9 Cisse, Papiss	Newcastle U	Shandong Luneng	Undisclosed
27 Clarke, Leon	Bury	Sheffield U	Undisclosed
19 Clarke, Peter	Bury	Oldham Ath	Free
20 Clifford, Billy	Boreham Wood	Crawley T	Free
11 Collins, James	Shrewsbury T	Crawley T	Free
5 Coloccini, Fabricio	Newcastle U	San Lorenzo	Free
2 Connolly, Mark	Kilmarnock	Crawley T	Free
5 Cook, Jordan	Walsall	Luton T	Free
8 Cook, Lewis	Leeds U	Bournemouth	Undisclosed
13 Cousins, Jordan	Charlton Ath	QPR	Undisclosed
16 Cox, Simon	Reading	Southend U	Free
22 Crofts, Andrew	Brighton & HA	Charlton Ath	Free
5 Dagnall, Chris	Hibernian	Crewe Alex	Free
21 Danns, Neil	Bolton W	Bury	Free
26 de Havilland, Will	Sheffield W	Wycombe W	Free
25 Delaney, Ryan	Wexford	Burton Alb	Free
13 Dieng, Timothee	Oldham Ath	Bradford C	Free
22 Dmitrovic, Marko	Charlton Ath	AD Alcorcon	Free
19 Dodoo, Joe	Leicester C	Rangers	Compensation
12 Doyle, Colin	Blackpool	Bradford C	£1
25 Dyer, Lloyd	Burnley	Burton Alb	Free
1 Eaves, Tom	Bolton W	Yeovil T	Free
1 Egan, John	Gillingham	Brentford	Undisclosed
15 El-Abd, Adam	Bristol C	Shrewsbury T	Free
2 Ezewele, Josh	WBA	Yeovil T	Free
5 Fer, Leroy	QPR	Swansea C	Undisclosed
26 Ferguson, Nathan	Burton Alb	Port Vale	Free
8 Fleck, John	Coventry C	Sheffield U	Free
12 Fletcher, Ashley	Manchester U	West Ham U	Free
1 Fletcher, Steven	Sunderland	Sheffield W	Free
13 Flynn, Ryan	Sheffield U	Oldham Ath	Undisclosed
12 Forrester, Anton	Blackburn R	Port Vale	Free
1 Forte, Jonathan	Oldham Ath	Notts Co	Free
22 Fox, David	Crewe Alex	Plymouth Arg	Free
8 Gamez, Jesus	Atletico Madrid	Newcastle U	Free
13 Garnett, Addison	QPR	Crawley T	Free
1 Gayle, Dwight	Crystal Palace	Newcastle U	£10m
16 Giaccherini, Emanuele	Sunderland	Napoli	Undisclosed
28 Green, Paul	Rotherham U	Oldham Ath	Free
6 Green, Robert	QPR	Leeds U	Free
19 Gudmundsson, Johann Berg	Charlton Ath	Burnley	Undisclosed
6 Guthrie, Kurtis	Forest Green R	Colchester U	Undisclosed
29 Guzan, Brad	Aston Villa	Middlesbrough	Free
19 Hall, Rob	Bolton W	Oxford U	Free
21 Hanley, Grant	Blackburn R	Newcastle U	Undisclosed
11 Hayden, Isaac	Arsenal	Newcastle U	Undisclosed
27 Hemmings, Kane	Dundee	Oxford U	Undisclosed
22 Henderson, Stephen	Charlton Ath	Nottingham F	Free
11 Hewitt, Steven	Burnley	Accrington S	Free
22 Holding, Rob	Bolton W	Arsenal	£2m
7 Holmes, Duane	Huddersfield T	Scunthorpe U	Free
12 Hornby-Forbes, Tyler	Fleetwood T	Brighton & HA	Undisclosed
13 Howard, Mark	Sheffield U	Bolton W	Free
6 Hyde, Jake	York C	Stevenage	Free
14 Ibe, Jordon	Liverpool	Bournemouth	£15m
18 Ijaha, David	Whitehawk	Plymouth Arg	Free
15 Irvine, Jackson	Ross Co	Burton Alb	Undisclosed
18 Jackson, Simeon	Blackburn R	Walsall	Free
4 Jurado, Jose Manuel	Watford	Espanyol	Undisclosed

16 Kante, N'Golo	Leicester C	Chelsea	£30m
18 Kean, Jake	Norwich C	Sheffield W	Free
2 Kelly, Liam	Oldham Ath	Leyton Orient	Undisclosed
12 Kettings, Chris	Crystal Palace	Oldham Ath	Free
29 Kinsella, Lewis	Aston Villa	Colchester U	Free
1 Knight-Percival, Nathaniel	Shrewsbury T	Bradford C	Free
21 Konchesky, Paul	Leicester C	Gillingham	Free
21 Lacey, Paddy	Barrow	Accrington S	Free
9 Law, Josh	Motherwell	Oldham Ath	Free
29 Lawless, Alex	Luton T	Yeovil T	Free
2 Lea, Joe	Southampton	Yeovil T	Free
1 Leigh, Greg	Bradford C	Bury	Undisclosed
4 Liburd, Rowan	Reading	Stevenage	Undisclosed
2 Lindegaard, Anders	WBA	Preston NE	Free
1 Loft, Doug	Gillingham	Colchester U	Free
14 Maddison, Jonny	Leicester C	Yeovil T	Free
4 Main, Curtis	Doncaster R	Portsmouth	Undisclosed
19 Malone, Scott	Cardiff C	Fulham	Swap
1 Mannion, Will	AFC Wimbledon	Hull C	Undisclosed
6 Martin, Lee	Millwall	Gillingham	Free
19 McAnuff, Jobi	Leyton Orient	Stevenage	Free
22 McDonald, Kevin	Wolverhampton W	Fulham	Undisclosed
12 McFadzean, Kyle	Milton Keynes D	Burton Alb	Undisclosed
19 McGovern, Michael	Hamilton A	Norwich C	Free
22 McGurk, Adam	Portsmouth	Cambridge U	Undisclosed
12 McNaughton, Kevin	Wigan Ath	Inverness CT	Free
4 Mellor, Kelvin	Plymouth Arg	Blackpool	Free
11 Moussa, Franck	Southend U	Walsall	Free
4 Nelson, Curtis	Plymouth Arg	Oxford U	Undisclosed
1 Nicholls, Alex	Exeter C	Barnet	Free
30 Nizic, Daniel	Burnley	Morecambe	Free
8 O'Connell, Jack	Brentford	Sheffield U	Undisclosed
14 O'Dowda, Callum	Oxford U	Bristol C	Undisclosed
29 Osei, Darius	Stalybridge Celtic	Oldham Ath	Undisclosed
12 O'Shaughnessy, Daniel	Brentford	Cheltenham T	Free
12 Oxley, Mark	Hibernian	Southend U	Free
17 Parkin, Jon	Forest Green R	Newport Co	Free
1 Parrett, Dean	Stevenage	AFC Wimbledon	Free
11 Pelle, Graziano	Southampton	Shandong Luneng	£12m
6 Phillips, Matt	QPR	WBA	£5.5m
8 Pigott, Joe	Charlton Ath	Cambridge U	Free
2 Poleon, Dominic	Oldham Ath	AFC Wimbledon	Free
19 Pope, Nick	Charlton Ath	Burnley	Undisclosed
12 Powell, Nick	Manchester U	Wigan Ath	Free
16 Price, Lewis	Sheffield W	Rotherham U	Free
5 Proctor, Jamie	Bradford C	Bolton W	Free
28 Pudil, Daniel	Watford	Sheffield W	Undisclosed
18 Pugh, Danny	Bury	Blackpool	Free
12 Reid, Tyler	Manchester U	Swansea C	Undisclosed
19 Richards, Jazz	Fulham	Cardiff C	Swap
1 Riley, Joe	Bury	Shrewsbury T	Undisclosed
1 Ritchie, Matt	Bournemouth	Newcastle U	£12m
4 Robinson, Callum	Aston Villa	Preston NE	Undisclosed
7 Roofe, Kemar	Oxford U	Leeds U	Undisclosed
4 Rooney, Paul	Bohemians	Millwall	Free
12 Rothwell, Joe	Manchester U	Oxford U	Free
1 Sawyers, Romaine	Walsall	Brentford	Free
14 Skrtel, Martin	Liverpool	Fenerbahce	£5m
7 Slater, Craig	Kilmarnock	Colchester U	Undisclosed
19 Slocombe, Sam	Oxford U	Blackpool	Free
4 Sloth, Casper	Leeds U	Aalborg	Undisclosed
27 Smith, Brad	Liverpool	Bournemouth	£3m
29 Sokolik, Jakub	Yeovil T	Southend U	Free
4 Sordell, Marvin	Colchester U	Coventry C	Free
1 Stekelenburg, Maarten	Fulham	Everton	Undisclosed
1 Stevens, Matty	Barnet	Peterborough U	Undisclosed
28 Sweeney, Pierce	Reading	Exeter C	Free
14 Swift, John	Chelsea	Reading	Free
1 Taylor, Andy	Walsall	Blackpool	Free
1 Taylor, Chris	Blackburn R	Bolton W	Free
4 Thomas, Conor	Coventry C	Swindon T	Free
12 Thomas, Jerome	Rotherham U	Port Vale	Free
1 Thomas, Kwame	Derby Co	Coventry C	Free
2 Threlkeld, Oscar	Bolton W	Plymouth Arg	Free
5 Tomkins, James	West Ham U	Crystal Palace	£10m
5 Tomlin, Lee	Bournemouth	Bristol C	Undisclosed
24 Toure, Kolo	Liverpool	Celtic	Free
1 Townsend, Andros	Newcastle U	Crystal Palace	£13m
4 Tozer, Ben	Yeovil T	Newport Co	Free
29 Traore, Armand	QPR	Nottingham F	Free
10 Tshibola, Aaron	Reading	Aston Villa	Undisclosed
10 Turner, Rhys	Oldham Ath	Morecambe	Free
7 Valdes, Victor	Manchester U	Middlesbrough	Free
23 Vassell, Isaac	Truro C	Luton T	Free
8 Vassell, Theo	Oldham Ath	Walsall	Free
22 Vaulks, Will	Falkirk	Rotherham U	Undisclosed
30 Vernon, Scott	Shrewsbury T	Grimsby T	Free
1 Vigouroux, Lawrence	Liverpool	Swindon T	Undisclosed
23 Vincelot, Romain	Coventry C	Bradford C	Undisclosed
7 Wagstaff, Scott	Bristol C	Gillingham	Free
22 Wall, Luke	Blackburn R	Accrington S	Free
1 Watson, Ryan	Leicester C	Barnet	Free
22 Wijnaldum, Georginio	Newcastle U	Liverpool	£25m

25	Williamson, Lee	Blackburn R	Burton Alb	Free
5	Wilson, James	Oldham Ath	Sheffield U	Free
11	Woodland, Luke	Bradford PA	Oldham Ath	Free
27	Woods, Gary	Leyton Orient	Hamilton A	Free
10	Wright, Jake	Oxford U	Sheffield U	Free

AUGUST 2016

8	Adams, Che	Sheffield U	Birmingham C	Undisclosed
31	Adomah, Albert	Middlesbrough	Aston Villa	Undisclosed
11	Agard, Kieran	Bristol C	Milton Keynes D	Undisclosed
2	Akpa, Jean-Louis	Shrewsbury T	Barnet	Free
31	Alberto, Luis	Liverpool	Lazio	£4.3m
31	Alnwick, Ben	Peterborough U	Bolton W	Free
31	Anderson, Paul	Bradford C	Northampton T	Free
31	Anya, Ikechi	Watford	Derby Co	Undisclosed
8	Ayew, Andre	Swansea C	West Ham U	£20.5m
11	Ayling, Luke	Bristol C	Leeds U	Undisclosed
12	Ball, Dominic	Tottenham H	Rotherham U	Undisclosed
31	Balotelli, Mario	Liverpool	Nice	Free
3	Barnett, Tyrone	Shrewsbury T	AFC Wimbledon	Free
31	Barton, Adam	Portsmouth	Partick Thistle	Undisclosed
27	Bennett, Joe	Aston Villa	Cardiff C	Undisclosed
20	Benteke, Christian	Liverpool	Crystal Palace	£32m
30	Best, Leon	Rotherham U	Ipswich T	Free
26	Bigirimana, Gael	Newcastle U	Coventry C	Undisclosed
22	Bingham, Rakish	Hartlepool U	Hamilton A	Free
2	Binnom-Williams, Jermone	Crystal Palace	Peterborough U	Undisclosed
22	Blackett, Tyler	Manchester U	Reading	Undisclosed
15	Bolasie, Yannick	Crystal Palace	Everton	£30m
16	Bridcutt, Liam	Sunderland	Leeds U	Undisclosed
5	Brown, Chris	Blackburn R	Bury	Free
28	Burke, Oliver	Nottingham F	Red Bull Leipzig	£13m
25	Butcher, Calum	Burton Alb	Millwall	Free
4	Buxton, Adam	Accrington S	Portsmouth	Free
5	Buxton, Lewis	Rotherham U	Bolton W	Free
31	Byrne, Nathan	Wolverhampton W	Wigan Ath	Undisclosed
4	Campbell-Ryce, Jamal	Sheffield U	Barnet	Free
31	Carayol, Mustapha	Middlesbrough	Nottingham F	Free
29	Chadli, Nacer	Tottenham H	WBA	£13m
30	Chicksen, Adam	Brighton & HA	Charlton Ath	Free
25	Chow, Tim	Wigan Ath	Ross Co	Undisclosed
24	Church, Simon	Milton Keynes D	Roda JC	Undisclosed
3	Clark, Ciaran	Aston Villa	Newcastle U	£5m
2	Clark, Jordan	Shrewsbury T	Accrington S	Free
31	Clark, Nicky	Bury	Dunfermline Ath	Free
10	Clay, Craig	Grimsby T	Motherwell	Free
24	Copp, Kyle	Swansea C	Yeovil T	Free
4	Crocombe, Max	Oxford U	Carlisle U	Free
1	Davies, Arron	Exeter C	Accrington S	Free
17	Davies, Steven	Bradford C	Rochdale	Free
23	De Laet, Ritchie	Leicester C	Aston Villa	Undisclosed
13	de, Dorus	Nottingham F	Celtic	Undisclosed
18	Delfouneso, Nathan	Blackburn R	Swindon T	Free
3	Diame, Mohamed	Hull C	Newcastle U	Undisclosed
5	Djilobodji, Papy	Chelsea	Sunderland	£8m
5	Donacien, Janoi	Aston Villa	Accrington S	Free
20	Donnelly, Liam	Fulham	Hartlepool U	Free
26	Duffy, Shane	Blackburn R	Brighton & HA	Undisclosed
31	Dummigan, Cameron	Burnley	Oldham Ath	Undisclosed
12	Dunne, Charles	Blackpool	Oldham Ath	Free
5	Eagles, Chris	Bury	Accrington S	Free
12	Fabio	Cardiff C	Middlesbrough	£2m
3	Fane, Ousmane	Kidderminster H	Oldham Ath	£50,000
27	Ferdinand, Anton	Reading	Southend U	Free
10	Fisher, Darnell	Celtic	Rotherham U	Undisclosed
5	Foley, Kevin	Ipswich T	Charlton Ath	Free
30	Gamboa, Cristian	WBA	Celtic	Undisclosed
20	Garner, Joe	Preston NE	Rangers	Undisclosed
31	Gnabry, Serge	Arsenal	Werder Bremen	Undisclosed
19	Gnanduillet, Armand	Leyton Orient	Blackpool	Undisclosed
17	Gomez, Jordi	Sunderland	Wigan Ath	Free
1	Gray, Jake	Crystal Palace	Luton T	Free
2	Greer, Gordon	Brighton & HA	Blackburn R	Free
2	Gueye, Idrissa	Aston Villa	Everton	Undisclosed
30	Halliday, Brad	Middlesbrough	Cambridge U	Undisclosed
5	Harriott, Callum	Charlton Ath	Reading	Undisclosed
3	Hendersen, Darius	Coventry C	Mansfield T	Free
31	Hendrick, Jeff	Derby Co	Burnley	£10.5m
31	Henry, Rico	Walsall	Brentford	£1.5m
19	Hollands, Danny	Portsmouth	Crewe Alex	Free
24	Holmes-Dennis, Tareiq	Charlton Ath	Huddersfield T	Undisclosed
12	Huws, Emyr	Wigan Ath	Cardiff C	Undisclosed
24	Ikpeazu, Uche	Watford	Cambridge U	Free
30	Jackson, Adam	Middlesbrough	Barnsley	Undisclosed
12	Jahraldo-Martin, Calaum	Hull C	Oldham Ath	Free
24	Janmaat, Daryl	Newcastle U	Watford	Undisclosed
17	Jedinak, Mile	Crystal Palace	Aston Villa	Undisclosed
26	Johansen, Stefan	Celtic	Fulham	Undisclosed
31	Johnson, Marvin	Motherwell	Oxford U	Undisclosed
16	Jones, David	Burnley	Sheffield W	Undisclosed
4	Jones, Paul	Portsmouth	Norwich C	Free
19	Kaboul, Younes	Sunderland	Watford	Undisclosed
31	Kashket, Scott	Leyton Orient	Wycombe W	Free
30	Keane, Will	Manchester U	Hull C	Undisclosed

1 Kelly, Sean	St Mirren	AFC Wimbledon	Free
1 Kilgallon, Matt	Blackburn R	Bradford C	Free
30 Kodjia, Jonathan	Bristol C	Aston Villa	£11m
31 Kpekawa, Cole	QPR	Barnsley	Undisclosed
31 Lambert, Rickie	WBA	Cardiff C	Undisclosed
30 Lavery, Caolan	Sheffield W	Sheffield U	Undisclosed
31 Ledesma, Emmanuel	Brentford	Panetolikos	Free
25 Ledson, Ryan	Everton	Oxford U	Undisclosed
29 Lescott, Joleon	Aston Villa	AEK Athens	Undisclosed
10 Logan, Conrad	Hibernian	Rochdale	Free
11 Love, Donald	Manchester U	Sunderland	Combined £5.5m
31 Lyness, Dean	Burton Alb	Blackpool	Free
2 MacDonald, Angus	Torquay U	Barnsley	Undisclosed
13 MacDonald, Shaun	Bournemouth	Wigan Ath	Undisclosed
11 Magennis, Josh	Kilmarnock	Charlton Ath	Undisclosed
31 Margetts, Jonny	Lincoln C	Scunthorpe U	Undisclosed
30 Mariappa, Adrian	Crystal Palace	Watford	Free
30 Marshall, David	Cardiff C	Hull C	Undisclosed
30 Mason, Ryan	Tottenham H	Hull C	£13m
30 Mawson, Alfie	Barnsley	Swansea C	Undisclosed
1 McCallum, Marc	Livingston	Plymouth Arg	Free
1 McCarthy, Alex	Crystal Palace	Southampton	Undisclosed
4 McCormack, Ross	Fulham	Aston Villa	£12m
31 McJannett, Cameron	Luton T	Stoke C	Undisclosed
30 McKeown, Rory	Raith R	Accrington S	Free
8 McLaughlin, Ryan	Liverpool	Oldham Ath	Free
25 McLeod, Izale	Notts Co	Yeovil T	Free
11 McNair, Paddy	Manchester U	Sunderland	Combined £5.5m
20 Moore, Liam	Leicester C	Reading	Undisclosed
19 Moore, Simon	Cardiff C	Sheffield U	Undisclosed
5 Mugabi, Bevis	Southampton	Yeovil T	Free
31 Mulgrew, Charlie	Celtic	Blackburn R	Free
28 Murphy, Daryl	Ipswich T	Newcastle U	Undisclosed
31 Murray, Sean	Watford	Swindon T	Free
3 Nicholls, Lee	Wigan Ath	Milton Keynes D	Undisclosed
6 Norris, Luke	Gillingham	Swindon T	Undisclosed
3 Norwood, Oliver	Reading	Brighton & HA	Undisclosed
31 Ntlhe, Kgosi	Peterborough U	Stevenage	Undisclosed
31 Nyom, Allan	Watford	WBA	Undisclosed
12 O'Hara, Jamie	Fulham	Gillingham	Free
31 O'Kane, Eunan	Bournemouth	Leeds U	Undisclosed
27 Paterson, Jamie	Nottingham F	Bristol C	Undisclosed
26 Paterson, Martin	Blackpool	Port Vale	Free
25 Payne, Jack	Peterborough U	Blackpool	Free
4 Pearce, Jason	Wigan Ath	Charlton Ath	Undisclosed
19 Pienaar, Steven	Everton	Sunderland	Free
4 Pritchard, Alex	Tottenham H	Norwich C	Undisclosed
6 Rachubka, Paul	Bolton W	Bury	Free
31 Reach, Adam	Middlesbrough	Sheffield W	Undisclosed
30 Richardson, Frazer	Rotherham U	Doncaster R	Free
31 Robson-Kanu, Hal	Reading	WBA	Free
1 Rose, Michael	Rochdale	Morecambe	Free
30 Rosicky, Tomas	Arsenal	Sparta Prague	Free
3 Salah, Mohamed	Chelsea	Roma	Undisclosed
31 Senior, Jack	Huddersfield T	Luton T	Undisclosed
7 Sinclair, Scott	Aston Villa	Celtic	Undisclosed
31 Sissoko, Moussa	Newcastle U	Tottenham H	£30m
9 Smith, Harry	Folkestone Invicta	Millwall	Undisclosed
12 Sonupe, Emmanuel	Tottenham H	Northampton T	Free
12 Stewart, Greg	Dundee	Birmingham C	£500,000
9 Stones, John	Everton	Manchester C	£47.5m
5 Sweeney, Ryan	AFC Wimbledon	Stoke C	Undisclosed
3 Taylor, Jon	Peterborough U	Rotherham U	£500,000
1 Taylor, Matt	Burnley	Northampton T	Free
1 Taylor, Steven	Newcastle U	Portland Timbers	Free
7 Thompson, Joe	Carlisle U	Rochdale	Free
31 Traore, Adama	Aston Villa	Middlesbrough	Undisclosed
15 Turnbull, Jordan	Southampton	Coventry C	Undisclosed
24 Vaughan, James	Birmingham C	Bury	Free
31 Veldwijk, Lars	Nottingham F	KV Kortrijk	Undisclosed
31 Vermijl, Marnick	Sheffield W	Preston NE	Undisclosed
27 Vydra, Matej	Watford	Derby Co	£8m
1 Ward, Grant	Tottenham H	Ipswich T	Undisclosed
31 Weale, Chris	Yeovil T	Derby Co	Free
31 Weir, James	Manchester U	Hull C	Undisclosed
10 Williams, Ashley	Swansea C	Everton	£12m
26 Williams, Derrick	Bristol C	Blackburn R	Undisclosed
2 Wilson, Kelvin	Nottingham F	Rotherham U	Free
15 Wilson, Marc	Stoke C	Bournemouth	£2m
31 Woolery, Kaiyne	Bolton W	Wigan Ath	Undisclosed
20 Woolford, Martyn	Sheffield U	Fleetwood T	Free
24 Yedlin, DeAndre	Tottenham H	Newcastle U	Undisclosed

SEPTEMBER 2016

13 Cox, Dean	Leyton Orient	Crawley T	Free*

**Not available to play until 2 January 2017.*

JANUARY 2017

27 Adams, Blair	Cambridge U	Hamilton A	Free
1 Akinola, Simeon	Braintree T	Barnet	£40,000
30 Alnwick, Jak	Port Vale	Rangers	Undisclosed
20 Amadi-Holloway, Aaron	Fleetwood T	Oldham Ath	Undisclosed
18 Asante, Akwasi	Solihull Moors	Grimsby T	Undisclosed
31 Ayew, Jordan	Aston Villa	Swansea C	Undisclosed

18 Bamford, Patrick	Chelsea	Middlesbrough	£5.5m
1 Barkhuizen, Tom	Morecambe	Preston NE	Compensation
1 Beavon, Stuart	Burton Alb	Coventry C	Free
31 Bedeau, Jacob	Bury	Aston Villa	Undisclosed
20 Berahino, Saido	WBA	Stoke C	£12m
23 Bird, Ryan	Eastleigh	Newport Co	Undisclosed
5 Blissett, Nathan	Torquay U	Plymouth Arg	£15,000
31 Bogle, Omar	Grimsby T	Wigan Ath	Undisclosed
1 Boyle, Andy	Dundalk	Preston NE	Free
9 Boyle, Will	Huddersfield T	Cheltenham T	Free
31 Brady, Robbie	Norwich C	Burnley	Undisclosed
10 Bramall, Cohen	Hednesford T	Arsenal	£40,000
25 Bree, James	Barnsley	Aston Villa	Undisclosed
31 Brill, Dean	Motherwell	Colchester U	Free
6 Brown, Reece	Sheffield U	Bury	Free
26 Burn, Jonny	Middlesbrough	Bristol R	Undisclosed
19 Burns, Wes	Bristol C	Fleetwood T	Undisclosed
12 Bus, Sergiu	Sheffield W	Astra Giurgiu	Free
1 Byrom, Joel	Northampton T	Mansfield T	Free
31 Canos, Sergi	Norwich C	Brentford	Undisclosed
12 Carroll, Jake	Hartlepool U	Cambridge U	Undisclosed
17 Carroll, Tom	Tottenham H	Swansea C	£4.5m
3 Carruthers, Samir	Milton Keynes D	Sheffield U	Undisclosed
24 Chery, Tjaronn	QPR	Guizhou Hengfeng Zhicheng	Undisclosed
1 Clarke, Nathan	Bradford C	Coventry C	Free
19 Clements, Chris	Mansfield T	Grimsby T	Undisclosed
23 Clough, Charlie	Forest Green R	Barnet	Undisclosed
31 Clough, Zach	Bolton W	Nottingham F	£2.5m
27 Conroy, Dion	Chelsea	Swindon T	Undisclosed
31 Correia, Raul	Radcliffe Bor	Blackpool	Undisclosed
17 Coulson, Luke	Eastleigh	Barnet	Undisclosed
6 D'Ath, Lawson	Northampton T	Luton T	Undisclosed
7 Davies, Craig	Wigan Ath	Scunthorpe U	Undisclosed
21 Delfouneso, Nathan	Swindon T	Blackpool	Free
20 Depay, Memphis	Manchester U	Lyon	£16m
11 Eagles, Chris	Accrington S	Port Vale	Free
12 Eardley, Neal	Hibernian	Northampton T	Free
6 Foley, Kevin	Charlton Ath	Coventry C	Free
20 Fonte, Jose	Southampton	West Ham U	£8m
5 Forster-Caskey, Jake	Brighton & HA	Charlton Ath	Undisclosed
6 Fox, Morgan	Charlton Ath	Sheffield W	Undisclosed
30 Freeman, Luke	Bristol C	QPR	Undisclosed
31 Gabbiadini, Manolo	Napoli	Southampton	£14m
16 Gambin, Luke	Barnet	Luton T	Undisclosed
7 Gape, Dominic	Southampton	Wycombe W	Free
4 Gestede, Rudy	Aston Villa	Middlesbrough	Undisclosed
30 Gibson, Darron	Everton	Sunderland	Undisclosed
31 Gilks, Matt	Rangers	Wigan Ath	Undisclosed
12 Glendon, George	Manchester C	Fleetwood T	Undisclosed
20 Gobern, Oscar	Mansfield T	Ross Co	Free
31 Gomez, Jordi	Wigan Ath	Rayo Vallecano	Undisclosed
13 Goodship, Brandon	Bournemouth	Yeovil T	Free
28 Goss, Sean	Manchester U	QPR	£500,000
31 Grant, Anthony	Port Vale	Peterborough U	Undisclosed
4 Grant, Lee	Derby Co	Stoke C	£1.3m
31 Guedioura, Adlene	Watford	Middlesbrough	Undisclosed
6 Halford, Greg	Rotherham U	Cardiff C	Undisclosed
24 Hanson, James	Bradford C	Sheffield U	Undisclosed
31 Hedges, Ryan	Swansea C	Barnsley	Undisclosed
24 Hernandez, Luis	Leicester C	Malaga	Undisclosed
31 Hogan, Scott	Brentford	Aston Villa	£12m
22 Holland, Nathan	Everton	West Ham U	Undisclosed
1 Horgan, Daryl	Dundalk	Preston NE	Free
26 Hourihane, Conor	Barnsley	Aston Villa	Undisclosed
1 Humphrey, Chris	Preston NE	Hibernian	Free
31 Ighalo, Odion	Watford	Changchun Yatai	£20m
9 Ilori, Tiago	Liverpool	Reading	Undisclosed
31 Jakupovic, Arnel	Middlesbrough	Empoli	Undisclosed
13 James, Tom	Cardiff C	Yeovil T	Free
5 Jones, Alex	Birmingham C	Bradford C	Undisclosed
31 Jonsson, Eggert	Fleetwood T	Soenderjyske	Undisclosed
27 Jozefzoon, Florian	PSV Eindhoven	Brentford	Undisclosed
3 Jutkiewicz, Lukas	Burnley	Birmingham C	£1m
18 Kabamba, Nicke	Hampton & Richmond Bor	Portsmouth	Undisclosed
3 Keane, Keith	Cambridge U	Rochdale	Free
31 King, Jack	Scunthorpe U	Stevenage	Free
31 Kitching, Mark	Middlesbrough	Rochdale	Undisclosed
31 Klok, Marc	Oldham Ath	Dundee	Free
13 Lafferty, Daniel	Burnley	Sheffield U	Undisclosed
20 Lansbury, Henri	Nottingham F	Aston Villa	£2.75m
31 Laurent, Josh	Hartlepool U	Wigan Ath	Undisclosed
13 Lawlor, Ian	Manchester C	Doncaster R	Undisclosed
13 Lewis, Paul	Macclesfield T	Cambridge U	Undisclosed
13 Liddle, Gary	Chesterfield	Carlisle U	Undisclosed
20 Livermore, Jake	Hull C	WBA	£10m
5 Lookman, Ademola	Charlton Ath	Everton	£11m
24 Lowe, Ryan	Crewe Alex	Bury	Free
31 MacDonald, Alex	Oxford U	Mansfield T	Free
1 Mackreth, Jack	Macclesfield T	Bury	Undisclosed
13 Maguire, Joe	Liverpool	Fleetwood T	Undisclosed
31 Mandron, Mikael	Eastleigh	Wigan Ath	Undisclosed
31 Marshall, Ben	Blackburn R	Wolverhampton W	Undisclosed
1 May, Alfie	Hythe T	Doncaster R	Undisclosed

27 McAllister, Kyle	St Mirren	Derby Co	Undisclosed
6 Meite, Ibrahim	Harrow Bor	Cardiff C	Undisclosed
6 Mikel, John Obi	Chelsea	Tianjin TEDA	Undisclosed
16 Moore, Kieffer	Forest Green R	Ipswich T	Undisclosed
1 Morias, Junior	St Albans	Peterborough U	Undisclosed
20 Morris, Bryn	Middlesbrough	Shrewsbury T	Free
27 Mowatt, Alex	Leeds U	Barnsley	Undisclosed
19 Muirhead, Robbie	Hearts	Milton Keynes D	Undisclosed
31 Murray, Glenn	Bournemouth	Brighton & HA	Undisclosed
31 Murray, Sean	Swindon T	Colchester U	Free
20 Ngoo, Michael	Bromley	Oldham Ath	Free
18 Nouble, Frank	Gillingham	Southend U	Free
1 Nsiala, Aristote	Hartlepool U	Shrewsbury T	Undisclosed
18 Nsue, Emilio	Middlesbrough	Birmingham C	Undisclosed
9 Nugent, David	Middlesbrough	Derby Co	Undisclosed
19 O'Donnell, Richard	Bristol C	Rotherham U	Undisclosed
17 Olsson, Martin	Norwich C	Swansea C	£4m
31 O'Neil, Liam	Chesterfield	Cambridge U	Undisclosed
18 Osborne, Jamey	Solihull Moors	Grimsby T	Undisclosed
16 Osborne, Karleigh	Plymouth Arg	Kilmarnock	Free
1 Oscar	Chelsea	Shanghai SIPG	£60m
30 O'Sullivan, John	Blackburn R	Carlisle U	Free
20 O'Sullivan, Tommy	Cardiff C	Colchester U	Undisclosed
30 Oviedo, Bryan	Everton	Sunderland	Undisclosed
6 Page, Lewis	West Ham U	Charlton Ath	Undisclosed
13 Partington, Joe	Eastleigh	Bristol R	Undisclosed
30 Payet, Dimitri	West Ham U	Marseille	£25m
18 Phipps, Eli	Cardiff C	Colchester U	Undisclosed
12 Polter, Sebastian	QPR	Union Berlin	Undisclosed
31 Potter, Alfie	Northampton T	Mansfield T	Free
30 Purrington, Ben	Plymouth Arg	Rotherham U	Undisclosed
6 Reid, Craig	Gloucester C	Newport Co	Undisclosed
31 Robinson, Theo	Lincoln C	Southend U	Undisclosed
5 Rodman, Alex	Notts Co	Shrewsbury T	Undisclosed
20 Rose, Mitchell	Mansfield T	Newport Co	Free
27 Rowe, Danny	Macclesfield T	Ipswich T	Undisclosed
11 Sandro	QPR	Antalyaspor	Undisclosed
1 Santos, Ricardo Almeida	Peterborough U	Barnet	£100,000
20 Saunders, Sam	Brentford	Wycombe W	Free
23 Scarr, Dan	Stourbridge	Birmingham C	Undisclosed
13 Schlupp, Jeffrey	Leicester C	Crystal Palace	£12m
12 Schneiderlin, Morgan	Manchester U	Everton	£20m
9 Simpson, Jay	Leyton Orient	Philadelphia Union	Undisclosed
31 Smith, Matt	Fulham	QPR	Undisclosed
27 Snodgrass, Robert	Hull C	West Ham U	£10.2m
31 Soares, Tom	Bury	AFC Wimbledon	Undisclosed
1 Sordell, Marvin	Coventry C	Burton Alb	Free
24 Spector, Jonathan	Birmingham C	Orlando C	Free
31 Starkey, Jesse	Brighton & HA	Swindon T	Undisclosed
1 Sweeney, Dan	Maidstone U	Barnet	Undisclosed
27 Tanser, Scott	Rochdale	Port Vale	Free
31 Taylor, Matty	Bristol R	Bristol C	Undisclosed
31 Taylor, Neil	Swansea C	Aston Villa	Undisclosed
30 Taylor, Ryan	Oxford U	Plymouth Arg	Free
1 Tutonda, David	Cardiff C	Barnet	Free
4 Varney, Luke	Ipswich T	Burton Alb	Free
31 Westwood, Ashley	Aston Villa	Burnley	Undisclosed
31 Wildschut, Yanic	Wigan Ath	Norwich C	£7m
1 Williams, Aaron	Peterborough U	Newport Co	Undisclosed
12 Winchester, Carl	Oldham Ath	Cheltenham T	Free
13 Winnall, Sam	Barnsley	Sheffield W	Undisclosed
6 Wright, Bailey	Preston NE	Bristol C	Undisclosed
31 Wyke, Charlie	Carlisle U	Bradford C	Undisclosed
30 Yeates, Mark	Blackpool	Notts Co	Undisclosed
1 Yussuf, Adi	Mansfield T	Grimsby T	Free
FEBRUARY 2017			
2 Coates, Sebastian	Sunderland	Sporting Lisbon	Undisclosed
9 Tiote, Cheick	Newcastle U	Beijing Enterprises Group	Undisclosed
MARCH 2017			
28 Ajayi, Semi	Cardiff C	Rotherham U	Undisclosed
6 Bendtner, Nicklas	Nottingham F	Rosenborg	Undisclosed
10 Bray, Alex	Swansea C	Rotherham U	Undisclosed
31 Cleverley, Tom	Everton	Watford	Undisclosed
30 Lobjoit, Leon	Buckingham T	Northampton T	Undisclosed
31 Murphy, Joe	Huddersfield T	Bury	Free
23 Olsson, Jonas	WBA	Djurgarden	Free
9 Pawlett, Peter	Aberdeen	Milton Keynes D	Free
21 Schweinsteiger, Bastian	Manchester U	Chicago Fire	Free
MAY 2017			
30 Ainsworth, Lionel	Motherwell	Plymouth Arg	Free
26 Alessandra, Lewis	Hartlepool U	Notts Co	Undisclosed
24 Amoo, David	Partick Thistle	Cambridge U	Free
16 Anderson, Paul	Northampton T	Mansfield T	Free
17 Angol, Lee	Peterborough U	Mansfield T	Undisclosed
19 Anyon, Joe	Scunthorpe U	Chesterfield	Free
31 Appiah, Kwesi	Crystal Palace	AFC Wimbledon	Free
28 Atangana, Nigel	Leyton Orient	Cheltenham T	Free
30 Atkinson, Will	Southend U	Mansfield T	Free
24 Atsu, Christian	Chelsea	Newcastle U	Undisclosed

31 Barnett, Leon	Bury	Northampton T	Free
18 Barry, Brad	Swindon T	Chesterfield	Free
12 Beckford, Jermaine	Preston NE	Bury	Free
30 Begovic, Asmir	Chelsea	Bournemouth	Undisclosed
31 Bennett, Ryan	Norwich C	Wolverhampton W	Free
23 Berra, Christophe	Ipswich T	Hearts	Free
23 Bowery, Jordan	Leyton Orient	Crewe Alex	Free
25 Brown, Reece	Bury	Rochdale	Free
19 Bulman, Dannie	AFC Wimbledon	Crawley T	Free
17 Collins, Lee	Mansfield T	Forest Green R	Free
22 Cuadrado, Juan	Chelsea	Juventus	£17m
24 Daniels, Luke	Scunthorpe U	Brentford	Free
17 Dawson, Kevin	Yeovil T	Cheltenham T	Free
16 Dawson, Stephen	Scunthorpe U	Bury	Free
19 Dempsey, Kyle	Huddersfield T	Fleetwood T	Undisclosed
12 Diamond, Zander	Northampton T	Mansfield T	Free
16 Digby, Paul	Ipswich T	Mansfield T	Free
11 Doyle, Michael	Portsmouth	Coventry C	Free
14 Edwards, Phil	Burton Alb	Bury	Free
30 Etheridge, Neil	Walsall	Cardiff C	Free
22 Evans, Callum	Barnsley	Forest Green R	Free
8 Evans, Ched	Chesterfield	Sheffield U	Undisclosed
12 Ferry, James	Brentford	Stevenage	Undisclosed
22 Foley, Sam	Port Vale	Northampton T	Free
11 Gardner, Craig	WBA	Birmingham C	Undisclosed
24 Gnahoua, Arthur	Kidderminster H	Shewsbury T	Free
18 Grimes, Jamie	Dover Ath	Cheltenham T	Free
18 Hawkridge, Terry	Lincoln C	Notts Co	Free
23 Hunt, Johnny	Chester	Mansfield T	Free
24 Hyam, Dominic	Reading	Coventry C	Free
26 Ibehre, Jabo	Carlisle U	Cambridge U	Free
25 Ihiekwe, Michael	Tranmere R	Rotherham U	Free
26 John-Lewis, Lenell	Newport Co	Shrewsbury T	Free
22 Kelly, Liam	Leyton Orient	Coventry C	Free
31 Kelly, Sam	Port Vale	Grimsby T	Free
23 Lacey, Alex	Yeovil T	Gillingham	Free
8 Lloyd, Danny	Stockport Co	Peterborough U	Free
10 Logan, Conrad	Rochdale	Mansfield T	Free
19 Lund, Matty	Rochdale	Burton Alb	Free
18 Mallan, Stevie	St Mirren	Barnsley	Undisclosed
8 Mason, Niall	Aston Villa	Doncaster R	Undisclosed
19 McDonald, Rod	Northampton T	Coventry C	Undisclosed
18 McGrandles, Conor	Norwich C	Milton Keynes D	Free
19 Mellis, Jacob	Bury	Mansfield T	Free
30 Mendez-Laing, Nathaniel	Rochdale	Cardiff C	Free
29 Meredith, James	Bradford C	Millwall	Free
3 Miller, Ricky	Dover Ath	Peterborough U	Free
23 Mirfin, David	Scunthorpe U	Mansfield T	Free
15 Nolan, Liam	Southport	Accrington S	Undisclosed
24 O'Brien, Liam	Portsmouth	Coventry C	Free
31 Osadebe, Emmanuel	Gillingham	Cambridge U	Free
18 Pope, Tom	Bury	Port Vale	Free
31 Porter, Chris	Colchester U	Crewe Alex	Free
5 Powell, Daniel	Milton Keynes D	Northampton T	
26 Raynes, Michael	Carlisle U	Crewe Alex	Free
26 Reilly, Callum	Burton Alb	Bury	Free
22 Rose, Mitch	Newport Co	Grimsby T	Free
9 Samuel, Alex	Swansea C	Stevenage	Free
31 Sercombe, Liam	Oxford U	Bristol R	Undisclosed
16 Shearer, Scott	Mansfield T	Oxford U	Free
17 Smith, George	Gateshead	Northampton T	Undisclosed
30 Solanke, Dominic	Chelsea	Liverpool	Compensation
16 Spencer, Jimmy	Plymouth Arg	Mansfield T	Free
22 Stevens, Enda	Portsmouth	Sheffield U	Free
25 Taylor, Andrew	Wigan Ath	Bolton W	Free
15 Thomas, Nathan	Hartlepool U	Sheffield U	Undisclosed
17 Tibbetts, Jordan	Birmingham C	Peterborough U	Free
25 Ugwu, Gozie	Woking	Chesterfield	Free
17 White, Hayden	Peterborough U	Mansfield T	Undisclosed
19 Wiseman, Scott	Scunthorpe U	Chesterfield	Free
26 Zabaleta, Pablo	Manchester C	West Ham U	Free

THE NEW FOREIGN LEGION 2016–17

JUNE 2016	*From*	*To*	*Fee in £*
28 Antonsson, Marcus	Kalmar	Leeds U	Undisclosed
8 Bailly, Eric	Villarreal	Manchester U	£30m
29 Berg, Joey van den	Heerenveen	Reading	Free
22 Borysiuk, Ariel	Legia Warsaw	QPR	Undisclosed
29 Bulvitis, Nauris	Spartaks Jurmala	Plymouth Arg	Free
30 Cicilia, Rigino	Roda JC	Port Vale	Free
15 Espinosa, Bernardo	Sporting Gijon	Middlesbrough	Free
14 Feghouli, Sofiane	Valencia	West Ham U	Undisclosed

2 Gundogan, Ilkay	Borussia Dortmund	Manchester C	£20m
21 Hernandez, Luis	Sporting Gijon	Leicester C	Free
24 Kachunga, Elias	Ingolstadt	Huddersfield T	Loan
28 Knops, Kjell	Maastricht	Port Vale	Undisclosed
23 Kranjcar, Niko	New York Cosmos	Rangers	Free
7 Makienok, Simon	Palermo	Preston NE	Loan
7 Mersin, Yusuf	Kasimpasa	Crawley T	Free
30 Mousset, Lys	Le Havre	Bournemouth	Undisclosed
16 Myrie-Williams, Jennison	Sligo Rovers	Newport Co	Free
7 Paurevic, Ivan	FC Ufa	Huddersfield T	Undisclosed
29 Schindler, Christopher	TSV 1860 Munich	Huddersfield T	Undisclosed
29 Sels, Matz	Gent	Newcastle U	£5m
29 Vellios, Apostolos	Iraklis Thessaloniki	Nottingham F	£1m
JULY 2016			
20 Amoros, Sebastien	Monaco	Port Vale	Free
1 Ayite, Floyd	Bastia	Fulham	Undisclosed
15 Barragan, Antonio	Valencia	Middlesbrough	Undisclosed
3 Batshuayi, Michy	Marseille	Chelsea	£33m
15 Beerens, Roy	Hertha Berlin	Reading	Undisclosed
18 Birighitti, Mark	Newcastle Jets	Swansea C	Free
29 Costa, Helder	Benfica	Wolverhampton W	Loan
1 de Freitas, Anthony	Monaco	Port Vale	Free
5 de Roon, Marten	Atalanta	Middlesbrough	£12m
21 Djedje, Brice Dja	Marseille	Watford	Undisclosed
1 Erichot, Yvan	Sint-Truiden	Leyton Orient	Free
1 Fischer, Viktor	Ajax	Middlesbrough	Undisclosed
8 Gollini, Pierluigi	Hellas Verona	Aston Villa	Undisclosed
1 Gounongbe, Frederic	KVC Westerlo	Cardiff C	Free
11 Hojbjerg, Pierre-Emile	Bayern Munich	Southampton	£12.8m
1 Ibrahimovic, Zlatan	Paris Saint-Germain	Manchester U	Free
11 Jaakkola, Anssi	Ajax Cape Town	Reading	Undisclosed
12 Janssen, Vincent	AZ Alkmaar	Tottenham H	£17m
1 Kabasele, Christian	Genk	Watford	£6m
5 Kiko	Vitoria Setubal	Port Vale	Free
12 Kip, Ricardo	Almere C	Fleetwood T	Free
20 Klavan, Ragnar	Augsburg	Liverpool	£4.2m
13 Klok, Marc	Cherno More	Oldham Ath	Undisclosed
8 Lam, Thomas	PEC Zwolle	Nottingham F	Free
27 Lucic, Ivan	Bayern Munich	Bristol C	Undisclosed
1 Mac-Intisch, Calvin	SC Cambuur	Port Vale	Free
13 Magnusson, Hordur	Juventus	Bristol C	Undisclosed
1 Mandanda, Steve	Marseille	Crystal Palace	Undisclosed
22 Manninger, Alex	Augsburg	Liverpool	Free
11 Mbamba, Christopher	Hamarkameratene	Port Vale	Undisclosed
29 Meite, Yakou	Paris Saint-Germain	Reading	Undisclosed
8 Mendes, Joseph	Le Havre	Reading	Undisclosed
3 Mendy, Nampalys	Nice	Leicester C	Undisclosed
6 Mkhitaryan, Henrikh	Borussia Dortmund	Manchester U	Undisclosed
8 Musa, Ahmed	CSKA Moscow	Leicester C	£16m
20 Negredo, Alvaro	Valencia	Middlesbrough	Loan
1 Nolito	Celta Vigo	Manchester C	£13.8m
14 Odoi, Denis	Lokeren	Fulham	Undisclosed
22 Pereira, Hildeberto	Benfica	Nottingham F	Loan
1 Pereira, Quentin	Epernay Champagne	Port Vale	Free
22 Perquis, Damien	Toronto	Nottingham F	Free
6 Saadi, Idris	KV Kortrijk	Cardiff C	Loan
5 Sacko, Hadi	Sporting Lisbon	Leeds U	Loan
5 Saleiro, Carlos	Clube Oriental de Lisboa	Port Vale	Free
22 Sattelmaier, Rouven	Stuttgart Kickers	Bradford C	Free
30 Silvio	Atletico Madrid	Wolverhampton W	Undisclosed
25 Sobhi, Ramadan	Al Ahly	Stoke C	£5m
8 Stankovic, Jon Gorenc	Borussia Dortmund	Huddersfield T	Undisclosed
1 Success, Isaac	Granada	Watford	£12.5m
5 Tavares, Paulo	Vitoria Setubal	Port Vale	Free
11 Tore, Gokhan	Besiktas	West Ham U	Loan
2 Tursun, Alper	Alanyaspor	Crawley T	Free
6 van der Hoorn, Mike	Ajax	Swansea C	Undisclosed
4 Zinchenko, Oleksandr	FC Ufa	Manchester C	Undisclosed
6 Zohore, Kenneth	KV Kortrijk	Cardiff C	Undisclosed
16 Zuniga, Juan Camilo	Napoli	Watford	Loan
AUGUST 2016			
31 Alonso, Marcos	Fiorentina	Chelsea	£23m
2 Aneke, Chuks	Zulte Waregem	Milton Keynes D	Free
31 Arbeloa, Alvaro	Real Madrid	West Ham U	Free
11 Baston, Borja	Atletico Madrid	Swansea C	£15.5m
29 Boufal, Sofiane	Lille	Southampton	£16m
25 Bravo, Claudio	Barcelona	Manchester C	£15.4m
11 Calleri, Jonathan	Deportivo Maldonado	West Ham U	Loan
31 Cavaleiro, Ivan	Monaco	Wolverhampton W	Undisclosed
2 Dadi, Jon	Kaiserslautern	Wolverhampton W	Undisclosed
11 D'Almeida, Sessi	Paris Saint-Germain	Barnsley	Free
16 Defour, Steven	Anderlecht	Burnley	£7.35m
31 Djalo, Aliu	PS Kemi	Crawley T	Free
31 Dumitru, Nicolao	Napoli	Nottingham F	Loan
25 Eduardo	Dinamo Zagreb	Chelsea	Undisclosed
31 Engvall, Gustav	IFK Gothenburg	Bristol C	Undisclosed
26 Gladon, Paul	Heracles	Wolverhampton W	Undisclosed
31 Henriksen, Markus	AZ Alkmaar	Hull C	Loan
1 Hernandez, Pablo	Al-Arabi	Leeds U	Loan
18 Jansson, Pontus	Torino	Leeds U	Loan
3 Jesus, Gabriel	Palmeiras	Manchester C	£27m
22 John, Ola	Benfica	Wolverhampton W	Loan

12	Jozabed	Rayo Vallecano	Fulham	Undisclosed
3	Kapustka, Bartosz	Cracovia	Leicester C	£7.5m
3	Kasami, Pajtim	Olympiacos	Nottingham F	Loan
26	Kebano, Neeskens	Genk	Fulham	Undisclosed
28	Lazaar, Achraf	Palermo	Newcastle U	Undisclosed
31	Lica	Porto	Nottingham F	Undisclosed
5	Llorente, Fernando	Sevilla	Swansea C	Undisclosed
31	Lopez, Pau	Espanyol	Tottenham H	Loan
31	Luiz, David	Paris Saint-Germain	Chelsea	£34m
1	Makris, Andreas	Anorthosis Famagusta	Walsall	Undisclosed
25	Manquillo, Javier	Atletico Madrid	Sunderland	Loan
8	Masuaku, Arthur	Olympiacos	West Ham U	£6m
31	Mbokani, Dieumerci	Dynamo Kyiv	Hull C	Loan
19	McBean, Jack	LA Galaxy	Coventry C	Loan
2	McCann, Chris	Atlanta U	Coventry C	Loan
29	Mezague, Teddy	Royal Excel Mouscron	Leyton Orient	Free
25	Moore, Taylor	Lens	Bristol C	Undisclosed
6	Moreno, Marlos	Atletico Nacional	Manchester C	£4.75m
30	Mustafi, Shkodran	Valencia	Arsenal	Around £35m
31	Ndong, Didier	Lorient	Sunderland	£13.6m
6	Ngbakoto, Yeni	Metz	QPR	Undisclosed
31	Nkoudou, Georges-Kevin	Marseille	Tottenham H	£9m
31	N'Nomo, Ulrich	Chateauroux	Leyton Orient	Undisclosed
29	Okaka, Stefano	Anderlecht	Watford	Undisclosed
30	Oliveira, Nelson	Benfica	Norwich C	Undisclosed
15	Oniangue, Prince	Reims	Wolverhampton W	Undisclosed
19	Pereyra, Roberto	Juventus	Watford	£13m
30	Perez, Lucas	Deportivo La Coruna	Arsenal	£17.1m
1	Pied, Jeremy	Nice	Southampton	Free
9	Pogba, Paul	Juventus	Manchester U	£89.3m
16	Rabieg, Vincent	Red Bull Leipzig	Bradford C	Free
30	Saiss, Romain	Angers	Wolverhampton W	Undisclosed
2	Sane, Leroy	Schalke	Manchester C	£37m
19	Sasso, Vincent	Braga	Sheffield W	Undisclosed
23	Sigurdsson, Ragnar	FC Krasnodar	Fulham	Undisclosed
31	Slimani, Islam	Sporting Lisbon	Leicester C	£29.7m
1	Song, Alex	Barcelona	Rubin Kazan	Free
24	Stojkovic, Vladimir	Maccabi Haifa	Nottingham F	Undisclosed
30	Sylla, Idrissa	Anderlecht	QPR	Undisclosed
2	Teixeira, Joao	Benfica	Wolverhampton W	Loan
18	Wieser, Sandro	FC Thun	Reading	Free
31	Wszolek, Pawel	Hellas Verona	QPR	Loan
SEPTEMBER 2016				
7	Mika	Boavista	Sunderland	Undisclosed
JANUARY 2017				
1	Arquin, Yoann	Syrianska	Mansfield T	Free
25	Bjarnason, Birkir	FC Basel	Aston Villa	Undisclosed
30	Costa, Helder	Benfica	Wolverhampton W	£13m
31	Cyriac, Gohi	KV Oostende	Fulham	Loan
31	Dijks, Mitchell	Ajax	Norwich C	Loan
4	Djuric, Milan	Cesena	Bristol C	Undisclosed
20	Elabdellaoui, Omar	Olympiacos	Hull C	Loan
13	Evandro	Porto	Hull C	Undisclosed
20	Frei, Kerim	Besiktas	Birmingham C	£2.2m
19	Giefer, Fabian	Schalke	Bristol C	Loan
31	Hassen, Mouez	Nice	Southampton	Loan
4	Hegeler, Jens	Hertha Berlin	Bristol C	Undisclosed
6	Henriksen, Markus	AZ Alkmaar	Hull C	Undisclosed
9	Hernandez, Pablo	Al-Arabi	Leeds U	Undisclosed
20	Holy, Tomas	Sparta Prague	Gillingham	Undisclosed
19	Keita, Cheick	Virtus Entella	Birmingham C	Undisclosed
31	Milivojevic, Luka	Olympiacos	Crystal Palace	Undisclosed
31	Morrison, Ravel	Lazio	QPR	Loan
12	Narsingh, Luciano	PSV Eindhoven	Swansea C	Undisclosed
31	N'Diaye, Alfred	Villarreal	Hull C	Loan
5	Ndidi, Wilfred	Genk	Leicester C	£15m
30	Ngombo, Maecky	Fortuna Dusseldorf	Milton Keynes D	Loan
26	Niang, M'Baye	AC Milan	Watford	Loan
31	Pedraza, Alfonso	Villarreal	Leeds U	Loan
26	Petsos, Thanos	Werder Bremen	Fulham	Loan
30	Popa, Adrian	Steaua Bucharest	Reading	Undisclosed
20	Quaner, Collin	Union Berlin	Huddersfield T	Undisclosed
31	Ranocchia, Andrea	Inter Milan	Hull C	Loan
20	Schwabl, Markus	VfR Aalen	Fleetwood T	Undisclosed
27	Teixeira, Joao	Benfica	Nottingham F	Loan
31	Wague, Molla	Udinese	Leicester C	Loan
31	Wszolek, Pawel	Hellas Verona	QPR	Undisclosed
25	Zarate, Mauro	Fiorentina	Watford	Undisclosed
FEBRUARY 2017				
24	Bentaleb, Nabil	Schalke 04	Tottenham H	Undisclosed
2	Jansson, Pontus	Torino	Leeds U	Undisclosed
MARCH 2017				
22	Kachunga, Elias	Ingolstadt	Huddersfield T	£1.1m
MAY 2017				
23	Dalsgaard, Henrik	Zulte Waregem	Brentford	Undisclosed
19	Gross, Pascal	Ingolstadt	Brighton & HA	Undisclosed
26	Silva, Bernardo	Monaco	Manchester C	£43m

ENGLISH LEAGUE HONOURS 1888–2017

**Won or placed on goal average (ratio), goal difference or most goals scored. ‡Not promoted after play-offs. No official competition during 1915–19 and 1939–46, regional leagues operated.*

FOOTBALL LEAGUE (1888–89 to 1891–92) – TIER 1

MAXIMUM POINTS: *a* 44; *b* 60.

1	1888–89*a*	Preston NE	40	Aston Villa	29	Wolverhampton W	28
1	1889–90*a*	Preston NE	33	Everton	31	Blackburn R	27
1	1890–91*a*	Everton	29	Preston NE	27	Notts Co	26
1	1891–92*b*	Sunderland	42	Preston NE	37	Bolton W	36

DIVISION 1 (1892–93 to 1991–92)

MAXIMUM POINTS: *a* 44; *b* 52; *c* 60; *d* 68; *e* 76; *f* 84; *g* 126; *h* 120; *k* 114.

1	1892–93*c*	Sunderland	48	Preston NE	37	Everton	36
1	1893–94*c*	Aston Villa	44	Sunderland	38	Derby Co	36
1	1894–95*c*	Sunderland	47	Everton	42	Aston Villa	39
1	1895–96*c*	Aston Villa	45	Derby Co	41	Everton	39
1	1896–97*c*	Aston Villa	47	Sheffield U*	36	Derby Co	36
1	1897–98*c*	Sheffield U	42	Sunderland	37	Wolverhampton W*	35
1	1898–99*d*	Aston Villa	45	Liverpool	43	Burnley	39
1	1899–1900*d*	Aston Villa	50	Sheffield U	48	Sunderland	41
1	1900–01*d*	Liverpool	45	Sunderland	43	Notts Co	40
1	1901–02*d*	Sunderland	44	Everton	41	Newcastle U	37
1	1902–03*d*	The Wednesday	42	Aston Villa*	41	Sunderland	41
1	1903–04*d*	The Wednesday	47	Manchester C	44	Everton	43
1	1904–05*d*	Newcastle U	48	Everton	47	Manchester C	46
1	1905–06*e*	Liverpool	51	Preston NE	47	The Wednesday	44
1	1906–07*e*	Newcastle U	51	Bristol C	48	Everton*	45
1	1907–08*e*	Manchester U	52	Aston Villa*	43	Manchester C	43
1	1908–09*e*	Newcastle U	53	Everton	46	Sunderland	44
1	1909–10*e*	Aston Villa	53	Liverpool	48	Blackburn R*	45
1	1910–11*e*	Manchester U	52	Aston Villa	51	Sunderland*	45
1	1911–12*e*	Blackburn R	49	Everton	46	Newcastle U	44
1	1912–13*e*	Sunderland	54	Aston Villa	50	Sheffield W	49
1	1913–14*e*	Blackburn R	51	Aston Villa	44	Middlesbrough*	43
1	1914–15*e*	Everton	46	Oldham Ath	45	Blackburn R*	43
1	1919–20*f*	WBA	60	Burnley	51	Chelsea	49
1	1920–21*f*	Burnley	59	Manchester C	54	Bolton W	52
1	1921–22*f*	Liverpool	57	Tottenham H	51	Burnley	49
1	1922–23*f*	Liverpool	60	Sunderland	54	Huddersfield T	53
1	1923–24*f*	Huddersfield T*	57	Cardiff C	57	Sunderland	53
1	1924–25*f*	Huddersfield T	58	WBA	56	Bolton W	55
1	1925–26*f*	Huddersfield T	57	Arsenal	52	Sunderland	48
1	1926–27*f*	Newcastle U	56	Huddersfield T	51	Sunderland	49
1	1927–28*f*	Everton	53	Huddersfield T	51	Leicester C	48
1	1928–29*f*	Sheffield W	52	Leicester C	51	Aston Villa	50
1	1929–30*f*	Sheffield W	60	Derby Co	50	Manchester C*	47
1	1930–31*f*	Arsenal	66	Aston Villa	59	Sheffield W	52
1	1931–32*f*	Everton	56	Arsenal	54	Sheffield W	50
1	1932–33*f*	Arsenal	58	Aston Villa	54	Sheffield W	51
1	1933–34*f*	Arsenal	59	Huddersfield T	56	Tottenham H	49
1	1934–35*f*	Arsenal	58	Sunderland	54	Sheffield W	49
1	1935–36*f*	Sunderland	56	Derby Co*	48	Huddersfield T	48
1	1936–37*f*	Manchester C	57	Charlton Ath	54	Arsenal	52
1	1937–38*f*	Arsenal	52	Wolverhampton W	51	Preston NE	49
1	1938–39*f*	Everton	59	Wolverhampton W	55	Charlton Ath	50
1	1946–47*f*	Liverpool	57	Manchester U*	56	Wolverhampton W	56
1	1947–48*f*	Arsenal	59	Manchester U*	52	Burnley	52
1	1948–49*f*	Portsmouth	58	Manchester U*	53	Derby Co	53
1	1949–50*f*	Portsmouth*	53	Wolverhampton W	53	Sunderland	52
1	1950–51*f*	Tottenham H	60	Manchester U	56	Blackpool	50
1	1951–52*f*	Manchester U	57	Tottenham H*	53	Arsenal	53
1	1952–53*f*	Arsenal*	54	Preston NE	54	Wolverhampton W	51
1	1953–54*f*	Wolverhampton W	57	WBA	53	Huddersfield T	51
1	1954–55*f*	Chelsea	52	Wolverhampton W*	48	Portsmouth*	48
1	1955–56*f*	Manchester U	60	Blackpool*	49	Wolverhampton W	49
1	1956–57*f*	Manchester U	64	Tottenham H*	56	Preston NE	56
1	1957–58*f*	Wolverhampton W	64	Preston NE	59	Tottenham H	51
1	1958–59*f*	Wolverhampton W	61	Manchester U	55	Arsenal*	50
1	1959–60*f*	Burnley	55	Wolverhampton W	54	Tottenham H	53
1	1960–61*f*	Tottenham H	66	Sheffield W	58	Wolverhampton W	57
1	1961–62*f*	Ipswich T	56	Burnley	53	Tottenham H	52
1	1962–63*f*	Everton	61	Tottenham H	55	Burnley	54
1	1963–64*f*	Liverpool	57	Manchester U	53	Everton	52
1	1964–65*f*	Manchester U*	61	Leeds U	61	Chelsea	56

1	1965–66*f*	Liverpool	61	Leeds U*	55	Burnley	55
1	1966–67*f*	Manchester U	60	Nottingham F*	56	Tottenham H	56
1	1967–68*f*	Manchester C	58	Manchester U	56	Liverpool	55
1	1968–69*f*	Leeds U	67	Liverpool	61	Everton	57
1	1969–70*f*	Everton	66	Leeds U	57	Chelsea	55
1	1970–71*f*	Arsenal	65	Leeds U	64	Tottenham H*	52
1	1971–72*f*	Derby Co	58	Leeds U*	57	Liverpool*	57
1	1972–73*f*	Liverpool	60	Arsenal	57	Leeds U	53
1	1973–74*f*	Leeds U	62	Liverpool	57	Derby Co	48
1	1974–75*f*	Derby Co	53	Liverpool*	51	Ipswich T	51
1	1975–76*f*	Liverpool	60	QPR	59	Manchester U	56
1	1976–77*f*	Liverpool	57	Manchester C	56	Ipswich T	52
1	1977–78*f*	Nottingham F	64	Liverpool	57	Everton	55
1	1978–79*f*	Liverpool	68	Nottingham F	60	WBA	59
1	1979–80*f*	Liverpool	60	Manchester U	58	Ipswich T	53
1	1980–81*f*	Aston Villa	60	Ipswich T	56	Arsenal	53
1	1981–82*g*	Liverpool	87	Ipswich T	83	Manchester U	78
1	1982–83*g*	Liverpool	82	Watford	71	Manchester U	70
1	1983–84*g*	Liverpool	80	Southampton	77	Nottingham F*	74
1	1984–85*g*	Everton	90	Liverpool*	77	Tottenham H	77
1	1985–86g	Liverpool	88	Everton	86	West Ham U	84
1	1986–87*g*	Everton	86	Liverpool	77	Tottenham H	71
1	1987–88*h*	Liverpool	90	Manchester U	81	Nottingham F	73
1	1988–89*k*	Arsenal*	76	Liverpool	76	Nottingham F	64
1	1989–90*k*	Liverpool	79	Aston Villa	70	Tottenham H	63
1	1990–91*k*	Arsenal[1]	83	Liverpool	76	Crystal Palace	69
1	1991–92*g*	Leeds U	82	Manchester U	78	Sheffield W	75

[1]*Arsenal deducted 2pts due to player misconduct in match on 20/10/1990 v Manchester U at Old Trafford.*

FA PREMIER LEAGUE (1992–93 to 2016–17)

MAXIMUM POINTS: *a* 126; *b* 114.

1	1992–93*a*	Manchester U	84	Aston Villa	74	Norwich C	72
1	1993–94*a*	Manchester U	92	Blackburn R	84	Newcastle U	77
1	1994–95*a*	Blackburn R	89	Manchester U	88	Nottingham F	77
1	1995–96*b*	Manchester U	82	Newcastle U	78	Liverpool	71
1	1996–97*b*	Manchester U	75	Newcastle U*	68	Arsenal*	68
1	1997–98*b*	Arsenal	78	Manchester U	77	Liverpool	65
1	1998–99*b*	Manchester U	79	Arsenal	78	Chelsea	75
1	1999–2000*b*	Manchester U	91	Arsenal	73	Leeds U	69
1	2000–01*b*	Manchester U	80	Arsenal	70	Liverpool	69
1	2001–02*b*	Arsenal	87	Liverpool	80	Manchester U	77
1	2002–03*b*	Manchester U	83	Arsenal	78	Newcastle U	69
1	2003–04*b*	Arsenal	90	Chelsea	79	Manchester U	75
1	2004–05*b*	Chelsea	95	Arsenal	83	Manchester U	77
1	2005–06*b*	Chelsea	91	Manchester U	83	Liverpool	82
1	2006–07*b*	Manchester U	89	Chelsea	83	Liverpool*	68
1	2007–08*b*	Manchester U	87	Chelsea	85	Arsenal	83
1	2008–09*b*	Manchester U	90	Liverpool	86	Chelsea	83
1	2009–10*b*	Chelsea	86	Manchester U	85	Arsenal	75
1	2010–11*b*	Manchester U	80	Chelsea*	71	Manchester C	71
1	2011–12*b*	Manchester C*	89	Manchester U	89	Arsenal	70
1	2012–13*b*	Manchester U	89	Manchester C	78	Chelsea	75
1	2013–14*b*	Manchester C	86	Liverpool	84	Chelsea	82
1	2014–15*b*	Chelsea	87	Manchester C	79	Arsenal	75
1	2015–16*b*	Leicester C	81	Arsenal	71	Tottenham H	70
1	2016–17*b*	Chelsea	93	Tottenham H	86	Manchester C	78

DIVISION 2 (1892–93 to 1991–92) – TIER 2

MAXIMUM POINTS: *a* 44; *b* 56; *c* 60; *d* 68; *e* 76; *f* 84; *g* 126; *h* 132; *k* 138.

2	1892–93*a*	Small Heath	36	Sheffield U	35	Darwen	30
2	1893–94*b*	Liverpool	50	Small Heath	42	Notts Co	39
2	1894–95*c*	Bury	48	Notts Co	39	Newton Heath*	38
2	1895–96*c*	Liverpool*	46	Manchester C	46	Grimsby T*	42
2	1896–97*c*	Notts Co	42	Newton Heath	39	Grimsby T	38
2	1897–98*c*	Burnley	48	Newcastle U	45	Manchester C	39
2	1898–99*d*	Manchester C	52	Glossop NE	46	Leicester Fosse	45
2	1899–1900*d*	The Wednesday	54	Bolton W	52	Small Heath	46
2	1900–01*d*	Grimsby T	49	Small Heath	48	Burnley	44
2	1901–02*d*	WBA	55	Middlesbrough	51	Preston NE*	42
2	1902–03*d*	Manchester C	54	Small Heath	51	Woolwich A	48
2	1903–04*d*	Preston NE	50	Woolwich A	49	Manchester U	48
2	1904–05*d*	Liverpool	58	Bolton W	56	Manchester U	53
2	1905–06*e*	Bristol C	66	Manchester U	62	Chelsea	53
2	1906–07*e*	Nottingham F	60	Chelsea	57	Leicester Fosse	48
2	1907–08*e*	Bradford C	54	Leicester Fosse	52	Oldham Ath	50
2	1908–09*e*	Bolton W	52	Tottenham H*	51	WBA	51
2	1909–10*e*	Manchester C	54	Oldham Ath*	53	Hull C*	53
2	1910–11*e*	WBA	53	Bolton W	51	Chelsea	49

2	1911–12*e*	Derby Co*	54	Chelsea	54	Burnley	52
2	1912–13*e*	Preston NE	53	Burnley	50	Birmingham	46
2	1913–14*e*	Notts Co	53	Bradford PA*	49	Woolwich A	49
2	1914–15*e*	Derby Co	53	Preston NE	50	Barnsley	47
2	1919–20*f*	Tottenham H	70	Huddersfield T	64	Birmingham	56
2	1920–21*f*	Birmingham*	58	Cardiff C	58	Bristol C	51
2	1921–22*f*	Nottingham F	56	Stoke C*	52	Barnsley	52
2	1922–23*f*	Notts Co	53	West Ham U*	51	Leicester C	51
2	1923–24*f*	Leeds U	54	Bury*	51	Derby Co	51
2	1924–25*f*	Leicester C	59	Manchester U	57	Derby Co	55
2	1925–26*f*	Sheffield W	60	Derby Co	57	Chelsea	52
2	1926–27*f*	Middlesbrough	62	Portsmouth*	54	Manchester C	54
2	1927–28*f*	Manchester C	59	Leeds U	57	Chelsea	54
2	1928–29*f*	Middlesbrough	55	Grimsby T	53	Bradford PA*	48
2	1929–30*f*	Blackpool	58	Chelsea	55	Oldham Ath	53
2	1930–31*f*	Everton	61	WBA	54	Tottenham H	51
2	1931–32*f*	Wolverhampton W	56	Leeds U	54	Stoke C	52
2	1932–33*f*	Stoke C	56	Tottenham H	55	Fulham	50
2	1933–34*f*	Grimsby T	59	Preston NE	52	Bolton W*	51
2	1934–35*f*	Brentford	61	Bolton W*	56	West Ham U	56
2	1935–36*f*	Manchester U	56	Charlton Ath	55	Sheffield U*	52
2	1936–37*f*	Leicester C	56	Blackpool	55	Bury	52
2	1937–38*f*	Aston Villa	57	Manchester U*	53	Sheffield U	53
2	1938–39*f*	Blackburn R	55	Sheffield U	54	Sheffield W	53
2	1946–47*f*	Manchester C	62	Burnley	58	Birmingham C	55
2	1947–48*f*	Birmingham C	59	Newcastle U	56	Southampton	52
2	1948–49*f*	Fulham	57	WBA	56	Southampton	55
2	1949–50*f*	Tottenham H	61	Sheffield W*	52	Sheffield U*	52
2	1950–51*f*	Preston NE	57	Manchester C	52	Cardiff C	50
2	1951–52*f*	Sheffield W	53	Cardiff C*	51	Birmingham C	51
2	1952–53*f*	Sheffield U	60	Huddersfield T	58	Luton T	52
2	1953–54*f*	Leicester C*	56	Everton	56	Blackburn R	55
2	1954–55*f*	Birmingham C*	54	Luton T*	54	Rotherham U	54
2	1955–56*f*	Sheffield W	55	Leeds U	52	Liverpool*	48
2	1956–57*f*	Leicester C	61	Nottingham F	54	Liverpool	53
2	1957–58*f*	West Ham U	57	Blackburn R	56	Charlton Ath	55
2	1958–59*f*	Sheffield W	62	Fulham	60	Sheffield U*	53
2	1959–60*f*	Aston Villa	59	Cardiff C	58	Liverpool*	50
2	1960–61*f*	Ipswich T	59	Sheffield U	58	Liverpool	52
2	1961–62*f*	Liverpool	62	Leyton Orient	54	Sunderland	53
2	1962–63*f*	Stoke C	53	Chelsea*	52	Sunderland	52
2	1963–64*f*	Leeds U	63	Sunderland	61	Preston NE	56
2	1964–65*f*	Newcastle U	57	Northampton T	56	Bolton W	50
2	1965–66*f*	Manchester C	59	Southampton	54	Coventry C	53
2	1966–67*f*	Coventry C	59	Wolverhampton W	58	Carlisle U	52
2	1967–68*f*	Ipswich T	59	QPR*	58	Blackpool	58
2	1968–69*f*	Derby Co	63	Crystal Palace	56	Charlton Ath	50
2	1969–70*f*	Huddersfield T	60	Blackpool	53	Leicester C	51
2	1970–71*f*	Leicester C	59	Sheffield U	56	Cardiff C*	53
2	1971–72*f*	Norwich C	57	Birmingham C	56	Millwall	55
2	1972–73*f*	Burnley	62	QPR	61	Aston Villa	50
2	1973–74*f*	Middlesbrough	65	Luton T	50	Carlisle U	49
2	1974–75*f*	Manchester U	61	Aston Villa	58	Norwich C	53
2	1975–76*f*	Sunderland	56	Bristol C*	53	WBA	53
2	1976–77*f*	Wolverhampton W	57	Chelsea	55	Nottingham F	52
2	1977–78*f*	Bolton W	58	Southampton	57	Tottenham H*	56
2	1978–79*f*	Crystal Palace	57	Brighton & HA*	56	Stoke C	56
2	1979–80*f*	Leicester C	55	Sunderland	54	Birmingham C*	53
2	1980–81*f*	West Ham U	66	Notts Co	53	Swansea C*	50
2	1981–82*g*	Luton T	88	Watford	80	Norwich C	71
2	1982–83*g*	QPR	85	Wolverhampton W	75	Leicester C	70
2	1983–84*g*	Chelsea*	88	Sheffield W	88	Newcastle U	80
2	1984–85*g*	Oxford U	84	Birmingham C	82	Manchester C*	74
2	1985–86*g*	Norwich C	84	Charlton Ath	77	Wimbledon	76
2	1986–87*g*	Derby Co	84	Portsmouth	78	Oldham Ath‡	75
2	1987–88*h*	Millwall	82	Aston Villa*	78	Middlesbrough	78
2	1988–89*k*	Chelsea	99	Manchester C	82	Crystal Palace	81
2	1989–90*k*	Leeds U*	85	Sheffield U	85	Newcastle U‡	80
2	1990–91*k*	Oldham Ath	88	West Ham U	87	Sheffield W	82
2	1991–92*k*	Ipswich T	84	Middlesbrough	80	Derby Co	78

FIRST DIVISION (1992–93 to 2003–04)

MAXIMUM POINTS: 138

2	1992–93	Newcastle U	96	West Ham U*	88	Portsmouth‡	88
2	1993–94	Crystal Palace	90	Nottingham F	83	Millwall‡	74
2	1994–95	Middlesbrough	82	Reading‡	79	Bolton W	77
2	1995–96	Sunderland	83	Derby Co	79	Crystal Palace‡	75
2	1996–97	Bolton W	98	Barnsley	80	Wolverhampton W‡	76

2	1997–98	Nottingham F	94	Middlesbrough	91	Sunderland‡	90
2	1998–99	Sunderland	105	Bradford C	87	Ipswich T‡	86
2	1999–2000	Charlton Ath	91	Manchester C	89	Ipswich T	87
2	2000–01	Fulham	101	Blackburn R	91	Bolton W	87
2	2001–02	Manchester C	99	WBA	89	Wolverhampton W‡	86
2	2002–03	Portsmouth	98	Leicester C	92	Sheffield U‡	80
2	2003–04	Norwich C	94	WBA	86	Sunderland‡	79

FOOTBALL LEAGUE CHAMPIONSHIP (2004–05 to 2016–17)

MAXIMUM POINTS: 138

2	2004–05	Sunderland	94	Wigan Ath	87	Ipswich T‡	85
2	2005–06	Reading	106	Sheffield U	90	Watford	81
2	2006–07	Sunderland	88	Birmingham C	86	Derby Co	84
2	2007–08	WBA	81	Stoke C	79	Hull C	75
2	2008–09	Wolverhampton W	90	Birmingham C	83	Sheffield U‡	80
2	2009–10	Newcastle U	102	WBA	91	Nottingham F‡	79
2	2010–11	QPR	88	Norwich C	84	Swansea C*	80
2	2011–12	Reading	89	Southampton	88	West Ham U	86
2	2012–13	Cardiff C	87	Hull C	79	Watford‡	77
2	2013–14	Leicester C	102	Burnley	93	Derby Co‡	85
2	2014–15	Bournemouth	90	Watford	89	Norwich C	86
2	2015–16	Burnley	93	Middlesbrough*	89	Brighton & HA‡	89
2	2015–16	Burnley	93	Middlesbrough*	89	Brighton & HA‡	89
2	2016–17	Newcastle U	94	Brighton & HA	93	Reading‡	85

DIVISION 3 (1920–1921) – TIER 3

MAXIMUM POINTS: ***a*** **84.**

3	1920–21*a*	Crystal Palace	59	Southampton	54	QPR	53

DIVISION 3—SOUTH (1921–22 to 1957–58)

MAXIMUM POINTS: ***a*** **84;** ***b*** **92.**

3	1921–22*a*	Southampton*	61	Plymouth Arg	61	Portsmouth	53
3	1922–23*a*	Bristol C	59	Plymouth Arg*	53	Swansea T	53
3	1923–24*a*	Portsmouth	59	Plymouth Arg	55	Millwall	54
3	1924–25*a*	Swansea T	57	Plymouth Arg	56	Bristol C	53
3	1925–26*a*	Reading	57	Plymouth Arg	56	Millwall	53
3	1926–27*a*	Bristol C	62	Plymouth Arg	60	Millwall	56
3	1927–28*a*	Millwall	65	Northampton T	55	Plymouth Arg	53
3	1928–29*a*	Charlton Ath*	54	Crystal Palace	54	Northampton T*	52
3	1929–30*a*	Plymouth Arg	68	Brentford	61	QPR	51
3	1930–31*a*	Notts Co	59	Crystal Palace	51	Brentford	50
3	1931–32*a*	Fulham	57	Reading	55	Southend U	53
3	1932–33*a*	Brentford	62	Exeter C	58	Norwich C	57
3	1933–34*a*	Norwich C	61	Coventry C*	54	Reading*	54
3	1934–35*a*	Charlton Ath	61	Reading	53	Coventry C	51
3	1935–36*a*	Coventry C	57	Luton T	56	Reading	54
3	1936–37*a*	Luton T	58	Notts Co	56	Brighton & HA	53
3	1937–38*a*	Millwall	56	Bristol C	55	QPR*	53
3	1938–39*a*	Newport Co	55	Crystal Palace	52	Brighton & HA	49
3	1946–47*a*	Cardiff C	66	QPR	57	Bristol C	51
3	1947–48*a*	QPR	61	Bournemouth	57	Walsall	51
3	1948–49*a*	Swansea T	62	Reading	55	Bournemouth	52
3	1949–50*a*	Notts Co	58	Northampton T*	51	Southend U	51
3	1950–51*b*	Nottingham F	70	Norwich C	64	Reading*	57
3	1951–52*b*	Plymouth Arg	66	Reading*	61	Norwich C	61
3	1952–53*b*	Bristol R	64	Millwall*	62	Northampton T	62
3	1953–54*b*	Ipswich T	64	Brighton & HA	61	Bristol C	56
3	1954–55*b*	Bristol C	70	Leyton Orient	61	Southampton	59
3	1955–56*b*	Leyton Orient	66	Brighton & HA	65	Ipswich T	64
3	1956–57*b*	Ipswich T*	59	Torquay U	59	Colchester U	58
3	1957–58*b*	Brighton & HA	60	Brentford*	58	Plymouth Arg	58

DIVISION 3—NORTH (1921–22 to 1957–58)

MAXIMUM POINTS: ***a*** **76;** ***b*** **84;** ***c*** **80;** ***d*** **92.**

3	1921–22*a*	Stockport Co	56	Darlington*	50	Grimsby T	50
3	1922–23*a*	Nelson	51	Bradford PA	47	Walsall	46
3	1923–24*b*	Wolverhampton W	63	Rochdale	62	Chesterfield	54
3	1924–25*b*	Darlington	58	Nelson*	53	New Brighton	53
3	1925–26*b*	Grimsby T	61	Bradford PA	60	Rochdale	59
3	1926–27*b*	Stoke C	63	Rochdale	58	Bradford PA	55
3	1927–28*b*	Bradford PA	63	Lincoln C	55	Stockport Co	54
3	1928–29*b*	Bradford C	63	Stockport Co	62	Wrexham	52
3	1929–30*b*	Port Vale	67	Stockport Co	63	Darlington*	50
3	1930–31*b*	Chesterfield	58	Lincoln C	57	Wrexham*	54
3	1931–32*c*	Lincoln C*	57	Gateshead	57	Chester	50
3	1932–33*b*	Hull C	59	Wrexham	57	Stockport Co	54

3	1933–34*b*	Barnsley	62	Chesterfield	61	Stockport Co	59
3	1934–35*b*	Doncaster R	57	Halifax T	55	Chester	54
3	1935–36*b*	Chesterfield	60	Chester*	55	Tranmere R	55
3	1936–37*b*	Stockport Co	60	Lincoln C	57	Chester	53
3	1937–38*b*	Tranmere R	56	Doncaster R	54	Hull C	53
3	1938–39*b*	Barnsley	67	Doncaster R	56	Bradford C	52
3	1946–47*b*	Doncaster R	72	Rotherham U	64	Chester	56
3	1947–48*b*	Lincoln C	60	Rotherham U	59	Wrexham	50
3	1948–49*b*	Hull C	65	Rotherham U	62	Doncaster R	50
3	1949–50*b*	Doncaster R	55	Gateshead	53	Rochdale*	51
3	1950–51*d*	Rotherham U	71	Mansfield T	64	Carlisle U	62
3	1951–52*d*	Lincoln C	69	Grimsby T	66	Stockport Co	59
3	1952–53*d*	Oldham Ath	59	Port Vale	58	Wrexham	56
3	1953–54*d*	Port Vale	69	Barnsley	58	Scunthorpe U	57
3	1954–55*d*	Barnsley	65	Accrington S	61	Scunthorpe U*	58
3	1955–56*d*	Grimsby T	68	Derby Co	63	Accrington S	59
3	1956–57*d*	Derby Co	63	Hartlepools U	59	Accrington S*	58
3	1957–58*d*	Scunthorpe U	66	Accrington S	59	Bradford C	57

DIVISION 3 (1958–59 to 1991–92)

MAXIMUM POINTS: 92; 138 FROM 1981–82.

3	1958–59	Plymouth Arg	62	Hull C	61	Brentford*	57
3	1959–60	Southampton	61	Norwich C	59	Shrewsbury T*	52
3	1960–61	Bury	68	Walsall	62	QPR	60
3	1961–62	Portsmouth	65	Grimsby T	62	Bournemouth*	59
3	1962–63	Northampton T	62	Swindon T	58	Port Vale	54
3	1963–64	Coventry C*	60	Crystal Palace	60	Watford	58
3	1964–65	Carlisle U	60	Bristol C*	59	Mansfield T	59
3	1965–66	Hull C	69	Millwall	65	QPR	57
3	1966–67	QPR	67	Middlesbrough	55	Watford	54
3	1967–68	Oxford U	57	Bury	56	Shrewsbury T	55
3	1968–69	Watford*	64	Swindon T	64	Luton T	61
3	1969–70	Orient	62	Luton T	60	Bristol R	56
3	1970–71	Preston NE	61	Fulham	60	Halifax T	56
3	1971–72	Aston Villa	70	Brighton & HA	65	Bournemouth*	62
3	1972–73	Bolton W	61	Notts Co	57	Blackburn R	55
3	1973–74	Oldham Ath	62	Bristol R*	61	York C	61
3	1974–75	Blackburn R	60	Plymouth Arg	59	Charlton Ath	55
3	1975–76	Hereford U	63	Cardiff C	57	Millwall	56
3	1976–77	Mansfield T	64	Brighton & HA	61	Crystal Palace*	59
3	1977–78	Wrexham	61	Cambridge U	58	Preston NE*	56
3	1978–79	Shrewsbury T	61	Watford*	60	Swansea C	60
3	1979–80	Grimsby T	62	Blackburn R	59	Sheffield W	58
3	1980–81	Rotherham U	61	Barnsley*	59	Charlton Ath	59
3	1981–82	Burnley*	80	Carlisle U	80	Fulham	78
3	1982–83	Portsmouth	91	Cardiff C	86	Huddersfield T	82
3	1983–84	Oxford U	95	Wimbledon	87	Sheffield U*	83
3	1984–85	Bradford C	94	Millwall	90	Hull C	87
3	1985–86	Reading	94	Plymouth Arg	87	Derby Co	84
3	1986–87	Bournemouth	97	Middlesbrough	94	Swindon T	87
3	1987–88	Sunderland	93	Brighton & HA	84	Walsall	82
3	1988–89	Wolverhampton W	92	Sheffield U*	84	Port Vale	84
3	1989–90	Bristol R	93	Bristol C	91	Notts Co	87
3	1990–91	Cambridge U	86	Southend U	85	Grimsby T*	83
3	1991–92	Brentford	82	Birmingham C	81	Huddersfield T‡	78

SECOND DIVISION (1992–93 to 2003–04)

MAXIMUM POINTS: 138

3	1992–93	Stoke C	93	Bolton W	90	Port Vale‡	89
3	1993–94	Reading	89	Port Vale	88	Plymouth Arg*‡	85
3	1994–95	Birmingham C	89	Brentford‡	85	Crewe Alex‡	83
3	1995–96	Swindon T	92	Oxford U	83	Blackpool‡	82
3	1996–97	Bury	84	Stockport Co	82	Luton T‡	78
3	1997–98	Watford	88	Bristol C	85	Grimsby T	72
3	1998–99	Fulham	101	Walsall	87	Manchester C	82
3	1999–2000	Preston NE	95	Burnley	88	Gillingham	85
3	2000–01	Millwall	93	Rotherham U	91	Reading‡	86
3	2001–02	Brighton & HA	90	Reading	84	Brentford*‡	83
3	2002–03	Wigan Ath	100	Crewe Alex	86	Bristol C*‡	83
3	2003–04	Plymouth Arg	90	QPR	83	Bristol C‡	82

FOOTBALL LEAGUE 1 (2004–05 to 2016–17)

MAXIMUM POINTS: 138

3	2004–05	Luton T	98	Hull C	86	Tranmere R‡	79
3	2005–06	Southend U	82	Colchester U	79	Brentford‡	76
3	2006–07	Scunthorpe U	91	Bristol C	85	Blackpool	83
3	2007–08	Swansea C	92	Nottingham F	82	Doncaster R*	80
3	2008–09	Leicester C	96	Peterborough U	89	Milton Keynes D‡	87
3	2009–10	Norwich C	95	Leeds U	86	Millwall	85

3	2010–11	Brighton & HA	95	Southampton	92	Huddersfield T‡	87		
3	2011–12	Charlton Ath	101	Sheffield W	93	Sheffield U‡	90		
3	2012–13	Doncaster R	84	Bournemouth	83	Brentford‡	79		
3	2013–14	Wolverhampton W	103	Brentford	94	Leyton Orient‡	86		
3	2014–15	Bristol C	99	Milton Keynes D	91	Preston NE	89		
3	2015–16	Wigan Ath	87	Burton Alb	85	Walsall‡	84		
3	2016–17	Sheffield U	100	Bolton W	86	Scunthorpe U*‡	82		

DIVISION 4 (1958–59 to 1991–92) – TIER 4

MAXIMUM POINTS: 92; 138 FROM 1981–82.

4	1958–59	Port Vale	64	Coventry C*	60	York C	60	Shrewsbury T	58
4	1959–60	Walsall	65	Notts Co*	60	Torquay U	60	Watford	57
4	1960–61	Peterborough U	66	Crystal Palace	64	Northampton T*	60	Bradford PA	60
4	1961–62[2]	Millwall	56	Colchester U	55	Wrexham	53	Carlisle U	52
4	1962–63	Brentford	62	Oldham Ath*	59	Crewe Alex	59	Mansfield T*	57
4	1963–64	Gillingham*	60	Carlisle U	60	Workington	59	Exeter C	58
4	1964–65	Brighton & HA	63	Millwall*	62	York C	62	Oxford U	61
4	1965–66	Doncaster R*	59	Darlington	59	Torquay U	58	Colchester U*	56
4	1966–67	Stockport Co	64	Southport*	59	Barrow	59	Tranmere R	58
4	1967–68	Luton T	66	Barnsley	61	Hartlepools U	60	Crewe Alex	58
4	1968–69	Doncaster R	59	Halifax T	57	Rochdale*	56	Bradford C	56
4	1969–70	Chesterfield	64	Wrexham	61	Swansea C	60	Port Vale	59
4	1970–71	Notts Co	69	Bournemouth	60	Oldham Ath	59	York C	56
4	1971–72	Grimsby T	63	Southend U	60	Brentford	59	Scunthorpe U	57
4	1972–73	Southport	62	Hereford U	58	Cambridge U	57	Aldershot*	56
4	1973–74	Peterborough U	65	Gillingham	62	Colchester U	60	Bury	59
4	1974–75	Mansfield T	68	Shrewsbury T	62	Rotherham U	59	Chester*	57
4	1975–76	Lincoln C	74	Northampton T	68	Reading	60	Tranmere R	58
4	1976–77	Cambridge U	65	Exeter C	62	Colchester U*	59	Bradford C	59
4	1977–78	Watford	71	Southend U	60	Swansea C*	56	Brentford	56
4	1978–79	Reading	65	Grimsby T*	61	Wimbledon*	61	Barnsley	61
4	1979–80	Huddersfield T	66	Walsall	64	Newport Co	61	Portsmouth*	60
4	1980–81	Southend U	67	Lincoln C	65	Doncaster R	56	Wimbledon	55
4	1981–82	Sheffield U	96	Bradford C*	91	Wigan Ath	91	Bournemouth	88
4	1982–83	Wimbledon	98	Hull C	90	Port Vale	88	Scunthorpe U	83
4	1983–84	York C	101	Doncaster R	85	Reading*	82	Bristol C	82
4	1984–85	Chesterfield	91	Blackpool	86	Darlington	85	Bury	84
4	1985–86	Swindon T	102	Chester C	84	Mansfield T	81	Port Vale	79
4	1986–87	Northampton T	99	Preston NE	90	Southend U	80	Wolverhampton W‡	79
4	1987–88	Wolverhampton W	90	Cardiff C	85	Bolton W	78	Scunthorpe U*‡	77
4	1988–89	Rotherham U	82	Tranmere R	80	Crewe Alex	78	Scunthorpe U*‡	77
4	1989–90	Exeter C	89	Grimsby T	79	Southend U	75	Stockport Co‡	74
4	1990–91	Darlington	83	Stockport Co*	82	Hartlepool U	82	Peterborough U	80
4	1991–92[3]	Burnley	83	Rotherham U*	77	Mansfield T	77	Blackpool	76

[2]*Maximum points:* 88 owing to Accrington Stanley's resignation.
[3]*Maximum points:* 126 owing to Aldershot being expelled (and only 23 teams started the competition).

THIRD DIVISION (1992–93 to 2003–04)

MAXIMUM POINTS: *a* 126; *b* 138.

4	1992–93*a*	Cardiff C	83	Wrexham	80	Barnet	79	York C	75
4	1993–94*a*	Shrewsbury T	79	Chester C	74	Crewe Alex	73	Wycombe W	70
4	1994–95*a*	Carlisle U	91	Walsall	83	Chesterfield	81	Bury‡	80
4	1995–96*b*	Preston NE	86	Gillingham	83	Bury	79	Plymouth Arg*	78
4	1996–97*b*	Wigan Ath*	87	Fulham	87	Carlisle U	84	Northampton T	72
4	1997–98*b*	Notts Co	99	Macclesfield T	82	Lincoln C	72	Colchester U*	74
4	1998–99*b*	Brentford	85	Cambridge U	81	Cardiff C	80	Scunthorpe U	74
4	1999–2000*b*	Swansea C	85	Rotherham U	84	Northampton T	82	Darlington‡	79
4	2000–01*b*	Brighton & HA	92	Cardiff C	82	Chesterfield[4]	80	Hartlepool U‡	77
4	2001–02*b*	Plymouth Arg	102	Luton T	97	Mansfield T	79	Cheltenham T	78
4	2002–03*b*	Rushden & D	87	Hartlepool U	85	Wrexham	84	Bournemouth	74
4	2003–04*b*	Doncaster R	92	Hull C	88	Torquay U*	81	Huddersfield T	81

[4]*Chesterfield deducted 9pts for irregularities.*

FOOTBALL LEAGUE 2 (2004–05 to 2016–17)

MAXIMUM POINTS: 138

4	2004–05	Yeovil T	83	Scunthorpe U*	80	Swansea C	80	Southend U	80
4	2005–06	Carlisle U	86	Northampton T	83	Leyton Orient	81	Grimsby T‡	78
4	2006–07	Walsall	89	Hartlepool U	88	Swindon T	85	Milton Keynes D‡	84
4	2007–08	Milton Keynes D	97	Peterborough U	92	Hereford U	88	Stockport Co	82
4	2008–09	Brentford	85	Exeter C	79	Wycombe W*	78	Bury‡	78
4	2009–10	Notts Co	93	Bournemouth	83	Rochdale	82	Morecambe*‡	73
4	2010–11	Chesterfield	86	Bury	81	Wycombe W	80	Shrewsbury T‡	79
4	2011–12	Swindon T	93	Shrewsbury T	88	Crawley T	84	Southend U‡	83
4	2012–13	Gillingham	83	Rotherham U	79	Port Vale	78	Burton Alb	76
4	2013–14	Chesterfield	84	Scunthorpe U*	81	Rochdale	81	Fleetwood T	76
4	2014–15	Burton Alb	94	Shrewsbury T	89	Bury	85	Wycombe W*‡	84
4	2015–16	Northampton T	99	Oxford U	86	Bristol R*	85	Accrington S‡	85
4	2016–17	Portsmouth*	87	Plymouth Arg	87	Doncaster R	85	Luton T‡	77

LEAGUE TITLE WINS

DIVISION 1 (1888–89 to 1991–92) – TIER 1
Liverpool 18, Arsenal 10, Everton 9, Aston Villa 7, Manchester U 7, Sunderland 6, Newcastle U 4, Sheffield W 4 (2 as The Wednesday), Huddersfield T 3, Leeds U 3, Wolverhampton W 3, Blackburn R 2, Burnley 2, Derby Co 2, Manchester C 2, Portsmouth 2, Preston NE 2, Tottenham H 2, Chelsea 1, Ipswich T 1, Nottingham F 1, Sheffield U 1, WBA 1.

FA PREMIER LEAGUE (1992–93 to 2016–17) – TIER 1
Manchester U 13, Chelsea 5, Arsenal 3, Manchester C 2, Blackburn R 1, Leicester C 1.

DIVISION 2 (1892–93 TO 1991–92) – TIER 2
Leicester C 6, Manchester C 6, Sheffield W 5 (1 as The Wednesday), Birmingham C 4 (1 as Small Heath), Derby Co 4, Liverpool 4, Ipswich T 3, Leeds U 3, Middlesbrough 3, Notts Co 3, Preston NE 3, Aston Villa 2, Bolton W 2, Burnley 2, Chelsea 2, Grimsby T 2, Manchester U 2, Norwich C 2, Nottingham F 2, Stoke C 2, Tottenham H 2, WBA 2, West Ham U 2, Wolverhampton W 2, Blackburn R 1, Blackpool 1, Bradford C 1, Brentford 1, Bristol C 1, Bury 1, Coventry C 1, Crystal Palace 1, Everton 1, Fulham 1, Huddersfield T 1, Luton T 1, Millwall 1, Newcastle U 1, Oldham Ath 1, Oxford U 1, QPR 1, Sheffield U 1, Sunderland 1.

FIRST DIVISION (1992–93 to 2003–04) – TIER 2
Sunderland 1, Bolton W 1, Charlton Ath 1, Crystal Palace 1, Fulham 1, Manchester C 1, Middlesbrough 1, Newcastle U 1, Norwich C 1, Nottingham F 1, Portsmouth 1.

FOOTBALL LEAGUE CHAMPIONSHIP (2004–05 to 2016–17) – TIER 2
Newcastle U 2, Reading 2, Sunderland 2, Bournemouth 1, Burnley 1, Cardiff C 1, Leicester C 1, QPR 1, WBA 1, Wolverhampton W 1.

DIVISION 3—SOUTH (1920–21 to 1957–58) – TIER 3
Bristol C 3, Charlton Ath 2, Ipswich T 2, Millwall 2, Notts Co 2, Plymouth Arg 2, Swansea T 2, Brentford 1, Brighton & HA 1, Bristol R 1, Cardiff C 1, Coventry C 1, Crystal Palace 1, Fulham 1, Leyton Orient 1, Luton T 1, Newport Co 1, Norwich C 1, Nottingham F 1, Portsmouth 1, QPR 1, Reading 1, Southampton 1.

DIVISION 3—NORTH (1921–22 to 1957–58) – TIER 3
Barnsley 3, Doncaster R 3, Lincoln C 3, Chesterfield 2, Grimsby T 2, Hull C 2, Port Vale 2, Stockport Co 2, Bradford C 1, Bradford PA 1, Darlington 1, Derby Co 1, Nelson 1, Oldham Ath 1, Rotherham U 1, Scunthorpe U 1, Stoke C 1, Tranmere R 1, Wolverhampton W 1.

DIVISION 3 (1958–59 to 1991–92) – TIER 3
Oxford U 2, Portsmouth 2, Aston Villa 1, Blackburn R 1, Bolton W 1, Bournemouth 1, Bradford C 1, Brentford 1, Bristol R 1, Burnley 1, Bury 1, Cambridge U 1, Carlisle U 1, Coventry C 1, Grimsby T 1, Hereford U 1, Hull C 1, Mansfield T 1, Northampton T 1, Oldham Ath 1, Orient 1, Plymouth Arg 1, Preston NE 1, QPR 1, Reading 1, Rotherham U 1, Shrewsbury T 1, Southampton 1, Sunderland 1, Watford 1, Wolverhampton W 1, Wrexham 1.

SECOND DIVISION (1992–93 to 2003–04) – TIER 3
Birmingham C 1, Brighton & HA 1, Bury 1, Fulham 1, Millwall 1, Plymouth Arg 1, Preston NE 1, Reading 1, Stoke C 1, Swindon T 1, Watford 1, Wigan Ath 1.

FOOTBALL LEAGUE 1 (2004–05 to 2016–17) – TIER 3
Brighton & HA 1, Bristol C 1, Charlton Ath 1, Doncaster R 1, Leicester C 1, Luton T 1, Norwich C 1, Scunthorpe U 1, Sheffield U 1, Southend U 1, Swansea C 1, Wigan Ath 1, Wolverhampton W 1.

DIVISION 4 (1958–59 to 1991–92) – TIER 4
Chesterfield 2, Doncaster R 2, Peterborough U 2, Brentford 1, Brighton & HA 1, Burnley 1, Cambridge U 1, Darlington 1, Exeter C 1, Gillingham 1, Grimsby T 1, Huddersfield T 1, Lincoln C 1, Luton T 1, Mansfield T 1, Millwall 1, Northampton T 1, Notts Co 1, Port Vale 1, Reading 1, Rotherham U 1, Sheffield U 1, Southend U 1, Southport 1, Stockport Co 1, Swindon T 1, Walsall 1, Watford 1, Wimbledon 1, Wolverhampton W 1, York C 1.

THIRD DIVISION (1992–93 to 2003–04) – TIER 4
Brentford 1, Brighton & HA 1, Cardiff C 1, Carlisle U 1, Doncaster R 1, Notts Co 1, Plymouth Arg 1, Preston NE 1, Rushden & D 1, Shrewsbury T 1, Swansea C 1, Wigan Ath 1.

FOOTBALL LEAGUE 2 (2004–05 to 2016–17) – TIER 4
Chesterfield 2, Brentford 1, Burton Alb 1, Carlisle U 1, Gillingham 1, Milton Keynes D 1, Northampton T 1, Notts Co 1, Portsmouth 1, Swindon T 1, Walsall 1, Yeovil T 1.

PROMOTED AFTER PLAY-OFFS

1986–87	Charlton Ath to Division 1; Swindon T to Division 2; Aldershot to Division 3
1987–88	Middlesbrough to Division 1; Walsall to Division 2; Swansea C to Division 3
1988–89	Crystal Palace to Division 1; Port Vale to Division 2; Leyton Orient to Division 3
1989–90	Sunderland to Division 1; Notts Co to Division 2; Cambridge U to Division 3
1990–91	Notts Co to Division 1; Tranmere R to Division 2; Torquay U to Division 3
1991–92	Blackburn R to Premier League; Peterborough U to First Division; Blackpool to Second Division
1992–93	Swindon T to Premier League; WBA to First Division; York C to Second Division
1993–94	Leicester C to Premier League; Burnley to First Division; Wycombe W to Second Division
1994–95	Bolton W to Premier League; Huddersfield T to First Division; Wycome Wanderers to Second Division
1995–96	Leicester C to Premier League; Bradford C to First Division; Plymouth Arg to Second Division
1996–97	Crystal Palace to Premier League; Crewe Alex to First Division; Northampton T to Second Division
1997–98	Charlton Ath to Premier League; Grimsby T to First Division; Colchester U to Second Division
1998–99	Watford to Premier League; Manchester C to First Division; Scunthorpe U to Second Division
1999–2000	Ipswich to Premier League; Gillingham to First Division; Peterborough U to Second Division
2000–01	Bolton W to Premier league; Walsall to First Division; Blackpool to Second Division
2001–02	Birmingham C to Premier League; Stoke C to First Division; Cheltenham T to Second Division
2002–03	Wolverhampton W to Premier League; Cardiff C to First Division; Bournemouth to Second Division
2003–04	Crystal Palace to Premier League; Brighton & HA to First Division; Huddersfield T to Second Division
2004–05	West Ham U to Premier League; Sheffield W to Championship; Southend U to Football League 1
2005–06	Watford to Premier League; Barnsley to Championship; Cheltenham T to Football League 1
2006–07	Derby Co to Premier League; Blackpool to Championship; Bristol R to Football League 1
2007–08	Hull C to Premier League; Doncaster R to Championship; Stockport Co to Football League 1
2008–09	Burnley to Premier League; Scunthorpe U to Championship; Gillingham to Football League 1
2009–10	Blackpool to Premier League; Millwall to Championship; Dagenham & R to Football League 1
2010–11	Swansea C to Premier League; Peterborough U to Championship; Stevenage to Football League 1
2011–12	West Ham U to Premier League; Huddersfield T to Championship; Crewe Alex to Football League 1
2012–13	Crystal Palace to Premier League; Yeovil T to Championship; Bradford C to Football League 1
2013–14	QPR to Premier League; Rotherham U to Championship; Fleetwood T to Football League 1
2014–15	Norwich C to Premier League; Preston NE to Championship; Southend U to Football League 1
2015–16	Hull C to Premier League; Barnsley to Championship; AFC Wimbledon to Football League 1
2016–17	Huddersfield T to Premier League; Millwall to Championship; Blackpool to Football League 1

RELEGATED CLUBS

1891–92 League extended. Newton Heath, Sheffield W and Nottingham F admitted. *Second Division formed* including Darwen.
1892–93 In Test matches, Sheffield U and Darwen won promotion in place of Notts Co and Accrington S.
1893–94 In Tests, Liverpool and Small Heath won promotion. Newton Heath and Darwen relegated.
1894–95 After Tests, Bury promoted, Liverpool relegated.
1895–96 After Tests, Liverpool promoted, Small Heath relegated.
1896–97 After Tests, Notts Co promoted, Burnley relegated.
1897–98 Test system abolished after success of Stoke C and Burnley. League extended. Blackburn R and Newcastle U elected to First Division. *Automatic promotion and relegation introduced.*

DIVISION 1 TO DIVISION 2 (1898–99 to 1991–92)

1898–99 Bolton W and Sheffield W
1899–1900 Burnley and Glossop
1900–01 Preston NE and WBA
1901–02 Small Heath and Manchester C
1902–03 Grimsby T and Bolton W
1903–04 Liverpool and WBA
1904–05 League extended. Bury and Notts Co, two bottom clubs in First Division, re-elected.
1905–06 Nottingham F and Wolverhampton W
1906–07 Derby Co and Stoke C
1907–08 Bolton W and Birmingham C
1908–09 Manchester C and Leicester Fosse
1909–10 Bolton W and Chelsea
1910–11 Bristol C and Nottingham F
1911–12 Preston NE and Bury
1912–13 Notts Co and Woolwich Arsenal
1913–14 Preston NE and Derby Co
1914–15 Tottenham H and Chelsea*
1919–20 Notts Co and Sheffield W
1920–21 Derby Co and Bradford PA
1921–22 Bradford C and Manchester U
1922–23 Stoke C and Oldham Ath
1923–24 Chelsea and Middlesbrough
1924–25 Preston NE and Nottingham F
1925–26 Manchester C and Notts Co
1926–27 Leeds U and WBA
1927–28 Tottenham H and Middlesbrough
1928–29 Bury and Cardiff C
1929–30 Burnley and Everton
1930–31 Leeds U and Manchester U
1931–32 Grimsby T and West Ham U
1932–33 Bolton W and Blackpool
1933–34 Newcastle U and Sheffield U
1934–35 Leicester C and Tottenham H
1935–36 Aston Villa and Blackburn R
1936–37 Manchester U and Sheffield W
1937–38 Manchester C and WBA
1938–39 Birmingham C and Leicester C
1946–47 Brentford and Leeds U
1947–48 Blackburn R and Grimsby T
1948–49 Preston NE and Sheffield U
1949–50 Manchester C and Birmingham C
1950–51 Sheffield W and Everton
1951–52 Huddersfield T and Fulham
1952–53 Stoke C and Derby Co
1953–54 Middlesbrough and Liverpool
1954–55 Leicester C and Sheffield W
1955–56 Huddersfield T and Sheffield U
1956–57 Charlton Ath and Cardiff C
1957–58 Sheffield W and Sunderland
1958–59 Portsmouth and Aston Villa
1959–60 Luton T and Leeds U
1960–61 Preston NE and Newcastle U
1961–62 Chelsea and Cardiff C
1962–63 Manchester C and Leyton Orient
1963–64 Bolton W and Ipswich T
1964–65 Wolverhampton W and Birmingham C
1965–66 Northampton T and Blackburn R
1966–67 Aston Villa and Blackpool
1967–68 Fulham and Sheffield U
1968–69 Leicester C and QPR
1969–70 Sunderland and Sheffield W
1970–71 Burnley and Blackpool
1971–72 Huddersfield T and Nottingham F
1972–73 Crystal Palace and WBA
1973–74 Southampton, Manchester U, Norwich C
1974–75 Luton T, Chelsea, Carlisle U
1975–76 Wolverhampton W, Burnley, Sheffield U
1976–77 Sunderland, Stoke C, Tottenham H
1977–78 West Ham U, Newcastle U, Leicester C
1978–79 QPR, Birmingham C, Chelsea
1979–80 Bristol C, Derby Co, Bolton W
1980–81 Norwich C, Leicester C, Crystal Palace
1981–82 Leeds U, Wolverhampton W, Middlesbrough
1982–83 Manchester C, Swansea C, Brighton & HA
1983–84 Birmingham C, Notts Co, Wolverhampton W
1984–85 Norwich C, Sunderland, Stoke C
1985–86 Ipswich T, Birmingham C, WBA
1986–87 Leicester C, Manchester C, Aston Villa
1987–88 Chelsea**, Portsmouth, Watford, Oxford U
1988–89 Middlesbrough, West Ham U, Newcastle U
1989–90 Sheffield W, Charlton Ath, Millwall
1990–91 Sunderland and Derby Co
1991–92 Luton T, Notts Co, West Ham U

***Relegated after play-offs.*
**Subsequently re-elected to Division 1 when League was extended after the War.*

FA PREMIER LEAGUE TO DIVISION 1 (1992–93 to 2003–04)

1992–93 Crystal Palace, Middlesbrough, Nottingham F
1993–94 Sheffield U, Oldham Ath, Swindon T
1994–95 Crystal Palace, Norwich C, Leicester C, Ipswich T
1995–96 Manchester C, QPR, Bolton W
1996–97 Sunderland, Middlesbrough, Nottingham F
1997–98 Bolton W, Barnsley, Crystal Palace
1998–99 Charlton Ath, Blackburn R, Nottingham F
1999–2000 Wimbledon, Sheffield W, Watford
2000–01 Manchester C, Coventry C, Bradford C
2001–02 Ipswich T, Derby Co, Leicester C
2002–03 West Ham U, WBA, Sunderland
2003–04 Leicester C, Leeds U, Wolverhampton W

FA PREMIER LEAGUE TO CHAMPIONSHIP (2004–05 to 2016–17)

2004–05 Crystal Palace, Norwich C, Southampton
2005–06 Birmingham C, WBA, Sunderland
2006–07 Sheffield U, Charlton Ath, Watford
2007–08 Reading, Birmingham C, Derby Co
2008–09 Newcastle U, Middlesbrough, WBA
2009–10 Burnley, Hull C, Portsmouth
2010–11 Birmingham C, Blackpool, West Ham U
2011–12 Bolton W, Blackburn R, Wolverhampton W
2012–13 Wigan Ath, Reading, QPR
2013–14 Norwich C, Fulham, Cardiff C
2014–15 Hull C, Burnley, QPR
2015–16 Newcastle U, Norwich C, Aston Villa
2016–17 Hull C, Middlesbrough, Sunderland

DIVISION 2 TO DIVISION 3 (1920–21 to 1991–92)

1920–21 Stockport Co
1921–22 Bradford PA and Bristol C
1922–23 Rotherham Co and Wolverhampton W
1923–24 Nelson and Bristol C
1924–25 Crystal Palace and Coventry C
1925–26 Stoke C and Stockport Co

1926–27 Darlington and Bradford C
1927–28 Fulham and South Shields
1928–29 Port Vale and Clapton Orient
1929–30 Hull C and Notts Co
1930–31 Reading and Cardiff C
1931–32 Barnsley and Bristol C
1932–33 Chesterfield and Charlton Ath
1933–34 Millwall and Lincoln C
1934–35 Oldham Ath and Notts Co
1935–36 Port Vale and Hull C
1936–37 Doncaster R and Bradford C
1937–38 Barnsley and Stockport Co
1938–39 Norwich C and Tranmere R
1946–47 Swansea T and Newport Co
1947–48 Doncaster R and Millwall
1948–49 Nottingham F and Lincoln C
1949–50 Plymouth Arg and Bradford PA
1950–51 Grimsby T and Chesterfield
1951–52 Coventry C and QPR
1952–53 Southampton and Barnsley
1953–54 Brentford and Oldham Ath
1954–55 Ipswich T and Derby Co
1955–56 Plymouth Arg and Hull C
1956–57 Port Vale and Bury
1957–58 Doncaster R and Notts Co
1958–59 Barnsley and Grimsby T
1959–60 Bristol C and Hull C
1960–61 Lincoln C and Portsmouth
1961–62 Brighton & HA and Bristol R
1962–63 Walsall and Luton T
1963–64 Grimsby T and Scunthorpe U
1964–65 Swindon T and Swansea T
1965–66 Middlesbrough and Leyton Orient
1966–67 Northampton T and Bury
1967–68 Plymouth Arg and Rotherham U
1968–69 Fulham and Bury
1969–70 Preston NE and Aston Villa
1970–71 Blackburn R and Bolton W
1971–72 Charlton Ath and Watford
1972–73 Huddersfield T and Brighton & HA
1973–74 Crystal Palace, Preston NE, Swindon T
1974–75 Millwall, Cardiff C, Sheffield W
1975–76 Oxford U, York C, Portsmouth
1976–77 Carlisle U, Plymouth Arg, Hereford U
1977–78 Blackpool, Mansfield T, Hull C
1978–79 Sheffield U, Millwall, Blackburn R
1979–80 Fulham, Burnley, Charlton Ath
1980–81 Preston NE, Bristol C, Bristol R
1981–82 Cardiff C, Wrexham, Orient
1982–83 Rotherham U, Burnley, Bolton W
1983–84 Derby Co, Swansea C, Cambridge U
1984–85 Notts Co, Cardiff C, Wolverhampton W
1985–86 Carlisle U, Middlesbrough, Fulham
1986–87 Sunderland**, Grimsby T, Brighton & HA
1987–88 Huddersfield T, Reading, Sheffield U**
1988–89 Shrewsbury T, Birmingham C, Walsall
1989–90 Bournemouth, Bradford C, Stoke C
1990–91 WBA and Hull C
1991–92 Plymouth Arg, Brighton & HA, Port Vale

FIRST DIVISION TO SECOND DIVISION (1992–93 to 2003–04)

1992–93 Brentford, Cambridge U, Bristol R
1993–94 Birmingham C, Oxford U, Peterborough U
1994–95 Swindon T, Burnley, Bristol C, Notts Co
1995–96 Millwall, Watford, Luton T
1996–97 Grimsby T, Oldham Ath, Southend U
1997–98 Manchester C, Stoke C, Reading
1998–99 Bury, Oxford U, Bristol C
1999–2000 Walsall, Port Vale, Swindon T
2000–01 Huddersfield T, QPR, Tranmere R
2001–02 Crewe Alex, Barnsley, Stockport Co
2002–03 Sheffield W, Brighton & HA, Grimsby T
2003–04 Walsall, Bradford C, Wimbledon

FOOTBALL LEAGUE CHAMPIONSHIP TO FOOTBALL LEAGUE 1 (2004–05 to 2016–17)

2004–05 Gillingham, Nottingham F, Rotherham U
2005–06 Crewe Alex, Millwall, Brighton & HA
2006–07 Southend U, Luton T, Leeds U
2007–08 Leicester C, Scunthorpe U, Colchester U
2008–09 Norwich C, Southampton, Charlton Ath
2009–10 Sheffield W, Plymouth Arg, Peterborough U
2010–11 Preston NE, Sheffield U, Scunthorpe U
2011–12 Portsmouth, Coventry C, Doncaster R
2012–13 Peterborough U, Wolverhampton W, Bristol C
2013–14 Doncaster R, Barnsley, Yeovil T
2014–15 Millwall, Wigan Ath, Blackpool
2015–16 Charlton Ath, Milton Keynes D, Bolton W
2016–17 Blackburn R, Wigan Ath, Rotherham U

DIVISION 3 TO DIVISION 4 (1958–59 to 1991–92)

1958–59 Stockport Co, Doncaster R, Notts Co, Rochdale
1959–60 York C, Mansfield T, Wrexham, Accrington S
1960–61 Tranmere R, Bradford C, Colchester U, Chesterfield
1961–62 Torquay U, Lincoln C, Brentford, Newport Co
1962–63 Bradford PA, Brighton & HA, Carlisle U, Halifax T
1963–64 Millwall, Crewe Alex, Wrexham, Notts Co
1964–65 Luton T, Port Vale, Colchester U, Barnsley
1965–66 Southend U, Exeter C, Brentford, York C
1966–67 Swansea T, Darlington, Doncaster R, Workington
1967–68 Grimsby T, Colchester U, Scunthorpe U, Peterborough U (demoted)
1968–69 Northampton T, Hartlepool, Crewe Alex, Oldham Ath
1969–70 Bournemouth, Southport, Barrow, Stockport Co
1970–71 Reading, Bury, Doncaster R, Gillingham
1971–72 Mansfield T, Barnsley, Torquay U, Bradford C
1972–73 Rotherham U, Brentford, Swansea C, Scunthorpe U
1973–74 Cambridge U, Shrewsbury T, Southport, Rochdale
1974–75 Bournemouth, Tranmere R, Watford, Huddersfield T
1975–76 Aldershot, Colchester U, Southend U, Halifax T
1976–77 Reading, Northampton T, Grimsby T, York C
1977–78 Port Vale, Bradford C, Hereford U, Portsmouth
1978–79 Peterborough U, Walsall, Tranmere R, Lincoln C
1979–80 Bury, Southend U, Mansfield T, Wimbledon
1980–81 Sheffield U, Colchester U, Blackpool, Hull C
1981–82 Wimbledon, Swindon T, Bristol C, Chester
1982–83 Reading, Wrexham, Doncaster R, Chesterfield
1983–84 Scunthorpe U, Southend U, Port Vale, Exeter C
1984–85 Burnley, Orient, Preston NE, Cambridge U
1985–86 Lincoln C, Cardiff C, Wolverhampton W, Swansea C
1986–87 Bolton W**, Carlisle U, Darlington, Newport Co
1987–88 Rotherham U**, Grimsby T, York C, Doncaster R
1988–89 Southend U, Chesterfield, Gillingham, Aldershot
1989–90 Cardiff C, Northampton T, Blackpool, Walsall
1990–91 Crewe Alex, Rotherham U, Mansfield T
1991–92 Bury, Shrewsbury T, Torquay U, Darlington

** *Relegated after play-offs.*

SECOND DIVISION TO THIRD DIVISION (1992–93 to 2003–04)

1992–93 Preston NE, Mansfield T, Wigan Ath, Chester C
1993–94 Fulham, Exeter C, Hartlepool U, Barnet
1994–95 Cambridge U, Plymouth Arg, Cardiff C, Chester C, Leyton Orient
1995–96 Carlisle U, Swansea C, Brighton & HA, Hull C
1996–97 Peterborough U, Shrewsbury T, Rotherham U, Notts Co
1997–98 Brentford, Plymouth Arg, Carlisle U, Southend U
1998–99 York C, Northampton T, Lincoln C, Macclesfield T

1999–2000 Cardiff C, Blackpool, Scunthorpe U, Chesterfield
2000–01 Bristol R, Luton T, Swansea C, Oxford U
2001–02 Bournemouth, Bury, Wrexham, Cambridge U
2002–03 Cheltenham T, Huddersfield T, Mansfield T Northampton T
2003–04 Grimsby T, Rushden & D, Notts Co, Wycombe W

FOOTBALL LEAGUE 1 TO FOOTBALL LEAGUE 2 (2004–05 to 2016–17)

2004–05 Torquay U, Wrexham, Peterborough U, Stockport Co
2005–06 Hartlepool U, Milton Keynes D, Swindon T, Walsall
2006–07 Chesterfield, Bradford C, Rotherham U, Brentford
2007–08 Bournemouth, Gillingham, Port Vale, Luton T
2008–09 Northampton T, Crewe Alex, Cheltenham T, Hereford U
2009–10 Gillingham, Wycombe W, Southend U, Stockport Co
2010–11 Dagenham & R, Bristol R, Plymouth Arg, Swindon T
2011–12 Wycombe W, Chesterfield, Exeter C, Rochdale
2012–13 Scunthorpe U, Bury, Hartlepool U, Portsmouth
2013–14 Tranmere R, Carlisle U, Shrewsbury T, Stevenage
2014–15 Notts Co, Crawley T, Leyton Orient, Yeovil T
2015–16 Doncaster R, Blackpool, Colchester U, Crewe Alex
2016–17 Port Vale, Swindon T, Coventry C, Chesterfield

LEAGUE STATUS FROM 1986–87

RELEGATED FROM LEAGUE

1986–87 Lincoln C
1987–88 Newport Co
1988–89 Darlington
1989–90 Colchester U
1990–91 —
1991–92 —
1992–93 Halifax T
1993–94 —
1994–95 —
1995–96 —
1996–97 Hereford U
1997–98 Doncaster R
1998–99 Scarborough
1999–2000 Chester C
2000–01 Barnet
2001–02 Halifax T
2002–03 Shrewsbury T, Exeter C
2003–04 Carlisle U, York C
2004–05 Kidderminster H, Cambridge U
2005–06 Oxford U, Rushden & D
2006–07 Boston U, Torquay U
2007–08 Mansfield T, Wrexham
2008–09 Chester C, Luton T
2009–10 Grimsby T, Darlington
2010–11 Lincoln C, Stockport Co
2011–12 Hereford U, Macclesfield T
2012–13 Barnet, Aldershot T
2013–14 Bristol R, Torquay U
2014–15 Cheltenham T, Tranmere R
2015–16 Dagenham & R, York C
2016–17 Hartlepool U, Leyton Orient

PROMOTED TO LEAGUE

1986–87 Scarborough
1987–88 Lincoln C
1988–89 Maidstone U
1989–90 Darlington
1990–91 Barnet
1991–92 Colchester U
1992–93 Wycombe W
1993–94 —
1994–95 —
1995–96 —
1996–97 Macclesfield T
1997–98 Halifax T
1998–99 Cheltenham T
1999–2000 Kidderminster H
2000–01 Rushden & D
2001–02 Boston U
2002–03 Yeovil T, Doncaster R
2003–04 Chester C, Shrewsbury T
2004–05 Barnet, Carlisle U
2005–06 Accrington S, Hereford U
2006–07 Dagenham & R, Morecambe
2007–08 Aldershot T, Exeter C
2008–09 Burton Alb, Torquay U
2009–10 Stevenage B, Oxford U
2010–11 Crawley T, AFC Wimbledon
2011–12 Fleetwood T, York C
2012–13 Mansfield T, Newport Co
2013–14 Luton T, Cambridge U
2014–15 Barnet, Bristol R
2015–16 Cheltenham T, Grimsby T
2016–17 Lincoln C, Forest Green R

APPLICATIONS FOR RE-ELECTION

FOURTH DIVISION

Eleven: Hartlepool U.
Seven: Crewe Alex.
Six: Barrow (lost League place to Hereford U 1972), Halifax T, Rochdale, Southport (lost League place to Wigan Ath 1978), York C.
Five: Chester C, Darlington, Lincoln C, Stockport Co, Workington (lost League place to Wimbledon 1977).
Four: Bradford PA (lost League place to Cambridge U 1970), Newport Co, Northampton T.
Three: Doncaster R, Hereford U.
Two: Bradford C, Exeter C, Oldham Ath, Scunthorpe U, Torquay U.
One: Aldershot, Colchester U, Gateshead (lost League place to Peterborough U 1960), Grimsby T, Swansea C, Tranmere R, Wrexham, Blackpool, Cambridge U, Preston NE.

Accrington S resigned and Oxford U were elected 1962.
Port Vale were forced to re-apply following expulsion in 1968.
Aldershot expelled March 1992. Maidstone U resigned August 1992.

THIRD DIVISIONS NORTH & SOUTH

Seven: Walsall.
Six: Exeter C, Halifax T, Newport Co.
Five: Accrington S, Barrow, Gillingham, New Brighton, Southport.
Four: Rochdale, Norwich C.
Three: Crystal Palace, Crewe Alex, Darlington, Hartlepool U, Merthyr T, Swindon T.
Two: Aberdare Ath, Aldershot, Ashington, Bournemouth, Brentford, Chester, Colchester U, Durham C, Millwall, Nelson, QPR, Rotherham U, Southend U, Tranmere R, Watford, Workington.
One: Bradford C, Bradford PA, Brighton & HA, Bristol R, Cardiff C, Carlisle U, Charlton Ath, Gateshead, Grimsby T, Mansfield T, Shrewsbury T, Torquay U, York C.

LEAGUE ATTENDANCES SINCE 1946–47

Season	*Matches*	*Total*	*Div. 1*	*Div. 2*	*Div. 3 (S)*	*Div. 3 (N)*
1946–47	1848	35,604,606	15,005,316	11,071,572	5,664,004	3,863,714
1947–48	1848	40,259,130	16,732,341	12,286,350	6,653,610	4,586,829
1948–49	1848	41,271,414	17,914,667	11,353,237	6,998,429	5,005,081
1949–50	1848	40,517,865	17,278,625	11,694,158	7,104,155	4,440,927
1950–51	2028	39,584,967	16,679,454	10,780,580	7,367,884	4,757,109
1951–52	2028	39,015,866	16,110,322	11,066,189	6,958,927	4,880,428
1952–53	2028	37,149,966	16,050,278	9,686,654	6,704,299	4,708,735
1953–54	2028	36,174,590	16,154,915	9,510,053	6,311,508	4,198,114
1954–55	2028	34,133,103	15,087,221	8,988,794	5,996,017	4,051,071
1955–56	2028	33,150,809	14,108,961	9,080,002	5,692,479	4,269,367
1956–57	2028	32,744,405	13,803,037	8,718,162	5,622,189	4,601,017
1957–58	2028	33,562,208	14,468,652	8,663,712	6,097,183	4,332,661
		Total	*Div. 1*	*Div. 2*	*Div. 3*	*Div. 4*
1958–59	2028	33,610,985	14,727,691	8,641,997	5,946,600	4,276,697
1959–60	2028	32,538,611	14,391,227	8,399,627	5,739,707	4,008,050
1960–61	2028	28,619,754	12,926,948	7,033,936	4,784,256	3,874,614
1961–62	2015	27,979,902	12,061,194	7,453,089	5,199,106	3,266,513
1962–63	2028	28,885,852	12,490,239	7,792,770	5,341,362	3,261,481
1963–64	2028	28,535,022	12,486,626	7,594,158	5,419,157	3,035,081
1964–65	2028	27,641,168	12,708,752	6,984,104	4,436,245	3,512,067
1965–66	2028	27,206,980	12,480,644	6,914,757	4,779,150	3,032,429
1966–67	2028	28,902,596	14,242,957	7,253,819	4,421,172	2,984,648
1967–68	2028	30,107,298	15,289,410	7,450,410	4,013,087	3,354,391
1968–69	2028	29,382,172	14,584,851	7,382,390	4,339,656	3,075,275
1969–70	2028	29,600,972	14,868,754	7,581,728	4,223,761	2,926,729
1970–71	2028	28,194,146	13,954,337	7,098,265	4,377,213	2,764,331
1971–72	2028	28,700,729	14,484,603	6,769,308	4,697,392	2,749,426
1972–73	2028	25,448,642	13,998,154	5,631,730	3,737,252	2,081,506
1973–74	2027	24,982,203	13,070,991	6,326,108	3,421,624	2,163,480
1974–75	2028	25,577,977	12,613,178	6,955,970	4,086,145	1,992,684
1975–76	2028	24,896,053	13,089,861	5,798,405	3,948,449	2,059,338
1976–77	2028	26,182,800	13,647,585	6,250,597	4,152,218	2,132,400
1977–78	2028	25,392,872	13,255,677	6,474,763	3,332,042	2,330,390
1978–79	2028	24,540,627	12,704,549	6,153,223	3,374,558	2,308,297
1979–80	2028	24,623,975	12,163,002	6,112,025	3,999,328	2,349,620
1980–81	2028	21,907,569	11,392,894	5,175,442	3,637,854	1,701,379
1981–82	2028	20,006,961	10,420,793	4,750,463	2,836,915	1,998,790
1982–83	2028	18,766,158	9,295,613	4,974,937	2,943,568	1,552,040
1983–84	2028	18,358,631	8,711,448	5,359,757	2,729,942	1,557,484
1984–85	2028	17,849,835	9,761,404	4,030,823	2,667,008	1,390,600
1985–86	2028	16,488,577	9,037,854	3,551,968	2,490,481	1,408,274
1986–87	2028	17,379,218	9,144,676	4,168,131	2,350,970	1,715,441
1987–88	2030	17,959,732	8,094,571	5,341,599	2,751,275	1,772,287
1988–89	2036	18,464,192	7,809,993	5,887,805	3,035,327	1,791,067
1989–90	2036	19,445,442	7,883,039	6,867,674	2,803,551	1,891,178
1990–91	2036	19,508,202	8,618,709	6,285,068	2,835,759	1,768,666
1991–92	2064*	20,487,273	9,989,160	5,809,787	2,993,352	1,694,974
		Total	*FA Premier*	*Div. 1*	*Div. 2*	*Div. 3*
1992–93	2028	20,657,327	9,759,809	5,874,017	3,483,073	1,540,428
1993–94	2028	21,683,381	10,644,551	6,487,104	2,972,702	1,579,024
1994–95	2028	21,856,020	11,213,168	6,044,293	3,037,752	1,560,807
1995–96	2036	21,844,416	10,469,107	6,566,349	2,843,652	1,965,308
1996–97	2036	22,783,163	10,804,762	6,931,539	3,195,223	1,851,639
1997–98	2036	24,692,608	11,092,106	8,330,018	3,503,264	1,767,220
1998–99	2036	25,435,542	11,620,326	7,543,369	4,169,697	2,102,150
1999–2000	2036	25,341,090	11,668,497	7,810,208	3,700,433	2,161,952
2000–01	2036	26,030,167	12,472,094	7,909,512	3,488,166	2,160,395
2001–02	2036	27,756,977	13,043,118	8,352,128	3,963,153	2,398,578
2002–03	2036	28,343,386	13,468,965	8,521,017	3,892,469	2,460,935
2003–04	2036	29,197,510	13,303,136	8,772,780	4,146,495	2,975,099
		Total	*FA Premier*	*Championship*	*League 1*	*League 2*
2004–05	2036	29,245,870	12,878,791	9,612,761	4,270,674	2,483,644
2005–06	2036	29,089,084	12,871,643	9,719,204	4,183,011	2,315,226
2006–07	2036	29,541,949	13,058,115	10,057,813	4,135,599	2,290,422
2007–08	2036	29,914,212	13,708,875	9,397,036	4,412,023	2,396,278
2008–09	2036	29,881,966	13,527,815	9,877,552	4,171,834	2,304,765
2009–10	2036	30,057,892	12,977,251	9,909,882	5,043,099	2,127,660
2010–11	2036	29,459,105	13,406,990	9,595,236	4,150,547	2,306,332
2011–12	2036	29,454,401	13,148,465	9,784,100	4,091,897	2,429,939
2012–13	2036	29,225,443	13,653,958	9,662,232	3,485,290	2,423,963
2013–14	2036	29,629,309	13,930,810	9,168,922	4,126,701	2,402,876
2014–15	2036	30,052,575	13,746,753	9,838,940	3,884,414	2,582,468
2015–16	2036	30,207,923	13,852,291	9,705,865	3,955,385	2,694,382
2016–17	2036	31,727,248	13,612,316	11,106,918	4,385,178	2,622,836

**Figures include matches played by Aldershot.*

Football League official total for their three divisions in 2001–02 was 14,716,162.

ENGLISH LEAGUE ATTENDANCES 2016–17

PREMIER LEAGUE ATTENDANCES

	Average Gate			*Season 2016–17*	
	2015–16	*2016–17*	*+/–%*	*Highest*	*Lowest*
Arsenal	59,944	59,957	+0.02	60,055	59,510
Bournemouth	11,189	11,182	–0.06	11,388	10,890
Burnley	16,709	20,558	+23.04	21,870	18,519
Chelsea	41,500	41,508	+0.02	41,622	41,168
Crystal Palace	24,636	25,161	+2.13	25,648	23,503
Everton	38,124	39,310	+3.11	39,595	38,550
Hull C	17,199	20,761	+20.72	24,822	17,403
Leicester C	32,021	31,893	–0.40	32,072	31,351
Liverpool	43,910	53,016	+20.74	53,292	51,232
Manchester C	54,041	54,019	–0.04	54,512	51,527
Manchester U	75,279	75,290	+0.01	75,397	75,245
Middlesbrough	24,627	30,449	+23.64	32,704	27,316
Southampton	30,782	30,936	+0.50	31,891	28,976
Stoke City	27,534	27,433	–0.37	27,815	26,602
Sunderland	43,071	41,287	–4.14	46,494	38,394
Swansea C	20,711	20,619	–0.44	20,938	20,024
Tottenham H	35,776	31,639	–11.56	31,962	31,211
Watford	20,594	20,571	–0.11	21,118	20,022
WBA	24,631	23,876	–3.07	26,308	21,467
West Ham U	34,910	56,972	+63.20	56,996	56,864

TOTAL ATTENDANCES: 13,612,316 (380 games)
Average 35,822 (–1.73%)
HIGHEST: 75,397 Manchester U v WBA
LOWEST: 10,890 Bournemouth v Middlesbrough
HIGHEST AVERAGE: 75,290 Manchester U
LOWEST AVERAGE: 11,182 Bournemouth

SKY BET FOOTBALL LEAGUE: CHAMPIONSHIP ATTENDANCES

	Average Gate			*Season 2016–17*	
	2015–16	*2016–17*	*+/–%*	*Highest*	*Lowest*
Aston Villa	33,690	32,107	–4.70	41,337	26,435
Barnsley	9,499	13,857	+45.89	18,597	10,814
Birmingham C	17,603	18,717	+6.33	29,656	15,212
Blackburn R	14,131	12,688	–10.21	21,884	9,976
Brentford	10,310	10,467	+1.53	12,052	8,732
Brighton & HA	25,583	27,996	+9.43	30,338	24,166
Bristol C	15,292	19,256	+25.93	25,404	16,444
Burton Alb	4,089	5,228	+27.84	6,746	3,725
Cardiff C	16,463	16,564	+0.61	23,153	13,894
Derby Co	29,663	29,085	–1.95	32,616	26,301
Fulham	17,566	19,199	+9.29	24,594	13,735
Huddersfield T	12,755	20,343	+59.49	23,213	18,333
Ipswich T	18,989	16,981	–10.58	25,684	14,661
Leeds U	22,446	27,698	+23.40	36,002	19,009
Newcastle U	49,754	51,106	+2.72	52,301	47,907
Norwich C	26,972	26,354	–2.29	27,107	25,275
Nottingham F	19,676	20,333	+3.34	28,249	15,770
Preston NE	13,035	12,607	–3.28	21,255	9,216
QPR	15,994	14,616	–8.62	17,404	11,635
Reading	17,285	17,505	+1.27	23,121	12,655
Rotherham U	10,025	9,783	–2.42	11,653	8,266
Sheffield W	22,641	27,129	+19.82	33,681	24,151
Wigan Ath	9,467	11,722	+23.82	15,280	10,071
Wolverhampton W	20,157	21,570	+7.01	27,541	17,156

TOTAL ATTENDANCES: 11,106,918 (552 games)
Average 20,121 (+14.44%)
HIGHEST: 52,301 Newcastle U v Leeds U
LOWEST: 3,725 Burton Alb v Fulham
HIGHEST AVERAGE: 51,106 Newcastle U
LOWEST AVERAGE: 5,228 Burton Alb

Premier League and Football League attendance averages and highest crowd figures for 2016–17 are unofficial.

SKY BET FOOTBALL LEAGUE: DIVISION 1 ATTENDANCES

	Average Gate			Season 2016–17	
	2015–16	2016–17	+/–%	Highest	Lowest
AFC Wimbledon	4,138	4,477	+8.18	4,867	3,812
Bolton W	15,056	15,194	+0.92	23,376	12,290
Bradford C	18,090	18,167	+0.42	21,874	15,935
Bristol R	8,096	9,302	+14.90	11,750	7,805
Bury	3,751	3,845	+2.50	8,007	2,005
Charlton Ath	15,632	11,162	–28.60	15,315	8,745
Chesterfield	6,676	5,929	–11.20	8,451	4,598
Coventry C	12,570	9,118	–27.46	11,946	7,646
Fleetwood T	3,308	3,245	–1.90	5,123	2,111
Gillingham	6,316	6,129	–2.95	8,760	4,595
Millwall	9,108	9,340	+2.55	14,395	7,032
Milton Keynes D	13,158	10,307	–21.67	21,545	7,429
Northampton T	5,279	6,245	+18.30	7,675	4,686
Oldham Ath	4,361	4,514	+3.51	8,788	2,911
Oxford U	7,211	8,297	+15.06	11,790	6,552
Peterborough U	5,447	5,581	+2.46	10,258	3,964
Port Vale	4,993	4,813	–3.61	8,999	3,152
Rochdale	3,098	3,556	+14.77	6,876	1,907
Scunthorpe U	3,907	4,536	+16.10	6,243	3,168
Sheffield U	19,803	21,892	+10.54	31,003	17,410
Shrewsbury T	5,407	5,507	+1.85	7,532	4,314
Southend U	7,001	7,406	+5.79	10,329	5,507
Swindon T	7,409	7,026	–5.17	10,658	6,048
Walsall	5,382	5,072	–5.75	6,899	3,890

TOTAL ATTENDANCES: 4,385,178 (552 games)
Average 7,944 (+10.86%)
HIGHEST: 31,003 Sheffield U v Chesterfield
LOWEST: 1,907 Rochdale v Walsall
HIGHEST AVERAGE: 21,892 Sheffield U
LOWEST AVERAGE: 3,245 Fleetwood T.

SKY BET FOOTBALL LEAGUE: DIVISION 2 ATTENDANCES

	Average Gate			Season 2016–17	
	2015–16	2016–17	+/–%	Highest	Lowest
Accrington S	1,834	1,699	–7.36	2,754	1,045
Barnet	2,358	2,260	–4.16	4,571	1,164
Blackpool	7,052	3,456	–50.98	5,471	2,080
Cambridge U	5,274	4,737	–10.17	6,397	3,556
Carlisle U	4,838	5,114	+5.70	7,333	4,052
Cheltenham T	3,006	3,323	+10.55	5,606	2,238
Colchester U	4,136	3,973	–3.92	7,003	2,526
Crawley T	2,405	2,492	+3.60	5,350	1,566
Crewe Alex	4,551	3,882	–14.70	5,016	2,844
Doncaster R	6,553	6,021	–8.11	10,084	4,327
Exeter C	4,008	4,166	+3.95	6,774	2,660
Grimsby T	4,345	5,259	+21.05	6,866	4,061
Hartlepool U	3,890	3,788	–2.63	6,799	2,514
Leyton Orient	5,332	4,663	–12.54	6,854	2,660
Luton T	8,226	8,043	–2.22	9,164	6,708
Mansfield T	3,439	3,774	+9.73	6,819	2,503
Morecambe	1,572	1,703	+8.36	3,773	1,080
Newport Co	2,731	2,854	+4.50	7,326	1,868
Notts Co	4,860	5,970	+22.84	12,184	2,736
Plymouth Arg	8,798	9,652	+9.71	14,671	6,935
Portsmouth	16,391	16,823	+2.63	18,625	15,132
Stevenage	3,349	2,899	–13.44	4,185	1,930
Wycombe W	3,984	3,917	–1.69	6,313	2,572
Yeovil T	3,936	3,567	–9.38	6,306	2,749

TOTAL ATTENDANCES: 2,622,836 (552 games)
Average 4,752 (–2.65%)
HIGHEST: 18,625 Portsmouth v Plymouth Arg
LOWEST: 1,045 Accrington S v Wycombe W
HIGHEST AVERAGE: 16,823 Portsmouth
LOWEST AVERAGE: 1,699 Accrington S

LEAGUE CUP FINALS 1961–2017

Played as a two-leg final until 1966. All subsequent finals played at Wembley except between 2001 and 2007 (inclusive) which were played at Millennium Stadium, Cardiff.

FOOTBALL LEAGUE CUP

1961	Rotherham U v Aston Villa	2-0
	Aston Villa v Rotherham U	3-0*
	Aston Villa won 3-2 on aggregate.	
1962	Rochdale v Norwich C	0-3
	Norwich C v Rochdale	1-0
	Norwich C won 4-0 on aggregate.	
1963	Birmingham C v Aston Villa	3-1
	Aston Villa v Birmingham C	0-0
	Birmingham C won 3-1 on aggregate.	
1964	Stoke C v Leicester C	1-1
	Leicester C v Stoke C	3-2
	Leicester C won 4-3 on aggregate.	
1965	Chelsea v Leicester C	3-2
	Leicester C v Chelsea	0-0
	Chelsea won 3-2 on aggregate.	
1966	West Ham U v WBA	2-1
	WBA v West Ham U	4-1
	WBA won 5-3 on aggregate.	
1967	QPR v WBA	3-2
1968	Leeds U v Arsenal	1-0
1969	Swindon T v Arsenal	3-1*
1970	Manchester C v WBA	2-1*
1971	Tottenham H v Aston Villa	2-0
1972	Stoke C v Chelsea	2-1
1973	Tottenham H v Norwich C	1-0
1974	Wolverhampton W v Manchester C	2-1
1975	Aston Villa v Norwich C	1-0
1976	Manchester C v Newcastle U	2-1
1977	Aston Villa v Everton	0-0
Replay	Aston Villa v Everton	1-1*
	(at Hillsborough)	
Replay	Aston Villa v Everton	3-2*
	(at Old Trafford)	
1978	Nottingham F v Liverpool	0-0*
Replay	Nottingham F v Liverpool	1-0
	(at Old Trafford)	
1979	Nottingham F v Southampton	3-2
1980	Wolverhampton W v Nottingham F	1-0
1981	Liverpool v West Ham U	1-1*
Replay	Liverpool v West Ham U	2-1
	(at Villa Park)	

MILK CUP

1982	Liverpool v Tottenham H	3-1*
1983	Liverpool v Manchester U	2-1*
1984	Liverpool v Everton	0-0*
Replay	Liverpool v Everton	1-0
	(at Maine Road)	
1985	Norwich C v Sunderland	1-0
1986	Oxford U v QPR	3-0

LITTLEWOODS CUP

1987	Arsenal v Liverpool	2-1
1988	Luton T v Arsenal	3-2
1989	Nottingham F v Luton T	3-1
1990	Nottingham F v Oldham Ath	1-0

RUMBELOWS LEAGUE CUP

1991	Sheffield W v Manchester U	1-0
1992	Manchester U v Nottingham F	1-0

COCA-COLA CUP

1993	Arsenal v Sheffield W	2-1
1994	Aston Villa v Manchester U	3-1
1995	Liverpool v Bolton W	2-1
1996	Aston Villa v Leeds U	3-0
1997	Leicester C v Middlesbrough	1-1*
Replay	Leicester C v Middlesbrough	1-0*
	(at Hillsborough)	
1998	Chelsea v Middlesbrough	2-0*

WORTHINGTON CUP

1999	Tottenham H v Leicester C	1-0
2000	Leicester C v Tranmere R	2-1
2001	Liverpool v Birmingham C	1-1*
	Liverpool won 5-4 on penalties.	
2002	Blackburn R v Tottenham H	2-1
2003	Liverpool v Manchester U	2-0

CARLING CUP

2004	Middlesbrough v Bolton W	2-1
2005	Chelsea v Liverpool	3-2*
2006	Manchester U v Wigan Ath	4-0
2007	Chelsea v Arsenal	2-1
2008	Tottenham H v Chelsea	2-1*
2009	Manchester U v Tottenham H	0-0*
	Manchester U won 4-1 on penalties.	
2010	Manchester U v Aston Villa	2-1
2011	Birmingham C v Arsenal	2-1
2012	Liverpool v Cardiff C	2-2*
	Liverpool won 3-2 on penalties.	

CAPITAL ONE CUP

2013	Swansea C v Bradford C	5-0
2014	Manchester C v Sunderland	3-1
2015	Chelsea v Tottenham H	2-0
2016	Manchester C v Liverpool	1-1*
	Manchester C won 3-1 on penalties.	

EFL CUP

2017	Manchester U v Southampton	3-2

**After extra time.*

LEAGUE CUP WINS
Liverpool 8, Aston Villa 5, Chelsea 5, Manchester U 5, Manchester C 4, Nottingham F 4, Tottenham H 4, Leicester C 3, Arsenal 2, Birmingham C 2, Norwich C 2, Wolverhampton W 2, Blackburn R 1, Leeds U 1, Luton T 1, Middlesbrough 1, Oxford U 1, QPR 1, Sheffield W 1, Stoke C 1, Swansea C 1, Swindon T 1, WBA 1.

APPEARANCES IN FINALS
Liverpool 12, Manchester U 9, Aston Villa 8, Tottenham H 8, Arsenal 7, Chelsea 7, Nottingham F 6, Leicester C 5, Manchester C 5, Norwich C 4, Birmingham C 3, Middlesbrough 3, WBA 3, Bolton W 2, Everton 2, Leeds U 2, Luton T 2, QPR 2, Sheffield W 2, Southampton 2, Stoke C 2, Sunderland 2, West Ham U 2, Wolverhampton W 2, Blackburn R 1, Bradford C 1, Cardiff C 1, Newcastle U 1, Oldham Ath 1, Oxford U 1, Rochdale 1, Rotherham U 1, Swansea C 1, Swindon T 1, Tranmere R 1, Wigan Ath 1.

APPEARANCES IN SEMI-FINALS
Liverpool 17, Arsenal 14, Aston Villa 14, Manchester U 14, Tottenham H 14, Chelsea 12, Manchester C 9, West Ham U 9, Blackburn R 6, Nottingham F 6, Birmingham C 5, Everton 5, Leeds U 5, Leicester C 5, Middlesbrough 5, Norwich C 5, Bolton W 4, Burnley 4, Crystal Palace 4, Ipswich T 4, Sheffield W 4, Sunderland 4, WBA 4, QPR 3, Southampton 3, Stoke C 3, Swindon T 3, Wolverhampton W 3, Bristol C 2, Cardiff C 2, Coventry C 2, Derby Co 2, Luton T 2, Oxford U 2, Plymouth Arg 2, Sheffield U 2, Tranmere R 2, Watford 2, Wimbledon 2, Blackpool 1, Bradford C 1, Bury 1, Carlisle U 1, Chester C 1, Huddersfield T 1, Hull C 1, Newcastle U 1, Oldham Ath 1, Peterborough U 1, Rochdale 1, Rotherham U 1, Shrewsbury T 1, Stockport Co 1, Swansea C 1, Walsall 1, Wigan Ath 1, Wycombe W 1.

EFL CUP 2016–17

■ *Denotes player sent off.*

FIRST ROUND

Tuesday, 9 August 2016

Accrington S (0) 0

Bradford C (0) 0 1936

Accrington S: (4411) Parish■; Donacien, Hughes, Beckles, Pearson; Clark, Davies (Chapman 76), Conneely, O'Sullivan; Eagles (Hewitt 80); Gornell (McCartan 68).
Bradford C: (4411) Doyle; McMahon, Knight-Percival, Vincelot, Meredith; Anderson (Morais 65), Devine, Law, Hiwula (Webb-Foster 110); Clarke B (Marshall 66); Hanson.
aet; Accrington S won 11-10 on penalties.
Referee: David Webb.

Barnet (0) 0

Millwall (2) 4 *(Akinde J 23 (og), O'Brien 35, Morison 74, Onyedinma 81 (pen))* 1410

Barnet: (442) Vickers; Dembele, Nelson, N'Gala, Weston; Johnson, Togwell, Watson, Nicholls (Amaluzor 72); Akinde J (Gash 55), Akpa Akpro (Gambin 59).
Millwall: (442) Archer; Martin (Ferguson 83), Webster, Craig, Nelson; Wylde, Thompson, Abdou, O'Brien (Worrall 68); Onyedinma, Morison (Philpot 80).
Referee: Dean Whitestone.

Barnsley (1) 1 *(Scowen 21)*

Northampton T (0) 2 *(Davies 52 (og), O'Toole 114)* 4455

Barnsley: (442) Davies; Bree (Yiadom 95), Roberts, Mawson, White; Hammill, Scowen, Hourihane, Moncur (Kent 61); Bradshaw (Payne 82), Watkins.
Northampton T: (4411) Smith A; Phillips, Zakuani, Diamond, Buchanan; Gorre, Beautyman (D'Ath 79), O'Toole, Potter (Hoskins 65); Taylor M; Revell.
aet.
Referee: Carl Boyeson.

Birmingham C (0) 0

Oxford U (0) 1 *(Sercombe 120)* 7202

Birmingham C: (442) Legzdins; Dacres-Cogley, Morrison, Robinson, Grounds; Caddis (Maghoma 78), Tesche, Kieftenbeld (Gleeson 74), Solomon-Otabor; Vaughan, Storer (Donaldson 79).
Oxford U: (442) Eastwood; Long, Martin, Nelson, Skarz; MacDonald (Roberts T 108), Sercombe, Lundstram, Maguire; Thomas (Hemmings 28), Taylor (Crowley 74).
aet.
Referee: Darren Handley.

Blackpool (0) 4 *(Mellor 74, Potts 78, McAlister 109, Herron 115)*

Bolton W (1) 2 *(Proctor 45, Woolery 90)* 3633

Blackpool: (532) Slocombe; Mellor, Aimson, Nolan, Robertson, Daniel; Cain, McAlister, Yeates (Herron 106); Cullen (Cameron 90), Matt (Potts 17).
Bolton W: (433) Amos; Wilson, Beevers, Finney, Moxey; Trotter, Osede (Vela 25), Davies; Walker (Woolery 80), Proctor (Madine 63), Taylor C.
aet.
Referee: Darren Bond.

Brighton & HA (0) 4 *(Baldock 64, Murphy 70, 86, Manu 74)*

Colchester U (0) 0 6895

Brighton & HA: (442) Maenpaa; Hunt, Ince, White, Adekugbe; Murphy, Norwood, Holla, LuaLua; Manu, Baldock.
Colchester U: (442) Barnes; Wynter, Prosser, Kent, Vincent-Young; Szmodics (Bonne 72), Loft, Lapslie (Dunne 75), Dickenson; Johnstone, Guthrie (Slater 75).
Referee: James Linington.

Cambridge U (0) 2 *(Mingoia 90, Berry 118)*

Sheffield W (0) 1 *(Lucas Joao 52)* 4170

Cambridge U: (442) Gregory; Long, Coulson, Dallison, Adams (Taylor 96); Mingoia, Dunne (Newton 59), Berry, Elito (Maris 58); Pigott, Williamson.
Sheffield W: (433) Wildsmith; Palmer, Vermijl, O'Grady, Helan; Buckley, Semedo, Wallace (Murphy 86); Sougou (Hooper 46), Nuhiu, Lucas Joao (Hirst 92).
aet.
Referee: Keith Stroud.

Carlisle U (2) 2 *(Wyke 27, Miller S 41)*

Port Vale (0) 1 *(Grant 51)* 3363

Carlisle U: (442) Gillespie; Miller T (Atkinson 64), Raynes, Ellis, Grainger; Lambe, Jones, Joyce, Adams; Wyke, Miller S (Kennedy 70).
Port Vale: (433) Alnwick; Purkiss, MacIntosh, Smith, Knops; Grant, de Freitas (Hooper 46), Foley; Mbamba (Carlos Saleiro 73), Forrester, Kelly (Thomas 46).
Referee: Mark Haywood.

Cheltenham T (1) 1 *(Pell 17)*

Charlton Ath (0) 0 2106

Cheltenham T: (442) Griffiths; Suliman, O'Shaughnessy, Parslow, Cranston (Jennings 89); Waters (Barthram 89), Pell, Whitehead, Morgan-Smith (Rowe 90); Wright, Holman.
Charlton Ath: (442) Rudd; Foley, Johnson, Konsa, Fox; Holmes (Ahearne-Grant 68), Crofts, Jackson, Lookman; Ajose, Hanlan (Holmes-Dennis 80).
Referee: Brendan Malone.

Coventry C (0) 3 *(Haynes 60, Gadzhev 82, Rose 106)*

Portsmouth (1) 2 *(Main 20 (pen), Naismith 85)* 4976

Coventry C: (343) Charles-Cook; Willis (Finch 76), Ricketts, Harries; Stevenson, Rose, Gadzhev, Haynes; Lameiras, Tudgay (Reid 69), Thomas G (Jones 46).
Portsmouth: (4231) Bass; Buxton (Talbot 77), Davies, Barton, Naismith; Linganzi, May; Evans (Chaplin 64), Bennett, Tollitt; Main (Hunt 84).
aet.
Referee: Andrew Madley.

Derby Co (0) 1 *(Keogh 60)*

Grimsby T (0) 0 11,692

Derby Co: (442) Carson; Forsyth, Keogh, Pearce, Christie; Russell, Hughes (Hendrick 82), Bryson, Blackman (Ince 71); Martin (Butterfield 71), Bent.
Grimsby T: (442) McKeown; Andrew, Boyce, Pearson, Davies; Vose (Jackson 73), Summerfield, McAllister (Browne 55), Berrett; Bogle, Chambers (Bolarinwa 81).
Referee: Ben Toner.

Doncaster R (0) 1 *(Mandeville 69)*

Nottingham F (1) 2 *(Vaughan 11, Ward 90)* 5160

Doncaster R: (352) Marosi; Wright, Butler (Calder 46), Mason; Blair, Middleton (Mandeville 63), Houghton, Rowe, Garrett; Williams, Marquis.
Nottingham F: (4411) Henderson; Lichaj, Mills, Perquis, Traore; Burke (Osborn 75), Cohen (Kasami 67), Vaughan, Paterson; Ward (Veldwijk 90); Vellios.
Referee: Andy Haines.

Exeter C (0) 1 *(Harley 100)*

Brentford (0) 0 2633

Exeter C: (4132) Olejnik; McCready, Sweeney, Ampadu, Moore-Taylor; James; Harley, Taylor, Riley-Lowe (McAlinden 70); Watkins, Simpson (Wheeler 71).
Brentford: (4141) Bonham; Holldack, Egan, Dean, Field; McCormack (Woods 12); Clarke, Yennaris, Ledesma (Shaibu 102), Saunders; Hofmann (Hogan 77).
aet.
Referee: Kevin Johnson.

Ipswich T (0) 0

Stevenage (0) 1 *(Kennedy 53)* 6858

Ipswich T: (433) Gerken; Chambers, Smith, Digby, Knudsen; Bru (Bishop 69), Grant, Douglas; Ward, Sears, Dozzell (McGoldrick 46).
Stevenage: (442) Jones; Henry, Wilkinson, Wells (Fox 61), Franks; Conlon (Tonge 88), Lee, Gorman, McAnuff; Liburd (Godden 72), Kennedy.
Referee: Charles Breakspear.

Leyton Orient (0) 2 *(McCallum 73, 81)*
Fulham (1) 3 *(Adeniran 29, Woodrow 51, 54)* 3855
Leyton Orient: (442) Sargeant; Hunt, Pollock, Erichot, Kennedy; Massey, Weir (Atangana 74), Kelly, Semedo (Cox 62); Palmer, Cornick (McCallum 61).
Fulham: (433) Joronen; Kavanagh, Stearman, Ream, Sessegnon; Christensen, Parker, Adeniran (Tunnicliffe 64); De La Torre (Cairney 88), Woodrow, Edun.
Referee: Andy Davies.

Mansfield T (0) 1 *(Rose M 48)*
Blackburn R (1) 3 *(Stokes 29, 55, Duffy 54)* 2885
Mansfield T: (442) Shearer; Bennett, Benning, Howkins, Collins; Chapman, Clements (Hakeem 76), Hamilton (Green 70), Baxendale (Rose D 71); Rose M, Hemmings.
Blackburn R: (442) Steele; Lowe, Duffy, Greer, Hendrie (Henley 73); Marshall, Lenihan, Byrne, Conway (Feeney 69); Stokes, Graham (Mahoney 80).
Referee: Stephen Martin.

Newport Co (1) 2 *(Jackson 31, Randall 55 (pen))*
Milton Keynes D (0) 3 *(Bowditch 63 (pen), 90, Tilney 70)* 1402
Newport Co: (532) Day; Barnum-Bobb, Turley, Bennett, Jones, Butler; Labadie, Randall, Compton (Tozer 4); Jackson (Myrie-Williams 88), Rigg (Green 74).
Milton Keynes D: (4231) Nicholls; George B Williams, Wootton, Jackson, Tilney; Kasumu (Bowditch 62), Osei-Bonsu; Furlong (Powell 61), Rasulo, Thomas-Asante; Tshimanga (George C Williams 80).
Referee: Oliver Langford.

Oldham Ath (1) 2 *(Flynn 18, Law 83)*
Wigan Ath (1) 1 *(Grigg 34)* 2554
Oldham Ath: (451) Ripley; Law, Clarke, Burgess, Wilson; Mantack (Croft 46), Klok (Banks 62), Green, Fane, Flynn; Erwin (Cassidy 87).
Wigan Ath: (343) Jaaskelainen; Buxton■, Daniels, Warnock; Chow (O'Brien 87), Perkins, Power, Flores; Colclough (Cosgrove 87), Grigg (Barrigan 70), Jacobs.
Referee: Geoff Eltringham.

Peterborough U (0) 3 *(Nichols 64, 90, Taylor P 68)*
AFC Wimbledon (1) 2 *(Whelpdale 34, Taylor 78)* 2850
Peterborough U: (442) Alnwick; Hughes (Binnom-Williams 56), Bostwick, Baldwin, White; Maddison, Da Silva Lopes, Edwards G, Forrester (Chettle 73); Taylor P, Coulthirst (Nichols 56).
AFC Wimbledon: (442) Clarke; Fuller, Charles, Robinson, Kelly; Whelpdale (Beere 46), Parrett, Reeves, Barcham; Poleon (Elliott 69), Barnett (Taylor 69).
Referee: Ollie Yates.

Preston NE (0) 1 *(Doyle 90)*
Hartlepool U (0) 0 4509
Preston NE: (442) Lindegaard; Grimshaw, Huntington, Wright, Cunningham; Pringle (Humphrey 81), Browne, Johnson (Robinson 63), Gallagher; Garner (Hugill 63), Doyle.
Hartlepool U: (433) Bartlett; Magnay, Nsiala, Bates, Carroll; Laurent, Woods, Deverdics; Alessandra, Amond, Thomas.
Referee: Andy Woolmer.

Reading (2) 2 *(van den Berg 16, Beerens 28)*
Plymouth Arg (0) 0 6979
Reading: (4231) Jaakkola; Gunter, Cooper, van den Berg, Watson; Williams, Evans; Beerens, Swift, Harriott (Meite 57); Kermorgant.
Plymouth Arg: (433) Dorel; Miller, Songo'o, Bradley, Sawyer; Threlkeld, Carey, Fox (Donaldson 80); Jervis, Slew (Smith 73), Goodwillie (Spencer 72).
Referee: Simon Hooper.

Rochdale (0) 3 *(Henderson 47, Cannon 53, Mendez-Laing 78)*
Chesterfield (1) 1 *(McGinn 30)* 1436
Rochdale: (433) Lillis; Rafferty, Canavan, McGahey, McNulty; Allen, McDermott (Thomson 80), Cannon; Henderson, Andrew (Bunney 90), Odelusi (Mendez-Laing 68).
Chesterfield: (4411) Fulton; McGinn, Hird, Evatt (Raglan 60), Donohue; Ariyibi, Liddle, Dimaio, Mitchell (Morrison 64); O'Shea (Simons 71); Evans.
Referee: Nigel Miller.

Rotherham U (0) 4 *(Halford 59 (pen), Yates 81, 120, Forde 83)*
Morecambe (1) 5 *(Stockton 6, Dunn 68, 90 (pen), 118, Ellison 113)* 3793
Rotherham U: (433) Price; Thorpe, Halford, Wilson (Wood 46), Warren; Vaulks, Allan (Forde 76), Smallwood; Forster-Caskey (Ward D 63), Yates, Taylor.
Morecambe: (4231) Roche; Wakefield, Edwards, Whitmore, Conlan; Kenyon (Fleming 87), Rose; Barkhuizen, Mullin (Dunn 63), Molyneux; Stockton (Ellison 88).
aet.
Referee: Seb Stockbridge.

Scunthorpe U (0) 2 *(van Veen 100, 115)*
Notts Co (0) 0 2158
Scunthorpe U: (442) Daniels; Clarke, Wallace, Mirfin, Townsend; Holmes (Mantom 114), Ness, Dawson, Williams (Adelakun 106); Wootton (Morris 66), van Veen.
Notts Co: (442) Collin; Audel, Hollis, Duffy, Dickinson; Burke, Tootle, Smith (Atkinson 76), Rodman; Stead (Campbell A 67), Oliver.
aet.
Referee: Scott Duncan.

Sheffield U (1) 1 *(Clarke 6)*
Crewe Alex (0) 2 *(Lowe 89, 100)* 8305
Sheffield U: (442) Long; Brayford, Wilson, O'Connell, Hussey; Duffy, Fleck, Basham, Done (Scougall 76); Clarke (Calvert-Lewin 83), Sharp (McNulty 70).
Crewe Alex: (442) Garratt; Turton, Ray, Nugent, Bakayogo; Cooper, Bingham (Ng 46), Jones, Kirk (Kiwomya 59); Dagnall, Saunders (Lowe 68).
aet.
Referee: James Adcock.

Shrewsbury T (1) 2 *(Leitch-Smith 1, Dodds 77)*
Huddersfield T (1) 1 *(Kachunga 39)* 2862
Shrewsbury T: (4231) Leutwiler; Riley, McGivern, El-Abd, Brown; Deegan, Sarcevic; O'Brien, Dodds (Ogogo 79), Whalley (Jones 74); Leitch-Smith (Toney 46).
Huddersfield T: (4231) Ward; Cranie, Schindler, Stankovic, Lowe (Hefele 84); Payne (Palmer 58), Hogg (Paurevic 46); van La Parra, Mooy, Scannell; Kachunga.
Referee: Graham Salisbury.

Southend U (1) 1 *(McLaughlin 34)*
Gillingham (0) 3 *(McDonald 56, Emmanuel-Thomas 74, 88)* 2816
Southend U: (442) Oxley; Demetriou, White, Sokolik, Coker; O'Neill, Leonard, King (Williams 88), McLaughlin (McGlashan 79); Mooney (Bridge 79), Cox.
Gillingham: (41212) Nelson; Jackson, Ehmer (Oshilaja 17), Pask, Konchesky; Wright; Hessenthaler, Knott; Dack (Osadebe 30); McDonald, Quigley (Emmanuel-Thomas 63).
Referee: Tim Robinson.

Walsall (0) 0
Yeovil T (0) 2 *(Bakayoko 103 (og), Dolan 111)* 2699
Walsall: (4231) Etheridge; Edwards, Preston, McCarthy, Henry; Chambers, Dobson (Kinsella 69); Morris, Oztumer (Bakayoko 69), Ginnelly (Makris 63); Jackson.
Yeovil T: (433) Krysiak; Shephard (Mugabi 54), Butcher, Lacey, Dickson; Dolan, Dawson, Lawless; Hedges, Eaves (Sowunmi 115), Khan (Campbell 101).
aet.
Referee: Rob Jones.

Wolverhampton W (1) 2 *(Mason 7, Coady 76)*
Crawley T (1) 1 *(Boldewijn 13)* 8252
Wolverhampton W: (433) Lonergan; Coady, Batth, Hause, Doherty; Joao Teixeira (Edwards 84), Price, Evans; Wallace (Bodvarsson 46), Mason, Henry (Helder Costa 46).
Crawley T: (4231) Mersin; Young, McNerney, Connolly■, Arthur; Payne, Smith; Boldewijn, Banton (Harrold 82), Roberts (Yussuf 26 (Bawling 72)); Collins.
Referee: Ross Joyce.

Wycombe W (0) 0
Bristol C (1) 1 *(Abraham 27)* 1842
Wycombe W: (442) Dawson; Jombati, De Havilland (Pierre 68), Stewart, Jacobson; Harriman, McGinn, Bloomfield, Wood; Akinfenwa, Southwell (Thompson 67).

Bristol C: (41212) O'Donnell; Matthews (Bryan 65), Flint, Williams, Golbourne; Pack; Reid, Freeman; Tomlin; Wilbraham (Little 66), Abraham (Garita 66).
Referee: Lee Collins.

Wednesday, 10 August 2016

Burton Alb (1) 3 *(Reilly 36, Beavon 105, Butcher 113)*

Bury (0) 2 *(Pope 48, Maher 120)* 1523

Burton Alb: (442) McLaughlin; Edwards, Naylor, McFadzean (Flanagan 80), McCrory; Harness, Choudhury, Irvine (Palmer 74), Reilly (Akins 85); Beavon, Butcher.
Bury: (4231) Williams; Jones, Cameron, Kay, Leigh; Etuhu, Soares; Ismail (Maher 61), Mayor (Clark 81), Hope (Mellis 56); Pope.
aet. Referee: Mark Heywood.

Fleetwood T (1) 2 *(Holloway 13, Hunter 111)*

Leeds U (0) 2 *(Antonsson 89, Wood 94 (pen))* 3332

Fleetwood T: (433) Neal; McLaughlin, Bolger, Eastham, Bell; Jonsson, Ryan, Nirennold; Holloway (Hunter 60), Cole (Pond 81), Ball (Grant 72).
Leeds U: (4231) Green; Coyle, Bartley, Cooper (Bamba 46), Taylor; Vieira (Antonsson 76), Phillips; Sacko (Mowatt 65), Hernandez, Roofe; Wood.
aet; Leeds U won 5-4 on penalties. Referee: David Coote.

Luton T (1) 3 *(Gray 35, McGeehan 53, Okore 66 (og))*

Aston Villa (1) 1 *(Ayew 13)* 7412

Luton T: (442) Walton; Justin, Rea, Mullins, O'Donnell; Gray (Smith 87), Lee (Cuthbert 84), McGeehan, Ruddock; Hylton, Marriott (Vassell 90).
Aston Villa: (442) Bunn; Amavi, Okore, Richards, Baker (Hutton 46); Green, Tshibola, Gardner, Grealish; McCormack (Gestede 46), Ayew.
Referee: Gavin Ward.

QPR (0) 2 *(Ngbakoto 58, Washington 93)*

Swindon T (0) 2 *(Stewart 72, Brophy 107)* 5440

QPR: (4231) Ingram; Furlong, Onuoha, Lynch (Polter 78), Perch; Cousins, Henry; Ngbakoto (Kpekawa 71), El Khayati, Shodipo (Chery 58); Washington.
Swindon T: (352) Vigouroux; Thompson N (Iandolo 61), Sendles-White, Norris; Barry, Jones, Thomas, Rodgers, Brophy; Kasim (Smith 65), Hylton (Stewart 65).
aet; QPR won 4-2 on penalties. Referee: Tony Harrington.

Thursday, 11 August 2016

Bristol R (0) 1 *(Lines 115)*

Cardiff C (0) 0 4851

Bristol R: (532) Mildenhall; Leadbitter (Montano 94), Lockyer, Clarke J, Hartley, Brown; Clarke O, Lines, Sinclair (Bodin 78); Taylor, Harrison (Gaffney 78).
Cardiff C: (532) Moore; Richards, Ecuele Manga, Morrison, Connolly (Kennedy 87), John; O'Keefe, Gunnarsson, Ralls; Noone (Gounongbe 74), Zohore (Pilkington 63).
aet.
Referee: Chris Kavanagh.

SECOND ROUND

Tuesday, 23 August 2016

Blackburn R (1) 4 *(Akpan 42, Wharton 69, Conway 88, Duffy 97)*

Crewe Alex (2) 3 *(Bingham 8, Dagnall 39, 90)* 3448

Blackburn R: (442) Raya; Lowe (Marshall 70), Duffy, Wharton, Hendrie; Feeney, Byrne (Guthrie 56), Akpan, Conway; Gallagher, Stokes (Graham 56).
Crewe Alex: (442) Garratt; Turton, Guthrie, Davis, Bakayogo; Cooper (Ray 79), Bingham, Hollands (Jones 77), Kiwomya; Dagnall, Saunders (Lowe 65).
aet.
Referee: Geoff Eltringham.

Burton Alb (0) 0

Liverpool (2) 5 *(Origi 15, Firmino 22, Naylor 61 (og), Sturridge 78, 83)* 6450

Burton Alb: (352) Bywater; Naylor, McFadzean, McCrory; Akins (Harness 65), Williamson, Choudhury, Irvine (Palmer 46), Dyer (Fox 65); Beavon, Butcher.
Liverpool: (433) Mignolet; Clyne, Matip, Lovren, Milner; Lallana (Wijnaldum 64), Can (Stewart 71), Henderson; Mane, Origi, Firmino (Sturridge 64).
Referee: Simon Hooper.

Chelsea (3) 3 *(Batshuayi 29, 41, Moses 31)*

Bristol R (1) 2 *(Hartley 35, Harrison 48 (pen))* 39,276

Chelsea: (4231) Begovic; Aina (Terry 77), Ivanovic, Cahill, Azpilicueta; Fabregas, Matic; Moses, Loftus-Cheek (Oscar 82), Pedro (Hazard 75); Batshuayi.
Bristol R: (4231) Mildenhall; Leadbitter, Lockyer, Hartley, Brown; Clarke O, Sinclair; Bodin (Easter 46), Lines, James (Taylor 46); Harrison (Gaffney 66).
Referee: Keith Stroud.

Crystal Palace (1) 2 *(Dann 25, Wickham 47)*

Blackpool (0) 0 7533

Crystal Palace: (4231) Mandanda; Kelly, Dann, Tomkins, Souare; McArthur (Lee 61), Cabaye (Zaha 73); Puncheon, Mutch, Townsend; Benteke C (Wickham 46).
Blackpool: (532) Slocombe; Mellor, Aldred, Robertson, Aimson, Daniel; Nolan, McAlister (Herron 61), Cain; Potts (Yeates 61), Gnanduillet (Samuel 70).
Referee: Andrew Madley.

Derby Co (0) 1 *(Bent 56)*

Carlisle U (0) 1 *(Jones 90)* 9860

Derby Co: (442) Carson; Baird, Keogh, Pearce, Olsson (Elsnik 72); Camara (Ince 66), Butterfield, Johnson, Lowe; Blackman, Bent (Hughes 66).
Carlisle U: (442) Gillespie; Miller T, Raynes, Gillesphey, Grainger; Devitt, Joyce, Jones, Ellis (Ibehre 65); Adams (McKee 55), Miller S (Wyke 65).
aet; Derby Co won 14-13 on penalties.
Referee: Darren England.

Everton (1) 4 *(Lennon 28, Barkley 69, Kone 83, 90)*

Yeovil T (0) 0 24,617

Everton: (532) Stekelenburg; Lennon, Holgate (Cleverley 66), Williams A, Funes Mori, Oviedo; Gana, Barkley (Kone 79), McCarthy (Gibson 66); Bolasie, Lukaku.
Yeovil T: (433) Krysiak; Shephard, Smith, Butcher, Mugabi; Dawson (Lea 76), Lawless, Dolan; Hedges, Eaves, Khan (Campbell 63).
Referee: Chris Kavanagh.

Exeter C (1) 1 *(Taylor 24)*

Hull C (1) 3 *(Diomande 26, 77, Snodgrass 81)* 4037

Exeter C: (442) Pym; Woodman (Riley-Lowe 83), Brown, Ampadu, Sweeney; Harley (Watkins 74), Tillson, James, Taylor (Wheeler 83); McAlinden, Grant.
Hull C: (433) Kuciak; Elmohamady, Maguire, Livermore, Tymon (Robertson 32); Maloney (Snodgrass 77), Meyler, Bowen; Olley, Luer (Huddlestone 57), Diomande.
Referee: Andy Woolmer.

Luton T (0) 0

Leeds U (1) 1 *(Denton 23)* 7498

Luton T: (41212) Walton; O'Donnell, Rea, Mullins, Potts; Lee (Vassell 75); Gray (Cook 56), Smith; McGeehan; Hylton (Ruddock 66), Marriott.
Leeds U: (442) Silvestri; Coyle, Jansson (Cooper 74), Bamba, Denton; Dallas, Grimes, Murphy (Phillips 58), Hernandez (Mowatt 68); Doukara, Roofe.
Referee: Kevin Johnson.

Millwall (0) 1 *(Williams 77)*

Nottingham F (1) 2 *(Paterson 35, Veldwijk 87)* 4009

Millwall: (442) King; Romeo, Nelson, Webster, Ferguson; Onyedinma (Worrall 45), Abdou, Thompson (Williams 73), Wylde; Philpot, O'Brien (Morison 60).
Nottingham F: (433) Henderson; Lam (Pereira 68), Mills, Perquis, Lichaj; Lansbury, Vaughan, Paterson (Cash 89); Thorne (Burke 46), Veldwijk, Ward.
Referee: Gavin Ward.

Newcastle U (1) 2 *(Perez 45, 47)*

Cheltenham T (0) 0 21,972

Newcastle U: (4411) Darlow; Sterry, Lascelles, Hanley, Jesus Gamez; Aarons (Gouffran 24), Shelvey, Colback, Perez; Diame; Mitrovic (Gayle 38 (Anita 59)).
Cheltenham T: (352) Griffiths; Parslow, O'Shaughnessy, Suliman (Smith 68); Hall, Rowe, Pell, Dayton (Arthur 68), Cranston; Waters, Wright (Morgan-Smith 77).
Referee: Stephen Martin.

Northampton T (1) 2 *(Diamond 36, Revell 82)*

WBA (1) 2 *(McClean 45, McAuley 47)* 5516

Northampton T: (4231) Smith A; Moloney (Phillips 90), Nyatanga, Diamond, Buchanan; McCourt (Hoskins 75), Taylor M; Beautyman (Potter 75), O'Toole, Gorre; Revell.
WBA: (4411) Myhill; Dawson, McAuley, Olsson, Galloway (Wilson 70); Phillips, Morrison, Field, McClean (Fletcher 62); Berahino; Lambert (Rondon 85).
aet; Northampton T won 4-3 on penalties.
Referee: Darren Bond.

Norwich C (2) 6 *(Lafferty 25, Canos 36, 80, Martin 58, Jacob Murphy 63, Godfrey 86)*

Coventry C (0) 1 *(Lameiras 56 (pen))* 10,510

Norwich C: (4231) Jones; Whittaker (Godfrey 65), Martin, Bassong, Toffolo; Andreu, Canos; Thompson, Maddison, Jacob Murphy (Josh Murphy 65); Lafferty (Mulumbu 74).
Coventry C: (352) Charles-Cook; Willis, Ricketts, Harries; Dion Kelly-Evans, Stevenson (Devon Kelly-Evans 67), Gadzhev, McCann, Page; Reid (Lameiras 46), Agyei (Spence 67).
Referee: David Webb.

Oxford U (1) 2 *(Thomas 28, Crowley 90)*

Brighton & HA (1) 4 *(Adekugbe 2, LuaLua 76, Manu 81, Hemed 85)* 3189

Oxford U: (442) Eastwood; Long, Ruffels, Dunkley, Skarz; Roberts T (MacDonald 72), Sercombe, Lundstram, Rothwell; Hemmings (Taylor 77), Thomas (Crowley 82).
Brighton & HA: (442) Maenpaa; Hunt, Hunemeier (Hemed 62), White, Adekugbe; Norwood, Ince, Holla, Murphy; LuaLua (Baldock 85), Manu (Tilley 87).
Referee: Andy Davies.

Peterborough U (0) 1 *(Da Silva Lopes 75)*

Swansea C (3) 3 *(Fulton 15, McBurnie 41, 44)* 4727

Peterborough U: (442) Tyler; Smith, Bostwick, Santos, Hughes; Maddison, Forrester (Chettle 74), Anderson (Da Silva Lopes 58), Edwards G; Taylor P (Coulthirst 65), Nichols.
Swansea C: (4231) Nordfeldt; Rangel, Amat (Fernandez 46), van der Hoorn, Taylor; Britton (Fer 80), Fulton; Dyer, Ki, Montero; McBurnie (Llorente 66).
Referee: James Adcock.

Preston NE (0) 2 *(Doyle 66, Hugill 81)*

Oldham Ath (0) 0 5075

Preston NE: (352) Maxwell; Clarke, Huntington, Cunningham; Humphrey, Pringle (Browne 27), Welsh (Robinson 60), Pearson, Spurr; Makienok (Doyle 61), Hugill.
Oldham Ath: (442) Ripley; Dunne, Burgess, Clarke, Law (McLaughlin 67); Wilson, Klok (Green 46), Fane, Banks (Osei 70); Erwin, Cassidy.
Referee: Scott Duncan.

QPR (1) 2 *(Sandro 41, 74)*

Rochdale (1) 1 *(Lund 5)* 3928

QPR: (4231) Ingram; Perch, Onuoha, Hall, Bidwell; Borysiuk (Luongo 61), Sandro; Kakay (Polter 73), El Khayati (Chery 40), Shodipo; Washington.
Rochdale: (433) Logan; Rafferty (Andrew 78), McGahey, Canavan, McNulty; Lund, Allen, Cannon (Mendez-Laing 62); McDermott, Henderson, Thompson (Davies 63).
Referee: Dean Whitestone.

Reading (0) 2 *(Harriott 68, 114)*

Milton Keynes D (1) 2 *(Bowditch 34 (pen), Tshimanga 118)* 6848

Reading: (433) Jaakkola; Watson, Cooper, Moore, Obita; Quinn, Gravenberch (Williams 75), Kelly (Evans 52); Harriott, Mendes, Rakels (Beerens 21).
Milton Keynes D: (442) Nicholls; George B Williams, Downing, Wootton, Tilney; Jackson (Reeves 46), Upson, Rasulo, Thomas-Asante (George C Williams 70); Tshimanga, Bowditch (Carruthers 63).
aet; Reading won 4-2 on penalties.
Referee: Charles Breakspear.

Scunthorpe U (0) 1 *(Morris 60 (pen))*

Bristol C (1) 2 *(Reid 35, Abraham 97)* 2397

Scunthorpe U: (442) Daniels; Clarke, Goode, Wallace, Townsend; Adelakun (Holmes 61), Dawson, Bishop, Morris; Hopper (Wootton 87), van Veen.
Bristol C: (4231) Fielding; Little, Flint, Williams, Golbourne; Brownhill, Pack; O'Dowda, Reid (Tomlin 68), Freeman (De Girolamo 101); Wilbraham (Abraham 67).
aet.
Referee: Ross Joyce.

Stevenage (0) 0

Stoke C (2) 4 *(Crouch 14, 48, 70, Bardsley 32)* 3363

Stevenage: (442) Jones; Henry, Wilkinson, Franks, Fox; Hunte (McAnuff 58), Lee (Tonge 67), Gorman, Pett; Hyde (Godden 58), Liburd.
Stoke C: (4231) Given; Bardsley, Shawcross (Pieters 74), Cameron, Muniesa; Whelan, Allen (Krkic 85); Walters, Adam, Arnautovic (Sobhi 61); Crouch.
Referee: Oliver Langford.

Watford (0) 1 *(Ighalo 57)*

Gillingham (0) 2 *(Byrne 82, Dack 102)* 7004

Watford: (352) Pantilimon; Hoban, Kabasele, Paredes; Nyom, Guedioura (Ighalo 56), Watson, Doucoure, Anya (Zuniga 94); Deeney, Vydra (Capoue 66).
Gillingham: (352) Nelson; Ehmer, Pask, Oshilaja; Osadebe, Knott, Wright (Oldaker 74), Byrne, Konchesky (List 66); McDonald, Emmanuel-Thomas (Dack 66).
aet.
Referee: James Linington.

Wolverhampton W (2) 2 *(Helder Costa 6, Wallace 13)*

Cambridge U (1) 1 *(Elito 14)* 9500

Wolverhampton W: (4411) Lonergan; Coady, Iorfa, Hause, Saville; Henry, Oniangue (Edwards 62), Price, Wallace; Joao Teixeira (Doherty 57); Helder Costa (Bodvarsson 70).
Cambridge U: (451) Norris; Taylor, Coulson, Legge, Adams; Mingoia, Clark (Gosling 70), Dunne (Newton 46), Elito (Pigott 64), Berry; Williamson.
Referee: Brendan Malone.

Wednesday, 24 August 2016

Accrington S (0) 1 *(Pearson 120)*

Burnley (0) 0 3170

Accrington S: (4411) Parish; Donacien, Beckles, Hughes, Pearson; O'Sullivan (Davies 101), Hewitt, Conneely, McConville; McCartan (Boco 68); Kee (Lacey 84).
Burnley: (442) Pope; Darikwa, Long, Tarkowski, Flanagan; Gudmundsson, Ulvestad, O'Neill, Kightly (Arfield 81); Vokes (Gray 67), Jutkiewicz (Boyd 106).
aet.
Referee: Tony Harrington.

Fulham (0) 2 *(de Sart 54 (og), Christensen 113)*

Middlesbrough (1) 1 *(Nugent 8)* 8522

Fulham: (4231) Joronen; Grimmer (Kavanagh 56), Stearman, Ream, Malone; Tunnicliffe, Adeniran; Christensen, Jozabed (De La Torre 104), Edun; Woodrow (Smith 94).
Middlesbrough: (4231) Guzan; Baptiste, Ayala, Gibson, Da Silva (Friend 10 (Stuani 90)); Clayton, de Sart; Nugent, Nsue, Downing; Fischer (Forshaw 80).
aet.
Referee: David Coote.

Morecambe (1) 1 *(Stockton 14)*

Bournemouth (1) 2 *(Gradel 8, Wilson M 54)* 2542

Morecambe: (4231) Roche; Wakefield, Edwards, Whitmore, Conlan; Fleming, Rose; Barkhuizen, Dunn (Mullin 80), Molyneux (Ellison 73); Stockton (Turner 80).
Bournemouth: (442) Federici; Francis, Wilson M, Ake, Smith B; Stanislas (Pugh 61), Cook L, Gosling, Gradel (Hyndman 90); Afobe, Grabban (Mousset 77).
Referee: Peter Bankes.

Sunderland (0) 1 *(Januzaj 83)*

Shrewsbury T (0) 0 13,979

Sunderland: (442) Pickford; Love, McNair, Djilobodji, Van Aanholt; Khazri, Rodwell, Pienaar (Watmore 61), Gooch; Asoro, Januzaj.
Shrewsbury T: (41212) Leutwiler; El-Abd, McGivern, Lancashire, Riley; Ogogo; Deegan, Brown; Sarcevic (O'Brien 64); Toney (Waring 79), Dodds (Mangan 73).
Referee: Jeremy Simpson.

THIRD ROUND

Tuesday, 20 September 2016

Bournemouth (0) 2 *(Grabban 53 (pen), Gosling 76)*

Preston NE (1) 3 *(Makienok 10, 85, 111)* 7595

Bournemouth: (451) Federici; Ake, Wilson M (Mousset 46), Mings (Jordan 106), Smith B; Gradel, Grabban, Gosling, Cook L, Fraser (Hyndman 89); Afobe.
Preston NE: (532) Maxwell; Huntington, Humphrey (Robinson 102), Pearson, Wright, Cunningham (Clarke 67); Davies, Welsh, Johnson (Doyle 76); Pringle, Makienok.
aet.
Referee: Simon Hooper.

Brighton & HA (0) 1 *(Hemed 85)*

Reading (1) 2 *(Quinn 32, Swift 54)* 6235

Brighton & HA: (442) Maenpaa; Hunt, Hunemeier, Goldson, Pocognoli (Skalak 69); Norwood, Sidwell, Ince (Hemed 62), Manu (Murphy 73); Baldock, Murray.
Reading: (4231) Jaakkola; Watson, Moore (Gunter 61), Blackett■, Obita; Kelly, Swift (Evans 76); Samuel (Gravenberch 43), Quinn, Harriott; Mendes.
Referee: Lee Probert.

Derby Co (0) 0

Liverpool (1) 3 *(Klavan 24, Coutinho 50, Origi 54)* 26,245

Derby Co: (451) Mitchell; Christie, Keogh, Pearce, Olsson (Lowe 64); Butterfield, Hughes, Baird (Ince 46), Johnson, Weimann (Elsnik 55); Bent.
Liverpool: (433) Karius; Clyne, Matip, Klavan, Moreno; Henderson (Can 57), Lucas, Grujic; Firmino (Ejaria 77), Origi, Coutinho (Ings 64).
Referee: Graham Scott.

Everton (0) 0

Norwich C (1) 2 *(Naismith 41, Josh Murphy 74)* 29,550

Everton: (4231) Stekelenburg; Coleman, Holgate (Kone 83), Williams A, Funes Mori; Cleverley, Gana; Lennon (Bolasie 68), Barkley, Valencia; Deulofeu (Mirallas 68).
Norwich C: (4231) Ruddy; Whittaker, Bennett, Bassong, Brady; Thompson, Mulumbu (Godfrey 90); Josh Murphy, Naismith, Pritchard (Turner 89); Oliveira (Lafferty 46).
Referee: Andrew Madley.

Leeds U (0) 1 *(Wood 85)*

Blackburn R (0) 0 8488

Leeds U: (433) Silvestri; Coyle, Bartley, Cooper, Taylor; O'Kane, Phillips, Vieira (Hernandez 59); Roofe, Antonsson (Wood 71), Mowatt (Grimes 83).
Blackburn R: (442) Raya; Lowe, Wharton (Nyambe 8), Lenihan, Hendrie; Feeney, Byrne, Akpan, Samuelsen (Mahoney 62); Gallagher (Emnes 62), Bennett.
Referee: Darren Deadman.

Leicester C (2) 2 *(Okazaki 17, 34)*

Chelsea (1) 4 *(Cahill 45, Azpilicueta 49, Fabregas 92, 94)* 29,899

Leicester C: (4411) Zieler; Simpson, Wasilewski■, Morgan, Chilwell; Gray (Amartey 90), King, Drinkwater, Schlupp; Okazaki (Ulloa 75); Musa (Vardy 76).
Chelsea: (4231) Begovic; Azpilicueta, Cahill, Luiz, Alonso; Matic, Fabregas; Moses, Loftus-Cheek (Costa 67), Pedro (Hazard 89); Batshuayi (Chalobah 80).
aet.
Referee: Robert Madley.

Newcastle U (2) 2 *(Ritchie 29, Gouffran 31)*

Wolverhampton W (0) 0 34,735

Newcastle U: (4231) Darlow; Yedlin, Hanley, Clark, Lazaar; Shelvey, Colback; Ritchie (Lascelles 86), Diame (Perez 72), Gouffran (Atsu 74); Murphy.
Wolverhampton W: (433) Lonergan; Silvio, Hause, Iorfa, Borthwick-Jackson; Saville, Joao Teixeira (John 46), Coady; Wallace (Bodvarsson 78), Gladon, Mason (Price 62).
Referee: Andy Woolmer.

Nottingham F (0) 0

Arsenal (1) 4 *(Xhaka 23, Lucas Perez 60 (pen), 71, Oxlade-Chamberlain 90)* 28,567

Nottingham F: (4141) Stojkovic; Pereira, Mancienne, Mills, Lichaj; Cohen; Dumitru (Lica 81), Lansbury, Kasami (Carayol 68), Osborn; Bendtner (Vellios 80).
Arsenal: (4231) Martinez; Maitland-Niles (Bielik 87), Holding, Gabriel, Gibbs; Xhaka, Elneny; Oxlade-Chamberlain, Reine-Adelaide (Zelalem 83), Akpom (Willock 83); Lucas Perez.
Referee: Paul Tierney.

Wednesday, 21 September 2016

Fulham (1) 1 *(Piazon 14)*

Bristol C (1) 2 *(Wilbraham 45, Abraham 90)* 6017

Fulham: (451) Joronen; Malone, Madl, Ream, Edun (De La Torre 69); Piazon, Christensen (Kebano 85), Johansen, Tunnicliffe, Adeniran; Woodrow.
Bristol C: (442) Lucic; Golbourne, Moore, Flint, Matthews (Little 46); Freeman, Pack, Brownhill, O'Dowda; Engvall (Abraham 62), Wilbraham (Reid 79).
Referee: Andy Davies.

Northampton T (1) 1 *(Revell 42 (pen))*

Manchester U (1) 3 *(Carrick 17, Ander Herrera 68, Rashford 75)* 7798

Northampton T: (4141) Smith A; Moloney, Diamond, Zakuani, Buchanan; McCourt (Richards 73); Hoskins, Beautyman (O'Toole 54), Taylor M, Gorre (Potter 66); Revell.
Manchester U: (4231) Romero; Fosu-Mensah (Rashford 55), Smalling, Blind, Rojo; Carrick, Schneiderlin (Fellaini 73); Young, Ander Herrera, Depay (Ibrahimovic 55); Rooney.
Referee: Stuart Attwell.

QPR (0) 1 *(Sandro 60)*

Sunderland (0) 2 *(McNair 70, 80)* 14,301

QPR: (451) Ingram; Kakay, Lynch, Caulker, Hamalainen; Sylla (Polter 74), Cousins (Chery 85), Sandro, Wszolek, El Khayati; Washington (Luongo 79).
Sunderland: (4411) Pickford; Denayer (Love 69), O'Shea, Djilobodji, Van Aanholt; Ndong, Kirchhoff, McNair, Gooch (Cattermole 69); Watmore; Asoro (Maja 69).
Referee: Peter Bankes.

Southampton (1) 2 *(Austin 33 (pen), Hesketh 63)*

Crystal Palace (0) 0 14,080

Southampton: (4312) McCarthy; Martina, Fonte, Yoshida, Targett; Ward-Prowse, Reed, Clasie; Hesketh (Hojbjerg 77); Long (Tadic 89), Austin (Redmond 57).
Crystal Palace: (442) Hennessey; Ward, Dann (Kelly 18), Delaney, Fryers; Zaha, Cabaye, Mutch (Puncheon 70), Lee; Wickham, Sako (Benteke C 64).
Referee: James Adcock.

Stoke C (1) 1 *(Arnautovic 24)*

Hull C (1) 2 *(Mason 45, Henriksen 90)* 10,550

Stoke C: (433) Grant; Johnson, Shawcross, Martins Indi, Pieters; Cameron, Allen, Imbula (Adam 69); Arnautovic, Bony (Diouf 69), Sobhi.
Hull C: (442) Marshall; Meyler (Huddlestone 79), Maguire, Davies, Robertson; Weir, Mason (Elmohamady 68), Henriksen, Maloney (Diomande 90); Mbokani, Keane.
Referee: Chris Kavanagh.

Swansea C (0) 1 *(Sigurdsson 90)*

Manchester C (0) 2 *(Clichy 49, Garcia 67)* 18,237

Swansea C: (4231) Nordfeldt; Rangel, van der Hoorn, Amat, Taylor; Cork (Fer 55), Britton; Naughton (Sigurdsson 61), Fulton, Routledge; Borja Baston (Barrow 75).
Manchester C: (4231) Caballero; Zabaleta, Kompany, Stones, Clichy; Tasende (De Bruyne 58), Fernando; Garcia (Adarabioyo 90), Jesus Navas, Sane; Iheanacho (Diaz 80).
Referee: Keith Stroud.

Tottenham H (1) 5 *(Eriksen 31, 48, Janssen 51 (pen), Onomah 65, Lamela 68)*
Gillingham (0) 0 26,244
Tottenham H: (4231) Vorm; Trippier, Carter-Vickers, Wimmer, Davies (Walkes 80); Winks, Carroll; Lamela, Eriksen (Nkoudou 60), Onomah; Janssen (Edwards 75).
Gillingham: (4411) Bond (Nelson 16); Jackson, Ehmer, Oshilaja, Konchesky; Emmanuel-Thomas (Wagstaff 60), Wright, Byrne, Osadebe; Dack (Knott 81); McDonald.
Referee: David Coote.

West Ham U (0) 1 *(Payet 90)*
Accrington S (0) 0 39,877
West Ham U: (4231) Randolph; Arbeloa, Nordtveit, Ogbonna, Masuaku; Obiang, Fernandes; Feghouli (Payet 46), Calleri (Antonio 70), Tore (Lanzini 46); Zaza.
Accrington S: (4231) Parish; Vyner, Pearson, Beckles, Donacien; Brown (Hughes 77), Conneely (Boco 84); O'Sullivan (Eagles 66), Clark, McConville; Kee.
Referee: Stephen Martin.

FOURTH ROUND

Tuesday, 25 October 2016

Arsenal (1) 2 *(Oxlade-Chamberlain 33, 78)*
Reading (0) 0 59,865
Arsenal: (4231) Martinez; Jenkinson, Gabriel, Holding, Gibbs; Elneny, Maitland-Niles; Oxlade-Chamberlain (Zelalem 80), Iwobi, Reine-Adelaide (Giroud 66); Lucas Perez (Willock 72).
Reading: (433) Al Habsi; Watson (Gravenberch 68), Moore, Blackett, Obita; van den Berg (Quinn 80), Kelly, Evans; McCleary, Samuel, Harriott (Kermorgant 56).
Referee: Graham Scott.

Bristol C (0) 1 *(Tomlin 90)*
Hull C (1) 2 *(Maguire 44, Dawson 47)* 16,149
Bristol C: (4231) O'Donnell; Little, Flint, Moore, Golbourne; Pack, Reid; O'Dowda, Engvall (McClousky 76), Bryan (Abraham 60); Wilbraham (Tomlin 59).
Hull C: (3412) Jakupovic; Maguire, Dawson, Davies; Elmohamady, Livermore, Mason (Huddlestone 79), Tymon; Henriksen; Diomande, Hernandez (Meyler 89).
Referee: Keith Stroud.

Leeds U (1) 2 *(Antonsson 43, Wood 109)*
Norwich C (1) 2 *(Pritchard 14, Oliveira 99)* 22,222
Leeds U: (4231) Silvestri; Coyle, Bartley, Cooper, Berardi; Grimes, Vieira; Doukara (Phillips 81), Mowatt (Sacko 76), Roofe; Antonsson (Wood 67).
Norwich C: (4231) Ruddy; Godfrey (Turner 77), Bennett, Bassong, Brady; Tettey (Dorrans 46), Thompson; Josh Murphy (Canos 71), Naismith, Pritchard; Oliveira.
aet; Leeds U won 3-2 on penalties.
Referee: Andy Woolmer.

Liverpool (1) 2 *(Sturridge 9, 64)*
Tottenham H (0) 1 *(Janssen 76 (pen))* 53,051
Liverpool: (4312) Mignolet; Alexander-Arnold (Clyne 68), Lucas, Klavan, Moreno; Wijnaldum, Stewart, Ejaria; Grujic (Can 89); Sturridge, Origi (Ings 68).
Tottenham H: (4231) Vorm; Trippier, Carter-Vickers, Wimmer, Davies; Dier (Wanyama 67), Winks; Onomah, Carroll (Lamela 61), Nkoudou (Harrison 83); Janssen.
Referee: Jon Moss.

Newcastle U (2) 6 *(Mitrovic 19, 55, Diame 38, 87, Ritchie 53 (pen), Perez 90)*
Preston NE (0) 0 49,042
Newcastle U: (4411) Sels; Yedlin, Mbemba, Hanley, Dummett (Anita 58); Ritchie (Perez 76), Hayden, Colback (Shelvey 32), Atsu; Diame; Mitrovic.
Preston NE: (352) Lindegaard; Wright, Davies (Clarke 46), Huntington; Humphrey, Browne■, Pringle (Gallagher 46), Grimshaw, Spurr; Doyle, Makienok (Johnson 63).
Referee: Andrew Madley.

Wednesday, 26 October 2016

Manchester U (0) 1 *(Mata 54)*
Manchester C (0) 0 75,196
Manchester U: (4231) de Gea; Valencia, Blind, Rojo, Shaw; Carrick, Ander Herrera; Mata (Schneiderlin 73), Pogba, Rashford (Lingard 81); Ibrahimovic.
Manchester C: (4411) Caballero; Maffeo, Kompany (Kolarov 46), Otamendi, Clichy; Jesus Navas, Garcia, Fernando, Nolito (Aguero 71); Sane (Sterling 63); Iheanacho.
Referee: Micheal Dean.

Southampton (0) 1 *(Boufal 66)*
Sunderland (0) 0 21,460
Southampton: (433) McCarthy; Yoshida, Fonte, Stephens, McQueen; Reed (Clasie 82), Ward-Prowse, Hojbjerg; Boufal, Rodriguez (Olomola 26), Isgrove (Redmond 72).
Sunderland: (433) Pickford; Jones, Kone, Djilobodji, Van Aanholt; Rodwell, McNair (Pienaar 87), Ndong; Watmore (Gooch 87), Anichebe, Khazri (Defoe 72).
Referee: Chris Kavanagh.

West Ham U (1) 2 *(Kouyate 11, Fernandes 48)*
Chelsea (0) 1 *(Cahill 90)* 45,957
West Ham U: (343) Randolph; Kouyate, Reid, Ogbonna; Fernandes (Feghouli 66), Noble, Obiang, Cresswell; Antonio (Zaza 82), Payet, Lanzini (Ayew 78).
Chelsea: (343) Begovic; Luiz, Cahill, Terry; Aina (Pedro 67), Kante, Chalobah (Hazard 63), Azpilicueta; Willian, Batshuayi (Costa 54), Oscar.
Referee: Craig Pawson.

QUARTER-FINALS

Tuesday, 29 November 2016

Hull C (0) 1 *(Snodgrass 99)*
Newcastle U (0) 1 *(Diame 98)* 16,243
Hull C: (433) Jakupovic; Elmohamady (Weir 79), Maguire, Dawson, Robertson (Tymon 79); Huddlestone, Livermore (Henriksen 79), Meyler; Snodgrass, Mbokani■, Diomande.
Newcastle U: (4411) Sels; Anita (Yedlin 109), Lascelles, Clark, Lazaar; Ritchie (Atsu 81), Shelvey, Hayden (Murphy 106), Gouffran; Diame; Gayle.
aet; Hull C won 3-1 on penalties.
Referee: Neil Swarbrick.

Liverpool (0) 2 *(Origi 76, Woodburn 81)*
Leeds U (0) 0 52,012
Liverpool: (433) Mignolet; Alexander-Arnold, Lucas, Klavan, Moreno; Ejaria (Milner 82), Stewart (Woodburn 67), Can; Mane, Origi (Grujic 90), Wijnaldum.
Leeds U: (4231) Silvestri; Berardi, Bartley, Cooper (Ayling 46), Taylor; Vieira, O'Kane (Phillips 28); Sacko, Roofe, Dallas (Wood 62); Doukara.
Referee: Andre Marriner.

Wednesday, 30 November 2016

Arsenal (0) 0
Southampton (2) 2 *(Clasie 13, Bertrand 38)* 59,013
Arsenal: (4231) Martinez; Jenkinson (Maitland-Niles 64), Gabriel, Holding, Gibbs; Coquelin, Elneny (Xhaka 43); Reine-Adelaide (Oxlade-Chamberlain 62), Ramsey, Iwobi; Lucas Perez.
Southampton: (433) Forster; Martina, Yoshida, van Dijk, Bertrand; Clasie, Reed (Hojbjerg 65), Davis; McQueen, Long, Boufal (Sims 66).
Referee: Kevin Friend.

Manchester U (1) 4 *(Ibrahimovic 2, 90, Martial 48, 62)*
West Ham U (1) 1 *(Fletcher 35)* 65,269
Manchester U: (4231) de Gea; Valencia, Jones, Rojo, Shaw (Blind 46); Ander Herrera, Carrick; Mkhitaryan (Rashford 90), Rooney, Martial (Schweinsteiger 86); Ibrahimovic.
West Ham U: (343) Adrian; Kouyate, Reid, Ogbonna; Antonio (Lanzini 58), Obiang, Fernandes, Cresswell (Masuaku 45); Feghouli, Fletcher, Payet (Zaza 76).
Referee: Mike Jones.

SEMI-FINALS FIRST LEG

Tuesday, 10 January 2017

Manchester U (0) 2 *(Mata 56, Fellaini 87)*

Hull C (0) 0 65,798

Manchester U: (4231) de Gea; Valencia, Smalling, Jones, Darmian; Ander Herrera, Pogba; Mata (Fellaini 79), Rooney (Martial 59), Mkhitaryan (Lingard 71); Rashford.
Hull C: (4141) Jakupovic; Meyler, Maguire, Huddlestone, Robertson; Mason; Snodgrass, Henriksen (Hernandez 19), Clucas, Tymon (Weir 90); Diomande (Maloney 74).
Referee: Kevin Friend.

Wednesday, 11 January 2017

Southampton (1) 1 *(Redmond 20)*

Liverpool (0) 0 31,480

Southampton: (433) Forster; Cedric, Yoshida, van Dijk, Bertrand; Clasie (Hojbjerg 73), Romeu, Davis (Ward-Prowse 82); Redmond, Rodriguez (Long 82), Tadic.
Liverpool: (433) Karius; Clyne, Lovren, Klavan, Milner; Wijnaldum (Coutinho 61), Lucas, Can; Lallana, Sturridge, Firmino (Origi 83).
Referee: Neil Swarbrick.

SEMI-FINALS SECOND LEG

Wednesday, 25 January 2017

Liverpool (0) 0

Southampton (0) 1 *(Long 90)* 52,238

Liverpool: (433) Karius; Alexander-Arnold, Matip, Lovren, Milner; Can (Origi 78), Henderson, Lallana; Firmino, Sturridge, Coutinho (Wijnaldum 87).
Southampton: (433) Forster; Cedric, Stephens, Yoshida, Bertrand; Ward-Prowse (Hojbjerg 59), Romeu, Davis; Redmond (Sims 81), Rodriguez (Long 46), Tadic.
Southampton won 2-0 on aggregate
Referee: Martin Atkinson.

Thursday, 26 January 2017

Hull C (1) 2 *(Huddlestone 35 (pen), Niasse 85)*

Manchester U (0) 1 *(Pogba 66)* 16,831

Hull C: (4231) Marshall; Meyler, Dawson, Maguire, Tymon; Huddlestone, Clucas; Bowen (Markovic 59), Maloney (Evandro 64), Diomande (Hernandez 70); Niasse.
Manchester U: (433) de Gea; Darmian, Smalling, Jones, Rojo; Ander Herrera, Carrick, Pogba; Lingard (Rooney 79), Ibrahimovic, Rashford (Fellaini 90).
Manchester U won 3-2 on aggregate
Referee: Jon Moss.

EFL CUP FINAL 2016

Sunday, 26 February 2017

(at Wembley Stadium, attendance 85,264)

Manchester U (2) 3 **Southampton (1) 2**

Manchester U: (4231) de Gea; Valencia, Bailly, Smalling, Rojo; Ander Herrera, Pogba; Mata (Carrick 46), Lingard (Rashford 77), Martial (Fellaini 90); Ibrahimovic.
Scorers: Ibrahimovic 19, 87, Lingard 38.

Southampton: (4411) Forster; Cedric, Stephens, Yoshida, Bertrand; Ward-Prowse, Romeu, Davis (Rodriguez 90), Redmond; Tadic (Boufal 77); Gabbiadini (Long 83).
Scorers: Gabbiadini 45, 48.

Referee: Andre Marriner.

Zlatan Ibrahimovic made a huge impact for Manchester United, scoring 17 goals in the Premier League, and scoring two goals in a 3-2 victory over Southampton in the EFL Cup final. This is the opening goal of the game. (Reuters/Darren Staples Livepic)

LEAGUE CUP ATTENDANCES 1960–2017

Season	*Attendances*	*Games*	*Average*
1960–61	1,204,580	112	10,755
1961–62	1,030,534	104	9,909
1962–63	1,029,893	102	10,097
1963–64	945,265	104	9,089
1964–65	962,802	98	9,825
1965–66	1,205,876	106	11,376
1966–67	1,394,553	118	11,818
1967–68	1,671,326	110	15,194
1968–69	2,064,647	118	17,497
1969–70	2,299,819	122	18,851
1970–71	2,035,315	116	17,546
1971–72	2,397,154	123	19,489
1972–73	1,935,474	120	16,129
1973–74	1,722,629	132	13,050
1974–75	1,901,094	127	14,969
1975–76	1,841,735	140	13,155
1976–77	2,236,636	147	15,215
1977–78	2,038,295	148	13,772
1978–79	1,825,643	139	13,134
1979–80	2,322,866	169	13,745
1980–81	2,051,576	161	12,743
1981–82	1,880,682	161	11,681
1982–83	1,679,756	160	10,498
1983–84	1,900,491	168	11,312
1984–85	1,876,429	167	11,236
1985–86	1,579,916	163	9,693
1986–87	1,531,498	157	9,755
1987–88	1,539,253	158	9,742
1988–89	1,552,780	162	9,585
1989–90	1,836,916	168	10,934
1990–91	1,675,496	159	10,538
1991–92	1,622,337	164	9,892
1992–93	1,558,031	161	9,677
1993–94	1,744,120	163	10,700
1994–95	1,530,478	157	9,748
1995–96	1,776,060	162	10,963
1996–97	1,529,321	163	9,382
1997–98	1,484,297	153	9,701
1998–99	1,555,856	153	10,169
1999–2000	1,354,233	153	8,851
2000–01	1,501,304	154	9,749
2001–02	1,076,390	93	11,574
2002–03	1,242,478	92	13,505
2003–04	1,267,729	93	13,631
2004–05	1,313,693	93	14,216
2005–06	1,072,362	93	11,531
2006–07	1,098,403	93	11,811
2007–08	1,332,841	94	14,179
2008–09	1,329,753	93	14,298
2009–10	1,376,405	93	14,800
2010–11	1,197,917	93	12,881
2011–12	1,209,684	93	13,007
2012–13	1,210,031	93	13,011
2013–14	1,362,360	93	14,649
2014–15	1,274,413	93	13,690
2015–16	1,430,554	93	15,382
2016–17	1,462,722	93	15,728

EFL CUP 2016–17

Round	*Aggregate*	*Games*	*Average*
One	148,244	35	4,236
Two	218,970	25	8,759
Three	308,418	16	19,276
Four	342,942	8	42,868
Quarter-finals	192,537	4	48,134
Semi-finals	166,347	4	41,587
Final	85,264	1	85,264
Total	1,462,722	93	15,728

FOOTBALL LEAGUE TROPHY FINALS 1984–2017

The 1984 final was played at Boothferry Park, Hull. All subsequent finals played at Wembley except between 2001 and 2007 (inclusive) which were played at Millennium Stadium, Cardiff.

ASSOCIATE MEMBERS' CUP

1984	Bournemouth v Hull C	2-1

FREIGHT ROVER TROPHY

1985	Wigan Ath v Brentford	3-1
1986	Bristol C v Bolton W	3-0
1987	Mansfield T v Bristol C	1-1*
	Mansfield T won 5-4 on penalties	

SHERPA VANS TROPHY

1988	Wolverhampton W v Burnley	2-0
1989	Bolton W v Torquay U	4-1

LEYLAND DAF CUP

1990	Tranmere R v Bristol R	2-1
1991	Birmingham C v Tranmere R	3-2

AUTOGLASS TROPHY

1992	Stoke C v Stockport Co	1-0
1993	Port Vale v Stockport Co	2-1
1994	Swansea C v Huddersfield T	1-1*
	Swansea C won 3-1 on penalties	

AUTO WINDSCREENS SHIELD

1995	Birmingham C v Carlisle U	1-0*
1996	Rotherham U v Shrewsbury T	2-1
1997	Carlisle U v Colchester U	0-0*
	Carlisle U won 4-3 on penalties	
1998	Grimsby T v Bournemouth	2-1
1999	Wigan Ath v Millwall	1-0
2000	Stoke C v Bristol C	2-1

LDV VANS TROPHY

2001	Port Vale v Brentford	2-1
2002	Blackpool v Cambridge U	4-1
2003	Bristol C v Carlisle U	2-0
2004	Blackpool v Southend U	2-0
2005	Wrexham v Southend U	2-0*

FOOTBALL LEAGUE TROPHY

2006	Swansea C v Carlisle U	2-1

JOHNSTONE'S PAINT TROPHY

2007	Doncaster R v Bristol R	3-2*
2008	Milton Keynes D v Grimsby T	2-0
2009	Luton T v Scunthorpe U	3-2*
2010	Southampton v Carlisle U	4-1
2011	Carlisle U v Brentford	1-0
2012	Chesterfield v Swindon T	2-0
2013	Crewe Alex v Southend U	2-0
2014	Peterborough U v Chesterfield	3-1
2015	Bristol C v Walsall	2-0
2016	Barnsley v Oxford U	3-2

EFL CHECKATRADE TROPHY

2017	Coventry C v Oxford U	2-1

**After extra time.*

FOOTBALL LEAGUE TROPHY WINS

Bristol C 3, Birmingham C 2, Blackpool 2, Carlisle U 2, Port Vale 2, Stoke C 2, Swansea C 2, Wigan Ath 2, Barnsley 1, Bolton W 1, Bournemouth 1, Chesterfield 1, Coventry C 1, Crewe Alex 1, Doncaster R 1, Grimsby T 1, Luton T 1, Mansfield T 1, Milton Keynes D 1, Peterborough U 1, Rotherham U 1, Southampton 1, Tranmere R 1, Wolverhampton W 1, Wrexham 1.

APPEARANCES IN FINALS

Carlisle U 6, Bristol C 5, Brentford 3, Southend U 3, Birmingham C 2, Blackpool 2, Bolton W 2, Bournemouth 2, Bristol R 2, Chesterfield 2, Grimsby T 2, Oxford U 2, Port Vale 2, Stockport Co 2, Stoke C 2, Swansea C 2, Tranmere R 2, Wigan Ath 2, Barnsley 1, Burnley 1, Cambridge U 1, Colchester U 1, Coventry C 1, Crewe Alex 1, Doncaster R 1, Huddersfield T 1, Hull C 1, Luton T 1, Mansfield T 1, Millwall 1, Milton Keynes D 1, Peterborough U 1, Rotherham U 1, Scunthorpe U 1, Shrewsbury T 1, Southampton 1, Swindon T 1, Torquay U 1, Walsall 1, Wolverhampton W 1, Wrexham 1.

EFL TROPHY ATTENDANCES 2016–17

Round	*Aggregate*	*Games*	*Average*
One	117,823	96	1,227
Two	20,010	16	1,251
Three	10,374	8	1,297
Quarter-finals	10,085	4	2,521
Semi-finals	18,573	2	9,287
Final	74,434	1	74,434
Total	251,299	127	1,979

EFL CHECKATRADE TROPHY 2016–17

▪ *Denotes player sent off.*
In the group stages an additional point was awarded to the team that won on penalties when a match was drawn after 90 minutes.

NORTHERN SECTION GROUP A

Tuesday, 30 August 2016

Blackpool (0) 2 *(Vassell 56, 58)*

Cheltenham T (1) 1 *(Jennings 20)* 760

Blackpool: (442) Boney; Higham, Robertson, Aimson, Nolan; Daniel (Cameron 59), Yeates, Cain, Potts (Payne 46); Cullen, Gnanduillet (Vassell 46).
Cheltenham T: (352) Kitscha; O'Shaughnessy (Rowe 46), Parslow, Dickie; Jennings (Wright 74), Smith, Whitehead, Pell (Hall 46), Barthram; Morgan-Smith, Arthur.
Referee: Ben Toner.

Bolton W (0) 0

Everton U21 (1) 2 *(Dyson 22, McAleny 79)* 1540

Bolton W: (4411) Howard; Wilson, Taylor A, Beevers, Perry (Spearing 70); Buxton, Earing, Vela (Madine 70), Proctor (Wilkinson 20); Woolery; Taylor C.
Everton U21: (433) Hewelt; Yates (Brewster 83), Foulds, Yarney, Robinson; Bainbridge, Beningime, Walsh; Sambou (McAleny 64), Dyson, Henen (Broadhead 64).
Referee: David Webb.

Tuesday, 4 October 2016

Bolton W (1) 1 *(Ameobi 4)*

Blackpool (0) 0 1589

Bolton W: (442) Alnwick; Wilson, Osede, Wheater, Taylor A; Henry, Thorpe, Ameobi, Vela (Spearing 89); Proctor (Samizadeh 82), Clough (Madine 69).
Blackpool: (442) Lyness; Daniel, Nolan, Aimson, Higham; Potts (Samuel 46), Cain, McAlister, Philliskirk (Yeates 46); Cullen (Vassell 81), Matt.
Referee: Kevin Friend.

Cheltenham T (0) 2 *(Waters 82, Wright 84 (pen))*

Everton U21 (1) 1 *(Kitscha 5 (og))* 1023

Cheltenham T: (442) Kitscha; Barthram, Dickie, Parslow, Cranston (O'Shaughnessy 37); Dayton, Munns, Hall (Pell 56), Morgan-Smith (Wright 70); Waters, Smith.
Everton U21: (442) Hewelt; Bainbridge, Yarney, Foulds, Robinson; Henen (Sambou 76), Williams J (Brewster 85), Beningime, Dyson; Niasse (McAleny 57), Walsh.
Referee: Lee Probert.

Tuesday, 8 November 2016

Cheltenham T (0) 1 *(Morgan-Smith 90 (pen))*

Bolton W (0) 0 1038

Cheltenham T: (352) Kitscha; O'Shaughnessy, Downes, Parslow; Dickie, Munns (Whitehead 88), Pell, Dayton, Cranston; Waters (Holman 79), Wright (Morgan-Smith 79).
Bolton W: (442) Alnwick; Wilson, Wheater, Buxton, Moxey; Henry (Ameobi 80), Trotter, Vela, Taylor C (Clough 80); Proctor, Anderson (Clayton 80).
Referee: Kevin Friend.

Everton U21 (0) 1 *(Charsley 79)*

Blackpool (0) 1 *(Gnanduillet 48)* 527

Everton U21: (532) Hewelt; Jones, Yarney, Browning (Bainbridge 46), Foulds (Evans 61), Robinson; Charsley, Beningime, Henen; Gibson, Dyson (Duffus 61).
Blackpool: (442) Slocombe (Boney 13); Wilson, Aimson, Nolan, Daniel; Yeates, McAlister, Cain, Samuel (Philliskirk 66); Cullen, Gnanduillet.
Blackpool won 5-4 on penalties.
Referee: Chris Kavanagh.

Northern Group A	P	W	D	L	F	A	GD	Pts
Cheltenham T	3	2	0	1	4	3	1	6
Blackpool	3	1	1	1	3	3	0	5
Everton U21	3	1	1	1	4	3	1	4
Bolton W	3	1	0	2	1	3	–2	3

NORTHERN SECTION GROUP B

Tuesday, 30 August 2016

Accrington S (0) 0

Crewe Alex (0) 3 *(Ainley 47, Cooper 76, Udoh 90)* 585

Accrington S: (4411) Parish; Jones, Sykes, Pearson, McKeown; O'Sullivan, Lacey, Davies, McConville (Wall 61); Hery (Webb 61); Kee (Boco 69).
Crewe Alex: (4231) Garratt; Turton, Ray, Nugent, Bakayogo (Guthrie 87); Jones, Hollands; Kirk, Ainley (Udoh 72), Cooper; Saunders.
Referee: Darren Handley.

Chesterfield (1) 2 *(Ebanks-Blake 24, Dennis 76)*

Wolverhampton W U21 (0) 1 *(Herc 74)* 950

Chesterfield: (4231) Allinson; Graham, Raglan, Evatt, Donohue; Dimaio, Nolan (Maguire 80); Ariyibi (Daly 46), Simons (Dennis 61), Gardner; Ebanks-Blake.
Wolverhampton W U21: (442) Flatt; Simpson, Ebanks-Landell▪, Johnson, O'Hanlon; Gibbs-White (Hayden 31), Ronan, Herc, Randall; Dicko (Wilson 65), Enobakhare (Collins 82).
Referee: Seb Stockbridge.

Tuesday, 4 October 2016

Chesterfield (0) 1 *(Dennis 61)*

Accrington S (3) 4 *(Taylor-Fletcher 14, Gornell 21, 66, Clark 42)* 976

Chesterfield: (4141) Allinson; Ofoegbu, Anderson, Evatt, Maguire; Humphreys (German 46); Ariyibi, Liddle, Nolan, Gardner (Dennis 46); O'Shea (Mitchell 65).
Accrington S: (442) Chapman; Donacien, Hughes, Sykes, Jones; Clark (McCartan 78), Lacey (Davies 57), Hewitt, McConville; Gornell, Taylor-Fletcher (Eagles 55).
Referee: David Coote.

Crewe Alex (0) 2 *(Dagnall 69, Lowe 82)*

Wolverhampton W U21 (2) 3 *(Dicko 7, 45, Enobakhare 88)* 963

Crewe Alex: (442) Garratt; Turton, Guthrie, Ray, Bakayogo; Bingham, Wintle (Lowery 79), Cooper, Ainley (Kirk 61); Dagnall, Udoh (Lowe 70).
Wolverhampton W U21: (442) Lonergan; Silvio, Johnson, Leak, Deslandes; Finnie (McKenna 87), Saville, Wallace, Randall (Breslin 61); Enobakhare, Dicko (Wilson 78).
Referee: David Webb.

Tuesday, 8 November 2016

Crewe Alex (0) 0

Chesterfield (1) 2 *(O'Shea 22, Dimaio 81 (pen))* 929

Crewe Alex: (442) Garratt; Ng, Davis, Nugent, Bakayogo; Cooper, Hollands (Kirk 78), Ainley, Kiwomya; Lowe (Saunders 16), Udoh (Lowery 64).
Chesterfield: (532) Allinson; Ariyibi, Evatt, Anderson, Maguire, Mitchell; Dimaio, O'Shea (Ofoegbu 63), Nolan; Dennis (Humphreys 78), Simons (German 64).
Referee: Roger East.

Wolverhampton W U21 (3) 4 *(Herc 18, Wilson 37, Ronan 45 (pen), Enobakhare 67)*

Accrington S (0) 0 547

Wolverhampton W U21: (433) Burgoyne; Simpson, Johnson (Breslin 63), Upton, Deslandes; Wilson (Delacoe 78), Herc, Ronan; Enobakhare, White, Randall (Carnat 81).
Accrington S: (4411) Chapman; Pearson, Sykes, Conneely (Ogle 56), Hughes; Clark, Lacey, McConville (Eagles 62), Hewitt; Taylor-Fletcher; Kee (Boco 59).
Referee: David Webb.

Northern Group B	P	W	D	L	F	A	GD	Pts
Wolverhampton W U21	3	2	0	1	8	4	4	6
Chesterfield	3	2	0	1	5	5	0	6
Crewe Alex	3	1	0	2	5	5	0	3
Accrington S	3	1	0	2	4	8	–4	3

NORTHERN SECTION GROUP C

Tuesday, 30 August 2016

Bradford C (1) 1 *(Dieng 38)*

Stoke C U21 (0) 0 1444

Bradford C: (442) Sattelmaier; Darby, Knight-Percival, Dieng, Meredith (Kilgallon 46); Morais (Windle 73), Devine, Boateng, Webb-Foster; Hiwula, Rabiega (Hudson 33).
Stoke C U21: (4231) Isted; Banks■, Muniesa, Renne-Pringle (Edwards T 89), Edwards L; Lecygne, Adam; Verlinden, Shenton, Taylor; Ngoy.
Referee: Michael Salisbury.

Bury (1) 4 *(Ismail 3 (pen), Pope 49, 90, Kay 81)*

Morecambe (1) 1 *(Mullin 43)* 1154

Bury: (442) Williams; Jones (Maher 53), Kay, Barnett, Leigh; Ismail (Hope 64), Mellis, Soares, Mayor (Obi 85); Pope, Dudley.
Morecambe: (442) Nizic; Wakefield (Dunn 71), Edwards, Whitmore, McGowan; Fleming (Murphy 84), Kenyon, Molyneux, Ellison (Barkhuizen 59); Mullin, Turner.
Referee: Rob Jones.

Tuesday, 4 October 2016

Bradford C (2) 2 *(Vuckic 31, Hiwula 35)*

Bury (0) 1 *(Walker 69)* 1865

Bradford C: (4411) Doyle (Sattelmaier 3); Darby (Windle 60), Clarke N, Kilgallon, McArdle; Morais, Devine, Dieng (Boateng 60), Rabiega; Vuckic; Hiwula.
Bury: (442) Williams; Etuhu, Bryan, Maher, Leigh; Tutte (Burgess S 75), Mellis, Soares, Walker; Dudley (Pope 61), Hope (Harker 89).
Referee: Ben Toner.

Morecambe (3) 3 *(Dunn 3, Stockton 21, Murphy 44)*

Stoke C U21 (0) 1 *(Adam 48)* 686

Morecambe: (4231) Nizic; McGowan, Edwards (Barkhuizen 54), Winnard, Whitmore; Murphy, Kenyon (Rose 69); Wildig (Turner 48), Dunn, Molyneux; Stockton.
Stoke C U21: (442) Haugaard; Bardsley, Edwards L■, Muniesa, Taylor; Renne-Pringle, Molina, Adam, Diouf; Shenton (Telford 72), Ngoy.
Referee: Andy Haines.

Tuesday, 8 November 2016

Stoke C U21 (0) 1 *(Krkic 86)*

Bury (0) 1 *(Miller G 68)* 698

Stoke C U21: (4231) Haugaard; Edwards T, Banks, Muniesa, Taylor; Lecygne, Imbula; Verlinden (Campbell 80), Krkic, Ngoy; Crouch.
Bury: (442) Williams; Danns, Kay, Maher, Leigh; Mayor, Tutte, Mellis (Soares 80), Walker; Hope (Dudley 84), Vaughan (Miller G 67).
Stoke C U21 won 4-3 on penalties.
Referee: Ben Toner.

Wednesday, 9 November 2016

Morecambe (0) 3 *(Mullin 54, Stockton 66, 68)*

Bradford C (0) 2 *(Vuckic 52, 83)* 827

Morecambe: (4231) Nizic; Conlan, Whitmore, Edwards, Wakefield; McGowan, Murphy (Rose 46); Molyneux (Mullin 46), Dunn (Turner 77), Fleming; Stockton.
Bradford C: (442) Sattelmaier; Meredith (Wright 69), McArdle, Clarke N, Windle; Hudson (Rabiega 76), Devine, King, Morais; McNulty, Vuckic.
Referee: Tony Harrington.

Northern Group C	P	W	D	L	F	A	GD	Pts
Bradford C	3	2	0	1	5	4	1	6
Morecambe	3	2	0	1	7	7	0	6
Bury	3	1	1	1	6	4	2	4
Stoke C U21	3	0	1	2	2	5	–3	2

NORTHERN SECTION GROUP D

Tuesday, 30 August 2016

Fleetwood T (1) 1 *(Cole 45)*

Blackburn R U21 (0) 0 392

Fleetwood T: (433) Neal; Duckworth, Bolger, Eastham, Davis; Dempsey, Jonsson (Glendon 32), Woolford; Grant (Nirennold 68), Cole (Kip 61), Hunter.
Blackburn R U21: (451) Raya; Nyambe, Platt, Wharton, Doyle J; Thomson (Rittenberg 87), Hardcastle, Tomlinson, Rankin-Costello, Mahoney; Mansell.
Referee: Ross Joyce.

Oldham Ath (1) 4 *(McKay 16, Osei 48, 49, Banks 66)*

Carlisle U (3) 5 *(Raynes 18, Lambe 22, Burgess 28 (og), Miller T 74, Wyke 89)* 1897

Oldham Ath: (442) Kettings; Wilson, Burgess, Edmundson, Dunne; Flynn, Banks, Woodland (Croft 46), McLaughlin (Osei 46); McKay (Winchester 75), Ladapo.
Carlisle U: (532) Crocombe; Miller T, Raynes, Brisley (Wyke 53), Grainger, Gillesphey■; Joyce, Jones (Penn 90), Lambe; Devitt, Miller S (Brough 77).
Referee: Peter Bankes.

Tuesday, 4 October 2016

Carlisle U (1) 2 *(Miller S 39, Grainger 88 (pen))*

Blackburn R U21 (0) 0 1253

Carlisle U: (442) Crocombe; Miller T, Ellis, Brisley, Grainger; Lambe, Kennedy, Joyce, Devitt; Miller S (Wyke 68 (Salkeld 78)), Ibehre (McKee 89).
Blackburn R U21: (442) Raya; Nyambe, Brown W, Wharton, Doyle J; Bennett, Hardcastle, Tomlinson, Mahoney; Stokes, Mansell.
Referee: Richard Clarke.

Fleetwood T (0) 0

Oldham Ath (2) 2 *(McKay 32, Erwin 38)* 793

Fleetwood T: (433) Neal; Duckworth, Bolger, Eastham, Wallace; Grant (Hunter 46), Jonsson (Glendon 63), Nirennold; Ball (Cole 32), Jakubiak, Woolford.
Oldham Ath: (442) Ripley; Wilson, Clarke, Burgess, Reckord; Flynn, Green (Banks 73), Winchester (Croft 73), Fane; McKay (Ladapo 77), Erwin.
Referee: Darren Bond.

Tuesday, 8 November 2016

Blackburn R U21 (1) 2 *(Stokes 22, Feeney 61)*

Oldham Ath (0) 2 *(Ladapo 49, Wilson 67)* 471

Blackburn R U21: (442) Raya; Nyambe, Brown W, Wharton, Hendrie (Doyle C 65); Mahoney, Hardcastle, Tomlinson, Bennett; Stokes, Feeney.
Oldham Ath: (352) Ripley; Wilson, Burgess, Reckord (Croft 46); Dunne, Flynn (McLaughlin 65), Banks, Fane, Law; McKay, Jahraldo-Martin (Ladapo 46).
Oldham Ath won 5-4 on penalties.
Referee: Rob Jones.

Wednesday, 9 November 2016

Carlisle U (3) 4 *(McKee 14, Wyke 18, Grainger 41 (pen), Salkeld 73)*

Fleetwood T (0) 2 *(Sowerby 48, Jakubiak 64)* 1420

Carlisle U: (442) Crocombe; Ellis (Miller T 53), Gillesphey, Brisley, Grainger; Lambe, Joyce (Salkeld 46), McKee, Devitt; Wyke, Asamoah.
Fleetwood T: (433) Cairns; Nirennold, Eastham, Davis, Wallace; Glendon, Roberts, Osbourne (Sowerby 46); Jakubiak, Holloway, Woolford (Charles 9 (Deacon 77)).
Referee: Christopher Sarginson.

Northern Group D	P	W	D	L	F	A	GD	Pts
Carlisle U	3	3	0	0	11	6	5	9
Oldham Ath	3	1	1	1	8	7	1	5
Fleetwood T	3	1	0	2	3	6	–3	3
Blackburn R U21	3	0	1	2	2	5	–3	1

NORTHERN SECTION GROUP E

Tuesday, 30 August 2016

Mansfield T (0) 0

Doncaster R (0) 2 *(Beestin 72, Calder 86)* 1461

Mansfield T: (442) Shearer; Bennett, Pearce, Taft, Howkins (Collins 59); Chapman, McGuire (Hurst 43), Baxendale (Hoban 53), Hamilton; Hemmings, Rose D.
Doncaster R: (343) Etheridge; Blair (Amos 71), Wright, Evina; Fielding, Houghton, Calder, Middleton; Williams (Pugh 71), Mandeville, Beestin (Longbottom 87).
Referee: Neil Swarbrick.

Port Vale (0) 1 *(Smith 80)*

Derby Co U21 (0) 0 1198

Port Vale: (442) Alnwick; Purkiss, Streete, Smith, Kiko; Mbamba (Turner 81), Pereira, Amoros, Hart (Ferguson 40); Forrester (Cicilia 58), Paterson.
Derby Co U21: (352) Ravas; Rawson, Cover, Wassall (Gordon 71); Stabana, Hanson, Guy, Santos (Walker 85), MacDonald; Venam, Babos (Jakobsen 86).
Referee: Mark Heywood.

Tuesday, 4 October 2016

Doncaster R (0) 2 *(Mandeville 53, Longbottom 82)*

Derby Co U21 (1) 2 *(Wilson 8, Weimann 90)* 1515

Doncaster R: (41212) Marosi; Mason, Wright (Fielding 31), Baudry, Evina (Garrett 30); Keegan; Middleton, Calder; Mandeville (Longbottom 74); Marquis, Beestin.
Derby Co U21: (4231) Ravas; Santos, Cover, Rawson, Stabana; Guy, Venam (Bennett 65); Russell (Gordon 78), Wilson (Camara 65), Weimann; Blackman.
Doncaster R won 4-2 on penalties.
Referee: Carl Boyeson.

Port Vale (0) 0

Mansfield T (0) 1 *(Green 66)* 1025

Port Vale: (4411) Miguel Santos; Purkiss, MacIntosh, Smith, Hart; Jones, Amoros, Tavares (Shalaj 46), Kiko (Mbamba 85); Pereira; Cicilia.
Mansfield T: (442) Shearer; Bennett, Pearce, Collins, Benning; Hamilton, Clements (McGuire 61), Gobern, Hemmings; Henderson (Green 64), Marriott (Rose M 70).
Referee: Michael Salisbury.

Tuesday, 8 November 2016

Derby Co U21 (1) 2 *(Hanson 24, Weimann 84)*

Mansfield T (2) 3 *(Hemmings 2, Henderson 5, Clements 90)* 870

Derby Co U21: (433) Weale; Baird, Rawson, Shackell, Stabana; Guy, Hanson, Venam (Walker 79); Gordon (Santos 67), Bennett (Jakobsen 85), Weimann.
Mansfield T: (442) Shearer; Bennett, Pearce, Howkins, Benning; Baxendale (Hamilton 59), Clements, Thomas (Rose M 49), Hemmings; Gobern, Henderson (Green 74).
Referee: Trevor Kettle.

Doncaster R (0) 0

Port Vale (0) 0 1495

Doncaster R: (352) Etheridge; Baudry, Alcock (Richardson 46), Garrett; Mason, Keegan, Calder, Beestin (Houghton 65), Evina; Longbottom, Mandeville.
Port Vale: (4141) Miguel Santos; MacIntosh, Streete, Smith, Hart; Grant; Pereira, de Freitas (Tavares 78), Kiko (Mbamba 59), Kelly (Cicilia 69); Turner.
Port Vale won 4-3 on penalties.
Referee: Geoff Eltringham.

Northern Group E	P	W	D	L	F	A	GD	Pts
Doncaster R	3	1	2	0	4	2	2	6
Mansfield T	3	2	0	1	4	4	0	6
Port Vale	3	1	1	1	1	1	0	5
Derby Co U21	3	0	1	2	4	6	–2	1

NORTHERN SECTION GROUP F

Wednesday, 31 August 2016

Notts Co (2) 2 *(Snijders 20, Burke 36 (pen))*

Hartlepool U (1) 1 *(Oates 29)* 1095

Notts Co: (442) Loach; Audel, Laing, Hollis, Dickinson; Rodman (Hewitt 55), Aborah (Atkinson■ 70), Richards, Snijders; Campbell A (Milsom 64), Burke.
Hartlepool U: (4312) Bartlett; Richards, Nsiala■, Harrison, Carroll (Martin 74); Deverdics, Hawkins, Laurent; Alessandra (Green 46); Paynter (Smith 46), Oates.
Referee: Darren England.

Tuesday, 6 September 2016

Rochdale (0) 1 *(Henderson 57)*

Sunderland U21 (0) 1 *(Embleton 51)* 1184

Rochdale: (4231) Lillis; Rafferty, Tanser, Canavan, McGahey; Lund (Mendez-Laing 65), Camps; Vincenti (Davies 65), Allen, Bunney; Henderson (Odelusi 82).
Sunderland U21: (442) Stryjek; Robson J, Robson T, Ledger, Denayer; Robson E, Kirchhoff, Embleton (Molyneux 84), Honeyman; Greenwood, Maja (Nelson 73).
Rochdale won 4-2 on penalties.
Referee: Graham Salisbury.

Tuesday, 4 October 2016

Hartlepool U (0) 0

Sunderland U21 (0) 1 *(Love 63)* 1295

Hartlepool U: (433) Bartlett; Richards, Harrison, Martin, Pollock; Laurent (Green 68), Featherstone, Hawkins (Walker 7); Fewster (Orrell 25), Paynter, Heardman.
Sunderland U21: (442) Mika; Jones, Ledger (Lawson 53), Beadling, Robson T; Honeyman, Love, Robson E, Greenwood (Molyneux 85); Maja, Brady.
Referee: John Brooks.

Rochdale (0) 2 *(Odelusi 61, Davies 69)*

Notts Co (1) 1 *(Forte 25)* 1147

Rochdale: (433) Lillis; Rafferty, Canavan, McGahey, Tanser; Camps (Rathbone 50), Noble-Lazarus (Mendez-Laing 75), Morley; Odelusi, Cannon, Thompson (Davies 46).
Notts Co: (442) Loach; Hewitt, Laing, Hollis, Milsom; Campbell A, Aborah (Audel 67), Richards, Burke; Oliver, Forte (Snijders 46).
Referee: Jeremy Simpson.

Wednesday, 9 November 2016

Hartlepool U (0) 1 *(Oates 85)*

Rochdale (1) 2 *(Noble-Lazarus 21, Gillam 67)* 380

Hartlepool U: (433) Bartlett; Richards, Harrison, Bates (Wise 46), Martin (Pollock 73); Walker, Woods, Donnelly; Orrell, Paynter, Deverdics (Oates 64).
Rochdale: (442) Lillis; Rafferty, McNulty, McGahey, Tanser; Gillam, Thompson (Barry-Murphy 56 (Bunney 77)), Morley, Rathbone; Noble-Lazarus, Cannon (Mendez-Laing 60).
Referee: Scott Duncan.

Sunderland U21 (0) 2 *(Maja 84, Hollis 90 (og))*

Notts Co (0) 1 *(Campbell A 49)* 633

Sunderland U21: (442) Mannone; Robson J (Molyneux 78), Robson T, Brady, Ledger; Love, Larsson, Denayer, Honeyman; Greenwood, Asoro (Maja 58).
Notts Co: (442) Loach; Tootle, Laing, Duffy, Dickinson; Hollis, Hewitt, Smith (Oliver 75), Burke (Milsom 79); Campbell A, Snijders (Forte 90).
Referee: Ross Joyce.

Northern Group F	P	W	D	L	F	A	GD	Pts
Rochdale	3	2	1	0	5	3	2	8
Sunderland U21	3	2	1	0	4	2	2	7
Notts Co	3	1	0	2	4	5	–1	3
Hartlepool U	3	0	0	3	2	5	–3	0

NORTHERN SECTION GROUP G

Tuesday, 30 August 2016

Scunthorpe U (0) 2 *(Wallace 63, Adelakun 73)*

Middlesbrough U21 (0) 1 *(Cooke 71)* 1200

Scunthorpe U: (442) Anyon; Clarke, Goode, Wallace, Butroid; Adelakun, Mantom (van Veen 82), Holmes (Sutton 48), Morris; Hopper, Madden (Wootton 76).
Middlesbrough U21: (4231) Fryer; Johnson, Elsdon, Bernardo, Kitching; Morris, Tinkler; Cooke, Pattison, Tavernier (Mondal 70); Morelli (McAloon 83).
Referee: Andrew Madley.

Shrewsbury T (0) 0

Cambridge U (1) 1 *(Pigott 20)* 1187

Shrewsbury T: (442) Leutwiler; Brown, Lancashire, Sadler, Riley; Jones (Mangan 62), Black (Deegan 60), Ogogo, El Ouriachi; Leitch-Smith (Dodds 57), Waring.
Cambridge U: (442) Norris; Clark, Legge, Dallison, Taylor; Gosling, Elito (Mingoia 64), Newton, Davies (Long 64); Williamson (Ikpeazu 64), Pigott.
Referee: Christopher Sarginson.

Tuesday, 4 October 2016

Cambridge U (1) 2 *(Ikpeazu 12, Elsdon 55 (og))*

Middlesbrough U21 (1) 1 *(Tavernier 34)* 693

Cambridge U: (442) Norris; Long, Legge, Coulson, Halliday; Mingoia (Newton 46), Dunne (Davies 61), Clark, Gosling; Pigott (Williamson 78), Ikpeazu.
Middlesbrough U21: (4411) Fryer; Johnson, Elsdon, McGoldrick, Tavernier; McAloon (Kitching 64), Tinkler, Morris, Mondal; Pattison; Morelli.
Referee: John Busby.

Scunthorpe U (1) 2 *(Lancashire 10 (og), Margetts 56)*

Shrewsbury T (0) 0 1316

Scunthorpe U: (433) Anyon; Mantom, Wallace, Goode, Townsend; Dawson (Adelakun 46), Ness, Sutton; van Veen, Hopper (Margetts 24), Madden.
Shrewsbury T: (352) Halstead; Lancashire, El-Abd, Sarcevic (Waring 62); Brown, Black, O'Brien, Deegan, Grimmer; Toney (Leitch-Smith 89), El Ouriachi (Mangan 46).
Referee: Nigel Miller.

Tuesday, 8 November 2016

Cambridge U (0) 0

Scunthorpe U (1) 2 *(Williams 36, Adelakun 90)* 666

Cambridge U: (442) Norris; Long, Dallison, Coulson, Adams (Davies 31); Elito, Clark, Dunne (Darling 46), Maris; Williamson, Pigott (Foy 23).
Scunthorpe U: (442) Anyon; Clarke, Wallace, Goode, Townsend; Adelakun, Ness, Mantom, Williams; van Veen (Smallwood 81), Hopper (Margetts 63).
Referee: Darren Deadman.

Middlesbrough U21 (0) 0

Shrewsbury T (2) 3 *(Leitch-Smith 10, 59, Toney 14)* 308

Middlesbrough U21: (4231) Fryer; Johnson, McGoldrick, Elsdon, Da Silva; Morris, Maloney (Wheatley 64); Morelli (Coulson 84), Cooke, Mondal (McAloon 64); De Pena.
Shrewsbury T: (4231) Halstead; Grimmer, Smith, Lancashire, Brown (Sadler 64); Deegan, Ogogo; Whalley (O'Brien 79), Leitch-Smith (Jones 62), Dodds; Toney.
Referee: Darren Handley.

Northern Group G	P	W	D	L	F	A	GD	Pts
Scunthorpe U	3	3	0	0	6	1	5	9
Cambridge U	3	2	0	1	3	3	0	6
Shrewsbury T	3	1	0	2	3	3	0	3
Middlesbrough U21	3	0	0	3	2	7	–5	0

NORTHERN SECTION GROUP H

Tuesday, 30 August 2016

Sheffield U (0) 0

Leicester C U21 (0) 0 3632

Sheffield U: (442) Moore; Freeman, Wilson, O'Connell, Hussey; Chapman, Coutts, Fleck, Reed; Sharp (Duffy 46), Done (Brooks 63).
Leicester C U21: (442) Hamer (Bramley 24); Hernandez, Benalouane (Moore 46), Wasilewski, Chilwell; Rowe, Miles, James (Barnes 75), Ndukwu; Gray, Muskwe.
Leicester C U21 won 5-4 on penalties.
Referee: Nigel Miller.

Walsall (3) 5 *(Bakayoko 18, 39, 45, Morris 61, Kouhyar 71)*

Grimsby T (1) 2 *(Boyce 5, Summerfield 67)* 1022

Walsall: (4411) MacGillivray; Edwards, McCarthy, Preston, Kouhyar (Ginnelly 72); Morris, Kinsella, Dobson, Cockerill-Mollett; Oztumer; Bakayoko.
Grimsby T: (352) McKeown; Pearson, Gowling (Bolarinwa 46), Boyce; Mills, Venney (Chambers 46), Disley, Summerfield, Andrew; Vernon, Bogle (Vose 46).
Referee: Andy Woolmer.

Tuesday, 4 October 2016

Grimsby T (0) 0

Leicester C U21 (0) 1 *(Mitchell 64)* 609

Grimsby T: (442) McKeown■; Mills, Pearson, Gowling, Andrew; Bolarinwa (Jones 61), Disley, Berrett, Vose (Summerfield 71); Tuton (Vernon 72), Jackson.
Leicester C U21: (451) Hamer; Knight (Rubio 46), Moore, Benalouane, Debayo; Barnes, Sheriff, Domej, Watts (Miles 60), Mitchell; Muskwe.
Referee: Mark Haywood.

Sheffield U (0) 1 *(Coutts 78)*

Walsall (1) 2 *(Laird 16, Bakayoko 66)* 2619

Sheffield U: (451) Moore; O'Connell, Wilson (Whiteman 80), Brown (Freeman 69), Hussey; Scougall (Coutts 58), Brooks, Basham, Fleck, Duffy; Done.
Walsall: (4231) MacGillivray; McCarthy, Preston, Toner, Laird; Dobson (Chambers 84), Edwards; Ginnelly (Shorrock 74), Oztumer, Moussa; Bakayoko.
Referee: Mark Haywood.

Tuesday, 8 November 2016

Leicester C U21 (0) 0

Walsall (0) 1 *(Bakayoko 58)* 839

Leicester C U21: (433) Hamer; Pascanu (Wood 78), Wasilewski, Benalouane, Debayo; James, Miles, Barnes; Ndukwu (Rubio 65), Ulloa, Muskwe.
Walsall: (541) MacGillivray; Ginnelly (Shorrock 89), McCarthy, Preston, Toner, Cockerill-Mollett; Bakayoko (Sangha 78), Dobson, Osbourne, Kinsella; Moussa.
Referee: Mark Haywood.

Wednesday, 9 November 2016

Grimsby T (1) 2 *(Jackson 14, Disley 81)*

Sheffield U (0) 4 *(Slater 53, Boyce 74 (og), O'Connell 78, Clarke 87)* 597

Grimsby T: (442) Warrington; Mills, Pearson, Boyce, Jones; Chambers (Tuton 77), Comley, Disley, Berrett (Bolarinwa 57); Jackson, Vernon (Browne 56).
Sheffield U: (343) Long; O'Connell, Brown, Basham (Cummings 76); Kelly, Slater, Whiteman, Freeman (Done 46); Brooks, Lavery (Clarke 64), Hallam.
Referee: Richard Clark.

Northern Group H	P	W	D	L	F	A	GD	Pts
Walsall	3	3	0	0	8	3	5	9
Leicester C U21	3	1	1	1	1	1	0	5
Sheffield U	3	1	1	1	5	4	1	4
Grimsby T	3	0	0	3	4	10	–6	0

SOUTHERN SECTION GROUP A

Tuesday, 30 August 2016

Bristol R (0) 2 *(Taylor 60, Easter 81)*

Reading U21 (1) 3 *(Stacey 33, Sheppard 76, Mendes 84 (pen))* 1418

Bristol R: (442) Roos; Leadbitter, Clarke J, McChrystal, Brown; Bodin (Taylor 46), Sinclair, Lawrence (Lines 28), Montano (Clarke O 46); Easter, Gaffney.
Reading U21: (433) Jaakkola; Watson, McIntyre, Osho, Griffin; Rinomhota, Barrett (Frost 65), Stacey; Samuel (Sheppard 65), Mendes (Cardwell 85), Fosu.
Referee: Brett Huxtable.

Yeovil T (4) 4 *(Mugabi 14, Eaves 22, 39, McLeod 27)*

Portsmouth (2) 3 *(Smith 10, 37, 54)* 1534

Yeovil T: (433) Maddison; Shephard, Smith, Mugabi, Butcher; Whitfield (Lea 75), Lawless, Dolan; Khan (Copp 89), Eaves, McLeod.
Portsmouth: (433) O'Brien; Close, Barton, Clarke (Davies 61), Naismith; May, Bennett, Linganzi; Tollitt (Chaplin 56), Smith (Hunt 73), Evans.
Referee: Kevin Johnson.

Tuesday, 4 October 2016

Bristol R (0) 0

Yeovil T (0) 0 2117

Bristol R: (442) Roos; Leadbitter, Clarke J, Hartley, Brown (Colkett 66); Montano, Boateng, Sinclair, Moore (Bodin 77); James, Gaffney (Taylor 67).
Yeovil T: (433) Maddison; Mugabi, Lacey, Smith, Dickson; Dolan, Lawless, Whitfield (McLeod 55); Campbell, Hedges, Khan (Dawson■ 60).
Bristol R won 5-3 on penalties.
Referee: James Adcock.

Portsmouth (0) 2 *(Main 57, 63)*

Reading U21 (1) 2 *(Novakovich 6, Mendes 52 (pen))* 1355

Portsmouth: (442) O'Brien; Buxton (Evans 45), Whatmough, Clarke, Haunstrup; Lalkovic, Linganzi, Close (May 73), Bennett; Main (Naismith 69), Smith.
Reading U21: (433) Jaakkola; Watson, McIntyre (Griffin 19), Gravenberch, Blackett; Frost, Kelly, Rinomhota; Samuel, Mendes, Novakovich (Richards 79).
Reading U21 won 4-3 on penalties.
Referee: Oliver Langford.

Tuesday, 8 November 2016

Portsmouth (0) 1 *(Naismith 88)*

Bristol R (0) 0 1200

Portsmouth: (4231) O'Brien; Buxton (Rose 73), Davies, Whatmough, Talbot; Close (Evans 73), Linganzi; Naismith, Lalkovic, Bennett (Hunt 77); Smith.
Bristol R: (442) Roos (Puddy 3); Roberts, Hartley, McChrystal, Leadbitter; Easter (Clarke O 78), Mansell, Boateng, Colkett; James, Gaffney (Harrison 80).
Referee: Nick Kinseley.

Wednesday, 9 November 2016

Reading U21 (0) 0

Yeovil T (0) 2 *(Eaves 48, Zoko 89)* 739

Reading U21: (433) Moore; Watson, McIntyre, Gravenberch, Cooper; Rinomhota, Richards (Smith 79), Frost; Kelly (Barrett 46), Samuel (Keown 63), Novakovich.
Yeovil T: (433) Maddison; Shephard, Lacey, Mugabi, Smith; Butcher (Ezewele 81), Whitfield, Dolan; Hedges, Campbell (Eaves 46), Khan (Zoko 70).
Referee: John Busby.

Southern Group A	P	W	D	L	F	A	GD	Pts
Yeovil T	3	2	1	0	6	3	3	7
Reading U21	3	1	1	1	5	6	–1	5
Portsmouth	3	1	1	1	6	6	0	4
Bristol R	3	0	1	2	2	4	–2	2

SOUTHERN SECTION GROUP B

Tuesday, 30 August 2016

AFC Wimbledon (1) 3 *(Barcham 38, Poleon 57, 67)*

Swansea C U21 (0) 0 461

AFC Wimbledon: (442) Clarke; Fuller, Nightingale, Francomb, Kelly; Beere, Parrett, Reeves (Bulman 65), Barcham (Fitzpatrick 65); Poleon, Barnett.
Swansea C U21: (451) Tremmel; Lewis, Davies, Reid, Tabanou; Emnes, Blair (Holland 65), Bray (Garrick 87), Fulton, Jones (Byers 65); Bia Bi.
Referee: Simon Hooper.

Plymouth Arg (0) 4 *(Slew 51, Jervis 58, Bulvitis 69, Tanner 90)*

Newport Co (1) 1 *(Green 19)* 2349

Plymouth Arg: (433) Dorel (McCallum 82); Miller, Bulvitis, Bradley, Purrington; Tanner, Fox, Smith (Ijaha 61); Jervis (Donaldson 70), Slew, Goodwillie.
Newport Co: (442) Day; Bignot, Angel, Bennett (Butler 67), Barnum-Bobb; Compton (Rigg 74), Tozer, Owen-Evans, Myrie-Williams; Green, Parkin (Jackson 59).
Referee: Andy Davies.

Tuesday, 4 October 2016

AFC Wimbledon (0) 2 *(Taylor 65, Barnett 68)*

Plymouth Arg (1) 1 *(Smith 7)* 936

AFC Wimbledon: (433) Shea; Francomb, Nightingale, Robertson, Kelly; Beere, Reeves (Bulman 30), Parrett (Egan 46); Taylor, Poleon (Elliott 78), Barnett.
Plymouth Arg: (4231) Dorel; Miller, Bulvitis, Songo'o, Purrington; Ijaha, Threlkeld (Donaldson 52); Tanner (Carey 72), Smith, Slew (Spencer 72); Goodwillie.
Referee: Graham Horwood.

Newport Co (0) 1 *(Myrie-Williams 90)*

Swansea C U21 (1) 2 *(Bia Bi 35, Samuel 88)* 807

Newport Co: (442) Day; Barnum-Bobb, Bignot, Bennett (Myrie-Williams 46), Butler; Grego-Cox, Randall (Green 65), Tozer, Compton (Jackson 57); Healey, Rigg.
Swansea C U21: (4231) Birighitti; Reid, Mawson, Davies, Kingsley; Fulton, Blair; Bia Bi, Byers (Maric 64), Bray (Holland 85); Samuel.
Referee: Brett Huxtable.

Tuesday, 8 November 2016

Newport Co (1) 2 *(Bennett 7, Barnum-Bobb 85)*

AFC Wimbledon (0) 0 368

Newport Co: (442) Day; Barnum-Bobb, Jones, Bennett, Butler; Sheehan (Bignot 81), Labadie (Owen-Evans 27), Tozer, Jebb (Wood 52); O'Hanlon, Healey.
AFC Wimbledon: (442) Shea (McDonnell 11); Francomb, Robertson, Nightingale, Owens; Parrett, Beere (Fitzpatrick 58), Egan, Whelpdale; Barnett, Poleon (Oakley 72).
Referee: Andy Davies.

Swansea C U21 (2) 2 *(James 13, McBurnie 20)*

Plymouth Arg (0) 0 641

Swansea C U21: (4231) Nordfeldt; Reid, Rodon, Davies, Naughton; Cork, Blair; James, Byers (Holland 86), Samuel (Bray 78); McBurnie.
Plymouth Arg: (433) Dorel (McCallum 84); Bentley■, Bulvitis, Bradley, Purrington (Osborne 53); Ijaha, Carey, Donaldson; Jervis, Goodwillie, Slew (Tanner 74).
Referee: Brendan Malone.

Southern Group B	P	W	D	L	F	A	GD	Pts
AFC Wimbledon	3	2	0	1	5	3	2	6
Swansea C U21	3	2	0	1	4	4	0	6
Plymouth Arg	3	1	0	2	5	5	0	3
Newport Co	3	1	0	2	4	6	–2	3

SOUTHERN SECTION GROUP C

Tuesday, 30 August 2016

Oxford U (2) 4 *(Roberts T 12, Maguire 36 (pen), Taylor 68, MacDonald 71)*

Exeter C (1) 2 *(Jay 43, McAlinden 61)* 1575

Oxford U: (451) Eastwood; Long, Ruffels, Dunkley, Edwards; Roberts T (Roberts J 79), Crowley, Lundstram (Sercombe 46), Rothwell, Maguire (MacDonald 62); Taylor.
Exeter C: (442) Olejnik; Egan, Sweeney (Storey 62), Oakley (Ampadu 46), Riley-Lowe; Smallcombe, Jay, James (Down 62), Byrne; McAlinden, Grant.
Referee: James Adcock.

Tuesday, 13 September 2016

Swindon T (1) 2 *(Branco 18, Delfouneso 60)*

Chelsea U21 (0) 1 *(Ali 80)* 1961

Swindon T: (352) Henry; Branco, Sendles-White, Jones; Furlong, Smith, Murray, Goddard (Iandolo 58), Ormonde-Ottewill; Norris (Delfouneso 46), Hylton (Obika 73).
Chelsea U21: (4231) Collins; Sterling, Chalobah, Tomori, Dasilva; Quintero (Ali 73), Scott (Taylor-Crossdale 65); Wakefield, Mount, Christie-Davies; Ugbo (Colley 57).
Referee: Graham Horwood.

Tuesday, 4 October 2016

Swindon T (0) 0

Oxford U (0) 0 2698

Swindon T: (352) Henry; Thomas, Branco, Furlong; Brophy, Iandolo (Murray 67), Rodgers (Goddard 67), Smith, Ormonde-Ottewill; Delfouneso, Norris.
Oxford U: (4411) Eastwood; Edwards, Martin, Long, Skarz; Roberts T (Johnson 63), Rothwell (Sercombe 86), Ruffels, MacDonald■; Crowley (Thomas 87); Taylor.
Swindon T won 3-1 on penalties.
Referee: Paul Tierney.

Tuesday, 18 October 2016

Exeter C (2) 3 *(Watkins 2, Wheeler 24, McAlinden 50)*

Chelsea U21 (0) 2 *(Ugbo 72, 90)* 1979

Exeter C: (442) Pym; Moore-Taylor (Riley-Lowe 69), Ampadu, Croll, Sweeney; Grant, Oakley, Watkins, Wheeler (Taylor 62); Reid, McAlinden (Jay 80).
Chelsea U21: (433) Collins; Dasilva, Colley (Scott 46), Tomori, Dabo; Mount (Taylor-Crossdale 84), Chalobah, Sammut; Sterling, Ugbo, Wakefield (Maddox 36).
Referee: Christopher Sarginson.

Tuesday, 8 November 2016

Chelsea U21 (1) 1 *(Quintero 44)*

Oxford U (0) 1 *(Hemmings 90)* 5200

Chelsea U21: (343) Collins; Colley, Zouma, Aina; James (Grant 72), Ali, van Ginkel, Dabo; Mount (Maddox 90), Ugbo, Quintero.
Oxford U: (442) Eastwood; Edwards, Martin, Nelson, Skarz; Sercombe (Johnson 55), Lundstram, Rothwell, Hall (Hemmings 67); Crowley (Thomas 78), Maguire.
Chelsea U21 won 13-12 on penalties.
Referee: Dean Whitestone.

Exeter C (0) 1 *(Wheeler 59)*

Swindon T (1) 1 *(Norris 30)* 729

Exeter C: (442) Hamon; Sweeney, Oakley, Simpson, Woodman; Wheeler (Taylor 66), James, Watkins, Grant; Reid (Jay 58), McAlinden (Holmes 77).
Swindon T: (442) Henry; Barry, Branco, Jones, Brophy; Goddard, Rodgers (Doughty 46), Smith (Kasim 68), Iandolo (Evans 56); Delfouneso, Norris.
Swindon T won 4-2 on penalties.
Referee: Brett Huxtable.

Southern Group C	P	W	D	L	F	A	GD	Pts
Swindon T	3	1	2	0	3	2	1	7
Oxford U	3	1	2	0	5	3	2	5
Exeter C	3	1	1	1	6	7	–1	4
Chelsea U21	3	0	1	2	4	6	–2	2

SOUTHERN SECTION GROUP D

Tuesday, 30 August 2016

Coventry C (1) 4 *(Turnbull 35, 75, Lameiras 48, Willis 73)*

West Ham U U21 (1) 2 *(Martinez 33, 90)* 2091

Coventry C: (343) Burge; Willis, Harries, Turnbull; Dion Kelly-Evans■, Bigirimana, McCann (Stevenson 61), Haynes; Lameiras (Tudgay 72), Sordell (Jones 66), Agyei.
West Ham U U21: (442) Spiegel; Pike, Lewis (Eggleton 66), Rice, Neufville; Diangana (Gordon 78), Makasi, Quina (Powell 62), Sylvestra; Browne, Martinez.
Referee: Keith Stroud.

Northampton T (0) 0

Wycombe W (1) 3 *(Rowe 18, Hayes 47, Thompson 90)* 1408

Northampton T: (442) Cornell; Phillips, Nyatanga, Diamond, Buchanan; D'Ath (Sonupe 74), Byrom, McCourt, Beautyman (Gorre 57); Revell, Hooper (Hanley 57).
Wycombe W: (4141) Blackman; Jombati, Stewart, De Havilland, Harriman; McGinn; Southwell (Ainsworth 85), Bloomfield, Rowe, Freeman; Hayes (Thompson 74).
Referee: Paul Tierney.

Tuesday, 4 October 2016

Coventry C (2) 3 *(Agyei 1, Jones 8, Lameiras 66)*

Northampton T (1) 1 *(Richards 2)* 2085

Coventry C: (4231) Burge; Sterry, Willis, Turnbull, Page (Ricketts 69); Bigirimana, Gadzhev (Lameiras 65); Jones, McCann, Agyei (Tudgay 81); Sordell.
Northampton T: (442) Cornell; Phillips, Nyatanga, McDonald, Buchanan; Sonupe (Beautyman 46 (D'Ath 81)), McCourt, O'Toole, Gorre; Richards (Hoskins 68), Hooper.
Referee: Ollie Yates.

Wycombe W (1) 3 *(Akinfenwa 7, Kashket 47, Freeman 68)*

West Ham U U21 (0) 0 1060

Wycombe W: (442) Blackman; Jombati, De Havilland, Pierre (Stewart 46), Harriman; Freeman, Rowe (Bean 59), McGinn, Wood; Akinfenwa (Hayes 69), Kashket.
West Ham U U21: (4231) Howes; Sylvestra (Eggleton 75), Pike, Akinola, Neufville; Makasi, Lewis; Kemp (Parfitt-Williams 63), Browne, Diangana; Gordon (Hector-Ingram 56).
Referee: Darren Deadman.

Tuesday, 8 November 2016

Northampton T (1) 1 *(Beautyman 23)*

West Ham U U21 (1) 1 *(Parfitt-Williams 39)* 762

Northampton T: (4231) Cornell; Phillips, Diamond (McDonald 46), Nyatanga, Buchanan (Hanley 46); O'Toole, Byrom; Potter, Beautyman, Sonupe; Revell (Iaciofano 74).
West Ham U U21: (4231) Spiegel; Akinola, Pike, Rice, Parfitt-Williams (Powell 65); Makasi, Lewis; Kemp, Browne, Westley (Neufville 78); Hector-Ingram.
West Ham U U21 won 3-2 on penalties.
Referee: Graham Salisbury.

Wednesday, 9 November 2016

Wycombe W (1) 2 *(McGinn 32, Kashket 53)*

Coventry C (0) 4 *(Haynes 57, 60, Thomas G 63, Bigirimana 86)* 912

Wycombe W: (442) Brown; Jombati, Stewart, Pierre, Harriman (Cowan-Hall 69); Freeman (O'Nien 82), McGinn, Bean, Thompson; Kashket, Weston.
Coventry C: (343) Charles-Cook; Maycock, Harries, Turnbull; Sterry (Haynes 46), Rose (Bigirimana 46), Finch, Dion Kelly-Evans; Lameiras (Jones 46), Thomas G, McBean.
Referee: Charles Breakspear.

Southern Group D	P	W	D	L	F	A	GD	Pts
Coventry C	3	3	0	0	11	5	6	9
Wycombe W	3	2	0	1	8	4	4	6
West Ham U U21	3	0	1	2	3	8	–5	2
Northampton T	3	0	1	2	2	7	–5	1

SOUTHERN SECTION GROUP E

Tuesday, 30 August 2016

Charlton Ath (0) 0

Southampton U21 (0) 0 1336

Charlton Ath: (41212) Phillips; Konsa, Johnson, Lennon, Fox (Chicksen 66); Crofts (Charles 84); Solly, Foley; Hanlan; Ahearne-Grant, Ajose (Umerah 55).
Southampton U21: (442) McCarthy; Johnson, Gape (O'Connor 88), Stephens, Valery; Olomola (N'Lundulu 87), Reed, McQueen, Jones; Hesketh, Sims.
Charlton Ath won 5-4 on penalties.
Referee: Andy Haines.

Crawley T (1) 1 *(Collins 34)*

Colchester U (0) 0 881

Crawley T: (433) Beeney; Young, Connolly, Davey, Arthur; Yorwerth, Banton (Clifford 71), Tajbakhsh; Bawling, Collins (Boldewijn 67), Yussuf (Blackman 75).
Colchester U: (4141) Walker; Vincent-Young, Wynter, Eastman, Kinsella; Lapslie (Diaz Wright 62); Sembie-Ferris, Bonne, Szmodics (Peter 64), Drey Wright (Dickenson 73); Johnstone.
Referee: Tim Robinson.

Tuesday, 4 October 2016

Charlton Ath (0) 0

Crawley T (1) 2 *(Yussuf 44, Collins 50)* 1186

Charlton Ath: (442) Phillips; Konsa, Johnson, Lennon, Fox (Ahearne-Grant 61); Holmes, Ulvestad, Crofts (Aribo 61), Chicksen; Novak, Ajose (Hanlan 81).
Crawley T: (4231) Beeney; Young, Connolly (Pappoe 82), Davey, Arthur; Djalo (Smith 46), Tajbakhsh; Bawling, Clifford, Banton; Yussuf (Collins 48).
Referee: James Linington.

Colchester U (1) 1 *(Sembie-Ferris 23)*

Southampton U21 (1) 2 *(McQueen 8, Olomola 51)* 791

Colchester U: (4411) Bransgrove; Vincent-Young, Wynter, Prosser, Kinsella; Drey Wright (James 72), Slater, Kamara, Sembie-Ferris (Issa 46); Szmodics; Johnstone (Porter 64).
Southampton U21: (4231) Lewis; Valery, Jones, Cook, McQueen; Reed, O'Connor; Sims, Hesketh, Johnson; Olomola.
Referee: Stephen Martin.

Tuesday, 8 November 2016

Colchester U (1) 1 *(Bonne 42)*

Charlton Ath (1) 1 *(Ajose 32)* 548

Colchester U: (4231) Barnes; Vincent-Young (Brindley 46), Kent, Eastman, Wynter; Lapslie (Slater 60), Kamara; Drey Wright, Guthrie, Dickenson (Dunne 46); Bonne.
Charlton Ath: (3412) Phillips; Teixeira, Johnson, Lennon; Konsa, Foley (Ahearne-Grant 75), Crofts (Ulvestad 47), Chicksen; Aribo; Ajose (Novak 46), Hanlan.
Colchester U won 4-3 on penalties.
Referee: John Brooks.

Wednesday, 9 November 2016

Southampton U21 (3) 4 *(Mersin 3 (og), Mdlalose 9, Slattery 34, Olomola 78)*

Crawley T (0) 0 495

Southampton U21: (4231) Lewis; Valery (Flannigan 46), Gardos, Rowthorn, Vokins; Jones, Slattery; Sims (Johnson 87), Mdlalose (Smallbone 82), Isgrove; Olomola.
Crawley T: (4231) Mersin; Tajbakhsh, Pappoe, Arthur (Garnett 46), Blackman; Bawling, Djalo; Boldewijn (Roberts 64), Clifford (Harrold 53), Banton; Yussuf.
Referee: Keith Stroud.

Southern Group E	P	W	D	L	F	A	GD	Pts
Southampton U21	3	2	1	0	6	1	5	7
Crawley T	3	2	0	1	3	4	–1	6
Charlton Ath	3	0	2	1	1	3	–2	3
Colchester U	3	0	1	2	2	4	–2	2

SOUTHERN SECTION GROUP F

Tuesday, 30 August 2016

Milton Keynes D (1) 2 *(Reeves 17, Walsh 82)*

Barnet (0) 2 *(Nicholls 62, Weston 72)* 2114

Milton Keynes D: (4231) Nicholls; Baldock (George B Williams 54), Walsh, Wootton (Jackson 65), Lewington; Potter, Carruthers; Bowditch, Reeves (Thomas-Asante 62), Powell; Maynard.
Barnet: (442) Vickers; Taylor H (Amaluzor 46), N'Gala, Nelson, Johnson; Vilhete, Weston, Togwell, Muggleton (Akpa Akpro 46); Akinde J (Tomlinson 79), Nicholls.
Milton Keynes D won 5-3 on penalties.
Referee: John Brooks.

Peterborough U (0) 1 *(Anderson 52)*

Norwich C U21 (4) 6 *(Josh Murphy 6, 82, Andreu 8, 45, 56, Maddison 24)* 1696

Peterborough U: (442) Tyler; Anderson, Tafazolli, Santos, Binnom-Williams; Maddison (Penfold 72), Bostwick, Chettle, Nabi (Da Silva Lopes 46); Coulthirst (Moore 46), Nichols.
Norwich C U21: (4231) Killip; Ramsey, Godfrey, Efete, Toffolo; Grant (Cantwell 78), Thompson; Maddison, Andreu, Josh Murphy; Morris.
Referee: Dean Whitestone.

Tuesday, 4 October 2016

Barnet (0) 0

Norwich C U21 (1) 5 *(Josh Murphy 45, 56, 89, Canos 68, Oliveira 79)* 457

Barnet: (532) Vickers; Vilhete, Sesay, N'Gala■, Dembele, Johnson; Taylor J, Watson (Muggleton 66), Kyei; Shomotun (Tomlinson 46), Amaluzor (Mason-Clark 59).
Norwich C U21: (4231) Jones; Efete, Godfrey, Odusina, Ramsey; Thompson, Grant; Canos (Morris 78), Pritchard, Josh Murphy; Oliveira (Jaiyesimi 85).
Referee: Kevin Johnson.

Peterborough U (0) 0

Milton Keynes D (1) 1 *(Agard 40)* 1793

Peterborough U: (442) McGee; Hughes, Tafazolli, Baldwin, White; Edwards G (Taylor P 46), Da Silva Lopes, Forrester, Maddison; Moore (Nichols 61), Moncur (Oduwa 71).
Milton Keynes D: (442) Nicholls; Tilney, Hendry, Downing, George B Williams; Thomas-Asante, Reeves (Rasulo 71), Upson, Carruthers; Bowditch (Colclough 76), Agard (Tshimanga 66).
Referee: Trevor Kettle.

Tuesday, 8 November 2016

Barnet (0) 1 *(Amaluzor 68)*

Peterborough U (1) 2 *(Taylor P 6, Moncur 84)* 393

Barnet: (442) Stephens; Pascal, Sesay, Dembele, Muggleton (Payne 10); Nicholls, Kyei, Fonguck (Mason-Clark 59), Tomlinson; Shomotun (Amaluzor 53), Akpa Akpro.
Peterborough U: (41212) McGee; White, Tafazolli, Santos, Binnom-Williams; Nabi (Stevens 72); Chettle, Edwards G (Oduwa 61); Moncur; Angol, Taylor P (Douglas 88).
Referee: Gavin Ward.

Norwich C U21 (2) 4 *(Morris 11, Oliveira 38 (pen), 63, Adams 87)*

Milton Keynes D (0) 1 *(Tapp 84)* 1042

Norwich C U21: (442) Killip; Whittaker (Efete 46), Turner, Godfrey, Ramsey; Canos, Adams, Grant, Jacob Murphy; Oliveira (Jaiyesimi 86), Morris (Cantwell 79).
Milton Keynes D: (4231) Nicholls; George B Williams (Brittain 86), Hendry (Tapp 76), Downing (Jackson 76), Tilney; Rasulo, Osei- Bonsu; Powell, Thomas-Asante, George C Williams; Tshimanga.
Referee: Andy Haines.

Southern Group F	P	W	D	L	F	A	GD	Pts
Norwich C U21	3	3	0	0	15	2	13	9
Milton Keynes D	3	1	1	1	4	6	–2	5
Peterborough U	3	1	0	2	3	8	–5	3
Barnet	3	0	1	2	3	9	–6	1

SOUTHERN SECTION GROUP G

Tuesday, 30 August 2016

Leyton Orient (1) 3 *(McCallum 33, 70, Semedo 54)*

Stevenage (0) 1 *(Franks 58)* 876

Leyton Orient: (442) Sargeant; Hunt, Pollock, Parkes, Kennedy; Cornick (Koroma 78), Weir, Atangana (Kelly 46), Semedo; McCallum, Bowery (Dalby 74).
Stevenage: (442) Jones; Lee, Franks, Wells■, Henry (Kerr 77); Fox, Cowans, King, Pett; Godden (Liburd 69), Hyde (Hunte 60).
Referee: Gavin Ward.

Southend U (1) 2 *(Mooney 35, Kyprianou 49)*

Brighton & HA U21 (0) 0 1275

Southend U: (442) Smith; Ferdinand (Alawode-Williams 66), White, Thompson, Sokolik (Matsuzaka 88); Atkinson, Leonard, King, Kyprianou; Cox, Mooney.
Brighton & HA U21: (442) Sanchez; Hunemeier, Goldson (Tilley 64), White, Cadman; Hornby-Forbes (Barclay 70), Hutchinson, Molumby, Collar; Starkey (Harper 64), Ward.
Referee: Darren Deadman.

Tuesday, 4 October 2016

Southend U (0) 1 *(Fortune 82)*

Leyton Orient (0) 0 2383

Southend U: (532) Oxley; O'Neill (Bridge 81), White, Inniss, Thompson, Coker; Leonard, King (Atkinson 59), Wordsworth (McLaughlin 58); Cox, Fortune.
Leyton Orient: (442) Sargeant; Hunt, Parkes (Dunne 46), Pollock, Kennedy; Massey (Janse 46), Weir (Simpson 87), Kelly, N'Nomo; Bowery, Palmer.
Referee: Andy Woolmer.

Stevenage (0) 2 *(Walker 60, McKirdy 87)*

Brighton & HA U21 (1) 2 *(Ince 1, Starkey 83)* 486

Stevenage: (4312) Preston; Henry, Fox, Wilkinson (Tonge 51), Ntlhe; Gorman, King, Cowans; Schumacher (Hyde 61); Hunte, Walker (McKirdy 70).
Brighton & HA U21: (442) Sanchez; Hunt, Goldson, Hunemeier, Pocognoli; Collar, Ince, Hutchinson (Tilley 76), Starkey; Manu (Ayunga 76), Ward (Tighe 88).
Brighton & HA U21 won 4-3 on penalties.
Referee: Nick Kingsley.

Tuesday, 8 November 2016

Brighton & HA U21 (1) 1 *(Towell 16)*

Leyton Orient (0) 0 549

Brighton & HA U21: (4231) Ankergren; Hunt, White, Hunemeier (Hall 24), Hornby-Forbes (Molumby 46); Hutchinson, Collar; March, Towell (LuaLua 46), Starkey; Manu.
Leyton Orient: (442) Cisak; Janse (Judd 53), Pollock, Dunne, Kennedy; Koroma, Collins, Benedicic (Ochieng 81), Semedo; Simpson (Adeboyejo 46), McCallum.
Referee: Lee Probert.

Stevenage (2) 4 *(Schumacher 8, Godden 18, Liburd 64, 90)*

Southend U (0) 0 559

Stevenage: (442) Day; Kerr, Franks, Wilkinson, Fox (Cowans 61); Gorman, Schumacher (Slater 77), Tonge, Pett; Godden (Kennedy 67), Liburd.
Southend U: (442) Smith; White, Thompson (Sokolik 46), King, Kyprianou; McGlashan, Fortune, Timlin (Wordsworth 62), O'Neill; Cox (Bridge 9), Barrett.
Referee: Graham Horwood.

Southern Group G	P	W	D	L	F	A	GD	Pts
Southend U	3	2	0	1	3	4	–1	6
Brighton & HA U21	3	1	1	1	3	4	–1	5
Stevenage	3	1	1	1	7	5	2	4
Leyton Orient	3	1	0	2	3	3	0	3

SOUTHERN SECTION GROUP H

Tuesday, 30 August 2016

Gillingham (0) 1 *(Oldaker 90)*

Luton T (2) 2 *(Musonda 10, Smith 24)* 2128

Gillingham: (352) Nelson; Pask, Ehmer, Dickenson (Stevenson 60); Osadebe, Hessenthaler, Dack (O'Hara 46), Oldaker, List; McDonald, Emmanuel-Thomas (Donnelly 46).
Luton T: (41212) King; Cotter, Musonda, Famewo, Justin; Bakinson; Smith, Gray; Banton (Tomlinson 90); Vassell, McQuoid (Atkinson 84).
Referee: John Busby.

Millwall (0) 2 *(Abdou 63, Morison 75 (pen))*

WBA U21 (0) 0 2054

Millwall: (442) King; Romeo, Nelson, Craig, Chesmain; Twardek (Worrall 67), Abdou, Williams (Thompson 67), Wylde; O'Brien (Morison 66), Philpot.
WBA U21: (433) Rose; Wilson, Fitzwater (Piggott 90), O'Shea, McCourt; Sweeney, Donnellan (Elbouzedi 46), Nabi; Harper, Wright, Smith (Pritchatt 76).
Referee: Brendan Malone.

Tuesday, 4 October 2016

Luton T (0) 2 *(Gilliead 60, Gray 62)*

WBA U21 (0) 0 1454

Luton T: (41212) King; O'Donnell, Musonda, Famewo, Senior; Bakinson; Smith, Gray; Gilliead (Bean 90); Banton (Hinds 86), McQuoid (Vassell 73).
WBA U21: (433) Myhill; Fitzwater, Donnellan, Olsson, McCourt (Morrison 75); Harper, Smith (Walker 67), Gardner; McManaman, Tulloch, Sweeney (Barbir 63).
Referee: Andy Davies.

Millwall (1) 2 *(Onyedinma 45, Morison 88)*

Gillingham (1) 1 *(Wright 17)* 2104

Millwall: (442) King; Brown (Abdou 54), Nelson, Craig, Chesmain (Martin 46); Wylde (Morison 46), Williams, Butcher, Thompson; Gregory, Onyedinma.
Gillingham: (352) Nelson; Pask (Dickenson 46), Ehmer, Oshilaja; Jackson (Knott 71), Hessenthaler, Wright, Herd (Byrne 61), Osadebe; Donnelly, List.
Referee: Christopher Sarginson.

Tuesday, 8 November 2016

Luton T (0) 1 *(Hutchinson 58 (og))*

Millwall (0) 3 *(Onyedinma 72, Smith 81, 87)* 2251

Luton T: (41212) King; O'Donnell, Musonda, Famewo, Senior; Bakinson (Hinds 86); Smith, Gray (Down 90); McQuoid; Mackail-Smith (Banton 66), Vassell.
Millwall: (442) King; Cummings, Hutchinson (Craig 84), Rooney, Martin; Worrall (Twardek 89), Butcher, Farrell, Wylde; O'Brien (Onyedinma 62), Smith.
Referee: Oliver Langford.

WBA U21 (0) 0

Gillingham (1) 2 *(Oldaker 45, Emmanuel-Thomas 55 (pen))* 274

WBA U21: (442) Palmer; Wilson, Fitzwater, Donnellan, McCourt; Sweeney, Harper, Nabi, Bradley (Soule 85); Elbouzedi (Pritchatt 71), Forss (Pierce 61).
Gillingham: (352) Nelson; Pask, Oshilaja, Cargill (Dickenson 61); Osadebe, Oldaker, Knott, Byrne, Garmston (Jackson 46 (Cundle 74)); Emmanuel-Thomas, Donnelly.
Referee: Nigel Miller.

Southern Group H	P	W	D	L	F	A	GD	Pts
Millwall	3	3	0	0	7	2	5	9
Luton T	3	2	0	1	5	4	1	6
Gillingham	3	1	0	2	4	4	0	3
WBA U21	3	0	0	3	0	6	–6	0

NORTHERN SECTION SECOND ROUND

Monday, 5 December 2016

Wolverhampton W U21 (1) 1 *(Enobakhare 13)*

Sunderland U21 (1) 1 *(Beadling 17)* 1118

Wolverhampton W U21: (433) Burgoyne; Simpson, Deslandes, Ronan, Upton (Breslin 28); Herc, Johnson, Carnat; Randall, Enobakhare, Gibbs-White.
Sunderland U21: (442) Mannone; Robson J, Robson T, Ledger, Brady; Beadling (Molyneux 80), Robson E, Embleton (Nelson 72), Honeyman; Asoro (Casey 90), Maja.
Wolverhampton W U21 won 4-3 on penalties.
Referee: Mark Heywood.

Tuesday, 6 December 2016

Carlisle U (0) 2 *(Miller S 72, Wyke 80)*

Mansfield T (2) 3 *(Pearce 15, Green 30, Rose D 86)* 1126

Carlisle U: (352) Crocombe; Miller T, Brisley, Gillesphey; McQueen (Wyke 46), McKee (Wright 45), Joyce, Lambe (Asamoah 71), Grainger; Devitt, Miller S.
Mansfield T: (442) Shearer; Bennett, Collins, Pearce, Benning; McGuire, Clements, Hamilton, Baxendale (Rose D 79); Green (Thomas 89), Hemmings (Hurst 71).
Referee: David Webb.

Doncaster R (0) 1 *(Williams 52)*

Blackpool (1) 1 *(Gnanduillet 24)* 1549

Doncaster R: (343) Marosi; Mason, Wright, Garrett (Baudry 46); Calder, Middleton, Keegan, Evina (Houghton 46); Williams (Mandeville 71), Beestin, Longbottom.
Blackpool: (3412) Lyness; Aimson, Nolan, Higham; Philliskirk, Cain (Roache 84), McAlister, Samuel (Cameron 78); Yeates; Gnanduillet (Redshaw 71), Cullen.
Blackpool won 8-7 on penalties.
Referee: David Coote.

Rochdale (0) 0

Chesterfield (1) 2 *(Maguire 24, Evans 59)* 995

Rochdale: (4231) Logan; McNulty■, Canavan, McGahey, Bunney; Lund, Morley; Odelusi (Allen 54), Noble-Lazarus (Davies 46), Mendez-Laing (McDermott 54); Henderson.
Chesterfield: (4411) Allinson; Liddle, Anderson■, Maguire, Donohue; Simons (Evatt 69), Nolan, Dimaio, Gardner (Ariyibi 65); Beesley; Evans (Dennis 65).
Referee: Graham Salisbury.

Scunthorpe U (1) 1 *(Mantom 3)*

Morecambe (0) 1 *(Edwards 53)* 987

Scunthorpe U: (442) Anyon; Townsend (Morris 90), Wallace, Goode, Clarke; Williams, Smallwood (van Veen 82), Mantom, Holmes (Bishop 51); Madden, Adelakun.
Morecambe: (3412) Nizic; Winnard, Edwards, Whitmore; Conlan (Molyneux 84), Rose, Murphy, McGowan; Wildig (Mullin 78); Ellison (Turner 71), Stockton.
Scunthorpe U won 5-3 on penalties.
Referee: Darren Drysdale.

Wednesday, 7 December 2016

Bradford C (0) 1 *(Law 64)*

Cambridge U (0) 0 1360

Bradford C: (4411) Sattelmaier; Darby (McMahon 25), Clarke N, McArdle, Kilgallon; Marshall, Dieng (Devine 46), Law, Morais; Vuckic (Cullen 64); Hiwula.
Cambridge U: (442) Norris; Long (Davies 20), Legge, Dallison, Adams; Mingoia (Ikpeazu 56), Dunne, Maris (Berry 57), Clark; Williamson, Dunk.
Referee: Rob Lewis.

Tuesday, 13 December 2016

Walsall (1) 1 *(Bakayoko 44)*

Oldham Ath (0) 3 *(Croft 69, Burgess 73, Erwin 89)* 925

Walsall: (352) MacGillivray; McCarthy, Preston, Toner; Kinsella (Moussa 65), Dobson (Edwards 71), Cuvelier, Osbourne, Laird; Jackson, Bakayoko (Makris 87).
Oldham Ath: (442) Ripley; Law, Burgess, Clarke, Dunne; Flynn (Winchester 46), Fane, Banks, McLaughlin (Croft 46); Ladapo (Erwin 73), McKay.
Referee: Nigel Miller.

Tuesday, 10 January 2017

Cheltenham T (3) 6 *(De Girolamo 9, 36, 87, O'Shaughnessy 31, Waters 65, Morgan-Smith 79)*

Leicester C U21 (1) 1 *(Kapustka 10)* 1028

Cheltenham T: (3412) Kitscha; Onariase, Boyle, O'Shaughnessy; Barthram, Rowe (Morgan-Smith 73), Pell, Cranston; Waters (Dayton 73); Wright (Munns 73), De Girolamo.
Leicester C U21: (4321) Hamer (Bramley 33); Pascanu, Johnson, Debayo (Wood 70), Kipre (Mitchell 60); Barnes, Miles, Choudhury; Kapustka, Ndukwu; Muskwe.
Referee: Brett Huxtable.

SOUTHERN SECTION SECOND ROUND

Tuesday, 6 December 2016

AFC Wimbledon (0) 1 *(Barnett 68)*

Brighton & HA U21 (2) 2 *(Manu 38, Towell 45 (pen))* 497

AFC Wimbledon: (433) McDonnell; Francomb, Nightingale, Kelly, Owens; Egan, Beere, Parrett (Reeves 46); Whelpdale, Barnett, Poleon (Elliott 46).
Brighton & HA U21: (433) Maenpaa; Collar, Hall, Ince, Hunt; Starkey (Molumby 59), Hutchinson, Towell; Bjordal (Ward 74), Manu (Tilley 77), LuaLua■.
Referee: Charles Breakspear.

Norwich C U21 (0) 0

Swansea C U21 (0) 1 *(McBurnie 74)* 785

Norwich C U21: (4231) Killip; Whittaker, Klose, Godfrey■, Ramsey; Mulumbu, Grant; Canos, Josh Murphy (Jaiyesimi 77), Jarvis (Crowe 46); Morris.
Swansea C U21: (4231) Tremmel; Rodon, Davies, Mawson, Reid; Evans (Holland 66), Blair; James, Byers, Samuel (Bray 59); McBurnie.
Referee: Darren Deadman.

Southend U (0) 1 *(Wordsworth 86)*

Oxford U (0) 1 *(Maguire 81)* 2004

Southend U: (442) Oxley; Demetriou, Thompson, Ferdinand, Timlin; Atkinson (O'Neill 54), Leonard, Wordsworth, McLaughlin; Ranger (Fortune 78), Cox.
Oxford U: (442) Eastwood; Edwards, Nelson, Martin, Johnson; Maguire, Lundstram, Ruffels, Hall (Roberts T 78); Hemmings, Taylor.
Oxford U won 4-3 on penalties.
Referee: Trevor Kettle.

Swindon T (1) 2 *(Norris 6, Iandolo 62)*

Luton T (2) 3 *(McQuoid 9, 19, Vassell 69)* 1692

Swindon T: (4141) Henry; Furlong, Thomas, Sharpe, Ormonde-Ottewill (Hylton 46); Rodgers (Iandolo 46); Goddard, Murray, Evans, Delfouneso; Norris (Young 46).
Luton T: (451) King; Justin, Musonda, Potts, Senior; Lee, Ruddock, Smith, Gray (Bakinson 85), Vassell; McQuoid (Mackail-Smith 74).
Referee: Roger East.

Yeovil T (0) 4 *(Dawson 49 (pen), Zoko 62 (pen), Lacey 73, Whitfield 79)*

Milton Keynes D (1) 1 *(Lacey 24 (og))* 1308

Yeovil T: (433) Maddison; Shephard, Smith, Lacey, Dickson; Dawson (Lawless 83), Butcher, Whitfield; Campbell, Zoko (Eaves 80), Hedges (Khan 86).
Milton Keynes D: (4231) Nicholls; George B Williams, Hendry, Downing, Tilney; Carruthers■, George C Williams; Powell, Aneke (Agard 59), Colclough (Reeves 59); Tshimanga (Baldock 71).
Referee: Lee Swabey.

Wednesday, 7 December 2016

Coventry C (1) 1 *(Sordell 28)*

Crawley T (0) 0 1338

Coventry C: (4231) Charles-Cook; Page (Maycock 56), Turnbull, Willis, Rose; McCann, Bigirimana (Gadzhev 83); Sordell, Thomas G, Jones; McBean (Tudgay 71).
Crawley T: (4231) Beeney; Arthur, Yorwerth, Connolly, Young; Djalo, Tajbakhsh; Watt (Boldewijn 59), Clifford (Banton 46), Yussuf; Collins (Henderson 46).
Referee: Graham Horwood.

Millwall (0) 1 *(Worrall 53)*

Wycombe W (0) 3 *(Akinfenwa 51 (pen), Thompson 85, 90)* 1619

Millwall: (442) King; Cummings, Nelson (Ferguson 87), Craig, Martin; Worrall, Twardek, Abdou, Thompson (Butcher 66); Onyedinma, O'Brien (Smith 66).
Wycombe W: (433) Blackman; Harriman, De Havilland, Muller (Pierre 59), Jombati; Rowe, Bean, McGinn (Kashket 75); Thompson, Hayes (Akinfenwa 46), Wood.
Referee: Dean Whitestone.

Wednesday, 21 December 2016

Southampton U21 (1) 1 *(Isgrove 30)*

Reading U21 (0) 1 *(Keown 50)* 1679

Southampton U21: (442) Lewis; Vokins, Jones, Cook, Valery; O'Connor, Little, Slattery, Isgrove; Afolabi, Johnson (Mdlalose 69).
Reading U21: (433) Jaakkola; Medford-Smith, Keown, Cooper, Watson; Wieser, Barrett, Rinomhota; Loader, Smith (Frost 68), Meite.
Reading U21 won 4-3 on penalties.
Referee: Lee Collins.

THIRD ROUND

Tuesday, 10 January 2017

Blackpool (1) 1 *(Mellor 9)*

Wycombe W (0) 1 *(Stewart 77)* 766

Blackpool: (41212) Slocombe; Mellor (Turenne Des Pres 67), Aimson, Robertson, Pugh; Cain; Philliskirk, Samuel (Payne 73); Yeates; Cullen (Redshaw 46), Gnanduillet.
Wycombe W: (433) Blackman; Stewart, Muller, De Havilland, Jacobson; Bean, O'Nien, Wood; Thompson, Hayes (Akinfenwa 71), Weston (Cowan-Hall 76).
Wycombe W won 5-4 on penalties.
Referee: Eddie Ilderton.

Coventry C (1) 3 *(Lameiras 41, Thomas G 51, Haynes 88)*

Brighton & HA U21 (0) 0 2085

Coventry C: (4231) Charles-Cook; Dion Kelly-Evans, Harries, Stokes (Finch 46), Haynes; Bigirimana, Gadzhev (Stevenson 77); Thomas G, Lameiras, Jones; Beavon (Tudgay 59).
Brighton & HA U21: (4312) Sanchez; Rosenior (White 46), Hall, Barclay, Cox; Ince, Hutchinson (Ward 81), Bjordal; Molumby; Tilley, Tighe (Mandroiu 68).
Referee: Rob Lewis.

Luton T (2) 4 *(Mackail-Smith 23 (pen), Marriott 25, 51, Vassell 86)*

Chesterfield (0) 0 1655

Luton T: (41212) Walton; O'Donnell, Musonda, Rea, Senior; Smith; Ruddock, Gray (Lee 62); Cook; Marriott (Vassell 77), Mackail-Smith (Banton 77).
Chesterfield: (442) Allinson; O'Neil, Hird, Evatt, Maguire; Simons (Dennis 56), Dimaio, O'Shea, Ariyibi (Nolan 56); Beesley, Gardner (Mitchell 75).
Referee: Charles Breakspear.

Mansfield T (0) 2 *(Hoban 84, 90)*

Oldham Ath (0) 0 1343

Mansfield T: (4132) Kean; Bennett, Howkins (Rose M 70), Pearce, Benning; Collins; Baxendale, Clements (Thomas 83), Hamilton; Hoban, Arquin (Green 83).
Oldham Ath: (451) Ripley; Law, Clarke, Edmundson, Wilson; Croft (McKay 61), Green (Winchester 70), Flynn (Banks 61), Fane, McLaughlin; Osei.
Referee: Darren Drysdale.

Oxford U (2) 4 *(Johnson 19, Hemmings 23, 50 (pen), 90)*

Scunthorpe U (1) 1 *(Williams 11 (pen))* 1383

Oxford U: (442) Eastwood; Skarz (Carroll 89), Dunkley, Edwards, Johnson; Hall, Rothwell, Sercombe (Maguire 73), Ruffels; Taylor (Lundstram 81), Hemmings.
Scunthorpe U: (433) Anyon; Goode, Wallace, Clarke, Wiseman (Morris 63); Sutton, Holmes, Mantom; Williams, Davies (Hopper 66), van Veen (Margetts 56).
Referee: Gavin Ward.

Swansea C U21 (0) 2 *(McBurnie 47, 87)*

Wolverhampton W U21 (1) 1 *(Herc 13)* 980

Swansea C U21: (4231) Tremmel; Reid, Davies, Rodon, Lewis; Maric, Holland (Evans 77); Barrow (Jones 28), Byers, James; McBurnie.
Wolverhampton W U21: (4231) Burgoyne; Simpson (O'Hanlon 63), Hayden, Johnson, Breslin; Levingston (McKenna 77), White; Randall, Herc, Carnat; Collins (Reid 67).
Referee: Tim Robinson.

Yeovil T (2) 4 *(Khan 24, Zoko 32, Sowunmi 65, Sheppard 88 (og))*

Reading U21 (1) 2 *(Novakovich 45, Barrett 90 (pen))* 1081

Yeovil T: (433) Maddison; Shephard, Smith, Lacey, Dickson; Dolan, Lawless (Butcher 46), Dawson (Mugabi 89); Whitfield, Khan (Sowunmi 56), Zoko.
Reading U21: (41212) Moore; Sheppard, Gravenberch (Griffin 62), Hyam, Medford-Smith; Wieser■; Rinomhota, Barrett; Frost; Novakovich (Smith 75), Cardwell (Loader 72).
Referee: John Brooks.

Tuesday, 17 January 2017

Cheltenham T (0) 0

Bradford C (0) 1 *(Hiwula 64)* 1081

Cheltenham T: (3412) Kitscha; Onariase, Boyle, O'Shaughnessy; Barthram (Dayton 72), Pell, Rowe, Cranston; Waters (Munns 85); Wright, De Girolamo (Holman 72).
Bradford C: (433) Sattelmaier; McMahon, McArdle, Kilgallon, Darby; Devine, Vincelot (Cullen 46), Dieng; Marshall (Clarke B 68), James Hanson (Knight-Percival 77), Hiwula.
Referee: Brendan Malone.

QUARTER-FINALS

Tuesday, 24 January 2017

Mansfield T (1) 1 *(Green 34 (pen))*

Wycombe W (0) 2 *(Kashket 73, Akinfenwa 81)* 2047

Mansfield T: (4132) Kean; Collins (Hoban 88), Pearce, Bennett, Benning; McGuire; Thomas, Baxendale (Hemmings 82), Hamilton; Green, Arquin (Rose D 82).
Wycombe W: (4321) Blackman; Jombati, Jacobson, De Havilland, Muller; Bean (Wood 84), O'Nien, Saunders; Cowan-Hall (Kashket 66), Thompson (Akinfenwa 66); Weston.
Referee: David Webb.

Swansea C U21 (0) 1 *(McBurnie 70 (pen))*

Coventry C (0) 1 *(Willis 85)* 3356

Swansea C U21: (4231) Tremmel; Reid, Davies, Rodon, Lewis; Fulton (Maric 46), Blair; Jones (Garrick 71), Byers, Bray (Bia Bi 90); McBurnie.
Coventry C: (4231) Charles-Cook; Dion Kelly-Evans, Willis, Turnbull, Haynes; Reilly (Bigirimana 76), Stevenson (Gadzhev 89); Lameiras, Rose (Jones 71), Reid; Thomas G.
Coventry C won 4-2 on penalties.
Referee: Mark Haywood.

Tuesday, 31 January 2017

Oxford U (0) 2 *(Maguire 53 (pen), Johnson 55)*

Bradford C (0) 1 *(Hiwula 85)* 2274

Oxford U: (4411) Eastwood; Edwards, Dunkley, Nelson, Johnson; Rothwell, Sercombe, Ruffels (Ledson 77), Hall (Carroll 85); Maguire; Hemmings (Lundstram 65).
Bradford C: (442) Sattelmaier; Darby, Vincelot, McArdle (Devine 57), Meredith; Law, Dieng, Cullen, Marshall; Clarke B (Hudson 73), Hiwula.
Referee: Dean Whitestone.

Tuesday, 7 February 2017

Luton T (1) 5 *(Cook 12, Sheehan 50, Vassell 60, 90, Hylton 66)*

Yeovil T (0) 2 *(Zoko 58, Sowunmi 65)* 2408

Luton T: (442) Macey; O'Donnell, Mullins, Sheehan, Senior; Rea, Smith, Ruddock, Cook (Cuthbert 64); Vassell (Marriott 90), Hylton (Justin 90).
Yeovil T: (442) Maddison; Smith, Dickson (James 79), Mugabi, Butcher; Dawson, Dolan, Whitfield (Goodship 81), Harrison; Eaves (Sowunmi 53), Zoko.
Referee: Ben Toner.

SEMI-FINALS

Tuesday, 7 February 2017

Coventry C (2) 2 *(Beavon 11, Thomas G 19)*

Wycombe W (0) 1 *(Akinfenwa 55)* 11,672

Coventry C: (442) Charles-Cook; Dion Kelly-Evans, Harries, Turnbull, Haynes; Thomas G, Rose, Reilly, Reid (Finch 64); Beavon (Jones 46), Tudgay.
Wycombe W: (433) Blackman; Jombati (Akinfenwa 46), Stewart, De Havilland, Jacobson; Bean, Harriman, O'Nien; Weston (Wood 85), Thompson (Kashket 59), Saunders.
Referee: Darren England.

Wednesday, 1 March 2017

Luton T (0) 2 *(Vassell 72, Hylton 82)*

Oxford U (1) 3 *(Edwards 10, Ruddock 69 (og), Johnson 85)* 6901

Luton T: (41212) Macey; Justin (Cuthbert 90), Mullins, Sheehan, Senior (Gambin 46); Rea; Gray (Marriott 80), Ruddock; Cook; Hylton, Vassell.
Oxford U: (442) Eastwood; Edwards, Nelson, Dunkley, Skarz; Johnson, Lundstram, Ledson, Sercombe; Maguire (Rothwell 27), Hemmings.
Referee: Nigel Miller.

EFL CHECKATRADE TROPHY FINAL 2017

Sunday, 2 April 2017

(at Wembley Stadium, attendance 74,434)

Coventry C (1) 2 Oxford U (0) 1

Coventry C: (4411) Burge; Willis (Dion Kelly-Evans 60), Stokes, Turnbull, Haynes; Thomas G (Jones 82), Stevenson, Bigirimana, Reid; Lameiras; Beavon (Tudgay 90).

Scorers: Bigirimana 11, Thomas G 55.

Oxford U: (4411) Eastwood; Edwards, Nelson, Dunkley, Johnson; Hall, Lundstram, Ledson (Sercombe 57), Rothwell (Ruffels 90); Maguire; Hemmings.

Scorer: Sercombe 75.

Referee: Christopher Sarginson.

FA CUP FINALS 1872–2017

VENUES

1872 and 1874–92	Kennington Oval	1895–1914	Crystal Palace
1873	Lillie Bridge	1915	Old Trafford, Manchester
1893	Fallowfield, Manchester	1920–22	Stamford Bridge
1894	Everton	2001–06	Millennium Stadium, Cardiff
1923–2000	Wembley Stadium (old)	2007 to date	Wembley Stadium (new)

THE FA CUP

1872	Wanderers v Royal Engineers	1-0
1873	Wanderers v Oxford University	2-0
1874	Oxford University v Royal Engineers	2-0
1875	Royal Engineers v Old Etonians	1-1*
Replay	Royal Engineers v Old Etonians	2-0
1876	Wanderers v Old Etonians	1-1*
Replay	Wanderers v Old Etonians	3-0
1877	Wanderers v Oxford University	2-1*
1878	Wanderers v Royal Engineers	3-1

Wanderers won the cup outright, but it was restored to the Football Association.

1879	Old Etonians v Clapham R	1-0
1880	Clapham R v Oxford University	1-0
1881	Old Carthusians v Old Etonians	3-0
1882	Old Etonians v Blackburn R	1-0
1883	Blackburn Olympic v Old Etonians	2-1*
1884	Blackburn R v Queen's Park, Glasgow	2-1
1885	Blackburn R v Queen's Park, Glasgow	2-0
1886	Blackburn R v WBA	0-0
Replay	Blackburn R v WBA	2-0
	(at Racecourse Ground, Derby Co)	

A special trophy was awarded to Blackburn R for third consecutive win.

1887	Aston Villa v WBA	2-0
1888	WBA v Preston NE	2-1
1889	Preston NE v Wolverhampton W	3-0
1890	Blackburn R v The Wednesday	6-1
1891	Blackburn R v Notts Co	3-1
1892	WBA v Aston Villa	3-0
1893	Wolverhampton W v Everton	1-0
1894	Notts Co v Bolton W	4-1
1895	Aston Villa v WBA	1-0

FA Cup was stolen from a shop window in Birmingham and never found.

1896	The Wednesday v Wolverhampton W	2-1
1897	Aston Villa v Everton	3-2
1898	Nottingham F v Derby Co	3-1
1899	Sheffield U v Derby Co	4-1
1900	Bury v Southampton	4-0
1901	Tottenham H v Sheffield U	2-2
Replay	Tottenham H v Sheffield U	3-1
	(at Burnden Park, Bolton W)	
1902	Sheffield U v Southampton	1-1
Replay	Sheffield U v Southampton	2-1
1903	Bury v Derby Co	6-0
1904	Manchester C v Bolton W	1-0
1905	Aston Villa v Newcastle U	2-0
1906	Everton v Newcastle U	1-0
1907	The Wednesday v Everton	2-1
1908	Wolverhampton W v Newcastle U	3-1
1909	Manchester U v Bristol C	1-0
1910	Newcastle U v Barnsley	1-1
Replay	Newcastle U v Barnsley	2-0
	(at Goodison Park, Everton)	
1911	Bradford C v Newcastle U	0-0
Replay	Bradford C v Newcastle U	1-0
	(at Old Trafford, Manchester U)	

Trophy was given to Lord Kinnaird – he made nine FA Cup Final appearances – for services to football.

1912	Barnsley v WBA	0-0
Replay	Barnsley v WBA	1-0
	(at Bramall Lane, Sheffield U)	
1913	Aston Villa v Sunderland	1-0
1914	Burnley v Liverpool	1-0
1915	Sheffield U v Chelsea	3-0
1920	Aston Villa v Huddersfield T	1-0*
1921	Tottenham H v Wolverhampton W	1-0
1922	Huddersfield T v Preston NE	1-0
1923	Bolton W v West Ham U	2-0
1924	Newcastle U v Aston Villa	2-0
1925	Sheffield U v Cardiff C	1-0
1926	Bolton W v Manchester C	1-0
1927	Cardiff C v Arsenal	1-0
1928	Blackburn R v Huddersfield T	3-1
1929	Bolton W v Portsmouth	2-0
1930	Arsenal v Huddersfield T	2-0
1931	WBA v Birmingham	2-1
1932	Newcastle U v Arsenal	2-1
1933	Everton v Manchester C	3-0
1934	Manchester C v Portsmouth	2-1
1935	Sheffield W v WBA	4-2
1936	Arsenal v Sheffield U	1-0
1937	Sunderland v Preston NE	3-1
1938	Preston NE v Huddersfield T	1-0*
1939	Portsmouth v Wolverhampton W	4-1
1946	Derby Co v Charlton Ath	4-1*
1947	Charlton Ath v Burnley	1-0*
1948	Manchester U v Blackpool	4-2
1949	Wolverhampton W v Leicester C	3-1
1950	Arsenal v Liverpool	2-0
1951	Newcastle U v Blackpool	2-0
1952	Newcastle U v Arsenal	1-0
1953	Blackpool v Bolton W	4-3
1954	WBA v Preston NE	3-2
1955	Newcastle U v Manchester C	3-1
1956	Manchester C v Birmingham C	3-1
1957	Aston Villa v Manchester U	2-1
1958	Bolton W v Manchester U	2-0
1959	Nottingham F v Luton T	2-1
1960	Wolverhampton W v Blackburn R	3-0
1961	Tottenham H v Leicester C	2-0
1962	Tottenham H v Burnley	3-1
1963	Manchester U v Leicester C	3-1
1964	West Ham U v Preston NE	3-2
1965	Liverpool v Leeds U	2-1*
1966	Everton v Sheffield W	3-2
1967	Tottenham H v Chelsea	2-1
1968	WBA v Everton	1-0*
1969	Manchester C v Leicester C	1-0
1970	Chelsea v Leeds U	2-2*
Replay	Chelsea v Leeds U	2-1
	(at Old Trafford, Manchester U)	
1971	Arsenal v Liverpool	2-1*
1972	Leeds U v Arsenal	1-0
1973	Sunderland v Leeds U	1-0
1974	Liverpool v Newcastle U	3-0
1975	West Ham U v Fulham	2-0
1976	Southampton v Manchester U	1-0
1977	Manchester U v Liverpool	2-1
1978	Ipswich T v Arsenal	1-0
1979	Arsenal v Manchester U	3-2
1980	West Ham U v Arsenal	1-0
1981	Tottenham H v Manchester C	1-1*
Replay	Tottenham H v Manchester C	3-2

1982	Tottenham H v QPR	1-1*
Replay	Tottenham H v QPR	1-0
1983	Manchester U v Brighton & HA	2-2*
Replay	Manchester U v Brighton & HA	4-0
1984	Everton v Watford	2-0
1985	Manchester U v Everton	1-0*
1986	Liverpool v Everton	3-1
1987	Coventry C v Tottenham H	3-2*
1988	Wimbledon v Liverpool	1-0
1989	Liverpool v Everton	3-2*
1990	Manchester U v Crystal Palace	3-3*
Replay	Manchester U v Crystal Palace	1-0
1991	Tottenham H v Nottingham F	2-1*
1992	Liverpool v Sunderland	2-0
1993	Arsenal v Sheffield W	1-1*
Replay	Arsenal v Sheffield W	2-1*
1994	Manchester U v Chelsea	4-0

THE FA CUP SPONSORED BY LITTLEWOODS POOLS

1995	Everton v Manchester U	1-0
1996	Manchester U v Liverpool	1-0
1997	Chelsea v Middlesbrough	2-0
1998	Arsenal v Newcastle U	2-0

THE AXA-SPONSORED FA CUP

1999	Manchester U v Newcastle U	2-0
2000	Chelsea v Aston Villa	1-0
2001	Liverpool v Arsenal	2-1
2002	Arsenal v Chelsea	2-0

THE FA CUP

2003	Arsenal v Southampton	1-0
2004	Manchester U v Millwall	3-0
2005	Arsenal v Manchester U	0-0*
	Arsenal won 5-4 on penalties.	
2006	Liverpool v West Ham U	3-3*
	Liverpool won 3-1 on penalties.	

THE FA CUP SPONSORED BY E.ON

2007	Chelsea v Manchester U	1-0*
2008	Portsmouth v Cardiff C	1-0
2009	Chelsea v Everton	2-1
2010	Chelsea v Portsmouth	1-0
2011	Manchester C v Stoke C	1-0

THE FA CUP WITH BUDWEISER

2012	Chelsea v Liverpool	2-1
2013	Wigan Ath v Manchester C	1-0
2014	Arsenal v Hull C	3-2*

THE FA CUP

2015	Arsenal v Aston Villa	4-0

THE EMIRATES FA CUP

2016	Manchester U v Crystal Palace	2-1*
2017	Arsenal v Chelsea	2-1

**After extra time.*

FA CUP WINS

Arsenal 13, Manchester U 12, Tottenham H 8, Aston Villa 7, Chelsea 7, Liverpool 7, Blackburn R 6, Newcastle U 6, Everton 5, Manchester C 5, The Wanderers 5, WBA 5, Bolton W 4, Sheffield U 4, Wolverhampton W 4, Sheffield W 3, West Ham U 3, Bury 2, Nottingham F 2, Old Etonians 2, Portsmouth 2, Preston NE 2, Sunderland 2, Barnsley 1, Blackburn Olympic 1, Blackpool 1, Bradford C 1, Burnley 1, Cardiff C 1, Charlton Ath 1, Clapham R 1, Coventry C 1, Derby Co 1, Huddersfield T 1, Ipswich T 1, Leeds U 1, Notts Co 1, Old Carthusians 1, Oxford University 1, Royal Engineers 1, Southampton 1, Wigan Ath 1, Wimbledon 1.

APPEARANCES IN FINALS

Arsenal 20, Manchester U 19, Liverpool 14, Everton 13, Newcastle U 13, Chelsea 12, Aston Villa 11, Manchester C 10, WBA 10, Tottenham H 9, Blackburn R 8, Wolverhampton W 8, Bolton W 7, Preston NE 7, Old Etonians 6, Sheffield U 6, Sheffield W 6, Huddersfield T 5, Portsmouth 5, *The Wanderers 5, West Ham U 5, Derby Co 4, Leeds U 4, Leicester C 4, Oxford University 4, Royal Engineers 4, Southampton 4, Sunderland 4, Blackpool 3, Burnley 3, Cardiff C 3, Nottingham F 3, Barnsley 2, Birmingham C 2, *Bury 2, Charlton Ath 2, Clapham R 2, Crystal Palace 2, Notts Co 2, Queen's Park (Glasgow) 2, *Blackburn Olympic 1, *Bradford C 1, Brighton & HA 1, Bristol C 1, *Coventry C 1, Fulham 1, Hull C 1, *Ipswich T 1, Luton T 1, Middlesbrough 1, Millwall 1, *Old Carthusians 1, QPR 1, Stoke C 1, Watford 1, *Wigan Ath 1, *Wimbledon 1.

* *Denotes undefeated in final.*

APPEARANCES IN SEMI-FINALS

Arsenal 29, Manchester U 28, Everton 26, Liverpool 24, Chelsea 22, Aston Villa 21, Tottenham H 20, WBA 20, Blackburn R 18, Newcastle U 17, Sheffield W 16, Bolton W 14, Sheffield U 14, Wolverhampton W 14, Derby Co 13, Manchester C 13, Nottingham F 12, Sunderland 12, Southampton 11, Preston NE 10, Birmingham C 9, Burnley 8, Leeds U 8, Huddersfield T 7, Leicester C 7, Portsmouth 7, West Ham U 7, Old Etonians 6, Fulham 6, Oxford University 6, Watford 6, Millwall 5, Notts Co 5, The Wanderers 5, Cardiff C 4, Crystal Palace (professional club) 4, Luton T 4, Queen's Park (Glasgow) 4, Royal Engineers 4, Stoke C 4, Barnsley 3, Blackpool 3, Clapham R 3, Ipswich T 3, Middlesbrough 3, Norwich C 3, Old Carthusians 3, Oldham Ath 3, The Swifts 3, Blackburn Olympic 2, Bristol C 2, Bury 2, Charlton Ath 2, Grimsby T 2, Hull C 2, Reading 2, Swansea T 2, Swindon T 2, Wigan Ath 2, Wimbledon 2, Bradford C 1, Brighton & HA 1, Cambridge University 1, Chesterfield 1, Coventry C 1, Crewe Alex 1, Crystal Palace (amateur club) 1, Darwen 1, Derby Junction 1, Glasgow R 1, Marlow 1, Old Harrovians 1, Orient 1, Plymouth Arg 1, Port Vale 1, QPR 1, Shropshire W 1, Wycombe W 1, York C 1.

FA CUP ATTENDANCES 1969–2017

	1st Round	*2nd Round*	*3rd Round*	*4th Round*	*5th Round*	*6th Round*	*Semi-finals & Final*	*Total*	*No. of matches*	*Average per match*
1969–70	345,229	195,102	925,930	651,374	319,893	198,537	390,700	3,026,765	170	17,805
1970–71	329,687	230,942	956,683	757,852	360,687	304,937	279,644	3,220,432	162	19,879
1971–72	277,726	236,127	986,094	711,399	486,378	230,292	248,546	3,158,562	160	19,741
1972–73	259,432	169,114	938,741	735,825	357,386	241,934	226,543	2,928,975	160	18,306
1973–74	214,236	125,295	840,142	747,909	346,012	233,307	273,051	2,779,952	167	16,646
1974–75	283,956	170,466	914,994	646,434	393,323	268,361	291,369	2,968,903	172	17,261
1975–76	255,533	178,099	867,880	573,843	471,925	206,851	205,810	2,759,941	161	17,142
1976–77	379,230	192,159	942,523	631,265	373,330	205,379	258,216	2,982,102	174	17,139
1977–78	258,248	178,930	881,406	540,164	400,751	137,059	198,020	2,594,578	160	16,216
1978–79	243,773	185,343	880,345	537,748	243,683	263,213	249,897	2,604,002	166	15,687
1979–80	267,121	204,759	804,701	507,725	364,039	157,530	355,541	2,661,416	163	16,328
1980–81	246,824	194,502	832,578	534,402	320,530	288,714	339,250	2,756,800	169	16,312
1981–82	236,220	127,300	513,185	356,987	203,334	124,308	279,621	1,840,955	160	11,506
1982–83	191,312	150,046	670,503	452,688	260,069	193,845	291,162	2,209,625	154	14,348
1983–84	192,276	151,647	625,965	417,298	181,832	185,382	187,000	1,941,400	166	11,695
1984–85	174,604	137,078	616,229	320,772	269,232	148,690	242,754	1,909,359	157	12,162
1985–86	171,142	130,034	486,838	495,526	311,833	184,262	192,316	1,971,951	168	11,738
1986–87	209,290	146,761	593,520	349,342	263,550	119,396	195,533	1,877,400	165	11,378
1987–88	204,411	104,561	720,121	443,133	281,461	119,313	177,585	2,050,585	155	13,229
1988–89	212,775	121,326	690,199	421,255	206,781	176,629	167,353	1,966,318	164	12,173
1989–90	209,542	133,483	683,047	412,483	351,423	123,065	277,420	2,190,463	170	12,885
1990–91	194,195	121,450	594,592	530,279	276,112	124,826	196,434	2,038,518	162	12,583
1991–92	231,940	117,078	586,014	372,576	270,537	155,603	201,592	1,935,340	160	12,095
1992–93	241,968	174,702	612,494	377,211	198,379	149,675	293,241	2,047,670	161	12,718
1993–94	190,683	118,031	691,064	430,234	172,196	134,705	228,233	1,965,146	159	12,359
1994–95	219,511	125,629	640,017	438,596	257,650	159,787	174,059	2,015,249	161	12,517
1995–96	185,538	115,669	748,997	391,218	274,055	174,142	156,500	2,046,199	167	12,252
1996–97	209,521	122,324	651,139	402,293	199,873	67,035	191,813	1,843,998	151	12,211
1997–98	204,803	130,261	629,127	455,557	341,290	192,651	172,007	2,125,696	165	12,883
1998–99	191,954	132,341	609,486	431,613	359,398	181,005	202,150	2,107,947	155	13,599
1999–2000	181,485	127,728	514,030	374,795	182,511	105,443	214,921	1,700,913	158	10,765
2000–01	171,689	122,061	577,204	398,241	256,899	100,663	177,778	1,804,535	151	11,951
2001–02	198,369	119,781	566,284	330,434	249,190	173,757	171,278	1,809,093	148	12,224
2002–03	189,905	104,103	577,494	404,599	242,483	156,244	175,498	1,850,326	150	12,336
2003–04	162,738	117,967	624,732	347,964	292,521	156,780	167,401	1,870,103	149	12,551
2004–05	161,197	98,702	602,152	477,472	339,082	127,914	193,233	1,999,752	146	13,697
2005–06	188,876	107,456	654,570	388,339	286,225	163,449	177,723	1,966,638	160	12,291
2006–07	168,884	113,924	708,628	478,924	340,612	230,064	177,810	2,218,846	158	14,043
2007–08	175,195	99,528	704,300	356,404	276,903	142,780	256,210	2,011,320	152	13,232
2008–09	161,526	96,923	631,070	529,585	297,364	149,566	264,635	2,131,669	163	13,078
2009–10	147,078	100,476	613,113	335,426	288,604	144,918	254,806	1,884,421	151	12,480
2010–11	169,259	101,291	637,202	390,524	284,311	164,092	250,256	1,996,935	150	13,313
2011–12	155,858	92,267	640,700	391,214	250,666	194,971	262,064	1,987,740	151	13,164
2012–13	135,642	115,965	645,676	373,892	288,509	221,216	234,210	2,015,110	156	12,917
2013–14	144,709	75,903	668,242	346,706	254,084	156,630	243,350	1,889,624	149	12,682
2014–15	156,621	111,434	609,368	515,229	208,908	233,341	258,780	2,093,681	153	13,684
2015–16	134,914	94,855	755,187	397,217	235,433	227,262	253,793	2,098,661	149	14,085
2016–17	147,448	97,784	685,467	409,084	212,842	163,620	261,552	1,977,797	156	12,678

THE EMIRATES FA CUP 2016–17

PRELIMINARY AND QUALIFYING ROUNDS

EXTRA PRELIMINARY ROUND

Ashington v Nelson	1-2
Heaton Stannington v West Auckland T	2-3
Harrogate Railway Ath v Albion Sports	1-1, 3-0
Easington Colliery v Northallerton T	0-1
West Allotment Celtic v Consett	0-2
Shildon v Bedlington Terriers	6-1
Seaham Red Star v Morpeth T	1-3
Thornaby v Bishop Auckland	0-4
Liversedge v Guisborough T	2-5
North Shields v Jarrow Roofing Boldon CA	0-0, 2-0
Bridlington T v Silsden	1-1, 3-1
Newcastle Benfield v Thackley	2-0
Whitley Bay v Norton & Stockton Ancients	2-2, 1-2
Chester-le-Street T v Garforth T	3-0
Sunderland Ryhope CW v Pickering T	2-2, 3-3
aet; Pickering T won 2-1 on penalties.	
Padiham v Team Northumbria	1-0
Marske U v South Shields	3-1
Penrith v Sunderland RCA	1-0
Washington v Newton Aycliffe	2-2, 2-0
Durham C v Billingham Synthonia	0-4
Barnoldswick T v Dunston UTS	2-2, 0-4
Armthorpe Welfare v Handsworth Parramore	0-2
Maltby Main v Squires Gate	0-1
Penistone Church v Cheadle T	1-3
Alsager T v Barton T Old Boys	4-1
Pontefract Collieries v Runcorn T	3-2
Parkgate v Irlam	2-1
Maine Road v Nostell MW	3-3, 3-2
Congleton T v New Mills	3-0
West Didsbury & Chorlton v Liverpool	0-0, 1-0
Hemsworth MW v Runcorn Linnets	2-1
AFC Blackpool v Ashton Ath	0-1
Atherton Colleries v Bacup Bor	3-2
AFC Emley v Athersley Recreation	2-1
AFC Darwen v Cammell Laird 1907	3-3, 2-3
Abbey Hey v Bootle	1-3
1874 Northwich v Barnton	2-1
Worksop T v Hallam	4-2
Staveley MW v Winsford U	1-2
Lichfield C v Wolverhampton Casuals	0-0, 2-1
Haughmond v Alvechurch	0-2
AFC Bridgnorth v Boldmere St Michaels	0-3
Heath Hayes v Bromsgrove Sporting	0-3
Coleshill T v Cradley T	2-2, 4-1
Brocton v Walsall Wood	2-1
Lye T v Wulfrunians	3-2
Sporting Khalsa v Hanley T	1-1, 3-1
Tividale v Wolverhampton SC	2-1
Coventry Sphinx v Highgate U	0-5
Stourport Swifts v Westfields	3-4
Coventry U v Shawbury U	1-1
Tie abandoned 82 minutes and tie awarded to Coventry U – Shawbury U removed.	
Dudley Sports v Nuneaton Griff	1-1, 3-3
aet; Dudley Sports won 6-5 on penalties.	
Malvern T v Rocester	1-2
Brigg T v Clipstone	2-1
Oadby T v Long Eaton U	1-2
Loughborough University v Shirebrook T	4-4, 3-0
Bottesford T v Radford	1-0
South Normanton Ath v Aylestone Park	2-0
Shepshed Dynamo v AFC Mansfield	0-4
Hinckley v Heanor T	1-1, 1-5
aet; (1-1 at the end of normal time).	
Blaby & Whetstone Ath v St Andrews	2-0
Leicester Nirvana v Dunkirk	1-2
Anstey Nomads v Harborough T	1-3
Retford U v Leicester Road	1-1, 2-4
Ashby Ivanhoe v Quorn	4-3
Bardon Hill (withdrawn) v Kirby Muxloe (walkover)	
Rainworth MW v Cleethorpes T	1-3
Holbeach U v Swaffham T	4-1
Boston T v Wisbech T	1-4
Kirkley & Pakefield v Walsham Le Willows	0-0, 2-1
Peterborough Sports v Gorleston	8-0
Harrowby U v Thetford T	2-1
Yaxley v Huntingdon T	12-0
Ely C v Deeping Rangers	1-4
Fakenham T v Sleaford T	0-1
Godmanchester R v Great Yarmouth T	2-0
Eynesbury R v Peterborough Northern Star	3-1
Haverhill R v Hertford T	1-2
Redbridge v Waltham Forest	1-5
Brantham Ath v Hadley	0-1
Enfield 1893 v Tower Hamlets	2-4
FC Clacton v Eton Manor	3-5
Sporting Bengal U v Ipswich W	0-0, 2-0
Wivenhoe T v Hullbridge Sports	0-2
Barkingside v Hadleigh U	2-1
Whitton U v Basildon U	0-0, 0-5
London Bari v Clapton	1-3
Barking v Takeley	2-0
Sawbridgeworth T v Southend Manor	0-0, 2-2
aet; Sawbridgeworth T won 4-3 on penalties.	
Stanway R v Romania	1-0
Ilford v Burnham Ramblers	9-0
FC Broxbourne Bor v Felixstowe & Walton U	1-5
Halstead T v Newmarket T	A-A, 2-1
First match abandoned due to serious injury to Newmarket T player Matt Hayden.	
St Margaretsbury v Long Melford	2-5
Hoddesdon T v Stansted	1-0
Saffron Walden T v Mildenhall T	1-0
Edgware T v Holmer Green	5-1
Flackwell Heath v Baldock T	6-3
Crawley Green v Rothwell Corinthians	2-1
London Tigers v Sun Sports	1-1, 0-2
Leighton T v Northampton Sileby Rangers	1-2
Tring Ath v Desborough T	0-1
Wellingborough T v Stotfold	1-3
Burnham v Oxhey Jets	0-2
Cogenhoe U v Berkhamsted	1-0
Bedford v Welwyn Garden C	1-2
Cockfosters v Harpenden T	1-2
Newport Pagnell T v Biggleswade U	0-1
Wembley v Daventry T	4-0
Harefield U v Northampton On Chenecks	1-1, 1-1
aet; Harefield U won 9-8 on penalties.	
Leverstock Green v London Colney	1-2
Ascot U v Milton U	2-0
Abingdon U v Hayes	0-0, 1-6
Thame U v Abbey Rangers	3-0
Binfield v North Greenford U	0-1
Thatcham T v Bracknell T	2-3
Spelthorne Sports v Hartley Wintney	4-3
Carterton v Highmoor Ibis	1-2
Camberley T v Cove	6-1
Chertsey T v Hook Norton	2-0
Brimscombe & Thrupp v Henley T	3-1
Longlevens v Bedfont & Feltham	4-2
Bedfont Sports v Windsor	3-2
Ardley U v Tuffley R	3-2
Highworth T v Tadley Calleva	2-1
Andover T v Royal Wootton Bassett T	5-2
Hanworth Villa v Knaphill	2-2, 3-2
Fairford T v CB Hounslow U	1-5
Horsham YMCA v Hollands & Blair	2-3
Sevenoaks T v Sporting Club Thamesmead	2-1
Holmesdale v Haywards Heath T	0-2
Chessington & Hook U v Wick	3-1
Littlehampton T v Pagham	1-3
Hailsham T v Crawley Down Gatwick	5-7
Beckenham T v Lancing	1-1, 4-3
Colliers Wood U v Croydon Ath	5-2
Croydon v Uckfield T	2-1
Epsom & Ewell v Gravesham Bor	5-2
Erith & Belvedere v Loxwood	0-1
Deal T v Banstead Ath	0-1
Peacehaven & Telscombe v Lordswood	3-3, 3-1
Tunbridge Wells v Eastbourne U	1-1, 1-2
Newhaven v Rochester U	0-0, 4-1
Mile Oak v Guildford C	0-3
Bridon Ropes v Canterbury C	0-3
Raynes Park Vale v Eastbourne T	0-2

Worthing U v Shoreham 0-3
East Preston v Horley T 4-1
Whitstable T v Oakwood 4-0
Southwick v Cray Valley (PM) 0-4
Crowborough Ath v Farnham T 1-3
Redhill v St Francis Rangers 4-1
Sheppey U v Badshot Lea 0-1
Ashford U v Corinthian 2-0
Erith T v Sutton Common R 2-2, 2-0
Westfield v Walton & Hersham 0-1
Arundel v Chichester C 4-3
Moneyfields v Christchurch 4-3
Sholing v Bournemouth 4-1
Bemerton Heath Harlequins v Keynsham T 1-0
Cadbury Heath v Folland Sports 7-0
Hengrove Ath v Verwood T 2-2, 1-3
Oldland Abbotonians v Newport (IW) 1-0
Lydney T v Team Solent 0-6
Lymington T v Hamworthy U 0-0, 0-1
Bradford T v Fareham T 1-3
Whitchurch U v Cribbs 0-0, 1-0
Brockenhurst v Laverstock & Ford 2-1
United Services Portsmouth v Melksham T 2-1
Odd Down v Longwell Green Sports 2-0
Sherborne T v Amesbury T 0-2
Bashley v Horndean 2-1
Cowes Sports v Brislington 0-3
Fawley v AFC Portchester 0-3
Bridport v Alresford T 1-2
Blackfield & Langley v Hallen 2-0
Bristol Manor Farm v Gillingham T 1-1, 3-4
Welton R v Bitton 0-2
AFC St Austell v Street 2-2, 0-3
Clevedon T v Ashton & Backwell U 2-1
Wells C v Portishead T 2-2, 1-2
Shepton Mallet v Willand R 1-1, 2-0
Buckland Ath v Plymouth Parkway 2-3
Bodmin T v Cheddar 2-2, 3-2
aet; (1-1 at the end of normal time).

PRELIMINARY ROUND
Harrogate Railway Ath v Norton & Stockton Ancients 3-1
Billingham Synthonia v Northallerton T 6-0
Dunston UTS v Penrith 3-3, 2-1
Shildon v Kendal T 2-0
Padiham v Newcastle Benfield 1-2
Nelson v Bishop Auckland 1-4
Chester-le-Street T v Marske U 0-4
West Auckland T v Lancaster C 1-5
Clitheroe v Consett 0-1
Guisborough T v Bridlington T 2-3
Washington v Pickering T 2-2, 2-1
Tadcaster Alb v Scarborough Ath 3-2
North Shields v Morpeth T 0-1
Droylsden v Radcliffe Bor 4-4, 1-2
Prescot Cables v Trafford 0-1
Handsworth Parramore v Stocksbridge Park Steels 4-1
Congleton T v Farsley Celtic 0-6
Alsager T v Winsford U 1-6
Ramsbottom U v Sheffield 1-2
Worksop T v Ashton Ath 2-2, 2-2
aet; Ashton Ath won 4-1 on penalties.
Parkgate v Burscough 1-4
Ossett T v Goole 2-1
West Didsbury & Chorlton v Squires Gate 2-3
Atherton Collieries v Witton Alb 1-3
Mossley v Hemsworth MW 4-0
Hyde U v Cammell Laird 1907 4-0
Glossop North End v Brighouse T 2-2, 2-4
Maine Road v AFC Emley 3-2
Shaw Lane Association v Colwyn Bay 0-1
Colne v 1874 Northwich 2-2, 3-1
Northwich Vic v Cheadle T 2-4
Bamber Bridge v Ossett Alb 2-5
Pontefract Collieries v Bootle 2-1
Coleshill T v Dudley Sports 4-0
Bedworth U v Rocester 3-2
Kidsgrove Ath v Lye T 2-0
Coventry U v Lichfield C 5-1
Hereford v Alvechurch 4-2
Rugby T v Bromsgrove Sporting 1-0
Leek T v Newcastle T 3-2
Highgate U v Boldmere St Michaels 1-0
Market Drayton T v Evesham U 0-2
Sporting Khalsa v Romulus 1-2
Chasetown v Brocton 9-0
Westfields v Tividale 5-1
Dunkirk v Cleethorpes T 2-0
Heanor T v Long Eaton U 3-2
Lincoln U v Carlton T 2-1
Loughborough Dynamo v Ashby Ivanhoe 1-3
Basford U v Belper T 2-4
AFC Mansfield v South Normanton Ath 2-0
Brigg T v Blaby & Whetstone Ath 2-1
Leicester Road v Harborough T 3-1
Bottesford T v Kirby Muxloe 1-2
Loughborough University v Gresley 1-4
Sleaford T v Stamford 0-3
Yaxley v Dereham T 4-4, 0-1
Soham Town Rangers v Harrowby U 4-1
Kirkley & Pakefield v Holbeach U 3-4
Deeping Rangers v Wroxham 2-1
Wisbech T v Peterborough Sports 1-4
Norwich U v Histon 1-2
Eynesbury R v Godmanchester R 1-1, 3-1
Bury T v Spalding U 0-3
Ware v Maldon & Tiptree 0-2
Thurrock v Halstead T 2-3
Witham T v Eton Manor 3-0
Waltham Forest v Hoddesdon T 4-0
Haringey Bor v Barkingside 7-2
Waltham Abbey v Bowers & Pitsea 2-2, 4-2
Brentwood T v Tilbury 1-2
Sporting Bengal U v Clapton 2-0
Long Melford v Saffron Walden T 0-2
Romford v Hullbridge Sports 4-3
Barking v Stanway R 0-0, 2-3
Ilford v Felixstowe & Walton U 0-2
Brightlingsea Regent v Great Wakering R 2-1
Sawbridgeworth T v Tower Hamlets 4-2
Aveley v Hornchurch 0-1
Hertford T v Hadley 0-1
Royston T v Heybridge Swifts 1-4
Cheshunt v Basildon U 8-0
Kempston R v Oxhey Jets 1-0
Stotfold v Welwyn Garden C 3-2
Crawley Green v Uxbridge 0-3
Bedford T v AFC Dunstable 1-2
Sun Sports v Northwood 2-0
Arlesey T v Potters Bar T 1-1, 1-4
AFC Rushden & Diamonds v Northampton Sileby Rangers 4-3
Desborough T v London Colney 0-1
Chalfont St Peter v Harpenden T 2-0
Edgware T v Barton R 1-3
Aylesbury U v Biggleswade U 0-1
Cogenhoe U v Flackwell Heath 1-5
Beaconsfield SYCOB v Marlow 2-2, 3-3
aet; Beaconsfield SYCOB won 4-3 on penalties.
Aylesbury v Hanwell T 1-3
Wembley v Harefield U 1-1, 1-2
Bishop's Cleeve v Camberley T 1-1, 0-2
Highmoor Ibis v Brimscombe & Thrupp 1-2
Thame U v North Leigh 1-7
Wantage T v Hanworth Villa 4-2
North Greenford U v Kidlington 4-1
CB Hounslow U v Petersfield T 2-1
Egham T v Bracknell T 2-1
Spelthorne Sports v Andover T 2-3
Farnborough v Longlevens 5-1
Ascot U v Didcot T 4-3
Slimbridge v Bedfont Sports 3-0
Chertsey T v Hayes 3-0
Yate T v Fleet T 1-2
Shortwood U v Ashford T (Middlesex) 0-2
Ardley U v Highworth T 0-3
Canterbury C v Pagham 1-1, 1-2
aet; (1-1 at the end of normal time)
Cray Valley (PM) v Hastings U 0-2
Shoreham v Dorking W 3-4
Greenwich Bor v Walton & Hersham 1-1, 3-0
Hollands & Blair v Whyteleafe 1-1, 2-4
Peacehaven & Telscombe v Haywards Heath T 2-0
Redhill v Lewes 1-6
Badshot Lea v Cray W 0-4
Crawley Down Gatwick v Corinthian Casuals 2-3

Loxwood v Arundel 0-2
Carshalton Ath v Farnham T 3-0
Whitstable T v Eastbourne T 0-0, 1-1
aet; Eastbourne T won 3-1 on penalties.
Chipstead v Beckenham T 2-1
South Park v Phoenix Sports 2-0
Eastbourne U v Newhaven 2-2, 2-1
Ashford U v Three Bridges 1-0
Herne Bay v East Grinstead T 1-0
Molesey v Godalming T 0-2
Faversham T v Epsom & Ewell 2-1
VCD Ath v Croydon 0-0, 2-1
Sevenoaks T v Horsham 4-2
Tooting & Mitcham U v East Preston 0-1
Guernsey v Thamesmead T 2-2, 1-1
aet; Thamesmead T won 4-2 on penalties.
Walton Casuals v Chatham T 3-3, 2-1
Ramsgate v Erith T 1-0
Banstead Ath v Colliers Wood U 3-3, 0-3
Sittingbourne v Hythe T 1-1, 0-5
Guildford C v Chessington & Hook U 1-1, 2-1
Gillingham T v Totton 2-0
Bashley v Sholing 1-2
Amesbury T v Bemerton Heath Harlequins 1-3
Blackfield & Langley v Paulton R 1-2
Cadbury Heath v Team Solent 4-1
AFC Portchester v Mangotsfield U 2-0
Whitchurch U v Moneyfields 0-3
Wimborne T v Alresford T 1-1, 0-1
aet; (0-0 at the end of normal time).
United Services Portsmouth v Winchester C 0-3
Verwood T v Fareham T 2-2, 0-4
Swindon Supermarine v Odd Down 5-1
Oldland Abbotonians v Brislington 2-3
Hamworthy U v Brockenhurst 2-1
Salisbury v Bitton 5-0
Street v Larkhall Ath 4-2
Bideford v Bodmin T 1-1, 2-1
Taunton T v Tiverton T 4-4, 2-0
Bridgwater T v Plymouth Parkway 0-6
Portishead T v Shepton Mallet 2-0
Clevedon T v Barnstaple T 0-1

FIRST QUALIFYING ROUND
Washington v Shildon 2-5
Ashton U v Nantwich T 0-3
Brighouse T v Lancaster C 0-3
Blyth Spartans v Frickley Ath 3-1
Hyde U v Colne 1-0
Bishop Auckland v Ossett Alb 5-1
Whitby T v Winsford U 3-3, 2-1
Sheffield v Farsley Celtic 0-3
Marske U v Marine 0-2
Newcastle Benfield v Bridlington T 0-2
Morpeth T v Colwyn Bay 4-1
Harrogate Railway Ath v Consett 0-5
Dunston UTS v Skelmersdale U 2-2, 2-1
Ashton Ath v Mossley 7-2
Squires Gate v Handsworth Parramore 2-5
Witton Alb v Buxton 3-0
Billingham Synthonia v Ossett T 2-2, 2-3
Pontefract Collieries v Tadcaster Alb 2-3
Burscough v Maine Road 4-3
Trafford v Cheadle T 5-2
Workington v Warrington T 3-0
Radcliffe Bor v Spennymoor T 3-5
Leek T v Kettering T 2-3
Hednesford T v Belper T 1-2
King's Lynn T v Brigg T 6-1
AFC Mansfield v Stratford T 2-1
Rushall Olympic v Soham Town Rangers 2-2, 1-0
Matlock T v Heanor T 4-2
Chasetown v Grantham T 1-1, 2-2
aet; Chasetown won 6-5 on penalties.
Evesham U v Barwell 2-2, 0-2
Peterborough Sports v Stourbridge 1-3
Ashby Ivanhoe v Ilkeston 0-6
St Neots T v Stamford 1-1, 1-4
Westfields v St Ives T 4-0
Lincoln U v Dunkirk 6-1
Halesowen T v Coleshill T 3-0
Highgate U v Leamington 3-1
Leicester Road v Kirby Muxloe 0-0, 2-3
aet; (2-2 at the end of normal time).

Coalville T v Redditch U 2-1
Coventry U v Bedworth U 0-2
Mickleover Sports v Spalding U 3-2
Deeping Rangers v Gresley 2-6
Romulus v Hereford 1-1, 0-3
Rugby T v Corby T 1-0
Dereham T v Holbeach U 2-1
Eynesbury R v Sutton Coldfield T 1-3
Stafford Rangers v Kidsgrove Ath 1-2
Brightlingsea Regent v Billericay T 1-2
Hadley v London Colney 1-0
Haringey Bor v Witham T 0-3
Kempston R v Harefield U 3-2
Hanwell T v Enfield T 1-0
Sun Sports v Hayes & Yeading U 0-2
Hendon v Cheshunt 5-2
Maldon & Tiptree v Biggleswade T 0-1
Heybridge Swifts v AFC Dunstable 2-2, 1-2
Chesham U v Saffron Walden T 5-0
Harrow Bor v Sawbridgeworth T 4-1
AFC Sudbury v Halstead T 6-0
Kings Langley v Sporting Bengal U 6-1
Felixstowe & Walton U v Tilbury 2-1
Chalfont St Peter v Potters Bar T 0-3
Uxbridge v Needham Market 2-0
Cambridge C v Flackwell Heath 3-1
Harlow T v Romford 3-1
Stanway R v Barton R 0-1
Canvey Island v Dunstable T 2-1
Hitchin T v Biggleswade U 4-2
Leiston v Grays Ath 4-1
Waltham Forest v Stotfold 2-1
AFC Rushden & Diamonds v Hornchurch 2-0
Lowestoft T v Histon 0-2
Waltham Abbey v Wingate & Finchley 0-5
Colliers Wood U v Eastbourne T 2-0
Hythe T v Leatherhead 1-0
East Preston v Merstham 1-4
Camberley T v Hastings U 0-2
South Park v Dorking W 2-1
Walton Casuals v Greenwich Bor 3-2
Burgess Hill T v Ashford U 2-1
Fleet T v Slimbridge 1-1, 0-1
aet; (0-0 at the end of normal time).
Andover T v Farnborough 0-5
Brimscombe & Thrupp v Peacehaven & Telscombe 3-0
Staines T v Godalming T 4-0
CB Hounslow U v Metropolitan Police 1-3
Herne Bay v Ashford T (Middlesex) 3-1
Eastbourne U v Highworth T 0-3
Faversham T v Cray W 1-0
Pagham v Dulwich Hamlet 0-3
Ascot U v Tonbridge Angels 2-2, 0-7
Arundel v Egham T 1-5
Worthing v Carshalton Ath 3-3, 6-2
Lewes v Sevenoaks T 0-0, 1-2
Wantage T v Beaconsfield SYCOB 1-1, 1-6
VCD Ath v Kingstonian 4-1
Slough T v Chipstead 6-1
Thamesmead T v Chertsey T 1-0
Corinthian Casuals v North Leigh 2-3
Folkestone Invicta v North Greenford U 3-1
Bognor Regis T v Guildford C 5-1
Ramsgate v Whyteleafe 1-2
Taunton T v Cinderford T 2-0
Alresford T v Fareham T 1-1, 4-2
Barnstaple T v Merthyr T 0-4
Weymouth v Paulton R A-A, 2-1
First match abandoned after 50 minutes due to waterlogged pitch, 1-1.
Winchester C v Street 4-2
Sholing v Havant & Waterlooville 0-2
Salisbury v Frome T 2-0
Portishead T v Swindon Supermarine 1-4
Gillingham T v Cirencester T 0-2
Cadbury Heath v Plymouth Parkway 3-0
Chippenham T v Moneyfields 9-0
Basingstoke T v Bemerton Heath Harlequins 4-0
Dorchester T v Banbury U 0-3
Bideford v AFC Portchester 1-2
Brislington v Hamworthy U 5-2

SECOND QUALIFYING ROUND

Bridlington T v Harrogate T 1-1, 2-3
Handsworth Parramore v Burscough 2-0
Witton Alb v Stalybridge Celtic 1-1, 1-2
Blyth Spartans v Morpeth T 2-4
Bishop Auckland v Trafford 1-0
Nantwich T v Marine 2-2, 3-2
Ashton Ath v FC Halifax T 0-5
Curzon Ashton v Consett 1-1, 1-0
Altrincham v Gainsborough Trinity 3-2
Kidsgrove Ath v Matlock T 1-2
Lancaster C v Darlington 1883 2-1
Alfreton T v Fylde 1-0
Tadcaster Alb v Farsley Celtic 0-2
Bradford (Park Avenue) v Salford C 0-1
Workington v Shildon 3-1
Dunston UTS v Chorley 0-2
Stockport Co v Hyde U 2-0
Ossett T v FC United of Manchester 1-7
Spennymoor T v Whitby T 1-0
Rushall Olympic v Kettering T 1-2
Kirby Muxloe v Boston U 1-2
Sutton Coldfield T v Hereford 2-3
Brackley T v Rugby T 6-0
Coalville T v AFC Mansfield 0-1
Mickleover Sports v Stourbridge 1-2
Westfields v Highgate U 4-2
Kidderminster H v Tamworth 4-0
Nuneaton T v Lincoln U 1-2
Halesowen T v Belper T 1-0
Gresley v Stamford 1-1, 0-1
Barwell v Ilkeston 0-1
Chasetown v Bedworth U 0-1
Worcester C v Telford U 0-0, 3-1
Sevenoaks T v Chesham U 2-2, 1-2
Concord Rangers v AFC Rushden & Diamonds 1-3
Beaconsfield SYCOB v Witham T 3-1
Egham T v VCD Ath 2-1
Dulwich Hamlet v Hendon 0-2
Hythe T v Walton Casuals 2-4
Dereham T v St Albans C 1-2
Wingate & Finchley v Tonbridge Angels 0-3
AFC Dunstable v Hampton & Richmond Bor 1-7
Wealdstone v Histon 4-0
Chelmsford C v Dartford 2-3
Staines T v Maidenhead U 1-0
Hayes & Yeading U v Worthing 0-2
Hemel Hempstead T v Herne Bay 1-1, 5-1
Eastbourne Bor v Metropolitan Police 2-1
Kempston R v Burgess Hill T 1-1, 1-3
South Park v Leiston 1-4
Hadley v Kings Langley 2-1
Ebbsfleet U v AFC Sudbury 5-0
Felixstowe & Walton U v Bishop's Stortford 2-1
Cambridge C v Slough T 1-3
Folkestone Invicta v Waltham Forest 3-1
Uxbridge v Harrow Bor 1-2
East Thurrock U v Whitehawk 2-3
Canvey Island v Potters Bar T 2-2, 2-3
Whyteleafe v Welling U 0-2
King's Lynn T v Harlow T 1-0
Billericay T v Bognor Regis T 2-1
Faversham T v Hitchin T 2-2, 1-0
Hanwell T v Thamesmead T 1-1, 2-4
aet; (2-2 at the end of normal time).
Merstham v Colliers Wood U 0-0, 2-1
aet; (1-1 at the end of normal time).
Margate v Biggleswade T 2-0
Barton R v Hastings U 0-1
Swindon Supermarine v Farnborough 1-0
Winchester C v Truro C 4-0
Havant & Waterlooville v Highworth T 5-1
Alresford T v Cadbury Heath 1-3
Chippenham T v Poole T 4-1
Salisbury v Gloucester C 1-2
Cirencester T v Banbury U 1-6
Basingstoke T v Hungerford T 0-1
Weymouth v Gosport Bor 3-2
AFC Portchester v Merthyr T 0-2
Taunton T v Slimbridge 2-0
Brislington v Brimscombe & Thrupp 1-2
Bath C v Oxford C 1-1, 2-1
aet; (1-1 at the end of normal time).
North Leigh v Weston-super-Mare 2-1

THIRD QUALIFYING ROUND

Halesowen T v Nantwich T 1-1, 1-2
Kettering T v Boston U 2-0
Lincoln U v Handsworth Parramore 3-1
Farsley Celtic v Bishop Auckland 0-1
FC Halifax T v Stalybridge Celtic 2-1
Worcester C v Brackley T 0-3
King's Lynn T v Alfreton T 0-2
Curzon Ashton v Bedworth U 4-0
Ilkeston v Stourbridge 1-2
Lancaster C v Kidderminster H 2-3
Matlock T v Workington 1-1, 3-1
Stockport Co v Salford C 2-0
Spennymoor T v Chorley 1-0
FC United of Manchester v Harrogate T 3-3, 0-2
Altrincham v Morpeth T 3-0
AFC Mansfield v Stamford 1-2
Faversham T v Egham T 1-1, 0-1
North Leigh v Folkestone Invicta 3-1
Ebbsfleet U v Havant & Waterlooville 7-0
Hungerford T v Leiston 1-4
Potters Bar T v Bath C 0-0, 1-1
aet; Potters Bar T won 4-3 on penalties.
Hendon v AFC Rushden & Diamonds 3-0
Margate v Hastings U 2-2, 2-1
aet; (1-1 at the end of normal time).
Taunton T v Hampton & Richmond Bor 2-1
Weymouth v Brimscombe & Thrupp 6-0
St Albans C v Worthing 6-0
Wealdstone v Banbury U 2-1
Tonbridge Angels v Hereford 4-2
Beaconsfield SYCOB v Felixstowe & Walton U 3-0
Whitehawk v Merthyr T 2-0
Chesham U v Staines T 2-0
Burgess Hill T v Cadbury Heath 6-1
Slough T v Dartford 2-3
Billericay T v Chippenham T 3-2
Welling U v Swindon Supermarine 7-1
Gloucester C v Hemel Hempstead T 2-2, 0-2
Westfields v Walton Casuals 4-0
Eastbourne Bor v Hadley 0-0, 4-1
Merstham v Thamesmead T 5-1
Harrow Bor v Winchester C 2-1

FOURTH QUALIFYING ROUND

Southport v Chester FC 1-0
Alfreton T v Gateshead 2-2, 3-2
aet; (2-2 at the end of normal time).
North Ferriby U v Macclesfield T 1-4
Harrogate T v FC Halifax T 0-2
Stockport Co v Bishop Auckland 2-0
Barrow v Tranmere R 2-1
Nantwich T v Stourbridge 1-3
Altrincham v Matlock T 3-1
Lincoln C v Guiseley 0-0, 2-1
Lincoln U v Spennymoor T 0-3
Stamford v Wrexham 1-1, 3-2
aet; (2-2 at the end of normal time).
York C v Curzon Ashton 1-1, 1-2
Welling U v Whitehawk 0-1
Westfields v Leiston 2-1
Sutton U v Forest Green R 2-1
Chesham U v Potters Bar T 1-0
Dagenham & Redbridge v Wealdstone 3-1
Torquay U v Woking 1-1, 1-2
Taunton T v Hemel Hempstead T 0-0, 1-0
Braintree T v Bromley 4-2
Beaconsfield SYCOB v Brackley T 0-5
Tonbridge Angels v Dartford 0-3
Egham T v St Albans C 0-1
Boreham Wood v Hendon 3-0
Aldershot T v Eastbourne Bor 1-2
Harrow Bor v Margate 2-2, 3-1
Maidstone U v Billericay T 3-1
Kidderminster H v Weymouth 6-0
Solihull Moors v Kettering T 3-1
Burgess Hill T v Dover Ath 0-5
Merstham v Ebbsfleet U 2-1
Eastleigh v North Leigh 6-0

THE EMIRATES FA CUP 2016–17

COMPETITION PROPER

▪ *Denotes player sent off.*

FIRST ROUND

Friday, 4 November 2016

Eastleigh (0) 1 *(Mandron 64)*

Swindon T (0) 1 *(Doughty 69 (pen))* 3312

Eastleigh: (442) Clarke; Pipe (Obileye 79), Essam, Johnson, Green; Howells, Drury, Taylor, Coulson; Mandron (Wilson 88), Constable.
Swindon T: (3142) Vigouroux; Branco, Thompson N (Goddard 27), Jones; Kasim; Barry, Murray (Stewart 83), Doughty, Ormonde-Ottewill; Delfouneso, Norris.
Referee: Oliver Langford.

Millwall (0) 1 *(Romeo 88)*

Southend U (0) 0 4502

Millwall: (442) Archer; Craig, Webster, Hutchinson, Romeo; Ferguson (Worrall 76), Williams, Thompson (Butcher 46), Onyedinma; Morison (Gregory 43), O'Brien.
Southend U: (442) Oxley; Coker, Inniss (Sokolik 81), Thompson, Demetriou; McLaughlin (McGlashan 73), Leonard, Wordsworth, Atkinson; Cox, Fortune.
Referee: James Linington.

Saturday, 5 November 2016

Bolton W (1) 1 *(Trotter 20)*

Grimsby T (0) 0 6649

Bolton W: (4231) Howard; Wilson, Wheater, Beevers, Taylor A; Trotter, Perry (Moxey 85); Ameobi, Taylor C (Henry 75), Clough; Proctor (Anderson 66).
Grimsby T: (4141) McKeown; Mills, Gowling, Collins, Andrew; Disley; Berrett (Browne 79), Summerfield, Comley (Bolarinwa 75), Bogle (Jackson 84); Vernon.
Referee: Trevor Kettle.

Bradford C (0) 1 *(Conneely 72 (og))*

Accrington S (1) 2 *(Boco 30, Clark 80)* 4985

Bradford C: (442) Doyle; Darby, McArdle, Clarke N, Kilgallon; Marshall (Clarke B 62), Dieng, Devine, Morais (Law 63); Vuckic (Hiwula 46), James Hanson.
Accrington S: (4411) Parish; Lacey, Hughes, Beckles, Pearson; Boco, Conneely, Brown, McConville; Clark (McCartan 85 (Hewitt 90)); Gornell.
Referee: Graham Salisbury.

Braintree T (3) 7 *(Patterson 6, Elokobi 11, 83, Muldoon 21, Barnard 68, 74 (pen), Akinola 88)*

Eastbourne Bor (0) 0 645

Braintree T: (442) Beasant; Okimo, Elokobi, Goodman, Clohessy; Akinola, Lee, Muldoon (Hall-Johnson 80), Patterson (Matthews 62); Cheek (Midson 72), Barnard.
Eastbourne Bor: (541) Carey; Smith, O'Reilly, Khinda-John, Stone, Hare; McCallum, Dutton (Tate 85), Hughes (Baptista 67), Taylor (Pinney 59); Romain.
Referee: Stephen Ross.

Bury (2) 2 *(Hope 27, 29)*

AFC Wimbledon (0) 2 *(Taylor 61, Elliott 67)* 2346

Bury: (442) Williams; Danns, Kay, Soares, Leigh; Ismail (Miller G 85), Tutte, Mellis, Walker; Hope, Vaughan.
AFC Wimbledon: (442) Shea; Fuller, Robinson, Robertson, Meades; Francomb (Whelpdale 64), Reeves, Beere (Parrett 64), Barcham; Barnett (Elliott 55), Taylor.
Referee: Jeremy Simpson.

Cambridge U (1) 1 *(Mingoia 38)*

Dover Ath (0) 1 *(Miller 82)* 2620

Cambridge U: (433) Norris; Halliday, Legge, Roberts, Taylor; Dunne (Pigott 84), Clark (Williamson 68), Berry; Mingoia, Ikpeazu, Dunk (Elito 68).
Dover Ath: (541) Walker; Magri, Sterling, Parkinson, Grimes, Thomas (Orlu 75); Miller, Kinnear, Stevenson, Modeste (Emmanuel 74); Lafayette.
Referee: Nicholas Kinsley.

Charlton Ath (2) 3 *(Lookman 34, 83, Jackson 40)*

Scunthorpe U (0) 1 *(Hopper 52)* 4123

Charlton Ath: (442) Rudd; Foley, Bauer, Konsa, Fox; Holmes (Lookman 27), Ulvestad, Crofts, Jackson (Botaka 89); Magennis, Ajose (Novak 73).
Scunthorpe U: (442) Daniels; Wiseman, Goode, Wallace, Townsend; Holmes (Williams 68), Smallwood (Mantom 77), Dawson, Morris; Madden (Hopper 42), van Veen.
Referee: Christopher Sarginson.

Cheltenham T (0) 1 *(Waters 58)*

Crewe Alex (0) 1 *(Jones 73)* 2880

Cheltenham T: (352) Griffiths; Dickie, Downes, Parslow; Barthram (Munns 46), Storer▪, Dayton (Whitehead 88), Pell, Cranston; Wright (Morgan-Smith 88), Waters.
Crewe Alex: (442) Garratt; Turton (Ng 65), Davis, Guthrie, Bakayogo; Cooper, Jones, Hollands, Kiwomya; Dagnall (Udoh 46), Lowe.
Referee: Michael Salisbury.

Colchester U (0) 1 *(Fosu 46)*

Chesterfield (1) 2 *(O'Shea 23, Evans 50)* 1840

Colchester U: (4411) Walker; Brindley, Eastman, Prosser, Wynter (Dunne 89); Vincent-Young (Fosu 46), Slater, Guthrie, Drey Wright; Szmodics (Bonne 79); Johnstone.
Chesterfield: (3412) Fulton; Liddle, Evatt, Anderson; Ariyibi, Dimaio, O'Neil (Nolan 67), Donohue; O'Shea; Evans, Dennis (Graham 81).
Referee: Lee Probert.

Crawley T (1) 1 *(Clifford 35)*

Bristol R (1) 1 *(Brown 15)* 2281

Crawley T: (4231) Morris; Young, Connolly, Davey, Blackman▪; Smith, Djalo; Boldewijn (Yussuf 46), Clifford, Bawling (Tajbakhsh 86); Collins (Harrold 89).
Bristol R: (41212) Roos; Roberts, Lockyer, Hartley, Brown; Clarke O; Sinclair (Moore 61), Boateng; Easter (James 73); Harrison, Taylor (Montano 60).
Referee: Darren Deadman.

Dagenham & R (0) 0

FC Halifax T (0) 0 1387

Dagenham & R: (4231) Cousins; Widdowson, Doe, Staunton, Raymond; Boucaud, Robinson; Whitely, Guttridge (Benson 84), Maguire-Drew (Ling 74); Hawkins.
FC Halifax T: (442) Drench; Roberts, Hotte, Garner, Wilde; MacDonald, King, Lynch, Simmons; Denton, Sinnott (Hibbs 76).
Referee: Neil Hair.

Dartford (2) 3 *(Bradbrook 5, 17 (pen), Ofori-Acheampong 51)*

Sutton U (3) 6 *(Biamou 1, 23, Deacon 15, 71, Stearn 58, 90)* 1689

Dartford: (442) Ibrahim; Harris, Gardiner, Brown A, Wynter (Wood 79); Hayes, Bonner, Bradbrook, Wanadio (Noble 84); Pugh, Ofori-Acheampong (Brown E 83).
Sutton U: (442) Worner; Amankwaah, Stearn, Eastmond, Collins; Bailey, Fitchett (Dickson 82), McLennan (Spence 59), Downer; Biamou (Burge 74), Deacon.
Referee: Samuel Allison.

Exeter C (1) 1 *(Reid 39)*

Luton T (1) 3 *(Hylton 11 (pen), 86 (pen), Rea 71)* 2972

Exeter C: (442) Olejnik; Sweeney, Ampadu (Oakley 87), Moore-Taylor, Woodman; Wheeler (Archibald-Henville 82), Stacey, Taylor, Holmes; Simpson (Grant 67), Reid.
Luton T: (4231) Walton; Justin (O'Donnell 87), Rea, Cuthbert, Sheehan; Lee, McGeehan; Gilliead (Smith 62), Ruddock▪, Cook (Mackail-Smith 70); Hylton.
Referee: John Busby.

Gillingham (2) 2 *(Nouble 28, 45)*
Brackley T (2) 2 *(Gudger 13, Armson 27)* 2410
Gillingham: (433) Nelson; Osadebe, Ehmer, Oshilaja, Konchesky; Hessenthaler, Wright, Knott; Emmanuel-Thomas, McDonald (Donnelly 81), Nouble (List 56).
Brackley T: (442) Walker L; Myles, Graham, Dean, Gudger; Walker A, Armson, Byrne, Walker G; Ndlovu (Pitt 90), Diggin (Moyo 78).
Referee: Brendan Malone.

Lincoln C (1) 2 *(Raggett 21, Power 59)*
Altrincham (0) 1 *(Cyrus 75)* 3529
Lincoln C: (442) Farman; Wood, Waterfall, Raggett, Habergham; Anderson, Power, Woodyard, Arnold; Robinson (Muldoon 57), Rhead (Hawkridge 73).
Altrincham: (451) Dawber; Obeng (Marsh 65), Cyrus, Hannigan, McWilliams; Lawrie, Moult (Patterson 46), Lenighan (Richman 64), Wilkinson, Miller; Reeves.
Referee: Steven Rushton.

Mansfield T (0) 1 *(Hemmings 58)*
Plymouth Arg (1) 2 *(Slew 14, Fox 80)* 2318
Mansfield T: (4231) Jensen; Bennett, Pearce, Collins (Rose D 88), Benning; McGuire, Clements; Rose M (Thomas 73), Baxendale (Henderson 81), Hemmings; Green.
Plymouth Arg: (4231) McCormick; Miller, Bulvitis, Bradley, Purrington; Songo'o, Fox; Carey, Tanner (Donaldson 61), Slew (Ijaha 83); Spencer.
Referee: Dean Whitestone.

Merstham (0) 0
Oxford U (2) 5 *(MacDonald 12, Ruffels 45, Hemmings 62, 90, Roberts T 63)* 1920
Merstham: (4411) Wilson; Abnett, Okoye, Douglas, Campbell; Addai, Kavanagh, Samuels (Folkes 54), Hall (Hector 53); Vidal (Henriques 65); Bennett.
Oxford U: (41212) Eastwood; Sercombe, Martin, Dunkley, Johnson; Ledson; Roberts T (Rothwell 69), MacDonald; Ruffels; Hemmings, Taylor.
Referee: John Brooks.

Milton Keynes D (3) 3 *(Reeves 8, Thomas-Asante 12, Agard 14)*
Spennymoor T (1) 2 *(Tait 19, Johnson 84)* 4099
Milton Keynes D: (4231) Nicholls; George B Williams, Hendry, Walsh, Lewington; Upson, Reeves; Agard, Bowditch, Thomas-Asante (Colclough 70); Maynard (Tshimanga 70).
Spennymoor T: (451) Lowson; Griffiths, Tait, Curtis, Mason; Ramshaw (Johnson 63), Chandler, Henry, Gott, Anderson (Mitchell 77); Armstrong (Dowson 64).
Referee: Constantine Hatzidakis.

Northampton T (2) 6 *(Anderson 6, Richards 11, 54, O'Toole 70, Taylor M 82, Hooper 90)*
Harrow Bor (0) 0 3406
Northampton T: (4231) Smith A; Moloney, Diamond, Zakuani, Buchanan; McCourt (O'Toole 47), Taylor M; Anderson P (Potter 81), Hoskins, Hooper; Richards (Revell 66).
Harrow Bor: (442) Williams; Ochoa, Peacock, Preddie, Bryan; Nicholas, Webb, Newman (Meite 60), Driver (Turl 74); Charles-Smith (Babalola 75), Holland.
Referee: Ross Joyce.

Oldham Ath (1) 2 *(Flynn 45, McKay 53)*
Doncaster R (0) 1 *(Mandeville 90 (pen))* 2984
Oldham Ath: (442) Ripley; Dummigan, Clarke, Burgess, Dunne; McLaughlin, Banks, Green (Fane 29), Winchester (Flynn 9); McKay, Erwin (Law 77).
Doncaster R: (41212) Marosi; Richardson, Alcock, Wright (Butler 63), Garrett (Evina 46); Baudry; Blair, Middleton (Keegan 57); Mandeville; Beestin, Marquis.
Referee: David Webb.

Peterborough U (1) 2 *(Coulthirst 40, 70)*
Chesham U (0) 1 *(Blake 80)* 4328
Peterborough U: (442) McGee; Smith, Santos, Tafazolli, Hughes; Maddison (Taylor P 77), Bostwick, Forrester, Da Silva Lopes (Edwards 61); Coulthirst, Nichols (Angol 73).
Chesham U: (442) Jones; Crilley, Mitchel-King, Purse, Wilson (Little 79); Pearce, Martin, Youngs (Hayles 79), Taylor; Wadkins, Roberts (Blake 69).
Referee: Darren Handley.

Port Vale (1) 1 *(Streete 38)*
Stevenage (0) 0 3093
Port Vale: (4411) Alnwick; Kiko (de Freitas 68), Streete, Smith, Knops; Thomas, Tavares, Grant, Taylor; Kelly (Hart 63); Paterson (Cicilia 79).
Stevenage: (433) Jones; Henry, Wilkinson (Godden 66), Franks, Ntlhe; King, Lee, Gorman (Pett 46); Kennedy (Liburd 88), McKirdy, Cowans.
Referee: Mark Haywood.

Portsmouth (0) 1 *(Evans 47)*
Wycombe W (1) 2 *(Cowan-Hall 27, Akinfenwa 84)* 8130
Portsmouth: (4231) Forde; Buxton (Baker 65), Burgess, Clarke, Stevens; Close, Rose; Evans, Roberts, Lalkovic (Bennett 64); Hunt (Chaplin 75).
Wycombe W: (4321) Blackman; Harriman, Pierre, Stewart, Jacobson; Gape, Bloomfield, O'Nien; Hayes (Thompson 77), Cowan-Hall (Weston 72); Akinfenwa (Bean 89).
Referee: Gavin Ward.

Shrewsbury T (2) 3 *(Sadler 27, Leitch-Smith 32, Grimmer 57)*
Barnet (0) 0 3120
Shrewsbury T: (442) Leutwiler; Grimmer, Sadler, El-Abd, Brown; Dodds (Whalley 83), Ogogo, Deegan, O'Brien; Toney (Waring 85), Leitch-Smith.
Barnet: (532) Stephens; Johnson (Gambin 46), Dembele, Nelson, N'Gala, Vilhete; Weston, Champion (Watson 46), Muggleton; Akpa Akpro, Tomlinson (Amaluzor 46).
Referee: Ben Toner.

Stockport Co (2) 2 *(Ball 9, 45)*
Woking (2) 4 *(Jones 18, Ugwu 32, 59, Saraiva 90)* 4025
Stockport Co: (433) Hinchliffe; Ross, Clarke, Smalley, Cartwright; Minihan (Hooper 67), Montrose, Stopforth; Ball (Marsden 80), Amis (Odejayi 81), Lloyd.
Woking: (442) Hall B; Jones, Saah, Yakubu, Jefford (Saraiva 62); Lewis, Murtagh, Sutherland (Carter 57), Ralph; Ugwu, Sam-Yorke (Thomas 90).
Referee: Ben Toner.

Walsall (0) 0
Macclesfield T (1) 1 *(McCombe 23)* 2334
Walsall: (4231) Etheridge; Laird, Toner, Preston, McCarthy; Chambers, Edwards; Moussa (Bakayoko 64), Oztumer, Ginnelly (Makris 76); Jackson.
Macclesfield T: (451) Mendy; Byrne (Hancox 46), Pilkington, McCombe, Fitzpatrick; Rowe, Lewis, Halls, James, Whitaker; Sampson.
Referee: Brett Huxtable.

Westfields (1) 1 *(Jones 9 (pen))*
Curzon Ashton (0) 1 *(Morgan 81)* 1178
Westfields: (451) Blackburn; Kahaki, Glover, Febery (Saunston 90), Archer-Plane; Grant (Ham 58), Reeve, Bonella, Jones, Thomas (Gwynne 67); Greaves.
Curzon Ashton: (4411) Burton; Baillie, Hunt, Stott, Hampson; Hall (Gorman 64), Clark, Brown, Guest; Howard (Morgan 66); Cummins (Ennis 87).
Referee: Tom Nield.

Whitehawk (1) 1 *(Southam 12)*
Stourbridge (0) 1 *(Scarr 52)* 767
Whitehawk: (442) Flitney; West (Rodrigues 90), Strevens, Reid, Harding; Masterton (Torres 70), M'Boungou, Southam, Abdulla; Connolly (Favarel 76), Mills.
Stourbridge: (4411) Gould; Green, Westlake, Tonks (Dodd 83), Smickle; Brown, Scarr, Broadhurst, Lait (Canavan 67); Gater; Benbow (Duggan 90).
Referee: Robert Whitton.

Yeovil T (1) 2 *(Hedges 8, Khan 52)*
Solihull Moors (0) 2 *(Byrne 57, 63)* 2118
Yeovil T: (433) Krysiak; Shephard, Lacey, Ward, Smith; Dawson■, Whitfield (Mugabi 59), Dolan; Hedges, Eaves, Khan (Zoko 69).
Solihull Moors: (3412) Lewis; Daly, Gough, Fagbola; Murombedzi, Byrne, Osborne, Franklin; Jones (Sterling-James 76); Brown, White (Asante 77).
Referee: David Rock.

Sunday, 6 November 2016

Alfreton T (0) 1 *(Kennedy 74)*

Newport Co (0) 1 *(Sheehan 65)* 1109

Alfreton T: (442) Spiess; Mantack, McGowan, Kennedy, Heaton; Nyoni, Wilson, Marshall (Allan 73), Monkhouse; Westcarr, Priestley (Hearn 86).
Newport Co: (4141) Day; Bignot, Jones, Bennett, Cameron; Tozer; Barnum-Bobb, Sheehan, Rigg, Myrie-Williams (Butler 61); Healey.
Referee: Graham Horwood.

Blackpool (2) 2 *(Matt 27, Potts 37)*

Kidderminster H (0) 0 1963

Blackpool: (442) Slocombe; Taylor, Nolan, Robertson, Mellor; Potts, Cain, McAlister, Yeates (Daniel 80); Vassell (Cullen 80), Matt (Philliskirk 34).
Kidderminster H: (4231) Hornby; Francis-Angol (Truslove 46), Tunnicliffe, Lowe, Williams; McQuilkin, Carter; Ngwatala (Brown 64), Gnahoua (Austin 73), Waite; Dieseruvwe.
Referee: Martin Coy.

Boreham Wood (1) 2 *(Ferrier 31, Balanta 50)*

Notts Co (0) 2 *(Campbell A 60, 83)* 1201

Boreham Wood: (4231) Smith; Nunn, Devera, Paine, Ilesanmi; Jerneic, Davis (Clifford 65); Andrade (Woodards 90), Balanta, Jeffrey; Ferrier (Lucas 76).
Notts Co: (442) Collin; Tootle, Laing, Hollis, Dickinson; Rodman (Campbell A 46), Richards (Forte 46), O'Connor, Milsom (Hewitt 73); Collins, Oliver.
Referee: Mark Heywood.

Hartlepool U (0) 3 *(Deverdics 65, Gordon 82 (og), Paynter 85)*

Stamford (0) 0 2461

Hartlepool U: (433) Carson; Richards, Nsiala, Bates, Carroll; Woods (Hawkins 80), Featherstone (Orrell 86), Laurent; Alessandra (Paynter 81), Amond, Deverdics.
Stamford: (442) Donkin; Gordon, Salt, Miller (Robbins 63), Luto (King 71); Beeson, Duffy, Hill, Challinor; Brown (Sandy 59), Smith.
Referee: Anthony Backhouse.

Maidstone U (1) 1 *(Taylor B 21 (pen))*

Rochdale (0) 1 *(Camps 90)* 2227

Maidstone U: (41212) Worgan; Nana Ofori-Twumasi, Lokko, Acheampong, Mills; Rogers; Flisher, Taylor B; Paxman; Enver-Marum (Odubade 85), Loza (Sweeney 82).
Rochdale: (433) Lillis; Rafferty, Canavan, McGahey, Bunney; Lund (McNulty 64), Camps, Cannon; Rathbone (McDermott 64), Davies, Mendez-Laing (Noble-Lazarus 86).
Referee: Charles Breakspear.

Morecambe (0) 1 *(Winnard 59)*

Coventry C (0) 1 *(Sterry 72)* 1732

Morecambe: (4231) Roche; McGowan, Winnard, Whitmore, Jennings; Murphy, Rose; Barkhuizen, Wildig (Mullin 67), Molyneux (Dunn 76); Stockton.
Coventry C: (4231) Burge; Dion Kelly-Evans, Willis, Turnbull, Sterry; Rose, Stevenson; Sordell, Lameiras, Reid (McBean 46); Wright (Maycock 78).
Referee: Charles Breakspear.

Sheffield U (3) 6 *(Basham 22, Scougall 39, Freeman 45, Chapman 54, 69, 90)*

Leyton Orient (0) 0 6099

Sheffield U: (352) Ramsdale; Basham, O'Connell, Wright; Freeman, Coutts (Whiteman 72), Duffy (Brooks 60), Fleck, Lafferty; Scougall (Lavery 46), Chapman.
Leyton Orient: (442) Cisak; Dunne, Parkes (Janse 81), Hunt, Kennedy; Massey, Atangana, Weir, Semedo; Simpson (McCallum 70), Palmer (Bowery 35).
Referee: Nigel Miller.

St Albans C (1) 3 *(Morias 4, 65, Theophanous 86)*

Carlisle U (1) 5 *(Grainger 20 (pen), Kennedy 57, Ibehre 71, 81, Lambe 83)* 3473

St Albans C: (442) Russell; Casey (Lucien 63), Martin, Hill, Bender; Herd, Thomas (Ball 84), Noble (Merson 75), Chappell; Theophanous, Morias.
Carlisle U: (442) Gillespie; Brisley, Raynes (Lambe 42), Ellis, Grainger; Kennedy, Joyce, Jones, Adams (Miller T 74); Wyke (Miller S 70), Ibehre.
Referee: Simon Hooper.

Taunton T (2) 2 *(Wright 14, Villis 37)*

Barrow (2) 2 *(Harrison 35 (pen), Bennett 43)* 2297

Taunton T: (352) Irish L; Irish O, Palmer, Villis; Mitchell, White, Trowbridge, Chamberlain, Batley (Searle 73); Wright, Rogers.
Barrow: (442) Dixon; Beeley, Livesey, Diarra, Anderton; Hughes■, Harvey, Yates, Williams J; Bennett, Harrison.
Referee: Craig Hicks.

Monday, 7 November 2016

Southport (0) 0

Fleetwood T (0) 0 2265

Southport: (4132) Norman; Higgins R, Howe, Thompson, Ashton; Weeks; Lussey (Ferguson 81), Nolan, Caton (Cofie 77); Andrai Jones, Allen.
Fleetwood T: (442) Neal; Ekpolo, Pond, Bolger, Bell; Sowerby (Woolford 46), Ryan, Dempsey, Grant (Cole 76); Ball (Hunter 63), Long.
Referee: Darren England.

FIRST ROUND REPLAYS

Monday, 14 November 2016

Curzon Ashton (2) 3 *(Morgan 23, 34, Cummins 70)*

Westfields (0) 1 *(Harrhy 90)* 1075

Curzon Ashton: (442) Burton; Baillie, Stott, Hunt, Hampson; Howard, Clark (Brown 73), Tomsett (Wright 82), Guest; Cummins, Morgan (Hall 87).
Westfields: (4411) Blackburn; Reeve, Glover, Febery, Archer-Plane; Polan (Miller 58), Bonella, Gwynne, Thomas (Ham 79); Jones; Greaves (Harrhy 76).
Referee: Karl Evans.

Stourbridge (0) 3 *(Lait 51, Benbow 60, 76)*

Whitehawk (0) 0 1993

Stourbridge: (442) Gould; Green, Westlake, Scarr, Smickle; Dodd (Canavan 83), Tonks (Birch 68), Broadhurst, Lait; Brown (Duggan 68), Benbow.
Whitehawk: (442) Munzo; Southam, M'Boungou (Marimon 83), Reid, Hamilton; Connolly (Rodrigues 72), Strevens, Torres (West 81), Favarel; Mills, Abdulla.
Referee: Tom Nield.

Tuesday, 15 November 2016

AFC Wimbledon (3) 5 *(Robinson 27, Parrett 32, Poleon 45, 72, Taylor 80)*

Bury (0) 0 2316

AFC Wimbledon: (4321) Shea; Fuller (Owens 67), Robertson, Robinson, Francomb; Parrett, Reeves, Bulman (Beere 75); Whelpdale, Barcham (Poleon 24); Taylor.
Bury: (442) Williams; Danns, Barnett (Maher 46), Kay, Leigh (Miller G 37); Mayor, Soares, Mellis, Tutte; Vaughan, Hope (Walker 75).
Referee: John Brooks.

Barrow (0) 2 *(Williams J 48, Yates 75)*

Taunton T (0) 1 *(Palmer 73)* 1717

Barrow: (442) Dixon; Beeley, Livesey, Anderton, Anderton; Hughes, Harvey, Yates, Williams J; Bennett, Harrison (Hannah 40).
Taunton T: (442) Irish L; Batley, Irish O, Palmer, Searle; White, Villis, Trowbridge (Buse 84), Chamberlain (Kelly 69); Wright, Rogers (Veal 59).
Referee: Martin Coy.

Bristol R (1) 4 *(Taylor 34, 102 (pen), Gaffney 52, 96)*

Crawley T (1) 2 *(Roberts 45, Harrold 65)* 3676

Bristol R: (442) Roos; Roberts, Hartley (Clarke-Salter 91), Lockyer, Brown; Montano (James 86), Sinclair, Lines, Moore (Bodin 46); Taylor, Gaffney.
Crawley T: (442) Morris; Young, Garnett, Davey, Arthur (Boldewijn 65); Smith, Djalo (Harrold 59), Roberts (Henderson 75), Clifford; Collins, Yussuf.
aet.
Referee: Ben Toner.

Coventry C (1) 2 *(Sordell 39, 57)*

Morecambe (1) 1 *(Winnard 10)* 2175

Coventry C: (343) Burge; Willis (Rose 46), Turnbull, Harries; Sterry, Bigirimana, Gadzhev (Stevenson 74), Haynes; Jones (Thomas G 90), Sordell, Reid.
Morecambe: (4231) Roche; Winnard, Edwards, Whitmore (Mullin 62), Jennings; Fleming (Murphy 70), Rose; Molyneux, Wildig (McGowan 55), Ellison; Stockton.
Referee: Mark Haywood.

Crewe Alex (0) 1 *(Lowe 64)*

Cheltenham T (2) 4 *(Pell 19, Barthram 36, Waters 52, Holman 61)* 1711

Crewe Alex: (4141) Garratt; Ng, Davis, Nugent, Guthrie; Hollands (Wintle 67); Cooper, Jones, Ainley, Kiwomya (Lowe 46); Udoh (Saunders 62).
Cheltenham T: (3412) Griffiths; Parslow, Downes, O'Shaughnessy; Dickie, Pell, Dayton (Munns 58), Barthram; Waters (Rowe 80); Wright, Holman (Morgan-Smith 70).
Referee: Seb Stockbridge.

FC Halifax T (1) 2 *(Denton 35, Kosylo 90)*

Dagenham & R (0) 1 *(Whitely 73)* 1465

FC Halifax T: (4231) Drench; Roberts, Garner, Hotte, Wilde; Lynch, Sinnott (Hibbs 73); MacDonald, King, Simmons (Kosylo 67); Denton.
Dagenham & R: (442) Cousins; Widdowson, Doe, Staunton, Raymond; Maguire-Drew (White 90), Hyde, Guttridge, Whitely; Benson, Hawkins■.
Referee: Thomas Bramall.

Fleetwood T (1) 4 *(Holloway 34, Bolger 94, Hunter 96, Bell 101)*

Southport (0) 1 *(Grimes 87)* 1609

Fleetwood T: (433) Cairns; Nirennold, Pond, Eastham, Bell; Dempsey, Glendon, Grant (Jonsson 73); Cole, Holloway (Bolger 78), Ball (Hunter 60).
Southport: (4132) Norman; Higgins R (White 105), Howe, Thompson, Ashton; Weeks; Lussey, Nolan, Ferguson (Grimes 69); Allen, Andrai Jones (Gray 85).
aet. Referee: David Webb.

Newport Co (0) 4 *(Healey 68, Green 97, Sheehan 110, Barnum-Bobb 117)*

Alfreton T (0) 1 *(Priestley 74)* 1189

Newport Co: (442) Day; Barnum-Bobb, Jones, Bennett, Butler; Myrie-Williams (Green 78), Tozer, Sheehan, Compton (Wood 36 (Cameron 109)); Rigg, Healey.
Alfreton T: (442) Spiess; Mantack, McGowan, Kennedy (Allan 99), Heaton; Smith A, Wilson, Nyoni, Monkhouse; Priestley (Smith S 89), Clayton (Hearn 89).
aet. Referee: Brett Huxtable.

Notts Co (1) 2 *(Forte 24, Collins 90)*

Boreham Wood (0) 0 1762

Notts Co: (4231) Collin; Laing, Duffy, Hollis, Dickinson; Milsom, Aborah; Burke, Campbell A (Smith 84), Snijders (Collins 84); Forte.
Boreham Wood: (442) Smith; Nunn, Paine, Devera, Ilesanmi; Ferrier (Lucas 74), Davis, Jerneic (Stephens 88), Jeffrey; Andrade, Balanta (Uchechi 74).
Referee: Richard Clark.

Rochdale (2) 2 *(Davies 14, 22 (pen))*

Maidstone U (0) 0 1350

Rochdale: (433) Logan; Rafferty, McGahey, McNulty, Bunney; Thompson, Camps, Cannon (Rathbone 46); Mendez-Laing, Davies (Tanser 70), Noble-Lazarus (Morley 85).
Maidstone U: (442) Worgan; Nana Ofori-Twumasi, Lokko, Acheampong, Mills; Taylor B, Evans, Rogers (Paxman 59), Flisher (Greenhalgh 71); Odubade (Murphy 76), Loza.
Referee: Nigel Miller.

Solihull Moors (0) 1 *(Asante 99 (pen))*

Yeovil T (0) 1 *(Zoko 93)* 1460

Solihull Moors: (433) Vaughan (Lewis 67); Franklin, Gough, Daly, Murombedzi; Fagbola, Byrne, Osborne; Knights (Jones 81), Brown (Asante 96), Sterling-James.
Yeovil T: (433) Krysiak; Dickson, Ward, Lacey, Shephard; Whitfield (Butcher 78), Dawson, Dolan; Hedges, Eaves, Khan (Zoko 77).
aet; Solihull Moors won 4-2 on penalties.
Referee: Carl Boyeson.

Swindon T (0) 1 *(Delfouneso 79)*

Eastleigh (2) 3 *(Reason 16, Drury 35, Mandron 74 (pen))* 4321

Swindon T: (4231) Vigouroux; Furlong, Branco, Jones, Ormonde-Ottewill; Thomas (Delfouneso 57), Kasim (Rodgers 37); Murray, Doughty, Goddard; Norris.
Eastleigh: (442) Clarke; Partington, Essam, Johnson, Green; Drury, Reason, Taylor, Coulson; Wilson, Mandron.
Referee: Christopher Sarginson.

Wednesday, 16 November 2016

Brackley T (2) 4 *(Armson 17, 26, 105, Nelson 96 (og))*

Gillingham (1) 3 *(Hessenthaler 36, Wagstaff 67, McDonald 113)* 1654

Brackley T: (532) Walker L; Myles, Dean, Graham, Gudger, Walker G; Byrne, Walker A, Armson; Diggin (Moyo 89), Ndlovu (Lowe 104).
Gillingham: (433) Nelson; Jackson, Ehmer, Oshilaja, Garmston (Wagstaff 66); Hessenthaler, Herd (Wright 46), Knott; Emmanuel-Thomas, McDonald, Dack (Donnelly 64).
aet. Referee: Rob Jones.

Thursday, 17 November 2016

Dover Ath (0) 2 *(Miller 70, Thomas 102)*

Cambridge U (0) 4 *(Roberts 90, Legge 110, Elito 118, Williamson 120)* 1158

Dover Ath: (343) Walker; Grimes, Orlu, Sterling; Magri, Kinnear (Fazakerley 90), Stevenson, Thomas; Miller (Pinnock 85), Lafayette, Modeste.
Cambridge U: (4411) Norris; Halliday, Legge, Roberts, Taylor (Adams 103); Mingoia (Coulson 120), Dunne, Elito, Dunk (Williamson 66); Berry; Ikpeazu.
aet. Referee: Charles Breakspear.

SECOND ROUND

Friday, 2 December 2016

Macclesfield T (0) 0

Oxford U (0) 0 2566

Macclesfield T: (451) Mendy; Halls, McCombe, Pilkington, Fitzpatrick; Mackreth, Lewis, Hancox, Whitaker, Rowe; Holroyd.
Oxford U: (442) Eastwood; Edwards, Martin, Dunkley, Skarz (Ruffels 51); MacDonald, Ledson, Rothwell (Taylor 64), Johnson; Roberts T (Hemmings 79), Maguire.
Referee: Sebastian Stockbridge.

Saturday, 3 December 2016

Blackpool (1) 1 *(Matt 6)*

Brackley T (0) 0 1764

Blackpool: (442) Slocombe; Mellor, Aldred, Robertson, Taylor; Potts, Payne, Pugh, Samuel (Yeates 66); Vassell (McAlister 79), Matt (Gnanduillet 71).
Brackley T: (352) Walker L; Dean, Graham (Lowe 81), Gudger; Myles, Byrne, Armson, Walker A, Walker G; Diggin (Moyo 87), Ndlovu (Pitt 87).
Referee: Ross Joyce.

Carlisle U (0) 0

Rochdale (0) 2 *(Davies 48, Mendez-Laing 90)* 4426

Carlisle U: (433) Gillespie; Miller T, Raynes, Brisley (Asamoah 82), Grainger; Kennedy (Miller S 60), Joyce, Jones; Lambe (Devitt 60), Wyke, Adams.
Rochdale: (4231) Logan; Rafferty, Canavan (McNulty 46), Keane, Bunney (Mendez-Laing 87); Lund, Camps; Thompson, Rathbone, Henderson; Davies (McGahey 78).
Referee: Mark Haywood.

Charlton Ath (0) 0

Milton Keynes D (0) 0 4982

Charlton Ath: (442) Phillips; Konsa (Teixeira 30), Bauer, Pearce, Fox; Botaka (Novak 90), Crofts, Ulvestad, Lookman; Magennis, Ajose (Hanlan 90).
Milton Keynes D: (433) Martin; Baldock, Downing, Walsh, Lewington; Carruthers (Powell 78), Potter, Upson; Reeves, Agard (Colclough 78), Bowditch.
Referee: Darren England.

Chesterfield (0) 0

Wycombe W (2) 5 *(Hayes 21, Kashket 24, 70, 77, Stewart 74)* 3685

Chesterfield: (343) Fulton; Liddle, Evatt, Anderson; Mitchell (Evans 33), O'Neil, Nolan■, Donohue; O'Shea, Beesley (Dennis 60), Ariyibi.
Wycombe W: (442) Blackman; Harriman, Stewart, Pierre, Jacobson; Bloomfield (Wood 78), O'Nien, Gape (Bean 73), Kashket (Cowan-Hall 81); Hayes, Akinfenwa.
Referee: Michael Salisbury.

Luton T (0) 6 *(Hylton 51, Mullins 54, O'Donnell 59, 89, Marriott 63, 90)*

Solihull Moors (2) 2 *(Osborne 5, 35)* 3512

Luton T: (41212) Walton; Justin (O'Donnell 46), Cuthbert, Mullins, Sheehan; Rea; McGeehan, Gilliead (Potts 76); Cook; Hylton (Vassell 82), Marriott.
Solihull Moors: (532) Lewis; Murombedzi, Daly, Gough, Fagbola, Franklin (Morris 72); Byrne, Jones (Knights 82), Osborne; Sterling-James (White 82), Asante.
Referee: Christopher Sarginson.

Plymouth Arg (0) 0

Newport Co (0) 0 5071

Plymouth Arg: (4231) McCormick; Miller (Donaldson 55), Songo'o, Bradley, Threlkeld; Smith, Fox; Jervis, Tanner (Fletcher 79), Carey; Goodwillie (Rooney 59).
Newport Co: (442) Day; Barnum-Bobb, Meite, Bennett, Butler; Green (Jebb 46), Tozer, Sheehan, Rigg■; O'Hanlon (Myrie-Williams 32), Healey (Jackson 82).
Referee: John Brooks.

Shrewsbury T (0) 0

Fleetwood T (0) 0 2886

Shrewsbury T: (4231) Leutwiler; Smith, El-Abd, Sadler, McGivern; Brown, Black (Waring 82); Deegan, Dodds, O'Brien; Toney (Jones 90).
Fleetwood T: (442) Cairns; Davis (Nirennold 64), McLaughlin, Pond, Bolger; Grant, Dempsey, Bell, Glendon (Hunter 64); Ball, Cole (Long 72).
Referee: Trevor Kettle.

Sutton U (0) 2 *(Tubbs 46, Deacon 90)*

Cheltenham T (1) 1 *(Wright 35)* 2224

Sutton U: (442) Worner; Amankwaah, Collins, Downer, Spence; Gomis, Bailey, Eastmond, Deacon; Biamou, Tubbs (May 90).
Cheltenham T: (442) Griffiths; Dickie, Parslow, O'Shaughnessy, Cranston (Suliman 70); Dayton, Pell, Storer, Munns (Smith 82); Waters, Wright.
Referee: Robert Jones.

Sunday, 4 December 2016

Bolton W (1) 3 *(Madine 44, Ameobi 46, Vela 84)*

Sheffield U (0) 2 *(Coutts 64, O'Connell 86)* 7027

Bolton W: (4231) Alnwick; Wilson, Wheater, Beevers, Taylor A; Thorpe (Osede 76), Spearing; Ameobi (Taylor C 82), Vela, Clough; Madine (Proctor 85).
Sheffield U: (352) Ramsdale; Brown (Duffy 49), Basham, O'Connell; Freeman, Coutts, Scougall (Sharp 85), Fleck, Hussey; Lavery, Clarke.
Referee: Lee Probert.

Bristol R (1) 1 *(Gaffney 10)*

Barrow (1) 2 *(Harrison 16, 61)* 4570

Bristol R: (352) Roos; Lockyer, Hartley, Clarke J (Harrison 46); Leadbitter, Clarke O, Sinclair (Montano 64), Lines, Brown; Gaffney, James (Bodin 64).
Barrow: (442) Erlandsson; Beeley, Livesey, Diarra, Anderton; Hughes, Yates, Harvey, Williams J (Meikle 89); Bennett (Wright 82), Harrison.
Referee: Dean Whitestone.

Cambridge U (3) 4 *(Berry 7, 29 (pen), 38, 86)*

Coventry C (0) 0 4283

Cambridge U: (4231) Norris; Halliday, Legge, Roberts, Taylor; Dunne, Clark; Mingoia, Berry (Dunk 87), Maris (Williamson 77); Ikpeazu (Pigott 90).
Coventry C: (433) Burge; Willis, Turnbull, Harries (McCann 46), Page; Maycock (Reid 46), Gadzhev, Bigirimana; Lameiras (Jones 75), Sordell, McBean.
Referee: Keith Stroud.

Curzon Ashton (2) 3 *(Morgan 1, 21, 62)*

AFC Wimbledon (0) 4 *(Elliott 80, 90, Poleon 81, Barnett 82)* 1731

Curzon Ashton: (4411) Burton; Baillie, Woodford, Hunt, Hampson; Howard, Clark, Brown (Rowney 86), Guest (Wright 84); Morgan (Tomsett 90); Cummins.
AFC Wimbledon: (433) Shea; Fuller, Robinson, Robertson, Meades; Parrett (Barnett 66), Reeves, Bulman; Poleon, Elliott, Taylor.
Referee: James Adcock.

Eastleigh (1) 3 *(Mandron 18, 90, Wilson 74)*

FC Halifax T (0) 3 *(Sinnott 62, Garner 67, Peniket 72)* 2098

Eastleigh: (442) Huddart; Partington, Johnson, Taylor (Santos 46 (Bird 75)), Green; Essam, Pipe, Reason, Coulson; Constable (Wilson 67), Mandron.
FC Halifax T: (451) Drench; Moyo, Hotte, Garner, Wilde; MacDonald (Hibbs 71), King, Lynch, Sinnott, Simmons (Peniket 52); Denton.
Referee: Brendan Malone.

Millwall (3) 5 *(Smith 17, 21, 48, Ferguson 25, O'Brien 90)*

Braintree T (2) 2 *(Cheek 16, Midson 34)* 3345

Millwall: (442) Archer; Romeo, Webster, Nelson (Craig 65), Martin; Worrall, Williams, Butcher, Ferguson; Smith (O'Brien 78), Gregory (Onyedinma 86).
Braintree T: (442) Beasant; Clohessy, Gayle (Barnard 84), Jules, Okimo; Patterson (Matthews 63), Isaac (Maybanks 89), Lee, Akinola; Cheek, Midson.
Referee: Darren Deadman.

Notts Co (1) 2 *(Campbell A 42, Laing 90)*

Peterborough U (2) 2 *(Da Silva Lopes 3, Edwards G 15)* 3940

Notts Co: (442) Collin; Dickinson, Milsom, Duffy, Tootle; Burke (Stead 72), Laing, O'Connor, Campbell A; Oliver (Collins 77), Forte.
Peterborough U: (442) McGee; Hughes, Bostwick, Tafazolli, Smith; Edwards G, Forrester, Da Silva Lopes, Maddison (Nichols 58); Angol■, Taylor (Coulthirst 58).
Referee: Ben Toner.

Port Vale (3) 4 *(Cicilia 12, Carroll 14 (og), Jones 31, Taylor 56 (pen))*

Hartlepool U (0) 0 3514

Port Vale: (4411) Alnwick; Taylor, Streete, Smith, Kiko; Jones (Shalaj 71), Amoros, Tavares (Gibbons 60), de Freitas; Kelly (Mbamba 82); Cicilia.
Hartlepool U: (433) Carson; Bates, Jones (Richards 66), Nsiala, Carroll; Laurent, Deverdics, Woods; Alessandra (Paynter 53), Amond, Featherstone (Hawkins 53).
Referee: Darren Handley.

Woking (0) 0

Accrington S (2) 3 *(Kee 34, 42, O'Sullivan 61)* 3718

Woking: (3511) Hall B; Yakubu (Edgar 72), Thomas, Saah; Caprice, Saraiva, Jones, Carter■, Shaw (Sutherland 70); Lewis (Sam-Yorke 59); Ugwu.
Accrington S: (4411) Chapman; Pearson, Beckles, Hughes, McConville; O'Sullivan, Brown (Davies 88), Conneely, Clark; Lacey (Boco 58); Kee (Gornell 72).
Referee: Nicholas Kinseley.

Monday, 5 December 2016

Lincoln C (2) 3 *(Robinson 22, 47, Hawkridge 24)*

Oldham Ath (0) 2 *(Clarke 70, McKay 73)* 7012

Lincoln C: (442) Farman; Wood, Waterfall, McCombe, Habergham; Arnold, Power, Woodyard, Hawkridge (Anderson 72); Rhead, Robinson (Muldoon 81).
Oldham Ath: (442) Ripley; Dummigan, Clarke, Burgess, Reckord (McKay 66); McLaughlin, Green, Banks, Winchester (Croft 55); Erwin, Ladapo (Osei 77).
Referee: Gavin Ward.

Tuesday, 13 December 2016

Stourbridge (0) 1 *(Duggan 86)*

Northampton T (0) 0 2520

Stourbridge: (442) Gould; Green, Duggan, Scarr, Westlake; Dodd (Canavan 90), Tonks, Broadhurst, Lait (Gater 82); Benbow, Brown.
Northampton T: (442) Cornell; Phillips, Zakuani, Nyatanga, Buchanan; Anderson P (Hanley 77), McCourt (Iaciofano 90), Taylor M, Hoskins; Richards, Revell.
Referee: Andy Davies.

SECOND ROUND REPLAYS

Tuesday, 13 December 2016

FC Halifax T (0) 0

Eastleigh (2) 2 *(Wilson 43, Mandron 45 (pen))* 1539

FC Halifax T: (442) Drench; Moyo, Hotte, Garner■, Wilde; Kosylo (Simmons 60), Lynch, King (Hibbs 70), Peniket; Denton, Sinnott (MacDonald 33).
Eastleigh: (442) Huddart; Partington, Pipe, Coulson (Obileye 77), Green; Wilson (Dugdale 65), Essam, Johnson, Mandron (Bird 59); Constable, Reason.
Referee: Richard Clark.

Fleetwood T (0) 3 *(Cole 63, 77, Hunter 90)*

Shrewsbury T (1) 2 *(O'Brien 43, Dodds 60)* 1157

Fleetwood T: (352) Cairns; Davis (Holloway 46), Pond (Glendon 59), Bolger; McLaughlin, Sowerby (Hunter 66), Jonsson, Grant, Bell; Cole, Long.
Shrewsbury T: (442) Leutwiler; Smith, Lancashire, El-Abd■, Sadler; O'Brien (Black 73), Ogogo, Deegan, Brown; Dodds, Toney.
Referee: Mark Heywood.

Milton Keynes D (1) 3 *(Powell 6, Reeves 94, Bowditch 97)*

Charlton Ath (1) 1 *(Chicksen 24)* 3655

Milton Keynes D: (4231) Nicholls; Baldock (Hendry 59), Downing, Lewington, George B Williams; Upson, Potter; Colclough, Bowditch, Aneke (Agard 61); Powell (Reeves 47).
Charlton Ath: (41212) Phillips; Foley, Konsa, Teixeira, Chicksen; Jackson (Johnson 80); Aribo, Botaka; Lookman; Hanlan (Ajose 73), Novak (Fox 40).
aet. Referee: Rob Jones.

Oxford U (1) 3 *(Taylor 10, Rothwell 47, Hemmings 78)*

Macclesfield T (0) 0 3642

Oxford U: (442) Eastwood; Edwards (Carroll 80), Nelson, Martin (Dunkley 4), Johnson; MacDonald, Rothwell, Ruffels, Hall (Hemmings 68); Roberts T, Taylor.
Macclesfield T: (451) Mendy; Halls, Pilkington, McCombe, Fitzpatrick; Mackreth (Sampson 53), James (Lewis 53), Hancox■, Whitaker, Rowe (Byrne 79); Holroyd.
Referee: Carl Boyeson.

Tuesday, 20 December 2016

Peterborough U (2) 2 *(Edwards G 2, Taylor P 8)*

Notts Co (0) 0 7796

Peterborough U: (41212) McGee; Smith, Bostwick, Tafazolli, Hughes; Forrester; Da Silva Lopes, Edwards G (Binnom-Williams 88); Taylor P (Inman 35); Coulthirst (Oduwa 74), Nichols.
Notts Co: (442) Loach; Tootle, Duffy, Hollis, Audel; Richards (Campbell A 58), Thompson, Smith (Collins 73), Milsom; Stead (Oliver 68), Forte.
Referee: Darren England.

Wednesday, 21 December 2016

Newport Co (0) 0

Plymouth Arg (0) 1 *(Carey 113 (pen))* 5121

Newport Co: (4222) Day; Barnum-Bobb, Jones, Bennett, Myrie-Williams; Tozer, Labadie (Meite 116); Sheehan, Wood (Green 67); Jackson (O'Hanlon 67), Healey.
Plymouth Arg: (4231) McCormick; Miller, Songo'o, Bradley, Threlkeld; Fox, Smith; Carey, Tanner (Garita 69), Jervis (Goodwillie 69); Slew.
aet. Referee: Dean Whitestone.

THIRD ROUND

Friday, 6 January 2017

West Ham U (0) 0

Manchester C (3) 5 *(Toure 33 (pen), Nordtveit 41 (og), Silva 43, Aguero 50, Stones 84)* 56,975

West Ham U: (4231) Adrian; Nordtveit, Reid, Ogbonna, Cresswell; Obiang, Fernandes; Feghouli, Lanzini (Noble 58), Antonio (Fletcher 72); Carroll (Payet 58).
Manchester C: (442) Caballero; Sagna, Otamendi, Stones, Clichy; Silva (Nolito 58), Zabaleta, Toure (Delph 78), De Bruyne (Garcia 68); Aguero, Sterling.
Referee: Michael Oliver.

Saturday, 7 January 2017

Accrington S (1) 2 *(McConville 45, Beckles 57)*

Luton T (0) 1 *(Gray 54)* 1717

Accrington S: (4411) Chapman; Pearson, Beckles, Hughes, Donacien; O'Sullivan (Clark 72), Conneely, Brown, McConville; Edwards (Boco 68); Kee.
Luton T: (352) Walton; Rea■, Cuthbert (O'Donnell 41), Mullins; Justin, Smith (Ruddock 58), Lee (Marriott 52), Gray, Sheehan; McQuoid, Vassell.
Referee: Darren Deadman.

Barrow (0) 0

Rochdale (1) 2 *(Henderson 17, 62)* 4414

Barrow: (442) Flatt; Beeley, Livesey, Diarra, Anderton; Hughes (Haworth 72), Harvey, Rowe (Wright 71), Williams J; Harrison, Bennett (Hannah 77).
Rochdale: (433) Logan; McGahey, Keane (Canavan 90), McNulty, Rafferty; Lund, Camps, Rathbone (Allen 87); Henderson (Cannon 81), Davies, Andrew.
Referee: David Webb.

Birmingham C (1) 1 *(Jutkiewicz 42)*

Newcastle U (1) 1 *(Murphy 6)* 13,171

Birmingham C: (4231) Legzdins; Spector (Dacres-Cogley 44), Shotton, Robinson, Grounds; Kieftenbeld, Gleeson; Davis, Adams, Fabbrini (Stewart 79); Jutkiewicz.
Newcastle U: (442) Sels; Yedlin, Lascelles, Hanley, Haidara (Ritchie 70); Anita, Colback, Tiote (Hayden 65), Lazaar; Murphy, Mitrovic (Gouffran 10).
Referee: Neil Swarbrick.

Blackpool (0) 0

Barnsley (0) 0 4875

Blackpool: (532) Slocombe; Mellor, Aldred, Aimson, Taylor, Robertson; Payne (Pugh 74), Potts, McAlister; Cullen (Samuel 68), Vassell (Matt 69).
Barnsley: (442) Davies; Bree, Roberts, MacDonald, White; Watkins, Hourihane, Scowen, Hammill (Kent 75); Winnall, Bradshaw (Payne 75).
Referee: Christopher Sarginson.

Bolton W (0) 0

Crystal Palace (0) 0 11,683

Bolton W: (4231) Alnwick; Wilson, Wheater, Beevers, Taylor A; Thorpe, Spearing; Clough (Clayton 80), Vela, Henry (Taylor C 86); Madine (Proctor 80).
Crystal Palace: (442) Speroni; Ward, Delaney, Kelly, Fryers; Lee, Ledley (Townsend 66), Flamini, Mutch; Remy (Cabaye 46), Campbell (KaiKai 80).
Referee: Roger East.

Brentford (5) 5 *(Barbet 9 (pen), Field 17, 38, Vibe 23, Sawyers 45)*

Eastleigh (1) 1 *(Obileye 29)* 7537

Brentford: (3511) Bentley; Dean (Mepham 80), Egan, Barbet; Colin (Clarke 46), McEachran, Yennaris (Jota 61), Woods, Field; Sawyers; Vibe.
Eastleigh: (352) Stack; Dugdale, Essam, Hoyte (Reason 9); Odoffin, Obileye, Togwell, Coulson, Green; Constable (Wilson 55), Bird (Mandron 62).
Referee: Peter Bankes.

Brighton & HA (1) 2 *(Kayal 9, Hemed 72)*

Milton Keynes D (0) 0 11,091

Brighton & HA: (4231) Maenpaa; Hunt, Hunemeier, Goldson, Adekugbe; Kayal (Ince 78), Sidwell; March, Towell, Murphy; Hemed.
Milton Keynes D: (4231) Martin; Baldock, George B Williams, Walsh, Lewington; Upson, Potter; Agard (Powell 79), Aneke (Brittain 83), Reeves; Maynard.
Referee: James Linington.

Bristol C (0) 0

Fleetwood T (0) 0 10,301

Bristol C: (3412) Fielding (O'Donnell 46); Hegeler, Flint, Wright; Little, Brownhill, Smith (Pack 44), Bryan; Tomlin (Paterson 80); Djuric, Abraham.
Fleetwood T: (532) Cairns; McLaughlin, Bolger, Pond, Davies, Bell; Dempsey (Long 68), Glendon (Nirennold 77), Grant; Ball, Cole (Hunter 60).
Referee: Stephen Martin.

Everton (0) 1 *(Lukaku 63)*
Leicester C (0) 2 *(Musa 66, 71)* 35,493
Everton: (352) Robles; Funes Mori, Williams A, Holgate (Deulofeu 46); Coleman, Davies, Barry, Barkley (Kone 75), Baines; Lukaku, Valencia (Mirallas 62).
Leicester C: (433) Schmeichel; Simpson, Huth, Morgan, Chilwell; Mendy, Ndidi, Drinkwater; Gray (Fuchs 77), Ulloa (Musa 35), Albrighton (Kapustka 84).
Referee: Martin Atkinson.

Huddersfield T (1) 4 *(Payne 28, 84, Palmer 73, Bunn 80)*
Port Vale (0) 0 11,715
Huddersfield T: (4231) Coleman; Cranie, Hudson, Stankovic, Holmes-Dennis; Billing (Mooy 67), Whitehead; Payne, Palmer, Lolley (Bunn 57); Brown (Smith 71).
Port Vale: (442) Alnwick (Miguel Santos 59); Purkiss, Streete (Hart 39), Smith, Knops; de Freitas, Grant, Kelly, Taylor; Thomas (Forrester 75), Cicilia.
Referee: Geoff Eltringham.

Hull C (0) 2 *(Hernandez 78, Tymon 90)*
Swansea C (0) 0 6608
Hull C: (4411) Jakupovic; Meyler, Livermore, Dawson (Maloney 70), Robertson; Henriksen (Hernandez 64), Huddlestone, Mason, Clucas; Snodgrass; Diomande (Tymon 89).
Swansea C: (433) Nordfeldt; Naughton, van der Hoorn, Fernandez, Kingsley (Rangel 67); Fer, Cork, Ki; Dyer (Routledge 63), Borja Baston (Llorente 62), Sigurdsson.
Referee: Anthony Taylor.

Ipswich T (1) 2 *(Lawrence 12, 86)*
Lincoln C (1) 2 *(Robinson 7, 65)* 16,027
Ipswich T: (442) Gerken; Emmanuel, Webster, Berra, Knudsen; Ward, Bru, Dozzell, Lawrence; Pitman, Sears.
Lincoln C: (442) Farman; Wood, Waterfall, Raggett, Habergham; Hawkridge, Woodyard, Power, Arnold; Robinson (Muldoon 81), Rhead (Long 90).
Referee: Lee Probert.

Manchester U (2) 4 *(Rooney 7, Martial 15, Rashford 75, 79)*
Reading (0) 0 74,396
Manchester U: (4231) Romero; Young, Smalling, Rojo (Jones 19), Blind; Fellaini, Carrick (Fosu-Mensah 78); Mata (Schweinsteiger 78), Rooney, Martial; Rashford.
Reading: (4231) Al Habsi; Gunter, Moore, van den Berg, Blackett (Obita 46); Williams, Evans (Swift 57); McCleary, Kelly, Beerens; Kermorgant (Samuel 77).
Referee: Andre Marriner.

Millwall (1) 3 *(Morison 26, Cummings 50, Ferguson 90)*
Bournemouth (0) 0 9471
Millwall: (442) Archer; Webster, Cummings, Hutchinson, Craig; Onyedinma (Worrall 75), Thompson, Williams, O'Brien (Ferguson 53); Gregory (Butcher 84), Morison.
Bournemouth: (4411) Federici; Lee (Wilson C 46), Wilson M, Mings, Smith (Cook S 74); Surman, Hyndman (Gosling 56), Pugh, Ibe; Grabban; Mousset.
Referee: Andrew Madley.

Norwich C (0) 2 *(Whittaker 52 (pen), Naismith 90)*
Southampton (1) 2 *(van Dijk 38, Yoshida 67)* 12,479
Norwich C: (4231) McGovern; Whittaker, Martin, Klose (Bennett 69), Olsson; Tettey, Howson; Josh Murphy (Jacob Murphy 69), Pritchard (Lafferty 79), Naismith; Jerome.
Southampton: (433) Lewis; Stephens, Yoshida, van Dijk, Bertrand; Reed (Romeu 63), Hojbjerg, Ward-Prowse; Sims (Redmond 79), Long (Rodriguez 63), Tadic.
Referee: Chris Kavanagh.

Preston NE (1) 1 *(Robinson 7)*
Arsenal (0) 2 *(Ramsey 46, Giroud 89)* 22,185
Preston NE: (442) Maxwell; Vermijl, Clarke, Huntington, Cunningham; Gallagher (Browne 60), Pearson, Johnson (Horgan 81), McGeady; Hugill (Makienok 75), Robinson.
Arsenal: (4231) Ospina; Maitland-Niles (Holding 90), Mustafi, Gabriel, Monreal; Ramsey, Xhaka; Lucas Perez (Reine-Adelaide 90), Iwobi, Oxlade-Chamberlain (Welbeck 83); Giroud.
Referee: Robert Madley.

QPR (0) 1 *(Bidwell 61 (pen))*
Blackburn R (1) 2 *(Lynch 8 (og), Feeney 58)* 7482
QPR: (352) Ingram; Hall, Onuoha, Lynch; Perch, Wszolek, Luongo (Cousins 82), Gladwin (Shodipo 56), Bidwell; Mackie, Eze (Ngbakoto 18).
Blackburn R: (442) Raya; Mulgrew, Greer, Williams, Bennett; Feeney, Akpan (Nyambe 74), Lowe, Marshall; Gallagher (Brown 90), Graham (Stokes 87).
Referee: Simon Hooper.

Rotherham U (0) 2 *(Ward D 51, Adeyemi 90)*
Oxford U (1) 3 *(Taylor 41, Edwards 80, Hemmings 88)* 5618
Rotherham U: (442) Price; Fisher, Broadfoot, Wood, Mattock; Forde, Adeyemi, Vaulks, Newell; Ward D, Blackstock (Yates 53).
Oxford U: (442) Eastwood; Edwards, Nelson, Dunkley, Johnson; Hall (Sercombe 74), Lundstram, Ledson, MacDonald; Taylor (Hemmings 81), Maguire (Rothwell 81).
Referee: James Adcock.

Stoke C (0) 0
Wolverhampton W (1) 2 *(Helder Costa 29, Doherty 80)* 21,479
Stoke C: (4231) Grant; Johnson, Shawcross, Martins Indi, Pieters; Afellay, Imbula (Adam 46); Shaqiri (Ngoy 72), Krkic (Allen 46), Arnautovic; Crouch.
Wolverhampton W: (4231) Ikeme; Iorfa (Dicko 77), Hause, Williamson, Doherty; Saville, Evans; Helder Costa, Enobakhare (Edwards 72), Mason (White 62); Bodvarsson.
Referee: Mike Jones.

Sunderland (0) 0
Burnley (0) 0 17,632
Sunderland: (433) Mannone; Love, Manquillo, Djilobodji, Van Aanholt; Denayer, Rodwell, Larsson (O'Shea 84); Januzaj, Defoe, Borini.
Burnley: (442) Pope; Darikwa, Tarkowski, Keane, Ward; Gudmundsson (Hendrick 72), Defour, Barton, Arfield (Kightly 60); Gray (Barnes 72), Vokes.
Referee: Stuart Attwell.

Sutton U (0) 0
AFC Wimbledon (0) 0 5013
Sutton U: (4411) Worner; Downer (Hudson-Odoi 82), Beckwith, Collins, Amankwaah; Deacon, Bailey, Eastmond, Gomis; Biamou (Monakana 90); Tubbs (Fitchett 72).
AFC Wimbledon: (442) Shea; Fuller, Robinson, Charles, Kelly; Parrett (Francomb 90), Reeves, Bulman, Barcham; Elliott, Taylor.
Referee: Keith Stroud.

Watford (1) 2 *(Kabasele 21, Sinclair 77)*
Burton Alb (0) 0 13,270
Watford: (442) Pantilimon; Cathcart (Prodl 16), Kaboul (Dja Djedje 60), Britos, Mason; Kabasele, Doucoure, Capoue, Sinclair (Stewart 90); Ighalo, Deeney.
Burton Alb: (352) McLaughlin; Brayford, McFadzean, Flanagan; Harness, Palmer (Murphy 81), Naylor, Williamson, Dyer; Miller (Ward 32), Varney (Akins 70).
Referee: Lee Mason.

WBA (1) 1 *(Phillips 35)*
Derby Co (0) 2 *(Bent 51, Ince 54)* 25,288
WBA: (4231) Myhill; Dawson, McAuley, Olsson (Chadli 78), Galloway (Robson-Kanu 68); Yacob, Fletcher; Phillips, Morrison, McClean; Rondon.
Derby Co: (433) Carson; Baird, Keogh, Shackell, Hanson (Pearce 82); de Sart, Bryson (Vernam 88), Johnson; Ince, Bent, Camara (Vydra 86).
Referee: Jon Moss.

Wigan Ath (1) 2 *(Grigg 45, Wildschut 57)*
Nottingham F (0) 0 5163
Wigan Ath: (442) Haugaard; Power, Buxton, Burn, Warnock; Powell (Gomez 9), Morsy, MacDonald, Jacobs; Grigg (Flores 88), Wildschut (Le Fondre 69).
Nottingham F: (442) Henderson; Cash, Hobbs, Mancienne, Lichaj; Dumitru (Carayol 63), Lam, Pereira, Osborn; Bendtner (Vellios 82), Assombalonga (Lica 56).
Referee: Oliver Langford.

Wycombe W (0) 2 *(Wood 47, Akinfenwa 83)*
Stourbridge (0) 1 *(Scarr 70)* 6312
Wycombe W: (433) Blackman; Jombati, Stewart, Pierre, Jacobson; Bloomfield (Wood 39), Gape, O'Nien; Cowan-Hall (Hayes 66), Akinfenwa, Kashket (Weston 84).
Stourbridge: (4411) Gould; Green, Scarr, Duggan (Knight 89), Westlake; Dodd, Broadhurst, Tonks, Lait (Canavan 84); Brown (Gater 77); Benbow.
Referee: Darren England.

Sunday, 8 January 2017

Cardiff C (1) 1 *(Pilkington 8)*
Fulham (2) 2 *(Johansen 14, Sessegnon 33)* 5199
Cardiff C: (3421) Murphy; Morrison, Halford (Harris M 69), Bamba; Richards, Ralls, Huws, Bennett; Pilkington, Harris K (Noone 80); Lambert (O'Keefe 69).
Fulham: (4231) Bettinelli; Odoi, Sigurdsson, Ream, Sessegnon (Malone 90); McDonald, Johansen (Adeniran 81); Fredericks, Cairney, Piazon; Aluko (Humphrys 85).
Referee: Andy Woolmer.

Chelsea (2) 4 *(Pedro 18, 75, Batshuayi 43, Willian 52)*
Peterborough U (0) 1 *(Nichols 70)* 41,003
Chelsea: (352) Begovic; Zouma, Terry■, Cahill (Aina 57); Ivanovic, Chalobah, Fabregas, Loftus-Cheek (Azpilicueta 70), Pedro; Willian (Kante 73), Batshuayi.
Peterborough U: (442) McGee; Smith, Bostwick, Tafazolli, Hughes (Binnom-Williams 83); Maddison (Taylor 57), Da Silva Lopes, Forrester, Edwards G (Samuelsen 58); Nichols, Angol.
Referee: Kevin Friend.

Liverpool (0) 0
Plymouth Arg (0) 0 52,692
Liverpool: (433) Karius; Alexander-Arnold, Gomez, Lucas, Moreno; Can (Sturridge 63), Stewart, Ejaria (Lallana 75); Ojo, Origi, Woodburn (Firmino 75).
Plymouth Arg: (4141) McCormick; Miller (Smith 76), Songo'o, Bradley, Purrington; Fox; Jervis, Threlkeld, Carey, Slew; Garita (Tanner 65).
Referee: Paul Tierney.

Middlesbrough (0) 3 *(Leadbitter 58, Negredo 67, de Roon 90)*
Sheffield W (0) 0 23,661
Middlesbrough: (433) Guzan; Chambers, Ayala■, Bernardo, Friend; de Roon, Clayton (Downing 62), Leadbitter; Stuani, Negredo, Traore (Da Silva 62).
Sheffield W: (4411) Wildsmith; Palmer (Lucas Joao 72), Lees, Loovens, Pudil; Wallace (McManaman 46), Jones, Bannan, Reach; Forestieri; Fletcher (Nuhiu 71).
Referee: David Coote.

Tottenham H (0) 2 *(Davies 71, Son 80)*
Aston Villa (0) 0 31,182
Tottenham H: (343) Vorm; Carter-Vickers, Alderweireld (Nkoudou 70), Wimmer; Trippier, Dier, Winks, Davies; Sissoko (Onomah 84), Janssen (Alli 60), Son.
Aston Villa: (4411) Johnstone; Hutton, Chester, Baker, Amavi; Adomah (Green 77), Tshibola, Jedinak (Davis 77), Bacuna; Grealish; Agbonlahor (McCormack 77).
Referee: Mike Dean.

Monday, 9 January 2017

Cambridge U (1) 1 *(Ikpeazu 25)*
Leeds U (0) 2 *(Dallas 56, Mowatt 63)* 7973
Cambridge U: (4231) Norris; Taylor, Legge, Roberts, Adams; Newton (Dunk 66), Dunne; Mingoia, Berry, Clark (Williamson 88); Ikpeazu.
Leeds U: (4231) Silvestri; Berardi (Coyle 46), Jansson, Cooper (Bartley 71), Denton; Grimes, Phillips; Dallas, Mowatt, Doukara (Roofe 59); Antonsson.
Referee: Craig Pawson.

THIRD ROUND REPLAYS

Tuesday, 17 January 2017

AFC Wimbledon (1) 1 *(Elliott 10)*
Sutton U (0) 3 *(Deacon 75, Biamou 90, Fitchett 90)* 4768
AFC Wimbledon: (433) Shea; Kelly, Robinson■, Charles, Fuller; Reeves, Bulman, Parrett; Taylor (Whelpdale 70), Elliott (Barnett 83), Poleon (Robertson 16).
Sutton U: (442) Worner; Amankwaah, Downer (Hudson-Odoi 66), Beckwith, Spence; Gomis (May 66), Eastmond, Collins, Deacon; Tubbs (Fitchett 75), Biamou.
Referee: Darren Drysdale.

Barnsley (0) 1 *(MacDonald 49)*
Blackpool (1) 2 *(Mellor 30, Samuel 120)* 5558
Barnsley: (442) Davies; Bree, Roberts (Jackson 29), MacDonald, White; Hammill, Scowen, Hourihane, Kent (Williams 76); Armstrong (Watkins 76), Bradshaw.
Blackpool: (532) Slocombe; Mellor, Aldred, Aimson, Taylor (Philliskirk 46), Robertson; Payne (Yeates 62), McAlister, Pugh; Cullen, Vassell (Samuel 41).
aet. Referee: Roger East.

Burnley (1) 2 *(Vokes 44, Gray 83)*
Sunderland (0) 0 12,257
Burnley: (451) Pope; Darikwa, Keane, Tarkowski, Flanagan; Boyd (O'Neill 90), Hendrick, Barton, Defour, Kightly (Gray 77); Vokes.
Sunderland: (442) Mannone; Jones, Djilobodji, Manquillo, Van Aanholt; Love (Defoe 63), Denayer, Honeyman, Larsson; Januzaj, Borini (Asoro 80).
Referee: Michael Jones.

Crystal Palace (0) 2 *(Benteke C 68, 77)*
Bolton W (0) 1 *(Henry 48)* 7149
Crystal Palace: (433) Speroni; Ward, Kelly, Delaney (Tomkins 62), Fryers; Lee, Flamini, Ledley (Puncheon 63); Townsend, Remy (Benteke C 63), KaiKai.
Bolton W: (442) Alnwick; Wilson, Wheater, Beevers, Taylor A; Spearing, Thorpe, Henry (Taylor C 89), Vela; Clough (Clayton 88), Madine (Proctor 77).
Referee: Stuart Attwell.

Fleetwood T (0) 0
Bristol C (1) 1 *(Paterson 17)* 2115
Fleetwood T: (352) Cairns; Eastham (Hunter 74), Bolger, Davies; McLaughlin, Sowerby (Nirennold 55), Jonsson (Ball 63), Dempsey, Bell; Cole, Long.
Bristol C: (3412) Fielding; Wright, Flint, Magnusson; Little (O'Dowda 77), O'Neil, Hegeler, Bryan; Paterson; Engvall (Abraham 68), Djuric (Brownhill 82).
Referee: Carl Boyeson.

Lincoln C (0) 1 *(Arnold 90)*
Ipswich T (0) 0 9054
Lincoln C: (442) Farman; Wood, Waterfall, Raggett, Habergham; Arnold (Muldoon 90), Woodyard, Power, Hawkridge (McCombe 90); Robinson (Marriott 80), Rhead.
Ipswich T: (352) Gerken; Digby, Chambers, Berra; Emmanuel, Ward (Dozzell 75), Douglas, Skuse, Knudsen; Best (Sears 75), Lawrence.
Referee: Ben Toner.

Wednesday, 18 January 2017

Newcastle U (2) 3 *(Ritchie 9 (pen), 90, Gouffran 34)*
Birmingham C (0) 1 *(Cotterill 71)* 34,896
Newcastle U: (4231) Sels; Yedlin (Hayden 76), Hanley, Findlay, Lazaar; Shelvey, Tiote (Colback 83); Ritchie, El-Mhanni (Perez 70), Barlaser; Gouffran.
Birmingham C: (433) Legzdins; Dacres-Cogley, Robinson, Shotton, Grounds; Kieftenbeld (Fabbrini 80), Davis (Brown 64), Tesche; Adams, Solomon-Otabor (Jutkiewicz 64), Cotterill.
Referee: Lee Probert.

Plymouth Arg (0) 0
Liverpool (1) 1 *(Lucas 18)* 17,048
Plymouth Arg: (4141) McCormick; Threlkeld, Songo'o, Bradley, Purrington; Fox; Jervis, Donaldson (Tanner 67), Carey, Slew (Bulvitis 80); Garita (Rooney 72).
Liverpool: (433) Karius; Alexander-Arnold, Gomez, Lucas, Moreno; Coutinho (Wilson 65), Stewart, Ejaria; Sturridge (Ojo 76), Origi, Woodburn.
Referee: Graham Scott.

Southampton (0) 1 *(Long 90)*
Norwich C (0) 0 13,517
Southampton: (433) Lewis; Martina, Yoshida, Stephens, McQueen; Ward-Prowse, Clasie, Reed (Romeu 71); Sims, Long, Rodriguez (Redmond 70).

Norwich C: (541) McGovern; Ivo Pinto, Bennett, Klose, Bassong, Martin; Josh Murphy (Jacob Murphy 73), Godfrey (Grant 86), Brady, Pritchard; Lafferty (Canos 80).
Referee: Jonathan Moss.

FOURTH ROUND

Friday, 27 January 2017

Derby Co (2) 2 *(Bent 21, Bryson 40)*

Leicester C (1) 2 *(Bent 8 (og), Morgan 86)* 25,079

Derby Co: (433) Carson; Baird, Keogh, Pearce, Olsson; Hughes (Butterfield 63), Johnson, Bryson (Camara 89); Ince, Bent, Russell (Vydra 84).
Leicester C: (442) Schmeichel; Simpson, Morgan, Huth, Fuchs (Gray 46); Albrighton (Musa 74), Drinkwater, King, Chilwell; Okazaki (Mahrez 64), Vardy.
Referee: Mark Clattenburg.

Saturday, 28 January 2017

Blackburn R (2) 2 *(Gallagher 9, Bennett 22)*

Blackpool (0) 0 9327

Blackburn R: (442) Steele; Nyambe, Greer, Lenihan, Williams; Bennett, Lowe, Akpan (Guthrie 67), Conway; Graham (Mahoney 72), Gallagher.
Blackpool: (352) Slocombe; Aimson, Aldred, Robertson; Mellor■, Payne (Yeates 63), McAlister, Pugh, Taylor; Samuel (Matt 55), Cullen (Odelusi 55).
Referee: Peter Bankes.

Burnley (1) 2 *(Vokes 45, Defour 68)*

Bristol C (0) 0 14,921

Burnley: (451) Pope; Darikwa, Keane, Mee, Flanagan; Gudmundsson, Barton (Hendrick 70), Tarkowski, Defour (Kightly 78), Arfield (Barnes 70); Vokes.
Bristol C: (4231) Giefer; Vyner, Wright, Flint, Golbourne; Hegeler (Pack 76), Brownhill; O'Dowda, Reid, Bryan (Abraham 61); Djuric (Engvall 61).
Referee: Andre Marriner.

Chelsea (2) 4 *(Willian 14, Pedro 21, Ivanovic 69, Batshuayi 81 (pen))*

Brentford (0) 0 41,042

Chelsea: (343) Begovic; Zouma, Terry, Azpilicueta (Kenedy 71); Pedro (Costa 76), Fabregas, Chalobah, Ake; Willian (Ivanovic 64), Batshuayi, Loftus-Cheek.
Brentford: (3511) Bentley; Egan, Dean, Bjelland; Colin, Yennaris, McEachran (Kerschbaumer 78), Woods, Barbet; Sawyers (Hogan 64); Vibe (Jota 65).
Referee: Michael Oliver.

Crystal Palace (0) 0

Manchester C (1) 3 *(Sterling 43, Sane 71, Toure 90)* 13,979

Crystal Palace: (4231) Hennessey; Ward, Kelly, Tomkins, Schlupp (Fryers 76); Flamini, Ledley; Lee, Mutch (McArthur 65), Townsend; Benteke C (Remy 46).
Manchester C: (4231) Caballero; Clichy, Kolarov, Kompany, Sagna; Delph, Toure; Sterling (Jesus Navas 66), Silva (Fernando 79), Sane (Nolito 84); Gabriel Jesus.
Referee: Mike Jones.

Lincoln C (0) 3 *(Power 57 (pen), Tomori 62 (og), Robinson 85)*

Brighton & HA (1) 1 *(Towell 24)* 9469

Lincoln C: (442) Farman; Wood, Waterfall, Raggett, Habergham; Arnold, Power (McCombe 90), Woodyard, Hawkridge; Rhead (Long 88), Robinson (Muldoon 87).
Brighton & HA: (4231) Maenpaa (Ankergren 56); Tomori, Goldson, Hunemeier, Adekugbe; Norwood, Sidwell; Skalak (Murphy 68), Towell (Hemed 68), March; Murray.
Referee: Andrew Madley.

Liverpool (0) 1 *(Origi 86)*

Wolverhampton W (2) 2 *(Stearman 1, Weimann 41)* 52,469

Liverpool: (433) Karius; Randall (Coutinho 46), Gomez, Klavan, Moreno; Ejaria (Can 74), Lucas, Wijnaldum; Woodburn, Origi, Firmino (Sturridge 65).
Wolverhampton W: (4231) Burgoyne; Coady, Stearman, Hause, Doherty; Evans, Saville; Helder Costa (Ronan 67), Edwards, Weimann (Mason 77); Dicko (Bodvarsson 71).
Referee: Craig Pawson.

Middlesbrough (0) 1 *(Downing 69)*

Accrington S (0) 0 24,040

Middlesbrough: (442) Konstantopoulos; Friend (Fry 9), Bernardo, Gibson, Da Silva; Fischer (Traore 61), Clayton, Leadbitter, Downing; Bamford (Stuani 70), Gestede.
Accrington S: (442) Rodak; Rodgers, Hughes, Beckles (Gornell 90), Donacien; Davies (Clark 74), Clare, Conneely, Boco (McCartan 74); Kee, McConville.
Referee: Anthony Taylor.

Oxford U (0) 3 *(Hemmings 46, Nelson 79, Martinez 87)*

Newcastle U (0) 0 11,810

Oxford U: (4411) Eastwood; Edwards, Dunkley, Nelson, Skarz; Maguire (Martinez 70), Lundstram, Ledson, Johnson; Hall; Hemmings (Sercombe 83).
Newcastle U: (442) Sels; Jesus Gamez, Hanley, Lazaar, Haidara (Ritchie 77); Good, Hayden, Barlaser, El-Mhanni (Gouffran 68); Perez, Mitrovic.
Referee: David Coote.

Rochdale (0) 0

Huddersfield T (1) 4 *(Quaner 42, Brown 66 (pen), Hefele 72, 84)* 7431

Rochdale: (451) Logan; Rafferty, McGahey, McNulty, Keane; Allen (Redshaw 67), Andrew (Kitching 12), Camps, Vincenti, Noble-Lazarus (Mendez-Laing 67); Henderson.
Huddersfield T: (4231) Coleman; Cranie, Hudson, Stankovic, Holmes-Dennis; Whitehead (Mooy 69), Billing; Kachunga (Hefele 46), Brown, Bunn (Hogg 46); Quaner.
Referee: Oliver Langford.

Southampton (0) 0

Arsenal (3) 5 *(Welbeck 15, 22, Walcott 35, 69, 84)* 31,288

Southampton: (433) Lewis; Martina, Gardos, Stephens, McQueen; Hojbjerg, Reed, Clasie; Sims, Long (Redmond 65), Isgrove (Tadic 64).
Arsenal: (433) Ospina; Bellerin, Mustafi, Holding, Gibbs; Oxlade-Chamberlain, Maitland-Niles, Reine-Adelaide (Iwobi 72); Walcott, Lucas Perez, Welbeck (Sanchez 65).
Referee: Kevin Friend.

Tottenham H (0) 4 *(Son 60, 90, Janssen 64 (pen), Alli 89)*

Wycombe W (2) 3 *(Hayes 23, 36 (pen), Thompson 83)* 31,440

Tottenham H: (4231) Vorm; Trippier, Carter-Vickers, Wimmer (Dembele 61), Davies; Winks, Dier; Sissoko, Onomah (Alli 61), Nkoudou (Janssen 46); Son.
Wycombe W: (433) Blackman; Jombati, Stewart, Pierre, Jacobson; Wood, Gape, O'Nien; Kashket (Saunders 77), Akinfenwa (Weston 68), Hayes (Thompson 77).
Referee: Roger East.

Sunday, 29 January 2017

Fulham (1) 4 *(Aluko 17, Martin 54, Sessegnon 66, Johansen 78)*

Hull C (0) 1 *(Evandro 49)* 15,143

Fulham: (4231) Bettinelli; Sessegnon, Ream, Kalas, Odoi; McDonald, Johansen; Aluko (Ayite 80), Cairney (Fredericks 88), Piazon; Martin (Petsos 83).
Hull C: (4231) Jakupovic; Elabdellaoui, Davies (Maguire 10), Huddlestone, Robertson; Evandro (Tymon 74), Meyler (Niasse 62); Markovic, Diomande, Clucas; Hernandez.
Referee: Paul Tierney.

Manchester U (1) 4 *(Fellaini 44, Smalling 57, Mkhitaryan 74, Schweinsteiger 81)*

Wigan Ath (0) 0 75,229

Manchester U: (4231) Romero (Joel Pereira 80); Fosu-Mensah (Tuanzebe 68), Smalling, Rojo, Shaw; Fellaini (Ander Herrera 70), Schweinsteiger; Mata, Rooney, Mkhitaryan; Martial.
Wigan Ath: (4141) Haugaard; Connolly, Buxton, Burn, Warnock; MacDonald (Browne 76); Perkins (Wildschut 59), Power, Morsy, Jacobs; Grigg (Tunnicliffe 71).
Referee: Neil Swarbrick.

Millwall (0) 1 *(Morison 85)*

Watford (0) 0 9772

Millwall: (442) Archer; Cummings, Webster, Cooper, Craig; Onyedinma (Wallace 72), Thompson, Williams, O'Brien (Ferguson 71); Gregory (Abdou 90), Morison.
Watford: (352) Pantilimon (Gomes 42); Kaboul, Mariappa, Britos; Dja Djedje (Janmaat 69), Doucoure, Watson, Guedioura, Mason; Okaka, Sinclair (Deeney 77).
Referee: Martin Atkinson.

Sutton U (0) 1 *(Collins 53 (pen))*

Leeds U (0) 0 4997

Sutton U: (451) Worner; Amankwaah, Downer, Collins, Spence; Biamou, Eastmond (Traore 90), Bailey, May, Deacon; Gomis.
Leeds U: (41212) Silvestri; Coyle, McKay, Cooper■, Denton; Grimes; Whitehouse (Roofe 73), Dallas (Sacko 57); Phillips; Doukara (Wilks 64), Antonsson.
Referee: Stuart Attwell.

FOURTH ROUND REPLAY

Wednesday, 8 February 2017

Leicester C (0) 3 *(King 46, Ndidi 94, Gray 114)*

Derby Co (0) 1 *(Camara 61)* 31,648

Leicester C: (4231) Zieler; Amartey, Wasilewski, Benalouane, Chilwell; King, Mendy (Ndidi 91); Albrighton, Kapustka (Mahrez 81), Gray; Musa (Slimani 91).
Derby Co: (433) Mitchell; Christie, Keogh, Shackell, Lowe; Butterfield, de Sart, Johnson (Vydra 53); Camara (Russell 74), Blackman (Nugent 82), Anya.
aet.
Referee: Mike Jones.

FIFTH ROUND

Saturday, 18 February 2017

Burnley (0) 0

Lincoln C (0) 1 *(Raggett 89)* 19,185

Burnley: (442) Heaton; Darikwa, Keane, Tarkowski, Flanagan; Gudmundsson (Boyd 20), Westwood, Barton, Arfield; Gray, Vokes (Barnes 73).
Lincoln C: (442) Farman; Wood, Waterfall, Raggett, Habergham; Arnold, Woodyard, Power, Hawkridge (Ward 81); Muldoon (Southwell 64), Rhead (McCombe 90).
Referee: Graham Scott.

Huddersfield T (0) 0

Manchester C (0) 0 24,129

Huddersfield T: (4231) Coleman; Cranie, Hudson, Stankovic, Holmes-Dennis; Whitehead, Billing; Lolley (Wells 59), Payne (Brown 72), van La Parra (Kachunga 59); Quaner.
Manchester C: (433) Bravo; Zabaleta, Stones, Otamendi, Kolarov (Sagna 78); Fernandinho, Fernando, Delph (De Bruyne 69); Jesus Navas, Aguero, Nolito (Sane 69).
Referee: Anthony Taylor.

Middlesbrough (2) 3 *(Leadbitter 26 (pen), Gestede 34, Stuani 86)*

Oxford U (0) 2 *(Maguire 64, Martinez 65)* 28,198

Middlesbrough: (433) Guzan; Chambers, Ayala, Bernardo, Da Silva; Leadbitter, Clayton, Downing; Traore (Stuani 72), Gestede (Negredo 86), Fischer (Ramirez 72).
Oxford U: (442) Eastwood; Edwards, Dunkley, Nelson, Johnson; Hall, Ledson, Lundstram, Maguire; Hemmings (McAleny 67), Martinez (Sercombe 85).
Referee: Andre Marriner.

Millwall (0) 1 *(Cummings 90)*

Leicester C (0) 0 18,012

Millwall: (442) Archer; Cummings, Webster, Cooper■, Craig; O'Brien (Gregory 79), Butcher (Abdou 75), Williams, Ferguson (Romeo 86); Onyedinma, Morison.
Leicester C: (4231) Zieler; Amartey, Wague (Wasilewski 70), Benalouane, Chilwell; King, Mendy; Musa, Kapustka (Albrighton 64), Gray (Vardy 73); Okazaki.
Referee: Craig Pawson.

Wolverhampton W (0) 0

Chelsea (0) 2 *(Pedro 65, Costa 89)* 30,193

Wolverhampton W: (433) Ikeme; Coady, Batth, Hause, Doherty; Edwards, Price, Saville (Saiss 84); Helder Costa, Bodvarsson (Ronan 84), Weimann (Wilson 76).
Chelsea: (343) Begovic; Zouma, Terry, Ake; Moses, Fabregas, Chalobah, Pedro (Azpilicueta 73); Willian (Kante 80), Costa, Hazard (Loftus-Cheek 86).
Referee: Jonathan Moss.

Sunday, 19 February 2017

Blackburn R (1) 1 *(Graham 17)*

Manchester U (1) 2 *(Rashford 27, Ibrahimovic 75)* 23,130

Blackburn R: (442) Steele; Lowe, Greer, Lenihan, Williams; Feeney (Mahoney 73), Guthrie (Tomlinson 81), Mulgrew, Conway; Emnes, Graham (Stokes 77).
Manchester U: (4231) Romero; Young, Smalling, Rojo, Darmian; Ander Herrera, Carrick; Lingard (Pogba 62), Mkhitaryan, Martial (Ibrahimovic 62); Rashford (Mata 89).
Referee: Martin Atkinson.

Fulham (0) 0

Tottenham H (1) 3 *(Kane 16, 51, 73)* 22,557

Fulham: (4231) Bettinelli; Odoi, Kalas, Ream, Malone; McDonald (Parker 74), Johansen; Aluko (Cyriac 66), Cairney, Ayite (Sessegnon 56); Kebano.
Tottenham H: (4231) Vorm; Trippier, Alderweireld, Vertonghen, Davies; Winks (Dembele 79), Wanyama; Eriksen, Alli (Onomah 86), Son; Kane (Sissoko 75).
Referee: Robert Madley.

Monday, 20 February 2017

Sutton U (0) 0

Arsenal (1) 2 *(Lucas Perez 26, Walcott 55)* 5013

Sutton U: (4132) Worner; Downer, Beckwith (Spence 70), Collins, Amankwaah; Bailey; May (Hudson-Odoi 71), Eastmond, Gomis; Deacon, Biamou (Fitchett 82).
Arsenal: (433) Ospina; Gabriel, Mustafi, Holding, Monreal; Elneny (Oxlade-Chamberlain 46), Xhaka, Reine-Adelaide (Maitland-Niles 74); Walcott, Lucas Perez, Iwobi (Sanchez 74).
Referee: Michael Oliver.

FIFTH ROUND REPLAY

Wednesday, 1 March 2017

Manchester C (3) 5 *(Sane 30, Aguero 35 (pen), 73, Zabaleta 38, Iheanacho 90)*

Huddersfield T (1) 1 *(Bunn 7)* 42,425

Manchester C: (4141) Bravo; Zabaleta, Stones, Otamendi, Clichy; Fernandinho; Sterling, De Bruyne (Delph 75), Garcia, Sane (Jesus Navas 81); Aguero (Iheanacho 79).
Huddersfield T: (4231) Coleman; Cranie, Hudson, Stankovic, Holmes-Dennis; Whitehead, Billing (Hogg 67); Lolley (Smith 61), Payne, Bunn (van La Parra 54); Quaner.
Referee: Paul Tierney.

SIXTH ROUND

Saturday, 11 March 2017

Arsenal (1) 5 *(Walcott 45, Giroud 53, Waterfall 58 (og), Sanchez 72, Ramsey 75)*

Lincoln C (0) 0 59,454

Arsenal: (433) Cech; Bellerin, Mustafi, Koscielny, Gibbs; Oxlade-Chamberlain (Ozil 27), Xhaka (Coquelin 61), Ramsey; Walcott, Giroud (Lucas Perez 65), Sanchez.
Lincoln C: (442) Farman; Wood, Waterfall, Raggett, Habergham; Arnold, Woodyard, Power, Hawkridge (Marriott 78); Rhead (Ward 66), Muldoon (Margetts 54).
Referee: Anthony Taylor.

Middlesbrough (0) 0

Manchester C (1) 2 *(Silva 3, Aguero 67)* 32,228

Middlesbrough: (433) Guzan; Barragan, Bernardo (Fry 50), Gibson, Da Silva; de Roon, Clayton, Leadbitter (Ramirez 66); Traore, Gestede (Negredo 26), Stuani.
Manchester C: (4141) Bravo; Zabaleta, Stones, Otamendi, Clichy; Toure (Fernando 86); Sterling, De Bruyne, Silva, Sane (Nolito 70); Aguero (Iheanacho 90).
Referee: Mike Dean.

Sunday, 12 March 2017

Tottenham H (2) 6 *(Eriksen 31, Son 41, 54, 90, Alli 72, Janssen 79)*

Millwall (0) 0 31,137

Tottenham H: (3421) Vorm; Dier, Alderweireld, Vertonghen; Trippier, Wanyama (Sissoko 78), Winks, Davies; Son, Alli (Janssen 74); Kane (Eriksen 10).
Millwall: (442) King; Cummings, Webster, Cooper, Craig; Wallace (Ferguson 70), Thompson (Butcher 46), Williams, O'Brien; Gregory, Morison (Onyedinma 58).
Referee: Martin Atkinson.

Monday, 13 March 2017

Chelsea (0) 1 *(Kante 51)*

Manchester U (0) 0 40,801

Chelsea: (343) Courtois; Azpilicueta, Luiz, Cahill; Moses (Zouma 89), Kante, Matic, Alonso; Willian (Fabregas 81), Costa (Batshuayi 90), Hazard.
Manchester U: (343) de Gea; Jones, Smalling, Rojo; Valencia, Ander Herrera■, Pogba, Darmian; Mkhitaryan (Fellaini 37), Rashford, Young (Lingard 81).
Referee: Michael Oliver.

SEMI-FINALS

Saturday, 22 April 2017

Chelsea (2) 4 *(Willian 5, 43 (pen), Hazard 75, Matic 80)*

Tottenham H (1) 2 *(Kane 18, Alli 52)* 86,355

Chelsea: (343) Courtois; Azpilicueta, Luiz, Ake; Moses, Kante, Matic, Alonso; Willian (Hazard 61), Batshuayi (Costa 61), Pedro (Fabregas 74).
Tottenham H: (3421) Lloris; Dier, Alderweireld, Vertonghen; Trippier, Wanyama (Nkoudou 80), Dembele, Son (Walker 68); Eriksen, Alli; Kane.
Referee: Martin Atkinson.

Sunday, 23 April 2017

Arsenal (0) 2 *(Monreal 71, Sanchez 101)*

Manchester C (0) 1 *(Aguero 62)* 85,725

Arsenal: (3421) Cech; Gabriel, Koscielny, Holding; Oxlade-Chamberlain (Bellerin 105), Xhaka, Ramsey, Monreal; Ozil (Coquelin 119), Sanchez; Giroud (Welbeck 83).
Manchester C: (4231) Bravo; Jesus Navas, Kompany, Otamendi, Clichy; Fernandinho (Fernando 99), Toure; De Bruyne, Silva (Sterling 23 (Iheanacho 106)), Sane; Aguero (Delph 99).
aet.
Referee: Craig Pawson.

THE FA CUP FINAL 2017

Saturday, 27 May 2017

(at Wembley Stadium, attendance 89,472)

Arsenal (1) 2 Chelsea (0) 1

Arsenal: (3421) Ospina; Holding, Mertesacker, Monreal; Bellerin, Ramsey, Xhaka, Oxlade-Chamberlain (Coquelin 82); Ozil, Sanchez (Elneny 90); Welbeck (Giroud 78).
Scorers: Sanchez 4, Ramsey 79.

Chelsea: (343) Courtois; Azpilicueta, Luiz, Cahill; Moses■, Kante, Matic (Fabregas 61), Alonso; Pedro (Willian 72), Costa (Batshuayi 88), Hazard.
Scorer: Costa 76.

Referee: Anthony Taylor.

Arsenal's Aaron Ramsay salvaged the Gunners' season with this winning goal in their 2-1 FA Cup final defeat of Chelsea at Wembley Stadium. (Nick Potts/PA Wire/PA Images)

NATIONAL LEAGUE 2016–17

(P) Promoted into division at end of 2015–16 season. (R) Relegated into division at end of 2015–16 season.

			Home					Away					Total						
		P	W	D	L	F	A	W	D	L	F	A	W	D	L	F	A	GD	Pts
1	Lincoln C	46	17	4	2	48	17	13	5	5	35	23	30	9	7	83	40	43	99
2	Tranmere R	46	16	3	4	43	19	13	5	5	36	20	29	8	9	79	39	40	95
3	Forest Green R¶	46	12	9	2	46	25	13	2	8	42	31	25	11	10	88	56	32	86
4	Dagenham & R (R)	46	12	5	6	37	28	14	1	8	42	25	26	6	14	79	53	26	84
5	Aldershot T	46	15	5	3	38	13	8	8	7	28	24	23	13	10	66	37	29	82
6	Dover Ath	46	13	5	5	48	28	11	2	10	37	35	24	7	15	85	63	22	79
7	Barrow	46	12	8	3	40	20	8	7	8	32	33	20	15	11	72	53	19	75
8	Gateshead	46	9	9	5	38	23	10	4	9	34	28	19	13	14	72	51	21	70
9	Macclesfield T	46	9	3	11	30	29	11	5	7	34	28	20	8	18	64	57	7	68
10	Bromley	46	11	3	9	33	37	7	5	11	26	29	18	8	20	59	66	–7	62
11	Boreham Wood	46	8	7	8	23	21	7	6	10	26	27	15	13	18	49	48	1	58
12	Sutton U (P)	46	13	6	4	41	25	2	7	14	20	38	15	13	18	61	63	–2	58
13	Wrexham	46	10	5	8	23	24	5	8	10	24	37	15	13	18	47	61	–14	58
14	Maidstone U (P)	46	8	5	10	29	39	8	5	10	30	36	16	10	20	59	75	–16	58
15	Eastleigh	46	8	7	8	28	26	6	8	9	28	37	14	15	17	56	63	–7	57
16	Solihull Moors (P)	46	8	3	12	35	38	7	7	9	27	37	15	10	21	62	75	–13	55
17	Torquay U	46	9	5	9	34	28	5	6	12	20	33	14	11	21	54	61	–7	53
18	Woking	46	9	7	7	32	30	5	4	14	34	50	14	11	21	66	80	–14	53
19	Chester FC	46	8	3	12	37	35	6	7	10	26	36	14	10	22	63	71	–8	52
20	Guiseley	46	9	6	8	32	31	4	6	13	18	36	13	12	21	50	67	–17	51
21	York C (R)	46	7	8	8	33	31	4	9	10	22	39	11	17	18	55	70	–15	50
22	Braintree T	46	6	4	13	23	36	7	5	11	28	40	13	9	24	51	76	–25	48
23	Southport	46	7	5	11	32	41	3	4	16	20	56	10	9	27	52	97	–45	39
24	North Ferriby U (P)	46	6	2	15	17	40	6	1	16	15	42	12	3	31	32	82	–50	39

¶Forest Green R promoted via play-offs.

NATIONAL LEAGUE PLAY-OFFS 2016–17

▪ *Denotes player sent off.*

SEMI-FINALS FIRST LEG

Wednesday 3 May 2017

Aldershot T (0) 0

Tranmere R (1) 3 *(Stockton 3, 76, Norwood 48)* 5614

Aldershot T: Cole; Evans, Arnold, Alexander, Reynolds, Benyu (Oyeleke 63), Gallagher, Mensah, Kellerman (Fenelon 48), Kanu, McClure (Rendell 63).
Tranmere R: Davies; Buxton, McNulty, Ihiekwe, Ridehalgh, Maynard (Mangan 88), Hughes, Wallace, Norwood (Dunn 90), Jennings C, Stockton (Cook 86).
Referee: Craig Hicks.

Thursday 4 May 2017

Dagenham & R (1) 1 *(Maguire-Drew 45)*

Forest Green R (1) 1 *(Noble 29 (pen))* 2208

Dagenham & R: Cousins; Doe, Widdowson, Staunton (Howell 23), Donnellan, Boucaud, Robson, Benson, Okenabirhie (Hawkins 75), Whitely, Maguire-Drew.
Forest Green R: Russell; Ellis, Bennett, Monthe, Traore (Pinnock 71), Noble (Marsh-Brown 79), Woolery, Cooper, Whishart, Doidge, Bugiel (Mullings 68).
Referee: Anthony Coggins.

SEMI-FINALS SECOND LEG

Saturday 6 May 2017

Tranmere R (1) 2 *(Stockton 31, Norwood 90)*

Aldershot T (1) 2 *(Mensah 43, Hughes 50 (og))* 10,241

Tranmere R: Davies; McNulty, Ridehalgh, Buxton, Ihiekwe, Maynard, Hughes, Wallace (Mangan 69), Jennings C, Norwood, Stockton.
Aldershot T: Cole; Reynolds, Evans, Arnold, Straker, Gallagher (Kellerman 72), Oyeleke, Rendell, McClure, Mensah, Kanu (Fenelon 72).
Referee: Scott Oldham.
Tranmere R won 5-2 on aggregate.

Sunday 7 May 2017

Forest Green R (2) 2 *(Doidge 34, Marsh-Brown 45)*

Dagenham & R (0) 0 3237

Forest Green R: Russell; Ellis, Bennett, Monthe, Pinnock, Traore (Wedgbury 71), Noble, Marsh-Brown (Wishart 66), Woolery, Cooper, Doidge (Mullings 80).
Dagenham & R: Cousins; Doe, Widdowson, Williams, Donnellan, Boucaud, Robson, Benson (Hawkins 59), Okenabirhie (Guttridge 46), Whitely, Maguire-Drew (Howell 59).
Referee: Martin Coy.
Forest Green R won 3-1 on aggregate.

FINAL

Wembley, Sunday 14 May 2017

Forest Green R (3) 3 *(Woolery 11, 44, Doidge 41)*

Tranmere R (1) 1 *(Jennings C 22)* 18,801

Forest Green R: Russell; Ellis, Bennett, Monthe, Pinnock, Traore (Wedgbury 81), Noble, Marsh-Brown (Wishart 61), Woolery, Cooper, Doidge (Mullings 76).
Tranmere R: Davies; McNulty, Ridehalgh, Buxton, Ihiekwe, Maynard, Hughes, Mangan (Dunne 53), Jennings C (Cook 61), Norwood, Stockton.
Referee: Anthony Backhouse.
Forest Green R promoted to EFL League Two.

NATIONAL LEAGUE PROMOTED TEAMS ROLL CALL 2016–17

LINCOLN CITY

Player	H	W	DOB
Acar, Jenk (F)			06/09/1997
Andersen, Luke (M)			15/10/1998
Angol, Lee (F)	5 10	11 05	04/08/1994
Arnold, Nathan (M)	5 7	10 03	26/07/1987
Beevers, Lee (D)	6 1	13 12	04/12/1983
Calder, Riccardo (M)	6 0	12 06	26/01/1996
Etheridge, Ross (G)	6 2	11 00	14/09/1994
Everington, Kegan (M)			17/12/1995
Farman, Paul (G)	6 5	14 07	02/11/1989
Fixter, Jack (D)			24/05/1998
Habergham, Sam (D)	6 0	11 07	20/02/1992
Hawkridge, Terry (M)	5 9	11 00	23/02/1990
Howe, Callum (D)	6 0	11 07	09/04/1994
Margetts, Jonny (F)	5 9		28/09/1993
Marriott, Adam (F)	5 9	11 03	14/04/1991
McCombe, Jamie (D)	6 5	12 06	01/01/1983
McMenemy, Jack (F)			22/11/1998
Moyses, Archie (M)			21/07/1998
Muldoon, Jack (F)	5 10	10 12	19/05/1989
Power, Alan (M)	5 7	11 07	23/01/1988
Raggett, Sean (D)	5 11	12 04	17/04/1993
Rhead, Matt (F)	6 1	14 09	31/05/1984
Simmons, Alex (F)			13/03/1996
Walker, Jimmy (G)	5 11	13 05	09/07/1973
Waterfall, Luke (D)	6 2	13 03	30/07/1990
Weatherell, Jack (M)			05/04/1998
Whitehouse, Elliott (M)	5 11	12 08	27/10/1993
Wood, Bradley (D)	5 9	11 00	02/09/1991
Woodyard, Alex (M)	5 9	9 02	16/11/1992
Wright, Andy (M)			17/09/1996

FOREST GREEN ROVERS

Player	H	W	DOB
Bennett, Dale (D)	5 10	12 01	06/01/1990
Bugiel, Omar (F)			25/09/1994
Cooper, Charlie (M)			01/05/1997
Davies, Blake (F)			24/03/1998
Doidge, Christian (F)	6 1	12 02	25/08/1992
Gosling, Jake (M)	5 9	10 10	11/08/1993
Kelly, Marcus (M)	5 7	10 06	16/03/1986
Lefebvre, Simon (G)			06/05/1997
Marsh-Brown, Keanu (M)	5 11	12 04	10/08/1992
Mehew, Olly (F)			03/11/1997
Monthe, Manny (D)			26/01/1995
Mullings, Shamir (F)			30/10/1993
Noble, Liam (M)	5 8	8 09	08/05/1991
Pinnock, Ethan (D)			29/05/1993
Poke, Michael (G)	6 1	13 10	21/11/1985
Robert, Fabien (F)	5 9	10 08	06/01/1989
Russell, Sam (G)	6 0	10 12	04/10/1982
Sinclair, Rob (M)	5 10	11 03	29/08/1989
Stokes, Joe (M)			08/12/1997
Tilt, Curtis (D)			04/08/1991
Traore, Drissa (M)	5 9	11 11	25/03/1992
Wedgbury, Sam (M)	5 10	12 08	26/02/1989
Wishart, Daniel (F)			28/05/1992
Woolery, Kaiyne (F)	5 10	11 07	11/01/1995

NATIONAL LEAGUE ATTENDANCES BY CLUB 2016–17

	Aggregate 2016–17	Average 2016–17	Highest Attendance 2016–17
Tranmere R	118,990	5,173	7,790 v Chester FC
Lincoln C	118,717	5,162	10,031 v Macclesfield T
Wrexham	89,885	3,908	5,603 v Dover Ath
York C	59,108	2,570	4,091 v Wrexham
Maidstone U	54,877	2,386	3,409 v Tranmere R
Aldershot T	52,815	2,296	3,977 v Braintree T
Eastleigh	52,107	2,266	4,114 v Maidstone U
Chester FC	46,052	2,002	3,961 v Wrexham
Torquay U	43,429	1,888	4,026 v North Ferriby U
Forest Green R	40,324	1,753	2,383 v Torquay U
Sutton U	38,173	1,660	2,246 v Lincoln C
Macclesfield T	33,504	1,457	3,317 v Tranmere R
Woking	32,883	1,430	3,224 v Aldershot T
Dagenham & R	31,724	1,379	2,055 v Guiseley
Dover Ath	30,073	1,308	3,018 v Guiseley
Barrow	29,645	1,289	2,123 v Gateshead
Bromley	26,575	1,155	2,036 v Sutton U
Southport	26,238	1,141	3,462 v Lincoln C
Guiseley	23,732	1,032	2,446 v Lincoln C
Solihull Moors	23,194	1,008	1,995 v Tranmere R
Gateshead	20,923	910	3,770 v Lincoln C
Braintree T	16,648	724	1,353 v Dagenham & R
North Ferriby U	14,161	616	2,389 v Lincoln C
Boreham Wood	10,974	477	1,002 v Lincoln C

VANARAMA NATIONAL LEAGUE LEADING GOALSCORERS 2016–17

Player	Club	League	FA Cup	FA Trophy	Play-Offs	Total
Ricky Miller	Dover Ath	40	2	1	0	43
Christian Doidge	Forest Green R	25	0	0	2	27
Andy Cook	Tranmere R	23	0	0	0	23
Michael Cheek	Braintree T	19	1	3	0	23
Byron Harrison	Barrow	19	3	0	0	22
Richard Bennett	Barrow	15	1	5	0	21
Gozie Ugwu	Woking	17	2	0	0	19
Oliver Hawkins	Dagenham & R	18	0	0	0	18
Danny Johnson	Gateshead	18	0	0	0	18
James Alabi	Chester FC	17	0	1	0	18
Corey Whitely	Dagenham & R	15	1	0	0	16
Jon Parkin	York C	13	0	3	0	16
Matt Rhead	Lincoln C	15	0	0	0	15
Jordan Maguire-Drew	Dagenham & R	14	0	0	1	15
James Norwood	Tranmere R	13	0	0	2	15
Scott Rendell	Aldershot T	13	0	0	0	13
Chris Holroyd	Macclesfield T	13	0	0	0	13

NATIONAL LEAGUE NORTH 2016–17

(P) *Promoted into division at end of 2015–16 season.* (R) *Relegated into division at end of 2015–16 season.*

			Home					*Away*					*Total*						
		P	*W*	*D*	*L*	*F*	*A*	*W*	*D*	*L*	*F*	*A*	*W*	*D*	*L*	*F*	*A*	*GD*	*Pts*
1	AFC Fylde	42	13	7	1	58	26	13	3	5	51	34	26	10	6	109	60	49	88
2	Kidderminster H (R)	42	16	2	3	43	15	9	5	7	33	26	25	7	10	76	41	35	82
3	FC Halifax Town (R)¶	42	12	5	4	37	16	12	3	6	44	27	24	8	10	81	43	38	80
4	Salford C (P)	42	13	7	1	45	17	9	4	8	34	27	22	11	9	79	44	35	77
5	Darlington 1883* (P)	42	14	2	5	50	29	8	8	5	39	38	22	10	10	89	67	22	76
6	Chorley	42	13	4	4	34	20	7	10	4	26	21	20	14	8	60	41	19	74
7	Brackley T	42	9	6	6	27	21	11	7	3	39	22	20	13	9	66	43	23	73
8	Stockport Co	42	9	8	4	34	26	10	8	3	25	15	19	16	7	59	41	18	73
9	Tamworth	42	15	2	4	43	28	6	4	11	30	39	21	6	15	73	67	6	69
10	Gloucester C	42	10	3	8	41	30	8	7	6	28	31	18	10	14	69	61	8	64
11	Harrogate T	42	10	4	7	44	38	6	7	8	27	25	16	11	15	71	63	8	59
12	Nuneaton T	42	7	8	6	33	29	7	5	9	34	40	14	13	15	67	69	–2	55
13	FC United of Manchester	42	6	8	7	35	35	8	4	9	34	33	14	12	16	69	68	1	54
14	Curzon Ashton	42	6	6	9	31	36	8	4	9	32	36	14	10	18	63	72	–9	52
15	Boston U	42	7	4	10	29	33	5	7	9	25	39	12	11	19	54	72	–18	47
16	Bradford Park Avenue	42	4	5	12	22	38	8	2	11	24	36	12	7	23	46	74	–28	43
17	AFC Telford U	42	8	5	8	19	25	2	7	12	19	32	10	12	20	38	57	–19	42
18	Alfreton T	42	7	7	7	30	34	4	2	15	32	61	11	9	22	62	95	–33	42
19	Gainsborough Trinity	42	5	8	8	27	31	3	4	14	24	53	8	12	22	51	84	–33	36
20	Worcester C	42	4	8	9	30	30	3	6	12	14	33	7	14	21	44	63	–19	35
21	Stalybridge Celtic	42	5	1	15	23	48	3	4	14	17	41	8	5	29	40	89	–49	29
22	Altrincham (R)	42	1	5	15	19	46	3	4	14	20	45	4	9	29	39	91	–52	21

*¶FC Halifax T promoted via play-offs. *Darlington 1883 barred from play-offs due to failing ground-size regulations.*

NATIONAL LEAGUE NORTH PLAY-OFFS 2016–17

SEMI-FINALS FIRST LEG

Wednesday 3 May 2017

Chorley (0) 0

Kidderminster H (0) 1 *(Gnahoua 77)* 2487

Chorley: Branagan; Challoner, Teague, Leather, Charnock (O'Keefe 83), Blakeman (Roscoe 59), Whitham, Jarvis (Beesley 83), Carver, Walker.
Kidderminster H: Hornby; Hodgkiss, Francis-Angol, Lowe, Tunnicliffe, McQuilkin, Croasdale, Waite, Ironside, Gnahoua (Carter 81), Brown.
Referee: Marc Edwards.

Salford C (0) 1 *(Poole 86)*

FC Halifax T (1) 1 *(Peniket 37)* 2175

Salford C: Lynch; Nottingham, O'Halloran, Walker, Grand, Horsfall, Hulme, Johnston (Poole 64), Phenix (Allen 77), Norris, Hine.
FC Halifax T: Johnson; Roberts, Wilde, Peniket, Hotte, Brown, Kosylo, Lynch, Denton, Sinnott, Garner.
Referee: Peter Gibbons.

SEMI-FINALS SECOND LEG

Sunday 7 May 2017

Kidderminster H (0) 0

Chorley (1) 2 *(Carver 19, Roscoe 90)* 3407

Kidderminster H: Hornby; Hodgkiss (Knights 90), Lowe, Francis-Angol, Tunnicliffe, McQuilkin, Croasdale, Gnahoua, Waite (Sonupe 79), Ironside, Browne.
Chorley: Branagan; Jordan (Roscoe 76), Leather, Blakeman, Challoner, Teague, O'Keefe (Jarvis 59), Cottrell, Whitham, Walker, Carver (Charnock 85).
Referee: Joe Hull.
Chorley won 2-1 on aggregate.

FC Halifax T (0) 1 *(Peniket 96)*

Salford C (0) 1 *(Nottingham 106)* 3655

FC Halifax T: Johnson; Roberts, Garner, Wilde, Brown, Lynch (Clarke 76), Hotte, Sinnott, Denton, Charles (Peniket 89), Kosylo.
Salford C: Lynch; O'Halloran, Grand, Nottingham, Horsfall, Norris, Phenix (Johnson 91), Walker, Haughton (Poole 54), Hine (Allen 59), Hulme.
Referee: Paul Marsden.
aet; FC Halifax T won 3-0 on penalties.

FINAL

Saturday 13 May 2017

FC Halifax T (0) 2 *(Roberts 46, Garner 103)*

Chorley (0) 1 *(Blakeman)* 7920

FC Halifax T: Johnson; Roberts, Garner, Wilde (Denton 24), Brown, Lynch (Clarke 78), Hotte, Sinnott, Peniket, Charles (Moyo 62), Kosylo.
Chorley: Branagan; Jordan (Charnock 38), Leather, Blackman, Challoner, Teague, O'Keefe (Walker 58), Cottrell, Whitham (Roscoe 105), Carver, Sampson.
Referee: Daniel Middleton.
aet; FC Halifax T promoted to National League.

NATIONAL LEAGUE SOUTH 2016–17

(P) *Promoted into division at end of 2015–16 season.* (R) *Relegated into division at end of 2015–16 season.*

			Home					Away					Total						
		P	*W*	*D*	*L*	*F*	*A*	*W*	*D*	*L*	*F*	*A*	*W*	*D*	*L*	*F*	*A*	*GD*	*Pts*
1	Maidenhead U	42	16	4	1	53	11	14	4	3	40	18	30	8	4	93	29	64	98
2	Ebbsfleet U¶	42	17	3	1	62	15	12	6	3	34	15	29	9	4	96	30	66	96
3	Dartford	42	16	3	2	49	20	9	6	6	34	25	25	9	8	83	45	38	84
4	Chelmsford C	42	14	6	1	54	23	9	7	5	35	24	23	13	6	89	47	42	82
5	Poole T (P)	42	12	6	3	38	19	8	5	8	25	30	20	11	11	63	49	14	71
6	Hungerford T (P)	42	12	6	3	37	17	7	7	7	30	32	19	13	10	67	49	18	70
7	Hampton & Richmond Bor (P)	42	9	5	7	36	28	10	7	4	45	28	19	12	11	81	56	25	69
8	Wealdstone	42	7	7	7	30	31	11	5	5	32	27	18	12	12	62	58	4	66
9	Bath C	42	10	5	6	41	24	8	3	10	30	28	18	8	16	71	52	19	62
10	St Albans C	42	11	4	6	43	31	5	7	9	29	35	16	11	15	72	66	6	59
11	Eastbourne Bor	42	12	4	5	51	30	4	6	11	31	40	16	10	16	82	70	12	58
12	Hemel Hempstead T	42	9	6	6	34	36	6	6	9	40	47	15	12	15	74	83	–9	57
13	East Thurrock U (P)	42	7	9	5	37	25	7	5	9	36	40	14	14	14	73	65	8	56
14	Oxford City	42	8	5	8	21	32	7	2	12	27	41	15	7	20	48	73	–25	52
15	Weston-Super-Mare	42	6	4	11	33	35	8	2	11	30	34	14	6	22	63	69	–6	48
16	Welling U (R)	42	9	2	10	36	26	3	5	13	28	43	12	7	23	64	69	–5	43
17	Whitehawk	42	6	5	10	24	32	6	2	13	27	40	12	7	23	51	72	–21	43
18	Concord Rangers	42	6	7	8	28	37	4	5	12	29	38	10	12	20	57	75	–18	42
19	Truro C	42	7	5	9	29	41	4	2	15	24	58	11	7	24	53	99	–46	40
20	Gosport Bor	42	6	3	12	23	47	3	6	12	22	54	9	9	24	45	101	–56	36
21	Bishops Stortford	42	3	1	17	14	51	5	2	14	15	53	8	3	31	29	104	–75	27
22	Margate	42	6	2	13	17	41	1	2	18	9	40	7	4	31	26	81	–55	25

¶*Ebbsfleet U promoted via play-offs.*

NATIONAL LEAGUE SOUTH PLAY-OFFS 2016–17

SEMI-FINALS FIRST LEG

Wednesday 3 May 2017

Chelmsford C (0) 0

Dartford (0) 0 1653

Chelmsford C: Fitzsimons; Hill, Daley, Porter, Bush, Haines, Willmott, Church, Theophanous (Jeffers 84), Dickson Rees.
Dartford: Ibrahim; Wood (Harris 76), Wynter, Bonner, Vint, Brown, Hayes, Bradbrook, Ofori-Acheampong, Noble, Wanadio (Murphy 76).
Referee: Savvas Yianni.

Hampton & Richmond Bor (1) 1 *(McLean 45 (og))*

Ebbsfleet U (2) 2 *(Rance 6, McLean 44)* 1689

Hampton & Richmond Bor: Howes, Kamara, Casey, Collier, Murphy, Solomon (Rivic 81), Jelley, Odametey (Gallagher 16), Culley, Jolley, Kiernan (Hippolyte-Patrick 70).
Ebbsfleet U: Ashmore, Cook, Connors, McCoy, Winfield, Clark, Powell, Drury, McLean (Kedwell 90), Rance, Deering.
Referee: Chris Pollard.

SEMI-FINALS SECOND LEG

Sunday 7 May 2017

Dartford (0) 1 *(Ofori-Acheampong 90)*

Chelmsford C (0) 2 *(Theophanous 70, Dixon 85)* 2622

Dartford: Ibrahim; Bonner, Wynter, Vint, Harris, Bradbrook, Hayes, Brown (Noble 55), Wanadio (Murphy 75), Pugh (Pavey 75), Ofori-Acheampong.
Chelmsford C: Fitzsimons; Haines, Bush, Hill, Willmott, Porter, Rees, Dickson, Daley (Graham 46), Jeffers, Theophanous.
Referee: Gary Parsons.
Chelmsford C won 2-1 on aggregate.

Ebbsfleet U (1) 2 *(Clark 34, McQueen 89)*

Hampton & Richmond Bor (0) 1 *(Federico 61)* 2102

Ebbsfleet U: Ashmore; Clark, Winfield, McCoy, Connors, Drury, Cook (Shields 90), Deering, Rance, Powell (Kedwell 76), McLean (McQueen 68).
Hampton & Richmond Bor: Howes; Solomon (Culley 82), Murphy, Hicks, Jelley (Hippolyte-Patrick 46), Rivic (Federico 46), Kamara, Casey, Collier, Kiernan, Jolley.
Referee: Alan Dale.
Ebbsfleet U won 4-2 on aggregate.

FINAL

Saturday 13 May 2017

Ebbsfleet U (0) 2 *(Winfield 72, McQueen 75)*

Chelmsford C (0) 1 *(Graham 55)* 3134

Ebbsfleet U: Ashmore; Clark, Winfield, McCoy, Connors, Drury, Cook, Deering (Mambo 83), Rance (McQueen 70), Kedwell (Powell 46), McLean.
Chelmsford C: Fitzsimons; Spillane, Haines, Bush, Willmott, Porter, Rees (Church 82), Dickson, Jeffers (Daley 82), Graham (Buchanan 55), Theophanous.
Referee: Richard Hulme.
Ebbsfleet U promoted to National League.

ALDERSHOT TOWN

Ground: The EBB Stadium at the Recreation Ground, High Street, Aldershot, Hampshire GU11 1TW.
Tel: (01252) 320211. *Website:* www.theshots.co.uk *Email:* admin@theshots.co.uk *Year Formed:* 1926.
Record Attendance: 19,138 v Carlisle U, FA Cup 4th rd (replay), 28 January 1970. *Nickname:* 'The Shots'.
Manager: Gary Waddock. *Colours:* Red shirts with white trim, blue shorts with white trim, red socks.

ALDERSHOT TOWN – NATIONAL LEAGUE 2016–17 LEAGUE RECORD

Match No.	Date		Venue	Opponents	Result		H/T Score	Lg Pos.	Goalscorers	Attendance
1	Aug	6	A	Barrow	L	0-1	0-1	19		1664
2		9	H	Maidstone U	W	1-0	0-0	12	Mensah [88]	2355
3		13	H	Wrexham	W	2-0	1-0	8	Fenelon [3], Rendell [58]	1907
4		16	A	Bromley	D	2-2	2-1	9	Rendell [14], McClure [21]	906
5		20	A	Braintree T	L	0-2	0-1	13		677
6		27	H	North Ferriby U	W	2-0	2-0	5	Mensah [15], Bellamy [26]	1527
7		29	A	Dover Ath	W	2-1	2-1	5	Fenelon [21], Bellamy [41]	1093
8	Sept	3	H	Tranmere R	W	3-1	1-1	3	Mensah [3], Rendell (pen) [79], Evans [82]	2585
9		10	H	Chester FC	D	0-0	0-0	5		2445
10		13	A	Boreham Wood	D	1-1	0-0	6	McClure [66]	547
11		17	A	Southport	D	1-1	0-0	7	Evans [79]	772
12		24	H	Gateshead	W	3-0	0-0	7	Allen [50], McClure (pen) [60], Walker, C [90]	1647
13	Oct	1	A	York C	W	1-0	1-0	5	Mensah [29]	2188
14		4	H	Forest Green R	L	0-4	0-4	7		2195
15		8	H	Solihull Moors	W	2-0	0-0	6	Fenelon [64], Rendell [82]	1712
16		22	A	Torquay U	D	0-0	0-0	7		1788
17		25	A	Dagenham & R	L	0-1	0-0	9		1371
18		29	H	Guiseley	W	1-0	0-0	5	Walker, C [74]	1731
19	Nov	5	A	Forest Green R	L	1-2	0-1	6	Gallagher [88]	1638
20		12	A	Lincoln C	D	3-3	1-2	7	Mensah [8], Alexander [51], Rendell [72]	3461
21		19	H	Macclesfield T	L	1-2	0-1	9	Evans [69]	1636
22		22	H	Eastleigh	L	0-1	0-1	11		1609
23		26	A	Sutton U	L	0-2	0-0	11		1847
24	Dec	3	H	Boreham Wood	W	2-0	1-0	9	Rendell [35], Kanu [76]	1390
25		17	A	Chester FC	L	0-2	0-1	10		1937
26		26	H	Woking	W	4-0	4-0	8	Rendell 3 [8, 25, 45], Fenelon [10]	3456
27	Jan	1	A	Woking	W	2-1	0-0	7	Rendell [63], Gallagher [90]	3224
28		7	H	Southport	W	2-1	1-0	7	Fenelon [45], Gallagher [70]	1772
29		21	A	Gateshead	D	1-1	1-1	7	Rendell [41]	653
30		28	H	York C	D	0-0	0-0	7		2230
31	Feb	4	A	Maidstone U	W	2-0	1-0	6	Benyu [19], Gallagher [86]	2293
32		11	H	Barrow	D	2-2	2-0	6	McClure [1], Evans [26]	1858
33		18	A	Wrexham	W	2-0	0-0	7	Rendell [71], Kellermann [81]	4308
34		25	H	Bromley	W	4-0	2-0	6	Arnold [37], Fenelon [45], Gallagher [47], McClure [83]	2014
35		28	A	Eastleigh	D	1-1	1-0	6	Kanu [42]	2522
36	Mar	4	H	Lincoln C	D	0-0	0-0	6		3595
37		11	A	Guiseley	L	0-1	0-0	7		1009
38		18	H	Sutton U	W	2-0	1-0	7	Puddy (og) [42], Mensah [90]	2197
39		21	H	Dagenham & R	W	3-1	2-0	6	Fenelon [17], Mensah [38], McClure [83]	2113
40		25	A	Macclesfield T	W	2-0	0-0	5	Benyu [59], McClure [83]	1586
41	Apr	1	A	Solihull Moors	W	2-0	1-0	5	Benyu 2 [27, 61]	1238
42		8	H	Torquay U	D	1-1	0-1	5	Benyu [76]	3007
43		14	A	Tranmere R	D	2-2	2-2	6	McClure [3], Mensah [40]	6324
44		17	H	Dover Ath	W	1-0	0-0	5	McClure (pen) [73]	3857
45		22	A	North Ferriby U	W	3-0	1-0	5	Mensah 2 [31, 62], Rendell [82]	562
46		29	H	Braintree T	W	2-0	0-0	5	Evans [55], Mensah [59]	3977

Final League Position: 5

GOALSCORERS

League (66): Rendell 13 (1 pen), Mensah 11, McClure 9 (2 pens), Fenelon 7, Benyu 5, Evans 5, Gallagher 5, Bellamy 2, Kanu 2, Walker, C 2, Alexander 1, Allen 1, Arnold 1, Kellermann 1, own goal 1.
FA Cup (1): Kanu 1.
National League Play-Offs (2): Mensah 1, own goal 1.
FA Trophy (4): Mensah 2, McClure 1, Walker, C 1.

Cole 37	Alexander 42	Evans 36 + 2	Saville 6 + 2	Straker 23 + 10	Reynolds 44	Gallagher 43 + 1	Bellamy 13 + 1	Fenelon 31 + 7	Mensah 40 + 2	McClure 24 + 15	Rendell 36 + 7	Allen 9 + 13	Kellermann 15 + 13	Smith M 9	Arnold 25 + 4	Wakefield 7 + 10	Conroy 13 + 2	Walker C 3 + 10	Kanu 24 + 5	Benyu 21 + 1	Giles — + 9	Buckley 3 + 1	Hyam 1 + 2	Oyeleke 1 + 3	Match No.
1	2	3^{1}	4	5	6	7^{3}	8	9	10^{2}	11	12	13	14												1
1	8		4	2	11	10	3	5^{2}	12	7	6	9^{1}	13												2
	5	3			4	6	7	8^{2}	11^{1}	10	9^{3}	13	12	1	2	14									3
	5	3		2	4	8	7		6^{2}	11	10	12	9^{1}	1	13										4
	5		3		4	8			10	11	9	6^{1}	12	1	2	7									5
	9	4		2	11		3	5^{1}	8^{2}	7	6	12	13	1	14	10^{3}									6
1	5	3		13	4	6^{3}	7	11	9	10	14		8^{2}		2^{1}	12									7
1	9	4		2^{3}	11	10	3	5	8^{1}	7^{2}	6	12			13	14									8
1	4	2		14	3	7	6^{3}	8^{1}	11	10	9	13			5^{2}	12									9
1	6	5		4	2	9		11^{1}		10	12	7				8^{2}	3	13							10
1	2	6		5	4	8		9		11	10^{2}	12				7	3^{1}	13							11
1	5	3			4	8	6	10^{3}	9^{2}	11^{1}		7			2	14	13	12							12
1	2	6			3	10	5^{3}	7^{2}	11^{1}	8	13	9			4	14	12								13
1	9	5■			3	10		6^{1}	11	7^{3}		8^{2}	12		4	13	2	14							14
	7		3	2	11	10		12	6^{3}		5	8^{2}	13	1		9		4^{1}	14						15
1	2		4	5	3	8	9^{2}	6^{1}	11	12	10	14				7^{3}		13							16
1	3	4		2	5	6	7^{2}		11	10	9	12						13	8^{1}						17
1	2	5			4	7	13		8^{1}		10	12			3	6		9	11^{2}						18
1	3	5		14	4	7	6	11^{2}		13	9	8^{1}			2			10^{3}	12						19
1	2	3	13		4	8			6	10^{2}	11		12		5		7		9^{1}						20
1	2	3	13		4^{3}	8			6	11^{2}	10	12			5		7^{1}	14	9						21
		3		5		7			9	10^{3}	11	6^{2}	8^{1}	1	2	14	4	12	13						22
	2		4^{2}	5		8■			9^{1}	10^{3}	11	14	7	1		12	3	13	6						23
	4	3		2	6			11^{2}	8^{1}	12	10		7	1		13	5		9						24
	5^{2}	4^{1}		2	3	7		8	10^{3}		9	14		1			6	13	11	12					25
1	5	14		2	3	7		9^{2}	10	12	11^{3}		13				4		8	6^{1}					26
1	5	14		4	3	6		11^{2}	8	12	9		13				2		10^{3}	7^{1}					27
1	6			2	11	7		3^{2}	5		4		13				8		9	10^{1}	12				28
1	2			3	4	9		11^{2}	7^{1}	12	6						5		10	8	13				29
1	5	3		2	4	6		8^{1}	10		9		12						11	7					30
1	2	3			4	6		9^{1}	11^{3}	10	13		7						12	8^{2}	14	5			31
1	6	2			10	7		14	5^{3}	4^{1}	3		12						8	9^{2}	13	11			32
1	6	3			11	7		12	5^{1}		4		8		2				9	10^{2}	13				33
1	5	4			2	6		11	12	13	10^{3}		7		3				9^{2}	8^{1}	14				34
1	6^{2}	3		2	11	7		12	5^{1}		4		8■		13				9	10					35
1	5^{3}	3		12	4	6		8^{2}	9	14	10^{1}				2				11	7	13				36
1	2^{1}	4			3	6		10		9	11				5				8^{2}	7	12	13			37
1	4	3		14	5	7		9^{2}	10	13	12				2				11^{1}	8		6^{3}			38
1	4^{3}	3		13	5	6		8	10^{1}	12	9				2				11^{2}	7	14				39
1		4		3	5	6		12	9^{1}	13	10		7		2				11^{2}	8^{3}			14		40
1		4		3	11^{3}	8		5	7	13	6		9^{1}		2					10^{2}			14	12	41
1	3			13	5	6		12	10^{1}	14	9		7^{2}		2^{3}				11	8			4		42
1		5		4	2	7		12	11	9			8^{1}		3				10^{2}	6				13	43
1	5	2		14	3	8		9	11	13	10^{3}		6^{2}		4^{1}				12■	7					44
1	4	3		14	5	8		10^{2}	9	11	12		6^{1}		2^{3}					7				13	45
1	5	4		13	2	12		9	11^{2}	14	10				3				7^{3}	8^{1}				6	46

FA Cup
Fourth Qualifying Eastbourne Bor (h) 1-2

National League Play-Offs
Semi-Final 1st leg Tranmere R (h) 0-3
Semi-Final 2nd leg Tranmere R (a) 2-2
Tranmere R won 5-2 on aggregate.

FA Trophy
First Round East Thurrock U (a) 1-1
Replay East Thurrock U (h) 3-4
aet.

BARROW

Ground: Furness Building Society Stadium, Wilkie Road, Barrow-in-Furness, Cumbria LA14 5UW.
Tel: (01229) 666010. *Website:* www.barrowafc.com *Email:* office@barrowafc.com *Year Formed:* 1901.
Record Attendance: 16,854 v Swansea T, FA Cup 3rd rd, 9 January 1954. *Nickname:* 'The Bluebirds'.
Manager: Paul Cox. *Colours:* White shirts with blue trim, blue shorts, white socks with blue trim.

BARROW – VANARAMA PREMIER 2016–17 LEAGUE RECORD

Match No.	*Date*	*Venue*	*Opponents*	*Result*		*H/T Score*	*Lg Pos.*	*Goalscorers*	*Attendance*
1	Aug 6	H	Aldershot T	W	1-0	1-0	6	Hughes [7]	1664
2	9	A	Tranmere R	L	0-2	0-1	13		4977
3	13	A	Torquay U	D	1-1	0-1	16	Bennett [90]	2207
4	16	H	Chester FC	W	3-2	2-0	12	Hannah [37], Williams, J 2 [39, 57]	1251
5	20	A	Dover Ath	L	1-3	0-1	14	Hannah (pen) [89]	826
6	27	H	Braintree T	W	2-1	1-1	8	Bennett [42], Harrison [87]	966
7	29	A	North Ferriby U	W	1-0	0-0	7	Bennett [90]	581
8	Sept 3	H	Bromley	D	1-1	1-0	8	Harrison [12]	1096
9	10	H	Boreham Wood	D	1-1	0-0	8	Harrison (pen) [69]	1041
10	13	A	Southport	W	4-1	2-0	7	Harrison 2 (1 pen) [6, 27 (p)], Bennett [51], Hughes [59]	848
11	17	A	Lincoln C	W	2-1	1-1	4	Bennett [14], Harrison [85]	3578
12	24	H	York C	W	2-0	0-0	3	Livesey [57], Fry (og) [65]	1628
13	Oct 1	A	Forest Green R	D	0-0	0-0	6		2236
14	4	H	Macclesfield T	D	1-1	0-0	6	Livesey [79]	1442
15	8	H	Maidstone U	W	3-0	1-0	4	Turnbull [38], Williams, J [57], Bennett [60]	1402
16	22	A	Woking	D	1-1	1-0	5	Harrison [20]	1351
17	25	A	Wrexham	D	2-2	1-1	5	Harrison [9], Yates [88]	3616
18	29	H	Eastleigh	W	4-0	0-0	3	Harrison 3 (1 pen) [47 (p), 74, 90], Anderton [62]	1795
19	Nov 12	A	Sutton U	D	0-0	0-0	5		1588
20	19	H	Solihull Moors	W	2-1	2-0	3	Diarra [12], Harrison [15]	1184
21	22	H	Guiseley	W	3-0	2-0	4	Williams, J [41], Harrison 2 (1 pen) [44, 66 (p)]	1070
22	26	A	Dagenham & R	W	4-1	2-0	3	Hughes [41], Harrison 2 (1 pen) [45, 77 (p)], Bennett [63]	1228
23	Dec 17	A	Boreham Wood	D	1-1	0-0	5	Harrison [75]	401
24	26	H	Gateshead	D	0-0	0-0	4		2123
25	31	A	Gateshead	L	1-4	1-2	4	Livesey [7]	871
26	Jan 10	H	Southport	L	0-1	0-1	6		956
27	21	A	York C	L	1-2	0-1	6	Williams, J [74]	2430
28	24	H	Lincoln C	W	3-0	1-0	5	Harrison [9], Bennett [60], Hannah (pen) [90]	1152
29	28	H	Forest Green R	L	2-3	1-1	6	Bennett [33], Hannah [88]	1422
30	Feb 11	A	Aldershot T	D	2-2	0-2	7	Tuton [73], Hannah [90]	1858
31	15	A	Macclesfield T	W	1-0	0-0	5	Bennett (pen) [66]	1246
32	18	H	Torquay U	D	0-0	0-0	6		1391
33	28	A	Guiseley	L	0-1	0-1	8		642
34	Mar 4	H	Sutton U	D	0-0	0-0	8		1145
35	7	H	Tranmere R	W	2-1	0-1	8	Effiong [63], Williams, J [71]	1251
36	11	A	Eastleigh	L	0-2	0-1	8		2039
37	18	H	Dagenham & R	W	2-1	1-1	8	Hughes (pen) [39], Diarra [57]	1102
38	21	H	Wrexham	D	1-1	0-0	8	Diarra [90]	1009
39	25	A	Solihull Moors	W	4-2	3-0	8	Diarra [26], Williams, J [27], Hughes [29], Bennett (pen) [55]	1820
40	28	A	Chester FC	W	2-1	1-0	6	Bennett [2], Williams, J [76]	1501
41	Apr 1	A	Maidstone U	L	1-2	1-1	7	Turnbull [9]	2803
42	8	H	Woking	D	2-2	0-1	7	Williams, J [51], Bennett [83]	1326
43	14	A	Bromley	L	1-4	1-3	7	Bennett (pen) [18]	1049
44	17	H	North Ferriby U	W	3-1	3-1	7	Bennett [11], Beeley [40], Williams, J [43]	1017
45	22	A	Braintree T	W	2-0	0-0	7	Harrison [64], Wright [70]	778
46	29	H	Dover Ath	L	2-3	1-1	7	Williams, J [20], Diarra [67]	1212

Final League Position: 7

GOALSCORERS

League (72): Harrison 19 (5 pens), Bennett 15 (3 pens), Williams, J 11, Diarra 5, Hannah 5 (2 pens), Hughes 5 (1 pen), Livesey 3, Turnbull 2, Anderton 1, Beeley 1, Effiong 1, Tuton 1, Wright 1, Yates 1, own goal 1.
FA Cup (8): Harrison 3 (1 pen), Bennett 2, Turnbull 1, Williams, J 1, Yates 1.
FA Trophy (12): Bennett 5, Williams, J 2, Wright 2, Hannah 1, Livesay 1, Meikle 1.

Dixon 21	Beeley 34	Livesey 42 + 1	Diarra 46	Anderton 43	Turnbull 27 + 4	Harvey 39 + 2	Hughes 34 + 4	Williams J 40	Hannah 10 + 23	Harrison 28 + 2	Parry 2 + 2	Meikle 13 + 14	Bennett 37 + 7	Murray 4 + 2	Haworth — + 15	Smith 6	Yates 16	Wright 12 + 12	Erlandsson 2	Coughlin 2	Flatt 21	Rowe 8 + 1	Tuton 7 + 5	Thomas 2 + 3	Burke 2	Thomson 1 + 1	Effiong 1 + 6	Platt 6 + 2	Panayiotou — + 1	Newby E — + 1	Match No.
1	2	3	4	5	6	7	8^{1}	9	10^{2}	11^{3}	12	13	14																		1
1	2	4^{3}	5	3	7	6^{1}	8	11	9	10^{2}			13	12	14																2
1	2		4	3	8^{3}	5	9	7	6^{1}	11^{2}		12	13	10	14																3
1	2^{1}		4	3		6	7	8	9^{2}	10	12	11^{3}	14	5	13																4
1		4	5	3	7^{1}	6	8	9	12	10^{2}		11^{3}	14		13	2															5
1		4	5	3		8	13	11		10^{1}	7	6^{2}	9		12	2															6
1		4	5^{3}	3	7		6	9	10^{2}	11^{1}	2		13	12	14		8														7
1		4	5	3		7	8	6		11		9^{1}	10	2	12																8
1		4	5	3	13	6	7	11	12	10			9^{2}			2	8^{1}														9
1		4	5	3	13	6^{1}	7	9	12	11^{3}		14	10^{2}			2	8														10
1		3	4	2		6	8	7^{1}	12	11		13	10^{2}			5	9														11
1		4	5	3	6		7^{2}	8	12	11		13	10^{1}			2	9														12
1	2	4	5	3	6	12	7	8		11^{1}			10^{2}		13		9														13
1	2	4	5	3	6		7	11		10			9^{1}		12		8														14
1	2	3	4	5	7		6	9^{1}	12	11		13	10^{2}				8														15
1	2	4	5	3	7		6		12	10		13	11^{1}				8	9^{2}													16
1	2	4	5	3	7^{3}	12	6^{2}	11	14	10			9^{1}				8	13													17
1	2	4	5	3		7	6^{1}	11	12	10^{3}		14	9^{2}		13		8														18
1		3	4	2		5	8	7	6^{1}	10			12	9			11														19
1	2	4	5	3		7^{1}	6	11^{2}		10		14	9^{3}		13		8	12													20
1	2	3	4	5		7	6	9^{1}	12	11^{2}			10		13		8^{3}	14													21
	2	3	4	5		7	6	9^{1}	12	11^{2}		13	10				8		1												22
	2	4	5	3	13	6		7■		10^{1}		12	11				8^{2}	9	1												23
	2	4	5	3		7	6			10		11	9					8		1											24
	2	4	5	3		6	14	8	12	11^{3}		10^{1}	9^{2}		13			7		1											25
	2	4	5	3		6		11^{1}	13	10		14	9^{3}		12			8			1	7^{2}									26
	2	4	5	3	8	6	9^{1}	7^{2}		11		13	10					12			1										27
	2	4	5	3	7	8	12	11^{2}	13	10^{1}			9					6			1										28
	2	3	4	5	8^{2}	7	11^{1}		13			12	10		14			6^{3}			1	9									29
	2■	4	5	3■	10^{3}	7	11^{1}	9^{2}	14				8					12			1		6	13							30
		4	5		8	7	12		9				11					6■			1	2	10^{1}		3						31
		4	5	3		7		11	12				10^{1}								1		9	8	2	6^{2}	13				32
	2	4	5	3		7	6^{2}	11	10				9^{1}								1	8	13				12				33
	2	4^{2}	5	3	13	7	6	11	10^{1}				9								1	8	14					12^{3}			34
	3		5	4	9	7		8	11^{1}									12			1	2^{2}	10				13	6			35
	2	14	4	3	8	7^{1}		6										9			1		10			12	11^{2}	5^{3}	13		36
	2	4	5	3	8	7	6^{1}					11	10^{3}					13			1		9^{2}	14			12				37
	2	4	5	3	8	7	6					11^{2}	10^{1}					13			1		9				12				38
	2^{3}	4	5	3■	8	6	9	7				10^{2}	11^{1}					14			1	12	13								39
		4	5		8	7^{2}	6	9	13			11^{1}	10^{3}					12			1	3	14					2			40
	2	4	5		9	8^{1}	6^{3}	7	14			11^{2}	10					12			1	3	13								41
	2^{1}	4	5	3	8■	6	9^{2}	7	14			11^{3}	10								1			12				13			42
	2	4	5	3		7	6^{3}	10	12			11^{1}	9^{2}					14			1			8			13				43
	2	4	5	3	8	7		10		12			11^{1}					9			1							6			44
	2	4	5	3	9	7		8^{3}	13	12			11^{2}					10			1							6^{1}		14	45
	2	3	4	5	8	7		11	12				10					9^{1}			1							6			46

FA Cup

Fourth Qualifying	Tranmere R	(h)	2-1
First Round	Taunton T	(a)	2-2
Replay	Taunton T	(h)	2-1
Second Round	Bristol R	(a)	2-1
Third Round	Rochdale	(h)	0-2

FA Trophy

First Round	Harrogate T	(a)	3-3
Replay	Harrogate T	(h)	4-2
aet.			
Second Round	Matlock T	(h)	3-2
Third Round	Kidderminster H	(h)	1-0
Fourth Round	Tranmere R	(a)	1-5

BOREHAM WOOD

Ground: Meadow Park, Broughinge Road, Borehamwood, Hertfordshire WD6 5AL. *Tel:* (02089) 535097.
Website: borehamwoodfootballclub.co.uk *Email:* see website. *Year Formed:* 1948.
Record Attendance: 4,030 v Arsenal, Friendly, 13 July 2001. *Nickname:* 'The Wood' *Manager:* Luke Garrard.
Colours: White shirts with black trim, black shorts with white trim, white socks.

BOREHAM WOOD – NATIONAL LEAGUE 2016–17 LEAGUE RECORD

Match No.	*Date*	*Venue*	*Opponents*	*Result*		*H/T Score*	*Lg Pos.*	*Goalscorers*	*Attendance*
1	Aug 6	H	Forest Green R	W	1-0	1-0	7	Shakes [30]	504
2	9	A	Dover Ath	W	4-1	0-1	3	Davis (pen) [62], Andrade 2 [67, 77], Balanta [69]	1024
3	13	A	York C	D	1-1	0-0	2	Shakes [89]	2169
4	16	H	Tranmere R	L	0-1	0-1	5		801
5	20	H	Chester FC	D	1-1	1-0	10	Ferrier [5]	335
6	27	A	Gateshead	D	1-1	1-1	11	Balanta [6]	732
7	29	H	Maidstone U	L	0-1	0-0	15		637
8	Sept 3	A	Dagenham & R	W	2-0	0-0	12	Ferrier [49], Davis [90]	1312
9	10	A	Barrow	D	1-1	0-0	10	Ferrier [90]	1041
10	13	H	Aldershot T	D	1-1	0-0	12	Ferrier [64]	547
11	17	H	Torquay U	W	2-0	2-0	10	Jeffrey [9], Ferrier [12]	605
12	24	A	Solihull Moors	D	1-1	0-0	10	Balanta [54]	618
13	Oct 1	H	Wrexham	L	0-1	0-0	12		458
14	4	A	Braintree T	W	2-1	1-0	12	Ferrier 2 [26, 73]	533
15	8	A	Macclesfield T	W	2-0	0-0	11	Davis (pen) [70], Ferrier [82]	1386
16	22	H	North Ferriby U	W	1-0	0-0	11	Jeffrey [47]	313
17	25	A	Lincoln C	L	0-2	0-1	11		3014
18	29	H	Woking	W	2-1	0-1	9	Balanta [55], Andrade [60]	405
19	Nov 12	A	Bromley	L	0-1	0-1	10		818
20	19	H	Southport	W	2-0	1-0	7	Davis [30], Lucas [77]	314
21	22	H	Sutton U	W	1-0	1-0	7	Jeffrey [22]	371
22	26	A	Guiseley	L	1-3	0-0	7	Davis [69]	749
23	Dec 3	A	Aldershot T	L	0-2	0-1	8		1390
24	17	H	Barrow	D	1-1	0-0	9	Balanta [53]	401
25	20	H	Braintree T	L	0-1	0-0	9		313
26	27	A	Eastleigh	D	2-2	0-1	9	Ferrier [51], Woodards [90]	2213
27	31	H	Eastleigh	L	0-1	0-0	10		445
28	Jan 7	A	Torquay U	W	1-0	0-0	10	Andrade [62]	1789
29	21	H	Solihull Moors	D	0-0	0-0	11		322
30	28	A	Wrexham	L	1-2	0-1	11	Ferrier (pen) [76]	3664
31	Feb 11	A	Forest Green R	L	0-2	0-0	14		1575
32	18	H	York C	D	1-1	1-1	13	Ferrier [28]	656
33	21	A	Tranmere R	L	1-2	0-2	13	Andrade [89]	4107
34	28	A	Sutton U	L	0-1	0-1	13		1441
35	Mar 4	H	Bromley	D	0-0	0-0	13		401
36	11	A	Woking	D	0-0	0-0	14		1157
37	14	H	Dover Ath	W	5-0	0-0	12	Andrade 2 [56, 73], Shakes 3 [67, 83, 86]	314
38	18	H	Guiseley	D	0-0	0-0	11		375
39	21	H	Lincoln C	W	2-0	0-0	11	Shakes [64], Andrade [80]	1002
40	25	A	Southport	L	0-1	0-0	12		1010
41	Apr 1	H	Macclesfield T	L	2-4	1-4	12	Stephens [14], Andrade [74]	340
42	8	A	North Ferriby U	W	4-2	2-0	10	Ferrier [10], Gray (og) [28], Andrade [68], Emerton (og) [81]	357
43	14	H	Dagenham & R	L	1-3	1-1	11	Shakes [17]	801
44	17	A	Maidstone U	L	0-1	0-0	14		2880
45	22	H	Gateshead	L	0-4	0-2	14		314
46	29	A	Chester FC	W	2-0	1-0	11	Davis [45], Balanta [61]	2013

Final League Position: 11

GOALSCORERS

League (49): Ferrier 12 (1 pen), Andrade 10, Shakes 7, Balanta 6, Davis 6 (2 pens), Jeffrey 3, Lucas 1, Stephens 1, Woodards 1, own goals 2.
FA Cup (5): Balanta 2, Ferrier 2, Andrade 1.
FA Trophy (10): Davis 3, Jeffrey 3, Balanta 2, Andrade 1, Ferrier 1.

Smith 46	Devera 41	Nunn 32 + 3	Paine 40 + 3	Stephens 21	Andrade 30 + 6	Ricketts 36 + 2	Shakes 21 + 8	Davis 38 + 4	Moke 6 + 3	Balanta 38 + 4	Clifford C 14 + 6	Ferrier 22 + 8	Woodards 26 + 5	Jeffrey 19 + 5	Ilesanmi 42 + 1	Chiedozie 1 + 3	Kuhl 5 + 3	Lucas 2 + 8	Uchechi 4 + 4	Murrell-Williamson — + 4	Boal — + 1	Williams 2 + 5	Hitchcock 5 + 6	Reason 12 + 3	Goodliffe 2 + 2	Keita 1 + 1	Morgan — + 1	Sach — + 1	Match No.
1	2	3	4	5²	6	7	8	9³	10	11¹	12	13	14																1
1	3	4	2		7	6	8	9³	10²	11¹	14	13	5	12															2
1	11	2	5		9²	4	6	7³	8¹	10	12	13	3		14														3
1	3	2	5			6	7	8¹	11²	10	9■	13	4			12													4
1	4	2	5			7	6	8¹	9	11		10²			3	13	12												5
1	2		4			6	7	8		11	9	10¹	5		3	12													6
1	5	2	4			7		8	9	10¹	12	13			3	11²	6												7
1	4	12	3			9		8	14	10	6	11³	2¹		5		7²	13											8
1	11		4			3	12	5		9	8¹	6	2	13	7		10²												9
1	4		2			6		7		10	9	11	5	8¹	3				12										10
1	11	2	4			3		5		10	9	6¹		7²	8				12	13									11
1	3	2	4		12	8		6		11²	9		13	7	5		10¹												12
1	4	2	3		6			10		11	9			8	5		7¹	12											13
1	5²	2	4		7¹	8		6		11	9	10³	12	13	3				14										14
1		3	5		7²			6	12	9	8³	11	4	13	2		14		10¹										15
1	3	2	5		8	7	13	6	12	10				9¹	4				11²										16
1	11		4		7	3¹	5³	6²		10	9		2	12	8		14	13											17
1		2	5		8	6		7¹		11	10		4	9	3			12											18
1	11	2	4		5	3		12		10	9²	6¹		7	8			13											19
1	11	2		4	6	3		5		10		7²	13	8¹	9			12											20
1	11	2	13	4	7¹	3		5²		10	12			8	9			6											21
1	2	5	4			6²		7		9	13			8	3			10	11¹		12								22
1	3	5	14	4	9²	6	7¹	8		11	10³				2			12		13									23
1	11		4	5	7¹	3		6		10			2	8	9					12									24
1	11		4	5■	7¹	3	12	6²		10³		13	2	8	9					14									25
1	11	2	4		6	3		5		10²		7¹	13	8	9			12											26
1	4	2²		5	13	7	12	8¹		11		10	3	9	6														27
1	11	14	13	4	6¹	3³	12	5		9			2	7	8							10²							28
1	11	2	5			4		6		10		7	3¹	8	9								12						29
1	4	2	5		13	6	12	7¹		11		9		8	3								10²						30
1		2	3		7	12	4	5		11³		8¹			9				14				13	6²	10				31
1	2		4		7	5	12			9		10		8	3								11	6¹					32
1		5	4		14	6²	7	13		12					2				11¹				10³	8	3	9			33
1		13	3	4	7	9		8²		14		11¹	2	6³	5							12		10					34
1	3	2	4	6	12	8	9¹			11²					5							13	10	7	14³				35
1	4	2	6	7	13	8¹	14	9		12			5		3							11²	10³						36
1	11	2	4	5	9		6³	7²					3¹		10							12	13	8	14				37
1	5	2	4	7	11		8	9					3		6									10					38
1	7	2	4	5	11¹		8	9				12	3		6								13	10²					39
1	6		3	4	10		7	8				11²	2		5							13	12	9¹					40
1	7³	2²	4	5	11	12	8	9¹		14		13	3		6									10					41
1	11		4	5	7	3²	6	13		10¹		8³	2		9								14	12					42
1	4		3	2	9	7	8			11²		10	6¹		5							13		12					43
1	5			3	8	9	6			11		10	2		4									7					44
1	5	2	6	7	10		8	12		11²			3¹		4									9		13			45
1	11³	2	3	4	7²		5	6		10		8¹			9									12			13	14	46

FA Cup

Fourth Qualifying	Hendon	(h)	3-0
First Round	Notts Co	(h)	2-2
Replay	Notts Co	(a)	0-2

FA Trophy

First Round	Maidstone U	(h)	0-0
Replay	Maidstone U	(a)	3-2
Second Round	Alfreton T	(h)	2-1
Third Round	Sutton U	(a)	0-0
Replay	Sutton U	(h)	5-0
Fourth Round	Lincoln C	(h)	0-2

BRAINTREE TOWN

Ground: The Ironmongery*Direct* Stadium, off Clockhouse Way, Braintree, Essex CM7 3RD. *Tel:* (01376) 345 617.
Website: www.braintreetownfc.org.uk *Email:* braintreeTFC@aol.com *Year Formed:* 1898.
Record Attendance: 4,000 v Tottenham H, Friendly, 8 May 1952. *Nickname:* 'The Iron'. *Manager:* Brad Quinton.
Colours: Orange shirts with white trim, blue shorts, blue socks.

BRAINTREE TOWN – NATIONAL LEAGUE 2016–17 LEAGUE RECORD

Match No.	*Date*	*Venue*	*Opponents*	*Result*	*H/T Score*	*Lg Pos.*	*Goalscorers*	*Attendance*
1	Aug 6	A	North Ferriby U	D 0-0	0-0	12		557
2	9	H	Eastleigh	D 1-1	0-0	15	Barnard [71]	766
3	13	H	Macclesfield T	L 1-3	0-2	20	Barnard (pen) [81]	703
4	16	A	Maidstone U	L 1-2	0-2	21	Maybanks [90]	2252
5	20	H	Aldershot T	W 2-0	1-0	16	Goodman [8], Akinola [76]	677
6	27	A	Barrow	L 1-2	1-1	17	Isaac (pen) [21]	966
7	29	H	Torquay U	L 1-3	1-2	21	Braham-Barrett [32]	892
8	Sept 3	A	Guiseley	D 0-0	0-0	21		704
9	10	H	Gateshead	L 1-4	0-1	21	Cheek [57]	519
10	13	A	Sutton U	W 2-1	1-1	21	Isaac 2 (1 pen) [45 (p), 90]	922
11	17	A	Chester FC	L 0-1	0-1	21		1590
12	24	H	Forest Green R	L 0-1	0-1	22		621
13	Oct 1	A	Lincoln C	L 0-3	0-1	22		3554
14	4	H	Boreham Wood	L 1-2	0-1	22	Akinola [63]	533
15	8	H	York C	D 1-1	0-1	21	Barnard (pen) [88]	728
16	22	A	Dover Ath	L 1-6	1-5	21	Matthews [12]	1073
17	25	A	Woking	W 3-2	1-2	21	Muldoon [2], Cheek [52], Akinola [82]	1362
18	29	H	Solihull Moors	L 0-1	0-0	22		625
19	Nov 12	A	Wrexham	W 1-0	1-0	21	Cheek [22]	3413
20	19	H	Tranmere R	L 0-1	0-0	21		964
21	22	H	Bromley	D 2-2	1-1	21	Hall-Johnson [3], Cheek [68]	521
22	26	A	Southport	W 5-4	4-3	20	Cheek 2 [1, 45], Parry [30], Muldoon [36], Midson [64]	866
23	Dec 17	A	Gateshead	D 1-1	0-0	20	Cheek [62]	501
24	20	A	Boreham Wood	W 1-0	0-0	20	Cheek [63]	313
25	26	H	Dagenham & R	W 3-2	2-1	17	Cheek [36], Akinola 2 (1 pen) [45 (p), 64]	1353
26	Jan 2	A	Dagenham & R	L 0-3	0-2	18		1261
27	7	H	Chester FC	L 1-2	1-0	18	Midson [31]	707
28	10	H	Sutton U	W 1-0	1-0	18	Cheek [36]	568
29	21	A	Forest Green R	D 1-1	1-0	17	Cheek [14]	1735
30	Feb 11	H	North Ferriby U	W 1-0	0-0	17	Hall-Johnson [78]	410
31	14	A	Eastleigh	W 2-0	1-0	16	Cheek 2 [28, 75]	1702
32	18	A	Macclesfield T	L 0-2	0-0	16		1267
33	25	H	Maidstone U	D 0-0	0-0	17		1002
34	28	A	Bromley	W 5-0	3-0	17	Cheek (pen) [5], Midson (pen) [33], Hall-Johnson 2 [45, 73], Patterson [70]	437
35	Mar 4	H	Wrexham	L 1-2	1-1	18	Cheek [1]	698
36	7	H	Lincoln C	L 0-4	0-2	18		1182
37	11	A	Solihull Moors	D 3-3	3-1	18	Hall-Johnson [6], Cheek 2 (1 pen) [17, 23 (p)]	556
38	18	H	Southport	W 2-0	1-0	17	Corne 2 [42, 57]	501
39	21	H	Woking	L 1-3	1-2	18	Corne [21]	572
40	25	A	Tranmere R	L 0-1	0-0	18		4514
41	Apr 1	A	York C	L 0-3	0-2	19		2825
42	8	H	Dover Ath	L 1-2	1-0	21	Cheek [7]	704
43	14	H	Guiseley	W 2-0	0-0	21	Okimo [57], Cheek [71]	624
44	17	A	Torquay U	L 1-3	1-1	21	Parry [8]	2580
45	22	H	Barrow	L 0-2	0-0	22		778
46	29	A	Aldershot T	L 0-2	0-0	22		3977

Final League Position: 22

GOALSCORERS

League (51): Cheek 19 (2 pens), Akinola 5 (1 pen), Hall-Johnson 5, Barnard 3 (2 pens), Corne 3, Isaac 3 (2 pens), Midson 3 (1 pen), Muldoon 2, Parry 2, Braham-Barrett 1, Goodman 1, Matthews 1, Maybanks 1, Okimo 1, Patterson 1.
FA Cup (13): Cheek 3, Barnard 2 (1 pen), Elokobi 2, Akinola 1, Isaac 1, Lee 1, Midson 1, Muldoon 1, Patterson 1.
FA Trophy (9): Cheek 3, Midson 3, Barnard 1, Okimo 1, Parry 1.

Butler 6	Okimo 46	Lee 29 + 4	Gayle 19 + 3	Ashton 13 + 2	Midson 34 + 5	Isaac 37 + 3	Barnard 16 + 19	Akinola 24 + 1	Braham-Barrett 11 + 4	Cheek 42 + 2	Goodman 21 + 4	Williams 11 + 1	Fagan 2	Gordon 2 + 3	Corne 19 + 7	Fitzsimons 1	Maybanks 1 + 14	Beasant 28	Goodship 3 + 2	Matthews 9 + 2 / Musonda 3	Cowgill 3 + 1	Puddy 4 / McNamara 5	Muldoon 10	Elokobi 7 / Mbulu 3	Hall-Johnson 17 + 7	Taylor J 1	Lincoln 1	Patterson 10 + 1	Dias — + 2	Clohessy 26	Parry 24	Rumens 1	Jules 1 + 2	Adams 2 + 1	Twardek 9 + 3	Henshall 1 + 6	Farrell 4 + 5	*Match No.*
1	2	3	4	5	6	7	8	9	10^{1}	11	12																											1
1	3	4	5	6	7		8	9		11		2	10																									2
1■	5	7	3	4	8		9	10		11^{2}		2	6^{1}	12	13																						3
	3	7	4	5■	11		9^{1}	10		12		2		8^{2}	6	1	13																					4
1	4	6	3		7^{3}	8^{2}	10	9^{1}	14	11	5	2		12	13																						5
1	5	8		3	9	7		11	12	10^{1}	4	2			6																						6
1	3	8^{3}	4^{2}	6		9	11	10	5^{1}		12	2		13	7		14																					7
	5	7		4		8	9	10	3		6	2						12	1	11^{1}																				8
	3	6		5		8	11^{2}	9		10	4	2		7^{1}				1	12	13																			9
	2		3■	12		6	13	9	5	11	4^{3}				7		14	1	10^{1}	8^{2}																			10
	2				5		6	12	10	4	9^{1}					8		13	1	11	7^{2}	3																		11
	3	6				7		11	2	10	4				8				12	9^{1}	5	1																	12
	5	6		2^{2}	10	7	14	11	3	9	4^{3}	13									12	1	8^{1}																13
	3	6	12		9^{1}	8	13	10	2	11												5^{2}	1	7	4															14
	3	6^{1}	4		10^{2}	7	14	11		12		2								9		1	8^{3}	5	13														15
	5	7^{3}	3	12	13	6		10		11		2^{2}					14			9^{1}			8	4		1													16
	2	12	4		14	6	9	11		10^{2}	3									8^{1}			7^{3}	5			1	13										17
	2		3^{2}		14	6	7^{3}	10		11	4							1		12			9	5				8^{1}	13									18
	3	6			12	13	10^{1}	9		11^{3}	5							1		7^{2}			8	2	14					4							19
	3	6			13	14	10^{1}	9		11	4						12	1		7^{3}			8^{2}	5						2							20
	3	6		5	10	12	14	13		11	4^{3}							1		7^{2}			8		9^{1}					2							21
	2	7			8		12	9		10^{1}								1						6				11		4	3	5					22
	2	3			4	5^{3}	14	6		8^{1}								1							12			9^{2}		10	11		7	13				23
	5		2		9	7	12	10		11^{1}								1							8					3	4			6				24
	3	12	4^{2}		10	7		9		11								1							8^{1}					2	5		13	6■				25
	2	3^{1}	4		5	6	14			9^{3}					13		7^{2}	1							8■					10	11		12					26
	3	13	4		8	6^{1}	10			11^{2}					9^{3}		14	1												2	5				7	12		27
	3	13	4		6	7	10^{3}			11	12				8^{1}			1												2	5^{2}				9		14	28
	2				11	6	14			10^{2}	3				8^{3}			1							12					4	5				9	7^{1}	13	29
	3				10	7				11	4	2			13			1							12			9			5				8^{1}		6^{2}	30
	2		12		3	4	14			7^{1}	6				13			1							5			8		9^{2}	10						11^{3}	31
	2		12			3	4			7	6^{1}							1							5^{3}			8	14	9	10					13	11^{2}	32
	3	6	4		9	7				10								1							8			11		2	5							33
	2	6	5■		9	7^{1}	12			10^{3}					13		14	1							8			11^{2}		4	3							34
	3	7			10	8^{3}				11							14	1		4						6^{2}			9^{1}		2	5				12	13		35
	3	6			10					11					7^{2}		13	1		4						8			9^{1}		2	5					12		36
	2	3	4		5		13			8^{3}					7^{2}		14			11		1			6						10				9^{1}		12	37
	3				10	7	13			11^{2}					6								1		4	8^{1}					2	5				9	12		38
	3				10	7	14			11					6^{3}		13						1		4	8^{2}					2	5				9^{1}	12		39
	3				11	7	10^{1}			9	12				8								1		5	6					4	2^{2}				13			40
	2				3	4				8	6				7^{1}		12	1							5					10	11				9^{2}		13	41
	4	9			10	8			2■	11	5				7^{1}			1							12					3	6							42
	4	9			10	8			2^{1}	11	5				7^{2}			1												3	6				12		13	43
	2	3			4	5	13		6^{2}	9	7				8^{1}			1							12					10	11							44
	3			5	10	7	13		12	11	4				6			1							9^{1}					2					8^{2}			45
	5	6^{2}		3	11	7	13		14	10					12							1			8					4^{1}	2						9^{3}	46

FA Cup

Fourth Qualifying	Bromley	(h)	4-2
First Round	Eastbourne Bor	(h)	7-0
Second Round	Millwall	(a)	2-5

FA Trophy

First Round	Torquay U	(h)	2-0
Second Round	East Thurrock U	(a)	5-2
Third Round	Dulwich Hamlet	(h)	0-0
Replay	Dulwich Hamlet	(a)	2-5

BROMLEY

Ground: The Stadium, Hayes Lane, Bromley BR2 9EF. *Tel:* (02084) 605291. *Website:* bromleyfc.tv
Email: info@bromleyfc.co.uk *Year Formed:* 1892. *Record Attendance:* 10,798 v Nigeria, Friendly, 24 September 1949.
Nickname: 'The Ravens', 'The Lillywhites'. *Manager:* Neil Smith. *Colours:* White shirts with black trim, black shorts with white trim, white socks.

BROMLEY – NATIONAL LEAGUE 2016–17 LEAGUE RECORD

Match No.	Date	Venue	Opponents	Result		H/T Score	Lg Pos.	Goalscorers	Attendance
1	Aug 6	H	Tranmere R	L	0-2	0-2	21		2000
2	9	A	Torquay U	L	0-1	0-1	23		2279
3	13	A	Solihull Moors	L	0-1	0-1	24		756
4	16	H	Aldershot T	D	2-2	1-2	23	Sho-Silva 44, Dennis 74	906
5	20	H	Gateshead	W	3-2	3-1	20	Sho-Silva 2 6, 11, Anderson 36	1128
6	27	A	Guiseley	W	4-1	0-0	17	Turgott 51, Dennis (pen) 54, Porter, M 71, Goldberg 88	565
7	29	H	Eastleigh	L	0-5	0-2	19		1100
8	Sept 3	A	Barrow	D	1-1	0-1	18	Turgott 85	1096
9	10	H	Macclesfield T	L	0-1	0-1	19		1011
10	13	A	Maidstone U	W	2-0	1-0	18	Porter, G 24, Sho-Silva 55	2358
11	17	A	Forest Green R	L	0-1	0-0	19		1371
12	24	H	Dagenham & R	L	1-3	0-1	20	Swaine 50	1558
13	Oct 1	A	Southport	W	2-1	2-0	18	Cunnington 11, Higgs 24	744
14	4	H	Woking	W	2-1	1-1	18	Turgott 35, Minshull 89	808
15	8	H	Lincoln C	D	1-1	0-0	16	Turgott 65	1511
16	22	A	Wrexham	L	1-2	0-1	17	Turgott 56	3531
17	25	H	Dover Ath	L	0-2	0-2	17		1052
18	29	A	North Ferriby U	W	2-1	0-0	17	Porter, G 57, Turgott 89	354
19	Nov 12	H	Boreham Wood	W	1-0	1-0	15	Martin 42	818
20	19	A	Chester FC	D	1-1	1-0	14	Turgott 15	1827
21	22	A	Braintree T	D	2-2	1-1	14	Sho-Silva 7, Minshull 51	521
22	26	H	York C	W	3-0	2-0	14	Holland 5, Porter, G 25, Cunnington 79	1203
23	29	A	Woking	L	1-2	1-1	13	Turgott (pen) 34	1057
24	Dec 3	H	Maidstone U	W	2-0	1-0	13	Cunnington 1, Porter, G 65	1676
25	17	A	Macclesfield T	W	2-1	1-0	13	Sho-Silva 35, Turgott 85	1213
26	26	H	Sutton U	W	1-0	0-0	9	Dennis 90	2036
27	Jan 1	A	Sutton U	L	0-2	0-1	13		1766
28	7	H	Forest Green R	L	1-5	0-2	13	Swaine 50	1247
29	28	H	Southport	W	3-1	1-1	14	Hanlan 2 24, 54, Dennis 49	953
30	Feb 4	H	Torquay U	W	1-0	1-0	11	Turgott (pen) 13	889
31	11	A	Tranmere R	D	2-2	0-2	11	Hanlan 64, Holland 87	4425
32	18	H	Solihull Moors	L	0-1	0-1	11		1109
33	21	A	Dagenham & R	L	1-2	1-1	11	Hanlan 7	1202
34	25	A	Aldershot T	L	0-4	0-2	12		2014
35	28	H	Braintree T	L	0-5	0-3	12		437
36	Mar 4	A	Boreham Wood	D	0-0	0-0	12		401
37	11	H	North Ferriby U	W	3-0	1-0	11	Goldberg 34, Porter, G 78, Wynter 90	905
38	18	A	Dover Ath	L	0-1	0-0	13		988
39	25	H	Chester FC	L	0-1	0-0	14		1237
40	Apr 1	A	Lincoln C	L	0-1	0-0	16		6843
41	4	A	York C	W	2-0	1-0	14	Dennis 2, Sho-Silva 57	3000
42	8	H	Wrexham	W	4-3	2-0	11	Sho-Silva 2 9, 48, Higgs 21, Turgott 83	1006
43	14	H	Barrow	W	4-1	3-1	10	Porter, G 9, Turgott (pen) 22, Sho-Silva 2 35, 85	1049
44	17	A	Eastleigh	L	1-2	0-1	10	Higgs 83	1830
45	22	H	Guiseley	D	1-1	1-0	10	Goldberg 4	936
46	29	A	Gateshead	W	2-0	0-0	10	Dennis 2 78, 85	701

Final League Position: 10

GOALSCORERS

League (59): Turgott 12 (3 pens), Sho-Silva 11, Dennis 7 (1 pen), Porter, G 6, Hanlan 4, Cunnington 3, Goldberg 3, Higgs 3, Holland 2, Minshull 2, Swaine 2, Anderson 1, Martin 1, Porter, M 1, Wynter 1.
FA Cup (2): Turgott 1, own goal 1.
FA Trophy (7): Cunnington 3, Turgott 2, Holland 1, Porter, G 1.

Julian 31	Howe 9 + 1	Anderson 41	Chorley 24 + 2	Holland 42 + 1	Martin 26 + 3	Prestedge 10 + 3	Turgott 40 + 3	Porter M 12	Cunnington 15 + 6	Sho-Silva 30 + 8	Dymond 22 + 12	Porter G 22 + 10	Swaine 23 + 1	Goldberg 13 + 15	Dennis 16 + 9	Johnson 23 + 5	Pavey 5 + 2	Minshull 25 + 6	Higgs 25 + 7	Ajakaiye — + 3	Philpot 3	Ngoo — + 1	Wynter 5 + 7	Dunne 14 + 2	Hanlan 8	Flitney 14	Granger 1	Hall 2 + 4	McLoughlin 5 + 2	Omofe — + 3	Enver — + 1	*Match No.*
1	2^{3}	3	4	5	6	7^{1}	8	9^{2}	10	11	12	13	14																			1
1	2	3	4	5	7^{1}	6	9	8^{2}	10	11	13			12																		2
1		6	5	2		7^{2}	9	8	4^{1}	11	12		3^{3}	10	13	14																3
1		2	3	5	6		8	7		10^{2}	13		4	9^{1}	12		11															4
1		3	2	5	6^{1}	13	7	8^{3}		10■	12		4		9^{2}	14	11															5
1		8		4			9	10			7	5^{2}	3	13	6	2	11^{1}	12														6
1	12	2		5^{2}			8^{3}	9	14	13	7■	6	4		11	3	10^{1}															7
1	2	4	3		12	7^{3}	14	8	9^{2}	11		6	5		10^{1}		13															8
1	2	5	3		6		8^{2}	9	10^{1}	11		7	4	13			12															9
1	2	3	4	5	6	8	9	10		11		7^{1}		12																		10
1		4	3	5	6	7	8	9^{2}	13	11	12		2	10^{1}																		11
1		6	2	4	5	7	8	9^{2}		10	12		3■	13			11^{1}															12
1	2	7		4	5^{1}	9	10		6^{2}	11^{3}				14		3		12	8	13												13
1	2	5				7^{2}	8		9	11	14		4	10^{1}		3		12	6^{3}	13												14
1	2	5		14	7^{3}	8^{1}	9		11^{2}	10			4			3		12	6	13												15
1		8		4	5	13	10		7	12			3			2		6^{2}	9		11^{1}											16
1		5		4	6				9^{3}	10	13	12	3	14		2■		7	8^{2}		11^{1}											17
1	2	8		4	5^{1}		9			14	7	13	3	10				6^{3}	12		11^{2}											18
1		5		4	6^{1}		10		13	11	9	8^{2}	3			2		7	12													19
1		2		5	6	14	10			11^{3}	9	8^{1}	4			3		7^{2}	12			13										20
1		9		4	5		10		12	11^{2}	8^{1}	7	3			2		6	13													21
1		5	12	4	6		9		13	11^{3}	8	10^{1}	3^{2}		14	2		7														22
1		5	3	4	6^{1}		9		12	11	8	10^{3}			14	2		7^{2}	13													23
1		4		5	9		6		11^{2}	12	8	10^{1}	3			2		7	13													24
1		2	12	5			9		11	10^{1}	7	6^{2}	4			3			8				13									25
1		5		4	6^{2}		9		11		7	10^{1}	3	13	12	2			8													26
1		9		4	5^{3}		11		7		8	6^{1}	3	12	13	2^{2}			10				14									27
1		5	3^{2}	6	7^{1}		9		10			13	4■		11			12	8				2									28
1		3	2	5	6		9^{2}					13			10	12		7	8					4^{1}	11							29
1		2	4	5	6^{1}		11				13	12			9^{3}			7	8^{2}				14	3	10							30
1		4	3	5	6		9				8	10^{1}		12				7						2	11							31
		8	2	4			10^{2}				7^{3}	6		14	12			5^{1}	9				13	3	11	1						32
		4	2	5			8			12				10^{3}	9			6	7					3	11	1						33
		2	3	5	12		8^{3}			13				9	11^{2}	14		6	7					4^{1}	10		1					34
		5	3	4	14		8			13	12			9^{3}	10	2■		6■	7^{1}						11^{2}	1						35
		4	3	8	5^{2}					14	6			10^{1}	9			7	12					2	11^{3}	1		13				36
		4	3	5						11^{2}	8	12		10^{3}	9			7	6^{1}				14	2		1		13				37
		4	3	6			13			10	8^{3}	12		11^{2}	9^{1}			7	5					2		1		14				38
		8	2	4			10^{3}			11	12	13			7			5^{2}	9					3		1		6^{1}	14			39
		3	2^{2}	6			10^{3}			11		8		14	13	12		7	9					4		1			5^{1}			40
		2		5			9			11^{2}	7	6			10^{1}	3			8				13	4^{3}		1			12	14		41
				5			10			11^{2}	8^{3}	6		13		3		12	9^{1}				4			1		7	2	14		42
				4			9			10	7	6^{1}		13		3		5	8				2	12		1			11^{2}			43
				2			9			11	5^{1}	6^{2}		12		3		8	7				4	14		1			10^{3}	13		44
				3			12			11^{3}	6	9		8	13	5		4	7^{1}				14	2		1			10^{2}			45
				5			8^{3}			11^{1}		12		10^{2}	9	3		6	7				2	4		1		13			14	46

FA Cup

Fourth Qualifying	Braintree T	(a)	2-4

FA Trophy

First Round	Leiston	(h)	1-1
Replay	Leiston	(a)	5-3
Second Round	Welling U	(h)	1-2

CHESTER FC

Ground: Lookers Vauxhall Stadium, Bumpers Lane, Chester CH1 4LT. *Tel:* (01244) 371376.
Website: www.chesterfc.com *Email:* info@chesterfc.com *Year Formed:* 1885, renamed Chester City 1983, reformed as Chester FC 2010. *Record Attendance:* 20,500 v Chelsea, FA Cup 3rd rd (replay), 16 January 1952 (at Sealand Road). *Nickname:* 'The Blues'. *Manager:* Jon McCarthy. *Colours:* Blue and white striped shirts, white shorts with blue trim, white socks with blue trim.

CHESTER FC – NATIONAL LEAGUE 2016–17 LEAGUE RECORD

Match No.	Date	Venue	Opponents	Result	H/T Score	Lg Pos.	Goalscorers	Attendance
1	Aug 6	A	Gateshead	L 0-3	0-0	23		991
2	9	H	Dagenham & R	W 3-0	2-0	10	Durrell [12], Shaw [24], Alabi [59]	1841
3	13	H	Maidstone U	L 1-3	1-1	18	Alabi [31]	1912
4	16	A	Barrow	L 2-3	0-2	19	Akintunde [66], Vassell [69]	1251
5	20	A	Boreham Wood	D 1-1	0-1	19	Durrell [83]	335
6	27	H	Sutton U	W 4-0	2-0	14	Hudson [3], Lloyd [7], Shaw (pen) [85], Richards [90]	1625
7	29	A	Woking	L 1-3	1-2	18	Lloyd [26]	1271
8	Sept 3	H	Forest Green R	L 1-2	0-1	19	Durrell [79]	1820
9	10	A	Aldershot T	D 0-0	0-0	18		2445
10	13	H	Guiseley	W 2-0	0-0	17	Richards [50], Shaw (pen) [58]	1578
11	17	H	Braintree T	W 1-0	1-0	14	Hughes [16]	1590
12	24	A	Wrexham	D 0-0	0-0	15		5058
13	Oct 1	H	Dover Ath	W 5-0	0-0	11	Hunt [51], Alabi [52], Durrell (pen) [79], Mahon [85], Akintunde [90]	1686
14	4	A	North Ferriby U	W 1-0	0-0	10	Akintunde [75]	476
15	8	H	Torquay U	W 1-0	1-0	10	Lloyd [26]	2201
16	22	A	York C	D 1-1	0-0	12	Richards [90]	2639
17	25	A	Macclesfield T	D 0-0	0-0	12		1922
18	29	H	Lincoln C	L 2-5	2-2	12	Astles [33], Shaw (pen) [44]	2586
19	Nov 12	A	Tranmere R	D 2-2	0-2	12	Shaw [50], Astles [90]	7790
20	19	H	Bromley	D 1-1	0-1	12	Shaw (pen) [69]	1827
21	22	H	Southport	D 2-2	2-0	12	Richards [12], Alabi [31]	1752
22	26	A	Eastleigh	W 3-0	1-0	12	Richards [20], Durrell [72], Chapell [90]	1932
23	29	H	North Ferriby U	W 3-0	0-0	8	Richards [52], Alabi 2 (1 pen) [54 (p), 88]	1392
24	Dec 3	A	Guiseley	D 1-1	1-0	7	Alabi [29]	957
25	17	H	Aldershot T	W 2-0	1-0	7	Chapell [44], Alabi [53]	1937
26	26	A	Solihull Moors	L 2-3	1-1	7	Durrell [18], Richards [90]	1475
27	Jan 1	H	Solihull Moors	L 0-3	0-1	9		2244
28	7	A	Braintree T	W 2-1	0-1	9	Alabi 2 [60, 84]	707
29	21	H	Wrexham	D 1-1	0-0	9	Alabi (pen) [60]	3961
30	28	A	Dover Ath	L 1-3	1-1	10	Alabi [30]	1183
31	Feb 4	A	Dagenham & R	L 2-3	0-1	12	George [50], Shaw [58]	1250
32	11	H	Gateshead	L 1-2	1-1	12	Hudson [32]	2095
33	18	A	Maidstone U	L 2-4	0-4	12	Alabi (pen) [52], Hughes [67]	2120
34	25	A	Southport	W 1-0	0-0	11	Horwood [67]	1496
35	Mar 3	H	Tranmere R	L 2-3	1-0	11	Alabi (pen) [5], Astles [68]	3696
36	18	H	Eastleigh	L 0-1	0-0	15		988
37	21	H	Macclesfield T	L 2-3	1-2	15	Alabi [6], Richards [75]	1802
38	25	A	Bromley	W 1-0	0-0	13	Durrell [88]	1237
39	28	H	Barrow	L 1-2	0-1	13	Shaw [88]	1501
40	Apr 1	A	Torquay U	W 1-0	0-0	13	Hughes [80]	1881
41	8	H	York C	L 0-2	0-1	14		2235
42	11	A	Lincoln C	L 0-1	0-1	14		7401
43	14	A	Forest Green R	L 0-2	0-0	16		1936
44	17	H	Woking	L 2-3	0-0	16	Davies [55], Durrell [82]	1770
45	22	A	Sutton U	L 2-5	0-3	17	Alabi 2 [79, 82]	2082
46	29	H	Boreham Wood	L 0-2	0-1	19		2013

Final League Position: 19

GOALSCORERS

League (63): Alabi 17 (4 pens), Durrell 8 (1 pen), Richards 8, Shaw 8 (4 pens), Akintunde 3, Astles 3, Hughes 3, Lloyd 3, Chapell 2, Hudson 2, Davies 1, George 1, Horwood 1, Hunt 1, Mahon 1, Vassell 1.
FA Cup (0).
FA Trophy (3): Alabi 1, Chapell 1, Durrell 1.

Roberts 15	Vassell 26 + 5	Astles 46	Hudson 30 + 2	Hunt 37 + 2	Chapell 11 + 13	George 21 + 3	Shaw 40 + 3	Durrell 42 + 4	Alabi 40 + 2	Richards 31 + 8	Akintunde 6 + 10	Mahon 19 + 6	Hughes 31 + 5	Horwood 17 + 4	Waters 2 + 10	Joyce 11 + 19	Lloyd 39 + 2	Worsnop 4	Lynch 27	Killock — + 2	Marsh — + 2	O'Brien 1 + 3	Dawson 7 + 4	Davies 3	*Match No.*
1	2	3	4	5^{7}	6^{3}	7	8^{1}	9	10	11	12	13	14												1
1	3	5	4	2	12	8	9	7^{3}	11^{1}	10		13		6^{2}	14										2
1	2	4	3	9	12	8	7^{2}	6	11■	10^{1}	14	13		5^{3}											3
1	2	5	3	4^{1}	10		8	9^{2}		11	13			6		7	12								4
1	4	5	3		7^{1}		6	12		11^{2}		9	13	2		8	10								5
	2^{1}	4	3	14	12	6	7	8^{2}		11		10^{3}		5		13	9	1							6
		4	3^{3}	5^{2}	9^{1}	8	7	13	10	11	14		12	2			6	1							7
		3	2	4	13	7	6^{2}	9	10^{1}	11		5			12		8	1							8
1	3^{3}	5	4	2	14		7	8^{1}	10	11^{2}		6			12	13	9								9
	2	3		4	12		6	9^{3}		11	10^{2}	5^{1}	8		14	13	7	1							10
1	2	4		3			7	6^{3}	12	11^{1}	10^{2}	9	5	13		14	8								11
1	2	4	3	5	12		7	6^{3}	10^{1}	11^{2}	14	9	13				8								12
1	2	4^{1}		5		12	7^{3}	6	10	11^{2}	14	9	3			13	8								13
1	2	3		4		12	6^{1}	5	14	11^{3}	10	9	7			13	8^{2}								14
1	2	4		5	13	7		6^{3}	11	12	10^{1}	9	3			14	8^{2}								15
1	10	3		9	7^{1}	2		6	5	12		4	8				11								16
	2^{1}	4	14	5	6		7	11	10^{2}		13	9	3				8		1	12^{3}					17
		4	2	5	6		7	10	11^{1}	12	13	9^{2}	3				8		1						18
		4	3	5			7	6	10	11		9	2				8		1						19
		3	2	4	12		8	9^{2}	10	11		6^{1}	5			13	7		1						20
		3	2	4	12		7	6^{2}	10	11		9^{1}	5			13	8		1						21
		4	3	5	12		7	6	10	11^{1}		9	2				8		1						22
		4	3	5	12		7	6^{1}	10	11^{2}		9^{3}	2			13	8		1		14				23
		3	2	4	13		7	6	10	11^{2}		9^{1}	5			12	8		1						24
		4		5	11	2	7	6^{2}	10^{3}				3	9^{1}	13	12	8		1		14				25
		3		2■	8	5	6	7^{2}	11^{1}	12			9	4^{3}	14	13	10		1						26
	12	3			9	4	6	8	10	11			5	2^{1}			7		1						27
		4	3		9^{2}	2	7	6^{1}	11	10				5	12	13	8		1						28
	2	4	3	5		6■	7	9	10	11							8		1						29
1	2	4	3	5^{2}			7	6	10	11^{1}		14		13	8^{3}	12	9								30
1	2	4	3	5■		8	7	6^{1}	11				12	10^{2}		9						13			31
1	2^{2}	5	3			8	7	10	11	13			6	4^{1}		9	12								32
		4	3			9	7^{2}	6	11	13			2	5		8^{1}	10		1	12					33
	12	4		5		2^{1}	6^{3}	13	10	11		14	3	9^{2}		7	8		1						34
		4	3	5				6^{2}	10	11^{1}		14	2	9^{3}		7	8		1			12	13		35
	5	4	3^{3}	9			12	6	11	10^{2}			2	14			8		1			13	7^{1}		36
	13	4	3^{1}	9			6	10	11	12			2				8		1			5^{2}	7		37
	2	4	12	5^{3}			7	6	10	11			3^{1}	13		14	8		1				9^{2}		38
	2^{1}	5	3	6			8	7	10	11				4^{2}		13	9		1				12		39
		4	3	5			14	13	10	11^{2}			7	2^{3}	12	6^{1}	9		1				8		40
	14	3	2^{2}	4^{3}		12	7	6	11	13			5		10		8		1				9^{1}		41
	12	3	2^{1}	14		4	5	6	11	10■			7			8^{2}	9^{3}		1				13		42
	2	4		5^{2}		6	14	10	11^{1}		13		3		12	7			1				8^{3}	9	43
	2	3				4	7	10	11		12		5			6^{1}	8		1					9	44
	3	2				4	5	6	11		8		7^{1}			12	9		1				10		45
	4	3		2			7^{3}	6^{1}	10		11		5		12	14	8		1				13	9^{2}	46

FA Cup

Fourth Qualifying	Southport	(a)	0-1

FA Trophy

First Round	Witton Alb	(a)	1-1
Replay	Witton Alb	(h)	2-1
Second Round	Forest Green R	(h)	0-2

DAGENHAM & REDBRIDGE

Ground: The London Borough of Barking and Dagenham Stadium, Victoria Road, Dagenham, Essex RM10 7XL.
Tel: (020) 8592 1549. *Website:* www.daggers.co.uk *Email:* info@daggers.co.uk *Year Formed:* 1992.
Record Attendance: 5,949 v Ipswich T, FA Cup 3rd rd, 5 January 2002. *Nickname:* 'The Daggers'.
Manager: John Still. *Colours:* Red shirts with blue stripes, blue shorts with red trim, blue socks.

DAGENHAM & REDBRIDGE – NATIONAL LEAGUE 2016–17 LEAGUE RECORD

Match No.	Date	Venue	Opponents	Result		H/T Score	Lg Pos.	Goalscorers	Attendance
1	Aug 6	H	Southport	W	3-0	2-0	1	Okenabirhie [15], Guttridge [23], Maguire-Drew [67]	1296
2	9	A	Chester FC	L	0-3	0-2	11		1841
3	13	A	Guiseley	W	2-0	1-0	7	Assombalonga [6], Hawkins [76]	680
4	16	H	Lincoln C	W	1-0	1-0	4	Guttridge [26]	1399
5	20	A	Woking	W	3-1	3-0	2	Robson [11], Maguire-Drew [16], Okenabirhie [19]	1153
6	27	H	Wrexham	W	3-0	3-0	1	Hawkins 3 (1 pen) [10, 22, 45 (p)]	1256
7	29	A	Sutton U	L	0-1	0-1	4		1951
8	Sept 3	H	Boreham Wood	L	0-2	0-0	6		1312
9	10	A	Solihull Moors	W	5-2	2-0	4	Hawkins 3 (1 pen) [24, 64, 90 (p)], Okenabirhie [39], Maguire-Drew [55]	716
10	13	H	Dover Ath	W	2-0	2-0	2	Maguire-Drew [2], Hawkins (pen) [39]	1269
11	17	H	North Ferriby U	W	2-0	1-0	1	Hawkins [36], Howell [86]	1119
12	24	A	Bromley	W	3-1	1-0	1	Whitely [15], Maguire-Drew [53], Hawkins (pen) [56]	1558
13	Oct 1	H	Tranmere R	D	0-0	0-0	1		1554
14	4	A	Torquay U	L	0-1	0-1	3		1638
15	8	A	Eastleigh	W	1-0	0-0	2	Whitely [73]	2209
16	22	H	Macclesfield T	D	1-1	1-0	2	Okenabirhie [18]	1214
17	25	H	Aldershot T	W	1-0	0-0	2	Whitely [81]	1371
18	29	A	Forest Green R	D	1-1	0-0	3	Hawkins [74]	2268
19	Nov 12	H	Gateshead	L	0-5	0-1	4		1354
20	19	A	York C	W	2-0	2-0	4	Hawkins [28], Guttridge [45]	2410
21	22	A	Maidstone U	W	1-0	1-0	3	Guttridge [26]	1970
22	26	H	Barrow	L	1-4	0-2	5	Whitely [65]	1228
23	29	H	Torquay U	L	0-1	0-0	6		1072
24	Dec 3	A	Dover Ath	W	2-1	2-0	4	Maguire-Drew [11], Benson [41]	1234
25	17	H	Solihull Moors	D	4-4	2-3	4	Doe [34], Hyde [41], Hawkins [83], Whitely [85]	1112
26	26	A	Braintree T	L	2-3	1-2	5	Hawkins [32], Maguire-Drew [47]	1353
27	Jan 2	H	Braintree T	W	3-0	2-0	4	Maguire-Drew [11], Guttridge [42], Whitely [80]	1261
28	7	A	North Ferriby U	W	4-0	3-0	4	Okenabirhie [15], Hawkins 2 [17, 64], Guttridge [34]	453
29	28	A	Tranmere R	W	2-0	1-0	3	Whitely [24], Hawkins [47]	5293
30	Feb 4	H	Chester FC	W	3-2	1-0	2	Sheppard [45], Whitely (pen) [86], Maguire-Drew [90]	1250
31	11	A	Southport	W	4-1	3-1	2	Maguire-Drew [34], Cundy (og) [37], Okenabirhie [42], Whitely (pen) [77]	845
32	18	H	Guiseley	L	1-2	0-1	2	Hawkins [90]	2055
33	21	H	Bromley	W	2-1	1-1	2	Okenabirhie [40], Sheppard [88]	1202
34	28	H	Maidstone U	L	0-2	0-1	2		1456
35	Mar 4	A	Gateshead	L	0-1	0-0	4		1030
36	11	H	Forest Green R	W	2-1	0-0	2	Maguire-Drew [53], Doe [89]	1459
37	18	A	Barrow	L	1-2	1-1	4	Whitely [11]	1102
38	21	A	Aldershot T	L	1-3	0-2	4	Doe [57]	2113
39	25	H	York C	W	1-0	0-0	4	Raymond [82]	1659
40	Apr 1	H	Eastleigh	W	4-0	3-0	4	Whitely 3 (1 pen) [26, 30, 61 (p)], Benson [28]	1332
41	3	A	Lincoln C	L	0-2	0-0	4		7173
42	8	A	Macclesfield T	W	4-1	1-1	4	Guttridge [41], Whitely (pen) [65], Maguire-Drew 2 [78, 89]	1281
43	14	A	Boreham Wood	W	3-1	1-1	4	Benson 2 [29, 51], Whitely [78]	801
44	17	H	Sutton U	D	2-2	2-0	4	Guttridge [27], Maguire-Drew [38]	1634
45	22	A	Wrexham	W	1-0	1-0	4	Benson [23]	3653
46	29	H	Woking	D	1-1	0-1	4	Heard [83]	1860

Final League Position: 4

GOALSCORERS

League (79): Hawkins 18 (4 pens), Whitely 15 (4 pens), Maguire-Drew 14, Guttridge 8, Okenabirhie 7, Benson 5, Doe 3, Sheppard 2, Assombalonga 1, Heard 1, Howell 1, Hyde 1, Raymond 1, Robson 1, own goal 1.
FA Cup (4): Hawkins 1, Maguire-Drew 1, Okenabirhie 1, Whitely 1.
National League Play-Offs (1): Maguire-Drew 1.
FA Trophy (1): Benson 1.

Justham 43	Williams 10	Widdowson 45	Robson 29	Doe 36 + 3	Boucaud 36	Robinson 20	Guttridge 25 + 2	Okenabirhie 27 + 2	Hawkins 37 + 1	Maguire-Drew 36 + 6	Assombalonga 3 + 9	Staunton 26 + 9	Raymond 29 + 7	Benson 8 + 24	Whitely 35 + 2	Howell 6 + 12	Ling 7 + 4	Barnwell — + 1	Heard 2 + 7	Hyde 2 + 3	Shepherd 2	Okuonghae 3 + 1	Donnellan S 16 + 2	White — + 1	Donnellan L 1 + 1	Sheppard 10	Howells 2 + 2	Grant 1 + 2	Cousins 3	Romain 5 + 5	Pennell 1	*Match No.*
1	2	3	4	5	6	7^{3}	8^{1}	9	10	11^{2}	12	13	14																			1
1	2	3	5	4	8^{2}	6	7^{1}	11	9^{3}	10	13	12		14																		2
1	2	5	4	3	7	6	8	9	11	12	10^{1}																					3
1	2	3	5	4	7	6	8	9	10^{1}		11^{2}	12		13																		4
1	2	3	5	4	11	6	7^{1}	8		10^{2}		13		9	12																	5
1		2	4	3	10	5	6^{2}	7	8	9^{1}		11	13		12																	6
1		2	4	3		6	12	9^{3}	10^{2}	11	14	5	7	13	8^{1}																	7
1		2	4	3		6		9^{1}	10	11	12	5	8		7																	8
1		2		3	7^{2}	5		9	10^{1}	11		4	6	13	8	12																9
1		3		4	5	6		9	10	11^{1}		2	7		8^{2}	13	12															10
1		3		4	7	5		9^{1}	10^{3}	11^{2}	13	2	6	14	8	12																11
1		2		3	9^{1}	4		6	7	8		11	5		10	12																12
1		3		4	7	5		11^{2}	10	9^{1}	13	2	6		8	12																13
1		2	4	3■		6		9^{2}	11	10^{1}	13	12	5		8	7^{3}	14															14
1		5	3			8		12	11	6		4	10		9	7	2^{1}															15
1		2	4^{1}	3	9	5		10^{3}	11	8^{2}		13	6		7	12		14														16
1		2		3	6	7			10	11		5	8		9		4^{1}		12													17
1		2		4	6	7	5^{1}		10	11^{2}		3	9	13	8		12															18
1		2		3		4	6		7^{3}	8^{2}		11	5	13	10		9^{1}		12	14												19
1		2		3	8		5		6	7^{1}		11	4	12	10				9													20
1		2		3^{1}	7		9		11	10		5	6	12	8						4											21
1		5					9		11^{2}	8	12	4	6	13	10				7^{1}	14	2^{3}	3										22
1		2		3	8		7		10^{2}	11^{1}	13	4	6	12	9							5										23
1		3		4	9		6			8	5^{1}	11		7	10					12		2										24
1		2		3	8		5		6	7^{2}		11	4	12	10				13	9^{1}												25
1		2		3■	7				5	6^{3}		10	4	14	9		8^{1}		13	11^{2}		12										26
1		2			7		4^{3}	13	5^{1}	6		11	3	14	9		8^{2}		12				10									27
1		6	5				8	9^{2}	10	11^{1}		2	7^{3}				4		13				3	12	14							28
1		4	5	14	8		7	10^{1}	11	13			6		9^{2}	12							2			3^{3}						29
1		2	3		8		7^{2}	10^{1}	11	13			6^{3}	14	9	12							4			5						30
1		2	4		7			9	11	10^{2}			6	13	8^{1}								5			3	12					31
1		2	4	12	7			11^{1}	10	9^{2}				13	6■								5			3	14	8^{3}				32
1		2	3	14	7			9	10^{3}	11^{2}		13	6	12									8			4	5^{1}					33
		2	5^{2}	3	8			9	10	11^{3}			7	12			13						4			6^{1}		14	1			34
1		2^{3}	4	3	9		6^{2}	7	8^{1}	12			5	13									10			11		14				35
1		2	5	6	8			10	11^{2}	9^{1}		12	13	14	7								3^{3}			4						36
1		2	5	3	8			9^{2}	10	11^{1}		13			7								6			4				12		37
1		2	5	3				9^{2}	10^{1}	11^{3}			7	14	8	13							6			4				12		38
1	11	2	4	3			7^{1}					9	12	10	8	5														6		39
1	2^{3}	3	5	4	9		8^{2}		14			6		11^{1}	10	13							12							7		40
1		2	4	3	9				11^{3}	13		6	14	12	10	7^{1}							5							8^{2}		41
1	2	3	5	4	9^{2}		7			12			14	8	10^{3}	13							11							6^{1}		42
1	3	4	6	5	9		7^{3}			11			14	10^{1}	8^{2}	12							2							13		43
1		4	6	5	8		7^{1}			10		3		11	9								2							12		44
	2	3	5	4	9		12			8^{2}				7^{1}	10	6									11				1	13		45
						2	6^{1}	7^{3}				11	4	14		3	9		12				13				10^{2}		1	5	8	46

FA Cup

Fourth Qualifying	Wealdstone	(h)	3-1
First Round	FC Halifax T	(h)	0-0
Replay	FC Halifax T	(a)	1-2

FA Trophy

First Round	Worthing	(h)	1-2

National League Play-Offs

Semi-Final 1st leg	Forest Green R	(h)	1-1
Semi-Final 2nd leg	Forest Green R	(1)	0-2

Forest Green R won 3-1 on aggregate.

DOVER ATHLETIC

Ground: Crabbie Athletic Ground, Lewisham Road, River, Dover, Kent CT17 0JB. *Tel:* (01304) 822373. *Website:* doverathletic.com *Email:* enquiries@doverathletic.com *Year Formed:* 1894 as Dover FC, reformed as Dover Ath 1983. *Record Attendance:* 7,000 v Folkestone, 13 October 1951 (Dover FC); 5,645 v Crystal Palace, FA Cup 3rd rd, 4 January 2015 (Dover Ath). *Nickname:* 'The Whites'. *Manager:* Chris Kinnear. *Colours:* White shirts with grey trim, black shorts, black socks.

DOVER ATHLETIC – NATIONAL LEAGUE 2016–17 LEAGUE RECORD

Match No.	*Date*	*Venue*	*Opponents*	*Result*		*H/T Score*	*Lg Pos.*	*Goalscorers*	*Attendance*
1	Aug 6	A	Wrexham	D	0-0	0-0	13		5603
2	9	H	Boreham Wood	L	1-4	1-0	20	Miller (pen) [20]	1024
3	13	H	North Ferriby U	W	2-0	1-0	14	Emmanuel [34], Lafayette [75]	726
4	16	A	Eastleigh	W	4-2	0-0	10	Huddart (og) [51], Lafayette [60], Stevenson [87], Miller [89]	1854
5	20	H	Barrow	W	3-1	1-0	4	Emmanuel [30], Lafayette [56], Magri [82]	826
6	27	A	Torquay U	L	1-2	0-0	6	Miller [75]	1793
7	29	H	Aldershot T	L	1-2	1-2	11	Lafayette [45]	1093
8	Sept 3	A	Southport	W	1-0	1-0	10	Modeste [3]	760
9	10	H	Forest Green R	W	4-3	1-1	7	Miller 3 (1 pen) [12, 47 (p), 87], Lafayette [68]	785
10	13	A	Dagenham & R	L	0-2	0-2	10		1269
11	17	A	York C	W	1-0	1-0	8	Miller [24]	2137
12	24	H	Lincoln C	W	2-0	1-0	8	Grimes [4], Emmanuel [53]	1509
13	Oct 1	A	Chester FC	L	0-5	0-0	9		1686
14	4	H	Sutton U	W	3-1	1-0	8	Miller 2 [2, 57], Stevenson [85]	821
15	8	A	Gateshead	L	2-4	1-2	8	Parkinson [35], Miller [57]	688
16	22	H	Braintree T	W	6-1	5-1	8	Thomas [18], Miller 4 [22, 26, 33, 48], Parkinson [40]	1073
17	25	A	Bromley	W	2-0	2-0	6	Miller [25], Lafayette [28]	1052
18	29	H	Tranmere R	L	1-4	1-1	7	Thomas [22]	1534
19	Nov 12	A	Solihull Moors	W	3-2	0-1	6	Miller 3 [53, 60, 74]	837
20	19	H	Guiseley	W	2-0	0-0	5	Miller [46], Emmanuel [49]	3018
21	22	H	Woking	W	3-1	2-0	6	Lafayette 2 [20, 46], Emmanuel [42]	823
22	29	A	Sutton U	W	6-0	4-0	5	Miller 2 [7, 70], Emmanuel 3 [32, 45, 53], Lafayette [36]	1091
23	Dec 3	H	Dagenham & R	L	1-2	0-2	6	Miller [82]	1234
24	17	A	Forest Green R	D	1-1	0-0	6	Emmanuel [70]	1818
25	26	H	Maidstone U	D	1-1	1-0	6	Miller (pen) [16]	2369
26	Jan 1	A	Maidstone U	W	4-1	1-0	4	Emmanuel 2 [29, 55], Lafayette [74], Miller [90]	2257
27	7	H	York C	D	2-2	1-1	5	Grimes [6], Miller (pen) [72]	1308
28	10	A	Macclesfield T	L	1-2	1-0	5	Grimes [8]	1020
29	20	A	Lincoln C	L	0-2	0-1	5		6491
30	28	H	Chester FC	W	3-1	1-1	5	Miller 2 (1 pen) [26 (p), 49], Healy [58]	1183
31	Feb 11	H	Wrexham	D	1-1	0-0	5	Healy [65]	1057
32	18	A	North Ferriby U	W	2-1	0-0	5	Healy [55], Thomas [71]	465
33	25	H	Eastleigh	W	3-0	1-0	5	Miller 3 [4, 72, 80]	1164
34	28	A	Woking	L	0-1	0-0	5		1092
35	Mar 4	H	Solihull Moors	D	0-0	0-0	5		1104
36	14	A	Boreham Wood	L	0-5	0-0	6		314
37	18	H	Bromley	W	1-0	0-0	6	Healy [59]	988
38	25	A	Guiseley	W	4-0	1-0	6	Miller 2 (1 pen) [15, 80 (p)], Modeste [67], Lafayette (pen) [90]	1261
39	28	A	Tranmere R	L	0-1	0-0	8		4281
40	Apr 1	H	Gateshead	W	2-0	1-0	6	Miller 2 [34, 78]	2507
41	8	A	Braintree T	W	2-1	0-1	6	Essam [64], Miller [89]	704
42	14	H	Southport	W	3-0	1-0	5	Modeste 2 [28, 73], Miller [71]	1563
43	17	A	Aldershot T	L	0-1	0-0	6		3857
44	22	H	Torquay U	L	1-2	0-1	6	Thomas [71]	1432
45	25	H	Macclesfield T	D	2-2	1-1	6	Miller (pen) [40], Lafayette [87]	932
46	29	A	Barrow	W	3-2	1-1	6	Miller 3 (1 pen) [22, 47 (p), 90]	1212

Final League Position: 6

GOALSCORERS

League (85): Miller 40 (8 pens), Lafayette 12 (1 pen), Emmanuel 11, Healy 4, Modeste 4, Thomas 4, Grimes 3, Parkinson 2, Stevenson 2, Essam 1, Magri 1, own goal 1.
FA Cup (8): Miller 4, Marsh 1, Modeste 1, Pinnock 1, Thomas 1.
FA Trophy (2): Miller 1, Stevenson 1.

Arnold 30	Magri 42 + 1	Grimes 46	Thomas 38 + 6	Kinnear 11 + 12	Orlu 37	Parkinson 24 + 2	Stevenson 24 + 3	Miller 38 + 3	Marsh T 1 + 7	Modeste 33 + 1	Emmanuel 25 + 10	Sterling 29 + 8	Lafayette 37 + 7	Fazakerley 4 + 4	Pinnock 3 + 20	Moore 16 + 4	Jackson — + 4	Obileye — + 3	Walker 16	Healy 17 + 2	Hurst 10 + 4	Essam 15 + 1	Deverdics 5	N'Gala 5	*Match No.*
1	2	3[2]	4	5	6	7	8	9	10[1]	11	12	13													1
1	4[2]	3[1]	5	6	2	7	8	9■		11	10[3]	12	13	14											2
1	2	4	6	8		5	9		13	7[1]	11[2]	3	10		12										3
1	2	8	3	4	5	10	7	12		6	9[1]		11												4
1	2	4	5	6	3	8	7		12	10[2]	9[1]		11		13										5
1	2[3]	3	5	6[1]	4	8	7	14	12	10	11[2]		9			13									6
1	2	3	5	7[2]	4	8[3]	6	12	14	11	9[1]		10			13									7
1	2	5	3	13	4	7	6	11[2]		9	12		10			8[1]									8
1	2[2]	3	5		4	8	6	9		11		12	10	13		7[1]									9
1	2	4	5		3[1]	6	8	10		11[3]	14	12	9[2]			7	13								10
1	2	4	3	12		8	7	9		10[2]		5	11	13		6[1]									11
1	2	4	3			8	7	10			9[1]	5	11		12	6									12
1	2	3	5			6[3]	7	10			9[1]	4	11		14	8[2]	12	13							13
	2	3	5	7		8[3]	6	11[2]			9■	4	10[1]		12		14	13	1						14
		3	2	5[1]		9	6	10				4	11	8	7	12			1						15
	2	4	5			8	6	9[1]		10[3]		3[2]	11		13	7	14	12	1						16
	2	4	3			7	8	11[1]		9		5	10		12	6			1						17
	3	4	2			6[1]	7	10		9	12	5	11			8			1						18
		7	2	13	3	10■	5	6[1]		4		8	11		12	9[2]			1						19
1	2[1]	3	12		4	8	6	11			10	5			9	7									20
1	2	3	4	13	5		8				10[1]	6	11		7	9[2]				12					21
1	2	5	3		4	12	6	9[3]	14		10	7	11[2]		13	8[1]									22
1	2	7	3[2]	11[1]	4	13	5	6			9	8	10		12										23
1	2	3	4	12	6	7		8		10	9[1]	5	11												24
1	2	7	3		4	10[1]	12	6		5	9[2]	8	11			13									25
1	2	6	3	14	4	10[2]	12	5[1]			8[3]	7	11		13	9									26
1	2	4	5		3		8	9		12	10[1]	6	11			7[2]					13				27
1	3	6	4	12	5		13	10[1]	14	9[2]		7	11			8					2[3]				28
1	2	7	5		6			11	13		9[1]	8	10							12	3[2]	4			29
1	6	4	5	13	3	7		11[2]		9[3]	12	14	10							8[1]		2			30
1	2	8	3		5			7		6			9							10		4	11		31
1	2	6	3		5			10[1]		9	12	14	11[3]		13					7[2]		4	8		32
1	2	5	6[3]		3			11[1]		7[2]	13	14	10							9	12		8	4	33
1	2	6	4		5			10		11[1]	12		9[2]							8	13		7	3	34
1	2	7	3		4[1]			6		5		13	9							10		12	11	8[2]	35
1	2	7	3		5[2]					6	8[1]		10		12					11	13	4		9	36
	2	6	12		5					10[1]	11[2]	7	9		13				1	8	3	4			37
		4		14	3			10[2]		9	11[3]	5	12	7	13				1	8	6[1]	2			38
	13	7	12		3			5		4	9[1]	8	14	6[3]					1	10	11[2]	2			39
	8	4		12	3			10		9	11[1]	6	13	2[2]	14				1	7[3]		5			40
	2[1]	5	12	8	4			10		11[3]	9[2]	6	13		14				1	7		3			41
	2	5	12	13	4[2]			11[1]		7	10	6	14						1	9	8[3]	3			42
	4[3]	3	5	12	8			11		10		2	14		13				1	9[1]	7[2]	6			43
	6	4	14		3[3]			11		9[1]	12	5[2]	10		13				1	8	7	2			44
	3	7	4[1]		6			10			14	8[2]	11	13	12				1	9	2[3]	5			45
	2	7	3		6			11					10						1	9	4	5		8	46

FA Cup

Fourth Qualifying	Burgess Hill T	(a)	5-0
First Round	Cambridge U	(a)	1-1
Replay	Cambridge U	(h)	2-4

aet.

FA Trophy

First Round	Dartford	(a)	1-1
Replay	Dartford	(h)	1-2

EASTLEIGH

Ground: The Silverlake Stadium, Ten Acres, Stoneham Lane, Eastleigh, Hampshire SO50 9HT. *Tel:* (02380) 613361.
Website: eastleighfc.com *Email:* admin@eastleighfc.com *Year Formed:* 1946.
Record Attendance: 5,250 v Bolton W, FA Cup 3rd rd, 9 January 2016. *Nickname:* 'Spitfires'.
Manager: Richard Hill. *Colours:* Blue shirts with white trim, white shorts, blue socks.

EASTLEIGH – NATIONAL LEAGUE 2016–17 LEAGUE RECORD

Match No.	*Date*	*Venue*	*Opponents*	*Result*		*H/T Score*	*Lg Pos.*	*Goalscorers*	*Attendance*
1	Aug 6	H	Guiseley	W	2-1	2-0	5	Drury [11], Partington [44]	2407
2	9	A	Braintree T	D	1-1	0-0	6	Gayle (og) [64]	766
3	13	A	Tranmere R	L	1-2	1-1	12	Dugdale [30]	4619
4	16	H	Dover Ath	L	2-4	0-0	16	Bird [81], Drury [86]	1854
5	20	A	Wrexham	D	0-0	0-0	17		4034
6	27	H	Solihull Moors	W	2-0	0-0	13	Cresswell [58], Johnson [65]	1632
7	29	A	Bromley	W	5-0	2-0	9	Mandron 3 [5, 26, 65], Howells [58], Dawson [71]	1100
8	Sept 3	H	North Ferriby U	W	2-0	1-0	7	Drury [4], Johnson [51]	1883
9	10	H	Southport	D	1-1	0-0	9	Mandron [51]	1878
10	13	A	Forest Green R	D	1-1	0-0	9	Mandron [50]	1442
11	17	A	Macclesfield T	W	1-0	0-0	6	Coulson [50]	1287
12	24	H	Sutton U	W	2-1	0-0	6	Coulson 2 [48, 50]	2853
13	Oct 1	A	Woking	D	3-3	3-1	8	Coulson [7], Dugdale [29], Partington [45]	1403
14	4	H	Maidstone U	W	3-0	2-0	5	Coulson 2 [29, 85], Bird [39]	4114
15	8	H	Dagenham & R	L	0-1	0-0	7		2209
16	22	A	Lincoln C	D	0-0	0-0	10		3180
17	25	H	Torquay U	W	3-0	0-0	7	Cureton [48], Drury [89], Bird [90]	2116
18	29	A	Barrow	L	0-4	0-0	8		1795
19	Nov 12	H	York C	D	1-1	0-0	9	Mandron [52]	2431
20	19	A	Gateshead	D	2-2	2-0	11	Wilson [25], Mandron (pen) [45]	703
21	22	A	Aldershot T	W	1-0	1-0	8	Mandron [45]	1609
22	26	H	Chester FC	L	0-3	0-1	8		1932
23	29	A	Maidstone U	L	1-2	0-1	9	Mandron (pen) [49]	1714
24	Dec 17	A	Southport	L	3-4	1-2	12	Johnson [32], Constable 2 [58, 86]	769
25	27	H	Boreham Wood	D	2-2	1-0	13	Constable [8], Mandron (pen) [81]	2213
26	31	A	Boreham Wood	W	1-0	0-0	8	Wilson [47]	445
27	Jan 10	H	Forest Green R	D	1-1	1-1	12	Obileye [34]	1917
28	21	A	Sutton U	D	1-1	1-0	12	Garrett [6]	2179
29	28	H	Woking	L	0-1	0-1	13		2036
30	Feb 11	A	Guiseley	D	1-1	1-0	13	Constable [45]	609
31	14	H	Braintree T	L	0-2	0-1	13		1702
32	18	H	Tranmere R	L	0-2	0-0	15		2475
33	21	H	Macclesfield T	L	0-1	0-1	15		2345
34	25	A	Dover Ath	L	0-3	0-1	15		1164
35	28	H	Aldershot T	D	1-1	0-1	14	McAllister [80]	2522
36	Mar 4	A	York C	L	1-3	1-2	15	Stearn [16]	2406
37	11	H	Barrow	W	2-0	1-0	13	Togwell [20], Tubbs [46]	2039
38	18	A	Chester FC	W	1-0	0-0	12	Wilson [90]	988
39	21	A	Torquay U	W	3-2	1-0	12	Matthews 2 [17, 66], Obileye [55]	1528
40	25	H	Gateshead	D	1-1	0-0	10	Obileye [59]	2393
41	Apr 1	A	Dagenham & R	L	0-4	0-3	11		1332
42	8	H	Lincoln C	L	0-1	0-0	13		2738
43	14	A	North Ferriby U	L	1-2	0-1	14	Stearn [77]	364
44	17	H	Bromley	W	2-1	1-0	12	Wilson [9], Matthews [82]	1830
45	22	A	Solihull Moors	L	0-2	0-2	14		893
46	29	H	Wrexham	D	1-1	0-0	15	Tubbs [73]	2588

Final League Position: 15

GOALSCORERS

League (56): Mandron 10 (3 pens), Coulson 6, Constable 4, Drury 4, Wilson 4, Bird 3, Johnson 3, Matthews 3, Obileye 3, Dugdale 2, Partington 2, Stearn 2, Tubbs 2, Cresswell 1, Cureton 1, Dawson 1, Garrett 1, Howells 1, McAllister 1, Togwell 1, own goal 1.
FA Cup (16): Mandron 5 (2 pens), Bird 4, Drury 2, Wilson 2, Constable 1, Obileye 1, Reason 1.
FA Trophy (0).

Flitney 9	Howells 13+1	Cresswell 15 / Cole 4+2	Green 39	Essam 10+1 / Close 8+1	Pipe 6+3	Partington 20+1 / Matthews 9+4	Drury 18	Reason 17+6 / McAllister 12+3	Mandron 24+4	Constable 26+16	Bird 7+10	Dawson 6+5 / Reid 10	Wilson 10+21	Huddart 5 / Burge 5	Dugdale 18	Coulson 17+3 / Tubbs 8+1	Odubade 1+1	Taylor 20 / Barnes 2	Johnson 21	Clarke 11	Cureton 3+4	Granger —+1	Santos 1+3	Stearn 11+7	Brown 3	N'Gala 9 / Masterton 1	Togwell 23	Odoffin 19+1	Strevens 10+4	Childs 2 / Bearwish —+1	Hoyte 14	Garrett 10+1	Stack 14	Obileye 9+7	Henderson 2+1	Muggleton 2+3	Leacock-McLeod 2+3	Match No.
1	2	3	4	5	6	7	8	9^{3}	10^{2}	11^{1}	12	13	14																									1
1	9	11	3	4	5	2^{3}	6	8	10^{1}	7^{2}	14	12	13																									2
	7	10	2		4		5	13	9	6	11^{2}		12	1	3	8^{1}																						3
	8	10	2		4^{2}		6	12	9	7	14		13	1	3		5^{1}	11^{3}																				4
1	7	9	2	3			5	6^{2}	14	13	10^{3}	8^{1}			4		12	11																				5
1	6	3	5	2			8^{1}	13	10	12	11^{2}	9						7	4																			6
1	2^{1}	3	4	5^{3}		12	7^{2}	13	10	11		8	14		6			9																				7
1	2	3	5			6	9		11	10^{1}	13	7^{2}				12		8	4																			8
1	5	3	4			9	7		10	11^{1}	13	6^{2}				12		8	2																			9
1	4	3	6			9	8		10	11^{1}	12					2		7	5																			10
1	3^{1}	5	2			7		8	11	10		12				4		9	6																			11
	6	4	5			8		7	10	11^{1}	12					2		9	3	1																		12
			3			2	5	7^{2}	9	6^{1}		12			4	8		11	10	1	13																	13
	6^{1}		3		13	7		8	10	14	11^{2}	12^{3}			5	4		9	2■	1																		14
			5		2	3		7	11	14	10^{1}	9^{3}			4^{2}	6		8		1	13	12																15
	12	4	3			9	6	7	11^{2}	13	10^{1}			1		5		8	2																			16
		3	5			2	8	6	13	10^{1}	12					9		7	4	1	11^{2}																	17
		8■	3	4	12	2	5	6^{2}	14		9^{3}		13			7		10		1	11^{1}																	18
			3	4		2	9^{2}	14	10	11^{1}	12					6		7	5	1	13		8^{3}															19
			5	3		2	8^{2}	9	10^{1}	13			11	1		6		7	4					12														20
			4	5		7		6	11	13			10^{2}			2		8					12	9^{1}	1	3												21
			5			2	8		10				11^{2}			9		7	4		12		13	6^{1}	1	3												22
			5	4		2	8		10^{3}	14			12			9		7			11^{2}		13	6^{1}	1	3												23
			3^{2}		7^{3}	2■		11	10	6			12	1		13			5							4	8^{1}	9■	14									24
					12			8^{2}	10	11			13			7^{3}			4^{1}					14		3	6		9	1	2	5						25
			2	12				8^{3}		11	13		10^{1}		3									7^{2}		6	9	5	14	1		4						26
						8		13	10	11^{2}			14			5										2	7^{3}	6^{1}	9			4	1	3	12			27
									10^{1}	12			13		4									7		3	8	2	9^{3}			6	1	14	11^{2}	5		28
			5^{2}					7	12	10^{1}					4									6		3	8	2				9^{3}	1		11	13	14	29
		2^{1}		8^{2}		9				10^{3}			11		3				4								7	5	13			6	1	14		12		30
		2		8^{1}						13			10		3				4^{2}								9	5	11			6^{3}	1	12		14	7	31
		14				12		9^{1}		13			10^{3}		3									8			7	2	11				1	4		5	6^{2}	32
		2		14				10^{3}		9^{1}			12		3					1				7			8^{2}	5	11			6		4			13	33
			5					11		10^{1}			12		3^{2}					1				6^{3}			7	14	8		2	9		4			13	34
			5			13		10		12			11						4	1				9^{2}			8		7		2	6^{1}		3				35
			5	6^{1}		14		10^{3}		9			13						3	1				7^{2}			8		11		4	12		2				36
			6	7				11				5	13	9^{2}		10^{1}			3								8	2	12		4		1					37
			5	9		13		11				3	12	7^{3}		10^{2}			4^{1}								8	6			2		1	14				38
			2			7^{3}		14		10		5	13	9		11^{2}								12			8	4^{1}			6		1	3				39
			2			7		13		10^{1}		3	12	9^{2}		11^{3}								14			8	6			4		1	5				40
		13	2^{1}			7		11		14		3		9^{3}		10								12			8	6			4		1	5^{2}				41
			6	7^{1}		9^{3}		11		14		4	10^{2}		5	12											8	2			3		1	13				42
			2			6		9^{3}		4		8	12		3	5^{2}								13			7	11^{1}			10		1	14				43
			3			8^{2}		11		12		2	10^{1}		4												7	6	9		5		1	13				44
			2	3		6		12		4^{3}		8^{1}	14			5^{2}		1						13		10	7	11			9							45
			3	7		8		11^{2}		12		4^{1}	13			10^{3}		1									9	6		14	5							46

FA Cup

Fourth Qualifying	North Leigh	(h)	6-0
First Round	Swindon T	(h)	1-1
Replay	Swindon T	(a)	3-1
Second Round	FC Halifax T	(h)	3-3
Replay	FC Halifax T	(a)	2-0
Third Round	Brentford	(a)	1-5

FA Trophy

First Round	Harlow T	(a)	0-2

FOREST GREEN ROVERS

Ground: The New Lawn Stadium, Another Way, Nailsworth, Gloucestershire GL6 0FG. *Tel:* (01453) 834 860.
Website: www.forestgreenroversfc.com *Email:* reception@forestgreenrovers.com. *Year Formed:* 1889.
Record Attendance: 4,836 v Derby Co, FA Cup 3rd rd, 3 January 2009. *Nickname:* 'The Rovers'.
Manager: Mark Cooper. *Colours:* Green and black hooped shirts, green shorts with black trim, green and black hooped socks.

FOREST GREEN ROVERS – NATIONAL LEAGUE 2016–17 LEAGUE RECORD

Match No.	*Date*	*Venue*	*Opponents*	*Result*		*H/T Score*	*Lg Pos.*	*Goalscorers*	*Attendance*
1	Aug 6	A	Boreham Wood	L	0-1	0-1	20		504
2	9	H	Sutton U	D	1-1	1-0	16	Tubbs [7]	1370
3	13	H	Gateshead	W	1-0	0-0	13	Bennett [90]	1143
4	16	A	Woking	W	1-0	1-0	11	Marsh-Brown [19]	864
5	20	H	York C	W	2-1	1-1	6	Murphy [40], Tubbs (pen) [90]	1396
6	27	A	Maidstone U	W	4-1	2-1	3	Carter [5], Doidge [45], Murphy 2 [75, 79]	2274
7	29	H	Southport	W	5-1	2-0	1	Moore 2 [6, 78], Chemlal [10], Clough [61], Murphy [86]	1621
8	Sept 3	A	Chester FC	W	2-1	1-0	1	Noble [24], Carter [52]	1820
9	10	A	Dover Ath	L	3-4	1-1	1	Noble [7], Murphy [49], Doidge [85]	785
10	13	H	Eastleigh	D	1-1	0-0	3	Murphy [57]	1442
11	17	H	Bromley	W	1-0	0-0	2	Marsh-Brown [73]	1371
12	24	A	Braintree T	W	1-0	1-0	2	Marsh-Brown [38]	621
13	Oct 1	H	Barrow	D	0-0	0-0	2		2236
14	4	A	Aldershot T	W	4-0	4-0	1	Robert 2 [5, 27], Moore 2 [8, 45]	2195
15	8	A	North Ferriby U	W	3-0	1-0	1	Pinnock [43], Clough [75], Doidge [90]	501
16	22	H	Guiseley	W	3-0	1-0	1	Carter [20], Doidge [47], Lawlor (og) [58]	1723
17	25	A	Solihull Moors	W	1-0	0-0	1	Daly (og) [59]	919
18	29	H	Dagenham & R	D	1-1	0-0	1	Murphy [48]	2268
19	Nov 5	H	Aldershot T	W	2-1	1-0	1	Doidge 2 [17, 90]	1638
20	12	A	Macclesfield T	W	1-0	1-0	1	Marsh-Brown [2]	1749
21	19	H	Lincoln C	L	2-3	1-0	1	Doidge [25], Marsh-Brown [65]	2164
22	22	H	Tranmere R	D	2-2	2-1	1	Doidge [3], Noble [29]	2040
23	26	A	Wrexham	L	1-3	0-2	1	Carter [68]	3472
24	Dec 17	H	Dover Ath	D	1-1	0-0	3	Moore [90]	1818
25	26	A	Torquay U	L	3-4	0-0	3	Doidge [73], Clough [74], Pinnock [77]	2540
26	Jan 1	H	Torquay U	D	5-5	2-3	3	Marsh-Brown 2 [4, 29], Doidge 2 [62, 83], Moore, B (og) [88]	2383
27	7	A	Bromley	W	5-1	2-0	3	Frear [28], Doidge 2 [43, 90], Marsh-Brown [51], Pinnock [54]	1247
28	10	A	Eastleigh	D	1-1	1-1	2	Doidge [24]	1917
29	21	H	Braintree T	D	1-1	0-1	2	Clough [59]	1735
30	28	A	Barrow	W	3-2	1-1	2	Noble [6], Doidge [64], Monthe [90]	1422
31	Feb 11	H	Boreham Wood	W	2-0	0-0	3	Doidge [83], Bugiel [88]	1575
32	18	A	Gateshead	L	1-3	0-2	3	Woolery [49]	916
33	25	H	Woking	W	4-3	1-1	3	Marsh-Brown [37], Doidge [56], Bugiel 2 [88, 90]	1566
34	Mar 4	H	Macclesfield T	W	3-0	1-0	2	Doidge [12], Noble [52], Ellis [71]	1569
35	11	A	Dagenham & R	L	1-2	0-0	3	Doidge [81]	1459
36	14	A	Sutton U	W	2-1	2-0	2	Ellis [32], Doidge [35]	1446
37	18	H	Wrexham	W	3-0	1-0	2	Bennett [45], Noble (pen) [47], Doidge [64]	2146
38	21	H	Solihull Moors	W	2-1	1-0	1	Robert [40], Doidge [90]	1445
39	25	A	Lincoln C	L	1-3	1-0	2	Doidge [10]	6798
40	Apr 1	H	North Ferriby U	L	0-1	0-0	3		1709
41	8	A	Guiseley	W	1-0	1-0	3	Doidge [26]	760
42	11	A	Tranmere R	W	1-0	0-0	3	Woolery [85]	6907
43	14	H	Chester FC	W	2-0	0-0	3	Doidge [50], Noble [74]	1936
44	17	A	Southport	L	0-2	0-0	3		844
45	22	H	Maidstone U	D	2-2	1-0	3	Marsh-Brown [11], Lokko (og) [55]	2030
46	29	A	York C	D	2-2	2-1	3	Bugiel 2 [6, 35]	3984

Final League Position: 3

GOALSCORERS

League (88): Doidge 25, Marsh-Brown 10, Murphy 7, Noble 7 (1 pen), Bugiel 5, Moore 5, Carter 4, Clough 4, Pinnock 3, Robert 3, Bennett 2, Ellis 2, Tubbs 2 (1 pen), Woolery 2, Chemlal 1, Frear 1, Monthe 1, own goals 4.
FA Cup (1): Noble 1.
National League Play-Offs (6): Doidge 2, Woolery 2, Noble 1 (1 pen), Marsh-Brown 1.
FA Trophy (4): Kelly 2, Carter 1, Marsh-Brown 1.

Russell 46	Traore 27 + 3	Pinnock 37	Clough 25	Bennett 41 + 1	Frear 7 + 12	Carter 25 + 4	Sinclair 19 + 4	Chemlal 5 + 1	Doidge 35 + 5	Murphy 12 + 5	Tubbs 6 + 5	Robert 10 + 13	Racine 12 + 1	Marsh-Brown 22 + 11	Moore 10 + 7	Jefford 9	Noble 39 + 1	Kelly 9 + 11	Wishart 27 + 2	Monthe 11 + 2	Cooper 19 + 2	Mullings 5 + 7	Woolery 10 + 6	Gosling 4 + 3	Ellis 17	Bugiel 6 + 10	Wedgbury 6 + 4	Tilt 5 + 2	Mehew — + 1	*Match No.*
1	2	3	4	5	6	7^{2}	8	9	10	11^{1}	12	13																		1
1	6^{1}	4	2	3	12		13	8			10	11^{2}	5	7	9															2
1	7^{3}	4		3		13	14	6^{2}	9	12	10	11^{1}	5	8		2														3
1	7	2		3		12	8^{2}		10^{3}	11^{1}	13		4	9	14	5	6													4
1	3^{1}	7		4				10	12	11^{2}	8	13	9	5		2	6													5
1	6^{3}	3		4	12	8			10^{1}	11		14	5	7^{2}	13	2	9													6
1	2^{3}	8	3	4	5	13		11^{2}		14	9^{1}	12	10		6		7													7
1		3	5	6	12	9				11^{3}	13	14	2	7^{2}	10	4^{1}	8													8
1	6^{2}	5	3	2	13	7			12	11^{1}	10^{3}	9	4		14		8													9
1	6^{3}	4	5	2	12	8			10	11^{2}	14			7^{1}		3	9	13												10
1	13	10	3	4	7	8			14	11^{2}				5^{1}	12	2	9	6^{3}												11
1		5	4	2	9	10			11			12	14	8^{1}	13	3	6^{3}	7^{2}												12
1	8^{2}	3	5	6	12	9			11	13		14	2	7^{3}		4^{1}	10													13
1	3	2	4	5		6^{2}		12		11^{3}		10^{1}		14	7		8	13	9											14
1	5	4	3	2	14	7			13	10^{1}		8^{3}		12	9^{2}		6		11											15
1	5	3	2	4		6^{2}			10	13		11^{3}		12	7^{1}		8	14	9											16
1	6^{2}	2	3	4		5			10			11^{1}		12	8		7	13	9											17
1	5	2	3	4	13	7			10	11^{2}				6^{1}	12		8		9											18
1	5^{2}	4	3		14	6^{1}	12		9	11^{3}	10		2	13			7		8											19
1		8	2		5	6^{1}	10		4^{2}				11	3	12		7	13	9											20
1	12	3	2	13	6^{1}	7	9		10				4	5			8^{2}		11											21
1	3	2	4	5		7	9		10^{2}	13	12			6^{1}			8		11											22
1	8	2	3	4		6	9		11^{2}			13		5			7		10^{1}	12										23
1	14	4	3		13	7^{3}	6^{2}							12	11		8	5^{1}		2	9	10								24
1	2^{3}	7	3	4	13		10		12					14	5		6		8^{2}		11^{1}	9								25
1		9	2	3	12	6^{2}	11		5					4	7^{1}		8		10			13								26
1		5	3	4	7^{1}		9^{3}		11			12		6^{2}			8		10	2	13	14								27
1		5	3	4			8^{1}		10					6^{2}			7	13	11	2	9	12								28
1		4	3	5			9		11					6^{2}			8	7		2^{1}	10		12	13						29
1		7		3			9		4					13			6		8^{1}	12	10		5	11^{2}	2					30
1		7		3			9^{2}		4					12			6		8		10^{1}		5^{3}	11	2	13	14			31
1		4		5					9					13			6		12	2^{3}	7	14	10	8^{1}	3	11^{2}				32
1		8				6^{2}	10		5					3^{1}			7		9		11			13	2	12	4			33
1		8		3		5	10^{3}		4								7^{2}	14	9^{1}		11		6		2	12	13			34
1		3^{3}		4		5^{2}	7^{1}		9			14					6	12	11		8		10		2	13				35
1	5^{1}	4		3					9			14					8	7^{3}	11		13		12		2	10^{2}	6			36
1	2^{2}	3^{3}		5		6	14		10^{1}								7	8			9		11		4	13	12			37
1				3			9		5			11					7	13	8^{1}		10^{2}		12	14	2	6^{3}	4			38
1	4^{2}			3		7			10			14					8	6			9		11^{3}		2	13	5^{1}	12		39
1	7^{3}			4			8		11			10^{2}						6^{1}	12		9		14	5	3	13		2		40
1	4^{1}			6		14			7			12							9	3	11	10^{2}	13		5	8^{3}		2		41
1				5					9									8^{2}	10	3	7	11^{1}	12		4	13	6	2		42
1	4			6					7								12	13	10^{1}	3	11	14	9^{3}		5	8^{2}		2		43
1				5					9					13			7		11^{3}	3	8^{1}	12	10		4	14	6	2^{2}		44
1	5^{2}			3					9^{3}					6^{1}			7		10	2	8	14	11		4	13	12			45
1	7^{1}			4^{3}								10		5^{2}			6	12	8	2		9			3	11		13	14	46

FA Cup
Fourth Qualifying Sutton U (a) 1-2

National League Play-Offs
Semi-Final 1st leg Dagenham & R (a) 1-1
Semi-Final 2nd leg Dagenham & R (h) 2-0
Forest Green R won 3-1 on aggregate.
Final Tranmere R (Wembley) 3-1

FA Trophy
First Round Truro C (h) 1-1
Replay Truro C (a) 1-0
aet.
Second Round Chester FC (a) 2-0
Third Round Macclesfield T (a) 0-1

GATESHEAD

Ground: Gateshead International Stadium, Neilson Road, Gateshead, Tyne and Wear NE10 0EF.
Tel: (0191) 4783883. *Website:* www.gateshead-fc.com *Email:* info@gateshead-fc.com
Year Formed: 1889 (Reformed 1977). *Record Attendance:* 20,752 v Lincoln C, Division 3N (at Redheugh Park), 25 September 1937. *Nickname:* 'The Tynesiders', 'The Heed'. *Manager:* Neil Aspin.
Colours: White shirts with black trim, black shorts, white socks with black trim.

GATESHEAD – NATIONAL LEAGUE 2016–17 LEAGUE RECORD

Match No.	Date	Venue	Opponents	Result		H/T Score	Lg Pos.	Goalscorers	Attendance
1	Aug 6	H	Chester FC	W	3-0	0-0	2	York 2 [62, 82], Smith, M [88]	991
2	9	A	Southport	W	3-0	1-0	2	Johnson, D [45], York [87], Brundle [90]	926
3	13	A	Forest Green R	L	0-1	0-0	5		1143
4	16	H	York C	W	6-1	1-1	2	Bowman 2 [17, 56], Johnson, D [47], Ajala [75], Fyfield [80], Jones, S [84]	1331
5	20	A	Bromley	L	2-3	1-3	7	Bolton [5], Johnson, D (pen) [81]	1128
6	27	H	Boreham Wood	D	1-1	1-1	5	Bowman [8]	732
7	29	A	Lincoln C	L	0-3	0-1	10		3687
8	Sept 3	H	Sutton U	W	1-0	0-0	9	Oates [65]	890
9	10	A	Braintree T	W	4-1	1-0	6	Styche 2 [23, 52], McLaughlin [70], York [82]	519
10	13	H	North Ferriby U	L	0-1	0-0	8		614
11	17	H	Solihull Moors	D	0-0	0-0	9		541
12	24	A	Aldershot T	L	0-3	0-0	12		1647
13	Oct 1	H	Torquay U	D	0-0	0-0	13		693
14	4	A	Tranmere R	W	1-0	0-0	11	Jones, S [51]	4048
15	8	H	Dover Ath	W	4-2	2-1	9	York [36], Jones, S 2 [44, 59], McLaughlin [48]	688
16	22	A	Maidstone U	W	2-0	1-0	9	Johnson, D 2 [45, 70]	2208
17	25	A	Guiseley	D	1-1	0-0	10	Johnson, D [86]	762
18	29	H	Wrexham	D	2-2	1-0	11	Jones, S [36], Johnson, D [49]	832
19	Nov 12	A	Dagenham & R	W	5-0	1-0	8	Jones, S 2 [20, 60], Brundle [47], Johnson, D (pen) [62], Smith, M [64]	1354
20	19	H	Eastleigh	D	2-2	0-2	7	Jones, S [71], Johnson, D (pen) [79]	703
21	22	H	Macclesfield T	D	1-1	1-1	9	Johnson, D [12]	491
22	26	A	Woking	L	0-3	0-1	9		1062
23	29	H	Tranmere R	L	0-1	0-1	10		723
24	Dec 3	A	North Ferriby U	L	0-1	0-1	11		498
25	17	H	Braintree T	D	1-1	0-0	11	McLaughlin (pen) [85]	501
26	26	A	Barrow	D	0-0	0-0	12		2123
27	31	H	Barrow	W	4-1	2-1	7	Hannant [26], Bell, N [39], Burrow [49], York [70]	871
28	Jan 7	A	Solihull Moors	W	2-0	1-0	8	Bell, N [22], Jones, S [90]	750
29	21	H	Aldershot T	D	1-1	1-1	8	Burrow [35]	653
30	28	A	Torquay U	L	1-3	0-1	9	McLaughlin (pen) [54]	1555
31	Feb 4	H	Southport	W	3-0	2-0	8	Burrow [27], Smith, G [43], Johnson, D [62]	620
32	11	A	Chester FC	W	2-1	1-1	8	Johnson, D [36], Burrow [63]	2095
33	18	H	Forest Green R	W	3-1	2-0	8	Johnson, D 2 [21, 30], York [56]	916
34	21	A	York C	W	3-1	2-1	6	Johnson, D [1], McLaughlin (pen) [44], York [76]	2320
35	Mar 4	H	Dagenham & R	W	1-0	0-0	7	Johnson, D [48]	1030
36	11	A	Wrexham	W	2-0	0-0	5	Burrow [53], Johnson, D [90]	3986
37	14	A	Macclesfield T	D	1-1	0-0	5	Smith, M [75]	993
38	18	H	Woking	W	2-1	0-1	5	Johnson, D [52], York [90]	832
39	21	H	Guiseley	D	1-1	0-1	5	York [62]	833
40	25	A	Eastleigh	D	1-1	0-0	5	Mafuta [57]	2393
41	Apr 1	A	Dover Ath	L	0-2	0-1	8		2507
42	8	H	Maidstone U	L	1-2	1-0	8	Burrow [26]	967
43	14	A	Sutton U	L	0-3	0-1	8		1889
44	17	H	Lincoln C	L	1-2	1-0	8	McLaughlin (pen) [29]	3770
45	22	A	Boreham Wood	W	4-0	2-0	8	York [13], Hannant [16], Smith, M [86], Fyfield [90]	314
46	29	H	Bromley	L	0-2	0-0	8		701

Final League Position: 8

GOALSCORERS

League (72): Johnson, D 18 (3 pens), York 11, Jones, S 9, Burrow 6, McLaughlin 6 (4 pens), Smith, M 4, Bowman 3, Bell, N 2, Brundle 2, Fyfield 2, Hannant 2, Styche 2, Ajala 1, Bolton 1, Mafuta 1, Oates 1, Smith, G 1.
FA Cup (4): Jones, S 2, Brundle 1, own goal 1.
FA Trophy (3): Burrow 2, Smith 1.

Johnson S 10	Bolton 37 + 2	Smith G 34 + 4	Smith M 44	Hogan 44	Fyfield 37	Mafuta 29 + 8	McLaughlin 44	York 36 + 7	Johnson D 32 + 6	Styche 6 + 11	Bowman 4 + 3	Ajala 1 + 6	Jones S 18 + 8	Brundle 25 + 9	Sweeney — + 1	Oates 2 + 4	Wrightson — + 3	Hanford 24 + 1	Penn 15	Bell N 5 + 4	Jones D 3	Hannant 10 + 8	Atkinson 6 + 1	Burrow 22 + 1	Montgomery 12	Beere 1 + 6	Green 1	White — + 1	Wright — + 4	O'Donnell 4	Mellish — + 1	*Match No.*
1	2	3	4	5	6	7	8	9^{1}	10^{3}	11^{2}	12	13	14																			1
1	2	3	4	5	6	10	11	7	8^{2}	9^{1}	12			13																		2
1	2	4	5	6	7	9	10	8^{3}	13	11^{1}	12			3^{2}	14																	3
1	2	3	4	5	6	10	11	7^{1}	8^{2}		9	12	13																			4
1	2	3	4■	5	6^{2}	8	9		11	13	10^{1}	12	7^{3}	14																		5
1	2	3		4	5	8	9	6	10^{1}		11	7^{2}	12	13																		6
1	2	3^{3}	4	5	6	10	11	7	8^{2}	13	9^{1}	12	14																			7
1	2	6	4	3	5	7	8	10^{1}	11^{2}	12				9		13																8
1	2	3	4	5		13	11	6	12	10^{1}			8	7		9^{2}																9
1	2^{1}	4	5	6		13	7	8	12	11			9^{2}	3		10^{3}	14															10
	2	3	4	5		8	9	7	10^{1}	11^{2}			12	6^{3}		14	13	1														11
	2	3	5	6		8^{1}	7	10	11	12			13	4^{2}		14		1	9^{3}													12
	2^{1}	6	4	3	5		8	10	11■	12			9^{2}			13		1	7													13
		5^{1}	9	3	4	12	7	6		13			10	2				1	8	11^{2}												14
			2	3	4	13	10	8^{1}		12			7	6				1	9	11^{2}	5											15
		2	3	5				7^{1}	11	12			9	6				1	8		4	10										16
		2^{1}	3	4				5	7	13			8	6				1	10		9	11^{2}	12									17
		3	4			13	5	6^{2}	11^{3}	12			7	2			14	1	9			10	8^{1}									18
	2^{2}	12	3	4	5		11	14	7^{3}				8	6				1	10^{1}			13	9									19
	5^{1}	12	4^{2}	3	6		9	13	11				10	7				1	8				2									20
	2^{2}	3		4	5		10	12	11	13			7^{1}	6				1	9				8									21
	2		3	4	5		10	12	11				7	6				1	9				8^{1}									22
	2	3	4	5		13	10	12	11				7	6				1	9^{2}				8^{1}									23
	2^{3}	3	4	5	6		11^{2}	12	8				9	7				1	10^{1}			14		13								24
	2		3	4	5	14	8	12	11^{2}				9^{3}	6				1	7^{1}			13		10								25
	2	14	3	4	5	9	11		13			12	6^{1}					1	7^{3}			10^{2}		8								26
	4		3	2	5	7	8	6	13			12						1		11^{1}		9^{2}		10								27
	2		3	4	5	9	11	6					12					1		8^{1}		10		7								28
	2		3	4	6	9	10	7					8^{1}	5				1		12				11								29
	3		4	5	6	9	8^{1}	7	13				14	2^{2}				1		10^{3}		12		11								30
	2	3	4	5	6	8	9	7	10^{1}											12				11	1							31
	2	3	4	5	6	8	9	7	10^{1}															11	1	12						32
	2	3^{3}	4	5	6	9	8	7^{1}	11^{2}					13						14				10	1	12						33
	2	3^{2}	4	5	6	8	9	7	10^{1}					13										11	1	12						34
	5	8^{2}	3	2	4	6	7	11^{1}	9					13										10	1	12						35
	2	4^{1}	3	5	6^{2}	8	9	7	10					13										11	1	12						36
	2	3^{1}	4	5	6	9	7	8	10															11	1	12						37
	2^{2}	5	4	3		7	8	11	9					13								12		10	1	6^{1}						38
		8	3	2	4	6^{1}	7	11	9					5								12		10	1							39
	12	2^{1}	3	4	5	8	9	7	10					6										11	1							40
	13	9^{1}	3	2	4	6^{2}	8		10					5								12		11	1		7^{3}	14				41
	2		3	4	5	10	11	6	8^{1}					7^{3}				14				13		9	1^{2}				12			42
		12	3	2	4	8	9	7						5^{1}				1				6		11					13	10^{2}		43
	2	3	4	5	6		9	7						12				1				8		11						10^{1}		44
	2	3	4	5	6	12	9	7^{1}										1				8		11					13	10^{2}		45
	2	9^{2}	3		4	7^{3}	6	11										1		13		5		10					12	8^{1}	14	46

FA Cup

Fourth Qualifying	Alfreton T	(a)	2-2
Replay	Alfreton T	(h)	2-3

aet.

FA Trophy

First Round	King's Lynn T	(h)	2-0
Second Round	Lincoln C	(h)	1-3

GUISELEY

Ground: Nethermoor Park, Otley Road, Guiseley, Leeds LS20 8BT. *Tel:* (01943) 873223. *Website:* guiseleyafc.co.uk
Email: see website. *Year Formed:* 1909. *Record Attendance:* 6,548 v Carlisle U, FA Cup 1st rd, 13 November 1994 (at Valley Parade); 2,486 v Bridlington T, FA Vase Semi-Final 1st leg, 24 March 1990 (at Nethermoor Park).
Nickname: 'The Lions'. *Manager:* Adam Lockwood. *Colours:* White shirts with blue trim, blue shorts with white trim, blue socks with white trim.

GUISELEY – NATIONAL LEAGUE 2016–17 LEAGUE RECORD

Match No.	*Date*	*Venue*	*Opponents*	*Result*	*H/T Score*	*Lg Pos.*	*Goalscorers*	*Attendance*
1	Aug 6	A	Eastleigh	L 1-2	0-2	18	Rankine [57]	2407
2	9	H	Wrexham	L 2-3	1-1	22	Rankine [12], Lawlor [83]	1130
3	13	H	Dagenham & R	L 0-2	0-1	23		680
4	16	A	North Ferriby U	L 2-3	1-2	24	Johnson 2 [29, 83]	487
5	20	A	Solihull Moors	L 2-3	1-1	24	Hatfield [41], Boyes [77]	554
6	27	H	Bromley	L 1-4	0-0	24	Smith [86]	565
7	29	A	Tranmere R	L 0-1	0-1	24		4798
8	Sept 3	H	Braintree T	D 0-0	0-0	24		704
9	10	H	Woking	D 1-1	0-0	24	Boyes [47]	649
10	13	A	Chester FC	L 0-2	0-0	24		1578
11	17	A	Maidstone U	D 1-1	0-1	24	Webb-Foster [65]	2106
12	24	H	Macclesfield T	L 1-2	1-2	24	Preston [36]	891
13	Oct 1	A	Sutton U	L 0-1	0-1	24		1282
14	4	H	York C	W 6-1	4-1	24	Cassidy [18], Purver 2 [21, 23], Preston [30], Hylton [55], Atkinson, R [82]	1626
15	8	H	Southport	W 2-1	0-0	23	Cassidy [49], Rankine [82]	1046
16	22	A	Forest Green R	L 0-3	0-1	24		1723
17	25	H	Gateshead	D 1-1	0-0	23	Walton (pen) [65]	762
18	29	A	Aldershot T	L 0-1	0-0	23		1731
19	Nov 12	H	Torquay U	W 2-0	2-0	21	Preston [14], Cassidy [19]	924
20	19	A	Dover Ath	L 0-2	0-0	23		3018
21	22	A	Barrow	L 0-3	0-2	24		1070
22	26	H	Boreham Wood	W 3-1	0-0	22	Atkinson, R [47], Hatfield [50], Cassidy [80]	749
23	29	A	York C	D 1-1	0-0	22	Cassidy [85]	1907
24	Dec 3	H	Chester FC	D 1-1	0-1	22	Walton (pen) [52]	957
25	17	A	Woking	D 0-0	0-0	23		969
26	26	H	Lincoln C	W 2-1	1-1	22	Hatfield 2 [12, 90]	2446
27	Jan 1	A	Lincoln C	L 1-3	1-0	22	Habergham (og) [12]	5148
28	7	H	Maidstone U	W 2-1	1-0	21	Walton (pen) [32], Rankine [83]	1040
29	21	A	Macclesfield T	W 2-1	1-1	21	Rankine 2 (1 pen) [29 (p), 48]	1349
30	Feb 4	A	Wrexham	L 1-3	1-1	22	Cassidy [11]	3730
31	11	H	Eastleigh	D 1-1	0-1	22	Lawlor [90]	609
32	14	H	Sutton U	W 2-1	1-1	20	Cassidy [7], Rooney [90]	664
33	18	A	Dagenham & R	W 2-1	1-0	19	Preston 2 [12, 52]	2055
34	25	H	North Ferriby U	L 1-2	1-0	19	Hatfield [13]	951
35	28	H	Barrow	W 1-0	1-0	18	Hurst, K [13]	642
36	Mar 4	A	Torquay U	W 2-1	0-1	17	Cassidy [64], Hatfield [72]	1446
37	11	H	Aldershot T	W 1-0	0-0	17	Preston [54]	1009
38	18	A	Boreham Wood	D 0-0	0-0	16		375
39	21	A	Gateshead	D 1-1	1-0	16	Lawlor [15]	833
40	25	H	Dover Ath	L 0-4	0-1	16		1261
41	Apr 1	A	Southport	W 1-0	0-0	15	Hurst, K [72]	981
42	8	H	Forest Green R	L 0-1	0-1	17		760
43	14	A	Braintree T	L 0-2	0-0	17		624
44	17	H	Tranmere R	L 1-2	1-0	19	Asamoah [33]	2148
45	22	A	Bromley	D 1-1	0-1	20	Preston [50]	936
46	29	H	Solihull Moors	D 1-1	0-1	20	Lowe [90]	1519

Final League Position: 20

GOALSCORERS

League (50): Cassidy 8, Preston 7, Hatfield 6, Rankine 6 (1 pen), Lawlor 3, Walton 3 (3 pens), Atkinson, R 2, Boyes 2, Hurst, K 2, Johnson 2, Purver 2, Asamoah 1, Hylton 1, Lowe 1, Rooney 1, Smith 1, Webb-Foster 1, own goal 1.
FA Cup (1): Boyes 1.
FA Trophy (2): Rankine 2.

Atkinson D 9	Williams 27 + 3	East 14 + 2	Palmer 30 + 4	Vidal 10 + 2	Lockwood 2	Lawlor 32 + 1	Hatfield 43 + 1	Clee 9 + 5	Preston 31 + 12	Rankine 18 + 21	Johnson 7 + 4	Smith 3 + 4	Boyes 12 + 23	Syers 1 + 1	Atkinson R 22 + 1	Boshell D — + 1	Deasy 1	Purver 19 + 7	Porritt 1 + 4	Maxted 36	Webb-Foster 4 + 1	Walton 33 + 1	Lowe 28	Whitehouse 1	Brown 31	Hylton 3	Cassidy 30	Wesolowski 12	Logan — + 9	Green 6 + 2	Asamoah 9 + 6	Hurst K 15 + 1	Rooney 7	Wells — + 1	Match No.
1	2	3	4	5^{3}	6	7	8	9^{1}	10^{2}	11	12	13	14																						1
1	10	11	9	2	3	4	5		14	7^{1}	6^{2}	13	12	8^{3}																					2
1	4	5	3	2		7	9			11	10^{1}	8	12	13	6^{2}																				3
1	2	3	5	14		6^{2}	8		11	10^{1}	9	7^{3}	12		4	13																			4
	4	5	3	2^{1}		13	7^{3}		11^{2}	10	9	14	12		6		1	8																	5
1	2		3	5			9^{2}	14	11	10^{1}	6^{3}	12	8		4			7	13																6
1			7	2		3	5^{3}	8	13	14	12	4^{2}	6^{1}		11			10	9																7
			4	3		6	7	10	11	13	9^{2}		8^{1}		2			5	12	1															8
	12		3	2		5	7	10	11	13			9^{1}		4			6		1	8^{2}														9
			2	4		6^{1}	7■	9	10^{2}	14			8		3			5	13	1	11^{3}	12													10
			13	3^{1}		5		11	12	10^{2}	9^{3}		8		4			6		1	14	7	2												11
			4			5	12	9^{3}	10				14		2			6	13	1	11	7^{2}	3	8^{1}											12
						4	5	12	7	13			6		10			8		1	11^{2}	9^{1}	3		2										13
						5	6	12	9	13			14		4			7		1		8	2		3^{3}	10^{1}	11^{2}								14
						4	6	12	9^{3}	14			13		3			7		1		8	5		2	11^{1}	10^{2}								15
1		4^{1}	14			5	6	13	10^{2}				12		3			7				8	2			11^{3}	9								16
		7				3	4	5^{1}					12		9			6		1		8	2				10	11							17
		3	4			6■	7	10^{3}	12	14	13		9^{1}		2			8		1			5				11^{2}								18
	12	9	6				4		7^{3}	14			5^{1}		11			8		1			3		2		10^{2}		13						19
		4	5				8		10^{1}	13			9^{2}		3			6		1			7		2		11		12						20
1	7^{3}	8	6				4^{1}		13	5					10			14				9	3		2		11^{2}		12						21
		3	4				7^{1}		10	12					2			8		1		9	6		5		11^{2}		13						22
		6^{1}	5				7^{2}		10^{3}	12			14		3			8		1		9	4		2		11		13						23
	12	3	2				7		11						4^{1}			8		1		9	6		5		10								24
	8		6				4		7^{1}	5										1		9	3		2		10	11	12						25
	2		5				6^{2}		10^{3}	9■	13		12					14		1		7	4		3		11^{1}	8							26
	8		6				4		7^{1}				5■							1		9	3■		2		10	11		12					27
	3		4				6		11^{1}	10										1		7			5		9	8	12	2					28
						5	6		12	9			13							1		7	4		2		10^{2}	8^{1}		3	11				29
	2					5	7		12	11			13							1		8	4		3		9^{3}		14		10^{1}	6^{2}			30
	4					5	7		12	9^{1}			13							1		8	3		2		10				11^{2}	6			31
	8					4	6		12	13			14							1		9	3		2		10^{1}				11^{2}	5^{3}	7		32
	2					5	7		9^{1}	12			13							1		6	4		3		10^{3}		14		11^{2}		8		33
	9					4	5		8^{3}	7^{2}			14							1		10	3■		2		11^{1}			13		12	6		34
	8					3	5		7^{2}	13										1		9			2		10			11	12	4^{1}	6		35
	3		12	14		5■	8^{1}		10^{2}				13							1		7			4		11^{3}			2		6	9		36
	3		5				8		10^{1}				12							1		7			4		11^{2}			2	13	6	9		37
	3		4				7		10	13										1		9			5		11			2^{2}	12	6^{3}	8^{1}	14	38
	9		7			4	6		8^{3}	14			13							1		10	3		2		11^{2}				12	5^{1}			39
	4		5^{3}			6	8		10	14								12		1		9^{2}	3		2		11				13	7^{1}			40
	8					4	6		7^{2}	14			13					12		1		9	3		2		10^{1}	11^{3}				5			41
	7		14			4	6			13								12		1		8^{1}	3^{3}		2		9■	10			11	5^{2}			42
	2		3			5	7		11^{3}	13			10^{2}					14		1		8^{1}			4			9			12	6			43
	8^{1}		7			3	5		13	6								12		1		9			2			10^{2}			11	4			44
	8^{2}	14	7			3^{1}	5^{3}		12	6					13					1		9			2			10			11	4			45
1		13	7^{2}			4			12	6^{3}			14									8	3		2		9	10			11	5^{1}			46

FA Cup

Fourth Qualifying	Lincoln C	(a)	0-0
Replay	Lincoln C	(h)	1-2

FA Trophy

First Round	Chorley	(a)	1-0
Second Round	Nuneaton T	(a)	1-6

LINCOLN CITY

Ground: Sincil Bank Stadium, Sincil Bank, Lincoln LN5 8LD. *Tel:* (01522) 880 011.
Website: www.redimps.com *Email:* info@lincolncityfc.co.uk *Year Formed:* 1884.
Record Attendance: 23,196 v Derby Co, League Cup 4th rd (replay), 15 November 1967. *Nickname:* 'The Red Imps'.
Manager: Danny Cowley. *Colours:* Red and white striped shirts, black shorts with white trim, red socks.

LINCOLN CITY – NATIONAL LEAGUE 2016–17 LEAGUE RECORD

Match No.	*Date*	*Venue*	*Opponents*	*Result*		*H/T Score*	*Lg Pos.*	*Goalscorers*	*Attendance*
1	Aug 6	A	Woking	W	3-1	1-0	3	Marriott ^{28}, Rhead 2 (1 pen) $^{60, 73 (p)}$	1592
2	9	H	North Ferriby U	W	6-1	4-1	1	Rhead 2 (1 pen) $^{2, 24 (p)}$, Arnold ^{5}, Waterfall ^{16}, Margetts ^{51}, Wood ^{66}	3622
3	13	H	Sutton U	L	1-3	0-1	4	Habergham ^{51}	3195
4	16	A	Dagenham & R	L	0-1	0-1	14		1399
5	20	H	Southport	W	4-0	3-0	8	Margetts 4 (1 pen) $^{16, 30, 45, 79 (p)}$	2440
6	27	A	Macclesfield T	W	2-1	0-1	4	Anderson ^{56}, Marriott ^{75}	1650
7	29	H	Gateshead	W	3-0	1-0	3	Raggett ^{6}, Arnold ^{50}, Marriott ^{83}	3687
8	Sept 3	A	Torquay U	W	2-1	1-1	3	Rhead 2 (1 pen) $^{2 (p), 90}$	2061
9	10	A	Tranmere R	W	1-0	0-0	1	Bonne ^{67}	5274
10	13	H	Solihull Moors	D	0-0	0-0	1		4049
11	17	H	Barrow	L	1-2	1-1	3	Arnold ^{33}	3578
12	24	A	Dover Ath	L	0-2	0-1	5		1509
13	Oct 1	H	Braintree T	W	3-0	1-0	4	Arnold ^{3}, Waterfall ^{52}, Muldoon ^{89}	3554
14	4	A	Wrexham	W	2-1	2-0	2	Waterfall ^{30}, Anderson ^{44}	3847
15	8	A	Bromley	D	1-1	0-0	3	Anderson ^{46}	1511
16	22	H	Eastleigh	D	0-0	0-0	3		3180
17	25	H	Boreham Wood	W	2-0	1-0	3	Arnold ^{45}, Rhead ^{73}	3014
18	29	A	Chester FC	W	5-2	2-2	2	Rhead 2 $^{42, 48}$, Raggett ^{45}, Muldoon ^{81}, Anderson ^{83}	2586
19	Nov 12	H	Aldershot T	D	3-3	2-1	2	Arnold 2 $^{21, 30}$, Rhead ^{90}	3461
20	19	A	Forest Green R	W	3-2	0-1	2	Woodyard ^{69}, Waterfall ^{89}, Raggett ^{90}	2164
21	22	A	York C	W	4-1	2-0	2	Whitehouse ^{24}, Arnold ^{29}, Waterfall ^{61}, Wood ^{74}	2889
22	26	H	Maidstone U	W	2-0	0-0	2	Robinson ^{52}, Rhead ^{54}	3917
23	29	H	Wrexham	W	1-0	1-0	1	Whitehouse ^{14}	3344
24	Dec 17	H	Tranmere R	W	2-1	1-1	1	Arnold ^{3}, Marriott ^{81}	6335
25	26	A	Guiseley	L	1-2	1-1	1	Waterfall ^{26}	2446
26	Jan 1	H	Guiseley	W	3-1	0-1	1	Power (pen) ^{57}, Raggett ^{87}, Arnold ^{90}	5148
27	20	H	Dover Ath	W	2-0	1-0	1	Sterling (og) ^{9}, Hawkridge ^{83}	6491
28	24	A	Barrow	L	0-3	0-1	1		1152
29	31	A	Solihull Moors	W	1-0	0-0	1	Muldoon ^{52}	1650
30	Feb 11	H	Woking	W	3-2	1-1	1	Rhead 2 $^{9, 60}$, Thomas (og) ^{51}	5553
31	21	A	North Ferriby U	W	1-0	1-0	1	Waterfall ^{21}	2389
32	28	H	York C	D	1-1	0-1	1	Power ^{76}	6892
33	Mar 4	A	Aldershot T	D	0-0	0-0	1		3595
34	7	A	Braintree T	W	4-0	2-0	1	Angol 3 (1 pen) $^{14, 22, 82 (p)}$, Arnold ^{85}	1182
35	21	A	Boreham Wood	L	0-2	0-0	2		1002
36	25	H	Forest Green R	W	3-1	0-1	1	Angol ^{55}, Kelly (og) ^{61}, Habergham ^{76}	6798
37	28	A	Sutton U	D	1-1	0-0	1	Whitehouse ^{81}	2246
38	Apr 1	H	Bromley	W	1-0	0-0	1	Knott ^{65}	6843
39	3	H	Dagenham & R	W	2-0	0-0	1	Whitehouse ^{47}, Rhead ^{68}	7173
40	8	A	Eastleigh	W	1-0	0-0	1	Raggett ^{77}	2738
41	11	H	Chester FC	W	1-0	1-0	1	Anderson ^{35}	7401
42	14	H	Torquay U	W	2-1	0-0	1	Anderson ^{86}, Habergham ^{88}	9011
43	17	A	Gateshead	W	2-1	0-1	1	Arnold ^{90}, Rhead (pen) ^{90}	3770
44	22	H	Macclesfield T	W	2-1	1-1	1	Hawkridge 2 $^{29, 76}$	10,031
45	25	A	Maidstone U	D	0-0	0-0	1		3014
46	29	A	Southport	D	1-1	1-0	1	Angol ^{32}	3462

Final League Position: 1

GOALSCORERS

League (83): Rhead 15 (4 pens), Arnold 12, Waterfall 7, Anderson 6, Angol 5 (1 pen), Margetts 5 (1 pen), Raggett 5, Marriott 4, Whitehouse 4, Habergham 3, Hawkridge 3, Muldoon 3, Power 2 (1 pen), Wood 2, Bonne 1, Knott 1, Robinson 1, Woodyard 1, own goals 3.
FA Cup (14): Robinson 7, Power 2 (1 pen), Raggett 2, Arnold 1, Hawkridge 1, own goal 1.
FA Trophy (12): Ward 3, Hawkridge 2, Whitehouse 2, Angol 1, Habergham 1, Raggett 1, Southwell 1, own goal 1.

Farman 44	Wood 32 + 2	Habergham 43	Waterfall 44	Beevers 14 + 1	McCombe 3 + 4	Arnold 43 + 2	Woodyard 44 + 1	Muldoon 10 + 15	Marriott 8 + 17	Rhead 40 + 3	Margetts 7 + 3	Miles — + 1	Hodge — + 2	Raggett 41	Simmons — + 2	Hawkridge 24 + 8	Power 14 + 16	Anderson 13 + 12	Bonne 5 + 3	Champion 3 + 2	Robinson 12 + 2	Whitehouse 14 + 14	Andersen 1	Howe 4 + 4	Long 12 + 2	Ward — + 2	Knott 8 + 5	Southwell 2	Ginnelly 7 + 6	Angol 11	Etheridge 2	Calder 1	*Match No.*
1	2	3	4	5	6	7^{1}	8	9	10^{2}	11	12	13^{3}	14																				1
1	2	3	4	5	14	7^{3}	8	9^{1}		10^{2}	11		13	6	12																		2
1	2■	3	4	5^{1}	14	8^{2}	7	9	12	10^{3}	11			6		13																	3
1		2		3	5	7	8	9	10^{2}		11			4		12	6^{1}	13															4
1		2	5	3	14	8^{3}	11	12	9^{1}		10			4^{2}		6	13	7															5
1		2	3	4	5	8^{2}	9		13	10^{1}	11					6	12	7															6
1	2	3	4	8		10^{3}	11		6^{1}	5^{2}	12			9		13	14	7															7
1	2	3	4	8		10^{2}	11		6^{3}	5				9		12	14	7^{1}	13														8
1	2^{3}	3	4	7		9^{2}	11		13	5				8		6	14	12	10^{1}														9
1	2	3	5			8	9		11^{1}	10				4		6^{2}		13	12	7													10
1	2	3	4			8	9	13	14	10				5			12	6^{3}	11^{1}	7^{2}													11
1	2	3	4	12		7	8	10^{2}	13	9^{1}				5^{3}				14	11	6													12
1	4	5	6	3		8	9	12		11^{2}				2		7^{1}		13	10														13
1	2^{1}	6	3	5		7	9	12		10^{2}				4			13	8	11^{3}	14													14
1	2^{3}	3	4	5		8^{1}	9	10		11^{2}				6				7	13	12	14												15
1	2	3	4	5		7	8	13		10^{1}				6				9^{2}			11	12											16
1	2	3	4	7^{1}		9	10	14		5^{2}				8			12				11^{3}	13	6										17
1	2	3	4			9	10	12		7^{1}				8		14	5^{3}	6			11^{2}	13											18
1	2	3	4			9^{3}	10	12		6				8		13	5^{2}	7^{1}			11	14											19
1	2	5	3			6	7		13	10				4		12	8^{2}	9^{1}			11^{3}	14											20
1	2	3	4			8^{1}	9	12	14	10^{2}						7	13				11^{3}	6		5									21
1	2	3	5			8^{1}	9	12	14	11^{2}				4		7	6				10^{3}	13											22
1	2	3	5			8	9	14		10^{2}				4■		7^{1}	13				11^{3}	6		12									23
1	2	3	5		14	9	10		13	7^{3}						8^{1}		12			11^{2}	4		6									24
1	2^{2}	3	5			8	9	12	13	10				4		6^{1}					11	7■											25
1	2	3	4			9	10	13	12	6^{2}				8		7	5^{3}				11^{1}			14									26
1	14	2	3			8	9		11^{2}	10^{3}				4		6^{1}	13				12	7			5								27
1	2		4			8	9		14	10^{2}				5		7^{3}	6^{1}				11	12			3	13							28
1	2	3	4			8^{3}	9	10^{1}	12	11^{2}				5		7	13					6			14								29
1	2	3	4			7	8			11				5		6^{2}	14					13					9^{1}	10^{3}	12				30
1		2	3			6	8	14		12				5			13					7^{3}			4		9^{2}	11^{1}	10				31
1	12	4	5			7	8			11				2^{3}			6							14	3^{2}	13	9^{1}		10				32
1	2	3	4			8	9	14		10	11^{2}			5		7^{3}	6^{1}										12		13				33
1	4	5	3^{1}			14	9			13	10^{3}			2		7						6		12					8^{2}	11			34
1		2	4			7	8			12	14			6		13						3			5		9^{1}		10^{2}	11^{3}			35
1		4	5			8	9			10				3		7^{2}	6	12				13			2					11^{1}			36
1		5	3			6	8		14	10				4		9^{1}	7^{3}	12				13			2					11^{2}			37
1		2	5			8	9			10^{2}				4			6^{1}	7^{3}				14			3		13		12	11			38
1	2	5	4			8	9		14	10^{2}				3		6^{3}		13				7					12			11^{1}			39
1	2	3	4			8^{1}	9			10				5		7^{2}	14	13				6^{3}					12			11			40
1	2	3	4			7	8			11				5			14■	12				6^{2}					9^{1}		13	10^{3}			41
1		2	3			8	9	4^{3}	14	5				7				13				12			6		10^{2}		11^{1}				42
1		2	3			8	9		12	10				5				7^{1}				6			4				13	11^{2}			43
1	3	5	4			8^{1}	9			11^{3}				2		7						6^{2}			14		13		12	10			44
								11	10^{2}					2	13	6	5					12		4	3		8		9^{1}		1	7	45
			3			13	14	9		10						6	5^{1}					12		4	2		7^{2}		8^{3}	11	1		46

FA Cup

Fourth Qualifying	Guiseley	(h)	0-0
Replay	Guiseley	(a)	2-1
First Round	Altrincham	(h)	2-1
Second Round	Oldham Ath	(h)	3-2
Third Round	Ipswich T	(a)	2-2
Replay	Ipswich T	(h)	1-0
Fourth Round	Brighton & HA	(h)	3-1
Fifth Round	Burnley	(a)	1-0
Sixth Round	Arsenal	(a)	0-5

FA Trophy

First Round	Nantwich T	(a)	2-1
Second Round	Gateshead	(a)	3-1
Third Round	Welling U	(a)	3-1
Fourth Round	Boreham Wood	(a)	2-0
Semi-Final 1st leg	York C	(a)	1-2
Semi-Final 2nd leg	York C	(h)	1-1

aet.

MACCLESFIELD TOWN

Ground: Moss Rose Stadium, London Road, Macclesfield, Cheshire SK11 7SP. *Tel:* (01625) 264 686.
Website: www.mtfc.co.uk *Email:* reception@mtfc.co.uk *Year Formed:* 1874.
Record Attendance: 9,008 v Winsford U, Cheshire Senior Cup 2nd rd, 4 February 1948.
Nickname: 'The Silkmen'. *Manager:* John Askey. *Colours:* Blue shirts with white trim, white shorts, blue socks with white trim.

MACCLESFIELD TOWN – NATIONAL LEAGUE 2016–17 LEAGUE RECORD

Match No.	Date	Venue	Opponents	Result		H/T Score	Lg Pos.	Goalscorers	Attendance
1	Aug 6	H	Torquay U	W	2-0	1-0	3	Norburn [24], Holroyd [65]	1501
2	9	A	York C	L	0-1	0-0	9		2468
3	13	A	Braintree T	W	3-1	2-0	6	Rowe [10], Holroyd [31], Sampson [73]	703
4	16	H	Southport	W	3-1	3-0	3	Whitaker [5], Lewis [9], James [25]	1329
5	20	A	Sutton U	L	0-2	0-2	9		1255
6	27	H	Lincoln C	L	1-2	1-0	12	James [43]	1650
7	29	A	Solihull Moors	W	3-2	1-2	8	James 2 (2 pens) [41, 48], Norburn [90]	970
8	Sept 3	H	Woking	W	3-1	2-0	5	Whitaker [28], Rowe [37], Holroyd [90]	1221
9	10	A	Bromley	W	1-0	1-0	4	Rowe [21]	1011
10	17	H	Eastleigh	L	0-1	0-0	8		1287
11	24	A	Guiseley	W	2-1	2-1	9	Holroyd [14], Norburn [26]	891
12	27	H	Wrexham	W	3-0	1-0	3	Whitaker 2 [35, 53], Lewis [47]	1579
13	Oct 1	H	North Ferriby U	W	1-0	1-0	3	Whitaker (pen) [22]	1476
14	4	A	Barrow	D	1-1	0-0	4	Byrne [82]	1442
15	8	H	Boreham Wood	L	0-2	0-0	5		1386
16	22	A	Dagenham & R	D	1-1	0-1	6	Holroyd [90]	1214
17	25	H	Chester FC	D	0-0	0-0	8		1922
18	29	A	Maidstone U	L	1-2	1-1	10	Holroyd [8]	2114
19	Nov 12	H	Forest Green R	L	0-1	0-1	11		1749
20	19	A	Aldershot T	W	2-1	1-0	8	Holroyd 2 [27, 49]	1636
21	22	A	Gateshead	D	1-1	1-1	10	Rowe [25]	491
22	Dec 6	A	Wrexham	W	3-0	0-0	7	Rowe [52], Hancox [65], Whitaker [89]	3204
23	17	H	Bromley	L	1-2	0-1	8	Lewis [84]	1213
24	26	A	Tranmere R	L	0-1	0-0	10		7274
25	Jan 1	H	Tranmere R	W	4-2	1-2	7	Lewis 3 (1 pen) [12, 50, 82 (p)], Rowe [71]	3317
26	10	H	Dover Ath	W	2-1	0-1	8	Holroyd 2 [69, 75]	1020
27	21	H	Guiseley	L	1-2	1-1	10	Holroyd [31]	1349
28	28	A	North Ferriby U	W	2-0	2-0	8	Pilkington [17], Whitehead [27]	429
29	Feb 11	A	Torquay U	D	1-1	1-0	9	James [35]	1400
30	15	H	Barrow	L	0-1	0-0	9		1246
31	18	H	Braintree T	W	2-0	0-0	9	Jennings [71], Holroyd [73]	1267
32	21	A	Eastleigh	W	1-0	1-0	9	Browne [7]	2345
33	Mar 4	A	Forest Green R	L	0-3	0-1	9		1569
34	14	H	Gateshead	D	1-1	0-0	9	McCombe [82]	993
35	21	A	Chester FC	W	3-2	2-1	9	Halls [23], Dudley [43], Norburn [85]	1802
36	25	H	Aldershot T	L	0-2	0-0	9		1586
37	28	H	York C	L	1-3	0-2	9	Whitaker (pen) [58]	1318
38	Apr 1	A	Boreham Wood	W	4-2	4-1	9	Dudley [6], Hancox 3 [27, 45, 45]	340
39	4	A	Southport	W	2-1	2-1	9	Byrne [13], Dudley [15]	792
40	8	H	Dagenham & R	L	1-4	1-1	9	Hancox [14]	1281
41	11	H	Maidstone U	W	3-0	1-0	9	Browne [1], Whitaker (pen) [86], Mackreth [88]	988
42	14	A	Woking	L	0-1	0-0	9		2068
43	17	H	Solihull Moors	L	1-3	0-0	9	Holroyd [47]	1166
44	22	A	Lincoln C	L	1-2	1-1	9	Hancox [23]	10,031
45	25	A	Dover Ath	D	2-2	1-1	9	Norburn [32], Dudley [73]	932
46	29	H	Sutton U	D	0-0	0-0	9		1660

Final League Position: 9

GOALSCORERS

League (64): Holroyd 13, Whitaker 8 (3 pens), Hancox 6, Lewis 6 (1 pen), Rowe 6, James 5 (2 pens), Norburn 5, Dudley 4, Browne 2, Byrne 2, Halls 1, Jennings 1, Mackreth 1, McCombe 1, Pilkington 1, Sampson 1, Whitehead 1.
FA Cup (5): Whitaker 2 (1 pen), Holroyd 1, Mackreth 1, McCombe 1.
FA Trophy (15): Browne 4, Norburn 3, Summerfield 2, Dudley 1, James 1, Rowe 1, Sampson 1, Whitaker 1, Whitehead 1.

Ross 22	Halls 34 + 3	Pilkington 41 + 1	McCombe 35 + 1	Mackreth 19 + 12	Holroyd 39 + 3	Sampson 15 + 6	Rowe 23 + 2	Norburn 21 + 3	Hancox 34 + 4	Whitaker 37 + 6	Byrne 26 + 6	Lewis 16 + 5	James 34 + 2	Fitzpatrick 33 + 4	Branagan 1	Cowan 1 + 3	Flinders 23	Sutherland — + 1	Madeley — + 2	Brodie 1 + 3	Wellens — + 2	Bell — + 2	Dudley 8 + 4	Perel 1	Whitehead 5 + 4	Browne 13 + 4	Summerfield 13 + 5	Jennings 5	Haworth 1 + 1	Evans 2	Thorne 3 + 3	Okosieme — + 1	*Match No.*
1	2	3	4^2	5^1	6	7	8	9	10	11	12	13																					1
1	2	3^1	4	5	6	7	8	9^3	10	11^2	12	14	13																				2
1	2	4	5	12	10^3	11	7		3■	9^1	13	6^2	8	14																			3
1	2	4	5	12	10	11^2	7			9^1	13	6	8	3																			4
1	2■	3	4	12	10	11^1	9^3	13		8^2	14	7	6	5																			5
		4	5	13	10	11	7	12		9^1		6^2	8	2	1	3																	6
1		3	5^1	6	14	11^3	8	10	4	13	2	7	9^2			12																	7
1		3	5	6	10		8	9	4	11	2	7																					8
1	2	3	5	6	11^2	12	8	9^1	4	10		7		13																			9
1	14	3	4	13	10	11	9		5^2	7^1	2^3	8	6	12																			10
	2	4	5	6	11	13	7^1	9	12	10			8	3^2			1																11
	2	5	6	13	11^2	12	8^1		4	10	3	7	9				1																12
	3	5	6■		11	13	7^2	9	2	10^1	4	12	8				1																13
		4		12	10	11^1	6	8	2	9	3	5	7				1																14
	12	4	5	13	11		7	9^1	2^3	10	3^2	6	8	14			1																15
1	2	3	4	6	10	11				9^1		7	8	5				12															16
1	2	4	5	6^1	7	8	12		10	11			9	3																			17
1	2	5		6	11^1	10	12			9^2	4	7	8	3					13														18
1	2	4	5	12		7^2	8		10	11		6^1	9	3					13														19
1	2	3	4	6	11^1	12	7^2		9	10			8	5						13													20
1	2	5	6	7	11		8		3	10		12	9^1	4																			21
1	2	4	5	7^2	11^1	13	8		6	10			9	3						12													22
1	2	4	5	6^2	11		8			10		7	9^1	3						12	13												23
1	2	4	5		6^1		7		9	11		12	8^2	3						10	13												24
1	2	4	5^1		7	8	9		11		12	6	10	3^2								13											25
		5	6		10^1	11^2	7		2	9	4		8	3			1					13	12										26
		5	6		11			8^3	3	9^1	4		7	2			1						13	10^2	12	14							27
	2	5			7			12	9	10	4		8	3			1						11		6^1								28
	2	6			10				3	8	5		7	4			1										9	11					29
	3^1	6	12^3		10				2	8	5		7	4			1									14	13	11	9^2				30
		4			6				8	12	3		7	2			1									5^1	10	9		11			31
		4			10				5	12	3		8	2			1									7^1	9	11		6			32
	2	4			11				6^2	10^1	3		8	5			1									12	9	7^3	14		13		33
		4	5^2	9^3	11			8	12		3		7^1	2		14	1									6	10				13		34
	2		5	8	12			7		9	4			3			1						10^1			6	11						35
	2	5		9^2	11			8		13	4		7^1	3			1						12			6	10						36
	2	4	5	12	11			8	3	9							1						10			6	7^1						37
	2		5	13				9^2	6	10	4		8^3	3		14	1						11			7^1	12						38
	2		5	9				7	6	8	4			3			1						11				10						39
	2	12	5^2	14				7	8	9	4■			3			1						10		13	6^1	11^3						40
1	3	5	6	9	11				2	10				4											8^1	7	12						41
1	2	4	5	9^2	11			7^1	12	8				3											14	6	10^3				13		42
1	14	4	3		10				9	12	2^2		8	5											7^1	6	13				11^3		43
	2	6			11			9^3	3^2	13	5		8	4			1						12		14	7	10^1						44
	3		5		12			8	2	9^2	4						1						10		7	6^1	13				11^3	14	45
	2	5			7			8^3	14		4		12	3			1						9		6	13	10^1				11^2		46

FA Trophy

First Round	Altrincham	(a)	1-1
Replay	Altrincham	(h)	2-1
Second Round	AFC Sudbury	(a)	3-1
Third Round	Forest Green R	(h)	1-0
Fourth Round	Dulwich Hamlet	(a)	2-2
Replay	Dulwich Hamlet	(h)	2-0
Semi-Final 1st leg	Tranmere R	(h)	1-1
Semi-Final 2nd leg	Tranmere R	(a)	1-0
Final	York C	(Wembley)	2-3

FA Cup

Fourth Qualifying	North Ferriby U	(a)	4-1
First Round	Walsall	(a)	1-0
Second Round	Oxford U	(h)	0-0
Replay	Oxford U	(a)	0-3

MAIDSTONE UNITED

Ground: Gallagher Stadium, James Whatman Way, Maidstone ME14 1LQ. *Tel:* (01622) 753817.
Website: www.maidstoneunited.co.uk *Email:* See website. *Year Formed:* 1897. Reformed 1992.
Record Attendance: 3,030 v Sutton U, National League South, 5 April 2016 (Gallagher Stadium).
Nickname: 'The Stones'. *Manager:* Jay Saunders. *Colours:* Amber shirts with black trim, black shorts with amber trim, black socks with amber trim.

MAIDSTONE UNITED – NATIONAL LEAGUE 2016–17 LEAGUE RECORD

Match No.	Date	Venue	Opponents	Result		H/T Score	Lg Pos.	Goalscorers	Attendance
1	Aug 6	H	York C	D	1-1	1-0	8	Taylor, B [22]	2495
2	9	A	Aldershot T	L	0-1	0-0	17		2355
3	13	A	Chester FC	W	3-1	1-1	10	Acheampong [20], Greenhalgh [57], Flisher [64]	1912
4	16	H	Braintree T	W	2-1	2-0	7	Taylor, B 2 [4, 30]	2252
5	20	A	Tranmere R	L	1-2	0-1	12	Flisher [61]	4797
6	27	H	Forest Green R	L	1-4	1-2	18	Evans [12]	2274
7	29	A	Boreham Wood	W	1-0	0-0	13	Lokko [90]	637
8	Sept 3	H	Wrexham	D	2-2	1-1	14	Greenhalgh [21], Enver-Marum [77]	2550
9	10	A	North Ferriby U	W	2-0	1-0	12	Enver-Marum [11], Flisher [49]	479
10	13	H	Bromley	L	0-2	0-1	13		2358
11	17	H	Guiseley	D	1-1	1-0	12	Flisher [14]	2106
12	24	A	Torquay U	W	3-2	2-1	11	Odubade 2 [15, 48], Enver-Marum [19]	2026
13	Oct 1	H	Solihull Moors	L	2-4	2-3	15	Enver-Marum [20], Sweeney [40]	2119
14	4	A	Eastleigh	L	0-3	0-2	16		4114
15	8	A	Barrow	L	0-3	0-1	17		1402
16	22	H	Gateshead	L	0-2	0-1	18		2208
17	25	A	Sutton U	D	2-2	2-2	16	Taylor, B (pen) [25], Loza [45]	1609
18	29	H	Macclesfield T	W	2-1	1-1	16	Enver-Marum [16], Odubade [89]	2114
19	Nov 12	A	Southport	L	2-3	0-2	17	Odubade [59], Taylor, B [90]	932
20	19	H	Woking	L	0-3	0-2	17		2147
21	22	H	Dagenham & R	L	0-1	0-1	18		1970
22	26	A	Lincoln C	L	0-2	0-0	18		3917
23	29	H	Eastleigh	W	2-1	1-0	18	Sweeney [5], Taylor, B (pen) [59]	1714
24	Dec 3	A	Bromley	L	0-2	0-1	18		1676
25	17	H	North Ferriby U	L	1-2	0-2	18	Paxman [60]	2006
26	26	A	Dover Ath	D	1-1	0-1	19	Loza [60]	2369
27	Jan 1	H	Dover Ath	L	1-4	0-1	19	Karagiannis [61]	2257
28	7	A	Guiseley	L	1-2	0-1	20	Taylor, B (pen) [64]	1040
29	21	H	Torquay U	W	2-1	0-0	20	Sam-Yorke [53], Paxman [69]	2455
30	28	A	Solihull Moors	L	0-2	0-2	21		1003
31	Feb 4	H	Aldershot T	L	0-2	0-1	21		2293
32	11	A	York C	D	1-1	0-1	20	Prestedge [47]	2816
33	18	H	Chester FC	W	4-2	4-0	21	Lokko 2 [2, 44], Sam-Yorke [5], Pigott [14]	2120
34	25	A	Braintree T	D	0-0	0-0	21		1002
35	28	A	Dagenham & R	W	2-0	1-0	20	Pigott [6], Sam-Yorke [85]	1456
36	Mar 4	H	Southport	W	4-2	2-1	19	Loza 2 (1 pen) [38, 45 (p)], Pigott [60], Lokko [70]	2404
37	21	H	Sutton U	D	1-1	0-0	20	Loza (pen) [68]	2929
38	25	A	Woking	W	4-2	1-2	19	Loza 3 [29, 68, 76], Odubade [83]	2088
39	Apr 1	H	Barrow	W	2-1	1-1	18	Pigott [45], Lewis [62]	2803
40	8	A	Gateshead	W	2-1	0-1	16	Hogan (og) [73], Taylor, B [76]	967
41	11	A	Macclesfield T	L	0-3	0-1	16		988
42	14	A	Wrexham	W	3-1	1-1	15	Pigott [31], Loza [52], Flisher [82]	3379
43	17	H	Boreham Wood	W	1-0	0-0	13	Odubade [90]	2880
44	22	A	Forest Green R	D	2-2	0-1	12	Phipps [61], Pigott [81]	2030
45	25	H	Lincoln C	D	0-0	0-0	11		3014
46	29	H	Tranmere R	L	0-1	0-0	14		3409

Final League Position: 14

GOALSCORERS

League (59): Loza 9 (2 pens), Taylor, B 8 (3 pens), Odubade 6, Pigott 6, Enver-Marum 5, Flisher 5, Lokko 4, Sam-Yorke 3, Greenhalgh 2, Paxman 2, Sweeney 2, Acheampong 1, Evans 1, Karagiannis 1, Lewis 1, Phipps 1, Prestedge 1, own goal 1.
FA Cup (4): Flisher 2, Murphy 1, Taylor, B 1 (1 pen).
FA Trophy (2): Loza 1, Greenhalgh 1.

Worgan 46	Driver 6	Mills 44	Lokko 41	Rogers 22 + 3	Sweeney 18 + 5	Flisher 34 + 5	Murphy 11 + 6	Acheampong 19 + 1	Taylor B 29 + 12	Greenhalgh 10 + 11	Karagiannis 4 + 4	Dumaka — + 6	Paxman 34 + 10	Evans 14 + 3	Hall-Johnson 2 + 5	Coyle 29 + 1	Mavila 2 + 4	Enver-Marum 9 + 6	May — + 2	Odubade 17 + 13	Nana Ofori-Twumasi 27	Loza 20 + 4	Hudson-Odoi 2 + 2	N'Guessan — + 2	Sam-Yorke 7 + 1	Prestedge 19	Lewis 15	Pigott 16 + 1	McCarthy 1 + 3	Phipps 2 + 5	Oakley 1 + 3	Okuonghae 5	Richards — + 2	*Match No.*
1	2	3	4	5	6^{1}	7^{2}	8^{3}	9	10	11	12	13	14																					1
1	2^{2}	3	4	5	6	7	8	9	10	11^{1}		13	12																					2
1		2	3	4	13	6	8	9	10^{2}	11^{3}		12	5^{1}	7	14																			3
1		2	3	6	12	8	9^{2}	5	10^{1}	11	14		7^{3}	4	13																			4
1		4	5	6^{2}	13	8	9^{1}	2	10	11		12	7	3																				5
1		2	4	6^{1}	7^{3}	11	12	5	8^{2}	10		14	9	3	13																			6
1		2	6	7	14	8	9	5^{2}	12	10^{1}		13		4^{3}	11	3																		7
1		2	5		6	8	9^{3}		10	11^{2}			7	4^{1}	14	3	12	13																8
1		2	4	13	6	8	9^{1}		10				7^{2}	5■	12	3	14	11^{3}																9
1			4^{2}		5	7	8^{3}	13	9^{1}	12			6		10	2	3	11	14															10
1		2			7	9	12	5	10^{1}	14			8	4		3	6^{3}	11^{2}		13														11
1		2	4	6	7	8^{2}	13		9	14			12	5		3		11^{1}		10^{3}														12
1		2	4	5^{3}	6				8	9^{1}			12	7^{2}		3	13	11	14	10														13
1		2	3	8	7		14		10^{1}	6^{2}			9^{3}	4		5	13	12		11														14
1		2	3	4^{3}	5	6	12	8	9^{2}	14			13	7				11^{1}		10														15
1		6	5	7^{3}		9^{2}	14	3	12				8	4				13		10^{1}	2	11												16
1		5	4	6	7		8^{3}	3	9	12				14				11^{2}		13	2	10^{1}												17
1		2	5	6	7^{2}		8^{3}	3	9	12			13					10^{1}		14	4	11												18
1					4^{1}	7		8	9	13			6	12		3		14		10	2^{2}	11	5^{3}											19
1	2	3	5	6		9			10^{1}	13			8			4				12		11	7^{2}											20
1		2	4	6^{2}	7	9			10^{3}				8			3		14		12	5	11^{1}	13											21
1		2	5	6	7^{3}				9^{2}	13			8			4		10		14	3	11^{1}	12											22
1		2	4	5	11	7			8				6			3		12		10^{1}	9													23
1		3	5	6	7	9			10^{1}	13			8^{3}	14		4				11^{2}	2	12												24
1	2	3		5^{2}	14	12		8	9^{1}		6		13	7^{3}		4				10		11												25
1	5	2	3	7		6			12		9^{1}		8			4				11^{2}		10		13										26
1	2^{2}	3	5	6^{3}		9			14	13	7		8			4				10^{1}		11		12										27
1		5^{1}	4	13		6		2	12		8		7								3	9			10	11^{2}								28
1		2		13		12		4	6				9^{1}			3					5	10^{2}			11	8	7							29
1		4	5			8		3	10^{1}		13		7^{2}								2	11				9	6	12						30
1		2				13		4	5^{1}		14		8^{2}			3					9	10^{3}			12	6	7	11						31
1		2	6			12		4^{1}	13				8^{2}			3					5				11	9	7	10						32
1		2	4			8			12				7^{2}			3					10	13			6^{1}	9	5	11^{3}	14					33
1		2	3			9							8^{2}			4				12	5	13			10	6	7	11^{1}						34
1		2	4						12				7^{3}			3				14	5	10^{2}			9	8	6■	11^{1}	13					35
1		2	4						13				6			3				14	9	10^{2}			5^{3}	7		11	8^{1}	12				36
1		2	4			12							7^{2}			3				13	9	10				8	5	11			6^{1}			37
1		2	5			8							7^{2}			4				12	3	10^{3}				9	6	11^{1}		13	14			38
1		2	3			9							8^{1}			4				13	5	10^{2}				6	7	11		12				39
1		2	4			7			12				6^{2}			3				10^{1}	9					8	5	11			13			40
1		3	5			8^{2}			10^{3}				7^{1}			4				12	2	13				9	6	11			14			41
1		2	3			7			12				6^{2}							9^{3}	4	10^{1}				8		11	14	13		5		42
1		2	3			7			10^{1}				12							9	4					8	6	11				5		43
1		2	3			9							8^{1}							10	4					6		11		7		5	12	44
1		4	5			7			12				13							10^{1}	2					8	6^{3}	11		9^{2}		3	14	45
1		2	3			5			7				12			13				9	8					6^{1}	4	11^{2}		14		10^{3}		46

FA Cup

Fourth Qualifying	Billericay T	(h)	3-1
First Round	Rochdale	(h)	1-1
Replay	Rochdale	(a)	0-2

FA Trophy

First Round	Boreham Wood	(a)	0-0
Replay	Boreham Wood	(h)	2-3

NORTH FERRIBY UNITED

Ground: Eon Visual Media Stadium, Grange Lane, North Ferriby, East Yorkshire HU14 3AB.
Tel: (01482) 634601. *Website:* www.northferribyunited.com *Email:* info@northferribyunitedfc.co.uk
Year Formed: 1934. *Record Attendance:* 2,389 v Lincoln C, National League, 21 February 2017.
Nickname: 'The Villagers'. *Manager:* Steve Housham. *Colours:* Green and white hooped shirts, green shorts, green socks.

NORTH FERRIBY UNITED – NATIONAL LEAGUE 2016–17 LEAGUE RECORD

Match No.	*Date*	*Venue*	*Opponents*	*Result*		*H/T Score*	*Lg Pos.*	*Goalscorers*	*Attendance*
1	Aug 6	H	Braintree T	D	0-0	0-0	14		557
2	9	A	Lincoln C	L	1-6	1-4	21	Bateson 28	3622
3	13	A	Dover Ath	L	0-2	0-1	22		726
4	16	H	Guiseley	W	3-2	2-1	18	Kendall 8, Emerton 21, Russell 88	487
5	20	H	Torquay U	W	1-0	0-0	15	Clarke 69	505
6	27	A	Aldershot T	L	0-2	0-2	16		1527
7	29	H	Barrow	L	0-1	0-0	20		581
8	Sept 3	A	Eastleigh	L	0-2	0-1	20		1883
9	10	H	Maidstone U	L	0-2	0-1	20		479
10	13	A	Gateshead	W	1-0	0-0	20	Thompson 49	614
11	17	A	Dagenham & R	L	0-2	0-1	20		1119
12	24	H	Southport	L	0-1	0-1	21		451
13	Oct 1	A	Macclesfield T	L	0-1	0-1	21		1476
14	4	H	Chester FC	L	0-1	0-0	21		476
15	8	H	Forest Green R	L	0-3	0-1	22		501
16	22	A	Boreham Wood	L	0-1	0-0	22		313
17	25	A	Tranmere R	L	0-1	0-0	24		4326
18	29	H	Bromley	L	1-2	0-0	24	Thompson 52	354
19	Nov 5	H	Wrexham	D	0-0	0-0	23		528
20	12	A	Woking	D	1-1	1-0	24	Brogan 45	1357
21	19	H	Sutton U	W	2-1	1-0	23	Topliss 11, Thompson 46	372
22	26	A	Solihull Moors	L	0-2	0-1	24		526
23	29	A	Chester FC	L	0-3	0-0	24		1392
24	Dec 3	H	Gateshead	W	1-0	1-0	23	Thompson 28	498
25	17	A	Maidstone U	W	2-1	2-0	22	Wootton 16, Brogan (pen) 38	2006
26	26	H	York C	L	0-1	0-1	24		1950
27	Jan 1	A	York C	W	1-0	1-0	22	Thompson 28	3182
28	7	H	Dagenham & R	L	0-4	0-3	23		453
29	14	A	Wrexham	L	0-1	0-1	23		3625
30	21	A	Southport	W	4-2	1-0	23	Bateson 8, Oliver 69, Kendall 85, Thompson 89	795
31	28	H	Macclesfield T	L	0-2	0-2	23		429
32	Feb 11	A	Braintree T	L	0-1	0-0	23		410
33	18	H	Dover Ath	L	1-2	0-0	24	Bateson 49	465
34	21	H	Lincoln C	L	0-1	0-1	24		2389
35	25	A	Guiseley	W	2-1	0-1	23	Thompson 57, Skelton 86	951
36	Mar 4	H	Woking	W	2-1	1-1	22	Skelton 5, Thompson 69	402
37	11	A	Bromley	L	0-3	0-1	23		905
38	18	H	Solihull Moors	L	1-4	1-1	23	Tinkler 43	363
39	21	H	Tranmere R	L	1-4	1-2	23	Gray 12	638
40	25	A	Sutton U	L	1-5	0-3	24	Tinkler 48	1664
41	Apr 1	A	Forest Green R	W	1-0	0-0	23	Thompson 68	1709
42	8	H	Boreham Wood	L	2-4	0-2	23	Tinkler 67, Thompson 90	357
43	14	H	Eastleigh	W	2-1	1-0	23	Tinkler 22, Thompson 88	364
44	17	A	Barrow	L	1-3	1-3	23	Thompson 4	1017
45	22	H	Aldershot T	L	0-3	0-1	23		562
46	29	A	Torquay U	L	0-2	0-0	24		4026

Final League Position: 24

GOALSCORERS

League (32): Thompson 12, Tinkler 4, Bateson 3, Brogan 2 (1 pen), Kendall 2, Skelton 2, Clarke 1, Emerton 1, Gray 1, Oliver 1, Russell 1, Topliss 1, Wootton 1.
FA Cup (1): Mukendi 1.
FA Trophy (0).

Watson 40	Topliss 39	Skelton 30 + 1	Gray 39	Brogan 15	Oliver 29 + 4	Russell 20	Clarke 18	Robinson 7 + 8	Bateson 17 + 6	Fosu-Mensah 1 + 2	Mukendi 4 + 10	Kendall 8 + 23	Middleton 39 + 1	Emerton 32 + 9	Fallowfield 20 + 8	Slade 4	Hare 39	Bruce 1	Thompson 35 + 3	Wootton 14	Armstrong 9 + 7	Sutton 6	Stamp — + 4	Templeton 2 + 7	Cosgrove 3 + 11	Tinkler 15	Dixon 14 + 1	Keyi — + 3	Bell — + 2	Evans 6	Cooke — + 4	Bolton — + 1	Douglas — + 1	*Match No.*
1	2	3	4	5	6	7	8	9^1	10	11^2	12	13																						1
1		4	3	6	5^2	7	8	10^1	9		11^3	12	2■	13	14																			2
1	2		3	5	7	8	6	11^2	9		13	12		10^1		4																		3
1		3		5^3	6	7	9	13	11^2		14	10^1	12	8			2	4																4
1			4		8	6	9	12	11		13	10^1	2	7^2		5	3																	5
1			3		2	8	5	7^2	6^3	14	12	13	10	4^1		11	9																	6
1			4		8	6	9	12	11		13	10^1	2	7^2		5	3																	7
1		5	4		6	7	10	13	9^3	14	11^2		2	8^1			3		12															8
1		5	4		6^1	8	9				10^2	12	2	7	13		3		11															9
1	2	4^3	3		7	8	9	10^2				13	5	12	14		6		11^1															10
1	2	5	7		3	8	10^3	9^2			13	14	4		12		6		11^1															11
1	2^2	6	3		7	8		10^1				13	4	12	9		5		11															12
1	5	3^1	6		9	7		13			14		2^3	12	8^2		4		11	10														13
1	2	6	3		7^3	9	10				14	12	4■	13			5		11^2	8^1														14
1	3	2	4	5	6	8^1	9				11			12					10	7^2	13													15
1	2^1	5		8	6	7	9^2						4	12	13		3		11	10														16
1	2	4		9	6^1	7	10					11^2	5		13		3		12	8														17
1	2	6		5		9	8				13	14	4	12	7^3		3		11^2	10^1														18
1	3	2		6		8	10	12				13	5		7^3		4		11^1	9^2	14													19
1	2	6^3		5		8^1	7	14	13				4	12	11		3		10^2	9														20
1	2		3	6				12	13				4	9^1	7		5		11^2	10	8													21
1	2^2		3	6					12■			13	5	7	9		4			10^1	11^3	8	14											22
1	3		6	4								11	5	10^2	8		2		12		7^1	9	13											23
1	2	14	3	6	13				12				4	9^1	7^3		5		11	10	8^2													24
1	2^2		6	3					13				5	9	12		4		11^1	10	8	7												25
1	5^2	3	4									14	2	8^3	12		9		11	10	7^1	6	13											26
1	2		4		3				13			12	9	5	8^1		7		11^2	10		6												27
1	2^2		3		6				10			12	4	9	7^1		5		11		13	8												28
1	2	4	3		6				11^2			13		9	8		5		10		7^1			12										29
1	2	4	3		8				11			14		9^2	7^1		5		10		12			6^3	13									30
1	2	4	3		6^2				7			12		11			5		9		8		13		10^1									31
1	2	4	3						11^1			13	5	8			6		10		9^2					7	12							32
1	2	6							9^1			10^2	4	7^3			3		11		14			12	13	5	8							33
1	2	6	3^1		14				9^3			12	4				5		11					13	10^2	7	8							34
1	2	9	3^2						5			12	7	4			6		11^1						13	8	10							35
1	2	5	3						11^3			12	4	9^2			6		10^1		14				13	7	8							36
1	2	5	4		14							11^1	6	9^2			3■		10					13	12	8^3	7							37
1	2	5	3		12							11^1	4	9					10		14			8^3	13	6	7^2							38
1	2	5	3		11							12	4	9^1	8^2				10^3					13	14	6	7							39
1	2	3	4^2										5	8^3	7				11^1					12	10	6	9	13	14					40
	2		3		7^1								5	8	9^3		4		11^2						13	6	10	12		1	14			41
	2		3		6								4	10	9^1		5		11					13^3	12	7	8^2	14		1				42
	2		3		6								4	10	9		5		11							7	8			1				43
	2	3^1	7		8								6	10			5		11^2						13	4	9			1	12			44
	2^3		3		7								4	10	9^1		5		11						13	6^2	8			1	12	14		45
	3		6		7								5	10	9		4^1		11^2							2	8		13	1^3	12		14	46

FA Cup
Fourth Qualifying Macclesfield T (h) 1-4

FA Trophy
First Round Alfreton T (a) 0-1

SOLIHULL MOORS

Ground: The Automated Technology Group Stadium, Damson Parkway, Solihull, West Midlands B91 2PP.
Tel: (0121) 205 6770. *Website:* www.solihullmoorsfc.co.uk *Email:* info@solihullmoorsfc.co.uk *Year Formed:* 2007.
Record Attendance: 1,995 v Tranmere R, National League, 22 October 2016. *Nickname:* 'Moors'.
Manager: Liam McDonald. *Colours:* Yellow and blue hooped shirts, blue shorts, blue socks, with yellow trim.

SOLIHULL MOORS – NATIONAL LEAGUE 2016–17 LEAGUE RECORD

Match No.	Date	Venue	Opponents	Result		H/T Score	Lg Pos.	Goalscorers	Attendance
1	Aug 6	A	Sutton U	W	3-1	1-1	4	Beswick [37], Sterling-James [55], Brown [77]	1305
2	9	H	Woking	D	2-2	0-1	5	White [73], Fagbola [80]	699
3	13	H	Bromley	W	1-0	1-0	3	Daly [4]	756
4	16	A	Wrexham	L	0-1	0-0	8		4017
5	20	H	Guiseley	W	3-2	1-1	5	Brown 2 [13, 80], White [84]	554
6	27	A	Eastleigh	L	0-2	0-0	8		1632
7	29	H	Macclesfield T	L	2-3	2-1	12	Murombedzi [22], Asante (pen) [45]	970
8	Sept 3	A	York C	L	0-4	0-1	17		2105
9	10	H	Dagenham & R	L	2-5	0-2	17	Brown [78], Osborne [81]	716
10	13	A	Lincoln C	D	0-0	0-0	19		4049
11	17	A	Gateshead	D	0-0	0-0	18		541
12	24	H	Boreham Wood	D	1-1	0-0	17	Osborne [48]	618
13	Oct 1	A	Maidstone U	W	4-2	3-2	16	Sterling-James [26], Asante 3 (1 pen) [34 (p), 38, 64]	2119
14	4	H	Southport	W	4-0	0-0	13	Asante 3 [50, 74, 82], Sterling-James [70]	772
15	8	A	Aldershot T	L	0-2	0-0	14		1712
16	22	H	Tranmere R	L	0-3	0-1	15		1995
17	25	H	Forest Green R	L	0-1	0-0	15		919
18	29	A	Braintree T	W	1-0	0-0	15	White (pen) [86]	625
19	Nov 12	H	Dover Ath	L	2-3	1-0	16	Brown [43], Asante [90]	837
20	19	A	Barrow	L	1-2	0-2	16	Asante [52]	1184
21	22	A	Torquay U	L	0-3	0-1	17		1272
22	26	H	North Ferriby U	W	2-0	1-0	16	Asante 2 [31, 75]	526
23	29	A	Southport	D	0-0	0-0	16		703
24	Dec 17	A	Dagenham & R	D	4-4	3-2	16	White [3], Sterling-James 2 [19, 49], Byrne [25]	1112
25	26	H	Chester FC	W	3-2	1-1	16	Sterling-James 2 [45, 69], White [56]	1475
26	Jan 1	A	Chester FC	W	3-0	1-0	14	Osborne [17], Daly [55], White (pen) [78]	2244
27	7	H	Gateshead	L	0-2	0-1	16		750
28	21	A	Boreham Wood	D	0-0	0-0	16		322
29	28	H	Maidstone U	W	2-0	2-0	15	Kettle [7], Carline [30]	1003
30	31	H	Lincoln C	L	0-1	0-0	15		1650
31	Feb 11	H	Sutton U	W	3-0	2-0	15	Charles-Cook 2 [2, 45], Afolayan [70]	671
32	14	A	Woking	L	1-2	0-1	15	Murombedzi [59]	1000
33	18	A	Bromley	W	1-0	1-0	14	White [9]	1109
34	25	H	Wrexham	L	0-1	0-1	14		1349
35	Mar 4	A	Dover Ath	D	0-0	0-0	14		1104
36	11	H	Braintree T	D	3-3	1-3	15	Maye [26], Afolayan [79], Carline [86]	556
37	18	A	North Ferriby U	W	4-1	1-1	14	Maye [40], Sterling-James [63], Carline [76], Nortey [90]	363
38	21	A	Forest Green R	L	1-2	0-1	14	Afolayan [59]	1445
39	25	H	Barrow	L	2-4	0-3	15	Green [65], Afolayan [74]	1820
40	28	H	Torquay U	L	0-1	0-0	16		857
41	Apr 1	H	Aldershot T	L	0-2	0-1	17		1238
42	8	A	Tranmere R	L	0-9	0-3	18		5001
43	14	H	York C	L	1-2	1-2	20	White [45]	1570
44	17	A	Macclesfield T	W	3-1	0-0	18	Carline [78], Byrne [85], Charles-Cook [90]	1166
45	22	H	Eastleigh	W	2-0	2-0	16	Charles-Cook [11], Maye [22]	893
46	29	A	Guiseley	D	1-1	1-0	16	Sterling-James [26]	1519

Final League Position: 16

GOALSCORERS

League (62): Asante 11 (2 pens), Sterling-James 9, White 8 (2 pens), Brown 5, Afolayan 4, Carline 4, Charles-Cook 4, Maye 3, Osborne 3, Byrne 2, Daly 2, Murombedzi 2, Beswick 1, Fagbola 1, Green 1, Kettle 1, Nortey 1.
FA Cup (8): Brown 2, Byrne 2, Osborne 2, Asante 1 (1 pen), Beswick 1.
FA Trophy (1): White 1.

Lewis 21	Fagbola 22 + 1	Daly 39	Gough 18 + 1	Franklin 33 + 2	Murombedzi 35 + 2	Beswick 12 + 4	Knights 11 + 8	Sterling-James 27 + 15	Brown 14 + 8	Moore 4 + 5	Asante 13 + 8	Moseley 1 + 1	White 18 + 15	Osborne 22	Byrne 32 + 4	Vaughan 8	Koue Niate 8	Dielna 3 + 1	Jones 5 + 2	Obeng 3 + 1	Carline 25	Nortey 12 + 6	Kettle 23	Maye 19 + 2	Flanagan 11 + 1	Mwamyongo — + 6	Baxter 17	Green 19	Rodgers — + 3	Sammons 10 + 3	Charles-Cook 10 + 3	Afolayan 10 + 5	Udoh — + 4	Coyle — + 3	Sanusi 1 + 2	Shade — + 2	Endall — + 1	*Match No.*
1	2	3	4	5	6	7	8[3]	9	10[2]	11[1]	12	13	14																									1
1	5	3	4	2	7	6		9	10[1]	11			12	8																								2
1	2	4	5	3	7	14	12	9[2]	11[1]	10[3]			13	8	6																							3
1	2	3	4	5	6	12	9	14	13		10[1]		11[2]	8[3]	7																							4
1	5	3	4	2	7[2]	14	8	12	10		11[3]		13	9	6[1]																							5
	6	2	3[3]	14	12	8	9[1]	10	11	13		4[2]			7	1	5																					6
1	2	4	5	3	8[1]	14	7[2]	12		13	10		11[3]	9	6																							7
1	2[1]	4	5	3	7	8	9[3]	14	11	12	10[2]		13	6																								8
	3	5	6[1]	4	7[2]	8	13	12	10	11				9		1	2																					9
	4	2		5	6	7	8[2]	10[1]	12	14			11[3]	9	13	1	3■																					10
	2	4		3	6	7	8	10[2]	11[1]	13			12	9	5	1																						11
	4	3	5	2	6	8	9[2]	13			12		11[1]	10	7	1																						12
	9	4	5	3	2	8	13	11[1]			6[2]		12	10	7	1																						13
	2	4	5	3	6[1]	8	12	10			11			9	7	1																						14
	9	4	5	3	2	8	14	11[3]	12		6[1]		13	10[2]	7	1																						15
1	9	4	14	3[3]	2	7	13	11[2]	6		12			10	5		8[1]																					16
1	3	2	6	13	12		8■				11		10		7		4	5[1]	9[2]																			17
1	9	4		3	2			11[1]	7		5[2]		12	10	6		8		13																			18
1	9	4		3[1]	2			11[2]	6		12		14	10	5		8	13	7[3]																			19
1	3		5	4	6		8[1]	12			11		13	10	7		2		9[2]																			20
1	3	5	6	2	7		13	10[1]			11[2]		12	9	8					4																		21
1	12	5	6	4	7		13				11[1]		14	9[2]				3	8[3]	2	10																	22
1		3	4	2				12			5			9	6			11[1]	7	8	10																	23
1		5		4	2			9[2]			13		11[1]		7				12		10	3	6	8														24
1	3	5		2	7[1]			9			13		11[2]		8						10	4	6		12													25
1		2			5			9[3]			13		11[1]	8	7[2]					12	10	4	6		3	14												26
1		3			2			9			14		7[3]	8[1]	6						10	11[2]	4	13	5	12												27
		3			7[3]			11[2]					10[1]		6						9	13	4	8	5		1	2	12	14								28
		3			8[2]			9[1]					11[3]		6						10	13	4	7	5	14	1	2	12									29
		4			8			12					11[2]								7	3[3]	5	10	6	14	1	2	13	9[1]								30
		3			2								8[2]								9[3]	10	4	7	5	14	1	6		13	11[1]	12						31
		3			10[2]			8					13		12						9	2[1]	4	7[3]	5		1	6			11	14						32
		3			2								9[2]		6						10		4	8	5		1	7			11[1]	12	13■					33
		3			2			12					8[1]		6■						9	10[2]	4	14	5		1	7			11[3]	13						34
		3[1]			2			10[2]													11	14	4	8	5		1	7		6	12	9[3]	13					35
		3			2			12													9	10[3]	4	7			1	6		5	11[1]	8[2]	13	14				36
				3	2[3]			10[1]													11	12	4	8[2]	5		1	7		6	14	9	13					37
		4		3	2[3]			14							12						10	13	5	8			1	7		6[1]	11[2]	9						38
		3		5[1]				13	12						7						9		4	8			1	2		6	10[2]	11						39
		4		3				6[1]	12						9[2]						8		5	10			1	2			7■	11			13			40
1		3		2				12	7[1]						6[2]						11		4	9				8		5[3]		10		14	13			41
1				2				8[3]	13				10[1]		12						9	4	3	7				5		6		11[2]				14		42
				2[1]				14	5				9		4						10	11[2]	3	7			1	6		13		12			8[3]			43
				2				10[1]	12				9[3]		5						11	14	3	7			1	6		4	13	8[2]						44
				2				9[2]	13				12		5						10		3	7			1	6		4	11[1]	8[3]					14	45
				2				9[3]	6						5						10	11[1]	3	8		12	1	7			4[2]			13		14		46

FA Cup

Fourth Qualifying	Kettering T	(h)	3-1
First Round	Yeovil T	(a)	2-2
Replay	Yeovil T	(h)	1-1
Second Round	Luton T	(a)	2-6

FA Trophy

First Round	Matlock T	(h)	1-2

SOUTHPORT

Ground: Merseyrail Community Stadium, Haig Avenue, Southport, Lancashire PR8 6JZ. *Tel:* (01704) 533 422.
Website: southportfc.net *Email:* secretary@southportfc.net *Year Formed:* 1881.
Record Attendance: 20,010 v Newcastle U, FA Cup 4th rd (replay), 26 January 1932. *Nickname:* 'The Sandgrounders'.
Manager: Alan Lewer. *Colours:* Yellow shirts with black trim, yellow shorts with black trim, yellow socks with black trim.

SOUTHPORT – NATIONAL LEAGUE 2016–17 LEAGUE RECORD

Match No.	Date	Venue	Opponents	Result		H/T Score	Lg Pos.	Goalscorers	Attendance
1	Aug 6	A	Dagenham & R	L	0-3	0-2	24		1296
2	9	H	Gateshead	L	0-3	0-1	24		926
3	13	H	Woking	W	2-1	1-1	19	Almond 2 (1 pen) [19 (p), 88]	702
4	16	A	Macclesfield T	L	1-3	0-3	20	Grimes [83]	1329
5	20	A	Lincoln C	L	0-4	0-3	22		2440
6	27	H	Tranmere R	D	1-1	0-0	22	Almond [62]	3046
7	29	A	Forest Green R	L	1-5	0-2	22	Bishop [50]	1621
8	Sept 3	H	Dover Ath	L	0-1	0-1	23		760
9	10	A	Eastleigh	D	1-1	0-0	23	Gray [71]	1878
10	13	H	Barrow	L	1-4	0-2	23	Caton [85]	848
11	17	H	Aldershot T	D	1-1	0-0	23	Gray [70]	772
12	24	A	North Ferriby U	W	1-0	1-0	23	Nolan [45]	451
13	Oct 1	H	Bromley	L	1-2	0-2	23	Lussey [57]	744
14	4	A	Solihull Moors	L	0-4	0-0	23		772
15	8	A	Guiseley	L	1-2	0-0	24	Allen [69]	1046
16	22	H	Sutton U	D	1-1	1-0	23	Jones, Andrai [37]	864
17	25	H	York C	W	2-0	0-0	22	Allen 2 (1 pen) [48 (p), 90]	856
18	29	A	Torquay U	W	2-1	0-1	19	Howe [67], Caton [75]	1490
19	Nov 12	H	Maidstone U	W	3-2	2-0	18	Allen 2 [5, 52], Nolan [45]	932
20	19	A	Boreham Wood	L	0-2	0-1	18		314
21	22	A	Chester FC	D	2-2	0-2	19	Jones, Andrai [60], Allen [79]	1752
22	26	H	Braintree T	L	4-5	3-4	21	Higgins, J [16], Thompson [27], Jones, Andrai [28], Allen (pen) [56]	866
23	29	H	Solihull Moors	D	0-0	0-0	20		703
24	Dec 17	H	Eastleigh	W	4-3	2-1	20	Jones, Andrai [4], Nolan [30], Weeks [48], Allen (pen) [75]	769
25	26	A	Wrexham	L	0-1	0-0	21		4317
26	Jan 1	H	Wrexham	W	3-2	2-1	19	Nolan 2 [36, 88], Brewster, D [45]	2066
27	7	A	Aldershot T	L	1-2	0-1	19	Jones, Andrai [90]	1772
28	10	A	Barrow	W	1-0	1-0	19	McKenna [14]	956
29	21	H	North Ferriby U	L	2-4	0-1	19	McKeown [50], Weeks [90]	795
30	28	A	Bromley	L	1-3	1-1	20	Wright, J [22]	953
31	Feb 4	A	Gateshead	L	0-3	0-2	20		620
32	11	H	Dagenham & R	L	1-4	1-3	21	Allen (pen) [24]	845
33	18	A	Woking	D	0-0	0-0	22		1386
34	25	H	Chester FC	L	0-1	0-0	22		1496
35	Mar 4	A	Maidstone U	L	2-4	1-2	24	McKenna [3], Allen [51]	2404
36	11	H	Torquay U	L	1-2	0-1	24	Stevenson [47]	1159
37	18	A	Braintree T	L	0-2	0-1	24		501
38	21	A	York C	L	3-5	3-2	24	Almond 2 [19, 41], McKeown [20]	2482
39	25	H	Boreham Wood	W	1-0	0-0	23	Nolan [81]	1010
40	Apr 1	H	Guiseley	L	0-1	0-0	24		981
41	4	H	Macclesfield T	L	1-2	1-2	24	Higgins, R [42]	792
42	8	A	Sutton U	D	2-2	0-1	24	Spence (og) [68], Ashton [74]	1807
43	14	A	Dover Ath	L	0-3	0-1	24		1563
44	17	H	Forest Green R	W	2-0	0-0	24	Cundy [62], McKeown [71]	844
45	22	A	Tranmere R	L	1-4	0-1	24	Myers [61]	6159
46	29	H	Lincoln C	D	1-1	0-1	23	Ashton [88]	3462

Final League Position: 23

GOALSCORERS

League (52): Allen 10 (4 pens), Nolan 6, Almond 5 (1 pen), Jones, Andrai 5, McKeown 3, Ashton 2, Caton 2, Gray 2, McKenna 2, Weeks 2, Bishop 1, Brewster, D 1, Cundy 1, Grimes 1, Higgins, J 1, Higgins, R 1, Howe 1, Lussey 1, Myers 1, Stevenson 1, Thompson 1, Wright, J 1, own goal 1.
FA Cup (2): Grimes 1, Weeks 1.
FA Trophy (5): Allen 1, Caton 1, Higgins, R 1, Lussey 1, Wright, J 1.

Belford 9 / Wright J 2 + 1	Kearns 1 + 1	Ashton 35 + 1	Nolan 39	Thompson 24 / Murray 12	O'Brien K 2 + 2	Jones Andrai 37 + 7	Caton 13 + 10	Jones G 11 + 1 / Springthorpe 1	Gray 7 + 6	Almond 14 + 5	Grimes 4 + 14	White 20 + 4	Allen 33 + 2	Cofie 3 + 5 / Stevenson 10 + 1	McCarthy 1 + 4	Bishop 3 + 1 / Meikle 4	Royle 3	Howe 15 / King 6	Stanley 5	Crump 1 / Coly Jean-Charles 1 + 3	O'Brien M 5	Moseley 2 + 3 / Brodie 3 + 4	Norman 23	Higgins R 36	Lussey 12	Weeks 26 + 3	Mulhern — + 1	Ferguson 4 / Cheetham 6	Hynes 15 + 8	Higgins J 8 + 1	McKenna 10 + 8	Jerome 1 + 3 / Myers 3 + 1	Jones Aaron 4 + 1	Brewster D 3 / Monteiro — + 3	McKeown 17 + 1	Onovwigun — + 1 / Grimshaw — + 1	Cundy 12	Match No.
1	2	3	4	5	6^{1}	7	8	9	10	11^{2}	12	13																										1
1		3	4^{3}	5		6	11	8	9^{2}	10^{1}	14	2	7	12	13																							2
1		3	4	5	14	2	7^{1}	9	8^{3}	10	13	6	11^{2}			12																						3
1		3		4	13	5	7	8	10^{1}	9	14	2^{3}	11		12		6^{2}																					4
1	14	3		4	5	8	10^{3}	11	13	12	7■	2	6^{2}				9^{1}																					5
1		5	8	3		2	11^{1}	6		13			12		9	10^{2}		4	7																			6
1		3	4	5			12	8	13	7		2	6^{3}		14	9^{1}		11	10^{2}																			7
		4		2		5	9^{2}	7		10				12	13	11^{1}	6	3	8	1																		8
1		2^{1}	3	4		7^{2}	12	8	13	10		14		11^{3}				5	9		6																	9
1			6			13	7	8^{1}	14	11	12^{3}	2		10				5	9		3^{2}	4																10
			2	4		7	9		10^{2}		12		11					5				6	1	3	8^{1}	13												11
		5	8			6	9^{2}		10^{3}				11^{1}	14				3			4	12	1	2	7		13											12
		5	7^{2}			6	9^{3}	12	11^{1}				10	13				4			3	14	1	2	8													13
		2				7	9^{3}	8	12				10	11^{1}				4			5	13	1	6	3^{2}	14												14
		5		6		10						3	11					4					1	2	8	7		9^{1}	12									15
		5	10	6		8	13				14		9^{1}					7					1	2	11	4^{2}		3^{3}	12									16
		6	2	5		10	13						11					4					1	3	7^{2}	8		9^{1}	12									17
		2	3	4		7	12				13		5^{2}					9					1	10		8		11^{1}	6									18
		6	4	3		7^{3}	9^{2}				14		11	13				5					1	2	10^{1}	8			12									19
		2	3	4		7					12		6					10					1	11	8	9			5^{1}									20
		6	3	5		10^{1}	13				9^{2}		11										1	2		7				4	8	12						21
		3	4	6		8	13		14		7^{1}		11										1	2		9^{3}			12	5	10^{2}							22
			4	6		7	12					3	5										1	2	9^{2}	11			8^{1}	10		13						23
		3	4^{3}	5		7^{2}							6										1	2	8	9^{1}			10■	11	12	13	14					24
		5	6	4		10	12						11										1	2	7	8					9^{1}		3					25
		2	3	4		7	12						5^{2}										1	10		8				9	14		11^{3}	6^{1}	13			26
		2	3	4		7						14											1	11		8^{2}					12	5^{1}	9	6^{3}	10	13		27
12		2	3	4		9																	1	7					8		10			11^{1}	5		6	28
11		2	3			9																	1	4		12			10		8		7		6^{1}		5	29
11^{1}		3	7	5		9							8										1	2		10			6		12						4	30
		2	3	4		8					13		11^{2}										1	7		9^{1}			10		12				5		6	31
		3	4	5		8		1				12	11											2		9					10^{1}				6		7■	32
			3	4		8						2	10	9		11							1	6					7						5			33
			7^{2}	4		11^{1}				12	14	3	10	8		9^{3}							1	2					6		13				5			34
		2	3^{2}	4		13				12	14		5^{3}	9		8		1						11					6		7^{1}						10	35
				3		9^{3}				11	12	2		8		10^{1}		1		13				5					6	14	7^{2}				4			36
			3	4^{1}		13				10	5^{2}	2		8				1		12				11		6				7					9			37
			3			12				11		2		10^{2}				1		7^{1}				4		9			8		13				6		5	38
		14	3	4		12				10^{3}		2		9^{2}				1				11^{1}		5		8			13	7					6			39
			3	4		13				9		2	14	7^{2}				1				11^{3}		10		5^{1}			12	6					8			40
			3	4		13				10		2	11^{1}	12								14		5		9^{2}		1	7^{3}		8	6						41
		6	7			8						5	11^{1}	10								12		2		9		1							3		4	42
		5	7			8						3	10^{2}							12		11^{1}		2		9		1						13	6		4	43
		3	4			8^{2}						2	11^{3}	10								13		7		9^{1}		1				12		14	5		6	44
		3	4			9^{3}						2	11											7		10^{2}		1	12		13	8^{1}		14	5		6	45
		6		5						12			11^{1}									13		2		9^{2}		1	7		8	10^{3}			3	14	4	46

FA Cup

Fourth Qualifying	Chester	(h)	1-0
First Round	Fleetwood T	(h)	0-0
Replay	Fleetwood T	(a)	1-4

aet.

FA Trophy

First Round	Farsley Celtic	(a)	4-0
Second Round	Wealdstone	(h)	1-2

SUTTON UNITED

Ground: Borough Sports Ground, Gander Green Lane, Sutton, Surrey SM1 2EY. *Tel:* (0208) 644 4440.
Website: www.suttonunited.net *Email:* info@suttonunited.net *Year Formed:* 1898.
Record Attendance: 14,000 v Leeds U, FA Cup 4th rd, 24th January 1970. *Nickname:* 'The U's'.
Manager: Paul Doswell. *Colours:* Amber shirts with chocolate trim, amber shorts with chocolate trim, amber socks with chocolate trim.

SUTTON UNITED – NATIONAL LEAGUE 2016–17 LEAGUE RECORD

Match No.	*Date*	*Venue*	*Opponents*	*Result*		*H/T Score*	*Lg Pos.*	*Goalscorers*	*Attendance*
1	Aug 6	H	Solihull Moors	L	1-3	1-1	19	Beckwith [42]	1305
2	9	A	Forest Green R	D	1-1	0-1	19	Bailey (pen) [55]	1370
3	13	A	Lincoln C	W	3-1	1-0	11	Wishart [23], Collins [83], Deacon [90]	3195
4	16	H	Torquay U	W	2-0	1-0	6	Biamou [4], Bailey (pen) [55]	1625
5	20	H	Macclesfield T	W	2-0	2-0	3	Stearn [25], Gomis [37]	1255
6	27	A	Chester FC	L	0-4	0-2	7		1625
7	29	H	Dagenham & R	W	1-0	1-0	6	Hudson-Odoi [11]	1951
8	Sept 3	A	Gateshead	L	0-1	0-0	11		890
9	10	A	Wrexham	L	0-1	0-0	15		3890
10	13	H	Braintree T	L	1-2	1-1	14	Bailey (pen) [35]	922
11	17	H	Tranmere R	W	1-0	0-0	12	Fitchett [47]	1680
12	24	A	Eastleigh	L	1-2	0-0	13	Stearn [82]	2853
13	Oct 1	H	Guiseley	W	1-0	1-0	10	Brown (og) [34]	1282
14	4	A	Dover Ath	L	1-3	0-1	14	Amankwaah [75]	821
15	8	H	Woking	W	4-1	2-0	13	Deacon [22], Stearn [42], Bailey [47], McAllister [52]	1714
16	22	A	Southport	D	1-1	0-1	13	Collins (pen) [57]	864
17	25	H	Maidstone U	D	2-2	2-2	13	Fitchett [17], Bailey [23]	1609
18	29	A	York C	D	2-2	1-1	13	Collins 2 (2 pens) [17, 88]	2037
19	Nov 12	H	Barrow	D	0-0	0-0	13		1588
20	19	A	North Ferriby U	L	1-2	0-1	13	Biamou [75]	372
21	22	A	Boreham Wood	L	0-1	0-1	13		371
22	26	H	Aldershot T	W	2-0	0-0	13	Collins 2 [58, 80]	1847
23	29	H	Dover Ath	L	0-6	0-4	14		1091
24	Dec 17	H	Wrexham	W	1-0	1-0	14	Riley (og) [4]	1613
25	26	A	Bromley	L	0-1	0-0	14		2036
26	Jan 1	H	Bromley	W	2-0	1-0	14	Biamou [45], Hudson-Odoi [62]	1766
27	10	A	Braintree T	L	0-1	0-1	14		568
28	21	H	Eastleigh	D	1-1	0-1	15	Tubbs [73]	2179
29	Feb 11	A	Solihull Moors	L	0-3	0-2	16		671
30	14	A	Guiseley	L	1-2	1-1	17	Tubbs (pen) [37]	664
31	25	A	Torquay U	W	3-2	1-1	16	Deacon [30], Biamou [47], Beckwith [79]	1646
32	28	H	Boreham Wood	W	1-0	1-0	16	Biamou [31]	1441
33	Mar 4	A	Barrow	D	0-0	0-0	16		1145
34	11	H	York C	D	2-2	0-0	16	Bailey [74], Newton (og) [87]	2171
35	14	H	Forest Green R	L	1-2	0-2	16	Cadogan [90]	1446
36	18	A	Aldershot T	L	0-2	0-1	18		2197
37	21	A	Maidstone U	D	1-1	0-0	17	Coyle (og) [51]	2929
38	25	H	North Ferriby U	W	5-1	3-0	16	Deacon [14], Collins [23], Biamou [34], Cadogan 2 [63, 83]	1664
39	28	H	Lincoln C	D	1-1	0-0	14	Deacon [90]	2246
40	Apr 1	A	Woking	L	1-2	0-1	14	Cadogan [62]	1537
41	4	A	Tranmere R	L	2-3	0-1	15	Jebb [77], Gueye [81]	4694
42	8	H	Southport	D	2-2	1-0	15	Cadogan [25], Deacon [90]	1807
43	14	H	Gateshead	W	3-0	1-0	13	Deacon (pen) [42], Biamou 2 [60, 83]	1889
44	17	A	Dagenham & R	D	2-2	0-2	15	Biamou 2 [51, 53]	1634
45	22	H	Chester FC	W	5-2	3-0	11	Coombes 2 [5, 46], May [8], Collins [41], Bailey [71]	2082
46	29	A	Macclesfield T	D	0-0	0-0	12		1660

Final League Position: 12

GOALSCORERS

League (61): Biamou 10, Collins 8 (3 pens), Bailey 7 (3 pens), Deacon 7 (1 pen), Cadogan 5, Stearn 3, Beckwith 2, Coombes 2, Fitchett 2, Hudson-Odoi 2, Tubbs 2 (1 pen), Amankwaah 1, Gomis 1, Gueye 1, Jebb 1, May 1, McAllister 1, Wishart 1, own goals 4.
FA Cup (14): Deacon 5, Biamou 3, Stearn 3, Collins 1 (1 pen), Fitchett 1, Tubbs 1.
FA Trophy (6): May 2, Beckwith 1, Deacon 1, Jefford 1, McAlister 1.

Worner 31	Downer 18 + 1	Beckwith 30	Collins 43	Wishart 8 + 1	Eastmond 36 + 1	Bailey 37 + 1	Gomis 34 + 9	Stearn 14 + 4	Fitchett 14 + 11	Deacon 37 + 5	Dickson 9 + 11	Biamou 29 + 10	Hudson-Odoi 6 + 5	Amankwaah 33 + 2	Burge 7 + 5	Cooper — + 2	Morrell — + 3	Spence 19 + 5	John Louis 13 + 2	McAllister 6 + 6	McLennan 2 + 1	Dundas 7 + 12	Haunstrup 1 + 2	May 11 + 9	Jefford 10 + 2	Alves 1	Tubbs 3 + 2	Monakana 3 + 1	Traore — + 1	Gueye — + 3	Jebb 5 + 8	Smith — + 1	Coker — + 1	Coombes 12 + 1	Puddy 15	Cadogan 12 + 2	Wright — + 1	Match No.
1	2^{2}	3	4	5	6	7	8	9	10^{1}	11^{3}	12	13	14																									1
1		3	4	5		8	6^{1}	7^{2}	11^{3}	9	12	14		2	10	13																						2
1	11^{3}	3	4	6		8	5^{1}	7		9	14	10^{2}		2	12		13																					3
1		3	4	5^{2}	6	7^{1}		12		9	14	11	10^{3}	2	8		13																					4
1	5^{2}	3	4		8	7	9^{1}	6		10	13	11^{3}		2	12		14																					5
1		3	4		7	12	6^{1}	14	11	8	10^{3}	13		2	9^{2}			5																				6
1	5■	3	4		8	9	12	7		13	14	11^{3}	6^{2}	2	10^{1}																							7
1		3	5		8	9	6	7^{2}	14	10^{3}	13	11^{1}		2	12			4																				8
1		3	4	14	6	7	5^{2}		12	13	9	11^{1}		2	10			8^{3}																				9
1			5	3	9^{1}	10	7^{3}	8		12	11	13	6^{2}	2	14				4																			10
1	2		4	5	7	8	6	13	10^{1}	9	12	11^{2}		3																								11
1	2		4	5	7		6	12	11^{3}	8	14	10^{2}	13	3	9^{1}																							12
1	11		4	3	8		5	7	6^{1}	10	9^{2}	12		2				13																				13
1			4		8		7	9	13	11	10^{1}		6	2				5^{2}	3	12																		14
1		3^{2}	4		7	8		9	14	6	10^{1}	13		2		12		5		11^{3}																		15
1		3	4			9	6	8			12	11^{1}	5^{2}	2						7	10^{3}	13	14															16
1		3	4		8	6	12	10^{1}	11	9				2						14	13		5^{2}	7^{3}														17
1		3■	4		8	9	13	6	11	10^{3}		12		2							5^{2}		14	7^{1}														18
1	11	3	4		9		5	8^{1}	7^{2}	10				2	12					6		13																19
1		4	5		8		6^{2}		7^{3}	9	12	11		2	10^{1}					14		13			3													20
1	11	3			6	7	13		14	12	9^{2}	10^{1}						8		4				5^{3}	2													21
1	3		4		8	7^{1}	6		13	9	10^{2}	11^{3}		2				5		12				14														22
1		4■	5		12		6			14	9^{1}			13				2		10^{3}		8		7	3	11^{2}												23
1	10		4		6	7	5^{2}		14	8		9^{1}		2						13		12			3		11^{3}											24
1	4		3		6	7	12		13	8		14	5^{1}							10		9^{2}			2		11^{3}											25
1	11	3	4		7^{1}	8	5		6	9		10	12^{3}											13	2^{2}			14										26
1		3					5		9	7		11^{3}		2				6	4	12		10^{1}		13			14	8^{2}										27
1		3				7^{3}	9^{1}		11^{2}	6		10	12	2				5	4					8			13		14									28
1			6			8	7^{1}		11	9				3^{3}				2^{2}	5			10		14	4					12	13							29
1	10		3			7	4^{2}		13	9^{3}									2			6		5			11^{1}				8	12	14					30
1^{2}	2	4	5		7	8	12			9		10	13					3						6^{1}							14			11^{3}				31
	4		5		6	7	12			9		10^{2}		2				3				13									8			11^{1}	1			32
		3	4			7	5			9■		10^{2}		2				8				14		6^{1}							13			11^{3}	1	12		33
		3	4			7	6		13			10^{2}		2				5						14	12						8^{3}			11	1	9^{1}		34
	14	3	4		6	7	5^{1}			9		10		2^{3}				8^{2}						13										11	1	12		35
	4^{2}	2	3		7	8	5		14	9		12		13										6^{3}										11^{1}	1	10		36
	9^{1}	3	4		6	7	5^{2}			8^{3}		13		2				12													14			10	1	11		37
			4		6	7	5^{3}			8		10		2^{2}				12	3			14			13									11^{1}	1	9		38
			4		8	5	7^{1}			6		10		2^{2}				12	3			14		13										11^{3}	1	9		39
			5		6	8	12			9		10						3	4						2									11^{1}	1	7		40
			4		7		6			8		10^{2}						5	3			11^{1}			2					14	13				1	9^{3}	12	41
			5		7	8	6^{2}			9		11^{1}		2^{3}				4	3			13									14			12	1	10		42
		3^{3}	4		6^{2}	7	5			9		11		2					14			13		12							8^{1}				1	10		43
		3	4		7	8	5^{1}			10		11							13			12		14	2^{2}						9^{3}				1	6		44
		2^{2}	4		6	7						10^{3}						14	3			13		5				8^{1}			12			11	1	9		45
		2	4		7	8	13												3			6^{1}		5^{2}				9^{3}		14	12			10	1	11		46

FA Cup

Fourth Qualifying	Forest Green R	(h)	2-1
First Round	Dartford	(a)	6-3
Second Round	Cheltenham T	(h)	2-1
Third Round	AFC Wimbledon	(h)	0-0
Replay	AFC Wimbledon	(a)	3-1
Fourth Round	Leeds U	(h)	1-0
Fifth Round	Arsenal	(h)	0-2

FA Trophy

First Round	Bath C	(h)	1-0
Second Round	Worthing	(a)	2-2
Replay	Worthing	(h)	3-2
aet.			
Third Round	Boreham Wood	(h)	0-0
Replay	Boreham Wood	(a)	0-5

TORQUAY UNITED

Ground: The Launa Windows Stadium, Plainmoor, Marnham Road, Torquay, Devon TQ1 3PS.
Tel: (01803) 328666. *Website:* www.torquayunited.com *Email:* reception@torquayunited.com
Year Formed: 1899. *Record Attendance:* 21,908 v Huddersfield T, FA Cup 4th rd, 29 January 1955.
Nickname: 'The Gulls'. *Manager:* Kevin Nicholson. *Colours:* Yellow shirts with blue trim, blue shorts with yellow trim, yellow socks with blue trim.

TORQUAY UNITED – NATIONAL LEAGUE 2016–17 LEAGUE RECORD

Match No.	*Date*	*Venue*	*Opponents*	*Result*		*H/T Score*	*Lg Pos.*	*Goalscorers*	*Attendance*
1	Aug 6	A	Macclesfield T	L	0-2	0-1	22		1501
2	9	H	Bromley	W	1-0	1-0	14	Gerring [42]	2279
3	13	H	Barrow	D	1-1	1-0	17	Williams [39]	2207
4	16	A	Sutton U	L	0-2	0-1	17		1625
5	20	A	North Ferriby U	L	0-1	0-0	21		505
6	27	H	Dover Ath	W	2-1	0-0	19	Reid [46], Sparkes [76]	1793
7	29	A	Braintree T	W	3-1	2-1	14	Reid [21], Gallifuoco [35], Young [75]	892
8	Sept 3	H	Lincoln C	L	1-2	1-1	16	Gallifuoco [21]	2061
9	10	H	York C	W	2-0	2-0	14	Blissett 2 [6, 29]	1989
10	13	A	Woking	L	1-3	1-0	15	Gallifuoco [28]	1115
11	17	A	Boreham Wood	L	0-2	0-2	16		605
12	24	H	Maidstone U	L	2-3	1-2	16	Blissett [38], Sparkes [54]	2026
13	Oct 1	A	Gateshead	D	0-0	0-0	17		693
14	4	H	Dagenham & R	W	1-0	1-0	17	Reid [23]	1638
15	8	A	Chester FC	L	0-1	0-1	18		2201
16	22	H	Aldershot T	D	0-0	0-0	16		1788
17	25	A	Eastleigh	L	0-3	0-0	18		2116
18	29	H	Southport	L	1-2	1-0	18	Williams [25]	1490
19	Nov 12	A	Guiseley	L	0-2	0-2	19		924
20	19	H	Wrexham	D	1-1	0-1	18	Moore, K [88]	1484
21	22	H	Solihull Moors	W	3-0	1-0	16	Moore, K 3 [30, 60, 71]	1272
22	26	A	Tranmere R	L	1-2	0-1	17	Sparkes [65]	4449
23	29	A	Dagenham & R	W	1-0	0-0	17	Moore, K [76]	1072
24	Dec 17	A	York C	D	0-0	0-0	17		2272
25	26	H	Forest Green R	W	4-3	0-0	17	Blissett [55], Fitzpatrick [66], McGinty [69], Gerring [81]	2540
26	Jan 1	A	Forest Green R	D	5-5	3-2	17	Sparkes 2 [15, 21], Verma [40], Pinnock (og) [50], Fitzpatrick [66]	2383
27	7	H	Boreham Wood	L	0-1	0-0	17		1789
28	14	H	Woking	L	1-2	0-2	17	Williams [86]	1593
29	21	A	Maidstone U	L	1-2	0-0	18	Williams [63]	2455
30	28	H	Gateshead	W	3-1	1-0	17	Fitzpatrick [34], Rooney [59], Williams [90]	1555
31	Feb 4	A	Bromley	L	0-1	0-1	17		889
32	11	H	Macclesfield T	D	1-1	0-1	17	McGinty [50]	1400
33	18	A	Barrow	D	0-0	0-0	18		1391
34	25	H	Sutton U	L	2-3	1-1	18	Young [14], Williams [46]	1646
35	Mar 4	H	Guiseley	L	1-2	1-0	21	Verma [25]	1446
36	11	A	Southport	W	2-1	1-0	20	Young [36], Keating [90]	1159
37	14	H	Tranmere R	D	0-0	0-0	20		1418
38	21	H	Eastleigh	L	2-3	0-1	21	Young [50], Harrad [63]	1528
39	25	A	Wrexham	D	1-1	0-0	21	Reid (pen) [78]	3328
40	28	A	Solihull Moors	W	1-0	0-0	20	Sparkes [88]	857
41	Apr 1	H	Chester FC	L	0-1	0-0	21		1881
42	8	A	Aldershot T	D	1-1	1-0	22	Keating [33]	3007
43	14	A	Lincoln C	L	1-2	0-0	22	Keating [78]	9011
44	17	H	Braintree T	W	3-1	1-1	22	Williams 2 [41, 52], Lee [90]	2580
45	22	A	Dover Ath	W	2-1	1-0	19	Williams 2 [43, 68]	1432
46	29	H	North Ferriby U	W	2-0	0-0	17	Verma [58], Anderson [86]	4026

Final League Position: 17

GOALSCORERS

League (54): Williams 10, Sparkes 6, Moore, K 5, Blissett 4, Reid 4 (1 pen), Young 4, Fitzpatrick 3, Gallifuoco 3, Keating 3, Verma 3, Gerring 2, McGinty 2, Anderson 1, Harrad 1, Lee 1, Rooney 1, own goal 1.
FA Cup (2): Chaney 1, Young 1.
FA Trophy (0).

Moore B 46	Rowe-Turner 46	Lathrope 21 + 3	Gerring 14 + 4	Young 39 + 1	Blissett 21 + 3	Richards 29	Sparkes 34 + 1	Verma 40 + 1	Williams 21 + 18	McGinty 46	Chaney 12 + 19	Reid 31 + 15	Gallifuoco 30 + 5	Scrivens — + 6	Chamberlain — + 5	Ward 12 + 5	Ambalu — + 1	Nicholson 1 + 2	Fitzpatrick 12 + 1	Moore K 4	McCoulsky — + 2	Rooney 3 + 3	Harrad 7 + 8	Lee 6 + 3	Racine 1	Hodgkiss 8	Anderson 14	Keating 8 + 7	Hancox — + 1	*Match No.*
1	2	3^{1}	4	5	6	7	8	9	10^{2}	11	12	13																		1
1	2	3^{2}	4	5	6	7	8	9	10^{1}	11	12	13																		2
1	2	13	3	6	10	7^{1}	8	9	11^{2}	4	5^{3}	12	14																	3
1	2	7	4■	9^{1}	10^{3}		5	6	11^{2}	3	8	13	12	14																4
1	3	4^{3}		7	10		8	5	11^{1}	2	6^{2}	12	9		13	14														5
1	2			5	10	6	7	8	12	3		11^{1}	4			9														6
1	3			8	11^{2}		5	4	12	2	7^{1}	10^{3}	6	13	14	9														7
1	2			4	5^{3}	6	7^{1}	8	14	9	12	10	3	13		11^{2}														8
1	2			5	11	7	8^{1}	9	12	3	13	10^{2}	4	14		6^{3}														9
1	5			7	11	6	9^{2}	3	13	2	14	10^{1}	4	12		8^{3}														10
1	2		14	4	5	6^{2}	7	8	13	9^{3}	12	10	3			11^{1}														11
1	2	6^{3}		7	11	8^{1}	9	4		3	12	10^{2}	5	14		13														12
1	2	9	4■	6	11	7		8^{3}	13	3	5^{2}	10^{1}	12		14															13
1	2	4		6	10	7	8^{2}		13	3	12	11^{1}	5			9														14
1	2	8		7	11	6				3	9^{2}	10	5			4^{1}	12	13												15
1	3	4^{1}		7		8		9^{2}	10	2	6	11	5			12		13												16
1	3			8	10	7^{2}			11	4	12	9	2		13	6^{1}		5												17
1	2		4	5	6^{2}	7			8	9	12	10	3		13	11^{1}														18
1	5		3	8	11	7^{1}			9	4	6^{2}	10	2			13			12											19
1	2			4	5^{1}	6	7^{2}	8		9	12	14	3			10^{3}				11	13									20
1	2			5	14	6	7^{3}	8		3	12	10	4						9^{2}	11^{1}	13									21
1	5		12	8^{2}	13		9	2		4	14	11^{1}	3			7			6^{3}	10										22
1	2		3		12	5	6	8		4		10^{1}	9						7	11										23
1	2		4		5	6	7	8	12	9		10^{2}	3						11^{1}			13								24
1	2		4		6	7	8^{3}	9		10	5^{2}	13	3^{1}			14			11			12								25
1	2		3			5	6	7	12	8	4^{1}	10							11			9								26
1	2		3			5	6	7	13	8	4^{2}	10^{1}							11			9	12							27
1	5		3			8	9	7	13	4	12	10							6				11^{1}	2^{2}						28
1	5		3^{1}	9^{2}		8	11	7	13	4	14	12							6			2	10^{3}							29
1	5	13		6^{2}		7	9^{3}	10	11	3		14							8			12			2^{1}	4				30
1	3			9^{1}		8	11	7	10	4		12	5						6							2				31
1	5	8^{1}		10^{2}		7	6	13	11^{3}	3		12							9							2	4	14		32
1	3	5		12		6^{2}	7	8	9^{1}	2		10														11	4	13		33
1	2^{2}	6^{3}		7			8	9	11^{1}	5	13	10											12			3	4	14		34
1	4^{3}	7^{2}		6			8	9	10	2	13	11^{1}	5										12				3	14		35
1	5	6		7			11^{1}	8	10^{2}	4		12	14										9^{3}			2	3	13		36
1	2	7		3			8	9	11^{1}	4		13	14										10^{3}			6	5^{2}	12		37
1	5	6^{2}		8			7	9	11^{3}	4	14	13											10^{1}			2	3	12		38
1	4	5^{3}		7			8	9	12	3		13	6										10^{1}	14			2	11^{2}		39
1	4	5		7			8	9^{3}	14	3		10^{2}	6										13	12			2	11^{1}		40
1	4	5		7				8	13	3		10	6										9^{1}	12			2■	11^{2}		41
1	2	5		8^{2}				9	12	3	7^{3}	10	6										14	4				11^{1}	13	42
1	2	3^{3}	12	5				6	14	7		9	4										13	11			8^{2}	10^{1}		43
1	2			4				5	6	7		9	3											11			8	10		44
1	2	13	14	6^{3}				5	7^{1}	4		9	3										12	11			8	10^{2}		45
1	5			7			12	8	9^{1}	2	13	10^{2}	6										14	3^{3}			4	11		46

FA Cup

Fourth Qualifying	Woking	(h)	1-1
Replay	Woking	(a)	1-2

FA Trophy

First Round	Braintree T	(a)	0-2

TRANMERE ROVERS

Ground: Prenton Park, Prenton Road West, Prenton, Wirral CH42 9PY. *Tel:* (03330) 144452.
Website: www.tranmererovers.co.uk *Email:* customerservice@tranmererovers.co.uk *Year Formed:* 1884.
Record Attendance: 24,424 v Stoke C, FA Cup 4th rd, 5 February 1972. *Nickname:* 'Rovers' *Manager:* Micky Mellon.
Colours: White shirts with blue trim, white shorts with blue trim, white socks with blue trim.

TRANMERE ROVERS – NATIONAL LEAGUE 2016–17 LEAGUE RECORD

Match No.	*Date*	*Venue*	*Opponents*	*Result*		*H/T Score*	*Lg Pos.*	*Goalscorers*	*Attendance*
1	Aug 6	A	Bromley	W	2-0	2-0	4	Norwood 2 [9, 44]	2000
2	9	H	Barrow	W	2-0	1-0	4	Cook [40], Norwood (pen) [86]	4977
3	13	H	Eastleigh	W	2-1	1-1	1	Jennings, S [24], Norwood [90]	4619
4	16	A	Boreham Wood	W	1-0	1-0	1	Jennings, C [33]	801
5	20	H	Maidstone U	W	2-1	1-0	1	Cook [40], McNulty [80]	4797
6	27	A	Southport	D	1-1	0-0	1	Cook [47]	3046
7	29	H	Guiseley	W	1-0	1-0	1	Norwood [40]	4798
8	Sept 3	A	Aldershot T	L	1-3	1-1	2	Cook [37]	2585
9	10	H	Lincoln C	L	0-1	0-0	3		5274
10	13	A	York C	D	0-0	0-0	4		2379
11	17	A	Sutton U	L	0-1	0-0	5		1680
12	24	H	Woking	W	3-1	1-0	4	Cook 2 [33, 49], Norwood [69]	4214
13	Oct 1	A	Dagenham & R	D	0-0	0-0	5		1554
14	4	H	Gateshead	L	0-1	0-0	9		4048
15	8	H	Wrexham	W	2-0	0-0	7	Jalal (og) [64], Cook [90]	5644
16	22	A	Solihull Moors	W	3-0	1-0	4	Kirby 2 [17, 81], Norwood [90]	1995
17	25	H	North Ferriby U	W	1-0	0-0	4	Cook [90]	4326
18	29	A	Dover Ath	W	4-1	1-1	4	Cook 2 [31, 60], Walker (og) [65], Tollitt [79]	1534
19	Nov 12	H	Chester FC	D	2-2	2-0	3	Cook [29], Tollitt [35]	7790
20	19	A	Braintree T	W	1-0	0-0	2	Cook [76]	964
21	22	A	Forest Green R	D	2-2	1-2	5	Maynard [5], Norwood [66]	2040
22	26	H	Torquay U	W	2-1	1-0	4	Mangan 2 [12, 46]	4449
23	29	A	Gateshead	W	1-0	1-0	3	Tollitt [3]	723
24	Dec 3	H	York C	W	1-0	0-0	1	Norwood [90]	5075
25	17	A	Lincoln C	L	1-2	1-1	2	Hughes (pen) [29]	6335
26	26	H	Macclesfield T	W	1-0	0-0	1	Hughes [83]	7274
27	Jan 1	A	Macclesfield T	L	2-4	2-1	2	McNulty [10], Sutton [36]	3317
28	28	H	Dagenham & R	L	0-2	0-1	4		5293
29	31	A	Woking	W	3-0	0-0	3	Cook [51], Tollitt 2 [53, 78]	860
30	Feb 11	H	Bromley	D	2-2	2-0	4	Cook 2 [8, 15]	4425
31	18	A	Eastleigh	W	2-0	0-0	4	Tollitt 2 [60, 86]	2475
32	21	H	Boreham Wood	W	2-1	2-0	3	Cook 2 [1, 13]	4107
33	Mar 3	A	Chester FC	W	3-2	0-1	2	Harris [54], Norwood [81], Cook [89]	3696
34	7	A	Barrow	L	1-2	1-0	3	Cook [33]	1251
35	14	A	Torquay U	D	0-0	0-0	4		1418
36	21	A	North Ferriby U	W	4-1	2-1	3	Harris 3 [22, 45, 90], Cook [60]	638
37	25	H	Braintree T	W	1-0	0-0	3	Cook [54]	4514
38	28	H	Dover Ath	W	1-0	0-0	2	Stockton [68]	4281
39	Apr 1	A	Wrexham	W	1-0	1-0	2	Marx (og) [10]	4630
40	4	H	Sutton U	W	3-2	1-0	2	Ihiekwe 2 [29, 90], Eastmond (og) [60]	4694
41	8	H	Solihull Moors	W	9-0	3-0	2	Stockton 3 [20, 25, 45], Jennings, C 3 [48, 50, 90], Cook [68], Ridehalgh [84], Collins [90]	5001
42	11	H	Forest Green R	L	0-1	0-0	2		6907
43	14	H	Aldershot T	D	2-2	2-2	2	Stockton [12], Jennings, C [23]	6324
44	17	A	Guiseley	W	2-1	0-1	2	Norwood [49], Cook [58]	2148
45	22	H	Southport	W	4-1	1-0	2	Norwood 2 [25, 46], Jennings, C 2 [50, 71]	6159
46	29	A	Maidstone U	W	1-0	0-0	2	Ilesanmi [56]	3409

Final League Position: 2

GOALSCORERS

League (79): Cook 23, Norwood 13 (1 pen), Jennings, C 7, Tollitt 7, Stockton 5, Harris 4, Hughes 2 (1 pen), Ihiekwe 2, Kirby 2, Mangan 2, McNulty 2, Collins 1, Ilesanmi 1, Jennings, S 1, Maynard 1, Ridehalgh 1, Sutton 1, own goals 4.
FA Cup (1): own goal 1.
National League Play-Offs (6): Stockton 3, Norwood 2, Jennings 1.
FA Trophy (16): Stockton 5, Kirby 3, Sutton 3, Hughes 2, Ihiekwe 1, Mangan 1, own goal 1.

Davies S 45	Maynard 26 + 4	Ridehalgh 38 + 1	McNulty 45	Ihiekwe 35 + 4	Harris 28 + 3	Hughes 40	Jennings S 16	Cook 32 + 10	Norwood 32 + 8	Jennings C 20 + 3	Mekki 4 + 15	Kirby 13 + 13	Vaughan 34 + 1	Stephenson 3 + 8	Jones 1 + 4	Sutton 21	Tollitt 15 + 3	Almond 5	Duggan 2 + 2	Osborne 1 + 2 / Divine — + 1	Mangan 12 + 8	Dawson 2 + 2	Wallace 7 + 2	Stockton 8 + 8	Buxton 9	Dunn 3 + 2	Collins 1 + 1	Sousa 1 + 3	Pilling 1	Solomon-Davies 1	Drysdale 1	Lucy 1	Ilesanmi 1	Gumbs 1	Clarke 1	Flemming — + 1	Coughan — + 1	Match No.
1	2	3	4	5	6	7	8	9^1	10^2	11	12	13																										1
1	2	5^1	3	4	7	8	6	9	10^2	11		13	12																									2
1	10		4	5	6^2	11	3	7^1	8	9		12	2	13																								3
1	5		3	4	7	8	6	9	10	11			2																									4
1	2		5	3	8	6	7	9	10^2	11^1	13	12	4																									5
1	7	13	3	4	8^3	5	6	10	9	11^2	12	14	2^1																									6
1	10	2	4	5	6^1	11	3	7	8	9	12																											7
1	2	5	3	4		7	8	10^2	11	9	6^1	13		12																								8
1	10		4	5	6^3	11	3	7^1	8	9^2	14	12	2	13																								9
1	6	3	4	5		8▮	7	9	10				2	11																								10
1	3	4	5	6	9^3		7	13	10		12	8^1	2	11^2	14																							11
1	4	2	3	5			7	9^2	10					12	14	6	8^3	11^1	13																			12
1	2	3	4	5▮			8	10	9^3			7^2			14	6		11^1	12	13																		13
1		5	3		7			10				9^2		13	11	4	12	6^1	2	8																		14
1		2	4	5	7		6	11				8^1		12		3	9^2		10	13																		15
1	8	3	4		13	6	7^1	11^3	12			10	2	14		5		9^2																				16
1	6	3	4		7^2	9		10	12▮			8^1	2	14		5	13	11^3																				17
1	4	6	5	13	7	8		10^1			12		2^3	11^2	14	3	9																					18
1		3	4	12	8	9		10			13	6^1	2			5	7▮				11^2																	19
1	13	3	4	14	5^2	10		6			12	8^1	2			7					9	11^3																20
1	2	6	4	3		8		10^1	12			9				5	7				11																	21
1	6	3^3	4	12	7^1	9		11	13			14	2			5	8				10^2																	22
1	3		5	4	8	9		11^1	12			7				2	6^3				10^2	14	13															23
1	6^1		4	5	7^2	9		13	11			12	3			2	8				10^3	14																24
1	10	3	4		5^1	11			6			12	2			7	8				9																	25
1	13	3	4			10			5	12		7^1	2			6	8				9^2		11															26
1	14	3	4			10			5	13	12	7^1	2			6	8				9^2		11^3															27
1		5	4	3		8	6^1	10	13			7^3	2				12				11^2		9	14														28
1	3	6	4	5	12	7		11^1	10^3			13	2				9						8^2	14														29
1	12	2	3^1	4		7		9	11								6				13		8		5▮	10^2												30
1	3	4	5	6		8		9	11			12	2				7									10^1												31
1	2	4	5	6		8		11^3	10			12	3				7^2				13			14		9^1												32
1	7^2	5	3	4	12	6		13	14		8		2			9					11^1			10^3														33
1		3	4	5	8^1	9		10	11	13	7^2		2			6^3					12			14														34
1		3	4	5	7	8		13	12	9			2			6					10^2			11^1														35
1		3	2	5	7	8		10^2	11^3	9^1	14		6			4					12			13														36
1		4	5	6	7	8		9^1	10	11^2	12		2			3								13														37
1		3	4	5	6	11		7^2	8^1	9^3	14		2								13			12	10													38
1		9	3	4	6	7		14	11^1	8^3	12		5								13			10^2	2													39
1		3	4	5	7	8		13	9	10^2	12		2											11^1	6													40
1		4	5	6	8^3	7		12	9^2	10			2											11^1	3		13	14										41
1		4	5	6	7^3	8		13	9	10			3^2										12	11^1	2			14										42
1	6	3	4	7		8		13	9	10			2											11^2	5^1			12										43
1		3	4	5		7		10^1	11^3	8^2			2								14		9	13	6	12												44
1		3	4	5		7		14	9^1	10			2^2								13		8	11^3	6	12												45
											11^3									14		8					3	10	1	2	4	5	6^2	7	9^1	12	13	46

FA Cup

Fourth Qualifying	Barrow	(a)	1-2

National League Play-Offs

Semi-Final 1st leg	Aldershot T	(a)	3-0
Semi-Final 2nd leg	Aldershot T	(h)	2-2
Tranmere R won 5-2 on aggregate.			
Final	Forest Green R	(Wembley)	1-3

FA Trophy

First Round	Wrexham	(a)	1-0
Second Round	South Park	(h)	4-1
Third Round	Chelmsford C	(h)	1-1
Replay	Chelmsford C	(a)	4-1
Fourth Round	Barrow	(h)	5-1
Semi-Final 1st leg	Macclesfield T	(a)	1-1
Semi-Final 2nd leg	Macclesfield T	(h)	0-1

WOKING

Ground: The Laithwaite Community Stadium, Kingfield, Woking, Surrey GU22 9AA. *Tel:* (01483) 722 470. *Website:* wokingfc.co.uk *Email:* admin@wokingfc.co.uk *Year Formed:* 1889. *Record Attendance:* 6,064 v Coventry C, FA Cup 3rd rd, 4 February 1997. *Nickname:* 'The Cardinals'. *Manager:* Anthony Limbrick. *Colours:* Red and white halved shirts, black shorts with red trim, white socks with red trim.

WOKING – NATIONAL LEAGUE 2016–17 LEAGUE RECORD

Match No.	Date	Venue	Opponents	Result		H/T Score	Lg Pos.	Goalscorers	Attendance
1	Aug 6	H	Lincoln C	L	1-3	0-1	20	Yakubu ^{46}	1592
2	9	A	Solihull Moors	D	2-2	1-0	18	Ralph ^{31}, Ansah ^{49}	699
3	13	A	Southport	L	1-2	1-1	21	Lewis ^{13}	702
4	16	H	Forest Green R	L	0-1	0-1	22		864
5	20	H	Dagenham & R	L	1-3	0-3	23	Edgar ^{48}	1153
6	27	A	York C	L	1-4	1-4	23	Ugwu ^{8}	1972
7	29	H	Chester FC	W	3-1	2-1	22	Murtagh ^{17}, Jones ^{28}, Ugwu ^{75}	1271
8	Sept 3	A	Macclesfield T	L	1-3	0-2	22	Lewis ^{59}	1221
9	10	A	Guiseley	D	1-1	0-0	22	Lewis ^{82}	649
10	13	H	Torquay U	W	3-1	0-1	22	Sam-Yorke 2 $^{50, 59}$, Lewis ^{86}	1115
11	17	H	Wrexham	W	2-0	0-0	19	Saraiva ^{81}, Kandi ^{89}	1213
12	24	A	Tranmere R	L	1-3	0-1	19	Saraiva ^{68}	4214
13	Oct 1	H	Eastleigh	D	3-3	1-3	20	Tubbs ^{23}, Sam-Yorke ^{59}, Kandi ^{79}	1403
14	4	A	Bromley	L	1-2	1-1	19	Saraiva ^{3}	808
15	8	A	Sutton U	L	1-4	0-2	20	Tubbs ^{75}	1714
16	22	H	Barrow	D	1-1	0-1	20	Tubbs (pen) ^{51}	1351
17	25	H	Braintree T	L	2-3	2-1	20	Jones ^{25}, Saraiva ^{30}	1362
18	29	A	Boreham Wood	L	1-2	1-0	21	Jones ^{20}	405
19	Nov 12	H	North Ferriby U	D	1-1	0-1	21	Kandi ^{90}	1357
20	19	A	Maidstone U	W	3-0	2-0	20	Saraiva ^{30}, Ugwu 2 $^{34, 72}$	2147
21	22	A	Dover Ath	L	1-3	0-2	20	Ugwu ^{56}	823
22	26	H	Gateshead	W	3-0	1-0	19	Ugwu 3 $^{9, 56, 72}$	1062
23	29	H	Bromley	W	2-1	1-1	19	Ugwu ^{31}, Saraiva ^{81}	1057
24	Dec 17	H	Guiseley	D	0-0	0-0	19		969
25	26	A	Aldershot T	L	0-4	0-4	19		3456
26	Jan 1	H	Aldershot T	L	1-2	0-0	21	Kretzschmar ^{65}	3224
27	7	A	Wrexham	L	1-2	0-0	22	Saraiva ^{55}	3575
28	14	A	Torquay U	W	2-1	2-0	20	Saraiva (pen) ^{6}, Saah ^{35}	1593
29	28	A	Eastleigh	W	1-0	1-0	19	Ugwu ^{16}	2036
30	31	H	Tranmere R	L	0-3	0-0	19		860
31	Feb 11	A	Lincoln C	L	2-3	1-1	19	Ugwu ^{11}, Saraiva (pen) ^{75}	5553
32	14	H	Solihull Moors	W	2-1	1-0	19	Thomas ^{3}, Saraiva ^{74}	1000
33	18	H	Southport	D	0-0	0-0	20		1386
34	25	A	Forest Green R	L	3-4	1-1	20	Jones ^{44}, Ugwu ^{54}, Thomas ^{90}	1566
35	28	H	Dover Ath	W	1-0	0-0	19	Kretzschmar ^{66}	1092
36	Mar 4	A	North Ferriby U	L	1-2	1-1	20	Ugwu ^{26}	402
37	11	H	Boreham Wood	D	0-0	0-0	21		1157
38	18	A	Gateshead	L	1-2	1-0	21	Thomas ^{21}	832
39	21	A	Braintree T	W	3-1	2-1	19	Sam-Yorke 2 $^{23, 25}$, Murtagh ^{69}	572
40	25	H	Maidstone U	L	2-4	2-1	20	Sam-Yorke ^{13}, Lucas ^{25}	2088
41	Apr 1	H	Sutton U	W	2-1	1-0	20	Sam-Yorke ^{5}, Ugwu ^{83}	1537
42	8	A	Barrow	D	2-2	1-0	20	Lucas (pen) ^{45}, Murtagh ^{70}	1326
43	14	H	Macclesfield T	W	1-0	0-0	19	Ugwu (pen) ^{61}	2068
44	17	A	Chester FC	W	3-2	0-0	17	Saah ^{54}, Hall, C ^{85}, Ugwu (pen) ^{90}	1770
45	22	H	York C	D	1-1	0-0	18	Ugwu (pen) ^{66}	2702
46	29	A	Dagenham & R	D	1-1	1-0	18	Kretzschmar ^{12}	1860

Final League Position: 18

GOALSCORERS

League (66): Ugwu 17 (3 pens), Saraiva 10 (2 pens), Sam-Yorke 7, Jones 4, Lewis 4, Kandi 3, Kretzschmar 3, Murtagh 3, Thomas 3, Tubbs 3 (1 pen), Lucas 2 (1 pen), Saah 2, Ansah 1, Edgar 1, Hall, C 1, Ralph 1, Yakubu 1.
FA Cup (7): Ugwu 4, Edgar 1, Jones 1, Saraiva 1.
FA Trophy (1): Winfield 1.

Poke 35	Caprice 37 + 2	Gordon 6	Jones 44 + 1	Saah 38	Ralph 31	Murtagh 40	Saraiva 30 + 11	Lewis 21 + 6	Ugwu 37 + 6	Ansah 5 + 6	Yakubu 22 + 4	Penny 3 + 7	Kretzschmar 9 + 13	Carter 16 + 15	Kandi 3 + 13	Edgar 2 + 15	Essam 6	Sam-Yorke 19 + 7	Sutherland 7 + 5	Tubbs 6	Hall B 11	Thomas 29 + 1	Jefford 2	Shaw 5	Ferdinand 22	Hall C 3 + 5	Bonne 5 + 2	Arthur 6 + 1	Morris — + 2	Lucas 6 + 3	Match No.
1	2	3[2]	4	5	6	7	8[1]	9[3]	10	11	12	13	14																		1
1	2	3	6	4	9	7	13	8[2]	10	11[3]	5[1]	12		14																	2
1	2	3[3]	4	5	9	6	10	11	7[2]	8[1]		12			13	14															3
1	2	3	4	5	6	7	8[3]	9[1]	10[2]	11		12	14			13															4
1	2	8[2]	4	5	3	10	12		13	14		6	11[3]	9[1]		7															5
1	2		3	4	5	6	9		10[1]	11[3]		12	13	8	14	7[2]															6
1	2	3	6	4		7	14	9	11	12	5[3]	10[1]	8[2]	13																	7
1	2		4	5	3	7	14	9	10	13	6[2]	11[3]	8[1]	12																	8
1	2[1]		4	5	3	7	13	9	10			14	8[2]		12		6	11[3]													9
1	2		4	5	3	7	8[3]	9	10[2]			14		13	12		6	11[1]													10
1	2		4	5	3	7	8	9	10						12		6	11[1]													11
1			2■	3	4	6[2]	8	9	10[1]	14				7	12	13	5	11[3]													12
1			4	5		7	3	2			6[1]		14	8[2]	13	12		11	9[3]	10											13
1			2	3	6	5	7	8						12	13	14	10	9[3]	11[1]	4[2]											14
	2[1]		3[3]	4	6	7[2]	8	9					13	12		14	5	11		10	1										15
	2		4		3	6	12	9	11					7		13		14	8[3]	10[1]	1	5[2]									16
	2		4		3		7	9[1]	11[2]				14	6		12		13	8[3]	10	1	5									17
			5		4	6	12	8[3]	10					7[1]		13		14	9	11[2]	1	2	3								18
	2[2]		3	4		6	9		7		5		14	8[3]	12	13		10			1		11[1]								19
	2		3[3]	4		5	8		6[2]					7	9[1]	14		12	13		1	10		11							20
	2		3	4		9	7		10		12			8[3]	11			14	13		1	5[1]		6[2]							21
	4		5[3]	6		8[2]	9	10[1]	11		7					13		14	12		1	3		2							22
	2			5			8[1]		9		13			7	11[2]	12		10	6		1	4		3							23
	2[2]		7	5	3		9	12	10		4				13			11[1]	8		1	6									24
	2		6	5	10[2]	7[3]	12		11		4[1]			8		13					1	14		3	9						25
1			4	5	2	6	7[1]	9	11				8[2]			12			13			3			10						26
1			3	4[3]	7	5	8	9	6					13	12				14			2			10[1]	11[2]					27
1			3	4	5[1]	6	7	8	10					12	13							2			9	11[2]					28
1	13		5	6[3]		7	3	2■	10		12		14	8[1]								4			9		11[2]				29
1	2		4			7[3]	6		10		5		12	8[2]								3			9	13	11[1]	14			30
1	2		5			7[3]	8		10		6[2]		13	12	14							4			9[1]		11	3			31
1	2		5		3[1]	7	9		11		4			12								6			8	13	10[2]				32
1	2		4			6	7	13	11		5[3]		8[2]									3			9	14	12	10[1]			33
1	2[1]		4		8	6	9	13	7		5[2]		14	12								3			10		11[3]				34
1	2		4	5			8[2]		11		6		10[1]	12								3			9		13	7			35
1	2		5	4	3		12	14	10	13	6[2]		11[3]	7[1]								8			9						36
1	2		14	4		6	8[3]		10		5[1]		12					11[2]				3			9			7	13		37
1	2		6	4	8		9		7[1]		5[3]			13				14				3			10				12	11[2]	38
1	2		4	6		7[1]			12		5			13				11				3			8			9		10[2]	39
1	2[2]		6	4		7	13		12	14	5[3]							10				3			8			9		11[1]	40
1	14		7[1]	5	3	8			12		6			2[2]				10				4			9	13				11[3]	41
1	2		4	5	7	8			12		6							10				3			9					11[1]	42
1	2		3	4	8	7			12		5[2]			13				10				6			9					11[1]	43
1	3[1]		5	6	2	8	9[3]		11				13					10[2]				4			7	14				12	44
1	3[1]		6	7	4	8		13	10									11				5			9	2[2]				12	45
1	2[3]		4	5	8	6	12	14	7[2]				9[1]					10				3			11					13	46

FA Cup

Fourth Qualifying	Torquay U	(a)	1-1
Replay	Torquay U	(h)	2-1
First Round	Stockport Co	(a)	4-2
Second Round	Accrington S	(h)	0-3

FA Trophy

First Round	Ebbsfleet U	(a)	1-1
Replay	Ebbsfleet U	(h)	0-1

WREXHAM

Ground: Racecourse Ground, Mold Road, Wrexham, Wales LL11 2AH. *Tel:* (01978) 891 864.
Website: wrexhamafc.co.uk *Email:* see website. *Year Formed:* 1872.
Record Attendance: 34,445 v Manchester U, FA Cup 4th rd, 26 January 1957. *Nickname:* 'Red Dragons'.
Manager: Dean Keates. *Colours:* Red shirts with white trim, white shorts with red trim, red socks.

WREXHAM – NATIONAL LEAGUE 2016–17 LEAGUE RECORD

Match No.	Date		Venue	Opponents	Result		H/T Score	Lg Pos.	Goalscorers	Attendance
1	Aug	6	H	Dover Ath	D	0-0	0-0	15		5603
2		9	A	Guiseley	W	3-2	1-1	7	Rooney (pen) ^{25}, McDonagh ^{65}, Rutherford ^{90}	1130
3		13	A	Aldershot T	L	0-2	0-1	15		1907
4		16	H	Solihull Moors	W	1-0	0-0	13	Carrington ^{90}	4017
5		20	H	Eastleigh	D	0-0	0-0	11		4034
6		27	A	Dagenham & R	L	0-3	0-3	13		1256
7		29	H	York C	W	2-1	1-1	10	Rooney (pen) ^{16}, Newton ^{63}	4005
8	Sept	3	A	Maidstone U	D	2-2	1-1	13	Powell 2 $^{38, 66}$	2550
9		10	H	Sutton U	W	1-0	0-0	11	Newton ^{64}	3890
10		17	A	Woking	L	0-2	0-0	14		1213
11		24	H	Chester FC	D	0-0	0-0	14		5058
12		27	A	Macclesfield T	L	0-3	0-1	14		1579
13	Oct	1	A	Boreham Wood	W	1-0	0-0	10	Rooney ^{57}	458
14		4	H	Lincoln C	L	1-2	0-2	15	Bencherif ^{81}	3847
15		8	A	Tranmere R	L	0-2	0-0	15		5644
16		22	H	Bromley	W	2-1	1-0	14	Harrad ^{44}, McDonagh ^{80}	3531
17		25	H	Barrow	D	2-2	1-1	14	Tilt ^{25}, Rooney ^{78}	3616
18		29	A	Gateshead	D	2-2	0-1	14	Rooney ^{59}, Bencherif ^{69}	832
19	Nov	5	A	North Ferriby U	D	0-0	0-0	14		528
20		12	H	Braintree T	L	0-1	0-1	14		3413
21		19	A	Torquay U	D	1-1	1-0	14	McDonagh ^{10}	1484
22		26	H	Forest Green R	W	3-1	2-0	15	Harrad ^{15}, McDonagh 2 $^{30, 90}$	3472
23		29	A	Lincoln C	L	0-1	0-1	15		3344
24	Dec	6	H	Macclesfield T	L	0-3	0-0	15		3204
25		17	A	Sutton U	L	0-1	0-1	15		1613
26		26	H	Southport	W	1-0	0-0	15	Edwards ^{88}	4317
27	Jan	1	A	Southport	L	2-3	1-2	16	White, J ^{6}, Rooney (pen) ^{67}	2066
28		7	H	Woking	W	2-1	0-0	15	Rooney ^{51}, Evans, R ^{60}	3575
29		14	H	North Ferriby U	W	1-0	1-0	14	McLeod ^{28}	3625
30		21	A	Chester FC	D	1-1	0-0	13	Rooney ^{53}	3961
31		28	H	Boreham Wood	W	2-1	1-0	12	Barry (pen) ^{27}, Rooney (pen) ^{90}	3664
32	Feb	4	H	Guiseley	W	3-1	1-1	10	Massanka ^{31}, Rooney 2 $^{62, 90}$	3730
33		11	A	Dover Ath	D	1-1	0-0	10	White, J ^{81}	1057
34		18	H	Aldershot T	L	0-2	0-0	10		4308
35		25	A	Solihull Moors	W	1-0	1-0	10	Barry (pen) ^{7}	1349
36	Mar	4	A	Braintree T	W	2-1	1-1	10	Massanka ^{4}, Shenton ^{64}	698
37		11	H	Gateshead	L	0-2	0-0	10		3986
38		18	A	Forest Green R	L	0-3	0-1	10		2146
39		21	A	Barrow	D	1-1	0-0	10	Rutherford ^{90}	1009
40		25	H	Torquay U	D	1-1	0-0	10	Harry (pen) ^{47}	3328
41	Apr	1	H	Tranmere R	L	0-1	0-1	10		4630
42		8	A	Bromley	L	3-4	0-2	12	White, J ^{52}, Massanka 2 $^{58, 86}$	1006
43		14	H	Maidstone U	L	1-3	1-1	12	White, J ^{9}	3379
44		17	A	York C	W	3-1	1-1	11	White, J 2 $^{30, 58}$, Smith, L ^{90}	4091
45		22	H	Dagenham & R	L	0-1	0-1	12		3653
46		29	A	Eastleigh	D	1-1	0-0	13	White, J ^{47}	2588

Final League Position: 13

GOALSCORERS

League (47): Rooney 11 (4 pens), White, J 7, McDonagh 5, Massanka 4, Barry 2 (2 pens), Bencherif 2, Harrad 2, Newton 2, Powell 2, Rutherford 2, Carrington 1, Edwards 1, Evans, R 1, Harry 1 (1 pen), McLeod 1, Shenton 1, Smith, L 1, Tilt 1.
FA Cup (3): Harrod 2, Evans, J 1.
FA Trophy (0).

Dunn 17 + 2	Evans J 21 + 1	Bencherif 24 + 2	Riley 29 + 1	Barry 24 + 7	Rooney 29 + 4	Newton 15	Carrington 43 + 1	Rutherford 37 + 1	Harrad 14 + 4	Harvey 9 + 2	Bakare 3 + 5	Powell 7 + 17	Edwards 20 + 2	McDonagh 15 + 7	Nortey 1 + 5	Jalal 24	Tilt 36	Reid 1 + 1	Evans R 19 + 10	Smith L 11 + 9	Bailey-Nicholls — + 3	Coddington 5	Pyke 1 + 2	White J 16 + 8	Harry 2 + 3	Jennings J 15	McLeod 13 + 2	Penn 16	Massanka 11 + 7	Shenton 14 + 3	Lund 4	Allen 3 + 4	Marx 7	Match No.
1	2	3	4	5^2	6	7	8	9	10^3	11^1	12	13	14																					1
1	9^1	2	3	4	5	6	7	8	10^2	11^3		13		12	14																			2
1	4^3	2	3	6^1	7	5	8	9		11^2	12	13		10	14																			3
		7	3	6^2	10	5	8	9			12	13	2	11^1		1	4																	4
		2	3		7	5	8^2	9		13	11^3	12	6	10	14	1	4^1																	5
		2	3^3		5	6	8	9	12	13		14	7	10^2		1	4	11^1																6
		2		4	5	6	8	9	10^2	11^1		12	7	13		1	3																	7
		5		6^2	7	2	8	9	11^1		13	10	3		12	1	4																	8
	8	2			4	5	6	7	12		13	9^2	14	10^1	11^3	1	3																	9
	2	7	3		6^3	5	8	9	10^1	11^2				12		1	4	13	14															10
	12	7	3		5	2	6	8^1	10^2		11^3	13		14		1	4		9															11
	4	7			8^1	3	6	9	12		11^2	14	5^3	13		1	2		10															12
	9	3			8	5	2	11		10			6			1	4		7															13
	9	7			6^1	5	2	11	12	10		13	3			1	4		8^2															14
	4	6		13	7^2	2	8	9^1		11		14	3	12		1	5		10^3															15
	8	2		4^3	12		6		9	11^2		14	5	10		1	3		7^1	13														16
	5	3			8		6		10			11	2	9	12	1	4			7^1														17
	3	8			7		6		10^1			9	2	11		1	5			4	12													18
12	3	5		13	7		8		10			9	2	11^1		1^2	6			4^3	14													19
	5	6		7^3	8		9		11^2			10	3	14			2		13	4^1	12	1												20
	8	2			4		6		10			9	5	11			3		7			1												21
	3	9			5		6	7^1	10^2			12	2	11			4		8	13		1												22
	4	5		13	6^1		7	8				14	3^2	11^3			2		9			1	10	12										23
	2^3	5		13	6		7	8^1	10				4	11^2			3		9			1	12	14										24
	10		2	4^1	6		8^2	9				14	7			1	3		12	11^3			13	5										25
	6		2		7			8					5	11		1	4		9	3				10^1	12									26
13	9	14	2	6	5			7^2				12		10		1^1	3		8	11^3				4										27
1			4	6	8		2					12					5		9	7^1				11		3	10							28
1		14	3	5^3	6		7	8^2									4			13				10		2	11^1	9	12					29
1			3	5^1	7		9	10									4							6		2	8^2	11	12	13				30
1			3	5^3	14		6	7									4		12					10		2	11^1	8^2	13	9				31
1			4	6^1	12		7	8^3									5		13					14		3	11^2		10	9	2			32
1			4		13		7	8									5		14					12		3	6^1	9	10	11^2	2^3			33
1			4	12			6	7^2									5		13					14		3	11	9	10	8^1	2^3			34
1			3	5^2			7	8^3									4		12	14				13			6^1	9	10	11	2			35
1			3	5			7	8									4		14	13				12		2	11^1	9	10^3	6^2				36
1			3	5			6	7^1									4			12				13	14	2	10^2	8	11	9^3				37
1			3	5^3			6	7									4		14					11		2	10^1	8^2	13	9		12		38
1			3	6^1			13	12									4^2		7	5				10	14	2			11^3	9			8	39
1			3	12			4	5^3											6	2^2				10	9^1		11	7	13	8		14		40
1			3	7^1			2	6^2											8	14				11^3			13	9	10	5		12	4	41
			2				4	5								1			6	13				10			11^2	7	12	8		3^1	9	42
			4	13			6	5								1			8^1					10		2		9	11	12		7^2	3	43
			3	4			6	7								1				12				5		2		8	9	10^1			11	44
			3^3	4			6	7								1				10^1				5		2^2	14	8	9	12		13	11	45
			12	6			7									1			8					10	11^2	3		9^1	13	4		2	5	46

FA Cup
Fourth Qualifying Stamford (a) 1-1
Replay Stamford (h) 2-3
aet.

FA Trophy
First Round Tranmere R (h) 0-1

YORK CITY

Ground: Bootham Crescent, York YO30 7AQ. *Tel:* (01904) 624 447. *Website:* www.yorkcityfootballclub.co.uk
Email: enquiries@yorkcityfootballclub.co.uk *Year Formed:* 1922.
Record Attendance: 28,123 v Huddersfield T, FA Cup 6th rd, 5 March 1938. *Nickname:* 'Minstermen'.
Manager: Gary Mills. *Colours:* Red shirts with white trim, blue shorts, white socks.

YORK CITY – NATIONAL LEAGUE 2016–17 LEAGUE RECORD

Match No.	Date	Venue	Opponents	Result	H/T Score	Lg Pos.	Goalscorers	Attendance
1	Aug 6	A	Maidstone U	D 1-1	0-1	9	Kamdjo [69]	2495
2	9	H	Macclesfield T	W 1-0	0-0	8	Fry [57]	2468
3	13	H	Boreham Wood	D 1-1	0-0	9	Heslop [88]	2169
4	16	A	Gateshead	L 1-6	1-1	15	Brodie (pen) [45]	1331
5	20	A	Forest Green R	L 1-2	1-1	18	Brodie [20]	1396
6	27	H	Woking	W 4-1	4-1	14	Brodie [9], Klukowski [13], Wright [20], Connolly [26]	1972
7	29	A	Wrexham	L 1-2	1-1	17	Brodie [24]	4005
8	Sept 3	H	Solihull Moors	W 4-0	1-0	14	Brodie [9], Connolly 2 [84, 90], Fenwick [90]	2105
9	10	A	Torquay U	L 0-2	0-2	16		1989
10	13	H	Tranmere R	D 0-0	0-0	16		2379
11	17	H	Dover Ath	L 0-1	0-1	17		2137
12	24	A	Barrow	L 0-2	0-0	18		1628
13	Oct 1	H	Aldershot T	L 0-1	0-1	19		2188
14	4	A	Guiseley	L 1-6	1-4	20	Fry [11]	1626
15	8	A	Braintree T	D 1-1	1-0	19	Heslop [5]	728
16	22	H	Chester FC	D 1-1	0-0	19	Fry [70]	2639
17	25	A	Southport	L 0-2	0-0	19		856
18	29	H	Sutton U	D 2-2	1-1	20	Nti [24], Galbraith [64]	2037
19	Nov 12	A	Eastleigh	D 1-1	0-0	20	Heslop [77]	2431
20	19	H	Dagenham & R	L 0-2	0-2	21		2410
21	22	H	Lincoln C	L 1-4	0-2	22	Klukowski [69]	2889
22	26	A	Bromley	L 0-3	0-2	23		1203
23	29	H	Guiseley	D 1-1	0-0	23	Rzonca [59]	1907
24	Dec 3	A	Tranmere R	L 0-1	0-0	24		5075
25	17	H	Torquay U	D 0-0	0-0	24		2272
26	26	A	North Ferriby U	W 1-0	1-0	23	Racine [13]	1950
27	Jan 1	H	North Ferriby U	L 0-1	0-1	24		3182
28	7	A	Dover Ath	D 2-2	1-1	24	Parkin [36], Rooney [77]	1308
29	21	H	Barrow	W 2-1	1-0	24	Morgan-Smith [22], Newton [90]	2430
30	28	A	Aldershot T	D 0-0	0-0	24		2230
31	Feb 11	H	Maidstone U	D 1-1	1-0	23	Parkin [3]	2816
32	18	A	Boreham Wood	D 1-1	1-1	23	Morgan-Smith [7]	656
33	21	H	Gateshead	L 1-3	1-2	23	Oliver [14]	2320
34	28	A	Lincoln C	D 1-1	1-0	24	Parkin [14]	6892
35	Mar 4	H	Eastleigh	W 3-1	2-1	23	Parkin 2 [7, 13], Oliver [80]	2406
36	11	A	Sutton U	D 2-2	0-0	22	Fenwick [89], Klukowski [90]	2171
37	21	H	Southport	W 5-3	2-3	22	Newton [4], Oliver [45], Parkin 2 [64, 78], Morgan-Smith [72]	2482
38	25	A	Dagenham & R	L 0-1	0-0	22		1659
39	28	A	Macclesfield T	W 3-1	2-0	22	Heslop [7], Oliver [15], Parkin [82]	1318
40	Apr 1	H	Braintree T	W 3-0	2-0	22	Parkin [11], Hall [45], Morgan-Smith [75]	2825
41	4	H	Bromley	L 0-2	0-1	22		3000
42	8	A	Chester FC	W 2-0	1-0	19	Oliver [25], Holmes [75]	2235
43	14	A	Solihull Moors	W 2-1	2-1	18	Oliver 2 [15, 31]	1570
44	17	H	Wrexham	L 1-3	1-1	20	Parkin [2]	4091
45	22	A	Woking	D 1-1	0-0	21	Parkin [75]	2702
46	29	H	Forest Green R	D 2-2	1-2	21	Parkin 2 [33, 48]	3984

Final League Position: 21

GOALSCORERS

League (55): Parkin 13, Oliver 7, Brodie 5 (1 pen), Heslop 4, Morgan-Smith 4, Connolly 3, Fry 3, Klukowski 3, Fenwick 2, Newton 2, Galbraith 1, Hall 1, Holmes 1, Kamdjo 1, Nti 1, Racine 1, Rooney 1, Rzonca 1, Wright 1.
FA Cup (2): Brodie 2 (1 pen).
FA Trophy (15): Oliver 3, Parkin 3, Connolly 2, Morgan-Smith 2, Murphy 2, Fenwick 1, Heslop 1, Newton 1.

Flinders 8 + 1 / Murphy 5	Rooney 27 + 3	Whittle 38 + 3	Kamdjo 13 + 2	Higgins 15 / Parkin 23	Fry 20 + 1	Heslop 44	Klukowski 22 + 3	Connolly 15 + 5	Clappison 9	Fenwick 9 + 15	Brodie 11 + 6	Robinson 2 + 3 / Racine 4	Felix 5 + 7	Nti 6 + 10	Dixon 10 + 3	Wright 6 + 1 / Parslow 18	Simpson 1 + 1	Letheren 28	Thompson — + 1	Rzonca 1 + 9	Johnson 2 + 3	Walton — + 1 / Bencherif 17	Murdoch — + 2	Galbraith 5 + 2 / Morgan-Smith 18	Barber 1	Oyebanjo 3 + 1	Fielding 1	Clarke 1 + 1 / Oliver 17 + 1	Newton 28	Cooper 5 / Hall 13	Holmes 16 + 5	McDaid 5 + 1 / Muggleton 1 + 7	Moke 14 + 4	Lappin 7	Woodland 1 + 1	Charles 2 / Loach 9	Bruton — + 1	Match No.
1	2^{1}	3	4	5	6	7	8^{3}	9	10	11^{2}	12	13	14																									1
1	2	3	4	5	6^{3}	7	8^{1}	9	10	11^{2}	13	14		12																								2
1	2	3	4	5		6	10^{3}	7	8^{1}	11^{2}	12	9	14	13																								3
1	2^{1}	3	4^{2}	5	6	8					9	10	11	7	12	13																						4
	2	3	13	4		5■	7	8^{3}	9	14	6^{1}			12	10	11^{2}	1																					5
	2	3	4^{3}		5		6	8	7	14	11^{2}			12	9	10^{1}		1	13																			6
	2	3	12		4	5	7^{3}	8	9	14	6				10^{2}	11^{1}		1		13																		7
	2	5		4	3	7		6		14	11^{3}		13	12	8	10^{1}		1			9^{2}																	8
	2	3		4	5	7	8^{3}	9^{1}		10^{2}	11		12		6			1			14	13																9
	2	3		4	5	7				13	8		10	6^{2}	9	11^{1}		1			12																	10
		5		4	3	8		7^{1}	2	13	11		10	6^{2}	9			1			12																	11
	2^{1}	5	8	3	4	9		6			11^{3}	12	14		7	10^{2}		1					13															12
	2	3^{3}	4	5	6	7		8^{2}		11	14		10^{1}	12	13			1						9														13
	3		2		4	9	13		5^{3}	11^{1}			14		8			1			10^{2}		12	7	6													14
	3	5	8	4	13	7	9				11^{1}			12				1						10		2^{2}	6											15
		2	3	4	5	7	14			8^{1}	13			6				1		10^{3}				12		11		9^{2}										16
12		3	4	5^{1}	6	7	8^{3}		2	11			10					1^{2}		14				9				13										17
1	2	5	3	4^{1}		9					11^{2}		13	8	10									12					6	7								18
1	12	2^{1}	3		4	6	7				13									14				8^{3}						9^{2}	5	10	11					19
1					2	3	4	5		6^{1}				12						13									9	7	11	8^{2}	10■					20
1	2	12			4^{3}	6	7	8^{2}						13■						14									5	10^{1}	3	11		9				21
	2	3				6	10^{3}			12								1		13									4	9^{1}	5	11^{2}			7	8	14	22
	2	9			3	7	4	6		13					14			1		12^{3}									5		8	11^{1}				10^{2}		23
10^{1}	2	5		11	6	7	8											1											3		4	12	9					24
10	5			11		7	8					2		6^{1}				1		12									4		3		9					25
10	2	12		11		6	7^{1}					4						1											3		5		9	8				26
10	2	12		6		3	4					11						1		13									7		9^{1}		8^{2}	5				27
11^{1}	2	3		10	4^{2}	7	8					6		13				1											5					9	12			28
	2^{2}	3		10		6	7			14						4		1				9		11				13	5		12^{3}			8^{1}				29
		2		9■		5	6									4		1				8		11				10	3					7				30
		2		11		5	6									4		1				8		9		12		10	3					7^{1}				31
	13	5		9^{1}		6				14						4		1				7		11		2		8^{2}	3		12		10^{3}					32
	2^{1}	3		11^{2}		7		13								6		1				8		9				10	4		5		12					33
		4		9		5				12						3		1				6		11				8^{1}	2	7			10					34
		3		10		5										2		1				7		8				9	4	6	12		11^{1}					35
		2^{2}		10		5	13	12		14						4		1				7		11				8	3	6^{3}			9^{1}					36
	2			11		5		7^{3}								4	14	1^{2}				6		9				10	3	8^{1}		13	12					37
		2		7		3		13		14						10						11		4^{2}				6	8	5^{3}		12	9^{1}			1		38
		4		10		5^{1}										2						6		8				9^{2}	3	7	12	13	11			1		39
		2		6^{1}												10						11		3				5	7	4	9	12	8			1		40
		4^{3}		11		5				14						3						7		10				8	2	6^{1}	13	12	9^{2}			1		41
		2		10		6										5						8		11^{1}				9	3	7	4		12			1		42
	12	2		7		3										10						11		4				6	8	5	9^{1}					1		43
	2^{2}	3		8		4		13								11								5				7	9	6^{1}	10	12				1		44
		2^{1}		10		8										3						4		9^{2}				11	5	7	6	12	13			1		45
				10		7		12		13						5						6		11^{1}				9	3	8^{2}	4	2				1		46

FA Cup

Fourth Qualifying	Curzon Ashton	(h)	1-1
Replay	Curzon Ashton	(a)	1-2

FA Trophy

First Round	Worcester C	(h)	3-1
Second Round	Harlow T	(a)	2-1
Third Round	Nuneaton T	(a)	3-0
Fourth Round	Brackley T	(h)	1-0
Semi-Final 1st leg	Lincoln C	(h)	2-1
Semi-Final 2nd leg	Lincoln C	(a)	1-1
aet.			
Final	Macclesfield T	(Wembley)	3-2

SCOTTISH LEAGUE TABLES 2016–17

(P) *Promoted into division at end of 2015–16 season.* (R) *Relegated into division at end of 2015–16 season.*

SPFL LADBROKES PREMIERSHIP 2016–17

			Home					*Away*					*Total*						
		P	*W*	*D*	*L*	*F*	*A*	*W*	*D*	*L*	*F*	*A*	*W*	*D*	*L*	*F*	*A*	*GD*	*Pts*
1	Celtic	38	17	2	0	47	8	17	2	0	59	17	34	4	0	106	25	81	106
2	Aberdeen	38	12	3	4	34	16	12	1	6	40	19	24	4	10	74	35	39	76
3	Rangers (P)	38	11	5	3	31	18	8	5	6	25	26	19	10	9	56	44	12	67
4	St Johnstone	38	8	3	8	25	25	9	4	6	25	21	17	7	14	50	46	4	58
5	Hearts	38	9	5	5	36	20	3	5	11	19	32	12	10	16	55	52	3	46
6	Partick Thistle	38	6	5	9	21	32	4	7	7	17	22	10	12	16	38	54	–16	42
7	Ross Co	38	6	5	7	28	31	5	8	7	20	27	11	13	14	48	58	–10	46
8	Kilmarnock	38	4	7	8	18	23	5	7	7	18	33	9	14	15	36	56	–20	41
9	Motherwell	38	5	3	11	27	37	5	5	9	19	32	10	8	20	46	69	–23	38
10	Dundee	38	5	5	9	19	30	5	2	12	19	32	10	7	21	38	62	–24	37
11	Hamilton A	38	6	7	6	22	20	1	7	11	15	36	7	14	17	37	56	–19	35
12	Inverness CT	38	5	8	6	27	33	2	5	12	17	38	7	13	18	44	71	–27	34

Top 6 teams split after 33 games, teams in the bottom six cannot pass teams in the top six after the split. Hamilton A not relegated after play-offs.

SPFL LADBROKES CHAMPIONSHIP 2016–17

			Home					*Away*					*Total*						
		P	*W*	*D*	*L*	*F*	*A*	*W*	*D*	*L*	*F*	*A*	*W*	*D*	*L*	*F*	*A*	*GD*	*Pts*
1	Hibernian	36	9	8	1	35	15	10	6	2	24	10	19	14	3	59	25	34	71
2	Falkirk	36	8	6	4	31	22	8	6	4	27	18	16	12	8	58	40	18	60
3	Dundee U (R)	36	11	6	1	31	17	4	6	8	19	25	15	12	9	50	42	8	57
4	Greenock Morton	36	8	8	2	23	17	5	5	8	21	24	13	13	10	44	41	3	52
5	Dunfermline Ath (P)	36	6	7	5	28	25	6	5	7	18	18	12	12	12	46	43	3	48
6	Queen of the South	36	6	3	9	25	29	5	7	6	21	23	11	10	15	46	52	–6	43
7	St Mirren	36	5	6	7	24	23	4	6	8	28	33	9	12	15	52	56	–4	39
8	Dumbarton	36	5	6	7	17	20	4	6	8	29	36	9	12	15	46	56	–10	39
9	Raith R®	36	8	5	5	22	20	2	4	12	13	32	10	9	17	35	52	–17	39
10	Ayr U	36	4	4	10	13	32	3	8	7	20	30	7	12	17	33	62	–29	33

Dundee U not promoted after play-offs. ®Raith R relegated after play-offs.

SPFL LADBROKES LEAGUE ONE 2016–17

			Home					*Away*					*Total*						
		P	*W*	*D*	*L*	*F*	*A*	*W*	*D*	*L*	*F*	*A*	*W*	*D*	*L*	*F*	*A*	*GD*	*Pts*
1	Livingston (R)	36	13	1	4	43	16	13	2	3	37	16	26	3	7	80	32	48	81
2	Alloa Ath (R)	36	8	6	4	35	21	9	5	4	34	23	17	11	8	69	44	25	62
3	Airdrieonians	36	8	2	8	27	32	8	2	8	34	34	16	4	16	61	66	–5	52
4	Brechin C¶	36	8	3	7	22	20	7	2	9	21	29	15	5	16	43	49	–6	50
5	East Fife (P)	36	7	5	6	22	20	5	5	8	19	24	12	10	14	41	44	–3	46
6	Queen's Park (P)	36	7	4	7	18	21	5	6	7	19	30	12	10	14	37	51	–14	46
7	Stranraer	36	8	3	7	29	25	4	5	9	17	25	12	8	16	46	50	–4	44
8	Albion R	36	6	4	8	21	22	5	5	8	20	26	11	9	16	41	48	–7	42
9	Peterhead®	36	4	6	8	25	29	6	4	8	19	30	10	10	16	44	59	–15	40
10	Stenhousemuir	36	5	4	9	23	36	6	2	10	22	28	11	6	19	45	64	–19	39

¶Brechin C promoted after play-offs. ®Peterhead relegated after play-offs.

SPFL LADBROKES LEAGUE TWO 2016–17

			Home					*Away*					*Total*						
		P	*W*	*D*	*L*	*F*	*A*	*W*	*D*	*L*	*F*	*A*	*W*	*D*	*L*	*F*	*A*	*GD*	*Pts*
1	Arbroath	36	8	5	5	30	18	10	7	1	33	18	18	12	6	63	36	27	66
2	Forfar Ath¶ (R)	36	8	5	5	38	28	10	5	3	31	21	18	10	8	69	49	20	64
3	Annan Ath	36	12	1	5	35	23	6	3	9	26	35	18	4	14	61	58	3	58
4	Montrose	36	5	6	7	22	30	9	4	5	22	23	14	10	12	44	53	–9	52
5	Elgin C	36	7	7	4	36	22	7	2	9	31	25	14	9	13	67	47	20	51
6	Stirling Alb	36	6	6	6	20	25	6	5	7	30	34	12	11	13	50	59	–9	47
7	Edinburgh C (P)	36	5	6	7	21	20	6	4	8	17	25	11	10	15	38	45	–7	43
8	Berwick Rangers	36	6	3	9	28	32	4	7	7	22	33	10	10	16	50	65	–15	40
9	Clyde	36	8	4	6	33	30	2	4	12	16	34	10	8	18	49	64	–15	38
10	Cowdenbeath (R)	36	4	3	11	15	25	5	5	8	25	30	9	8	19	40	55	–15	35

¶Forfar Ath promoted after play-offs. Cowdenbeath not relegated after play-offs.

SCOTTISH LEAGUE ATTENDANCES 2016–17

SPFL LADBROKES PREMIERSHIP ATTENDANCES

	Average Gate			*Season 2016–17*	
	2015–16	*2016–17*	*+/–%*	*Highest*	*Lowest*
Aberdeen	13,094	12,641	–3.46	19,332	8,195
Celtic	44,850	54,624	+21.79	58,967	37,404
Dundee	6,122	6,432	+5.05	9,702	4,708
Hamilton A	3,027	2,531	–16.39	5,292	1,548
Hearts	16,423	16,326	–0.59	16,803	15,470
Inverness CT	3,839	3,946	+2.79	7,012	2,473
Kilmarnock	3,993	4,964	+24.31	11,800	3,056
Motherwell	4,912	4,486	–8.68	8,535	3,131
Partick Thistle	3,800	4,282	+12.70	7,951	2,257
Rangers	45,325	48,893	+7.87	50,126	46,563
Ross Co	4,034	4,103	+1.73	6,590	2,511
St Johnstone	3,880	4,392	+13.21	7,979	2,549

SPFL LADBROKES CHAMPIONSHIP ATTENDANCES

	Average Gate			*Season 2016–17*	
	2015–16	*2016–17*	*+/–%*	*Highest*	*Lowest*
Ayr U	1,297	1,866	+43.92	3,100	1,103
Dumbarton	1,041	1,130	+8.57	1,660	600
Dundee U	7,969	6,584	–17.38	10,925	4,661
Dunfermline Ath	3,497	4,438	+26.91	7,622	2,653
Falkirk	4,670	5,032	+7.77	6,747	4,160
Greenock Morton	2,731	2,362	–13.51	4,609	1,451
Hibernian	9,339	15,394	+64.84	19,764	13,604
Queen of the South	2,115	1,857	–12.22	3,703	1,147
Raith R	2,317	2,631	+13.59	5,899	1,161
St Mirren	3,549	3,599	+1.41	4,997	2,126

SPFL LADBROKES LEAGUE ONE ATTENDANCES

	Average Gate			*Season 2016–17*	
	2015–16	*2016–17*	*+/–%*	*Highest*	*Lowest*
Airdrieonians	861	830	–3.62	1,633	482
Albion R	555	450	–18.97	1,199	228
Alloa Ath	1,121	531	–52.63	712	307
Brechin C	540	429	–20.69	553	283
East Fife	625	626	+0.20	918	412
Livingston	1,765	797	–54.84	1,099	531
Peterhead	637	505	–20.75	681	365
Queen's Park	518	645	+24.36	957	481
Stenhousemuir	566	429	–24.30	604	331
Stranraer	507	409	–19.21	523	317

SPFL LADBROKES LEAGUE TWO ATTENDANCES

	Average Gate			*Season 2016–17*	
	2015–16	*2016–17*	*+/–%*	*Highest*	*Lowest*
Annan Ath	447	386	–13.58	461	241
Arbroath	651	727	+11.58	1,731	482
Berwick R	461	427	–7.46	695	302
Clyde	612	526	–14.05	738	365
Cowdenbeath	596	345	–42.02	571	258
Edinburgh C	N/A	401	N/A	590	256
Elgin C	737	687	–6.72	1,091	519
Forfar Ath	698	654	–6.26	1,564	337
Montrose	566	606	+7.06	1,324	283
Stirling Alb	616	639	+3.77	1,748	412

ABERDEEN

Year Formed: 1903. *Ground & Address:* Pittodrie Stadium, Pittodrie St, Aberdeen AB24 5QH. *Telephone:* 01224 650400. *Fax:* 01224 644173. *E-mail:* feedback@afc.co.uk *Website:* www.afc.co.uk
Ground Capacity: 20,961 (all seated). *Size of Pitch:* 105m × 66m.
Chairman: Stewart Milne. *Chief Executive:* Duncan Fraser.
Manager: Derek McInnes. *Assistant Manager:* Tony Docherty. *U-20 Coach:* Paul Sheerin.
Club Nicknames: 'The Dons', 'The Reds', 'The Dandies'.
Previous Grounds: None.
Record Attendance: 45,061 v Hearts, Scottish Cup 4th rd, 13 March 1954.
Record Transfer Fee received: £1,750,000 for Eoin Jess to Coventry C (February 1996).
Record Transfer Fee paid: £1,000,000+ for Paul Bernard from Oldham Ath (September 1995).
Record Victory: 13-0 v Peterhead, Scottish Cup 3rd rd, 10 February 1923.
Record Defeat: 0-9 v Celtic, Premier League, 6 November 2010.
Most Capped Player: Alex McLeish, 77 (Scotland).
Most League Appearances: 556: Willie Miller, 1973-90.
Most League Goals in Season (Individual): 38: Benny Yorston, Division I, 1929-30.
Most Goals Overall (Individual): 199: Joe Harper, 1969-72; 1976-81.

ABERDEEN – SPFL LADBROKES PREMIERSHIP 2016–17 LEAGUE RECORD

Match No.	Date	Venue	Opponents	Result		H/T Score	Lg Pos.	Goalscorers	Attendance
1	Aug 7	A	St Johnstone	D	0-0	0-0	4		5728
2	13	H	Hearts	D	0-0	0-0	3		13,559
3	20	H	Partick Thistle	W	2-1	1-0	2	McGinn ^{28}, Storey ^{58}	11,049
4	27	A	Celtic	L	1-4	1-2	4	Rooney ^{32}	57,758
5	Sept 10	H	Inverness CT	D	1-1	0-0	4	McGinn ^{51}	11,356
6	18	A	Dundee	W	3-1	1-1	4	Maddison ^{19}, Stockley ^{77}, McLean (pen) ^{88}	6321
7	25	H	Rangers	W	2-1	0-0	2	Hayes ^{46}, Maddison ^{90}	19,263
8	Oct 1	A	Kilmarnock	W	4-0	1-0	2	Rooney 2 (1 pen) $^{25 (p), 72}$, Considine ^{50}, Taylor ^{67}	4592
9	15	H	Ross Co	W	4-0	2-0	2	Hayes ^{20}, Logan ^{32}, McGinn ^{68}, Stockley ^{78}	10,091
10	25	A	Hamilton A	L	0-1	0-1	2		2315
11	29	H	Celtic	L	0-1	0-1	2		17,105
12	Nov 4	A	Partick Thistle	W	2-1	1-0	2	O'Connor ^{39}, Stockley ^{53}	3974
13	19	A	Inverness CT	W	3-1	2-1	2	McLean 2 $^{28, 89}$, Rooney (pen) ^{33}	4867
14	Dec 3	A	Rangers	L	1-2	0-0	4	Considine ^{90}	50,003
15	6	H	Kilmarnock	W	5-1	3-0	3	Pawlett ^{20}, O'Connor ^{30}, Hayes 2 $^{37, 85}$, McGinn ^{69}	8195
16	10	H	St Johnstone	D	0-0	0-0	3		11,501
17	17	A	Ross Co	L	1-2	0-1	3	McGinn ^{68}	4467
18	23	A	Motherwell	W	3-1	2-1	3	Shinnie ^{6}, Rooney ^{25}, McGinn ^{90}	3428
19	27	H	Hamilton A	W	2-1	1-1	3	Taylor ^{34}, Rooney ^{68}	13,131
20	30	A	Hearts	W	1-0	0-0	3	Hayes ^{66}	16,630
21	Jan 27	H	Dundee	W	3-0	2-0	2	Jack ^{29}, McGinn 2 $^{45, 80}$	10,512
22	Feb 1	A	Celtic	L	0-1	0-0	3		53,958
23	4	H	Partick Thistle	W	2-0	0-0	2	Stockley ^{72}, Christie ^{90}	10,094
24	15	H	Motherwell	W	7-2	4-0	2	Hayes ^{2}, Considine ^{32}, Rooney 3 (1 pen) $^{34, 64 (p), 69}$, Christie ^{40}, Pawlett ^{83}	10,384
25	19	A	Kilmarnock	W	2-1	0-1	2	Stockley ^{83}, Pawlett ^{85}	3972
26	25	H	Ross Co	W	1-0	0-0	2	Rooney ^{69}	11,774
27	28	A	Hamilton A	L	0-1	0-1	2		2006
28	Mar 11	H	Motherwell	W	1-0	0-0	2	McGinn ^{90}	12,524
29	18	H	Hearts	W	2-0	1-0	2	Logan ^{21}, Hayes ^{60}	12,178
30	31	A	Dundee	W	7-0	4-0	2	Considine 3 $^{17, 39, 83}$, Rooney ^{25}, McLean ^{34}, Jack ^{51}, McGinn ^{73}	7314
31	Apr 4	H	Inverness CT	W	1-0	1-0	2	Warren (og) ^{22}	11,507
32	9	H	Rangers	L	0-3	0-0	2		19,332
33	15	A	St Johnstone	W	2-1	2-0	2	Christie ^{19}, Scobbie (og) ^{32}	5132
34	29	H	St Johnstone	L	0-2	0-0	2		10,606
35	May 7	A	Hearts	W	2-1	1-0	2	Rooney ^{21}, O'Connor ^{64}	16,522
36	12	H	Celtic	L	1-3	1-3	2	Hayes ^{12}	16,015
37	17	A	Rangers	W	2-1	1-0	2	Shinnie ^{9}, Christie ^{51}	48,289
38	21	A	Partick Thistle	W	6-0	5-0	2	Christie 2 $^{7, 45}$, Wright 3 $^{11, 17, 51}$, Hayes ^{26}	3924

Final League Position: 2

Honours
League Champions: Division I 1954-55. Premier Division 1979-80, 1983-84, 1984-85; *Runners-up:* Premiership 2014-15, 2015-16, 2016-17. Division I 1910-11, 1936-37, 1955-56, 1970-71, 1971-72. Premier Division 1977-78, 1980-81, 1981-82, 1988-89, 1989-90, 1990-91, 1992-93, 1993-94.
Scottish Cup Winners: 1947, 1970, 1982, 1983, 1984, 1986, 1990; *Runners-up:* 1937, 1953, 1954, 1959, 1967, 1978, 1993, 2000, 2017.
League Cup Winners: 1955-56, 1976-77, 1985-86, 1989-90, 1995-96, 2013-14; *Runners-up:* 1946-47, 1978-79, 1979-80, 1987-88, 1988-89, 1992-93, 1999-2000, 2016-17.
Drybrough Cup Winners: 1971, 1980.

European: *European Cup:* 12 matches (1980-81, 1984-85, 1985-86); *Cup Winners' Cup:* 39 matches (1967-68, 1970-71, 1978-79, 1982-83 winners, 1983-84 semi-finals, 1986-87, 1990-91, 1993-94); *UEFA Cup:* 56 matches (*Fairs Cup:* 1968-69. *UEFA Cup:* 1971-72, 1972-73, 1973-74, 1977-78, 1979-80, 1981-82, 1987-88, 1988-89, 1989-90, 1991-92, 1994-95, 1996-97, 2000-01, 2002-03, 2007-08). *Europa League:* 20 matches (2009-10, 2014-15, 2015-16, 2016-17).

Club colours: All red with white trim.

Goalscorers: *League (74):* Rooney 12 (3 pens), McGinn 10, Hayes 9, Christie 6, Considine 6, Stockley 5, McLean 4 (1 pen), O'Connor 3, Pawlett 3, Wright 3, Jack 2, Logan 2, Maddison 2, Shinnie 2, Taylor 2, Storey 1, own goals 2.
William Hill Scottish FA Cup (10): Rooney 3 (1 pen), McGinn 2, Christie 1, Hayes 1, Logan 1, Shinnie 1, own goal 1.
Betfred Scottish League Cup (5): Rooney 2, McGinn 1, McLean 1, own goal 1.
IRN-BRU Scottish League Challenge Cup (6): Wright 3, Norris 1, Nuttall 1, Omolokun 1.
UEFA Europa League (8): Rooney 3 (1 pen), Burns 1, Hayes 1, Logan 1, McGinn 1, Stockley 1.

Lewis J 38	Logan S 37 + 1	Reynolds M 22 + 4	O'Connor A 25 + 7	Considine A 36	Shinnie G 35 + 1	Jack R 25 + 1	McLean K 37 + 1	Burns W 7 + 6	Stockley J 8 + 19	Storey M 2 + 12	Rooney A 32 + 6	McGinn N 30 + 6	Taylor A 28 + 3	Pawlett P 6 + 12	Storie C — + 2	Hayes J 32	Maddison J 10 + 4	Christie R 7 + 6	Wright S 1 + 4	Ross F — + 3	Campbell D — + 1	*Match No.*
1	2	3	4	5	6	7	8	9^{2}	10	11^{1}	12	13										1
1	2	5	4		8	7	12	6^{1}	11^{3}	14	13	10	3	9^{2}								2
1	2	4	3	5	8		7	12	14	11^{2}	10^{1}	9	13	6^{3}								3
1	2	5■	3^{3}	6	9		8	7	13	12	11^{2}	10^{1}	4		14							4
1	3		2	5	6^{1}		10	7^{2}	14		11	8	4	13		9^{3}	12					5
1	2		4	5	8		7	12	13		10^{2}	6^{1}	3		14	9	11^{3}					6
1	2	4	3	5	8		7	13			11^{2}	9^{3}	14	10^{1}		6	12					7
1	2		4	5	7		6	12	14	13	11^{3}	8^{2}	3			10^{1}	9					8
1	2	12	4	5	8		10		13		11^{2}	9^{1}	3^{3}	14		6	7					9
1	2	4^{3}	3	5	7		6	8^{2}		13	11	12		14		10	9^{1}					10
1	5	3	4	2	6	7^{2}	9	11^{3}	14		13	8^{1}				10	12					11
1	2	13	3	4	5	7	8		11^{1}		10	12				9	6^{2}					12
1	2	14	4	3	5^{2}	8	7		10^{3}		11	12	13			9	6^{1}					13
1	2	4		5	7^{2}	6■	9^{1}		11^{3}		12	13	3	14		8	10					14
1	2	12	3	4	5		7	13	14		11^{1}	9		6^{2}		10	8^{3}					15
1	12		3	4	5^{3}	2	8	14	13		11	9^{2}		10^{1}		6	7					16
1	2		3	4	5	6^{1}	7	8^{2}	11^{3}	14	13	12				10	9					17
1	2	4	12	5	7	6	9				11	8	3			10^{1}						18
1	2	4	13	5^{1}	8	7	10				11	6^{2}	3			9	12					19
1	2	4	12	5	7	6	9				11	8^{1}	3			10						20
1	2	4		5	8	7	10			13	11^{2}	6^{1}	3			9^{3}		12	14			21
1	2^{3}	5^{2}		3	9	7	8		13	12	11^{1}	6	4	14		10						22
1	2^{3}	4^{1}	14	5	8	7	10		13		11^{2}	9	3			6		12				23
1	2	4		5		7	8		12	14	11^{1}	9^{3}	3	13		6		10^{2}				24
1	2	4^{1}		5^{2}	12	7	8		13		11	6	3	14		9		10^{3}				25
1	2	4^{2}	13	5	8	7	10			12	11	6^{3}	3	14		9^{1}						26
1	2	4^{3}	14	5	7	6^{1}	9			13	11	8	3	12				10^{2}				27
1	2		4^{1}		5	6	7		11	13	9^{2}	10	3			8		12				28
1	2		4	5	7	6	9		12■		11^{2}	8^{3}	3			10^{1}		13		14		29
1	5		2	4	8	6	7^{3}				11	9^{1}	3			10^{2}		12	13	14		30
1	2		4	5	8	6	7			12	10^{1}	11^{2}	3			9		13				31
1	2		4^{1}	5	7	6	9		12		11	10	3			8						32
1	2		4	5	7	6	9		13		11		3	12		10^{2}		8^{1}				33
1	2			4	5	6	7		12		11^{2}	10	3	13		8^{3}		9^{1}	14			34
1	2	4	12	5	6		7		13		11^{1}	10	3	9^{2}		8						35
1	5	3^{1}	4	8	7		6		11^{3}		12	9^{2}	2			10			13		14	36
1	5	3	4	6	7		8		12■		11^{1}	9	2					10				37
1	2	4^{3}	6	5		12	7^{1}				11		3	13		8^{2}		9	10	14		38

AIRDRIEONIANS

Year Formed: 2002. *Ground & Address:* Excelsior Stadium, New Broomfield, Craigneuk Avenue, Airdrie ML6 8QZ.
Telephone: (Stadium) 01236 622000. *Fax:* 0141 221 1497. *Postal Address:* 60 St Enoch Square, Glasgow G1 4AG.
E-mail: enquiries@airdriefc.com *Website:* www.airdriefc.com
Ground Capacity: 10,101 (all seated). *Size of Pitch:* 105m × 67m.
Chairman: Jim Ballantyne. *Secretary:* Ann Marie Ballantyne.
Director of Football: Gordon Dalziel. *Head Coach:* TBC.
Club Nickname: 'The Diamonds'.
Record Attendance: 9,044 v Rangers, League 1, 23 August 2013.
Record Victory: 11-0 v Gala Fairydean, Scottish Cup 3rd rd, 19 November 2011.
Record Defeat: 0-7 v Partick Thistle, First Division, 20 October 2012.
Most League Appearances: 222, Paul Lovering 2004-12.
Most League Goals in Season (Individual): 23: Andy Ryan, 2016-17.
Most Goals Overall (Individual): 43: Bryan Prunty, 2005-08, 2015-16.

AIRDRIEONIANS – SPFL LADBROKES LEAGUE ONE 2016–17 LEAGUE RECORD

Match No.	Date		Venue	Opponents	Result		H/T Score	Lg Pos.	Goalscorers	Attendance
1	Aug	6	A	Queen's Park	W	3-1	1-0	3	Russell, I (pen) [29], Fitzpatrick [51], Brown [90]	957
2		13	H	Livingston	L	2-4	0-2	5	Ryan 2 [53, 65]	1048
3		20	H	Stranraer	W	1-0	1-0	4	Ryan [26]	812
4		27	A	Stenhousemuir	D	2-2	0-1	4	Russell, I (pen) [52], Brown [65]	597
5	Sept	10	A	Brechin C	L	2-3	1-1	5	Ryan [38], Stewart [71]	466
6		17	H	East Fife	D	1-1	0-1	5	Russell, I (pen) [59]	814
7		24	H	Albion R	L	0-2	0-2	7		972
8	Oct	1	A	Alloa Ath	W	2-1	1-0	6	Ryan [28], Conroy [52]	644
9		15	H	Peterhead	L	1-3	0-0	6	Russell, I [55]	482
10		22	H	Queen's Park	W	4-1	3-1	5	Russell, I 3 (3 pens) [9, 28, 74], Stewart [45]	702
11		29	A	East Fife	W	1-0	1-0	4	Ryan [10]	706
12	Nov	5	A	Albion R	W	2-1	2-0	4	Ryan [7], Russell, I [32]	1199
13		12	H	Brechin C	W	1-0	0-0	4	Russell, I (pen) [53]	739
14		19	H	Alloa Ath	W	2-1	2-0	2	Goodwin (og) [30], Ryan [45]	790
15	Dec	3	A	Peterhead	W	4-2	3-1	2	Ryan 2 [13, 90], McIntosh [14], Russell, I [19]	475
16		10	H	Stenhousemuir	L	0-5	0-3	2		791
17		17	A	Livingston	L	0-2	0-1	2		989
18		24	A	Stranraer	W	2-1	1-1	2	Brown [10], Ryan [77]	317
19	Jan	2	H	Albion R	L	1-2	1-2	2	Brown [24]	1633
20		7	A	Queen's Park	L	1-2	1-1	3	Russell, I [39]	922
21		14	H	East Fife	D	2-2	1-1	3	Ryan [26], Leitch [89]	833
22		28	A	Stenhousemuir	L	2-4	1-1	3	Ryan [42], Gorman [70]	604
23	Feb	4	H	Peterhead	W	4-1	0-1	2	McKay [69], Conroy [71], Ryan [76], Stewart [90]	599
24		18	H	Livingston	L	0-4	0-1	3		1012
25		25	A	Alloa Ath	L	1-2	1-2	3	Russell, I [22]	540
26	Mar	4	H	Stranraer	L	1-2	0-0	4	Ryan [90]	706
27		11	A	Albion R	W	4-3	1-0	4	Leitch [15], Ryan [49], Russell, I [76], McIntosh [90]	873
28		14	A	Brechin C	L	0-3	0-1	5		346
29		18	H	Stenhousemuir	W	1-0	0-0	5	Russell, I [56]	568
30		25	A	Livingston	L	2-4	1-2	5	Conroy [34], Ryan (pen) [90]	832
31	Apr	1	A	Peterhead	D	1-1	1-1	5	McIntosh [35]	524
32		8	H	Brechin C	W	3-1	2-1	3	Russell, I 2 [20, 56], MacDonald [23]	676
33		15	A	Stranraer	L	1-2	0-1	4	Ryan [72]	489
34		22	H	Alloa Ath	L	0-1	0-0	5		757
35		29	A	East Fife	W	4-0	1-0	3	Ryan 3 (1 pen) [16, 51 (p), 59], Russell, I [79]	918
36	May	6	H	Queen's Park	W	3-2	1-1	3	Ryan 2 [41, 46], Russell, I [54]	1011

Final League Position: 3

Honours
League Champions: Second Division 2003-04; *Runners-up:* Second Division 2007-08.
League Challenge Cup Winners: 2008-09; *Runners-up:* 2003-04.

Club colours: Shirt: White with red diamond. Shorts: White with red trim. Socks: White with red trim.

Goalscorers: *League (61):* Ryan 23 (2 pens), Russell I 18 (7 pens), Brown 4, Conroy 3, McIntosh 3, Stewart 3, Leitch 2, Fitzpatrick 1, Gorman 1, MacDonald 1, McKay 1, own goal 1.
William Hill Scottish FA Cup (1): Ryan 1.
Betfred Scottish League Cup (5): Brown 3, Russell I 1, Ryan 1.
IRN-BRU Scottish League Challenge Cup (4): Conroy 1, Russell I 1, Ryan 1, own goal 1.
Play-Offs (1): Ryan 1.

Ferguson R 36	Stewart S 28 + 2	McIntosh S 25 + 3	Gorman J 25 + 3	MacDonald K 35	Conroy R 34	Fitzpatrick M 14	Leitch J 29 + 2	Brown A 29 + 7	Schmidt K 5 + 9	Russell I 32 + 1	Loudon M — + 6	Scullion C 1 + 8	Boateng D 19 + 1	Ryan A 32	Daly J — + 2	McLaughlin C 2 + 3	Leighton R — + 8	Hutton K 20	Cairns D 1 + 1	McKay J 7 + 8	Mensing S 15	McGregor J 7 + 1	Thomson S — + 1	Match No.
1	2	3	4	5	6	7	8	9	10^{2}	11^{1}	12	13												1
1	2	3		5	7^{2}	8	9	6^{1}	12	11			4	10	13									2
1	2			5	7	4	8	6	9^{1}	11		12	3	10										3
1	2	7		5	8	4		6		10	12	9^{1}	3	11										4
1	2			5	6	4	7	8	10^{1}			12	3	11		9^{2}	13							5
1	2			5	7	4	6	8^{1}	12	10		13	3	11		9^{2}								6
1	2	9^{2}	12	5	7^{1}	4	6	8	13	10■			3	11										7
1	2		4	5	9^{2}	7	8	6	11^{1}			13	3	10^{3}	14		12							8
1	2		4	3	9	8	7^{1}	6^{2}	12	11			5	10		13								9
1	2		4	5	7	8	6^{2}	9	12■	11^{3}		13	3	10^{1}		14								10
1	2^{1}	12■	4	5	6	7	8	9		11			3	10^{2}			13							11
1		2	4	5	7	8	6	9		11			3	10^{1}			12							12
1		2	4	5	7	8	6	9	13	11^{2}		12	3	10^{1}										13
1	2		4	5	7	8^{1}	6	9		11			3	10		12								14
1		2	4	5	8		11	6^{1}	12	9			3	10				7						15
1		2	4	5	6		9^{3}	8^{2}		10^{1}		12	3■	11			14	7	13					16
1	2	3	4	5	7		9^{1}	6	10^{2}	11	12						13	8						17
1	6	2	4	5	7		9	11	12				3	10^{1}				8						18
1		2	4	5	8			6	13	9^{2}	12		3	11					7	10^{1}				19
1		2	4	5	8		6^{2}	9		11	13		3^{1}	10				7		12				20
1	8	2	4	5	7		9	10^{2}		12			3^{1}	11				6		13				21
1	2^{1}	5	4		7		9■	8		10				11				6		12	3			22
1	13	2	12	5	7			6		9^{2}				10^{3}			14	8		11	3	4^{1}		23
1	12	2	4^{1}	5	8■			6^{2}		9				11				7		10	3		13	24
1	7^{1}	2		5			10	6^{2}		9				11			13	8		12	4	3		25
1	7	2		5			10	12		9^{1}				11				8		6	4	3		26
1	2	13	14	4	7		8^{3}	12		9				10				6■		11^{1}	3	5^{2}		27
1	6	2		5^{2}	7		8	12		10			13	11						9^{1}	4	3		28
1	2		5	6	9		10	7		11								8			4	3		29
1	2	12	8	3	9			6^{1}		11				10				7			4	5		30
1	2	3	7	5	9		8	12		10								6		11^{1}	4			31
1	2	7^{3}	4	5	9		8	13		10^{2}				11^{1}				6		14	3	12		32
1	2	7	4^{2}	5	9		8^{1}	12		10				11				6		13	3			33
1	2^{1}	7	3	5	9		8^{2}	12		10				11				6		13	4			34
1	2	7	4	5	9		12	6		11^{1}	14			10^{3}				8^{2}		13	3			35
1	2	3	5	9	8		12	6		11^{1}				10				7			4			36

ALBION ROVERS

Year Formed: 1882. *Ground & Address:* Cliftonhill Stadium, Main St, Coatbridge ML5 3RB. *Telephone/Fax:* 01236 606334.
E-mail: general@albionroversfc.co.uk *Website:* albionroversfc.co.uk
Ground capacity: 1,572 (seated: 489). *Size of Pitch:* 101m × 66m.
Chairman Ronnie Boyd. *Director of Football:* David Caldwell.
Manager: Brian Kerr. *Assistant Manager:* Stuart Malcolm.
Club Nickname: 'The Wee Rovers'.
Previous Grounds: Cowheath Park, Meadow Park, Whifflet.
Record Attendance: 27,381 v Rangers, Scottish Cup 2nd rd, 8 February 1936.
Record Transfer Fee received: £40,000 from Motherwell for Bruce Cleland (1979).
Record Transfer Fee paid: £7000 for Gerry McTeague to Stirling Alb, September 1989.
Record Victory: 12-0 v Airdriehill, Scottish Cup 1st rd, 3 September 1887.
Record Defeat: 1-11 v Partick Thistle, League Cup 2nd rd, 11 August 1993.
Most Capped Player: Jock White, 1 (2), Scotland.
Most League Appearances: 399: Murdy Walls, 1921-36.
Most League Goals in Season (Individual): 41: Jim Renwick, Division II, 1932-33.
Most Goals Overall (Individual): 105: Bunty Weir, 1928-31.

ALBION ROVERS – SPFL LADBROKES LEAGUE ONE 2016–17 LEAGUE RECORD

Match No.	Date	Venue	Opponents	Result		H/T Score	Lg Pos.	Goalscorers	Attendance
1	Aug 6	A	East Fife	D	2-2	1-2	5	Ferguson [15], Wallace [65]	682
2	13	H	Brechin C	L	0-2	0-1	7		228
3	20	A	Peterhead	D	2-2	0-1	7	Stewart II 2 [64, 74]	503
4	27	H	Alloa Ath	L	0-4	0-0	8		411
5	Sept 10	H	Stenhousemuir	W	4-0	0-0	7	Boyd [65], Willis [69], Wallace [74], Hamilton (og) [80]	301
6	17	A	Stranraer	L	2-3	0-2	8	Stewart II [60], Willis (pen) [90]	402
7	24	A	Airdrieonians	W	2-0	2-0	6	Willis [2], Ferry [33]	972
8	Oct 1	H	Queen's Park	W	2-0	1-0	5	Boyd [30], Wallace [90]	444
9	15	A	Livingston	W	2-1	1-0	4	Boyd [18], Wallace [70]	702
10	22	H	Peterhead	L	0-1	0-0	4		360
11	29	A	Alloa Ath	D	0-0	0-0	5		453
12	Nov 5	H	Airdrieonians	L	1-2	0-2	5	Stewart II [90]	1199
13	12	H	Stranraer	W	3-2	2-1	5	Stewart II [15], Wallace 2 (1 pen) [44 (p), 77]	321
14	Dec 3	H	Livingston	L	0-1	0-0	6		413
15	6	A	Brechin C	W	2-1	1-1	5	Stewart II 2 [39, 70]	283
16	10	A	Queen's Park	L	1-2	1-2	6	Stewart II [3]	662
17	17	A	Stenhousemuir	L	0-1	0-0	6		371
18	Jan 2	A	Airdrieonians	W	2-1	2-1	7	Boyd 2 [15, 44]	1633
19	7	H	Brechin C	W	1-0	0-0	7	Dunlop, M [71]	332
20	28	H	Alloa Ath	D	1-1	0-1	7	Stewart II [70]	348
21	Feb 4	A	Stranraer	L	0-3	0-1	7		364
22	11	A	Peterhead	D	1-1	0-1	7	Stewart II [56]	423
23	18	H	Stenhousemuir	D	1-1	1-0	7	Dunlop, M [29]	327
24	Mar 4	A	East Fife	L	0-2	0-0	9		539
25	7	A	Livingston	L	0-3	0-1	9		548
26	11	H	Airdrieonians	L	3-4	0-1	9	Davidson [47], Wallace 2 (1 pen) [61 (p), 89]	873
27	18	H	Peterhead	D	0-0	0-0	9		285
28	25	A	Stenhousemuir	W	3-0	0-0	8	Stewart II 2 [58, 63], McBride [90]	433
29	28	H	East Fife	W	1-0	0-0	7	Wallace [55]	419
30	Apr 1	A	Alloa Ath	D	1-1	1-1	7	Willis [45]	606
31	4	H	Queen's Park	D	1-1	1-0	7	Wallace [20]	512
32	8	H	Stranraer	W	3-0	1-0	7	Willis [34], Wallace [75], Neill (og) [81]	377
33	15	A	Queen's Park	L	0-2	0-1	7		677
34	22	H	East Fife	L	0-1	0-0	7		488
35	29	A	Brechin C	L	0-1	0-0	7		422
36	May 6	H	Livingston	L	0-2	0-2	8		454

Final League Position: 8

Honours
League Champions: Division II 1933-34, Second Division 1988-89. League Two 2014-15; *Runners-up:* Division II 1913-14, 1937-38, 1947-48. *Promoted to Second Division:* 2010-11 (play-offs).
Scottish Cup Runners-up: 1920.

Club colours: Shirt: Yellow with white trim. Shorts: Red. Socks: Red.

Goalscorers: *League (41):* Ross Stewart II 12, Wallace 11 (2 pens), Boyd 5, Willis 5 (1 pen), Dunlop M 2, Davidson 1, Ferguson 1, Ferry 1, McBride 1, own goals 2.
William Hill Scottish FA Cup (2): Dunlop M 1, Ferguson 1.
Betfred Scottish League Cup (1): Davidson 1.
IRN-BRU Scottish League Challenge Cup (5): Dunlop R 3, Dunlop M 1, Ferry 1.

Stewart Ross I 35	Reid A 32	Dunlop R 36	Dunlop M 35	Turnbull K 16 + 9	Fisher G 26 + 6	Ferry M 29 + 2	Willis P 28 + 4	Wallace R 27	Davidson R 24 + 2	Ferguson C 6 + 15	McBride S 24 + 5	Stewart Ross II 22 + 4	Lightbody D 1 + 7	Gilmour R 10 + 15	Boyd S 15	Shields C 6 + 12	Archibald P — + 2	McCann K 13 + 6	Gallagher J — + 1	Archibald T 11 + 3	Smith B — + 2	Munro J — + 1	*Match No.*
1	2	3	4	5	6	7^{1}	8	9	10	11^{2}	12	13											1
1	2	4	3	5	8	6	10	11	7^{1}	9^{2}			12	13									2
1	2	3	4	5	7	6^{2}	10			12	9	11		13	8^{1}								3
1	2	4	3	5	7^{2}	6	10^{3}			12	11	9^{1}	14	13	8								4
1	2	4	3	5		7	8^{2}	11			9	10^{1}		12	6	13							5
1	2	3	4	5^{2}		7^{1}	8	11			9	10		12	6		13						6
1	2	3	4		13	6	9	10^{1}	7		5	12		8^{3}	11^{2}			14					7
1	2	4	3		12	8^{1}	10	11	7		9	14		5^{2}	6^{3}			13					8
1	2	3	4	12	13	7	9	11^{1}	8		5	6^{2}			10^{3}	14							9
1	2^{2}	3	4	14		7^{3}	9	11	8		5	6^{1}			10	12		13					10
1	2	3	4	13	12	6^{3}	10^{1}	11	7		5	9^{2}				8		14					11
1	2	3	4	13	12	7^{1}	9		8	14	5	6			11^{2}	10^{3}							12
1	2	4	3	13	5		10^{2}	8^{3}	7	14	11	9			6^{1}			12					13
1	2■	4	3		7		10	11	8	12	5	13		6^{1}	9^{2}								14
1		4	3		7	6	13	10^{1}	8^{3}	14	5	11		12	9			2^{2}					15
1	2	3	4		8	7^{3}	13	9		12	5	10^{1}		6	11^{2}				14				16
1	2	4	8	5	3	6^{1}					9			7	11	10	12						17
1	2	3	4	5	8	13	7^{2}		6	14	9^{3}			12	10	11^{1}							18
1	2	4	3	5	8^{3}	6	10		7	12	11^{2}		14	13		9^{1}							19
1	2	4	3	5	7		10^{2}		8^{1}	12	9^{3}	11		14				13		6			20
1	2	3	4	5	7^{3}		10		8^{1}	12	13	11		14				6^{2}		9			21
1		3	4	5	8	12			7	10^{1}		9		6		13		2^{2}		11			22
1	2	4	3		7	6		10^{1}	8	9^{2}		11		5		12				13			23
1	5	3	4	13	8^{2}			10	7	11^{1}		6		2^{3}		14				9	12		24
1	2	3	4	5	8^{2}	7	12	11^{1}	13	14		10						6^{3}		9			25
1	2	4	3	5^{1}	7^{3}	8	13	10	12	14		11^{2}						6		9			26
1	5	4	3		7^{1}	6	10	11	8		13			12				2^{2}		9^{3}	14		27
1	5	3	4	14	7	6	11^{3}	10^{1}	8		13	9^{2}		12				2					28
1	5	4	3	12	7^{3}	6	10	11^{1}			8	9	14	13				2^{2}					29
1	2	3	4	5^{2}	13	6	10	11			8	9^{1}		7^{3}		12				14			30
1	2	3	4		6^{2}	7	9	11	8		5			13		12				10^{1}			31
1		3	4	13	7	6	9	11	8^{3}	12	5^{2}					14		2		10^{1}			32
1		3			6	7^{1}	10	11	9	12	5^{2}		14	4		13		2		8^{3}			33
	5	4	3		7	6^{2}	10	11		9^{1}	13	1	14			8^{3}		2		12			34
1	5	3	4		6	7^{2}	10	11	8^{1}				13			12		2		9			35
1	2^{3}	4	3	5^{2}		6	10	11			9^{1}		7	12		13		8				14	36

ALLOA ATHLETIC

Year Formed: 1878. *Ground & Address:* Indodrill Stadium, Recreation Park, Clackmannan Rd, Alloa FK10 1RY.
Telephone: 01259 722695. *Fax:* 01259 210886. *E-mail:* fcadmin@alloaatheltic.co.uk *Website:* www.alloaathletic.co.uk
Ground Capacity: 3,100 (seated: 919). *Size of Pitch:* 102m × 69m.
Chairman: Mike Mulraney. *Secretary:* Ewen Cameron.
Player/Manager: Jim Goodwin. *Assistant Manager:* Paddy Connolly.
Club Nicknames: 'The Wasps', 'The Hornets'.
Previous Grounds: West End Public Park, Gabberston Park, Bellevue Park.
Record Attendance: 13,000 v Dunfermline Ath, Scottish Cup 3rd rd replay, 26 February 1939.
Record Transfer Fee received: £100,000 for Martin Cameron to Bristol R (July 2000).
Record Transfer Fee paid: £26,000 for Ross Hamilton from Stenhousemuir (July 2000).
Record Victory: 9-0 v Selkirk, Scottish Cup 1st rd, 28 November 2005.
Record Defeat: 0-10 v Dundee, Division II, 8 March 1947; v Third Lanark, League Cup, 8 August 1953.
Most Capped Player: Jock Hepburn, 1, Scotland.
Most League Appearances: 239: Peter Smith 1960-69.
Most League Goals in Season (Individual): 49: 'Wee' Willie Crilley, Division II, 1921-22.
Most Goals Overall (Individual): 91: Willie Irvine, 1996-2001.

ALLOA ATHLETIC – SPFL LADBROKES LEAGUE ONE 2016–17 LEAGUE RECORD

Match No.	*Date*	*Venue*	*Opponents*	*Result*		*H/T Score*	*Lg Pos.*	*Goalscorers*	*Attendance*
1	Aug 6	H	Peterhead	W	4-0	3-0	2	Kirkpatrick 2 [9, 43], Cawley [14], Layne [69]	504
2	13	A	Stranraer	W	5-2	5-1	1	Spence 2 [17, 33], Flannigan [23], Kirkpatrick 2 [29, 40]	448
3	20	H	East Fife	W	2-1	2-0	2	Flannigan [37], Spence [40]	652
4	27	A	Albion R	W	4-0	0-0	1	Kirkpatrick [57], Waters [62], Donnelly [68], Dunlop, M (og) [74]	411
5	Sept 10	H	Livingston	L	1-3	0-3	2	Spence (pen) [65]	712
6	17	A	Queen's Park	W	2-1	0-0	1	Spence (pen) [79], Flannigan [86]	664
7	24	A	Stenhousemuir	D	2-2	1-0	1	Kerr (og) [3], Goodwin [51]	466
8	Oct 1	H	Airdrieonians	L	1-2	0-1	3	Spence [54]	644
9	15	A	Brechin C	W	1-0	0-0	1	Marr [68]	413
10	22	A	Livingston	L	1-3	0-0	3	Spence (pen) [90]	977
11	29	H	Albion R	D	0-0	0-0	3		453
12	Nov 5	H	Stenhousemuir	W	4-1	3-1	3	Spence [8], Graham [29], Longworth [35], Cawley [60]	458
13	15	A	East Fife	D	2-2	0-1	3	Longworth [57], Hynd [89]	412
14	19	A	Airdrieonians	L	1-2	0-2	4	Taggart [67]	790
15	Dec 10	A	Peterhead	D	1-1	0-0	3	Kirkpatrick [76]	365
16	13	H	Stranraer	D	2-2	1-1	3	Kirkpatrick [23], Spence [82]	307
17	17	H	Queen's Park	D	1-1	0-0	4	Spence [69]	442
18	24	H	Brechin C	L	1-2	0-1	4	Kirkpatrick [54]	386
19	31	A	Stenhousemuir	W	4-2	3-1	4	Cawley [24], Spence [29], Kirkpatrick 2 [44, 71]	335
20	Jan 7	A	Stranraer	W	2-1	0-1	2	Flannigan [70], Robertson [73]	383
21	14	H	Peterhead	L	0-1	0-0	2		504
22	28	A	Albion R	D	1-1	1-0	2	Taggart [35]	348
23	Feb 4	H	Livingston	D	2-2	1-1	3	Kirkpatrick [25], Mackin [86]	565
24	18	A	Queen's Park	W	2-0	1-0	2	Spence [4], Kirkpatrick [85]	657
25	25	H	Airdrieonians	W	2-1	2-1	2	Graham 2 [4, 17]	540
26	28	H	East Fife	W	3-0	2-0	2	Spence [11], Cawley [38], Longworth [80]	436
27	Mar 11	H	Stenhousemuir	W	2-1	1-0	2	Mackin [40], Spence (pen) [86]	508
28	18	A	East Fife	D	0-0	0-0	2		612
29	21	A	Brechin C	W	2-1	1-0	2	Cawley [41], Graham [90]	372
30	25	H	Queen's Park	D	2-2	1-1	2	Flannigan [18], Taggart [54]	675
31	Apr 1	H	Albion R	D	1-1	1-1	2	Kirkpatrick [21]	606
32	8	A	Livingston	L	1-2	0-1	2	Mackin [67]	1099
33	15	H	Brechin C	W	6-1	2-1	2	McCluskey [25], Spence 2 (1 pen) [32, 65 (p)], Marr [47], Flannigan 2 [69, 83]	662
34	22	A	Airdrieonians	W	1-0	0-0	2	Kirkpatrick [66]	757
35	29	H	Stranraer	W	1-0	0-0	2	Cawley [90]	507
36	May 6	A	Peterhead	L	2-3	1-0	2	Flannigan [29], Martin [59]	681

Final League Position: 2

Honours
League Champions: Division II 1921-22; Third Division 1997-98, 2011-12.
Runners-up: Division II 1938-39; Second Division 1976-77, 1981-82, 1984-85, 1988-89, 1999-2000, 2001-02, 2009-10, 2012-13 (promoted via play-offs); League One 2016-17.
League Challenge Cup Winners: 1999-2000; *Runners-up:* 2001-02, 2014-15.

Club colours: Shirt: Gold and black hoops. Shorts: Black. Socks: Black with gold hoops.

Goalscorers: *League (69):* Spence 16 (5 pens), Kirkpatrick 14, Flannigan 8, Cawley 6, Graham 4, Longworth 3, Mackin 3, Taggart 3, Marr 2, Donnelly 1, Goodwin 1, Hynd 1, Layne 1, Martin 1, McCluskey 1, Robertson 1, Waters 1, own goals 2.
William Hill Scottish FA Cup (3): Longworth 1, McCluskey 1, Spence 1.
Betfred Scottish League Cup (11): Spence 3, Kirkpatrick 2, Layne 2, Graham 1, Marr 1, Robertson 1, Waters 1.
IRN-BRU Scottish League Challenge Cup (7): Spence 3, Cawley 1, Kirkpatrick 1, Robertson 1, Waters 1.
Play-Offs (5): Spence 3 (1 pen), Mackin 1, Robertson 1.

Parry N 29	Taggart S 36	Graham A 34	Marr J 24 + 1	Waters C 36	Holmes G 19 + 8	Kirkpatrick J 32 + 2	Robertson J 23 + 7	Flannigan I 22 + 6	Cawley K 32 + 3	Spence G 33 + 2	Layne I — + 6	Hetherington S 12 + 9	Longworth J 8 + 23	Goodwin J 14	Hoggan R 1 + 5	Donnelly L — + 6	Gordon B 3	Martin A 2 + 4	Scullion P — + 1	Hynd S — + 4	McKeown F 11 + 1	Wilson A 1	McCluskey S 7 + 5	Mackin D 11 + 1	McDowall C 6	*Match No.*
1	2	3	4	5	6	7^3	8	9^2	10	11^1	12	13	14													1
1	2	3	4	5	12	6	8^2	9	11^1	10	14	13		7^3												2
1	2	3	4	5	8^3	9		7^2	11	10^1	12	13		6	14											3
1	2	3	4^2	5	8	9^3	12	6	11^1	10		14		7		13										4
1	2	3	4^2	5	8^1	10	6		9	11			12	7		13										5
1	2	3		5	14	9^2	8	6	11^3	10^1			12	7		13	4									6
1	2	3	14	5	12	10^1	7	8	9^2	11^3			13	6■			4									7
1	2		3^2	5	7	9^1	8	6	11^3	10			12		14	13	4									8
1	3	2	5	4	12	8^1	6	9	11	10				7^2				13								9
1	2	3^3	4	5		10	7		9	11			13	8^2		14		6^1	12							10
1	2	3	4	5		10^1	8	6	9	11			12	7												11
1	2	3	4	5	12	10^2	7		8	11^1			9	6^3		13		14								12
1	2	3	4	5	7^2	12	8	9	6	11			10^1							13						13
1	2	4	3^3	5		9	7	8^2	10^1	11			13	6■	12					14						14
1	5	3	2	9	7	12	6	8^1		10	13		11		4^2											15
1	2	4	3	5	6^1	10	7		8	11	12		9													16
1	2	3	4	5		8	9		7	11	12		10^1	6												17
1	2	4	3	5		7^2	8	9	6	11		10^1	12							13						18
1	2	4	3	5	14	8	7	13	6^1	11^2		10^3	12	9												19
1	2	4	3	5	13	10^1	7	12	6	11		9^2	14	8^3												20
1	2	4	3^1	5		11	8	9	6	10		7^2	12								13					21
	2	4		5	7^3	10	14		6	9		12	11^2								3	1	8^1	13		22
	2	4		5	7	10		12	6^1	13		8^2	14								3		9^3	11	1	23
	2	4		5	7	6^2	8	12	13	10^3		9^1	14								3			11	1	24
	2	4		5	7^3	9	14	13	6	10^1		12									3		8^2	11	1	25
	2	4		5	14	9	13	8	6^2	10^1		7	12								3			11^3	1	26
1	2	4		5	7	8		6^1	9^2	10^3			13		14						3		12	11		27
1	2	4		5	6	10		7	8^1	11^3		12	14								3		13	9^2		28
	2	4		5		9	8	12	6	14		7^3	13								3		11^2	10^1	1	29
1	2	4		5	7	11^1		8	6	10^2		13	12								3			9		30
1	2	4		5	6^1	10^2		8	9	11		7	13								3		12			31
1	2	4	3	5	8	9^3	12		6^1	10^2		7	14										13	11		32
1	2	4	3	5	8^1		13	7	6	11			14					12					9^2	10^3		33
1	2	4	3	5		9	6	7^3	13	10		8^2	14										12	11^1		34
1	2	4	3	5	7^1	8	13		6	11^3		12	10					14					9^2			35
	2		3	5^1			7	9^3	12			8	10		13			11		14	4		6^2		1	36

ANNAN ATHLETIC

Year Formed: 1942. *Ground & Address:* Galabank, North Street, Annan DG12 5DQ. *Telephone:* 01461 204108.
E-mail: annanathletic.enquiries@btconnect.com *Website:* www.annanathleticfc.com
Ground capacity: 2,517 (seated: 500). *Size of Pitch:* 100m × 62m.
Chairman: Henry McClelland.
Secretary: Alan Irving.
Player/Manager: Peter Murphy.
Assistant Manager: John Joyce.
Coaches: Peter Weatherson and Bill Bentley.
Club Nicknames: 'Galabankies', 'Black and Golds'.
Previous Ground: Mafeking Park.
Record attendance: 2,517, v Rangers, Third Division, 15 September 2012.
Record Victory: 6-0 v Elgin C, Third Division, 7 March 2009.
Record Defeat: 1-8 v Inverness CT, Scottish Cup 3rd rd, 24 January 1998.
Most League Appearances: 240: Peter Watson, 2008-17.
Most League Goals in Season (Individual): 22: Peter Weatherson, 2014-15.
Most Goals Overall (Individual): 56: Peter Weatherson, 2013-17.

ANNAN ATHLETIC – SPFL LADBROKES LEAGUE TWO 2016–17 LEAGUE RECORD

Match No.	*Date*	*Venue*	*Opponents*	*Result*	*H/T Score*	*Lg Pos.*	*Goalscorers*	*Attendance*
1	Aug 6	H	Stirling Alb	W 3-2	3-1	1	Forsyth (og) [18], McKenna [31], Smith [42]	421
2	13	A	Berwick R	L 0-2	0-1	5		366
3	20	H	Clyde	W 3-2	1-0	3	McKenna [38], Ramsay [70], Omar [82]	421
4	27	A	Montrose	D 2-2	2-0	5	Ramsay [2], Wright [7]	340
5	Sept 10	H	Forfar Ath	L 1-2	1-0	6	Wright (pen) [22]	403
6	17	A	Arbroath	D 1-1	0-0	6	McKenna [58]	482
7	24	H	Edinburgh C	D 1-1	1-0	6	McKenna [29]	351
8	Oct 1	A	Elgin C	W 2-0	1-0	5	Ramsay [3], McKenna (pen) [47]	583
9	15	A	Cowdenbeath	D 2-2	2-0	6	Cuddihy [22], McKenna [37]	331
10	Nov 5	H	Arbroath	L 1-2	1-0	6	Swinglehurst [45]	326
11	8	H	Montrose	L 2-3	1-2	6	Campbell, I (og) [69], Ramsay [30]	289
12	12	A	Edinburgh C	L 0-1	0-0	6		256
13	19	H	Elgin C	W 1-0	1-0	5	McKenna [5]	353
14	Dec 10	H	Cowdenbeath	W 2-0	1-0	5	Ramsay [16], Swinglehurst [61]	241
15	13	A	Forfar Ath	L 1-5	0-3	5	Smith [60]	337
16	17	A	Stirling Alb	L 1-3	1-2	5	Wright (pen) [1]	694
17	24	H	Berwick R	W 3-1	3-1	5	McKenna [5], Watson [30], Omar [39]	430
18	31	A	Clyde	W 3-2	0-1	5	McKenna 2 [52, 63], Smith [88]	467
19	Jan 7	H	Forfar Ath	L 1-2	1-1	4	Wright (pen) [23]	432
20	14	A	Elgin C	L 2-3	0-3	4	Weatherson [70], Osadolor [83]	638
21	21	A	Arbroath	W 2-1	1-1	4	Ramsay (pen) [40], Krissian [68]	566
22	28	H	Stirling Alb	W 4-1	1-1	4	Osadolor 2 [45, 56], Wright 2 [74, 90]	420
23	Feb 4	A	Berwick R	L 1-4	1-2	4	Weatherson [26]	355
24	11	H	Edinburgh C	W 1-0	1-0	4	Weatherson [15]	379
25	18	A	Cowdenbeath	W 1-0	0-0	4	Ramsay [52]	258
26	25	H	Clyde	W 1-0	0-0	4	Wright [74]	398
27	Mar 4	A	Montrose	W 3-2	3-1	4	Omar [5], Wright [15], Swinglehurst [23]	384
28	11	H	Elgin C	W 1-0	1-0	3	McKenna (pen) [19]	328
29	18	A	Stirling Alb	L 0-1	0-0	4		531
30	25	H	Cowdenbeath	W 1-0	0-0	3	Smith [76]	386
31	Apr 1	H	Arbroath	L 2-5	2-2	3	Weatherson [14], Stewart [24]	456
32	8	A	Clyde	L 1-2	1-1	4	Smith [16]	462
33	15	H	Berwick R	W 2-1	0-0	3	Ramsay (pen) [52], Smith [70]	460
34	22	A	Edinburgh C	L 0-2	0-1	3		378
35	29	H	Montrose	W 5-1	4-0	3	Omar [6], Cuddihy [11], Swinglehurst [13], Krissian [17], Weatherson [50]	461
36	May 6	A	Forfar Ath	W 4-2	3-1	3	Watson [14], Osadolor [36], Wright [39], Smith [89]	917

Final League Position: 3

Honours
League Two Runners-up: 2013-14.
League Challenge Cup: Semi-finals: 2009-10, 2011-12.

Club colours: Shirt: Gold with black trim. Shorts: Black. Socks: Gold with black and white rings.

Goalscorers: *League (61):* McKenna 11 (2 pens), Wright 9 (3 pens), Ramsay 8 (2 pens), Smith 7, Weatherson 5, Omar 4, Osadolor 4, Swinglehurst 4, Cuddihy 2, Krissian 2, Watson 2, Stewart 1, own goals 2.
William Hill Scottish FA Cup (2): Asghar 1, McKenna 1.
Betfred Scottish League Cup (4): Dachnowicz 1, Finnie 1, Omar 1, Wright 1 (1 pen).
IRN-BRU Scottish League Challenge Cup (1): Omar 1.
Play-Offs (4): Smith 2 (1 pen), Ramsay 1, Weatherson 1.

Currie B 35	Black S 12	Watson P 19 + 3	Krissian R 22 + 2	Lucas J 30 + 3	Omar R 23 + 8	Finnie R 12	Ramsay D 29 + 2	Wright M 26 + 7	McKenna D 24 + 9	Smith A 14 + 19	Park L — + 4	Dachnowicz P 1 + 6	Robertson W 2 + 3	Bradbury A — + 2	Norman S — + 1	Cuddihy B 19 + 3	Asghar A 3 + 4	Swinglehurst S 25	Sinnamon R 8 + 1	Bronsky S 10 + 1	Home C 11 + 5	Pearson E — + 1	Nade C 3	Flanagan N 20 + 2	Ribeiro T — + 1	Skelton G 19	Osadolor S 5 + 6	Weatherson P 14 + 2	Stewart J 9	Fry T — + 3	Mitchell A 1	*Match No.*
1	2	3	4	5	6[1]	7	8	9	10[2]	11	12	13																				1
1	2	3	4	5[2]		7	6	9	10[3]	11[1]		14	8	12	13																	2
1	2	3	4	5	10	6	7	9	11[2]		13					8[1]	12															3
1	2	3	4	5	10	6	7	9	11[1]	12						8																4
1	2	3	4	13	10	6[2]	8	9	11[1]	12			14			7		5[3]														5
1	2	3	4[3]		10■	7	8[2]	9	11[1]	12	14		13			6		5														6
1	2	3	4			7	8[2]	10[3]	11[1]	12	13	14	9			6		5														7
1	2	3			6	7	9[2]	13	10[1]	11			12			8		5	4													8
1	2	4		13	6	8	9[1]	12	10[2]	11						7		5	3													9
1		3		5	13	6[1]	8[2]	9	10	11		14				7[3]	12	4	2													10
1		12		2	10	7	9[1]	6[3]	13	11							8■	4[2]	5	3	14											11
1			4	5	9	6[2]	8[3]	13	10	11		14				7			2[1]	3		12										12
1			12	2	6		8	9[3]	10[1]					13		7		4	5	3	14		11[2]									13
1		12		2			6		10[1]	13						8	7	4	5	3	9[3]		11[2]	14								14
1		8		2			9	12	10[1]	11						7	6[2]	4	5	3[3]				13	14							15
1		13		2	12		8[1]	9[2]	14	11						7		4		3	5		10[3]	6								16
1		3		5	10		8[3]	9[1]	11[2]	12						7	14	4	13		2			6								17
1		3		5	10[2]		13	8	11[1]	12						7		4			2			6		9						18
1		4	3	5[1]	7			9[2]	10[3]	12		13					14				2			6		8	11					19
1		3	12	5	6		13	11[2]	10[3]									4[1]			2			9		8	14	7				20
1		4	3	5[2]	6		8	13	14	12											2			9[3]		7	11[1]	10				21
1		4	3	5	9		8[3]	12	14	13											2			6[1]		7	11[2]	10				22
1		4		5	9[3]		8	14	13	12								3			2			6		7[1]	11[2]	10				23
1	3			2	12		7	6	11[3]	13								4						9[2]		8	14	10[1]	5			24
1			3	2[1]	13		8	6	11[3]	14								4			12			9[2]		7		10	5			25
1			3	2	13		7	6	11[2]	12								4						9[1]		8		10	5			26
1			3	2	10		7■	6[3]	11[1]	13						14		4						9[2]		8			5	12		27
1			3	2	10[1]			6	11[2]	13						7		4						9		8		12	5			28
1			3	2	11			6[1]	14	13						7[3]		4						9		8[2]		10	5	12		29
1			3	2	11[1]		7	6[2]		12						13		4						9		8		10	5			30
1			3	2[3]			7[1]	6		10								4■			13			9[2]		8	14	11	5	12		31
1			4	2	14		8[1]	6		11						13				3	12			9[2]		7		10	5[3]			32
1	2		3	5	12		7	6[3]	13	11										4				9[2]		8	14	10[1]				33
1	2		4	12	6		7■		13	11								5		3[1]				9[3]		8[2]	14	10				34
1			3	5	6				12	11						7[2]		4		14	2			9[3]		8	13	10[1]				35
		4		5	12			6[1]	10	14		9[3]				8				3	2					7	11[2]	13			1	36

ARBROATH

Year Formed: 1878. *Ground & Address:* Gayfield Park, Arbroath DD11 1QB. *Telephone:* 01241 872157. *Fax:* 01241 431125. *E-mail:* afc@gayfield.fsnet.co.uk *Website:* www.arbroathfc.co.uk
Ground Capacity: 6,600 (seated: 861). *Size of Pitch:* 105m × 65m.
Chairman: Mike Caird. *Secretary:* Dr Gary Callon.
Manager: Dick Campbell. *Assistant Manager:* Ian Campbell.
Club Nickname: 'The Red Lichties'.
Previous Grounds: Lesser Gayfield.
Record Attendance: 13,510 v Rangers, Scottish Cup 3rd rd, 23 February 1952.
Record Transfer Fee received: £120,000 for Paul Tosh to Dundee (August 1993).
Record Transfer Fee paid: £20,000 for Douglas Robb from Montrose (1981).
Record Victory: 36-0 v Bon Accord, Scottish Cup 1st rd, 12 September 1885.
Record Defeat: 0-8 v Kilmarnock, Division II, 3 January 1949; 1-9 v Celtic, League Cup 3rd rd, 25 August 1993.
Most Capped Player: Ned Doig, 2 (5), Scotland.
Most League Appearances: 445: Tom Cargill, 1966-81.
Most League Goals in Season (Individual): 45: Dave Easson, Division II, 1958-59.
Most Goals Overall (Individual): 120: Jimmy Jack, 1966-71.

ARBROATH – SPFL LADBROKES LEAGUE TWO 2016–17 LEAGUE RECORD

Match No.	*Date*	*Venue*	*Opponents*	*Result*		*H/T Score*	*Lg Pos.*	*Goalscorers*	*Attendance*
1	Aug 6	H	Berwick R	D	1-1	0-0	5	Scott ^{58}	502
2	13	A	Montrose	D	1-1	1-0	6	McCord ^{34}	794
3	20	A	Elgin C	W	1-0	0-0	4	Skelly ^{86}	519
4	27	H	Stirling Alb	W	5-3	1-1	2	Skelly ^{31}, Linn 3 (1 pen) $^{58, 67 (p), 72}$, Kader ^{78}	601
5	Sept 10	A	Clyde	L	2-3	2-2	4	Skelly ^{12}, Linn ^{44}	559
6	17	H	Annan Ath	D	1-1	0-0	4	McCord ^{90}	482
7	24	H	Cowdenbeath	D	0-0	0-0	5		558
8	Oct 1	A	Edinburgh C	D	3-3	1-1	6	Kader ^{8}, Little ^{47}, Scott ^{79}	590
9	15	H	Forfar Ath	W	2-0	0-0	4	Cox (og) ^{51}, Scott ^{77}	862
10	29	A	Berwick R	D	1-1	1-0	4	Gold ^{20}	390
11	Nov 5	A	Annan Ath	W	2-1	0-1	4	Whatley ^{47}, Skelly ^{90}	326
12	12	H	Clyde	W	4-0	1-0	3	Linn ^{31}, Scott 2 $^{70, 72}$, McCord ^{87}	615
13	19	A	Stirling Alb	D	2-2	1-0	3	Doris ^{40}, Kader ^{68}	605
14	Dec 3	H	Edinburgh C	L	0-1	0-0	4		582
15	10	A	Forfar Ath	W	1-0	0-0	3	McCord ^{85}	786
16	17	H	Elgin C	W	3-2	0-1	2	Prunty ^{54}, Doris 2 (1 pen) $^{55, 90 (p)}$	584
17	24	A	Cowdenbeath	W	2-0	0-0	2	Skelly ^{74}, Doris ^{87}	317
18	Jan 2	H	Montrose	D	0-0	0-0	2		1731
19	7	A	Edinburgh C	W	2-0	1-0	2	Ferns ^{10}, Kader ^{64}	481
20	14	H	Berwick R	W	4-1	0-1	2	McCord 2 $^{64, 74}$, Scott ^{79}, Malin ^{90}	539
21	21	H	Annan Ath	L	1-2	1-1	2	Doris ^{12}	566
22	28	A	Clyde	W	2-1	1-0	2	Hamilton ^{26}, Little ^{72}	465
23	Feb 4	H	Forfar Ath	L	0-1	0-1	2		1008
24	11	A	Montrose	W	3-1	0-1	2	Smyth ^{54}, McCord ^{70}, Kader ^{90}	1002
25	18	H	Stirling Alb	D	1-1	0-0	2	Doris ^{64}	625
26	25	H	Cowdenbeath	W	4-1	2-0	2	Scott ^{5}, Doris ^{30}, Henderson (og) ^{54}, Malin ^{73}	519
27	Mar 4	A	Elgin C	D	0-0	0-0	2		640
28	11	H	Clyde	W	1-0	1-0	2	Whatley ^{41}	566
29	18	A	Berwick R	W	2-0	1-0	2	Doris (pen) ^{38}, Scott ^{90}	425
30	25	H	Montrose	L	0-1	0-0	2		1156
31	Apr 1	A	Annan Ath	W	5-2	2-2	2	McCord ^{2}, Doris 3 $^{42, 60, 90}$, Prunty ^{74}	456
32	8	A	Forfar Ath	D	1-1	0-0	2	McCord ^{65}	1564
33	15	H	Edinburgh C	L	0-1	0-0	2		775
34	22	A	Cowdenbeath	W	2-1	1-0	2	Doris ^{20}, McCord ^{48}	501
35	29	H	Elgin C	W	3-2	1-0	1	McCord 3 $^{38, 63, 80}$	807
36	May 6	A	Stirling Alb	D	1-1	1-0	1	Scott ^{5}	1748

Final League Position: 1

Honours
League Champions: Third Division 2010-11; League Two 2016-17. *Runners-up:* Division II 1934-35, 1958-59, 1967-68, 1971-72; Second Division 2000-01; Third Division 1997-98, 2007-08 (promoted via play-offs).
Scottish Cup: Quarter-finals 1993.

Club colours: Shirt: Maroon with white trim. Shorts: Maroon. Socks: Maroon.

Goalscorers: *League (63):* McCord 13, Doris 12 (2 pens), Scott 9, Kader 5, Linn 5 (1 pen), Skelly 5, Little 2, Malin 2, Prunty 2, Whatley 2, Ferns 1, Gold 1, Hamilton 1, Smyth 1, own goals 2.
William Hill Scottish FA Cup (3): Doris 1, Hamilton 1, Linn 1.
Betfred Scottish League Cup (1): Hamilton 1.
IRN-BRU Scottish League Challenge Cup (5): Hamilton 1, Hester 1, Kader 1, Little 1, Scott 1.

Mutch R 8	Whatley M 35	Dunlop M 3 + 3	Little R 34	Hamilton C 36	Kader O 20 + 13	McCord R 30 + 1	Scott M 22 + 4	Linn B 36	Doris S 30 + 6	Prunty B 11 + 17	Hester K 1 + 8	Gold D 28 + 4	Sukar J 23 + 3	Skelly J 13 + 9	Phillips G 7 + 1	Callaghan L 2 + 4	Brown J 3 + 1	Gomes R 28 + 1	Malin G 3 + 12	Ferns E 5 + 7	McCallum D — + 5	Hodge B 14	Smyth M 4 + 4	*Match No.*
1	2	3	4	5	6	7	8	9	10^{1}	11^{2}	12	13												1
1	7	2	3	5	9	8■		6^{3}	10^{2}	11^{1}	14	12	4	13										2
1	7	14	2	4	13			6^{2}	12		10^{3}	8	3	11	5^{1}	9								3
1	8		2	3	6			9	10^{3}	13	14	7	4	11^{1}	5^{2}		12							4
1	8^{3}		2	5	6		7	9	11^{2}	13	14	12	4	10^{1}			3							5
1			2	4	6^{2}	7	8	9	12	10^{1}	14	13		11^{3}	5		3							6
1	8^{3}		3	4	12	7	10	9	14		13		5	11^{1}		6^{2}	2							7
1^{1}	2		3	4	6	7	8	9	13	10^{3}	14		5■	11^{2}				12						8
	7		3	4	6	8^{1}	9	11^{3}	10^{2}	14		2		13	5			1	12					9
	7^{3}		3	4	6	8	11	9^{1}	10^{2}	14	12	2			5	13		1						10
	7		3	4	6^{1}	8^{2}	10	9	13	11^{3}		2	5	14		12		1						11
	7		3	4	6	8	11^{2}	9^{1}	12	10^{3}		2	5	13				1	14					12
	8		3■	4	6^{3}	7^{1}	11	9^{2}	10			2	5		14	13		1	12					13
	7	3		4	6^{2}	8^{1}	11	9	10^{3}	14		2	5	12				1	13					14
	7	13	3	4	12	8	11^{2}	9^{1}	10	14		2^{3}	5	6				1						15
	8	14	3	4	13	7^{2}		6^{3}	10	11^{1}		2	5■	9				1	12					16
	7		3	4	12	8^{1}		6^{2}	10	11^{3}		2		9	5	14		1	13					17
	7		3	4	12	8^{1}	13	6	10	11^{2}		2		9^{3}	5			1	14					18
	7		3	4	9	8^{2}	14	6	10^{1}	13		2	5					1	12	11^{3}				19
	7		3	4	6^{1}	8^{3}	13	9	10			2	5	12				1	14	11^{2}				20
	7		3	4	6^{1}	8	12	9	10			2	5^{3}	13				1		11^{2}	14			21
	7		3	4	13		11^{1}	9^{2}	10^{3}	12		2	5	6				1	14			8		22
	8		3	4	13			9	10			2	5	6^{2}				1		11^{1}	12	7		23
	8			4	14	12		9^{1}	11	13		2	5^{3}	6				1		10^{2}		7	3	24
	7		3	4	6	8		9^{3}	10	11^{1}		2^{2}		14				1		13		5	12	25
	8		3	4		7^{1}	11^{2}	9	10				5	12				1	2		13	6^{3}	14	26
	8		4■	3	12	7	10^{2}	9	11^{3}				5					1	2^{1}	14		6	13	27
	8		3	4	12	7	11^{1}	6^{3}	10	13		2	5					1		14		9^{2}		28
	8		4	3	13	7^{3}	11	6	10^{2}	14		2						1	9^{1}			5	12	29
	7		3	4	11^{3}	8		6^{2}	10	12		2	5					1		14	13	9^{1}		30
	8		3	4	6	7		9^{3}	10	11^{1}		2	12					1		13	14	5^{2}		31
	8		3	4	6^{3}	7^{2}	11^{1}	9	10	12		2						1	14	13		5		32
	8		3	4	6	7	11^{1}	9	10	12		2	5					1						33
	7		3	4		8^{2}	10^{1}	9^{3}	11	14		2						1	13	12		5	6	34
	8		3	4		7^{2}	11	9	10^{1}	13		2	12					1				5	6	35
	8		3	4	13	6	11^{3}	9^{2}	10	14		2	12					1				5^{1}	7	36

AYR UNITED

Year Formed: 1910. *Ground & Address:* Somerset Park, Tryfield Place, Ayr KA8 9NB. *Telephone:* 01292 263435. *Fax:* 01292 281314. *E-mail:* info@ayrunitedfc.co.uk *Website:* ayrunitedfc.co.uk
Ground Capacity: 10,185 (seated: 1,597). *Size of Pitch:* 101m × 66m.
Chairman: Lachlan Cameron.
Managing Director: Lewis Grant.
Manager: Ian McCall. *Assistant Manager:* Neil Scally.
Club Nickname: 'The Honest Men'.
Previous Grounds: None.
Record Attendance: 25,225 v Rangers, Division I, 13 September 1969.
Record Transfer Fee received: £300,000 for Steven Nicol to Liverpool (October 1981).
Record Transfer Fee paid: £90,000 for Mark Campbell from Stranraer (March 1999).
Record Victory: 11-1 v Dumbarton, League Cup, 13 August 1952.
Record Defeat: 0-9 in Division I v Rangers (1929); v Hearts (1931); B Division v Third Lanark (1954).
Most Capped Player: Jim Nisbet, 3, Scotland.
Most League Appearances: 459: John Murphy, 1963-78.
Most League League and Cup Goals in Season (Individual): 66: Jimmy Smith, 1927-28.
Most League and Cup Goals Overall (Individual): 213: Peter Price, 1955-61.

AYR UNITED – SPFL LADBROKES CHAMPIONSHIP 2016–17 LEAGUE RECORD

Match No.	*Date*	*Venue*	*Opponents*	*Result*		*H/T Score*	*Lg Pos.*	*Goalscorers*	*Atten-dance*
1	Aug 6	H	Raith R	L	0-2	0-1	10		1550
2	13	A	Queen of the South	L	1-4	0-2	10	Nisbet, K ^{61}	1982
3	20	A	Dundee U	L	0-3	0-2	10		6427
4	27	H	St Mirren	D	1-1	1-0	10	Adams ^{14}	2165
5	Sept 10	H	Greenock Morton	W	2-1	0-0	7	Cairney ^{47}, Forrest ^{69}	1441
6	17	A	Hibernian	W	2-1	0-0	6	Balatoni ^{74}, Gilmour ^{80}	15,056
7	24	A	Falkirk	L	0-2	0-0	6		4345
8	Oct 1	H	Dunfermline Ath	D	0-0	0-0	7		2883
9	15	A	Dumbarton	W	3-0	1-0	7	Forrest 3 (1 pen) $^{2, 50, 62 (p)}$	1005
10	22	H	Queen of the South	W	1-0	0-0	6	Cairney ^{52}	1842
11	29	A	Greenock Morton	L	1-2	1-0	7	Nisbet, K ^{37}	1859
12	Nov 5	H	Hibernian	L	0-3	0-1	7		3100
13	19	H	Falkirk	L	0-1	0-1	7		1414
14	22	A	Raith R	D	1-1	0-1	7	Harkins ^{88}	1241
15	Dec 3	A	Dunfermline Ath	D	1-1	0-1	7	Forrest (pen) ^{50}	3250
16	10	H	Dundee U	L	0-1	0-1	8		2049
17	17	A	St Mirren	D	1-1	0-0	9	Cairney ^{63}	3124
18	24	H	Dumbarton	D	4-4	2-1	8	McKenna ^{31}, Harkins ^{43}, Forrest (pen) ^{74}, Cairney ^{85}	1441
19	31	A	Queen of the South	D	0-0	0-0	8		1594
20	Jan 7	H	Dunfermline Ath	L	0-2	0-2	9		2261
21	14	A	Falkirk	D	1-1	1-1	9	Harkins ^{24}	5038
22	28	H	Greenock Morton	L	1-4	1-3	9	Adams ^{36}	1576
23	Feb 4	A	Hibernian	D	1-1	1-0	9	Crawford ^{4}	14,349
24	18	A	Dumbarton	D	2-2	0-0	9	Moore (pen) ^{90}, Rose ^{90}	1198
25	25	H	St Mirren	L	0-2	0-0	9		2712
26	28	H	Raith R	W	1-0	0-0	9	El Alagui ^{62}	1103
27	Mar 11	H	Falkirk	L	1-4	0-1	9	Harkins ^{64}	1614
28	18	A	Dunfermline Ath	W	1-0	0-0	9	Docherty ^{49}	3276
29	25	H	Dumbarton	W	2-1	1-1	9	El Alagui ^{45}, Crawford ^{51}	1608
30	28	A	Dundee U	L	1-2	0-1	9	Harkins (pen) ^{51}	4661
31	Apr 1	A	St Mirren	L	2-6	0-4	9	Cairney ^{74}, El Alagui ^{87}	4620
32	8	H	Queen of the South	L	0-2	0-0	10		1476
33	15	H	Dundee U	D	0-0	0-0	10		1205
34	22	A	Greenock Morton	D	1-1	1-1	10	Moore ^{45}	2390
35	29	H	Hibernian	L	0-4	0-2	10		2152
36	May 6	A	Raith R	L	1-2	0-1	10	Docherty ^{70}	3064

Final League Position: 10

Honours
League Champions: Division II 1911-12, 1912-13, 1927-28, 1936-37, 1958-59, 1965-66. Second Division 1987-88, 1996-97; *Runners-up:* Division II 1910-11, 1955-56, 1968-69. Second Division 2008-09. League One 2015-16. *Promoted to First Division:* 2008-09 (play-offs). *Promoted to First Division:* 2010-11 (play-offs). *Promoted to Championship:* 2015-16 (play-offs).
Scottish Cup: Semi-finals 2002.
League Cup: Runners-up: 2001-02.
League Challenge Cup Runners-up: 1990-91, 1991-92.

Club colours: Shirt: White with black hoops. Shorts: Black. Socks: White.

Goalscorers: *League (33):* Forrest 6 (3 pens), Cairney 5, Harkins 5 (1 pen), El Alagui 3, Adams 2, Crawford 2, Docherty 2, Moore 2 (1 pen), Nisbet K 2, Balatoni 1, Gilmour 1, McKenna 1, Rose 1.
William Hill Scottish FA Cup (7): Balatoni 1, Cairney 1, McDaid 1, McGuffie 1, Moore 1, O'Connell 1, Wardrope 1.
Betfred Scottish League Cup (6): Forrest 2 (1 pen), Crawford 1, Gilmour 1, McGuffie 1, Murphy 1.
IRN-BRU Scottish League Challenge Cup (5): Balatoni 1, Forrest 1, Harkins 1, McGuffie 1, O'Connell 1.

Fleming G 36	Devlin N 34	Murphy P 9	Meggatt D 31	Boyle P 26 + 3	Crawford R 24 + 3	Docherty R 29	Adams J 16 + 2	Donald M 1 + 5	Cairney P 27 + 3	Forrest A 24 + 10	McGuffie C 6 + 20	Thomas J — + 3	O'Connell A 1 + 7	Rose M 10 + 10	Harkins G 30 + 2	Gilmour B 19 + 6	Nisbet K 11 + 9	Balatoni C 30	McKenna S 11	Wardrope M 2 + 3	Moore C 9 + 4	McDaid D 2 + 5	El Alagui F 8 + 3	Hart J — + 1	*Match No.*
1	2	3	4	5	6^{1}	7	8^{3}	9^{2}	10	11	12	13	14												1
1	2		4	5	11^{3}	7	13		9^{2}	12	14			3	6^{1}	8	10								2
1	2	3		5	6^{3}	8	4		7	9^{2}	14	13			10	12	11^{1}								3
1	2	3	4	5	13	8	7		9^{1}	12					10	6	11^{2}								4
1	2		4	5		8	7		9^{1}	11	13		14		10^{2}	6^{3}	12	3							5
1	2		4	5	14	7	8		9^{3}	11^{1}	13				10^{2}	6	12	3							6
1	2		4	5	7	8			12	9^{2}	14	13			10^{3}	6	11^{1}	3							7
1	2		4	5	10^{3}	8	7^{2}		14	11^{1}	13				9	6	12	3							8
1	2	3	5		8	7		13	9^{3}	10^{2}	14				11^{1}	6	12	4							9
1	2	3	5		7^{2}	8	14	13	9^{3}	11^{1}					10	6	12	4							10
1	2	4	5		12	8	7^{2}	13	9^{1}	14					10	6	11^{3}	3							11
1	2		4	5		7	8^{3}		9	11	12		14		10^{1}	6^{2}	13	3							12
1	2			5	7^{1}				8	6^{2}	9		12	13	10		11	3	4						13
1	2		5		7				8■	12	9^{3}		14	13	10		11^{2}	3	4	6^{1}					14
1	2			5	6	7	8^{1}			10			13		9	12	11^{2}	3	4						15
1	2		5		6^{2}	7	8^{3}		9^{1}	10			12		11	14	13	3	4						16
1	2		5^{3}	12	6	8	7■		9	11^{1}				14	10^{2}		13	3	4						17
1			5	12	6	8			9	13			11^{1}	2	7		10^{2}	3	4						18
1			5	2	7	8		14	9^{2}	11^{3}	13				10	6^{1}	12	3	4						19
1	2			5	6		7^{3}	14	8	10^{1}				13	9	12	11^{2}	4	3						20
1	2			5	7	8			9	13				12	10	6^{2}	11^{1}	3	4						21
1	2		5		6^{1}		8		9^{2}	13	12			7^{3}	10			3	4	14	11				22
1	2		5	4	6	11	8^{3}		9^{2}		13			14	10^{1}	12		3				7			23
1	2		4	5		7■	6		8		14			13	9^{2}			3			12	10^{3}	11^{1}		24
1	5	3^{3}	4	9^{1}			7^{2}		6	14				12	8			2		13	11		10		25
1	2		5	14					7^{2}	10	9^{1}			12		6		4	3	8^{3}	13		11		26
1	2		4	5	8					13	6^{2}			12	9	7^{3}		3			10^{1}	14	11		27
1	2		4	5	6	8^{2}				10^{1}	12			7	14	9		3			13		11^{3}		28
1	2		4	5	9	7^{2}				10^{1}	12			8		6		3			13		11		29
1	2		3	5	6^{3}	9				13	14			8	10^{1}	7		4			11^{2}		12		30
1	2		4	5	8^{1}	7			13	10	12			9		6^{2}		3^{3}		14			11		31
1	2	4	3	5	6	7			8^{3}	9^{1}	13				12						10	14	11^{2}		32
1	2	4	5			8			7	6	9^{1}			3	10						11	12			33
1	2		4	5		7			9^{1}	6^{2}	12			8	10			3			11	13			34
1	2		4	5		7			9^{3}	6^{2}	12			8^{1}	10	14		3			11		13		35
1^{3}	2		4	5		7				9	6^{1}				10	8		3			11^{2}	12	13	14	36

BERWICK RANGERS

Year Formed: 1881. *Ground & Address:* Shielfield Park, Tweedmouth, Berwick-upon-Tweed TD15 2EF. *Telephone:* 01289 307424. *Fax:* 01289 309424. *Email:* club@berwickrangers.com *Website:* berwickrangers.com
Ground Capacity: 4,131 (seated: 1,366). *Size of Pitch:* 101m × 64m.
Chairman: Len Eyre. *Vice-Chairman:* John Bell. *Football Secretary:* Dennis McCleary.
Manager: John Coughlin. *First-Team Coach:* Myles Allan.
Club Nicknames: 'The Borderers', 'Black and Gold', 'The Wee Gers'.
Previous Grounds: Bull Stob Close, Pier Field, Meadow Field, Union Park, Old Shielfield.
Record Transfer Fee received: £80,000 for John Hughes to Swansea C (November 1989).
Record Transfer Fee paid: £27,000 for Sandy Ross from Cowdenbeath (March 1991).
Record Attendance: 13,283 v Rangers, Scottish Cup 1st rd, 28 January 1967.
Record Victory: 8-1 v Forfar Ath, Division II, 25 December 1965; v Vale of Leithen, Scottish Cup, December 1966.
Record Defeat: 1-9 v Hamilton A, First Division, 9 August 1980.
Most League Appearances: 439: Eric Tait, 1970-87.
Most League Goals in Season (Individual): 33: Ken Bowron, Division II, 1963-64.
Most Goals Overall (Individual): 114: Eric Tait, 1970-87.

BERWICK RANGERS – SPFL LADBROKES LEAGUE TWO 2016–17 LEAGUE RECORD

Match No.	*Date*	*Venue*	*Opponents*	*Result*		*H/T Score*	*Lg Pos.*	*Goalscorers*	*Attendance*
1	Aug 6	A	Arbroath	D	1-1	0-0	6	Thomson ^{69}	502
2	13	H	Annan Ath	W	2-0	1-0	3	Thomson ^{4}, McKenna ^{65}	366
3	20	H	Forfar Ath	L	1-2	0-1	6	Sheerin ^{62}	421
4	27	A	Edinburgh C	W	2-1	0-0	4	Sheerin 2 (1 pen) $^{74 (p), 78}$	408
5	Sept 10	H	Elgin C	L	2-4	1-2	5	Hurst 2 $^{45, 79}$	407
6	17	A	Cowdenbeath	W	2-0	2-0	3	Thomson 2 $^{27, 35}$	327
7	24	A	Montrose	D	0-0	0-0	4		283
8	Oct 1	H	Clyde	D	1-1	1-1	4	Thomson ^{44}	469
9	15	A	Stirling Alb	D	0-0	0-0	5		517
10	29	H	Arbroath	D	1-1	0-1	5	Thomson ^{48}	390
11	Nov 5	H	Cowdenbeath	D	1-1	1-0	5	Rutherford ^{19}	454
12	12	A	Forfar Ath	L	0-2	0-1	5		477
13	19	A	Clyde	L	2-3	0-1	6	Rutherford ^{58}, Hurst ^{62}	546
14	Dec 6	H	Stirling Alb	W	3-2	2-2	5	Hurst ^{7}, Sheerin 2 (1 pen) $^{36 (p), 81}$	302
15	10	A	Elgin C	L	0-6	0-2	6		535
16	17	H	Montrose	L	1-2	0-0	8	McKenna ^{64}	361
17	24	A	Annan Ath	L	1-3	1-3	9	Scullion ^{7}	430
18	31	H	Edinburgh C	L	1-3	0-2	9	Sheerin ^{72}	515
19	Jan 7	A	Cowdenbeath	W	1-0	0-0	8	Thomson ^{84}	343
20	14	A	Arbroath	L	1-4	1-0	9	McKenna ^{13}	539
21	28	A	Montrose	L	1-2	0-0	9	McKenna ^{51}	1222
22	Feb 4	H	Annan Ath	W	4-1	2-1	7	Thomson 3 $^{13, 19, 90}$, Orru ^{87}	355
23	11	A	Stirling Alb	D	2-2	2-0	7	Hamilton ^{6}, Murrell ^{34}	515
24	18	H	Forfar Ath	W	3-2	1-2	6	Lavery ^{10}, Bain (og) ^{70}, Phillips ^{89}	480
25	25	H	Elgin C	L	0-1	0-1	6		403
26	Mar 7	H	Clyde	W	4-3	3-2	7	Phillips ^{16}, Rutherford 2 $^{29, 71}$, Thomson ^{37}	336
27	11	H	Cowdenbeath	L	1-3	0-1	7	Rutherford ^{79}	408
28	15	A	Edinburgh C	D	2-2	1-0	7	Rutherford ^{31}, Thomson ^{80}	423
29	18	H	Arbroath	L	0-2	0-1	7		425
30	25	A	Forfar Ath	W	3-2	1-1	7	Scullion ^{7}, Murrell ^{74}, Rutherford ^{76}	477
31	Apr 1	A	Elgin C	D	2-2	2-1	7	Rutherford ^{41}, Murrell ^{42}	588
32	8	H	Stirling Alb	L	0-1	0-1	7		440
33	15	A	Annan Ath	L	1-2	0-0	9	Thomson ^{68}	460
34	22	H	Montrose	L	0-1	0-1	9		452
35	29	A	Clyde	D	1-1	0-1	9	Fairbairn ^{55}	710
36	May 6	H	Edinburgh C	W	3-2	2-0	8	Lavery ^{16}, Rutherford ^{28}, Verlaque ^{90}	695

Final League Position: 8

Honours
League Champions: Second Division 1978-79. Third Division 2006-07; *Runners-up:* Second Division 1993-94. Third Division 1999-2000, 2005-06.
Scottish Cup: Quarter-finals 1953-54, 1979-80.
League Cup: Semi-finals 1963-64.
League Challenge Cup: Quarter-finals 2004-05.

Club colours: Shirt: Black with gold vertical stripes. Shorts: Black. Socks: Black.

Goalscorers: *League (50):* Thomson 13, Rutherford 9, Sheerin 6 (2 pens), Hurst 4, McKenna 4, Murrell 3, Lavery 2, Phillips 2, Scullion 2, Fairbairn 1, Hamilton 1, Orru 1, Verlaque 1, own goal 1.
William Hill Scottish FA Cup (2): McKenna 1, Rutherford 1.
Betfred Scottish League Cup (3): Fairbairn 1, Mackie 1, Sheerin 1.
IRN-BRU Scottish League Challenge Cup (0).

Walker K 19	Hamilton L 24 + 3	Fairbairn J 18 + 3	Martin B 18	McKinlay K 25 + 2	Thomson S 32 + 1	Stirling B 8 + 3	Notman S 28 + 2	Sheerin J 18 + 2	Walker A 4 + 1	Lavery D 28 + 4	Beveridge G 8 + 5	McKenna M 26 + 1	Wilson R 7 + 2	Orru J 1 + 14	Hogg B — + 5	Hurst G 9 + 1	Bauld E — + 2	Brennan S 14 + 1	Watt D — + 8	Rutherford G 25 + 1	Perez S 1 + 6	Mackie S 2 + 1	Scullion P 21	Phillips G 15 + 2	Dunlop M 1	Spark E 16	Murrell A 11 + 5	MacKay D 4	Kessels R 1 + 5	Donkor R 1	McKirdy S 7 + 2	Verlaque D 3 + 7	Page G 1 + 1	*Match No.*
1	2	3	4	5	6	7	8^{1}	9	10	11	12																							1
1	2	3■	4	5	9^{1}	7	8	10^{3}	6^{2}	14		11	12	13																				2
1	2^{1}		4	5	9	6	7	11	8^{2}	12		10■	3		13																			3
1	2^{3}		3	5	7	6^{2}	8	11	12	9			4	13		10^{1}	14																	4
1		3	4	5^{3}	8^{1}	2	6	11	7^{2}	10	14		12	13		9																		5
1		3	4	9	8		5	11		12	6	7^{1}	2	13		10^{2}																		6
1		3	4	5	8			10		9	6	7	2			11																		7
1^{1}		3		4	8		6	11		9	5	7■	2	13		10^{2}		12																8
1		4	7	5■	6		8	9		10	2		3			11^{1}			12															9
1	5^{2}	3	4		7	13	6^{3}	10^{1}		9	8		2	14		12				11														10
1	2	3	4	5	8■		7■	11^{1}		6	12	9^{2}			13					10														11
1	2^{2}	3	4	5^{3}		7		11^{1}			6	9		12	13	8			14	10														12
1	2	4	3		6	8		9^{2}		11■	5^{1}			14	12	7^{3}			13	10														13
1	2	3		4			6	10^{2}			5	7^{1}			14	9^{3}		11	13	8	12													14
1	2	4	3	5	6^{1}		7	11			12	8		14					13		9^{3}	10^{2}												15
1	2^{1}		4	5	6		7	11		8^{2}	12	9								10	13		3											16
	2		4	5	9^{1}	13	7^{3}	11^{2}		6		8						1		10	14	12	3											17
1	5^{2}	3	4^{3}		7^{1}	6	12	13		11		9								10	14	8	2											18
1	2	4		5^{2}	7^{3}	13	6	12		9		11		14						10^{1}			3	8										19
			4	5	9		6			7		8						1	13	11^{2}	12		3	10	2^{1}									20
	13		4^{2}	5	10^{1}		7			8		6						1		11^{3}	14		3	9		2	12							21
	2			4^{3}	6			11^{2}		7		8		12						10^{1}			3	9		5	13	1	14					22
	7				6					10		8		4^{2}			12			11			3	5		2	9^{1}	1	13					23
	5			14	11					6		9								12			3	8		4	10^{1}	1		2^{2}	7^{3}	13■		24
	2^{3}			12	9^{2}		7			8		6■		14						10			3	5		4	11^{1}	1	13					25
1	5			4	8^{2}		6^{3}			7				12					13	10			3	9		2	11^{1}				14			26
	2	13			10		6			9								1		11			3^{3}	5^{2}		4	12		7^{1}		8	14		27
	2			5	9		13			8								1		11			3	12		4	10				7^{2}	6^{1}		28
	2^{2}	12		5	9		7			8		6						1		10			3	14		4^{1}	11^{3}					13		29
				5			7			8^{1}		6		12				1		10			3	9		4	11^{2}		14		2^{3}	13		30
		12		5^{3}	14		7					6						1		11			3^{2}	9		4	10				8^{1}	2	13	31
	12				9^{2}		7			13		6						1	14	10			3			4	11^{3}				8^{1}	2	5	32
	2			5^{2}	10		8			6		12						1		11			3	9^{1}		4	14				7^{3}	13		33
	5^{1}	2			6^{3}		7^{2}			8		11						1		10			3	9		4	12		13			14		34
		3			6		7			8		9						1		10			4	5		2	11							35
	12	4			9^{3}		7			8		6						1		10^{1}			3	5		2	11^{2}				14	13		36

BRECHIN CITY

Year Formed: 1906. *Ground & Address:* Glebe Park, Trinity Rd, Brechin, Angus DD9 6BJ. *Telephone:* 01356 622856. *Fax:* 01382 206331. *E-mail:* secretary@brechincityfc.com *Website:* www.brechincity.com
Ground Capacity: 4,123 (seated: 1,528). *Size of Pitch:* 101m × 61m.
Chairman: Ken Ferguson. *Vice-Chairman:* Martin Smith. *Secretary:* Gus Fairlie.
Manager: Darren Dods. *Assistant Manager:* Lee Bailey.
Club Nicknames: 'The City', 'The Hedgemen'.
Previous Grounds: Nursery Park.
Record Attendance: 8,122 v Aberdeen, Scottish Cup 3rd rd, 3 February 1973.
Record Transfer Fee received: £100,000 for Scott Thomson to Aberdeen (1991) and Chris Templeman to Morton (2004).
Record Transfer Fee paid: £16,000 for Sandy Ross from Berwick R (1991).
Record Victory: 12-1 v Thornhill, Scottish Cup 1st rd, 28 January 1926.
Record Defeat: 0-10 v Airdrieonians, Albion R and Cowdenbeath, all in Division II, 1937-38.
Most League Appearances: 459: David Watt, 1975-89.
Most League Goals in Season (Individual): 26: Ronald McIntosh, Division II, 1959-60.
Most Goals Overall (Individual): 131: Ian Campbell, 1977-85.

BRECHIN CITY – SPFL LADBROKES LEAGUE ONE 2016–17 LEAGUE RECORD

Match No.	Date	Venue	Opponents	Result	H/T Score	Lg Pos.	Goalscorers	Attendance
1	Aug 6	H	Stenhousemuir	W 2-1	1-0	4	Trouten [35], Caldwell [79]	402
2	13	A	Albion R	W 2-0	1-0	3	Trouten (pen) [29], Jackson, A [49]	228
3	20	H	Queen's Park	D 0-0	0-0	3		447
4	27	A	East Fife	W 2-1	1-1	2	Caldwell [4], Graham [50]	609
5	Sept 10	H	Airdrieonians	W 3-2	1-1	1	Love [10], Jackson, A [68], Hill [78]	466
6	17	A	Livingston	L 1-2	0-1	3	Trouten [72]	858
7	24	H	Peterhead	W 2-1	1-1	2	Love [43], Jackson, A [84]	431
8	Oct 1	A	Stranraer	W 1-0	0-0	1	Jackson, A [75]	402
9	15	H	Alloa Ath	L 0-1	0-0	2		413
10	22	A	Stenhousemuir	W 3-1	0-0	1	Love [60], McLean [62], McCormack [84]	352
11	29	H	Livingston	L 0-3	0-0	2		517
12	Nov 5	A	Peterhead	W 3-1	1-0	2	Caldwell 3 [23, 53, 65]	621
13	12	A	Airdrieonians	L 0-1	0-0	2		739
14	Dec 3	A	Queen's Park	L 0-2	0-1	3		632
15	6	H	Albion R	L 1-2	1-1	3	Stewart I, Ross (og) [25]	283
16	10	H	East Fife	L 0-1	0-1	3		414
17	17	H	Stranraer	W 2-0	2-0	3	Love [15], McLennan [38]	402
18	24	A	Alloa Ath	W 2-1	1-0	2	Trouten (pen) [41], Love [58]	386
19	Jan 2	H	Peterhead	L 0-1	0-0	3		553
20	7	A	Albion R	L 0-1	0-0	4		332
21	28	A	Livingston	L 0-3	0-2	4		746
22	Feb 4	H	Stenhousemuir	D 2-2	1-2	4	Jackson, A [3], Hill [49]	403
23	18	A	East Fife	L 2-3	1-2	6	Jackson, A [34], Dyer [54]	642
24	25	A	Stranraer	L 0-2	0-1	6		340
25	28	H	Queen's Park	W 3-1	2-1	5	Love [8], Hill [26], Jackson, A [90]	393
26	Mar 11	A	Peterhead	W 1-0	0-0	5	Jackson, A [60]	483
27	14	H	Airdrieonians	W 3-0	1-0	4	Love 2 (1 pen) [45 (p), 68], Jackson, A [86]	346
28	18	A	Queen's Park	D 1-1	0-0	4	Jackson, A [84]	481
29	21	H	Alloa Ath	L 1-2	0-1	4	Jackson, A [76]	372
30	25	H	East Fife	W 2-1	1-0	3	Watt [20], Jackson, A [90]	525
31	Apr 1	H	Livingston	L 0-2	0-1	3		523
32	8	A	Airdrieonians	L 1-3	1-2	4	Leitch (og) [45]	676
33	15	A	Alloa Ath	L 1-6	1-2	5	Jackson, A [23]	662
34	22	H	Stranraer	D 0-0	0-0	4		403
35	29	H	Albion R	W 1-0	0-0	4	McLean [46]	422
36	May 6	A	Stenhousemuir	D 1-1	1-0	4	Trouten (pen) [5]	557

Final League Position: 4

Honours
League Champions: Second Division 1982-83, 1989-90, 2004-05. Third Division 2001-02. C Division 1953-54;
Runners-up: Second Division 1992-93, 2002-03. Third Division 1995-96. *Promoted to Championship:* 2016-17 (play-offs).
League Challenge Cup Runners-up: 2002-03.

Club colours: Shirt: Red with black trim. Shorts: Black with red trim. Socks: Black with red trim.

Goalscorers: *League (43):* Jackson A 13, Love 8 (1 pen), Caldwell 5, Trouten 5 (3 pens), Hill 3, McLean 2, Dyer 1, Graham 1, McCormack 1, McLennan 1, Watt 1, own goals 2.
William Hill Scottish FA Cup (0).
Betfred Scottish League Cup (5): Trouten 2 (1 pen), Dyer 1, Jackson A 1, Love 1.
IRN-BRU Scottish League Challenge Cup (5): Jackson A 2, Caldwell 1, Graham 1, Love 1.
Play-Offs (8): Caldwell 2 (1 pen), Watt 2, Dale 1, Ford 1, McLean 1, Trouten 1.

Smith G 34	Rodger G 13 + 5	Hill D 32	Smith E 18	Dyer W 28	Graham F 27 + 5	O'Neil C 19	Dale J 28 + 1	Love A 31 + 3	Trouten A 20 + 6	Jackson A 28 + 1	Caldwell R 11 + 16	McLean P 27 + 2	Fusco G 18 + 3	Lynas A 17 + 9	O'Neil P 2 + 3	Ford E 8 + 9	McCormack D 5 + 5	Spence L 7	Buchanan R 3 + 1	McLennan C 3	Watt L 17	Dods D — + 1	Match No.
1	2	3	4	5	6	7	8	9[1]	10	11	12												1
1	4	3[1]	7	5	8	2[2]	11	9[3]	6	10	12	13	14										2
1	4	3	2	8	6	5	7	10[1]	9	11	12												3
1	4	3	2	8	6[1]	5[2]	7	10		9	11	12		13									4
1[1]	14	4	3	9[3]	7	5[2]	6	8		10	11	2			12	13							5
1		4[3]	3	5	8[1]	7[2]	6	9	13	11	10	2				12	14						6
1		4[3]	2	9	13		7	8[1]	10	11		3		14		5	12	6[2]					7
1		4	2	9			7	8[1]	10[3]	11	13	3		14		5[2]	12	6					8
1		3	4	9	13		6	8[1]	10	11	12	2				5		7[2]					9
1		4	7[3]	8	12		6	11[2]	5	10	13	2				14	3	9[1]					10
1		4	3	9	13		6	8	11	10	12					2[2]	5	7[1]					11
1	12	4	2	8	6		7	10	9		11[1]			13			3[2]	5					12
1	8	4	3	5			7	9	6[1]		10	2■		12				11					13
1	4	3	7	5	13			9[2]	12	14	10[3]		8[1]	6		2			11				14
1	3		4	8	6[2]			12	9[3]	10	13		14	7		5	2		11[1]				15
1	5[1]	4	3	6	8			13	7		11			9		2■	12		10[2]				16
1[3]		4	2	9	6			8[1]	10			5	7	12	13		3[2]		14	11			17
1	12	4	3[2]	5	10			9	6		13	2	8	7						11[1]			18
1	3	4		9	8[2]			10	6		13	2	7	5		12				11[1]			19
1	4			9	7[1]			11	6		10	2	3	5							8	12	20
1	3	4			7	8[1]	12	9		11[2]	13	2	6	5							10		21
1	4	3				8	7	10	12	11		2	6[1]	5							9		22
1	4	2		8	6	3[1]	7		9■	11	12	5				13					10[2]		23
1	12	4		8	5	6[1]	7[2]	9		11		2	3	13							10		24
1		4		5	9	2	7	10[1]		11		3	6	12							8		25
1	12	4[1]		5	10[2]	2	8	9		11		3	7	13							6		26
1		4			8	5	7	10[1]		11		3	6	2		12					9		27
1		4			6[2]	5	8	11		10	13	3	7[1]	2		12					9		28
1		4			9[2]	5	7	10[1]		11	12	3	6	2		13					8		29
1		4			9	5	7			11	10	3	6	2							8		30
1		4			8	5	7	13	12	9	11[1]	3	6[2]	2							10		31
1		3		5	8	4	7	10[2]	13	11	12	2	6[1]								9		32
1■		4			7[1]	3[2]	8	9	14	11	10[3]	2		5	13		12				6		33
				5	8		7	11	6	10		3	4	2	1						9		34
				5			7	10[1]	9	11	12	4	3	2	1	8					6		35
1		4		5	7		6	10[1]	8[2]	11		2	13	3		12					9		36

CELTIC

Year Formed: 1888. *Ground & Address:* Celtic Park, Glasgow G40 3RE. *Telephone:* 0871 226 1888. *Fax:* 0141 551 8106.
E-mail: customerservices@celticfc.co.uk *Website:* www.celticfc.net
Ground Capacity: 60,832 (all seated). *Size of Pitch:* 105m × 68m.
Chairman: Ian Bankier. *Chief Executive:* Peter Lawwell.
Manager: Brendan Rodgers. *Assistant Manager:* Chris Davies. *First Team Coach:* John Kennedy.
Club Nicknames: 'The Bhoys', 'The Hoops', 'The Celts'. *Previous Grounds:* None.
Record Attendance: 92,000 v Rangers, Division I, 1 January 1938.
Record Transfer Fee received: £12,500,000 for Victor Wanyama to Southampton (July 2013).
Record Transfer Fee paid: £6,000,000 for Chris Sutton from Chelsea (July 2000) and for John Hartson from Coventry C (August 2001).
Record Victory: 11-0 Dundee, Division I, 26 October 1895. *Record Defeat:* 0-8 v Motherwell, Division I, 30 April 1937.
Most Capped Player: Pat Bonner 80, Republic of Ireland. *Most League Appearances:* 486: Billy McNeill, 1957-75.
Most League Goals in Season (Individual): 50: James McGrory, Division I, 1935-36.
Most Goals Overall (Individual): 397: James McGrory, 1922-39.

Honours
League Champions: (48 times) Division I 1892-93, 1893-94, 1895-96, 1897-98, 1904-05, 1905-06, 1906-07, 1907-08, 1908-09, 1909-10, 1913-14, 1914-15, 1915-16, 1916-17, 1918-19, 1921-22, 1925-26, 1935-36, 1937-38, 1953-54, 1965-66, 1966-67, 1967-68, 1968-69, 1969-70, 1970-71, 1971-72, 1972-73, 1973-74. Premier Division 1976-77, 1978-79, 1980-81, 1981-82, 1985-86, 1987-88, 1997-98, 2000-01, 2001-02, 2003-04, 2005-06, 2006-07, 2007-08, 2011-12, 2012-13; Premiership 2013-14, 2014-15, 2015-16, 2016-17. *Runners-up:* 31 times.
Scottish Cup Winners: (37 times) 1892, 1899, 1900, 1904, 1907, 1908, 1911, 1912, 1914, 1923, 1925, 1927, 1931, 1933, 1937, 1951, 1954, 1965, 1967, 1969, 1971, 1972, 1974, 1975, 1977, 1980, 1985, 1988, 1989, 1995, 2001, 2004, 2005, 2007, 2011, 2013, 2017.
Runners-up: 18 times.

CELTIC – SPFL LADBROKES PREMIERSHIP 2016–17 LEAGUE RECORD

Match No.	Date	Venue	Opponents	Result	H/T Score	Lg Pos.	Goalscorers	Attendance
1	Aug 7	A	Hearts	W 2-1	1-1	2	Forrest [8], Sinclair [81]	16,777
2	20	A	St Johnstone	W 4-2	3-0	2	Griffiths [28], Sinclair [40], Forrest [44], Christie [90]	6823
3	27	H	Aberdeen	W 4-1	2-1	1	Griffiths [13], Forrest [42], Sinclair (pen) [87], Rogic [90]	57,758
4	Sept 10	H	Rangers	W 5-1	2-1	1	Dembele 3 [33, 42, 83], Sinclair [61], Armstrong [90]	58,348
5	18	A	Inverness CT	D 2-2	2-1	1	Rogic [17], Sinclair [34]	6061
6	24	H	Kilmarnock	W 6-1	2-1	1	Dembele 2 [35, 38], Forrest [52], Griffiths [66], Sinclair (pen) [72], Rogic [85]	53,532
7	Oct 1	A	Dundee	W 1-0	0-0	1	Brown [47]	8827
8	15	H	Motherwell	W 2-0	1-0	1	Sinclair [18], Dembele (pen) [87]	54,159
9	26	A	Ross Co	W 4-0	1-0	1	Roberts [3], Armstrong [83], Dembele [90], Sinclair [90]	6290
10	29	A	Aberdeen	W 1-0	1-0	1	Rogic [23]	17,105
11	Nov 5	H	Inverness CT	W 3-0	0-0	1	Sinclair [48], Griffiths [63], Rogic [83]	54,152
12	18	A	Kilmarnock	W 1-0	1-0	1	Armstrong [44]	10,962
13	Dec 3	A	Motherwell	W 4-3	0-2	1	McGregor [48], Roberts [70], Armstrong [72], Rogic [90]	8535
14	9	A	Partick Thistle	W 4-1	1-0	1	Armstrong 2 [39, 49], Griffiths [50], McGregor [82]	7609
15	13	H	Hamilton A	W 1-0	1-0	1	Griffiths [36]	55,076
16	17	H	Dundee	W 2-1	1-0	1	Griffiths [45], Bitton [57]	37,404
17	20	H	Partick Thistle	W 1-0	1-0	1	Sinclair [16]	55,733
18	24	A	Hamilton A	W 3-0	1-0	1	Griffiths [41], Armstrong [54], Dembele [84]	5003
19	28	H	Ross Co	W 2-0	2-0	1	Sviatchenko [38], Armstrong [45]	55,355
20	31	A	Rangers	W 2-1	1-1	1	Dembele [33], Sinclair [70]	50,126
21	Jan 25	H	St Johnstone	W 1-0	0-0	1	Boyata [72]	51,057
22	29	H	Hearts	W 4-0	1-0	1	McGregor [29], Sinclair 2 (1 pen) [77, 90 (p)], Roberts [80]	58,247
23	Feb 1	H	Aberdeen	W 1-0	0-0	1	Boyata [57]	53,958
24	5	A	St Johnstone	W 5-2	1-2	1	Henderson [6], Dembele 3 (1 pen) [61 (p), 75, 85], Sinclair [81]	6548
25	18	H	Motherwell	W 2-0	2-0	1	Dembele (pen) [34], Forrest [41]	56,366
26	25	H	Hamilton A	W 2-0	1-0	1	Dembele 2 (1 pen) [45, 59 (p)]	54,685
27	Mar 1	A	Inverness CT	W 4-0	1-0	1	Sinclair [43], Dembele 2 [46, 73], Armstrong [66]	5948
28	12	H	Rangers	D 1-1	1-0	1	Armstrong [35]	58,545
29	19	A	Dundee	W 2-1	1-0	1	Simunovic [45], Armstrong [52]	8968
30	Apr 2	A	Hearts	W 5-0	2-0	1	Sinclair 3 (1 pen) [24, 27, 84 (p)], Armstrong [55], Roberts [61]	16,539
31	5	H	Partick Thistle	D 1-1	0-0	1	Sinclair [50]	54,047
32	8	H	Kilmarnock	W 3-1	1-0	1	Armstrong [22], Sinclair [71], Forrest [76]	57,679
33	16	A	Ross Co	D 2-2	1-0	1	Tierney [34], Roberts [78]	6205
34	29	A	Rangers	W 5-1	2-0	1	Sinclair (pen) [7], Griffiths [18], McGregor [52], Boyata [66], Lustig [87]	49,822
35	May 6	H	St Johnstone	W 4-1	0-0	1	Roberts 2 [47, 62], Boyata [52], McGregor [71]	52,796
36	12	A	Aberdeen	W 3-1	3-1	1	Boyata [3], Armstrong [8], Griffiths [11]	16,015
37	18	A	Partick Thistle	W 5-0	3-0	1	Griffiths (pen) [18], Rogic [26], Roberts 2 [41, 84], McGregor [82]	7847
38	21	H	Hearts	W 2-0	0-0	1	Griffiths [50], Armstrong [76]	58,967

Final League Position: 1

League Cup Winners: (16 times) 1956-57, 1957-58, 1965-66, 1966-67, 1967-68, 1968-69, 1969-70, 1974-75, 1982-83, 1997-98, 1999-2000, 2000-01, 2005-06, 2008-09, 2014-15, 2016-17; *Runners-up:* 15 times.

European: *European Cup/Champions League:* 188 matches (1966-67 winners, 1967-68, 1968-69, 1969-70 runners-up, 1970-71, 1971-72, 1972-73, 1973-74 semi-finals, 1974-75, 1977-78, 1979-80, 1981-82, 1982-83, 1986-87, 1988-89, 1998-99, 2001-02, 2002-03, 2003-04, 2004-05, 2005-06, 2006-07, 2007-08, 2008-09, 2009-10, 2010-11, 2012-13, 2013-14, 2014-15, 2015-16, 2016-17). *Cup Winners' Cup:* 38 matches (1963-64 semi-finals, 1965-66 semi-finals, 1975-76, 1980-81, 1984-85, 1985-86, 1989-90, 1995-96). *UEFA Cup:* 75 matches (*Fairs Cup:* 1962-63, 1964-65. *UEFA Cup:* 1976-77, 1983-84, 1987-88, 1991-92, 1992-93, 1993-94, 1996-97, 1997-98, 1998-99, 1999-2000, 2000-01, 2001-02, 2002-03 runners-up, 2003-04 quarter-finals). *Europa League:* 30 matches (2009-10, 2010-11, 2011-12, 2014-15, 2015-16).

Club colours: Shirt: Green and white hoops. Shorts: White. Socks: White with green hoop.

Goalscorers: *League (106):* Sinclair 21 (5 pens), Dembele 17 (4 pens), Armstrong 15, Griffiths 12 (1 pen), Roberts 9, Rogic 7, Forrest 6, McGregor 6, Boyata 5, Bitton 1, Brown 1, Christie 1, Henderson 1, Lustig 1, Simunovic 1, Sviatchenko 1, Tierney 1.
William Hill Scottish FA Cup (17): Dembele 5, Sinclair 3 (1 pen), Armstrong 2, Lustig 2, Brown 1, Griffiths 1, McGregor 1, Rogic 1, Tierney 1.
Betfred Scottish League Cup (11): Dembele 5 (2 pens), Rogic 3, Forrest 2, Sinclair 1.
IRN-BRU Scottish League Challenge Cup (8): Aitchison 2, Crossan 2, Hendry 2, Nesbitt 2.
UEFA Champions League (16): Dembele 5 (2 pens), Griffiths 5 (1 pen), Roberts 2, Brown 1, Lustig 1, Rogic 1, own goal 1.

Gordon C 34 + 1	Tierney K 24	O'Connell E 2	Toure K 5 + 4	Lustig M 28 + 1	McGregor C 20 + 11	Armstrong S 25 + 6	Brown S 33	Forrest J 23 + 5	Griffiths L 15 + 8	Dembele M 20 + 9	Sinclair S 30 + 5	Rogic T 15 + 7	Janko S 1 + 1	Bitton N 16 + 10	Henderson L 5 + 5	Christie R 3 + 2	De Vries D 4	Sviatchenko E 23 + 5	Roberts P 20 + 12	Gamboa C 13 + 4	Simunovic J 24 + 1	Izaguirre E 10 + 2	Boyata D 17	Mackay-Steven G 4 + 4	Miller C 1	Aitchison J — + 2	Ciftci N — + 1	Eboue K 1 + 3	Ralston A 1	Johnston M 1	*Match No.*
1	2	3[3]	4	5	6	7[1]	8	9	10[2]	11	12	13	14																		1
1	5	4	3				6	8[2]	11[1]	12	10	9	2	7[3]	13	14															2
	5		3	2	14		6	8[3]	11[1]	13	10	9		7[2]			1	4	12												3
	5		4	2	14	12	6[3]	8[1]		11	10	9[2]		7			1	3	13												4
	5			4	9	14	8	13		11	10	7[2]					1	3	6[1]	2[3]	12										5
12	5			2			6	10	13	11[1]	8[3]	9		7			1[2]	3	14		4										6
1	5			2		14	6	8[3]	12	11	10[2]	9[1]		7				4	13		3										7
1	5		14			8[1]	7	9[3]	12	10	11				6			4	13	2[2]	3										8
1				3	6	10			11[3]	12	13			14	7[2]	9[1]		4	8	2		5									9
1				5[3]		9	7	10[1]		11	8	6[2]		12				4	13	14	3	2									10
1				2[1]	8	7	6[3]		10	11[2]	9	14		13				4	5		3	12									11
1				2	8	7	6	9[2]		10	11	12		13				4	5[1]				3								12
1			4	2	12	6	7	10[3]		11		9		13					8[1]	14	3	5[2]									13
1				4	13	8	6		11	14		9[2]				12		3	10[3]	5		2		7[1]							14
1				2	9[2]	8	7		10	11[1]		6		13				4	5		3			12							15
1					12	7			11[3]	14	13	9[2]		8		6		4		2	3	5		10[1]							16
1				3	9	13	8		14	11[1]	10[2]				7				6	2	4	12			5[3]						17
1				3	9■	7	6	14	11[3]	12	10[1]			13				4	8[2]	2		5									18
1				2		8	7	9[2]	10[1]	13	11				12	6[3]		3	14		4	5									19
1				5	9[1]	6	7	10[2]		11	8			13				3	12		4	2									20
1	5					9	6	8[3]	13	11[2]	10			7				14	12	2[1]	3		4								21
1	5			13	8		6	9[2]			10			7	12				11[1]	2[3]	3		4			14					22
1	5			2	6[2]		7	9[1]			11			8	13			14	10[3]		4		3	12							23
1	5			2	13		7			12	11			6	9[2]			4	8[1]				3	10[3]			14				24
1	5			2	13	12	7	8		11	10			6[2]	9[1]						4		3								25
1	5				14	9[1]	7	8[3]	13	11[2]	10			6				4		2			3	12							26
1	5			2	12	9	6[2]			11	10			7	13			4					3	8[1]							27
1	5			2	12	9[2]	7	8[3]	14	11	10			6[1]				4	13				3								28
1	5			2	6[3]	7	8	9[1]		11	10[2]							14	13		4		3					12			29
1	5		14	2[2]	8	6	7	11			9								10[1]	13	3		4[3]	12							30
1				2	8[2]	12					10	13		7				4	11	5	3	9[1]				14		6[3]			31
1	5			2	7[2]	9[1]	6	8		12	10	13							11[3]		3		4					14			32
1	4				6	7	8■	5[3]	13	11[1]	10	9[2]						3	14	12	2										33
1	5			2	9	7[2]	6[1]	12	11		10	13							8[3]		3		4					14			34
1	5				13	7		14	11		12	9[2]		6					8[1]		3		4						2	10[3]	35
1	5			2[3]	9	6		13	11[2]		10	7[1]		12				14	8		3		4								36
1			13		7		6	10[2]	11[1]		12	9		14				3	8	2		5	4[3]								37
1	5		13		9	7[2]	6		11		10	12						14	8	2[1]	3[3]		4								38

CLYDE

Year Formed: 1877. *Ground & Address:* Broadwood Stadium, Cumbernauld, G68 9NE. *Telephone:* 01236 451511. *Fax:* 01236 733490. *E-mail:* info@clydefc.co.uk *Website:* www.clydefc.co.uk
Ground Capacity: 8,006 (all seated). *Size of Pitch:* 100m × 68m.
Chairman: Norrie Innes. *Vice Chairman:* John Taylor. *Secretary:* Gordon Thomson.
Manager: Jim Chapman. *Assistant Manager:* John Joyce.
Club Nickname: 'The Bully Wee'.
Previous Grounds: Barrowfield Park 1877-98, Shawfield Stadium 1898-1986, Firhill Stadium 1986-91, Douglas Park 1991-94.
Record Attendance: 52,000 v Rangers, Division I, 21 November 1908.
Record Transfer Fee received: £200,000 from Blackburn R for Gordon Greer (May 2001).
Record Transfer Fee paid: £14,000 for Harry Hood from Sunderland (1966).
Record Victory: 11-1 v Cowdenbeath, Division II, 6 October 1951.
Record Defeat: 0-11 v Dumbarton, Scottish Cup 4th rd, 22 November, 1879; v Rangers, Scottish Cup 4th rd, 13 November 1880.
Most Capped Player: Tommy Ring, 12, Scotland.
Most League Appearances: 420: Brian Ahern, 1971-81; 1987-88.
Most League Goals in Season (Individual): 32: Bill Boyd, 1932-33.
Most Goals Overall (Individual): 124: Tommy Ring, 1950-60.

CLYDE – SPFL LADBROKES LEAGUE TWO 2016–17 LEAGUE RECORD

Match No.	Date	Venue	Opponents	Result		H/T Score	Lg Pos.	Goalscorers	Attendance
1	Aug 6	H	Montrose	W	2-1	1-0	3	Easton [25], Flynn [75]	445
2	13	A	Stirling Alb	D	1-1	0-0	4	Higgins [73]	777
3	20	A	Annan Ath	L	2-3	0-1	7	MacDonald 2 [51, 77]	421
4	27	H	Cowdenbeath	W	5-3	3-2	3	Smith 2 [13, 73], Higgins 2 [33, 59], Sives (og) [43]	538
5	Sept 10	H	Arbroath	W	3-2	2-2	2	Linton [6], McNiff [24], MacDonald [71]	559
6	17	A	Elgin C	W	2-0	2-0	2	Higgins [2], MacDonald [41]	713
7	24	H	Forfar Ath	L	0-1	0-1	2		660
8	Oct 1	A	Berwick R	D	1-1	1-1	2	Higgins [18]	469
9	15	A	Edinburgh C	W	1-0	0-0	3	Higgins [70]	438
10	29	H	Stirling Alb	D	1-1	1-1	3	MacDonald [29]	738
11	Nov 5	H	Elgin C	W	2-1	2-0	3	Gormley [2], MacDonald [6]	616
12	12	A	Arbroath	L	0-4	0-1	4		615
13	19	H	Berwick R	W	3-2	1-0	2	MacDonald [23], Gormley [54], Smith [81]	546
14	Dec 3	A	Cowdenbeath	L	0-1	0-0	3		309
15	10	A	Montrose	L	1-2	0-1	4	MacDonald (pen) [52]	396
16	17	H	Edinburgh C	D	0-0	0-0	4		461
17	26	A	Forfar Ath	L	3-4	2-1	4	McNeil [20], Gormley [43], MacDonald (pen) [68]	659
18	31	H	Annan Ath	L	2-3	1-0	4	MacDonald 2 (1 pen) [12, 80 (p)]	467
19	Jan 7	A	Stirling Alb	L	0-3	0-1	5		718
20	28	H	Arbroath	L	1-2	0-1	6	MacDonald [65]	465
21	Feb 4	A	Edinburgh C	D	0-0	0-0	6		302
22	18	A	Elgin C	L	1-4	0-1	7	Higgins [76]	881
23	25	A	Annan Ath	L	0-1	0-0	8		398
24	28	H	Montrose	L	1-2	0-2	9	MacDonald [74]	365
25	Mar 4	H	Forfar Ath	D	2-2	0-1	8	MacDonald (pen) [53], Gormley [61]	490
26	7	A	Berwick R	L	3-4	2-3	8	Smith [32], Scullion (og) [35], Gormley [82]	336
27	11	A	Arbroath	L	0-1	0-1	9		566
28	18	H	Edinburgh C	W	3-1	0-1	8	Flynn [51], MacDonald 2 [57, 77]	484
29	21	H	Cowdenbeath	L	0-2	0-1	9		395
30	25	H	Stirling Alb	L	2-3	1-0	9	MacDonald [25], Gormley (pen) [63]	606
31	Apr 1	A	Cowdenbeath	L	0-1	0-0	9		460
32	8	H	Annan Ath	W	2-1	1-1	9	Smith [4], Gormley [81]	462
33	15	H	Elgin C	W	3-2	0-2	8	Goodwillie 3 [52, 57, 64]	465
34	22	A	Forfar Ath	L	0-3	0-1	8		741
35	29	H	Berwick R	D	1-1	1-0	8	Gormley (pen) [33]	710
36	May 6	A	Montrose	D	1-1	1-0	9	Goodwillie [26]	1324

Final League Position: 9

Honours
League Champions: Division II 1904-05, 1951-52, 1956-57, 1961-62, 1972-73. Second Division 1977-78, 1981-82, 1992-93, 1999-2000.
Runners-up: Division II 1903-04, 1905-06, 1925-26, 1963-64. First Division 2002-03, 2003-04.
Scottish Cup Winners: 1939, 1955, 1958; *Runners-up:* 1910, 1912, 1949.
League Challenge Cup Runners-up: 2006-07.

Club colours: Shirt: White with red trim. Shorts: Black. Socks: Red.

Goalscorers: *League (49):* MacDonald 17 (4 pens), Gormley 8 (2 pens), Higgins 7, Smith 5, Goodwillie 4, Flynn 2, Easton 1, Linton 1, McNeil 1, McNiff 1, own goals 2.
William Hill Scottish FA Cup (14): Gormley 8, MacDonald 4 (2 pens), Flynn 1, McLaughlin 1.
Betfred Scottish League Cup (4): Easton 1 (1 pen), MacDonald 1, McNeil 1, Watson 1.
IRN-BRU Scottish League Challenge Cup (0).

Gibson J 25	McNeil E 33	McNiff M 30 + 1	Oliver M 4 + 1	Lowdon J 3	Linton S 21 + 2	Easton D 5	McLaughlin S 35 + 1	Johnston P 29 + 2	Gormley D 28 + 7	MacDonald P 30 + 1	Flynn M 20 + 9	Higgins S 24 + 7	Smith C 25 + 3	Marsh D — + 1	Watson J — + 2	Ferguson S 7 + 17	Perry R 20 + 1	Tiffoney S 3 + 3	Miller D 4 + 2	Long B 1	Millar A — + 5	McMillan J 11	McKenzie M 5 + 6	Finnie R 3 + 4	Quinn C 3	Lochhead S 2 + 2	McMillan M 1	Rutkiewicz K 1 + 1	Gourlay K 6	Waddell K 6	Intakie K 1	Goodwillie D 5 + 1	McGovern J 5	*Match No.*
1	2	3	4^{1}	5	6	7	8	9	10	11	12																							1
1	2	3		5	6	7	8	9	10^{1}	11	4	12																						2
1	3	4		5^{2}	7	9	6	2	13	10	8^{1}	11^{3}	12	14																				3
1	2	3	4		7	8	6		13	10^{1}	9	11^{2}	5		12																			4
1	3	4			9	8	7	2^{1}	13	11	6^{3}	10^{2}	5			12	14																	5
1	6	5■			8		7	2	12	11^{2}	9	10^{1}	4			13	3																	6
1	5				9		8	2	10^{2}	11	7^{1}	6	3		13	12	4																	7
1	2	5			9		8	6	13	11	7^{1}	10^{2}	3			12	4																	8
1	2	5			9		7	6^{1}	10^{2}	11	13	8	4			12	3																	9
1	9	4^{2}			8		7	5	12	10	6^{1}	11	3			13	2																	10
1	2	5	13		7		6	8	10^{2}	11		9	4			12	3^{1}																	11
1	5	3			8		7	2	9^{2}	10^{1}	14	11	4			13		6^{3}	12															12
1	2				6		7	3^{1}	11^{2}	9	14	10	13			12	4	8^{3}	5															13
1	2	4					7		9	10		11	5			12	3	8^{1}	6															14
1	2	3			8^{1}		6		9	10		11	4			12	5	13	7^{2}															15
1	2	3			8		6^{1}	12	9	10		11^{2}	4			7^{3}	5	13	14															16
1	2	3			8		6	7	11	10	9		4				5																	17
1	7		3		5		8	2	10	11	6^{1}					12	4	13	9^{2}															18
	2	5	4		9^{2}		7^{1}	6	10	11	12	8					3			1	13													19
1	2	4					8		9	11^{1}	13	10^{2}	3			12						5	6	7■										20
1	4	5					8	2	11	10^{2}	12	9^{1}	3								13	6	7											21
		5^{1}			12		14	2	11^{2}	10	7^{3}	8	4			13	3					9■	6		1									22
	3				5		6	2	11^{1}	10		8	4			7							9	12	1									23
1	2	12			5		9	14	13	11		8	4^{1}			7^{2}	3					6	10^{3}											24
1	2	4			14		8	9	10	11	12		13			6^{1}	5					3^{3}		7^{2}										25
1	2	5			9^{1}		7	6	10		8	11^{2}	4				3				13		12											26
1	2	5					7	9^{2}	10^{3}	11	8^{1}	12				6	4					3	14			13								27
	7	5					9	2	11	10^{1}	8	12	4			6^{2}						3	13		1									28
	5						8	9^{2}		11	7	10	4			6					14	3^{3}	12	2^{1}			1	13						29
1		9					8	5	11	10	7^{1}	13	4				2^{3}				14			12		6^{2}		3						30
		9					8	5	10	11^{1}	6^{3}					14						4		12		7^{2}			1	2	3	13		31
	4	9					6	5	10		8^{1}	13	3													12			1	2		11^{2}	7	32
	6	3					8	5^{2}	11		9	13	4			12													1	2		10^{1}	7	33
	6^{2}	3					8		11^{1}		9	14				12	4^{3}					5		13					1	2		10	7	34
	3	9					7	5	10^{1}	14	13	8^{2}	4										12						1	2^{3}		11	6	35
	5	4					8	6^{1}	10			9										3	12						1	2		11	7	36

COWDENBEATH

Year Formed: 1882. *Ground & Address:* Central Park, Cowdenbeath KY4 9QQ. *Telephone:* 01383 610166. *Fax:* 01383 512132.
E-mail: office@cowdenbeathfc.com *Website:* www.cowdenbeathfc.com
Ground Capacity: 4,370 (seated: 1,431). *Size of Pitch:* 95m × 60m.
Chairman: Donald Findlay QC. *Finance Director:* David Allan. *Operations:* John Cameron.
Club Nicknames: 'The Blue Brazil', 'Cowden', 'The Miners'.
Manager: Billy Brown. *First-Team Coach:* Neil Irvine.
Previous Grounds: North End Park.
Record Attendance: 25,586 v Rangers, League Cup quarter-final, 21 September 1949.
Record Transfer Fee received: £30,000 for Nicky Henderson to Falkirk (March 1994).
Record Victory: 12-0 v Johnstone, Scottish Cup 1st rd, 21 January 1928.
Record Defeat: 1-11 v Clyde, Division II, 6 October 1951; 0-10 v Hearts, Championship, 28 February 2015.
Most Capped Player: Jim Paterson, 3, Scotland.
Most League and Cup Appearances: 491, Ray Allan 1972-75, 1979-89.
Most League Goals in Season (Individual): 54, Rab Walls, Division II, 1938-39.
Most Goals Overall (Individual): 127, Willie Devlin, 1922-26, 1929-30.

COWDENBEATH – SPFL LADBROKES LEAGUE TWO 2016–17 LEAGUE RECORD

Match No.	Date	Venue	Opponents	Result		H/T Score	Lg Pos.	Goalscorers	Attendance
1	Aug 6	H	Elgin C	L	0-1	0-0	10		315
2	13	A	Forfar Ath	L	3-4	1-2	9	Sives [17], Todorov [59], Moore [80]	516
3	20	H	Edinburgh C	W	2-0	1-0	8	Renton, K [34], Moore [88]	325
4	27	A	Clyde	L	3-5	2-3	8	Brett (pen) [31], Ross, B [42], Gormley (og) [85]	538
5	Sept 10	A	Montrose	W	2-1	1-1	7	Glen [45], Renton, K [54]	393
6	17	H	Berwick R	L	0-2	0-2	7		327
7	24	A	Arbroath	D	0-0	0-0	7		558
8	Oct 1	H	Stirling Alb	L	0-2	0-1	9		342
9	15	H	Annan Ath	D	2-2	0-2	9	Miller [51], Todorov [81]	331
10	29	A	Elgin C	L	1-3	0-2	9	Ross, B [87]	650
11	Nov 5	A	Berwick R	D	1-1	0-1	8	Muirhead [90]	454
12	12	H	Montrose	W	2-0	1-0	8	Todorov (pen) [20], Renton, K [57]	270
13	19	A	Edinburgh C	D	1-1	1-0	8	Renton, K [38]	311
14	Dec 3	H	Clyde	W	1-0	0-0	6	Renton, K [86]	309
15	10	A	Annan Ath	L	0-2	0-1	8		241
16	17	H	Forfar Ath	L	3-4	1-2	10	Mullen 2 [27, 56], Renton, K [68]	277
17	24	H	Arbroath	L	0-2	0-0	10		317
18	31	A	Stirling Alb	W	2-1	0-0	8	Renton, K [50], Moore [64]	538
19	Jan 7	H	Berwick R	L	0-1	0-0	10		343
20	21	A	Montrose	L	1-2	0-1	10	Brett [85]	432
21	28	A	Forfar Ath	L	1-3	1-0	10	Carrick [17]	547
22	Feb 18	H	Annan Ath	L	0-1	0-0	10		258
23	25	A	Arbroath	L	1-4	0-2	10	Rumsby [90]	519
24	28	H	Edinburgh C	L	1-2	1-1	10	Carrick [12]	309
25	Mar 4	H	Stirling Alb	L	0-2	0-1	10		381
26	11	A	Berwick R	W	3-1	1-0	10	Buchanan [16], Ross, B [46], Renton, K [67]	408
27	14	H	Elgin C	D	1-1	0-1	10	Carrick [54]	278
28	18	H	Montrose	L	0-2	0-1	10		302
29	21	A	Clyde	W	2-0	1-0	10	Miller [43], Syme [51]	395
30	25	A	Annan Ath	L	0-1	0-0	10		386
31	Apr 1	H	Clyde	W	1-0	0-0	10	Carrick [52]	460
32	8	A	Edinburgh C	D	1-1	0-1	10	Renton, K [90]	567
33	15	A	Stirling Alb	W	3-0	2-0	10	Carrick 2 [4, 68], Renton, K [21]	638
34	22	H	Arbroath	L	1-2	0-1	10	Rumsby [62]	501
35	29	H	Forfar Ath	D	1-1	0-0	10	Buchanan [47]	571
36	May 6	A	Elgin C	D	0-0	0-0	10		909

Final League Position: 10

Honours
League Champions: Division II 1913-14, 1914-15, 1938-39. Second Division 2011-12. Third Division 2005-06. *Runners-up:* Division II 1921-22, 1923-24, 1969-70. Second Division 1991-92. Third Division 2000-01, 2008-09. *Promoted to First Division:* 2009-10 (play-offs).
Scottish Cup: Quarter-finals 1931.
League Cup: Semi-finals 1959-60, 1970-71.

Club colours: Shirt: Royal blue with white trim. Shorts: White. Socks: Red.

Goalscorers: *League (40):* Renton K 10, Carrick 6, Moore 3, Ross B 3, Todorov 3 (1 pen), Brett 2 (1 pen), Buchanan 2, Miller 2, Mullen 2, Rumsby 2, Glen 1, Muirhead 1, Sives 1, Syme 1, own goal 1.
William Hill Scottish FA Cup (0).
Betfred Scottish League Cup (4): Brett 1, Johnston 1, Todorov 1, Turner 1.
IRN-BRU Scottish League Challenge Cup (1): Todorov 1.
Play-Offs (1): Mullen 1.

McGurn D 21	Mullen F 31 + 2	Ross G 5	Sives C 8	Rutherford S 24 + 3	Brett D 19	O'Brien B 10 + 2	Turner C 7 + 2	Miller K 26 + 5	Todorov N 17 + 2	Glen G 6 + 5	Moore L 21 + 11	Ross B 19 + 6	Johnston C 8 + 8	Renton K 32	McLauchlan G 25	Creaney J 5 + 1	Robertson David 2 + 5	Murrell A — + 5	Pyper J 22	Renton G 1	Muirhead C 2 + 13	Swan H — + 1	Henderson L 17	Rumsby S 16	Carrick D 16	Sneddon J 15	Buchanan R 10 + 2	Rooney M 1 + 1	Syme D 10	*Match No.*
1	2^{3}	3	4	5	6	7^{1}	8^{2}	9	10	11	12	13	14																	1
1	2	4	3	5	8		9		10^{1}	11	6	7	12																	2
1	6	3	4	5	2		8	12	10	13	9	7^{1}		11^{2}																3
1	6	7	4	5	2		10^{2}	13	12	8^{1}	9	3		11																4
1	3				2		12	7	10	9^{1}		8		11	4	5	6^{2}	13												5
1	2				6		13	9^{3}	3	10	12	8^{1}		11	4	5	7^{2}	14												6
1	7		3		2		9		10^{1}	12	6	8		11	4	5														7
1	2		3		6^{1}		8^{3}	12	10^{2}	13	9	7		11	4	5		14												8
1	6		3	5		8		7	13	10^{1}		9			4			12	2	11^{2}										9
1	2		3			7^{1}	6	9^{2}	11		5^{3}	13		10		8	12	14	4											10
1					2	8		5	11^{2}		6	7^{1}	9	10	3		12		4		13									11
1	13				2	7^{1}		5	10		9^{2}	8	6^{3}	11	3	14			4		12									12
1	12	8			2	7^{1}		5	11		9		6^{2}	10	3				4		13									13
1	7			13	2			5	10		9^{1}	8	6^{2}	11	4				3		12									14
1	7			14	2^{3}			5	10		9	8^{2}	6^{1}	11	4		13		3		12									15
1	7			12	2			8	3		9	6	13	11	5				4^{2}		10^{1}									16
1	7			5	2			8	3		9	6^{1}	13	11	4		12				10^{2}									17
1	3			7	2			8	10		6	5	9^{1}	11	4		12													18
1				5	2	8^{2}		7	3		9	6	10^{1}	11	4						13	12								19
1	6			5	8			9			10		11^{1}	7	3						12		2	4						20
1	8			5	2^{1}	12		7			9			10					3				6	4	11					21
	2			5				6			8^{2}	13		10	4								7^{1}	3	11	1	9	12		22
	2					13		7			6^{1}	12		9^{2}	4						14		8	3	11	1	10	5^{3}		23
	7■			5							12	9		11	3				2				8	4	10	1	6^{1}			24
				5				12			9^{1}	8^{2}		11	4				2		13		7	3	10	1	6			25
	7			5						14	13	8	12	11^{3}	4				2				9	3	10^{1}	1	6^{2}			26
	7			5							12			10	4				6				9	3	11	1	8^{1}		2	27
	8			5				14			12		13	10	4				2				9^{1}	3	11	1	6^{3}		7^{2}	28
	8			5				6				12		11	4				2		13		9^{1}	3	10^{2}	1			7	29
	8^{2}			5				7		12	13			11	4				2				9^{3}	3	10^{1}	1	14		6	30
	6			5				8^{1}				12		11	3				2				9	4	10	1			7	31
	2			5		8^{1}		7			12		14	10					3		13		9^{3}		11	1	6^{2}		4	32
	4^{1}			9		8		7			12			11					5				6	3	10	1			2	33
	6			5		8^{2}		7			10^{3}		12						2		14		9^{1}	4	11	1	13		3	34
	7			5■				8			12			11					2				9	4	10	1	6		3^{1}	35
	7^{1}			5				8			12			11					2		13		9	4	10	1	6^{2}		3	36

DUMBARTON

Year Formed: 1872. *Ground:* Dumbarton Football Stadium, Castle Road, Dumbarton G82 1JJ. *Telephone/Fax:* 01389 762569. *E-mail:* enquiries@dumbartonfc.com *Website:* www.dumbartonfootballclub.com
Ground Capacity: total: 2,025 (all seated). *Size of Pitch:* 98m × 67m.
Chairman: Les Hope. *Vice-Chairman:* Colin Hosie.
Manager: Stephen Aitken. *Assistant Manager:* Ian Durrant.
Club Nickname: 'The Sons', 'Sons of the Rock'.
Previous Grounds: Broadmeadow, Ropework Lane, Townend Ground, Boghead Park, Cliftonhill Stadium.
Record Attendance: 18,000 v Raith R, Scottish Cup, 2 March 1957.
Record Transfer Fee received: £300,000 for Neill Collins to Sunderland (July 2004).
Record Transfer Fee paid: £50,000 for Charlie Gibson from Stirling Alb (1989).
Record Victory: 13-1 v Kirkintilloch Central, Scottish Cup 1st rd, 1 September 1888.
Record Defeat: 1-11 v Albion R, Division II, 30 January 1926: v Ayr U, League Cup, 13 August 1952.
Most Capped Player: James McAulay, 9, Scotland.
Most League Appearances: 298: Andy Jardine, 1957-67.
Most Goals in Season (Individual): 38: Kenny Wilson, Division II, 1971-72. *(League and Cup):* 46 Hughie Gallacher, 1955-56.
Most Goals Overall (Individual): 202: Hughie Gallacher, 1954-62

DUMBARTON – SPFL LADBROKES CHAMPIONSHIP 2016–17 LEAGUE RECORD

Match No.	Date	Venue	Opponents	Result		H/T Score	Lg Pos.	Goalscorers	Attendance
1	Aug 6	A	Dunfermline Ath	L	3-4	1-2	8	Thomson, R [18], Docherty 2 (2 pens) [90, 90]	3496
2	13	H	Dundee U	W	1-0	0-0	5	Docherty (pen) [54]	1475
3	20	A	Greenock Morton	D	1-1	1-0	5	Gaston (og) [28]	1586
4	27	A	Falkirk	L	0-1	0-0	5		4311
5	Sept 10	H	Hibernian	L	0-1	0-1	6		1339
6	17	H	St Mirren	D	1-1	1-1	6	Stirling [15]	1101
7	24	A	Raith R	L	2-3	0-3	9	Stevenson [71], Thomson, R [77]	1636
8	Oct 1	H	Queen of the South	D	0-0	0-0	9		840
9	15	H	Ayr U	L	0-3	0-1	9		1005
10	22	A	Dundee U	L	1-2	0-0	9	Thomson, R [73]	5979
11	29	H	Dunfermline Ath	D	2-2	1-0	9	Thomson, J [37], Fleming [82]	1018
12	Nov 5	A	St Mirren	W	1-0	0-0	8	Fleming [63]	2758
13	12	H	Greenock Morton	L	0-2	0-0	8		1147
14	19	H	Raith R	D	0-0	0-0	8		600
15	Dec 3	A	Queen of the South	W	2-1	2-0	8	Stevenson [32], Fleming (pen) [42]	1261
16	10	A	Hibernian	L	0-2	0-1	9		13,881
17	17	H	Falkirk	W	2-1	1-0	7	Muirhead (og) [44], Fleming [68]	832
18	24	A	Ayr U	D	4-4	1-2	7	Thomson, R [45], Harvie [52], Thomson, J [84], Stevenson [88]	1441
19	31	H	Dundee U	W	1-0	1-0	6	Docherty [27]	1221
20	Jan 7	A	Greenock Morton	L	1-2	0-1	8	Stirling [69]	2094
21	14	H	Hibernian	L	0-1	0-1	8		1523
22	21	H	Queen of the South	L	1-2	0-1	8	Nade [61]	825
23	28	A	Raith R	W	3-1	0-1	8	Nade [49], Harvie [57], Buchanan [63]	1413
24	Feb 4	H	St Mirren	D	2-2	0-1	8	Nade [56], Thomson, R [80]	1377
25	18	H	Ayr U	D	2-2	0-0	7	Stanton 2 [62, 75]	1198
26	25	A	Falkirk	D	2-2	1-1	6	Vaughan [38], Stirling [51]	4160
27	Mar 4	A	Dunfermline Ath	L	1-5	0-2	7	Harvie [86]	3320
28	11	H	Raith R	W	4-0	2-0	7	Thomson, R 2 [6, 44], Stanton [47], Fleming [90]	719
29	18	A	Hibernian	D	2-2	1-0	8	Nade (pen) [37], Thomson, R [62]	14,093
30	25	A	Ayr U	L	1-2	1-1	8	Thomson, R [21]	1608
31	Apr 1	H	Greenock Morton	W	1-0	0-0	7	Vaughan [59]	1323
32	8	A	St Mirren	D	1-1	1-1	7	Vaughan [37]	3906
33	15	H	Dunfermline Ath	L	0-2	0-0	9		1142
34	22	A	Queen of the South	W	2-1	2-1	7	Stanton [20], Thomson, R [39]	1289
35	29	A	Dundee U	D	2-2	1-1	7	Thomson, R [35], Vaughan [65]	5107
36	May 6	H	Falkirk	L	0-1	0-0	8		1660

Final League Position: 8

Honours
League Champions: Division I 1890-91 (shared with Rangers), 1891-92. Division II 1910-11, 1971-72. Second Division 1991-92. Third Division 2008-09.
Runners-up: First Division 1983-84. Division II 1907-08. Second Division 1994-95. Third Division 2001-02.
Scottish Cup Winners: 1883; *Runners-up:* 1881, 1882, 1887, 1891, 1897.

Club colours: Shirt: White with yellow and black horizontal stripe. Shorts: White. Socks: White.

Goalscorers: *League (46):* Thomson R 11, Fleming 5 (1 pen), Docherty 4 (3 pens), Nade 4 (1 pen), Stanton 4, Vaughan 4, Harvie 3, Stevenson 3, Stirling 3, Thomson J 2, Buchanan 1, own goals 2.
William Hill Scottish FA Cup (0).
Betfred Scottish League Cup (7): Buchanan 1, Fleming 1 (1 pen), Gallagher 1, Smith 1, Stevenson 1 (1 pen), Thomson 1, Wright 1.
IRN-BRU Scottish League Challenge Cup (0).

Martin A 36	Pettigrew C 10 + 2	Buchanan G 33	Wright F 2	Harvie D 34	Smith D 34 + 2	Stevenson R 9 + 8	Todd J 16 + 4	Thomson J 18	Thomson R 35 + 1	Stirling A 26 + 8	McCallum D 1 + 6	Docherty M 23 + 6	Gallagher G 6	Barr D 31 + 1	Fleming G 13 + 16	Stanton S 22 + 4	Lyden R — + 2	Brown M — + 1	Nade C 10 + 5	Vaughan L 11 + 4	Carswell S 16	Lang T 1 + 5	Gallagher C 3 + 4	McCrorie R 6 + 3	Prior K — + 1	Nuttall J — + 2	*Match No.*
1	2	3	4^{1}	5	6	7^{2}	8	9	10	11	12	13															1
1	3	4		2	10	9	7	8	11	12		5	6^{1}														2
1	2	3		5	9^{1}	10	6	8	11	12		4	7														3
1	2	3		5	9^{3}	10^{1}	6	8^{2}	11	12		4	7	13	14												4
1	2	3		5	9^{2}	10^{1}	6	7	11		13	14	8^{3}	4	12												5
1	2	3		5	10^{1}		6	7	11	9^{2}			8	4	12	13											6
1	2^{3}	3■		5	6	14	13	7	11	9^{1}			8	4	10^{2}	12											7
1	2			5	6	10	8	7^{2}	11	12		4		3	13	9^{1}											8
1	2			5	9^{1}	10	6^{2}	7^{3}	11	12	13	4		3	14	8											9
1		2		3	8	13	6^{3}	7^{1}	11	12	14	5		4	10^{2}	9											10
1		3		2	9	13	6	7	11^{1}	12		5		4	10	8^{2}											11
1		3		5	2	13	12	8	10	7^{2}		6		4	11^{1}	9											12
1	13	3	4^{1}	5	2		12	8^{2}	10	7	14	6^{3}			11	9											13
1		3		5	2	8	7		11^{2}	13	10^{1}	6		4	12	9											14
1	12	3		5	2	9^{2}	6	8	11	7^{1}	13			4	10^{3}		14										15
1		3		8	7	12	10	2	6	9		5		4	11^{1}												16
1		4		2	6	13	12	8	11	9^{2}		5		3	10^{1}	7											17
1		3		5	2	12	6^{1}	8	11	9■		7		4	10												18
1		3		5	2	12	6	9	8			7		4	11^{1}	10											19
1^{1}	5	4			2		8		10^{2}	7		6^{3}		3	11	9		12	13	14							20
1		3		5	2				9^{2}	6		7		4	11				12	10	8^{1}	13					21
1		3		5	2^{2}				14	6		7		4	13	9			11^{1}	10	8^{3}		12				22
1		3		5	2				10	6^{3}		7		4		9^{1}			11^{2}		8	14	12	13			23
1		3		5	2				7	10		6		4^{1}	14	9^{2}			11	13	8^{3}	12					24
1		3		5	2^{1}				9	11		7		4	13	8^{3}			10^{2}	14	6			12			25
1		3		5	2				10	7^{2}		6		4	13	12			11^{3}	9^{1}	8			14			26
1		4		5	2				9	6		8^{3}		3	14	12			11^{2}	10	7^{1}	13					27
1				5	2				9	6^{3}				4	12	8	14		11^{1}		7	3	10^{2}		13		28
1		4		5	2				10	9				3	13				11^{2}	12	7		8^{1}	6			29
1		4			2				11	9		5		3^{1}	12■	8				10	7	13	6^{2}				30
1		4		5	2				11	6^{3}		14		3		9^{2}				10^{1}	7		13	8		12	31
1		4		5	2				11	6				3		9			12	10^{1}	7			8			32
1		4		5	2				11	10				3		9			12	8^{2}	6^{1}			7		13	33
1		3		5	14				11	6^{1}		13		4	12	8			10^{2}	9^{3}	7			2			34
1		3		5	14				10	8		12		4	13	7^{1}			11^{3}	9^{2}	6			2			35
1		3		5	2				10	8		14		4	11^{1}	7			12	9^{3}	6^{2}		13				36

DUNDEE

Year Formed: 1893. *Ground & Address:* Dens Park Stadium, Sandeman St, Dundee DD3 7JY. *Telephone:* 01382 889966.
Fax: 01382 832284. *E-mail:* reception@dundeefc.co.uk *Website:* www.dundeefc.co.uk
Ground Capacity: 11,850 (all seated). *Size of Pitch:* 101m × 66m.
Chairmain: Tim Keyes. *Managing Director:* John Nelms.
Manager: Neil McCann. *Assistant Manager:* Graham Gartland. *Youth Development:* Jimmy Boyle.
Club Nicknames: 'The Dark Blues' or 'The Dee'.
Previous Grounds: Carolina Port 1893-98.
Record Attendance: 43,024 v Rangers, Scottish Cup 2nd rd, 7 February 1953.
Record Transfer Fee received: £1,500,000 for Robert Douglas to Celtic (October 2000).
Record Transfer Fee paid: £600,000 for Fabian Caballero from Sol de América (Paraguay) (July 2000).
Record Victory: 10-0 Division II v Alloa Ath, 9 March 1947 and v Dunfermline Ath, 22 March 1947.
Record Defeat: 0-11 v Celtic, Division I, 26 October 1895.
Most Capped Player: Alex Hamilton, 24, Scotland.
Most League Appearances: 400: Barry Smith, 1995-2006.
Most League Goals in Season (Individual): 52: Alan Gilzean, 1960-64.
Most Goals Overall (Individual): 113: Alan Gilzean 1960-64.

DUNDEE – SPFL LADBROKES PREMIERSHIP 2016–17 LEAGUE RECORD

Match No.	*Date*	*Venue*	*Opponents*	*Result*		*H/T Score*	*Lg Pos.*	*Goalscorers*	*Attendance*
1	Aug 6	A	Ross Co	W	3-1	2-0	7	Loy 2 (1 pen) 13, 41 (p), McGowan 62	3669
2	13	H	Rangers	L	1-2	1-2	7	O'Hara 44	9702
3	19	H	Hamilton A	D	1-1	1-1	7	O'Hara 17	5287
4	27	A	Motherwell	D	0-0	0-0	8		4078
5	Sept 10	H	Kilmarnock	D	1-1	1-1	8	El Bakhtaoui 7	5111
6	18	H	Aberdeen	L	1-3	1-1	9	Holt 13	6321
7	24	A	Inverness CT	L	1-3	0-2	10	Low 84	2884
8	Oct 1	H	Celtic	L	0-1	0-0	10		8827
9	15	A	Hearts	L	0-2	0-0	12		16,512
10	23	A	St Johnstone	L	1-2	0-0	12	Loy (pen) 88	3646
11	26	H	Partick Thistle	L	0-2	0-1	12		4783
12	29	A	Hamilton A	W	1-0	0-0	12	McGowan 62	1853
13	Nov 5	H	Motherwell	W	2-0	1-0	11	Kerr 40, Haber 80	5471
14	19	A	Rangers	L	0-1	0-0	12		48,773
15	26	H	Inverness CT	W	2-1	1-0	8	Wighton 25, Gadzhalov 60	5094
16	Dec 3	A	Kilmarnock	L	0-2	0-1	10		3615
17	10	H	Ross Co	D	0-0	0-0	11		4742
18	17	A	Celtic	L	1-2	0-1	11	Haber 69	37,404
19	23	H	Hearts	W	3-2	0-1	8	O'Dea 54, McGowan 71, Haber 90	6160
20	28	A	Partick Thistle	L	0-2	0-2	9		3758
21	31	H	St Johnstone	W	3-0	2-0	7	El Bakhtaoui 15, Gadzhalov 42, Anderson (og) 57	6492
22	Jan 27	A	Aberdeen	L	0-3	0-2	8		10,512
23	Feb 4	A	Inverness CT	D	2-2	2-0	9	Haber 37, O'Dea 43	2606
24	11	H	Kilmarnock	D	1-1	1-1	8	Holt 27	4708
25	19	H	Rangers	W	2-1	2-0	7	O'Hara 13, Holt 41	9017
26	25	A	Motherwell	W	5-1	5-1	7	Jules (og) 7, Haber 2 27, 45, O'Hara 31, Wighton 35	4002
27	Mar 1	H	Partick Thistle	L	0-1	0-1	7		5328
28	11	A	St Johnstone	L	0-2	0-2	8		4195
29	19	H	Celtic	L	1-2	0-1	8	El Bakhtaoui 76	8968
30	31	H	Aberdeen	L	0-7	0-4	8		7314
31	Apr 4	A	Ross Co	L	1-2	1-1	9	O'Dea (pen) 45	2819
32	8	A	Hearts	L	0-1	0-1	9		16,304
33	15	H	Hamilton A	L	0-2	0-1	11		6489
34	29	A	Motherwell	W	3-2	1-0	9	O'Hara 45, Haber 2 49, 56	4919
35	May 6	A	Kilmarnock	W	1-0	0-0	9	Haber 55	4040
36	13	H	Ross Co	D	1-1	0-1	9	O'Dea (pen) 76	6812
37	17	H	Inverness CT	L	0-2	0-2	10		5574
38	20	A	Hamilton A	L	0-4	0-2	10		2616

Final League Position: 10

Honours
League Champions: Division I 1961-62. First Division 1978-79, 1991-92, 1997-98. Championship 2013-14. Division II 1946-47.
Runners-up: Division I 1902-03, 1906-07, 1908-09, 1948-49. First Division 1980-81, 2007-08, 2009-10, 2011-12.
Scottish Cup Winners: 1910; *Runners-up:* 1925, 1952, 1964, 2003.
League Cup Winners: 1951-52, 1952-53, 1973-74; *Runners-up:* 1967-68, 1980-81, 1995-96.
League Challenge Cup Winners: 1990-91, 2009-10.

European: *European Cup:* 8 matches (1962-63 semi-finals). *Cup Winners' Cup:* 2 matches: (1964-65).
UEFA Cup: 22 matches: (*Fairs Cup:* 1967-68 semi-finals. *UEFA Cup:* 1971-72, 1973-74, 1974-75, 2003-04).

Club colours: Shirt: Navy blue with white trim. Shorts: White with navy trim. Socks: Navy blue.

Goalscorers: *League (38):* Haber 9, O'Hara 5, O'Dea 4 (2 pens), El Bakhtaoui 3, Holt 3, Loy 3 (2 pens), McGowan 3, Gadzhalov 2, Wighton 2, Kerr 1, Low 1, own goals 2.
William Hill Scottish FA Cup (0).
Betfred Scottish League Cup (15): Stewart 6, Hemmings 3, Duffy 1, Etxabeguren Leanizbarrutia 1, Loy 1, McGowan 1, O'Dea 1, Teijsse 1.
IRN-BRU Scottish League Challenge Cup (1): Warwick 1.

Bain S 36	Kerr C 35 + 1	Etxabeguren Leanizbarrutia J 14 + 3	O'Dea D 35	Holt K 37	O'Hara M 26 + 2	Vincent J 27 + 1	McGowan P 35 + 1	Williams D 11 + 12	Duffy M 4 + 4	Loy R 4 + 9	El Bakhtaoui F 15 + 15	Ross N 11 + 8	Teijsse Y 3 + 6	Gomis K 22	Hateley T 26 + 1	Wighton C 19 + 12	Low N 2	Gadzhalov K 15 + 3	Haber M 27	Mitchell D 2	Curran J 1	Ojamaa H 9 + 5	Klok M — + 2	Higgins D 2 + 2	*Match No.*
1	2	3	4	5	6	7	8	9^2	10^1	11	12	13													1
1	2	4	5	3	10	6^1	8	9	7^2	11^3	13	12	14												2
1	5	3	4	2	9	6^1		7		10	11	8	12												3
1	2		4	5	8		6	9^1	10	12	11	7		3											4
1	2	12	4^1	5	10		7			14	11	6	13	3■	8^3	9^2									5
1	2	3	4	5	7■		9	10^1	13	14	11	8^3			6^2	12									6
1	2	3	4	5			9	14	8^3	12	11	7^1	13		6^2		10								7
1	5		3	4	8		6	9^1		14	11^3	13	10	2		12	7^2								8
1	13			4	8	7^3	6	9	12	14	10		11	3	5^1			2^2							9
1			3	2		7	6	5	12	14	11^3	8^2	10	4	9^1	13									10
1	5		3	4			7	9^2	13	10^1			14	2^3	6	8		12	11						11
	5	4	3	9		7	8^1					12	13		6	11		2	10^2	1					12
	2		4	6		7	8	12						5^1	9	10		3	11	1					13
1	6		3	9		7	8	13			12			2	5	11^1		4	10^2						14
1	5	13	3	9		7^2	8	12						2	6	11		4	10^1						15
1	5	2	3	9		7^3	8	12		14	13				6	11^2		4^1	10						16
1	5		4	9		13	7				12			3	6^2	11		2	10		8^1				17
1	2		4	6	12	9		10^1			13			5	8^2	7		3	11						18
1	9	12	3	5	6^1	8	13							2^2	7	10		4	11						19
1	5	2^1	3	9		6^2	7			13	12				8	11		4	10						20
1	2	4		5	8^1		7	13			9^2	12			6	11		3	10						21
1	5	2^1			9		8				12	6		3	7	10		4	11						22
1	6	2	4	5	7		8				13			3	10^2				11			9^1	12		23
1	5		4	9	6		7				14			2^3	8^1	13		3	10			11^2	12		24
1	2	4	5	3	6	8	9	12								7			11			10^1			25
1	2	3	4	5	6^3	7	8	12			14				13	9^1			10			11^2			26
1	5	3^3	4	2	6	8	7	13			12					9^1		14	11			10^2			27
1	2		3	5	7	9	8	13			12					6^1		4	10			11^2			28
1	2		4	5	6	7^3	8				14	13		3	9^1	12			10			11^2			29
1	2		4	5	6	9	7				11	10^1		3	8^2	13						12			30
1	2		4	5	6	7	8	9■						3		12			10			11^1			31
1	9		3	4	8	7	6								5	12			11			10^1		2	32
1	5^2		3	4	12	8^1	7				11				6	9			10			13		2	33
1			4	5	6^2	7	8	12			14	9^3		3	2	10^1			11					13	34
1	2		4	5	6	7	8^2				10^1	13		3	9	12			11^3			14			35
1	2		4	5	6	7	10				9^2	12		3^3	8^1	14		13	11						36
1	2		4	5	8	6	9				10^2	7		3^3		14			11^1			13		12	37
1	2		4	5	6^2	8	9	14			10	7^3				12		3	11^1			13			38

DUNDEE UNITED

Year Formed: 1909 (1923). *Ground & Address:* Tannadice Park, Tannadice St, Dundee DD3 7JW. *Telephone:* 01382 833166. *Fax:* 01382 889398. *E-mail:* admin@dundeeunited.co.uk *Website:* www.dufc.co
Ground Capacity: 14,223 (all seated). *Size of Pitch:* 100m × 66m.
Chairman: Stephen Thompson, OBE.
Manager: Ray McKinnon. *Assistant Manager:* Laurie Ellis.
Club Nicknames: 'The Terrors', 'The Arabs'.
Previous Grounds: None.
Record Attendance: 28,000 v Barcelona, Fairs Cup, 16 November 1966.
Record Transfer Fee received: £4,000,000 for Duncan Ferguson from Rangers (July 1993).
Record Transfer Fee paid: £750,000 for Steven Pressley from Coventry C (July 1995).
Record Victory: 14-0 v Nithsdale Wanderers, Scottish Cup 1st rd, 17 January 1931.
Record Defeat: 1-12 v Motherwell, Division II, 23 January 1954.
Most Capped Player: Maurice Malpas, 55, Scotland.
Most League Appearances: 618, Maurice Malpas, 1980-2000.
Most Appearances in European Matches: 76, Dave Narey (record for Scottish player).
Most League Goals in Season (Individual): 40: John Coyle, Division II, 1955-56.
Most Goals Overall (Individual): 199: Peter McKay, 1947-54.

DUNDEE UNITED – SPFL LADBROKES CHAMPIONSHIP 2016–17 LEAGUE RECORD

Match No.	*Date*	*Venue*	*Opponents*	*Result*		*H/T Score*	*Lg Pos.*	*Goalscorers*	*Attendance*
1	Aug 6	H	Queen of the South	D	1-1	0-1	4	Van der Velden [58]	7058
2	13	A	Dumbarton	L	0-1	0-0	8		1475
3	20	H	Ayr U	W	3-0	2-0	4	Murray [13], Robson [37], Flood [76]	6427
4	27	H	Raith R	D	2-2	2-1	4	Flood [17], Smith, C (pen) [23]	7434
5	Sept 10	A	Dunfermline Ath	W	3-1	1-0	4	Murray [21], Andreu 2 [46, 90]	5563
6	17	A	Falkirk	L	1-3	1-1	5	Obadeyi [33]	5488
7	24	H	Greenock Morton	W	2-1	0-0	3	Andreu 2 [64, 90]	5829
8	Oct 2	A	Hibernian	D	1-1	0-1	5	Edjenguele [68]	15,492
9	15	A	St Mirren	W	2-0	1-0	4	Fraser [38], Andreu [74]	3612
10	22	H	Dumbarton	W	2-1	0-0	2	Buchanan (og) [53], Edjenguele [66]	5979
11	29	H	Falkirk	W	1-0	0-0	2	Durnan [82]	7046
12	Nov 5	A	Queen of the South	W	4-1	2-1	2	Durnan [14], Andreu [22], Fraser [57], Murray [77]	2316
13	8	H	Dunfermline Ath	W	1-0	0-0	2	Murray [79]	5996
14	19	A	Greenock Morton	D	0-0	0-0	2		2578
15	Dec 2	H	Hibernian	W	1-0	0-0	2	Andreu (pen) [73]	10,925
16	10	A	Ayr U	W	1-0	1-0	2	Obadeyi [6]	2049
17	17	A	Raith R	D	0-0	0-0	2		4361
18	24	H	St Mirren	W	2-1	2-1	1	Fraser [28], Murray [45]	7247
19	31	A	Dumbarton	L	0-1	0-1	1		1221
20	Jan 6	A	Hibernian	L	0-3	0-2	2		18,786
21	14	H	Queen of the South	D	3-3	1-1	2	Murray 2 [4, 89], Fraser [77]	6136
22	28	A	Dunfermline Ath	D	1-1	1-1	2	Andreu [18]	4670
23	Feb 4	H	Raith R	W	3-0	1-0	2	Mikkelsen 2 [45, 53], Andreu [48]	5232
24	11	A	Falkirk	L	0-3	0-1	2		5028
25	25	H	Greenock Morton	D	1-1	0-1	2	Durnan [83]	6065
26	Mar 10	H	Hibernian	L	0-1	0-1	3		9532
27	15	A	St Mirren	L	2-3	1-2	4	Andreu 2 [33, 69]	2766
28	18	A	Raith R	L	1-2	0-1	4	Murray [81]	2192
29	28	H	Ayr U	W	2-1	1-0	4	Murray [23], Durnan [78]	4661
30	Apr 1	A	Queen of the South	L	2-4	1-2	4	Mikkelsen 2 [27, 55]	1514
31	8	H	Falkirk	D	1-1	0-0	4	Murray [50]	6313
32	11	H	Dunfermline Ath	W	1-0	1-0	3	Mikkelsen [30]	5304
33	15	A	Ayr U	D	0-0	0-0	3		1205
34	22	H	St Mirren	W	3-2	1-1	3	Mikkelsen [7], Andreu [66], Spittal [90]	6225
35	29	H	Dumbarton	D	2-2	1-1	3	Andreu [22], Mikkelsen [79]	5107
36	May 6	A	Greenock Morton	D	1-1	0-0	3	Spittal [63]	2158

Final League Position: 3

Honours: *League Champions:* Premier Division 1982-83.
Division II 1924-25, 1928-29.
Runners-up: Division II 1930-31, 1959-60. First Division 1995-96.
Scottish Cup Winners: 1994, 2010; *Runners-up:* 1974, 1981, 1985, 1987, 1988, 1991, 2005, 2014.
League Cup Winners: 1979-80, 1980-81; *Runners-up:* 1981-82, 1984-85, 1997-98, 2007-08, 2014-15.
League Challenge Cup Winners, 2016-17. *Runners-up:* 1995-96.

European: *European Cup:* 8 matches (1983-84, semi-finals). *Cup Winners' Cup:* 10 matches (1974-75, 1988-89, 1994-95). *UEFA Cup:* 86 matches (*Fairs Cup:* 1966-67, 1969-70, 1970-71. *UEFA Cup:* 1975-76, 1977-78, 1978-79, 1979-80, 1980-81, 1981-82, 1982-83, 1984-85, 1985-86, 1986-87 runners-up, 1987-88, 1989-90, 1990-91, 1993-94, 1997-98, 2005-06). *Europa League:* 6 matches (2010-2011, 2011-12, 2012-13).

Club colours: Shirt: Tangerine with black trim. Shorts: Tangerine. Socks: Tangerine.

Goalscorers: *League (50):* Andreu 13 (1 pen), Murray 10, Mikkelsen 7, Durnan 4, Fraser 4, Edjenguele 2, Flood 2, Obadeyi 2, Spittal 2, Robson 1, Smith C 1 (1 pen), Van der Velden 1, own goal 1.
William Hill Scottish FA Cup (2): Andreu 2.
Betfred Scottish League Cup (14): Murray 4, Smith C 4 (1 pen), Anier 2, Fraser 1, Murdoch 1, Toshney 1, Van der Velden 1.
IRN-BRU Scottish League Challenge Cup (10): Andreu 4, Telfer 2, Durnan 1, Fraser 1, Mikkelsen 1, Van der Velden 1.
Play-Offs (9): Murray 4, Spittal 3, Dixon 1, Kuate 1.

Bell C 35	Dillon S 6 + 4	Durnan M 31	Donaldson C 7 + 7	Robson J 19 + 2	Flood W 32	Murdoch S 16 + 2	Smith C 5 + 11	Van der Velden N 14 + 10	Obadeyi T 11 + 7	Murray S 24 + 8	Anier H — + 1	Johnson J — + 1	Toshney L 18 + 2	Spittal B 18 + 6	Fraser S 23 + 2	Telfer C 17 + 8	Edjenguele W 29	van der Struijk F 16	Dixon P 17	Andreu T 31	Coote A 2 + 7	Zwick L 1 + 3	Mikkelsen T 14 + 3	Nicholls A 4 + 5	Kuate W 2 + 2	Allardice S 4 + 1	*Match No.*
1	2	3	4	5	6	7	8	9[1]	10	11[2]	12	13															1
1		3	4	5	9	7	8[1]	13	11[3]	12			2	6[2]	10	14											2
1	3		4	5	6[2]	7	9[1]	8	13	11			2	12	10[3]	14											3
1	3		4	5	6	7	9	8	12	11[1]			2	13	10[2]												4
1			14	12	6		13	8[2]	10[3]	11[1]			2			7	3	4	5■	9							5
1	12			5	8[1]		14	6	9	10			4[2]		13	7	3	2		11[3]							6
1	14	4					9[1]	8[3]	12	11			6	7[2]	13		3	2	5	10							7
1		3					13	10[1]	14	11[3]			6[2]	7	9	12	4	2	5	8							8
1		3■	14		9			8[2]	11[1]	13				12	7	6	4	2	5	10[3]							9
1			3		7			9	10[1]						8	6	4	2	5	11	12						10
1		4	14		6		13	9[2]	10[3]	12					8[1]	7	3	2	5	11							11
1[1]		4[2]	14	12	7				9	11					6	8	3	2	5[3]	10		13					12
1		3		5	6		13	12	10[1]	11[3]				14	8	7[2]	4	2		9							13
1		3		5	6		14	13		11[1]			12	8	10	7	4	2[3]		9[2]							14
1		4		2	7	13	14	11[3]		12			5	10[2]	8	6	3			9[1]							15
1		3		5	8		12	13	11[2]				2	6	9[1]	7	4			10							16
1	12	4		5	7				11[1]	13			2■	8	10	6[2]	3			9							17
1	2	3[3]	12		6		14	13		11[1]				8	9	7[2]	4		5	10							18
1	2	3	14		7	8	12	10	13	11[2]				6[3]	9[1]		4		5								19
1		3			7	6[2]	13	11[3]	12				2		9	8[1]	4		5	10			14				20
1		3			8	7[3]			12	10			2	13	9	14	4		5	6[2]			11[1]				21
1[2]		3			7					13			6	10	8		4	2	5	9		12	11[1]				22
1		3						12		10			7[3]	9	6	14	4	2	5	8[2]			11[1]	13			23
	13	3			7	14				12			4[2]	8[3]	6[1]			2	5	9		1	11	10			24
1		3			6			10[1]		12					8	7	4	2	5	9	13		11[2]				25
1		3			7			13		11			6■		8[2]		4	2	5	9[1]			12	10			26
1	2	3		5	7			14		11[3]					8[2]	6	4			9	13		12	10[1]			27
1		2		4	7	6[3]		13		10			8				3	5[1]		9	14		11[2]	12			28
1		3		5	6	2				10[2]						7	4			9	12		11	8[1]	13		29
1[3]		3			6	2				11				12		7	4		5	10	8[2]	13	9[1]	14			30
1		3		5	6	2				10				8[1]		13	4			9			11	12		7[2]	31
1		3		5	6	2		13		10			12	8[1]			4			9	14		11[3]			7[2]	32
1		3		5		2				10			8[1]	6		12	4			11			9			7	33
1		3	13	5	7	2				10				6[1]			4			9			11		12	8[2]	34
1		3	4	5	7	2				10				8						9	12		11		6[1]		35
1		3	4	5	7[1]	2								8		12				9	10[2]		11	14	6[3]	13	36

DUNFERMLINE ATHLETIC

Year Formed: 1885. *Ground & Address:* East End Park, Halbeath Road, Dunfermline KY12 7RB.
Telephone: 01383 724295. *Fax:* 01383 745 959. *E-mail:* enquiries@dafc.co.uk
Website: www.dafc.co.uk
Ground Capacity: 11,380 (all seated). *Size of Pitch:* 105m × 65m.
Chairman: Bob Garmony. *Vice-Chairman:* Billy Braisby.
Manager: Allan Johnston. *Assistant Manager:* Sandy Clark. *Head Coach:* John Potter.
Club Nickname: 'The Pars'.
Previous Grounds: None.
Record Attendance: 27,816 v Celtic, Division I, 30 April 1968.
Record Transfer Fee received: £650,000 for Jackie McNamara to Celtic (October 1995).
Record Transfer Fee paid: £540,000 for Istvan Kozma from Bordeaux (September 1989).
Record Victory: 11-2 v Stenhousemuir, Division II, 27 September 1930.
Record Defeat: 1-13 v St. Bernard's, Scottish Cup, 1st rd; 15 September 1883.
Most Capped Player: Colin Miller 16 (61), Canada.
Most League Appearances: 497: Norrie McCathie, 1981-96.
Most League Goals in Season (Individual): 53: Bobby Skinner, Division II, 1925-26.
Most Goals Overall (Individual): 212: Charles Dickson, 1954-64.

DUNFERMLINE ATHLETIC – SPFL LADBROKES CHAMPIONSHIP 2016–17 LEAGUE RECORD

Match No.	*Date*	*Venue*	*Opponents*		*Result*	*H/T Score*	*Lg Pos.*	*Goalscorers*	*Attendance*
1	Aug 6	H	Dumbarton	W	4-3	2-1	2	Cardle 3 23, 26, 66, Hopkirk 81	3496
2	13	A	Hibernian	L	1-2	0-1	4	Reilly 58	16,477
3	20	A	Raith R	L	0-2	0-0	7		5114
4	27	H	Queen of the South	L	0-1	0-1	7		3973
5	Sept 10	H	Dundee U	L	1-3	0-1	8	Paton 50	5563
6	17	A	Greenock Morton	L	1-2	1-1	9	Clark 30	1756
7	24	H	St Mirren	W	4-3	1-2	7	Clark 2 40, 77, Webster (og) 62, El Alagui 85	2732
8	Oct 1	A	Ayr U	D	0-0	0-0	8		2883
9	15	A	Falkirk	L	1-2	0-1	8	El Alagui 75	6377
10	22	H	Hibernian	L	1-3	1-0	8	Higginbotham (pen) 22	7622
11	29	A	Dumbarton	D	2-2	0-1	8	Clark 50, Cardle 80	1018
12	Nov 5	H	Raith R	D	0-0	0-0	9		5649
13	8	A	Dundee U	L	0-1	0-0	9		5996
14	19	A	St Mirren	W	1-0	1-0	8	Clark 26	2126
15	Dec 3	H	Ayr U	D	1-1	1-0	9	Clark 30	3250
16	10	H	Greenock Morton	W	2-1	2-1	7	Moffat 2 12, 23	3101
17	17	A	Queen of the South	D	2-2	0-1	7	Talbot 61, Higginbotham 73	1561
18	26	H	Falkirk	D	1-1	0-1	7	McCabe (pen) 59	6134
19	Jan 2	A	Raith R	W	2-0	1-0	6	Clark 11, Ashcroft 77	5899
20	7	A	Ayr U	W	2-0	2-0	6	Clark 26, Geggan 33	2261
21	14	H	St Mirren	D	1-1	1-0	5	Higginbotham (pen) 37	4108
22	28	H	Dundee U	D	1-1	1-1	6	Herron 28	4670
23	Feb 4	A	Falkirk	L	0-2	0-1	6		5953
24	25	A	Hibernian	D	2-2	1-2	6	McMullan 26, Higginbotham 46	14,437
25	Mar 4	H	Dumbarton	W	5-1	2-0	6	Clark 4 7, 60, 79, 84, McMullan 27	3320
26	7	H	Queen of the South	D	1-1	1-1	6	Moffat 17	2653
27	11	A	St Mirren	D	0-0	0-0	6		4582
28	18	H	Ayr U	L	0-1	0-0	6		3276
29	25	A	Greenock Morton	W	1-0	1-0	6	Wedderburn 16	2670
30	Apr 1	H	Hibernian	D	1-1	0-1	6	Higginbotham (pen) 59	7058
31	8	H	Raith R	W	1-0	0-0	6	Higginbotham (pen) 49	4865
32	11	A	Dundee U	L	0-1	0-1	6		5304
33	15	A	Dumbarton	W	2-0	0-0	5	McCabe 80, Hopkirk 85	1142
34	22	H	Falkirk	L	1-2	1-0	5	Clark 35	5076
35	29	H	Greenock Morton	W	3-1	1-1	5	Clark 3, Moffat 51, McCabe 85	3339
36	May 6	A	Queen of the South	W	1-0	0-0	5	Clark 90	1849

Final League Position: 5

Honours
League Champions: First Division 1988-89, 1995-96, 2010-11. Division II 1925-26. Second Division 1985-86. League One 2015-16. *Runners-up:* First Division 1986-87, 1993-94, 1994-95, 1999-2000. Division II 1912-13, 1933-34, 1954-55, 1957-58, 1972-73. Second Division 1978-79. League One 2013-14.
Scottish Cup Winners: 1961, 1968; *Runners-up:* 1965, 2004, 2007.
League Cup Runners-up: 1949-50, 1991-92, 2005-06.
League Challenge Cup Runners-up: 2007-08.

European: *Cup Winners' Cup:* 14 matches (1961-62, 1968-69 semi-finals). *UEFA Cup:* 32 matches (*Fairs Cup:* 1962-63, 1964-65, 1965-66, 1966-67, 1969-70. *UEFA Cup:* 2004-05, 2007-08).

Club colours: Shirt: Black and white stripes. Shorts: Black. Socks: Black with white trim.

Goalscorers: *League (46):* Clark 15, Higginbotham 6 (4 pens), Cardle 4, Moffat 4, McCabe 3 (1 pen), El Alagui 2, Hopkirk 2, McMullan 2, Ashcroft 1, Geggan 1, Herron 1, Paton 1, Reilly 1, Talbot 1, Wedderburn 1, own goal 1.
William Hill Scottish FA Cup (10): McMullan 4, Cardle 1, Clark 1, Higginbotham 1, Morris 1, Paton 1 (1 pen), own goal 1.
Betfred Scottish League Cup (7): Geggan 4, Moffat 2, Ashcroft 1.
IRN-BRU Scottish League Challenge Cup (7): Ashcroft 2, El Alagui 2, McMullan 1, Reilly 1, own goal 1.

Hutton D 6 + 1	Williamson R 11 + 3	Ashcroft L 35	Richards-Everton B 6	Martin L 16 + 2	Higginbotham K 31 + 1	Geggan A 29	McCabe R 18 + 5	Cardle J 9 + 14	Moffat M 24 + 5	Reilly G 11 + 11	McMullan P 23 + 6	Paton M 10 + 8	Hopkirk D 1 + 10	Fordyce C 13	Talbot J 30 + 1	Spence L — + 2	Clark N 30	El Alagui F 6 + 7	Murdoch S 30	Herron J 20	Wedderburn N 23 + 1	Duthie C 1 + 1	Morris C 13	Smith C — + 2	*Match No.*
1	2	3■	4	5	6^{1}	7	8	9	10^{3}	11^{2}	12	13	14												1
1	2		4	5	6	7	8	9	10^{1}	11			12	3											2
1	2	3	4	5^{2}	6	8	7^{3}	9	11^{1}	10		13	12		14										3
1	2	3	4	13	9^{3}	8	7^{1}		10^{2}	11	12	6			5■	14									4
1	2^{2}	3		4^{1}		7	8	13		11	9	6		5			10	12							5
1		3	4	5	13	8	7	12		11^{1}	9^{2}	6^{3}		2			10	14							6
	12	3		2		7		9^{2}		10^{1}	14	6		4^{3}	5		11	13	1	8					7
	2	3		4		6	12	9	14	10^{1}		7			5		11^{3}	13	1	8^{2}					8
	2	4		3	11	8	7^{2}			13		6^{1}	12		5		9	10	1						9
		4	3	2	9^{3}	7			13■	10	14	6^{1}	12		5			11^{2}	1		8				10
	2	3		4	9	7		12	13	11^{1}		6^{2}			5		10		1		8				11
		3		4	6	2		9							5		10	11	1	7	8				12
		3		4	6^{2}	2	12	9^{1}			13				5		10	11	1	7	8■				13
		3		2	6		8		13		12	7^{2}		4	5		10	11^{1}	1	9					14
		4		2■	6		8		13		9			3	5		10^{2}	11^{1}	1	7		12			15
	13	4			6		8		10		9			3	5		11^{1}	14	1	7^{2}	12	2^{3}			16
		4		2	6		8	12	10		9^{1}			3	5		11		1		7				17
		4		3		2	8	9^{3}	10^{1}	12	6	13			5		11^{2}	14	1	7					18
		4			6	2		12	10	13	9^{1}			3	5		11^{2}		1	7	8				19
		4			6^{2}	2		13	10^{3}	12	9			3	5		11^{1}	14	1	7	8				20
		4			6	2		12	10		9^{1}			3	5		11		1	8	7				21
		4			6^{3}	2		12	10^{2}	13	9^{1}		14		5		11		1	8	7		3		22
		4			9	2		14	10^{2}	12	6^{3}		13		5		11		1	8^{1}	7		3		23
		4			9	2			10		6				5		11		1	7	8		3		24
		4			6	2	12		10^{3}	14	9				5	13	11		1	7^{1}	8^{2}		3		25
		4			6^{3}	2		12	10^{1}	14	9^{2}	13			5		11		1	7	8		3		26
		4			6^{1}	2			10		9	12			5		11		1	8	7		3		27
	2	4			6^{3}			9^{2}	10^{1}	14		13	12		5		11		1	7	8		3		28
		4			6	2	12	14	11^{3}		9^{2}		13		5		10		1	7^{1}	8		3		29
		3			6	2	12		11		9				5		10		1	8^{1}	7		4		30
		4			6	2	8	12	11		9^{1}				5		10		1		7		3		31
	13	4			6	2^{1}	8	14	10^{2}	12	9^{3}				5		11		1		7		3		32
		4			6	2	7		11^{1}	10^{2}	9	13	12		5				1		8		3		33
12		4		13■	6	2	7				9		11		5		10		1^{2}		8		3^{1}		34
	2	4			6		7		10^{2}	14	9^{1}	12		3	5		11^{3}		1		8			13	35
	5	3			6		8	12	11^{2}		9^{1}	2		4			10		1		7			13	36

EAST FIFE

Year Formed: 1903. *Ground & Address:* Bayview Stadium, Harbour View, Methil, Fife KY8 3RW. *Telephone:* 01333 426323. *Fax:* 01333 426376. *E-mail:* office@eastfifefc.info. *Website:* www.eastfifefc.info
Ground Capacity: 1,992. *Size of Pitch:* 105m × 65m.
Chairman: Jim Stevenson. *Vice-Chairman:* David Marshall.
Manager: Darren Young. *Assistant Manager:* Tony McMinn.
Club Nickname: 'The Fifers'.
Previous Ground: Bayview Park.
Record Attendance: 22,515 v Raith Rovers, Division I, 2 January 1950 (Bayview Park); 4,700 v Rangers, League One, 26 October 2013 (Bayview Stadium).
Record Transfer Fee received: £150,000 for Paul Hunter from Hull C (March 1990).
Record Transfer Fee paid: £70,000 for John Sludden from Kilmarnock (July 1991).
Record Victory: 13-2 v Edinburgh C, Division II, 11 December 1937.
Record Defeat: 0-9 v Hearts, Division I, 5 October 1957.
Most Capped Player: George Aitken, 5 (8), Scotland.
Most League Appearances: 517: David Clarke, 1968-86.
Most League Goals in Season (Individual): 41: Jock Wood, Division II; 1926-27 and Henry Morris, Division II, 1947-48.
Most Goals Overall (Individual): 225: Phil Weir, 1922-35.

EAST FIFE – SPFL LADBROKES LEAGUE ONE 2016–17 LEAGUE RECORD

Match No.	*Date*	*Venue*	*Opponents*	*Result*		*H/T Score*	*Lg Pos.*	*Goalscorers*	*Attendance*
1	Aug 6	H	Albion R	D	2-2	2-1	6	Smith 4, Kerr 45	682
2	13	A	Peterhead	W	3-0	2-0	4	Kerr 5, Smith 45, Lamont 66	492
3	20	A	Alloa Ath	L	1-2	0-2	5	O'Hara 90	652
4	27	H	Brechin C	L	1-2	1-1	6	Robinson 33	609
5	Sept 10	H	Stranraer	W	2-0	1-0	4	Insall 2 38, 60	555
6	17	A	Airdrieonians	D	1-1	1-0	4	Smith 14	814
7	24	H	Livingston	W	3-1	3-0	4	Insall 2 9, 34, Kane 11	784
8	Oct 1	H	Stenhousemuir	L	0-1	0-0	4		563
9	15	A	Queen's Park	L	0-1	0-1	6		571
10	22	A	Stranraer	D	1-1	1-0	7	Brown 28	428
11	29	H	Airdrieonians	L	0-1	0-1	8		706
12	Nov 5	A	Livingston	L	1-3	0-1	9	Smith 53	907
13	15	H	Alloa Ath	D	2-2	1-0	8	Smith 31, Taggart (og) 74	412
14	19	H	Queen's Park	L	1-2	1-1	9	Insall 45	557
15	Dec 10	A	Brechin C	W	1-0	1-0	8	Robinson 11	414
16	17	H	Peterhead	W	2-0	0-0	7	Kerr 48, O'Hara 56	486
17	20	A	Stenhousemuir	W	1-0	1-0	6	O'Hara 11	356
18	31	H	Livingston	W	2-1	0-1	6	Insall 74, Robinson 77	661
19	Jan 7	H	Stenhousemuir	W	1-0	1-0	6	Robinson 22	635
20	14	A	Airdrieonians	D	2-2	1-1	6	Kerr 45, Brown 74	833
21	28	H	Stranraer	D	0-0	0-0	5		584
22	Feb 4	A	Queen's Park	D	2-2	0-2	5	Duggan 49, Robinson 72	566
23	18	H	Brechin C	W	3-2	2-1	4	Smith 28, Kane 31, Duggan (pen) 68	642
24	25	A	Peterhead	D	1-1	0-0	4	Smith 49	495
25	28	A	Alloa Ath	L	0-3	0-2	4		436
26	Mar 4	H	Albion R	W	2-0	0-0	3	Duggan 2 52, 59	539
27	11	A	Livingston	W	1-0	0-0	3	Kerr 85	773
28	18	H	Alloa Ath	D	0-0	0-0	3		612
29	25	A	Brechin C	L	1-2	0-1	4	Duggan (pen) 56	525
30	28	A	Albion R	L	0-1	0-0	4		419
31	Apr 1	H	Queen's Park	D	0-0	0-0	4		692
32	8	A	Stenhousemuir	L	1-3	0-1	5	Kane 56	455
33	15	H	Peterhead	L	1-2	1-1	6	Kerr 31	636
34	22	A	Albion R	W	1-0	0-0	3	Kerr 63	488
35	29	H	Airdrieonians	L	0-4	0-1	5		918
36	May 6	A	Stranraer	L	1-2	0-0	5	Kerr 76	462

Final League Position: 5

Honours
League Champions: Division II 1947-48. Third Division 2007-08. League Two 2015-16.
Runners-up: Division II 1929-30, 1970-71. Second Division 1983-84, 1995-96. Third Division 2002-03.
Scottish Cup Winners: 1938; *Runners-up:* 1927, 1950.
League Cup Winners: 1947-48, 1949-50, 1953-54.

Club colours: Shirt: Gold and black stripes. Shorts: White. Socks: Black.

Goalscorers: *League (41):* Kerr 8, Smith 7, Insall 6, Duggan 5 (2 pens), Robinson 5, Kane 3, O'Hara 3, Brown 2, Lamont 1, own goal 1.
William Hill Scottish FA Cup (5): Duggan 2 (2 pens), Kane 1, Kerr 1, Paterson 1.
Betfred Scottish League Cup (5): McManus 2 (1 pen), Smith 2, Page 1.
IRN-BRU Scottish League Challenge Cup (3): McManus 1 (1 pen), Page 1, Smith 1.

Muir W 3	Mercer S 16 + 2	Kerr J 31 + 2	Page J 27	Slattery P 29 + 1	Robinson S 22 + 1	Kane C 34	Lamont M 13 + 6	Wilkie K 18	Smith K 24 + 5	McManus P 4 + 5	Wallace T 7 + 9	O'Hara K 6 + 10	Brown R 32 + 1	Mutch R — + 1	Naysmith G 10 + 2	Goodfellow R 10 + 1	Austin J 7 + 8	Hurst M 23 + 1	Insall J 12 + 12	Penrice J 18	Paterson N 15	Duggan C 13 + 3	Watt L 2 + 1	Reilly B 1 + 5	Curran J 11 + 1	Cooper A 3 + 3	Duffie K 5 + 1	*Match No.*
1	2	3	4	5^{2}	6	7	8	9	10	11^{1}	12	13																1
1	5	3	4		7	8^{3}	6	9^{2}	10	11^{1}	13	12	2	14														2
1	2	4	3		6	7^{2}	12	9	11	10^{3}	14	13	8^{1}		5													3
	2	3	4		8	7^{2}	6	9		10	12	11^{1}			5	1	13											4
	2		4	7	6^{2}	3	8^{1}	9	10		12	14	13		5			1	11^{3}									5
	2		4	7		3	8^{2}	9	10^{1}	14	13	12	6		5			1	11^{3}									6
	2	14	4	7^{3}		3	8^{2}	9	10^{1}		13	12	6		5			1	11									7
	2		4	7^{3}		3	8^{1}	9	10	13	14	12	6^{2}		5			1	11									8
	2^{1}	12	4	8^{2}	13	3		9	11		6	14	7^{3}		5			1	10									9
	2	6	4	9		3		10	11	13	7^{2}		8^{1}		5			1	12									10
	2^{3}	3	4■	7		6	12	9^{1}	10	14	13		8^{2}		5			1	11									11
	2	3		8		4		7	11^{1}	13■	9^{2}	10^{3}	6		5	12		1■	14									12
	12	2	4	8		3	9^{2}	7	10		6^{1}		5		13	1	14		11^{3}									13
	13	2	4	7^{2}		3^{1}	8	6	10		9^{3}	14	5		12			1	11									14
	5	8	4	7	6■	3		10			9	13	2^{1}			1	11^{2}		12									15
	5	6	4	7		3		10			8^{1}	9	2			1	11		12									16
	5	2	4	9	7^{2}	3		6				10	8			1^{1}	11	12	13									17
		3	4	7	9	2	12	6^{2}				10	8				11^{1}	1	13	5								18
	8	3	4	7	9	2			12			10^{1}	6				13	1	11^{2}	5								19
		3	4	7	9	2^{1}	8^{3}		12				10				14	1	11^{2}	5	6	13						20
		3	4	7	9	2	13		10				8^{2}			1			11^{1}	5	6	12						21
		4	3	9	8				10^{1}				7			1	13		12	5	6	11^{2}	2					22
		3	4	7		2	8^{1}		10				6^{2}			1			12	5	9■	11		13				23
		3	4	8^{1}	7	2	6^{2}		11				9			1			13	5		10		12				24
		4	3		7	2	12						9			1	11^{1}		10	5		13		6^{2}	8			25
		3	4		9	2			10				8					1		5	7	11		12	6^{1}			26
		3	4	12	9^{2}	2			10				8					1	13	5	6	11^{1}			7			27
		3		7	9	4			10^{1}				2					1		5	8	11			6	12		28
		3	4^{2}	7	9	2			10				6					1	14	5	8^{3}	11^{1}			12	13		29
		3		6	10	7							2				13	1	12	5	9	11^{1}			8	4^{2}		30
		3		7	9	4			10^{2}				2					1		5^{1}	6	11			8	12	13	31
		4			9^{1}	3	13		10^{2}				6				12	1			7	11			8	5	2	32
		3		7			10^{1}		12				6				13	1		5	9	11			8	2^{2}	4	33
		4		9		3			12				7				10^{1}	1		5	6	11■			8		2	34
		3		7		2■			10^{2}				8^{1}				11	1		5	6		12	13	9		4	35
		3		10	9	2			13									1		5	6^{2}	11	7^{1}	12	8		4	36

EDINBURGH CITY

Year formed: 1928 (disbanded 1955, reformed from Postal United in 1986).
Ground & Address: Ainslie Park Stadium, 94 Pilton Drive, Edinburgh EH5 2HF (for 3 seasons from 2017-18 whilst Meadowbank Stadium is redeveloped).
Telephone: 0845 463 1932. *Postal Address:* 74 Lochend Road South, Edinburgh EH7 6DR.
E-mail: admin@edinburghcityfc.com *Website:* edinburghcityfc.com
Ground Capacity: 3,127. *Size of Pitch:* 96m × 66m
Chairman: Jim Brown. *Secretary:* Gavin Kennedy.
Manager: Gary Jardine. *Assistant Manager:* Ross MacNamara.
Previous names: Postal United.
Club Nickname: 'The Citizens'.
Previous Grounds: City Park 1928-55; Fernieside 1986-95; Meadowbank Stadium 1996-2017.
Record victory: 5-0 v King's Park, Division II (1935-36); 6-1 and 7-2 v Brechin City, Division II (1937-38).
Record defeat: 1-11 v Rangers, Scottish Cup, 19 January 1929.

EDINBURGH CITY – SPFL LADBROKES LEAGUE TWO 2016–17 LEAGUE RECORD

Match No.	*Date*	*Venue*	*Opponents*	*Result*		*H/T Score*	*Lg Pos.*	*Goalscorers*	*Attendance*
1	Aug 6	H	Forfar Ath	L	2-3	1-2	7	Beattie [20], Guthrie [90]	547
2	13	A	Elgin C	L	0-3	0-3	10		610
3	20	A	Cowdenbeath	L	0-2	0-1	10		325
4	27	H	Berwick R	L	1-2	0-0	10	See [65]	408
5	Sept 10	A	Stirling Alb	D	1-1	0-0	10	Allum [84]	465
6	17	H	Montrose	L	0-1	0-0	10		309
7	24	A	Annan Ath	D	1-1	0-1	10	Swinglehurst (og) [48]	351
8	Oct 1	H	Arbroath	D	3-3	1-1	10	Laird [10], See 2 [53, 74]	590
9	8	H	Elgin C	L	1-2	0-2	10	Gair (pen) [77]	352
10	15	H	Clyde	L	0-1	0-0	10		438
11	29	A	Forfar Ath	D	1-1	1-0	10	See [25]	491
12	Nov 5	A	Montrose	W	1-0	0-0	10	Gair (pen) [64]	388
13	12	H	Annan Ath	W	1-0	0-0	10	Porteous [81]	256
14	19	H	Cowdenbeath	D	1-1	0-1	10	Gair [79]	311
15	Dec 3	A	Arbroath	W	1-0	0-0	8	See [82]	582
16	10	H	Stirling Alb	W	2-0	1-0	7	See [29], Gair [86]	368
17	17	A	Clyde	D	0-0	0-0	7		461
18	31	A	Berwick R	W	3-1	2-0	6	McKee [1], Gair [3], Beattie (pen) [71]	515
19	Jan 7	H	Arbroath	L	0-2	0-1	6		481
20	21	H	Forfar Ath	L	0-1	0-1	8		352
21	28	A	Elgin C	L	1-3	0-2	8	Beattie [70]	563
22	Feb 4	H	Clyde	D	0-0	0-0	8		302
23	11	A	Annan Ath	L	0-1	0-1	9		379
24	18	H	Montrose	D	1-1	1-0	9	Walker [30]	346
25	25	A	Stirling Alb	L	0-1	0-1	9		501
26	28	A	Cowdenbeath	W	2-1	1-1	8	Gair (pen) [17], Walker [64]	309
27	Mar 11	A	Forfar Ath	W	2-1	0-1	8	Riordan [76], Allan [89]	446
28	15	H	Berwick R	D	2-2	0-1	8	Riordan [48], Gair [71]	423
29	18	A	Clyde	L	1-3	1-0	9	Allan [22]	484
30	25	H	Elgin C	W	3-0	1-0	8	Gair 2 (1 pen) [37, 48 (p)], Caddow [85]	396
31	Apr 1	A	Montrose	L	0-3	0-1	8		454
32	8	H	Cowdenbeath	D	1-1	1-0	8	Walker [29]	567
33	15	A	Arbroath	W	1-0	0-0	7	Porteous [90]	775
34	22	H	Annan Ath	W	2-0	1-0	7	Beattie [45], Allan [59]	378
35	29	H	Stirling Alb	W	1-0	0-0	7	Riordan [90]	388
36	May 6	A	Berwick R	L	2-3	0-2	7	Allan [74], Porteous [85]	695

Final League Position: 7

Honours
Scottish Lowland League Champions: 2014-15, 2015-16 (promoted to League Two via play-offs).

Club colours: Shirt: White with diagonal black band. Shorts: Black. Socks: White.

Goalscorers: *League (38):* Gair 9 (4 pens), See 6, Allan 4, Beattie 4 (1 pen), Porteous 3, Riordan 3, Walker 3, Allum 1, Caddow 1, Guthrie 1, Laird 1, McKee 1, own goal 1.
William Hill Scottish FA Cup (2): Allum 1, See 1.
Betfred Scottish League Cup (2): Allum 2.
IRN-BRU Scottish League Challenge Cup (1): Cummings 1.

Antell C 13	Harrison S 14 + 1	Mbu J 30	McKee C 29	Caddow J 13 + 9	Muhsin S 2 + 5	McFarland I 24 + 4	McConnell M 13 + 15	Donaldson G 13 + 5	Beattie C 15 + 8	Gibson N 1 + 1	Cummings D 14 + 7	Guthrie R 11 + 12	Dunn J 22 + 3	Porteous R 23	Martyniuk N 2	Dunsmore A 30 + 1	Allum R 6 + 9	See O 15 + 5	MacDonald J — + 1	Gair D 23 + 9	Stobie A 23	Laird M 24	Walker J 16	Allan L 13 + 1	Riordan D 7	Mafoko S — + 1	*Match No.*
1	2	3■	4	5	6[1]	7[2]	8	9	10[3]	11	12	13	14														1
1			4		13	6[1]		9	10	12	7	11[3]	8	2[2]	3	5	14										2
1			5	6		7[2]	14				9	8[1]	10	3	4[3]	2	11	12	13								3
1		4	5	2		8[1]	13				7[2]		9	3		6	10	11		12							4
1		4	7	2		6[1]	9[3]		14		8		11	3		5[2]	10	13		12							5
1		3	7	2	14	6[2]	9[1]		12		8		11	4		5[3]	10	13									6
	5	3	7	14	4	13			10[3]				11[2]			2	12	6[1]		8	1	9					7
	4	3	5			7	13		10[1]				6			2	12	11		9	1	8[2]					8
	4	3[1]	5	13		7	12		10[2]			8[3]	6			2	14	11		9	1						9
			3[2]	5		7[3]	12	4	13			10[1]	6	2			14	11		9	1	8					10
		3	5	2	12	7	9[3]		10[2]			14		4			13	11[1]		8	1	6					11
	4	3	5		13	7	9[1]		10[3]			14				2	12	11[2]		8	1	6					12
	4	3	5			7	13				12	9[2]		8		2	11	10[3]		14	1	6[1]					13
	4[1]	3		14		7	9[3]				13	11[2]		5		2	10	12		8	1	6					14
		3	4	2	12	8[1]	6[3]	5[2]			11		9				13	10		14	1	7					15
		3	8			6	9[1]	5			11			4		2		10		12	1	7					16
		3	7			6	9[2]	5			10[1]	13		4		2		11		12	1	8					17
		3	5			7	10[1]	6	13				12	4		2		11		8[2]	1	9					18
		3	5[1]			7[3]	10[2]	6	13		14			4		2	12	11		8	1	9					19
	3	4	9			8[1]	14	5[3]	12		10[2]		6			2		11		13	1	7					20
	3	4		13		8[2]		9	12		10[1]	11[3]	6			2		14		7	1		5				21
	2	3[2]		5		14	7	12				13	8[3]			4		10[1]		9	1		6	11			22
	3		8	14		13	12					9[1]	6	5		2				7[3]	1	11[2]	4	10			23
	3		4	5		13	12				14	11[2]	6			2				9	1	7[1]	8	10[3]			24
	3[2]		4	14		10[3]		9			8	12		2		5[1]				13	1	7	6	11			25
		3	4	13			12	14			10[1]		8	2		5[3]				9	1	7	6	11[2]			26
		4	3[1]	2			6[3]	5	10		8	14	9							13	1		7[2]	12	11		27
		3					13	4	9[2]				12	2		5				8	1	7	6	11	10[1]		28
		3		5				12	13			14	9	7		4[3]				8	1	2	6[1]	10	11[2]		29
1		3	5	12		6[1]	13		10[3]			14	9			2				7		4	8[2]	11			30
1		3	4			6[1]	13		11[2]			12	2			5				7		8	9	10			31
1	12	3	4[2]	14					10		13		5[3]	2		6				9		7	8	11[1]			32
1		3	4						10[1]			13	5	2		12				9		6	7	11	8[2]		33
1		3	4■						10[1]			12		2		5				9		6	7	11	8		34
1	3	4				9[3]	12	14	11[2]		13	6[1]		5		2				8			7		10		35
1		4		3			13	12			9[3]	6[2]		5		2[1]				8			7	10	11	14	36

ELGIN CITY

Year Formed: 1893. *Ground and Address:* Borough Briggs, Borough Briggs Road, Elgin IV30 1AP.
Telephone: 01343 551114. *Fax:* 01343 547921. *E-mail:* office@elgincity.com *Website:* www.elgincity.net
Ground Capacity: 3,927 (seated: 478). *Size of pitch:* 102m × 68m.
Chairman: Graham Tatters. *Secretary:* Kate Taylor.
Manager: Jim Weir. *Assistant Manager:* Gavin Price.
Previous names: 1900-03 Elgin City United.
Club Nicknames: 'City', 'The Black & Whites'.
Previous Grounds: Association Park 1893-95; Milnfield Park 1895-1909; Station Park 1909-19; Cooper Park 1919-21.
Record Attendance: 12,608 v Arbroath, Scottish Cup, 17 February 1968.
Record Transfer Fee received: £32,000 for Michael Teasdale to Dundee (January 1994).
Record Transfer Fee paid: £10,000 for Russell McBride from Fraserburgh (July 2001).
Record Victory: 18-1 v Brora Rangers, North of Scotland Cup, 6 February 1960.
Record Defeat: 1-14 v Hearts, Scottish Cup, 4 February 1939.
Most League Appearances: 306: Mark Nicholson, 2007-17.
Most League Goals in Season (Individual): 21: Craig Gunn, 2015-16.
Most Goals Overall (Individual): 128: Craig Gunn, 2009-17.

ELGIN CITY – SPFL LADBROKES LEAGUE TWO 2016–17 LEAGUE RECORD

Match No.	*Date*	*Venue*	*Opponents*	*Result*	*H/T Score*	*Lg Pos.*	*Goalscorers*	*Atten-dance*
1	Aug 6	A	Cowdenbeath	W 1-0	0-0	4	McLeish [51]	315
2	13	H	Edinburgh C	W 3-0	3-0	1	Gunn [17], Sutherland, S 2 [21, 25]	610
3	20	H	Arbroath	L 0-1	0-0	2		519
4	27	A	Forfar Ath	L 2-3	2-1	6	McLeish 2 [22, 42]	537
5	Sept 10	A	Berwick R	W 4-2	2-1	3	Sutherland, S [11], Reid [24], Gunn 2 [75, 86]	407
6	17	H	Clyde	L 0-2	0-2	5		713
7	24	A	Stirling Alb	W 4-0	3-0	3	Sutherland, S 2 [5, 30], Dodd [8], Gunn [89]	457
8	Oct 1	H	Annan Ath	L 0-2	0-1	3		583
9	8	A	Edinburgh C	W 2-1	2-0	2	Dodd [3], Reilly [31]	352
10	15	A	Montrose	W 5-0	3-0	2	McHardy 2 [2, 19], Cameron 2 [30, 83], Sutherland, S [51]	302
11	29	H	Cowdenbeath	W 3-1	2-0	2	Cameron [26], MacPhee [33], Sutherland, S [81]	650
12	Nov 5	A	Clyde	L 1-2	0-2	2	McHardy [60]	616
13	12	H	Stirling Alb	L 2-3	1-0	2	McHardy [29], Cameron [76]	585
14	19	A	Annan Ath	L 0-1	0-1	4		353
15	Dec 3	H	Montrose	W 4-1	0-0	2	MacPhee [54], McLeish [62], Sutherland, S [68], Cameron [88]	586
16	10	H	Berwick R	W 6-0	2-0	2	Sutherland, S 3 (1 pen) [9, 54 (p), 70], Cameron 2 [14, 63], Moore [66]	535
17	17	A	Arbroath	L 2-3	1-0	3	Cameron [18], McLeish [51]	584
18	Jan 2	H	Forfar Ath	D 2-2	2-1	3	McLeish [20], McHardy [40]	1091
19	7	A	Montrose	W 3-0	2-0	3	Dodd [29], Sutherland, S 2 [40, 87]	562
20	14	H	Annan Ath	W 3-2	3-0	3	Cameron [17], Sutherland, S [28], McLeish [41]	638
21	28	H	Edinburgh C	W 3-1	2-0	3	Sutherland, S 3 (1 pen) [15, 42, 73 (p)]	563
22	Feb 11	A	Forfar Ath	D 1-1	0-1	3	Cameron [65]	551
23	18	H	Clyde	W 4-1	1-0	3	Nicolson [22], Sutherland, S (pen) [48], Perry (og) [56], Gunn [80]	881
24	25	A	Berwick R	W 1-0	1-0	3	McLeish [31]	403
25	28	A	Stirling Alb	L 0-1	0-0	3		412
26	Mar 4	H	Arbroath	D 0-0	0-0	3		640
27	11	A	Annan Ath	L 0-1	0-1	4		328
28	14	A	Cowdenbeath	D 1-1	1-0	3	Cameron [20]	278
29	18	H	Forfar Ath	D 1-1	0-0	3	McHardy [49]	709
30	25	A	Edinburgh C	L 0-3	0-1	4		396
31	Apr 1	H	Berwick R	D 2-2	1-2	4	Reilly [44], Cameron (pen) [82]	588
32	8	H	Montrose	D 1-1	1-0	3	Cameron [10]	781
33	15	A	Clyde	L 2-3	2-0	4	McLeish [6], Dodd [27]	465
34	22	H	Stirling Alb	D 2-2	0-0	5	Reid [69], MacPhee [88]	785
35	29	A	Arbroath	L 2-3	0-1	5	Reid [58], Sukar (og) [86]	807
36	May 6	H	Cowdenbeath	D 0-0	0-0	5		909

Final League Position: 5

Honours
Runners-up: League Two 2015-16.
Scottish Cup: Quarter-finals 1968.
Highland League Champions: winners 15 times.

Club colours: Shirt: Black and white stripes. Shorts: Black. Socks: White.

Goalscorers: *League (67):* Sutherland S 18 (3 pens), Cameron 13 (1 pen), McLeish 9, McHardy 6, Gunn 5, Dodd 4, MacPhee 3, Reid 3, Reilly 2, Moore 1, Nicolson 1, own goals 2.
William Hill Scottish FA Cup (13): Sutherland S 5, Cameron 3, McLeish 2, Gunn 1, Nicolson 1, own goal 1.
Betfred Scottish League Cup (6): Gunn 2 (1 pen), Duff 1, MacLeod 1, McHardy 1, Moore 1.
IRN-BRU Scottish League Challenge Cup (3): MacLeod 1, Nicolson 1, Sutherland S 1.

Black S 3	Cooper M 28	Nicolson M 31 + 1	Stewart K 14 + 13	MacPhee A 34	McLeish C 34 + 2	Reilly T 35	Cameron B 35	Moore D 22 + 11	Gunn C 12 + 22	Sutherland S 23 + 1	MacLeod K — + 12	Smith S 2 + 4	Dodd C 25 + 6	Meckay C 12	McHardy D 32 + 2	Reid J 12 + 14	Crawford D 1	Waters M 14 + 1	Bruce R — + 4	Brownlie D 13	Sutherland A 5 + 8	Mackay C 6	Sinnamon R 2	Finnamon R 1	*Match No.*
1	2	3	4	5	6^{2}	7	8	9^{3}	10^{1}	11	12	13	14												1
	2	3	4	5	10	8	7^{1}	9	11^{2}	6	13	12^{3}	14	1											2
	2	3	4	5	10	8	7	9^{2}	11^{1}	6	12			1	13										3
	2	3	4	5	6	7^{3}	8	9^{1}	10^{2}	11	12			1	13	14									4
1	2	3	14	5	10^{3}	7	8	12	13	11			9^{1}		4	6^{2}									5
1	2	3	13	5	12	8	7	9^{1}	10^{2}	11			14		4	6^{3}									6
	2	4		5^{2}	10^{3}	7	8	12	13	11	14		9		3	6^{1}	1								7
	2	3		5	10^{1}	8	7	12	13	11	14		9^{2}		4	6^{3}		1							8
	2	4	12	5	10^{2}	7	8	13		11	14		9^{3}		3	6^{1}		1							9
	2	4	12	5	10^{1}	7^{2}	8		13	11			9^{3}		3	6		1	14						10
	2	3	14	4	10^{1}	7	8	12	13	11			9^{2}		5	6^{3}		1							11
	2		4	5	11^{3}	7	8	12	14	10	13		9^{1}		3	6^{2}		1							12
	2	3		5	10^{2}	8	7	14	13	11	12		9^{1}		4	6^{3}		1							13
	2		3	5	6^{1}	7^{2}	8	9	11^{3}	10	13		12		4	14		1							14
		3	2	5	10^{1}	8	7	9	12	11^{2}	14		6^{3}	1	4	13									15
		3	2	5	10^{1}	8	7	9	12	11^{3}	14		6^{2}	1	4	13									16
		3	2	5^{2}	10^{1}	8■	7	9	12	11			6	1	4	13									17
	2	3		5	10^{1}		7	9	12	11			6^{2}	1	4	8			13						18
	2	3	13	5	10^{2}	6	7	9^{1}	14	11			8^{3}	1	4	12									19
	2	3	13	5	10^{3}	8	7	9^{2}		11			6^{1}	1	4	12			14						20
	2		13	5	10^{2}	8	7	9^{1}	12	11			6^{3}	1	4	14				3					21
	2	4		9	10^{1}	7	8	6	12	11					5			1		3■					22
	2	3		5	10^{1}	8	7	9	12	11^{3}			6^{2}	1	4	13					14				23
	2		12	5	10^{2}	8^{1}	7	9^{3}	11				6	1	4	14				3	13				24
	2	8	13	5	14	7^{2}	11	9^{1}	10^{3}				6		3			12		4		1			25
	2	9		5	10^{2}	7	8	12	11				6^{1}		3					4	13	1			26
	2	3	13	6	10^{3}	7	8	9^{1}	11^{2}						5				14	4	12	1			27
	2^{2}	12	9	5	10	7	8		14	13^{3}			6		4					3	11^{1}	1			28
		2	6	9	10	8	7	13	11^{2}				5^{1}		4					3	12	1			29
		2	6^{1}		10^{2}	8	7	12	14				9		4	13				3	11^{3}	1	5		30
		7	12	5	11	8	10	9	14						4	6^{3}		1		3^{2}	13			2^{1}	31
		7	2	5	11	8	10	9^{1}	13				12		4	14		1		3^{3}	6^{2}				32
		7	4		10	8		9	13			14	6^{1}		5	12		1		3	11^{3}		2^{2}		33
	2	3		5	10	8	7	9^{1}	11^{2}			14	6^{3}		4	12		1			13				34
	5	3		9	10^{1}	6^{3}	8		12			11	14		4	7■		1		2^{2}	13				35
	2	3	14	5	11^{3}	8	10	12	13			7	6^{2}		4			1			9^{1}				36

FALKIRK

Year Formed: 1876. *Ground & Address:* The Falkirk Stadium, 4 Stadium Way, Falkirk FK2 9EE. *Telephone:* 01324 624121. *Fax:* 01324 612418. *Email:* post@falkirkfc.co.uk *Website:* www.falkirkfc.co.uk
Ground Capacity: 8,750 (all seated). *Size of Pitch:* 105m × 68m.
Acting Chair: Margaret Lang. *Chief Executive:* Craig Campbell.
Manager: Peter Houston. *Assistant Manager:* James McDonaugh.
Club Nickname: 'The Bairns'.
Previous Grounds: Randyford 1876-81; Blinkbonny Grounds 1881-83; Brockville Park 1883-2003.
Record Attendance: 23,100 v Celtic, Scottish Cup 3rd rd, 21 February 1953.
Record Transfer Fee received: £945,000 for Conor McGrandles to Norwich C (August 2014).
Record Transfer Fee paid: £225,000 to Chelsea for Kevin McAllister (August 1991).
Record Victory: 11-1 v Tillicoultry, Scottish Cup 1st rd, 7 Sep 1889.
Record Defeat: 1-11 v Airdrieonians, Division I, 28 April 1951.
Most Capped Player: Alex Parker, 14 (15), Scotland.
Most League Appearances: 451: Tom Ferguson, 1919-32.
Most League Goals in Season (Individual): 43: Evelyn Morrison, Division I, 1928-29.
Most Goals Overall (Individual): 154: Kenneth Dawson, 1934-51.

FALKIRK – SPFL LADBROKES CHAMPIONSHIP 2016–17 LEAGUE RECORD

Match No.	Date	Venue	Opponents	Result		H/T Score	Lg Pos.	Goalscorers	Attendance
1	Aug 6	H	Hibernian	L	1-2	1-1	9	Sibbald [9]	6458
2	13	A	Greenock Morton	D	1-1	0-1	7	Leahy [90]	2079
3	20	A	Queen of the South	L	0-2	0-1	8		1841
4	27	H	Dumbarton	W	1-0	0-0	6	Miller [86]	4311
5	Sept 10	A	Raith R	W	2-0	1-0	5	Baird [30], Taiwo [72]	2320
6	17	H	Dundee U	W	3-1	1-1	4	Baird [18], Hippolyte [87], Miller [89]	5488
7	24	H	Ayr U	W	2-0	0-0	3	Meggatt (og) [78], Miller [90]	4345
8	Oct 1	A	St Mirren	D	1-1	1-0	3	Sibbald [9]	2334
9	15	H	Dunfermline Ath	W	2-1	1-0	3	Sibbald [27], Hippolyte [52]	6377
10	22	H	Raith R	L	2-4	1-2	5	Baird [18], Miller [75]	4773
11	29	A	Dundee U	L	0-1	0-0	5		7046
12	Nov 5	H	Greenock Morton	D	1-1	0-0	5	Miller [90]	4432
13	12	A	Hibernian	D	1-1	0-0	5	Baird [78]	14,551
14	19	A	Ayr U	W	1-0	1-0	5	Craigen [15]	1414
15	Dec 3	H	St Mirren	W	3-1	0-1	3	Miller [47], McHugh [78], Hippolyte [83]	4486
16	10	H	Queen of the South	D	2-2	1-1	3	Hippolyte 2 [45, 54]	4170
17	17	A	Dumbarton	L	1-2	0-1	3	Sibbald [66]	832
18	26	A	Dunfermline Ath	D	1-1	1-0	4	Hippolyte [10]	6134
19	31	H	Hibernian	L	1-2	1-1	4	Sibbald [15]	6747
20	Jan 7	A	Raith R	W	4-1	3-1	4	Hippolyte [16], McHugh [25], Sibbald 2 [38, 48]	2202
21	14	H	Ayr U	D	1-1	1-1	4	Grant [45]	5038
22	28	A	St Mirren	W	2-1	1-0	4	Baird 2 [11, 63]	3316
23	Feb 4	H	Dunfermline Ath	W	2-0	1-0	3	Baird [34], Miller [77]	5953
24	11	H	Dundee U	W	3-0	1-0	3	Baird [5], Muirhead (pen) [53], Craigen [60]	5028
25	18	A	Greenock Morton	D	2-2	1-1	3	Craigen [43], Muirhead (pen) [50]	2397
26	25	H	Dumbarton	D	2-2	1-1	3	Leahy [37], Austin [59]	4160
27	Mar 4	A	Queen of the South	W	2-0	1-0	2	Kidd [45], Sibbald (pen) [79]	1995
28	11	A	Ayr U	W	4-1	1-0	2	Austin 2 [8, 63], Aird [90], Sibbald [90]	1614
29	18	H	Greenock Morton	L	0-1	0-0	2		4584
30	25	A	Hibernian	L	1-2	0-0	2	Sibbald [77]	16,140
31	Apr 1	H	Raith R	W	1-0	0-0	2	Miller [71]	4823
32	8	A	Dundee U	D	1-1	0-0	2	Leahy [83]	6313
33	15	H	St Mirren	D	2-2	1-1	2	Miller [20], McHugh [77]	4734
34	22	A	Dunfermline Ath	W	2-1	0-1	2	Muirhead (pen) [53], Austin [70]	5076
35	29	H	Queen of the South	D	2-2	1-1	2	Austin [31], Muirhead (pen) [71]	4673
36	May 6	A	Dumbarton	W	1-0	0-0	2	Austin [85]	1660

Final League Position: 2

Honours
League Champions: Division II 1935-36, 1969-70, 1974-75. First Division 1990-91, 1993-94, 2002-03, 2004-05. Second Division 1979-80;
Runners-up: Division I 1907-08, 1909-10. First Division 1985-86, 1988-89, 1997-98, 1998-99. Division II 1904-05, 1951-52, 1960-61. Championship: 2015-16, 2016-17.
Scottish Cup Winners: 1913, 1957; *Runners-up:* 1997, 2009, 2015.
League Cup Runners-up: 1947-48.
League Challenge Cup Winners: 1993-94, 1997-98, 2004-05, 2011-12.

European: *Europa League:* 2 matches (2009-10).

Club colours: Shirt: Navy blue with red and white vertical stripes. Shorts: Navy blue. Socks: Navy blue.

Goalscorers: *League (58):* Sibbald 10 (1 pen), Miller 9, Baird 8, Hippolyte 7, Austin 6, Muirhead 4 (4 pens), Craigen 3, Leahy 3, McHugh 3, Aird 1, Grant 1, Kidd 1, Taiwo 1, own goal 1.
William Hill Scottish FA Cup (0).
Betfred Scottish League Cup (5): Austin 1, Gasparotto 1, McHugh 1, Miller 1, Vaulks 1.
IRN-BRU Scottish League Challenge Cup (6): Baird 2, McHugh 2, Hippolyte 1, McCracken 1.
Play-Offs (3): Craigen 2, McKee 1.

Rogers D 28	McCracken D 16	Watson P 10 + 1	Gasparotto L 27 + 2	Muirhead A 24 + 2	Taiwo T 30 + 1	Rankin J 7 + 6	Sibbald C 35 + 1	Leahy L 31	McHugh B 15 + 18	Baird J 32 + 2	Austin N 7 + 10	Craigen J 13 + 14	Miller L 16 + 14	Mehmet D 1	Hippolyte M 22 + 8	Kerr M 29 + 1	Kidd L 12 + 2	Shepherd S 2 + 9	Grant P 20 + 1	Gallacher T 5 + 1	Aird F 5 + 7	McKee J 2 + 1	Thomson R 7	*Match No.*
1	2	3	4	5	6^1	7	8^3	9	10	11^2	12	13	14											1
		3	4	2	6	8	9	5	10^1	12	14	7^2	11^3	1	13									2
1		3	4	2	6^2	8^1	9^3	5	11	10	14	13			12	7								3
1	3		4	14	6^3		8	5	10	11^2		12	13		9	7	2^1							4
1	3		4		6	12	7^1	5	11	10^2		14	13		9^3	8	2							5
1	3		4		6^3	12	8^2	5	11^1	10		13	14		9	7	2							6
1	3		4		6	12	8^2	5	10^1	11			13		9	7^3	2	14						7
1	3		4		8^1	6	7^3	5	11^2	10		13	12		14	9	2							8
1	3	12	4		7^2	13	8	5	11	10					9^1	6	2^3	14						9
1	3	2	4		6^1		7	5	11^2	10		13	12		9^3	8		14						10
1	3		4	2	6	7^2	9^3	5	13	10^1		14	11		12	8								11
1	3		4	2	7^2		9	5	13	11^3		12	10		8	6								12
1	3		4	2	8■	12	6^1	5	13	11			10^2		9^3	7			14					13
1	3		4	2		7	9^2	5	14	10^1	13	6	11^3		12	8								14
1	3		4	2		7^1	12	5	14	11^2		6^3	10		9	8		13						15
1	3		4	2	14		8	5	13	11^2		6^3	10		9	7^1		12						16
1	3			2	6^2		9			10		12	11^1		8	7		13	4	5				17
1			3	2	7^2	14	9		12	10			13		6^1	8		11^3	4	5				18
1			3	2	7		10		12	11^2			13		9	8		6^1	4	5				19
1		3^1	13	2	8		9		7	11^2					10	6		12	4	5				20
1	3			2	6^2		8		11^1	10^3		12	13		9	7		14	4	5				21
1		3	14	2			8	5	12	10^3			11^1		9	7	13		4		6^2			22
1		3		2			6	5^1	13	11^2	14	8	10^3		9				4	12		7		23
1		3		2	6^1		7	5		11^2	12	8	10^3		9		13		4		14			24
1		3		2	7		8	5	12		10	6^3	11^1		9^2	13			4		14			25
1		3		2	6		8	5	14	13	10^2	7	11^1		9^3				4		12			26
1			3		6		9	5	13	11^3	10^2	8^1	14			7	2		4		12			27
1			3		7		9	5	13	10^2	11^1		12			8	2		4		6			28
1			3		6		8	5	13	10^3	11	14			12	7^2	2		4		9^1			29
			4	14	7^2		9	5	8^3	11	13				12	6	2^1		3		10		1	30
			4		7		8	5	11	10^2		13	12		9		2		3		6^1		1	31
			4	2	8		6	5	11^1	10^2	12	13			9^3	7		14	3				1	32
			4	2	8		6	5	14	10^1	12	11	9^2			7^3			3		13		1	33
			4	2	6^2		9	5		11	13	8	10^1		12	7^3			3			14	1	34
				3	6		8	5	12	10^2	11	9^1	14			7	2^3		4		13		1	35
			3	2			8	5	13		10^2	9^1	11			7			4		12	6	1	36

FORFAR ATHLETIC

Year Formed: 1885. *Ground & Address:* Station Park, Carseview Road, Forfar DD8 3BT. *Telephone:* 01307 463576.
Fax: 01307 466956. *E-mail:* info@forfarathletic.co.uk *Website:* www.forfarathletic.co.uk
Ground Capacity: 6,777 (seated: 739). *Size of Pitch:* 103m × 64m.
Chairman: Ken Stewart. *Vice-Chairman:* Dennis Fenton. *Secretary:* David McGregor.
Manager: Gary Bollan. *Assistant Manager:* Stuart Balmer.
Club Nicknames: 'The Loons', 'The Sky Blues'.
Previous Grounds: None.
Record Attendance: 10,780 v Rangers, Scottish Cup 2nd rd, 2 February 1970.
Record Transfer Fee received: £65,000 for David Bingham to Dunfermline Ath (September 1995).
Record Transfer Fee paid: £50,000 for Ian McPhee from Airdrieonians (1991).
Record Victory: 14-1 v Lindertis, Scottish Cup 1st rd, 1 September 1888.
Record Defeat: 2-12 v King's Park, Division II, 2 January 1930.
Most League Appearances: 463: Ian McPhee, 1978-88 and 1991-98.
Most League Goals in Season (Individual): 46: Dave Kilgour, Division II, 1929-30.
Most Goals Overall: 125: John Clark, 1978-91.

FORFAR ATHLETIC – SPFL LADBROKES LEAGUE TWO 2016–17 LEAGUE RECORD

Match No.	Date	Venue	Opponents	Result		H/T Score	Lg Pos.	Goalscorers	Attendance
1	Aug 6	A	Edinburgh C	W	3-2	2-1	2	Cox (pen) [10], Milne [41], Lister, James [81]	547
2	13	H	Cowdenbeath	W	4-3	2-1	2	Lister, James [20], Denholm [24], Peters [51], Swankie [87]	516
3	20	A	Berwick R	W	2-1	1-0	1	Milne [10], Peters [53]	421
4	27	H	Elgin C	W	3-2	1-2	1	O'Brien 2 [38, 65], Peters [50]	537
5	Sept 10	A	Annan Ath	W	2-1	0-1	1	Munro [61], Milne [84]	403
6	17	H	Stirling Alb	W	4-1	1-1	1	Munro [25], Peters 2 [61, 88], Denholm [90]	635
7	24	A	Clyde	W	1-0	1-0	1	O'Brien [40]	660
8	Oct 1	H	Montrose	L	1-3	0-1	1	Denholm [90]	740
9	15	A	Arbroath	L	0-2	0-0	1		862
10	29	H	Edinburgh C	D	1-1	0-1	1	Denholm [68]	491
11	Nov 5	A	Stirling Alb	W	3-0	1-0	1	Munro [7], Swankie [54], Cox [69]	663
12	12	H	Berwick R	W	2-0	1-0	1	Cox [45], Milne [86]	477
13	19	A	Montrose	D	1-1	1-1	1	Denholm [45]	630
14	Dec 10	H	Arbroath	L	0-1	0-0	1		786
15	13	H	Annan Ath	W	5-1	3-0	1	Cox [4], O'Brien [27], Denholm [44], Milne 2 [49, 83]	337
16	17	A	Cowdenbeath	W	4-3	2-1	1	Milne [32], Swankie 2 [42, 90], Peters [70]	277
17	26	H	Clyde	W	4-3	1-2	1	Swankie [9], Fotheringham [51], Lister, James [80], Cox [90]	659
18	Jan 2	A	Elgin C	D	2-2	1-2	1	Cox [18], Swankie [65]	1091
19	7	A	Annan Ath	W	2-1	1-1	1	Lister, James [38], Home (og) [48]	432
20	14	H	Stirling Alb	D	1-1	1-1	1	Cox [37]	632
21	21	A	Edinburgh C	W	1-0	1-0	1	Cox (pen) [37]	352
22	28	H	Cowdenbeath	W	3-1	0-1	1	Peters [54], O'Brien [69], Milne [77]	547
23	Feb 4	A	Arbroath	W	1-0	1-0	1	Peters [34]	1008
24	11	H	Elgin C	D	1-1	1-0	1	Peters [7]	551
25	18	A	Berwick R	L	2-3	2-1	1	Cox [13], Peters [21]	480
26	25	H	Montrose	D	0-0	0-0	1		725
27	Mar 4	A	Clyde	D	2-2	1-0	1	Denholm [25], Lister, James [73]	490
28	11	H	Edinburgh C	L	1-2	1-0	1	Lister, James [42]	446
29	18	A	Elgin C	D	1-1	0-0	1	Lister, James [71]	709
30	25	H	Berwick R	L	2-3	1-1	1	Denholm [45], Cox (pen) [84]	477
31	Apr 1	A	Stirling Alb	W	3-0	2-0	1	Lister, James [14], Denholm 2 [27, 57]	738
32	8	H	Arbroath	D	1-1	0-0	1	Peters [46]	1564
33	15	A	Montrose	L	0-1	0-1	1		984
34	22	H	Clyde	W	3-0	1-0	1	Denholm [21], Cox [52], O'Brien [79]	741
35	29	A	Cowdenbeath	D	1-1	0-0	2	Denholm [69]	571
36	May 6	H	Annan Ath	L	2-4	1-3	2	Travis [41], O'Brien [54]	917

Final League Position: 2

Honours
League Champions: Second Division 1983-84. Third Division 1994-95; C Division 1948-49.
Runners-up: Third Division 1996-97, 2009-10 (promoted via play-offs). League Two 2016-17 (promoted via play-offs).
Scottish Cup: Semi-finals 1982.
League Cup: Semi-finals 1977-78.
League Challenge Cup: Semi-finals 2004-05.

Club colours: All navy blue with sky blue trim.

Goalscorers: *League (69):* Denholm 12, Cox 11 (3 pens), Peters 11, James Lister 8, Milne 8, O'Brien 7, Swankie 6, Munro 3, Fotheringham 1, Travis 1, own goal 1.
William Hill Scottish FA Cup (0).
Betfred Scottish League Cup (4): James Lister 1, Munro 1, O'Brien 1, Peters 1.
IRN-BRU Scottish League Challenge Cup (7): Peters 4, Malcolm 1, Milne 1, Smith 1.
Play-Offs (13): Denholm 2, Fotheringham 2, Swankie 2, Travis 2, Bain 1, Cox 1, Malone A 1, Milne 1, Peters 1.

Adam G 35	MacKintosh M 8	Munro A 21 + 3	Malcolm S 19 + 1	Bain J 33	Cox D 33	O'Brien T 34	Milne L 29 + 2	Denholm D 30 + 4	Lister James 22 + 8	Swankie G 32	Scott M 6 + 22	Peters J 23 + 10	Smith A 1 + 8	Kennedy M 9 + 1	Fotheringham M 11 + 4	Warwick G 1	McCawl E 3 + 5	Aitken M — + 1	McCall O 1 + 2	Travis M 17 + 1	Malone E 12	McLaughlin C 14	Malone A 1 + 7	Halliwell B 1	*Match No.*
1	2	3	4	5	6■	7	8^{1}	9	10	11	12														1
1	2	3	4	5		7	8^{1}	9	11	10	12	6^{2}	13												2
1	2	3	4	5	6	7	8		11	9^{2}	12	10^{1}	13												3
1	2	3	4	5	9^{2}	8	6	13	11	7	12	10^{1}													4
1		3	4	2	9	6	7	8	11			10^{1}	12	5											5
1		3	4	2	6^{2}	8	7	12	10	9^{1}	13	11		5											6
1		3	4	2	9^{2}	7	8	13	11^{1}	6	12	10^{3}	14	5											7
1		3	4	2		8	7^{1}	9	10	6	12		11^{2}	5	13										8
1		3	4	2■	6	7^{2}	8^{1}	12	10	9	13	11^{3}	14	5											9
1		3	4		6	2		9^{2}	10	11	13	12			7	5^{1}	8								10
1	2	3^{1}	12	5	10	4	8	9^{2}		11	6		13		7										11
1	2		3	5	10	4	8	9^{1}	13	11^{2}	6	12			7										12
1	2		3	5	6	4	8	9	12	11	10^{2}	13			7^{1}										13
1	2^{2}		3	5	10	4	8	9		11	6^{1}	12	13				7								14
1			3	2	11^{2}	4	6^{1}	9^{3}		8	13	10	12	5	7			14							15
1			3	2	11	4	7^{2}	6^{1}		9	12	10		5	8		13								16
1			3	2	10	4	7^{3}	6	13	9^{1}	14	11^{2}		5	8		12								17
1		4	3■	2	11			6	13	9^{1}		10^{2}		5	8				7	12					18
1		4		5	10	3	8^{1}	6	9	11		13			7^{2}				12	2					19
1		4		5	9	2	7	6^{2}	10^{1}	8	12	11							13	3					20
1		4		2	11	3	6	9		8^{2}	12	10^{1}					13			7	5				21
1		3		2	10	7	8	9			6^{1}	11					12			4	5				22
1				2	6	4	8	9	12	10		11^{1}								3	7	5			23
1				2	11	4	8	6	12	9^{2}		10^{1}					13			3	7■	5			24
1		7		2	11	4	8^{3}	6■	14	9^{2}	12	10^{1}								3		5	13		25
1				2	11	4	8^{2}		12	9	13	10			7		6^{1}			3		5			26
1■			4	2	10	7	8^{1}	9	11		13	6^{3}		12	14					3		5^{2}			27
			4	2	10	7	14	6	11^{3}		13	12			8^{2}					3	9^{1}	5		1	28
1		12		2	10	4	7	6^{2}	11	8^{3}	13	14								3		5^{1}	9		29
1		12		2	10	4	7	6	11^{1}	9		13								3^{3}	8	5^{2}	14		30
1		4			6	3		9^{3}	10^{2}	8	12	11^{1}			14					2	7	5	13		31
1		3		2				9	10	8	6	11^{1}								4	7	5	12		32
1		3			6	4	14	9^{3}	11	8	13	10^{1}								2	7^{2}	5	12		33
1				2	6	4	7^{1}	9	10^{2}	11		13								3	8	5	12		34
1		3		2^{2}	6	4	7^{1}	9	10	11		12									8	5	13		35
1		12		2^{3}	6^{1}	4		9	11	8	14	10			13					3	7^{2}	5			36

GREENOCK MORTON

Year Formed: 1874. *Ground & Address:* Cappielow Park, Sinclair St, Greenock PA15 2TY. *Telephone:* 01475 723571. *Fax:* 01475 781084. *E-mail:* info@gmfc.net *Website:* www.gmfc.net
Ground Capacity: 11,612 (seated: 6,062). *Size of Pitch:* 100m × 65m.
Chairman: Douglas Rae OBE. *Chief Executive:* Warren Hawke.
Manager: Jim Duffy. *Assistant Manager:* Craig McPherson.
Club Nickname: 'The Ton'.
Previous Grounds: Grant Street 1874, Garvel Park 1875, Cappielow Park 1879, Ladyburn Park 1882, Cappielow Park 1883.
Record Attendance: 23,500 v Celtic, 29 April 1922.
Record Transfer Fee received: £500,000 for Derek Lilley to Leeds U (March 1997).
Record Transfer Fee paid: £250,000 for Janne Lindberg and Marko Rajamäki from MyPa, Finland (November 1994).
Record Victory: 11-0 v Carfin Shamrock, Scottish Cup 4th rd, 13 November 1886.
Record Defeat: 1-10 v Port Glasgow Ath, Division II, 5 May, 1894 and v St Bernards, Division II, 14 October 1933.
Most Capped Player: Jimmy Cowan, 25, Scotland.
Most League Appearances: 534: Derek Collins, 1987-98, 2001-05.
Most League Goals in Season (Individual): 58: Allan McGraw, Division II, 1963-64.
Most Goals Overall (Individual): 136: Andy Ritchie, 1976-83.

GREENOCK MORTON – SPFL LADBROKES CHAMPIONSHIP 2016–17 LEAGUE RECORD

Match No.	Date	Venue	Opponents	Result		H/T Score	Lg Pos.	Goalscorers	Attendance
1	Aug 6	A	St Mirren	D	1-1	1-0	5	O'Ware 17	4997
2	13	H	Falkirk	D	1-1	1-0	6	Kilday 25	2079
3	20	H	Dumbarton	D	1-1	0-1	6	Oyenuga 62	1586
4	27	A	Hibernian	L	0-4	0-2	8		14,508
5	Sept 10	A	Ayr U	L	1-2	0-0	9	Forbes 86	1441
6	17	H	Dunfermline Ath	W	2-1	1-1	7	Oliver 24, Quitongo 84	1756
7	24	A	Dundee U	L	1-2	0-0	7	Dillon (og) 90	5829
8	Oct 1	H	Raith R	W	1-0	1-0	6	Forbes 18	1528
9	15	A	Queen of the South	W	5-0	3-0	6	Forbes 6, McDonagh 33, Oliver 36, Quitongo 64, O'Ware (pen) 72	1695
10	29	H	Ayr U	W	2-1	0-1	6	O'Ware 73, Oliver 89	1859
11	Nov 1	H	St Mirren	W	3-1	2-0	4	O'Ware 15, Forbes 27, Oliver 68	3378
12	5	A	Falkirk	D	1-1	0-0	4	Kilday 87	4432
13	12	A	Dumbarton	W	2-0	0-0	3	Russell 69, Oyenuga 76	1147
14	19	H	Dundee U	D	0-0	0-0	3		2578
15	Dec 10	A	Dunfermline Ath	L	1-2	1-2	4	Nesbitt 43	3101
16	17	H	Hibernian	D	1-1	0-0	4	Oliver 79	2156
17	24	H	Queen of the South	W	1-0	1-0	3	O'Ware 17	1638
18	31	A	St Mirren	D	1-1	0-1	3	Lamie 90	4902
19	Jan 7	H	Dumbarton	W	2-1	1-0	3	Buchanan (og) 19, Tidser (pen) 66	2094
20	14	H	Raith R	W	2-0	1-0	3	Forbes 27, Shankland 67	1957
21	28	A	Ayr U	W	4-1	3-1	3	Forbes 2 11, 19, Oliver 2 31, 65	1576
22	Feb 4	A	Queen of the South	L	0-3	0-0	4		1588
23	7	A	Raith R	W	1-0	0-0	3	Kilday 53	1161
24	18	H	Falkirk	D	2-2	1-1	4	O'Ware 13, Forbes 68	2397
25	25	A	Dundee U	D	1-1	1-0	4	Kilday 39	6065
26	Mar 11	H	Queen of the South	W	1-0	0-0	3	Forbes 55	1451
27	18	A	Falkirk	W	1-0	0-0	3	Oyenuga 79	4584
28	25	H	Dunfermline Ath	L	0-1	0-1	3		2670
29	29	A	Hibernian	D	0-0	0-0	2		15,149
30	Apr 1	A	Dumbarton	L	0-1	0-0	3		1323
31	8	H	Hibernian	D	1-1	0-1	3	Shankland (pen) 66	4229
32	11	H	St Mirren	L	1-4	1-1	4	Murdoch 29	4609
33	15	A	Raith R	L	0-2	0-1	4		1720
34	22	H	Ayr U	D	1-1	1-1	4	Shankland 38	2390
35	29	A	Dunfermline Ath	L	1-3	1-1	4	Shankland 37	3339
36	May 6	H	Dundee U	D	1-1	0-0	4	Oyenuga 52	2158

Final League Position: 4

Honours
League Champions: First Division 1977-78, 1983-84, 1986-87. Division II 1949-50, 1963-64, 1966-67. Second Division 1994-95, 2006-07. League One: 2014–15. Third Division 2002-03.
Runners-up: Division 1 1916-17. First Division 2012-13. Division II 1899-1900, 1928-29, 1936-37.
Scottish Cup Winners: 1922; *Runners-up:* 1948.
League Cup Runners-up: 1963-64.
League Challenge Cup Runners-up: 1992-93.

European: *UEFA Cup:* 2 matches (*Fairs Cup:* 1968-69).

Club colours: Shirt: Blue and white hoops. Shorts: White with blue trim. Socks: White.

Goalscorers: *League (44):* Forbes 9, Oliver 7, O'Ware 6 (1 pen), Kilday 4, Oyenuga 4, Shankland 4 (1 pen), Quitongo 2, Lamie 1, McDonagh 1, Murdoch 1, Nesbitt 1, Russell 1, Tidser 1 (1 pen), own goals 2.
William Hill Scottish FA Cup (9): Forbes 2, Lindsay 2, O'Ware 2, Tidser 2, McDonagh 1.
Betfred Scottish League Cup (9): Quitongo 4, O'Ware 2, Forbes 1, Lindsay 1, Oliver 1.
IRN-BRU Scottish League Challenge Cup (0).
Play-Offs (1): O'Ware 1.

Gaston D 29 + 1	Doyle M 27 + 2	Kilday L 18 + 4	O'Ware T 35	Lamie R 24 + 4	Forbes R 33 + 1	Lindsay J 29 + 2	Tidser M 16 + 12	McDonagh J 19 + 6	Oliver G 29 + 1	Quitongo J 14	Russell M 27 + 3	Tiffoney S 3 + 5	McAleer C — + 5	Nesbitt A 24 + 6	Oyenuga K 8 + 16	Scullion J 1 + 8	McNeil A 6 + 1	Orr T — + 3	Gunning G 10	Murdoch A 26 + 2	Shankland L 13 + 3	Donnelly L 2 + 4	Strapp L 2	Armour B — + 1	Halliwell B 1	McGowan J — + 1	*Match No.*
1	2	3	4	5	6	7^{3}	8	9	10^{2}	11^{1}	12	13	14														1
1	2	3	4	5	7	6^{3}	8	13	10	11^{1}			14	9^{2}	12												2
1	2	3	4	5	7	6^{2}	8		10^{1}	11		9			12	13											3
1^{3}	2	3	4		7	6	8		10^{2}	11^{1}	5		14	9	12		13										4
	2	3	8	4^{1}	7	6		13	9^{2}	10	5■			12	11^{3}		1	14									5
	5	3^{3}	6		8	12		2	11^{1}	10		13		7^{2}	9		1	14	4								6
	2		3		8	7^{1}		6	10	11	5	12		9^{2}			1		4	13							7
14	2		3		8	7		6	11	10	5	13		9^{1}			1^{3}		4^{2}	12							8
1	3		4		8^{1}	7		2	11	10^{2}	5	14		9^{3}	12	13				6							9
	14		3	4	6	8		2	10^{2}	11	5			9^{3}	13	12	1			7^{1}							10
1			3	4	8^{2}	7	13	2	10	11^{1}	5			9	12					6							11
1	2	13	3		8	7	14		11	10^{3}	5			12	9^{2}				4	6^{1}							12
1		14	6	4	7^{3}	9	13	2^{2}	10		5		12		11^{1}				3	8							13
1	2		3	5	6	8	13		10	11^{2}	9				12				4	7^{1}							14
1			3		6	8^{3}	12	2	10	11^{2}	5		14	9	13				4	7^{1}							15
1	13	12	3	5	6		7	2	11		9				10^{2}				4	8^{1}							16
	2		3	12	6	8	13	11^{1}	10		5			9^{2}			1		4	7							17
1	2		3	5	6	7^{3}	14	11■	10^{1}		9			13	12				4	8^{2}							18
1	2	3	4		6	9	8				5			10^{1}	11^{2}	12		13		7							19
1	2	3	4	13	6	7	12		10		5			9^{1}						8	11^{2}						20
1	2	3	4	5^{2}	6^{1}		8	13	10		12			9		14				7	11^{3}						21
1	2	12	3	4	6^{2}	8		13	10^{3}		5^{1}			9		14				7	11						22
1	2	3	4	5		7	8	6			9			12							10	11^{1}					23
1		3	4	5	6		8	2^{1}			9			10^{2}	13					7	11	12					24
1		3	4	5	6		8	2			9^{1}			10	13					7	11^{2}	12					25
1	5	3	4	12	6	7	9^{1}	2^{2}						10	13					8	11						26
1		2	3	4	7	8			10^{2}		5			9	12					6	11^{1}	13					27
1	2	3^{2}	4	12	6	7^{1}	13		10		5			9	14					8	11^{3}						28
1	2		3	4	6^{1}	7	9		10^{2}		5			11	12■					8	13						29
1	2		3	4	12	8	9^{1}		14		5	6^{2}		13						7	11	10^{3}					30
1	2		3	4	6	8	9^{2}	13	11^{1}		5			10						7	12						31
1	2		3	4	6	8^{1}	12		11		5			9						7	10^{2}	13					32
1		3	4	5	6	7^{1}	13	2	10^{2}					9	11	12				8^{3}	14						33
1	2	3	4	5	6	14	8^{1}	12	11		13			9^{3}						7	10^{2}						34
1	2^{2}	3		4		7	8	6	10^{1}			9			12	13					11^{3}		5	14			35
	2		3	4	8^{1}		12	6			9			14	11^{3}	10				7			5		1^{2}	13	36

HAMILTON ACADEMICAL

Year Formed: 1874. *Ground:* New Douglas Park, Cadzow Avenue, Hamilton ML3 0FT. *Telephone:* 01698 368652. *Fax:* 01698 285422. *E-mail:* office@acciesfc.co.uk *Website:* www.hamiltonacciesfc.co.uk
Ground Capacity: 6,078 (all seated). *Size of Pitch:* 105m × 68m.
Chairman: Les Gray. *Vice-Chairman:* Ronnie MacDonald.
Player Manager: Martin Canning. *First Team Coach:* Guillaume Beuzelin.
Club Nickname: 'The Accies'.
Previous Grounds: Bent Farm, South Avenue, South Haugh, Douglas Park, Cliftonhill Stadium, Firhill Stadium.
Record Attendance: 28,690 v Hearts, Scottish Cup 3rd rd, 3 March 1937 (at Douglas Park); 5,895 v Rangers, 28 February 2009 (at New Douglas Park).
Record Transfer Fee received: £1,200,000 for James McCarthy to Wigan Ath (July 2009).
Record Transfer Fee paid: £180,000 for Tomas Cerny from Sigma Olomouc (July 2009).
Record Victory: 10-2 v Greenock Morton, Scottish Championship, 3 May 2014.
Record Defeat: 1-11 v Hibernian, Division I, 6 November 1965.
Most Capped Player: Colin Miller, 29 (61), Canada, 1988-94.
Most League Appearances: 452: Rikki Ferguson, 1974-88.
Most League Goals in Season (Individual): 35: David Wilson, Division I; 1936-37.
Most Goals Overall (Individual): 246: David Wilson, 1928-39.

HAMILTON ACADEMICAL – SPFL LADBROKES PREMIERSHIP 2016–17 LEAGUE RECORD

Match No.	*Date*	*Venue*	*Opponents*	*Result*		*H/T Score*	*Lg Pos.*	*Goalscorers*	*Attendance*
1	Aug 6	A	Rangers	D	1-1	1-0	8	Crawford [30]	49,125
2	13	H	Kilmarnock	L	1-2	1-0	11	Longridge [26]	2228
3	19	A	Dundee	D	1-1	1-1	11	Lyon [13]	5287
4	27	H	Ross Co	W	1-0	0-0	9	Imrie [74]	1609
5	Sept 10	A	Hearts	L	1-3	0-0	10	Crawford [50]	15,947
6	17	A	Motherwell	L	2-4	1-3	11	Crawford 2 [36, 64]	4514
7	25	H	St Johnstone	D	1-1	1-0	11	Docherty [37]	1705
8	Oct 1	H	Inverness CT	D	1-1	1-0	10	D'Acol [18]	1611
9	15	A	Partick Thistle	D	2-2	1-2	11	Donati [14], Brophy [83]	2843
10	25	H	Aberdeen	W	1-0	1-0	7	D'Acol (pen) [6]	2315
11	29	H	Dundee	L	0-1	0-0	10		1853
12	Nov 5	A	Kilmarnock	D	0-0	0-0	9		3387
13	21	H	Hearts	D	3-3	1-1	11	Crawford [24], Bingham 2 [46, 68]	2339
14	26	A	Ross Co	D	1-1	0-1	10	Crawford [77]	3275
15	Dec 3	H	Partick Thistle	D	1-1	1-0	8	D'Acol [15]	2210
16	10	A	Inverness CT	D	1-1	1-0	9	Crawford [16]	2473
17	13	A	Celtic	L	0-1	0-1	9		55,076
18	16	H	Rangers	L	1-2	0-1	9	Imrie [77]	5292
19	24	H	Celtic	L	0-3	0-1	11		5003
20	27	A	Aberdeen	L	1-2	1-1	11	Imrie (pen) [38]	13,131
21	31	H	Motherwell	D	1-1	0-0	11	D'Acol [54]	3526
22	Jan 28	A	St Johnstone	L	0-3	0-0	11		3279
23	31	H	Inverness CT	W	3-0	1-0	11	D'Acol [11], Gillespie [47], Bingham [61]	1745
24	Feb 4	H	Kilmarnock	D	1-1	1-1	11	Brophy [43]	2159
25	18	A	Partick Thistle	L	0-2	0-0	11		3057
26	25	A	Celtic	L	0-2	0-1	12		54,685
27	28	H	Aberdeen	W	1-0	1-0	9	Devlin [9]	2006
28	Mar 11	A	Hearts	L	0-4	0-1	11		15,881
29	18	A	Rangers	L	0-4	0-2	12		49,090
30	Apr 1	H	St Johnstone	W	1-0	0-0	11	D'Acol [89]	1662
31	5	A	Motherwell	D	0-0	0-0	11		4644
32	8	H	Ross Co	D	1-1	1-0	10	Donati [3]	1548
33	15	A	Dundee	W	2-0	1-0	9	D'Acol (pen) [23], Devlin [84]	6489
34	29	H	Kilmarnock	L	0-2	0-2	10		2482
35	May 6	A	Inverness CT	L	1-2	0-2	10	Redmond [90]	2478
36	13	H	Motherwell	L	0-1	0-0	11		4173
37	16	A	Ross Co	L	2-3	1-1	11	Bingham [26], Templeton [75]	4871
38	20	H	Dundee	W	4-0	2-0	11	Bingham [23], Skondras [25], Imrie (pen) [56], Crawford [76]	2616

Final League Position: 11

Honours
League Champions: Division II 1903-04. First Division 1985-86, 1987-88, 2007-08; Third Division 2000-01.
Runners-up: Division II 1952-53, 1964-65; Second Division 1996-97, 2003-04; Championship 2013-14 (promoted via play-offs).
Scottish Cup Runners-up: 1911, 1935. *League Cup:* Semi-finalists three times.
League Challenge Cup Winners: 1991-92, 1992-93. *Runners-up:* 2005-06, 2011-12.

Club colours: Shirt: Red and white hoops. Shorts: White. Socks: White.

Goalscorers: *League (37):* Crawford 8, D'Acol 7 (2 pens), Bingham 5, Imrie 4 (2 pens), Brophy 2, Devlin 2, Donati 2, Docherty 1, Gillespie 1, Longridge 1, Lyon 1, Redmond 1, Skondras 1, Templeton 1.
William Hill Scottish FA Cup (3): Bingham 2 (2 pens), Redmond 1.
Betfred Scottish League Cup (11): Imrie 3 (2 pens), Crawford 2, D'Acol 2, Longridge 2, Donati 1, McGregor 1.
IRN-BRU Scottish League Challenge Cup (3): Boyd 1, Cunningham 1, Tierney 1.
Play-Offs (1): Docherty 1.

Matthews R 17	Gillespie G 28 + 3	Kurakins A 1	Sarris G 30	Devlin M 28	Donati M 26 + 5	Imrie D 36 + 1	Docherty G 23 + 6	Crawford A 31 + 2	Longridge L 9 + 7	D'Acol A 24 + 5	Brophy E 7 + 21	Lyon D 5 + 1	Hughes R — + 2	Roy R — + 1	MacKinnon D 32 + 1	Kurtaj G 5 + 9	Redmond D 15 + 12	Seaborne D 10 + 1	Want S — + 2	Bingham R 23 + 7	McMann S 21 + 2	Thomson R — + 1	Woods G 21	Sowah L 6 + 1	Cunningham R — + 2	Watson C 2	Adams B 2 + 3	Boyd S 1 + 2	Skondras G 11 + 2	Gogic A 3 + 4	Tierney R — + 2	Templeton D 1 + 2	*Match No.*
1	2	3	4	5	6^{3}	7	8^{1}	9	10	11^{2}	12	13	14																				1
1	5		4	3	7	9^{2}	6	8	11	10^{1}	12	2		13																			2
1	2		4	3	6^{2}	10	14	9	7^{1}	11^{3}	12	5			8	13																	3
1	5		4	3	6	7	9^{1}			11^{2}	13	2			8	10^{3}	12	14															4
1	5		3		6	7	8^{1}	10		11^{3}		2			9		14	4^{2}	12	13													5
1	5^{2}		3	4	6	8		10	7		11	2^{3}			9^{1}	14	13			12													6
1	2		3		7	5	8	9	12	11^{1}	10^{2}				6			4		13													7
1^{2}	5		4			6	7	10	9^{1}	11^{3}					8			3	14	12	2	13											8
	2		3		4	7	8^{3}	9		11^{2}	12				6	14				10^{1}	13		1	5									9
	2		3	4		7	8^{1}	9^{3}	14	11	10^{2}				6	12	13						1	5									10
	2		3	4		8	6^{1}	9		10^{2}	11^{3}				7	13	14			12			1	5									11
	5		2	4	3	9^{1}	6	11	13		12				7	8^{2}				10^{3}	14		1										12
	2^{1}		3	4	6	7^{2}	12	9		13					8	11		5		10^{3}			1	14									13
	6		2	3	5^{3}	13	12	7		14					8	10^{1}		4^{2}		11			1	9									14
	5			2	3^{1}	7	12	6		11	13				8			4		10^{2}			1	9									15
	5		4			9	8	7	10^{1}	11^{2}					6		13	3		12	2		1										16
	2		3		4	10	8	9^{1}	13		12				6		7^{3}			11^{2}	5		1		14								17
	2		4	3	12	10	7^{2}	9		11^{3}	14				6		8^{1}			13	5		1										18
			4	3	2	5		7	11	13	12				6		9^{2}			10^{1}	8		1										19
	2		3	4	14	9		10	6^{1}	13	12				8^{2}		7			11^{3}	5■		1										20
	2		4^{1}	3	6			11	12	10	7^{3}				14	13	9^{2}	5					1	8									21
	2					9		8		10	12				7		5^{2}	3		11^{1}	4		1		13	6							22
	5			2	3	8		9^{2}		10^{3}	14				7		6			11^{1}	4		1				12	13					23
	6			2	3^{1}	8				10^{3}	12		13		7		9^{2}	4		11			1				5	14					24
	12			3	6^{1}	8					10^{2}				9	14	7^{3}			11	5		1			4	13		2				25
	7			3	4	9	12				14				8	13	6^{1}			10^{3}	5		1					11^{2}	2				26
	7		2	3	14	9	13	12							6■	10^{2}	8^{3}			11^{1}	4		1						5				27
	13		5		4	9^{3}	6	8			10^{2}						7			11^{1}	3		1						2	12	14		28
	5^{3}		2		3	11	8^{1}	10		12					7	14	6^{2}				9		1						13	4			29
1	2^{3}		3	4		9	6^{2}	8		11	13				7		14			10^{1}	5								12				30
1			4	3	13	7^{3}	8	9^{2}		10					6■		12			11^{1}	5								2	14			31
1			3	4	6	7	8	9^{2}		11^{1}	14									10^{3}	5						12		2■	13			32
1			3	4	7	6	9^{2}			10^{1}	14				8		12			11^{3}	5								2	13			33
1			3	4	7	6^{2}	8	9^{3}	13	10	14						12			11	5						2^{1}						34
1			3	4	6^{1}	7	9^{2}	12		11	14				8		13			10^{3}	5								2				35
1	5		3	4		9	6^{2}	8		10	12				7		11^{1}												2			13	36
1					7	6	10^{2}	8	4^{3}						11		14			9^{1}	3								2	5	13	12	37
1	14			3^{3}	12	7		9	13						8		6^{1}			11	5								2	4		10^{2}	38

HEART OF MIDLOTHIAN

Year Formed: 1874. *Ground & Address:* Tynecastle Stadium, McLeod Street, Edinburgh EH11 2NL. *Telephone:* 0871 663 1874. *Fax:* 0131 200 7222. *E-mail:* supporterservices@homplc.co.uk *Website:* www.heartsfc.co.uk
Ground Capacity: 17,529. *Size of Pitch:* 100m × 64m.
Chief Executive and Chairwoman: Ann Budge. *Director of Football:* Craig Levein.
Head Coach: Ian Cathro. *Assistant Head Coach:* Austin MacPhee.
Club Nicknames: 'Hearts', 'Jambos', 'Jam Tarts'.
Previous Grounds: The Meadows 1874, Powderhall 1878, Old Tynecastle 1881 Tynecastle Park, 1886.
Record Attendance: 53,396 v Rangers, Scottish Cup 3rd rd, 13 February 1932 (57,857 v Barcelona, 28 July 2007 at Murrayfield).
Record Transfer Fee received: £9,000,000 for Craig Gordon to Sunderland (August 2008).
Record of Transfer paid: £850,000 for Mirsad Beslija to Genk (January 2006).
Record Victory: 15-0 v King's Park, Scottish Cup 2nd rd, 13 February 1937 (21-0 v Anchor, EFA Cup, 30 October 1880).
Record Defeat: 1-8 v Vale of Leven, Scottish Cup 3rd rd, 1883; 0-7 v Celtic, Scottish Cup 4th rd, 1 December 2013.
Most Capped Player: Steven Pressley, 32, Scotland.
Most League Appearances: 515: Gary Mackay, 1980-97.
Most League Goals in Season (Individual): 44: Barney Battles, 1930-31.
Most Goals Overall (Individual): 214: John Robertson, 1983-98.

HEART OF MIDLOTHIAN – SPFL LADBROKES PREMIERSHIP 2016–17 LEAGUE RECORD

Match No.	Date	Venue	Opponents	Result		H/T Score	Lg Pos.	Goalscorers	Attendance
1	Aug 7	H	Celtic	L	1-2	1-1	6	Walker (pen) [36]	16,777
2	13	A	Aberdeen	D	0-0	0-0	6		13,559
3	20	H	Inverness CT	W	5-1	2-0	3	Cowie 2 [7, 47], Sammon [18], Nicholson 2 [78, 79]	15,880
4	27	A	Partick Thistle	W	2-1	1-0	3	Paterson [16], Watt [90]	4919
5	Sept 10	H	Hamilton A	W	3-1	0-0	2	Walker 2 (1 pen) [69, 81 (p)], Nicholson [90]	15,947
6	17	A	St Johnstone	L	0-1	0-0	2		5456
7	24	H	Ross Co	D	0-0	0-0	2		16,321
8	30	A	Motherwell	W	3-1	1-0	2	McManus (og) [45], Paterson [67], Djoum [84]	4666
9	Oct 15	H	Dundee	W	2-0	0-0	3	Paterson [68], Johnsen [89]	16,512
10	26	A	Kilmarnock	L	0-2	0-1	4		3917
11	29	A	Inverness CT	D	3-3	1-2	3	Johnsen [38], Rherras [51], Djoum [74]	3565
12	Nov 5	H	St Johnstone	D	2-2	1-1	3	Buaben [25], Paterson [87]	16,421
13	21	A	Hamilton A	D	3-3	1-1	4	Walker 2 (1 pen) [8, 73 (p)], Paterson [86]	2339
14	26	H	Motherwell	W	3-0	1-0	3	Johnsen 2 [31, 49], Walker [66]	16,199
15	30	H	Rangers	W	2-0	1-0	2	Muirhead 2 [44, 60]	16,803
16	Dec 3	A	Ross Co	D	2-2	0-1	3	Djoum [66], Paterson [67]	4042
17	10	A	Rangers	L	0-2	0-1	4		50,039
18	17	H	Partick Thistle	D	1-1	1-0	4	Johnsen [17]	16,418
19	23	A	Dundee	L	2-3	1-0	4	Walker (pen) [3], Paterson [48]	6160
20	27	H	Kilmarnock	W	4-0	2-0	4	Paterson [8], Djoum [42], Walker 2 [48, 70]	16,696
21	30	H	Aberdeen	L	0-1	0-0	4		16,630
22	Jan 29	A	Celtic	L	0-4	0-1	4		58,247
23	Feb 1	H	Rangers	W	4-1	1-1	4	Nowak [4], Walker 2 [49, 63], Cowie [54]	16,570
24	4	A	Motherwell	W	3-0	0-0	4	Tziolis [59], Goncalves 2 [84, 88]	4651
25	18	H	Inverness CT	D	1-1	0-1	4	Djoum [64]	16,372
26	25	A	Partick Thistle	L	0-2	0-1	4		4143
27	Mar 1	H	Ross Co	L	0-1	0-0	4		15,470
28	11	H	Hamilton A	W	4-0	1-0	4	Djoum [45], Goncalves [55], Walker [58], Martin [88]	15,881
29	18	A	Aberdeen	L	0-2	0-1	4		12,178
30	Apr 2	H	Celtic	L	0-5	0-2	5		16,539
31	5	A	St Johnstone	L	0-1	0-0	5		4197
32	8	H	Dundee	W	1-0	1-0	5	Goncalves [13]	16,304
33	14	A	Kilmarnock	D	0-0	0-0	5		4110
34	29	H	Partick Thistle	D	2-2	0-0	5	Goncalves (pen) [69], Struna [88]	15,930
35	May 7	H	Aberdeen	L	1-2	0-1	5	Goncalves [61]	16,522
36	13	A	Rangers	L	1-2	0-1	5	Goncalves [51]	47,809
37	17	A	St Johnstone	L	0-1	0-1	5		3141
38	21	A	Celtic	L	0-2	0-0	5		58,967

Final League Position: 5

Honours
League Champions: Division I 1894-95, 1896-97, 1957-58, 1959-60. First Division 1979-80. Championship 2014-15.
Runners-up: Division I 1893-94, 1898-99, 1903-04, 1905-06, 1914-15, 1937-38, 1953-54, 1956-57, 1958-59, 1964-65. Premier Division 1985-86, 1987-88, 1991-92, 2005-06. First Division 1977-78, 1982-83.
Scottish Cup Winners: 1891, 1896, 1901, 1906, 1956, 1998, 2006, 2012; *Runners-up:* 1903, 1907, 1968, 1976, 1986, 1996.
League Cup Winners: 1954-55, 1958-59, 1959-60, 1962-63; *Runners-up:* 1961-62, 1996-97, 2012-13.

European: *European Cup:* 8 matches (1958-59, 1960-61, 2006-07). *Cup Winners' Cup:* 10 matches (1976-77, 1996-97, 1998-99). *UEFA Cup:* 46 matches (*Fairs Cup:* 1961-62, 1963-64, 1965-66. *UEFA Cup:* 1984-85, 1986-87, 1988-89, 1990-91, 1992-93, 1993-94, 2000-01, 2003-04, 2004-05, 2006-07). *Europa League:* 12 matches (2010-11, 2011-12, 2012-13, 2016-17).

Club colours: Shirt: Maroon. Shorts: White with maroon trim. Socks: Maroon.

Goalscorers: *League (55):* Walker 12 (4 pens), Paterson 8, Goncalves 7 (1 pen), Djoum 6, Johnsen 5, Cowie 3, Nicholson 3, Muirhead 2, Buaben 1, Martin 1, Nowak 1, Rherras 1, Sammon 1, Struna 1, Tziolis 1, Watt 1, own goal 1.
William Hill Scottish FA Cup (6): Walker 2 (1 pen), Currie 1, Goncalves 1, Johnsen 1, Martin 1 (1 pen).
Betfred Scottish League Cup (2): Paterson 1, Walker 1 (1 pen).
IRN-BRU Scottish League Challenge Cup (3): Jones 1, McLean 1, Roy 1.
UEFA Europa League (7): Rossi 2, Buaben 1 (1 pen), Paterson 1, Ozturk 1, Sammon 1, own goal 1.

Hamilton J 35	Rherras F 17 + 2	Igor Rossi B 20	Souttar J 22	Paterson C 20	Walker J 28 + 6	Djoum A 30 + 3	Cowie D 34	Nicholson S 13 + 6	Watt T 12 + 4	Sammon C 9 + 10	Muirhead R 6 + 12	Buaben P 11 + 9	Kitchen P 26 + 3	Smith L 12 + 8	Johnsen B 22 + 12	Ozturk A 2 + 3	Currie R 1 + 8	Nowak K 17	Zanatta D — + 1	Hughes A 8	Sowah L 11	Martin M 5 + 8	Choulay M 3 + 8	Beith A — + 2	Struna A 13	Goncalves E 15	Tziolis A 14 + 2	Avlonitis A 8 + 1	Bikey D — + 2	Noring V 3	Brandon J 1	Henderson E — + 1	Match No.
1	2	3	4	5	6	7	8	9	10^{2}	11^{3}	12	13																					1
1	5^{2}	3	4	2		6	8	9^{3}	10	11	14	7^{1}	12	13																			2
1	5	4	3	2		6	7^{1}	9	10	11^{3}	14	12	8^{2}		13																		3
1	5	4	3	2	13	6	7	9^{2}	10^{1}	11^{3}			8	14	12																		4
1	5	4	3	2	9	6^{1}	8	13	11^{3}	10^{2}	14		7		12																		5
1	5	4	3	2	6	12	8^{1}	9	11^{3}	13	14		7		10^{2}																		6
1	5	4	3^{2}	2	13	6	8^{3}	9	11	10^{1}			7		14	12																	7
1	5	4	3	2	9^{1}	8		6^{3}	11	10^{2}	14	13	7		12																		8
1		5	4	2	9	7	8^{1}		11^{2}	10^{3}	12	14	6		13	3																	9
1	5	4	3	2	13	6	8		11^{2}	10^{1}	9	14	7^{3}		12																		10
1	5^{3}	3	4	2	10	8	6		12	14	9^{2}		7		11^{1}	13																	11
1		4	3	2	9	12	6		11^{1}	14	13	8^{2}	7	5	10^{3}																		12
1	14		4	2	9	12	7		11^{1}	13		6^{2}	8	5	10^{3}	3																	13
1	5	4	3	2^{2}	9	6	8^{1}			13	10		7	12	11^{3}		14																14
1	5	4	3	2	6	10	7^{3}			14	9^{2}	12	8	13	11^{1}																		15
1	5	4^{3}	3	2	8	9	6^{2}			12	10^{1}	14	7		11	13																	16
1	5	4	3	2	8^{1}	9	7^{2}		12	13	10^{3}		6	14	11																		17
1		4	3	2	10^{2}	7	6		13	12	14	9^{3}	8	5	11^{1}																		18
1	13	3	4	5	8^{2}	9	10^{1}		14		12		7	2^{3}	11			6															19
1	5	4	3	2^{1}	10^{2}	6					13	9^{3}	7	12	11			8	14														20
1	5	4^{2}	3		9	10^{1}	6				13		8	2	11		12	7															21
1			4		6		8	10^{1}		13			3^{2}	7	11					2	5	9^{3}	12	14									22
1					6		7	13					8		10^{2}			3^{1}		4	5	9^{3}			2	11	12	14					23
1					9^{3}		6	14					13		11^{1}					4	5	8^{2}	12		2	10	3	7					24
1					12	6							7^{3}		10^{1}		13			4	5	14	9^{2}		2	11	8	3					25
1	5^{1}				7^{2}	9		12									11^{3}	6			4		14		2	10■	8	3	13				26
1						9	6^{1}	8							11^{3}		12	4			5	14	10^{2}		2		7	3	13				27
1					7^{3}	9^{1}	8	10^{2}							14			4			5	12	13		2	11	6	3					28
1					10^{3}	9^{2}	6	8					13		12			3			5	14			2	11	7^{1}	4					29
1					10^{1}		9					12	6		8			3			5	13		14	2	11^{3}	7^{2}	4					30
1					10		9	13■				12	6	14	8^{3}			4			5^{1}				2	11	7	3^{2}					31
1					10^{3}	8^{1}	6					3	7	2	14		13	4				12			5	11^{2}	9						32
1					10^{2}	8	9^{3}					3^{1}	6	2			12	4				14	13		5	11	7						33
1					11	8	7	13				3		2	12			4					6^{2}		9	10	5^{1}						34
1					10■	6	8^{2}					3		12	14			4		2	9^{3}		13		5^{1}	11	7						35
						9	6	5^{3}				3■		8	10^{1}		13	4		2		7^{2}	14			11	12			1			36
					13	8	6	9^{1}						5	10^{3}		12	2		4		7^{2}	14			11	3			1			37
					13	8	6					3^{1}		9	11			2		4		12				10^{2}	7^{3}			1	5	14	38

HIBERNIAN

Year Formed: 1875. *Ground & Address:* Easter Road Stadium, 12 Albion Place, Edinburgh EH7 5QG. *Telephone:* 0131 661 2159. *Fax:* 0131 659 6488. *E-mail:* club@hibernianfc.co.uk *Website:* www.hibernianfc.co.uk
Ground Capacity: 20,421 (all seated). *Size of Pitch:* 105m × 68m.
Chairman: Rod Petrie. *Chief Executive:* Leean Dempster.
Head Coach: Neil Lennon. *Assistant Head Coach:* Garry Parker.
Club Nickname: 'Hibs', 'Hibees'.
Previous Grounds: Meadows 1875-78, Powderhall 1878-79, Mayfield 1879-80, First Easter Road 1880-92, Second Easter Road 1892-.
Record Attendance: 65,860 v Hearts, Division I, 2 January 1950.
Record Transfer Fee received: £4,400,000 for Scott Brown from Celtic (2007).
Record of Transfer paid: £700,000 for Ulises de la Cruz to LDU Quito (2001).
Record Victory: 15-1 v Pebbles Rovers, Scottish Cup 2nd rd, 11 February 1961.
Record Defeat: 0-10 v Rangers, Division I, 24 December 1898.
Most Capped Player: Lawrie Reilly, 38, Scotland.
Most League Appearances: 446: Arthur Duncan, 1969-84.
Most League Goals in Season (Individual): 42: Joe Baker, 1959-60.
Most Goals Overall (Individual): 233: Lawrie Reilly, 1945-58.

HIBERNIAN – SPFL LADBROKES CHAMPIONSHIP 2016–17 LEAGUE RECORD

Match No.	Date	Venue	Opponents	Result	H/T Score	Lg Pos.	Goalscorers	Attendance
1	Aug 6	A	Falkirk	W 2-1	1-1	3	Cummings 2 [2, 48]	6458
2	13	H	Dunfermline Ath	W 2-1	1-0	2	Richards-Everton (og) [33], Cummings [78]	16,477
3	20	A	St Mirren	W 2-0	2-0	2	Cummings 2 [22, 32]	4517
4	27	H	Greenock Morton	W 4-0	2-0	1	Shinnie [29], Holt [41], Cummings [54], Graham [74]	14,508
5	Sept 10	A	Dumbarton	W 1-0	1-0	1	Cummings (pen) [32]	1339
6	17	H	Ayr U	L 1-2	0-0	2	Cummings [50]	15,056
7	24	A	Queen of the South	D 0-0	0-0	2		3703
8	Oct 2	H	Dundee U	D 1-1	1-0	2	Keatings [35]	15,492
9	15	A	Raith R	D 0-0	0-0	1		3753
10	22	A	Dunfermline Ath	W 3-1	0-1	1	Ashcroft (og) [55], Holt (pen) [66], Graham [90]	7622
11	29	H	St Mirren	W 2-0	2-0	1	Boyle [8], Holt [34]	14,485
12	Nov 5	A	Ayr U	W 3-0	1-0	1	Boyle 2 [28, 77], McGinn [84]	3100
13	12	H	Falkirk	D 1-1	0-0	1	Hanlon [83]	14,551
14	19	H	Queen of the South	W 4-0	2-0	1	Graham [8], Higgins (og) [42], Gray [52], Boyle [65]	13,861
15	Dec 2	A	Dundee U	L 0-1	0-0	1		10,925
16	10	H	Dumbarton	W 2-0	1-0	1	Hanlon [45], Graham [76]	13,881
17	17	A	Greenock Morton	D 1-1	0-0	1	Cummings [81]	2156
18	24	H	Raith R	D 1-1	0-0	2	Boyle [88]	15,409
19	31	A	Falkirk	W 2-1	1-1	1	Cummings [17], Commons [87]	6747
20	Jan 6	H	Dundee U	W 3-0	2-0	1	Cummings 2 [6, 26], McGinn [81]	18,786
21	14	A	Dumbarton	W 1-0	1-0	1	Commons [14]	1523
22	28	A	Queen of the South	W 1-0	0-0	1	McGinn [52]	3007
23	Feb 4	H	Ayr U	D 1-1	0-1	1	Cummings [74]	14,349
24	18	A	Raith R	D 1-1	0-0	1	Cummings [60]	4172
25	25	H	Dunfermline Ath	D 2-2	2-1	1	Boyle [6], Cummings (pen) [24]	14,437
26	Mar 1	A	St Mirren	L 0-2	0-1	1		3441
27	10	A	Dundee U	W 1-0	1-0	1	Cummings [39]	9532
28	18	H	Dumbarton	D 2-2	0-1	1	Harvie (og) [57], Boyle [83]	14,093
29	25	H	Falkirk	W 2-1	0-0	1	Ambrose [75], Keatings [90]	16,140
30	29	H	Greenock Morton	D 0-0	0-0	1		15,149
31	Apr 1	A	Dunfermline Ath	D 1-1	1-0	1	McGinn [12]	7058
32	8	A	Greenock Morton	D 1-1	1-0	1	Cummings [34]	4229
33	15	H	Queen of the South	W 3-0	2-0	1	McGregor 2 [13, 38], Gray [48]	17,054
34	26	H	Raith R	W 3-2	1-0	1	Keatings 2 [41, 90], Holt [81]	13,604
35	29	A	Ayr U	W 4-0	2-0	1	Cummings 2 [27, 72], Boyle [30], Keatings [66]	2152
36	May 6	H	St Mirren	D 1-1	0-0	1	Holt [49]	19,764

Final League Position: 1

Honours
League Champions: Division I 1902-03, 1947-48, 1950-51, 1951-52. First Division 1980-81, 1998-99. Championship 2016-17. Division II 1893-94, 1894-95, 1932-33.
Runners-up: Division I 1896-97, 1946-47, 1949-50, 1952-53, 1973-74, 1974-75. Championship 2014-15.
Scottish Cup Winners: 1887, 1902, 2016; *Runners-up:* 1896, 1914, 1923, 1924, 1947, 1958, 1972, 1979, 2001, 2012, 2013.
League Cup Winners: 1972-73, 1991-92, 2006-07; *Runners-up:* 1950-51, 1968-69, 1974-75, 1985-86, 1993-94, 2003-04, 2015-16.
Drybrough Cup Winners: 1972-73, 1973-74.

European: *European Cup:* 6 matches (1955-56 semi-finals). *Cup Winners' Cup:* 6 matches (1972-73). *UEFA Cup:* 64 matches (*Fairs Cup:* 1960-61 semi-finals, 1961-62, 1962-63, 1965-66, 1967-68, 1968-69, 1970-71. *UEFA Cup:* 1973-74, 1974-75, 1975-76, 1976-77, 1978-79, 1989-90, 1992-93, 2001-02, 2005-06. *Europa League:* 4 matches 2010-11, 2013-14).

Club colours: Shirt: Green with white sleeves. Shorts: White. Socks: Green.

Goalscorers: *League (59):* Cummings 19 (2 pens), Boyle 8, Holt 5 (1 pen), Keatings 5, Graham 4, McGinn 4, Commons 2, Gray 2, Hanlon 2, McGregor 2, Ambrose 1, Shinnie 1, own goals 4.
William Hill Scottish FA Cup (16): Cummings 4 (1 pen), Keatings 3, Holt 2, Shinnie 2, Forster 1, Humphrey 1, McGeouch 1, McGinn 1, Stevenson 1.
Betfred Scottish League Cup (1): Hanlon 1.
IRN-BRU Scottish League Challenge Cup (4): Boyle 1, Graham 1, Harris 1, Murray F 1.
UEFA Europa League (1): Gray 1.

Laidlaw R 15	McGregor D 35	Hanlon P 21 + 1	Fontaine L 15	Gray D 32 + 1	Martin S 4	McGinn J 27 + 2	Keatings J 12 + 12	Stevenson L 34	Cummings J 26 + 6	Holt G 22 + 8	Bartley M 21 + 7	Boyle M 22 + 12	Forster J 4 + 12	McGeouch D 11 + 7	Shinnie A 24 + 3	Graham B 8 + 20	Marciano O 21	Fyvie F 18 + 3	Eardley N — + 2	Harris A 1 + 4	Commons K 5	Humphrey C 5 + 1	Crane C — + 1	Ambrose E 10	McLean B 2	Murray F 1 + 1	Mackie S — + 1	*Match No.*
1	2²	3	4	5	6³	7	8¹	9	10	11	12	13	14															1
1	2	3	4²	5		7	9	8	10	11¹	6³	12	14	13														2
1	4	3		2		7	9¹	5	11³	10²	6	14		8	12	13												3
	3	4		2		8	13	5	11³	10¹	6²	14			9	12	1	7										4
	3	4		2		7		5	11³	10	6¹		14	12	9²	13	1	8										5
	3	4		2		9	14	5	10²	11³	7■	13			8¹	12	1	6										6
	3	4		2		7	14	5■	10³		6	9²	12	8¹		11	1	13										7
	3	5		2³		9	11		10²			13	4	6	8¹	14	1	7	12									8
	3	4		2		8	9²	5	11	10¹	7■	12				13	1	6										9
	4	3	2	5		7	10²	8		11¹		12			9	13	1	6										10
	2	3	4	5		7¹		8		11³	12	10²			9	13	1	6		14								11
	2	3	4	5		6³		9	13	10²	14	11			8¹	12	1	7										12
1	2	3	4¹	5³		7		8	13	10		11		14	9²			6		12								13
	2	3	4	5		7¹		8	13		14	11²		12	9	10	1	6³										14
	5	4	3¹	6				2	12	10	8²	11³		9	7	13	1		14									15
1	2	3	4	5				9	11		7¹	8		12	6	10												16
1	2	3	4²	5				8	13	12	7	11¹	14		6	10³					9							17
1	3	4		2	7		12	5	11²	10		13		6¹	8	14					9³							18
1	3	4		2	6			5	11²	10³		12	14	7	8	13					9¹							19
1	3	4		2		12	13	5	11²		6	10		7		14					9¹	8³						20
1	4		3	2		12		5	11²	13	8	6	14					7			9³	10¹						21
1	3		4	2		6	8²	5	11¹	10³		12	14		9	13		7										22
1	3		4	2		8	10	5	13	12		11¹			6²	14		7				9³						23
	3		4	2		8	9²	5	11	14	6	13				10¹	1	7³				12						24
	3		4¹	2		8	14	5	11	10	12	6			9³		1	7²					13					25
	3			2		8	13	5	11	12	7¹	10³			9²	14	1	6						4				26
	3			2		8		5	11■	10³	7¹	6²	14		9	13	1	12						4				27
	3			2²		8	11	5		10	7³	6	13	12	9¹	14	1							4				28
1	3	14					12	5	11	10³	8	9	4¹	6	7²	13								2				29
	3■	4¹				8	9	5	11³	10²	7	6	14	13		12	1							2				30
	3			14		8	12	5	10¹	13	9	6²		7		11³	1							2	4			31
	3			2		8		5	11	12	7	6²		9¹	14	10³	1			13				4				32
	3			2		9	13	5	10		14	11¹		7²	6³		1	8		12				4				33
1					5		11			13	12		3		9²	10³				8		7		4	6	2¹	14	34
1	3			2		10²	12	5	11	8		6³	4		13			7				9¹				14		35
	3			2³		8	14	5	11	10	7²	9	12		6¹		1	13						4				36

INVERNESS CALEDONIAN THISTLE

Year Formed: 1994. *Ground & Address:* Tulloch Caledonian Stadium, Stadium Road, Inverness IV1 1FF. *Telephone:* 01463 222880. *Fax:* 01463 227479. *E-mail:* info@ictfc.co.uk *Website:* www.ictfc.co.uk
Ground Capacity: 7,780 (all seated). *Size of Pitch:* 105m × 68m.
Chairman: Wllie Finlayson. *Club Secretary:* Ian MacDonald.
Club Nicknames: 'Caley Thistle', 'Caley Jags', 'ICT'.
Manager: John Robertson. *Assistant Manager:* Brian Rice.
Record Attendance: 7,753 v Rangers, SPL, 20 January 2008.
Record Transfer Fee received: £400,000 for Marius Niculae to Dinamo Bucharest (July 2008).
Record of Transfer paid: £65,000 for John Rankin from Ross Co (July 2006).
Record Victory: 8-1 v Annan Ath, Scottish Cup 3rd rd, 24 January 1998; 7-0 v Ayr U, First Division, 24 April 2010; 7-0 v Arbroath, League Cup Northern Section Group C, 30 July 2016.
Record Defeats: 0-6 v Airdrieonians, First Division, 21 Sep 2000; 0-6 v Celtic, League Cup 3rd rd, 22 Sep 2010; 0-6 v Celtic, Scottish Premiership, 27 April 2014; 0-6 v Celtic, Scottish Cup 5th rd, 11 February 2017.
Most Capped Player: Richard Hastings, 38 (59), Canada.
Most League Appearances: 490: Ross Tokely, 1995-2012.
Most League Goals in Season: 27: Iain Stewart, 1996-97; Denis Wyness, 2002-03.
Most Goals Overall (Individual): 118: Denis Wyness, 2000-03, 2005-08.

INVERNESS CALEDONIAN TH – SPFL LADBROKES PREMIERSHIP 2016–17 LEAGUE RECORD

Match No.	Date	Venue	Opponents	Result		H/T Score	Lg Pos.	Goalscorers	Attendance
1	Aug 6	A	Partick Thistle	L	0-2	0-1	12		2943
2	13	H	Ross Co	L	2-3	1-2	12	Boden 45, Draper 65	4204
3	20	A	Hearts	L	1-5	0-2	12	Draper 87	15,880
4	27	H	St Johnstone	W	2-1	0-0	12	Draper 59, Meekings 90	2729
5	Sept 10	A	Aberdeen	D	1-1	0-0	12	Vigurs 68	11,356
6	18	H	Celtic	D	2-2	1-2	12	King 28, Fisher 89	6061
7	24	H	Dundee	W	3-1	2-0	9	Doumbouya 8, Tansey (pen) 17, Polworth 51	2884
8	Oct 1	A	Hamilton A	D	1-1	0-1	9	Polworth 90	1611
9	14	H	Rangers	L	0-1	0-1	9		7012
10	22	H	Kilmarnock	D	1-1	0-1	7	Doumbouya 86	2591
11	26	A	Motherwell	W	3-0	0-0	7	Tremarco 57, Doumbouya 71, Polworth 83	3131
12	29	H	Hearts	D	3-3	2-1	7	Raven 15, Doumbouya 32, Doran 55	3565
13	Nov 5	A	Celtic	L	0-3	0-0	7		54,152
14	19	H	Aberdeen	L	1-3	1-2	8	Doumbouya 15	4867
15	26	A	Dundee	L	1-2	0-1	9	Tremarco 81	5094
16	Dec 3	A	St Johnstone	L	0-3	0-1	12		2549
17	10	H	Hamilton A	D	1-1	0-1	12	Cole 51	2473
18	17	A	Kilmarnock	D	1-1	0-0	12	Warren 84	3294
19	24	A	Rangers	L	0-1	0-1	12		48,528
20	28	H	Motherwell	L	1-2	0-0	12	Tansey 90	3097
21	31	A	Ross Co	L	2-3	1-2	12	Tremarco 28, Fisher 81	5111
22	Jan 28	H	Partick Thistle	D	0-0	0-0	12		2823
23	31	A	Hamilton A	L	0-3	0-1	12		1745
24	Feb 4	H	Dundee	D	2-2	0-2	12	McKay, Billy (pen) 53, Tansey 79	2606
25	18	A	Hearts	D	1-1	1-0	12	Tremarco 24	16,372
26	24	H	Rangers	W	2-1	1-0	11	Tansey 45, McKay, Billy 89	6415
27	Mar 1	H	Celtic	L	0-4	0-1	12		5948
28	11	A	Partick Thistle	D	1-1	0-0	12	Warren 90	3082
29	18	H	Ross Co	D	1-1	0-0	11	Tansey 48	4123
30	Apr 1	H	Kilmarnock	D	1-1	1-1	12	McKay, Billy 25	2780
31	4	A	Aberdeen	L	0-1	0-1	12		11,507
32	8	H	St Johnstone	L	0-3	0-1	12		2961
33	15	A	Motherwell	L	2-4	1-2	12	Fisher 2 21, 54	3696
34	28	A	Ross Co	L	0-4	0-2	12		4928
35	May 6	H	Hamilton A	W	2-1	2-0	12	McKay, Brad 10, Tansey (pen) 36	2478
36	13	A	Kilmarnock	L	1-2	0-1	12	Fisher 71	3137
37	17	A	Dundee	W	2-0	2-0	12	McKay, Billy 2, Fisher 10	5574
38	20	H	Motherwell	W	3-2	0-0	12	Tansey 64, Fisher 2 66, 67	5351

Final League Position: 12

Honours
League Champions: First Division 2003-04, 2009-10. Third Division 1996-97. *Runners-up:* Second Division 1998-99.
Scottish Cup Winners: 2015; Semi-finals 2003, 2004; Quarter-finals 1996.
League Cup Runners-up: 2013-14.
League Challenge Cup Winners: 2003-04; *Runners-up:* 1999-2000, 2009-10.

European: *Europa League:* 4 matches (2015-16).

Club colours: Shirt: Blue with vertical red stripes. Shorts: Blue. Socks: Blue with red stripes.

Goalscorers: *League (44):* Fisher 8, Tansey 7 (2 pens), Doumbouya 5, Billy McKay 4 (1 pen), Tremarco 4, Draper 3, Polworth 3, Warren 2, Boden 1, Brad McKay 1, Cole 1, Doran 1, King 1, Meekings 1, Raven 1, Vigurs 1.
William Hill Scottish FA Cup (2): Cole 1, Doumbouya 1.
Betfred Scottish League Cup (15): Boden 4, Vigurs 4, Tremarco 3, King 2, Draper 1, Warren 1.
IRN-BRU Scottish League Challenge Cup (0).

Fon Williams O 31	Raven D 19 + 2	Warren G 33	McNaughton K 5 + 4	Tremarco C 29	Polworth L 26 + 6	Tansey G 37	Mulraney J 10 + 16	Vigurs I 28 + 4	King B 17 + 9	Boden S 3 + 10	Draper R 35 + 2	Fisher A 9 + 12	Horner L 5 + 5	Doran A 6 + 11	Meekings J 18	Doumbouya L 17 + 2	McKay Brad 25 + 1	Cole L 13 + 8	Mackay C 1	Sutherland A — + 1	Gilchrist C — + 1	Anier H 8 + 5	McKay Billy 14 + 1	Ebbe D — + 3	Esson R 6	McCart J 9 + 2	Laing L 14	*Match No.*
1	2	3	4	5	6	7	8^{1}	9^{2}	10	11	12	13																1
1	2	3	4^{2}	5	6	8	13	10^{1}	9^{3}	11	7		12	14														2
1	2^{2}	3		5	8	6	10^{1}	9		11^{3}	7	12	13	14	4													3
1		3		5	8	6	14	7^{1}	10^{3}	13	9	11^{2}	2		4	12												4
1		3		5	8	6		7^{1}	10^{2}		9	11^{3}	14	13	2	12	4											5
1		3		5	8^{3}	6	13	7^{1}	10		9	14		12	4	11^{2}	2											6
1		3		5	6	7	8^{1}		10^{2}		9	12		13	4	11^{3}	2	14										7
1		3		5	6	8^{2}	13	9^{1}	10^{3}	12	7				4	11	2	14										8
1	2	3		5	8	6	13	7^{3}	10^{2}		9	14		12		11^{1}	4											9
1		3		5	8	6	10^{2}	7	13	14	9^{1}			12	4	11	2^{3}											10
1	13	3		5	8	6		7	12	14	9			10^{3}	4^{1}	11^{2}	2											11
	12	3		5^{1}	7	6	13	9^{3}			8		14	10^{2}	4	11	2		1									12
1		3			10^{3}	7■	13	9	8^{1}		6	12	2		4	11^{2}	5	14										13
1		3		5			12	7	10^{2}		6	14	13	8	4	11	2^{1}	9^{3}										14
1		3		5		9	12	7^{1}	10^{3}	13	6		2■	8^{2}	4	11		14										15
1		3■		5^{1}		9	12	7	10		6			8^{3}	4	11^{2}		2		13	14							16
1				5		6	8	9	12		7		2^{1}		4	11	3	10										17
1		3		2	13	7		10	14		6	12	8^{2}		4	11^{1}	5^{3}	9										18
1		3		5	7	6		10^{3}		14	8	13		12	4	11^{2}	2	9^{1}										19
1		3		5	8^{1}	6	14	9			7	13		12	4	11^{2}	2	10^{3}										20
1		3		5		7		9^{3}	12	14	6	13		10	4	11^{1}	2	8^{2}										21
1	2	3		5	8	7	13	12			6^{1}			14		11^{2}	4	10^{3}				9						22
1	2	3		5	6	7		9			8^{2}						4	12				10^{1}	11	13				23
	2	3		8	13	6	12	7^{2}	5^{1}		9											10	11		1	4		24
1	2			5	8	6	10^{1}				7			12				9				13	11^{2}			4	3	25
1	2			5^{2}	10	7	8^{3}	14	13		6^{1}						12	9					11			4	3	26
1	5	4			10	7		12	8		6						2	9^{2}				13	11^{1}				3	27
1	5	3			9^{3}	8		10^{1}	12	14							2	13				7^{2}	11			4	6	28
1	2	3		6	12	7		9^{2}			8											11^{1}	10	13		5	4	29
1	5	3	12		14	8	13		7^{1}		9						2^{3}	10^{2}					11			4	6	30
1	2	3	4^{2}	5	9	8					7^{1}	14						12				10^{3}	11	13			6	31
1		3	5^{1}	9	12	7			13	14	8^{2}	10						6■					11			4^{3}	2	32
1			12	5^{1}	6	8	13	9^{2}	10^{3}		7	11					2					14				4	3	33
	5^{1}		2		9■	6	10	7^{3}	8^{2}		14	11										13	12		1	4	3	34
	5	3	13			7	10^{2}		14	12	6	11^{1}					2^{3}					8	9		1		4	35
	5	4			13	7	10^{2}	12			6^{1}	11					2	14				8^{3}	9		1		3	36
	2	3	13		8	7		9^{2}			6	10^{1}					5					12	11^{3}		1	14	4	37
	5	3			10^{1}	9	12	6^{2}			8	7					2						11		1	13	4	38

KILMARNOCK

Year Formed: 1869. *Ground & Address:* Rugby Park, Kilmarnock KA1 2DP. *Telephone:* 01563 545300. *Fax:* 01563 522181. *Email:* info@kilmarnockfc.co.uk *Website:* www.kilmarnockfc.co.uk
Ground Capacity: 18,128 (all seated). *Size of Pitch:* 102m × 67m.
Chief Executive: Kirsten Callaghan. *Director:* Billy Bowie.
Manager: Lee McCulloch. *First-Team Coach:* Peter Leven.
Club Nickname: 'Killie'.
Previous Grounds: Rugby Park (Dundonald Road); The Grange; Holm Quarry; Rugby Park 1899.
Record Attendance: 35,995 v Rangers, Scottish Cup Quarter-final, 10 March 1962.
Record Transfer Fee received: £1,900,000 for Steven Naismith to Rangers (2007).
Record Transfer Fee paid: £340,000 for Paul Wright from St Johnstone (1995).
Record Victory: 11-1 v Paisley Academical, Scottish Cup 1st rd, 18 January 1930.
Record Defeat: 1-9 v Celtic, Division I, 13 August 1938.
Most Capped Player: Joe Nibloe, 11, Scotland.
Most League Appearances: 481: Alan Robertson, 1972-88.
Most League Goals in Season (Individual): 34: Harry 'Peerie' Cunningham 1927-28; Andy Kerr 1960-61.
Most Goals Overall (Individual): 148: Willy Culley, 1912-23.

KILMARNOCK – SPFL LADBROKES PREMIERSHIP 2016–17 LEAGUE RECORD

Match No.	Date		Venue	Opponents	Result		H/T Score	Lg Pos.	Goalscorers	Attendance
1	Aug	6	H	Motherwell	L	1-2	0-1	11	Smith, M 81	4308
2		13	A	Hamilton A	W	2-1	0-1	8	Boyd, K 71, Coulibaly 73	2228
3		20	A	Ross Co	L	0-2	0-1	10		3263
4		26	H	Rangers	D	1-1	1-0	9	Boyd, K 29	11,800
5	Sept	10	A	Dundee	D	1-1	1-1	11	Coulibaly 32	5111
6		17	H	Partick Thistle	D	2-2	1-1	10	Boyd, K 17, Coulibaly 65	4169
7		24	A	Celtic	L	1-6	1-2	11	Coulibaly 32	53,532
8	Oct	1	H	Aberdeen	L	0-4	0-1	12		4592
9		15	A	St Johnstone	W	1-0	0-0	10	Boyd, S 76	2930
10		22	A	Inverness CT	D	1-1	1-0	9	Coulibaly (pen) 7	2591
11		26	H	Hearts	W	2-0	1-0	8	Coulibaly 22, Smith, S 71	3917
12		29	A	Rangers	L	0-3	0-2	8		49,302
13	Nov	5	H	Hamilton A	D	0-0	0-0	8		3387
14		18	H	Celtic	L	0-1	0-1	8		10,962
15	Dec	3	H	Dundee	W	2-0	1-0	7	McKenzie 22, Coulibaly 70	3615
16		6	A	Aberdeen	L	1-5	0-3	7	McKenzie 77	8195
17		10	A	Motherwell	D	0-0	0-0	7		3684
18		17	H	Inverness CT	D	1-1	0-0	8	Coulibaly 73	3294
19		23	H	St Johnstone	L	0-1	0-1	9		3056
20		27	A	Hearts	L	0-4	0-2	9		16,696
21		31	A	Partick Thistle	D	0-0	0-0	10		3584
22	Jan	28	H	Ross Co	W	3-2	1-2	8	Boyd, K 1, Dicker 61, Longstaff 90	3207
23	Feb	4	A	Hamilton A	D	1-1	1-1	8	Longstaff 7	2159
24		11	A	Dundee	D	1-1	1-1	7	Boyd, K 9	4708
25		19	H	Aberdeen	L	1-2	1-0	8	McKenzie 41	3972
26		25	A	St Johnstone	W	2-0	1-0	8	McKenzie 11, Sammon 71	2933
27	Mar	4	H	Motherwell	L	1-2	1-0	8	Boyd, K 32	4726
28		11	A	Ross Co	W	2-1	0-0	7	Sammon 47, Boyd, K 85	3380
29		18	H	Partick Thistle	D	1-1	0-0	7	Sammon 87	4519
30	Apr	1	A	Inverness CT	D	1-1	1-1	7	Boyd, K (pen) 19	2780
31		5	H	Rangers	D	0-0	0-0	7		9548
32		8	A	Celtic	L	1-3	0-1	7	Jones 65	57,679
33		14	H	Hearts	D	0-0	0-0	7		4110
34		29	A	Hamilton A	W	2-0	2-0	7	Sammon 11, Jones 23	2482
35	May	6	H	Dundee	L	0-1	0-0	8		4040
36		13	H	Inverness CT	W	2-1	1-0	7	Longstaff 17, Jones 57	3137
37		16	A	Motherwell	L	1-3	1-1	8	Frizzell 17	5246
38		20	H	Ross Co	L	1-2	1-1	8	Sammon (pen) 10	3951

Final League Position: 8

Honours
League Champions: Division I 1964-65. Division II 1897-98, 1898-99; *Runners-up:* Division I 1959-60, 1960-61, 1962-63, 1963-64. First Division 1975-76, 1978-79, 1981-82, 1992-93. Division II 1953-54, 1973-74. Second Division 1989-90.
Scottish Cup Winners: 1920, 1929, 1997; *Runners-up:* 1898, 1932, 1938, 1957, 1960.
League Cup Winners: 2011-12; *Runners-up:* 1952-53, 1960-61, 1962-63, 2000-01, 2006-07.

European: *European Cup:* 4 matches (1965-66). *Cup Winners' Cup:* 4 matches (1997-98). *UEFA Cup:* 32 matches (*Fairs Cup:* 1964-65, 1966-67 semi-finals, 1969-70, 1970-71. *UEFA Cup:* 1998-99, 1999-2000, 2001-02).

Club colours: Shirts: Blue with white stripes. Shorts: Blue. Socks: White.

Goalscorers: *League (36):* Boyd K 8 (1 pen), Coulibaly 8 (1 pen), Sammon 5 (1 pen), McKenzie 4, Jones 3, Longstaff 3, Boyd S 1, Dicker 1, Frizzell 1, Smith M 1, Smith S 1.
William Hill Scottish FA Cup (0).
Betfred Scottish League Cup (5): Coulibaly 3, Boyle 1, McKenzie 1.
IRN-BRU Scottish League Challenge Cup (2): Hawkshaw 1, Queen 1.

MacDonald J 24	Boyle W 11	McFadzean C 1+3	Addison M 8+3	Smith S 25+1	Dicker G 36	Hawkshaw D 7+8	Taylor G 34	McKenzie R 25+3	Coulibaly S 18+3	Kiltie G 7+4	Boyd K 22+5	Jones J 29+8	Smith M 7+3	Green G 2+2	Waddington M —+1	Hendrie L 32	Adams C 4+5	Burn J 6+2	Frizzell A 8+7	Boyd S 18+1	Tyson N 11+6	Morrison L —+1	Bojaj F 2	Wilson I 16+4	Cameron I —+2	Webb J —+1	Woodman F 14	Ajer K 16	Osborne K 1	Longstaff S 16	Roberts C 4+6	Umerah J —+4	Sammon C 14+1	Graham W —+3	Match No.
1	2	3	4	5	6	7^3	8	9^1	10	11^2	12	13	14																						1
1	4	13	3	5	7		2	11	12		10	9^2	6^1	8^3	14																				2
1	4	13	3^2	5		14			11		10	9	8	6^3		2	7^1	12																	3
1	3			2	6	9	7■		14	8^2	11^1			13		5	12	4	10^3																4
1				5	9	10^2		6	8		11	12		14		2	13^3	3	7^1	4															5
1				5^1	8	9		6	10		11	14	12^3			2		3	7^2	4	13														6
1					8	9^1	5	6^3	7		11	13				2	12	3		4	10^2	14													7
1			14		8		5	9	11	6^1	10	13				2	7^3	3^2		4	12														8
1			3		8		5	6	11^2			9	7			2	13	4^1		12	10														9
1			3	12	7		8	6	10^2		13	9	5^1			2				4	11														10
1			3	7	6		5	9	8		12	10^2				2			13	4	11^1														11
1			3	7	6		5	9	8		12	10				2				4	11^1														12
1			3^2	7^1	6		5	9	8		11	10				2		12	13	4															13
1	3	14		7	6^1		5	9	13			10^2				2			8	4	12		11^3												14
1	4			7	6		5	9	8			10^1				2			12	3	11														15
1	4			6	7		5	9	8^2			10^3				2	14		11^1	3	12			13											16
1	4			5	6	12	10	7	11			8^1				2				3	9														17
1	4			7	6		5	9	8			10				2					11			3											18
1	4			7^2	6	12	5	9^1	8		13	10				2■					11^3			3	14										19
1	4^3			5	7	13	2		9		11^1	12	8^2				6				10			3		14									20
1				5	7	8^2	2		11			13				4	6		12		9^1		10	3											21
				8	7		5	6			10^2	13				2					14			12			1	3	4^1	9	11^3				22
				7^3	6	12	5	8			11^2	10^1				2								3			1	4		9		13	14		23
			12		7		5	6			11^2	9^1				2^3					13			4			1	3		8	14		10		24
			12	7^2	3		5	9			11	6				2								13			1	4		8^1		14	10^3		25
					2		9	6			11	8	12			5				4							1	3		7^1			10		26
					7		5	9			10	6				2				3							1	4		8^1	12		11		27
						12	5				11^2	7				2				3				6			1	4		9	8^1	13	10		28
					6		5	9			11	8^1				2				3				12			1	4		7^2		13	10		29
					6		5	8^1		12	11	7^2								3				2			1	4		9	13		10		30
					6		5			9^1	11	8				2								3			1	4		7	12		10		31
					4	12	6				10^1		8			2			13	5				3			1			9^2	7^3		11	14	32
					3	12	5			13	11	10	6^2			2			14					7			1	4		9^1	8^3				33
				7	3		5			12	10	9^2				2			13					6			1	4		8^1			11		34
				8	3		5			12	11	6^1				2								7^2			1	4		9	13		10		35
1				5	3			12		9^1		10				2			8					6				4		7			11		36
1				5	3	2^3	8	13		10^2		7							9					6^1				4			12		11	14	37
1				5	3		2	12		10^2		7^3							9					6^1	13			4		8			11	14	38

LIVINGSTON

Year Formed: 1974. *Ground:* Tony Macaroni Arena, Almondvale Stadium, Alderstone Road, Livingston EH54 7DN.
Telephone: 01506 417000. *Fax:* 01506 429948.
Email: lfcreception@livingstonfc.co.uk *Website:* www.livingstonfc.co.uk
Ground Capacity: 9,865 (all seated). *Size of Pitch:* 98m × 69m.
Chairman: Robert Wilson. *Secretary:* Brian Ewing.
Head Coach: David Hopkin. *Assistant Coach:* David Martindale.
Club Nickname: 'Livi Lions'.
Previous Grounds: Meadowbank Stadium (as Meadowbank Thistle).
Record Attendance: 10,024 v Celtic, Premier League, 18 August 2001.
Record Transfer Fee received: £1,000,000 for David Fernandez to Celtic (June 2002).
Record Transfer Fee paid: £120,000 for Wes Hoolahan from Shelbourne (December 2005).
Record Victory: 8-0 v Stranraer, League Cup, 1st rd, 31 July 2012.
Record Defeat: 0-8 v Hamilton A. Division II, 14 December 1974.
Most Capped Player (under 18): Ian Little.
Most League Appearances: 446: Walter Boyd, 1979-89.
Most League Goals in Season (Individual): 22: Leigh Griffiths, 2008-09; Iain Russell, 2010-11; Liam Buchanan, 2016-17.
Most Goals Overall (Individual): 64: David Roseburgh, 1986-93.

LIVINGSTON – SPFL LADBROKES LEAGUE ONE 2016–17 LEAGUE RECORD

Match No.	*Date*	*Venue*	*Opponents*	*Result*	*H/T Score*	*Lg Pos.*	*Goalscorers*	*Attendance*
1	Aug 6	H	Stranraer	W 5-1	2-0	1	Pitman 2 $^{5, 90}$, Mullen ^{24}, Buchanan 2 (1 pen) $^{72 (p), 87}$	693
2	13	A	Airdrieonians	W 4-2	2-0	2	Mullen ^{13}, Buchanan ^{37}, Boateng (og) ^{58}, Mullin ^{90}	1048
3	20	H	Stenhousemuir	W 4-1	2-0	1	Mullen 2 $^{4, 49}$, Pitman ^{23}, Longridge ^{78}	769
4	27	A	Queen's Park	L 0-1	0-1	3		698
5	Sept 10	A	Alloa Ath	W 3-1	3-0	3	Pitman ^{24}, Buchanan ^{34}, Miller ^{39}	712
6	17	H	Brechin C	W 2-1	1-0	2	Mullen ^{34}, Pitman ^{65}	858
7	24	A	East Fife	L 1-3	0-3	3	Mullin ^{59}	784
8	Oct 1	A	Peterhead	W 2-1	1-1	2	Mullen 2 $^{25, 58}$	569
9	15	H	Albion R	L 1-2	0-1	3	Buchanan (pen) ^{90}	702
10	22	H	Alloa Ath	W 3-1	0-0	2	Miller ^{55}, Buchanan 2 $^{62, 90}$	977
11	29	A	Brechin C	W 3-0	0-0	1	Buchanan ^{66}, Longridge ^{69}, Byrne ^{86}	517
12	Nov 5	H	East Fife	W 3-1	1-0	1	Buchanan 2 (1 pen) $^{45, 66 (p)}$, Miller ^{49}	907
13	19	H	Peterhead	L 1-2	0-1	1	Buchanan ^{80}	712
14	Dec 3	A	Albion R	W 1-0	0-0	1	Cadden (pen) ^{89}	413
15	10	A	Stranraer	W 2-1	0-1	1	Carrick ^{77}, De Vita ^{84}	333
16	13	A	Stenhousemuir	W 4-0	1-0	1	Summers (og) ^{16}, De Vita ^{70}, Buchanan ^{81}, Carrick ^{90}	334
17	17	H	Airdrieonians	W 2-0	1-0	1	Carrick ^{10}, Cadden ^{89}	989
18	24	H	Queen's Park	L 1-2	1-0	1	Buchanan ^{40}	819
19	31	A	East Fife	L 1-2	1-0	1	Buchanan ^{14}	661
20	Jan 7	A	Peterhead	W 3-2	0-0	1	Gallagher ^{50}, Buchanan ^{53}, Byrne ^{79}	582
21	28	H	Brechin C	W 3-0	2-0	1	Buchanan ^{1}, Halkett ^{29}, Cadden ^{56}	746
22	Feb 4	A	Alloa Ath	D 2-2	1-1	1	Mullen ^{36}, Buchanan ^{48}	565
23	11	H	Stranraer	D 0-0	0-0	1		677
24	18	A	Airdrieonians	W 4-0	1-0	1	Crighton ^{34}, Gorman (og) ^{50}, Mullen ^{78}, Cadden ^{81}	1012
25	Mar 4	A	Queen's Park	D 1-1	1-1	1	Pitman ^{11}	701
26	7	H	Albion R	W 3-0	1-0	1	Todorov 2 $^{34, 90}$, Mullen ^{88}	548
27	11	H	East Fife	L 0-1	0-0	1		773
28	18	A	Stranraer	W 1-0	0-0	1	Buchanan ^{84}	523
29	21	H	Stenhousemuir	W 1-0	1-0	1	Todorov ^{24}	531
30	25	H	Airdrieonians	W 4-2	2-1	1	Mullen 2 $^{8, 62}$, Gallagher ^{10}, Cadden ^{85}	832
31	Apr 1	A	Brechin C	W 2-0	1-0	1	Buchanan 2 $^{11, 59}$	523
32	8	H	Alloa Ath	W 2-1	1-0	1	Pitman ^{16}, Longridge ^{49}	1099
33	15	A	Stenhousemuir	W 1-0	0-0	1	Buchanan ^{54}	472
34	22	H	Queen's Park	W 4-0	1-0	1	Todorov ^{18}, Mullen ^{70}, Mullin ^{80}, Cadden ^{90}	821
35	29	H	Peterhead	W 4-1	3-0	1	Buchanan ^{12}, Pitman ^{21}, Mullin ^{42}, Mullen ^{81}	891
36	May 6	A	Albion R	W 2-0	2-0	1	Pitman ^{19}, De Vita ^{44}	454

Final League Position: 1

Honours
League Champions: First Division 2000-01. Second Division 1986-87, 1998-99, 2010-11. League One 2016-17. Third Division 1995-96, 2009-10; *Runners-up:* Second Division 1982-83. First Division 1987-88.
Scottish Cup: Semi-finals 2001, 2004.
League Cup Winners: 2003-04. Semi-finals 1984-85. *B&Q Cup:* Semi-finals 1992-93, 1993-94, 2001.
League Challenge Cup Winners: 2014-15. *Runners-up:* 2000-01.

European: *UEFA Cup:* 4 matches (2002-03).

Club colours: Shirt: Yellow with black trim. Shorts: Black with yellow trim. Socks: Yellow with black tops.

Goalscorers: *League (80):* Buchanan 22 (3 pens), Mullen 14, Pitman 9, Cadden 6 (1 pen), Mullin 4, Todorov 4, Carrick 3, De Vita 3, Longridge 3, Miller 3, Byrne 2, Gallagher 2, Crighton 1, Halkett 1, own goals 3.
William Hill Scottish FA Cup (2): Cadden 1, Mullen 1.
Betfred Scottish League Cup (6): Buchanan 1, Cadden 1, Carrick 1, Mullen 1, Mullin 1, own goal 1.
IRN-BRU Scottish League Challenge Cup (8): Buchanan 3 (1 pen), Cadden 1, Crighton 1, De Vita 1, Longridge 1, Mullen 1.

Kelly L 34	Neill M 3 + 4	Lithgow A 31	Crighton S 29 + 3	Longridge J 24 + 6	Byrne S 26 + 4	Miller M 13 + 1	Mullin J 18 + 9	Pitman S 36	Cadden N 22 + 12	Mullen D 28 + 4	Buchanan L 32 + 4	Sinclair J 2 + 4	Watt L 2 + 9	Halkett C 33	Allan L — + 3	Orr T — + 1	Carrick D 4 + 10	Knox M 3 + 5	De Vita R 18 + 5	Currie R — + 2	Ogilvie J — + 3	Gallagher D 14 + 1	Millar M 12 + 1	Todorov N 7 + 7	Sampson K — + 3	Jacobs K 3 + 1	Maley G 2	*Match No.*
1	2	3	4	5	6^{2}	7	8^{1}	9	10	11^{3}	12	13	14															1
1		3	4	5	6^{2}	2	13	9	10^{1}	8	11		12	7														2
1		4	3	5	6	7		9	10^{3}	8^{2}	11^{1}		12	2	13	14												3
1	13	4	3	5	7^{3}	6	12	9	10^{2}	8^{1}	11		14	2														4
1		3	4		12	2	6	7	9	11^{1}	10^{2}	8^{3}		5	14		13											5
1		4	3		6	7	5^{2}	8	9^{3}	10	11^{1}	13	12	2	14													6
1		3■	4	13	7^{2}	2■	6	8	9^{1}	11	10			5			12											7
1	4		3	5		7	6^{3}	8	9^{1}	11	10	14	12	2^{2}			13											8
1			3	5	7	2	6^{2}	8^{1}	9^{3}	11	10		12	4			14	13										9
1		4	3	5	14	7	12	6	8^{2}	10^{3}	11		13	2					9^{1}									10
1		4	3	5	12	8^{1}		7	9^{3}	10	11^{2}		13	2			14		6									11
1	7		3	5	12	2		6	9^{1}	11	10^{2}			4			14		8^{3}	13								12
1		4	3	5^{1}	9^{3}	8	6^{2}	7	12	11	10			2			13	14										13
1	13	4	3	5	6			7	11		10^{1}		8^{2}	2			12		9									14
1		4	3	5	6		13	8	10^{1}		9^{2}		7^{3}	2			12		11		14							15
1		3	4	2	8		9^{2}	7	13		12			5			11	10^{3}	6^{1}	14								16
1	14	4	3	5^{2}	8		6	7	12	13	10^{1}			2			11^{3}		9									17
1	14	2	5	12	4		9^{3}	7	6^{2}	13	11			3			10^{1}		8									18
1		3	4	2	6		12	7		8	11			5			9^{1}		10									19
1		4	3	14	8			6	12	9^{1}	10^{2}			2			13		11^{3}			5	7					20
1		4	3		8			7	9^{1}	11^{3}	10^{2}	14		2					13			5	6	12				21
1		3	2		7		14	8	9^{1}	11^{2}	10^{3}			5					12			4	6	13				22
1		4	3		8		13	7	9^{2}	11	10			2					12			5	6^{1}					23
1		4	5	9	8			7	14	10^{2}	11^{1}			2					12			3^{3}	6	13				24
1		4	2	5	7^{2}		12	6	14	11	10^{1}			3					9^{3}				8	13				25
1		5	2	13	8		14	6	9^{1}	12	10^{3}			3								4	7^{2}	11				26
1			2	5	8^{1}		6	7	12	10^{2}	14			3					9^{3}			4	13	11				27
1		3	13	5			6	7	12	9^{3}	11^{2}			2								4	8	10^{1}	14			28
1		5		14	7		2	6	12	13	10^{3}			3					9			4	8^{1}	11^{2}				29
1		4		5	8		6^{1}	7	13	11^{3}	10^{2}			2				14	9			3		12				30
1		2	5	14	6			8	9^{2}	11^{3}	10			4					7^{1}			3		13		12		31
1		4	12	5^{2}	8		6^{1}	7	13	11^{3}	10			3					9			2		14				32
1		4		5				6	9		10^{2}	2^{3}						8^{1}	13		14		7	11	12	3		33
			2^{3}	5			6	7	9	11^{2}	13			3				10			14	12		4^{1}		8	1	34
1		4	12	5			6^{2}	7	13^{3}	11	10			3				14	9			2^{1}	8					35
		2				14	6	8		10^{2}	11							12	9^{3}			4	7^{1}	3	13	5	1	36

MONTROSE

Year Formed: 1879. *Ground & Address:* Links Park, Wellington St, Montrose DD10 8QD. *Telephone:* 01674 673200. *Fax:* 01674 677311. *E-mail:* office@montrosefc.co.uk *Website:* www.montrosefc.co.uk
Ground Capacity: total: 4,936, (seated: 1,338). *Size of Pitch:* 100m × 64m.
Chairman (Interim): John Crawford. *Secretary:* Brian Petrie.
Manager: Stewart Petrie. *Assistant Manager:* Ross Campbell.
Club Nickname: 'The Gable Endies'.
Previous Grounds: None.
Record Attendance: 8,983 v Dundee, Scottish Cup 3rd rd, 17 March 1973.
Record Transfer Fee received: £50,000 for Gary Murray to Hibernian (December 1980).
Record Transfer Fee paid: £17,500 for Jim Smith from Airdrieonians (February 1992).
Record Victory: 12-0 v Vale of Leithen, Scottish Cup 2nd rd, 4 January 1975.
Record Defeat: 0-13 v Aberdeen, 17 March 1951.
Most Capped Player: Alexander Keillor, 2 (6), Scotland.
Most League Appearances: 432: David Larter, 1987-98.
Most League Goals in Season (Individual): 28: Brian Third, Division II, 1972-73.
Most Goals Overall (Individual): 126: Bobby Livingstone, 1967-79.

MONTROSE – SPFL LADBROKES LEAGUE TWO 2016–17 LEAGUE RECORD

Match No.	*Date*	*Venue*	*Opponents*	*Result*		*H/T Score*	*Lg Pos.*	*Goalscorers*	*Attendance*
1	Aug 6	A	Clyde	L	1-2	0-1	9	Templeman 55	445
2	13	H	Arbroath	D	1-1	0-1	8	Dunlop (og) 77	794
3	20	A	Stirling Alb	L	0-2	0-0	9		497
4	27	H	Annan Ath	D	2-2	0-2	9	McDonald 54, Fraser 63	340
5	Sept 10	H	Cowdenbeath	L	1-2	1-1	9	Fraser (pen) 44	393
6	17	A	Edinburgh C	W	1-0	0-0	8	Fraser 61	309
7	24	H	Berwick R	D	0-0	0-0	8		283
8	Oct 1	A	Forfar Ath	W	3-1	1-0	7	Fraser 2 (1 pen) 43, 66 (p), Templeman 48	740
9	15	H	Elgin C	L	0-5	0-3	8		302
10	Nov 5	H	Edinburgh C	L	0-1	0-0	9		388
11	8	A	Annan Ath	W	3-2	2-1	7	Campbell, I 24, Watson 27, Bolochoweckyj 86	289
12	12	A	Cowdenbeath	L	0-2	0-1	9		270
13	19	H	Forfar Ath	D	1-1	1-1	9	Fraser 29	630
14	Dec 3	A	Elgin C	L	1-4	0-0	10	Bolochoweckyj 78	586
15	10	H	Clyde	W	2-1	1-0	9	Fraser (pen) 26, Webster 71	396
16	17	A	Berwick R	W	2-1	0-0	6	Ferguson 56, Court 79	361
17	24	H	Stirling Alb	D	2-2	0-1	6	Masson 57, Fraser 60	610
18	Jan 2	A	Arbroath	D	0-0	0-0	7		1731
19	7	H	Elgin C	L	0-3	0-2	9		562
20	21	H	Cowdenbeath	W	2-1	1-0	6	McLauchlan (og) 39, Fraser (pen) 88	432
21	28	H	Berwick R	W	2-1	0-0	5	Templeman 60, Ferguson 70	1222
22	Feb 4	A	Stirling Alb	W	2-1	0-1	5	Templeman 74, Webster (pen) 81	494
23	11	H	Arbroath	L	1-3	1-0	5	Smith 26	1002
24	18	A	Edinburgh C	D	1-1	0-1	5	Ballantyne 89	346
25	25	A	Forfar Ath	D	0-0	0-0	5		725
26	28	A	Clyde	W	2-1	2-0	5	Hay 5, Pascazio 42	365
27	Mar 4	H	Annan Ath	L	2-3	1-3	5	Fraser 7, Hay 56	384
28	11	H	Stirling Alb	L	1-3	0-1	6	Hay 87	401
29	18	A	Cowdenbeath	W	2-0	1-0	6	Bolochoweckyj 31, Smith 77	302
30	25	A	Arbroath	W	1-0	0-0	6	Fraser 85	1156
31	Apr 1	H	Edinburgh C	W	3-0	1-0	5	Steeves 43, Watson 53, Templeman 71	454
32	8	A	Elgin C	D	1-1	0-1	6	Templeman 60	781
33	15	H	Forfar Ath	W	1-0	1-0	5	Templeman 7	984
34	22	A	Berwick R	W	1-0	1-0	4	Templeman 38	452
35	29	A	Annan Ath	L	1-5	0-4	4	Hay 82	461
36	May 6	H	Clyde	D	1-1	0-1	4	Templeman 81	1324

Final League Position: 4

Honours
League Champions: Second Division 1984-85; *Runners-up:* Second Division 1990-91. Third Division 1994-95.
Scottish Cup: Quarter-finals 1973, 1976.
League Cup: Semi-finals 1975-76.
League Challenge Cup: Semi-finals 1992-93, 1996-97.

Club colours: Shirt: Blue. Shorts: Blue. Socks: Blue.

Goalscorers: *League (44):* Fraser 11 (4 pens), Templeman 9, Hay 4, Bolochoweckyj 3, Ferguson 2, Smith 2, Watson 2, Webster 2 (1 pen), Ballantyne 1, Campbell I 1, Court 1, Masson 1, McDonald 1, Pascazio 1, Steeves 1, own goals 2.
William Hill Scottish FA Cup (3): Court 1, Fraser 1 (1 pen), Templeman 1.
Betfred Scottish League Cup (1): Bolochoweckyj 1.
IRN-BRU Scottish League Challenge Cup (3): Ferguson 1, Masson 1, Webster 1.
Play-Offs (1): Templeman 1.

Millar J 16	McWalter K 21 + 5	McDonald C 3	Lennie R 1 + 5	Campbell I 15 + 3	Webster G 28 + 4	Watson P 21 + 1	Steeves A 32	Ferguson R 19 + 6	Fraser G 29 + 4	Templeman C 29 + 5	Campbell R 7 + 8	Anderson G 10 + 5	Masson T 32	Bolochoweckyj M 25 + 1	Pascazio G 10 + 2	Milne D — + 1	Fleming A 20	McKay D 1	Ballantyne C 27 + 3	Hynd S 1 + 5	MacDonald C 13 + 3	Court J 2 + 9	Thomas D 2 + 7	Smith M 11 + 5	Callaghan L 5 + 6	Hay K 6 + 6	Allan M 10 + 1	*Match No.*
1	2	3	4	5	6	7^{2}	8	9^{1}	10	11	12	13																1
1	6	3	13	5	7		4	9^{1}	10^{2}	11	12	2	8															2
1	6^{1}		12	5	9	8		13	10^{3}		11	2	7	3	4^{2}	14												3
	6	3	12	9	11	7	2^{2}	13	10		5^{1}		8	4			1											4
	6^{2}			5			4		10	11	12	13	7	3			1	2^{1}	8	9								5
	8			5	9		4	6^{1}	11	10	2		7■	3			1			12								6
	7			5	9	8^{3}	4	6^{1}	11	10	2	12		3^{2}			1		14	13								7
	6			5	9			8^{3}	10^{1}	11		3	7	4			1		12	13	2^{2}	14						8
	8			5	6			9^{2}	10■	11^{3}		3	7^{1}	4			1		12	14	2■	13						9
	8			5	9^{3}	14	4	6^{1}		11^{2}	12	3	7				1		2	13		10						10
	7^{1}			5	9	6^{2}	8		10	13	11^{3}	4	3	12			1		2			14						11
	7		13	5	9	6^{1}	4		14	11^{2}	10^{3}		8	3			1		2■			12						12
	8^{1}		12		6		5	9	10^{2}	13		2	7	4			1				3	11						13
	12				6	8^{2}	5	9^{1}	10	11	13		7■	3			1		2		4							14
1					7	8	5	9	10^{1}	11^{3}	12	13	6	3					2^{2}		4	14						15
1	8^{2}				9	7	5	11	10^{1}	13			6	3					2		4	12						16
1					6	8	5	9	10	11^{1}			7	4					2		3	12						17
1					9	8	5	6	11^{1}	10^{2}	13	4	7	3^{3}	12				2			14						18
1					6	8^{2}	5	9	10^{1}	11^{3}	12	4	7	3					2			14	13					19
1	7				6		5	9	14■	11^{1}		4^{3}			3				2		12		8^{2}	10■	13			20
1	7				6		5	9^{1}		12	11^{3}	13	10		3				2		4		14		8^{2}			21
1	6^{3}				8		5	10		11^{1}			7		3				2		4		14	12	9^{2}	13		22
1					6		5	9^{1}	13	10			8^{2}		3				2		4			11		12	7	23
1					6^{1}		5	13	10	12			7	3	4^{2}				2					11	9	14	8^{3}	24
1	8				6^{3}		5^{2}	9^{1}	10	11			7	3	4				2					14		13	12	25
1	8				12				13	11^{2}			7	3	4				2		14		6^{1}	10	5	9^{3}		26
1	8^{1}				14		5		10	11			7	3	4^{3}				2		12			6^{2}	13	9		27
	14				12	8^{2}	5		10	11			7	4			1		2		3^{1}			6^{3}	13	9		28
				12		7	5		10^{2}	11			8^{3}	4			1		2		3		14	13	9^{1}		6	29
	12			9^{1}		8	5		10	11^{2}			7	4			1		2^{3}		3		13	14			6	30
				13	6	8^{3}	5		10^{1}	11^{2}			7	4			1		2					12	14	9	3	31
	8^{2}				6^{1}	7	5		10	11				4			1		2				12	9		13	3	32
				12	6^{3}	7	5	14	10^{2}	11			8	3^{1}			1		2					9		13	4	33
	14			5	6^{1}	7^{3}	4	12	9	10			8^{2}				1		2				13	11			3	34
	12			5■		7^{1}	4		10^{2}	11			8^{3}		14		1		2					9	13	6	3	35
					13	8	5	12	10^{1}	11			7^{3}		3		1		2					9	14	6^{2}	4	36

MOTHERWELL

Year Formed: 1886. *Ground & Address:* Fir Park Stadium, Motherwell ML1 2QN. *Telephone:* 01698 333333. *Fax:* 01698 338001.
E-mail: mfcenquiries@motherwellfc.co.uk *Website:* www.motherwellfc.co.uk
Ground Capacity: 13,742 (all seated). *Size of Pitch:* 105m × 65m.
Chairman: Jim McMahon. *Vice-Chairman:* Douglas Dickie.
Manager: Stephen Robinson. *Assistant Manager:* Keith Lasley.
Club Nicknames: 'The Well', 'The Steelmen'.
Previous Grounds: The Meadows, Dalziel Park.
Record Attendance: 35,632 v Rangers, Scottish Cup 4th rd replay, 12 March 1952.
Record Transfer Fee received: £1,750,000 for Phil O'Donnell to Celtic (September 1994).
Record Transfer Fee paid: £500,000 for John Spencer from Everton (January 1999).
Record Victory: 12-1 v Dundee U, Division II, 23 January 1954.
Record Defeat: 0-8 v Aberdeen, Premier Division, 26 March 1979.
Most Capped Player: Stephen Craigan, 54, Northern Ireland.
Most League Appearances: 626: Bobby Ferrier, 1918-37.
Most League Goals in Season (Individual): 52: Willie McFadyen, Division I, 1931-32.
Most Goals Overall (Individual): 283: Hugh Ferguson, 1916-25.

MOTHERWELL – SPFL LADBROKES PREMIERSHIP 2016–17 LEAGUE RECORD

Match No.	*Date*	*Venue*	*Opponents*	*Result*	*H/T Score*	*Lg Pos.*	*Goalscorers*	*Attendance*
1	Aug 6	A	Kilmarnock	W 2-1	1-0	7	Ainsworth [41], Johnson [46]	4308
2	13	H	St Johnstone	L 1-2	0-0	9	Cadden [47]	3739
3	20	A	Rangers	L 1-2	1-0	9	McDonald [19]	48,716
4	27	H	Dundee	D 0-0	0-0	10		4078
5	Sept 10	A	Ross Co	D 1-1	0-0	9	Moult (pen) [67]	3019
6	17	H	Hamilton A	W 4-2	3-1	7	Moult 4 (1 pen) [8, 13, 21, 50 (p)]	4514
7	24	A	Partick Thistle	D 1-1	0-1	7	McDonald [83]	3227
8	30	H	Hearts	L 1-3	0-1	8	McFadden [90]	4666
9	Oct 15	A	Celtic	L 0-2	0-1	7		54,159
10	26	H	Inverness CT	L 0-3	0-0	11		3131
11	29	H	Ross Co	W 4-1	2-0	9	McDonald [8], van der Weg (og) [32], Tait [51], Ainsworth [62]	3177
12	Nov 5	A	Dundee	L 0-2	0-1	10		5471
13	19	H	Partick Thistle	W 2-0	2-0	7	Moult [14], McDonald [38]	3759
14	26	A	Hearts	L 0-3	0-1	7		16,199
15	Dec 3	H	Celtic	L 3-4	2-0	9	Moult 2 [3, 35], Ainsworth [71]	8535
16	10	H	Kilmarnock	D 0-0	0-0	10		3684
17	17	A	St Johnstone	D 1-1	1-0	9	Clark (og) [12]	2836
18	23	H	Aberdeen	L 1-3	1-2	10	McDonald [16]	3428
19	28	A	Inverness CT	W 2-1	0-0	7	Clay [50], McDonald [87]	3097
20	31	A	Hamilton A	D 1-1	0-0	8	Moult [90]	3526
21	Jan 28	H	Rangers	L 0-2	0-0	10		7902
22	31	A	Ross Co	W 2-1	1-1	7	McDonald [28], Moult [54]	2511
23	Feb 4	H	Hearts	L 0-3	0-0	7		4651
24	15	A	Aberdeen	L 2-7	0-4	10	Bowman [73], Pearson [82]	10,384
25	18	A	Celtic	L 0-2	0-2	10		56,366
26	25	H	Dundee	L 1-5	1-5	10	Moult [22]	4002
27	Mar 4	A	Kilmarnock	W 2-1	0-1	10	McHugh [51], Jules [76]	4726
28	11	A	Aberdeen	L 0-1	0-0	10		12,524
29	18	H	St Johnstone	L 1-2	1-1	10	McDonald [44]	3588
30	Apr 1	A	Rangers	D 1-1	1-0	10	Moult [3]	49,198
31	5	H	Hamilton A	D 0-0	0-0	10		4644
32	8	A	Partick Thistle	L 0-1	0-1	11		3920
33	15	H	Inverness CT	W 4-2	2-1	10	Cadden [7], Moult [9], McDonald [65], Campbell [70]	3696
34	29	H	Dundee	L 2-3	0-1	11	Moult [50], Cadden [80]	4919
35	May 6	H	Ross Co	L 0-1	0-0	11		3870
36	13	A	Hamilton A	W 1-0	0-0	10	Moult [66]	4173
37	16	H	Kilmarnock	W 3-1	1-1	9	McHugh [1], Ainsworth [53], Frear [78]	5246
38	20	A	Inverness CT	L 2-3	0-0	9	McFadden [73], Bowman (pen) [90]	5351

Final League Position: 9

Honours
League Champions: Division I 1931-32. First Division 1981-82, 1984-85. Division II 1953-54, 1968-69.
Runners-up: Premier Division 1994-95, 2012-13. Premiership 2013-14. Division I 1926-27, 1929-30, 1932-33, 1933-34. Division II 1894-95, 1902-03.
Scottish Cup: 1952, 1991; *Runners-up:* 1931, 1933, 1939, 1951, 2011.
League Cup Winners: 1950-51; *Runners-up:* 1954-55, 2004-05.

European: *Champions League:* 2 matches (2012-13). *Cup Winners' Cup:* 2 matches (1991-92). *UEFA Cup:* 8 matches (1994-95, 1995-96, 2008-09). *Europa League:* 18 matches (2009-10, 2010-11, 2012-13, 2013-14, 2014-15).

Club colours: Shirt: Amber with maroon band. Shorts: Amber. Socks: Amber with maroon band.

Goalscorers: *League (46):* Moult 15 (2 pens), McDonald 9, Ainsworth 4, Cadden 3, Bowman 2 (1 pen), McFadden 2, McHugh 2, Campbell 1, Clay 1, Frear 1, Johnson 1, Jules 1, Pearson 1, Tait 1, own goals 2.
William Hill Scottish FA Cup (1): Moult 1.
Betfred Scottish League Cup (9): Johnson 3, Cadden 2, McDonald 2, Moult 2.
IRN-BRU Scottish League Challenge Cup (3): Mackin 2, Fry 1.

Samson C 34	Tait R 25	Heneghan B 37	McManus S 25	Hammell S 24 + 1	Ainsworth L 10 + 20	Cadden C 36	McHugh C 19	Clay C 31 + 4	Johnson M 4	McDonald S 34 + 1	Chalmers J 7 + 1	MacLean R 4 + 3	Lasley K 25 + 3	Blyth J 1 + 7	Thomas D — + 4	McFadden J — + 6	Bowman R 11 + 13	Moult L 30 + 1	Lucas L 6 + 4	McMillan J 9 + 5	Ferguson D 7 + 3	Hastie J — + 3	Campbell A 6 + 1	Frear E 11 + 4	Jules Z 6 + 4	Pearson S 10 + 1	Gordon S 2 + 2	Griffiths R 4	Livingstone A — + 2	*Match No.*
1	2	3	4	5	6^1	7	8^2	9	10	11	12	13																		1
1	2	3	4		6^2	9^1		8	10	11	5		7	12	13															2
1	2	3	4		6	9		7^1	10	11	5		8	12																3
1	2	3	4		6^1	9		8	10	11	5		7			12														4
1	2	3	4	5	12	8		9		11	10^3		6^2			14	7^1	13												5
1	2	3	4	5	12	6		8		10			7				9	11^1												6
1	2	3	4	5	13	6		8		10			7^1			12	9	11^2												7
1	2	3	4	5	13	6^1		8		9			7^3			14	11^2	10	12											8
1	2	3	4			6		8		10^3		9^1	7				12	11		5^2	13	14								9
1	2	3	4		14	6		8^1		12		9^2	7			13	11^3	10		5										10
1	2	3	4		9^1	6		7		10		13						11	8^2	5			12							11
1	2	3	4	5^3	7^2	6		9		11		13	8^1		14			10		12										12
1	2	3	4			6		8		10			7					11		5	9									13
1	5	2	3	13	12	6^2		8		11			7					10		9^1	4^3	14								14
1	2^2	3	4	5	12	6^3		8		10		9^1	7				14	11		13										15
1	2	3	4		6^1			8		10		9^3	7^2		14			11	12		5	13								16
1	2	3	4		13	6		8		11			7^3				14	10	12	9^2	5^1									17
1	2	3	4^3	5	13	6^1		8		10			7^2		12		14	11	9											18
1	2	3	4	5^2	12	6^1	8	7		10								11	9	13										19
1	2	3	4		12		6	8		11								10	7■	9^1			5							20
1	2^2	3	4	5		6^3	7	8		10■	9^1						14	11		12				13						21
1	2	4	3	5^3	14	6	8	12		10			7					11^2	9^1						13					22
1	5^3	2	3	8^2	9^1	10	7■						6					11	13	12					4	14				23
1	2	3	4	5		10		13					7				12	11	8^2					6^1		9				24
1		3	4^1			6^2		8		10	5		7				13	11		2					12	9				25
1		3				6	7	8		10	5^1							11		2				12	4	9				26
1	2^2	3		5^3		6	8			10			7^1				12	11			14			13	4	9				27
1		3		5^2		6	7	8		10				12			11^1				2			13	4	9				28
1				5^2	13	6	4	7		10				14			12	11			2			9^1	3^3	8				29
1		3		4	14	5	2	6^1		10			12	13			9^2	11^3						7		8				30
1		3		4	14	5	2	6^2		9			12	11^3			10							8^1		7	13			31
1		4			12	5	3	6^1		10			13	14			11							8^2	2	7	9^3			32
1		2		4^3	12	5	3			10				13			8^2	11^1					6	9	14	7				33
1		2		4	12	5	3	14		9^2			6^1				10^3	11					7	8			13			34
		2		4^2	9^1	5	3	14		10			6				13	11					7^3	8	12			1		35
		3		5	12	2	4	6		11			8^2				13	10^1			14		7	9^3				1		36
		3		5	12^3	6	4	8		10			7				13	11^1			2^2			9				1	14	37
		3		5	8^3	2	4	6								14	13	9^1					7	10			11^2	1	12	38

PARTICK THISTLE

Year Formed: 1876. *Ground & Address:* Firhill Stadium, 80 Firhill Rd, Glasgow G20 7AL. *Telephone:* 0141 579 1971. *Fax:* 0141 945 1525. *E-mail:* mail@ptfc.co.uk *Website:* ptfc.co.uk
Ground Capacity: 10,102 (all seated). *Size of Pitch:* 105m × 68m.
Chairman: David Beattie. *Managing Director:* Ian Maxwell.
Manager: Alan Archibald. *Assistant Manager:* Scott Paterson.
Club Nickname: 'The Jags'.
Previous Grounds: Overnewton Park; Jordanvale Park; Muirpark; Inchview; Meadowside Park.
Record Attendance: 49,838 v Rangers, Division I, 18 February 1922. *Ground Record:* 54,728, Scotland v Ireland, 25 February 1928.
Record Transfer Fee received: £200,000 for Mo Johnston to Watford (July 1981).
Record Transfer Fee paid: £85,000 for Andy Murdoch from Celtic (February 1991).
Record Victory: 16-0 v Royal Albert, Scottish Cup 1st rd, 17 January 1931.
Record Defeat: 0-10 v Queen's Park, Scottish Cup 5th rd, 3 December 1881.
Most Capped Player: Alan Rough, 51 (53), Scotland.
Most League Appearances: 410: Alan Rough, 1969-82.
Most League Goals in Season (Individual): 41: Alex Hair, Division I, 1926-27.
Most Goals Overall (Individual): 229: Willie Sharp, 1939-57.

PARTICK THISTLE – SPFL LADBROKES PREMIERSHIP 2016–17 LEAGUE RECORD

Match No.	Date	Venue	Opponents	Result	H/T Score	Lg Pos.	Goalscorers	Attendance
1	Aug 6	H	Inverness CT	W 2-0	1-0	1	Erskine 36, Amoo 60	2943
2	20	A	Aberdeen	L 1-2	0-1	5	Erskine 90	11,049
3	27	H	Hearts	L 1-2	0-1	6	Lindsay 55	4919
4	Sept 10	H	St Johnstone	L 0-2	0-1	6		2885
5	17	A	Kilmarnock	D 2-2	1-1	6	Lawless 32, Lindsay 82	4169
6	24	H	Motherwell	D 1-1	1-0	6	Erskine 31	3227
7	Oct 1	A	Rangers	L 0-2	0-2	6		49,680
8	15	H	Hamilton A	D 2-2	2-1	6	Edwards 22, Lindsay 43	2843
9	22	H	Ross Co	D 1-1	1-0	6	Welsh (pen) 24	3777
10	26	A	Dundee	W 2-0	1-0	6	Azeez 29, Doolan 62	4783
11	29	A	St Johnstone	W 2-1	1-1	6	Doolan 17, Osman 90	3096
12	Nov 4	H	Aberdeen	L 1-2	0-1	6	Barton 51	3974
13	19	A	Motherwell	L 0-2	0-2	6		3759
14	26	H	Rangers	L 1-2	0-0	6	Doolan 76	7951
15	Dec 3	A	Hamilton A	D 1-1	0-1	6	Welsh 61	2210
16	9	H	Celtic	L 1-4	0-1	6	Lindsay 61	7609
17	17	A	Hearts	D 1-1	0-1	6	Welsh 47	16,418
18	20	A	Celtic	L 0-1	0-1	6		55,733
19	23	A	Ross Co	W 3-1	0-0	6	Lindsay 50, Doolan 62, Erskine 78	2935
20	28	H	Dundee	W 2-0	2-0	6	Booth 16, Doolan 44	3758
21	31	H	Kilmarnock	D 0-0	0-0	6		3584
22	Jan 28	A	Inverness CT	D 0-0	0-0	6		2823
23	Feb 1	H	St Johnstone	L 0-1	0-1	6		2257
24	4	A	Aberdeen	L 0-2	0-0	6		10,094
25	18	H	Hamilton A	W 2-0	0-0	6	Doolan 2 68, 79	3057
26	25	H	Hearts	W 2-0	1-0	6	Doolan 5, Lindsay 73	4143
27	Mar 1	A	Dundee	W 1-0	1-0	6	Etxabeguren Leanizbarrutia (og) 30	5328
28	11	H	Inverness CT	D 1-1	0-0	6	Doolan 56	3082
29	18	A	Kilmarnock	D 1-1	0-0	6	Erskine 73	4519
30	Apr 1	H	Ross Co	W 2-1	0-0	6	Doolan 2 64, 79	3149
31	5	A	Celtic	D 1-1	0-0	6	Azeez 64	54,047
32	8	H	Motherwell	W 1-0	1-0	6	Doolan 11	3920
33	15	A	Rangers	L 0-2	0-1	6		49,748
34	29	A	Hearts	D 2-2	0-0	6	Doolan 50, Lawless 72	15,930
35	May 7	H	Rangers	L 1-2	1-0	6	Doolan 14	6799
36	13	A	St Johnstone	L 0-1	0-1	6		3630
37	18	H	Celtic	L 0-5	0-3	6		7847
38	21	H	Aberdeen	L 0-6	0-5	6		3924

Final League Position: 6

Honours
League Champions: First Division 1975-76, 2001-02, 2012-13; Division II 1896-97, 1899-1900, 1970-71; Second Division 2000-01.
Runners-up: First Division 1991-92, 2008-09. Division II 1901-02. *Promoted to First Division:* 2005-06 (play-offs).
Scottish Cup Winners: 1921; *Runners-up:* 1930.
League Cup Winners: 1971-72; *Runners-up:* 1953-54, 1956-57, 1958-59.
League Challenge Cup Runners-up: 2012-13.

European: *Fairs Cup:* 4 matches (1963-64). *UEFA Cup:* 2 matches (1972-73). *Intertoto Cup:* 4 matches (1995-96).

Club colours: Shirt: Yellow with red front panel and black trim. Shorts: Black. Socks: Black.

Goalscorers: *League (38):* Doolan 14, Lindsay 6, Erskine 5, Welsh 3 (1 pen), Azeez 2, Lawless 2, Amoo 1, Barton 1, Booth 1, Edwards 1, Osman 1, own goal 1.
William Hill Scottish FA Cup (5): Erskine 2, Barton 1, Lawless 1, Osman 1.
Betfred Scottish League Cup (10): Erskine 2, Welsh 2 (2 pens), Amoo 1, Azeez 1, Doolan 1, Lawless 1, Lindsay 1, Pogba 1.
IRN-BRU Scottish League Challenge Cup (6): Nisbet 3, McLaughlin 1, McMullin 1, Penrice 1.

Cerny T 27	Gordon Z 12 + 2	Devine D 28 + 2	Lindsay L 36	Booth C 31	Welsh S 18 + 3	Osman A 30 + 1	Amoo D 14 + 11	Erskine C 25 + 11	Lawless S 24 + 6	Doolan K 29 + 8	Edwards R 33 + 5	Azeez A 19 + 19	Pogba M — + 2	Scully R 6 + 1	Elliot C 26 + 5	Barton A 30 + 1	McDaid D — + 3	Stuckmann T 4 + 1	Wilson D — + 1	Keown N 14	Dumbuya M 8	Nisbet K — + 3	McCarthy A 3 + 2	Ridgers M 1 + 1	Fleming R — + 1	Lamont M — + 1	McLaughlin N — + 1	Match No.
1	2	3	4^{2}	5	6	7	8	9^{1}	10	11	12	13																1
1	2	3	4	5	7■	6	8^{2}	12	10	13	9^{3}	11^{1}	14															2
1	2	3	4	5		7	12	9	10	11^{1}	6	8^{2}	13															3
1^{1}	2	3	4	5	8^{2}	7	14	6	9	10	13	11^{3}		12														4
	2	3	4	5	13	6■	8^{2}	9^{3}	10	11^{1}	7	12		1	14													5
	2	3	4		12		8	9^{2}	10^{1}	13	6	11		1	5	7												6
	2	3	4	5	13	7	8^{3}	11^{1}	10		6	9^{2}		1	12		14											7
	2	3	4	5		6	12	9^{2}	10^{1}	11^{3}	7	13		1	14	8												8
	12	3	4^{1}	5	7	6	13			11^{2}	9	8		1	2	10												9
		3	4	5	7	6^{2}				11	9	8		1^{1}	2	10		12	13									10
		2	4	9	8	7	13	12		11^{2}	6	10^{1}			5	3		1										11
		2	4	9	8	7	13	12		11^{3}	6^{2}	10^{1}			5	3	14	1										12
		3	5	6	9	8	14	10^{2}	13	12	7^{3}	11			2^{1}	4		1										13
	2		4	5	7	6	8^{3}	9^{2}	13	11^{1}	12	14			10	3		1										14
1	2		4	5	7	6		12		11	9	8^{1}			10	3												15
1	5		3	2	6	7	10^{3}	9^{2}	13	11^{1}	12	14			8	4												16
1		4	3	9	7	6		12		11	8	10^{1}			5	2												17
1	2	3	4	5	6^{2}	8	10^{1}	12	9	14	7	11^{3}				13												18
1		3	2	4	8	7	13	9	5^{1}	10^{2}	11	12			6													19
1	12	3	4^{2}	5	10	6		8^{1}		11	9	13			2	7												20
1		3		5	7	6	12	8^{3}	10^{1}	11	9^{2}	13			2	4	14											21
1			4	5	7			10	9	12	6	11^{1}			2	8				3								22
1			4	5	7^{2}	13	14	8^{1}	10	11^{3}	9	12			2■	6				3								23
1		3	4			6	8^{3}	13	10	11^{2}	9^{1}	12			5	7					2	14						24
1		3	4	5		7	8^{1}	13	10	12	9	11^{2}				6					2							25
1		3	4	9		7		11^{1}	13	10^{2}	6	14			12	8				2	5^{3}							26
1		3	2	8		6		11^{2}	12	9^{1}	10	13			5	7				4								27
1			4	5		7^{1}	12	8^{2}	10^{3}	11	9	13			14	6				3	2							28
1		12	4			6		8^{1}	10^{2}	11	9	13			5	7				3	2							29
1		12	4			6^{1}		8^{2}	10	11	9	13			5	7				3	2							30
1		3	4	9			10^{2}	13		12	8	11			5	6				2			7^{1}					31
1		3	4					10^{2}	9^{1}	11	7	12			8	6				2	5		13					32
1		4	5				7^{2}	12	8^{3}	13	6	11^{1}			10	9				3	2	14						33
1		2■		9				6^{1}	10	11	8	12			5	3				4			7					34
1			4	5		8		10^{2}	7	11	9^{1}	12			2	6				3			13					35
1		3^{3}	4	5		7		13	12	11	9^{1}	10^{2}			6	8				2		14						36
1^{3}		3	4	5		6^{2}	8	9^{1}	10	11	12	14			2	7								13				37
			4				5^{2}	6	9^{1}	10	8	11				3				2			7^{3}	1	12	13	14	38

PETERHEAD

Year Formed: 1891. *Ground and Address:* Balmoor Stadium, Balmoor Terrace, Peterhead AB42 1EU.
Telephone: 01779 478256. *Fax:* 01779 490682. *E-mail:* office@peterheadfc.co.uk *Website:* www.peterheadfc.com
Ground Capacity: 3,150 (seated: 1,000). *Size of Pitch:* 101m × 64m.
Chairman: Rodger Morrison. *Vice-Chairman:* Ian Grant.
Manager: Jim McInally. *Assistant Coach:* David Nicholls.
Club Nickname: 'Blue Toon'.
Previous Ground: Recreation Park.
Record Attendance: 8,643 v Raith R, Scottish Cup 4th rd replay, 25 February 1987 (Recreation Park); 4,855 v Rangers, Third Division, 19 January 2013 (at Balmoor).
Record Victory: 8-0 v Forfar Athletic, Second Division, 30 Sep 2006.
Record Defeat: 0-13 v Aberdeen, Scottish Cup 3rd rd, 10 February 1923.
Most League Appearances: 275: Martin Bavidge, 2003-13.
Most League Goals in Season (Individual): 32: Rory McAllister, 2013-14.
Most Goals Overall (Individual): 119: Rory McAllister, 2011-16.

PETERHEAD – SPFL LADBROKES LEAGUE ONE 2016–17 LEAGUE RECORD

Match No.	*Date*	*Venue*	*Opponents*	*Result*		*H/T Score*	*Lg Pos.*	*Goalscorers*	*Atten-dance*
1	Aug 6	A	Alloa Ath	L	0-4	0-3	10		504
2	13	H	East Fife	L	0-3	0-2	10		492
3	20	H	Albion R	D	2-2	1-0	8	Baptie [40], McAllister [60]	503
4	27	A	Stranraer	L	0-1	0-1	10		376
5	Sept 10	H	Queen's Park	W	2-0	0-0	8	Redman [47], Riley [61]	519
6	17	A	Stenhousemuir	D	2-2	2-0	9	Riley [17], Dzierzawski [21]	331
7	24	A	Brechin C	L	1-2	1-1	9	McAllister [32]	431
8	Oct 1	H	Livingston	L	1-2	1-1	10	Kelleher [7]	569
9	15	A	Airdrieonians	W	3-1	0-0	8	Kelleher [66], McAllister [67], McIntosh [90]	482
10	22	A	Albion R	W	1-0	0-0	8	Brown, J [79]	360
11	29	H	Stranraer	W	2-0	0-0	6	McAllister [64], Brown, S [87]	444
12	Nov 5	H	Brechin C	L	1-3	0-1	6	McAllister [76]	621
13	12	A	Queen's Park	D	0-0	0-0	6		524
14	19	A	Livingston	W	2-1	1-0	6	McIntosh [39], Brown, S [74]	712
15	Dec 3	H	Airdrieonians	L	2-4	1-3	7	Riley [32], McIntosh (pen) [85]	475
16	10	H	Alloa Ath	D	1-1	0-0	7	Kelleher [67]	365
17	17	A	East Fife	L	0-2	0-0	8		486
18	26	H	Stenhousemuir	L	0-2	0-0	8		427
19	Jan 2	A	Brechin C	W	1-0	0-0	8	McAllister [77]	553
20	7	H	Livingston	L	2-3	0-0	8	Riley [52], McAllister [62]	582
21	14	A	Alloa Ath	W	1-0	0-0	8	McIntosh [49]	504
22	28	H	Queen's Park	W	4-0	3-0	8	Strachan [10], Anderson [25], McAllister 2 (1 pen) [32 (p), 63]	442
23	Feb 4	A	Airdrieonians	L	1-4	1-0	8	McAllister [36]	599
24	11	H	Albion R	D	1-1	1-0	8	McAllister [37]	423
25	18	A	Stranraer	D	3-3	1-2	8	McAllister 2 [12, 55], Anderson [67]	459
26	25	H	East Fife	D	1-1	0-0	7	Brown, J [64]	495
27	Mar 4	A	Stenhousemuir	L	1-3	0-2	8	Brown, J [47]	362
28	11	H	Brechin C	L	0-1	0-0	8		483
29	18	A	Albion R	D	0-0	0-0	8		285
30	25	H	Stranraer	D	2-2	1-2	9	McAllister [8], Redman [90]	449
31	Apr 1	H	Airdrieonians	D	1-1	1-1	9	McAllister [8]	524
32	8	A	Queen's Park	L	0-2	0-1	9		501
33	15	A	East Fife	W	2-1	1-1	9	Redman [25], Reid, Craig [55]	636
34	22	H	Stenhousemuir	L	0-1	0-1	9		587
35	29	A	Livingston	L	1-4	0-3	10	Redman [61]	891
36	May 6	H	Alloa Ath	W	3-2	0-1	9	McAllister [53], Anderson [68], Brown, J [81]	681

Final League Position: 9

Honours
League Champions: League Two 2013-14.
Runners up: Third Division 2004-05, 2012-13.
Scottish Cup: Quarter-finals 2001.
League Challenge Cup: Runners up: 2015-16.

Club colours: Shirt: Royal blue with white trim. Shorts: Royal blue with white trim. Socks: Royal blue.

Goalscorers: *League (44):* McAllister 16 (1 pen), Brown J 4, McIntosh 4 (1 pen), Redman 4, Riley 4, Anderson 3, Kelleher 3, Brown S 2, Baptie 1, Dzierzawski 1, Craig Reid 1, Strachan 1.
William Hill Scottish FA Cup (0).
Betfred Scottish League Cup (8): McAllister 4 (3 pens), Brown 1, Dzierzawski 1, McIntosh 1, own goal 1.
IRN-BRU Scottish League Challenge Cup (5): McAllister 3, Brown J 1, McIntosh 1.
Play-Offs (6): McAllister 3 (1 pen), Brown J 1, Brown S 1, Strachan 1.

Smith G 26	Ross S 23 + 4	Kelleher F 19	Rumsby S 4 + 6	Noble S 27 + 1	Strachan R 27 + 1	Stevenson J 28 + 2	Redman J 18 + 8	Dzierzawski K 10 + 10	McAllister R 33	Brown J 16 + 17	McIntosh L 6 + 21	Blockley N 8 + 4	Riley N 23 + 9	Ferry S 26 + 2	Nassor S — + 1	Hobday F 10	Baptie R 3 + 1	McCluskey S 8 + 2	Brown S 32	Comrie A 14 + 2	McMullin M 8 + 3	Anderson G 12 + 2	Smith A — + 7	Gordon L 7	Reid Craig 8	Match No.
1	2	3	4	5	6[2]	7	8[3]	9[1]	10	11	12	13	14													1
1	3	4		5	2	6[1]	9[2]	8	10	13	12		11[3]	7	14											2
	2	4	3[3]		5		13	6	11	8[1]	10[2]		14	7		1	9	12								3
	3	4			9			12	10	11[1]	14	2[2]	13	7[3]		1	5	6	8							4
	3[3]	4	12	5	2		6	8	10[2]	14	13		11[1]			1		9	7							5
		2	4	5	3	14	6[2]	8	10		12		11[1]	13		1		9[3]	7							6
1		3		5	4	2	9[1]	6[2]	11	14	12		10[3]	8				13	7							7
1		4		5	3[1]	2	14	8	10	13	12		11[2]	7				9[3]	6							8
1		3		9	2	5	13	4[1]	10	12	14		6[2]	11				8[3]	7							9
1		3	14	5	4	2	8[3]	13	10	7[1]			12	11				9[2]	6							10
1	12	4		5[1]	3	2		14	10	8	13		11[2]	7[3]				9	6							11
1	13	3		5	4	2			10	8[2]	12	14	9[3]	7				11[1]	6							12
1	3[2]	4	14	5	12	2		13		7[3]	11	6	10[1]	9■					8							13
1	4	3	14	5	6	2[3]		12	11[1]	10[2]	7	9	13						8							14
1	3	4	14	5		2[2]	13	12		9[3]	10	6	11	8[1]					7							15
1	3	4		5			6[1]	2	10	12	11		9[2]	7			13		8							16
	2	3	14	5			9[1]	6[2]	11	10[3]	13	12	8	7		1			4							17
	3	4		5		2	6[1]		11	13	12		10	7		1	9[2]		8							18
1	3	4		5		6	13	14	11[2]	9[1]	12		10[3]	8					7	2						19
1	3		4	5		6			10	9[1]	12	13	11[2]	8					7	2						20
1	3			5		11		13	10[1]	14	12■	8[2]	9[3]	6					7	2	4					21
1				5	4	9[2]	14		10	13		6[3]		8[1]					7	2	3	11	12			22
1	13			5	4	9[2]			10	14	12	6[3]		8[1]					7	2	3	11				23
1	2[3]			5[2]	8	11			10		13	6[1]							7	12	3	9	14	4		24
1	5				8[3]	11[1]	13	14	10		12		6[2]						7	2	3	9		4		25
1					4	6[1]		14	10	12			11[2]	7[3]					8	2	5	9	13	3		26
1	4[1]			13	8	10[3]	14		11■	7	12			9[2]						2	5	6		3		27
1				5[2]		9[3]	7[1]			11	13		10						8	2	12	6	14	4	3	28
1	13				7[2]	9[3]	8		11	12			14						6	5	4[1]	10		2	3	29
1	2				8		9		10	14			11	13					7	5[2]	12[3]	6		3[1]	4	30
1				5	4	14	9[1]		10	13			11[2]	8					7	2	12	6			3[3]	31
	4			5	3	2	8[3]		11	7[1]			12	10		1			9	13		6[2]	14			32
	4				3	10[1]	6		11[3]	14			8[2]	9		1			7	5		12	13		2	33
	3				4	6	9		11	13			12	8		1			7[2]	2[1]		10[3]	14		5	34
	3			5	4	6	8		10	13	12		11[1]	9[2]		1			7						2	35
1	3			5[2]	4	6	9		10	8	11[1]		13						7			12			2	36

QUEEN OF THE SOUTH

Year Formed: 1919. *Ground & Address:* Palmerston Park, Dumfries DG2 9BA. *Telephone:* 01387 254853.
Fax: 01387 240470. *E-mail:* admin@qosfc.com *Website:* www.qosfc.com
Ground Capacity: 8,690 (seated: 3,377) *Size of Pitch:* 102m × 66m.
Chairman: Billy Hewitson. *Vice-Chairman:* Craig Paterson. *Football Administration:* Ewan Lithgow.
Player/Manager: Gary Naysmith. *Assistant Manager:* Dougie Anderson. *Coach:* Lee Robinson.
Club Nickname: 'The Doonhamers'.
Previous Grounds: None.
Record Attendance: 26,552 v Hearts, Scottish Cup 3rd rd, 23 February 1952.
Record Transfer Fee received: £250,000 for Andy Thomson to Southend U (July 1994).
Record Transfer Fee paid: £30,000 for Jim Butter from Alloa Ath (1995).
Record Victory: 11-1 v Stranraer, Scottish Cup 1st rd, 16 January 1932.
Record Defeat: 2-10 v Dundee, Division I, 1 December 1962.
Most Capped Player: Billy Houliston, 3, Scotland.
Most League Appearances: 731: Allan Ball, 1963-82.
Most League Goals in Season (Individual): 37: Jimmy Gray, Division II, 1927-28.
Most Goals in Season: 41: Jimmy Rutherford, 1931-32; Nicky Clark, 2012-13.
Most Goals Overall (Individual): 251: Jim Patterson, 1949-63.

QUEEN OF THE SOUTH – SPFL LADBROKES CHAMPIONSHIP 2016–17 LEAGUE RECORD

Match No.	*Date*	*Venue*	*Opponents*	*Result*	*H/T Score*	*Lg Pos.*	*Goalscorers*	*Attendance*
1	Aug 6	A	Dundee U	D 1-1	1-0	6	Millar [40]	7058
2	13	H	Ayr U	W 4-1	2-0	3	Lyle 2 [12, 53], Dobbie [44], Dykes [74]	1982
3	20	H	Falkirk	W 2-0	1-0	3	Dobbie 2 [34, 50]	1841
4	27	A	Dunfermline Ath	W 1-0	1-0	3	Lyle [45]	3973
5	Sept 10	A	St Mirren	W 3-1	2-1	2	Lyle 2 [12, 43], Dobbie [55]	3102
6	17	H	Raith R	W 3-1	0-0	1	Dobbie 2 [52, 68], Brotherston [80]	1864
7	24	H	Hibernian	D 0-0	0-0	1		3703
8	Oct 1	A	Dumbarton	D 0-0	0-0	1		840
9	15	H	Greenock Morton	L 0-5	0-3	2		1695
10	22	A	Ayr U	L 0-1	0-0	3		1842
11	29	A	Raith R	L 0-1	0-0	4		1244
12	Nov 5	H	Dundee U	L 1-4	1-2	6	Anderson [45]	2316
13	19	A	Hibernian	L 0-4	0-2	6		13,861
14	Dec 3	H	Dumbarton	L 1-2	0-2	6	Lyle [80]	1261
15	6	H	St Mirren	L 2-3	2-1	6	Dobbie 2 [17, 42]	1147
16	10	A	Falkirk	D 2-2	1-1	6	Dobbie [34], Lyle [60]	4170
17	17	H	Dunfermline Ath	D 2-2	1-0	6	Ashcroft (og) [39], Dobbie [78]	1561
18	24	A	Greenock Morton	L 0-1	0-1	6		1638
19	31	H	Ayr U	D 0-0	0-0	6		1594
20	Jan 7	A	St Mirren	W 3-0	1-0	7	Dobbie [45], Thomson, J [81], MacKenzie (og) [88]	3105
21	14	A	Dundee U	D 3-3	1-1	7	Dobbie [28], Thomson, J [53], Thomas [65]	6136
22	21	A	Dumbarton	W 2-1	1-0	5	Thomas 2 [24, 68]	825
23	28	H	Hibernian	L 0-1	0-0	5		3007
24	Feb 4	H	Greenock Morton	W 3-0	0-0	5	Lyle [71], Jacobs [83], Thomson, J [90]	1588
25	25	H	Raith R	W 2-1	2-0	5	Rankin [7], Lyle [36]	1484
26	Mar 4	H	Falkirk	L 0-2	0-1	5		1995
27	7	A	Dunfermline Ath	D 1-1	1-1	5	Thomson, J [28]	2653
28	11	A	Greenock Morton	L 0-1	0-0	5		1451
29	18	H	St Mirren	L 0-2	0-1	5		1728
30	25	A	Raith R	D 1-1	1-1	5	Dobbie [24]	1609
31	Apr 1	H	Dundee U	W 4-2	2-1	5	Lyle [19], Dobbie [43], Dykes [81], Hilson [89]	1514
32	8	A	Ayr U	W 2-0	0-0	5	Dobbie 2 [71, 76]	1476
33	15	A	Hibernian	L 0-3	0-2	6		17,054
34	22	H	Dumbarton	L 1-2	1-2	6	Dobbie [15]	1289
35	29	A	Falkirk	D 2-2	1-1	6	Dobbie 2 [9, 78]	4673
36	May 6	H	Dunfermline Ath	L 0-1	0-0	6		1849

Final League Position: 6

Honours
League Champions: Division II 1950-51. Second Division 2001-02, 2012-13.
Runners-up: Division II 1932-33, 1961-62, 1974-75. Second Division 1980-81, 1985-86.
Scottish Cup Runners-up: 2007-08.
League Cup: semi-finals 1950-51, 1960-61.
League Challenge Cup Winners: 2002-03, 2012-13; *Runners-up:* 1997-98, 2010-11.

European: *UEFA Cup:* 2 matches (2008-09).

Club colours: Shirt: Royal blue with white trim. Shorts: White. Socks: Royal blue.

Goalscorers: *League (46):* Dobbie 19, Lyle 10, Thomson J 4, Thomas 3, Dykes 2, Anderson 1, Brotherston 1, Hilson 1, Jacobs 1, Millar 1, Rankin 1, own goals 2.
William Hill Scottish FA Cup (1): Hamill 1.
Betfred Scottish League Cup (9): Lyle 2, Anderson 1, Dobbie 1, Dowie 1, Dykes 1, Hamill 1, Pickard 1, own goal 1.
IRN-BRU Scottish League Challenge Cup (13): Dobbie 6, Lyle 2 (1 pen), Rigg 2, Anderson 1, Dykes 1, Hilson 1.

Robinson L 35	Hamill J 18 + 3	Dowie A 27	Higgins C 23	Marshall J 31	Anderson G 16 + 3	Millar M 17 + 1	Jacobs K 33	Dykes L 20 + 10	Hilson D 5 + 9	Lyle D 19 + 8	Brownlie D 34 + 1	Dobbie S 34 + 1	Tapping C 2 + 3	Brotherston D 1 + 9	Pickard J 5 + 6	Rigg S 3 + 7	Moxon O — + 5	Hooper S — + 1	Fergusson R — + 6	Carmichael D 11 + 8	Bell O 1 + 2	Rankin J 17	Thomson J 16 + 1	Thomas D 14 + 3	Murray Connor 1 + 7	Mercer S 11	Atkinson J 1	McManus C 1 + 3	*Match No.*
1	2	3	4²	5	6	7	8	9	10¹	11³	12	13	14																1
1	2	3		5	6		7	9		10³	4	11¹	8²	12	13	14													2
1	2	3		5	6	7³	8	9	12	11²	4	10¹			13		14												3
1	2	3		5	6	7³	8	9²	12	10¹	4	11	14			13													4
1	2	3		5	6³	7¹	8		9	10²	4	11		14	12	13													5
1	2	3		5	6²	7	9	12	8¹	10³	4	11		13		14													6
1	5	3	4		13	7	8¹	6	9	10²	2	11			12														7
1	4	2	5		6²	7	8	9			3	11		12	13	10¹													8
1	2	4		5	6¹	7³		9			3	11		13	8	10²		12	14										9
1		4	3	5	12	8	7	11			2	10		6¹	9²	13													10
1		4	3	5	6²	13	7	9			2	10		12	8¹	11													11
1	14	3	4	5	6²	7	8¹	9		11³	2	10		13		12													12
1		3	4	5	6²	7	8	9		10¹	2			12	11	13													13
1	2	3		5	6²	7¹		11		12	4	10			8		13			9									14
1	5	2	4	9	6¹	7		8²		10	3	11		14	12³					13									15
1	2	8	4	5	6¹	7²	9			10³	3	11					14		13	12									16
1	6	3	4	5	9³	7	8¹			10²	2	11					13		14	12									17
1	7	3	4³	5	6¹	9²	8			10	2	11							14	12	13								18
1	2	3		5	14	8³	6			10	4	11²					12		13	9	7¹								19
1	2	4		5			6	12		13	3	10¹								9²		7	8	11³	14				20
1	13	3		5			8	12			4	11²								6¹		9	7	10		2			21
1		3	5				8			12	4	11								6¹		7	10	9		2			22
1		4		5			7¹	13		12	3	10								9²		8	11	6		2			23
1	14		4	5			7	12		11²	3	10³										8	9	6¹	13	2			24
1		4		5			9	12		11³	3	10²							14	13		8	7	6¹		2			25
1		3		5			7	12	14	11²	4	10¹								13		6³	9	8		2			26
1	2		4				7	6¹	12	13	3	11²									14	8	9³	10		5			27
1	2		4				7²	11¹	13	14	3	10³								12		8	9	6		5			28
		3	4	5			7	11¹	13	12		10										8³	9	6²	14	2	1		29
1		2	4	9			7	14		11²	3	10										6	8¹	12		5³		13	30
1			4	5			2	12	14	10²	3	11								9¹		8	7	6³	13				31
1			3	5			2	10¹	13		4	11								6²		8	7	9³	12			14	32
1			4	5			2	11¹	14		3	10								6³		8	7	9²	12			13	33
1			4	5			2	12	10²		3	11								13		8	6³	14	9¹			7	34
1			4	5			7	10			3	11	13							9		8	6¹	12		2²			35
1			4	5			2	11³		13	3	10	7²							9¹		8	12	6	14				36

QUEEN'S PARK

Year Formed: 1867. *Ground & Address:* Hampden Park, Mount Florida, Glasgow G42 9BA. *Telephone:* 0141 632 1275. *Fax:* 0141 636 1612. *E-mail:* secretary@queensparkfc.co.uk *Website:* queensparkfc.co.uk
Ground Capacity: 51,866 (all seated). *Size of Pitch:* 105m × 68m.
President: Alan Hutchinson. *Secretary:* Christine Wright. *Treasurer:* David Gordon.
Head Coach: Gus MacPherson. *Assistant Head Coach:* Tony Quinn.
Club Nickname: 'The Spiders'.
Previous Grounds: 1st Hampden (Recreation Ground); (Titwood Park was used as an interim measure between 1st & 2nd Hampdens); 2nd Hampden (Cathkin); 3rd Hampden.
Record Attendance: 95,772 v Rangers, Scottish Cup 1st rd, 18 January 1930.
Record for Ground: 149,547 Scotland v England, 1937.
Record Transfer Fees: Not applicable due to amateur status.
Record Victory: 16-0 v St. Peter's, Scottish Cup 1st rd, 12 Sep 1885.
Record Defeat: 0-9 v Motherwell, Division I, 26 April 1930.
Most Capped Player: Walter Arnott, 14, Scotland.
Most League Appearances: 532: Ross Caven, 1982-2002.
Most League Goals in Season (Individual): 30: William Martin, Division I, 1937-38.
Most Goals Overall (Individual): 163: James B. McAlpine, 1919-33.

QUEEN'S PARK – SPFL LADBROKES LEAGUE ONE 2016–17 LEAGUE RECORD

Match No.	Date	Venue	Opponents	Result		H/T Score	Lg Pos.	Goalscorers	Attendance
1	Aug 6	H	Airdrieonians	L	1-3	0-1	8	Fitzpatrick (og) 82	957
2	13	A	Stenhousemuir	W	2-1	0-1	6	Miller, D (pen) 73, Watt 90	534
3	20	A	Brechin C	D	0-0	0-0	6		447
4	27	H	Livingston	W	1-0	1-0	5	Malone 25	698
5	Sept 10	A	Peterhead	L	0-2	0-0	6		519
6	17	H	Alloa Ath	L	1-2	0-0	6	Millen (pen) 54	664
7	24	H	Stranraer	L	0-2	0-1	8		534
8	Oct 1	A	Albion R	L	0-2	0-1	8		444
9	15	H	East Fife	W	1-0	1-0	8	Fotheringham 15	571
10	22	A	Airdrieonians	L	1-4	1-3	9	Millen (pen) 23	702
11	29	H	Stenhousemuir	L	0-3	0-1	9		538
12	Nov 5	A	Stranraer	W	2-0	1-0	8	Zanatta 44, Brady 87	446
13	12	H	Peterhead	D	0-0	0-0	7		524
14	19	A	East Fife	W	2-1	1-1	7	Cummins 22, Millen (pen) 54	557
15	Dec 3	H	Brechin C	W	2-0	1-0	5	Millen (pen) 39, McGeever 75	632
16	10	H	Albion R	W	2-1	2-1	5	Millen (pen) 15, Woods 37	662
17	17	A	Alloa Ath	D	1-1	0-0	5	Millen 62	442
18	24	A	Livingston	W	2-1	0-1	5	McKernon (pen) 55, Cummins 58	819
19	31	H	Stranraer	L	0-1	0-0	5		556
20	Jan 7	H	Airdrieonians	W	2-1	1-1	5	Fotheringham 21, McGeever 78	922
21	28	A	Peterhead	L	0-4	0-3	6		442
22	Feb 4	H	East Fife	D	2-2	2-0	6	Zanatta 28, Brady 35	566
23	11	A	Stenhousemuir	W	2-0	1-0	4	Zanatta 32, Brady 90	423
24	18	H	Alloa Ath	L	0-2	0-1	5		657
25	28	A	Brechin C	L	1-3	1-2	6	Wharton 4	393
26	Mar 4	H	Livingston	D	1-1	1-1	6	Zanatta 20	701
27	11	A	Stranraer	D	1-1	1-0	6	Millen (pen) 32	434
28	18	H	Brechin C	D	1-1	0-0	6	McGeever 90	481
29	25	A	Alloa Ath	D	2-2	1-1	6	Galt 28, MacPherson 90	675
30	Apr 1	A	East Fife	D	0-0	0-0	6		692
31	4	A	Albion R	D	1-1	0-1	6	Brady 90	512
32	8	H	Peterhead	W	2-0	1-0	6	Zanatta 29, McGeever 73	501
33	15	H	Albion R	W	2-0	1-0	3	MacPherson 41, Galt 46	677
34	22	A	Livingston	L	0-4	0-1	6		821
35	29	H	Stenhousemuir	L	0-2	0-1	6		764
36	May 6	A	Airdrieonians	L	2-3	1-1	6	Zanatta 15, Orsi 53	1011

Final League Position: 6

Honours
League Champions: Division II 1922-23. B Division 1955-56. Second Division 1980-81. Third Division 1999-2000. *Runners-up:* Third Division 2011-12. League Two 2014-15. *Promoted to Second Division:* 2006-07 (play-offs). *Promoted to League One:* 2015-16 (play-offs).
Scottish Cup Winners: 1874, 1875, 1876, 1880, 1881, 1882, 1884, 1886, 1890, 1893; *Runners-up:* 1892, 1900.
FA Cup Runners-up: 1884, 1885.
FA Charity Shield: 1899 (shared with Aston Villa).

Club colours: Shirt: Black and white thin hoops. Shorts: White. Socks: Black.

Goalscorers: *League (37):* Millen 7 (6 pens), Zanatta 6, Brady 4, McGeever 4, Cummins 2, Fotheringham 2, Galt 2, MacPherson 2, Malone 1, McKernon 1 (1 pen), Miller D 1 (1 pen), Orsi 1, Watt 1, Wharton 1, Woods 1, own goal 1.
William Hill Scottish FA Cup (4): Woods 2, Galt 1, Wharton 1.
Betfred Scottish League Cup (5): Burns 2, Cummins 1, Malone 1, McVey 1.
IRN-BRU Scottish League Challenge Cup (9): Galt 2, Brown 1, Carter 1, Cummins 1, MacPherson 1 (1 pen), McGeever 1, Wharton 1, own goal 1.

Murphy A 5	Millen R 27	McGeever R 34	Cummins A 32 + 1	Gibson S 17	Miller D 10	McVey C 14 + 5	Woods P 24 + 1	Galt D 19 + 9	Brady A 26 + 7	Malone A 9 + 6	MacPherson E 4 + 12	Brown L 5 + 11	Watt J 2 + 4	Burns S 29 + 1	Carter J 3 + 9	Muir W 31	Fotheringham G 14 + 1	Wharton B 15 + 1	Zanatta D 24	McLeish C 4	McKernon J 23 + 1	Mitchell G 5 + 3	Mortimer W — + 3	McIlduff A 4 + 3	Docherty D 6 + 3	Orsi K 3 + 8	Foy C 7	Miller A — + 1	*Match No.*
1	2	3	4	5^{1}	6	7	8^{3}	9^{2}	10	11	12	13	14																1
1	2	4	8	5	7		6^{1}	11	9		12	3^{3}	13	10^{2}	14														2
1	2	3	4	5	8	7	6	12		13			10	9^{1}	11^{2}														3
1	5	2	3	4	7	6	11^{1}	12	14	10^{3}			8^{2}	9	13														4
1	2	4	3^{3}	5	8	7	10^{1}	6	12	11^{2}	14			9	13														5
	5	3	2	4^{1}	7	13	10	14	8					9^{3}	11	1	6^{2}	12											6
	5	3	2	4^{3}	7■		14	11^{2}	8^{1}	12		13		9		1	6		10										7
	2	3	4	5			6		11^{2}	12	14	13			10^{1}	1	7^{3}		8	9									8
	2	4	3		8		6		14	11^{2}		9^{1}		12	13	1	7		10^{3}	5									9
	2	3	4		6		8		13	11		9^{1}	12			1	7		10	5^{2}									10
	2	3	4		6^{3}		8^{1}		14	11^{2}		9	13			1	7■		10	5	12								11
	2	3	4	5		12	6^{1}		9	14				10	13^{3}	1	8^{2}		11		7								12
	5	3	2	4			10^{1}	13	8	11^{2}		14		9	12	1	6^{3}				7								13
	5	3	2	4		13	11^{1}	12	8^{3}					9	14	1	6		10^{2}		7								14
	5	3	2	4		13	11	9^{2}	12					8	14	1	7		10^{1}		6^{3}								15
	5	3	2			14	9^{3}	11^{2}	12					8	13	1	7	4	10^{1}		6								16
	5		2	3			10		8^{1}	12				9		1	6	4	11		7								17
		4	3	5		9	6	12	7	11^{1}				10		1		2			8								18
		4	3	5^{2}			6	10	7	11^{1}	12	13		9		1		2			8								19
	5	3	12	4^{1}			9		11	13	10^{2}			8		1	7	2			6								20
	5	3■	4			8	11	10				14		9^{1}		1	6^{2}	2			7^{3}	12	13						21
	5		4				7	13	9^{3}			8				1		3	11^{1}		6	2^{2}		10	12	14			22
	5■	3	4				11^{1}		8							1	12	2	10^{3}		7	13		9	6^{2}	14			23
		3					8^{2}	10	9		13	12		5		1		4			6	2			7	11^{1}			24
	2^{3}	3	8				6^{1}	13	9^{2}					5		1		4	11		7			14	10	12			25
	5	3	4			8		12	7					9		1		2	11		6					10^{1}			26
	2^{1}	3	4■			9		6^{2}	8		13			10		1		5	11		7			12					27
		3				6		10^{1}	8		13			5		1		4	11^{3}		7			9	14	12	2^{2}		28
	2	3	4			6		10^{1}			14	13		9		1			11		7		12		8^{3}		5^{2}		29
	2	4	5			7		11	9					6		1			10		8						3		30
	5^{3}	3	4			8^{2}		10	6		13	14		9^{1}		1			11		7	12					2		31
		3	4					8	7		11^{1}			9		1			10			5			6	12	2		32
		3	4					6	8		11^{2}			9		1			10^{1}		7	5	13			12	2		33
		4	7			11		6	8		12			9^{2}		1			10		3	2^{1}		13		14	5^{3}		34
		3		4^{2}				6	8		10^{1}	13		9		1		2	11^{3}		7			5	14	12			35
		3	2			7^{1}		5	8		14	13		9		1		4^{3}	11						6	10^{2}		12	36

RAITH ROVERS

Year Formed: 1883. *Ground & Address:* Stark's Park, Pratt St, Kirkcaldy KY1 1SA. *Telephone:* 01592 263514. *Fax:* 01592 642833. *E-mail:* info@raithrovers.net *Website:* www.raithrovers.net
Ground Capacity: 8,473 (all seated). *Size of Pitch:* 103m × 64m.
Chairman: Alan Young. *Chief Executive:* Eric Drysdale.
Manager: Barry Smith. *Coach:* Craig Easton.
Club Nickname: 'Rovers'.
Previous Grounds: Robbie's Park.
Record Attendance: 31,306 v Hearts, Scottish Cup 2nd rd, 7 February 1953.
Record Transfer Fee received: £900,000 for Steve McAnespie to Bolton W (September 1995).
Record Transfer Fee paid: £225,000 for Paul Harvey from Airdrieonians (July 1996).
Record Victory: 10-1 v Coldstream, Scottish Cup 2nd rd, 13 February 1954.
Record Defeat: 2-11 v Morton, Division II, 18 March 1936.
Most Capped Player: David Morris, 6, Scotland.
Most League Appearances: 430: Willie McNaught, 1946-51.
Most League Goals in Season (Individual): 38: Norman Haywood, Division II, 1937-38.
Most Goals Overall (Individual): 154: Gordon Dalziel (League), 1987-94.

RAITH ROVERS – SPFL LADBROKES CHAMPIONSHIP 2016–17 LEAGUE RECORD

Match No.	*Date*	*Venue*	*Opponents*	*Result*		*H/T Score*	*Lg Pos.*	*Goalscorers*	*Attendance*
1	Aug 6	A	Ayr U	W	2-0	1-0	1	Callachan [19], Matthews [75]	1550
2	13	H	St Mirren	W	3-1	1-0	1	McManus 2 [17, 51], Callachan [50]	2140
3	20	H	Dunfermline Ath	W	2-0	0-0	1	Barr, B [71], Stewart [79]	5114
4	27	A	Dundee U	D	2-2	1-2	2	Thompson [38], McHattie [72]	7434
5	Sept 10	H	Falkirk	L	0-2	0-1	3		2320
6	17	A	Queen of the South	L	1-3	0-0	3	Hamill (og) [90]	1864
7	24	H	Dumbarton	W	3-2	3-0	4	McHattie [15], Callachan [34], Roberts [35]	1636
8	Oct 1	A	Greenock Morton	L	0-1	0-1	4		1528
9	15	H	Hibernian	D	0-0	0-0	5		3753
10	22	A	Falkirk	W	4-2	2-1	4	Davidson [17], Stewart 2 [37, 79], McManus [72]	4773
11	29	H	Queen of the South	W	1-0	0-0	3	Stewart [90]	1244
12	Nov 5	A	Dunfermline Ath	D	0-0	0-0	3		5649
13	19	A	Dumbarton	D	0-0	0-0	4		600
14	22	H	Ayr U	D	1-1	1-0	4	Coustrain [17]	1241
15	Dec 10	A	St Mirren	L	0-1	0-0	5		2630
16	17	H	Dundee U	D	0-0	0-0	5		4361
17	24	A	Hibernian	D	1-1	0-0	5	Mvoto [49]	15,409
18	Jan 2	H	Dunfermline Ath	L	0-2	0-1	5		5899
19	7	H	Falkirk	L	1-4	1-3	5	Johnston [9]	2202
20	14	A	Greenock Morton	L	0-2	0-1	6		1957
21	28	H	Dumbarton	L	1-3	1-0	7	Hardie [27]	1413
22	Feb 4	A	Dundee U	L	0-3	0-1	8		5232
23	7	H	Greenock Morton	L	0-1	0-0	8		1161
24	18	H	Hibernian	D	1-1	0-0	8	Stevenson, Ryan [52]	4172
25	25	A	Queen of the South	L	1-2	0-2	8	Mvoto [60]	1484
26	28	A	Ayr U	L	0-1	0-0	8		1103
27	Mar 8	H	St Mirren	W	2-0	0-0	7	Hardie 2 [74, 80]	2124
28	11	A	Dumbarton	L	0-4	0-2	8		719
29	18	H	Dundee U	W	2-1	1-0	7	Barr, C [41], Hardie [49]	2192
30	25	H	Queen of the South	D	1-1	1-1	7	Hardie [10]	1609
31	Apr 1	A	Falkirk	L	0-1	0-0	8		4823
32	8	A	Dunfermline Ath	L	0-1	0-0	8		4865
33	15	H	Greenock Morton	W	2-0	1-0	7	Barr, C [28], Matthews [59]	1720
34	26	A	Hibernian	L	2-3	0-1	8	McManus [67], Hardie [85]	13,604
35	29	A	St Mirren	L	0-5	0-2	9		4937
36	May 6	H	Ayr U	W	2-1	1-0	9	Court [37], McManus [90]	3064

Final League Position: 9

Honours
League Champions: First Division 1992-93, 1994-95. Second Division 2002-03, 2008-09. Division II 1907-08, 1909-10 (shared), 1937-38, 1948-49.
Runners-up: Division II 1908-09, 1926-27, 1966-67. Second Division 1975-76, 1977-78, 1986-87.
Scottish Cup Runners-up: 1913.
League Cup Winners: 1994-95. *Runners-up:* 1948-49.
League Challenge Cup Winners: 2013-14.

European: *UEFA Cup:* 6 matches (1995-96).

Club colours: Shirt: Navy with white sleeves. Shorts: White with navy trim. Socks: Navy.

Goalscorers: *League (35):* Hardie 6, McManus 5, Stewart 4, Callachan 3, Barr C 2, Matthews 2, McHattie 2, Mvoto 2, Barr B 1, Court 1, Coustrain 1, Davidson 1, Johnston 1, Roberts 1, Ryan Stevenson 1, Thompson 1, own goal 1.
William Hill Scottish FA Cup (3): Barr 1, Hardie 1, McManus 1.
Betfred Scottish League Cup (5): Vaughan 2 (1 pen), Benedictus 1, Johnston 1, own goal 1.
IRN-BRU Scottish League Challenge Cup (2): McManus 1, Stewart 1.
Play-Offs (4): McManus 2, Hardie 1, Mvoto 1.

Cuthbert K 17	Thomson J 23	Mvoto J 34	Benedictus K 30	McHattie K 27	Thompson J 26 + 3	Callachan R 30	Matthews R 23 + 1	Barr B 24 + 5	Vaughan L 5 + 7	McManus D 28 + 6	Skacel R 10 + 14	Stewart M 12 + 17	Robertson S — + 1	Lennox A 2	Roberts S 5 + 12	Brennan C 6 + 2	Davidson I 25 + 1	Coustrain J 1 + 5	Smith L 2	Johnston C 20 + 7	Barr C 14 + 1	Hardie R 11 + 7	Stevenson Ryan 6 + 3	Penksa P 10	Osei-Opoku Y — + 1	Handling D 4 + 1	Court J 1 + 3	*Match No.*
1	2	3	4	5	6	7	8	9[3]	10[2]	11[1]	12	13	14															1
	2	3	4	5	8[1]	7	6	9	10[3]	11[2]	12	13		1	14													2
	2	3	4	5	8[2]	7	6	9	10[3]	11[1]	12	13		1	14													3
	2	3	4	5	8[3]	7	6	9	10[2]	11[1]	12	13				1	14											4
	2		4	5	8[3]	7	6[2]	9	10[1]	11	13				12	1	3	14										5
		3	4	5	8[2]	7	6[1]	9	12	10	14	13			11[3]	1	2											6
1		3	4	5	14	9		10		11[1]	8[2]	12			7[3]		6		2	13								7
1		3	4	5	14	8		7		11	9[3]	12			10[1]		6		2[2]	13								8
1		3	4	5	7[3]	8	6	9	12	11[2]	10[1]	13					2			14								9
1		3	4	5	7	8	6	9[1]	14	11[2]		10[3]			13		2			12								10
1		3	4	5	7[3]	8	6		12	11[2]	14	10			13		2			9[1]								11
1		3	4	5	8	7	6			11	13	10[1]			12		2			9[2]								12
1		3	4	5	7[2]	8	6		14	11		10[1]			12		2	13		9[3]								13
1		3	4■	5	12	7	8			11	13	10[1]			6[2]		2	9[3]		14								14
1		3		5	8	7	2[1]	12	13	11	14	10[2]			9[3]		4			6								15
1		3	4	5	6	7		11[1]	13	10[3]	8[2]	12					2	14		9								16
1	5	3	4		8[2]		7	6		11	10[1]	12					2			9	13							17
1	2	4		5	8	7		9		11[3]	10[2]	14					3			6[1]		12	13					18
1	2		4	5[1]	8	7		9		12		13					3			6		11	10[2]					19
1		3	4	5	8	7		9		13		12			14		2			6[3]		11[1]	10[2]					20
1	2[2]	3	4	5		7	8	9[3]			14	10			13					6[1]		11	12					21
1[1]	2	4	3	5		7	6[2]	9		10[3]		11				12	8					13	14					22
	2[1]	3	4		9	7[3]		6		12	14	13				1	8				5	11	10[2]					23
	2	3	4[1]		6	8	7	10		14		11[2]				1		13		12	5		9[3]					24
	9	2	3		6[2]	7		8[1]		12		10				1	5			14	4	13	11[3]					25
	5	3	2[2]	9		8		13		11[1]		14					7	12		6[3]	4	10	1					26
	2	3	5			8	12	9		11		10[1]					7[2]			6	4	13		1				27
	2	4	5			8	7[3]	9		10	12				14					6[1]	3	11[2]		1	13			28
	2	4	5		9	8	7			11										6	3	10		1				29
	2	4	5[2]		10	6	7	13		8[1]	12				14					9[3]	3	11		1				30
		3	2[2]	5	8	6[1]				10					13		7			9	4	11		1		12		31
	2	4		5	7[2]			12			8[1]						6			10	3	11		1		9	13	32
	2	4		5			6	12		13	8	14					7			9[3]	3	10[1]		1		11[2]		33
	2	4		5	8		7	9		11		10[2]								6[1]	3	13		1			12	34
	2	3		5	6			9[3]		11	7[1]	14								10[2]	4	13		1		8	12	35
	2[1]	4	5				6			11	9[2]					12	7				3	13		1■		8	10	36

RANGERS

Year Formed: 1873. *Ground & Address:* Ibrox Stadium, 150 Edmiston Drive, Glasgow G51 2XD.
Telephone: 0871 702 1972. *Fax:* 0870 600 1978. *Website:* rangers.co.uk
Ground Capacity: 51,082 (all seated). *Size of Pitch:* 105m × 68m.
Chairman: Dave King. *Secretary:* James Blair.
Manager: Pedro Caixinha. *First-Team Coaches:* Helder Baptista, Jonatan Johannson, Pedro Malta. *Managing Director:* Stewart Robertson.
Club Nickname: 'The Gers', 'The Teddy Bears'.
Previous Grounds: Flesher's Haugh, Burnbank, Kinning Park, Old Ibrox.
Record Attendance: 118,567 v Celtic, Division I, 2 January 1939.
Record Transfer Fee received: £8,500,000 for Giovanni van Bronckhorst to Arsenal (July 2001).
Record Transfer Fee paid: £12,000,000 for Tore Andre Flo from Chelsea (November 2000).
Record Victory: 14-2 v Blairgowrie, Scottish Cup 1st rd, 20 January, 1934.
Record Defeat: 1-7 v Celtic, League Cup Final, 19 October 1957.
Most Capped Player: Ally McCoist, 60, Scotland. *Most League Appearances:* 496: John Greig, 1962-78.
Most League Goals in Season (Individual): 44: Sam English, Division I, 1931-32.
Most Goals Overall (Individual): 355: Ally McCoist; 1985-98.

Honours
League Champions: (54 times) Division I 1890-91 (shared), 1898-99, 1899-1900, 1900-01, 1901-02, 1910-11, 1911-12, 1912-13, 1917-18, 1919-20, 1920-21, 1922-23, 1923-24, 1924-25, 1926-27, 1927-28, 1928-29, 1929-30, 1930-31, 1932-33, 1933-34, 1934-35, 1936-37, 1938-39, 1946-47, 1948-49, 1949-50, 1952-53, 1955-56, 1956-57, 1958-59, 1960-61, 1962-63, 1963-64, 1974-75. Premier Division: 1975-76, 1977-78, 1986-87, 1988-89, 1989-90, 1990-91, 1991-92, 1992-93, 1993-94, 1994-95, 1995-96, 1996-97, 1998-99, 1999-2000, 2002-03, 2004-05, 2008-09, 2009-10, 2010-11. *Runners-up:* 30 times. Championship 2015-16. League One 2013-14. Third Division 2012-13.
Scottish Cup Winners: (33 times) 1894, 1897, 1898, 1903, 1928, 1930, 1932, 1934, 1935, 1936, 1948, 1949, 1950, 1953, 1960, 1962, 1963, 1964, 1966, 1973, 1976, 1978, 1979, 1981, 1992, 1993, 1996, 1999, 2000, 2002, 2003, 2008, 2009; *Runners-up:* 18 times.

RANGERS – SPFL LADBROKES PREMIERSHIP 2016–17 LEAGUE RECORD

Match No.	*Date*	*Venue*	*Opponents*	*Result*		*H/T Score*	*Lg Pos.*	*Goalscorers*	*Attendance*
1	Aug 6	H	Hamilton A	D	1-1	0-1	2	Waghorn 62	49,125
2	13	A	Dundee	W	2-1	2-1	1	Forrester 14, Miller 39	9702
3	20	H	Motherwell	W	2-1	0-1	1	Forrester 64, Miller 90	48,716
4	26	A	Kilmarnock	D	1-1	0-1	1	Tavernier 59	11,800
5	Sept 10	A	Celtic	L	1-5	1-2	2	Garner 44	58,348
6	17	H	Ross Co	D	0-0	0-0	4		47,935
7	25	A	Aberdeen	L	1-2	0-0	5	Halliday (pen) 79	19,263
8	Oct 1	H	Partick Thistle	W	2-0	2-0	5	Kranjcar 33, Halliday 40	49,680
9	14	A	Inverness CT	W	1-0	1-0	3	Miller 22	7012
10	26	H	St Johnstone	D	1-1	1-1	5	Garner 37	46,563
11	29	H	Kilmarnock	W	3-0	2-0	2	Wallace 16, Halliday (pen) 29, Garner 47	49,302
12	Nov 6	A	Ross Co	D	1-1	1-1	3	Hill 8	6590
13	19	H	Dundee	W	1-0	0-0	3	Forrester 90	48,773
14	26	A	Partick Thistle	W	2-1	0-0	2	Dodoo 2 81, 90	7951
15	30	A	Hearts	L	0-2	0-1	3		16,803
16	Dec 3	H	Aberdeen	W	2-1	0-0	2	Miller 52, Hodson 70	50,003
17	10	H	Hearts	W	2-0	1-0	2	Kiernan 29, McKay 51	50,039
18	16	A	Hamilton A	W	2-1	1-0	2	Waghorn 2 45, 52	5292
19	24	H	Inverness CT	W	1-0	1-0	2	McKay, Brad (og) 13	48,528
20	28	A	St Johnstone	D	1-1	1-1	2	McKay 23	7979
21	31	H	Celtic	L	1-2	1-1	2	Miller 12	50,126
22	Jan 28	A	Motherwell	W	2-0	0-0	2	Miller 72, Hyndman 87	7902
23	Feb 1	A	Hearts	L	1-4	1-1	2	Hyndman 36	16,570
24	4	H	Ross Co	D	1-1	0-1	3	Wallace 71	49,428
25	19	A	Dundee	L	1-2	0-2	3	Garner 62	9017
26	24	A	Inverness CT	L	1-2	0-1	3	Waghorn (pen) 67	6415
27	Mar 1	H	St Johnstone	W	3-2	1-0	3	McKay 22, Waghorn 48, Hyndman 90	46,800
28	12	A	Celtic	D	1-1	0-1	3	Hill 87	58,545
29	18	H	Hamilton A	W	4-0	2-0	3	Hyndman 26, Hill 41, Waghorn (pen) 55, Wallace 74	49,090
30	Apr 1	H	Motherwell	D	1-1	0-1	3	Garner 61	49,198
31	5	A	Kilmarnock	D	0-0	0-0	3		9548
32	9	A	Aberdeen	W	3-0	0-0	3	Miller 2 79, 81, Dodoo 83	19,332
33	15	H	Partick Thistle	W	2-0	1-0	3	Miller 39, Toral 54	49,748
34	29	H	Celtic	L	1-5	0-2	3	Miller 81	49,822
35	May 7	A	Partick Thistle	W	2-1	0-1	3	McKay 83, Garner 90	6799
36	13	H	Hearts	W	2-1	1-0	3	Garner 6, McKay 53	47,809
37	17	H	Aberdeen	L	1-2	0-1	3	Waghorn 61	48,289
38	21	A	St Johnstone	W	2-1	1-0	3	Miller 40, Toral 53	6799

Final League Position: 3

League Cup Winners: (27 times) 1946-47, 1948-49, 1960-61, 1961-62, 1963-64, 1964-65, 1970-71, 1975-76, 1977-78, 1978-79, 1981-82, 1983-84, 1984-85, 1986-87, 1987-88, 1988-89, 1990-91, 1992-93, 1993-94, 1996-97, 1998-99, 2001-02, 2002-03, 2004-05, 2007-08, 2009-10, 2010-11; *Runners-up:* 7 times.
League Challenge Cup Winners: 2015-16. *Runners-up:* 2013-14.

European: *European Cup:* 161 matches (1956-57, 1957-58, 1959-60 semi-finals, 1961-62, 1963-64, 1964-65, 1975-76, 1976-77, 1978-79, 1987-88, 1989-90, 1990-91, 1991-92, 1992-93 final pool, 1993-94, 1994-95, 1995-96; 1996-97, 1997-98, 1999-2000, 2000-01, 2001-02, 2003-04, 2004-05, 2005-06, 2007-08, 2008-09, 2009-10, 2010-11, 2011-12).
Cup Winners' Cup: 54 matches (1960-61 runners-up, 1962-63, 1966-67 runners-up, 1969-70, 1971-72 winners, 1973-74, 1977-78, 1979-80, 1981-82, 1983-84).
UEFA Cup: 88 matches (*Fairs Cup:* 1967-68, 1968-69 semi-finals, 1970-71. *UEFA Cup:* 1982-83, 1984-85, 1985-86, 1986-87, 1988-89, 1997-98, 1998-99, 1999-2000, 2000-01, 2001-02, 2002-03, 2004-05, 2006-07, 2007-08 runners-up). *Europa League:* 6 matches (2010-11, 2011-12).

Club colours: Shirt: Royal blue with white trim. Shorts: White with blue trim. Socks: Black with red tops.

Goalscorers: *League (56):* Miller 11, Garner 7, Waghorn 7 (2 pens), McKay 5, Hyndman 4, Dodoo 3, Forrester 3, Halliday 3 (2 pens), Hill 3, Wallace 3, Toral 2, Hodson 1, Kiernan 1, Kranjcar 1, Tavernier 1, own goal 1.
William Hill Scottish FA Cup (10): Garner 3, Miller 3, Waghorn 2 (1 pen), Hill 1, Toral 1.
Betfred Scottish League Cup (20): Waghorn 7 (1 pen), Dodoo 2, Halliday 2 (1 pen), Hill 2, Kranjcar 2, Holt 1, McKay 1, Tavernier 1, Windass 1, own goal 1.
IRN-BRU Scottish League Challenge Cup (5): Hardie 2, Jeffries 2, Burt 1.

Foderingham W 37	Tavernier J 35 + 1	Kiernan R 24	Hill C 23 + 1	Wallace L 27	Kranjcar N 4 + 5	Barton J 5	Halliday A 24 + 8	Waghorn M 20 + 12	Miller K 32 + 5	McKay B 28 + 7	O'Halloran M 6 + 10	Forrester H 7 + 14	Rossiter J 3 + 1	Wilson D 19 + 2	Dodoo J 5 + 15	Garner J 21 + 10	Senderos P 3	Windass J 14 + 7	Holt J 28 + 3	Hodson L 10 + 1	Crooks M 1 + 1	Burt L — + 1	Toral J 12	Hyndman E 13	Bates D 7	Beerman M 6 + 1	Barjonas J 1 + 3	Wilson Aiden 2	Alnwick J 1	Bradley K — + 1	*Match No.*
1	2	3	4	5	6¹	7	8³	9	10²	11	12	13	14																		1
1	2	4		5	13	7	11³		10²	6	14	9¹	8	3	12																2
1	2	3		5	12	7	8²		10	11¹	14	9³	6	4	13																3
1	5	3	4	2	13	7²	14		11	6		9	8³		10¹	12															4
1	2	3²		5	9¹	6	12	13	7³	10		14				11	4▮	8													5
1	2		4	5	14		7	9³	12	11	13			3		10¹		8	6²												6
1	2		4	5	12		7	9¹	14	11	13	8²		3		10³			6												7
1	2			5	7¹		6	9³	10	11²		14		4	13	12	3		8												8
1	2	4	3	5	7²		6	10¹	11	9³					13	12		14	8												9
1		3	4	5			8	14	12	13	9	11²				10¹		7³	6	2											10
1	2	3	4	5			8	13	11¹		9				12	10²		7³	6		14										11
1	2	3	4	5			7	12	9²	13	11³				14	10¹		6	8												12
1	2	3	4	5			7		11²	12	9¹	14			13	10		8³	6												13
1	2	3		5			7		11	12	14	9³		4	13	10¹		6²	8												14
1	2	3		5			7		11	14	12	9¹		4	10²	13			8		6³										15
1	12	3	4▮	5			7	13	11²	8¹	9³	14				10			6	2											16
1	6	3		5			7	12	9³	11²				4	13	10¹			8	2		14									17
1	7	3		5			8	11¹		9		12		4		10			6	2											18
1	6³	3	4	5			7	9²	12	11¹		14				10		13	8	2											19
1	2	3	4²				8	12	9³	11	14			5		10¹		6	7	13											20
1	9	4	3				7	12	10	5		14		2	13	11²		6¹	8³												21
1	2	3	4	5			7	12	11²	10¹	8▮	13						14					6³	9							22
1	2	3	4	5			7	9³	10	11		12						13	14				6²	8¹							23
1	2		4	5				13	9	11²		12				10¹	3		6				8	7							24
1	2	4	5³				6²	11	10	8¹		14		12		9			13	3				7							25
1	2	4		5			6¹	11	10	9				3		13			12				8²	7							26
1	2	3▮	4	5			14	9³	10²	11				13		12			6				7¹	8							27
1	6		3	5				9³	10	11²	14	13		4				12	7¹	2				8							28
1	2		4	5				11¹	9²	10³		14		3	13	12			6				7	8							29
1		3	4¹	5³			13	11	9	10	14					12			6	2²			7	8							30
1	2						7	8²	12	10				4	13	11³		14	6					9¹	3	5					31
1	2						14	11¹	9					4	13	8²		12	6				7	10³	3	5					32
1	2						14	8³	11	10³				4	12	13			6				7²	9	3	5					33
1	2		4				12	10	9					3	11²	13		6	7					8¹		5					34
1	2		12					6²	10	14				4³	9	11		8	7¹						3	5	13				35
1	2		4					14	8	10					12	11		9¹	6²	5			7³		3		13				36
1	2							13	6	11					9³	10		8		5²			7¹		3	12	14	4			37
	2						14	9²	10	12								8	6				7¹		3	5	11³	4	1	13	38

ROSS COUNTY

Year Formed: 1929. *Ground & Address:* The Global Energy Stadium, Victoria Park, Dingwall IV15 9QZ. *Telephone:* 01349 860860. *Fax:* 01349 866277. *E-mail:* info@rosscountyfootballclub.co.uk
Website: www.rosscountyfootballclub.co.uk
Ground Capacity: 6,700 (all seated). *Size of Ground:* 105 × 68m.
Chairman: Roy MacGregor. *Club Secretary:* Fiona MacBean.
Manager: Jim McIntyre. *Assistant Manager:* Billy Dodds.
Club Nickname: 'The Staggies'.
Record Attendance: 6,110 v Celtic, Premier League, 18 August 2012.
Record Transfer Fee received: circa. £300,000 for Jackson Irvine to Burton Albion (July 2016).
Record Transfer Fee paid: £50,000 for Derek Holmes from Hearts (October 1999).
Record Victory: 11-0 v St Cuthbert Wanderers, Scottish Cup 1st rd, 11 December 1993.
Record Defeat: 0-7 v Kilmarnock, Scottish Cup 3rd rd, 17 February 1962.
Most League Appearances: 230: Mark McCulloch, 2002-09.
Most League Goals in Season: 24: Andrew Barrowman, 2007-08.
Most League Goals (Overall): 48: Liam Boyce, 2014-17.

ROSS COUNTY – SPFL LADBROKES PREMIERSHIP 2016–17 LEAGUE RECORD

Match No.	Date	Venue	Opponents	Result	H/T Score	Lg Pos.	Goalscorers	Attendance
1	Aug 6	H	Dundee	L 1-3	0-2	11	Curran [67]	3669
2	13	A	Inverness CT	W 3-2	2-1	10	Boyce 3 [7, 26, 47]	4204
3	20	H	Kilmarnock	W 2-0	1-0	7	Boyce 2 [29, 74]	3263
4	27	A	Hamilton A	L 0-1	0-0	7		1609
5	Sept 10	H	Motherwell	D 1-1	0-0	7	Boyce [61]	3019
6	17	A	Rangers	D 0-0	0-0	8		47,935
7	24	A	Hearts	D 0-0	0-0	8		16,321
8	Oct 1	H	St Johnstone	L 0-2	0-1	8		3299
9	15	A	Aberdeen	L 0-4	0-2	9		10,091
10	22	A	Partick Thistle	D 1-1	0-1	8	Burke [90]	3777
11	26	H	Celtic	L 0-4	0-1	10		6290
12	29	A	Motherwell	L 1-4	0-2	11	Schalk [78]	3177
13	Nov 6	H	Rangers	D 1-1	1-1	12	Davies [26]	6590
14	19	A	St Johnstone	W 4-2	2-0	9	McEveley [24], Routis [38], Curran [63], Boyce [83]	2554
15	26	H	Hamilton A	D 1-1	1-0	9	Boyce [39]	3275
16	Dec 3	H	Hearts	D 2-2	1-0	8	McEveley [43], Boyce (pen) [86]	4042
17	10	A	Dundee	D 0-0	0-0	8		4742
18	17	H	Aberdeen	W 2-1	1-0	7	Boyce [26], Dow [88]	4467
19	23	H	Partick Thistle	L 1-3	0-0	7	Boyce [83]	2935
20	28	A	Celtic	L 0-2	0-2	8		55,355
21	31	H	Inverness CT	W 3-2	2-1	7	Boyce 2 [2, 35], Woods [61]	5111
22	Jan 28	A	Kilmarnock	L 2-3	2-1	7	Routis [7], Schalk [11]	3207
23	31	H	Motherwell	L 1-2	1-1	8	McEveley [34]	2511
24	Feb 4	A	Rangers	D 1-1	1-0	8	Schalk [18]	49,428
25	18	H	St Johnstone	L 1-2	0-1	9	Curran [73]	3187
26	25	A	Aberdeen	L 0-1	0-0	9		11,774
27	Mar 1	A	Hearts	W 1-0	0-0	9	Schalk [51]	15,470
28	11	H	Kilmarnock	L 1-2	0-0	9	Boyce [58]	3380
29	18	A	Inverness CT	D 1-1	0-0	9	Schalk [86]	4123
30	Apr 1	A	Partick Thistle	L 1-2	0-0	9	Curran [58]	3149
31	4	H	Dundee	W 2-1	1-1	8	Chow [7], Boyce (pen) [90]	2819
32	8	A	Hamilton A	D 1-1	0-1	8	Curran [60]	1548
33	16	H	Celtic	D 2-2	0-1	8	Gardyne [50], Boyce (pen) [90]	6205
34	28	H	Inverness CT	W 4-0	2-0	7	Boyce 4 (2 pens) [21, 34, 49 (p), 60 (p)]	4928
35	May 6	A	Motherwell	W 1-0	0-0	7	Routis [72]	3870
36	13	A	Dundee	D 1-1	1-0	8	Boyce [4]	6812
37	16	H	Hamilton A	W 3-2	1-1	7	Gardyne [3], Matthews (og) [73], Franks [90]	4871
38	20	A	Kilmarnock	W 2-1	1-1	7	Boyce 2 [42, 70]	3951

Final League Position: 7

Honours
League Champions: First Division 2011-12. Second Division 2007-08. Third Division 1998-99.
Scottish Cup Runners-up: 2010.
League Cup Winners: 2015-16.
League Challenge Cup Winners: 2006-07, 2010-11; *Runners-up:* 2004-05, 2008-09.

Club colours: Shirt: Navy blue with white and red trim. Shorts: Navy blue with white trim. Socks: Navy blue with white tops.

Goalscorers: *League (48):* Boyce 23 (5 pens), Curran 5, Schalk 5, McEveley 3, Routis 3, Gardyne 2, Burke 1, Chow 1, Davies 1, Dow 1, Franks 1, Woods 1, own goal 1.
William Hill Scottish FA Cup (6): Routis 2, Boyce 1, Chow 1, O'Brien 1, Quinn 1.
Betfred Scottish League Cup (11): Graham 6 (2 pens), Schalk 3, Curran 2.
IRN-BRU Scottish League Challenge Cup (2): Morrison G 1, Wallace 1.

Fox S 35	Quinn P 19	Davies A 31	McEveley J 19 + 3	Schalk A 15 + 17	Gardyne M 28 + 5	Routis C 23 + 7	Woods M 27 + 2	van der Weg K 29 + 4	Boyce L 34	Graham B 1	McShane I 5 + 3	Franks J 9 + 9	Curran C 26 + 8	Foster R 1	Cikos E 5	Dingwall T 4 + 10	Morrison G 1 + 4	Chow T 26 + 4	Fraser M 33	Burke C 4 + 2	Dow R 13 + 10	McCarey A 3 + 1	McLaughlin C — + 1	Tumility R 2 + 6	O'Brien J 8 + 8	Lalkovic M 2 + 4	Naismith J 14 + 2	Dykes D — + 2	Malcolm B 1	Dingwall R — + 1	*Match No.*
1	2	3	4	5	6	7	8^{1}	9^{2}	10	11^{3}	12	13	14																		1
1	4	3	5	12	6^{3}	8	7		11^{1}		14	13	10^{2}	2	9																2
1	3	4	5	12	9^{2}	8	7		10			6^{3}	11^{1}		2	13	14														3
1	3	4	5	12	9	7^{3}	8		10			6^{1}	11^{2}		2	14		13													4
1	4	3	5■	10^{3}	9^{2}	7	8	12	11			6^{1}	13		2			14													5
1	3	4		11^{3}	9	7	8	5				6^{2}	10^{1}			13	14	12	2												6
1	3	4^{3}	14		10	8	7	5	11^{1}		9■	6^{2}	13			12			2												7
1	3		4		9	7^{3}	8	5	11			6^{2}					10^{1}	14	2	12	13										8
1	3	4			10	13	7	5			9^{1}	6^{3}	11^{2}			12		8■	2		14										9
1	3	4		6^{3}	9		8	5			7		11^{1}			14	12		2^{2}	13	10										10
1	4^{3}	3	12	14	6		8	5	10		7					13			2^{2}	9^{1}	11										11
1	3	4		13	9^{1}		8	5	11^{2}		7		12						2	6	10										12
1		3	4	13		9		12	11				10^{1}		5^{3}	14		7	2	6	8^{2}										13
1^{2}		3	4	13	9	8		5	11				10^{1}					7	2	6^{3}	14	12									14
1		3	4	12	9^{1}	7		5	10			13	11^{3}			14		8	2		6^{2}										15
1		3	4	12	9	7	13	5	10				11^{1}			8^{3}		6^{4}	2		14										16
1		4	3	12	9^{1}	7		5	10			14	11^{2}			8^{3}		6	2		13										17
1	3	4		14	9^{2}	7		5■	10			13	11^{3}			6^{1}		8	2		12										18
1	3	4	5	12		7			10			13	11^{1}			6^{2}		8	2		9^{3}		14								19
1	3	4	5	10^{3}		7^{2}	8		11^{1}		13		9				14	6	2					12							20
1		3	4	11^{3}		8	6^{1}	5	10			13	12			14		7	2		9^{2}										21
1	3		5	11^{2}	14	8^{1}	7	4	10				13					6	2		9^{3}				12						22
1	3		4^{1}	11	14	10^{2}	8	5	7									6	2						9^{3}	12	13				23
1		3		11^{2}	13		8	4	7				14					6	2		12				9^{1}	10^{3}	5				24
1		3	4	14	9^{2}		7	5^{1}	11				10					8^{3}	2						13	6	12				25
1	4^{2}	3		6	9		7	12	11				10^{1}					8^{3}	5						13	14	2				26
1		2	3^{3}	9^{1}	14		7^{2}	4	11				10					8	6					13	12		5				27
	3			9	6^{1}	12	7^{3}	5	11				10^{2}					8	4		13	1			14		2				28
		4		10	9^{3}	6^{2}		5	7				11^{1}					8	3		14	1			12	13	2				29
1		3	4^{3}	10	12	8^{1}	6	9	7				11^{2}						2		14				13		5				30
1		3^{1}	13^{3}		6	12	7^{2}	5	10				11					8	4					14	9■		2				31
1		4		12	6	13	8	5	10				11^{3}					7^{1}	3		9^{2}					14	2				32
1		4		12	7^{3}	13		6	11			14						8	5		10			2^{1}	9^{2}		3				33
1					5	12	6^{3}	4	10^{1}				11					7^{2}	3		9			13	8		2	14			34
1		4			7	12	8	5^{1}				14	11					6	2		10^{2}			13	9^{3}		3				35
1		3		14	11		6	12	10				5^{3}					7	4		9^{2}			13	8^{1}		2				36
1				11^{1}	6^{2}	8	12^{3}	5	10			9	14					7	4					2	13		3				37
				13		8		4	10			9	11^{2}					7^{3}	3			1			6^{1}		2	12	5	14	38

ST JOHNSTONE

Year Formed: 1884. *Ground & Address:* McDiarmid Park, Crieff Road, Perth PH1 2SJ. *Telephone:* 01738 459090. *Fax:* 01738 625 771. *Email:* enquiries@perthsaints.co.uk *Website:* www.perthstjohnstonefc.co.uk
Ground Capacity: 10,673 (all seated). *Size of Pitch:* 105m × 68m.
Chairman: Steve Brown. *Vice-Chairman:* Charlie Fraser.
Manager: Tommy Wright. *Assistant Manager:* Callum Davidson.
Club Nickname: 'Saints'.
Previous Grounds: Recreation Grounds, Muirton Park.
Record Attendance: 29,972 v Dundee, Scottish Cup 2nd rd, 10 February 1951 (Muirton Park): 10,545 v Dundee, Premier Division, 23 May 1999 (McDiarmid Park).
Record Transfer Fee received: £1,750,000 for Callum Davidson to Blackburn R (March 1998).
Record Transfer Fee paid: £400,000 for Billy Dodds from Dundee (January 1994).
Record Victory: 9-0 v Albion R, League Cup, 9 March 1946.
Record Defeat: 1-10 v Third Lanark, Scottish Cup 1st rd, 24 January 1903.
Most Capped Player: Nick Dasovic, 26, Canada.
Most League Appearances: 325: Steven Anderson, 2004-17.
Most League Goals in Season (Individual): 36: Jimmy Benson, Division II, 1931-32.
Most Goals Overall (Individual): 140: John Brogan, 1977-83.

ST JOHNSTONE – SPFL LADBROKES PREMIERSHIP 2016–17 LEAGUE RECORD

Match No.	*Date*	*Venue*	*Opponents*	*Result*		*H/T Score*	*Lg Pos.*	*Goalscorers*	*Attendance*
1	Aug 7	H	Aberdeen	D	0-0	0-0	5		5728
2	13	A	Motherwell	W	2-1	0-0	2	Swanson 56, MacLean 75	3739
3	20	H	Celtic	L	2-4	0-3	5	Swanson (pen) 83, MacLean 89	6823
4	27	A	Inverness CT	L	1-2	0-0	5	Foster 79	2729
5	Sept 10	A	Partick Thistle	W	2-0	1-0	4	Anderson 21, MacLean 64	2885
6	17	H	Hearts	W	1-0	0-0	3	Cummins 57	5456
7	25	A	Hamilton A	D	1-1	0-1	4	Craig 82	1705
8	Oct 1	A	Ross Co	W	2-0	1-0	4	Swanson (pen) 42, Kane 73	3299
9	15	H	Kilmarnock	L	0-1	0-0	5		2930
10	23	H	Dundee	W	2-1	0-0	4	Anderson 62, Swanson (pen) 75	3646
11	26	A	Rangers	D	1-1	1-1	3	Alston 5	46,563
12	29	H	Partick Thistle	L	1-2	1-1	5	MacLean 18	3096
13	Nov 5	A	Hearts	D	2-2	1-1	5	Swanson 41, Kane 85	16,421
14	19	H	Ross Co	L	2-4	0-2	5	Swanson (pen) 65, MacLean 80	2554
15	Dec 3	H	Inverness CT	W	3-0	1-0	5	Craig 14, Davidson 62, Swanson 81	2549
16	10	A	Aberdeen	D	0-0	0-0	5		11,501
17	17	H	Motherwell	D	1-1	0-1	5	Kane 62	2836
18	23	A	Kilmarnock	W	1-0	1-0	5	Davidson 43	3056
19	28	H	Rangers	D	1-1	1-1	5	MacLean 28	7979
20	31	A	Dundee	L	0-3	0-2	5		6492
21	Jan 25	A	Celtic	L	0-1	0-0	5		51,057
22	28	H	Hamilton A	W	3-0	0-0	5	Cummins 2 53, 59, Davidson 74	3279
23	Feb 1	A	Partick Thistle	W	1-0	1-0	5	MacLean 40	2257
24	5	H	Celtic	L	2-5	2-1	5	Watson 31, Boyata (og) 43	6548
25	18	A	Ross Co	W	2-1	1-0	5	McEveley (og) 31, Kane 90	3187
26	25	H	Kilmarnock	L	0-2	0-1	5		2933
27	Mar 1	A	Rangers	L	2-3	0-1	5	Wotherspoon 74, Anderson 87	46,800
28	11	H	Dundee	W	2-0	2-0	5	Paton 12, Alston 19	4195
29	18	A	Motherwell	W	2-1	1-1	4	Craig 2 8, 66	3588
30	Apr 1	A	Hamilton A	L	0-1	0-0	4		1662
31	5	H	Hearts	W	1-0	0-0	4	Shaughnessy 73	4197
32	8	A	Inverness CT	W	3-0	1-0	4	MacLean 40, Craig (pen) 88, Cummins 90	2961
33	15	H	Aberdeen	L	1-2	0-2	4	Swanson (pen) 48	5132
34	29	A	Aberdeen	W	2-0	0-0	4	Swanson 80, Thomson 83	10,606
35	May 6	A	Celtic	L	1-4	0-0	4	MacLean 49	52,796
36	13	H	Partick Thistle	W	1-0	1-0	4	Swanson (pen) 33	3630
37	17	H	Hearts	W	1-0	1-0	4	Kane 26	3141
38	21	H	Rangers	L	1-2	0-1	4	Cummins 76	6799

Final League Position: 4

Honours
League Champions: First Division 1982-83, 1989-90, 1996-97, 2008-09. Division II 1923-24, 1959-60, 1962-63.
Runners-up: Division II 1931-32. First Division 2005-06, 2006-07. Second Division 1987-88.
Scottish Cup Winners: 2014.
League Cup Runners-up: 1969-70, 1998-99.
League Challenge Cup Winners: 2007-08; *Runners-up:* 1996-97.

European: *UEFA Cup:* 10 matches (1971-72, 1999-2000). *Europa League:* 12 matches (2012-13, 2013-14, 2014-15, 2015-16).

Club colours: Shirt: Blue with white sleeves. Short: White. Socks: Blue.

Goalscorers: *League (50):* Swanson 10 (6 pens), MacLean 9, Craig 5 (1 pen), Cummins 5, Kane 5, Anderson 3, Davidson 3, Alston 2, Foster 1, Paton 1, Shaughnessy 1, Thomson 1, Watson 1, Wotherspoon 1, own goals 2.
William Hill Scottish FA Cup (2): Alston 1, MacLean 1.
Betfred Scottish League Cup (14): Swanson 5 (3 pens), MacLean 2, Anderson 1, Craig 1, Cummins 1, Kane 1, McKay 1, Shaughnessy 1, Wotherspoon 1.
IRN-BRU Scottish League Challenge Cup (1): Hurst 1.

Mannus A 12 + 2	Shaughnessy J 38	Anderson S 26	Scobbie T 14 + 2	Easton B 37	Alston B 25 + 10	Davidson M 19 + 4	Craig L 27 + 9	Swanson D 28 + 2	MacLean S 30 + 2	Cummins G 17 + 13	Kane C 14 + 11	Wotherspoon D 20 + 13	Coulson M 7 + 7	McKay B 2	Millar C 14 + 3	Paton P 22 + 6	Foster R 33	Clark Z 26	Comrie A — + 1	Gormley J — + 1	Watson K 3 + 1	Thomson C 2 + 7	Smith C 2 + 1	Hurst G — + 1	*Match No.*
1	2	3	4	5	6^{1}	7	8	9	10^{2}	11^{3}	12	13	14												1
1	2	4		5	6^{3}	8	14	10^{2}	11		9	12		3	7^{1}	13									2
1	3			5	8^{3}	7	12	10	11	14	13	9^{2}		4^{1}		6	2								3
1	4	3		5	6^{2}	12	14	8	11	13	10^{3}	9				7^{1}	2								4
	3	4		5			6	9^{2}	10	12	11^{1}	13			7	8	2	1							5
	3	4		5	14	7	9		10^{2}	11^{3}	13	12	6^{1}			8	2	1							6
	3	4		5	6	7	8	9		11^{3}	14		10^{2}				2^{1}	1	12	13					7
	3	4		5	6^{1}	7	8	9^{2}	11		10	12				13	2	1							8
	3	4		5	7^{3}	8	6^{2}	9	11	13	10^{1}	12	14				2	1							9
	4	3		2		8	7	6^{1}	10		11^{2}	9	12			13	5	1							10
	4	3		5	8		6	10		12	11^{1}	13			7^{2}	9	2	1							11
	4	3		5	14		8	6^{1}	10	11^{2}	12	9^{3}	13			7	2	1							12
	4	3		5	8		12	9^{2}	10		13	6			11^{1}	7	2	1							13
14	3^{2}	4	13	5	6		8^{3}	10	11		12	9				7	2	1^{1}							14
	3	4		5	12	8	9	7^{1}	11^{3}	13	14	10	6^{2}				2	1							15
	4	3		5	12	7	8		11	13	10^{1}	6	9^{2}				2	1							16
	3		4	5	12	8			10	14	11^{1}	9	6^{2}		7^{3}	13	2	1							17
	3	4		5	6	8	13	10^{1}		12	11^{2}	9			7		2	1							18
	3	4	12	5	6^{2}		13	14	10	11		9^{1}			7^{3}	8	2	1							19
	3	4		5	6	8	9^{3}	10	11^{1}	14	12	13				7^{2}	2	1							20
	3	4	5		12		9	10^{1}	13	14	11^{3}	6^{2}			7	8		1			2				21
	3	4		5	6	7	13	9^{1}	11^{2}	10		12				8	2	1							22
	4	3		5		8	9	6^{1}	11	10		12			7		2	1							23
	3		4	5	12	7	14	10^{1}	13	11		9^{2}				8	2^{3}	1			6				24
	3	4		5	10	6^{2}	7		11^{1}		13	8			9		2	1			12				25
	2	3	4^{2}	9	6^{3}				10		11	8	13		7^{1}	12	5	1				14			26
	3	4		5	8^{3}		9	10^{2}	11	12		13	14			6	7	1			2^{1}				27
	3		4	5	6^{1}	12	8	9^{2}	10	11						7	2	1				13			28
12	3		4	5	6^{1}	13	8	9	10	11						7	2	1^{2}							29
1	3		4	5	6^{1}	7	9^{2}	10■		11					13	8	2■						12		30
1	3		4	5	6		8		10	11		9^{1}			12	7							2		31
1	4		3	5	6^{1}		8		11^{2}	10		12	9^{3}		13	7						14	2		32
1	3		4	5	6^{1}	13	8^{2}	12	11			9	10^{3}			7	2					14			33
1	3	4		5	14	7	8	10^{3}		11		9^{1}			6^{2}	12	2					13			34
	4	3		5	6^{3}		8	9^{1}	10	11^{2}	14	13				7	2	1				12			35
1	3		4	5	12		8	9^{2}	10	11		6^{1}				7	2					13			36
1	3		4	5	12		14	9^{1}		10	11	7	13		8^{2}		2					6^{3}			37
1	3		4	5	6		8		11	12	10^{2}				7		2					9^{1}		13	38

ST MIRREN

Year Formed: 1877. *Ground & Address:* St Mirren Park, Greenhill Road, Paisley PA3 1RU. *Telephone:* 0141 889 2558. *Fax:* 0141 848 6444. *E-mail:* info@stmirren.com *Website:* www.stmirren.com
Ground Capacity: 8,023 (all seated). *Size of Pitch:* 105m × 68m.
Chairman: Gordon Scott. *Chief Executive:* Tony Fitzpatrick.
Manager: Jack Ross. *Assistant Manager:* James Fowler.
Club Nickname: 'The Buddies'.
Previous Grounds: Shortroods 1877-79, Thistle Park Greenhill 1879-83, Westmarch 1883-94, Love Street 1894-2009.
Record Attendance: 47,438 v Celtic, League Cup, 20 August 1949.
Record Transfer Fee received: £850,000 for Ian Ferguson to Rangers (February 1988).
Record Transfer Fee paid: £400,000 for Thomas Stickroth from Bayer Uerdingen (March 1990).
Record Victory: 15-0 v Glasgow University, Scottish Cup 1st rd, 30 January 1960.
Record Defeat: 0-9 v Rangers, Division I, 4 December 1897.
Most Capped Player: Godmundur Torfason, 29, Iceland.
Most League Appearances: 399: Hugh Murray, 1997-2012.
Most League Goals in Season (Individual): 45: Dunky Walker, Division I, 1921-22.
Most Goals Overall (Individual): 221: David McCrae, 1923-34.

ST MIRREN – SPFL LADBROKES CHAMPIONSHIP 2016–17 LEAGUE RECORD

Match No.	*Date*	*Venue*	*Opponents*	*Result*	*H/T Score*	*Lg Pos.*	*Goalscorers*	*Attendance*
1	Aug 6	H	Greenock Morton	D 1-1	0-1	7	Sutton [83]	4997
2	13	A	Raith R	L 1-3	0-1	9	Hardie [63]	2140
3	20	H	Hibernian	L 0-2	0-2	9		4517
4	27	A	Ayr U	D 1-1	0-1	9	Walsh [89]	2165
5	Sept 10	H	Queen of the South	L 1-3	1-2	10	Walsh [41]	3102
6	17	A	Dumbarton	D 1-1	1-1	10	Hardie [41]	1101
7	24	A	Dunfermline Ath	L 3-4	2-1	10	Sutton 2 [31, 45], Hardie [81]	2732
8	Oct 1	H	Falkirk	D 1-1	0-1	10	Walsh [87]	2334
9	15	H	Dundee U	L 0-2	0-1	10		3612
10	29	A	Hibernian	L 0-2	0-2	10		14,485
11	Nov 1	A	Greenock Morton	L 1-3	0-2	10	Gordon [86]	3378
12	5	H	Dumbarton	L 0-1	0-0	10		2758
13	19	H	Dunfermline Ath	L 0-1	0-1	10		2126
14	Dec 3	A	Falkirk	L 1-3	1-0	10	Morgan [17]	4486
15	6	A	Queen of the South	W 3-2	1-2	10	Magennis [20], Gordon [57], Mallan [90]	1147
16	10	H	Raith R	W 1-0	0-0	10	Morgan [47]	2630
17	17	H	Ayr U	D 1-1	0-0	10	Sutton [81]	3124
18	24	A	Dundee U	L 1-2	1-2	10	Sutton [27]	7247
19	31	H	Greenock Morton	D 1-1	1-0	10	MacKenzie [30]	4902
20	Jan 7	H	Queen of the South	L 0-3	0-1	10		3105
21	14	A	Dunfermline Ath	D 1-1	0-1	10	MacKenzie [46]	4108
22	28	H	Falkirk	L 1-2	0-1	10	Loy [77]	3316
23	Feb 4	A	Dumbarton	D 2-2	1-0	10	Clarkson [35], Davis [71]	1377
24	25	A	Ayr U	W 2-0	0-0	10	Sutton [51], Morgan [82]	2712
25	Mar 1	H	Hibernian	W 2-0	1-0	10	Demetriou 2 [35, 46]	3441
26	8	A	Raith R	L 0-2	0-0	10		2124
27	11	H	Dunfermline Ath	D 0-0	0-0	10		4582
28	15	H	Dundee U	W 3-2	2-1	10	Davis [2], Mallan [37], Morgan [59]	2766
29	18	A	Queen of the South	W 2-0	1-0	10	Mallan [44], Loy (pen) [54]	1728
30	Apr 1	H	Ayr U	W 6-2	4-0	10	Mallan [5], MacKenzie [20], McGinn [23], Magennis [36], Morgan [52], Smith [88]	4620
31	8	H	Dumbarton	D 1-1	1-1	9	Magennis [10]	3906
32	11	A	Greenock Morton	W 4-1	1-1	8	Demetriou [20], Mallan [46], Sutton [56], MacKenzie [80]	4609
33	15	A	Falkirk	D 2-2	1-1	8	Loy [5], McGinn [59]	4734
34	22	A	Dundee U	L 2-3	1-1	9	MacKenzie [38], Todd [86]	6225
35	29	H	Raith R	W 5-0	2-0	8	Mallan 2 [27, 59], McManus (og) [39], Loy [48], Morgan [87]	4937
36	May 6	A	Hibernian	D 1-1	0-0	7	Loy [60]	19,764

Final League Position: 7

Honours
League Champions: First Division 1976-77, 1999-2000, 2005-06. Division II 1967-68.
Runners-up: First Division 2004-05; Division II 1935-36.
Scottish Cup Winners: 1926, 1959, 1987; *Runners-up:* 1908, 1934, 1962.
League Cup Winners: 2012-13; *Runners-up:* 1955-56, 2009-10.
League Challenge Cup Winners: 2005-06; *Runners-up:* 2016-17.
B&Q Cup Runners-up: 1993-94. *Anglo-Scottish Cup:* 1979-80.

European: *Cup Winners' Cup:* 4 matches (1987-88). *UEFA Cup:* 10 matches (1980-81, 1983-84, 1985-86).

Club colours: Shirt: Black and thin vertical white stripes. Shorts: Black with red trim. Socks: White with black trim.

Goalscorers: *League (52):* Mallan 7, Sutton 7, Morgan 6, Loy 5 (1 pen), MacKenzie 5, Demetriou 3, Hardie 3, Magennis 3, Walsh 3, Davis 2, Gordon 2, McGinn 2, Clarkson 1, Smith 1, Todd 1, own goal 1.
William Hill Scottish FA Cup (11): Morgan 2, Shankland 2, Sutton 2, Baird 1, Davis 1, Mallan 1, McAllister 1, Smith 1.
Betfred Scottish League Cup (7): Baird 2, Clarkson 2, Morgan 1, Shankland 1, Walsh 1.
IRN-BRU Scottish League Challenge Cup (13): Sutton 4, Mallan 3, Loy 2, Clarkson 1, McGinn 1, Morgan 1, Shankland 1.

Langfield J 9	Naismith J 21	Baird J 21 + 4	Webster A 10 + 5	Irvine G 33	Gallagher C 2 + 6	Mallan S 34	Hutton K 11	Morgan L 31 + 2	Clarkson D 7 + 9	Shankland L 7 + 10	Hardie R 8 + 8	Walsh T 4 + 6	Sutton J 24 + 11	Gallacher S 12	Stewart J 1 + 2	MacKenzie G 29	Gordon B 6 + 2	Whyte D — + 1	Quinn R 11 + 3	Magennis K 21 + 4	McAllister K 10	McLear L — + 3	Storie C 3 + 4	Loy R 11 + 2	O'Brien B 15	Fjelde P 1 + 2	Smith C 15	McGinn S 14 + 1	Todd J 1 + 10	Davis H 6	Eckersley A 12	Demetriou S 6 + 6	*Match No.*
1	2	3	4	5^{1}	6^{2}	7	8	9	10^{3}	11	12	13	14																				1
1	2^{1}	4	3	5	9^{3}	8^{2}	7	6	14	11	10	12	13																				2
	2	3	4	5		7	8	6^{1}	13	11^{3}	12	9	10^{2}	1	14																		3
	2	3	4	5		7	8^{2}		11	13	9	12	10	1	6^{1}																		4
1	2^{3}		4^{1}	5		8	7	9	13	12	11	6	10^{2}			3	14																5
	2	4		5	12	7	8^{1}	9^{2}		14	10^{3}	6	11	1		3		13															6
	2	3	12	5		8	7	10^{2}			6	13	11	1		4^{1}			9														7
1	2	4		5		9	6^{1}	10	13		8	12	11			3			7^{2}														8
1	2	4		5		8^{2}	6	9	14	12	11^{1}	13	10			3^{3}			7														9
1	2	4		5	14	7	8^{3}	9	11^{2}	10	6^{1}		13				3			12													10
1	2	3		5		8	7^{1}	9	10	11^{2}	14	6^{3}	13				4			12													11
1	2			5	14	7		10	9^{3}	12	13		11			3	4^{2}			6	8^{1}												12
	2	4		5		6		10	9^{2}	12	13		11	1			3^{3}			7^{1}	8	14											13
	2	4■		5	14	9		10		13			11^{1}	1	12	3			6^{2}	7	8^{3}												14
	2			5	14	9		10		12	13		11^{1}	1		3	4		7^{3}	8	6^{2}												15
	2		12	5				9		10	14		11^{2}	1		4	3^{1}		7^{3}	8	6	13											16
	2		4^{2}	5		9		10	13	11^{1}	14		12	1		3			6^{3}	7	8												17
	2	12	4	5		9		10	13	14			11	1		3^{2}			8^{3}	7	6^{1}												18
	2		3	5	14	9		10	13				11	1		4			6^{2}	7^{1}	8^{3}	12											19
	2		3^{1}	5		9		10	12	13			11	1		4			6	7^{2}	8												20
1	2	12	3^{3}	5		9		13					10			4			8^{1}	14	6^{2}		7	11									21
		4	12	5		6^{2}		8					11			3^{1}							7^{3}	9	1	2	10	13	14				22
				2				6^{2}	11^{1}				12			3				8			7		1		9	10	14	4	5^{3}	13	23
						10^{2}		9					11			3				7					1	13	6^{1}	8	12	4	5	2	24
		14		5^{2}		7		9					11			4				6^{1}					1	12	10^{3}	8	13	3		2	25
						9		10					11			3				6^{1}				13	1		8	7	12	4	5	2^{2}	26
				2		6		10					11			3								12	1		9^{1}	7	8^{2}	4	5	13	27
		12		2		6		10					11			3				13			14	8^{3}	1		9^{1}	7		4^{2}	5		28
		4		2		7		9					12			3				6^{1}			13	11^{2}	1		10^{3}	8			5	14	29
		3	14			7^{2}		9^{3}					12			4^{1}				6				10	1		11	8	13		5	2	30
		3		2		8							12			4	14			6^{1}				10^{3}	1		11	7	13		5■	9^{2}	31
		3		2		7^{2}							11			4			14	6			12	10^{1}	1		9^{3}	8	13			5	32
		3		2		8		12					10^{2}			4				6			13	11^{3}	1		9^{1}	7	14		5		33
		4		2^{1}		7		9					12			3				6				11^{2}	1		10^{3}	8	14		5	13	34
		3	14	2		8		9								4^{2}			13	6^{3}				11	1		10^{1}	7			5	12	35
		3		4^{1}		7		11					14			2			13	10				8^{3}	1		9^{2}	6			5	12	36

STENHOUSEMUIR

Year Formed: 1884. *Ground & Address:* Ochilview Park, Gladstone Rd, Stenhousemuir FK5 4QL. *Telephone:* 01324 562992. *Fax:* 01324 562980. *E-mail:* info@stenhousemuirfc.com *Website:* www.stenhousemuirfc.com
Ground Capacity: 3,776 (seated: 626). *Size of Pitch:* 101m × 66m.
Chairman: Gordon Thompson. *Vice-Chairman:* David Reid. *Secretary/General Manager:* Margaret Kilpatrick.
Manager: Brown Ferguson. *Assistant Manager:* Jim Paterson.
Club Nickname: 'The Warriors'.
Previous Grounds: Tryst Ground 1884-86, Goschen Park 1886-90.
Record Attendance: 12,500 v East Fife, Scottish Cup Quarter-final, 11 March 1950.
Record Transfer Fee received: £70,000 for Euan Donaldson to St Johnstone (May 1995).
Record Transfer Fee paid: £20,000 to Livingston for Ian Little (June 1995); £20,000 to East Fife for Paul Hunter (September 1995).
Record Victory: 9-2 v Dundee U, Division II, 16 April 1937.
Record Defeat: 2-11 v Dunfermline Ath, Division II, 27 September 1930.
Most League Appearances: 434: Jimmy Richardson, 1957-73.
Most League Goals in Season (Individual): 32: Robert Taylor, Division II, 1925-26.

STENHOUSEMUIR – SPFL LADBROKES LEAGUE ONE 2016–17 LEAGUE RECORD

Match No.	Date		Venue	Opponents	Result		H/T Score	Lg Pos.	Goalscorers	Attendance
1	Aug	6	A	Brechin C	L	1-2	0-1	7	Kerr [67]	402
2		13	H	Queen's Park	L	1-2	1-0	8	Stirling [34]	534
3		20	A	Livingston	L	1-4	0-2	9	McMenamin (pen) [90]	769
4		27	H	Airdrieonians	D	2-2	1-0	9	McMenamin [15], Kerr [87]	597
5	Sept	10	A	Albion R	L	0-4	0-0	10		301
6		17	H	Peterhead	D	2-2	0-2	10	McCormack [68], Kerr [78]	331
7		24	H	Alloa Ath	D	2-2	0-1	10	Furtado [79], Shaw [90]	466
8	Oct	1	A	East Fife	W	1-0	0-0	9	McMenamin (pen) [58]	563
9		15	H	Stranraer	L	0-5	0-3	10		341
10		22	H	Brechin C	L	1-3	0-0	10	Gilhaney [56]	352
11		29	A	Queen's Park	W	3-0	1-0	10	Gilhaney [28], McMenamin (pen) [49], Roy, Alistair [67]	538
12	Nov	5	A	Alloa Ath	L	1-4	1-3	10	Roy, Alistair [36]	458
13		19	A	Stranraer	L	1-3	1-1	10	Roy, Alistair [45]	323
14	Dec	10	A	Airdrieonians	W	5-0	3-0	10	Furtado [32], Marsh 2 [35, 56], Cook [44], Martinez [66]	791
15		13	H	Livingston	L	0-4	0-1	10		334
16		17	H	Albion R	W	1-0	0-0	10	Furtado [74]	371
17		20	H	East Fife	L	0-1	0-1	10		356
18		26	A	Peterhead	W	2-0	0-0	9	McAllister (og) [70], McCormack [79]	427
19		31	H	Alloa Ath	L	2-4	1-3	10	Cook [9], Shaw [90]	335
20	Jan	7	A	East Fife	L	0-1	0-1	10		635
21		14	H	Stranraer	W	1-0	0-0	9	Millar [68]	392
22		28	H	Airdrieonians	W	4-2	1-1	9	Cook 2 [30, 62], McMenamin [86], Martinez [90]	604
23	Feb	4	A	Brechin C	D	2-2	2-1	9	Furtado [7], Shaw [16]	403
24		11	H	Queen's Park	L	0-2	0-1	10		423
25		18	A	Albion R	D	1-1	0-1	10	Robertson, M [83]	327
26	Mar	4	H	Peterhead	W	3-1	2-0	10	Cook [10], Robertson, M [16], McMenamin [64]	362
27		11	A	Alloa Ath	L	1-2	0-1	10	Grant [61]	508
28		18	A	Airdrieonians	L	0-1	0-0	10		568
29		21	A	Livingston	L	0-1	0-1	10		531
30		25	H	Albion R	L	0-3	0-0	10		433
31	Apr	1	A	Stranraer	L	0-3	0-1	10		440
32		8	H	East Fife	W	3-1	1-0	10	Furtado 2 [44, 79], McMenamin (pen) [61]	455
33		15	H	Livingston	L	0-1	0-0	10		472
34		22	A	Peterhead	W	1-0	1-0	10	Shaw [12]	587
35		29	A	Queen's Park	W	2-0	1-0	9	Shaw 2 [22, 52]	764
36	May	6	H	Brechin C	D	1-1	0-1	10	Shaw [62]	557

Final League Position: 10

Honours
League Champions: Third Division runners-up: 1998-99. *Promoted to Second Division:* 2008-09 (play-offs).
Scottish Cup: Semi-finals 1902-03. Quarter-finals 1948-49, 1949-50, 1994-95.
League Cup: Quarter-finals 1947-48, 1960-61, 1975-76.
League Challenge Cup Winners: 1995-96.

Club colours: Shirt: Maroon with light blue trim. Shorts: Maroon with light blue trim. Socks: Maroon.

Goalscorers: *League (45):* McMenamin 7 (4 pens), Shaw 7, Furtado 6, Cook 5, Kerr 3, Alistair Roy 3, Gilhaney 2, Marsh 2, Martinez 2, McCormack 2, Robertson M 2, Grant 1, Millar 1, Stirling 1, own goal 1.
William Hill Scottish FA Cup (5): McMenamin 3, Furtado 1, Kerr 1.
Betfred Scottish League Cup (2): Gilhaney 1, McCroary 1.
IRN-BRU Scottish League Challenge Cup (4): Cook 2, McMenamin 1, own goal 1.

McCabe C 20 + 1	McCormack J 22 + 4	Meechan R 28 + 5	Kerr F 32	Hamilton G 6	Berry V 31	Gilhaney M 14 + 7	Stirling S 9 + 3	Millar K 31 + 1	Cook A 30	McMenamin C 32 + 4	Howarth J — + 3	Smith J — + 7	Shaw O 16 + 8	McCroary L 2 + 5	Roy Alistair 12 + 16	Sinclair D — + 2	Summers C 23 + 2	Paterson J 1	Furtado W 24 + 5	Allan M 1	Marsh D 23	Crawford D 10	Martinez C 1 + 12	Walker S — + 1	Robertson M 11 + 1	Duthie C 10 + 1	Grant T 1 + 3	Bowman G 6 + 1	*Match No.*
1	2	3	4	5	6	7	8[2]	9	10[1]	11	12	13																	1
1	2	3	4	5	8	6	7[1]		9	10[2]		13	11	12															2
1	5[2]	2	4	3	8[3]	10	6[1]	7	9	11			14		12	13													3
1	2	3	4■			6[2]	8	7[3]	9	10[1]		14	11		12	13	5												4
1	2	3		4			8	13		12			10	7	11[2]			5[1]	6	9									5
1	3	5[1]	4			13	7		9	12			10	8	11[2]				6		2								6
1	2	3	5		8	12	7[1]		9	10			11		13				6		4[2]								7
1	2	5	3		7	12		8	9	10[3]			11[1]	14	13				6[2]		4								8
1	2	5	3		8	14	12	7[2]	9[3]	10			11[1]		13				6		4								9
1	2	3	4		8	6[3]		7[2]		10		12	11[1]	14	13		5		9■										10
		2	4		7	6		8[1]	9[3]	10[2]	12	14		13	11		5				3	1							11
13	12	2	4		7	6		8[3]	9[1]	10	14				11		5				3	1[2]							12
1	12	2	4[3]		7	6[2]		8	9	11[1]					10		5		13		3		14						13
1	2[2]	14	4		8			7	9[3]	10[1]			13		11		5		6		3		12						14
1	5	13	3		8			7	6	10					11[2]		2		9		4[1]		12						15
1	2	3	4		8			7	9	10			12		6[1]		5		11										16
1	2	3	4		8	12		7[2]	9	10					6[3]		5[1]		11				13	14					17
1	2			4	7	11[1]		8	9[2]	10			12	14	13		5		6[3]		3								18
1	2	3		4	8	10[2]		7	9[3]	11			12		14		5		6[1]				13						19
1	2[1]	3			7			8	9	10			11				5		6		4		12						20
1	12	2	4		8			7	9	10			11[1]				5		6		3								21
1		2	4		8[2]		14	7	9[1]	10			11[3]		13		5		6		3		12						22
	13	2	4		7			8	9[3]	10[1]			11		12		5		6[2]		3■	1	14						23
	2	3[1]	4		8		7[2]		9	10		14	11[3]		12		5		6			1	13						24
	2		4		7			8	9	10[1]		14			11[3]		5		6[2]		3	1	13		12				25
		2	4		7[3]		14	8	9	10[2]							5		12		3	1			11	6[1]	13		26
		2	4		7		10[3]	8	9	13					14		5				3	1			11[1]	6[2]	12		27
		2	4		6			7	10	9					13		5[1]		8[2]		3■	1			11	12			28
	2	3	4		7	14		8[2]		13					11		5		12			1			10[3]	9	6[1]		29
	2	3	4		7			8	9	10					13		5[1]		12			1[3]			11[2]	6		14	30
	2■	3	4			14		8	9[1]	10			13		7[3]		5[2]		12						11	6		1	31
		12	4		6	11[1]		7	9[2]	10			13						5[3]		3		14		2	8		1	32
		6[2]	4			11[1]		7	9	10			12		14				5[3]		3		13		2	8		1	33
		12	4		6	9[2]		7		10			11				13		5[1]		3				2	8		1	34
		13	4		7	6[1]		8■		11			10				14		9		3[2]				2	5	12[3]	1	35
			4		8			7		10			11		12				9		3		6[1]		2	5		1	36

STIRLING ALBION

Year Formed: 1945. *Ground & Address:* Forthbank Stadium, Springkerse, Stirling FK7 7UJ. *Telephone:* 01786 450399.
Fax: 01786 448592. *Email:* office@stirlingalbionfc.co.uk *Website:* www.stirlingalbionfc.co.uk
Ground Capacity: 3,808 (seated: 2,508). *Size of Pitch:* 101m × 68m.
Chairman: Stuart Brown. *Administrator:* Neil Mackay.
Manager: Dave Mackay. *Assistant Manager:* Frazer Wright.
Club Nickname: 'The Binos'.
Previous Grounds: Annfield 1945-92.
Record Attendance: 26,400 v Celtic, Scottish Cup 4th rd, 14 March 1959 (Annfield); 3,808 v Aberdeen, Scottish Cup 4th rd, 15 February 1996 (Forthbank).
Record Transfer Fee received: £90,000 for Stephen Nicholas to Motherwell (March 1999).
Record Transfer Fee paid: £25,000 for Craig Taggart from Falkirk (August 1994).
Record Victory: 20-0 v Selkirk, Scottish Cup 1st rd, 8 December 1984.
Record Defeat: 0-9 v Dundee U, Division I, 30 December 1967; 0-9 v Ross Co, Scottish Cup 5th rd, 6 February 2010.
Most League Appearances: 504: Matt McPhee, 1967-81.
Most League Goals in Season (Individual): 27: Joe Hughes, Division II, 1969-70.
Most Goals Overall (Individual): 129: Billy Steele, 1971-83.

STIRLING ALBION – SPFL LADBROKES LEAGUE TWO 2016–17 LEAGUE RECORD

Match No.	*Date*	*Venue*	*Opponents*	*Result*	*H/T Score*	*Lg Pos.*	*Goalscorers*	*Attendance*
1	Aug 6	A	Annan Ath	L 2-3	1-3	8	Dickson [12], McKenzie, M [57]	421
2	13	H	Clyde	D 1-1	0-0	7	Forsyth [79]	777
3	20	H	Montrose	W 2-0	0-0	5	Smith, D [59], McKenzie, M [90]	497
4	27	A	Arbroath	L 3-5	1-1	7	Sukar (og) [34], Henderson [54], Ferns [70]	601
5	Sept 10	H	Edinburgh C	D 1-1	0-0	8	McMillan [55]	465
6	17	A	Forfar Ath	L 1-4	1-1	9	Dickson [45]	635
7	24	H	Elgin C	L 0-4	0-3	9		457
8	Oct 1	A	Cowdenbeath	W 2-0	1-0	8	Layne [7], Smith, D [63]	342
9	15	H	Berwick R	D 0-0	0-0	7		517
10	29	A	Clyde	D 1-1	1-1	7	McKenzie, M [9]	738
11	Nov 5	H	Forfar Ath	L 0-3	0-1	7		663
12	12	A	Elgin C	W 3-2	0-1	7	McKenzie, M [46], Henderson [59], Mills [89]	585
13	19	H	Arbroath	D 2-2	0-1	7	Dickson 2 [90, 90]	605
14	Dec 6	A	Berwick R	L 2-3	2-2	9	Bikey 2 [6, 23]	302
15	10	A	Edinburgh C	L 0-2	0-1	10		368
16	17	H	Annan Ath	W 3-1	2-1	9	Smith, D [12], McMillan [17], Bikey [75]	694
17	24	A	Montrose	D 2-2	1-0	8	Steeves (og) [25], Smith, R [79]	610
18	31	H	Cowdenbeath	L 1-2	0-0	9	Bikey [54]	538
19	Jan 7	H	Clyde	W 3-0	1-0	7	Kavanagh [29], Bikey 2 [66, 74]	718
20	14	A	Forfar Ath	D 1-1	1-1	6	Smith, D [20]	632
21	28	A	Annan Ath	L 1-4	1-1	7	Henderson [7]	420
22	Feb 4	H	Montrose	L 1-2	1-0	9	Henderson (pen) [16]	494
23	11	H	Berwick R	D 2-2	0-2	8	Malone [86], Dickson [88]	515
24	18	A	Arbroath	D 1-1	0-0	8	Smith, D [57]	625
25	25	H	Edinburgh C	W 1-0	1-0	7	Kavanagh [17]	501
26	28	H	Elgin C	W 1-0	0-0	6	Dickson [90]	412
27	Mar 4	A	Cowdenbeath	W 2-0	1-0	6	Smith, R [20], Dickson [47]	381
28	11	A	Montrose	W 3-1	1-0	5	Smith, D [5], Kavanagh [60], McLaren [86]	401
29	18	H	Annan Ath	W 1-0	0-0	5	Smith, D [74]	531
30	25	A	Clyde	W 3-2	0-1	5	Smith, D 2 [53, 81], Kavanagh [78]	606
31	Apr 1	H	Forfar Ath	L 0-3	0-2	6		738
32	8	A	Berwick R	W 1-0	1-0	5	Smith, D [17]	440
33	15	H	Cowdenbeath	L 0-3	0-2	6		638
34	22	A	Elgin C	D 2-2	0-0	6	Smith, D [53], Bikey [57]	785
35	29	A	Edinburgh C	L 0-1	0-0	6		388
36	May 6	H	Arbroath	D 1-1	0-1	6	Henderson (pen) [76]	1748

Final League Position: 6

Honours

League Champions: Division II 1952-53, 1957-58, 1960-61, 1964-65. Second Division 1976-77, 1990-91, 1995-96, 2009-10; *Runners-up:* Division II 1948-49, 1950-51. Second Division 2006-07. Third Division 2003-04. *Promoted to First Division:* 2006-07 (play-offs). *Promoted to League One:* 2013-14 (play-offs).
League Cup: Semi-finals 1961-62.
League Challenge Cup: Semi-finals 1995-96, 1999-2000.

Club colours: Shirt: Red with white trim. Shorts: Red. Socks: Red with white trim.

Goalscorers: *League (50):* Smith D 11, Bikey 7, Dickson 7, Henderson 5 (2 pens), Kavanagh 4, McKenzie 4, McMillan 2, Smith R 2, Ferns 1, Forsyth 1, Layne 1, Malone 1, McLaren 1, Mills 1, own goals 2.
William Hill Scottish FA Cup (9): Bikey 3, Henderson 3 (2 pens), Ferns 1, McKenzie M 1, Olanrewaju 1.
Betfred Scottish League Cup (6): Henderson 4 (2 pens), Ferns 1, Smith D 1.
IRN-BRU Scottish League Challenge Cup (2): McKenzie M 2.

Binnie C 5	Mills J 4 + 1	Davidson Scott 12 + 3	Verlaque D 6 + 3	Forsyth R 12 + 2	McKenzie M 14 + 2	Hodge B 9 + 1	Dickson S 26 + 4	Smith D 28 + 3	Henderson B 22 + 9	Ferns E 11 + 5	McCue J 6 + 2	Fowler J 1 + 1	Smith C 31	Smith R 14	McMillan R 23	Olanrewaju M 1 + 6	Morrison C 7 + 8	Layne I 7 + 1 / McMullan C 6 + 1	McGeachie R 22 + 1	Mazel A — + 1	Docherty A — + 1	Petrie D 12 + 3	Kavanagh R 12 + 11	Beith A 10 / Vezza A — + 1	Robertson W 8	Colquhoun C 13 + 1	Bikey D 10 + 3	Caddis L 16	Wright F 7 + 2	Quigley C 17	McLaren C 11 + 5	Jeffries J 2 + 3	Cameron R — + 2	Black A 11 + 2	Malone A — + 1	Little A — + 5	Johnstone A — + 3	*Match No.*
1	2^{1}	3	4^{2}	5	6	7	8	9	10	11	12	13																										1
			4	5	6^{2}	2	8	9	10^{1}	11	12		1	3■	7	13																						2
		3	2	5	6	8	7	11^{1}	10^{2}	13	9^{3}		1		4	12	14																					3
			2	5		7	8	6	11	9^{1}			1	3	4	12	13	10^{2}																				4
		4		5^{1}	6		7	9^{3}	11	8			1		3		13	10^{2}	2	12	14																	5
		5	2^{2}		7		8	9	13	10			1		3	11		12	4			6^{1}																6
		4	2		6		5	9	10^{2}	13	8		1		3		12	11^{1}				7																7
			13		6^{1}		7	10		9		8	1	3	4			11^{2}	2			5	12															8
		4			6	7	8	9^{2}	13	10^{1}			1		3	12		11^{3}	2			5	14															9
		5			6	7	9			11^{1}	4		1		3	13		10^{2}				8	12	2														10
		4	12		6	8	9			10	2^{3}		1		3	13		11^{1}				5^{2}	14	7														11
	14	4	13		6^{2}	8	9		10^{1}	11			1		3							5	12	7	2^{3}													12
		3			8	7^{2}	9		11	10^{1}			1		4				13			5	12	2	6													13
		4				14	12		10	13			1		3				2			5■	11^{1}	8	7^{2}	6^{3}	9											14
				4	6^{3}		7^{1}	13	9^{2}	14			1	3	5				2				12	10		8	11											15
	9	13			14			11^{1}					1	3^{3}	4		6^{2}		2			5	10	8		7	12											16
1	5	12			13			10		14				3	4		6^{1}		2^{2}			9^{3}		8■		7	11											17
1	9^{1}	13			5		6	10^{3}	14					3^{2}	4		12		2			8				7	11											18
1							14	12	13						4								10^{2}	9	7	8	11^{1}	2	3	5	6^{3}							19
1							13	10	12						4									9^{2}	7^{1}	8	11	2	3	5	6							20
		3					12	10	11				1												8^{1}	7^{2}		2	4	5	9	6^{3}	13	14				21
							9	11^{1}	10				1		4							12			8^{2}	7■		2	3	5	6		13					22
				4			8	10	11		7^{3}		1	2	3^{2}				5									6^{1}	12	9	14				13			23
							8	11	10^{3}		7^{2}		1	2					5				14			6			3	4	9^{1}					12	13	24
							8	6^{1}	11				1	4					3				10^{2}			7		2		5	9^{3}			14		13	12	25
				5			8	12	10^{1}				1	4				7	3				11					2			9^{2}			6			13	26
				14			8	6^{2}	11				1	4				7^{1}	3				10			13^{3}		2		5	12			9				27
							8	9	11^{1}				1	4				7^{2}	3			14	10^{3}					2■		5	12	13		6				28
							8	7	13				1	4^{2}			12	9	3				11						14	5	10^{3}	6^{1}		2				29
				14			8	6	10^{2}				1				12		2				11^{1}					7	4	5	9^{3}			3		13		30
				3				9	12				1				6^{2}	7^{1}				13	11^{3}				10	2	4	5				8		14		31
				3			7	9^{3}	10^{1}				1				6^{2}		4				13				11	2		5	14			8		12		32
				4			7	9	11				1				8^{2}		3				10^{3}				12	2		5	13	14		6^{1}				33
								9	13				1		4		8^{2}		3				14			7	11^{1}	2		5	10^{3}	12		6				34
								9^{2}	13				1		4		8^{1}	14	3				12			7	11^{3}	2		5	10			6				35
				4				9	10^{3}				1				13	7^{1}	3				11	14	8^{2}		12	2		5				6				36

STRANRAER

Year Formed: 1870. *Ground & Address:* Stair Park, London Rd, Stranraer DG9 8BS. *Telephone and Fax:* 01776 703271.
E-mail: secretary@stranraerfc.org *Website:* www.stranraerfc.org
Ground Capacity: 4,178 (seated: 1,830). *Size of Pitch:* 103m × 64m.
Chairman: Iain Dougan. *Vice-Chairman:* Bill Paton.
Manager: Stevie Farrell. *Assistant Manager:* Chris Aitken.
Club Nicknames: 'The Blues', 'The Clayholers'.
Previous Grounds: None.
Record Attendance: 6,500 v Rangers, Scottish Cup 1st rd, 24 January 1948.
Record Transfer Fee received: £90,000 for Mark Campbell to Ayr U (1999).
Record Transfer Fee paid: £35,000 for Michael Moore from St Johnstone (March 2005).
Record Victory: 9-0 v St Cuthbert Wanderers, Scottish Cup 2nd rd, 23 October 2010; 9-0 v Wigtown & Bladnoch, Scottish Cup 2nd rd, 22 October 2011.
Record Defeat: 1-11 v Queen of the South, Scottish Cup 1st rd, 16 January 1932.
Most League Appearances: 301: Keith Knox, 1986-90; 1999-2001.
Most League Goals in Season (Individual): 27: Derek Frye, 1977-78.
Most Goals Overall (Individual): 136: Jim Campbell, 1965-75.

STRANRAER – SPFL LADBROKES LEAGUE ONE 2016–17 LEAGUE RECORD

Match No.	Date	Venue	Opponents	Result		H/T Score	Lg Pos.	Goalscorers	Attendance
1	Aug 6	A	Livingston	L	1-5	0-2	9	Malcolm ^{55}	693
2	13	H	Alloa Ath	L	2-5	1-5	9	Malcolm 2 $^{4, 47}$	448
3	20	A	Airdrieonians	L	0-1	0-1	10		812
4	27	H	Peterhead	W	1-0	1-0	7	McGuigan ^{26}	376
5	Sept 10	A	East Fife	L	0-2	0-1	9		555
6	17	H	Albion R	W	3-2	2-0	7	Thomson, C 2 $^{17, 45}$, McGuigan ^{56}	402
7	24	A	Queen's Park	W	2-0	1-0	5	Dick ^{39}, Malcolm ^{63}	534
8	Oct 1	H	Brechin C	L	0-1	0-0	7		402
9	15	A	Stenhousemuir	W	5-0	3-0	5	Gibson ^{11}, Turner ^{28}, Malcolm 2 $^{33, 80}$, Nade ^{78}	341
10	22	H	East Fife	D	1-1	0-1	6	Bell ^{70}	428
11	29	A	Peterhead	L	0-2	0-0	7		444
12	Nov 5	H	Queen's Park	L	0-2	0-1	7		446
13	12	A	Albion R	L	2-3	1-2	8	Gibson ^{38}, Nuttall ^{72}	321
14	19	H	Stenhousemuir	W	3-1	1-1	8	Bell ^{36}, Thomson, R ^{69}, Nuttall ^{82}	323
15	Dec 10	H	Livingston	L	1-2	1-0	9	Gibson ^{5}	333
16	13	A	Alloa Ath	D	2-2	1-1	8	Agnew ^{9}, Gibson ^{72}	307
17	17	A	Brechin C	L	0-2	0-2	9		402
18	24	H	Airdrieonians	L	1-2	1-1	9	Agnew ^{22}	317
19	31	A	Queen's Park	W	1-0	0-0	8	Gibson ^{60}	556
20	Jan 7	H	Alloa Ath	L	1-2	1-0	9	Thomson, C ^{20}	383
21	14	A	Stenhousemuir	L	0-1	0-0	10		392
22	28	A	East Fife	D	0-0	0-0	10		584
23	Feb 4	H	Albion R	W	3-0	1-0	10	Malcolm 2 $^{21, 79}$, Bell ^{88}	364
24	11	A	Livingston	D	0-0	0-0	9		677
25	18	H	Peterhead	D	3-3	2-1	9	Thomson, R ^{19}, Gibson 2 $^{33, 72}$	459
26	25	H	Brechin C	W	2-0	1-0	9	Gibson ^{22}, Malcolm ^{78}	340
27	Mar 4	A	Airdrieonians	W	2-1	0-0	7	Malcolm ^{53}, Thomson, R ^{69}	706
28	11	H	Queen's Park	D	1-1	0-1	7	Malcolm ^{76}	434
29	18	H	Livingston	L	0-1	0-0	7		523
30	25	A	Peterhead	D	2-2	2-1	7	Malcolm ^{18}, Robertson ^{24}	449
31	Apr 1	H	Stenhousemuir	W	3-0	1-0	8	Agnew ^{37}, Thomson, R ^{56}, Kassarate ^{87}	440
32	8	A	Albion R	L	0-3	0-1	8		377
33	15	H	Airdrieonians	W	2-1	1-0	8	McGuigan ^{12}, Turner ^{64}	489
34	22	A	Brechin C	D	0-0	0-0	8		403
35	29	A	Alloa Ath	L	0-1	0-0	8		507
36	May 6	H	East Fife	W	2-1	0-0	7	Malcolm ^{63}, Kassarate ^{84}	462

Final League Position: 7

Honours
League Champions: Second Division 1993-94, 1997-98. Third Division 2003-04.
Runners-up: Second Division 2004-05, Third Division 2007-08. League One: 2014-15. Promoted to Second Division 2011-12 (play-offs).
Scottish Cup: Quarter-finals 2003
League Challenge Cup Winners: 1996-97. Semi-finals: 2000-01, 2014-15.

Club colours: Shirt: Blue with white trim. Shorts: White. Socks: Blue.

Goalscorers: *League (46):* Malcolm 13, Gibson 8, Thomson R 4, Agnew 3, Bell 3, McGuigan 3, Thomson C 3, Kassarate 2, Nuttall 2, Turner 2, Dick 1, Nade 1, Robertson 1.
William Hill Scottish FA Cup (2): Gibson 1 (1 pen), own goal 1.
Betfred Scottish League Cup (5): McKeown 2, Malcolm 1, Nade 1, Turner 1.
IRN-BRU Scottish League Challenge Cup (8): Malcolm 4, McGuigan 2 (1 pen), Gibson 1, Turner 1.

Belford C 36	Robertson S 33 + 1	McKeown F 6 + 5	Bell S 32	Dick L 34	Turner K 20 + 8	Agnew S 28 + 5	Kemp C 1 + 3	McGuigan M 12 + 15	Malcolm C 31 + 3	Nade C 4 + 2	McCloskey S — + 1	Morena G 12 + 4	Barbour R 1	Thomson C 17 + 2	Thomson R 22 + 7	Gibson W 32 + 1	Barron D 24 + 1	Watt L 6 + 6	Nuttall J 8 + 1	Johnstone A — + 1	Wilson D 6 + 7	Neill M 12 + 1	Pettigrew C 10	Whittaker J — + 1	Donald M 9 + 3	Kassarate A — + 13	McGowan C — + 1	*Match No.*
1	2	3	4	5	6	7	8^{1}	9	10	11^{2}	12	13																1
1	3		4	5	13	8	14	12	10	11^{2}			2^{3}	6^{1}	7	9												2
1	2	3	4	5	12	7		11^{2}	10			13		6^{1}	8	9												3
1		3	4	5	12	8	14	11^{3}	10			13		6^{1}	7	9	2^{2}											4
1	2	3^{1}	4	5	6^{2}	8		11	10^{3}	12				13	7	9	14											5
1	3		4	5	6	13		11	10			8^{1}		7		9	2^{2}	12										6
1	2	14	3	5	8			11^{2}	10^{1}			7		6	12	9	4^{3}	13										7
1	2		3	5^{2}	8	14		11	10			7^{3}		6^{1}	13	9	4	12										8
1	3	14	4	5	8			11^{3}	10	13		7		6^{2}		9	2^{1}	12										9
1	2		3	5	7	13			10	11^{2}		8^{1}		6	12	9		4										10
1	2	12	3	5	7^{2}	14			10	11^{1}		8^{3}		6	13	9■		4										11
1	3	4^{1}	7	5	6	11		13	10			12		9	8^{2}			2										12
1	4		3	5	12			13	10			8^{1}		6^{2}	7	9		2	11									13
1	3	13	4	5	7^{1}	14		6	10^{2}					12	8	9	2^{3}		11									14
1	3		4	5	8	10^{1}		12				7		6		9	2^{2}	13	11									15
1	2		4		8	9		12				6		5	7	10		3	11^{1}									16
1	4	14	3■	5	8	10		13	12			7^{3}		6^{2}		9		2	11^{1}									17
1	3	4		5	8^{2}	10			12			7		6^{1}	2	9			11	13								18
1	3		4	5	7	10			12			8		6^{2}		9	2	13	11^{1}									19
1	3		4	5	7	10			11					6^{2}	13	9^{1}	2		12		8							20
1	2			5	7^{3}	8		12	10						13		3		9^{1}		6	4	11^{2}	14				21
1	6		7	5		8		12	10^{1}						9^{2}	11	2					4	3		13			22
1	2		6	5	12	9^{1}		13	11^{3}						7	8	3				14	4			10^{2}			23
1	3		6	5	12	9			11^{1}						7	8	4						2		10^{2}	13		24
1	3		7	5		9		13	11^{1}						6	8	4					14	2^{3}		10^{2}	12		25
1	2		7	5	12	9		14	11^{2}						6	8^{1}	3					4			10^{3}	13		26
1	2		7	5		9			11^{2}						6	8	3				13	4■			10^{1}	12		27
1	3		6^{3}		8^{1}	9		14	11						7	10	4				12		2		5^{2}	13		28
1	2		4	5	12	9	14	8^{2}	11^{3}						6	10					7^{1}		3			13		29
1	2		4	5		9^{3}		14	11^{1}						6	10	3				7^{2}	8			12	13		30
1			6	5		10		12	11^{2}						9	8^{3}	3				7^{1}	4	2		14	13		31
1	12		7^{2}	5		9			11						6	14	3				8^{3}	4	2		10^{1}	13		32
1	4			5	8	10		11^{1}	6							9^{2}	7				13	3	2			12		33
1	4			5	6^{3}	7		11^{1}	8						12	10	9				14	3	2^{2}			13		34
1	2		8	5		9		14	11^{3}						7	6^{2}	3				13	4			10^{1}	12		35
1	2		6	5^{3}		10			11^{1}						7	8	3				12	4			9^{2}	13	14	36

SCOTTISH LEAGUE HONOURS 1890–2017

*=Until 1921–22 season teams were equal if level on points, unless a play-off took place. §Not promoted after play-offs. *Won or placed on goal average (ratio), goal difference or most goals scored (goal average from 1921–22 until 1971–72 when it was replaced by goal difference). No official competition during 1939–46; Regional Leagues operated.*

DIVISION 1 (1890–91 to 1974–75) – TIER 1

Tier	Season	Max Pts	First	Pts	Second	Pts	Third	Pts
1	1890–91	36	Dumbarton=	29	Rangers=	29	Celtic	21
	Dumbarton and Rangers held title jointly after indecisive play-off ended 2-2. Celtic deducted 4 points for fielding an ineligible player.							
1	1891–92	44	Dumbarton	37	Celtic	35	Hearts	34
1	1892–93	36	Celtic	29	Rangers	28	St Mirren	20
1	1893–94	36	Celtic	29	Hearts	26	St Bernard's	23
1	1894–95	36	Hearts	31	Celtic	26	Rangers	22
1	1895–96	36	Celtic	30	Rangers	26	Hibernian	24
1	1896–97	36	Hearts	28	Hibernian	26	Rangers	25
1	1897–98	36	Celtic	33	Rangers	29	Hibernian	22
1	1898–99	36	Rangers	36	Hearts	26	Celtic	24
1	1899–1900	36	Rangers	32	Celtic	25	Hibernian	24
1	1900–01	40	Rangers	35	Celtic	29	Hibernian	25
1	1901–02	36	Rangers	28	Celtic	26	Hearts	22
1	1902–03	44	Hibernian	37	Dundee	31	Rangers	29
1	1903–04	52	Third Lanark	43	Hearts	39	Celtic / Rangers=	38
1	1904–05	52	Celtic=	41	Rangers=	41	Third Lanark	35
	Celtic won title after beating Rangers 2-1 in play-off.							
1	1905–06	60	Celtic	49	Hearts	43	Airdrieonians	38
1	1906–07	68	Celtic	55	Dundee	48	Rangers	45
1	1907–08	68	Celtic	55	Falkirk	51	Rangers	50
1	1908–09	68	Celtic	51	Dundee	50	Clyde	48
1	1909–10	68	Celtic	54	Falkirk	52	Rangers	46
1	1910–11	68	Rangers	52	Aberdeen	48	Falkirk	44
1	1911–12	68	Rangers	51	Celtic	45	Clyde	42
1	1912–13	68	Rangers	53	Celtic	49	Hearts / Airdrieonians=	41
1	1913–14	76	Celtic	65	Rangers	59	Hearts / Morton=	54
1	1914–15	76	Celtic	65	Hearts	61	Rangers	50
1	1915–16	76	Celtic	67	Rangers	56	Morton	51
1	1916–17	76	Celtic	64	Morton	54	Rangers	53
1	1917–18	68	Rangers	56	Celtic	55	Kilmarnock / Morton=	43
1	1918–19	68	Celtic	58	Rangers	57	Morton	47
1	1919–20	84	Rangers	71	Celtic	68	Motherwell	57
1	1920–21	84	Rangers	76	Celtic	66	Hearts	50
1	1921–22	84	Celtic	67	Rangers	66	Raith R	51
1	1922–23	76	Rangers	55	Airdrieonians	50	Celtic	46
1	1923–24	76	Rangers	59	Airdrieonians	50	Celtic	46
1	1924–25	76	Rangers	60	Airdrieonians	57	Hibernian	52
1	1925–26	76	Celtic	58	Airdrieonians*	50	Hearts	50
1	1926–27	76	Rangers	56	Motherwell	51	Celtic	49
1	1927–28	76	Rangers	60	Celtic*	55	Motherwell	55
1	1928–29	76	Rangers	67	Celtic	51	Motherwell	50
1	1929–30	76	Rangers	60	Motherwell	55	Aberdeen	53
1	1930–31	76	Rangers	60	Celtic	58	Motherwell	56
1	1931–32	76	Motherwell	66	Rangers	61	Celtic	48
1	1932–33	76	Rangers	62	Motherwell	59	Hearts	50
1	1933–34	76	Rangers	66	Motherwell	62	Celtic	47
1	1934–35	76	Rangers	55	Celtic	52	Hearts	50
1	1935–36	76	Celtic	66	Rangers*	61	Aberdeen	61
1	1936–37	76	Rangers	61	Aberdeen	54	Celtic	52
1	1937–38	76	Celtic	61	Hearts	58	Rangers	49
1	1938–39	76	Rangers	59	Celtic	48	Aberdeen	46
1	1946–47	60	Rangers	46	Hibernian	44	Aberdeen	39
1	1947–48	60	Hibernian	48	Rangers	46	Partick Thistle	36
1	1948–49	60	Rangers	46	Dundee	45	Hibernian	39
1	1949–50	60	Rangers	50	Hibernian	49	Hearts	43
1	1950–51	60	Hibernian	48	Rangers*	38	Dundee	38
1	1951–52	60	Hibernian	45	Rangers	41	East Fife	37
1	1952–53	60	Rangers*	43	Hibernian	43	East Fife	39
1	1953–54	60	Celtic	43	Hearts	38	Partick Thistle	35
1	1954–55	60	Aberdeen	49	Celtic	46	Rangers	41
1	1955–56	68	Rangers	52	Aberdeen	46	Hearts*	45
1	1956–57	68	Rangers	55	Hearts	53	Kilmarnock	42
1	1957–58	68	Hearts	62	Rangers	49	Celtic	46
1	1958–59	68	Rangers	50	Hearts	48	Motherwell	44
1	1959–60	68	Hearts	54	Kilmarnock	50	Rangers*	42
1	1960–61	68	Rangers	51	Kilmarnock	50	Third Lanark	42
1	1961–62	68	Dundee	54	Rangers	51	Celtic	46
1	1962–63	68	Rangers	57	Kilmarnock	48	Partick Thistle	46

1	1963–64	68	Rangers	55	Kilmarnock	49	Celtic*	47
1	1964–65	68	Kilmarnock*	50	Hearts	50	Dunfermline Ath	49
1	1965–66	68	Celtic	57	Rangers	55	Kilmarnock	45
1	1966–67	68	Celtic	58	Rangers	55	Clyde	46
1	1967–68	68	Celtic	63	Rangers	61	Hibernian	45
1	1968–69	68	Celtic	54	Rangers	49	Dunfermline Ath	45
1	1969–70	68	Celtic	57	Rangers	45	Hibernian	44
1	1970–71	68	Celtic	56	Aberdeen	54	St Johnstone	44
1	1971–72	68	Celtic	60	Aberdeen	50	Rangers	44
1	1972–73	68	Celtic	57	Rangers	56	Hibernian	45
1	1973–74	68	Celtic	53	Hibernian	49	Rangers	48
1	1974–75	68	Rangers	56	Hibernian	49	Celtic*	45

PREMIER DIVISION (1975–76 to 1997–98)

1	1975–76	72	Rangers	54	Celtic	48	Hibernian	43
1	1976–77	72	Celtic	55	Rangers	46	Aberdeen	43
1	1977–78	72	Rangers	55	Aberdeen	53	Dundee U	40
1	1978–79	72	Celtic	48	Rangers	45	Dundee U	44
1	1979–80	72	Aberdeen	48	Celtic	47	St Mirren	42
1	1980–81	72	Celtic	56	Aberdeen	49	Rangers*	44
1	1981–82	72	Celtic	55	Aberdeen	53	Rangers	43
1	1982–83	72	Dundee U	56	Celtic*	55	Aberdeen	55
1	1983–84	72	Aberdeen	57	Celtic	50	Dundee U	47
1	1984–85	72	Aberdeen	59	Celtic	52	Dundee U	47
1	1985–86	72	Celtic*	50	Hearts	50	Dundee U	47
1	1986–87	88	Rangers	69	Celtic	63	Dundee U	60
1	1987–88	88	Celtic	72	Hearts	62	Rangers	60
1	1988–89	72	Rangers	56	Aberdeen	50	Celtic	46
1	1989–90	72	Rangers	51	Aberdeen*	44	Hearts	44
1	1990–91	72	Rangers	55	Aberdeen	53	Celtic*	41
1	1991–92	88	Rangers	72	Hearts	63	Celtic	62
1	1992–93	88	Rangers	73	Aberdeen	64	Celtic	60
1	1993–94	88	Rangers	58	Aberdeen	55	Motherwell	54
1	1994–95	108	Rangers	69	Motherwell	54	Hibernian	53
1	1995–96	108	Rangers	87	Celtic	83	Aberdeen*	55
1	1996–97	108	Rangers	80	Celtic	75	Dundee U	60
1	1997–98	108	Celtic	74	Rangers	72	Hearts	67

PREMIER LEAGUE (1998–99 to 2012–13)

1	1998–99	108	Rangers	77	Celtic	71	St Johnstone	57
1	1999–2000	108	Rangers	90	Celtic	69	Hearts	54
1	2000–01	114	Celtic	97	Rangers	82	Hibernian	66
1	2001–02	114	Celtic	103	Rangers	85	Livingston	58
1	2002–03	114	Rangers*	97	Celtic	97	Hearts	63
1	2003–04	114	Celtic	98	Rangers	81	Hearts	68
1	2004–05	114	Rangers	93	Celtic	92	Hibernian*	61
1	2005–06	114	Celtic	91	Hearts	74	Rangers	73
1	2006–07	114	Celtic	84	Rangers	72	Aberdeen	65
1	2007–08	114	Celtic	89	Rangers	86	Motherwell	60
1	2008–09	114	Rangers	86	Celtic	82	Hearts	59
1	2009–10	114	Rangers	87	Celtic	81	Dundee U	63
1	2010–11	114	Rangers	93	Celtic	92	Hearts	63
1	2011–12	114	Celtic	93	Rangers	73	Motherwell	62
	Rangers deducted 10 points for entering administration.							
1	2012–13	114	Celtic	79	Motherwell	63	St Johnstone	56

SPFL SCOTTISH PREMIERSHIP (2013–14 to 2016–17)

1	2013–14	114	Celtic	99	Motherwell	70	Aberdeen	68
1	2014–15	114	Celtic	92	Aberdeen	75	Inverness CT	65
1	2015–16	114	Celtic	86	Aberdeen	71	Hearts	65
1	2016–17	114	Celtic	106	Aberdeen	76	Rangers	67

DIVISION 2 (1893–93 to 1974–75) – TIER 2

Tier	*Season*	*Max Pts*	*First*	*Pts*	*Second*	*Pts*	*Third*	*Pts*
2	1893–94	36	Hibernian	29	Cowlairs	27	Clyde	24
2	1894–95	36	Hibernian	30	Motherwell	22	Port Glasgow Ath	20
2	1895–96	36	Abercorn	27	Leith Ath	23	Renton / Kilmarnock=	21
2	1896–97	36	Partick Thistle	31	Leith Ath	27	Airdrieonians / Kilmarnock=	21
2	1897–98	36	Kilmarnock	29	Port Glasgow Ath	25	Morton	22
2	1898–99	36	Kilmarnock	32	Leith Ath	27	Port Glasgow Ath	25
2	1899–1900	36	Partick Thistle	29	Morton	28	Port Glasgow Ath	20
2	1900–01	36	St Bernard's	26	Airdrieonians	23	Abercorn	21
2	1901–02	44	Port Glasgow Ath	32	Partick Thistle	30	Motherwell	26
2	1902–03	44	Airdrieonians	35	Motherwell	28	Ayr U / Leith Ath=	27
2	1903–04	44	Hamilton A	37	Clyde	29	Ayr U	28
2	1904–05	44	Clyde	32	Falkirk	28	Hamilton A	27

2	1905–06	44	Leith Ath	34	Clyde	31	Albion R	27
2	1906–07	44	St Bernard's	32	Vale of Leven=	27	Arthurlie=	27
2	1907–08	44	Raith R	30	Dumbarton=	27	Ayr U=	27

Dumbarton deducted 2 points for registration irregularities.

2	1908–09	44	Abercorn	31	Raith R=	28	Vale of Leven=	28
2	1909–10	44	Leith Ath=	33	Raith R=	33	St Bernard's	27

Leith Ath and Raith R held title jointly, no play-off game played.

2	1910–11	44	Dumbarton	31	Ayr U	27	Albion R	25
2	1911–12	44	Ayr U	35	Abercorn	30	Dumbarton	27
2	1912–13	52	Ayr U	34	Dunfermline Ath	33	East Stirling	32
2	1913–14	44	Cowdenbeath	31	Albion R	27	Dunfermline Ath / Dundee U=	26
2	1914–15	52	Cowdenbeath=	37	St Bernard's=	37	Leith Ath=	37

Cowdenbeath won title after a round robin tournament between the three tied clubs.

2	1921–22	76	Alloa Ath	60	Cowdenbeath	47	Armadale	45
2	1922–23	76	Queen's Park	57	Clydebank	50	St Johnstone	48

Clydebank and St Johnstone both deducted 2 points for fielding an ineligible player.

2	1923–24	76	St Johnstone	56	Cowdenbeath	55	Bathgate	44
2	1924–25	76	Dundee U	50	Clydebank	48	Clyde	47
2	1925–26	76	Dunfermline Ath	59	Clyde	53	Ayr U	52
2	1926–27	76	Bo'ness	56	Raith R	49	Clydebank	45
2	1927–28	76	Ayr U	54	Third Lanark	45	King's Park	44
2	1928–29	72	Dundee U	51	Morton	50	Arbroath	47
2	1929–30	76	Leith Ath*	57	East Fife	57	Albion R	54
2	1930–31	76	Third Lanark	61	Dundee U	50	Dunfermline Ath	47
2	1931–32	76	East Stirling*	55	St Johnstone	55	Raith R*	46
2	1932–33	68	Hibernian	54	Queen of the South	49	Dunfermline Ath	47

Armadale and Bo'ness were expelled for failing to meet match guarantees. Their records were expunged.

2	1933–34	68	Albion R	45	Dunfermline Ath*	44	Arbroath	44
2	1934–35	68	Third Lanark	52	Arbroath	50	St Bernard's	47
2	1935–36	68	Falkirk	59	St Mirren	52	Morton	48
2	1936–37	68	Ayr U	54	Morton	51	St Bernard's	48
2	1937–38	68	Raith R	59	Albion R	48	Airdrieonians	47
2	1938–39	68	Cowdenbeath	60	Alloa Ath*	48	East Fife	48
2	1946–47	52	Dundee	45	Airdrieonians	42	East Fife	31
2	1947–48	60	East Fife	53	Albion R	42	Hamilton A	40
2	1948–49	60	Raith R*	42	Stirling Alb	42	Airdrieonians*	41
2	1949–50	60	Morton	47	Airdrieonians	44	Dunfermline Ath*	36
2	1950–51	60	Queen of the South*	45	Stirling Alb	45	Ayr U*	36
2	1951–52	60	Clyde	44	Falkirk	43	Ayr U	39
2	1952–53	60	Stirling Alb	44	Hamilton A	43	Queen's Park	37
2	1953–54	60	Motherwell	45	Kilmarnock	42	Third Lanark*	36
2	1954–55	60	Airdrieonians	46	Dunfermline Ath	42	Hamilton A	39
2	1955–56	72	Queen's Park	54	Ayr U	51	St Johnstone	49
2	1956–57	72	Clyde	64	Third Lanark	51	Cowdenbeath	45
2	1957–58	72	Stirling Alb	55	Dunfermline Ath	53	Arbroath	47
2	1958–59	72	Ayr U	60	Arbroath	51	Stenhousemuir	46
2	1959–60	72	St Johnstone	53	Dundee U	50	Queen of the South	49
2	1960–61	72	Stirling Alb	55	Falkirk	54	Stenhousemuir	50
2	1961–62	72	Clyde	54	Queen of the South	53	Morton	44
2	1962–63	72	St Johnstone	55	East Stirling	49	Morton	48
2	1963–64	72	Morton	67	Clyde	53	Arbroath	46
2	1964–65	72	Stirling Alb	59	Hamilton A	50	Queen of the South	45
2	1965–66	72	Ayr U	53	Airdrieonians	50	Queen of the South	47
2	1966–67	76	Morton	69	Raith R	58	Arbroath	57
2	1967–68	72	St Mirren	62	Arbroath	53	East Fife	49
2	1968–69	72	Motherwell	64	Ayr U	53	East Fife*	48
2	1969–70	72	Falkirk	56	Cowdenbeath	55	Queen of the South	50
2	1970–71	72	Partick Thistle	56	East Fife	51	Arbroath	46
2	1971–72	72	Dumbarton*	52	Arbroath	52	Stirling Alb*	50
2	1972–73	72	Clyde	56	Dumfermline Ath	52	Raith R*	47
2	1973–74	72	Airdrieonians	60	Kilmarnock	58	Hamilton A	55
2	1974–75	76	Falkirk	54	Queen of the South*	53	Montrose	53

Elected to First Division: 1894 Clyde; 1895 Hibernian; 1896 Abercorn; 1897 Partick Thistle; 1899 Kilmarnock; 1900 Morton and Partick Thistle; 1902 Port Glasgow and Partick Thistle; 1903 Airdrieonians and Motherwell; 1905 Falkirk and Aberdeen; 1906 Clyde and Hamilton A; 1910 Raith R; 1913 Ayr U and Dumbarton.

FIRST DIVISION (1975–76 to 2012–13)

2	1975–76	52	Partick Thistle	41	Kilmarnock	35	Montrose	30
2	1976–77	78	St Mirren	62	Clydebank	58	Dundee	51
2	1977–78	78	Morton*	58	Hearts	58	Dundee	57
2	1978–79	78	Dundee	55	Kilmarnock*	54	Clydebank	54
2	1979–80	78	Hearts	53	Airdrieonians	51	Ayr U*	44
2	1980–81	78	Hibernian	57	Dundee	52	St Johnstone	51
2	1981–82	78	Motherwell	61	Kilmarnock	51	Hearts	50
2	1982–83	78	St Johnstone	55	Hearts	54	Clydebank	50
2	1983–84	78	Morton	54	Dumbarton	51	Partick Thistle	46
2	1984–85	78	Motherwell	50	Clydebank	48	Falkirk	45
2	1985–86	78	Hamilton A	56	Falkirk	45	Kilmarnock*	44
2	1986–87	88	Morton	57	Dunfermline Ath	56	Dumbarton	53

2	1987–88	88	Hamilton A	56	Meadowbank Thistle	52	Clydebank	49
2	1988–89	78	Dunfermline Ath	54	Falkirk	52	Clydebank	48
2	1989–90	78	St Johnstone	58	Airdrieonians	54	Clydebank	44
2	1990–91	78	Falkirk	54	Airdrieonians	53	Dundee	52
2	1991–92	88	Dundee	58	Partick Thistle*	57	Hamilton A	57
2	1992–93	88	Raith R	65	Kilmarnock	54	Dunfermline Ath	52
2	1993–94	88	Falkirk	66	Dunfermline Ath	65	Airdrieonians	54
2	1994–95	108	Raith R	69	Dunfermline Ath*	68	Dundee	68
2	1995–96	108	Dunfermline Ath	71	Dundee U*	67	Greenock Morton	67
2	1996–97	108	St Johnstone	80	Airdrieonians	60	Dundee*	58
2	1997–98	108	Dundee	70	Falkirk	65	Raith R*	60
2	1998–99	108	Hibernian	89	Falkirk	66	Ayr U	62
2	1999–2000	108	St Mirren	76	Dunfermline Ath	71	Falkirk	68
2	2000–01	108	Livingston	76	Ayr U	69	Falkirk	56
2	2001–02	108	Partick Thistle	66	Airdrieonians	56	Ayr U*	52
2	2002–03	108	Falkirk	81	Clyde	72	St Johnstone	67
2	2003–04	108	Inverness CT	70	Clyde	69	St Johnstone	57
2	2004–05	108	Falkirk	75	St Mirren*	60	Clyde	60
2	2005–06	108	St Mirren	76	St Johnstone	66	Hamilton A	59
2	2006–07	108	Gretna	66	St Johnstone	65	Dundee*	53
2	2007–08	108	Hamilton A	76	Dundee	69	St Johnstone	58
2	2008–09	108	St Johnstone	65	Partick Thistle	55	Dunfermline Ath	51
2	2009–10	108	Inverness CT	73	Dundee	61	Dunfermline Ath	58
2	2010–11	108	Dunfermline Ath	70	Raith R	60	Falkirk	58
2	2011–12	108	Ross Co	79	Dundee	55	Falkirk	52
2	2012–13	108	Partick Thistle	78	Greenock Morton	67	Falkirk	53

SPFL SCOTTISH CHAMPIONSHIP (2013–14 to 2016–17)

2	2013–14	108	Dundee	69	Hamilton A	67	Falkirk§	66
2	2014–15	108	Hearts	91	Hibernian§	70	Rangers§	67
2	2015–16	108	Rangers	81	Falkirk*§	70	Hibernian§	70
2	2016–17	108	Hibernian	71	Falkirk§	60	Dundee U§	57

SECOND DIVISION (1975–76 to 2012–13) – TIER 3

Tier	*Season*	*Max Pts*	*First*	*Pts*	*Second*	*Pts*	*Third*	*Pts*
3	1975–76	52	Clydebank*	40	Raith R	40	Alloa Ath	35
3	1976–77	78	Stirling Alb	55	Alloa Ath	51	Dunfermline Ath	50
3	1977–78	78	Clyde*	53	Raith R	53	Dunfermline Ath*	48
3	1978–79	78	Berwick R	54	Dunfermline Ath	52	Falkirk	50
3	1979–80	78	Falkirk	50	East Stirling	49	Forfar Ath	46
3	1980–81	78	Queen's Park	50	Queen of the South	46	Cowdenbeath	45
3	1981–82	78	Clyde	59	Alloa Ath*	50	Arbroath	50
3	1982–83	78	Brechin C	55	Meadowbank Thistle	54	Arbroath	49
3	1983–84	78	Forfar Ath	63	East Fife	47	Berwick R	43
3	1984–85	78	Montrose	53	Alloa Ath	50	Dunfermline Ath	49
3	1985–86	78	Dunfermline Ath	57	Queen of the South	55	Meadowbank Thistle	49
3	1986–87	78	Meadowbank Thistle	55	Raith R*	52	Stirling Alb*	52
3	1987–88	78	Ayr U	61	St Johnstone	59	Queen's Park	51
3	1988–89	78	Albion R	50	Alloa Ath	45	Brechin C	43
3	1989–90	78	Brechin C	49	Kilmarnock	48	Stirling Alb	47
3	1990–91	78	Stirling Alb	54	Montrose	46	Cowdenbeath	45
3	1991–92	78	Dumbarton	52	Cowdenbeath	51	Alloa Ath	50
3	1992–93	78	Clyde	54	Brechin C*	53	Stranraer	53
3	1993–94	78	Stranraer	56	Berwick R	48	Stenhousemuir*	47
3	1994–95	108	Greenock Morton	64	Dumbarton	60	Stirling Alb	58
3	1995–96	108	Stirling Alb	81	East Fife	67	Berwick R	60
3	1996–97	108	Ayr U	77	Hamilton A	74	Livingston	64
3	1997–98	108	Stranraer	61	Clydebank	60	Livingston	59
3	1998–99	108	Livingston	77	Inverness CT	72	Clyde	53
3	1999–2000	108	Clyde	65	Alloa Ath	64	Ross Co	62
3	2000–01	108	Partick Thistle	75	Arbroath	58	Berwick R*	54
3	2001–02	108	Queen of the South	67	Alloa Ath	59	Forfar Ath	53
3	2002–03	108	Raith R	59	Brechin C	55	Airdrie U	54
3	2003–04	108	Airdrie U	70	Hamilton A	62	Dumbarton	60
3	2004–05	108	Brechin C	72	Stranraer	63	Greenock Morton	62
3	2005–06	108	Gretna	88	Greenock Morton§	70	Peterhead*§	57
3	2006–07	108	Greenock Morton	77	Stirling Alb	69	Raith R§	62
3	2007–08	108	Ross Co	73	Airdrie U	66	Raith R§	60
3	2008–09	108	Raith R	76	Ayr U	74	Brechin C§	62
3	2009–10	108	Stirling Alb*	65	Alloa Ath§	65	Cowdenbeath	59
3	2010–11	108	Livingston	82	Ayr U*	59	Forfar Ath§	59
3	2011–12	108	Cowdenbeath	71	Arbroath§	63	Dumbarton	58
3	2012–13	108	Queen of the South	92	Alloa Ath	67	Brechin C	61

SPFL SCOTTISH LEAGUE ONE (2013–14 to 2016–17)

3	2013–14	108	Rangers	102	Dunfermline Ath§	63	Stranraer§	51
3	2014–15	108	Greenock Morton	69	Stranraer§	67	Forfar Ath	66
3	2015–16	108	Dunfermline Ath	79	Ayr U	61	Peterhead§	59
3	2016–17	108	Livingston	81	Alloa Ath§	62	Airdrieonians§	52

THIRD DIVISION (1994–95 to 2012–13) – TIER 4

Tier	Season	Max Pts	First	Pts	Second	Pts	Third	Pts
4	1994–95	108	Forfar Ath	80	Montrose	67	Ross Co	60
4	1995–96	108	Livingston	72	Brechin C	63	Inverness CT	57
4	1996–97	108	Inverness CT	76	Forfar Ath*	67	Ross Co	67
4	1997–98	108	Alloa Ath	76	Arbroath	68	Ross Co	67
4	1998–99	108	Ross Co	77	Stenhousemuir	64	Brechin C	59
4	1999–2000	108	Queen's Park	69	Berwick R	66	Forfar Ath	61
4	2000–01	108	Hamilton A*	76	Cowdenbeath	76	Brechin C	72
4	2001–02	108	Brechin C	73	Dumbarton	61	Albion R	59
4	2002–03	108	Greenock Morton	72	East Fife	71	Albion R	70
4	2003–04	108	Stranraer	79	Stirling Alb	77	Gretna	68
4	2004–05	108	Gretna	98	Peterhead	78	Cowdenbeath	51
4	2005–06	108	Cowdenbeath*	76	Berwick R§	76	Stenhousemuir§	73
4	2006–07	108	Berwick R	75	Arbroath§	70	Queen's Park	68
4	2007–08	108	East Fife	88	Stranraer	65	Montrose§	59
4	2008–09	108	Dumbarton	67	Cowdenbeath	63	East Stirling§	61
4	2009–10	108	Livingston	78	Forfar Ath	63	East Stirling§	61
4	2010–11	108	Arbroath	66	Albion R	61	Queen's Park*§	59
4	2011–12	108	Alloa Ath	77	Queen's Park§	63	Stranraer	58
4	2012–13	108	Rangers	83	Peterhead§	59	Queen's Park§	56

SPFL SCOTTISH LEAGUE TWO (2013–14 to 2016–17)

Tier	Season	Max Pts	First	Pts	Second	Pts	Third	Pts
4	2013–14	108	Peterhead	76	Annan Ath§	63	Stirling Alb	57
4	2014–15	108	Albion R	71	Queen's Park§	61	Arbroath§	56
4	2015–16	108	East Fife	62	Elgin C§	59	Clyde§	56
4	2016–17	108	Abroath	66	Forfar Ath	64	Annan Ath§	58

RELEGATED CLUBS

RELEGATED FROM DIVISION I (1921–22 to 1973–74)

1921–22 *Dumbarton, Queen's Park, Clydebank
1922–23 Albion R, Alloa Ath
1923–24 Clyde, Clydebank
1924–25 Ayr U, Third Lanark
1925–26 Raith R, Clydebank
1926–27 Morton, Dundee U
1927–28 Bo'ness, Dunfermline Ath
1928–29 Third Lanark, Raith R
1929–30 Dundee U, St Johnstone
1930–31 Hibernian, East Fife
1931–32 Dundee U, Leith Ath
1932–33 Morton, East Stirling
1933–34 Third Lanark, Cowdenbeath
1934–35 St Mirren, Falkirk
1935–36 Airdrieonians, Ayr U
1936–37 Dunfermline Ath, Albion R
1937–38 Dundee, Morton
1938–39 Queen's Park, Raith R
1946–47 Kilmarnock, Hamilton A
1947–48 Airdrieonians, Queen's Park
1948–49 Morton, Albion R
1949–50 Queen of the South, Stirling Alb
1950–51 Clyde, Falkirk
1951–52 Morton, Stirling Alb
1952–53 Motherwell, Third Lanark
1953–54 Airdrieonians, Hamilton A
1954–55 *No clubs relegated as league extended to 18 teams*
1955–56 Clyde, Stirling Alb
1956–57 Dunfermline Ath, Ayr U
1957–58 East Fife, Queen's Park
1958–59 Falkirk, Queen of the South
1959–60 Stirling Alb, Arbroath
1960–61 Clyde, Ayr U
1961–62 St Johnstone, Stirling Alb
1962–63 Clyde, Raith R
1963–64 Queen of the South, East Stirling
1964–65 Airdrieonians, Third Lanark
1965–66 Morton, Hamilton A
1966–67 St Mirren, Ayr U
1967–68 Motherwell, Stirling Alb
1968–69 Falkirk, Arbroath
1969–70 Raith R, Partick Thistle
1970–71 St Mirren, Cowdenbeath
1971–72 Clyde, Dunfermline Ath
1972–73 Kilmarnock, Airdrieonians
1973–74 East Fife, Falkirk

**Season 1921–22 – only 1 club promoted, 3 clubs relegated.*

RELEGATED FROM PREMIER DIVISION (1974–75 to 1997–98)

1974–75 *No relegation due to League reorganisation*
1975–76 Dundee, St Johnstone
1976–77 Hearts, Kilmarnock
1977–78 Ayr U, Clydebank
1978–79 Hearts, Motherwell
1979–80 Dundee, Hibernian
1980–81 Kilmarnock, Hearts
1981–82 Partick Thistle, Airdrieonians
1982–83 Morton, Kilmarnock
1983–84 St Johnstone, Motherwell
1984–85 Dumbarton, Morton
1985–86 *No relegation due to League reorganisation*
1986–87 Clydebank, Hamilton A
1987–88 Falkirk, Dunfermline Ath, Morton
1988–89 Hamilton A
1989–90 Dundee
1990–91 *No clubs relegated*
1991–92 St Mirren, Dunfermline Ath
1992–93 Falkirk, Airdrieonians
1993–94 St Johnstone, Raith R, Dundee
1994–95 Dundee U
1995–96 Partick Thistle, Falkirk
1996–97 Raith R
1997–98 Hibernian

RELEGATED FROM PREMIER LEAGUE (1998–99 to 2012–13)

1998–99 Dunfermline Ath
1999–2000 *No relegation due to League reorganisation*
2000–01 St Mirren
2001–02 St Johnstone
2002–03 *No clubs relegated*
2003–04 Partick Thistle
2005–06 Livingston
2006–07 Dunfermline Ath
2007–08 Gretna
2008–09 Inverness CT
2009–10 Falkirk
2010–11 Hamilton A
2011–12 Dunfermline Ath, Rangers (demoted to Third Division)
2012–13 Dundee

RELEGATED FROM SPFL SCOTTISH PREMIERSHIP (2013–14 to 2016–17)

2013–14 Hibernian, Hearts
2014–15 St Mirren
2015–16 Dundee U
2016–17 Inverness CT

RELEGATED FROM FIRST DIVISION (1975–76 to 2012–13)

1975–76 Dunfermline Ath, Clyde
1976–77 Raith R, Falkirk
1977–78 Alloa Ath, East Fife
1978–79 Montrose, Queen of the South
1979–80 Arbroath, Clyde
1980–81 Stirling Alb, Berwick R
1981–82 East Stirling, Queen of the South
1982–83 Dunfermline Ath, Queen's Park
1983–84 Raith R, Alloa Ath
1984–85 Meadowbank Thistle, St Johnstone
1985–86 Ayr U, Alloa Ath
1986–87 Brechin C, Montrose
1987–88 East Fife, Dumbarton
1988–89 Kilmarnock, Queen of the South
1989–90 Albion R, Alloa Ath
1990–91 Clyde, Brechin C
1991–92 Montrose, Forfar Ath
1992–93 Meadowbank Thistle, Cowdenbeath
1993–94 Dumbarton, Stirling Alb, Clyde, Morton, Brechin C
1994–95 Ayr U, Stranraer
1995–96 Hamilton A, Dumbarton
1996–97 Clydebank, East Fife
1997–98 Partick Thistle, Stirling Alb
1998–99 Hamilton A, Stranraer
1999–2000 Clydebank
2000–01 Greenock Morton, Alloa Ath
2001–02 Raith R
2002–03 Alloa Ath, Arbroath
2003–04 Ayr U, Brechin C
2004–05 Partick Thistle, Raith R
2005–06 Stranraer, Brechin C
2006–07 Airdrie U, Ross Co
2007–08 Stirling Alb
2008–09 Livingstone *(for breaching rules)*, Clyde
2009–10 Airdrie U, Ayr U
2010–11 Cowdenbeath, Stirling Alb
2011–12 Ayr U, Queen of the South
2012–13 Dunfermline Ath, Airdrie U

RELEGATED FROM SPFL SCOTTISH CHAMPIONSHIP (2013–14 to 2016–17)

2013–14 Greenock Morton
2014–15 Cowdenbeath
2015–16 Livingston, Alloa Ath
2016–17 Raith R, Ayr U

RELEGATED FROM SECOND DIVISION (1993–94 to 2012–13)

1993–94 Alloa Ath, Forfar Ath, East Stirlingshire, Montrose, Queen's Park, Arbroath, Albion R, Cowdenbeath
1994–95 Meadowbank Thistle, Brechin C
1995–96 Forfar Ath, Montrose
1996–97 Dumbarton, Berwick R
1997–98 Stenhousemuir, Brechin C
1998–99 East Fife, Forfar Ath
1999–2000 Hamilton A *(after being deducted 15 points)*
2000–01 Queen's Park, Stirling Alb
2001–02 Greenock Morton
2002–03 Stranraer, Cowdenbeath
2003–04 East Fife, Stenhousemuir
2004–05 Arbroath, Berwick R
2005–06 Dumbarton
2006–07 Stranraer, Forfar Ath
2007–08 Cowdenbeath, Berwick R
2008–09 Queen's Park, Stranraer
2009–10 Arbroath, Clyde
2010–11 Alloa Ath, Peterhead
2011–12 Stirling Alb
2012–13 Albion R

RELEGATED FROM SPFL SCOTTISH LEAGUE ONE (2013–14 to 2016–17)

2013–14 East Fife, Arbroath
2014–15 Stirling Alb
2015–16 Cowdenbeath, Forfar Ath
2016–17 Peterhead, Stenhousmuir

RELEGATED FROM SPFL SCOTTISH LEAGUE TWO (2015–16 to 2016–17)

2015–16 East Stirlingshire
2016–17 None

SCOTTISH LEAGUE CHAMPIONSHIP WINS

Rangers 54, Celtic 48, Aberdeen 4, Hearts 4, Hibernian 4, Dumbarton 2, Dundee 1, Dundee U 1, Kilmarnock 1, Motherwell 1, Third Lanark 1.

The totals for Rangers and Dumbarton each include the shared championship of 1890–91.

Since the formation of the Scottish Football League in 1890, there have been periodic reorganisations of the leagues to allow for expansion, improve competition and commercial aspects of the game. The table below lists the league names by tier and chronology. This table can be used to assist when studying the records.

Tier	Division	
1	Scottish League Division I	1890–1939
	Scottish League Division A	1946–1956
	Scottish League Division I	1956–1975
	Premier Division	1975–1998
	Scottish Premier League	1998–2013
	SPFL Premiership	2013–
2	Scottish League Division II	1893–1939
	Scottish League Division B	1946–1956
	Scottish League Division II	1956–1975
	First Division	1975–2013
	SPFL Championship	2013–
3	Scottish League Division III	1923–1926
	Scottish League Division C	1946–1949
	Second Division	1975–2013
	SPFL League One	2013–
4	Third Division	1994–2013
	SPFL League Two	2013–

In 2013–14 the SPFL introduced play-offs to determine a second promotion/relegation place for the Premiership, Championship and League One.

The team finishing second bottom of the Premiership plays two legs against the team from the Championship that won the eliminator games played between the teams finishing second, third and fourth.

For both the Championship and League One, the team finishing second bottom joins the teams from second, third and fourth places of the lower league in a play-off series of two-legged semi-finals and finals.

In 2014–15 a play-off was introduced for promotion/relegation from League Two. The team finishing bottom of League Two plays two legs against the victors of the eliminator games between the winners of the Highland and Lowland leagues.

SCOTTISH LEAGUE PLAY-OFFS 2016–17

▪ *Denotes player sent off.*

PREMIERSHIP QUARTER-FINAL FIRST LEG

Tuesday, 9 May 2017

Greenock Morton (1) 1 *(O'Ware 7)*

Dundee U (0) 2 *(Murray 51, Spittal 65)* 3306

Greenock Morton: (442) Gaston; McDonagh, O'Ware, Lamie, Russell; Forbes (Doyle 76), Murdoch, Lindsay, Tidser (Tiffoney 90); Oliver, Shankland (Oyenuga 81).
Dundee U: (442) Bell; Murdoch, Durnan, Edjenguele, Robson; Andreu, Kuate, Flood, Spittal; Murray (Coote 90), Mikkelsen (Allardice 85).
Referee: William Collum.

PREMIERSHIP QUARTER-FINAL SECOND LEG

Friday, 12 May 2017

Dundee U (0) 3 *(Murray 52, Kuate 64, Spittal 81)*

Greenock Morton (0) 0 6606

Dundee U: (442) Bell; Murdoch, Durnan, Edjenguele, Robson; Spittal, Flood (Telfer 66), Kuate, Andreu; Murray (Coote 84), Mikkelsen (Fraser 84).
Greenock Morton: (442) McGowan; Doyle, Lamie, O'Ware, Russell; Nesbitt (McDonagh 72), Murdoch, Lindsay (Shankland 69), Forbes (Tidser 63); Oliver, Oyenuga.
Dundee U won 5-1 on aggregate.
Referee: Andrew Dallas.

PREMIERSHIP SEMI-FINAL FIRST LEG

Tuesday, 16 May 2017

Dundee U (1) 2 *(Murray 16, Spittal 53)*

Falkirk (1) 2 *(Craigen 27, McKee 59)* 7034

Dundee U: (4231) Bell; Murdoch (Dillon 8), Durnan, Edjenguele, Robson (Dixon 80); Kuate (Telfer 64), Flood; Spittal, Andreu, Murray; Mikkelsen.
Falkirk: (442) Thomson; Muirhead, Gasparotto, Grant, Leahy; Craigen, McKee, Kerr, Sibbald (Taiwo 75); Austin (McHugh 80), Miller (Baird 64).
Referee: Bobby Madden.

PREMIERSHIP SEMI-FINAL SECOND LEG

Friday, 19 May 2017

Falkirk (1) 1 *(Craigen 11)*

Dundee U (0) 2 *(Murray 76, Dixon 87)* 7926

Falkirk: (442) Thomson; Muirhead, Watson, Gasparotto, Leahy; Craigen (Hippolyte 79), McKee (Taiwo 54), Kerr, Sibbald; Baird (McHugh 61), Austin.
Dundee U: (442) Bell; Dillon, Durnan, Edjenguele, Dixon; Andreu, Kuate, Flood (Telfer 70), Spittal; Murray, Mikkelsen (Fraser 70 (Nicholls 79)).
Dundee U won 4-3 on aggregate.
Referee: Kevin Clancy.

PREMIERSHIP FINAL FIRST LEG

Thursday, 25 May 2017

Dundee U (0) 0

Hamilton A (0) 0 9386

Dundee U: (442) Bell; Dillon, Durnan, Edjenguele, Dixon; Andreu (Nicholls 88), Kuate (Telfer 57), Flood, Spittal; Murray▪, Mikkelsen.
Hamilton A: (442) Matthews; Skondras, Gogic, Donati, McMann; Imrie, Redmond (Docherty 74), MacKinnon, Crawford; Bingham (D'Acol 80), Templeton (Longridge 63).
Referee: Steven McLean.

PREMIERSHIP FINAL SECOND LEG

Sunday, 28 May 2017

Hamilton A (0) 1 *(Docherty 64)*

Dundee U (0) 0 5027

Hamilton A: (4231) Matthews; Skondras, Gillespie, Gogic, McMann; Docherty (Lyon 78), Redmond; Imrie, Crawford, Templeton (Longridge 55); Bingham (Sarris 87).
Dundee U: (4312) Bell; Dillon, Durnan, Edjenguele, Dixon; Spittal, Flood, Telfer (Fraser 71); Andreu; Murray, Mikkelsen.
Hamilton A won 1-0 on aggregate.
Referee: Craig Thomson.

CHAMPIONSHIP SEMI-FINALS FIRST LEG

Wednesday, 10 May 2017

Airdrieonians (0) 1 *(Ryan 52)*

Alloa Ath (0) 0 1199

Airdrieonians: (3421) Ferguson; McIntosh, Mensing, Gorman; Stewart, Hutton, Conroy, MacDonald; Brown, Russell I (Leitch 86); Ryan (McKay 90).
Alloa Ath: (442) Parry; Taggart, McKeown, Graham, Waters; Cawley, Flannigan, Kirkpatrick (McCluskey 78), Holmes (Robertson 67); Spence, Mackin (Hetherington 63).
Referee: Stephen Finnie.

Brechin C (1) 1 *(Caldwell 45 (pen))*

Raith R (0) 1 *(McManus 70)* 1022

Brechin C: (4411) Smith G; Lynas, Fusco, McLean, Dyer; Ford, Graham, Dale, Watt; Jackson A; Caldwell.
Raith R: (442) Brennan; Thomson, Mvoto, Barr C, Benedictus; Matthews, Davidson, Skacel (Hardie 57), Handling; McManus, Court (Johnston 68).
Referee: Don Robertson.

CHAMPIONSHIP SEMI-FINALS SECOND LEG

Saturday, 13 May 2017

Alloa Ath (0) 1 *(Robertson 50)*

Airdrieonians (0) 0 1181

Alloa Ath: (442) Parry; Taggart, McKeown, Graham, Waters; Cawley (Martin 106), Robertson, Flannigan (McCluskey 86), Kirkpatrick; Spence (Hetherington 74), Mackin.
Airdrieonians: (352) Ferguson; McIntosh, Gorman, Mensing (Boateng 90); Stewart, Brown (Leitch 63), Hutton, Conroy (Loudon 107), MacDonald; Ryan, Russell I.
aet; Alloa Ath won 4-3 on penalties.
Referee: Barry Cook.

Raith R (0) 3 *(Mvoto 68, McManus 90, Hardie 103)*

Brechin C (0) 3 *(Caldwell 51, Trouten 84, Watt 115)* 2932

Raith R: (442) Brennan; Thomson, Barr C, Mvoto, Benedictus (Robertson 65); Matthews (Thompson 65), Davidson, Handling, McManus; Hardie, Court (Barr B 64).
Brechin C: (442) Smith G; Lynas, Fusco, McLean, Dyer; Watt, Graham (Love 100), Dale, Ford (O'Neil 75); Jackson A, Caldwell (Trouten 76).
aet; Brechin C won 4-3 on penalties.
Referee: Alan Muir.

CHAMPIONSHIP FINAL FIRST LEG

Wednesday, 17 May 2017

Brechin C (0) 1 *(Ford 56)*

Alloa Ath (0) 0 702

Brechin C: (442) Smith G; Lynas, Fusco, McLean, Dyer; Watt, Graham, Dale, Ford; Jackson A, Caldwell (Love 90).
Alloa Ath: (451) Parry; Taggart, Graham, McKeown, Waters; Cawley (Spence 64), Kirkpatrick, Hetherington (McCluskey 64), Robertson, Flannigan (Martin 81); Mackin.
Referee: Euan Anderson.

CHAMPIONSHIP FINAL SECOND LEG
Saturday, 20 May 2017
Alloa Ath (2) 4 *(Spence 36 (pen), 40, 74, Mackin 79)*
Brechin C (1) 3 *(Dale 34, McLean 54, Watt 78)* 1204
Alloa Ath: (442) Parry; Taggart, McKeown, Graham, Waters; Cawley (McCluskey 65), Robertson (Holmes 71), Kirkpatrick, Flannigan; Spence, Mackin (Martin 95).
Brechin C: (442) Smith G; Lynas, McLean, Fusco, Dyer; Watt, Graham (Love 80), Dale, Ford (Trouten 46); Jackson A, Caldwell (Hill 46).
aet; Brechin C won 5-4 on penalties.
Referee: Nick Walsh.

LEAGUE ONE SEMI-FINALS FIRST LEG
Wednesday, 10 May 2017
Annan Ath (2) 2 *(Weatherson 4, Smith 16)*
Forfar Ath (0) 2 *(Travis 81, Fotheringham 82)* 629
Annan Ath: (442) Currie; Home, Krissian, Swinglehurst, Lucas; Omar, Cuddihy, Skelton (Wright 48), Flanagan (McKenna 86); Weatherson (Osadolor 73), Smith.
Forfar Ath: (3421) Adam; Munro, O'Brien, Travis; Bain, Swankie, Fotheringham, McLaughlin; Cox, Denholm; James Lister.
Referee: Crawford Allan.

Montrose (1) 1 *(Templeman 14)*
Peterhead (1) 1 *(Strachan 10)* 1251
Montrose: (442) Fleming; Ballantyne, Pascazio, Allan, Steeves; Webster (Masson 69), Watson (Campbell I 80), Callaghan, Smith; Templeman, Fraser (Hay 69).
Peterhead: (442) Smith G; Craig Reid, Strachan, Ross (Gordon 71), Noble; Stevenson, Brown S, Redman, Anderson (McIntosh 74); McAllister, Brown J (Riley 67).
Referee: Mat Northcroft.

LEAGUE ONE SEMI-FINALS SECOND LEG
Saturday, 13 May 2017
Forfar Ath (3) 4 *(Swankie 12, 37, Denholm 32, Bain 73)*
Annan Ath (0) 2 *(Smith 50 (pen), Ramsay 67)* 665
Forfar Ath: (3421) Adam; Travis, O'Brien, Malone E; Bain, Swankie, Fotheringham (Milne 88), McLaughlin; Cox, Denholm (Malone A 84); James Lister (Scott 84).
Annan Ath: (442) Currie; Home, Krissian, Swinglehurst, Stewart (McKenna 74); Omar, Skelton (Wright 84), Cuddihy, Flanagan (Ramsay 57); Weatherson, Smith.
Forfar Ath won 6-4 on aggregate.
Referee: John McKendrick.

Peterhead (1) 3 *(McAllister 34, 51 (pen), Brown J 90)*
Montrose (0) 0 1096
Peterhead: (4231) Smith G; Craig Reid, Strachan, Gordon, McMullin; Brown S (Redman 23), Ferry (Anderson 76); Stevenson, Brown J, Riley (McIntosh 73); McAllister.
Montrose: (442) Fleming; Ballantyne, Allan, Pascazio, Steeves; Webster (McWalter 70), Masson, Watson, Callaghan (Ferguson 46); Smith■, Templeman (Hay 77).
Peterhead won 4-1 on aggregate.
Referee: Steven Kirkland.

LEAGUE ONE FINAL FIRST LEG
Wednesday, 17 May 2017
Forfar Ath (0) 2 *(Fotheringham 54, Travis 74)*
Peterhead (1) 1 *(McAllister 3)* 958
Forfar Ath: (442) Adam; Bain, O'Brien, Travis, McLaughlin; Cox, Malone E, Fotheringham (Peters 85), Denholm; James Lister (Milne 85), Swankie (Malone A 65).
Peterhead: (4411) Smith G; Craig Reid (McIntosh 57), Strachan, Gordon, McMullin■; Stevenson (Blockley 61), Brown S, Redman, Anderson; Brown J (Ross 52); McAllister.
Referee: Stephen Finnie.

LEAGUE ONE FINAL SECOND LEG
Saturday, 20 May 2017
Peterhead (0) 1 *(Brown S 78)*
Forfar Ath (2) 5 *(Milne 5, Cox 17, Denholm 51, Malone A 68, Peters 83)* 1084
Peterhead: (442) Smith G; Strachan (Blockley 76), Ross, Gordon, McMullin (Anderson 53); Stevenson, Brown S, Ferry, Redman (Smith A 64); Riley, McIntosh.
Forfar Ath: (442) Adam; Bain, O'Brien, Travis, McLaughlin; Cox, Malone E, Fotheringham (Malone A 34 (Peters 83)), Denholm (Scott 64); James Lister, Milne.
Forfar Ath won 7-2 on aggregate.
Referee: Gavin Duncan.

LEAGUE TWO SEMI-FINAL FIRST LEG
Saturday, 29 April 2017
Buckie Thistle (2) 2 *(Angus 9, Urquhart 34 (pen))*
East Kilbride (1) 2 *(Woods 45, McLean R 84)*
Buckie Thistle: (4231) Bell; Wood, Munro, MacKinnon, Maitland (Carrol 36); Fraser K, McLean C; Taylor, Angus, Urquhart; McLeod (Ross 75).
East Kilbride: (442) McGinley; Capuano, Proctor, Howie, Russell; Winter (McLean R 77), McLeish (McBride 60), Gibbons, Strachan; Woods, Victoria.
Referee: David Munro.

LEAGUE TWO SEMI-FINAL SECOND LEG
Saturday, 6 May 2017
East Kilbride (2) 2 *(Winter 5, Victoria 21)*
Buckie Thistle (1) 1 *(Proctor 32 (og))*
East Kilbride: (442) McGinley; Capuano (Stevenson 84), Proctor, Howie, Russell; Winter, McLeish, Gibbons (Hughes 66), Strachan; Woods (McLean R 81), Victoria.
Buckie Thistle: (4231) Bell; Copeland■, Munro, MacKinnon, Carrol; Fraser K, McLean C; Taylor, Angus■, Urquhart (Fraser J 88); McLeod (Ross 64).
East Kilbride won 4-3 on aggregate.
Referee: Euan Anderson.

LEAGUE TWO FINAL FIRST LEG
Saturday, 13 May 2017
East Kilbride (0) 0
Cowdenbeath (0) 0 548
East Kilbride: (442) McGinley; Capuano (Stevenson 90), Proctor, Howie, Russell; Winter, Gibbons, Strachan, McLeish; Woods (McLean R 90), Victoria.
Cowdenbeath: (442) Sneddon; Rumsby, McLauchlan, Syme, Mullen; Moore, Carrick, Henderson (Buchanan 82), Miller; Kris Renton, Pyper.
Referee: Gavin Duncan.

LEAGUE TWO FINAL SECOND LEG
Saturday, 20 May 2017
Cowdenbeath (1) 1 *(Mullen 3)*
East Kilbride (0) 1 *(Gibbons 64)* 1676
Cowdenbeath: (442) Sneddon; Syme, Rumsby, McLauchlan, Pyper; Buchanan (Moore 85), Mullen, Miller (O'Brien 85), Henderson; Kris Renton, Carrick (Johnston 110).
East Kilbride: (4411) McGinley; Stevenson (McLaren 90), Proctor, Howie, Russell (Coll 107); Winter (McLean R 115), McLeish, Gibbons, Strachan; Victoria; Woods.
aet; Cowdenbeath won 5-3 on penalties.
Referee: Craig Charleston.

SCOTTISH LEAGUE CUP FINALS 1946–2017

SCOTTISH LEAGUE CUP

1946–47	Rangers v Aberdeen	4-0
1947–48	East Fife v Falkirk	0-0*
Replay	East Fife v Falkirk	4-1
1948–49	Rangers v Raith R	2-0
1949–50	East Fife v Dunfermline Ath	3-0
1950–51	Motherwell v Hibernian	3-0
1951–52	Dundee v Rangers	3-2
1952–53	Dundee v Kilmarnock	2-0
1953–54	East Fife v Partick Thistle	3-2
1954–55	Hearts v Motherwell	4-2
1955–56	Aberdeen v St Mirren	2-1
1956–57	Celtic v Partick Thistle	0-0*
Replay	Celtic v Partick Thistle	3-0
1957–58	Celtic v Rangers	7-1
1958–59	Hearts v Partick Thistle	5-1
1959–60	Hearts v Third Lanark	2-1
1960–61	Rangers v Kilmarnock	2-0
1961–62	Rangers v Hearts	1-1*
Replay	Rangers v Hearts	3-1
1962–63	Hearts v Kilmarnock	1-0
1963–64	Rangers v Morton	5-0
1964–65	Rangers v Celtic	2-1
1965–66	Celtic v Rangers	2-1
1966–67	Celtic v Rangers	1-0
1967–68	Celtic v Dundee	5-3
1968–69	Celtic v Hibernian	6-2
1969–70	Celtic v St Johnstone	1-0
1970–71	Rangers v Celtic	1-0
1971–72	Partick Thistle v Celtic	4-1
1972–73	Hibernian v Celtic	2-1
1973–74	Dundee v Celtic	1-0
1974–75	Celtic v Hibernian	6-3
1975–76	Rangers v Celtic	1-0
1976–77	Aberdeen v Celtic	2-1*
1977–78	Rangers v Celtic	2-1*
1978–79	Rangers v Aberdeen	2-1

BELL'S LEAGUE CUP

1979–80	Dundee U v Aberdeen	0-0*
Replay	Dundee U v Aberdeen	3-0
1980–81	Dundee U v Dundee	3-0

SCOTTISH LEAGUE CUP

1981–82	Rangers v Dundee U	2-1
1982–83	Celtic v Rangers	2-1
1983–84	Rangers v Celtic	3-2*

SKOL CUP

1984–85	Rangers v Dundee U	1-0
1985–86	Aberdeen v Hibernian	3-0
1986–87	Rangers v Celtic	2-1
1987–88	Rangers v Aberdeen	3-3*
	Rangers won 5-3 on penalties.	
1988–89	Rangers v Aberdeen	3-2
1989–90	Aberdeen v Rangers	2-1*
1990–91	Rangers v Celtic	2-1*
1991–92	Hibernian v Dunfermline Ath	2-0
1992–93	Rangers v Aberdeen	2-1*

SCOTTISH LEAGUE CUP

1993–94	Rangers v Hibernian	2-1

COCA-COLA CUP

1994–95	Raith R v Celtic	2-2*
	Raith R won 6-5 on penalties.	
1995–96	Aberdeen v Dundee	2-0
1996–97	Rangers v Hearts	4-3
1997–98	Celtic v Dundee U	3-0

SCOTTISH LEAGUE CUP

1998–99	Rangers v St Johnstone	2-1

CIS INSURANCE CUP

1999–2000	Celtic v Aberdeen	2-0
2000–01	Celtic v Kilmarnock	3-0
2001–02	Rangers v Ayr U	4-0
2002–03	Rangers v Celtic	2-1
2003–04	Livingston v Hibernian	2-0
2004–05	Rangers v Motherwell	5-1
2005–06	Celtic v Dunfermline Ath	3-0
2006–07	Hibernian v Kilmarnock	5-1
2007–08	Rangers v Dundee U	2-2*
	Rangers won 3-2 on penalties.	

CO-OPERATIVE INSURANCE CUP

2008–09	Celtic v Rangers	2-0*
2009–10	Rangers v St Mirren	1-0
2010–11	Rangers v Celtic	2-1*

SCOTTISH COMMUNITIES LEAGUE CUP

2011–12	Kilmarnock v Celtic	1-0
2012–13	St Mirren v Hearts	3-2
2013–14	Aberdeen v Inverness CT	0-0*
	Aberdeen won 4-2 on penalties.	

SCOTTISH LEAGUE CUP PRESENTED BY QTS

2014–15	Celtic v Dundee U	2-0
2015–16	Ross Co v Hibernian	2-1

BETFRED SCOTTISH LEAGUE CUP

2016–17	Celtic v Aberdeen	3-0

**After extra time.*

SCOTTISH LEAGUE CUP WINS

Rangers 27, Celtic 16 Aberdeen 6, Hearts 4, Dundee 3, East Fife 3, Hibernian 3, Dundee U 2, Kilmarnock 1, Livingston 1, Motherwell 1, Partick Thistle 1, Raith R 1, Ross Co 1, St Mirren 1.

APPEARANCES IN FINALS

Rangers 34, Celtic 31 Aberdeen 14, Hibernian 10, Dundee U 7, Hearts 7, Dundee 6, Kilmarnock 6, Partick Thistle 4, Dunfermline Ath 3, East Fife 3, Motherwell 3, St Mirren 3, Raith R 2, St Johnstone 2, Ayr U 1, Falkirk 1, Inverness CT 1, Livingston 1, Morton 1, Ross Co 1, Third Lanark 1.

BETFRED SCOTTISH LEAGUE CUP 2016–17

▪ *Denotes player sent off.*
PW = won on penalties. PL = lost on penalties.

FIRST ROUND

NORTH SECTION – GROUP A

Saturday, 16 July 2016

East Fife (0) 1 *(Smith 78)*
Dundee (1) 1 *(Hemmings 36)* 1407
East Fife won 4-2 on penalties.

Forfar Ath (1) 2 *(Peters 36, O'Brien 62)*
Dumbarton (0) 2 *(Gallagher 54, Fleming 69 (pen))* 426
Forfar Ath won 5-3 on penalties.

Tuesday, 19 July 2016

Dumbarton (0) 0
East Fife (2) 2 *(Smith 19, McManus 39)* 452

Peterhead (2) 2 *(Munro 20 (og), McAllister 34 (pen))*
Forfar Ath (0) 0 508

Saturday, 23 July 2016

Dundee (1) 6 *(Stewart 16, 74, 80, Hemmings 48, 85, O'Dea 73)*
Dumbarton (2) 2 *(Wright 26, Buchanan 33)* 2319

East Fife (1) 2 *(Page 38, McManus 50 (pen))*
Peterhead (1) 1 *(Brown J 26)* 532

Tuesday, 26 July 2016

Forfar Ath (1) 2 *(James Lister 20, Munro 50)*
East Fife (0) 0 565

Peterhead (0) 2 *(McAllister 62, 88 (pen))*
Dundee (0) 1 *(Stewart 90)* 998

Saturday, 30 July 2016

Dumbarton (2) 3 *(Thomson R 21, Smith 36, Stevenson 48 (pen))*
Peterhead (1) 3 *(Dzierzawski 16, McIntosh 57, McAllister 69 (pen))* 305
Peterhead won 6-5 on penalties.

Dundee (3) 7 *(McGowan 18, Duffy 34, Stewart 39, 64, Etxabeguren Leanizbarrutia 55, Loy 72, Teijsse 88)*
Forfar Ath (0) 0 2219

Group A – Table	P	W	PW	PL	L	F	A	GD	Pts
Peterhead	4	2	1	0	1	8	6	2	8
East Fife	4	2	1	0	1	5	4	1	8
Dundee	4	2	0	1	1	15	5	10	7
Forfar Ath	4	1	1	0	2	4	11	–7	5
Dumbarton	4	0	0	2	2	7	13	–6	2

NORTH SECTION – GROUP B

Saturday, 16 July 2016

Elgin C (0) 1 *(Duff 48)*
St Johnstone (1) 3 *(Swanson 16, Cummins 71, MacLean 79)* 1046

Stirling Alb (1) 1 *(Smith D 41)*
Falkirk (0) 0 1315

Tuesday, 19 July 2016

Brechin C (1) 2 *(Love 14, Trouten 87)*
Stirling Alb (1) 1 *(Henderson 38 (pen))* 362

Falkirk (2) 3 *(Vaulks 28, Miller 36, McHugh 88)*
Elgin C (0) 0 1278

Saturday, 23 July 2016

Elgin C (2) 4 *(Gunn 11, 45 (pen), Moore 61, McHardy 66)*
Brechin C (1) 2 *(Dyer 30, Trouten 68 (pen))* 506

St Johnstone (2) 3 *(Swanson 25 (pen), 38 (pen), Shaughnessy 68)*
Falkirk (0) 0 2725

Tuesday, 26 July 2016

Brechin C (1) 1 *(Jackson A 35)*
St Johnstone (0) 1 *(Kane 86)* 912
Brechin C won 4-2 on penalties.

Stirling Alb (1) 4 *(Ferns 11, Henderson 48, 71, 74 (pen))*
Elgin C (1) 1 *(MacLeod 12)* 522

Saturday, 30 July 2016

Falkirk (0) 2 *(Gasparotto 50, Austin 53)*
Brechin C (0) 0 1073

St Johnstone (3) 4 *(Anderson 4, MacLean 33, Craig 43, Wotherspoon 90)*
Stirling Alb (0) 0 2858

Group B – Table	P	W	PW	PL	L	F	A	GD	Pts
St Johnstone	4	3	0	1	0	11	2	9	10
Falkirk	4	2	0	0	2	5	4	1	6
Stirling Alb	4	2	0	0	2	6	7	–1	6
Brechin C	4	1	1	0	2	5	8	–3	5
Elgin C	4	1	0	0	3	6	12	–6	3

NORTH SECTION – GROUP C

Friday, 15 July 2016

Arbroath (0) 1 *(Hamilton 90)*
Dundee U (0) 1 *(Anier 85)* 3124
Dundee U won 5-3 on penalties.

Saturday, 16 July 2016

Cowdenbeath (1) 1 *(Brett 23)*
Inverness CT (1) 2 *(Draper 13, Warren 74)* 487

Tuesday, 19 July 2016

Dundee U (4) 6 *(Murray 4, 32, 72, Toshney 9, Smith C 21, Anier 88)*
Cowdenbeath (1) 1 *(Turner 25)* 3360

Dunfermline Ath (1) 3 *(Moffat 44, 66, Geggan 62)*
Arbroath (0) 0 1974

Saturday, 23 July 2016

Cowdenbeath (0) 0
Dunfermline Ath (0) 3 *(Geggan 57, 85, Ashcroft 68)* 1481

Inverness CT (1) 1 *(Boden 35)*
Dundee U (0) 1 *(Murdoch 46)* 1839
Dundee U won 4-1 on penalties.

Tuesday, 26 July 2016

Dunfermline Ath (1) 1 *(Geggan 28)*
Inverness CT (2) 5 *(Vigurs 16, 42, 66, King 54, Tremarco 89)* 2580

Wednesday, 27 July 2016

Arbroath (0) 0
Cowdenbeath (2) 2 *(Johnston 14, Todorov 42)* 421

Saturday, 30 July 2016

Inverness CT (4) 7 *(King 10, Boden 18, 25, 71, Tremarco 37, 87, Vigurs 47)*
Arbroath (0) 0 1316

Sunday, 31 July 2016

Dundee U (0) 2 *(Murray 49, Fraser 83)*
Dunfermline Ath (0) 0 4951

Group C – Table	P	W	PW	PL	L	F	A	GD	Pts
Inverness CT	4	3	0	1	0	15	3	12	10
Dundee U	4	2	2	0	0	10	3	7	10
Dunfermline Ath	4	2	0	0	2	7	7	0	6
Cowdenbeath	4	1	0	0	3	4	11	–7	3
Arbroath	4	0	0	1	3	1	13	–12	1

NORTH SECTION – GROUP D

Friday, 15 July 2016

Cove R (1) 1 *(Stott 32)*
Raith R (1) 2 *(Benedictus 36, Vaughan 56)* 362

Saturday, 16 July 2016

Montrose (0) 0
Ross Co (0) 1 *(Graham 86 (pen))* 557

Tuesday, 19 July 2016

Alloa Ath (1) 4 *(Spence 23, Graham 51, Kirkpatrick 64, Layne 83)*
Cove R (0) 0 213

Raith R (1) 2 *(Johnston 12, Vaughan 87 (pen))*
Montrose (0) 1 *(Bolochoweckyj 58)* 1147

Saturday, 23 July 2016

Montrose (0) 0
Alloa Ath (1) 2 *(Spence 33, Layne 50)* 358

Ross Co (0) 1 *(Graham 75 (pen))*
Raith R (1) 1 *(Cikos 18 (og))* 1173
Raith R won 4-3 on penalties.

Tuesday, 26 July 2016

Alloa Ath (2) 3 *(Kirkpatrick 2, Robertson 11, Waters 72)*
Ross Co (2) 2 *(Graham 14, Schalk 21)* 319

Wednesday, 27 July 2016

Cove R (1) 3 *(Walker 14, Megginson 59, Park 78)*
Montrose (0) 0 189

Saturday, 30 July 2016

Raith R (0) 0
Alloa Ath (1) 1 *(Spence 34)* 1674

Ross Co (1) 7 *(Schalk 24, 49, Graham 47, 56, 89, Curran 65, 81)*
Cove R (0) 0 722

Group D – Table	P	W	PW	PL	L	F	A	GD	Pts
Alloa Ath	4	4	0	0	0	10	2	8	12
Raith R	4	2	1	0	1	5	4	1	8
Ross Co	4	2	0	1	1	11	4	7	7
Cove R	4	1	0	0	3	4	13	–9	3
Montrose	4	0	0	0	4	1	8	–7	0

SOUTH SECTION – GROUP E

Friday, 15 July 2016

Airdrieonians (0) 0
Partick Thistle (0) 1 *(Doolan 55)* 1632

Saturday, 16 July 2016

Queen's Park (0) 0
Queen of the South (2) 2 *(Pickard 29, Dowie 34)* 410

Tuesday, 19 July 2016

Queen of the South (2) 2 *(Lyle 9, 24)*
Airdrieonians (0) 0 1036

Stenhousemuir (0) 0
Queen's Park (1) 2 *(Burns 40, McVey 81)* 273

Saturday, 23 July 2016

Airdrieonians (1) 2 *(Brown 13, 67)*
Stenhousemuir (0) 1 *(Gilhaney 56)* 532

Partick Thistle (0) 2 *(Erskine 82, Lawless 90)*
Queen of the South (0) 1 *(Lindsay 48 (og))* 2358

Tuesday, 26 July 2016

Queen's Park (1) 3 *(Cummins 3, Malone 48, Burns 79)*
Airdrieonians (3) 3 *(Ryan 19, Brown 20, Russell I 31)* 553
Airdrieonians won 8-7 on penalties.

Stenhousemuir (0) 1 *(McCroary 73)*
Partick Thistle (2) 4 *(Pogba 20, Welsh 22 (pen), Amoo 85, Azeez 86)* 1433

Saturday, 30 July 2016

Partick Thistle (1) 2 *(Erskine 6, Lindsay 78)*
Queen's Park (0) 0 2250

Queen of the South (0) 1 *(Hamill 78)*
Stenhousemuir (0) 0 1013

Group E – Table	P	W	PW	PL	L	F	A	GD	Pts
Partick Thistle	4	4	0	0	0	9	2	7	12
Queen of the South	4	3	0	0	1	6	2	4	9
Airdrieonians	4	1	1	0	2	5	7	–2	5
Queen's Park	4	1	0	1	2	5	7	–2	4
Stenhousemuir	4	0	0	0	4	2	9	–7	0

SOUTH SECTION – GROUP F

Saturday, 16 July 2016

Annan Ath (0) 1 *(Dachnowicz 87)*
Stranraer (0) 2 *(Nade 59, McKeown 76)* 418

Motherwell (0) 0
Rangers (0) 2 *(Tavernier 48, Waghorn 90)* 6951

Tuesday, 19 July 2016

Rangers (1) 2 *(McKay 30, Waghorn 74)*
Annan Ath (0) 0 31,628

Stranraer (0) 3 *(Malcolm 64, Turner 90, McKeown 90)*
East Stirling (0) 1 *(Glasgow 60)* 373

Friday, 22 July 2016

East Stirling (0) 0
Rangers (2) 3 *(Halliday 10 (pen), Windass 35, Dodoo 90)* 2246

Saturday, 23 July 2016

Annan Ath (1) 1 *(Omar 44)*
Motherwell (1) 3 *(Johnson 16, Moult 61, 63)* 956

Monday, 25 July 2016

Rangers (2) 3 *(Waghorn 5 (pen), 16, Kranjcar 53)*
Stranraer (0) 0 29,575

Tuesday, 26 July 2016

Motherwell (0) 3 *(Johnson 53, McDonald 76, Cadden 87)*
East Stirling (0) 0 2503

Saturday, 30 July 2016

East Stirling (0) 0
Annan Ath (0) 2 *(Finnie 56, Wright 90 (pen))* 134

Stranraer (0) 0
Motherwell (0) 3 *(Cadden 51, Johnson 84, McDonald 86)* 953

Group F – Table	P	W	PW	PL	L	F	A	GD	Pts
Rangers	4	4	0	0	0	10	0	10	12
Motherwell	4	3	0	0	1	9	3	6	9
Stranraer	4	2	0	0	2	5	8	–3	6
Annan Ath	4	1	0	0	3	4	7	–3	3
East Stirlingshire	4	0	0	0	4	1	11	–10	0

SOUTH SECTION – GROUP G

Saturday, 16 July 2016

Ayr U (1) 2 *(Forrest 2 (pen), Crawford 49)*
Hamilton A (0) 1 *(Longridge 90)* 994

Livingston (0) 2 *(Cadden 50, Carrick 68)*
St Mirren (1) 3 *(Clarkson 13, 81, Morgan 74)* 894

Tuesday, 19 July 2016

St Mirren (0) 1 *(Baird 90)*
Ayr U (0) 0 2098

Wednesday, 20 July 2016

Edinburgh C (0) 0
Livingston (2) 3 *(Mullin 27, Mullen 45, Buchanan 76)* 525

Saturday, 23 July 2016

Ayr U (1) 1 *(Gilmour 11)*
Edinburgh C (0) 0 862

Hamilton A (1) 3 *(Crawford 13, Imrie 51, Donati 70)*
St Mirren (0) 0 1379

Tuesday, 26 July 2016

Livingston (0) 0
Ayr U (1) 2 *(Murphy 19, McGuffie 78)* 643

Wednesday, 27 July 2016

Edinburgh C (2) 2 *(Allum 17, 19)*
Hamilton A (2) 4 *(Crawford 22, D'Acol 26, McGregor 66, Imrie 71 (pen))* 459

Saturday, 30 July 2016

Hamilton A (1) 2 *(D'Acol 22, Longridge 55)*
Livingston (1) 1 *(Matthews 41 (og))* 764

St Mirren (3) 3 *(Shankland 12, Walsh 30, Baird 33)*
Edinburgh C (0) 0 1800

Group G – Table	P	W	PW	PL	L	F	A	GD	Pts
Hamilton A	4	3	0	0	1	10	5	5	9
Ayr U	4	3	0	0	1	5	2	3	9
St Mirren	4	3	0	0	1	7	5	2	9
Livingston	4	1	0	0	3	6	7	–1	3
Edinburgh C	4	0	0	0	4	2	11	–9	0

SOUTH SECTION – GROUP H

Saturday, 16 July 2016

Albion R (0) 0
Greenock Morton (0) 0 431
Greenock Morton won 4-3 on penalties

Clyde (0) 1 *(Watson 87)*
Kilmarnock (0) 2 *(Coulibaly 69, Boyle 76)* 1303

Tuesday, 19 July 2016

Berwick R (0) 0
Albion R (0) 0 323
Albion R won 5-4 on penalties.

Greenock Morton (0) 1 *(O'Ware 77)*
Clyde (0) 0 931

Saturday, 23 July 2016

Clyde (0) 1 *(MacDonald 49)*
Berwick R (0) 1 *(Sheerin 64)* 397
Clyde won 6-5 on penalties.

Kilmarnock (0) 0
Greenock Morton (1) 2 *(Oliver 7, Quitongo 67)* 3020

Tuesday, 26 July 2016

Albion R (0) 1 *(Davidson 59)*
Clyde (0) 2 *(McNeil 73, Easton 90 (pen))* 377

Berwick R (1) 2 *(Fairbairn 11, Mackie 56)*
Kilmarnock (0) 3 *(Coulibaly 65, 70, McKenzie 85)* 609

Saturday, 30 July 2016

Greenock Morton (2) 2 *(Lindsay 2, Quitongo 16)*
Berwick R (0) 0 1044

Kilmarnock (0) 0
Albion R (0) 0 2219
Albion R won 5-3 on penalties.

Group H – Table	P	W	PW	PL	L	F	A	GD	Pts
Greenock Morton	4	3	1	0	0	5	0	5	11
Kilmarnock	4	2	0	1	1	5	5	0	7
Clyde	4	1	1	0	2	4	5	–1	5
Albion R	4	0	2	1	1	1	2	–1	5
Berwick R	4	0	0	2	2	3	6	–3	2

SECOND ROUND

Tuesday, 9 August 2016

Alloa Ath (1) 1 *(Marr 28)*
Inverness CT (0) 0 613
Alloa Ath: (4411) Parry; Taggart, Graham, Marr, Waters; Kirkpatrick (Holmes 76), Goodwin, Robertson, Flannigan; Longworth (Cawley 46); Spence (Layne 81).
Inverness CT: (4231) Fon Williams; Raven, Warren, McNaughton, Tremarco; Polworth (Doran 74), Tansey; Mulraney (Draper 46), Vigurs, King; Boden (Fisher 60).
Referee: Don Robertson.

Dundee U (3) 3 *(Smith C 10, 27, 30 (pen))*
Partick Thistle (0) 1 *(Welsh 65 (pen))* 5036
Dundee U: (4231) Bell; Toshney (Dillon 74), Durnan, Donaldson, Robson; Flood, Murdoch; Spittal, Fraser (Telfer 86), Obadeyi; Smith C (Murray 78).
Partick Thistle: (4231) Scully; Gordon, Devine, Syme (Edwards 58), Booth; Welsh, Osman; Amoo (Azeez 39), Erskine, Lawless; Doolan (Pogba 78).
Referee: Steven McLean.

Hamilton A (1) 1 *(Imrie 8 (pen))*
Greenock Morton (0) 2 *(Forbes 59, Quitongo 63)* 1112
Hamilton A: (4411) Matthews; Gillespie, Sarris, Devlin, Kurakins (Lyon 33); Imrie, MacKinnon (Roy 75), Docherty, Longridge; Crawford; Boyd (Donati 46).
Greenock Morton: (4411) Gaston; Doyle, Kilday, O'Ware, Lamie; Forbes, Lindsay, Tidser, Nesbitt (Tiffoney 90); Oliver (McAleer 90); Quitongo (McDonagh 80).
Referee: Stephen Finnie.

Hibernian (1) 1 *(Hanlon 22)*
Queen of the South (0) 3 *(Dobbie 66, Anderson 82, Dykes 86)* 7646
Hibernian: (352) Laidlaw; McGregor (Harris 86), Fontaine, Hanlon; Gray, Keatings, Bartley, McGinn, Stevenson; Holt (Boyle 81), Cummings (Forster 90).
Queen of the South: (442) Robinson; Hamill (Brotherston 65), Brownlie, Dowie, Hooper; Anderson, Millar, Jacobs, Dykes; Hilson (Dobbie 48), Lyle (Rigg 81).
Referee: Euan Anderson.

Rangers (2) 5 *(Kranjcar 19, Hill 35, 56, Kelleher 48 (og), Dodoo 65)*
Peterhead (0) 0 27,076
Rangers: (433) Gilks; Tavernier, Kiernan, Hill, Hodson; Kranjcar (McKay 62), Barton (Holt 62), Rossiter (Halliday 62); O'Halloran, Dodoo, Forrester.
Peterhead: (4141) Smith G; Strachan, Ross (McIntosh 54), Rumsby, Noble; Kelleher; Stevenson (Riley 53), Ferry, Blockley■, Redman (Nassor 61); McAllister.
Referee: Andrew Dallas.

Wednesday, 10 August 2016

Ayr U (1) 1 *(Forrest 41)*
Aberdeen (2) 2 *(Meggatt 3 (og), McGinn 30)* 2653
Ayr U: (433) Fleming; Devlin, Murphy, Meggatt, Boyle; Crawford (Johnston 84), Cairney, Adams; McGuffie (O'Connell 74), Thomas (Gilmour 60), Forrest.
Aberdeen: (433) Lewis; Logan, O'Connor, Reynolds, Considine; McLean (McKenna 90), Jack, Shinnie; Burns, Rooney (Stockley 60), McGinn.
Referee: Alan Muir.

Celtic (2) 5 *(Rogic 20, 76, Dembele 34 (pen), 64, Sinclair 61)*
Motherwell (0) 0 20,165
Celtic: (433) Gordon; Janko (Ralston 82), Lustig (McCart 69), O'Connell, Izaguirre; Brown (Henderson 73), Rogic, McGregor; Forrest, Dembele, Sinclair.
Motherwell: (451) Samson; Tait, Heneghan, McManus, Hammell (Ainsworth 46); Cadden, Lasley, Clay, Chalmers, Johnson; McDonald.
Referee: Kevin Clancy.

St Johnstone (1) 3 *(Swanson 10, 75 (pen), McKay 80)*
Hearts (2) 2 *(Paterson 43, Walker 45 (pen))* 4214
St Johnstone: (4411) Mannus; Easton, Scobbie (McKay 46), Anderson, Shaughnessy; Swanson, Craig (MacLean 67), Paton, Alston; Wotherspoon; Kane.

Hearts: (442) Hamilton; Igor Rossi, Ozturk, Souttar, Paterson; Walker (Watt 62), Djoum, Buaben (Smith 83), Cowie; Sammon, Muirhead (Nicholson 63).
Referee: Crawford Allan.

QUARTER-FINALS

Tuesday, 20 September 2016

Greenock Morton (2) 2 *(Quitongo 24, O'Ware 31)*

Dundee U (0) 1 *(Van der Velden 55)* 2149

Greenock Morton: (442) McNeil; Doyle, O'Ware, Gunning, Russell; McDonagh, Lindsay, Forbes, Oyenuga (McAleer 76); Quitongo (Nesbitt 81), Oliver (Tiffoney 90).
Dundee U: (4231) Bell; Toshney, van der Struijk (Donaldson 76), Edjenguele, Dixon; Murdoch, Fraser (Murray 65); Van der Velden, Smith C, Spittal; Obadeyi (Coote 84).
Referee: Andrew Dallas.

Rangers (1) 5 *(Holt 33, Halliday 62, Waghorn 63, 71, 83)*

Queen of the South (0) 0 26,079

Rangers: (433) Gilks; Tavernier, Hill, Wilson, Hodson; Holt (McKay 46), Halliday, Kranjcar; O'Halloran (Miller 77), Waghorn, Forrester (Crooks 72).
Queen of the South: (442) Robinson; Hamill, Dowie, Brownlie, Marshall; Anderson (Dykes 50), Millar, Hilson, Jacobs (Pickard 68); Dobbie, Lyle (Brotherston 69).
Referee: Don Robertson.

Wednesday, 21 September 2016

Celtic (0) 2 *(Forrest 83, Dembele 90)*

Alloa Ath (0) 0 15,900

Celtic: (4231) Gordon; Lustig, Toure, Simunovic (Christie 71), Tierney; Brown, Armstrong; Roberts (Sinclair 46), Rogic (Sviatchenko 85), Forrest; Dembele.
Alloa Ath: (451) Parry; Taggart, Gordon, Graham, Waters; Cawley (Holmes 78), Flannigan, Goodwin (Longworth 84), Robertson, Kirkpatrick; Spence.
Referee: Alan Muir.

Thursday, 22 September 2016

Aberdeen (0) 1 *(Rooney 90)*

St Johnstone (0) 0 8829

Aberdeen: (4411) Lewis; Logan, Taylor, O'Connor, Considine; McGinn, Maddison (Reynolds 90), Shinnie, Burns (Pawlett 72); McLean; Stockley (Rooney 73).
St Johnstone: (4411) Clark; Gordon, Shaughnessy, Anderson, Easton; Wotherspoon, Davidson, Paton (Kane 90), Swanson (Craig 77); Gormley (Coulson 49); MacLean.
Referee: Craig Thomson.

SEMI-FINALS

Saturday, 22 October 2016

Greenock Morton (0) 0

Aberdeen (0) 2 *(Rooney 69, McLean 88)* 16,183

Greenock Morton: (4411) McNeil; Doyle, O'Ware, Gunning, Russell; McDonagh (Tiffoney 77), Lindsay (Kilday 89), Murdoch, Oyenuga (Nesbitt 72); Oliver; Quitongo.
Aberdeen: (4231) Lewis; Logan, O'Connor, Reynolds, Considine; McLean, Shinnie (Burns 90); McGinn (Storey 90), Maddison (Jack 85), Hayes; Rooney.
Referee: Kevin Clancy.

Sunday, 23 October 2016

Rangers (0) 0

Celtic (0) 1 *(Dembele 87)* 50,697

Rangers: (433) Gilks; Hodson, Kiernan, Hill, Wallace; Windass (Garner 70), Halliday, Holt; Tavernier, Miller (Waghorn 70), McKay (Dodoo 78).
Celtic: (4231) Gordon; Lustig, Simunovic, Sviatchenko, Tierney; Brown, Bitton (Armstrong 63); Forrest (Gamboa 90), Rogic (Griffiths 70), Sinclair; Dembele.
Referee: Craig Thomson.

BETFRED SCOTTISH LEAGUE CUP FINAL 2016–17

Sunday, 27 November 2016

(at Hampden Park, attendance 49,629)

Aberdeen (0) 0 Celtic (2) 3

Aberdeen: (4231) Lewis; Logan, Taylor, O'Connor (Stockley 65), Considine; Jack, Shinnie; Hayes (McGinn 71), McLean, Maddison; Rooney (Burns 79).

Celtic: (4231) Gordon; Lustig, Simunovic, Sviatchenko, Izaguirre; Brown, Armstrong; Roberts (Bitton 65), Rogic (McGregor 77), Forrest (Griffiths 90); Dembele.
Scorers: Rogic 16, Forrest 37, Dembele 64 (pen).

Referee: John Beaton.

Moussa Dembele of Celtic scores the Glasgow club's third goal from the penalty spot as they secure the Scottish League Cup with a 3-0 victory over Aberdeen at Hampden Park (Reuters/Russell Cheyne Livepic)

IRN-BRU SCOTTISH LEAGUE CHALLENGE CUP 2016–17

■ *Denotes player sent off.*

ROUND ONE – NORTH

Tuesday, 2 August 2016

Cove R (0) 2 *(Buchan 78, Scully 84)*
Dundee U20 (1) 1 *(Warwick 29)* 190

East Stirling (0) 0
Montrose (1) 3 *(Masson 29, Webster 61, Ferguson 83)* 149

Formartine U (0) 2 *(Gauld 81, Rodger 83)*
Aberdeen U20 (1) 5 *(Wright 27, 53, 65, Norris 50, Nuttall 66)* 305

Inverness CT U20 (0) 0
Arbroath (2) 3 *(Kader 17, Hamilton 21, Scott 77)* 296

Ross Co U20 (0) 2 *(Morrison G 52, Wallace 76)*
Brora R (1) 3 *(Pollock 33, Mackay 80, Campbell 103)* 350
aet.

St Johnstone U20 (1) 1 *(Hurst 19)*
Turriff U (0) 2 *(Booth C 51, Booth D 86)* 320

Stirling Alb (2) 2 *(McKenzie M 4, 34)*
Hearts U20 (0) 3 *(Jones 47, Roy 50, McLean 67)* 476

ROUND ONE – SOUTH

Tuesday, 2 August 2016

Berwick R (0) 0
Spartans (2) 3 *(Maxwell 11, Dishington 45, Stevenson 50)* 302

Celtic U20 (3) 5 *(Nesbitt 21, 71, Hendry 25, Aitchison 40, Crossan 82)*
Annan Ath (1) 1 *(Omar 1)* 216

Clyde (0) 0
Partick Thistle U20 (0) 5 *(Nisbet 52, 67, 76, Penrice 64, McLaughlin 80)* 351

Motherwell U20 (1) 2 *(Mackin 37, Fry 60)*
Edinburgh C (0) 1 *(Cummings 73)* 402

Queen's Park (3) 5 *(Brown 2, Wharton 15, McGeever 39, Galt 60, MacPherson 86 (pen))*
Kilmarnock U20 (2) 2 *(Hawkshaw 1, Queen 45)* 299

Wednesday, 3 August 2016

Cumbernauld Colts (0) 0
Hamilton A U20 (1) 3 *(Cunningham 17, Boyd 46, Tierney 84)* 119

Wednesday, 10 August 2016

Rangers U20 (4) 4 *(Jeffries 6, 26, Hardie 18, Burt 28)*
Stirling Uni (0) 0 493

ROUND TWO – NORTH

Tuesday, 16 August 2016

Aberdeen U20 (0) 1 *(Omolokun 89)*
Forfar Ath (1) 3 *(Peters 33, 90, Smith 54)* 221

Brechin C (2) 4 *(Graham 16, Jackson A 36, 90, Caldwell 60)*
Cove R (1) 1 *(Milne 2)* 242

Elgin C (1) 2 *(Sutherland S 34, MacLeod 56)*
Hearts U20 (0) 0 350

Peterhead (0) 3 *(Brown J 74, McAllister 77, McIntosh 80)*
Brora R (1) 2 *(Sutherland 18, Brindle 48)* 399

Wednesday, 17 August 2016

Arbroath (1) 2 *(Little 34, Hester 83)*
East Fife (0) 3 *(Page 62, Smith 87, McManus 113 (pen))*
aet. 335

Turriff U (0) 1 *(Kleczkowski 59)*
Montrose (0) 0 180

ROUND TWO – SOUTH

Tuesday, 16 August 2016

Albion R (1) 2 *(Dunlop R 18, Ferry 55)*
Hamilton A U20 (0) 0 114

Cowdenbeath (1) 1 *(Todorov 30)*
Celtic U20 (0) 2 *(Aitchison 52, Crossan 71)* 449

Motherwell U20 (0) 1 *(Mackin 54)*
Airdrieonians (1) 2 *(Russell I 45, Ryan 49)* 1007

Partick Thistle U20 (0) 1 *(McMullin 48)*
Queen's Park (0) 1 *(Carter 88)* 436
aet; Queen's Park won 6-5 on penalties.

Stranraer (3) 7 *(Malcolm 27, 40, 43, 55, McGuigan 49 (pen), Gibson 58, Turner 84)*
Spartans (0) 1 *(Malone 86)* 326

Wednesday, 17 August 2016

Rangers U20 (0) 1 *(Hardie 62)*
Stenhousemuir (2) 3 *(McMenamin 7, Cook 38, Robby McCrorie 58 (og))* 324

ROUND THREE – NORTH

Saturday, 3 September 2016

Alloa Ath (3) 3 *(Kirkpatrick 12, Waters 16, Spence 45)*
East Fife (0) 0 444

Brechin C (1) 1 *(Love 27)*
Dunfermline Ath (2) 5 *(Ashcroft 17, 90, Hill 25 (og), McMullan 49, Reilly 80)* 577

Dundee U (2) 3 *(Telfer 1, Van der Velden 34, Andreu 116)*
Peterhead (2) 2 *(McAllister 28, 35)* 3520
aet.

Falkirk (3) 6 *(McHugh 5, 55, Hippolyte 32, Baird 43, 71, McCracken 48)*
Elgin C (1) 1 *(Nicolson 38)* 1591

Forfar Ath (2) 3 *(Milne 31, Peters 37, 57)*
Raith R (1) 2 *(Stewart 19, McManus 67)* 690

Sunday, 4 September 2016

Turriff U (0) 0
Hibernian (2) 3 *(Murray F 16, Graham 21, Boyle 76)* 1791

ROUND THREE – SOUTH

Saturday, 3 September 2016

Albion R (3) 3 *(Dunlop R 6, 40, Dunlop M 13)*

St Mirren (3) 4 *(Morgan 30, Mallan 35, Sutton 38, Shankland 98)* 711

aet.

Livingston (5) 5 *(Buchanan 5, 14 (pen), Crighton 17, Mullen 35, Longridge 40)*

Celtic U20 (1) 1 *(Hendry 43)* 1214

Queen of the South (4) 7 *(Hilson 6, Anderson 10, Dobbie 33, 46, Lyle 38 (pen), Rigg 66, 79)*

Stenhousemuir (0) 1 *(Cook 81)* 1158

Queen's Park (1) 2 *(Cummins 44, Galt 46)*

Greenock Morton (0) 0 1085

Stranraer (0) 1 *(McGuigan 84)*

Dumbarton (0) 0 401

Sunday, 4 September 2016

Ayr U (2) 3 *(McGuffie 35, Forrest 45, Balatoni 97)*

Airdrieonians (1) 2 *(Conroy 14, Balatoni 49 (og))* 1135

aet.

ROUND FOUR

Friday, 7 October 2016

Ayr U (0) 1 *(Harkins 114)*

Falkirk (0) 0 1247

Ayr U: (4411) Fleming; Devlin, Balatoni, Murphy, Meggatt; Gilmour (Donald 76), Cairney (Crawford 91), Docherty, McGuffie (O'Connell 69); Harkins; Forrest.
Falkirk: (442) Mehmet; Kidd, Watson, Gasparotto, Leahy; Shepherd (Baird 80), Kerr (Blues 110), Rankin, Hippolyte; Miller, McHugh (Sibbald 68).
aet.
Referee: Alan Muir.

Saturday, 8 October 2016

Bala T (0) 2 *(Hunt 60 (pen), Jones S 73)*

Alloa Ath (3) 4 *(Spence 10, 45, Robertson 43, Cawley 65)* 591

Bala T: (442) Morris; Valentine (Edwards 79), Stuart Jones Sr., Stuart Jones Jr., Stephens; Sheridan (Thompson 72), Burke, Jones M (Wade 46), Smith; Hunt, Venables.
Alloa Ath: (4231) Parry; Taggart, Marr, Gordon, Waters; Holmes, Robertson; Cawley (Donnelly 67), Kirkpatrick (Longworth 84), Flannigan (Martin 90); Spence.
Referee: Steven Taylor.

Dunfermline Ath (0) 2 *(El Alagui 48, 62)*

Queen's Park (0) 1 *(El Alagui 70 (og))* 1930

Dunfermline Ath: (442) Murdoch; Williamson, Martin, Ashcroft, Talbot; Paton, McCabe (Higginbotham 64), Geggan, Cardle; Reilly (El Alagui 46), Clark (Hopkirk 81).
Queen's Park: (4231) Muir; Millen, Cummins, McGeever, McLeish; Miller D, Fotheringham (MacPherson 86); Brady (Brown 71), Woods, Burns; Carter (Malone 58).
Referee: Nick Walsh.

Forfar Ath (1) 1 *(Malcolm 38)*

The New Saints (1) 3 *(Draper 24, 80, 87)* 691

Forfar Ath: (442) Adam; Bain, Munro, Malcolm, Kennedy; Scott (Smith 84), Fotheringham, Swankie, Denholm; Peters, James Lister.
The New Saints: (442) Harrison; Spender, Baker, Rawlinson, Marriott; Brobbel, Routledge, Edwards, Mullan (Parry 59); Darlington, Draper (Fletcher 90).
Referee: Evan Boyce.

Hibernian (1) 1 *(Harris 37)*

St Mirren (1) 2 *(Mallan 41, Clarkson 82)* 4393

Hibernian: (4141) Marciano; Gray, McGregor, Forster, Hanlon; Fyvie; Harris (Holt 84), McGeouch, Shinnie (Bartley 69), Boyle (Cummings 69); Keatings.
St Mirren: (4411) Langfield; Naismith, MacKenzie, Baird, Irvine; Walsh (Gallagher 74), Quinn (Clarkson 63), Hutton, Morgan; Mallan; Sutton (Shankland 82).
Referee: William Collum.

Stranraer (0) 0

Dundee U (0) 1 *(Andreu 68)* 629

Stranraer: (442) Belford; Robertson, Barron, Bell, Dick; Thomson C (Nade 70), Morena (Thomson R 81), Turner (McKeown 88), Gibson; Malcolm, McGuigan.
Dundee U: (4321) Zwick; Dillon, Durnan, Edjenguele, Dixon; Spittal, Telfer, Fraser; Andreu, Murray; Smith C (Coote 81).
Referee: Greg Aitken.

Sunday, 9 October 2016

Queen of the South (0) 2 *(Dykes 102, Dobbie 109)*

Linfield (0) 0 2358

Queen of the South: (442) Robinson; Marshall, Brownlie, Dowie, Hamill; Dykes, Pickard, Jacobs (Millar 36), Anderson (Brotherston 58); Dobbie, Rigg (Moxon 106).
Linfield: (442) Carroll; Callacher, Haughey, Clingan, Clarke (Fallon 106); Burns (Strain 74), Carson (Quinn 58), Mulgrew, Waterworth; Casement, Millar.
aet.
Referee: Iwan Griffith.

Tuesday, 1 November 2016

Crusaders (0) 0

Livingston (0) 3 *(Cadden 66, De Vita 74, Buchanan 89)* 479

Crusaders: (442) Dougherty; Kerr, McAnulty, McCreery, McClean; Carvill (Mitchell 76), Gault, Forsyth (Smith 74), Cushley (Nimack 86); Soares, Jallow.
Livingston: (4231) Maley; Halkett, Crighton, Lithgow, Neill; Sinclair (Buchanan 77), Mullin; Watt (Mullen 64), Byrne, Cadden (De Vita 67); Carrick.
Referee: Nick Pratt.

QUARTER-FINALS

Saturday, 12 November 2016

Dunfermline Ath (0) 0

Dundee U (1) 1 *(Durnan 8)* 2576

Dunfermline Ath: (442) Murdoch; Geggan, Martin■, Ashcroft, Talbot; Higginbotham, McCabe, Herron, Cardle (Fordyce 60); Moffat (El Alagui 67), Clark (McMullan 70).
Dundee U: (3412) Zwick; Durnan, Dillon, Donaldson; Spittal, Toshney (Murdoch 87), Smith B, Robson; Smith C (Taylor 81); Murray (Coote 63), Van der Velden.
Referee: Willie Collum.

Queen of the South (1) 2 *(Dobbie 41, 76)*

Alloa Ath (0) 0 1180

Queen of the South: (442) Robinson; Hamill, Brownlie, Dowie, Marshall; Anderson, Jacobs, Millar (Pickard 77), Dykes; Lyle (Brotherston 69), Dobbie.
Alloa Ath: (442) Parry; Taggart, Graham, Marr, Waters; Cawley, Goodwin (Holmes 70), Robertson (Martin 83), Kirkpatrick; Spence, Longworth (Donnelly 72).
Referee: Euan Anderson.

Sunday, 13 November 2016

Livingston (0) 0

The New Saints (1) 3 *(Parry 36, Saunders 58, Quigley 70)* 733

Livingston: (442) Maley; Halkett, Crighton, Lithgow, Longridge (Mullin 63); Cadden (Carrick 68), Pitman, Miller, De Vita; Buchanan (Byrne 76), Mullen.
The New Saints: (4141) Harrison; Spender, Rawlinson, Saunders, Pryce; Routledge; Brobbel (Quigley 67), Edwards, Seargeant (Darlington 89), Parry; Draper (Fletcher 71).
Referee: Raymond Crangle.

St Mirren (0) 2 *(Sutton 83, 85)*

Ayr U (0) 1 *(O'Connell 68)* 2199

St Mirren: (4231) Gallacher; Naismith, MacKenzie, Baird (Walsh 72), Irvine; Magennis, Mallan; McAllister (Stewart 88), Clarkson (Shankland 57), Morgan; Sutton.
Ayr U: (4411) Fleming; Devlin, Balatoni, McKenna, Boyle (Meggatt 26); Cairney, Docherty, Crawford, McGuffie (Donald 77); Harkins; Forrest (O'Connell 59).
Referee: Crawford Allan.

SEMI-FINALS

Saturday, 18 February 2017

Queen of the South (0) 2 *(Dobbie 51, Lyle 90)*

Dundee U (3) 3 *(Telfer 3, Fraser 11, Andreu 35)* 1526

Queen of the South: (4411) Robinson; Brownlie, Dowie, Higgins, Marshall; Hamill (Carmichael 85), Jacobs, Thomas, Murray (Dykes 58); Dobbie; Lyle.
Dundee U: (442) Zwick; van der Struijk, Dillon, Edjenguele, Dixon; Fraser, Flood, Telfer, Andreu; Nicholls (Coote 73), Murray (Mikkelsen 68).
Referee: Nick Walsh.

Sunday, 19 February 2017

St Mirren (0) 4 *(McGinn 60, Mallan 65, Sutton 80, Loy 90)*

The New Saints (1) 1 *(Brobbel 41)* 2044

St Mirren: (442) O'Brien; Demetriou, Baird, Davis, Eckersley (Irvine 90); Magennis, Storie (Morgan 46), McGinn (Fjelde 87), Mallan; Loy, Sutton.
The New Saints: (4141) Harrison; Spender, Saunders■, Rawlinson, Marriott; Baker; Mullan, Edwards, Brobbel (Seargeant 68), Cieslewicz (Quigley 68); Fletcher (Draper 81).
Referee: Keith Kennedy.

IRN-BRU SCOTTISH LEAGUE CHALLENGE CUP FINAL 2016–17

Saturday, 25 March 2017

(at Fir Park, attendance 8089)

Dundee U (1) 2 St Mirren (1) 1

Dundee U: (4231) Bell; Murdoch, Edjenguele, Durnan, Robson; Telfer, Flood; Coote (Donaldson 89), Andreu, Van der Velden (Mikkelsen 58); Murray (Nicholls 80).
Scorers: Andreu 37, Mikkelsen 75.

St Mirren: (442) O'Brien; Irvine, MacKenzie, Baird, Eckersley; Magennis (O'Keefe 84), Mallan, McGinn, Morgan; Loy, Sutton.
Scorer: Loy 38.

Referee: Nick Walsh.

LEAGUE CHALLENGE FINALS 1991–2017

B&Q CENTENARY CUP

1990–91	Dundee v Ayr U	3-2*

B&Q CUP

1991–92	Hamilton A v Ayr U	1-0
1992–93	Hamilton A v Morton	3-2
1993–94	Falkirk v St Mirren	3-0
1994–95	Airdrieonians v Dundee	3-2*

SCOTTISH LEAGUE CHALLENGE CUP

1995–96	Stenhousemuir v Dundee U	0-0*
	Stenhousemuir won 5-4 on penalties.	
1996–97	Stranraer v St Johnstone	1-0
1997–98	Falkirk v Queen of the South	1-0
1998–99	*No competition.*	
	Suspended due to lack of sponsorship.	

BELL'S CHALLENGE CUP

1999–2000	Alloa Ath v Inverness CT	4-4*
	Alloa Ath won 5-4 on penalties.	
2000–01	Airdrieonians v Livingston	2-2*
	Airdrieonians won 3-2 on penalties.	
2001–02	Airdrieonians v Alloa Ath	2-1

BELL'S CUP

2002–03	Queen of the South v Brechin C	2-0
2003–04	Inverness CT v Airdrie U	2-0
2004–05	Falkirk v Ross Co	2-1
2005–06	St Mirren v Hamilton A	2-1

SCOTTISH LEAGUE CHALLENGE CUP

2006–07	Ross Co v Clyde	1-1*
	Ross Co won 5-4 on penalties.	
2007–08	St Johnstone v Dunfermline Ath	3-2

ALBA CHALLENGE CUP

2008–09	Airdrie U v Ross Co	2-2*
	Airdrie U won 3-2 on penalties.	
2009–10	Dundee v Inverness CT	3-2
2010–11	Ross Co v Queen of the South	2-0

RAMSDENS CUP

2011–12	Falkirk v Hamilton A	1-0
2012–13	Queen of the South v Partick Thistle	1-1*
	Queen of the South won 6-5 on penalties.	
2013–14	Raith R v Rangers	1-0*

PETROFAC TRAINING SCOTTISH LEAGUE CHALLENGE CUP

2014–15	Livingston v Alloa Athletic	4-0
2015–16	Rangers v Peterhead	4-0

IRN-BRU SCOTTISH LEAGUE CHALLENGE CUP

2016–17	Dundee U v St Mirren	2-1

**After extra time.*

SCOTTISH CUP FINALS 1874–2017

SCOTTISH FA CUP

1874	Queen's Park v Clydesdale	2-0
1875	Queen's Park v Renton	3-0
1876	Queen's Park v Third Lanark	1-1
Replay	Queen's Park v Third Lanark	2-0
1877	Vale of Leven v Rangers	1-1
Replay	Vale of Leven v Rangers	1-1
2nd Replay	Vale of Leven v Rangers	3-2
1878	Vale of Leven v Third Lanark	1-0
1879	Vale of Leven v Rangers	1-1
	Vale of Leven awarded cup, Rangers failing to appear for replay.	
1880	Queen's Park v Thornliebank	3-0
1881	Queen's Park v Dumbarton	2-1
Replay	Queen's Park v Dumbarton	3-1
	After Dumbarton protested the first game.	
1882	Queen's Park v Dumbarton	2-2
Replay	Queen's Park v Dumbarton	4-1
1883	Dumbarton v Vale of Leven	2-2
Replay	Dumbarton v Vale of Leven	2-1
1884	Queen's Park v Vale of Leven	
	Queen's Park awarded cup, Vale of Leven failing to appear.	
1885	Renton v Vale of Leven	0-0
Replay	Renton v Vale of Leven	3-1
1886	Queen's Park v Renton	3-1
1887	Hibernian v Dumbarton	2-1
1888	Renton v Cambuslang	6-1
1889	Third Lanark v Celtic	3-0
Replay	Third Lanark v Celtic	2-1
	Replay by order of Scottish FA because of playing conditions in first match.	
1890	Queen's Park v Vale of Leven	1-1
Replay	Queen's Park v Vale of Leven	2-1
1891	Hearts v Dumbarton	1-0
1892	Celtic v Queen's Park	1-0
Replay	Celtic v Queen's Park	5-1
	After mutually protested first match.	
1893	Queen's Park v Celtic	0-1
Replay	Queen's Park v Celtic	2-1
	Replay by order of Scottish FA because of playing conditions in first match.	
1894	Rangers v Celtic	3-1
1895	St Bernard's v Renton	2-1
1896	Hearts v Hibernian	3-1
1897	Rangers v Dumbarton	5-1
1898	Rangers v Kilmarnock	2-0
1899	Celtic v Rangers	2-0
1900	Celtic v Queen's Park	4-3
1901	Hearts v Celtic	4-3
1902	Hibernian v Celtic	1-0
1903	Rangers v Hearts	1-1
Replay	Rangers v Hearts	0-0
2nd Replay	Rangers v Hearts	2-0
1904	Celtic v Rangers	3-2
1905	Third Lanark v Rangers	0-0
Replay	Third Lanark v Rangers	3-1
1906	Hearts v Third Lanark	1-0
1907	Celtic v Hearts	3-0
1908	Celtic v St Mirren	5-1
1909	Celtic v Rangers	2-2
Replay	Celtic v Rangers	1-1
	Owing to riot, the cup was withheld.	
1910	Dundee v Clyde	2-2
Replay	Dundee v Clyde	0-0*
2nd Replay	Dundee v Clyde	2-1
1911	Celtic v Hamilton A	0-0
Replay	Celtic v Hamilton A	2-0
1912	Celtic v Clyde	2-0
1913	Falkirk v Raith R	2-0
1914	Celtic v Hibernian	0-0
Replay	Celtic v Hibernian	4-1
1920	Kilmarnock v Albion R	3-2
1921	Partick Thistle v Rangers	1-0
1922	Morton v Rangers	1-0
1923	Celtic v Hibernian	1-0
1924	Airdrieonians v Hibernian	2-0
1925	Celtic v Dundee	2-1
1926	St Mirren v Celtic	2-0
1927	Celtic v East Fife	3-1
1928	Rangers v Celtic	4-0
1929	Kilmarnock v Rangers	2-0
1930	Rangers v Partick Thistle	0-0
Replay	Rangers v Partick Thistle	2-1
1931	Celtic v Motherwell	2-2
Replay	Celtic v Motherwell	4-2
1932	Rangers v Kilmarnock	1-1
Replay	Rangers v Kilmarnock	3-0
1933	Celtic v Motherwell	1-0
1934	Rangers v St Mirren	5-0
1935	Rangers v Hamilton A	2-1
1936	Rangers v Third Lanark	1-0
1937	Celtic v Aberdeen	2-1
1938	East Fife v Kilmarnock	1-1
Replay	East Fife v Kilmarnock	4-2*
1939	Clyde v Motherwell	4-0
1947	Aberdeen v Hibernian	2-1
1948	Rangers v Morton	1-1*
Replay	Rangers v Morton	1-0*
1949	Rangers v Clyde	4-1
1950	Rangers v East Fife	3-0
1951	Celtic v Motherwell	1-0
1952	Motherwell v Dundee	4-0
1953	Rangers v Aberdeen	1-1
Replay	Rangers v Aberdeen	1-0
1954	Celtic v Aberdeen	2-1
1955	Clyde v Celtic	1-1
Replay	Clyde v Celtic	1-0
1956	Hearts v Celtic	3-1
1957	Falkirk v Kilmarnock	1-1
Replay	Falkirk v Kilmarnock	2-1*
1958	Clyde v Hibernian	1-0
1959	St Mirren v Aberdeen	3-1
1960	Rangers v Kilmarnock	2-0
1961	Dunfermline Ath v Celtic	0-0
Replay	Dunfermline Ath v Celtic	2-0
1962	Rangers v St Mirren	2-0
1963	Rangers v Celtic	1-1
Replay	Rangers v Celtic	3-0
1964	Rangers v Dundee	3-1
1965	Celtic v Dunfermline Ath	3-2
1966	Rangers v Celtic	0-0
Replay	Rangers v Celtic	1-0
1967	Celtic v Aberdeen	2-0
1968	Dunfermline Ath v Hearts	3-1
1969	Celtic v Rangers	4-0
1970	Aberdeen v Celtic	3-1
1971	Celtic v Rangers	1-1
Replay	Celtic v Rangers	2-1
1972	Celtic v Hibernian	6-1
1973	Rangers v Celtic	3-2
1974	Celtic v Dundee U	3-0
1975	Celtic v Airdrieonians	3-1
1976	Rangers v Hearts	3-1
1977	Celtic v Rangers	1-0
1978	Rangers v Aberdeen	2-1
1979	Rangers v Hibernian	0-0
Replay	Rangers v Hibernian	0-0*
2nd Replay	Rangers v Hibernian	3-2*
1980	Celtic v Rangers	1-0*
1981	Rangers v Dundee U	0-0*
Replay	Rangers v Dundee U	4-1
1982	Aberdeen v Rangers	4-1*
1983	Aberdeen v Rangers	1-0*
1984	Aberdeen v Celtic	2-1*
1985	Celtic v Dundee U	2-1
1986	Aberdeen v Hearts	3-0
1987	St Mirren v Dundee U	1-0*
1988	Celtic v Dundee U	2-1
1989	Celtic v Rangers	1-0

TENNENTS SCOTTISH CUP

1990	Aberdeen v Celtic	0-0*
	Aberdeen won 9-8 on penalties.	
1991	Motherwell v Dundee U	4-3*
1992	Rangers v Airdrieonians	2-1
1993	Rangers v Aberdeen	2-1
1994	Dundee U v Rangers	1-0
1995	Celtic v Airdrieonians	1-0
1996	Rangers v Hearts	5-1
1997	Kilmarnock v Falkirk	1-0
1998	Hearts v Rangers	2-1
1999	Rangers v Celtic	1-0
2000	Rangers v Aberdeen	4-0
2001	Celtic v Hibernian	3-0
2002	Rangers v Celtic	3-2
2003	Rangers v Dundee	1-0
2004	Celtic v Dunfermline Ath	3-1
2005	Celtic v Dundee U	1-0
2006	Hearts v Gretna	1-1*
	Hearts won 4-2 on penalties.	
2007	Celtic v Dunfermline Ath	1-0

SCOTTISH FA CUP

2008	Rangers v Queen of the South	3-2

HOMECOMING SCOTTISH CUP

2009	Rangers v Falkirk	1-0

ACTIVE NATION SCOTTISH CUP

2010	Dundee U v Ross Co	3-0

SCOTTISH FA CUP

2011	Celtic v Motherwell	3-0

WILLIAM HILL SCOTTISH CUP

2012	Hearts v Hibernian	5-1
2013	Celtic v Hibernian	3-0
2014	St Johnstone v Dundee U	2-0
2015	Inverness CT v Falkirk	2-1
2016	Hibernian v Rangers	3-2
2017	Celtic v Aberdeen	2-1

**After extra time.*

SCOTTISH CUP WINS

Celtic 37, Rangers 33, Queen's Park 10, Hearts 8, Aberdeen 7, Clyde 3, Hibernian 3, Kilmarnock 3, St Mirren 3, Vale of Leven 3, Dundee U 2, Dunfermline Ath 2, Falkirk 2, Motherwell 2, Renton 2, Third Lanark 2, Airdrieonians 1, Dumbarton 1, Dundee 1, East Fife 1, Inverness CT 1, Morton 1, Partick Thistle 1, St Bernard's 1, St Johnstone 1.

APPEARANCES IN FINAL

Celtic 55, Rangers 51, Aberdeen 16, Hearts 14, Hibernian 14, Queen's Park 12, Dundee U 10, Kilmarnock 8, Motherwell 7, Vale of Leven 7, Clyde 6, Dumbarton 6, St Mirren 6, Third Lanark 6, Dundee 5, Dunfermline Ath 5, Falkirk 5, Renton 5, Airdrieonians 4, East Fife 3, Hamilton A 2, Morton 2, Partick Thistle 2, Albion R 1, Cambuslang 1, Clydesdale 1, Gretna 1, Inverness CT 1, Queen of the South 1, Raith R 1, Ross Co 1, St Bernard's 1, St Johnstone 1, Thornliebank 1.

WILLIAM HILL SCOTTISH FA CUP 2016–17

■ *Denotes player sent off.*

FIRST PRELIMINARY ROUND

Edusport Academy v Colville Park	2–2, 0-1
Newton Stewart v Beith Juniors	0–4
Wigtown & Bladnoch v Auchinleck Talbot	0–4
St Cuthbert W v Leith Ath	0–3
Glasgow University v Bonnyrigg Rose	2–8

SECOND PRELIMINARY ROUND

Leith Ath v Coldstream	1–0
Bonnyrigg Rose v Burntisland Shipyard	14–0
Colville Park v Girvan	0-1
Beith Juniors v Auchinleck Talbot	2–2, 3-0
Threave R v Linlithgow Rose	1–2
Banks O'Dee v Golspie Sutherland	4–0

FIRST ROUND

Turriff U v Bonnyrigg Rose	1–1, 1-4
Fort William v Brora Rangers	1–4
Forres Mechanics v Lossiemouth	2–2, 4-0
East Kilbride v Vale of Leithen	9–1
BSC Glasgow v Rothes	3–1
Deveronvale v Gretna 2008	0–3
Keith v Banks O' Dee	0–1
Edinburgh University v Whitehill Welfare	0–1
Gala Fairydean R v Fraserburgh	3–1
Beith Juniors v Strathspey	6–0
Civil Service Strollers v Hawick Royal Albert	1–1, 2-6
Nairn County v Preston Ath	2–3
Inverurie Loco Works v Buckie Thistle	0–6
Clachnacuddin v Stirling University	1–2
Dalbeattie Star v Wick Academy	1–3
Selkirk v Linlithgow Rose	0–3
Girvan v Huntly	1–2
Leith Ath v Cumbernauld Colts	0–0, 0-1

SECOND ROUND

Annan Ath v East Stirlingshire	0–0, 2-1
Banks O' Dee v Formartine U	2–2, 2-7
Brora Rangers v Clyde	0–2
BSC Glasgow v Beith Juniors	0–1
Bonnyrigg Rose v Cove Rangers	2–1
Berwick Rangers v Hawick Royal Albert	2–3
Linlithgow Rose v Stirling Albion	0–3
Wick Academy v Whitehill Welfare	4–1
Preston Ath v Montrose	0–3
Huntly v Spartans	0–2
Edinburgh C v Forfar Ath	0–0, 1-0
Cowdenbeath v East Kilbride	0–1
Cumbernauld Colts v Forres Mechanics	2–2, 0-4
Arbroath v Stirling University	3–1
Gala Fairydean R v Elgin C	0–4
Buckie Thistle v Gretna 2008	1–1, 6-2

THIRD ROUND

Saturday, 26 November 2016

Airdrieonians (1) 1 *(Ryan 18)*

Livingston (1) 2 *(Cadden 30, Mullen 62)* 780

Airdrieonians: (442) Ferguson; McIntosh, Boateng, Gorman, MacDonald; Brown, Conroy, Stewart (Scullion 67), Leitch; Russell I (Schmidt 75), Ryan.
Livingston: (352) Kelly; Halkett, Crighton, Lithgow; Mullin, Pitman, Miller (Cadden 10), Byrne, Longridge; Buchanan (De Vita 77), Mullen.
Referee: Barry Cook.

Bonnyrigg Rose (0) 0

Dumbarton (0) 0 1552

Bonnyrigg Rose: (433) Andrews; Horne, Young, Hoskins, Donaldson; Kidd, Stewart, Nelson (Gray 85); Turner, McGachie, McIntosh (McLaren 85).
Dumbarton: (4132) Martin; Smith, Barr, Buchanan, Pettigrew; Docherty; Stirling, Todd, Stevenson; Fleming, McCallum (Thomson R 66).
Referee: Stephen Finnie.

Buckie Thistle (2) 3 *(Mcloud 14, Angus 33, 68)*

Dunfermline Ath (2) 5 *(Munro 12 (og), Paton 16 (pen), Higginbotham 58, McMullan 60, 90)* 1440

Buckie Thistle: (4411) Salmon; Cheyne, MacKinnon, Munro, Dorrat; Fraser, McLean (Wood 44), Copeland (Milne 81), Urquhart; Angus; Mcloud.
Dunfermline Ath: (442) Murdoch; Martin, Ashcroft, Fordyce, Duthie; McMullan, McCabe (Herron 82), Wedderburn, Paton (Higginbotham 46); Clark (El Alagui 78), Moffat.
Referee: Craig Charleston.

Elgin C (3) 8 *(Sutherland S 6, 24, 40, 73, McLeish 53, Cameron 64, 89, Gunn 76)*

Hawick Royal Albert (1) 1 *(Mitchell 32)* 549

Elgin C: (442) Waters; Stewart, Nicolson, McHardy, MacPhee; Dodd, Cameron, Reilly (Cooper 65), Moore (Reid 75); McLeish (Gunn 68), Sutherland S.
Hawick Royal Albert: (442) Ranking; McPartlin (McInally 63), Johnstone (Darling 74), Saunderson (Spence 9), Hunter; Stevenson, Hughes, Conaghan, Meikle; Morris, Mitchell.
Referee: Matt Northcroft.

Forres Mechanics (1) 2 *(Allan 27, Fraser L 66)*

Stenhousemuir (1) 2 *(Kerr 45, Furtado 47)* 369

Forres Mechanics: (442) Knight; Allan, Grant, Fraser G, Finlayson; Khutsishvili, MacPherson (Cameron 78), Soane, McGovern (Groat 80); Fraser L, Graham (Baxter 83).
Stenhousemuir: (4411) McCabe; McCormack, Marsh, Kerr, Summers; Gilhaney (Nash 75), Berry (Martinez 75), Millar, Furtado; McMenamin; Alistair Roy.
Referee: Scott Millar.

Peterhead (0) 0

Alloa Ath (0) 1 *(Longworth 74)* 563

Peterhead: (4411) Smith G; Stevenson (Dzierzawski 59), Kelleher, Ross, Noble; Brown S (Redman 80), Ferry, Blockley, Riley (Brown J 55); McIntosh; McAllister.
Alloa Ath: (4231) Parry; Taggart, Hoggan, Graham, Waters; Goodwin, Robertson; Flannigan, Kirkpatrick (Longworth 66), Cawley; Spence.
Referee: Euan Anderson.

Tuesday, 29 November 2016

Albion R (1) 2 *(Dunlop M 16, Ferguson 90)*

Queen of the South (0) 1 *(Hamill 76)* 387

Albion R: (4411) Ross Stewart I; Reid, Dunlop M, Dunlop R, McBride; McCann (Willis 88), Fisher (Ferguson 81), Davidson, Boyd (Gilmour 62); Wallace■; Ross Stewart II.
Queen of the South: (352) Robinson; Dowie (Hamill 60), Brownlie, Higgins; Anderson, Millar, Pickard (Carmichael 72), Dykes, Marshall; Lyle, Dobbie.
Referee: Alan Newlands.

Brechin C (0) 0

Ayr U (0) 1 *(O'Connell 70)* 308

Brechin C: (442) Smith G; Fusco, Smith E, Hill, Dyer; Ford, Rodger, Lynas, Love; Caldwell, Buchanan (McCormack 81).
Ayr U: (442) Fleming; Devlin, Meggatt, Balatoni, Boyle; Crawford, Adams (Forrest 63), Docherty, McGuffie (Gilmour 72); Harkins, O'Connell (Rose 81).
Referee: Alan Muir.

East Fife (0) 1 *(Kerr 64)*

Edinburgh C (1) 1 *(See 40)* 339

East Fife: (352) Goodfellow; Mercer, Kane, Page; Wilkie, Lamont, Brown (Kerr 63), Robinson (Slattery 67), Naysmith; Insall (Wallace 51), Smith.
Edinburgh C: (352) Stobie; Dunsmore (Allum 78), Mbu, Harrison; McFarland (Caddow 79), Gair, Laird, McKee, Cummings; See, Guthrie (Dunn 63).
Referee: David Lowe.

Queen's Park (1) 2 *(Galt 15, Woods 54)*
Montrose (0) 0 348
Queen's Park: (352) Muir; Cummins, McGeever, Gibson; Millen, Woods, McKernon, Brady (Brown 85), Burns; Carter (Malone 70), Galt (Fotheringham 85).
Montrose: (442) Fleming; Anderson (Watson 69), Bolochoweckyj, MacDonald, Steeves; Webster (Campbell R 90), Masson, McWalter, Ferguson; Fraser, Court (Templeman 52).
Referee: Steven Reid.

St Mirren (3) 5 *(Shankland 15, 68, Mallan 20, McAllister 32, Sutton 63)*
Spartans (0) 1 *(Beesley 73)* 1147
St Mirren: (442) Gallacher; Naismith, MacKenzie (Baird 64), Gordon (Quinn 59), Irvine; McAllister, Mallan, Magennis, Morgan; Sutton (Orsi 82), Shankland.
Spartans: (352) Carswell; Herd, Townsley, Thomson; Dishington, Tolmie (Gabiola 74), Malone, Stevenson, Brown; Haye (Beesley 64), Mair (Maxwell 46).
Referee: Kevin Graham.

Saturday, 3 December 2016

Beith (0) 0
Greenock Morton (3) 6 *(Forbes 11, Tidser 17, McDonagh 42, O'Ware 51, 90, Lindsay 78)* 1693
Beith: (442) Grindlay; McGlinchey, Sheridan, McDonald, McLaughlin; Mcgowan, Wilson, Frize, Burke (Watt 60); Christie (McLean 60), McPherson (Collins 64).
Greenock Morton: (442) Gaston; Kilday, O'Ware, Lamie, Russell; Forbes (McAleer 83), Lindsay, Tidser (Nesbitt 86), McDonagh; Quitongo (Oyenuga 74), Oliver.
Referee: John McKendrick.

Formartine U (0) 4 *(Gethins 56, 59, 72, Barbour 69)*
Annan Ath (0) 0 345
Formartine U: (442) MacDonald; Michie, Jamieson, Smith, Dingwall; Rodger (Lawrence 88), Young (Burnett 82), Anderson, Masson; Gethins (Gauld 73), Barbour.
Annan Ath: (4411) Currie; Lucas, Swinglehurst, Bronsky, Sinnamon (Bradbury 66); Wright, Cuddihy, Ramsay (Dachnowicz 80), Omar; Krissian (Asghar 70); McKenna.
Referee: Colin Steven.

Stirling Alb (1) 2 *(Henderson 43, Bikey 84)*
Wick Academy (0) 0 572
Stirling Alb: (442) Smith C; McGeachie, McMillan (Smith R 46), Davidson, Forsyth; McKenzie M, Colquhoun, Petrie (Ferns 83), Dickson; Kavanagh (Bikey 64), Henderson.
Wick Academy: (442) McCarthy; Steven M (Hardwick 83), Farquhar, Mackay D, Steven G; Manson, Allan, Pickles, Mackay S; Weir (Macadie 79), Anderson.
Referee: Stephen Finnie.

Stranraer (1) 2 *(Gibson 26 (pen), Strachan 89 (og))*
East Kilbride (1) 1 *(Winter 14)* 331
Stranraer: (442) Belford; Barron, Robertson, Bell, Dick; McGuigan (Agnew 38), Turner, Thomson R, Gibson; Malcolm (Morena 90), Nuttall.
East Kilbride: (442) Kean; Capuano (McLaren 90), Howie, Proctor, Russell; Winter, Hughes, Marenghi (McBride 76), Victoria; Coll (Smith 62), Strachan.
Referee: Steven Kirkland.

Tuesday, 6 December 2016

Clyde (3) 5 *(MacDonald 14 (pen), 45 (pen), McLaughlin 21, Gormley 73, 90)*
Arbroath (0) 0 390
Clyde: (433) Gibson; McNeil, Perry, Smith, McNiff; Miller (Flynn■ 62), McLaughlin, Linton (Ferguson K 90); MacDonald, Gormley, Higgins (Ferguson S 71).
Arbroath: (442) Gomes; Gold, Little, Hamilton, Sukar; Kader (Prunty 76), Whatley, McCord (Phillips 64), Linn; Doris (Skelly 71), Scott.
Referee: Gavin Duncan.

THIRD ROUND REPLAYS

Saturday, 3 December 2016

Stenhousemuir (2) 3 *(McMenamin 12, 15, 81)*
Forres Mechanics (0) 1 *(Baxter 87 (pen))* 289
Stenhousemuir: (442) McCabe; McCormack, Marsh■, Kerr, Summers; Gilhaney (Cook 64), Millar, Berry, Furtado (Meechan 89); Alistair Roy, McMenamin (McCroary 86).
Forres Mechanics: (442) Knight; Finlayson (Groat 46), Grant, Fraser G, Allan; Graham, MacPherson, Khutsishvili (Cameron 76), Soane (Baxter 74); Fraser L, McGovern■.
Referee: Scott Millar.

Tuesday, 6 December 2016

Dumbarton (0) 0
Bonnyrigg Rose (0) 1 *(Nelson 86)* 632
Dumbarton: (4141) Martin; Smith, Barr, Buchanan, Docherty; Thomson J; Todd, Stevenson (Pettigrew 68), Stirling, Thomson R (McCallum 68); Fleming.
Bonnyrigg Rose: (442) Andrews; Horne, Hoskins, Young, Donaldson; Turner, Kidd (Gray 80), Stewart, Nelson; McGachie (Moyes 90), McIntosh (McLaren 81).
Referee: Greg Aitken.

Wednesday, 7 December 2016

Edinburgh C (0) 0
East Fife (0) 1 *(Kane 54)* 397
Edinburgh C: (532) Stobie; Dunsmore, Caddow, Harrison, Mbu, Gair; Laird, Muhsin (Cummings 72), McFarland (McConnell 72); Guthrie (See 72), Allum.
East Fife: (4141) Goodfellow; Mercer, Page, Kerr, Slattery; Kane; Wilkie, Robinson (Wallace 67), Brown, Smith; Insall (Austin 88).
Referee: David Lowe.

FOURTH ROUND

Saturday, 21 January 2017

Aberdeen (2) 4 *(Rooney 30, 50 (pen), McGinn 35, 54)*
Stranraer (0) 0 8960
Aberdeen: (4411) Lewis; Logan, Taylor, Reynolds, Considine (Wright 74); McGinn, Jack, Shinnie, Hayes (Pawlett 64); McLean (Ross 83); Rooney.
Stranraer: (442) Belford; Robertson, Barron (Turner 57), Bell, Dick; Agnew, Gibson, Thomson R (Morena 73), Neill; McGuigan (Wilson 64), Malcolm.
Referee: Don Robertson.

Alloa Ath (0) 2 *(McCluskey 68, Spence 90)*
Dunfermline Ath (2) 3 *(Clark 12, McMullan 44, Cardle 60)* 1871
Alloa Ath: (4411) Parry; Taggart, McKeown, Graham, Waters; Cawley, Hetherington (McCluskey 67), Holmes, Kirkpatrick; Flannigan (Longworth 66); Spence.
Dunfermline Ath: (442) Murdoch; Martin, Ashcroft, Geggan, Morris; Herron (McCabe 79), Wedderburn, McMullan, Higginbotham (Cardle 46); Clark (Moffat 73), Reilly.
Referee: Alan Newlands.

Ayr U (0) 0
Queen's Park (0) 0 1326
Ayr U: (442) Fleming; Devlin, Balatoni, McKenna, Boyle; Gilmour (Forrest 46), Crawford, Docherty, Cairney (Adams 63); Moore (McGuffie 75), Harkins.
Queen's Park: (4411) Muir; Millen, Cummins, McGeever, Wharton; Woods (Malone 69), Fotheringham, McKernon, Burns; Brady; MacPherson (Galt 70).
Referee: Barry Cook.

Bonnyrigg Rose (1) 1 *(Hoskins 33 (pen))*
Hibernian (3) 8 *(Shinnie 11, Keatings 15, 76, Humphrey 24, Cummings 52, 72, Stevenson 61, Forster 82)* 1552
Bonnyrigg Rose: (433) Andrews; Horne, Young, Hoskins, Donaldson; Kidd, Stewart (Brown 79), Nelson; Turner (Gray 60), McGachie, McIntosh (McLaren 64).
Hibernian: (352) Marciano (Laidlaw 20); Forster, McGregor, Fontaine; Humphrey, McGinn (Fyvie 64), Keatings, Shinnie, Stevenson; Cummings (Boyle 75), Holt.
Referee: Alan Muir.

Dundee (0) 0

St Mirren (1) 2 *(Sutton 25, Baird 50)* 3622

Dundee: (4231) Bain; Holt, Etxabeguren Leanizbarrutia, Gadzhalov, Kerr; McGowan, Hateley (Duffy 58); El Bakhtaoui (Williams 58), O'Hara, Wighton; Haber.
St Mirren: (4231) O'Brien; Irvine, Baird, MacKenzie, Magennis (Whyte 74); Fjelde, Storie; McAllister (McAtherson 90), Mallan, Morgan; Sutton (Clarkson 85).
Referee: Bobby Madden.

Elgin C (1) 1 *(Nicolson 25)*

Inverness CT (1) 2 *(Cole 32, Doumbouya 66)* 3624

Elgin C: (4411) Waters; Cooper, McHardy, Nicolson (Stewart 29), MacPhee; Dodd (Reid 64), Reilly, Cameron, Moore (Gunn 73); Sutherland S; McLeish.
Inverness CT: (352) Fon Williams; Brad McKay, Warren, Tremarco; Polworth, Doran, Tansey, Cole, Vigurs; Doumbouya, Boden (Anier 79).
Referee: John McKendrick.

Greenock Morton (1) 2 *(Lindsay 39, Forbes 47)*

Falkirk (0) 0 2349

Greenock Morton: (4411) Gaston; Doyle, Kilday, O'Ware, Lamie; Forbes, Lindsay, Murdoch, Russell; Nesbitt (McDonagh 90); Oliver.
Falkirk: (4411) Rogers; Muirhead, McCracken, Watson, Gallacher; Aird, Kerr, Sibbald, Hippolyte (Baird 69); Craigen (McHugh 54); Miller.
Referee: Greg Aitken.

Kilmarnock (0) 0

Hamilton A (0) 1 *(Bingham 90 (pen))* 2944

Kilmarnock: (442) Woodman; Hendrie, Osborne, Ajer, Taylor; McKenzie (Smith S 60), Dicker, Jones, Roberts (Coulibaly 64); Tyson (Boyd K 64), Longstaff.
Hamilton A: (352) Woods; Gillespie, Devlin, McMann; Redmond, MacKinnon, Crawford, Donati, Imrie; Brophy (Bingham 67), D'Acol (Longridge 81).
Referee: Crawford Allan.

Livingston (0) 0

East Fife (1) 1 *(Paterson 27)* 726

Livingston: (442) Kelly; Halkett, Crighton, Lithgow, Gallagher; Cadden (Carrick 83), Pitman, Byrne, De Vita (Mullin 66); Mullen, Buchanan.
East Fife: (433) Goodfellow; Kane, Kerr, Page, Penrice; Paterson, Robinson, Slattery; Smith, Insall (Duggan 82), Brown (Lamont 76).
Referee: Colin Steven.

Partick Thistle (3) 4 *(Erskine 10, 31, Lawless 30, Osman 64)*

Formartine United (0) 0 2782

Partick Thistle: (433) Cerny; Elliot, Devine, Barton, Booth (Dumbuya 46); Osman, Erskine, Welsh (McCarthy 76); Amoo (Azeez 63), Doolan, Lawless.
Formartine United: (4411) MacDonald; Young (Dingwall 46), Crawford, Ferries, Smith; Rodger (Gauld 82), Lawson, Masson, Anderson (Gethins 72); Barbour; Wood.
Referee: Craig Charleston.

Rangers (0) 2 *(Miller 84, 89)*

Motherwell (0) 1 *(Moult 74)* 31,921

Rangers: (4231) Foderingham; Hodson, Kiernan, Hill, Wallace; Toral (Windass 63), Halliday; O'Halloran (Waghorn 71), Holt (Hyndman 73), McKay; Miller.
Motherwell: (451) Samson; Tait, Heneghan, McManus, Hammell; Cadden (McMillan 81), Lasley, McHugh, Clay, Chalmers (McDonald 63); Moult.
Referee: Craig Thomson.

Ross Co (4) 6 *(Routis 6, 76, Quinn 16, Chow 28, Boyce 30, O'Brien 90)*

Dundee U (2) 2 *(Andreu 13, 45)* 2440

Ross Co: (442) Fox; Fraser, Quinn, McEveley (Tumility 46), van der Weg; Dow, Woods (O'Brien 46), Routis, Chow; Boyce, Schalk (Lalkovic 79).
Dundee U: (4231) Bell; van der Struijk, Edjenguele, Durnan, Robson; Telfer, Murdoch (Flood 46); Fraser, Andreu, Obadeyi (Mikkelsen 46); Murray (Spittal 67).
Referee: Kevin Clancy.

St Johnstone (2) 2 *(MacLean 6, Alston 32)*

Stenhousemuir (0) 0 2441

St Johnstone: (442) Clark; Watson, Shaughnessy, Anderson, Easton; Alston, Wotherspoon, Millar, Swanson (Craig 78); MacLean, Cummins (Kane 82).
Stenhousemuir: (442) McCabe; McCormack, Kerr, Meechan, Summers; Furtado (Martinez 73), Berry, Millar (McCroary 89), Cook; Shaw, McMenamin (Howarth 82).
Referee: Euan Anderson.

Stirling Alb (1) 2 *(Bikey 9, 84)*

Clyde (1) 2 *(MacDonald 24, 62)* 869

Stirling Alb: (442) Binnie; Black (Henderson 62), Davidson, Wright, Quigley; Caddis, Colquhoun (Dickson 79), Robertson, McLaren; Smith D, Bikey.
Clyde: (442) Gibson; Johnston, Perry, Smith, McNiff; McNeil, McMillan, McLaughlin, Higgins; MacDonald, Gormley (Ferguson S 81).
Referee: Mat Northcroft.

Sunday, 22 January 2017

Albion R (0) 0

Celtic (1) 3 *(Sinclair 30, Dembele 77, Armstrong 90)* 8319

Albion R: (4231) Ross Stewart I; Turnbull (McCann 79), Dunlop M, Dunlop R, Reid; Fisher, Davidson; McBride, Ferry (Gilmour 74), Ross Stewart II (Ferguson 65); Willis.
Celtic: (4231) Gordon; Tierney (McGregor 62), Boyata, Lustig (Simunovic 46), Gamboa; Bitton, Brown; Sinclair, Armstrong, Forrest (Roberts 75); Dembele.
Referee: William Collum.

Raith R (0) 1 *(McManus 89)*

Hearts (1) 1 *(Walker 37)* 5036

Raith R: (4141) Cuthbert; Davidson, Mvoto, Benedictus, McHattie; Matthews; Barr, Callachan, Thompson (Skacel 81), Johnston (Hardie 69); Stewart (McManus 81).
Hearts: (4411) Hamilton; Struna, Hughes, Souttar, Sowah; Cowie, Nowak, Kitchen, Walker (Zanatta 86); Martin; Johnsen (Sammon 90).
Referee: John Beaton.

FOURTH ROUND REPLAYS

Tuesday, 24 January 2017

Queen's Park (2) 2 *(Woods 4, Wharton 32)*

Ayr U (1) 2 *(Moore 26, Balatoni 83)* 1026

Queen's Park: (352) Muir; Wharton, McGeever, Cummins; Millen, Fotheringham, McKernon, Brady (McVey 74), Burns■; Woods (Galt 81), MacPherson (Malone 61).
Ayr U: (4411) Fleming; Devlin (Rose 120), Balatoni, Murphy, Boyle; Docherty, Crawford, Gilmour (Cairney 58), Donald (Forrest 71); Harkins; Moore (McGuffie 71).
aet; Ayr U won 5-4 on penalties.
Referee: Barry Cook.

Wednesday, 25 January 2017

Hearts (1) 4 *(Currie 35, Martin 94 (pen), Walker 105 (pen), Johnsen 114)*

Raith R (1) 2 *(Barr B 14, Hardie 101)* 10,740

Hearts: (442) Hamilton; Struna (Smith 91), Souttar, Hughes, Sowah; Martin, Kitchen, Buaben (Nicholson 46 (Sammon 107)), Walker; Currie (Zanatta 99), Johnsen.
Raith R: (442) Cuthbert; Davidson (Thomson 71), Mvoto, Benedictus, McHattie; Matthews, Callachan, Thompson (Hardie 79), Barr B (Skacel 99); Stewart, McManus (Johnston 99).
aet.
Referee: John Beaton.

Tuesday, 31 January 2017

Clyde (3) 3 *(Gormley 5, 10, 39)*

Stirling Alb (1) 2 *(Henderson 4 (pen), 82 (pen))* 625

Clyde: (4132) Gibson■; Johnston, McNeil, Smith, McNiff; McMillan; Ferguson S (Flynn 58), Higgins, McLaughlin; MacDonald (Caddis 81), Gormley.
Stirling Alb: (451) Smith C; Black (Dickson 46), Wright (Smith R 85), McMillan, Quigley; Caddis, Colquhoun (Cameron 78), Robertson, McLaren, Smith D; Henderson.
Referee: Mat Northcroft.

FIFTH ROUND

Saturday, 11 February 2017

Ayr U (0) 1 *(Cairney 70)*

Clyde (0) 1 *(Gormley 55)* 1554

Ayr U: (442) Fleming; Devlin, Meggatt, Balatoni, Boyle (Murphy 27); McGuffie (Forrest 67), Adams (Gilmour 41), Docherty, Cairney; Harkins, McDaid.
Clyde: (433) Quinn; McNeil, Smith, McMillan (Perry 56), McNiff; Ferguson S (Flynn 73), McLaughlin, Johnston; Higgins, Gormley, MacDonald (Millar 85).
Referee: Stephen Finnie.

Celtic (2) 6 *(Lustig 20, Dembele 45, 50, 59, Tierney 86, Brown 90)*

Inverness CT (0) 0 25,577

Celtic: (4231) Gordon; Lustig, Boyata (Toure 89), Sviatchenko, Tierney; Bitton, Brown; Forrest, Henderson (McGregor 66), Sinclair; Dembele (Ciftci 82).
Inverness CT: (451) Fon Williams; Raven, Warren, Brad McKay, Tremarco; King (Mulraney 54), Tansey, Draper (Cole 64), Vigurs, Anier; Billy McKay (Ebbe 64).
Referee: Kevin Clancy.

Dunfermline Ath (1) 1 *(McMullan 30)*

Hamilton A (0) 1 *(Redmond 74)* 2945

Dunfermline Ath: (442) Murdoch; Geggan (Talbot 39), Morris, Ashcroft, Martin; McMullan, Wedderburn, Herron, Higginbotham; Clark, Moffat (Hopkirk 87).
Hamilton A: (4132) Matthews; Skondras (McMann 54), Devlin, Seaborne, Adams; Donati; Redmond, MacKinnon, Gillespie (Imrie 46); Brophy (Kurtaj 78), Bingham.
Referee: Craig Thomson.

East Fife (0) 2 *(Duggan 54 (pen), 90 (pen))*

St Mirren (1) 3 *(Smith 33, Morgan 70, 84)* 1483

East Fife: (4231) Goodfellow; Watt (Kane 12), Kerr, Page, Penrice; Paterson, Slattery; Brown (Insall 75), Robinson, Smith (Lamont 66); Duggan.
St Mirren: (4231) O'Brien; Demetriou, MacKenzie, Davis, Eckersley; Storie (Morgan 66), Magennis; Mallan, McGinn, Smith (Fjelde 90); Loy (Sutton 57).
Referee: Don Robertson.

Ross Co (0) 0

Aberdeen (0) 1 *(Logan 87)* 4671

Ross Co: (4141) Fox; Fraser, Davies, McEveley, van der Weg; Chow (Gobern 46); Gardyne (Lalkovic 53), Woods, Boyce, O'Brien; Schalk (Curran 66).
Aberdeen: (4231) Lewis; Logan, Taylor, Reynolds (O'Connor 62), Considine; Jack, Shinnie; McGinn, McLean, Hayes; Rooney (Stockley 73).
Referee: Bobby Madden.

St Johnstone (0) 0

Partick Thistle (1) 1 *(Barton 7)* 2884

St Johnstone: (442) Clark; Foster, Shaughnessy, Anderson, Easton; Wotherspoon (Alston 46), Millar (Craig 74), Davidson, Swanson; MacLean, Cummins (Kane 74).
Partick Thistle: (3511) Cerny; Keown, Devine, Lindsay; Amoo, Barton, Osman, Welsh, Lawless; Edwards; Azeez (Doolan 84).
Referee: Steven McLean.

Sunday, 12 February 2017

Hearts (0) 0

Hibernian (0) 0 16,971

Hearts: (4411) Hamilton; Struna, Avlonitis, Hughes, Sowah; Nicholson (Djoum 65), Cowie (Nowak 79), Tziolis, Walker; Martin (Johnsen 46); Goncalves.
Hibernian: (41212) Marciano; Gray, McGregor, Forster (Fontaine 54), Stevenson; Bartley; Fyvie, McGinn; Keatings; Holt (Graham 79), Cummings.
Referee: William Collum.

Rangers (1) 2 *(Miller 13, Waghorn 61)*

Greenock Morton (1) 1 *(Tidser 7)* 30,295

Rangers: (433) Foderingham; Tavernier, Senderos, Hill, Wallace (Hodson 83); Hyndman (Toral 80), Halliday, Holt (O'Halloran 62); Waghorn, Miller, McKay.
Greenock Morton: (4411) Gaston; Kilday, Doyle (McDonagh 39), O'Ware, Lamie (Donnelly 71); Forbes, Murdoch, Lindsay, Russell; Tidser; Nesbitt.
Referee: Andrew Dallas.

FIFTH ROUND REPLAYS

Tuesday, 14 February 2017

Clyde (0) 1 *(Gormley 88)*

Ayr U (1) 2 *(McDaid 11, Wardrope 117)* 965

Clyde: (442) Quinn; Johnston, Perry, Smith, McNiff (Flynn 69); Ferguson S (Millar 85), McNeil, Higgins (McGovern 111), McLaughlin (Linton 77); MacDonald, Gormley.
Ayr U: (442) Fleming; Devlin, Murphy, Balatoni, Meggatt; Gilmour (McKenzie 99), Docherty, Cairney (Wardrope 106), Harkins (McGuffie 86); Forrest (Rose 58), McDaid.
aet.
Referee: Stephen Finnie.

Hamilton A (0) 1 *(Bingham 87 (pen))*

Dunfermline Ath (1) 1 *(Morris 25)* 1222

Hamilton A: (3412) Matthews; Devlin, Seaborne (Donati 29), McMann; Watson, MacKinnon, Gillespie (Skondras 68), Imrie; Redmond; Bingham (Cunningham 114), Kurtaj (Brophy 54).
Dunfermline Ath: (442) Murdoch; Martin, Morris, Ashcroft, Talbot; Higginbotham (Cardle 96), Herron, Wedderburn, McMullan (Paton 96); Clark (Reilly 69), Moffat (McCabe 83).
aet; Hamilton A won 3-0 on penalties.
Referee: Craig Thomson.

Wednesday, 22 February 2017

Hibernian (2) 3 *(Cummings 21, Holt 37, Shinnie 63)*

Hearts (0) 1 *(Goncalves 70)* 20,205

Hibernian: (442) Marciano; Gray, McGregor, Fontaine, Stevenson; Humphrey (Shinnie 5), Bartley, McGinn, Boyle; Holt (Graham 76), Cummings (Fyvie 89).
Hearts: (4141) Hamilton; Struna (Choulay 77), Avlonitis, Hughes, Sowah; Kitchen (Nicholson 46); Walker, Tziolis, Martin (Currie 46), Djoum; Goncalves.
Referee: Steven McLean.

QUARTER-FINALS

Saturday, 4 March 2017

Hibernian (2) 3 *(McGinn 7, Cummings 12 (pen), Keatings 79)*

Ayr U (1) 1 *(McGuffie 33)* 13,602

Hibernian: (442) Marciano; Gray, Forster, Ambrose, Stevenson; Boyle, Bartley (Fyvie 83), McGinn, Shinnie; Holt (Graham 87), Cummings (Keatings 77).
Ayr U: (442) Fleming; Devlin, McKenna■, Balatoni, Meggatt; Gilmour, Docherty (Rose 68), McGuffie (Wardrope 77), Boyle; Moore (Forrest 66), Harkins.
Referee: Nick Walsh.

Rangers (1) 6 *(Waghorn 33 (pen), Garner 48, 88, 90, Toral 77, Hill 82)*

Hamilton A (0) 0 27,287

Rangers: (433) Foderingham; Tavernier, Kiernan, Hill, Wallace; Holt, Toral, Hyndman (Forrester 82); Waghorn (O'Halloran 75), Miller (Garner 46), McKay.
Hamilton A: (4231) Matthews; Skondras, Devlin, Sarris (Watson 40), Adams (McMann 62); Donati, Gillespie; Imrie, Crawford, Kurtaj (Docherty 67); Bingham.
Referee: John Beaton.

Sunday, 5 March 2017

Aberdeen (1) 1 *(Shinnie 43)*

Partick Thistle (0) 0 11,333

Aberdeen: (442) Lewis; Logan, Taylor, Considine, Shinnie; Pawlett (O'Connor 75), Hayes, McLean, McGinn (Christie 88); Stockley, Rooney (Storey 80).
Partick Thistle: (352) Cerny; Devine■, Keown, Lindsay; Elliot, Edwards, Barton (Lawless 54), Osman, Booth; Erskine (Azeez 60), Doolan (Nisbet 79).
Referee: Craig Thomson.

Celtic (0) 4 *(Lustig 58, Sinclair 59, Dembele 68, Griffiths 78)*

St Mirren (1) 1 *(Davis 13)* 27,455

Celtic: (4231) Gordon; Lustig, Boyata, Sviatchenko, Tierney; Brown, Bitton (Griffiths 54); Mackay-Steven (Roberts 46), Armstrong (Eboue 77), Sinclair; Dembele.
St Mirren: (4411) O'Brien; Demetriou, Davis, MacKenzie (Baird 75), Irvine; Magennis (Storie 83), Mallan, McGinn, Morgan; Smith; Sutton (Loy 70).
Referee: Steven McLean.

SEMI-FINALS (at Hampden Park)

Saturday, 22 April 2017

Hibernian (1) 2 *(Holt 36, McGeouch 60)*

Aberdeen (2) 3 *(Rooney 1, Christie 25, McGregor 86 (og))* 31,969

Hibernian: (4231) Marciano; Gray, McGregor, Ambrose (Graham 88), Stevenson; Bartley, Fyvie (Holt 34); Boyle, McGeouch (Shinnie 63), McGinn; Cummings.
Aberdeen: (4231) Lewis; Logan, Taylor, Reynolds (McGinn 69), Considine; Jack, Shinnie; Christie (O'Connor 59), McLean, Hayes; Rooney.
Referee: John Beaton.

Sunday, 23 April 2017

Celtic (1) 2 *(McGregor 11, Sinclair 51 (pen))*

Rangers (0) 0 49,643

Celtic: (4231) Gordon; Lustig, Boyata, Simunovic, Tierney; Brown, McGregor (Rogic 75); Roberts (Forrest 82), Armstrong, Sinclair; Dembele (Griffiths 34).
Rangers: (433) Foderingham; Tavernier, Wilson, Bates, Beerman; Hyndman (Windass 70), Holt, Halliday (McKay 46); Garner (Dodoo 46), Miller, Waghorn.
Referee: William Collum.

WILLIAM HILL SCOTTISH CUP FINAL 2017

Saturday, 27 May 2017

(at Hampden Park, attendance 48,713)

Celtic (1) 2 Aberdeen (1) 1

Celtic: (433) Gordon; Lustig, Simunovic, Boyata, Tierney (Rogic 27); McGregor, Brown, Armstrong; Roberts (Sviatchenko 90), Griffiths, Sinclair.
Scorers: Armstrong 11, Rogic 90.

Aberdeen: (4231) Lewis; Logan, Reynolds, Taylor, Considine; Jack (Wright 90), Shinnie; Hayes, McLean, McGinn (O'Connor 75); Stockley (Rooney 62).
Scorer: Hayes 9.

Referee: Boddy Madden.

Stuart Armstrong drives home Celtic's opening goal as they beat Aberdeen 2-1 in the Scottish Cup final. Celtic completed an historic treble. (Jane Barlow/PA Wire/PA Images)

SCOTTISH FOOTBALL PYRAMID 2016–17

PRESS & JOURNAL HIGHLAND LEAGUE

	P	W	D	L	F	A	GD	Pts
Buckie Thistle	34	26	4	4	130	36	94	82
Cove Rangers	34	25	7	2	109	30	79	82
Brora Rangers	34	26	3	5	116	36	80	81
Formartine U	34	22	7	5	82	47	35	73
Fraserburgh	34	19	6	9	77	48	29	63
Forres Mechanics	34	17	7	10	84	63	21	58
Turriff U	34	18	4	12	56	42	14	58
Wick Academy	34	15	8	11	75	52	23	53
Inverurie Loco Works	34	14	8	12	71	53	18	50
Keith	34	15	2	17	74	88	−14	47
Clachnacuddin	34	11	8	15	53	77	−24	41
Lossiemouth	34	11	5	18	52	70	−18	38
Nairn Co	34	9	7	18	57	74	−17	34
Huntly	34	9	7	18	54	97	−43	34
Deveronvale	34	9	3	22	51	75	−24	30
Rothes	34	7	5	22	37	106	−69	26
Fort William	34	3	2	29	44	136	−92	11
Strathspey Thistle	34	2	3	29	28	120	−92	9

FERRARI PACKAGING LOWLAND LEAGUE

	P	W	D	L	F	A	GD	Pts
East Kilbride	30	24	3	3	89	21	68	75
East Stirlingshire	30	21	5	4	107	43	64	68
Spartans	30	17	5	8	69	30	39	56
Stirling University	30	16	5	9	60	53	7	53
Dalbeattie Star	30	14	5	11	60	50	10	47
Cumbernauld Colts	30	13	8	9	51	43	8	47
BSC Glasgow	30	12	6	12	63	56	7	42
Whitehill Welfare	30	13	1	16	53	64	−11	40
Gretna 2008	30	12	4	14	44	65	−21	40
Gala Fairydean R	30	11	7	12	55	77	−22	40
Edinburgh University	30	10	7	13	40	42	−2	37
Civil Service Strollers	30	10	7	13	59	68	−9	37
Vale of Leithen	30	11	4	15	52	66	−14	37
Hawick Royal Albert	30	8	1	21	58	93	−35	25
Selkirk	30	6	5	19	58	86	−28	23
Preston Ath	30	5	1	24	41	102	−61	16

East Kilbride won play-off with Buckie Thistle (4-3 on aggregate) for the right to play a further play-off with League Two Cowdenbeath, which Cowdenbeath won 5-3 on penalties (1-1 after extra time).

CENTRAL TAXIS EAST OF SCOTLAND LEAGUE

	P	W	D	L	F	A	GD	Pts
Lothian Thistle Hutchison Vale	20	17	2	1	85	16	69	53
Leith Ath	20	15	2	3	80	18	62	47
Tynecastle	20	14	1	5	56	26	30	43
Heriot Watt University	20	12	3	5	61	30	31	39
Coldstream	20	9	4	7	39	51	−12	31
Stirling University	20	9	3	8	55	36	19	30
Eyemouth U	20	7	2	11	34	53	−19	23
Peebles R	20	6	1	13	28	45	−17	19
Ormiston	20	4	0	16	25	57	−32	12
Tweedmouth Rangers	20	3	3	14	28	77	−49	12
Burntisland Shipyard	20	3	1	16	12	94	−82	10

Duns resigned membership, record expunged.

SOUTH OF SCOTLAND FOOTBALL LEAGUE

	P	W	D	L	F	A	GD	Pts
Edusport Academy	26	22	2	2	88	28	60	68
Wigtown and Bladnoch	26	21	3	2	74	29	45	66
St Cuthbert W	26	19	3	4	110	54	56	60
Threave R	26	11	7	8	62	32	30	40
Mid Annandale	26	12	4	10	79	72	7	40
Newton Stewart	26	12	3	11	70	59	11	39
Heston R	26	12	2	12	68	61	7	38
Abbey Vale	26	11	5	10	61	54	7	38
Lochar Thistle	26	11	2	13	62	52	10	35
Creetown	26	10	1	15	49	67	−18	31
Lochmaben	26	8	2	16	46	65	−19	26
Upper Annandale	26	5	6	15	45	69	−24	21
Nithsdale W	26	6	3	17	53	84	−31	21
Dumfries YMCA	26	0	1	25	22	163	−141	1

NORTH CALEDONIAN FOOTBALL LEAGUE

	P	W	D	L	F	A	GD	Pts
Invergordon	14	11	1	2	34	18	16	34
Orkney	14	10	1	3	29	13	16	31
Halkirk U	14	9	1	4	33	17	16	28
Golspie Sutherland	14	6	2	6	33	33	0	20
Thurso	14	5	3	6	22	18	4	18
St Duthus	14	4	2	8	22	30	−8	14
Inverness Ath	14	2	2	10	27	39	−12	8
Alness U	14	2	2	10	19	51	−32	8

WELSH FOOTBALL 2016–17

THE DAFABET WELSH PREMIER LEAGUE 2016–17

			Home					*Away*					*Total*						
		P	*W*	*D*	*L*	*F*	*A*	*W*	*D*	*L*	*F*	*A*	*W*	*D*	*L*	*F*	*A*	*GD*	*Pts*
1	The New Saints	32	16	0	0	55	6	12	1	3	46	20	28	1	3	101	26	75	85
2	Connah's Quay Nomads	32	9	5	2	25	11	7	5	4	20	13	16	10	6	45	24	21	58
3	Bala T	32	8	6	2	33	18	8	3	5	28	28	16	9	7	61	46	15	57
4	Bangor C	32	11	0	5	30	20	5	4	7	23	33	16	4	12	53	53	0	52
5	Newtown	32	5	8	3	34	26	7	1	8	25	15	12	9	11	59	41	18	45
6	Carmarthen T	32	4	4	8	21	29	6	5	5	19	17	10	9	13	40	46	–6	39
7	Cefn Druids	32	6	5	5	27	27	3	7	6	13	21	9	12	11	40	48	–8	39
8	Cardiff Met University	32	6	3	7	28	23	4	3	9	13	18	10	6	16	41	41	0	36
9	Llandudno	32	3	6	7	12	21	4	8	4	19	24	7	14	11	31	45	–14	35
10	Aberystwyth	32	5	2	9	19	29	5	2	9	22	34	10	4	18	41	63	–22	34
11	Rhyl	32	6	3	7	18	21	2	3	11	20	55	8	6	18	38	76	–38	30
12	Airbus UK Broughton	32	4	3	9	18	36	1	3	12	19	42	5	6	21	37	78	–41	21

Top 6 teams split after 22 games.

PREVIOUS WELSH LEAGUE WINNERS

1993	Cwmbran Town	2000	TNS	2007	TNS	2014	The New Saints
1994	Bangor City	2001	Barry Town	2008	Llanelli	2015	The New Saints
1995	Bangor City	2002	Barry Town	2009	Rhyl	2016	The New Saints
1996	Barry Town	2003	Barry Town	2010	The New Saints	2017	The New Saints
1997	Barry Town	2004	Rhyl	2011	Bangor C		
1998	Barry Town	2005	TNS	2012	The New Saints		
1999	Barry Town	2006	TNS	2013	The New Saints		

NATHANIEL CAR SALES WELSH LEAGUE 2016–17

			Home					*Away*					*Total*						
		P	*W*	*D*	*L*	*F*	*A*	*W*	*D*	*L*	*F*	*A*	*W*	*D*	*L*	*F*	*A*	*GD*	*Pts*
1	Barry Town U	30	11	3	1	45	8	9	3	3	24	10	20	6	4	69	18	51	66
2	Penybont	30	11	1	3	41	18	8	3	4	32	23	19	4	7	73	41	32	61
3	Goytre	30	9	3	3	41	24	9	1	5	39	25	18	4	8	80	49	31	58
4	Haverfordwest Co	30	7	5	3	22	18	9	1	5	33	29	16	6	8	55	47	8	54
5	Caerau (Ely)	30	10	4	1	38	21	3	5	7	19	29	13	9	8	57	50	7	48
6	Cwmbran Celtic	30	10	1	4	41	23	4	2	9	19	27	14	3	13	60	50	10	45
7	Undy Ath	30	9	0	6	31	16	4	2	9	22	37	13	2	15	53	53	0	41
8	Afan Lido*	30	6	3	6	20	20	7	2	6	26	29	13	5	12	46	49	–3	41
9	Taff's Well	30	8	1	6	26	24	4	3	8	14	24	12	4	14	40	48	–8	40
10	Goytre U	30	4	3	8	21	19	6	6	3	23	18	10	9	11	44	37	7	39
11	Cambrian & Clydach Vale	30	1	6	8	16	28	9	1	5	25	21	10	7	13	41	49	–8	37
12	Ton Pentre	30	7	3	5	31	22	3	3	9	20	39	10	6	14	51	61	–10	36
13	Port Talbot T	30	8	2	5	29	24	2	3	10	12	33	10	5	15	41	57	–16	35
14	Monmouth T	30	6	4	5	34	30	3	2	10	15	44	9	6	15	49	74	–25	33
15	Caldicot T	30	4	1	10	16	29	3	1	11	20	36	7	2	21	36	65	–29	23
16	Risca U	30	4	0	11	21	36	2	2	11	17	49	6	2	22	38	85	–47	20

**Afan Lido deducted 3pts for fielding an ineligible player.*

HUWS GRAY CYMRU ALLIANCE LEAGUE 2016–17

			Home					*Away*					*Total*						
		P	*W*	*D*	*L*	*F*	*A*	*W*	*D*	*L*	*F*	*A*	*W*	*D*	*L*	*F*	*A*	*GD*	*Pts*
1	Prestatyn T	30	13	1	1	50	18	13	1	1	64	17	26	2	2	114	35	79	80
2	Caernarfon T	30	10	3	2	46	22	9	4	2	37	23	19	7	4	83	45	38	64
3	Gresford Ath	30	9	2	4	39	22	9	0	6	28	25	18	2	10	67	47	20	56
4	Porthmadog	30	7	1	7	25	26	9	1	5	39	22	16	2	12	64	48	16	50
5	Holywell T	30	8	4	3	27	21	6	4	5	25	24	14	8	8	52	45	7	50
6	Flint Town U	30	7	2	6	25	22	7	4	4	37	25	14	6	10	62	47	15	48
7	Caersws	30	6	1	8	23	30	9	2	4	38	29	15	3	12	61	59	2	48
8	Guilsfield	30	8	2	5	28	16	4	5	6	26	30	12	7	11	54	46	8	43
9	Holyhead H	30	7	1	7	33	26	5	5	5	24	26	12	6	12	57	52	5	42
10	Denbigh T	30	5	4	6	30	32	5	4	6	27	30	10	8	12	57	62	–5	38
11	Ruthin T	30	6	3	6	27	29	4	0	11	22	43	10	3	17	49	72	–23	33
12	Penrhyncoch*	30	4	4	7	20	23	5	3	7	19	25	9	7	14	39	48	–9	31
13	Llanfair U	30	3	3	9	18	35	4	1	10	18	34	7	4	19	36	69	–33	25
14	Mold Alex	30	4	2	9	25	52	3	2	10	19	39	7	4	19	44	91	–47	25
15	Conwy Bor	30	3	2	10	27	43	4	1	10	26	40	7	3	20	53	83	–30	24
16	Buckley T	30	4	3	8	26	44	2	1	12	12	37	6	4	20	38	81	–43	22

**Penrhyncoch deducted 3pts for fielding an ineligible player.*

JD WELSH FA CUP 2016–17

**After extra time.*

QUALIFYING ROUND 1 – CENTRAL
Berriew v Trewern 5-0
Brecon Corries v Kerry 3-1
Llansantffraid Village v Abermule 3-4
Montgomery T v Tywyn Bryncrug 3-2
Presteigne St Andrews v Borth U 2-3
Waterloo R v Newbridge-on-Wye 4-4*
Newbridge-on-Wye won 7-6 on penalties

QUALIFYING ROUND 1 – NORTH EAST
AFC Brynford v Cefn Alb 6-3
Coedpoeth U v Acton 3-2
FC Penley v Sychdyn 1-2
Lex Glyndwr v Rhostyllen 4-1
Llangollen T v Llanuwchllyn 3-4
Mynydd Isa Spartans v Greenfield 1-5
Rhydymwyn v Castell Alun Colts 4-1

QUALIFYING ROUND 1 – NORTH WEST
Amlwch T v Mochdre Sports 1-2
Cemaes Bay v Blaenau Ffestiniog 4-2
Dyffryn Nantlle v Pwllheli 3-2
Gaerwen v Llanfairfechan 3-2*
Llandudno Alb v Llanfairpwll 7-1
Llanllyfni v Llanystumdwy 7-3
Llanrwst U v Penmaenmawr Phoenix 1-4
Meliden v Pentraeth 1-3
Mynydd Llandegai v Menai Bridge Tigers 5-0
Prestatyn Sports (walkover) v Gwalchmai (withdrawn)
Y Felinheli v Llandyrnog U 6-5

QUALIFYING ROUND 1 – SOUTH EAST
Abergavenny T v Chepstow T 6-4
Abertillery Bluebirds v Treowen Stars 2-3
AFC Perthcelyn v Aber Valley 0-4
Blaenrhondda v Ynysddu Welfare 1-0
Bridgend Street v AFC Butetown 4-1
Caerleon v Cwm Welfare 5-3
Dynamo Aber v Penrhiwceiber Rangers 5-3
Gelli Hibernian v Dinas Powys 0-6
Llanrumney U v Cwmbran T 2-1*
Merthyr Saints v Cardiff Hibernian 5-2
Newport YMCA v Cardiff Corinthians 4-1
Risca Whiteheads v Nelson Cavaliers 0-3
RTB Ebbw Vale v Newport C 3-1
STM Sports v Llantwit Fardre 2-0
Sully Sports v Clwb Cymric 4-0
Tiger Bay v Blaenavon Blues 2-1
Trethomas Bluebirds v Panteg 3-2
Wattsville v Tredegar T 0-4

QUALIFYING ROUND 1 – SOUTH WEST
Bettws (walkover) v CP Suburbs (withdrawn)
Caerau v West End 1-0
Cefn Cribbwr v Trefelin BGC 2-4
Ely Rangers v Llandovery 7-0
Hirwaun v Penlan Social 0-2
Llangynwyd Rangers v Pontyclun 1-2
Llantwit Major v Garw 2-0
Newcastle Emlyn v Porthcawl Town Ath 0-6
Penrhiwfer v Hirwaun Sports 2-5
Pontypridd T v Team Swansea 4-0
Ynysgerwyn v Treforest 4-1

QUALIFYING ROUND 2 – CENTRAL
Aberaeron v Montgomery T 2-1
Abermule v Llanuwchllyn 1-6
Borth U v Welshpool T 1-3
Bow Street v Brecon Corries 0-2
Carno v Knighton T 3-0
Hay St Marys v Llanrhaeadr Ym Mochnant 1-2
Llanidloes T v Berriew 4-2
Newbridge-on-Wye v Llandrindod Wells 2-6
Rhayader T v Machynlleth 6-2

QUALIFYING ROUND 2 – NORTH
Abergele T v Pentraeth 7-3
Brymbo v Llay Welfare 6-1
Cemaes Bay v Prestatyn Sports 1-5
Coedpoeth U v AFC Brynford 2-0
Corwen v FC Queens Park 4-1
Dyffryn Nantlle v Glan Conwy 5-3
FC Nomads of Connah's Quay v Brickfield Rangers 3-1
Gaerwen v Llangefni T 0-1
Lex Glyndwr v Chirk AAA 3-2
Llanberis v Penmaenmawr Phoenix 7-2
Llandudno Alb v Llanllyfni 4-2
Llandudno Junction v Mynydd Llandegai 2-3
Llanrug U v Penrhyndeudraeth 4-0
Mochdre Sports v St Asaph C 0-3
Rhydymwyn v Hawarden Rangers 1-3
Saltney T v Penycae 2-4
Sychdyn v Greenfield 0-7
Trearddur Bay U v Glantraeth 0-1
Y Felinheli v Barmouth & Dyffryn U 2-3

QUALIFYING ROUND 2 – SOUTH
Aberbargoed Buds v Dynamo Aber 4-2
Aberdare T v Trethomas Bluebirds 0-1
Abergavenny T v Aber Valley 4-3*
AFC Porth v AFC Llywdcoed 2-1*
Ammanford v Ynysgerwyn 0-1
Bettws v Trefelin BGC 1-11
Bridgend Street v STM Sports 2-0
Caerau v Briton Ferry Llansawel 2-0
Cwmamman U v Porthcawl Town Ath 5-1
Dinas Powys v Merthyr Saints 0-1
Ely Rangers v Croesyceiliog 1-4
Hirwaun Sports v Pontardawe T 2-2*
Pontardawe T won 4-3 on penalties
Llanelli T v Pontypridd T 3-1
Llantwit Major v Penlan Social 2-1*
Nelson Cavaliers v Blaenrhondda 0-4
Newport YMCA v Caerleon 3-2
Pontyclun v Garden Village 4-3*
RTB Ebbw Vale v Llanrumney U 2-1
Sully Sports v Tiger Bay 4-1
Treowen Stars v Tredegar T 1-0

FIRST ROUND – NORTH
Abergele T v Llanrug U 0-2
Barmouth & Dyffryn U v Buckley T 0-2
Coedpoeth U v Holywell T 0-8
Conwy Borough v Caernarfon T 1-5
Dyffryn Nantlle Vale v Holyhead H 0-3
Flint Town U v Penycae 6-0
Glantraeth v Mynydd Llandegai 3-5
Greenfield v Llandudno Alb 3-2
Gresford Ath v Denbigh T 3-0
Guilsfield v Welshpool T 6-3
Hawarden Rangers v Carno 2-1
Lex Glyndwr v Corwen 1-2
Llangefni T v Brymbo 4-0
Llanidloes T v Llanfair U 0-2
Llanrhaeadr y Mochnant v Prestatyn Sports 5-3
Llanuwchlyn v Ruthin T 0-3
Mold Alex v Llanberis 4-0
Penrhyncoch v FC Nomads of Connah's Quay 2-0
Porthmadog v Caersws 4-0
St. Asaph C v Prestatyn T 0-8

FIRST ROUND – SOUTH
Aberaeron v Caldicot T 1-4
Aberbargoed Buds v Barry Town U 0-5
Afan Lido v Pontyclun 4-1
Bridgend Street v Goytre (Gwent) 2-2*
Goytre (Gwent) won 5-4 on penalties
Cambrian & Clydach Vale v Trefelin BGC 1-3
Croesyceiliog v Goytre U 1-1*
Goytre U won 4-2 on penalties
Cwmamman U v Caerau 2-0
Merthyr Saints v Llandrindod Wells 2-3
Monmouth T v Brecon Corries 1-0
Newport YMCA v Haverfordwest Co 1-2
Pen-y-Bont v AFC Porth 3-1
Pontardawe T v Cwmbran Celtic 1-0

Rhayader T v Caerau (Ely) 4-3
RTB Ebbw Vale v Ynysygerwyn 1-2
Sully Sports v Llantwit Major 2-6
Taff's Well v Port Talbot T 0-0*
Taff's Well won 5-3 on penalties
Ton Pentre v Abergavenny T 4-2
Treowen Stars v Risca U 4-1
Trethomas Bluebirds v Llanelli T 0-6
Undy Ath v Blaenrhondda 3-0

SECOND ROUND – NORTH
Buckley T v Corwen 1-6
Flint Town U v Llanfair U 3-4
Hawarden Rangers v Prestatyn T 1-4
Holyhead H v Llanrug U 2-1
Holywell T v Llanrhaeadr y Mochnant 6-0
Llangefni T v Caernarfon T 4-4*
Caernarfon T won 4-3 on penalties
Mold Alex v Guilsfield 2-4*
Mynydd Llandegai v Greenfield 0-3
Penrhyncoch v Ruthin T 3-0
Porthmadog v Gresford Ath 2-2*
Porthmadog won 3-1 on penalties

SECOND ROUND – SOUTH
Afan Lido v Pontardawe T 1-0
Barry Town U v Pen-y-Bont 0-3
Caldicot T v Cwmamman U 2-0
Haverfordwest Co v Undy Ath 3-2
Llantwit Major v Llandrindod Wells 1-0
Rhayader T v Goytre (Gwent) 1-2
Taff's Well v Llanelli T 2-3
Trefelin BGC v Goytre U 0-1*
Treowen Stars v Ton Pentre 1-2
Ynysygerwyn v Monmouth T 7-3

THIRD ROUND
Aberystwyth T v Holywell T 2-0
Bala T v Caldicot T 6-1
Caernarfon T v Carmarthen T 3-1
Cardiff Met University v Porthmadog 4-0
Cefn Druids v Llantwit Major 2-0
Connah's Quay Nomads v Goytre U 3-2
Greenfield v Guilsfield 0-3
Haverfordwest Co v Afan Lido 1-0
Llandudno v Goytre (Gwent) 0-2
Goytre (Gwent) removed for fielding an ineligible player. Llandudno reinstated.
Llanelli T v Ynysygerwyn 5-1
Llanfair U v Corwen 1-0
Newtown v The New Saints 0-3
Pen-y-Bont v Airbus UK Broughton 4-1
Prestatyn T v Holyhead H 2-1
Rhyl v Penrhyncoch 6-0
Ton Pentre v Bangor C 0-2

FOURTH ROUND
Aberystwyth T v Prestatyn T 1-5
Bala T v Pen-y-Bont 4-1
Bangor C v Llandudno 4-0
Caernarfon T v Rhyl 3-2
Guilsfield v Cardiff Met University 4-2
Haverfordwest Co v Connah's Quay Nomads 1-5
Llanfair U v Cefn Druids 4-1
The New Saints v Llanelli T 7-0

QUARTER-FINALS
Guilsfield v Bala T 0-3
Llanfair U v Caernarfon T 0-7
Prestatyn T v Connah's Quay Nomads 2-2*
Connah's Quay Nomads won 4-3 on penalties
The New Saints v Bangor C 2-1*

SEMI-FINALS
Caernarfon T v Bala T 1-3
Connah's Quay Nomads v The New Saints 0-3

JD WELSH FA CUP FINAL 2017
Bangor, Sunday 30 April 2017
Bala T (0) 2 *(Evans 77, Smith 85)*
The New Saints (0) 1 *(Draper 55)* 1110
Bala T: Morris; Stephens, Stuart Jones, Stuart J. Jones, Sheridan (Wade 71), Smith, Hunt (Evans 65), Venables, Irving, Thompson, Burke.
The New Saints: Harrison; Spender, Marriott, Routledge, Brobbel (Darlington 87) Draper (Quigley 74), Mullan (Seargeant 87), Saunders, Rawlinson, Cieslewicz, Edwards.
Referee: Huw Jones.

PREVIOUS WELSH CUP WINNERS

1878	Wrexham	1911	Wrexham	1954	Flint Town United	1987	Merthyr Tydfil
1879	Newtown White Star	1912	Cardiff City	1955	Barry Town	1988	Cardiff City
1880	Druids	1913	Swansea Town	1956	Cardiff City	1989	Swansea City
1881	Druids	1914	Wrexham	1957	Wrexham	1990	Hereford United
1882	Druids	1915	Wrexham	1958	Wrexham	1991	Swansea City
1883	Wrexham	1920	Cardiff City	1959	Cardiff City	1992	Cardiff City
1884	Oswestry White Stars	1921	Wrexham	1960	Wrexham	1993	Cardiff City
1885	Druids	1922	Cardiff City	1961	Swansea Town	1994	Barry Town
1886	Druids	1923	Cardiff City	1962	Bangor City	1995	Wrexham
1887	Chirk	1924	Wrexham	1963	Borough United	1996	TNS
1888	Chirk	1925	Wrexham	1964	Cardiff City	1997	Barry Town
1889	Bangor	1926	Ebbw Vale	1965	Cardiff City	1998	Bangor City
1890	Chirk	1927	Cardiff City	1966	Swansea Town	1999	Inter Cable-Tel
1891	Shrewsbury Town	1928	Cardiff City	1967	Cardiff City	2000	Bangor City
1892	Chirk	1929	Connah's Quay	1968	Cardiff City	2001	Barry Town
1893	Wrexham	1930	Cardiff City	1969	Cardiff City	2002	Barry Town
1894	Chirk	1931	Wrexham	1970	Cardiff City	2003	Barry Town
1895	Newtown	1932	Swansea Town	1971	Cardiff City	2004	Rhyl
1896	Bangor	1933	Chester	1972	Wrexham	2005	TNS
1897	Wrexham	1934	Bristol City	1973	Cardiff City	2006	Rhyl
1898	Druids	1935	Tranmere Rovers	1974	Cardiff City	2007	Carmarthen Town
1899	Druids	1936	Crewe Alexandra	1975	Wrexham	2008	Bangor City
1900	Aberystwyth Town	1937	Crewe Alexandra	1976	Cardiff City	2009	Bangor City
1901	Oswestry United	1938	Shrewsbury Town	1977	Shrewsbury Town	2010	Bangor City
1902	Wellington Town	1939	South Liverpool	1978	Wrexham	2011	Llanelli
1903	Wrexham	1940	Wellington Town	1979	Shrewsbury Town	2012	The New Saints
1904	Druids	1947	Chester	1980	Newport County	2013	Prestatyn Town
1905	Wrexham	1948	Lovell's Athletic	1981	Swansea City	2014	The New Saints
1906	Wellington Town	1949	Merthyr Tydfil	1982	Swansea City	2015	The New Saints
1907	Oswestry United	1950	Swansea Town	1983	Swansea City	2016	The New Saints
1908	Chester	1951	Merthyr Tydfil	1984	Shrewsbury Town	2017	Bala Town
1909	Wrexham	1952	Rhyl	1985	Shrewsbury Town		
1910	Wrexham	1953	Rhyl	1986	Wrexham		

NATHANIEL MG WELSH LEAGUE CUP 2016–17

**After extra time.*

FIRST ROUND

Abergavenny Town v Goytre (Gwent)	1-2*
Cambrian & Clydach Vale v Barry Town U	1-3*
Flint Town U v Bala T	1-5
Guilsfield v Airbus UK	2-1
Haverfordwest Co v Port Talbot T	6-2
Llandudno v Holyhead H	2-1
Caernarfon T v Rhyl	1-5
Cardiff Metropolitan v Taff's Well	5-0
Holywell T v Cefn Druids	3-5
Penrhyncoch v Aberystwyth T	1-2
Pontypridd T v Newtown	2-4
Prestatyn T v Bangor C	4-4*
Bangor C won 3-1 on penalties.	

SECOND ROUND

Barry Town U v Cardiff Metropolitan	1-0
Haverfordwest Co v Aberystwyth T	1-0
Llandudno v Rhyl	0-1
The New Saints v Bala T	2-1
Carmarthen T v Goytre (Gwent)	4-2
Cefn Druids v Bangor C	2-3
Connah's Quay Nomads v Denbigh T	3-1
Guilsfield v Newtown	0-3

QUARTER-FINALS

Bangor C v The New Saints	0-2
Barry Town U v Haverfordwest Co	7-1
Connah's Quay Nomads v Rhyl	2-1
Newtown v Carmarthen T	2-3*

SEMI-FINALS

Barry Town U v Carmarthen T	1-0
Connah's Quay Nomads v The New Saints	0-1

WELSH NATHANIEL MG CUP FINAL

Cyncoed Campus, Cardiff, Saturday 21 January 2017

The New Saints (0) 4 *(Seargeant 78, 84, 89, Cieslewicz 80)*

Barry Town U (0) 0 1116

The New Saints: Harrison; Marriott, Saunders, Rawlinson, Pryce, Edwards, Routledge, Cieslewicz (Mullan 87), Brobbel, Draper (Quigley 46), Darlington (Seargeant 46).

Barry Town U: Lewis; Watkins, Evans, Cooper, Hugh, Hartley (Gerrard 74), Saddler, Fahiya (Sainty 81), Nagi, Morgan (Dixon 81), Cotterill.

Referee: Iwan Griffiths (Conwy).

THE FAW TROPHY 2016–17

**After extra time.*

ROUND 3

Abergele T v Trearddur Bay	2-4
AC Pontymister v Sully Sports	1-2
Baglan Dragons v Penlan Club	1-2*
Blaenavon Blues v Pontlottyn	3-1
Brymbo v Corwen	1-2
Carno v Llanidloes T	2-1
Cefn Mawr Rangers v Rhostyllen	4-2
Chirk AAA v AFC Brynford	5-1
Churchstoke v Radnor Valley	1-6
Goodwick U v Hakin U	2-0
Grange Alb v Clwb Cymric	3-1
Hawarden Rangers v Cefn Alb	3-1
Lex Glyndwr v Penycae	1-2
Llandudno Junction v Blaenau Ffestiniog	6-1
Llandyrnog U v St Asaph City	2-2*
St Asaph C won 5-3 on penalties.	
Llangefni T v Meliden	3-1
Llangynnwyd Rangers v Brecon Corries	1-2
Llanllyfni v Aberffraw	2-5
Llanrwst U v Penrhyndeudraeth	1-0
Llanuwchllyn v Llanrhaeadr	2-3
Maltsters Sports v FC Cwmaman	2-1
Merlins Bridge v Trefelin	1-3
Mynydd Llandegai v Llandudno Alb	3-2
Pencoed Ath v Morriston Olympic	6-0
Pwllheli v Mochdre Sports	2-0
Queens Park v Rhos Aelwyd	5-3
RTB Ebbw Vale v Villa Dino Christchurch	6-3
STM Sports v Lucas Cwmbran	5-3
Team Swansea v Garw SGBC	6-4
Ton & Gelli BC v Treharris Ath Western	2-1
Tywyn Bryncrug v Machynlleth	1-2
Greenfield v FC Nomads of Connah's Quay	1-3

ROUND 4

Aberffraw v Llanrwst U	1-3
Cefn Mawr Rangers v FC Nomads of Connah's Quay	3-6*
Goodwick U v Pencoed Ath	0-1
Hawarden Rangers v Mynydd Llandegai	6-2
Llandudno Junction v Corwen	1-2
Llangefni T v Pwllheli	4-1
Llanrhaeadr v Brecon Corries	2-4
Machynlleth v Trearddur Bay	2-4
Penycae v Carno	0-3
Radnor Valley v Chirk AAA	1-3
St Asaph C v Queens Park	2-1
STM Sports v RTB Ebbw Vale	6-3
Sully Sports v Maltsters Sports	3-2
Team Swansea v Grange Alb	9-1
Ton & Gelli BC v Penlan Club	0-2
Trefelin v Blaenavon Blues	5-1

ROUND 5

Hawarden Rangers v FC Nomads of Connah's Quay	0-1
Llangefni T v St Asaph C	10-0
Llanrwst U v Chirk AAA	1-2
Pencoed Ath v Trefelin	0-0*
Trefelin won 4-3 on penalties.	
Penlan Club v STM Sports	3-2
Sully Sports v Carno	4-1
Team Swansea v Brecon Corries	5-4
Trearddur Bay v Corwen	1-2

QUARTER-FINALS

Corwen v Chirk AAA	1-2
Sully Sports v Team Swansea	1-0
Trefelin v Penlan Club	1-1*
Penlan Club won 4-1 on penalties.	
Llangefni T v FC Nomads of Connah's Quay	1-0

SEMI-FINALS

Sully Sports v Penlan Club	0-1
Llangefni T v Chirk AAA	0-1

FAW TROPHY FINAL 2016–17

Aberystwyth, Saturday 8 April 2017

Chirk AAA (0) 2 *(Thomas 71, Bennion 98)*

Penlan Club (1) 1 *(Chappel 20)*

Chirk AAA: Bebbington; Salisbury, Hughes, Lavender, Pearce, Bennion, Williams N, Ashton Williams (Adam Williams 82), Thomas, Roberts (Evans 112), Middlehurst (Woods 90).

Penlan Club: Collins; Rowe, Otten, Roberts, Davies (Blundell 46), James, Doyle (Sillitoe 78), Charles (Beer 84), Rowe, Chappel, Mucha.

aet.

Referee: Rob Jenkins (Guilsfield).

NORTHERN IRISH FOOTBALL 2016–17

NIFL DANSKE BANK PREMIERSHIP 2016–17

	P	Home W	D	L	F	A	Away W	D	L	F	A	Total W	D	L	F	A	GD	Pts
1 Linfield	38	11	5	2	39	10	16	3	1	48	14	27	8	3	87	24	63	89
2 Crusaders	38	15	2	1	49	17	12	4	4	34	19	27	6	5	83	36	47	87
3 Coleraine	38	11	8	2	40	23	7	3	7	16	19	18	11	9	56	42	14	65
4 Ballymena U	38	12	2	6	49	34	6	3	9	26	39	18	5	15	75	73	2	59
5 Cliftonville	38	12	3	5	28	19	5	4	9	27	31	17	7	14	55	50	5	58
6 Glenavon	38	9	4	5	33	17	4	9	7	22	38	13	13	12	55	55	0	52
7 Dungannon Swifts	38	7	6	6	38	29	7	4	8	29	30	14	10	14	67	59	8	52
8 Ards	38	8	3	8	34	35	5	5	9	27	35	13	8	17	61	70	–9	47
9 Glentoran	38	5	6	8	18	22	7	4	8	27	31	12	10	16	45	53	–8	46
10 Ballinamallard U	38	7	1	12	26	31	3	4	11	19	41	10	5	23	45	72	–27	35
11 Carrick Rangers	38	2	6	10	17	34	3	1	16	14	45	5	7	26	31	79	–48	22
12 Portadown*	38	6	1	11	16	30	1	3	16	12	45	7	4	27	28	75	–47	13

Top 6 teams split after 33 games.
**Portadown deducted 12pts for breach of rule. Linfield qualify for Champions League first qualifying round.*
Crusaders and Coleraine qualify for Europa League first qualifying round.
Europa League play-off: Ballymena U 2 Glenavon 1.
Relegation/promotion play-off: Carrick Rangers 5 Institute 2 (agg). Carrick Rangers retain Premiership status.

LEADING GOALSCORERS (League goals only)

25	Andrew Mitchell	Dungannon Swifts
21	Paul Heatley	Crusaders
20	Jordan Owens	Crusaders
20	Andy Waterworth	Linfield
18	Curtis Allen	Glentoran
16	Cathair Friel	Ballymena U
14	Tony Kane	Ballymena U
14	Jamie McGonigle	Coleraine
14	Aaron Burns	Linfield
13	Johnny McMurray	Ballymena U
11	Michael Ruddy	Ards
11	Adam Lecky	Ballinamallard U
11	Gregory Moorhouse	Glenavon
10	James McLaughlin	Coleraine
10	Gavin Whyte	Crusaders
9	Guillaume Keke	Ards
9	Ryan Mayse	Ballinamallard U
9	Jay Donnelly	Cliftonville
9	Eoin Bradley	Coleraine

IRISH LEAGUE CHAMPIONSHIP WINNERS

1891 Linfield
1892 Linfield
1893 Linfield
1894 Glentoran
1895 Linfield
1896 Distillery
1897 Glentoran
1898 Linfield
1899 Distillery
1900 Belfast Celtic
1901 Distillery
1902 Linfield
1903 Distillery
1904 Linfield
1905 Glentoran
1906 Cliftonville/ Distillery (shared)
1907 Linfield
1908 Linfield
1909 Linfield
1910 Cliftonville
1911 Linfield
1912 Glentoran
1913 Glentoran
1914 Linfield
1915 Belfast Celtic
1920 Belfast Celtic
1921 Glentoran
1922 Linfield
1923 Linfield
1924 Queen's Island
1925 Glentoran
1926 Belfast Celtic
1927 Belfast Celtic
1928 Belfast Celtic
1929 Belfast Celtic
1930 Linfield
1931 Glentoran
1932 Linfield
1933 Belfast Celtic
1934 Linfield
1935 Linfield
1936 Belfast Celtic
1937 Belfast Celtic
1938 Belfast Celtic
1939 Belfast Celtic
1940 Belfast Celtic
1948 Belfast Celtic
1949 Linfield
1950 Linfield
1951 Glentoran
1952 Glenavon
1953 Glentoran
1954 Linfield
1955 Linfield
1956 Linfield
1957 Glentoran
1958 Ards
1959 Linfield
1960 Glenavon
1961 Linfield
1962 Linfield
1963 Distillery
1964 Glentoran
1965 Derry City
1966 Linfield
1967 Glentoran
1968 Glentoran
1969 Linfield
1970 Glentoran
1971 Linfield
1972 Glentoran
1973 Crusaders
1974 Coleraine
1975 Linfield
1976 Crusaders
1977 Glentoran
1978 Linfield
1979 Linfield
1980 Linfield
1981 Glentoran
1982 Linfield
1983 Linfield
1984 Linfield
1985 Linfield
1986 Linfield
1987 Linfield
1988 Glentoran
1989 Linfield
1990 Portadown
1991 Portadown
1992 Glentoran
1993 Linfield
1994 Linfield
1995 Crusaders
1996 Portadown
1997 Crusaders
1998 Cliftonville
1999 Glentoran
2000 Linfield
2001 Linfield
2002 Portadown
2003 Glentoran
2004 Linfield
2005 Glentoran
2006 Linfield
2007 Linfield
2008 Linfield
2009 Glentoran
2010 Linfield
2011 Linfield
2012 Linfield
2013 Cliftonville
2014 Cliftonville
2015 Crusaders
2016 Crusaders
2017 Linfield

NIFL CHAMPIONSHIP 2016–17

			Home					Away					Total						
		P	W	D	L	F	A	W	D	L	F	A	W	D	L	F	A	GD	Pts
1	Warrenpoint T	32	13	3	0	48	15	9	3	4	30	20	22	6	4	78	35	43	72
2	Institute	32	9	5	2	30	12	7	4	5	34	27	16	9	7	64	39	25	57
3	Ballyclare Comrades	32	10	2	4	34	26	5	4	7	30	30	15	6	11	64	56	8	51
4	PSNI	32	9	4	3	29	17	4	6	6	20	27	13	10	9	49	44	5	49
5	Dergview	32	8	2	6	36	23	4	4	8	31	32	12	6	14	67	55	12	42
6	Loughgall	32	8	2	6	32	26	4	1	11	22	33	12	3	17	54	59	–5	39
7	H&W Welders	32	6	5	5	22	18	9	1	6	30	23	15	6	11	52	41	11	51
8	Knockbreda	32	6	3	7	26	24	8	1	7	30	28	14	4	14	56	52	4	46
9	Larne	32	10	1	5	36	21	1	6	9	16	30	11	7	14	52	51	1	40
10	Lurgan Celtic	32	7	2	7	33	35	5	1	10	23	36	12	3	17	56	71	–15	39
11	Armagh C	32	6	3	7	26	26	3	4	9	15	29	9	7	16	41	55	–14	34
12	Annagh U	32	2	5	9	20	50	2	2	12	12	57	4	7	21	32	107	–75	19

Top 6 teams split after 22 games. Promotion play-off: Institute 3 Ballyclare Comrades 2 (agg).
Premiership relegation/promotion play-off: Carrick Rangers 5 Institute 2 (agg). Institute not promoted.
Championship relegation/promotion play-off: First Leg: Newry C 4 Armagh C 0;
Second Leg: Armagh C 1 Newry C 3; Newry C win 7-1 on aggregate and are promoted to Championship.
Armagh C relegated to Premier Intermediate.

NIFL CHAMPIONSHIP WINNERS

1996 Coleraine
1997 Ballymena United
1998 Newry Town
1999 Distillery
2000 Omagh Town
2001 Ards
2002 Lisburn Distillery
2003 Dungannon Swifts
2004 Loughgall
2005 Armagh City
2006 Crusaders
2007 Institute
2008 Loughgall
2009 Portadown
2010 Loughgall
2011 Carrick Rangers
2012 Ballinamallard U
2013 Ards
2014 Institute
2015 Carrick Rangers
2016 Ards
2017 Warrenpoint T

NIFL PREMIER INTERMEDIATE 2016–17

			Home					Away					Total						
		P	W	D	L	F	A	W	D	L	F	A	W	D	L	F	A	GD	Pts
1	Limavady U	27	11	0	2	35	12	7	4	3	30	14	18	4	5	65	26	39	58
2	Newry C	27	7	2	4	30	16	8	1	5	27	18	15	3	9	57	34	23	48
3	Donegal Celtic	27	8	2	4	26	21	5	4	4	25	23	13	6	8	51	44	7	45
4	Moyola Park	27	9	4	1	27	12	4	1	8	18	26	13	5	9	45	38	7	44
5	Tobermore U	27	8	2	3	25	16	3	2	9	15	29	11	4	12	40	45	–5	37
6	Banbridge T	27	7	0	7	20	20	4	2	7	16	21	11	2	14	36	41	–5	35
7	Dundela	27	2	7	5	24	27	7	1	5	21	20	9	8	10	45	47	–2	35
8	Queens University	27	7	1	5	18	14	4	0	10	16	28	11	1	15	34	42	–8	34
9	Lisburn Distillery	27	6	1	7	26	29	4	3	6	17	24	10	4	13	43	53	–10	34
10	Newington YC	27	5	1	7	20	21	5	2	7	16	28	10	3	14	36	49	–13	33
11	Sports & Leisure Swifts	27	5	1	7	12	20	4	2	8	20	32	9	3	15	32	52	–20	30
12	Bangor	27	5	3	6	28	31	3	2	8	18	28	8	5	14	46	59	–13	29

Top 6 teams split after 22 games. Championship relegation/promotion play-off: First Leg: Newry C 4 Armagh C 0; Second Leg: Armagh C 1 Newry C 3; Newry C win 7-1 on aggregate and are promoted to Championship. Armagh C relegated to Premier Intermediate.

IFA DEVELOPMENT LEAGUES 2016–17

Premiership Development League

	P	W	D	L	F	A	GD	Pts
Linfield	33	26	5	2	120	24	96	83
Ballymena U	33	26	0	7	87	41	46	78
Cliftonville	32	24	2	6	88	38	50	74
Crusaders	33	15	5	13	97	72	25	50
Glentoran	33	15	5	13	67	67	0	50
Portadown	33	13	6	14	65	64	1	45
Glenavon	33	12	8	13	92	75	17	44
Coleraine	33	10	6	17	62	94	–32	36
Ballinamallard U	32	9	2	21	58	95	–37	29
Ards	33	8	3	22	54	124	–70	27
Dungannon Swifts	33	7	5	21	65	107	–42	26
Carrick Rangers	33	6	5	22	41	95	–54	23

Game between Cliftonville and Ballinamallard U not fulfilled. Awaiting Committee decision in respect of result.

Development League North

	P	W	D	L	F	A	GD	Pts
Institute	22	15	4	3	82	30	52	49
Ballyclare Comrades	22	14	1	7	58	42	16	43
Dundela	22	12	6	4	63	30	33	42
PSNI	22	10	4	8	41	32	9	34
H&W Welders	22	9	6	7	51	43	8	33
Bangor	22	9	5	8	67	67	0	32
Newington	22	9	5	8	47	50	–3	32
Larne	21	7	3	11	53	54	–1	24
Knockbreda	22	3	1	18	38	86	–48	10
Moyola Park	21	2	3	16	23	90	–67	9

Game between Larne and Moyola Park not fulfilled. Awaiting Committee decision in respect of result.

Development League South

	P	W	D	L	F	A	GD	Pts
Banbridge T	24	17	2	5	82	34	48	53
Lisburn Distillery	24	13	4	7	53	57	–4	43
Donegal Celtic	24	12	1	11	69	66	3	37
Loughgall	24	8	3	13	47	53	–6	27
Annagh U	24	9	6	9	68	45	23	33
Armagh C	24	9	2	13	42	67	–25	29
Warrenpoint T	24	8	3	13	69	66	3	27
Lurgan Celtic	24	8	3	13	49	91	–42	27

TENNENT'S IRISH FA CUP 2016–17

**After extra time.*

FIRST ROUND

Newington v Bangor	3-2
Windmill Stars v Tullyvallen Rangers	5-0
Brantwood v Comber Rec	3-3*
Comber Rec won 3-1 on penalties	
Desertmartin v Newcastle	2-0
East Belfast v Dundonald	5-2
Lisburn Distillery v Rosario YC	4-0
Sirocco Works v Hanover	2-2*
Sirrocco Works won 4-1 on penalties	
Coagh U v Malachians	2-1
Glebe Rangers v Iveagh U	4-0
Trojans v Immaculata	3-1
Ballynure OB v Albert Foundry	4-1
St. Patrick's v Markethill Swifts	5-4
Dungiven v Saintfield U	1-0
UUJ v Dungannon R	4-0
Portaferry R v AFC Silverwood	2-3
Rathfriland Rangers v Moyola Park	3-3*
Rathfriland Rangers won 4-2 on penalties	
Ballywalter Rec v Ardstraw	1-2
Banbridge Rangers v Derriaghy CC	4-4*
Derriaghy CC won 4-3 on penalties	
Queen's University v Dromore Amateurs	14-0
Dollingstown v Newbuildings U	4-2
Craigavon C v Grove U	1-6
Chimney Corner v Crewe U	0-5
Sport & Leisure Swifts v Ballynahinch Olympic	3-2
Newry C v Oxford Sunnyside	7-0
Bloomfield v Seapatrick	3-4
Donegal Celtic v Oxford U Stars	1-3
Downshire YM v Rathfern Rangers	4-0
Abbey Villa v Holywood	5-0
Limavady U v Banbridge T	2-0
18th Newtownabbey OB v Bangor Amateurs	5-3
Islandmagee v Ballymacash Rangers	4-1
Moneyslane v Magherafelt Sky Blues	6-1
Valley Rangers v Newtowne	3-1
Shankill U v Crumlin U	0-4
Lurgan T v Laurelvale	2-1
Sofia Farmer v Lower Maze	2-1
Fivemiletown U walkover v Killymoon Rangers withdrew	

SECOND ROUND

18th Newtownabbey OB v Ballynahinch U	2-1
Abbey Villa v Dungiven	4-1
Ards Rangers v Lurgan T	2-0
Barn U v Dundela	1-2
Camlough R v Dromara Village	0-5
Coagh U v Derriaghy CC	1-1*
Derriaghy CC won 3-2 on penalties	
Comber Rec v Ardstraw	5-2
Crewe U v Ardglass	5-1
Crumlin Star v Trojans	1-2
Downshire YM v UUJ	2-2*
Downshire YM won 3-2 on penalties	
Fivemiletown U v Sirocco Works	4-1
Glebe Rangers v AFC Silverwood	3-2
Grove U v Rathfriland Rangers	4-4*
Grove U won 3-1 on penalties	
Islandmagee v Killyleagh YC	5-3
Islandmagee withdrew after fielding an ineligible player; Killyleagh YC reinstated	
Larne Tech OB v Wakehurst	1-2
Lisburn Rangers v Ballynure OB	4-2
Moneyslane v Portstewart	0-2
Mossley v St. Luke's	1-4
Newry C v Newington	1-3
Seapatrick v Drumaness Mills	0-2
Shorts v Dunloy	8-0
Sofia Farmer v Limavady U	2-0
Sport & Leisure Swifts v St. Patrick's	2-1
St. Mary's YC v Oxford U Stars	4-5
Strabane Ath v East Belfast	4-5
Tobermore U v Desertmartin	6-0
Valley Rangers v Seagoe	7-0
Crumlin U v Ballymoney U	2-3
Queen's University v Lisburn Distillery	0-1
Richhill walkover v Nortel withdrew	
Windmill Stars walkover v Donard Hospital dissolved	
Bye: Dollingstown	

THIRD ROUND

Abbey Villa v Dollingstown	2-3
Comber Rec v St. Luke's	2-3
Derriaghy CC v Valley Rangers	2-0
Dromara Village v Drumaness Mills	1-2
Dundela v Downshire YM	3-2
East Belfast v Shorts	0-2
Glebe Rangers v Grove U	0-0*
Grove U won 4-3 on penalties	
Killyleagh YC v Portstewart	0-5
Lisburn Rangers v Lisburn Distillery	0-1
Richhill v Oxford U Stars	1-0
Sofia Farmer v Windmill Stars	0-2
Sport & Leisure Swifts v Ards Rangers	3-2
Tobermore U v Wakehurst	2-1
Crewe U v Ballymoney U	3-1
Fivemiletown U v Newington	5-4
Trojans walkover v 18th Newtownabbey	

FOURTH ROUND

Derriaghy CC v Portstewart	2-4
Dundela v Fivemiletown U	3-4
Lisburn Distillery v St. Luke's	3-0
Richhill v Grove U	6-2
Sport & Leisure Swifts v Dollingstown	1-3
Tobermore U v Shorts	6-0
Trojans v Drumaness Mills	3-1
Windmill Stars v Crewe U	3-4

FIFTH ROUND

H&W Welders v Lurgan Celtic	1-0
Knockbreda v Crewe U	1-2
PSNI v Lisburn Distillery	2-1
Richhill v Dollingstown	1-4
Annagh U v Tobermore U	0-2
Armagh C v Trojans	2-1
Ballyclare Comrades v Institute	2-4
Ballymena U v Cliftonville	1-1*
Ballymena U won 4-3 on penalties	
Coleraine v Carrick Rangers	5-1
Dungannon Swifts v Dergview	3-0
Glenavon v Portstewart	4-1
Glentoran v Linfield	1-2*
Larne v Portadown	1-2
Loughgall v Fivemiletown U	3-0
Warrenpoint T v Ballinamallard U	0-0*
Warrenpoint T won 5-4 on penalties	
Crusaders v Ards	2-0

SIXTH ROUND

H&W Welders v Ballymena U	1-3
Armagh C v Glenavon	0-2
Coleraine v Tobermore U	1-0
Crusaders v PSNI	2-0
Dungannon Swifts v Dollingstown	4-1
Institute v Linfield	0-2
Loughgall v Portadown	1-2
Warrenpoint T v Crewe U	5-0

QUARTER-FINALS

Ballymena U v Coleraine	0-4
Crusaders v Linfield	0-2
Dungannon Swifts v Warrenpoint T	2-1*
Portadown v Glenavon	0-5

SEMI-FINALS

Coleraine v Glenavon	2-1
Dungannon Swifts v Linfield	0-1

TENNENT'S NORTHERN IRISH FA CUP FINAL 2017

Windsor Park, Belfast, Saturday 6 May 2017

Linfield (2) 3 *(Waterworth 29, 33, 87)*

Coleraine (0) 0

Linfield: Carroll; Stafford, Haughey, Callacher, Waterworth, Lowry, Burns (Stewart 82), Clarke, Mulgrew, Quinn, Smyth (Casement 89).
Coleraine: Johns; Kane, Mullan, Harkin, Ogilby, McCauley, McLaughlin (Parkhill 57), McConaghie, Lyons, McGonigle (Allan 82), Bradley.
Referee: Keith Kennedy.

IRISH CUP FINALS (from 1946–47)

1946–47 Belfast Celtic 1, Glentoran 0
1947–48 Linfield 3, Coleraine 0
1948–49 Derry City 3, Glentoran 1
1949–50 Linfield 2, Distillery 1
1950–51 Glentoran 3, Ballymena U 1
1951–52 Ards 1, Glentoran 0
1952–53 Linfield 5, Coleraine 0
1953–54 Derry City 1, Glentoran 0
1954–55 Dundela 3, Glenavon 0
1955–56 Distillery 1, Glentoran 0
1956–57 Glenavon 2, Derry City 0
1957–58 Ballymena U 2, Linfield 0
1958–59 Glenavon 2, Ballymena U 0
1959–60 Linfield 5, Ards 1
1960–61 Glenavon 5, Linfield 1
1961–62 Linfield 4, Portadown 0
1962–63 Linfield 2, Distillery 1
1963–64 Derry City 2, Glentoran 0
1964–65 Coleraine 2, Glenavon 1
1965–66 Glentoran 2, Linfield 0
1966–67 Crusaders 3, Glentoran 1
1967–68 Crusaders 2, Linfield 0
1968–69 Ards 4, Distillery 2
1969–70 Linfield 2, Ballymena U 1
1970–71 Distillery 3, Derry City
1971–72 Coleraine 2, Portadown 1
1972–73 Glentoran 3, Linfield 2
1973–74 Ards 2, Ballymena U 1
1974–75 Coleraine 1:0:1, Linfield 1:0:0
1975–76 Carrick Rangers 2, Linfield 1
1976–77 Coleraine 4, Linfield 1
1977–78 Linfield 3, Ballymena U 1
1978–79 Cliftonville 3, Portadown 2
1979–80 Linfield 2, Crusaders 0
1980–81 Ballymena U 1, Glenavon 0
1981–82 Linfield 2, Coleraine 1
1982–83 Glentoran 1:2, Linfield 1:1
1983–84 Ballymena U 4, Carrick Rangers 1
1984–85 Glentoran 1:1, Linfield 1:0
1985–86 Glentoran 2, Coleraine 1
1986–87 Glentoran 1, Larne 0
1987–88 Glentoran 1, Glenavon 0
1988–89 Ballymena U 1, Larne 0
1989–90 Glentoran 3, Portadown 0
1990–91 Portadown 2, Glenavon 1
1991–92 Glenavon 2, Linfield 1
1992–93 Bangor 1:1:1, Ards 1:1:0
1993–94 Linfield 2, Bangor 0
1994–95 Linfield 3, Carrick Rangers 1
1995–96 Glentoran 1, Glenavon 0
1996–97 Glenavon 1, Cliftonville 0
1997–98 Glentoran 1, Glenavon 0
1998–99 *Portadown awarded trophy after Cliftonville were eliminated for using an ineligible player in semi-final.*
1999–2000 Glentoran 1, Portadown 0
2000–01 Glentoran 1, Linfield 0
2001–02 Linfield 2, Portadown 1
2002–03 Coleraine 1, Glentoran 0
2003–04 Glentoran 1, Coleraine 0
2004–05 Portadown 5, Larne 1
2005–06 Linfield 2, Glentoran 1
2006–07 Linfield 2, Dungannon Swifts 2
(aet; Linfield won 3-2 on penalties).
2007–08 Linfield 2, Coleraine 1
2008–09 Crusaders 1, Cliftonville 0
2009–10 Linfield 2, Portadown 1
2010–11 Linfield 2, Crusaders 1
2011–12 Linfield 4, Crusaders 1
2012–13 Glentoran 3, Cliftonville 1
2013–14 Glenavon 2, Balymena U 1
2014–15 Glentoran 1, Portadown 0
2015–16 Glenavon 2, Linfield 0
2016–17 Linfield 3, Coleraine 0

JBE NORTHERN IRELAND LEAGUE CUP 2016–17

**After extra time.*

ROUND 1

Limavady U v Queens University	2-1*
Lurgan Celtic v Bangor	1-1*
Lurgan Celtic won 5-4 on penalties.	
Moyola Park v Institute	1-3
PSNI v Banbridge T	0-1

ROUND 2

Annagh U v Glentoran	3-2
Ards v Newry C	3-1
Armagh C v Dergview	3-1*
Ballinamallard U v Dundela	3-0
Ballyclare Comrades v Carrick Rangers	0-2
Ballymena U v Newington YC	4-1
Cliftonville v Lisburn Distillery	11-1
Coleraine v Limavady U	3-0
Crusaders v Loughgall	3-1
Dungannon Swifts v S&L Swifts	6-2
Glenavon v Tobermore U	5-0
Institute v H&W Welders	0-2*
Linfield v Larne	5-0
Portadown v Donegal Celtic	6-1
Warrenpoint T v Banbridge T	4-2*
Knockbreda v Lurgan Celtic	4-3

ROUND 3

Annagh U v Cliftonville	0-6
Ards v Warrenpoint T	2-4*
Armagh C v Carrick Rangers	0-2
Ballymena U v Linfield	4-1
Coleraine v Knockbreda	3-0
Dungannon Swifts v Ballinamallard U	6-1
Glenavon v H&W Welders	4-2
Portadown v Crusaders	3-4

QUARTER-FINALS

Carrick Rangers v Dungannon Swifts	2-0
Coleraine v Crusaders	1-1*
Coleraine won 5-4 on penalties.	
Glenavon v Cliftonville	3-2*
Warrenpoint T v Ballymena U	0-2

SEMI-FINALS

Ballymena U v Coleraine	3-0*
Glenavon v Carrick Rangers	0-1

NORTHERN IRISH LEAGUE CUP FINAL 2017

Seaview, Belfast, Saturday February 18 2017

Ballymena U (1) 2 *(Jenkins 45, McCloskey 90)*

Carrick Rangers (0) 0 12,551

Ballymena U: Glendinning; Kane T (Thompson 90), Owens, Jenkins, Faulkner, Friel, Ervin, Millar, McMurray (Henderson 90), McCaffrey (McCloskey 81), Loughran.

Carrick Rangers: Neeson; Chapman, McCullough, Surgenor, McNally, Clarke (Salley 61), McAllister (McConnell 80), Murray TJ, Kelly, Murray M (Morrow 84), Noble.

Referee: Ian McNabb.

ROLL OF HONOUR SEASON 2016–17

Competition	*Winner*	*Runner-up*
NIFL Danske Bank Premier League	Linfield	Crusaders
Tennent's Irish FA Cup	Linfield	Coleraine
NIFL Championship	Warrenpoint T	Institute
NIFL Premier Intermediate	Limavady U	Newry C
JBE League Cup	Ballymena T	Carrick Rangers
County Antrim Shield	Linfield	Crusaders
Steel & Sons Cup	Dundela	Linfield Swifts
Co Antrim Junior Shield	Suffolk	Woodvale
Irish Junior Cup	Enniskillen Rangers	Hill Street
Mid Ulster Cup (Senior)	Warrenpoint T	Armagh C
Harry Cavan Youth Cup	Linfield Rangers	Ballinmallard U Thirds
George Wilson Memorial Cup	Cliftonville Olympics	Ballyclare Comrades
North West Senior Cup	Institute	Coleraine
The Fermanagh Mulhern Cup	Strathroy Harps	Beragh Swifts
Intermediate Cup	Linfield Swifts	Dundela

NORTHERN IRELAND FOOTBALL WRITERS ASSOCIATION AWARDS 2016–17

MANAGER OF THE YEAR
David Healy (Linfield)

PLAYER OF THE YEAR
Jamie Mulgrew (Linfield)

BELLEEK CHAMPIONSHIP PLAYER OF THE YEAR
John McGuigan (Warrenpoint Town)

EVENT EXHIBITION YOUNG PLAYER OF THE YEAR
Paul Smyth (Linfield)

UHISPORT GOALKEEPER OF THE YEAR
Roy Carroll (Linfield)

INTERNATIONAL PERSONALITY OF THE YEAR
Gareth McAuley (WBA and Northern Ireland)

BELLEEK NON-SENIOR TEAM OF THE YEAR
Limavady United

MERIT AWARD
Andy Kerr (Linfield)

EVENTSEC GOAL OF THE SEASON 2016–17
James McLaughlin of Coleraine v Crusaders

WOMEN'S PERSONALITY OF THE YEAR
Marissa Callaghan

DR MALCOLM BRODIE HALL OF FAME
Sammy McIlroy

TEAM OF THE SEASON
Roy Carroll (Linfield)
Lyndon Kane (Coleraine)
Howard Beverland (Crusaders)
Jimmy Callacher (Linfield)
Levi Ives (Cliftonville)
Paul Smyth (Linfield)
Jamie Mulgrew (Linfield)
Stephen Lowry (Linfield)
Paul Heatley (Crusaders)
Andy Waterworth (Linfield)
Andy Mitchell (Dungannon)

NIFWA PREMIERSHIP PLAYER OF THE MONTH 2016–17

Month	*Player*	*Team*
August	Gavin Whyte	Crusaders
September	Aaron Burns	Linfield
October	Michael Doherty	Coleraine
November	James Mulgrew	Linfield
December	Jimmy Callagher	Linfield
January	Howard Beverland	Crusaders
February	Tony Kane	Ballymena United
March	Steven Lowry	Linfield
April	Andrew Waterworth	Linfield

NIFWA MANAGER OF THE MONTH 2016–17

Month	*Player*	*Team*
August	Niall Curry	Ards
September	David Jeffrey	Ballymena United
October	Gavin Haveron	Glentoran
November	Gerard Lyttle	Cliftonville
December	David Healy	Linfield
January	Oran Kearney	Coleraine
February	David Jeffrey	Ballymena United
March	Oran Kearney	Coleraine
April	David Healy	Linfield

NIFWA NIFL CHAMPIONSHIP PLAYER OF THE MONTH 2016–17

Month	*Player*	*Team*
August	Philip Donnelly	Amagh City
September	Ryan Campbell	Dergview
October	John McGuigan	Warrenpoint Town
November	Lukasz Adamczyk	PSNI
December	John Uprichard	Loughall
January	Corey McMullan	Ballyclare
February	Davy Rainey	H&W Welders
March	Stephen Murray	Warrenpoint Town
April	Stephen Murray	Warrenpoint Town

EUROPEAN CUP FINALS

EUROPEAN CUP FINALS 1956–1992

Year	Winners v Runners-up		Venue	Attendance	Referee
1956	Real Madrid v Reims	4-3	Paris	38,239	A. Ellis (England)
1957	Real Madrid v Fiorentina	2-0	Madrid	124,000	L. Horn (Netherlands)
1958	Real Madrid v AC Milan	3-2*	Brussels	67,000	A. Alsteen (Belgium)
1959	Real Madrid v Reims	2-0	Stuttgart	72,000	A. Dutsch (West Germany)
1960	Real Madrid v Eintracht Frankfurt	7-3	Glasgow	127,621	J. Mowat (Scotland)
1961	Benfica v Barcelona	3-2	Berne	26,732	G. Dienst (Switzerland)
1962	Benfica v Real Madrid	5-3	Amsterdam	61,257	L. Horn (Netherlands)
1963	AC Milan v Benfica	2-1	Wembley	45,715	A. Holland (England)
1964	Internazionale v Real Madrid	3-1	Vienna	71,333	J. Stoll (Austria)
1965	Internazionale v Benfica	1-0	Milan	89,000	G. Dienst (Switzerland)
1966	Real Madrid v Partizan Belgrade	2-1	Brussels	46,745	R. Kreitlein (West Germany)
1967	Celtic v Internazionale	2-1	Lisbon	45,000	K. Tschenscher (West Germany)
1968	Manchester U v Benfica	4-1*	Wembley	92,225	C. Lo Bello (Italy)
1969	AC Milan v Ajax	4-1	Madrid	31,782	J. Ortiz de Mendibil (Spain)
1970	Feyenoord v Celtic	2-1*	Milan	53,187	C. Lo Bello (Italy)
1971	Ajax v Panathinaikos	2-0	Wembley	90,000	J. Taylor (England)
1972	Ajax v Internazionale	2-0	Rotterdam	61,354	R. Helies (France)
1973	Ajax v Juventus	1-0	Belgrade	89,484	M. Guglovic (Yugoslavia)
1974	Bayern Munich v Atletico Madrid	1-1	Brussels	48,722	V. Loraux (Belgium)
Replay	Bayern Munich v Atletico Madrid	4-0	Brussels	23,325	A. Delcourt (Belgium)
1975	Bayern Munich v Leeds U	2-0	Paris	48,374	M. Kitabdjian (France)
1976	Bayern Munich v Saint-Etienne	1-0	Glasgow	54,864	K. Palotai (Hungary)
1977	Liverpool v Moenchengladbach	3-1	Rome	52,078	R. Wurtz (France)
1978	Liverpool v Club Brugge	1-0	Wembley	92,500	C. Corver (Netherlands)
1979	Nottingham F v Malmo	1-0	Munich	57,500	E. Linemayr (Austria)
1980	Nottingham F v Hamburger SV	1-0	Madrid	51,000	A. Garrido (Portugal)
1981	Liverpool v Real Madrid	1-0	Paris	48,360	K. Palotai (Hungary)
1982	Aston Villa v Bayern Munich	1-0	Rotterdam	46,000	G. Konrath (France)
1983	Hamburg v Juventus	1-0	Athens	73,500	N. Rainea (Romania)
1984	Liverpool v Roma	1-1*	Rome	69,693	E. Fredriksson (Sweden)
	(Liverpool won 4-2 on penalties)				
1985	Juventus v Liverpool	1-0	Brussels	58,000	A. Daina (Switzerland)
1986	Steaua Bucharest v Barcelona	0-0*	Seville	70,000	M. Vautrot (France)
	(Steaua won 2-0 on penalties)				
1987	FC Porto v Bayern Munich	2-1	Vienna	57,500	A. Ponnet (Belgium)
1988	PSV Eindhoven v Benfica	0-0*	Stuttgart	68,000	L. Agnolin (Italy)
	(PSV won 6-5 on penalties)				
1989	AC Milan v Steaua Bucharest	4-0	Barcelona	97,000	K.-H. Tritschler (West Germany)
1990	AC Milan v Benfica	1-0	Vienna	57,500	H. Kohl (Austria)
1991	Crvena Zvezda v Olympique Marseille	0-0*	Bari	56,000	T. Lanese (Italy)
	(Crvena Zvezda won 5-3 on penalties)				
1992	Barcelona v Sampdoria	1-0*	Wembley	70,827	A. Schmidhuber (Germany)

UEFA CHAMPIONS LEAGUE FINALS 1993–2017

Year	Winners v Runners-up		Venue	Attendance	Referee
1993	Marseille† v AC Milan	1-0	Munich	64,400	K. Rothlisberger (Switzerland)
1994	AC Milan v Barcelona	4-0	Athens	70,000	P. Don (England)
1995	Ajax v AC Milan	1-0	Vienna	49,730	I. Craciunescu (Romania)
1996	Juventus v Ajax	1-1*	Rome	70,000	M. D. Vega (Spain)
	(Juventus won 4-2 on penalties)				
1997	Borussia Dortmund v Juventus	3-1	Munich	59,000	S. Puhl (Hungary)
1998	Real Madrid v Juventus	1-0	Amsterdam	48,500	H. Krug (Germany)
1999	Manchester U v Bayern Munich	2-1	Barcelona	90,245	P. Collina (Italy)
2000	Real Madrid v Valencia	3-0	Paris	80,000	S. Braschi (Italy)
2001	Bayern Munich v Valencia	1-1*	Milan	79,000	D. Jol (Netherlands)
	(Bayern Munich won 5-4 on penalties)				
2002	Real Madrid v Leverkusen	2-1	Glasgow	50,499	U. Meier (Switzerland)
2003	AC Milan v Juventus	0-0*	Manchester	62,315	M. Merk (Germany)
	(AC Milan won 3-2 on penalties)				
2004	FC Porto v Monaco	3-0	Gelsenkirchen	53,053	K. M. Nielsen (Denmark)
2005	Liverpool v AC Milan	3-3*	Istanbul	65,000	M. M. González (Spain)
	(Liverpool won 3-2 on penalties)				
2006	Barcelona v Arsenal	2-1	Paris	79,610	T. Hauge (Norway)
2007	AC Milan v Liverpool	2-1	Athens	74,000	H. Fandel (Germany)
2008	Manchester U v Chelsea	1-1*	Moscow	67,310	L. Michel (Slovakia)
	(Manchester U won 6-5 on penalties)				
2009	Barcelona v Manchester U	2-0	Rome	62,467	M. Busacca (Switzerland)
2010	Internazionale v Bayern Munich	2-0	Madrid	73,490	H. Webb (England)
2011	Barcelona v Manchester U	3-1	Wembley	87,695	V. Kassai (Hungary)
2012	Chelsea v Bayern Munich	1-1*	Munich	62,500	P. Proença (Portugal)
	(Chelsea won 4-3 on penalties)				
2013	Bayern Munich v Borussia Dortmund	2-1	Wembley	86,298	N. Rizzoli (Italy)
2014	Real Madrid v Atletico Madrid	4-1*	Lisbon	60,000	B. Kuipers (Netherlands)
2015	Barcelona v Juventus	3-1	Berlin	70,442	C. Cakir (Turkey)
2016	Real Madrid v Atletico Madrid	1-1*	Milan	71,942	M. Clattenburg (England)
	(Real Madrid won 5-3 on penalties)				
2017	Real Madrid v Juventus	4-1	Cardiff	65,842	F. Brych (Germany)

†Subsequently stripped of title.
**After extra time.*

UEFA CHAMPIONS LEAGUE 2016–17

■ *Denotes player sent off.*

FIRST QUALIFYING ROUND FIRST LEG

Tuesday, 28 June 2016

Flora Tallinn (1) 2 *(Alliku 35, Sappinen 49)*
Lincoln Red Imps (0) 1 *(Chipolina J 57)* 886

Flora Tallinn: (442) Toom; Kams, Jurgenson, Baranov, Vihmann; Alliku, Beglarishvili (Prosa 71), Gussev (Saliste 85), Sappinen; Ainsalu (Lepistu 68), Kokla.
Lincoln Red Imps: (442) Walker; Navas, Chipolina J, Bernardo Lopes, Chipolina R; Casciaro R, Garcia, Yeray, Bardon (Calderon 63); Casciaro K, Casciaro L (Juanfri 63).

FC Santa Coloma (0) 0
Alashkert (0) 0 600

FC Santa Coloma: (442) Casals; Armero (Lain 66), Capdevila, Gonzalez, Lima; Martinez, Pujol, Ramos A, Rebes (Conde 61); Rodriguez (Toscano 80), Wagner.
Alashkert: (442) Grigoryan (Gyozalyan 84); Kasparov, Khovbosha, Manasyan, Minasyan; Muradyan, Poghosyan, Savin (Dashyan 69), Tasic; Veranyan, Artak Yedigaryan (Avagyan 76).

The New Saints (2) 2 *(Quigley 13, Mullan 40)*
Tre Penne (1) 1 *(Fraternali 16)* 712

The New Saints: (4231) Harrison; Spender, Baker, Rawlinson, Marriott; Edwards, Routledge; Mullan, Brobbel, Cieslewicz (Parry 71); Quigley (Draper 85).
Tre Penne: (433) Migani; Capicchioni, Fraternali, Rossi, Merendino; Calzolari, Patregnani, Gai; Valli (Palazzi 28), Agostinelli (Friguglietti 81), Censoni (Chiaruzzi 73).

Valletta (0) 1 *(Falcone 69)*
B36 Torshavn (0) 0 1151

Valletta: (442) Aguirre; Azzopardi, Bonello, Briffa, Caruana; Cremona (Malano 57), Falcone (Mifsud Triganza 87), Gill, Jhonnattann (Borg J 80); Pani, Romeu.
B36 Torshavn: (442) Askham H; Askham T, Borg (Pingel 82), Dam, Eriksen; Eysturoy, Faero, Jakobsen, Mellemgaard (Cieslewicz 74); Naes, Thorleifsson (Agnarsson 71).

FIRST QUALIFYING ROUND SECOND LEG

Tuesday, 5 July 2016

Alashkert (1) 3 *(Minasyan 12, Gyozalyan 84, Artur Yedigaryan 88)*
FC Santa Coloma (0) 0 2100

Alashkert: (442) Kasparov; Poghosyan, Minasyan, Artak Yedigaryan, Tasic; Veranyan (Ghazaryan 78), Dashyan (Gyozalyan 72), Savin (Artur Yedigaryan 87), Muradyan; Manasyan■, Grigoryan.
FC Santa Coloma: (442) Casals; Capdevila, Lima, Rebes (Noguerol 20), Ramos A (Mercade 11); Ramos R (Juanfer 23), Rodriguez, Martinez■, Armero; Gonzalez■, Parra.

B36 Torshavn (1) 2 *(Thorleifsson 11, Agnarsson 66)*
Valletta (1) 1 *(Falcone 24)* 850

B36 Torshavn: (442) Askham T; Faero, Mellemgaard (Petersen 89), Naes, Jakobsen; Thorleifsson (Pingel 81), Eysturoy, Askham H, Eriksen; Borg (Agnarsson 62), Cieslewicz.
Valletta: (442) Bonello; Caruana, Azzopardi, Aguirre (Borg J 90), Gill; Pani, Briffa, Romeu, Malano; Falcone, Jhonnattann (Mifsud 88).

Tre Penne (0) 0
The New Saints (1) 3 *(Quigley 45, Edwards 47, Draper 90)* 743

Tre Penne: (4141) Migani; Capicchioni (Cesarini 72), Fraternali, Rossi, Merendino; Patregnani; Gasperoni (Friguglietti 79), Chiaruzzi (Calzolari 52), Gai, Palazzi; Agostinelli.
The New Saints: (4141) Harrison; Spender (Pryce 76), Baker, Rawlinson, Marriott; Routledge; Mullan, Edwards, Brobbel (Seargeant 88), Cieslewicz; Quigley (Draper 82).

Wednesday, 6 July 2016

Lincoln Red Imps (1) 2 *(Chipolina J 15 (pen), Calderon 79)*
Flora Tallinn (0) 0 1020

Lincoln Red Imps: (442) Navas; Garcia, Chipolina J, Bardon (Calderon 71), Casciaro R; Bernardo Lopes, Casciaro L (Cabrera 64), Casciaro K, Chipolina R; Patino (Chipolina K 78), Walker.
Flora Tallinn: (442) Toom; Kokla (Slein 82), Alliku, Lepistu, Sappinen; Jurgenson, Kams, Gussev, Vihmann (Tamm 60); Baranov, Beglarishvili (Prosa 53).

SECOND QUALIFYING ROUND FIRST LEG

Tuesday, 12 July 2016

BATE Borisov (1) 2 *(Kendysh 32, Rodionov 68)*
SJK (0) 0 9247

BATE Borisov: (442) Veremko; Palyakow, Hayduchyk, Pikk, Zhavnerchik; Stasevich, Valadzko A (Ivanic 74), Kendysh, Karnitskiy (Gvilia 84); Rodionov, Gordeichuk (Ryas 69).
SJK: (433) Aksalu; Meite, Aalto, Hurme, Laaksonen; Vasara (Klinga 76), Hetemaj, Hradecky; Riski, Penninkangas (Rahimi 90), Nguekam (Tahvanainen 76).

Dinamo Tbilisi (0) 2 *(Kiteishvili 55, Kvilitaia 69 (pen))*
Alashkert (0) 0 11,769

Dinamo Tbilisi: (442) Scribe; Amisulashvili, Spicic, Lobzhanidze (Kiteishvili 50), Rene; Velev, Parunashvili, Jigauri, Dvalishvili (Coureur 84); Tchanturishvili, Kvilitaia (Papunashvili 10).
Alashkert: (442) Kasparov; Poghosyan, Minasyan, Artak Yedigaryan, Tasic (Bareghamyan 46); Dashyan, Savin (Artur Yedigaryan 64), Voskanyan, Muradyan; Gyozalyan (Melkonyan 83), Grigoryan.

Hapoel Beer Sheva (1) 3 *(Ogu 43, Barad 52 (pen), Radi 90 (pen))*
Sheriff (1) 2 *(Ivancic 22, Brezovec 64)* 15,939

Hapoel Beer Sheva: (442) Goresh; William Soares, Davidadze, Biton (Radi 64), Taha; Hoban (Sahar 70), Ogu, Buzaglo (Ohayon 90), Melikson; Barad, Nwakaeme.
Sheriff: (433) Mitrev; Skvorc, Susic, Savic (Dupovac 46), Aliti■; Brezovec, Ginsari (Metoua 31), Yahaya; Kvrzic, Ricardinho, Ivancic (Subotic 74).

Lincoln Red Imps (0) 1 *(Casciaro L 48)*
Celtic (0) 0 1632

Lincoln Red Imps: (4141) Navas; Garcia, Chipolina R, Casciaro R, Chipolina J; Bernardo Lopes; Patino (Chipolina K 90), Walker (Bardon 86), Casciaro K, Calderon; Casciaro L (Cabrera 74).
Celtic: (433) Gordon; Janko, Ambrose, Sviatchenko, Tierney; Rogic (Armstrong 58), Brown, Bitton; Griffiths, Dembele (Ciftci 73), Christie (Forrest 58).

Qarabag (2) 2 *(Almeida 10 (pen), 27)*
F91 Dudelange (0) 0 18,600

Qarabag: (442) Sehic; Garayev, Medvedev, Michel, Muarem (Ismayilov 74); Mammadov (Reynaldo 63), Sadygov, Almeida, Agolli; Guseynov, Quintana (Amirguliyev 83).
F91 Dudelange: (442) Joubert; Schnell, Pokar (N'Diaye 56), Da Mota Alves, Dikaba; Stolz, Nakache (Stelvio Cruz 81), Prempeh, Melisse; Malget (Moreira 67), Turpel.

Red Bull Salzburg (0) 1 *(Soriano 83)*
FK Liepaja (0) 0 6917

Red Bull Salzburg: (442) Walke; Ulmer, Schiemer, Paulo Miranda, Hinteregger; Berisha, Lazaro (Lainer 70), Laimer (Samassekou 65), da Silva; Soriano, Dabbur.
FK Liepaja: (433) Dorosevs; Gorkss, Ivanovs, Klava, Kluk; Kamess, Torres (Afanasjevs 70), Mickevics (Kurtiss 61); Brtan, Karklins, Strumia (Gucs 28).

The New Saints (0) 0

APOEL (0) 0 1056

The New Saints: (4411) Harrison; Marriott, Baker, Routledge, Brobbel (Williams 72); Mullan, Rawlinson, Cieslewicz (Parry 89), Quigley; Edwards (Seargeant 36); Pryce.
APOEL: (4231) Waterman; Carlao, Efrem (Aloneftis 83), De Vincenti, Alexandrou; Vinicius (Orlandi 71), Sotiriou; Milanov, Astiz, Morais; Vander.

Valletta (1) 1 *(Falcone 15)*

Crvena Zvezda (0) 2 *(Katai 66, Sikimic 75)* 1098

Valletta: (433) Bonello; Caruana, Azzopardi (Umeh 83), Aguirre, Borg S; Gill, Pani, Briffa (Cremona 78); Romeu, Falcone (Malano 42), Jhonnattann.
Crvena Zvezda: (442) Kahriman; Lukovic, Phibel, Ibanez, Cvetkovic; Donald, Le Tallec, Srnic (Mouche 46), Kanga; Vieira (Sikimic 65), Katai (Ruiz 83).

Vardar (0) 1 *(Asani 54)*

Dinamo Zagreb (2) 2 *(Mijuskovic 22 (og), Rog 30)* 17,000

Vardar: (442) Pacovski; Grncarov, Popov, Hambardzumyan, Mijuskovic; Gligorov (Velkovski 46), Spirovski, Kojasevic, Petkovski (Balotelli 46); Asani (Obregon 71), Juan Felipe.
Dinamo Zagreb: (433) Jezina; Sigali, Schildenfeld, Matel (Sosa 66), Paulo Machado; Antolic, Stojanovic, Rog (Sovsic 80); Fernandes, Soudani, Henriquez (Coric 66).

Zrinjski Mostar (0) 1 *(Katanec 57)*

Legia Warsaw (0) 1 *(Nikolic 49)* 5500

Zrinjski Mostar: (442) Kozic; Peko (Zeravica 81), Tomic, Baric, Stojkic; Todorovic (Filipovic 69), Mesanovic, Petrak, Jakovljevic; Katanec, Bilbja (Arezina 87).
Legia Warsaw: (532) Malarz (Cierzniak 46); Jodlowiec, Lewczuk, Guilherme, Nikolic (Prijovic 76), Duda (Aleksandrov 60); Hlousek, Kucharczyk, Rzezniczak; Broz, Moulin.

Wednesday, 13 July 2016

Crusaders (0) 0

FC Copenhagen (2) 3 *(Santander 6, Cornelius 40, Jensen 53)* 2069

Crusaders: (442) O'Neill; Burns, Bererland, Coates, McClean; Clarke (Cushley 53), Caddell (Mitchell 61), Heatley, Snoddy (Gault 74); Owens, Whyte.
FC Copenhagen: (442) Olsen; Jorgensen, Johansson, Ankersen, Augustinsson; Kvist Jorgensen (Gregus 59), Delaney, Kusk (Toutouh 76), Santander (Kadrii 73); Jensen, Cornelius.

Dundalk (0) 1 *(McMillan 66)*

Hafnarfjordur (0) 1 *(Lennon 77)* 3111

Dundalk: (442) Rogers; Boyle, Finn, Gannon, Gartland (Barrett 43); Horgan, Massey, McEleney, McMillan (Kilduff 78); Mountney (Benson 81), O'Donnell.
Hafnarfjordur: (442) Nielsen; Bodvarsson, Doumbia, Hendrickx, Lennon; Olafsson, Palsson, Valdimarsson, Vidarsson B; Vidarsson D (Vidarsson P 87), Gudnason (Hewson 79).

Ludogorets Razgrad (2) 2 *(Moti 13 (pen), Lukoki 26)*

Mladost Podgorica (0) 0 6000

Ludogorets Razgrad: (442) Stoyanov; Moti, Cicinho, Plastun, Dyakov (Andrianantenaina 90); Wanderson (Keseru 80), Natanael, Quixada (Sasha 81), Marcelinho; Lukoki, Cafu.
Mladost Podgorica: (442) Ljuljanovic; Lakic, Novovic, Boris Kopitovic (Lazarevic 46), Raicevic; Igumanovic, Vlaisavljevic, Burzanovic (Stijepovic 90), Djurisic; Petrovic Z (Bukorac 71), Boris Kopitovic.

Olimpija Ljubljana (2) 3 *(Velikonja 34, Zajc 43, Eleke 89)*

Trencin (4) 4 *(Lawrence 4, Kalu 6, Janga 20, Holubek 32)* 5950

Olimpija Ljubljana: (442) Seliga; Bajric, Kirm (Krefl 80), Kelhar, Klinar; Matic, Novak (Alves 75), Velikonja, Wobay (Eleke 51); Zajc, Zarifovic.
Trencin: (442) Semrinec; Bero, Holubek (Diks 78), Janga (Udeh 90), Kalu; Klescik, Lawrence (Janco 39), Skovajsa, Sulek; Ibrahim, Madu.

Partizani Tirana (0) 1 *(Fili 47)*

Ferencvaros (0) 1 *(Bode 71)* 1700

Partizani Tirana: (442) Hoxha; Arapi, Krasniqi, Kalari, Ibrahimi; Vila (Atanda 82), Trashi, Batha, Fili (Volas 85); Ramadani, Torassa (Ekuban 67).
Ferencvaros: (442) Dibusz; Pinter, Dilaver, Leandro, Ramirez; Nalepa, Nagy (Trinks 88), Gera, Djuricin (Bode 66); Lovrencsics, Rado (Sestak 66).

Rosenborg (0) 3 *(Eyjolfsson 48, Helland 62, de Lanlay 65)*

IFK Norrkoping (0) 1 *(Andersson 70)* 11,595

Rosenborg: (442) Londak; Reginiussen, Eyjolfsson, Skjelvik, Svensson; Jensen, Konradsen, Midtsjoe (Thorarinsson 88), Helland; Gytkjaer (Vilhjalmsson 80), de Lanlay (Gersbach 86).
IFK Norrkoping: (442) Vaikla; Fjoluson, Wahlqvist, Johansson, Telo; Sjolund, Blomqvist (Citaku 90), Tekie (Smith 67), Barkroth (Hadenius 68); Andersson, Nyman.

Zalgiris (0) 0

Astana (0) 0 4100

Zalgiris: (442) Klevinskas; Klimavicius, Vaitkunas, Mbodj, Mikoliunas (Elivelto 64); Slijngard, Pilibaitis (Ljujic 59), Luksa, Kuklys; Blagojevic, Kaluderovic.
Astana: (442) Eric; Logvinenko, Anicic, Shitov, Shomko; Canas, Muzhikov, Maksimovic, Ibraimi (Tagybergen 80); Nuserbaev (Kabananga 71), Twumasi (Despotovic 90).

SECOND QUALIFYING ROUND SECOND LEG

Tuesday, 19 July 2016

Alashkert (0) 1 *(Gyozalyan 51)*

Dinamo Tbilisi (1) 1 *(Jigauri 21)* 4600

Alashkert: (442) Kasparov; Minasyan, Tasic, Voskanyan, Artak Yedigaryan; Muradyan, Dashyan (Ghazaryan 76), Artur Yedigaryan (Melkonyan 65), Kvekveskiri; Grigoryan, Gyozalyan.
Dinamo Tbilisi: (442) Scribe; Lobzhanidze, Rene, Amisulashvili, Tchelidze; Jigauri, Kiteishvili (Papunashvili 68), Parunashvili, Tchanturishvili (Coureur 84); Kvilitaia (Tsintsadze 62), Dvalishvili.

APOEL (0) 3 *(Alexandrou 54, Sotiriou 73, De Vincenti 90 (pen))*

The New Saints (0) 0 10,548

APOEL: (442) Waterman; Carlao, Morais, Mario Sergio (Milanov 85), Astiz; De Vincenti, Alexandrou, Vinicius (Bressan 58), Vander; Efrem (Orlandi 77), Sotiriou.
The New Saints: (442) Harrison; Spender, Marriott, Baker, Rawlinson; Routledge, Seargeant, Brobbel (Parry 90), Cieslewicz (Saunders 79); Mullan (Draper 86), Quigley.

Crvena Zvezda (1) 2 *(Donald 30, Katai 76)*

Valletta (1) 1 *(Caruana 11)* 31,112

Crvena Zvezda: (3331) Kahriman; Cvetkovic, Phibel, Ibanez; Donald, Rendulic, Le Tallec; Katai, Mouche (Srnic 65), Kanga (Ruiz 85); Hugo Vieira (Sikimic 71).
Valletta: (442) Bartolo; Borg S, Caruana, Gill, Azzopardi (Umeh 79); Romeu (Santiago 72), Briffa (Cremona 90), Pani, Aguirre; Mifsud, Jhonnattann.

FC Copenhagen (2) 6 *(Pavlovic 15, Mitchell 45 (og), Cornelius 48, 76, Jensen 58, Gregus 68)*

Crusaders (0) 0 6924

FC Copenhagen: (442) Andersen; Remmer, Jorgensen (Keita 63), Antonsson, Augustinsson; Kusk, Toutouh, Gregus, Jensen (Amankwaa 63); Cornelius, Pavlovic (Kadrii 63).
Crusaders: (4141) O'Neill; Mitchell, Burns, Bererland, McClean; Gault (Snoddy 68); Carvill, Lowry (Owens 60), Caddell, Forsyth; Cushley (Heatley 57).

FK Liepaja (0) 0

Red Bull Salzburg (1) 2 *(Berisha 35, da Silva 65)* 3633

FK Liepaja: (532) Dorosevs; Kluk, Klava, Ivanovs, Gorkss, Karklins; Brtan, Torres, Gucs (Mickevics 71); Kamess (Afanasjevs 57), Grebis (Gauracs 65).
Red Bull Salzburg: (442) Walke; Schwegler, Paulo Miranda (Caleta-Car 83), Hinteregger, Ulmer; Lazaro, Laimer (Samassekou 59), da Silva (Upamecano 87), Berisha; Soriano, Dabbur.

Legia Warsaw (1) 2 *(Nikolic 28 (pen), 62)*
Zrinjski Mostar (0) 0 12,784
Legia Warsaw: (4141) Malarz; Broz, Pazdan, Lewczuk, Hlousek; Jodlowiec; Aleksandrov, Moulin, Guilherme (Hamalainen 15), Kucharczyk (Brzyski 84); Nikolic (Kopczynski 75).
Zrinjski Mostar: (4231) Kozic; Baric, Jakovljevic, Katanec (Radeljic 45), Stojkic; Petrak, Tomic; Peko, Bilbja (Zeravica 75), Todorovic (Filipovic 78); Mesanovic.

Mladost Podgorica (0) 0
Ludogorets Razgrad (1) 3 *(Lukoki 39, 64, Wanderson 48)* 4300
Mladost Podgorica: (4411) Ljuljanovic; Djurisic, Lakic, Boris Kopitovic, Igumanovic (Petrovic Z 60); Raicevic (Petrovic G 83), Bukorac, Lazarevic (Stijepovic 75), Novovic; Burzanovic; Vlaisavljevic.
Ludogorets Razgrad: (4231) Stoyanov; Natanael, Moti, Plastun, Minev; Lukoki, Wanderson (Keseru 65); Dyakov, Sasha (Abel 84), Marcelinho (Prepelita 76); Cafu.

Sheriff (0) 0
Hapoel Beer Sheva (0) 0 8184
Sheriff: (442) Mitrev; Susic, Savic, Skvorc, Metoua; Kvrzic, Oancea (Puntus 82), Brezovec, Ginsari; Ivancic, Subotic (Ricardinho 57).
Hapoel Beer Sheva: (433) Goresh; Bitton, William Soares, Vitor, Davidadze; Hoban■, Ogu, Radi (Shabtai 74); Melikson (Buzaglo 90), Sahar (Barda 61), Nwakaeme.

SJK (1) 2 *(Nguekam 44, Riski 61)*
BATE Borisov (2) 2 *(Karnitskiy 15, Ryas 29)* 5817
SJK: (4411) Aksalu; Tahvanainen (Kane 46), Meite, Aalto, Hurme; Vasara, Laaksonen, Hetemaj, Hradecky (Ahde 75); Nguekam; Riski.
BATE Borisov: (4411) Veremko; Zhavnerchik, Gaiduchik, Palyakow, Pikk; Ryas (Gordeichuk 69), Valadzko A (Ivanic 54), Kendysh, Stasevich; Karnitskiy; Rodionov (Valadzko M 85).

Wednesday, 20 July 2016

Astana (1) 2 *(Anicic 31, 90)*
Zalgiris (0) 1 *(Elivelto 57)* 18,449
Astana: (4321) Eric; Anicic, Maksimovic, Ibraimi (Despotovic 72), Shitov; Nuserbaev (Muzhikov 55), Twumasi (Beisebekov 90), Logvinenko; Kabananga, Shomko; Canas.
Zalgiris: (442) Klevinskas; Slijngard, Klimavicius, Mbodj, Blagojevic; Vaitkunas, Luksa, Mikoliunas (Atajic 54), Elivelto (Ljujic 77); Kuklys, Kaluderovic (Zaliukas 85).

Celtic (3) 3 *(Lustig 23, Griffiths 25, Roberts 29)*
Lincoln Red Imps (0) 0 55,632
Celtic: (334) Gordon; Lustig, Sviatchenko, Tierney (Ajer 59); Forrest (Izaguirre 63), Brown, Roberts; McGregor, Armstrong, Dembele (Ciftci 76), Griffiths.
Lincoln Red Imps: (433) Navas; Garcia, Casciaro R, Chipolina R, Chipolina J; Patino, Bernardo Lopes, Calderon (Bardon 89); Walker (Livramento 89), Casciaro L (Cabrera 89), Casciaro K.

Dinamo Zagreb (0) 3 *(Pjaca 55 (pen), 70 (pen), Paulo Machado 78)*
Vardar (1) 2 *(Velkovski 39, 63)* 10,142
Dinamo Zagreb: (3421) Jezina; Soudani, Antolic, Paulo Machado; Hodzic (Benkovic 68), Pjaca (Pivaric 85), Sigali, Schildenfeld; Rog (Fernandes 81), Stojanovic; Matel.
Vardar: (4231) Aleksovski; Grncarov, Spirovski, Kojasevic, Asani (Nikolov 67); Velkovski (Petkovski 71), Hambardzumyan; Novak, Glisic, Juan Felipe; Balotelli (Obregon 75).

F91 Dudelange (0) 1 *(N'Diaye 72)*
Qarabag (0) 1 *(Reynaldo 90)* 891
F91 Dudelange: (442) Joubert; Moreira, Schnell, Da Mota Alves (Lauriente 80), Dikaba; Stolz, Nakache (Pokar 66), Prempeh, Melisse; Turpel, N'Diaye (Ibrahimovic 86).
Qarabag: (451) Sehic; Garayev (Diniyev 82), Medvedev, Michel, Reynaldo; Muarem (Madatov 70), Sadygov, Almeida, Agolli, Guseynov; Quintana (Ismayilov 90).

Ferencvaros (1) 1 *(Gera 14 (pen))*
Partizani Tirana (1) 1 *(Husing 40 (og))* 8752
Ferencvaros: (4411) Dibusz; Husing, Lovrencsics, Bode, Leandro; Pinter (Sestak 46), Gera, Trinks (Djuricin 35), Dilaver; Ramirez; Varga (Nagy 46).
Partizani Tirana: (451) Hoxha; Arapi, Krasniqi, Fili (Bardhi 82), Batha (Ekuban 26); Ramadani, Trashi, Ibrahimi, Torassa (Atanda 71), Vila; Kalari.
aet; Partizani Tirana won 3-1 on penalties.

Hafnarfjordur (1) 2 *(Hewson 19, Finnbogason 78)*
Dundalk (0) 2 *(McMillan 52, 62)* 1850
Hafnarfjordur: (433) Nielsen; Olafsson, Hewson (Bjornsson 77), Lennon, Palsson (Vidarsson P 66); Valdimarsson, Vidarsson D, Vidarsson B (Finnbogason 66); Doumbia, Bodvarsson, Hendrickx.
Dundalk: (4141) Rogers; Gannon, Boyle, O'Donnell, Horgan; Mountney (Benson 46); McMillan (Kilduff 82), Finn, McEleney (Shields 79), Massey; Barrett.
Dundalk won on away goals.

IFK Norrkoping (0) 3 *(Andersson 57, 77, Nyman 59)*
Rosenborg (1) 2 *(Gytkjaer 36 (pen), de Lanlay 55)* 10,372
IFK Norrkoping: (442) Vaikla; Fjoluson (Dagerstal 90), Johansson, Nyman, Wahlqvist; Blomqvist (Hadenius 74), Barkroth, Telo, Smith (Tekie 59); Andersson, Sjolund.
Rosenborg: (433) Londak; Svensson, Reginiussen, Eyjolfsson, Jensen; Konradsen, Gytkjaer (Bjordal 90), de Lanlay (Thorarinsson 84); Skjelvik, Midtsjoe (Vilhjalmsson 67), Helland.

Trencin (2) 2 *(Janga 13, Bero 20)*
Olimpija Ljubljana (2) 3 *(Kelhar 41, Eleke 45, Klinar 79)* 3750
Trencin: (433) Semrinec; Skovajsa, Sulek, Bala (Diks 74), Ibrahim (Rafael 90); Janga (Udeh 85), Holubek, Madu; Kalu, Bero, Klescik.
Olimpija Ljubljana: (3142) Seliga; Klinar, Kelhar, Zajc; Matic; Eleke, Velikonja, Alves (Wobay 65), Kirm (Krefl 81); Zarifovic, Bajric.
Trencin won on away goals.

THIRD QUALIFYING ROUND FIRST LEG

Tuesday, 26 July 2016

Ajax (0) 1 *(Dolberg 58)*
PAOK Salonika (1) 1 *(Djalma 27)* 45,640
Ajax: (433) Cillessen; Tete, Veltman, Viergever, Dijks; van de Beek (Schone 77), Riedewald, Klaassen; El Ghazi (Cerny 88), Dolberg, Casierra (Younes 58).
PAOK Salonika: (433) Glykos; Leo Matos, Crespo, Tzavelas, Leovac; Charisis (Tziolis 69), Shakhov, Cimirot; Rodrigues (Mystakidis 83), Athanasiadis (Koulouris 90), Djalma.

BATE Borisov (0) 1 *(Gordeichuk 71)*
Dundalk (0) 0 11,321
BATE Borisov: (442) Veremko; Dubra, Palyakow, Ivanic (Gordeichuk 68), Pikk; Zhavnerchik (Hleb 60), Karnitskiy (Valadzko A 88), Ryas, Stasevich; Rodionov, Kendysh.
Dundalk: (442) Rogers; Boyle, Massey, Barrett, Benson (Mountney 46); Gannon, O'Donnell, Horgan, Finn; McEleney (Shields 46), McMillan (Kilduff 78).

Dinamo Zagreb (2) 2 *(Soudani 39, Coric 42)*
Dinamo Tbilisi (0) 0 10,258
Dinamo Zagreb: (343) Eduardo; Stojanovic, Sigali, Benkovic; Rog, Paulo Machado (Fernandes 9), Antolic, Pivaric; Soudani, Coric (Henriquez 74), Hodzic (Jonas 62).
Dinamo Tbilisi: (4231) Scribe; Lobzhanidze, Rene, Amisulashvili, Chelidze; Papunashvili (Coureur 56), Jigauri; Parunashvili, Tchanturishvili, Kiteishvili (Gelashvili 46); Dvalishvili (Tsintsadze 78).

Ludogorets Razgrad (1) 2 *(Cafu 43, Keseru 76)*
Crvena Zvezda (0) 2 *(Katai 48, Kanga 66)* 7759
Ludogorets Razgrad: (442) Stoyanov; Cafu, Minev, Moti, Natanael; Sasha (Quixada 75), Dyakov, Plastun, Marcelinho; Wanderson, Lukoki (Keseru 67).
Crvena Zvezda: (442) Kahriman; Cvetkovic, Rendulic, Ibanez, Phibel; Kanga, Donald, Srnic, Le Tallec; Katai (Sikimic 88), Mouche (Ruiz 67).

Partizani Tirana (0) 0

Red Bull Salzburg (0) 1 *(Soriano 70 (pen))* 4000

Partizani Tirana: (442) Hoxha; Arapi, Krasniqi, Kalari■, Ibrahimi; Vila, Fili (Batha 57), Ramadani, Trashi; Torassa (Bardhi 82), Ekuban.
Red Bull Salzburg: (442) Walke; Caleta-Car, Schwegler, Ulmer, Hinteregger; Samassekou■, Lazaro (Lainer 89), Berisha, Soriano (Gulbrandsen 74); Dabbur (Laimer 55), da Silva.

Rostov (1) 2 *(Ezatolahi 16, Poloz 60 (pen))*

Anderlecht (1) 2 *(Hanni 3, Tielemans 52)* 14,770

Rostov: (442) Dzanaev; Kalachev, Ezatolahi (Terentjev 82), Bastos, Noboa; Novoseltsev, Kudryashov, Cesar Navas, Gatcan; Poloz (Kireev 74), Bukharov (Azmoun 56).
Anderlecht: (442) Roef; De Maio, Chipciu (Acheampong 69), Appiah, Nuytinck; Defour (Heylen 90), N'Sakala, Tielemans, Dendoncker; Sylla, Hanni (Hassan 80).

Shakhtar Donetsk (1) 2 *(Bernard 27, Seleznyov 75)*

Young Boys (0) 0 7477

Shakhtar Donetsk: (442) Pyatov; Srna, Kryvtsov, Ordets, Ismaily; Marlos, Fred, Stepanenko, Bernard; Eduardo (Seleznyov 71), Taison (Dentinho 77).
Young Boys: (442) Mvogo; Sutter (Hadergjonaj 81), Vilotic■, Rochat, Lecjaks; Sulejmani (Wuthrich 58), Sanogo, Bertone, Ravet; Gerndt (Kubo 49), Hoarau.

Sparta Prague (1) 1 *(Sural 35)*

Steaua Bucharest (0) 1 *(Stanciu 75)* 13,257

Sparta Prague: (442) Bicik; Kadlec Michal, Brabec, Dockal, Frydek; Cermak (Matejovsky 63), Konate, Holek, Zahustel (Nhamoinesu 80); Lafata, Sural (Fatai 59).
Steaua Bucharest: (442) Nita; Tamas, Pintilii, Stanciu, Tosca; Momcilovic, Aganovic (Sulley 62), Achim (Popescu D 89), Enache; Tudorie (Popa 55), Golubovic.

Viktoria Plzen (0) 0

Qarabag (0) 0 10,269

Viktoria Plzen: (442) Kozacik; Mateju, Hubnik, Horava, Limbersky; Petrzela, Duris (Krmencik 62), Hrosovsky, Kovarik (Kopic 72); Baranek■, Kolar (Hejda 79).
Qarabag: (442) Sehic; Garayev, Medvedev, Michel, Sadygov; Almeida, Agolli (Gurbanov 79), Guseynov, Quintana (Ismayilov 67); Reynaldo, Madatov (Muarem 46).

Wednesday, 27 July 2016

Astana (1) 1 *(Logvinenko 19)*

Celtic (0) 1 *(Griffiths 78)* 29,000

Astana: (4231) Eric; Shitov, Logvinenko, Anicic, Shomko; Maksimovic, Canas; Beisebekov (Ibraimi 84), Nurgaliev (Muzhikov 61), Twumasi; Kabananga (Despotovic 86).
Celtic: (442) Gordon; Lustig, Ambrose, O'Connell, Tierney; Roberts, McGregor (Rogic 77), Brown, Armstrong (Forrest 72); Dembele (Bitton 62), Griffiths.

Astra Giurgiu (1) 1 *(Teixeira 7)*

FC Copenhagen (0) 1 *(Delaney 64)* 2381

Astra Giurgiu: (451) Lung; Vangjeli, Alves, Fabricio, Maranhao; Lovin, Teixeira, Seto (William Amorim 72), Boldrin, Boudjemaa (Sapunaru 60); Nicorescu.
FC Copenhagen: (424) Olsen; Jorgensen, Johansson, Ankersen, Augustinsson; Kvist Jorgensen, Delaney; Toutouh (Jensen 61), Verbic (Amankwaa 80), Santander, Cornelius.

Fenerbahce (1) 2 *(Emenike 39, 61)*

Monaco (1) 1 *(Falcao 42)* 12,223

Fenerbahce: (334) Taskiran; Neustadter, Skrtel, Kjaer; Ucan (Ozbayrakli 82), Souza, Tufan; van der Wiel (Stoch 90), Emenike (Chahechouhe 71), Fernandao, Kaldirim.
Monaco: (442) De Sanctis (Badiashile 13); Sidibe, Jemerson, Raggi, Mendy; Dirar (Bernardo Silva 76), Fabinho, Bakayoko, Lemar; Falcao, Germain (Ivan Cavaleiro 86).

Olympiacos (0) 0

Hapoel Beer Sheva (0) 0 20,531

Olympiacos: (442) Kapino; Maniatis (Bouchalakis 63), Botia, Milivojevic, Fortounis; Durmaz (Dominguez 58), Siovas (da Costa 40), De la Bella, Diogo Figueiras; Seba, Ideye.
Hapoel Beer Sheva: (442) Goresh; Bitton, Vitor, Davidadze, Broun; Taha, Melikson (Radi 76), William Soares, Ogu; Barda (Sahar 69), Nwakaeme (Shabtai 90).

Rosenborg (2) 2 *(Gytkjaer 23, Skjelvik 45)*

APOEL (0) 1 *(Efrem 67)* 13,281

Rosenborg: (442) Kwarasey; Svensson, Reginiussen, Eyjolfsson, Jensen; Konradsen, de Lanlay (Bakenga 75), Skjelvik, Midtsjoe (Vilhjalmsson 79); Helland, Gytkjaer.
APOEL: (442) Waterman; Carlao, Artymatas (Orlandi 59), Alexandrou, Vinicius; Milanov, Astiz, Morais, Vander (Efrem 65); Sotiriou (de Camargo 77), Gianniotas.

Trencin (0) 0

Legia Warsaw (0) 1 *(Nikolic 69)* 5866

Trencin: (4141) Chovan; Sulek, Udeh, Klescik, Holubek; Lawrence; Kalu, Ibrahim, Bero, Bala (Diks 79); Janga (Prekop 85).
Legia Warsaw: (4321) Malarz; Bereszynski, Lewczuk, Pazdan, Brzyski; Jodlowiec (Hamalainen 85), Kopczynski, Kucharczyk; Moulin, Aleksandrov (Broz 89); Nikolic (Prijovic 75).

THIRD QUALIFYING ROUND SECOND LEG

Tuesday, 2 August 2016

APOEL (0) 3 *(Vander 90, De Vincenti 90, Gianniotas 90)*

Rosenborg (0) 0 15,559

APOEL: (433) Waterman; Milanov, Astiz, Carlao, Alexandrou; Efrem (Vander 71), De Vincenti, Morais; Vinicius (Orlandi 71), Gianniotas, Sotiriou (de Camargo 77).
Rosenborg: (433) Kwarasey; Svensson, Eyjolfsson, Reginiussen, Skjelvik; Jensen (Bjordal 87), Konradsen, Midtsjoe (Vilhjalmsson 76); Helland (Rashani 81), Gytkjaer, de Lanlay.

Crvena Zvezda (1) 2 *(Donald 17, Ibanez 62 (pen))*

Ludogorets Razgrad (2) 4 *(Cafu 24, Wanderson 40, 92, 97)* 50,223

Crvena Zvezda: (442) Kahriman; Rendulic, Ibanez, Phibel, Cvetkovic; Kanga, Donald, Srnic (Hugo Vieira 53), Le Tallec (Ristic 106); Katai, Mouche (Ruiz 57).
Ludogorets Razgrad: (442) Stoyanov; Cafu (Misidjan 70), Minev, Moti, Natanael; Abel, Dyakov, Plastun■, Marcelinho (Sasha 101); Wanderson, Keseru (Palomino 46).
aet.

Dinamo Tbilisi (0) 0

Dinamo Zagreb (1) 1 *(Rog 8)* 21,510

Dinamo Tbilisi: (442) Scribe; Lobzhanidze, Amisulashvili, Tchanturishvili, Dvalishvili; Papunashvili (Mikel Alvaro 72), Parunashvili, Coureur (Gelashvili 46), Rene; Jigauri, Spicic (Kiteishvili 46).
Dinamo Zagreb: (442) Eduardo; Soudani, Jonas (Coric 77), Antolic, Fernandes (Pavicic 72); Sigali, Schildenfeld, Benkovic, Rog; Stojanovic, Sosa (Matel 53).

Dundalk (1) 3 *(McMillan 45, 59, Benson 90)*

BATE Borisov (0) 0 4645

Dundalk: (4141) Rogers; Gannon, Barrett, Boyle, Massey; Shields; Mountney, Finn (McEleney 32), O'Donnell, Horgan (Kilduff 90); McMillan (Benson 78).
BATE Borisov: (4231) Veremko; Zhavnerchik (Signevich 81), Dubra, Palyakow, Pikk (Gordeichuk 65); Karnitskiy (Hleb 46), Kendysh; Ryas, Ivanic, Stasevich; Rodionov.

Qarabag (1) 1 *(Muarem 28)*

Viktoria Plzen (0) 1 *(Krmencik 85)* 30,792

Qarabag: (433) Sehic; Medvedev, Guseynov, Sadygov, Agolli; Michel, Garayev, Almeida (Yunuszadze 84); Quintana (El Jadeyaoui 82), Reynaldo, Muarem (Ismayilov 70).
Viktoria Plzen: (4411) Kozacik; Mateju, Hubnik, Hejda, Limbersky; Petrzela, Horava, Hrosovsky, Kovarik (Kopic 57); Kolar (Krmencik 63); Duris (Bakos 79).
Viktoria Plzen won on away goals.

Wednesday, 3 August 2016

Anderlecht (0) 0

Rostov (1) 2 *(Noboa 28, Azmoun 47)* 19,464

Anderlecht: (442) Roef; De Maio, Chipciu, Appiah, Nuytinck (Kabasele 60); Defour, N'Sakala (Acheampong 54), Tielemans, Dendoncker; Sylla, Hanni (Hassan 78).
Rostov: (442) Dzanaev; Kalachev, Terentjev, Bastos, Noboa; Novoseltsev, Kudryashov, Cesar Navas, Gatcan; Bukharov (Ezatolahi 74), Azmoun (Poloz 57).

Celtic (1) 2 *(Griffiths 45 (pen), Dembele 90 (pen))*

Astana (0) 1 *(Ibraimi 62)* 52,952

Celtic: (451) Gordon; Janko, Lustig, O'Connell, Tierney; Brown, McGregor, Armstrong (Toure 61), Roberts (Johansen 32), Forrest (Dembele 75); Griffiths.
Astana: (433) Eric; Anicic, Muzhikov, Nurgaliev (Ibraimi 56), Shitov■; Beisebekov, Logvinenko, Shomko; Canas, Twumasi, Kabananga.

FC Copenhagen (3) 3 *(Cornelius 14, 45, Santander 34)*

Astra Giurgiu (0) 0 16,853

FC Copenhagen: (442) Olsen; Ankersen, Jorgensen, Johansson, Augustinsson; Verbic, Kvist Jorgensen, Delaney (Toutouh 70), Jensen; Santander (Kusk 84), Cornelius (Pavlovic 61).
Astra Giurgiu: (451) Lung; Sapunaru (Seto 76), Geraldo Alves, Fabricio, Junior Morais; Boudjemaa (William Amorim 57), Stan, Lovin, Boldrin, Teixeira; Niculae (Florea 76).

Hapoel Beer Sheva (0) 1 *(Tzedek 79)*

Olympiacos (0) 0 15,500

Hapoel Beer Sheva: (433) Goresh; Bitton, Vitor, Tzedek, Davidadze; Broun (Radi 66), Ogu, Hoban; Melikson (Taha 83), Barda (Maranhao 61), Nwakaeme.
Olympiacos: (4231) Kapino; Diogo Figueiras (Maniatis 51), Botia (Pulido 82), da Costa, De la Bella; Cambiasso, Milivojevic; Dominguez (Masuaku 60), Fortounis, Bouchalakis; Ideye.

Legia Warsaw (0) 0

Trencin (0) 0 21,850

Legia Warsaw: (433) Malarz; Jodlowiec, Lewczuk, Pazdan, Bereszynski (Broz 56); Hlousek, Kopczynski, Kucharczyk; Langil (Aleksandrov 69), Moulin, Nikolic (Prijovic 78).
Trencin: (532) Chovan; Bero, Klescik, Lawrence, Sulek, Udeh (Rafael 90); Holubek, Janco (Prekop 77), Bala; Janga, Kalu.

Monaco (2) 3 *(Germain 3, 65, Falcao 19 (pen))*

Fenerbahce (0) 1 *(Emenike 54)* 8403

Monaco: (442) Subasic; Fabinho, Jemerson, Mendy, Sidibe; Raggi, Dirar, Bakayoko, Falcao (Carrillo 45); Germain (Glik 90), Lemar (Bernardo Silva 81).
Fenerbahce: (442) Taskiran; Kaldirim (Stoch 79), Kjaer (Topal 36), Souza (Chahechouhe 69), van der Wiel; Skrtel, Tufan, Neustadter, Ucan; Fernandao, Emenike.

PAOK Salonika (1) 1 *(Athanasiadis 4)*

Ajax (1) 2 *(Klaassen 45 (pen), 88)* 24,930

PAOK Salonika: (442) Glykos; Leo Matos, Leovac, Charisis (Biseswar 84), Crespo; Cimirot, Shakhov (Koulouris 89), Tzavelas, Djalma; Rodrigues (Mystakidis 70), Athanasiadis.
Ajax: (442) Cillessen; Tete, Veltman, Riedewald, Klaassen; Westermann, Viergever, Gudelj, Dijks; Casierra, Dolberg (El Ghazi 63).

Red Bull Salzburg (0) 2 *(Soriano 76, Wanderson 81)*

Partizani Tirana (0) 0 7853

Red Bull Salzburg: (442) Walke; Caleta-Car, Schwegler, Dabbur (Wanderson 45), Lazaro (Lainer 74); Berisha, Ulmer, Soriano (Gulbrandsen 84), Laimer; Hinteregger, da Silva.
Partizani Tirana: (442) Hoxha; Arapi, Krasniqi, Fili (Volas 78), Ramadani; Trashi, Ibrahimi, Torassa (Batha 63), Atanda; Ekuban, Vila.

Steaua Bucharest (1) 2 *(Stanciu 31, 62)*

Sparta Prague (0) 0 37,127

Steaua Bucharest: (4231) Nita; Enache, Tamas, Tosca, Momcilovic; Pintilii, Achim (Sulley 64); Popa, Stanciu (Aganovic 81), Hamroun; Golubovic (Tudorie 88).
Sparta Prague: (3142) Bicik; Brabec■, Nhamoinesu, Kadlec Michal; Vacha; Zahustel, Frydek, Dockal, Konate; Sural (Julis 63), Lafata (Marecek 83).

Young Boys (0) 2 *(Kubo 54, 60)*

Shakhtar Donetsk (0) 0 9365

Young Boys: (442) Mvogo; von Bergen, Bertone (Gajic 111), Lecjaks, Rochat; Sutter (Obexer 116), Sanogo, Kubo, Sulejmani; Ravet (Hadergjonaj 88), Hoarau.
Shakhtar Donetsk: (442) Pyatov; Ordets, Stepanenko, Fred, Marlos; Ismaily, Srna, Kryvtsov (Rakitskiy 120), Dentinho (Wellington Nem 75); Eduardo (Seleznyov 62), Taison.
aet; Young Boys won 4-2 on penalties.

PLAY-OFF ROUND FIRST LEG

Tuesday, 16 August 2016

Ajax (1) 1 *(Klaassen 38 (pen))*

Rostov (1) 1 *(Noboa 13)* 51,463

Ajax: (433) Cillessen; Veltman, Sanchez, Riedewald, Dijks; Bazoer, Gudelj, Klaassen; El Ghazi, Traore (Dolberg 82), Younes (Casierra 69).
Rostov: (532) Dzanaev; Kalachev, Terentjev, Cesar Navas, Novoseltsev, Kudryashov; Noboa, Gatcan, Erokhin (Ezatolahi 67); Bukharov (Azmoun 57), Poloz (Bayramyan 87).

Dinamo Zagreb (0) 1 *(Rog 76 (pen))*

Red Bull Salzburg (0) 1 *(Lazaro 59)* 13,784

Dinamo Zagreb: (433) Eduardo; Stojanovic, Sigali, Benkovic, Matel; Knezevic (Pavicic 57), Antolic (Coric 65), Jonas; Soudani, Rog, Fernandes (Henriquez 78).
Red Bull Salzburg: (442) Walke; Schwegler, Caleta-Car, Hinteregger, Ulmer; Lazaro, Laimer, Bernardo, Berisha; Wanderson (Lainer 78), Soriano (Gulbrandsen 63).

FC Copenhagen (1) 1 *(Pavlovic 43)*

APOEL (0) 0 20,519

FC Copenhagen: (442) Olsen; Ankersen, Jorgensen, Johansson, Augustinsson; Verbic (Gregus 88), Kvist Jorgensen, Delaney, Jensen (Toutouh 79); Santander, Pavlovic (Cornelius 67).
APOEL: (451) Waterman; Milanov, Astiz, Carlao (Merkis 46), Alexandrou; Efrem (Vander 56), Vinicius, Morais, Orlandi, Gianniotas; Sotiriou (de Camargo 75).

Steaua Bucharest (0) 0

Manchester C (2) 5 *(Silva 13, Aguero 41, 78, 89, Nolito 49)* 45,327

Steaua Bucharest: (4231) Nita; Enache, Tamas, Tosca, Momcilovic; Achim (Bourceanu 46), Sulley (Popescu O 66); Popa, Stanciu, Hamroun; Golubovic (Tudorie 46).
Manchester C: (433) Caballero; Zabaleta (Sagna 69), Otamendi, Stones, Kolarov (Clichy 75); De Bruyne (Fernando 80), Fernandinho, Silva; Sterling, Aguero, Nolito.

Young Boys (0) 1 *(Sulejmani 56)*

Borussia Munchengladbach (1) 3 *(Raffael 11, 70, Hahn 67)* 30,224

Young Boys: (442) Mvogo; Vilotic, Bertone, Sulejmani (Schick 86), Lecjaks; Ravet, Gajic (Zakaria 73), Rochat, Sutter; Kubo (Frey 73), Hoarau.
Borussia Munchengladbach: (442) Sommer; Christensen, Strobl, Kramer, Hazard (Hahn 66); Raffael, Stindl (Johnson 81), Traore (Vestergaard 79), Wendt; Jantschke, Elvedi.

Wednesday, 17 August 2016

Celtic (3) 5 *(Rogic 9, Griffiths 40, 45, Dembele 73, Brown 85)*

Hapoel Beer Sheva (0) 2 *(Maranhao 55, Melikson 57)* 52,659

Celtic: (451) Gordon; Lustig (Janko 62), Toure, O'Connell, Tierney; Forrest, Brown, Rogic (Dembele 70), McGregor (Bitton 60), Sinclair; Griffiths.
Hapoel Beer Sheva: (541) Goresh; Biton, Hoban (Buzaglo 79), Taha, Tzedek, Davidadze; Melikson, Radi (Broun 84), Ogu, Nwakaeme; Maranhao (Sahar 69).

Dundalk (0) 0

Legia Warsaw (0) 2 *(Nikolic 56 (pen), Prijovic 90)* 30,417

Dundalk: (4231) Rogers; Gannon, Barrett, Boyle, Massey; O'Donnell, Shields (Benson 77); Mountney (Finn 64), McEleney, Horgan; McMillan (Kilduff 80).
Legia Warsaw: (451) Malarz; Broz, Pazdan, Lewczuk, Hlousek; Langil (Aleksandrov 88), Odjidja-Ofoe (Kopczynski 76), Jodlowiec, Moulin, Kucharczyk; Nikolic (Prijovic 83).

Ludogorets Razgrad (0) 2 *(Moti 51 (pen), Misidjan 64)*

Viktoria Plzen (0) 0 11,812

Ludogorets Razgrad: (442) Stoyanov; Palomino, Minev, Moti, Natanael; Sasha, Dyakov, Marcelinho, Cafu (Quixada 90); Wanderson (Campanharo 90), Misidjan (Keseru 81).
Viktoria Plzen: (442) Kozacik; Hejda, Mateju, Hubnik, Limbersky; Kopic, Duris (Horava 68), Hrosovsky, Kovarik; Hromada (Kolar 83), Bakos (Krmencik 77).

Porto (0) 1 *(Andre Silva 61 (pen))*

Roma (1) 1 *(Felipe 21 (og))* 46,310

Porto: (4231) Casillas; Maxi Pereira, Felipe, Marcano, Alex Telles; Herrera, Danilo Pereira; Adrian (Corona 76), Otavio (Evandro 85), Andre Andre (Layun 66); Andre Silva.
Roma: (433) Alisson; Florenzi (Paredes 85), Manolas, Vermaelen■, Juan Jesus; Nainggolan, De Rossi, Strootman; Salah (Fazio 77), Dzeko, Perotti (Emerson 44).

Villarreal (1) 1 *(Alexandre Pato 36)*

Monaco (1) 2 *(Fabinho 3 (pen), Bernardo Silva 72)* 19,516

Villarreal: (442) Sergio Asenjo; Mario, N'Diaye, Musacchio, Jose Angel; Soriano, Trigueros, Bruno, Castillejo; Borre (Gonzalez 76), Alexandre Pato.
Monaco: (442) Subasic; Raggi, Glik, Jemerson, Mendy■; Bernardo Silva (Joao Moutinho 81), Fabinho, Bakayoko, Lemar; Dirar, Germain (Carrillo 69).

PLAY-OFF ROUND SECOND LEG

Tuesday, 23 August 2016

Hapoel Beer Sheva (1) 2 *(Sahar 21, Hoban 48)*

Celtic (0) 0 15,383

Hapoel Beer Sheva: (433) Goresh; Bitton, Vitor (Shabtai 75), Tzedek, Davidadze; Radi, Ogu, Hoban; Melikson (Buzaglo 34), Nwakaeme, Maranhao (Sahar 19).
Celtic: (3511) Gordon; Lustig, Toure, Tierney; Janko, Bitton, Brown, McGregor (Sviatchenko 65), Sinclair; Forrest (Rogic 46); Griffiths (Dembele 57).

Legia Warsaw (0) 1 *(Kucharczyk 90)*

Dundalk (1) 1 *(Benson 19)* 29,066

Legia Warsaw: (451) Malarz; Broz, Lewczuk, Pazdan, Hlousek■; Langil (Guilherme 65), Jodlowiec, Odjidja-Ofoe, Moulin (Prijovic 90), Kucharczyk; Nikolic (Bereszynski 71).
Dundalk: (451) Rogers; Gannon, Barrett, Boyle, Massey; McEleney (O'Connor 88), Finn, Shields (Meenan 83), Benson, Horgan; McMillan.

Monaco (0) 1 *(Fabinho 90 (pen))*

Villarreal (0) 0 8750

Monaco: (4231) Subasic; Raggi, Glik, Jemerson, Sidibe; Bakayoko, Fabinho; Dirar, Bernardo Silva, Lemar (Joao Moutinho 68); Germain (Carrillo 81).
Villarreal: (442) Sergio Asenjo; Mario, Musacchio, Victor Ruiz, Jose Angel (Jaume 67); Castillejo, Trigueros, Bruno, Soriano (N'Diaye 80); Borre (Suarez 75), Alexandre Pato.

Roma (0) 0

Porto (1) 3 *(Felipe 8, Layun 73, Corona 75)* 39,866

Roma: (4411) Szczesny; Bruno Peres, Manolas, De Rossi■, Juan Jesus; Salah, Strootman, Paredes (Emerson■ 42), Perotti (Gerson 86); Nainggolan; Dzeko (Iturbe 59).
Porto: (4411) Casillas; Maxi Pereira (Layun 45), Felipe, Marcano, Alex Telles; Corona, Herrera, Danilo Pereira, Andre Andre; Otavio (Sergio Oliveira 57); Andre Silva (Adrian 66).

Viktoria Plzen (1) 2 *(Duris 7, Mateju 64)*

Ludogorets Razgrad (1) 2 *(Misidjan 17, Keseru 90)* 10,312

Viktoria Plzen: (442) Kozacik; Mateju, Hejda, Hubnik, Limbersky; Petrzela (Kovarik 83), Hromada, Horava (Baranek 88), Kopic; Duris (Krmencik 84), Bakos.
Ludogorets Razgrad: (4411) Stoyanov; Minev, Moti, Palomino, Natanael; Wanderson (Plastun 85), Dyakov (Campanharo 80), Sasha, Misidjan (Keseru 76); Marcelinho; Cafu.

Wednesday, 24 August 2016

APOEL (0) 1 *(Sotiriou 69)*

FC Copenhagen (0) 1 *(Santander 86)* 17,310

APOEL: (4141) Waterman; Milanov, Astiz, Carlao, Alexandrou (de Camargo 89); Morais; Gianniotas, Vinicius, Orlandi (Bressan 75), Efrem (Vander 49); Sotiriou.
FC Copenhagen: (442) Olsen; Ankersen, Jorgensen, Johansson, Augustinsson; Verbic (Gregus 88), Kvist Jorgensen, Delaney, Jensen (Toutouh 46); Cornelius (Pavlovic 80), Santander.

Borussia Munchengladbach (3) 6 *(Hazard 9, 64, 84, Raffael 33, 40, 77)*

Young Boys (0) 1 *(Ravet 79)* 43,302

Borussia Munchengladbach: (343) Sommer; Elvedi, Christensen, Jantschke (Korb 72); Herrmann, Kramer (Dahoud 59), Strobl (Vestergaard 53), Johnson; Hazard, Stindl, Raffael.
Young Boys: (541) Mvogo; Sutter, Wuthrich, von Bergen (Kubo 46), Rochat, Lecjaks; Ravet, Bertone, Zakaria, Sulejmani (Schick 46); Frey (Duah 69).

Manchester C (0) 1 *(Delph 56)*

Steaua Bucharest (0) 0 40,064

Manchester C: (433) Hart; Maffeo, Stones (Adarabioyo 59), Kolarov, Clichy; Toure, Fernando, Delph; Jesus Navas, Iheanacho (Fernandinho 76), Nolito (Tasende 60).
Steaua Bucharest: (4141) Cojocaru; Aganovic (Stanciu 53), Tamas, Mitrea, Momcilovic; Enache; Sulley (Achim 61), Bourceanu, Popescu O (Popa 53), Hamroun; Tudorie.

Red Bull Salzburg (1) 1 *(Lazaro 22)*

Dinamo Zagreb (0) 2 *(Fernandes 87, Soudani 95)* 23,451

Red Bull Salzburg: (442) Walke; Schwegler (Lainer 46), Caleta-Car, Hinteregger, Ulmer; Lazaro (Samassekou 61), da Silva, Laimer, Berisha; Wanderson (Minamino 67), Soriano.
Dinamo Zagreb: (442) Eduardo; Stojanovic, Sigali, Benkovic, Pivaric; Soudani, Rog, Jonas (Pavicic 73), Antolic (Schildenfeld 83); Henriquez (Coric 62), Fernandes.
aet.

Rostov (1) 4 *(Azmoun 34, Erokhin 52, Noboa 60, Poloz 66)*

Ajax (0) 1 *(Klaassen 84 (pen))* 15,320

Rostov: (532) Dzanaev; Terentjev, Novoseltsev, Cesar Navas, Kudryashov■, Kalachev; Gatcan, Noboa, Erokhin (Ezatolahi 79); Azmoun (Bukharov 73), Poloz (Doumbia 87).
Ajax: (442) Cillessen; Veltman, Viergever, Riedewald, Tete; Bazoer (Dolberg 58), Gudelj, Klaassen, El Ghazi (Schone 46); Traore, Younes (Casierra 77).

GROUP STAGE

GROUP A

Tuesday, 13 September 2016

FC Basel (0) 1 *(Steffen 80)*

Ludogorets Razgrad (1) 1 *(Cafu 45)* 30,852

FC Basel: (4231) Vaclik; Lang, Suchy, Balanta, Traore; Xhaka, Zuffi (Fransson 70); Bjarnason, Delgado (Calla 81), Steffen; Janko (Doumbia 39).
Ludogorets Razgrad: (4231) Stoyanov; Minev, Moti, Palomino, Natanael (Vitinha 82); Abel, Dyakov (Sasha 90); Misidjan, Marcelinho, Wanderson (Plastun 85); Cafu.

Paris Saint-Germain (1) 1 *(Cavani 1)*

Arsenal (0) 1 *(Sanchez 78)* 46,440

Paris Saint-Germain: (433) Areola; Aurier (Meunier 84), Marquinhos, Thiago Silva, Maxwell; Verratti■, Krychowiak (Pastore 80), Rabiot (Thiago Motta 73); Di Maria, Cavani, Matuidi.
Arsenal: (451) Ospina; Bellerin, Mustafi, Koscielny, Monreal; Iwobi, Coquelin (Xhaka 71), Ozil (Elneny 85), Cazorla, Oxlade-Chamberlain (Giroud■ 63); Sanchez.

Wednesday, 28 September 2016

Arsenal (2) 2 *(Walcott 7, 26)*

FC Basel (0) 0 59,993

Arsenal: (451) Ospina; Bellerin, Mustafi, Koscielny, Monreal (Gibbs 75); Walcott (Oxlade-Chamberlain 70), Cazorla, Xhaka, Iwobi (Elneny 70), Ozil; Sanchez.
FC Basel: (532) Vaclik; Lang, Suchy, Xhaka, Balanta, Traore; Bjarnason (Delgado 79), Zuffi (Elyounoussi 71), Fransson; Doumbia (Sporar 58), Steffen.

Ludogorets Razgrad (1) 1 *(Natanael 16)*

Paris Saint-Germain (1) 3 *(Matuidi 41, Cavani 56, 60)* 17,155

Ludogorets Razgrad: (4231) Stoyanov; Minev, Moti, Palomino, Natanael; Wanderson (Keseru 88), Dyakov; Abel, Misidjan (Lukoki 73), Marcelinho; Cafu.
Paris Saint-Germain: (433) Areola; Aurier, Marquinhos, Thiago Silva, Maxwell; Verratti (Krychowiak 80), Thiago Motta, Matuidi; Lucas Moura, Cavani (Augustin 90), Di Maria (Ikone 88).

Wednesday, 19 October 2016

Arsenal (2) 6 *(Sanchez 12, Walcott 42, Oxlade-Chamberlain 46, Ozil 56, 83, 87)*

Ludogorets Razgrad (0) 0 59,944

Arsenal: (4231) Ospina; Bellerin, Mustafi, Koscielny, Gibbs; Coquelin, Cazorla (Elneny 57); Walcott (Lucas Perez 61), Ozil, Oxlade-Chamberlain; Sanchez (Iwobi 73).
Ludogorets Razgrad: (4231) Stoyanov; Minev, Moti, Palomino, Natanael; Dyakov, Abel; Wanderson (Lukoki 79), Marcelinho, Misidjan (Keseru 69); Cafu.

Paris Saint-Germain (1) 3 *(Di Maria 40, Lucas Moura 62, Cavani 90 (pen))*

FC Basel (0) 0 46,488

Paris Saint-Germain: (433) Areola; Aurier, Marquinhos, Thiago Silva, Kurzawa; Matuidi (Krychowiak 83), Verratti, Rabiot; Lucas Moura (Ben Arfa 81), Cavani, Di Maria (Jese 85).
FC Basel: (451) Vaclik; Lang, Suchy, Balanta, Traore; Bjarnason, Xhaka, Delgado (Zuffi 70), Die (Janko 78), Steffen; Doumbia (Sporar 61).

Tuesday, 1 November 2016

FC Basel (0) 1 *(Zuffi 76)*

Paris Saint-Germain (1) 2 *(Matuidi 44, Meunier 90)* 34,639

FC Basel: (4141) Vaclik; Gaber (Sporar 69), Suchy, Balanta, Traore; Bjarnason; Die■, Xhaka, Delgado (Zuffi 59), Steffen; Doumbia (Janko 59).
Paris Saint-Germain: (433) Areola; Meunier, Thiago Silva (Krychowiak 46), Marquinhos, Kurzawa; Thiago Motta, Verratti, Matuidi (Rabiot 82); Lucas Moura (Jese 83), Cavani, Di Maria.

Ludogorets Razgrad (2) 2 *(Cafu 12, Keseru 15)*

Arsenal (2) 3 *(Xhaka 20, Giroud 41, Ozil 87)* 30,862

Ludogorets Razgrad: (4231) Borjan; Minev, Palomino, Moti, Natanael; Abel, Dyakov; Cafu, Marcelinho, Wanderson; Keseru (Misidjan 79).
Arsenal: (4231) Ospina; Jenkinson, Mustafi, Koscielny, Gibbs; Coquelin, Xhaka (Elneny 87); Ramsey (Oxlade-Chamberlain 75), Ozil, Sanchez (Iwobi 90); Giroud.

Wednesday, 23 November 2016

Arsenal (1) 2 *(Giroud 45 (pen), Verratti 60 (og))*

Paris Saint-Germain (1) 2 *(Cavani 18, Lucas Moura 77)* 59,628

Arsenal: (4411) Ospina; Jenkinson (Oxlade-Chamberlain 81), Mustafi, Koscielny, Gibbs; Sanchez, Ramsey, Coquelin (Walcott 80), Iwobi (Xhaka 78); Ozil; Giroud.
Paris Saint-Germain: (433) Areola; Meunier, Marquinhos, Thiago Silva, Maxwell; Verratti, Krychowiak (Ben Arfa 67), Thiago Motta; Lucas Moura (Jese 88), Cavani, Matuidi.

Ludogorets Razgrad (0) 0

FC Basel (0) 0 20,821

Ludogorets Razgrad: (4411) Stoyanov; Cicinho, Palomino, Natanael, Abel; Dyakov, Cafu, Moti, Keseru (Plastun 90); Wanderson (Campanharo 90); Misidjan (Lukoki 84).
FC Basel: (451) Vaclik; Traore, Lang, Zuffi, Bjarnason (Calla 84); Delgado (Sporar 79), Suchy, Balanta, Elyounoussi, Xhaka; Doumbia (Janko 79).

Tuesday, 6 December 2016

FC Basel (0) 1 *(Doumbia 78)*

Arsenal (2) 4 *(Lucas Perez 8, 16, 47, Iwobi 53)* 36,000

FC Basel: (4231) Vaclik; Lang, Suchy, Balanta, Traore; Die (Zuffi 74), Xhaka; Elyounoussi (Calla 59), Delgado (Doumbia 55), Steffen; Janko.
Arsenal: (4231) Ospina; Gabriel, Holding, Koscielny, Gibbs; Ramsey (Giroud 73), Xhaka; Iwobi, Ozil (Walcott 74), Lucas Perez; Sanchez (Elneny 69).

Paris Saint-Germain (0) 2 *(Cavani 61, Di Maria 90)*

Ludogorets Razgrad (1) 2 *(Misidjan 15, Wanderson 69)* 42,650

Paris Saint-Germain: (451) Areola; Maxwell (Kurzawa 80), Thiago Silva, Marquinhos, Meunier (Aurier 88); Lucas Moura (Jese 84), Matuidi, Ben Arfa, Thiago Motta, Di Maria; Cavani.
Ludogorets Razgrad: (433) Stoyanov; Cicinho, Plastun, Moti, Natanael; Dyakov, Marcelinho (Campanharo 85), Abel; Misidjan (Lukoki 71), Cafu, Wanderson (Keseru 90).

Group A	*P*	*W*	*D*	*L*	*F*	*A*	*GD*	*Pts*
Arsenal	6	4	2	0	18	6	12	14
Paris Saint-Germain	6	3	3	0	13	7	6	12
Ludogorets Razgrad	6	0	3	3	6	15	–9	3
FC Basel	6	0	2	4	3	12	–9	2

GROUP B

Tuesday, 13 September 2016

Benfica (1) 1 *(Cervi 12)*

Besiktas (0) 1 *(Anderson Talisca 90)* 42,126

Benfica: (4231) Ederson Moraes; Nelson Semedo, Lopez, Lindelof, Grimaldo; Andre Horta, Fejsa (Celis 88); Salvio, Cervi (Samaris 70), Pizzi; Goncalo Guedes.
Besiktas: (4231) Zengin; Beck, Marcelo, Tosic, Adriano (Tosun 63); Inler, Hutchinson; Quaresma, Ozyakup (Anderson Talisca 46), Erkin; Aboubakar (Sahan 81).

Dynamo Kyiv (1) 1 *(Harmash 26)*

Napoli (2) 2 *(Milik 36, 45)* 35,137

Dynamo Kyiv: (451) Shovkovskiy; Makarenko, Vida, Khacheridi, Antunes; Yarmolenko, Sydorchuk■, Rybalka (Korzun 82), Harmash, Tsyhankov (Husyev 73); Junior Moraes (Hladkyy 86).
Napoli: (433) Reina; Hysaj, Albiol, Koulibaly, Ghoulam; Allan, Jorginho, Hamsik (Zielinski 62); Callejon, Milik (Gabbiadini 82), Mertens (Insigne 72).

Wednesday, 28 September 2016

Besiktas (1) 1 *(Quaresma 29)*

Dynamo Kyiv (0) 1 *(Tsyhankov 65)* 33,938

Besiktas: (4231) Fabri; Beck, Marcelo, Tosic, Erkin; Arslan (Inler 77), Hutchinson; Quaresma, Anderson Talisca, Adriano (Tosun 68); Aboubakar (Frei 85).
Dynamo Kyiv: (451) Rudko; Morozyuk, Khacheridi, Vida, Antunes; Yarmolenko, Harmash, Rybalka, Buyalsky (Korzun 22), Gonzalez (Tsyhankov 62); Junior Moraes (Hladkyy 78).

Napoli (1) 4 *(Hamsik 20, Mertens 51, 58, Milik 54 (pen))*

Benfica (0) 2 *(Goncalo Guedes 70, Salvio 86)* 41,281

Napoli: (451) Reina; Hysaj, Albiol (Maksimovic 11), Koulibaly, Ghoulam; Callejon (Insigne 69), Allan, Jorginho, Hamsik, Mertens (Giaccherini 82); Milik.
Benfica: (442) Julio Cesar; Andre Almeida, Lopez, Lindelof, Grimaldo; Nelson Semedo, Andre Horta (Salvio 56), Fejsa (Gomes 82), Pizzi; Carrillo (Goncalo Guedes 66), Mitroglou.

Wednesday, 19 October 2016

Dynamo Kyiv (0) 0

Benfica (1) 2 *(Salvio 9 (pen), Cervi 55)* 25,991

Dynamo Kyiv: (451) Rudko; Antunes, Vida, Khacheridi, Danilo Silva; Gonzalez (Tsyhankov 70), Fedorchuk (Buyalsky 56), Korzun, Sydorchuk (Hladkyy 80), Yarmolenko; Junior Moraes.
Benfica: (442) Ederson Moraes; Nelson Semedo, Luisao, Lindelof, Grimaldo; Salvio, Pizzi, Fejsa, Cervi (Celis 83); Goncalo Guedes (Eliseu 89), Mitroglou (Jimenez 71).

Napoli (1) 2 *(Mertens 30, Gabbiadini 69 (pen))*

Besiktas (2) 3 *(Adriano 13, Aboubakar 38, 86)* 28,502

Napoli: (433) Reina; Maggio, Chiriches, Koulibaly, Ghoulam; Zielinski (Allan 82), Jorginho (Diawara 69), Hamsik; Callejon, Mertens, Insigne (Gabbiadini 65).
Besiktas: (4231) Fabri; Beck, Marcelo, Tosic, Erkin; Uysal (Anderson Talisca 89), Hutchinson; Quaresma, Arslan (Tosun 75), Adriano (Inler 70); Aboubakar.

Tuesday, 1 November 2016

Benfica (1) 1 *(Salvio 45 (pen))*

Dynamo Kyiv (0) 0 51,641

Benfica: (4411) Ederson Moraes; Nelson Semedo, Luisao, Lindelof, Grimaldo; Salvio, Pizzi, Fejsa (Samaris 58), Cervi; Goncalo Guedes (Andre Almeida 87); Mitroglou (Jimenez 70).
Dynamo Kyiv: (451) Rudko; Morozyuk, Khacheridi, Vida, Makarenko; Tsyhankov (Besyedin 60), Sydorchuk (Orikhovskiy 76), Rybalka, Buyalsky (Gromov 87), Gonzalez; Junior Moraes.

Besiktas (0) 1 *(Quaresma 79 (pen))*

Napoli (0) 1 *(Hamsik 82)* 35,552

Besiktas: (4231) Fabri; Tosic (Tosun 23), Rhodolfo, Marcelo, Beck; Inler (Ozyakup 65), Hutchinson; Adriano, Arslan, Quaresma; Aboubakar.
Napoli: (433) Reina; Hysaj, Maksimovic, Koulibaly, Ghoulam; Allan (Zielinski 81), Jorginho (Diawara 79), Hamsik; Callejon, Gabbiadini (Mertens 63), Insigne.

Wednesday, 23 November 2016

Besiktas (0) 3 *(Tosun 58, Quaresma 83 (pen), Aboubakar 89)*

Benfica (3) 3 *(Goncalo Guedes 10, Nelson Semedo 25, Fejsa 32)* 36,063

Besiktas: (4231) Fabri; Gonul (Tosun 46), Marcelo, Tosic (Nukan 60), Beck; Arslan (Inler 46), Hutchinson; Quaresma, Ozyakup, Adriano; Aboubakar.
Benfica: (4231) Ederson Moraes; Nelson Semedo, Luisao, Lindelof, Eliseu; Pizzi, Fejsa; Salvio, Goncalo Guedes (Samaris 74), Cervi (Rafa Silva 63); Mitroglou (Jimenez 86).

Napoli (0) 0

Dynamo Kyiv (0) 0 33,736

Napoli: (433) Reina; Ghoulam, Koulibaly, Albiol, Hysaj; Hamsik, Diawara, Zielinski (Allan 78); Insigne (Gabbiadini 66), Mertens (Giaccherini 86), Callejon.
Dynamo Kyiv: (451) Rudko; Morozyuk, Khacheridi, Vida, Makarenko; Yarmolenko, Sydorchuk (Orikhovskiy 67), Rybalka, Harmash, Tsyhankov (Gonzalez 60); Besyedin (Junior Moraes 81).

Tuesday, 6 December 2016

Benfica (0) 1 *(Jimenez 87)*

Napoli (0) 2 *(Callejon 60, Mertens 79)* 55,634

Benfica: (442) Ederson Moraes; Nelson Semedo, Luisao, Lindelof, Andre Almeida; Salvio (Mitroglou 80), Pizzi, Fejsa, Cervi (Carrillo 69); Jimenez, Goncalo Guedes (Rafa Silva 57).
Napoli: (433) Reina; Hysaj, Albiol, Koulibaly, Ghoulam; Allan, Diawara, Hamsik (Zielinski 72); Callejon, Gabbiadini (Mertens 57), Insigne (Rog 81).

Dynamo Kyiv (4) 6 *(Besyedin 9, Yarmolenko 31 (pen), Buyalsky 33, Gonzalez 45, Sydorchuk 60, Junior Moraes 77)*

Besiktas (0) 0 14,036

Dynamo Kyiv: (4141) Rudko; Burda, Khacheridi, Vida, Antunes; Rybalka; Yarmolenko, Sydorchuk (Korzun 66), Buyalsky, Gonzalez (Tsyhankov 69); Besyedin (Junior Moraes 76).
Besiktas: (433) Fabri; Beck■, Marcelo, Tosic, Adriano; Arslan (Tosun 46), Ozyakup, Hutchinson; Quaresma (Frei 70), Aboubakar■, Sahan (Gonul 46).

Group B	P	W	D	L	F	A	GD	Pts
Napoli	6	3	2	1	11	8	3	11
Benfica	6	2	2	2	10	10	0	8
Besiktas	6	1	4	1	9	14	–5	7
Dynamo Kyiv	6	1	2	3	8	6	2	5

GROUP C

Tuesday, 13 September 2016

Barcelona (2) 7 *(Messi 4, 28, 61, Neymar 50, Iniesta 59, Suarez L 76, 89)*

Celtic (0) 0 73,290

Barcelona: (433) ter Stegen; Sergi Roberto, Pique, Umtiti, Jordi Alba; Rakitic (Iniesta 46), Busquets (Rafinha 62), Andre Gomes; Messi, Suarez L, Neymar.
Celtic: (451) De Vries; Lustig, Toure, Sviatchenko (O'Connell 68), Tierney; Roberts (Armstrong 68), Gamboa, Bitton (McGregor 76), Brown, Sinclair; Dembele.

Wednesday, 14 September 2016

Manchester C (2) 4 *(Aguero 8, 28 (pen), 77, Iheanacho 90)*

Borussia Munchengladbach (0) 0 30,270

Manchester C: (4141) Bravo; Zabaleta, Otamendi, Stones, Kolarov; Fernandinho; Jesus Navas, De Bruyne, Gundogan (Clichy 81), Sterling (Sane 79); Aguero (Iheanacho 83).
Borussia Munchengladbach: (343) Sommer; Elvedi, Christensen, Strobl; Johnson, Dahoud, Kramer (Korb 38), Wendt; Stindl (Traore 81), Raffael, Hahn (Hazard 59).

Wednesday, 28 September 2016

Borussia Munchengladbach (1) 1 *(Hazard 34)*

Barcelona (0) 2 *(Turan 65, Pique 74)* 46,283

Borussia Munchengladbach: (4231) Sommer; Korb, Christensen, Elvedi, Wendt; Kramer, Dahoud; Traore, Stindl (Hahn 83), Hazard (Herrmann 79); Raffael (Johnson 48).
Barcelona: (433) ter Stegen; Sergi Roberto, Pique, Mascherano, Jordi Alba; Rakitic (Turan 59), Busquets, Iniesta; Alcacer (Rafinha 54), Suarez L, Neymar.

Celtic (2) 3 *(Dembele 3, 47, Sterling 20 (og))*

Manchester C (2) 3 *(Fernandinho 11, Sterling 28, Nolito 55)* 57,592

Celtic: (433) Gordon; Lustig, Toure, Sviatchenko, Tierney; Brown, Rogic (Armstrong 57), Bitton (Griffiths 84); Sinclair, Dembele, Forrest (Roberts 80).
Manchester C: (451) Bravo; Zabaleta, Otamendi, Kolarov, Clichy (Stones 73); Sterling, Gundogan, Fernandinho, Silva, Nolito (Fernando 76); Aguero.

Wednesday, 19 October 2016

Barcelona (1) 4 *(Messi 17, 61, 69, Neymar 89)*

Manchester C (0) 0 96,290

Barcelona: (433) ter Stegen; Mascherano, Pique (Mathieu■ 39), Umtiti, Jordi Alba (Digne 9); Rakitic, Busquets, Iniesta (Andre Gomes 80); Suarez L, Messi, Neymar.
Manchester C: (433) Bravo■; Zabaleta (Clichy 57), Otamendi, Stones, Kolarov; Gundogan (Aguero 79), Fernandinho, Silva; Sterling, De Bruyne, Nolito (Caballero 56).

Celtic (0) 0

Borussia Munchengladbach (0) 2 *(Stindl 57, Hahn 77)* 57,814

Celtic: (4411) Gordon; Lustig, Toure, Sviatchenko, Tierney; Forrest (Roberts 72), Brown, Bitton (McGregor 64), Sinclair; Rogic (Griffiths 71); Dembele.
Borussia Munchengladbach: (4411) Sommer; Korb, Vestergaard, Elvedi, Wendt; Traore (Schulz 86), Kramer, Strobl, Hofmann; Stindl; Hahn (Herrmann 89).

Tuesday, 1 November 2016

Borussia Munchengladbach (1) 1 *(Stindl 32)*

Celtic (0) 1 *(Dembele 76 (pen))* 46,283

Borussia Munchengladbach: (4132) Sommer; Korb■, Strobl (Jantschke 77), Vestergaard, Elvedi; Kramer; Johnson, Stindl (Raffael 81), Wendt; Hazard (Herrmann 69), Hahn.
Celtic: (4411) Gordon; Gamboa (Henderson 84), Lustig, Sviatchenko, Izaguirre; Forrest (Roberts 61), Armstrong, Brown, Sinclair; Rogic (McGregor 69); Dembele.

Manchester C (1) 3 *(Gundogan 39, 74, De Bruyne 51)*

Barcelona (1) 1 *(Messi 21)* 53,340

Manchester C: (451) Caballero; Zabaleta, Otamendi, Stones, Kolarov; Sterling (Jesus Navas 70), De Bruyne (Nolito 88), Fernandinho (Fernando 60), Gundogan, Silva; Aguero.
Barcelona: (433) ter Stegen; Sergi Roberto, Mascherano, Umtiti, Digne; Rakitic (Turan 61), Busquets, Andre Gomes (Rafinha 76); Messi, Suarez L, Neymar.

Wednesday, 23 November 2016

Borussia Munchengladbach (1) 1 *(Raffael 23)*

Manchester C (1) 1 *(Silva 45)* 45,921

Borussia Munchengladbach: (4411) Sommer; Elvedi, Christensen, Jantschke, Wendt; Traore (Hofmann 41), Dahoud (Vestergaard 60), Strobl, Johnson; Stindl■; Raffael (Hahn 84).
Manchester C: (433) Bravo; Otamendi, Fernandinho■, Stones, Kolarov; De Bruyne, Gundogan, Silva; Jesus Navas, Aguero, Sterling (Sagna 68).

Celtic (0) 0

Barcelona (1) 2 *(Messi 24, 56 (pen))* 57,937

Celtic: (4411) Gordon; Lustig, Simunovic, Sviatchenko, Izaguirre; McGregor (Roberts 71), Armstrong, Brown, Sinclair (Forrest 46); Rogic (Bitton 64); Dembele.
Barcelona: (433) ter Stegen; Sergi Roberto, Mascherano, Pique (Marlon 72), Jordi Alba (Digne 65); Rakitic, Busquets, Andre Gomes; Messi, Suarez L, Neymar (Turan 76).

Tuesday, 6 December 2016

Barcelona (1) 4 *(Messi 16, Turan 50, 53, 67)*

Borussia Munchengladbach (0) 0 67,157

Barcelona: (433) Cillessen; Aleix Vidal, Mascherano, Umtiti, Digne; Suarez D, Andre Gomes, Iniesta (Rafinha 60); Messi, Alcacer, Turan (Cardona 74).
Borussia Munchengladbach: (442) Sommer; Christensen, Vestergaard, Jantschke, Elvedi; Korb, Strobl, Dahoud (Kramer 58), Schulz (Johnson 58); Hazard (Raffael 72), Hahn.

Manchester C (1) 1 *(Iheanacho 8)*

Celtic (1) 1 *(Roberts 4)* 51,297

Manchester C: (433) Caballero; Sagna, Maffeo (Jesus Navas 61), Adarabioyo, Clichy; Zabaleta, Fernando, Gundogan; Nolito, Iheanacho, Sane.
Celtic: (4411) Gordon; Lustig, Simunovic, Sviatchenko, Izaguirre; Roberts, Brown, Armstrong, Rogic; Forrest (Mackay-Steven 50); Dembele (Griffiths 73).

Group C	*P*	*W*	*D*	*L*	*F*	*A*	*GD*	*Pts*
Barcelona	6	5	0	1	20	4	16	15
Manchester C	6	2	3	1	12	10	2	9
Borussia M'gladbach	6	1	2	3	5	12	–7	5
Celtic	6	0	3	3	5	16	–11	3

GROUP D

Tuesday, 13 September 2016

Bayern Munich (2) 5 *(Lewandowski 28 (pen), Muller 45, Kimmich 54, 61, Bernat 90)*

Rostov (0) 0 70,000

Bayern Munich: (433) Neuer; Rafinha, Javi Martinez, Hummels (Bernat 50), Alaba; Kimmich, Vidal, Thiago (Renato Sanches 71); Muller, Lewandowski, Douglas Costa (Ribery 64).
Rostov: (532) Dzanaev; Terentjev, Mevlja, Cesar Navas, Granat, Kalachev; Erokhin, Gatcan, Noboa; Azmoun (Prepelita 64), Poloz (Doumbia 46).

PSV Eindhoven (0) 0

Atletico Madrid (1) 1 *(Saul 43)* 33,989

PSV Eindhoven: (442) Zoet; Brenet, Isimat-Mirin, Moreno, Willems; Propper, Hendrix (Ramselaar 67), Schwaab (Pereiro 80), Guardado; Narsingh (Bergwijn 80), de Jong L.
Atletico Madrid: (442) Oblak; Juanfran, Godin, Gimenez, Filipe Luis; Gaitan (Tiago 60), Saul (Torres 77), Gabi, Koke; Gameiro (Carrasco 65), Griezmann.

Wednesday, 28 September 2016

Atletico Madrid (1) 1 *(Carrasco 35)*

Bayern Munich (0) 0 48,242

Atletico Madrid: (442) Oblak; Juanfran, Godin, Savic, Filipe Luis; Carrasco (Gameiro 71), Gabi, Saul, Koke; Torres (Gaitan 79), Griezmann (Thomas 90).
Bayern Munich: (433) Neuer; Lahm, Boateng (Hummels 64), Javi Martinez, Alaba; Alonso, Vidal, Thiago (Kimmich 66); Muller (Robben 59), Lewandowski, Ribery.

Rostov (2) 2 *(Poloz 8, 37)*

PSV Eindhoven (2) 2 *(Propper 14, de Jong L 45)* 12,646

Rostov: (442) Dzanaev; Terentjev, Mevlja, Cesar Navas, Granat; Kalachev, Gatcan, Noboa, Erokhin; Azmoun (Doumbia 77), Poloz (Prepelita 90).
PSV Eindhoven: (4132) Zoet; Arias, Moreno, Isimat-Mirin, Willems; Schwaab; Propper, Hendrix (Bergwijn 64), Guardado; Narsingh (De Jong S 73), de Jong L.

Wednesday, 19 October 2016

Bayern Munich (2) 4 *(Muller 13, Kimmich 21, Lewandowski 60, Robben 84)*

PSV Eindhoven (1) 1 *(Narsingh 41)* 70,000

Bayern Munich: (4321) Neuer; Lahm, Boateng, Hummels, Alaba; Kimmich (Javi Martinez 85), Alonso, Thiago; Robben (Renato Sanches 86), Muller; Lewandowski (Douglas Costa 72).
PSV Eindhoven: (442) Zoet; Brenet, Schwaab (Zinchenko 85), Moreno, Willems; Propper, De Jong S, Pereiro (Bergwijn 77), Narsingh; de Jong L, Guardado (Isimat-Mirin 61).

Rostov (0) 0

Atletico Madrid (0) 1 *(Carrasco 62)* 15,400

Rostov: (532) Dzanaev; Kireev, Mevlja, Cesar Navas, Granat, Kudryashov; Gatcan, Erokhin, Noboa; Azmoun (Prepelita 74), Poloz (Doumbia 77).
Atletico Madrid: (442) Oblak; Juanfran, Godin, Savic, Filipe Luis; Correa (Gameiro 57), Gabi, Koke, Carrasco (Saul 89); Torres, Griezmann (Tiago 90).

Tuesday, 1 November 2016

Atletico Madrid (1) 2 *(Griezmann 28, 90)*

Rostov (1) 1 *(Azmoun 30)* 40,392

Atletico Madrid: (442) Oblak; Vrsaljko, Godin, Savic, Filipe Luis; Saul (Gameiro 58), Gabi, Koke, Carrasco (Correa 79); Griezmann, Torres.
Rostov: (532) Dzanaev; Kalachev (Terentjev 73), Mevlja, Cesar Navas, Granat, Kudryashov; Noboa, Erokhin (Prepelita 45), Gatcan; Azmoun (Doumbia 70), Poloz.

PSV Eindhoven (1) 1 *(Arias 16)*

Bayern Munich (1) 2 *(Lewandowski 34 (pen), 74)* 35,000

PSV Eindhoven: (451) Pasveer; Arias, Isimat-Mirin, Moreno, Willems (Brenet 46); Propper, Ramselaar (Zinchenko 76), Schwaab, Guardado, Pereiro (Bergwijn 67); de Jong L.
Bayern Munich: (4132) Neuer; Lahm, Hummels, Boateng, Alaba; Alonso; Robben (Douglas Costa 65), Kimmich (Coman 64), Vidal; Lewandowski, Muller (Renato Sanches 85).

Wednesday, 23 November 2016

Atletico Madrid (0) 2 *(Gameiro 55, Griezmann 66)*

PSV Eindhoven (0) 0 37,891

Atletico Madrid: (442) Oblak; Vrsaljko, Gimenez, Godin, Filipe Luis (Juanfran 75); Koke, Tiago (Saul 75), Gabi, Carrasco; Gameiro, Griezmann.
PSV Eindhoven: (442) Zoet; Arias, Isimat-Mirin, Moreno, Willems (De Wijs 46); Zinchenko, Propper (Lundqvist 84), Schwaab, Ramselaar; Pereiro, Bergwijn (Narsingh 61).

Rostov (1) 3 *(Azmoun 44, Poloz 50 (pen), Noboa 67)*

Bayern Munich (1) 2 *(Douglas Costa 35, Bernat 52)* 15,211

Rostov: (532) Dzanaev; Kalachev (Terentjev 87), Mevlja, Cesar Navas, Granat, Kudryashov; Erokhin, Gatcan, Noboa; Azmoun (Grigorev 82), Poloz (Ezatolahi 90).
Bayern Munich: (451) Ulreich; Rafinha, Badstuber, Boateng (Hummels 58), Bernat; Douglas Costa, Lahm, Thiago, Renato Sanches (Muller 73), Ribery; Lewandowski.

Tuesday, 6 December 2016

Bayern Munich (1) 1 *(Lewandowski 28)*

Atletico Madrid (0) 0 70,000

Bayern Munich: (433) Neuer; Rafinha, Hummels, Alaba, Bernat; Thiago, Vidal, Renato Sanches; Robben (Kimmich 83), Lewandowski (Muller 80), Douglas Costa (Javi Martinez 87).
Atletico Madrid: (442) Oblak; Vrsaljko, Godin, Savic, Lucas; Saul, Gabi, Koke (Thomas 68), Gaitan (Correa 60); Griezmann, Carrasco (Gameiro 60).

PSV Eindhoven (0) 0

Rostov (0) 0 33,400

PSV Eindhoven: (532) Zoet; Arias (Pereiro 62), Isimat-Mirin (Narsingh 76), Schwaab, Moreno, Brenet; Ramselaar, Propper, Zinchenko (De Jong S 61); de Jong L, Bergwijn.
Rostov: (532) Dzanaev; Kalachev (Terentjev 80), Mevlja, Cesar Navas, Granat, Kudryashov; Erokhin, Noboa, Gatcan; Azmoun (Ezatolahi 89), Poloz (Bukharov 88).

Group D	P	W	D	L	F	A	GD	Pts
Atletico Madrid	6	5	0	1	7	2	5	15
Bayern Munich	6	4	0	2	14	6	8	12
Rostov	6	1	2	3	6	12	–6	5
PSV Eindhoven	6	0	2	4	4	11	–7	2

GROUP E

Wednesday, 14 September 2016

Bayer Leverkusen (2) 2 *(Mehmedi 9, Calhanoglu 15)*

CSKA Moscow (2) 2 *(Dzagoev 36, Eremenko 38)* 23,459

Bayer Leverkusen: (4411) Leno; Henrichs, Tah, Toprak, Wendell; Brandt, Bender (Volland 50), Kampl, Mehmedi; Calhanoglu (Aranguiz 46); Hernandez (Pohjanpalo 46).
CSKA Moscow: (451) Akinfeev; Fernandes, Berezutski V, Ignashevich, Schennikov; Ionov (Milanov 78), Dzagoev, Eremenko, Wernbloom, Golovin (Berezutski A 90); Traore (Strandberg 73).

Tottenham H (1) 1 *(Alderweireld 45)*

Monaco (2) 2 *(Bernardo Silva 15, Lemar 31)* 85,011

Tottenham H: (4231) Lloris; Walker, Alderweireld, Vertonghen, Davies; Dier (Sissoko 81), Alli; Son (Dembele 46), Eriksen, Lamela (Janssen 71); Kane.
Monaco: (4231) Subasic; Raggi, Glik, Jemerson, Sidibe; Fabinho, Bakayoko; Dirar (Lemar 5), Joao Moutinho, Bernardo Silva; Falcao (Germain 81).

Tuesday, 27 September 2016

CSKA Moscow (0) 0

Tottenham H (0) 1 *(Son 71)* 26,153

CSKA Moscow: (4231) Akinfeev; Fernandes, Berezutski V (Berezutski A 46), Ignashevich, Schennikov; Golovin, Wernbloom; Tosic (Natcho 72), Eremenko, Milanov; Traore.
Tottenham H: (433) Lloris; Trippier, Alderweireld, Vertonghen, Davies; Eriksen, Wanyama, Alli (Winks 81); Lamela, Janssen (Nkoudou 66), Son.

Monaco (0) 1 *(Glik 90)*

Bayer Leverkusen (0) 1 *(Hernandez 73)* 8100

Monaco: (433) Subasic; Sidibe, Glik, Jemerson, Raggi; Joao Moutinho, Bakayoko (Mbappe-Lottin 77), Fabinho; Bernardo Silva (Boschilia 81), Germain (Carrillo 73), Lemar.
Bayer Leverkusen: (4411) Leno; Henrichs, Tah, Toprak, Bender; Volland (Mehmedi 73), Aranguiz, Kampl, Brandt (Kiessling 63); Calhanoglu; Hernandez (Baumgartlinger 89).

Tuesday, 18 October 2016

Bayer Leverkusen (0) 0

Tottenham H (0) 0 28,887

Bayer Leverkusen: (442) Leno; Bender (Jedvaj 74), Tah, Toprak, Henrichs; Mehmedi, Aranguiz, Kampl, Calhanoglu (Baumgartlinger 46); Kiessling, Hernandez (Brandt 86).
Tottenham H: (4231) Lloris; Trippier, Dier, Vertonghen, Rose; Alli, Wanyama; Lamela (Sissoko 71), Eriksen, Son (Onomah 90); Janssen (Dembele 64).

CSKA Moscow (1) 1 *(Traore 34)*

Monaco (0) 1 *(Bernardo Silva 87)* 24,125

CSKA Moscow: (4411) Akinfeev; Fernandes, Berezutski V, Ignashevich, Schennikov; Tosic (Gordyushenko 74), Wernbloom, Natcho, Golovin; Ionov (Milanov 46); Traore (Strandberg 83).
Monaco: (433) Subasic; Sidibe, Glik, Jemerson, Raggi (Mendy 69); Fabinho, Bakayoko (Mbappe-Lottin 83), Joao Moutinho (Carrillo 40); Lemar, Germain, Bernardo Silva.

Wednesday, 2 November 2016

Monaco (3) 3 *(Germain 12, Falcao 29, 41)*

CSKA Moscow (0) 0 10,029

Monaco: (442) Subasic; Sidibe, Glik (Raggi 89), Jemerson, Mendy; Lemar, Bakayoko, Fabinho, Bernardo Silva; Falcao (Carrillo 74), Germain (Mbappe-Lottin 84).
CSKA Moscow: (4231) Akinfeev; Fernandes, Ignashevich, Berezutski A, Schennikov (Nababkin 90); Wernbloom, Natcho; Tosic (Milanov 71), Golovin, Ionov; Strandberg (Traore 63).

Tottenham H (0) 0

Bayer Leverkusen (0) 1 *(Kampl 65)* 85,512

Tottenham H: (4411) Lloris; Walker, Dier, Vertonghen, Davies; Sissoko, Wanyama, Dembele (Janssen 30), Eriksen (Winks 65); Alli; Son (Nkoudou 73).
Bayer Leverkusen: (442) Leno; Henrichs, Toprak, Tah, Wendell; Kampl (Volland 84), Baumgartlinger, Aranguiz (Havertz 86), Brandt (Calhanoglu 70); Mehmedi, Hernandez.

Tuesday, 22 November 2016

CSKA Moscow (0) 1 *(Natcho 76 (pen))*

Bayer Leverkusen (1) 1 *(Volland 16)* 19,164

CSKA Moscow: (4411) Akinfeev; Fernandes, Berezutski A, Berezutski V, Schennikov; Milanov, Wernbloom, Dzagoev (Traore 82), Golovin; Natcho; Chalov (Strandberg 90).
Bayer Leverkusen: (442) Leno; Jedvaj, Tah, Toprak, Henrichs; Volland, Aranguiz, Kampl (Mehmedi 90), Brandt (Havertz 70); Calhanoglu, Hernandez (Baumgartlinger 81).

Monaco (0) 2 *(Sidibe 49, Lemar 53)*

Tottenham H (0) 1 *(Kane 52 (pen))* 13,100

Monaco: (433) Subasic; Sidibe, Glik, Jemerson, Mendy; Fabinho, Bakayoko, Lemar (Joao Moutinho 81); Bernardo Silva, Falcao (Raggi 89), Germain (Carrillo 77).
Tottenham H: (4411) Lloris; Trippier, Dier, Wimmer, Rose; Alli, Wanyama, Dembele (Eriksen 65), Son (Janssen 64); Winks (Sissoko 76); Kane.

Wednesday, 7 December 2016

Bayer Leverkusen (1) 3 *(Yurchenko 30, Brandt 48, De Sanctis 82 (og))*

Monaco (0) 0 21,928

Bayer Leverkusen: (442) Ozcan; Wendell, Dragovic, Jedvaj, Da Costa; Calhanoglu (Aranguiz 67), Yurchenko (Henrichs 77), Baumgartlinger, Brandt (Kruse 71); Hernandez, Kiessling.
Monaco: (433) De Sanctis; Toure, Raggi, Jemerson, Diallo; Joao Moutinho, N'Doram, Boschilia (Traore 66); Dirar, Carrillo (Lemar 79), Jean (Germain 76).

Tottenham H (2) 3 *(Alli 38, Kane 45, Akinfeev 77 (og))*

CSKA Moscow (1) 1 *(Dzagoev 33)* 62,034

Tottenham H: (4411) Lloris; Walker, Dier, Vertonghen, Rose; Son (Nkoudou 61), Wanyama (Alderweireld 68), Winks, Eriksen; Alli; Kane (Onomah 82).
CSKA Moscow: (4411) Akinfeev; Nababkin, Berezutski V, Berezutski A, Schennikov; Tosic (Gordyushenko 70), Dzagoev, Natcho, Milanov; Golovin (Chalov 46); Traore (Strandberg 79).

Group E	P	W	D	L	F	A	GD	Pts
Monaco	6	3	2	1	9	7	2	11
Bayer Leverkusen	6	2	4	0	8	4	4	10
Tottenham H	6	2	1	3	6	6	0	7
CSKA Moscow	6	0	3	3	5	11	–6	3

GROUP F

Wednesday, 14 September 2016

Legia Warsaw (0) 0

Borussia Dortmund (3) 6 *(Gotze 7, Papastathopoulos 16, Bartra 18, Guerreiro 51, Castro 76, Aubameyang 87)* 27,304

Legia Warsaw: (433) Malarz; Bereszynski, Dabrowski, Czerwinski, Guilherme; Jodlowiec, Odjidja-Ofoe, Moulin (Radovic 76); Langil, Prijovic (Nikolic 63), Qazaishvili (Aleksandrov 66).
Borussia Dortmund: (4141) Burki; Piszczek, Papastathopoulos, Bartra, Schmelzer; Pulisic; Gotze (Castro 75), Weigl (Ginter 78), Guerreiro, Dembele (Mor 75); Aubameyang.

Real Madrid (0) 2 *(Ronaldo 89, Morata 90)*

Sporting Lisbon (0) 1 *(Bruno Cesar 47)* 72,179

Real Madrid: (433) Casilla; Carvajal, Varane, Sergio Ramos, Marcelo; Modric, Casemiro, Kroos (Rodriguez 77); Bale (Lucas 67), Benzema (Morata 68), Ronaldo.
Sporting Lisbon: (442) Rui Patricio; Joao Pereira, Semedo, Coates, Zeegelaar; Martins (Markovic 70), Adrien Silva (Elias 73), William Carvalho, Bruno Cesar; Dost, Ruiz (Campbell 90).

Tuesday, 27 September 2016

Borussia Dortmund (1) 2 *(Aubameyang 43, Schurrle 87)*

Real Madrid (1) 2 *(Ronaldo 17, Varane 68)* 65,849

Borussia Dortmund: (4141) Burki; Piszczek, Papastathopoulos, Ginter, Schmelzer; Weigl; Dembele (Pulisic 73), Gotze (Schurrle 58), Castro, Guerreiro (Mor 79); Aubameyang.
Real Madrid: (433) Navas; Carvajal, Varane, Sergio Ramos, Danilo; Modric, Kroos, Rodriguez (Kovacic 71); Bale, Benzema (Morata 88), Ronaldo.

Sporting Lisbon (2) 2 *(Ruiz 28, Dost 37)*

Legia Warsaw (0) 0 40,094

Sporting Lisbon: (442) Rui Patricio; Joao Pereira, Semedo, Coates, Jefferson; Bruno Cesar (Markovic 66), Adrien Silva, William Carvalho, Martins (Campbell 76); Dost, Ruiz (Petrovic 87).
Legia Warsaw: (4231) Malarz; Bereszynski, Czerwinski, Rzezniczak, Hlousek; Jodlowiec, Moulin (Kopczynski 86); Langil (Aleksandrov 47), Radovic, Guilherme; Nikolic (Odjidja-Ofoe 60).

Tuesday, 18 October 2016

Real Madrid (3) 5 *(Bale 16, Jodlowiec 20 (og), Marco 37, Lucas 68, Morata 84)*

Legia Warsaw (1) 1 *(Radovic 22 (pen))* 70,251

Real Madrid: (433) Navas; Marcelo, Varane, Pepe, Danilo; Rodriguez (Lucas 63), Marco (Kovacic 79), Kroos; Ronaldo, Benzema, Bale (Morata 63).
Legia Warsaw: (4231) Malarz; Bereszynski, Czerwinski, Rzezniczak, Hlousek; Jodlowiec, Moulin (Kopczynski 81); Guilherme (Qazaishvili 73), Odjidja-Ofoe, Kucharczyk; Radovic (Nikolic 74).

Sporting Lisbon (0) 1 *(Bruno Cesar 67)*

Borussia Dortmund (2) 2 *(Aubameyang 9, Weigl 43)* 46,609

Sporting Lisbon: (4231) Rui Patricio; Schelotto, Coates, Semedo, Zeegelaar; William Carvalho, Elias (Bruno Cesar 60); Martins, Markovic (Campbell 65), Ruiz (Andre Felipe 79); Dost.
Borussia Dortmund: (4141) Burki; Ginter (Rode 71), Papastathopoulos, Bartra (Piszczek 68), Passlack (Burnic 90); Weigl; Pulisic, Kagawa, Gotze, Dembele; Aubameyang.

Wednesday, 2 November 2016

Borussia Dortmund (1) 1 *(Ramos 12)*

Sporting Lisbon (0) 0 65,849

Borussia Dortmund: (451) Burki; Ginter, Papastathopoulos, Bartra, Guerreiro; Pulisic, Castro (Piszczek 69), Weigl, Gotze (Rode 69), Dembele (Schurrle 46); Ramos.
Sporting Lisbon: (4411) Rui Patricio; Paulo Oliveira, Semedo, Coates, Zeegelaar; Schelotto, William Carvalho, Bruno Cesar (Adrien Silva 58), Martins; Ruiz (Markovic 78); Castaignos (Dost 46).

Legia Warsaw (1) 3 *(Odjidja-Ofoe 40, Radovic 58, Moulin 83)*

Real Madrid (2) 3 *(Bale 1, Benzema 35, Kovacic 85)* 0

Legia Warsaw: (4231) Malarz; Bereszynski, Rzezniczak, Pazdan, Hlousek; Kopczynski, Moulin; Guilherme, Odjidja-Ofoe (Jodlowiec 87), Radovic (Prijovic 77); Nikolic (Kucharczyk 69).
Real Madrid: (442) Navas; Carvajal, Nacho, Varane, Fabio Coentrao (Marco 77); Bale, Kovacic, Kroos, Ronaldo; Morata (Mariano 85), Benzema (Lucas 65).
Behind closed doors.

Tuesday, 22 November 2016

Borussia Dortmund (5) 8 *(Kagawa 17, 18, Sahin 20, Dembele 29, Reus 32, 52, Passlack 81, Rzezniczak 90 (og))*

Legia Warsaw (2) 4 *(Prijovic 10, 24, Kucharczyk 57, Nikolic 83)* 55,094

Borussia Dortmund: (451) Weidenfeller; Rode, Ginter, Bartra (Durm 61), Passlack; Pulisic, Kagawa, Sahin (Aubameyang 70), Castro, Dembele (Schurrle 72); Reus.
Legia Warsaw: (4231) Cierzniak; Bereszynski, Czerwinski, Pazdan, Rzezniczak; Kopczynski, Guilherme (Jodlowiec 55); Kucharczyk, Radovic, Odjidja-Ofoe (Nikolic 75); Prijovic (Wieteska 69).

Sporting Lisbon (0) 1 *(Adrien Silva 81 (pen))*

Real Madrid (1) 2 *(Varane 29, Benzema 87)* 50,046

Sporting Lisbon: (442) Rui Patricio; Joao Pereira■, Coates, Semedo, Zeegelaar; Martins, William Carvalho, Adrien Silva, Ruiz (Schelotto 67); Dost (Andre Felipe 76), Bruno Cesar (Campbell 62).
Real Madrid: (442) Navas; Carvajal, Varane, Sergio Ramos, Marcelo (Fabio Coentrao 71); Lucas, Modric, Kovacic, Bale (Marco 58); Isco (Benzema 67), Ronaldo.

Wednesday, 7 December 2016

Legia Warsaw (1) 1 *(Guilherme 30)*

Sporting Lisbon (0) 0 28,232

Legia Warsaw: (4231) Malarz; Bereszynski, Rzezniczak, Pazdan, Hlousek; Moulin, Kopczynski; Guilherme (Kucharczyk 61), Odjidja-Ofoe, Radovic (Dabrowski 90); Prijovic (Hamalainen 86).

Sporting Lisbon: (442) Rui Patricio; Paulo Oliveira (Ricardo Esgaio 58), Coates, Semedo, Zeegelaar (Andre Felipe 68); Martins, Adrien Silva, William Carvalho■, Bruno Cesar; Markovic (Ruiz 58), Dost.

Real Madrid (1) 2 *(Benzema 28, 53)*

Borussia Dortmund (0) 2 *(Aubameyang 60, Reus 88)* 76,894

Real Madrid: (433) Navas; Carvajal, Varane, Sergio Ramos, Marcelo; Modric (Kroos 63), Casemiro, Rodriguez; Lucas, Benzema (Morata 85), Ronaldo.
Borussia Dortmund: (433) Weidenfeller; Piszczek, Papastathopoulos, Bartra, Schmelzer; Castro (Rode 80), Weigl, Pulisic (Mor 63); Dembele, Aubameyang, Schurrle (Reus 63).

Group F	P	W	D	L	F	A	GD	Pts
Borussia Dortmund	6	4	2	0	21	9	12	14
Real Madrid	6	3	3	0	16	10	6	12
Legia Warsaw	6	1	1	4	9	24	–15	4
Sporting Lisbon	6	1	0	5	5	8	–3	3

GROUP G

Wednesday, 14 September 2016

Club Brugge (0) 0

Leicester C (2) 3 *(Albrighton 5, Mahrez 29, 61 (pen))* 20,970

Club Brugge: (442) Butelle; De Bock, Denswil, Engels (Poulain 53), Van Rhijn; Vanaken, Pina, Simons, Vormer; Diaby (Vossen 63), Izquierdo (Felipe Gedoz 77).
Leicester C: (442) Schmeichel; Hernandez, Morgan, Huth, Fuchs; Albrighton, Drinkwater, Amartey, Mahrez (Gray 80); Slimani (Ulloa 62), Vardy (Musa 70).

Porto (1) 1 *(Otavio 13)*

FC Copenhagen (0) 1 *(Cornelius 52)* 34,325

Porto: (433) Casillas; Layun, Felipe, Marcano, Alex Telles; Herrera (Brahimi 70), Danilo Pereira, Torres; Corona (Depoitre 62), Andre Silva, Otavio (Diogo Jota 82).
FC Copenhagen: (442) Olsen; Ankersen, Jorgensen, Johansson, Augustinsson; Gregus■, Delaney, Kvist Jorgensen (Antonsson 90), Toutouh (Jensen 77); Santander (Verbic 69), Cornelius.

Tuesday, 27 September 2016

FC Copenhagen (0) 4 *(Denswil 54 (og), Delaney 64, Santander 69, Jorgensen 90)*

Club Brugge (0) 0 25,605

FC Copenhagen: (442) Olsen; Ankersen, Jorgensen, Johansson, Augustinsson; Verbic (Toutouh 67), Kvist Jorgensen, Delaney, Jensen (Amankwaa 86); Santander (Pavlovic 79), Cornelius.
Club Brugge: (442) Butelle; Van Rhijn, Poulain, Denswil, De Bock; Vormer, Claudemir, Simons, Vanaken (Limbombe 46); Vossen (Wesley 63), Izquierdo (Felipe Gedoz 79).

Leicester C (1) 1 *(Slimani 25)*

Porto (0) 0 31,805

Leicester C: (442) Schmeichel; Hernandez, Morgan, Huth, Fuchs; Mahrez (Gray 89), Drinkwater, Amartey, Albrighton; Slimani (King 82), Vardy (Musa 90).
Porto: (433) Casillas; Layun, Felipe, Marcano, Alex Telles; Andre Andre (Herrera 63), Danilo Pereira, Torres; Andre Silva, Adrian (Diogo Jota 63), Otavio.

Tuesday, 18 October 2016

Club Brugge (1) 1 *(Vossen 12)*

Porto (0) 2 *(Layun 68, Andre Silva 90 (pen))* 23,372

Club Brugge: (3421) Butelle; Poulain, Simons, Denswil; Van Rhijn, Pina (Felipe Gedoz 78), Claudemir, Limbombe (Bolingoli Mbombo 82); Vormer, Vanaken; Vossen (Wesley 84).
Porto: (4132) Casillas; Layun, Felipe, Marcano, Alex Telles; Danilo Pereira; Torres, Herrera (Brahimi 59), Otavio (Andre Andre 72); Andre Silva, Diogo Jota (Corona 59).

Leicester C (1) 1 *(Mahrez 41)*

FC Copenhagen (0) 0 31,037

Leicester C: (442) Schmeichel; Simpson, Morgan, Huth, Fuchs; Mahrez (Amartey 90), King, Drinkwater, Albrighton; Slimani (Ulloa 88), Vardy (Okazaki 85).
FC Copenhagen: (442) Olsen; Ankersen (Gregus 87), Jorgensen, Johansson, Augustinsson; Verbic (Jensen 66), Kvist Jorgensen, Delaney, Toutouh (Pavlovic 85); Santander, Cornelius.

Wednesday, 2 November 2016

FC Copenhagen (0) 0

Leicester C (0) 0 34,146

FC Copenhagen: (442) Olsen; Ankersen, Jorgensen, Johansson, Augustinsson; Verbic (Kusk 83), Kvist Jorgensen, Delaney, Jensen (Toutouh 65); Santander, Cornelius.
Leicester C: (442) Schmeichel; Hernandez, Huth, Morgan, Fuchs; Mahrez, Amartey, Drinkwater, Schlupp (Okazaki 71); Vardy, Musa.

Porto (1) 1 *(Andre Silva 37)*

Club Brugge (0) 0 32,310

Porto: (4132) Casillas; Alex Telles, Marcano, Felipe, Maxi Pereira; Danilo Pereira; Otavio (Layun 79), Torres, Herrera (Ruben Neves 62); Diogo Jota (Corona 71), Andre Silva.
Club Brugge: (442) Butelle; Van Rhijn, Poulain, Denswil, Cools; Vormer, Claudemir, Pina, Bolingoli Mbombo (Vanaken 65); Diaby (Limbombe 46), Wesley (Izquierdo 77).

Tuesday, 22 November 2016

FC Copenhagen (0) 0

Porto (0) 0 32,036

FC Copenhagen: (442) Olsen; Ankersen, Jorgensen, Johansson, Augustinsson; Jensen (Kusk 76), Delaney, Kvist Jorgensen, Toutouh (Gregus 75); Pavlovic, Verbic.
Porto: (4132) Casillas; Maxi Pereira, Felipe, Marcano, Alex Telles; Danilo Pereira; Corona (Varela 89), Torres, Otavio (Evandro 84); Diogo Jota, Andre Silva.

Leicester C (2) 2 *(Okazaki 5, Mahrez 30 (pen))*

Club Brugge (0) 1 *(Izquierdo 52)* 31,443

Leicester C: (442) Zieler; Fuchs, Morgan, Huth, Simpson; Albrighton (Amartey 77), Drinkwater, King, Mahrez (Schlupp 68); Okazaki (Gray 68), Vardy.
Club Brugge: (442) Butelle; Cools, Poulain, Mechele, De Bock (Van Rhijn 70); Claudemir (Wesley 84), Simons, Pina (Limbombe 61), Vanaken; Vossen, Izquierdo.

Wednesday, 7 December 2016

Club Brugge (0) 0

FC Copenhagen (2) 2 *(Mechele 9 (og), Jorgensen 15)* 18,981

Club Brugge: (433) Butelle; Van Rhijn (Vormer 77), Mechele, Denswil, Cools; Pina, Claudemir, Bolingoli Mbombo; Rafaelov (Vanaken 66), Wesley, Felipe Gedoz.
FC Copenhagen: (442) Olsen; Ankersen (Hogli 89), Jorgensen, Johansson, Augustinsson; Jensen (Gregus 57), Kvist Jorgensen, Delaney, Toutouh; Pavlovic (Keita 88), Cornelius.

Porto (3) 5 *(Andre Silva 6, 64 (pen), Corona 26, Brahimi 44, Diogo Jota 77)*

Leicester C (0) 0 39,310

Porto: (4132) Casillas; Maxi Pereira, Felipe, Marcano, Alex Telles; Danilo Pereira (Ruben Neves 75); Corona (Herrera 76), Torres, Brahimi; Andre Silva (Rui Pedro 78), Diogo Jota.
Leicester C: (442) Hamer; Hernandez, Morgan, Wasilewski, Chilwell; Gray, Mendy, Drinkwater (Barnes 76), Schlupp (Albrighton 46); Musa (Ulloa 46), Okazaki.

Group G	P	W	D	L	F	A	GD	Pts
Leicester C	6	4	1	1	7	6	1	13
Porto	6	3	2	1	9	3	6	11
FC Copenhagen	6	2	3	1	7	2	5	9
Club Brugge	6	0	0	6	2	14	–12	0

GROUP H

Wednesday, 14 September 2016

Juventus (0) 0

Sevilla (0) 0 33,261

Juventus: (532) Buffon; Bonucci, Barzagli, Chiellini, Dani Alves, Lemina; Evra (Alex Sandro 68), Khedira, Asamoah (Pjanic 68); Dybala (Pjaca 86), Higuain.
Sevilla: (4312) Sergio Rico; Mercado, Rami, Pareja, Escudero; Nzonzi, Kranevitter (Mariano 78), Iborra; Vazquez (Carrico 90); Vitolo, Sarabia (Correa 64).

Lyon (1) 3 *(Tolisso 13, Ferri 49, Cornet 57)*

Dinamo Zagreb (0) 0 43,700

Lyon: (3511) Lopes; Yanga-Mbiwa, N'Koulou, Morel; Da Silva, Ferri, Gonalons (Tousart 32), Darder, Rybus; Tolisso (Ghezzal 78); Cornet (Kalulu 72).
Dinamo Zagreb: (442) Semper; Stojanovic, Benkovic, Schildenfeld, Pivaric; Pavicic, Jonas (Gojak 85), Paulo Machado (Situm 68), Coric (Fiolic 53); Soudani, Fernandes.

Tuesday, 27 September 2016

Dinamo Zagreb (0) 0

Juventus (2) 4 *(Pjanic 24, Higuain 31, Dybala 57, Dani Alves 85)* 23,875

Dinamo Zagreb: (433) Semper; Situm, Sigali, Schildenfeld, Pivaric; Antolic (Paulo Machado 72), Benkovic, Jonas (Fiolic 48); Soudani, Fernandes (Hodzic 58), Pavicic.
Juventus: (352) Buffon; Barzagli (Pjaca 68), Bonucci, Chiellini; Dani Alves, Hernanes, Evra, Khedira, Pjanic (Cuadrado 46); Dybala, Higuain (Mandzukic 70).

Sevilla (0) 1 *(Ben Yedder 53)*

Lyon (0) 0 36,741

Sevilla: (442) Sergio Rico; Mariano, Mercado (Kolodziejczak 87), Pareja, Escudero; Nasri, Nzonzi, Vazquez (Iborra 59), Vitolo; Vietto, Ben Yedder (Sarabia 82).
Lyon: (352) Lopes; Yanga-Mbiwa (Valbuena 70), N'Koulou, Morel; Gaspar (Ghezzal 78), Tolisso, Gonalons, Darder, Rybus; Fekir (Kalulu 70), Cornet.

Tuesday, 18 October 2016

Dinamo Zagreb (0) 0

Sevilla (1) 1 *(Nasri 37)* 6021

Dinamo Zagreb: (442) Livakovic; Stojanovic, Sigali, Schildenfeld, Sosa; Pavicic (Jonas 51), Benkovic, Knezevic (Henriquez 87), Antolic (Fiolic 15); Soudani, Fernandes.
Sevilla: (442) Sergio Rico; Mercado, Rami, Pareja, Escudero; Mariano, Nzonzi, Nasri, Vitolo; Vietto (Ben Yedder 65), Vazquez (Iborra 89).

Lyon (0) 0

Juventus (0) 1 *(Cuadrado 76)* 53,907

Lyon: (532) Lopes; Da Silva, Yanga-Mbiwa (Ghezzal 82), N'Koulou, Diakhaby, Morel; Darder (Ferri 64), Gonalons, Tolisso; Fekir, Lacazette (Cornet 72).
Juventus: (3511) Buffon; Barzagli, Bonucci, Evra; Dani Alves (Benatia 83), Khedira (Sturaro 75), Lemina■, Pjanic, Alex Sandro; Dybala (Cuadrado 69); Higuain.

Wednesday, 2 November 2016

Juventus (1) 1 *(Higuain 14 (pen))*

Lyon (0) 1 *(Tolisso 85)* 40,356

Juventus: (4312) Buffon; Dani Alves, Barzagli, Bonucci (Benatia 67), Evra; Khedira, Marchisio, Sturaro; Pjanic (Alex Sandro 68); Higuain (Cuadrado 83), Mandzukic.
Lyon: (4411) Lopes; Da Silva, Diakhaby, Mammana, Morel; Ghezzal, Gonalons, Tolisso, Rybus (Cornet 70); Fekir (Darder 77); Lacazette.

Sevilla (1) 4 *(Vietto 31, Escudero 66, Nzonzi 80, Ben Yedder 87)*

Dinamo Zagreb (0) 0 35,215

Sevilla: (4231) Sergio Rico; Mariano, Mercado, Rami, Escudero; Kranevitter, Nzonzi; Vazquez (Ben Yedder 60), Ganso (Kiyotake 75), Vitolo (Sarabia 75); Vietto.
Dinamo Zagreb: (541) Livakovic; Stojanovic■, Sigali, Schildenfeld, Benkovic, Pivaric; Soudani (Matel 46), Paulo Machado (Peric 60), Pavicic, Coric (Situm 53); Fernandes.

Tuesday, 22 November 2016

Dinamo Zagreb (0) 0

Lyon (0) 1 *(Lacazette 72)* 7834

Dinamo Zagreb: (4141) Livakovic; Matel (Henriquez 14), Sigali, Benkovic, Pivaric; Knezevic; Situm, Pavicic (Paulo Machado 74), Gojak, Coric (Jonas 52); Fernandes.
Lyon: (433) Lopes; Da Silva, Yanga-Mbiwa, N'Koulou, Morel; Ferri, Gonalons, Darder (Tolisso 66); Cornet (Fekir 66), Lacazette, Valbuena (Rybus 87).

Sevilla (1) 1 *(Pareja 10)*

Juventus (1) 3 *(Marchisio 45 (pen), Bonucci 84, Mandzukic 90)* 38,942

Sevilla: (3142) Sergio Rico; Rami, Pareja, Mercado; Nzonzi; Mariano (Kranevitter 76), Iborra, Vitolo, Escudero; Vazquez■, Vietto (Sarabia 46).
Juventus: (433) Buffon; Dani Alves, Bonucci, Rugani, Evra (Sturaro 72); Khedira, Marchisio, Pjanic (Kean 84); Cuadrado (Chiellini 86), Mandzukic, Alex Sandro.

Wednesday, 7 December 2016

Juventus (0) 2 *(Higuain 52, Rugani 73)*

Dinamo Zagreb (0) 0 39,380

Juventus: (352) Neto; Benatia, Rugani, Evra; Cuadrado, Lemina, Marchisio (Sturaro 74), Pjanic (Dybala 80), Asamoah; Higuain, Mandzukic (Hernanes 85).
Dinamo Zagreb: (433) Livakovic; Situm, Sigali, Schildenfeld, Pivaric; Moro (Matel 86), Knezevic, Gojak (Fiolic 57); Soudani (Stojanovic 74), Coric, Fernandes.

Lyon (0) 0

Sevilla (0) 0 52,423

Lyon: (433) Lopes; Da Silva, Yanga-Mbiwa, Diakhaby, Morel; Darder (Cornet 72), Gonalons, Tolisso (Grenier 78); Ghezzal (Fekir 69), Lacazette, Valbuena.
Sevilla: (343) Sergio Rico; Mercado, Pareja, Rami; Mariano, Nzonzi, Iborra, Escudero; Vitolo, Sarabia (Ben Yedder 65), Nasri (Kranevitter 87).

Group H	P	W	D	L	F	A	GD	Pts
Juventus	6	4	2	0	11	2	9	14
Sevilla	6	3	2	1	7	3	4	11
Lyon	6	2	2	2	5	3	2	8
Dinamo Zagreb	6	0	0	6	0	15	–15	0

KNOCK-OUT STAGE

ROUND OF 16 FIRST LEG

Tuesday, 14 February 2017

Benfica (0) 1 *(Mitroglou 49)*

Borussia Dortmund (0) 0 55,124

Benfica: (442) Ederson; Nelson Semedo, Luisao, Lindelof, Eliseu; Salvio, Pizzi, Fejsa, Carrillo (Filipe Augusto 46); Rafa Silva (Cervi 67), Mitroglou (Jimenez 75).
Borussia Dortmund: (532) Burki; Piszczek, Papastathopoulos, Bartra, Schmelzer, Durm; Dembele, Weigl, Guerreiro (Castro 82); Reus (Pulisic 82), Aubameyang (Schurrle 62).

Paris Saint-Germain (2) 4 *(Di Maria 18, 55, Draxler 40, Cavani 71)*

Barcelona (0) 0 46,484

Paris Saint-Germain: (4231) Trapp; Meunier, Marquinhos, Kimpembe, Kurzawa; Verratti (Nkunku 69), Rabiot; Di Maria (Lucas Moura 61), Matuidi, Draxler (Pastore 86); Cavani.
Barcelona: (433) ter Stegen; Sergi Roberto, Pique, Umtiti, Jordi Alba; Andre Gomes (Rafinha 58), Busquets, Iniesta (Rakitic 73); Messi, Suarez, Neymar.

Wednesday, 15 February 2017

Bayern Munich (1) 5 *(Robben 11, Lewandowski 53, Thiago 56, 64, Muller 88)*

Arsenal (1) 1 *(Sanchez 30)* 70,000

Bayern Munich: (433) Neuer; Lahm, Javi Martinez, Hummels, Alaba; Alonso, Thiago, Vidal; Robben (Rafinha 87), Douglas Costa (Kimmich 83), Lewandowski (Muller 86).
Arsenal: (4231) Ospina; Bellerin, Mustafi, Koscielny (Gabriel 48), Gibbs; Coquelin (Giroud 77), Xhaka; Iwobi (Walcott 65), Ozil, Oxlade-Chamberlain; Sanchez.

Real Madrid (1) 3 *(Benzema 19, Kroos 49, Casemiro 54)*

Napoli (1) 1 *(Insigne 8)* 78,000

Real Madrid: (433) Navas; Carvajal, Sergio Ramos (Pepe 71), Varane, Marcelo; Modric, Casemiro, Kroos; Rodriguez (Lucas 76), Benzema (Morata 82), Ronaldo.
Napoli: (433) Reina; Hysaj, Albiol, Koulibaly, Ghoulam; Zielinski (Allan 75), Diawara, Hamsik (Milik 83); Callejon, Mertens, Insigne.

Tuesday, 21 February 2017

Bayer Leverkusen (0) 2 *(Bellarabi 48, Savic 68 (og))*

Atletico Madrid (2) 4 *(Saul 17, Griezmann 25, Gameiro 59 (pen), Torres 86)* 29,300

Bayer Leverkusen: (442) Leno; Henrichs, Dragovic, Toprak, Wendell; Bellarabi (Pohjanpalo 66), Aranguiz, Kampl, Brandt (Bailey 88); Havertz (Volland 56), Hernandez.
Atletico Madrid: (442) Moya; Vrsaljko, Savic, Gimenez, Filipe Luis; Koke, Gabi, Saul, Carrasco (Torres 78); Griezmann (Correa 78), Gameiro (Thomas 71).

Manchester C (1) 5 *(Sterling 27, Aguero 58, 71, Stones 77, Sane 82)*

Monaco (2) 3 *(Falcao 32, 61, Mbappe-Lottin 41)* 53,351

Manchester C: (433) Caballero; Fernandinho (Zabaleta 62), Stones, Otamendi, Sagna; De Bruyne, Toure, Silva; Sterling (Jesus Navas 89), Aguero (Fernando 86), Sane.
Monaco: (4231) Subasic; Mendy, Raggi, Glik, Sidibe; Bakayoko (Dirar 88), Fabinho; Mbappe-Lottin (Germain 79), Lemar, Bernardo Silva (Joao Moutinho 85); Falcao.

Wednesday, 22 February 2017

Porto (0) 0

Juventus (0) 2 *(Pjaca 72, Dani Alves 74)* 49,229

Porto: (4132) Casillas; Maxi Pereira, Felipe, Marcano, Alex Telles■; Danilo Pereira; Herrera, Ruben Neves (Corona 60), Brahimi (Diogo Jota 73); Andre Silva (Layun 30), Tiquinho Soares.
Juventus: (4231) Buffon; Lichtsteiner (Dani Alves 73), Barzagli, Chiellini, Alex Sandro; Khedira, Pjanic; Cuadrado (Pjaca 67), Dybala (Marchisio 86), Mandzukic; Higuain.

Sevilla (1) 2 *(Sarabia 25, Correa 62)*

Leicester C (0) 1 *(Vardy 73)* 38,834

Sevilla: (352) Sergio Rico; Rami, Lenglet (Carrico 55), Escudero; Mariano, Nzonzi, Sarabia, Nasri, Vitolo; Jovetic, Correa (Iborra 63).
Leicester C: (4411) Schmeichel; Simpson, Morgan, Huth, Fuchs; Albrighton (Amartey 87), Drinkwater, Ndidi, Mahrez; Musa (Gray 57); Vardy.

ROUND OF 16 SECOND LEG

Tuesday, 7 March 2017

Arsenal (1) 1 *(Walcott 20)*

Bayern Munich (0) 5 *(Lewandowski 55 (pen), Robben 68, Douglas Costa 78, Vidal 80, 85)* 59,911

Arsenal: (433) Ospina; Monreal, Koscielny■, Mustafi, Bellerin; Ramsey (Coquelin 72), Xhaka, Oxlade-Chamberlain; Giroud (Ozil 72), Sanchez (Lucas Perez 73), Walcott.
Bayern Munich: (4231) Neuer; Rafinha, Javi Martinez, Hummels, Alaba; Vidal, Alonso; Robben (Douglas Costa 70), Thiago (Kimmich 80), Ribery (Renato Sanches 79); Lewandowski.

Napoli (1) 1 *(Mertens 24)*

Real Madrid (0) 3 *(Sergio Ramos 51, 57, Morata 90)* 56,695

Napoli: (433) Reina; Hysaj, Albiol, Koulibaly, Ghoulam; Allan (Rog 55), Diawara, Hamsik (Zielinski 75); Callejon, Mertens, Insigne (Milik 70).
Real Madrid: (433) Navas; Carvajal, Pepe, Sergio Ramos, Marcelo; Modric (Isco 80), Casemiro, Kroos; Bale (Lucas 68), Benzema (Morata 77), Ronaldo.

Wednesday, 8 March 2017

Barcelona (2) 6 *(Suarez 3, Kurzawa 41 (og), Messi 50 (pen), Neymar 88, 90 (pen), Sergi Roberto 90)*

Paris Saint-Germain (0) 1 *(Cavani 62)* 96,290

Barcelona: (433) ter Stegen; Rafinha (Sergi Roberto 76), Umtiti, Pique, Mascherano; Iniesta (Turan 65), Busquets, Rakitic (Andre Gomes 84); Neymar, Suarez, Messi.
Paris Saint-Germain: (4411) Trapp; Meunier (Krychowiak 90), Marquinhos, Thiago Silva, Kurzawa; Lucas Moura (Di Maria 55), Rabiot, Matuidi, Draxler (Aurier 75); Verratti; Cavani.

Borussia Dortmund (1) 4 *(Aubameyang 4, 61, 85, Pulisic 59)*

Benfica (0) 0 65,849

Borussia Dortmund: (532) Burki; Durm, Piszczek, Papastathopoulos (Ginter 88), Bartra, Schmelzer; Castro, Weigl, Dembele (Kagawa 81); Aubameyang (Schurrle 86), Pulisic.
Benfica: (442) Ederson; Nelson Semedo, Luisao, Lindelof, Eliseu; Salvio (Jonas 64), Samaris (Zivkovic 74), Pizzi, Andre Almeida; Mitroglou, Cervi (Jimenez 82).

Tuesday, 14 March 2017

Juventus (1) 1 *(Dybala 42 (pen))*

Porto (0) 0 41,161

Juventus: (4411) Buffon; Dani Alves, Bonucci, Benatia (Barzagli 60), Alex Sandro; Cuadrado (Pjaca 46), Khedira, Marchisio, Mandzukic; Dybala (Rincon 78); Higuain.
Porto: (4132) Casillas; Maxi Pereira■, Felipe, Marcano, Layun; Danilo Pereira; Andre Andre, Torres (Otavio 70), Brahimi (Diogo Jota 67); Tiquinho Soares, Andre Silva (Boly 46).

Leicester C (1) 2 *(Morgan 27, Albrighton 55)*

Sevilla (0) 0 31,520

Leicester C: (442) Schmeichel; Simpson, Morgan, Huth, Fuchs; Mahrez (Amartey 89), Drinkwater, Ndidi, Albrighton; Okazaki (Slimani 63), Vardy.
Sevilla: (343) Sergio Rico; Mercado (Mariano 46), Pareja, Rami; Sarabia (Jovetic 45), Iborra, Nzonzi, Escudero; Vitolo, Ben Yedder (Correa 68), Nasri■.

Wednesday, 15 March 2017

Atletico Madrid (0) 0

Bayer Leverkusen (0) 0 49,133

Atletico Madrid: (442) Oblak; Vrsaljko, Gimenez, Godin, Lucas; Saul, Thomas, Koke, Carrasco (Savic 71); Correa (Gaitan 64), Griezmann.
Bayer Leverkusen: (4411) Leno; Hilbert, Jedvaj, Dragovic, Wendell; Bellarabi, Baumgartlinger, Kampl, Brandt (Bailey 78); Volland (Aranguiz 88); Hernandez (Mehmedi 81).

Monaco (2) 3 *(Mbappe-Lottin 8, Fabinho 29, Bakayoko 77)*

Manchester C (0) 1 *(Sane 71)* 15,700

Monaco: (433) Subasic; Sidibe, Raggi (Toure 69), Jemerson, Mendy; Fabinho, Bakayoko, Lemar; Bernardo Silva, Germain (Dirar 90), Mbappe-Lottin (Joao Moutinho 80).
Manchester C: (433) Caballero; Sagna, Stones, Clichy (Iheanacho 84), Kolarov; Sane, Fernandinho, Silva; De Bruyne, Aguero, Sterling.
Monaco won on away goals rule.

QUARTER-FINALS FIRST LEG

Tuesday, 11 April 2017

Juventus (2) 3 *(Dybala 7, 22, Chiellini 55)*
Barcelona (0) 0 41,092

Juventus: (4231) Buffon; Dani Alves, Bonucci, Chiellini, Alex Sandro; Pjanic (Barzagli 89), Khedira; Cuadrado (Lemina 73), Dybala (Rincon 81), Mandzukic; Higuain.
Barcelona: (433) ter Stegen; Sergi Roberto, Pique, Umtiti, Mathieu (Andre Gomes 46); Rakitic, Mascherano, Iniesta; Messi, Suarez, Neymar.

Wednesday, 12 April 2017

Atletico Madrid (1) 1 *(Griezmann 28 (pen))*
Leicester C (0) 0 51,423

Atletico Madrid: (442) Oblak; Juanfran, Savic, Godin, Filipe Luis; Saul, Gabi, Koke, Carrasco (Correa 65); Torres (Thomas 75), Griezmann.
Leicester C: (442) Schmeichel; Simpson, Benalouane, Huth, Fuchs; Mahrez, Drinkwater, Ndidi, Albrighton; Vardy (Slimani 77), Okazaki (King 46).

Bayern Munich (1) 1 *(Vidal 26)*
Real Madrid (0) 2 *(Ronaldo 47, 77)* 70,000

Bayern Munich: (4231) Neuer; Lahm, Javi Martinez■, Boateng, Alaba; Alonso (Bernat 63), Vidal; Robben, Thiago, Ribery (Douglas Costa 66); Muller (Coman 81).
Real Madrid: (433) Navas; Carvajal, Nacho, Sergio Ramos, Marcelo; Modric (Kovacic 90), Casemiro, Kroos; Bale (Asensio 58), Benzema (Rodriguez 83), Ronaldo.

Borussia Dortmund (0) 2 *(Dembele 57, Kagawa 84)*
Monaco (2) 3 *(Mbappe-Lottin 19, 79, Bender 35 (og))* 65,849

Borussia Dortmund: (343) Burki; Ginter, Papastathopoulos, Bender (Sahin 46); Piszczek, Kagawa, Weigl, Schmelzer (Pulisic 46); Dembele, Aubameyang, Guerreiro.
Monaco: (442) Subasic; Toure, Glik, Jemerson, Raggi; Bernardo Silva (Dirar 66), Fabinho, Joao Moutinho, Lemar; Falcao (Germain 85), Mbappe-Lottin.

QUARTER-FINALS SECOND LEG

Tuesday, 18 April 2017

Leicester C (0) 1 *(Vardy 61)*
Atletico Madrid (1) 1 *(Saul 26)* 31,548

Leicester C: (4411) Schmeichel; Simpson, Morgan (Amartey 83), Benalouane (Chilwell 46), Fuchs; Mahrez, Ndidi, Drinkwater, Albrighton; Okazaki (Ulloa 46); Vardy.
Atletico Madrid: (442) Oblak; Juanfran (Lucas 55), Savic, Godin, Filipe Luis (Correa 74); Saul, Gabi, Gimenez, Koke; Carrasco (Torres 69), Griezmann.

Real Madrid (0) 4 *(Ronaldo 76, 105, 109, Asensio 112)*
Bayern Munich (0) 2 *(Lewandowski 53 (pen), Sergio Ramos 78 (og))* 78,346

Real Madrid: (433) Navas; Carvajal, Nacho, Sergio Ramos, Marcelo; Modric, Casemiro, Kroos (Kovacic 114); Isco (Lucas 71), Benzema (Asensio 64), Ronaldo.
Bayern Munich: (451) Neuer; Lahm, Hummels, Boateng, Alaba; Robben, Vidal■, Alonso (Muller 75), Thiago, Ribery (Douglas Costa 71); Lewandowski (Kimmich 88).
aet.

Wednesday, 19 April 2017

Barcelona (0) 0
Juventus (0) 0 96,290

Barcelona: (433) ter Stegen; Sergi Roberto (Mascherano 78), Pique, Umtiti, Jordi Alba; Rakitic (Alcacer 58), Busquets, Iniesta; Messi, Suarez, Neymar.
Juventus: (4231) Buffon; Dani Alves, Bonucci, Chiellini, Alex Sandro; Khedira, Pjanic; Cuadrado (Lemina 83), Dybala (Barzagli 74), Mandzukic; Higuain (Asamoah 88).

Monaco (2) 3 *(Mbappe-Lottin 3, Falcao 17, Germain 81)*
Borussia Dortmund (0) 1 *(Reus 48)* 17,135

Monaco: (442) Subasic; Toure, Glik, Jemerson, Mendy; Bernardo Silva (Raggi 90), Joao Moutinho, Bakayoko, Lemar; Mbappe-Lottin (Germain 81), Falcao (Dirar 67).
Borussia Dortmund: (4141) Burki; Piszczek, Papastathopoulos, Ginter, Guerreiro (Pulisic 72); Weigl; Durm (Dembele 26), Kagawa, Sahin (Schmelzer 46), Reus; Aubameyang.

SEMI-FINALS FIRST LEG

Tuesday, 2 May 2017

Real Madrid (1) 3 *(Ronaldo 10, 73, 86)*
Atletico Madrid (0) 0 77,609

Real Madrid: (433) Navas; Carvajal (Nacho 46), Sergio Ramos, Varane, Marcelo; Kroos, Casemiro, Modric; Isco (Asensio 67), Benzema (Lucas 77), Ronaldo.
Atletico Madrid: (442) Oblak; Lucas, Savic, Godin, Filipe Luis; Koke, Gabi, Saul (Gaitan 57), Carrasco (Correa 68); Griezmann, Gameiro (Torres 57).

Wednesday, 3 May 2017

Monaco (0) 0
Juventus (1) 2 *(Higuain 29, 59)* 16,762

Monaco: (442) Subasic; Fabinho, Glik, Jemerson, Sidibe; Dirar, Bernardo Silva (Toure 82), Bakayoko (Joao Moutinho 66), Lemar (Badiashile 67); Falcao, Mbappe-Lottin.
Juventus: (343) Buffon; Barzagli, Bonucci, Chiellini; Dani Alves, Marchisio (Rincon 81), Pjanic (Lemina 89), Alex Sandro; Higuain (Cuadrado 77), Dybala, Mandzukic.

SEMI-FINALS SECOND LEG

Tuesday, 9 May 2017

Juventus (2) 2 *(Mandzukic 33, Dani Alves 44)*
Monaco (0) 1 *(Mbappe-Lottin 69)* 40,244

Juventus: (343) Buffon; Barzagli (Benatia 85), Bonucci, Chiellini; Dani Alves, Pjanic, Khedira (Marchisio 10), Alex Sandro; Dybala (Cuadrado 54), Higuain, Mandzukic.
Monaco: (442) Subasic; Raggi, Glik, Jemerson, Sidibe; Mendy (Fabinho 55), Bakayoko (Germain 78), Joao Moutinho, Bernardo Silva (Lemar 69); Falcao, Mbappe-Lottin.

Wednesday, 10 May 2017

Atletico Madrid (2) 2 *(Saul 12, Griezmann 16 (pen))*
Real Madrid (1) 1 *(Isco 42)* 53,422

Atletico Madrid: (442) Oblak; Gimenez (Thomas 57), Savic, Godin, Filipe Luis; Koke (Correa 76), Gabi, Saul, Carrasco; Torres (Gameiro 56), Griezmann.
Real Madrid: (4312) Navas; Danilo, Sergio Ramos, Varane, Marcelo; Kroos, Casemiro (Lucas 76), Modric; Isco (Morata 87); Benzema (Asensio 77), Ronaldo.

CHAMPIONS LEAGUE FINAL 2017

Saturday, 3 June 2017

(in Cardiff, 65,842)

Juventus (1) 1 *(Mandzukic 27)* **Real Madrid (1) 4** *(Ronaldo 20, 64, Casemiro 61, Asensio 90)*

Juventus: (352) Buffon; Dani Alves, Barzagli (Cuadrado■ 66), Bonucci; Chiellini, Alex Sandro, Pjanic (Marchisio 71), Khedira, Higuain; Dybala (Lemina 78), Mandzukic.

Real Madrid: (433) Navas; Carvajal, Sergio Ramos, Varane, Marcelo; Kroos (Morata 88), Casemiro, Modric; Isco (Asensio 82), Benzema (Bale 77), Ronaldo.

Referee: Felix Brych.

EUROPEAN CUP-WINNERS' CUP FINALS 1961–99

Year	Winners v Runners-up		Venue	Attendance	Referee
1961	1st Leg Fiorentina v Rangers	2-0	Glasgow	80,000	C. E. Steiner (Austria)
	2nd Leg Fiorentina v Rangers	2-1	Florence	50,000	V. Hernadi (Hungary)
1962	Atletico Madrid v Fiorentina	1-1	Glasgow	27,389	T. Wharton (Scotland)
Replay	Atletico Madrid v Fiorentina	3-0	Stuttgart	38,000	K. Tschenscher (West Germany)
1963	Tottenham Hotspur v Atletico Madrid	5-1	Rotterdam	49,000	A. van Leuwen (Netherlands)
1964	Sporting Lisbon v MTK Budapest	3-3*	Brussels	3,208	L. van Nuffel (Belgium)
Replay	Sporting Lisbon v MTK Budapest	1-0	Antwerp	13,924	G. Versyp (Belgium)
1965	West Ham U v Munich 1860	2-0	Wembley	7,974	I. Zsolt (Hungary)
1966	Borussia Dortmund v Liverpool	2-1*	Glasgow	41,657	P. Schwinte (France)
1967	Bayern Munich v Rangers	1-0*	Nuremberg	69,480	C. Lo Bello (Italy)
1968	AC Milan v Hamburg	2-0	Rotterdam	53,000	J. Ortiz de Mendibil (Spain)
1969	Slovan Bratislava v Barcelona	3-2	Basle	19,000	L. van Ravens (Netherlands)
1970	Manchester C v Gornik Zabrze	2-1	Vienna	7,968	P. Schiller (Austria)
1971	Chelsea v Real Madrid	1-1*	Athens	45,000	R. Scheurer (Switzerland)
Replay	Chelsea v Real Madrid	2-1*	Athens	19,917	R. Scheurer (Switzerland)
1972	Rangers v Dynamo Moscow	3-2	Barcelona	24,701	J. Ortiz de Mendibil (Spain)
1973	AC Milan v Leeds U	1-0	Salonika	40,154	C. Mihas (Greece)
1974	Magdeburg v AC Milan	2-0	Rotterdam	4,641	A. van Gemert (Netherlands)
1975	Dynamo Kyiv v Ferencvaros	3-0	Basle	13,000	R. Davidson (Scotland)
1976	Anderlecht v West Ham U	4-2	Brussels	51,296	R. Wurtz (France)
1977	Hamburger SV v Anderlecht	2-0	Amsterdam	66,000	P. Partridge (England)
1978	Anderlecht v Austria/WAC	4-0	Paris	48,679	H. Adlinger (West Germany)
1979	Barcelona v Fortuna Dusseldorf	4-3*	Basel	58,000	K. Palotai (Hungary)
1980	Valencia v Arsenal *(Valencia won 5-4 on penalties)*	0-0*	Brussels	40,000	V. Christov (Czechoslovakia)
1981	Dinamo Tbilisi v Carl Zeiss Jena	2-1	Dusseldorf	4,750	R. Lattanzi (Italy)
1982	Barcelona v Standard Liege	2-1	Barcelona	80,000	W. Eschweiler (West Germany)
1983	Aberdeen v Real Madrid	2-1*	Gothenburg	17,804	G. Menegali (Italy)
1984	Juventus v Porto	2-1	Basel	55,000	A. Prokop (Egypt)
1985	Everton v Rapid Vienna	3-1	Rotterdam	38,500	P. Casarin (Italy)
1986	Dynamo Kyiv v Atletico Madrid	3-0	Lyon	50,000	F. Wohrer (Austria)
1987	Ajax v Lokomotiv Leipzig	1-0	Athens	35,107	L. Agnolin (Italy)
1988	Mechelen v Ajax	1-0	Strasbourg	39,446	D. Pauly (West Germany)
1989	Barcelona v Sampdoria	2-0	Berne	42,707	G. Courtney (England)
1990	Sampdoria v Anderlecht	2-0*	Gothenburg	20,103	B. Galler (Switzerland)
1991	Manchester U v Barcelona	2-1	Rotterdam	43,500	B. Karlsson (Sweden)
1992	Werder Bremen v Monaco	2-0	Lisbon	16,000	P. D'Elia (Italy)
1993	Parma v Antwerp	3-1	Wembley	37,393	K.-J. Assenmacher (Germany)
1994	Arsenal v Parma	1-0	Copenhagen	33,765	V. Krondl (Czech Republic)
1995	Real Zaragoza v Arsenal	2-1	Paris	42,424	P. Ceccarini (Italy)
1996	Paris Saint-Germain v Rapid Vienna	1-0	Brussels	37,000	P. Pairetto (Italy)
1997	Barcelona v Paris Saint-Germain	1-0	Rotterdam	52,000	M. Merk (Germany)
1998	Chelsea v VfB Stuttgart	1-0	Stockholm	30,216	S. Braschi (Italy)
1999	Lazio v Mallorca	2-1	Villa Park	33,021	G. Benko (Austria)

INTER-CITIES FAIRS CUP FINALS 1958–71

Year	1st Leg		Attendance	2nd Leg	Attendance	Agg	Winner
1958	London XI v Barcelona	2-2	45,466	0-6	70,000	2-8	Barcelona
1960	Birmingham C v Barcelona	0-0	40,524	1-4	70,000	1-4	Barcelona
1961	Birmingham C v Roma	2-2	21,005	0-2	60,000	2-4	Roma
1962	Valencia v Barcelona	6-2	65,000	1-1	60,000	7-3	Valencia
1963	Dinamo Zagreb v Valencia	1-2	40,000	0-2	55,000	1-4	Valencia
1964	Real Zaragoza v Valencia	2-1	50,000	(in Barcelona, one match only)			Real Zaragoza
1965	Ferencvaros v Juventus	1-0	25,000	(in Turin, one match only)			Ferencvaros
1966	Barcelona v Real Zaragoza	0-1	70,000	4-2*	70,000	4-3	Barcelona
1967	Dinamo Zagreb v Leeds U	2-0	40,000	0-0	35,604	2-0	Dynamo Zagreb
1968	Leeds U v Ferencvaros	1-0	25,368	0-0	70,000	1-0	Leeds U
1969	Newcastle U v Ujpest Dozsa	3-0	60,000	3-2	37,000	6-2	Newcastle U
1970	Anderlecht v Arsenal	3-1	37,000	0-3	51,612	3-4	Arsenal
1971	Juventus v Leeds U	0-0	*(abandoned 51 minutes)*		42,000		
	Juventus v Leeds U *Leeds U won on away goals rule.*	2-2	42,000	1-1	42,483	3-3	Leeds U

Trophy Play-Off – *between first and last winners to decide who would have possession of the original trophy*

1971	Barcelona v Leeds U	2-1	50,000	(in Barcelona, one match only)

*After extra time.

UEFA CUP FINALS 1972–97

Year	1st Leg		Attendance	2nd Leg	Attendance	Agg	Winner
1972	Wolverhampton W v Tottenham H	1-2	38,562	1-1	54,303	2-3	Tottenham H
1973	Liverpool v Moenchengladbach	0-0	*(abandoned after 27 minutes)*		44,967		
	Liverpool v Moenchengladbach	3-0	41,169	0-2	35,000	3-2	Liverpool
1974	Tottenham H v Feyenoord	2-2	46,281	0-2	59,317	2-4	Feyenoord
1975	Moenchengladbach v FC Twente	0-0	42,368	5-1	21,767	5-1	Moenchengladbach
1976	Liverpool v Club Brugge	3-2	49,981	1-1	29,423	4-3	Liverpool
1977	Juventus v Athletic Bilbao	1-0	66,000	1-2	39,700	2-2	Juventus
	Juventus won on away goals rule.						
1978	Bastia v PSV Eindhoven	0-0	8,006	0-3	28,000	0-3	PSV Eindhoven
1979	RS Belgrade v Moenchengladbach	1-1	65,000	0-1	45,000	1-2	Moenchengladbach
1980	Moenchengladbach v E. Frankfurt	3-2	25,000	0-1	59,000	3-3	E. Frankfurt
	Eintracht Frankfurt won on away goals rule.						
1981	Ipswich T v AZ 67 Alkmaar	3-0	27,532	2-4	22,291	5-4	Ipswich T
1982	IFK Gothenburg v Hamburger SV	1-0	42,548	3-0	57,312	4-0	IFK Gothenburg
1983	Anderlecht v Benfica	1-0	55,000	1-1	70,000	2-1	Anderlecht
1984	Anderlecht v Tottenham H	1-1	33,000	1-1*	46,258	2-2	Tottenham H
	Tottenham H won 4-3 on penalties.						
1985	Videoton v Real Madrid	0-3	30,000	1-0	80,000	1-3	Real Madrid
1986	Real Madrid v Cologne	5-1	60,000	0-2	22,000	5-3	Real Madrid
1987	IFK Gothenburg v Dundee U	1-0	48,614	1-1	20,900	2-1	IFK Gothenburg
1988	Espanol v Bayer Leverkusen	3-0	31,180	0-3*	21,600	3-3	Bayer Leverkusen
	Bayer Leverkusen won 3-2 on penalties.						
1989	Napoli v VfB Stuttgart	2-1	81,093	3-3	64,000	5-4	Napoli
1990	Juventus v Fiorentina	3-1	47,519	0-0	30,999	3-1	Juventus
1991	Internazionale v Roma	2-0	68,887	0-1	70,901	2-1	Internazionale
1992	Torino v Ajax	2-2	65,377	0-0	40,000	2-2	Ajax
	Ajax won on away goals rule.						
1993	Borussia Dortmund v Juventus	1-3	37,000	0-3	62,781	1-6	Juventus
1994	Salzburg v Internazionale	0-1	43,000	0-1	80,345	0-2	Internazionale
1995	Parma v Juventus	1-0	22,057	1-1	80,000	2-1	Parma
1996	Bayern Munich v Bordeaux	2-0	63,000	3-1	30,000	5-1	Bayern Munich
1997	Schalke 04 v Internazionale	1-0	57,000	0-1*	81,675	1-1	Schalke 04
	Schalke 04 won 4-1 on penalties.						

UEFA CUP FINALS 1998–2009

Year	Winners v Runners-up		Venue	Attendance	Referee
1998	Internazionale v Lazio	3-0	Paris	44,412	A. L. Nieto (Spain)
1999	Parma v Olympique Marseille	3-0	Moscow	61,000	H. Dallas (Scotland)
2000	Galatasaray v Arsenal	0-0*	Copenhagen	38,919	A. L. Nieto (Spain)
	Galatasaray won 4-1 on penalties.				
2001	Liverpool v Alaves	5-4*	Dortmund	48,050	G. Veissiere (France)
	Liverpool won on sudden death 'golden goal'.				
2002	Feyenoord v Borussia Dortmund	3-2	Rotterdam	45,611	V. M. M. Pereira (Portugal)
2003	FC Porto v Celtic	3-2*	Seville	52,140	L. Michel (Slovakia)
2004	Valencia v Olympique Marseille	2-0	Gothenburg	39,000	P. Collina (Italy)
2005	CSKA Moscow v Sporting Lisbon	3-1	Lisbon	47,085	G. Poll (England)
2006	Sevilla v Middlesbrough	4-0	Eindhoven	32,100	H. Fandel (Germany)
2007	Sevilla v Espanyol	2-2*	Glasgow	47,602	M. Busacca (Switzerland)
	Sevilla won 3-1 on penalties.				
2008	Zenit St Petersburg v Rangers	2-0	Manchester	43,878	P. Fröjdfeldt (Sweden)
2009	Shakhtar Donetsk v Werder Bremen	2-1*	Istanbul	37,357	L. M. Chantalejo (Spain)

UEFA EUROPA LEAGUE FINALS 2010–17

Year	Winners v Runners-up		Venue	Attendance	Referee
2010	Atletico Madrid v Fulham	2-1*	Hamburg	49,000	N. Rizzoli (Italy)
2011	FC Porto v Braga	1-0	Dublin	45,391	V. Carballo (Spain)
2012	Atletico Madrid v Athletic Bilbao	3-0	Bucharest	52,347	W. Stark (Germany)
2013	Chelsea v Benfica	2-1	Amsterdam	46,163	B. Kuipers (Netherlands)
2014	Sevilla v Benfica	0-0*	Turin	33,120	F. Brych (Germany)
	Sevilla won 4-2 on penalties.				
2015	Sevilla v Dnipro Dnipropetrovsk	3-2	Warsaw	45,000	M. Atkinson (England)
2016	Sevilla v Liverpool	3-1	Basel	34,429	J. Eriksson (Sweden)
2017	Manchester U v Ajax	2-0	Stockholm	46,961	D. Skomina (Slovenia)

**After extra time.*

UEFA EUROPA LEAGUE 2016–17

▪ *Denotes player sent off.*

FIRST QUALIFYING ROUND FIRST LEG

Tuesday, 28 June 2016

Kapaz (0) 0

Dacia (0) 0 2000

Kapaz: (442) Simatis; Axundov, Baybalaev (Javadov 73), Daniyev, Dario Junior; Ebah, Gurbanov (Aliyev O 70), Rahimov, Renan; Serginho (Qurbatov 79), Aliyev S.
Dacia: (442) Celeadnic; Bugaev (Mani 61), Bulgaru, Bejan (Bugneac 83), Cociuc; Feshchuk, Kozhanov, Mamah, Posmac; Slinkin, Valeev (Havrylenko 40).

Partizani Tirana (0) 0

Slovan Bratislava (0) 0 1350

Partizani Tirana: (442) Hoxha; Arapi, Batha, Fili (Jaupaj 87), Ibrahimi; Kalari (Atanda 87), Krasniqi, Ramadani, Torassa (Bardhi 83); Trashi, Vila.
Slovan Bratislava: (442) Mucha; Burnet, de Kamps, De Sa (Kubik 76), Lasik (Savicevic 61); Ligeon, Salata, Schet, Sekulic; Soumah, Zrelak.
Second leg cancelled. Partizani Tirana replaced Skenderbeu (disqualified for match fixing) in Champions League second qualifying round; Slovan Bratislava received bye into next round.

Rabotnicki Kometal (0) 1 *(Sahiti 80)*

Buducnost Podgorica (1) 1 *(Janketic 36)* 1500

Rabotnicki Kometal: (442) Altiparmakovski; Cikarski, Galic (Duranski 54), Markoshi (Herera 77), Mitrev; Najdovski L, Najdovski B (Elmas 62), Sahiti, Siljanovski; Siskovski, Trajcevski.
Buducnost Podgorica: (442) Dragojevic; Djalovic, Hocko, Janketic (Camaj 63), Mirkovic; Mitrovic, Pejakovic, Raickovic (Markovic 87), Seratlic; Vukcevic A, Vusurovic.

St Patrick's Ath (1) 1 *(Fagan 10)*

Jeunesse Esch (0) 0 1200

St Patrick's Ath: (442) Clarke; O'Brien, Hoare, Dennehy D, Bermingham; Kelly, Treacy, Cawley, Byrne (Timlin 60); Fagan, Dennehy B.
Jeunesse Esch: (433) Oberweis; Todorovic, Delgado, Portier, Lapierre; Ontiveros (Deidda 80), Peters, Pinna; Corral (Sardaryan 24), Stumpf, Mertinitz.

Thursday, 30 June 2016

Aberdeen (0) 3 *(Logan 68, McGinn 90, Rooney 90 (pen))*

Fola Esch (0) 1 *(Klein 70)* 12,750

Aberdeen: (4141) Lewis; Logan, Taylor, Considine, Shinnie; Flood (Rooney 55); McGinn, Jack, McLean, Hayes; Stockley.
Fola Esch: (4141) Hym; Martino, Klein, Bernard (Sacras 70), Bensi; Muharemovic; Laterza (Rodrigues 67), Kirch (Mahmutovic 82), Dallevedove, Francoise; Hadji.

Admira Wacker Modling (1) 1 *(Bajrami 34)*

Spartak Myjava (0) 1 *(Kona 73)* 1200

Admira Wacker Modling: (442) Siebenhandl; Zwierschitz, Lackner, Ebner, Wostry; Toth, Knasmullner, Bajrami, Spiridonovic; Starkl (Pavic 74), Monschein (Vastic 59).
Spartak Myjava: (442) Hruska; Machovec, Kukol, Beno, Mehremic; Ostojic, Kona, Daniel, Bilovsky (Marcek 89); Duga (Pekar 65), Kolar (Sladek 64).

AEK Larnaca (3) 3 *(Trickovski 22, 34, Alves 31)*

Folgore/Falciano (0) 0 2100

AEK Larnaca: (442) Taudul; Charalambous (Englezou 84), Catala, Mintikkis, Mojsov (Murillo 74); Laban, Trickovski, Jorge, Tomas; Alves, Tete (Charalambidis 63).
Folgore/Falciano: (442) Montanari; Quintavalla, Righi (Brolli 69), Genestreti, Bezzi (Rossi 86); Camillini, Nucci (Angelini 59), Muccini, Perrotta; Hirsch, Traini.

AIK Solna (1) 2 *(Affane 27, Johansson 52)*

Bala T (0) 0 6127

AIK Solna: (442) Carlgren; Karlsson, Johansson, Sundgren, Kpozo; Ishizaki, Affane (Blomberg 68), Ofori, Gravius (Saletros 74); Isak, Strandberg.
Bala T: (433) Morris; Stuart Jones Snr, Valentine, Stephens, Stuart Jones Jnr; Davies, Connolly (Jones M 69), Thompson (Hayes 56); Burke (Jamie 82), Sheridan, Smith.

Aktobe (1) 1 *(Zhalmukan 44 (pen))*

MTK Budapest (1) 1 *(Torghelle 30)* 8600

Aktobe: (442) Otarbaev; Tsveiba, Sorokin, Kouadja, Kairov; Mitosevic, Kryukov, Sitdikov, Bocharov; Zhalmukan (Shestakov 84), Dao (Golubov 62).
MTK Budapest: (442) Hegedus; Vadnai, Grgic, Poor, Baki; Vass, Kanta, Szatmari (Borbely 88), Torghelle; Nikac (Deutsch 90), Gera.

Atlantas (0) 0

HJK Helsinki (0) 2 *(Morelos 53, 85)* 2500

Atlantas: (442) Valincius; Gnedojus, Epifanov, Beneta, Baravykas; Gedminas (Kazlauskas 68), Verbickas, Simkus (Bartkus 68), Dmitriev (Papsys 77); Sylla, Maksimov.
HJK Helsinki: (442) Dahne; Taiwo, Jalasto, Rexhepi, Tatomirovic; Tanaka, Kamara, Malolo, Alho (Gadze 24 (Sorsa 83)); Oduamadi (Kolehmainen 88), Morelos.

Balzan (0) 0

Neftchi (1) 2 *(Haciyev 14, Qurbanov 84 (pen))* 357

Balzan: (442) Janjusevic; Serrano, Bezzina, Guimaraes de Oliveira, Fenech; Brincat (Grioli 74), Grima (Arab 82), de Barros, Manevski (Micallef 66); Effiong, Kaljevic.
Neftchi: (442) Santini; Shikov, Isayev, Jairo, Melnjak; Abdullayev A (Muradbayli 81), Haciyev (Imamverdiyev 75), Castillo (Mammadov 90), Agaev; Qurbanov, Abdullayev E.

Banants Yerevan (0) 0

Omonia Nicosia (1) 1 *(Derbyshire 26)* 1520

Banants Yerevan: (442) Ghazaryan; Drobarov, Kachmazov, Adams, Hakobyan; Badoyan (Movsesyan 85), Ayvazyan (Avetisyan 81), Poghosyan (Oganisyan 78), Torrejon; Buraev, Kalmanov.
Omonia Nicosia: (442) Panagi; Panteliadis, Carlitos, Florescu, Orsulic; Christofi (Agaiev 15), Margaca, Fylaktou, Derbyshire; Sheridan (Cleyton 70), Badibanga (Panayiotou 90).

Beroe (0) 0

Radnik Bijeljina (0) 0 2918

Beroe: (442) Makendzhiev; Penev, Vasilev V, Milanov, Hubchev; Milisavljevic (Dryanov 55), Panayotov (Tom 71), Pochanski, Vasilev A (Pedro Marques 83); Bozhilov, Kolev.
Radnik Bijeljina: (442) Lucic; Kojic, Celebic (Ostojic 59), Zelijkovic, Stokic; Duric (Jankovic 65), Martinovic, Vasic, Besirovic; Memisevic, Obradovic.

Bokelj (1) 1 *(Djenic 5)*

Vojvodina (1) 1 *(Meleg 6)* 1403

Bokelj: (442) Mijatovic; Ognjanovic, Todorovic, Mladenovic, Tomic (Kotorac 64); Zlaticanin, Bogdanovic, Macanovic, Djenic; Vucinic (Maras 72), Pepic (Pajovic 76).
Vojvodina: (442) Kordic; Kovacevic V, Miletic, Antic, Kovacevic N (Micic 60); Puskaric, Trujic, Malbasic, Meleg; Jovancic (Palocevic 60), Babic (Asceric 70).

Breidablik (1) 2 *(Bamberg 13, Sigurjonsson 90)*

Jelgava (3) 3 *(Kluskins 10, Redjko 33, Grigaravicius 44)* 531

Breidablik: (442) Gunnleifsson; Muminovic, Helgason, Sampsted, Bamberg; Yeoman (Hlynsson 78), Sigurjonsson, Olafsson, Hreinsson; Atlason (Eyjolfsson 62), Glenn (Leifsson 62).
Jelgava: (442) Ikstens; Bogdaskins (Malasenoks 90), Freimanis, Smirnovs, Redjko; Diallo, Lazdins, Kluskins, Grigaravicius (Sorokins 78); Nakano, Turkovs (Silich 70).

Connah's Quay Nomads (0) 0
Stabaek (0) 0 573
Connah's Quay Nomads: (442) Danby; Disney, Kearney, Baynes, Horan; Harrison, Morris, Owen J, Short; Woolfe, Wilde (Davies 89).
Stabaek: (442) Sandhu (Sayouba 30); Skjonsberg, Naess, Nije (Mehmeti 65), Moe; Meling, Grossman, Gorozia, Issah; Omoijuanfo, Asante.

Cukaricki (0) 3 *(Matic 49, 68, Kajevic 52)*
Ordabasy (0) 0 2214
Cukaricki: (442) Stevanovic; Lucas, Stojkovic, Lagator, Duric; Zivkovic, Fofana, Kajevic, Knezevic (Masovic A 71); Jankovic B (Docic 60), Mandic (Matic 46).
Ordabasy: (442) Boichenko; Simcevic, Abdulin, Mukhtarov■, Adyrbekov; Gogua, Chatto (Beysenov 86), Diakhate, Tolebek (Geynrikh 59); Kasalica (Khozhabaev 84), Tungyshbayev.

Differdange 03 (1) 1 *(Er Rafik 38)*
Cliftonville (0) 1 *(Lavery 89)* 1355
Differdange 03: (4231) Weber; Franzoni, Siebenaler (Bukvic 71), Vandenbroeck, Rodrigues; May, Janisch; Pedro Ribeiro (Sinani 67), Yeye (Lascak 81), Er Rafik; Luisi.
Cliftonville: (442) Mooney; Knowles, McGuinness, Bonner, Ives; Curran (Murray D 85), Catney, Winchester, Donnelly M (Lavery 67); Donnelly J, Hughes (McDaid 56).

Dila Gori (1) 1 *(Modebadze 36)*
Shirak (0) 0 2512
Dila Gori: (442) Mujrishvili; Kvirkvelia, Ghonghadze, Karkuzashvili, Samkharadze; Razmadze, Dolidze, Eristavi (Sabadze 79), Tsikaridze (KIkabidze 68); Nonikashvili (Katamadze 89), Modebadze.
Shirak: (442) Ayvazov; Hovanisian, Mikaelyan, Hovhannisyan, Darbinyan; Stoskovic, Hakobyan (Brou 78), Hovsepyan (Diarrassouba 58), Udo; Kaba, Kouakou (Muradyan 87).

Dinamo Minsk (1) 2 *(Bykov 18, 81)*
Spartaks Jurmala (0) 1 *(Ulimbashevs 79)* 1700
Dinamo Minsk: (442) Ignatovich; Ostroukh, Zhukouski (Shramchenko 86), Korytko (Rotkovic 66), Habovda; Noyok, Premudrov, Bykov, Kaplenko; Khvashchynskiy, Rassadkin.
Spartaks Jurmala: (442) Kurakins; Mihadjuks, Slampe, Platonov (Ulimbashevs 36), Kozeka; Pushnyakov, Yaghoubi, Kazacoks, Kozlovs; Kozlov, Adeyemo.

Domzale (3) 3 *(Dobrovoljc 11, Horic 26, Crnic 43)*
Lusitanos (1) 1 *(Luis Henrique 5)* 1000
Domzale: (442) Golubovic; Horic, Sirok, Dobrovoljc, Trajkovski; Zinko, Horvat (Repas 57), Crnic, Majer; Morel (Volaric 87), Vuk (Juninho 75).
Lusitanos: (442) Jesus Coca; Maciel, San Nicolas M, Acosta (Pousa 66), Munoz; Bruninho, Pinto (Lucas Sousa 56), Aguilar, Molina; Luis Miguel, Luis Henrique (San Nicolas L 84).

Europa (2) 2 *(Carrion 32, Lopez 39)*
Pyunik (0) 0 850
Europa: (442) Javi Munoz; Merino, Vazquez, Moya, Toscano; Quillo (Eloy 67), Roldan, Toni Garcia (Joselinho 59), Belfortti; Lopez, Carrion (Copi 77).
Pyunik: (442) Manukyan; Voskanyan, Grigoryan■, Manucharyan, Kartashyan; Yuspashyan (Minasyan 73), Manoyan, Hovhannisyan, Satumyan (Harutunyan 46); Arakelyan, Razmik Hakobyan (Petrosyan 46).

Hearts (2) 2 *(Buaben 28 (pen), Kalimulin 36 (og))*
FCI Tallinn (1) 1 *(Harin 21)* 14,417
Hearts: (442) Hamilton; Rherras, Paterson, Souttar, Ozturk; Buaben (Kitchen 79), Nicholson, Djoum, Walker; Sammon, Delgado (King 65).
FCI Tallinn: (442) Igonen; Appiah, Kalimulin, Avilov, Volodin; Dmitrijev, Mosnikov, Kruglov, Harin (Kulinits 83); Mashicev (Dramani 61), Voskoboinikov.

IFK Gothenburg (3) 5 *(Engvall 11, Rieks 12, Salomonsson 36, Hysen 79, 81)*
Llandudno (0) 0 6074
IFK Gothenburg: (442) Alvbage; Salomonsson, Bjarsmyr, Rogne, Aleesami; Smedberg-Dalence (Lagemyr 53), Albaek, Eriksson (Pettersson 76), Rieks; Boman (Hysen 65), Engvall.
Llandudno: (442) Roberts; Taylor, Shaw, Mike Williams, Joyce (Tierney 77); Thomas (Dawson 57), Hughes, Dix, Reed; Marc Williams, Buckley (Owen 70).

KR Reykjavik (1) 2 *(Palmason 40, Fridjonsson 78 (pen))*
Glenavon (1) 1 *(Kelly 14)* 502
KR Reykjavik: (4411) Magnusson; Beck Andersen, Fridgeirsson (Josepsson 82), Sigurdsson, Gunnarsson; Chopart, Praest, Margeirsson, Hauksson (Fazlagic 87); Palmason; Beck (Fridjonsson 72).
Glenavon: (442) Tuffey; Patton, Kelly, Lindsay (Doyle 56), Martyn (Kilmartin 82); Hall, Bradley, Marshall, Sykes; Moorhouse (Hamilton 71), Cooper.

Kukesi (1) 1 *(Rangel 32)*
Rudar Pljevlja (0) 1 *(Radanovic 71 (pen))* 104
Kukesi: (442) Kolici; Hallaci, Mici, Malota, Muca (Greca 81); Shameti, Jean Carioca (Guimaraes 75), Musolli, Dvornekovic (Dema 66); Emini, Rangel.
Rudar Pljevlja: (442) Radanovic; Nestorovic, Zivkovic, Radisic, Alic; Bozovic (Jovanovic 78), Soppo, Vlahovic, Brnovic; Ivanovic (Reljic 90), Noma (Markovic 90).

La Fiorita (0) 0
Debrecen (2) 5 *(Szakaly 5, 83, Tisza 34, 49, Sekulic 89)* 402
La Fiorita: (442) Vivan; Bollini (Mazzola 75), Martini A, Bugli, Gasperoni; Tommasi, Cavalli (Parma 65), Zafferani (Guidi 89), Cangini; Martini M, Rinaldi.
Debrecen: (442) Radosevic; Meszaros N, Brkovic, Szakaly, Varga; Jovanovic, Ferenczi, Holman, Meszaros K (Delmic 58); Tisza (Sekulic 68), Castillon (Kulcsar 46).

Levadia Tallinn (0) 1 *(Marin 65)*
Torshavn (1) 1 *(Jespersen 21)* 730
Levadia Tallinn: (442) Lepmets; Morozov, Podholjuzin, Tabi, Ratnikov; Antonov, Marin, Miranchuk (Gatagov 69), Gando; Kobzar (Luts 46), Hunt.
Torshavn: (442) Gestsson; Johan Davidsen, Jogvan Davidsen, Benjaminsen, Jespersen (Justinussen 90); Mouritsen, Egilsson (Wardum 67), Jensen, Jonsson; Jacobsen, Olsen (Joensen 85).

Linfield (0) 0
Cork C (0) 1 *(Maguire 63 (pen))* 2093
Linfield: (442) Carroll; Glendinning, Haughey, Stafford, Quinn; Millar (Clarke R 84), Mulgrew (Kee 56), Lowry, Gaynor; Waterworth, Smyth (Burns 72).
Cork C: (433) McNulty; Beattie, Browne, Bennett, O'Connor; Morrissey G, Buckley (O'Sullivan 60), Bolger; Sheppard (Morrissey D 45), Maguire (Healy 90), Dooley.

Maccabi Tel Aviv (2) 3 *(Igiebor 14, 69, Orlando Sa 45)*
Gorica (0) 0 7982
Maccabi Tel Aviv: (442) Rajkovic; Carlos Garcia, Ben Haroush (Rikan 82), Tibi, Medunjanin; Alberman, Igiebor, Micha, Peretz D; Orlando Sa (Itzhaki 70), Ben Chaim I (Ben Basat 78).
Gorica: (442) Sorcan; Jogan, Skarabot, Gregoric, Kavcic; Kolenc, Osuji (Nagode 70), Kapic, Kotnik; Burgic (Wilson 85), Franciosi (Arcon 58).

Midtjylland (0) 1 *(Onuachu 56)*
Suduva (0) 0 4347
Midtjylland: (442) Dahlin; Hansen, Novak, Banggaard, Nissen; Poulsen, Sparv (Halsti 90), Olsson (Duelund 55), Sisto (Kadlec V 77); Pusic, Onuachu.
Suduva: (442) Kardum; Jankauskas A, Jablan, Leimonas, Slavickas; Pavlovic, Svrljuga, Jamak, Jankauskas E (Antanavicius 90); Kecap, Laukzemis (Janusauskas 51).

NSI Runavik (0) 0
Shakhtyor Soligorsk (1) 2 *(Starhorodskyi 45 (pen), 83 (pen))* 350
NSI Runavik: (442) Hansen; Justinussen, Jacobsen J, Joensen■, Langgaard; Madsen, Mortensen J (Olsen J 71), Jacobsen M, Kohlert; Knudsen (Benjaminsen 88), Olsen K (Olsen M 52).
Shakhtyor Soligorsk: (442) Bushma; Yurevich, Rybak, Kuzmyanok, Matsveychyk; Ignjatijevic, Burko (Shlbun 65), Starhorodskyi, Rudyka (Pavlov 58); Kovalev, Osipenko (Elizarenko 79).

Odd (0) 2 *(Grogaard 63, Occean 86)*
IFK Mariehamn (0) 0 3701
Odd: (442) Rossbach; Eriksen, Ruud, Hagen, Nilsen; Grogaard (Jensen 75), Nordkvelle, Berg (Zehninki 55), Bentley; Halvorsen, Johansen (Occean 56).
IFK Mariehamn: (442) Viitala; Friberg da Cruz, Lyyski, Kojola, Granlund; Petrovic, Ekhalie (Wirtanen 90), Span, Dafaa (Sparrdal Mantilla 59); Diego Assis (Kangaskolkka 59), Orgill.

Qabala (3) 5 *(Stankovic 16, Zenjov 19, Weeks 30, 69, 72)*
Samtredia (0) 1 *(Shergelashvili 59)* 5850
Qabala: (442) Bezotosnyi; Ricardinho, Vernydub, Stankovic, Abbasov; Sadiqov, Weeks (Aliyev 86), Kvekveskiri, Ozobic; Zenjov (Mutallimov 83), Dabo (Eyyubov 78).
Samtredia: (442) Migineishvili; Gogiashvili, Sandokhadze, Mtchedlishvili, Shergelashvili; Datunaishvili, Razhamashvili, Mandzhgaladze (Tsnobiladze 71), Arabuli; Zivzivadze (Markozashvili 58), Jikia (Gamkrelidze 46).

Shamrock R (0) 0
RoPS Rovaniemi (1) 2 *(Lahdenmaki 27, Saksela 74)* 1908
Shamrock R: (4321) Hyland; Madden, Cornwall, Heaney, O'Connor; Miele, Brennan G (Clarke D 56), McPhail (Boyd 86); Cregg, Brennan K (McCabe 75); Shaw.
RoPS Rovaniemi: (451) Reguero; Lahdenmaki, Hamalainen, Jammeh, Pirinen; Saksela, Saine (Makitalo 82), Mravec, Nganbe (Muinonen 70), Taylor; John (Kokko 68).

Siroki Brijeg (1) 1 *(Baraban 45)*
Birkirkara (1) 1 *(Attard 15)* 3000
Siroki Brijeg: (442) Soldo; Pandza, Brekalo, Coric, Markovic; Sesar, Ivankovic (Plazonic 70), Crnov, Corluka (Wagner 46); Baraban (Menalo 85), Krstanovic.
Birkirkara: (442) Kopric; Zerafa (Guillaumier 63), Bubalovic, Jovic, Sciberras; Scicluna (Bilbao 76), Dimitrov, Camenzuli (Bajada 57), Attard; Plut, Emerson.

Shkendija Tetovo (1) 2 *(Ibraimi 41, Junior 68)*
Cracovia (0) 0 4539
Shkendija Tetovo: (442) Zahov; Cuculi, Bejtulai, Alimi (Polozani 73), Todorovski; Hasani (Juffo 87), Vujcic, Demiri, Ibraimi; Junior (Taipi 84), Radeski.
Cracovia: (442) Sandomierski; Deleu, Wolakiewicz (Karachanakov 72), Bejan, Litauszki; Wojcicki, Cetnarski (Covilo 61), Budzinski, Dabrowski; Jendrisek, Vestenicky (Wdowiak 61).

Slavia Sofia (0) 1 *(Serderov 85)*
Zaglebie Lubin (0) 0 1160
Slavia Sofia: (442) Kirev; Martinov, Sergeev, Velkov (Hristov 90), Khamis; Baldjiski (Karabelyov 57), Pashov, Vasev, Yomov; Serderov, Krastev (Dimitrov 57).
Zaglebie Lubin: (442) Polacek; Guldan, Cotra, Dabrowski, Todorovski; Janoszka (Janus 75), Piatek L, Vlasko (Rakowski 83), Kubicki; Woznaik, Piatek K (Papadopulos 68).

Sloboda Tuzla (0) 0
Beitar Jerusalem (0) 0 2762
Sloboda Tuzla: (442) Piric; Merzic, Kostic, Dzidic, Zeba; Stjepanovic, Efendic, Ordagic, Govedarica (Veselinovic 80); Mehidic (Grahovac 85), Karic.
Beitar Jerusalem: (442) Klaiman; Rueda, Mori, Magbo, Mishan; Moyal (Cohen 66), Claudemir, Einbinder, Atzili; Shechter (Brihon 80), Valpoort (Nachmani 89).

Spartak Trnava (2) 3 *(Tambe 7, 83, Mikovic 40)*
Hibernians (0) 0 0
Spartak Trnava: (442) Jakubech; Conka, Godal, Cogley, Deket (Paukner 46); Gressak, Bello, Mikovic, Halilovic (Privat 71); Schranz (Jirka 81), Tambe.
Hibernians: (442) Haber; Pearson, Agius, Soares, Mbele (Renan 62); Cohen, Failla, Lima, Bezzina (Mbong 88); Varea (Farrugia 76), Dias.
Behind closed doors.

Teuta (0) 0
Kairat Almaty (0) 1 *(Arshavin 70)* 500
Teuta: (442) Mocka; Hoxha E, Hoxha R, Kotobelli, Shkalla; Hodo (Gripshi 82), Lena (Lamcja 65), Musta, Hila; Cybja, Magani (Rraboshta 76).
Kairat Almaty: (442) Plotnikov; Tesak, Markovic, Kuantayev, Tymoschuk; Bakaev, Isael (Kuat 80), Islamkhan, Arshavin (Acevedo 78); Gohou (Tawamba Kana 90), Lunin.

Trakai (0) 2 *(Valskis 69, Arshakiyan 78)*
Nomme Kalju (1) 1 *(Wakui 6 (pen))* 500
Trakai: (442) Rapalis; Janusevskis, Cesnauskis, Silenas, Valskis (Masenzovas 87); Rekish (Kochanauskas 76), Bychenok, Zasavitchi, Gurenko (Vitukynas 79); Vorobjovas, Arshakiyan.
Nomme Kalju: (442) Teles; Sidorenkov, Mool, Ugge, Mbu Alidor; Rodrigues, Dmitrijev, Toomet (Jarva 76), Wakui; Quintieri (Sinyavskiy 46), Klein (Neemelo 80).

UE Santa Coloma (0) 1 *(Reis 90)*
Lokomotiva Zagreb (1) 3 *(Maric 20, 73, Prenga 65)* 250
UE Santa Coloma: (442) Perianes Meca; Ruiz, Codina (Bousenine 74), Martinez, Jesus Rubio; Ayala, Aloy (Orosa 81), Bernat, Reis; Alonso, Salomo (Jordi Rubio 62).
Lokomotiva Zagreb: (442) Filipovic; Brucic, Prenga, Capan, Peric; Bartolec, Cekici, Fiolic, Grezda (Majer 76); Ivanusec (Coric 60), Maric (Puljic 79).

Vaduz (2) 3 *(Costanzo 37, 45, Grippo 90)*
Sileks (0) 1 *(Mickov 86)* 928
Vaduz: (442) Jehle; Grippo, Buhler, Borgmann, Muntwiler (Hasler 76); Ciccone, Kukuruzovic, Brunner, Janjatovic (Avdijaj 63); Zarate (Mathys 70), Costanzo.
Sileks: (442) Vujanac; Dzhonov, Ivanov, Gligorov, Mickov; Tanushev (Stojchevski 90), Acevski (Kalanoski 61), Panovski, Timovski (Filipovski 52); Gucev, Nedeljkovic.

Valur Reykjavik (0) 1 *(Ingvarsson 90)*
Brondby (0) 4 *(Wilczek 47, 54, Pukki 61, Jakobsen 79)* 728
Valur Reykjavik: (442) Einarsson; Christiansen, Stefansson, Eiriksson, Omarsson; Lydsson (Ingvarsson 66), Sigurdsson H (Sturluson 77), Sigurdsson K, Larusson; Halldorsson (Toft 73), Hansen.
Brondby: (442) Ronnow; Juelsgaard, Rocker, Larsson, Crone; Boysen (Phiri 46), Norgaard, Hjulsager (Holst 83), Jakobsen; Pukki (Borring 69), Wilczek.

Ventspils (2) 2 *(Karlsons 5, 37)*
Vikingur (0) 0 1982
Ventspils: (442) Uvarenko; Jemelins, Boranijasevic, Kolesovs, Recickis; Sinelnikovs, Rugins, Paulius, Alekseev (Mujeci 46); Tidenbergs, Karlsons (Svarups 90).
Vikingur: (442) Tamas; Hansen G, Gregersen, Djurhuus, Jacobsen; Hansen B, Samuelsen (Anghel 62), Vatnhamar, Djordjevic (Olsen J 86); Olsen A (Poulsen 75), Justinussen.

Videoton (1) 3 *(Geresi 18, Feczesin 88, 90)*
Zaria Balti (0) 0 2321
Videoton: (442) Kovacsik; Fejes, Nego, Vinicius, Szolnoki; Patkai, Barczi (Feczesin 72), Simon, Bodi; Suljic, Geresi.
Zaria Balti: (442) Pascenco; Golovatenco, Erhan, Novicov, Gomez Garcia; Tigirlas, Grosu (Suvorov■ 73), Mihaliov, Onica (Rata 81); Ovsianicov (Boghiu 70), Picusciac■.

Zimbru Chisinau (0) 0

Chikhura Sachkhere (1) 1 *(Tatanashvili 40)* 2500

Zimbru Chisinau: (442) Rusu; Jardan, Emerson, Luan, Izaldo; Diego Lima (Zagaevschii 46), Spataru (Kabi 86), Anton■, Bruno; Coulibaly (Erick 81), Amancio Fortes.
Chikhura Sachkhere: (442) Hamzic; Kashia, Rekhviashvili, Kakubava, Chikvaidze; Grigalashvili, Ganugrava■, Lobzhanidze (Lekvtadze 66), Tatanashvili; Ivanishvili (Dekanoidze 90), Gabedava (Dobrovolski 57).

FIRST QUALIFYING ROUND SECOND LEG

Tuesday, 5 July 2016

Birkirkara (1) 2 *(Dimitrov 29, Markovic 76 (og))*

Siroki Brijeg (0) 0 1152

Birkirkara: (442) Kopric; Zerafa, Bubalovic, Jovic (Camenzuli 79), Sciberras; Bajada, Scicluna (Guillaumier 65), Dimitrov (Bilbao 75), Attard; Plut, Emerson.
Siroki Brijeg: (442) Soldo; Pandza (Barisic 46), Brekalo, Coric, Markovic; Sesar, Wagner, Crnov, Plazonic (Ivankovic 46); Baraban (Menalo 78), Krstanovic.

Chikhura Sachkhere (1) 2 *(Ivanishvili 13, Kakubava 55)*

Zimbru Chisinau (1) 3 *(Emerson 45, 90, Jardan 61)* 1500

Chikhura Sachkhere: (442) Hamzic; Kashia, Rekhviashvili, Kakubava, Chikvaidze; Grigalashvili, Dobrovolski, Koripadze, Lobzhanidze (Dekanoidze 78); Tatanashvili (Mumladze 90), Ivanishvili (Lekvtadze 71).
Zimbru Chisinau: (442) Rusu; Jardan, Emerson, Luan, Izaldo; Erick (Zagaevschii 80), Spataru, Bruno, Coulibaly (Diego Lima 39); Amancio Fortes (Burghiu 88), Damascan.

Jeunesse Esch (1) 2 *(Stumpf 22, 87)*

St Patrick's Ath (0) 1 *(Dennehy D 73)* 1378

Jeunesse Esch: (4231) Oberweis; Todorovic, Portier■, Delgado, Lapierre (Sardaryan 80); Peters, Kuhne; Mertinitz, Ontiveros (Deidda 88), Pinna; Stumpf.
St Patrick's Ath: (433) Clarke; O'Brien, Dennehy D, Hoare, Bermingham; Dennehy B, Treacy (Verdon 82), Cawley; Byrne, Fagan, Timlin (Kelly 79).

Wednesday, 6 July 2016

FCI Tallinn (0) 2 *(Harin 51, Voskoboinikov 63)*

Hearts (3) 4 *(Paterson 2, Igor Rossi 9, 52, Ozturk 45)* 1354

FCI Tallinn: (541) Igonen; Volodin (Kulinits 75), Appiah, Kalimulin, Avilov (Domov 46), Kruglov; Mashicev, Dmitrijev, Mosnikov (Dramani 46), Harin; Voskoboinikov.
Hearts: (4312) Hamilton; Smith, Paterson, Ozturk, Igor Rossi; Rherras, Djoum (Lloria 89), Kitchen; Buaben (Souttar 74); Walker (Nicholson 70), Sammon.

Thursday, 7 July 2016

Bala T (0) 0

AIK Solna (2) 2 *(Avdic 8, Strandberg 24)* 890

Bala T: (4411) Morris; Valentine, Stuart Jones Snr, Stuart Jones Jnr, Stephens; Smith (Hayes 74), Burke, Davies (Jamie 65), Sheridan; Jones M (Thompson 65); Connolly.
AIK Solna: (433) Carlgren; Sundgren, Vaisanen, Saletros, Johansson; Kpozo, Ishizaki (Yasin 46), Ofori (Affane 72); Blomberg, Strandberg (Isak 63), Avdic.

Beitar Jerusalem (0) 1 *(Atzili 66 (pen))*

Sloboda Tuzla (0) 0 9010

Beitar Jerusalem: (442) Atzili; Klaiman, Rueda, Mori, Magbo; Mishan, Moyal (Cohen 86), Claudemir, Einbinder; Shechter, Valpoort (Brihon 73).
Sloboda Tuzla: (442) Piric; Merzic, Kostic, Dzidic■, Zeba; Stjepanovic (Krpic 82), Efendic, Ordagic, Veselinovic; Mehidic (Govedarica 74), Karic.

Brondby (3) 6 *(Wilczek 5, Hjulsager 15, Pukki 26, 51, Stuckler 71, 90)*

Valur Reykjavik (0) 0 6227

Brondby: (442) Ronnow; Wilczek (Stuckler 46), Hjulsager, Pukki, Juelsgaard; Rocker, Larsson, Crone, Norgaard; Phiri (Holst 61), Jakobsen (Da Silva 73).
Valur Reykjavik: (442) Kale; Christiansen, Stefansson, Eiriksson, Omarsson; Lydsson, Sigurdsson K (Ingvarsson 76), Larusson (Bergsson 77), Halldorsson; Hansen (Toft 61), Sigurdsson H.

Buducnost Podgorica (1) 1 *(Radanovic 18 (pen))*

Rabotnicki Kometal (0) 0 2000

Buducnost Podgorica: (442) Radanovic (Markovic 81); Dragojevic, Vukovic, Mirkovic (Janketic 78), Radunovic; Mitrovic, Pejakovic (Seratlic 72), Hocko, Raicevic; Djalovic, Vusurovic.
Rabotnicki Kometal: (451) Siskovski; Siljanovski (Tomas 46), Mitrev, Cikarski, Najdovski L■; Herera (Elmas 56), Duranski (Galic 74), Najdovski B, Trajcevski, Sahiti; Altiparmakovski.

Cliftonville (1) 2 *(McDaid 2, Donnelly J 75)*

Differdange 03 (0) 0 1168

Cliftonville: (4312) Mooney; Cosgrove, McGuinness, Bonner, Ives (Lavery 66); Curran, Catney, Donnelly M; Winchester (Knowles 73); McDaid (Hughes 84), Donnelly J.
Differdange 03: (433) Weber; Franzoni, Vandenbroeck, Siebenaler■, Rodrigues; Pedro Ribeiro (Luisi 78), May, Sinani (Lascak 49); Yeye, Er Rafik, Caron.

Cork C (0) 1 *(Maguire 49 (pen))*

Linfield (0) 1 *(Stafford 52)* 3521

Cork C: (433) McNulty; McSweeney (O'Sullivan 56), Browne, Bennett, O'Connor; Morrissey G, Buckley (Healy 65), Holohan (Morrissey D 56); Beattie, Maguire, Dooley.
Linfield: (532) Carroll; Clarke M (McLellan 88), Stafford, Haughey, Quinn, Lowry; Millar (Burns 78), Mulgrew, Gaynor; Waterworth, Smyth.

Cracovia (0) 1 *(Cetnarski 68)*

Shkendija Tetovo (1) 2 *(Ibraimi 13, Hasani 90)* 7122

Cracovia: (442) Sandomierski; Deleu, Polczak, Wolakiewicz, Wojcicki; Budzinski, Dabrowski (Stepniowski 46), Covilo, Karachanakov (Steblecki 17); Jendrisek, Vestenicky (Cetnarski 46).
Shkendija Tetovo: (442) Zahov; Cuculi, Bejtulai, Alimi (Polozani 71), Todorovski; Hasani, Vujcic, Demiri, Ibraimi (Juffo 88); Junior, Radeski (Taipi 84).

Dacia (0) 0

Kapaz (0) 1 *(Dario Junior 57)* 620

Dacia: (442) Celeadnic; Slinkin, Bulgaru, Posmac, Bejan (Bugneac 72); Kozhanov (Bugaev 77), Mani (Valeev 67), Cociuc, Gavrylenko; Mamah, Feshchuk.
Kapaz: (4411) Simaitis; Daniyev, Baybalaev (Javadov 68), Dario Junior, Rahimov; Gurbanov, Akhundov, Aliyev S, Renan; Serginho (Qurbanov 73 (Karimov 82)); Ebah.

Debrecen (1) 2 *(Tisza 41, Holman 51)*

La Fiorita (0) 0 8632

Debrecen: (442) Radosevic; Korhut, Brkovic, Szatmari, Szakaly; Varga, Jovanovic, Delmic, Holman; Tisza, Castillon.
La Fiorita: (442) Vivan; Bollini, Bugli, Gasperoni, Tommasi; Zafferani, Cangini, Martini M, Selva; Rinaldi, Parma.

Fola Esch (1) 1 *(Hadji 45)*

Aberdeen (0) 0 1789

Fola Esch: (442) Hym; Laterza, Klein, Bernard, Kirch; Klapp (Rodrigues 71), Dallevedove, Muharemovic (Rocha 87), Francoise (Camerling 78); Hadji, Bensi.
Aberdeen: (4231) Lewis; Logan, Taylor, Considine, Shinnie; Jack, O'Connor (Reynolds 46); Pawlett (Flood 46), McLean, Hayes; Stockley (Rooney 63).

Folgore/Falciano (1) 1 *(Traini 35)*

AEK Larnaca (0) 3 *(Trickovski 51, 55, Alves 65 (pen))* 319

Folgore/Falciano: (442) Montanari; Quintavalla, Genestreti, Bezzi, Camillini; Berardi (Brolli 67), Nucci (Rossi 72), Muccini, Perrotta; Angelini (Delle Valle 87), Traini.

AEK Larnaca: (442) Taudul; Murillo, Charalambous (Tete 68), Catala, Mintikkis; Laban (Boljevic 74), Trickovski (Konstantinou 86), Jorge, Tomas; Charalambidis, Alves.

Glenavon (0) 0

KR Reykjavik (2) 6 *(Chopart 6, 29, Fridjonsson 53 (pen), Beck 68, Hauksson 78, Fazlagic 80)* 1250

Glenavon: (451) Tuffey; Doyle, Kelly, Marshall, Cooper; Bradley, Hall (O'Mahony 79), Patton, Sykes, Martyn (Kilmartin 71); Hamilton (Moorhouse 64).
KR Reykjavik: (433) Magnusson; Beck Andersen, Sigurdsson, Josepsson, Praest (Michaelsson 80); Gunnarsson, Margeirsson, Palmason; Chopart (Fazlagic 58), Fridjonsson (Beck 56), Hauksson.

Gorica (0) 0

Maccabi Tel Aviv (1) 1 *(Benayoun 10)* 700

Gorica: (442) Sorcan; Skarabot, Gregoric, Boben, Kavcic; Kolenc, Kapic, Kotnik (Grudina 71), Marinic (Arcon 77); Burgic (Wilson 66), Nagode.
Maccabi Tel Aviv: (442) Rajkovic; Ben Haim I, Ben Haroush, Tibi (Filipenko 64), Medunjanin; Benayoun, Alberman, Igiebor, Micha (Ben Haim II (71); Peretz D, Orlando Sa (Ben Basat 46).

Hibernians (0) 0

Spartak Trnava (1) 3 *(Mikovic 5, Oravec 58, Bello 90)* 322

Hibernians: (442) Haber; Pearson, Agius (Mbele 30), Soares, Failla (Mbong 72); Lima, Kristensen, Varea (Degabriele 80), Renan; Dias, Jorginho.
Spartak Trnava: (442) Jakubech; Conka (Kadlec 44), Godal, Cogley, Eder (Oravec 51); Gressak, Bello, Mikovic, Halilovic; Schranz (Jirka 64), Tambe.

HJK Helsinki (1) 1 *(Taiwo 30 (pen))*

Atlantas (0) 1 *(Papsys 76)* 3501

HJK Helsinki: (442) Dahne; Taiwo, Jalasto, Rexhepi, Tatomirovic; Kamara, Kolehmainen, Malolo, Alho (Sorsa 82); Morelos (Forssell 67), Gadze (Oduamadi 75).
Atlantas: (442) Adamonis; Epifanov, Gaspuitis, Beneta, Baravykas; Bartkus (Kazlauskas 67), Verbickas, Dmitriev (Simkus 55), Sylla; Maksimov, Rakauskas (Papsys 40).

IFK Mariehamn (1) 1 *(Sparrdal Mantilla 4)*

Odd (0) 1 *(Akabueze 78)* 1402

IFK Mariehamn: (442) Viitala; Friberg da Cruz, Lyyski, Kojola, Granlund; Sparrdal Mantilla (Makinen 88), Petrovic (Diego Assis 25), Ekhalie, Span (Sid 71); Kangaskolkka, Orgill.
Odd: (442) Rossbach; Eriksen, Ruud, Hagen, Nilsen; Semb Berge (Bergan 86), Jensen (Occean 82), Berg, Halvorsen; Johansen, Zehninki (Akabueze 73).

Jelgava (1) 2 *(Turkovs 15, Diallo 70)*

Breidablik (2) 2 *(Hreinsson 31, Bamberg 33 (pen))* 1560

Jelgava: (442) Ikstens; Smirnovs (Savcenkovs 46), Freimanis, Nakano, Redjko; Bogdaskins, Turkovs (Kovalovs 84), Diallo, Grigaravicius; Kluskins, Lazdins.
Breidablik: (442) Gunnleifsson; Sigurjonsson, Muminovic, Helgason, Atlason; Eyjolfsson (Glenn 83), Olafsson, Hreinsson, Bamberg (Sigurgeirsson 77); Adalsteinsson, Yeoman (Hlynsson 77).

Kairat Almaty (2) 5 *(Gohou 27, 61, Bakaev 45, Tawamba Kana 72, Turysbek 79)*

Teuta (0) 0 20,700

Kairat Almaty: (442) Plotnikov; Vorogovskiy, Markovic, Kuat, Bakaev; Islamkhan (Acevedo 67), Isael, Gohou (Tawamba Kana 70), Lunin; Arshavin (Turysbek 77), Tymoschuk.
Teuta: (442) Mocka; Shkalla (Gripshi 67), Hoxha R (Shehi 54), Cybja (Rraboshta 52), Kotobelli; Magani, Hila, Musta, Lena; Hoxha E, Hodo.

Llandudno (0) 1 *(Hughes 72)*

IFK Gothenburg (1) 2 *(Smedberg-Dalence 36, Skold 54)* 841

Llandudno: (442) Roberts; Mike Williams, Taylor, Joyce, Shaw (Peate 58); Evans (Dawson 70), Hughes, Marc Williams, Owen (Riley 65); Dix, Buckley.
IFK Gothenburg: (433) Dahlberg; Jonsson, Nordstrom, Bjarsmyr, Pettersson; Albaek (Eriksson 63), Hysen (Boman 80), Smedberg-Dalence; Skold, Lagemyr (Rieks 80), Leksell.

Lokomotiva Zagreb (3) 4 *(Coric 8, Prenga 18 (pen), Maric 48, Peric 57)*

UE Santa Coloma (0) 1 *(Salomo 89)* 294

Lokomotiva Zagreb: (442) Filipovic; Bartolec, Karacic, Maric, Fiolic; Peric, Coric, Cekici (Dolezal 72), Grezda; Prenga (Oluic 82), Capan (Majer 62).
UE Santa Coloma: (451) Fernandez; Jesus Rubio, Maneiro (Salomo 69), Martinez, Jordi Rubio; Boris, Bernat (Pereira 60), Ruiz, Crespo (Nazzaro 63), Bousenine; Orosa.

Lusitanos (1) 1 *(Luizao 18)*

Domzale (2) 2 *(Majer 5, Morel 42)* 500

Lusitanos: (442) Jesus Coca; Maciel, San Nicolas M, Munoz, Lucas Sousa; Bruninho (San Nicolas 82), Pousa (Acosta 69), Pinto, Aguilar; Molina, Luizao (Luis Miguel 70).
Domzale: (442) Golubovic; Horic, Sirok, Dobrovoljc Blazic 49), Trajkovski; Zinko (Juninho 84), Crnic, Husmani (Horvat 65), Majer; Morel, Mance.

MTK Budapest (1) 2 *(Nikac 7, Borbely 84)*

Aktobe (0) 0 601

MTK Budapest: (442) Hegedus; Baki, Grgic, Nikac (Hrepka 84), Szatmari (Borbely 62); Torghelle, Bese, Kanta (Jakab 90), Poor; Gera, Vass.
Aktobe: (451) Otarbaev; Sitdikov, Kouadja, Kairov, Kryukov; Zhalmukan, Tsveiba, Mitosevic, Bocharov, Dao (Golubov 58 (Abdukarimov 81)); Sorokin.

Neftchi (1) 1 *(Jairo 20)*

Balzan (0) 2 *(Micallef 51, 67)* 7650

Neftchi: (442) Santini; Shikov, Isayev, Jairo, Melnjak; Abdullayev A (Muradbayli 77), Haciyev, Castillo, Agaev; Qurbanov (Imamverdiyev 69), Abdullayev E (Mammadov 90).
Balzan: (442) Cassar; Serrano, Bezzina, Guimaraes de Oliveira, Grioli; Fenech, Grima (Brincat 82), Darmanin, Manevski (Micallef 46); Effiong, Kaljevic.

Nomme Kalju (0) 4 *(Rodrigues 66, Sidorenkov 69, Neemelo 87, 90)*

Trakai (1) 1 *(Arshakiyan 14)* 465

Nomme Kalju: (442) Teles; Ugge, Rodrigues, Mbu Alidor, Dmitrijev; Toomet, Klein (Neemelo 46), Sidorenkov, Mool; Wakui (Puri 66), Quintieri (Purje 59).
Trakai: (442) Rapalis; Vorobjovas, Cesnauskis, Rekish, Arshakiyan; Vitukynas, Janusevskis, Silenas, Zachazevskij; Gurenko (Kochanauskas 89), Bychenok.

Omonia Nicosia (0) 4 *(Roushias 93, 108, Derbyshire 114, Cleyton 120)*

Banants Yerevan (0) 1 *(Buraev 71)* 8042

Omonia Nicosia: (442) Panagi; Panteliadis, Carlitos, Florescu (Katelaris 74), Orsulic; Margaca, Fylaktou, Agaiev (Roushias 86), Derbyshire; Sheridan, Badibanga (Cleyton 74).
Banants Yerevan: (442) Ghazaryan; Mecinovikj, Drobarov, Kachmazov (Avetisyan 101), Adams; Hakobyan, Badoyan (Mosesyan 89), Poghosyan (Ayvazyan 57), Torrejon; Buraev, Kalmanov.
aet.

Ordabasy (1) 3 *(Geynrikh 45, Tungyshbayev 67, Erlanov 90)*

Cukaricki (3) 3 *(Mandic 10, 14, Kajevic 21)* 5100

Ordabasy: (442) Boichenko; Simcevic, Trajkovic, Adyrbekov, Erlanov; Chatto, Geynrikh, Diakhate (Gogua 46), Tolebek; Tungyshbayev (Beysenov 78), Kaykibasov (Kasalica 45).
Cukaricki: (442) Stevanovic; Lucas, Jankovic N, Lagator, Duric; Zivkovic, Fofana (Jovanovic 79), Kajevic, Knezevic; Srnic (Masovic E 75), Mandic (Matic 59).

Pyunik (1) 2 *(Arakelyan 25, Minasyan 56)*
Europa (1) 1 *(Joselinho 10)* 2000
Pyunik: (442) Manukyan; Kartashyan, Manucharyan, Hovhannisyan, Pogosyan; Manoyan, Yuspashyan (Razmik Hakobyan 55), Robert Hakobyan, Arakelyan; Minasyan (Satumyan 65), Harutunyan (Aslanyan 90).
Europa: (442) Javi Munoz; Moya (Joselinho 6 (Copi 75)), Toni Garcia, Lopez, Carrion (Villodres 61); Toscano, Roldan, Quillo, Vazquez; Belfortti, Sanchez.

Radnik Bijeljina (0) 0
Beroe (0) 2 *(Pochanski 79, 80)* 2832
Radnik Bijeljina: (442) Lucic; Kojic, Celebic, Zelijkovic, Stokic (Peco 76); Duric, Martinovic, Vasic, Besirovic (Jankovic 76); Memisevic, Obradovic.
Beroe: (442) Makendzhiev; Penev, Vasilev V, Ivanov, Milanov; Milisavljevic, Tom (Dinkov 85), Panayotov, Pochanski (Kolev 90); Pedro Marques (Vasilev A 89), Bozhilov.

RoPS Rovaniemi (1) 1 *(Muinonen 26)*
Shamrock R (1) 1 *(McCabe 22 (pen))* 1525
RoPS Rovaniemi: (442) Reguero; Pirinen, Jammeh, Saksela, Lahdenmaki; Hamalainen, Muinonen, Taylor, Mravec; Saine (Makitalo 46 (Nganbe 53)), John (Kokko 46).
Shamrock R: (442) Hyland; Madden, Cornwall, Heaney, Cregg; McCabe, Brennan K, Brennan G, Miele (Clarke T 67); Shaw (Dobbs 74), Clarke D (Boyd 73).

Rudar Pljevlja (0) 0
Kukesi (0) 1 *(Guri 79)* 486
Rudar Pljevlja: (442) Radanovic; Nestorovic, Zivkovic, Radisic (Vukovic 86), Alic; Bozovic, Soppo (Markovic 81), Vlahovic, Brnovic; Ivanovic, Noma (Jovanovic 73).
Kukesi: (442) Kolici; Hallaci, Mici, Malota, Shameti; Jean Carioca, Dema (Greca■ 54), Musolli (Muca 77), Dvornekovic (Guri 63); Emini, Rangel.

Samtredia (1) 2 *(Zivzivadze 14 (pen), Shergelashvili 90)*
Qabala (1) 1 *(Weeks 42)* 847
Samtredia: (442) Migineishvili; Gogiashvili (Mandzhgaladze 46), Sandokhadze, Arabuli, Zivzivadze; Tsnobiladze (Razhamashvili 76), Shergelashvili, Mtchedlishvili, Datunaishvili; Gorgiashvili, Gamkrelidze (Jikia 63).
Qabala: (442) Bezotosnyi; Stankovic, Sadiqov (Jamalov 69), Kvekveskiri, Zenjov; Vernydub (Rafael Santos 46), Dabo, Ozobic (Mutallimov 52), Ricardinho; Weeks, Abbasov.

Shakhtyor Soligorsk (2) 5 *(Burko 20, Rudyka 42, Shlbun 81 (pen), Elizarenko 86, Yurevich 90)*
NSI Runavik (0) 0 1100
Shakhtyor Soligorsk: (442) Bushma; Yurevich (Elizarenko 67), Rybak, Kuzmyanok, Ignjatijevic; Yanushkevich, Burko (Shlbun 69), Starhorodskyi, Rudyka; Kovalev, Osipenko (Pavlov 79).
NSI Runavik: (442) Gango; Justinussen, Langgaard, Jacobsen M, Madsen (Gaardbo 85); Mortensen J (Benjaminsen 75), Jacobsen J, Kohlert, Knudsen (Mortensen M 88); Olsen M, Olsen K.

Shirak (0) 1 *(Bichakhchyan 84)*
Dila Gori (0) 0 2400
Shirak: (4411) Ayvazov; Mikaelyan, Hovsepyan, Kouakou (Ayvazyan 69), Hakobyan; Udo, Hovanisian, Darbinyan, Davoyan (Hovhannisyan 71); Diarrassouba; Stoskovic (Bichakhchyan 65).
Dila Gori: (343) Mujrishvili; Samkharadze, Razmadze, Tsikaridze (Sharikadze 72); Japaridze (KIkabidze 91), Modebadze, Kvirkvelia, Eristavi (Nonikashvili 68); Ghonghadze, Dolidze, Karkuzashvili.
aet; Shirak won 4-1 on penalties.

Sileks (1) 1 *(Mickov 31)*
Vaduz (0) 2 *(Costanzo 89 (pen), Messaoud 90)* 450
Sileks: (442) Vujanac; Dzhonov, Ivanov, Gligorov, Mickov; Tanushev, Panovski (Georgiev 84), Filipovski (Biljali 73), Gucev; Nedeljkovic, Kalanoski (Acevski 57).
Vaduz: (442) Siegrist; Grippo, Buhler, Borgmann, Ciccone; Mathys (Schurpf 72), Kukuruzovic, Hasler (Avdijaj 62), Brunner; Zarate (Messaoud 82), Costanzo.

Spartak Myjava (1) 2 *(Daniel 30, Pekar 89)*
Admira Wacker Modling (2) 3 *(Wostry 2, Starkl 27, Zwierschitz 57)* 2057
Spartak Myjava: (442) Bilovsky; Daniel, Duga (Sladek 46), Hruska, Kolar; Kona, Kukol (Cernacek 84), Machovec, Marcek (Pekar 46); Mehremic, Ostojic.
Admira Wacker Modling: (442) Bajrami; Ebner, Grozurek (Sax 46), Knasmullner (Toth 67), Lackner; Pavic, Siebenhandl, Starkl (Monschein 81), Strauss; Wostry, Zwierschitz.

Spartaks Jurmala (0) 0
Dinamo Minsk (1) 2 *(Khvashchynskiy 11, El Monir 90)* 1100
Spartaks Jurmala: (442) Kurakins; Ulimbashevs (Stuglis 72), Kazacoks, Adeyemo (Platonov 81), Kozlov; Yaghoubi, Pushnyakov, Kozeka, Kozlovs (Korzans 67); Mihadjuks, Slampe.
Dinamo Minsk: (451) Ignatovich; Ostroukh, Premudrov, Bykov, Rassadkin (Rotkovic 90); Korytko, Zhukouski (El Monir 83), Noyok, Habovda, Khvashchynskiy (Shramchenko 69); Kaplenko.

Stabaek (0) 0
Connah's Quay Nomads (1) 1 *(Morris 15)* 384
Stabaek: (442) Sayouba; Skjonsberg (Haugsdal 72), Moe (Eghan 66), Nije, Meling; Naess, Gorozia (Mehmeti 54), Issah■, Omoijuanfo; Grossman, Asante.
Connah's Quay Nomads: (442) Danby; Disney■ (Owen M 68), Baynes, Kearney, Short; Horan, Harrison, Morris, Owen J; Woolfe (Smith 80), Wilde (Davies 84).

Suduva (0) 0
Midtjylland (1) 1 *(Novak 16)* 1738
Suduva: (442) Kardum; Jankauskas A, Jablan, Janusauskas, Leimonas; Slavickas, Pavlovic (Laukzemis 90), Svrljuga, Jamak (Jankauskas E 46); Radzinevicius (Veliulis 63), Kecap.
Midtjylland: (442) Dahlin; Halsti (Romer 77), Hansen (Riis 65), Novak, Banggaard; Nissen, Poulsen, Hassan (Kadlec V 56), Olsson; Sisto, Pusic.

Torshavn (0) 0
Levadia Tallinn (0) 2 *(Kobzar 71, Miranchuk 90)* 580
Torshavn: (442) Gestsson; Johan Davidsen, Jogvan Davidsen, Benjaminsen, Mouritsen (Wardum 37); Egilsson, Jensen, Jonsson, Jacobsen; Justinussen (Dalbud 79), Olsen (Joensen 78).
Levadia Tallinn: (442) Lepmets; Morozov, Podholjuzin, Tabi, Luts; Kaljumae, Antonov, Miranchuk, Gando; Kobzar (Raudsepp 75), Hunt.

Vikingur (0) 0
Ventspils (0) 2 *(Jemelins 57 (pen), Karlsons 90)* 369
Vikingur: (442) Tamas; Hansen G, Gregersen, Djurhuus, Jacobsen; Hansen B, Vatnhamar, Djordjevic (Olsen J 68), Anghel (Vatuhamar 71); Olsen A, Justinussen.
Ventspils: (442) Uvarenko; Jemelins, Boranijasevic, Kolesovs, Recickis (Alfa 63)); Sinelnikovs (Zigajevs 64), Rugins, Paulius, Alekseev (Obuobi 76); Tidenbergs, Karlsons.

Vojvodina (2) 5 *(Malbasic 9, 42, Meleg 60, Trujic 63, 87)*
Bokelj (0) 0 4388
Vojvodina: (442) Kordic; Miletic, Antic, Maksimovic, Puskaric; Trujic, Malbasic (Durisic 68), Meleg, Lakicevic; Palocevic (Zlicic 69), Babic (Stamenic 70).
Bokelj: (442) Mijatovic; Ognjanovic, Todorovic, Mladenovic, Tomic (Nikezic 65); Zlaticanin, Bogdanovic, Macanovic (Kotorac 52), Djenic; Vucinic, Pepic (Maras 52).

Zaglebie Lubin (1) 3 *(Guldan 20, Piatek L 64, Dabrowski 81)*
Slavia Sofia (0) 0 5817
Zaglebie Lubin: (442) Polacek; Guldan, Cotra, Dabrowski, Todorovski; Janoszka (Tosik 85), Piatek L, Vlasko (Rakowski 62), Kubicki; Woznaik, Piatek K (Papadopoulos 77).
Slavia Sofia: (442) Kirev; Martinov (Krastv 82), Sergeev, Velkov, Khamis; Baldzhiski, Pashov, Vasev, Karabelyov (Yomov 46); Dimitrov (Stankev 67), Serderov.

Zaria Balti (2) 2 *(Mihaliov 9, Ovsianicov 29)*
Videoton (0) 0 2097
Zaria Balti: (442) Pascenco; Golovatenco, Erhan, Novicov, Gomez Garcia; Tigirlas, Grosu, Mihaliov, Onica; Boghiu, Ovsianicov.
Videoton: (442) Kovacsik; Nego, Vinicius, Szolnoki, Stopira; Lang, Oliveira (Fejes 87), Simon, Bodi (Feczesin 67); Suljic, Geresi.

SECOND QUALIFYING ROUND FIRST LEG

Thursday, 14 July 2016

Aberdeen (0) 3 *(Stockley 72, Rooney 76, Burns 90)*
Ventspils (0) 0 10,672
Aberdeen: (541) Lewis; Jack, Logan, Shinnie, Considine, Taylor; Reynolds, McLean (Stockley 68), McGinn, Hayes; Rooney (Burns 89).
Ventspils: (451) Uvarenko; Jemelins, Sinelnikovs, Kolesovs, Alekseev (Svarups 87); Paulius, Tidenbergs (Zulevs 81), Recickis, Boranijasevic, Rugins; Karlsons.

Admira Wacker Modling (1) 1 *(Starkl 41)*
Kapaz (0) 0 956
Admira Wacker Modling: (442) Siebenhandl; Strauss, Zwierschitz, Ebner, Lackner; Sax (Spiridonovic 58), Knasmullner, Starkl (Monschein 75), Pavic; Wostry, Bajrami.
Kapaz: (442) Simaitis; Daniyev, Baybalaev (Javadov 73), Dario Junior, Rahimov; Gurbanov (Aliyev O 73), Akhundov, Aliyev S, Renan; Serginho (Qurbatov 88), Ebah.

AIK Solna (0) 1 *(Strandberg 89)*
Europa (0) 0 5250
AIK Solna: (442) Carlgren; Hauksson (Sundgren 78), Karlsson, Avdic, Ofori; Ishizaki, Hooiveld, Gravius (Strandberg 46), Kpozo; Isak, Affane (Blomberg 68).
Europa: (442) Munoz; Moya, Toni Garcia (Pinero 89), Carrion (Gonzalez 66), Toscano; Roldan, Quillo (Copi 75), Yahaya, Vazquez; Belfortti, Sanchez.

Austria Vienna (1) 1 *(Pires 24)*
Kukesi (0) 0 4312
Austria Vienna: (442) Hadzikic; Filipovic, Kayode (Vukojevic 90), Venuto, Serbest; Prokop (Kvasina 69), Larsen, Holzhauser, Martschinko; Rotpuller, Pires (De Paula 85).
Kukesi: (442) Kolici; Shameti, Lilaj, Mici, Jean Carioca (Emini 73); Hallaci, Latifi, Rangel (Guri 70), Musolli; Malota, Fukui (Dvornekovic 81).

Beitar Jerusalem (0) 1 *(Abuhazira 71)*
Omonia Nicosia (0) 0 9200
Beitar Jerusalem: (442) Klaiman; Keltjens, Mori, Khila, Atzili; Vered (Moyal 72), Einbinder, Claudemir, Valpoort (Shechter 85); Brihon (Abuhazira 64), Magbo.
Omonia Nicosia: (442) Panagi; Carlitos, Panteliadis, Sheridan, Cleyton; Agaiev (Toure 68), Fylaktou, Derbyshire, Margaca; Florescu, Orsulic.

Beroe (0) 1 *(Penev 49)*
HJK Helsinki (1) 1 *(Morelos 38)* 4424
Beroe: (442) Makendzhiev; Kato, Ivanov, Kirilov, Milisavljevic (Kolev 89); Bozhilov, Vasilev V (Vasilev A 76), Penev, Tom (Panayotov 89); Milanov, Pochanski.
HJK Helsinki: (442) Dahne; Taiwo, Medo (Annan 80), Rexhepi, Alho (Malolo 73); Tanaka, Morelos, Tatomirovic, Jalasto; Sorsa, Dahlstrom.

Birkirkara (0) 0
Hearts (0) 0 1868
Birkirkara: (4132) Kopric; Attard, Bubalovic, Emerson, Zerafa; Sciberras; Guillaumier, Bajada (Temile 81), Scicluna (Marotti 90); Dimitrov (Bilbao 90), Plut.
Hearts: (3331) Hamilton; Paterson, Ozturk, Igor Rossi; Smith, Kitchen (Cowie 30), Rherras; Djoum, Buaben, Sammon (Delgado 74); Walker (Nicholson 82).

Cliftonville (1) 2 *(McGuinness 18, Donnelly J 50)*
AEK Larnaca (0) 3 *(Trickovski 59, Charalambous 64, Tomas 77)* 1352
Cliftonville: (442) Mooney; Cosgrove, Bonner, McGuinness, Ives; Curran, Winchester (Garrett 88), Knowles, Donnelly M (Lavery 82); McDaid (Hughes 74), Donnelly J.
AEK Larnaca: (433) Mino; Ortiz, Mojsov, Catala, Charalambous; Jorge, Laban (Boljevic 81), Tomas; Tete (Englezou 84), Alves (Charalambidis 72), Trickovski.

CSMS Iasi (2) 2 *(Cristea 19, Piccioni 23)*
Hajduk Split (0) 2 *(Ohandza 48, Said 90)* 8004
CSMS Iasi: (442) Grahovac; Mihalache, Gheorghe, Cristea, Piccioni (Roman 83); Voicu, Bole, Mitic, Frasinescu; Tiganasu (Madalin 78), Ciucur (Ciuca 64).
Hajduk Split: (442) Stipica; Jefferson, Vlasic, Mastelic (Ohandza 46), Juranovic; Kozulj, Milic, Nizic, Basic (Mujan 57); Tudor (Said 68), Cosic.

Debrecen (1) 1 *(Tisza 2)*
Torpedo Zhodino (1) 2 *(Zagynaylov 23, Klopotskiy 88)* 6015
Debrecen: (442) Radosevic; Brkovic, Castillon (Takacs 57), Holman (Ferenczi 82), Jovanovic; Korhut, Meszaros K, Meszaros N (Delmic 63), Szakaly; Tisza, Varga.
Torpedo Zhodino: (442) Fomichev; Pankavets, Chelyadzinsky, Shcherbo (Chelyadko 85), Lutsevich; Klopotskiy, Afanasyev, Khachaturyan (Pavlykovets 80), Demidovich; Zagynaylov (Trapashko 69), Shapoval.

Dinamo Minsk (1) 1 *(Korytko 25)*
St Patrick's Ath (0) 1 *(Fagan 54)* 1286
Dinamo Minsk: (442) Ignatovich; Habovda, Noyok, Kaplenko, Ostroukh; Zhukouski (Rotkovic 70), Bykov, Premudrov, Khvashchynskiy (El Monir 57); Korytko (Shramchenko 79), Rassadkin.
St Patrick's Ath: (442) Clarke; Dennehy D, Hoare, O'Brien, Bermingham; Byrne, Dennehy B, Kelly, Timlin (Verdon 79); Treacy (Cawley 72), Fagan (Corcoran 79).

Genk (1) 2 *(Kebano 17 (pen), Samatta 79)*
Buducnost Podgorica (0) 0 10,450
Genk: (442) Bizot; Dewaest, Kumordzi, Buffel, Uronen; Ndidi, Bailey, Castagne, Buyens (Heynen 74); Samatta (Trossard 88), Kebano (Karelis 76).
Buducnost Podgorica: (442) Dragojevic; Radunovic, Vukovic, Vusurovic (Camaj 85), Mitrovic; Raickovic (Janketic 60), Raspopovic, Pejakovic (Seratlic 75), Hocko; Mirkovic, Djalovic.

Hacken (0) 1 *(Owoeri 83)*
Cork C (0) 1 *(Maguire 64 (pen))* 2022
Hacken: (433) Abrahamsson; Sudic, Wahlstrom, Schuller, Paulinho; Mensah■, Ericsson (Savage 57), Arkivuo (Binaku 78); Owoeri, Mohammed (Andersson 66), Gustafsson.
Cork C: (433) McNulty; Browne, O'Connor, McSweeney, Bennett; Bolger, Dooley, Maguire (Healy 90); Buckley (O'Sullivan 85), Beattie (Sheppard 75), Morrissey G.

Hibernian (0) 0
Brondby (1) 1 *(Wilczek 1)* 13,454
Hibernian: (433) Virtanen; McGregor, Gray, Hanlon, Bartley (Fontaine 65); McGinn, McGeouch (Keatings 65), Stevenson; Boyle (Harris 77), Holt, Cummings.
Brondby: (442) Ronnow; Da Silva, Larsson, Holst, Rocker; Albrechtsen, Austin (Hjulsager 43), Norgaard, Jakobsen (Juelsgaard 84); Wilczek, Stuckler (Pukki 52).

Kairat Almaty (1) 1 *(Arshavin 29)*
Maccabi Tel Aviv (0) 1 *(Benayoun 90)* 22,500
Kairat Almaty: (442) Plotnikov; Markovic, Kuantayev, Suyumbayev, Tymoschuk; Bakaev, Isael, Islamkhan■, Arshavin (Kuat 77); Gohou (Tawamba Kana 83), Lunin.
Maccabi Tel Aviv: (442) Rajkovic; Ben Haim I, Tibi, Medunjanin (Golasa 90), Alberman; Igiebor (Itzhaki 86), Rikan, Micha, Peretz D; Orlando Sa, Ben Haim II (Benayoun 73).

KR Reykjavik (0) 3 *(Beck Andersen 46, 50, Hauksson 77 (pen))*

Grasshoppers (2) 3 *(Munsy 18, Gjorgjev 36, Caio 59)* 767

KR Reykjavik: (442) Magnusson; Beck, Praest, Gunnarsson, Margeirsson; Fridjonsson (Beck Andersen 46), Palmason (Fazlagic 76), Sigurdsson, Chopart; Josepsson, Hauksson (Tryggvason 90).
Grasshoppers: (442) Mall; Pnishi, Sigurjonsson, Basic, Brahimi (Kamberi 68); Lavanchy, Munsy (Tabakovic 78), Caio, Bamert; Luthi, Gjorgjev (Andersen 62).

Levadia Tallinn (1) 3 *(Hunt 35, Gando 67, Antonov 90)*

Slavia Prague (0) 1 *(Mingazov 63)* 2750

Levadia Tallinn: (442) Lepmets; Morozov, Podholjuzin, Tabi, Luts; Kaljumae, Antonov, Miranchuk, Gando; Kobzar (Raudsepp 68), Hunt.
Slavia Prague: (442) Berkovec; Boril, Ngadjui-Ngadjui, Soucek, Holik; Husbauer, Mingazov (Mihalik 69), Zmrhal, Deli; Barak (Kenia 61), Mesanovic (van Buren 78).

Maccabi Haifa (0) 1 *(Vermouth 70)*

Nomme Kalju (0) 1 *(Toomet 47)* 6500

Maccabi Haifa: (442) Levita; Valiente, Abu Abaid, Kagelmacher (Gozlan 65), Obraniak; Rukavytsya, Vermouth, Menachem, Magharbeh (Raiyan 78); Meshumar (Habashi 84), Lavi.
Nomme Kalju: (442) Teles; Ugge, Rodrigues, Mbu Alidor, Dmitrijev; Purje (Neemelo 79), Toomet (Subbotin 68), Valikaev, Sidorenkov; Mool, Quintieri (Puri 59).

Maribor (0) 0

Levski Sofia (0) 0 7345

Maribor: (442) Handanovic; Hodzic, Janza, Suler, Vrhovec (Vrsic 46); Sallalich (Bajde 46), Tavares, Hotic, Novakovic (Omoregie 76); Kabha, Sme.
Levski Sofia: (442) Jorgacevic; Pirgov, Alexandrov, Narh, de Nooijer; Hristov (Adeniji 71), Minev, Prochazka, Anete (Orachev 85); Aleksandrov, Kostadinov.

Midtjylland (1) 3 *(Sisto 20, 82, Onuachu 73)*

Vaduz (0) 0 4455

Midtjylland: (442) Dahlin; Hansen, Halsti, Poulsen, Pusic (Onuachu 68); Banggaard, Sisto (Duelund 87), Hassan (Kadlec V 72), Nissen; Novak, Olsson.
Vaduz: (442) Jehle; Grippo, Ciccone, Zarate (Avdijaj 80), Costanzo; Mathys (Messaoud 65), Borgmann, Brunner (Pfrunder 80), Kukuruzovic; Muntwiler, Buhler.

MTK Budapest (0) 1 *(Torghelle 70)*

Qabala (1) 2 *(Kvekveskiri 25, Ozobic 63)* 501

MTK Budapest: (442) Hegedus; Baki, Grgic, Nikac (Varga 65), Torghelle; Bese, Kanta, Poor, Borbely (Szatmari 74); Gera (Jakab 78), Vass.
Qabala: (442) Bezotosnyi; Stankovic, Sadiqov, Kvekveskiri, Zenjov; Vernydub, Mirzabekov, Dabo (Mammadov 85), Ozobic; Ricardinho, Weeks.

Neftchi (0) 0

Shkendija Tetovo (0) 0 6891

Neftchi: (442) Santini; Shikov, Isayev, Jairo, Melnjak; Abdullayev A, Haciyev, Castillo, Agaev (Imamverdiyev 78); Muradbayli, Qurbanov (Abdullayev E 86).
Shkendija Tetovo: (442) Zahov; Cuculi, Bejtulai, Alimi, Todorovski; Hasani, Vujcic, Demiri, Ibraimi (Polozani 90); Junior, Radeski.

Partizan Belgrade (0) 0

Zaglebie Lubin (0) 0 15,870

Partizan Belgrade: (442) Saranov; Vulicevic, Mihajlovic, Brasanac (Marjanovic 75), Radovic; Bogosavac, Everton Bilher, Milenkovic, Djudjic (Bojinov 69); Gogoua, Jankovic (Stevanovic 83).
Zaglebie Lubin: (442) Polacek; Dabrowski, Cotra, Todorovski (Tosik 73), Woznaik; Janoszka (Vlasko 82), Rakowski (Piatek K 66), Kubicki, Papadopulos■; Piatek L, Guldan.

PAS Giannina (2) 3 *(Michail 7, Acosta 31, 68)*

Odd (0) 0 5615

PAS Giannina: (442) Paschalakis; Lila, Berios, Michail, Giakos (Donis 80); Tzimopoulos, Acosta (Skondras 90), Ferfelis (Conde 77), Fonsi; Karanikas, Kozoronis.
Odd: (442) Rossbach; Ruud, Grogaard, Berg (Jensen 46), Halvorsen; Johansen, Nordkvelle (Bergan 86), Nilsen (Haugen 73), Hagen; Eriksen, Akabueze.

Piast Gliwice (0) 0

IFK Gothenburg (2) 3 *(Rogne 2, Hysen 35, Engvall 86)* 5629

Piast Gliwice: (442) Szmatula; Mraz, Pietrowski, Murawski, Barisic (Mak 72); Zivec, Mokwa (Maslowski 46), Szeliga (Jankowski 61), Bukata; Hebert, Girdvainis.
IFK Gothenburg: (442) Alvbage; Salomonsson, Aleesami, Eriksson, Albaek; Rieks, Ankersen (Smedberg-Dalence 82), Hysen (Engvall 80), Boman (Pettersson 87); Rogne, Bjarsmyr.

RoPS Rovaniemi (0) 1 *(Jammeh 87)*

Lokomotiva Zagreb (0) 1 *(Jammeh 73 (og))* 1812

RoPS Rovaniemi: (442) Reguero; Saksela, Hamalainen, Jammeh, John (Osei 81); Kokko (Heikkila 60), Mravec, Muinonen, Nganbe (Okkonen 74); Pirinen, Taylor.
Lokomotiva Zagreb: (442) Bartolec; Capan, Cekici, Coric (Sunjic 82), Filipovic; Fiolic (Puljic 90), Grezda (Bockaj 66), Maric, Peric; Prenga, Rozman.

Shakhtyor Soligorsk (1) 1 *(Ignjatijevic 35)*

Domzale (0) 1 *(Trajkovski 52)* 2100

Shakhtyor Soligorsk: (442) Bushma; Yanushkevich, Yurevich, Burko, Osipenko (Yanush 55); Rudyka (Laptev 75), Starhorodskyi, Ignjatijevic, Rybak; Kuzmyanok, Kovalev (Yelezarenko 66).
Domzale: (442) Maraval; Alvaro Brachi, Horic, Crnic (Repas 70), Horvat; Trajkovski, Dobrovoljc, Majer (Alvir 78), Zinko; Morel (Juninho 83), Mance.

Shirak (1) 1 *(Hakobyan 16)*

Spartak Trnava (0) 1 *(Jirka 87)* 2747

Shirak: (442) Ayvazov; Darbinyan, Davoyan (Hovhannisyan 84), Diarrassouba (Poghosyan 75), Hakobyan; Hovanisian, Kaba, Kouakou, Mikaelyan; Stoskovic (Bichakhchyan 64), Udo.
Spartak Trnava: (442) Godal; Gressak, Halilovic (Oravec 90), Hornik, Jakubech; Kadlec, Mikovic, Privat (Jirka 59), Schranz (Paukner 76); Sloboda, Eder.

Slovan Bratislava (0) 0

Jelgava (0) 0 1451

Slovan Bratislava: (442) Mucha; Sekulic, Savicevic (Pliatsikas 90), Burnet, de Kamps; Kubik (Lasik 87), Zrelak, Soumah, Ligeon; Salata, Schet.
Jelgava: (442) Ikstens; Savcenkovs, Freimanis, Nakano (Sorokins 82), Redjko; Bogdaskins, Turkovs (Malasenoks 72), Diallo, Grigaravicius (Kovalovs 62); Kluskins, Lazdins.

SonderjyskE (1) 2 *(Klove 9, Uhre 82)*

Stromsgodset (1) 1 *(Pedersen 16)* 4795

SonderjyskE: (4141) Skender; Pedersen, Kanstrup, Maak, Dal Hende; Drachmann; Kroon, Romer (Uhre 63), Guira, Klove (Olesen 56); Bechmann (Ritter 76).
Stromsgodset: (433) Pettersen; Vilsvik, Madsen, Valsvik, Hamoud; Boateng, Abu, Junior; Kastrati (Parr 75), Pedersen, Keita.

Videoton (0) 2 *(Bodi 58, Suljic 90)*

Cukaricki (0) 0 1858

Videoton: (442) Kovacsik; Vinicius, Nego■, Patkai, Lang; Stopira, Bodi, Szolnoki, Barczi (Filipe Oliveira 81); Geresi (Feczesin 84), Suljic.
Cukaricki: (442) Stevanovic; Piasentin, Docic, Mandic (Jovanovic 56), Fofana; Kajevic (Matic 46), Jankovic N, Djuric, Zivkovic; Lagator, Knezevic.

Vojvodina (0) 1 *(Palocevic 86)*

Connah's Quay Nomads (0) 0 4276

Vojvodina: (4132) Kordic; Lakicevic (Jovancic 57), Miletic, Puskaric, Antic; Maksimovic; Palocevic, Meleg, Malbasic (Zlicic 82); Trujic, Babic (Asceric 57).
Connah's Quay Nomads: (4321) Danby; Baynes, Kearney, Horan, Smith; Woolfe, Harrison, Short; Owen J (Owen M 89), Morris; Wilde (Davies 81).

Zimbru Chisinau (1) 2 *(Zagaevschii 24, Damascan 62)*

Osmanlispor (1) 2 *(Curusku 12, Bekdemir 77)* 4160

Zimbru Chisinau: (442) Rusu; Diego Lima (Burghiu 74), Amancio Fortes (Rusnac 90), Zagaevschii, Erick; Luan, Bruno, Hugo Moreira, Damascan (Izaldo 85); Emerson, Jardan.
Osmanlispor: (442) Karcemarskas; Vrsajevic, Guven, Lawal (Rusescu 64), Webo (Bekdemir 76); Ndiaye, Prochazka, Umar, Delarge (Kilicaslan 87); Bayir, Curusku.

SECOND QUALIFYING ROUND SECOND LEG

Wednesday, 20 July 2016

Kapaz (0) 0

Admira Wacker Modling (1) 2 *(Knasmullner 17, Schmidt 76)* 1650

Kapaz: (442) Simaitis; Daniyev, Baybalaev (Javadov 46), Dario Junior, Rahimov; Gurbanov (Aliyev O 69), Akhundov, Aliyev S, Renan; Serginho (Qurbatov 82), Ebah.
Admira Wacker Modling: (442) Siebenhandl; Zwierschitz, Ebner, Lackner, Sax (Ayyildiz 54); Knasmullner (Fischerauer 75), Toth, Starkl (Schmidt 38), Pavic; Wostry, Bajrami.

Thursday, 21 July 2016

AEK Larnaca (1) 2 *(Boljevic 45, Tomas 48)*

Cliftonville (0) 0 2112

AEK Larnaca: (442) Mino; Mojsov (Alves 46), Catala, Jorge, Tomas; Tete (Ioannou 77), Trickovski (Englezou 68), Boljevic, Ortiz; Murillo, Charalambidis.
Cliftonville: (442) Mooney; McGovern, Ives, Bonner■, Curran (Murray M 74); Knowles, McDaid (Ramsey 14), Catney, Winchester (Garrett 55); Donnelly J, Cosgrove.

Brondby (0) 0

Hibernian (0) 1 *(Gray 62)* 11,548

Brondby: (4312) Ronnow; Larsson, Albrechtsen, Rocker, Crone; Hjulsager, Norgaard, Phiri (Corlu 102); Jakobsen (Holst 64); Wilczek, Pukki (Stuckler 114).
Hibernian: (532) Laidlaw; Gray (Boyle 77), McGregor, Hanlon, Fontaine, Stevenson; McGeouch, Bartley (Forster 104), McGinn; Holt, Cummings (Keatings 90).
aet; Brondby won 5-3 on penalties.

Buducnost Podgorica (2) 2 *(Djalovic 1, Raickovic 42)*

Genk (0) 0 4500

Buducnost Podgorica: (442) Dragojevic; Vukcevic N, Mirkovic, Radunovic, Raspopovic; Mitrovic, Raickovic (Hocko 64), Janketic (Pejakovic 53), Vujovic (Raicevic 92); Djalovic, Vusurovic.
Genk: (442) Bizot; Dewaest, Uronen, Castagne (Walsh 67), Ndidi; Buffel, Buyens (Heynen 46), Kumordzi■, Karelis (Wouters 75); Samatta, Bailey.
aet; Genk won 4-2 on penalties.

Connah's Quay Nomads (0) 1 *(Wilde 65)*

Vojvodina (1) 2 *(Meleg 8, 49 (pen))* 809

Connah's Quay Nomads: (442) Danby; Disney (Davies 55), Kearney, Horan, Smith; Baynes, Short, Morris, Owen J (Owen M 71); Woolfe, Wilde (Ruane 84).
Vojvodina: (442) Kordic; Kovacevic V, Puskaric, Antic, Miletic; Jovancic (Micic 68), Meleg (Zlicic 82), Palocevic, Malbasic; Trujic (Stamenic 73), Maksimovic.

Cork C (1) 1 *(O'Connor 26)*

Hacken (0) 0 5334

Cork C: (442) McNulty; Bennett, O'Connor, McSweeney, Browne; Bolger, Buckley, Dooley, Beattie; Morrissey G (Holohan 79), Maguire (O'Sullivan 90).
Hacken: (442) Abrahamsson; Sudic, Wahlstrom, Arkivuo, Schuller (Ericsson 64); Paulinho, Abubakari, Gustafsson, Andersson; Owoeri (Jeremejeff 74), Mohammed (Savage 45).

Cukaricki (1) 1 *(Fofana 13)*

Videoton (0) 1 *(Geresi 76)* 1653

Cukaricki: (442) Stevanovic; Jankovic N, Djuric, Zivkovic, Tomic; Fofana, Matic, Regan (Srnic 86), Docic (Radonjic 65); Masovic E, Masovic A (Mandic 65).
Videoton: (442) Kovacsik; Vinicius, Szolnoki, Stopira, Lang; Patkai, Barczi, Simon (Filipe Oliveira 79), Bodi; Suljic, Geresi (Feczesin 79).

Domzale (1) 2 *(Alvir 35, Majer 69)*

Shakhtyor Soligorsk (0) 1 *(Laptev 61)* 1800

Domzale: (442) Maraval; Horic, Brachi, Balkovec, Dobrovoljc; Horvat, Crnic (Repas 64), Majer (Zuzek 89), Alvir; Morel, Mance (Juninho 84).
Shakhtyor Soligorsk: (442) Bushma; Yurevich, Rybak (Osipenko 72), Kuzmyanok, Ignjatijevic; Burko, Shlbun (Laptev 46), Starhorodskyi, Kovalev; Elizarenko (Rudyka 77), Yanush.

Europa (0) 0

AIK Solna (0) 1 *(Markkanen 55)* 1145

Europa: (442) Javi Munoz; Merino, Vazquez, Moya, Toscano; Quillo (Joselinho 39), Roldan, Toni Garcia (Copi 67), Belfortti; Yahaya, Carrion.
AIK Solna: (442) Carlgren; Hooiveld, Johansson, Hauksson, Sundgren; Vaisanen (Kpozo 88), Blomberg, Affane (Ishizaki 46), Saletros; Ofori, Markkanen (Yasin 78).

Grasshoppers (1) 2 *(Sigurjonsson 45, 68)*

KR Reykjavik (0) 1 *(Beck Andersen 52)* 3940

Grasshoppers: (442) Mall; Luthi, Pnishi (Kallstrom 63), Lavanchy, Bamert; Caio (Gjorgjev 66), Sigurjonsson, Basic, Andersen (Kamberi 73); Brahimi, Munsy.
KR Reykjavik: (442) Magnusson; Gunnarsson, Sigurdsson, Josepsson, Hauksson (Tryggvason 81); Palmason, Margeirsson, Praest (Fazlagic 72), Chopart; Beck, Beck Andersen.

Hajduk Split (1) 2 *(Tudor 22, Ohandza 90)*

CSMS Iasi (1) 1 *(Ciucur 26)* 16,798

Hajduk Split: (442) Stipica; Nizic, Milic, Susic (Basic 60), Cosic; Kozulj, Jefferson (Bilyi 68), Vlasic, Juranovic; Tudor, Said (Ohandza 46).
CSMS Iasi: (442) Grahovac; Frasinescu, Voicu, Mitic, Ciucur (Florin Martin 62); Mihalache, Gheorghe (Cretu 76), Bole, Tiganasu; Cristea (Roman 81), Piccioni.

Hearts (0) 1 *(Sammon 74)*

Birkirkara (0) 2 *(Bubalovic 55, Herrera 67)* 14,301

Hearts: (343) Hamilton; Ozturk, Rherras, Igor Rossi (Muirhead 74); Smith (Delgado 57), Walker, Buaben (Cowie 81), Djoum; Nicholson, Sammon, Paterson.
Birkirkara: (4141) Kopric; Attard, Bubalovic, Emerson, Zerafa; Sciberras; Herrera, Scicluna (Camenzuli 90), Bajada (Jovic 66), Dimitrov (Guillaumier 73); Plut.

HJK Helsinki (1) 1 *(Tanaka 25)*

Beroe (0) 0 3872

HJK Helsinki: (442) Dahne; Taiwo (Sorsa 79), Jalasto, Rexhepi, Tatomirovic; Tanaka, Annan, Kamara (Dahlstrom 90), Alho; Oduamadi, Morelos.
Beroe: (442) Makendzhiev; Penev, Vasilev V, Ivanov, Milanov; Milisavljevic (Pedro Marques 65), Tom (Dryanov 84), Pochanski, Kato; Bozhilov, Kirilov (Kolev 84).

IFK Gothenburg (0) 0

Piast Gliwice (0) 0 7276

IFK Gothenburg: (442) Alvbage; Salomonsson, Aleesami, Albaek (Eriksson 69), Rieks (Ankersen 63); Hysen (Skold 78), Smedberg-Dalence, Engvall, Pettersson; Rogne, Bjarsmyr.
Piast Gliwice: (442) Rusov; Flis (Szeliga 69), Jankowski (Barisic 81), Moskwik, Maslowski (Murawski 73); Mak, Badia Cortes, Mokwa, Sedlar; Bukata, Korun.

Jelgava (1) 3 *(Kluskins 27 (pen), Bogdaskins 48, Malasenoks 85)*

Slovan Bratislava (0) 0 1560

Jelgava: (442) Ikstens; Bogdaskins, Freimanis, Savcenkovs, Redjko; Diallo■, Lazdins, Kluskins (Osipovs 65), Grigaravicius (Kovalovs 83); Nakano, Malasenoks (Smirnovs 90).
Slovan Bratislava: (442) Mucha; Salata, Ligeon, Burnet, Sekulic; Schet, Kubik (Priskin 50), Soumah, de Kamps (Lasik 72); Savicevic (Scott 72), Zrelak.

Kukesi (0) 1 *(Hallaci 78)*
Austria Vienna (1) 4 *(Kayode 16, 58, Holzhauser 67, Martschinko 90)* 1580
Kukesi: (442) Kolici; Hallaci, Mici, Malota, Shameti; Jean Carioca (Dvornekovic 46), Lilaj, Musolli, Latifi; Fukui (Guri 61), Rangel (Emini 33).
Austria Vienna: (442) Almer; Rotpuller, Larsen, Filipovic, Martschinko; Holzhauser (Vukojevic 79), Kahat, Serbest, Venuto; Kayode (Kvasina 70), Pires (Tajouri 79).

Levski Sofia (1) 1 *(Narh 22)*
Maribor (0) 1 *(Tavares 68)* 17,600
Levski Sofia: (442) Jorgacevic; Aleksandrov, Alexandrov, Minev, Pirgov; Prochazka, Kostadinov (Adeniji 79), de Nooijer, Hristov; Anete (Deza 86), Narh.
Maribor: (442) Handanovic; Suler, Janza, Sme, Hodzic; Kabha, Vrhovec (Vrsic 54), Hotic (Mertelj 76), Novakovic; Tavares, Bohar (Bajde 68).
Maribor won on away goals.

Lokomotiva Zagreb (1) 3 *(Fiolic 44, Maric 49, 83)*
RoPS Rovaniemi (0) 0 630
Lokomotiva Zagreb: (442) Filipovic; Prenga, Peric, Bartolec, Rozman; Grezda, Capan (Sunjic 71), Cekici (Bockaj 65), Coric (Antunovic 85); Fiolic, Maric.
RoPS Rovaniemi: (442) Hamalainen; Jammeh■, John, Kokko (Okkonen 45), Makitalo (Nganbe 62); Mravec (Lahdenmaki 75), Muinonen, Pirinen■, Reguero; Saksela, Taylor.

Maccabi Tel Aviv (1) 2 *(Ben Haim II 5, Alberman 86)*
Kairat Almaty (0) 1 *(Gohou 64)* 9832
Maccabi Tel Aviv: (442) Rajkovic; Ben Haim I, Tibi, Medunjanin (Filipenko 90), Alberman; Igiebor, Rikan, Micha, Peretz D (Dasa 69); Orlando Sa, Ben Haim II (Benayoun 75).
Kairat Almaty: (442) Plotnikov; Arzo (Kuantayev 80), Markovic, Suyumbayev, Tymoschuk; Bakaev, Acevedo (Kuat 46), Isael (Tawamba Kana 88), Arshavin; Gohou, Lunin.

Nomme Kalju (0) 1 *(Neemelo 90)*
Maccabi Haifa (1) 1 *(Rukavytsya 34 (pen))* 2273
Nomme Kalju: (442) Teles; Sidorenkov, Mool, Ugge, Rodrigues; Dmitrijev, Valikaev (Wakui 84), Toomet (Subbotin 71), Mbu Alidor; Quintieri (Neemelo 63), Purje.
Maccabi Haifa: (442) Levita; Valiente, Kagelmacher, Meshumar (Keinan 71), Lavi; Abu Abaid, Obraniak, Vermouth (Zenati 89), Menachem; Rukavytsya, Mugrabi (Gozlan 77).
aet; Nomme Kalju won 5-3 on penalties.

Odd (0) 3 *(Nordkvelle 55 (pen), Akabueze 57, Ruud 89)*
PAS Giannina (0) 1 *(Koutris 98)* 3184
Odd: (442) Rossbach; Ruud, Hagen, Semb Berge, Grogaard; Samuelsen (Berg 63), Nordkvelle (Messoudi 84), Jensen (Nilsen 101), Akabueze; Johansen, Zehninki.
PAS Giannina: (442) Paschalakis; Tzimopoulos, Fonsi, Michail, Berios; Karanikas, Lila, Acosta, Kozoronis (Donis 94); Giakos (Maboulou 79), Ferfelis (Koutris 66).
aet.

Omonia Nicosia (2) 3 *(Agaiev 26, Sheridan 45 (pen), Roushias 81)*
Beitar Jerusalem (2) 2 *(Atzili 17, 45 (pen))* 14,383
Omonia Nicosia: (442) Panagi; Bruno, Carlitos, Cleyton, Florescu; Orsulic, Margaca, Fylaktou (Soiledis 55), Agaiev (Toure 55); Derbyshire, Sheridan (Roushias 65).
Beitar Jerusalem: (442) Klaiman; Rueda, Mori, Magbo, Keltjens; Moyal (Rali 64), Claudemir, Einbinder, Atzili; Shechter (Abuhazira 78), Valpoort (Vered 58).
Beitar Jerusalem won on away goals.

Osmanlispor (2) 5 *(Umar 16 (pen), 26, 50, Kilicaslan 74, Rusescu 83)*
Zimbru Chisinau (0) 0 6382
Osmanlispor: (442) Karcemarskas; Prochazka, Vrsajevic, Tiago Pinto, Curusku; Guven, Cagiran (Bekdemir 14 (Kilicaslan 38)), Ndiaye, Webo (Rusescu 75); Delarge, Umar.
Zimbru Chisinau: (442) Rusu; Jardan, Emerson, Luan, Hugo Moreira; Erick (Spataru 46 (Jalo 76)), Diego Lima, Bruno, Amancio Fortes; Zagaevschii (Anton 57), Damascan.

Qabala (2) 2 *(Zenjov 7, Weeks 37)*
MTK Budapest (0) 0 5550
Qabala: (442) Bezotosnyi; Ricardinho, Vernydub, Stankovic (Rafael Santos 88), Sadiqov; Weeks, Kvekveskiri (Jamalov 79), Ozobic, Mirzabekov; Zenjov (Mammadov 77), Dabo.
MTK Budapest: (442) Hegedus; Vadnai, Grgic, Bese (Varga 78), Poor; Baki, Vass, Kanta (Borbely 73), Szatmari; Torghelle, Nikac (Hrepka 52).

Shkendija Tetovo (1) 1 *(Ibraimi 31)*
Neftchi (0) 0 9510
Shkendija Tetovo: (442) Zahov; Cuculi, Bejtulai, Alimi (Juffo 90), Todorovski; Hasani (Taipi 90), Vujcic, Demiri, Ibraimi (Polozani 87); Junior, Radeski.
Neftchi: (442) Santini; Shikov■, Isayev, Jairo, Melnjak; Abdullayev A, Haciyev (Imamverdiyev 80), Castillo, Agaev; Muradbayli (Qurbanli 85), Qurbanov (Mammadov 87).

Slavia Prague (1) 2 *(Skoda 10, Van Kessel 67)*
Levadia Tallinn (0) 0 14,856
Slavia Prague: (442) Pavlenka; Bilek (Ngadjui-Ngadjui 75), Boril, Mikula, Soucek; Husbauer, Kenia, Zmrhal (Mihalik 61), Deli; Skoda, Van Kessel (Barak 71).
Levadia Tallinn: (442) Lepmets; Morozov, Podholjuzin, Tabi, Luts; Kaljumae (Raudsepp 80), Antonov, Miranchuk, Gando; Kobzar (Gatagov 80), Hunt.

Spartak Trnava (0) 2 *(Schranz 57, Tambe 61)*
Shirak (0) 0 6129
Spartak Trnava: (442) Jakubech; Gressak, Godal, Kadlec, Hornik; Sloboda, Bello, Mikovic, Halilovic (Paukner 80); Schranz (Kostal 87), Tambe (Jirka 76).
Shirak: (442) Ayvazov; Hovanisian, Mikaelyan, Hovhannisyan (Davoyan 76), Darbinyan; Stoskovic (Ayvazyan 65), Hovsepyan (Poghosyan 65), Udo, Kaba; Diarrassouba, Kouakou.

St Patrick's Ath (0) 0
Dinamo Minsk (1) 1 *(Rassadkin 18)* 2400
St Patrick's Ath: (442) Clarke; O'Brien, Bermingham, Dennehy D, Hoare; Treacy, Byrne (Corcoran 90), Dennehy B, Kelly (Cawley 69); Fagan, Timlin (McGrath 62).
Dinamo Minsk: (442) Ignatovich; Ostroukh, Zhukouski (Shramchenko 79), Sverchinskiy, Bykov; Korytko, El Monir (Premudrov 90), Noyok, Kaplenko; Habovda, Rassadkin (Rotkovic 58).

Stromsgodset (2) 2 *(Keita 17, 45)*
SonderjyskE (0) 2 *(Uhre 69, Klove 120)* 3875
Stromsgodset: (442) Pettersen; Madsen, Hamoud, Valsvik, Vilsvik; Storflor (Kastrati 66), Keita (Parr 96), Abu, Junior (Moen 72); Boateng, Pedersen.
SonderjyskE: (442) Skender; Pedersen (Hedegaard 118), Kanstrup, Dal Hende, Maak; Drachmann, Absalonsen (Klove 71), Romer, Guira; Kroon, Uhre (Bechmann 80).
aet.

Torpedo Zhodino (1) 1 *(Demidovich 25)*
Debrecen (0) 0 2650
Torpedo Zhodino: (442) Fomichev; Pankavets, Chelyadzinsky, Lutsevich, Klopotskiy; Afanasyev (Bialevich 87), Khachaturyan, Demidovich, Golenkov (Chelyadko 66); Zagynaylov (Trapashko 78), Shapoval.
Debrecen: (442) Radosevic; Meszaros N, Korhut, Brkovic, Szakaly (Ferenczi 65); Varga, Jovanovic, Sekulic, Holman (Horvath 59); Tisza, Castillon (Takacs 57).

Vaduz (0) 2 *(Brunner 83, Costanzo 86 (pen))*
Midtjylland (1) 2 *(Sisto 41, 68)* 842
Vaduz: (442) Siegrist; Grippo, Strohmaier, Borgmann, Pfrunder; Muntwiler, Ciccone, Mathys (Burgmeier 80), Kukuruzovic (Hasler 65); Zarate (Brunner 65), Costanzo.
Midtjylland: (442) Dahlin; Halsti (Olsson 69), Hansen (Riis 57), Banggaard, Romer; Nissen, Poulsen■, Hassan, Sisto; Kadlec V, Onuachu (Duelund 57).

Ventspils (0) 0

Aberdeen (0) 1 *(Rooney 79)* 2100

Ventspils: (4231) Uvarenko; Boranijasevic, Kolesovs, Jemelins, Obuobi; Recickis (Alfa 86), Paulius; Rugins, Alekseev (Svarups 81), Sinelnikovs (Tidenbergs 65); Karlsons.
Aberdeen: (4231) Lewis; Logan, Taylor, Reynolds, Considine; Jack, Shinnie; McGinn (Stockley 71), McLean, Hayes (Storey 82); Rooney (Burns 80).

Zaglebie Lubin (0) 0

Partizan Belgrade (0) 0 11,279

Zaglebie Lubin: (442) Polacek; Guldan, Cotra, Dabrowski, Todorovski; Janoszka (Janus 74), Piatek L, Rakowski (Vlasko 61), Kubicki; Woznaik, Piatek K (Tosik 101).
Partizan Belgrade: (442) Saranov; Vulicevic, Bogosavac (Djurickovic 120), Gogoua, Milenkovic; Radovic (Ilic 91), Everton Bilher, Brasanac, Jankovic; Djudjic (Vlahovic 70), Mihajlovic.
aet; Zaglebie Lubin won 4-3 on penalties.

THIRD QUALIFYING ROUND FIRST LEG

Thursday, 28 July 2016

Aberdeen (0) 1 *(Hayes 88)*

Maribor (0) 1 *(Novakovic 83)* 17,105

Aberdeen: (442) Lewis; Logan, Taylor, Reynolds, Considine; McGinn, Jack, Shinnie (Burns 72), Hayes; Stockley (McLean 72), Rooney.
Maribor: (4141) Handanovic; Sme, Defendi, Suler, Janza; Vrhovec (Pihler 68); Vrsic (Bajde 84), Tavares, Kabha, Hotic (Bohar 46); Novakovic.

Admira Wacker Modling (1) 1 *(Knasmullner 7)*

Slovan Liberec (1) 2 *(Vuch 11, 69)* 2245

Admira Wacker Modling: (4411) Kuttin; Zwierschitz, Strauss, Wostry, Ebner; Lackner, Toth (Spiridonovic 60), Sax, Knasmullner; Bajrami (Vastic■ 60); Starkl.
Slovan Liberec: (4141) Dubravka; Coufal, Hovorka, Pokorny, Sykora; Breite; Vuch (Navratil 88), Folprecht, Sevcik, Bartl (Nitriansky 80); Komlichenko (Baros 60).

AEK Larnaca (0) 1 *(Alves 65)*

Spartak Moscow (1) 1 *(Ananidze 38)* 4323

AEK Larnaca: (442) Mino; Mojsov, Catala, Charalambous (Ioannou 84), Jorge; Tete (Charalambidis 76), Boljevic, Tomas, Trickovski; Ortiz, Alves.
Spartak Moscow: (442) Rebrov; Eshchenko, Kombarov, Kutepov, Bocchetti; Ananidze (Melkadze 72), Glushakov, Zobnin, Popov (Zuev 59); Promes, Ze Luis.

Austria Vienna (0) 0

Spartak Trnava (0) 1 *(Tambe 46)* 6835

Austria Vienna: (442) Almer; Filipovic, Venuto, Serbest, Larsen; Kahat (Grunwald 61), Holzhauser, Martschinko, Rotpuller; Pires (Tajouri 72), Kayode (Friesenbicher 85).
Spartak Trnava: (442) Jakubech; Kadlec, Hornik, Bello, Mikovic (Privat 88); Godal, Sloboda, Schranz, Halilovic (Jirka 61); Tambe (Paukner 72), Gressak.

AZ Alkmaar (1) 1 *(Luckassen 36)*

PAS Giannina (0) 0 9156

AZ Alkmaar: (433) Rochet; Johansson, Luckassen, Vlaar, Haps; van Overeem (Seuntjens 87), Henriksen, Wuytens; Jahanbakhsh (Garcia 63), Weghorst (Fred Friday 63), dos Santos Souza.
PAS Giannina: (532) Paschalakis; Karanikas, Tzimopoulos, Berios, Michail, Fonsi; Kozoronis (Koutris 61), Lila, Acosta; Giakos (Donis 74), Ferfelis (Maboulou 50).

Birkirkara (0) 0

Krasnodar (1) 3 *(Granqvist 45, Smolov 75 (pen), Laborde 89)* 1560

Birkirkara: (541) Kopric; Scicluna■, Attard, Emerson, Bubalovic, Zerafa; Djordjevic (Andjelkovic 62), Dimitrov (Guillaumier 83), Bajada (Temile 62), Sciberras; Plut.
Krasnodar: (433) Kritsyuk; Jedrzejczyk, Strandberg, Granqvist, Torbinski; Ahmedov (Joaozinho 83), Gazinski, Izmailov; Pereyra (Laborde 64), Smolov, Ari (Wanderson 76).

Domzale (1) 2 *(Crnic 11 (pen), 49)*

West Ham U (1) 1 *(Noble 18 (pen))* 8458

Domzale: (451) Maraval; Brachi, Horic, Dobrovoljc, Balkovec; Morel (Repas 77), Alvir, Horvat, Majer (Vetrih 85), Crnic (Juninho 90); Mance.
West Ham U: (451) Adrian; Antonio (Quina 80), Nordtveit, Reid, Byram; Feghouli, Kouyate, Noble, Obiang, Valencia; Carroll.

Genk (1) 1 *(Bailey 31)*

Cork C (0) 0 7765

Genk: (442) Bizot; Walsh, Dewaest, Wouters, Ndidi; Uronen, Buffel, Pozuelo (Heynen 82), Samatta; Karelis (Kebano 73), Bailey.
Cork C: (442) McNulty; O'Connor, Bennett, Browne, Bolger; Dooley, McSweeney, Maguire (O'Sullivan 86), Buckley; Morrissey G, Beattie (Morrissey D 83).

Grasshoppers (1) 2 *(Tabakovic 11, Lavanchy 90)*

Apollon Limassol (0) 1 *(Guie Guie 76)* 2330

Grasshoppers: (4321) Mall; Luthi, Bamert, Pnishi, Antonov; Basic, Kallstrom, Sigurjonsson; Andersen (Brahimi 77), Kamberi (Lavanchy 71); Tabakovic (Munsy 46).
Apollon Limassol: (442) Bruno Vale; Vasiliou, Vinicius, Angeli, Pittas (Sachetti■ 63); Stylianou, Alex, Kyriakou, Joao Pedro; Guie Guie (Maglica 83), Bedoya (Barbaro 90).

Heracles Almelo (0) 1 *(Gladon 53)*

Arouca (0) 1 *(Gege 90)* 11,670

Heracles Almelo: (433) Castro; Breukers, te Wierik (Propper 74), Zomer, Gosens; Pelupessy, Bruns, Bel Hassani; Kuwas, Gladon, Navratil (Darri 81).
Arouca: (433) Rafael Bracali; Gege, Jubal Junior, Hugo Basto, Nelsinho; Adilson Goiano (Andre Santos 55), Nuno Coelho, Artur Moreira (Pintassilgo 50); Mateus, Gonzalez, Zequinha (Rafael Crivellaro 88).

Hertha Berlin (1) 1 *(Ibisevic 28)*

Brondby (0) 0 18,454

Hertha Berlin: (442) Jarstein; Pekarik, Skjelbred, Darida, Langkamp; Plattenhardt, Weiser, Brooks, Lustenberger (Stark 90); Kalou (Haraguchi 73), Ibisevic (Schieber 87).
Brondby: (442) Ronnow; Rocker, Albrechtsen, Holst (Mukhtar 58), Larsson; Phiri, Norgaard (Austin 78), Hjulsager, Crone; Wilczek (Jakobsen 84), Pukki.

IFK Gothenburg (0) 1 *(Salomonsson 73)*

HJK Helsinki (0) 2 *(Tanaka 47, Morelos 75)* 9046

IFK Gothenburg: (442) Alvbage; Salomonsson, Bjarsmyr (Jonsson 46), Rogne, Aleesami; Albaek, Eriksson, Smedberg-Dalence (Lagemyr 65), Hysen (Engvall 79); Rieks, Ankersen.
HJK Helsinki: (4231) Dahne; Sorsa, Tatomirovic, Rexhepi, Jalasto; Annan, Medo; Gadze (Malolo 87), Tanaka (Kolehmainen 77), Alho; Morelos.

Istanbul Basaksehir (0) 0

Rijeka (0) 0 5768

Istanbul Basaksehir: (442) Babacan; Ayhan, Epureanu, Ucar, Emre; Albayrak, Visca, Tekdemir, Holmen (Mossoro 59); Doka Madureira (Under 76), Batdal (Cikalleshi 85).
Rijeka: (442) Prskalo; Ristovski, Zuta, Mitrovic, Tomasov (Misic 80); Elaz, Males, Bradaric, Vesovic (Handzic 86); Gavranovic (Matei 61), Bezjak.

Jelgava (0) 1 *(Smirnovs 70)*

Beitar Jerusalem (1) 1 *(Vered 25)* 2886

Jelgava: (442) Ikstens; Savcenkovs, Smirnovs, Freimanis, Nakano; Redjko (Osipovs 28), Bogdaskins, Grigaravicius (Kovalovs 71), Kluskins (Pereplotkins 55); Lazdins, Malasenoks.
Beitar Jerusalem: (442) Klaiman; Rueda, Mori, Atzili, Einbinder; Claudemir, Cohen (Abuhazira 73), Rali (Benish 69), Magbo; Vered, Shechter (Heister 80).

KAA Gent (2) 5 *(Mitrovic 16, Coulibaly 37, 50, Depoitre 56, Renato Neto 66)*

Viitorul Constanta (0) 0 12,332

KAA Gent: (442) Rinne; Matton (Milicevic 65), Renato Neto, Mitrovic, Kums (Schoofs R 76); Saief, Nielsen, Foket, Gershon; Coulibaly, Depoitre (Perbet 69).
Viitorul Constanta: (442) Rimniceanu; Filip (Hodorogea 46), Benzar, Tanase, Iancu (Nedelcu 46); Ionut Tiru, Marin, Ganea, Chitu; Purece, Carp (Casap 70).

Lille (0) 1 *(Mendes 47)*

Qabala (1) 1 *(Vernydub 13)* 8265

Lille: (451) Enyeama; Corchia, Civelli, Basa, Palmieri; Mavuba (Amadou 62), Amalfitano, Obbadi (Benzia 27), Lopes, Mendes (Bissouma 76); Bautheac.
Qabala: (4141) Bezotosnyi; Mirzabekov, Vernydub, Stankovic (Rafael Santos 76), Ricardinho; Sadiqov; Zenjov (Mammadov 81), Weeks, Kvekveskiri, Ozobic; Dabo (Eyyubov 90).

Lokomotiva Zagreb (0) 0

Vorskla (0) 0 328

Lokomotiva Zagreb: (451) Radelic-Zarkov; Bartolec, Majstorovic, Peric, Rozman; Grezda (Cekici 89), Coric, Capan (Sunjic 81), Ivanusec, Fiolic; Maric (Radonjic 67).
Vorskla: (4231) Shust; Siminin (Sapai 72), Dytiatiev, Chesnakov, Perduta; Thachuk, Sklyar; Kobakhidze, Zarichnyuk (Kolomoets 56), Rebenok (Bartulovic 66); Khlyobas.

Luzern (1) 1 *(Schneuwly M 8)*

Sassuolo (1) 1 *(Berardi 42 (pen))* 10,555

Luzern: (442) Zibung; Hyka (Grether 54), Ricardo Costa, Puljic, Lustenberger; Neumayr, Schneuwly C, Jantscher, Haas; Itten (Juric 63), Schneuwly M.
Sassuolo: (433) Consigli; Gazzola, Cannavaro, Acerbi, Peluso; Biondini, Magnanelli, Duncan; Berardi (Mazzitelli 90), Defrel, Sansone (Politano 72).

Oleksandriya (0) 0

Hajduk Split (0) 3 *(Cosic 53, Erceg 82, Ohandza 90)* 6800

Oleksandriya: (451) Levanidov; Mikitsey, Basov, Gitchenko, Shendrik; Zhychykov (Leonov 77), Banada, Zaporoshan, Ponomar, Kozak (Hrytsuk 73); Kulish (Yaremchuk 62).
Hajduk Split: (451) Kalinic; Juranovic, Cosic, Nizic, Milic; Susic, Kozulj, Bilyi (Basic 64), Jefferson, Vlasic (Erceg 71); Said (Ohandza 68).

Osmanlispor (0) 1 *(Tiago Pinto 74)*

Nomme Kalju (0) 0 8634

Osmanlispor: (433) Karcemarskas; Prochazka, Tiago Pinto, Curusku, Vrsajevic; Guven, Ndiaye, Webo (Diabate 81); Kilicaslan (Rusescu 71), Umar, Delarge (Lawal 89).
Nomme Kalju: (451) Teles; Ugge, Sidorenkov, Rodrigues, Mbu Alidor; Purje (Neemelo 67), Toomet (Puri 75), Valikaev, Mool, Quintieri (Subbotin 64); Dmitrijev.

Panathinaikos (0) 1 *(Rodrigo Moledo 79)*

AIK Solna (0) 0 12,021

Panathinaikos: (343) Steele; Koutroubis (Villafanez 46), Ibarbo (Lod 87), Berg; Zeca, Wakaso (Leto 71), Hult, Ledesma; Mesto, Rodrigo Moledo, Ivanov.
AIK Solna: (442) Carlgren; Hauksson, Karlsson, Johansson, Blomberg; Avdic (Saletros 87), Markkanen, Ofori, Sundgren; Ishizaki (Yasin 65), Kpozo.

Pandurii Targu Jiu (1) 1 *(Herea 30)*

Maccabi Tel Aviv (1) 3 *(Ben Haim II 7, Igiebor 49, Micha 77)* 4058

Pandurii Targu Jiu: (4231) Stanca; Bunoza, Vasiljevic, Voiculet, Hora; Herea (Buijs 62), Ungurusan; Grecu, Mrzljak (Obodo 62), Pleasca (Trifu 80); Rauta.
Maccabi Tel Aviv: (433) Rajkovic; Medunjanin (Peretz E 68), Alberman, Ben Haim II, Micha; Tibi, Filipenko, Rikan; Igiebor (Itzhaki 79), Peretz D, Orlando Sa (Ben Basat 75).

Saint-Etienne (0) 0

AEK Athens (0) 0 30,438

Saint-Etienne: (433) Ruffier; Theophile-Catherine, Perrin, Pogba, Polomat; Pajot (Dabo 69), Selnaes, Lemoine; Tannane (Beric 64), Roux, Hamouma (Monnet-Paquet 86).
AEK Athens: (4231) Anestis; Rodrigo Galo, Chygrynskiy, Kolovetsios, Didac; Johansson, Andre Simoes; Vargas (Galanopoulos 67), Mantalos (Platellas 82), Helder Barbosa; Pekhart (Bakasetas 46).

Shkendija Tetovo (0) 2 *(Junior 69, Hasani 75)*

Mlada Boleslav (0) 0 11,717

Shkendija Tetovo: (442) Zahov; Bejtulai, Cuculi, Alimi (Juffo 66), Ibraimi (Imeri 81); Radeski (Taipi 46), Demiri, Todorovski, Vujcic; Hasani, Junior.
Mlada Boleslav: (442) Divis; Fleisman, Pauschek, Hulka■, Kalabiska; Kudela, Rada, Janos, Vukadinovic; Mebrahtu (Chramostra 46 (Kerestes 59)), Magera (Takacs 82).

Slavia Prague (0) 0

Rio Ave (0) 0 15,082

Slavia Prague: (4231) Pavlenka; Mikula, Deli, Bilek, Boril; Husbauer, Soucek; Van Kessel, Kenia (Scuk 81), Mihalik (Zmrhal 60); Skoda.
Rio Ave: (4312) Cassio; Cassama, Roderick Miranda, Marcelo, Rafa; Joao Novais, Wakaso, Ruben Ribeiro (Tarantini 82); Krovinovic (Helder Guedes 69); Gil Dias, Yazalde (Heldon 59).

Torpedo Zhodino (0) 0

Rapid Vienna (0) 0 3940

Torpedo Zhodino: (442) Fomichev; Chelyadzinsky, Afanasyev (Shcherbo 87), Klopotskiy, Pankavets; Shapoval, Khachaturyan, Lutsevich, Zagynaylov (Golenkov 71); Imerekov, Demidovich (Bialevich 90).
Rapid Vienna: (451) Novota; Schosswendter, Schrammel, Dibon, Pavelic; Schobesberger (Traustason 70), Schwab, Schaub, Grahovac, Murg (Mocinic 85); Joelinton.

Videoton (0) 0

Midtjylland (0) 1 *(Novak 55)* 2899

Videoton: (4231) Kovacsik; Szolnoki, Stopira, Nego, Lang; Bodi (Oliveira 61), Geresi (Barczi 83); Patkai, Suljic, Lazovic (Feczesin 46); Vinicius.
Midtjylland: (4141) Dahlin; Banggaard, Halsti, Hansen, Hassan; Kadlec V (Romer 71); Nissen, Novak, Olsson, Onuachu; Sisto (Duelund 88).

Vojvodina (1) 1 *(Babic 29)*

Dinamo Minsk (0) 1 *(Bykov 83)* 8346

Vojvodina: (451) Kordic; Kovacevic V, Meleg, Puskaric, Palocevic (Zlicic 87); Babic, Antic, Malbasic (Trifunovic 71), Maksimovic, Miletic; Trujic (Jovancic 79).
Dinamo Minsk: (343) Ignatovich; Ostroukh, Bykov, Korytko; Zhukouski (Karpovich 64), El Monir (Shramchenko 84), Noyok, Habovda; Kantsavy, Sverchinskiy, Rotkovic (Budnik 64).

Zaglebie Lubin (1) 1 *(Janoszka 45)*

SonderjyskE (2) 2 *(Kroon 19, Dal Hende 36)* 10,271

Zaglebie Lubin: (442) Polacek; Dabrowski, Cotra, Todorovski, Guldan; Kubicki, Vlasko (Starzynski 46), Woznaik, Janoszka (Janus 73); Piatek K (Papadopulos 79), Piatek L.
SonderjyskE: (442) Skender; Pedersen, Kanstrup, Maak, Kroon (Klove 68); Drachmann, Guira, Romer (Madsen 74), Dal Hende; Bechmann (Uhre 64), Absalonsen.

THIRD QUALIFYING ROUND SECOND LEG

Wednesday, 3 August 2016

Slovan Liberec (2) 2 *(Coufal 20, Komlichenko 34 (pen))*

Admira Wacker Modling (0) 0 6125

Slovan Liberec: (451) Dubravka; Coufal, Hovorka, Pokorny, Sykora; Vuch, Folprecht, Breite, Sevcik (Lesniak 83), Bartl (Navratil 76); Komlichenko (Baros 62).

Admira Wacker Modling: (4231) Kuttin; Zwierschitz, Strauss, Wostry, Posch; Lackner (Roguljic 88), Ebner; Bajrami, Knasmullner, Spiridonovic; Starkl (Grozurek 62).

Thursday, 4 August 2016

AEK Athens (0) 0

Saint-Etienne (1) 1 *(Beric 23)* 25,004

AEK Athens: (4411) Anestis; Rodrigo Galo, Chygrynskiy, Kolovetsios, Didac; Helder Barbosa (Aravidis 61), Lampropoulos, Andre Simoes (Almeida 67), Vargas (Platellas 53); Mantalos; Bakasetas.
Saint-Etienne: (451) Ruffier; Theophile-Catherine, Perrin, Pogba, Polomat; Hamouma (Roux 84), Dabo (Pajot 30), Selnaes, Lemoine (Monnet-Paquet 79), Tannane; Beric.

AIK Solna (0) 0

Panathinaikos (0) 2 *(Ibarbo 46, Berg 73)* 15,175

AIK Solna: (523) Carlgren; Hauksson, Karlsson, Hooiveld, Johansson, Sundgren; Ofori, Blomberg (Yasin 61); Affane (Avdic 62), Ishizaki (Saletros 78), Markkanen.
Panathinaikos: (3142) Steele; Koutroubis, Ivanov, Rodrigo Moledo; Ledesma (Nano 67); Mesto, Zeca, Lod (Villafanez 84), Wakaso; Ibarbo (Leto 70), Berg.

Apollon Limassol (0) 3 *(Vinicius 73, Papoulis 87, Guie Guie 101)*

Grasshoppers (0) 3 *(Andersen 77, Caio 103, Gjorgjev 120)* 5887

Apollon Limassol: (4321) Bruno Vale; Stylianou, Angeli, Vinicius, Vasiliou (Dudu Paraiba 84); Pedro Silva, Maglica (Piech 39), Kyriakou (Papoulis 68); Alex, Guie Guie; Bedoya.
Grasshoppers: (343) Mall; Luthi, Bamert, Pnishi; Lavanchy, Basic, Kallstrom (Gjorgjev 91), Andersen; Caio, Munsy (Tabakovic 86), Sigurjonsson (Brahimi 90).
aet.

Arouca (0) 0

Heracles Amelo (0) 0 2750

Arouca: (4132) Rafael Bracali; Gege, Jubal Junior, Hugo Basto, Anderson Luis; Nuno Coelho; Nuno Valente (Adilson Goiano 90), Andre Santos (De Jesus 78), Mateus; Gonzalez (Rafael Crivellaro 69), Zequinha.
Heracles Amelo: (4132) Castro; Breukers, te Wierik, Zomer (Hoogma 46), Gosens; Pelupessy; Bruns (Propper 82), Bel Hassani, Kuwas (Van Mieghem 61); Gladon, Navratil.
Arouca won on away goals.

Beitar Jerusalem (2) 3 *(Atzili 16 (pen), Shechter 29, Heister 47)*

Jelgava (0) 0 16,175

Beitar Jerusalem: (433) Klaiman; Rali, Mori, Rueda, Heister (Magbo 57); Vered (Abuhazira 76), Einbinder, Claudemir; Atzili, Shechter, Cohen (Keltjens 66).
Jelgava: (442) Ikstens; Freimanis, Smirnovs, Savcenkovs, Osipovs; Grigaravicius (Labanovskis 71), Lazdins, Nakano, Bogdaskins; Kluskins (Malasenoks 63), Pereplotkins (Kovalovs 54).

Brondby (2) 3 *(Pukki 3, 34, 52)*

Hertha Berlin (1) 1 *(Ibisevic 30)* 17,102

Brondby: (4312) Ronnow; Larsson, Albrechtsen, Rocker, Crone; Phiri, Norgaard (Austin 76), Hjulsager; Mukhtar (Jakobsen 67); Pukki (Urena 76), Wilczek.
Hertha Berlin: (433) Kraft; Pekarik (Stocker 84), Langkamp, Brooks, Plattenhardt; Skjelbred (Stark 62), Darida, Lustenberger (Allagui 62); Weiser, Ibisevic, Kalou.

Cork C (0) 1 *(Bennett 63)*

Genk (2) 2 *(Buffel 13, Dewaest 41)* 6745

Cork C: (433) McNulty; McSweeney (Morrissey D 46), Browne, Bennett, O'Connor; Morrissey G (O'Sullivan 46), Bolger, Buckley; Beattie, Maguire (Sheppard 56), Dooley.
Genk: (4411) Bizot; Walsh, Dewaest, Wouters, Uronen; Buffel (Tshimanga 83), Pozuelo, Ndidi, Bailey (Trossard 65); Kebano; Samatta (Heynen 77).

Dinamo Minsk (0) 0

Vojvodina (1) 2 *(Babic 32, Antic 81)* 7500

Dinamo Minsk: (442) Ignatovich; Ostroukh, Karpovich, Sverchinskiy, Bykov; Budnik (Rotkovic 84), Korytko (Zhukouski 70), El Monir■, Noyok; Habovda, Kontsevoi.
Vojvodina: (442) Kordic; Kovacevic V, Puskaric, Meleg (Jovancic 85), Palocevic; Babic (Trifunovic 74), Trujic (Micic 84), Malbasic, Maksimovic; Antic, Miletic.

Hajduk Split (1) 3 *(Nizic 21, Susic 52 (pen), 56)*

Oleksandriya (1) 1 *(Starenkiy 13)* 25,000

Hajduk Split: (4411) Kalinic; Juranovic, Cosic, Nizic, Milic; Susic (Tudor 77), Jefferson, Bilyi (Basic 61), Vlasic; Kozulj; Said (Ohandza 66).
Oleksandriya: (442) Novak; Mikitsey, Gitchenko, Shendrik, Tsurikov; Kozak, Banada, Myagkov, Starenkiy (Putrash 57); Yaremchuk (Kulish 73), Ponomar (Hrytsuk 46).

HJK Helsinki (0) 0

IFK Gothenburg (1) 2 *(Boman 35, Ankersen 82)* 10,107

HJK Helsinki: (442) Dahne; Sorsa, Tatomirovic, Halme, Jalasto; Alho, Annan, Medo, Gadze (Kolehmainen 67); Oduamadi, Morelos.
IFK Gothenburg: (442) Alvbage; Salomonsson, Bjarsmyr, Rogne, Aleesami; Smedberg-Dalence (Pettersson 86), Albaek, Eriksson, Ankersen; Boman, Rieks.

Krasnodar (3) 3 *(Eboue 15, Joaozinho 37, Laborde 38)*

Birkirkara (0) 1 *(Jovic 61)* 7256

Krasnodar: (433) Sinitsyn; Bystrov, Martynovich, Strandberg, Petrov; Torbinski (Pereyra 79), Kabore (Gazinski 69), Eboue; Laborde (Ari 40), Wanderson, Joaozinho.
Birkirkara: (433) Kopric; Attard, Bubalovic, Emerson (Temile 46), Zerafa; Andjelkovic, Bajada (Jovic 46), Sciberras; Dimitrov (Djordjevic 77), Plut, Herrera.

Maccabi Tel Aviv (1) 2 *(Igiebor 24, Benayoun 80)*

Pandurii Targu Jiu (0) 1 *(Pleasca 57)* 8126

Maccabi Tel Aviv: (442) Rajkovic; Dasa, Tibi, Filipenko, Medunjanin; Benayoun (Ben Basat 82), Alberman (Scarione 59), Micha, Rikan; Igiebor, Orlando Sa (Itzhaki 72).
Pandurii Targu Jiu: (442) Lazar; Pleasca, Bunoza, Vasiljevic, Buijs (Trifu 71); Munteanu (Voiculet 46), Herea, Pitian, Mrzljak; Pircalabu (Grecu 79), Rauta.

Maribor (0) 1 *(Shinnie 90 (og))*

Aberdeen (0) 0 9796

Maribor: (4231) Handanovic; Sme, Suler, Defendi, Janza; Pihler (Kabha 77), Vrhovec; Vrsic (Sallalich 88), Tavares, Bohar (Bajde 73); Novakovic.
Aberdeen: (433) Lewis; Logan, Reynolds, Taylor, Considine; Jack, McLean (Storey 66), Shinnie; McGinn (Wright 84), Rooney, Burns (Stockley■ 51).

Midtjylland (0) 1 *(Novak 104)*

Videoton (0) 1 *(Kovacs 75)* 6258

Midtjylland: (4141) Dahlin; Nissen, Hansen, Banggaard, Novak; Halsti; Kadlec V (Duelund 69), Olsson (Larsen 109), Romer (Pusic 80), Hassan; Onuachu.
Videoton: (4411) Kovacsik; Nego, Vinicius■, Lang, Stopira (Bodi 12); Juhasz, Szolnoki, Patkai, Barczi; Kovacs (Suljic 91); Geresi (Feczesin 67).
aet.

Mlada Boleslav (0) 1 *(Magera 82)*

Shkendija Tetovo (0) 0 3528

Mlada Boleslav: (442) Divis; Fleisman, Douglas., Janos, Kalabiska (Kerestes 61); Kudela, Chramostra, Pauschek (Mebrahtu 46), Rada; Vukadinovic (Takacs 69), Magera.
Shkendija Tetovo: (442) Zahov; Bejtulai, Alimi (Polozani 54), Cuculi, Ibraimi; Hasani, Radeski (Taipi 75), Demiri, Todorovski; Vujcic, Junior (Bojku 85).

Nomme Kalju (0) 0

Osmanlispor (2) 2 *(Curusku 4, Delarge 29)* 2235

Nomme Kalju: (4411) Teles; Mool, Rodrigues, Ugge, Sidorenkov; Toomet (Subbotin 46), Mbu Alidor, Dmitrijev, Quintieri (Neemelo 63); Valikaev (Wakui 79); Purje.
Osmanlispor: (433) Karcemarskas; Vrsajevic, Curusku, Prochazka, Tiago Pinto; Ndiaye (Lawal 54), Guven, Kilicaslan; Umar (Diabate 70), Rusescu (Kacar 79), Delarge.

PAS Giannina (1) 1 *(Conde 9)*

AZ Alkmaar (2) 2 *(dos Santos Souza 29, Luckassen 36)* 3373

PAS Giannina: (532) Paschalakis; Lila, Berios, Michail, Fonsi, Conde; Tzimopoulos (Skondras 46), Acosta, Karanikas; Kozoronis (Donis 78), Giakos (Maboulou 51).
AZ Alkmaar: (433) Rochet; Van Eijden, Vlaar, Haps, Luckassen; van Overeem (Til 71), Henriksen, dos Santos Souza (Garcia 79); Wuytens, Jahanbakhsh, Weghorst.

Qabala (1) 1 *(Ozobic 34)*

Lille (0) 0 10,550

Qabala: (433) Bezotosnyi; Mirzabekov, Vernydub, Stankovic, Ricardinho; Kvekveskiri, Sadiqov, Weeks; Ozobic (Mammadov 77), Dabo, Zenjov.
Lille: (433) Enyeama; Corchia, Civelli, Soumaoro, Palmieri; Obbadi (Sankhare 64), Amadou, Amalfitano (Benzia 73); Lopes, Eder, Bautheac (Mendes 64).

Rapid Vienna (2) 3 *(Pavelic 26, Schrammel 36, Schaub 90)*

Torpedo Zhodino (0) 0 18,600

Rapid Vienna: (442) Novota; Schosswendter, Schrammel, Schaub, Dibon; Pavelic, Schwab, Traustason (Grahovac 68), Mocinic (Szanto 80); Murg, Joelinton (Schobesberger 71).
Torpedo Zhodino: (442) Fomichev; Chelyadzinsky, Afanasyev (Chelyadko 66), Klopotskiy, Pankavets (Shcherbo 46); Shapoval, Khachaturyan, Lutsevich, Zagynaylov (Trapashko 57); Imerekov, Demidovich.

Rijeka (1) 2 *(Bezjak 25, 50 (pen))*

Istanbul Basaksehir (1) 2 *(Visca 42, 74)* 5524

Rijeka: (442) Prskalo; Ristovski (Canadjija 90), Mitrovic, Elaz, Zuta; Vesovic (Matei 67), Males, Misic (Handzic 83), Tomasov; Gavranovic, Bezjak.
Istanbul Basaksehir: (433) Babacan; Ucar (Alkilic 64), Ayhan, Epureanu, Albayrak; Tekdemir, Mossoro (Holmen 84), Emre; Visca, Batdal, Doka Madureira (Under 64).
Istanbul Basaksehir won on away goals.

Rio Ave (0) 1 *(Ruben Ribeiro 57)*

Slavia Prague (1) 1 *(Husbauer 22)* 6081

Rio Ave: (442) Cassio; Cassama■, Roderick Miranda, Marcelo, Krovinovic (Pedrinho 46); Joao Novais (Heldon 61), Wakaso, Gil Dias, Ruben Ribeiro; Rafa, Yazalde (Tarantini 46).
Slavia Prague: (442) Pavlenka; Mikula, Ngadjui-Ngadjui (Barak 90), Boril, Bilek; Zmrhal (Mihalik 90), Husbauer, Deli, Soucek; Skoda, Van Kessel (Scuk 66).
Slavia Prague won on away goals.

Sassuolo (2) 3 *(Berardi 19, 39 (pen), Defrel 64)*

Luzern (0) 0 13,415

Sassuolo: (451) Consigli; Gazzola, Acerbi, Cannavaro, Peluso; Berardi (Politano 73), Biondini (Sensi 72), Magnanelli, Duncan, Sansone; Defrel (Falcinelli 82).
Luzern: (4411) Zibung; Schneuwly C, Ricardo Costa■, Puljic (Sarr 11), Lustenberger; Hyka (Joao Oliveira 72), Haas, Kryeziu, Jantscher; Neumayr (Arnold 72); Schneuwly M.

SonderjyskE (0) 1 *(Pedersen 65)*

Zaglebie Lubin (1) 1 *(Janus 22)* 4795

SonderjyskE: (442) Skender; Pedersen, Kroon (Klove 76), Dal Hende, Drachmann; Bechmann (Uhre 81), Guira, Kanstrup, Romer; Maak, Absalonsen.
Zaglebie Lubin: (442) Polacek; Dabrowski, Cotra, Todorovski, Janus (Janoszka 67); Starzynski, Kubicki, Piatek K (Papadopulos 72), Guldan; Vlasko (Tosik 85), Piatek L.

Spartak Moscow (0) 0

AEK Larnaca (0) 1 *(Trickovski 89)* 24,017

Spartak Moscow: (442) Rebrov; Kutepov, Kombarov, Bocchetti, Eshchenko (Melgarejo 90); Ananidze (Glushakov 46), Fernando, Zobnin (Romulo 68), Makeev; Ze Luis, Promes.
AEK Larnaca: (433) Mino; Murillo (Charalambidis 81), Mojsov, Catala, Jorge; Tomas, Tete (Englezou 88), Boljevic (Acoran 84); Ortiz, Trickovski, Alves.

Spartak Trnava (0) 0

Austria Vienna (0) 1 *(Friesenbicher 88)* 17,152

Spartak Trnava: (4411) Jakubech; Kadlec, Gressak, Godal, Hornik; Schranz, Bello, Sloboda, Mikovic; Halilovic (Jirka 97); Tambe (Hladik 79).
Austria Vienna: (4411) Almer; Larsen, Filipovic, Rotpuller, Martschinko; Venuto (Kvasina 86), Holzhauser (Friesenbicher 71), Serbest, Pires (Tajouri 71); Grunwald; Kayode.
aet; Austria Vienna win 5-4 on penalties.

Viitorul Constanta (0) 0

KAA Gent (0) 0 1294

Viitorul Constanta: (433) Buzbuchi; Radoi, Carp, Casap (Marin 65), Nedelcu; Iancu (Dumitrescu 77), Lopez, Brandan; Rusu (Tanase 46), Hodorogea, Nimley.
KAA Gent: (442) Thoelen; Gershon, Mitrovic (Nielsen 46), Horemans, Renato Neto (Schoofs L 64); Saief, Schoofs R, Perbet, Foket (Ndongala 72); Kujovic, Milicevic.

Vorskla (0) 2 *(Peric 49 (og), Chesnakov 74)*

Lokomotiva Zagreb (1) 3 *(Bockaj 1, Fiolic 53, Peric 64)* 12,000

Vorskla: (442) Shust; Perduta, Sklyar (Golodyuk 70), Kobakhidze, Thachuk; Bartulovic, Khlyobas (Zarichnyuk 74), Chesnakov, Sapai (Rebenok 60); Kolomoets, Dytiatiev.
Lokomotiva Zagreb: (442) Radelic-Zarkov; Bartolec, Rozman, Maric (Radonjic 65), Fiolic (Sunjic 81); Peric, Coric, Grezda, Capan; Bockaj (Cekici 68), Majstorovic.

West Ham U (2) 3 *(Kouyate 8, 25, Feghouli 81)*

Domzale (0) 0 53,914

West Ham U: (451) Randolph; Antonio, Oxford, Reid, Byram; Feghouli (Quina 87), Noble, Nordtveit, Kouyate (Obiang 78), Valencia; Carroll (Fletcher 90).
Domzale: (4141) Maraval; Brachi, Horic, Dobrovoljc, Balkovec; Horvat (Husmani 62); Morel, Alvir, Majer (Juninho 77), Crnic; Mance (Bratanovic 68).

PLAY-OFF ROUND FIRST LEG

Wednesday, 17 August 2016

Beitar Jerusalem (1) 1 *(Vered 8)*

Saint-Etienne (2) 2 *(Lemoine 15, Pogba 30)* 25,049

Beitar Jerusalem: (433) Klaiman; Rali, Mori, Rueda, Heister; Vered (Keltjens 82), Claudemir, Einbinder; Atzili, Shechter (Audel 82), Cohen (Abuhazira 59).
Saint-Etienne: (433) Ruffier; Theophile-Catherine, Perrin, Pogba, Polomat; Lemoine, Selnaes, Hamouma (Roux 46); Monnet-Paquet, Beric (Tannane 78), Pajot.

Thursday, 18 August 2016

AEK Larnaca (0) 0

Slovan Liberec (1) 1 *(Coufal 29)* 4645

AEK Larnaca: (433) Mino; Ortiz■, Murillo, Mojsov, Tete (Acoran 82); Boljevic, Truyols (Charalambous 34), Trickovski; Jorge, Tomas, Alves (Charalambidis 75).
Slovan Liberec: (4411) Dubravka; Coufal, Hovorka, Pokorny, Bartosak (Sukennik 70); Bartl, Folprecht, Breite, Sykora; Vuch (Navratil 60); Komlichenko.

Arouca (0) 0

Olympiacos (1) 1 *(Seba 27)* 1950

Arouca: (433) Rafael Bracali; Anderson Luis, Jubal Junior, Hugo Basto, Thiago Carleto (De Jesus 59); Nuno Valente, Nuno Coelho, Adilson Goiano (Rafael Crivellaro 75); Artur Moreira (Andre Santos 68), Gonzalez, Mateus.

Olympiacos: (4231) Kapino; Diogo Figueiras, da Costa, Botia, De la Bella; Cambiasso, Milivojevic; Pardo (Zdjelar 90), Dominguez (Androutsos A 72), Seba (Durmaz 88); Ideye.

Astana (0) 2 *(Kabananga 70, Nurgaliev 80)*

BATE Borisov (0) 0 17,536

Astana: (4411) Eric; Beisebekov, Anicic, Maliy, Logvinenko; Twumasi (Tagybergen 89), Canas, Maksimovic, Ibraimi (Nurgaliev 63); Muzhikov; Kabananga (Despotovic 83).
BATE Borisov: (4411) Veremko; Ryas, Gaiduchik, Palyakow, Zhavnerchik; Gvilia (Yablonskiy 46), Karnitskiy (Signevich 80), Kendysh, Gordeichuk; Hleb (Ivanic 39); Rodionov.

Astra Giurgiu (0) 1 *(Alibec 83)*

West Ham U (1) 1 *(Noble 45 (pen))* 3360

Astra Giurgiu: (4231) Lung; Vangjeli (Alibec 58), Geraldo Alves, Fabricio, Junior Morais; Sapunaru, Lovin; Ionita II (Florea 85), Seto, Teixeira (Balaure 90); Niculae.
West Ham U: (442) Randolph; Byram, Oxford, Ogbonna, Burke; Tore (Browne 75), Noble, Obiang, Antonio; Calleri (Collins 63), Valencia (Carroll 62).

Austria Vienna (0) 2 *(Grunwald 51, Pires 53)*

Rosenborg (0) 1 *(Reginiussen 90)* 6090

Austria Vienna: (4231) Almer; Larsen, Rotpuller, Filipovic, Martschinko; Serbest, Holzhauser; Venuto (De Paula 84), Grunwald (Windbichler 81), Pires; Kayode (Friesenbicher 90).
Rosenborg: (433) Kwarasey; Svensson, Reginiussen, Eyjolfsson, Skjelvik (Rashani 71); Jensen, Konradsen, Midtsjoe (Vilhjalmsson 77); Helland, Gytkjaer, Gersbach.

Dinamo Tbilisi (0) 0

PAOK Salonika (1) 3 *(Leo Matos 20, Crespo 71, Pereyra 83)* 12,006

Dinamo Tbilisi: (4411) Scribe; Lobzhanidze (Tevzadze 58), Rene, Amisulashvili, Chelidze; Jigauri, Parunashvili, Tsintsadze (Mikel Alvaro 70), Tchanturishvili; Kiteishvili; Papunashvili (Dvalishvili 63).
PAOK Salonika: (4411) Glykos; Leovac, Tzavelas, Crespo, Leo Matos; Rodrigues, Cimirot, Shakhov (Biseswar 68), Djalma (Pereyra 81); Charisis (Canas 46); Athanasiadis.

Fenerbahce (1) 3 *(Chahechouhe 4, Stoch 72, 90)*

Grasshoppers (0) 0 16,280

Fenerbahce: (442) Demirel; van der Wiel, Kaldirim, Skrtel, Topal; Tufan, Neustadter, Ucan, Chahechouhe (Stoch 68); Fernandao (van Persie 68), Emenike.
Grasshoppers: (442) Vasic; Pnishi, Basic, Bamert, Luthi; Kallstrom, Sigurjonsson (Brahimi 84), Lavanchy, Caio (Kamberi 74); Gjorgjev (Andersen 64), Munsy.

IFK Gothenburg (0) 1 *(Albaek 56)*

Qarabag (0) 0 11,458

IFK Gothenburg: (442) Alvbage; Salomonsson, Bjarsmyr, Rogne, Jamieson; Rieks (Nordstrom 88), Albaek, Pettersson, Ankersen; Hysen (Smedberg-Dalence 83), Boman.
Qarabag: (451) Sehic; Medvedev, Guseynov, Sadygov, Agolli; Quintana, Michel, Garayev, Almeida, Muarem (Aleskerov 72); Reynaldo.

Istanbul Basaksehir (0) 1 *(Emre 56 (pen))*

Shakhtar Donetsk (2) 2 *(Cikalleshi 25 (og), Kovalenko 41)* 3016

Istanbul Basaksehir: (4231) Babacan; Alkilic (Dieng 72), Ayhan, Epureanu, Oztorun; Tekdemir, Emre (Holmen 75); Visca, Mossoro, Doka Madureira (Under 46); Cikalleshi.
Shakhtar Donetsk: (4231) Pyatov; Srna, Kucher, Rakitskiy, Ismaily; Fred, Stepanenko; Marlos, Kovalenko (Malyshev 87), Taison (Wellington Nem 80); Ferreyra (Eduardo 70).

KAA Gent (1) 2 *(Matton 45, Coulibaly 90)*

Skendija Tetovo (1) 1 *(Ibraimi 9)* 13,416

KAA Gent: (343) Rinne; Mitrovic, Gershon (Perbet 85), Nielsen; Foket, Renato Neto, Kums, Saief; Kujovic (Milicevic 64), Matton (Simon 73), Coulibaly.
Skendija Tetovo: (4132) Zahov; Todorovski, Bejtulai, Cuculi, Demiri; Vujcic; Polozani, Alimi (Taipi 82), Junior; Hasani, Ibraimi (Imeri 90).

Krasnodar (3) 4 *(Joaozinho 18 (pen), Smolov 27, Jedrzejczyk 45, Ari 73)*

Partizani Tirana (0) 0 11,575

Krasnodar: (433) Kritsyuk; Kaleshin, Martynovich, Granqvist, Jedrzejczyk; Ahmedov (Eboue 66), Kabore, Pereyra (Gazinski 62); Ari, Smolov (Torbinski 76), Joaozinho.
Partizani Tirana: (442) Hoxha; Ibrahimi (Fejzullahu 64), Krasniqi, Arapi, Vila; Trashi, Ramadani, Batha, Torassa; Ekuban, Bardhi (Fazliu 64).

Lokomotiva Zagreb (0) 2 *(Maric 52 (pen), Fiolic 59)*

Genk (1) 2 *(Bailey 35 (pen), Samatta 47)* 1700

Lokomotiva Zagreb: (4141) Zagorac; Bartolec, Majstorovic, Peric, Rozman; Sunjic; Grezda, Fiolic, Coric (Ivanusec 46), Bockaj (Cekici 87); Maric.
Genk: (4411) Bizot; Walsh, Dewaest, Colley, Uronen; Buffel (Trossard 42), Heynen, Ndidi, Bailey; Pozuelo; Samatta (Karelis 83).

Maccabi Tel Aviv (1) 2 *(Alberman 9, Scarione 77)*

Hajduk Split (0) 1 *(Said 56)* 9932

Maccabi Tel Aviv: (451) Rajkovic; Peretz D (Dasa 63), Tibi, Filipenko, Rikan; Micha, Igiebor, Alberman (Ben Basat 68), Medunjanin, Ben Chaim II; Scarione (Benayoun 84).
Hajduk Split: (4231) Kalinic; Ismajli, Nizic, Cosic, Memolla; Jefferson, Kozulj (Bilyi 73); Susic, Gentzoglou (Basic 87), Vlasic; Said (Ohandza 62).

Midtjylland (0) 0

Osmanlispor (1) 1 *(Banggaard 20 (og))* 7003

Midtjylland: (4141) Dahlin; Nissen, Hansen, Banggaard, Novak; Halsti (Romer 61); Kadlec, Poulsen, Olsson (Pusic 53), Hassan; Onuachu (Duelund 78).
Osmanlispor: (4141) Karcemarskas; Vrsajevic, Curusku, Prochazka, Tiago Pinto; Guven; Delarge, Lawal (Cagiran 61), Ndiaye, Webo (Rusescu 77); Kilicaslan (Bayir 77).

Panathinaikos (1) 3 *(Berg 45, 82, Ledesma 54 (pen))*

Brondby (0) 0 11,072

Panathinaikos: (442) Steele; Koutroubis (Leto 58), Ivanov, Rodrigo Moledo, Mesto; Zeca, Ledesma, Hult, Ibarbo; Wakaso (Villafanez 73), Berg (Rinaldi 86).
Brondby: (442) Ronnow■; Larsson, Albrechtsen, Rocker, Crone■; Phiri, Norgaard, Hjulsager, Mukhtar (Juelsgaard 46); Pukki (Toppel 52), Wilczek (Hermannsson 72).

Qabala (1) 3 *(Zenjov 37, Dabo 50, 52)*

Maribor (1) 1 *(Tavares 17)* 4723

Qabala: (4132) Bezotosnyi; Mirzabekov, Rafael Santos, Stankovic, Ricardinho; Vernydub (Jamalov 90); Kvekveskiri, Weeks (Eyyubov 90), Ozobic (Mammadov 80); Dabo, Zenjov.
Maribor: (4231) Handanovic; Sme, Suler, Defendi, Janza; Pihler, Vrhovec; Vrsic (Bajde 72), Tavares (Omoregie 80), Bohar (Sallalich 72); Novakovic.

Sassuolo (2) 3 *(Berardi 17, Politano 41, Defrel 69)*

Crvena Zvezda (0) 0 6861

Sassuolo: (433) Consigli; Gazzola, Cannavaro, Acerbi, Peluso; Biondini, Magnanelli, Duncan; Berardi (Falcinelli 69), Defrel (Trotta 76), Politano (Sensi 84).
Crvena Zvezda: (541) Kahriman; Phibel, Donald, Cvetkovic, Le Tallec, Ristic; Ruiz (Plavsic 57), Katai, Poletanovic, Mouche (Srnic 71); Hugo Vieira (Sikimic 84).

Slavia Prague (0) 0

Anderlecht (0) 3 *(Sylla 49, Teodorczyk 61, Hanni 71)* 16,096

Slavia Prague: (4231) Pavlenka; Mikula (Frydrych 9), Bilek, Deli, Boril; Ngadjui-Ngadjui, Barak (Mingazov 67); Van Kessel, Kenia (Mesanovic 78), Svento; Skoda.
Anderlecht: (4132) Roef; Appiah (Heylen 73), Dendoncker, Nuytinck, Acheampong; Tielemans; Chipciu, Hanni, Praet (Badji 68); Teodorczyk, Sylla (Diego Capel 78).

SonderjyskE (0) 0

Sparta Prague (0) 0 4795

SonderjyskE: (442) Skender; Pedersen, Kanstrup, Maak, Dal Hende; Absalonsen, Drachmann, Romer (Kroon 73), Madsen; Guira, Uhre (Klove 74).
Sparta Prague: (433) Koubek; Zahustel, Mazuch, Michal Kadlec, Nhamoinesu; Dockal, Vacha, Marecek; Sural (Pulkrab 80), Julis, Holzer (Frydek 46).

Trencin (0) 0

Rapid Vienna (1) 4 *(Schaub 32, 54, 83, Schwab 73)* 4069

Trencin: (433) Chovan; Sulek, Udeh, Klescik, Holubek; Paur, Lawrence (Ket 80), Janco (Ibrahim 62); Kalu, Janga, Bala (Prekop 63).
Rapid Vienna: (451) Novota; Pavelic, Schosswendter, Dibon, Schrammel; Schaub (Auer 85), Grahovac, Schwab, Mocinic, Schobesberger (Murg 50); Joelinton (Entrup 84).

Vojvodina (0) 0

AZ Alkmaar (2) 3 *(Wuytens 32, 83, Fred Friday 45)* 10,473

Vojvodina: (4141) Kordic; Miletic, Kovacevic V, Puskaric, Antic; Maksimovic; Malbasic, Palocevic (Zlicic 80), Meleg, Babic (Jovancic 46); Trujic (Trifunovic 63).
AZ Alkmaar: (4231) Rochet; Johansson, Van Eijden, Vlaar, Haps; Luckassen, Wuytens (Til 86); Jahanbakhsh, Henriksen, Garcia (dos Santos Souza 74); Fred Friday (Weghorst 79).

PLAY-OFF ROUND SECOND LEG

Thursday, 25 August 2016

Anderlecht (2) 3 *(Tielemans 22 (pen), Teodorczyk 40 (pen), Heylen 61)*

Slavia Prague (0) 0 13,075

Anderlecht: (4411) Roef; Heylen, Dendoncker, Nuytinck, Acheampong; Chipciu, Badji, Tielemans (Doumbia 62), Diego Capel; Hanni (Sowah 70); Teodorczyk (Sylla 56).
Slavia Prague: (4231) Berkovec; Mikula, Ngadjui-Ngadjui, Frydrych, Jablonsky; Soucek, Husbauer (Bilek 69); Van Kessel, Barak (Mihalik 46), Zmrhal; Mesanovic (van Buren 46).

AZ Alkmaar (0) 0

Vojvodina (0) 0 8401

AZ Alkmaar: (4231) Rochet; Johansson, Van Eijden, Vlaar, Haps; Luckassen, Wuytens; Jahanbakhsh (van Overeem 76), Henriksen, Garcia (dos Santos Souza 65); Fred Friday (Weghorst 70).
Vojvodina: (4231) Kordic; Miletic, Planic, Puskaric, Antic; Micic, Maksimovic (Vukasovic 71); Palocevic, Meleg, Malbasic (Trifunovic 77); Asceric (Babic 60).

BATE Borisov (1) 2 *(Gordeichuk 27, Stasevich 89 (pen))*

Astana (0) 2 *(Maksimovic 50, Tagybergen 76)* 9516

BATE Borisov: (451) Soroko; Zhavnerchik, Gaiduchik, Palyakow, Valadzko M (Signevich 55); Ryas■, Stasevich, Kendysh, Ivanic, Gordeichuk (Mozolewski 73); Rodionov (Pikk 86).
Astana: (4411) Mokin; Shitov, Anicic, Logvinenko (Maliy 46), Shomko; Twumasi, Maksimovic, Canas, Muzhikov (Tagybergen 85); Nurgaliev (Beisebekov 46); Kabananga.

Brondby (1) 1 *(Mukhtar 35)*

Panathinaikos (0) 1 *(Ivanov 65)* 13,521

Brondby: (4312) Toppel; Holst (Urena 67), Rocker, Hermannsson, Larsson; Hjulsager, Norgaard, Phiri (Corlu 75); Mukhtar; Wilczek, Pukki (Jakobsen 83).
Panathinaikos: (343) Steele; Koutroubis, Ivanov, Rodrigo Moledo; Mesto, Ledesma (Lod 59), Zeca, Hult (Villafanez 85); Ibarbo (Leto 46), Berg, Wakaso.

Crvena Zvezda (0) 1 *(Katai 54)*

Sassuolo (1) 1 *(Berardi 28)* 22,314

Crvena Zvezda: (442) Kahriman; Cvetkovic (Babunski 80), Phibel, Donald, Ristic; Poletanovic, Le Tallec (Rendulic 57), Ruiz (Srnic 85), Katai; Mouche, Hugo Vieira.
Sassuolo: (442) Consigli; Peluso, Acerbi, Lirola, Cannavaro; Magnanelli, Biondini, Duncan, Matri (Trotta 83); Politano (Falcinelli 62), Berardi (Letschert 72).

Genk (1) 2 *(Samatta 2, Bailey 50)*

Lokomotiva Zagreb (0) 0 8166

Genk: (4231) Bizot; Walsh, Dewaest, Colley, Uronen; Pozuelo (Kumordzi 82), Ndidi; Bailey (Kebano 74), Heynen, Trossard; Samatta (Karelis 80).
Lokomotiva Zagreb: (4231) Zagorac; Bartolec, Majstorovic, Peric, Rozman; Capan (Ivanusec 66), Sunjic; Grezda (Coric 46), Fiolic, Bockaj (Cekici 72); Maric.

Grasshoppers (0) 0

Fenerbahce (0) 2 *(Fernandao 77, Stoch 84)* 14,400

Grasshoppers: (4321) Mall; Luthi, Pnishi, Rhyner, Antonov; Gubari (Kamberi 68), Sigurjonsson, Gjorgjev; Andersen (Alpsoy 81), Brahimi; Tabakovic.
Fenerbahce: (4231) Demirel; van der Wiel, Kjaer, Skrtel, Kaldirim (Koybasi 73); Topal, Tufan; Ucan (Chahechouhe 53), Potuk, Stoch; van Persie (Fernandao 68).

Hajduk Split (1) 2 *(Cosic 40, 59)*

Maccabi Tel Aviv (0) 1 *(Scarione 52)* 21,102

Hajduk Split: (442) Kalinic; Simic, Said (Ohandza 63), Jefferson, Vlasic; Kozulj (Tudor 69), Memolla, Susic, Ismajli; Cosic, Gentzoglou.
Maccabi Tel Aviv: (442) Rajkovic; Dasa, Tibi, Ben Haim I, Ben Haroush; Medunjanin, Scarione, Benayoun (Orlando Sa 81), Micha (Itzhaki 114); Ben Basat (Rikan 106), Igiebor.
aet; Maccabi Tel Aviv won 4-3 on penalties.

Maribor (0) 1 *(Tavares 66)*

Qabala (0) 0 9000

Maribor: (442) Handanovic; Janza, Suler, Defendi (Bajde 85), Vrhovec (Kabha 46); Pihler (Sallalich 63), Vrsic, Bohar, Tavares; Novakovic, Sme.
Qabala: (442) Bezotosnyi; Stankovic, Vernydub, Ricardinho, Rafael Santos; Kvekveskiri, Mirzabekov, Ozobic, Weeks■; Zenjov (Mammadov 86), Dabo (Eyyubov 90).

Olympiacos (0) 2 *(Dominguez 94, Ideye 113)*

Arouca (0) 1 *(Gege 80)* 18,348

Olympiacos: (4231) Kapino; Retsos, Botia, da Costa, De la Bella; Cambiasso (Dominguez 91), Milivojevic; Pardo (Manthatis 99), Fortounis (Andre Martins 72), Seba; Ideye.
Arouca: (433) Rafael Bracali; Gege (Bruno Lopes 112), Jubal Junior, Velazquez, Hugo Basto; Artur Moreira (Nuno Valente 90), Andre Santos, Rafael Crivellaro; Zequinha (Mateus 77), De Jesus, Gonzalez.
aet.

Osmanlispor (1) 2 *(Tiago Pinto 20, 50)*

Midtjylland (0) 0 12,116

Osmanlispor: (451) Karcemarskas; Altinay (Bayir 82), Prochazka, Curusku, Tiago Pinto; Umar, Ndiaye, Lawal, Cagiran, Delarge (Kilicaslan 75); Webo (Diabate 66).
Midtjylland: (451) Dahlin; Nissen, Hansen, Banggaard, Novak (Duelund 62); Kadlec (van der Vaart 72), Poulsen (Pusic 55), Halsti, Olsson, Hassan; Romer.

PAOK Salonika (2) 2 *(Rodrigues 5, Tzavelas 45)*

Dinamo Tbilisi (0) 0 14,821

PAOK Salonika: (433) Glykos; Leovac (Kitsiou 65), Crespo (Varela 76), Tzavelas, Leo Matos; Cimirot, Canas, Shakhov (Biseswar 57); Djalma, Pereyra, Rodrigues.
Dinamo Tbilisi: (451) Scribe; Lobzhanidze, Rene, Amisulashvili, Spicic; Papunashvili, Tsintsadze (Velev 74), Mikel Alvaro, Parunashvili, Kiteishvili (Tchanturishvili 62); Dvalishvili (Mikeltadze 77).

Partizani Tirana (0) 0

Krasnodar (0) 0 1550

Partizani Tirana: (442) Hoxha; Ibrahimi, Atanda, Krasniqi, Fejzullahu (Bardhi 64); Vila, Trashi (Vatnikaj 74), Batha, Ramadani (Bertoni 22); Torassa, Ekuban.
Krasnodar: (442) Sinitsyn; Torbinski, Granqvist, Martynovich, Eboue; Pereyra (Ahmedov 46), Petrov, Joaozinho, Podberezkin (Jedrzejczyk 46); Ari (Vorobyev 64), Bystrov.

Qarabag (2) 3 *(Sadygov 19, Muarem 26, Quintana 51)*

IFK Gothenburg (0) 0 25,500

Qarabag: (433) Sehic; Medvedev, Yunuszadze, Sadygov, Agolli; Michel, Garayev, Almeida (Amirguliyev 88); Quintana, Reynaldo (Aleskerov 90), Muarem (Ndlovu 83).
IFK Gothenburg: (442) Alvbage; Salomonsson, Bjarsmyr, Rogne, Jamieson; Rieks, Albaek, Eriksson (Smedberg-Dalence 83), Ankersen; Hysen (Omarsson 72), Boman (Pettersson 72).

Rapid Vienna (0) 0

Trencin (2) 2 *(Lawrence 12, Paur 35)* 21,200

Rapid Vienna: (4231) Novota; Pavelic, Dibon, Hofmann M, Auer; Mocinic, Grahovac; Schaub (Hofmann S 90), Murg (Schwab 46), Traustason (Schrammel 83); Joelinton.
Trencin: (433) Semrinec; Sulek, Udeh, Klescik, Holubek (Halgos 84); Ket (Madu 64), Janco■, Lawrence; Paur, Janga, Bala (Prekop 79).

Rosenborg (0) 1 *(Gytkjaer 59 (pen))*

Austria Vienna (0) 2 *(Grunwald 58, Kayode 69)* 11,692

Rosenborg: (433) Kwarasey; Svensson, Reginiussen, Eyjolfsson, Skjelvik (Gersbach 70); Jensen, Konradsen, Midtsjoe; Helland (Vilhjalmsson 26), Gytkjaer, Rashani.
Austria Vienna: (4411) Almer; Larsen (Tajouri 89), Filipovic, Rotpuller, Martschinko; Venuto (De Paula 76), Serbest, Holzhauser, Pires; Grunwald; Kayode (Friesenbicher 78).

Saint-Etienne (0) 0

Beitar Jerusalem (0) 0 20,354

Saint-Etienne: (442) Ruffier■; Theophile-Catherine, Perrin, Pogba, Malcuit; Saint-Louis (Moulin 45), Lemoine, Selnaes, Monnet-Paquet (Tannane 53); Roux (Pajot 86), Beric.
Beitar Jerusalem: (541) Klaiman; Rali (Benish 59), Mori, Keltjens (Atzili 46), Rueda, Heister; Vered, Einbinder, Claudemir, Cohen (Audel 69); Shechter.

Shakhtar Donetsk (1) 2 *(Attamah 23 (og), Marlos 71 (pen))*

Istanbul Basaksehir (0) 0 7014

Shakhtar Donetsk: (4231) Pyatov; Srna, Kucher, Rakitskiy, Ismaily; Fred (Malyshev 72), Stepanenko; Marlos, Kovalenko (Wellington Nem 83), Taison; Ferreyra (Eduardo 77).
Istanbul Basaksehir: (4141) Babacan; Alkilic (Ucar 46), Epureanu, Attamah, Oztorun; Rotman; Under, Ozmert (Mossoro 78), Emre (Holmen 28), Albayrak; Cikalleshi.

Skendija Tetovo (0) 0

KAA Gent (0) 4 *(Coulibaly 60, 69, Perbet 81, Renato Neto 86)* 30,252

Skendija Tetovo: (433) Zahov; Todorovski, Bejtulai, Cuculi, Demiri; Taipi (Radeski 40), Polozani, Junior (Juffo 66); Hasani, Alimi (Totre 74), Ibraimi.
KAA Gent: (343) Rinne; Nielsen (Asare 46), Gershon, Mitrovic; Foket, Renato Neto, Kums, Saief; Milicevic (Matton 71), Coulibaly (Perbet 75), Simon.

Slovan Liberec (3) 3 *(Sykora 8, 15, 41)*

AEK Larnaca (0) 0 7570

Slovan Liberec: (4141) Dubravka; Coufal, Hovorka, Pokorny, Bartosak; Breite; Bartl (Navratil 79), Folprecht, Sykora, Vuch (Sukennik 89); Baros (Komlichenko 83).
AEK Larnaca: (4411) Mino; Mintikkis (Charalambidis 46), Murillo■, Mojsov, Charalambous (Acoran 46); Tete (Englezou 59), Boljevic, Jorge, Trickovski; Tomas; Alves.

Sparta Prague (1) 3 *(Lafata 44, Sural 69, Brabec 85)*

SonderjyskE (2) 2 *(Uhre 35, Klove 40)* 13,685

Sparta Prague: (442) Koubek; Karavaev (Brabec 85), Holek, Michal Kadlec, Nhamoinesu; Sural, Marecek (Julis 46), Vacha, Frydek; Pulkrab (Zahustel 82), Lafata.
SonderjyskE: (442) Skender; Pedersen, Kanstrup, Maak, Dal Hende; Klove (Kroon 76), Drachmann, Romer (Mattila 83), Absalonsen (Luyckx 87); Madsen, Uhre.

West Ham U (0) 0

Astra Giurgiu (1) 1 *(Teixeira 45)* 56,932

West Ham U: (4141) Randolph; Byram, Reid, Ogbonna, Burke (Collins 88); Nordtveit (Valencia 46); Tore, Obiang, Kouyate, Antonio; Calleri (Fletcher 60).
Astra Giurgiu: (442) Lung; Sapunaru, Fabricio, Geraldo Alves, Junior Morais; Ionita II (Stan 75), Lovin (Florea 88), Seto, Teixeira; Alibec, Niculae (Oros 57).

GROUP STAGE

GROUP A

Thursday, 15 September 2016

Feyenoord (0) 1 *(Vilhena 79)*

Manchester U (0) 0 31,000

Feyenoord: (433) Jones; Karsdorp (Nieuwkoop 90), Botteghin, Kongolo, Van Der Heijden; Kuyt, El Ahmadi, Vilhena; Toornstra, Jorgensen, Berghuis (Basacikoglu 68).
Manchester U: (433) de Gea; Darmian, Smalling, Bailly, Rojo; Schneiderlin, Pogba, Ander Herrera; Mata (Young 64), Rashford (Ibrahimovic 63), Martial (Depay 63).

Zorya Luhansk (0) 1 *(Grechyshkin 53)*

Fenerbahce (0) 1 *(Kjaer 90)* 16,000

Zorya Luhansk: (451) Shevchenko; Kamenyuka, Sivakov, Forster, Sobol; Karavayev, Grechyshkin, Ljubenovic (Opanasenko 82), Chaykovsky, Petryak (Paulinho 73); Kulach (Hordiyenko 87).
Fenerbahce: (433) Demirel; Ozbayrakli, Kjaer, Skrtel, Kaldirim; Ucan (Tufan 46), Topal, Souza; Potuk (Emenike 73), Sow, Stoch (van Persie 58).

Thursday, 29 September 2016

Fenerbahce (1) 1 *(Emenike 17)*

Feyenoord (0) 0 16,500

Fenerbahce: (433) Demirel; van der Wiel, Skrtel, Kjaer, Kaldirim (Koybasi 76); Tufan, Topal, Souza; Lens (Potuk 85), Emenike (van Persie 77), Sow.
Feyenoord: (433) Jones; Karsdorp, Botteghin (Kramer 82), Kongolo, Van Der Heijden; Kuyt, El Ahmadi, Vilhena; Toornstra, Jorgensen, Berghuis (Basacikoglu 57).

Manchester U (0) 1 *(Ibrahimovic 69)*

Zorya Luhansk (0) 0 58,179

Manchester U: (4231) Romero; Fosu-Mensah (Martial 74), Bailly, Smalling, Rojo; Fellaini, Pogba; Lingard (Rooney 67), Mata (Young 73), Rashford; Ibrahimovic.
Zorya Luhansk: (4411) Shevchenko; Sivakov, Chaykovsky (Hordiyenko 79), Kamenyuka, Petryak; Kulach (Paulinho 59), Forster, Karavayev, Ljubenovic (Lipartia 76); Grechyshkin; Sobol.

Thursday, 20 October 2016

Feyenoord (0) 1 *(Jorgensen 55)*

Zorya Luhansk (0) 0 35,000

Feyenoord: (433) Jones; Karsdorp, Van Der Heijden, Botteghin, Kongolo; El Ahmadi, Vilhena, Tapia; Toornstra, Jorgensen (Kramer 81), Basacikoglu.
Zorya Luhansk: (4411) Shevchenko; Kamenyuka, Sivakov, Forster, Sobol; Karavayev, Grechyshkin, Hordiyenko (Kharatin 65), Petryak (Paulinho 58); Lipartia; Kulach (Ljubenovic 46).

Manchester U (3) 4 *(Pogba 31 (pen), 45, Martial 34 (pen), Lingard 48)*

Fenerbahce (0) 1 *(van Persie 83)* 73,063

Manchester U: (4231) de Gea; Darmian, Smalling (Rojo 46), Bailly, Shaw; Carrick, Pogba (Fosu-Mensah 75); Lingard (Depay 66), Mata, Martial; Rooney.
Fenerbahce: (433) Demirel; Ozbayrakli, Skrtel, Kjaer (Emenike 46), Souza; Topal, Kaldirim, Neustadter; Potuk, van Persie, Sen (Koybasi 69).

Thursday, 3 November 2016

Fenerbahce (1) 2 *(Sow 2, Lens 59)*

Manchester U (0) 1 *(Rooney 89)* 35,378

Fenerbahce: (433) Demirel; Ozbayrakli, Skrtel, Kjaer, Kaldirim; Souza, Potuk (Neustadter 81), Topal; Lens, Sow (Koybasi 86), Sen (Emenike 67).
Manchester U: (4231) de Gea; Darmian, Rojo, Blind, Shaw; Schneiderlin (Mata 46), Ander Herrera; Rashford (Mkhitaryan 61), Pogba (Ibrahimovic 30), Martial; Rooney.

Zorya Luhansk (1) 1 *(Forster 45)*

Feyenoord (1) 1 *(Jorgensen 15)* 16,855

Zorya Luhansk: (4411) Shevchenko; Opanasenko (Kamenyuka 30), Grechyshkin, Forster, Sobol; Karavayev, Kharatin, Chaykovsky, Petryak; Ljubenovic (Paulinho 63); Bonaventure (Kulach 55).
Feyenoord: (451) Jones; Karsdorp, Botteghin■, Van Der Heijden, Kongolo; Toornstra (Nieuwkoop 81), Kuyt (Basacikoglu 70), Tapia, Vejinovic, Elia; Jorgensen (Nelom 46).

Thursday, 24 November 2016

Fenerbahce (0) 2 *(Stoch 59, Kjaer 67)*

Zorya Luhansk (0) 0 16,145

Fenerbahce: (433) Demirel; Kaldirim, Kjaer, Skrtel, Ozbayrakli; Topal, Potuk, Souza; Sen (Neustadter 72), Sow (Ucan 86), Emenike (Stoch 46).
Zorya Luhansk: (451) Shevchenko; Kamenyuka (Opanasenko 35), Sivakov, Forster, Sobol■; Karavayev, Grechyshkin, Kharatin, Chaykovsky, Petryak (Bonaventure 57); Kulach (Paulinho 69).

Manchester U (1) 4 *(Rooney 35, Mata 69, Jones 75 (og), Lingard 90)*

Feyenoord (0) 0 64,628

Manchester U: (4231) Romero; Valencia, Jones, Blind, Shaw; Pogba, Carrick; Mata (Rashford 70), Rooney (Depay 82), Mkhitaryan (Lingard 84); Ibrahimovic.
Feyenoord: (433) Jones; Karsdorp, Dammers, Van Der Heijden, Nelom; Tapia, Kuyt (Berghuis 61), Vilhena; Toornstra (Basacikoglu 78), Elia, Jorgensen (Kramer 73).

Thursday, 8 December 2016

Feyenoord (0) 0

Fenerbahce (1) 1 *(Sow 22)* 32,000

Feyenoord: (4231) Jones; Karsdorp, Botteghin, Van Der Heijden, Nelom; El Ahmadi, Vilhena (Kramer 76); Kuyt, Toornstra (Basacikoglu 46), Jorgensen; Elia.
Fenerbahce: (433) Demirel; Ozbayrakli, Skrtel, Kjaer, Kaldirim; Souza, Potuk, Topal (Neustadter 86); Lens (Sen 70), Sow, van Persie (Emenike 75).

Zorya Luhansk (0) 0

Manchester U (0) 2 *(Mkhitaryan 48, Ibrahimovic 88)* 25,900

Zorya Luhansk: (4411) Levchenko; Opanasenko, Sivakov, Forster, Sukhotsky; Karavayev, Kharatin (Grechyshkin 57), Chaykovsky, Petryak; Ljubenovic (Lipartia 72); Bezborodko (Bonaventure 54).
Manchester U: (4231) Romero; Young, Bailly, Rojo, Blind; Pogba, Ander Herrera; Mkhitaryan (Fosu-Mensah 85), Rooney (Fellaini 70), Mata (Lingard 65); Ibrahimovic.

Group A	*P*	*W*	*D*	*L*	*F*	*A*	*GD*	*Pts*
Fenerbahce	6	4	1	1	8	6	2	13
Manchester U	6	4	0	2	12	4	8	12
Feyenoord	6	2	1	3	3	7	–4	7
Zorya Luhansk	6	0	2	4	2	8	–6	2

GROUP B

Thursday, 15 September 2016

APOEL Nicosia (0) 2 *(Vinicius 75, de Camargo 87)*

Astana (1) 1 *(Maksimovic 45)* 12,008

APOEL Nicosia: (451) Waterman; Milanov, Astiz, Carlao, Roberto Lago; Gianniotas (Vander 78), Vinicius, Morais, Orlandi (Bertoglio 56), Efrem (de Camargo 70); Sotiriou.
Astana: (4411) Eric; Shitov, Maliy, Anicic, Shomko; Beisebekov, Maksimovic, Canas, Muzhikov (Tagybergen 77); Despotovic (Twumasi 57); Kabananga (Nuserbaev 70).

Young Boys (0) 0

Olympiacos (1) 1 *(Cambiasso 42)* 11,132

Young Boys: (442) Mvogo; Sutter, Rochat, von Bergen, Lecjaks; Ravet (Duah 86), Zakaria, Bertone, Sulejmani; Kubo, Frey (Schick 78).
Olympiacos: (433) Leali; Diogo Figueiras, da Costa, Botia, De la Bella; Milivojevic, Cambiasso, Marin (Andre Martins 62); Elyounoussi (Romao 90), Ideye (Cardozo 81), Seba.

Thursday, 29 September 2016

Astana (0) 0

Young Boys (0) 0 21,328

Astana: (4411) Eric; Shitov, Maliy, Anicic, Shomko; Beisebekov, Canas, Maksimovic, Muzhikov (Nurgaliev 84); Despotovic (Nuserbaev 74); Kabananga (Tagybergen 84).
Young Boys: (433) Mvogo; Lecjaks, von Bergen, Nuhu, Sutter; Zakaria, Bertone, Sulejmani (Schick 81); Ravet, Frey (Duah 81), Kubo (Aebischer 90).

Olympiacos (0) 0

APOEL Nicosia (1) 1 *(Sotiriou 10)* 24,378

Olympiacos: (4231) Leali; Diogo Figueiras, da Costa, Botia, De la Bella; Cambiasso (Andre Martins 78), Milivojevic; Fortounis (Elyounoussi 64), Seba, Marin (Cardozo 78); Ideye.
APOEL Nicosia: (433) Waterman; Milanov, Merkis, Carlao, Roberto Lago; Bertoglio (Artymatas 64), Morais, Vinicius; Gianniotas (Astiz 82), Sotiriou, Vander (Efrem 68).

Thursday, 20 October 2016

Olympiacos (3) 4 *(Diogo Figueiras 25, Elyounoussi 33, Seba 34, 64)*

Astana (0) 1 *(Kabananga 53)* 21,480

Olympiacos: (4231) Leali; Diogo Figueiras, da Costa, Botia, Retsos; Andre Martins, Milivojevic (Cambiasso 73); Elyounoussi (Manthatis 68), Fortounis (Bouchalakis 78), Seba; Cardozo.
Astana: (532) Eric; Beisebekov, Maliy, Anicic, Logvinenko, Shomko; Twumasi, Tagybergen (Muzhikov 63), Canas■; Nuserbaev (Shitov 58), Kabananga (Despotovic 72).

Young Boys (1) 3 *(Hoarau 18, 52, 82 (pen))*

APOEL Nicosia (1) 1 *(Efrem 14)* 9553

Young Boys: (442) Mvogo; Sutter, Nuhu, von Bergen, Lecjaks; Schick (Bertone 80), Zakaria, Sanogo, Ravet (Duah 88); Hoarau (Frey 84), Kubo.
APOEL Nicosia: (4141) Waterman; Milanov, Astiz, Carlao (Merkis 50), Roberto Lago; Morais; Efrem, Bertoglio (Bressan 78), Vinicius, Vander (Gianniotas 68); Sotiriou.

Thursday, 3 November 2016

APOEL Nicosia (0) 1 *(Sotiriou 69)*

Young Boys (0) 0 12,761

APOEL Nicosia: (4231) Waterman; Milanov, Astiz, Carlao, Roberto Lago; Morais, Vinicius; Efrem, Bressan (Bertoglio 59), Aloneftis (Gianniotas 66); Sotiriou (de Camargo 83).
Young Boys: (442) Mvogo; Sutter, von Bergen, Nuhu, Lecjaks; Schick, Zakaria (Bertone 80), Sanogo, Ravet (Mbabu■ 65); Hoarau, Kubo (Frey 80).

Astana (1) 1 *(Despotovic 8)*

Olympiacos (1) 1 *(Seba 30)* 12,158

Astana: (541) Eric; Shitov, Beisebekov, Maliy, Logvinenko, Shomko; Twumasi (Najarian 90), Muzhikov, Maksimovic, Despotovic (Kulbekov 81); Kabananga.

Olympiacos: (4231) Leali; Elabdellaoui, Botia, Viana, Retsos; Bouchalakis, Cambiasso (Romao 80); Manthatis (Elyounoussi 63), Andre Martins (Androutsos A 90), Seba; Cardozo.

Thursday, 24 November 2016

Astana (0) 2 *(Anicic 59, Despotovic 84)*

APOEL Nicosia (1) 1 *(Efrem 31)* 9143

Astana: (352) Eric; Shitov (Nuserbaev 78), Logvinenko, Anicic; Beisebekov, Maksimovic, Canas, Muzhikov (Nurgaliev 81), Shomko; Despotovic, Kabananga (Maliy 90).

APOEL Nicosia: (532) Waterman; Milanov, Astiz■, Morais, Carlao, Roberto Lago; de Camargo (Vander 63), Vinicius, Efrem (Gianniotas 80); Sotiriou, Aloneftis (Artymatas 35).

Olympiacos (0) 1 *(Fortounis 48)*

Young Boys (0) 1 *(Hoarau 57)* 24,131

Olympiacos: (4231) Leali; Diogo Figueiras, Botia, da Costa, Retsos; Andre Martins, Milivojevic; Elyounoussi (Manthatis 85), Fortounis, Seba; Ideye.

Young Boys: (442) Mvogo; Sutter, von Bergen, Benito, Lecjaks; Sulejmani (Gerndt 58), Sanogo (Duah 77), Zakaria, Schick (Frey 89); Hoarau, Bertone.

Thursday, 8 December 2016

APOEL Nicosia (1) 2 *(da Costa 20 (og), de Camargo 83)*

Olympiacos (0) 0 14,779

APOEL Nicosia: (433) Waterman; Milanov, Merkis, Carlao, Alexandrou; Morais, Bertoglio (Orlandi 67), Vinicius; Efrem (Gianniotas 59), Sotiriou (de Camargo 80), Aloneftis.

Olympiacos: (4231) Leali; Diogo Figueiras, Viana, da Costa, De la Bella (Manthatis 76); Andre Martins (Androutsos T 66), Romao; Elyounoussi, Fortounis (Dominguez 76), Seba; Ideye.

Young Boys (0) 3 *(Frey 62, Hoarau 66, Schick 71)*

Astana (0) 0 7616

Young Boys: (4141) Mvogo; Sutter, von Bergen, Nuhu, Obexer (Benito 67); Sanogo; Schick, Bertone, Aebischer (Frey 61), Gerndt; Hoarau (Duah 78).

Astana: (4231) Eric; Beisebekov, Shitov, Logvinenko (Maliy 56), Shomko; Canas, Maksimovic; Twumasi, Despotovic (Najarian 77), Muzhikov (Zhunussov 87); Kabananga.

Group B	*P*	*W*	*D*	*L*	*F*	*A*	*GD*	*Pts*
APOEL Nicosia	6	4	0	2	8	6	2	12
Olympiacos	6	2	2	2	7	6	1	8
Young Boys	6	2	2	2	7	4	3	8
Astana	6	1	2	3	5	11	–6	5

GROUP C

Thursday, 15 September 2016

Anderlecht (2) 3 *(Teodorczyk 14, Rafael Santos 42 (og), Diego Capel 77)*

Qabala (1) 1 *(Dabo 20)* 11,638

Anderlecht: (4411) Roef; Spajic, Mbodji, Nuytinck, Acheampong; Chipciu (Diego Capel 72), Dendoncker, Tielemans (Badji 17), Hanni; Stanciu; Teodorczyk (Harbaoui 80).

Qabala: (352) Bezotosnyi; Rafael Santos, Vernydub (Franjic 59), Stankovic; Mirzabekov, Gurbanov (Mammadov 46), Sadiqov, Zenjov (Eyyubov 90), Ricardinho; Ozobic, Dabo.

Mainz 05 (0) 1 *(Bungert 57)*

Saint-Etienne (0) 1 *(Beric 88)* 20,275

Mainz 05: (433) Lossl; Donati, Bell, Bungert, Bussmann; Clemens (Oztunali 84), Serdar (Frei 71), Gbamin; Malli, De Blasis, Muto (Cordoba 69).

Saint-Etienne: (433) Moulin; Malcuit, Theophile-Catherine, Perrin, Pogba; Dabo (Tannane 58), Selnaes, Lemoine (Veretout 67); Hamouma, Beric, Saivet (Soderlund 80).

Thursday, 29 September 2016

Qabala (0) 2 *(Gurbanov 57 (pen), Zenjov 62)*

Mainz 05 (1) 3 *(Muto 41, Cordoba 68, Oztunali 78)* 6500

Qabala: (451) Bezotosnyi; Mirzabekov, Stankovic, Rafael Santos, Ricardinho; Gurbanov (Franjic 81), Sadiqov (Mammadov 81), Vernydub (Jamalov 86), Ozobic, Zenjov; Dabo.

Mainz 05: (433) Lossl; Brosinski, Hack, Bell, Bussmann; Clemens (Oztunali 67), Frei, Rodriguez (Cordoba 67); Malli, De Blasis, Muto (Serdar 84).

Saint-Etienne (0) 1 *(Roux 90)*

Anderlecht (0) 1 *(Tielemans 62 (pen))* 23,258

Saint-Etienne: (352) Moulin; Karamoko, Lacroix, Dabo (Tannane 77); Malcuit, Pajot (Soderlund 76), Clement (Corgnet 86), Veretout, Monnet-Paquet; Hamouma, Roux.

Anderlecht: (4411) Roef; Spajic, Mbodji, Nuytinck, Acheampong; Chipciu, Dendoncker, Tielemans, Hanni (Badji 74); Stanciu (Diego Capel 82); Teodorczyk (Harbaoui 69).

Thursday, 20 October 2016

Mainz 05 (1) 1 *(Malli 11 (pen))*

Anderlecht (0) 1 *(Teodorczyk 65)* 21,317

Mainz 05: (433) Lossl; Donati, Bungert, Bell, Bussmann; Gbamin, Malli, Serdar (Brosinski 58); De Blasis (Jairo 76), Onisiwo (Oztunali 80), Cordoba.

Anderlecht: (343) Roef; Deschacht, Mbodji, Nuytinck; Sowah (Bruno 82), Dendoncker, Tielemans, Acheampong; Stanciu (Diego Capel 60), Teodorczyk (Badji 75), Hanni.

Saint-Etienne (0) 1 *(Ricardinho 70 (og))*

Qabala (0) 0 22,855

Saint-Etienne: (442) Moulin; Theophile-Catherine, Perrin, M'Bengue, Pogba; Saivet (Pajot 90), Selnaes, Veretout, Monnet-Paquet; Tannane (Beric 62), Roux.

Qabala: (4141) Bezotosnyi; Mirzabekov, Vernydub, Stankovic, Abbasov; Ricardinho; Mammadov (Eyyubov 80), Ozobic, Weeks, Zenjov (Franjic 80); Gurbanov.

Thursday, 3 November 2016

Anderlecht (2) 6 *(Stanciu 9, 41, Tielemans 63, Teodorczyk 89, 90 (pen), Bruno 90)*

Mainz 05 (1) 1 *(De Blasis 15)* 13,275

Anderlecht: (4411) Roef; Sowah, Mbodji, Deschacht, Acheampong; Chipciu (Diego Capel 56), Dendoncker, Tielemans (Bruno 88), Hanni; Stanciu (Badji 67); Teodorczyk.

Mainz 05: (433) Lossl; Donati (Oztunali 80), Balogun, Bell, Brosinski; Serdar (Jairo 67), Malli, Gbamin; De Blasis, Onisiwo, Cordoba.

Qabala (1) 1 *(Gurbanov 39)*

Saint-Etienne (1) 2 *(Tannane 45, Beric 53)* 5600

Qabala: (4411) Bezotosnyi; Mirzabekov, Vernydub, Stankovic, Ricardinho; Gurbanov, Ozobic, Sadiqov (Kvekveskiri 84), Eyyubov (Franjic 65); Weeks; Zenjov (Mammadov 61).

Saint-Etienne: (433) Ruffier; Malcuit, Perrin, Pogba, M'Bengue; Veretout, Selnaes, Saivet (Pajot 74); Tannane (Roux 84), Beric (Soderlund 62), Monnet-Paquet.

Thursday, 24 November 2016

Qabala (1) 1 *(Ricardinho 15 (pen))*

Anderlecht (1) 3 *(Tielemans 10, Bruno 90, Teodorczyk 90)* 4500

Qabala: (4231) Bezotosnyi; Abbasov, Vernydub, Rafael Santos, Ricardinho; Eyyubov■, Kvekveskiri; Mammadov, Weeks, Ozobic; Dabo (Gurbanov 52).

Anderlecht: (4141) Boeckx; Sowah, Spajic, Nuytinck, Obradovic; Dendoncker; Diego Capel (Bruno 60), Tielemans, Stanciu (Hanni 70), Acheampong (Doumbia 90); Teodorczyk.

Saint-Etienne (0) 0

Mainz 05 (0) 0 21,750

Saint-Etienne: (352) Ruffier; Theophile-Catherine, Perrin, Pogba; Monnet-Paquet (Nordin 58), Veretout (Lacroix 90), Selnaes, Saivet, Polomat; Tannane, Roux (Pajot 83).
Mainz 05: (343) Lossl; Bell, Ramalho Silva (Frei 65), Balogun; Brosinski, Malli, Gbamin (Seydel 83), Bussmann (Jairo 82); Onisiwo, Cordoba, Oztunali.

Thursday, 8 December 2016

Anderlecht (2) 2 *(Chipciu 21, Stanciu 31)*

Saint-Etienne (0) 3 *(Soderlund 62, 67, Monnet-Paquet 75)* 13,583

Anderlecht: (451) Roef; Sowah, Spajic, Nuytinck, Obradovic; Chipciu (Najar 59), Stanciu, Dendoncker, Badji, Acheampong (Hanni 65); Vancamp (Teodorczyk 60).
Saint-Etienne: (433) Ruffier; Polomat, Pogba, Lacroix, Theophile-Catherine; Soderlund (Tannane 76), Malcuit, Dabo; Nordin (Hamouma 64), Monnet-Paquet, Saivet (Pajot 63).

Mainz 05 (2) 2 *(Hack 29, De Blasis 40)*

Qabala (0) 0 12,860

Mainz 05: (433) Huth; Donati, Bell, Hack, Bussmann; Gbamin (Malli 69), Frei, Ramalho Silva; De Blasis (Oztunali 87), Cordoba (Seydel 81), Jairo.
Qabala: (4231) Bezotosnyi; Abbasov, Stankovic, Vernydub, Ricardinho; Kvekveskiri, Sadiqov (Gurbanov 46); Mammadov, Weeks (Jamalov 86), Ozobic; Zenjov (Huseynov 77).

Group C	P	W	D	L	F	A	GD	Pts
Saint-Etienne	6	3	3	0	8	5	3	12
Anderlecht	6	3	2	1	16	8	8	11
Mainz 05	6	2	3	1	8	10	–2	9
Qabala	6	0	0	6	5	14	–9	0

GROUP D

Thursday, 15 September 2016

AZ Alkmaar (0) 1 *(Wuytens 61)*

Dundalk (0) 1 *(Kilduff 89)* 10,003

AZ Alkmaar: (4231) Rochet; Johansson, Van Eijden, Vlaar, Haps; Luckassen, Wuytens (Rienstra 66); Jahanbakhsh (Bel Hassani 75), van Overeem, dos Santos Souza; Fred Friday (Weghorst 55).
Dundalk: (442) Rogers; Gannon, Gartland, Boyle, Massey; Mountney (Benson 77), O'Donnell■, Finn, Horgan; McMillan (Shields 75), McEleney (Kilduff 84).

Maccabi Tel Aviv (1) 3 *(Medunjanin 26, 70, Kjartansson 50)*

Zenit St Petersburg (0) 4 *(Kokorin 76, Mak 85, Giuliano 86, Djordjevic 90)* 10,855

Maccabi Tel Aviv: (433) Rajkovic; Dasa■, Ben Haim I, Filipenko, Ben Haroush; Medunjanin, Alberman, Igiebor; Benayoun (Micha 78), Kjartansson (Ben Basat 73), Ben Haim II (Peretz D 85).
Zenit St Petersburg: (442) Lodygin; Smolnikov, Luis Neto, Javi Garcia (Mauricio 71), Criscito; Kokorin, Witsel, Giuliano, Zhirkov (Novoseltsev 90); Mak, Kerzhakov A (Djordjevic 60).

Thursday, 29 September 2016

Dundalk (0) 1 *(Kilduff 73)*

Maccabi Tel Aviv (0) 0 5543

Dundalk: (442) Rogers; Gannon, Gartland, Boyle, Massey; Benson (Shiels 85), Finn, Shields, Horgan; McEleney (Mountney 75), McMillan (Kilduff 64).
Maccabi Tel Aviv: (433) Rajkovic; Peretz D, Ben Haim I, Tibi, Ben Haroush; Igiebor (Micha 59), Alberman (Itzhaki 75), Medunjanin; Scarione, Kjartansson, Ben Haim II (Benayoun 81).

Zenit St Petersburg (1) 5 *(Kokorin 25, 59, Giuliano 48, Criscito 66 (pen), Shatov 80)*

AZ Alkmaar (0) 0 15,275

Zenit St Petersburg: (442) Lodygin; Smolnikov, Luis Neto, Lombaerts, Criscito; Mak (Djordjevic 69), Witsel, Javi Garcia (Mauricio 63), Giuliano; Dzjuba (Shatov 63), Kokorin.
AZ Alkmaar: (442) Rochet; Lewis, Van Eijden, Vlaar (Rienstra 57), Haps; van Overeem, Luckassen, Wuytens, dos Santos Souza (Bel Hassani 73); Fred Friday, Weghorst (Seuntjens 26).

Thursday, 20 October 2016

AZ Alkmaar (0) 1 *(Muhren 72)*

Maccabi Tel Aviv (1) 2 *(Scarione 24, Golasa 82)* 12,016

AZ Alkmaar: (433) Rochet; Johansson, Van Eijden, Wuytens, Haps; van Overeem (Garcia 61), Luckassen (Weghorst 84), Rienstra (Til 57); Fred Friday, Bel Hassani, Muhren.
Maccabi Tel Aviv: (433) Rajkovic; Dasa, Ben Haim I, Tibi, Ben Haroush; Alberman (Igiebor 79), Medunjanin, Golasa; Scarione (Filipenko 84), Kjartansson, Ben Haim II (Micha 69).

Dundalk (0) 1 *(Benson 52)*

Zenit St Petersburg (0) 2 *(Mak 71, Giuliano 77)* 5500

Dundalk: (442) Sava; Gannon, Gartland, Boyle, Massey; Benson (Mountney 79), Finn, Shields (Shiels 86), Horgan; McEleney, McMillan (Kilduff 72).
Zenit St Petersburg: (442) Lodygin; Aniukov, Luis Neto, Lombaerts, Criscito; Shatov (Kokorin 62), Javi Garcia (Mauricio 71), Witsel, Mak (Djordjevic 78); Dzjuba, Giuliano.

Thursday, 3 November 2016

Maccabi Tel Aviv (0) 0

AZ Alkmaar (0) 0 11,356

Maccabi Tel Aviv: (433) Rajkovic; Dasa, Ben Haim I, Tibi, Ben Haroush (Rikan 71); Medunjanin, Alberman, Scarione; Micha (Benayoun 81), Kjartansson (Igiebor 72), Ben Haim II.
AZ Alkmaar: (433) Rochet; Johansson, Van Eijden (Muhren 55), Vlaar, Haps; Luckassen, Wuytens, Rienstra; Bel Hassani (dos Santos Souza 61), Weghorst (Fred Friday 76), Garcia.

Zenit St Petersburg (1) 2 *(Giuliano 42, 78)*

Dundalk (0) 1 *(Horgan 52)* 17,723

Zenit St Petersburg: (433) Kerzhakov M; Aniukov, Luis Neto, Lombaerts (Zhirkov 88), Criscito; Witsel, Giuliano, Mauricio; Kokorin, Kerzhakov A (Djordjevic 90), Shatov (Mak 67).
Dundalk: (4141) Rogers; Gannon, Boyle, Gartland, Massey; Shields; Mountney (O'Donnell 46), McEleney (Shiels 83), Finn, Horgan; McMillan (Kilduff 65).

Thursday, 24 November 2016

Dundalk (0) 0

AZ Alkmaar (1) 1 *(Weghorst 9)* 5500

Dundalk: (451) Rogers; Gannon, Boyle, Gartland, Massey; Benson, McEleney (Shiels 80), O'Donnell (Mountney 41), Finn, Horgan; Kilduff (McMillan 77).
AZ Alkmaar: (433) Rochet; Johansson, Vlaar, Wuytens, Haps; Luckassen, Seuntjens, Rienstra; Jahanbakhsh (dos Santos Souza 75), Weghorst (Fred Friday 87), Tankovic (Ouwejan 79).

Zenit St Petersburg (1) 2 *(Kokorin 44, Kerzhakov A 90)*

Maccabi Tel Aviv (0) 0 15,843

Zenit St Petersburg: (442) Lodygin; Criscito, Javi Garcia, Novoseltsev, Luis Neto; Djordjevic (Dzjuba 46), Witsel, Mak, Zhirkov (Lombaerts 74); Giuliano, Kokorin (Kerzhakov A 66).
Maccabi Tel Aviv: (433) Rajkovic; Dasa, Tibi, Filipenko, Ben Haroush; Igiebor, Golasa, Medunjanin (Peretz E 82); Ben Basat, Scarione (Benayoun 46), Ben Haim II (Yehezkel 46).

Thursday, 8 December 2016

AZ Alkmaar (2) 3 *(Rienstra 7, Haps 43, Tankovic 68)*

Zenit St Petersburg (0) 2 *(Giuliano 58, Luckassen 81 (og))* 13,713

AZ Alkmaar: (433) Rochet; Johansson, Luckassen, Wuytens, Haps; Seuntjens (van Overeem 74), Muhren, Rienstra; Bel Hassani (Jahanbakhsh 69), Weghorst, Tankovic (dos Santos Souza 69).
Zenit St Petersburg: (433) Lodygin; Aniukov, Novoseltsev, Lombaerts, Zhirkov; Javi Garcia (Yusupov 60), Giuliano, Witsel; Djordjevic (Kokorin 46), Dzjuba, Mak.

Maccabi Tel Aviv (2) 2 *(Ben Haim II 21 (pen), Micha 38)*

Dundalk (1) 1 *(Dasa 28 (og))* 9891

Maccabi Tel Aviv: (433) Rajkovic; Dasa, Ben Haim I, Tibi, Ben Haroush; Igiebor (Benayoun 84), Golasa (Alberman 82), Medunjanin; Micha, Kjartansson, Ben Haim II (Ben Basat 88).
Dundalk: (451) Rogers; Gannon (O'Donnell 68), Boyle, Gartland (Barrett 46), Massey; Benson, Finn, Shields, McEleney (Kilduff 80), Horgan; McMillan.

Group D	P	W	D	L	F	A	GD	Pts
Zenit St Petersburg	6	5	0	1	17	8	9	15
AZ Alkmaar	6	2	2	2	6	10	–4	8
Maccabi Tel Aviv	6	2	1	3	7	9	–2	7
Dundalk	6	1	1	4	5	8	–3	4

GROUP E

Thursday, 15 September 2016

Astra Giurgiu (1) 2 *(Alibec 18, Sapunaru 74)*

Austria Vienna (2) 3 *(Holzhauser 17 (pen), Friesenbicher 33, Grunwald 59)* 3300

Astra Giurgiu: (4141) Lung; Sapunaru, Alves, Fabricio, Maranhao; Lovin (Nicoara 46); Boudjemaa (Florea 76), Niculae (Seto 46), Budescu, Teixeira; Alibec.
Austria Vienna: (433) Hadzikic; De Paula (Larsen 37), Rotpuller■, Filipovic, Salamon; Holzhauser, Grunwald, Serbest; Tajouri, Friesenbicher (Kayode 81), Pires (Venuto 62).

Viktoria Plzen (1) 1 *(Bakos 11)*

Roma (1) 1 *(Perotti 4 (pen))* 10,326

Viktoria Plzen: (442) Bolek; Mateju, Hejda, Hubnik, Limbersky; Kopic, Kace, Horava, Zeman (Petrzela 73); Duris (Krmencik 78), Bakos (Poznar 84).
Roma: (433) Alisson; Bruno Peres, Manolas, Fazio, Juan Jesus; Nainggolan, Paredes, Perotti; Iturbe (Florenzi 71), Gerson (Dzeko 46), El Shaarawy (Totti 72).

Thursday, 29 September 2016

Austria Vienna (0) 0

Viktoria Plzen (0) 0 16,509

Austria Vienna: (4231) Almer; Larsen, Stronati, Filipovic, Martschinko; Serbest, Holzhauser; Venuto (Tajouri 80), Grunwald, Pires; Kayode (Friesenbicher 86).
Viktoria Plzen: (442) Kozacik; Mateju, Hejda, Hubnik, Limbersky; Petrzela (Kopic 58), Horava, Kace (Hromada 90), Zeman; Poznar, Bakos (Krmencik 66).

Roma (2) 4 *(Strootman 15, Fazio 45, Fabricio 47 (og), Salah 54)*

Astra Giurgiu (0) 0 13,509

Roma: (4231) Alisson; Bruno Peres (Florenzi 63), Manolas, Fazio, Juan Jesus; Paredes, Strootman (Gerson 68); Salah (Nainggolan 56), Totti, Perotti; Iturbe.
Astra Giurgiu: (433) Lung; Lazic (Niculae 60), Fabricio, Geraldo Alves, Junior Morais; Mansaly (Lovin 47), Seto, Sapunaru; Teixeira, Alibec, Nicoara (Budescu 61).

Thursday, 20 October 2016

Roma (2) 3 *(El Shaarawy 19, 34, Florenzi 70)*

Austria Vienna (1) 3 *(Holzhauser 16, Prokop 82, Kayode 84)* 16,478

Roma: (433) Alisson; Florenzi (Emerson 76), Manolas, Fazio, Juan Jesus; Nainggolan, Paredes, Gerson; Iturbe (Dzeko 81), Totti, El Shaarawy (Salah 64).
Austria Vienna: (4231) Almer (Hadzikic 24); Larsen, Stronati, Filipovic, Martschinko; Holzhauser, Serbest; Grunwald (Prokop 78), Venuto (Tajouri 77), Kayode; Pires.

Viktoria Plzen (0) 1 *(Horava 86)*

Astra Giurgiu (1) 2 *(Alibec 41, Horava 65 (og))* 9440

Viktoria Plzen: (442) Kozacik; Reznik, Hejda, Baranek, Limbersky; Petrzela, Kace, Horava, Zeman (Kovarik 76); Duris (Poznar 53), Bakos (Krmencik 66).
Astra Giurgiu: (532) Lung; Sapunaru, Alves, Fabricio, Maranhao, Seto; Lovin (Oros 90), Mansaly, Lazic; Alibec (Florea 90), Budescu (Ionita II 84).

Thursday, 3 November 2016

Astra Giurgiu (1) 1 *(Stan 20)*

Viktoria Plzen (1) 1 *(Krmencik 25)* 1450

Astra Giurgiu: (3421) Lung; Sapunaru, Alves, Oros; Stan, Mansaly, Lovin (Nicoara 55), Junior Morais; Seto, Teixeira (Ionita II 88); Budescu (Niculae 75).
Viktoria Plzen: (4231) Kozacik; Reznik, Hejda, Hubnik, Mateju; Hromada (Bakos 87), Hrosovsky; Petrzela, Kace (Horava 62), Kovarik (Kopic 67); Krmencik.

Austria Vienna (1) 2 *(Kayode 2, Grunwald 90)*

Roma (2) 4 *(Dzeko 4, 66, De Rossi 17, Nainggolan 79)* 32,751

Austria Vienna: (4231) Hadzikic; Larsen, Rotpuller, Filipovic, Martschinko; Holzhauser, Serbest (Prokop 84); Pires, Grunwald, Venuto (Tajouri 87); Kayode (Friesenbicher 71).
Roma: (433) Alisson; Bruno Peres, Rudiger, De Rossi, Juan Jesus; Paredes, Nainggolan, Strootman; El Shaarawy (Gerson 71), Dzeko, Perotti (Iturbe 85).

Thursday, 24 November 2016

Austria Vienna (0) 1 *(Rotpuller 57)*

Astra Giurgiu (0) 2 *(Florea 78, Budescu 88 (pen))* 14,127

Austria Vienna: (4231) Hadzikic; Larsen, Rotpuller, Filipovic, Martschinko; Holzhauser, Serbest; Venuto (Tajouri 90), Grunwald■, Pires; Kayode (Friesenbicher 90).
Astra Giurgiu: (433) Lung; Stan, Oros (Florea 61), Geraldo Alves, Junior Morais; Seto, Sapunaru, Mansaly (Lovin 71); Budescu (Nicoara 90), Teixeira, Alibec.

Roma (1) 4 *(Dzeko 11, 61, 88, Perotti 82)*

Viktoria Plzen (1) 1 *(Zeman 19)* 13,789

Roma: (4411) Alisson; Bruno Peres, Rudiger, Fazio, Emerson; Iturbe (Perotti 62), Dzeko, Salah (De Rossi 84), Nainggolan; Paredes; Strootman (Gerson 89).
Viktoria Plzen: (4231) Kozacik; Mateju, Hejda, Limbersky, Kovarik; Hrosovsky, Hromada; Petrzela, Kopic (Duris 63), Zeman; Krmencik (Bakos 74).

Thursday, 8 December 2016

Astra Giurgiu (0) 0

Roma (0) 0 7100

Astra Giurgiu: (442) Lung; Sapunaru, Oros, Fabricio (Florea 72), Stan; Nicoara, Seto, Lovin, Teixeira; Alibec (Niculae 90), Budescu (Mansaly 89).
Roma: (4231) Alisson; Bruno Peres, Vermaelen, Juan Jesus, Seck; Strootman (Nainggolan 70), Gerson; El Shaarawy (Dzeko 70), Iturbe, Emerson (Marchizza 90); Totti.

Viktoria Plzen (1) 3 *(Horava 44, Duris 72, 84)*

Austria Vienna (2) 2 *(Holzhauser 19 (pen), Rotpuller 40)* 9117

Viktoria Plzen: (4411) Kozacik; Petrzela, Reznik, Hejda■, Kovarik; Hrosovsky, Hromada, Kopic (Bakos 83), Horava (Poznar 90); Zeman; Krmencik (Duris 58).
Austria Vienna: (4231) Hadzikic; Larsen, Rotpuller, Filipovic, Martschinko; Serbest, Holzhauser; Pires (Tajouri 77), Prokop (Friesenbicher 70), Venuto (Kvasina 85); Kayode.

Group E	P	W	D	L	F	A	GD	Pts
Roma	6	3	3	0	16	7	9	12
Astra Giurgiu	6	2	2	2	7	10	–3	8
Viktoria Plzen	6	1	3	2	7	10	–3	6
Austria Vienna	6	1	2	3	11	14	–3	5

GROUP F

Thursday, 15 September 2016

Rapid Vienna (0) 3 *(Schwab 51, Joelinton 59, Colley 61 (og))*

Genk (1) 2 *(Bailey 29, 90 (pen))* 21,800

Rapid Vienna: (4231) Strebinger; Pavelic, Dibon, Schosswendter, Schrammel; Mocinic, Schwab; Schaub, Szanto (Hofmann S 63), Traustason (Murg 79); Joelinton (Kvilitaia 86).
Genk: (4411) Bizot; Walsh, Dewaest, Colley, Uronen; Bailey, Heynen (Susic 78), Ndidi, Buffel (Trossard 66); Pozuelo; Samatta (Karelis 78).

Sassuolo (0) 3 *(Lirola 59, Defrel 75, Politano 82)*

Athletic Bilbao (0) 0 7032

Sassuolo: (433) Consigli; Lirola, Cannavaro, Acerbi, Letschert; Biondini, Magnanelli, Mazzitelli (Duncan 73); Politano, Defrel (Matri 83), Ricci (Ragusa 54).
Athletic Bilbao: (4231) Herrerin; De Marcos, Yeray, Laporte, Balenziaga (Lekue 77); Benat, San Jose; Williams (Susaeta 54), Raul Garcia, Merino; Muniain (Aduriz 54).

Thursday, 29 September 2016

Athletic Bilbao (0) 1 *(Benat 59)*

Rapid Vienna (0) 0 34,039

Athletic Bilbao: (4231) Herrerin; De Marcos, Yeray, Laporte, Balenziaga; Benat (Mikel Rico 80), Iturraspe (San Jose 59); Williams, Raul Garcia, Susaeta (Muniain 59); Aduriz.
Rapid Vienna: (4231) Strebinger; Pavelic, Schosswendter, Dibon, Schrammel; Grahovac, Mocinic (Hofmann S 67); Schaub, Schwab, Traustason (Szanto 71); Joelinton (Kvilitaia 84).

Genk (2) 3 *(Karelis 8, Bailey 26, Buffel 61)*

Sassuolo (0) 1 *(Politano 65)* 9130

Genk: (433) Bizot; Walsh, Brabec, Colley, Nastic; Pozuelo, Ndidi, Susic (Kumordzi 82); Bailey, Karelis (Samatta 75), Buffel (Trossard 87).
Sassuolo: (433) Consigli; Lirola, Letschert, Acerbi, Peluso; Biondini (Ragusa 59), Magnanelli, Pellegrini (Mazzitelli 66); Ricci (Caputo 79), Defrel, Politano.

Thursday, 20 October 2016

Genk (1) 2 *(Brabec 40, Ndidi 83)*

Athletic Bilbao (0) 0 9530

Genk: (433) Bizot; Castagne, Brabec, Colley, Nastic; Susic (Heynen 77), Ndidi, Pozuelo; Bailey, Karelis (Trossard 84), Buffel (Samatta 55).
Athletic Bilbao: (4231) Herrerin; Lekue, Yeray, Laporte, Balenziaga (Saborit 46); Iturraspe, San Jose (Elustondo 80); Williams (Susaeta 80), Raul Garcia, Muniain; Aduriz.

Rapid Vienna (1) 1 *(Schaub 7)*

Sassuolo (0) 1 *(Schrammel 66 (og))* 22,200

Rapid Vienna: (4231) Strebinger; Pavelic, Schosswendter, Dibon (Hofmann M 46), Schrammel; Mocinic, Schwab; Murg (Grahovac 63), Schaub, Traustason (Jelic 73); Joelinton.
Sassuolo: (433) Consigli; Lirola, Antei, Acerbi, Peluso; Mazzitelli, Magnanelli, Pellegrini; Politano (Adjapong 87), Matri (Ricci 78), Ragusa (Defrel 58).

Thursday, 3 November 2016

Athletic Bilbao (3) 5 *(Aduriz 8, 24 (pen), 44 (pen), 74, 90 (pen))*

Genk (1) 3 *(Bailey 28, Ndidi 50, Susic 79)* 33,417

Athletic Bilbao: (4231) Herrerin; De Marcos, Yeray, Laporte, Balenziaga; Iturraspe, Mikel Rico; Susaeta (Williams 77), Raul Garcia (Eraso 88), Muniain (Merino 82); Aduriz.
Genk: (4141) Bizot; Castagne, Brabec, Colley, Nastic (Walsh 75); Ndidi; Buffel (Trossard 75), Susic, Pozuelo, Bailey; Samatta (Karelis 83).

Sassuolo (2) 2 *(Defrel 34, Ragusa 45)*

Rapid Vienna (0) 2 *(Jelic 85, Kvilitaia 90)* 7838

Sassuolo: (532) Consigli; Lirola, Gazzola, Acerbi, Peluso, Adjapong; Biondini, Pellegrini, Ragusa (Ricci 81); Defrel (Franchini 90), Matri (Politano 64).
Rapid Vienna: (4411) Strebinger; Thurnwald, Sonnleitner, Hofmann M, Schrammel; Schaub, Grahovac, Mocinic (Szanto 85), Traustason; Murg (Jelic 61); Joelinton (Kvilitaia 60).

Thursday, 24 November 2016

Athletic Bilbao (1) 3 *(Raul Garcia 10, Aduriz 58, Lekue 79)*

Sassuolo (1) 2 *(Balenziaga 2 (og), Ragusa 83)* 37,806

Athletic Bilbao: (4231) Herrerin; Lekue, Yeray, Laporte, Balenziaga; San Jose, Benat; Williams (Boveda 61), Raul Garcia, Muniain (Mikel Rico 72); Aduriz (Merino 88).
Sassuolo: (433) Consigli; Lirola, Cannavaro, Acerbi, Gazzola; Magnanelli, Pellegrini (Missiroli 70), Biondini (Matri 71); Ricci, Defrel (Politano 78), Ragusa.

Genk (1) 1 *(Brabec 12)*

Rapid Vienna (0) 0 9406

Genk: (433) Bizot; Castagne, Brabec, Colley, Nastic; Susic (Heynen 78), Ndidi, Pozuelo; Buffel (Trossard 89), Karelis (Samatta 84), Bailey.
Rapid Vienna: (352) Novota; Sonnleitner, Schosswendter, Dibon; Thurnwald (Kvilitaia 72), Grahovac, Schaub (Jelic 84), Wober, Schrammel; Joelinton (Schobesberger 63), Traustason.

Thursday, 8 December 2016

Rapid Vienna (0) 1 *(Joelinton 72)*

Athletic Bilbao (0) 1 *(Saborit 85)* 21,500

Rapid Vienna: (352) Knoflach; Hofmann M, Sonnleitner, Wober; Auer, Grahovac, Dibon (Schaub 69), Malicsek, Schrammel; Tomi Correa (Kvilitaia 57), Jelic (Joelinton 57).
Athletic Bilbao: (4231) Iraizoz; Lekue, Yeray, Etxeita, Saborit; Mikel Rico (Benat 64), Vesga; Eraso (Susaeta 74), Muniain, Merino (Villalibre 78); Williams.

Friday, 9 December 2016

Sassuolo (0) 0

Genk (0) 2 *(Heynen 58, Trossard 80)* 1154

Sassuolo: (433) Pegolo; Lirola, Antei, Cannavaro, Acerbi; Mazzitelli, Missiroli (Pellegrini 46), Adjapong; Caputo (Magnanelli 74), Matri, Ragusa (Ricci 46).
Genk: (4231) Jackers; Castagne, Dewaest, Brabec, Walsh; Heynen (Kumordzi 89), Ndidi; Bailey (Buffel 81), Samatta, Trossard; Karelis (Sabak 90).

Group F	P	W	D	L	F	A	GD	Pts
Genk	6	4	0	2	13	9	4	12
Athletic Bilbao	6	3	1	2	10	11	–1	10
Rapid Vienna	6	1	3	2	7	8	–1	6
Sassuolo	6	1	2	3	9	11	–2	5

GROUP G

Thursday, 15 September 2016

Panathinaikos (1) 1 *(Berg 5)*

Ajax (1) 2 *(Traore 34, Riedewald 67)* 13,019

Panathinaikos: (523) Steele; Mesto, Koutroubis (Villafanez 68), Rodrigo Moledo, Ivanov■, Hult; Zeca, Ledesma (Leto 65); Lod (Samba 73), Berg, Wakaso■.
Ajax: (532) Onana; Viergever, Sanchez, Veltman, Riedewald, Dijks; Ziyech■, Gudelj, Younes (Sinkgraven 86); Klaassen (Schone 89), Traore (Dolberg 72).

Standard Liege (1) 1 *(Dossevi 3)*

Celta Vigo (1) 1 *(Rossi 13)* 10,723

Standard Liege: (442) Gillet; Echiejile (Fiore 86), Scholz, Laifis, Fai; Dossevi, Enoh, Trebel, Junior; Raman (Mbenza 68), Belfodil (Orlando Sa 82).
Celta Vigo: (433) Sergio; Lemos, Costas, Sergi Gomez, Jonny; Cabral, Radoja, Hernandez; Rossi (Aspas 86), Sisto (Bongonda 82), Naranjo (Wass 71).

Thursday, 29 September 2016

Ajax (1) 1 *(Dolberg 28)*

Standard Liege (0) 0 31,352

Ajax: (433) Onana; Veltman, Sanchez, Viergever, Sinkgraven; Schone (Riedewald 61), Gudelj, Klaassen; Traore, Dolberg (Casierra 69), Younes (El Ghazi 85).
Standard Liege: (442) Gillet; Fai, Scholz, Laifis, Andrade; Dossevi (Legear 80), Enoh, Trebel, Junior (Mbenza 69); Raman (Dompe 69), Belfodil.

Celta Vigo (0) 2 *(Guidetti 84, Wass 89)*

Panathinaikos (0) 0 15,726

Celta Vigo: (433) Sergio; Hugo Mallo, Cabral, Fontas, Jonny; Rossi (Aspas 79), Diaz, Hernandez; Sene (Wass 71), Guidetti, Naranjo (Sisto 60).
Panathinaikos: (3412) Steele; Koutroubis (M'Poku 88), Samba, Rodrigo Moledo; Coulibaly, Zeca, Ledesma, Lod; Villafanez; Ibarbo, Berg.

Thursday, 20 October 2016

Celta Vigo (1) 2 *(Fontas 29, Orellana 82)*

Ajax (1) 2 *(Ziyech 22, Younes 71)* 18,397

Celta Vigo: (433) Ruben; Roncaglia, Fontas, Sergi Gomez, Planas; Radoja, Hernandez (Wass 76), Sene; Sisto, Guidetti (Rossi 73), Lemos (Orellana 63).
Ajax: (433) Onana; Veltman, Sanchez, Viergever, Sinkgraven; Klaassen, Ziyech (Bazoer 77), Gudelj; Traore, Dolberg, Younes (Casierra 77).

Standard Liege (1) 2 *(Junior 45 (pen), Belfodil 82)*

Panathinaikos (2) 2 *(Ibarbo 12, 35)* 14,463

Standard Liege: (442) Gillet; Fai, Scholz, Laifis, Andrade; Dossevi (Mbenza 64), Trebel, Cisse (Enoh 72), Junior; Orlando Sa, Belfodil.
Panathinaikos: (433) Steele; Rodrigo Moledo, Samba (Ivanov 46), Koutroubis, Coulibaly; Zeca (M'Poku 78), Villafanez, Ledesma; Hult, Ibarbo, Leto (Lod 74).

Thursday, 3 November 2016

Ajax (1) 3 *(Dolberg 41, Ziyech 67, Younes 71)*

Celta Vigo (0) 2 *(Guidetti 80, Aspas 86)* 44,545

Ajax: (433) Onana; Veltman, Sanchez, Riedewald, Sinkgraven; Schone, Klaassen, Ziyech (Gudelj 77); Traore, Dolberg (Casierra 83), Younes.
Celta Vigo: (433) Ruben; Hugo Mallo, Sergi Gomez, Fontas, Planas; Diaz, Radoja, Sene (Aspas 73); Lemos (Wass 54), Rossi (Guidetti 78), Bongonda.

Panathinaikos (0) 0

Standard Liege (0) 3 *(Cisse 61, Belfodil 76, 90)* 10,837

Panathinaikos: (4312) Steele; Mesto (Chatzigiovanis 77), Rodrigo Moledo, Ivanov, Chouchoumis; Coulibaly, Koutroubis, M'Poku■; Lod; Ibarbo (Rinaldi 86), Berg (Leto 29).
Standard Liege: (433) Hubert; Fai, Scholz, Laifis, Echiejile (Fiore 46); Raman (Badibanga 63), Trebel, Cisse; Junior (Mbenza 88), Belfodil, Orlando Sa.

Thursday, 24 November 2016

Ajax (1) 2 *(Schone 39, Tete 50)*

Panathinaikos (0) 0 41,011

Ajax: (433) Onana; Tete, Westermann, de Ligt, Dijks; van de Beek, Schone (De Jong 69), Nouri; Cerny, Casierra, Younes (Clement 62).
Panathinaikos: (343) Steele; Koutroubis, Samba (Ivanov 57), Rodrigo Moledo; Coulibaly, Zeca, Lod, Hult; Villafanez (Ledesma 63), Ibarbo (Rinaldi 75), Wakaso.

Celta Vigo (1) 1 *(Aspas 8)*

Standard Liege (0) 1 *(Laifis 81)* 16,470

Celta Vigo: (433) Ruben; Hugo Mallo, Cabral, Roncaglia, Jonny (Sergi Gomez 83); Wass (Rossi 84), Diaz (Radoja 62), Hernandez; Aspas■, Guidetti, Sisto.
Standard Liege: (442) Hubert; Fai, Scholz, Laifis, Fiore; Junior (Mbenza 62), Trebel, Cisse, Raman (Badibanga 88); Orlando Sa, Belfodil.

Thursday, 8 December 2016

Panathinaikos (0) 0

Celta Vigo (1) 2 *(Guidetti 4, Orellana 76 (pen))* 4005

Panathinaikos: (4411) Steele; Mesto, Rodrigo Moledo, Ivanov, Chouchoumis; M'Poku, Zeca, Lod (Koutroubis 83), Wakaso; Villafanez (Leto 70); Rinaldi (Ibarbo 60).
Celta Vigo: (433) Ruben; Hugo Mallo, Cabral, Roncaglia, Jonny; Wass (Diaz 63), Radoja, Hernandez; Bongonda, Guidetti (Sergi Gomez 90), Orellana (Sisto 82).

Standard Liege (0) 1 *(Raman 84)*

Ajax (1) 1 *(El Ghazi 27)* 20,344

Standard Liege: (433) Hubert; Goreux, Scholz, Laifis, Fiore (Echiejile 57); Trebel, Dompe (Raman 56), Enoh; Mbenza, Orlando Sa, Junior (Badibanga 66).
Ajax: (433) Boer; Tete, de Ligt, Riedewald, Dijks; Klaassen, van de Beek, Nouri (Ziyech 78); El Ghazi, Casierra, Younes (Dolberg 66).

Group G	P	W	D	L	F	A	GD	Pts
Ajax	6	4	2	0	11	6	5	14
Celta Vigo	6	2	3	1	10	7	3	9
Standard Liege	6	1	4	1	8	6	2	7
Panathinaikos	6	0	1	5	3	13	–10	1

GROUP H

Thursday, 15 September 2016

Braga (1) 1 *(Andre Pinto 24)*

KAA Gent (1) 1 *(Milicevic 6)* 8903

Braga: (4231) Matheus Magalhaes; Baiano, Andre Pinto, Rosic, Goiano; Mauro, Bakic (Vukcevic N 73); Pedro Santos (Stoiljkovic 76), Pedro Tiba, Wilson Eduardo (Alan 84); Hassan.
KAA Gent: (343) Rinne; Mitrovic, Gershon, Asare; Foket, Esiti, Renato Neto, Saief; Milicevic, Perbet (Davidadze 70), Simon (Coulibaly 39).

Konyaspor (0) 0

Shakhtar Donetsk (0) 1 *(Ferreyra 76)* 26,860

Konyaspor: (442) Kirintili; Skubic, Turan, Vukovic, Douglas; Sahiner, Jonsson (Sonmez 85), Camdali, Hadziahmetovic; Milosevic (Meha 77), Bajic (Hora 70).
Shakhtar Donetsk: (433) Pyatov; Butko, Kucher, Rakitskiy, Ismaily; Stepanenko, Kovalenko (Malyshev 90), Fred; Marlos, Ferreyra (Eduardo 90), Bernard (Taison 67).

Thursday, 29 September 2016

KAA Gent (2) 2 *(Saief 17, Renato Neto 34)*

Konyaspor (0) 0 15,870

KAA Gent: (343) Rinne; Mitrovic, Gershon, Nielsen; Saief (Davidadze 88), Renato Neto, Vanderbruggen, Asare; Ndongala (Esiti 71), Coulibaly, Milicevic (Perbet 46).
Konyaspor: (442) Kirintili; Skubic, Turan, Vukovic, Douglas; Sahiner, Jonsson (Findikli 41), Camdali, Hadziahmetovic (Meha 65); Milosevic (Sonmez 80), Bajic.

Shakhtar Donetsk (1) 2 *(Stepanenko 5, Kovalenko 56)*

Braga (0) 0 11,938

Shakhtar Donetsk: (4411) Pyatov; Butko, Kucher, Ordets, Ismaily; Marlos (Taison 74), Stepanenko, Fred■, Bernard; Ferreyra (Dentinho 85); Kovalenko (Malyshev 90).
Braga: (433) Marafona; Baiano, Artur Jorge, Rosic, Marcelo Goiano; Vukcevic N, Mauro, Pedro Santos (Bakic 67); Ricardo Horta (Stoiljkovic 58), Hassan, Wilson Eduardo (Martinez 67).

Thursday, 20 October 2016

Konyaspor (1) 1 *(Milosevic 9)*

Braga (0) 1 *(Hassan 54)* 24,968

Konyaspor: (442) Kirintili; Skubic, Turan, Vukovic, Douglas; Sahiner (Meha 46), Findikli, Camdali, Hadziahmetovic (Sonmez 82); Milosevic, Bajic.
Braga: (433) Matheus Magalhaes; Baiano, Velazquez, Rosic, Marcelo Goiano; Alan (Rui Fonte 74), Vukcevic N, Mauro; Wilson Eduardo (Ricardo Horta 66), Hassan (Stoiljkovic 74), Pedro Santos.

Shakhtar Donetsk (2) 5 *(Kovalenko 13, Ferreyra 30, Bernard 46, Taison 75, Malyshev 85)*

KAA Gent (0) 0 10,505

Shakhtar Donetsk: (4411) Pyatov; Srna, Kucher, Rakitskiy, Ismaily; Marlos, Stepanenko, Malyshev, Bernard (Taison 74); Kovalenko (Dentinho 38); Ferreyra (Eduardo 81).
KAA Gent: (343) Rinne; Mitrovic, Gershon, Foket; Saief, Renato Neto, Vanderbruggen (Ibrahim 65), Asare; Simon, Perbet (Coulibaly 46), Milicevic (Dejaegere 73).

Thursday, 3 November 2016

KAA Gent (1) 3 *(Coulibaly 1, Perbet 84, Milicevic 89)*

Shakhtar Donetsk (3) 5 *(Marlos 37 (pen), Taison 42, Stepanenko 45, Fred 68, Ferreyra 87)* 14,526

KAA Gent: (343) Rinne; Nielsen, Gershon, Foket; Esiti, Renato Neto, Dejaegere (Saief 70), Asare; Simon (Ndongala 77), Milicevic, Coulibaly (Perbet 75).
Shakhtar Donetsk: (4411) Pyatov; Srna, Kucher, Rakitskiy (Ordets 78), Ismaily; Marlos, Stepanenko (Malyshev 72), Fred, Bernard; Taison (Dentinho 71); Ferreyra.

Braga (2) 3 *(Velazquez 34, Wilson Eduardo 45, Ricardo Horta 90)*

Konyaspor (1) 1 *(Rangelov 30)* 7729

Braga: (451) Matheus Magalhaes; Marcelo Goiano, Velazquez (Alan 73), Rosic, Baiano; Rui Fonte (Pedro Tiba 43), Ricardo Horta, Vukcevic N, Mauro■, Wilson Eduardo (Pedro Santos 69); Hassan.
Konyaspor: (442) Kirintili; Skubic■, Turan (Camdali 46), Bardakci, Uslu; Meha, Findikli, Guven, Fuchs (Sahiner 46); Rangelov (Bajic 76), Milosevic.

Thursday, 24 November 2016

KAA Gent (2) 2 *(Coulibaly 32, Milicevic 40)*

Braga (2) 2 *(Stoiljkovic 14, Hassan 36)* 19,650

KAA Gent: (352) Thoelen; Nielsen, Mitrovic, Asare; Foket, Renato Neto, Milicevic, Esiti (Perbet 85), Saief (Matton 90); Coulibaly, Simon (Dejaegere 70).
Braga: (433) Matheus Magalhaes; Baiano, Rosic, Andre Pinto (Artur Jorge 65), Marcelo Goiano; Ricardo Horta (Pedro Santos 89), Pedro Tiba, Vukcevic N; Stoiljkovic, Hassan (Rui Fonte 76), Wilson Eduardo.

Shakhtar Donetsk (2) 4 *(Bardakci 11 (og), Dentinho 36, Eduardo 66, Bernard 74)*

Konyaspor (0) 0 10,021

Shakhtar Donetsk: (4411) Shevchenko; Srna, Ordets, Kryvtsov, Matviyenko; Taison (Eduardo 63), Malyshev, Kovalenko (Tankovskiy 46), Bernard; Dentinho; Boriachuk (Stepanenko 78).
Konyaspor: (442) Kirintili; Sahiner, Ay, Bardakci, Uslu; Mbamba, Camdali (Meha 16), Findikli, Hadziahmetovic; Milosevic (Sonmez 63), Hora (Bajic 82).

Thursday, 8 December 2016

Braga (1) 2 *(Stoiljkovic 43, Vukcevic N 89)*

Shakhtar Donetsk (2) 4 *(Kryvtsov 22, 62, Taison 39, 66)* 15,084

Braga: (433) Marafona; Marcelo Goiano, Andre Pinto, Rosic, Baiano; Vukcevic N, Pedro Tiba, Wilson Eduardo (Benitez 67); Ricardo Horta, Rui Fonte (Hassan 58), Stoiljkovic (Alan 70).
Shakhtar Donetsk: (442) Shevchenko; Butko, Kryvtsov, Ordets, Matviyenko; Marlos (Bernard 58), Tankovskiy (Fred 61), Malyshev, Taison; Boryachuk (Ferreyra 69), Dentinho.

Konyaspor (0) 0

KAA Gent (0) 1 *(Coulibaly 90)* 10,720

Konyaspor: (451) Kirintili; Skubic, Ay, Vukovic, Douglas; Findikli, Sahiner (Milosevic 73), Mbamba, Meha (Hadziahmetovic 87), Jonsson; Hora (Bajic 66).
KAA Gent: (4411) Rinne; Foket, Nielsen, Mitrovic, Gershon; Matton (Dejaegere 66), Renato Neto (Esiti 69), Vanderbruggen, Saief; Milicevic; Perbet (Coulibaly 67).

Group H	P	W	D	L	F	A	GD	Pts
Shakhtar Donetsk	6	6	0	0	21	5	16	18
KAA Gent	6	2	2	2	9	13	–4	8
Braga	6	1	3	2	9	11	–2	6
Konyaspor	6	0	1	5	2	12	–10	1

GROUP I

Thursday, 15 September 2016

Nice (0) 0

Schalke 04 (0) 1 *(Rahman 76)* 21,378

Nice: (442) Cardinale; Ricardo Pereira, Baysse, Dante, Dalbert (Belhanda 81); Sarr, Koziello (Bodmer 67), Seri, Cyprien; Plea, Balotelli.
Schalke 04: (433) Fahrmann; Howedes, Naldo, Nastasic, Rahman; Goretzka (Kolasinac 90), Stambouli (Meyer 59), Bentaleb; Schopf (Konoplyanka 53), Embolo, Choupo-Moting.

Red Bull Salzburg (0) 0

Krasnodar (1) 1 *(Joaozinho 37)* 6507

Red Bull Salzburg: (433) Walke; Wisdom (Lainer 30 (Wanderson 79)), Paulo Miranda, Caleta-Car, Ulmer; Samassekou (Dabbur 73), Berisha, Upamecano; Lazaro, Soriano, Minamino.
Krasnodar: (433) Kritsyuk; Jedrzejczyk, Granqvist, Naldo, Petrov■; Ahmedov (Gazinski 62), Kabore, Eboue; Podberezkin (Laborde 60), Smolov, Joaozinho (Kaleshin 73).

Thursday, 29 September 2016

Krasnodar (2) 5 *(Smolov 22, Joaozinho 33, 65 (pen), Ari 86, 90)*

Nice (1) 2 *(Balotelli 42, Cyprien 71)* 10,750

Krasnodar: (433) Kritsyuk; Jedrzejczyk, Granqvist, Naldo, Torbinski; Eboue, Podberezkin (Laborde 74), Kabore; Ahmedov (Gazinski 59), Smolov (Ari 29), Joaozinho.
Nice: (433) Cardinale; Ricardo Pereira, Baysse, Dante, Sarr; Koziello (Walter 79), Seri, Eysseric; Belhanda, Balotelli (Plea 46), Dalbert (Cyprien 66).

Schalke 04 (1) 3 *(Goretzka 15, Caleta-Car 47 (og), Howedes 58)*

Red Bull Salzburg (0) 1 *(Soriano 72)* 48,374

Schalke 04: (4231) Fahrmann; Howedes, Naldo, Nastasic, Bentaleb; Geis, Kolasinac (Baba 80); Schopf, Goretzka (Konoplyanka 67), Meyer (Stambouli 88); Embolo.
Red Bull Salzburg: (4231) Walke; Lainer, Paulo Miranda, Caleta-Car, Ulmer; Laimer (Radosevic 66), Upamecano; Wanderson (Rzatkowski 89), Berisha, Lazaro (Minamino 66); Soriano.

Thursday, 20 October 2016

Krasnodar (0) 0

Schalke 04 (1) 1 *(Konoplyanka 11)* 33,550

Krasnodar: (433) Kritsyuk; Jedrzejczyk, Martynovich, Granqvist, Petrov; Eboue (Gazinski 55), Podberezkin (Laborde 67), Kabore; Ahmedov (Mamaev 74), Ari, Joaozinho.
Schalke 04: (4411) Fahrmann; Howedes, Naldo, Nastasic, Baba; Junior Caicara, Stambouli, Aogo, Konoplyanka (Schopf 67); Meyer (Huntelaar 77); Di Santo (Kehrer 90).

Red Bull Salzburg (0) 0

Nice (1) 1 *(Plea 12)* 9473

Red Bull Salzburg: (442) Walke; Lainer, Paulo Miranda, Wisdom, Ulmer; Rzatkowski, Laimer, Radosevic, Lazaro (Minamino 79); Gulbrandsen (Hwang 83), Soriano (Dabbur 83).
Nice: (532) Cardinale; Ricardo Pereira, Dante, Baysse, Sarr, Dalbert (Belhanda 77); Koziello (Cyprien 73), Bodmer (Seri 73), Walter; Plea, Eysseric.

Thursday, 3 November 2016

Nice (0) 0

Red Bull Salzburg (0) 2 *(Hwang 72, 73)* 17,582

Nice: (433) Cardinale; Souquet, Sarr, Dante, Ricardo Pereira; Koziello, Seri (Walter 76), Belhanda; Cyprien (Donis 78), Balotelli, Plea (Eysseric 71).
Red Bull Salzburg: (442) Walke; Wisdom, Paulo Miranda, Upamecano, Ulmer; Rzatkowski (Lainer 76), Laimer, Radosevic, Lazaro; Dabbur (Soriano 83), Gulbrandsen (Hwang 62).

Schalke 04 (2) 2 *(Junior Caicara 24, Bentaleb 28)*

Krasnodar (0) 0 42,210

Schalke 04: (352) Fahrmann; Howedes, Naldo, Nastasic; Stambouli, Bentaleb (Goretzka 57), Aogo, Junior Caicara, Baba (Kolasinac 69); Konoplyanka (Schopf 81), Choupo-Moting.
Krasnodar: (433) Kritsyuk; Jedrzejczyk (Kaleshin 75), Naldo, Granqvist, Petrov; Eboue, Pereyra, Kabore; Ahmedov (Izmailov 62), Podberezkin (Laborde 12), Joaozinho.

Thursday, 24 November 2016

Krasnodar (0) 1 *(Smolov 85)*

Red Bull Salzburg (1) 1 *(Dabbur 37)* 19,150

Krasnodar: (433) Kritsyuk; Kaleshin, Naldo, Granqvist, Torbinski; Eboue (Gazinski 46), Kabore, Pereyra (Laborde 58); Ahmedov, Smolov, Joaozinho (Izmailov 74).
Red Bull Salzburg: (442) Walke; Wisdom, Paulo Miranda, Upamecano, Ulmer; Berisha (Schlager 88), Samassekou, Radosevic, Lazaro; Dabbur, Gulbrandsen (Hwang 73).

Schalke 04 (1) 2 *(Konoplyanka 14, Aogo 80 (pen))*

Nice (0) 0 51,504

Schalke 04: (532) Fahrmann; Junior Caicara, Riether, Naldo, Kehrer, Baba; Stambouli, Meyer (Reese 46), Aogo; Tekpetey■, Konoplyanka (Bentaleb 61 (Avdijaj 81)).
Nice: (352) Cardinale; Souquet, Dante, Bodmer; Ricardo Pereira (Plea 66), Walter (Marcel 69), Boscagli, Koziello, Dalbert; Donis, Belhanda (Eysseric 65).

Thursday, 8 December 2016

Nice (0) 2 *(Bosetti 64 (pen), Le Marchand 77)*

Krasnodar (0) 1 *(Smolov 51)* 12,722

Nice: (442) Benitez; Boscagli, Bodmer, Le Marchand, Burner; Souquet (Rafetraniaina 75), Lusamba, Marcel, Perraud; Balotelli (Bosetti 46), Donis (Mahou 68).
Krasnodar: (433) Sinitsyn; Naldo, Martynovich, Granqvist■, Jedrzejczyk; Gazinski, Eboue, Ahmedov; Torbinski (Kaleshin 65), Smolov, Joaozinho.

Red Bull Salzburg (1) 2 *(Schlager 22, Radosevic 90)*

Schalke 04 (0) 0 21,000

Red Bull Salzburg: (442) Stankovic; Caleta-Car, Schwegler, Lazaro (Wolf 75), Rzatkowski; Minamino, Lainer, Radosevic, Laimer (Samassekou 60); Schlager (Yabo 86), Wisdom.
Schalke 04: (433) Giefer; Riether (Uchida 83), Howedes, Kehrer, Junior Caicara; Stambouli, Aogo, Baba; Reese (Schopf 58), Avdijaj, Konoplyanka (Sam 75).

Group I	P	W	D	L	F	A	GD	Pts
Schalke 04	6	5	0	1	9	3	6	15
Krasnodar	6	2	1	3	8	8	0	7
Red Bull Salzburg	6	2	1	3	6	6	0	7
Nice	6	2	0	4	5	11	–6	6

GROUP J

Thursday, 15 September 2016

PAOK Salonika (0) 0

Fiorentina (0) 0 20,904

PAOK Salonika: (433) Glykos; Matos, Varela, Tzavelas, Leovac; Cimirot, Canas, Pelkas (Shakhov 57); Djalma (Crespo 58), Athanasiadis (Thiam 79), Rodrigues.
Fiorentina: (532) Tatarusanu; Salcedo (Bernarderschi 74), Tomovic, Rodriguez, Astori, Olivera; Valero, Badelj, Ilicic (Sanchez 63); El Babacar (Tello 77), Kalinic.

Qarabag (1) 2 *(Michel 7, Sadygov 90)*

Slovan Liberec (1) 2 *(Sykora 1, Baros 68)* 6200

Qarabag: (433) Sehic; Medvedev, Yunuszadze, Sadygov, Agolli (Madatov 86); Michel, Garayev (Ismayilov 77), Almeida; Quintana, Ndlovu (Muarem 67), Reynaldo.
Slovan Liberec: (4411) Dubravka; Coufal, Hovorka, Latka, Bartosak; Bartl (Karafiat 65), Folprecht, Breite, Vuch; Sykora (Nitriansky 85); Baros (Sukennik 75).

Thursday, 29 September 2016

Fiorentina (3) 5 *(El Babacar 39, 45, Kalinic 43, Zarate 63, 78)*

Qarabag (0) 1 *(Ndlovu 90)* 14,145

Fiorentina: (343) Tatarusanu; Tomovic, De Maio, Salcedo; Tello, Sanchez (Vecino 46), Cristoforo, Olivera; Bernarderschi (Chiesa 61), El Babacar, Kalinic (Zarate 61).
Qarabag: (4231) Sehic; Medvedev, Yunuszadze■, Sadygov, Agolli; Michel, Almeida; Ismayilov (Muarem 62), Amirguliyev, Quintana (Guseynov 46); Reynaldo (Ndlovu 84).

Slovan Liberec (1) 1 *(Komlichenko 1)*

PAOK Salonika (1) 2 *(Athanasiadis 10 (pen), 82)* 8883

Slovan Liberec: (4231) Dubravka; Coufal, Latka, Hovorka, Bartosak (Baros 79); Breite, Folprecht (Karafiat 73); Bartl (Ekpai 46), Sykora, Vuch; Komlichenko.
PAOK Salonika: (4231) Glykos; Matos, Varela, Tzavelas, Leovac; Canas, Cimirot; Rodrigues, Shakhov (Thiam 73), Djalma (Mystakidis 59); Athanasiadis (Crespo 85).

Thursday, 20 October 2016

Qarabag (0) 2 *(Quintana 56, Amirguliyev 87)*

PAOK Salonika (0) 0 26,784

Qarabag: (4312) Sehic; Medvedev, Guseynov, Sadygov, Agolli; Garayev, Almeida, Quintana (Aleskerov 90); Amirguliyev; Muarem (Nadirov 90), Ndlovu (Madatov 77).
PAOK Salonika: (433) Glykos; Matos, Crespo, Varela, Leovac; Shakhov, Canas (Biseswar 59), Cimirot; Djalma (Koulouris 77), Thiam (Pereyra 66), Rodrigues.

Slovan Liberec (0) 1 *(Sevcik 58)*

Fiorentina (2) 3 *(Kalinic 8, 23, El Babacar 70)* 9037

Slovan Liberec: (4141) Dubravka; Coufal, Hovorka, Karafiat, Sykora (Bartosak 68); Vuch; Sevcik, Breite■, Folprecht, Navratil (Bartl 72); Komlichenko (Markovic 78).
Fiorentina: (352) Tatarusanu; Tomovic, Astori, Rodriguez; Cristoforo (Bernarderschi 62), Badelj, Valero, Vecino, Olivera; El Babacar (Sanchez 78), Kalinic (Tello 52).

Thursday, 3 November 2016

Fiorentina (2) 3 *(Ilicic 30 (pen), Kalinic 42, Cristoforo 73)*

Slovan Liberec (0) 0 11,583

Fiorentina: (4411) Tatarusanu; Tomovic, Rodriguez, De Maio, Milic; Sanchez, Valero (El Babacar 79), Cristoforo, Chiesa; Ilicic (Vecino 69); Kalinic (Bernarderschi 86).
Slovan Liberec: (4231) Hladk˝; Sukennik, Coufal, Hovorka (Nitriansky 16), Bartosak; Folprecht, Sykora (Navratil 79); Bartl, Sevcik, Vuch; Markovic (Komlichenko 59).

PAOK Salonika (0) 0

Qarabag (0) 1 *(Michel 69)* 11,476

PAOK Salonika: (4411) Glykos; Matos, Varela, Tzavelas, Leovac; Mystakidis (Pereyra 61), Canas, Cimirot (Shakhov 81), Rodrigues; Biseswar (Thiam 73); Athanasiadis.
Qarabag: (433) Sehic; Medvedev, Guseynov, Sadygov, Agolli; Amirguliyev (Michel 64), Garayev, Almeida; Quintana, Ndlovu (Reynaldo 76), Muarem (Ismayilov 88).

Thursday, 24 November 2016

Fiorentina (1) 2 *(Bernarderschi 33, El Babacar 50)*

PAOK Salonika (2) 3 *(Shakhov 6, Djalma 26, Rodrigues 90)* 12,793

Fiorentina: (4231) Lezzerini; Tomovic, Astori, Rodriguez, Milic (Chiesa 51); Cristoforo (Sanchez 66), Badelj; Tello (Ilicic 83), Vecino, Bernarderschi; El Babacar.
PAOK Salonika: (433) Brkic; Matos, Crespo, Varela, Leovac; Shakhov (Mystakidis 82), Canas, Cimirot; Djalma (Pelkas 71), Koulouris (Thiam 61), Rodrigues.

Slovan Liberec (1) 3 *(Vuch 11, Komlichenko 57 (pen), 63)*

Qarabag (0) 0 4942

Slovan Liberec: (4231) Dubravka; Karafiat, Coufal, Pokorny, Bartosak; Breite, Folprecht; Ekpai, Sevcik (Navratil 80), Vuch (Blaha 90); Komlichenko (Bartl 86).
Qarabag: (433) Sehic; Agolli, Medvedev, Guseynov, Dashdemirov; Almeida, Garayev, Michel (Ismayilov 53); Quintana, Ndlovu, Muarem (Reynaldo 60).

Thursday, 8 December 2016

PAOK Salonika (1) 2 *(Rodrigues 29, Pelkas 67)*

Slovan Liberec (0) 0 11,463

PAOK Salonika: (433) Glykos; Matos, Varela, Crespo, Leovac (Malezas 82); Cimirot, Pelkas (Shakhov 80), Canas; Djalma, Athanasiadis (Koulouris 71), Rodrigues.
Slovan Liberec: (4141) Dubravka; Karafiat (Bartl 46), Coufal, Pokorny, Bartosak; Breite; Vuch, Sevcik, Folprecht (Kubyshkin 79), Ekpai (Sykora 64); Komlichenko.

Qarabag (0) 1 *(Reynaldo 73)*

Fiorentina (0) 2 *(Vecino 60, Chiesa 76)* 21,750

Qarabag: (433) Sehic; Gurbanov, Guseynov, Sadygov, Agolli; Amirguliyev (Reynaldo 62), Garayev, Almeida; Quintana, Ndlovu (Madatov 71), Muarem (Ismayilov 46).

Fiorentina: (4231) Tatarusanu; Tomovic, Rodriguez, Astori, Olivera; Badelj, Vecino; Chiesa■, Cristoforo (Valero 61), Bernarderschi (Sanchez 82); El Babacar (Kalinic 51).

Group J	P	W	D	L	F	A	GD	Pts
Fiorentina	6	4	1	1	15	6	9	13
PAOK Salonika	6	3	1	2	7	6	1	10
Qarabag	6	2	1	3	7	12	–5	7
Slovan Liberec	6	1	1	4	7	12	–5	4

GROUP K

Thursday, 15 September 2016

Internazionale (0) 0

Hapoel Beer Sheva (0) 2 *(Vitor 54, Buzaglo 69)* 16,778

Internazionale: (433) Handanovic; D'Ambrosio, Ranocchia, Murillo, Nagatomo; Medel, Brozovic (Banega 46), Felipe Melo (Icardi 73); Biabiany (Candreva 58), Palacio, Eder.
Hapoel Beer Sheva: (532) Goresh; Biton, Vitor, Tzedek, Taha, Korhut (Turjeman 85); Hoban, Ogu, Nwakaeme; Buzaglo (Sahar 77), Maranhao (Melikson 66).

Southampton (2) 3 *(Austin 5 (pen), 27, Rodriguez 90)*

Sparta Prague (0) 0 25,125

Southampton: (442) Forster; Martina, van Dijk, Targett, Yoshida; Hojbjerg, Romeu (Davis 83), Ward-Prowse, Tadic (Redmond 70); Austin (Rodriguez 76), Long.
Sparta Prague: (352) Koubek; Holek, Nhamoinesu, Michal Kadlec; Karavaev, Frydek, Sacek, Vacha (Marecek 64), Sural (Pulkrab 74); Kadlec V, Julis (Lafata 47).

Thursday, 29 September 2016

Hapoel Beer Sheva (0) 0

Southampton (0) 0 16,138

Hapoel Beer Sheva: (352) Goresh; Biton, Vitor, Taha; Tzedek, Korhut, Nwakaeme, Radi (Hoban 80), Ogu; Melikson (Buzaglo 70), Maranhao (Sahar 63).
Southampton: (4231) Forster; Martina, van Dijk, Targett, Yoshida; Clasie, Ward-Prowse; Romeu, Redmond (Hojbjerg 85), Hesketh (Tadic 34); Long.

Sparta Prague (2) 3 *(Kadlec V 7, 25, Holek 76)*

Internazionale (0) 1 *(Palacio 71)* 14,651

Sparta Prague: (4411) Koubek; Karavaev, Mazuch, Holek, Michal Kadlec (Pulkrab 73); Cermak (Lafata 87), Frydek (Julis 66), Sacek, Holzer; Dockal; Kadlec V.
Internazionale: (433) Handanovic; D'Ambrosio (Ansaldi 56), Ranocchia■, Murillo, Miangue; Gnoukouri (Icardi 70), Banega, Felipe Melo; Candreva (Perisic 63), Palacio, Eder.

Thursday, 20 October 2016

Hapoel Beer Sheva (0) 0

Sparta Prague (0) 1 *(Pulkrab 71)* 15,607

Hapoel Beer Sheva: (433) Goresh; Bitton, Vitor, Tzedek, Korhut; Radi (Buzaglo 68), Ogu, Hoban (Sahar 73); Melikson, Maranhao (Ghadir 82), Nwakaeme.
Sparta Prague: (442) Koubek; Karavaev, Mazuch, Holek, Michal Kadlec; Holzer (Pulkrab 46), Marecek, Dockal, Zahustel; Julis (Lafata 77), Kadlec V (Dudl 90).

Internazionale (0) 1 *(Candreva 67)*

Southampton (0) 0 26,719

Internazionale: (433) Handanovic; Nagatomo (D'Ambrosio 90), Miranda, Murillo, Santon; Gnoukouri, Medel, Brozovic■; Candreva (Ansaldi 81), Icardi, Eder (Perisic 86).
Southampton: (4312) Forster; Martina, Yoshida, van Dijk, McQueen; Hojbjerg, Romeu, Ward-Prowse; Tadic (Boufal 73); Rodriguez (Davis 78), Long (Austin 48).

Thursday, 3 November 2016

Southampton (0) 2 *(van Dijk 65, Nagatomo 69 (og))*

Internazionale (1) 1 *(Icardi 33)* 30,389

Southampton: (4231) Forster; Martina, Yoshida, van Dijk, McQueen; Romeu, Ward-Prowse; Hojbjerg, Redmond, Tadic (Davis 77); Rodriguez (Austin 59).
Internazionale: (4411) Handanovic; D'Ambrosio, Ranocchia, Miranda, Nagatomo; Candreva (Biabiany 89), Medel (Eder 74), Gnoukouri (Felipe Melo 82), Perisic; Banega; Icardi.

Sparta Prague (2) 2 *(Biton 24 (og), Lafata 38)*

Hapoel Beer Sheva (0) 0 12,891

Sparta Prague: (442) Koubek; Karavaev, Michal Kadlec, Mazuch, Nhamoinesu; Julis (Dudl 72), Holek, Marecek, Holzer (Milan Kadlec 90); Dockal, Lafata (Pulkrab 79).
Hapoel Beer Sheva: (352) Goresh; Taha, Vitor (Shabtai 46), Tzedek; Biton, Hoban, Radi, Buzaglo (Ghadir 62), Korhut; Melikson, Maranhao (Sahar 73).

Thursday, 24 November 2016

Hapoel Beer Sheva (0) 3 *(Maranhao 58, Nwakaeme 71 (pen), Sahar 90)*

Internazionale (2) 2 *(Icardi 12, Brozovic 25)* 15,973

Hapoel Beer Sheva: (541) Goresh; Bitton, Taha (Radi 35), Vitor, Tzedek, Korhut; Buzaglo, Hoban (Ghadir 81), Ogu, Nwakaeme; Maranhao (Sahar 75).
Internazionale: (433) Handanovic■; D'Ambrosio, Miranda, Murillo, Nagatomo; Felipe Melo (Gnoukouri 62), Banega (Carrizo 69), Brozovic; Candreva, Icardi, Eder (Perisic 60).

Sparta Prague (1) 1 *(Nhamoinesu 11)*

Southampton (0) 0 17,429

Sparta Prague: (442) Koubek; Karavaev, Mazuch, Michal Kadlec, Nhamoinesu; Julis (Kostl 90), Holek, Marecek, Holzer (Dudl 90); Dockal, Lafata (Havelka 87).
Southampton: (433) Forster; Martina, Yoshida, van Dijk, McQueen; Clasie (Austin 72), Hojbjerg (Romeu 54), Ward-Prowse; Rodriguez (Boufal 55), Redmond, Long.

Thursday, 8 December 2016

Internazionale (1) 2 *(Eder 24, 90)*

Sparta Prague (0) 1 *(Marecek 54)* 6449

Internazionale: (442) Carrizo; Murillo, Andreolli, Ranocchia, Miangue; Eder, Ansaldi, Felipe Melo, Biabiany; Pinamonti (Bakayoko 79), Palacio (Perisic 46).
Sparta Prague: (442) Koubek; Karavaev, Mazuch, Michal Kadlec, Nhamoinesu; Julis (Dudl 89), Holek, Marecek, Cermak (Sacek 78); Dockal, Lafata (Pulkrab 73).

Southampton (0) 1 *(van Dijk 90)*

Hapoel Beer Sheva (0) 1 *(Buzaglo 78)* 30,416

Southampton: (433) Forster; Cedric, van Dijk, Yoshida, Bertrand; Romeu, Davis, Hojbjerg (Ward-Prowse 82); Sims (Tadic 59), Austin (Long 39), Redmond.
Hapoel Beer Sheva: (433) Goresh; Bitton, Vitor, Tzedek, Korhut (Shabtai 77); Radi, Ogu, Hoban (Ghadir 56); Buzaglo, Sahar (Maranhao 68), Nwakaeme.

Group K	P	W	D	L	F	A	GD	Pts
Sparta Prague	6	4	0	2	8	6	2	12
Hapoel Beer Sheva	6	2	2	2	6	6	0	8
Southampton	6	2	2	2	6	4	2	8
Internazionale	6	2	0	4	7	11	–4	6

GROUP L

Thursday, 15 September 2016

Osmanlispor (0) 2 *(Diabate 64 (pen), Umar 74)*

Steaua Bucharest (0) 0 11,807

Osmanlispor: (4231) Karcemarskas; Altinay, Curusku, Demir, Tiago Pinto; Lawal, Cagiran (Maher 83); Umar (Delarge 75), Ndiaye, Regattin; Diabate (Rusescu 78).
Steaua Bucharest: (4231) Nita; Enache■, Tamas, Moke, Tosca; Bourceanu, Aganovic; Popa, Boldrin (Tanase 61), William (Jakolis 67); Golubovic (Mitrea 46).

Villarreal (2) 2 *(Alexandre Pato 28, Jonathan 45)*

FC Zurich (1) 1 *(Sadiku 2)* 16,384

Villarreal: (442) Fernandez; Rukavina, Alvaro, Victor Ruiz, Jose Angel; Jonathan (Castillejo 71), N'Diaye, Bruno, Cheryshev (Soriano 80); Borre (Sansone 67), Alexandre Pato.
FC Zurich: (4411) Vanins; Bangura, Nef, Kecojevic, Brunner; Voser, Sarr (Yapi Yapo 57), Kukeli, Winter (Schonbachler 65); Rodriguez (Cavusevic 84); Sadiku.

Thursday, 29 September 2016

FC Zurich (1) 2 *(Schonbachler 45, Cavusevic 80)*

Osmanlispor (0) 1 *(Maher 74)* 7473

FC Zurich: (451) Vanins; Brunner, Nef, Kecojevic, Voser; Kone (Rodriguez 56), Buff (Yapi Yapo 89), Kukeli, Sarr, Schonbachler (Winter 71); Cavusevic.
Osmanlispor: (4231) Karcemarskas; Vrsajevic, Curusku, Demir, Tiago Pinto; Cagiran (Maher 62), Lawal; Delarge (Umar 68), Ndiaye, Regattin; Rusescu (Diabate 72).

Steaua Bucharest (1) 1 *(Sulley 19)*

Villarreal (1) 1 *(Borre 9)* 13,231

Steaua Bucharest: (442) Nita; Tamas, Moke, Tosca, Momcilovic; Popa (Jakolis 77), Bourceanu, Sulley, William (Popescu 89); Boldrin, Golubovic (Tanase 77).
Villarreal: (442) Fernandez; Rukavina, Musacchio, Bonera, Jose Angel; Jonathan, N'Diaye, Bruno, Cheryshev (Soriano 73); Borre (Bakambu 82), Alexandre Pato (Castillejo 63).

Thursday, 20 October 2016

Osmanlispor (2) 2 *(Rusescu 24, 26)*

Villarreal (0) 2 *(N'Diaye 56, Alexandre Pato 74)* 11,692

Osmanlispor: (4231) Arikan; Vrsajevic, Curusku, Demir, Tiago Pinto; Ndiaye, Lawal (Guven■ 39); Umar, Maher (Prochazka 58), Delarge; Rusescu (Regattin 79).
Villarreal: (442) Fernandez; Rukavina, Alvaro, Bonera, Jose Angel; Jonathan (Soriano 70), N'Diaye (Sansone 82), Bruno, Castillejo; Borre (Bakambu 65), Alexandre Pato.

Steaua Bucharest (0) 1 *(Golubovic 62)*

FC Zurich (0) 1 *(Kone 85)* 13,154

Steaua Bucharest: (4231) Nita; Popescu, Tamas, Tosca, Momcilovic; Bourceanu, Sulley (Jakolis 82); Popa, Boldrin, William; Golubovic (Tudorie 79).
FC Zurich: (343) Vanins; Brunner (Marchesano 84), Kecojevic, Nef; Buff, Yapi Yapo, Sarr (Cavusevic 78), Voser; Winter (Schonbachler 73), Kone, Rodriguez.

Thursday, 3 November 2016

FC Zurich (0) 0

Steaua Bucharest (0) 0 8060

FC Zurich: (4141) Vanins; Brunner, Kecojevic, Nef, Voser (Stettler 29); Kukeli; Winter (Kone 65), Buff (Schonbachler 75), Sarr, Rodriguez; Cavusevic.
Steaua Bucharest: (4231) Nita; Tamas, Moke, Tosca, Momcilovic; Bourceanu (Aganovic 63), Sulley (Tudorie 84); Popa, Boldrin, William; Golubovic (Achim 72).

Villarreal (0) 1 *(Rodri 48)*

Osmanlispor (1) 2 *(Webo 7, Rusescu 75)* 15,386

Villarreal: (442) Fernandez; Rukavina, Alvaro, Victor Ruiz, Jose Angel; Jonathan (Sansone 86), Rodri, Bruno, Cheryshev (Castillejo 69); Bakambu, Borre (Alexandre Pato 63).
Osmanlispor: (4231) Arikan; Bayir, Curusku, Prochazka, Tiago Pinto; Cagiran (Guzel 86), Ndiaye; Umar, Maher, Delarge (Regattin 67); Webo (Rusescu 72).

Thursday, 24 November 2016

FC Zurich (0) 1 *(Rodriguez 87 (pen))*

Villarreal (1) 1 *(Bruno 14)* 10,069

FC Zurich: (352) Vanins; Bangura, Kecojevic, Nef; Brunner (Rodriguez 69), Marchesano, Sarr, Kukeli (Sadiku 80), Voser (Winter 69); Kone, Schonbachler.
Villarreal: (442) Sergio Asenjo; Rukavina, Musacchio, Victor Ruiz, Jose Angel; Jonathan, Trigueros, Bruno, Cheryshev (Castillejo 70); Bakambu (Rodri 82), Alexandre Pato (Sansone 78).

Steaua Bucharest (0) 2 *(Momcilovic 68, Tamas 86)*

Osmanlispor (1) 1 *(Ndiaye 30)* 6020

Steaua Bucharest: (4411) Nita; Tamas, Moke, Tosca, Momcilovic; Pintilii (Bourceanu 46), Sulley (Achim 63), Enache (Golubovic 46), Boldrin; William; Popa.
Osmanlispor: (4231) Karcemarskas; Vrsajevic (Bayir 75), Curusku, Prochazka, Tiago Pinto; Cagiran, Maher (Lawal 61); Regattin, Ndiaye, Delarge (Kilicaslan 70); Rusescu.

Thursday, 8 December 2016

Osmanlispor (0) 2 *(Delarge 73, Kilicaslan 90)*

FC Zurich (0) 0 10,250

Osmanlispor: (4231) Karcemarskas; Vrsajevic, Curusku, Prochazka, Tiago Pinto; Guven, Ndiaye; Delarge (Umar 74), Maher, Regattin (Kilicaslan 87); Webo (Rusescu 77).
FC Zurich: (343) Vanins; Nef, Bangura, Kecojevic; Brunner (Sadiku 60), Sarr, Kukeli, Voser (Kone 77); Winter, Cavusevic (Schonbachler 68), Rodriguez.

Villarreal (1) 2 *(Sansone 16, Trigueros 87)*

Steaua Bucharest (0) 1 *(Achim 55)* 19,471

Villarreal: (442) Sergio Asenjo; Mario, Musacchio (Alvaro 39), Victor Ruiz, Jaume; Jonathan, Trigueros, Bruno, Soriano; Bakambu (Rodri 85), Sansone (Borre 79).
Steaua Bucharest: (442) Nita; Tamas■, Moke, Tosca, Momcilovic; Enache (Golubovic 46), Pintilii (Achim 54), Bourceanu, William; Popa, Boldrin (Popescu 76).

Group L	P	W	D	L	F	A	GD	Pts
Osmanlispor	6	3	1	2	10	7	3	10
Villarreal	6	2	3	1	9	8	1	9
FC Zurich	6	1	3	2	5	7	–2	6
Steaua Bucharest	6	1	3	2	5	7	–2	6

KNOCKOUT STAGE

ROUND OF 32 FIRST LEG

Thursday, 16 February 2017

Anderlecht (2) 2 *(Acheampong 5, 31)*

Zenit St Petersburg (0) 0 13,415

Anderlecht: (4231) Ruben Martinez; Obradovic, Deschacht, Spajic, Najar; Tielemans, Dendoncker; Acheampong (Chipciu 60), Stanciu (Hanni 74), Bruno; Thelin (Teodorczyk 81).
Zenit St Petersburg: (442) Lodygin; Ivanovic, Luis Neto, Javi Garcia, Criscito; Junior, Giuliano (Yusupov 80), Shatov (Mak 65), Zhirkov; Dzjuba, Kokorin (Danny 71).

Astra Giurgiu (1) 2 *(Budescu 43, Seto 90)*

Genk (1) 2 *(Castagne 25, Trossard 83)* 3775

Astra Giurgiu: (343) Lung; Geraldo Alves, Sapunaru, Fabricio; Stan, Seto, Teixeira, Junior Morais; Ionita II (Florea 64), Niculae (Bus 65 (Nicoara 80)), Budescu.
Genk: (4231) Ryan; Castagne, Brabec, Colley, Uronen; Kumordzi (Berge 65), Heynen; Schrijvers, Pozuelo (Boetius 75), Trossard (Buffel 88); Samatta.

Athletic Bilbao (1) 3 *(Merkis 38 (og), Aduriz 61, Williams 71)*

APOEL Nicosia (1) 2 *(Efrem 36, Gianniotas 89)* 32,675

Athletic Bilbao: (4231) Iraizoz; Balenziaga (Lekue 56), Laporte, Yeray, De Marcos; Benat, Iturraspe (San Jose 56); Muniain, Raul Garcia, Williams (Susaeta 77); Aduriz.
APOEL Nicosia: (4231) Waterman; Milanov, Merkis, Choco, Ioannou; Morais, Vinicius; Gianniotas, Bertoglio (de Camargo 59), Efrem (Aloneftis 73); Sotiriou (Astiz 77).

AZ Alkmaar (0) 1 *(Jahanbakhsh 69 (pen))*

Lyon (2) 4 *(Tousart 26, Lacazette 45, 57, Ferri 90)* 16,098

AZ Alkmaar: (433) Krul; Luckassen, Van Eijden, Wuytens, Haps; Seuntjens (van Overeem 74), Jahanbakhsh, Rienstra; Bel Hassani, Weghorst (Fred Friday 65), Tankovic (Garcia 65).
Lyon: (4312) Lopes; Jallet, Mammana, Diakhaby, Rybus; Tousart (Ferri 67), Gonalons, Tolisso; Darder (Aouar 84); Fekir, Lacazette (Cornet 66).

Borussia Munchengladbach (0) 0

Fiorentina (1) 1 *(Bernarderschi 44)* 41,863

Borussia Munchengladbach: (442) Sommer; Jantschke (Drmic 64), Christensen, Vestergaard, Wendt; Herrmann (Hahn 77), Kramer, Dahoud, Johnson (Korb 77); Hazard, Stindl.
Fiorentina: (343) Tatarusanu; Sanchez, Astori, Rodriguez; Badelj, Vecino, Olivera, Tello (Tomovic 85); Valero, Bernarderschi (Cristoforo 64), Kalinic (El Babacar 77).

Celta Vigo (0) 0

Shakhtar Donetsk (1) 1 *(Blanco Leschuk 26)* 18,318

Celta Vigo: (433) Sergio; Hugo Mallo, Cabral, Roncaglia, Jonny; Hernandez, Wass, Radoja (Jozabed 74); Aspas, Guidetti (Rossi 85), Bongonda (Sisto 58).
Shakhtar Donetsk: (4411) Pyatov; Ismaily, Rakitskiy, Ordets, Srna; Taison (Bernard 84), Fred, Malyshev, Marlos (Azevedo 90); Dentinho (Kovalenko 46); Blanco Leschuk.

Hapoel Beer Sheva (1) 1 *(Barda 44)*

Besiktas (1) 3 *(William Soares 43 (og), Tosun 60, Hutchinson 90)* 15,347

Hapoel Beer Sheva: (4141) Goresh; Bitton, William Soares, Tzedek, Turjeman; Ogu; Melikson (Ghadir 58), Hoban (Ohana 67), Radi, Nwakaeme; Barda (Sahar 79).
Besiktas: (4231) Fabri; Gonul, Marcelo, Mitrovic, Tosic; Uysal, Hutchinson; Quaresma (Inler 90), Arslan (Anderson Talisca 74), Babel; Tosun (Sismanoglu 90).

KAA Gent (0) 1 *(Perbet 59)*

Tottenham H (0) 0 19,267

KAA Gent: (433) Kalinic; Mitrovic, Asare (Gershon 80), Dejaegere, Gigot; Saief, Esiti, Foket; Simon (Kalu 74), Perbet (Coulibaly 74), Milicevic.
Tottenham H: (4231) Lloris; Walker, Alderweireld, Dier, Davies; Wanyama, Dembele (Son 68); Sissoko (Nkoudou 72), Alli, Winks (Eriksen 80); Kane.

Krasnodar (1) 1 *(Claesson 4)*

Fenerbahce (0) 0 32,460

Krasnodar: (433) Kritsyuk; Kaleshin, Martynovich, Naldo, Ramirez; Gazinski, Kabore, Podberezkin (Pereyra 70); Wanderson (Laborde 66), Smolov, Claesson.
Fenerbahce: (433) Demirel; Ozbayrakli, Neustadter, Kjaer, Kaldirim; Souza, Potuk, Topal; Lens, Emenike (Fernandao 73), Sow (Tufan 73).

Legia Warsaw (0) 0

Ajax (0) 0 28,742

Legia Warsaw: (4231) Malarz; Broz, Dabrowski, Pazdan, Hlousek; Kopczynski, Jodlowiec; Radovic, Odjidja-Ofoe (Hamalainen 82), Qazaishvili (Guilherme 59); Necid (Kucharczyk 58).
Ajax: (433) Onana; Tete■, Sanchez, Viergever, Sinkgraven; Klaassen, Schone, Ziyech (van de Beek 81); Traore (Kluivert 73 (Westermann 86)), Dolberg, Younes.

Ludogorets Razgrad (0) 1 *(Keseru 81)*

FC Copenhagen (1) 2 *(Abel 3 (og), Toutouh 53)* 14,500

Ludogorets Razgrad: (433) Stoyanov; Minev, Palomino, Moti, Natanael; Dyakov, Marcelinho, Abel; Wanderson (Paulo 80), Cafu, Misidjan (Keseru 62).
FC Copenhagen: (442) Olsen; Ankersen, Jorgensen, Johansson, Augustinsson; Jensen (Gregus■ 72), Matic, Kvist Jorgensen, Toutouh (Hogli 90); Santander (Pavlovic 71), Cornelius.

Manchester U (1) 3 *(Ibrahimovic 15, 75, 88 (pen))*

Saint-Etienne (0) 0 67,192

Manchester U: (4411) Romero; Valencia, Smalling, Bailly, Blind; Mata (Rashford 70), Ander Herrera, Fellaini (Lingard 46), Martial (Young 84); Pogba; Ibrahimovic.
Saint-Etienne: (442) Ruffier; Malcuit, Perrin, Theophile-Catherine, Pogba (Beric 79); Jorginho (Roux 65), Veretout, Pajot (Selnaes 72), Monnet-Paquet; Saivet, Hamouma.

Olympiacos (0) 0

Osmanlispor (0) 0 24,478

Olympiacos: (4231) Leali; Diogo Figueiras, Botia, Bruno Viana■, Cissokho; Andre Martins (Ansarifard 88), Retsos; Seba, Fortounis (Manthatis 71), Androutsos; Cardozo (Romao 76).
Osmanlispor: (4231) Karcemarskas; Vrsajevic, Curusku, Prochazka, Tiago Pinto; Carlos (Maher 87), Cagiran; Thievy (Guven 90), Ndiaye, Regattin; Delarge (Rusescu 81).

PAOK Salonika (0) 0

Schalke 04 (1) 3 *(Burgstaller 27, Meyer 82, Huntelaar 90)* 25,593

PAOK Salonika: (532) Glykos; Leo Matos, Crespo, Malezas, Varela, Leovac; Shakhov, Cimirot, Biseswar (Pedro Henrique 77); Mystakidis (Djalma 55), Athanasiadis (Warda 85).
Schalke 04: (532) Fahrmann; Schopf (Kehrer 46), Howedes, Naldo, Nastasic, Kolasinac; Goretzka, Stambouli, Meyer; Burgstaller (Huntelaar 84), Caligiuri (Konoplyanka 78).

Rostov (3) 4 *(Mevlja 15, Poloz 37, Noboa 40, Azmoun 68)*

Sparta Prague (0) 0 6160

Rostov: (541) Medvedev; Kalachev, Mevlja, Cesar Navas, Granat, Kudryashov; Noboa, Gatcan, Erokhin (Prepelita 83), Bukharov (Azmoun 67); Poloz (Devic 74).
Sparta Prague: (433) Koubek; Karavaev, Mazuch, Kadlec, Costa; Vacha (Holek 80), Dockal (Lafata 87), Sacek; Albiach (Hybs 76), Julis, Konate■.

Villarreal (0) 0

Roma (1) 4 *(Emerson 32, Dzeko 65, 79, 86)* 17,960

Villarreal: (442) Sergio Asenjo; Mario, Musacchio, Victor Ruiz, Jaume; Jonathan, Trigueros, Bruno, Castillejo (Cheryshev 67); Bakambu (Adrian 66), Sansone (Borre 82).
Roma: (3421) Alisson; Manolas, Fazio, Rudiger (Juan Jesus 71); Bruno Peres, De Rossi, Strootman, Emerson; Nainggolan (Paredes 90), El Shaarawy (Salah 62); Dzeko.

ROUND OF 32 SECOND LEG

Wednesday, 22 February 2017

Fenerbahce (1) 1 *(Souza 41)*

Krasnodar (1) 1 *(Smolov 7)* 21,788

Fenerbahce: (433) Demirel (Fabiano 69); Ozbayrakli (Sen 70), Kjaer, Skrtel, Koybasi; Topal, Potuk, Souza; Lens, van Persie, Sow (Fernandao 70).
Krasnodar: (433) Kritsyuk; Kaleshin, Naldo, Granqvist, Ramirez; Gazinski, Kabore, Podberezkin (Pereyra 79); Wanderson (Laborde 63), Smolov, Claesson.

Saint-Etienne (0) 0

Manchester U (1) 1 *(Mkhitaryan 16)* 41,492

Saint-Etienne: (442) Ruffier; Malcuit, Theophile-Catherine, Perrin, Pogba; Veretout (Lemoine 68), Pajot, Hamouma, Saivet (Jorginho 53); Monnet-Paquet, Beric (Roux 59).
Manchester U: (4231) Romero; Young, Bailly■, Smalling, Blind; Mkhitaryan (Rashford 25), Pogba; Carrick (Schweinsteiger 61), Fellaini, Mata (Rojo 64); Ibrahimovic.

Schalke 04 (1) 1 *(Schopf 23)*

PAOK Salonika (1) 1 *(Nastasic 26 (og))* 50,619

Schalke 04: (352) Fahrmann; Howedes, Naldo (Badstuber 70), Nastasic; Schopf, Meyer, Geis, Bentaleb (Kehrer 84), Kolasinac; Huntelaar, Choupo-Moting (Goretzka 56).
PAOK Salonika: (4231) Glykos; Kitsiou, Malezas, Crespo, Poungouras; Cimirot, Shakhov; Djalma (Pelkas 77), Warda (Biseswar 68), Mystakidis (Pedro Henrique 62); Koulouris.

Thursday, 23 February 2017

Ajax (0) 1 *(Viergever 49)*

Legia Warsaw (0) 0 52,851

Ajax: (433) Onana; Veltman, Sanchez, Riedewald, Viergever; Klaassen, Schone, Ziyech; Traore, Dolberg (Nouri 82), Younes.
Legia Warsaw: (4411) Malarz; Broz, Dabrowski, Pazdan, Hlousek; Guilherme (Necid 73), Kopczynski (Chukwu 82), Jodlowiec (Moulin 58), Qazaishvili; Odjidja-Ofoe; Kucharczyk.

APOEL Nicosia (0) 2 *(Sotiriou 46, Gianniotas 54 (pen))*

Athletic Bilbao (0) 0 15,275

APOEL Nicosia: (442) Waterman; Milanov, Merkis, Astiz, Ioannou; Gianniotas, Morais, Vinicius (Ebecilio 76), Efrem (Vander 71); Barral (de Camargo 60), Sotiriou■.
Athletic Bilbao: (4231) Iraizoz; De Marcos (Merino 79), Yeray, Etxeita (Iturraspe■ 70), Balenziaga; San Jose, Benat; Williams, Muniain, Susaeta (Villalibre 57); Raul Garcia.

Besiktas (1) 2 *(Aboubakar 17, Tosun 87)*

Hapoel Beer Sheva (0) 1 *(Nwakaeme 64)* 34,000

Besiktas: (4231) Fabri; Beck, Marcelo, Nukan, Tosic; Quaresma (Arslan 61), Inler; Uysal (Ozyakup 72), Babel, Anderson Talisca; Aboubakar (Tosun 79).
Hapoel Beer Sheva: (532) Goresh; Ohayon, Hoban, William Soares, Tzedek, Turjeman; Ogu, Brown (Buzaglo 57), Nwakaeme; Ghadir (Melikson 65), Sahar (Barda 70).

FC Copenhagen (0) 0

Ludogorets Razgrad (0) 0 17,064

FC Copenhagen: (442) Olsen; Ankersen, Jorgensen, Johansson, Augustinsson; Jensen (Boilesen 89), Matic, Keita (Kusk 65), Toutouh; Santander (Pavlovic 79), Cornelius.
Ludogorets Razgrad: (433) Stoyanov; Minev, Palomino, Moti, Natanael; Dyakov, Marcelinho, Abel (Quixada 65); Wanderson (Paulo 83), Cafu (Misidjan 75), Keseru.

Fiorentina (2) 2 *(Kalinic 15, Valero 29)*

Borussia Munchengladbach (1) 4 *(Stindl 44 (pen), 47, 55, Christensen 60)* 24,712

Fiorentina: (3421) Tatarusanu; Sanchez, Astori, Rodriguez; Chiesa, Badelj (El Babacar 64), Vecino, Olivera; Bernarderschi (Ilicic 63), Valero; Kalinic.
Borussia Munchengladbach: (442) Sommer; Jantschke, Christensen, Vestergaard, Wendt; Herrmann, Kramer, Dahoud (Strobl 79), Hofmann (Johnson 72); Hazard (Drmic 27), Stindl.

Genk (0) 1 *(Pozuelo 66)*

Astra Giurgiu (0) 0 8804

Genk: (4231) Ryan; Castagne, Brabec, Colley, Uronen; Berge, Malinovsky (Boetius 89); Schrijvers (Buffel 76), Pozuelo (Kumordzi 89), Trossard; Samatta.
Astra Giurgiu: (433) Lung; Stan, Sapunaru, Geraldo Alves, Moise; Lovin (Florea 68), Mansaly, Seto (Ionita II 81); Teixeira, Niculae (Bus 70), Budescu.

Lyon (4) 7 *(Fekir 4, 27, 78, Cornet 17, Darder 34, Aouar 86, Diakhaby 89)*

AZ Alkmaar (1) 1 *(Garcia 26)* 25,743

Lyon: (433) Lopes; Da Silva, Yanga-Mbiwa, Diakhaby, Jallet; Ferri, Tousart (Tolisso 80), Darder; Ghezzal (Lacazette 76), Fekir, Cornet (Aouar 63).
AZ Alkmaar: (433) Krul; Johansson, Vlaar (Van Eijden 46), Wuytens, Haps; Luckassen, Rienstra, Jahanbakhsh (Seuntjens 71); Bel Hassani, Fred Friday (Weghorst 76), Garcia.

Osmanlispor (0) 0

Olympiacos (0) 3 *(Ansarifard 47, 86, Elyounoussi 70)* 17,500

Osmanlispor: (4231) Karcemarskas; Vrsajevic, Curusku, Prochazka, Tiago Pinto (Bayir 66); Ndiaye, Cagiran (Guven 74); Bifouma, Maher, Regattin (Delarge 75); Webo.
Olympiacos: (4231) Leali; Diogo Figueiras, da Costa, Botia, Cissokho; Retsos, Andre Martins (Androutsos 65); Seba, Fortounis (Romao 86), Elyounoussi (Manthatis 81); Ansarifard.

Roma (0) 0

Villarreal (1) 1 *(Borre 15)* 19,495

Roma: (343) Alisson; Vermaelen, Manolas (Rudiger■ 46), Juan Jesus; Bruno Peres (Fazio 84), Paredes, De Rossi (Nainggolan 76), Rui; Perotti, Totti, El Shaarawy.
Villarreal: (442) Fernandez; Rukavina, Alvaro, Bonera, Jose Angel; Soriano, Rodri, Bruno (Jonathan 77), Cheryshev (Bakambu 73); Soldado (Adrian 66), Borre.

Shakhtar Donetsk (0) 0

Celta Vigo (0) 2 *(Aspas 90 (pen), Cabral 108)* 33,117

Shakhtar Donetsk: (4411) Pyatov; Srna, Ordets, Rakitskiy, Ismaily; Marlos, Malyshev (Boryachuk 112), Fred, Taison (Bernard 83); Kovalenko (Stepanenko 73); Blanco Leschuk.
Celta Vigo: (433) Sergio; Jonny, Fontas, Cabral, Roncaglia (Jozabed 58); Hernandez, Wass (Bongonda 81), Hugo Mallo; Aspas, Guidetti, Sisto (Rossi 85).
aet.

Sparta Prague (0) 1 *(Karavaev 83)*

Rostov (1) 1 *(Poloz 13)* 13,413

Sparta Prague: (442) Koubek; Karavaev, Mazuch (Havelka 46), Kadlec, Nhamoinesu■; Sacek, Cermak, Holek, Albiach (Hybs 72); Julis, Pulkrab (Sural 40).
Rostov: (532) Medvedev; Kalachev, Mevlja, Cesar Navas, Granat (Terentjev 70), Kudryashov; Noboa, Erokhin, Gatcan (Prepelita 46); Bukharov (Azmoun 46), Poloz.

Tottenham H (1) 2 *(Eriksen 10, Wanyama 61)*

KAA Gent (1) 2 *(Kane 21 (og), Perbet 82)* 80,465

Tottenham H: (4231) Lloris; Walker, Alderweireld, Vertonghen, Davies (Son 58); Dier (Janssen 90), Wanyama; Dembele (Winks 75), Eriksen, Alli■; Kane.
KAA Gent: (4231) Kalinic; Mitrovic, Gershon, Dejaegere (Verstraete 55), Gigot; Simon (Perbet 75), Saief; Foket, Milicevic (Matton 46), Esiti; Coulibaly.

Zenit St Petersburg (1) 3 *(Giuliano 24, 78, Dzjuba 72)*

Anderlecht (0) 1 *(Thelin 90)* 17,992

Zenit St Petersburg: (433) Lodygin; Aniukov, Luis Neto, Criscito, Zhirkov; Javi Garcia, Giuliano, Mauricio; Danny (Mak 88), Dzjuba, Kokorin.
Anderlecht: (451) Ruben Martinez; Najar, Spajic, Deschacht, Obradovic; Chipciu (Nuytinck 84), Stanciu (Bruno 73), Dendoncker, Tielemans, Acheampong (Diego Capel 89); Thelin.
Anderlecht won on away goals rule.

ROUND OF 16 FIRST LEG

Thursday, 9 March 2017

APOEL Nicosia (0) 0

Anderlecht (1) 1 *(Stanciu 29)* 19,327

APOEL Nicosia: (4411) Waterman; Milanov, Merkis, Astiz (Roberto Lago 40), Ioannou; Gianniotas, Morais, Ebecilio (Artymatas 72), Efrem (Vander 55); Barral; de Camargo.
Anderlecht: (451) Ruben Martinez; Appiah, Spajic, Nuytinck, Najar; Chipciu (Bruno 88), Stanciu (Acheampong 80), Dendoncker, Tielemans, Hanni; Teodorczyk (Thelin 59).

Celta Vigo (0) 2 *(Wass 50, Beauvue 89)*

Krasnodar (0) 1 *(Claesson 56)* 18,414

Celta Vigo: (442) Sergio; Hugo Mallo, Fontas, Cabral, Jonny; Diaz, Radoja, Wass (Jozabed 70), Aspas; Guidetti (Beauvue 78), Sisto.
Krasnodar: (442) Kritsyuk; Martynovich, Naldo, Granqvist, Ramirez; Zhigulyov (Torbinski 82), Gazinski, Pereyra, Podberezkin (Mamaev 75); Wanderson (Laborde 78), Claesson.

FC Copenhagen (1) 2 *(Jensen 1, Cornelius 59)*

Ajax (1) 1 *(Dolberg 32)* 31,189

FC Copenhagen: (442) Olsen; Augustinsson, Johansson, Jorgensen, Ankersen; Toutouh, Kvist Jorgensen, Matic, Jensen; Cornelius, Santander (Pavlovic 63).
Ajax: (433) Onana; Tete, Savastano, Viergever, Sinkgraven; Klaassen, Schone, van de Beek (Ziyech 77); Traore (Neres 77), Dolberg, Younes.

KAA Gent (1) 2 *(Kalu 27, Coulibaly 61)*

Genk (4) 5 *(Malinovsky 22, Colley 33, Samatta 41, 72, Uronen 45)* 17,112

KAA Gent: (343) Kalinic; Mitrovic, Gigot, Gershon; Verstraete (Ibrahim 46), Esiti■, Matton, Saief (Simon 75); Perbet (Foket 75), Coulibaly, Kalu.
Genk: (433) Ryan; Castagne, Brabec, Colley, Uronen; Pozuelo, Berge, Malinovsky (Heynen 80); Schrijvers (Trossard 90), Samatta, Boetius (Buffel 46).

Lyon (1) 4 *(Diakhaby 9, Tolisso 47, Fekir 74, Lacazette 90)*

Roma (2) 2 *(Salah 20, Fazio 33)* 50,588

Lyon: (433) Lopes; Da Silva (Jallet 46), Mammana (Fekir 71), Diakhaby, Morel; Tolisso, Gonalons, Tousart; Ghezzal (Cornet 76), Lacazette, Valbuena.
Roma: (343) Alisson; Manolas, Fazio, Juan Jesus; Bruno Peres, De Rossi (Paredes 82), Strootman, Emerson; Nainggolan (Perotti 84), Dzeko, Salah.

Olympiacos (1) 1 *(Cambiasso 36)*

Besiktas (0) 1 *(Aboubakar 53)* 25,515

Olympiacos: (4231) Leali; Diogo Figueiras, Retsos, Botia (da Costa 64), Cissokho; Cambiasso (Andre Martins 70), Romao; Elyounoussi, Fortounis (Marin 74), Manthatis; Ansarifard.
Besiktas: (4231) Fabri; Gonul, Marcelo, Tosic, Adriano; Arslan (Ozyakup 45), Hutchinson; Quaresma, Anderson Talisca (Inler 90), Babel; Aboubakar (Tosun 81).

Rostov (0) 1 *(Bukharov 53)*

Manchester U (1) 1 *(Mkhitaryan 35)* 14,223

Rostov: (532) Medvedev; Kalachev, Mevlja, Cesar Navas, Granat (Terentjev 18), Kudryashov; Noboa, Erokhin, Gatcan; Poloz, Bukharov (Azmoun 74).
Manchester U: (433) Romero; Rojo, Jones, Smalling, Blind (Valencia 90); Ander Herrera (Carrick 90), Pogba, Fellaini; Mkhitaryan (Martial 67), Young, Ibrahimovic.

Schalke 04 (1) 1 *(Burgstaller 25)*

Borussia Munchengladbach (1) 1 *(Hofmann 15)* 52,412

Schalke 04: (352) Fahrmann; Howedes, Nastasic, Kehrer; Schopf (Choupo-Moting 72), Stambouli (Bentaleb 55), Goretzka, Geis, Kolasinac; Burgstaller (Di Santo 84), Caligiuri.
Borussia Munchengladbach: (442) Sommer; Jantschke, Vestergaard, Kolodziejczak, Wendt; Hofmann (Schulz 83), Strobl, Dahoud, Johnson (Hahn 65); Stindl, Raffael (Herrmann 79).

ROUND OF 16 SECOND LEG

Thursday, 16 March 2017

Ajax (2) 2 *(Traore 23, Dolberg 45 (pen))*

FC Copenhagen (0) 0 52,270

Ajax: (433) Onana; Veltman (Tete 20), Sanchez, de Ligt, Viergever; van de Beek (De Jong 76), Schone, Ziyech; Traore (Kluivert 81), Dolberg, Younes.
FC Copenhagen: (442) Olsen; Ankersen, Okore (Boilesen 47), Johansson, Augustinsson; Gregus (Verbic 57), Matic, Kvist Jorgensen, Toutouh (Kusk 78); Santander, Cornelius.

Anderlecht (0) 1 *(Acheampong 65)*

APOEL Nicosia (0) 0 15,662

Anderlecht: (451) Ruben Martinez; Appiah, Mbodji, Spajic, Najar; Chipciu (Bruno 89), Stanciu (Acheampong 64), Dendoncker, Tielemans, Hanni; Teodorczyk (Thelin 75).
APOEL Nicosia: (442) Waterman; Milanov, Merkis, Roberto Lago, Ioannou; Gianniotas, Artymatas, Ebecilio (Yambere 57), Barral (Vander 77); de Camargo (Bertoglio 72), Sotiriou.

Besiktas (2) 4 *(Aboubakar 11, Babel 22, 75, Tosun 84)*

Olympiacos (1) 1 *(Elyounoussi 31)* 37,966

Besiktas: (4231) Fabri; Gonul, Mitrovic, Tosic, Adriano; Hutchinson, Ozyakup (Uysal 60); Quaresma (Tosun 82), Anderson Talisca (Inler 90), Babel; Aboubakar■.
Olympiacos: (4231) Leali; Diogo Figueiras, da Costa, Retsos, Cissokho; Cambiasso (Marin 67), Romao (Andre Martins 76); Elyounoussi, Fortounis, Manthatis (Seba 56); Ansarifard.

Borussia Munchengladbach (2) 2 *(Christensen 27, Dahoud 45)*

Schalke 04 (0) 2 *(Goretzka 54, Bentaleb 68 (pen))* 46,283

Borussia Munchengladbach: (442) Sommer; Jantschke, Christensen, Vestergaard, Wendt; Herrmann, Dahoud, Kramer (Strobl 46), Johnson (Hofmann 16); Drmic, Raffael.
Schalke 04: (4411) Fahrmann; Kehrer, Howedes, Nastasic, Kolasinac; Caligiuri (Schopf 88), Geis (Meyer 46), Bentaleb (Stambouli 79), Choupo-Moting; Goretzka; Burgstaller.
Schalke 04 won on away goals.

Genk (1) 1 *(Castagne 20)*

KAA Gent (0) 1 *(Verstraete 84)* 16,028

Genk: (4231) Ryan; Castagne, Brabec, Colley, Uronen (Janssens 81); Pozuelo (Schrijvers 46), Berge; Buffel (Trossard 73), Malinovsky, Boetius; Samatta.
KAA Gent: (343) Kalinic; Gigot, Mitrovic, De Smet; Foket, Dejaegere, Ibrahim, Simon; Kalu, Perbet (Verstraete 62), Coulibaly.

Krasnodar (0) 0

Celta Vigo (0) 2 *(Hugo Mallo 52, Aspas 80)* 34,200

Krasnodar: (433) Sinitsyn; Martynovich, Naldo, Granqvist, Petrov; Gazinski, Kabore■, Pereyra (Laborde 70); Podberezkin (Mamaev 46), Wanderson, Claesson (Joaozinho 59).
Celta Vigo: (433) Sergio; Hugo Mallo, Cabral, Fontas, Jonny; Wass (Jozabed 74), Radoja, Hernandez (Beauvue 85); Aspas (Roncaglia 82), Guidetti, Sisto.

Manchester U (0) 1 *(Mata 70)*

Rostov (0) 0 64,361

Manchester U: (451) Romero; Valencia, Bailly, Smalling, Rojo; Mata, Ander Herrera, Blind (Jones 64), Pogba (Fellaini 48), Mkhitaryan; Ibrahimovic.
Rostov: (532) Medvedev; Bayramyan (Kireev 81), Mevlja, Cesar Navas, Kudryashov, Terentjev; Noboa, Prepelita (Devic 79), Erokhin; Azmoun (Bukharov 61), Poloz.

Roma (1) 2 *(Strootman 18, Tousart 60 (og))*

Lyon (1) 1 *(Diakhaby 16)* 46,453

Roma: (3421) Alisson; Rudiger, Manolas, Fazio; Bruno Peres (El Shaarawy 59), De Rossi (Totti 84), Strootman, Rui (Perotti 76); Salah, Nainggolan; Dzeko.
Lyon: (4231) Lopes; Jallet, Mammana (Yanga-Mbiwa 78), Diakhaby, Morel; Tousart, Gonalons; Cornet, Tolisso, Valbuena (Da Silva 90); Lacazette (Ferri 84).

QUARTER-FINALS FIRST LEG

Thursday, 13 April 2017

Ajax (1) 2 *(Klaassen 23 (pen), 52)*

Schalke 04 (0) 0 52,384

Ajax: (433) Onana; Veltman, Sanchez, Viergever, Sinkgraven (de Ligt 46); Ziyech, van de Beek (De Jong 87), Klaassen; Kluivert (Neres 74), Traore, Younes.
Schalke 04: (433) Fahrmann; Kehrer, Howedes, Nastasic, Aogo; Meyer (Stambouli 59), Goretzka, Bentaleb; Schopf (Huntelaar 71), Burgstaller, Caligiuri (Konoplyanka 83).

Anderlecht (0) 1 *(Dendoncker 87)*

Manchester U (1) 1 *(Mkhitaryan 37)* 20,060

Anderlecht: (451) Ruben Martinez; Appiah, Mbodji, Nuytinck, Obradovic; Bruno (Chipciu 58), Tielemans, Dendoncker, Stanciu (Hanni 64), Acheampong; Thelin (Teodorczyk 75).
Manchester U: (4231) Romero; Valencia, Bailly, Rojo, Darmian; Carrick, Pogba; Mkhitaryan (Fosu-Mensah 90), Lingard (Martial 62), Rashford (Fellaini 75); Ibrahimovic.

Celta Vigo (3) 3 *(Sisto 14, Aspas 17, Guidetti 38)*

Genk (1) 2 *(Boetius 10, Buffel 68)* 21,608

Celta Vigo: (433) Sergio; Hugo Mallo, Cabral, Fontas, Jonny; Wass (Jozabed 78), Radoja, Hernandez; Aspas, Guidetti (Beauvue 66), Sisto.
Genk: (4312) Ryan; Castagne, Brabec, Colley, Uronen; Pozuelo, Malinovsky (Heynen 90), Berge; Trossard (Schrijvers 82); Samatta, Boetius (Buffel 62).

Lyon (0) 2 *(Tolisso 83, Morel 84)*

Besiktas (1) 1 *(Babel 15)* 55,452

Lyon: (4231) Lopes; Da Silva (Jallet 53), Mammana, Diakhaby, Morel; Tousart, Tolisso; Ghezzal (Cornet 52), Fekir, Valbuena; Lacazette.
Besiktas: (4231) Fabri; Gonul, Mitrovic (Uysal 64), Marcelo, Tosic; Ozyakup (Arslan 74), Hutchinson; Babel, Anderson Talisca, Adriano; Tosun (Inler 87).

QUARTER-FINALS SECOND LEG

Thursday, 20 April 2017

Besiktas (1) 2 *(Anderson Talisca 27, 58)*

Lyon (1) 1 *(Lacazette 34)* 39,623

Besiktas: (4231) Fabri; Gonul, Mitrovic, Tosic, Adriano (Beck 77); Ozyakup (Uysal 94), Hutchinson; Quaresma (Arslan 116), Anderson Talisca, Babel; Tosun.
Lyon: (433) Lopes; Jallet, N'Koulou, Diakhaby, Morel (Rybus 120); Tousart, Gonalons, Tolisso; Cornet (Fekir 77), Lacazette (Ghezzal 90), Valbuena.
aet; Lyon won 7-6 on penalties.

Genk (0) 1 *(Trossard 67)*

Celta Vigo (0) 1 *(Sisto 63)* 18,833

Genk: (433) Ryan; Castagne, Brabec (Dewaest 81), Colley, Uronen; Berge, Pozuelo, Malinovsky (Boetius 72); Trossard, Samatta, Buffel (Schrijvers 72).
Celta Vigo: (433) Sergio; Hugo Mallo, Cabral, Fontas, Jonny; Wass (Jozabed 80), Radoja, Hernandez; Aspas, Guidetti (Beauvue 42 (Roncaglia 90)), Sisto.

Manchester U (1) 2 *(Mkhitaryan 10, Rashford 107)*

Anderlecht (1) 1 *(Hanni 32)* 71,496

Manchester U: (451) Romero; Valencia, Bailly, Rojo (Blind 23), Shaw; Mkhitaryan, Lingard (Fellaini 60), Carrick, Pogba, Rashford; Ibrahimovic (Martial 91).
Anderlecht: (451) Ruben Martinez; Appiah, Mbodji, Spajic, Obradovic; Chipciu (Bruno 63), Tielemans, Dendoncker, Hanni (Stanciu 63), Acheampong; Teodorczyk (Thelin 78).
aet.

Schalke 04 (0) 3 *(Goretzka 53, Burgstaller 56, Caligiuri 101)*

Ajax (0) 2 *(Viergever 111, Younes 120)* 53,701

Schalke 04: (4411) Fahrmann; Riether (Avdijaj 112), Howedes, Nastasic, Kolasinac; Caligiuri, Stambouli (Huntelaar 54), Bentaleb, Meyer; Goretzka (Geis 84); Burgstaller.
Ajax: (433) Onana; Veltman■, Sanchez, de Ligt, Viergever; Ziyech, Schone (van de Beek 73), Klaassen; Kluivert (Dolberg 61), Traore (Tete 82), Younes.
aet.

SEMI-FINALS FIRST LEG

Wednesday, 3 May 2017

Ajax (2) 4 *(Traore 25, 71, Dolberg 34, Younes 49)*

Lyon (0) 1 *(Valbuena 66)* 52,141

Ajax: (433) Onana; Tete, Sanchez, de Ligt, Riedewald; Klaassen, Schone (van de Beek 72), Ziyech; Traore, Dolberg (Neres 88), Younes (Kluivert 79).
Lyon: (4231) Lopes; Jallet (Da Silva 69), N'Koulou, Diakhaby, Morel; Tousart (Ghezzal 58), Gonalons; Cornet (Lacazette 76), Tolisso, Valbuena; Fekir.

Thursday, 4 May 2017

Celta Vigo (0) 0

Manchester U (0) 1 *(Rashford 67)* 26,202

Celta Vigo: (433) Sergio; Hugo Mallo (Beauvue 90), Cabral, Roncaglia, Jonny; Wass (Jozabed 74), Radoja, Hernandez; Aspas, Guidetti, Sisto.
Manchester U: (4231) Romero; Valencia, Bailly, Blind, Darmian; Ander Herrera, Fellaini; Lingard, Pogba, Mkhitaryan (Young 78 (Smalling 89)); Rashford (Martial 79).

SEMI-FINALS SECOND LEG

Thursday, 11 May 2017

Lyon (2) 3 *(Lacazette 45, 45 (pen), Viergever 81 (og))*

Ajax (1) 1 *(Dolberg 27)* 53,810

Lyon: (4231) Lopes; Da Silva, N'Koulou, Diakhaby, Morel (Rybus 74); Tolisso, Gonalons; Cornet, Fekir, Valbuena (Ghezzal 77); Lacazette.
Ajax: (433) Onana; Veltman (Tete 64), Sanchez, de Ligt, Viergever■; Ziyech, Schone (van de Beek 58), Klaassen; Traore, Dolberg, Younes (Kluivert 82).

Manchester U (1) 1 *(Fellaini 17)*

Celta Vigo (0) 1 *(Roncaglia 85)* 75,138

Manchester U: (433) Romero; Valencia, Bailly■, Blind, Darmian; Fellaini, Ander Herrera, Pogba; Mkhitaryan (Carrick 77), Rashford (Smalling 89), Lingard (Rooney 86).
Celta Vigo: (433) Sergio; Hugo Mallo, Cabral, Roncaglia■, Jonny; Wass (Jozabed 46), Radoja (Bongonda 68), Hernandez; Aspas, Guidetti, Sisto (Beauvue 80).

EUROPA LEAGUE FINAL 2017

Wednesday, 24 May 2017

(in Stockholm, attendance 46,961)

Ajax (0) 0 Manchester U (1) 2

Ajax: (433) Onana; Veltman, Sanchez, de Ligt, Riedewald (De Jong 82); Klaassen, Schone (van de Beek 70), Ziyech; Traore, Dolberg (Neres 62), Younes.

Manchester U: (4411) Romero; Valencia, Smalling, Blind, Darmian; Ander Herrera, Mata (Rooney 90), Fellaini, Pogba; Mkhitaryan (Lingard 73); Rashford (Martial 84).

Scorers: Pogba 18, Mkhitaryan 48.

Referee: Damir Skomina.

Henrikh Mkhitaryan scores Manchester United's second goal in a 2-0 defeat of Ajax to win the Europa League final in Stockholm (Reuters/Phil Noble Livepic)

UEFA CHAMPIONS LEAGUE 2017–18

PARTICIPATING CLUBS
The list below is provisional and is subject to pending legal proceedings and final confirmation from UEFA.

GROUP STAGE
Anderlecht (BEL)
Atletico Madrid (ESP)
Barcelona (ESP)
Bayern Munich (GER)
Benfica (POR)
Besiktas (TUR)
Borussia Dortmund (GER)
Chelsea (ENG)
FC Basel (SUI)
Feyenoord (NED)
Juventus (ITA)
Manchester C (ENG)
Manchester U (ENG)
Monaco (FRA)
Paris Saint-Germain (FRA)
Porto (POR)
RB Leipzig (GER)
Real Madrid (ESP)
Roma (ITA)
Shakhtar Donetsk (UKR)
Spartak Moscow (RUS)
Tottenham H (ENG)

PLAY-OFF – CHAMPIONS ROUTE
10 third qualifying round winners

PLAY-OFF – LEAGUE ROUTE
1899 Hoffenheim (GER)
Liverpool (ENG)
Napoli (ITA)
Sevilla (ESP)
Sporting Lisbon (POR)

THIRD QUALIFYING ROUND – CHAMPIONS ROUTE
Slavia Prague (CZE)
Olympiacos (GRE)
Viitorul Constanta (ROM)

THIRD QUALIFYING ROUND – LEAGUE ROUTE
AEK Athens (GRE)
Ajax (NED)
Club Brugge (NED)
CSKA Moscow (RUS)
Dynamo Kyiv (UKR)
Istanbul Basaksehir (TUR)
Nice (FRA)
Steaua Bucharest (ROM)
Viktoria Plzen (CZE)
Young Boys (SUI)

SECOND QUALIFYING ROUND
APOEL (CYP)
Astana (KAZ)
BATE Borisov (BLR)
Budapest Honved (HUN)
Buducnost Podgorica (MNE)
Celtic (SCO)
Dundalk (IRL)
F91 Dudelange (LUX)
FC Copenhagen (DEN)
FH Hafnarfjordur (ICE)
Hapoel Be'er Sheva (ISR)
IFK Mariehamn (FIN)
Kukesi (ALB)
Legia Warsaw (POL)
Ludogorets Razgrad (BUL)
Malmo (SWE)
Maribor (SVN)
Partizan Belgrade (SER)
Qarabag (AZE)
Red Bull Salzburg (AUS)
Rijeka (CRO)
Rosenborg (NOR)
Samtredia (GEO)
Sheriff Tiraspol (MDA)
Spartaks Jurmala (LVA)
Vardar (MDA)
Zalgiris Vilnius (LTU)
Zilina (SVK)
Zrinjski Mostar (BIH)

FIRST QUALIFYING ROUND
Alashkert (ARM)
Europa (GIB)
FC Santa Coloma (AND)
FCI Tallinn (EST)
Hibernians (MLT)
La Fiorita (SMR)
Linfield (NIR)
The New Saints (WAL)
Trepca '89 (KOS)
Vikingur Gota (FRO)

UEFA EUROPA LEAGUE 2017–18

PARTICIPATING CLUBS
The list below is provisional and is subject to pending legal proceedings and final confirmation from UEFA.

KNOCKOUT STAGE
8 third-placed teams from UEFA Champions League group stage

GROUP STAGE
1. FC Cologne (GER)
Arsenal (ENG)
Atalanta (ITA)
Fastav Zlin (CZE)
Hertha Berlin (GER)
Konyaspor (TUR)
Lazio (ITA)
Lokomotiv Moscow (RUS)
Lugano (SUI)
Lyon (FRA)
Real Sociedad (ESP)
Villarreal (ESP)
Vitesse (NED)
Vitoria de Guimaraes (POR)
Zorya Luhansk (UKR)
Zulte Waregem (BEL)
10 losers from UEFA Champions League play-off round

UEFA EUROPA LEAGUE PLAY-OFFS
29 third qualifying round winners
15 transfer from UEFA Champions League second qualifying round

THIRD QUALIFYING ROUND
AC Milan (ITA)
Arka Gdynia (POL)
Athletic Bilbao (ESP)
Austria Vienna (AUS)
Bordeaux (FRA)
Braga (POR)
CS U Craiova (ROU)
Dinamo Bucharest (ROU)
Dinamo Zagreb (CRO)
Everton (ENG)
Fenerbahce (TUR)
KAA Gent (BEL)
Krasnodar (RUS)
Maritimo (POR)
Marseille (FRA)
Oleksandria (UKR)
Olimpik Donetsk (UKR)
Oostende (BEL)
Panathinaikos (GRE)
PAOK Salonika (GRE)
PSV Eindhoven (NED)
SC Freiburg (GER)
Sion (SUI)
Sparta Prague (CZE)
Zenit St Petersburg (RUS)

SECOND QUALIFYING ROUND
Aberdeen (SCO)
Apollon Limassol (CYP)
Astra Giurgiu (ROU)
Bnei Yehuda (ISR)
Brann (NOR)
Brondby (DEN)
Dinamo Brest (BLR)
Galatasaray (TUR)
Hajduk Split (CRO)
Luzern (SUI)
Mlada Boleslav (CZE)
Panionios (GRE)
Qabala (AZE)
Sturm Graz (AUT)
Utrecht (NED)
Ostersund (SWE)

FIRST QUALIFYING ROUND
AEK Larnaca (CYP)
AEL Limassol (CYP)
AIK Solna (SWE)
Atlantas (LTU)
B36 Torshavn (FRO)
Bala Town (WAL)
Ballymena U (NIR)
Balzan (MLT)
Bangor C (WAL)
Beitar Jerusalem (ISR)
Botev Plovdiv (BUL)
Chikhura Sachkhere (GEO)
Coleraine (NIR)
Connah's Quay Nomads (WAL)
Cork C (IRL)
Crusaders (NIR)
Crvena Zvezda (SRB)
Dacia Chisinau (MDA)
Derry C (IRL)
Differdange 03 (LUX)
Dinamo Batumi (GEO)
Dinamo Minsk (BLR)
Domzale (SVN)
Dunav Ruse (BUL)
Ferencvaros (HUN)
FK Liepaja (LVA)
Flora Tallinn (EST)
Floriana (MLT)
Fola Esch (LUX)
Folgore Falciano (SMR)
Gandzasar (ARM)
Gorica (SVN)
Haugesund (NOR)
HJK Helsinki (FIN)
IFK Norrkoping (SWE)
Inter Baku (AZE)
Irtysh Pavlodar (KAZ)
Jagiellonia Bialystok (POL)
Jelgava (LVA)
Kairat (KAZ)
KI Klaksvik (FRO)
KR Reykjavik (ISL)
Lech Poznan (POL)
Levadia Tallinn (EST)
Levski Sofia (BUL)
Lincoln Red Imps (GIB)
Lyngby (DEN)
Maccabi Tel Aviv (ISR)
Midtjylland (DEN)
Milsami Orhei (MDA)
Mladost Lucani (SRB)
Mladost Podgorica (MNE)
Nomme Kalju (EST)
NSI Runavík (FRO)
Odd (NOR)
Olimpija Ljubljana (SVN)
Ordabasy (KAZ)
Osijek (CRO)
Partizani Tirana (ALB)
Pelister (MKD)
Prishtina (KOS)
Progres Niederkorn (LUX)
Pyunik (ARM)
Rabotnicki (MKD)
Rangers (SCO)
Rheindorf Altach (AUT)
Ruzomberok (SVK)
Sant Julia (AND)
Sarajevo (BIH)
Shakhtyor Soligorsk (BLR)
Shamrock Rovers (IRL)
Shirak (ARM)
Shkendija (MKD)
Siroki Brijeg (BIH)
SJK Seinajoki (FIN)
Skenderbeu (ALB)
Slovan Bratislava (SVK)
St Johnstone (SCO)
St Joseph's (GIB)
Stjarnan (ISL)
Suduva Marijampole (LTU)
Sutjeska Niksic (MNE)
Tirana (ALB)
Torpedo Kutaisi (GEO)
Trakai (LTU)
Tre Penne (SMR)
Trencin (SVK)
UE Santa Coloma (AND)
Vaduz (LIE)
Valletta (MLT)
Valur (ISL)
Vasas Budapest (HUN)
Ventspils (LVA)
Videoton (HUN)
Vojvodina (SRB)
VPS Vaasa (FIN)
Zeta (MNE)
Zira (AZE)
Zaria Balti (MDA)
Zeljeznicar Sarajevo (BIH)

BRITISH AND IRISH CLUBS IN EUROPE

SUMMARY OF APPEARANCES

EUROPEAN CUP AND CHAMPIONS LEAGUE (1955–2017)

(Winners in brackets) (SE = seasons entered).

ENGLAND	*SE*	*P*	*W*	*D*	*L*	*F*	*A*
Manchester U (3)	26	261	145	64	52	483	248
Liverpool (5)	21	181	100	41	40	322	153
Arsenal	21	201	101	43	57	332	218
Chelsea (1)	14	152	77	43	32	257	130
Manchester C	7	52	21	13	18	88	72
Leeds U	4	40	22	6	12	76	41
Nottingham F (2)	3	20	12	4	4	32	14
Newcastle U	3	24	11	3	10	33	33
Tottenham H	3	26	11	5	10	52	38
Everton	3	10	2	5	3	14	10
Aston Villa (1)	2	15	9	3	3	24	10
Derby Co	2	12	6	2	4	18	12
Wolverhampton W	2	8	2	2	4	12	16
Blackburn R	1	6	1	1	4	5	8
Ipswich T	1	4	3	0	1	16	5
Burnley	1	4	2	0	2	8	8
Leicester C	1	10	5	2	3	11	10
SCOTLAND							
Celtic (1)	31	188	88	32	68	277	217
Rangers	30	161	62	40	59	232	218
Aberdeen	3	12	5	4	3	14	12
Hearts	3	8	2	1	5	8	16
Dundee U	1	8	5	1	2	14	5
Dundee	1	8	5	0	3	20	14
Hibernian	1	6	3	1	2	9	5
Kilmarnock	1	4	1	2	1	4	7
Motherwell	1	2	0	0	2	0	5
WALES							
The New Saints	10	26	6	4	16	24	43
Barry T	6	14	4	1	9	11	38
Rhyl	2	4	0	0	4	1	19
Cwmbran T	1	2	1	0	1	4	4
Llanelli	1	2	1	0	1	1	4
Bangor C	1	2	0	0	2	0	13
NORTHERN IRELAND							
Linfield	27	63	6	22	35	55	112
Glentoran	12	28	3	7	18	20	59
Crusaders	5	12	1	2	9	7	43
Portadown	3	6	0	1	5	3	24
Cliftonville	3	6	0	1	5	1	20
Glenavon	1	2	0	1	1	0	3
Lisburn Distillery	1	2	0	1	1	3	8
Ards	1	2	0	0	2	3	10
Coleraine	1	2	0	0	2	1	11
REPUBLIC OF IRELAND							
Dundalk	9	26	4	8	14	21	50
Shamrock R	9	20	1	6	13	9	33
Shelbourne	6	20	4	8	8	21	31
Bohemians	6	18	4	4	10	13	29
Waterford U	6	14	3	0	11	15	47
Derry C	4	9	1	1	7	9	26
St Patrick's Ath	4	8	0	3	5	2	23
Dublin C	3	6	1	0	5	3	25
Cork C	2	8	2	1	5	7	12
Athlone T	2	4	0	2	2	7	14
Sligo R	2	4	0	0	4	0	9
Limerick	2	4	0	0	4	4	16
Drogheda U	1	4	2	1	1	6	5
Cork Hibernians	1	2	0	0	2	1	7
Cork Celtic	1	2	0	0	2	1	7

UEFA CUP AND EUROPA LEAGUE 1971–2017

ENGLAND	*SE*	*P*	*W*	*D*	*L*	*F*	*A*
Tottenham H (2)	15	140	78	36	26	278	121
Liverpool (3)	14	124	66	34	24	186	94
Aston Villa	13	56	24	14	18	77	60
Ipswich T (1)	10	52	30	10	12	98	53
Manchester U (1)	9	43	18	14	11	57	37
Newcastle U	8	72	42	17	13	123	60
Manchester C	8	52	28	13	11	84	51
Leeds U	8	46	20	10	16	66	48
Everton	8	42	23	6	13	75	48
Southampton	7	22	6	9	7	23	20
Arsenal	6	25	12	4	9	45	32
Blackburn R	6	22	7	8	7	27	26
Chelsea (1)	4	17	10	2	5	28	20
Wolverhampton W	4	20	13	3	4	41	23
West Ham U	4	16	6	3	7	19	16
Fulham	3	39	21	10	8	64	31
Nottingham F	3	20	10	5	5	18	16
Stoke C	3	16	8	4	4	21	16
WBA	3	12	5	2	5	15	13
Middlesbrough	2	25	13	4	8	36	24
Bolton W	2	18	6	10	2	18	14
QPR	2	12	8	1	3	39	18
Derby Co	2	10	5	2	3	32	17
Leicester C	2	4	0	1	3	3	8
Birmingham C	1	8	4	2	2	11	8
Norwich C	1	6	2	2	2	6	4
Portsmouth	1	6	2	2	2	11	10
Watford	1	6	2	1	3	10	12
Wigan Ath	1	6	1	2	3	6	7
Sheffield W	1	4	2	1	1	13	7
Millwall	1	2	0	1	1	2	4
Hull C	1	4	2	1	1	4	3
SCOTLAND							
Celtic	19	99	40	25	34	155	112
Dundee U	19	82	33	25	24	134	89
Aberdeen	19	72	22	24	26	91	93
Rangers	16	76	31	23	22	99	77
Hearts	14	50	21	10	19	61	62
Hibernian	12	34	12	9	13	41	52
Motherwell	8	26	8	2	16	33	34
St Johnstone	6	22	7	7	8	24	27
Dundee	4	14	6	0	8	24	24
Kilmarnock	3	12	4	2	6	7	14
St Mirren	3	10	2	3	5	9	12
Dunfermline Ath	2	4	0	2	2	4	6
Raith R	1	6	2	1	3	10	8
Livingston	1	4	1	2	1	7	9
Falkirk	1	2	1	0	1	1	2
Gretna	1	2	0	1	1	3	7
Queen of the South	1	2	0	0	2	2	4
Partick Thistle	1	2	0	0	2	0	4
Inverness CT	1	2	0	1	1	0	1
WALES							
Bangor C	9	20	2	2	16	10	57
The New Saints	8	18	1	2	15	12	49
Llanelli	5	12	3	3	6	12	24
Rhyl	3	8	2	1	5	9	12
UWIC Inter Cardiff	3	6	1	0	5	1	18
Cwmbran T	3	6	0	0	6	0	21
Newtown	3	8	2	1	5	6	21
Air UK Broughton	3	6	0	4	2	6	9
Bala T	3	6	2	0	4	5	11
Barry T	2	8	2	2	4	10	16
Carmarthen T	2	6	1	0	5	8	21
Prestatyn T	1	4	1	0	3	3	11
Afan Lido	1	2	0	1	1	1	2
Cefn Druids	1	2	0	1	1	0	5
Port Talbot T	1	2	0	0	2	1	7
Neath	1	2	0	0	2	1	6
Haverfordwest Co	1	2	0	0	2	1	4
Swansea C	1	12	4	4	4	17	10
Aberystwith T	1	2	0	0	2	0	9
Llandudno T	1	2	0	0	2	0	6
Connah's Quay Nomads	1	4	1	1	2	2	3
NORTHERN IRELAND							
Glentoran	18	40	3	8	29	22	97
Linfield	12	34	9	8	17	37	63
Portadown	11	28	3	7	18	16	62
Crusaders	8	18	3	3	12	16	45

	SE	P	W	D	L	F	A
Glenavon	8	18	1	2	15	7	43
Coleraine	7	14	1	3	10	8	36
Cliftonville	5	14	3	3	8	9	28
Ards	1	2	1	0	1	4	8
Ballymena U	1	2	1	0	1	2	4
Dungannon Swifts	1	2	1	0	1	1	4
Lisburn Distillery	1	2	0	0	2	1	11
Bangor	1	2	0	0	2	0	6

REPUBLIC OF IRELAND

	SE	P	W	D	L	F	A
Bohemians	14	30	3	9	18	16	56
St Patrick's Ath	10	38	10	7	21	34	57
Cork C	8	24	4	7	13	15	34
Shamrock R	7	26	5	4	17	22	50
Derry C	7	22	6	5	11	26	32
Shelbourne	6	12	0	2	10	8	28
Dundalk	6	16	4	2	10	12	35
Drogheda U	4	12	3	4	5	10	24
Sligo R	4	10	2	4	4	11	13
Longford T	3	6	1	1	4	6	12
Finn Harps	3	6	0	0	6	3	33
Athlone T	1	4	1	2	1	4	5
Limerick	1	2	0	1	1	1	4
Sporting Fingal	1	2	0	0	2	4	6
Galway U	1	2	0	0	2	2	8
Bray W	1	2	0	0	2	0	8
University College Dublin	1	4	1	0	3	3	8

EUROPEAN CUP WINNERS' CUP 1960–1999

ENGLAND

	SE	*P*	*W*	*D*	*L*	*F*	*A*
Tottenham H (1)	6	33	20	5	8	65	34
Chelsea (2)	5	39	23	10	6	81	28
Liverpool	5	29	16	5	8	57	29
Manchester U (1)	5	31	16	9	6	55	35
West Ham U (1)	4	30	15	6	9	58	42
Arsenal (1)	3	27	15	10	2	48	20
Everton (1)	3	17	11	4	2	25	9
Manchester C (1)	2	18	11	2	5	32	13
Ipswich T	1	6	3	2	1	6	3
Leeds U	1	9	5	3	1	13	3
Leicester C	1	4	2	1	1	8	5
Newcastle U	1	2	1	0	1	2	2
Southampton	1	6	4	0	2	16	8
Sunderland	1	4	3	0	1	5	3
WBA	1	6	2	2	2	8	5
Wolverhampton W	1	4	1	1	2	6	5

SCOTLAND

	SE	P	W	D	L	F	A
Rangers (1)	10	54	27	11	16	100	62
Aberdeen (1)	8	39	22	5	12	79	37
Celtic	8	38	21	4	13	75	37
Dundee U	3	10	3	3	4	9	10
Hearts	3	10	3	3	4	16	14
Dunfermline Ath	2	14	7	2	5	34	14
Airdrieonians	1	2	0	0	2	1	3
Dundee	1	2	0	1	1	3	4
Hibernian	1	6	3	1	2	19	10
Kilmarnock	1	4	1	2	1	5	6
Motherwell	1	2	1	0	1	3	3
St Mirren	1	4	1	2	1	1	2

WALES

	SE	P	W	D	L	F	A
Cardiff C	14	49	16	14	19	67	61
Wrexham	8	28	10	8	10	34	35
Swansea C	7	18	3	4	11	32	37
Bangor C	3	9	1	2	6	5	12
Barry T	1	2	0	0	2	0	7
Borough U	1	4	1	1	2	2	4
Cwmbran T	1	2	0	0	2	2	12
Merthyr Tydfil	1	2	1	0	1	2	3
Newport Co	1	6	2	3	1	12	3
The New Saints (Llansantfraid)	1	2	0	1	1	1	6

NORTHERN IRELAND

	SE	P	W	D	L	F	A
Glentoran	9	22	3	7	12	18	46
Glenavon	5	10	1	3	6	11	25
Ballymena U	4	8	0	0	8	1	25
Coleraine	4	8	0	1	7	7	34
Crusaders	3	6	0	2	4	5	18
Derry C	3	6	1	1	4	4	11
Linfield	3	6	2	0	4	6	11
Ards	2	4	0	1	3	2	17
Bangor	2	4	0	1	3	2	8
Carrick Rangers	1	4	1	0	3	7	12
Cliftonville	1	2	0	0	2	0	8
Distillery	1	2	0	0	2	1	7
Portadown	1	2	1	0	1	4	7

REPUBLIC OF IRELAND

	SE	P	W	D	L	F	A
Shamrock R	6	16	5	2	9	19	27
Shelbourne	4	10	1	1	8	9	20
Bohemians	3	8	2	2	4	6	13
Dundalk	3	8	2	1	5	7	14
Limerick U	3	6	0	1	5	2	11
Waterford U	3	8	1	1	6	6	14
Cork C	2	4	1	0	3	2	9
Cork Hibernians	2	6	2	1	3	7	8
Galway U	2	4	0	0	4	2	11
Sligo R	2	6	1	1	4	5	11
Bray W	1	2	0	1	1	1	3
Cork Celtic	1	2	0	1	1	1	3
Finn Harps	1	2	0	1	1	2	4
Home Farm	1	2	0	1	1	1	7
St Patrick's Ath	1	2	0	0	2	1	8
University College Dublin	1	2	0	1	1	0	1

INTER-CITIES FAIRS CUP 1955–1970

ENGLAND

	SE	*P*	*W*	*D*	*L*	*F*	*A*
Leeds U (2)	5	53	28	17	8	92	40
Birmingham C	4	25	14	6	5	51	38
Liverpool	4	22	12	4	6	46	15
Arsenal (1)	3	24	12	5	7	46	19
Chelsea	3	20	10	5	5	33	24
Everton	3	12	7	2	3	22	15
Newcastle U (1)	3	24	13	6	5	37	21
Nottingham F	2	6	3	0	3	8	9
Sheffield W	2	10	5	0	5	25	18
Burnley	1	8	4	3	1	16	5
Coventry C	1	4	3	0	1	9	8
London XI	1	8	4	1	3	14	13
Manchester U	1	11	6	3	2	29	10
Southampton	1	6	2	3	1	11	6
WBA	1	4	1	1	2	7	9

SCOTLAND

	SE	P	W	D	L	F	A
Hibernian	7	36	18	5	13	66	60
Dunfermline Ath	5	28	16	3	9	49	31
Kilmarnock	4	20	8	3	9	34	32
Dundee U	3	10	5	1	4	11	12
Hearts	3	12	4	4	4	20	20
Rangers	3	18	8	4	6	27	17
Celtic	2	6	1	3	2	9	10
Aberdeen	1	4	2	1	1	4	4
Dundee	1	8	5	1	2	14	6
Morton	1	2	0	0	2	3	9
Partick Thistle	1	4	3	0	1	10	7

NORTHERN IRELAND

	SE	P	W	D	L	F	A
Glentoran	4	8	1	1	6	7	22
Coleraine	2	8	2	1	5	15	23
Linfield	2	4	1	0	3	3	11

REPUBLIC OF IRELAND

	SE	P	W	D	L	F	A
Drumcondra	2	6	2	0	4	8	19
Dundalk	2	6	1	1	4	4	25
Shamrock R	2	4	0	2	2	4	6
Cork Hibernians	1	2	0	0	2	1	6
Shelbourne	1	5	1	2	2	3	4
St Patrick's Ath	1	2	0	0	2	4	9

FIFA CLUB WORLD CUP 2016

Formerly known as the FIFA Club World Championship, this tournament is played annually between the champion clubs from all 6 continental confederations, although since 2007 the champions of Oceania must play a qualifying play-off against the champion club of the host country.

(Finals in Japan)

QUARTER-FINALS
Thursday 8 December 2016

Kashima Antlers (0) 2 *(Akasaki 67, Kanazaki 88)*

Auckland City (0) 1 *(Kim Daewook 50)* 17,667

Kashima Antlers: Sogahata; Nishi, Seokho, Shoji, Yamamoto (Akasaki 54), Endo (Nakamura 84), Ogasawara (Kanazaki 87), Nagaki, Shibasaki, Fabricio, Doi.
Auckland City: Zubikarai; White, Kim Daewook, Berlanga, Iwata, Riera, Tade, Tavano, Lewis, De Vries (Leaalafa 83), Moreira (Berry 90).
Referee: Janny Sikazwe (Zambia).

QUARTER-FINALS
Sunday 11 December 2016

Jeonbuk Hyundai Motors (1) 1 *(Kim Bokyung 23)*

Club America (0) 2 *(Romero 58, 74)* 14,587

Jeonbuk Hyundai Motors: Hong Jungnam; Lim Jongeun, Shin Hyungmin, Choi Chulsoon, Kim Changsoo (Go Mooyeol 77), Kim Bokyung, Jung Hyuk (Leonardo 66), Lee Jaesung, Park Wonjae, Edu (Lee Donggook 76), Kim Shinwook.
Club America: Munoz; Valdez, Alvarez (Arroyo 46), Goltz, Aguilar, Samudio, Martinez (Guerrro 46), Da Silva, Peralta, Quintero (Alvarado 70), Romero.
Referee: Viktor Kassai (Hungary).

Mamelodi Sundowns (0) 0

Kashima Antlers (0) 2 *(Endo 63, Kanazki 88)* 21,702

Mamelodi Sundowns: Onyango; Morena (Laffor 71), Arendse, Ricardo Nascimento, Langerman, Kekana, Mabunda, Dolly, Tau, Billiat (Vilakazi 70), Castro (Zwane 65).
Kashima Antlers: Sogahata; Nishi, Ueda, Shoji, Yamamoto, Endo (Sugimoto 89), Nagaki, Shibasaki, Nakamura (Kanazaki 61), Akasaki (Suzuki 84), Doi.
Referee: Roberto Garcia (Mexico).

MATCH FOR FIFTH PLACE
Wednesday 14 December 2016

Jeonbuk Hyundai Motors (3) 4 *(Kim Bokyung 18, Lee Jongho 29, Ricardo Nascimento 41 (og), Kim Shinwook 89)*

Mamelodi Sundowns (0) 1 *(Tau 48)* 5938

Jeonbuk Hyundai Motors: Hong Jungnam; Choi Chulsoon, Kim Youngchan, Lim Jongeun, Park Wonjae, Jang Yunho (Lee Hando 72), Han Kyowon, Kim Bokyung, Lee Jaesung, Go Mooyeol (Leonardo 62), Lee Jongho (Kim Shinwook 78).
Mamelodi Sundowns: Onyango; Morena (Mohomi 81), Arendse, Ricardo Nascimento, Langerman, Kekana, Mabunda, Billiat (Mbekile 75), Tau, Dolly, Castro (Vilakazi 46).
Referee: Nawaf Shukralla (Bahrain).

SEMI-FINALS
Wednesday 14 December 2016

Atletico Nacional (0) 0

Kashima Antlers (1) 3 *(Doi 33 (pen), Endo 83, Suzuki 85)* 15,050

Atletico Nacional: Armani; Bocanegra, Aguilar, Charales, Diaz, Uribe, Arias (Guerra 60), Berrio (Rodriguez 87), Torres, Mosquera (Dajome 67), Borja.
Kashima Antlers: Sogahata; Nishi, Ueda, Shoji, Yamamoto, Endo, Shibasaki, Ogasawara (Nagaki 58), Nakamura (Suzuki 85), Doi, Akasaki (Kanazaki 54).
Referee: Viktor Kassai (Hungary).

Thursday 15 December 2016

Club America (0) 0

Real Madrid (1) 2 *(Benzema 45, Ronaldo 90)* 50,117

Club America: Munoz; Valdez, Alvarado (Guerrero 54), Goltz, Aguilar, Samudio, Ibarra (Quintero 61), Da Silva, Sambueza, Peralta, Romero (Arroyo 79).
Real Madrid: Navas; Carvajal, Varane, Nacho, Marcelo, Modric, Casemiro, Kroos (Rodriguez 72), Vazquez, Benzema (Morata 80), Ronaldo.
Referee: Enrique Caceres (Paraguay).

MATCH FOR THIRD PLACE
Sunday 18 December 2016

Club America (1) 2 *(Arroyo 38, Peralta 66 (pen))*

Atletico Nacional (2) 2 *(Samudio 6 (og), Guerra 26)* 44,625

Club America: Munoz; Alvarado (Quintero 46), Valdez, Aguilar, Pimentel, Samudio, Guerrero, Da Silva, Sambueza (Martinez 70), Arroyo, Romero (Peralta 59).
Atletico Nacional: Armani; Bocanegra, Aguilar, Charales, Diaz, Uribe (Nieto 70), Arias, Berrio (Rodriguez 89), Torres, Mosquera, Guerra (Borja 78).
Atletico Nacional won 4-3 on penalties.
Referee: Nawaf Shukralla (Bahrain).

FIFA CLUB WORLD CUP FINAL 2016

Yokohama, Sunday 18 December 2016 (attendance 68,714)

Real Madrid (1) 4 *(Benzema 9, Ronaldo 60 (pen), 98, 104)* **Kashima Antlers (1) 2** *(Shibasaki 44, 52)*

Real Madrid: Navas; Carvajal, Varane, Ramos (Nacho 108), Marcelo, Modric (Kovacic 105), Casemiro, Kroos, Vazquez (Isco 81), Benzema, Ronaldo (Morata 112).
Kashima Antlers: Soghata; Nishi, Ueda, Shoji, Yamamoto, Endo (Ito 103), Nagaki (Akasaki 114), Ogasawara (Fabricio 68), Shibasaki, Kanazaki, Doi (Suzuki 88).
aet.
Referee: Janny Sikazwe (Zambia).

PREVIOUS FINALS

2000 Corinthians beat Vasco da Gama 4-3 on penalties after 0-0 draw
2001–04 Not contested
2005 Sao Paulo beat Liverpool 1-0
2006 Internacional beat Barcelona 1-0
2007 AC Milan beat Boca Juniors 4-2
2008 Manchester U beat Liga De Quito 1-0
2009 Barcelona beat Estudiantes 2-1
2010 Internazionale beat TP Mazembe Englebert 3-0
2011 Barcelona beat Santos 4-0
2012 Corinthians beat Chelsea 1-0
2013 Bayern Munich beat Raja Casablanca 2-0
2014 Real Madrid beat San Lorenzo 2-0
2015 Barcelona beat River Plate 3-0
2016 Real Madrid beat Kashima Antlers 4-2 (*aet.*)

WORLD CLUB CHAMPIONSHIP

Played annually up to 1974 and intermittently since then between the winners of the European Cup and the winners of the South American Champions Cup — known as the Copa Libertadores. In 1980 the winners were decided by one match arranged in Tokyo in February 1981 which remained the venue until 2004, when the match was superseded by the FIFA Club World Championship. AC Milan replaced Marseille who had been stripped of their European Cup title in 1993.

1960 Real Madrid beat Penarol 0-0, 5-1
1961 Penarol beat Benfica 0-1, 5-0, 2-1
1962 Santos beat Benfica 3-2, 5-2
1963 Santos beat AC Milan 2-4, 4-2, 1-0
1964 Inter-Milan beat Independiente 0-1, 2-0, 1-0
1965 Inter-Milan beat Independiente 3-0, 0-0
1966 Penarol beat Real Madrid 2-0, 2-0
1967 Racing Club beat Celtic 0-1, 2-1, 1-0
1968 Estudiantes beat Manchester United 1-0, 1-1
1969 AC Milan beat Estudiantes 3-0, 1-2
1970 Feyenoord beat Estudiantes 2-2, 1-0
1971 Nacional beat Panathinaikos* 1-1, 2-1
1972 Ajax beat Independiente 1-1, 3-0
1973 Independiente beat Juventus* 1-0
1974 Atlético Madrid* beat Independiente 0-1, 2-0
1975 Independiente and Bayern Munich could not agree dates; no matches.
1976 Bayern Munich beat Cruzeiro 2-0, 0-0
1977 Boca Juniors beat Borussia Moenchengladbach* 2-2, 3-0
1978 Not contested
1979 Olimpia beat Malmö* 1-0, 2-1
1980 Nacional beat Nottingham Forest 1-0
1981 Flamengo beat Liverpool 3-0
1982 Penarol beat Aston Villa 2-0
1983 Gremio Porto Alegre beat SV Hamburg 2-1
1984 Independiente beat Liverpool 1-0
1985 Juventus beat Argentinos Juniors 4-2 on penalties after 2-2 draw
1986 River Plate beat Steaua Bucharest 1-0
1987 FC Porto beat Penarol 2-1 after extra time
1988 Nacional (Uru) beat PSV Eindhoven 7-6 on penalties after 1-1 draw
1989 AC Milan beat Atletico Nacional (Col) 1-0 after extra time
1990 AC Milan beat Olimpia 3-0
1991 Crvena Zvezda beat Colo Colo 3-0
1992 Sao Paulo beat Barcelona 2-1
1993 Sao Paulo beat AC Milan 3-2
1994 Velez Sarsfield beat AC Milan 2-0
1995 Ajax beat Gremio Porto Alegre 4-3 on penalties after 0-0 draw
1996 Juventus beat River Plate 1-0
1997 Borussia Dortmund beat Cruzeiro 2-0
1998 Real Madrid beat Vasco da Gama 2-1
1999 Manchester U beat Palmeiras 1-0
2000 Boca Juniors beat Real Madrid 2-1
2001 Bayern Munich beat Boca Juniors 1-0 after extra time
2002 Real Madrid beat Olimpia 2-0
2003 Boca Juniors beat AC Milan 3-1 on penalties after 1-1 draw
2004 Porto beat Once Caldas 8-7 on penalties after 0-0 draw

**European Cup runners-up; winners declined to take part.*

EUROPEAN SUPER CUP 2016

Played annually between the winners of the European Champions' Cup and the European Cup-Winners' Cup (UEFA Cup from 2000; UEFA Europa League from 2010). AC Milan replaced Marseille in 1993–94.

Trondheim, Tuesday 9 August 2016, attendance 17,939

Real Madrid (1) 3 *(Asensio 21, Ramos 90, Carvajal 119)*

Sevilla (1) 2 *(Vazquez 41, Konoplyanka 72 (pen))*

Real Madrid: Casilla; Carvajal, Varane, Sergio Ramos, Marcelo, Kovacic (James 72), Casemiro, Isco (Modric 66), Lucas, Morata (Benzema 62), Asensio.
Sevilla: Sergio Rico; Pareja, Kolodziejczak, Carrico (Rami 51), Kiyotake, Iborra (Kranevitter 74), Vazquez, Nzonzi, Mariano, Vietto (Konoplyanka 67), Vitolo.
aet.
Referee: Milorad Mazic (Serbia).

PREVIOUS MATCHES

1972 Ajax beat Rangers 3-1, 3-2
1973 Ajax beat AC Milan 0-1, 6-0
1974 Not contested
1975 Dynamo Kyiv beat Bayern Munich 1-0, 2-0
1976 Anderlecht beat Bayern Munich 4-1, 1-2
1977 Liverpool beat Hamburg 1-1, 6-0
1978 Anderlecht beat Liverpool 3-1, 1-2
1979 Nottingham F beat Barcelona 1-0, 1-1
1980 Valencia beat Nottingham F 1-0, 1-2
1981 Not contested
1982 Aston Villa beat Barcelona 0-1, 3-0
1983 Aberdeen beat Hamburg 0-0, 2-0
1984 Juventus beat Liverpool 2-0
1985 Juventus v Everton not contested due to UEFA ban on English clubs
1986 Steaua Bucharest beat Dynamo Kyiv 1-0
1987 FC Porto beat Ajax 1-0, 1-0
1988 KV Mechelen beat PSV Eindhoven 3-0, 0-1
1989 AC Milan beat Barcelona 1-1, 1-0
1990 AC Milan beat Sampdoria 1-1, 2-0
1991 Manchester U beat Crvena Zvezda 1-0
1992 Barcelona beat Werder Bremen 1-1, 2-1
1993 Parma beat AC Milan 0-1, 2-0
1994 AC Milan beat Arsenal 0-0, 2-0
1995 Ajax beat Zaragoza 1-1, 4-0
1996 Juventus beat Paris St Germain 6-1, 3-1
1997 Barcelona beat Borussia Dortmund 2-0, 1-1
1998 Chelsea beat Real Madrid 1-0
1999 Lazio beat Manchester U 1-0
2000 Galatasaray beat Real Madrid 2-1
2001 Liverpool beat Bayern Munich 3-2
2002 Real Madrid beat Feyenoord 3-1
2003 AC Milan beat Porto 1-0
2004 Valencia beat Porto 2-1
2005 Liverpool beat CSKA Moscow 3-1
2006 Sevilla beat Barcelona 3-0
2007 AC Milan beat Sevilla 3-1
2008 Zenit beat Manchester U 2-1
2009 Barcelona beat Shakhtar Donetsk 1-0
2010 Atletico Madrid beat Internazionale 2-0
2011 Barcelona beat Porto 2-0
2012 Atletico Madrid beat Chelsea 4-1
2013 Bayern Munch beat Chelsea 5-4 on penalties after 2-2 draw
2014 Real Madrid beat Sevilla 2-0
2015 Barcelona beat Sevilla 5-4
2016 Real Madrid beat Sevilla 3-2

INTERNATIONAL DIRECTORY

The latest available information has been given regarding numbers of clubs and players registered with FIFA, the world governing body. Where known, official colours are listed. With European countries, League tables show a number of signs: * team relegated, *+ team relegated after play-offs, + team not relegated after play-offs.

There are 211 member associations in the six FIFA Confederations, indicated in brackets after the regional heading. The four home countries, England, Scotland, Northern Ireland and Wales, are dealt with elsewhere in the Yearbook; but basic details appear in this directory. Gibraltar was admitted to full UEFA membership in 2013; Northern Cyprus is not a member of FIFA or UEFA and is the subject of an international territorial dispute. From March 2014 FIFA permitted Kosovo to play friendlies against full member nations; Kosovo was granted full membership of both FIFA and UEFA in May 2016 and entered World Cup 2018 qualification in September 2016. Gozo is included here for its close links with Maltese football. *N.B. In this edition international results for 2016–17 include matches played from 11 July 2016 to 2 July 2017.*

There are 12 associate members and others who have affiliation to their confederations; the most recent admission to full membership was South Sudan in 2011. The current associate members are as follows: AFC: Northern Mariana Islands; CAF: Reunion, Zanzibar; CONCACAF: Bonaire, French Guiana, Guadeloupe, Martinique, Saint-Martin, Sint Maarten; OFC: Kiribati, Niue, Tuvalu. Matches between full members and associate members are indicated with †.

EUROPE (UEFA)

ALBANIA

Football Association of Albania, Rruga e Elbasanit, 1000 Tirana.
Founded: 1930. *FIFA:* 1932; *UEFA:* 1954. *National Colours:* Red shirts with white trim, black shorts, red socks.

International matches 2016–17

Morocco (h) 0-0, Macedonia (h) 2-1, Liechtenstein (a) 2-0, Spain (h) 0-2, Israel (h) 0-3, Italy (a) 0-2, Bosnia-Herzegovina (h) 1-2, Luxembourg (a) 1-2, Israel (a) 3-0.

League Championship wins (1930–37; 1945–2017)

KF Tirana 24 (formerly SK Tirana; includes 17 Nentori 8); Dinamo Tirana 18; Partizani Tirana 15; Vllaznia 9; Skenderbeu 7; Elbasani 2 (including Labinoti 1); Flamurtari 1; Teuta 1; Kukesi 1.

Cup wins (1948–2017)

KF Tirana 16 (formerly SK Tirana; includes 17 Nentori 8); Partizani Tirana 15; Dinamo Tirana 13; Vllaznia 6; Flamurtari 4; Teuta 3; Elbasani 2 (including Labinoti 1); Besa 2; Laci 2; Apolonia 1; Kukesi 1.

Albanian Superliga 2016–17

	P	*W*	*D*	*L*	*F*	*A*	*GD*	*Pts*
Kukesi	36	20	15	1	51	18	33	75
Partizani Tirana	36	19	15	2	46	17	29	72
Skenderbeu	36	21	9	6	45	22	23	72
Luftetari Gjirokaster	36	11	11	14	37	45	–8	44
Teuta	36	10	10	16	27	34	–7	40
Laci	36	10	10	16	23	35	–12	40
Vllaznia	36	8	16	12	29	35	–6	40
Flamurtari (–6)	36	12	10	14	42	34	8	40
KF Tirana*	36	8	15	13	29	32	–3	39
Korabi Peshkopi*	36	2	7	27	11	68	–57	13

Top scorer: Pejic (Kukesi) 28.
Cup Final: KF Tirana 3, Skenderbeu 1 *aet*.

ANDORRA

Federacio Andorrana de Futbol, Avda Carlemany 67, 3er Pis, Apartado postal 65, Escaldes-Engordany.
Founded: 1994. *FIFA:* 1996; *UEFA:* 1996. *National Colours:* All red.

International matches 2016–17

Latvia (a) 0-1, Portugal (a) 0-6, Switzerland (h) 1-2, Hungary (a) 0-4, San Marino (a) 2-0, Faroe Islands (h) 0-0, Hungary (h) 1-0.

League Championship wins (1996–2017)

FC Santa Coloma 11; Principat 3; Encamp 2; Sant Julia 2; Ranger's 2; Lusitanos 2; Constel-lacio 1.

Cup wins (1991, 1994–2017)

FC Santa Coloma 9*; Principat 6*; Sant Julia 5; UE Santa Coloma 3; Constel-lacio 1; Lusitanos 1.
* *Includes one unofficial title.*

Andorran Primera Divisio Qualifying Table 2016–17

	P	*W*	*D*	*L*	*F*	*A*	*GD*	*Pts*
FC Santa Coloma	21	15	3	3	44	14	30	48
Sant Julia	21	13	5	3	49	16	33	44
UE Santa Coloma	21	13	5	3	54	22	32	44
Lusitanos	21	11	6	4	40	20	20	39
Engordany	21	8	6	7	35	27	8	30
Encamp	21	4	3	14	18	31	–13	15
Ordino	21	3	3	15	24	49	–25	12
Jenlai (–3)	21	1	1	19	10	95	–85	1

Championship Round 2016–17

	P	*W*	*D*	*L*	*F*	*A*	*GD*	*Pts*
FC Santa Coloma	27	18	6	3	57	21	36	60
Sant Julia	27	14	8	5	55	23	32	50
UE Santa Coloma	27	14	6	7	62	34	28	48
Lusitanos	27	13	9	5	49	30	19	48

Relegation Round 2016–17

	P	*W*	*D*	*L*	*F*	*A*	*GD*	*Pts*
Engordany	27	10	6	11	46	39	7	36
Encamp	27	8	3	16	45	37	8	27
Ordino*	27	8	3	16	45	56	–11	27
Jenlai*+ (–3)	27	2	1	24	18	137	–119	4

Top scorer: Bernat (UE Santa Coloma) 18.
Cup Final: UE Santa Coloma 1, FC Santa Coloma 0.

ARMENIA

Football Federation of Armenia, Khanjyan Street 27, 0010 Yerevan.
Founded: 1992. *FIFA:* 1992; *UEFA:* 1993. *National Colours:* Red shirts with white trim, red shorts, red socks.

International matches 2016–17

Czech Republic (a) 0-3, Denmark (a) 0-1, Romania (h) 0-5, Poland (a) 1-2, Montenegro (h) 3-2, Kazakhstan (h) 2-0, St Kitts & Nevis (h) 5-0, Montenegro (a) 1-4.

League Championship wins (1992–2017)

Pyunik 14 (including Homenetmen 1); Shirak 5*; Ararat Yerevan 2*; Araks 2 (including Tsement 1); Alashkert 2; FK Yerevan 1; Ulisses 1; Banants 1.
* *Includes one unofficial shared title.*

Cup wins (1992–2017)

Pyunik (including Homenetmen 1) 8; Mika 6; Ararat Yerevan 5; Banants 3; Tsement 2; Shirak 2.

Armenian Premier League 2016–17

	P	*W*	*D*	*L*	*F*	*A*	*GD*	*Pts*
Alashkert	30	19	7	4	59	26	33	64
Gandzasar	30	17	6	7	38	24	14	57
Shirak	30	16	5	9	31	24	7	53
Pyunik	30	12	9	9	35	27	8	45
Banants	30	5	6	19	18	44	–26	21
Ararat Yerevan*	30	3	3	24	17	53	–36	12

Top scorers (joint): Manasyan (Alashkert), Artak Yedigaryan (Alashkert) 13.
Cup Final: Shirak 3, Pyunik 0.

AUSTRIA

Oesterreichischer Fussball-Bund, Ernst-Happel Stadion, Sektor A/F, Meiereistrasse 7, Wien 1021.
Founded: 1904. *FIFA:* 1905; *UEFA:* 1954. *National Colours:* Red shirts, white shorts, red socks.

International matches 2016–17

Georgia (a) 2-1, Wales (h) 2-2, Serbia (a) 2-3, Republic of Ireland (h) 0-1, Slovakia (h) 0-0, Moldova (h) 2-0, Finland (h) 1-1, Republic of Ireland (a) 1-1.

League Championship wins (1912–2017)
Rapid Vienna 32; FK Austria Vienna (formerly Amateure) 24; Red Bull Salzburg 11 (incl. Austria Salzburg 3); Wacker Innsbruck 10 (incl. Swarovski Tirol 2, Tirol Innsbruck 3); Admira Vienna (now Admira Wacker Modling) 9 (incl. Wacker Vienna 1); First Vienna 6; Wiener Sportklub 3; Sturm Graz 3; WAF 1; WAC 1; Floridsdorfer 1; Hakoah 1; LASK Linz 1; Voest Linz 1; GAK Graz 1.

Cup wins (1919–2017)
FK Austria Vienna (formerly Amateure) 27; Rapid Vienna 14; Wacker Innsbruck 7 (incl. Swarovski Tirol 1, Tirol Innsbruck); Admira Vienna (now Admira Wacker Modling) 6 (including Wacker Vienna 1); Red Bull Salzburg 5; GAK Graz 4; Sturm Graz 4; First Vienna 3; WAC 2; Ried 2; WAF 1; Wiener Sportklub 1; Linz ASK 1; Kremser 1; Stockerau 1; Karnten 1; Horn 1; Pasching 1.

Austrian Bundesliga 2016–17

	P	*W*	*D*	*L*	*F*	*A*	*GD*	*Pts*
Red Bull Salzburg	36	25	6	5	74	24	50	81
Austria Vienna	36	20	3	13	72	50	22	63
Sturm Graz	36	19	3	14	55	39	16	60
Rheindorf Altach	36	15	8	13	46	49	–3	53
Rapid Vienna	36	12	10	14	52	42	10	46
Admira Wacker Modling	36	13	7	16	36	55	–19	46
Mattersburg	36	12	7	17	39	54	–15	43
Wolfsberger	36	11	9	16	40	59	–19	42
St Polten	36	9	10	17	41	60	–19	37
Ried*	36	10	5	21	33	56	–23	35

Top scorer: Kayode (Austria Vienna) 17.
Cup Final: Red Bull Salzburg 2, Rapid Vienna 1.

AZERBAIJAN

Association of Football Federations of Azerbaijan, 2208 Nobel prospekti, 1025 Baku.
Founded: 1992. *FIFA:* 1994; *UEFA:* 1994. *National Colours:* All red.

International matches 2016–17
San Marino (a) 1-0, Norway (h) 1-0, Czech Republic (a) 0-0, Northern Ireland (a) 0-4, Qatar (a) 2-1, Germany (h) 1-4, Northern Ireland (h) 0-1.

League Championship wins (1992–2017)
Neftchi 8; Qarabag 5; Kapaz 3; Shamkir 3*; FK Baku 2; Inter Baku 2; Turan 1; Khazar Lankaran 1.
* *Includes one unofficial title.*

Cup wins (1992–2017)
Neftchi 7*; Qarabag 6; Kapaz 4; FK Baku 3; Khazar Lankaran 3; Inshatchi 1; Shafa 1.
* *Includes one title awarded by forfeit.*

Azerbaijani Premier League 2016–17

	P	*W*	*D*	*L*	*F*	*A*	*GD*	*Pts*
Qarabag	28	19	5	4	46	14	32	62
Qabala	28	14	10	4	48	21	27	52
Inter Baku	28	11	10	7	39	33	6	43
Zira	28	10	9	9	29	26	3	39
Kapaz	28	9	9	10	24	27	–3	36
Sumqayit	28	9	8	11	28	35	–7	35
Neftci	28	9	2	17	24	45	–21	29
AZAL-Olympik Suvalan*	28	1	7	20	13	50	–37	10

Top scorers (joint): Aliyev (Inter Baku), Ozobic (Qabala) 13.
Cup Final: Qarabag 2, Qabala 0.

BELARUS

Belarus Football Federation, Prospekt Pobeditelei 20/3, 220020 Minsk.
Founded: 1989. *FIFA:* 1992; *UEFA:* 1993. *National Colours:* All red with white trim.

International matches 2016–17
Norway (a) 1-0, France (h) 0-0, Netherlands (a) 1-4, Luxembourg (h) 1-1, Greece (a) 1-0, Bulgaria (a) 0-1, Sweden (a) 0-4, FYR Macedonia (a) 0-3, Switzerland (a) 0-1, Bulgaria (h) 2-1, New Zealand (h) 1-0.

League Championship wins (1992–2016)
BATE Borisov 13; Dinamo Minsk 7; Slavia Mozyr (incl. MPKC 1) 2; Dnepr Mogilev 1; Belshina Bobruisk 1; Gomel 1; Shakhtyor Soligorsk 1.

Cup wins (1992–2017)
Dinamo Minsk 3; Belshina Bobruisk 3; BATE Borisov 3; Slavia Mozyr (formerly MPKC) 2; Gomel 2; Shakhtyor Soligorsk 2; MTZ-RIPA (now Partizan Minsk) 2; Dinamo Brest 2; Naftan Novopolotsk 2; Neman Grodno 1; Dinamo 93 Minsk 1; Lokomotiv 96 1; FC Minsk 1; Torpedo Zhodino 1.

Belarussian Premier League 2016

	P	*W*	*D*	*L*	*F*	*A*	*GD*	*Pts*
BATE Borisov	30	22	4	4	73	25	48	70
Shakhtyor Soligorsk	30	17	8	5	46	20	26	59
Dinamo Minsk	30	15	10	5	46	28	18	55
Minsk	30	15	8	7	49	24	25	53
Torpedo Zhodino	30	13	9	8	47	33	14	48
Vitebsk	30	12	6	12	30	26	4	42
Isloch	30	11	8	11	33	39	–6	41
Dinamo Brest	30	11	7	12	38	38	0	40
Gorodeya	30	8	14	8	36	39	–3	38
Slavia Mozyr	30	9	8	13	33	49	–16	35
Krumkachy	30	9	6	15	24	39	–15	33
Slutsk	30	6	12	12	22	34	–12	30
Naftan Novopolotsk	30	7	8	15	25	46	–21	29
Neman Grodno	30	7	8	15	21	36	–15	29
Belshina Bobruisk*	30	5	10	15	34	45	–11	25
Granit*	30	5	10	15	20	56	–36	25

Top scorers (joint): Gordeichuk (BATE Borisov), Rodionov (BATE Borisov) 15.
Cup Final: Dinamo Brest 1, Shakhtyor Soligorsk 1.
aet; Dinamo Brest won 10-9 on penalties.

BELGIUM

Union Royale Belge des Societes de Football-Association, 145 Avenue Houba de Strooper, B-1020 Bruxelles.
Founded: 1895. *FIFA:* 1904; *UEFA:* 1954. *National Colours:* All red.

International matches 2016–17
Spain (h) 0-2, Cyprus (a) 3-0, Bosnia-Herzegovina (h) 4-0, Gibraltar (n) 6-0, Netherlands (a) 1-1, Estonia (h) 8-1, Greece (h) 1-1, Russia (a) 3-3, Czech Republic (h) 2-1, Estonia (a) 2-0.

League Championship wins (1896–2017)
Anderlecht 34; Club Brugge 14; Union St Gilloise 11; Standard Liege 10; Beerschot VAC (became Germinal) 7; RC Brussels 6; RFC Liege 5; Daring Brussels 5; Antwerp 4; Lierse 4; Mechelen 4; Cercle Brugge 3; Genk 3; Beveren 2; RWD Molenbeek 1; KAA Gent 1.

Cup wins (1912–14; 1927; 1935; 1954–2017)
Club Brugge 11; Anderlecht 9; Standard Liege 7; Genk 4; KAA Gent 3; Union Saint- Gilloise 2; Waterschei (became Racing Genk) 2; Beveren 2; Cercle Brugge 2; Antwerp 2; Lierse 2; Beerschot VAC (became Germinal) 2; Beerschot Antwerpen Club (incl. Germinal Ekeren) 2; Lokeren 2; Zulte Waregem 2; Racing 1; Daring 1; Tournai 1; Mechelen 1; FC Liege 1; Westerlo 1; La Louviere 1.

Belgian First Division A Qualifying Table 2016–17

	P	*W*	*D*	*L*	*F*	*A*	*GD*	*Pts*
Anderlecht	30	18	7	5	67	30	37	61
Club Brugge	30	18	5	7	56	24	32	59
Zulte Waregem	30	15	9	6	49	38	11	54
KAA Gent	30	14	8	8	45	29	16	50
Oostende	30	14	8	8	52	37	15	50
Sporting Charleroi	30	13	10	7	34	29	5	49
Mechelen	30	14	6	10	41	36	5	48
Genk	30	14	6	10	40	35	5	48
Standard Liege (–3)	30	10	12	8	47	38	9	39
Kortrijk	30	8	7	15	38	55	–17	31
Lokeren	30	7	10	13	24	34	–10	31
Sint-Truiden	30	8	6	16	35	48	–13	30
Eupen	30	8	6	16	40	64	–24	30
Waasland-Beveren	30	7	9	14	28	43	–15	30
Royal Excel Mouscron	30	7	3	20	29	53	–24	24
Westerlo*	30	5	8	17	33	65	–32	23

NB: Points earned in Qualifying phase are halved and rounded up at start of Championship Play-off phase.

Championship Play-off

	P	*W*	*D*	*L*	*F*	*A*	*GD*	*Pts*
Anderlecht	10	6	3	1	14	6	8	52
Club Brugge	10	4	3	3	16	14	2	45
KAA Gent	10	4	4	2	16	11	5	41
Oostende	10	3	3	4	14	17	–3	37
Sporting Charleroi	10	2	4	4	10	13	–3	35
Zulte Waregem	10	1	3	6	12	21	–9	33

Top scorer: Teodorczyk (Anderlecht) 20.
Cup Final: Zulte Waregem 3, Oostende 3.
aet; Zulte Waregem won 4-2 on penalties.

BOSNIA-HERZEGOVINA

Football Federation of Bosnia & Herzegovina, Ferhadija 30, 71000 Sarajevo.
Founded: 1992. *FIFA:* 1996; *UEFA:* 1998. *National Colours:* Blue shirts, blue shorts, blue socks with white tops.

International matches 2016–17

Estonia (h) 5-0, Belgium (a) 0-4, Cyprus (h) 2-0, Greece (a) 1-1, Gibraltar (h) 5-0, Albania (a) 2-1, Greece (h) 0-0.

League Championship wins (1998–2017)

Zeljeznicar 6; Zrinjski 5; FK Sarajevo 3; Siroki Brijeg 2; Brotnjo 1; Leotar 1; Modrica 1; Borac Banja Luka 1.

Cup wins (1998; 2000–16)

Zeljeznicar 5; FK Sarajevo 4; Siroki Brijeg 2; Modrica 1; Orasje 1; Zrinjski 1; Slavija 1; Borac Banja Luka 1; Olimpic Sarajevo 1; Radnik Bijeljina 1.

Bosnian-Herzegovinian Premier League 2016–17

	P	*W*	*D*	*L*	*F*	*A*	*GD*	*Pts*
Zrinjski	22	13	6	3	38	19	19	45
Zeljeznicar	22	13	5	4	28	14	14	44
FK Sarajevo	22	12	7	3	30	16	14	43
Radnik Bijeljina	22	10	7	5	31	22	9	37
Sloboda Tuzla	22	9	8	5	31	24	7	35
Krupa na Vrbasu	22	9	5	8	27	22	5	32
Siroki Brijeg	22	7	7	8	23	26	–3	28
Mladost Doboj Kakanj	22	6	8	8	27	26	1	26
Vitez	22	5	8	9	12	19	–7	23
Metalleghe	22	6	3	13	20	29	–9	21
Celik Zenica	22	2	7	13	14	34	–20	13
Olimpic Sarajevo	22	2	5	15	15	45	–30	11

Championship Round 2016–17

	P	*W*	*D*	*L*	*F*	*A*	*GD*	*Pts*
Zrinjski	32	18	10	4	54	25	29	64
Zeljeznicar	32	18	9	5	41	22	19	63
FK Sarajevo	32	16	11	5	41	22	19	59
Krupa na Vrbasu	32	12	10	10	40	34	6	46
Sloboda Tuzla	32	11	10	11	39	42	–3	43
Radnik Bijeljina	32	10	10	12	37	39	–2	40

Relegation Round 2016–17

	P	*W*	*D*	*L*	*F*	*A*	*GD*	*Pts*
Siroki Brijeg	32	9	10	13	34	35	–1	37
Mladost Doboj Kakanj	32	8	13	11	42	45	–3	37
Vitez	32	8	11	13	20	30	–10	35
Celik Zenica	32	8	11	13	28	39	–11	35
Metalleghe*	32	7	11	14	25	34	–9	32
Olimpic Sarajevo*	32	5	8	19	28	62	–34	23

Top scorer: Lendric (Zeljeznicar) 19.
Cup Final: FK Sarajevo 0, 1, Siroki Brijeg 1, 0 (agg. 1-1).
Siroki Brijeg won 4-2 on penalties.

BULGARIA

Bulgarian Football Union, 26 Tzar Ivan Assen II Str., 1124 Sofia.
Founded: 1923. *FIFA:* 1992; *UEFA:* 1954. *National Colours:* White shirts, green shorts, red socks.

International matches 2016–17

Luxembourg (h) 4-3, France (a) 1-4, Sweden (a) 0-3, Belarus (h) 1-0, Netherlands (h) 2-0, Belarus (a) 1-2.

League Championship wins (1925–2017)

CSKA Sofia 31; Levski Sofia 26; Slavia Sofia 7; Ludogorets Razgrad 6; Lokomotiv Sofia 4; Litex Lovech 4; Vladislav Varna (now Cherno More Varna) 3; Botev Plovdiv (includes Trakija) 2; Athletic Slava 1923 1; Sokol Varna (now Spartak Varna) 1; Sportklub Sofia (now Septemvri Sofia) 1; Ticha Varna (now Cherno More Varna) 1; Spartak Plovdiv 1; Beroe Stara Zagora 1; FC Etar 1; Lokomotiv Plovdiv 1.

Cup wins (1946–2017)

Levski Sofia (incl. Vitosha 1) 24; CSKA Sofia (incl. Sredets 3) 20; Slavia Sofia 7; Lokomotiv Sofia 4; Litex Lovech 4; Botev Plovdiv (includes Trakija) 3; Beroe Stara Zagora 2; Ludogorets Razgrad 2; Spartak Plovdiv 1; Septemvri Sofia 1; Spartak Sofia 1; Marek Dupnitsa 1; Sliven 1; Cherno More Varna 1.

Bulgarian First League 2016–17

	P	*W*	*D*	*L*	*F*	*A*	*GD*	*Pts*
Ludogorets Razgrad	26	21	4	1	69	19	50	67
Levski Sofia	26	15	6	5	38	17	21	51
CSKA Sofia	26	13	7	6	35	16	19	46
Cherno More Varna	26	12	7	7	30	24	6	43
Lokomotiv Plovdiv	26	10	9	7	35	30	5	39
Dunav 2010	26	10	8	8	32	31	1	38
Botev Plovdiv	26	10	5	11	36	42	–6	35
Beroe	26	10	5	11	27	28	–1	35
Pirin Blagoevgrad	26	10	4	12	30	36	–6	34
Vereya	26	8	6	12	22	36	–14	30
Slavia Sofia	26	8	4	14	30	45	–15	28
Neftochimic	26	7	5	14	27	37	–10	26
L'tiv Gorna Orjahovica	26	5	7	14	22	39	–17	22
Montana	26	3	3	20	16	49	–33	12

Championship Round 2016–17

	P	*W*	*D*	*L*	*F*	*A*	*GD*	*Pts*
Ludogorets Razgrad	36	25	8	3	87	28	59	83
CSKA Sofia	36	19	10	7	51	21	30	67
Levski Sofia	36	18	9	9	50	31	19	63
Dunav 2010	36	15	10	11	46	44	2	55
Lokomotiv Plovdiv	36	14	10	12	50	52	-2	52
Cherno More Varna	36	13	8	15	39	45	-6	47

Relegation Round 2016–17

Group A

	P	*W*	*D*	*L*	*F*	*A*	*GD*	*Pts*
Vereya	32	13	6	13	31	40	–9	45
Botev Plovdiv	32	13	5	14	51	50	1	44
Slavia Sofia+	32	11	4	17	37	55	–18	37
Montana*+	32	4	3	25	24	66	–42	15

Group B

	P	*W*	*D*	*L*	*F*	*A*	*GD*	*Pts*
Beroe	32	12	8	12	35	33	2	44
Pirin Blagoevgrad	32	12	7	13	41	44	–3	43
Neftochimic*+	32	8	7	17	33	47	–14	31
L'tiv Gorna Orjahovica*	32	7	9	16	32	51	–19	30

Top scorer: Keseru (Ludogorets Razgrad) 22.
Cup Final: Botev Plovdiv 2, Ludogorets Razgrad 1.

CHANNEL ISLANDS

Guernsey

League Championship wins (1894–2017)

Northerners 32; Guernsey Rangers 17; Vale Recreation 15; St Martin's 13; Sylvans 10; Belgrave Wanderers 8; 2nd Bn Manchesters 3; 2nd Bn Royal Irish Regt 2; 2nd Bn Wiltshires 2; 10th Comp W Div Royal Artillery 1; 2nd Bn Leicesters 1; 2nd Bn PA Somerset Light Infantry 1; 2nd Middlesex Regt 1; Athletics 1; Band Comp 2nd Bn Royal Fusiliers 1; G&H Comp Royal Fusiliers 1; Grange 1; Yorkshire Regt (Green Howards); Guernsey Rovers 1.

Guernsey Priaulx League 2016–17

	P	*W*	*D*	*L*	*F*	*A*	*GD*	*Pts*
Guernsey Rovers	21	14	3	4	65	35	30	45
Northerners	21	13	5	3	47	29	18	44
St Martins	21	13	4	4	52	24	28	43
Sylvans	21	8	5	8	58	46	12	29
Alderney	21	8	3	10	35	45	–10	27
Guernsey Rangers	21	6	5	10	46	56	–10	23
Vale Recreation	21	5	6	10	48	44	4	21

Jersey

League Championship wins (1894–2017)

Jersey Wanderers 20; First Tower United 19; St Paul's 18; Jersey Scottish 10; Beeches Old Boys 5; Magpies 4; 2nd Bn King's Own Regt 3; Oaklands 3; St Peter 3; 1st Batt Devon Regt 2; 1st Bn East Surrey Regt 2; Georgetown 2; Mechanics 2; YMCA 2; 2nd Bn East Surrey Regt 1; 20th Comp Royal Garrison Artillery 1; National Rovers 1; Sporting Academics 1; Trinity 1.

Jersey Football Combination 2016–17

	P	*W*	*D*	*L*	*F*	*A*	*GD*	*Pts*
St Paul's (–3)	21	18	3	0	88	17	71	54
Jersey Wanderers	21	13	1	7	47	31	16	40
Jersey Scottish	21	10	4	7	54	27	27	34
St Ouen	21	10	1	10	46	45	1	31
St Peter	21	6	7	8	38	39	–1	25
Rozel Rovers	21	6	4	11	35	51	–16	22
Trinity	21	5	5	11	30	58	–28	20
Jersey Portuguese	21	2	3	16	18	88	–70	9

Upton Park Trophy 2017 (For Guernsey & Jersey League Champions)

St Paul's 3, Rovers 0.

Upton Park Trophy wins (1907–2017)

Northerners 17 (including 1 shared); First Tower United 12; Jersey Wanderers 11 (including 1 shared); St Martin's 11; St Paul's 10; Jersey Scottish 6; Guernsey Rangers 5; Vale Recreation 4; Belgrave Wanderers 4; Beeches Old

Boys 3; Old St Paul's 3; Magpies 3; Sylvans 3; St Peter 2; Jersey Mechanics 1; Jersey YMCA 1; National Rovers 1; Sporting Academics 1; Trinity 1.

CROATIA

Croatian Football Federation, Vukovarska 269A, 10000 Zagreb.
Founded: 1912. *FIFA:* 1992; *UEFA:* 1993. *National Colours:* Red and white check shirts, white shorts, blue socks.

International matches 2016–17
Turkey (h) 1-1*, Kosovo (n) 6-0, Finland (a) 1-0, Iceland (h) 2-0, Northern Ireland (a) 3-0, Chile (n) 1-1 (1-4p), China PR (a) 1-1 (3-4p), Ukraine (h) 1-0, Estonia (a) 0-3, Mexico (n) 2-1, Iceland (h) 0-1.
* *Behind closed doors.*

League Championship wins (1992–2017)
Dinamo Zagreb (incl. Croatia Zagreb 3) 18; Hajduk Split 6; NK Zagreb 1; Rijeka 1.

Cup wins (1992–2017)
Dinamo Zagreb (incl. Croatia Zagreb 4) 14; Hajduk Split 6; Rijeka 4; Inter Zapresic 1; Osijek 1.

Croatian Prva HNL 2016–17

	P	*W*	*D*	*L*	*F*	*A*	*GD*	*Pts*
Rijeka	36	27	7	2	71	23	48	88
Dinamo Zagreb	36	27	5	4	68	24	44	86
Hajduk Split	36	20	9	7	70	31	39	69
Osijek	36	20	6	10	52	37	15	66
Lokomotiva Zagreb	36	12	8	16	41	38	3	44
Istra 1961	36	10	9	17	33	49	–16	39
Slaven Koprivnica	36	9	11	16	36	45	–9	38
Inter Zapresic	36	5	13	18	26	57	–31	28
Cibalia+	36	4	9	23	26	79	–53	21
RNK Split*	36	3	9	24	12	52	–40	18

Top scorer: Futacs (Hajduk Split) 18.
Cup Final: Rijeka 3, Dinamo Zagreb 1.

CYPRUS

Cyprus Football Association, 10 Achaion Street, 2413 Engomi, PO Box 25071, 1306 Nicosia.
Founded: 1934. *FIFA:* 1948; *UEFA:* 1962. *National Colours:* All blue with white trim.

International matches 2016–17
Belgium (h) 0-3, Greece (a) 0-2, Bosnia-Herzegovina (a) 0-2, Gibraltar (h) 3-1, Kazakhstan (h) 3-1, Estonia (h) 0-0, Portugal (a) 0-4, Gibraltar (a) 2-1.

League Championship wins (1935–2017)
APOEL 26; Omonia 20; Anorthosis 13; AEL Limassol 6; EPA Larnaca 3; Olympiakos Nicosia 3; Apollon Limassol 3; Pezoporikos Larnaca 2; Trast 1; Cetinkaya 1.

Cup wins (1935–2017)
APOEL 21; Omonia 14; Anorthosis 10; Apollon Limassol 9; AEL Limassol 6; EPA Larnaca 5; Trast 3; Cetinkaya 2; Pezoporikos Larnaca 1; Olympiakos Nicosia 1; Nea Salamis Famagusta 1; AEK Larnaca 1; APOP Kinyras 1.

Cypriot First Division 2016–17

	P	*W*	*D*	*L*	*F*	*A*	*GD*	*Pts*
APOEL	26	19	5	2	62	16	46	62
AEK Larnaca	26	17	7	2	54	19	35	58
Apollon Limassol	26	17	6	3	56	19	37	57
AEL Limassol	26	15	6	5	40	22	18	51
Omonia	26	15	5	6	56	37	19	50
Anorthosis Famagusta	26	10	9	7	39	27	12	39
Ermis Aradippou	26	10	5	11	35	41	–6	35
Nea Salamis Famagusta	26	8	7	11	22	33	–11	31
Ethnikos Achnas	26	8	6	12	42	46	–4	30
Karmiotissa	26	7	6	13	30	53	–23	27
Aris Limassol	26	6	6	14	30	52	–22	24
Doxa Katokopia	26	5	5	16	20	38	–18	20
Anagennisi Deryneia*	26	0	7	19	18	58	–40	7
AE Zakakiou* (–6)	26	1	8	17	20	63	–43	5

Championship Round 2016–17

	P	*W*	*D*	*L*	*F*	*A*	*GD*	*Pts*
APOEL	36	24	8	4	77	24	53	80
AEK Larnaca	36	22	10	4	66	28	38	76
Apollon Limassol	36	21	10	5	71	30	41	73
AEL Limassol	36	19	9	8	53	36	17	66
Omonia	36	17	6	13	68	57	11	57
Anorthosis Famagusta	36	12	11	13	48	41	7	47

Relegation Round 2016–17

	P	*W*	*D*	*L*	*F*	*A*	*GD*	*Pts*
Nea Salamis Famagusta	36	12	9	15	33	44	–11	45
Ethnikos Achna	36	11	10	15	57	66	–9	43
Ermis Aradippou (–6)	36	14	6	16	51	61	–10	42
Aris Limassol	36	11	8	17	47	65	–18	41
Doxa Katokopia	36	10	7	19	40	52	–12	37
Karmiotissa*	36	10	7	19	47	71	–24	37

Top scorer: Derbyshire (Omonia) 24.
Cup Final: APOEL 0, Apollon Limassol 1.

CZECH REPUBLIC

Fotbalova Asociace Ceske Republiky, Diskarska 2431/4, PO Box 11, Praha 6 16017.
Founded: 1901. *FIFA:* 1907; *UEFA:* 1954. *National Colours:* All red.

International matches 2016–17
Armenia (h) 3-0, Northern Ireland (h) 0-0, Germany (a) 0-3, Azerbaijan (h) 0-0, Norway (h) 2-1, Denmark (h) 1-1, Lithuania (h) 3-0, San Marino (a) 6-0, Belgium (a) 1-2, Norway (a) 1-1.

League Championship wins – Czechoslovakia (1925–93)
Sparta Prague 21; Slavia Prague 13; Dukla Prague (prev. UDA, now Marila Pribram) 11; Slovan Bratislava (formerly NV Bratislava) 8; Spartak Trnava 5; Banik Ostrava 3; Viktoria Zizkov 1; Inter-Bratislava 1; Spartak Hradec Kralove 1; Zbrojovka Brno 1; Bohemians 1; Vitkovice 1.

Cup wins – Czechoslovakia (1961–93)
Dukla Prague 8; Sparta Prague 8; Slovan Bratislava 5; Spartak Trnava 4; Banik Ostrava 3; Lokomotiva Kosice 2; TJ Gottwaldov 1; Lokomotiva Kosice 1; Dunajska Streda 1.

League Championship wins – Czech Republic (1994–2017)
Sparta Prague 12; Viktoria Plzen 4; Slavia Prague 4; Slovan Liberec 3; Banik Ostrava 1.

Cup wins – Czech Republic (1994–2017)
Sparta Prague 6; Slavia Prague 3; Viktoria Zizkov 2; Jablonec 2; Slovan Liberec 2; Teplice 2; Mlada Boleslav 2; Hradec Kralove (formerly Spartak) 1; Banik Ostrava 1; Viktoria Plzen 1; Sigma Olomouc 1; Fastav Zlin 1.

Czech First League 2016–17

	P	*W*	*D*	*L*	*F*	*A*	*GD*	*Pts*
Slavia Prague	30	20	9	1	65	22	43	69
Viktoria Plzen	30	20	7	3	47	21	26	67
Sparta Prague	30	16	9	5	47	26	21	57
Mlada Boleslav	30	13	10	7	47	37	10	49
Teplice	30	13	9	8	38	25	13	48
Fastav Zlin	30	11	8	11	34	35	–1	41
Dukla Prague	30	11	7	12	39	35	4	40
Jablonec	30	9	12	9	43	38	5	39
Slovan Liberec	30	10	9	11	31	28	3	39
Karvina	30	9	7	14	39	49	–10	34
Slovacko	30	6	14	10	29	38	–9	32
Zbrojovka Brno	30	6	14	10	32	45	–13	32
Bohemians 1905	30	7	7	16	22	39	–17	28
Vysocina Jihlava	30	6	9	15	26	47	–21	27
Hradec Kralove*	30	8	3	19	29	51	–22	27
Pribram*	30	6	4	20	29	61	–32	22

Top scorers (joint): Lafata (Sparta Prague), Skoda (Slavia Prague) 15.
Cup Final: Fastav Zlin 1, Opava 0.

DENMARK

Dansk Boldspil-Union, Idraettens Hus, DBU Alle 1, DK-2605, Brondby.
Founded: 1889. *FIFA:* 1904; *UEFA:* 1954. *National Colours:* Red shirts, white shorts, red socks.

International matches 2016–17
Liechtenstein (h) 5-0, Armenia (h) 1-0, Poland (a) 2-3, Montenegro (h) 0-1, Kazakhstan (h) 4-1, Czech Republic (a) 1-1, Romania (a) 0-0, Germany (h) 1-1, Kazakhstan (a) 3-1.

League Championship wins (1913–2017)
KB Copenhagen 15; FC Copenhagen 12; Brondby 10; B 93 Copenhagen 9; AB (Akademisk) 9; B 1903 Copenhagen 7; Frem 6; AGF Aarhus 5; Vejle 5; Esbjerg 5; AaB Aalborg 4; Hvidovre 3; OB Odense 3; Koge 2; B 1909 Odense 2; Lyngby 2; Silkeborg 1; Herfolge 1; Nordsjaelland 1; Midtjylland 1.

Cup wins (1955–2017)
AGF Aarhus 9; FC Copenhagen 8; Vejle 6; Brondby 6; OB Odense 5; Esbjerg 3; AaB Aalborg 3; Randers Freja 3; Lyngby 3; Frem 2; B 1909 Odense 2; B 1903 Copenhagen 2; Nordsjaelland 2; B 1913 Odense 1; KB Copenhagen 1; Vanlose 1; Hvidovre 1; B 93 Copenhagen 1; AB (Akademisk) 1; Viborg 1; Silkeborg 1; Randers 1.

Danish Superliga 2016–17

	P	*W*	*D*	*L*	*F*	*A*	*GD*	*Pts*
FC Copenhagen	26	19	7	0	57	10	47	64
Brondby	26	15	7	4	52	23	29	52
Lyngby	26	11	6	9	25	23	2	39
SonderjyskE	26	10	9	7	30	32	–2	39
Midtjylland	26	10	8	8	44	29	15	38
Nordsjaelland	26	9	8	9	41	41	0	35
Randers	26	9	6	11	26	32	–6	33
AaB Aalborg	26	9	6	11	28	38	–10	33
Silkeborg	26	7	9	10	31	46	–15	30
Horsens	26	7	8	11	29	45	–16	29
OB Odense	26	7	7	12	26	32	–6	28
AGF Aarhus	26	6	7	13	33	40	–7	25

Championship Round 2016–17

	P	*W*	*D*	*L*	*F*	*A*	*GD*	*Pts*
FC Copenhagen	36	25	9	2	74	20	54	84
Brondby	36	18	8	10	62	40	22	62
Lyngby	36	17	7	12	42	35	7	58
Midtjylland	36	15	9	12	67	53	14	54
Nordsjaelland	36	13	10	13	59	55	4	49
SonderjyskE	36	12	10	14	44	54	–10	46

Relegation Round 2016–17

Group 1

	P	*W*	*D*	*L*	*F*	*A*	*GD*	*Pts*
Randers	32	11	8	13	33	35	–2	41
OB Odense	32	10	9	13	33	38	–5	39
Horsens+	32	9	9	14	34	53	–19	36
Esbjerg*+	32	6	12	14	32	54	–22	30

Group 2

	P	*W*	*D*	*L*	*F*	*A*	*GD*	*Pts*
Silkeborg	32	9	11	12	36	51	–15	38
AaB Aalborg	32	10	8	14	30	45	–15	38
AGF Aarhus+	32	10	7	15	45	46	–1	37
Viborg*+	32	8	9	15	35	47	–12	33

Top scorers: Ingvartsen (Nordsjaelland) 23.
Cup Final: FC Copenhagen 3, Brondby 1.

ENGLAND

The Football Association, Wembley Stadium, PO Box 1966, London SW1P 9EQ.
Founded: 1863. *FIFA:* 1905; *UEFA:* 1954. *National Colours:* White shirts with light blue trim, white shorts, red socks.

ESTONIA

Eesti Jalgpalli Liit, A. Le Coq Arena, Asula 4c, 11312 Tallinn.
Founded: 1921. *FIFA:* 1923; *UEFA:* 1992. *National Colours:* Blue shirts, black shorts, white socks.

International matches 2016–17
Malta (h) 1-1, Bosnia-Herzegovina (a) 0-5, Gibraltar (h) 4-0, Greece (h) 0-2, Belgium (a) 1-8, St Kitts & Nevis (a) 1-1, Antigua & Barbuda (a) 1-0, Cyprus (a) 0-0, Croatia (h) 3-0, Belgium (h) 0-2, Latvia (a) 2-1.

League Championship wins (1921–40; 1992–2016)
Flora 10; Sport 9; Levadia Tallinn (formerly Levadia Maardu) 9; Estonia 5; Tallinna JK 2; Norma 2; Lantana (formerly Nikol) 2; Sillamae Kalev 2; Olimpia Tartu 1; TVMK Tallinn 1; Nomme Kalju 1; FCI Tallinn 1.

Cup wins (1993–2017)
Levadia Tallinn (formerly Levadia Maardu) 8; Flora 7; Tallinna Sadam 2; TVMK Tallinn 2; Lantana (formerly Nikol) 1; Norma 1; Narva Trans 1; Levadia Tallinn (pre-2004) 1; Nomme Kalju 1; FCI Tallinn 1.

Estonian Meistriliiga 2016

	P	*W*	*D*	*L*	*F*	*A*	*GD*	*Pts*
FCI Tallinn	36	24	8	4	74	33	41	80
Levadia Tallinn	36	24	6	6	77	30	47	78
Nomme Kalju	36	22	9	5	70	28	42	75
Flora Tallinn	36	21	10	5	96	31	65	73
Sillamae Kalev	36	14	9	13	65	55	10	51
Paide Linnameeskond	36	14	6	16	58	61	–3	48
Tartu Tammeka	36	12	5	19	43	65	–22	41
Narva Trans	36	11	8	17	60	68	–8	41
Parnu Linnameeskond+	36	5	2	29	24	98	–74	17
Rakvere Tarvas*	36	0	3	33	15	113	–98	3

Top scorer: Kabaev (Sillamae Kalev) 25.
Cup Final: FCI Tallinn 2, Tartu Tammeka 0.

FAROE ISLANDS

Fotboltssamband Foroya, Gundadalur, PO Box 3028, 110 Torshavn.
Founded: 1979. *FIFA:* 1988; *UEFA:* 1990. *National Colours:* White shirts with blue trim, white shorts, white socks.

International matches 2016–17
Hungary (h) 0-0, Latvia (a) 2-0, Portugal (h) 0-6, Switzerland (a) 0-2, Andorra (a) 0-0, Switzerland (h) 0-2.

League Championship wins (1942–2016)
HB Torshavn 22; KI Klaksvik 17; B36 Torshavn 11; TB Tvoroyri 7; GI Gota 6; B68 Toftir 3; EB/Streymur 2; SI Sorvagur 1; IF Fuglafjordur 1; B71 Sandur 1; VB Vagur 1; NSI Runavik 1; Vikingur 1.

Cup wins (1955–2016)
HB Torshavn 26; KI Klaksvik 6; GI Gota 6; TB Tvoroyri 5; B36 Torshavn 5; Vikingur 5; EB/Streymur 4; NSI Runavik 2; VB Vagur 1; B71 Sandur 1.

Faroese Premier League 2016

	P	*W*	*D*	*L*	*F*	*A*	*GD*	*Pts*
Vikingur	27	19	4	4	59	25	34	61
KI Klaksvik	27	19	3	5	64	26	38	60
NSI Runavik	27	18	1	8	60	36	24	55
B36 Torshavn	27	14	7	6	46	28	18	49
HB Torshavn	27	12	7	8	44	30	14	43
IF Fuglafjordur	27	9	5	13	42	59	–17	32
TB Tvoroyri	27	7	6	14	31	48	–17	27
Skala Itrottarfelag	27	6	8	13	25	41	–16	26
AB Argir*	27	4	6	17	31	49	–18	18
B68 Toftir*	27	0	7	20	20	80	–60	7

Top scorer: Olsen (NSI Runavik) 23.
Cup Final: KI Klaksvik 1, Víkingur 1.
aet; KI Klaksvik won 5-3 on penalties.

FINLAND

Suomen Palloliitto Finlands Bollfoerbund, Urheilukatu 5, PO Box 191, 00251 Helsinki.
Founded: 1907. *FIFA:* 1908; *UEFA:* 1954. *National Colours:* White shirts with blue trim, white shorts, white socks.

International matches 2016–17
Germany (a) 0-2, Kosovo (h) 1-1, Iceland (a) 2-3, Croatia (h) 0-1, Ukraine (a) 0-1, Morocco (n) 1-0, Slovenia (n) 0-2, Turkey (a) 0-2, Austria (a) 1-1, Liechtenstein (h) 1-1, Ukraine (h) 1-2.

League Championship wins (1908–2016)
HJK Helsinki 27; HPS Helsinki 9; Haka Valkeakoski 9; TPS Turku 8; HIFK Helsinki 7; KuPS Kuopio 5; Kuusysi Lahti 5; KIF Helsinki 4; AIFK Turku 3; VIFK Vaasa 3; Reipas Lahti 3; Tampere United 3; VPS Vaasa 2; KTP Kotka 2; OPS Oulu 2; Jazz Pori 2; Unitas Helsinki 1; PUS Helsinki 1; Sudet Viipuri 1; HT Helsinki 1; Ilves-Kissat 1; Pyrkiva Turku 1; KPV Kokkola 1; Ilves Tampere 1; TPV Tampere 1; MyPa Anjalankoski (renamed MYPA-47) 1; Inter Turku 1; SJK Seinajoki 1; IFK Mariehamn 1.

Cup wins (1955–2016)
Haka Valkeakoski 12; HJK Helsinki 12; Reipas Lahti 7; KTP Kotka 4; TPS Turku 3; MyPa Anjalankoski (renamed MYPA-47) 3; KuPS Kuopio 2; Mikkeli 2; Ilves Tampere 2; Kuusysi Lahti 2; RoPS Rovaniemi 2; Pallo-Pojat 1; Drott (renamed Jaro) 1; HPS Helsinki 1; AIFK Turku 1; Jokerit (formerly PK-35) 1; Atlantis 1; Tampere United 1; Inter Turku 1; FC Honka 1; IFK Mariehamn 1; SJK Seinajoki 1.

Finnish Veikkausliiga 2016

	P	*W*	*D*	*L*	*F*	*A*	*GD*	*Pts*
IFK Mariehamn	33	17	10	6	40	25	15	61
HJK Helsinki	33	16	10	7	52	36	16	58
SJK Seinajoki	33	17	6	10	49	36	13	57
VPS Vaasa	33	15	8	10	36	27	9	53
Ilves	33	15	7	11	36	35	1	52
RoPS Rovaniemi	33	13	11	9	43	33	10	50
KuPS Kuopio	33	14	7	12	37	31	6	49
Lahti	33	10	12	11	42	43	–1	42
PS Kemi	33	10	5	18	29	48	–19	35
HIFK Helsinki	33	8	10	15	35	39	–4	34

Inter Turku+	33	7	11	15	28	41	–13	32
PK-35 Vantaa* (–6)	33	4	7	22	32	65	–33	13

Top scorer: Riski (SJK Seinajoki) 17.
Cup Final: SJK Seinajoki 1, HJK Helsinki 1.
aet; SJK Seinajoki won 7-6 on penalties.

FRANCE

Federation Francaise de Football, 87 Boulevard de Grenelle, 75738 Paris Cedex 15.
Founded: 1919. *FIFA:* 1904; *UEFA:* 1954. *National Colours:* Blue shirts, white shorts, red socks.

International matches 2016–17

Italy (a) 3-1, Belarus (a) 0-0, Bulgaria (h) 4-1, Netherlands (a) 1-0, Sweden (h) 2-1, Ivory Coast (h) 0-0, Luxembourg (a) 3-1, Spain (h) 0-2, Paraguay (h) 5-0, Sweden (a) 1-2, England (h) 3-2.

League Championship wins (1933–2017)

Saint-Etienne 10; Olympique Marseille 9; AS Monaco 8; Nantes 8; Olympique Lyonnais 7; Stade de Reims 6; Bordeaux 6; Paris Saint-Germain 6; OGC Nice 4; Lille OSC (includes Olympique Lillois) 4; FC Sete 2; Sochaux 2; Racing Club Paris 1; Roubaix-Tourcoing 1; Strasbourg 1; Auxerre 1; Lens 1; Montpellier 1.

Cup wins (1918–2017)

Paris Saint-Germain 11; Olympique Marseille 10; Lille OSC 6; Saint-Etienne 6; Red Star 5; Racing Club Paris 5; AS Monaco 5; Olympique Lyonnais 5; Bordeaux 4; Auxerre 4; Strasbourg 3; OGC Nice 3; Nantes 3; CAS Genereaux 2; Montpellier 2; FC Sete 2; Sochaux 2; Stade de Reims 2; Sedan 2; Stade Rennais 2; Metz 2; Guingamp 2; Olympique de Pantin 1; CA Paris 1; Club Français 1; AS Cannes 1; Excelsior Roubaix 1; EF Nancy-Lorraine 1; Toulouse 1; Le Havre 1; AS Nancy 1; Bastia 1; Lorient 1.

French Ligue 1 2016–17

	P	*W*	*D*	*L*	*F*	*A*	*GD*	*Pts*
AS Monaco	38	30	5	3	107	31	76	95
Paris Saint-Germain	38	27	6	5	83	27	56	87
Nice	38	22	12	4	63	36	27	78
Olympique Lyonnais	38	21	4	13	77	48	29	67
Olympique Marseille	38	17	11	10	57	41	16	62
Bordeaux	38	15	14	9	53	43	10	59
Nantes	38	14	9	15	40	54	–14	51
Saint-Etienne	38	12	14	12	41	42	–1	50
Rennes	38	12	14	12	36	42	–6	50
Guingamp	38	14	8	16	46	53	–7	50
Lille OSC	38	13	7	18	40	47	–7	46
Angers	38	13	7	18	40	49	–9	46
Toulouse	38	10	14	14	37	41	–4	44
Metz	38	11	10	17	39	72	–33	43
Montpellier	38	10	9	19	48	66	–18	39
Dijon	38	8	13	17	46	58	–12	37
Caen	38	10	7	21	36	65	–29	37
Lorient*+	38	10	6	22	44	70	–26	36
Nancy*	38	9	8	21	29	52	–23	35
Bastia*	38	8	10	20	29	54	–25	34

Top scorer: Cavani (Paris Saint-Germain) 35.
Cup Final: Paris Saint-Germain 1, Angers SCO 0.

FYR MACEDONIA

Football Federation of the Former Yugoslav Republic of Macedonia, 8-ma Udarna Brigada 31-A, PO Box 84, 1000 Skopje.
Founded: 1948. *FIFA:* 1994; *UEFA:* 1994. *National Colours:* All red.

International matches 2016–171

Albania (a) 1-2, Israel (h) 1-2, Italy (h) 2-3, Spain (a) 0-4, Liechtenstein (a) 3-0, Belarus (h) 3-0, Turkey (h) 0-0, Spain (h) 1-2.

League Championship wins (1992–2017)

Vardar 10; Rabotnicki 4; Sileks 3; Sloga Jugomagnat 3; Pobeda 2; Makedonija GjP 1; Renova 1; Shkendija 1.

Cup wins (1992–2017)

Vardar 5; Rabotnicki 4; Sloga Jugomagnat 3; Sileks 2; Pelister 2; Teteks 2; Pobeda 1; Cementarnica 55 1; Bashkimi 1; Makedonija GjP 1; Metalurg 1; Renova 1; Shkendija 1.

Macedonian First League Table 2016–17

	P	*W*	*D*	*L*	*F*	*A*	*GD*	*Pts*
Vardar	36	25	8	3	75	24	51	83
Shkendija	36	20	10	6	71	39	32	70
Rabotnicki	36	14	12	10	49	41	8	54
Pelister	36	14	10	12	44	35	9	52
Renova	36	13	13	10	42	37	5	52
Sileks	36	11	14	11	41	43	–2	47
Pobeda	36	10	11	15	34	50	–16	41
Shkupi+	36	8	13	15	27	39	–12	37
Bregalnica Stip*	36	4	12	20	39	69	–30	24
Makedonija GjP*	36	4	11	21	35	80	–45	23

Top scorer: Ibraimi (Shkendija) 20.
Cup Final: Pelister 0, Shkendija 0.
aet; Pelister won 4-3 on penalties.

GEORGIA

Georgian Football Federation, 76A Chavchavadze Avenue, 0179 Tbilisi.
Founded: 1990. *FIFA:* 1992; *UEFA:* 1992. *National Colours:* All white with red trim.

International matches 2016–17

Austria (h) 1-2, Republic of Ireland (a) 0-1, Wales (a) 1-1, Moldova (h) 1-1, Uzbekistan (n) 2-2, Jordan (n) 0-1, Serbia (h) 1-3, Latvia (h) 5-0, St Kitts & Nevis (h) 3-0, Moldova (a) 2-2.

League Championship wins (1990–2016)

Dinamo Tbilisi 16; Torpedo Kutaisi 3; WIT Georgia 2; Metalurgi Rustavi (formerly Olimpi) 2; Zestafoni 2; Sioni Bolnisi 1; Dila Gori 1; Samtredia 1.

Cup wins (1990–2016)

Dinamo Tbilisi 13; Torpedo Kutaisi 3; Lokomotivi 3; Ameri 2; Guria Lanchkhuti 1; Dinamo Batumi 1; Zestafoni 1; WIT Georgia 1; Gagra 1; Dila Gori 1.

Macedonian Umaglesi Liga 2016

Group Red

	P	*W*	*D*	*L*	*F*	*A*	*GD*	*Pts*
Samtredia	12	8	3	1	27	9	18	27
Dinamo Batumi	12	5	5	2	20	5	15	20
Saburtalo	12	5	4	3	17	12	5	19
Kolkheti Poti	12	6	0	6	10	18	–8	18
Dila Gori+	12	5	2	5	13	12	1	17
Sioni Bolnisi*+	12	3	2	7	13	19	–6	11
Zugdidi*	12	2	0	10	5	30	–25	6

Group White

	P	*W*	*D*	*L*	*F*	*A*	*GD*	*Pts*
Chikhura Sachkhere	12	9	2	1	27	11	16	29
Dinamo Tbilisi	12	6	5	1	17	5	12	23
Torpedo Kutaisi	12	4	3	5	16	12	4	15
Lokomotivi Tbilisi	12	4	3	5	11	18	–7	15
Shukura Kobuleti+	12	2	6	4	10	13	–3	12
Guria Lanchkhuti*+	12	3	2	7	8	21	–13	11
Tskhinvali*	12	2	3	7	12	21	–9	9

Championship Play-off

Samtredia 2, 2, Chikhura Sachkhere 0, 2 (agg. 4-2).
Top scorer: Zivzivadze (Samtredia) 11.
Cup Final: Torpedo Kutaisi 2, Merani Martvili 1.

GERMANY

Deutscher Fussball-Bund, Hermann-Neuberger-Haus, Otto-Fleck-Schneise 6, 60528 Frankfurt Am Main.
Founded: 1900. *FIFA:* 1904; *UEFA:* 1954. *National Colours:* White shirts with red and black trim, white shorts, white socks with red tops.

International matches 2016–17

Finland (h) 2-0, Norway (a) 3-0, Czech Republic (h) 3-0, Northern Ireland (h) 2-0, San Marino (a) 8-0, Italy (a) 0-0, England (h) 1-0, Azerbaijan (a) 4-1, Denmark (a) 1-1, San Marino (h) 7-0, Australia (n) 3-2, Chile (n) 1-1, Cameroon (n) 3-1, Mexico (n) 4-1, Chile (n) 1-0.

League Championship wins (1903–2017)

Bayern Munich 27; 1.FC Nuremberg 9; Borussia Dortmund 8; Schalke 04 7; Hamburger SV 6; VfB Stuttgart 5; Borussia Moenchengladbach 5; 1.FC Kaiserslautern 4; Werder Bremen 4; 1.FC Lokomotive Leipzig 3; SpVgg Greuther Furth 3; 1.FC Cologne 3; Viktoria Berlin 2; Hertha Berlin 2; Hannover 96 2; Dresden SC 2; Union Berlin 1; Freiburger FC 1; Phoenix Karlsruhe 1; Karlsruher FV 1; Holstein Kiel 1; Fortuna Dusseldorf 1; Rapid Vienna 1; VfR Mannheim 1; Rot-Weiss Essen 1; Eintracht Frankfurt 1; Munich 1860 1; Eintracht Braunschweig 1; VfL Wolfsburg 1.

Cup wins (1935–2017)

Bayern Munich 18; Werder Bremen 6; Schalke 04 5; 1.FC Nuremberg 4; Borussia Dortmund 4; 1.FC Cologne 4; Eintracht Frankfurt 4; VfB Stuttgart 3; Borussia Moenchengladbach 3; Hamburger SV 3; Dresden SC 2;

Munich 1860 2; Karlsruhe SC 2; Fortuna Dusseldorf 2; 1.FC Kaiserslautern 2; 1.FC Lokomotive Leipzig 1; Rapid Vienna 1; First Vienna 1; Rot-Weiss Essen 1; SW Essen 1; Kickers Offenbach 1; Bayer Uerdingen 1; Hannover 96 1; Bayer Leverkusen 1; VfLWolfsburg 1.

German Bundesliga 2016–17

	P	*W*	*D*	*L*	*F*	*A*	*GD*	*Pts*
Bayern Munich	34	25	7	2	89	22	67	82
RB Leipzig	34	20	7	7	66	39	27	67
Borussia Dortmund	34	18	10	6	72	40	32	64
TSG 1899 Hoffenheim	34	16	14	4	64	37	27	62
1.FC Cologne	34	12	13	9	51	42	9	49
Hertha Berlin	34	15	4	15	43	47	–4	49
Freiburg	34	14	6	14	42	60	–18	48
Werder Bremen	34	13	6	15	61	64	–3	45
Borussia M'gladbach	34	12	9	13	45	49	–4	45
Schalke 04	34	11	10	13	45	40	5	43
Eintracht Frankfurt	34	11	9	14	36	43	–7	42
Bayer Leverkusen	34	11	8	15	53	55	–2	41
Augsburg	34	9	11	14	35	51	–16	38
Hamburger SV	34	10	8	16	33	61	–28	38
1.FSV Mainz 05	34	10	7	17	44	55	–11	37
VfL Wolfsburg+	34	10	7	17	34	52	–18	37
Ingolstadt*	34	8	8	18	36	57	–21	32
Darmstadt 98*	34	7	4	23	28	63	–35	25

Top scorer: Aubameyang (Borussia Dortmund) 31.
Cup Final: Borussia Dortmund 2, Eintracht Frankfurt 1.

GIBRALTAR

Gibraltar Football Association, Bayside Sports Complex, PO Box 513, Gibraltar GX11 1AA.
Founded: 1895. *UEFA:* 2013. *National Colours:* Red shirts with white trim, red shorts, red socks.

International matches 2016–17
Portugal (a) 0-5, Greece (h) 1-4, Estonia (a) 0-4, Belgium (h) 0-6, Cyprus (a) 1-3, Bosnia-Herzegovina (a) 0-5, Cyprus (h) 1-2.

League Championship wins (1896–2017)
Lincoln Red Imps 22 (incl. Newcastle United 5; 1 title shared); Prince of Wales 19; Glacis United 17 (incl. 1 shared); Britannia (now Britannia XI) 14; Gibraltar United 11; Europa 7; Manchester United (now Manchester 62) 7; St Theresa's 3; Chief Construction 2; Jubilee 2; Exiles 2; South United 2; Gibraltar FC 2; Albion 1; Athletic 1; Royal Sovereign 1; Commander of the Yard 1; St Joseph's 1.

Cup wins (1895–2017)
Lincoln Red Imps (incl. Newcastle United 4) 17; St Joseph's 9; Europa 6; Glacis United 5; Britannia (now Britannia XI) 3; Gibraltar United 3; Manchester United (now Manchester 62) 3; Gibraltar FC 1; HMS Hood 1; 2nd Bn The King's Regt 1; AARA 1; RAF New Camp 1; 4th Bn Royal Scots 1; Prince of Wales 1; Manchester United Reserves 1; 2nd Bn Royal Green Jackets 1; RAF Gibraltar 1; St Theresa's 1.

Gibraltarian Premier Division 2016–17

	P	*W*	*D*	*L*	*F*	*A*	*GD*	*Pts*
Europa	27	24	1	2	93	18	75	73
Lincoln Red Imps	27	23	3	1	100	16	84	72
St Joseph's	27	16	6	5	53	18	35	54
Glacis United	27	12	8	7	42	34	8	44
Mons Calpe	27	13	3	11	44	35	9	42
Lynx	27	8	4	15	33	46	–13	28
Gibraltar United	27	4	9	14	20	43	–23	21
Lions Gibraltar	27	4	9	14	17	54	–37	21
Manchester 62+	27	4	5	18	27	60	–33	17
Europa Point*	27	2	2	23	14	119	–105	8

Top scorer: Gomez (Europa) 30.
Cup Final: Europa 3, Lincoln Red Imps 0.

GOZO

Gozo Football Association, GFA Headquarters, Mgarr Road, Xewkija, XWK 9014, Malta. (Not a member of FIFA or UEFA.)
Founded: 1936.

League Championship wins (1938–2016)
Victoria Hotspurs 11; Nadur Youngsters 11; Sannat Lions 10; Xewkija Tigers 8; Ghajnsielem 7; Xaghra United 6 (incl. Xaghra Blue Stars 1, Xaghra Young Stars 1); Salesian Youths (renamed Oratory Youths) 6; Victoria Athletics 4; Victoria Stars 1; Victoria City 1; Calypcians 1; Victoria United (renamed Victoria Wanderers) 1; Kercem Ajax 1; Zebbug Rovers 1.

Cup wins (1972–2017)
Xewkija Tigers 10; Sannat Lions 9; Nadur Youngsters 8; Ghajnsielem 6; Xaghra United 4; Kercem Ajax 2; Calypsians 1; Calypsians Bosco Youths 1; Victoria Hotspurs 1; Qala St Joseph 1; Victoria Wanderers 1.

Gozitan First Division 2016–17

	P	*W*	*D*	*L*	*F*	*A*	*GD*	*Pts*
Xewkija Tigers	21	15	3	3	38	16	22	48
Nadur Youngsters	21	15	2	4	50	23	27	47
Ghajnsielem	21	12	3	6	42	20	22	39
Kercem Ajax	21	9	4	8	40	30	10	31
Victoria Hotspurs	21	8	6	7	27	28	–1	30
Oratory Youths	21	6	5	10	25	41	–16	23
Victoria Wanderers	21	3	7	11	20	36	–16	16
Xaghra United	21	0	2	19	13	61	–48	2

Top scorers (joint): Dos Santos (Xewkija Tigers), Maciel (Victoria Hotspurs) 14.
Cup Final: Ghajnsielem 5, Oratory Youths 0.

GREECE

Hellenic Football Federation, Parko Goudi, PO Box 14161, 11510 Athens.
Founded: 1926. *FIFA:* 1927; *UEFA:* 1954. *National Colours:* All white.

International matches 2016–17
Netherlands (a) 2-1, Gibraltar (n) 4-1, Cyprus (h) 2-0, Estonia (a) 2-0, Belarus (h) 0-1, Bosnia-Herzegovina (h) 1-1, Belgium (a) 1-1, Bosnia-Herzegovina (a) 0-0.

League Championship wins (1927–2017)
Olympiacos 44; Panathinaikos 20; AEK Athens 11; Aris Salonika 3; PAOK 2; Larissa 1.

Cup wins (1932–2016)
Olympiacos 27; Panathinaikos 18; AEK Athens 15; PAOK 5; Panionios 2; Larissa 2; Ethnikos 1; Aris Salonika 1; Iraklis 1; Kastoria 1; OFI Crete 1.

Superleague Greece 2016–17

	P	*W*	*D*	*L*	*F*	*A*	*GD*	*Pts*
Olympiacos	30	21	4	5	57	16	41	67
PAOK (–3)	30	20	4	6	52	19	33	61
Panathinaikos	30	16	9	5	45	19	26	57
AEK Athens	30	14	11	5	54	23	31	53
Panionios	30	15	7	8	35	23	12	52
Xanthi	30	13	9	8	34	25	9	48
Platanias	30	11	9	10	34	38	–4	42
Atromitos	30	11	6	13	29	38	–9	39
PAS Giannina	30	8	12	10	30	37	–7	36
Kerkyra	30	8	8	14	22	43	–21	32
Panaitolikos	30	8	7	15	29	40	–11	31
Asteras Tripolis	30	6	10	14	34	49	–15	28
Larissa	30	6	10	14	23	42	–19	28
Levadiakos	30	6	8	16	27	49	–22	26
Iraklis* (–3)	30	6	11	13	28	39	–11	26
Veria*	30	5	7	18	23	56	–33	22

Champions League/Europa League Play-offs

	P	*W*	*D*	*L*	*F*	*A*	*GD*	*Pts*
AEK Athens	6	4	0	2	5	3	2	12
Panathinaikos (–2)	6	3	1	2	6	7	–1	8
PAOK (–4)	6	3	0	3	7	5	2	5
Panionios	6	1	1	4	3	6	–3	4

Top scorer: Berg (Panathinaikos) 22.
Cup Final: PAOK 2, AEK Athens 1.

HUNGARY

Magyar Labdarugo Szovetseg, Kanai ut 2. D, 1112 Budapest.
Founded: 1901. *FIFA:* 1907; *UEFA:* 1954. *National Colours:* Red shirts, white shorts, green socks.

International matches 2016–17
Faroe Islands (a) 0-0, Switzerland (h) 2-3, Latvia (a) 2-0, Andorra (h) 4-0, Sweden (h) 0-2, Portugal (a) 0-3, Russia (h) 0-3, Andorra (a) 0-1.

League Championship wins (1901–2017)
Ferencvaros 29; MTK Budapest 23; Ujpest 20; Budapest Honved 14 (incl. Kispest Honved); Debrecen 7; Vasas 6; Csepel 4; Gyor 4; Budapesti TC 2; Videoton 2; Nagyvarad 1; Vac 1; Dunaferr (renamed Dunaujvaros) 1; Zalaegerszeg 1.

Cup wins (1910–2017)
Ferencvaros 23; MTK Budapest 12; Ujpest 9; Budapest Honved 7 (inc. Kispest Honved); Debrecen 6; Vasas 4; Gyor 4; Diosgyor 2; Bocskai 1; III Ker 1; Soroksar 1; Szolnoki MAV 1; Siofoki Banyasz 1; Bekescsaba 1;

Pecsi 1; Sopron 1; Fehervar (renamed Videoton) 1; Kecskemet 1.
Cup not regularly held until 1964.

Nemzeti Bajnoksag I 2016–17

	P	*W*	*D*	*L*	*F*	*A*	*GD*	*Pts*
Budapest Honved	33	20	5	8	55	30	25	65
Videoton	33	18	8	7	65	28	37	62
Vasas	33	15	7	11	50	40	10	52
Ferencvaros	33	14	10	9	54	44	10	52
Paksi SE	33	11	12	10	41	37	4	45
Szombathelyi Haladas	33	12	7	14	42	46	–4	43
Ujpest	33	10	12	11	47	51	–4	42
Debrecen	33	11	8	14	42	46	–4	41
Mezokovesd-Zsory	33	10	10	13	39	54	–15	40
Diosgyor	33	10	7	16	39	58	–19	37
MTK Budapest*	33	8	13	12	26	36	–10	37
Gyirmot*	33	5	9	19	21	51	–30	24

Top scorer: Eppel (Budapest Honved) 16.
Cup Final: Ferencvaros 1, Vasas 1.
aet; Ferencvaros won 5-4 on penalties.

ICELAND

Knattspyrnusamband Islands, Laugardal, 104 Reykjavik.
Founded: 1947. *FIFA:* 1947; *UEFA:* 1954. *National Colours:* All blue.

International matches 2016–17
Ukraine (a) 1-1, Finland (h) 3-2, Turkey (h) 2-0, Croatia (a) 0-2, Malta (a) 2-0, China PR (a) 2-0, Chile (n) 0-1, Mexico (n) 0-1, Kosovo (a) 2-1, Republic of Ireland (a) 1-0, Croatia (n) 1-0.

League Championship wins (1912–2016)
KR Reykjavik 26; Valur 20; Fram 18; IA Akranes 18; FH Hafnarfjordur 8; Vikingur 5; IBK Keflavik 4; IBV Vestmannaeyjar 3; KA Akureyri 1; Breidablik 1 ; Stjarnan 1.

Cup wins (1960–2016)
KR Reykjavik 14; Valur 11; IA Akranes 9; Fram 8; IBV Vestmannaeyjar 4; IBK Keflavik 4; Fylkir 2; FH Hafnarfjordur 2; IBA Akureyri 1; Vikingur 1; Breidablik 1.

Urvalsdeild 2016

	P	*W*	*D*	*L*	*F*	*A*	*GD*	*Pts*
FH Hafnarfjordur	22	12	7	3	32	17	15	43
Stjarnan	22	12	3	7	43	31	12	39
KR Reykjavik	22	11	5	6	29	20	9	38
Fjolnir	22	11	4	7	42	25	17	37
Valur	22	10	5	7	41	28	13	35
Breidablik	22	10	5	7	27	20	7	35
Víkingur Reykjavik	22	9	5	8	29	32	–3	32
IA Akranes	22	10	1	11	28	33	–5	31
IBV Vestmannaeyjar	22	6	5	11	23	27	–4	23
Vikingur Olafsvik	22	5	6	11	23	38	–15	21
Fylkir*	22	4	7	11	25	40	–15	19
Throttur Reykjavik*	22	3	5	14	19	50	–31	14

Top scorer: Gunnlaugsson (IA Akranes) 14.
Cup Final: Valur 2, IBV Vestmannaeyjar 0.

ISRAEL

Israel Football Association, Ramat Gan Stadium, 299 Aba Hilell Street, PO Box 3591, Ramat Gan 52134.
Founded: 1928. *FIFA:* 1929; *UEFA:* 1994. *National Colours:* Blue shirts with white trim, blue shorts, blue socks.

International matches 2016–17
Italy (h) 1-3, FYR Macedonia (a) 2-1, Liechtenstein (h) 2-1, Albania (a) 3-0, Spain (a) 1-4, Moldova (h) 1-1, Albania (h) 0-3.

League Championship wins (1932–2017)
Maccabi Tel Aviv 21; Hapoel Tel Aviv 14 (incl. 1 shared); Maccabi Haifa 12; Hapoel Petah Tikva 6; Beitar Jerusalem 6; Maccabi Netanya 5; Hapoel Be'er Sheva 4; Hakoah Ramat Gan 2; British Police 1; Beitar Tel Aviv 1 (shared); Hapoel Ramat Gan 1; Hapoel Kfar Saba 1; Bnei Yehuda 1; Hapoel Haifa 1; Ironi Kiryat Shmona 1.

Cup wins (1928–2017)
Maccabi Tel Aviv 23; Hapoel Tel Aviv 15; Beitar Jerusalem 7; Maccabi Haifa 6; Hapoel Haifa 3; Bnei Yehuda 3; Hapoel Kfar Saba 3; Maccabi Petah Tikva 2; Beitar Tel Aviv 2; Hapoel Petah Tikva 2; Hakoah Amidar Ramat Gan 2; Hapoel Ramat Gan 2; Maccabi Hashmonai Jerusalem 1; British Police 1; Hapoel Jerusalem 1; Maccabi Netanya 1; Hapoel Yehud 1; Hapoel Lod 1; Hapoel Be'er Sheba 1; Bnei Sakhnin 1; Ironi Kiryat Shmona 1.

Israeli Premier League Qualifying Table 2016–17

	P	*W*	*D*	*L*	*F*	*A*	*GD*	*Pts*
Hapoel Be'er Sheva	26	18	5	3	54	13	41	59
Maccabi Tel Aviv	26	17	5	4	45	19	26	56
Maccabi Petah Tikva	26	13	9	4	36	23	13	48
Bnei Sakhnin	26	10	9	7	26	26	0	39
Beitar Jerusalem (–2)	26	10	10	6	34	27	7	38
Maccabi Haifa	26	10	8	8	30	25	5	38
Ironi Kiryat Shmona	26	9	8	9	35	33	2	35
Hapoel Haifa	26	8	4	14	29	36	–7	28
Ashdod	26	6	10	10	15	26	–11	28
Hapoel Ra'anana	26	7	7	12	14	29	–15	28
Bnei Yehuda	26	5	10	11	20	32	–12	25
Hapoel Kfar Saba	26	4	9	13	17	34	–17	21
Hapoel Ashkelon	26	3	9	14	15	39	–24	18
Hapoel Tel Aviv (–9)	26	5	11	10	18	26	–8	17

Championship Round 2016–17

	P	*W*	*D*	*L*	*F*	*A*	*GD*	*Pts*
Hapoel Be'er Sheva	36	26	7	3	73	18	55	85
Maccabi Tel Aviv	36	22	6	8	61	28	33	72
Beitar Jerusalem	36	16	12	8	53	36	17	60
Maccabi Petah Tikva	36	15	11	10	42	34	8	56
Bnei Sakhnin	36	13	9	14	32	46	–14	48
Maccabi Haifa	36	12	9	15	34	41	–7	45

Relegation Round 2016–17

	P	*W*	*D*	*L*	*F*	*A*	*GD*	*Pts*
Ironi Kiryat Shmona	33	10	9	14	44	48	–4	39
Hapoel Haifa	33	10	7	16	39	46	–7	37
Ashdod	33	7	15	11	22	32	–10	36
Hapoel Ra'anana	33	9	9	15	22	40	–18	36
Bnei Yehuda	33	8	11	14	26	39	–13	35
Hapoel Ashkelon	33	7	11	15	24	42	–18	32
Hapoel Kfar Saba*	33	7	10	16	23	40	–17	31
Hapoel Tel Aviv* (–9)	33	8	14	11	29	34	–5	29

Top scorer: Kjartansson (Maccabi Tel Aviv) 19.
Cup Final: Bnei Yehuda 0, Maccabi Tel Aviv 0.
aet; Bnei Yehuda won 4-3 on penalties.

ITALY

Federazione Italiana Giuoco Calcio, Via Gregorio Allegri 14, 00198 Roma.
Founded: 1898. *FIFA:* 1905; *UEFA:* 1954. *National Colours:* Blue shirts, white shorts, blue socks with white tops.

International matches 2016–17
France (h) 1-3, Israel (a) 3-1, Spain (h) 1-1, FYR Macedonia (a) 3-2, Liechtenstein (a) 4-0, Germany (h) 0-0, Albania (h) 2-0, Netherlands (a) 2-1, San Marino (h) 8-0, Uruguay (n) 3-0, Liechtenstein (h) 5-0.

League Championship wins (1898–2017)
Juventus 33 (excludes two titles revoked); AC Milan 18; Internazionale 18 (includes one title awarded); Genoa 9; Pro Vercelli 7; Bologna 7; Torino 7 (excludes one title revoked); Roma 3; Fiorentina 2; Lazio 2; Napoli 2; Casale 1; Novese 1; Cagliari 1; Hellas Verona 1; Sampdoria 1.

Cup wins (1928–2017)
Juventus 12; Roma 9; Internazionale 7; Fiorentina 6; Lazio 6; Torino 5; Napoli 5; AC Milan 5; Sampdoria 4; Parma 3; Bologna 2; Vado 1; Genoa 1; Venezia 1; Atalanta 1; Vicenza 1.

Italian Serie A 2016–17

	P	*W*	*D*	*L*	*F*	*A*	*GD*	*Pts*
Juventus	38	29	4	5	77	27	50	91
Roma	38	28	3	7	90	38	52	87
Napoli	38	26	8	4	94	39	55	86
Atalanta	38	21	9	8	62	41	21	72
Lazio	38	21	7	10	74	51	23	70
AC Milan	38	18	9	11	57	45	12	63
Internazionale	38	19	5	14	72	49	23	62
Fiorentina	38	16	12	10	63	57	6	60
Torino	38	13	14	11	71	66	5	53
Sampdoria	38	12	12	14	49	55	–6	48
Cagliari	38	14	5	19	55	76	–21	47
Sassuolo	38	13	7	18	58	63	–5	46
Udinese	38	12	9	17	47	56	–9	45
Chievo	38	12	7	19	43	61	–18	43
Bologna	38	11	8	19	40	58	–18	41
Genoa	38	9	9	20	38	64	–26	36
Crotone	38	9	7	22	34	58	–24	34

	P	W	D	L	F	A	GD	Pts
Empoli*	38	8	8	22	29	61	–32	32
Palermo*	38	6	8	24	33	77	–44	26
Pescara*	38	3	9	26	37	81	–44	18

Top scorer: Djeko (Roma) 29.
Cup Final: Juventus 2, Lazio 0.

KAZAKHSTAN

Football Federation of Kazakhstan, 29 Syganak Street, 9th floor, 010000 Astana.
Founded: 1914. *FIFA:* 1994; *UEFA:* 2002. *National Colours:* All yellow.

International matches 2016–17

Kyrgyzstan (a) 0-2, Poland (h) 2-2, Montenegro (h) 0-5, Romania (a) 0-0, Denmark (a) 1-4, Cyprus (a) 1-3, Armenia (a) 0-2, Denmark (h) 1-3.

League Championship wins (1992–2016)

Irtysh (includes Ansat) 5; Aktobe 5; Yelimay (renamed Spartak Semey) 3; FC Astana-64 (includes Zhenis) 3; Astana 3; Kairat 2; Shakhter Karagandy 2; Taraz 1; Tobol 1.

Cup wins (1992–2016)

Kairat 7; FC Astana-64 (incl. Zhenis) 3; Astana (incl. Lokomotiv) 3; Dostyk 1; Vostok 1; Yelimay (renamed Spartak Semey) 1; Irtysh 1; Kaisar 1; Taraz 1; Almaty 1; Tobol 1; Aktobe 1; Atirau 1; Ordabasy 1; Shakhter Karagandy 1.

Kazakh Premier League Qualifying Table 2016

	P	W	D	L	F	A	GD	Pts
Astana	22	17	2	3	34	14	20	53
Kairat	22	14	4	4	50	22	28	46
Irtysh	22	12	5	5	37	18	19	41
Okzhetpes	22	11	4	7	33	23	10	37
Ordabasy	22	9	6	7	26	27	–1	33
Aktobe	22	7	7	8	23	32	–9	28
Tobol	22	8	4	10	28	26	2	28
Atyrau	22	7	7	8	21	23	–2	28
Zhetysu	22	6	5	11	22	32	–10	23
Shakhter Karagandy	22	5	6	11	10	27	–17	21
Taraz	22	5	4	13	22	30	–8	19
Akzhayik	22	3	2	17	12	44	–32	11

NB: Points earned in Qualifying phase are halved and rounded up at start of Championship and Relegation Play-off phase.

Championship Round 2016

	P	W	D	L	F	A	GD	Pts
Astana	32	23	4	5	47	21	26	73
Kairat	32	22	5	5	75	30	45	71
Irtysh	32	14	7	11	52	36	16	49
Ordabasy	32	13	9	10	41	44	–3	48
Okzhetpes	32	13	6	13	42	44	–2	45
Aktobe	32	9	9	14	37	52	–15	36

Relegation Round 2016

	P	W	D	L	F	A	GD	Pts
Tobol	32	12	5	15	40	40	0	41
Atyrau	32	10	9	13	35	39	–4	39
Shakhter Karagandy	32	10	6	16	25	40	–15	36
Akzhayik	32	11	2	19	27	50	–23	35
Taraz*+	32	10	5	17	33	42	–9	35
Zhetysu*	32	8	7	17	37	53	–16	31

Top scorer: Gohou (Kairat) 22.
Cup Final: Astana 1, Kairat 0.

KOSOVO

Football Federation of Kosovo, Rruga Agim Ramadani 45, Prishtina, Kosovo 10000. *Founded:* 1946. *FIFA:* 2016; *UEFA:* 2016. *National Colours:* All blue.

International matches 2016–17

Finland (a) 1-1, Croatia (n) 0-6, Ukraine (n) 0-3, Turkey (a) 0-2, Iceland (h) 1-2, Turkey (h) 1-4.

League Championship wins (1945–217)

Prishtina 14; Vellaznimi 9; KF Trepca 7; Liria 5; Buduqnosti 4; Rudari 3; Red Star 3; Besa Peje 3; Jedinstvo 2; Kosova Prishtina 2; Slloga 2; Obiliqi 2; Fushe-Kosova 2; Feronikeli 2; Proletari 1; KXEK Kosova 1; Rudniku 1; KNI Ramiz Sadiku 1; Dukagjini 1; Besiana 1; Drita 1; Hysi 1; Kosova Vushtrri 1; Trepca'89 1.

Cup wins (1992–2016)

Prishtina 4; Liria 3; Besa Peje 3; Flamurtari 2; Feronikeli 2; KF Trepca 1; KF 2 Korriku 1; Gjilani 1; Drita 1; Besiana 1; KEK-u 1; Kosova Prishtina 1; Vellaznimi 1; Hysi 1; Trepca'89 1.

Kosovar Superliga 2016–17

	P	W	D	L	F	A	GD	Pts
Trepca'89	33	24	5	4	72	24	48	77
Prishtina	33	22	6	5	46	18	28	72
Llapi	33	21	5	7	44	30	14	68
Feronikeli	33	20	5	8	61	27	34	65
Gjilani	33	13	9	11	36	28	8	48
Besa Peje	33	13	8	12	42	39	3	47
Drenica Skenderaj	33	10	10	13	37	47	–10	40
Liria Prizren	33	10	7	16	41	39	2	37
Drita+	33	9	8	16	21	34	–13	35
Ferizaj*+	33	6	13	14	24	36	–12	31
Trepca Mitrovice*	33	5	8	20	37	64	–27	23
Hajvalia*	33	1	4	28	12	87	–75	7

Top scorer: John (Trepca'89) 27.
Cup Final: Besa Peje 1, Llapi 1.
aet; Besa Peje won 4-2 on penalties.

LATVIA

Latvijas Futbola Federacija, Olympic Sports Centre, Grostonas Street 6B, 1013 Riga.
Founded: 1921. *FIFA:* 1922; *UEFA:* 1992. *National Colours:* All carmine red.

International matches 2016–17

Luxembourg (h) 3-1, Andorra (a) 1-0, Faroe Islands (h) 0-2, Hungary (h) 0-2, Portugal (a) 1-4, Switzerland (a) 0-1, Georgia (a) 0-5, Portugal (h) 0-3, Estonia (h) 1-2.

League Championship wins (1922–2016)

Skonto Riga 15; ASK Riga (incl. AVN 2) 11; Sarkanais Metalurgs Liepaja 9; RFK Riga 8; Olympija Liepaya 7; VEF Riga 6; Ventspils 6; Energija Riga (incl. ESR Riga 2) 4; Elektrons Riga (incl. Alfa 1) 4; Torpedo Riga 3; Keisermezhs Riga 2; Khimikis Daugavpils 2; RAF Yelgava 2; Daugava Liepaja 2; Liepajas Metalurgs 2; Dinamo Riga 1; Zhmilyeva Team 1; Darba Rezervi 1; RER Riga 1; Starts Brotseni 1; Venta Ventspils 1; Jumieks Riga 1; Gauja Valmiera 1; Daugava Daugavpils 1; FK Liepaja 1; Spartaks Jurmala 1.

Cup wins (1937–2017)

Skonto Riga 8; ASK Riga 7 (includes AVN 3); Elektrons Riga 7; Ventspils 7; Sarkanais Metalurgs Liepaja 4; Jelgava 4; VEF Riga 3; Tseltnieks Riga 3; RAF Yelgava 3; RFK Riga 2; Daugava Liepaja 2; Starts Brotseni 2; Selmash Liepaya 2; Yurnieks Riga 2; Khimikis Daugavpils 2; Rigas Vilki 1; Dinamo Liepaya 1; Dinamo Riga 1; RER Riga 1; Voulkan Kouldiga 1; Baltika Liepaja 1; Venta Ventspils 1; Pilots Riga 1; Lielupe Yurmala 1; Energija Riga (formerly ESR Riga) 1; Torpedo Riga 1; Daugava SKIF Riga 1; Tseltnieks Daugavpils 1; Olympija Riga 1; FK Riga 1; Liepajas Metalurgs 1; Daugava Daugavpils 1.

Virsliga 2016

	P	W	D	L	F	A	GD	Pts
Spartaks Jurmala	28	17	4	7	46	22	24	55
Jelgava	28	16	3	9	37	24	13	51
Ventspils	28	15	6	7	47	28	19	51
Liepaja	28	12	6	10	38	31	7	42
Riga	28	8	12	8	28	24	4	36
Rigas FS	28	9	8	11	22	31	–9	35
Metta/LU+	28	8	6	14	32	47	–15	30
BFC Daugavpils*	28	2	5	21	13	56	–43	11

Top scorer: Karlsons (Ventspils) 17.
Cup Final: Ventspils 2, Riga 2.
aet; Ventspils won 6-5 on penalties.

LIECHTENSTEIN

Liechtensteiner Fussballverband, Landstrasse 149, 9494 Schaan.
Founded: 1934. *FIFA:* 1974; *UEFA:* 1974. *National Colours:* Blue shirts, red shorts, blue socks.

International matches 2016–17

Denmark (a) 0-5, Spain (a) 0-8, Albania (h) 0-2, Israel (a) 1-2, Italy (h) 0-4, FYR Macedonia (h) 0-3, Finland (a) 1-1, Italy (a) 0-5.
Liechtenstein has no national league. Teams compete in Swiss regional leagues.

Cup wins (1937–2016)

Vaduz 45; Balzers 11; Triesen 8; 5; FC Schaan 3.
Cup Final: Vaduz 5, Eschen/Meuren 1.

LITHUANIA

Lietuvos Futbolo Federacija, Stadiono g. 2, 02106 Vilnius.
Founded: 1922. *FIFA:* 1923; *UEFA:* 1992. *National Colours:* Yellow shirts, green shorts, yellow socks.

International matches 2016–17

Slovenia (h) 2-2, Scotland (a) 1-1, Malta (h) 2-0, Slovakia (a) 0-4, Czech Republic (a) 0-3, England (a) 0-2, Slovakia (h) 1-2.

League Championship wins (1990–2016)

FBK Kaunas 8 (including Zalgiris Kaunas 1); Zalgiris Vilnius 7; Ekranas 7; Inkaras Kaunas 2; Kareda 2; Sirijus Klaipeda 1; Mazeikiai 1.

Cup wins (1990–2016)

Zalgiris Vilnius 11; Ekranas 4; FBK Kaunas 4; Kareda 2; Atlantas 2; Suduva 2; Sirijus Klaipeda 1; Lietuvos Makabi Vilnius (renamed Neris Vilnius) 1; Inkaras Kaunas 1.

Lithuanian A Lyga Qualifying Table 2016

	P	*W*	*D*	*L*	*F*	*A*	*GD*	*Pts*
Zalgiris Vilnius	28	21	3	4	62	22	40	66
Trakai	28	18	4	6	47	22	25	58
Suduva	28	15	6	7	42	32	10	51
Atlantas	28	15	6	7	38	25	13	51
Jonava	28	7	8	13	28	44	–16	29
Stumbras	28	7	6	15	35	52	–17	27
Utenis Utena+	28	4	4	20	24	47	–23	16
Kauno Zalgiris*	28	2	9	17	23	55	–32	15

Championship Round 2016

	P	*W*	*D*	*L*	*F*	*A*	*GD*	*Pts*
Zalgiris Vilnius	33	24	4	5	74	29	45	76
Trakai	33	20	7	6	55	26	29	67
Suduva	33	17	7	9	55	41	14	58
Atlantas	33	16	8	9	42	32	10	56
Stumbras	33	8	9	16	43	63	–20	33
Jonava	33	8	8	17	35	58	–23	32

Top scorer: Kaluderovic (Zalgiris Vilnius) 20.
Cup Final: Zalgiris Vilnius 2, Suduvai 0.

LUXEMBOURG

Federation Luxembourgeoise de Football, BP 5 Rue de Limpach, 3932 Mondercange.
Founded: 1908. *FIFA:* 1910; *UEFA:* 1954. *National Colours:* White shirts with blue trim, white shorts, white socks.

International matches 2016–17

Latvia (a) 1-3, Bulgaria (a) 3-4, Sweden (h) 0-1, Belarus (a) 1-1, Netherlands (h) 1-3, France (h) 1-3, Cape Verde Islands (h) 0-2, Albania (h) 2-1, Netherlands (a) 0-5.

League Championship wins (1910–2017)

Jeunesse Esch 28; F91 Dudelange 13; Spora Luxembourg 11; Stade Dudelange 10; Fola Esch 7; Red Boys Differdange 6; Union Luxembourg 6; Avenir Beggen 6; US Hollerich-Bonnevoie 5; Progres Niedercorn 3; Aris Bonnevoie 3; Sporting Club 2; Racing Club 1; National Schifflange 1; Grevenmacher 1.

Cup wins (1922–2017)

Red Boys Differdange 15; Jeunesse Esch 13; Union Luxembourg 10; Spora Luxembourg 8; Avenir Beggen 7; F91 Dudelange 7; Progres Niedercorn 4; Stade Dudelange 4; Grevenmacher 4; Differdange 03 4; Fola Esch 3; Alliance Dudelange 2; US Rumelange 2; Racing Club 1; US Dudelange 1; SC Tetange 1; National Schifflange 1; Aris Bonnevoie 1; Jeunesse Hautcharage 1; Swift Hesperange 1; Etzella Ettelbruck 1; CS Petange 1.

Luxembourger National Division 2016–17

	P	*W*	*D*	*L*	*F*	*A*	*GD*	*Pts*
F91 Dudelange	26	20	5	1	68	14	54	65
Differdange 03	26	20	5	1	65	21	44	65
Fola Esch	26	16	8	2	69	34	35	56
Progres Niederkorn	26	13	5	8	57	38	19	44
UNA Strassen	26	11	4	11	39	47	–8	37
UT Petange	26	10	5	11	38	33	5	35
Mondorf-les-Bains	26	9	3	14	29	45	–16	30
Jeunesse Esch	26	7	8	11	38	49	–11	29
Victoria Rosport	26	8	4	14	38	54	–16	28
Racing	26	8	3	15	38	52	–14	27
RM Hamm Benfica	26	7	5	14	29	47	–18	26
Jeunesse Canach*+	26	5	8	13	30	54	–24	23
Rumelange*	26	5	8	13	29	53	–24	23
UN Kaerjeng*	26	7	1	18	37	63	–26	22

Top scorer: Er Rafik (Differdange 03) 26.
Cup Final: F91 Dudelange 4, Fola Esch 1.

MALTA

Malta Football Association, Millennium Stand, Floor 2, National Stadium, Ta'Qali ATD4000.
Founded: 1900. *FIFA:* 1959; *UEFA:* 1960. *National Colours:* Red shirts, white shorts, red socks.

International matches 2016–17

Estonia (a) 1-1, Scotland (h) 1-5, England (a) 0-2, Lithuania (a) 0-2, Slovenia (h) 0-1, Iceland (h) 0-2, Slovakia (h) 1-3, Ukraine (n) 1-0, Slovenia (a) 0-2.

League Championship wins (1910–2017)

Sliema Wanderers 26; Floriana 25; Valletta 23; Hibernians 12; Hamrun Spartans 7; Birkirkara 4; Rabat Ajax 2; St George's 1; KOMR 1; Marsaxlokk 1.

Cup wins (1935–2017)

Sliema Wanderers 21; Floriana 20; Valletta 13; Hibernians 10; Hamrun Spartans 6; Birkirkara 5; Melita 1; Gzira United 1; Zurrieq 1; Rabat Ajax 1.

Maltese Premier League 2016–17

	P	*W*	*D*	*L*	*F*	*A*	*GD*	*Pts*
Hibernians	33	22	5	6	64	31	33	71
Balzan	33	19	7	7	66	40	26	64
Birkirkara	33	18	8	7	64	30	34	62
Valletta	33	16	11	6	51	29	22	59
Floriana	33	15	9	9	51	37	14	54
Sliema Wanderers	33	15	7	11	47	37	10	52
Gzira United	33	10	7	16	43	51	–8	37
St Andrews	33	9	10	14	45	51	–6	37
Tarxien Rainbows	33	8	11	14	38	48	–10	35
Hamrun Spartans	33	9	6	18	44	61	–17	33
Mosta+ (–5)	33	7	5	21	29	71	–42	21
Pembroke Athleta*	33	4	6	23	28	84	–56	18

Top scorer: Kaljevic (Balzan) 23.
Cup Final: Floriana 2, Sliema Wanderers 0.

MOLDOVA

Federatia Moldoveneasca de Fotbal, Str. Tricolorului 39, 2012 Chisinau.
Founded: 1990. *FIFA:* 1994; *UEFA:* 1993. *National Colours:* All blue.

International matches 2016–17

Wales (a) 0-4, Serbia (h) 0-3, Republic of Ireland (h) 1-3, Georgia (a) 1-1, Qatar (a) 1-1, San Marino (a) 2-0, Austria (a) 0-2, Turkey (a) 1-3, Israel (a) 1-1, Georgia (h) 2-2.

League Championship wins (1992–2017)

Sheriff 15; Zimbru Chisinau 8; Constructorul 1; Dacia Chisinau 1; Milsami Orhei 1.

Cup wins (1992–2017)

Sheriff 9; Zimbru Chisinau 6; Tiligul 3; Tiraspol 3 (incl. Constructorul 2); Comrat 1; Nistru Otaci 1; Iskra-Stal 1; Milsami Orhei 1; Zaria Balti 1.

Moldovan National Division 2016–17

	P	*W*	*D*	*L*	*F*	*A*	*GD*	*Pts*
Sheriff (P)	30	22	3	5	71	15	56	69
Dacia Chisinau (P)	30	22	3	5	54	15	39	69
Milsami Orhei	30	22	2	6	57	20	37	68
Zaria Balti	30	20	5	5	56	21	35	65
Zimbru Chisinau	30	13	7	10	32	29	3	46
Petrocub	30	8	10	12	31	38	–7	34
Speranta Nisporeni	30	7	8	15	24	35	–11	29
Academia Chisinau	30	8	3	19	21	52	–31	27
Dinamo-Auto	30	5	8	17	31	58	–27	23
Saxan	30	5	4	21	23	57	–34	19
Ungheni*	30	4	5	21	19	79	–60	17

(P) *Equal points total; clubs qualified for Championship play-off.*

Championship Play-off

Sheriff 1, Dacia Chisinau 1.
aet; Sheriff won 3-0 on penalties.
Top scorer: Ricardinho (Sheriff) 15.
Cup Final: Sheriff 5, Zaria Balti 0.

MONTENEGRO

Fudbalski Savez Crne Gore, Ulica 19. Decembar 13, PO Box 275, 81000 Podgorica.
Founded: 1931 *FIFA:* 2007; *UEFA:* 2007. *National Colours:* All red with gold trim.

International matches 2016–17

Romania (a) 1-1, Kazakhstan (h) 5-0, Denmark (a) 1-0, Armenia (a) 2-3, Poland (h) 1-2, Iran (h) 1-2, Armenia (h) 4-1.

League Championship wins (2006–17)
Buducnost Podgorica 3; Mogren 2; Rudar Pljevlja 2; Sutjeska 2; Zeta 1; Mladost Podgorica 1.

Cup wins (2006–17)
Rudar Pljevlja 4; Mogren 1; Petrovac 1; Celik 1; Buducnost Podgorica 1; Lovcen 1: Mladost Podgorica 1; Sutjeska 1.

Montenegrin First League 2016–17

	P	W	D	L	F	A	GD	Pts
Buducnost Podgorica	33	17	6	10	52	28	24	57
Zeta (–6)	33	19	6	8	38	17	21	57
Mladost Podgorica	33	16	9	8	46	22	24	57
Sutjeska	33	15	10	8	43	25	18	55
Decic	33	14	8	11	27	32	–5	50
Iskra	33	14	7	12	29	32	–3	49
Grbalj	33	11	13	9	28	25	3	46
Rudar Pljevlja+	33	11	9	13	35	31	4	42
Petrovac+	33	11	6	16	30	50	–20	39
Bokelj*	33	8	12	13	28	34	–6	36
Lovcen* (–3)	33	10	7	16	25	36	–11	34
Jedinstvo*	33	3	5	25	20	69	–49	14

Top scorer: Petrovic (Mladost Podgorica) 14.
Cup Final: Sutjeska 1, Grbalj 0.

NETHERLANDS

Koninklijke Nederlandse Voetbalbond, Woudenbergseweg 56–58, Postbus 515, 3700 AM Zeist.
Founded: 1889. *FIFA:* 1904; *UEFA:* 1954. *National Colours:* Orange shirts, white shorts, orange socks.

International matches 2016–17
Greece (h) 1-2, Sweden (a) 1-1, Belarus (h) 4-1, France (h) 0-1, Belgium (h) 1-1, Luxembourg (a) 3-1, Bulgaria (a) 0-2, Italy (h) 1-2, Morocco (a) 2-1, Ivory Coast (h) 5-0, Luxembourg (h) 5-0.

League Championship wins (1889–2017)
Ajax 33; PSV Eindhoven 23; Feyenoord 15; HVV The Hague 10; Sparta Rotterdam 6; RAP Amsterdam 5; Go Ahead Eagles Deventer 4; HFC Haarlem 3; HBS Craeyenhout 3; Willem II Tilburg 3; RCH Heemstede 2; Heracles 2; ADO Den Haag 2; AZ 67 Alkmaar 2; VV Concordia 1; Quick Den Haag 1; Be Quick Groningen 1; NAC Breda 1; SC Enschede 1; Volewijckers Amsterdam 1; Haarlem 1; BVV Den Bosch 1; Schiedam 1; Limburgia 1; EVV Eindhoven 1; SVV Rapid JC Den Heerlen 1; DOS Utrecht 1; DWS Amsterdam 1; FC Twente 1.

Cup wins (1899–2017)
Ajax 18; Feyenoord 12; PSV Eindhoven 9; Quick The Hague 4; AZ 67 Alkmaar 4; HFC Haarlem 3; Sparta Rotterdam 3; FC Twente 3; Utrecht 3; Haarlem 2; VOC 2; HBS Craeyenhout 2; DFC 2; RCH Haarlem 2; Wageningen 2; Willem II Tilburg 2; Fortuna 54 2; FC Den Haag (includes ADO) 2; Roda JC 2; RAP Amsterdam 1; Velocitas Breda 1; HVV Den Haag 1; Concordia Delft 1; CVV 1; Schoten 1; ZFC Zaandam 1; Longa 1; VUC 1; Velocitas Groningen 1; Roermond 1; FC Eindhoven 1; VSV 1; Quick 1888 Nijmegen 1; VVV Groningen 1; NAC Breda 1; Heerenveen 1; PEC Zwolle 1; FC Groningen 1; Vitesse 1.

Dutch Eredivisie 2016–17

	P	W	D	L	F	A	GD	Pts
Feyenoord	34	26	4	4	86	25	61	82
Ajax	34	25	6	3	79	23	56	81
PSV Eindhoven	34	22	10	2	68	23	45	76
Utrecht	34	18	8	8	54	38	16	62
Vitesse	34	15	6	13	51	40	11	51
AZ Alkmaar	34	12	13	9	56	52	4	49
FC Twente	34	12	9	13	48	50	–2	45
FC Groningen	34	10	13	11	55	51	4	43
Heerenveen	34	12	7	15	54	53	1	43
Heracles Almelo	34	12	7	15	53	55	–2	43
ADO Den Haag	34	11	5	18	37	59	–22	38
SBV Excelsior	34	9	10	15	43	60	–17	37
Willem II Tilburg	34	9	9	16	29	44	–15	36
PEC Zwolle	34	9	8	17	39	67	–28	35
Sparta Rotterdam	34	9	7	18	42	61	–19	34
NEC*+	34	9	7	18	32	59	–27	34
Roda JC+	34	7	12	15	26	51	–25	33
Go Ahead Eagles*	34	6	5	23	32	73	–41	23

Top scorer: Jorgensen (Feyenoord) 21.
Cup Final: Vitesse 2, AZ Alkmaar 0.

NORTHERN CYPRUS

Cyprus Turkish Football Federation, 7 Memduh Asaf Street, 107 Koskluciftlik, Lefkosa. (Not a member of FIFA or UEFA.)
Founded: 1955; *National Colours:* Red shirts with white trim, red shorts, red socks.

League Championship wins (1956–63; 1969–74; 1976–2017)
Cetinkaya 14; Gonyeli 9; Magusa 8; Yenicami Agdelen 8; Dogan 7; Baf Ulku 4; Kucuk Kaymakli 4; Akincilar 1; Binatli 1.

Cup wins (1956–2017)
Cetinkaya 17; Gonyeli 8; Yenicami Agdelen 7; Kucuk Kaymakli 7; Magusa 5; Turk Ocagi 5; Lefke 2; Dogan 2; Genclik Gucu 1; Yalova 1; Binatli 1.

Birinc Lig 2016–17

	P	W	D	L	F	A	GD	Pts
Yenicami Agdelen	30	22	6	2	84	21	63	72
Dogan	30	17	5	8	53	28	25	56
Cihangir	30	15	9	6	54	36	18	54
Gencler Birligi	30	16	5	9	52	36	16	53
Kucuk Kaymakli	30	14	9	7	47	36	11	51
Yalova	30	12	11	7	55	42	13	47
Turk Ocagi	30	14	4	12	60	44	16	46
Cetinkaya	30	13	4	13	55	46	9	43
Lefke	30	12	6	12	45	50	–5	42
Genclik	30	11	5	14	38	49	–11	38
Ulku Yurdu	30	11	3	16	46	61	–15	36
Binatli	30	9	8	13	50	59	–9	35
Magusa	30	9	7	14	36	45	–9	34
Degirmenlik*	30	7	5	18	30	67	–37	26
Dumlupinar*	30	5	5	20	36	76	–40	20
Mormenekse*	30	5	4	21	36	81	–45	19

Top scorer: Taskiran (Turk Ocagi) 24.
Cup Final: Turk Ocagi 1, Yalova 0.

NORTHERN IRELAND

Irish Football Association, 20 Windsor Avenue, Belfast BT9 6EG.
Founded: 1880. *FIFA:* 1911; *UEFA:* 1954. *National Colours:* Green shirts, white shorts, green socks.

NORWAY

Norges Fotballforbund, Ullevaal Stadion, Serviceboks 1, 0840 Oslo.
Founded: 1902. *FIFA:* 1908; *UEFA:* 1954. *National Colours:* Red shirts, white shorts, red socks.

International matches 2016–17
Belarus (h) 0-1, Germany (h) 0-3, Azerbaijan (a) 0-1, San Marino (h) 4-1, Czech Republic (a) 1-2, Northern Ireland (a) 0-2, Czech Republic (h) 1-1, Sweden (h) 1-1.

League Championship wins (1938–2016)
Rosenborg 24; Fredrikstad 9; Viking Stavanger 8; Lillestrom 5; Valerenga 5; Larvik Turn 3; Brann 3; Molde 3; Lyn Oslo 2; Stromsgodset 2; IK Start 2; Freidig 1; Fram 1; Skeid 1; Moss 1; Stabaek 1.

Cup wins (1902–2016)
Odd Grenland 12; Fredrikstad 11; Rosenborg 11; Lyn Oslo 8; Skeid 8; Sarpsborg 6; Brann 6; Viking Stavanger 5; Stromsgodset 5; Lillestrom 5; Orn-Horten 4; Valerenga 4; Molde 4; Frigg 3; Mjondalen 3; Mercantile 2; Bodo/Glimt 2; Tromso 2; Aalesund 2; Grane Nordstrand 1; Kvik Halden 1; Sparta 1; Gjovik/Lyn 1; Moss 1; Bryne 1; Stabaek 1; Hodd 1.
(Known as the Norwegian Championship for HM The King's Trophy.)

Norwegian Tippeligaen 2016

	P	W	D	L	F	A	GD	Pts
Rosenborg	30	21	6	3	65	25	40	69
Brann	30	16	6	8	42	27	15	54
Odd	30	15	6	9	44	35	9	51
Haugesund	30	12	10	8	47	43	4	46
Molde	30	13	6	11	48	42	6	45
Sarpsborg 08	30	12	9	9	35	37	–2	45
Stromsgodset	30	12	8	10	44	40	4	44
Viking	30	12	7	11	33	35	–2	43
Aalesund	30	12	6	12	46	51	–5	42
Valerenga	30	10	8	12	41	39	2	38
Sogndal	30	8	12	10	33	37	–4	36
Lillestrom	30	8	10	12	45	50	–5	34
Tromso	30	9	7	14	36	46	–10	34

Team	P	W	D	L	F	A	GD	Pts
Stabaek+	30	8	7	15	35	42	–7	31
Bodo/Glimt*	30	8	6	16	36	45	–9	30
Start*	30	2	10	18	23	59	–36	16

Top scorer: Gytkjaer (Rosenborg) 19.
Cup Final: Rosenborg 4, Kongsvinger 0.

POLAND

Polski Zwiazek Pilki Noznej, ul. Bitwy Warszawskiej 1920r. 7, 02-366 Warszawa.
Founded: 1919. *FIFA:* 1923; *UEFA:* 1954. *National Colours:* White shirts with red vertical band, red shorts, white socks.

International matches 2016–17
Kazakhstan (a) 2-2, Denmark (h) 3-2, Armenia (h) 2-1, Romania (a) 3-0, Slovenia (h) 1-1, Montenegro (a) 2-1, Romania (h) 3-1.

League Championship wins (1921–2017)
Ruch Chorzow 14; Gornik Zabrze 14; Wisla Krakow 13; Legia Warsaw 12; Lech Poznan 7; Cracovia 5; Pogon Lwow 4; Widzew Lodz 4; Warta Poznan 2; Polonia Warsaw 2; Polonia Bytom 2; LKS Lodz 2; Stal Mielec 2; Slask Wroclaw 2; Zaglebie Lubin 2; Garbarnia Krakow 1; Szombierki Bytom 1.

Cup wins (1926; 1951–2017)
Legia Warsaw 18; Gornik Zabrze 6; Lech Poznan 5; Wisla Krakow 4; Zaglebie Sosnowiec 4; Ruch Chorzow 3; GKS Katowice 3; Amica Wronki 3; Polonia Warsaw 2; Slask Wroclaw 2; Arka Gdynia 2; Dyskobolia Grodzisk 2; Gwardia Warsaw 1; LKS Lodz 1; Stal Rzeszow 1; Lechia Gdansk 1; Widzew Lodz 1; Miedz Legnica 1; Wisla Plock 1; Jagiellonia Bialystok 1; Zawisza Bydgoszcz 1.

Polish Ekstraklasa Qualifying Table 2016–17

	P	W	D	L	F	A	GD	Pts
Jagiellonia Bialystok	30	18	5	7	56	31	25	59
Legia Warsaw	30	17	7	6	58	30	28	58
Lech Poznan	30	16	7	7	50	22	28	55
Lechia Gdansk	30	16	5	9	46	37	9	53
Wisla Krakow	30	13	5	12	45	46	–1	44
Pogon Szczecin	30	10	12	8	47	40	7	42
Nieciecza	30	12	6	12	31	38	–7	42
Korona Kielce	30	12	3	15	39	55	–16	39
Wisla Plock	30	10	9	11	42	44	–2	39
Zaglebie Lubin	30	10	9	11	37	36	1	39
Slask Wroclaw	30	8	10	12	34	45	–11	34
Arka Gdynia	30	8	7	15	37	50	–13	31
Cracovia Krakow	30	6	13	11	38	43	–5	31
Ruch Chorzow	30	10	4	16	37	46	–9	30
Piast Gliwice	30	7	9	14	31	49	–18	30
Gornik Leczna	30	7	9	14	36	52	–16	30

NB: Points earned in Qualifying phase are halved and rounded up at start of Championship and Relegation Play-off phase.

Championship Round 2016–17

	P	W	D	L	F	A	GD	Pts
Legia Warsaw	37	21	10	6	70	31	39	44
Jagiellonia Bialystok	37	21	8	8	64	39	25	42
Lech Poznan	37	20	9	8	62	29	33	42
Lechia Gdansk	37	20	8	9	57	37	20	42
Korona Kielce	37	14	5	18	47	65	–18	28
Wisla Krakow	37	14	6	17	54	57	–3	26
Pogon Szczecin	37	11	13	13	51	54	–3	25
Nieciecza	37	13	7	17	35	55	–20	25

Relegation Round 2016–17

	P	W	D	L	F	A	GD	Pts
Zaglebie Lubin	37	14	11	12	51	45	6	34
Piast Gliwice	37	12	10	15	45	54	–9	31
Slask Wroclaw	37	12	10	15	49	52	–3	29
Wisla Plock	37	12	11	14	49	57	–8	28
Arka Gdynia	37	10	9	18	44	60	–16	24
Cracovia Krakow	37	8	15	14	45	52	–7	24
Gornik Leczna*	37	9	10	18	47	63	–16	22
Ruch Chorzow*	37	10	8	19	42	62	–20	19

Top scorers (joint): Paixao (Lechia Gdansk), Vieira (Lech Poznan) 18.
Cup Final: Arka Gdynia 2, Lech Poznan 1 *aet.*

PORTUGAL

Federacao Portuguesa de Futebol, Rua Alexandre Herculano No. 58, Apartado postal 24013, Lisboa 1250-012.
Founded: 1914. *FIFA:* 1923; *UEFA:* 1954. *National Colours:* Carmine shirts with , red shorts, red and green socks.

International matches 2016–17
Gibraltar (h) 5-0, Switzerland (a) 0-2, Andorra (h) 6-0, Faroe Islands (a) 6-0, Latvia (a) 4-1, Hungary (h) 3-0, Sweden (h) 2-3, Cyprus (h) 4-0, Latvia (a) 3-0, Mexico (n) 2-2, Russia (a) 1-0, New Zealand (n) 4-0, Chile (n) 0-0 (0-3p), Mexico (n) 2-1.

League Championship wins (1935–2017)
Benfica 36; Porto 27; Sporting Lisbon 18; Belenenses 1; Boavista 1.

Cup wins (1939–2017)
Benfica 26; Sporting Lisbon 16; Porto 16; Boavista 5; Belenenses 3; Vitoria de Setubal 3; Academica de Coimbra 2; Braga 2; Leixoes 1; Estrela da Amadora 1; Beira-Mar 1; Vitoria de Guimaraes 1.

Portuguese Primeira Liga 2016–17

	P	W	D	L	F	A	GD	Pts
Benfica	34	25	7	2	72	18	54	82
Porto	34	22	10	2	71	19	52	76
Sporting Lisbon	34	21	7	6	68	36	32	70
Vitoria de Guimaraes	34	18	8	8	50	39	11	62
Braga	34	15	9	10	51	36	15	54
Maritimo	34	13	11	10	34	32	2	50
Rio Ave	34	14	7	13	41	39	2	49
Feirense	34	14	6	14	31	45	–14	48
Boavista	34	10	13	11	33	36	–3	43
Estoril	34	10	8	16	36	42	–6	38
Chaves	34	8	14	12	35	42	–7	38
Vitoria Setubal	34	10	8	16	30	39	–9	38
Pacos de Ferreira	34	8	12	14	32	45	–13	36
Belenenses	34	9	9	16	27	45	–18	36
Moreirense	34	8	9	17	33	48	–15	33
Tondela	34	8	8	18	29	52	–23	32
Arouca*	34	9	5	20	33	57	–24	32
Nacional*	34	4	9	21	22	58	–36	21

Top scorer: Dost (Sporting Lisbon) 34.
Cup Final: Benfica 2, Vitoria de Guimaraes 1.

REPUBLIC OF IRELAND

Football Association of Ireland (Cumann Peile na hEireann), National Sports Campus, Abbotstown, Dublin 15.
Founded: 1921. *FIFA:* 1923; *UEFA:* 1954. *National Colours:* Green shirts, green shorts, green socks with white tops.

League Championship wins (1922–2016)
Shamrock Rovers 17; Shelbourne 13; Dundalk 12; Bohemians 11; St Patrick's Athletic 8; Waterford United 6; Cork United 5; Drumcondra 5; Sligo Rovers 3; St James's Gate 2; Cork Athletic 2; Limerick 2; Athlone Town 2; Derry City 2; Cork City 2; Dolphin 1; Cork Hibernians 1; Cork Celtic 1; Drogheda United 1.

Cup wins (1922–2016)
Shamrock Rovers 24; Dundalk 10; Bohemians 7; Shelbourne 7; Drumcondra 5; Sligo Rovers 5; Derry City 5; St Patrick's Athletic 3; Cork City 3; St James's Gate 2; Cork (incl. Fordsons 1) 2; Waterford United 2; Cork United 2; Cork Athletic 2; Limerick 2; Cork Hibernians 2; Bray Wanderers 2; Longford Town 2; Alton United 1; Athlone Town 1; Transport 1; Finn Harps 1; Home Farm 1; UC Dublin 1; Galway United 1; Drogheda United 1; Sporting Fingal 1.

Irish Premier Division 2016

	P	W	D	L	F	A	GD	Pts
Dundalk	33	25	2	6	73	28	45	77
Cork City	33	21	7	5	65	23	42	70
Derry City	33	17	11	5	48	29	19	62
Shamrock Rovers	33	16	7	10	46	34	12	55
Sligo Rovers	33	13	10	10	42	35	7	49
Bray Wanderers	33	13	7	13	39	40	–1	46
St Patrick's Athletic	33	13	6	14	45	41	4	45
Bohemians	33	12	5	16	30	37	–7	41
Galway United	33	10	8	15	44	54	–10	38
Finn Harps	33	8	8	17	23	49	–26	32
Wexford*	33	6	5	22	31	70	–39	23
Longford Town*	33	2	8	23	25	71	–46	14

Top scorers: Maguire (Cork City) 18.
Cup Final: Cork City 1, Dundalk 0 *aet.*

ROMANIA

Federatia Romana de Fotbal, House of Football, Str. Sergent Serbanica Vasile 12, 22186 Bucuresti.
Founded: 1909. *FIFA:* 1923; *UEFA:* 1954. *National Colours:* All yellow.

International matches 2016–17
Montenegro (h) 1-1, Armenia (a) 5-0, Kazakhstan (a) 0-0, Poland (h) 0-3, Russia (a) 0-1, Denmark (h) 0-0, Poland (a) 1-3, Chile (h) 3-2.

League Championship wins (1910–2017)
Steaua Bucharest (renamed FCSB) 26; Dinamo Bucharest 18; Venus Bucharest 8; Chinezul Timisoara 6; UTA Arad 6; Petrolul Ploiesti 4; Ripensia Timisoara 4; Universitatea Craiova 4; Rapid Bucharest 3; CFR Cluj 3; Olimpia Bucharest 2; United Ploiesti 2 (incl. Prahova Ploiesti 1); Colentina Bucharest 2; Arges Pitesti 2; Romano-Americana Bucharest 1; Coltea Brasov 1; Metalochimia Resita 1; Unirea Tricolor 1; CA Oradea 1; Unirea Urziceni 1; Otelul Galati 1; Astra Giurgiu 1; Viitorul Constanta 1.

Cup wins (1934–2017)
Steaua Bucharest (renamed FCSB) 23; Rapid Bucharest 13; Dinamo Bucharest 13; Universitatea Craiova 6; CFR Cluj 4; Petrolul Ploiesti 3; Ripensia Timisoara 2; UTA Arad 2; Politehnica Timisoara 2; CFR Turnu Severin 1; Metalochimia Resita 1; Universitatea Cluj (includes Stiinta) 1; Progresul Oradea (formerly ICO) 1; Progresul Bucharest 1; Ariesul Turda 1; Chimia Ramnicu Vilcea 1; Jiul Petrosani 1; Gloria Bistrita 1; Astra Giurgiu 1; Voluntari 1.

Romanian Liga 1 Qualifying Table 2016–17
	P	*W*	*D*	*L*	*F*	*A*	*GD*	*Pts*
Viitorul Constanta	26	16	3	7	39	22	17	51
FCSB	26	13	8	5	34	22	12	47
Astra Giurgiu	26	13	5	8	32	28	4	44
Universitatea Craiova	26	13	4	9	36	26	10	43
CFR Cluj (–6)	26	14	7	5	42	23	19	43
Dinamo Bucharest	26	12	5	9	40	33	7	41
Gaz Metan Medias	26	10	9	7	36	27	9	39
Botosani	26	9	5	12	30	31	–1	32
Voluntari	26	8	6	12	30	37	–7	30
CSMS Iasi	26	8	5	13	28	31	–3	29
Concordia Chiajna	26	6	7	13	17	32	–15	25
Pandurii Targu Jiu (–6)	26	6	7	13	24	42	–18	19
ACS Poli Timisoara (–14)	26	7	7	12	25	42	–17	14
Targu Mures (–9)	26	5	6	15	20	37	–17	12

Championship Round 2016–17
	P	*W*	*D*	*L*	*F*	*A*	*GD*	*Pts*
Viitorul Constanta	10	5	3	2	12	8	4	44
FCSB	10	6	2	2	15	7	8	44
Dinamo Bucharest	10	5	4	1	15	8	7	40
CFR Cluj	10	3	2	5	8	14	–6	33
Universitatea Craiova	10	2	3	5	8	14	–6	31
Astra Giurgiu	10	1	2	7	10	17	–7	27

Relegation Round 2016–17
	P	*W*	*D*	*L*	*F*	*A*	*GD*	*Pts*
CSMS Iasi	14	7	7	0	16	5	11	43
Gaz Metan Medias	14	4	7	3	17	11	6	39
Voluntari	14	6	4	4	17	16	1	37
Botosani	14	4	5	5	15	12	3	33
Concordia Chiajna	14	4	4	6	14	18	–4	29
ACS Poli Timisoara+	14	5	5	4	16	14	2	27
Pandurii Targu Jiu *	14	4	5	5	12	18	–6	27
Targu Mures*	14	1	5	8	5	18	–13	14

Top scorer: Llullaku (Gaz Metan Medias) 16.
Cup Final: Voluntari 1, Astra Giurgiu 1.
aet; Voluntari won 5-3 on penalties.

RUSSIA

Russian Football Union, Ulitsa Narodnaya 7, 115 172 Moscow.
Founded: 1912. *FIFA:* 1912; *UEFA:* 1954. *National Colours:* All brick red.

International matches 2016–17
Turkey (a) 0-0, Ghana (h) 1-0, Costa Rica (h) 3-4, Qatar (a) 1-2, Romania (h) 1-0, Ivory Coast (h) 0-2, Belgium (h) 3-3, Hungary (a) 3-0, Chile (h) 1-1, New Zealand (h) 2-0, Portugal (h) 0-1, Mexico (h) 1-2.

League Championship wins (1936–2017)
Spartak Moscow 22; Dynamo Kyiv 13; CSKA Moscow 13; Dynamo Moscow 11; Zenit St Petersburg (formerly Zenit Leningrad) 5; Torpedo Moscow 3; Dinamo Tbilisi 2; Dnepr Dnepropetrovsk 2; Lokomotiv Moscow 2; Rubin Kazan 2; Saria Voroshilovgrad 1; Ararat Erevan 1; Dynamo Minsk 1; Spartak Vladikavkaz (renamed Alania) 1.

Cup wins (1936–2017)
Spartak Moscow 13; CSKA Moscow 12; Dynamo Kyiv 9; Lokomotiv Moscow 9; Torpedo Moscow 7; Dynamo Moscow 7; Zenit St Petersburg (formerly Zenit Leningrad) 4; Shakhtar Donetsk 4; Dinamo Tbilisi 2; Ararat Erevan 2; Karpaty Lvov 1; SKA Rostov-on-Don 1; Metalist Kharkov 1; Dnepr 1; Terek Grozny 1; Rubin Kazan 1; Rostov 1.

Russian Premier League 2016–17
	P	*W*	*D*	*L*	*F*	*A*	*GD*	*Pts*
Spartak Moscow	30	22	3	5	46	27	19	69
CSKA Moscow	30	18	8	4	47	15	32	62
Zenit St Petersburg	30	18	7	5	50	19	31	61
Krasnodar	30	12	13	5	40	22	18	49
Terek Grozny	30	14	6	10	38	35	3	48
Rostov	30	13	9	8	36	18	18	48
Ufa	30	12	7	11	22	25	–3	43
Lokomotiv Moscow	30	10	12	8	39	27	12	42
Rubin Kazan	30	10	8	12	30	34	–4	38
Amkar Perm	30	8	11	11	25	29	–4	35
Ural Sverdlovsk Oblast	30	8	6	16	24	44	–20	30
Anzhi	30	7	9	14	24	38	–14	30
Orenburg*	30	7	9	14	25	36	–11	30
Arsenal Tula+	30	7	7	16	18	40	–22	28
Krylya Sovetov*	30	6	10	14	31	39	–8	28
Tom Tomsk*	30	3	5	22	17	64	–47	14

Top scorer: Smolov (Krasnodar) 18.
Cup Final: Lokomotiv Moscow 2, Ural Sverdlovsk Oblast 0.

SAN MARINO

Federazione Sammarinese Giuoco Calcio, Strada di Montecchio 17, 47890 San Marino.
Founded: 1931. *FIFA:* 1988; *UEFA:* 1988. *National Colours:* Cobalt blue shirts with white trim, white shorts, cobalt blue socks.

International matches 2016–17
Azerbaijan (h) 0-1, Northern Ireland (a) 0-4, Norway (a) 1-4, Germany (h) 0-8, Andorra (h) 0-2, Moldova (h) 0-2, Czech Republic (h) 0-6, Italy (a) 0-8, Germany (a) 0-7.

League Championship wins (1986–2017)
Tre Fiori 7; La Fiorita 4; Domagnano 4; Folgore/Falciano 4; Faetano 3; Murata 3; Tre Penne 3; Montevito 1; Libertas 1; Cosmos 1; Pennarossa 1.

Cup wins (1937–2017)
Libertas 11; Domagnano 8; Tre Fiori 6; Tre Penne 6; Juvenes 5; Cosmos 4; La Fiorita 4; Faetano 3; Murata 3; Dogana 2; Pennarossa 2; Juvenes/Dogana 2; Folgore/Falciano 1.

Campionato Sammarinese Qualifying Table 2016–17

Group A
	P	*W*	*D*	*L*	*F*	*A*	*GD*	*Pts*
La Fiorita	20	14	2	4	51	22	29	44
Virtus	20	12	5	3	38	19	19	41
Juvenes/Dogana	20	8	7	5	27	22	5	31
Fiorentino	20	7	9	4	22	18	4	30
Cosmos	20	8	4	8	36	36	0	28
Tre Fiori	20	6	4	10	31	41	–10	22
Faetano	20	4	4	12	16	33	–17	16
La Fiorita	20	14	2	4	51	22	29	44

Group B
	P	*W*	*D*	*L*	*F*	*A*	*GD*	*Pts*
Libertas	21	14	5	2	37	13	24	47
Tre Penne	21	12	7	2	43	15	28	43
Folgore/Falciano	21	13	4	4	53	15	38	43
Domagnano	21	11	3	7	44	26	18	36
Murata	21	6	2	13	28	50	–22	20
Pennarossa	21	2	4	15	23	61	–38	10
Cailungo	21	2	3	16	20	52	–32	9
San Giovanni	21	1	5	15	15	61	–46	8

Play-offs
Top three in each group qualify for Play-offs; double-elimination format (eliminated teams shown in italics); group winners receive byes in first two rounds.
Rnd 1: Virtus 1, Folgore/Falciano 2; Tre Penne 2, Juvenes/Dogana 3
Rnd 2: Folgore/Falciano 0, Juvenes/Dogana 0 (aet; 3-0p); *Virtus* 0, Tre Penne 1
Rnd 3: Libertas 0, La Fiorita 1; Tre Penne 3, *Juvenes/Dogana* 1
Rnd 4: La Fiorita 2, Folgore/Falciano 0 (aet); Tre Penne 2, *Libertas* 0

Semi-final: Tre Penne 1, *Folgore/Falciano* 0
Final: La Fiorita 2, Tre Penne 1 (aet)
Top scorer: Martini (La Fiorita) 26.
Cup Final: Tre Penne 2, La Fiorita 0.

SCOTLAND

Scottish Football Association, Hampden Park, Glasgow G42 9AY.
Founded: 1873. *FIFA:* 1910; *UEFA:* 1954. *National Colours:* Dark blue shirts, dark blue shorts, red socks.

SERBIA

Football Association of Serbia, Terazije 35, PO Box 263, 11000 Beograd.
Founded: 1919. *FIFA:* 1921; *UEFA:* 1954. *National Colours:* Red shirts, blue shorts, white socks.

International matches 2016–17

Republic of Ireland (h) 2-2, Moldova (a) 3-0, Austria (h) 3-2, Wales (a) 1-1, Ukraine (a) 0-2, USA (a) 0-0, Georgia (a) 3-1, Wales (h) 1-1.

League Championship wins (1923–2017)

Partizan Belgrade 27; Crvena Zvezda (Red Star Belgrade) 27; Hajduk Split 9; Gradjanski Zagreb 5; BSK Belgrade (renamed OFK) 5; Dinamo Zagreb 4; Jugoslavija Belgrade 2; Concordia Zagreb 2; FC Sarajevo 2; Vojvodina Novi Sad 2; HASK Zagreb 1; Zeljeznicar 1; Obilic 1.

Cup wins (1947–2017)

Crvena Zvezda (Red Star Belgrade) 24; Partizan Belgrade 14; Hajduk Split 9; Dinamo Zagreb 7; OFK Belgrade (incl. BSK 3) 5; Rijeka 2; Velez Mostar 2; Vardar Skopje 1; Borac Banjaluka 1; Sartid 1; Zeleznik 1; Jagodina 1; Vojvodina 1; Cukaricki 1.

Serbian SuperLiga Qualifying Table 2016–17

	P	*W*	*D*	*L*	*F*	*A*	*GD*	*Pts*
Crvena Zvezda	30	25	4	1	75	25	50	79
Partizan Belgrade	30	23	4	3	59	17	42	73
Vojvodina	30	18	5	7	51	26	25	59
Napredak	30	15	7	8	35	23	12	52
Mladost Lucani	30	14	6	10	35	29	6	48
Radnicki Nis	30	12	8	10	37	36	1	44
Vozdovac	30	13	4	13	35	38	–3	43
Javor Ivanjica	30	11	9	10	32	37	–5	42
Cukaricki	30	11	7	12	40	42	–2	40
Spartak Subotica	30	10	8	12	38	47	–9	38
Rad	30	9	8	13	26	37	–11	35
Backa Palanka	30	8	3	19	17	37	–20	27
Metalac GM	30	6	9	15	20	34	–14	27
Radnik Surdulica	30	6	7	17	24	42	–18	25
Novi Pazar	30	5	5	20	22	53	–31	20
Borac Cacak	30	4	6	20	22	45	–23	18

NB: Points earned in Qualifying phase are halved and rounded up at start of Championship and Relegation Play-off phase.

Championship Round 2016–17

	P	*W*	*D*	*L*	*F*	*A*	*GD*	*Pts*
Partizan Belgrade	37	30	4	3	78	22	56	58
Crvena Zvezda	37	30	4	3	93	33	60	55
Vojvodina	37	22	6	9	58	31	27	43
Mladost Lucani	37	18	6	13	46	44	2	36
Radnicki Nis	37	15	9	13	47	46	1	32
Napredak	37	16	8	13	44	36	8	30
Vozdovac	37	14	6	17	41	51	–10	27
Javor Ivanjica	37	11	10	16	34	50	–16	22

Relegation Round 2016–17

	P	*W*	*D*	*L*	*F*	*A*	*GD*	*Pts*
Cukaricki	37	15	7	15	54	49	5	32
Spartak Subotica	37	14	9	14	47	55	–8	32
Rad	37	11	9	17	29	45	–16	25
Radnik Surdulica	37	9	10	18	35	48	–13	25
Backa Palanka	37	11	3	23	27	46	–19	23
Borac Cacak	37	8	7	22	29	51	–22	22
Metalac GM*	37	8	10	19	27	43	–16	21
Novi Pazar*	37	7	6	24	29	68	–39	17

Top scorers (joint): Djurdjevic (Partizan), Leonardo (Partizan) 21.
Cup Final: Partizan Belgrade 1, Crvena Zvezda 0.

SLOVAKIA

Slovensky Futbalovy Zvaz, Trnavska cesta 100, 821 01 Bratislava.
Founded: 1938. *FIFA:* 1994; *UEFA:* 1993. *National Colours:* White shirts with blue trim, white shorts, white socks.

International matches 2016–17

England (h) 0-1, Slovenia (a) 0-1, Scotland (h) 3-0, Lithuania (h) 4-0, Austria (a) 0-0, Uganda (n) 1-3, Sweden (n) 0-6, Malta (a) 3-1, Lithuania (a) 2-1.

League Championship wins (1939–44; 1994–2017)

Slovan Bratislava 12; Zilina 7; Kosice 2; Inter Bratislava 2; Artmedia Petrzalka 2; Trencin 2; Dukla Banska Bystrica 1; OAP Bratislava 1; Ruzomberok 1.
See also Czech Republic section for Slovak club honours in Czechoslovak era 1925–93.

Cup wins (1993–2017)

Slovan Bratislava 7; Inter Bratislava 3; Artmedia Petrzalka 2; Kosice 2; Trencin 2; Humenne 1; Spartak Trnava 1; Koba Senec 1; Matador Puchov 1; Dukla Banska Bystrica 1; Ruzomberok 1; ViOn Zlate Moravce 1; Zilina 1.

Slovak Super Liga 2016–17

	P	*W*	*D*	*L*	*F*	*A*	*GD*	*Pts*
Zilina	30	23	4	3	82	25	57	73
Slovan Bratislava	30	18	3	9	54	34	20	57
Ruzomberok	30	15	7	8	55	38	17	52
Trencin	30	14	5	11	53	48	5	47
Sport Podbrezova	30	12	9	9	34	31	3	45
Spartak Trnava	30	12	7	11	34	37	–3	43
DAC Dunajska Streda	30	10	12	8	37	34	3	42
Zemplin Michalovce	30	8	5	17	35	55	–20	29
Senica	30	7	7	16	25	35	–10	28
ViOn Zlate Moravce	30	5	7	18	29	55	–26	22
Tatran Predov	30	3	10	17	17	63	–46	19
Spartak Myjava†	0	0	0	0	0	0	0	0

† Spartak Myjava withdrew, results expunged.
Top scorers (joint): Hlohovsky (Zilina), Soumah (Slovan Bratislava) 20.
Cup Final: Slovan Bratislava 3, Skalica 0.

SLOVENIA

Nogometna Zveza Slovenije, Brnciceva 41g, PP 3986, 1001 Ljubljana.
Founded: 1920. *FIFA:* 1992; *UEFA:* 1992. *National Colours:* White shirts with blue trim, white shorts, white socks.

International matches 2016–17

Lithuania (a) 2-2, Slovakia (h) 1-0, England (h) 0-0, Malta (a) 1-0, Poland (a) 1-1, Saudi Arabia (n) 0-0, Finland (n) 2-0, Scotland (a) 0-1, Malta (h) 2-0.

League Championship wins (1991–2017)

Maribor 14; Olimpija (pre-2005) 4; Gorica 4; Domzale 2; Koper 1; Olimpija Ljubljana 1.

Cup wins (1991–2017)

Maribor 9; Olimpija (pre-2005) 4; Gorica 3; Koper 3; Interblock 2; Domzale 2, Mura (pre-2004) 1; Rudar Velenje 1; Celje 1.

Slovenian PrvaLiga 2016–17

	P	*W*	*D*	*L*	*F*	*A*	*GD*	*Pts*
Maribor	36	21	10	5	63	30	33	73
Gorica	36	16	12	8	48	39	9	60
Olimpija Ljubljana	36	17	9	10	49	35	14	60
Domzale	36	16	8	12	63	45	18	56
Celje	36	15	10	11	48	39	9	55
Koper*†	36	12	14	10	43	40	3	50
Rudar Velenje	36	10	11	15	49	53	–4	41
Krsko	36	8	15	13	39	50	–11	39
Aluminij	36	9	11	16	38	52	–14	38
Radomlje*	36	1	10	25	23	80	–57	13

† Koper relegated due to inability to obtain licence.
Top scorer: Mary (Rudar Velenje) 17.
Cup Final: Domzale 1, Olimpija Ljubljana 0.

SPAIN

Real Federacion Espanola de Futbol, Calle Ramon y Cajal s/n, Apartado postale 385, 28230 Las Rozas, Madrid.
Founded: 1913. *FIFA:* 1913; *UEFA:* 1954. *National Colours:* All red with yellow trim.

International matches 2016–17

Belgium (a) 2-0, Liechtenstein (h) 8-0, Italy (a) 1-1, Albania (a) 2-0, FYR Macedonia (h) 4-0, England (a) 2-2, Israel (h) 4-1, France (a) 2-0, Colombia (h) 2-2, FYR Macedonia (a) 2-1.

League Championship wins (1929–36; 1940–2017)

Real Madrid 33; Barcelona 24; Atletico Madrid 10; Athletic Bilbao 8; Valencia 6; Real Sociedad 2; Real Betis 1; Sevilla 1; Deportivo La Coruna 1.

Cup wins (1903–2017)
Barcelona 29; Athletic Bilbao (includes Vizcaya Bilbao 1) 23; Real Madrid 19; Atletico Madrid 10; Valencia 7; Real Zaragoza 6; Sevilla 5; Espanyol 4; Real Union de Irun 3; Real Betis 2; Real Sociedad (includes Ciclista) 2; Deportivo La Coruna 2; Arenas 1; Racing de Irun 1; Mallorca 1.

Spanish Liga 2016–17

	P	W	D	L	F	A	GD	Pts
Real Madrid	38	29	6	3	106	41	65	93
Barcelona	38	28	6	4	116	37	79	90
Atletico Madrid	38	23	9	6	70	27	43	78
Sevilla	38	21	9	8	69	49	20	72
Villarreal	38	19	10	9	56	33	23	67
Real Sociedad	38	19	7	12	59	53	6	64
Athletic Bilbao	38	19	6	13	53	43	10	63
Espanyol	38	15	11	12	49	50	–1	56
Alaves	38	14	13	11	41	43	–2	55
Eibar	38	15	9	14	56	51	5	54
Malaga	38	12	10	16	49	55	–6	46
Valencia	38	13	7	18	56	65	–9	46
Celta Vigo	38	13	6	19	53	69	–16	45
Las Palmas	38	10	9	19	53	74	–21	39
Real Betis	38	10	9	19	41	64	–23	39
Deportivo La Coruna	38	8	12	18	43	61	–18	36
Leganes	38	8	11	19	36	55	–19	35
Sporting Gijon*	38	7	10	21	42	72	–30	31
Osasuna*	38	4	10	24	40	94	–54	22
Granada*	38	4	8	26	30	82	–52	20

Top scorer: Messi (Barcelona) 37.
Cup Final: Barcelona 3, Alaves 0.

SWEDEN

Svenska Fotbollfoerbundet, Evenemangsgatan 31, PO Box 1216, SE-171 23 Solna.
Founded: 1904. *FIFA:* 1904; *UEFA:* 1954. *National Colours:* Yellow shirts with blue trim, blue shorts, yellow socks.

International matches 2016–17
Netherlands (h) 1-1, Luxembourg (a) 1-0, Bulgaria (h) 3-0, France (a) 1-2, Hungary (a) 2-0, Ivory Coast (n) 1-2, Slovakia (n) 6-0, Belarus (h) 4-0, Portugal (a) 3-2, France (h) 2-1, Norway (a) 1-1.

League Championship wins (1896–2016)
Malmo 19; IFK Gothenburg 18; IFK Norrkoping 13; Orgryte 12; AIK Stockholm 11; Djurgaarden 11; IF Elfsborg 6; Helsingborg 5; GAIS Gothenburg 4; Oster Vaxjo 4; Halmstad 4; Atvidaberg 2; Gothenburg IF 1; IFK Eskilstuna 1; Fassbergs 1; IF Gavic Brynas 1; IK Sleipner 1; Hammarby 1; Kalmar 1.
(Played in cup format from 1896–1925.)

Cup wins (1941–2017)
Malmo 14; AIK Stockholm 8; IFK Gothenburg 7; IFK Norrkoping 6; Helsingborg 5; Djurgaarden 4; Kalmar 3; IF Elfsborg 3; Atvidaberg 2; GAIS Gothenburg 1; IF Raa 1; Landskrona 1; Oster Vaxjo 1; Degerfors 1; Halmstad 1; Orgryte 1; Hacken 1; Ostersund 1.

Swedish Allsvenskan 2016

	P	W	D	L	F	A	GD	Pts
Malmo	30	20	4	6	57	26	31	64
AIK Solna	30	17	9	4	52	26	26	60
IFK Norrkoping	30	18	6	6	59	37	22	60
IFK Gothenburg	30	14	9	7	56	44	12	51
Elfsborg	30	13	9	8	58	38	20	48
Kalmar	30	12	8	10	45	40	5	44
Djurgarden	30	14	1	15	48	47	1	43
Ostersunds FK	30	12	6	12	44	46	–2	42
Örebro	30	11	8	11	48	51	–3	41
Hacken	30	11	7	12	58	45	13	40
Hammarby	30	10	9	11	46	49	–3	39
Jonkopings Sodra	30	8	11	11	32	39	–7	35
GIF Sundsvall	30	7	9	14	38	54	–16	30
Helsingborg*+	30	8	5	17	34	52	–18	29
Gefle*	30	6	9	15	34	56	–22	27
Falkenberg*	30	2	4	24	25	84	–59	10

Top scorer: Owoeri (Hacken) 17.
Cup Final: Ostersund 4, IFK Norrkoping 1.

SWITZERLAND

Schweizerisher Fussballverband, Worbstrasse 48, Postfach 3000, Bern 15.
Founded: 1895. *FIFA:* 1904; *UEFA:* 1954. *National Colours:* Red shirts, white shorts, red socks.

International matches 2016–17
Portugal (h) 2-0, Hungary (a) 3-2, Andorra (a) 2-1, Faroe Islands (h) 2-0, Latvia (h) 1-0, Belarus (h) 1-0, Faroe Islands (a) 2-0.

League Championship wins (1897–2017)
Grasshoppers 27; FC Basel 20; Servette 17; FC Zurich 12; Young Boys 11; Lausanne-Sport 7; Winterthur 3; Aarau 3; Lugano 3; La Chaux-de-Fonds 3; St Gallen 2; Neuchatel Xamax 2; Sion 2; Anglo-American Club 1; Brühl 1; Cantonal-Neuchatel 1; Etoile La Chaux-de-Fonds 1; Biel-Bienne 1; Bellinzona 1; Luzern 1.

Cup wins (1926–2016)
Grasshoppers 19; Sion 13; FC Basel 12; Lausanne-Sport 9; FC Zurich 9; Servette 7; Young Boys 6; La Chaux-de-Fonds 6; Lugano 3; Luzern 2; Urania Geneva 1; Young Fellows Zurich 1; FC Grenchen 1; St Gallen 1; Aarau 1; Wil 1.

Swiss Super League 2016–17

	P	W	D	L	F	A	GD	Pts
FC Basel	36	26	8	2	92	35	57	86
Young Boys	36	20	9	7	72	44	28	69
Lugano	36	15	8	13	52	61	–9	53
Sion	36	15	6	15	60	55	5	51
Luzern	36	14	8	14	62	66	–4	50
Thun	36	11	12	13	58	63	–5	45
St Gallen	36	11	8	17	43	57	–14	41
Grasshoppers	36	10	8	18	47	61	–14	38
Lausanne-Sport	36	9	8	19	51	62	–11	35
Vaduz*	36	7	9	20	45	78	–33	30

Top scorer: Doumbia (FC Basel) 20.
Cup Final: FC Basel 3, Sion 0.

TURKEY

Turkiye Futbol Federasyonu, Hasan Dogan Milli Takimlar, Kamp ve Egitim Tesisleri, Riva, Beykoz, Istanbul.
Founded: 1923. *FIFA:* 1923; *UEFA:* 1962. *National Colours:* All red.

International matches 2016–17
Russia (h) 0-0, Croatia (a) 1-1*, Ukraine (h) 2-2, Iceland (a) 0-2, Kosovo (h) 2-0, Finland (h) 2-0, Moldova (h) 3-1, FYR Macedonia (a) 0-0, Kosovo (a) 4-1.
* *Behind closed doors.*

League Championship wins (1959–2017)
Galatasaray 20; Fenerbahce 19; Besiktas 13; Trabzonspor 6; Bursaspor 1.

Cup wins (1963–2017)
Galatasaray 17; Besiktas 9; Trabzonspor 8; Fenerbahce 6; Altay Izmir 2; Goztepe Izmir 2; Ankaragucu 2; Genclerbirligi 2; Kocaelispor 2; Eskisehirspor 1; Bursaspor 1; Sakaryaspor 1; Kayseri 1; Konyaspor 1.

Turkish Super Lig 2016–17

	P	W	D	L	F	A	GD	Pts
Besiktas	33	22	8	3	69	30	39	74
Istanbul Basaksehir	33	20	10	3	62	28	34	70
Fenerbahce	33	17	10	6	57	31	26	61
Galatasaray	33	19	4	10	63	39	24	61
Antalyaspor	33	16	7	10	43	39	4	55
Trabzonspor	33	14	9	10	38	32	6	51
Akhisar Belediyespor	33	14	6	13	44	39	5	48
Genclerbirligi	33	11	10	12	32	34	–2	43
Kasimpasa	33	12	7	14	46	49	–3	43
Konyaspor	33	11	10	12	39	43	–4	43
Alanyaspor	33	12	4	17	54	64	–10	40
Karabukspor	33	11	7	15	35	46	–11	40
Osmanlispor	33	9	11	13	37	41	–4	38
Kayserispor	33	10	8	15	47	57	–10	38
Bursaspor	33	10	5	18	32	57	–25	35
Rizespor*	33	9	6	18	43	53	–10	33
Gaziantepspor*	33	7	5	21	29	61	–32	26
Adanaspor*	33	6	7	20	32	59	–27	25

Top scorer: Vagner Love (Alanyaspor) 23.
Cup Final: Konyaspor 0, Istanbul Basaksehir 0.
aet; Konyaspor won 4-1 on penalties.

UKRAINE

Football Federation of Ukraine, Provulok Laboratornyi 7-A, PO Box 55, 01133 Kyiv.
Founded: 1991. *FIFA:* 1992; *UEFA:* 1992. *National Colours:* All yellow with blue trim.

International matches 2016–17
Iceland (h) 1-1, Turkey (a) 2-2, Kosovo (n) 3-0, Finland (h) 1-0, Serbia (h) 2-0, Croatia (a) 0-1, Malta (n) 0-1, Finland (a) 2-1.

League Championship wins (1992–2017)
Dynamo Kyiv 15; Shakhtar Donetsk 10; Tavriya Simferopol 1.

Cup wins (1992–2017)
Dynamo Kyiv 11; Shakhtar Donetsk 11; Chornomorets Odessa 2; Vorskla Poltava 1; Tavriya Simferopol 1.

Ukrainian Premier League 2016–17

	P	*W*	*D*	*L*	*F*	*A*	*GD*	*Pts*
Shakhtar Donetsk	22	19	3	0	47	14	33	60
Dynamo Kyiv	22	14	4	4	43	23	20	46
Zorya Luhansk	22	12	4	6	34	21	13	40
Olimpik Donetsk	22	9	7	6	28	30	–2	34
Oleksandria	22	9	6	7	37	28	9	33
Chornomorets Odessa	22	7	6	9	17	23	–6	27
Vorskla Poltava	22	6	6	10	24	28	–4	24
Stal Kamianske	22	6	6	10	20	25	–5	24
Zirka	22	6	5	11	20	33	–13	23
Karpaty Lviv (–6)	22	4	7	11	21	30	–9	13
Dnipro Dnipropetrovsk (–12)	22	4	10	8	21	30	–9	10
Volyn Lutsk	22	2	4	16	13	40	–27	10

Championship Round 2016–17

	P	*W*	*D*	*L*	*F*	*A*	*GD*	*Pts*
Shakhtar Donetsk	32	25	5	2	66	24	42	80
Dynamo Kyiv	32	21	4	7	69	33	36	67
Zorya Luhansk	32	16	6	10	45	31	14	54
Olimpik Donetsk	32	11	11	10	33	44	–11	44
Oleksandria	32	10	10	12	41	43	–2	40
Chornomorets Odessa	32	10	8	14	25	37	–12	38

Relegation Round 2016–17

	P	*W*	*D*	*L*	*F*	*A*	*GD*	*Pts*
Vorskla Poltava	32	11	9	12	32	32	0	42
Stal Kamianske	32	11	8	13	27	31	–4	41
Zirka	32	9	7	16	29	43	–14	34
Karpaty Lviv (–6)	32	9	9	14	35	41	–6	30
Dnipro Dnipropropetrovsk* (–15)	31	8	13	10	31	37	–6	22
Volyn Lutsk* (–6)	31	3	4	24	14	51	–37	7

Top scorer: Yarmolenko (Dynamo Kyiv) 15.
Cup Final: Shakhtar Donetsk 1, Dynamo Kyiv 0.

WALES

Football Association of Wales, 11/12 Neptune Court, Vanguard Way, Cardiff CF24 5PJ.
Founded: 1876. *FIFA:* 1910; *UEFA:* 1954. *National Colours:* All red with green trim.

SOUTH AMERICA (CONMEBOL)

ARGENTINA

Asociacion del Futbol Argentina, Viamonte 1366/76, Buenos Aires 1053.
Founded: 1893. *FIFA:* 1912; *CONMEBOL:* 1916.
National Colours: Light blue and white vertical striped shirts, white shorts, white socks.
International matches 2016–17
Uruguay (h) 1-0, Venezuela (a) 2-2, Peru (a) 2-2, Paraguay (h) 0-1, Brazil (a) 0-3, Colombia (h) 3-0, Chile (h) 1-0, Bolivia (a) 0-2, Brazil (n) 1-0, Singapore (a) 6-0.
League champions 2016–17: Boca Juniors. *Cup winners 2016:* River Plate.

BOLIVIA

Federacion Boliviana de Futbol, Avenida Libertador Bolivar 1168, Casilla 484, Cochabamba.
Founded: 1925. *FIFA:* 1926; *CONMEBOL:* 1926.
National Colours: Green shirts, white shorts, white socks.
International matches 2016–17
Peru (h) 0-3*, Chile (a) 0-3*, Brazil (a) 0-5, Ecuador (h) 2-2, Venezuela (a) 0-5, Paraguay (h) 1-0, Colombia (a) 0-1, Argentina (h) 2-0, Nicaragua (a) 1-0, Nicaragua (h) 3-2.
* *Match awarded 3-0 due to breach of FIFA rule.*
League champions 2016–17: The Strongest (Apertura 2016); Bolivar (Apertura 2017). *Cup winners:* No competition.

BRAZIL

Confederacao Brasileira de Futebol, Avenida Luis Carlos Prestes 130, Barra da Tijuca, Rio de Janeiro 22775-055.
Founded: 1914. *FIFA:* 1923; *CONMEBOL:* 1916.
National Colours: Yellow shirts with green collar and cuffs, blue shorts, white socks.
International matches 2016–17
Ecuador (a) 3-0, Colombia (h) 2-1, Bolivia (h) 5-0, Venezuela (a) 2-0, Argentina (h) 3-0, Peru (a) 2-0, Colombia (h) 1-0, Uruguay (a) 4-1, Paraguay (h) 3-0, Argentina (n) 0-1, Australia (a) 4-0.
League champions 2016: Palmeiras. *Cup winners 2016:* Gremio.

CHILE

Federacion de Futbol de Chile, Avenida Quilin 5635, Comuna Penalolen, Casilla 3733, Santiago de Chile.
Founded: 1895. *FIFA:* 1913; *CONMEBOL:* 1916.
National Colours: Red shirts with blue collars, blue shorts, white socks.
International matches 2016–17
Paraguay (a) 1-2, Bolivia (h) 3-0*, Ecuador (a) 0-3, Peru (h) 2-1, Colombia (a) 0-0, Uruguay (h) 3-1, Croatia (n) 1-1 (4-1p), Iceland (n) 1-0, Argentina (a) 0-1, Venezuela (h) 3-1, Burkina Faso (h) 3-0, Russia (a) 1-1, Romania (a) 2-3, Cameroon (n) 2-0, Germany (n) 1-1, Australia (a) 1-1, Portugal (n) 0-0 (3-0p), Germany (n) 0-1.
* *Match awarded 3-0 due to breach of FIFA rule.*
League champions 2016–17: Universidad Catolica (Apertura); Universidad de Chile (Clausura). *Cup winners 2016:* Colo-Colo.

COLOMBIA

Federacion Colombiana de Futbol, Avenida 32 No. 16–22, Bogota.
Founded: 1924. *FIFA:* 1936; *CONMEBOL:* 1936.
National Colours: Yellow shirts with blue trim, white shorts, white socks.
International matches 2016–17
Venezuela (h) 2-0, Brazil (a) 1-2, Paraguay (a) 1-0, Uruguay (h) 2-2, Chile (h) 0-0, Argentina (a) 0-3, Brazil (a) 0-1, Bolivia (h) 1-0, Ecuador (a) 2-0, Spain (a) 2-2, Cameroon (n) 4-0.
League champions 2016: Medellin (Apertura); Santa Fe (Finalizacion). *Cup winners 2016:* Atletico Nacional.

ECUADOR

Federacion Ecuatoriana del Futbol, Avenida Las Aguas y Calle Alianza, PO Box 09-01-7447, Guayaquil 593.
Founded: 1925. *FIFA:* 1927; *CONMEBOL:* 1927.
National Colours: Yellow shirts, blue shorts, red socks.
International matches 2016–17
Brazil (h) 0-3, Peru (a) 1-2, Chile (h) 3-0, Bolivia (a) 2-2, Uruguay (a) 1-2, Venezuela (h) 3-0, Honduras (h) 3-1, Paraguay (a) 1-2, Colombia (h) 0-2, Venezuela (n) 1-1, El Salvador (n) 3-0.
League champions 2015: Barcelona. *Cup winners:* No competition.

PARAGUAY

Asociacion Paraguaya de Futbol, Calle Mayor Martinez 1393, Asuncion.
Founded: 1906. *FIFA:* 1925; *CONMEBOL:* 1921.
National Colours: Red and white striped shirts, blue shorts, blue socks.
International matches 2016–17
Chile (h) 2-1, Uruguay (a) 0-4, Colombia (h) 0-1, Argentina (a) 1-0, Peru (h) 1-4, Bolivia (a) 0-1, Ecuador (h) 2-1, Brazil (a) 0-3, France (a) 0-5, Peru (a) 0-1, Mexico (n) 1-2.
League champions 2016: Libertad (Apertura); Guarani (Clausura). *Cup winners:* No competition.

PERU

Federacion Peruana de Futbol, Avenida Aviacion 2085, San Luis, Lima 30.
Founded: 1922. *FIFA:* 1924; *CONMEBOL:* 1925.
National Colours: White shirts with red sash, white shorts, white socks.
International matches 2016–17
Bolivia (a) 3-0*, Ecuador (h) 2-1, Argentina (h) 2-2, Chile (a) 1-2, Paraguay (a) 4-1, Brazil (h) 0-2, Venezuela (a) 2-2, Uruguay (h) 2-1, Paraguay (h) 1-0, Jamaica (h) 3-1.
* *Match awarded 3-0 due to breach of FIFA rule.*
League champions 2016: Sporting Cristal. *Cup winners 2016:* Sport Rosario.

URUGUAY

Asociacion Uruguaya de Futbol, Guayabo 1531, Montevideo 11200.
Founded: 1900. *FIFA:* 1923; *CONMEBOL:* 1916. *National Colours:* Sky blue shirts, black shorts, black socks with sky blue tops.
International matches 2016–17
Argentina (a) 0-1, Paraguay (h) 4-0, Venezuela (h) 3-0, Colombia (a) 2-2, Ecuador (h) 2-1, Chile (a) 1-3, Brazil (a) 1-4, Peru (h) 1-2, Republic of Ireland (a) 1-3, Italia (h) 0-3.
League champions 2016: Nacional. *Cup winners:* No competition.

VENEZUELA

Federacion Venezolana de Futbol, Avenida Santos Erminy 1ra Calle las Delicias, Torre Mega II, P.H.B. Sabana Grande, 1050 Caracas.
Founded: 1926. *FIFA:* 1952; *CONMEBOL:* 1952. *National Colours:* All burgundy.
International matches 2016–17
Colombia (a) 0-2, Argentina (h) 2-2, Uruguay (a) 0-3, Brazil (h) 0-2, Bolivia (h) 5-0, Ecuador (a) 0-3, Peru (h) 2-2, Chile (a) 1-3, USA (a) 1-1, Ecuador (n) 1-1.
League champions 2016: Zamora. *Cup winners 2016:* Zulia.

ASIA (AFC)

AFGHANISTAN

Afghanistan Football Federation, PO Box 128, Kabul.
Founded: 1933. *FIFA:* 1948; *AFC:* 1954. *National Colours:* All red.
International matches 2016–17
Lebanon (a) 0-2, Malaysia (a) 1-1, Tajikistan (a) 0-1, Singapore (n) 2-1, Vietnam (n) 1-1, Maldives (n) 2-1, Cambodia (a) 0-1.
League champions 2016: Shaheen Asmayee. Cup winners: No competition.

AUSTRALIA

Football Federation Australia Ltd, Locked Bag A4071, Sydney South, NSW 1235.
Founded: 1961. *FIFA:* 1963; *AFC:* 2006. *National Colours:* Gold shirts, green shorts, white socks.
International matches 2016–17
Iraq (h) 2-0, UAE (a) 1-0, Saudi Arabia (a) 2-2, Japan (h) 1-1, Thailand (a) 2-2, Iraq (n) 1-1, UAE (h) 0-2, Saudi Arabia (h) 3-2, Brazil (h) 0-4, Germany (n) 2-3, Cameroon (n) 1-1, Chile (n) 1-1.
League champions 2016–17: Sydney. *Cup winners 2016:* Melbourne City.

BAHRAIN

Bahrain Football Association, PO Box 5464, Building 315, Road 2407, Block 934, East Riffa.
Founded: 1957. *FIFA:* 1968; *AFC:* 1969. *National Colours:* All red.
International matches 2016–17
Singapore (h) 3-1, Jordan (h) 0-0, Philippines (a) 3-1, Oman (a) 2-2, UAE (a) 0-2, Kyrgyzstan (h) 0-0, Tajikistan (h) 1-1, Singapore (h) 0-0, Palestine (h) 0-2, Turkmenistan (a) 2-1.
League champions 2016–17: Malkiya. *Cup winners 2016:* Muharraq.

BANGLADESH

Bangladesh Football Federation, BFF House, Motijheel Commercial Area, Dhaka 1000.
Founded: 1972. *FIFA:* 1976; *AFC:* 1974. *National Colours:* Green shirts, white shorts, green socks.
International matches 2016–17
Maldives (a) 0-5, Bhutan (h) 0-0, Bhutan (a) 1-3.
League champions 2016–17: Dhaka Abahani. *Cup winners 2017:* Dhaka Abahani.

BHUTAN

Bhutan Football Federation, PO Box 365, Changiiji, Thimphu 11001.
Founded: 1983. *FIFA:* 2000; *AFC:* 2000. *National Colours:* Yellow and orange shirts, white shorts, orange socks.
International matches 2016–17
India (h) 0-3, Bangladesh (a) 0-0, Bangladesh (h) 3-1, Bhutan (a) 0-14, Bhutan (h) 0-2.
League champions 2016: Thimphu City. *Cup winners:* No competition.

BRUNEI

National Football Association of Brunei Darussalam, NFABD House, Jalan Pusat Persidangan, Bandar Seri Begawan BB4313.
Founded: 1959. *FIFA:* 1972; *AFC:* 1969. *National Colours:* Yellow and black shirts, white shorts, yellow socks.
International matches 2016–17
Timor-Leste (n) 2-1, Cambodia (a) 0-3*, Laos (n) 3-4, Timor-Leste (n) 4-0, Nepal (n) 0-3, Macau (n) 1-1 (3-4p), Laos (n) 2-3.
League champions 2016: MS ABDB. *Cup winners 2016:* MS ABDB.

CAMBODIA

Football Federation of Cambodia, National Football Centre, Road Kabsrov Sangkat Samrongkrom, Khan Dangkor, Phnom Penh 2327 PPT3.
Founded: 1933. *FIFA:* 1954; *AFC:* 1954. *National Colours:* Red and blue shirts, blue shorts, red socks.
International matches 2016–17
Singapore (h) 2-1, Hong Kong (a) 2-4, Hong Kong (h) 0-2, Sri Lanka (h) 4-0, Laos (h) 2-1, Brunei (h) 3-0*, Timor-Leste (h) 3-2, Singapore (a) 0-1, Malaysia (n) 2-3, Myanmar (a) 1-3, Vietnam (n) 1-2, Saudi Arabia (n) 2-7, India (h) 2-3, Jordan (a) 0-7, Indonesia (h) 0-2, Afghanistan (h) 1-0.
League champions 2016: Boeung Ket. *Cup winners 2016:* National Defense.

CHINA PR

Football Association of the People's Republic of China, Building A, Dongjiudasha Mansion, Xizhaosi Street, Dongcheng, Beijing 100061.
Founded: 1924. *FIFA:* 1931, rejoined 1980; *AFC:* 1974. *National Colours:* All red.
International matches 2016–17
Korea Republic (a) 2-3, Iran (h) 0-0, Syria (h) 0-1, Uzbekistan (a) 0-2, Qatar (h) 0-0, Iceland (h) 0-2, Croatia (h) 1-1 (4-3p), Korea Republic (h) 1-0, Iran (a) 0-1, Philippines (h) 8-1, Syria (n) 2-2.
League champions 2016: Guangzhou Evergrande. *Cup winners 2016:* Guangzhou Evergrande.

CHINESE TAIPEI

Chinese Taipei Football Association, Room 210, 2F, 55 Chang Chi Street, Tatung, Taipei 10363.
Founded: 1936. *FIFA:* 1954; *AFC:* 1954. *National Colours:* All blue with white trim.
International matches 2016–17
Timor-Leste (a) 2-1*, Timor-Leste (h) 2-1, Korea DPR (n) 0-2, Hong Kong (a) 2-4, Guam (n) 2-0, Vietnam (a) 1-1, Turkmenistan (h) 1-3, Singapore (a) 2-1.
** Match played in Chinese Taipei.*
League champions 2015–16: Taipower. *Cup winners:* No competition.

GUAM

Guam Football Association, PO Box 20008, Barrigada, Guam 96921.
Founded: 1975. *FIFA:* 1996; *AFC:* 1996. *National Colours:* Blue shirts with white sleeves, blue shorts, blue socks.
International matches 2016–17
Hong Kong (a) 2-3, Korea DPR (n) 0-2, Chinese Taipei (n) 0-2.
League champions 2016–17: Rovers. *Cup winners 2017:* Guam Shipyard.

HONG KONG

Hong Kong Football Association Ltd, 55 Fat Kwong Street, Ho Man Tin, Kowloon, Hong Kong.
Founded: 1914. *FIFA:* 1954; *AFC:* 1954. *National Colours:* All red with white trim.
International matches 2016–17
Cambodia (h) 4-2, Cambodia (a) 2-0, Singapore (h) 2-0, Guam (h) 3-2, Chinese Taipei (h) 4-2, Korea DPR (h) 0-1, Jordan (a) 0-4, Lebanon (a) 0-2, Jordan (h) 0-0, Korea DPR (h) 1-1.
League champions 2016–17: Kitchee. *Cup winners 2016–17:* Kitchee.

INDIA

All India Football Federation, Football House, Sector 19, Phase 1 Dwarka, New Delhi 110075.
Founded: 1937. *FIFA:* 1948; *AFC:* 1954. *National Colours:* Sky blue and navy shirts, navy shorts, sky blue and navy socks.
International matches 2016–17
Bhutan (a) 3-0, Puerto Rico (h) 4-1, Cambodia (a) 3-2, Myanmar (a) 1-0, Nepal (h) 2-0, Kyrgyzstan (h) 1-0.
League champions 2017: Aizawl. *Cup winners 2017:* Bengaluru.

INDONESIA

Football Association of Indonesia, Gelora Bung Karno Pintu X–XI, PO Box
2305, Senayan, Jakarta 10023.
Founded: 1930. *FIFA:* 1952; *AFC:* 1954. *National Colours:* Red shirts with green trim, red shorts, red socks.
International matches 2016–17
Malaysia (h) 3-0, Vietnam (h) 2-2, Myanmar (a) 0-0, Vietnam (a) 2-3, Thailand (n) 2-4, Philippines (a) 2-2, Singapore (n) 2-1, Vietnam (h) 2-1, Vietnam (a) 2-2, Thailand (h) 2-1, Thailand (a) 0-2, Myanmar (h) 1-3, Cambodia (a) 0-2, Puerto Rico (h) 0-0.
League champions 2017: No competition since 2014. *Cup winners:* No competition since 2012.

IRAN

Football Federation IR Iran, No. 4 Third St., Seoul Avenue, Tehran 19958-73591.
Founded: 1920. *FIFA:* 1948; *AFC:* 1954. *National Colours:* All white.
International matches 2016–17
Qatar (h) 2-0, China PR (a) 0-0, Uzbekistan (a) 1-0, Korea Republic (h) 1-0, Papua New Guinea (n) 8-1, Syria (n) 0-0, Iraq (h) 0-1, Qatar (a) 1-0, China PR (h) 1-0, Montenegro (a) 2-1, Uzbekistan (h) 2-0.
League champions 2016–17: Persepolis. *Cup winners 2016–17:* Naft Tehran.

IRAQ

Iraq Football Association, Al-Shaab Stadium, PO Box 484, Baghdad.
Founded: 1948. *FIFA:* 1950; *AFC:* 1970. *National Colours:* All white.
International matches 2016–17
Uzbekistan (a) 1-2, Qatar (a) 1-2, Korea DPR (n) 1-1, Australia (a) 0-2, Saudi Arabia (n) 1-2, Japan (a) 1-2, Thailand (n) 4-0, Jordan (a) 0-0, UAE (a) 0-2, Iran (a) 1-0, Australia (n) 1-1, Saudi Arabia (a) 0-1, Jordan (h) 1-0, Korea Republic (n) 0-0, Japan (n) 1-1.
League champions 2015–16: Al-Zawra'a. *Cup winners 2015–16:* Al-Quwa Al-Juwiya.

JAPAN

Japan Football Association, JFA House, Football Ave., Bunkyo-ku, Tokyo 113-8311.
Founded: 1921. *FIFA:* 1929, rejoined 1950; *AFC:* 1954. *National Colours:* Blue shirts, white shorts, blue socks.
International matches 2016–17
UAE (h) 1-2, Thailand (a) 2-0, Iraq (h) 2-1, Australia (a) 1-1, Oman (h) 4-0, Saudi Arabia (h) 2-1, UAE (a) 2-0, Thailand (h) 4-0, Syria (h) 1-1, Iraq (n) 1-1.
League champions 2016: Kashima Antlers. *Cup winners 2016:* Kashima Antlers.

JORDAN

Jordan Football Association, PO Box 962024, Al-Hussein Youth City, Amman 11196.
Founded: 1949. *FIFA:* 1956; *AFC:* 1970. *National Colours:* All white with red trim.
International matches 2016–17
Qatar (n) 2-3, Lebanon (a) 1-1, Bahrain (a) 0-0, Oman (a) 1-1, Iraq (h) 0-0, Uzbekistan (a) 0-1, Lebanon (h) 0-0, Georgia (n) 1-0, Hong Kong (h) 4-0, Cambodia (h) 7-0, Iraq (a) 0-1, Hong Kong (a) 0-0, Vietnam (a) 0-0.
League champions 2016–17: Al-Faisaly. *Cup winners 2016–17:* Al-Faisaly.

KOREA DPR

DPR Korea Football Association, Kumsongdong, Kwangbok Street, Mangyongdae, PO Box 818, Pyongyang.
Founded: 1945. *FIFA:* 1958; *AFC:* 1974. *National Colours:* All red.
International matches 2016–17
Iraq (n) 1-1, UAE (n) 2-0, Vietnam (a) 2-5, Philippines (a) 3-1, Chinese Taipei (n) 2-0, Guam (n) 2-0, Hong Kong (a) 1-0, Qatar (n) 2-2, Hong Kong (a) 1-1.
No elite club competitions.

KOREA REPUBLIC

Korea Football Association, KFA House 21, Gyeonghuigung-gil 46, Jongno-Gu, Seoul 110-062.
Founded: 1933, 1948. *FIFA:* 1948; *AFC:* 1954. *National Colours:* Red shirts, blue shorts, red socks.
International matches 2016–17
China PR (h) 3-2, Syria (n) 0-0, Qatar (h) 3-2, Iran (a) 0-1, Canada (h) 2-0, Uzbekistan (h) 2-1, China PR (a) 0-1, Syria (h) 1-0, Iraq (n) 0-0, Qatar (a) 2-3.
League champions 2016: FC Seoul. *Cup winners 2016:* Suwon Bluewings.

KUWAIT

Kuwait Football Association, Block 5, Street 101, Building 141A, Jabriya, PO Box Hawalli 4020, Kuwait 32071.
Founded: 1952. *FIFA:* 1964; *AFC:* 1964. *National Colours:* All blue with white trim.
International matches 2016–17
None played.
League champions 2016–17: Al-Kuwait. *Cup winners 2016–17:* Al-Kuwait.

KYRGYZSTAN

Football Federation of Kyrgyz Republic, Mederova Street 1 'B', PO Box 1484, Bishkek 720082.
Founded: 1992. *FIFA:* 1994; *AFC:* 1994. *National Colours:* Red shirts, red shorts, red socks with yellow tops.
International matches 2016–17
Kazakhstan (h) 2-0, Philippines (h) 1-2, Lebanon (h) 0-0, Turkmenistan (h) 1-0, Philippines (a) 0-1, Bahrain (a) 0-0, Macau (h) 1-0, India (a) 0-1.
League champions 2016: Alay Osh. *Cup winners 2016:* Dordoi Bishkek.

LAOS

Lao Football Federation, FIFA Training Centre, Ban Houayhong, Chanthabuly, PO Box 1800, Vientiane 856-21.
Founded: 1951. *FIFA:* 1952; *AFC:* 1968. *National Colours:* All red with white trim.
International matches 2016–17
Saudi Arabia (n) 0-4, Maldives (a) 0-4, Maldives (h) 1-1, Cambodia (a) 1-2, Timor-Leste (n) 2-1, Brunei (n) 4-3, Sri Lanka (n) 2-1, Macau (n) 1-4, Mongolia (n) 3-0, Nepal (n) 2-2 (3-0p), Brunei (n) 3-2, UAE (n) 0-4.
League champions 2016: Lanexang United. *Cup winners:* No competition.

LEBANON

Association Libanaise de Football, Verdun Street, Bristol Radwan Centre, PO Box 4732, Beirut.
Founded: 1933. *FIFA:* 1936; *AFC:* 1964. *National Colours:* All red.
International matches 2016–17
Jordan (h) 1-1, Afghanistan (h) 2-0, Kyrgyzstan (a) 0-0, Equatorial Guinea (h) 1-1, Palestine (h) 1-1, Jordan (a) 0-0, Hong Kong (h) 2-0, Malaysia (a) 2-1.
League champions 2016–17: Al-Ahed. *Cup winners 2017:* Al-Ansar.

MACAU

Associacao de Futebol de Macau, Avenida Wai Leong, Taipa University of Science and Technology, Football Field Block 1, Taipa.
Founded: 1939. *FIFA:* 1978; *AFC:* 1978. *National Colours:* White shirts, black shorts, green socks.
International matches 2016–17
Mongolia (n) 2-1, Laos (n) 4-1, Sri Lanka (n) 1-1, Brunei (n) 1-1 (4-3p), Nepal (n) 0-1, Kyrgyzstan (a) 0-1, Myanmar (h) 0-4.
League champions 2017: Benfica de Macau. *Cup winners 2016:* Tak Chun Ka I.

MALAYSIA

Football Association of Malaysia, 3rd Floor, Wisma FAM, Jalan SS5A/9, Kelana Jaya, Petaling Jaya 47301, Selangor Darul Ehsan.
Founded: 1933. *FIFA:* 1954; *AFC:* 1954. *National Colours:* Yellow and black shirts, black shorts, black socks.

International matches 2016–17
Indonesia (h) 0-3, Singapore (a) 0-0, Afghanistan (h) 1-1, Papua New Guinea (h) 2-1, Cambodia (n) 3-2, Vietnam (n) 0-1, Myanmar (a) 0-1, Philippines (a) 0-0, Lebanon (h) 1-2.
League champions 2016: Johor Darul Ta'zim. *Cup winners 2017:* Kedah.

MALDIVES

Football Association of Maldives, FAM House, Ujaalahingun, Male 20388.
Founded: 1982. *FIFA:* 1986; *AFC:* 1984. *National Colours:* Red and white shirts, white shorts, red socks.
International matches 2016–17
Bangladesh (h) 5-0, Laos (h) 4-0, Laos (a) 1-1, Palestine (h) 0-3, Afghanistan (n) 1-2, Bhutan (a) 2-0.
League champions 2016: Maziya. *Cup winners:* No competition.

MONGOLIA

Mongolian Football Federation, PO Box 259, 15th Khoroo, Khan-Uul, Ulan Bator 210646.
Founded: 1959. *FIFA:* 1998; *AFC:* 1998. *National Colours:* Red shirts, blue shorts, red socks.
International matches 2016–17
Macau (n) 1-2, Sri Lanka (n) 2-0, Laos (n) 0-3.
League champions 2016: Erchim. *Cup winners:* No competition.

MYANMAR

Myanmar Football Federation, National Football Training Centre, Waizayanta Road, Thuwunna, Thingankyun Township, Yangon 11070.
Founded: 1947. *FIFA:* 1948; *AFC:* 1954. *National Colours:* All red.
International matches 2016–17
Indonesia (h) 0-0, Oman (h) 0-3, Vietnam (h) 1-2, Cambodia (h) 3-1, Malaysia (h) 1-0, Thailand (h) 0-2, Thailand (a) 0-4, Indonesia (a) 3-1, India (h) 0-1, Singapore (a) 1-1, Macau (a) 4-0.
League champions 2016: Yadanarbon. *Cup winners 2016:* Magwe.

NEPAL

All Nepal Football Association, ANFA House, Satdobato, Lalitpur-17, PO Box 12582, Kathmandu.
Founded: 1951. *FIFA:* 1972; *AFC:* 1954. *National Colours:* All red with white trim.
International matches 2016–17
Timor-Leste (n) 0-0, Brunei (n) 3-0, Laos (n) 2-2 (3-0p), Macau (n) 1-0, Philippines (a) 1-4, India (a) 0-2, Yemen (h) 0-0.
League champions 2015: Three Star Club. *Cup winners 2016:* Manang Marshyangdi Club.

OMAN

Oman Football Association, Seeb Sports Stadium, PO Box 3462, 112 Ruwi, Muscat.
Founded: 1978. *FIFA:* 1980; *AFC:* 1980. *National Colours:* All red.
International matches 2016–17
Turkmenistan (h) 1-0, Republic of Ireland (a) 0-4, Jordan (h) 1-1, Bahrain (h) 2-2, Japan (a) 0-4, Myanmar (a) 3-0, Bhutan (h) 14-0, Syria (h) 1-1, Palestine (a) 1-2.
League champions 2016–17: Dhofar. *Cup winners 2016–17:* Al-Suwaiq.

PAKISTAN

Pakistan Football Federation, PFF Football House, Ferozepur Road, Lahore 54600, Punjab.
Founded: 1947. *FIFA:* 1948; *AFC:* 1954. *National Colours:* All green and white.
International matches 2016–17
None played.
League champions 2014–15: K-Electric (league currently suspended). *Cup winners 2016:* KRL.

PALESTINE

Palestinian Football Association, Nr. Faisal Al-Husseini Stadium, PO Box 4373, Jerusalem-al-Ram.
Founded: 1928. *FIFA:* 1998; *AFC:* 1998. *National Colours:* All red with white trim.
International matches 2016–17
Tajikistan (h) 1-1, Tajikistan (a) 3-3, Lebanon (a) 1-1, Yemen (n) 1-0, Maldives (a) 3-0, Bahrain (a) 2-0, Oman (h) 2-1.
League champions 2016–17: Hilal Al-Quds. *Cup winners 2016–17:* Ahli Al-Khalil.

PHILIPPINES

Philippine Football Federation, 27 Danny Floro–corner Capt. Henry Javier Streets, Oranbo, Pasig City 1600.
Founded: 1907. *FIFA:* 1930; *AFC:* 1954. *National Colours:* All blue with white trim.
International matches 2016–17
Kyrgyzstan (a) 2-1, Bahrain (h) 1-3, Korea DPR (h) 1-3, Kyrgyzstan (h) 1-0, Singapore (h) 0-0, Indonesia (h) 2-2, Thailand (h) 0-1, Malaysia (h) 0-0, Nepal (h) 4-1, China PR (a) 1-8, Tajikistan (a) 4-3.
League champions 2016: Global. *Cup winners 2016:* Global.

QATAR

Qatar Football Association, 28th Floor, Al Bidda Tower, Corniche Street, West Bay, PO Box 5333, Doha.
Founded: 1960. *FIFA:* 1972; *AFC:* 1974. *National Colours:* All burgundy.
International matches 2016–17
Iraq (h) 2-1, Jordan (n) 3-2, Thailand (h) 3-0, Iran (a) 0-2, Uzbekistan (h) 0-1, Korea Republic (a) 2-3, Syria (h) 1-0, Russia (h) 2-1, China PR (a) 0-0, Moldova (h) 1-1, Azerbaijan (h) 1-2, Iran (h) 0-1, Uzbekistan (a) 0-1, Korea DPR (h) 2-2, Korea Republic (h) 3-2.
League champions 2016–17: Lekhwiya. *Cup winners 2017:* Al-Sadd.

SAUDI ARABIA

Saudi Arabian Football Federation, Al Mather Quarter, Prince Faisal Bin Fahad Street, PO Box 5844, Riyadh 11432.
Founded: 1956. *FIFA:* 1956; *AFC:* 1972. *National Colours:* White shirts with green trim, white shorts, white socks.
International matches 2016–17
Laos (n) 4-0, Thailand (h) 1-0, Iraq (n) 2-1, Australia (h) 2-2, UAE (h) 3-0, Japan (a) 1-2, Slovenia (n) 0-0, Cambodia (n) 7-2, Thailand (h) 3-0, Iraq (n) 1-0, Australia (h) 2-3.
League champions 2016–17: Al-Hilal. *Cup winners 2017:* Al-Hilal.

SINGAPORE

Football Association of Singapore, Jalan Besar Stadium, 100 Tyrwhitt Road, Singapore 207542.
Founded: 1892. *FIFA:* 1956; *AFC:* 1954. *National Colours:* All red.
International matches 2016–17
Cambodia (a) 1-2, Bahrain (a) 1-3, Malaysia (h) 0-0, Hong Kong (a) 0-2, Syria (n) 0-2, Cambodia (h) 1-0, Philippines (a) 0-0, Thailand (n) 0-1, Indonesia (n) 1-2, Afghanistan (n) 1-2, Bahrain (a) 0-0, Myanmar (h) 1-1, Chinese Taipei (h) 1-2, Argentina (h) 0-6.
League champions 2016: Albirex Niigata Singapore. *Cup winners 2016:* Albirex Niigata Singapore.

SRI LANKA

Football Federation of Sri Lanka, 100/9 Independence Avenue, Colombo 07.
Founded: 1939. *FIFA:* 1952; *AFC:* 1954. *National Colours:* All red with white trim.
International matches 2016–17
Cambodia (a) 0-4, Laos (n) 1-2, Mongolia (n) 0-2, Macau (n) 1-1.
League champions 2016–17: Colombo. *Cup winners 2016–17:* Army.

SYRIA

Syrian Arab Federation for Football, Al Faihaa Sports Complex, PO Box 421, Damascus.
Founded: 1936. *FIFA:* 1937; *AFC:* 1970. *National Colours:* All red.
International matches 2016–17
Tajikistan (a) 0-0, Uzbekistan (a) 0-1, Korea Republic (n) 0-0, China PR (h) 1-0, Qatar (a) 0-1, Singapore (n) 2-0, Iran (n) 0-0, Uzbekistan (n) 1-0, Korea Republic (a) 0-1, Oman (a) 1-1, Japan (a) 1-1, China PR (n) 2-2.
League champions 2015–16: Al-Jaish. *Cup winners 2016:* Al-Wahda.

TAJIKISTAN

Tajikistan Football Federation, 14/3 Ayni Street, Dushanbe 734 025.
Founded: 1936. *FIFA:* 1994; *AFC:* 1994. *National Colours:* Red, white and green shirts, white and red shorts, red and green socks.

International matches 2016–17
Syria (h) 0-0, Palestine (a) 1-1, Palestine (h) 3-3, Turkmenistan (h) 3-0, Afghanistan (h) 1-0, Bahrain (a) 1-1, Yemen (n) 1-2, Philippines (h) 3-4.
League champions 2016: Istiklol. *Cup winners 2016:* Istiklol.

THAILAND

Football Association of Thailand, National Stadium, Gate 3, Rama 1 Road, Patumwan, Bangkok 10330.
Founded: 1916. *FIFA:* 1925; *AFC:* 1954. *National Colours:* All red.
International matches 2016–17
Qatar (a) 0-3, Saudi Arabia (a) 0-1, Japan (h) 0-2, UAE (a) 1-3, Iraq (n) 0-4, Australia (h) 2-2, Indonesia (n) 4-2, Singapore (n) 1-0, Philippines (a) 1-0, Myanmar (a) 2-0, Myanmar (h) 4-0, Indonesia (a) 1-2, Indonesia (h) 2-0, Saudi Arabia (h) 0-3, Japan (a) 0-4, Uzbekistan (a) 0-2, UAE (h) 1-1.
League champions 2016: Muangthong United. *Cup winners 2016:* Competition abandoned; title shared four ways.

TIMOR-LESTE

Federacao Futebol de Timor-Leste, Campo Democracia, Avenida Bairo Formosa, Dili.
Founded: 2002. *FIFA:* 2005; *AFC:* 2005. *National Colours:* Red shirts with black trim, red shorts, red socks.
International matches 2016–17
Chinese Taipei (h) 1-2,* Chinese Taipei (a) 1-2, Brunei (n) 1-2, Laos (n) 1-2, Cambodia (a) 2-3, Brunei (n) 0-4, Nepal (n) 0-0.
* *Match played in Chinese Taipei.*
League champions 2016: Sport Laulara e Benfica. *Cup winners 2016:* Ponta Leste.

TURKMENISTAN

Football Federation of Turkmenistan, Stadium Kopetdag, 245 A. Niyazov Street, Ashgabat 744 001.
Founded: 1992. *FIFA:* 1994; *AFC:* 1994. *National Colours:* All white.
International matches 2016–17
Oman (a) 0-1, Kyrgyzstan (a) 0-1, Tajikistan (a) 0-3, Chinese Taipei (a) 3-1, Bahrain (h) 1-2.
League champions 2016: Altyn Asyr. *Cup winners 2016:* Altyn Asyr.

UNITED ARAB EMIRATES

United Arab Emirates Football Association, Zayed Sports City, PO Box 916, Abu Dhabi.
Founded: 1971. *FIFA:* 1974; *AFC:* 1974. *National Colours:* All white with red trim.
International matches 2016–17
Korea DPR (n) 0-2, Japan (a) 2-1, Australia (h) 0-1, Thailand (h) 3-1, Saudi Arabia (a) 0-3, Bahrain (h) 2-0, Iraq (h) 2-0, Japan (h) 0-2, Australia (a) 0-2, Laos (n) 4-0,Thailand (h) 1-1.
League champions 2016–17: Al-Jazira. *Cup winners 2016–17:* Al-Wahda.

UZBEKISTAN

Uzbekistan Football Federation, Massiv Almazar Furkat Street 15/1, Tashkent 700 003.
Founded: 1946. *FIFA:* 1994; *AFC:* 1994. *National Colours:* All white with blue trim.
International matches 2016–17
Iraq (h) 2-1, Burkina Faso (h) 1-0, Syria (h) 1-0, Qatar (a) 1-0, Iran (h) 0-1, China PR (h) 2-0, Jordan (h) 1-0, Korea Republic (a) 1-2, Georgia (n) 2-2, Syria (n) 0-1, Qatar (n) 1-0, Thailand (h) 2-0, Iran (a) 0-2.
League champions 2016: Lokomotiv Tashkent. *Cup winners 2016:* Lokomotiv Tashkent.

VIETNAM

Vietnam Football Federation, Le Quang Dao Street, Phu Do Ward, Nam Tu Liem District, Hanoi 844.
Founded: 1960 (NV). *FIFA:* 1952 (SV), 1964 (NV); *AFC:* 1954 (SV), 1978 (SRV). *National Colours:* All red.
International matches 2016–17
Korea DPR (h) 5-2, Indonesia (a) 2-2, Indonesia (h) 3-2, Myanmar (a) 2-1, Malaysia (n) 1-0, Cambodia (n) 2-1, Indonesia (a) 1-2, Indonesia (h) 2-2, Chinese Taipei (h) 1-1, Afghanistan (n) 1-1, Jordan (h) 0-0.
League champions 2016: Ha Noi. *Cup winners 2016:* Than Quang Ninh.

YEMEN

Yemen Football Association, Quarter of Sport Al Jeraf (Ali Mohsen Al-Muraisi Stadium), PO Box 908, Al-Thawra City, Sana'a.
Founded: 1940 (SY), 1962 (NY). *FIFA:* 1967 (SY), 1980 (NY); *AFC:* 1972 (SY), 1980 (NY). *National Colours:* Red shirts, white shorts, black socks.
International matches 2016–17
Palestine (n) 0-1, Tajikistan (n) 2-1, Egypt (a) 0-1, Nepal (a) 0-0.
No club competitions since January 2015 due to civil war.

NORTH AND CENTRAL AMERICA AND CARIBBEAN (CONCACAF)

ANGUILLA

Anguilla Football Association, 2 Queen Elizabeth Avenue, PO Box 1318, The Valley, AI-2640.
Founded: 1990. *FIFA:* 1996; *CONCACAF:* 1996. *National Colours:* Turquoise and white shirts, orange and blue and shorts, turquoise and orange socks.
International matches 2016–17
None played.
League champions 2015–16: Salsa Ballers. *Cup winners:* No competition.

ANTIGUA & BARBUDA

Antigua & Barbuda Football Association, Ground Floor, Sydney Walling Stand, Antigua Recreation Ground, PO Box 773, St John's.
Founded: 1928. *FIFA:* 1970; *CONCACAF:* 1972. *National Colours:* Yellow shirts with black, red and blue stripe, yellow shorts, yellow socks.
International matches 2016–17
Curacao (a) 0-3, Puerto Rico (h) 2-0, Estonia (h) 0-1.
League champions 2016–17: Parham. *Cup winners:* No competition.

ARUBA

Arubaanse Voetbal Bond, Technical Centre Angel Botta, Shaba 24, PO Box 376, Noord.
Founded: 1932. *FIFA:* 1988; *CONCACAF:* 1986. *National Colours:* Yellow shirts with sky blue sleeves, yellow shorts, yellow socks.
International matches 2016–17
None played.
League champions 2016–17: Nacional. *Cup winners 2017:* Britannia.

BAHAMAS

Bahamas Football Association, Rosetta Street, PO Box N-8434, Nassau, NP.
Founded: 1967. *FIFA:* 1968; *CONCACAF:* 1981. *National Colours:* Yellow shirts, black shorts, yellow socks.
International matches 2016–17
None played.
League champions 2016–17: Western Warriors. *Cup winners 2016:* Western Warriors.

BARBADOS

Barbados Football Association, Bottom Floor, ABC Marble Complex, PO Box 1362, Fontabelle, St Michael.
Founded: 1910. *FIFA:* 1968; *CONCACAF:* 1967. *National Colours:* Gold shirts with royal blue sleeves, gold shorts, white socks with gold tops.
International matches 2016–17
Trinidad & Tobago (a) 0-2, St Kitts & Nevis (a) 1-2, French Guiana† (a) 0-3, Dominica (n) 1-2.
League champions 2017: Weymouth Wales. *Cup winners 2016:* Weymouth Wales.

BELIZE

Football Federation of Belize, 26 Hummingbird Highway, Belmopan, PO Box 1742, Belize City.
Founded: 1980. *FIFA:* 1986; *CONCACAF:* 1986. *National Colours:* Blue shirts with white trim, red shorts, blue socks with white tops.
International matches 2016–17
Honduras (h) 1-2, Honduras (a) 0-5, Panama (a) 0-0, Costa Rica (n) 0-3, El Salvador (n) 1-3, Nicaragua (n) 1-3, Honduras (h) 0-1.
League champions 2016–17: Belmopan Bandits (Opening); Belmopan Bandits (Closing). *Cup winners:* No competition.

BERMUDA

Bermuda Football Association, 48 Cedar Avenue, PO Box HM 745, Hamilton HM11.
Founded: 1928. *FIFA:* 1962; *CONCACAF:* 1967. *National Colours:* All red.
International matches 2016–17
Canada (h) 2-4, Grenada (a) 2-1.
League champions 2016–17: Robin Hood. *Cup winners 2016–17:* PHC Zebras.

BRITISH VIRGIN ISLANDS

British Virgin Islands Football Association, Botanic Station, PO Box 4269, Road Town, Tortola VG 1110.
Founded: 1974. *FIFA:* 1996; *CONCACAF:* 1996. *National Colours:* Green shirts with gold trim, gold shorts, green socks.
International matches 2016–17
None played.
League champions 2016–17: Islanders. *Cup winners:* No competition.

CANADA

Canadian Soccer Association, Place Soccer Canada, 237 Metcalfe Street, Ottawa, Ontario K2P 1R2.
Founded: 1912. *FIFA:* 1912; *CONCACAF:* 1961. *National Colours:* All red.
International matches 2016–17
Honduras (a) 1-2, El Salvador (h) 3-1, Mauritania (n) 4-0, Morocco (a) 0-4, Korea Republic (a) 0-2, Bermuda (a) 4-2, Scotland (a) 1-1, Curacao (h) 2-1.
No national professional league. Canadian teams compete in MLS and NASL. Cup winners 2017: Toronto.

CAYMAN ISLANDS

Cayman Islands Football Association, PO Box 178, Poindexter Road, Prospect, George Town, Grand Cayman KY1-1104.
Founded: 1966. *FIFA:* 1992; *CONCACAF:* 1990. *National Colours:* Red and white shirts, red shorts, red socks with white tops.
International matches 2016–17
None played.
League champions 2016–17: Bodden Town. *Cup winners 2016–17:* Bodden Town.

COSTA RICA

Federacion Costarricense de Futbol, 600 mts sur del Cruce de la Panasonic, San Rafael de Alajuela, Radial a Santa Ana, San Jose 670-1000.
Founded: 1921. *FIFA:* 1927; *CONCACAF:* 1961. *National Colours:* Red shirts, blue shorts, white socks.
International matches 2016–17
Haiti (a) 1-0, Panama (h) 3-1, Russia (a) 4-3, Trinidad & Tobago (a) 2-0, USA (h) 4-0, El Salvador (n) 0-0, Belize (n) 3-0, Nicaragua (n) 0-0, Honduras (n) 1-1, Panama (a) 0-1, Mexico (a) 0-2, Honduras (a) 1-1, Panama (h) 0-0, Trinidad & Tobago (h) 2-1.
League champions 2016–17: Deportivo Saprissa (Invierno); Herediano (Verano). *Cup winners:* No competition.

CUBA

Asociacion de Futbol de Cuba, Estadio Pedro Marrero Escuela Nacional de
Futbol – Mario Lopez, Avenida 41 no. 44 y 46, La Habana.
Founded: 1924. *FIFA:* 1932; *CONCACAF:* 1961. *National Colours:* All red.
International matches 2016–17
USA (h) 0-2.
League champions 2016: Villa Clara. *Cup winners:* No competition.

CURACAO

Curacao Football Federation, Bonamweg 49, PO Box 341, Willemstad.
Founded: 1921 (Netherlands Antilles), 2010. *FIFA:* 1932, 2010; *CONCACAF:* 1961, 2010. *National Colours:* All blue.
International matches 2016–17
Antigua & Barbuda (h) 3-0, Puerto Rico (a) 4-2, El Salvador (a) 1-1, Canada (a) 1-2, Nicaragua (h) 0-0, Martinique† (a) 2-1, Jamaica (n) 2-1.
League champions 2016: Centro Dominguito. *Cup winners:* No competition.

DOMINICA

Dominica Football Association, Patrick John Football House, Bath Estate, PO Box 1080, Roseau.
Founded: 1970. *FIFA:* 1994; *CONCACAF:* 1994. *National Colours:* Emerald green shirts with black sleeves, black shorts, emerald green socks.
International matches 2016–17
Grenada (a) 1-1, Barbados (n) 2-1.
League champions 2016–17: Dublanc. *Cup winners:* No competition.

DOMINICAN REPUBLIC

Federacion Dominicana de Futbol, Centro Olimpico Juan Pablo Duarte, Apartado Postal 1953, Santo Domingo.
Founded: 1953. *FIFA:* 1958; *CONCACAF:* 1964. *National Colours:* All navy blue.
International matches 2016–17
Bermuda (a) 1-0*, French Guiana† (h) 2-1*, Puerto Rico (h) 5-0, Puerto Rico (a) 1-0, Trinidad & Tobago (a) 0-4, Martinique† (h) 1-2.
** Played 05/07.06.2015, results omitted from last edition.*
League champions 2016: Club Barcelona Atletico. *Cup winners:* No competition.

EL SALVADOR

Federacion Salvadorena de Futbol, Avenida Jose Matias Delgado, Frente al Centro Espanol Colonia Escalon, Zona 10, San Salvador 1029.
Founded: 1935. *FIFA:* 1938; *CONCACAF:* 1961. *National Colours:* All blue.
International matches 2016–17
Mexico (h) 1-3, Canada (a) 1-3, Costa Rica (n) 0-0, Honduras (n) 1-2, Belize (n) 3-1, Panama (a) 0-1, Nicaragua (n) 1-0, Curacao (h) 1-1, Honduras (n) 2-2, Ecuador (n) 0-3.
League champions 2016–17: Santa Tecla (Apertura); Santa Tecla (Clausura). *Cup winners 2014–15:* Aguila.

GRENADA

Grenada Football Association, National Stadium, PO Box 326, St George's.
Founded: 1924. *FIFA:* 1978; *CONCACAF:* 1969. *National Colours:* Yellow shirts, yellow shorts, green socks.
International matches 2016–17
Trinidad & Tobago (h) 2-2, Bermuda (h) 1-2, Dominica (h) 1-1, St Lucia (h) 2-0.
League champions 2016: Paradise. *Cup winners:* No competition.

GUATEMALA

Federacion Nacional de Futbol de Guatemala, 2a Calle 15-57, Zona 15, Boulevard Vista Hermosa, Guatemala City 01015.
Founded: 1919. *FIFA:* 1946; *CONCACAF:* 1961. *National Colours:* Blue shirts with white sash, blue shorts, blue socks.
International matches 2016–17
Panama (a) 0-0, Trinidad & Tobago (a) 2-2, St Vincent/Grenadines (h) 9-3.
League champions 2016–17: Antigua GFC (Apertura); Municipal (Clausura). *Cup winners:* No competition.

GUYANA

Guyana Football Federation, Lot 17, Dadanawa Street Section 'K', Campbellville, PO Box 10727, Georgetown.
Founded: 1902. *FIFA:* 1970; *CONCACAF:* 1961. *National Colours:* Green shirts with white trim, green shorts, green socks.
International matches 2016–17
Suriname (a) 2-3, Jamaica (h) 2-4.
League champions 2016–17: Guyana Defence Force. *Cup winners:* No competition since 2015.

HAITI

Federation Haitienne de Football, Stade Sylvio Cator, Rue Oswald Durand, Port-au-Prince.
Founded: 1904. *FIFA:* 1933; *CONCACAF:* 1961. *National Colours:* Blue shirts, red shorts, blue socks.
International matches 2016–17
Costa Rica (h) 0-1, Jamaica (a) 2-0, French Guiana† (h) 2-5*, St Kitts & Nevis (a) 2-0, Suriname (n) 4-2, Trinidad & Tobago (a) 4-3, Nicaragua (h) 3-1, Nicaragua (a) 0-3.
League champions 2016: Racing (Ouverture); FICA (Cloture). *Cup winners:* No competition.

HONDURAS

Federacion Nacional Autonoma de Futbol de Honduras, Colonia Florencia Norte, Edificio Plaza America Ave. Roble, 1 y 2 Nivle, PO Box 827, Tegucigalpa 504.
Founded: 1935. *FIFA:* 1946; *CONCACAF:* 1961. *National Colours:* All white.
International matches 2016–17
Nicaragua (h) 1-0, Canada (h) 2-1, Mexico (a) 0-0, Belize (a) 2-1, Belize (h) 5-0, Panama (h) 0-1, Trinidad & Tobago (h) 3-1, Nicaragua (n) 2-1, El Salvador (n) 2-1, Panama (a) 1-0, Costa Rica (n) 1-1, Belize (n) 1-0, Jamaica (n) 0-1, Ecuador (a) 1-3, Nicaragua (h) 2-0, USA (a) 0-6, Costa Rica (h) 1-1, El Salvador (n) 2-2, Mexico (a) 0-3, Panama (a) 2-2.
League champions 2016–17: Motagua (Apertura); Motagua (Clausura). *Cup winners 2016–17:* Marathon.

JAMAICA

Jamaica Football Federation Ltd, 20 St Lucia Crescent, Kingston 5.
Founded: 1910. *FIFA:* 1962; *CONCACAF:* 1963. *National Colours:* Gold shirts, black shorts, gold socks with green tops.
International matches 2016–17
Panama (a) 0-2, Haiti (h) 0-2, Guyana (a) 4-2, Suriname (h) 1-0, USA (a) 0-1, Honduras (n) 1-0, Peru (a) 1-3, French Guiana† (n) 1-1, Curacao (n) 1-2.
League champions 2016–17: Arnett Gardens. *Cup winners:* No competition.

MEXICO

Federacion Mexicana de Futbol Asociacion, A.C., Colima No. 373, Colonia Roma, Delegacion Cuauhtemoc, Mexico DF 06700.
Founded: 1927. *FIFA:* 1929; *CONCACAF:* 1961. *National Colours:* All black with green trim.
International matches 2016–17
El Salvador (a) 3-1, Honduras (h) 0-0, New Zealand (n) 2-1, Panama (n) 1-0, USA (a) 2-1, Panama (a) 0-0, Iceland (n) 1-0, Costa Rica (h) 2-0, Trinidad & Tobago (a) 1-0, Croatia (n) 1-2, Republic of Ireland (n) 3-1, Honduras (h) 3-0, USA (h) 1-1 Portugal (n) 2-2, New Zealand (n) 2-1, Russia (a) 2-1, Ghana (n) 1-0, Germany (n) 1-4, Paraguay (n) 2-1, Portugal (n) 1-2.
League champions 2016–17: Tigres UANL (Apertura); Guadalajara (Clausura). *Cup winners 2016–17:* Queretaro (Apertura); Guadalajara (Clausura).

MONTSERRAT

Montserrat Football Association Inc., PO Box 505, Blakes, Montserrat.
Founded: 1994. *FIFA:* 1996; *CONCACAF:* 1996. *National Colours:* Black shirts with red stripes, black shorts, black socks.
International matches 2016–17
None played.
No senior club competitions since 2004.

NICARAGUA

Federacion Nicaraguense de Futbol, Porton Principal del Hospital Bautista 1 Cuadra Abajo, 1 Cuadra al Sur y 1/2 Cuadra Abajo, Apartado Postal 976, Managua.
Founded: 1931. *FIFA:* 1950; *CONCACAF:* 1961. *National Colours:* All blue.
International matches 2016–17
Honduras (a) 0-1, Trinidad & Tobago (h) 2-1, Trinidad & Tobago (h) 1-3, Honduras (n) 1-2, Panama (a) 1-2, Costa Rica (n) 0-0, Belize (n) 3-1, El Salvador (n) 0-1, Honduras (a) 0-2, Haiti (a) 1-3, Haiti (h) 3-0, Bolivia (h) 0-1, Bolivia (a) 2-3, Curacao (a) 2-4.
League champions 2016–17: Real Esteli (Apertura); Real Esteli (Clausura). *Cup winners:* No competition.

PANAMA

Federacion Panamena de Futbol, Ciudad Deportiva Irving Saladino, Corregimiento de Juan Diaz, Apartado Postal 0827-00391, Zona 8, Panama City.
Founded: 1937. *FIFA:* 1938; *CONCACAF:* 1961. *National Colours:* All red.
International matches 2016–17
Guatemala (h) 0-0, Jamaica (h) 2-0, Costa Rica (a) 1-3, Mexico (n) 0-1, Honduras (a) 1-0, Mexico (h) 0-0, Belize (h) 0-0, Nicaragua (h) 2-1, Honduras (h) 0-1, El Salvador (h) 1-0, Costa Rica (h) 1-0, Trinidad & Tobago (a) 0-1, USA (h) 1-1, Costa Rica (a) 0-0, Honduras (h) 2-2.
League champions 2016–17: Arabe Unido (Apertura); Tauro (Clausura). *Cup winners:* No competition.

PUERTO RICO

Federacion Puertorriquena de Futbol, PO Box 367567, San Juan 00936.
Founded: 1940. *FIFA:* 1960; *CONCACAF:* 1961. *National Colours:* Red and white striped shirts, blue shorts, blue socks.
International matches 2016–17
Dominican Republic (a) 0-5, Dominican Republic (h) 0-1, India (a) 1-4, Antigua & Barbuda (a) 0-2, Curacao (h) 2-4, Indonesia (a) 0-0.
No senior club competitions since 2015. .

ST KITTS & NEVIS

St Kitts & Nevis Football Association, PO Box 465, Lozack Road, Basseterre.
Founded: 1932. *FIFA:* 1992; *CONCACAF:* 1992. *National Colours:* Green and red shirts, red shorts, green socks.
International matches 2016–17
French Guiana† (a) 0-1, Haiti (h) 0-2, Estonia (h) 1-1, Barbados (h) 2-1, Arrmenia (a) 0-5, Georgia (a) 0-3.
League champions 2016–17: Cayon Rockets. *Cup winners 2015–16:* Garden Hotspurs.

ST LUCIA

St Lucia National Football Association, Barnard Hill, PO Box 255, Castries.
Founded: 1979. *FIFA:* 1988; *CONCACAF:* 1986. *National Colours:* Sky blue shirts with yellow sleeves, sky blue shorts, white socks.
International matches 2016–17
St Vincent/Grenadines (n) 2-1, Grenada (a) 0-2.
League champions 2016: Survivals. *Cup winners:* No competition since 2013.

ST VINCENT & THE GRENADINES

St Vincent & the Grenadines Football Federation, PO Box 1278, Nichols Building (2nd Floor), Bentinck Square, Victoria Park, Kingstown.
Founded: 1979. *FIFA:* 1988; *CONCACAF:* 1986. *National Colours:* Yellow shirts, blue shorts, blue socks.
International matches 2016–17
USA (h) 0-6, Guatemala (a) 3-9, St Lucia (n) 1-2.
League champions 2014: System 3. *Cup winners:* No competition.

SURINAME

Surinaamse Voetbal Bond, Letitia Vriesdelaan 7, PO Box 1223, Paramaribo.
Founded: 1920. *FIFA:* 1929; *CONCACAF:* 1961. *National Colours:* White shirts with green cuffs, white shorts, white socks.
International matches 2016–17
Guyana (h) 3-2, Jamaica (a) 0-1, Trinidad & Tobago (a) 2-1, Haiti (n) 2-4
League champions 2016–17: Inter Moengotapoe. *Cup winners 2016:* SV Robinhood.

TRINIDAD & TOBAGO

Trinidad & Tobago Football Association, 24–26 Dundonald Street, PO Box 400, Port of Spain.
Founded: 1908. *FIFA:* 1964; *CONCACAF:* 1962. *National Colours:* Red shirts with black trim, black shorts with red trim, red socks.
International matches 2016–17
Guatemala (h) 2-2, USA (a) 0-4, Dominican Republic (h) 4-0, Martinique† (a) 0-2, Costa Rica (h) 0-2, Honduras (a) 1-3, Nicaragua (a) 1-2, Nicaragua (a) 3-1, Suriname (h) 1-2, Haiti (h) 3-4, Barbados (h) 2-0, Panama (h) 1-0, Mexico (h) 0-1, Grenada (a) 2-2, USA (a) 0-2, Costa Rica (a) 1-2.
League champions 2016–17: Central. *Cup winners 2017:* Defence Force.

TURKS & CAICOS ISLANDS

Turks & Caicos Islands Football Association, TCIFA National Academy, Venetian Road, PO Box 626, Providenciales.
Founded: 1996. *FIFA:* 1998; *CONCACAF:* 1996. *National Colours:* All white.
International matches 2016–17
None played.
League champions 2017: Beaches. *Cup winners:* No competition.

UNITED STATES

US Soccer Federation, US Soccer House, 1801 S. Prairie Avenue, Chicago, IL 60616.
Founded: 1913. *FIFA:* 1914; *CONCACAF:* 1961. *National Colours:* All white.
International matches 2016–17
St Vincent/Grenadines (a) 6-0, Trinidad & Tobago (h) 4-0, Cuba (a) 2-0, New Zealand (h) 1-1, Mexico (h) 1-2, Costa Rica (a) 0-4, Serbia (h) 0-0, Jamaica (h) 1-0, Honduras (h) 6-0, Panama (a) 1-1, Venezuela (h) 1-1, Trinidad & Tobago (h) 2-0, Mexico (a) 1-1, Ghana (h) 2-1.
League champions 2016: Seattle Sounders. (N.B. Teams from USA and Canada compete in MLS.) *Cup winners 2016:* FC Dallas.

US VIRGIN ISLANDS

USVI Soccer Federation Inc., 498D Strawberry, PO Box 2346, Christiansted, St Croix 00851.
Founded: 1987. *FIFA:* 1998; *CONCACAF:* 1987. *National Colours:* Gold shirts with royal blue trim, gold shorts, gold socks.
International matches 2016–17
None played.
League champions 2016–17: Raymix. *Cup winners:* No competition.

OCEANIA (OFC)

AMERICAN SAMOA

Football Federation American Samoa, PO Box 982 413, Pago Pago AS 96799.
Founded: 1984. *FIFA:* 1998; *OFC:* 1998. *National Colours:* Navy blue shirts, red shorts, white socks.
International matches 2016–17
None played.
League champions 2015: Pago Youth. *Cup winners:* No competition since 2014.

COOK ISLANDS

Cook Islands Football Association, Matavera Main Road, PO Box 29, Avarua, Rarotonga.
Founded: 1971. *FIFA:* 1994; *OFC:* 1994. *National Colours:* Green shirts with white trim, green shorts, white socks.
International matches 2016–17
None played.
League champions 2016: Puaikura. *Cup winners:* No competition since 2015.

FIJI

Fiji Football Association, PO Box 2514, Government Buildings, Suva.
Founded: 1938. *FIFA:* 1964; *OFC:* 1966. *National Colours:* White shirts, black shorts, white socks.
International matches 2016–17
New Zealand (h) 0-2, New Zealand (a) 0-2, Solomon Islands (h) 1-1, Solomon Islands (h) 1-0, New Caledonia (h) 2-2, New Caledonia (a) 1-2.
League champions 2016: Ba. *Cup winners 2017:* Rewa.

NEW CALEDONIA

Federation Caledonienne de Football, 7 bis, Rue Suffren Quartien latin, BP 560, Noumea 99845.
Founded: 1928. *FIFA:* 2004; *OFC:* 2004. *National Colours:* Grey shirts, red shorts, grey socks.
International matches 2016–17
Solomon Islands (a) 3-0, Solomon Islands (a) 1-0, New Zealand (a) 0-2, New Zealand (h) 0-0, Fiji (a) 2-2, Fiji (h) 2-1.
League champions 2016: AS Magenta. *Cup winners 2016:* AS Magenta.

NEW ZEALAND

New Zealand Football, PO Box 301-043, Albany, Auckland.
Founded: 1891. *FIFA:* 1948; *OFC:* 1966. *National Colours:* All white.
International matches 2016–17
Mexico (n) 1-2, USA (a) 1-1, New Caledonia (h) 2-0, New Caledonia (a) 0-0, Fiji (a) 2-0, Fiji (h) 2-0, Northern Ireland (a) 0-1, Belarus (a) 0-1, Russia (a) 0-2, Mexico (n) 1-2, Portugal (n) 0-4.
League champions 2016–17: Auckland City. *Cup winners 2016:* Birkenhead United.

PAPUA NEW GUINEA

Papua New Guinea Football Association, PO Box 957, Lae 411, Morobe Province.
Founded: 1962. *FIFA:* 1966; *OFC:* 1966. *National Colours:* Red shirts with black trim, red shorts, yellow socks.
International matches 2016–17
Iran (h) 1-8, Malaysia (a) 1-2, Tahiti (h) 1-3, Tahiti (a) 2-1, Solomon Islands (a) 2-3, Solomon Islands (h) 1-2.
League champions 2015–16: Lae City Dwellers. *Cup winners:* No competition.

SAMOA

Football Federation Samoa, PO Box 1682, Tuanimato, Apia.
Founded: 1968. *FIFA:* 1986; *OFC:* 1986. *National Colours:* Blue, white and red shirts, blue and white shorts, red and blue socks.
International matches 2016–17
None played.
League champions 2016: Lupe o le Soaga. *Cup winners:* No competition since 2014.

SOLOMON ISLANDS

Solomon Islands Football Federation, Allan Boso Complex, Panatina Academy, PO Box 584, Honiara.
Founded: 1978. *FIFA:* 1988; *OFC:* 1988. *National Colours:* Green, gold and blue shirts, blue and white shorts, white and blue socks.
International matches 2016–17
New Caledonia (h) 0-3, New Caledonia (h) 0-1, Tahiti (a) 0-3, Tahiti (h) 1-0, Fiji (a) 1-1, Fiji (a) 0-1, Papua New Guinea (h) 3-2, Papua New Guinea (a) 2-1.
League champions 2015: Marist Fire. *Cup winners:* No competition.

TAHITI

Federation Tahitienne de Football, Rue Gerald Coppenrath, Complexe de Fautaua, PO Box 50358, Pirae 98716.
Founded: 1989. *FIFA:* 1990; *OFC:* 1990. *National Colours:* White shirts with red trim, white shorts, white socks.
International matches 2016–17
Solomon Islands (h) 3-0, Solomon Islands (a) 0-1, Papua New Guinea (a) 3-1, Papua New Guinea (a) 1-2.
League champions 2016–17: Tefana. *Cup winners 2016:* Tefana.

TONGA

Tonga Football Association, Loto-Tonga Soka Centre, Valungafulu Road, Atele, PO Box 852, Nuku'alofa.
Founded: 1965. *FIFA:* 1994; *OFC:* 1994. *National Colours:* All red.
International matches 2016–17
None played.
League champions 2016: Veitongo. *Cup winners:* No competition since 2003.

VANUATU

Vanuatu Football Federation, VFF House, Lini Highway, PO Box 266, Port Vila.
Founded: 1934. *FIFA:* 1988; *OFC:* 1988. *National Colours:* Gold and white shirts with green sleeves, green shorts, black socks with white tops.
International matches 2016–17
None played.
League champions 2016: Naikutan. *Cup winners:* No competition.

AFRICA (CAF)

ALGERIA

Federation Algerienne De Football, Chemin Ahmed Ouaked, BP 39, Dely-Ibrahim, Algiers 16000.
Founded: 1962. *FIFA:* 1963; *CAF:* 1964. *National Colours:* All white.
International matches 2016–17
Lesotho (h) 6-0, Cameroon (h) 1-1, Nigeria (a) 1-3, Mauritania (h) 3-1, Zimbabwe (n) 2-2, Tunisia (n) 1-2, Senegal (n) 2-2, Guinea (h) 2-1, Togo (h) 1-0.
League champions 2016–17: ES Setif. *Cup winners 2016–17:* CR Belouizdad.

ANGOLA

Federacao Angolana de Futetbol, Senado de Compl. da Cidadela Desportiva, BP 3449, Luanda.
Founded: 1979. *FIFA:* 1980; *CAF:* 1980. *National Colours:* Red shirts with yellow trim, black shorts, red socks.
International matches 2016–17
Madagascar (h) 1-1, Botswana (a) 1-1 (0-3p), Mozambique (a) 0-2, South Africa (a) 0-0, Burkina Faso (h) 1-3, Mauritius (n) 1-0, Tanzania (a) 0-0, Malawi (h) 0-0.
League champions 2016: Primeiro de Agosto. *Cup winners 2016:* Recreativo do Libolo.

BENIN

Federation Beninoise de Football, Rue du boulevard Djassain, BP 112, 3-eme Arrondissement de Porto-Novo 01.
Founded: 1962. *FIFA:* 1962; *CAF:* 1962. *National Colours:* All yellow.
International matches 2016–17
Mali (a) 2-5, Mauritania (a) 0-1, Burkina Faso (a) 1-1, Burkina Faso (h) 2-2, Ghana (a) 1-1, Ivory Coast (a) 1-1, Gambia (h) 1-0.
No senior club competitions since 2014.

BOTSWANA

Botswana Football Association, PO Box 1396, Gaborone.
Founded: 1970. *FIFA:* 1978; *CAF:* 1976. *National Colours:* Blue, white and black shirts, blue shorts, blue socks.
International matches 2016–17
Burkina Faso (a) 1-2, Angola (h) 1-1 (3-0p), Tanzania (a) 0-2, Congo DR (n) 0-2, Mauritania (h) 0-1, Zambia (n) 1-2.
League champions 2016–17: Township Rollers. *Cup winners:* No competition since 2012.

BURKINA FASO

Federation Burkinabe de Foot-Ball, Centre Technique National Ouaga 2000, BP 57, Ouagadougou 01.
Founded: 1960. *FIFA:* 1964; *CAF:* 1964. *National Colours:* Green shirts with red sleeves, green shorts, green socks.
International matches 2016–17
Uzbekistan (a) 0-1, Botswana (h) 2-1, South Africa (h) 1-1, Cape Verde Islands (a) 2-0, Morocco (a) 0-1, Mali (n) 1-2, Cameroon (n) 1-1, Gabon (a) 1-1, Guinea-Bissau (n) 2-0, Tunisia (n) 2-0, Egypt (n) 1-1 (3-4p), Ghana (n) 1-0, Morocco (a) 0-2, Benin (h) 1-1, Benin (a) 2-2, Chile (a) 0-3, Angola (h) 3-1.
League champions 2015–16: Rail Club du Kadiogo. *Cup winners 2016:* Rail Club du Kadiogo.

BURUNDI

Federation de Football du Burundi, Avenue Muyinga, BP 3426, Bujumbura.
Founded: 1948. *FIFA:* 1972; *CAF:* 1972. *National Colours:* All red with white trim.
International matches 2016–17
Niger (a) 1-3, Djibouti (h) 7-0, Djibouti (h) 1-0, Tanzania (a) 1-2, South Sudan (h) 3-0.
League champions 2016–17: LLB Academic. *Cup winners 2016:* Le Messager Ngozi.

CAMEROON

Federation Camerounaise de Football, Avenue du 27 aout 1940, Tsinga-Yaounde, BP 1116, Yaounde.
Founded: 1959. *FIFA:* 1962; *CAF:* 1963. *National Colours:* Green shirts, red shorts, yellow socks.
International matches 2016–17
Gambia (h) 2-0, Gabon (h) 2-1, Algeria (a) 1-1, Zambia (h) 1-1, Congo DR (h) 2-0, Zimbabwe (n) 1-1, Burkina Faso (n) 1-1, Guinea-Bissau (n) 2-1, Gabon (a) 0-0, Senegal (n) 0-0 (5-4p), Ghana (n) 2-0, Egypt (n) 2-1, Tunisia (a) 1-0, Guinea (n) 1-2, Morocco (h) 1-0, Colombia (n) 0-4, Chile (n) 0-2, Australia (a) 1-1, Germany (h) 1-3.
League champions 2016: UMS de Loum. *Cup winners 2016:* APEJES Academy.

CAPE VERDE ISLANDS

Federacao Caboverdiana de Futebol, Praia Cabo Verde, FCF CX, PO Box 234, Praia.
Founded: 1982. *FIFA:* 1986; *CAF:* 2000. *National Colours:* All blue with white trim.
International matches 2016–17
Libya (h) 0-1, Senegal (a) 0-2, Burkina Faso (h) 0-2, Luxembourg (a) 2-0, Uganda (h) 0-1.
League champions 2016: CS Mindelense. *Cup winners:* No competition since 2012.

CENTRAL AFRICAN REPUBLIC

Federation Centrafricaine de Football, Avenue des Martyrs, BP 344, Bangui.
Founded: 1961. *FIFA:* 1964; *CAF:* 1965. *National Colours:* All white with blue trim.
International matches 2016–17
Congo DR (a) 1-4, Gambia (n) 1-2, Rwanda (h) 2-1.
League champions 2016: Olympique Real de Bangui. *Cup winners:* No competition since 2012.

CHAD

Federation Tchadienne de Football, BP 886, N'Djamena.
Founded: 1962. *FIFA:* 1964; *CAF:* 1964. *National Colours:* Blue shirts, yellow shorts, red socks.
International matches 2016–17
None played.
League champions 2015: AS CotonTchad. *Cup winners:* No competition since 2014.

COMOROS

Federation Comorienne de Football, Route d'Itsandra, BP 798, Moroni.
Founded: 1979. *FIFA:* 2005; *CAF:* 2003. *National Colours:* All green.
International matches 2016–17
Uganda (a) 0-1, Togo (n) 2-2, Gabon (n) 1-1, Gabon (n) 1-1, Mauritius (h) 2-0, Mauritius (a) 1-1, Togo (n) 0-2, Malawi (a) 0-1.
League champions 2016: Ngaya Club de Mde. *Cup winners 2016:* Volcan Club.

CONGO

Federation Congolaise de Football, 80 Rue Eugene Etienne, Centre Ville, BP Box 11, Brazzaville 00 242.
Founded: 1962. *FIFA:* 1964; *CAF:* 1965. *National Colours:* Green shirts, yellow shorts, red socks.
International matches 2016–17
Guinea-Bissau (h) 1-0, Egypt (h) 1-2, Uganda (a) 0-1, Senegal (h) 0-2, Mauritania (a) 1-2, Congo DR (a) 1-3.
League champions 2016: AC Leopards. *Cup winners 2016:* AC Leopards.

CONGO DR

Federation Congolaise de Football-Association, 31 Avenue de la Justice Kinshasa-Gombe, BP 1284, Kinshasa 1.
Founded: 1919. *FIFA:* 1964; *CAF:* 1964. *National Colours:* Blue shirts with red sleeves, blue shorts, blue socks.
International matches 2016–17
Central African Republic (h) 4-1, Kenya (h) 0-1, Libya (h) 4-0, Guinea (a) 2-1, Cameroon (a) 0-2, Morocco (n) 1-0, Ivory Coast (n) 2-2, Togo (n) 3-1, Ghana (n) 1-2, Kenya (a) 1-2, Botswana (n) 2-0, Congo (h) 3-1.
League champions 2015–16: TP Mazembe. *Cup winners 2016:* FC Renaissance.

DJIBOUTI

Federation Djiboutienne de Football, Centre Technique National, BP 2694, Ville de Djibouti.
Founded: 1979. *FIFA:* 1994; *CAF:* 1994. *National Colours:* Green shirts, white shorts, blue socks.
International matches 2016–17
Togo (a) 0-5, Burundi (a) 0-7, Burundi (a) 0-1, South Sudan (h) 2-0, South Sudan (a) 0-6.
League champions 2016–17: AS Ali Sabieh Djibouti Telecom. *Cup winners 2016:* AS Ali Sabieh Djibouti Telecom.

EGYPT

Egyptian Football Association, 5 Gabalaya Street, Gezira El Borg Post Office, Cairo.
Founded: 1921. *FIFA:* 1923; *CAF:* 1957. *National Colours:* Red shirts with white trim, white shorts, black socks.
International matches 2016–17
Guinea (h) 1-1, South Africa (a) 0-1, Congo (a) 2-1, Ghana (h) 2-0, Tunisia (h) 1-0, Mali (n) 0-0, Uganda (n) 1-0, Ghana (n) 1-0, Morocco (n) 1-0, Burkina Faso (n) 1-1 (4-3p), Cameroon (n) 1-2, Togo (h) 3-0, Yemen (h) 1-0, Libya (h) 1-0, Tunisia (a) 0-1.
League champions 2016–17: Al Ahly. *Cup winners 2016:* Zamalek.

EQUATORIAL GUINEA

Federacion Ecuatoguineana de Futbol, Avenida de Hassan II, Apartado de correo 1017, Malabo.
Founded: 1957. *FIFA:* 1986; *CAF:* 1986. *National Colours:* All red.
International matches 2016–17
South Sudan (h) 4-0, Lebanon (a) 1-1, Senegal (a) 0-3.
League champions 2015–16: CD Ela Nguema. *Cup winners 2016:* Racing de Micomeseng.

ERITREA

Eritrean National Football Federation, Sematat Avenue 29–31, PO Box 3665, Asmara.
Founded: 1996. *FIFA:* 1998; *CAF:* 1998. *National Colours:* Blue shirts, red shorts, green socks.
International matches 2016–17
None played.
No senior club competitions since 2014.

ETHIOPIA

Ethiopia Football Federation, Addis Ababa Stadium, PO Box 1080, Addis Ababa.
Founded: 1943. *FIFA:* 1952; *CAF:* 1957. *National Colours:* Green shirts, yellow shorts, red socks.
International matches 2016–17
Seychelles (a) 2-1, Ghana (a) 0-5.
League champions 2016–17: Saint George. *Cup winners 2016:* Saint George.

GABON

Federation Gabonaise de Football, BP 181, Libreville.
Founded: 1962. *FIFA:* 1966; *CAF:* 1967. *National Colours:* Yellow shirts, blue shorts with yellow trim, blue socks with yellow tops.
International matches 2016–17
Sudan (a) 2-1, Cameroon (a) 1-2, Morocco (h) 0-0, Mali (a) 0-0, Comoros (n) 1-1, Guinea-Bissau (h) 1-1, Burkina Faso (h) 1-1, Cameroon (h) 0-0, Guinea (n) 2-2, Zambia (h) 0-0, Mali (a) 1-2.
League champions 2015–16: CF Mounana. *Cup winners 2016:* CF Mounana.

GAMBIA

Gambia Football Association, Kafining Layout, Bakau, PO Box 523, Banjul.
Founded: 1952. *FIFA:* 1968; *CAF:* 1966. *National Colours:* Red shirts, blue shorts, green socks.
International matches 2016–17
South Africa (h) 0-4*, Cameroon (a) 0-2, Central African Republic (n) 2-1, Benin (a) 0-1.
** Played 04.06.2016, result incorrect in last edition.*
League champions 2016–17: Armed Forces. *Cup winners 2017:* Hawks.

GHANA

Ghana Football Association, General Secretariat, South East Ridge, PO Box AN 19338, Accra.
Founded: 1957. *FIFA:* 1958; *CAF:* 1958. *National Colours:* All white.
International matches 2016–17
Rwanda (h) 1-1, Russia (a) 0-1, Uganda (h) 0-0, South Africa (a) 1-1, Egypt (a) 0-2, Uganda (n) 1-0, Mali (n) 1-0, Egypt (n) 0-1, Congo (n) 2-1, Cameroon (n) 0-2, Burkina Faso (n) 0-1, Benin (h) 1-1, Ethiopia (h) 5-0, Mexico (n) 0-1, USA (a) 1-2.
League champions 2016–17: Wa All Stars. *Cup winners 2016:* Bechem United.

GUINEA

Federation Guineenne de Football, Annexe 1 du Palais du Peuple, PO Box 3645, Conakry.
Founded: 1960. *FIFA:* 1962; *CAF:* 1963. *National Colours:* Red shirts, yellow shorts, green socks.
International matches 2016–17
Egypt (a) 1-1, Zimbabwe (h) 1-0, Tunisia (a) 0-2, Congo (h) 1-2, Gabon (n) 2-2, Cameroon (n) 2-1, Algeria (a) 1-2, Ivory Coast (a) 3-2.
League champions 2015–16: Horoya. *Cup winners 2016:* Horoya.

GUINEA-BISSAU

Federacao de Futebol da Guine-Bissau, Alto Bandim (Nova Sede), BP 375, Bissau 1035.
Founded: 1974. *FIFA:* 1986; *CAF:* 1986. *National Colours:* Red shirts with green and yellow trim, red shorts, red socks.
International matches 2016–17
Congo (a) 0-1, Gabon (a) 1-1, Cameroon (n) 1-2, Burkina Faso (n) 0-2, South Africa (a) 1-3, Namibia (h) 1-0.
League champions 2016–17: Sport Bissau e Benfica. *Cup winners 2015–16:* Sport Bissau e Benfica.

IVORY COAST

Federation Ivoirienne de Football, Treichville Avenue 1, 01, BP 1202, Abidjan 01.
Founded: 1960. *FIFA:* 1964; *CAF:* 1960. *National Colours:* All orange.
International matches 2016–17
Sierra Leone (h) 1-1, Mali (h) 3-1, Morocco (a) 0-0, France (a) 0-0, Zimbabwe (h) 0-0, Sweden (n) 2-1, Uganda (n) 3-0, Togo (n) 0-0, Congo DR (n) 2-2, Morocco (n) 0-1, Russia (a) 2-0, Benin (h) 1-1, Netherlands (a) 0-5, Guinea (h) 2-3.
League champions 2016–17: ASEC Mimosas. *Cup winners 2016:* Sewe Sport de San-Pedro.

KENYA

Football Kenya Federation, Nyayo Sports Complex, Kasarani, PO Box 12705, 00400 Nairobi.
Founded: 1960 (KFF); 2011 (FKF). *FIFA:* 1960 (2012); *CAF:* 1968 (2012). *National Colours:* All red.
International matches 2016–17
Uganda (a) 0-0, Zambia (a) 1-1, Congo DR (a) 1-0, Mozambique (h) 1-0, Liberia (h) 1-0, Uganda (h) 1-1, Congo DR (h) 2-1, Malawi (h) 0-0, Sierra Leone (a) 1-2.
League champions 2016: Tusker. *Cup winners 2015:* Bandari.

LESOTHO

Lesotho Football Association, Bambatha Tsita Sports Arena, Old Polo Ground, PO Box 1879, Maseru 100.
Founded: 1932. *FIFA:* 1964; *CAF:* 1964. *National Colours:* Blue shirts, green shorts, white socks.
International matches 2016–17
Algeria (a) 0-6, Mozambique (a) 0-1, Mauritania (h) 1-0, Tanzania (a) 1-1, Namibia (n) 0-0 (5-4p).
League champions 2016–17: Bantu. *Cup winners 2016:* Lioli.

LIBERIA

Liberia Football Association, Professional Building, Benson Street, PO Box 10-1066, Monrovia 1000.
Founded: 1936. *FIFA:* 1964; *CAF:* 1960. *National Colours:* Red and white shirts with black trim, red shorts, red socks with blue.
International matches 2016–17
Tunisia (a) 1-4, Kenya (a) 0-1, Sierra Leone (h) 1-0, Zimbabwe (n) 0-3.
League champions 2016: Barrack Young Controllers. *Cup winners 2016:* Monrovia Club Breweries.

LIBYA

Libyan Football Federation, General Sports Federation Building, Sports City, Goriji, PO Box 5137, Tripoli.
Founded: 1962. *FIFA:* 1964; *CAF:* 1965. *National Colours:* Red shirts, black shorts, black socks.
International matches 2016–17
Cape Verde Islands (a) 1-0, Congo DR (a) 0-4, Tunisia (n) 0-1, Senegal (n) 1-2, Togo (n) 0-0, Egypt (a) 0-1, Seychelles (n) 5-1.
League champions 2015–16: Al-Ahli Tripoli. *Cup winners 2016:* Al-Ahli Tripoli.

MADAGASCAR

Federation Malagasy de Football, 29 Rue de Russie Isoraka, PO Box 4409, Antananarivo 101.
Founded: 1961. *FIFA:* 1964; *CAF:* 1963. *National Colours:* All green and white.
International matches 2016–17
Angola (a) 1-1, Sao Tome & Principe (a) 1-0, Sao Tome & Principe (h) 3-2, Malawi (h) 1-0, Malawi (a) 1-0, Sudan (a) 3-1, Seychelles (n) 2-0, Zimbabwe (n) 0-0, Mozambique (n) 4-1.
League champions 2016: CNaPS Sport. *Cup winners 2016:* CNaPS Sport.

MALAWI

Football Association of Malawi, Chiwembe Technical Centre, Off Chiwembe Road, PO Box 51657, Limbe.
Founded: 1966. *FIFA:* 1968; *CAF:* 1968. *National Colours:* All red.

International matches 2016–17
Lesotho (n) 0-1*, Swaziland (h) 1-0, Kenya (a) 0-0, Madagascar (a) 0-1, Madagascar (h) 0-1, Comoros (h) 1-0, Tanzania (n) 0-2, Mauritius (n) 0-0, Angola (n) 0-0.
* *Played 16.06.2016, result incorrect in last edition.*
League champions 2016: Kamuzu Barracks. *Cup winners 2015:* CIVO United.

MALI

Federation Malienne de Football, Avenue du Mali, Hamdallaye ACI 2000, BP 1020, Bamako 0000.
Founded: 1960. *FIFA:* 1964; *CAF:* 1963. *National Colours:* All yellow.
International matches 2016–17
Benin (h) 5-2, Ivory Coast (a) 1-3, Gabon (h) 0-0, Burkina Faso (n) 2-1, Egypt (n) 0-0, Ghana (n) 0-1, Uganda (n) 1-1, Gabon (h) 2-1.
League champions 2015–16: Stade Malien. *Cup winners 2016:* Onze Createurs.

MAURITANIA

Federation de Foot-Ball de la Rep. Islamique de Mauritanie, Route de l'Espoire, BP 566, Nouakchott.
Founded: 1961. *FIFA:* 1970; *CAF:* 1968. *National Colours:* All green with yellow trim.
International matches 2016–17
South Africa (a) 1-1, Canada (n) 0-4, Tunisia (h) 0-0, Algeria (a) 1-3, Benin (h) 1-0, Congo (h) 2-1, Senegal (a) 0-2, Lesotho (a) 0-1, Botswana (n) 1-0.
League champions 2016–17: ASAC Concorde. *Cup winners 2016:* FC Nouadhibou.

MAURITIUS

Mauritius Football Association, Sepp Blatter House, Trianon.
Founded: 1952. *FIFA:* 1964; *CAF:* 1963. *National Colours:* All white with red trim.
International matches 2016–17
Mozambique (a) 0-1, Comoros (a) 0-2, Comoros (h) 1-1, Seychelles (h) 2-1, Seychelles (a) 1-1, Angola (n) 0-1, Malawi (n) 0-0, Tanzania (n) 1-1.
League champions 2016–17: Pamplemousses. *Cup winners 2016:* Pamplemousses.

MOROCCO

Federation Royale Marocaine de Football, 51 bis, Avenue Ibn Sina, Agdal BP 51, Rabat 10 000.
Founded: 1955. *FIFA:* 1960; *CAF:* 1959. *National Colours:* Red shirts with green trim, white shorts, red socks with green trim.
International matches 2016–17
Albania (a) 0-0, Sao Tome & Principe (h) 2-0, Gabon (a) 0-0, Canada (h) 4-0, Ivory Coast (h) 0-0, Togo (h) 2-1, Burkina Faso (h) 1-0, Finland (n) 0-1, Congo DR (n) 0-1, Togo (n) 3-1, Ivory Coast (n) 1-0, Egypt (n) 0-1, Burkina Faso (h) 2-0, Tunisia (h) 1-0, Netherlands (h) 1-2, Cameroon (a) 0-1.
League champions 2016–17: Wydad Casablanca. *Cup winners 2016:* MAS Fez.

MOZAMBIQUE

Federacao Mocambicana de Futebol, Avenida Samora Machel 11, Caixa Postal 1467, Maputo.
Founded: 1976. *FIFA:* 1980; *CAF:* 1980. *National Colours:* Red shirts, black shorts, black socks with red tops.
International matches 2016–17
Mauritius (h) 1-0, Togo (a) 0-2, Kenya (a) 0-1, South Africa (h) 1-1, Angola (h) 2-0, Lesotho (h) 1-0, Zambia (a) 1-0, Zimbabwe (n) 0-4, Seychelles (n) 2-1, Madagascar (n) 1-4.
League champions 2016: Ferroviario Beira. *Cup winners 2016:* Uniao Desportiva do Songo.

NAMIBIA

Namibia Football Association, Richard Kamuhuka Str., Soccer House, Katutura, PO Box 1345, Windhoek 9000.
Founded: 1990. *FIFA:* 1992; *CAF:* 1992. *National Colours:* All red.
International matches 2016–17
Senegal (a) 0-2, Guinea-Bissau (a) 0-1, Lesotho (n) 0-0 (4-5p), Swaziland (n) 1-0.
League champions 2015–16: Tigers (2016–17 competition cancelled). *Cup winners 2015:* Tigers.

NIGER

Federation Nigerienne de Football, Avenue Francois Mitterand, BP 10299, Niamey.
Founded: 1961. *FIFA:* 1964; *CAF:* 1964. *National Colours:* White shirts, white shorts, orange socks.
International matches 2016–17
Burundi (h) 3-1, Swaziland (h) 0-0.
League champions 2016–17: AS FAN. *Cup winners 2016:* AS Douanes.

NIGERIA

Nigeria Football Federation, Plot 2033, Olusegun Obasanjo Way, Zone 7, Wuse Abuja, PO Box 5101 Garki, Abuja.
Founded: 1945. *FIFA:* 1960; *CAF:* 1960. *National Colours:* All green with white trim.
International matches 2016–17
Tanzania (h) 1-0, Zambia (a) 2-1, Algeria (h) 3-1, Senegal (n) 1-1, Togo (n) 3-0, South Africa (h) 0-2.
League champions 2016: Enugu Rangers. *Cup winners 2016:* Ifeanyi Ubah.

RWANDA

Federation Rwandaise de Football Association, BP 2000, Kigali.
Founded: 1972. *FIFA:* 1978; *CAF:* 1976. *National Colours:* Green and yellow hooped shirts, blue shorts, green socks.
International matches 2016–17
Ghana (a) 1-1, Central African Republic (a) 1-4.
League champions 2016–17: Rayon Sports. *Cup winners 2016:* APR.

SAO TOME & PRINCIPE

Federacao Santomense de Futebol, Rua Ex-Joao de Deus No. QXXIII-426/26, BP 440, Sao Tome.
Founded: 1975. *FIFA:* 1986; *CAF:* 1986. *National Colours:* Green and red shirts, black shorts, green socks.
International matches 2016–17
Morocco (a) 0-2, Madagascar (h) 0-1, Madagascar (a) 2-3.
League champions 2016: Sporting Praia Cruz. *Cup winners 2016:* UDRA.

SENEGAL

Federation Senegalaise de Football, VDN Ouest-Foire en face du Cicesi, BP 13021, Dakar.
Founded: 1960. *FIFA:* 1964; *CAF:* 1964. *National Colours:* All white with yellow trim.
International matches 2016–17
Namibia (h) 2-0, Cape Verde Islands (h) 2-0, South Africa (a) 1-2, Libya (n) 2-1, Congo (a) 2-0, Tunisia (n) 2-0, Zimbabwe (n) 2-0, Algeria (n) 2-2, Cameroon (n) 0-0 (4-5p), Nigeria (n) 1-1, Mauritania (h) 2-0, Uganda (h) 0-0, Equatorial Guinea (h) 3-0.
League champions 2016–17: Generation Foot. *Cup winners 2016:* ASC Niarry-Tally.

SEYCHELLES

Seychelles Football Federation, Maison Football, Roche Caiman, PO Box 843, Mahe.
Founded: 1979. *FIFA:* 1986; *CAF:* 1986. *National Colours:* Red shirts, blue shorts, blue socks.
International matches 2016–17
Ethiopia (a) 1-2, Mauritius (a) 1-2, Mauritius (h) 1-1, Libya (n) 1-5, Madagascar (n) 0-2, Mozambique (n) 1-2, Zimbabwe (n) 0-6.
League champions 2015: Cote d'O. *Cup winners 2016:* Saint Michel United.

SIERRA LEONE

Sierra Leone Football Association, 21 Battery Street, Kingtom, PO Box 672, Freetown.
Founded: 1960. *FIFA:* 1960; *CAF:* 1960. *National Colours:* Green shirts, white shorts, blue socks.
International matches 2016–17
Ivory Coast (a) 1-1, Liberia (a) 0-1, Kenya (h) 2-1.
No senior club football since 2014.

SOMALIA

Somali Football Federation, Mogadishu BN 03040 (DHL only).
Founded: 1951. *FIFA:* 1962; *CAF:* 1968. *National Colours:* All blue with white trim.
International matches 2016–17
South Sudan (n) 1-2, South Sudan (a) 0-2.
League champions 2015–16: Banadir. *Cup winners 2016:* Jeenyo United.

SOUTH AFRICA

South African Football Association, 76 Nasrec Road, Nasrec, Johannesburg 2000.
Founded: 1991. *FIFA:* 1992; *CAF:* 1992. *National Colours:* Yellow shirts with green trim, green shorts with yellow trim, yellow socks with green tops.
International matches 2016–17
Mauritania (h) 1-3, Egypt (h) 1-0, Burkina Faso (a) 1-1, Ghana (h) 1-1, Senegal (h) 2-1, Mozambique (a) 1-1, Guinea-Bissau (h) 3-1, Angola (h) 0-0, Nigeria (a) 2-0, Zambia (h) 1-2, Tanzania (h) 0-1.
League champions 2016–17: Bidvest Wits. *Cup winners 2016–17:* SuperSport United.

SOUTH SUDAN

South Sudan Football Association, Juba National Stadium, Hai Himra, Talata, Juba.
Founded: 2011. *FIFA:* 2012; *CAF:* 2012. *National Colours:* All blue.
International matches 2016–17
Equatorial Guinea (a) 0-4, Djibouti (a) 0-2, Djibouti (h) 6-0, Somalia (n) 2-1, Somalia (h) 2-0, Burundi (a) 0-3.
League champions 2015: Atlabara (league suspended from 2016). *Cup winners* 2016*:* Wau Salaam.

SUDAN

Sudan Football Association, Baladia Street, PO Box 437, 11111 Khartoum.
Founded: 1936. *FIFA:* 1948; *CAF:* 1957. *National Colours:* All red.
International matches 2016–17
Gabon (h) 1-2, Madagascar (h) 1-3.
League champions 2016: Al-Hilal Omdurman. *Cup winners 2016:* Al-Hilal Omdurman.

SWAZILAND

National Football Association of Swaziland, Sigwaca House, Plot 582, Sheffield Road, PO Box 641, Mbabane H100.
Founded: 1968. *FIFA:* 1978; *CAF:* 1976. *National Colours:* Blue and red shirts, blue shorts, blue socks.
International matches 2016–17
Malawi (a) 0-1, Niger (a) 0-0, Zimbabwe (n) 1-2.
League champions 2016–17: Mbabane Swallows. *Cup winners 2017:* Young Buffaloes.

TANZANIA

Tanzania Football Federation, Karume Memorial Stadium, Uhuru/Shauri Moyo Road, PO Box 1574, Ilala/Dar Es Salaam.
Founded: 1930. *FIFA:* 1964; *CAF:* 1964. *National Colours:* Blue shirts, black shorts, blue socks.
International matches 2016–17
Nigeria (a) 0-1, Zimbabwe (a) 0-3, Botswana (h) 2-0, Burundi (h) 2-1, Lesotho (h) 1-1, Malawi (n) 2-0, Angola (n) 0-0, Mauritius (n) 1-1, South Africa (a) 1-0.
League champions 2016–17: Young Africans. *Cup winners 2016–17:* Simba SC.

TOGO

Federation Togolaise de Football, Route de Kegoue, BP 05, Lome.
Founded: 1960. *FIFA:* 1964; *CAF:* 1964. *National Colours:* Yellow shirts, green shorts, yellow socks.
International matches 2016–17
Djibouti (h) 5-0, Uganda (h) 1-0, Mozambique (h) 2-0, Comoros (n) 2-2, Morocco (a) 1-2, Ivory Coast (n) 0-0, Morocco (n) 1-3, Congo DR (n) 1-3, Libya (n) 0-0, Egypt (a) 0-3, Nigeria (n) 0-3, Comoros (a) 2-0, Algeria (a) 0-1.
League champions 2016–17: AS Togo Port. *Cup winners 2017:* AS Togo Port.

TUNISIA

Federation Tunisienne de Football, Stade Annexe d'El Menzah, Cite Olympique, El Menzah 1003.
Founded: 1957. *FIFA:* 1960; *CAF:* 1960. *National Colours:* All white with red trim.
International matches 2016–17
Liberia (h) 4-1, Guinea (h) 2-0, Libya (n) 1-0, Mauritania (h) 0-0, Uganda (h) 2-0, Egypt (a) 0-1, Senegal (n) 0-2, Algeria (n) 2-1, Zimbabwe (n) 4-2, Burkina Faso (n) 0-2, Cameroon (h) 0-1, Morocco (a) 0-1, Egypt (h) 1-0.
League champions 2016–17: Esperance de Tunis. *Cup winners 2016–17:* Club Africain.

UGANDA

Federation of Uganda Football Associations, FUFA House, Plot No. 879, Wakaliga Road, Mengo, PO Box 22518, Kampala.
Founded: 1924. *FIFA:* 1960; *CAF:* 1960. *National Colours:* Yellow shirts, black shorts, yellow socks.
International matches 2016–17
Kenya (h) 0-0, Comoros (h) 1-0, Togo (a) 0-1, Ghana (a) 0-0, Zambia (h) 0-1, Congo (h) 1-0, Tunisia (a) 0-2, Slovakia (n) 3-1, Ivory Coast (n) 0-3, Ghana (n) 0-1, Egypt (n) 0-1, Mali (n) 1-1, Kenya (n) 1-1, Senegal (a) 0-0, Cape Verde Islands (a) 1-0.
League champions 2016–17: KCCA. *Cup winners 2016–17:* KCCA.

ZAMBIA

Football Association of Zambia, Football House, Alick Nkhata Road, Long Acres, PO Box 34751, Lusaka.
Founded: 1929. *FIFA:* 1964; *CAF:* 1964. *National Colours:* Green shirts, green shorts, green and orange socks.
International matches 2016–17
Kenya (h) 1-1, Nigeria (h) 1-2, Zimbabwe (a) 0-1, Uganda (a) 1-0, Cameroon (a) 1-1, Zimbabwe (a) 0-0, Gabon (a) 0-0, Mozambique (h) 0-1, South Africa (a) 2-1, Botswana (n) 2-1.
League champions 2016: Zanaco. *Cup winners:* No competition.

ZIMBABWE

Zimbabwe Football Association, ZIFA House, 53 Livingston Avenue, PO Box CY 114, Causeway, Harare.
Founded: 1965. *FIFA:* 1965; *CAF:* 1980. *National Colours:* Gold shirts, gold shorts, green socks.
International matches 2016–17
Guinea (a) 0-1, Zambia (h) 1-0, Tanzania (h) 3-0, Ivory Coast (a) 0-0, Cameroon (a) 1-1, Algeria (n) 2-2, Senegal (n) 0-2, Tunisia (n) 2-4, Zambia (h) 0-0, Liberia (h) 3-0, Mozambique (n) 4-0, Madagascar (n) 0-0, Seychelles (n) 6-0, Swaziland (n) 2-1.
League champions 2016: CAPS United. *Cup winners 2016:* Ngezi Platinum.

FIFA WORLD CUP 2018 QUALIFYING COMPETITION – EUROPE

■ *Denotes player sent off.*

GROUP A

Tuesday, 6 September 2016

Belarus (0) 0

France (0) 0 12,920

Belarus: (451) Gorbunov; Palyakow, Sivakov, Bordachev, Politevich; Korzun, Stasevich (Krivets 69), Gordeichuk (Volodko 85), Maewski, Kalachev; Signevich (Kornilenko 80).
France: (433) Mandanda; Sidibe, Varane, Koscielny, Kurzawa; Sissoko (Dembele 70), Kante, Pogba; Griezmann, Giroud (Gameiro 82), Martial (Payet 57).

Bulgaria (1) 4 *(Rangelov 16, Marcelinho 66, Popov I 80, Tonev 90)*

Luxembourg (0) 3 *(Joachim 60, 63, Bohnert 90)* 1000

Bulgaria: (4231) Stoyanov; Popov S, Ivanov, Chorbadzhiyski, Nedyalkov; Dyakov, Marcelinho; Milanov G (Tonev 65), Popov I (Bozhilov 85), Aleksandrov M (Chochev 55); Rangelov.
Luxembourg: (442) Joubert; Jans, Martins Pereira, Chanot, Malget; Mutsch, Gerson, Philipps (Deville 84), Da Mota Alves (Bohnert 68); Joachim, Thill V (Turpel 58).

Sweden (1) 1 *(Berg 43)*

Netherlands (0) 1 *(Sneijder 67)* 36,128

Sweden: (4231) Olsen; Wendt, Lustig, Lindelof, Granqvist; Rohden (Kujovic 76), Forsberg; Hiljemark, Fransson, Guidetti (Nyman 64); Berg (Durmaz 88).
Netherlands: (433) Zoet; Janmaat, Bruma, van Dijk, Blind; Klaassen, Strootman, Wijnaldum (Dost 66); Promes (Berghuis 78), Janssen, Sneijder.

Friday, 7 October 2016

France (3) 4 *(Gameiro 23, 59, Payet 26, Griezmann 38)*

Bulgaria (1) 1 *(Aleksandrov M 6 (pen))* 65,475

France: (4231) Lloris; Sagna (Sidibe 27), Varane, Koscielny, Kurzawa; Pogba, Matuidi; Sissoko, Griezmann (Fekir 83), Payet; Gameiro (Gignac 72).
Bulgaria: (442) Stoyanov; Popov S, Aleksandrov A, Pirgov, Milanov Z; Milanov G, Dyakov, Kostadinov, Aleksandrov M (Nedelev 76); Marcelinho (Rangelov 62), Popov I (Tonev 67).

Netherlands (2) 4 *(Promes 15, 32, Klaassen 55, Janssen 64)*

Belarus (0) 1 *(Rios 48)* 41,200

Netherlands: (4411) Stekelenburg; Karsdorp, van Dijk, Bruma, Blind; Promes, Strootman (Clasie 79), Wijnaldum, Sneijder (Propper 46); Klaassen; Janssen (Dost 83).
Belarus: (4411) Gorbunov; Palyakow, Sivakov, Politevich, Bordachev; Gordeichuk (Valadzko 74), Maewski (Hleb 46), Korzun, Rios; Krivets (Kislyak 68); Kornilenko.

Luxembourg (0) 0

Sweden (0) 1 *(Lustig 58)* 2500

Luxembourg: (433) Moris; Jans, Philipps, Malget■, Carlson; Thill V (Turpel 67), Martins Pereira, Bohnert; Deville (Da Mota Alves 66), Mutsch, Joachim.
Sweden: (442) Olsen; Lustig, Lindelof, Granqvist, Olsson; Durmaz (Nyman 89), Hiljemark, Ekdal (Fransson 80), Forsberg; Guidetti (Toivonen 71), Berg.

Monday, 10 October 2016

Belarus (0) 1 *(Savitskiy 80)*

Luxembourg (0) 1 *(Joachim 85)* 9011

Belarus: (451) Gorbunov; Palyakow, Martynovich, Filipenko, Bordachev (Valadzko 79); Kalachev, Maewski (Savitskiy 71), Korzun, Hleb, Gordeichuk; Signevich (Kornilenko 60).
Luxembourg: (451) Moris; Delgado, Philipps, Martins Pereira (Veiga 34), Carlson■; Jans, Thill V (Janisch 45), Mutsch, Da Mota Alves, Bohnert (Turpel 72); Joachim.

Netherlands (0) 0

France (1) 1 *(Pogba 30)* 50,220

Netherlands: (4231) Stekelenburg; Karsdorp, Bruma, van Dijk, Blind; Strootman, Wijnaldum (Dost 62); Promes (Depay 16), Propper (Willems 84), Klaassen; Janssen.
France: (4231) Lloris; Sidibe, Varane, Koscielny, Kurzawa; Pogba, Matuidi; Sissoko, Griezmann (Kante 90), Payet (Martial 67); Gameiro (Gignac 79).

Sweden (2) 3 *(Toivonen 39, Hiljemark 45, Lindelof 58)*

Bulgaria (0) 0 21,777

Sweden: (442) Olsen; Krafth, Lindelof, Granqvist, Olsson (Augustinsson 63); Durmaz, Hiljemark, Ekdal, Forsberg (Wendt 74); Berg (Guidetti 85), Toivonen.
Bulgaria: (4411) Stoyanov; Popov S, Aleksandrov A, Bozhikov, Nedyalkov; Kostadinov (Aleksandrov M 54), Slavchev (Raynov 89), Chochev (Marcelinho 72), Milanov G; Dyakov; Popov I.

Friday, 11 November 2016

France (0) 2 *(Pogba 58, Payet 65)*

Sweden (0) 1 *(Forsberg 55)* 80,000

France: (4411) Lloris; Sidibe, Varane, Koscielny, Evra; Sissoko, Pogba, Matuidi, Payet; Griezmann (Kante 88); Giroud.
Sweden: (442) Olsen; Krafth, Lindelof, Granqvist, Augustinsson; Durmaz (Jansson 87), Johansson, Ekdal (Hiljemark 66), Forsberg; Guidetti (Thelin 73), Toivonen.

Sunday, 13 November 2016

Bulgaria (1) 1 *(Popov I 10)*

Belarus (0) 0 1994

Bulgaria: (442) Stoyanov; Popov S, Aleksandrov A, Bozhikov, Zanev; Milanov G (Chochev 53), Dyakov, Slavchev, Tonev (Kirilov 66); Delev, Popov I (Yordanov 75).
Belarus: (451) Gorbunov; Politevich, Martynovich (Shitov 35), Filipenko, Palyakow; Gordeichuk, Hleb■, Kendysh, Maewski (Kornilenko 74), Nekhaychik (Savitskiy 61); Laptsew.

Luxembourg (1) 1 *(Chanot 44 (pen))*

Netherlands (1) 3 *(Robben 36, Depay 58, 84)* 8000

Luxembourg: (541) Schon; Jans (Janisch 26), Malget, Chanot, Mahmutovic, Da Mota Alves (Kerger 75); Bohnert, Bensi (Thill V 82), Philipps, Mutsch; Turpel.
Netherlands: (433) Stekelenburg; Brenet, Bruma, van Dijk, Blind; Klaassen, Wijnaldum, Ramselaar (de Roon 88); Robben (Berghuis 45), Dost, Sneijder (Depay 45).

Saturday, 25 March 2017

Bulgaria (2) 2 *(Delev 5, 20)*

Netherlands (0) 0 10,900

Bulgaria: (4141) Mihailov; Popov S, Chorbadzhiyski, Bozhikov, Zanev (Nedyalkov 86); Manolev; Kostadinov, Slavchev, Popov I (Kraev 68), Tonev; Delev (Bodurov 88).
Netherlands: (4411) Zoet; Karsdorp, Martins Indi, de Ligt (Hoedt 46), Blind; Strootman, Klaassen, Robben, Promes (de Jong 69); Wijnaldum (Sneijder 46); Dost.

Luxembourg (1) 1 *(Joachim 34 (pen))*

France (2) 3 *(Giroud 28, 77, Griezmann 38 (pen))* 8000

Luxembourg: (4141) Moris (Schon 20); Jans, Martins Pereira, Chanot, Malget; Philipps; Bensi, Gerson, Mutsch, Da Mota Alves (Rodrigues 82); Joachim.
France: (4411) Lloris; Sidibe (Jallet 62), Koscielny, Umtiti, Mendy; Dembele, Kante, Matuidi (Rabiot 83), Payet (Mbappe-Lottin 79); Griezmann; Giroud.

Sweden (1) 4 *(Forsberg 19 (pen), 49, Berg 57, Thelin 78)*

Belarus (0) 0 31,243

Sweden: (442) Olsen; Lustig, Jansson, Granqvist, Augustinsson; Durmaz (Claesson 85), Hiljemark, Ekdal (Johansson 68), Forsberg; Berg, Toivonen (Thelin 73).

Belarus: (442) Gorbunov; Shitov, Martynovich, Politevich, Filipenko; Bordachev (Valadzko 69), Bressan, Maewski (Dragun 65), Rios; Signevich (Rodionov 70), Gordeichuk.

Friday, 9 June 2017

Belarus (1) 2 *(Sivakov 34 (pen), Savitskiy 80)*

Bulgaria (0) 1 *(Kostadinov 90)* 6150

Belarus: (352) Chernik; Politevich, Filipenko, Sivakov; Aliseiko, Maewski (Gordeichuk 88), Dragun, Balanovich, Matsveychyk; Laptev (Bykov 73), Savitskiy (Skavysh 82).
Bulgaria: (433) Mihailov; Popov S, Chorbadzhiyski, Bozhikov, Zanev; Dyakov, Popov I (Chochev 64), Kostadinov; Manolev (Milanov G 81), Delev (Galabinov 54), Tonev.

Netherlands (2) 5 *(Robben 21, Sneijder 34, Wijnaldum 62, Promes 70, Janssen 83 (pen))*

Luxembourg (0) 0 41,300

Netherlands: (433) Cillessen; Veltman, de Vrij, Hoedt, Blind; Wijnaldum, Sneijder (Ake 82), Strootman; Robben (Lens 72), Janssen, Depay (Promes 66).
Luxembourg: (451) Schon; Jans, Chanot (Delgado 25), Mahmutovic, Malget; Bensi, Rodrigues (Bohnert 85), Martins Pereira, Thill V (Gerson 54), Thill S; Turpel.

Sweden (1) 2 *(Durmaz 43, Toivonen 90)*

France (1) 1 *(Giroud 37)* 48,783

Sweden: (442) Olsen; Lustig, Lindelof, Granqvist, Augustinsson; Durmaz (Claesson 76), Johansson, Ekdal (Larsson 77), Forsberg; Berg (Guidetti 88), Toivonen.
France: (4231) Lloris; Sidibe, Varane, Koscielny, Mendy; Pogba, Matuidi; Sissoko, Griezmann (Mbappe-Lottin 76), Payet (Lemar 76); Giroud.

Group A Table	P	W	D	L	F	A	GD	Pts
Sweden	6	4	1	1	12	4	8	13
France	6	4	1	1	11	5	6	13
Netherlands	6	3	1	2	13	6	7	10
Bulgaria	6	3	0	3	9	12	–3	9
Belarus	6	1	2	3	4	11	–7	5
Luxembourg	6	0	1	5	6	17	–11	1

GROUP B

Tuesday, 6 September 2016

Andorra (0) 0

Latvia (0) 1 *(Sabala 48)* 1000

Andorra: (451) Pol; Jordi Rubio, Llovera, Lima, Garcia M; Clemente (Pujol 78), Alaez, Vales, Vieira, Martinez C (Moreira 85); Riera (Rebes 30).
Latvia: (451) Vanins; Maksimenko, Gabovs, Gorkss, Jagodinskis; Ikaunieks D (Torres.. 63), Ikaunieks J, Lazdins (Laizans 45), Zjuzins (Karasausks 74), Visnakovs; Sabala.

Faroe Islands (0) 0

Hungary (0) 0 4066

Faroe Islands: (433) Nielsen; Hansen, Gregersen, Nattestad, Davidsen V; Vatnhamar, Benjaminsen, Joensen; Henriksen Olsen, Edmundsson, Hansson (Vatnsdal 90).
Hungary: (433) Gulacsi; Fiola, Guzmics, Lang, Kadar; Nemeth (Nikolic 70), Nagy A, Dzsudzsak; Kleinheisler (Stieber 80), Priskin (Szalai 27), Elek.

Switzerland (2) 2 *(Embolo 24, Mehmedi 30)*

Portugal (0) 0 36,000

Switzerland: (4231) Sommer; Lichtsteiner (Widmer 69), Schar, Djourou, Rodriguez; Behrami, Xhaka■; Embolo, Dzemaili (Fernandes G 88), Mehmedi; Seferovic (Derdiyok 78).
Portugal: (433) Rui Patricio; Cedric, Pepe, Fonte, Guerreiro; Joao Moutinho (Quaresma 68), William Carvalho (Joao Mario 45), Adrien Silva; Nani, Eder (Andre Silva 45), Bernardo Silva.

Friday, 7 October 2016

Hungary (0) 2 *(Szalai 54, 71)*

Switzerland (0) 3 *(Seferovic 51, Rodriguez 67, Stocker 89)* 21,668

Hungary: (4231) Gulacsi; Fiola, Guzmics, Lang, Kadar; Nagy A, Gera; Dzsudzsak, Kleinheisler (Nemeth 76), Stieber; Szalai (Nikolic 87).
Switzerland: (4231) Sommer; Lichtsteiner, Schar, Elvedi, Rodriguez; Behrami, Dzemaili; Embolo, Shaqiri (Fernandes G 81), Mehmedi (Stocker 88); Seferovic (Derdiyok 73).

Latvia (0) 0

Faroe Islands (1) 2 *(Nattestad 19, Edmundsson 70)* 4823

Latvia: (442) Vanins; Gabovs, Jagodinskis, Gorkss, Maksimenko; Visnakovs, Kluskins (Zjuzins 72), Laizans, Lukjanovs (Ikaunieks J 76); Gutkovskis (Karlsons 64), Sabala.
Faroe Islands: (451) Nielsen; Davidsen V, Nattestad, Gregersen, Naes; Vatnhamar, Henriksen Olsen (Justinussen P 87), Benjaminsen, Hansson, Joensen (Sorensen 72); Edmundsson (Klettskard 90).

Portugal (3) 6 *(Ronaldo 2, 4, 47, 68, Joao Cancelo 44, Andre Silva 86)*

Andorra (0) 0 25,120

Portugal: (442) Rui Patricio; Joao Cancelo, Fonte, Pepe (Gelson Martins 72), Guerreiro (Antunes 52); Quaresma, Andre Gomes (Joao Mario 66), Joao Moutinho, Bernardo Silva; Ronaldo, Andre Silva.
Andorra: (541) Gomes; Jordi Rubio■, Lima, Vales, Llovera, Garcia M (San Nicolas 49); Rodriguez, Vieira, Rebes■, Martinez C (Moreira 76); Alaez (Pujol 73).

Monday, 10 October 2016

Andorra (0) 1 *(Martinez A 90)*

Switzerland (1) 2 *(Schar 19 (pen), Mehmedi 76)* 2014

Andorra: (532) Gomes; Jesus Rubio, Garcia E, Lima, Llovera, San Nicolas; Rodriguez, Vales, Clemente (Martinez A 72); Vieira (Martinez C 79), Pujol (Riera 83).
Switzerland: (4411) Burki; Lang, Schar, Klose (Elvedi 45), Rodriguez; Shaqiri (Stocker 79), Fernandes G (Zakaria 65), Xhaka, Mehmedi; Embolo; Seferovic.

Faroe Islands (0) 0

Portugal (3) 6 *(Andre Silva 12, 22, 37, Ronaldo 65, Joao Cancelo 90, Joao Moutinho 90)* 4780

Faroe Islands: (4411) Nielsen; Hansen, Gregersen (Davidsen J 73), Nattestad, Davidsen V; Vatnhamar, Benjaminsen, Hansson, Sorensen (Joensen 66); Henriksen Olsen (Bartalsstovu 79); Edmundsson.
Portugal: (442) Rui Patricio; Joao Cancelo, Fonte, Pepe, Antunes; Quaresma (Gelson Martins 67), Andre Gomes, William Carvalho, Joao Mario (Joao Moutinho 81); Ronaldo, Andre Silva (Eder 79).

Latvia (0) 0

Hungary (1) 2 *(Gyurcso 9, Szalai 77)* 4715

Latvia: (4141) Vanins; Gabovs, Jagodinskis, Gorkss, Maksimenko; Tarasovs; Visnakovs (Zjuzins 57), Kluskins (Ikaunieks J 69), Laizans (Karasausks 79), Ikaunieks D; Sabala.
Hungary: (442) Gulacsi; Bese, Guzmics, Kadar, Korhut; Gyurcso, Gera (Vida 84), Nagy A, Dzsudzsak; Szalai, Nikolic (Kleinheisler 45).

Sunday, 13 November 2016

Hungary (2) 4 *(Gera 33, Lang 43, Gyurcso 73, Szalai 88)*

Andorra (0) 0 20,479

Hungary: (4411) Gulacsi; Bese, Lang, Guzmics, Korhut; Gyurcso (Nemeth 81), Nagy A, Gera (Bode 84), Dzsudzsak; Kleinheisler (Stieber 73); Szalai.
Andorra: (532) Gomes; Jesus Rubio, Garcia E, Vales, Llovera, San Nicolas; Rodriguez (Moreira 82), Vieira, Martinez C (Martinez A 67); Pujol (Sanchez Soto 87), Alaez.

Portugal (1) 4 *(Ronaldo 28 (pen), 85, William Carvalho 69, Bruno Alves 90)*

Latvia (0) 1 *(Zjuzins 68)* 20,744

Portugal: (4141) Rui Patricio; Joao Cancelo, Fonte, Bruno Alves, Guerreiro; William Carvalho; Nani (Quaresma 65), Joao Mario (Gelson Martins 71), Andre Gomes (Sanches 87), Ronaldo; Andre Silva.
Latvia: (442) Vanins; Freimanis, Jagodinskis, Gorkss, Maksimenko; Gabovs, Tarasovs, Laizans, Kluskins (Visnakovs 79); Rudnevs (Gutkovskis 87), Ikaunieks D (Zjuzins 59).

Switzerland (1) 2 *(Derdiyok 27, Lichtsteiner 83)*

Faroe Islands (0) 0 14,800

Switzerland: (433) Sommer; Lichtsteiner, Schar, Djourou, Rodriguez; Behrami, Dzemaili (Steffen 80), Xhaka; Mehmedi, Derdiyok (Seferovic 87), Stocker (Fernandes E 69).
Faroe Islands: (433) Nielsen; Naes, Nattestad, Gregersen, Hansen; Henriksen Olsen, Benjaminsen (Faero 89), Hansson; Vatnhamar (Olsen A 81), Rolantsson (Joensen 78), Edmundsson.

Saturday, 25 March 2017

Andorra (0) 0

Faroe Islands (0) 0 1755

Andorra: (4411) Gomes; Jesus Rubio (Garcia M 45), Llovera, Lima, San Nicolas; Jordi Rubio (Clemente 77), Pujol (Martinez A 54), Vales, Martinez C; Vieira; Alaez.
Faroe Islands: (433) Nielsen; Naes, Davidsen V, Gregersen, Klettskard; Davidsen J, Bartalsstovu (Hansen 70), Hansson; Edmundsson■, Vatnhamar, Sorensen (Justinussen P 82).

Portugal (2) 3 *(Andre Silva 32, Ronaldo 36, 64)*

Hungary (0) 0 57,816

Portugal: (4132) Rui Patricio; Cedric, Pepe, Fonte, Guerreiro; William Carvalho; Joao Mario (Joao Moutinho 83), Andre Gomes (Pizzi 86), Quaresma; Andre Silva (Bernardo Silva 67), Ronaldo.
Hungary: (4141) Gulacsi; Lang (Lovrencsics 46), Vinicius, Kadar, Korhut; Nagy A; Bese, Gyurcso (Kalmar 69), Gera (Pinter 85), Dzsudzsak; Szalai.

Switzerland (0) 1 *(Drmic 66)*

Latvia (0) 0 25,000

Switzerland: (4231) Sommer; Lichtsteiner, Schar, Djourou, Moubandje; Fernandes G (Drmic 64), Xhaka; Shaqiri (Zuber 78), Dzemaili, Mehmedi; Seferovic (Freuler 83).
Latvia: (442) Vanins; Freimanis, Jagodinskis, Gorkss, Solovjovs; Visnakovs (Gabovs 55), Lazdins (Gutkovskis 77), Laizans, Kluskins; Sabala, Ikaunieks D (Rakels 69).

Friday, 9 June 2017

Andorra (1) 1 *(Rebes 26)*

Hungary (0) 0 2407

Andorra: (4411) Gomes; Jesus Rubio, Llovera, Lima, San Nicolas; Clemente (Riera 82), Vales, Rebes, Martinez A; Pujol (Ayala 88); Alaez (Maneiro 67).
Hungary: (4411) Gulacsi; Bese, Lang (Balogh 56), Toth, Vinicius; Gyurcso (Sallai 71), Nagy A, Stieber (Nagy D 21), Dzsudzsak; Kleinheisler; Eppel.

Faroe Islands (0) 0

Switzerland (1) 2 *(Xhaka 36, Shaqiri 59)* 4594

Faroe Islands: (442) Nielsen; Naes, Davidsen V, Gregersen, Davidsen J (Faero 70); Hansson (Lokin 66), Benjaminsen, Olsen K (Joensen 60), Sorensen; Vatnhamar, Justinussen F.
Switzerland: (442) Sommer; Lichtsteiner, Moubandje, Seferovic (Derdiyok 78), Xhaka; Behrami, Akanji, Dzemaili (Freuler 85), Mehmedi (Zuber 61); Djourou, Shaqiri.

Latvia (0) 0

Portugal (1) 3 *(Ronaldo 42, 63, Andre Silva 67)* 8087

Latvia: (4411) Vanins; Jagodinskis, Kolesovs, Gorkss, Maksimenko; Kluskins (Indrans 62), Kazacoks (Vardanjans 72), Laizans, Solovjovs; Sabala; Ikaunieks D (Rakels 68).
Portugal: (433) Rui Patricio; Bruno Alves, Cedric (Nelson Semedo 71), Fonte, Guerreiro; Joao Moutinho, William Carvalho, Andre Gomes; Gelson Martins (Quaresma 58), Andre Silva (Nani 80), Ronaldo.

Group B Table	P	W	D	L	F	A	GD	Pts
Switzerland	6	6	0	0	12	3	9	18
Portugal	6	5	0	1	22	3	19	15
Hungary	6	2	1	3	8	7	1	7
Faroe Islands	6	1	2	3	2	10	–8	5
Andorra	6	1	1	4	2	13	–11	4
Latvia	6	1	0	5	2	12	–10	3

GROUP C

Sunday, 4 September 2016

Czech Republic (0) 0

Northern Ireland (0) 0 10,731

Czech Republic: (442) Vaclik; Kaderabek, Suchy, Kadlec M, Novak; Skalak (Kopic 77), Pavelka, Darida, Krejci; Skoda (Necid 68), Kadlec V (Vydra 83).
Northern Ireland: (433) McGovern; McLaughlin, Evans J, McAuley, Ferguson; Norwood (Hodson 66), Davis, Dallas; Ward (McGinn 74), Lafferty K (Magennis 59), McNair.

Norway (0) 0

Germany (2) 3 *(Muller 16, 60, Kimmich 45)* 26,793

Norway: (442) Jarstein; Svensson, Hovland, Nordtveit, Aleesami; Diomande, Johansen (Jenssen 67), Tettey, Berisha; King (Sorloth 72), Henriksen (Selnaes 61).
Germany: (343) Neuer; Kimmich, Howedes, Hummels; Muller, Khedira (Weigl 84), Kroos, Hector; Ozil, Gotze (Brandt 73), Draxler (Meyer 84).

San Marino (0) 0

Azerbaijan (1) 1 *(Gurbanov 45)* 886

San Marino: (541) Simoncini A; Cesarini, Brolli■, Simoncini D, Vitaioli M (Valentini 85), Hirsch J; Palazzi, Tosi, Berardi M, Berardi F (Rinaldi 73); Chiaruzzi (Gasperoni L 53).
Azerbaijan: (4141) Agayev K; Garayev, Mirzabekov, Medvedev, Gurbanov (Alasgarov 69); Nazarov (Makhmudov 78); Rashad Sadygov, Ramazanov (Sheydayev 89), Amirguliev, Dashdemirov; Ismayilov.

Saturday, 8 October 2016

Azerbaijan (1) 1 *(Medvedev 11)*

Norway (0) 0 35,000

Azerbaijan: (433) Agayev K; Mirzabekov, Medvedev, Rashad Sadygov, Dashdemirov; Eddy (Alasgarov 65), Garayev, Amirguliev; Gurbanov (Sheydayev 80), Ramazanov (Guseynov 90), Nazarov.
Norway: (442) Jarstein; Svensson, Strandberg, Hovland, Aleesami; Helland (Berget 71), Skjelbred (Johansen 84), Selnaes, Diomande; King (Sorloth 61), Henriksen.

Germany (1) 3 *(Muller 13, 65, Kroos 49)*

Czech Republic (0) 0 53,000

Germany: (4231) Neuer; Kimmich, Boateng, Hummels, Hector (Howedes 67); Khedira, Kroos (Gundogan 75); Muller, Ozil, Draxler (Brandt 80); Gotze.
Czech Republic: (4231) Vaclik; Kaderabek, Sivok, Suchy, Novak; Pavelka (Droppa 63), Horava; Petrzela (Skalak 69), Dockal, Krejci; Vydra (Kadlec V 77).

Northern Ireland (1) 4 *(Davis 26 (pen), Lafferty K 79, 90, Ward 85)*

San Marino (0) 0 18,234

Northern Ireland: (4411) McGovern; McLaughlin (McNair 77), Evans J, McAuley, Ferguson; McGinn, Davis, Norwood, Dallas (Washington 65); Ward; Magennis (Lafferty K 72).
San Marino: (541) Simoncini A; Berardi M, Vitaioli F, Simoncini D, Della Valle, Palazzi■; Hirsch A (Cesarini 55), Tosi, Coppini (Golinucci E 70), Vitaioli M; Stefanelli (Zafferani 87).

Tuesday, 11 October 2016

Czech Republic (0) 0

Azerbaijan (0) 0 12,148

Czech Republic: (442) Vaclik; Gebre Selassie, Brabec, Sivok, Sykora; Skalak (Zmrhal 74), Droppa, Dockal, Krejci (Petrzela 63); Schick (Skoda 66), Kadlec V.
Azerbaijan: (4141) Agayev K; Mirzabekov, Medvedev, Guseynov, Dashdemirov; Garayev; Alasgarov (Ramazanov 70), Amirguliev, Nazarov, Gurbanov (Abdullayev 87); Sheydayev (Eddy 90).

Germany (2) 2 *(Draxler 13, Khedira 17)*

Northern Ireland (0) 0 42,132

Germany: (4231) Neuer; Kimmich, Boateng (Mustafi 69), Hummels, Hector (Volland 80); Khedira, Kroos; Muller, Ozil (Gundogan 45), Draxler; Gotze.
Northern Ireland: (532) McGovern; Hodson, Hughes, McAuley, Evans J, Ferguson; Evans C, Davis, Norwood (McNair 72); Ward (McGinn 60), Magennis (Lafferty K 76).

Norway (1) 4 *(Simoncini D 11 (og), Diomande 77, Samuelsen 81, King 83)*

San Marino (0) 1 *(Stefanelli 54)* 8298

Norway: (442) Jarstein; Svensson, Strandberg, Hovland, Aleesami; Skjelbred, Selnaes, Tettey (Samuelsen 67), Berget (Sorloth 73); Henriksen (Diomande 45), King.
San Marino: (532) Simoncini A; Brolli, Vitaioli F, Simoncini D, Della Valle, Rinaldi (Berardi M 45); Valentini (Hirsch J 67), Tosi, Mazza; Zafferani, Stefanelli (Selva 82).

Friday, 11 November 2016

Czech Republic (1) 2 *(Krmencik 11, Zmrhal 47)*

Norway (0) 1 *(King 87)* 16,411

Czech Republic: (4141) Vaclik; Kaderabek, Sivok, Brabec, Novak; Droppa (Pavelka 81); Krejci (Skalak 86), Dockal, Horava, Zmrhal; Krmencik (Schick 81).
Norway: (442) Jarstein; Elabdellaoui, Hovland, Forren, Aleesami; Skjelbred (Daehli 50), Tettey, Johansen, Berget (Elyounoussi T 71); Henriksen (Diomande 60), King.

Northern Ireland (2) 4 *(Lafferty K 27, McAuley 40, McLaughlin 67, Brunt 83)*

Azerbaijan (0) 0 18,404

Northern Ireland: (442) McGovern; McLaughlin, McAuley, Evans J, Brunt; Evans C (McNair 81), Norwood, Davis, Ferguson (McGinn 73); Lafferty K (Grigg 61), Magennis.
Azerbaijan: (451) Agayev K; Mirzabekov, Medvedev, Guseynov, Dashdemirov; Ismayilov, Makhmudov (Nazarov 70), Garayev, Amirguliev, Qurbanov (Ramazanov 75); Sheydayev (Yilmaz 45).

San Marino (0) 0

Germany (3) 8 *(Khedira 7, Gnabry 9, 58, 76, Hector 32, 65, Stefanelli 82 (og), Volland 85)* 3851

San Marino: (541) Simoncini A; Palazzi, Cesarini, Simoncini D, Vitaioli F, Berardi M; Zafferani (Brolli 83), Gasperoni A, Tosi (Domeniconi 59), Vitaioli M (Hirsch A 90); Stefanelli.
Germany: (4231) ter Stegen; Henrichs, Kimmich, Hummels, Hector; Khedira (Goretzka 77), Gundogan; Muller, Gnabry, Gotze (Meyer 71); Gomez (Volland 71).

Sunday, 26 March 2017

Azerbaijan (1) 1 *(Nazarov 31)*

Germany (3) 4 *(Schurrle 19, 80, Muller 36, Gomez 45)* 30,000

Azerbaijan: (4231) Agayev K; Pashaev, Guseynov, Rashad Sadygov, Mirzabekov; Garayev, Amirguliev (Eddy 87); Ismayilov (Qurbanov 82), Huseynov, Nazarov; Sheydayev (Yilmaz 67).
Germany: (4231) Leno; Kimmich, Hummels, Howedes, Hector; Khedira, Kroos (Rudy 89); Schurrle, Muller, Draxler (Sane 85); Gomez (Ozil 61).

Northern Ireland (2) 2 *(Ward 2, Washington 32)*

Norway (0) 0 18,161

Northern Ireland: (4231) McGovern; McLaughlin, Evans J, McAuley, Cathcart; Davis, Norwood; Ward (McGinn 80), Brunt, Dallas (Lund 88); Washington (Lafferty K 85).
Norway: (4231) Jarstein; Skjelvik, Elabdellaoui, Valsvik, Hovland; Johansen (Berge 74), Nordtveit; Elyounoussi M, King, Elyounoussi T (Daehli 53); Soderlund (Diomande 63).

San Marino (0) 0

Czech Republic (5) 6 *(Barak 17, 24, Darida 19, 77 (pen), Gebre Selassie 25, Krmencik 43)* 1000

San Marino: (541) Simoncini A; Palazzi, Cesarini, Simoncini D, Vitaioli F, Rinaldi (Tomassini 61); Vitaioli M, Domeniconi, Zafferani, Cervellini (Battistini 90); Stefanelli (Mazza 84).
Czech Republic: (4231) Vaclik; Gebre Selassie, Sivok, Brabec, Novak; Darida, Dockal; Jankto (Zmrhal 67), Krejci, Barak (Horava 75); Krmencik (Skoda 67).

Saturday, 10 June 2017

Azerbaijan (0) 0

Northern Ireland (0) 1 *(Dallas 90)* 27,978

Azerbaijan: (433) Agayev K; Medvedev, Guseynov, Rashad Sadygov, Pashaev; Huseynov, Garayev, Almeida; Ismayilov (Amirguliev 84), Sheydayev (Abdullayev 90), Nazarov (Aleskerov 76).
Northern Ireland: (532) McGovern; McLaughlin, Hughes, McAuley (McGinn 25 (Hodson 86)), Evans J, Dallas; Brunt, Norwood, Davis; Boyce (Lafferty K 77), Magennis.

Germany (4) 7 *(Draxler 11, Wagner 16, 29, 85, Younes 39, Mustafi 47, Brandt 72)*

San Marino (0) 0 32,467

Germany: (3142) ter Stegen; Kimmich, Mustafi, Hector (Plattenhardt 55); Can; Brandt, Goretzka, Draxler (Demme 75), Younes; Wagner, Stindl (Werner 55).
San Marino: (4141) Benedettini; Bonini, Della Valle, Biordi, Cesarini (Brolli 87); Cervellini; Golinucci A, Mazza (Bernardi 69), Zafferani, Palazzi; Rinaldi (Hirsch A 78).

Norway (0) 1 *(Soderlund 56 (pen))*

Czech Republic (1) 1 *(Gebre Selassie 36)* 12,179

Norway: (442) Jarstein; Svensson, Nordtveit, Reginiussen (Valsvik 33), Aleesami; Elyounoussi M, Berge, Johansen, Berget (Daehli 61); Elyounoussi T, Soderlund (Johnsen 71).
Czech Republic: (4411) Vaclik; Kaderabek, Sivok, Brabec, Gebre Selassie; Krejci, Darida (Horava 80), Soucek, Zmrhal (Jankto 43); Dockal; Krmencik (Schick 63).

Group C Table	*P*	*W*	*D*	*L*	*F*	*A*	*GD*	*Pts*
Germany	6	6	0	0	27	1	26	18
Northern Ireland	6	4	1	1	11	2	9	13
Czech Republic	6	2	3	1	9	5	4	9
Azerbaijan	6	2	1	3	3	9	–6	7
Norway	6	1	1	4	6	10	–4	4
San Marino	6	0	0	6	1	30	–29	0

GROUP D

Monday, 5 September 2016

Georgia (0) 1 *(Ananidze 78)*

Austria (2) 2 *(Hinteregger 16, Janko 42)* 28,500

Georgia: (4312) Loria; Lobjanidze (Chanturia 84), Kvirkvelia, Amisulashvili (Okriashvili 76), Navalovski; Kashia, Daushvili, Jigauri; Ananidze; Qazaishvili, Dvalishvili (Skhirtladze 63).
Austria: (4411) Almer; Klein, Dragovic, Hinteregger, Suttner; Harnik (Sabitzer 71), Baumgartlinger, Alaba, Arnautovic; Junuzovic (Schopf 67); Janko (Gregoritsch 76).

Serbia (0) 2 *(Kostic 62, Tadic 69 (pen))*

Republic of Ireland (1) 2 *(Hendrick 3, Murphy 81)* 7896

Serbia: (343) Rajkovic; Ivanovic, Nastasic, Vukovic; Rukavina, Milivojevic, Gudelj, Mladenovic (Tosic D 76); Tadic, Mitrovic A (Pavlovic 59), Kostic (Katai 82).
Republic of Ireland: (433) Randolph; Coleman, O'Shea, Keogh, Ward (Quinn 71); Hendrick (Murphy 75), Whelan, Brady; Walters, Long S (Clark 90), McClean.

Wales (2) 4 *(Vokes 38, Allen 44, Bale 51, 90 (pen))*

Moldova (0) 0 31,731

Wales: (532) Hennessey; Gunter, Chester, Williams (Collins 82), Davies, Taylor; Ledley (Huws 67), Allen, King; Vokes (Robson-Kanu 75), Bale.
Moldova: (532) Cebanu; Cojocari, Cascaval, Epureanu, Armas, Jardan; Gatcan, Cebotaru (Sidorenco 75), Ionita; Ginsari (Bugaev 75), Dedov (Mihaliov 84).

Thursday, 6 October 2016

Austria (1) 2 *(Arnautovic 28, 48)*

Wales (2) 2 *(Allen 22, Wimmer 45 (og))* 44,200

Austria: (4411) Almer (Ozcan 58); Klein, Dragovic, Hinteregger, Wimmer; Sabitzer, Baumgartlinger, Alaba, Arnautovic (Schaub 87); Junuzovic (Schopf 79); Janko.
Wales: (532) Hennessey; Gunter, Chester, Davies, Williams, Taylor (Huws 90); Ledley, Allen (Edwards 56), King; Bale, Vokes (Robson-Kanu 77).

Moldova (0) 0

Serbia (2) 3 *(Kostic 20, Ivanovic 38, Tadic 59)* 8500

Moldova: (4231) Cebanu; Racu, Carp, Epureanu, Bolohan; Cojocari, Gatcan; Andronic (Mihaliov 68), Cebotaru (Ginsari 77), Dedov (Sidorenco 63); Bugaev.
Serbia: (3421) Stojkovic; Nastasic, Ivanovic, Vukovic (Mitrovic S 70); Rukavina, Gudelj, Milivojevic, Kolarov; Kostic (Tosic Z 71), Tadic; Pavlovic (Katai 45).

Republic of Ireland (0) 1 *(Coleman 56)*

Georgia (0) 0 39,793

Republic of Ireland: (433) Randolph; Coleman, Duffy, Clark, Ward; McCarthy, Hendrick, Brady (Whelan 81); Walters, Long S (O'Shea 90), McClean.
Georgia: (433) Loria; Kakabadze, Kvirkvelia, Kashia, Navalovski (Kobakhidze 89); Daushvili (Kacharava 90), Qazaishvili, Gvilia; Okriashvili, Mchedlidze, Ananidze (Skhirtladze 74).

Sunday, 9 October 2016

Moldova (1) 1 *(Bugaev 45)*

Republic of Ireland (1) 3 *(Long S 2, McClean 69, 76)* 6089

Moldova: (4231) Calancea; Bordiyan, Posmac, Armas (Golovatenco 36), Bolohan; Gatcan, Cojocari; Andronic (Sidorenco 83), Zasavitchi (Cebotaru 61), Dedov; Bugaev.
Republic of Ireland: (4231) Randolph; Coleman, Duffy, Clark, Ward; Whelan, McCarthy (Meyler 80); Walters, Hoolahan (O'Kane 86), McClean; Long S (O'Dowda 62).

Serbia (2) 3 *(Mitrovic A 5, 23, Tadic 74)*

Austria (1) 2 *(Sabitzer 15, Janko 62)* 29,000

Serbia: (3412) Stojkovic; Ivanovic, Mitrovic S, Nastasic; Rukavina (Maksimovic 90), Milivojevic, Fejsa, Kolarov; Tadic; Mitrovic A (Gudelj 77), Kostic (Katai 65).
Austria: (4231) Ozcan; Klein, Dragovic (Prodl 71), Hinteregger, Wimmer; Baumgartlinger (Ilsanker 58), Alaba; Sabitzer, Junuzovic (Schopf 64), Arnautovic; Janko.

Wales (1) 1 *(Bale 10)*

Georgia (0) 1 *(Okriashvili 57)* 32,652

Wales: (532) Hennessey; Gunter, Chester, Williams, Davies, Taylor (Cotterill 69); Edwards, Ledley (Huws 73), King (Robson-Kanu 61); Vokes, Bale.
Georgia: (4411) Loria; Kakabadze, Kvirkvelia, Kashia, Navalovski; Ananidze (Kacharava 90), Daushvili, Gvilia, Okriashvili (Jigauri 90); Qazaishvili; Mchedlidze (Dvalishvili 75).

Saturday, 12 November 2016

Austria (0) 0

Republic of Ireland (0) 1 *(McClean 48)* 48,500

Austria: (4231) Ozcan; Klein, Dragovic, Hinteregger, Wimmer (Ilsanker 78); Sabitzer (Harnik 73), Baumgartlinger; Alaba, Schopf (Schaub 57), Arnautovic; Janko.
Republic of Ireland: (4231) Randolph; Coleman, Duffy, Clark, Brady; Whelan (Meyler 24), Arter; Hendrick, Hoolahan (McGoldrick 78), McClean (McGeady 85); Walters.

Georgia (1) 1 *(Qazaishvili 16)*

Moldova (0) 1 *(Gatcan 78)* 40,642

Georgia: (4231) Loria; Kakabadze, Kvirkvelia, Kashia, Navalovski; Gvilia (Dvalishvili 71), Daushvili; Chanturia, Qazaishvili (Skhirtladze 80), Okriashvili; Kvilitaia (Kankava 64).
Moldova: (4231) Cebanu; Racu (Golovatenco 42), Posmac, Epureanu, Bolohan; Bordiyan, Gatcan; Jardan, Mihaliov (Andronic 77), Sidorenco (Antoniuc 70); Bugaev.

Wales (1) 1 *(Bale 30)*

Serbia (0) 1 *(Mitrovic A 86)* 32,879

Wales: (442) Hennessey; Gunter, Chester, Williams, Taylor; Allen, Ledley (Edwards 83), Bale, Ramsey; Vokes, Robson-Kanu (Lawrence 68).
Serbia: (541) Stojkovic; Rukavina, Ivanovic, Maksimovic, Nastasic, Obradovic; Kostic (Katai 70), Matic, Milivojevic, Tadic; Mitrovic A (Gudelj 88).

Friday, 24 March 2017

Austria (0) 2 *(Sabitzer 75, Harnik 90)*

Moldova (0) 0 21,000

Austria: (3421) Lindner; Dragovic, Prodl, Hinteregger; Lazaro (Janko 69), Junuzovic, Ilsanker, Alaba; Arnautovic (Suttner 90), Sabitzer; Burgstaller (Harnik 82).
Moldova: (442) Namasco; Golovatenco, Posmac, Epureanu, Bolohan (Mihaliov 90); Dedov, Cebotaru, Gatcan, Antoniuc (Ionita 62); Ginsari (Racu 81), Bugaev.

Georgia (1) 1 *(Kacharava 5)*

Serbia (1) 3 *(Tadic 45 (pen), Mitrovic A 64, Gacinovic 86)* 31,328

Georgia: (451) Loria; Kakabadze (Arabidze 70), Kashia, Kvirkvelia, Navalovski; Qazaishvili (Kvilitaia 83), Gvilia (Jigauri 90), Kvekveskiri, Kankava, Ananidze; Kacharava.
Serbia: (343) Stojkovic; Ivanovic, Maksimovic, Kolarov; Rukavina, Milivojevic, Matic, Obradovic (Vukovic 45); Kostic (Gacinovic 81), Tadic, Mitrovic A (Gudelj 71).

Republic of Ireland (0) 0

Wales (0) 0 49,989

Republic of Ireland: (4141) Randolph; Coleman (Christie 72), Keogh, O'Shea, Ward; Walters; Whelan, Hendrick, McClean, Long S; Meyler (McGeady 80).
Wales: (532) Hennessey; Gunter, Chester, Williams, Davies, Taylor■; Ledley (Richards 72), Ramsey, Allen; Bale, Robson-Kanu (Vokes 45).

Sunday, 11 June 2017

Moldova (2) 2 *(Ginsari 15, Dedov 36)*

Georgia (0) 2 *(Merebashvili 65, Kazaishvili 70)* 4803

Moldova: (4231) Namasco; Tigirlas (Racu 77), Posmac, Epureanu, Bordian; Cebotaru, Carp (Cojocari 72); Antoniuc, Cociuc (Bugaev 73), Dedov; Ginsari.
Georgia: (343) Makaridze; Kvirkvelia, Kashia, Tabidze; Lobjanidze (Kvekveskiri 35), Kankava, Daushvili (Kazaishvili 45), Navalovski; Arabidze, Kacharava, Dvalishvili (Merebashvili 64).

Republic of Ireland (0) 1 *(Walters 85)*

Austria (1) 1 *(Hinteregger 31)* 50,000

Republic of Ireland: (4231) Randolph; Christie, Duffy, Long K, Ward (Murphy 55); Arter (Hoolahan 71), Whelan (McGeady 77); Brady, Hendrick, McClean; Walters.
Austria: (4321) Lindner; Lainer, Dragovic, Prodl, Hinteregger; Baumgartlinger, Junuzovic (Grillitsch 79), Alaba; Lazaro, Kainz (Gregoritsch 90); Burgstaller (Harnik 75).

Serbia (0) 1 *(Mitrovic A 73)*

Wales (1) 1 *(Ramsey 35 (pen))* 42,100

Serbia: (343) Stojkovic; Ivanovic, Nastasic, Vukovic; Rukavina, Milivojevic (Gudelj 63), Matic, Kolarov; Kostic (Prijovic 67), Mitrovic A, Tadic.
Wales: (352) Hennessey; Gunter, Chester, Williams; Davies, Richards, Allen, Edwards (Huws 73), Ledley; Ramsey, Vokes (Lawrence 85).

Group D Table	*P*	*W*	*D*	*L*	*F*	*A*	*GD*	*Pts*
Serbia	6	3	3	0	13	7	6	12
Republic of Ireland	6	3	3	0	8	4	4	12
Wales	6	1	5	0	9	5	4	8
Austria	6	2	2	2	9	8	1	8
Georgia	6	0	3	3	6	10	–4	3
Moldova	6	0	2	4	4	15	–11	2

GROUP E

Sunday, 4 September 2016

Denmark (1) 1 *(Eriksen 17)*

Armenia (0) 0 21,000

Denmark: (343) Ronnow; Kjaer, Christensen, Vestergaard; Ankersen, Kvist, Hojbjerg (Delaney 81), Durmisi; Fischer, Eriksen, Jorgensen N (Poulsen 66).
Armenia: (523) Beglaryan; Hambartsumyan, Haroyan, Mkoyan, Andonian, Hovhannisyan G; Yedigaryan, Malakyan (Manoyan 77); Ozbiliz (Ghazaryan 41), Arshakiyan (Pizzelli 70), Kadimyan.

Kazakhstan (0) 2 *(Khizhnichenko 51, 58)*

Poland (2) 2 *(Kapustka 9, Lewandowski 35 (pen))* 19,905

Kazakhstan: (532) Pokatilov; Beisebekov, Akhmetov (Abdulin 61), Maliy, Kislitsyn, Shomko; Muzhikov, Baizhanov (Nurgaliev 69), Kuat; Islamkhan (Tagybergen 79), Khizhnichenko.
Poland: (442) Fabianski; Piszczek, Glik, Salamon, Rybus; Blaszczykowski, Krychowiak, Zielinski, Kapustka (Linetty 82); Lewandowski, Milik.

Romania (0) 1 *(Popa 85)*

Montenegro (0) 1 *(Jovetic 87)* 25,468

Romania: (4231) Pantilimon; Benzar, Moti, Grigore, Filip; Hoban, Sapunaru; Bicfalvi (Popa 76), Stancu (Keseru 90), Stanciu; Andone (Torje 70).
Montenegro: (4411) Bozovic; Tomasevic, Savic, Simic, Vukcevic; Marusic, Vesovic (Kojasevic 80), Scekic, Bakic (Mugosa 68); Jovetic; Beciraj (Nikolic 90).

Saturday, 8 October 2016

Armenia (0) 0

Romania (4) 5 *(Stancu 5 (pen), Popa 10, Marin 12, Stanciu 29, Chipciu 59)* 5500

Armenia: (4231) Beglaryan; Mkoyan, Haroyan, Andonian (Voskanyan 38), Hayrapetyan; Grigoryan, Malakyan■; Ozbiliz (Hovhannisyan B 64), Pizzelli, Manoyan; Pogosyan (Muradyan 33).
Romania: (4231) Tatarusanu; Benzar, Sapunaru, Grigore, Latovlevici; Marin, Hoban; Popa, Stanciu (Bicfalvi 81), Chipciu (Rotariu 67); Stancu (Keseru 57).

Montenegro (1) 5 *(Tomasevic 24, Vukcevic 59, Jovetic 64, Beciraj 73, Savic 78)*

Kazakhstan (0) 0 8517

Montenegro: (442) Bozovic; Marusic, Savic, Simic, Tomasevic; Vesovic, Scekic (Bakic 83), Vukcevic (Nikolic 67), Kojasevic; Beciraj (Raicevic 75), Jovetic.
Kazakhstan: (4132) Pokatilov; Beisebekov, Kislitsyn, Logvinenko, Shomko; Maliy; Kuat (Tagybergen 76), Mukhutdinov, Nurgaliev; Khizhnichenko (Murtazaev 85), Islamkhan (Muzhikov 63).

Poland (2) 3 *(Lewandowski 20, 36 (pen), 47)*

Denmark (0) 2 *(Glik 49 (og), Poulsen 69)* 56,800

Poland: (442) Fabianski; Piszczek, Glik, Cionek, Jedrzejczyk; Blaszczykowski (Peszko 88), Krychowiak, Zielinski, Grosicki (Rybus 73); Milik (Linetty 45), Lewandowski.
Denmark: (3412) Schmeichel; Kjaer, Christensen, Vestergaard (Delaney 81); Ankersen, Kvist, Hojbjerg, Durmisi; Eriksen; Fischer (Sisto 74), Jorgensen N (Poulsen 45).

Tuesday, 11 October 2016

Denmark (0) 0

Montenegro (1) 1 *(Beciraj 32)* 24,962

Denmark: (3412) Schmeichel; Kjaer, Jorgensen M (Jorgensen N 83), Christensen; Ankersen, Hojbjerg (Sisto 63), Delaney, Durmisi; Eriksen; Fischer (Cornelius 70), Poulsen.
Montenegro: (442) Bozovic; Marusic, Simic (Sofranac 70), Savic, Tomasevic; Vesovic (Mijuskovic 90), Vukcevic, Scekic, Kojasevic (Jovovic 63); Jovetic, Beciraj.

Kazakhstan (0) 0

Romania (0) 0 12,346

Kazakhstan: (541) Pokatilov; Beisebekov, Akhmetov, Maliy, Logvinenko, Shomko; Smakov, Muzhikov, Kuat (Tagybergen 86), Baizhanov (Nurgaliev 66); Khizhnichenko (Murtazaev 82).
Romania: (4411) Tatarusanu; Benzar, Sapunaru, Grigore (Moti 26), Tosca; Hoban, Marin, Popa (Andone 84), Stanciu; Chipciu (Enache 45); Stancu.

Poland (0) 2 *(Mkoyan 47 (og), Lewandowski 90)*

Armenia (0) 1 *(Pizzelli 50)* 44,786

Poland: (442) Fabianski; Blaszczykowski, Glik, Cionek, Jedrzejczyk (Wszolek 33); Grosicki (Kapustka 70), Krychowiak, Zielinski, Rybus; Lewandowski, Teodorczyk (Wilczek 85).
Armenia: (541) Beglaryan; Minasian, Haroyan, Mkoyan, Andonian■, Hayrapetyan; Hovhannisyan K (Ozbiliz 60), Muradyan (Voskanyan 34), Grigoryan, Manoyan; Pizzelli (Hakobyan 84).

Friday, 11 November 2016

Armenia (0) 3 *(Grigoryan 50, Haroyan 74, Ghazaryan 90)*

Montenegro (2) 2 *(Kojasevic 36, Jovetic 38)* 3500

Armenia: (451) Beglaryan; Voskanyan, Haroyan, Mkoyan, Hayrapetyan; Ghazaryan, Grigoryan, Pizzelli (Hovhannisyan K 81), Malakyan, Mkhitaryan; Koryan (Sarkisov 59).
Montenegro: (4411) Bozovic; Marusic, Savic, Basa, Stojkovic; Vesovic (Mugosa 86), Scekic, Vukcevic (Zverotic 63), Kojasevic (Jovovic 76); Jovetic; Beciraj.

Denmark (2) 4 *(Cornelius 15, Eriksen 36 (pen), 90, Ankersen 78)*

Kazakhstan (1) 1 *(Suyumbayev 17)* 18,418

Denmark: (433) Ronnow; Ankersen, Kjaer, Bjelland, Durmisi; Kvist, Delaney, Eriksen; Poulsen, Jorgensen N, Cornelius (Dolberg 81).
Kazakhstan: (532) Pokatilov; Suyumbayev, Akhmetov, Logvinenko, Shomko, Maliy; Baizhanov, Mukhutdinov, Muzhikov (Tunggyshbayev 80); Khizhnichenko (Moldakaraev 59), Islamkhan (Murtazaev 70).

Romania (0) 0

Poland (1) 3 *(Grosicki 11, Lewandowski 82, 90 (pen))* 48,531

Romania: (4231) Tatarusanu; Benzar, Chiriches, Grigore, Tosca; Hoban (Prepelita 45), Marin; Popa (Andone 45), Stanciu (Keseru 82), Chipciu; Stancu.
Poland: (4321) Fabianski; Piszczek, Glik, Pazdan, Jedrzejczyk; Krychowiak, Blaszczykowski, Grosicki (Peszko 89); Zielinski (Teodorczyk 80), Linetty (Maczynski 69); Lewandowski.

Sunday, 26 March 2017

Armenia (0) 2 *(Mkhitaryan 73, Ozbiliz 75)*

Kazakhstan (0) 0 11,500

Armenia: (433) Beglaryan; Voskanyan, Haroyan, Andonian, Hayrapetyan; Mkhitaryan, Malakyan, Pizzelli (Manucharyan 65); Hovhannisyan K, Sarkisov (Ozbiliz 70), Ghazaryan (Barseghyan 5).
Kazakhstan: (352) Loria; Beisebekov, Maliy■, Shomko; Tunggyshbayev (Muzhikov 78), Kuat (Dmitrenko 81), Tagybergen, Islamkhan (Baizhanov 87), Suyumbayev; Nuserbaev, Nurgaliev.

Montenegro (0) 1 *(Mugosa 63)*

Poland (1) 2 *(Lewandowski 40, Piszczek 82)* 10,439

Montenegro: (442) Bozovic; Marusic (Vucinic 90), Savic, Sofranac, Stojkovic; Vesovic, Vukcevic, Scekic (Djordjevic 86), Kojasevic (Ivanic 76); Mugosa, Beciraj.
Poland: (451) Fabianski; Piszczek, Glik, Pazdan, Jedrzejczyk; Blaszczykowski, Linetty (Teodorczyk 79), Zielinski, Maczynski (Cionek 90), Grosicki (Peszko 90); Lewandowski.

Romania (0) 0

Denmark (0) 0 26,892

Romania: (3412) Tatarusanu; Sapunaru, Chiriches, Tosca; Benzar, Marin, Pintilii, Latovlevici (Rotariu 76); Stanciu; Chipciu (Ivan 86), Keseru (Alibec 63).
Denmark: (352) Schmeichel; Kjaer (Jorgensen M 46), Christensen, Vestergaard; Ankersen, Kvist, Schone (Braithwaite 69), Delaney, Durmisi; Eriksen, Cornelius.

Saturday, 10 June 2017

Kazakhstan (0) 1 *(Kuat 76)*

Denmark (1) 3 *(Jorgensen N 27, Eriksen 51 (pen), Dolberg 81)* 19,065

Kazakhstan: (451) Loria; Suyumbayev, Akhmetov, Logvinenko, Shomko (Vorogovskiy 67); Muzhikov, Zhukov, Kuat, Islamkhan■, Nurgaliev (Beisebekov 56); Nuserbaev (Tunggyshbayev 74).
Denmark: (433) Ronnow; Larsen (Dalsgaard 82), Kjaer, Vestergaard, Durmisi; Kvist (Schone 46), Eriksen, Delaney; Poulsen (Dolberg 68), Jorgensen N, Braithwaite.

Montenegro (2) 4 *(Beciraj 2, Jovetic 28, 54, 82)*

Armenia (0) 1 *(Koryan 89)* 6861

Montenegro: (4231) Petkovic; Marusic, Savic, Simic, Tomasevic (Klimenta 74); Vukcevic (Scekic 71), Kosovic; Jankovic, Jovetic, Jovovic (Haksabanovic 84); Beciraj.

Armenia: (4231) Beglaryan; Mkoyan, Voskanyan, Andonian, Daghbashyan; Mkhitaryan, Grigoryan; Hovhannisyan K, Pizzelli (Barseghyan 73), Ozbiliz (Manucharyan 60); Koryan.

Poland (1) 3 *(Lewandowski 29 (pen), 57, 62 (pen))*

Romania (0) 1 *(Stancu 77)* 57,128

Poland: (4411) Szczesny; Jedrzejczyk, Pazdan, Cionek, Piszczek; Grosicki, Linetty (Milik 73), Maczynski (Krychowiak 44), Blaszczykowski; Zielinski (Teodorczyk 81); Lewandowski.
Romania: (541) Tatarusanu; Latovlevici (Grozav 60), Tosca, Sapunaru, Chiriches, Benzar; Stancu, Pintilii, Marin (Hanca 79), Chipciu (Stanciu 60); Andone.

Group E Table	P	W	D	L	F	A	GD	Pts
Poland	6	5	1	0	15	7	8	16
Montenegro	6	3	1	2	14	7	7	10
Denmark	6	3	1	2	10	6	4	10
Romania	6	1	3	2	7	7	0	6
Armenia	6	2	0	4	7	14	–7	6
Kazakhstan	6	0	2	4	4	16	–12	2

GROUP F

Sunday, 4 September 2016

Lithuania (2) 2 *(Cernych 32, Slivka 34)*

Slovenia (0) 2 *(Krhin 77, Cesar 90)* 4114

Lithuania: (433) Setkus; Vaitkunas, Freidgeimas, Girdvainis, Slavickas; Cernych (Grigaravicius 70), Zulpa, Kuklys; Novikovas, Slivka (Chvedukas 78), Valskis (Matulevicius 84).
Slovenia: (442) Oblak; Skubic, Samardzic, Cesar, Jokic; Verbic (Novakovic 56), Krhin, Kampl, Birsa; Beric (Ilicic 46), Bezjak.

Malta (1) 1 *(Effiong 14)*

Scotland (1) 5 *(Snodgrass 10, 61 (pen), 85, Martin C 53, Fletcher S 78)* 15,069

Malta: (532) Hogg; Agius, Caruana■, Borg, Zerafa, Scicluna (Camilleri 79); Fenech P, Sciberras, Gambin■; Schembri (Briffa 66), Effiong (Mifsud 89).
Scotland: (442) Marshall; Martin R, Robertson, Paterson, Hanley; Fletcher D, Bannan, Ritchie (Anya 86), Snodgrass; Martin C (Fletcher S 68), Burke (Forrest 66).

Slovakia (0) 0

England (0) 1 *(Lallana 90)* 18,111

Slovakia: (451) Kozacik; Pekarik, Skrtel■, Durica, Hubocan; Mak (Kubik 71), Gregus, Pecovsky (Gyomber 56), Hamsik, Svento (Kiss 78); Duris.
England: (4231) Hart; Walker, Cahill, Stones, Rose; Henderson (Alli 64), Dier; Sterling (Walcott 70), Rooney, Lallana; Kane (Sturridge 82).

Saturday, 8 October 2016

England (2) 2 *(Sturridge 29, Alli 38)*

Malta (0) 0 81,787

England: (451) Hart; Walker, Cahill, Stones, Bertrand (Rose 19); Walcott (Rashford 68), Rooney, Henderson, Alli, Lingard; Sturridge (Vardy 73).
Malta: (532) Hogg; Borg, Muscat Z, Agius, Camilleri, Muscat A; Kristensen, Sciberras, Fenech P; Schembri (Muscat R 87), Effiong (Mifsud 76).

Scotland (0) 1 *(McArthur 89)*

Lithuania (0) 1 *(Cernych 58)* 35,966

Scotland: (442) Marshall; Paterson, Martin R, Hanley, Robertson; Snodgrass, Bannan, Fletcher D (McArthur 46), Ritchie (Griffiths 71); Burke (Forrest 57), Martin C.
Lithuania: (442) Setkus; Vaitkunas, Freidgeimas, Girdvainis, Slavickas (Andriuskevicius 63); Cernych, Zulpa (Chvedukas 65), Kuklys, Novikovas; Valskis (Grigaravicius 85), Slivka.

Slovenia (0) 1 *(Kronaveter 74)*

Slovakia (0) 0 10,492

Slovenia: (4132) Oblak; Struna, Samardzic, Cesar, Jokic; Krhin; Kurtic (Kronaveter 72), Birsa (Novakovic 68), Verbic; Ilicic, Bezjak (Mevlja 90).
Slovakia: (532) Kozacik; Pauschek (Sabo 79), Salata, Hubocan, Durica, Svento (Holubek 79); Kucka, Hrosovsky (Duris 79), Gregus; Mak, Hamsik.

Tuesday, 11 October 2016

Lithuania (0) 2 *(Cernych 75, Novikovas 84 (pen))*

Malta (0) 0 5067

Lithuania: (451) Setkus; Vaitkunas, Mikuckis, Freidgeimas, Andriuskevicius; Cernych, Zulpa, Slivka, Kuklys (Chvedukas 79), Novikovas (Grigaravicius 87); Valskis (Matulevicius 61).
Malta: (532) Hogg; Borg, Muscat Z, Agius, Caruana■, Zerafa; Kristensen (Effiong 80), Sciberras, Fenech P (Pisani 85); Mifsud, Schembri (Muscat R 83).

Slovakia (1) 3 *(Mak 18, 56, Nemec 68)*

Scotland (0) 0 11,098

Slovakia: (4231) Kozacik; Sabo, Skrtel, Durica, Holubek; Kucka, Skriniar; Duris, Hamsik (Kiss 87), Mak (Svento 80); Nemec (Bakos 69).
Scotland: (451) Marshall; Paterson, Martin R, Hanley, Tierney; Snodgrass, Bannan, Fletcher D (Griffiths 64), McArthur, Ritchie (Anya 64); Fletcher S (McGinn 76).

Slovenia (0) 0

England (0) 0 13,274

Slovenia: (442) Oblak; Struna, Samardzic, Cesar (Mevlja 68), Jokic; Kurtic, Krhin (Omladic 84), Birsa (Kronaveter 59), Verbic; Ilicic, Bezjak.
England: (433) Hart; Walker, Cahill, Stones, Rose; Henderson, Dier, Alli (Rooney 73); Walcott (Townsend 62), Sturridge (Rashford 81), Lingard.

Friday, 11 November 2016

England (1) 3 *(Sturridge 25, Lallana 51, Cahill 61)*

Scotland (0) 0 87,258

England: (4231) Hart; Rose, Stones, Cahill, Walker; Dier, Henderson; Lallana, Rooney, Sterling; Sturridge (Vardy 75).
Scotland: (4411) Gordon; Anya (Paterson 79), Wallace, Hanley, Berra; Morrison (McArthur 66), Brown, Fletcher D, Forrest; Snodgrass (Ritchie 82); Griffiths.

Malta (0) 0

Slovenia (0) 1 *(Verbic 47)* 4207

Malta: (532) Hogg; Muscat Z, Magri, Agius, Camilleri (Borg 68), Zerafa; Muscat R, Sciberras, Gambin; Schembri, Mifsud (Farrugia 78).
Slovenia: (4312) Oblak; Skubic, Samardzic, Cesar, Trajkovski (Jovic 63); Kurtic, Krhin, Verbic; Birsa (Omladic 71); Ilicic, Novakovic (Sporar 83).

Slovakia (3) 4 *(Nemec 12, Kucka 15, Skrtel 36, Hamsik 86)*

Lithuania (0) 0 9653

Slovakia: (451) Kozacik; Pekarik, Skrtel, Durica, Hubocan; Weiss (Bero 89), Kucka, Skriniar, Hamsik, Mak (Svento 83); Nemec (Duris 77).
Lithuania: (4411) Setkus; Vaitkunas, Girdvainis, Freidgeimas, Andriuskevicius; Novikovas, Zulpa (Chvedukas 33), Kuklys, Cernych; Slivka; Valskis (Ruzgis 87).

Sunday, 26 March 2017

England (1) 2 *(Defoe 22, Vardy 66)*

Lithuania (0) 0 77,690

England: (4141) Hart; Walker, Keane, Stones, Bertrand; Dier; Oxlade-Chamberlain, Lallana, Alli, Sterling (Rashford 60); Defoe (Vardy 59).
Lithuania: (4231) Setkus; Vaitkunas, Kijanskas, Klimavicius, Slavickas; Kuklys, Zulpa; Novikovas (Grigaravicius 54), Slivka (Paulius 87), Cernych; Valskis (Matulevicius 73).

Malta (1) 1 *(Farrugia 14)*

Slovakia (2) 3 *(Weiss 2, Gregus 41, Nemec 84)* 4980

Malta: (532) Hogg; Attard, Muscat Z, Magri, Camilleri (Baldacchino 80), Zerafa; Gambin (Kristensen 73), Sciberras, Fenech P; Farrugia■, Schembri (Montebello 90).
Slovakia: (4141) Kozacik; Pekarik, Skrtel, Skriniar, Hubocan; Hrosovsky; Mak (Hamsik 50), Kucka (Duris 74), Gregus, Weiss (Rusnak 86); Nemec■.

Scotland (0) 1 *(Martin C 88)*
Slovenia (0) 0 20,435
Scotland: (442) Gordon; Robertson, Martin R, Mulgrew, Tierney; Morrison (Martin C 82), Brown, Armstrong, Forrest; Snodgrass (Anya 75), Griffiths (Naismith 49).
Slovenia: (433) Oblak; Struna, Samardzic, Cesar, Jokic; Kurtic, Krhin, Kampl (Omladic 87); Ilicic, Birsa (Beric 69), Bezjak (Verbic 58).

Saturday, 10 June 2017

Lithuania (0) 1 *(Sernas 90)*
Slovakia (1) 2 *(Weiss 32, Hamsik 58)* 4083
Lithuania: (442) Zubas; Borovskij, Kijanskas, Klimavicius, Slavickas; Cernych, Slivka (Dapkus 75), Kuklys, Sernas; Valskis (Matulevicius 72), Novikovas.
Slovakia: (442) Dubravka; Pekarik, Skrtel, Durica, Hubocan (Gyomber 59); Mak (Rusnak 77), Gregus, Skriniar, Weiss; Hamsik, Duda (Benes 89).

Scotland (0) 2 *(Griffiths 87, 89)*
England (0) 2 *(Oxlade-Chamberlain 70, Kane 90)* 48,520
Scotland: (4231) Gordon; Berra, Mulgrew, Robertson, Tierney; Brown, Armstrong; Anya (Martin C 81), Snodgrass (Fraser 66), Griffiths; Morrison (McArthur 45).
England: (451) Hart; Walker, Cahill, Smalling, Bertrand; Rashford (Oxlade-Chamberlain 65), Lallana, Dier, Alli (Sterling 84), Livermore (Defoe 90); Kane.

Slovenia (1) 2 *(Ilicic 45, Novakovic 84)*
Malta (0) 0 7900
Slovenia: (4411) Oblak; Skubic (Palcic 88), Mlinar, Mevlja, Jokic; Bezjak (Omladic 59), Kurtic, Krhin, Verbic; Ilicic; Beric (Novakovic 64).
Malta: (532) Hogg; Muscat A, Muscat Z, Agius, Borg (Magri 89), Failla; Pisani, Kristensen (Gambin 46), Fenech R; Effiong, Schembri (Mifsud 62).

Group F Table	P	W	D	L	F	A	GD	Pts
England	6	4	2	0	10	2	8	14
Slovakia	6	4	0	2	12	4	8	12
Slovenia	6	3	2	1	6	3	3	11
Scotland	6	2	2	2	9	10	–1	8
Lithuania	6	1	2	3	6	11	–5	5
Malta	6	0	0	6	2	15	–13	0

GROUP G

Monday, 5 September 2016

Israel (1) 1 *(Ben Haim II 35)*
Italy (2) 3 *(Pelle 14, Candreva 31 (pen), Immobile 83)* 29,300
Israel: (433) Goresh; Bitton B, Tibi (Gershon 50), Tzedek, Davidadze; Kayal, Bitton N (Atzily 57), Yeini; Ben Haim II (Kahat 62), Hemed, Zahavi.
Italy: (532) Buffon; Candreva (Florenzi 67), Barzagli, Bonucci, Chiellini■, Antonelli; Parolo, Verratti, Bonaventura (Ogbonna 62); Eder (Immobile 70), Pelle.

Spain (1) 8 *(Costa 11, 67, Roberto 55, Silva 59, 90, Vitolo 60, Morata 82, 83)*
Liechtenstein (0) 0 12,139
Spain: (4231) de Gea; Roberto, Pique, Sergio Ramos, Jordi Alba; Busquets, Koke; Vitolo (Asensio 79), Thiago (Nolito 46), Silva; Costa (Morata 68).
Liechtenstein: (451) Jehle; Rechsteiner (Yildiz 71), Polverino, Kaufmann, Goppel; Salanovic (Wolfinger 77), Martin Buchel, Wieser, Marcel Buchel, Burgmeier; Hasler.

Tuesday, 6 September 2016

Albania (1) 2 *(Sadiku 9, Balaj 89)*
FYR Macedonia (0) 1 *(Alioski 51)* 14,667
Albania: (433) Berisha; Hysaj, Djimsiti, Mavraj, Agolli; Abrashi (Balaj 59), Kukeli, Xhaka; Gashi (Memushaj 60), Sadiku, Hyka (Roshi 66).
FYR Macedonia: (4231) Zahov; Ristevski, Sikov, Mojsov, Zuta; Ristovski, Alioski; Stjepanovic (Petrovic 61), Spirovski, Hasani (Gjorgjev 74); Pandev.

Thursday, 6 October 2016

FYR Macedonia (0) 1 *(Nestoroski 63)*
Israel (2) 2 *(Hemed 25, Ben Haim II 43)* 6500
FYR Macedonia: (532) Bogatinov; Ristovski, Mojsov, Sikov (Ibraimi 51), Ristevski, Zuta; Hasani, Petrovic (Spirovski 45), Alioski; Pandev (Jahovic 76), Nestoroski.
Israel: (433) Goresh; Dasa, Tzedek, Tibi■, Davidadze; Golasa (Einbinder 72), Bitton N, Cohen; Zahavi, Hemed (Abed 75), Ben Haim II (Buzaglo 68).

Italy (0) 1 *(De Rossi 82 (pen))*
Spain (0) 1 *(Vitolo 55)* 38,470
Italy: (352) Buffon; Barzagli, Bonucci, Romagnoli; Florenzi, De Rossi, Montolivo (Bonaventura 30), Parolo (Belotti 76), De Sciglio; Eder, Pelle (Immobile 59).
Spain: (433) de Gea; Jordi Alba (Nacho 22), Sergio Ramos, Pique, Carvajal; Iniesta, Busquets, Koke; Silva, Costa (Morata 66), Vitolo (Thiago 83).

Liechtenstein (0) 0
Albania (1) 2 *(Jehle 12 (og), Balaj 71)* 5684
Liechtenstein: (433) Jehle; Oehri, Polverino (Rechsteiner 45), Kaufmann, Goppel; Hasler, Wieser, Marcel Buchel; Burgmeier, Gubser (Frick 59), Salanovic (Kuhne 72).
Albania: (433) Berisha; Hysaj, Djimsiti, Mavraj, Aliji; Kukeli (Basha 44), Hyka, Abrashi (Lila 45); Roshi, Balaj, Llullaku (Cikalleshi 69).

Sunday, 9 October 2016

Albania (0) 0
Spain (0) 2 *(Costa 55, Nolito 63)* 15,245
Albania: (433) Berisha; Hysaj, Djimsiti, Mavraj, Agolli; Lila, Xhaka (Hyka 75), Memushaj (Basha 67); Roshi, Balaj, Lenjani (Aliji 45).
Spain: (4411) de Gea; Koke, Sergio Ramos (Martinez 80), Pique, Monreal; Vitolo (Nolito 59), Iniesta (Isco 77), Busquets, Silva; Thiago; Costa.

FYR Macedonia (0) 2 *(Nestoroski 57, Hasani 59)*
Italy (1) 3 *(Belotti 24, Immobile 75, 90)* 19,195
FYR Macedonia: (532) Bogatinov; Ristovski, Mojsov, Sikov, Ristevski, Zuta (Ibraimi 45); Hasani (Trajcevski 83), Spirovski, Alioski; Pandev, Nestoroski (Petrovic 67).
Italy: (532) Buffon; Candreva, Barzagli, Bonucci, Romagnoli, De Sciglio; Bernardeschi (Sansone 64), Verratti, Bonaventura (Parolo 64); Belotti (Eder 83), Immobile.

Israel (2) 2 *(Hemed 3, 16)*
Liechtenstein (0) 1 *(Goppel 49)* 9000
Israel: (442) Goresh; Dasa, Tzedek, Gershon, Ben Haroush; Ben Haim II (Dabour 81), Cohen, Golasa, Buzaglo (Atzily 63); Zahavi, Hemed (Kahat 76).
Liechtenstein: (3412) Jehle; Rechsteiner, Kaufmann, Goppel; Marcel Buchel (Salanovic 88), Martin Buchel, Wieser, Burgmeier (Kuhne 81); Hasler; Christen, Gubser (Frick 75).

Saturday, 12 November 2016

Albania (0) 0
Israel (1) 3 *(Zahavi 18 (pen), Einbinder 66, Atar 83)* 7600
Albania: (433) Berisha■; Hysaj (Cani 79), Djimsiti■, Mavraj, Agolli; Xhaka (Manaj 82), Kukeli, Memushaj; Roshi, Balaj, Llullaku (Hoxha 57).
Israel: (433) Goresh; Dasa, Tzedek, Tibi, Gershon; Einbinder (Hemed 70), Natcho, Cohen; Sahar (Buzaglo 64), Zahavi, Ben Haim II (Atar 75).

Liechtenstein (0) 0
Italy (4) 4 *(Belotti 11, 44, Immobile 12, Candreva 32)* 5864
Liechtenstein: (451) Jehle; Rechsteiner, Polverino, Kaufmann, Oehri; Christen, Martin Buchel, Wieser, Marcel Buchel, Burgmeier; Salanovic.
Italy: (424) Buffon; Zappacosta, Bonucci, Romagnoli, De Sciglio; De Rossi, Verratti; Candreva (Eder 74), Belotti, Immobile (Zaza 81), Bonaventura (Insigne 67).

Spain (1) 4 *(Velkoski 34 (og), Vitolo 63, Monreal 84, Aduriz 85)*
FYR Macedonia (0) 0 16,622
Spain: (451) de Gea; Carvajal, Bartra, Nacho, Monreal; Vitolo (Callejon 87), Koke (Isco 72), Busquets, Thiago, Silva; Morata (Aduriz 60).
FYR Macedonia: (352) Aleksovski; Velkoski, Mojsov, Ristevski; Ristovski, Hasani (Gjorgjev 87), Bardi, Spirovski (Zuta 60), Alioski; Pandev, Nestoroski (Ibraimi 82).

Friday, 24 March 2017

Italy (1) 2 *(De Rossi 12 (pen), Immobile 72)*
Albania (0) 0 33,136
Italy: (442) Buffon; Zappacosta, Barzagli, Bonucci, De Sciglio; Candreva, De Rossi, Verratti, Insigne; Immobile, Belotti.
Albania: (433) Strakosha; Hysaj, Veseli, Ajeti, Agolli; Basha (Latifi 89), Kukeli, Memushaj; Lila (Sadiku 69), Cikalleshi, Roshi (Grezda 80).

Liechtenstein (0) 0
FYR Macedonia (1) 3 *(Nikolov 43, Nestoroski 68, 72)* 4517
Liechtenstein: (4141) Jehle; Rechsteiner (Wolfinger 78), Gubser, Malin, Goppel; Martin Buchel (Sele 83); Burgmeier, Hasler, Marcel Buchel, Salanovic (Brandle 87); Frick.
FYR Macedonia: (442) Dimitrievski; Ristovski, Velkoski, Sikov, Ristevski; Trickovski (Babunski 77), Nikolov, Spirovski (Gjorgjev 85), Ibraimi (Trajkovski 64); Pandev, Nestoroski.

Spain (2) 4 *(Silva 13, Vitolo 45, Costa 51, Isco 88)*
Israel (0) 1 *(Rafaelov 77)* 20,321
Spain: (433) de Gea; Carvajal, Sergio Ramos, Pique, Jordi Alba; Busquets, Iniesta (Isco 70), Thiago (Koke 63); Vitolo (Aspas 83), Costa, Silva.
Israel: (433) Marciano; Dasa, Tzedek, Tibi (Tawatha 18), Gershon; Cohen, Natcho, Einbinder (Keltjens 60); Ben Haim II (Hemed 63), Zahavi, Rafaelov.

Sunday, 11 June 2017

FYR Macedonia (0) 1 *(Ristovski 66)*
Spain (2) 2 *(Silva 15, Costa 27)* 20,675
FYR Macedonia: (442) Dimitrievski; Tosevski (Trajkovski 74), Sikov, Mojsov (Trickovski 85), Ristevski; Ristovski, Stjepanovic (Elmas 45), Spirovski, Alioski; Nestoroski, Pandev.
Spain: (433) de Gea; Carvajal, Sergio Ramos, Pique, Jordi Alba; Iniesta (Saul 90), Busquets, Silva (Pedro 68); Isco, Costa, Thiago (Koke 73).

Israel (0) 0
Albania (2) 3 *(Sadiku 22, 44, Memushaj 71)* 15,150
Israel: (442) Goresh; Dasa, Tibi, Tzedek, Tawatha; Natcho, Golasa (Shechter 53), Cohen, Rafaelov (Vered 57); Sahar (Benayoun 67), Zahavi.
Albania: (532) Strakosha; Hysaj, Xhimshiti, Kukeli (Veseli 82), Mavraj, Aliji; Hyka, Memushaj, Roshi (Lila 53); Sadiku (Cikalleshi 69), Abrashi.

Italy (1) 5 *(Insigne 35, Belotti 52, Eder 74, Bernarderschi 82, Gabbiadini 90)*
Liechtenstein (0) 0 20,514
Italy: (442) Buffon; Darmian, Barzagli, Chiellini, Spinazzola; Candreva (Bernarderschi 60), Pellegrini, De Rossi, Insigne; Belotti (Gabbiadini 75), Immobile (Eder 66).
Liechtenstein: (451) Jehle; Rechsteiner, Malin, Gubser, Goppel; Salanovic (Brandle 59), Hasler, Polverino (Quintans 87), Martin Buchel, Burgmeier (Wolfinger 68); Frick.

Group G Table	P	W	D	L	F	A	GD	Pts
Spain	6	5	1	0	21	3	18	16
Italy	6	5	1	0	18	4	14	16
Albania	6	3	0	3	7	8	–1	9
Israel	6	3	0	3	9	12	–3	9
FYR Macedonia	6	1	0	5	8	13	–5	3
Liechtenstein	6	0	0	6	1	24	–23	0

GROUP H

Tuesday, 6 September 2016

Bosnia-Herzegovina (2) 5 *(Spahic 7, 90, Dzeko 23 (pen), Medunjanin 71, Ibisevic 83)*
Estonia (0) 0 8820
Bosnia-Herzegovina: (442) Begovic; Vranjes (Bicakcic 62), Zukanovic, Spahic, Kolasinac; Visca (Milicevic 75), Pjanic, Medunjanin, Lulic; Ibisevic, Dzeko (Djuric 81).
Estonia: (4411) Aksalu; Teniste, Baranov, Klavan, Pikk; Kams (Kruglov 45), Mets, Antonov (Sappinen 86), Kallaste; Vassiljev; Zenjov (Anier 71).

Cyprus (0) 0
Belgium (1) 3 *(Lukaku R 13, 61, Carrasco 81)* 12,029
Cyprus: (4411) Panagi; Demetriou, Junior, Laifis, Alexandrou; Kastanos (Makris 78), Charis Kyriakou, Laban (Artymatas 70), Efrem; Charalambidis; Sotiriou (Mitidis 69).
Belgium: (451) Courtois; Meunier, Alderweireld, Vermaelen, Vertonghen; Carrasco, Fellaini (Nainggolan 84), Witsel, De Bruyne, Hazard; Lukaku R (Batshuayi 73).

Gibraltar (1) 1 *(Walker 26)*
Greece (4) 4 *(Mitroglou 10, Wiseman 44 (og), Fortounis 45, Torosidis 45)* 300
Gibraltar: (3331) Perez; Wiseman, Chipolina R, Casciaro R; Garcia, Bosio (Casciaro K 71), Chipolina J; Hernandez, Coombes (Yome 85), Casciaro L; Walker.
Greece: (433) Karnezis; Tzavelas, Papastathopoulos, Manolas, Torosidis; Samaris, Maniatis (Tziolis 71), Fortounis; Mantalos (Gianniotas 62), Bakasetas, Mitroglou (Vellios 73).

Friday, 7 October 2016

Belgium (2) 4 *(Spahic 26 (og), Hazard 28, Alderweireld 60, Lukaku R 79)*
Bosnia-Herzegovina (0) 0 42,653
Belgium: (433) Courtois; Meunier, Alderweireld, Vertonghen, Lukaku J (Ciman 21); Mertens, Fellaini, Witsel; Hazard (Mirallas 87), Carrasco, Lukaku R (Benteke 82).
Bosnia-Herzegovina: (4321) Begovic; Bicakcic, Spahic, Zukanovic, Kolasinac; Lulic, Jajalo (Visca 73), Medunjanin; Pjanic (Cimirot 81), Dzeko; Ibisevic (Djuric 64).

Estonia (0) 4 *(Kait 47, 70, Vassiljev 52, Mosnikov 88)*
Gibraltar (0) 0 4678
Estonia: (4231) Aksalu; Teniste, Baranov, Klavan, Kruglov; Kait (Lepistu 80), Mets; Zenjov (Ojamaa 65), Vassiljev (Mosnikov 61), Luts; Anier.
Gibraltar: (442) Perez; Garcia, Casciaro R, Chipolina R, Chipolina J (Casciaro K 90); Bardon, Bosio (Payas 58), Walker, Olivero; Priestley (Coombes 65), Casciaro L.

Greece (2) 2 *(Mitroglou 12, Mantalos 42)*
Cyprus (0) 0 16,512
Greece: (4411) Karnezis; Torosidis, Papastathopoulos, Manolas, Tzavelas (Karelis 87); Mantalos, Maniatis, Stafylidis (Papadopoulos 70), Bakasetas (Holebas 77); Fortounis; Mitroglou.
Cyprus: (433) Panagi; Demetriou, Junior, Laifis, Charalambous; Artymatas (Charalambos Kyriakou 78), Laban, Kastanos; Charalambidis (Christofi 66), Mitidis (Makris 83), Efrem.

Monday, 10 October 2016

Bosnia-Herzegovina (0) 2 *(Dzeko 70, 81)*
Cyprus (0) 0 8900
Bosnia-Herzegovina: (442) Begovic; Vranjes, Sunjic, Spahic, Kolasinac (Hajrovic 64); Visca (Susic 78), Pjanic, Medunjanin, Lulic; Djuric (Ibisevic 83), Dzeko.
Cyprus: (433) Panagi; Demetriou, Junior, Laifis, Alexandrou; Artymatas (Mitidis 85), Kastanos, Laban; Christofi (Charalambidis 77), Sotiriou, Makris (Efrem 72).

Estonia (0) 0

Greece (1) 2 *(Torosidis 2, Stafylidis 61)* 4467

Estonia: (4411) Aksalu; Teniste (Kams 31), Baranov, Klavan, Kallaste; Marin, Aleksandr Dmitrijev (Mosnikov 79), Mets, Luts (Purje 69); Vassiljev; Zenjov.
Greece: (4411) Karnezis; Torosidis (Oikonomou 18), Papastathopoulos (Tachtsidis 6), Manolas, Stafylidis; Bakasetas, Maniatis (Tziolis 86), Papadopoulos, Karelis; Mantalos; Mitroglou.

Gibraltar (0) 0

Belgium (3) 6 *(Benteke 1, 43, 56, Witsel 19, Mertens 51, Hazard 79)* 1959

Gibraltar: (442) Ibrahim; Wiseman, Casciaro R, Chipolina R, Chipolina J; Garcia, Bosio (Payas 46), Walker (Bardon 81), Olivero; Casciaro K (Yome 86), Casciaro L.
Belgium: (343) Courtois; Alderweireld, Ciman, Vertonghen; Meunier, Witsel, Defour, Carrasco (Chadli 53); Mertens (Mirallas 64), Benteke (Batshuayi 81), Hazard.

Sunday, 13 November 2016

Belgium (3) 8 *(Meunier 8, Mertens 16, 68, Hazard 25, Carrasco 62, Klavan 65 (og), Lukaku R 83, 88)*

Estonia (1) 1 *(Anier 29)* 37,128

Belgium: (343) Courtois; Dendoncker, Ciman, Vertonghen; Meunier, De Bruyne, Witsel (Simons 87), Carrasco; Mertens (Tielemans 78), Lukaku R, Hazard (Mirallas 73).
Estonia: (4411) Aksalu; Teniste, Baranov, Klavan, Kallaste; Mosnikov (Kams 63), Aleksandr Dmitrijev, Mets, Luts (Marin 84); Vassiljev; Anier (Ojamaa 85).

Cyprus (1) 3 *(Laifis 29, Sotiriou 65, Sielis 87)*

Gibraltar (0) 1 *(Casciaro L 51)* 3151

Cyprus: (433) Panagi; Charalambous, Laifis, Sielis, Demetriou; Artymatas, Kastanos, Charalambos Kyriakou (Nicolaou 90); Efrem (Charalambidis 73), Sotiriou (Mitidis 86), Christofi.
Gibraltar: (451) Ibrahim; Garcia, Barnett, Casciaro R, Olivero■; Casciaro K (Garro 74), Walker, Casciaro L, Bardon (Hernandez 68), Chipolina J; Cabrera (Priestley 85).

Greece (0) 1 *(Tzavelas 90)*

Bosnia-Herzegovina (1) 1 *(Karnezis 33 (og))* 20,075

Greece: (4231) Karnezis; Torosidis, Papadopoulos■, Papastathopoulos, Tzavelas; Maniatis (Gianniotas 61), Samaris; Mantalos (Karelis 86), Fortounis, Stafylidis; Mitroglou.
Bosnia-Herzegovina: (4312) Begovic; Vranjes, Spahic (Sunjic 70), Zukanovic, Kolasinac; Hajrovic (Bicakcic 87), Jajalo, Lulic; Pjanic; Ibisevic (Djuric 84), Dzeko■.

Saturday, 25 March 2017

Belgium (0) 1 *(Lukaku R 90)*

Greece (0) 1 *(Mitroglou 47)* 42,281

Belgium: (3331) Courtois; Alderweireld, Ciman (Mirallas 84), Vertonghen; Fellaini (Dembele 65), Witsel, Nainggolan; Chadli, Mertens, Carrasco; Lukaku R.
Greece: (4411) Kapino; Torosidis, Manolas, Papastathopoulos, Tzavelas■; Mantalos (Zeca 84), Tachtsidis■, Samaris, Stafylidis; Fortounis (Tziolis 68); Mitroglou (Vellios 90).

Bosnia-Herzegovina (2) 5 *(Ibisevic 4, 43, Vrsajevic 52, Visca 56, Bicakcic 90)*

Gibraltar (0) 0 8285

Bosnia-Herzegovina: (442) Begovic; Bicakcic, Cocalic, Zukanovic, Kolasinac (Pavlovic 45); Vrsajevic (Bajic 75), Pjanic (Vrancic 57), Cimirot, Visca; Hodzic, Ibisevic.
Gibraltar: (442) Ibrahim; Chipolina K (Pusey 53), Payas, Chipolina J, Chipolina R; Garcia, Hernandez, Walker, Gulling (Bardon 75); Casciaro K (Duarte 87), Casciaro L.

Cyprus (0) 0

Estonia (0) 0 3864

Cyprus: (4231) Panagi; Stylianou (Avraam 71), Merkis, Laifis, Charalambous; Artymatas, Laban (Roushias 81); Christofi, Charalambos Kyriakou, Kastanos; Mitidis (Makris 88).
Estonia: (4411) Aksalu; Teniste, Baranov, Klavan, Kruglov; Aleksandr Dmitrijev, Mets, Kait, Vassiljev (Anier 90); Ojamaa (Luts 64); Zenjov (Toomet 78).

Friday, 9 June 2017

Bosnia-Herzegovina (0) 0

Greece (0) 0 11,000

Bosnia-Herzegovina: (4231) Begovic; Bicakcic, Vranjes, Sunjic (Dumic 69), Zukanovic; Pjanic, Jajalo; Visca, Ibisevic, Lulic (Kodro 21 (Besic 77)); Dzeko.
Greece: (4231) Karnezis; Torosidis, Manolas, Papastathopoulos, Stafylidis; Tziolis, Zeca; Mantalos (Kourmpelis 90), Fortounis (Maniatis 90), Bakasetas (Donis 50); Mitroglou.

Estonia (0) 0

Belgium (1) 2 *(Mertens 31, Chadli 86)* 10,176

Estonia: (442) Aksalu; Teniste, Baranov, Klavan, Pikk; Kait (Anier 86), Mets, Artjom Dmitrijev■, Zenjov (Ojamaa 79); Vassiljev, Luts (Kallaste 74).
Belgium: (3421) Courtois; Alderweireld, Vertonghen, Kompany; Fellaini, Witsel, Chadli, Mertens (Batshuayi 81); De Bruyne, Carrasco; Lukaku R.

Gibraltar (1) 1 *(Hernandez 30)*

Cyprus (1) 2 *(Chipolina R 10 (og), Sotiriou 87)* 488

Gibraltar: (433) Ibrahim; Garcia, Chipolina R, Casciaro R (Coombes 81), Chipolina J; Bardon (Casciaro K 90), Barnett, Olivero; Hernandez, Casciaro L, Walker.
Cyprus: (4231) Panagi; Demetriou, Makris, Laifis, Ioannou; Artymatas (Mitidis 81), Charalambos Kyriakou; Christofi (Merkis 73), Charalambidis, Margaca (Alexandrou 61); Sotiriou.

Group H Table	*P*	*W*	*D*	*L*	*F*	*A*	*GD*	*Pts*
Belgium	6	5	1	0	24	2	22	16
Greece	6	3	3	0	10	3	7	12
Bosnia and Herzegovina	6	3	2	1	13	5	8	11
Cyprus	6	2	1	3	5	9	–4	7
Estonia	6	1	1	4	5	17	–12	4
Gibraltar	6	0	0	6	3	24	–21	0

GROUP I

Monday, 5 September 2016

Croatia (1) 1 *(Rakitic 44 (pen))*

Turkey (1) 1 *(Calhanoglu 45)* 0

Croatia: (4231) Kalinic L; Vrsaljko, Corluka, Vida, Strinic; Pjaca (Kalinic N 79), Badelj; Modric, Perisic, Rakitic (Brozovic 64); Mandzukic (Kramaric 84).
Turkey: (451) Babacan; Ozbayrakli, Aziz, Topal, Koybasi; Ozan Tufan, Yokuslu, Ayhan (Yilmaz Calik 53), Mor (Sen 84), Calhanoglu; Tosun (Sahan 71).
Behind closed doors.

Finland (1) 1 *(Arajuuri 18)*

Kosovo (0) 1 *(Berisha V 60 (pen))* 7571

Finland: (352) Hradecky; Lam (Ring 65), Arajuuri, Moisander; Raitala, Lod (Schuller 88), Halsti, Eremenko, Uronen; Pukki (Hamalainen 73), Pohjanpalo.
Kosovo: (451) Ujkani; Perdedaj, Rrahmani, Pnishi, Paqarada; Rashica, Berisha V (Meha 90), Kryeziu, Alushi, Bernard Berisha (Halimi 81); Bunjaku (Celina 65).

Ukraine (1) 1 *(Yarmolenko 41)*

Iceland (1) 1 *(Finnbogason 6)* 0

Ukraine: (442) Pyatov; Butko, Rakitskiy, Kucher, Sobol; Yarmolenko, Sydorchuk (Zozulya 63), Stepanenko, Konoplyanka; Kovalenko, Zinchenko (Shakhov 90).
Iceland: (442) Halldorsson; Saevarsson, Arnason, Sigurdsson R, Skulason A (Magnusson 40); Gudmundsson (Hallfredsson 84), Gunnarsson, Sigurdsson G, Bjarnason B (Traustason 75); Finnbogason, Bodvarsson.
Behind closed doors.

Thursday, 6 October 2016

Iceland (1) 3 *(Arnason 37, Finnbogason 90, Sigurdsson R 90)*

Finland (2) 2 *(Pukki 21, Lod 39)* 9548

Iceland: (442) Kristinsson; Saevarsson (Bjarnason T 89), Arnason, Sigurdsson R, Skulason A; Bjarnason B, Gunnarsson, Sigurdsson G, Gudmundsson; Sigurdarson (Kjartansson 75), Finnbogason.
Finland: (442) Hradecky; Vaisanen, Halsti, Arajuuri, Moisander; Hetemaj, Ring (Schuller 90), Arkivuo, Lod; Hamalainen (Markkanen 55 (Raitala 85)), Pukki.

Kosovo (0) 0

Croatia (3) 6 *(Mandzukic 6, 24, 35, Mitrovic 68, Perisic 83, Kalinic N 90)* 14,612

Kosovo: (4231) Ujkani; Perdedaj, Pnishi, Pepa, Paqarada; Kryeziu, Berisha V; Rashica, Zeneli (Shala 77), Bernard Berisha (Halimi 58); Celina (Bunjaku 70).
Croatia: (442) Subasic; Vrsaljko, Corluka (Mitrovic 45), Vida, Pivaric; Brozovic, Kovacic, Badelj, Perisic; Kramaric (Rog 71), Mandzukic (Kalinic N 59).

Turkey (1) 2 *(Ozan Tufan 45, Calhanoglu 81 (pen))*

Ukraine (2) 2 *(Yarmolenko 25 (pen), Kravets 27)* 36,714

Turkey: (442) Babacan; Ozbayrakli, Toprak, Balta (Ayhan 45), Erkin; Ozan Tufan (Sen 77), Topal, Mor, Calhanoglu; Unal (Cigerci 45), Tosun.
Ukraine: (4141) Pyatov; Butko, Kucher, Ordets, Sobol; Stepanenko; Yarmolenko, Zinchenko (Sydorchuk 46), Kovalenko, Konoplyanka (Petryak 81); Kravets (Zozulya 73).

Sunday, 9 October 2016

Finland (0) 0

Croatia (1) 1 *(Mandzukic 18)* 15,567

Finland: (4321) Hradecky; Raitala, Ojala, Arajuuri, Vaisanen (Riski 86); Arkivuo (Schuller 45), Moisander, Saksela; Ring (Lam 67), Lod; Pukki.
Croatia: (442) Subasic; Vrsaljko, Mitrovic, Vida, Pivaric; Brozovic (Cop 71), Badelj, Kovacic, Perisic; Kramaric (Rog 81), Mandzukic (Kalinic N 87).

Iceland (2) 2 *(Toprak 42 (og), Finnbogason 45)*

Turkey (0) 0 9775

Iceland: (442) Halldorsson; Saevarsson, Arnason, Sigurdsson R, Skulason A; Bjarnason T (Magnusson 86), Sigurdsson G, Bjarnason B, Gudmundsson; Finnbogason (Kjartansson 68), Bodvarsson (Sigurdarson 62).
Turkey: (433) Babacan; Ozbayrakli, Toprak, Topal, Erkin; Ozan Tufan (Cigerci 44), Ayhan, Calhanoglu; Oztekin (Tosun 59), Mor, Sen (Erdinc 67).

Ukraine (1) 3 *(Kravets 30, Yarmolenko 81, Rotan 87)*

Kosovo (0) 0 999

Ukraine: (442) Pyatov; Butko, Ordets, Kucher, Sobol; Yarmolenko, Kovalenko, Stepanenko, Konoplyanka (Kryvtsov 78); Zinchenko (Rotan 63), Kravets (Zozulya 84).
Kosovo: (4231) Ujkani; Perdedaj (Sulejmani 77), Rrahmani, Pnishi, Paqarada; Kryeziu, Meha (Bernard Berisha 54); Rashica (Zeneli 66), Shala, Berisha V; Muriqi.

Saturday, 12 November 2016

Croatia (1) 2 *(Brozovic 15, 90)*

Iceland (0) 0 0

Croatia: (4231) Subasic; Vrsaljko, Corluka, Vida, Pivaric; Kovacic (Modric 45), Badelj; Brozovic, Rakitic (Kramaric 85), Perisic■; Mandzukic (Cop 90).
Iceland: (442) Halldorsson; Saevarsson, Sigurdsson R, Arnason, Magnusson; Gudmundsson, Sigurdsson G, Gunnarsson, Bjarnason T (Traustason 75); Bjarnason B, Bodvarsson (Kjartansson 75).
Behind closed doors.

Turkey (0) 2 *(Yilmaz 51, Sen 56)*

Kosovo (0) 0 26,555

Turkey: (451) Babacan; Gonul, Yilmaz Calik, Topal, Kaldirim; Sen (Under 77), Ozyakup (Malli 47), Inan, Calhanoglu, Turan; Yilmaz (Tosun 87).
Kosovo: (4141) Ujkani; Perdedaj, Rrahmani, Pnishi, Kololli; Alushi; Rashica, Shala, Berisha V, Zeneli; Muriqi.

Ukraine (1) 1 *(Kravets 25)*

Finland (0) 0 26,482

Ukraine: (4141) Pyatov; Butko, Kucher, Rakitskiy, Sobol; Stepanenko; Yarmolenko, Zinchenko (Rotan 67), Kovalenko (Shakhov 89), Konoplyanka (Tsyhankov 83); Kravets.
Finland: (523) Hradecky; Arkivuo, Vaisanen (Saksela 83), Arajuuri, Toivio, Raitala; Mattila, Halsti (Lam 63); Ring (Markkanen 46), Lod, Pukki.

Friday, 24 March 2017

Croatia (1) 1 *(Kalinic N 38)*

Ukraine (0) 0 33,000

Croatia: (433) Subasic; Jedvaj, Mitrovic, Vida, Pivaric; Modric, Rakitic (Kovacic 80), Badelj; Brozovic (Rog 90), Kalinic N (Kramaric 88), Mandzukic.
Ukraine: (4411) Pyatov; Butko, Ordets, Kucher, Matviyenko; Yarmolenko, Rotan (Sydorchuk 77), Stepanenko, Konoplyanka; Kovalenko (Besyedin 86); Kravets (Seleznyov 59).

Kosovo (0) 1 *(Nuhiu 53)*

Iceland (2) 2 *(Sigurdarson 25, Sigurdsson G 35 (pen))* 6832

Kosovo: (4411) Ujkani; Perdedaj (Avdijaj 74), Kololli, Pnishi, Shala; Rashica (Celina 64), Besart Berisha (Bernard Berisha 83), Rrahmani, Berisha V; Kryeziu; Nuhiu.
Iceland: (442) Halldorsson; Saevarsson, Sigurdsson R, Kjartansson (Bodvarsson 69), Sigurdsson G; Arnason, Gunnarsson, Hallfredsson, Traustason (Gislason 72); Sigurdarson (Skulason O 86), Skulason A.

Turkey (2) 2 *(Tosun 9, 13)*

Finland (0) 0 28,990

Turkey: (442) Babacan; Koybasi, Toprak, Gonul, Inan; Tosun (Unal 83), Turan, Sahan (Mor 72), Topal; Malli (Yokuslu 62), Sen.
Finland: (442) Hradecky; Arajuuri, Moisander, Ring (Forsell 84), Lod; Hetemaj, Pukki, Arkivuo, Mattila (Yaghoubi 67); Uronen, Pohjanpalo (Markkanen 72).

Sunday, 11 June 2017

Finland (0) 1 *(Pohjanpalo 72)*

Ukraine (0) 2 *(Konoplyanka 52, Besyedin 75)* 8723

Finland: (4411) Hradecky; Raitala, Moisander, Ojala, Arkivuo; Uronen (Markkanen 84), Yaghoubi, Lam, Lod (Jensen 68); Hamalainen; Pukki (Pohjanpalo 68).
Ukraine: (4411) Pyatov; Matviyenko, Rakitskiy, Ordets, Butko; Konoplyanka (Sobol 86), Malinovsky, Stepanenko, Yarmolenko; Kovalenko (Shepelyev 76); Seleznyov (Besyedin 64).

Iceland (0) 1 *(Magnusson 90)*

Croatia (0) 0 9800

Iceland: (442) Halldorsson; Saevarsson, Arnason, Sigurdsson R (Ingason 90), Magnusson; Gudmundsson, Gunnarsson, Hallfredsson, Bjarnason B (Gislason 80); Sigurdsson G, Finnbogason (Sigurdarson 76).
Croatia: (433) Kalinic L; Jedvaj, Lovren, Vida, Pivaric; Modric, Kovacic, Badelj; Perisic, Kalinic N (Brozovic 63), Mandzukic (Santini 88).

Kosovo (1) 1 *(Rrahmani 22)*

Turkey (2) 4 *(Sen 7, Under 31, Yilmaz 61, Ozan Tufan 83)* 6000

Kosovo: (541) Ujkani (Nurkovic 52); Vojvoda, Rrahmani, Alushi, Pnishi, Aliti; Zeneli (Bernard Berisha■ 53), Berisha V, Kryeziu, Avdijaj (Rashica 74); Nuhiu.
Turkey: (433) Babacan; Gonul, Topal, Soyuncu, Ali Kaldirim (Koybasi 85); Ozan Tufan, Inan, Ozyakup (Yazici 74); Under, Yilmaz, Sen (Mor 81).

Group I Table	*P*	*W*	*D*	*L*	*F*	*A*	*GD*	*Pts*
Croatia	6	4	1	1	11	2	9	13
Iceland	6	4	1	1	9	6	3	13
Turkey	6	3	2	1	11	6	5	11
Ukraine	6	3	2	1	9	5	4	11
Finland	6	0	1	5	4	10	−6	1
Kosovo	6	0	1	5	3	18	−15	1

FIFA WORLD CUP 2018 QUALIFYING COMPETITION – REST OF THE WORLD

SOUTH AMERICA (CONMEBOL)

Bolivia v Uruguay 0-2
Colombia v Peru 2-0
Venezuela v Paraguay 0-1
Chile v Brazil 2-0
Argentina v Ecuador 0-2
Ecuador v Bolivia 2-0
Uruguay v Colombia 3-0
Paraguay v Argentina 0-0
Brazil v Venezuela 3-1
Peru v Chile 3-4
Bolivia v Venezuela 4-2
Ecuador v Uruguay 2-1
Chile v Colombia 1-1
Argentina v Brazil 1-1
Peru v Paraguay 1-0
Colombia v Argentina 0-1
Venezuela v Ecuador 1-3
Paraguay v Bolivia 2-1
Uruguay v Chile 3-0
Brazil v Peru 3-0
Bolivia v Colombia 2-3
Ecuador v Paraguay 2-2
Chile v Argentina 1-2
Peru v Venezuela 2-2
Brazil v Uruguay 2-2
Colombia v Ecuador 3-1
Uruguay v Peru 1-0
Argentina v Bolivia 2-0
Venezuela v Chile 1-4
Paraguay v Brazil 2-2
Bolivia v Peru 0-3
Match awarded 3-0 to Peru after Bolivia fielded an ineligible player, original match Bolivia won 2-0.
Colombia v Venezuela 2-0
Ecuador v Brazil 0-3
Argentina v Uruguay 1-0
Paraguay v Chile 2-1
Uruguay v Paraguay 4-0
Chile v Bolivia 3-0
Match awarded 3-0 to Chile after Bolivia fielded an ineligible player, original match drawn 0-0.
Venezuela v Argentina 2-2
Brazil v Colombia 2-1
Peru v Ecuador 2-1
Ecuador v Chile 3-0
Uruguay v Venezuela 3-0
Paraguay v Colombia 0-1
Brazil v Bolivia 5-0
Peru v Argentina 2-2
Bolivia v Ecuador 2-2
Colombia v Uruguay 2-2
Chile v Peru 2-1
Argentina v Paraguay 0-1
Venezuela v Brazil 0-2
Colombia v Chile 0-0
Uruguay v Ecuador 2-1
Paraguay v Peru 1-4
Venezuela v Bolivia 5-0
Brazil v Argentina 3-0
Bolivia v Paraguay 1-0
Ecuador v Venezuela 3-0
Chile v Uruguay 3-1
Argentina v Colombia 3-0
Peru v Brazil 0-2
Colombia v Bolivia 1-0
Paraguay v Ecuador 2-1
Uruguay v Brazil 1-4
Argentina v Chile 1-0
Venezuela v Peru 2-2
Bolivia v Argentina 2-0
Ecuador v Colombia 0-2
Chile v Venezuela 3-1
Brazil v Paraguay 3-0
Peru v Uruguay 2-1

Latest Table	P	W	D	L	F	A	GD	Pts
Brazil	14	10	3	1	35	10	25	33
Colombia	14	7	3	4	18	15	3	24
Uruguay	14	7	2	5	26	17	9	23
Chile	14	7	2	5	24	19	5	23
Argentina	14	6	4	4	15	14	1	22
Ecuador	14	6	2	6	23	20	3	20
Peru	14	5	3	6	22	23	–1	18
Paraguay	14	5	3	6	13	21	–8	18
Bolivia	14	3	1	10	12	32	–20	10
Venezuela	14	1	3	10	17	34	–17	6

Top four qualify for Russia 2018; 5th placed team plays off against winners of OFC play-off.

AFRICA (CAF)

GROUP A
Congo DR v Libya 4-0
Tunisia v Guinea 2-0
Libya v Tunisia 0-1
Guinea v Congo DR 1-2

Group A Table	P	W	D	L	F	A	GD	Pts
Congo DR	2	2	0	0	6	1	5	6
Tunisia	2	2	0	0	3	0	3	6
Guinea	2	0	0	2	1	4	–3	0
Libya	2	0	0	2	0	5	–5	0

GROUP B
Zambia v Nigeria 1-2
Algeria v Cameroon 1-1
Cameroon v Zambia 1-1
Nigeria v Algeria 3-1

Group B Table	P	W	D	L	F	A	GD	Pts
Nigeria	2	2	0	0	5	2	3	6
Cameroon	2	0	2	0	2	2	0	2
Zambia	2	0	1	1	2	3	–1	1
Algeria	2	0	1	1	2	4	–2	1

GROUP C
Gabon v Morocco 0-0
Ivory Coast v Mali 3-1
Mali v Gabon 0-0
Morocco v Ivory Coast 0-0

Group A Table	P	W	D	L	F	A	GD	Pts
Ivory Coast	2	1	1	0	3	1	2	4
Gabon	2	0	2	0	0	0	0	2
Morocco	2	0	2	0	0	0	0	2
Mali	2	0	1	1	1	3	–2	1

GROUP D
Burkina Faso v South Africa 1-1
Senegal v Cape Verde 2-0
South Africa v Senegal 2-1
Cape Verde v Burkina Faso 0-2

Group D Table	P	W	D	L	F	A	GD	Pts
Burkina Faso	2	1	1	0	3	1	2	4
South Africa	2	1	1	0	3	2	1	4
Senegal	2	1	0	1	3	2	1	3
Cape Verde	2	0	0	2	0	4	–4	0

GROUP E
Ghana v Uganda 0-0
Congo v Egypt 1-2
Uganda v Congo 1-0
Egypt v Ghana 2-0

Group E Table	P	W	D	L	F	A	GD	Pts
Egypt	2	2	0	0	4	1	3	6
Uganda	2	1	1	0	1	0	1	4
Ghana	2	0	1	1	0	2	–2	1
Congo	2	0	0	2	1	3	–2	0

Each group winner qualifies for Russia 2018.

ASIA (AFC)

ROUND 3

GROUP A

Korea Republic v China PR	3-2
Uzbekistan v Syria	1-0
Iran v Qatar	2-0
China PR v Iran	0-0
Syria v Korea Republic	0-0
Qatar v Uzbekistan	0-1
Korea Republic v Qatar	3-2
China PR v Syria	0-1
Uzbekistan v Iran	0-1
Uzbekistan v China PR	2-0
Iran v Korea Republic	1-0
Qatar v Syria	1-0
Korea Republic v Uzbekistan	2-1
China PR v Qatar	0-0
Syria v Iran	0-0
China PR v Korea Republic	1-0
Syria v Uzbekistan	1-0
Qatar v Iran	0-1
Korea Republic v Syria	1-0
Iran v China PR	1-0
Uzbekistan v Qatar	1-0
Iran v Uzbekistan	2-0
Syria v China PR	2-2
Qatar v Korea Republic	3-2

Group A Table	P	W	D	L	F	A	GD	Pts
Iran	8	6	2	0	8	0	8	20
Korea Republic	8	4	1	3	11	10	1	13
Uzbekistan	8	4	0	4	6	6	0	12
Syria	8	2	3	3	4	5	–1	9
Qatar	8	2	1	5	6	10	–4	7
China PR	8	1	3	4	5	9	–4	6

GROUP B

Australia v Iraq	2-0
Japan v UA Emirates	1-2
Saudi Arabia v Thailand	1-0
Iraq v Saudi Arabia	1-2
Thailand v Japan	0-2
UA Emirates v Australia	0-1
Japan v Iraq	2-1
UA Emirates v Thailand	3-1
Saudi Arabia v Australia	2-2
Australia v Japan	1-1
Iraq v Thailand	4-0
Saudi Arabia v UA Emirates	3-0
Japan v Saudi Arabia	2-1
Thailand v Australia	2-2
UA Emirates v Iraq	2-0
Iraq v Australia	1-1
Thailand v Saudi Arabia	0-3
UA Emirates v Japan	0-2
Australia v UA Emirates	2-0
Japan v Thailand	4-0
Saudi Arabia v Iraq	1-0
Australia v Saudi Arabia	3-2
Thailand v UA Emirates	1-1
Iraq v Japan	1-1

Group B Table	P	W	D	L	F	A	GD	Pts
Japan	8	5	2	1	15	6	9	17
Saudi Arabia	8	5	1	2	15	8	7	16
Australia	8	4	4	0	14	8	6	16
UA Emirates	8	3	1	4	8	11	–3	10
Iraq	8	1	2	5	8	11	–3	5
Thailand	8	0	2	6	4	20	–16	2

Top two in each group qualify for Russia 2018; 3rd placed teams play each other, the winner playing off against 4th placed CONCACAF team.

NORTH, CENTRAL AMERICA AND CARIBBEAN (CONCACAF)

ROUND 5

Honduras v Panama	0-1
Trinidad & Tobago v Costa Rica	0-2
USA v Mexico	1-2
Honduras v Trinidad & Tobago	3-1
Costa Rica v USA	4-0
Panama v Mexico	0-0
Trinidad & Tobago v Panama	1-0
Mexico v Costa Rica	2-0
USA v Honduras	6-0
Honduras v Costa Rica	1-1
Trinidad & Tobago v Mexico	0-1
Panama v USA	1-1
USA v Trinidad & Tobago	2-0
Costa Rica v Panama	0-0
Mexico v Honduras	3-0
Mexico v USA	1-1
Panama v Honduras	2-2
Costa Rica v Trinidad & Tobago	2-1

Latest Table	P	W	D	L	F	A	GD	Pts
Mexico	6	4	2	0	9	2	7	14
Costa Rica	6	3	2	1	9	4	5	11
USA	6	2	2	2	11	8	3	8
Panama	6	1	4	1	4	4	0	7
Honduras	6	1	2	3	6	14	–8	5
Trinidad & Tobago	6	1	0	5	3	10	–7	3

Top three qualify for Russia 2018; 4th placed team plays off against winners of AFC play-off.

OCEANIA (OFC)

ROUND 3

GROUP A

New Zealand v New Caledonia	2-0
New Caledonia v New Zealand	0-0
Fiji v New Zealand	0-2
New Zealand v Fiji	2-0
Fiji v New Caledonia	2-2
New Caledonia v Fiji	2-1

Group A Table	P	W	D	L	F	A	GD	Pts
New Zealand	4	3	1	0	6	0	6	10
New Caledonia	4	1	2	1	4	5	–1	5
Fiji	4	0	1	3	3	8	–5	1

GROUP B

Tahiti v Solomon Islands	3-0
Solomon Islands v Tahiti	1-0
Papua New Guinea v Tahiti	1-3
Tahiti v Papua New Guinea	1-2
Solomon Islands v Papua New Guinea	3-2
Papua New Guinea v Solomon Islands	1-2

Group B Table	P	W	D	L	F	A	GD	Pts
Solomon Islands	4	3	0	1	6	6	0	9
Tahiti	4	2	0	2	7	4	3	6
Papua New Guinea	4	1	0	3	6	9	–3	3

Group winners play off for right to meet 5th placed CONMEBOL team for right to play at Russia 2018.

OLYMPICS – RIO 2016

MEN

GROUP A

Iraq v Denmark	0-0
Brazil v South Africa	0-0
Denmark v South Africa	1-0
Brazil v Iraq	0-0
Denmark v Brazil	0-4
South Africa v Iraq	1-1

Group A Table	P	W	D	L	F	A	GD	Pts
Brazil	3	1	2	0	4	0	4	5
Denmark	3	1	1	1	1	4	–3	4
Iraq	3	0	3	0	1	1	0	3
South Africa	3	0	2	1	1	2	–1	2

GROUP B

Sweden v Colombia	2-2
Nigeria v Japan	5-4
Sweden v Nigeria	0-1
Japan v Colombia	2-2
Japan v Sweden	1-0
Colombia v Nigeria	2-0

Group B Table	P	W	D	L	F	A	GD	Pts
Nigeria	3	2	0	1	6	6	0	6
Colombia	3	1	2	0	6	4	2	5
Japan	3	1	1	1	7	7	0	4
Sweden	3	0	1	2	2	4	–2	1

GROUP C

Mexico v Germany	2-2
Fiji v Korea Republic	0-8
Fiji v Mexico	1-5
Germany v Korea Republic	3-3
Germany v Fiji	10-0
Korea Republic v Mexico	1-0

Group C Table	P	W	D	L	F	A	GD	Pts
Korea Republic	3	2	1	0	12	3	9	7
Germany	3	1	2	0	15	5	10	5
Mexico	3	1	1	1	7	4	3	4
Fiji	3	0	0	3	1	23	–22	0

GROUP D

Honduras v Algeria	3-2
Portugal v Argentina	2-0
Honduras v Portugal	1-2
Argentina v Algeria	2-1
Argentina v Honduras	1-1
Algeria v Portugal	1-1

Group D Table	P	W	D	L	F	A	GD	Pts
Portugal	3	2	1	0	5	2	3	7
Honduras	3	1	1	1	5	5	0	4
Argentina	3	1	1	1	3	4	–1	4
Algeria	3	0	1	2	4	6	–2	1

QUARTER-FINALS

Brazil v Colombia	2-0
Korea Republic v Honduras	0-1
Nigeria v Denmark	2-0
Portugal v Germany	0-4

SEMI-FINALS

Brazil v Honduras	6-0
Nigeria v Germany	0-2

BRONZE MEDAL MATCH

Honduras v Nigeria	2-3

GOLD MEDAL MATCH

Rio de Janeiro, Saturday 20 August 2016

Brazil (1) 1 *(Neymar 27)*

Germany (0) 1 *(Meyer 59)* 63,707

Brazil: Weverton; Zeca, Rodrigo Caio, Marquinhos, Douglas Santos, Renato Augusto, Walace, Luan, Gabriel Barbosa (Felipe Anderson 70), Neymar, Gabriel Jesus (Rafinha 95).
Germany: Horn; Toljan, Klostermann, Ginter, Suele, Bender S, Meyer, Bender L (Promel 67), Brandt, Gnabry, Selke (Petersen 76).
Referee: Alireza Faghani (Iran).
aet; Brazil won 5-4 on penalties.

WOMEN

GROUP E

Sweden v South Africa	1-0
Brazil v China PR	3-0
South Africa v China PR	0-2
Brazil v Sweden	5-1
South Africa v Brazil	0-0
China PR v Sweden	0-0

Group E Table	P	W	D	L	F	A	GD	Pts
Brazil	3	2	1	0	8	1	7	7
China PR	3	1	1	1	2	3	–1	4
Sweden	3	1	1	1	2	5	–3	4
South Africa	3	0	1	2	0	3	–3	1

GROUP F

Canada v Australia	2-0
Zimbabwe v Germany	1-6
Canada v Zimbabwe	3-1
Germany v Australia	2-2
Germany v Canada	1-2
Australia v Zimbabwe	6-1

Group F Table	P	W	D	L	F	A	GD	Pts
Canada	3	3	0	0	7	2	5	9
Germany	3	1	1	1	9	5	4	4
Australia	3	1	1	1	8	5	3	4
Zimbabwe	3	0	0	3	3	15	–12	0

GROUP G

USA v New Zealand	2-0
France v Colombia	4-0
USA v France	1-0
Colombia v New Zealand	0-1
Colombia v USA	2-2
New Zealand v France	0-3

Group G Table	P	W	D	L	F	A	GD	Pts
USA	3	2	1	0	5	2	3	7
France	3	2	0	1	7	1	6	6
New Zealand	3	1	0	2	1	5	–4	3
Colombia	3	0	1	2	2	7	–5	1

QUARTER-FINALS

Brazil v Australia 0-0
aet; Brazil won 7-6 on penalties.
USA v Sweden 1-1
aet; Sweden won 4-3 on penalties.
Canada v France 1-0
China PR v Germany 0-1

SEMI-FINALS

Brazil v Sweden 0-0
aet; Sweden won 4-3 on penalties.
Canada v Germany 0-2

BRONZE MEDAL MATCH

Brazil v Canada 1-2

GOLD MEDAL MATCH

Rio de Janeiro, Friday 19 August 2016

Sweden (0) 1 *(Blackstenius 67)*

Germany (0) 2 *(Marozsan 48, Sembrant 62 (og))* 52,432

Sweden: Lindahl; Sembrant, Fischer, Samuelsson, Dahlkvist, Asllani (Hammarlund 66), Rubensson (Ericsson 70), Seger, Schelin, Jakobsson (Blackstenius 55), Schough.
Germany: Schult; Bartusiak, Maier, Krahn, Kemme, Behringer (Goessling 70), Daebritz (Huth 83), Leupolz, Popp, Marozsan, Mittag.
Referee: Carol Chenard (Canada).

OLYMPIC FOOTBALL PAST MEDALLISTS 1896–2016

* No official tournament. ** No official tournament but gold medal later awarded by IOC.

1896 Athens*
1 Denmark
2 Greece

1900 Paris*
1 Great Britain
2 France

1904 St Louis**
1 Canada
2 USA

1908 London
1 Great Britain
2 Denmark
3 Netherlands

1912 Stockholm
1 England
2 Denmark
3 Netherlands

1920 Antwerp
1 Belgium
2 Spain
3 Netherlands

1924 Paris
1 Uruguay
2 Switzerland
3 Sweden

1928 Amsterdam
1 Uruguay
2 Argentina
3 Italy

1932 Los Angeles
no tournament

1936 Berlin
1 Italy
2 Austria
3 Norway

1948 London
1 Sweden
2 Yugoslavia
3 Denmark

1952 Helsinki
1 Hungary
2 Yugoslavia
3 Sweden

1956 Melbourne
1 USSR
2 Yugoslavia
3 Bulgaria

1960 Rome
1 Yugoslavia
2 Denmark
3 Hungary

1964 Tokyo
1 Hungary
2 Czechoslovakia
3 East Germany

1968 Mexico City
1 Hungary
2 Bulgaria
3 Japan

1972 Munich
1 Poland
2 Hungary
3 E Germany/USSR

1976 Montreal
1 East Germany
2 Poland
3 USSR

1980 Moscow
1 Czechoslovakia
2 East Germany
3 USSR

1984 Los Angeles
1 France
2 Brazil
3 Yugoslavia

1988 Seoul
1 USSR
2 Brazil
3 West Germany

1992 Barcelona
1 Spain
2 Poland
3 Ghana

1996 Atlanta
1 Nigeria
2 Argentina
3 Brazil

2000 Sydney
1 Cameroon
2 Spain
3 Chile

2004 Athens
1 Argentina
2 Paraguay
3 Italy

2008 Beijing
1 Argentina
2 Nigeria
3 Brazil

2012 London
1 Mexico
2 Brazil
3 South Korea

2016 Rio
1 Brazil
2 Germany
3 Nigeria

EUROPEAN FOOTBALL CHAMPIONSHIP 1960–2016

(formerly EUROPEAN NATIONS' CUP)

Year	Winners v Runners-up		Venue	Attendance	Referee
1960	USSR v Yugoslavia	2-1*	Paris	17,966	A. E. Ellis (England)
	Winning Coach: Gavriil Kachalin				
1964	Spain v USSR	2-1	Madrid	79,115	A. E. Ellis (England)
	Winning Coach: Jose Villalonga				
1968	Italy v Yugoslavia	1-1	Rome	68,817	G. Dienst (Switzerland)
Replay	Italy v Yugoslavia	2-0	Rome	32,866	J. M. O. de Mendibil (Spain)
	Winning Coach: Ferruccio Valcareggi				
1972	West Germany v USSR	3-0	Brussels	43,066	F. Marschall (Austria)
	Winning Coach: Helmut Schon				
1976	Czechoslovakia v West Germany	2-2	Belgrade	30,790	S. Gonella (Italy)
	Czechoslovakia won 5-3 on penalties.				
	Winning Coach: Vaclav Jezek				
1980	West Germany v Belgium	2-1	Rome	47,860	N. Rainea (Romania)
	Winning Coach: Jupp Derwall				
1984	France v Spain	2-0	Paris	47,368	V. Christov (Slovakia)
	Winning Coach: Michel Hidalgo				
1988	Netherlands v USSR	2-0	Munich	62,770	M. Vautrot (France)
	Winning Coach: Rinus Michels				
1992	Denmark v Germany	2-0	Gothenburg	37,800	B. Galler (Switzerland)
	Winning Coach: Richard Moller Nielsen				
1996	Germany v Czech Republic	2-1*	Wembley	73,611	P. Pairetto (Italy)
	Germany won on sudden death 'golden goal'.				
	Winning Coach: Berti Vogts				
2000	France v Italy	2-1*	Rotterdam	48,200	A. Frisk (Sweden)
	France won on sudden death 'golden goal'.				
	Winning Coach: Roger Lemerre				
2004	Greece v Portugal	1-0	Lisbon	62,865	M. Merk (Germany)
	Winning Coach: Otto Rehhagel				
2008	Spain v Germany	1-0	Vienna	51,428	R. Rosetti (Italy)
	Winning Coach: Luis Aragones				
2012	Spain v Italy	4-0	Kiev	63,170	P. Proenca (Portugal)
	Winning Coach: Vicente del Bosque				
2016	Portugal v France	1-0*	Paris	75,868	M. Clattenburg (England)
	Winning Coach: Fernando Santos				

*(*After extra time)*

THE WORLD CUP 1930–2014

Year	Winners v Runners-up		Venue	Attendance	Referee
1930	Uruguay v Argentina	4-2	Montevideo	68,346	J. Langenus (Belgium)
	Winning Coach: Alberto Suppici				
1934	Italy v Czechoslovakia	2-1*	Rome	55,000	I. Eklind (Sweden)
	Winning Coach: Vittorio Pozzo				
1938	Italy v Hungary	4-2	Paris	45,000	G. Capdeville (France)
	Winning Coach: Vittorio Pozzo				
1950	Uruguay v Brazil	2-1	Rio de Janeiro	173,850	G. Reader (England)
	Winning Coach: Juan Lopez				
1954	West Germany v Hungary	3-2	Berne	62,500	W. Ling (England)
	Winning Coach: Sepp Herberger				
1958	Brazil v Sweden	5-2	Stockholm	49,737	M. Guigue (France)
	Winning Coach: Vicente Feola				
1962	Brazil v Czechoslovakia	3-1	Santiago	68,679	N. Latychev (USSR)
	Winning Coach: Aymore Moreira				
1966	England v West Germany	4-2*	Wembley	96,924	G. Dienst (Sweden)
	Winning Coach: Alf Ramsey				
1970	Brazil v Italy	4-1	Mexico City	107,412	R. Glockner (East Germany)
	Winning Coach: Mario Zagallo				
1974	West Germany v Netherlands	2-1	Munich	78,200	J. Taylor (England)
	Winning Coach: Helmut Schon				
1978	Argentina v Netherlands	3-1*	Buenos Aires	71,483	S. Gonella (Italy)
	Winning Coach: Cesar Luis Menotti				
1982	Italy v West Germany	3-1	Madrid	90,000	A. C. Coelho (Brazil)
	Winning Coach: Enzo Bearzot				
1986	Argentina v West Germany	3-2	Mexico City	114,600	R. A. Filho (Brazil)
	Winning Coach: Carlos Bilardo				
1990	West Germany v Argentina	1-0	Rome	73,603	E. C. Mendez (Mexico)
	Winning Coach: Franz Beckenbauer				
1994	Brazil v Italy	0-0*	Los Angeles	94,194	S. Puhl (Hungary)
	Brazil won 3-2 on penalties.				
	Winning Coach: Carlos Alberto Parreira				
1998	France v Brazil	3-0	Paris	80,000	S. Belqola (Morocco)
	Winning Coach: Aime Jacquet				
2002	Brazil v Germany	2-0	Yokohama	69,029	P. Collina (Italy)
	Winning Coach: Luiz Felipe Scolari				
2006	Italy v France	1-1*	Berlin	69,000	H. Elizondo (Argentina)
	Italy won 5-3 on penalties.				
	Winning Coach: Marcello Lippi				
2010	Spain v Netherlands	1-0	Johannesburg	84,490	H. Webb (England)
	Winning Coach: Vicente del Bosque				
2014	Germany v Argentina	1-0*	Rio de Janeiro	74,738	N. Rizzoli (Italy)
	Winning Coach: Joachim Low				

*(*After extra time)*

GOALSCORING AND ATTENDANCES IN WORLD CUP FINAL ROUNDS

Year	*Venue*	*Games*	*Goals (av)*	*Attendance (av)*
1930	Uruguay	18	70 (3.9)	590,549 (32,808)
1934	Italy	17	70 (4.1)	363,000 (21,352)
1938	France	18	84 (4.7)	375,700 (20,872)
1950	Brazil	22	88 (4.0)	1,045,246 (47,511)
1954	Switzerland	26	140 (5.4)	768,607 (29,562)
1958	Sweden	35	126 (3.6)	819,810 (23,423)
1962	Chile	32	89 (2.8)	893,172 (27,912)
1966	England	32	89 (2.8)	1,563,135 (48,848)
1970	Mexico	32	95 (3.0)	1,603,975 (50,124)
1974	West Germany	38	97 (2.6)	1,865,753 (49,098)
1978	Argentina	38	102 (2.7)	1,545,791 (40,678)
1982	Spain	52	146 (2.8)	2,109,723 (40,571)
1986	Mexico	52	132 (2.5)	2,394,031 (46,039)
1990	Italy	52	115 (2.2)	2,516,215 (48,388)
1994	USA	52	141 (2.7)	3,587,538 (68,991)
1998	France	64	171 (2.7)	2,785,100 (43,517)
2002	Japan/S. Korea	64	161 (2.5)	2,705,197 (42,268)
2006	Germany	64	147 (2.3)	3,359,439 (52,491)
2010	South Africa	64	145 (2.3)	3,178,856 (49,669)
2014	Brazil	64	171 (2.7)	3,367,727 (52,621)
Total		836	2379 (2.8)	37,438,564 (44,783)

LEADING GOALSCORERS

Year	*Player*	*Goals*
1930	Guillermo Stabile (Argentina)	8
1934	Oldrich Nejedly (Czechoslovakia)	5
1938	Leonidas da Silva (Brazil)	7
1950	Ademir (Brazil)	8
1954	Sandor Kocsis (Hungary)	11
1958	Just Fontaine (France)	13
1962	Valentin Ivanov (USSR), Leonel Sanchez (Chile), Garrincha (Brazil), Vava (Brazil), Florian Albert (Hungary), Drazen Jerkovic (Yugoslavia)	4
1966	Eusebio (Portugal)	9
1970	Gerd Muller (West Germany)	10
1974	Grzegorz Lato (Poland)	7
1978	Mario Kempes (Argentina)	6
1982	Paolo Rossi (Italy)	6
1986	Gary Lineker (England)	6
1990	Salvatore Schillaci (Italy)	6
1994	Oleg Salenko (Russia) Hristo Stoichkov (Bulgaria)	6
1998	Davor Suker (Croatia)	6
2002	Ronaldo (Brazil)	8
2006	Miroslav Klose (Germany)	5
2010	Thomas Muller (Germany), David Villa (Spain), Wesley Sneijder (Netherlands), Diego Forlan (Uruguay)	5
2014	James Rodriguez (Colombia)	6

BRITISH AND IRISH INTERNATIONAL RESULTS 1872–2017

Note: In the results that follow, WC=World Cup, EC=European Championship, UI=Umbro International Trophy. TF = Tournoi de France. NC = Nations Cup. Northern Ireland played as Ireland before 1921. *After extra time.

Bold type indicates matches played in season 2016–17.

ENGLAND v SCOTLAND

Played: 114; England won 48, Scotland won 41, Drawn 25. Goals: England 203, Scotland 174.

			E	*S*
1872	30 Nov	Glasgow	0	0
1873	8 Mar	Kennington Oval	4	2
1874	7 Mar	Glasgow	1	2
1875	6 Mar	Kennington Oval	2	2
1876	4 Mar	Glasgow	0	3
1877	3 Mar	Kennington Oval	1	3
1878	2 Mar	Glasgow	2	7
1879	5 Apr	Kennington Oval	5	4
1880	13 Mar	Glasgow	4	5
1881	12 Mar	Kennington Oval	1	6
1882	11 Mar	Glasgow	1	5
1883	10 Mar	Sheffield	2	3
1884	15 Mar	Glasgow	0	1
1885	21 Mar	Kennington Oval	1	1
1886	31 Mar	Glasgow	1	1
1887	19 Mar	Blackburn	2	3
1888	17 Mar	Glasgow	5	0
1889	13 Apr	Kennington Oval	2	3
1890	5 Apr	Glasgow	1	1
1891	6 Apr	Blackburn	2	1
1892	2 Apr	Glasgow	4	1
1893	1 Apr	Richmond	5	2
1894	7 Apr	Glasgow	2	2
1895	6 Apr	Everton	3	0
1896	4 Apr	Glasgow	1	2
1897	3 Apr	Crystal Palace	1	2
1898	2 Apr	Glasgow	3	1
1899	8 Apr	Aston Villa	2	1
1900	7 Apr	Glasgow	1	4
1901	30 Mar	Crystal Palace	2	2
1902	3 Mar	Aston Villa	2	2
1903	4 Apr	Sheffield	1	2
1904	9 Apr	Glasgow	1	0
1905	1 Apr	Crystal Palace	1	0
1906	7 Apr	Glasgow	1	2
1907	6 Apr	Newcastle	1	1
1908	4 Apr	Glasgow	1	1
1909	3 Apr	Crystal Palace	2	0
1910	2 Apr	Glasgow	0	2
1911	1 Apr	Everton	1	1
1912	23 Mar	Glasgow	1	1
1913	5 Apr	Chelsea	1	0
1914	14 Apr	Glasgow	1	3
1920	10 Apr	Sheffield	5	4
1921	9 Apr	Glasgow	0	3
1922	8 Apr	Aston Villa	0	1
1923	14 Apr	Glasgow	2	2
1924	12 Apr	Wembley	1	1
1925	4 Apr	Glasgow	0	2
1926	17 Apr	Manchester	0	1
1927	2 Apr	Glasgow	2	1
1928	31 Mar	Wembley	1	5
1929	13 Apr	Glasgow	0	1
1930	5 Apr	Wembley	5	2
1931	28 Mar	Glasgow	0	2
1932	9 Apr	Wembley	3	0
1933	1 Apr	Glasgow	1	2
1934	14 Apr	Wembley	3	0
1935	6 Apr	Glasgow	0	2
1936	4 Apr	Wembley	1	1
1937	17 Apr	Glasgow	1	3
1938	9 Apr	Wembley	0	1
1939	15 Apr	Glasgow	2	1
1947	12 Apr	Wembley	1	1
1948	10 Apr	Glasgow	2	0
1949	9 Apr	Wembley	1	3
WC1950	15 Apr	Glasgow	1	0
1951	14 Apr	Wembley	2	3
1952	5 Apr	Glasgow	2	1
1953	18 Apr	Wembley	2	2
WC1954	3 Apr	Glasgow	4	2
1955	2 Apr	Wembley	7	2
1956	14 Apr	Glasgow	1	1
1957	6 Apr	Wembley	2	1
1958	19 Apr	Glasgow	4	0
1959	11 Apr	Wembley	1	0
1960	9 Apr	Glasgow	1	1
1961	15 Apr	Wembley	9	3
1962	14 Apr	Glasgow	0	2
1963	6 Apr	Wembley	1	2
1964	11 Apr	Glasgow	0	1
1965	10 Apr	Wembley	2	2
1966	2 Apr	Glasgow	4	3
EC1967	15 Apr	Wembley	2	3
EC1968	24 Jan	Glasgow	1	1
1969	10 May	Wembley	4	1
1970	25 Apr	Glasgow	0	0
1971	22 May	Wembley	3	1
1972	27 May	Glasgow	1	0
1973	14 Feb	Glasgow	5	0
1973	19 May	Wembley	1	0
1974	18 May	Glasgow	0	2
1975	24 May	Wembley	5	1
1976	15 May	Glasgow	1	2
1977	4 June	Wembley	1	2
1978	20 May	Glasgow	1	0
1979	26 May	Wembley	3	1
1980	24 May	Glasgow	2	0
1981	23 May	Wembley	0	1
1982	29 May	Glasgow	1	0
1983	1 June	Wembley	2	0
1984	26 May	Glasgow	1	1
1985	25 May	Glasgow	0	1
1986	23 Apr	Wembley	2	1
1987	23 May	Glasgow	0	0
1988	21 May	Wembley	1	0
1989	27 May	Glasgow	2	0
EC1996	15 June	Wembley	2	0
EC1999	13 Nov	Glasgow	2	0
EC1999	17 Nov	Wembley	0	1
2013	14 Aug	Wembley	3	2
2014	18 Nov	Hampden	3	1
WC2016	**11 Nov**	**Wembley**	**3**	**0**
WC2017	**10 June**	**Hampden**	**2**	**2**

ENGLAND v WALES

Played: 102; England won 67, Wales won 14, Drawn 21. Goals: England 247, Wales 91.

			E	*W*
1879	18 Jan	Kennington Oval	2	1
1880	15 Mar	Wrexham	3	2
1881	26 Feb	Blackburn	0	1
1882	13 Mar	Wrexham	3	5
1883	3 Feb	Kennington Oval	5	0
1884	17 Mar	Wrexham	4	0
1885	14 Mar	Blackburn	1	1
1886	29 Mar	Wrexham	3	1
1887	26 Feb	Kennington Oval	4	0
1888	4 Feb	Crewe	5	1
1889	23 Feb	Stoke	4	1
1890	15 Mar	Wrexham	3	1
1891	7 May	Sunderland	4	1
1892	5 Mar	Wrexham	2	0
1893	13 Mar	Stoke	6	0
1894	12 Mar	Wrexham	5	1

			E	*W*
1895	18 Mar	Queen's Club, Kensington	1	1
1896	16 Mar	Cardiff	9	1
1897	29 Mar	Sheffield	4	0
1898	28 Mar	Wrexham	3	0
1899	20 Mar	Bristol	4	0
1900	26 Mar	Cardiff	1	1
1901	18 Mar	Newcastle	6	0
1902	3 Mar	Wrexham	0	0
1903	2 Mar	Portsmouth	2	1
1904	29 Feb	Wrexham	2	2
1905	27 Mar	Liverpool	3	1
1906	19 Mar	Cardiff	1	0
1907	18 Mar	Fulham	1	1
1908	16 Mar	Wrexham	7	1
1909	15 Mar	Nottingham	2	0
1910	14 Mar	Cardiff	1	0
1911	13 Mar	Millwall	3	0
1912	11 Mar	Wrexham	2	0
1913	17 Mar	Bristol	4	3
1914	16 Mar	Cardiff	2	0
1920	15 Mar	Highbury	1	2
1921	14 Mar	Cardiff	0	0
1922	13 Mar	Liverpool	1	0
1923	5 Mar	Cardiff	2	2
1924	3 Mar	Blackburn	1	2
1925	28 Feb	Swansea	2	1
1926	1 Mar	Crystal Palace	1	3
1927	12 Feb	Wrexham	3	3
1927	28 Nov	Burnley	1	2
1928	17 Nov	Swansea	3	2
1929	20 Nov	Chelsea	6	0
1930	22 Nov	Wrexham	4	0
1931	18 Nov	Liverpool	3	1
1932	16 Nov	Wrexham	0	0
1933	15 Nov	Newcastle	1	2
1934	29 Sept	Cardiff	4	0
1936	5 Feb	Wolverhampton	1	2
1936	17 Oct	Cardiff	1	2
1937	17 Nov	Middlesbrough	2	1
1938	22 Oct	Cardiff	2	4
1946	13 Nov	Manchester	3	0
1947	18 Oct	Cardiff	3	0
1948	10 Nov	Aston Villa	1	0
wc1949	15 Oct	Cardiff	4	1
1950	15 Nov	Sunderland	4	2
1951	20 Oct	Cardiff	1	1
1952	12 Nov	Wembley	5	2
wc1953	10 Oct	Cardiff	4	1
1954	10 Nov	Wembley	3	2
1955	27 Oct	Cardiff	1	2
1956	14 Nov	Wembley	3	1
1957	19 Oct	Cardiff	4	0
1958	26 Nov	Aston Villa	2	2
1959	17 Oct	Cardiff	1	1
1960	23 Nov	Wembley	5	1
1961	14 Oct	Cardiff	1	1
1962	21 Oct	Wembley	4	0
1963	12 Oct	Cardiff	4	0
1964	18 Nov	Wembley	2	1
1965	2 Oct	Cardiff	0	0
EC1966	16 Nov	Wembley	5	1
EC1967	21 Oct	Cardiff	3	0
1969	7 May	Wembley	2	1
1970	18 Apr	Cardiff	1	1
1971	19 May	Wembley	0	0
1972	20 May	Cardiff	3	0
wc1972	15 Nov	Cardiff	1	0
wc1973	24 Jan	Wembley	1	1
1973	15 May	Wembley	3	0
1974	11 May	Cardiff	2	0
1975	21 May	Wembley	2	2
1976	24 Mar	Wrexham	2	1
1976	8 May	Cardiff	1	0
1977	31 May	Wembley	0	1
1978	3 May	Cardiff	3	1
1979	23 May	Wembley	0	0
1980	17 May	Wrexham	1	4
1981	20 May	Wembley	0	0
1982	27 Apr	Cardiff	1	0
1983	23 Feb	Wembley	2	1
1984	2 May	Wrexham	0	1
wc2004	9 Oct	Old Trafford	2	0
wc2005	3 Sept	Cardiff	1	0
EC2011	26 Mar	Cardiff	2	0
EC2011	6 Sept	Wembley	1	0
EC2016	16 June	Lens	2	1

ENGLAND v NORTHERN IRELAND

Played: 98; England won 75, Northern Ireland won 7, Drawn 16. Goals: England 323, Northern Ireland 81.

			E	*NI*
1882	18 Feb	Belfast	13	0
1883	24 Feb	Liverpool	7	0
1884	23 Feb	Belfast	8	1
1885	28 Feb	Manchester	4	0
1886	13 Mar	Belfast	6	1
1887	5 Feb	Sheffield	7	0
1888	31 Mar	Belfast	5	1
1889	2 Mar	Everton	6	1
1890	15 Mar	Belfast	9	1
1891	7 Mar	Wolverhampton	6	1
1892	5 Mar	Belfast	2	0
1893	25 Feb	Birmingham	6	1
1894	3 Mar	Belfast	2	2
1895	9 Mar	Derby	9	0
1896	7 Mar	Belfast	2	0
1897	20 Feb	Nottingham	6	0
1898	5 Mar	Belfast	3	2
1899	18 Feb	Sunderland	13	2
1900	17 Mar	Dublin	2	0
1901	9 Mar	Southampton	3	0
1902	22 Mar	Belfast	1	0
1903	14 Feb	Wolverhampton	4	0
1904	12 Mar	Belfast	3	1
1905	25 Feb	Middlesbrough	1	1
1906	17 Feb	Belfast	5	0
1907	16 Feb	Everton	1	0
1908	15 Feb	Belfast	3	1
1909	13 Feb	Bradford	4	0
1910	12 Feb	Belfast	1	1
1911	11 Feb	Derby	2	1
1912	10 Feb	Dublin	6	1
1913	15 Feb	Belfast	1	2
1914	14 Feb	Middlesbrough	0	3
1919	25 Oct	Belfast	1	1
1920	23 Oct	Sunderland	2	0
1921	22 Oct	Belfast	1	1
1922	21 Oct	West Bromwich	2	0
1923	20 Oct	Belfast	1	2
1924	22 Oct	Everton	3	1
1925	24 Oct	Belfast	0	0
1926	20 Oct	Liverpool	3	3
1927	22 Oct	Belfast	0	2
1928	22 Oct	Everton	2	1
1929	19 Oct	Belfast	3	0
1930	20 Oct	Sheffield	5	1
1931	17 Oct	Belfast	6	2
1932	17 Oct	Blackpool	1	0
1933	14 Oct	Belfast	3	0
1935	6 Feb	Everton	2	1
1935	19 Oct	Belfast	3	1
1936	18 Nov	Stoke	3	1
1937	23 Oct	Belfast	5	1
1938	16 Nov	Manchester	7	0
1946	28 Sept	Belfast	7	2
1947	5 Nov	Everton	2	2
1948	9 Oct	Belfast	6	2
wc1949	16 Nov	Manchester	9	2
1950	7 Oct	Belfast	4	1
1951	14 Nov	Aston Villa	2	0
1952	4 Oct	Belfast	2	2
wc1953	11 Nov	Everton	3	1
1954	2 Oct	Belfast	2	0
1955	2 Nov	Wembley	3	0
1956	10 Oct	Belfast	1	1

			E	*NI*
1957	6 Nov	Wembley	2	3
1958	4 Oct	Belfast	3	3
1959	18 Nov	Wembley	2	1
1960	8 Oct	Belfast	5	2
1961	22 Nov	Wembley	1	1
1962	20 Oct	Belfast	3	1
1963	20 Nov	Wembley	8	3
1964	3 Oct	Belfast	4	3
1965	10 Nov	Wembley	2	1
EC1966	20 Oct	Belfast	2	0
EC1967	22 Nov	Wembley	2	0
1969	3 May	Belfast	3	1
1970	21 Apr	Wembley	3	1
1971	15 May	Belfast	1	0
1972	23 May	Wembley	0	1
1973	12 May	Everton	2	1
1974	15 May	Wembley	1	0
1975	17 May	Belfast	0	0
1976	11 May	Wembley	4	0
1977	28 May	Belfast	2	1
1978	16 May	Wembley	1	0
EC1979	7 Feb	Wembley	4	0
1979	19 May	Belfast	2	0
EC1979	17 Oct	Belfast	5	1
1980	20 May	Wembley	1	1
1982	23 Feb	Wembley	4	0
1983	28 May	Belfast	0	0
1984	24 Apr	Wembley	1	0
WC1985	27 Feb	Belfast	1	0
WC1985	13 Nov	Wembley	0	0
EC1986	15 Oct	Wembley	3	0
EC1987	1 Apr	Belfast	2	0
WC2005	26 Mar	Old Trafford	4	0
WC2005	7 Sept	Belfast	0	1

SCOTLAND v WALES

Played: 107; Scotland won 61, Wales won 23, Drawn 23. Goals: Scotland 243, Wales 124.

			S	*W*
1876	25 Mar	Glasgow	4	0
1877	5 Mar	Wrexham	2	0
1878	23 Mar	Glasgow	9	0
1879	7 Apr	Wrexham	3	0
1880	3 Apr	Glasgow	5	1
1881	14 Mar	Wrexham	5	1
1882	25 Mar	Glasgow	5	0
1883	12 Mar	Wrexham	3	0
1884	29 Mar	Glasgow	4	1
1885	23 Mar	Wrexham	8	1
1886	10 Apr	Glasgow	4	1
1887	21 Mar	Wrexham	2	0
1888	10 Mar	Easter Road	5	1
1889	15 Apr	Wrexham	0	0
1890	22 Mar	Paisley	5	0
1891	21 Mar	Wrexham	4	3
1892	26 Mar	Tynecastle	6	1
1893	18 Mar	Wrexham	8	0
1894	24 Mar	Kilmarnock	5	2
1895	23 Mar	Wrexham	2	2
1896	21 Mar	Dundee	4	0
1897	20 Mar	Wrexham	2	2
1898	19 Mar	Motherwell	5	2
1899	18 Mar	Wrexham	6	0
1900	3 Feb	Aberdeen	5	2
1901	2 Mar	Wrexham	1	1
1902	15 Mar	Greenock	5	1
1903	9 Mar	Cardiff	1	0
1904	12 Mar	Dundee	1	1
1905	6 Mar	Wrexham	1	3
1906	3 Mar	Tynecastle	0	2
1907	4 Mar	Wrexham	0	1
1908	7 Mar	Dundee	2	1
1909	1 Mar	Wrexham	2	3
1910	5 Mar	Kilmarnock	1	0
1911	6 Mar	Cardiff	2	2
1912	2 Mar	Tynecastle	1	0
1913	3 Mar	Wrexham	0	0
1914	28 Feb	Glasgow	0	0
1920	26 Feb	Cardiff	1	1
1921	12 Feb	Aberdeen	2	1
1922	4 Feb	Wrexham	1	2
1923	17 Mar	Paisley	2	0
1924	16 Feb	Cardiff	0	2
1925	14 Feb	Tynecastle	3	1
1925	31 Oct	Cardiff	3	0
1926	30 Oct	Glasgow	3	0
1927	29 Oct	Wrexham	2	2
1928	27 Oct	Glasgow	4	2
1929	26 Oct	Cardiff	4	2
1930	25 Oct	Glasgow	1	1
1931	31 Oct	Wrexham	3	2
1932	26 Oct	Tynecastle	2	5
1933	4 Oct	Cardiff	2	3
1934	21 Nov	Aberdeen	3	2
1935	5 Oct	Cardiff	1	1
1936	2 Dec	Dundee	1	2
1937	30 Oct	Cardiff	1	2
1938	9 Nov	Tynecastle	3	2
1946	19 Oct	Wrexham	1	3
1947	12 Nov	Glasgow	1	2
1948	23 Oct	Cardiff	3	1
WC1949	9 Nov	Glasgow	2	0
1950	21 Oct	Cardiff	3	1
1951	14 Nov	Glasgow	0	1
1952	18 Oct	Cardiff	2	1
WC1953	4 Nov	Glasgow	3	3
1954	16 Oct	Cardiff	1	0
1955	9 Nov	Glasgow	2	0
1956	20 Oct	Cardiff	2	2
1957	13 Nov	Glasgow	1	1
1958	18 Oct	Cardiff	3	0
1959	4 Nov	Glasgow	1	1
1960	20 Oct	Cardiff	0	2
1961	8 Nov	Glasgow	2	0
1962	20 Oct	Cardiff	3	2
1963	20 Nov	Glasgow	2	1
1964	3 Oct	Cardiff	2	3
EC1965	24 Nov	Glasgow	4	1
EC1966	22 Oct	Cardiff	1	1
1967	22 Nov	Glasgow	3	2
1969	3 May	Wrexham	5	3
1970	22 Apr	Glasgow	0	0
1971	15 May	Cardiff	0	0
1972	24 May	Glasgow	1	0
1973	12 May	Wrexham	2	0
1974	14 May	Glasgow	2	0
1975	17 May	Cardiff	2	2
1976	6 May	Glasgow	3	1
WC1976	17 Nov	Glasgow	1	0
1977	28 May	Wrexham	0	0
WC1977	12 Oct	Liverpool	2	0
1978	17 May	Glasgow	1	1
1979	19 May	Cardiff	0	3
1980	21 May	Glasgow	1	0
1981	16 May	Swansea	0	2
1982	24 May	Glasgow	1	0
1983	28 May	Cardiff	2	0
1984	28 Feb	Glasgow	2	1
WC1985	27 Mar	Glasgow	0	1
WC1985	10 Sept	Cardiff	1	1
1997	27 May	Kilmarnock	0	1
2004	18 Feb	Cardiff	0	4
2009	14 Nov	Cardiff	0	3
NC2011	25 May	Dublin	3	1
WC2012	12 Oct	Cardiff	1	2
WC2013	22 Mar	Glasgow	1	2

SCOTLAND v NORTHERN IRELAND

Played: 96; Scotland won 64, Northern Ireland won 15, Drawn 17. Goals: Scotland 261, Northern Ireland 81.

			S	*NI*
1884	26 Jan	Belfast	5	0
1885	14 Mar	Glasgow	8	2
1886	20 Mar	Belfast	7	2
1887	19 Feb	Glasgow	4	1
1888	24 Mar	Belfast	10	2
1889	9 Mar	Glasgow	7	0
1890	29 Mar	Belfast	4	1
1891	28 Mar	Glasgow	2	1
1892	19 Mar	Belfast	3	2
1893	25 Mar	Glasgow	6	1
1894	31 Mar	Belfast	2	1
1895	30 Mar	Glasgow	3	1
1896	28 Mar	Belfast	3	3
1897	27 Mar	Glasgow	5	1
1898	26 Mar	Belfast	3	0
1899	25 Mar	Glasgow	9	1
1900	3 Mar	Belfast	3	0
1901	23 Feb	Glasgow	11	0
1902	1 Mar	Belfast	5	1
1902	9 Aug	Belfast	3	0
1903	21 Mar	Glasgow	0	2
1904	26 Mar	Dublin	1	1
1905	18 Mar	Glasgow	4	0
1906	17 Mar	Dublin	1	0
1907	16 Mar	Glasgow	3	0
1908	14 Mar	Dublin	5	0
1909	15 Mar	Glasgow	5	0
1910	19 Mar	Belfast	0	1
1911	18 Mar	Glasgow	2	0
1912	16 Mar	Belfast	4	1
1913	15 Mar	Dublin	2	1
1914	14 Mar	Belfast	1	1
1920	13 Mar	Glasgow	3	0
1921	26 Feb	Belfast	2	0
1922	4 Mar	Glasgow	2	1
1923	3 Mar	Belfast	1	0
1924	1 Mar	Glasgow	2	0
1925	28 Feb	Belfast	3	0
1926	27 Feb	Glasgow	4	0
1927	26 Feb	Belfast	2	0
1928	25 Feb	Glasgow	0	1
1929	23 Feb	Belfast	7	3
1930	22 Feb	Glasgow	3	1
1931	21 Feb	Belfast	0	0
1931	19 Sept	Glasgow	3	1
1932	12 Sept	Belfast	4	0
1933	16 Sept	Glasgow	1	2
1934	20 Oct	Belfast	1	2
1935	13 Nov	Tynecastle	2	1
1936	31 Oct	Belfast	3	1
1937	10 Nov	Aberdeen	1	1
1938	8 Oct	Belfast	2	0
1946	27 Nov	Glasgow	0	0
1947	4 Oct	Belfast	0	2
1948	17 Nov	Glasgow	3	2
WC1949	1 Oct	Belfast	8	2
1950	1 Nov	Glasgow	6	1
1951	6 Oct	Belfast	3	0
1952	5 Nov	Glasgow	1	1
WC1953	3 Oct	Belfast	3	1
1954	3 Nov	Glasgow	2	2
1955	8 Oct	Belfast	1	2
1956	7 Nov	Glasgow	1	0
1957	5 Oct	Belfast	1	1
1958	5 Nov	Glasgow	2	2
1959	3 Oct	Belfast	4	0
1960	9 Nov	Glasgow	5	2
1961	7 Oct	Belfast	6	1
1962	7 Nov	Glasgow	5	1
1963	12 Oct	Belfast	1	2
1964	25 Nov	Glasgow	3	2
1965	2 Oct	Belfast	2	3
1966	16 Nov	Glasgow	2	1
1967	21 Oct	Belfast	0	1
1969	6 May	Glasgow	1	1
1970	18 Apr	Belfast	1	0
1971	18 May	Glasgow	0	1
1972	20 May	Glasgow	2	0
1973	16 May	Glasgow	1	2
1974	11 May	Glasgow	0	1
1975	20 May	Glasgow	3	0
1976	8 May	Glasgow	3	0
1977	1 June	Glasgow	3	0
1978	13 May	Glasgow	1	1
1979	22 May	Glasgow	1	0
1980	17 May	Belfast	0	1
WC1981	25 Mar	Glasgow	1	1
1981	19 May	Glasgow	2	0
WC1981	14 Oct	Belfast	0	0
1982	28 Apr	Belfast	1	1
1983	24 May	Glasgow	0	0
1983	13 Dec	Belfast	0	2
1992	19 Feb	Glasgow	1	0
2008	20 Aug	Glasgow	0	0
NC2011	9 Feb	Dublin	3	0
2015	25 Mar	Hampden	1	0

WALES v NORTHERN IRELAND

Played: 96; Wales won 45, Northern Ireland won 27, Drawn 24. Goals: Wales 191, Northern Ireland 132.

			W	*NI*
1882	25 Feb	Wrexham	7	1
1883	17 Mar	Belfast	1	1
1884	9 Feb	Wrexham	6	0
1885	11 Apr	Belfast	8	2
1886	27 Feb	Wrexham	5	0
1887	12 Mar	Belfast	1	4
1888	3 Mar	Wrexham	11	0
1889	27 Apr	Belfast	3	1
1890	8 Feb	Shrewsbury	5	2
1891	7 Feb	Belfast	2	7
1892	27 Feb	Bangor	1	1
1893	8 Apr	Belfast	3	4
1894	24 Feb	Swansea	4	1
1895	16 Mar	Belfast	2	2
1896	29 Feb	Wrexham	6	1
1897	6 Mar	Belfast	3	4
1898	19 Feb	Llandudno	0	1
1899	4 Mar	Belfast	0	1
1900	24 Feb	Llandudno	2	0
1901	23 Mar	Belfast	1	0
1902	22 Mar	Cardiff	0	3
1903	28 Mar	Belfast	0	2
1904	21 Mar	Bangor	0	1
1905	18 Apr	Belfast	2	2
1906	2 Apr	Wrexham	4	4
1907	23 Feb	Belfast	3	2
1908	11 Apr	Aberdare	0	1
1909	20 Mar	Belfast	3	2
1910	11 Apr	Wrexham	4	1
1911	28 Jan	Belfast	2	1
1912	13 Apr	Cardiff	2	3
1913	18 Jan	Belfast	1	0
1914	19 Jan	Wrexham	1	2
1920	14 Feb	Belfast	2	2
1921	9 Apr	Swansea	2	1
1922	4 Apr	Belfast	1	1
1923	14 Apr	Wrexham	0	3
1924	15 Mar	Belfast	1	0
1925	18 Apr	Wrexham	0	0
1926	13 Feb	Belfast	0	3
1927	9 Apr	Cardiff	2	2
1928	4 Feb	Belfast	2	1
1929	2 Feb	Wrexham	2	2
1930	1 Feb	Belfast	0	7
1931	22 Apr	Wrexham	3	2
1931	5 Dec	Belfast	0	4
1932	7 Dec	Wrexham	4	1
1933	4 Nov	Belfast	1	1

			W	NI
1935	27 Mar	Wrexham	3	1
1936	11 Mar	Belfast	2	3
1937	17 Mar	Wrexham	4	1
1938	16 Mar	Belfast	0	1
1939	15 Mar	Wrexham	3	1
1947	16 Apr	Belfast	1	2
1948	10 Mar	Wrexham	2	0
1949	9 Mar	Belfast	2	0
wc1950	8 Mar	Wrexham	0	0
1951	7 Mar	Belfast	2	1
1952	19 Mar	Swansea	3	0
1953	15 Apr	Belfast	3	2
wc1954	31 Mar	Wrexham	1	2
1955	20 Apr	Belfast	3	2
1956	11 Apr	Cardiff	1	1
1957	10 Apr	Belfast	0	0
1958	16 Apr	Cardiff	1	1
1959	22 Apr	Belfast	1	4
1960	6 Apr	Wrexham	3	2
1961	12 Apr	Belfast	5	1
1962	11 Apr	Cardiff	4	0
1963	3 Apr	Belfast	4	1
1964	15 Apr	Swansea	2	3
1965	31 Mar	Belfast	5	0

			W	NI
1966	30 Mar	Cardiff	1	4
EC1967	12 Apr	Belfast	0	0
EC1968	28 Feb	Wrexham	2	0
1969	10 May	Belfast	0	0
1970	25 Apr	Swansea	1	0
1971	22 May	Belfast	0	1
1972	27 May	Wrexham	0	0
1973	19 May	Everton	0	1
1974	18 May	Wrexham	1	0
1975	23 May	Belfast	0	1
1976	14 May	Swansea	1	0
1977	3 June	Belfast	1	1
1978	19 May	Wrexham	1	0
1979	25 May	Belfast	1	1
1980	23 May	Cardiff	0	1
1982	27 May	Wrexham	3	0
1983	31 May	Belfast	1	0
1984	22 May	Swansea	1	1
wc2004	8 Sept	Cardiff	2	2
wc2005	8 Oct	Belfast	3	2
2007	6 Feb	Belfast	0	0
NC2011	27 May	Dublin	2	0
2016	24 Mar	Cardiff	1	1
EC2016	25 June	Paris	1	0

OTHER BRITISH INTERNATIONAL RESULTS 1908–2017

ENGLAND

		v ALBANIA	E	A
wc1989	8 Mar	Tirana	2	0
wc1989	26 Apr	Wembley	5	0
wc2001	28 Mar	Tirana	3	1
wc2001	5 Sept	Newcastle	2	0

		v ALGERIA	E	A
wc2010	18 June	Cape Town	0	0

		v ANDORRA	E	A
EC2006	2 Sept	Old Trafford	5	0
EC2007	28 Mar	Barcelona	3	0
wc2008	6 Sept	Barcelona	2	0
wc2009	10 June	Wembley	6	0

		v ARGENTINA	E	A
1951	9 May	Wembley	2	1
1953	17 May	Buenos Aires	0	0
(abandoned after 21 mins)				
wc1962	2 June	Rancagua	3	1
1964	6 June	Rio de Janeiro	0	1
wc1966	23 July	Wembley	1	0
1974	22 May	Wembley	2	2
1977	12 June	Buenos Aires	1	1
1980	13 May	Wembley	3	1
wc1986	22 June	Mexico City	1	2
1991	25 May	Wembley	2	2
wc1998	30 June	St Etienne	2	2
2000	23 Feb	Wembley	0	0
wc2002	7 June	Sapporo	1	0
2005	12 Nov	Geneva	3	2

		v AUSTRALIA	E	A
1980	31 May	Sydney	2	1
1983	11 June	Sydney	0	0
1983	15 June	Brisbane	1	0
1983	18 June	Melbourne	1	1
1991	1 June	Sydney	1	0
2003	12 Feb	West Ham	1	3
2016	27 May	Sunderland	2	1

		v AUSTRIA	E	A
1908	6 June	Vienna	6	1
1908	8 June	Vienna	11	1
1909	1 June	Vienna	8	1
1930	14 May	Vienna	0	0
1932	7 Dec	Chelsea	4	3
1936	6 May	Vienna	1	2
1951	28 Nov	Wembley	2	2
1952	25 May	Vienna	3	2
wc1958	15 June	Boras	2	2
1961	27 May	Vienna	1	3
1962	4 Apr	Wembley	3	1
1965	20 Oct	Wembley	2	3
1967	27 May	Vienna	1	0
1973	26 Sept	Wembley	7	0
1979	13 June	Vienna	3	4
wc2004	4 Sept	Vienna	2	2
wc2005	8 Oct	Old Trafford	1	0
2007	16 Nov	Vienna	1	0

		v AZERBAIJAN	E	A
wc2004	13 Oct	Baku	1	0
wc2005	30 Mar	Newcastle	2	0

		v BELARUS	E	B
wc2008	15 Oct	Minsk	3	1
wc2009	14 Oct	Wembley	3	0

		v BELGIUM	E	B
1921	21 May	Brussels	2	0
1923	19 Mar	Highbury	6	1
1923	1 Nov	Antwerp	2	2
1924	8 Dec	West Bromwich	4	0
1926	24 May	Antwerp	5	3
1927	11 May	Brussels	9	1
1928	19 May	Antwerp	3	1
1929	11 May	Brussels	5	1
1931	16 May	Brussels	4	1
1936	9 May	Brussels	2	3
1947	21 Sept	Brussels	5	2
1950	18 May	Brussels	4	1
1952	26 Nov	Wembley	5	0
wc1954	17 June	Basle	4	4*
1964	21 Oct	Wembley	2	2
1970	25 Feb	Brussels	3	1
EC1980	12 June	Turin	1	1
wc1990	27 June	Bologna	1	0*
1998	29 May	Casablanca	0	0
1999	10 Oct	Sunderland	2	1
2012	2 June	Wembley	1	0

		v BOHEMIA	E	B
1908	13 June	Prague	4	0

		v BRAZIL	E	B
1956	9 May	Wembley	4	2
wc1958	11 June	Gothenburg	0	0
1959	13 May	Rio de Janeiro	0	2
wc1962	10 June	Vina del Mar	1	3
1963	8 May	Wembley	1	1
1964	30 May	Rio de Janeiro	1	5
1969	12 June	Rio de Janeiro	1	2
wc1970	7 June	Guadalajara	0	1
1976	23 May	Los Angeles	0	1
1977	8 June	Rio de Janeiro	0	0

			E	*B*
1978	19 Apr	Wembley	1	1
1981	12 May	Wembley	0	1
1984	10 June	Rio de Janeiro	2	0
1987	19 May	Wembley	1	1
1990	28 Mar	Wembley	1	0
1992	17 May	Wembley	1	1
1993	13 June	Washington	1	1
UI1995	11 June	Wembley	1	3
TF1997	10 June	Paris	0	1
2000	27 May	Wembley	1	1
WC2002	21 June	Shizuoka	1	2
2007	1 June	Wembley	1	1
2009	14 Nov	Doha	0	1
2013	6 Feb	Wembley	2	1
2013	2 June	Rio de Janeiro	2	2

		v BULGARIA	*E*	*B*
WC1962	7 June	Rancagua	0	0
1968	11 Dec	Wembley	1	1
1974	1 June	Sofia	1	0
EC1979	6 June	Sofia	3	0
EC1979	22 Nov	Wembley	2	0
1996	27 Mar	Wembley	1	0
EC1998	10 Oct	Wembley	0	0
EC1999	9 June	Sofia	1	1
EC2010	3 Sept	Wembley	4	0
EC2011	2 Sept	Sofia	3	0

		v CAMEROON	*E*	*C*
WC1990	1 July	Naples	3	2*
1991	6 Feb	Wembley	2	0
1997	15 Nov	Wembley	2	0
2002	26 May	Kobe	2	2

		v CANADA	*E*	*C*
1986	24 May	Burnaby	1	0

		v CHILE	*E*	*C*
WC1950	25 June	Rio de Janeiro	2	0
1953	24 May	Santiago	2	1
1984	17 June	Santiago	0	0
1989	23 May	Wembley	0	0
1998	11 Feb	Wembley	0	2
2013	15 Nov	Wembley	0	2

		v CHINA PR	*E*	*CPR*
1996	23 May	Beijing	3	0

		v CIS	*E*	*C*
1992	29 Apr	Moscow	2	2

		v COLOMBIA	*E*	*C*
1970	20 May	Bogota	4	0
1988	24 May	Wembley	1	1
1995	6 Sept	Wembley	0	0
WC1998	26 June	Lens	2	0
2005	31 May	New Jersey	3	2

		v COSTA RICA	*E*	*C*
WC2014	26 June	Belo Horizonte	0	0

		v CROATIA	*E*	*C*
1996	24 Apr	Wembley	0	0
2003	20 Aug	Ipswich	3	1
EC2004	21 June	Lisbon	4	2
EC2006	11 Oct	Zagreb	0	2
EC2007	21 Nov	Wembley	2	3
WC2008	10 Sept	Zagreb	4	1
WC2009	9 Sept	Wembley	5	1

		v CYPRUS	*E*	*C*
EC1975	16 Apr	Wembley	5	0
EC1975	11 May	Limassol	1	0

		v CZECHOSLOVAKIA	*E*	*C*
1934	16 May	Prague	1	2
1937	1 Dec	Tottenham	5	4
1963	29 May	Bratislava	4	2
1966	2 Nov	Wembley	0	0
WC1970	11 June	Guadalajara	1	0
1973	27 May	Prague	1	1
EC1974	30 Oct	Wembley	3	0
EC1975	30 Oct	Bratislava	1	2
1978	29 Nov	Wembley	1	0
WC1982	20 June	Bilbao	2	0
1990	25 Apr	Wembley	4	2
1992	25 Mar	Prague	2	2

		v CZECH REPUBLIC	*E*	*C*
1998	18 Nov	Wembley	2	0
2008	20 Aug	Wembley	2	2

		v DENMARK	*E*	*D*
1948	26 Sept	Copenhagen	0	0
1955	2 Oct	Copenhagen	5	1
WC1956	5 Dec	Wolverhampton	5	2
WC1957	15 May	Copenhagen	4	1
1966	3 July	Copenhagen	2	0
EC1978	20 Sept	Copenhagen	4	3
EC1979	12 Sept	Wembley	1	0
EC1982	22 Sept	Copenhagen	2	2
EC1983	21 Sept	Wembley	0	1
1988	14 Sept	Wembley	1	0
1989	7 June	Copenhagen	1	1
1990	15 May	Wembley	1	0
EC1992	11 June	Malmo	0	0
1994	9 Mar	Wembley	1	0
WC2002	15 June	Niigata	3	0
2003	16 Nov	Old Trafford	2	3
2005	17 Aug	Copenhagen	1	4
2011	9 Feb	Copenhagen	2	1
2014	5 Mar	Wembley	1	0

		v ECUADOR	*E*	*Ec*
1970	24 May	Quito	2	0
WC2006	25 June	Stuttgart	1	0
2014	4 June	Miami	2	2

		v EGYPT	*E*	*Eg*
1986	29 Jan	Cairo	4	0
WC1990	21 June	Cagliari	1	0
2010	3 Mar	Wembley	3	1

		v ESTONIA	*E*	*Es*
EC2007	6 June	Tallinn	3	0
EC2007	13 Oct	Wembley	3	0
EC2014	12 Oct	Tallinn	1	0
EC2015	9 Oct	Wembley	2	0

		v FIFA	*E*	*FIFA*
1938	26 Oct	Highbury	3	0
1953	21 Oct	Wembley	4	4
1963	23 Oct	Wembley	2	1

		v FINLAND	*E*	*F*
1937	20 May	Helsinki	8	0
1956	20 May	Helsinki	5	1
1966	26 June	Helsinki	3	0
WC1976	13 June	Helsinki	4	1
WC1976	13 Oct	Wembley	2	1
1982	3 June	Helsinki	4	1
WC1984	17 Oct	Wembley	5	0
WC1985	22 May	Helsinki	1	1
1992	3 June	Helsinki	2	1
WC2000	11 Oct	Helsinki	0	0
WC2001	24 Mar	Liverpool	2	1

		v FRANCE	*E*	*F*
1923	10 May	Paris	4	1
1924	17 May	Paris	3	1
1925	21 May	Paris	3	2
1927	26 May	Paris	6	0
1928	17 May	Paris	5	1
1929	9 May	Paris	4	1
1931	14 May	Paris	2	5
1933	6 Dec	Tottenham	4	1
1938	26 May	Paris	4	2
1947	3 May	Highbury	3	0
1949	22 May	Paris	3	1
1951	3 Oct	Highbury	2	2
1955	15 May	Paris	0	1
1957	27 Nov	Wembley	4	0
EC1962	3 Oct	Sheffield	1	1
EC1963	27 Feb	Paris	2	5
WC1966	20 July	Wembley	2	0
1969	12 Mar	Wembley	5	0
WC1982	16 June	Bilbao	3	1
1984	29 Feb	Paris	0	2
1992	19 Feb	Wembley	2	0
EC1992	14 June	Malmo	0	0
TF1997	7 June	Montpellier	1	0
1999	10 Feb	Wembley	0	2
2000	2 Sept	Paris	1	1
EC2004	13 June	Lisbon	1	2
2008	26 Mar	Paris	0	1
2010	17 Nov	Wembley	1	2

			E	*F*
EC2012	11 June	Donetsk	1	1
2015	17 Nov	Wembley	2	0
2017	**13 June**	**Paris**	**2**	**3**

		v FYR MACEDONIA	*E*	*M*
EC2002	16 Oct	Southampton	2	2
EC2003	6 Sept	Skopje	2	1
EC2006	6 Sept	Skopje	1	0

		v GEORGIA	*E*	*G*
WC1996	9 Nov	Tbilisi	2	0
WC1997	30 Apr	Wembley	2	0

		v GERMANY	*E*	*G*
1930	10 May	Berlin	3	3
1935	4 Dec	Tottenham	3	0
1938	14 May	Berlin	6	3
1991	11 Sept	Wembley	0	1
1993	19 June	Detroit	1	2
EC1996	26 June	Wembley	1	1*
EC2000	17 June	Charleroi	1	0
WC2000	7 Oct	Wembley	0	1
WC2001	1 Sept	Munich	5	1
2007	22 Aug	Wembley	1	2
2008	19 Nov	Berlin	2	1
WC2010	27 June	Bloemfontein	1	4
2013	19 Nov	Wembley	0	1
2016	26 Mar	Berlin	3	2
2017	**22 Mar**	**Dortmund**	**0**	**1**

		v EAST GERMANY	*E*	*EG*
1963	2 June	Leipzig	2	1
1970	25 Nov	Wembley	3	1
1974	29 May	Leipzig	1	1
1984	12 Sept	Wembley	1	0

		v WEST GERMANY	*E*	*WG*
1954	1 Dec	Wembley	3	1
1956	26 May	Berlin	3	1
1965	12 May	Nuremberg	1	0
1966	23 Feb	Wembley	1	0
WC1966	30 July	Wembley	4	2*
1968	1 June	Hanover	0	1
WC1970	14 June	Leon	2	3*
EC1972	29 Apr	Wembley	1	3
EC1972	13 May	Berlin	0	0
1975	12 Mar	Wembley	2	0
1978	22 Feb	Munich	1	2
WC1982	29 June	Madrid	0	0
1982	13 Oct	Wembley	1	2
1985	12 June	Mexico City	3	0
1987	9 Sept	Dusseldorf	1	3
WC1990	4 July	Turin	1	1*

		v GHANA	*E*	*G*
2011	29 Mar	Wembley	1	1

		v GREECE	*E*	*G*
EC1971	21 Apr	Wembley	3	0
EC1971	1 Dec	Piraeus	2	0
EC1982	17 Nov	Salonika	3	0
EC1983	30 Mar	Wembley	0	0
1989	8 Feb	Athens	2	1
1994	17 May	Wembley	5	0
WC2001	6 June	Athens	2	0
WC2001	6 Oct	Old Trafford	2	2
2006	16 Aug	Old Trafford	4	0

		v HONDURAS	*E*	*H*
2014	7 June	Miami	0	0

		v HUNGARY	*E*	*H*
1908	10 June	Budapest	7	0
1909	29 May	Budapest	4	2
1909	31 May	Budapest	8	2
1934	10 May	Budapest	1	2
1936	2 Dec	Highbury	6	2
1953	25 Nov	Wembley	3	6
1954	23 May	Budapest	1	7
1960	22 May	Budapest	0	2
WC1962	31 May	Rancagua	1	2
1965	5 May	Wembley	1	0
1978	24 May	Wembley	4	1
WC1981	6 June	Budapest	3	1
WC1982	18 Nov	Wembley	1	0
EC1983	27 Apr	Wembley	2	0
EC1983	12 Oct	Budapest	3	0
1988	27 Apr	Budapest	0	0
1990	12 Sept	Wembley	1	0

			E	*H*
1992	12 May	Budapest	1	0
1996	18 May	Wembley	3	0
1999	28 Apr	Budapest	1	1
2006	30 May	Old Trafford	3	1
2010	11 Aug	Wembley	2	1

		v ICELAND	*E*	*I*
1982	2 June	Reykjavik	1	1
2004	5 June	City of Manchester	6	1
EC2016	27 June	Nice	1	2

		v ISRAEL	*E*	*I*
1986	26 Feb	Ramat Gan	2	1
1988	17 Feb	Tel Aviv	0	0
EC2007	24 Mar	Tel Aviv	0	0
EC2007	8 Sept	Wembley	3	0

		v ITALY	*E*	*I*
1933	13 May	Rome	1	1
1934	14 Nov	Highbury	3	2
1939	13 May	Milan	2	2
1948	16 May	Turin	4	0
1949	30 Nov	Tottenham	2	0
1952	18 May	Florence	1	1
1959	6 May	Wembley	2	2
1961	24 May	Rome	3	2
1973	14 June	Turin	0	2
1973	14 Nov	Wembley	0	1
1976	28 May	New York	3	2
WC1976	17 Nov	Rome	0	2
WC1977	16 Nov	Wembley	2	0
EC1980	15 June	Turin	0	1
1985	6 June	Mexico City	1	2
1989	15 Nov	Wembley	0	0
WC1990	7 July	Bari	1	2
WC1997	12 Feb	Wembley	0	1
TF1997	4 June	Nantes	2	0
WC1997	11 Oct	Rome	0	0
2000	15 Nov	Turin	0	1
2002	27 Mar	Leeds	1	2
EC2012	24 June	Kiev	0	0
2012	15 Aug	Berne	2	1
WC2014	14 June	Manaus	1	2
2015	31 Mar	Turin	1	1

		v JAMAICA	*E*	*J*
2006	3 June	Old Trafford	6	0

		v JAPAN	*E*	*J*
UI1995	3 June	Wembley	2	1
2004	1 June	City of Manchester	1	1
2010	30 May	Graz	2	1

		v KAZAKHSTAN	*E*	*K*
WC2008	11 Oct	Wembley	5	1
WC2009	6 June	Almaty	4	0

		v KOREA REPUBLIC	*E*	*KR*
2002	21 May	Seoguipo	1	1

		v KUWAIT	*E*	*K*
WC1982	25 June	Bilbao	1	0

		v LIECHTENSTEIN	*E*	*L*
EC2003	29 Mar	Vaduz	2	0
EC2003	10 Sept	Old Trafford	2	0

		v LITHUANIA	*E*	*L*
EC2015	27 Mar	Wembley	4	0
EC2015	12 Oct	Vilnius	3	0
WC2017	**26 Mar**	**Wembley**	**2**	**0**

		v LUXEMBOURG	*E*	*L*
1927	21 May	Esch-sur-Alzette	5	2
WC1960	19 Oct	Luxembourg	9	0
WC1961	28 Sept	Highbury	4	1
WC1977	30 Mar	Wembley	5	0
WC1977	12 Oct	Luxembourg	2	0
EC1982	15 Dec	Wembley	9	0
EC1983	16 Nov	Luxembourg	4	0
EC1998	14 Oct	Luxembourg	3	0
EC1999	4 Sept	Wembley	6	0
EC2006	7 Oct	Old Trafford	0	0

		v MALAYSIA	*E*	*M*
1991	12 June	Kuala Lumpur	4	2

		v MALTA	*E*	*M*
EC1971	3 Feb	Valletta	1	0
EC1971	12 May	Wembley	5	0
2000	3 June	Valletta	2	1
WC2016	**8 Oct**	**Wembley**	**2**	**0**

		v MEXICO	*E*	*M*
1959	24 May	Mexico City	1	2
1961	10 May	Wembley	8	0
wc1966	16 July	Wembley	2	0
1969	1 June	Mexico City	0	0
1985	9 June	Mexico City	0	1
1986	17 May	Los Angeles	3	0
1997	29 Mar	Wembley	2	0
2001	25 May	Derby	4	0
2010	24 May	Wembley	3	1

		v MOLDOVA	*E*	*M*
wc1996	1 Sept	Chisinau	3	0
wc1997	10 Sept	Wembley	4	0
wc2012	7 Sept	Chisinau	5	0
wc2013	6 Sept	Wembley	4	0

		v MONTENEGRO	*E*	*M*
ec1989	8 Mar	Tirana	2	0
2010	12 Oct	Wembley	0	0
ec2011	7 Oct	Podgorica	2	2
wc2013	26 Mar	Podgorica	1	1
wc2013	11 Oct	Wembley	4	1

		v MOROCCO	*E*	*M*
wc1986	6 June	Monterrey	0	0
1998	27 May	Casablanca	1	0

		v NETHERLANDS	*E*	*N*
1935	18 May	Amsterdam	1	0
1946	27 Nov	Huddersfield	8	2
1964	9 Dec	Amsterdam	1	1
1969	5 Nov	Amsterdam	1	0
1970	14 June	Wembley	0	0
1977	9 Feb	Wembley	0	2
1982	25 May	Wembley	2	0
1988	23 Mar	Wembley	2	2
ec1988	15 June	Dusseldorf	1	3
wc1990	16 June	Cagliari	0	0
2005	9 Feb	Villa Park	0	0
wc1993	28 Apr	Wembley	2	2
wc1993	13 Oct	Rotterdam	0	2
ec1996	18 June	Wembley	4	1
2001	15 Aug	Tottenham	0	2
2002	13 Feb	Amsterdam	1	1
2006	15 Nov	Amsterdam	1	1
2009	12 Aug	Amsterdam	2	2
2012	29 Feb	Wembley	2	3
2016	29 Mar	Wembley	1	2

		v NEW ZEALAND	*E*	*NZ*
1991	3 June	Auckland	1	0
1991	8 June	Wellington	2	0

		v NIGERIA	*E*	*N*
1994	16 Nov	Wembley	1	0
wc2002	12 June	Osaka	0	0

		v NORWAY	*E*	*N*
1937	14 May	Oslo	6	0
1938	9 Nov	Newcastle	4	0
1949	18 May	Oslo	4	1
1966	29 June	Oslo	6	1
wc1980	10 Sept	Wembley	4	0
wc1981	9 Sept	Oslo	1	2
wc1992	14 Oct	Wembley	1	1
wc1993	2 June	Oslo	0	2
1994	22 May	Wembley	0	0
1995	11 Oct	Oslo	0	0
2012	26 May	Oslo	1	0
2014	3 Sept	Wembley	1	0

		v PARAGUAY	*E*	*P*
wc1986	18 June	Mexico City	3	0
2002	17 Apr	Liverpool	4	0
wc2006	10 June	Frankfurt	1	0

		v PERU	*E*	*P*
1959	17 May	Lima	1	4
1962	20 May	Lima	4	0
2014	30 May	Wembley	3	0

		v POLAND	*E*	*P*
1966	5 Jan	Everton	1	1
1966	5 July	Chorzow	1	0
wc1973	6 June	Chorzow	0	2
wc1973	17 Oct	Wembley	1	1
wc1986	11 June	Monterrey	3	0
wc1989	3 June	Wembley	3	0
wc1989	11 Oct	Katowice	0	0
ec1990	17 Oct	Wembley	2	0
ec1991	13 Nov	Poznan	1	1
wc1993	29 May	Katowice	1	1
wc1993	8 Sept	Wembley	3	0
wc1996	9 Oct	Wembley	2	1
wc1997	31 May	Katowice	2	0
ec1999	27 Mar	Wembley	3	1
ec1999	8 Sept	Warsaw	0	0
wc2004	8 Sept	Katowice	2	1
wc2005	12 Oct	Old Trafford	2	1
wc2012	17 Oct	Warsaw	1	1
wc2013	15 Oct	Wembley	2	0

		v PORTUGAL	*E*	*P*
1947	25 May	Lisbon	10	0
1950	14 May	Lisbon	5	3
1951	19 May	Everton	5	2
1955	22 May	Oporto	1	3
1958	7 May	Wembley	2	1
wc1961	21 May	Lisbon	1	1
wc1961	25 Oct	Wembley	2	0
1964	17 May	Lisbon	4	3
1964	4 June	São Paulo	1	1
wc1966	26 July	Wembley	2	1
1969	10 Dec	Wembley	1	0
1974	3 Apr	Lisbon	0	0
ec1974	20 Nov	Wembley	0	0
ec1975	19 Nov	Lisbon	1	1
wc1986	3 June	Monterrey	0	1
1995	12 Dec	Wembley	1	1
1998	22 Apr	Wembley	3	0
ec2000	12 June	Eindhoven	2	3
2002	7 Sept	Villa Park	1	1
2004	18 Feb	Faro	1	1
ec2004	24 June	Lisbon	2	2*
wc2006	1 July	Gelsenkirchen	0	0
2016	2 June	Wembley	1	0

		v REPUBLIC OF IRELAND	*E*	*RI*
1946	30 Sept	Dublin	1	0
1949	21 Sept	Everton	0	2
wc1957	8 May	Wembley	5	1
wc1957	19 May	Dublin	1	1
1964	24 May	Dublin	3	1
1976	8 Sept	Wembley	1	1
ec1978	25 Oct	Dublin	1	1
ec1980	6 Feb	Wembley	2	0
1985	26 Mar	Wembley	2	1
ec1988	12 June	Stuttgart	0	1
wc1990	11 June	Cagliari	1	1
ec1990	14 Nov	Dublin	1	1
ec1991	27 Mar	Wembley	1	1
1995	15 Feb	Dublin	0	1
(abandoned after 27 mins)				
2013	29 May	Wembley	1	1
2015	7 June	Dublin	0	0

		v ROMANIA	*E*	*R*
1939	24 May	Bucharest	2	0
1968	6 Nov	Bucharest	0	0
1969	15 Jan	Wembley	1	1
wc1970	2 June	Guadalajara	1	0
wc1980	15 Oct	Bucharest	1	2
wc1981	29 April	Wembley	0	0
wc1985	1 May	Bucharest	0	0
wc1985	11 Sept	Wembley	1	1
1994	12 Oct	Wembley	1	1
wc1998	22 June	Toulouse	1	2
ec2000	20 June	Charleroi	2	3

		v RUSSIA	*E*	*R*
ec2007	12 Sept	Wembley	3	0
ec2007	17 Oct	Moscow	1	2
ec2016	11 June	Marseille	1	1

		v SAN MARINO	*E*	*SM*
wc1992	17 Feb	Wembley	6	0
wc1993	17 Nov	Bologna	7	1
wc2012	12 Oct	Wembley	5	0
wc2013	22 Mar	Serravalle	8	0
ec2014	9 Oct	Wembley	5	0
ec2015	5 Sept	Serravalle	6	0

		v SAUDI ARABIA	*E*	*SA*
1988	16 Nov	Riyadh	1	1
1998	23 May	Wembley	0	0

v SERBIA-MONTENEGRO			*E*	*SM*
2003	3 June	Leicester	2	1

v SLOVAKIA			*E*	*S*
EC2002	12 Oct	Bratislava	2	1
EC2003	11 June	Middlesbrough	2	1
2009	28 Mar	Wembley	4	0
EC2016	20 June	Lille	0	0
WC2016	**4 Sept**	**Trnava**	**1**	**0**

v SLOVENIA			*E*	*S*
2009	5 Sept	Wembley	2	1
WC2010	23 June	Port Elizabeth	1	0
EC2014	15 Nov	Wembley	3	1
EC2015	14 June	Ljubljana	3	2
WC2016	**11 Oct**	**Ljubljana**	**0**	**0**

v SOUTH AFRICA			*E*	*SA*
1997	24 May	Old Trafford	2	1
2003	22 May	Durban	2	1

v SPAIN			*E*	*S*
1929	15 May	Madrid	3	4
1931	9 Dec	Highbury	7	1
WC1950	2 July	Rio de Janeiro	0	1
1955	18 May	Madrid	1	1
1955	30 Nov	Wembley	4	1
1960	15 May	Madrid	0	3
1960	26 Oct	Wembley	4	2
1965	8 Dec	Madrid	2	0
1967	24 May	Wembley	2	0
EC1968	3 Apr	Wembley	1	0
EC1968	8 May	Madrid	2	1
1980	26 Mar	Barcelona	2	0
EC1980	18 June	Naples	2	1
1981	25 Mar	Wembley	1	2
WC1982	5 July	Madrid	0	0
1987	18 Feb	Madrid	4	2
1992	9 Sept	Santander	0	1
EC 1996	22 June	Wembley	0	0
2001	28 Feb	Villa Park	3	0
2004	17 Nov	Madrid	0	1
2007	7 Feb	Old Trafford	0	1
2009	11 Feb	Seville	0	2
2011	12 Nov	Wembley	1	0
2015	13 Nov	Alicante	0	2
2017	**15 Nov**	**Wembley**	**2**	**2**

v SWEDEN			*E*	*S*
1923	21 May	Stockholm	4	2
1923	24 May	Stockholm	3	1
1937	17 May	Stockholm	4	0
1947	19 Nov	Highbury	4	2
1949	13 May	Stockholm	1	3
1956	16 May	Stockholm	0	0
1959	28 Oct	Wembley	2	3
1965	16 May	Gothenburg	2	1
1968	22 May	Wembley	3	1
1979	10 June	Stockholm	0	0
1986	10 Sept	Stockholm	0	1
WC1988	19 Oct	Wembley	0	0
WC1989	6 Sept	Stockholm	0	0
EC1992	17 June	Stockholm	1	2
UI1995	8 June	Leeds	3	3
EC1998	5 Sept	Stockholm	1	2
EC1999	5 June	Wembley	0	0
2001	10 Nov	Old Trafford	1	1
WC2002	2 June	Saitama	1	1
2004	31 Mar	Gothenburg	0	1
WC2006	20 June	Cologne	2	2
2011	15 Nov	Wembley	1	0
EC2012	15 June	Kiev	3	2
2012	14 Nov	Stockholm	2	4

v SWITZERLAND			*E*	*S*
1933	20 May	Berne	4	0
1938	21 May	Zurich	1	2
1947	18 May	Zurich	0	1
1948	2 Dec	Highbury	6	0
1952	28 May	Zurich	3	0
WC1954	20 June	Berne	2	0
1962	9 May	Wembley	3	1
1963	5 June	Basle	8	1
EC1971	13 Oct	Basle	3	2
EC1971	10 Nov	Wembley	1	1
1975	3 Sept	Basle	2	1
1977	7 Sept	Wembley	0	0
WC1980	19 Nov	Wembley	2	1
WC1981	30 May	Basle	1	2
1988	28 May	Lausanne	1	0
1995	15 Nov	Wembley	3	1
EC1996	8 June	Wembley	1	1
1998	25 Mar	Berne	1	1
EC2004	17 June	Coimbra	3	0
2008	6 Feb	Wembley	2	1
EC1989	8 Mar	Tirana	2	0
EC2010	7 Sept	Basle	3	1
EC2011	4 June	Wembley	2	2
EC2014	8 Sept	Basel	2	0
EC2015	8 Sept	Wembley	2	0

v TRINIDAD & TOBAGO			*E*	*TT*
WC2006	15 June	Nuremberg	2	0
2008	2 June	Port of Spain	3	0

v TUNISIA			*E*	*T*
1990	2 June	Tunis	1	1
WC1998	15 June	Marseilles	2	0

v TURKEY			*E*	*T*
WC1984	14 Nov	Istanbul	8	0
WC1985	16 Oct	Wembley	5	0
EC1987	29 Apr	Izmir	0	0
EC1987	14 Oct	Wembley	8	0
EC1991	1 May	Izmir	1	0
EC1991	16 Oct	Wembley	1	0
WC1992	18 Nov	Wembley	4	0
WC1993	31 Mar	Izmir	2	0
EC2003	2 Apr	Sunderland	2	0
EC2003	11 Oct	Istanbul	0	0
2016	22 May	Etihad Stadium	2	1

v UKRAINE			*E*	*U*
2000	31 May	Wembley	2	0
2004	18 Aug	Newcastle	3	0
WC2009	1 Apr	Wembley	2	1
WC2009	10 Oct	Dnepr	0	1
EC2012	19 June	Donetsk	1	0
WC2012	11 Sept	Wembley	1	1
WC2013	10 Sept	Kiev	0	0

v URUGUAY			*E*	*U*
1953	31 May	Montevideo	1	2
WC1954	26 June	Basle	2	4
1964	6 May	Wembley	2	1
WC1966	11 July	Wembley	0	0
1969	8 June	Montevideo	2	1
1977	15 June	Montevideo	0	0
1984	13 June	Montevideo	0	2
1990	22 May	Wembley	1	2
1995	29 Mar	Wembley	0	0
2006	1 Mar	Liverpool	2	1
WC2014	19 June	Sao Paulo	1	2

v USA			*E*	*USA*
WC1950	29 June	Belo Horizonte	0	1
1953	8 June	New York	6	3
1959	28 May	Los Angeles	8	1
1964	27 May	New York	10	0
1985	16 June	Los Angeles	5	0
1993	9 June	Foxboro	0	2
1994	7 Sept	Wembley	2	0
2005	28 May	Chicago	2	1
2008	28 May	Wembley	2	0
WC2010	12 June	Rustenburg	1	1

v USSR			*E*	*USSR*
1958	18 May	Moscow	1	1
WC1958	8 June	Gothenburg	2	2
WC1958	17 June	Gothenburg	0	1
1958	22 Oct	Wembley	5	0
1967	6 Dec	Wembley	2	2
EC1968	8 June	Rome	2	0
1973	10 June	Moscow	2	1
1984	2 June	Wembley	0	2
1986	26 Mar	Tbilisi	1	0
EC1988	18 June	Frankfurt	1	3
1991	21 May	Wembley	3	1

v YUGOSLAVIA			*E*	*Y*
1939	18 May	Belgrade	1	2
1950	22 Nov	Highbury	2	2
1954	16 May	Belgrade	0	1
1956	28 Nov	Wembley	3	0
1958	11 May	Belgrade	0	5
1960	11 May	Wembley	3	3
1965	9 May	Belgrade	1	1
1966	4 May	Wembley	2	0

			E	*Y*
EC1968	5 June	Florence	0	1
1972	11 Oct	Wembley	1	1
1974	5 June	Belgrade	2	2
EC1986	12 Nov	Wembley	2	0
EC1987	11 Nov	Belgrade	4	1
1989	13 Dec	Wembley	2	1

SCOTLAND

		v ARGENTINA	*S*	*A*
1977	18 June	Buenos Aires	1	1
1979	2 June	Glasgow	1	3
1990	28 Mar	Glasgow	1	0
2008	19 Nov	Glasgow	0	1

		v AUSTRALIA	*S*	*A*
wc1985	20 Nov	Glasgow	2	0
wc1985	4 Dec	Melbourne	0	0
1996	27 Mar	Glasgow	1	0
2000	15 Nov	Glasgow	0	2
2012	15 Aug	Easter Road	3	1

		v AUSTRIA	*S*	*A*
1931	16 May	Vienna	0	5
1933	29 Nov	Glasgow	2	2
1937	9 May	Vienna	1	1
1950	13 Dec	Glasgow	0	1
1951	27 May	Vienna	0	4
wc1954	16 June	Zurich	0	1
1955	19 May	Vienna	4	1
1956	2 May	Glasgow	1	1
1960	29 May	Vienna	1	4
1963	8 May	Glasgow	4	1
(*abandoned after 79 mins*)				
wc1968	6 Nov	Glasgow	2	1
wc1969	5 Nov	Vienna	0	2
EC1978	20 Sept	Vienna	2	3
EC1979	17 Oct	Glasgow	1	1
1994	20 Apr	Vienna	2	1
wc1996	31 Aug	Vienna	0	0
wc1997	2 Apr	Celtic Park	2	0
2003	30 Apr	Glasgow	0	2
2005	17 Aug	Graz	2	2
2007	30 May	Vienna	1	0

		v BELARUS	*S*	*B*
wc1997	8 June	Minsk	1	0
wc1997	7 Sept	Aberdeen	4	1
wc2005	8 June	Minsk	0	0
wc2005	8 Oct	Glasgow	0	1

		v BELGIUM	*S*	*B*
1946	23 Jan	Glasgow	2	2
1947	18 May	Brussels	1	2
1948	28 Apr	Glasgow	2	0
1951	20 May	Brussels	5	0
EC1971	3 Feb	Liege	0	3
EC1971	10 Nov	Aberdeen	1	0
1974	1 June	Brussels	1	2
EC1979	21 Nov	Brussels	0	2
EC1979	19 Dec	Glasgow	1	3
EC1982	15 Dec	Brussels	2	3
EC1983	12 Oct	Glasgow	1	1
EC1987	1 Apr	Brussels	1	4
EC1987	14 Oct	Glasgow	2	0
wc2001	24 Mar	Glasgow	2	2
wc2001	5 Sept	Brussels	0	2
wc2012	16 Oct	Brussels	0	2
wc2013	6 Sept	Glasgow	0	2

		v BOSNIA-HERZEGOVINA	*S*	*BH*
EC1999	4 Sept	Sarajevo	2	1
EC1999	5 Oct	Ibrox	1	0

		v BRAZIL	*S*	*B*
1966	25 June	Glasgow	1	1
1972	5 July	Rio de Janeiro	0	1
1973	30 June	Glasgow	0	1
wc1974	18 June	Frankfurt	0	0
1977	23 June	Rio de Janeiro	0	2
wc1982	18 June	Seville	1	4
1987	26 May	Glasgow	0	2
wc1990	20 June	Turin	0	1
wc1998	10 June	St Denis	1	2
2011	27 Mar	Emirates	0	2

		v BULGARIA	*S*	*B*
1978	22 Feb	Glasgow	2	1
EC1986	10 Sept	Glasgow	0	0
EC1987	11 Nov	Sofia	1	0
EC1990	14 Nov	Sofia	1	1
EC1991	27 Mar	Glasgow	1	1
2006	11 May	Kobe	5	1

		v CANADA	*S*	*C*
1983	12 June	Vancouver	2	0
1983	16 June	Edmonton	3	0
1983	20 June	Toronto	2	0
1992	21 May	Toronto	3	1
2002	15 Oct	Easter Road	3	1
2017	**22 Mar**	**Easter Road**	**1**	**1**

		v CHILE	*S*	*C*
1977	15 June	Santiago	4	2
1989	30 May	Glasgow	2	0

		v CIS	*S*	*C*
EC1992	18 June	Norrkoping	3	0

		v COLOMBIA	*S*	*C*
1988	17 May	Glasgow	0	0
1996	29 May	Miami	0	1
1998	23 May	New York	2	2

		v COSTA RICA	*S*	*CR*
wc1990	11 June	Genoa	0	1

		v CROATIA	*S*	*C*
wc2000	11 Oct	Zagreb	1	1
wc2001	1 Sept	Glasgow	0	0
2008	26 Mar	Glasgow	1	1
wc2013	7 June	Zagreb	1	0
wc2013	15 Oct	Glasgow	2	0

		v CYPRUS	*S*	*C*
wc1968	11 Dec	Nicosia	5	0
wc1969	17 May	Glasgow	8	0
wc1989	8 Feb	Limassol	3	2
wc1989	26 Apr	Glasgow	2	1
2011	11 Nov	Larnaca	2	1

		v CZECHOSLOVAKIA	*S*	*C*
1937	15 May	Prague	3	1
1937	8 Dec	Glasgow	5	0
wc1961	14 May	Bratislava	0	4
wc1961	26 Sept	Glasgow	3	2
wc1961	29 Nov	Brussels	2	4*
1972	2 July	Porto Alegre	0	0
wc1973	26 Sept	Glasgow	2	1
wc1973	17 Oct	Bratislava	0	1
wc1976	13 Oct	Prague	0	2
wc1977	21 Sept	Glasgow	3	1

		v CZECH REPUBLIC	*S*	*C*
EC1999	31 Mar	Glasgow	1	2
EC1999	9 June	Prague	2	3
2008	30 May	Prague	1	3
2010	3 Mar	Glasgow	1	0
EC2010	8 Oct	Prague	0	1
EC2011	3 Sept	Glasgow	2	2
2016	24 Mar	Prague	1	0

		v DENMARK	*S*	*D*
1951	12 May	Glasgow	3	1
1952	25 May	Copenhagen	2	1
1968	16 Oct	Copenhagen	1	0
EC1970	11 Nov	Glasgow	1	0
EC1971	9 June	Copenhagen	0	1
wc1972	18 Oct	Copenhagen	4	1
wc1972	15 Nov	Glasgow	2	0
EC1975	3 Sept	Copenhagen	1	0
EC1975	29 Oct	Glasgow	3	1
wc1986	4 June	Nezahualcoyotl	0	1
1996	24 Apr	Copenhagen	0	2
1998	25 Mar	Ibrox	0	1
2002	21 Aug	Glasgow	0	1

			S	D
2004	28 Apr	Copenhagen	0	1
2011	10 Aug	Glasgow	2	1
2016	29 Mar	Glasgow	1	0

		v ECUADOR	S	E
1995	24 May	Toyama	2	1

		v EGYPT	S	E
1990	16 May	Aberdeen	1	3

		v ESTONIA	S	E
wc1993	19 May	Tallinn	3	0
wc1993	2 June	Aberdeen	3	1
wc1997	11 Feb	Monaco	0	0
wc1997	29 Mar	Kilmarnock	2	0
EC1998	10 Oct	Tynecastle	3	2
EC1999	8 Sept	Tallinn	0	0
2004	27 May	Tallinn	1	0
2013	6 Feb	Aberdeen	1	0

		v FAROE ISLANDS	S	F
EC1994	12 Oct	Glasgow	5	1
EC1995	7 June	Toftir	2	0
EC1998	14 Oct	Aberdeen	2	1
EC1999	5 June	Toftir	1	1
EC2002	7 Sept	Toftir	2	2
EC2003	6 Sept	Glasgow	3	1
EC2006	2 Sept	Celtic Park	6	0
EC2007	6 June	Toftir	2	0
2010	16 Nov	Aberdeen	3	0

		v FINLAND	S	F
1954	25 May	Helsinki	2	1
wc1964	21 Oct	Glasgow	3	1
wc1965	27 May	Helsinki	2	1
1976	8 Sept	Glasgow	6	0
1992	25 Mar	Glasgow	1	1
EC1994	7 Sept	Helsinki	2	0
EC1995	6 Sept	Glasgow	1	0
1998	22 Apr	Easter Road	1	1

		v FRANCE	S	F
1930	18 May	Paris	2	0
1932	8 May	Paris	3	1
1948	23 May	Paris	0	3
1949	27 Apr	Glasgow	2	0
1950	27 May	Paris	1	0
1951	16 May	Glasgow	1	0
wc1958	15 June	Orebro	1	2
1984	1 June	Marseilles	0	2
wc1989	8 Mar	Glasgow	2	0
wc1989	11 Oct	Paris	0	3
1997	12 Nov	St Etienne	1	2
2000	29 Mar	Glasgow	0	2
2002	27 Mar	Paris	0	5
EC2006	7 Oct	Glasgow	1	0
EC2007	12 Sept	Paris	1	0
2016	4 June	Metz	0	3

		v FYR MACEDONIA	S	M
wc2008	6 Sept	Skopje	0	1
wc2009	5 Sept	Glasgow	2	0
wc2012	11 Sept	Glasgow	1	1
wc2013	10 Sept	Skopje	2	1

		v GEORGIA	S	G
EC2007	24 Mar	Glasgow	2	1
EC2007	17 Oct	Tbilisi	0	2
EC2014	11 Oct	Ibrox	1	0
EC2015	4 Sept	Tblisi	0	1

		v GERMANY	S	G
1929	1 June	Berlin	1	1
1936	14 Oct	Glasgow	2	0
EC1992	15 June	Norrkoping	0	2
1993	24 Mar	Glasgow	0	1
1999	28 Apr	Bremen	1	0
EC2003	7 June	Glasgow	1	1
EC2003	10 Sept	Dortmund	1	2
EC2014	7 Sept	Dortmund	1	2
EC2015	7 Sept	Glasgow	2	3

		v EAST GERMANY	S	EG
1974	30 Oct	Glasgow	3	0
1977	7 Sept	East Berlin	0	1
EC1982	13 Oct	Glasgow	2	0
EC1983	16 Nov	Halle	1	2
1985	16 Oct	Glasgow	0	0
1990	25 Apr	Glasgow	0	1

		v WEST GERMANY	S	WG
1957	22 May	Stuttgart	3	1
1959	6 May	Glasgow	3	2
1964	12 May	Hanover	2	2
wc1969	16 Apr	Glasgow	1	1
wc1969	22 Oct	Hamburg	2	3
1973	14 Nov	Glasgow	1	1
1974	27 Mar	Frankfurt	1	2
wc1986	8 June	Queretaro	1	2

		v GIBRALTAR	S	G
EC2015	29 Mar	Hampden	6	1
EC2015	11 Oct	Faro	6	0

		v GREECE	S	G
EC1994	18 Dec	Athens	0	1
EC1995	16 Aug	Glasgow	1	0

		v HONG KONG XI	S	HK
†2002	23 May	Hong Kong	4	0

†match not recognised by FIFA

		v HUNGARY	S	H
1938	7 Dec	Ibrox	3	1
1954	8 Dec	Glasgow	2	4
1955	29 May	Budapest	1	3
1958	7 May	Glasgow	1	1
1960	5 June	Budapest	3	3
1980	31 May	Budapest	1	3
1987	9 Sept	Glasgow	2	0
2004	18 Aug	Glasgow	0	3

		v ICELAND	S	I
wc1984	17 Oct	Glasgow	3	0
wc1985	28 May	Reykjavik	1	0
EC2002	12 Oct	Reykjavik	2	0
EC2003	29 Mar	Glasgow	2	1
wc2008	10 Sept	Reykjavik	2	1
wc2009	1 Apr	Glasgow	2	1

		v IRAN	S	I
wc1978	7 June	Cordoba	1	1

		v ISRAEL	S	I
wc1981	25 Feb	Tel Aviv	1	0
wc1981	28 Apr	Glasgow	3	1
1986	28 Jan	Tel Aviv	1	0

		v ITALY	S	I
1931	20 May	Rome	0	3
wc1965	9 Nov	Glasgow	1	0
wc1965	7 Dec	Naples	0	3
1988	22 Dec	Perugia	0	2
wc1992	18 Nov	Ibrox	0	0
wc1993	13 Oct	Rome	1	3
wc2005	26 Mar	Milan	0	2
wc2005	3 Sept	Glasgow	1	1
EC2007	28 Mar	Bari	0	2
EC2007	17 Nov	Glasgow	1	2
2016	29 May	Ta'Qali	0	1

		v JAPAN	S	J
1995	21 May	Hiroshima	0	0
2006	13 May	Saitama	0	0
2009	10 Oct	Yokohama	0	2

		v KOREA REPUBLIC	S	KR
2002	16 May	Busan	1	4

		v LATVIA	S	L
wc1996	5 Oct	Riga	2	0
wc1997	11 Oct	Celtic Park	2	0
wc2000	2 Sept	Riga	1	0
wc2001	6 Oct	Glasgow	2	1

		v LIECHTENSTEIN	S	L
EC2010	7 Sept	Glasgow	2	1
EC2011	8 Oct	Vaduz	1	0

		v LITHUANIA	S	L
EC1998	5 Sept	Vilnius	0	0
EC1999	9 Oct	Glasgow	3	0
EC2003	2 Apr	Kaunas	0	1
EC2003	11 Oct	Glasgow	1	0
EC2006	6 Sept	Kaunas	2	1
EC2007	8 Sept	Glasgow	3	1
EC2010	3 Sept	Kaunas	0	0
EC2011	6 Sept	Glasgow	1	0
wc2016	**8 Oct**	**Hampden**	**1**	**1**

		v LUXEMBOURG	S	L
1947	24 May	Luxembourg	6	0
EC1986	12 Nov	Glasgow	3	0

			S	*L*
EC1987	2 Dec	Esch	0	0
2012	14 Nov	Luxembourg	2	1

v MALTA

			S	*M*
1988	22 Mar	Valletta	1	1
1990	28 May	Valletta	2	1
WC1993	17 Feb	Ibrox	3	0
WC1993	17 Nov	Valletta	2	0
1997	1 June	Valletta	3	2
WC2016	**4 Sept**	**Ta'Qali**	**5**	**1**

v MOLDOVA

			S	*M*
WC2004	13 Oct	Chisinau	1	1
WC2005	4 June	Glasgow	2	0

v MOROCCO

			S	*M*
WC1998	23 June	St Etienne	0	3

v NETHERLANDS

			S	*N*
1929	4 June	Amsterdam	2	0
1938	21 May	Amsterdam	3	1
1959	27 May	Amsterdam	2	1
1966	11 May	Glasgow	0	3
1968	30 May	Amsterdam	0	0
1971	1 Dec	Amsterdam	1	2
WC1978	11 June	Mendoza	3	2
1982	23 Mar	Glasgow	2	1
1986	29 Apr	Eindhoven	0	0
EC1992	12 June	Gothenburg	0	1
1994	23 Mar	Glasgow	0	1
1994	27 May	Utrecht	1	3
EC1996	10 June	Villa Park	0	0
2000	26 Apr	Arnhem	0	0
EC2003	15 Nov	Glasgow	1	0
EC2003	19 Nov	Amsterdam	0	6
WC2009	28 Mar	Amsterdam	0	3
WC2009	9 Sept	Glasgow	0	1

v NEW ZEALAND

			S	*NZ*
WC1982	15 June	Malaga	5	2
2003	27 May	Tynecastle	1	1

v NIGERIA

			S	*N*
2002	17 Apr	Aberdeen	1	2
2014	28 May	Craven Cottage	2	2

v NORWAY

			S	*N*
1929	26 May	Oslo	7	3
1954	5 May	Glasgow	1	0
1954	19 May	Oslo	1	1
1963	4 June	Bergen	3	4
1963	7 Nov	Glasgow	6	1
1974	6 June	Oslo	2	1
EC1978	25 Oct	Glasgow	3	2
EC1979	7 June	Oslo	4	0
WC1988	14 Sept	Oslo	2	1
WC1989	15 Nov	Glasgow	1	1
1992	3 June	Oslo	0	0
WC1998	16 June	Bordeaux	1	1
2003	20 Aug	Oslo	0	0
WC2004	9 Oct	Glasgow	0	1
WC2005	7 Sept	Oslo	2	1
WC2008	11 Oct	Glasgow	0	0
WC2009	12 Aug	Oslo	0	4
2013	19 Nov	Molde	1	0

v PARAGUAY

			S	*P*
WC1958	11 June	Norrkoping	2	3

v PERU

			S	*P*
1972	26 Apr	Glasgow	2	0
WC1978	3 June	Cordoba	1	3
1979	12 Sept	Glasgow	1	1

v POLAND

			S	*P*
1958	1 June	Warsaw	2	1
1960	4 May	Glasgow	2	3
WC1965	23 May	Chorzow	1	1
WC1965	13 Oct	Glasgow	1	2
1980	28 May	Poznan	0	1
1990	19 May	Glasgow	1	1
2001	25 Apr	Bydgoszcz	1	1
2014	5 Mar	Warsaw	1	0
EC2014	14 Oct	Warsaw	2	2
EC2015	8 Oct	Glasgow	2	2

v PORTUGAL

			S	*P*
1950	21 May	Lisbon	2	2
1955	4 May	Glasgow	3	0
1959	3 June	Lisbon	0	1
1966	18 June	Glasgow	0	1
EC1971	21 Apr	Lisbon	0	2
EC1971	13 Oct	Glasgow	2	1
1975	13 May	Glasgow	1	0
EC1978	29 Nov	Lisbon	0	1
EC1980	26 Mar	Glasgow	4	1
WC1980	15 Oct	Glasgow	0	0
WC1981	18 Nov	Lisbon	1	2
WC1992	14 Oct	Ibrox	0	0
WC1993	28 Apr	Lisbon	0	5
2002	20 Nov	Braga	0	2

v QATAR

			S	*Q*
2015	5 June	Easter Road	1	0

v REPUBLIC OF IRELAND

			S	*RI*
WC1961	3 May	Glasgow	4	1
WC1961	7 May	Dublin	3	0
1963	9 June	Dublin	0	1
1969	21 Sept	Dublin	1	1
EC1986	15 Oct	Dublin	0	0
EC1987	18 Feb	Glasgow	0	1
2000	30 May	Dublin	2	1
2003	12 Feb	Glasgow	0	2
NC2011	29 May	Dublin	0	1
EC2014	14 Nov	Hampden	1	0
EC2015	13 June	Dublin	1	1

v ROMANIA

			S	*R*
EC1975	1 June	Bucharest	1	1
EC1975	17 Dec	Glasgow	1	1
1986	26 Mar	Glasgow	3	0
EC1990	12 Sept	Glasgow	2	1
EC1991	16 Oct	Bucharest	0	1
2004	31 Mar	Glasgow	1	2

v RUSSIA

			S	*R*
EC1994	16 Nov	Glasgow	1	1
EC1995	29 Mar	Moscow	0	0

v SAN MARINO

			S	*SM*
EC1991	1 May	Serravalle	2	0
EC1991	13 Nov	Glasgow	4	0
EC1995	26 Apr	Serravalle	2	0
EC1995	15 Nov	Glasgow	5	0
WC2000	7 Oct	Serravalle	2	0
WC2001	28 Mar	Glasgow	4	0

v SAUDI ARABIA

			S	*SA*
1988	17 Feb	Riyadh	2	2

v SERBIA

			S	*Se*
WC2012	8 Sept	Glasgow	0	0
WC2013	26 Mar	Novi Sad	0	2

v SLOVAKIA

			S	*Sl*
WC2016	**11 Oct**	**Trnava**	**0**	**3**

v SLOVENIA

			S	*Sl*
WC2004	8 Sept	Glasgow	0	0
WC2005	12 Oct	Celje	3	0
2012	29 Feb	Koper	1	1
WC2017	**26 Mar**	**Hampden**	**1**	**0**

v SOUTH AFRICA

			S	*SA*
2002	20 May	Hong Kong	0	2
2007	22 Aug	Aberdeen	1	0

v SPAIN

			S	*Sp*
WC1957	8 May	Glasgow	4	2
WC1957	26 May	Madrid	1	4
1963	13 June	Madrid	6	2
1965	8 May	Glasgow	0	0
EC1974	20 Nov	Glasgow	1	2
EC1975	5 Feb	Valencia	1	1
1982	24 Feb	Valencia	0	3
WC1984	14 Nov	Glasgow	3	1
WC1985	27 Feb	Seville	0	1
1988	27 Apr	Madrid	0	0
2004	3 Sept	Valencia	1	1

Match abandoned after 60 minutes; floodlight failure.

			S	*Sp*
EC2010	12 Oct	Glasgow	2	3
EC2011	11 Oct	Alicante	1	3

v SWEDEN

			S	*Sw*
1952	30 May	Stockholm	1	3
1953	6 May	Glasgow	1	2
1975	16 Apr	Gothenburg	1	1
1977	27 Apr	Glasgow	3	1
WC1980	10 Sept	Stockholm	1	0

			S	*Sw*
wc1981	9 Sept	Glasgow	2	0
wc1990	16 June	Genoa	2	1
1995	11 Oct	Stockholm	0	2
wc1996	10 Nov	Ibrox	1	0
wc1997	30 Apr	Gothenburg	1	2
2004	17 Nov	Easter Road	1	4
2010	11 Aug	Stockholm	0	3

		v SWITZERLAND	*S*	*Sw*
1931	24 May	Geneva	3	2
1946	15 May	Glasgow	3	1
1948	17 May	Berne	1	2
1950	26 Apr	Glasgow	3	1
wc1957	19 May	Basle	2	1
wc1957	6 Nov	Glasgow	3	2
1973	22 June	Berne	0	1
1976	7 Apr	Glasgow	1	0
EC1982	17 Nov	Berne	0	2
EC1983	30 May	Glasgow	2	2
EC1990	17 Oct	Glasgow	2	1
EC1991	11 Sept	Berne	2	2
wc1992	9 Sept	Berne	1	3
wc1993	8 Sept	Aberdeen	1	1
wc1996	18 June	Villa Park	1	0
2006	1 Mar	Glasgow	1	3

		v TRINIDAD & TOBAGO	*S*	*TT*
2004	30 May	Easter Road	4	1

		v TURKEY	*S*	*T*
1960	8 June	Ankara	2	4

		v UKRAINE	*S*	*U*
EC2006	11 Oct	Kiev	0	2
EC2007	13 Oct	Glasgow	3	1

		v URUGUAY	*S*	*U*
wc1954	19 June	Basle	0	7
1962	2 May	Glasgow	2	3
1983	21 Sept	Glasgow	2	0
wc1986	13 June	Nezahualcoyotl	0	0

		v USA	*S*	*USA*
1952	30 Apr	Glasgow	6	0
1992	17 May	Denver	1	0
1996	26 May	New Britain	1	2
1998	30 May	Washington	0	0
2005	12 Nov	Glasgow	1	1
2012	26 May	Jacksonville	1	5
2013	15 Nov	Glasgow	0	0

		v USSR	*S*	*USSR*
1967	10 May	Glasgow	0	2
1971	14 June	Moscow	0	1
wc1982	22 June	Malaga	2	2
1991	6 Feb	Ibrox	0	1

		v YUGOSLAVIA	*S*	*Y*
1955	15 May	Belgrade	2	2
1956	21 Nov	Glasgow	2	0
wc1958	8 June	Vasteras	1	1
1972	29 June	Belo Horizonte	2	2
wc1974	22 June	Frankfurt	1	1
1984	12 Sept	Glasgow	6	1
wc1988	19 Oct	Glasgow	1	1
wc1989	6 Sept	Zagreb	1	3

		v ZAIRE	*S*	*Z*
wc1974	14 June	Dortmund	2	0

WALES

		v ALBANIA	*W*	*A*
EC1994	7 Sept	Cardiff	2	0
EC1995	15 Nov	Tirana	1	1

		v ANDORRA	*W*	*A*
EC2014	9 Sept	La Vella	2	1
EC2015	13 Oct	Cardiff	2	0

		v ARGENTINA	*W*	*A*
1992	3 June	Tokyo	0	1
2002	13 Feb	Cardiff	1	1

		v ARMENIA	*W*	*A*
wc2001	24 Mar	Erevan	2	2
wc2001	1 Sept	Cardiff	0	0

		v AUSTRALIA	*W*	*A*
2011	10 Aug	Cardiff	1	2

		v AUSTRIA	*W*	*A*
1954	9 May	Vienna	0	2
1955	23 Nov	Wrexham	1	2
EC1974	4 Sept	Vienna	1	2
1975	19 Nov	Wrexham	1	0
1992	29 Apr	Vienna	1	1
EC2005	26 Mar	Cardiff	0	2
EC2005	30 Mar	Vienna	0	1
2013	6 Feb	Swansea	2	1
wc2016	**6 Oct**	**Vienna**	**2**	**2**

		v AZERBAIJAN	*W*	*A*
EC2002	20 Nov	Baku	2	0
EC2003	29 Mar	Cardiff	4	0
wc2004	4 Sept	Baku	1	1
wc2005	12 Oct	Cardiff	2	0
wc2008	6 Sept	Cardiff	1	0
wc2009	6 June	Baku	1	0

		v BELARUS	*W*	*B*
EC1998	14 Oct	Cardiff	3	2
EC1999	4 Sept	Minsk	2	1
wc2000	2 Sept	Minsk	1	2
wc2001	6 Oct	Cardiff	1	0

		v BELGIUM	*W*	*B*
1949	22 May	Liege	1	3
1949	23 Nov	Cardiff	5	1
EC1990	17 Oct	Cardiff	3	1
EC1991	27 Mar	Brussels	1	1
wc1992	18 Nov	Brussels	0	2
wc1993	31 Mar	Cardiff	2	0
wc1997	29 Mar	Cardiff	1	2
wc1997	11 Oct	Brussels	2	3
wc2012	7 Sept	Cardiff	0	2
wc2013	15 Oct	Brussels	1	1
EC2014	16 Nov	Brussels	0	0
EC2015	12 June	Cardiff	1	0
EC2016	1 July	Lille	3	1

		v BOSNIA-HERZEGOVINA	*W*	*BH*
2003	12 Feb	Cardiff	2	2
2012	15 Aug	Llanelli	0	2
EC2014	10 Oct	Cardiff	0	0
EC2015	10 Oct	Zenica	0	2

		v BRAZIL	*W*	*B*
wc1958	19 June	Gothenburg	0	1
1962	12 May	Rio de Janeiro	1	3
1962	16 May	São Paulo	1	3
1966	14 May	Rio de Janeiro	1	3
1966	18 May	Belo Horizonte	0	1
1983	12 June	Cardiff	1	1
1991	11 Sept	Cardiff	1	0
1997	12 Nov	Brasilia	0	3
2000	23 May	Cardiff	0	3
2006	5 Sept	Cardiff	0	2

		v BULGARIA	*W*	*B*
EC1983	27 Apr	Wrexham	1	0
EC1983	16 Nov	Sofia	0	1
EC1994	14 Dec	Cardiff	0	3
EC1995	29 Mar	Sofia	1	3
2006	15 Aug	Swansea	0	0
2007	22 Aug	Burgas	1	0
EC2010	8 Oct	Cardiff	0	1
EC2011	12 Oct	Sofia	1	0

		v CANADA	*W*	*C*
1986	10 May	Toronto	0	2
1986	20 May	Vancouver	3	0
2004	30 May	Wrexham	1	0

		v CHILE	*W*	*C*
1966	22 May	Santiago	0	2
2014	4 June	Valparaiso	0	2

		v COSTA RICA	*W*	*CR*
1990	20 May	Cardiff	1	0
2012	29 Feb	Cardiff	0	1

		v CROATIA	*W*	*C*
2002	21 Aug	Varazdin	1	1
2010	23 May	Osijek	0	2
wc2012	16 Oct	Osijek	0	2
wc2013	26 Mar	Swansea	1	2

		v CYPRUS	*W*	*C*
wc1992	14 Oct	Limassol	1	0
wc1993	13 Oct	Cardiff	2	0
2005	16 Nov	Limassol	0	1
EC2006	11 Oct	Cardiff	3	1
EC2007	13 Oct	Nicosia	1	3
EC2014	13 Oct	Cardiff	2	1
EC2015	3 Sept	Nicosia	1	0

		v CZECHOSLOVAKIA	*W*	*C*
wc1957	1 May	Cardiff	1	0
wc1957	26 May	Prague	0	2
EC1971	21 Apr	Swansea	1	3
EC1971	27 Oct	Prague	0	1
wc1977	30 Mar	Wrexham	3	0
wc1977	16 Nov	Prague	0	1
wc1980	19 Nov	Cardiff	1	0
wc1981	9 Sept	Prague	0	2
EC1987	29 Apr	Wrexham	1	1
EC1987	11 Nov	Prague	0	2
wc1993	28 Apr	Ostrava†	1	1
wc1993	8 Sept	Cardiff†	2	2

†*Czechoslovakia played as RCS (Republic of Czechs and Slovaks).*

2008	19 Nov	Brondby	1	0

		v ESTONIA	*W*	*E*
1994	23 May	Tallinn	2	1
2009	29 May	Llanelli	1	0

		v FAROE ISLANDS	*W*	*F*
wc1992	9 Sept	Cardiff	6	0
wc1993	6 June	Toftir	3	0

		v FINLAND	*W*	*F*
EC1971	26 May	Helsinki	1	0
EC1971	13 Oct	Swansea	3	0
EC1987	10 Sept	Helsinki	1	1
EC1987	1 Apr	Wrexham	4	0
wc1988	19 Oct	Swansea	2	2
wc1989	6 Sept	Helsinki	0	1
2000	29 Mar	Cardiff	1	2
EC2002	7 Sept	Helsinki	2	0
EC2003	10 Sept	Cardiff	1	1
wc2009	28 Mar	Cardiff	0	2
wc2009	10 Oct	Helsinki	1	2
2013	16 Nov	Cardiff	1	1

		v FRANCE	*W*	*F*
1933	25 May	Paris	1	1
1939	20 May	Paris	1	2
1953	14 May	Paris	1	6
1982	2 June	Toulouse	1	0

		v FYR MACEDONIA	*W*	*M*
wc2013	6 Sept	Skopje	1	2
wc2013	11 Oct	Cardiff	1	0

		v GEORGIA	*W*	*G*
EC1994	16 Nov	Tbilisi	0	5
EC1995	7 June	Cardiff	0	1
2008	20 Aug	Swansea	1	2
wc2016	**9 Oct**	**Cardiff**	**1**	**1**

		v GERMANY	*W*	*G*
EC1995	26 Apr	Dusseldorf	1	1
EC1995	11 Oct	Cardiff	1	2
2002	14 May	Cardiff	1	0
EC2007	8 Sept	Cardiff	0	2
EC2007	21 Nov	Frankfurt	0	0
wc2008	15 Oct	Moenchengladbach	0	1
wc2009	1 Apr	Cardiff	0	2

		v EAST GERMANY	*W*	*EG*
wc1957	19 May	Leipzig	1	2
wc1957	25 Sept	Cardiff	4	1
wc1969	16 Apr	Dresden	1	2
wc1969	22 Oct	Cardiff	1	3

		v WEST GERMANY	*W*	*WG*
1968	8 May	Cardiff	1	1
1969	26 Mar	Frankfurt	1	1
1976	6 Oct	Cardiff	0	2
1977	14 Dec	Dortmund	1	1
EC1979	2 May	Wrexham	0	2
EC1979	17 Oct	Cologne	1	5
wc1989	31 May	Cardiff	0	0
wc1989	15 Nov	Cologne	1	2
EC1991	5 June	Cardiff	1	0
EC1991	16 Oct	Nuremberg	1	4

		v GREECE	*W*	*G*
wc1964	9 Dec	Athens	0	2
wc1965	17 Mar	Cardiff	4	1

		v HUNGARY	*W*	*H*
wc1958	8 June	Sanviken	1	1
wc1958	17 June	Stockholm	2	1
1961	28 May	Budapest	2	3
EC1962	7 Nov	Budapest	1	3
EC1963	20 Mar	Cardiff	1	1
EC1974	30 Oct	Cardiff	2	0
EC1975	16 Apr	Budapest	2	1
1985	16 Oct	Cardiff	0	3
2004	31 Mar	Budapest	2	1
2005	9 Feb	Cardiff	2	0

		v ICELAND	*W*	*I*
wc1980	2 June	Reykjavik	4	0
wc1981	14 Oct	Swansea	2	2
wc1984	12 Sept	Reykjavik	0	1
wc1984	14 Nov	Cardiff	2	1
1991	1 May	Cardiff	1	0
2008	28 May	Reykjavik	1	0
2014	5 Mar	Cardiff	3	1

		v IRAN	*W*	*I*
1978	18 Apr	Teheran	1	0

		v ISRAEL	*W*	*I*
wc1958	15 Jan	Tel Aviv	2	0
wc1958	5 Feb	Cardiff	2	0
1984	10 June	Tel Aviv	0	0
1989	8 Feb	Tel Aviv	3	3
EC2015	28 Mar	Haifa	3	0
EC2015	6 Sept	Cardiff	0	0

		v ITALY	*W*	*I*
1965	1 May	Florence	1	4
wc1968	23 Oct	Cardiff	0	1
wc1969	4 Nov	Rome	1	4
1988	4 June	Brescia	1	0
1996	24 Jan	Terni	0	3
EC1998	5 Sept	Liverpool	0	2
EC1999	5 June	Bologna	0	4
EC2002	16 Oct	Cardiff	2	1
EC2003	6 Sept	Milan	0	4

		v JAMAICA	*W*	*J*
1998	25 Mar	Cardiff	0	0

		v JAPAN	*W*	*J*
1992	7 June	Matsuyama	1	0

		v KUWAIT	*W*	*K*
1977	6 Sept	Wrexham	0	0
1977	20 Sept	Kuwait	0	0

		v LATVIA	*W*	*L*
2004	18 Aug	Riga	2	0

		v LIECHTENSTEIN	*W*	*L*
2006	14 Nov	Swansea	4	0
wc2008	11 Oct	Cardiff	2	0
wc2009	14 Oct	Vaduz	2	0

		v LUXEMBOURG	*W*	*L*
EC1974	20 Nov	Swansea	5	0
EC1975	1 May	Luxembourg	3	1
EC1990	14 Nov	Luxembourg	1	0
EC1991	13 Nov	Cardiff	1	0
2008	26 Mar	Luxembourg	2	0
2010	11 Aug	Llanelli	5	1

		v MALTA	*W*	*M*
EC1978	25 Oct	Wrexham	7	0
EC1979	2 June	Valletta	2	0

			W	M
1988	1 June	Valletta	3	2
1998	3 June	Valletta	3	0

v MEXICO

			W	M
WC1958	11 June	Stockholm	1	1
1962	22 May	Mexico City	1	2
2012	27 May	New Jersey	0	2

v MOLDOVA

			W	M
EC1994	12 Oct	Kishinev	2	3
EC1995	6 Sept	Cardiff	1	0
WC2016	**5 Sept**	**Cardiff**	**4**	**0**

v MONTENEGRO

			W	M
2009	12 Aug	Podgorica	1	2
EC2010	3 Sept	Podgorica	0	1
EC2011	2 Sept	Cardiff	2	1

v NETHERLANDS

			W	N
WC1988	14 Sept	Amsterdam	0	1
WC1989	11 Oct	Wrexham	1	2
1992	30 May	Utrecht	0	4
WC1996	5 Oct	Cardiff	1	3
WC1996	9 Nov	Eindhoven	1	7
2008	1 June	Rotterdam	0	2
2014	4 June	Amsterdam	0	2
2015	13 Nov	Cardiff	2	3

v NEW ZEALAND

			W	NZ
2007	26 May	Wrexham	2	2

v NORWAY

			W	N
EC1982	22 Sept	Swansea	1	0
EC1983	21 Sept	Oslo	0	0
1984	6 June	Trondheim	0	1
1985	26 Feb	Wrexham	1	1
1985	5 June	Bergen	2	4
1994	9 Mar	Cardiff	1	3
WC2000	7 Oct	Cardiff	1	1
WC2001	5 Sept	Oslo	2	3
2004	27 May	Oslo	0	0
2008	6 Feb	Wrexham	3	0
2011	12 Nov	Cardiff	4	1

v PARAGUAY

			W	P
2006	1 Mar	Cardiff	0	0

v POLAND

			W	P
WC1973	28 Mar	Cardiff	2	0
WC1973	26 Sept	Katowice	0	3
1991	29 May	Radom	0	0
WC2000	11 Oct	Warsaw	0	0
WC2001	2 June	Cardiff	1	2
WC2004	13 Oct	Cardiff	2	3
WC2005	7 Sept	Warsaw	0	1
2009	11 Feb	Vila Real	0	1

v PORTUGAL

			W	P
1949	15 May	Lisbon	2	3
1951	12 May	Cardiff	2	1
2000	2 June	Chaves	0	3
EC2016	6 July	Lille	0	2

v QATAR

			W	Q
2000	23 Feb	Doha	1	0

v REPUBLIC OF IRELAND

			W	RI
1960	28 Sept	Dublin	3	2
1979	11 Sept	Swansea	2	1
1981	24 Feb	Dublin	3	1
1986	26 Mar	Dublin	1	0
1990	28 Mar	Dublin	0	1
1991	6 Feb	Wrexham	0	3
1992	19 Feb	Dublin	1	0
1993	17 Feb	Dublin	1	2
1997	11 Feb	Cardiff	0	0
EC2007	24 Mar	Dublin	0	1
EC2007	17 Nov	Cardiff	2	2
NC2011	8 Feb	Dublin	0	3
2013	14 Aug	Cardiff	0	0
WC2017	**24 Mar**	**Dublin**	**0**	**0**

v ROMANIA

			W	R
EC1970	11 Nov	Cardiff	0	0
EC1971	24 Nov	Bucharest	0	2
1983	12 Oct	Wrexham	5	0
WC1992	20 May	Bucharest	1	5
WC1993	17 Nov	Cardiff	1	2

v RUSSIA

			W	R
EC2003	15 Nov	Moscow	0	0
EC2003	19 Nov	Cardiff	0	1
WC2008	10 Sept	Moscow	1	2
WC2009	9 Sept	Cardiff	1	3
EC2016	20 June	Toulouse	3	0

v SAN MARINO

			W	SM
WC1996	2 June	Serravalle	5	0
WC1996	31 Aug	Cardiff	6	0
EC2007	28 Mar	Cardiff	3	0
EC2007	17 Oct	Serravalle	2	1

v SAUDI ARABIA

			W	SA
1986	25 Feb	Dahran	2	1

v SERBIA

			W	S
WC2012	11 Sept	Novi Sad	1	6
WC2013	10 Sept	Cardiff	0	3
WC2016	**12 Nov**	**Cardiff**	**1**	**1**
WC2017	**11 June**	**Belgrade**	**1**	**1**

v SERBIA-MONTENEGRO

			W	SM
EC2003	20 Aug	Belgrade	0	1
EC2003	11 Oct	Cardiff	2	3

v SLOVAKIA

			W	S
EC2006	7 Oct	Cardiff	1	5
EC2007	12 Sept	Trnava	5	2
EC2016	11 June	Bordeaux	2	1

v SLOVENIA

			W	Sl
2005	17 Aug	Swansea	0	0

v SPAIN

			W	S
WC1961	19 Apr	Cardiff	1	2
WC1961	18 May	Madrid	1	1
1982	24 Mar	Valencia	1	1
WC1984	17 Oct	Seville	0	3
WC1985	30 Apr	Wrexham	3	0

v SWEDEN

			W	S
WC1958	15 June	Stockholm	0	0
1988	27 Apr	Stockholm	1	4
1989	26 Apr	Wrexham	0	2
1990	25 Apr	Stockholm	2	4
1994	20 Apr	Wrexham	0	2
2010	3 Mar	Swansea	0	1
2016	5 June	Stockholm	0	3

v SWITZERLAND

			W	S
1949	26 May	Berne	0	4
1951	16 May	Wrexham	3	2
1996	24 Apr	Lugano	0	2
EC1999	31 Mar	Zurich	0	2
EC1999	9 Oct	Wrexham	0	2
EC2010	12 Oct	Basle	1	4
EC2011	8 Oct	Swansea	2	0

v TRINIDAD & TOBAGO

			W	TT
2006	27 May	Graz	2	1

v TUNISIA

			W	T
1998	6 June	Tunis	0	4

v TURKEY

			W	T
EC1978	29 Nov	Wrexham	1	0
EC1979	21 Nov	Izmir	0	1
WC1980	15 Oct	Cardiff	4	0
WC1981	25 Mar	Ankara	1	0
WC1996	14 Dec	Cardiff	0	0
WC1997	20 Aug	Istanbul	4	6

v UKRAINE

			W	U
WC2001	28 Mar	Cardiff	1	1
WC2001	6 June	Kiev	1	1
2016	28 Mar	Kiev	0	1

v REST OF UNITED KINGDOM

			W	RUK
1951	5 Dec	Cardiff	3	2
1969	28 July	Cardiff	0	1

v URUGUAY

			W	U
1986	21 Apr	Wrexham	0	0

		v USA	*W*	*USA*
2003	27 May	San Jose	0	2

		v USSR	*W*	*USSR*
WC1965	30 May	Moscow	1	2
WC1965	27 Oct	Cardiff	2	1
WC1981	30 May	Wrexham	0	0
WC1981	18 Nov	Tbilisi	0	3
1987	18 Feb	Swansea	0	0

		v YUGOSLAVIA	*W*	*Y*
1953	21 May	Belgrade	2	5
1954	22 Nov	Cardiff	1	3
EC1976	24 Apr	Zagreb	0	2
EC1976	22 May	Cardiff	1	1
EC1982	15 Dec	Titograd	4	4
EC1983	14 Dec	Cardiff	1	1
1988	23 Mar	Swansea	1	2

NORTHERN IRELAND

		v ALBANIA	*NI*	*A*
WC1965	7 May	Belfast	4	1
WC1965	24 Nov	Tirana	1	1
EC1982	15 Dec	Tirana	0	0
EC1983	27 Apr	Belfast	1	0
WC1992	9 Sept	Belfast	3	0
WC1993	17 Feb	Tirana	2	1
WC1996	14 Dec	Belfast	2	0
WC1997	10 Sept	Zurich	0	1
2010	3 Mar	Tirana	0	1

		v ALGERIA	*NI*	*A*
WC1986	3 June	Guadalajara	1	1

		v ARGENTINA	*NI*	*A*
WC1958	11 June	Halmstad	1	3

		v ARMENIA	*NI*	*A*
WC1996	5 Oct	Belfast	1	1
WC1997	30 Apr	Erevan	0	0
EC2003	29 Mar	Erevan	0	1
EC2003	10 Sept	Belfast	0	1

		v AUSTRALIA	*NI*	*A*
1980	11 June	Sydney	2	1
1980	15 June	Melbourne	1	1
1980	18 June	Adelaide	2	1

		v AUSTRIA	*NI*	*A*
WC1982	1 July	Madrid	2	2
EC1982	13 Oct	Vienna	0	2
EC1983	21 Sept	Belfast	3	1
EC1990	14 Nov	Vienna	0	0
EC1991	16 Oct	Belfast	2	1
EC1994	12 Oct	Vienna	2	1
EC1995	15 Nov	Belfast	5	3
WC2004	13 Oct	Belfast	3	3
WC2005	12 Oct	Vienna	0	2

		v AZERBAIJAN	*NI*	*A*
WC2004	9 Oct	Baku	0	0
WC2005	3 Sept	Belfast	2	0
WC2012	14 Nov	Belfast	1	1
WC2013	11 Oct	Baku	0	2
WC2016	**11 Nov**	**Belfast**	**4**	**0**
WC2017	**10 June**	**Baku**	**1**	**0**

		v BARBADOS	*NI*	*B*
2004	30 May	Waterford	1	1

		v BELARUS	*NI*	*B*
2016	27 May	Belfast	3	0

		v BELGIUM	*NI*	*B*
WC1976	10 Nov	Liege	0	2
WC1977	16 Nov	Belfast	3	0
1997	11 Feb	Belfast	3	0

		v BRAZIL	*NI*	*B*
WC1986	12 June	Guadalajara	0	3

		v BULGARIA	*NI*	*B*
WC1972	18 Oct	Sofia	0	3
WC1973	26 Sept	Sheffield	0	0
EC1978	29 Nov	Sofia	2	0
EC1979	2 May	Belfast	2	0
WC2001	28 Mar	Sofia	3	4
WC2001	2 June	Belfast	0	1
2008	6 Feb	Belfast	0	1

		v CANADA	*NI*	*C*
1995	22 May	Edmonton	0	2
1999	27 Apr	Belfast	1	1
2005	9 Feb	Belfast	0	1

		v CHILE	*NI*	*C*
1989	26 May	Belfast	0	1
1995	25 May	Edmonton	1	2
2010	30 May	Chillan	0	1
2014	4 June	Valparaiso	0	2

		v COLOMBIA	*NI*	*C*
1994	4 June	Boston	0	2

		v CROATIA	*NI*	*C*
2016	**15 Nov**	**Belfast**	**0**	**3**

		v CYPRUS	*NI*	*C*
EC1971	3 Feb	Nicosia	3	0
EC1971	21 Apr	Belfast	5	0
WC1973	14 Feb	Nicosia	0	1
WC1973	8 May	London	3	0
2002	21 Aug	Belfast	0	0
2014	5 Mar	Nicosia	0	0

		v CZECHOSLOVAKIA	*NI*	*C*
WC1958	8 June	Halmstad	1	0
WC1958	17 June	Malmo	2	1*

**After extra time*

		v CZECH REPUBLIC	*NI*	*C*
WC2001	24 Mar	Belfast	0	1
WC2001	6 June	Teplice	1	3
WC2008	10 Sept	Belfast	0	0
WC2009	14 Oct	Prague	0	0
WC2016	**4 Sept**	**Prague**	**0**	**0**

		v DENMARK	*NI*	*D*
EC1978	25 Oct	Belfast	2	1
EC1979	6 June	Copenhagen	0	4
1986	26 Mar	Belfast	1	1
EC1990	17 Oct	Belfast	1	1
EC1991	13 Nov	Odense	1	2
WC1992	18 Nov	Belfast	0	1
WC1993	13 Oct	Copenhagen	0	1
WC2000	7 Oct	Belfast	1	1
WC2001	1 Sept	Copenhagen	1	1
EC2006	7 Oct	Copenhagen	0	0
EC2007	17 Nov	Belfast	2	1

		v ESTONIA	*NI*	*E*
2004	31 Mar	Tallinn	1	0
2006	1 Mar	Belfast	1	0
EC2011	6 Sept	Tallinn	1	4
EC2011	7 Oct	Belfast	1	2

		v FAROE ISLANDS	*NI*	*F*
EC1991	1 May	Belfast	1	1
EC1991	11 Sept	Landskrona	5	0
EC2010	12 Oct	Toftir	1	1
EC2011	10 Aug	Belfast	4	0
EC2014	11 Oct	Belfast	2	0
EC2015	4 Sept	Torshavn	3	1

		v FINLAND	*NI*	*F*
WC1984	27 May	Pori	0	1
WC1984	14 Nov	Belfast	2	1
EC1998	10 Oct	Belfast	1	0
EC1998	9 Oct	Helsinki	1	4
2003	12 Feb	Belfast	0	1
2006	16 Aug	Helsinki	2	1
2012	15 Aug	Belfast	3	3
EC2015	29 Mar	Belfast	2	1
EC2015	11 Oct	Helsinki	1	1

		v FRANCE	*NI*	*F*
1928	21 Feb	Paris	0	4
1951	12 May	Belfast	2	2
1952	11 Nov	Paris	1	3
WC1958	19 June	Norrkoping	0	4
1982	24 Mar	Paris	0	4

			NI	*F*
wc1982	4 July	Madrid	1	4
1986	26 Feb	Paris	0	0
1988	27 Apr	Belfast	0	0
1999	18 Aug	Belfast	0	1

		v GEORGIA	*NI*	*G*
2008	26 Mar	Belfast	4	1

		v GERMANY	*NI*	*G*
1992	2 June	Bremen	1	1
1996	29 May	Belfast	1	1
wc1996	9 Nov	Nuremberg	1	1
wc1997	20 Aug	Belfast	1	3
EC1999	27 Mar	Belfast	0	3
EC1999	8 Sept	Dortmund	0	4
2005	4 June	Belfast	1	4
EC2016	21 June	Paris	0	1
wc2016	**11 Oct**	**Hanover**	**0**	**2**

		v WEST GERMANY	*NI*	*WG*
wc1958	15 June	Malmo	2	2
wc1960	26 Oct	Belfast	3	4
wc1961	10 May	Hamburg	1	2
1966	7 May	Belfast	0	2
1977	27 Apr	Cologne	0	5
EC1982	17 Nov	Belfast	1	0
EC1983	16 Nov	Hamburg	1	0

		v GREECE	*NI*	*G*
wc1961	3 May	Athens	1	2
wc1961	17 Oct	Belfast	2	0
1988	17 Feb	Athens	2	3
EC2003	2 Apr	Belfast	0	2
EC2003	11 Oct	Athens	0	1
EC2014	14 Oct	Piraeus	2	0
EC2015	8 Oct	Belfast	3	1

		v HONDURAS	*NI*	*H*
wc1982	21 June	Zaragoza	1	1

		v HUNGARY	*NI*	*H*
wc1988	19 Oct	Budapest	0	1
wc1989	6 Sept	Belfast	1	2
2000	26 Apr	Belfast	0	1
2008	19 Nov	Belfast	0	2
EC2014	7 Sept	Budapest	2	1
EC2015	7 Sept	Belfast	1	1

		v ICELAND	*NI*	*I*
wc1977	11 June	Reykjavik	0	1
wc1977	21 Sept	Belfast	2	0
wc2000	11 Oct	Reykjavik	0	1
wc2001	5 Sept	Belfast	3	0
EC2006	2 Sept	Belfast	0	3
EC2007	12 Sept	Reykjavik	1	2

		v ISRAEL	*NI*	*I*
1968	10 Sept	Jaffa	3	2
1976	3 Mar	Tel Aviv	1	1
wc1980	26 Mar	Tel Aviv	0	0
wc1981	18 Nov	Belfast	1	0
1984	16 Oct	Belfast	3	0
1987	18 Feb	Tel Aviv	1	1
2009	12 Aug	Belfast	1	1
wc2013	26 Mar	Belfast	0	2
wc2013	15 Oct	Tel Aviv	1	1

		v ITALY	*NI*	*I*
wc1957	25 Apr	Rome	0	1
1957	4 Dec	Belfast	2	2
wc1958	15 Jan	Belfast	2	1
1961	25 Apr	Bologna	2	3
1997	22 Jan	Palermo	0	2
2003	3 June	Campobasso	0	2
2009	6 June	Pisa	0	3
EC2010	8 Oct	Belfast	0	0
EC2011	11 Oct	Pescara	0	3

		v LATVIA	*NI*	*L*
wc1993	2 June	Riga	2	1
wc1993	8 Sept	Belfast	2	0
EC1995	26 Apr	Riga	1	0
EC1995	7 June	Belfast	1	2
EC2006	11 Oct	Belfast	1	0
EC2007	8 Sept	Riga	0	1
2015	13 Nov	Belfast	1	0

		v LIECHTENSTEIN	*NI*	*L*
EC1994	20 Apr	Belfast	4	1
EC1995	11 Oct	Eschen	4	0
2002	27 Mar	Vaduz	0	0
EC2007	24 Mar	Vaduz	4	1
EC2007	22 Aug	Belfast	3	1

		v LITHUANIA	*NI*	*L*
wc1992	28 Apr	Belfast	2	2
wc1993	25 May	Vilnius	1	0

		v LUXEMBOURG	*NI*	*L*
2000	23 Feb	Luxembourg	3	1
wc2012	11 Sept	Belfast	1	1
wc2013	10 Sept	Luxembourg	2	3

		v MALTA	*NI*	*M*
wc1988	21 May	Belfast	3	0
wc1989	26 Apr	Valletta	2	0
2000	28 Mar	Valletta	3	0
wc2000	2 Sept	Belfast	1	0
wc2001	6 Oct	Valletta	1	0
2005	17 Aug	Ta'Qali	1	1
2013	6 Feb	Ta'Qali	0	0

		v MEXICO	*NI*	*M*
1966	22 June	Belfast	4	1
1994	11 June	Miami	0	3

		v MOLDOVA	*NI*	*M*
EC1998	18 Nov	Belfast	2	2
EC1999	31 Mar	Chisinau	0	0

		v MONTENEGRO	*NI*	*M*
2010	11 Aug	Podgorica	0	2

		v MOROCCO	*NI*	*M*
1986	23 Apr	Belfast	2	1
2010	17 Nov	Belfast	1	1

		v NETHERLANDS	*NI*	*N*
1962	9 May	Rotterdam	0	4
wc1965	17 Mar	Belfast	2	1
wc1965	7 Apr	Rotterdam	0	0
wc1976	13 Oct	Rotterdam	2	2
wc1977	12 Oct	Belfast	0	1
2012	2 June	Amsterdam	0	6

		v NEW ZEALAND	*NI*	*N*
2017	**2 June**	**Belfast**	**1**	**0**

		v NORWAY	*NI*	*N*
1922	25 May	Bergen	1	2
EC1974	4 Sept	Oslo	1	2
EC1975	29 Oct	Belfast	3	0
1990	27 Mar	Belfast	2	3
1996	27 Mar	Belfast	0	2
2001	28 Feb	Belfast	0	4
2004	18 Feb	Belfast	1	4
2012	29 Feb	Belfast	0	3
wc2017	**26 Mar**	**Belfast**	**2**	**0**

		v POLAND	*NI*	*P*
EC1962	10 Oct	Katowice	2	0
EC1962	28 Nov	Belfast	2	0
1988	23 Mar	Belfast	1	1
1991	5 Feb	Belfast	3	1
2002	13 Feb	Limassol	1	4
EC2004	4 Sept	Belfast	0	3
EC2005	30 Mar	Warsaw	0	1
wc2009	28 Mar	Belfast	3	2
wc2009	5 Sept	Chorzow	1	1
EC2016	12 June	Nice	0	1

		v PORTUGAL	*NI*	*P*
wc1957	16 Jan	Lisbon	1	1
wc1957	1 May	Belfast	3	0
wc1973	28 Mar	Coventry	1	1
wc1973	14 Nov	Lisbon	1	1
wc1980	19 Nov	Lisbon	0	1
wc1981	29 Apr	Belfast	1	0
EC1994	7 Sept	Belfast	1	2
EC1995	3 Sept	Lisbon	1	1
wc1997	29 Mar	Belfast	0	0
wc1997	11 Oct	Lisbon	0	1
2005	15 Nov	Belfast	1	1
wc2012	16 Oct	Porto	1	1
wc2013	6 Sept	Belfast	2	4

		v QATAR	*NI*	*Q*
2015	31 May	Crewe	1	1

		v REPUBLIC OF IRELAND	*NI*	*RI*
EC1978	20 Sept	Dublin	0	0
EC1979	21 Nov	Belfast	1	0
WC1988	14 Sept	Belfast	0	0
WC1989	11 Oct	Dublin	0	3
WC1993	31 Mar	Dublin	0	3
WC1993	17 Nov	Belfast	1	1
EC1994	16 Nov	Belfast	0	4
EC1995	29 Mar	Dublin	1	1
1999	29 May	Dublin	1	0
NC2011	24 May	Dublin	0	5

		v ROMANIA	*NI*	*R*
WC1984	12 Sept	Belfast	3	2
WC1985	16 Oct	Bucharest	1	0
1994	23 Mar	Belfast	2	0
2006	27 May	Chicago	0	2
EC2014	14 Nov	Bucharest	0	2
EC2015	13 June	Belfast	0	0

		v RUSSIA	*NI*	*R*
WC2012	7 Sept	Moscow	0	2
WC2013	14 Aug	Belfast	1	0

		v SAN MARINO	*NI*	*SM*
WC2008	15 Oct	Belfast	4	0
WC2009	11 Feb	Serravalle	3	0
WC2016	**8 Oct**	**Belfast**	**4**	**0**

		v ST KITTS & NEVIS	*NI*	*SK*
2004	2 June	Basseterre	2	0

		v SERBIA	*NI*	*S*
2009	14 Nov	Belfast	0	1
EC2011	25 Mar	Belgrade	1	2
EC2011	2 Sept	Belfast	0	1

		v SERBIA-MONTENEGRO	*NI*	*SM*
2004	28 Apr	Belfast	1	1

		v SLOVAKIA	*NI*	*S*
1998	25 Mar	Belfast	1	0
WC2008	6 Sept	Bratislava	1	2
WC2009	9 Sept	Belfast	0	2
2016	4 June	Trnava	0	0

		v SLOVENIA	*NI*	*S*
WC2008	11 Oct	Maribor	0	2
WC2009	1 Apr	Belfast	1	0
EC2010	3 Sept	Maribor	1	0
EC2011	29 Mar	Belfast	0	0
2016	28 Mar	Belfast	1	0

		v SOUTH AFRICA	*NI*	*SA*
1924	24 Sept	Belfast	1	2

		v SPAIN	*NI*	*S*
1958	15 Oct	Madrid	2	6
1963	30 May	Bilbao	1	1
1963	30 Oct	Belfast	0	1
EC1970	11 Nov	Seville	0	3
EC1972	16 Feb	Hull	1	1
WC1982	25 June	Valencia	1	0
1985	27 Mar	Palma	0	0
WC1986	7 June	Guadalajara	1	2
WC1988	21 Dec	Seville	0	4
WC1989	8 Feb	Belfast	0	2
WC1992	14 Oct	Belfast	0	0
WC1993	28 Apr	Seville	1	3
1998	2 June	Santander	1	4
2002	17 Apr	Belfast	0	5
EC2002	12 Oct	Albacete	0	3
EC2003	11 June	Belfast	0	0
EC2006	6 Sept	Belfast	3	2
EC2007	21 Nov	Las Palmas	0	1

		v SWEDEN	*NI*	*S*
EC1974	30 Oct	Solna	2	0
EC1975	3 Sept	Belfast	1	2
WC1980	15 Oct	Belfast	3	0
WC1981	3 June	Solna	0	1
1996	24 Apr	Belfast	1	2
EC2007	28 Mar	Belfast	2	1
EC2007	17 Oct	Stockholm	1	1

		v SWITZERLAND	*NI*	*S*
WC1964	14 Oct	Belfast	1	0
WC1964	14 Nov	Lausanne	1	2
1998	22 Apr	Belfast	1	0
2004	18 Aug	Zurich	0	0

		v THAILAND	*NI*	*T*
1997	21 May	Bangkok	0	0

		v TRINIDAD & TOBAGO	*NI*	*TT*
2004	6 June	Bacolet	3	0

		v TURKEY	*NI*	*T*
WC1968	23 Oct	Belfast	4	1
WC1968	11 Dec	Istanbul	3	0
2013	15 Nov	Adana	0	1
EC1983	30 Mar	Belfast	2	1
EC1983	12 Oct	Ankara	0	1
WC1985	1 May	Belfast	2	0
WC1985	11 Sept	Izmir	0	0
EC1986	12 Nov	Izmir	0	0
EC1987	11 Nov	Belfast	1	0
EC1998	5 Sept	Istanbul	0	3
EC1999	4 Sept	Belfast	0	3
2010	26 May	New Britain	0	2
2013	15 Nov	Adana	0	1

		v UKRAINE	*NI*	*U*
WC1996	31 Aug	Belfast	0	1
WC1997	2 Apr	Kiev	1	2
EC2002	16 Oct	Belfast	0	0
EC2003	6 Sept	Donetsk	0	0
EC2016	16 June	Lyon	2	0

		v URUGUAY	*NI*	*U*
1964	29 Apr	Belfast	3	0
1990	18 May	Belfast	1	0
2006	21 May	New Jersey	0	1
2014	30 May	Montevideo	0	1

		v USSR	*NI*	*USSR*
WC1969	19 Sept	Belfast	0	0
WC1969	22 Oct	Moscow	0	2
EC1971	22 Sept	Moscow	0	1
EC1971	13 Oct	Belfast	1	1

		v YUGOSLAVIA	*NI*	*Y*
EC1975	16 Mar	Belfast	1	0
EC1975	19 Nov	Belgrade	0	1
WC1982	17 June	Zaragoza	0	0
EC1987	29 Apr	Belfast	1	2
EC1987	14 Oct	Sarajevo	0	3
EC1990	12 Sept	Belfast	0	2
EC1991	27 Mar	Belgrade	1	4
2000	16 Aug	Belfast	1	2

REPUBLIC OF IRELAND

		v ALBANIA	*RI*	*A*
WC1992	26 May	Dublin	2	0
WC1993	26 May	Tirana	2	1
EC2003	2 Apr	Tirana	0	0
EC2003	7 June	Dublin	2	1

		v ALGERIA	*RI*	*A*
1982	28 Apr	Algiers	0	2
2010	28 May	Dublin	3	0

		v ANDORRA	*RI*	*A*
WC2001	28 Mar	Barcelona	3	0
WC2001	25 Apr	Dublin	3	1
EC2010	7 Sept	Dublin	3	1
EC2011	7 Oct	Andorra La Vella	2	0

		v ARGENTINA	*RI*	*A*
1951	13 May	Dublin	0	1
†1979	29 May	Dublin	0	0
1980	16 May	Dublin	0	1
1998	22 Apr	Dublin	0	2
2010	11 Aug	Dublin	0	1

†*Not considered a full international.*

		v ARMENIA	*RI*	*A*
EC2010	3 Sept	Erevan	1	0
EC2011	11 Oct	Dublin	2	1

		v AUSTRALIA	*RI*	*A*
2003	19 Aug	Dublin	2	1
2009	12 Aug	Limerick	0	3

		v AUSTRIA	*RI*	*A*
1952	7 May	Vienna	0	6
1953	25 Mar	Dublin	4	0
1958	14 Mar	Vienna	1	3
WC2013	10 Sept	Vienna	0	1
1962	8 Apr	Dublin	2	3
EC1963	25 Sept	Vienna	0	0
EC1963	13 Oct	Dublin	3	2
1966	22 May	Vienna	0	1
1968	10 Nov	Dublin	2	2
EC1971	30 May	Dublin	1	4
EC1971	10 Oct	Linz	0	6
EC1995	11 June	Dublin	1	3
EC1995	6 Sept	Vienna	1	3
WC2013	26 Mar	Dublin	2	2
WC2013	10 Sept	Vienna	0	1
WC2016	**12 Nov**	**Vienna**	**1**	**0**
WC2017	**11 June**	**Dublin**	**1**	**1**

		v BELARUS	*RI*	*B*
2016	31 May	Cork	1	2

		v BELGIUM	*RI*	*B*
1928	12 Feb	Liege	4	2
1929	30 Apr	Dublin	4	0
1930	11 May	Brussels	3	1
WC1934	25 Feb	Dublin	4	4
1949	24 Apr	Dublin	0	2
1950	10 May	Brussels	1	5
1965	24 Mar	Dublin	0	2
1966	25 May	Liege	3	2
WC1980	15 Oct	Dublin	1	1
WC1981	25 Mar	Brussels	0	1
EC1986	10 Sept	Brussels	2	2
EC1987	29 Apr	Dublin	0	0
WC1997	29 Oct	Dublin	1	1
WC1997	16 Nov	Brussels	1	2
EC2016	18 June	Bordeaux	0	3

		v BOLIVIA	*RI*	*B*
1994	24 May	Dublin	1	0
1996	15 June	New Jersey	3	0
2007	26 May	Boston	1	1

		v BOSNIA-HERZEGOVINA	*RI*	*BH*
2012	26 May	Dublin	1	0
EC2015	13 Nov	Zenica	1	1
EC2015	16 Nov	Dublin	2	0

		v BRAZIL	*RI*	*B*
1974	5 May	Rio de Janeiro	1	2
1982	27 May	Uberlandia	0	7
1987	23 May	Dublin	1	0
2004	18 Feb	Dublin	0	0
2008	6 Feb	Dublin	0	1
2010	2 Mar	Emirates	0	2

		v BULGARIA	*RI*	*B*
WC1977	1 June	Sofia	1	2
WC1977	12 Oct	Dublin	0	0
EC1979	19 May	Sofia	0	1
EC1979	17 Oct	Dublin	3	0
WC1987	1 Apr	Sofia	1	2
WC1987	14 Oct	Dublin	2	0
2004	18 Aug	Dublin	1	1
WC2009	28 Mar	Dublin	1	1
WC2009	6 June	Sofia	1	1

		v CAMEROON	*RI*	*C*
WC2002	1 June	Niigata	1	1

		v CANADA	*RI*	*C*
2003	18 Nov	Dublin	3	0

		v CHILE	*RI*	*C*
1960	30 Mar	Dublin	2	0
1972	21 June	Recife	1	2
1974	12 May	Santiago	2	1
1982	22 May	Santiago	0	1
1991	22 May	Dublin	1	1
2006	24 May	Dublin	0	1

		v CHINA PR	*RI*	*CPR*
1984	3 June	Sapporo	1	0
2005	29 Mar	Dublin	1	0

		v COLOMBIA	*RI*	*C*
2008	29 May	Fulham	1	0

		v COSTA RICA	*RI*	*C*
2014	6 June	Philadephia	1	1

		v CROATIA	*RI*	*C*
1996	2 June	Dublin	2	2
EC1998	5 Sept	Dublin	2	0
EC1999	4 Sept	Zagreb	0	1
2001	15 Aug	Dublin	2	2
2004	16 Nov	Dublin	1	0
2011	10 Aug	Dublin	0	0
EC2012	10 June	Poznan	1	3

		v CYPRUS	*RI*	*C*
WC1980	26 Mar	Nicosia	3	2
WC1980	19 Nov	Dublin	6	0
WC2001	24 Mar	Nicosia	4	0
WC2001	6 Oct	Dublin	4	0
WC2004	4 Sept	Dublin	3	0
WC2005	8 Oct	Nicosia	1	0
EC2006	7 Oct	Nicosia	2	5
EC2007	17 Oct	Dublin	1	1
2008	15 Oct	Dublin	1	0
WC2009	5 Sept	Nicosia	2	1

		v CZECHOSLOVAKIA	*RI*	*C*
1938	18 May	Prague	2	2
EC1959	5 Apr	Dublin	2	0
EC1959	10 May	Bratislava	0	4
WC1961	8 Oct	Dublin	1	3
WC1961	29 Oct	Prague	1	7
EC1967	21 May	Dublin	0	2
EC1967	22 Nov	Prague	2	1
WC1969	4 May	Dublin	1	2
WC1969	7 Oct	Prague	0	3
1979	26 Sept	Prague	1	4
1981	29 Apr	Dublin	3	1
1986	27 May	Reykjavik	1	0

		v CZECH REPUBLIC	*RI*	*C*
1994	5 June	Dublin	1	3
1996	24 Apr	Prague	0	2
1998	25 Mar	Olomouc	1	2
2000	23 Feb	Dublin	3	2
2004	31 Mar	Dublin	2	1
EC2006	11 Oct	Dublin	1	1
EC2007	12 Sept	Prague	0	1
2012	29 Feb	Dublin	1	1

		v DENMARK	*RI*	*D*
WC1956	3 Oct	Dublin	2	1
WC1957	2 Oct	Copenhagen	2	0
WC1968	4 Dec	Dublin	1	1
	(abandoned after 51 mins)			
WC1969	27 May	Copenhagen	0	2
WC1969	15 Oct	Dublin	1	1
EC1978	24 May	Copenhagen	3	3
EC1979	2 May	Dublin	2	0
WC1984	14 Nov	Copenhagen	0	3
WC1985	13 Nov	Dublin	1	4
WC1992	14 Oct	Copenhagen	0	0
WC1993	28 Apr	Dublin	1	1
2002	27 Mar	Dublin	3	0
2007	22 Aug	Copenhagen	4	0

		v ECUADOR	*RI*	*E*
1972	19 June	Natal	3	2
2007	23 May	New Jersey	1	1

		v EGYPT	*RI*	*E*
WC1990	17 June	Palermo	0	0

		v ENGLAND	*RI*	*E*
1946	30 Sept	Dublin	0	1
1949	21 Sept	Everton	2	0
WC1957	8 May	Wembley	1	5
WC1957	19 May	Dublin	1	1
1964	24 May	Dublin	1	3
1976	8 Sept	Wembley	1	1
EC1978	25 Oct	Dublin	1	1
EC1980	6 Feb	Wembley	0	2
1985	26 Mar	Wembley	1	2
EC1988	12 June	Stuttgart	1	0
WC1990	11 June	Cagliari	1	1
EC1990	14 Nov	Dublin	1	1
EC1991	27 Mar	Wembley	1	1
1995	15 Feb	Dublin	1	0
	(abandoned after 27 mins)			
2013	29 May	Wembley	1	1
2015	7 June	Dublin	0	0

		v ESTONIA	*RI*	*E*
wc2000	11 Oct	Dublin	2	0
wc2001	6 June	Tallinn	2	0
EC2011	11 Nov	Tallinn	4	0
EC2011	15 Nov	Dublin	1	1

		v FAROE ISLANDS	*RI*	*F*
EC2004	13 Oct	Dublin	2	0
EC2005	8 June	Toftir	2	0
wc2012	16 Oct	Torshavn	4	1
wc2013	7 June	Dublin	3	0

		v FINLAND	*RI*	*F*
wc1949	8 Sept	Dublin	3	0
wc1949	9 Oct	Helsinki	1	1
1990	16 May	Dublin	1	1
2000	15 Nov	Dublin	3	0
2002	21 Aug	Helsinki	3	0

		v FRANCE	*RI*	*F*
1937	23 May	Paris	2	0
1952	16 Nov	Dublin	1	1
wc1953	4 Oct	Dublin	3	5
wc1953	25 Nov	Paris	0	1
wc1972	15 Nov	Dublin	2	1
wc1973	19 May	Paris	1	1
wc1976	17 Nov	Paris	0	2
wc1977	30 Mar	Dublin	1	0
wc1980	28 Oct	Paris	0	2
wc1981	14 Oct	Dublin	3	2
1989	7 Feb	Dublin	0	0
wc2004	9 Oct	Paris	0	0
wc2005	7 Sept	Dublin	0	1
wc2009	14 Nov	Dublin	0	1
wc2009	18 Nov	Paris	1	1
EC2016	26 June	Lyon	1	2

		v FYR MACEDONIA	*RI*	*M*
wc1996	9 Oct	Dublin	3	0
wc1997	2 Apr	Skopje	2	3
EC1999	9 June	Dublin	1	0
EC1999	9 Oct	Skopje	1	1
EC2011	26 Mar	Dublin	2	1
EC2011	4 June	Podgorica	2	0

		v GEORGIA	*RI*	*G*
EC2003	29 Mar	Tbilisi	2	1
EC2003	11 June	Dublin	2	0
wc2008	6 Sept	Mainz	2	1
wc2009	11 Feb	Dublin	2	1
2013	2 June	Dublin	3	0
EC2014	7 Sept	Tbilisi	2	1
EC2015	7 Sept	Dublin	1	0
wc2016	**6 Oct**	**Dublin**	**1**	**0**

		v GERMANY	*RI*	*G*
1935	8 May	Dortmund	1	3
1936	17 Oct	Dublin	5	2
1939	23 May	Bremen	1	1
1994	29 May	Hanover	2	0
wc2002	5 June	Ibaraki	1	1
EC2006	2 Sept	Stuttgart	0	1
EC2007	13 Oct	Dublin	0	0
wc2012	12 Oct	Dublin	1	6
wc2013	11 Oct	Cologne	0	3
EC2014	14 Oct	Gelsenkirchen	1	1
EC2015	8 Oct	Dublin	1	0

		v WEST GERMANY	*RI*	*WG*
1951	17 Oct	Dublin	3	2
1952	4 May	Cologne	0	3
1955	28 May	Hamburg	1	2
1956	25 Nov	Dublin	3	0
1960	11 May	Dusseldorf	1	0
1966	4 May	Dublin	0	4
1970	9 May	Berlin	1	2
1975	1 Mar	Dublin	1	0†
1979	22 May	Dublin	1	3
1981	21 May	Bremen	0	3†
1989	6 Sept	Dublin	1	1

†*v West Germany 'B'*

		v GIBRALTAR	*RI*	*G*
EC2014	11 Oct	Dublin	7	0
EC2015	4 Sept	Faro	4	0

		v GREECE	*RI*	*G*
2000	26 Apr	Dublin	0	1
2002	20 Nov	Athens	0	0
2012	14 Nov	Dublin	0	1

		v HUNGARY	*RI*	*H*
1934	15 Dec	Dublin	2	4
1936	3 May	Budapest	3	3
1936	6 Dec	Dublin	2	3
1939	19 Mar	Cork	2	2
1939	18 May	Budapest	2	2
wc1969	8 June	Dublin	1	2
wc1969	5 Nov	Budapest	0	4
wc1989	8 Mar	Budapest	0	0
wc1989	4 June	Dublin	2	0
1991	11 Sept	Gyor	2	1
2012	4 June	Budapest	0	0

		v ICELAND	*RI*	*I*
EC1962	12 Aug	Dublin	4	2
EC1962	2 Sept	Reykjavik	1	1
EC1982	13 Oct	Dublin	2	0
EC1983	21 Sept	Reykjavik	3	0
1986	25 May	Reykjavik	2	1
wc1996	10 Nov	Dublin	0	0
wc1997	6 Sept	Reykjavik	4	2
2017	**28 Mar**	**Dublin**	**0**	**1**

		v IRAN	*RI*	*I*
1972	18 June	Recife	2	1
wc2001	10 Nov	Dublin	2	0
wc2001	15 Nov	Tehran	0	1

		v NORTHERN IRELAND	*RI*	*NI*
EC1978	20 Sept	Dublin	0	0
EC1979	21 Nov	Belfast	0	1
wc1988	14 Sept	Belfast	0	0
wc1989	11 Oct	Dublin	3	0
wc1993	31 Mar	Dublin	3	0
wc1993	17 Nov	Belfast	1	1
EC1994	16 Nov	Belfast	4	0
EC1995	29 Mar	Dublin	1	1
1999	29 May	Dublin	0	1
NC2011	24 May	Dublin	5	0

		v ISRAEL	*RI*	*I*
1984	4 Apr	Tel Aviv	0	3
1985	27 May	Tel Aviv	0	0
1987	10 Nov	Dublin	5	0
EC2005	26 Mar	Tel Aviv	1	1
EC2005	4 June	Dublin	2	2

		v ITALY	*RI*	*I*
1926	21 Mar	Turin	0	3
1927	23 Apr	Dublin	1	2
EC1970	8 Dec	Rome	0	3
EC1971	10 May	Dublin	1	2
1985	5 Feb	Dublin	1	2
wc1990	30 June	Rome	0	1
1992	4 June	Foxboro	0	2
wc1994	18 June	New York	1	0
2005	17 Aug	Dublin	1	2
wc2009	1 Apr	Bari	1	1
wc2009	10 Oct	Dublin	2	2
2011	7 June	Liege	2	0
EC2012	18 June	Poznan	0	2
2014	31 May	Craven Cottage	0	0
EC2016	22 June	Lille	1	0

		v JAMAICA	*RI*	*J*
2004	2 June	Charlton	1	0

		v KAZAKHSTAN	*RI*	*K*
wc2012	7 Sept	Astana	2	1
wc2013	15 Oct	Dublin	3	1

		v LATVIA	*RI*	*L*
wc1992	9 Sept	Dublin	4	0
wc1993	2 June	Riga	2	1
EC1994	7 Sept	Riga	3	0
EC1995	11 Oct	Dublin	2	1
2013	15 Nov	Dublin	3	0

		v LIECHTENSTEIN	*RI*	*L*
EC1994	12 Oct	Dublin	4	0
EC1995	3 June	Eschen	0	0
WC1996	31 Aug	Eschen	5	0
WC1997	21 May	Dublin	5	0

		v LITHUANIA	*RI*	*L*
WC1993	16 June	Vilnius	1	0
WC1993	8 Sept	Dublin	2	0
WC1997	20 Aug	Dublin	0	0
WC1997	10 Sept	Vilnius	2	1

		v LUXEMBOURG	*RI*	*L*
1936	9 May	Luxembourg	5	1
WC1953	28 Oct	Dublin	4	0
WC1954	7 Mar	Luxembourg	1	0
EC1987	28 May	Luxembourg	2	0
EC1987	9 Sept	Dublin	2	1

		v MALTA	*RI*	*M*
EC1983	30 Mar	Valletta	1	0
EC1983	16 Nov	Dublin	8	0
WC1989	28 May	Dublin	2	0
WC1989	15 Nov	Valletta	2	0
1990	2 June	Valletta	3	0
EC1998	14 Oct	Dublin	5	0
EC1999	8 Sept	Valletta	3	2

		v MEXICO	*RI*	*M*
1984	8 Aug	Dublin	0	0
WC1994	24 June	Orlando	1	2
1996	13 June	New Jersey	2	2
1998	23 May	Dublin	0	0
2000	4 June	Chicago	2	2
2017	**2 June**	**New Jersey**	**1**	**3**

		v MOLDOVA	*RI*	*M*
WC2016	**9 Oct**	**Chisinau**	**3**	**1**

		v MONTENEGRO	*RI*	*M*
WC2008	10 Sept	Podgorica	0	0
WC2009	14 Oct	Dublin	0	0

		v MOROCCO	*RI*	*M*
1990	12 Sept	Dublin	1	0

		v NETHERLANDS	*RI*	*N*
1932	8 May	Amsterdam	2	0
1934	8 Apr	Amsterdam	2	5
1935	8 Dec	Dublin	3	5
1955	1 May	Dublin	1	0
1956	10 May	Rotterdam	4	1
WC1980	10 Sept	Dublin	2	1
WC1981	9 Sept	Rotterdam	2	2
EC1982	22 Sept	Rotterdam	1	2
EC1983	12 Oct	Dublin	2	3
EC1988	18 June	Gelsenkirchen	0	1
WC1990	21 June	Palermo	1	1
1994	20 Apr	Tilburg	1	0
WC1994	4 July	Orlando	0	2
EC1995	13 Dec	Liverpool	0	2
1996	4 June	Rotterdam	1	3
WC2000	2 Sept	Amsterdam	2	2
WC2001	1 Sept	Dublin	1	0
2004	5 June	Amsterdam	1	0
2006	16 Aug	Dublin	0	4
2016	27 May	Dublin	1	1

		v NIGERIA	*RI*	*N*
2002	16 May	Dublin	1	2
2004	29 May	Charlton	0	3
2009	29 May	Fulham	1	1

		v NORWAY	*RI*	*N*
WC1937	10 Oct	Oslo	2	3
WC1937	7 Nov	Dublin	3	3
1950	26 Nov	Dublin	2	2
1951	30 May	Oslo	3	2
1954	8 Nov	Dublin	2	1
1955	25 May	Oslo	3	1
1960	6 Nov	Dublin	3	1
1964	13 May	Oslo	4	1
1973	6 June	Oslo	1	1
1976	24 Mar	Dublin	3	0
1978	21 May	Oslo	0	0

			RI	*N*
WC1984	17 Oct	Oslo	0	1
WC1985	1 May	Dublin	0	0
1988	1 June	Oslo	0	0
WC1994	28 June	New York	0	0
2003	30 Apr	Dublin	1	0
2008	20 Aug	Oslo	1	1
2010	17 Nov	Dublin	1	2

		v OMAN	*RI*	*O*
2012	11 Sept	London	4	1
2014	3 Sept	Dublin	2	0
2016	**31 Aug**	**Dublin**	**4**	**0**

		v PARAGUAY	*RI*	*P*
1999	10 Feb	Dublin	2	0
2010	25 May	Dublin	2	1

		v POLAND	*RI*	*P*
1938	22 May	Warsaw	0	6
1938	13 Nov	Dublin	3	2
1958	11 May	Katowice	2	2
1958	5 Oct	Dublin	2	2
1964	10 May	Kracow	1	3
1964	25 Oct	Dublin	3	2
1968	15 May	Dublin	2	2
1968	30 Oct	Katowice	0	1
1970	6 May	Dublin	1	2
1970	23 Sept	Dublin	0	2
1973	16 May	Wroclaw	0	2
1973	21 Oct	Dublin	1	0
1976	26 May	Poznan	2	0
1977	24 Apr	Dublin	0	0
1978	12 Apr	Lodz	0	3
1981	23 May	Bydgoszcz	0	3
1984	23 May	Dublin	0	0
1986	12 Nov	Warsaw	0	1
1988	22 May	Dublin	3	1
EC1991	1 May	Dublin	0	0
EC1991	16 Oct	Poznan	3	3
2004	28 Apr	Bydgoszcz	0	0
2013	19 Nov	Poznan	0	0
2008	19 Nov	Dublin	2	3
2013	6 Feb	Dublin	2	0
2013	19 Nov	Poznan	0	0
EC2015	29 Mar	Dublin	1	1
EC2015	11 Oct	Warsaw	1	2

		v PORTUGAL	*RI*	*P*
1946	16 June	Lisbon	1	3
1947	4 May	Dublin	0	2
1948	23 May	Lisbon	0	2
1949	22 May	Dublin	1	0
1972	25 June	Recife	1	2
1992	7 June	Boston	2	0
EC1995	26 Apr	Dublin	1	0
EC1995	15 Nov	Lisbon	0	3
1996	29 May	Dublin	0	1
WC2000	7 Oct	Lisbon	1	1
WC2001	2 June	Dublin	1	1
2005	9 Feb	Dublin	1	0
2014	10 June	New Jersey	1	5

		v ROMANIA	*RI*	*R*
1988	23 Mar	Dublin	2	0
WC1990	25 June	Genoa	0	0*
WC1997	30 Apr	Bucharest	0	1
WC1997	11 Oct	Dublin	1	1
2004	27 May	Dublin	1	0

		v RUSSIA	*RI*	*R*
1994	23 Mar	Dublin	0	0
1996	27 Mar	Dublin	0	2
2002	13 Feb	Dublin	2	0
EC2002	7 Sept	Moscow	2	4
EC2003	6 Sept	Dublin	1	1
EC2010	8 Oct	Dublin	2	3
EC2011	6 Sept	Moscow	0	0

		v SAN MARINO	*RI*	*SM*
EC2006	15 Nov	Dublin	5	0
EC2007	7 Feb	Serravalle	2	1

		v SAUDI ARABIA	*RI*	*SA*
WC2002	11 June	Yokohama	3	0

		v SCOTLAND	*RI*	*S*
WC1961	3 May	Glasgow	1	4
WC1961	7 May	Dublin	0	3
1963	9 June	Dublin	1	0
1969	21 Sept	Dublin	1	1
EC1986	15 Oct	Dublin	0	0
EC1987	18 Feb	Glasgow	1	0
2000	30 May	Dublin	1	2
2003	12 Feb	Glasgow	2	0
NC2011	29 May	Dublin	1	0
EC2014	14 Nov	Hampden	0	1
EC2015	13 June	Dublin	1	1

		v SERBIA	*RI*	*S*
2008	24 May	Dublin	1	1
2012	15 Aug	Belgrade	0	0
2014	5 Mar	Dublin	1	2
WC2016	**5 Sept**	**Belgrade**	**2**	**2**

		v SLOVAKIA	*RI*	*S*
EC2007	28 Mar	Dublin	1	0
EC2007	8 Sept	Bratislava	2	2
EC2010	12 Oct	Zilina	1	1
EC2011	2 Sept	Dublin	0	0
2016	29 Mar	Dublin	2	2

		v SOUTH AFRICA	*RI*	*SA*
2000	11 June	New Jersey	2	1
2009	8 Sept	Limerick	1	0

		v SPAIN	*RI*	*S*
1931	26 Apr	Barcelona	1	1
1931	13 Dec	Dublin	0	5
1946	23 June	Madrid	1	0
1947	2 Mar	Dublin	3	2
1948	30 May	Barcelona	1	2
1949	12 June	Dublin	1	4
1952	1 June	Madrid	0	6
1955	27 Nov	Dublin	2	2
EC1964	11 Mar	Seville	1	5
EC1964	8 Apr	Dublin	0	2
WC1965	5 May	Dublin	1	0
WC1965	27 Oct	Seville	1	4
WC1965	10 Nov	Paris	0	1

		v SPAIN	*RI*	*S*
EC1966	23 Oct	Dublin	0	0
EC1966	7 Dec	Valencia	0	2
1977	9 Feb	Dublin	0	1
EC1982	17 Nov	Dublin	3	3
EC1983	27 Apr	Zaragoza	0	2
1985	26 May	Cork	0	0
WC1988	16 Nov	Seville	0	2
WC1989	26 Apr	Dublin	1	0
WC1992	18 Nov	Seville	0	0
WC1993	13 Oct	Dublin	1	3
WC2002	16 June	Suwon	1	1
EC2012	14 June	Gdansk	0	4
2013	11 June	New York	0	2

		v SWEDEN	*RI*	*S*
WC1949	2 June	Stockholm	1	3
WC1949	13 Nov	Dublin	1	3
1959	1 Nov	Dublin	3	2
1960	18 May	Malmo	1	4
EC1970	14 Oct	Dublin	1	1
EC1970	28 Oct	Malmo	0	1
1999	28 Apr	Dublin	2	0
2006	1 Mar	Dublin	3	0
WC2013	22 Mar	Stockholm	0	0
WC2013	6 Sept	Dublin	1	2
EC2016	13 June	Paris	1	1

		v SWITZERLAND	*RI*	*S*
1935	5 May	Basle	0	1
1936	17 Mar	Dublin	1	0
1937	17 May	Berne	1	0
1938	18 Sept	Dublin	4	0
1948	5 Dec	Dublin	0	1
EC1975	11 May	Dublin	2	1
EC1975	21 May	Berne	0	1
1980	30 Apr	Dublin	2	0
WC1985	2 June	Dublin	3	0
WC1985	11 Sept	Berne	0	0
1992	25 Mar	Dublin	2	1
EC2002	16 Oct	Dublin	1	2
EC2003	11 Oct	Basle	0	2
WC2004	8 Sept	Basle	1	1
WC2005	12 Oct	Dublin	0	0
2016	25 Mar	Dublin	1	0

		v TRINIDAD & TOBAGO	*RI*	*TT*
1982	30 May	Port of Spain	1	2

		v TUNISIA	*RI*	*T*
1988	19 Oct	Dublin	4	0

		v TURKEY	*RI*	*T*
EC1966	16 Nov	Dublin	2	1
EC1967	22 Feb	Ankara	1	2
EC1974	20 Nov	Izmir	1	1
EC1975	29 Oct	Dublin	4	0
2014	25 May	Dublin	1	2
1976	13 Oct	Ankara	3	3
1978	5 Apr	Dublin	4	2
1990	26 May	Izmir	0	0
EC1990	17 Oct	Dublin	5	0
EC1991	13 Nov	Istanbul	3	1
EC2000	13 Nov	Dublin	1	1
EC2000	17 Nov	Bursa	0	0
2003	9 Sept	Dublin	2	2
2014	25 May	Dublin	1	2

		v URUGUAY	*RI*	*U*
1974	8 May	Montevideo	0	2
1986	23 Apr	Dublin	1	1
2011	29 Mar	Dublin	2	3
2017	**4 June**	**Dublin**	**3**	**1**

		v USA	*RI*	*USA*
1979	29 Oct	Dublin	3	2
1991	1 June	Boston	1	1
1992	29 Apr	Dublin	4	1
1992	30 May	Washington	1	3
1996	9 June	Boston	1	2
2000	6 June	Boston	1	1
2002	17 Apr	Dublin	2	1
2014	18 Nov	Dublin	4	1

		v USSR	*RI*	*USSR*
WC1972	18 Oct	Dublin	1	2
WC1973	13 May	Moscow	0	1
EC1974	30 Oct	Dublin	3	0
EC1975	18 May	Kiev	1	2
WC1984	12 Sept	Dublin	1	0
WC1985	16 Oct	Moscow	0	2
EC1988	15 June	Hanover	1	1
1990	25 Apr	Dublin	1	0

		v WALES	*RI*	*W*
1960	28 Sept	Dublin	2	3
1979	11 Sept	Swansea	1	2
1981	24 Feb	Dublin	1	3
1986	26 Mar	Dublin	0	1
1990	28 Mar	Dublin	1	0
1991	6 Feb	Wrexham	3	0
1992	19 Feb	Dublin	0	1
1993	17 Feb	Dublin	2	1
1997	11 Feb	Cardiff	0	0
EC2007	24 Mar	Dublin	1	0
EC2007	17 Nov	Cardiff	2	2
NC2011	8 Feb	Dublin	3	0
2013	14 Aug	Cardiff	0	0
WC2017	**24 Mar**	**Dublin**	**0**	**0**

		v YUGOSLAVIA	*RI*	*Y*
1955	19 Sept	Dublin	1	4
1988	27 Apr	Dublin	2	0
EC1998	18 Nov	Belgrade	0	1
EC1999	1 Sept	Dublin	2	1

OTHER BRITISH AND IRISH INTERNATIONAL MATCHES 2016–17

FRIENDLIES

■ *Denotes player sent off.*

ENGLAND

Tuesday, 15 November 2016

England (1) 2 *(Lallana 9 (pen), Vardy 48)*

Spain (0) 2 *(Aspas 89, Isco 90)* 83,716

England: (4231) Hart (Heaton 46); Clyne, Stones, Cahill (Jagielka 46), Rose (Cresswell 79); Dier, Henderson; Sterling (Townsend 65), Lallana (Walcott 26), Lingard; Vardy (Rashford 67).
Spain: (433) Reina; Carvajal, Martinez, Nacho, Azpilicueta; Mata (Koke 46), Busquets (Nolito 78), Thiago (Ander Herrera 56); Silva (Isco 63), Aduriz (Morata 63), Vitolo (Aspas 46).
Referee: Ovidiu Alin Hategan.

Wednesday, 22 March 2017

Germany (0) 1 *(Podolski 69)*

England (0) 0 60,109

Germany: (4231) ter Stegen; Kimmich, Rudiger, Hummels, Hector; Weigl (Can 66), Kroos; Brandt (Schurrle 59), Podolski (Rudy 84), Sane; Werner (Muller 77).
England: (3421) Hart; Keane, Cahill, Smalling (Stones 85); Walker, Livermore (Ward-Prowse 82), Dier, Bertrand (Shaw 83); Alli (Lingard 71), Lallana (Redmond 66); Vardy (Rashford 70).
Referee: Damir Skomina.

Tuesday, 13 June 2017

France (2) 3 *(Umtiti 22, Sidibe 43, Dembele 78)*

England (1) 2 *(Kane 9, 48 (pen))* 80,000

France: (442) Lloris; Mendy (Digne 21), Umtiti, Varane■, Sidibe (Jallet 89); Lemar, Pogba, Kante, Dembele; Mbappe-Lottin, Giroud (Koscielny 52).
England: (4231) Heaton (Butland 46); Trippier (Lallana 76), Jones (Cresswell 81), Cahill, Bertrand (Walker 46); Stones, Dier; Sterling, Alli, Oxlade-Chamberlain; Kane.
Referee: Davide Massa.

SCOTLAND

Wednesday, 22 March 2017

Scotland (1) 1 *(Naismith 35)*

Canada (1) 1 *(Aird 11)* 9158

Scotland: (4411) McGregor; Anya, Berra, Mulgrew, Wallace (Robertson 46); Burke (Bannan 46), Fletcher D, Cairney (McGinn 76), Naismith (Rhodes 62); Snodgrass; Martin C (Griffiths 62).
Canada: (4231) Thomas (Leutwiler 46); Ledgerwood, Straith, James, Tissot (Corbin-Ong 67); Arfield (Trafford 90), Piette; Aird, Bustos, Jackson (Fisk 76); Hoilett.
Referee: Jakob Kehlet.

NORTHERN IRELAND

Tuesday, 15 November 2016

Northern Ireland (0) 0

Croatia (2) 3 *(Mandzukic 9, Cop 34, Kramaric 68)* 17,000

Northern Ireland: (433) Mannus; McAuley (Davis 46), McNair, Evans J, Hodson; Brunt (McLaughlin 46), Lund (McGivern 46), Magennis (Lafferty K 55); Norwood, Boyce (Grigg 68), McGinn (Paton 62).
Croatia: (433) Kalinic (Vargic 82); Jedvaj, Leovac, Vida (Vrsaljko 59), Mitrovic; Badelj (Brozovic 51), Bradaric, Rog (Pivaric 87); Cop, Kramaric, Mandzukic (Coric 72).
Referee: Mark Clattenburg.

Friday, 2 June 2017

Northern Ireland (1) 1 *(Boyce 6)*

New Zealand (0) 0 16,815

Northern Ireland: (442) McGovern (Carroll 83); McLaughlin, Hughes, Flanagan, Evans J; Norwood, Brunt (Ferguson 48), Lund (Lafferty K 48), Dallas (Paton 74); Magennis (McCartan 83), Boyce (Davis 48).
New Zealand: (442) Marinovic; Boxall, Colvey (Barbarouses 63), Doyle (Wynne 72), Durante; Smith, Lewis (Tuiloma 46), McGlinchey, Rojas (Patterson 63); Thomas (Smeltz 79), Wood.
Referee: Laurent Kopriwa.

REPUBLIC OF IRELAND

Wednesday, 31 August 2016

Republic of Ireland (3) 4 *(Brady 7, Keane 29, Walters 34, 63)*

Oman (0) 0 27,000

Republic of Ireland: (433) Westwood (Randolph 46); Christie, Wilson, Clark, Brady (Ward 46); Quinn (O'Dowda 65), Whelan (Hendrick 46), Arter; Long S (McClean 46), Keane (Hoolahan 57), Walters.
Oman: (4411) Al-Rushaidi; Mabrook M (Al Saadi 47), Amur, Mabrook N, Abdulsalam (Al-Amri 59); Al Hadri (Al Yaqoobi 75), Al-Yahaya, Al-Sheyadi, Saleh; Al Khaldi (Mohammed 59); Al Muqbali.
Referee: Demetris Masias.

Tuesday, 28 March 2017

Republic of Ireland (0) 0

Iceland (1) 1 *(Magnusson 21)* 37,241

Republic of Ireland: (451) Westwood; Christie, Pearce, Egan (Boyle 63), Brady; McGeady (O'Dowda 72), Hendrick (Gleeson 63), Hourihane (O'Kane 63), Hayes (Horgan 62), McClean (Long S 72); Doyle.
Iceland: (442) Kristinsson; Saevarsson (Jonsson 85), Skulason O (Smarason 79), Ingason, Sigurdsson R (Eyjolfsson 52); Magnusson, Gislason (Skulason A 88), Gunnarsson, Sigurdarson (Omarsson 65); Finnbogason (Karlsson 71), Bodvarsson.
Referee: Jakob Kehlet.

Friday, 2 June 2017

Mexico (2) 3 *(Corona 16, Jimenez 25 (pen), Vela 54)*

Republic of Ireland (0) 1 *(Gleeson 77)* 42,017

Mexico: (433) Cota; Corona (Aquino 58), Gallardo, Jorge Hernandez, Herrera (Peralta 46); Jimenez, Jonathan (Pineda 58), Moreno (Alanis 46); Reyes, Salcedo (Layun 47), Vela (Marquez 68).
Republic of Ireland: (352) Randolph; Duffy, Keogh, Egan (Long K 64); Christie (Browne 73), Hourihane (O'Kane 64), Horgan (Gleeson 73), O'Dowda, McClean; Murphy (Hoolahan 64), McGoldrick.
Referee: Ted Unkel.

Sunday, 4 June 2017

Republic of Ireland (1) 3 *(Walters 28, Christie 52, McClean 78)*

Uruguay (1) 1 *(Gimenez 39)* 27,193

Republic of Ireland: (433) Randolph (Westwood 46); Christie, Long K, Duffy (Pearce 62), Ward; Hendrick (McClean 75), Whelan (Hoolahan 46), Arter; Hayes (McGeady 62), Walters (Murphy 63), Brady.
Uruguay: (352) Conde; Pereira (Ricca 64), Coates, Caceres; Gimenez, Rios (Gonzalez 46), Sanchez (Nandez 46), Vecino, Laxalt (Silva 46); Urreta, Cavani (Stuani 14).
Referee: Craig Thomson.

BRITISH AND IRISH INTERNATIONAL MANAGERS

England

Walter Winterbottom 1946–1962 (after period as coach); Alf Ramsey 1963–1974; Joe Mercer (caretaker) 1974; Don Revie 1974–1977; Ron Greenwood 1977–1982; Bobby Robson 1982–1990; Graham Taylor 1990–1993; Terry Venables (coach) 1994–1996; Glenn Hoddle 1996–1999; Kevin Keegan 1999–2000; Sven-Goran Eriksson 2001–2006; Steve McClaren 2006–2007; Fabio Capello 2008–2012; Roy Hodgson 2012–2016; Sam Allardyce 2016 for one match; Gareth Southgate from November 2016.

Northern Ireland

Peter Doherty 1951–1952; Bertie Peacock 1962–1967; Billy Bingham 1967–1971; Terry Neill 1971–1975; Dave Clements (player-manager) 1975–1976; Danny Blanchflower 1976–1979; Billy Bingham 1980–1994; Bryan Hamilton 1994–1998; Lawrie McMenemy 1998–1999; Sammy McIlroy 2000–2003; Lawrie Sanchez 2004–2007; Nigel Worthington 2007–2011; Michael O'Neill from December 2011.

Scotland (since 1967)

Bobby Brown 1967–1971; Tommy Docherty 1971–1972; Willie Ormond 1973–1977; Ally MacLeod 1977–1978; Jock Stein 1978–1985; Alex Ferguson (caretaker) 1985–1986 Andy Roxburgh (coach) 1986–1993; Craig Brown 1993–2001; Berti Vogts 2002–2004; Walter Smith 2004–2007; Alex McLeish 2007; George Burley 2008–2009; Craig Levein 2009–2012; Gordon Strachan from February 2013.

Wales (since 1974)

Mike Smith 1974–1979; Mike England 1980–1988; David Williams (caretaker) 1988; Terry Yorath 1988–1993; John Toshack 1994 for one match; Mike Smith 1994–1995; Bobby Gould 1995–1999; Mark Hughes 1999–2004; John Toshack 2004–2010; Gary Speed 2010–2011; Chris Coleman from January 2012.

Republic of Ireland

Liam Tuohy 1971–1972; Johnny Giles 1973–1980 (after period as player-manager); Eoin Hand 1980–1985; Jack Charlton 1986–1996; Mick McCarthy 1996–2002; Brian Kerr 2003–2006; Steve Staunton 2006–2007; Giovanni Trapattoni 2008–2013; Martin O'Neill from November 2013.

Gareth Southgate, England manager.

BRITISH AND IRISH INTERNATIONAL APPEARANCES 1872–2017

This is a list of full international appearances by Englishmen, Irishmen, Scotsmen and Welshmen in matches against the Home Countries and against foreign nations. It does not include unofficial matches against Commonwealth and Empire countries. The year indicated refers to the player's international debut season; i.e. 2017 is the 2016–17 season. **Bold** type indicates players who have made an international appearance in season 2016–17.

As at July 2017.

ENGLAND

Abbott, W. 1902 (Everton) 1
A'Court, A. 1958 (Liverpool) 5
Adams, T. A. 1987 (Arsenal) 66
Adcock, H. 1929 (Leicester C) 5
Agbonlahor, G. 2009 (Aston Villa) 3
Alcock, C. W. 1875 (Wanderers) 1
Alderson, J. T. 1923 (Crystal Palace) 1
Aldridge, A. 1888 (WBA, Walsall Town Swifts) 2
Allen, A. 1888 (Aston Villa) 1
Allen, A. 1960 (Stoke C) 3
Allen, C. 1984 (QPR, Tottenham H) 5
Allen, H. 1888 (Wolverhampton W) 5
Allen, J. P. 1934 (Portsmouth) 2
Allen, R. 1952 (WBA) 5
Alli, B. J. (Dele) 2016 (Tottenham H) 19
Alsford, W. J. 1935 (Tottenham H) 1
Amos, A. 1885 (Old Carthusians) 2
Anderson, R. D. 1879 (Old Etonians) 1
Anderson, S. 1962 (Sunderland) 2
Anderson, V. A. 1979 (Nottingham F, Arsenal, Manchester U) 30
Anderton, D. R. 1994 (Tottenham H) 30
Angus, J. 1961 (Burnley) 1
Armfield, J. C. 1959 (Blackpool) 43
Armitage, G. H. 1926 (Charlton Ath) 1
Armstrong, D. 1980 (Middlesbrough, Southampton) 3
Armstrong, K. 1955 (Chelsea) 1
Arnold, J. 1933 (Fulham) 1
Arthur, J. W. H. 1885 (Blackburn R) 7
Ashcroft, J. 1906 (Woolwich Arsenal) 3
Ashmore, G. S. 1926 (WBA) 1
Ashton, C. T. 1926 (Corinthians) 1
Ashton, D. 2008 (West Ham U) 1
Ashurst, W. 1923 (Notts Co) 5
Astall, G. 1956 (Birmingham C) 2
Astle, J. 1969 (WBA) 5
Aston, J. 1949 (Manchester U) 17
Athersmith, W. C. 1892 (Aston Villa) 12
Atyeo, P. J. W. 1956 (Bristol C) 6
Austin, S. W. 1926 (Manchester C) 1

Bach, P. 1899 (Sunderland) 1
Bache, J. W. 1903 (Aston Villa) 7
Baddeley, T. 1903 (Wolverhampton W) 5
Bagshaw, J. J. 1920 (Derby Co) 1
Bailey, G. R. 1985 (Manchester U) 2
Bailey, H. P. 1908 (Leicester Fosse) 5
Bailey, M. A. 1964 (Charlton Ath) 2
Bailey, N. C. 1878 (Clapham R) 19
Baily, E. F. 1950 (Tottenham H) 9
Bain, J. 1877 (Oxford University) 1
Baines, L. J. 2010 (Everton) 30
Baker, A. 1928 (Arsenal) 1
Baker, B. H. 1921 (Everton, Chelsea) 2
Baker, J. H. 1960 (Hibernian, Arsenal) 8
Ball, A. J. 1965 (Blackpool, Everton, Arsenal) 72
Ball, J. 1928 (Bury) 1
Ball, M. J. 2001 (Everton) 1
Balmer, W. 1905 (Everton) 1
Bamber, J. 1921 (Liverpool) 1
Bambridge, A. L. 1881 (Swifts) 3
Bambridge, E. C. 1879 (Swifts) 18
Bambridge, E. H. 1876 (Swifts) 1
Banks, G. 1963 (Leicester C, Stoke C) 73
Banks, H. E. 1901 (Millwall) 1
Banks, T. 1958 (Bolton W) 6
Bannister, W. 1901 (Burnley, Bolton W) 2
Barclay, R. 1932 (Sheffield U) 3
Bardsley, D. J. 1993 (QPR) 2
Barham, M. 1983 (Norwich C) 2
Barkas, S. 1936 (Manchester C) 5
Barker, J. 1935 (Derby Co) 11
Barker, R. 1872 (Herts Rangers) 1
Barker, R. R. 1895 (Casuals) 1
Barkley, R. 2013 (Everton) 22
Barlow, R. J. 1955 (WBA) 1
Barmby, N. J. 1995 (Tottenham H, Middlesbrough, Everton, Liverpool) 23
Barnes, J. 1983 (Watford, Liverpool) 79
Barnes, P. S. 1978 (Manchester C, WBA, Leeds U) 22
Barnet, H. H. 1882 (Royal Engineers) 1
Barrass, M. W. 1952 (Bolton W) 3
Barrett, A. F. 1930 (Fulham) 1
Barrett, E. D. 1991 (Oldham Ath, Aston Villa) 3
Barrett, J. W. 1929 (West Ham U) 1
Barry, G. 2000 (Aston Villa, Manchester C) 53
Barry, L. 1928 (Leicester C) 5
Barson, F. 1920 (Aston Villa) 1
Barton, J. 1890 (Blackburn R) 1
Barton, J. 2007 (Manchester C) 1
Barton, P. H. 1921 (Birmingham) 7
Barton, W. D. 1995 (Wimbledon, Newcastle U) 3
Bassett, W. I. 1888 (WBA) 16
Bastard, S. R. 1880 (Upton Park) 1
Bastin, C. S. 1932 (Arsenal) 21
Batty, D. 1991 (Leeds U, Blackburn R, Newcastle U, Leeds U) 42
Baugh, R. 1886 (Stafford Road, Wolverhampton W) 2
Bayliss, A. E. J. M. 1891 (WBA) 1
Baynham, R. L. 1956 (Luton T) 3
Beardsley, P. A. 1986 (Newcastle U, Liverpool, Newcastle U) 59
Beasant, D. J. 1990 (Chelsea) 2
Beasley, A. 1939 (Huddersfield T) 1
Beats, W. E. 1901 (Wolverhampton W) 2
Beattie, J. S. 2003 (Southampton) 5
Beattie, T. K. 1975 (Ipswich T) 9
Beckham, D. R. J. 1997 (Manchester U, Real Madrid, LA Galaxy) 115
Becton, F. 1895 (Preston NE, Liverpool) 2
Bedford, H. 1923 (Blackpool) 2
Bell, C. 1968 (Manchester C) 48
Bennett, W. 1901 (Sheffield U) 2
Benson, R. W. 1913 (Sheffield U) 1
Bent, D. A. 2006 (Charlton Ath, Tottenham H, Sunderland, Aston Villa) 13
Bentley, D. M. 2008 (Blackburn R, Tottenham H) 7
Bentley, R. T. F. 1949 (Chelsea) 12
Beresford, J. 1934 (Aston Villa) 1
Berry, A. 1909 (Oxford University) 1
Berry, J. J. 1953 (Manchester U) 4
Bertrand, R. 2013 (Chelsea, Southampton) 14
Bestall, J. G. 1935 (Grimsby T) 1
Betmead, H. A. 1937 (Grimsby T) 1
Betts, M. P. 1877 (Old Harrovians) 1
Betts, W. 1889 (Sheffield W) 1
Beverley, J. 1884 (Blackburn R) 3
Birkett, R. H. 1879 (Clapham R) 1
Birkett, R. J. E. 1936 (Middlesbrough) 1
Birley, F. H. 1874 (Oxford University, Wanderers) 2
Birtles, G. 1980 (Nottingham F) 3
Bishop, S. M. 1927 (Leicester C) 4
Blackburn, F. 1901 (Blackburn R) 3
Blackburn, G. F. 1924 (Aston Villa) 1
Blenkinsop, E. 1928 (Sheffield W) 26
Bliss, H. 1921 (Tottenham H) 1
Blissett, L. L. 1983 (Watford, AC Milan) 14
Blockley, J. P. 1973 (Arsenal) 1
Bloomer, S. 1895 (Derby Co, Middlesbrough) 23
Blunstone, F. 1955 (Chelsea) 5

Bond, R. 1905 (Preston NE, Bradford C) 8
Bonetti, P. P. 1966 (Chelsea) 7
Bonsor, A. G. 1873 (Wanderers) 2
Booth, F. 1905 (Manchester C) 1
Booth, T. 1898 (Blackburn R, Everton) 2
Bothroyd, J. 2011 (Cardiff C) 1
Bould, S. A. 1994 (Arsenal) 2
Bowden, E. R. 1935 (Arsenal) 6
Bower, A. G. 1924 (Corinthians) 5
Bowers, J. W. 1934 (Derby Co) 3
Bowles, S. 1974 (QPR) 5
Bowser, S. 1920 (WBA) 1
Bowyer, L. D. 2003 (Leeds U) 1
Boyer, P. J. 1976 (Norwich C) 1
Boyes, W. 1935 (WBA, Everton) 3
Boyle, T. W. 1913 (Burnley) 1
Brabrook, P. 1958 (Chelsea) 3
Bracewell, P. W. 1985 (Everton) 3
Bradford, G. R. W. 1956 (Bristol R) 1
Bradford, J. 1924 (Birmingham) 12
Bradley, W. 1959 (Manchester U) 3
Bradshaw, F. 1908 (Sheffield W) 1
Bradshaw, T. H. 1897 (Liverpool) 1
Bradshaw, W. 1910 (Blackburn R) 4
Brann, G. 1886 (Swifts) 3
Brawn, W. F. 1904 (Aston Villa) 2
Bray, J. 1935 (Manchester C) 6
Brayshaw, E. 1887 (Sheffield W) 1
Bridge W. M. 2002 (Southampton, Chelsea, Manchester C) 36
Bridges, B. J. 1965 (Chelsea) 4
Bridgett, A. 1905 (Sunderland) 11
Brindle, T. 1880 (Darwen) 2
Brittleton, J. T. 1912 (Sheffield W) 5
Britton, C. S. 1935 (Everton) 9
Broadbent, P. F. 1958 (Wolverhampton W) 7
Broadis, I. A. 1952 (Manchester C, Newcastle U) 14
Brockbank, J. 1872 (Cambridge University) 1
Brodie, J. B. 1889 (Wolverhampton W) 3
Bromilow, T. G. 1921 (Liverpool) 5
Bromley-Davenport, W. E. 1884 (Oxford University) 2
Brook, E. F. 1930 (Manchester C) 18
Brooking, T. D. 1974 (West Ham U) 47
Brooks, J. 1957 (Tottenham H) 3
Broome, F. H. 1938 (Aston Villa) 7
Brown, A. 1882 (Aston Villa) 3
Brown, A. 1971 (WBA) 1
Brown, A. S. 1904 (Sheffield U) 2
Brown, G. 1927 (Huddersfield T, Aston Villa) 9
Brown, J. 1881 (Blackburn R) 5
Brown, J. H. 1927 (Sheffield W) 6
Brown, K. 1960 (West Ham U) 1
Brown, W. 1924 (West Ham U) 1
Brown, W. M. 1999 (Manchester U) 23
Bruton, J. 1928 (Burnley) 3
Bryant, W. I. 1925 (Clapton) 1
Buchan, C. M. 1913 (Sunderland) 6
Buchanan, W. S. 1876 (Clapham R) 1
Buckley, F. C. 1914 (Derby Co) 1
Bull, S. G. 1989 (Wolverhampton W) 13
Bullock, F. E. 1921 (Huddersfield T) 1
Bullock, N. 1923 (Bury) 3
Burgess, H. 1904 (Manchester C) 4
Burgess, H. 1931 (Sheffield W) 4
Burnup, C. J. 1896 (Cambridge University) 1
Burrows, H. 1934 (Sheffield W) 3
Burton, F. E. 1889 (Nottingham F) 1
Bury, L. 1877 (Cambridge University, Old Etonians) 2
Butcher, T. 1980 (Ipswich T, Rangers) 77
Butland, J. 2013 (Birmingham C, Stoke C) 5
Butler, J. D. 1925 (Arsenal) 1
Butler, W. 1924 (Bolton W) 1
Butt, N. 1997 (Manchester U, Newcastle U) 39
Byrne, G. 1963 (Liverpool) 2
Byrne, J. J. 1962 (Crystal Palace, West Ham U) 11
Byrne, R. W. 1954 (Manchester U) 33

Cahill, G. J. 2011 (Bolton W, Chelsea) 55
Callaghan, I. R. 1966 (Liverpool) 4
Calvey, J. 1902 (Nottingham F) 1
Campbell, A. F. 1929 (Blackburn R, Huddersfield T) 8
Campbell, F. L. 2012 (Sunderland) 1
Campbell, S. 1996 (Tottenham H, Arsenal, Portsmouth) 73
Camsell, G. H. 1929 (Middlesbrough) 9
Capes, A. J. 1903 (Stoke) 1
Carr, J. 1905 (Newcastle U) 2
Carr, J. 1920 (Middlesbrough) 2
Carr, W. H. 1875 (Owlerton, Sheffield) 1
Carragher, J. L. 1999 (Liverpool) 38
Carrick, M. 2001 (West Ham U, Tottenham H, Manchester U) 34
Carroll, A. T. 2011 (Newcastle U, Liverpool) 9
Carson, S. P. 2008 (Liverpool, WBA) 4
Carter, H. S. 1934 (Sunderland, Derby Co) 13
Carter, J. H. 1926 (WBA) 3
Catlin, A. E. 1937 (Sheffield W) 5
Caulker, S. A. 2013 (Tottenham H) 1
Chadwick, A. 1900 (Southampton) 2
Chadwick, E. 1891 (Everton) 7
Chamberlain, M. 1983 (Stoke C) 8
Chambers, H. 1921 (Liverpool) 8
Chambers, C. 2015 (Arsenal) 3
Channon, M. R. 1973 (Southampton, Manchester C) 46
Charles, G. A. 1991 (Nottingham F) 2
Charlton, J. 1965 (Leeds U) 35
Charlton, R. 1958 (Manchester U) 106
Charnley, R. O. 1963 (Blackpool) 1
Charsley, C. C. 1893 (Small Heath) 1
Chedgzoy, S. 1920 (Everton) 8
Chenery, C. J. 1872 (Crystal Palace) 3
Cherry, T. J. 1976 (Leeds U) 27
Chilton, A. 1951 (Manchester U) 2
Chippendale, H. 1894 (Blackburn R) 1
Chivers, M. 1971 (Tottenham H) 24
Christian, E. 1879 (Old Etonians) 1
Clamp, E. 1958 (Wolverhampton W) 4
Clapton, D. R. 1959 (Arsenal) 1
Clare, T. 1889 (Stoke) 4
Clarke, A. J. 1970 (Leeds U) 19
Clarke, H. A. 1954 (Tottenham H) 1
Clay, T. 1920 (Tottenham H) 4
Clayton, R. 1956 (Blackburn R) 35
Clegg, J. C. 1872 (Sheffield W) 1
Clegg, W. E. 1873 (Sheffield W, Sheffield Alb) 2
Clemence, R. N. 1973 (Liverpool, Tottenham H) 61
Clement, D. T. 1976 (QPR) 5
Cleverley, T. W. 2013 (Manchester U) 13
Clough, B. H. 1960 (Middlesbrough) 2
Clough, N. H. 1989 (Nottingham F) 14
Clyne, N. E. 2015 (Southampton, Liverpool) 14
Coates, R. 1970 (Burnley, Tottenham H) 4
Cobbold, W. N. 1883 (Cambridge University, Old Carthusians) 9
Cock, J. G. 1920 (Huddersfield T, Chelsea) 2
Cockburn, H. 1947 (Manchester U) 13
Cohen, G. R. 1964 (Fulham) 37
Cole, A. 2001 (Arsenal, Chelsea) 107
Cole, A. A. 1995 (Manchester U) 15
Cole, C. 2009 (West Ham U) 7
Cole, J. J. 2001 (West Ham U, Chelsea) 56
Colclough, H. 1914 (Crystal Palace) 1
Coleman, E. H. 1921 (Dulwich Hamlet) 1
Coleman, J. 1907 (Woolwich Arsenal) 1
Collymore, S. V. 1995 (Nottingham F, Aston Villa) 3
Common, A. 1904 (Sheffield U, Middlesbrough) 3
Compton, L. H. 1951 (Arsenal) 2
Conlin, J. 1906 (Bradford C) 1
Connelly, J. M. 1960 (Burnley, Manchester U) 20
Cook, T. E. R. 1925 (Brighton) 1
Cooper, C. T. 1995 (Nottingham F) 2
Cooper, N. C. 1893 (Cambridge University) 1
Cooper, T. 1928 (Derby Co) 15
Cooper, T. 1969 (Leeds U) 20
Coppell, S. J. 1978 (Manchester U) 42
Copping, W. 1933 (Leeds U, Arsenal, Leeds U) 20
Corbett, B. O. 1901 (Corinthians) 1
Corbett, R. 1903 (Old Malvernians) 1
Corbett, W. S. 1908 (Birmingham) 3
Corrigan, J. T. 1976 (Manchester C) 9
Cottee, A. R. 1987 (West Ham U, Everton) 7
Cotterill, G. H. 1891 (Cambridge University, Old Brightonians) 4
Cottle, J. R. 1909 (Bristol C) 1
Cowan, S. 1926 (Manchester C) 3
Cowans, G. S. 1983 (Aston Villa, Bari, Aston Villa) 10
Cowell, A. 1910 (Blackburn R) 1
Cox, J. 1901 (Liverpool) 3

Cox, J. D. 1892 (Derby Co) 1
Crabtree, J. W. 1894 (Burnley, Aston Villa) 14
Crawford, J. F. 1931 (Chelsea) 1
Crawford, R. 1962 (Ipswich T) 2
Crawshaw, T. H. 1895 (Sheffield W) 10
Crayston, W. J. 1936 (Arsenal) 8
Creek, F. N. S. 1923 (Corinthians) 1
Cresswell, A. W. 2017 (West Ham U) 2
Cresswell, W. 1921 (South Shields, Sunderland, Everton) 7
Crompton, R. 1902 (Blackburn R) 41
Crooks, S. D. 1930 (Derby Co) 26
Crouch, P. J. 2005 (Southampton, Liverpool, Portsmouth, Tottenham H) 42
Crowe, C. 1963 (Wolverhampton W) 1
Cuggy, F. 1913 (Sunderland) 2
Cullis, S. 1938 (Wolverhampton W) 12
Cunliffe, A. 1933 (Blackburn R) 2
Cunliffe, D. 1900 (Portsmouth) 1
Cunliffe, J. N. 1936 (Everton) 1
Cunningham, L. 1979 (WBA, Real Madrid) 6
Curle, K. 1992 (Manchester C) 3
Currey, E. S. 1890 (Oxford University) 2
Currie, A. W. 1972 (Sheffield U, Leeds U) 17
Cursham, A. W. 1876 (Notts Co) 6
Cursham, H. A. 1880 (Notts Co) 8

Daft, H. B. 1889 (Notts Co) 5
Daley, A. M. 1992 (Aston Villa) 7
Danks, T. 1885 (Nottingham F) 1
Davenport, P. 1985 (Nottingham F) 1
Davenport, J. K. 1885 (Bolton W) 2
Davies, K. C. 2011 (Bolton W) 1
Davis, G. 1904 (Derby Co) 2
Davis, H. 1903 (Sheffield W) 3
Davison, J. E. 1922 (Sheffield W) 1
Dawson, J. 1922 (Burnley) 2
Dawson, M. R. 2011 (Tottenham H) 4
Day, S. H. 1906 (Old Malvernians) 3
Dean, W. R. 1927 (Everton) 16
Deane, B. C. 1991 (Sheffield U) 3
Deeley, N. V. 1959 (Wolverhampton W) 2
Defoe, J. C. 2004 (Tottenham H, Portsmouth, Tottenham H, Sunderland) 57
Delph, F. 2015 (Aston Villa, Manchester C) 9
Devey, J. H. G. 1892 (Aston Villa) 2
Devonshire, A. 1980 (West Ham U) 8
Dewhurst, F. 1886 (Preston NE) 9
Dewhurst, G. P. 1895 (Liverpool Ramblers) 1
Dickinson, J. W. 1949 (Portsmouth) 48
Dier, E. J. E. 2016 (Tottenham H) 19
Dimmock, J. H. 1921 (Tottenham H) 3
Ditchburn, E. G. 1949 (Tottenham H) 6
Dix, R. W. 1939 (Derby Co) 1
Dixon, J. A. 1885 (Notts Co) 1
Dixon, K. M. 1985 (Chelsea) 8
Dixon, L. M. 1990 (Arsenal) 22
Dobson, A. T. C. 1882 (Notts Co) 4
Dobson, C. F. 1886 (Notts Co) 1
Dobson, J. M. 1974 (Burnley, Everton) 5
Doggart, A. G. 1924 (Corinthians) 1
Dorigo, A. R. 1990 (Chelsea, Leeds U) 15
Dorrell, A. R. 1925 (Aston Villa) 4
Douglas, B. 1958 (Blackburn R) 36
Downing, S. 2005 (Middlesbrough, Aston Villa, Liverpool, West Ham U) 35
Downs, R. W. 1921 (Everton) 1
Doyle, M. 1976 (Manchester C) 5
Drake, E. J. 1935 (Arsenal) 5
Drinkwater, D. N. 2016 (Leicester C) 3
Dublin, D. 1998 (Coventry C, Aston Villa) 4
Ducat, A. 1910 (Woolwich Arsenal, Aston Villa) 6
Dunn, A. T. B. 1883 (Cambridge University, Old Etonians) 4
Dunn, D. J. I. 2003 (Blackburn R) 1
Duxbury, M. 1984 (Manchester U) 10
Dyer, K. C. 2000 (Newcastle U, West Ham U) 33

Earle, S. G. J. 1924 (Clapton, West Ham U) 2
Eastham, G. 1963 (Arsenal) 19
Eastham, G. R. 1935 (Bolton W) 1
Eckersley, W. 1950 (Blackburn R) 17
Edwards, D. 1955 (Manchester U) 18
Edwards, J. H. 1874 (Shropshire Wanderers) 1
Edwards, W. 1926 (Leeds U) 16
Ehiogu, U. 1996 (Aston Villa, Middlesbrough) 4
Ellerington, W. 1949 (Southampton) 2
Elliott, G. W. 1913 (Middlesbrough) 3
Elliott, W. H. 1952 (Burnley) 5
Evans, R. E. 1911 (Sheffield U) 4
Ewer, F. H. 1924 (Casuals) 2

Fairclough, P. 1878 (Old Foresters) 1
Fairhurst, D. 1934 (Newcastle U) 1
Fantham, J. 1962 (Sheffield W) 1
Fashanu, J. 1989 (Wimbledon) 2
Felton, W. 1925 (Sheffield W) 1
Fenton, M. 1938 (Middlesbrough) 1
Fenwick, T. W. 1984 (QPR, Tottenham H) 20
Ferdinand, L. 1993 (QPR, Newcastle U, Tottenham H) 17
Ferdinand, R. G. 1998 (West Ham U, Leeds U, Manchester U) 81
Field, E. 1876 (Clapham R) 2
Finney, T. 1947 (Preston NE) 76
Flanagan, J. P. 2014 (Liverpool) 1
Fleming, H. J. 1909 (Swindon T) 11
Fletcher, A. 1889 (Wolverhampton W) 2
Flowers, R. 1955 (Wolverhampton W) 49
Flowers, T. D. 1993 (Southampton, Blackburn R) 11
Forman, Frank 1898 (Nottingham F) 9
Forman, F. R. 1899 (Nottingham F) 3
Forrest, J. H. 1884 (Blackburn R) 11
Forster, F. G. 2013 (Celtic, Southampton) 6
Fort, J. 1921 (Millwall) 1
Foster, B. 2007 (Manchester U, Birmingham C, WBA) 8
Foster, R. E. 1900 (Oxford University, Corinthians) 5
Foster, S. 1982 (Brighton & HA) 3
Foulke, W. J. 1897 (Sheffield U) 1
Foulkes, W. A. 1955 (Manchester U) 1
Fowler, R. B. 1996 (Liverpool, Leeds U) 26
Fox, F. S. 1925 (Millwall) 1
Francis, G. C. J. 1975 (QPR) 12
Francis, T. 1977 (Birmingham C, Nottingham F, Manchester C, Sampdoria) 52
Franklin, C. F. 1947 (Stoke C) 27
Freeman, B. C. 1909 (Everton, Burnley) 5
Froggatt, J. 1950 (Portsmouth) 13
Froggatt, R. 1953 (Sheffield W) 4
Fry, C. B. 1901 (Corinthians) 1
Furness, W. I. 1933 (Leeds U) 1

Galley, T. 1937 (Wolverhampton W) 2
Gardner, A. 2004 (Tottenham H) 1
Gardner, T. 1934 (Aston Villa) 2
Garfield, B. 1898 (WBA) 1
Garraty, W. 1903 (Aston Villa) 1
Garrett, T. 1952 (Blackpool) 3
Gascoigne, P. J. 1989 (Tottenham H, Lazio, Rangers, Middlesbrough) 57
Gates, E. 1981 (Ipswich T) 2
Gay, L. H. 1893 (Cambridge University, Old Brightonians) 3
Geary, F. 1890 (Everton) 2
Geaves, R. L. 1875 (Clapham R) 1
Gee, C. W. 1932 (Everton) 3
Geldard, A. 1933 (Everton) 4
George, C. 1977 (Derby Co) 1
George, W. 1902 (Aston Villa) 3
Gerrard, S. G. 2000 (Liverpool) 114
Gibbins, W. V. T. 1924 (Clapton) 2
Gibbs, K. J. R. 2011 (Arsenal) 10
Gidman, J. 1977 (Aston Villa) 1
Gillard, I. T. 1975 (QPR) 3
Gilliat, W. E. 1893 (Old Carthusians) 1
Goddard, P. 1982 (West Ham U) 1
Goodall, F. R. 1926 (Huddersfield T) 25
Goodall, J. 1888 (Preston NE, Derby Co) 14
Goodhart, H. C. 1883 (Old Etonians) 3
Goodwyn, A. G. 1873 (Royal Engineers) 1
Goodyer, A. C. 1879 (Nottingham F) 1
Gosling, R. C. 1892 (Old Etonians) 5
Gosnell, A. A. 1906 (Newcastle U) 1
Gough, H. C. 1921 (Sheffield U) 1
Goulden, L. A. 1937 (West Ham U) 14
Graham, L. 1925 (Millwall) 2
Graham, T. 1931 (Nottingham F) 2
Grainger, C. 1956 (Sheffield U, Sunderland) 7
Gray, A. A. 1992 (Crystal Palace) 1
Gray, M. 1999 (Sunderland) 3

Greaves, J. 1959 (Chelsea, Tottenham H) 57
Green, F. T. 1876 (Wanderers) 1
Green, G. H. 1925 (Sheffield U) 8
Green, R. P. 2005 (Norwich C, West Ham U) 12
Greenhalgh, E. H. 1872 (Notts Co) 2
Greenhoff, B. 1976 (Manchester U, Leeds U) 18
Greenwood, D. H. 1882 (Blackburn R) 2
Gregory, J. 1983 (QPR) 6
Grimsdell, A. 1920 (Tottenham H) 6
Grosvenor, A. T. 1934 (Birmingham) 3
Gunn, W. 1884 (Notts Co) 2
Guppy, S. 2000 (Leicester C) 1
Gurney, R. 1935 (Sunderland) 1

Hacking, J. 1929 (Oldham Ath) 3
Hadley, H. 1903 (WBA) 1
Hagan, J. 1949 (Sheffield U) 1
Haines, J. T. W. 1949 (WBA) 1
Hall, A. E. 1910 (Aston Villa) 1
Hall, G. W. 1934 (Tottenham H) 10
Hall, J. 1956 (Birmingham C) 17
Halse, H. J. 1909 (Manchester U) 1
Hammond, H. E. D. 1889 (Oxford University) 1
Hampson, J. 1931 (Blackpool) 3
Hampton, H. 1913 (Aston Villa) 4
Hancocks, J. 1949 (Wolverhampton W) 3
Hapgood, E. 1933 (Arsenal) 30
Hardinge, H. T. W. 1910 (Sheffield U) 1
Hardman, H. P. 1905 (Everton) 4
Hardwick, G. F. M. 1947 (Middlesbrough) 13
Hardy, H. 1925 (Stockport Co) 1
Hardy, S. 1907 (Liverpool, Aston Villa) 21
Harford, M. G. 1988 (Luton T) 2
Hargreaves, F. W. 1880 (Blackburn R) 3
Hargreaves, J. 1881 (Blackburn R) 2
Hargreaves, O. 2002 (Bayern Munich, Manchester U) 42
Harper, E. C. 1926 (Blackburn R) 1
Harris, G. 1966 (Burnley) 1
Harris, P. P. 1950 (Portsmouth) 2
Harris, S. S. 1904 (Cambridge University, Old Westminsters) 6
Harrison, A. H. 1893 (Old Westminsters) 2
Harrison, G. 1921 (Everton) 2
Harrow, J. H. 1923 (Chelsea) 2
Hart, C. J. J. 2008 (Manchester C) 71
Hart, E. 1929 (Leeds U) 8
Hartley, F. 1923 (Oxford C) 1
Harvey, A. 1881 (Wednesbury Strollers) 1
Harvey, J. C. 1971 (Everton) 1
Hassall, H. W. 1951 (Huddersfield T, Bolton W) 5
Hateley, M. 1984 (Portsmouth, AC Milan, Monaco, Rangers) 32
Hawkes, R. M. 1907 (Luton T) 5
Haworth, G. 1887 (Accrington) 5
Hawtrey, J. P. 1881 (Old Etonians) 2
Haygarth, E. B. 1875 (Swifts) 1
Haynes, J. N. 1955 (Fulham) 56
Healless, H. 1925 (Blackburn R) 2
Heaton, T. 2016 (Burnley) 3
Hector, K. J. 1974 (Derby Co) 2
Hedley, G. A. 1901 (Sheffield U) 1
Hegan, K. E. 1923 (Corinthians) 4
Hellawell, M. S. 1963 (Birmingham C) 2
Henderson, J. B. 2011 (Sunderland, Liverpool) 32
Hendrie, L. A. 1999 (Aston Villa) 1
Henfrey, A. G. 1891 (Cambridge University, Corinthians) 5
Henry, R. P. 1963 (Tottenham H) 1
Heron, F. 1876 (Wanderers) 1
Heron, G. H. H. 1873 (Uxbridge, Wanderers) 5
Heskey, E. W. I. 1999 (Leicester C, Liverpool, Birmingham C, Wigan Ath, Aston Villa) 62
Hibbert, W. 1910 (Bury) 1
Hibbs, H. E. 1930 (Birmingham) 25
Hill, F. 1963 (Bolton W) 2
Hill, G. A. 1976 (Manchester U) 6
Hill, J. H. 1925 (Burnley, Newcastle U) 11
Hill, R. 1983 (Luton T) 3
Hill, R. H. 1926 (Millwall) 1
Hillman, J. 1899 (Burnley) 1
Hills, A. F. 1879 (Old Harrovians) 1
Hilsdon, G. R. 1907 (Chelsea) 8
Hinchcliffe, A. G. 1997 (Everton, Sheffield W) 7
Hine, E. W. 1929 (Leicester C) 6
Hinton, A. T. 1963 (Wolverhampton W, Nottingham F) 3
Hirst, D. E. 1991 (Sheffield W) 3
Hitchens, G. A. 1961 (Aston Villa, Internazionale) 7
Hobbis, H. H. F. 1936 (Charlton Ath) 2
Hoddle, G. 1980 (Tottenham H, Monaco) 53
Hodge, S. B. 1986 (Aston Villa, Tottenham H, Nottingham F) 24
Hodgetts, D. 1888 (Aston Villa) 6
Hodgkinson, A. 1957 (Sheffield U) 5
Hodgson, G. 1931 (Liverpool) 3
Hodkinson, J. 1913 (Blackburn R) 3
Hogg, W. 1902 (Sunderland) 3
Holdcroft, G. H. 1937 (Preston NE) 2
Holden, A. D. 1959 (Bolton W) 5
Holden, G. H. 1881 (Wednesbury OA) 4
Holden-White, C. 1888 (Corinthians) 2
Holford, T. 1903 (Stoke) 1
Holley, G. H. 1909 (Sunderland) 10
Holliday, E. 1960 (Middlesbrough) 3
Hollins, J. W. 1967 (Chelsea) 1
Holmes, R. 1888 (Preston NE) 7
Holt, J. 1890 (Everton, Reading) 10
Hopkinson, E. 1958 (Bolton W) 14
Hossack, A. H. 1892 (Corinthians) 2
Houghton, W. E. 1931 (Aston Villa) 7
Houlker, A. E. 1902 (Blackburn R, Portsmouth, Southampton) 5
Howarth, R. H. 1887 (Preston NE, Everton) 5
Howe, D. 1958 (WBA) 23
Howe, J. R. 1948 (Derby Co) 3
Howell, L. S. 1873 (Wanderers) 1
Howell, R. 1895 (Sheffield U, Liverpool) 2
Howey, S. N. 1995 (Newcastle U) 4
Huddlestone, T. A. 2010 (Tottenham H) 4
Hudson, A. A. 1975 (Stoke C) 2
Hudson, J. 1883 (Sheffield) 1
Hudspeth, F. C. 1926 (Newcastle U) 1
Hufton, A. E. 1924 (West Ham U) 6
Hughes, E. W. 1970 (Liverpool, Wolverhampton W) 62
Hughes, L. 1950 (Liverpool) 3
Hulme, J. H. A. 1927 (Arsenal) 9
Humphreys, P. 1903 (Notts Co) 1
Hunt, G. S. 1933 (Tottenham H) 3
Hunt, Rev. K. R. G. 1911 (Leyton) 2
Hunt, R. 1962 (Liverpool) 34
Hunt, S. 1984 (WBA) 2
Hunter, J. 1878 (Sheffield Heeley) 7
Hunter, N. 1966 (Leeds U) 28
Hurst, G. C. 1966 (West Ham U) 49

Ince, P. E. C. 1993 (Manchester U, Internazionale, Liverpool, Middlesbrough) 53
Ings, D. 2016 (Liverpool) 1
Iremonger, J. 1901 (Nottingham F) 2

Jack, D. N. B. 1924 (Bolton W, Arsenal) 9
Jackson, E. 1891 (Oxford University) 1
Jagielka, P. N. 2008 (Everton) 40
James. D. B. 1997 (Liverpool, Aston Villa, West Ham U, Manchester C, Portsmouth) 53
Jarrett, B. G. 1876 (Cambridge University) 3
Jarvis, M. T. 2011 (Wolverhampton W) 1
Jefferis, F. 1912 (Everton) 2
Jeffers, F. 2003 (Arsenal) 1
Jenas, J. A. 2003 (Newcastle U, Tottenham H) 21
Jenkinson, C. D. 2013 (Arsenal) 1
Jezzard, B. A. G. 1954 (Fulham) 2
Johnson, A. 2005 (Crystal Palace, Everton) 8
Johnson, A. 2010 (Manchester C) 12
Johnson, D. E. 1975 (Ipswich T, Liverpool) 8
Johnson, E. 1880 (Saltley College, Stoke) 2
Johnson, G. M. C. 2004 (Chelsea, Portsmouth, Liverpool) 54
Johnson, J. A. 1937 (Stoke C) 5
Johnson, S. A. M. 2001 (Derby Co) 1
Johnson, T. C. F. 1926 (Manchester C, Everton) 5
Johnson, W. H. 1900 (Sheffield U) 6
Johnston, H. 1947 (Blackpool) 10
Jones, A. 1882 (Walsall Swifts, Great Lever) 3
Jones, H. 1923 (Nottingham F) 1
Jones, H. 1927 (Blackburn R) 6
Jones, M. D. 1965 (Sheffield U, Leeds U) 3
Jones, P. A. 2012 (Manchester U) 21
Jones, R. 1992 (Liverpool) 8

Jones, W. 1901 (Bristol C) 1
Jones, W. H. 1950 (Liverpool) 2
Joy, B. 1936 (Casuals) 1

Kail, E. I. L. 1929 (Dulwich Hamlet) 3
Kane, H. E. 2015 (Tottenham H) 19
Kay, A. H. 1963 (Everton) 1
Kean, F. W. 1923 (Sheffield W, Bolton W) 9
Keane, M. V. 2017 (Burnley) 2
Keegan, J. K. 1973 (Liverpool, SV Hamburg, Southampton) 63
Keen, E. R. L. 1933 (Derby Co) 4
Kelly, M. R. 2012 (Liverpool) 1
Kelly, R. 1920 (Burnley, Sunderland, Huddersfield T) 14
Kennedy, A. 1984 (Liverpool) 2
Kennedy, R. 1976 (Liverpool) 17
Kenyon-Slaney, W. S. 1873 (Wanderers) 1
Keown, M. R. 1992 (Everton, Arsenal) 43
Kevan, D. T. 1957 (WBA) 14
Kidd, B. 1970 (Manchester U) 2
King, L. B. 2002 (Tottenham H) 21
King, R. S. 1882 (Oxford University) 1
Kingsford, R. K. 1874 (Wanderers) 1
Kingsley, M. 1901 (Newcastle U) 1
Kinsey, G. 1892 (Wolverhampton W, Derby Co) 4
Kirchen, A. J. 1937 (Arsenal) 3
Kirkland, C. E. 2007 (Liverpool) 1
Kirton, W. J. 1922 (Aston Villa) 1
Knight, A. E. 1920 (Portsmouth) 1
Knight, Z. 2005 (Fulham) 2
Knowles, C. 1968 (Tottenham H) 4
Konchesky, P. M. 2003 (Charlton Ath, West Ham U) 2

Labone, B. L. 1963 (Everton) 26
Lallana, A. D. 2013 (Southampton, Liverpool) 33
Lambert, R. L. 2013 (Southampton, Liverpool) 11
Lampard, F. J. 2000 (West Ham U, Chelsea) 106
Lampard, F. R. G. 1973 (West Ham U) 2
Langley, E. J. 1958 (Fulham) 3
Langton, R. 1947 (Blackburn R, Preston NE, Bolton W) 11
Latchford, R. D. 1978 (Everton) 12
Latheron, E. G. 1913 (Blackburn R) 2
Lawler, C. 1971 (Liverpool) 4
Lawton, T. 1939 (Everton, Chelsea, Notts Co) 23
Leach, T. 1931 (Sheffield W) 2
Leake, A. 1904 (Aston Villa) 5
Lee, E. A. 1904 (Southampton) 1
Lee, F. H. 1969 (Manchester C) 27
Lee, J. 1951 (Derby Co) 1
Lee, R. M. 1995 (Newcastle U) 21
Lee, S. 1983 (Liverpool) 14
Leighton, J. E. 1886 (Nottingham F) 1
Lennon, A. J. 2006 (Tottenham H) 21
Lescott, J. P. 2008 (Everton, Manchester C) 26
Le Saux, G. P. 1994 (Blackburn R, Chelsea) 36
Le Tissier, M. P. 1994 (Southampton) 8
Lilley, H. E. 1892 (Sheffield U) 1
Linacre, H. J. 1905 (Nottingham F) 2
Lindley, T. 1886 (Cambridge University, Nottingham F) 13
Lindsay, A. 1974 (Liverpool) 4
Lindsay, W. 1877 (Wanderers) 1
Lineker, G. 1984 (Leicester C, Everton, Barcelona, Tottenham H) 80
Lingard, J. E. 2017 (Manchester U) 4
Lintott, E. H. 1908 (QPR, Bradford C) 7
Lipsham, H. B. 1902 (Sheffield U) 1
Little, B. 1975 (Aston Villa) 1
Livermore, J. C. 2013 (Tottenham H, WBA) 3
Lloyd, L. V. 1971 (Liverpool, Nottingham F) 4
Lockett, A. 1903 (Stoke) 1
Lodge, L. V. 1894 (Cambridge University, Corinthians) 5
Lofthouse, J. M. 1885 (Blackburn R, Accrington, Blackburn R) 7
Lofthouse, N. 1951 (Bolton W) 33
Longworth, E. 1920 (Liverpool) 5
Lowder, A. 1889 (Wolverhampton W) 1
Lowe, E. 1947 (Aston Villa) 3
Lucas, T. 1922 (Liverpool) 3
Luntley, E. 1880 (Nottingham F) 2
Lyttelton, Hon. A. 1877 (Cambridge University) 1
Lyttelton, Hon. E. 1878 (Cambridge University) 1

Mabbutt, G. 1983 (Tottenham H) 16
Macaulay, R. H. 1881 (Cambridge University) 1
McCall, J. 1913 (Preston NE) 5
McCann, G. P. 2001 (Sunderland) 1
McDermott, T. 1978 (Liverpool) 25
McDonald, C. A. 1958 (Burnley) 8
Macdonald, M. 1972 (Newcastle U) 14
McFarland, R. L. 1971 (Derby Co) 28
McGarry, W. H. 1954 (Huddersfield T) 4
McGuinness, W. 1959 (Manchester U) 2
McInroy, A. 1927 (Sunderland) 1
McMahon, S. 1988 (Liverpool) 17
McManaman, S. 1995 (Liverpool, Real Madrid) 37
McNab, R. 1969 (Arsenal) 4
McNeal, R. 1914 (WBA) 2
McNeil, M. 1961 (Middlesbrough) 9
Macrae, S. 1883 (Notts Co) 5
Maddison, F. B. 1872 (Oxford University) 1
Madeley, P. E. 1971 (Leeds U) 24
Magee, T. P. 1923 (WBA) 5
Makepeace, H. 1906 (Everton) 4
Male, C. G. 1935 (Arsenal) 19
Mannion, W. J. 1947 (Middlesbrough) 26
Mariner, P. 1977 (Ipswich T, Arsenal) 35
Marsden, J. T. 1891 (Darwen) 1
Marsden, W. 1930 (Sheffield W) 3
Marsh, R. W. 1972 (QPR, Manchester C) 9
Marshall, T. 1880 (Darwen) 2
Martin, A. 1981 (West Ham U) 17
Martin, H. 1914 (Sunderland) 1
Martyn, A. N. 1992 (Crystal Palace, Leeds U) 23
Marwood, B. 1989 (Arsenal) 1
Maskrey, H. M. 1908 (Derby Co) 1
Mason, C. 1887 (Wolverhampton W) 3
Mason, R. G. 2015 (Tottenham H) 1
Matthews, R. D. 1956 (Coventry C) 5
Matthews, S. 1935 (Stoke C, Blackpool) 54
Matthews, V. 1928 (Sheffield U) 2
Maynard, W. J. 1872 (1st Surrey Rifles) 2
Meadows, J. 1955 (Manchester C) 1
Medley, L. D. 1951 (Tottenham H) 6
Meehan, T. 1924 (Chelsea) 1
Melia, J. 1963 (Liverpool) 2
Mercer, D. W. 1923 (Sheffield U) 2
Mercer, J. 1939 (Everton) 5
Merrick, G. H. 1952 (Birmingham C) 23
Merson, P. C. 1992 (Arsenal, Middlesbrough, Aston Villa) 21
Metcalfe, V. 1951 (Huddersfield T) 2
Mew, J. W. 1921 (Manchester U) 1
Middleditch, B. 1897 (Corinthians) 1
Milburn, J. E. T. 1949 (Newcastle U) 13
Miller, B. G. 1961 (Burnley) 1
Miller, H. S. 1923 (Charlton Ath) 1
Mills, D. J. 2001 (Leeds U) 19
Mills, G. R. 1938 (Chelsea) 3
Mills, M. D. 1973 (Ipswich T) 42
Milne, G. 1963 (Liverpool) 14
Milner, J. P. 2010 (Aston Villa, Manchester C, Liverpool) 61
Milton, C. A. 1952 (Arsenal) 1
Milward, A. 1891 (Everton) 4
Mitchell, C. 1880 (Upton Park) 5
Mitchell, J. F. 1925 (Manchester C) 1
Moffat, H. 1913 (Oldham Ath) 1
Molyneux, G. 1902 (Southampton) 4
Moon, W. R. 1888 (Old Westminsters) 7
Moore, H. T. 1883 (Notts Co) 2
Moore, J. 1923 (Derby Co) 1
Moore, R. F. 1962 (West Ham U) 108
Moore, W. G. B. 1923 (West Ham U) 1
Mordue, J. 1912 (Sunderland) 2
Morice, C. J. 1872 (Barnes) 1
Morley, A. 1982 (Aston Villa) 6
Morley, H. 1910 (Notts Co) 1
Morren, T. 1898 (Sheffield U) 1
Morris, F. 1920 (WBA) 2
Morris, J. 1949 (Derby Co) 3
Morris, W. W. 1939 (Wolverhampton W) 3
Morse, H. 1879 (Notts Co) 1
Mort, T. 1924 (Aston Villa) 3
Morten, A. 1873 (Crystal Palace) 1
Mortensen, S. H. 1947 (Blackpool) 25
Morton, J. R. 1938 (West Ham U) 1

Mosforth, W. 1877 (Sheffield W, Sheffield Alb, Sheffield W) 9
Moss, F. 1922 (Aston Villa) 5
Moss, F. 1934 (Arsenal) 4
Mosscrop, E. 1914 (Burnley) 2
Mozley, B. 1950 (Derby Co) 3
Mullen, J. 1947 (Wolverhampton W) 12
Mullery, A. P. 1965 (Tottenham H) 35
Murphy, D. B. 2002 (Liverpool) 9

Neal, P. G. 1976 (Liverpool) 50
Needham, E. 1894 (Sheffield U) 16
Neville, G. A. 1995 (Manchester U) 85
Neville, P. J. 1996 (Manchester U, Everton) 59
Newton, K. R. 1966 (Blackburn R, Everton) 27
Nicholls, J. 1954 (WBA) 2
Nicholson, W. E. 1951 (Tottenham H) 1
Nish, D. J. 1973 (Derby Co) 5
Norman, M. 1962 (Tottenham H) 23
Nugent, D. J. 2007 (Preston NE) 1
Nuttall, H. 1928 (Bolton W) 3

Oakley, W. J. 1895 (Oxford University, Corinthians) 16
O'Dowd, J. P. 1932 (Chelsea) 3
O'Grady, M. 1963 (Huddersfield T, Leeds U) 2
Ogilvie, R. A. M. M. 1874 (Clapham R) 1
Oliver, L. F. 1929 (Fulham) 1
Olney, B. A. 1928 (Aston Villa) 2
Osborne, F. R. 1923 (Fulham, Tottenham H) 4
Osborne, R. 1928 (Leicester C) 1
Osgood, P. L. 1970 (Chelsea) 4
Osman, L. 2013 (Everton) 2
Osman, R. 1980 (Ipswich T) 11
Ottaway, C. J. 1872 (Oxford University) 2
Owen, J. R. B. 1874 (Sheffield) 1
Owen, M. J. 1998 (Liverpool, Real Madrid, Newcastle U) 89
Owen, S. W. 1954 (Luton T) 3
Oxlade-Chamberlain, A. M. D. 2012 (Arsenal) 27

Page, L. A. 1927 (Burnley) 7
Paine, T. L. 1963 (Southampton) 19
Pallister, G. A. 1988 (Middlesbrough, Manchester U) 22
Palmer, C. L. 1992 (Sheffield W) 18
Pantling, H. H. 1924 (Sheffield U) 1
Paravicini, P. J. de 1883 (Cambridge University) 3
Parker, P. A. 1989 (QPR, Manchester U) 19
Parker, S. M. 2004 (Charlton Ath, Chelsea, Newcastle U, West Ham U, Tottenham H) 18
Parker, T. R. 1925 (Southampton) 1
Parkes, P. B. 1974 (QPR) 1
Parkinson, J. 1910 (Liverpool) 2
Parlour, R. 1999 (Arsenal) 10
Parr, P. C. 1882 (Oxford University) 1
Parry, E. H. 1879 (Old Carthusians) 3
Parry, R. A. 1960 (Bolton W) 2
Patchitt, B. C. A. 1923 (Corinthians) 2
Pawson, F. W. 1883 (Cambridge University, Swifts) 2
Payne, J. 1937 (Luton T) 1
Peacock, A. 1962 (Middlesbrough, Leeds U) 6
Peacock, J. 1929 (Middlesbrough) 3
Pearce, S. 1987 (Nottingham F, West Ham U) 78
Pearson, H. F. 1932 (WBA) 1
Pearson, J. H. 1892 (Crewe Alex) 1
Pearson, J. S. 1976 (Manchester U) 15
Pearson, S. C. 1948 (Manchester U) 8
Pease, W. H. 1927 (Middlesbrough) 1
Pegg, D. 1957 (Manchester U) 1
Pejic, M. 1974 (Stoke C) 4
Pelly, F. R. 1893 (Old Foresters) 3
Pennington, J. 1907 (WBA) 25
Pentland, F. B. 1909 (Middlesbrough) 5
Perry, C. 1890 (WBA) 3
Perry, T. 1898 (WBA) 1
Perry, W. 1956 (Blackpool) 3
Perryman, S. 1982 (Tottenham H) 1
Peters, M. 1966 (West Ham U, Tottenham H) 67
Phelan, M. C. 1990 (Manchester U) 1
Phillips, K. 1999 (Sunderland) 8
Phillips, L. H. 1952 (Portsmouth) 3
Pickering, F. 1964 (Everton) 3
Pickering, J. 1933 (Sheffield U) 1
Pickering, N. 1983 (Sunderland) 1
Pike, T. M. 1886 (Cambridge University) 1
Pilkington, B. 1955 (Burnley) 1
Plant, J. 1900 (Bury) 1
Platt, D. 1990 (Aston Villa, Bari, Juventus, Sampdoria, Arsenal) 62
Plum, S. L. 1923 (Charlton Ath) 1
Pointer, R. 1962 (Burnley) 3
Porteous, T. S. 1891 (Sunderland) 1
Powell, C. G. 2001 (Charlton Ath) 5
Priest, A. E. 1900 (Sheffield U) 1
Prinsep, J. F. M. 1879 (Clapham R) 1
Puddefoot, S. C. 1926 (Blackburn R) 2
Pye, J. 1950 (Wolverhampton W) 1
Pym, R. H. 1925 (Bolton W) 3

Quantrill, A. 1920 (Derby Co) 4
Quixall, A. 1954 (Sheffield W) 5

Radford, J. 1969 (Arsenal) 2
Raikes, G. B. 1895 (Oxford University) 4
Ramsey, A. E. 1949 (Southampton, Tottenham H) 32
Rashford, M. 2016 (Manchester U) 9
Rawlings, A. 1921 (Preston NE) 1
Rawlings, W. E. 1922 (Southampton) 2
Rawlinson, J. F. P. 1882 (Cambridge University) 1
Rawson, H. E. 1875 (Royal Engineers) 1
Rawson, W. S. 1875 (Oxford University) 2
Read, A. 1921 (Tufnell Park) 1
Reader, J. 1894 (WBA) 1
Reaney, P. 1969 (Leeds U) 3
Redknapp, J. F. 1996 (Liverpool) 17
Redmond, N. D. J. 2017 (Southampton) 1
Reeves, K. P. 1980 (Norwich C, Manchester C) 2
Regis, C. 1982 (WBA, Coventry C) 5
Reid, P. 1985 (Everton) 13
Revie, D. G. 1955 (Manchester C) 6
Reynolds, J. 1892 (WBA, Aston Villa) 8
Richards, C. H. 1898 (Nottingham F) 1
Richards, G. H. 1909 (Derby Co) 1
Richards, J. P. 1973 (Wolverhampton W) 1
Richards, M. 2007 (Manchester C) 13
Richardson, J. R. 1933 (Newcastle U) 2
Richardson, K. 1994 (Aston Villa) 1
Richardson, K. E. 2005 (Manchester U) 8
Richardson, W. G. 1935 (WBA) 1
Rickaby, S. 1954 (WBA) 1
Ricketts, M. B. 2002 (Bolton W) 1
Rigby, A. 1927 (Blackburn R) 5
Rimmer, E. J. 1930 (Sheffield W) 4
Rimmer, J. J. 1976 (Arsenal) 1
Ripley, S. E. 1994 (Blackburn R) 2
Rix, G. 1981 (Arsenal) 17
Robb, G. 1954 (Tottenham H) 1
Roberts, C. 1905 (Manchester U) 3
Roberts, F. 1925 (Manchester C) 4
Roberts, G. 1983 (Tottenham H) 6
Roberts, H. 1931 (Arsenal) 1
Roberts, H. 1931 (Millwall) 1
Roberts, R. 1887 (WBA) 3
Roberts, W. T. 1924 (Preston NE) 2
Robinson, J. 1937 (Sheffield W) 4
Robinson, J. W. 1897 (Derby Co, New Brighton Tower, Southampton) 11
Robinson, P. W. 2003 (Leeds U, Tottenham H, Blackburn R) 41
Robson, B. 1980 (WBA, Manchester U) 90
Robson, R. 1958 (WBA) 20
Rocastle, D. 1989 (Arsenal) 14
Rodriguez, J. E. 2013 (Southampton) 1
Rodwell, J. 2012 (Everton) 3
Rooney, W. M. 2003 (Everton, Manchester U) 119
Rose, D. L. 2016 (Tottenham H) 12
Rose, W. C. 1884 (Swifts, Preston NE, Wolverhampton W) 5
Rostron, T. 1881 (Darwen) 2
Rowe, A. 1934 (Tottenham H) 1
Rowley, J. F. 1949 (Manchester U) 6
Rowley, W. 1889 (Stoke) 2
Royle, J. 1971 (Everton, Manchester C) 6
Ruddlesdin, H. 1904 (Sheffield W) 3
Ruddock, N. 1995 (Liverpool) 1
Ruddy, J. T. G. 2013 (Norwich C) 1
Ruffell, J. W. 1926 (West Ham U) 6
Russell, B. B. 1883 (Royal Engineers) 1
Rutherford, J. 1904 (Newcastle U) 11

Sadler, D. 1968 (Manchester U) 4
Sagar, C. 1900 (Bury) 2
Sagar, E. 1936 (Everton) 4
Salako, J. A. 1991 (Crystal Palace) 5
Sandford, E. A. 1933 (WBA) 1
Sandilands, R. R. 1892 (Old Westminsters) 5
Sands, J. 1880 (Nottingham F) 1
Sansom, K. G. 1979 (Crystal Palace, Arsenal) 86
Saunders, F. E. 1888 (Swifts) 1
Savage, A. H. 1876 (Crystal Palace) 1
Sayer, J. 1887 (Stoke) 1
Scales, J. R. 1995 (Liverpool) 3
Scattergood, E. 1913 (Derby Co) 1
Schofield, J. 1892 (Stoke) 3
Scholes, P. 1997 (Manchester U) 66
Scott, L. 1947 (Arsenal) 17
Scott, W. R. 1937 (Brentford) 1
Seaman, D. A. 1989 (QPR, Arsenal) 75
Seddon, J. 1923 (Bolton W) 6
Seed, J. M. 1921 (Tottenham H) 5
Settle, J. 1899 (Bury, Everton) 6
Sewell, J. 1952 (Sheffield W) 6
Sewell, W. R. 1924 (Blackburn R) 1
Shackleton, L. F. 1949 (Sunderland) 5
Sharp, J. 1903 (Everton) 2
Sharpe, L. S. 1991 (Manchester U) 8
Shaw, G. E. 1932 (WBA) 1
Shaw, G. L. 1959 (Sheffield U) 5
Shaw, L. P. H. 2014 (Southampton, Manchester U) 7
Shawcross, R. J. 2013 (Stoke C) 1
Shea, D. 1914 (Blackburn R) 2
Shearer, A. 1992 (Southampton, Blackburn R, Newcastle U) 63
Shellito, K. J. 1963 (Chelsea) 1
Shelton A. 1889 (Notts Co) 6
Shelton, C. 1888 (Notts Rangers) 1
Shelvey, J. 2013 (Liverpool, Swansea C) 6
Shepherd, A. 1906 (Bolton W, Newcastle U) 2
Sheringham, E. P. 1993 (Tottenham H, Manchester U, Tottenham H) 51
Sherwood, T. A. 1999 (Tottenham H) 3
Shilton, P. L. 1971 (Leicester C, Stoke C, Nottingham F, Southampton, Derby Co) 125
Shimwell, E. 1949 (Blackpool) 1
Shorey, N. 2007 (Reading) 2
Shutt, G. 1886 (Stoke) 1
Silcock, J. 1921 (Manchester U) 3
Sillett, R. P. 1955 (Chelsea) 3
Simms, E. 1922 (Luton T) 1
Simpson, J. 1911 (Blackburn R) 8
Sinclair, T. 2002 (West Ham U, Manchester C) 12
Sinton, A. 1992 (QPR, Sheffield W) 12
Slater, W. J. 1955 (Wolverhampton W) 12
Smalley, T. 1937 (Wolverhampton W) 1
Smalling, C. L. 2012 (Manchester U) 31
Smart, T. 1921 (Aston Villa) 5
Smith, A. 1891 (Nottingham F) 3
Smith, A. 2001 (Leeds U, Manchester U, Newcastle U) 19
Smith, A. K. 1872 (Oxford University) 1
Smith, A. M. 1989 (Arsenal) 13
Smith, B. 1921 (Tottenham H) 2
Smith, C. E. 1876 (Crystal Palace) 1
Smith, G. O. 1893 (Oxford University, Old Carthusians, Corinthians) 20
Smith, H. 1905 (Reading) 4
Smith, J. 1920 (WBA) 2
Smith, Joe 1913 (Bolton W) 5
Smith, J. C. R. 1939 (Millwall) 2
Smith, J. W. 1932 (Portsmouth) 3
Smith, Leslie 1939 (Brentford) 1
Smith, Lionel 1951 (Arsenal) 6
Smith, R. A. 1961 (Tottenham H) 15
Smith, S. 1895 (Aston Villa) 1
Smith, S. C. 1936 (Leicester C) 1
Smith, T. 1960 (Birmingham C) 2
Smith, T. 1971 (Liverpool) 1
Smith, W. H. 1922 (Huddersfield T) 3
Sorby, T. H. 1879 (Thursday Wanderers, Sheffield) 1
Southgate, G. 1996 (Aston Villa, Middlesbrough) 57
Southworth, J. 1889 (Blackburn R) 3
Sparks, F. J. 1879 (Herts Rangers, Clapham R) 3
Spence, J. W. 1926 (Manchester U) 2
Spence, R. 1936 (Chelsea) 2
Spencer, C. W. 1924 (Newcastle U) 2
Spencer, H. 1897 (Aston Villa) 6
Spiksley, F. 1893 (Sheffield W) 7
Spilsbury, B. W. 1885 (Cambridge University) 3
Spink, N. 1983 (Aston Villa) 1
Spouncer, W. A. 1900 (Nottingham F) 1
Springett, R. D. G. 1960 (Sheffield W) 33
Sproston, B. 1937 (Leeds U, Tottenham H, Manchester C) 11
Squire, R. T. 1886 (Cambridge University) 3
Stanbrough, M. H. 1895 (Old Carthusians) 1
Staniforth, R. 1954 (Huddersfield T) 8
Starling, R. W. 1933 (Sheffield W, Aston Villa) 2
Statham, D. J. 1983 (WBA) 3
Steele, F. C. 1937 (Stoke C) 6
Stein, B. 1984 (Luton T) 1
Stephenson, C. 1924 (Huddersfield T) 1
Stephenson, G. T. 1928 (Derby Co, Sheffield W) 3
Stephenson, J. E. 1938 (Leeds U) 2
Stepney, A. C. 1968 (Manchester U) 1
Sterland, M. 1989 (Sheffield W) 1
Sterling, R. S. 2013 (Liverpool) 32
Steven, T. M. 1985 (Everton, Rangers, Marseille) 36
Stevens, G. A. 1985 (Tottenham H) 7
Stevens, M. G. 1985 (Everton, Rangers) 46
Stewart, J. 1907 (Sheffield W, Newcastle U) 3
Stewart, P. A. 1992 (Tottenham H) 3
Stiles, N. P. 1965 (Manchester U) 28
Stoker, J. 1933 (Birmingham) 3
Stone, S. B. 1996 (Nottingham F) 9
Stones, J. 2014 (Everton, Manchester C) 18
Storer, H. 1924 (Derby Co) 2
Storey, P. E. 1971 (Arsenal) 19
Storey-Moore, I. 1970 (Nottingham F) 1
Strange, A. H. 1930 (Sheffield W) 20
Stratford, A. H. 1874 (Wanderers) 1
Streten, B. 1950 (Luton T) 1
Sturgess, A. 1911 (Sheffield U) 2
Sturridge, D. A. 2012 (Chelsea, Liverpool) 25
Summerbee, M. G. 1968 (Manchester C) 8
Sunderland, A. 1980 (Arsenal) 1
Sutcliffe, J. W. 1893 (Bolton W, Millwall) 5
Sutton, C. R. 1998 (Blackburn R) 1
Swan, P. 1960 (Sheffield W) 19
Swepstone, H. A. 1880 (Pilgrims) 6
Swift, F. V. 1947 (Manchester C) 19

Tait, G. 1881 (Birmingham Excelsior) 1
Talbot, B. 1977 (Ipswich T, Arsenal) 6
Tambling, R. V. 1963 (Chelsea) 3
Tate, J. T. 1931 (Aston Villa) 3
Taylor, E. 1954 (Blackpool) 1
Taylor, E. H. 1923 (Huddersfield T) 8
Taylor, J. G. 1951 (Fulham) 2
Taylor, P. H. 1948 (Liverpool) 3
Taylor, P. J. 1976 (Crystal Palace) 4
Taylor, T. 1953 (Manchester U) 19
Temple, D. W. 1965 (Everton) 1
Terry, J. G. 2003 (Chelsea) 78
Thickett, H. 1899 (Sheffield U) 2
Thomas, D. 1975 (QPR) 8
Thomas, D. 1983 (Coventry C) 2
Thomas, G. R. 1991 (Crystal Palace) 9
Thomas, M. L. 1989 (Arsenal) 2
Thompson, A. 2004 (Celtic) 1
Thompson, P. 1964 (Liverpool) 16
Thompson, P. B. 1976 (Liverpool) 42
Thompson T. 1952 (Aston Villa, Preston NE) 2
Thomson, R. A. 1964 (Wolverhampton W) 8
Thornewell, G. 1923 (Derby Co) 4
Thornley, I. 1907 (Manchester C) 1
Tilson, S. F. 1934 (Manchester C) 4
Titmuss, F. 1922 (Southampton) 2
Todd, C. 1972 (Derby Co) 27
Toone, G. 1892 (Notts Co) 2
Topham, A. G. 1894 (Casuals) 1
Topham, R. 1893 (Wolverhampton W, Casuals) 2
Towers, M. A. 1976 (Sunderland) 3
Townley, W. J. 1889 (Blackburn R) 2
Townrow, J. E. 1925 (Clapton Orient) 2
Townsend, A. D. 2013 (Tottenham H, Newcastle U, Crystal Palace) 13
Tremelling, D. R. 1928 (Birmingham) 1
Tresadern, J. 1923 (West Ham U) 2
Trippier, K. J. 2017 (Tottenham H) 1

Tueart, D. 1975 (Manchester C) 6
Tunstall, F. E. 1923 (Sheffield U) 7
Turnbull, R. J. 1920 (Bradford) 1
Turner, A. 1900 (Southampton) 2
Turner, H. 1931 (Huddersfield T) 2
Turner, J. A. 1893 (Bolton W, Stoke, Derby Co) 3
Tweedy, G. J. 1937 (Grimsby T) 1

Ufton, D. G. 1954 (Charlton Ath) 1
Underwood, A. 1891 (Stoke C) 2
Unsworth, D. G. 1995 (Everton) 1
Upson, M. J. 2003 (Birmingham C, West Ham U) 21
Urwin, T. 1923 (Middlesbrough, Newcastle U) 4
Utley, G. 1913 (Barnsley) 1

Vardy, J. R. 2015 (Leicester C) 16
Vassell, D. 2002 (Aston Villa) 22
Vaughton, O. H. 1882 (Aston Villa) 5
Veitch, C. C. M. 1906 (Newcastle U) 6
Veitch, J. G. 1894 (Old Westminsters) 1
Venables, T. F. 1965 (Chelsea) 2
Venison, B. 1995 (Newcastle U) 2
Vidal, R. W. S. 1873 (Oxford University) 1
Viljoen, C. 1975 (Ipswich T) 2
Viollet, D. S. 1960 (Manchester U) 2
Von Donop 1873 (Royal Engineers) 2

Wace, H. 1878 (Wanderers) 3
Waddle, C. R. 1985 (Newcastle U, Tottenham H, Marseille) 62
Wadsworth, S. J. 1922 (Huddersfield T) 9
Wainscoat, W. R. 1929 (Leeds U) 1
Waiters, A. K. 1964 (Blackpool) 5
Walcott, T. J. 2006 (Arsenal) 47
Walden, F. I. 1914 (Tottenham H) 2
Walker, D. S. 1989 (Nottingham F, Sampdoria, Sheffield W) 59
Walker, I. M. 1996 (Tottenham H, Leicester C) 4
Walker, K. A. 2012 (Tottenham H) 27
Walker, W. H. 1921 (Aston Villa) 18
Wall, G. 1907 (Manchester U) 7
Wallace, C. W. 1913 (Aston Villa) 3
Wallace, D. L. 1986 (Southampton) 1
Walsh, P. A. 1983 (Luton T) 5
Walters, A. M. 1885 (Cambridge University, Old Carthusians) 9
Walters, K. M. 1991 (Rangers) 1
Walters, P. M. 1885 (Oxford University, Old Carthusians) 13
Walton, N. 1890 (Blackburn R) 1
Ward, J. T. 1885 (Blackburn Olympic) 1
Ward, P. 1980 (Brighton & HA) 1
Ward, T. V. 1948 (Derby Co) 2
Ward-Prowse, J. M. E. 2017 (Southampton) 1
Waring, T. 1931 (Aston Villa) 5
Warner, C. 1878 (Upton Park) 1
Warnock, S. 2008 (Blackburn R, Aston Villa) 2
Warren, B. 1906 (Derby Co, Chelsea) 22
Waterfield, G. S. 1927 (Burnley) 1
Watson, D. 1984 (Norwich C, Everton) 12
Watson, D. V. 1974 (Sunderland, Manchester C, Werder Bremen, Southampton, Stoke C) 65
Watson, V. M. 1923 (West Ham U) 5
Watson, W. 1913 (Burnley) 3
Watson, W. 1950 (Sunderland) 4
Weaver, S. 1932 (Newcastle U) 3
Webb, G. W. 1911 (West Ham U) 2
Webb, N. J. 1988 (Nottingham F, Manchester U) 26
Webster, M. 1930 (Middlesbrough) 3
Wedlock, W. J. 1907 (Bristol C) 26
Weir, D. 1889 (Bolton W) 2
Welbeck, D. 2011 (Manchester U, Arsenal) 34
Welch, R. de C. 1872 (Wanderers, Harrow Chequers) 2
Weller, K. 1974 (Leicester C) 4
Welsh, D. 1938 (Charlton Ath) 3
West, G. 1969 (Everton) 3
Westwood, R. W. 1935 (Bolton W) 6
Whateley, O. 1883 (Aston Villa) 2
Wheeler, J. E. 1955 (Bolton W) 1
Wheldon, G. F. 1897 (Aston Villa) 4
White, D. 1993 (Manchester C) 1
White, T. A. 1933 (Everton) 1
Whitehead, J. 1893 (Accrington, Blackburn R) 2
Whitfeld, H. 1879 (Old Etonians) 1
Whitham, M. 1892 (Sheffield U) 1
Whitworth, S. 1975 (Leicester C) 7
Whymark, T. J. 1978 (Ipswich T) 1
Widdowson, S. W. 1880 (Nottingham F) 1
Wignall, F. 1965 (Nottingham F) 2
Wilcox, J. M. 1996 (Blackburn R, Leeds U) 3
Wilkes, A. 1901 (Aston Villa) 5
Wilkins, R. C. 1976 (Chelsea, Manchester U, AC Milan) 84
Wilkinson, B. 1904 (Sheffield U) 1
Wilkinson, L. R. 1891 (Oxford University) 1
Williams, B. F. 1949 (Wolverhampton W) 24
Williams, O. 1923 (Clapton Orient) 2
Williams, S. 1983 (Southampton) 6
Williams, W. 1897 (WBA) 6
Williamson, E. C. 1923 (Arsenal) 2
Williamson, R. G. 1905 (Middlesbrough) 7
Willingham, C. K. 1937 (Huddersfield T) 12
Willis, A. 1952 (Tottenham H) 1
Wilshaw, D. J. 1954 (Wolverhampton W) 12
Wilshere, J. A. 2011 (Arsenal) 34
Wilson, C. P. 1884 (Hendon) 2
Wilson, C. W. 1879 (Oxford University) 2
Wilson, G. 1921 (Sheffield W) 12
Wilson, G. P. 1900 (Corinthians) 2
Wilson, R. 1960 (Huddersfield T, Everton) 63
Wilson, T. 1928 (Huddersfield T) 1
Winckworth, W. N. 1892 (Old Westminsters) 2
Windridge, J. E. 1908 (Chelsea) 8
Wingfield-Stratford, C. V. 1877 (Royal Engineers) 1
Winterburn, N. 1990 (Arsenal) 2
Wise, D. F. 1991 (Chelsea) 21
Withe, P. 1981 (Aston Villa) 11
Wollaston, C. H. R. 1874 (Wanderers) 4
Wolstenholme, S. 1904 (Everton, Blackburn R) 3
Wood, H. 1890 (Wolverhampton W) 3
Wood, R. E. 1955 (Manchester U) 3
Woodcock, A. S. 1978 (Nottingham F, Cologne, Arsenal) 42
Woodgate, J. S. 1999 (Leeds U, Newcastle U, Real Madrid, Tottenham H) 8
Woodger, G. 1911 (Oldham Ath) 1
Woodhall, G. 1888 (WBA) 2
Woodley, V. R. 1937 (Chelsea) 19
Woods, C. C. E. 1985 (Norwich C, Rangers, Sheffield W) 43
Woodward, V. J. 1903 (Tottenham H, Chelsea) 23
Woosnam, M. 1922 (Manchester C) 1
Worrall, F. 1935 (Portsmouth) 2
Worthington, F. S. 1974 (Leicester C) 8
Wreford-Brown, C. 1889 (Oxford University, Old Carthusians) 4
Wright, E. G. D. 1906 (Cambridge University) 1
Wright, I. E. 1991 (Crystal Palace, Arsenal, West Ham U) 33
Wright, J. D. 1939 (Newcastle U) 1
Wright, M. 1984 (Southampton, Derby Co, Liverpool) 45
Wright, R. I. 2000 (Ipswich T, Arsenal) 2
Wright, T. J. 1968 (Everton) 11
Wright, W. A. 1947 (Wolverhampton W) 105
Wright-Phillips, S. C. 2005 (Manchester C, Chelsea, Manchester C) 36
Wylie, J. G. 1878 (Wanderers) 1

Yates, J. 1889 (Burnley) 1
York, R. E. 1922 (Aston Villa) 2
Young, A. 1933 (Huddersfield T) 9
Young, A. S. 2008 (Aston Villa, Manchester U) 30
Young, G. M. 1965 (Sheffield W) 1
Young, L. P. 2005 (Charlton Ath) 7

Zaha, D. W. A. 2013 (Manchester U) 2
Zamora, R. L. 2011 (Fulham) 2

NORTHERN IRELAND

Addis, D. J. 1922 (Cliftonville) 1
Aherne, T. 1947 (Belfast Celtic, Luton T) 4
Alexander, T. E. 1895 (Cliftonville) 1
Allan, C. 1936 (Cliftonville) 1
Allen, J. 1887 (Limavady) 1
Anderson, J. 1925 (Distillery) 1
Anderson, T. 1973 (Manchester U, Swindon T, Peterborough U) 22
Anderson, W. 1898 (Linfield, Cliftonville) 4
Andrews, W. 1908 (Glentoran, Grimsby T) 3
Armstrong, G. J. 1977 (Tottenham H, Watford, Real Mallorca, WBA, Chesterfield) 63

Baird, C. P. 2003 (Southampton, Fulham, Reading, Burnley, WBA, Derby Co) 79
Baird, G. 1896 (Distillery) 3
Baird, H. C. 1939 (Huddersfield T) 1
Balfe, J. 1909 (Shelbourne) 2
Bambrick, J. 1929 (Linfield, Chelsea) 11
Banks, S. J. 1937 (Cliftonville) 1
Barr, H. H. 1962 (Linfield, Coventry C) 3
Barron, J. H. 1894 (Cliftonville) 7
Barry, J. 1888 (Cliftonville) 3
Barry, J. 1900 (Bohemians) 1
Barton, A. J. 2011 (Preston NE) 1
Baxter, R. A. 1887 (Distillery) 1
Baxter, S. N. 1887 (Cliftonville) 1
Bennett, L. V. 1889 (Dublin University) 1
Best, G. 1964 (Manchester U, Fulham) 37
Bingham, W. L. 1951 (Sunderland, Luton T, Everton, Port Vale) 56
Black, K. T. 1988 (Luton T, Nottingham F) 30
Black, T. 1901 (Glentoran) 1
Blair, H. 1928 (Portadown, Swansea T) 4
Blair, J. 1907 (Cliftonville) 5
Blair, R. V. 1975 (Oldham Ath) 5
Blanchflower, J. 1954 (Manchester U) 12
Blanchflower, R. D. 1950 (Barnsley, Aston Villa, Tottenham H) 56
Blayney, A. 2006 (Doncaster R, Linfield) 5
Bookman, L. J. O. 1914 (Bradford C, Luton T) 4
Bothwell, A. W. 1926 (Ards) 5
Bowler, G. C. 1950 (Hull C) 3
Boyce, L. 2011 (Werder Bremen, Ross Co) 10
Boyle, P. 1901 (Sheffield U) 5
Braithwaite, R. M. 1962 (Linfield, Middlesbrough) 10
Braniff, K. R. 2010 (Portadown) 2
Breen, T. 1935 (Belfast Celtic, Manchester U) 9
Brennan, B. 1912 (Bohemians) 1
Brennan, R. A. 1949 (Luton T, Birmingham C, Fulham) 5
Briggs, W. R. 1962 (Manchester U, Swansea T) 2
Brisby, D. 1891 (Distillery) 1
Brolly, T. H. 1937 (Millwall) 4
Brookes, E. A. 1920 (Shelbourne) 1
Brotherston, N. 1980 (Blackburn R) 27
Brown, J. 1921 (Glenavon, Tranmere R) 3
Brown, J. 1935 (Wolverhampton W, Coventry C, Birmingham C) 10
Brown, N. M. 1887 (Limavady) 1
Brown, W. G. 1926 (Glenavon) 1
Browne, F. 1887 (Cliftonville) 5
Browne, R. J. 1936 (Leeds U) 6
Bruce, A. 1925 (Belfast Celtic) 1
Bruce, A. S. 2013 (Hull C) 2
Bruce, W. 1961 (Glentoran) 2
Brunt, C. 2005 (Sheffield W, WBA) 59
Bryan, M. A. 2010 (Watford) 2
Buckle, H. R. 1903 (Cliftonville, Sunderland, Bristol R) 3
Buckle, J. 1882 (Cliftonville) 1
Burnett, J. 1894 (Distillery, Glentoran) 5
Burnison, J. 1901 (Distillery) 2
Burnison, S. 1908 (Distillery, Bradford, Distillery) 8
Burns, J. 1923 (Glenavon) 1
Burns, W. 1925 (Glentoran) 1
Butler, M. P. 1939 (Blackpool) 1

Camp, L. M. J. 2011 (Nottingham F) 9
Campbell, A. C. 1963 (Crusaders) 2
Campbell, D. A. 1986 (Nottingham F, Charlton Ath) 10
Campbell, James 1897 (Cliftonville) 14
Campbell, John 1896 (Cliftonville) 1
Campbell, J. P. 1951 (Fulham) 2
Campbell, R. M. 1982 (Bradford C) 2
Campbell, W. G. 1968 (Dundee) 6
Capaldi, A. C. 2004 (Plymouth Arg, Cardiff C) 22
Carey, J. J. 1947 (Manchester U) 7
Carroll, E. 1925 (Glenavon) 1
Carroll, R. E. 1997 (Wigan Ath, Manchester U, West Ham U, Olympiacos, Notts Co, Linfield) 45
Carson, J. G. 2011 (Ipswich T) 4
Carson, S. 2009 (Coleraine) 1
Casement, C. 2009 (Ipswich T) 1
Casey, T. 1955 (Newcastle U, Portsmouth) 12
Caskey, W. 1979 (Derby Co, Tulsa Roughnecks) 8
Cassidy, T. 1971 (Newcastle U, Burnley) 24
Cathcart, C. G. 2011 (Blackpool, Watford) 33
Caughey, M. 1986 (Linfield) 2
Chambers, R. J. 1921 (Distillery, Bury, Nottingham F) 12
Chatton, H. A. 1925 (Partick Thistle) 3
Christian, J. 1889 (Linfield) 1
Clarke, C. J. 1986 (Bournemouth, Southampton, QPR, Portsmouth) 38
Clarke, R. 1901 (Belfast Celtic) 2
Cleary, J. 1982 (Glentoran) 5
Clements, D. 1965 (Coventry C, Sheffield W, Everton, New York Cosmos) 48
Clingan, S. G. 2006 (Nottingham F, Norwich C, Coventry C, Kilmarnock) 39
Clugston, J. 1888 (Cliftonville) 14
Clyde, M. G. 2005 (Wolverhampton W) 3
Coates, C. 2009 (Crusaders) 6
Cochrane, D. 1939 (Leeds U) 12
Cochrane, G. 1903 (Cliftonville) 1
Cochrane, G. T. 1976 (Coleraine, Burnley, Middlesbrough, Gillingham) 26
Cochrane, M. 1898 (Distillery, Leicester Fosse) 8
Collins, F. 1922 (Celtic) 1
Collins, R. 1922 (Cliftonville) 1
Condy, J. 1882 (Distillery) 3
Connell, T. E. 1978 (Coleraine) 1
Connor, J. 1901 (Glentoran, Belfast Celtic) 13
Connor, M. J. 1903 (Brentford, Fulham) 3
Cook, W. 1933 (Celtic, Everton) 15
Cooke, S. 1889 (Belfast YMCA, Cliftonville) 3
Coote, A. 1999 (Norwich C) 6
Coulter, J. 1934 (Belfast Celtic, Everton, Grimsby T, Chelmsford C) 11
Cowan, J. 1970 (Newcastle U) 1
Cowan, T. S. 1925 (Queen's Island) 1
Coyle, F. 1956 (Coleraine, Nottingham F) 4
Coyle, L. 1989 (Derry C) 1
Coyle, R. I. 1973 (Sheffield W) 5
Craig, A. B. 1908 (Rangers, Morton) 9
Craig, D. J. 1967 (Newcastle U) 25
Craigan, S. J. 2003 (Partick Thistle, Motherwell) 54
Crawford, A. 1889 (Distillery, Cliftonville) 7
Croft, T. 1922 (Queen's Island) 3
Crone, R. 1889 (Distillery) 4
Crone, W. 1882 (Distillery) 12
Crooks, W. J. 1922 (Manchester U) 1
Crossan, E. 1950 (Blackburn R) 3
Crossan, J. A. 1960 (Sparta-Rotterdam, Sunderland, Manchester C, Middlesbrough) 24
Crothers, C. 1907 (Distillery) 1
Cumming, L. 1929 (Huddersfield T, Oldham Ath) 3
Cunningham, W. 1892 (Ulster) 4
Cunningham, W. E. 1951 (St Mirren, Leicester C, Dunfermline Ath) 30
Curran, S. 1926 (Belfast Celtic) 4
Curran, J. J. 1922 (Glenavon, Pontypridd, Glenavon) 5
Cush, W. W. 1951 (Glenavon, Leeds U, Portadown) 26

Dallas, S. A. 2011 (Crusaders, Brentford, Leeds U) 22
Dalrymple, J. 1922 (Distillery) 1
Dalton, W. 1888 (YMCA, Linfield) 11
D'Arcy, S. D. 1952 (Chelsea, Brentford) 5
Darling, J. 1897 (Linfield) 22
Davey, H. H. 1926 (Reading, Portsmouth) 5
Davis, S. 2005 (Aston Villa, Fulham, Rangers, Southampton) 95
Davis, T. L. 1937 (Oldham Ath) 1
Davison, A. J. 1996 (Bolton W, Bradford C, Grimsby T) 3
Davison, J. R. 1882 (Cliftonville) 8
Dennison, R. 1988 (Wolverhampton W) 18

Devine, A. O. 1886 (Limavady) 4
Devine, J. 1990 (Glentoran) 1
Dickson, D. 1970 (Coleraine) 4
Dickson, T. A. 1957 (Linfield) 1
Dickson, W. 1951 (Chelsea, Arsenal) 12
Diffin, W. J. 1931 (Belfast Celtic) 1
Dill, A. H. 1882 (Knock, Down Ath, Cliftonville) 9
Doherty, I. 1901 (Belfast Celtic) 1
Doherty, J. 1928 (Portadown) 1
Doherty, J. 1933 (Cliftonville) 2
Doherty, L. 1985 (Linfield) 2
Doherty, M. 1938 (Derry C) 1
Doherty, P. D. 1935 (Blackpool, Manchester C, Derby Co, Huddersfield T, Doncaster R) 16
Doherty, T. E. 2003 (Bristol C) 9
Donaghey, B. 1903 (Belfast Celtic) 1
Donaghy, M. M. 1980 (Luton T, Manchester U, Chelsea) 91
Donnelly, L. 1913 (Distillery) 1
Donnelly, L. F. P. 2014 (Fulham) 1
Donnelly, M. 2009 (Crusaders) 1
Doran, J. F. 1921 (Brighton) 3
Dougan, A. D. 1958 (Portsmouth, Blackburn R, Aston Villa, Leicester C, Wolverhampton W) 43
Douglas, J. P. 1947 (Belfast Celtic) 1
Dowd, H. O. 1974 (Glenavon, Sheffield W) 3
Dowie, I. 1990 (Luton T, West Ham U, Southampton, C Palace, West Ham U, QPR) 59
Duff, M. J. 2002 (Cheltenham T, Burnley) 24
Duggan, H. A. 1930 (Leeds U) 8
Dunlop, G. 1985 (Linfield) 4
Dunne, J. 1928 (Sheffield U) 7

Eames, W. L. E. 1885 (Dublin University) 3
Eglington, T. J. 1947 (Everton) 6
Elder, A. R. 1960 (Burnley, Stoke C) 40
Elleman, A. R. 1889 (Cliftonville) 2
Elliott, S. 2001 (Motherwell, Hull C) 39
Elwood, J. H. 1929 (Bradford) 2
Emerson, W. 1920 (Glentoran, Burnley) 11
English, S. 1933 (Rangers) 2
Enright, J. 1912 (Leeds C) 1
Evans, C. J. 2009 (Manchester U, Hull C, Blackburn R) 39
Evans, J. G. 2007 (Manchester U, WBA) 61

Falloon, E. 1931 (Aberdeen) 2
Farquharson, T. G. 1923 (Cardiff C) 7
Farrell, P. 1901 (Distillery) 2
Farrell, P. 1938 (Hibernian) 1
Farrell, P. D. 1947 (Everton) 7
Feeney, J. M. 1947 (Linfield, Swansea T) 2
Feeney, W. 1976 (Glentoran) 1
Feeney, W. J. 2002 (Bournemouth, Luton T, Cardiff C, Oldham Ath, Plymouth Arg) 46
Ferguson, G. 1999 (Linfield) 5
Ferguson, S. K. 2009 (Newcastle U, Millwall) 31
Ferguson, W. 1966 (Linfield) 2
Ferris, J. 1920 (Belfast Celtic, Chelsea, Belfast Celtic) 6
Ferris, R. O. 1950 (Birmingham C) 3
Fettis, A. W. 1992 (Hull C, Nottingham F, Blackburn R) 25
Finney, T. 1975 (Sunderland, Cambridge U) 14
Fitzpatrick, J. C. 1896 (Bohemians) 2
Flack, H. 1929 (Burnley) 1
Flanagan, T. M. 2017 (Burton Alb) 1
Fleming, J. G. 1987 (Nottingham F, Manchester C, Barnsley) 31
Forbes, G. 1888 (Limavady, Distillery) 3
Forde, J. T. 1959 (Ards) 4
Foreman, T. A. 1899 (Cliftonville) 1
Forsythe, J. 1888 (YMCA) 2
Fox, W. T. 1887 (Ulster) 2
Frame, T. 1925 (Linfield) 1
Fulton, R. P. 1928 (Larne, Belfast Celtic) 21

Gaffikin, G. 1890 (Linfield Ath) 15
Galbraith, W. 1890 (Distillery) 1
Gallagher, P. 1920 (Celtic, Falkirk) 11
Gallogly, C. 1951 (Huddersfield T) 2
Gara, A. 1902 (Preston NE) 3
Gardiner, A. 1930 (Cliftonville) 5
Garrett, J. 1925 (Distillery) 1
Garrett, R. 2009 (Linfield) 5
Gaston, R. 1969 (Oxford U) 1
Gaukrodger, G. 1895 (Linfield) 1
Gault, M. 2008 (Linfield) 1
Gaussen, A. D. 1884 (Moyola Park, Magherafelt) 6
Geary, J. 1931 (Glentoran) 2
Gibb, J. T. 1884 (Wellington Park, Cliftonville) 10
Gibb, T. J. 1936 (Cliftonville) 1
Gibson W. K. 1894 (Cliftonville) 14
Gillespie, K. R. 1995 (Manchester U, Newcastle U, Blackburn R, Leicester C, Sheffield U) 86
Gillespie, S. 1886 (Hertford) 6
Gillespie, W. 1889 (West Down) 1
Gillespie, W. 1913 (Sheffield U) 25
Goodall, A. L. 1899 (Derby Co, Glossop) 10
Goodbody, M. F. 1889 (Dublin University) 2
Gordon, H. 1895 (Linfield) 3
Gordon R. W. 1891 (Linfield) 7
Gordon, T. 1894 (Linfield) 2
Gorman, R. J. 2010 (Wolverhampton W) 9
Gorman, W. C. 1947 (Brentford) 4
Gough, J. 1925 (Queen's Island) 1
Gowdy, J. 1920 (Glentoran, Queen's Island, Falkirk) 6
Gowdy, W. A. 1932 (Hull C, Sheffield W, Linfield, Hibernian) 6
Graham, W. G. L. 1951 (Doncaster R) 14
Gray, P. 1993 (Luton T, Sunderland, Nancy, Luton T, Burnley, Oxford U) 26
Greer, W. 1909 (QPR) 3
Gregg, H. 1954 (Doncaster R, Manchester U) 25
Griffin, D. J. 1996 (St Johnstone, Dundee U, Stockport Co) 29
Grigg, W. D. 2012 (Walsall, Brentford, Milton Keynes D, Wigan Ath) 10

Hall, G. 1897 (Distillery) 1
Halligan, W. 1911 (Derby Co, Wolverhampton W) 2
Hamill, M. 1912 (Manchester U, Belfast Celtic, Manchester C) 7
Hamill, R. 1999 (Glentoran) 1
Hamilton, B. 1969 (Linfield, Ipswich T, Everton, Millwall, Swindon T) 50
Hamilton, G. 2003 (Portadown) 5
Hamilton, J. 1882 (Knock) 2
Hamilton, R. 1928 (Rangers) 5
Hamilton, W. D. 1885 (Dublin Association) 1
Hamilton, W. J. 1885 (Dublin Association) 1
Hamilton, W. J. 1908 (Distillery) 1
Hamilton, W. R. 1978 (QPR, Burnley, Oxford U) 41
Hampton, H. 1911 (Bradford C) 9
Hanna, J. 1912 (Nottingham F) 2
Hanna, J. D. 1899 (Royal Artillery, Portsmouth) 1
Hannon, D. J. 1908 (Bohemians) 6
Harkin, J. T. 1968 (Southport, Shrewsbury T) 5
Harland, A. I. 1922 (Linfield) 2
Harris, J. 1921 (Cliftonville, Glenavon) 2
Harris, V. 1906 (Shelbourne, Everton) 20
Harvey, M. 1961 (Sunderland) 34
Hastings, J. 1882 (Knock, Ulster) 7
Hatton, S. 1963 (Linfield) 2
Hayes, W. E. 1938 (Huddersfield T) 4
Healy, D. J. 2000 (Manchester U, Preston NE, Leeds U, Fulham, Sunderland, Rangers, Bury) 95
Healy, P. J. 1982 (Coleraine, Glentoran) 4
Hegan, D. 1970 (WBA, Wolverhampton W) 7
Henderson, J. 1885 (Ulster) 3
Hewison, G. 1885 (Moyola Park) 2
Hill, C. F. 1990 (Sheffield U, Leicester C, Trelleborg, Northampton T) 27
Hill, M. J. 1959 (Norwich C, Everton) 7
Hinton, E. 1947 (Fulham, Millwall) 7
Hodson, L. J. S. 2011 (Watford, Milton Keynes D, Rangers) 20
Holmes, S. P. 2002 (Wrexham) 1
Hopkins, J. 1926 (Brighton) 1
Horlock, K. 1995 (Swindon T, Manchester C) 32
Houston, J. 1912 (Linfield, Everton) 6
Houston, W. 1933 (Linfield) 1
Houston, W. J. 1885 (Moyola Park) 2
Hughes, A. W. 1998 (Newcastle U, Aston Villa, Fulham, QPR, Brighton & HA, Melbourne C, Kerala Blasters, Hearts) 106
Hughes, J. 2006 (Lincoln C) 2
Hughes, M. A. 2006 (Oldham Ath) 2
Hughes, M. E. 1992 (Manchester C, Strasbourg, West Ham U, Wimbledon, Crystal Palace) 71
Hughes, P. A. 1987 (Bury) 3

Hughes, W. 1951 (Bolton W) 1
Humphries, W. M. 1962 (Ards, Coventry C, Swansea T) 14
Hunter, A. 1905 (Distillery, Belfast Celtic) 8
Hunter, A. 1970 (Blackburn R, Ipswich T) 53
Hunter, B. V. 1995 (Wrexham, Reading) 15
Hunter, R. J. 1884 (Cliftonville) 3
Hunter, V. 1962 (Coleraine) 2

Ingham, M. G. 2005 (Sunderland, Wrexham) 3
Irvine, R. J. 1962 (Linfield, Stoke C) 8
Irvine, R. W. 1922 (Everton, Portsmouth, Connah's Quay, Derry C) 15
Irvine, W. J. 1963 (Burnley, Preston NE, Brighton & HA) 23
Irving, S. J. 1923 (Dundee, Cardiff C, Chelsea) 18

Jackson, T. A. 1969 (Everton, Nottingham F, Manchester U) 35
Jamison, J. 1976 (Glentoran) 1
Jenkins, I. 1997 (Chester C, Dundee U) 6
Jennings, P. A. 1964 (Watford, Tottenham H, Arsenal, Tottenham H) 119
Johnson, D. M. 1999 (Blackburn R, Birmingham C) 56
Johnston, H. 1927 (Portadown) 1
Johnston, R. S. 1882 (Distillery) 5
Johnston, R. S. 1905 (Distillery) 1
Johnston, S. 1890 (Linfield) 4
Johnston, W. 1885 (Oldpark) 2
Johnston, W. C. 1962 (Glenavon, Oldham Ath) 2
Jones, J. 1930 (Linfield, Hibernian, Glenavon) 23
Jones, J. 1956 (Glenavon) 3
Jones, S. 1934 (Distillery, Blackpool) 2
Jones, S. G. 2003 (Crewe Alex, Burnley) 29
Jordan, T. 1895 (Linfield) 2

Kavanagh, P. J. 1930 (Celtic) 1
Keane, T. R. 1949 (Swansea T) 1
Kearns, A. 1900 (Distillery) 6
Kee, P. V. 1990 (Oxford U, Ards) 9
Keith, R. M. 1958 (Newcastle U) 23
Kelly, H. R. 1950 (Fulham, Southampton) 4
Kelly, J. 1896 (Glentoran) 1
Kelly, J. 1932 (Derry C) 11
Kelly, P. J. 1921 (Manchester C) 1
Kelly, P. M. 1950 (Barnsley) 1
Kennedy, A. L. 1923 (Arsenal) 2
Kennedy, P. H. 1999 (Watford, Wigan Ath) 20
Kernaghan, N. 1936 (Belfast Celtic) 3
Kirk, A. R. 2000 (Hearts, Boston U, Northampton T, Dunfermline Ath) 11
Kirkwood, H. 1904 (Cliftonville) 1
Kirwan, J. 1900 (Tottenham H, Chelsea, Clyde) 17

Lacey, W. 1909 (Everton, Liverpool, New Brighton) 23
Lafferty, D. P. 2012 (Burnley) 13
Lafferty, K. 2006 (Burnley, Rangers, FC Sion, Palermo, Norwich C) 62
Lawrie, J. 2009 (Port Vale) 3
Lawther, R. 1888 (Glentoran) 2
Lawther, W. I. 1960 (Sunderland, Blackburn R) 4
Leatham, J. 1939 (Belfast Celtic) 1
Ledwidge, J. J. 1906 (Shelbourne) 2
Lemon, J. 1886 (Glentoran, Belfast YMCA) 3
Lennon, N. F. 1994 (Crewe Alex, Leicester C, Celtic) 40
Leslie, W. 1887 (YMCA) 1
Lewis, J. 1899 (Glentoran, Distillery) 4
Little, A. 2009 (Rangers) 9
Lockhart, H. 1884 (Rossall School) 1
Lockhart, N. H. 1947 (Linfield, Coventry C, Aston Villa) 8
Lomas, S. M. 1994 (Manchester C, West Ham U) 45
Loyal, J. 1891 (Clarence) 1
Lund, M. C. 2017 (Rochdale) 3
Lutton, R. J. 1970 (Wolverhampton W, West Ham U) 6
Lynas, R. 1925 (Cliftonville) 1
Lyner, D. R. 1920 (Glentoran, Manchester U, Kilmarnock) 6
Lytle, J. 1898 (Glentoran) 1

McAdams, W. J. 1954 (Manchester C, Bolton W, Leeds U) 15
McAlery, J. M. 1882 (Cliftonville) 2
McAlinden, J. 1938 (Belfast Celtic, Portsmouth, Southend U) 4
McAllen, J. 1898 (Linfield) 9
McAlpine, S. 1901 (Cliftonville) 1
McArdle, R. A. 2010 (Rochdale, Aberdeen, Bradford C) 7
McArthur, A. 1886 (Distillery) 1
McAuley, G. 2005 (Lincoln C, Leicester C, Ipswich T, WBA) 72
McAuley, J. L. 1911 (Huddersfield T) 6
McAuley, P. 1900 (Belfast Celtic) 1
McBride, S. D. 1991 (Glenavon) 4
McCabe, J. J. 1949 (Leeds U) 6
McCabe, W. 1891 (Ulster) 1
McCambridge, J. 1930 (Ballymena, Cardiff C) 4
McCandless, J. 1912 (Bradford) 5
McCandless, W. 1920 (Linfield, Rangers) 9
McCann, G. S. 2002 (West Ham U, Cheltenham T, Barnsley, Scunthorpe U, Peterborough U) 39
McCann, P. 1910 (Belfast Celtic, Glentoran) 7
McCartan, S. V. 2017 (Accrington S) 1
McCarthy, J. D. 1996 (Port Vale, Birmingham C) 18
McCartney, A. 1903 (Ulster, Linfield, Everton, Belfast Celtic, Glentoran) 15
McCartney, G. 2002 (Sunderland, West Ham U, Sunderland) 34
McCashin, J. W. 1896 (Cliftonville) 5
McCavana, W. T. 1955 (Coleraine) 3
McCaw, J. H. 1927 (Linfield) 6
McClatchey, J. 1886 (Distillery) 3
McClatchey, T. 1895 (Distillery) 1
McCleary, J. W. 1955 (Cliftonville) 1
McCleery, W. 1922 (Cliftonville, Linfield) 10
McClelland, J. 1980 (Mansfield T, Rangers, Watford, Leeds U) 53
McClelland, J. T. 1961 (Arsenal, Fulham) 6
McCluggage, A. 1922 (Cliftonville, Bradford, Burnley) 13
McClure, G. 1907 (Cliftonville, Distillery) 4
McConnell, E. 1904 (Cliftonville, Glentoran, Sunderland, Sheffield W) 12
McConnell, P. 1928 (Doncaster R, Southport) 2
McConnell, W. G. 1912 (Bohemians) 6
McConnell, W. H. 1925 (Reading) 8
McCourt, F. J. 1952 (Manchester C) 6
McCourt, P. J. 2002 (Rochdale, Celtic, Barnsley, Brighton & HA, Luton T) 18
McCoy, R. K. 1987 (Coleraine) 1
McCoy, S. 1896 (Distillery) 1
McCracken, E. 1928 (Barking) 1
McCracken, R. 1921 (Crystal Palace) 4
McCracken, R. 1922 (Linfield) 1
McCracken, W. R. 1902 (Distillery, Newcastle U, Hull C) 16
McCreery, D. 1976 (Manchester U, QPR, Tulsa Roughnecks, Newcastle U, Hearts) 67
McCrory, S. 1958 (Southend U) 1
McCullough, K. 1935 (Belfast Celtic, Manchester C) 5
McCullough, L. 2014 (Doncaster R) 5
McCullough, W. J. 1961 (Arsenal, Millwall) 10
McCurdy, C. 1980 (Linfield) 1
McDonald, A. 1986 (QPR) 52
McDonald, R. 1930 (Rangers) 2
McDonnell, J. 1911 (Bohemians) 4
McElhinney, G. M. A. 1984 (Bolton W) 6
McEvilly, L. R. 2002 (Rochdale) 1
McFaul, W. S. 1967 (Linfield, Newcastle U) 6
McGarry, J. K. 1951 (Cliftonville) 3
McGaughey, M. 1985 (Linfield) 1
McGibbon, P. C. G. 1995 (Manchester U, Wigan Ath) 7
McGinn, N. 2009 (Celtic, Aberdeen) 51
McGivern, R. 2009 (Manchester C, Hibernian, Port Vale, Shrewsbury) 24
McGovern, M. 2010 (Ross Co, Hamilton A, Norwich C) 22
McGrath, R. C. 1974 (Tottenham H, Manchester U) 21
McGregor, S. 1921 (Glentoran) 1
McGrillen, J. 1924 (Clyde, Belfast Celtic) 2
McGuire, E. 1907 (Distillery) 1
McGuire, J. 1928 (Linfield) 1
McIlroy, H. 1906 (Cliftonville) 1
McIlroy, J. 1952 (Burnley, Stoke C) 55
McIlroy, S. B. 1972 (Manchester U, Stoke C, Manchester C) 88
McIlvenny, P. 1924 (Distillery) 1
McIlvenny, R. 1890 (Distillery, Ulster) 2
McKay, W. R. 2013 (Inverness CT, Wigan Ath) 11
McKeag, W. 1968 (Glentoran) 2

McKeague, T. 1925 (Glentoran) 1
McKee, F. W. 1906 (Cliftonville, Belfast Celtic) 5
McKelvey, H. 1901 (Glentoran) 2
McKenna, J. 1950 (Huddersfield T) 7
McKenzie, H. 1922 (Distillery) 2
McKenzie, R. 1967 (Airdrieonians) 1
McKeown, N. 1892 (Linfield) 7
McKie, H. 1895 (Cliftonville) 3
Mackie, J. A. 1923 (Arsenal, Portsmouth) 3
McKinney, D. 1921 (Hull C, Bradford C) 2
McKinney, V. J. 1966 (Falkirk) 1
McKnight, A. D. 1988 (Celtic, West Ham U) 10
McKnight, J. 1912 (Preston NE, Glentoran) 2
McLaughlin, C. G. 2012 (Preston NE, Fleetwood T) 26
McLaughlin, J. C. 1962 (Shrewsbury T, Swansea T) 12
McLaughlin, R. 2014 (Liverpool) 3
McLean, B. S. 2006 (Rangers) 1
McLean, T. 1885 (Limavady) 1
McMahon, G. J. 1995 (Tottenham H, Stoke C) 17
McMahon, J. 1934 (Bohemians) 1
McMaster, G. 1897 (Glentoran) 3
McMichael, A. 1950 (Newcastle U) 40
McMillan, G. 1903 (Distillery) 2
McMillan, S. T. 1963 (Manchester U) 2
McMillen, W. S. 1934 (Manchester U, Chesterfield) 7
McMordie, A. S. 1969 (Middlesbrough) 21
McMorran, E. J. 1947 (Belfast Celtic, Barnsley, Doncaster R) 15
McMullan, D. 1926 (Liverpool) 3
McNair, P. J. C. 2015 (Manchester U, Sunderland) 16
McNally, B. A. 1986 (Shrewsbury T) 5
McNinch, J. 1931 (Ballymena) 3
McPake, J. 2012 (Coventry C) 1
McParland, P. J. 1954 (Aston Villa, Wolverhampton W) 34
McQuoid, J. J. B. 2011 (Millwall) 5
McShane, J. 1899 (Cliftonville) 4
McVeigh, P. M. 1999 (Tottenham H, Norwich C) 20
McVicker, J. 1888 (Linfield, Glentoran) 2
McWha, W. B. R. 1882 (Knock, Cliftonville) 7
Madden, O. 1938 (Norwich C) 1
Magee, G. 1885 (Wellington Park) 3
Magennis, J. B. D. 2010 (Cardiff C, Aberdeen, St Mirren, Kilmarnock, Charlton Ath) 29
Magill, E. J. 1962 (Arsenal, Brighton & HA) 26
Magilton, J. 1991 (Oxford U, Southampton, Sheffield W, Ipswich T) 52
Maginnis, H. 1900 (Linfield) 8
Mahood, J. 1926 (Belfast Celtic, Ballymena) 9
Mannus, A. 2004 (Linfield, St Johnstone) 9
Manderson, R. 1920 (Rangers) 5
Mansfield, J. 1901 (Dublin Freebooters) 1
Martin, C. 1882 (Cliftonville) 3
Martin, C. 1925 (Bo'ness) 1
Martin, C. J. 1947 (Glentoran, Leeds U, Aston Villa) 6
Martin, D. K. 1934 (Belfast Celtic, Wolverhampton W, Nottingham F) 10
Mathieson, A. 1921 (Luton T) 2
Maxwell, J. 1902 (Linfield, Glentoran, Belfast Celtic) 7
Meek, H. L. 1925 (Glentoran) 1
Mehaffy, J. A. C. 1922 (Queen's Island) 1
Meldon, P. A. 1899 (Dublin Freebooters) 2
Mercer, H. V. A. 1908 (Linfield) 1
Mercer, J. T. 1898 (Distillery, Linfield, Distillery, Derby Co) 12
Millar, W. 1932 (Barrow) 2
Miller, J. 1929 (Middlesbrough) 3
Milligan, D. 1939 (Chesterfield) 1
Milne, R. G. 1894 (Linfield) 28
Mitchell, E. J. 1933 (Cliftonville, Glentoran) 2
Mitchell, W. 1932 (Distillery, Chelsea) 15
Molyneux, T. B. 1883 (Ligoniel, Cliftonville) 11
Montgomery, F. J. 1955 (Coleraine) 1
Moore, C. 1949 (Glentoran) 1
Moore, P. 1933 (Aberdeen) 1
Moore, R. 1891 (Linfield Ath) 3
Moore, R. L. 1887 (Ulster) 2
Moore, W. 1923 (Falkirk) 1
Moorhead, F. W. 1885 (Dublin University) 1
Moorhead, G. 1923 (Linfield) 4
Moran, J. 1912 (Leeds C) 1
Moreland, V. 1979 (Derby Co) 6
Morgan, G. F. 1922 (Linfield, Nottingham F) 8
Morgan, S. 1972 (Port Vale, Aston Villa, Brighton & HA, Sparta Rotterdam) 18
Morrison, R. 1891 (Linfield Ath) 2
Morrison, T. 1895 (Glentoran, Burnley) 7
Morrogh, D. 1896 (Bohemians) 1
Morrow, S. J. 1990 (Arsenal, QPR) 39
Morrow, W. J. 1883 (Moyola Park) 3
Muir, R. 1885 (Oldpark) 2
Mulgrew, J. 2010 (Linfield) 2
Mulholland, T. S. 1906 (Belfast Celtic) 2
Mullan, G. 1983 (Glentoran) 4
Mulligan, J. 1921 (Manchester C) 1
Mulryne, P. P. 1997 (Manchester U, Norwich C, Cardiff C) 27
Murdock, C. J. 2000 (Preston NE, Hibernian, Crewe Alex, Rotherham U) 34
Murphy, J. 1910 (Bradford C) 3
Murphy, N. 1905 (QPR) 3
Murray, J. M. 1910 (Motherwell, Sheffield W) 3

Napier, R. J. 1966 (Bolton W) 1
Neill, W. J. T. 1961 (Arsenal, Hull C) 59
Nelis, P. 1923 (Nottingham F) 1
Nelson, S. 1970 (Arsenal, Brighton & HA) 51
Nicholl, C. J. 1975 (Aston Villa, Southampton, Grimsby T) 51
Nicholl, H. 1902 (Belfast Celtic) 3
Nicholl, J. M. 1976 (Manchester U, Toronto Blizzard, Sunderland, Toronto Blizzard, Rangers, Toronto Blizzard, WBA) 73
Nicholson, J. J. 1961 (Manchester U, Huddersfield T) 41
Nixon, R. 1914 (Linfield) 1
Nolan, I. R. 1997 (Sheffield W, Bradford C, Wigan Ath) 18
Nolan-Whelan, J. V. 1901 (Dublin Freebooters) 5
Norwood, O. J. 2011 (Manchester U, Huddersfield T, Reading, Brighton & HA) 46

O'Boyle, G. 1994 (Dunfermline Ath, St Johnstone) 13
O'Brien, M. T. 1921 (QPR, Leicester C, Hull C, Derby Co) 10
O'Connell, P. 1912 (Sheffield W, Hull C) 5
O'Connor, M. J. 2008 (Crewe Alex, Scunthorpe U, Rotherham U) 11
O'Doherty, A. 1970 (Coleraine) 2
O'Driscoll, J. F. 1949 (Swansea T) 3
O'Hagan, C. 1905 (Tottenham H, Aberdeen) 11
O'Hagan, W. 1920 (St Mirren) 2
O'Hehir, J. C. 1910 (Bohemians) 1
O'Kane, W. J. 1970 (Nottingham F) 20
O'Mahoney, M. T. 1939 (Bristol R) 1
O'Neill, C. 1989 (Motherwell) 3
O'Neill, J. 1962 (Sunderland) 1
O'Neill, J. P. 1980 (Leicester C) 39
O'Neill, M. A. M. 1988 (Newcastle U, Dundee U, Hibernian, Coventry C) 31
O'Neill, M. H. M. 1972 (Distillery, Nottingham F, Norwich C, Manchester C, Norwich C, Notts Co) 64
O'Reilly, H. 1901 (Dublin Freebooters) 3
Owens, J. 2011 (Crusaders) 1

Parke, J. 1964 (Linfield, Hibernian, Sunderland) 14
Paterson, M. A. 2008 (Scunthorpe U, Burnley, Huddersfield T) 22
Paton, P. R. 2014 (Dundee U) 4
Patterson, D. J. 1994 (Crystal Palace, Luton T, Dundee U) 17
Patterson, R. 2010 (Coleraine, Plymouth Arg) 5
Peacock, R. 1952 (Celtic, Coleraine) 31
Peden, J. 1887 (Linfield, Distillery) 24
Penney, S. 1985 (Brighton & HA) 17
Percy, J. C. 1889 (Belfast YMCA) 1
Platt, J. A. 1976 (Middlesbrough, Ballymena U, Coleraine) 23
Pollock, W. 1928 (Belfast Celtic) 1
Ponsonby, J. 1895 (Distillery) 9
Potts, R. M. C. 1883 (Cliftonville) 2
Priestley, T. J. M. 1933 (Coleraine, Chelsea) 2
Pyper, Jas. 1897 (Cliftonville) 7
Pyper, John 1897 (Cliftonville) 9
Pyper, M. 1932 (Linfield) 1

Quinn, J. M. 1985 (Blackburn R, Swindon T, Leicester C, Bradford C, West Ham U, Bournemouth, Reading) 46

Quinn, S. J. 1996 (Blackpool, WBA, Willem II, Sheffield W, Peterborough U, Northampton T) 50

Rafferty, P. 1980 (Linfield) 1
Ramsey, P. C. 1984 (Leicester C) 14
Rankine, J. 1883 (Alexander) 2
Rattray, D. 1882 (Avoniel) 3
Rea, R. 1901 (Glentoran) 1
Reeves, B. N. 2015 (Milton Keynes D) 2
Redmond, R. 1884 (Cliftonville) 1
Reid, G. H. 1923 (Cardiff C) 1
Reid, J. 1883 (Ulster) 6
Reid, S. E. 1934 (Derby Co) 3
Reid, W. 1931 (Hearts) 1
Reilly, M. M. 1900 (Portsmouth) 2
Renneville, W. T. J. 1910 (Leyton, Aston Villa) 4
Reynolds, J. 1890 (Distillery, Ulster) 5
Reynolds, R. 1905 (Bohemians) 1
Rice, P. J. 1969 (Arsenal) 49
Roberts, F. C. 1931 (Glentoran) 1
Robinson, P. 1920 (Distillery, Blackburn R) 2
Robinson, S. 1997 (Bournemouth, Luton T) 7
Rogan, A. 1988 (Celtic, Sunderland, Millwall) 18
Rollo, D. 1912 (Linfield, Blackburn R) 16
Roper, E. O. 1886 (Dublin University) 1
Rosbotham, A. 1887 (Cliftonville) 7
Ross, W. E. 1969 (Newcastle U) 1
Rowland, K. 1994 (West Ham U, QPR) 19
Rowley, R. W. M. 1929 (Southampton, Tottenham H) 6
Rushe, F. 1925 (Distillery) 1
Russell, A. 1947 (Linfield) 1
Russell, S. R. 1930 (Bradford C, Derry C) 3
Ryan, R. A. 1950 (WBA) 1

Sanchez, L. P. 1987 (Wimbledon) 3
Scott, E. 1920 (Liverpool, Belfast Celtic) 31
Scott, J. 1958 (Grimsby) 2
Scott, J. E. 1901 (Cliftonville) 1
Scott, L. J. 1895 (Dublin University) 2
Scott, P. W. 1975 (Everton, York C, Aldershot) 10
Scott, T. 1894 (Cliftonville) 13
Scott, W. 1903 (Linfield, Everton, Leeds C) 25
Scraggs, M. J. 1921 (Glentoran) 2
Seymour, H. C. 1914 (Bohemians) 1
Seymour, J. 1907 (Cliftonville) 2
Shanks, T. 1903 (Woolwich Arsenal, Brentford) 3
Sharkey, P. G. 1976 (Ipswich T) 1
Sheehan, Dr G. 1899 (Bohemians) 3
Sheridan, J. 1903 (Everton, Stoke C) 6
Sherrard, J. 1885 (Limavady) 3
Sherrard, W. C. 1895 (Cliftonville) 3
Sherry, J. J. 1906 (Bohemians) 2
Shields, R. J. 1957 (Southampton) 1
Shiels, D. 2006 (Hibernian, Doncaster R, Kilmarnock) 14
Silo, M. 1888 (Belfast YMCA) 1
Simpson, W. J. 1951 (Rangers) 12
Sinclair, J. 1882 (Knock) 2
Slemin, J. C. 1909 (Bohemians) 1
Sloan, A. S. 1925 (London Caledonians) 1
Sloan, D. 1969 (Oxford U) 2
Sloan, H. A. de B. 1903 (Bohemians) 8
Sloan, J. W. 1947 (Arsenal) 1
Sloan, T. 1926 (Cardiff C, Linfield) 11
Sloan, T. 1979 (Manchester U) 3
Small, J. M. 1887 (Clarence, Cliftonville) 4
Smith, A. W. 2003 (Glentoran, Preston NE) 18
Smith, E. E. 1921 (Cardiff C) 4
Smith, J. E. 1901 (Distillery) 2
Smith, M. 2016 (Peterborough U) 1
Smyth, R. H. 1886 (Dublin University) 1
Smyth, S. 1948 (Wolverhampton W, Stoke C) 9
Smyth, W. 1949 (Distillery) 4
Snape, A. 1920 (Airdrieonians) 1
Sonner, D. J. 1998 (Ipswich T, Sheffield W, Birmingham C, Nottingham F, Peterborough U) 13
Spence, D. W. 1975 (Bury, Blackpool, Southend U) 29
Spencer, S. 1890 (Distillery) 6
Spiller, E. A. 1883 (Cliftonville) 5
Sproule, I. 2006 (Hibernian, Bristol C) 11
Stanfield, O. M. 1887 (Distillery) 30
Steele, A. 1926 (Charlton Ath, Fulham) 4
Steele, J. 2013 (New York Red Bulls) 3
Stevenson, A. E. 1934 (Rangers, Everton) 17
Stewart, A. 1967 (Glentoran, Derby Co) 7
Stewart, D. C. 1978 (Hull C) 1
Stewart, I. 1982 (QPR, Newcastle U) 31
Stewart, R. K. 1890 (St Columb's Court, Cliftonville) 11
Stewart, T. C. 1961 (Linfield) 1
Swan, S. 1899 (Linfield) 1

Taggart, G. P. 1990 (Barnsley, Bolton W, Leicester C) 51
Taggart, J. 1899 (Walsall) 1
Taylor, M. S. 1999 (Fulham, Birmingham C, unattached) 88
Thompson, A. L. 2011 (Watford) 2
Thompson, F. W. 1910 (Cliftonville, Linfield, Bradford C, Clyde) 12
Thompson, J. 1897 (Distillery) 1
Thompson, P. 2006 (Linfield, Stockport Co) 8
Thompson, R. 1928 (Queen's Island) 1
Thompson, W. 1889 (Belfast Ath) 1
Thunder, P. J. 1911 (Bohemians) 1
Todd, S. J. 1966 (Burnley, Sheffield W) 11
Toner, C. 2003 (Leyton Orient) 2
Toner, J. 1922 (Arsenal, St Johnstone) 8
Torrans, R. 1893 (Linfield) 1
Torrans, S. 1889 (Linfield) 26
Trainor, D. 1967 (Crusaders) 1
Tuffey, J. 2009 (Partick Thistle, Inverness CT) 8
Tully, C. P. 1949 (Celtic) 10
Turner, A. 1896 (Cliftonville) 1
Turner, E. 1896 (Cliftonville) 1
Turner, W. 1886 (Cliftonville) 3
Twomey, J. F. 1938 (Leeds U) 2

Uprichard, W. N. M. C. 1952 (Swindon T, Portsmouth) 18

Vernon, J. 1947 (Belfast Celtic, WBA) 17

Waddell, T. M. R. 1906 (Cliftonville) 1
Walker, J. 1955 (Doncaster R) 1
Walker, T. 1911 (Bury) 1
Walsh, D. J. 1947 (WBA) 9
Walsh, W. 1948 (Manchester C) 5
Ward, J. J. 2012 (Derby Co, Nottingham F) 30
Waring, J. 1899 (Cliftonville) 1
Warren, P. 1913 (Shelbourne) 2
Washington, C. J. 2016 (QPR) 10
Watson, J. 1883 (Ulster) 9
Watson, P. 1971 (Distillery) 1
Watson, T. 1926 (Cardiff C) 1
Wattie, J. 1899 (Distillery) 1
Webb, C. G. 1909 (Brighton & HA) 3
Webb, S. M. 2006 (Ross Co) 4
Weir, E. 1939 (Clyde) 1
Welsh, E. 1966 (Carlisle U) 4
Whiteside, N. 1982 (Manchester U, Everton) 38
Whiteside, T. 1891 (Distillery) 1
Whitfield, E. R. 1886 (Dublin University) 1
Whitley, Jeff 1997 (Manchester C, Sunderland, Cardiff C) 20
Whitley, Jim 1998 (Manchester C) 3
Williams, J. R. 1886 (Ulster) 2
Williams, M. S. 1999 (Chesterfield, Watford, Wimbledon, Stoke C, Wimbledon, Milton Keynes D) 36
Williams, P. A. 1991 (WBA) 1
Williamson, J. 1890 (Cliftonville) 3
Willighan, T. 1933 (Burnley) 2
Willis, G. 1906 (Linfield) 4
Wilson, D. J. 1987 (Brighton & HA, Luton T, Sheffield W) 24
Wilson, H. 1925 (Linfield) 2
Wilson, K. J. 1987 (Ipswich T, Chelsea, Notts Co, Walsall) 42
Wilson, M. 1884 (Distillery) 3
Wilson, R. 1888 (Cliftonville) 1
Wilson, S. J. 1962 (Glenavon, Falkirk, Dundee) 12
Wilton, J. M. 1888 (St Columb's Court, Cliftonville, St Columb's Court) 7
Winchester, C. 2011 (Oldham Ath) 1
Wood, T. J. 1996 (Walsall) 1
Worthington, N. 1984 (Sheffield W, Leeds U, Stoke C) 66
Wright, J. 1906 (Cliftonville) 6
Wright, T. J. 1989 (Newcastle U, Nottingham F, Manchester C) 31

Young, S. 1907 (Linfield, Airdrieonians, Linfield) 9

SCOTLAND

Adam, C. G. 2007 (Rangers, Blackpool, Liverpool, Stoke C) 26
Adams, J. 1889 (Hearts) 3
Agnew, W. B. 1907 (Kilmarnock) 3
Aird, J. 1954 (Burnley) 4
Aitken, A. 1901 (Newcastle U, Middlesbrough, Leicester Fosse) 14
Aitken, G. G. 1949 (East Fife, Sunderland) 8
Aitken, R. 1886 (Dumbarton) 2
Aitken, R. 1980 (Celtic, Newcastle U, St Mirren) 57
Aitkenhead, W. A. C. 1912 (Blackburn R) 1
Albiston, A. 1982 (Manchester U) 14
Alexander, D. 1894 (East Stirlingshire) 2
Alexander, G. 2002 (Preston NE, Burnley) 40
Alexander, N. 2006 (Cardiff C) 3
Allan, D. S. 1885 (Queen's Park) 3
Allan, G. 1897 (Liverpool) 1
Allan, H. 1902 (Hearts) 1
Allan, J. 1887 (Queen's Park) 2
Allan, T. 1974 (Dundee) 2
Ancell, R. F. D. 1937 (Newcastle U) 2
Anderson, A. 1933 (Hearts) 23
Anderson, F. 1874 (Clydesdale) 1
Anderson, G. 1901 (Kilmarnock) 1
Anderson, H. A. 1914 (Raith R) 1
Anderson, J. 1954 (Leicester C) 1
Anderson, K. 1896 (Queen's Park) 3
Anderson, R. 2003 (Aberdeen, Sunderland) 11
Anderson, W. 1882 (Queen's Park) 6
Andrews, P. 1875 (Eastern) 1
Anya, I. 2013 (Watford, Derby Co) 27
Archibald, A. 1921 (Rangers) 8
Archibald, S. 1980 (Aberdeen, Tottenham H, Barcelona) 27
Armstrong, M. W. 1936 (Aberdeen) 3
Armstrong, S. 2017 (Celtic) 2
Arnott, W. 1883 (Queen's Park) 14
Auld, J. R. 1887 (Third Lanark) 3
Auld, R. 1959 (Celtic) 3

Baird, A. 1892 (Queen's Park) 2
Baird, D. 1890 (Hearts) 3
Baird, H. 1956 (Airdrieonians) 1
Baird, J. C. 1876 (Vale of Leven) 3
Baird, S. 1957 (Rangers) 7
Baird, W. U. 1897 (St Bernard) 1
Bannan, B. 2011 (Aston Villa, Crystal Palace, Sheffield W) 25
Bannon, E. J. 1980 (Dundee U) 11
Barbour, A. 1885 (Renton) 1
Bardsley, P. A. 2011 (Sunderland) 13
Barker, J. B. 1893 (Rangers) 2
Barr, D. 2009 (Falkirk) 1
Barrett, F. 1894 (Dundee) 2
Battles, B. 1901 (Celtic) 3
Battles, B. jun. 1931 (Hearts) 1
Bauld, W. 1950 (Hearts) 3
Baxter, J. C. 1961 (Rangers, Sunderland) 34
Baxter, R. D. 1939 (Middlesbrough) 3
Beattie, A. 1937 (Preston NE) 7
Beattie, C. 2006 (Celtic, WBA) 7
Beattie, R. 1939 (Preston NE) 1
Begbie, I. 1890 (Hearts) 4
Bell, A. 1912 (Manchester U) 1
Bell, C. 2011 (Kilmarnock) 1
Bell, J. 1890 (Dumbarton, Everton, Celtic) 10
Bell, M. 1901 (Hearts) 1
Bell, W. J. 1966 (Leeds U) 2
Bennett, A. 1904 (Celtic, Rangers) 11
Bennie, R. 1925 (Airdrieonians) 3
Bernard, P. R. J. 1995 (Oldham Ath) 2
Berra, C. D. 2008 (Hearts, Wolverhampton W, Ipswich T) 36
Berry, D. 1894 (Queen's Park) 3
Berry, W. H. 1888 (Queen's Park) 4
Bett, J. 1982 (Rangers, Lokeren, Aberdeen) 25
Beveridge, W. W. 1879 (Glasgow University) 3
Black, A. 1938 (Hearts) 3
Black, D. 1889 (Hurlford) 1
Black, E. 1988 (Metz) 2
Black, I. 2013 (Rangers) 1
Black, I. H. 1948 (Southampton) 1
Blackburn, J. E. 1873 (Royal Engineers) 1
Blacklaw, A. S. 1963 (Burnley) 3
Blackley, J. 1974 (Hibernian) 7
Blair, D. 1929 (Clyde, Aston Villa) 8
Blair, J. 1920 (Sheffield W, Cardiff C) 8
Blair, J. 1934 (Motherwell) 1
Blair, J. A. 1947 (Blackpool) 1
Blair, W. 1896 (Third Lanark) 1
Blessington, J. 1894 (Celtic) 4
Blyth, J. A. 1978 (Coventry C) 2
Bone, J. 1972 (Norwich C) 2
Booth, S. 1993 (Aberdeen, Borussia Dortmund, Twente) 21
Bowie, J. 1920 (Rangers) 2
Bowie, W. 1891 (Linthouse) 1
Bowman, D. 1992 (Dundee U) 6
Bowman, G. A. 1892 (Montrose) 1
Boyd, G. I. 2013 (Peterborough U, Hull C) 2
Boyd, J. M. 1934 (Newcastle U) 1
Boyd, K. 2006 (Rangers, Middlesbrough) 18
Boyd, R. 1889 (Mossend Swifts) 2
Boyd, T. 1991 (Motherwell, Chelsea, Celtic) 72
Boyd, W. G. 1931 (Clyde) 2
Bradshaw, T. 1928 (Bury) 1
Brand, R. 1961 (Rangers) 8
Brandon, T. 1896 (Blackburn R) 1
Brazil, A. 1980 (Ipswich T, Tottenham H) 13
Breckenridge, T. 1888 (Hearts) 1
Bremner, D. 1976 (Hibernian) 1
Bremner, W. J. 1965 (Leeds U) 54
Brennan, F. 1947 (Newcastle U) 7
Breslin, B. 1897 (Hibernian) 1
Brewster, G. 1921 (Everton) 1
Bridcutt, L. 2013 (Brighton & HA, Sunderland) 2
Broadfoot, K. 2009 (Rangers) 4
Brogan, J. 1971 (Celtic) 4
Brown, A. 1890 (St Mirren) 2
Brown, A. 1904 (Middlesbrough) 1
Brown, A. D. 1950 (East Fife, Blackpool) 14
Brown, G. C. P. 1931 (Rangers) 19
Brown, H. 1947 (Partick Thistle) 3
Brown, J. B. 1939 (Clyde) 1
Brown, J. G. 1975 (Sheffield U) 1
Brown, R. 1884 (Dumbarton) 2
Brown, R. 1890 (Cambuslang) 1
Brown, R. 1947 (Rangers) 3
Brown, R. jun. 1885 (Dumbarton) 1
Brown, S. 2006 (Hibernian, Celtic) 53
Brown, W. D. F. 1958 (Dundee, Tottenham H) 28
Browning, J. 1914 (Celtic) 1
Brownlie, J. 1909 (Third Lanark) 16
Brownlie, J. 1971 (Hibernian) 7
Bruce, D. 1890 (Vale of Leven) 1
Bruce, R. F. 1934 (Middlesbrough) 1
Bryson, C. 2011 (Kilmarnock, Derby Co) 3
Buchan, M. M. 1972 (Aberdeen, Manchester U) 34
Buchanan, J. 1889 (Cambuslang) 1
Buchanan, J. 1929 (Rangers) 2
Buchanan, P. S. 1938 (Chelsea) 1
Buchanan, R. 1891 (Abercorn) 1
Buckley, P. 1954 (Aberdeen) 3
Buick, A. 1902 (Hearts) 2
Burchill, M. J. 2000 (Celtic) 6
Burke, C. 2006 (Rangers, Birmingham C) 7
Burke O. J. 2016 (Nottingham F, RB Leipzig) 5
Burley, C. W. 1995 (Chelsea, Celtic, Derby Co) 46
Burley, G. E. 1979 (Ipswich T) 11
Burns, F. 1970 (Manchester U) 1
Burns, K. 1974 (Birmingham C, Nottingham F) 20
Burns, T. 1981 (Celtic) 8
Busby, M. W. 1934 (Manchester C) 1

Caddis, P. M. 2016 (Birmingham C) 1
Cairney, T. 2017 (Fulham) 1
Cairns, T. 1920 (Rangers) 8
Calderhead, D. 1889 (Q of S Wanderers) 1
Calderwood, C. 1995 (Tottenham H) 36
Calderwood, R. 1885 (Cartvale) 3
Caldow, E. 1957 (Rangers) 40
Caldwell, G. 2002 (Newcastle U, Hibernian, Celtic, Wigan Ath) 55

Caldwell, S. 2001 (Newcastle U, Sunderland, Burnley,Wigan Ath) 12
Callaghan, P. 1900 (Hibernian) 1
Callaghan, W. 1970 (Dunfermline Ath) 2
Cameron, C. 1999 (Hearts, Wolverhampton W) 28
Cameron, J. 1886 (Rangers) 1
Cameron, J. 1896 (Queen's Park) 1
Cameron, J. 1904 (St Mirren, Chelsea) 2
Campbell, C. 1874 (Queen's Park) 13
Campbell, H. 1889 (Renton) 1
Campbell, Jas 1913 (Sheffield W) 1
Campbell, J. 1880 (South Western) 1
Campbell, J. 1891 (Kilmarnock) 2
Campbell, John 1893 (Celtic) 12
Campbell, John 1899 (Rangers) 4
Campbell, K. 1920 (Liverpool, Partick Thistle) 8
Campbell, P. 1878 (Rangers) 2
Campbell, P. 1898 (Morton) 1
Campbell, R. 1947 (Falkirk, Chelsea) 5
Campbell, W. 1947 (Morton) 5
Canero, P. 2004 (Leicester C) 1
Carabine, J. 1938 (Third Lanark) 3
Carr, W. M. 1970 (Coventry C) 6
Cassidy, J. 1921 (Celtic) 4
Chalmers, S. 1965 (Celtic) 5
Chalmers, W. 1885 (Rangers) 1
Chalmers, W. S. 1929 (Queen's Park) 1
Chambers, T. 1894 (Hearts) 1
Chaplin, G. D. 1908 (Dundee) 1
Cheyne, A. G. 1929 (Aberdeen) 5
Christie, A. J. 1898 (Queen's Park) 3
Christie, R. M. 1884 (Queen's Park) 1
Clark, J. 1966 (Celtic) 4
Clark, R. B. 1968 (Aberdeen) 17
Clarke, S. 1988 (Chelsea) 6
Clarkson, D. 2008 (Motherwell) 2
Cleland, J. 1891 (Royal Albert) 1
Clements, R. 1891 (Leith Ath) 1
Clunas, W. L. 1924 (Sunderland) 2
Collier, W. 1922 (Raith R) 1
Collins, J. 1988 (Hibernian, Celtic, Monaco, Everton) 58
Collins, R. Y. 1951 (Celtic, Everton, Leeds U) 31
Collins, T. 1909 (Hearts) 1
Colman, D. 1911 (Aberdeen) 4
Colquhoun, E. P. 1972 (Sheffield U) 9
Colquhoun, J. 1988 (Hearts) 2
Combe, J. R. 1948 (Hibernian) 3
Commons, K. 2009 (Derby Co, Celtic) 12
Conn, A. 1956 (Hearts) 1
Conn, A. 1975 (Tottenham H) 2
Connachan, E. D. 1962 (Dunfermline Ath) 2
Connelly, G. 1974 (Celtic) 2
Connolly, J. 1973 (Everton) 1
Connor, J. 1886 (Airdrieonians) 1
Connor, J. 1930 (Sunderland) 4
Connor, R. 1986 (Dundee, Aberdeen) 4
Conway, C. 2010 (Dundee U, Cardiff C) 7
Cook, W. L. 1934 (Bolton W) 3
Cooke, C. 1966 (Dundee, Chelsea) 16
Cooper, D. 1980 (Rangers, Motherwell) 22
Cormack, P. B. 1966 (Hibernian, Nottingham F) 9
Cowan, J. 1896 (Aston Villa) 3
Cowan, J. 1948 (Morton) 25
Cowan, W, D. 1924 (Newcastle U) 1
Cowie, D. 1953 (Dundee) 20
Cowie, D. M. 2010 (Watford, Cardiff C) 10
Cox, C. J. 1948 (Hearts) 1
Cox, S. 1949 (Rangers) 24
Craig, A. 1929 (Motherwell) 3
Craig, J. 1977 (Celtic) 1
Craig, J. P. 1968 (Celtic) 1
Craig, T. 1927 (Rangers) 8
Craig, T. B. 1976 (Newcastle U) 1
Crainey, S. D. 2002 (Celtic, Southampton, Blackpool) 12
Crapnell, J. 1929 (Airdrieonians) 9
Crawford, D. 1894 (St Mirren, Rangers) 3
Crawford, J. 1932 (Queen's Park) 5
Crawford, S. 1995 (Raith R, Dunfermline Ath, Plymouth Arg) 25
Crerand, P. T. 1961 (Celtic, Manchester U) 16
Cringan, W. 1920 (Celtic) 5
Crosbie, J. A. 1920 (Ayr U, Birmingham) 2
Croal, J. A. 1913 (Falkirk) 3
Cropley, A. J. 1972 (Hibernian) 2
Cross, J. H. 1903 (Third Lanark) 1
Cruickshank, J. 1964 (Hearts) 6
Crum, J. 1936 (Celtic) 2
Cullen, M. J. 1956 (Luton T) 1
Cumming, D. S. 1938 (Middlesbrough) 1
Cumming, J. 1955 (Hearts) 9
Cummings, G. 1935 (Partick Thistle, Aston Villa) 9
Cummings, W. 2002 (Chelsea) 1
Cunningham, A. N. 1920 (Rangers) 12
Cunningham, W. C. 1954 (Preston NE) 8
Curran, H. P. 1970 (Wolverhampton W) 5

Dailly, C. 1997 (Derby Co, Blackburn R, West Ham U, Rangers) 67
Dalglish, K. 1972 (Celtic, Liverpool) 102
Davidson, C. I. 1999 (Blackburn R, Leicester C, Preston NE) 19
Davidson, D. 1878 (Queen's Park) 5
Davidson, J. A. 1954 (Partick Thistle) 8
Davidson, M. 2013 (St Johnstone) 1
Davidson, S. 1921 (Middlesbrough) 1
Dawson, A. 1980 (Rangers) 5
Dawson, J. 1935 (Rangers) 14
Deans, J. 1975 (Celtic) 2
Delaney, J. 1936 (Celtic, Manchester U) 13
Devine, A. 1910 (Falkirk) 1
Devlin, P. J. 2003 (Birmingham C) 10
Dewar, G. 1888 (Dumbarton) 2
Dewar, N. 1932 (Third Lanark) 3
Dick, J. 1959 (West Ham U) 1
Dickie, M. 1897 (Rangers) 3
Dickov, P. 2001 (Manchester C, Leicester C, Blackburn R) 10
Dickson, W. 1888 (Dundee Strathmore) 1
Dickson, W. 1970 (Kilmarnock) 5
Divers, J. 1895 (Celtic) 1
Divers, J. 1939 (Celtic) 1
Dixon, P. A. 2013 (Hudderfield T) 3
Dobie, R. S. 2002 (WBA) 6
Docherty, T. H. 1952 (Preston NE, Arsenal) 25
Dodds, D. 1984 (Dundee U) 2
Dodds, J. 1914 (Celtic) 3
Dodds, W. 1997 (Aberdeen, Dundee U, Rangers) 26
Doig, J. E. 1887 (Arbroath, Sunderland) 5
Donachie, W. 1972 (Manchester C) 35
Donaldson, A. 1914 (Bolton W) 6
Donnachie, J. 1913 (Oldham Ath) 3
Donnelly, S. 1997 (Celtic) 10
Dorrans, G. 2010 (WBA, Norwich C) 12
Dougal, J. 1939 (Preston NE) 1
Dougall, C. 1947 (Birmingham C) 1
Dougan, R. 1950 (Hearts) 1
Douglas, A. 1911 (Chelsea) 1
Douglas, J. 1880 (Renfrew) 1
Douglas, R. 2002 (Celtic, Leicester C) 19
Dowds, P. 1892 (Celtic) 1
Downie, R. 1892 (Third Lanark) 1
Doyle, D. 1892 (Celtic) 8
Doyle, J. 1976 (Ayr U) 1
Drummond, J. 1892 (Falkirk, Rangers) 14
Dunbar, M. 1886 (Cartvale) 1
Duncan, A. 1975 (Hibernian) 6
Duncan, D. 1933 (Derby Co) 14
Duncan, D. M. 1948 (East Fife) 3
Duncan, J. 1878 (Alexandra Ath) 2
Duncan, J. 1926 (Leicester C) 1
Duncanson, J. 1947 (Rangers) 1
Dunlop, J. 1890 (St Mirren) 1
Dunlop, W. 1906 (Liverpool) 1
Dunn, J. 1925 (Hibernian, Everton) 6
Durie, G. S. 1988 (Chelsea, Tottenham H, Rangers) 43
Durrant, I. 1988 (Rangers, Kilmarnock) 20
Dykes, J. 1938 (Hearts) 2

Easson, J. F. 1931 (Portsmouth) 3
Elliott, M. S. 1998 (Leicester C) 18
Ellis, J. 1892 (Mossend Swifts) 1
Evans, A. 1982 (Aston Villa) 4
Evans, R. 1949 (Celtic, Chelsea) 48
Ewart, J. 1921 (Bradford C) 1
Ewing, T. 1958 (Partick Thistle) 2

Farm, G. N. 1953 (Blackpool) 10
Ferguson, B. 1999 (Rangers, Blackburn R, Rangers) 45

Ferguson, D. 1988 (Rangers) 2
Ferguson, D. 1992 (Dundee U, Everton) 7
Ferguson, I. 1989 (Rangers) 9
Ferguson, J. 1874 (Vale of Leven) 6
Ferguson, R. 1966 (Kilmarnock) 7
Fernie, W. 1954 (Celtic) 12
Findlay, R. 1898 (Kilmarnock) 1
Fitchie, T. T. 1905 (Woolwich Arsenal, Queen's Park) 4
Flavell, R. 1947 (Airdrieonians) 2
Fleck, R. 1990 (Norwich C) 4
Fleming, C. 1954 (East Fife) 1
Fleming, J. W. 1929 (Rangers) 3
Fleming, R. 1886 (Morton) 1
Fletcher, D. B. 2004 (Manchester U, WBA) 78
Fletcher, S. K. 2008 (Hibernian, Burnley, Wolverhampton W, Sunderland, Sheffield W) 30
Forbes, A. R. 1947 (Sheffield U, Arsenal) 14
Forbes, J. 1884 (Vale of Leven) 5
Ford, D. 1974 (Hearts) 3
Forrest, J. 1958 (Motherwell) 1
Forrest, J. 1966 (Rangers, Aberdeen) 5
Forrest, J. 2011 (Celtic) 17
Forsyth, A. 1972 (Partick Thistle, Manchester U) 10
Forsyth, C. 2014 (Derby Co) 4
Forsyth, R. C. 1964 (Kilmarnock) 4
Forsyth, T. 1971 (Motherwell, Rangers) 22
Fox, D. J. 2010 (Burnley, Southampton) 4
Foyers, R. 1893 (St Bernards) 2
Fraser, D. M. 1968 (WBA) 2
Fraser, J. 1891 (Moffat) 1
Fraser, J. 1907 (Dundee) 1
Fraser, M. J. E. 1880 (Queen's Park) 5
Fraser, R. 2017 (Bournemouth) 1
Fraser, W. 1955 (Sunderland) 2
Freedman, D. A. 2002 (Crystal Palace) 2
Fulton, W. 1884 (Abercorn) 1
Fyfe, J. H. 1895 (Third Lanark) 1

Gabriel, J. 1961 (Everton) 2
Gallacher, H. K. 1924 (Airdrieonians, Newcastle U, Chelsea, Derby Co) 20
Gallacher, K. W. 1988 (Dundee U, Coventry C, Blackburn R, Newcastle U) 53
Gallacher, P. 1935 (Sunderland) 1
Gallacher, P. 2002 (Dundee U) 8
Gallagher, P. 2004 (Blackburn R) 1
Galloway, M. 1992 (Celtic) 1
Galt, J. H. 1908 (Rangers) 2
Gardiner, I. 1958 (Motherwell) 1
Gardner, D. R. 1897 (Third Lanark) 1
Gardner, R. 1872 (Queen's Park, Clydesdale) 5
Gemmell, T. 1955 (St Mirren) 2
Gemmell, T. 1966 (Celtic) 18
Gemmill, A. 1971 (Derby Co, Nottingham F, Birmingham C) 43
Gemmill, S. 1995 (Nottingham F, Everton) 26
Gibb, W. 1873 (Clydesdale) 1
Gibson, D. W. 1963 (Leicester C) 7
Gibson, J. D. 1926 (Partick Thistle, Aston Villa) 8
Gibson, N. 1895 (Rangers, Partick Thistle) 14
Gilchrist, J. E. 1922 (Celtic) 1
Gilhooley, M. 1922 (Hull C) 1
Gilks, M. 2013 (Blackpool) 3
Gillespie, G. 1880 (Rangers, Queen's Park) 7
Gillespie, G. T. 1988 (Liverpool) 13
Gillespie, Jas 1898 (Third Lanark) 1
Gillespie, John 1896 (Queen's Park) 1
Gillespie, R. 1927 (Queen's Park) 4
Gillick, T. 1937 (Everton) 5
Gilmour, J. 1931 (Dundee) 1
Gilzean, A. J. 1964 (Dundee, Tottenham H) 22
Glass, S. 1999 (Newcastle U) 1
Glavin, R. 1977 (Celtic) 1
Glen, A. 1956 (Aberdeen) 2
Glen, R. 1895 (Renton, Hibernian) 3
Goodwillie, D. 2011 (Dundee U, Blackburn R) 3
Goram, A. L. 1986 (Oldham Ath, Hibernian, Rangers) 43
Gordon, C. A. 2004 (Hearts, Sunderland, Celtic) 47
Gordon, J. E. 1912 (Rangers) 10
Gossland, J. 1884 (Rangers) 1
Goudie, J. 1884 (Abercorn) 1
Gough, C. R. 1983 (Dundee U, Tottenham H, Rangers) 61
Gould, J. 2000 (Celtic) 2
Gourlay, J. 1886 (Cambuslang) 2
Govan, J. 1948 (Hibernian) 6
Gow, D. R. 1888 (Rangers) 1
Gow, J. J. 1885 (Queen's Park) 1
Gow, J. R. 1888 (Rangers) 1
Graham, A. 1978 (Leeds U) 11
Graham, G. 1972 (Arsenal, Manchester U) 12
Graham, J. 1884 (Annbank) 1
Graham, J. A. 1921 (Arsenal) 1
Grant, J. 1959 (Hibernian) 2
Grant, P. 1989 (Celtic) 2
Gray, A. 1903 (Hibernian) 1
Gray, A. D. 2003 (Bradford C) 2
Gray, A. M. 1976 (Aston Villa, Wolverhampton W, Everton) 20
Gray, D. 1929 (Rangers) 10
Gray, E. 1969 (Leeds U) 12
Gray, F. T. 1976 (Leeds U, Nottingham F, Leeds U) 32
Gray, W. 1886 (Pollokshields Ath) 1
Green, A. 1971 (Blackpool, Newcastle U) 6
Greer, G. 2013 (Brighton & HA) 11
Greig, J. 1964 (Rangers) 44
Griffiths, L. 2013 (Hibernian, Celtic) 13
Groves, W. 1888 (Hibernian, Celtic) 3
Gulliland, W. 1891 (Queen's Park) 4
Gunn, B. 1990 (Norwich C) 6

Haddock, H. 1955 (Clyde) 6
Haddow, D. 1894 (Rangers) 1
Haffey, F. 1960 (Celtic) 2
Hamilton, A. 1885 (Queen's Park) 4
Hamilton, A. W. 1962 (Dundee) 24
Hamilton, G. 1906 (Port Glasgow Ath) 1
Hamilton, G. 1947 (Aberdeen) 5
Hamilton, J. 1892 (Queen's Park) 3
Hamilton, J. 1924 (St Mirren) 1
Hamilton, R. C. 1899 (Rangers, Dundee) 11
Hamilton, T. 1891 (Hurlford) 1
Hamilton, T. 1932 (Rangers) 1
Hamilton, W. M. 1965 (Hibernian) 1
Hammell, S. 2005 (Motherwell) 1
Hanley, G. C. 2011 (Blackburn R, Newcastle U) 27
Hannah, A. B. 1888 (Renton) 1
Hannah, J. 1889 (Third Lanark) 1
Hansen, A. D. 1979 (Liverpool) 26
Hansen, J. 1972 (Partick Thistle) 2
Harkness, J. D. 1927 (Queen's Park, Hearts) 12
Harper, J. M. 1973 (Aberdeen, Hibernian, Aberdeen) 4
Harper, W. 1923 (Hibernian, Arsenal) 11
Harris, J. 1921 (Partick Thistle) 2
Harris, N. 1924 (Newcastle U) 1
Harrower, W. 1882 (Queen's Park) 3
Hartford, R. A. 1972 (WBA, Manchester C, Everton, Manchester C) 50
Hartley, P. J. 2005 (Hearts, Celtic, Bristol C) 25
Harvey, D. 1973 (Leeds U) 16
Hastings, A. C. 1936 (Sunderland) 2
Haughney, M. 1954 (Celtic) 1
Hay, D. 1970 (Celtic) 27
Hay, J. 1905 (Celtic, Newcastle U) 11
Hegarty, P. 1979 (Dundee U) 8
Heggie, C. 1886 (Rangers) 1
Henderson, G. H. 1904 (Rangers) 1
Henderson, J. G. 1953 (Portsmouth, Arsenal) 7
Henderson, W. 1963 (Rangers) 29
Hendry, E. C. J. 1993 (Blackburn R, Rangers, Coventry C, Bolton W) 51
Hepburn, J. 1891 (Alloa Ath) 1
Hepburn, R. 1932 (Ayr U) 1
Herd, A. C. 1935 (Hearts) 1
Herd, D. G. 1959 (Arsenal) 5
Herd, G. 1958 (Clyde) 5
Herriot, J. 1969 (Birmingham C) 8
Hewie, J. D. 1956 (Charlton Ath) 19
Higgins, A. 1885 (Kilmarnock) 1
Higgins, A. 1910 (Newcastle U) 4
Highet, T. C. 1875 (Queen's Park) 4
Hill, D. 1881 (Rangers) 3
Hill, D. A. 1906 (Third Lanark) 1
Hill, F. R. 1930 (Aberdeen) 3
Hill, J. 1891 (Hearts) 2
Hogg, G. 1896 (Hearts) 2
Hogg, J. 1922 (Ayr U) 1
Hogg, R. M. 1937 (Celtic) 1
Holm, A. H. 1882 (Queen's Park) 3

Holt, D. D. 1963 (Hearts) 5
Holt, G. J. 2001 (Kilmarnock, Norwich C) 10
Holton, J. A. 1973 (Manchester U) 15
Hope, R. 1968 (WBA) 2
Hopkin, D. 1997 (Crystal Palace, Leeds U) 7
Houliston, W. 1949 (Queen of the South) 3
Houston, S. M. 1976 (Manchester U) 1
Howden, W. 1905 (Partick Thistle) 1
Howe, R. 1929 (Hamilton A) 2
Howie, H. 1949 (Hibernian) 1
Howie, J. 1905 (Newcastle U) 3
Howieson, J. 1927 (St Mirren) 1
Hughes, J. 1965 (Celtic) 8
Hughes, R. D. 2004 (Portsmouth) 5
Hughes, S. R. 2010 (Norwich C) 1
Hughes, W. 1975 (Sunderland) 1
Humphries, W. 1952 (Motherwell) 1
Hunter, A. 1972 (Kilmarnock, Celtic) 4
Hunter, J. 1909 (Dundee) 1
Hunter, J. 1874 (Third Lanark, Eastern, Third Lanark) 4
Hunter, W. 1960 (Motherwell) 3
Hunter, R. 1890 (St Mirren) 1
Husband, J. 1947 (Partick Thistle) 1
Hutchison, D. 1999 (Everton, Sunderland, West Ham U) 26
Hutchison, T. 1974 (Coventry C) 17
Hutton, A. 2007 (Rangers, Tottenham H, Aston Villa) 50
Hutton, J. 1887 (St Bernards) 1
Hutton, J. 1923 (Aberdeen, Blackburn R) 10
Hyslop, T. 1896 (Stoke, Rangers) 2

Imlach, J. J. S. 1958 (Nottingham F) 4
Imrie, W. N. 1929 (St Johnstone) 2
Inglis, J. 1883 (Rangers) 2
Inglis, J. 1884 (Kilmarnock Ath) 1
Irons, J. H. 1900 (Queen's Park) 1
Irvine, B. 1991 (Aberdeen) 9
Iwelumo, C.R. 2009 (Wolverhampton W, Burnley) 4

Jackson, A. 1886 (Cambuslang) 2
Jackson, A. 1925 (Aberdeen, Huddersfield T) 17
Jackson, C. 1975 (Rangers) 8
Jackson, D. 1995 (Hibernian, Celtic) 28
Jackson, J. 1931 (Partick Thistle, Chelsea) 8
Jackson, T. A. 1904 (St Mirren) 6
James, A. W. 1926 (Preston NE, Arsenal) 8
Jardine, A. 1971 (Rangers) 38
Jarvie, A. 1971 (Airdrieonians) 3
Jenkinson, T. 1887 (Hearts) 1
Jess, E. 1993 (Aberdeen, Coventry C, Aberdeen) 18
Johnston, A. 1999 (Sunderland, Rangers, Middlesbrough) 18
Johnston, L. H. 1948 (Clyde) 2
Johnston, M. 1984 (Watford, Celtic, Nantes, Rangers) 38
Johnston, R. 1938 (Sunderland) 1
Johnston, W. 1966 (Rangers, WBA) 22
Johnstone, D. 1973 (Rangers) 14
Johnstone, J. 1888 (Abercorn) 1
Johnstone, J. 1965 (Celtic) 23
Johnstone, Jas 1894 (Kilmarnock) 1
Johnstone, J. A. 1930 (Hearts) 3
Johnstone, R. 1951 (Hibernian, Manchester C) 17
Johnstone, W. 1887 (Third Lanark) 3
Jordan, J. 1973 (Leeds U, Manchester U, AC Milan) 52

Kay, J. L. 1880 (Queen's Park) 6
Keillor, A. 1891 (Montrose, Dundee) 6
Keir, L. 1885 (Dumbarton) 5
Kelly, H. T. 1952 (Blackpool) 1
Kelly, J. 1888 (Renton, Celtic) 8
Kelly, J. C. 1949 (Barnsley) 2
Kelly, L. M. 2013 (Kilmarnock) 1
Kelso, R. 1885 (Renton, Dundee) 7
Kelso, T. 1914 (Dundee) 1
Kennaway, J. 1934 (Celtic) 1
Kennedy, A. 1875 (Eastern, Third Lanark) 6
Kennedy, J. 1897 (Hibernian) 1
Kennedy, J. 1964 (Celtic) 6
Kennedy, J. 2004 (Celtic) 1
Kennedy, S. 1905 (Partick Thistle) 1
Kennedy, S. 1975 (Rangers) 5
Kennedy, S. 1978 (Aberdeen) 8
Kenneth, G. 2011 (Dundee U) 2
Ker, G. 1880 (Queen's Park) 5
Ker, W. 1872 (Queen's Park) 2
Kerr, A. 1955 (Partick Thistle) 2
Kerr, B. 2003 (Newcastle U) 3
Kerr, P. 1924 (Hibernian) 1
Key, G. 1902 (Hearts) 1
Key, W. 1907 (Queen's Park) 1
King, A. 1896 (Hearts, Celtic) 6
King, J. 1933 (Hamilton A) 2
King, W. S. 1929 (Queen's Park) 1
Kingsley, S. 2016 (Swansea C) 1
Kinloch, J. D. 1922 (Partick Thistle) 1
Kinnaird, A. F. 1873 (Wanderers) 1
Kinnear, D. 1938 (Rangers) 1
Kyle, K. 2002 (Sunderland, Kilmarnock) 10

Lambert, P. 1995 (Motherwell, Borussia Dortmund, Celtic) 40
Lambie, J. A. 1886 (Queen's Park) 3
Lambie, W. A. 1892 (Queen's Park) 9
Lamont, W. 1885 (Pilgrims) 1
Lang, A. 1880 (Dumbarton) 1
Lang, J. J. 1876 (Clydesdale, Third Lanark) 2
Latta, A. 1888 (Dumbarton) 2
Law, D. 1959 (Huddersfield T, Manchester C, Torino, Manchester U, Manchester C) 55
Law, G. 1910 (Rangers) 3
Law, T. 1928 (Chelsea) 2
Lawrence, J. 1911 (Newcastle U) 1
Lawrence, T. 1963 (Liverpool) 3
Lawson, D. 1923 (St Mirren) 1
Leckie, R. 1872 (Queen's Park) 1
Leggat, G. 1956 (Aberdeen, Fulham) 18
Leighton, J. 1983 (Aberdeen, Manchester U, Hibernian, Aberdeen) 91
Lennie, W. 1908 (Aberdeen) 2
Lennox, R. 1967 (Celtic) 10
Leslie, L. G. 1961 (Airdrieonians) 5
Levein, C. 1990 (Hearts) 16
Liddell, W. 1947 (Liverpool) 28
Liddle, D. 1931 (East Fife) 3
Lindsay, D. 1903 (St Mirren) 1
Lindsay, J. 1880 (Dumbarton) 8
Lindsay, J. 1888 (Renton) 3
Linwood, A. B. 1950 (Clyde) 1
Little, R. J. 1953 (Rangers) 1
Livingstone, G. T. 1906 (Manchester C, Rangers) 2
Lochhead, A. 1889 (Third Lanark) 1
Logan, J. 1891 (Ayr) 1
Logan, T. 1913 (Falkirk) 1
Logie, J. T. 1953 (Arsenal) 1
Loney, W. 1910 (Celtic) 2
Long, H. 1947 (Clyde) 1
Longair, W. 1894 (Dundee) 1
Lorimer, P. 1970 (Leeds U) 21
Love, A. 1931 (Aberdeen) 3
Low, A. 1934 (Falkirk) 1
Low, J. 1891 (Cambuslang) 1
Low, T. P. 1897 (Rangers) 1
Low, W. L. 1911 (Newcastle U) 5
Lowe, J. 1887 (St Bernards) 1
Lundie, J. 1886 (Hibernian) 1
Lyall, J. 1905 (Sheffield W) 1

McAdam, J. 1880 (Third Lanark) 1
McAllister, B. 1997 (Wimbledon) 3
McAllister, G. 1990 (Leicester C, Leeds U, Coventry C) 57
McAllister, J. R. 2004 (Livingston) 1
Macari, L. 1972 (Celtic, Manchester U) 24
McArthur, D. 1895 (Celtic) 3
McArthur, J. 2011 (Wigan Ath, Crystal Palace) 28
McAtee, A. 1913 (Celtic) 1
McAulay, J. 1884 (Arthurlie) 1
McAulay, J. D. 1882 (Dumbarton) 9
McAulay, R. 1932 (Rangers) 2
Macauley, A. R. 1947 (Brentford, Arsenal) 7
McAvennie, F. 1986 (West Ham U, Celtic) 5
McBain, E. 1894 (St Mirren) 1
McBain, N. 1922 (Manchester U, Everton) 3
McBride, J. 1967 (Celtic) 2
McBride, P. 1904 (Preston NE) 6
McCall, A. 1888 (Renton) 1
McCall, A. S. M. 1990 (Everton, Rangers) 40
McCall, J. 1886 (Renton) 5
McCalliog, J. 1967 (Sheffield W, Wolverhampton W) 5

McCallum, N. 1888 (Renton) 1
McCann, N. 1999 (Hearts, Rangers, Southampton) 26
McCann, R. J. 1959 (Motherwell) 5
McCartney, W. 1902 (Hibernian) 1
McClair, B. 1987 (Celtic, Manchester U) 30
McClory, A. 1927 (Motherwell) 3
McCloy, P. 1924 (Ayr U) 2
McCloy, P. 1973 (Rangers) 4
McCoist, A. 1986 (Rangers, Kilmarnock) 61
McColl, I. M. 1950 (Rangers) 14
McColl, R. S. 1896 (Queen's Park, Newcastle U, Queen's Park) 13
McColl, W. 1895 (Renton) 1
McCombie, A. 1903 (Sunderland, Newcastle U) 4
McCorkindale, J. 1891 (Partick Thistle) 1
McCormack, R. 2008 (Motherwell, Cardiff C, Leeds U, Fulham) 13
McCormick, R. 1886 (Abercorn) 1
McCrae, D. 1929 (St Mirren) 2
McCreadie, A. 1893 (Rangers) 2
McCreadie, E. G. 1965 (Chelsea) 23
McCulloch, D. 1935 (Hearts, Brentford, Derby Co) 7
McCulloch, L. 2005 (Wigan Ath, Rangers) 18
MacDonald, A. 1976 (Rangers) 1
McDonald, J. 1886 (Edinburgh University) 1
McDonald, J. 1956 (Sunderland) 2
MacDougall, E. J. 1975 (Norwich C) 7
McDougall, J. 1877 (Vale of Leven) 5
McDougall, J. 1926 (Airdrieonians) 1
McDougall, J. 1931 (Liverpool) 2
McEveley, J. 2008 (Derby Co) 3
McFadden, J. 2002 (Motherwell, Everton, Birmingham C) 48
McFadyen, W. 1934 (Motherwell) 2
Macfarlane, A. 1904 (Dundee) 5
Macfarlane, W. 1947 (Hearts) 1
McFarlane, R. 1896 (Greenock Morton) 1
McGarr, E. 1970 (Aberdeen) 2
McGarvey, F. P. 1979 (Liverpool, Celtic) 7
McGeoch, A. 1876 (Dumbreck) 4
McGhee, J. 1886 (Hibernian) 1
McGhee, M. 1983 (Aberdeen) 4
McGinn, J. 2016 (Hibernian) 3
McGinlay, J. 1994 (Bolton W) 13
McGonagle, W. 1933 (Celtic) 6
McGrain, D. 1973 (Celtic) 62
McGregor, A. J. 2007 (Rangers, Besiktas, Hull C) 36
McGregor, J. C. 1877 (Vale of Leven) 4
McGrory, J. 1928 (Celtic) 7
McGrory, J. E. 1965 (Kilmarnock) 3
McGuire, W. 1881 (Beith) 2
McGurk, F. 1934 (Birmingham) 1
McHardy, H. 1885 (Rangers) 1
McInally, A. 1989 (Aston Villa, Bayern Munich) 8
McInally, J. 1987 (Dundee U) 10
McInally, T. B. 1926 (Celtic) 2
McInnes, D. 2003 (WBA) 2
McInnes, T. 1889 (Cowlairs) 1
McIntosh, W. 1905 (Third Lanark) 1
McIntyre, A. 1878 (Vale of Leven) 2
McIntyre, H. 1880 (Rangers) 1
McIntyre, J. 1884 (Rangers) 1
MacKay, D. 1959 (Celtic) 14
Mackay, D. C. 1957 (Hearts, Tottenham H) 22
Mackay, G. 1988 (Hearts) 4
Mackay, M. 2004 (Norwich C) 5
McKay, B. 2016 (Rangers) 1
McKay, J. 1924 (Blackburn R) 1
McKay, R. 1928 (Newcastle U) 1
McKean, R. 1976 (Rangers) 1
McKenzie, D. 1938 (Brentford) 1
Mackenzie, J. A. 1954 (Partick Thistle) 9
McKeown, M. 1889 (Celtic) 2
McKie, J. 1898 (East Stirling) 1
McKillop, T. R. 1938 (Rangers) 1
McKimmie, S. 1989 (Aberdeen) 40
McKinlay, D. 1922 (Liverpool) 2
McKinlay, T. 1996 (Celtic) 22
McKinlay, W. 1994 (Dundee U, Blackburn R) 29
McKinnon, A. 1874 (Queen's Park) 1
McKinnon, R. 1966 (Rangers) 28
McKinnon, R. 1994 (Motherwell) 3
MacKinnon, W. 1883 (Dumbarton) 4
MacKinnon, W. W. 1872 (Queen's Park) 9
McLaren, A. 1929 (St Johnstone) 5
McLaren, A. 1947 (Preston NE) 4
McLaren, A. 1992 (Hearts, Rangers) 24
McLaren, A. 2001 (Kilmarnock) 1
McLaren, J. 1888 (Hibernian, Celtic) 3
McLean, A. 1926 (Celtic) 4
McLean, D. 1896 (St Bernards) 2
McLean, D. 1912 (Sheffield W) 1
McLean, G. 1968 (Dundee) 1
McLean, K. 2016 (Aberdeen) 1
McLean, T. 1969 (Kilmarnock) 6
McLeish, A. 1980 (Aberdeen) 77
McLeod, D. 1905 (Celtic) 4
McLeod, J. 1888 (Dumbarton) 5
MacLeod, J. M. 1961 (Hibernian) 4
MacLeod, M. 1985 (Celtic, Borussia Dortmund, Hibernian) 20
McLeod, W. 1886 (Cowlairs) 1
McLintock, A. 1875 (Vale of Leven) 3
McLintock, F. 1963 (Leicester C, Arsenal) 9
McLuckie, J. S. 1934 (Manchester C) 1
McMahon, A. 1892 (Celtic) 6
McManus, S. 2007 (Celtic, Middlesbrough) 26
McMenemy, J. 1905 (Celtic) 12
McMenemy, J. 1934 (Motherwell) 1
McMillan, I. L. 1952 (Airdrieonians, Rangers) 6
McMillan, J. 1897 (St Bernards) 1
McMillan, T. 1887 (Dumbarton) 1
McMullan, J. 1920 (Partick Thistle, Manchester C) 16
McNab, A. 1921 (Morton) 2
McNab, A. 1937 (Sunderland, WBA) 2
McNab, C. D. 1931 (Dundee) 6
McNab, J. S. 1923 (Liverpool) 1
McNair, A. 1906 (Celtic) 15
McNamara, J. 1997 (Celtic, Wolverhampton W) 33
McNamee, D. 2004 (Livingston) 4
McNaught, W. 1951 (Raith R) 5
McNaughton, K. 2002 (Aberdeen, Cardiff C) 4
McNeill, W. 1961 (Celtic) 29
McNiel, H. 1874 (Queen's Park) 10
McNiel, M. 1876 (Rangers) 2
McPhail, J. 1950 (Celtic) 5
McPhail, R. 1927 (Airdrieonians, Rangers) 17
McPherson, D. 1892 (Kilmarnock) 1
McPherson, D. 1989 (Hearts, Rangers) 27
McPherson, J. 1875 (Clydesdale) 1
McPherson, J. 1879 (Vale of Leven) 8
McPherson, J. 1888 (Kilmarnock, Cowlairs, Rangers) 9
McPherson, J. 1891 (Hearts) 1
McPherson, R. 1882 (Arthurlie) 1
McQueen, G. 1974 (Leeds U, Manchester U) 30
McQueen, M. 1890 (Leith Ath) 2
McRorie, D. M. 1931 (Morton) 1
McSpadyen, A. 1939 (Partick Thistle) 2
McStay, P. 1984 (Celtic) 76
McStay, W. 1921 (Celtic) 13
McSwegan, G. 2000 (Hearts) 2
McTavish, J. 1910 (Falkirk) 1
McWattie, G. C. 1901 (Queen's Park) 2
McWilliam, P. 1905 (Newcastle U) 8
Mackay-Steven, G. 2013 (Dundee U) 1
Mackail-Smith, C. 2011 (Peterborough U, Brighton & HA) 7
Mackie, J. C. 2011 (QPR) 9
Madden, J. 1893 (Celtic) 2
Maguire, C. 2011 (Aberdeen) 2
Main, F. R. 1938 (Rangers) 1
Main, J. 1909 (Hibernian) 1
Maley, W. 1893 (Celtic) 2
Maloney, S. R. 2006 (Celtic, Aston Villa, Celtic, Wigan Ath, Chicago Fire, Hull C) 47
Malpas, M. 1984 (Dundee U) 55
Marshall, D. J. 2005 (Celtic, Cardiff C, Hull C) 27
Marshall, G. 1992 (Celtic) 1
Marshall, H. 1899 (Celtic) 2
Marshall, J. 1885 (Third Lanark) 4
Marshall, J. 1921 (Middlesbrough, Llanelly) 7
Marshall, J. 1932 (Rangers) 3
Marshall, R. W. 1892 (Rangers) 2
Martin, B. 1995 (Motherwell) 2
Martin, C. H. 2014 (Derby Co) 13
Martin, F. 1954 (Aberdeen) 6
Martin, N. 1965 (Hibernian, Sunderland) 3
Martin, R. K. A. 2011 (Norwich C) 29

Martis, J. 1961 (Motherwell) 1
Mason, J. 1949 (Third Lanark) 7
Massie, A. 1932 (Hearts, Aston Villa) 18
Masson, D. S. 1976 (QPR, Derby Co) 17
Mathers, D. 1954 (Partick Thistle) 1
Matteo, D. 2001 (Leeds U) 6
Maxwell, W. S. 1898 (Stoke C) 1
May, J. 1906 (Rangers) 5
May, S. 2015 (Sheffield W) 1
Meechan, P. 1896 (Celtic) 1
Meiklejohn, D. D. 1922 (Rangers) 15
Menzies, A. 1906 (Hearts) 1
Mercer, R. 1912 (Hearts) 2
Middleton, R. 1930 (Cowdenbeath) 1
Millar, J. 1897 (Rangers) 3
Millar, J. 1963 (Rangers) 2
Miller, A. 1939 (Hearts) 1
Miller, C. 2001 (Dundee U) 1
Miller, J. 1931 (St Mirren) 5
Miller, K. 2001 (Rangers, Wolverhampton W, Celtic, Derby Co, Rangers, Bursaspor, Cardiff C, Vancouver Whitecaps) 69
Miller, L. 2006 (Dundee U, Aberdeen) 3
Miller, P. 1882 (Dumbarton) 3
Miller, T. 1920 (Liverpool, Manchester U) 3
Miller, W. 1876 (Third Lanark) 1
Miller, W. 1947 (Celtic) 6
Miller, W. 1975 (Aberdeen) 65
Mills, W. 1936 (Aberdeen) 3
Milne, J. V. 1938 (Middlesbrough) 2
Mitchell, D. 1890 (Rangers) 5
Mitchell, J. 1908 (Kilmarnock) 3
Mitchell, R. C. 1951 (Newcastle U) 2
Mochan, N. 1954 (Celtic) 3
Moir, W. 1950 (Bolton W) 1
Moncur, R. 1968 (Newcastle U) 16
Morgan, H. 1898 (St Mirren, Liverpool) 2
Morgan, W. 1968 (Burnley, Manchester U) 21
Morris, D. 1923 (Raith R) 6
Morris, H. 1950 (East Fife) 1
Morrison, J. C. 2008 (WBA) 44
Morrison, T. 1927 (St Mirren) 1
Morton, A. L. 1920 (Queen's Park, Rangers) 31
Morton, H. A. 1929 (Kilmarnock) 2
Mudie, J. K. 1957 (Blackpool) 17
Muir, W. 1907 (Dundee) 1
Muirhead, T. A. 1922 (Rangers) 8
Mulgrew, C. P. 2012 (Celtic, Blackburn R) 27
Mulhall, G. 1960 (Aberdeen, Sunderland) 3
Munro, A. D. 1937 (Hearts, Blackpool) 3
Munro, F. M. 1971 (Wolverhampton W) 9
Munro, I. 1979 (St Mirren) 7
Munro, N. 1888 (Abercorn) 2
Murdoch, J. 1931 (Motherwell) 1
Murdoch, R. 1966 (Celtic) 12
Murphy, F. 1938 (Celtic) 1
Murray, I. 2003 (Hibernian, Rangers) 6
Murray, J. 1895 (Renton) 1
Murray, J. 1958 (Hearts) 5
Murray, J. W. 1890 (Vale of Leven) 1
Murray, P. 1896 (Hibernian) 2
Murray, S. 1972 (Aberdeen) 1
Murty, G. S. 2004 (Reading) 4
Mutch, G. 1938 (Preston NE) 1

Naismith, S. J. 2007 (Kilmarnock, Rangers, Everton, Norwich C) 45
Napier, C. E. 1932 (Celtic, Derby Co) 5
Narey, D. 1977 (Dundee U) 35
Naysmith, G. A. 2000 (Hearts, Everton, Sheffield U) 46
Neil, R. G. 1896 (Hibernian, Rangers) 2
Neill, R. W. 1876 (Queen's Park) 5
Neilson, R. 2007 (Hearts) 1
Nellies, P. 1913 (Hearts) 2
Nelson, J. 1925 (Cardiff C) 4
Nevin, P. K. F. 1986 (Chelsea, Everton, Tranmere R) 28
Niblo, T. D. 1904 (Aston Villa) 1
Nibloe, J. 1929 (Kilmarnock) 11
Nicholas, C. 1983 (Celtic, Arsenal, Aberdeen) 20
Nicholson, B. 2001 (Dunfermline Ath) 3
Nicol, S. 1985 (Liverpool) 27
Nisbet, J. 1929 (Ayr U) 3
Niven, J. B. 1885 (Moffat) 1

O'Connor, G. 2002 (Hibernian, Lokomotiv Moscow, Birmingham C) 16
O'Donnell, F. 1937 (Preston NE, Blackpool) 6
O'Donnell, P. 1994 (Motherwell) 1
Ogilvie, D. H. 1934 (Motherwell) 1
O'Hare, J. 1970 (Derby Co) 13
O'Neil, B. 1996 (Celtic, Wolfsburg, Derby Co, Preston NE) 7
O'Neil, J. 2001 (Hibernian) 1
Ormond, W. E. 1954 (Hibernian) 6
O'Rourke, F. 1907 (Airdrieonians) 1
Orr, J. 1892 (Kilmarnock) 1
Orr, R. 1902 (Newcastle U) 2
Orr, T. 1952 (Morton) 2
Orr, W. 1900 (Celtic) 3
Orrock, R. 1913 (Falkirk) 1
Oswald, J. 1889 (Third Lanark, St Bernards, Rangers) 3

Parker, A. H. 1955 (Falkirk, Everton) 15
Parlane, D. 1973 (Rangers) 12
Parlane, R. 1878 (Vale of Leven) 3
Paterson, C. 2016 (Aberdeen) 5
Paterson, G. D. 1939 (Celtic) 1
Paterson, J. 1920 (Leicester C) 1
Paterson, J. 1931 (Cowdenbeath) 3
Paton, A. 1952 (Motherwell) 2
Paton, D. 1896 (St Bernards) 1
Paton, M. 1883 (Dumbarton) 5
Paton, R. 1879 (Vale of Leven) 2
Patrick, J. 1897 (St Mirren) 2
Paul, H. McD. 1909 (Queen's Park) 3
Paul, W. 1888 (Partick Thistle) 3
Paul, W. 1891 (Dykebar) 1
Pearson, S. P. 2004 (Motherwell, Celtic, Derby Co) 10
Pearson, T. 1947 (Newcastle U) 2
Penman, A. 1966 (Dundee) 1
Pettigrew, W. 1976 (Motherwell) 5
Phillips, J. 1877 (Queen's Park) 3
Phillips, M. 2012 (Blackpool, QPR) 4
Plenderleith, J. B. 1961 (Manchester C) 1
Porteous, W. 1903 (Hearts) 1
Pressley, S. J. 2000 (Hearts) 32
Pringle, C. 1921 (St Mirren) 1
Provan, D. 1964 (Rangers) 5
Provan, D. 1980 (Celtic) 10
Pursell, P. 1914 (Queen's Park) 1

Quashie, N. F. 2004 (Portsmouth, Southampton, WBA) 14
Quinn, J. 1905 (Celtic) 11
Quinn, P. 1961 (Motherwell) 4

Rae, G. 2001 (Dundee, Rangers, Cardiff C) 14
Rae, J. 1889 (Third Lanark) 2
Raeside, J. S. 1906 (Third Lanark) 1
Raisbeck, A. G. 1900 (Liverpool) 8
Rankin, G. 1890 (Vale of Leven) 2
Rankin, R. 1929 (St Mirren) 3
Redpath, W. 1949 (Motherwell) 9
Reid, J. G. 1914 (Airdrieonians) 3
Reid, R. 1938 (Brentford) 2
Reid, W. 1911 (Rangers) 9
Reilly, L. 1949 (Hibernian) 38
Rennie, H. G. 1900 (Hearts, Hibernian) 13
Renny-Tailyour, H. W. 1873 (Royal Engineers) 1
Rhind, A. 1872 (Queen's Park) 1
Rhodes, J. L. 2012 (Huddersfield T, Blackburn R, Sheffield W) 14
Richmond, A. 1906 (Queen's Park) 1
Richmond, J. T. 1877 (Clydesdale, Queen's Park) 3
Ring, T. 1953 (Clyde) 12
Rioch, B. D. 1975 (Derby Co, Everton, Derby Co) 24
Riordan, D. G. 2006 (Hibernian) 3
Ritchie, A. 1891 (East Stirlingshire) 1
Ritchie, H. 1923 (Hibernian) 2
Ritchie, J. 1897 (Queen's Park) 1
Ritchie, M. T. 2015 (Bournemouth, Newcastle U) 14
Ritchie, P. S. 1999 (Hearts, Bolton W, Walsall) 7
Ritchie, W. 1962 (Rangers) 1
Robb, D. T. 1971 (Aberdeen) 5
Robb, W. 1926 (Rangers, Hibernian) 2
Robertson, A. 1955 (Clyde) 5
Robertson, A. 2014 (Dundee U, Hull C) 15
Robertson, D. 1992 (Rangers) 3
Robertson, G. 1910 (Motherwell, Sheffield W) 4

Robertson, G. 1938 (Kilmarnock) 1
Robertson, H. 1962 (Dundee) 1
Robertson, J. 1931 (Dundee) 2
Robertson, J. 1991 (Hearts) 16
Robertson, J. N. 1978 (Nottingham F, Derby Co) 28
Robertson, J. G. 1965 (Tottenham H) 1
Robertson, J. T. 1898 (Everton, Southampton, Rangers) 16
Robertson, P. 1903 (Dundee) 1
Robertson, S. 2009 (Dundee U) 2
Robertson, T. 1889 (Queen's Park) 4
Robertson, T. 1898 (Hearts) 1
Robertson, W. 1887 (Dumbarton) 2
Robinson, R. 1974 (Dundee) 4
Robson, B. G. G. 2008 (Dundee U, Celtic, Middlesbrough) 17
Ross, M. 2002 (Rangers) 13
Rough, A. 1976 (Partick Thistle, Hibernian) 53
Rougvie, D. 1984 (Aberdeen) 1
Rowan, A. 1880 (Caledonian, Queen's Park) 2
Russell, D. 1895 (Hearts, Celtic) 6
Russell, J. 1890 (Cambuslang) 1
Russell, J. S. S. 2015 (Derby Co) 4
Russell, W. F. 1924 (Airdrieonians) 2
Rutherford, E. 1948 (Rangers) 1

St John, I. 1959 (Motherwell, Liverpool) 21
Saunders, S. 2011 (Motherwell) 1
Sawers, W. 1895 (Dundee) 1
Scarff, P. 1931 (Celtic) 1
Schaedler, E. 1974 (Hibernian) 1
Scott, A. S. 1957 (Rangers, Everton) 16
Scott, J. 1966 (Hibernian) 1
Scott, J. 1971 (Dundee) 2
Scott, M. 1898 (Airdrieonians) 1
Scott, R. 1894 (Airdrieonians) 1
Scoular, J. 1951 (Portsmouth) 9
Sellar, W. 1885 (Battlefield, Queen's Park) 9
Semple, W. 1886 (Cambuslang) 1
Severin, S. D. 2002 (Hearts, Aberdeen) 15
Shankly, W. 1938 (Preston NE) 5
Sharp, G. M. 1985 (Everton) 12
Sharp, J. 1904 (Dundee, Woolwich Arsenal, Fulham) 5
Shaw, D. 1947 (Hibernian) 8
Shaw, F. W. 1884 (Pollokshields Ath) 2
Shaw, J. 1947 (Rangers) 4
Shearer, D. 1994 (Aberdeen) 7
Shearer, R. 1961 (Rangers) 4
Shinnie, A. M. 2013 (Inverness CT) 1
Sillars, D. C. 1891 (Queen's Park) 5
Simpson, J. 1895 (Third Lanark) 3
Simpson, J. 1935 (Rangers) 14
Simpson, N. 1983 (Aberdeen) 5
Simpson, R. C. 1967 (Celtic) 5
Sinclair, G. L. 1910 (Hearts) 3
Sinclair, J. W. E. 1966 (Leicester C) 1
Skene, L. H. 1904 (Queen's Park) 1
Sloan, T. 1904 (Third Lanark) 1
Smellie, R. 1887 (Queen's Park) 6
Smith, A. 1898 (Rangers) 20
Smith, D. 1966 (Aberdeen, Rangers) 2
Smith, G. 1947 (Hibernian) 18
Smith, H. G. 1988 (Hearts) 3
Smith, J. 1924 (Ayr U) 1
Smith, J. 1935 (Rangers) 2
Smith, J. 1968 (Aberdeen, Newcastle U) 4
Smith, J. 2003 (Celtic) 2
Smith, J. E. 1959 (Celtic) 2
Smith, Jas 1872 (Queen's Park) 1
Smith, John 1877 (Mauchline, Edinburgh University, Queen's Park) 10
Smith, N. 1897 (Rangers) 12
Smith, R. 1872 (Queen's Park) 2
Smith, T. M. 1934 (Kilmarnock, Preston NE) 2
Snodgrass, R. 2011 (Leeds U, Norwich C, Hull C, West Ham U) 24
Somers, P. 1905 (Celtic) 4
Somers, W. S. 1879 (Third Lanark, Queen's Park) 3
Somerville, G. 1886 (Queen's Park) 1
Souness, G. J. 1975 (Middlesbrough, Liverpool, Sampdoria) 54
Speedie, D. R. 1985 (Chelsea, Coventry C) 10
Speedie, F. 1903 (Rangers) 3
Speirs, J. H. 1908 (Rangers) 1
Spencer, J. 1995 (Chelsea, QPR) 14

Stanton, P. 1966 (Hibernian) 16
Stark, J. 1909 (Rangers) 2
Steel, W. 1947 (Morton, Derby Co, Dundee) 30
Steele, D. M. 1923 (Huddersfield) 3
Stein, C. 1969 (Rangers, Coventry C) 21
Stephen, J. F. 1947 (Bradford) 2
Stevenson, G. 1928 (Motherwell) 12
Stewart, A. 1888 (Queen's Park) 2
Stewart, A. 1894 (Third Lanark) 1
Stewart, D. 1888 (Dumbarton) 1
Stewart, D. 1893 (Queen's Park) 3
Stewart, D. S. 1978 (Leeds U) 1
Stewart, G. 1906 (Hibernian, Manchester C) 4
Stewart, J. 1977 (Kilmarnock, Middlesbrough) 2
Stewart, M. J. 2002 (Manchester U, Hearts) 4
Stewart, R. 1981 (West Ham U) 10
Stewart, W. G. 1898 (Queen's Park) 2
Stockdale, R. K. 2002 (Middlesbrough) 5
Storrier, D. 1899 (Celtic) 3
Strachan, G. D. 1980 (Aberdeen, Manchester U, Leeds U) 50
Sturrock, P. 1981 (Dundee U) 20
Sullivan, N. 1997 (Wimbledon, Tottenham H) 28
Summers, W. 1926 (St Mirren) 1
Symon, J. S. 1939 (Rangers) 1

Tait, T. S. 1911 (Sunderland) 1
Taylor, J. 1872 (Queen's Park) 6
Taylor, J. D. 1892 (Dumbarton, St Mirren) 4
Taylor, W. 1892 (Hearts) 1
Teale, G. 2006 (Wigan Ath, Derby Co) 13
Telfer, P. N. 2000 (Coventry C) 1
Telfer, W. 1933 (Motherwell) 2
Telfer, W. D. 1954 (St Mirren) 1
Templeton, R. 1902 (Aston Villa, Newcastle U, Woolwich Arsenal, Kilmarnock) 11
Tierney, K. 2016 (Celtic) 4
Thompson, S. 2002 (Dundee U, Rangers) 16
Thomson, A. 1886 (Arthurlie) 1
Thomson, A. 1889 (Third Lanark) 1
Thomson, A. 1909 (Airdrieonians) 1
Thomson, A. 1926 (Celtic) 3
Thomson, C. 1904 (Hearts, Sunderland) 21
Thomson, C. 1937 (Sunderland) 1
Thomson, D. 1920 (Dundee) 1
Thomson, J. 1930 (Celtic) 4
Thomson, J. J. 1872 (Queen's Park) 3
Thomson, J. R. 1933 (Everton) 1
Thomson, K. 2009 (Rangers, Middlesbrough) 3
Thomson, R. 1932 (Celtic) 1
Thomson, R. W. 1927 (Falkirk) 1
Thomson, S. 1884 (Rangers) 2
Thomson, W. 1892 (Dumbarton) 4
Thomson, W. 1896 (Dundee) 1
Thomson, W. 1980 (St Mirren) 7
Thornton, W. 1947 (Rangers) 7
Toner, W. 1959 (Kilmarnock) 2
Townsley, T. 1926 (Falkirk) 1
Troup, A. 1920 (Dundee, Everton) 5
Turnbull, E. 1948 (Hibernian) 8
Turner, T. 1884 (Arthurlie) 1
Turner, W. 1885 (Pollokshields Ath) 2

Ure, J. F. 1962 (Dundee, Arsenal) 11
Urquhart, D. 1934 (Hibernian) 1

Vallance, T. 1877 (Rangers) 7
Venters, A. 1934 (Cowdenbeath, Rangers) 3

Waddell, T. S. 1891 (Queen's Park) 6
Waddell, W. 1947 (Rangers) 17
Wales, H. M. 1933 (Motherwell) 1
Walker, A. 1988 (Celtic) 3
Walker, F. 1922 (Third Lanark) 1
Walker, G. 1930 (St Mirren) 4
Walker, J. 1895 (Hearts, Rangers) 5
Walker, J. 1911 (Swindon T) 9
Walker, J. N. 1993 (Hearts, Partick Thistle) 2
Walker, R. 1900 (Hearts) 29
Walker, T. 1935 (Hearts) 20
Walker, W. 1909 (Clyde) 2
Wallace, I. A. 1978 (Coventry C) 3
Wallace, L. 2010 (Hearts, Rangers) 10
Wallace, R. 2010 (Preston NE) 1

Wallace, W. S. B. 1965 (Hearts, Celtic) 7
Wardhaugh, J. 1955 (Hearts) 2
Wark, J. 1979 (Ipswich T, Liverpool) 28
Watson, A. 1881 (Queen's Park) 3
Watson, J. 1903 (Sunderland, Middlesbrough) 6
Watson, J. 1948 (Motherwell, Huddersfield T) 2
Watson, J. A. K. 1878 (Rangers) 1
Watson, P. R. 1934 (Blackpool) 1
Watson, R. 1971 (Motherwell) 1
Watson, W. 1898 (Falkirk) 1
Watt, A. P. 2016 (Charlton Ath) 1
Watt, F. 1889 (Kilbirnie) 4
Watt, W. W. 1887 (Queen's Park) 1
Waugh, W. 1938 (Hearts) 1
Webster, A. 2003 (Hearts, Dundee U, Hearts) 28
Weir, A. 1959 (Motherwell) 6
Weir, D. G. 1997 (Hearts, Everton, Rangers) 69
Weir, J. 1887 (Third Lanark) 1
Weir, J. B. 1872 (Queen's Park) 4
Weir, P. 1980 (St Mirren, Aberdeen) 6
White, John 1922 (Albion R, Hearts) 2
White, J. A. 1959 (Falkirk, Tottenham H) 22
White, W. 1907 (Bolton W) 2
Whitelaw, A. 1887 (Vale of Leven) 2
Whittaker, S. G. 2010 (Rangers, Norwich C) 31
Whyte, D. 1988 (Celtic, Middlesbrough, Aberdeen) 12
Wilkie, L. 2002 (Dundee) 11
Williams, G. 2002 (Nottingham F) 5
Wilson, A. 1907 (Sheffield W) 6
Wilson, A. 1954 (Portsmouth) 1
Wilson, A. N. 1920 (Dunfermline, Middlesbrough) 12
Wilson, D. 1900 (Queen's Park) 1
Wilson, D. 1913 (Oldham Ath) 1
Wilson, D. 1961 (Rangers) 22
Wilson, D. 2011 (Liverpool) 5
Wilson, G. W. 1904 (Hearts, Everton, Newcastle U) 6
Wilson, Hugh 1890 (Newmilns, Sunderland, Third Lanark) 4
Wilson, I. A. 1987 (Leicester C, Everton) 5
Wilson, J. 1888 (Vale of Leven) 4
Wilson, M. 2011 (Celtic) 1
Wilson, P. 1926 (Celtic) 4
Wilson, P. 1975 (Celtic) 1
Wilson, R. P. 1972 (Arsenal) 2
Winters, R. 1999 (Aberdeen) 1
Wiseman, W. 1927 (Queen's Park) 2
Wood, G. 1979 (Everton, Arsenal) 4
Woodburn, W. A. 1947 (Rangers) 24
Wotherspoon, D. N. 1872 (Queen's Park) 2
Wright, K. 1992 (Hibernian) 1
Wright, S. 1993 (Aberdeen) 2
Wright, T. 1953 (Sunderland) 3
Wylie, T. G. 1890 (Rangers) 1

Yeats, R. 1965 (Liverpool) 2
Yorston, B. C. 1931 (Aberdeen) 1
Yorston, H. 1955 (Aberdeen) 1
Young, A. 1905 (Everton) 2
Young, A. 1960 (Hearts, Everton) 8
Young, G. L. 1947 (Rangers) 53
Young, J. 1906 (Celtic) 1
Younger, T. 1955 (Hibernian, Liverpool) 24

WALES

Adams, H. 1882 (Berwyn R, Druids) 4
Aizlewood, M. 1986 (Charlton Ath, Leeds U, Bradford C, Bristol C, Cardiff C) 39
Allchurch, I. J. 1951 (Swansea T, Newcastle U, Cardiff C, Swansea T) 68
Allchurch, L. 1955 (Swansea T, Sheffield U) 11
Allen, B. W. 1951 (Coventry C) 2
Allen, J. M. 2009 (Swansea C, Liverpool, Stoke C) 36
Allen, M. 1986 (Watford, Norwich C, Millwall, Newcastle U) 14
Arridge, S. 1892 (Bootle, Everton, New Brighton Tower) 8
Astley, D. J. 1931 (Charlton Ath, Aston Villa, Derby Co, Blackpool) 13
Atherton, R. W. 1899 (Hibernian, Middlesbrough) 9

Bailiff, W. E. 1913 (Llanelly) 4
Baker, C. W. 1958 (Cardiff C) 7
Baker, W. G. 1948 (Cardiff C) 1
Bale, G. F. 2006 (Southampton, Tottenham H, Real Madrid) 66
Bamford, T. 1931 (Wrexham) 5
Barnard, D. S. 1998 (Barnsley, Grimsby T) 22
Barnes, W. 1948 (Arsenal) 22
Bartley, T. 1898 (Glossop NE) 1
Bastock, A. M. 1892 (Shrewsbury T) 1
Beadles, G. H. 1925 (Cardiff C) 2
Bell, W. S. 1881 (Shrewsbury Engineers, Crewe Alex) 5
Bellamy, C. D. 1998 (Norwich C, Coventry C, Newcastle U, Blackburn R, Liverpool, West Ham U, Manchester C, Liverpool, Cardiff C) 78
Bennion, S. R. 1926 (Manchester U) 10
Berry, G. F. 1979 (Wolverhampton W, Stoke C) 5
Blackmore, C. G. 1985 (Manchester U, Middlesbrough) 39
Blake, D. J. 2011 (Cardiff C, Crystal Palace) 14
Blake, N. A. 1994 (Sheffield U, Bolton W, Blackburn R, Wolverhampton W) 29
Blew, H. 1899 (Wrexham) 22
Boden, T. 1880 (Wrexham) 1
Bodin, P. J. 1990 (Swindon T, Crystal Palace, Swindon T) 23
Boulter, L. M. 1939 (Brentford) 1
Bowdler, H. E. 1893 (Shrewsbury T) 1
Bowdler, J. C. H. 1890 (Shrewsbury T, Wolverhampton W, Shrewsbury T) 4
Bowen, D. L. 1955 (Arsenal) 19
Bowen, E. 1880 (Druids) 2
Bowen, J. P. 1994 (Swansea C, Birmingham C) 2
Bowen, M. R. 1986 (Tottenham H, Norwich C, West Ham U) 41
Bowsher, S. J. 1929 (Burnley) 1
Boyle, T. 1981 (Crystal Palace) 2
Bradley, M. S. 2010 (Walsall) 1
Bradshaw, T. W. C. 2016 (Walsall) 1
Britten, T. J. 1878 (Parkgrove, Presteigne) 2
Brookes, S. J. 1900 (Llandudno) 2
Brown, A. I. 1926 (Aberdare Ath) 1
Brown, J. R. 2006 (Gillingham, Blackburn R, Aberdeen) 3
Browning, M. T. 1996 (Bristol R, Huddersfield T) 5
Bryan, T. 1886 (Oswestry) 2
Buckland, T. 1899 (Bangor) 1
Burgess, W. A. R. 1947 (Tottenham H) 32
Burke, T. 1883 (Wrexham, Newton Heath) 8
Burnett, T. B. 1877 (Ruabon) 1
Burton, A. D. 1963 (Norwich C, Newcastle U) 9
Butler, J. 1893 (Chirk) 3
Butler, W. T. 1900 (Druids) 2

Cartwright, L. 1974 (Coventry C, Wrexham) 7
Carty, T. See McCarthy (Wrexham).
Challen, J. B. 1887 (Corinthians, Wellingborough GS) 4
Chapman, T. 1894 (Newtown, Manchester C, Grimsby T) 7
Charles, J. M. 1981 (Swansea C, QPR, Oxford U) 19
Charles, M. 1955 (Swansea T, Arsenal, Cardiff C) 31
Charles, W. J. 1950 (Leeds U, Juventus, Leeds U, Cardiff C) 38
Chester, J. G. 2014 (Hull C, WBA, Aston Villa) 23
Church, S. R. 2009 (Reading, Charlton Ath) 38
Clarke, R. J. 1949 (Manchester C) 22
Coleman, C. 1992 (Crystal Palace, Blackburn R, Fulham) 32
Collier, D. J. 1921 (Grimsby T) 1
Collins, D. L. 2005 (Sunderland, Stoke C) 12
Collins, J. M. 2004 (Cardiff C, West Ham U, Aston Villa, West Ham U) 51
Collins, W. S. 1931 (Llanelly) 1
Collison, J. D. 2008 (West Ham U) 16
Conde, C. 1884 (Chirk) 3
Cook, F. C. 1925 (Newport Co, Portsmouth) 8
Cornforth, J. M. 1995 (Swansea C) 2
Cotterill, D. R. G. B. 2006 (Bristol C, Wigan Ath, Sheffield U, Swansea C, Doncaster R, Birmingham C) 24
Coyne, D. 1996 (Tranmere R, Grimsby T, Leicester C, Burnley, Tranmere R) 16
Crofts, A. L. 2006 (Gillingham, Brighton & HA, Norwich C, Brighton & HA, Bolton W) 28
Crompton, W. 1931 (Wrexham) 3
Cross, E. A. 1876 (Wrexham) 2
Crosse, K. 1879 (Druids) 3

Crossley, M. G. 1997 (Nottingham F, Middlesbrough, Fulham) 8
Crowe, V. H. 1959 (Aston Villa) 16
Cumner, R. H. 1939 (Arsenal) 3
Curtis, A. T. 1976 (Swansea C, Leeds U, Swansea C, Southampton, Cardiff C) 35
Curtis, E. R. 1928 (Cardiff C, Birmingham) 3

Daniel, R. W. 1951 (Arsenal, Sunderland) 21
Darvell, S. 1897 (Oxford University) 2
Davies, A. 1876 (Wrexham) 2
Davies, A. 1904 (Druids, Middlesbrough) 2
Davies, A. 1983 (Manchester U, Newcastle U, Swansea C, Bradford C) 13
Davies, A. O. 1885 (Barmouth, Swifts, Wrexham, Crewe Alex) 9
Davies, A. R. 2006 (Yeovil T) 1
Davies, A. T. 1891 (Shrewsbury T) 1
Davies, B. T. 2013 (Swansea C, Tottenham H) 30
Davies, C. 1972 (Charlton Ath) 1
Davies, C. M. 2006 (Oxford U, Verona, Oldham Ath, Barnsley) 7
Davies, D. 1904 (Bolton W) 3
Davies, D. C. 1899 (Brecon, Hereford) 2
Davies, D. W. 1912 (Treharris, Oldham Ath) 2
Davies, E. Lloyd 1904 (Stoke, Northampton T) 16
Davies, E. R. 1953 (Newcastle U) 6
Davies, G. 1980 (Fulham, Manchester C) 16
Davies, Rev. H. 1928 (Wrexham) 1
Davies, Idwal 1923 (Liverpool Marine) 1
Davies, J. E. 1885 (Oswestry) 1
Davies, Jas 1878 (Wrexham) 1
Davies, John 1879 (Wrexham) 1
Davies, Jos 1888 (Newton Heath, Wolverhampton W) 7
Davies, Jos 1889 (Everton, Chirk, Ardwick, Sheffield U, Manchester C, Millwall, Reading) 11
Davies, J. P. 1883 (Druids) 2
Davies, Ll. 1907 (Wrexham, Everton, Wrexham) 13
Davies, L. S. 1922 (Cardiff C) 23
Davies, O. 1890 (Wrexham) 1
Davies, R. 1883 (Wrexham) 3
Davies, R. 1885 (Druids) 1
Davies, R. O. 1892 (Wrexham) 2
Davies, R. T. 1964 (Norwich C, Southampton, Portsmouth) 29
Davies, R. W. 1964 (Bolton W, Newcastle U, Manchester C, Manchester U, Blackpool) 34
Davies, S. 2001 (Tottenham H, Everton, Fulham) 58
Davies, S. I. 1996 (Manchester U) 1
Davies, Stanley 1920 (Preston NE, Everton, WBA, Rotherham U) 18
Davies, T. 1886 (Oswestry) 1
Davies, T. 1903 (Druids) 4
Davies, W. 1884 (Wrexham) 1
Davies, W. 1924 (Swansea T, Cardiff C, Notts Co) 17
Davies, William 1903 (Wrexham, Blackburn R) 11
Davies, W. C. 1908 (Crystal Palace, WBA, Crystal Palace) 4
Davies, W. D. 1975 (Everton, Wrexham, Swansea C) 52
Davies, W. H. 1876 (Oswestry) 4
Davis, G. 1978 (Wrexham) 3
Davis, W. O. 1913 (Millwall Ath) 5
Day, A. 1934 (Tottenham H) 1
Deacy, N. 1977 (PSV Eindhoven, Beringen) 12
Dearson, D. J. 1939 (Birmingham) 3
Delaney, M. A. 2000 (Aston Villa) 36
Derrett, S. C. 1969 (Cardiff C) 4
Dewey, F. T. 1931 (Cardiff Corinthians) 2
Dibble, A. 1986 (Luton T, Manchester C) 3
Dorman, A. 2010 (St Mirren, Crystal Palace) 3
Doughty, J. 1886 (Druids, Newton Heath) 8
Doughty, R. 1888 (Newton Heath) 2
Duffy, R. M. 2006 (Portsmouth) 13
Dummett, P. 2014 (Newcastle U) 2
Durban, A. 1966 (Derby Co) 27
Dwyer, P. J. 1978 (Cardiff C) 10

Eardley, N. 2008 (Oldham Ath, Blackpool) 16
Earnshaw, R. 2002 (Cardiff C, WBA, Norwich C, Derby Co, Nottingham F, Cardiff C) 59
Easter, J. M. 2007 (Wycombe W, Plymouth Arg, Milton Keynes D, Crystal Palace, Millwall) 12
Eastwood, F. 2008 (Wolverhampton W, Coventry C) 11
Edwards, C. 1878 (Wrexham) 1
Edwards, C. N. H. 1996 (Swansea C) 1
Edwards, D. A. 2008 (Luton T, Wolverhampton W) 39
Edwards, G. 1947 (Birmingham C, Cardiff C) 12
Edwards, H. 1878 (Wrexham Civil Service, Wrexham) 8
Edwards, J. H. 1876 (Wanderers) 1
Edwards, J. H. 1895 (Oswestry) 3
Edwards, J. H. 1898 (Aberystwyth) 1
Edwards, L. T. 1957 (Charlton Ath) 2
Edwards, R. I. 1978 (Chester, Wrexham) 4
Edwards, R. O. 2003 (Aston Villa, Wolverhampton W) 15
Edwards, R. W. 1998 (Bristol C) 4
Edwards, T. 1932 (Linfield) 1
Egan, W. 1892 (Chirk) 1
Ellis, B. 1932 (Motherwell) 6
Ellis, E. 1931 (Nunhead, Oswestry) 3
Emanuel, W. J. 1973 (Bristol C) 2
England, H. M. 1962 (Blackburn R, Tottenham H) 44
Evans, B. C. 1972 (Swansea C, Hereford U) 7
Evans, C. M. 2008 (Manchester C, Sheffield U) 13
Evans, D. G. 1926 (Reading, Huddersfield T) 4
Evans, H. P. 1922 (Cardiff C) 6
Evans, I. 1976 (Crystal Palace) 13
Evans, J. 1893 (Oswestry) 3
Evans, J. 1912 (Cardiff C) 8
Evans, J. H. 1922 (Southend U) 4
Evans, Len 1927 (Aberdare Ath, Cardiff C, Birmingham) 4
Evans, M. 1884 (Oswestry) 1
Evans, P. S. 2002 (Brentford, Bradford C) 2
Evans, R. 1902 (Clapton) 1
Evans, R. E. 1906 (Wrexham, Aston Villa, Sheffield U) 10
Evans, R. O. 1902 (Wrexham, Blackburn R, Coventry C) 10
Evans, R. S. 1964 (Swansea T) 1
Evans, S. J. 2007 (Wrexham) 7
Evans, T. J. 1927 (Clapton Orient, Newcastle U) 4
Evans, W. 1933 (Tottenham H) 6
Evans, W. A. W. 1876 (Oxford University) 2
Evans, W. G. 1890 (Bootle, Aston Villa) 3
Evelyn, E. C. 1887 (Crusaders) 1
Eyton-Jones, J. A. 1883 (Wrexham) 4

Farmer, G. 1885 (Oswestry) 2
Felgate, D. 1984 (Lincoln C) 1
Finnigan, R. J. 1930 (Wrexham) 1
Fletcher, C. N. 2004 (Bournemouth, West Ham U, Crystal Palace) 36
Flynn, B. 1975 (Burnley, Leeds U, Burnley) 66
Fon Williams, O. 2016 (Inverness CT) 1
Ford, T. 1947 (Swansea T, Aston Villa, Sunderland, Cardiff C) 38
Foulkes, H. E. 1932 (WBA) 1
Foulkes, W. I. 1952 (Newcastle U) 11
Foulkes, W. T. 1884 (Oswestry) 2
Fowler, J. 1925 (Swansea T) 6
Freestone, R. 2000 (Swansea C) 1

Gabbidon, D. L. 2002 (Cardiff C, West Ham U, QPR, Crystal Palace) 49
Garner, G. 2006 (Leyton Orient) 1
Garner, J. 1896 (Aberystwyth) 1
Giggs, R. J. 1992 (Manchester U) 64
Giles, D. C. 1980 (Swansea C, Crystal Palace) 12
Gillam, S. G. 1889 (Wrexham, Shrewsbury, Clapton) 5
Glascodine, G. 1879 (Wrexham) 1
Glover, E. M. 1932 (Grimsby T) 7
Godding, G. 1923 (Wrexham) 2
Godfrey, B. C. 1964 (Preston NE) 3
Goodwin, U. 1881 (Ruthin) 1
Goss, J. 1991 (Norwich C) 9
Gough, R. T. 1883 (Oswestry White Star) 1
Gray, A. 1924 (Oldham Ath, Manchester C, Manchester Central, Tranmere R, Chester) 24
Green, A. W. 1901 (Aston Villa, Notts Co, Nottingham F) 8
Green, C. R. 1965 (Birmingham C) 15
Green, G. H. 1938 (Charlton Ath) 4
Green, R. M. 1998 (Wolverhampton W) 2
Grey, Dr W. 1876 (Druids) 2
Griffiths, A. T. 1971 (Wrexham) 17
Griffiths, F. J. 1900 (Blackpool) 2
Griffiths, G. 1887 (Chirk) 1
Griffiths, J. H. 1953 (Swansea T) 1
Griffiths, L. 1902 (Wrexham) 1
Griffiths, M. W. 1947 (Leicester C) 11

Griffiths, P. 1884 (Chirk) 6
Griffiths, P. H. 1932 (Everton) 1
Griffiths, T. P. 1927 (Everton, Bolton W, Middlesbrough, Aston Villa) 21
Gunter, C. R. 2007 (Cardiff C, Tottenham H, Nottingham F, Reading) 79

Hall, G. D. 1988 (Chelsea) 9
Hallam, J. 1889 (Oswestry) 1
Hanford, H. 1934 (Swansea T, Sheffield W) 7
Harrington, A. C. 1956 (Cardiff C) 11
Harris, C. S. 1976 (Leeds U) 24
Harris, W. C. 1954 (Middlesbrough) 6
Harrison, W. C. 1899 (Wrexham) 5
Hartson, J. 1995 (Arsenal, West Ham U, Wimbledon, Coventry C, Celtic) 51
Haworth, S. O. 1997 (Cardiff C, Coventry C) 5
Hayes, A. 1890 (Wrexham) 2
Henley, A. D. 2016 (Blackburn R) 2
Hennessey, W. R. 2007 (Wolverhampton W, Crystal Palace) 68
Hennessey, W. T. 1962 (Birmingham C, Nottingham F, Derby Co) 39
Hersee, A. M. 1886 (Bangor) 2
Hersee, R. 1886 (Llandudno) 1
Hewitt, R. 1958 (Cardiff C) 5
Hewitt, T. J. 1911 (Wrexham, Chelsea, South Liverpool) 8
Heywood, D. 1879 (Druids) 1
Hibbott, H. 1880 (Newtown Excelsior, Newtown) 3
Higham, G. G. 1878 (Oswestry) 2
Hill, M. R. 1972 (Ipswich T) 2
Hockey, T. 1972 (Sheffield U, Norwich C, Aston Villa) 9
Hoddinott, T. F. 1921 (Watford) 2
Hodges, G. 1984 (Wimbledon, Newcastle U, Watford, Sheffield U) 18
Hodgkinson, A. V. 1908 (Southampton) 1
Holden, A. 1984 (Chester C) 1
Hole, B. G. 1963 (Cardiff C, Blackburn R, Aston Villa, Swansea C) 30
Hole, W. J. 1921 (Swansea T) 9
Hollins, D. M. 1962 (Newcastle U) 11
Hopkins, I. J. 1935 (Brentford) 12
Hopkins, J. 1983 (Fulham, Crystal Palace) 16
Hopkins, M. 1956 (Tottenham H) 34
Horne, B. 1988 (Portsmouth, Southampton, Everton, Birmingham C) 59
Howell, E. G. 1888 (Builth) 3
Howells, R. G. 1954 (Cardiff C) 2
Hugh, A. R. 1930 (Newport Co) 1
Hughes, A. 1894 (Rhos) 2
Hughes, A. 1907 (Chirk) 1
Hughes, C. M. 1992 (Luton T, Wimbledon) 8
Hughes, E. 1899 (Everton, Tottenham H) 14
Hughes, E. 1906 (Wrexham, Nottingham F, Wrexham, Manchester C) 16
Hughes, F. W. 1882 (Northwich Victoria) 6
Hughes, I. 1951 (Luton T) 4
Hughes, J. 1877 (Cambridge University, Aberystwyth) 2
Hughes, J. 1905 (Liverpool) 3
Hughes, J. I. 1935 (Blackburn R) 1
Hughes, L. M. 1984 (Manchester U, Barcelona, Manchester U, Chelsea, Southampton) 72
Hughes, P. W. 1887 (Bangor) 3
Hughes, W. 1891 (Bootle) 3
Hughes, W. A. 1949 (Blackburn R) 5
Hughes, W. M. 1938 (Birmingham) 10
Humphreys, J. V. 1947 (Everton) 1
Humphreys, R. 1888 (Druids) 1
Hunter, A. H. 1887 (FA of Wales Secretary) 1
Huws, E. W. 2014 (Manchester C, Wigan Ath, Cardiff C) 11

Isgrove, L. J. 2016 (Southampton) 1

Jackett, K. 1983 (Watford) 31
Jackson, W. 1899 (St Helens Rec) 1
James, E. 1893 (Chirk) 8
James, E. G. 1966 (Blackpool) 9
James, L. 1972 (Burnley, Derby Co, QPR, Burnley, Swansea C, Sunderland) 54
James, R. M. 1979 (Swansea C, Stoke C, QPR, Leicester C, Swansea C) 47
James, W. 1931 (West Ham U) 2
Jarrett, R. H. 1889 (Ruthin) 2
Jarvis, A. L. 1967 (Hull C) 3
Jenkins, E. 1925 (Lovell's Ath) 1
Jenkins, J. 1924 (Brighton & HA) 8
Jenkins, R. W. 1902 (Rhyl) 1
Jenkins, S. R. 1996 (Swansea C, Huddersfield T) 16
Jenkyns, C. A. L. 1892 (Small Heath, Woolwich Arsenal, Newton Heath, Walsall) 8
Jennings, W. 1914 (Bolton W) 11
John, D. C. 2013 (Cardiff C) 2
John, R. F. 1923 (Arsenal) 15
John, W. R. 1931 (Walsall, Stoke C, Preston NE, Sheffield U, Swansea T) 14
Johnson, A. J. 1999 (Nottingham F, WBA) 15
Johnson, M. G. 1964 (Swansea T) 1
Jones, A. 1987 (Port Vale, Charlton Ath) 6
Jones, A. F. 1877 (Oxford University) 1
Jones, A. T. 1905 (Nottingham F, Notts Co) 2
Jones, Bryn 1935 (Wolverhampton W, Arsenal) 17
Jones, B. S. 1963 (Swansea T, Plymouth Arg, Cardiff C) 15
Jones, Charlie 1926 (Nottingham F, Arsenal) 8
Jones, Cliff 1954 (Swansea T, Tottenham H, Fulham) 59
Jones, C. W. 1935 (Birmingham) 2
Jones, D. 1888 (Chirk, Bolton W, Manchester C) 14
Jones, D. E. 1976 (Norwich C) 8
Jones, D. O. 1934 (Leicester C) 7
Jones, Evan 1910 (Chelsea, Oldham Ath, Bolton W) 7
Jones, F. R. 1885 (Bangor) 3
Jones, F. W. 1893 (Small Heath) 1
Jones, G. P. 1907 (Wrexham) 2
Jones, H. 1902 (Aberaman) 1
Jones, Humphrey 1885 (Bangor, Queen's Park, East Stirlingshire, Queen's Park) 14
Jones, Ivor 1920 (Swansea T, WBA) 10
Jones, Jeffrey 1908 (Llandrindod Wells) 3
Jones, J. 1876 (Druids) 1
Jones, J. 1883 (Berwyn Rangers) 3
Jones, J. 1925 (Wrexham) 1
Jones, J. L. 1895 (Sheffield U, Tottenham H) 21
Jones, J. Love 1906 (Stoke, Middlesbrough) 2
Jones, J. O. 1901 (Bangor) 2
Jones, J. P. 1976 (Liverpool, Wrexham, Chelsea, Huddersfield T) 72
Jones, J. T. 1912 (Stoke, Crystal Palace) 15
Jones, K. 1950 (Aston Villa) 1
Jones, Leslie J. 1933 (Cardiff C, Coventry C, Arsenal 11
Jones, M. A. 2007 (Wrexham) 2
Jones, M. G. 2000 (Leeds U, Leicester C) 13
Jones, P. L. 1997 (Liverpool, Tranmere R) 2
Jones, P. S. 1997 (Stockport Co, Southampton, Wolverhampton W, QPR) 50
Jones, P. W. 1971 (Bristol R) 1
Jones, R. 1887 (Bangor, Crewe Alex) 3
Jones, R. 1898 (Leicester Fosse) 1
Jones, R. 1899 (Druids) 1
Jones, R. 1900 (Bangor) 2
Jones, R. 1906 (Millwall) 2
Jones, R. A. 1884 (Druids) 4
Jones, R. A. 1994 (Sheffield W) 1
Jones, R. S. 1894 (Everton) 1
Jones, S. 1887 (Wrexham, Chester) 2
Jones, S. 1893 (Wrexham, Burton Swifts, Druids) 6
Jones, T. 1926 (Manchester U) 4
Jones, T. D. 1908 (Aberdare) 1
Jones, T. G. 1938 (Everton) 17
Jones, T. J. 1932 (Sheffield W) 2
Jones, V. P. 1995 (Wimbledon) 9
Jones, W. E. A. 1947 (Swansea T, Tottenham H) 4
Jones, W. J. 1901 (Aberdare, West Ham U) 4
Jones, W. Lot 1905 (Manchester C, Southend U) 20
Jones, W. P. 1889 (Druids, Wynnstay) 4
Jones, W. R. 1897 (Aberystwyth) 1

Keenor, F. C. 1920 (Cardiff C, Crewe Alex) 32
Kelly, F. C. 1899 (Wrexham, Druids) 3
Kelsey, A. J. 1954 (Arsenal) 41
Kenrick, S. L. 1876 (Druids, Oswestry, Shropshire Wanderers) 5
Ketley, C. F. 1882 (Druids) 1
King, A. P. 2009 (Leicester C) 39
King, J. 1955 (Swansea T) 1
Kinsey, N. 1951 (Norwich C, Birmingham C) 7
Knill, A. R. 1989 (Swansea C) 1

Koumas, J. 2001 (Tranmere R, WBA, Wigan Ath) 34
Krzywicki, R. L. 1970 (WBA, Huddersfield T) 8

Lambert, R. 1947 (Liverpool) 5
Latham, G. 1905 (Liverpool, Southport Central, Cardiff C) 10
Law, B. J. 1990 (QPR) 1
Lawrence, E. 1930 (Clapton Orient, Notts Co) 2
Lawrence, S. 1932 (Swansea T) 8
Lawrence, T. M. 2016 (Leicester C) 6
Lea, A. 1889 (Wrexham) 4
Lea, C. 1965 (Ipswich T) 2
Leary, P. 1889 (Bangor) 1
Ledley, J. C. 2006 (Cardiff C, Celtic, Crystal Palace) 73
Leek, K. 1961 (Leicester C, Newcastle U, Birmingham C, Northampton T) 13
Legg, A. 1996 (Birmingham C, Cardiff C) 6
Lever, A. R. 1953 (Leicester C) 1
Lewis, B. 1891 (Chester, Wrexham, Middlesbrough, Wrexham) 10
Lewis, D. 1927 (Arsenal) 3
Lewis, D. 1983 (Swansea C) 1
Lewis, D. J. 1933 (Swansea T) 2
Lewis, D. M. 1890 (Bangor) 2
Lewis, J. 1906 (Bristol R) 1
Lewis, J. 1926 (Cardiff C) 1
Lewis, T. 1881 (Wrexham) 2
Lewis, W. 1885 (Bangor, Crewe Alex, Chester, Manchester C, Chester) 27
Lewis, W. L. 1927 (Swansea T, Huddersfield T) 6
Llewellyn, C. M. 1998 (Norwich C, Wrexham) 6
Lloyd, B. W. 1976 (Wrexham) 3
Lloyd, J. W. 1879 (Wrexham, Newtown) 2
Lloyd, R. A. 1891 (Ruthin) 2
Lockley, A. 1898 (Chirk) 1
Lovell, S. 1982 (Crystal Palace, Millwall) 6
Lowndes, S. R. 1983 (Newport Co, Millwall, Barnsley) 10
Lowrie, G. 1948 (Coventry C, Newcastle U) 4
Lucas, P. M. 1962 (Leyton Orient) 4
Lucas, W. H. 1949 (Swansea T) 7
Lumberg, A. 1929 (Wrexham, Wolverhampton W) 4
Lynch, J. J. 2013 (Hudderfield T) 1

MacDonald, S. B. 2011 (Swansea C, Bournemouth) 4
McCarthy, T. P. 1889 (Wrexham) 1
McMillan, R. 1881 (Shrewsbury Engineers) 2
Maguire, G. T. 1990 (Portsmouth) 7
Mahoney, J. F. 1968 (Stoke C, Middlesbrough, Swansea C) 51
Mardon, P. J. 1996 (WBA) 1
Margetson, M. W. 2004 (Cardiff C) 1
Marriott, A. 1996 (Wrexham) 5
Martin, T. J. 1930 (Newport Co) 1
Marustik, C. 1982 (Swansea C) 6
Mates, J. 1891 (Chirk) 3
Matthews, A. J. 2011 (Cardiff C, Celtic) 13
Matthews, R. W. 1921 (Liverpool, Bristol C, Bradford) 3
Matthews, W. 1905 (Chester) 2
Matthias, J. S. 1896 (Brymbo, Shrewsbury T, Wolverhampton W) 5
Matthias, T. J. 1914 (Wrexham) 12
Mays, A. W. 1929 (Wrexham) 1
Medwin, T. C. 1953 (Swansea T, Tottenham H) 30
Melville, A. K. 1990 (Swansea C, Oxford U, Sunderland, Fulham, West Ham U) 65
Meredith, S. 1900 (Chirk, Stoke, Leyton) 8
Meredith, W. H. 1895 (Manchester C, Manchester U) 48
Mielczarek, R. 1971 (Rotherham U) 1
Millership, H. 1920 (Rotherham Co) 6
Millington, A. H. 1963 (WBA, Crystal Palace, Peterborough U, Swansea C) 21
Mills, T. J. 1934 (Clapton Orient, Leicester C) 4
Mills-Roberts, R. H. 1885 (St Thomas' Hospital, Preston NE, Llanberis) 8
Moore, G. 1960 (Cardiff C, Chelsea, Manchester U, Northampton T, Charlton Ath) 21
Morgan, C. 2007 (Milton Keynes D, Peterborough U, Preston NE) 23
Morgan, J. R. 1877 (Cambridge University, Derby School Staff) 10
Morgan, J. T. 1905 (Wrexham) 1
Morgan-Owen, H. 1902 (Oxford University, Corinthians) 4
Morgan-Owen, M. M. 1897 (Oxford University, Corinthians) 13
Morison, S. W. 2011 (Millwall, Norwich C) 20
Morley, E. J. 1925 (Swansea T, Clapton Orient) 4
Morris, A. G. 1896 (Aberystwyth, Swindon T, Nottingham F) 21
Morris, C. 1900 (Chirk, Derby Co, Huddersfield T) 27
Morris, E. 1893 (Chirk) 3
Morris, H. 1894 (Sheffield U, Manchester C, Grimsby T) 3
Morris, J. 1887 (Oswestry) 1
Morris, J. 1898 (Chirk) 1
Morris, R. 1900 (Chirk, Shrewsbury T) 6
Morris, R. 1902 (Newtown, Druids, Liverpool, Leeds C, Grimsby T, Plymouth Arg) 11
Morris, S. 1937 (Birmingham) 5
Morris, W. 1947 (Burnley) 5
Moulsdale, J. R. B. 1925 (Corinthians) 1
Murphy, J. P. 1933 (WBA) 15
Myhill, G. O. 2008 (Hull C, WBA) 19

Nardiello, D. 1978 (Coventry C) 2
Nardiello, D. A. 2007 (Barnsley, QPR) 3
Neal, J. E. 1931 (Colwyn Bay) 2
Neilson, A. B. 1992 (Newcastle U, Southampton) 5
Newnes, J. 1926 (Nelson) 1
Newton, L. F. 1912 (Cardiff Corinthians) 1
Nicholas, D. S. 1923 (Stoke, Swansea T) 3
Nicholas, P. 1979 (Crystal Palace, Arsenal, Crystal Palace, Luton T, Aberdeen, Chelsea, Watford) 73
Nicholls, J. 1924 (Newport Co, Cardiff C) 4
Niedzwiecki, E. A. 1985 (Chelsea) 2
Nock, W. 1897 (Newtown) 1
Nogan, L. M. 1992 (Watford, Reading) 2
Norman, A. J. 1986 (Hull C) 5
Nurse, M. T. G. 1960 (Swansea T, Middlesbrough) 12
Nyatanga, L. J. 2006 (Derby Co, Bristol C) 34

O'Callaghan, E. 1929 (Tottenham H) 11
Oliver, A. 1905 (Bangor, Blackburn R) 2
Oster, J. M. 1998 (Everton, Sunderland) 13
O'Sullivan, P. A. 1973 (Brighton & HA) 3
Owen, D. 1879 (Oswestry) 1
Owen, E. 1884 (Ruthin Grammar School) 3
Owen, G. 1888 (Chirk, Newton Heath, Chirk) 4
Owen, J. 1892 (Newton Heath) 1
Owen, T. 1879 (Oswestry) 1
Owen, Trevor 1899 (Crewe Alex) 2
Owen, W. 1884 (Chirk) 16
Owen, W. P. 1880 (Ruthin) 12
Owens, J. 1902 (Wrexham) 1

Page, M. E. 1971 (Birmingham C) 28
Page, R. J. 1997 (Watford, Sheffield U, Cardiff C, Coventry C) 41
Palmer, D. 1957 (Swansea T) 3
Parris, J. E. 1932 (Bradford) 1
Parry, B. J. 1951 (Swansea T) 1
Parry, C. 1891 (Everton, Newtown) 13
Parry, E. 1922 (Liverpool) 5
Parry, M. 1901 (Liverpool) 16
Parry, P. I. 2004 (Cardiff C) 12
Parry, T. D. 1900 (Oswestry) 7
Parry, W. 1895 (Newtown) 1
Partridge, D. W. 2005 (Motherwell, Bristol C) 7
Pascoe, C. 1984 (Swansea C, Sunderland) 10
Paul, R. 1949 (Swansea T, Manchester C) 33
Peake, E. 1908 (Aberystwyth, Liverpool) 11
Peers, E. J. 1914 (Wolverhampton W, Port Vale) 12
Pembridge, M. A. 1992 (Luton T, Derby Co, Sheffield W, Benfica, Everton, Fulham) 54
Perry, E. 1938 (Doncaster R) 3
Perry, J. 1994 (Cardiff C) 1
Phennah, E. 1878 (Civil Service) 1
Phillips, C. 1931 (Wolverhampton W, Aston Villa) 13
Phillips, D. 1984 (Plymouth Arg, Manchester C, Coventry C, Norwich C, Nottingham F) 62
Phillips, L. 1971 (Cardiff C, Aston Villa, Swansea C, Charlton Ath) 58
Phillips, T. J. S. 1973 (Chelsea) 4
Phoenix, H. 1882 (Wrexham) 1
Pipe, D. R. 2003 (Coventry C) 1
Poland, G. 1939 (Wrexham) 2
Pontin, K. 1980 (Cardiff C) 2
Powell, A. 1947 (Leeds U, Everton, Birmingham C) 8
Powell, D. 1968 (Wrexham, Sheffield U) 11

Powell, I. V. 1947 (QPR, Aston Villa) 8
Powell, J. 1878 (Druids, Bolton W, Newton Heath) 15
Powell, Seth 1885 (Oswestry, WBA) 7
Price, H. 1907 (Aston Villa, Burton U, Wrexham) 5
Price, J. 1877 (Wrexham) 12
Price, L. P. 2006 (Ipswich T, Derby Co, Crystal Palace) 11
Price, P. 1980 (Luton T, Tottenham H) 25
Pring, K. D. 1966 (Rotherham U) 3
Pritchard, H. K. 1985 (Bristol C) 1
Pryce-Jones, A. W. 1895 (Newtown) 1
Pryce-Jones, W. E. 1887 (Cambridge University) 5
Pugh, A. 1889 (Rhostyllen) 1
Pugh, D. H. 1896 (Wrexham, Lincoln C) 7
Pugsley, J. 1930 (Charlton Ath) 1
Pullen, W. J. 1926 (Plymouth Arg) 1

Ramsey, A. J. 2009 (Arsenal) 47
Rankmore, F. E. J. 1966 (Peterborough U) 1
Ratcliffe, K. 1981 (Everton, Cardiff C) 59
Rea, J. C. 1894 (Aberystwyth) 9
Ready, K. 1997 (QPR) 5
Reece, G. I. 1966 (Sheffield U, Cardiff C) 29
Reed, W. G. 1955 (Ipswich T) 2
Rees, A. 1984 (Birmingham C) 1
Rees, J. M. 1992 (Luton T) 1
Rees, R. R. 1965 (Coventry C, WBA, Nottingham F) 39
Rees, W. 1949 (Cardiff C, Tottenham H) 4
Ribeiro, C. M. 2010 (Bristol C) 2
Richards, A. 1932 (Barnsley) 1
Richards, A. D. J. (Jazz) 2012 (Swansea C, Cardiff C) 12
Richards, D. 1931 (Wolverhampton W, Brentford, Birmingham) 21
Richards, G. 1899 (Druids, Oswestry, Shrewsbury T) 6
Richards, R. W. 1920 (Wolverhampton W, West Ham U, Mold) 9
Richards, S. V. 1947 (Cardiff C) 1
Richards, W. E. 1933 (Fulham) 1
Ricketts, S. D. 2005 (Swansea C, Hull C, Bolton W, Wolverhampton W) 52
Roach, J. 1885 (Oswestry) 1
Robbins, W. W. 1931 (Cardiff C, WBA) 11
Roberts, A. M. 1993 (QPR) 2
Roberts, D. F. 1973 (Oxford U, Hull C) 17
Roberts, G. W. 2000 (Tranmere R) 9
Roberts, I. W. 1990 (Watford, Huddersfield T, Leicester C, Norwich C) 15
Roberts, Jas 1913 (Wrexham) 2
Roberts, J. 1879 (Corwen, Berwyn R) 7
Roberts, J. 1881 (Ruthin) 2
Roberts, J. 1906 (Bradford C) 2
Roberts, J. G. 1971 (Arsenal, Birmingham C) 22
Roberts, J. H. 1949 (Bolton W) 1
Roberts, N. W. 2000 (Wrexham, Wigan Ath) 4
Roberts, P. S. 1974 (Portsmouth) 4
Roberts, R. 1884 (Druids, Bolton W, Preston NE) 9
Roberts, R. 1886 (Wrexham) 3
Roberts, R. 1891 (Rhos, Crewe Alex) 2
Roberts, R. L. 1890 (Chester) 1
Roberts, S. W. 2005 (Wrexham) 1
Roberts, W. 1879 (Llangollen, Berwyn R) 6
Roberts, W. 1883 (Rhyl) 1
Roberts, W. 1886 (Wrexham) 4
Roberts, W. H. 1882 (Ruthin, Rhyl) 6
Robinson, C. P. 2000 (Wolverhampton W, Portsmouth, Sunderland, Norwich C, Toronto Lynx) 52
Robinson, J. R. C. 1996 (Charlton Ath) 30
Robson-Kanu, T. H. 2010 (Reading, WBA) 40
Rodrigues, P. J. 1965 (Cardiff C, Leicester C, Sheffield W) 40
Rogers, J. P. 1896 (Wrexham) 3
Rogers, W. 1931 (Wrexham) 2
Roose, L. R. 1900 (Aberystwyth, London Welsh, Stoke, Everton, Stoke, Sunderland) 24
Rouse, R. V. 1959 (Crystal Palace) 1
Rowlands, A. C. 1914 (Tranmere R) 1
Rowley, T. 1959 (Tranmere R) 1
Rush, I. 1980 (Liverpool, Juventus, Liverpool) 73
Russell, M. R. 1912 (Merthyr T, Plymouth Arg) 23

Sabine, H. W. 1887 (Oswestry) 1
Saunders, D. 1986 (Brighton & HA, Oxford U, Derby Co, Liverpool, Aston Villa, Galatasaray, Nottingham F, Sheffield U, Benfica, Bradford C) 75
Savage, R. W. 1996 (Crewe Alex, Leicester C, Birmingham C) 39
Savin, G. 1878 (Oswestry) 1
Sayer, P. A. 1977 (Cardiff C) 7
Scrine, F. H. 1950 (Swansea T) 2
Sear, C. R. 1963 (Manchester C) 1
Shaw, E. G. 1882 (Oswestry) 3
Sherwood, A. T. 1947 (Cardiff C, Newport Co) 41
Shone, W. W. 1879 (Oswestry) 1
Shortt, W. W. 1947 (Plymouth Arg) 12
Showers, D. 1975 (Cardiff C) 2
Sidlow, C. 1947 (Liverpool) 7
Sisson, H. 1885 (Wrexham Olympic) 3
Slatter, N. 1983 (Bristol R, Oxford U) 22
Smallman, D. P. 1974 (Wrexham, Everton) 7
Southall, N. 1982 (Everton) 92
Speed, G. A. 1990 (Leeds U, Everton, Newcastle U, Bolton W) 85
Sprake, G. 1964 (Leeds U, Birmingham C) 37
Stansfield, F. 1949 (Cardiff C) 1
Stevenson, B. 1978 (Leeds U, Birmingham C) 15
Stevenson, N. 1982 (Swansea C) 4
Stitfall, R. F. 1953 (Cardiff C) 2
Stock, B. B. 2010 (Doncaster R) 3
Sullivan, D. 1953 (Cardiff C) 17
Symons, C. J. 1992 (Portsmouth, Manchester C, Fulham, Crystal Palace) 37

Tapscott, D. R. 1954 (Arsenal, Cardiff C) 14
Taylor, G. K. 1996 (Crystal Palace, Sheffield U, Burnley, Nottingham F) 15
Taylor, J. 1898 (Wrexham) 1
Taylor, J. W. T. 2015 (Reading) 1
Taylor, N. J. 2010 (Wrexham, Swansea C, Aston Villa) 39
Taylor, O. D. S. 1893 (Newtown) 4
Thatcher, B. D. 2004 (Leicester C, Manchester C) 7
Thomas, C. 1899 (Druids) 2
Thomas, D. A. 1957 (Swansea T) 2
Thomas, D. S. 1948 (Fulham) 4
Thomas, E. 1925 (Cardiff Corinthians) 1
Thomas, G. 1885 (Wrexham) 2
Thomas, H. 1927 (Manchester U) 1
Thomas, Martin R. 1987 (Newcastle U) 1
Thomas, Mickey 1977 (Wrexham, Manchester U, Everton, Brighton & HA, Stoke C, Chelsea, WBA) 51
Thomas, R. J. 1967 (Swindon T, Derby Co, Cardiff C) 50
Thomas, T. 1898 (Bangor) 2
Thomas, W. R. 1931 (Newport Co) 2
Thomson, D. 1876 (Druids) 1
Thomson, G. F. 1876 (Druids) 2
Toshack, J. B. 1969 (Cardiff C, Liverpool, Swansea C) 40
Townsend, W. 1887 (Newtown) 2
Trainer, H. 1895 (Wrexham) 3
Trainer, J. 1887 (Bolton W, Preston NE) 20
Trollope, P. J. 1997 (Derby Co, Fulham, Coventry C, Northampton T) 9
Tudur-Jones, O. 2008 (Swansea C, Norwich C, Hibernian) 7
Turner, H. G. 1937 (Charlton Ath) 8
Turner, J. 1892 (Wrexham) 1
Turner, R. E. 1891 (Wrexham) 2
Turner, W. H. 1887 (Wrexham) 5

Van Den Hauwe, P. W. R. 1985 (Everton) 13
Vaughan, D. O. 2003 (Crewe Alex, Real Sociedad, Blackpool, Sunderland, Nottingham F) 42
Vaughan, Jas 1893 (Druids) 4
Vaughan, John 1879 (Oswestry, Druids, Bolton W) 11
Vaughan, J. O. 1885 (Rhyl) 4
Vaughan, N. 1983 (Newport Co, Cardiff C) 10
Vaughan, T. 1885 (Rhyl) 1
Vearncombe, G. 1958 (Cardiff C) 2
Vernon, T. R. 1957 (Blackburn R, Everton, Stoke C) 32
Villars, A. K. 1974 (Cardiff C) 3
Vizard, E. T. 1911 (Bolton W) 22
Vokes, S. M. 2008 (Bournemouth, Wolverhampton W, Burnley) 50

Walley, J. T. 1971 (Watford) 1
Walsh, I. P. 1980 (Crystal Palace, Swansea C) 18
Ward, D. 1959 (Bristol R, Cardiff C) 2
Ward, D. 2000 (Notts Co, Nottingham F) 5
Ward, D. 2016 (Liverpool) 3
Warner, J. 1937 (Swansea T, Manchester U) 2

Warren, F. W. 1929 (Cardiff C, Middlesbrough, Hearts) 6
Watkins, A. E. 1898 (Leicester Fosse, Aston Villa, Millwall) 5
Watkins, W. M. 1902 (Stoke, Aston Villa, Sunderland, Stoke) 10
Webster, C. 1957 (Manchester U) 4
Weston, R. D. 2000 (Arsenal, Cardiff C) 7
Whatley, W. J. 1939 (Tottenham H) 2
White, P. F. 1896 (London Welsh) 1
Wilcock, A. R. 1890 (Oswestry) 1
Wilding, J. 1885 (Wrexham Olympians, Bootle, Wrexham) 9
Williams, A. 1994 (Reading, Wolverhampton W, Reading) 13
Williams, A. E. 2008 (Stockport Co, Swansea C, Everton) 71
Williams, A. L. 1931 (Wrexham) 1
Williams, A. P. 1998 (Southampton) 2
Williams, B. 1930 (Bristol C) 1
Williams, B. D. 1928 (Swansea T, Everton) 10
Williams, D. G. 1988 (Derby Co, Ipswich T) 13
Williams, D. M. 1986 (Norwich C) 5
Williams, D. R. 1921 (Merthyr T, Sheffield W, Manchester U) 8
Williams, E. 1893 (Crewe Alex) 2
Williams, E. 1901 (Druids) 5
Williams, G. 1893 (Chirk) 6
Williams, G. C. 2014 (Fulham) 7
Williams, G. E. 1960 (WBA) 26
Williams, G. G. 1961 (Swansea T) 5
Williams, G. J. 2006 (West Ham U, Ipswich T) 2
Williams, G. J. J. 1951 (Cardiff C) 1
Williams, G. O. 1907 (Wrexham) 1
Williams, H. J. 1965 (Swansea T) 3
Williams, H. T. 1949 (Newport Co, Leeds U) 4
Williams, J. H. 1884 (Oswestry) 1
Williams, J. J. 1939 (Wrexham) 1
Williams, J. P. 2013 (Crystal Palace) 16
Williams, J. T. 1925 (Middlesbrough) 1
Williams, J. W. 1912 (Crystal Palace) 2
Williams, R. 1935 (Newcastle U) 2
Williams, R. P. 1886 (Caernarvon) 1
Williams, S. G. 1954 (WBA, Southampton) 43
Williams, W. 1876 (Druids, Oswestry, Druids) 11
Williams, W. 1925 (Northampton T) 1
Wilson, H. 2013 (Liverpool) 1
Wilson, J. S. 2013 (Bristol C) 1
Witcomb, D. F. 1947 (WBA, Sheffield W) 3
Woosnam, A. P. 1959 (Leyton Orient, West Ham U, Aston Villa) 17
Woosnam, G. 1879 (Newtown Excelsior) 1
Worthington, T. 1894 (Newtown) 1
Wynn, G. A. 1909 (Wrexham, Manchester C) 11
Wynn, W. 1903 (Chirk) 1

Yorath, T. C. 1970 (Leeds U, Coventry C, Tottenham H, Vancouver Whitecaps) 59
Young, E. 1990 (Wimbledon, Crystal Palace, Wolverhampton W) 21

REPUBLIC OF IRELAND

Aherne, T. 1946 (Belfast Celtic, Luton T) 16
Aldridge, J. W. 1986 (Oxford U, Liverpool, Real Sociedad, Tranmere R) 69
Ambrose, P. 1955 (Shamrock R) 5
Anderson, J. 1980 (Preston NE, Newcastle U) 16
Andrews, K. J. 2009 (Blackburn R, WBA) 35
Andrews, P. 1936 (Bohemians) 1
Arrigan, T. 1938 (Waterford) 1
Arter, H. N. 2015 (Bournemouth) 6

Babb, P. A. 1994 (Coventry C, Liverpool, Sunderland) 35
Bailham, E. 1964 (Shamrock R) 1
Barber, E. 1966 (Shelbourne, Birmingham C) 2
Barrett, G. 2003 (Arsenal, Coventry C) 6
Barry, P. 1928 (Fordsons) 2
Beglin, J. 1984 (Liverpool) 15
Bennett, A. J. 2007 (Reading) 2
Bermingham, J. 1929 (Bohemians) 1
Bermingham, P. 1935 (St James' Gate) 1
Best, L. J. B. 2009 (Coventry C, Newcastle U) 7
Bonner, P. 1981 (Celtic) 80
Boyle, A. 2017 (Preston NE) 1
Braddish, S. 1978 (Dundalk) 2
Bradshaw, P. 1939 (St James' Gate) 5
Brady, F. 1926 (Fordsons) 2
Brady, R. 2013 (Hull C, Norwich C, Burnley) 34
Brady, T. R. 1964 (QPR) 6
Brady, W. L. 1975 (Arsenal, Juventus, Sampdoria, Internazionale, Ascoli, West Ham U) 72
Branagan, K. G. 1997 (Bolton W) 1
Breen, G. 1996 (Birmingham C, Coventry C, West Ham U, Sunderland) 63
Breen, T. 1937 (Manchester U, Shamrock R) 5
Brennan, F. 1965 (Drumcondra) 1
Brennan, S. A. 1965 (Manchester U, Waterford) 19
Browne, A. J. 2017 (Preston NE) 1
Brown, J. 1937 (Coventry C) 2
Browne, W. 1964 (Bohemians) 3
Bruce, A. S. 2007 (Ipswich T) 2
Buckley, L. 1984 (Shamrock R, Waregem) 2
Burke, F. 1952 (Cork Ath) 1
Burke, J. 1929 (Shamrock R) 1
Burke, J. 1934 (Cork) 1
Butler, P. J. 2000 (Sunderland) 1
Butler, T. 2003 (Sunderland) 2
Byrne, A. B. 1970 (Southampton) 14
Byrne, D. 1929 (Shelbourne, Shamrock R, Coleraine) 3
Byrne, J. 1928 (Bray Unknowns) 1
Byrne, J. 1985 (QPR, Le Havre, Brighton & HA, Sunderland, Millwall) 23
Byrne, J. 2004 (Shelbourne) 2
Byrne, P. 1931 (Dolphin, Shelbourne, Drumcondra) 3
Byrne, P. 1984 (Shamrock R) 8
Byrne, S. 1931 (Bohemians) 1

Campbell, A. 1985 (Santander) 3
Campbell, N. 1971 (St Patrick's Ath, Fortuna Cologne) 11
Cannon, H. 1926 (Bohemians) 2
Cantwell, N. 1954 (West Ham U, Manchester U) 36
Carey, B. P. 1992 (Manchester U, Leicester C) 3
Carey, J. J. 1938 (Manchester U) 29
Carolan, J. 1960 (Manchester U) 2
Carr, S. 1999 (Tottenham H, Newcastle U) 44
Carroll, B. 1949 (Shelbourne) 2
Carroll, T. R. 1968 (Ipswich T, Birmingham C) 17
Carsley, L. K. 1998 (Derby Co, Blackburn R, Coventry C, Everton) 39
Cascarino, A. G. 1986 (Gillingham, Millwall, Aston Villa, Celtic, Chelsea, Marseille, Nancy) 88
Chandler, J. 1980 (Leeds U) 2
Chatton, H. A. 1931 (Shelbourne, Dumbarton, Cork) 3
Christie, C. S. F. 2015 (Derby Co) 11
Clark, C. 2011 (Aston Villa, Newcastle U) 24
Clarke, C. R. 2004 (Stoke C) 2
Clarke, J. 1978 (Drogheda U) 1
Clarke, K. 1948 (Drumcondra) 2
Clarke, M. 1950 (Shamrock R) 1
Clinton, T. J. 1951 (Everton) 3
Coad, P. 1947 (Shamrock R) 11
Coffey, T. 1950 (Drumcondra) 1
Coleman, S. 2011 (Everton) 43
Colfer, M. D. 1950 (Shelbourne) 2
Colgan, N. 2002 (Hibernian, Barnsley) 9
Collins, F. 1927 (Jacobs) 1
Conmy, O. M. 1965 (Peterborough U) 5
Connolly, D. J. 1996 (Watford, Feyenoord, Wolverhampton W, Excelsior, Feyenoord, Wimbledon, West Ham U, Wigan Ath) 41
Connolly, H. 1937 (Cork) 1
Connolly, J. 1926 (Fordsons) 1
Conroy, G. A. 1970 (Stoke C) 27
Conway, J. P. 1967 (Fulham, Manchester C) 20
Corr, P. J. 1949 (Everton) 4
Courtney, E. 1946 (Cork U) 1
Cox, S. R. 2011 (WBA, Nottingham F) 30
Coyle, O. C. 1994 (Bolton W) 1
Coyne, T. 1992 (Celtic, Tranmere R, Motherwell) 22
Crowe, G. 2003 (Bohemians) 2
Cummins, G. P. 1954 (Luton T) 19
Cuneen, T. 1951 (Limerick) 1
Cunningham, G. R. 2010 (Manchester C, Bristol C) 4
Cunningham, K. 1996 (Wimbledon, Birmingham C) 72
Curtis, D. P. 1957 (Shelbourne, Bristol C, Ipswich T, Exeter C) 17

Cusack, S. 1953 (Limerick) 1

Daish, L. S. 1992 (Cambridge U, Coventry C) 5
Daly, G. A. 1973 (Manchester U, Derby Co, Coventry C, Birmingham C, Shrewsbury T) 48
Daly, J. 1932 (Shamrock R) 2
Daly, M. 1978 (Wolverhampton W) 2
Daly, P. 1950 (Shamrock R) 1
Davis, T. L. 1937 (Oldham Ath, Tranmere R) 4
Deacy, E. 1982 (Aston Villa) 4
Delaney, D. F. 2008 (QPR, Ipswich T, Crystal Palace) 9
Delap, R. J. 1998 (Derby Co, Southampton) 11
De Mange, K. J. P. P. 1987 (Liverpool, Hull C) 2
Dempsey, J. T. 1967 (Fulham, Chelsea) 19
Dennehy, J. 1972 (Cork Hibernians, Nottingham F, Walsall) 11
Desmond, P. 1950 (Middlesbrough) 4
Devine, J. 1980 (Arsenal, Norwich C) 13
Doherty, G. M. T. 2000 (Luton T, Tottenham H, Norwich C) 34
Donnelly, J. 1935 (Dundalk) 10
Donnelly, T. 1938 (Drumcondra, Shamrock R) 2
Donovan, D. C. 1955 (Everton) 5
Donovan, T. 1980 (Aston Villa) 2
Douglas, J. 2004 (Blackburn R, Leeds U) 8
Dowdall, C. 1928 (Fordsons, Barnsley, Cork) 3
Doyle, C. 1959 (Shelbourne) 1
Doyle, Colin 2007 (Birmingham C) 1
Doyle, D. 1926 (Shamrock R) 1
Doyle, K. E. 2006 (Reading, Wolverhampton W, Colorado Rapids) 63
Doyle, L. 1932 (Dolphin) 1
Doyle, M. P. 2004 (Coventry C) 1
Duff, D. A. 1998 (Blackburn R, Chelsea, Newcastle U, Fulham) 100
Duffy, B. 1950 (Shamrock R) 1
Duffy, S. P. M. 2014 (Everton, Blackburn R, Brighton & HA) 11
Duggan, H. A. 1927 (Leeds U, Newport Co) 5
Dunne, A. P. 1962 (Manchester U, Bolton W) 33
Dunne, J. 1930 (Sheffield U, Arsenal, Southampton, Shamrock R) 15
Dunne, J. C. 1971 (Fulham) 1
Dunne, L. 1935 (Manchester C) 2
Dunne, P. A. J. 1965 (Manchester U) 5
Dunne, R. P. 2000 (Everton, Manchester C, Aston Villa, QPR) 80
Dunne, S. 1953 (Luton T) 15
Dunne, T. 1956 (St Patrick's Ath) 3
Dunning, P. 1971 (Shelbourne) 2
Dunphy, E. M. 1966 (York C, Millwall) 23
Dwyer, N. M. 1960 (West Ham U, Swansea T) 14

Eccles, P. 1986 (Shamrock R) 1
Egan, J. 2017 (Brentford) 2
Egan, R. 1929 (Dundalk) 1
Eglington, T. J. 1946 (Shamrock R, Everton) 24
Elliot, R. 2014 (Newcastle U) 4
Elliott, S. W. 2005 (Sunderland) 9
Ellis, P. 1935 (Bohemians) 7
Evans, M. J. 1998 (Southampton) 1

Fagan, E. 1973 (Shamrock R) 1
Fagan, F. 1955 (Manchester C, Derby Co) 8
Fagan, J. 1926 (Shamrock R) 1
Fahey, K. D. 2010 (Birmingham C) 16
Fairclough, M. 1982 (Dundalk) 2
Fallon, S. 1951 (Celtic) 8
Fallon, W. J. 1935 (Notts Co, Sheffield W) 9
Farquharson, T. G. 1929 (Cardiff C) 4
Farrell, P. 1937 (Hibernian) 2
Farrell, P. D. 1946 (Shamrock R, Everton) 28
Farrelly, G. 1996 (Aston Villa, Everton, Bolton W) 6
Feenan, J. J. 1937 (Sunderland) 2
Finnan, S. 2000 (Fulham, Liverpool, Espanyol) 53
Finucane, A. 1967 (Limerick) 11
Fitzgerald, F. J. 1955 (Waterford) 2
Fitzgerald, P. J. 1961 (Leeds U, Chester) 5
Fitzpatrick, K. 1970 (Limerick) 1
Fitzsimons, A. G. 1950 (Middlesbrough, Lincoln C) 26
Fleming, C. 1996 (Middlesbrough) 10
Flood, J. J. 1926 (Shamrock R) 5
Fogarty, A. 1960 (Sunderland, Hartlepools U) 11
Folan, C. C. 2009 (Hull C) 7
Foley, D. J. 2000 (Watford) 6
Foley, J. 1934 (Cork, Celtic) 7
Foley, K. P. 2009 (Wolverhampton W) 8
Foley, M. 1926 (Shelbourne) 1
Foley, T. C. 1964 (Northampton T) 9
Forde, D. 2011 (Millwall) 24
Foy, T. 1938 (Shamrock R) 2
Fullam, J. 1961 (Preston NE, Shamrock R) 11
Fullam, R. 1926 (Shamrock R) 2

Gallagher, C. 1967 (Celtic) 2
Gallagher, M. 1954 (Hibernian) 1
Gallagher, P. 1932 (Falkirk) 1
Galvin, A. 1983 (Tottenham H, Sheffield W, Swindon T) 29
Gamble, J. 2007 (Cork C) 2
Gannon, E. 1949 (Notts Co, Sheffield W, Shelbourne) 14
Gannon, M. 1972 (Shelbourne) 1
Gaskins, P. 1934 (Shamrock R, St James' Gate) 7
Gavin, J. T. 1950 (Norwich C, Tottenham H, Norwich C) 7
Geoghegan, M. 1937 (St James' Gate) 2
Gibbons, A. 1952 (St Patrick's Ath) 4
Gibson, D. T. D. 2008 (Manchester U, Everton) 27
Gilbert, R. 1966 (Shamrock R) 1
Giles, C. 1951 (Doncaster R) 1
Giles, M. J. 1960 (Manchester U, Leeds U, WBA, Shamrock R) 59
Given, S. J. J. 1996 (Blackburn R, Newcastle U, Manchester C, Aston Villa, Stoke C) 134
Givens, D. J. 1969 (Manchester U, Luton T, QPR, Birmingham C, Neuchatel X) 56
Gleeson, S. M. 2007 (Wolverhampton W, Birmingham C) 4
Glen, W. 1927 (Shamrock R) 8
Glynn, D. 1952 (Drumcondra) 2
Godwin, T. F. 1949 (Shamrock R, Leicester C, Bournemouth) 13
Golding, J. 1928 (Shamrock R) 2
Goodman, J. 1997 (Wimbledon) 4
Goodwin, J. 2003 (Stockport Co) 1
Gorman, W. C. 1936 (Bury, Brentford) 13
Grace, J. 1926 (Drumcondra) 1
Grealish, A. 1976 (Orient, Luton T, Brighton & HA, WBA) 45
Green, P. J. 2010 (Derby Co, Leeds U) 20
Gregg, E. 1978 (Bohemians) 8
Griffith, R. 1935 (Walsall) 1
Grimes, A. A. 1978 (Manchester U, Coventry C, Luton T) 18

Hale, A. 1962 (Aston Villa, Doncaster R, Waterford) 14
Hamilton, T. 1959 (Shamrock R) 2
Hand, E. K. 1969 (Portsmouth) 20
Harrington, W. 1936 (Cork) 5
Harte, I. P. 1996 (Leeds U, Levante) 64
Hartnett, J. B. 1949 (Middlesbrough) 2
Haverty, J. 1956 (Arsenal, Blackburn R, Millwall, Celtic, Bristol R, Shelbourne) 32
Hayes, A. W. P. 1979 (Southampton) 1
Hayes, J. 2016 (Aberdeen) 4
Hayes, W. E. 1947 (Huddersfield T) 2
Hayes, W. J. 1949 (Limerick) 1
Healey, R. 1977 (Cardiff C) 2
Healy, C. 2002 (Celtic, Sunderland) 13
Heighway, S. D. 1971 (Liverpool, Minnesota K) 34
Henderson, B. 1948 (Drumcondra) 2
Henderson, W. C. P. 2006 (Brighton & HA, Preston NE) 6
Hendrick, J. P. 2013 (Derby Co, Burnley) 33
Hennessy, J. 1965 (Shelbourne, St Patrick's Ath) 5
Herrick, J. 1972 (Cork Hibernians, Shamrock R) 3
Higgins, J. 1951 (Birmingham C) 1
Holland, M. R. 2000 (Ipswich T, Charlton Ath) 49
Holmes, J. 1971 (Coventry C, Tottenham H, Vancouver Whitecaps) 30
Hoolahan, W. 2008 (Blackpool, Norwich C) 40
Horgan, D. J. 2017 (Preston NE) 2
Horlacher, A. F. 1930 (Bohemians) 7
Houghton, R. J. 1986 (Oxford U, Liverpool, Aston Villa, Crystal Palace, Reading) 73
Hourihane, C. 2017 (Aston Villa) 2
Howlett, G. 1984 (Brighton & HA) 1
Hoy, M. 1938 (Dundalk) 6

Hughton, C. 1980 (Tottenham H, West Ham U) 53
Hunt, N. 2009 (Reading) 3
Hunt, S. P. 2007 (Reading, Hull C, Wolverhampton W) 39
Hurley, C. J. 1957 (Millwall, Sunderland, Bolton W) 40
Hutchinson, F. 1935 (Drumcondra) 2

Ireland S .J. 2006 (Manchester C) 6
Irwin, D. J. 1991 (Manchester U) 56

Jordan, D. 1937 (Wolverhampton W) 2
Jordan, W. 1934 (Bohemians) 2
Judge, A. C. 2016 (Brentford) 1

Kavanagh, G. A. 1998 (Stoke C, Cardiff C, Wigan Ath) 16
Kavanagh, P. J. 1931 (Celtic) 2
Keane, R. D. 1998 (Wolverhampton W, Coventry C, Internazionale, Leeds U, Tottenham H, Liverpool, Tottenham H, LA Galaxy) 146
Keane, R. M. 1991 (Nottingham F, Manchester U) 67
Keane, T. R. 1949 (Swansea T) 4
Kearin, M. 1972 (Shamrock R) 1
Kearns, F. T. 1954 (West Ham U) 1
Kearns, M. 1971 (Oxford U, Walsall, Wolverhampton W) 18
Kelly, A. T. 1993 (Sheffield U, Blackburn R) 34
Kelly, D. T. 1988 (Walsall, West Ham U, Leicester C, Newcastle U, Wolverhampton W, Sunderland, Tranmere R) 26
Kelly, G. 1994 (Leeds U) 52
Kelly, J. 1932 (Derry C) 4
Kelly, J. A. 1957 (Drumcondra, Preston NE) 47
Kelly, J. P. V. 1961 (Wolverhampton W) 5
Kelly, M. J. 1988 (Portsmouth) 4
Kelly, N. 1954 (Nottingham F) 1
Kelly, S. M. 2006 (Tottenham H, Birmingham C, Fulham, Reading) 38
Kendrick, J. 1927 (Everton, Dolphin) 4
Kenna, J. J. 1995 (Blackburn R) 27
Kennedy, M. F. 1986 (Portsmouth) 2
Kennedy, M. J. 1996 (Liverpool, Wimbledon, Manchester C, Wolverhampton W) 34
Kennedy, W. 1932 (St James' Gate) 3
Kenny, P. 2004 (Sheffield U) 7
Keogh, A. D. 2007 (Wolverhampton W, Millwall) 30
Keogh, J. 1966 (Shamrock R) 1
Keogh, R. J. 2013 (Derby Co) 17
Keogh, S. 1959 (Shamrock R) 1
Kernaghan, A. N. 1993 (Middlesbrough, Manchester C) 22
Kiely, D. L. 2000 (Charlton Ath, WBA) 11
Kiernan, F. W. 1951 (Shamrock R, Southampton) 5
Kilbane, K. D. 1998 (WBA, Sunderland, Everton, Wigan Ath, Hull C) 110
Kinnear, J. P. 1967 (Tottenham H, Brighton & HA) 26
Kinsella, J. 1928 (Shelbourne) 1
Kinsella, M. A. 1998 (Charlton Ath, Aston Villa, WBA) 48
Kinsella, O. 1932 (Shamrock R) 2
Kirkland, A. 1927 (Shamrock R) 1

Lacey, W. 1927 (Shelbourne) 3
Langan, D. 1978 (Derby Co, Birmingham C, Oxford U) 26
Lapira, J. 2007 (Notre Dame) 1
Lawler, J. F. 1953 (Fulham) 8
Lawlor, J. C. 1949 (Drumcondra, Doncaster R) 3
Lawlor, M. 1971 (Shamrock R) 5
Lawrence, L. 2009 (Stoke C, Portsmouth) 15
Lawrenson, M. 1977 (Preston NE, Brighton & HA, Liverpool) 39
Lee, A. D. 2003 (Rotherham U, Cardiff C, Ipswich T) 10
Leech, M. 1969 (Shamrock R) 8
Lennon, C. 1935 (St James' Gate) 3
Lennox, G. 1931 (Dolphin) 2
Long, K. F. 2017 (Burnley) 3
Long, S. P. 2007 (Reading, WBA, Hull C, Southampton) 73
Lowry, D. 1962 (St Patrick's Ath) 1
Lunn, R. 1939 (Dundalk) 2
Lynch, J. 1934 (Cork Bohemians) 1

McAlinden, J. 1946 (Portsmouth) 2
McAteer, J. W. 1994 (Bolton W, Liverpool, Blackburn R, Sunderland) 52
McCann, J. 1957 (Shamrock R) 1
McCarthy, J. 1926 (Bohemians) 3
McCarthy, J. 2010 (Wigan Ath, Everton) 41
McCarthy, M. 1932 (Shamrock R) 1
McCarthy, M. 1984 (Manchester C, Celtic, Lyon, Millwall) 57
McClean, J. J. 2012 (Sunderland, Wigan Ath, WBA) 52
McConville, T. 1972 (Dundalk, Waterford) 6
McDonagh, Jacko 1984 (Shamrock R) 3
McDonagh, J. 1981 (Everton, Bolton W, Notts Co, Wichita Wings) 25
McEvoy, M. A. 1961 (Blackburn R) 17
McGeady, A. J. 2004 (Celtic, Spartak Moscow, Everton) 90
McGee, P. 1978 (QPR, Preston NE) 15
McGoldrick, D. J. 2015 (Ipswich T) 6
McGoldrick, E. J. 1992 (Crystal Palace, Arsenal) 15
McGowan, D. 1949 (West Ham U) 3
McGowan, J. 1947 (Cork U) 1
McGrath, M. 1958 (Blackburn R, Bradford) 22
McGrath, P. 1985 (Manchester U, Aston Villa, Derby Co) 83
McGuire, W. 1936 (Bohemians) 1
Macken, A. 1977 (Derby Co) 1
Macken J. P. 2005 (Manchester C) 1
McKenzie, G. 1938 (Southend U) 9
Mackey, G. 1957 (Shamrock R) 3
McLoughlin, A. F. 1990 (Swindon T, Southampton, Portsmouth) 42
McLoughlin, F. 1930 (Fordsons, Cork) 2
McMillan, W. 1946 (Belfast Celtic) 2
McNally, J. B. 1959 (Luton T) 3
McPhail, S. 2000 (Leeds U) 10
McShane, P. D. 2007 (WBA, Sunderland, Hull C, Reading) 33
Madden, O. 1936 (Cork) 1
Madden, P. 2013 (Scunthorpe U) 1
Maguire, J. 1929 (Shamrock R) 1
Mahon, A. J. 2000 (Tranmere R) 2
Malone, G. 1949 (Shelbourne) 1
Mancini, T. J. 1974 (QPR, Arsenal) 5
Martin, C. 1927 (Bo'ness) 1
Martin, C. J. 1946 (Glentoran, Leeds U, Aston Villa) 30
Martin, M. P. 1972 (Bohemians, Manchester U, WBA, Newcastle U) 52
Maybury, A. 1998 (Leeds U, Hearts, Leicester C) 10
Meagan, M. K. 1961 (Everton, Huddersfield T, Drogheda) 17
Meehan, P. 1934 (Drumcondra) 1
Meyler, D. J. 2013 (Sunderland, Hull C) 19
Miller, L. W. P. 2004 (Celtic, Manchester U, Sunderland, Hibernian) 21
Milligan, M. J. 1992 (Oldham Ath) 1
Monahan, P. 1935 (Sligo R) 2
Mooney, J. 1965 (Shamrock R) 2
Moore, A. 1996 (Middlesbrough) 8
Moore, P. 1931 (Shamrock R, Aberdeen, Shamrock R) 9
Moran, K. 1980 (Manchester U, Sporting Gijon, Blackburn R) 71
Moroney, T. 1948 (West Ham U, Evergreen U) 12
Morris, C. B. 1988 (Celtic, Middlesbrough) 35
Morrison, C. H. 2002 (Crystal Palace, Birmingham C, Crystal Palace) 36
Moulson, C. 1936 (Lincoln C, Notts Co) 5
Moulson, G. B. 1948 (Lincoln C) 3
Muckian, C. 1978 (Drogheda U) 1
Muldoon, T. 1927 (Aston Villa) 1
Mulligan, P. M. 1969 (Shamrock R, Chelsea, Crystal Palace, WBA, Shamrock R) 50
Munroe, L. 1954 (Shamrock R) 1
Murphy, A. 1956 (Clyde) 1
Murphy, B. 1986 (Bohemians) 1
Murphy, D. 2007 (Sunderland, Ipswich T, Newcastle U) 26
Murphy, J. 1980 (Crystal Palace) 3
Murphy, J. 2004 (WBA, Scunthorpe U) 2
Murphy, P. M. 2007 (Carlisle U) 1
Murray, T. 1950 (Dundalk) 1

Newman, W. 1969 (Shelbourne) 1
Nolan. E. W. 2009 (Preston NE) 3

Nolan, R. 1957 (Shamrock R) 10

O'Brien, A. 2007 (Newcastle U) 5
O'Brien, A. J. 2001 (Newcastle U, Portsmouth) 26
O'Brien, F. 1980 (Philadelphia F) 3
O'Brien J. M. 2006 (Bolton W, West Ham U) 5
O'Brien, L. 1986 (Shamrock R, Manchester U, Newcastle U, Tranmere R) 16
O'Brien, M. T. 1927 (Derby Co, Walsall, Norwich C, Watford) 4
O'Brien, R. 1976 (Notts Co) 5
O'Byrne, L. B. 1949 (Shamrock R) 1
O'Callaghan, B. R. 1979 (Stoke C) 6
O'Callaghan, K. 1981 (Ipswich T, Portsmouth) 21
O'Cearuill, J. 2007 (Arsenal) 2
O'Connell, A. 1967 (Dundalk, Bohemians) 2
O'Connor, T. 1950 (Shamrock R) 4
O'Connor, T. 1968 (Fulham, Dundalk, Bohemians) 7
O'Dea, D. 2010 (Celtic, Toronto, Metalurh Donetsk) 20
O'Dowda, C. J. R. 2016 (Oxford U, Bristol C) 5
O'Driscoll, J. F. 1949 (Swansea T) 3
O'Driscoll, S. 1982 (Fulham) 3
O'Farrell, F. 1952 (West Ham U, Preston NE) 9
O'Flanagan, K. P. 1938 (Bohemians, Arsenal) 10
O'Flanagan, M. 1947 (Bohemians) 1
O'Halloran, S. E. 2007 (Aston Villa) 2
O'Hanlon, K. G. 1988 (Rotherham U) 1
O'Kane, E. C. 2016 (Bournemouth, Leeds U) 7
O'Kane, P. 1935 (Bohemians) 3
O'Keefe, E. 1981 (Everton, Port Vale) 5
O'Keefe, T. 1934 (Cork, Waterford) 3
O'Leary, D. 1977 (Arsenal) 68
O'Leary, P. 1980 (Shamrock R) 7
O'Mahoney, M. T. 1938 (Bristol R) 6
O'Neill, F. S. 1962 (Shamrock R) 20
O'Neill, J. 1952 (Everton) 17
O'Neill, J. 1961 (Preston NE) 1
O'Neill, K. P. 1996 (Norwich C, Middlesbrough) 13
O'Neill, W. 1936 (Dundalk) 11
O'Regan, K. 1984 (Brighton & HA) 4
O'Reilly, J. 1932 (Brideville, Aberdeen, Brideville, St James' Gate) 20
O'Reilly, J. 1946 (Cork U) 2
O'Shea, J. F. 2002 (Manchester U, Sunderland) 117

Pearce, A. J. 2013 (Reading, Derby Co) 9
Peyton, G. 1977 (Fulham, Bournemouth, Everton) 33
Peyton, N. 1957 (Shamrock R, Leeds U) 6
Phelan, T. 1992 (Wimbledon, Manchester C, Chelsea, Everton, Fulham) 42
Pilkington, A. N. J. 2013 (Norwich C, Cardiff C) 9
Potter, D. M. 2007 (Wolverhampton W) 5

Quinn, A. 2003 (Sheffield W, Sheffield U) 8
Quinn, B. S. 2000 (Coventry C) 4
Quinn, N. J. 1986 (Arsenal, Manchester C, Sunderland) 91
Quinn, S. 2013 (Hull C, Reading) 18

Randolf, D. E. 2013 (Motherwell, West Ham U) 22
Reid, A. M. 2004 (Nottingham F, Tottenham H, Charlton Ath, Sunderland, Nottingham F) 29
Reid, C. 1931 (Brideville) 1
Reid, S. J. 2002 (Millwall, Blackburn R) 23
Richardson, D. J. 1972 (Shamrock R, Gillingham) 3
Rigby, A. 1935 (St James' Gate) 3
Ringstead, A. 1951 (Sheffield U) 20
Robinson, J. 1928 (Bohemians, Dolphin) 2
Robinson, M. 1981 (Brighton & HA, Liverpool, QPR) 24
Roche, P. J. 1972 (Shelbourne, Manchester U) 8
Rogers, E. 1968 (Blackburn R, Charlton Ath) 19
Rowlands, M. C. 2004 (QPR) 5
Ryan, G. 1978 (Derby Co, Brighton & HA) 18
Ryan, R. A. 1950 (WBA, Derby Co) 16

Sadlier, R. T. 2002 (Millwall) 1
Sammon, C. 2013 (Derby Co) 9
Savage, D. P. T. 1996 (Millwall) 5
Saward, P. 1954 (Millwall, Aston Villa, Huddersfield T) 18
Scannell, T. 1954 (Southend U) 1
Scully, P. J. 1989 (Arsenal) 1
Sheedy, K. 1984 (Everton, Newcastle U) 46
Sheridan, C. 2010 (Celtic, CSKA Sofia) 3
Sheridan, J. J. 1988 (Leeds U, Sheffield W) 34
Slaven, B. 1990 (Middlesbrough) 7
Sloan, J. W. 1946 (Arsenal) 2
Smyth, M. 1969 (Shamrock R) 1
Squires, J. 1934 (Shelbourne) 1
Stapleton, F. 1977 (Arsenal, Manchester U, Ajax, Le Havre, Blackburn R) 71
Staunton, S. 1989 (Liverpool, Aston Villa, Liverpool, Aston Villa) 102
St Ledger-Hall, S. P. 2009 (Preston NE, Leicester C) 37
Stevenson, A. E. 1932 (Dolphin, Everton) 7
Stokes, A. 2007 (Sunderland, Celtic) 9
Strahan, F. 1964 (Shelbourne) 5
Sullivan, J. 1928 (Fordsons) 1
Swan, M. M. G. 1960 (Drumcondra) 1
Synnott, N. 1978 (Shamrock R) 3

Taylor, T. 1959 (Waterford) 1
Thomas, P. 1974 (Waterford) 2
Thompson, J. 2004 (Nottingham F) 1
Townsend, A. D. 1989 (Norwich C, Chelsea, Aston Villa, Middlesbrough) 70
Traynor, T. J. 1954 (Southampton) 8
Treacy, K. 2011 (Preston NE, Burnley) 6
Treacy, R. C. P. 1966 (WBA, Charlton Ath, Swindon T, Preston NE, WBA, Shamrock R) 42
Tuohy, L. 1956 (Shamrock R, Newcastle U, Shamrock R) 8
Turner, C. J. 1936 (Southend U, West Ham U) 10
Turner, P. 1963 (Celtic) 2

Vernon, J. 1946 (Belfast Celtic) 2

Waddock, G. 1980 (QPR, Millwall) 21
Walsh, D. J. 1946 (Linfield, WBA, Aston Villa) 20
Walsh, J. 1982 (Limerick) 1
Walsh, M. 1976 (Blackpool, Everton, QPR, Porto) 21
Walsh, M. 1982 (Everton) 4
Walsh, W. 1947 (Manchester C) 9
Walters, J. R. 2011 (Stoke C) 49
Ward, S. R. 2011 (Wolverhampton W, Burnley) 43
Waters, J. 1977 (Grimsby T) 2
Watters, F. 1926 (Shelbourne) 1
Weir, E. 1939 (Clyde) 3
Westwood, K. 2009 (Coventry C, Sunderland, Sheffield W) 21
Whelan, G. D. 2008 (Stoke C) 81
Whelan, R. 1964 (St Patrick's Ath) 2
Whelan, R. 1981 (Liverpool, Southend U) 53
Whelan, W. 1956 (Manchester U) 4
White, J. J. 1928 (Bohemians) 1
Whittaker, R. 1959 (Chelsea) 1
Williams, J. 1938 (Shamrock R) 1
Wilson, M. D. 2011 (Stoke C, Bournemouth) 25

BRITISH AND IRISH INTERNATIONAL GOALSCORERS 1872–2017

Where two players with the same surname and initials have appeared for the same country, and one or both have scored, they have been distinguished by reference to the club which appears *first* against their name in the international appearances section.
Bold type indicates players who have scored international goals in season 2016–17.

ENGLAND

A'Court, A. 1
Adams, T. A. 5
Adcock, H. 1
Alcock, C. W. 1
Allen, A. 3
Allen, R. 2
Alli, B. J. (Dele) 2
Amos, A. 1
Anderson, V. 2
Anderton, D. R. 7
Astall, G. 1
Athersmith, W. C. 3
Atyeo, P. J. W. 5

Bache, J. W. 4
Bailey, N. C. 2
Baily, E. F. 5
Baines, L. J. 1
Baker, J. H. 3
Ball, A. J. 8
Bambridge, A. L. 1
Bambridge, E. C. 11
Barclay, R. 2
Barkley, R. 2
Barmby, N. J. 4
Barnes, J. 11
Barnes, P. S. 4
Barry, G. 3
Barton, J. 1
Bassett, W. I. 8
Bastin, C. S. 12
Beardsley, P. A. 9
Beasley, A. 1
Beattie, T. K. 1
Beckham, D. R. J. 17
Becton, F. 2
Bedford, H. 1
Bell, C. 9
Bent, D. A. 4
Bentley, R. T. F. 9
Bishop, S. M. 1
Blackburn, F. 1
Blissett, L. 3
Bloomer, S. 28
Bond, R. 2
Bonsor, A. G. 1
Bowden, E. R. 1
Bowers, J. W. 2
Bowles, S. 1
Bradford, G. R. W. 1
Bradford, J. 7
Bradley, W. 2
Bradshaw, F. 3
Brann, G. 1
Bridge, W. M. 1
Bridges, B. J. 1
Bridgett, A. 3
Brindle, T. 1
Britton, C. S. 1
Broadbent, P. F. 2
Broadis, I. A. 8
Brodie, J. B. 1
Bromley-Davenport, W. 2
Brook, E. F. 10
Brooking, T. D. 5
Brooks, J. 2
Broome, F. H. 3
Brown, A. 4
Brown, A. S. 1
Brown, G. 5
Brown, J. 3
Brown, W. 1
Brown, W. M. 1
Buchan, C. M. 4
Bull, S. G. 4
Bullock, N. 2
Burgess, H. 4
Butcher, T. 3
Byrne, J. J. 8

Cahill, G. J. 4
Campbell, S. J. 1
Camsell, G. H. 18
Carroll, A. T. 2
Carter, H. S. 7
Carter, J. H. 4
Caulker, S. A. 1
Chadwick, E. 3
Chamberlain, M. 1
Chambers, H. 5
Channon, M. R. 21
Charlton, J. 6
Charlton, R. 49
Chenery, C. J. 1
Chivers, M. 13
Clarke, A. J. 10
Cobbold, W. N. 6
Cock, J. G. 2
Cole, A. 1
Cole, J. J. 10
Common, A. 2
Connelly, J. M. 7
Coppell, S. J. 7
Cotterill, G. H. 2
Cowans, G. 2
Crawford, R. 1
Crawshaw, T. H. 1
Crayston, W. J. 1
Creek, F. N. S. 1
Crooks, S. D. 7
Crouch, P. J. 22
Currey, E. S. 2
Currie, A. W. 3
Cursham, A. W. 2
Cursham, H. A. 5

Daft, H. B. 3
Davenport, J. K. 2
Davis, G. 1
Davis, H. 1
Day, S. H. 2
Dean, W. R. 18
Defoe, J. C. 20
Devey, J. H. G. 1
Dewhurst, F. 11
Dier, E. J. E. 2
Dix, W. R. 1
Dixon, K. M. 4
Dixon, L. M. 1
Dorrell, A. R. 1
Douglas, B. 11
Drake, E. J. 6
Ducat, A. 1
Dunn, A. T. B. 2

Eastham, G. 2
Edwards, D. 5
Ehiogu, U. 1
Elliott, W. H. 3
Evans, R. E. 1

Ferdinand, L. 5
Ferdinand, R. G. 3
Finney, T. 30
Fleming, H. J. 9
Flowers, R. 10
Forman, Frank 1
Forman, Fred 3
Foster, R. E. 3
Fowler, R. B. 7
Francis, G. C. J. 3
Francis, T. 12
Freeman, B. C. 3
Froggatt, J. 2
Froggatt, R. 2

Galley, T. 1
Gascoigne, P. J. 10
Geary, F. 3
Gerrard, S. G. 21
Gibbins, W. V. T. 3
Gilliatt, W. E. 3
Goddard, P. 1
Goodall, J. 12
Goodyer, A. C. 1
Gosling, R. C. 2
Goulden, L. A. 4
Grainger, C. 3
Greaves, J. 44
Grovesnor, A. T. 2
Gunn, W. 1

Haines, J. T. W. 2
Hall, G. W. 9
Halse, H. J. 2
Hampson, J. 5
Hampton, H. 2
Hancocks, J. 2
Hardman, H. P. 1
Harris, S. S. 2
Hassall, H. W. 4
Hateley, M. 9
Haynes, J. N. 18
Hegan, K. E. 4
Henfrey, A. G. 2
Heskey, E. W. 7
Hilsdon, G. R. 14
Hine, E. W. 4
Hinton, A. T. 1
Hirst, D. E. 1
Hitchens, G. A. 5
Hobbis, H. H. F. 1
Hoddle, G. 8
Hodgetts, D. 1
Hodgson, G. 1
Holley, G. H. 8
Houghton, W. E. 5
Howell, R. 1
Hughes, E. W. 1
Hulme, J. H. A. 4
Hunt, G. S. 1
Hunt, R. 18
Hunter, N. 2
Hurst, G. C. 24

Ince, P. E. C. 2

Jack, D. N. B. 3
Jagielka, P. N. 3
Jeffers, F. 1
Jenas, J. A. 1
Johnson, A. 2
Johnson, D. E. 6
Johnson, E. 2
Johnson, G. M. C. 1
Johnson, J. A. 2
Johnson, T. C. F. 5
Johnson, W. H. 1

Kail, E. I. L. 2
Kane, H. E. 8
Kay, A. H. 1
Keegan, J. K. 21
Kelly, R. 8
Kennedy, R. 3
Kenyon-Slaney, W. S. 2
Keown, M. R. 2
Kevan, D. T. 8
Kidd, B. 1
King, L. B. 2
Kingsford, R. K. 1
Kirchen, A. J. 2
Kirton, W. J. 1

Lallana, A. D. 3
Lambert, R. L. 3
Lampard, F. J. 29
Langton, R. 1
Latchford, R. D. 5
Latheron, E. G. 1
Lawler, C. 1
Lawton, T. 22
Lee, F. 10
Lee, J. 1
Lee, R. M. 2
Lee, S. 2
Lescott, J. 1
Le Saux, G. P. 1
Lindley, T. 14
Lineker, G. 48
Lofthouse, J. M. 3
Lofthouse, N. 30
Hon. A. Lyttelton 1

Mabbutt, G. 1
Macdonald, M. 6
Mannion, W. J. 11
Mariner, P. 13
Marsh, R. W. 1
Matthews, S. 11
Matthews, V. 1
McCall, J. 1
McDermott, T. 3
McManaman, S. 3
Medley, L. D. 1
Melia, J. 1
Mercer, D. W. 1
Merson, P. C. 3
Milburn, J. E. T. 10
Miller, H. S. 1
Mills, G. R. 3
Milner, J. P. 1
Milward, A. 3
Mitchell, C. 5
Moore, J. 1
Moore, R. F. 2
Moore, W. G. B. 2
Morren, T. 1
Morris, F. 1

Morris, J. 3
Mortensen, S. H. 23
Morton, J. R. 1
Mosforth, W. 3
Mullen, J. 6
Mullery, A. P. 1
Murphy, D. B 1

Neal, P. G. 5
Needham, E. 3
Nicholls, J. 1
Nicholson, W. E. 1
Nugent, D. J. 1

O'Grady, M. 3
Osborne, F. R. 3
Owen, M. J. 40
Own goals 33
Oxlade-Chamberlain, A. M. D. 6

Page, L. A. 1
Paine, T. L. 7
Palmer, C. L. 1
Parry, E. H. 1
Parry, R. A. 1
Pawson, F. W. 1
Payne, J. 2
Peacock, A. 3
Pearce, S. 5
Pearson, J. S. 5
Pearson, S. C. 5
Perry, W. 2
Peters, M. 20
Pickering, F. 5
Platt, D. 27
Pointer, R. 2

Quantrill, A. 1

Ramsay, A. E. 3
Rashford, M. 1
Revie, D. G. 4
Redknapp, J. F. 1
Reynolds, J. 3
Richards, M. 1
Richardson, K. E. 2
Richardson, J. R. 2
Rigby, A. 3
Rimmer, E. J. 2
Roberts, F. 2
Roberts, H. 1
Roberts, W. T. 2
Robinson, J. 3
Robson, B. 26
Robson, R. 4
Rooney, W. M. 53
Rowley, J. F. 6
Royle, J. 2
Rutherford, J. 3

Sagar, C. 1
Sandilands, R. R. 3
Sansom, K. 1
Schofield, J. 1
Scholes, P. 14
Seed, J. M. 1
Settle, J. 6
Sewell, J. 3
Shackleton, L. F. 1
Sharp, J. 1
Shearer, A. 30
Shelton, A. 1
Shepherd, A. 2
Sheringham, E. P. 11
Simpson, J. 1
Smalling, C. L. 1
Smith, A. 1
Smith, A. M. 2
Smith, G. O. 11
Smith, Joe 1
Smith, J. R. 2
Smith, J. W. 4
Smith, R. 13
Smith, S. 1
Sorby, T. H. 1
Southgate, G. 2
Southworth, J. 3
Sparks, F. J. 3
Spence, J. W. 1
Spiksley, F. 5
Spilsbury, B. W. 5
Steele, F. C. 8
Stephenson, G. T. 2
Sterling, R. S. 2
Steven, T. M. 4
Stewart, J. 2
Stiles, N. P. 1
Storer, H. 1
Stone, S. B. 2
Sturridge, D. A. 8
Summerbee, M. G. 1

Tambling, R. V. 1
Taylor, P. J. 2
Taylor, T. 16
Terry, J. G. 6
Thompson, P. B. 1
Thornewell, G. 1
Tilson, S. F. 6
Townley, W. J. 2
Townsend, A. D. 3
Tueart, D. 2

Upson, M. J. 2

Vardy, J. R. 6
Vassell, D. 6
Vaughton, O. H. 6
Veitch, J. G. 3
Viollet, D. S. 1

Waddle, C. R. 6
Walcott, T. J. 8
Walker, W. H. 9
Wall, G. 2
Wallace, D. 1
Walsh, P. 1
Waring, T. 4
Warren, B. 2
Watson, D. V. 4
Watson, V. M. 4
Webb, G. W. 1
Webb, N. 4
Wedlock, W. J. 2
Welbeck, D. 14
Weller, K. 1
Welsh, D. 1
Whateley, O. 2
Wheldon, G. F. 6
Whitfield, H. 1
Wignall, F. 2
Wilkes, A. 1
Wilkins, R. G. 3
Willingham, C. K. 1
Wilshaw, D. J. 10
Wilshere J. A. 2
Wilson, G. P. 1
Winckworth, W. N. 1
Windridge, J. E. 7
Wise, D. F. 1
Withe, P. 1
Wollaston, C. H. R. 1
Wood, H. 1
Woodcock, T. 16
Woodhall, G. 1
Woodward, V. J. 29
Worrall, F. 2
Worthington, F. S. 2
Wright, I. E. 9
Wright, M. 1
Wright, W. A. 3
Wright-Phillips, S. C. 6
Wylie, J. G. 1

Yates, J. 3
Young, A. S. 7

NORTHERN IRELAND

Anderson, T. 4
Armstrong, G. 12

Bambrick, J. 12
Barr, H. H. 1
Barron, H. 3
Best, G. 9
Bingham, W. L. 10
Black, K. 1
Blanchflower, D. 2
Blanchflower, J. 1
Boyce, L. 1
Brennan, B. 1
Brennan, R. A. 1
Brotherston, N. 3
Brown, J. 1
Browne, F. 2
Brunt, C. 2

Campbell, J. 1
Campbell, W. G. 1
Casey, T. 2
Caskey, W. 1
Cassidy, T. 1
Cathcart, C. G. 2
Chambers, J. 3
Clarke, C. J. 13
Clements, D. 2
Cochrane, T. 1
Condy, J. 1
Connor, M. J. 1
Coulter, J. 1
Croft, T. 1
Crone, W. 1
Crossan, E. 1
Crossan, J. A. 10
Curran, S. 2
Cush, W. W. 5

Dallas, S. A. 2
Dalton, W. 4
D'Arcy, S. D. 1
Darling, J. 1
Davey, H. H. 1
Davis, S. 9
Davis, T. L. 1
Dill, A. H. 1
Doherty, L. 1
Doherty, P. D. 3
Dougan, A. D. 8
Dowie, I. 12
Dunne, J. 4

Elder, A. R. 1
Elliott, S. 4
Emerson, W. 1
English, S. 1
Evans, C. 1
Evans, J. G. 1

Feeney, W. 1
Feeney, W. J. 5
Ferguson, S. K. 1
Ferguson, W. 1
Ferris, J. 1
Ferris, R. O. 1
Finney, T. 2

Gaffkin, J. 4
Gara, A. 3
Gaukrodger, G. 1
Gibb, J. T. 2
Gibb, T. J. 1
Gibson, W. 1
Gillespie, K. R. 2
Gillespie, W. 13
Goodall, A. L. 2
Griffin, D. J. 1
Gray, P. 6
Grigg, W. D. 1

Halligan, W. 1
Hamill, M. 1
Hamilton, B. 4
Hamilton, W. R. 5
Hannon, D. J. 1
Harkin, J. T. 2
Harvey, M. 3
Healy, D. J. 36
Hill, C. F. 1
Hughes, A. 1
Hughes, M. E. 5
Humphries, W. 1
Hunter, A. (Distillery) 1
Hunter, A. (Blackburn R) 1
Hunter, B. V. 1

Irvine, R. W. 3
Irvine, W. J. 8

Johnston, H. 2
Johnston, S. 2
Johnston, W. C. 1
Jones, S. (Distillery) 1
Jones, S. (Crewe Alex) 1
Jones, J. 1

Kelly, J. 4
Kernaghan, N. 2
Kirwan, J. 2

Lacey, W. 3
Lafferty, K. 20
Lemon, J. 2
Lennon, N. F. 2
Lockhart, N. 3
Lomas, S. M. 3

Magennis, J. B. D. 1
Magilton, J. 5
Mahood, J. 2
Martin, D. K. 3
Maxwell, J. 2
McAdams, W. J. 7
McAllen, J. 1
McAuley, G. 9
Mcauley, J. L. 1
McCann, G. S. 4
McCartney, G. 1
McCandless, J. 2
McCandless, W. 1
McCaw, J. H. 1
McClelland, J. 1
McCluggage, A. 2
McCourt, P. 2
McCracken, W. 1
McCrory, S. 1
McCurdy, C. 1
McDonald, A. 3
McGarry, J. K. 1
McGrath, R. C. 4
McGinn, N. 3
McIlroy, J. 10
McIlroy, S. B. 5
McKenzie, H 1
McKnight, J. 2
McLaughlin, C. G. 1
McLaughlin, J. C. 6
McMahon, G. J. 2
McMordie, A. S. 3
McMorran, E. J. 4
McParland, P. J. 10
McWha, W. B. R. 1
Meldon, P. A 1
Mercer, J. T. 1
Millar, W. 1

Milligan, D. 1
Milne, R. G. 2
Molyneux, T. B. 1
Moreland, V. 1
Morgan, S. 3
Morrow, S. J. 1
Morrow, W. J. 1
Mulryne, P. P. 3
Murdock, C. J. 1
Murphy, N. 1

Neill, W. J. T. 2
Nelson, S. 1
Nicholl, C. J. 3
Nicholl, J. M. 1
Nicholson, J. J. 6

O'Boyle, G. 1
O'Hagan, C. 2
O'Kane, W. J. 1
O'Neill, J. 2
O'Neill, M. A. 4
O'Neill, M. H. 8
Own goals 10

Paterson, M. A. 3
Patterson, D. J. 1
Patterson, R. 1
Peacock, R. 2
Peden, J. 7
Penney, S. 2
Pyper, James 2
Pyper, John 1

Quinn, J. M. 12
Quinn, S. J. 4

Reynolds, J. 1
Rowland, K. 1
Rowley, R. W. M. 2
Rushe, F. 1

Sheridan, J. 2
Sherrard, J. 1
Sherrard, W. C. 2
Shields, D. 1
Simpson, W. J. 5
Sloan, H. A. de B. 4
Smyth, S. 5
Spence, D. W. 3
Sproule, I. 1
Stanfield, O. M. 11
Stevenson, A. E. 5
Stewart, I. 2

Taggart, G. P. 7
Thompson, F. W. 2
Torrans, S. 1
Tully, C. P. 3
Turner, A. 1

Walker, J. 1
Walsh, D. J. 5
Ward, J. J. 4
Washington, C. J. 3
Welsh, E. 1
Whiteside, N. 9
Whiteside, T. 1
Whitley, Jeff 2
Williams, J. R. 1
Williams, M. S. 1
Williamson, J. 1
Wilson, D. J. 1
Wilson, K. J. 6
Wilson, S. J. 7
Wilton, J. M. 2
Young, S. 1

N.B. In 1914 Young goal should be credited to Gillespie W v Wales

SCOTLAND

Aitken, R. (Celtic) 1
Aitken, R. (Dumbarton) 1
Aitkenhead, W. A. C. 2
Alexander, D. 1
Allan, D. S. 4
Allan, J. 2
Anderson, F. 1
Anderson, W. 4
Andrews, P. 1
Anya, I. 3
Archibald, A. 1
Archibald, S. 4

Baird, D. 2
Baird, J. C. 2
Baird, S. 2
Bannon, E. 1
Barbour, A. 1
Barker, J. B. 4
Battles, B. Jr 1
Bauld, W. 2
Baxter, J. C. 3
Beattie, C. 1
Bell, J. 5
Bennett, A. 2
Berra, C. D. 3
Berry, D. 1
Bett, J. 1
Beveridge, W. W. 1
Black, A. 3
Black, D. 1
Bone, J. 1
Booth, S. 6
Boyd, K 7
Boyd, R. 2
Boyd, T. 1
Boyd, W. G. 1
Brackenridge, T. 1
Brand, R. 8
Brazil, A. 1
Bremner, W. J. 3
Broadfoot, K. 1
Brown, A. D. 6
Brown, S. 4
Buchanan, P. S. 1
Buchanan, R. 1
Buckley, P. 1
Buick, A. 2
Burke, C. 2
Burley, C. W. 3
Burns, K. 1

Cairns, T. 1
Caldwell, G. 2
Calderwood, C. 1
Calderwood, R. 2
Caldow, E. 4
Cameron, C. 2
Campbell, C. 1
Campbell, John (Celtic) 5
Campbell, John (Rangers) 4
Campbell, J. (South Western) 1
Campbell, P. 2
Campbell, R. 1
Cassidy, J. 1
Chalmers, S. 3
Chambers, T. 1
Cheyne, A. G. 4
Christie, A. J. 1
Clarkson, D. 1
Clunas, W. L. 1
Collins, J. 12
Collins, R. Y. 10
Combe, J. R. 1
Commons, K. 2
Conn, A. 1
Cooper, D. 6
Craig, J. 1
Craig, T. 1
Crawford, S. 4
Cunningham, A. N. 5
Curran, H. P. 1

Dailly, C. 6
Dalglish, K. 30
Davidson, D. 1
Davidson, J. A. 1
Delaney, J. 3
Devine, A. 1
Dewar, G. 1
Dewar, N. 4
Dickov, P. 1
Dickson, W. 4
Divers, J. 1
Dobie, R. S. 1
Docherty, T. H. 1
Dodds, D. 1
Dodds, W. 7
Donaldson, A. 1
Donnachie, J. 1
Dougall, J. 1
Drummond, J. 2
Dunbar, M. 1
Duncan, D. 7
Duncan, D. M. 1
Duncan, J. 1
Dunn, J. 2
Durie, G. S. 7

Easson, J. F. 1
Elliott, M. S. 1
Ellis, J. 1

Ferguson, B. 3
Ferguson, J. 6
Fernie, W. 1
Fitchie, T. T. 1
Flavell, R. 2
Fleming, C. 2
Fleming, J. W. 3
Fletcher, D. 5
Fletcher, S. K. 9
Fraser, M. J. E. 3
Freedman, D. A. 1

Gallacher, H. K. 23
Gallacher, K. W. 9
Gallacher, P. 1
Galt, J. H. 1
Gemmell, T. (St Mirren) 1
Gemmell, T. (Celtic) 1
Gemmill, A. 8
Gemmill, S. 1
Gibb, W. 1
Gibson, D. W. 3
Gibson, J. D. 1
Gibson, N. 1
Gillespie, Jas. 3
Gillick, T. 3
Gilzean, A. J. 12
Goodwillie, D. 1
Gossland, J. 2
Goudie, J. 1
Gough, C. R. 6
Gourlay, J. 1
Graham, A. 2
Graham, G. 3
Gray, A. 7
Gray, E. 3
Gray, F. 1
Greig, J. 3
Griffiths, L. 2
Groves, W. 4

Hamilton, G. 4
Hamilton, J. (Queen's Park) 3
Hamilton, R. C. 15
Hanley, G. C. 1
Harper, J. M. 2
Hartley, P. J. 1
Harrower, W. 5
Hartford, R. A. 4
Heggie, C. W 4
Henderson, J. G. 1
Henderson, W. 5
Hendry, E. C. J. 3
Herd, D. G. 3
Herd, G. 1
Hewie, J. D. 2
Higgins, A. (Newcastle U) 1
Higgins, A. (Kilmarnock) 4
Highet, T. C. 1
Holt, G.J. 1
Holton, J. A. 2
Hopkin, D. 2
Houliston, W. 2
Howie, H. 1
Howie, J. 2
Hughes, J. 1
Hunter, W. 1
Hutchison, D. 6
Hutchison, T. 1
Hutton, J. 1
Hyslop, T. 1

Imrie, W. N. 1

Jackson, A. 8
Jackson, C. 1
Jackson, D. 4
James, A. W. 4
Jardine, A. 1
Jenkinson, T. 1
Jess, E. 2
Johnston, A. 2
Johnston, L. H. 1
Johnston, M. 14
Johnstone, D. 2
Johnstone, J. 4
Johnstone, Jas. 1
Johnstone, R. 10
Johnstone, W. 1
Jordan, J. 11

Kay, J. L. 5
Keillor, A. 3
Kelly, J. 1
Kelso, R. 1
Ker, G. 10
King, A. 1
King, J. 1
Kinnear, D. 1
Kyle, K. 1

Lambert, P. 1
Lambie, J. 1
Lambie, W. A. 5
Lang, J. J. 2
Latta, A. 2
Law, D. 30
Leggat, G. 8
Lennie, W. 1
Lennox, R. 3
Liddell, W. 6
Lindsay, J. 6
Linwood, A. B. 1
Logan, J. 1
Lorimer, P. 4
Love, A. 1
Low, J. (Cambuslang) 1
Lowe, J. (St Bernards) 1

Macari, L. 5
MacDougall, E. J. 3
MacFarlane, A. 1
MacLeod, M. 1
Mackay, D. C. 4

Mackay, G. 1
MacKenzie, J. A. 1
Mackail-Smith, C. 1
Mackie, J. C. 2
MacKinnon, W. W. 5
Madden, J. 5
Maloney, S. R. 7
Marshall, H. 1
Marshall, J. 1
Martin, C. H. 3
Mason, J. 4
Massie, A. 1
Masson, D. S. 5
McAdam, J. 1
McAllister, G. 5
McArthur, J. 3
McAulay, J. D. 1
McAvennie, F. 1
McCall, J. 1
McCall, S. M. 1
McCalliog, J. 1
McCallum, N. 1
McCann, N. 3
McClair, B. J. 2
McCoist, A. 19
McColl, R. S. 13
McCormack, R. 2
McCulloch, D. 3
McCulloch, L. 1
McDougall, J. 4
McFadden, J.* 15
McFadyen, W. 2
McGhee, M. 2
McGinlay, J. 4
McGregor, J. 1
McGrory, J. 6
McGuire, W. 1
McInally, A. 3
McInnes, T. 2
McKie, J. 2
McKimmie, S. 1
McKinlay, W. 4
McKinnon, A. 1
McKinnon, R. 1
McLaren, A. 4
McLaren, J. 1
McLean, A. 1
McLean, T. 1
McLintock, F. 1
McMahon, A. 6
McManus, S. 2
McMenemy, J. 5
McMillan, I. L. 2
McNeill, W. 3
McNiel, H. 5
McPhail, J. 3
McPhail, R. 7
McPherson, J. (Kilmarnock) 7
McPherson, J. (Vale of Leven) 1
McPherson, R. 1
McQueen, G. 5
McStay, P. 9
McSwegan, G. 1
Meiklejohn, D. D. 3
Millar, J. 2
Miller, K. 18
Miller, T. 2
Miller, W. 1
Mitchell, R. C. 1
Morgan, W. 1
Morris, D. 1
Morris, H. 3
Morrison, J. C. 3
Morton, A. L. 5
Mudie, J. K. 9
Mulgrew, C. P. 2
Mulhall, G. 1

Munro, A. D. 1
Munro, N. 2
Murdoch, R. 5
Murphy, F. 1
Murray, J. 1

Napier, C. E. 3
Narey, D. 1
Naismith, S. J. 7
Naysmith, G. A. 1
Neil, R. G. 2
Nevin, P. K. F. 5
Nicholas, C. 5
Nisbet, J. 2

O'Connor, G. 4
O'Donnell, F. 2
O'Hare, J. 5
Ormond, W. E. 2
O'Rourke, F. 1
Orr, R. 1
Orr, T. 1
Oswald, J. 1
Own goals 21

Parlane, D. 1
Paul, H. McD. 2
Paul, W. 5
Pettigrew, W. 2
Provan, D. 1

Quashie, N. F. 1
Quinn, J. 7
Quinn, P. 1

Rankin, G. 2
Rankin, R. 2
Reid, W. 4
Reilly, L. 22
Renny-Tailyour, H. W. 1
Rhodes, J. L. 3
Richmond, J. T. 1
Ring, T. 2
Rioch, B. D. 6
Ritchie, J. 1
Ritchie, M. T. 3
Ritchie, P. S. 1
Robertson, A. (Clyde) 2
Robertson, A. (Dundee U) 1
Robertson, J. 3
Robertson, J. N. 8
Robertson, J. T. 2
Robertson, T. 1
Robertson, W. 1
Russell, D. 1

Scott, A. S. 5
Sellar, W. 4
Sharp, G. 1
Shaw, F. W. 1
Shearer, D. 2
Simpson, J. 1
Smith, A. 5
Smith, G. 4
Smith, J. 1
Smith, John 13
Snodgrass, R. 6
Somerville, G. 1
Souness, G. J. 4
Speedie, F. 2
St John, I. 9
Steel, W. 12
Stein, C. 10
Stevenson, G. 4
Stewart, A. 1
Stewart, R. 1
Stewart, W. E. 1
Strachan, G. 5
Sturrock, P. 3

Taylor, J. D. 1
Templeton, R. 1
Thompson, S. 3
Thomson, A. 1
Thomson, C. 4
Thomson, R. 1
Thomson, W. 1
Thornton, W. 1

Waddell, T. S. 1
Waddell, W. 6
Walker, J. 2
Walker, R. 7
Walker, T. 9
Wallace, I. A. 1
Wark, J. 7
Watson, J. A. K. 1
Watt, F. 2
Watt, W. W. 1
Webster, A. 1
Weir, A. 1
Weir, D. 1
Weir, J. B. 2
White, J. A. 3
Wilkie, L. 1
Wilson, A. (Sheffield W) 2
Wilson, A. N. (Dunfermline Ath) 13
Wilson, D. (Liverpool) 1
Wilson, D. (Queen's Park) 2
Wilson, D. (Rangers) 9
Wilson, H. 1
Wylie, T. G. 1

Young, A. 5

WALES

Allchurch, I. J. 23
Allen, J. M. 2
Allen, M. 3
Astley, D. J. 12
Atherton, R. W. 2

Bale, G. F. 26
Bamford, T. 1
Barnes, W. 1
Bellamy, C. D. 19
Blackmore, C. G. 1
Blake, D. 1
Blake, N. A. 4
Bodin, P. J. 3
Boulter, L. M. 1
Bowdler, J. C. H. 3
Bowen, D. L. 1
Bowen, M. 3
Boyle, T. 1
Bryan, T. 1
Burgess, W. A. R. 1
Burke, T. 1
Butler, W. T. 1

Chapman, T. 2
Charles, J. 1
Charles, M. 6
Charles, W. J. 15
Church, S. R. 3
Clarke, R. J. 5
Coleman, C. 4
Collier, D. J. 1
Collins, J. 3
Cotterill, D. R. G. B. 2
Crosse, K. 1
Cumner, R. H. 1
Curtis, A. 6
Curtis, E. R. 3

Davies, D. W. 1
Davies, E. Lloyd 1
Davies, G. 2
Davies, L. S. 6
Davies, R. T. 9
Davies, R. W. 6
Davies, Simon 6
Davies, Stanley 5
Davies, W. 6
Davies, W. H. 1
Davies, William 5
Davis, W. O. 1
Deacy, N. 4
Doughty, J. 6
Doughty, R. 2
Durban, A. 2
Dwyer, P. 2

Earnshaw, R. 16
Eastwood, F. 4
Edwards, D. A. 3
Edwards, G. 2
Edwards, R. I. 4
England, H. M. 4
Evans, C. 2
Evans, I. 1
Evans, J. 1
Evans, R. E. 2
Evans, W. 1
Eyton-Jones, J. A. 1

Fletcher, C. 1
Flynn, B. 7
Ford, T. 23
Foulkes, W. I. 1
Fowler, J. 3

Giles, D. 2
Giggs, R. J. 12
Glover, E. M. 7
Godfrey, B. C. 2
Green, A. W. 3
Griffiths, A. T. 6
Griffiths, M. W. 2
Griffiths, T. P. 3

Harris, C. S. 1
Hartson, J. 14
Hersee, R. 1
Hewitt, R. 1
Hockey, T. 1
Hodges, G. 2
Hole, W. J. 1
Hopkins, I. J. 2
Horne, B. 2
Howell, E. G. 3
Hughes, L. M. 16
Huws, E. W. 1

James, E. 2
James, L. 10
James, R. 7
Jarrett, R. H. 3
Jenkyns, C. A. 1
Jones, A. 1
Jones, Bryn 6
Jones, B. S. 2
Jones, Cliff 16
Jones, C. W. 1
Jones, D. E. 1
Jones, Evan 1
Jones, H. 1
Jones, I. 1
Jones, J. L. 1
Jones, J. O. 1
Jones, J. P. 1
Jones, Leslie J. 1
Jones, R. A. 2
Jones, W. L. 6

** The Scottish FA officially changed Robsons's goal against Iceland on 10 September 2008 to McFadden.*

Keenor, F. C. 2
King, A. P. 2
Koumas, J. 10
Krzywicki, R. L. 1

Ledley, J. C. 4
Leek, K. 5
Lewis, B. 4
Lewis, D. M. 2
Lewis, W. 8
Lewis, W. L. 3
Llewelyn, C. M 1
Lovell, S. 1
Lowrie, G. 2

Mahoney, J. F. 1
Mays, A. W. 1
Medwin, T. C. 6
Melville, A. K 3
Meredith, W. H. 11
Mills, T. J. 1
Moore, G. 1
Morgan, J. R. 2
Morgan-Owen, H. 1
Morgan-Owen, M. M. 2
Morison, S. 1
Morris, A. G. 9
Morris, H. 2
Morris, R. 1
Morris, S. 2

Nicholas, P. 2

O'Callaghan, E. 3
O'Sullivan, P. A. 1
Owen, G. 2
Owen, W. 4
Owen, W. P. 6
Own goals 14

Palmer, D. 3
Parry, P. I. 1
Parry, T. D. 3
Paul, R. 1
Peake, E. 1
Pembridge, M. 6
Perry, E. 1
Phillips, C. 5
Phillips, D. 2
Powell, A. 1
Powell, D. 1
Price, J. 4
Price, P. 1
Pryce-Jones, W. E. 3
Pugh, D. H. 2

Ramsey, A. J. 12
Reece, G. I. 2
Rees, R. R. 3
Richards, R. W. 1
Roach, J. 2
Robbins, W. W. 4
Roberts, J. (Corwen) 1
Roberts, Jas. 1
Roberts, P. S. 1
Roberts, R. (Druids) 1
Roberts, W. (Llangollen) 2
Roberts, W. (Wrexham) 1
Roberts, W. H. 1
Robinson, C. P. 1
Robinson, J. R. C. 3
Robson-Kanu, T. H. 4
Rush, I. 28
Russell, M. R. 1

Sabine, H. W. 1
Saunders, D. 22
Savage, R. W. 2
Shaw, E. G. 2
Sisson, H. 4
Slatter, N. 2
Smallman, D. P. 1
Speed, G. A. 7
Symons, C. J. 2

Tapscott, D. R. 4
Taylor, G. K. 1
Taylor, N. J. 1
Thomas, M. 4
Thomas, T. 1
Toshack, J. B. 12
Trainer, H. 2

Vaughan, D. O. 1
Vaughan, John 2
Vernon, T. R. 8
Vizard, E. T. 1
Vokes, S. M. 8

Walsh, I. 7
Warren, F. W. 3
Watkins, W. M. 4
Wilding, J. 4
Williams, A. 1
Williams, A. E. 2
Williams, D. R. 2
Williams, G. E. 1
Williams, G. G. 1
Williams, W. 1
Woosnam, A. P. 3
Wynn, G. A. 1

Yorath, T. C. 2
Young, E. 1

REPUBLIC OF IRELAND

Aldridge, J. 19
Ambrose, P. 1
Anderson, J. 1
Andrews, K. 3

Barrett, G. 2
Bermingham, P. 1
Bradshaw, P. 4
Brady, L. 9
Brady, R. 7
Breen, G. 7
Brown, J. 1
Byrne, D. 1
Byrne, J. 4

Cantwell, N. 14
Carey, J. 3
Carroll, T. 1
Cascarino, A. 19
Christie, C. S. F. 2
Clark, C. 2
Coad, P. 3
Coleman, S. 1
Connolly, D. J. 9
Conroy, T. 2
Conway, J. 3
Cox, S. R. 4
Coyne, T. 6
Cummins, G. 5
Curtis, D. 8

Daly, G. 13
Davis, T. 4
Dempsey, J. 1
Dennehy, M. 2
Doherty, G. M. T. 4
Donnelly, J. 4
Donnelly, T. 1
Doyle, K. E. 14
Duff, D. A. 8
Duffy, B. 1
Duggan, H. 1
Dunne, J. 13
Dunne, L. 1
Dunne, R. P. 8

Eglington, T. 2
Elliott, S. W. 1
Ellis, P. 1

Fagan, F. 5
Fahey, K. 3
Fallon, S. 2
Fallon, W. 2
Farrell, P. 3
Finnan, S. 2
Fitzgerald, P. 2
Fitzgerald, J. 1
Fitzsimons, A. 7
Flood, J. J. 4
Fogarty, A. 3
Foley, D. 2
Fullam, J. 1
Fullam, R. 1

Galvin, A. 1
Gavin, J. 2
Geoghegan, M. 2
Gibson, D. T. D. 1
Giles, J. 5
Givens, D. 19
Gleeson, S. M. 1
Glynn, D. 1
Grealish, T. 8
Green, P. J. 1
Grimes, A. A. 1

Hale, A. 2
Hand, E. 2
Harte, I. P. 11
Haverty, J. 3
Healy, C. 1
Hendrick, J. P. 1
Holland, M. R. 5
Holmes, J. 1
Hoolahan, W. 3
Horlacher, A. 2
Houghton, R. 6
Hughton, C. 1
Hunt, S. P. 1
Hurley, C. 2

Ireland, S. J. 4
Irwin, D. 4

Jordan, D. 1

Kavanagh, G. A. 1
Keane, R. D. 68
Keane, R. M. 9
Kelly, D. 9
Kelly, G. 2
Kelly, J. 2
Kennedy, M. 4
Keogh, A. 2
Keogh, R. J. 1
Kernaghan, A. N. 1
Kilbane, K. D. 8
Kinsella, M. A. 3

Lacey, W. 1
Lawrence, L. 2
Lawrenson, M. 5
Leech, M. 2
Long, S. P. 17
McAteer, J. W. 3
McCann, J. 1
McCarthy, M. 2
McClean, J. J. 9
McEvoy, A. 6
McGeady, A. G. 5
McGee, P. 4
McGrath, P. 8
McLoughlin, A. F. 2
McPhail, S. J. P. 1
Mancini, T. 1
Martin, C. 6
Martin, M. 4
Miller, L. W. P. 1
Mooney, J. 1
Moore, P. 7
Moran, K. 6
Morrison, C. H. 9
Moroney, T. 1
Mulligan, P. 1
Murphy, D. 1

O'Brien, A. J. 1
O'Callaghan, K. 1
O'Connor, T. 2
O'Dea, D. 1
O'Farrell, F. 2
O'Flanagan, K. 3
O'Keefe, E. 1
O'Leary, D. A. 1
O'Neill, F. 1
O'Neill, K. P. 4
O'Reilly, J. (Brideville) 2
O'Reilly, J. (Cork) 1
O'Shea, J. F. 3
Own goals 14

Pearce, A. J. 2
Pilkington, A. N. J. 1

Quinn, N. 21

Reid, A. M. 4
Reid, S. J. 2
Ringstead, A. 7
Robinson, M. 4
Rogers, E. 5
Ryan, G. 1
Ryan, R. 3

St Ledger-Hall, S. 3
Sheedy, K. 9
Sheridan, J. 5
Slaven, B. 1
Sloan, J. 1
Squires, J. 1
Stapleton, F. 20
Staunton, S. 7
Strahan, J. 1
Sullivan, J. 1

Townsend, A. D. 7
Treacy, R. 5
Touhy, L. 4

Waddock, G. 3
Walsh, D. 5
Walsh, M. 3
Walters, J. R. 14
Ward, S. R. 3
Waters, J. 1
White, J. J. 2
Whelan, G. D. 2
Whelan, R. 3
Wilson, M. D. 1

SOUTH AMERICA

COPA SUDAMERICANA 2016

FIRST ROUND – FIRST LEG

SOUTH ZONE

Fenix v Cerro Porteno	1-0
Sportivo Luqueno v Penarol	0-0
Universidad de Concepcion v Bolivar	2-0
Real Potosi v Universidad Catolica	3-1
Blooming v Plaza Colonia	1-0
Sol de America v Jorge Wilstermann	1-1
Montevideo Wanderers v O'Higgins	0-0
Palestino v Libertad	1-0

NORTH ZONE

Universitario v Emelec	0-3
Aucas v Real Garcilaso	2-1
Deportivo Lara v Junior	1-3
Deportes Tolima v Deportivo La Guaira	0-0
Barcelona v Zamora	1-1
Independiente Medellin v Universidad Catolica	1-1
Deportivo Anzoategui v Sport Huancayo	2-1
Deportivo Municipal v Atletico Nacional	0-5

FIRST ROUND – SECOND LEG

SOUTH ZONE

Match	Score	(agg)
Cerro Porteno v Fenix	2-0	2-1
Penarol v Sportivo Luqueno	1-1	1-1
Sportivo Luqueno won on away goals.		
Bolivar v Universidad de Concepcion	3-0	3-2
Universidad Catolica v Real Potosi	1-1	2-4
Plaza Colonia v Blooming	1-0	1-1
Blooming won 4-1 on penalties.		
Jorge Wilstermann v Sol de America	1-1	2-2
Sol de America won 5-4 on penalties.		
O'Higgins v Montevideo Wanderers	0-0	0-0
Montevideo Wanderers won 5-4 on penalties.		
Libertad v Palestino	0-3	0-4

NORTH ZONE

Match	Score	(agg)
Emelec v Universitario	3-1	6-1
Real Garcilaso v Aucas	1-0	2-2
Real Garcilaso won on away goals.		
Junior v Deportivo Lara	2-1	5-2
Deportivo La Guaira v Deportes Tolima	1-0	1-0
Zamora v Barcelona	1-1	2-2
Zamora won 3-0 on penalties.		
Universidad Catolica v Independiente Medellin	0-1	1-2
Sport Huancayo v Deportivo Anzoategui	1-0	2-2
Sport Huancayo won on away goals.		
Atletico Nacional v Deportivo Municipal	1-0	6-0

SECOND ROUND – FIRST LEG

Santa Cruz v Sport Recife	0-0
Deportivo La Guaira v Emelec	4-2
Cuiaba v Chapecoense	1-0
Bolivar v Atletico Nacional	1-1
Estudiantes v Belgrano	1-0
Blooming v Junior	0-2
Figueirense v Flamengo	4-2
Cerro Porteno v Real Potosi	6-0
Real Garcilaso v Palestino	2-2
Zamora v Montevideo Wanderers	0-1
Vitoria v Coritiba	2-1
Sol de America v Sport Huancayo	1-0
Lanus v Independiente	0-2
Banfield v San Lorenzo	2-0
Independiente Medellin v Sportivo Luqueno	3-0

SECOND ROUND – SECOND LEG

Match	Score	(agg)
Sport Recife v Santa Cruz	0-1	0-1
Emelec v Deportivo La Guaira	0-0	2-4
Chapecoense v Cuiaba	3-1	3-2
Atletico Nacional v Bolivar	1-0	2-1
Belgrano v Estudiantes	2-0	2-1
Junior v Blooming	1-1	3-1
Flamengo v Figueirense	3-1	5-5
Flamengo won on away goals.		
Real Potosi v Cerro Porteno	0-1	0-7
Palestino v Real Garcilaso	1-0	3-2
Montevideo Wanderers v Zamora	1-0	2-0
Coritiba v Vitoria	1-0	2-2
Coritiba won on away goals.		
Sport Huancayo v Sol de America	1-1	1-2
Independiente v Lanus	1-0	3-0
San Lorenzo v Banfield	4-1	4-3
Sportivo Luqueno v Independiente Medellin	2-0	2-3

ROUND OF 16 – FIRST LEG

Independiente Medellin v Santa Cruz	2-0
San Lorenzo v Deportivo La Guaira	2-1
Independiente v Chapecoense	0-0
Sol de America v Atletico Nacional	1-1
Coritiba v Belgrano	1-2
Montevideo Wanderers v Junior	0-0
Palestino v Flamengo	0-1
Santa Fe v Cerro Porteno	2-0

ROUND OF 16 – SECOND LEG

Match	Score	(agg)
Santa Cruz v Independiente Medellin	3-1	3-3
Santa Cruz won on away goals.		
Deportivo La Guaira v San Lorenzo	0-2	1-4
Chapecoense v Independiente	0-0	0-0
Chapecoense won 5-4 on penalties.		
Atletico Nacional v Sol de America	2-0	3-1
Belgrano v Coritiba	1-2	3-3
Coritiba won 4-3 on penalties.		
Junior v Montevideo Wanderers	0-0	0-0
Junior won 4-3 on penalties.		
Flamengo v Palestino	1-2	2-2
Palestino won on away goals.		
Cerro Porteno v Santa Fe	4-1	4-3

QUARTER-FINALS – FIRST LEG

Independiente Medellin v Cerro Porteno	0-0
San Lorenzo v Palestino	2-0
Junior v Chapecoense	1-0
Coritiba v Atletico Nacional	1-1

QUARTER-FINALS – SECOND LEG

Match	Score	(agg)
Cerro Porteno v Independiente Medellin	2-0	2-0
Palestino v San Lorenzo	1-0	1-2
Chapecoense v Junior	3-0	3-1
Atletico Nacional v Coritiba	3-1	4-2

SEMI-FINALS – FIRST LEG

Cerro Porteno v Atletico Nacional	1-1
San Lorenzo v Chapecoense	1-1

SEMI-FINALS – SECOND LEG

Match	Score	(agg)
Atletico Nacional v Cerro Porteno	0-0	1-1
Atletico Nacional won on away goals.		
Chapecoense v San Lorenzo	0-0	1-1
Chapecoense won on away goals.		

FINAL

The two-legged final between Atletico National and Chapecoense was suspended on 29 November following the crash of LaMia Flight 2933. The flight was carrying the Chapecoense football team and officials to the first leg. Seventy-one people were killed in the crash virtually wiping out the Chapecoense football club.

The South American football confederation CONMEBOL awarded the title to Chapecoense on 5 December 2016. Opponents Atletico Nacional requested that Chapecoense were awarded the trophy were given a Fair Play award for their 'spirit of peace, understanding and fair play'.

RECOPA SUDAMERICANA 2016

FINAL – FIRST LEG

Santa Fe v River Plate	0-0

FINAL – SECOND LEG

Match	Score	(agg)
River Plate v Santa Fe	2-1	2-1

COPA BRIDGESTONE LIBERTADORES 2016

SEMI-FINALS – FIRST LEG
Sao Paulo v Atletico Nacional	0-2
Independiente de Valle v Boca Juniors	2-1

SEMI-FINALS – SECOND LEG
		(agg)
Atletico Nacional v Sao Paulo	2-1	4-1
Boca Juniors v Independiente de Valle	2-3	3-5

FINAL – FIRST LEG
Independiente de Valle v Atletico Nacional	1-1

FINAL – SECOND LEG
		(agg)
Atletico Nacional v Independiente de Valle	1-0	2-1

COPA BRIDGESTONE LIBERTADORES 2017

FIRST STAGE – FIRST LEG
Universitario v Montevideo Wanderers	3-2
Deportivo Municipal v Independiente del Valle	0-1
Deportivo Capiata v Deportivo Tachira	1-0

FIRST STAGE – SECOND LEG
		(agg)
Montevideo Wanderers v Universitario	5-2	7-5
Independiente del Valle v Deportivo Municipal	2-2	3-2
Deportivo Tachira v Deportivo Capiata	0-0	0-1

SECOND STAGE – FIRST LEG
Atletico Paranaense v Millonarios	1-0
Botafogo v Colo-Colo	2-1
Cerro v Union Espanola	2-3
Carabobo v Junior	0-1
Atletico Tucuman v El Nacional	2-2
Montevideo Wanderers v The Strongest	0-2
Independiente del Valle v Olimpia	1-0
Deportivo Capiata v Universitario	1-3

SECOND STAGE – SECOND LEG
		(agg)
Millonarios v Atletico Paranaense	1-0	1-1
Atletico Paranaense won 4-2 on penalties.		
Colo-Colo v Botafogo	1-1	2-3
Union Espanola v Cerro	2-0	5-2
Junior v Carabobo	3-0	4-0
El Nacional v Atletico Tucuman	0-1	2-3
The Strongest v Montevideo Wanderers	4-0	6-0
Olimpia v Independiente del Valle	3-1	3-2
Universitario v Deportivo Capiata	0-3	3-4

THIRD STAGE – FIRST LEG
Atletico Paranaense v Deportivo Capiata	3-3
Botafogo v Olimpia	1-0
Union Espanola v The Strongest	1-1
Junior v Atletico Tucuman	1-0

THIRD STAGE – SECOND LEG
		(agg)
Deportivo Capiata v Atletico Paranaense	0-1	3-4
Olimpia v Botafogo	1-0	1-1
Botafogo won 3-1 on penalties.		
The Strongest v Union Espanola	5-0	6-1
Atletico Tucuman v Junior	3-1	3-2

GROUP STAGE

GROUP 1
Group 1 Table	P	W	D	L	F	A	GD	Pts
Barcelona	6	3	1	2	8	8	0	10
Botafogo	6	3	1	2	6	5	1	10
Estudiantes	6	3	0	3	7	8	–1	9
Atletico Nacional	6	2	0	4	8	8	0	6

GROUP 2
Group 2 Table	P	W	D	L	F	A	GD	Pts
Santos	6	3	3	0	11	4	7	12
The Strongest	6	2	3	1	9	5	4	9
Santa Fe	6	2	2	2	8	6	2	8
Sporting Cristal	6	0	2	4	2	15	–13	2

GROUP 3
Group 3 Table	P	W	D	L	F	A	GD	Pts
River Plate	6	4	1	1	14	9	5	13
Emelec	6	3	1	2	8	5	3	10
Medellin	6	3	0	3	8	8	0	9
Melgar	6	1	0	5	6	14	–8	3

GROUP 4
Group 4 Table	P	W	D	L	F	A	GD	Pts
San Lorenzo	6	3	1	2	8	8	0	10
Atletico Paranaense	6	3	1	2	9	10	–1	10
Flamengo	6	3	0	3	11	7	4	9
Universidad Catolica	6	1	2	3	8	11	–3	5

GROUP 5
Group 5 Table	P	W	D	L	F	A	GD	Pts
Palmeiras	6	4	1	1	13	9	4	13
Wilstermann	6	3	0	3	12	10	2	9
Atletico Tucuman	6	2	1	3	8	10	–2	7
Penarol	6	2	0	4	11	15	–4	6

GROUP 6
Group 6 Table	P	W	D	L	F	A	GD	Pts
Atletico Mineiro	6	4	1	1	17	6	11	13
Godoy Cruz	6	3	2	1	10	8	2	11
Libertad	6	1	3	2	7	9	–2	6
Sport Boys	6	0	2	4	8	19	–11	2

GROUP 7
Group 7 Table	P	W	D	L	F	A	GD	Pts
Lanus	6	3	1	2	11	5	6	10
Chapecoense	6	3	1	2	8	10	–2	10
Nacional	6	2	2	2	5	3	2	8
Zulia	6	1	2	3	4	10	–6	5

GROUP 8
Group 8 Table	P	W	D	L	F	A	GD	Pts
Gremio	6	4	1	1	15	6	9	13
Guarani	6	3	2	1	9	7	2	11
Deportes Iquique	6	3	1	2	12	9	3	10
Zamora	6	0	0	6	6	20	–14	0

Competition still being played

NORTH AMERICA – MAJOR LEAGUE SOCCER 2016

EASTERN CONFERENCE

	P	W	D	L	F	A	GD	Pts
New York Red Bulls	34	16	9	9	61	44	17	57
New York City	34	15	9	10	62	57	5	54
Toronto	34	14	11	9	51	39	12	53
DC United	34	11	13	10	53	47	6	46
Montreal Impact	34	11	12	11	49	53	–4	45
Philadelphia Union	34	11	9	14	52	55	–3	42
NE Revolution	34	11	9	14	44	54	–10	42
Orlando City	34	9	14	11	55	60	–5	41
Columbus Crew	34	8	12	14	50	58	–8	36
Chicago Fire	34	7	10	17	42	58	–16	31

WESTERN CONFERENCE

	P	W	D	L	F	A	GD	Pts
FC Dallas	34	17	9	8	50	40	10	60
Colorado Rapids	34	15	13	6	39	32	7	58
LA Galaxy	34	12	16	6	54	39	15	52
Seattle Sounders	34	14	6	14	44	43	1	48
Sporting Kansas City	34	13	8	13	42	41	1	47
Real Salt Lake	34	12	10	12	44	46	–2	46
Portland Timbers	34	12	8	14	48	53	–5	44
Vancouver Whitecaps	34	10	9	15	45	52	–7	39
San Jose Earthquakes	34	8	14	12	32	40	–8	38
Houston Dynamo	34	7	13	14	39	45	–6	34

EASTERN KNOCKOUT ROUND

Toronto v Philadelphia Union 3-1
DC United v Montreal Impact 2-4

WESTERN KNOCKOUT ROUND

LA Galaxy v Real Salt Lake 3-1
Seattle Sounders v Sporting Kansas City 1-0

EASTERN SEMI-FINALS – FIRST LEG

Toronto v New York City 2-0
Montreal Impact v New York Red Bulls 1-0

EASTERN SEMI-FINALS – SECOND LEG *(agg)*

New York City v Toronto 0-5 0-7
New York Red Bulls v Montreal Impact 1-2 1-3

WESTERN SEMI-FINALS – FIRST LEG

LA Galaxy v Colorado Rapids 1-0
Seattle Sounders v FC Dallas 3-0

WESTERN SEMI-FINALS – SECOND LEG *(agg)*

Colorado Rapids v LA Galaxy 1-0 1-1
aet; Colorado Rapids won 3-1 on penalties.
FC Dallas v Seattle Sounders 2-1 2-4

EASTERN CHAMPIONSHIP – FIRST LEG

Montreal Impact v Toronto 3-2

EASTERN CHAMPIONSHIP – SECOND LEG *(agg)*

Toronto v Montreal Impact 5-2 7-5
aet.

WESTERN CHAMPIONSHIP – FIRST LEG

Seattle Sounders v Colorado Rapids 2-1

WESTERN CHAMPIONSHIP – SECOND LEG *(agg)*

Colorado Rapids v Seattle Sounders 0-1 1-3

MLS CUP FINAL 2015

Sunday 6 December 2015
Toronto (0) 0
Seattle Sounders (0) 0 36,045

Toronto: Irwin; Zavaleta, Moor, Hagglund, Beitashour, Cooper (Cheyrou 84), Bradley, Osorio (Johnson 77), Morrow, Altidore, Giovinco (Ricketts 103).
Seattle Sounders: Frei; Mears, Torres, Marshall, Jones, Alonso, Roldan, Lodeiro, Friberg (Fernandez 66), Morris (Evans 108), Valdez (Ivanschitz 73).
aet; Seattle Sounders won 5-4 on penalties.
Referee: Alan Kelly (Republic of Ireland).

FIFA CONFEDERATIONS CUP 2017 (RUSSIA)

GROUP A

Russia v New Zealand 2-0
Portugal v Mexico 2-2
Russia v Portugal 0-1
Mexico v New Zealand 2-1
Mexico v Russia 2-1
New Zealand v Portugal 0-4

Group A Table	P	W	D	L	F	A	GD	Pts
Portugal	3	2	1	0	7	2	5	7
Mexico	3	2	1	0	6	4	2	7
Russia	3	1	0	2	3	3	0	3
New Zealand	3	0	0	3	1	8	–7	0

GROUP B

Cameroon v Chile 0-2
Australia v Germany 2-3
Cameroon v Australia 1-1
Germany v Chile 1-1
Germany v Cameroon 3-1
Chile v Australia 1-1

Group B Table	P	W	D	L	F	A	GD	Pts
Germany	3	2	1	0	7	4	3	7
Chile	3	1	2	0	4	2	2	5
Australia	3	0	2	1	4	5	–1	2
Cameroon	3	0	1	2	2	6	–4	1

SEMI-FINALS

Portugal v Chile 0-0
aet; Chile won 3-0 on penalties.
Germany v Mexico 4-1

MATCH FOR THIRD PLACE

Portugal v Mexico 2-1
aet.

FIFA CONFEDERATIONS CUP FINAL 2017

St Petersburg, Sunday 2 July 2017
Chile (0) 0
Germany (1) 1 *(Stindl 20)* 57,268

Chile: Bravo; Isla, Medel, Jara, Beausejour, Aranguiz (Puch 81), Diaz (Valencia 53), Hernandez, Vidal, Vargas (Sagal 81), Sanchez.
Germany: Ter Stegen; Ginter, Mustafi, Ruediger, Stindl, Rudy, Kimmich, Hector, Goretzka (Sule 90), Draxler, Werner (Can 79).
Referee: Milorad Mazic (Serbia).

UEFA UNDER-21 CHAMPIONSHIP 2015–17

QUALIFYING ROUND

GROUP 1

Belgium v Moldova 2-1
Moldova v Malta 0-0
Montenegro v Moldova 1-0
Latvia v Malta 1-2
Moldova v Montenegro 1-0
Latvia v Belgium 0-2
Czech Republic v Malta 4-1
Latvia v Czech Republic 1-1
Montenegro v Malta 0-0
Belgium v Malta 2-0
Moldova v Latvia 0-3
Czech Republic v Montenegro 3-3
Czech Republic v Belgium 1-0
Montenegro v Latvia 3-3
Moldova v Czech Republic 1-3
Moldova v Belgium 0-2
Malta v Montenegro 0-1
Czech Republic v Latvia 2-1
Belgium v Montenegro 1-2
Malta v Czech Republic 0-7
Montenegro v Czech Republic 0-3
Latvia v Moldova 0-2
Malta v Belgium 2-3
Latvia v Montenegro 0-0
Belgium v Czech Republic 2-1
Malta v Latvia 1-0
Czech Republic v Moldova 4-1
Montenegro v Belgium 3-0
Malta v Moldova 3-2
Belgium v Latvia 0-1

Group 1 Table	P	W	D	L	F	A	GD	Pts
Czech Republic	10	7	2	1	29	10	19	23
Belgium	10	6	0	4	14	11	3	18
Montenegro	10	4	4	2	13	11	2	16
Malta	10	3	2	5	9	20	–11	11
Latvia	10	2	3	5	10	13	–3	9
Moldova	10	2	1	7	8	18	–10	7

GROUP 2

Republic of Ireland v Andorra 1-0
Slovenia v Andorra 4-0
Andorra v Lithuania 1-0
Slovenia v Lithuania 3-0
Andorra v Republic of Ireland 0-2
Italy v Slovenia 1-0
Serbia v Lithuania 5-0
Serbia v Andorra 5-0
Slovenia v Italy 0-3
Republic of Ireland v Lithuania 3-0
Italy v Republic of Ireland 1-0
Lithuania v Serbia 0-2
Andorra v Slovenia 0-5
Lithuania v Republic of Ireland 3-1
Serbia v Italy 1-1
Slovenia v Serbia 2-0
Italy v Lithuania 2-0
Republic of Ireland v Italy 1-4
Andorra v Serbia 0-4
Slovenia v Republic of Ireland 3-1
Andorra v Italy 0-1
Lithuania v Andorra 1-0
Italy v Serbia 1-1
Republic of Ireland v Slovenia 2-0
Serbia v Republic of Ireland 3-2
Italy v Andorra 3-0
Lithuania v Slovenia 1-0
Republic of Ireland v Serbia 1-3
Lithuania v Italy 0-0
Serbia v Slovenia 3-1

Group 2 Table	P	W	D	L	F	A	GD	Pts
Italy	10	7	3	0	17	3	14	24
Serbia	10	7	2	1	27	8	19	23
Slovenia	10	5	0	5	18	11	7	15
Republic of Ireland	10	4	0	6	14	17	–3	12
Lithuania	10	3	1	6	5	17	–12	10
Andorra	10	1	0	9	1	26	–25	3

GROUP 3

Iceland v FYR Macedonia 3-0
Northern Ireland v Scotland 1-2
Iceland v France 3-2
FYR Macedonia v Ukraine 1-0
Iceland v Northern Ireland 1-1
Ukraine v Iceland 0-1
Scotland v France 1-2
Northern Ireland v FYR Macedonia 1-2
Scotland v Iceland 0-0
France v Ukraine 2-0
France v Northern Ireland 1-0
Scotland v Ukraine 2-2
FYR Macedonia v France 2-2
Northern Ireland v Ukraine 1-2
FYR Macedonia v Iceland 0-0
France v Scotland 2-0
France v FYR Macedonia 1-1
Scotland v Northern Ireland 3-1
Ukraine v FYR Macedonia 0-2
Northern Ireland v Iceland 0-1
Scotland v FYR Macedonia 0-1
Ukraine v France 1-0
Ukraine v Scotland 4-0
FYR Macedonia v Northern Ireland 2-0
France v Iceland 2-0
Iceland v Scotland 2-0
Ukraine v Northern Ireland 1-1
Iceland v Ukraine 2-4
Northern Ireland v France 0-3
FYR Macedonia v Scotland 2-0

Group 3 Table	P	W	D	L	F	A	GD	Pts
FYR Macedonia	10	6	3	1	13	7	6	21
France	10	6	2	2	17	8	9	20
Iceland	10	5	3	2	13	9	4	18
Ukraine	10	4	2	4	14	12	2	14
Scotland	10	2	2	6	8	17	–9	8
Northern Ireland	10	0	2	8	6	18	–12	2

GROUP 4

Liechtenstein v Albania 0-2
Liechtenstein v Israel 0-4
Albania v Israel 1-1
Liechtenstein v Hungary 0-6
Liechtenstein v Greece 0-2
Albania v Portugal 1-6
Portugal v Hungary 2-0
Greece v Portugal 0-4
Hungary v Albania 2-2
Greece v Liechtenstein 5-0
Portugal v Albania 4-0
Israel v Hungary 3-0
Hungary v Greece 2-1
Albania v Liechtenstein 2-0
Israel v Portugal 0-3
Portugal v Liechtenstein 4-0
Albania v Greece 0-0
Hungary v Israel 0-0
Greece v Israel 0-1
Albania v Hungary 2-1
Hungary v Liechtenstein 4-0
Greece v Albania 2-1
Portugal v Israel 0-0
Portugal v Greece 1-0
Israel v Liechtenstein 4-0

Hungary v Portugal 3-3
Israel v Greece 4-0
Greece v Hungary 3-1
Israel v Albania 4-0
Liechtenstein v Portugal 1-7

Group 4 Table	P	W	D	L	F	A	GD	Pts
Portugal	10	8	2	0	34	5	29	26
Israel	10	6	3	1	21	4	17	21
Greece	10	4	1	5	13	14	–1	13
Albania	10	3	3	4	11	20	–9	12
Hungary	10	3	3	4	19	16	3	12
Liechtenstein	10	0	0	10	1	40	–39	0

GROUP 5

Wales v Bulgaria 3-1
Romania v Armenia 3-0
Luxembourg v Wales 1-3
Romania v Bulgaria 0-2
Armenia v Romania 2-3
Bulgaria v Luxembourg 3-0
Luxembourg v Romania 0-1
Bulgaria v Armenia 2-0
Denmark v Wales 0-0
Armenia v Luxembourg 1-1
Denmark v Bulgaria 1-0
Wales v Armenia 2-1
Romania v Denmark 0-3
Denmark v Armenia 2-0
Wales v Romania 1-1
Luxembourg v Denmark 0-1
Bulgaria v Wales 0-0
Armenia v Denmark 1-3
Romania v Wales 2-1
Luxembourg v Bulgaria 0-0
Wales v Denmark 0-4
Romania v Luxembourg 4-0
Armenia v Bulgaria 0-1
Wales v Luxembourg 1-1
Denmark v Romania 3-1
Luxembourg v Armenia 1-0
Bulgaria v Denmark 0-3
Bulgaria v Romania 2-0
Armenia v Wales 1-3
Denmark v Luxembourg 4-1

Group 5 Table	P	W	D	L	F	A	GD	Pts
Denmark	10	9	1	0	24	3	21	28
Bulgaria	10	5	2	3	11	7	4	17
Romania	10	5	1	4	15	14	1	16
Wales	10	4	4	2	14	12	2	16
Luxembourg	10	1	3	6	5	18	–13	6
Armenia	10	0	1	9	6	21	–15	1

GROUP 6

San Marino v Georgia 0-3
Estonia v San Marino 0-0
Estonia v Spain 0-2
Croatia v Georgia 1-0
Sweden v San Marino 3-0
Estonia v Croatia 0-4
Georgia v Spain 2-5
San Marino v Croatia 0-3
Sweden v Estonia 5-0
Georgia v Estonia 3-0
Spain v Sweden 1-1
Croatia v San Marino 4-0
Spain v Georgia 5-0
San Marino v Estonia 1-2
Georgia v Sweden 0-1
Croatia v Spain 2-3
Georgia v San Marino 4-0
Spain v Croatia 0-3
San Marino v Sweden 0-2
Croatia v Estonia 2-1
Sweden v Georgia 3-2
Estonia v Georgia 0-1
Croatia v Sweden 1-1
Spain v San Marino 6-0
Sweden v Spain 1-1
Georgia v Croatia 2-2
San Marino v Spain 0-3
Estonia v Sweden 0-3
Sweden v Croatia 4-2
Spain v Estonia 5-0

Group 6 Table	P	W	D	L	F	A	GD	Pts
Sweden	10	7	3	0	24	7	17	24
Spain	10	7	2	1	31	9	22	23
Croatia	10	6	2	2	24	11	13	20
Georgia	10	4	1	5	17	17	0	13
Estonia	10	1	1	8	3	26	–23	4
San Marino	10	0	1	9	1	30	–29	1

GROUP 7

Faroe Islands v Azerbaijan 0-1
Azerbaijan v Austria 0-2
Finland v Russia 2-0
Azerbaijan v Germany 0-3
Austria v Russia 4-3
Finland v Faroe Islands 3-0
Austria v Azerbaijan 7-0
Germany v Finland 4-0
Azerbaijan v Finland 0-1
Faroe Islands v Germany 0-6
Russia v Faroe Islands 2-0
Germany v Azerbaijan 3-1
Austria v Finland 2-0
Azerbaijan v Russia 3-0
Germany v Austria 4-2
Russia v Azerbaijan 2-2
Germany v Faroe Islands 4-1
Austria v Faroe Islands 1-0
Russia v Germany 0-2
Faroe Islands v Finland 1-6
Faroe Islands v Russia 0-3
Finland v Austria 0-1
Russia v Austria 1-1
Azerbaijan v Faroe Islands 1-1
Finland v Germany 0-1
Faroe Islands v Austria 0-1
Finland v Azerbaijan 0-0
Germany v Russia 4-3
Russia v Finland 1-1
Austria v Germany 1-4

Group 7 Table	P	W	D	L	F	A	GD	Pts
Germany	10	10	0	0	35	8	27	30
Austria	10	7	1	2	22	12	10	22
Finland	10	4	2	4	13	10	3	14
Azerbaijan	10	2	3	5	8	19	–11	9
Russia	10	2	3	5	15	19	–4	9
Faroe Islands	10	0	1	9	3	28	–25	1

GROUP 8

Netherlands v Cyprus 4-0
Belarus v Slovakia 1-0
Turkey v Netherlands 0-1
Slovakia v Cyprus 2-0
Belarus v Turkey 0-2
Netherlands v Slovakia 1-3
Cyprus v Belarus 0-1
Cyprus v Turkey 0-3
Netherlands v Belarus 1-0
Belarus v Cyprus 2-2
Slovakia v Netherlands 4-2
Slovakia v Turkey 5-0
Turkey v Cyprus 0-1
Belarus v Netherlands 2-2
Cyprus v Slovakia 0-3
Turkey v Belarus 1-0
Netherlands v Turkey 0-0
Slovakia v Belarus 3-1
Cyprus v Netherlands 1-4
Turkey v Slovakia 1-1

Group 8 Table	P	W	D	L	F	A	GD	Pts
Slovakia	8	6	1	1	21	6	15	19
Netherlands	8	4	2	2	15	10	5	14
Turkey	8	3	2	3	7	8	–1	11
Belarus	8	2	2	4	7	11	–4	8
Cyprus	8	1	1	6	4	19	–15	4

GROUP 9

Norway v Bosnia-Herzegovina	2-0
Bosnia-Herzegovina v Kazakhstan	1-2
Kazakhstan v Switzerland	0-1
Norway v England	0-1
Switzerland v Bosnia-Herzegovina	3-1
Norway v Kazakhstan	2-1
Switzerland v Norway	1-1
England v Kazakhstan	3-0
Bosnia-Herzegovina v England	0-0
England v Switzerland	3-1
Kazakhstan v Bosnia-Herzegovina	0-0
Switzerland v England	1-1
Bosnia-Herzegovina v Norway	0-1
Switzerland v Kazakhstan	3-0
Bosnia-Herzegovina v Switzerland	0-0
England v Norway	6-1
Kazakhstan v England	0-1
Norway v Switzerland	2-1
Kazakhstan v Norway	0-3
England v Bosnia-Herzegovina	5-0

Group 9 Table	P	W	D	L	F	A	GD	Pts
England	8	6	2	0	20	3	17	20
Norway	8	5	1	2	12	10	2	16
Switzerland	8	3	3	2	11	8	3	12
Kazakhstan	8	1	1	6	3	14	–11	4
Bosnia-Herzegovina	8	0	3	5	2	13	–11	3

PLAY-OFF FIRST LEG

Serbia v Norway	2-0
Austria v Spain	1-1

PLAY-OFF SECOND LEG

		(agg)
Norway v Serbia	1-0	1-2
Spain v Austria	0-0	1-1

Spain win on away goals.

UEFA UNDER-21 CHAMPIONSHIP 2015–17

FINALS IN POLAND

GROUP A

Sweden v England	0-0
Poland v Slovakia	1-2
Slovakia v England	1-2
Poland v Sweden	2-2
Slovakia v Sweden	3-0
England v Poland	3-0

Group A Table	P	W	D	L	F	A	GD	Pts
England	3	2	1	0	5	1	4	7
Slovakia	3	2	0	1	6	3	3	6
Sweden	3	0	2	1	2	5	–3	2
Poland	3	0	1	2	3	7	–4	1

GROUP B

Portugal v Serbia	2-0
Spain v FYR Macedonia	5-0
Serbia v FYR Macedonia	2-2
Portugal v Spain	1-3
Serbia v Spain	0-1
FYR Macedonia v Portugal	2-4

Group B Table	P	W	D	L	F	A	GD	Pts
Spain	3	3	0	0	9	1	8	9
Portugal	3	2	0	1	7	5	2	6
Serbia	3	0	1	2	2	5	–3	1
FYR Macedonia	3	0	1	2	4	11	–7	1

GROUP C

Germany v Czech Republic	2-0
Denmark v Italy	0-2
Czech Republic v Italy	3-1
Germany v Denmark	3-0
Czech Republic v Denmark	2-4
Italy v Germany	1-0

Group C Table	P	W	D	L	F	A	GD	Pts
Italy	3	2	0	1	4	3	1	6
Germany	3	2	0	1	5	1	4	6
Denmark	3	1	0	2	4	7	–3	3
Czech Republic	3	1	0	2	5	7	–2	3

SEMI-FINALS

England v Germany	2-2*
aet; Germany won 4-3 on penalties.	
Spain v Italy	3-1

UEFA UNDER-21 CHAMPIONSHIP FINAL

Krakow, Friday 30 June 2017

Germany (1) 1 *(Weiser 40)*

Spain (0) 0 14,059

Germany: Pollersbeck; Stark, Kempf, Toljan, Haberer (Kohr 82), Gerhadt, Weiser, Meyer, Arnold, Gnabry (Amiri 81), Philipp (Oztunali 87).

Spain: Arrizabalaga; Bellerin, Mere, Vallejo, Jonny (Gaya 51), Saul Nigueza, Llorente (Mayoral 83), Ceballos, Asensio, Sandro Ramirez (Williams 71), Deulofeu.

Referee: Benoit Bastien (France).

UEFA YOUTH LEAGUE 2016–17

CHAMPIONS LEAGUE PATH

GROUP A

FC Basel v Ludogorets Razgrad 1-0
Paris Saint-Germain v Arsenal 0-0
Ludogorets Razgrad v Paris Saint-Germain 1-8
Arsenal v FC Basel 1-2
Arsenal v Ludogorets Razgrad 3-0
Paris Saint-Germain v FC Basel 4-1
Ludogorets Razgrad v Arsenal 1-1
FC Basel v Paris Saint-Germain 2-3
Ludogorets Razgrad v FC Basel 0-4
Arsenal v Paris Saint-Germain 2-2
Paris Saint-Germain v Ludogorets Razgrad 4-1
FC Basel v Arsenal 1-1

Group A Table	P	W	D	L	F	A	GD	Pts
Paris Saint-Germain	6	4	2	0	21	7	14	14
FC Basel	6	3	1	2	11	9	2	10
Arsenal	6	1	4	1	8	6	2	7
Ludogorets Razgrad	6	0	1	5	3	21	–18	1

GROUP B

Dynamo Kyiv v Napoli 4-1
Benfica v Besiktas 0-0
Besiktas v Dynamo Kyiv 3-3
Napoli v Benfica 2-3
Dynamo Kyiv v Benfica 2-1
Napoli v Besiktas 2-2
Besiktas v Napoli 0-1
Benfica v Dynamo Kyiv 1-2
Besiktas v Benfica 0-3
Napoli v Dynamo Kyiv 0-2
Dynamo Kyiv v Besiktas 3-1
Benfica v Napoli 2-0

Group B Table	P	W	D	L	F	A	GD	Pts
Dynamo Kyiv	6	5	1	0	16	7	9	16
Benfica	6	3	1	2	10	6	4	10
Napoli	6	1	1	4	6	13	–7	4
Besiktas	6	0	3	3	6	12	–6	3

GROUP C

Barcelona v Celtic 2-1
Manchester C v Borussia Moenchengladbach 4-1
Borussia Moenchengladbach v Barcelona 1-3
Celtic v Manchester C 0-4
Celtic v Borussia Moenchengladbach 1-1
Barcelona v Manchester C 1-0
Borussia Moenchengladbach v Celtic 4-1
Manchester C v Barcelona 0-2
Celtic v Barcelona 1-4
Borussia Moenchengladbach v Manchester C 1-2
Manchester C v Celtic 3-2
Barcelona v Borussia Moenchengladbach 1-2

Group C Table	P	W	D	L	F	A	GD	Pts
Barcelona	6	5	0	1	13	5	8	15
Manchester C	6	4	0	2	13	7	6	12
Borussia Moenchengladbach	6	2	1	3	10	12	–2	7
Celtic	6	0	1	5	6	18	–12	1

GROUP D

Bayern Munich v Rostov 4-2
PSV Eindhoven v Atletico Madrid 0-0
Rostov v PSV Eindhoven 0-6
Atletico Madrid v Bayern Munich 1-3
Rostov v Atletico Madrid 1-3
Bayern Munich v PSV Eindhoven 0-2
Atletico Madrid v Rostov 1-0
PSV Eindhoven v Bayern Munich 2-0
Rostov v Bayern Munich 0-1
Atletico Madrid v PSV Eindhoven 2-0
Bayern Munich v Atletico Madrid 1-1
PSV Eindhoven v Rostov 6-0

Group D Table	P	W	D	L	F	A	GD	Pts
PSV Eindhoven	6	4	1	1	16	2	14	13
Atletico Madrid	6	3	2	1	8	5	3	11
Bayern Munich	6	3	1	2	9	8	1	10
Rostov	6	0	0	6	3	21	–18	0

GROUP E

Bayer Leverkusen v CSKA Moscow 2-1
Tottenham H v Monaco 2-3
CSKA Moscow v Tottenham H 3-2
Monaco v Bayer Leverkusen 2-1
CSKA Moscow v Monaco 4-1
Bayer Leverkusen v Tottenham H 3-1
Monaco v CSKA Moscow 0-5
Tottenham H v Bayer Leverkusen 2-1
CSKA Moscow v Bayer Leverkusen 2-1
Monaco v Tottenham H 2-1
Bayer Leverkusen v Monaco 1-2
Tottenham H v CSKA Moscow 0-0

Group E Table	P	W	D	L	F	A	GD	Pts
CSKA Moscow	6	4	1	1	15	6	9	13
Monaco	6	4	0	2	10	14	–4	12
Bayer Leverkusen	6	2	0	4	9	10	–1	6
Tottenham H	6	1	1	4	8	12	–4	4

GROUP F

Legia Warsaw v Borussia Dortmund 0-2
Real Madrid v Sporting Lisbon 1-1
Borussia Dortmund v Real Madrid 2-5
Sporting Lisbon v Legia Warsaw 2-2
Sporting Lisbon v Borussia Dortmund 1-1
Real Madrid v Legia Warsaw 3-2
Borussia Dortmund v Sporting Lisbon 0-1
Legia Warsaw v Real Madrid 1-2
Borussia Dortmund v Legia Warsaw 3-3
Sporting Lisbon v Real Madrid 1-3
Legia Warsaw v Sporting Lisbon 2-0
Real Madrid v Borussia Dortmund 1-3

Group F Table	P	W	D	L	F	A	GD	Pts
Real Madrid	6	4	1	1	15	10	5	13
Borussia Dortmund	6	2	2	2	11	11	0	8
Sporting Lisbon	6	1	3	2	6	9	–3	6
Legia Warsaw	6	1	2	3	10	12	–2	5

GROUP G

Club Brugge v Leicester C 2-1
Porto v FC Copenhagen 4-1
Leicester C v Porto 0-2
FC Copenhagen v Club Brugge 0-0
Club Brugge v Porto 0-2
Leicester C v FC Copenhagen 3-2
Porto v Club Brugge 1-3
FC Copenhagen v Leicester C 3-2
Leicester C v Club Brugge 2-3
FC Copenhagen v Porto 3-1
Porto v Leicester C 2-1
Club Brugge v FC Copenhagen 0-3

Group G Table	P	W	D	L	F	A	GD	Pts
Porto	6	4	0	2	12	8	4	12
FC Copenhagen	6	3	1	2	12	10	2	10
Club Brugge	6	3	1	2	8	9	–1	10
Leicester C	6	1	0	5	9	14	–5	3

GROUP H

Lyon v Dinamo Zagreb 2-0
Juventus v Sevilla 2-1
Sevilla v Lyon 2-1
Dinamo Zagreb v Juventus 2-1
Lyon v Juventus 0-3
Dinamo Zagreb v Sevilla 2-4
Sevilla v Dinamo Zagreb 1-1
Juventus v Lyon 0-1
Dinamo Zagreb v Lyon 1-2
Sevilla v Juventus 0-2
Juventus v Dinamo Zagreb 0-1
Lyon v Sevilla 0-1

Group H Table	P	W	D	L	F	A	GD	Pts
Sevilla	6	3	1	2	9	8	1	10
Juventus	6	3	0	3	8	5	3	9
Lyon	6	3	0	3	6	7	–1	9
Dinamo Zagreb	6	2	1	3	7	10	–3	7

DOMESTIC CHAMPIONS PATH

FIRST ROUND – FIRST LEG

Nitra v Malaga	2-3
Puskas Akademia v PAOK Salonika	1-1
APOEL v Roma	0-3
Domzale v Cukaricki	1-1
Breidablik v Ajax	0-3
HJK Helsinki v Cork C	0-0
Anderlecht v Midtjylland	0-0
Rosenborg v AIK	0-0
Viitorul Constanta v Sheriff Tiraspol	4-1
Zrinjski Mostar v FC Zurich	0-3
Red Bull Salzburg v Vardar	5-0
Sparta Prague v Mladost Podgorica	4-0
Qabala v Dynamo Moscow	0-2
Maccabi Haifa v Shakhtyor Soligorsk	5-0
Dinamo Tbilisi v Kairat	0-3
Altinordu v Levski Sofia	5-0

FIRST ROUND – SECOND LEG

		(agg)
Malaga v Nitra	5-0	8-2
PAOK Solonika v Puskas Akademia	0-0	1-1
PAOK Salonika won on away goals		
Roma v APOEL	6-1	9-1
Cukaricki v Domzale	4-1	5-2
Ajax v Breidablik	4-0	7-0
Cork C v HJK Helsinki	1-0	1-0
Midtjylland v Anderlecht	3-1	3-1
AIK v Rosenborg	1-3	1-3
Sheriff Tiraspol v Viitorul Constanta	0-1	1-5
FC Zurich v Zrinjski Mostar	6-0	9-0
Vardar v Red Bull Salzburg	0-3	0-8
Mladost Podgorica v Sparta Prague	0-5	0-9
Dynamo Moscow v Qabala	5-0	7-0
Shakhtyor Soligorsk v Maccabi Haifa	2-3	2-8
Kairat v Dinamo Tbilisi	5-1	8-1
Levski Sofia v Altinordu	1-1	1-6

SECOND ROUND – FIRST LEG

PAOK Salonika v Ajax	0-2
Cork C v Roma	1-3
Malaga v Midtjylland	2-0
Rosenborg v Cukaricki	0-1
Altinordu v Sparta Prague	6-2
Viitorul Constanta v FC Zurich	5-0
Maccabi Haifa v Dynamo Moscow	0-0
Red Bull Salzburg v Kairat	8-1

SECOND ROUND – SECOND LEG

		(agg
Ajax v PAOK Salonika	2-1	4-1
Roma v Cork C	1-0	4-1
Midtjylland v Malaga	4-0	4-2
Cukaricki v Rosenborg	0-2	1-2
Sparta Prague v Altinordu	3-2	5-8
FC Zurich v Viitorul Constanta	2-0	2-5
Dynamo Moscow v Maccabi Haifa	1-1	1-1
Maccabi Haifa won on away goals		
Kairat v Red Bull Salzburg	0-1	1-9

PLAY-OFFS

Midtjylland v Benfica	1-1
Benfica won 6-5 on penalties	
Maccabi Haifa v Borussia Dortmund	0-1
Ajax v Juventus	2-0
Roma v Monaco	1-2
Viitorul Constanta v FC Copenhagen	4-2
Altinordu v Atletico Madrid	0-2
Rosenborg v FC Basel	1-0
Red Bull Salzburg v Manchester C	1-1
Red Bull Salzburg won 4-3 on penalties	

KNOCKOUT STAGE

ROUND OF 16

Porto v Viitorul Constanta	3-0
Atletico Madrid v Sevilla	3-2
PSV Eindhoven v Benfica	1-1
Benfica won 5-4 on penalties	
Ajax v Dynamo Kyiv	3-0
Red Bull Salzburg v Paris Saint-Germain	5-0
CSKA Moscow v Rosenborg	2-1
Monaco v Real Madrid	3-4
Barcelona v Borussia Dortmund	4-1

QUARTER-FINALS

CSKA Moscow v Benfica	0-2
Red Bull Salzburg v Atletico Madrid	2-1
Barcelona v Porto	2-1
Real Madrid v Ajax	2-1

SEMI-FINALS

Barcelona v Red Bull Salzburg	1-2
Real Madrid v Benfica	2-4

UEFA YOUTH LEAGUE FINAL 2016–17

Nyon, Monday 24 April 2017

Red Bull Salzburg (0) 2 *(Patson 72, Schmidt 76)*

Benfica (1) 1 *(Gomes 29)*

Red Bull Salzburg: Zynel; Meisi, Gorzel, Berisha, Wolf (Lugonja 90), Sturm (Schmidt 68), Mensah, Haidara, Meister (Patson 55), Ingolitsch■, Dos Santos De Paulo.
Benfica: Duarte; Buta, Dias, Kalaica, Araujo (Dju 87), Florentino, Filipe (Jau 83), Fernandes, Gomes, Goncalves, Felix (Tavares 73).
Referee: Ali Palabiyik (Turkey).

UEFA UNDER-19 CHAMPIONSHIP 2015–16

FINALS IN GERMANY

GROUP A

Germany v Italy 0-1
Portugal v Austria 1-1
Italy v Austria 1-1
Germany v Portugal 3-4
Austria v Germany 0-3
Italy v Portugal 1-1

Group A Table	P	W	D	L	F	A	GD	Pts
Portugal	3	1	2	0	6	5	1	5
Italy	3	1	2	0	3	2	1	5
Germany	3	1	0	2	6	5	1	3
Austria	3	0	2	1	2	5	–3	2

GROUP B

Croatia v Netherlands 1-3
France v England 1-2
Netherlands v England 1-2
Croatia v France 0-2
Netherlands v France 1-5
England v Croatia 2-1

Group B Table	P	W	D	L	F	A	GD	Pts
England	3	3	0	0	6	3	3	9
France	3	2	0	1	8	3	5	6
Netherlands	3	1	0	2	5	8	–3	3
Croatia	3	0	0	3	2	7	–5	0

SEMI-FINALS

England v Italy 1-2
Portugal v France 1-3

FINAL

France v Italy 4-0

UEFA UNDER-19 CHAMPIONSHIP 2016–17

QUALIFYING ROUND

GROUP 1 (BELGIUM)

Russia v Finland 1-1
Kazakhstan v Belgium 0-5
Belgium v Finland 2-2
Russia v Kazakhstan 5-0
Belgium v Russia 2-2
Finland v Kazakhstan 6-0

Group 1 Table	P	W	D	L	F	A	GD	Pts
Belgium	3	1	2	0	9	4	5	5
Finland	3	1	2	0	9	3	6	5
Russia	3	1	2	0	8	3	5	5
Kazakhstan	3	0	0	3	0	16	–16	0

GROUP 2 (NETHERLANDS)

San Marino v Norway 0-9
Netherlands v Romania 2-1
Norway v Romania 3-1
Netherlands v San Marino 4-0
Romania v San Marino 6-0
Norway v Netherlands 0-1

Group 2 Table	P	W	D	L	F	A	GD	Pts
Netherlands	3	3	0	0	7	1	6	9
Norway	3	2	0	1	12	2	10	6
Romania	3	1	0	2	8	5	3	3
San Marino	3	0	0	3	0	19	–19	0

GROUP 3 (ANDORRA)

Liechtenstein v Scotland 0-1
Israel v Andorra 3-2
Israel v Liechtenstein 5-0
Scotland v Andorra 1-0
Andorra v Liechtenstein 4-2
Scotland v Israel 0-1

Group 3 Table	P	W	D	L	F	A	GD	Pts
Israel	3	3	0	0	9	2	7	9
Scotland	3	2	0	1	2	1	1	6
Andorra	3	1	0	2	6	6	0	3
Liechtenstein	3	0	0	3	2	10	–8	0

GROUP 4 (ALBANIA)

Albania v Republic of Ireland 0-1
Germany v Gibraltar 5-0
Republic of Ireland v Gibraltar 5-0
Germany v Albania 3-2
Gibraltar v Albania 0-1
Republic of Ireland v Germany 0-4

Group 4 Table	P	W	D	L	F	A	GD	Pts
Germany	3	3	0	0	12	2	10	9
Republic of Ireland	3	2	0	1	6	4	2	6
Albania	3	1	0	2	3	4	–1	3
Gibraltar	3	0	0	3	0	11	–11	0

GROUP 5 (LITHUANIA)

Austria v Azerbaijan 4-1
Lithuania v Bosnia-Herzegovina 0-3
Bosnia-Herzegovina v Azerbaijan 2-1
Austria v Lithuania 3-2
Azerbaijan v Lithuania 2-0
Bosnia-Herzegovina v Austria 1-3

Group 5 Table	P	W	D	L	F	A	GD	Pts
Austria	3	3	0	0	10	4	6	9
Bosnia-Herzegovina	3	2	0	1	6	4	2	6
Azerbaijan	3	1	0	2	4	6	–2	3
Lithuania	3	0	0	3	2	8	–6	0

GROUP 6 (WALES)

Wales v Greece 0-2
England v Luxembourg 2-0
Greece v Luxembourg 5-0
England v Wales 2-3
Luxembourg v Wales 2-6
Greece v England 0-2

Group 6 Table	P	W	D	L	F	A	GD	Pts
England	3	2	0	1	6	3	3	6
Greece	3	2	0	1	7	2	5	6
Wales	3	2	0	1	9	6	3	6
Luxembourg	3	0	0	3	2	13	–11	0

GROUP 7 (ARMENIA)

Switzerland v Armenia 4-0
Hungary v Italy 0-1
Italy v Armenia 2-1
Switzerland v Hungary 1-2
Armenia v Hungary 0-4
Italy v Switzerland 1-1

Group 7 Table	P	W	D	L	F	A	GD	Pts
Italy	3	2	1	0	4	2	2	7
Hungary	3	2	0	1	6	2	4	6
Switzerland	3	1	1	1	6	3	3	4
Armenia	3	0	0	3	1	10	–9	0

GROUP 8 (BULGARIA)

Bulgaria v Portugal 1-0
Denmark v Belarus 5-0
Portugal v Belarus 1-1
Denmark v Bulgaria 1-3
Portugal v Denmark 2-1
Belarus v Bulgaria 1-0

Group 8 Table	P	W	D	L	F	A	GD	Pts
Bulgaria	3	2	0	1	4	2	2	6
Portugal	3	1	1	1	3	3	0	4
Belarus	3	1	1	1	2	6	–4	4
Denmark	3	1	0	2	7	5	2	3

GROUP 9 (CZECH REPUBLIC)

France v Slovenia 1-1
Estonia v Czech Republic 0-5

France v Estonia 4-0
Czech Republic v Slovenia 2-1
Czech Republic v France 0-2
Slovenia v Estonia 5-0

Group 9 Table	P	W	D	L	F	A	GD	Pts
France	3	2	1	0	7	1	6	7
Czech Republic	3	2	0	1	7	3	4	6
Slovenia	3	1	1	1	7	3	4	4
Estonia	3	0	0	3	0	14	–14	0

GROUP 10 (SERBIA)
Moldova v Serbia 0-2
Sweden v Malta 4-0
Sweden v Moldova 1-0
Serbia v Malta 1-0
Serbia v Sweden 2-3
Malta v Moldova 1-0

Group 10 Table	P	W	D	L	F	A	GD	Pts
Sweden	3	3	0	0	8	2	6	9
Serbia	3	2	0	1	5	3	2	6
Malta	3	1	0	2	1	5	–4	3
Moldova	3	0	0	3	0	4	–4	0

GROUP 11 (POLAND)
Northern Ireland v Slovakia 0-1
FYR Macedonia v Poland 0-4
FYR Macedonia v Northern Ireland 1-2
Slovakia v Poland 1-0
Slovakia v FYR Macedonia 2-0
Poland v Northern Ireland 1-0

Group 11 Table	P	W	D	L	F	A	GD	Pts
Slovakia	3	3	0	0	4	0	4	9
Poland	3	2	0	1	5	1	4	6
Northern Ireland	3	1	0	2	2	3	–1	3
FYR Macedonia	3	0	0	3	1	8	–7	0

GROUP 12 (MONTENEGRO)
Croatia v Cyprus 4-0
Faroe Islands v Montenegro 2-1
Montenegro v Cyprus 0-1
Croatia v Faroe Islands 5-0
Cyprus v Faroe Islands 1-0
Montenegro v Croatia 1-2

Group 12 Table	P	W	D	L	F	A	GD	Pts
Croatia	3	3	0	0	11	1	10	9
Cyprus	3	2	0	1	2	4	–2	6
Faroe Islands	3	1	0	2	2	7	–5	3
Montenegro	3	0	0	3	2	5	–3	0

GROUP 13 (UKRAINE)
Ukraine v Iceland 2-0
Latvia v Turkey 2-2
Turkey v Iceland 2-1
Ukraine v Latvia 3-0
Turkey v Ukraine 3-1
Iceland v Latvia 2-0

Group 13 Table	P	W	D	L	F	A	GD	Pts
Turkey	3	2	1	0	7	4	3	7
Ukraine	3	2	0	1	6	3	3	6
Iceland	3	1	0	2	3	4	–1	3
Latvia	3	0	1	2	2	7	–5	1

ELITE ROUND

GROUP 1 (NETHERLANDS)
Netherlands v Finland 1-0
Ukraine v Greece 2-0
Greece v Finland 4-1
Netherlands v Ukraine 2-0
Finland v Ukraine 2-1
Greece v Netherlands 0-0

Group 1 Table	P	W	D	L	F	A	GD	Pts
Netherlands	3	2	1	0	3	0	3	7
Greece	3	1	1	1	4	3	1	4
Finland	3	1	0	2	3	6	–3	3
Ukraine	3	1	0	2	3	4	–1	3

GROUP 2 (GERMANY)
Germany v Cyprus 2-1
Serbia v Slovakia 1-0
Germany v Serbia 2-0
Slovakia v Cyprus 5-0
Cyprus v Serbia 0-0
Slovakia v Germany 0-4

Group 2 Table	P	W	D	L	F	A	GD	Pts
Germany	3	3	0	0	8	1	7	9
Serbia	3	1	1	1	1	2	–1	4
Slovakia	3	1	0	2	5	5	0	3
Cyprus	3	0	1	2	1	7	–6	1

GROUP 3 (ENGLAND)
England v Norway 3-0
Spain v Belarus 5-0
Norway v Belarus 2-1
Spain v England 0-3
Belarus v England 1-5
Norway v Spain 0-2

Group 3 Table	P	W	D	L	F	A	GD	Pts
England	3	3	0	0	11	1	10	9
Spain	3	2	0	1	7	3	4	6
Norway	3	1	0	2	2	6	–4	3
Belarus	3	0	0	3	2	12	–10	0

GROUP 4 (PORTUGAL)
Poland v Turkey 1-0
Croatia v Portugal 1-2
Croatia v Poland 2-0
Turkey v Portugal 2-1
Turkey v Croatia 0-0
Portugal v Poland 3-1

Group 4 Table	P	W	D	L	F	A	GD	Pts
Portugal	3	2	0	1	6	4	2	6
Croatia	3	1	1	1	3	2	1	4
Turkey	3	1	1	1	2	2	0	4
Poland	3	1	0	2	2	5	–3	3

GROUP 5 (FRANCE)
Bosnia-Herzegovina v France 2-0
Israel v Bulgaria 1-1
Israel v Bosnia-Herzegovina 1-1
France v Bulgaria 1-2
France v Israel 0-0
Bulgaria v Bosnia-Herzegovina 3-1

Group 5 Table	P	W	D	L	F	A	GD	Pts
Bulgaria	3	2	1	0	6	3	3	7
Bosnia-Herzegovina	3	1	1	1	4	4	0	4
Israel	3	0	3	0	2	2	0	3
France	3	0	1	2	1	4	–3	1

GROUP 6 (CZECH REPUBLIC)
Austria v Scotland 3-0
Hungary v Czech Republic 1-2
Austria v Hungary 1-3
Czech Republic v Scotland 1-0
Scotland v Hungary 1-2
Czech Republic v Austria 3-0

Group 6 Table	P	W	D	L	F	A	GD	Pts
Czech Republic	3	3	0	0	6	1	5	9
Hungary	3	2	0	1	6	4	2	6
Austria	3	1	0	2	4	6	–2	3
Scotland	3	0	0	3	1	6	–5	0

GROUP 7 (BELGIUM)
Sweden v Belgium 1-2
Republic of Ireland v Italy 2-0
Sweden v Republic of Ireland 3-0
Italy v Belgium 1-1
Italy v Sweden 0-1
Belgium v Republic of Ireland 0-1

Group 7 Table	P	W	D	L	F	A	GD	Pts
Sweden	3	2	0	1	5	2	3	6
Republic of Ireland	3	2	0	1	3	3	0	6
Belgium	3	1	1	1	3	3	0	4
Italy	3	0	1	2	1	4	–3	1

Final Tournament in Georgia 2–15 July.

UEFA UNDER-17 CHAMPIONSHIP 2016–17

QUALIFYING ROUND

GROUP 1 (MOLDOVA)

Bosnia-Herzegovina v Latvia	3-0
Moldova v Russia	0-5
Bosnia-Herzegovina v Moldova	1-0
Russia v Latvia	1-0
Russia v Bosnia-Herzegovina	2-1
Latvia v Moldova	2-0

Group 1 Table	P	W	D	L	F	A	GD	Pts
Russia	3	3	0	0	8	1	7	9
Bosnia-Herzegovina	3	2	0	1	5	2	3	6
Latvia	3	1	0	2	2	4	–2	3
Moldova	3	0	0	3	0	8	–8	0

GROUP 2 (ANDORRA)

Kazakhstan v Greece	0-1
Republic of Ireland v Andorra	5-1
Republic of Ireland v Kazakhstan	3-1
Greece v Andorra	3-0
Andorra v Kazakhstan	0-2
Greece v Republic of Ireland	0-1

Group 2 Table	P	W	D	L	F	A	GD	Pts
Republic of Ireland	3	3	0	0	9	2	7	9
Greece	3	2	0	1	4	1	3	6
Kazakhstan	3	1	0	2	3	4	–1	3
Andorra	3	0	0	3	1	10	–9	0

GROUP 3 (LUXEMBOURG)

Switzerland v Luxembourg	2-1
Faroe Islands v Czech Republic	2-0
Czech Republic v Luxembourg	2-0
Switzerland v Faroe Islands	3-0
Luxembourg v Faroe Islands	2-2
Czech Republic v Switzerland	3-3

Group 3 Table	P	W	D	L	F	A	GD	Pts
Switzerland	3	2	1	0	8	4	4	7
Faroe Islands	3	1	1	1	4	5	–1	4
Czech Republic	3	1	1	1	5	5	0	4
Luxembourg	3	0	1	2	3	6	–3	1

GROUP 4 (ITALY)

Serbia v FYR Macedonia	3-1
Albania v Italy	0-1
Serbia v Albania	2-0
Italy v FYR Macedonia	0-0
FYR Macedonia v Albania	2-1
Italy v Serbia	2-0

Group 4 Table	P	W	D	L	F	A	GD	Pts
Italy	3	2	1	0	3	0	3	7
Serbia	3	2	0	1	5	3	2	6
FYR Macedonia	3	1	1	1	3	4	–1	4
Albania	3	0	0	3	1	5	–4	0

GROUP 5 (SLOVENIA)

Slovenia v Estonia	4-1
Montenegro v France	1-2
France v Estonia	7-0
Slovenia v Montenegro	2-2
France v Slovenia	1-1
Estonia v Montenegro	1-2

Group 5 Table	P	W	D	L	F	A	GD	Pts
France	3	2	1	0	10	2	8	7
Slovenia	3	1	2	0	7	4	3	5
Montenegro	3	1	1	1	5	5	0	4
Estonia	3	0	0	3	2	13	–11	0

GROUP 6 (ROMANIA)

Romania v Austria	1-2
England v Azerbaijan	2-0
England v Romania	3-0
Austria v Azerbaijan	3-1
Azerbaijan v Romania	1-0
Austria v England	2-3

Group 6 Table	P	W	D	L	F	A	GD	Pts
England	3	3	0	0	8	2	6	9
Austria	3	2	0	1	7	5	2	6
Azerbaijan	3	1	0	2	2	5	–3	3
Romania	3	0	0	3	1	6	–5	0

GROUP 7 (HUNGARY)

Hungary v Liechtenstein	3-0
Denmark v Netherlands	0-2
Netherlands v Liechtenstein	9-0
Hungary v Denmark	3-1
Liechtenstein v Denmark	0-11
Netherlands v Hungary	4-0

Group 7 Table	P	W	D	L	F	A	GD	Pts
Netherlands	3	3	0	0	15	0	15	9
Hungary	3	2	0	1	6	5	1	6
Denmark	3	1	0	2	12	5	7	3
Liechtenstein	3	0	0	3	0	23	–23	0

GROUP 8 (FINLAND)

Georgia v Bulgaria	0-1
Finland v Sweden	0-5
Sweden v Bulgaria	3-1
Georgia v Finland	0-2
Bulgaria v Finland	0-1
Sweden v Georgia	4-0

Group 8 Table	P	W	D	L	F	A	GD	Pts
Sweden	3	3	0	0	12	1	11	9
Finland	3	2	0	1	3	5	–2	6
Bulgaria	3	1	0	2	2	4	–2	3
Georgia	3	0	0	3	0	7	–7	0

GROUP 9 (NORTHERN IRELAND)

San Marino v Slovakia	0-4
Spain v Northern Ireland	4-0
Spain v San Marino	3-0
Slovakia v Northern Ireland	4-3
Northern Ireland v San Marino	2-1
Slovakia v Spain	0-6

Group 9 Table	P	W	D	L	F	A	GD	Pts
Spain	3	3	0	0	13	0	13	9
Slovakia	3	2	0	1	8	9	–1	6
Northern Ireland	3	1	0	2	5	9	–4	3
San Marino	3	0	0	3	1	9	–8	0

GROUP 10 (PORTUGAL)

Scotland v Malta	6-0
Wales v Portugal	0-2
Scotland v Wales	1-0
Portugal v Malta	5-0
Portugal v Scotland	0-1
Malta v Wales	0-3

Group 10 Table	P	W	D	L	F	A	GD	Pts
Scotland	3	3	0	0	8	0	8	9
Portugal	3	2	0	1	7	1	6	6
Wales	3	1	0	2	3	3	0	3
Malta	3	0	0	3	0	14	–14	0

GROUP 11 (CYPRUS)

Gibraltar v Belgium	0-2
Belarus v Cyprus	0-1
Belgium v Cyprus	0-1
Belarus v Gibraltar	3-1
Belgium v Belarus	0-0
Cyprus v Gibraltar	2-0

Group 11 Table	P	W	D	L	F	A	GD	Pts
Cyprus	3	3	0	0	4	0	4	9
Belarus	3	1	1	1	3	2	1	4
Belgium	3	1	1	1	2	1	1	4
Gibraltar	3	0	0	3	1	7	–6	0

GROUP 12 (ISRAEL)

Poland v Armenia	1-1
Iceland v Israel	0-2
Poland v Iceland	2-0
Israel v Armenia	2-0
Israel v Poland	3-1
Armenia v Iceland	3-2

Group 12 Table	P	W	D	L	F	A	GD	Pts
Israel	3	3	0	0	7	1	6	9
Poland	3	1	1	1	4	4	0	4
Armenia	3	1	1	1	4	5	–1	4
Iceland	3	0	0	3	2	7	–5	0

GROUP 13 (LITHUANIA)

Turkey v Norway	2-0
Ukraine v Lithuania	1-1
Ukraine v Turkey	0-1
Norway v Lithuania	2-1
Lithuania v Turkey	0-1
Norway v Ukraine	2-2

Group 13 Table	P	W	D	L	F	A	GD	Pts
Turkey	3	3	0	0	4	0	4	9
Norway	3	1	1	1	4	5	–1	4
Ukraine	3	0	2	1	3	4	–1	2
Lithuania	3	0	1	2	2	4	–2	1

ELITE ROUND

GROUP 1 (TURKEY)

Germany v Armenia	10-1
Finland v Turkey	1-4
Germany v Finland	6-2
Turkey v Armenia	6-0
Turkey v Germany	1-3
Armenia v Finland	0-5

Group 1 Table	P	W	D	L	F	A	GD	Pts
Germany	3	3	0	0	19	4	15	9
Turkey	3	2	0	1	11	4	7	6
Finland	3	1	0	2	8	10	–2	3
Armenia	3	0	0	3	1	21	–20	0

GROUP 2 (HUNGARY)

Russia v Norway	2-2
Hungary v Israel	0-1
Israel v Norway	0-3
Russia v Hungary	1-2
Israel v Russia	0-0
Norway v Hungary	0-1

Group 2 Table	P	W	D	L	F	A	GD	Pts
Hungary	3	2	0	1	3	2	1	6
Norway	3	1	1	1	5	3	2	4
Israel	3	1	1	1	1	3	–2	4
Russia	3	0	2	1	3	4	–1	2

GROUP 3 (PORTUGAL)

Greece v Portugal	0-4
Spain v Poland	3-1
Portugal v Poland	3-3
Spain v Greece	0-1
Poland v Greece	3-0
Portugal v Spain	0-2

Group 3 Table	P	W	D	L	F	A	GD	Pts
Spain	3	2	0	1	5	2	3	6
Portugal	3	1	1	1	7	5	2	4
Poland	3	1	1	1	7	6	1	4
Greece	3	1	0	2	1	7	–6	3

GROUP 4 (SCOTLAND)

Serbia v Switzerland	2-1
Scotland v Montenegro	6-1
Switzerland v Montenegro	3-1
Scotland v Serbia	1-0
Switzerland v Scotland	0-1
Montenegro v Serbia	0-1

Group 4 Table	P	W	D	L	F	A	GD	Pts
Scotland	3	3	0	0	8	1	7	9
Serbia	3	2	0	1	3	2	1	6
Switzerland	3	1	0	2	4	4	0	3
Montenegro	3	0	0	3	2	10	–8	0

GROUP 5 (NETHERLANDS)

Netherlands v Belgium	2-0
Belarus v Italy	0-3
Italy v Belgium	1-0
Netherlands v Belarus	3-2
Belgium v Belarus	1-2
Italy v Netherlands	1-2

Group 5 Table	P	W	D	L	F	A	GD	Pts
Netherlands	3	3	0	0	7	3	4	9
Italy	3	2	0	1	5	2	3	6
Belarus	3	1	0	2	4	7	–3	3
Belgium	3	0	0	3	1	5	–4	0

GROUP 6 (AUSTRIA)

Sweden v Ukraine	1-2
Austria v France	1-1
France v Ukraine	3-1
Sweden v Austria	1-3
France v Sweden	2-0
Ukraine v Austria	2-1

Group 6 Table	P	W	D	L	F	A	GD	Pts
France	3	2	1	0	6	2	4	7
Ukraine	3	2	0	1	5	5	0	6
Austria	3	1	1	1	5	4	1	4
Sweden	3	0	0	3	2	7	–5	0

GROUP 7 (BOSNIA-HERZEGOVINA)

England v Czech Republic	5-3
Slovenia v Bosnia-Herzegovina	0-0
Bosnia-Herzegovina v Czech Republic	2-1
England v Slovenia	4-0
Bosnia-Herzegovina v England	0-1
Czech Republic v Slovenia	2-2

Group 7 Table	P	W	D	L	F	A	GD	Pts
England	3	3	0	0	10	3	7	9
Bosnia-Herzegovina	3	1	1	1	2	2	0	4
Slovenia	3	0	2	1	2	6	–4	2
Czech Republic	3	0	1	2	6	9	–3	1

GROUP 8 (CYPRUS)

Republic of Ireland v Faroe Islands	4-0
Slovakia v Cyprus	2-1
Cyprus v Faroe Islands	0-0
Republic of Ireland v Slovakia	1-0
Faroe Islands v Slovakia	2-1
Cyprus v Republic of Ireland	0-2

Group 8 Table	P	W	D	L	F	A	GD	Pts
Republic of Ireland	3	3	0	0	7	0	7	9
Faroe Islands	3	1	1	1	2	5	–3	4
Slovakia	3	1	0	2	3	4	–1	3
Cyprus	3	0	1	2	1	4	–3	1

FINAL TOURNAMENT (CROATIA)

GROUP A

Turkey v Spain	2-3
Croatia v Italy	0-1
Croatia v Turkey	1-4
Spain v Italy	3-1
Italy v Turkey	1-2
Spain v Croatia	1-1

Group A Table	P	W	D	L	F	A	GD	Pts
Spain	3	2	1	0	7	4	3	7
Turkey	3	2	0	1	8	5	3	6
Italy	3	1	0	2	3	5	–2	3
Croatia	3	0	1	2	2	6	–4	1

GROUP B

Scotland v Faroe Islands	2-0
Hungary v France	3-2
France v Faroe Islands	7-0
Scotland v Hungary	1-1
Faroe Islands v Hungary	0-4
France v Scotland	2-1

Group B Table	P	W	D	L	F	A	GD	Pts
Hungary	3	2	1	0	8	3	5	7
France	3	2	0	1	11	4	7	6
Scotland	3	1	1	1	4	3	1	4
Faroe Islands	3	0	0	3	0	13	–13	0

GROUP C

Germany v Bosnia-Herzegovina	5-0
Serbia v Republic of Ireland	1-0
Germany v Serbia	3-1
Republic of Ireland v Bosnia-Herzegovina	2-1
Bosnia-Herzegovina v Serbia	1-0
Republic of Ireland v Germany	0-7

Group C Table	P	W	D	L	F	A	GD	Pts
Germany	3	3	0	0	15	1	14	9
Republic of Ireland	3	1	0	2	2	9	–7	3
Bosnia-Herzegovina	3	1	0	2	2	7	–5	3
Serbia	3	1	0	2	2	4	–2	3

GROUP D

Netherlands v Ukraine 1-0
Norway v England 1-3
England v Ukraine 4-0
Netherlands v Norway 2-2
Ukraine v Norway 2-0
England v Netherlands 3-0

Group D Table	P	W	D	L	F	A	GD	Pts
England	3	3	0	0	10	1	9	9
Netherlands	3	1	1	1	3	5	–2	4
Ukraine	3	1	0	2	2	5	–3	3
Norway	3	0	1	2	3	7	–4	1

QUARTER-FINALS

Hungary v Turkey 0-1
Spain v France 3-1
England v Republic of Ireland 1-0
Germany v Netherlands 2-1

SEMI-FINALS

Turkey v England 1-2
Spain v Germany 0-0
Spain won 4-2 on penalties.

UEFA UNDER-17 CHAMPIONSHIP 2016–17 FINAL

Varazdin, Friday 19 May 2017

Spain (1) 2 *(Morey 38, Diaz 80)*

England (1) 2 *(Hudson-Odoi 18, Foden 58)* 8187

Spain: Fernandez; Morey, Miranda, Guillamon, Chust, Blanco (Alonso 60), Torres, Moha, Ruiz, Gomez, Orellana (Beotoa 56).
England: Bursik; Gibson, McEachran, Guehi, Panzo, Foden (Loader 80), Brewster, Hudson-Odoi (Barlow 77), Sancho (Vokins 80), Denny, Latibeaudiere.
Spain won 4-1 on penalties.

FIFA UNDER-20 WORLD CUP 2017

FINALS IN KOREA REPUBLIC

**After extra time.*

GROUP A

Argentina v England 0-3
Korea Republic v Guinea 3-0
England v Guinea 1-1
Korea Republic v Argentina 2-1
England v Korea Republic 1-0
Guinea v Argentina 0-5

Group A Table	P	W	D	L	F	A	GD	Pts
England	3	2	1	0	5	1	4	7
Korea Republic	3	2	0	1	5	2	3	6
Argentina	3	1	0	2	6	5	1	3
Guinea	3	0	1	2	1	9	–8	1

GROUP B

Venezuela v Germany 2-0
Vanuatu v Mexico 2-3
Venezuela v Vanuatu 7-0
Mexico v Germany 0-0
Mexico v Venezuela 0-1
Germany v Vanuatu 3-2

Group B Table	P	W	D	L	F	A	GD	Pts
Venezuela	3	3	0	0	10	0	10	9
Mexico	3	1	1	1	3	3	0	4
Germany	3	1	1	1	3	4	–1	4
Vanuatu	3	0	0	3	4	13	–9	0

GROUP C

Zambia v Portugal 2-1
Iran v Costa Rica 1-0
Zambia v Iran 4-2
Costa Rica v Portugal 1-1
Costa Rica v Zambia 1-0
Portugal v Iran 2-1

Group C Table	P	W	D	L	F	A	GD	Pts
Zambia	3	2	0	1	6	4	2	6
Portugal	3	1	1	1	4	4	0	4
Costa Rica	3	1	1	1	2	2	0	4
Iran	3	1	0	2	4	6	–2	3

GROUP D

South Africa v Japan 1-2
Italy v Uruguay 0-1
South Africa v Italy 0-2
Uruguay v Japan 2-0
Uruguay v South Africa 0-0
Japan v Italy 2-2

Group D Table	P	W	D	L	F	A	GD	Pts
Uruguay	3	2	1	0	3	0	3	7
Italy	3	1	1	1	4	3	1	4
Japan	3	1	1	1	4	5	–1	4
South Africa	3	0	1	2	1	4	–3	1

GROUP E

France v Honduras 3-0
Vietnam v New Zealand 0-0
France v Vietnam 4-0
New Zealand v Honduras 3-1
New Zealand v France 0-2
Honduras v Vietnam 2-0

Group E Table	P	W	D	L	F	A	GD	Pts
France	3	3	0	0	9	0	9	9
New Zealand	3	1	1	1	3	3	0	4
Honduras	3	1	0	2	3	6	–3	3
Vietnam	3	0	1	2	0	6	–6	1

GROUP F

Ecuador v USA 3-3
Saudi Arabia v Senegal 0-2
Ecuador v Saudi Arabia 1-2
Senegal v USA 0-1
Senegal v Ecuador 0-0
USA v Saudi Arabia 1-1

Group F Table	P	W	D	L	F	A	GD	Pts
United States	3	1	2	0	5	4	1	5
Senegal	3	1	1	1	2	1	1	4
Saudi Arabia	3	1	1	1	3	4	–1	4
Ecuador	3	0	2	1	4	5	–1	2

ROUND OF 16

Venezuela v Japan 1-0*
Korea Republic v Portugal 1-3
Uruguay v Saudi Arabia 1-0
England v Costa Rica 2-1
Zambia v Germany 4-3*
Mexico v Senegal 1-0
France v Italy 1-2
USA v New Zealand 6-0

QUARTER-FINALS

Venezuela v USA 2-1*
Portugal v Uruguay 2-2*
Uruguay won 5-4 on penalties.
Italy v Zambia 3-2*
Mexico v England 0-1

SEMI-FINALS

Uruguay v Venezuela 1-1*
Venezuela won 4-3 on penalties.
Italy v England 1-3

FIFA U20 WORLD CUP 2017 FINAL

Suwon World Cup Stadium, Sunday 11 June 2017

Venezuela (0) 0

England (1) 1 *(Calvert-Lewin 35)*

England: Woodman; Kenny, Tomori, Clarke-Salter, Walker-Peters, Cook, Onomah, Lookman (Maitland-Niles 76), Solanke, Dowell (Ojo 62), Calvert-Lewin.
Venezuela: Farinez; Velasquez, Ferraresi, Jose Hernandez, Ronald Hernandez, Herrera, Lucena, Penaranda (Hurtado 90), Pena, Chacon (Soteldo 52), Cordova (Sosa 72).

ENGLAND UNDER-21 RESULTS 1976–2017

EC *UEFA Competition for Under-21 Teams*

Bold type indicates matches played in season 2016–17.

Year	*Date*		*Venue*		
			v ALBANIA	*Eng*	*Alb*
EC1989	Mar	7	Shkroda	2	1
EC1989	April	25	Ipswich	2	0
EC2001	Mar	27	Tirana	1	0
EC2001	Sept	4	Middlesbrough	5	0
			v ANGOLA	*Eng*	*Ang*
1995	June	10	Toulon	1	0
1996	May	28	Toulon	0	2
			v ARGENTINA	*Eng*	*Arg*
1998	May	18	Toulon	0	2
2000	Feb	22	Fulham	1	0
			v AUSTRIA	*Eng*	*Aus*
1994	Oct	11	Kapfenberg	3	1
1995	Nov	14	Middlesbrough	2	1
EC2004	Sept	3	Krems	2	0
EC2005	Oct	7	Leeds	1	2
2013	June	26	Brighton	4	0
			v AZERBAIJAN	*Eng*	*Az*
EC2004	Oct	12	Baku	0	0
EC2005	Mar	29	Middlesbrough	2	0
2009	June	8	Milton Keynes	7	0
EC2011	Sept	1	Watford	6	0
EC2012	Sept	6	Baku	2	0
			v BELARUS	*Eng*	*Bel*
2015	June	11	Barnsley	1	0
			v BELGIUM	*Eng*	*Bel*
1994	June	5	Marseille	2	1
1996	May	24	Toulon	1	0
EC2011	Nov	14	Mons	1	2
EC2012	Feb	29	Middlesbrough	4	0
			v BOSNIA-HERZEGOVINA	*Eng*	*B-H*
EC2015	Nov	12	Sarajevo Canton	0	0
EC2016	**Oct**	**11**	**Walsall**	**5**	**0**
			v BRAZIL	*Eng*	*B*
1993	June	11	Toulon	0	0
1995	June	6	Toulon	0	2
1996	June	1	Toulon	1	2
			v BULGARIA	*Eng*	*Bul*
EC1979	June	5	Pernik	3	1
EC1979	Nov	20	Leicester	5	0
1989	June	5	Toulon	2	3
EC1998	Oct	9	West Ham	1	0
EC1999	June	8	Vratsa	1	0
EC2007	Sept	11	Sofia	2	0
EC2007	Nov	16	Milton Keynes	2	0
			v CROATIA	*Eng*	*Cro*
1996	Apr	23	Sunderland	0	1
2003	Aug	19	West Ham	0	3
EC2014	Oct	10	Wolverhampton	2	1
EC2014	Oct	14	Vinkovci	2	1
			v CZECHOSLOVAKIA	*Eng*	*Cz*
1990	May	28	Toulon	2	1
1992	May	26	Toulon	1	2
1993	June	9	Toulon	1	1
			v CZECH REPUBLIC	*Eng*	*CzR*
1998	Nov	17	Ipswich	0	1
EC2007	June	11	Arnhem	0	0
2008	Nov	18	Bramall Lane	2	0
EC2011	June	19	Viborg	1	2
2015	Mar	27	Prague	1	0
			v DENMARK	*Eng*	*Den*
EC1978	Sept	19	Hvidovre	2	1
EC1979	Sept	11	Watford	1	0
EC1982	Sept	21	Hvidovre	4	1
EC1983	Sept	20	Norwich	4	1
EC1986	Mar	12	Copenhagen	1	0
EC1986	Mar	26	Manchester	1	1
1988	Sept	13	Watford	0	0
1994	Mar	8	Brentford	1	0
1999	Oct	8	Bradford	4	1
2005	Aug	16	Herning	1	0
2011	Mar	24	Viborg	4	0
2017	**Mar**	**27**	**Randers**	**4**	**0**
			v EQUADOR	*Eng*	*E*
2009	Feb	10	Malaga	2	3
			v FINLAND	*Eng*	*Fin*
EC1977	May	26	Helsinki	1	0
EC1977	Oct	12	Hull	8	1
EC1984	Oct	16	Southampton	2	0
EC1985	May	21	Mikkeli	1	3
EC2000	Oct	10	Valkeakoski	2	2
EC2001	Mar	23	Barnsley	4	0
EC2009	June	15	Halmstad	2	1
EC2013	Sept	9	Tampere	1	1
EC2013	Nov	14	Milton Keynes	3	0
			v FRANCE	*Eng*	*Fra*
EC1984	Feb	28	Sheffield	6	1
EC1984	Mar	28	Rouen	1	0
1987	June	11	Toulon	0	2
EC1988	April	13	Besancon	2	4
EC1988	April	27	Highbury	2	2
1988	June	12	Toulon	2	4
1990	May	23	Toulon	7	3
1991	June	3	Toulon	1	0
1992	May	28	Toulon	0	0
1993	June	15	Toulon	1	0
1994	May	31	Aubagne	0	3
1995	June	10	Toulon	0	2
1998	May	14	Toulon	1	1
1999	Feb	9	Derby	2	1
EC2005	Nov	11	Tottenham	1	1
EC2005	Nov	15	Nancy	1	2
2009	Mar	31	Nottingham	0	2
2014	Nov	17	Paris	2	3
2016	May	29	Toulon	2	1
2017	**Nov**	**14**	**Bonddoufle**	**2**	**3**
			v FYR MACEDONIA	*Eng*	*M*
EC2002	Oct	15	Reading	3	1
EC2003	Sept	5	Skopje	1	1
EC2009	Sept	4	Prilep	2	1
EC2009	Oct	9	Coventry	6	3
			v GEORGIA	*Eng*	*Geo*
EC1996	Nov	8	Batumi	1	0
EC1997	April	29	Charlton	0	0
2000	Aug	31	Middlesbrough	6	1
			v GERMANY	*Eng*	*Ger*
1991	Sept	10	Scunthorpe	2	1
EC2000	Oct	6	Derby	1	1
EC2001	Aug	31	Frieburg	2	1
2005	Mar	25	Hull	2	2
2005	Sept	6	Mainz	1	1
EC2006	Oct	6	Coventry	1	0
EC2006	Oct	10	Leverkusen	2	0
EC2009	June	22	Halmstad	1	1
EC2009	June	29	Malmo	0	4
2010	Nov	16	Wiesbaden	0	2
2015	Mar	30	Middlesbrough	3	2
2017	**Mar**	**24**	**Wiesbaden**	**0**	**1**
EC2017	**June**	**27**	**Tychy**	**2**	**2**
			v EAST GERMANY	*Eng*	*EG*
EC1980	April	16	Sheffield	1	2
EC1980	April	23	Jena	0	1
			v WEST GERMANY	*Eng*	*WG*
EC1982	Sept	21	Sheffield	3	1
EC1982	Oct	12	Bremen	2	3
1987	Sept	8	Ludenscheid	0	2
			v GREECE	*Eng*	*Gre*
EC1982	Nov	16	Piraeus	0	1
EC1983	Mar	29	Portsmouth	2	1
1989	Feb	7	Patras	0	1
EC1997	Nov	13	Heraklion	0	2
EC1997	Dec	17	Norwich	4	2
EC2001	June	5	Athens	1	3
EC2001	Oct	5	Ewood Park	2	1
EC2009	Sept	8	Tripoli	1	1
EC2010	Mar	3	Doncaster	1	2
			v GUINEA	*Eng*	*Gui*
2016	May	23	Toulon	7	1

v HUNGARY

				Eng	*Hun*
EC1981	June	5	Keszthely	2	1
EC1981	Nov	17	Nottingham	2	0
EC1983	April	26	Newcastle	1	0
EC1983	Oct	11	Nyiregyhaza	2	0
1990	Sept	11	Southampton	3	1
1992	May	12	Budapest	2	2
1999	April	27	Budapest	2	2

v ICELAND

				Eng	*Ice*
2011	Mar	28	Preston	1	2
EC2011	Oct	6	Reykjavik	3	0
EC2011	Nov	10	Colchester	5	0

v ISRAEL

				Eng	*Isr*
1985	Feb	27	Tel Aviv	2	1
2011	Sept	5	Barnsley	4	1
EC2013	June	11	Jerusalem	0	1

v ITALY

				Eng	*Italy*
EC1978	Mar	8	Manchester	2	1
EC1978	April	5	Rome	0	0
EC1984	April	18	Manchester	3	1
EC1984	May	2	Florence	0	1
EC1986	April	9	Pisa	0	2
EC1986	April	23	Swindon	1	1
EC1997	Feb	12	Bristol	1	0
EC1997	Oct	10	Rieti	1	0
EC2000	May	27	Bratislava	0	2
2000	Nov	14	Monza*	0	0
2002	Mar	26	Valley Parade	1	1
EC2002	May	20	Basle	1	2
2003	Feb	11	Pisa	0	1
2007	Mar	24	Wembley	3	3
EC2007	June	14	Arnhem	2	2
2011	Feb	8	Empoli	0	1
EC2013	June	5	Tel Aviv	0	1
EC2015	June	24	Olomouc	1	3
2016	**Nov**	**10**	**Southampton**	**3**	**2**

**Abandoned 11 mins; fog.*

v JAPAN

				Eng	*Jap*
2016	May	27	Toulon	1	0

v KAZAKHSTAN

EC2015	Oct	13	Coventry	3	0
EC2016	**Oct**	**6**	**Aktobe**	**1**	**0**

v LATVIA

Year	Month	Day	Venue	*Eng*	*Lat*
1995	April	25	Riga	1	0
1995	June	7	Burnley	4	0

v LITHUANIA

Year	Month	Day	Venue	*Eng*	*Lith*
EC2009	Nov	17	Vilnius	0	0
EC2010	Sept	7	Colchester	3	0
EC2013	Oct	15	Ipswich	5	0
EC2014	Sept	5	Zaliakalnis	1	0

v LUXEMBOURG

Year	Month	Day	Venue	*Eng*	*Lux*
EC1998	Oct	13	Greven Macher	5	0
EC1999	Sept	3	Reading	5	0

v MALAYSIA

Year	Month	Day	Venue	*Eng*	*Mal*
1995	June	8	Toulon	2	0

v MEXICO

Year	Month	Day	Venue	*Eng*	*Mex*
1988	June	5	Toulon	2	1
1991	May	29	Toulon	6	0
1992	May	25	Toulon	1	1
2001	May	24	Leicester	3	0

v MOLDOVA

Year	Month	Day	Venue	*Eng*	*Mol*
EC1996	Aug	31	Chisinau	2	0
EC1997	Sept	9	Wycombe	1	0
EC2006	Aug	15	Ipswich	2	2
EC2013	Sept	5	Reading	1	0
EC2014	Sept	9	Tiraspol	3	0

v MONTENEGRO

				Eng	*M*
EC2007	Sept	7	Podgorica	3	0
EC2007	Oct	12	Leicester	1	0

v MOROCCO

Year	Month	Day	Venue	*Eng*	*Mor*
1987	June	7	Toulon	2	0
1988	June	9	Toulon	1	0

v NETHERLANDS

Year	Month	Day	Venue	*Eng*	*N*
EC1993	April	27	Portsmouth	3	0
EC1993	Oct	12	Utrecht	1	1
2001	Aug	14	Reading	4	0
EC2001	Nov	9	Utrecht	2	2
EC2001	Nov	13	Derby	1	0

Year	Month	Day	Venue	*Eng*	*N*
2004	Feb	17	Hull	3	2
2005	Feb	8	Derby	1	2
2006	Nov	14	Alkmaar	1	0
EC2007	June	20	Heerenveen	1	1
2009	Aug	11	Groningen	0	0

v NORTHERN IRELAND

Year	Month	Day	Venue	*Eng*	*NI*
2012	Nov	13	Blackpool	2	0

v NORWAY

Year	Month	Day	Venue	*Eng*	*Nor*
EC1977	June	1	Bergen	2	1
EC1977	Sept	6	Brighton	6	0
1980	Sept	9	Southampton	3	0
1981	Sept	8	Drammen	0	0
EC1992	Oct	13	Peterborough	0	2
EC1993	June	1	Stavanger	1	1
1995	Oct	10	Stavanger	2	2
2006	Feb	28	Reading	3	1
2009	Mar	27	Sandefjord	5	0
2011	June	5	Southampton	2	0
EC2011	Oct	10	Drammen	2	1
EC2012	Sept	10	Chesterfield	1	0
EC2013	June	8	Petah Tikva	1	3
EC2015	Sept	7	Drammen	1	0
EC2016	**Sept**	**6**	**Colchester**	**6**	**1**

v PARAGUAY

Year	Month	Day	Venue	*Eng*	*Par*
2016	May	25	Toulon	4	0

v POLAND

Year	Month	Day	Venue	*Eng*	*Pol*
EC1982	Mar	17	Warsaw	2	1
EC1982	April	7	West Ham	2	2
EC1989	June	2	Plymouth	2	1
EC1989	Oct	10	Jastrzebie	3	1
EC1990	Oct	16	Tottenham	0	1
EC1991	Nov	12	Pila	1	2
EC1993	May	28	Zdroj	4	1
EC1993	Sept	7	Millwall	1	2
EC1996	Oct	8	Wolverhampton	0	0
EC1997	May	30	Katowice	1	1
EC1999	Mar	26	Southampton	5	0
EC1999	Sept	7	Plock	1	3
EC2004	Sept	7	Rybnik	3	1
EC2005	Oct	11	Hillsborough	4	1
2008	Mar	25	Wolverhampton	0	0
EC2017	**June**	**22**	**Kielce**	**3**	**0**

v PORTUGAL

Year	Month	Day	Venue	*Eng*	*Por*
1987	June	13	Toulon	0	0
1990	May	21	Toulon	0	1
1993	June	7	Toulon	2	0
1994	June	7	Toulon	2	0
EC1994	Sept	6	Leicester	0	0
1995	Sept	2	Lisbon	0	2
1996	May	30	Toulon	1	3
2000	Apr	16	Stoke	0	1
EC2002	May	22	Zurich	1	3
EC2003	Mar	28	Rio Major	2	4
EC2003	Sept	9	Everton	1	2
EC2008	Nov	20	Agueda	1	1
2008	Sept	5	Wembley	2	0
EC2009	Nov	14	Wembley	1	0
EC2010	Sept	3	Barcelos	1	0
2014	Nov	13	Burnley	3	1
EC2015	June	18	Uherske Hradiste	0	1
2016	May	19	Toulon	1	0

v REPUBLIC OF IRELAND

Year	Month	Day	Venue	*Eng*	*RoI*
1981	Feb	25	Liverpool	1	0
1985	Mar	25	Portsmouth	3	2
1989	June	9	Toulon	0	0
EC1990	Nov	13	Cork	3	0
EC1991	Mar	26	Brentford	3	0
1994	Nov	15	Newcastle	1	0
1995	Mar	27	Dublin	2	0
EC2007	Oct	16	Cork	3	0
EC2008	Feb	5	Southampton	3	0

v ROMANIA

				Eng	*Rom*
EC1980	Oct	14	Ploesti	0	4
EC1981	April	28	Swindon	3	0
EC1985	April	30	Brasov	0	0
EC1985	Sept	10	Ipswich	3	0
2007	Aug	21	Bristol	1	1
EC2010	Oct	8	Norwich	2	1
EC2010	Oct	12	Botosani	0	0
2013	Mar	21	Wycombe	3	0

			v RUSSIA	*Eng*	*Rus*
1994	May	30	Bandol	2	0
			v SAN MARINO	*Eng*	*SM*
EC1993	Feb	16	Luton	6	0
EC1993	Nov	17	San Marino	4	0
EC2013	Oct	10	San Marino	4	0
EC2013	Nov	19	Shrewsbury	9	0
			v SCOTLAND	*Eng*	*Sco*
1977	April	27	Sheffield	1	0
EC1980	Feb	12	Coventry	2	1
EC1980	Mar	4	Aberdeen	0	0
EC1982	April	19	Glasgow	1	0
EC1982	April	28	Manchester	1	1
EC1988	Feb	16	Aberdeen	1	0
EC1988	Mar	22	Nottingham	1	0
1993	June	13	Toulon	1	0
2013	Aug	13	Sheffield	6	0
			v SENEGAL	*Eng*	*Sen*
1989	June	7	Toulon	6	1
1991	May	27	Toulon	2	1
			v SERBIA	*Eng*	*Ser*
EC2007	June	17	Nijmegen	2	0
EC2012	Oct	12	Norwich	1	0
EC2012	Oct	16	Krusevac	1	0
			v SERBIA-MONTENEGRO	*Eng*	*S-M*
2003	June	2	Hull	3	2
			v SLOVAKIA	*Eng*	*Slo*
EC2002	June	1	Bratislava	0	2
EC2002	Oct	11	Trnava	4	0
EC2003	June	10	Sunderland	2	0
2007	June	5	Norwich	5	0
EC2017	**June**	**19**	**Kielce**	**2**	**1**
			v SLOVENIA	*Eng*	*Slo*
2000	Feb	12	Nova Gorica	1	0
2008	Aug	19	Hull	2	1
			v SOUTH AFRICA	*Eng*	*SA*
1998	May	16	Toulon	3	1
			v SPAIN	*Eng*	*Spa*
EC1984	May	17	Seville	1	0
EC1984	May	24	Sheffield	2	0
1987	Feb	18	Burgos	2	1
1992	Sept	8	Burgos	1	0
2001	Feb	27	Birmingham	0	4
2004	Nov	16	Alcala	0	1
2007	Feb	6	Derby	2	2
EC2009	June	18	Gothenburg	2	0
EC2011	June	12	Herning	1	1
			v SWEDEN	*Eng*	*Swe*
1979	June	9	Vasteras	2	1
1986	Sept	9	Ostersund	1	1
EC1988	Oct	18	Coventry	1	1
EC1989	Sept	5	Uppsala	0	1
EC1998	Sept	4	Sundvall	2	0
EC1999	June	4	Huddersfield	3	0
2004	Mar	30	Kristiansund	2	2
EC2009	June	26	Gothenburg	3	3
2013	Feb	5	Walsall	4	0
				Eng	*Swe*
EC2015	Jun	21	Olomouc	1	0
EC2017	**June**	**16**	**Kielce**	**0**	**0**
			v SWITZERLAND	*Eng*	*Swit*
EC1980	Nov	18	Ipswich	5	0
EC1981	May	31	Neuenburg	0	0
1988	May	28	Lausanne	1	1
1996	April	1	Swindon	0	0
1998	Mar	24	Brugglifeld	0	2
EC2002	May	17	Zurich	2	1
EC2006	Sept	6	Lucerne	3	2
EC2015	Nov	16	Brighton	3	1
EC2016	Mar	26	Thun	1	1
			v TURKEY	*Eng*	*Tur*
EC1984	Nov	13	Bursa	0	0
EC1985	Oct	15	Bristol	3	0
EC1987	April	28	Izmir	0	0
EC1987	Oct	13	Sheffield	1	1
EC1991	April	30	Izmir	2	2
1991	Oct	15	Reading	2	0
EC1992	Nov	17	Orient	0	1
EC1993	Mar	30	Izmir	0	0
EC2000	May	29	Bratislava	6	0
EC2003	April	1	Newcastle	1	1
EC2003	Oct	10	Istanbul	0	1
			v UKRAINE	*Eng*	*Uk*
2004	Aug	17	Middlesbrough	3	1
EC2011	June	15	Herning	0	0
			v USA	*Eng*	*USA*
1989	June	11	Toulon	0	2
1994	June	2	Toulon	3	0
2015	Sept	3	Preston	1	0
			v USSR	*Eng*	*USSR*
1987	June	9	Toulon	0	0
1988	June	7	Toulon	1	0
1990	May	25	Toulon	2	1
1991	May	31	Toulon	2	1
			v UZBEKISTAN	*Eng*	*Uzb*
2010	Aug	10	Bristol	2	0
			v WALES	*Eng*	*Wales*
1976	Dec	15	Wolverhampton	0	0
1979	Feb	6	Swansea	1	0
1990	Dec	5	Tranmere	0	0
EC2004	Oct	8	Blackburn	2	0
EC2005	Sept	2	Wrexham	4	0
2008	May	5	Wrexham	2	0
EC2008	Oct	10	Cardiff	3	2
EC2008	Oct	14	Villa Park	2	2
EC2013	Mar	5	Derby	1	0
EC2013	May	19	Swansea	3	1
			v YUGOSLAVIA	*Eng*	*Yugo*
EC1978	April	19	Novi Sad	1	2
EC1978	May	2	Manchester	1	1
EC1986	Nov	11	Peterborough	1	1
EC1987	Nov	10	Zemun	5	1
EC2000	Mar	29	Barcelona	3	0
2002	Sept	6	Bolton	1	1

ENGLAND C 2016–17

INTERNATIONAL CHALLENGE TROPHY

Tallin, Tuesday 15 November 2016

Estonia U23 (1) 1 *(Domov 9)*

England C (2) 2 *(Whitehouse 7, Lowe 13)*

England C: Hall; Arnold, Holland, Pinnock, Wishart, Gallagher, Woodyard, James, Whitehouse (Moore 90), Lowe (Alexander 86), Hardy (Turgott 68).

FRIENDLY

Solihull Moors, Sunday 28 May 2017

England C (1) 2 *(McQueen 34, 62)*

Panjab FA (0) 0

England C: Montgomery; Wood, Howe (Tunnicliffe 88), Lokko, Ferguson, Mafuta (Powell 65), Croasdale, Okenabirhie, McQueen (Ironside 82), Taylor (Carline 85), Alabi (Ferrier 73).

THE JACKSONS' TROPHY

St Helier, Tuesday 30 May 2017

Jersey FA (0) 1 *(Queree 90)*

FA XI (0) 1 *(Okenabirhie 61)*

Jersey FA: Van Der Vielt; Le Quesne, Weir C, O'Shea (Curtis 74), Andre, Queree, Weir M (Kilshaw 70), Miley, Russell (Lester 83), Trotte (Hinds 65), Cannon.

FA XI: Fitzsimons; Carline, Tunnicliffe, Lokko, Ferguson, Powell, Croasdale, Vince, Ferrier (Okenabirhie 60), Ironside (Alabi 76), McQueen (Taylor 56).

Jersey FA won 4-3 on penalties.

BRITISH AND IRISH UNDER-21 TEAMS 2016–17

▪ *Denotes player sent off.*

ENGLAND

UEFA UNDER-21 CHAMPIONSHIPS 2015–17

QUALIFYING GROUP 9

Tuesday, 6 September 2016

England (2) 6 *(Rashford 29, 65, 72 (pen), Chalobah 37, Loftus-Cheek 64, Baker 86)*

Norway (0) 1 *(Zahid 68)*

England: (4231) Gunn; Iorfa, Chambers, Hause, Targett; Ward-Prowse, Chalobah; Redmond (Gray 80), Loftus-Cheek (Watmore 80), Baker; Rashford (Akpom 84).

Thursday, 6 October 2016

Kazakhstan (0) 0

England (1) 1 *(Gray 6)*

England: (451) Woodman; Holgate, Chambers, Holding, Galloway; Ward-Prowse, Redmond, Loftus-Cheek (Watmore 73), Baker, Chalobah; Gray (Abraham 85).

Tuesday, 11 October 2016

England (2) 5 *(Swift 14, Abraham 18, 68, Onomah 49, Watmore 62)*

Bosnia-Herzegovina (0) 0

England: (4231) Walton; Iorfa, Stephens, Chalobah (Chambers 46), Galloway; Swift, Hayden; Watmore, Grealish (Redmond 74), Onomah; Abraham (Gray 74).

FRIENDLIES

Thursday, 10 November 2016

England (1) 3 *(Gray 6, Baker 60, Stephens 90)*

Italy (2) 2 *(Galloway 14 (og), Di Francesco 29)*

England: (433) Gunn; Hayden, Stephens, Chambers, Galloway; Chalobah, Ward-Prowse, Baker (Abraham 77); Gray (Watmore 72), Swift (Hughes 30), Redmond.

Monday, 14 November 2016

France (1) 3 *(Dembele 18, 64, Cyprien 83)*

England (1) 2 *(Watmore 9, Baker 81)*

England: (433) Mitchell; Iorfa, Holding (Redmond 82), Mawson, Hause; Chalobah (Hayden 82), Winks (Ward-Prowse 65), Baker; Grealish (Hughes 88), Abraham, Watmore.

Friday, 24 March 2017

Germany (1) 1 *(Amiri 23)*

England (0) 0

England: (442) Pickford; Holgate, Chilwell, Chalobah, Stephens; Mawson, Gray (Loftus-Cheek 58), Winks (Swift 72), Abraham; Baker, Murphy.

Monday, 27 March 2017

Denmark (0) 0

England (2) 4 *(Loftus-Cheek 10, 69, March 15, Woodrow 61)*

England: (4231) Gunn; Gomez, Holding, Hause, McQueen; Hughes, Swift; March (Gray 61), Loftus-Cheek, Murphy (Grealish 38); Woodrow (Abraham 74).

UEFA UNDER-21 CHAMPIONSHIPS 2015–17

FINALS IN POLAND – GROUP A

Friday, 16 June 2017

Sweden (0) 0

England (0) 0

England: (442) Pickford; Holgate, Mawson, Chambers, Chilwell; Ward-Prowse, Baker, Chalobah, Murphy (Gray 70); Redmond, Abraham.

Monday, 19 June 2017

Slovakia (1) 1 *(Chrien 23)*

England (0) 2 *(Mawson 50, Redmond 61)*

England: (4231) Pickford; Holgate (Murphy 46), Chambers, Mawson, Chilwell; Ward-Prowse, Chalobah; Swift (Gray 79), Baker, Redmond; Abraham (Woodrow 88).

Thursday, 22 June 2017

England (1) 3 *(Gray 6, Murphy 69, Baker 83 (pen))*

Poland (0) 0

England: (4231) Pickford; Holgate, Chambers, Mawson, Chilwell; Chalobah (Hughes 39), Baker; Ward-Prowse (Abraham 72), Swift, Redmond (Murphy 46); Gray.

SEMI-FINALS

Tuesday, 27 June 2017

England (1) 2 *(Gray 41, Abraham 50)*

Germany (1) 2 *(Selke 35, Platte 70)*

England: (442) Pickford; Holgate (Iorfa 106), Chambers, Mawson, Chilwell; Ward-Prowse, Hughes (Swift 86), Chalobah (Murphy 66), Gray (Redmond 73); Baker, Abraham.
aet; Germany won 4-3 on penalties.

SCOTLAND

UEFA UNDER-21 CHAMPIONSHIPS 2015–17

QUALIFYING GROUP 3

Friday, 2 September 2016

Scotland (0) 0

FYR Macedonia (1) 1 *(Markoski 18)*

Scotland: (442) Kelly; Smith (Nicholson 75), McGhee, Souttar, Kingsley; Christie, Gauld, Slater (McBurnie 58), Fraser (King 87); Henderson, Cummings.

Tuesday, 6 September 2016

Ukraine (1) 4 *(Blyznychenko 26, Besyedin 69, 77, Boryachuk 90 (pen))*

Scotland (0) 0

Scotland: (4411) Kelly; McGhee, Souttar▪, Hyam, Chalmers; King, Cadden, Henderson, Nicholson (Cummings 65); Gauld (O'Hara 83); McBurnie.

Wednesday, 5 October 2016

Iceland (0) 2 *(Thrandarson 47, Omarsson E 66)*

Scotland (0) 0

Scotland: (4231) Fulton; McGhee, Jules, Iacovitti, Cameron; Henderson, Docherty (Burt 63); Jones, Nesbitt (Sammut 69), McBurnie (Wighton 78); Hardie.

Tuesday, 11 October 2016

FYR Macedonia (2) 2 *(Markoski 18, Bardhi 22)*

Scotland (0) 0

Scotland: (4231) Fulton; Sheppard (McCrorie 58), Iacovitti, Jules, Cameron; Jones (Sammut 88), Henderson; Hardie (MacDonald 81), Wighton, Burt; McBurnie.

FRIENDLIES

Wednesday, 9 November 2016

Slovakia (1) 4 *(Rusnak 8, Iacovitti 57 (og), Ninaj 78, Balaj 83)*

Scotland (0) 0

Scotland: Fulton; Smith (Sheppard 71), Cameron (MacDonald 71), Souttar, Iacovitti, Jules (Sammut 67), Henderson (Quitongo 46), Cadden (Nesbitt 67), Jones, Brophy (Hardy 46), Docherty (Forrest 67).

Tuesday, 28 March 2017

Scotland (0) 0

Estonia (0) 0

Scotland: Fulton (Ruddy 46); McCart, Taylor, Smith, McGhee (Iacovitti 59), Jones (Thomson 74), Henderson, Mallan, Morgan (Wighton 81), McMullan (Thomas 59), McBurnie (Hardy 59).

WALES

UEFA UNDER-21 CHAMPIONSHIPS 2015–17

QUALIFYING GROUP 5

Friday, 2 September 2016

Wales (0) 0

Denmark (2) 4 *(Ingvartsen 21, Sisto 40, 49, Dolberg 83)*

Wales: (433) O'Brien; Jones, Lockyer, Smith, Evans; Sheehan (Poole 61), Harrison (James 51), O'Sullivan; Wilson, Hedges, Burns (Charles 71).

Tuesday, 6 September 2016

Wales (0) 1 *(Charles 90)*

Luxembourg (1) 1 *(Kerger 15)*

Wales: (442) O'Brien; Jones, Lockyer, Rodon, Evans; Wilson, Poole, Sheehan, Hedges (O'Sullivan 46); Burns (Harrison 83), James (Charles 76).

Tuesday, 11 October 2016

Armenia (0) 1 *(Simonyan 69)*

Wales (1) 3 *(Harrison 19, Shakhnazaryan 69 (og), O'Sullivan 83)*

Wales: (433) Crowe; Jones, Rodon, Smith, John; Wilson, Poole (Roberts 86), Williams C (James 65); Sheehan, O'Sullivan, Harrison (Charles 73).

NORTHERN IRELAND

UEFA UNDER-21 CHAMPIONSHIPS 2015–17

QUALIFYING GROUP 3

Friday, 2 September 2016

Northern Ireland (0) 0

Iceland (0) 1 *(Aegisson 87)*

Northern Ireland: (442) Mitchell; Dummigan, Donnelly, Johnson (Sendles-White 62), Nolan; Whyte, Gorman, Thompson, Cooper (Charles 65); Lavery (Rooney 78), Marshall.

Tuesday, 6 September 2016

FYR Macedonia (1) 2 *(Doherty 37 (og), 85)*

Northern Ireland (0) 0

Northern Ireland: (442) Mitchell; Dummigan, Conlan, Sendles-White, Gorman (Paul 87); Thompson, Sykes, Smyth (Cooper 46), Doherty; Lavery (Whyte 75), Charles.

Thursday, 6 October 2016

Ukraine (1) 1 *(Besyedin 15)*

Northern Ireland (1) 1 *(Smyth 12)*

Northern Ireland: (433) Mitchell; Nolan, Dummigan, Donnelly, Conlan; Thompson (McKnight 90), Quigley, Sykes; Kennedy B, Smyth (Kennedy M 78), Duffy (Charles 90).

Tuesday, 11 October 2016

Northern Ireland (0) 0

France (2) 3 *(Augustin 16, 42, Dembele 89)*

Northern Ireland: (4411) Mitchell; Dummigan, Donnelly, Quigley (Duffy 46), Conlan; McLaughlin, McDermott, Nolan, Kennedy B (Kennedy M 86); Sykes (Gorman 65); Smyth.

Thursday, 8 June 2017

Estonia (0) 1 *(Sappinen 50)*

Northern Ireland (0) 2 *(Parkhouse 74, Donnelly 90 (pen))*

Northern Ireland: (442) Mitchell; Lewis, Dummigan, Donnelly, Johnson; Gorman (Cooper 64), Thompson, McDermott, Dunwoody (Gordon 79); Parkhouse, Smyth (McGonigle 75).

REPUBLIC OF IRELAND

UEFA UNDER-21 CHAMPIONSHIPS 2015–17

QUALIFYING GROUP 2

Friday, 2 September 2016

Republic of Ireland (0) 2 *(Charsley 87, Maguire 90 (pen))*

Slovenia (0) 0

Republic of Ireland: (4231) Rogers; O'Connell, Rea, Hoban, O'Connor; Cullen, Browne (Dimaio 90); Charsley, Byrne, Shodipo; Duffus (Maguire 89).

Tuesday, 6 September 2016

Serbia (1) 3 *(Djurdjevic 12, 72 (pen), Lazic 65)*

Republic of Ireland (0) 2 *(O'Dowda 69, Maguire 81)*

Republic of Ireland: (442) Rogers; Rea, O'Connor, Hoban, Lenihan; Charsley, Cullen, Duffus (Maguire 72), Byrne (Dimaio 76); O'Dowda, Shodipo (Mulraney 66).

Friday, 7 October 2016

Republic of Ireland (0) 1 *(Duffus 49)*

Serbia (0) 3 *(Mihajlovic 64, Gacinovic 67, Lukic 88)*

Republic of Ireland: (4231) Bossin; O'Connell, Hoban, Lenihan, O'Connor; Cullen, Byrne (Mulraney 71); Shodipo (Kavanagh 79), Browne, Charsley; Duffus (Maguire 72).

Saturday, 25 March 2017

Republic of Ireland (0) 1 *(Shodipo 56)*

Kosovo (0) 0

Republic of Ireland: (442) O'Hara; Kane, Whelan, Sweeney, Donnellan; Manning (Grego-Cox 67), Dimaio, Charsley, Curtis; Cullen, Shodipo.

BRITISH UNDER-21 APPEARANCES 1976–2017

Bold type indicates players who made an international appearance in season 2016–17.

ENGLAND

Ablett, G. 1988 (Liverpool) 1
Abraham, K. O. T. 2017 (Tammy) (Chelsea) 10
Akpom, C. A. 2015 (Arsenal) 5
Adams, N. 1987 (Everton) 1
Adams, T. A. 1985 (Arsenal) 5
Addison, M. 2010 (Derby Co) 1
Afobe, B. T. 2012 (Arsenal) 2
Agbonlahor, G. 2007 (Aston Villa) 16
Albrighton, M. K. 2011 (Aston Villa) 8
Alli, B. J. (Dele) 2015 (Tottenham H) 2
Allen, B. 1992 (QPR) 8
Allen, C. 1980 (QPR, Crystal Palace) 3
Allen, C. A. 1995 (Oxford U) 2
Allen, M. 1987 (QPR) 2
Allen, P. 1985 (West Ham U, Tottenham H) 3
Allen, R. W. 1998 (Tottenham H) 3
Alnwick, B. R. 2008 (Tottenham H) 1
Ambrose, D. P. F. 2003 (Ipswich T, Newcastle U, Charlton Ath) 10
Ameobi, F. 2001 (Newcastle U) 19
Ameobi, S. 2012 (Newcastle U) 5
Amos, B. P. 2012 (Manchester U) 3
Anderson, V. A. 1978 (Nottingham F) 1
Anderton, D. R. 1993 (Tottenham H) 12
Andrews, I. 1987 (Leicester C) 1
Ardley, N. C. 1993 (Wimbledon) 10
Ashcroft, L. 1992 (Preston NE) 1
Ashton, D. 2004 (Crewe Alex, Norwich C) 9
Atherton, P. 1992 (Coventry C) 1
Atkinson, B. 1991 (Sunderland) 6
Awford, A. T. 1993 (Portsmouth) 9

Bailey, G. R. 1979 (Manchester U) 14
Baines, L. J. 2005 (Wigan Ath) 16
Baker, G. E. 1981 (Southampton) 2
Baker, L. R. 2015 (Chelsea) 17
Baker, N. L. 2011 (Aston Villa) 3
Ball, M. J. 1999 (Everton) 7
Bamford, P. J. 2013 (Chelsea) 2
Bannister, G. 1982 (Sheffield W) 1
Barker, S. 1985 (Blackburn R) 4
Barkley, R. 2012 (Everton) 5
Barmby, N. J. 1994 (Tottenham H, Everton) 4
Barnes, J. 1983 (Watford) 2
Barnes, P. S. 1977 (Manchester C) 9
Barrett, E. D. 1990 (Oldham Ath) 4
Barry, G. 1999 (Aston Villa) 27
Barton, J. 2004 (Manchester C) 2
Bart-Williams, C. G. 1993 (Sheffield W) 16
Batty, D. 1988 (Leeds U) 7
Bazeley, D. S. 1992 (Watford) 1
Beagrie, P. 1988 (Sheffield U) 2
Beardsmore, R. 1989 (Manchester U) 5
Beattie, J. S. 1999 (Southampton) 5
Beckham, D. R. J. 1995 (Manchester U) 9
Berahino, S. 2013 (WBA) 11
Bennett, J. 2011 (Middlesbrough) 3
Bennett, R. 2012 (Norwich C) 2
Bent, D. A. 2003 (Ipswich T, Charlton Ath) 14
Bent, M. N. 1998 (Crystal Palace) 2
Bentley, D. M. 2004 (Arsenal, Blackburn R) 8
Beeston, C 1988 (Stoke C) 1
Benjamin, T. J. 2001 (Leicester C) 1
Bertrand, R. 2009 (Chelsea) 16
Bertschin, K. E. 1977 (Birmingham C) 3
Bettinelli, M. 2015 (Fulham) 1
Birtles, G. 1980 (Nottingham F) 2
Blackett, T. N. 2014 (Manchester U) 1
Blackstock, D. A. 2008 (QPR) 2
Blackwell, D. R. 1991 (Wimbledon) 6
Blake, M. A. 1990 (Aston Villa) 8
Blissett, L. L. 1979 (Watford) 4
Bond, J. H. 2013 (Watford) 5
Booth, A. D. 1995 (Huddersfield T) 3
Bothroyd, J. 2001 (Coventry C) 1
Bowyer, L. D. 1996 (Charlton Ath, Leeds U) 13
Bracewell, P. 1983 (Stoke C) 13
Bradbury, L. M. 1997 (Portsmouth, Manchester C) 3
Bramble, T. M. 2001 (Ipswich T, Newcastle U) 10
Branch, P. M. 1997 (Everton) 1
Bradshaw, P. W. 1977 (Wolverhampton W) 4
Breacker, T. 1986 (Luton T) 2
Brennan, M. 1987 (Ipswich T) 5
Bridge, W. M. 1999 (Southampton) 8
Bridges, M. 1997 (Sunderland, Leeds U) 3
Briggs, M. 2012 (Fulham) 2
Brightwell, I. 1989 (Manchester C) 4
Briscoe, L. S. 1996 (Sheffield W) 5
Brock, K. 1984 (Oxford U) 4
Broomes, M. C. 1997 (Blackburn R) 2
Brown, M. R. 1996 (Manchester C) 4
Brown, W. M. 1999 (Manchester U) 8
Bull, S. G. 1989 (Wolverhampton W) 5
Bullock, M. J. 1998 (Barnsley) 1
Burrows, D. 1989 (WBA, Liverpool) 7
Butcher, T. I. 1979 (Ipswich T) 7
Butland, J. 2012 (Birmingham C, Stoke C) 28
Butt, N. 1995 (Manchester U) 7
Butters, G. 1989 (Tottenham H) 3
Butterworth, I. 1985 (Coventry C, Nottingham F) 8
Bywater, S. 2001 (West Ham U) 6

Cadamarteri, D. L. 1999 (Everton) 3
Caesar, G. 1987 (Arsenal) 3
Cahill, G. J. 2007 (Aston Villa) 3
Callaghan, N. 1983 (Watford) 9
Camp, L. M. J. 2005 (Derby Co) 5
Campbell, A. P. 2000 (Middlesbrough) 4
Campbell, F. L. 2008 (Manchester U) 14
Campbell, K. J. 1991 (Arsenal) 4
Campbell, S. 1994 (Tottenham) 11
Carbon, M. P. 1996 (Derby Co) 4
Carr, C. 1985 (Fulham) 1
Carr, F. 1987 (Nottingham F) 9
Carragher, J. L. 1997 (Liverpool) 27
Carroll, A. T. 2010 (Newcastle U) 5
Carroll, T. J. 2013 (Tottenham H) 17
Carlisle, C. J. 2001 (QPR) 3
Carrick, M. 2001 (West Ham U) 14
Carson, S. P. 2004 (Leeds U, Liverpool) 29
Casper, C. M. 1995 (Manchester U) 1
Caton, T. 1982 (Manchester C) 14
Cattermole, L. B. 2008 (Middlesbrough, Wigan Ath, Sunderland) 16
Caulker, S. R. 2011 (Tottenham H) 10
Chadwick, L. H. 2000 (Manchester U) 13
Challis, T. M. 1996 (QPR) 2
Chalobah, N. N. 2012 (Chelsea) 40
Chamberlain, M. 1983 (Stoke C) 4
Chambers, C. 2015 (Arsenal) 22
Chaplow, R. D. 2004 (Burnley) 1
Chapman, L. 1981 (Stoke C) 1
Charles, G. A. 1991 (Nottingham F) 4
Chettle, S. 1988 (Nottingham F) 12
Chilwell, B. J. 2016 (Leicester C) 7
Chopra, R. M. 2004 (Newcastle U) 1
Clark, L. R. 1992 (Newcastle U) 11
Clarke, P. M. 2003 (Everton) 8
Christie, M. N. 2001 (Derby Co) 11
Clegg, M. J. 1998 (Manchester U) 2
Clemence, S. N. 1999 (Tottenham H) 1
Cleverley, T. W. 2010 (Manchester U) 16
Clough, N. H. 1986 (Nottingham F) 15
Clyne, N. E. 2012 (Crystal Palace) 8
Cole, A. 2001 (Arsenal) 4
Cole, A. A. 1992 (Arsenal, Bristol C, Newcastle U) 8
Cole, C. 2003 (Chelsea) 19
Cole, J. J. 2000 (West Ham U) 8
Coney, D. 1985 (Fulham) 4
Connor, T. 1987 (Brighton & HA) 1

Cooke, R. 1986 (Tottenham H) 1
Cooke, T. J. 1996 (Manchester U) 4
Cooper, C. T. 1988 (Middlesbrough) 8
Cork, J. F. P. 2009 (Chelsea) 13
Corrigan, J. T. 1978 (Manchester C) 3
Cort, C. E. R. 1999 (Wimbledon) 12
Cottee, A. R. 1985 (West Ham U) 8
Couzens, A. J. 1995 (Leeds U) 3
Cowans, G. S. 1979 (Aston Villa) 5
Cox, N. J. 1993 (Aston Villa) 6
Cranie, M. J. 2008 (Portsmouth) 16
Cranson, I. 1985 (Ipswich T) 5
Cresswell, R. P. W. 1999 (York C, Sheffield W) 4
Croft, G. 1995 (Grimsby T) 4
Crooks, G. 1980 (Stoke C) 4
Crossley, M. G. 1990 (Nottingham F) 3
Crouch, P. J. 2002 (Portsmouth, Aston Villa) 5
Cundy, J. V. 1991 (Chelsea) 3
Cunningham, L. 1977 (WBA) 6
Curbishley, L. C. 1981 (Birmingham C) 1
Curtis, J. C. K. 1998 (Manchester U) 16

Daniel, P. W. 1977 (Hull C) 7
Dann, S. 2008 (Coventry C) 2
Davenport, C. R. P. 2005 (Tottenham H) 8
Davies, A. J. 2004 (Middlesbrough) 1
Davies, C. E. 2006 (WBA) 3
Davies, K. C. 1998 (Southampton, Blackburn R, Southampton) 3
Davis, K. G. 1995 (Luton T) 3
Davis, P. 1982 (Arsenal) 11
Davis, S. 2001 (Fulham) 11
Dawson, C. 2012 (WBA) 15
Dawson, M. R. 2003 (Nottingham F, Tottenham H) 13
Day, C. N. 1996 (Tottenham H, Crystal Palace) 6
D'Avray, M. 1984 (Ipswich T) 2
Deehan, J. M. 1977 (Aston Villa) 7
Defoe, J. C. 2001 (West Ham U) 23
Delfouneso, N. 2010 (Aston Villa) 17
Delph, F. 2009 (Leeds U, Aston Villa) 4
Dennis, M. E. 1980 (Birmingham C) 3
Derbyshire, M. A. 2007 (Blackburn R) 14
Dichio, D. S. E. 1996 (QPR) 1
Dickens, A. 1985 (West Ham U) 1
Dicks, J. 1988 (West Ham U) 4
Dier, E. J. E. 2013 (Sporting Lisbon, Tottenham H) 9
Digby, F. 1987 (Swindon T) 5
Dillon, K. P. 1981 (Birmingham C) 1
Dixon, K. M. 1985 (Chelsea) 1
Dobson, A. 1989 (Coventry C) 4
Dodd, J. R. 1991 (Southampton) 8
Donowa, L. 1985 (Norwich C) 3
Dorigo, A. R. 1987 (Aston Villa) 11
Downing, S. 2004 (Middlesbrough) 8
Dozzell, J. 1987 (Ipswich T) 9
Draper, M. A. 1991 (Notts Co) 3
Driver, A. 2009 (Hearts) 1
Duberry, M. W. 1997 (Chelsea) 5
Dunn, D. J. I. 1999 (Blackburn R) 20
Duxbury, M. 1981 (Manchester U) 7
Dyer, B. A. 1994 (Crystal Palace) 10
Dyer, K. C. 1998 (Ipswich T, Newcastle U) 11
Dyson, P. I. 1981 (Coventry C) 4

Eadie, D. M. 1994 (Norwich C) 7
Ebanks-Blake, S. 2009 (Wolverhampton W) 1
Ebbrell, J. 1989 (Everton) 14
Edghill, R. A. 1994 (Manchester C) 3
Ehiogu, U. 1992 (Aston Villa) 15
Elliott, P. 1985 (Luton T) 3
Elliott, R. J. 1996 (Newcastle U) 2
Elliott, S. W. 1998 (Derby Co) 3
Etherington, N, 2002 (Tottenham H) 3
Euell, J. J. 1998 (Wimbledon) 6
Evans, R. 2003 (Chelsea) 2

Fairclough, C. 1985 (Nottingham F, Tottenham H) 7
Fairclough, D. 1977 (Liverpool) 1
Fashanu, J. 1980 (Norwich C, Nottingham F) 11
Fear, P. 1994 (Wimbledon) 3
Fenton, G. A. 1995 (Aston Villa) 1
Fenwick, T. W. 1981 (Crystal Palace, QPR) 11
Ferdinand, A. J. 2005 (West Ham U) 17
Ferdinand, R. G. 1997 (West Ham U) 5
Fereday, W. 1985 (QPR) 5
Fielding, F. D. 2009 (Blackburn R) 12
Flanagan, J. 2012 (Liverpool) 3
Flitcroft, G. W. 1993 (Manchester C) 10
Flowers, T. D. 1987 (Southampton) 3
Ford, M. 1996 (Leeds U) 2
Forster, N. M. 1995 (Brentford) 4
Forsyth, M. 1988 (Derby Co) 1
Forster-Caskey, J. D. 2014 (Brighton & HA) 14
Foster, S. 1980 (Brighton & HA) 1
Fowler, R. B. 1994 (Liverpool) 8
Fox, D. J. 2008 (Coventry C) 1
Froggatt, S. J. 1993 (Aston Villa) 2
Futcher, P. 1977 (Luton T, Manchester C) 11

Gabbiadini, M. 1989 (Sunderland) 2
Gale, A. 1982 (Fulham) 1
Gallen, K. A. 1995 (QPR) 4
Galloway, B. J. 2017 (Everton) 3
Garbutt, L. S. 2014 (Everton) 11
Gardner, A. 2002 (Tottenham H) 1
Gardner, C. 2008 (Aston Villa) 14
Gardner, G. 2012 (Aston Villa) 5
Gascoigne, P. J. 1987 (Newcastle U) 13
Gayle, H. 1984 (Birmingham C) 3
Gernon, T. 1983 (Ipswich T) 1
Gerrard, P. W. 1993 (Oldham Ath) 18
Gerrard, S. G. 2000 (Liverpool) 4
Gibbs, K. J. R. 2009 (Arsenal) 15
Gibbs, N. 1987 (Watford) 5
Gibson, B. J. 2014 (Middlesbrough) 10
Gibson, C. 1982 (Aston Villa) 1
Gilbert, W. A. 1979 (Crystal Palace) 11
Goddard, P. 1981 (West Ham U) 8
Gomez, J. D. 2015 (Liverpool) 4
Gordon, D. 1987 (Norwich C) 4
Gordon, D. D. 1994 (Crystal Palace) 13
Gosling, D. 2010 (Everton, Newcastle U) 3
Grant, A. J. 1996 (Everton) 1
Grant, L. A. 2003 (Derby Co) 4
Granville, D. P. 1997 (Chelsea) 3
Gray, A. 1988 (Aston Villa) 2
Gray, D. R. 2016 (Leicester C) 11
Grealish, J. 2016 (Aston Villa) 7
Greening, J. 1999 (Manchester U, Middlesbrough) 18
Griffin, A. 1999 (Newcastle U) 3
Grimes, M. J. 2016 (Swansea C) 4
Gunn, A. 2015 (Manchester C) 6
Guppy, S. A. 1998 (Leicester C) 1

Haigh, P. 1977 (Hull C) 1
Hall, M. T. J. 1997 (Coventry C) 8
Hall, R. A. 1992 (Southampton) 11
Hamilton, D. V. 1997 (Newcastle U) 1
Hammill, A. 2010 (Wolverhampton W) 1
Harding, D. A. 2005 (Brighton & HA) 4
Hardyman, P. 1985 (Portsmouth) 2
Hargreaves, O. 2001 (Bayern Munich) 3
Harley, J. 2000 (Chelsea) 3
Hart, C. 2007 (Manchester C) 21
Hateley, M. 1982 (Coventry C, Portsmouth) 10
Hause, K. P. D. 2015 (Wolverhampton W) 10
Hayden, I. 2017 (Newcastle U) 3
Hayes, M. 1987 (Arsenal) 3
Hazell, R. J. 1979 (Wolverhampton W) 1
Heaney, N. A. 1992 (Arsenal) 6
Heath, A. 1981 (Stoke C, Everton) 8
Heaton, T. D. 2008 (Manchester U) 3
Henderson, J. B. 2011 (Sunderland, Liverpool) 27
Hendon, I. M. 1992 (Tottenham H) 7
Hendrie, L. A. 1996 (Aston Villa) 13
Hesford, I. 1981 (Blackpool) 7
Heskey, E. W. I. 1997 (Leicester C, Liverpool) 16
Hilaire, V. 1980 (Crystal Palace) 9
Hill, D. R. L. 1995 (Tottenham H) 4
Hillier, D. 1991 (Arsenal) 1
Hinchcliffe, A. 1989 (Manchester C) 1
Hines, Z. 2010 (West Ham U) 2
Hinshelwood, P. A. 1978 (Crystal Palace) 2
Hirst, D. E. 1988 (Sheffield W) 7

Hislop, N. S. 1998 (Newcastle U) 1
Hoddle, G. 1977 (Tottenham H) 12
Hodge, S. B. 1983 (Nottingham F, Aston Villa) 8
Hodgson, D. J. 1981 (Middlesbrough) 6
Holding, R. S. 2016 (Bolton W, Arsenal) 5
Holdsworth, D. 1989 (Watford) 1
Holgate, M. 2017 (Everton) 6
Holland, C. J. 1995 (Newcastle U) 10
Holland, P. 1995 (Mansfield T) 4
Holloway, D. 1998 (Sunderland) 1
Horne, B. 1989 (Millwall) 5
Howe, E. J. F. 1998 (Bournemouth) 2
Howson, J. M. 2011 (Leeds U) 1
Hoyte, J. R. 2004 (Arsenal) 18
Hucker, P. 1984 (QPR) 2
Huckerby, D. 1997 (Coventry C) 4
Huddlestone, T. A. 2005 (Derby Co, Tottenham H) 33
Hughes, S. J. 1997 (Arsenal) 8
Hughes, W. J. 2012 (Derby Co) 22
Humphreys, R. J. 1997 (Sheffield W) 3
Hunt, N. B. 2004 (Bolton W) 10

Ibe, J. A. F. 2015 (Liverpool) 4
Impey, A. R. 1993 (QPR) 1
Ince, P. E. C. 1989 (West Ham U) 2
Ince, T. C. 2012 (Blackpool, Hull C) 18
Ings, D. W. J. 2013 (Burnley) 13
Iorfa, D. 2016 (Wolverhampton W) 13

Jackson, M. A. 1992 (Everton) 10
Jagielka, P. N. 2003 (Sheffield U) 6
James, D. B. 1991 (Watford) 10
James, J. C. 1990 (Luton T) 2
Jansen, M. B. 1999 (Crystal Palace, Blackburn R) 6
Jeffers, F. 2000 (Everton, Arsenal) 16
Jemson, N. B. 1991 (Nottingham F) 1
Jenas, J. A. 2002 (Newcastle U) 9
Jenkinson, C. D. 2013 (Arsenal) 14
Jerome, C. 2006 (Cardiff C, Birmingham C) 10
Joachim, J. K. 1994 (Leicester C) 9
Johnson, A. 2008 (Middlesbrough) 19
Johnson, G. M. C. 2003 (West Ham U, Chelsea) 14
Johnson, M. 2008 (Manchester C) 2
Johnson, S. A. M. 1999 (Crewe Alex, Derby Co, Leeds U) 15
Johnson, T. 1991 (Notts Co, Derby Co) 7
Johnston, C. P. 1981 (Middlesbrough) 2
Jones, D. R. 1977 (Everton) 1
Jones, C. H. 1978 (Tottenham H) 1
Jones, D. F. L. 2004 (Manchester U) 1
Jones, P. A. 2011 (Blackburn R) 9
Jones, R. 1993 (Liverpool) 2

Kane, H. E. 2013 (Tottenham H) 14
Keane, M. V. 2013 (Manchester U, Burnley) 16
Keane, W. D. 2012 (Manchester U) 3
Keegan, G. A. 1977 (Manchester C) 1
Kelly, M. R. 2011 (Liverpool) 8
Kenny, W. 1993 (Everton) 1
Keown, M. R. 1987 (Aston Villa) 8
Kerslake, D. 1986 (QPR) 1
Kightly, M. J. 2008 (Wolverhampton W) 7
Kilcline, B. 1983 (Notts C) 2
Kilgallon, M. 2004 (Leeds U) 5
King, A. E. 1977 (Everton) 2
King, L. B. 2000 (Tottenham H) 12
Kirkland, C. E. 2001 (Coventry C, Liverpool) 8
Kitson, P. 1991 (Leicester C, Derby Co) 7
Knight, A. 1983 (Portsmouth) 2
Knight, I. 1987 (Sheffield W) 2
Knight, Z. 2002 (Fulham) 4
Konchesky, P. M. 2002 (Charlton Ath) 15
Kozluk, R. 1998 (Derby Co) 2

Lake, P. 1989 (Manchester C) 5
Lallana, A. D. 2009 (Southampton) 1
Lampard, F. J. 1998 (West Ham U) 19
Langley, T. W. 1978 (Chelsea) 1
Lansbury, H. G. 2010 (Arsenal, Nottingham F) 16
Lascellas, J. 2014 (Newcastle U) 2
Leadbitter, G. 2008 (Sunderland) 3
Lee, D. J. 1990 (Chelsea) 10
Lee, R. M. 1986 (Charlton Ath) 2
Lee, S. 1981 (Liverpool) 6
Lees, T. J. 2012 (Leeds U) 6
Lennon, A. J. 2006 (Tottenham H) 5
Le Saux, G. P. 1990 (Chelsea) 4
Lescott, J. P. 2003 (Wolverhampton W) 2
Lewis, J. P. 2008 (Peterborough U) 5
Lingard, J. E. 2013 (Manchester U) 11
Lita, L. H. 2005 (Bristol C, Reading) 9
Loach, S. J. 2009 (Watford) 14
Loftus-Cheek, R. I. 2015 (Chelsea) 17
Lowe, D. 1988 (Ipswich T) 2
Lowe, J. J. 2012 (Blackburn R) 11
Lukic, J. 1981 (Leeds U) 7
Lund, G. 1985 (Grimsby T) 3

McCall, S. H. 1981 (Ipswich T) 6
McCarthy, A. S. 2011 (Reading) 3
McDonald, N. 1987 (Newcastle U) 5
McEachran, J. M. 2011 (Chelsea) 13
McEveley, J. 2003 (Blackburn R) 1
McGrath, L. 1986 (Coventry C) 1
MacKenzie, S. 1982 (WBA) 3
McLeary, A. 1988 (Millwall) 1
McLeod, I. M. 2006 (Milton Keynes D) 1
McMahon, S. 1981 (Everton, Aston Villa) 6
McManaman, S. 1991 (Liverpool) 7
McQueen, S. J. 2017 (Southampton) 1
Mabbutt, G. 1982 (Bristol R, Tottenham H) 7
Maguire, J. H. 2012 (Sheffield U) 1
Makin, C. 1994 (Oldham Ath) 5
Mancienne, M. I. 2008 (Chelsea) 30
March, S. B. 2015 (Brighton & HA) 3
Marney, D. E. 2005 (Tottenham H) 1
Marriott, A. 1992 (Nottingham F) 1
Marsh, S. T. 1998 (Oxford U) 1
Marshall, A. J. 1995 (Norwich C) 4
Marshall, B. 2012 (Leicester C) 2
Marshall, L. K. 1999 (Norwich C) 1
Martin, L. 1989 (Manchester U) 2
Martyn, A. N. 1988 (Bristol R) 11
Matteo, D. 1994 (Liverpool) 4
Mattock, J. W. 2008 (Leicester C) 5
Matthew, D. 1990 (Chelsea) 9
Mawson, A. R. J. 2017 (Swansea C) 6
May, A. 1986 (Manchester C) 1
Mee, B. 2011 (Manchester C) 2
Merson, P. C. 1989 (Arsenal) 4
Middleton, J. 1977 (Nottingham F, Derby Co) 3
Miller, A. 1988 (Arsenal) 4
Mills, D. J. 1999 (Charlton Ath, Leeds U) 14
Mills, G. R. 1981 (Nottingham F) 2
Milner, J. P. 2004 (Leeds U, Newcastle U, Aston Villa) 46
Mimms, R. 1985 (Rotherham U, Everton) 3
Minto, S. C. 1991 (Charlton Ath) 6
Mitchell, J. 2017 (Derby Co) 1
Moore, I. 1996 (Tranmere R, Nottingham F) 7
Moore, L. 2012 (Leicester C) 10
Moore, L. I. 2006 (Aston Villa) 5
Moran, S. 1982 (Southampton) 2
Morgan, S. 1987 (Leicester C) 2
Morris, J. 1997 (Chelsea) 7
Morrison, R. R. 2013 (West Ham U) 4
Mortimer, P. 1989 (Charlton Ath) 2
Moses, A. P. 1997 (Barnsley) 2
Moses, R. M. 1981 (WBA, Manchester U) 8
Moses, V. 2011 (Wigan Ath) 1
Mountfield, D. 1984 (Everton) 1
Muamba, F. N. 2008 (Birmingham C, Bolton W) 33
Muggleton, C. D. 1990 (Leicester C) 1
Mullins, H. I. 1999 (Crystal Palace) 3
Murphy, D. B. 1998 (Liverpool) 4
Murphy, Jacob K. 2017 (Norwich C) 6
Murray, P. 1997 (QPR) 4
Murray, M. W. 2003 (Wolverhampton W) 5
Mutch, A. 1989 (Wolverhampton W) 1
Mutch, J. J. E. S. 2011 (Birmingham C) 1
Myers. A. 1995 (Chelsea) 4

Naughton, K. 2009 (Sheffield U, Tottenham H) 9
Naylor, L. M. 2000 (Wolverhampton W) 3

Nethercott, S. H. 1994 (Tottenham H) 8
Neville, P. J. 1995 (Manchester U) 7
Newell, M. 1986 (Luton T) 4
Newton, A. L. 2001 (West Ham U) 1
Newton, E. J. I. 1993 (Chelsea) 2
Newton, S. O. 1997 (Charlton Ath) 3
Nicholls, A. 1994 (Plymouth Arg) 1
Noble, M. J. 2007 (West Ham U) 20
Nolan, K. A. J. 2003 (Bolton W) 1
Nugent, D. J. 2006 (Preston NE) 14

Oakes, M. C. 1994 (Aston Villa) 6
Oakes, S. J. 1993 (Luton T) 1
Oakley, M. 1997 (Southampton) 4
O'Brien, A. J. 1999 (Bradford C) 1
O'Connor, J. 1996 (Everton) 3
O'Hara, J. D. 2008 (Tottenham H) 7
Oldfield, D. 1989 (Luton T) 1
Olney, I. A. 1990 (Aston Villa) 10
O'Neil, G. P. 2005 (Portsmouth) 9
Onomah, J. O. P. 2017 (Tottenham H) 1
Onuoha, C. 2006 (Manchester C) 21
Ord, R. J. 1991 (Sunderland) 3
Osman, R. C. 1979 (Ipswich T) 7
Owen, G. A. 1977 (Manchester C, WBA) 22
Owen, M. J. 1998 (Liverpool) 1
Oxlade-Chamberlain, A. M. D. 2011 (Southampton, Arsenal) 8

Painter, I. 1986 (Stoke C) 1
Palmer, C. L. 1989 (Sheffield W) 4
Parker, G. 1986 (Hull C, Nottingham F) 6
Parker, P. A. 1985 (Fulham) 8
Parker, S. M. 2001 (Charlton Ath) 12
Parkes, P. B. F. 1979 (QPR) 1
Parkin, S. 1987 (Stoke C) 5
Palmer, K. R. 2016 (Chelsea) 4
Parlour, R. 1992 (Arsenal) 12
Parnaby, S. 2003 (Middlesbrough) 4
Peach, D. S. 1977 (Southampton) 6
Peake, A. 1982 (Leicester C) 1
Pearce, I. A. 1995 (Blackburn R) 3
Pearce, S. 1987 (Nottingham F) 1
Pennant, J. 2001 (Arsenal) 24
Pickering N. 1983 (Sunderland, Coventry C) 15
Pickford, J. L. 2015 (Sunderland) 14
Platt, D. 1988 (Aston Villa) 3
Plummer, C. S. 1996 (QPR) 5
Pollock, J. 1995 (Middlesbrough) 3
Porter, G. 1987 (Watford) 12
Potter, G. S. 1997 (Southampton) 1
Powell, N. E. 2012 (Manchester U) 2
Pressman, K. 1989 (Sheffield W) 1
Pritchard, A. D. 2014 (Tottenham H) 9
Proctor, M. 1981 (Middlesbrough, Nottingham F) 4
Prutton, D. T. 2001 (Nottingham F, Southampton) 25
Purse, D. J. 1998 (Birmingham C) 2

Quashie, N. F. 1997 (QPR) 4
Quinn, W. R. 1998 (Sheffield U) 2

Ramage, C. D. 1991 (Derby Co) 3
Ranson, R. 1980 (Manchester C) 10
Rashford, M. 2017 (Manchester U) 1
Redknapp, J. F. 1993 (Liverpool) 19
Redmond, N. D. J. 2013 (Birmingham C, Norwich C, Southampton) 38
Redmond, S. 1988 (Manchester C) 14
Reeves, K. P. 1978 (Norwich C, Manchester C) 10
Regis, C. 1979 (WBA) 6
Reid, N. S. 1981 (Manchester C) 6
Reid, P. 1977 (Bolton W) 6
Reo-Coker, N. S. A. 2004 (Wimbledon, West Ham U) 23
Richards, D. I. 1995 (Wolverhampton W) 4
Richards, J. P. 1977 (Wolverhampton W) 2
Richards, M. 2007 (Manchester C) 15
Richards, M. L. 2005 (Ipswich T) 1
Richardson, K. E. 2005 (Manchester U) 12
Rideout, P. 1985 (Aston Villa, Bari) 5
Ridgewell, L. M. 2004 (Aston Villa) 8
Riggott, C. M. 2001 (Derby Co) 8
Ripley, S. E. 1988 (Middlesbrough) 8
Ritchie, A. 1982 (Brighton & HA) 1
Rix, G. 1978 (Arsenal) 7
Roberts, A. J. 1995 (Millwall, Crystal Palace) 5
Roberts, B. J. 1997 (Middlesbrough) 1
Robins, M. G. 1990 (Manchester U) 6
Robinson, J. 2012 (Liverpool, QPR) 10
Robinson, P. P. 1999 (Watford) 3
Robinson, P. W. 2000 (Leeds U) 11
Robson, B. 1979 (WBA) 7
Robson, S. 1984 (Arsenal, West Ham U) 8
Rocastle, D. 1987 (Arsenal) 14
Roche, L. P. 2001 (Manchester U) 1
Rodger, G. 1987 (Coventry C) 4
Rodriguez, J. E. 2011 (Burnley) 1
Rodwell, J. 2009 (Everton) 21
Rogers, A. 1998 (Nottingham F) 3
Rosario, R. 1987 (Norwich C) 4
Rose, D. L. 2009 (Tottenham H) 29
Rose, M. 1997 (Arsenal) 2
Rosenior, L. J. 2005 (Fulham) 7
Routledge, W. 2005 (Crystal Palace, Tottenham H) 12
Rowell, G. 1977 (Sunderland) 1
Rudd, D. T. 2013 (Norwich C) 1
Ruddock, N. 1989 (Southampton) 4
Rufus, R. R. 1996 (Charlton Ath) 6
Ryan, J. 1983 (Oldham Ath) 1
Ryder, S. H. 1995 (Walsall) 3

Samuel, J. 2002 (Aston Villa) 7
Samways, V. 1988 (Tottenham H) 5
Sansom, K. G. 1979 (Crystal Palace) 8
Scimeca, R. 1996 (Aston Villa) 9
Scowcroft, J. B. 1997 (Ipswich T) 5
Seaman, D. A. 1985 (Birmingham C) 10
Sears, F. D. 2010 (West Ham U) 3
Sedgley, S. 1987 (Coventry C, Tottenham H) 11
Sellars, S. 1988 (Blackburn R) 3
Selley, I. 1994 (Arsenal) 3
Serrant, C. 1998 (Oldham Ath) 2
Sharpe, L. S. 1989 (Manchester U) 8
Shaw, L. P. H. 2013 (Southampton, Manchester U) 5
Shaw, G. R. 1981 (Aston Villa) 7
Shawcross, R. J. 2008 (Stoke C) 2
Shearer, A. 1991 (Southampton) 11
Shelton, G. 1985 (Sheffield W) 1
Shelvey, J. 2012 (Liverpool, Swansea C) 13
Sheringham, E. P. 1988 (Millwall) 1
Sheron, M. N. 1992 (Manchester C) 16
Sherwood, T. A. 1990 (Norwich C) 4
Shipperley, N. J. 1994 (Chelsea, Southampton) 7
Sidwell, S. J. 2003 (Reading) 5
Simonsen, S. P. A. 1998 (Tranmere R, Everton) 4
Simpson, P. 1986 (Manchester C) 5
Sims, S. 1977 (Leicester C) 10
Sinclair, S. A. 2011 (Swansea C) 7
Sinclair, T. 1994 (QPR, West Ham U) 5
Sinnott, L. 1985 (Watford) 1
Slade, S. A. 1996 (Tottenham H) 4
Slater, S. I. 1990 (West Ham U) 3
Small, B. 1993 (Aston Villa) 12
Smalling, C. L. 2010 (Fulham, Manchester U) 14
Smith, A. 2000 (Leeds U) 10
Smith, A. J. 2012 (Tottenham H) 11
Smith, D. 1988 (Coventry C) 10
Smith, M. 1981 (Sheffield W) 5
Smith, M. 1995 (Sunderland) 1
Smith, T. W. 2001 (Watford) 1
Snodin, I. 1985 (Doncaster R) 4
Soares, T. J. 2006 (Crystal Palace) 4
Solanke, D. A. 2015 (Chelsea) 3
Sordell, M. A. 2012 (Watford, Bolton W) 14
Spence, J. 2011 (West Ham U) 1
Stanislaus, F. J. 2010 (West Ham U) 2
Statham, B. 1988 (Tottenham H) 3
Statham, D. J. 1978 (WBA) 6
Stead, J. G. 2004 (Blackburn R, Sunderland) 11
Stearman, R. J. 2009 (Wolverhampton W) 4
Steele, J. 2011 (Middlesbrough) 7
Stein, B. 1984 (Luton T) 3
Stephens, J. 2015 (Southampton) 8
Sterland, M. 1984 (Sheffield W) 7
Sterling, R. S. 2012 (Liverpool) 8

Steven, T. M. 1985 (Everton) 2
Stevens, G. A. 1983 (Brighton & HA, Tottenham H) 8
Stewart, J. 2003 (Leicester C) 1
Stewart, P. 1988 (Manchester C) 1
Stockdale, R. K. 2001 (Middlesbrough) 1
Stones, J. 2013 (Everton) 12
Stuart, G. C. 1990 (Chelsea) 5
Stuart, J. C. 1996 (Charlton Ath) 4
Sturridge, D. A. 2010 (Chelsea) 15
Suckling, P. 1986 (Coventry C, Manchester C, Crystal Palace) 10
Summerbee, N. J. 1993 (Swindon T) 3
Sunderland, A. 1977 (Wolverhampton W) 1
Surman, A. R. E. 2008 (Southampton) 4
Sutch, D. 1992 (Norwich C) 4
Sutton, C. R. 1993 (Norwich C) 13
Swift, J. D. 2015 (Chelsea, Reading) 13
Swindlehurst, D. 1977 (Crystal Palace) 1

Talbot, B. 1977 (Ipswich T) 1
Targett, M. R. 2015 (Southampton) 12
Taylor, A. D. 2007 (Middlesbrough) 13
Taylor, M. 2001 (Blackburn R) 1
Taylor, M. S. 2003 (Portsmouth) 3
Taylor, R. A. 2006 (Wigan Ath) 4
Taylor, S. J. 2002 (Arsenal) 3
Taylor, S. V. 2004 (Newcastle U) 29
Terry, J. G. 2001 (Chelsea) 9
Thatcher, B. D. 1996 (Millwall, Wimbledon) 4
Thelwell, A. A. 2001 (Tottenham H) 1
Thirlwell, P. 2001 (Sunderland) 1
Thomas, D. 1981 (Coventry C, Tottenham H) 7
Thomas, J. W. 2006 (Charlton Ath) 2
Thomas, M. 1986 (Luton T) 3
Thomas, M. L. 1988 (Arsenal) 12
Thomas, R. E. 1990 (Watford) 1
Thompson, A. 1995 (Bolton W) 2
Thompson, D. A. 1997 (Liverpool) 7
Thompson, G. L. 1981 (Coventry C) 6
Thorn, A. 1988 (Wimbledon) 5
Thornley, B. L. 1996 (Manchester U) 3
Thorpe, T. J. 2013 (Manchester U) 1
Tiler, C. 1990 (Barnsley, Nottingham F) 13
Tomkins, J. O. C. 2009 (West Ham U) 10
Tonge, M. W. E. 2004 (Sheffield U) 2
Townsend, A. D. 2012 (Tottenham H) 3
Trippier, K. J. 2011 (Manchester C) 2

Unsworth, D. G. 1995 (Everton) 6
Upson, M. J. 1999 (Arsenal) 11

Vassell, D. 1999 (Aston Villa) 11
Vaughan, J. O. 2007 (Everton) 4
Venison, B. 1983 (Sunderland) 10
Vernazza, P. A. P. 2001 (Arsenal, Watford) 2
Vinnicombe, C. 1991 (Rangers) 12

Waddle, C. R. 1985 (Newcastle U) 1
Waghorn, M. T. 2012 (Leicester C) 5
Walcott, T. J. 2007 (Arsenal) 21
Wallace, D. L. 1983 (Southampton) 14
Wallace, Ray 1989 (Southampton) 4
Wallace, Rod 1989 (Southampton) 11
Walker, D. 1985 (Nottingham F) 7
Walker, I. M. 1991 (Tottenham H) 9
Walker, K. 2010 (Tottenham H) 7
Walsh, G. 1988 (Manchester U) 2
Walsh, P. A. 1983 (Luton T) 4
Walters, K. 1984 (Aston Villa) 9
Walton, C. T. 2017 (Brighton & HA) 1
Ward, P. 1978 (Brighton & HA) 2
Ward-Prowse, J. M. E. 2013 (Southampton) 31
Warhurst, P. 1991 (Oldham Ath, Sheffield W) 8
Watmore, D. I. 2015 (Sunderland) 13
Watson, B. 2007 (Crystal Palace) 1
Watson, D. 1984 (Norwich C) 7
Watson, D. N. 1994 (Barnsley) 5
Watson, G. 1991 (Sheffield W) 2
Watson, S. C. 1993 (Newcastle U) 12
Weaver, N. J. 2000 (Manchester C) 10
Webb, N. J. 1985 (Portsmouth, Nottingham F) 3
Welbeck, D. 2009 (Manchester U) 14
Welsh, J. J. 2004 (Liverpool, Hull C) 8
Wheater, D. J. 2008 (Middlesbrough) 11
Whelan, P. J. 1993 (Ipswich T) 3
Whelan, N. 1995 (Leeds U) 2
Whittingham, P. 2004 (Aston Villa, Cardiff C) 17
White, D. 1988 (Manchester C) 6
Whyte, C. 1982 (Arsenal) 4
Wickham, C. N. R. 2011 (Ipswich T, Sunderland) 17
Wicks, S. 1982 (QPR) 1
Wilkins, R. C. 1977 (Chelsea) 1
Wilkinson, P. 1985 (Grimsby T, Everton) 4
Williams, D. 1998 (Sunderland) 2
Williams, P. 1989 (Charlton Ath) 4
Williams, P. D. 1991 (Derby Co) 6
Williams, S. C. 1977 (Southampton) 14
Wilshere, J. A. 2010 (Arsenal) 7
Wilson, C. E. G. 2014 (Bournemouth) 1
Wilson, J. A. 2015 (Manchester U) 1
Wilson, M. A. 2001 (Manchester U, Middlesbrough) 6
Winks, H. 2017 (Tottenham H) 2
Winterburn, N. 1986 (Wimbledon) 1
Wisdom, A. 2012 (Liverpool) 10
Wise, D. F. 1988 (Wimbledon) 1
Woodcook, A. S. 1978 (Nottingham F) 2
Woodgate, J. S. 2000 (Leeds U) 1
Woodhouse, C. 1999 (Sheffield U) 4
Woodman, F. J. 2017 (Newcastle U) 1
Woodrow, C. 2014 (Fulham) 9
Woods, C. C. E. 1979 (Nottingham F, QPR, Norwich C) 6
Wright, A. G. 1993 (Blackburn R) 2
Wright, M. 1983 (Southampton) 4
Wright, R. I. 1997 (Ipswich T) 15
Wright, S. J. 2001 (Liverpool) 10
Wright, W. 1979 (Everton) 6
Wright-Phillips, S. C. 2002 (Manchester C) 6

Yates, D. 1989 (Notts Co) 5
Young, A. S. 2007 (Watford, Aston Villa) 10
Young, L. P. 1999 (Tottenham H, Charlton Ath) 12

Zaha, D. W. A. 2012 (Crystal Palace, Manchester U) 13
Zamora, R. L. 2002 (Brighton & HA) 6

NORTHERN IRELAND

Allen, C. 2009 (Lisburn Distillery) 1
Armstrong, D. T. 2007 (Hearts) 1

Bagnall, L. 2011 (Sunderland) 1
Bailie, N. 1990 (Linfield) 2
Baird, C. P. 2002 (Southampton) 6
Ball, D. 2013 (Tottenham H) 2
Ball, M. 2011 (Norwich C) 5
Beatty, S. 1990 (Chelsea, Linfield) 2
Black, J. 2003 (Tottenham H) 1
Black, K. T. 1990 (Luton T) 1
Black, R. Z. 2002 (Morecambe) 1
Blackledge, G. 1978 (Portadown) 1
Blake, R. G. 2011 (Brentford) 2
Blayney, A. 2003 (Southampton) 4
Boyce, L. 2010 (Cliftonville, Werder Bremen) 8
Boyle, W. S. 1998 (Leeds U) 7
Braniff, K. R. 2002 (Millwall) 11
Breeze, J. 2011 (Wigan Ath) 4
Brennan, C. 2013 (Kilmarnock) 13
Brobbel, R. 2013 (Middlesbrough) 9
Brotherston, N. 1978 (Blackburn R) 1
Browne, G. 2003 (Manchester C) 5
Brunt, C. 2005 (Sheffield W) 2
Bryan, M. A. 2010 (Watford) 4
Buchanan, D. T. H. 2006 (Bury) 15
Buchanan, W. B. 2002 (Bolton W, Lisburn Distillery) 5
Burns, A. 2014 (Linfield) 1
Burns, L. 1998 (Port Vale) 13

Callaghan, A. 2006 (Limavady U, Ballymena U, Derry C) 15
Campbell, S. 2003 (Ballymena U) 1
Camps, C. 2015 (Rochdale) 1

Capaldi, A. C. 2002 (Birmingham C, Plymouth Arg) 14
Carlisle, W. T. 2000 (Crystal Palace) 9
Carroll, R. E. 1998 (Wigan Ath) 11
Carson, J. G. 2011 (Ipswich T, York C) 12
Carson, S. 2000 (Rangers, Dundee U) 2
Carson, T. 2007 (Sunderland) 15
Carvill, M. D. 2008 (Wrexham, Linfield) 8
Casement, C. 2007 (Ipswich T, Dundee) 18
Cathcart, C. 2007 (Manchester U) 15
Catney, R. 2007 (Lisburn Distillery) 1
Chapman, A. 2008 (Sheffield U, Oxford U) 7
Charles, D. 2017 (Fleetwood T) 3
Clarke, L. 2003 (Peterborough U) 4
Clarke, R. 2006 (Newry C) 7
Clarke, R. D. J. 1999 (Portadown) 5
Clingan, S. G. 2003 (Wolverhampton W, Nottingham F) 11
Close, B. 2002 (Middlesbrough) 10
Clucas, M. S. 2011 (Preston NE, Bristol R) 11
Clyde, M. G. 2002 (Wolverhampton W) 5
Colligan, L. 2009 (Ballymena U) 1
Conlan, L. 2013 (Burnley, Morecambe) 11
Connell, T. E. 1978 (Coleraine) 1
Cooper, J. 2015 (Glenavon) 5
Coote, A. 1998 (Norwich C) 12
Convery, J. 2000 (Celtic) 4

Dallas, S. 2012 (Crusaders, Brentford) 2
Davey, H. 2004 (UCD) 3
Davis, S. 2004 (Aston Villa) 3
Devine, D. 1994 (Omagh T) 1
Devine, D. G. 2011 (Preston NE) 2
Devine, J. 1990 (Glentoran) 1
Devlin, C. 2011 (Manchester U, unattached, Cliftonville) 11
Dickson, H. 2002 (Wigan Ath) 1
Doherty, J. E. 2014 (Watford, Leyton O) 5
Doherty, M. 2007 (Hearts) 2
Dolan, J. 2000 (Millwall) 6
Donaghy, M. M. 1978 (Larne) 1
Donnelly, L. F. P. 2012 (Fulham, Hartlepool U) 14
Donnelly, M. 2007 (Sheffield U, Crusaders) 5
Donnelly, R. 2013 (Swansea C) 1
Dowie, I. 1990 (Luton T) 1
Drummond, W. 2011 (Rangers) 2
Dudgeon, J. P. 2010 (Manchester U) 4
Duff, S. 2003 (Cheltenham T) 1
Duffy, M. 2014 (Derry C, Celtic) 9
Duffy, S. P. M. 2010 (Everton) 3
Dummigan, C. 2014 (Burnley, Oldham Ath) 12
Dunwoody, J. 2017 (Stoke C) 1

Elliott, S. 1999 (Glentoran) 3
Ervin, J. 2005 (Linfield) 2
Evans, C. J. 2009 (Manchester U) 10
Evans, J. 2006 (Manchester U) 3

Feeney, L. 1998 (Linfield, Rangers) 8
Feeney, W. 2002 (Bournemouth) 8
Ferguson, M. 2000 (Glentoran) 2
Ferguson, S. 2009 (Newcastle U) 11
Fitzgerald, D. 1998 (Rangers) 4
Flanagan, T. M. 2012 (Milton Keynes D) 1
Flynn, J. J. 2009 (Blackburn R, Ross Co) 11
Fordyce, D. T. 2007 (Portsmouth, Glentoran) 12
Friars, E. C. 2005 (Notts Co) 7
Friars, S. M. 1998 (Liverpool, Ipswich T) 21

Garrett, R. 2007 (Stoke C, Linfield) 14
Gault, M. 2005 (Linfield) 2
Gibb, S. 2009 (Falkirk, Drogheda U) 2
Gilfillan, B. J. 2005 (Gretna, Peterhead) 9
Gillespie, K. R. 1994 (Manchester U) 1
Glendinning, M. 1994 (Bangor) 1
Glendinning, R. 2012 (Linfield) 3
Gordon, S. 2017 (Motherwell) 1
Gorman, D. A. 2015 (Stevenage) 6
Gorman, R. J. 2012 (Wolverhampton W, Leyton Orient) 4
Graham, G. L. 1999 (Crystal Palace) 5
Graham, R. S. 1999 (QPR) 15
Gray, J. P. 2012 (Accrington S) 11
Gray, P. 1990 (Luton T) 1
Griffin, D. J. 1998 (St Johnstone) 10
Grigg, W. D. 2011 (Walsall) 10

Hamilton, G. 2000 (Blackburn R, Portadown) 12
Hamilton, W. R. 1978 (Linfield) 1
Hanley, N. 2011 (Linfield) 1
Harkin, M. P. 2000 (Wycombe W) 9
Harney, J. J. 2014 (West Ham U) 1
Harvey, J. 1978 (Arsenal) 1
Hawe, S. 2001 (Blackburn R) 2
Hayes, T. 1978 (Luton T) 1
Hazley, M. 2007 (Stoke C) 3
Healy, D. J. 1999 (Manchester U) 8
Hegarty, C. 2011 (Rangers) 7
Herron, C. J. 2003 (QPR) 2
Higgins, R. 2006 (Derry C) 1
Hodson, L. J. S. 2010 (Watford) 10
Holmes, S. 2000 (Manchester C, Wrexham) 13
Howland, D. 2007 (Birmingham C) 4
Hughes, J. 2006 (Lincoln C) 7
Hughes, M. A. 2003 (Tottenham H, Oldham Ath) 12
Hughes, M. E. 1990 (Manchester C) 1
Hunter, M. 2002 (Glentoran) 1

Ingham, M. G. 2001 (Sunderland) 4

Jarvis, D. 2010 (Aberdeen) 2
Johns, C. 2014 (Southampton) 1
Johnson, D. M. 1998 (Blackburn R) 11
Johnson, R. A. 2015 (Stevenage) 5
Johnston, B. 1978 (Cliftonville) 1
Julian, A. A. 2005 (Brentford) 1

Kane, A. M. 2008 (Blackburn R) 5
Kane, M. 2012 (Glentoran) 1
Kee, B. R. 2010 (Leicester C, Torquay U, Burton Alb) 10
Kee, P. V. 1990 (Oxford U) 1
Kelly, D. 2000 (Derry C) 11
Kelly, N. 1990 (Oldham Ath) 1
Kennedy, B. J. 2017 (Stevenage) 2
Kennedy, M. C. P. 2015 (Charlton Ath) 7
Kirk, A. R. 1999 (Hearts) 9
Knowles, J. 2012 (Blackburn R) 2

Lafferty, D. 2009 (Celtic) 6
Lafferty, K. 2006 (Burnley) 2
Lavery, C. 2011 (Ipswich T, Sheffield W) 7
Lavery, S. 2017 (Everton) 2
Lawrie, J. 2009 (Port Vale, AFC Telford U) 9
Lennon, N. F. 1990 (Manchester C, Crewe Alex) 2
Lester, C. 2013 (Bolton W) 1
Lewis, J. 2017 (Norwich C) 1
Lindsay, K. 2006 (Larne) 1
Little, A. 2009 (Rangers) 6
Lowry, P. 2009 (Institute, Linfield) 6
Lund, M. 2011 (Stoke C) 6
Lyttle, G. 1998 (Celtic, Peterborough U) 8

McAlinden, L. J. 2012 (Wolverhampton W) 3
McAllister, M. 2007 (Dungannon Swifts) 4
McArdle, R. A. 2006 (Sheffield W, Rochdale) 19
McAreavey, P. 2000 (Swindon T) 7
McBride, J. 1994 (Glentoran) 1
McCaffrey, D. 2006 (Hibernian) 8
McCallion, E. 1998 (Coleraine) 1
McCann, G. S. 2000 (West Ham U) 11
McCann, P. 2003 (Portadown) 1
McCann, R. 2002 (Rangers, Linfield) 2
McCartan, S. V. 2013 (Accrington S) 9
McCartney, G. 2001 (Sunderland) 5
McCashin, S. 2011 (Jerez Industrial, unattached) 2
McChrystal, M. 2005 (Derry C) 9
McClean, J. 2010 (Derry C) 3
McClure, M. 2012 (Wycombe W) 1
McCourt, P. J. 2002 (Rochdale, Derry C) 8
McCoy, R. K. 1990 (Coleraine) 1
McCreery, D. 1978 (Manchester U) 1
McCullough, L. 2013 (Doncaster R) 8
McDaid, R. 2015 (Leeds U) 5
McDermott, C. 2017 (Coleraine) 2
McDonagh, J. 2015 (Sheffield U) 1
McEleney, S. 2012 (Derry C) 2
McElroy, P. 2013 (Hull C) 1

McEvilly, L. R. 2003 (Rochdale) 9
McFlynn, T. M. 2000 (QPR, Woking, Margate) 19
McGeehan, C. 2013 (Norwich C) 3
McGibbon, P. C. G. 1994 (Manchester U) 1
McGivern, R. 2010 (Manchester C) 6
McGlinchey, B. 1998 (Manchester C, Port Vale, Gillingham) 14
McGonigle, J. 2017 (Coleraine) 1
McGovern, M. 2005 (Celtic) 10
McGowan, M. V. 2006 (Clyde) 2
McGurk, A. 2010 (Aston Villa) 1
McIlroy, T. 1994 (Linfield) 1
McKay, W. 2009 (Leicester C, Northampton T) 7
McKenna, K. 2007 (Tottenham H) 6
McKeown, R. 2012 (Kilmarnock) 12
McKnight, D. 2015 (Shrewsbury T, Stalybridge Celtic) 5
McKnight, P. 1998 (Rangers) 3
McLaughlin, C. G. 2010 (Preston NE, Fleetwood T) 7
McLaughlin, P. 2010 (Newcastle U, York C) 10
McLaughlin, R. 2012 (Liverpool, Oldham Ath) 6
McLean, B. S. 2006 (Rangers) 1
McLean, J. 2009 (Derry C) 4
McLellan, M. 2012 (Preston NE) 1
McMahon, G. J. 2002 (Tottenham H) 1
McMenamin, L. A. 2009 (Sheffield W) 4
McNair, P. J. C. 2014 (Manchester U) 2
McNally, P. 2013 (Celtic) 1
McQuilken, J. 2009 (Tescoma Zlin) 1
McQuoid, J. J. B. 2009 (Bournemouth) 8
McVeigh, A. 2002 (Ayr U) 1
McVeigh, P. M. 1998 (Tottenham H) 11
McVey, K. 2006 (Coleraine) 8
Magee, J. 1994 (Bangor) 1
Magee, J. 2009 (Lisburn Distillery) 1
Magennis, J. B. D. 2010 (Cardiff C, Aberdeen) 16
Magilton, J. 1990 (Liverpool) 1
Magnay, C. 2010 (Chelsea) 1
Maloney, L. 2015 (Middlesbrough) 6
Marshall, R. 2017 (Glenavon) 1
Matthews, N. P. 1990 (Blackpool) 1
Meenan, D. 2007 (Finn Harps, Monaghan U) 3
Melaugh, G. M. 2002 (Aston Villa, Glentoran) 11
Millar, K. S. 2011 (Oldham Ath, Linfield) 11
Millar, W. P. 1990 (Port Vale) 1
Miskelly, D. T. 2000 (Oldham Ath) 10
Mitchell, A. 2012 (Rangers) 3
Mitchell, C. 2017 (Burnley) 5
Moreland, V. 1978 (Glentoran) 1
Morgan, D. 2012 (Nottingham F) 4
Morgan, M. P. T. 1999 (Preston NE) 1
Morris, E. J. 2002 (WBA, Glentoran) 8
Morrison, O. 2001 (Sheffield W, Sheffield U) 7
Morrow, A. 2001 (Northampton T) 1
Morrow, S. 2005 (Hibernian) 4
Mulgrew, J. 2007 (Linfield) 10
Mulryne, P. P. 1999 (Manchester U, Norwich C) 5
Murray, W. 1978 (Linfield) 1
Murtagh, C. 2005 (Hearts) 1

Nicholl, J. M. 1978 (Manchester U) 1
Nixon, C. 2000 (Glentoran) 1
Nolan, L. J. 2014 (Crewe Alex, Southport) 4
Norwood, O. J. 2010 (Manchester U) 11

O'Connor, M. J. 2008 (Crewe Alex) 3
O'Hara, G. 1994 (Leeds U) 1
O'Kane, E. 2009 (Everton, Torquay U) 4
O'Neill, J. P. 1978 (Leicester C) 1
O'Neill, M. A. M. 1994 (Hibernian) 1
O'Neill, S. 2009 (Ballymena U) 4

Parkhouse, D. 2017 (Sheffield U) 1
Paterson, M. A. 2007 (Stoke C) 2
Patterson, D. J. 1994 (Crystal Palace) 1
Paul, C. D. 2017 (QPR) 1

Quigley, C. 2017 (Dundee) 2
Quinn, S. J. 1994 (Blackpool) 1

Ramsey, C. 2011 (Portadown) 3
Ramsey, K. 2006 (Institute) 1
Reid, J. T. 2013 (Exeter C) 2
Robinson, S. 1994 (Tottenham H) 1
Rooney, L. J. 2017 (Plymouth Arg) 1

Scullion, D. 2006 (Dungannon Swifts) 8
Sendles-White J. 2013 (QPR, Hamilton A) 12
Sharpe, R. 2013 (Derby Co, Notts Co) 6
Shiels, D. 2005 (Hibernian) 6
Shields, S. P. 2013 (Dagenham & R) 2
Shroot, R. 2009 (Harrow B, Birmingham C) 4
Simms, G. 2001 (Hartlepool U) 14
Singleton, J. 2015 (Glenavon) 2
Skates, G. 2000 (Blackburn R) 4
Sloan, T. 1978 (Ballymena U) 1
Smylie, D. 2006 (Newcastle U, Livingston) 6
Smyth, P. 2017 (Linfield) 4
Stewart, J. 2015 (Swindon T) 2
Stewart, S. 2009 (Aberdeen) 1
Stewart, T. 2006 (Wolverhampton W, Linfield) 19
Sykes, M. 2017 (Glenavon) 3

Taylor, J. 2007 (Hearts, Glentoran) 10
Taylor, M. S. 1998 (Fulham) 1
Teggart, N. 2005 (Sunderland) 2
Tempest, G. 2013 (Notts Co) 6
Thompson, A. L. 2011 (Watford) 11
Thompson, J. 2017 (Rangers) 4
Thompson, P. 2006 (Linfield) 4
Toner, C. 2000 (Tottenham H, Leyton Orient) 17
Tuffey, J. 2007 (Partick Thistle) 13
Turner, C. 2007 (Sligo R, Bohemians) 12

Ward, J. J. 2006 (Aston Villa, Chesterfield) 7
Ward, M. 2006 (Dungannon Swifts) 1
Ward, S. 2005 (Glentoran) 10
Waterman, D. G. 1998 (Portsmouth) 14
Waterworth, A. 2008 (Lisburn Distillery, Hamilton A) 7
Webb, S. M. 2004 (Ross Co, St Johnstone, Ross Co) 6
Weir, R. J. 2009 (Sunderland) 8
Wells, D. P. 1999 (Barry T) 1
Whitley, J. 1998 (Manchester C) 17
Whyte, G. 2015 (Crusaders) 5
Willis, P. 2006 (Liverpool) 1
Winchester, C. 2011 (Oldham Ath) 13
Winchester, J. 2013 (Kilmarnock) 1

SCOTLAND

Adam, C. G. 2006 (Rangers) 5
Adam, G. 2011 (Rangers) 6
Adams, J. 2007 (Kilmarnock) 1
Aitken, R. 1977 (Celtic) 16
Albiston, A. 1977 (Manchester U) 5
Alexander, N. 1997 (Stenhousemuir, Livingston) 10
Allan, S. 2012 (WBA) 10
Anderson, I. 1997 (Dundee, Toulouse) 15
Anderson, R. 1997 (Aberdeen) 15
Andrews, M. 2011 (East Stirlingshire) 1
Anthony, M. 1997 (Celtic) 3
Archdeacon, O. 1987 (Celtic) 1
Archer, J. G. 2012 (Tottenham H) 14
Archibald, A. 1998 (Partick Thistle) 5
Archibald, S. 1980 (Aberdeen, Tottenham H) 5
Arfield, S. 2008 (Falkirk, Huddersfield T) 17
Armstrong, S. 2011 (Dundee U) 20

Bagen, D. 1997 (Kilmarnock) 4
Bain, K. 1993 (Dundee) 4
Baker, M. 1993 (St Mirren) 10
Baltacha, S. S. 2000 (St Mirren) 3
Bannan, B. 2009 (Aston Villa) 10
Bannigan, S. 2013 (Partick Thistle) 3
Bannon, E. J. 1979 (Hearts, Chelsea, Dundee U) 7
Barclay, J. 2011 (Falkirk) 1
Beattie, C. 2004 (Celtic) 7
Beattie, J. 1992 (St Mirren) 4
Beaumont, D. 1985 (Dundee U) 1
Bell, D. 1981 (Aberdeen) 2
Bernard, P. R. J. 1992 (Oldham Ath) 15
Berra, C. 2005 (Hearts) 6

Bett, J. 1981 (Rangers) 7
Black, E. 1983 (Aberdeen) 8
Blair, A. 1980 (Coventry C, Aston Villa) 5
Bollan, G. 1992 (Dundee U, Rangers) 17
Bonar, P. 1997 (Raith R) 4
Booth, C. 2011 (Hibernian) 4
Booth, S. 1991 (Aberdeen) 14
Bowes, M. J. 1992 (Dunfermline Ath) 1
Bowman, D. 1985 (Hearts) 1
Boyack, S. 1997 (Rangers) 1
Boyd, K. 2003 (Kilmarnock) 8
Boyd, T. 1987 (Motherwell) 5
Brazil, A. 1978 (Hibernian) 1
Brazil, A. 1979 (Ipswich T) 8
Brebner, G. I. 1997 (Manchester U, Reading, Hibernian) 18
Brighton, T. 2005 (Rangers, Clyde) 7
Broadfoot, K. 2005 (St Mirren) 5
Brophy, E. 2017 (Hamilton A) 1
Brough, J. 1981 (Hearts) 1
Brown, A. H. 2004 (Hibernian) 1
Brown, S. 2005 (Hibernian) 10
Browne, P. 1997 (Raith R) 1
Bryson, C. 2006 (Clyde) 1
Buchan, J. 1997 (Aberdeen) 13
Burchill, M. J. 1998 (Celtic) 15
Burke, A. 1997 (Kilmarnock) 4
Burke, C. 2004 (Rangers) 3
Burley, C. W. 1992 (Chelsea) 7
Burley, G. E. 1977 (Ipswich T) 5
Burns, H. 1985 (Rangers) 2
Burns, T. 1977 (Celtic) 5
Burt, L. 2017 (Rangers) 2

Cadden, C. 2017 (Motherwell) 2
Caddis, P. 2008 (Celtic, Dundee U, Celtic, Swindon T) 13
Cairney, T. 2011 (Hull C) 6
Caldwell, G. 2000 (Newcastle U) 19
Caldwell, S. 2001 (Newcastle U) 4
Cameron, G. 2008 (Dundee U) 3
Cameron, K. M. 2017 (Newcastle U) 3
Campbell, R. 2008 (Hibernian) 6
Campbell, S. 1989 (Dundee) 3
Campbell, S. P. 1998 (Leicester C) 15
Canero, P. 2000 (Kilmarnock) 17
Cardwell, H. 2014 (Reading) 1
Carey, L. A. 1998 (Bristol C) 1
Carrick, D. 2012 (Hearts) 1
Casey, J. 1978 (Celtic) 1
Chalmers, J. 2014 (Celtic, Motherwell) 2
Christie, M. 1992 (Dundee) 3
Christie, R. 2014 (Inverness CT, Celtic) 9
Clark, R. B. 1977 (Aberdeen) 3
Clarke, S. 1984 (St Mirren) 8
Clarkson, D. 2004 (Motherwell) 13
Cleland, A. 1990 (Dundee U) 11
Cole, D. 2011 (Rangers) 2
Collins, J. 1988 (Hibernian) 8
Collins, N. 2005 (Sunderland) 7
Connolly, P. 1991 (Dundee U) 3
Connor, R. 1981 (Ayr U) 2
Conroy, R. 2007 (Celtic) 4
Considine, A. 2007 (Aberdeen) 5
Cooper, D. 1977 (Clydebank, Rangers) 6
Cooper, N. 1982 (Aberdeen) 13
Coutts, P. A. 2009 (Peterborough U, Preston NE) 7
Crabbe, S. 1990 (Hearts) 2
Craig, M. 1998 (Aberdeen) 2
Craig, T. 1977 (Newcastle U) 1
Crainey, S. D. 2000 (Celtic) 7
Crainie, D. 1983 (Celtic) 1
Crawford, S. 1994 (Raith R) 19
Creaney, G. 1991 (Celtic) 11
Cummings, J. 2015 (Hibernian) 8
Cummings, W. 2000 (Chelsea) 8
Cuthbert, S. 2007 (Celtic, St Mirren) 13

Dailly, C. 1991 (Dundee U) 34
Dalglish, P. 1999 (Newcastle U, Norwich C) 6
Dargo, C. 1998 (Raith R) 10
Davidson, C. I. 1997 (St Johnstone) 2
Davidson, H. N. 2000 (Dundee U) 3
Davidson, M. 2011 (St Johnstone) 1
Dawson, A. 1979 (Rangers) 8
Deas, P. A. 1992 (St Johnstone) 2
Dempster, J. 2004 (Rushden & D) 1
Dennis, S. 1992 (Raith R) 1
Diamond, A. 2004 (Aberdeen) 12
Dickov, P. 1992 (Arsenal) 4
Dixon, P. 2008 (Dundee) 2
Docherty, G. 2017 (Hamilton A) 2
Dodds, D. 1978 (Dundee U) 1
Dods, D. 1997 (Hibernian) 5
Doig, C. R. 2000 (Nottingham F) 13
Donald, G. S. 1992 (Hibernian) 3
Donnelly, S. 1994 (Celtic) 11
Dorrans, G. 2007 (Livingston) 6
Dow, A. 1993 (Dundee, Chelsea) 3
Dowie, A. J. 2003 (Rangers, Partick Thistle) 14
Duff, J. 2009 (Inverness CT) 1
Duff, S. 2003 (Dundee U) 9
Duffie, K. 2011 (Falkirk) 6
Duffy, D. A. 2005 (Falkirk, Hull C) 8
Duffy, J. 1987 (Dundee) 1
Durie, G. S. 1987 (Chelsea) 4
Durrant, I. 1987 (Rangers) 4
Doyle, J. 1981 (Partick Thistle) 2

Easton, B. 2009 (Hamilton A) 3
Easton, C. 1997 (Dundee U) 21
Edwards, M. 2012 (Rochdale) 1
Elliot, B. 1998 (Celtic) 2
Elliot, C. 2006 (Hearts) 9
Esson, R. 2000 (Aberdeen) 7

Fagan, S. M. 2005 (Motherwell) 1
Ferguson, B. 1997 (Rangers) 12
Ferguson, D. 1987 (Rangers) 5
Ferguson, D. 1992 (Dundee U) 7
Ferguson, D. 1992 (Manchester U) 5
Ferguson, I. 1983 (Dundee) 4
Ferguson, I. 1987 (Clyde, St Mirren, Rangers) 6
Ferguson, R. 1977 (Hamilton A) 1
Feruz, I. 2012 (Chelsea) 4
Findlay, S. 2012 (Celtic) 13
Findlay, W. 1991 (Hibernian) 5
Fitzpatrick, A. 1977 (St Mirren) 5
Fitzpatrick, M. 2007 (Motherwell) 4
Flannigan, C. 1993 (Clydebank) 1
Fleck, J. 2009 (Rangers) 4
Fleck, R. 1987 (Rangers, Norwich C) 6
Fleming, G. 2008 (Gretna) 1
Fletcher, D. B. 2003 (Manchester U) 2
Fletcher, S. 2007 (Hibernian) 7
Forrest, A. 2017 (Ayr U) 1
Forrest, J. 2011 (Celtic) 4
Foster, R. M. 2005 (Aberdeen) 5
Fotheringham, M. M. 2004 (Dundee) 3
Fowler, J. 2002 (Kilmarnock) 3
Foy, R. A. 2004 (Liverpool) 5
Fraser, M. 2012 (Celtic) 5
Fraser, R. 2013 (Aberdeen, Bournemouth) 10
Fraser, S. T. 2000 (Luton T) 4
Freedman, D. A. 1995 (Barnet, Crystal Palace) 8
Fridge, L. 1989 (St Mirren) 2
Fullarton, J. 1993 (St Mirren) 17
Fulton, J. 2014 (Swansea C) 2
Fulton, R. 2017 (Liverpool) 4
Fulton, M. 1980 (St Mirren) 5
Fulton, S. 1991 (Celtic) 7
Fyvie, F. 2012 (Wigan Ath) 8

Gallacher, K. W. 1987 (Dundee U) 7
Gallacher, P. 1999 (Dundee U) 7
Gallacher, S. 2009 (Rangers) 2
Gallagher, P. 2003 (Blackburn R) 11
Galloway, M. 1989 (Hearts, Celtic) 2
Gardiner, J. 1993 (Hibernian) 1
Gauld, R. 2013 (Dundee U, Sporting Lisbon) 11
Geddes, R. 1982 (Dundee) 5
Gemmill, S. 1992 (Nottingham F) 4
Germaine, G. 1997 (WBA) 1
Gilles, R. 1997 (St Mirren) 7
Gillespie, G. T. 1979 (Coventry C) 8

Glass, S. 1995 (Aberdeen) 11
Glover, L. 1988 (Nottingham F) 3
Goodwillie, D. 2009 (Dundee U) 9
Goram, A. L. 1987 (Oldham Ath) 1
Gordon, C. S. 2003 (Hearts) 5
Gough, C. R. 1983 (Dundee U) 5
Graham, D. 1998 (Rangers) 8
Grant, P. 1985 (Celtic) 10
Gray, D. P. 2009 (Manchester U) 2
Gray, S. 1987 (Aberdeen) 1
Gray S. 1995 (Celtic) 7
Griffiths, L. 2010 (Dundee, Wolverhampton W) 11
Grimmer, J. 2014 (Fulham) 1
Gunn, B. 1984 (Aberdeen) 9

Hagen, D. 1992 (Rangers) 8
Hamill, J. 2008 (Kilmarnock) 11
Hamilton, B. 1989 (St Mirren) 4
Hamilton, J. 1995 (Dundee, Hearts) 14
Hamilton, J. 2014 (Hearts) 8
Hammell, S. 2001 (Motherwell) 11
Handling, D. 2014 (Hibernian) 3
Handyside, P. 1993 (Grimsby T) 7
Hanley, G. 2011 (Blackburn R) 1
Hanlon, P. 2009 (Hibernian) 23
Hannah, D. 1993 (Dundee U) 16
Hardy, R. 2017 (Rangers) 4
Harper, K. 1995 (Hibernian) 7
Hartford, R. A. 1977 (Manchester C) 1
Hartley, P. J. 1997 (Millwall) 1
Hegarty, P. 1987 (Dundee U) 6
Henderson, L. 2015 (Celtic) 9
Hendrie, S. 2014 (West Ham U) 3
Hendry, J. 1992 (Tottenham H) 1
Henly, J. 2014 (Reading) 1
Herron, J. 2012 (Celtic) 2
Hetherston, B. 1997 (St Mirren) 1
Hewitt, J. 1982 (Aberdeen) 6
Hogg, G. 1984 (Manchester U) 4
Holt, J. 2012 (Hearts) 7
Hood, G. 1993 (Ayr U) 3
Horn, R. 1997 (Hearts) 6
Howie, S. 1993 (Cowdenbeath) 5
Hughes, R. D. 1999 (Bournemouth) 9
Hughes, S. 2002 (Rangers) 12
Hunter, G. 1987 (Hibernian) 3
Hunter, P. 1989 (East Fife) 3
Hutton, A. 2004 (Rangers) 7
Hutton, K. 2011 (Rangers) 1
Hyam, D. J. 2014 (Reading) 5

Iacovitti, A. 2017 (Nottingham F) 4
Inman, B. 2011 (Newcastle U) 2
Irvine, G. 2006 (Celtic) 2

Jack, R. 2012 (Aberdeen) 19
James, K. F. 1997 (Falkirk) 1
Jardine, I. 1979 (Kilmarnock) 1
Jess, E. 1990 (Aberdeen) 14
Johnson, G. I. 1992 (Dundee U) 6
Johnston, A. 1994 (Hearts) 3
Johnston, F. 1993 (Falkirk) 1
Johnston, M. 1984 (Partick Thistle, Watford) 3
Jones, J. C. 2017 (Crewe Alex) 4
Jordan, A. J. 2000 (Bristol C) 3
Jules, Z. K. 2017 (Reading) 3
Jupp, D. A. 1995 (Fulham) 9

Kelly, L. A. 2017 (Reading) 11
Kelly, S. 2014 (St Mirren) 1
Kennedy, J. 2003 (Celtic) 15
Kennedy, M. 2012 (Kilmarnock) 1
Kenneth, G. 2008 (Dundee U) 8
Kerr, B. 2003 (Newcastle U) 14
Kerr, F. 2012 (Birmingham C) 3
Kerr, M. 2001 (Kilmarnock) 1
Kerr, S. 1993 (Celtic) 10
Kettings, C. D. 2012 (Blackpool) 3
King, A. 2014 (Swansea C) 1
King, C. M. 2014 (Norwich C) 1
King, W. 2015 (Hearts) 8
Kingsley, S. 2015 (Swansea C) 6
Kinniburgh, W. D. 2004 (Motherwell) 3
Kirkwood, D. 1990 (Hearts) 1
Kyle, K. 2001 (Sunderland) 12

Lambert, P. 1991 (St Mirren) 11
Langfield, J. 2000 (Dundee) 2
Lappin, S. 2004 (St Mirren) 10
Lauchlan, J. 1998 (Kilmarnock) 11
Lavety, B. 1993 (St Mirren) 9
Lavin, G. 1993 (Watford) 7
Lawson, P. 2004 (Celtic) 10
Leighton, J. 1982 (Aberdeen) 1
Lennon, S. 2008 (Rangers) 6
Levein, C. 1985 (Hearts) 2
Leven, P. 2005 (Kilmarnock) 2
Liddell, A. M. 1994 (Barnsley) 12
Lindsey, J. 1979 (Motherwell) 1
Locke, G. 1994 (Hearts) 10
Love, D. 2015 (Manchester U) 5
Love, G. 1995 (Hibernian) 1
Loy, R. 2009 (Dunfermline Ath, Rangers) 5
Lynch, S. 2003 (Celtic, Preston NE) 13

McAllister, G. 1990 (Leicester C) 1
McAllister, R. 2008 (Inverness CT) 2
McAlpine, H. 1983 (Dundee U) 5
McAnespie, K. 1998 (St Johnstone) 4
McArthur, J. 2008 (Hamilton A) 2
McAuley, S. 1993 (St Johnstone) 1
McAvennie, F. 1982 (St Mirren) 5
McBride, J. 1981 (Everton) 1
McBride, J. P. 1998 (Celtic) 2
McBurnie, O. 2015 (Swansea C) 8
McCabe, R. 2012 (Rangers, Sheffield W) 3
McCall, A. S. M. 1988 (Bradford C, Everton) 2
McCann, K. 2008 (Hibernian) 4
McCann, N. 1994 (Dundee) 9
McCart, J. 2017 (Celtic) 1
McClair, B. 1984 (Celtic) 8
McCluskey, G. 1979 (Celtic) 6
McCluskey, S. 1997 (St Johnstone) 14
McCoist, A. 1984 (Rangers) 1
McConnell, I. 1997 (Clyde) 1
McCormack, D. 2008 (Hibernian) 1
McCormack, R. 2006 (Rangers, Motherwell, Cardiff C) 13
McCracken, D. 2002 (Dundee U) 5
McCrorie, R. 2017 (Rangers) 1
McCulloch, A. 1981 (Kilmarnock) 1
McCulloch, I. 1982 (Notts Co) 2
McCulloch, L. 1997 (Motherwell) 14
McCunnie, J. 2001 (Dundee U, Ross Co, Dunfermline Ath) 20
MacDonald, A. 2011 (Burnley) 6
MacDonald, C. 2017 (Derby Co) 2
MacDonald, J. 1980 (Rangers) 8
MacDonald, J. 2007 (Hearts) 11
McDonald, C. 1995 (Falkirk) 5
McDonald, K. 2008 (Dundee, Burnley) 14
McEwan, C. 1997 (Clyde, Raith R) 17
McEwan, D. 2003 (Livingston) 2
McFadden, J. 2003 (Motherwell) 7
McFadzean C. 2015 (Sheffield U) 3
McFarlane, D. 1997 (Hamilton A) 3
McGarry, S. 1997 (St Mirren) 3
McGarvey, F. P. 1977 (St Mirren, Celtic) 3
McGarvey, S. 1982 (Manchester U) 4
McGeough, D. 2012 (Celtic) 10
McGhee, J. 2013 (Hearts) 20
McGhee, M. 1981 (Aberdeen) 1
McGinn, J. 2014 (St Mirren, Hibernian) 9
McGinn, S. 2009 (St Mirren, Watford) 8
McGinnis, G. 1985 (Dundee U) 1
McGlinchey, M. R. 2007 (Celtic) 1
McGregor, A. 2003 (Rangers) 6
McGregor, C. W. 2013 (Celtic) 5
McGrillen, P. 1994 (Motherwell) 2
McGuire, D. 2002 (Aberdeen) 2
McHattie, K. 2012 (Hearts) 6
McInally, J. 1989 (Dundee U) 1
McKay, B. 2012 (Rangers) 4
McKay, B. 2013 (Hearts) 1
McKean, K. 2011 (St Mirren) 1

McKenzie, R. 2013 (Kilmarnock) 4
McKenzie, R. 1997 (Hearts) 2
McKimmie, S. 1985 (Aberdeen) 3
McKinlay, T. 1984 (Dundee) 6
McKinlay, W. 1989 (Dundee U) 6
McKinnon, R. 1991 (Dundee U) 6
McLaren, A, 1989 (Hearts) 11
McLaren, A. 1993 (Dundee U) 4
McLaughlin, B. 1995 (Celtic) 8
McLaughlin, J. 1981 (Morton) 10
McLean, E. 2008 (Dundee U, St Johnstone) 2
McLean, S. 2003 (Rangers) 4
McLeish, A. 1978 (Aberdeen) 6
McLean, K. 2012 (St Mirren) 11
MacLeod, A. 1979 (Hibernian) 3
McLeod, J. 1989 (Dundee U) 2
MacLeod, L. 2012 (Rangers) 8
MacLeod, M. 1979 (Dumbarton, Celtic) 5
McManus, D. J. 2014 (Aberdeen, Fleetwood T) 4
McManus, T. 2001 (Hibernian) 14
McMillan, S. 1997 (Motherwell) 4
McMullan, P. 2017 (Celtic) 1
McNab, N. 1978 (Tottenham H) 1
McNally, M. 1991 (Celtic) 2
McNamara, J. 1994 (Dunfermline Ath, Celtic) 12
McNaughton, K. 2002 (Aberdeen) 1
McNeil, A. 2007 (Hibernian) 1
McNichol, J. 1979 (Brentford) 7
McNiven, D. 1977 (Leeds U) 3
McNiven, S. A. 1996 (Oldham Ath) 1
McParland, A. 2003 (Celtic) 1
McPhee, S. 2002 (Port Vale) 1
McPherson, D. 1984 (Rangers, Hearts) 4
McQuilken, J. 1993 (Celtic) 2
McStay, P. 1983 (Celtic) 5
McWhirter, N. 1991 (St Mirren) 1
Mackay-Steven, G. 2012 (Dundee U) 3
Maguire, C. 2009 (Aberdeen) 12
Main, A. 1988 (Dundee U) 3
Malcolm, R. 2001 (Rangers) 1
Mallan, S. 2017 (St Mirren) 1
Maloney, S. 2002 (Celtic) 21
Malpas, M. 1983 (Dundee U) 8
Marr, B. 2011 (Ross Co) 1
Marshall, D. J. 2004 (Celtic) 10
Marshall, S. R. 1995 (Arsenal) 5
Martin, A. 2009 (Leeds U, Ayr U) 12
Mason, G. R. 1999 (Manchester C, Dunfermline Ath) 2
Mathieson, D. 1997 (Queen of the South) 3
May, E. 1989 (Hibernian) 2
May, S. 2013 (St Johnstone, Sheffield W) 8
Meldrum, C. 1996 (Kilmarnock) 6
Melrose, J. 1977 (Partick Thistle) 8
Millar, M, 2009 (Celtic) 1
Miller, C. 1995 (Rangers) 8
Miller, J. 1987 (Aberdeen, Celtic) 7
Miller, K. 2000 (Hibernian, Rangers) 7
Miller, W. 1991 (Hibernian) 7
Miller, W. F. 1978 (Aberdeen) 2
Milne, K. 2000 (Hearts) 1
Milne, R. 1982 (Dundee U) 3
Mitchell, C. 2008 (Falkirk) 7
Money, I. C. 1987 (St Mirren) 3
Montgomery, N. A. 2003 (Sheffield U) 2
Morgan, L. 2017 (St Mirren) 1
Morrison, S. A. 2004 (Aberdeen, Dunfermline Ath) 12
Muir, L. 1977 (Hibernian) 1
Mulgrew, C. P. 2006 (Celtic, Wolverhampton W, Aberdeen) 14
Murphy J. 2009 (Motherwell) 13
Murray, H. 2000 (St Mirren) 3
Murray, I. 2001 (Hibernian) 15
Murray, N. 1993 (Rangers) 16
Murray, R. 1993 (Bournemouth) 1
Murray, S. 2004 (Kilmarnock) 2

Narey, D. 1977 (Dundee U) 4
Naismith, J. 2014 (St Mirren) 1
Naismith, S. J. 2006 (Kilmarnock, Rangers) 15
Naysmith, G. A. 1997 (Hearts) 22
Neilson, R. 2000 (Hearts) 1
Nesbitt, A. 2017 (Celtic) 2
Ness, J, 2011 (Rangers) 2
Nevin, P. 1985 (Chelsea) 5
Nicholas, C. 1981 (Celtic, Arsenal) 6
Nicholson, B. 1999 (Rangers) 7
Nicholson, S. 2015 (Hearts) 8
Nicol, S. 1981 (Ayr U, Liverpool) 14
Nisbet, S. 1989 (Rangers) 5
Noble, D. J. 2003 (West Ham U) 2
Notman, A. M. 1999 (Manchester U) 10

O'Brien, B. 1999 (Blackburn R, Livingston) 6
O'Connor, G. 2003 (Hibernian) 8
O'Donnell, P. 1992 (Motherwell) 8
O'Donnell, S. 2013 (Partick Thistle) 1
O'Halloran, M. 2012 (Bolton W) 2
O'Hara, M. 2015 (Kilmarnock, Dundee) 2
O'Leary, R. 2008 (Kilmarnock) 2
O'Neil, B. 1992 (Celtic) 7
O'Neil, J. 1991 (Dundee U) 1
O'Neill, M. 1995 (Clyde) 6
Orr, N. 1978 (Morton) 7

Palmer, L. J. 2011 (Sheffield W) 8
Park, C. 2012 (Middlesbrough) 1
Parker, K. 2001 (St Johnstone) 1
Parlane, D. 1977 (Rangers) 1
Paterson, C. 1981 (Hibernian) 2
Paterson, C. 2012 (Hearts) 12
Paterson, J. 1997 (Dundee U) 9
Pawlett, P. 2012 (Aberdeen) 7
Payne, G. 1978 (Dundee U) 3
Peacock, L. A. 1997 (Carlisle U) 1
Pearce, A. J. 2008 (Reading) 2
Pearson, S. P. 2003 (Motherwell) 8
Perry, R. 2010 (Rangers, Falkirk, Rangers) 16
Polworth, L. 2016 (Inverness CT) 1
Pressley, S. J. 1993 (Rangers, Coventry C, Dundee U) 26
Provan, D. 1977 (Kilmarnock) 1
Prunty, B. 2004 (Aberdeen) 6

Quinn, P. C. 2004 (Motherwell) 3
Quinn, R. 2006 (Celtic) 9
Quitongo, J. 2017 (Hamilton A) 1

Rae, A. 1991 (Millwall) 8
Rae, G. 1999 (Dundee) 6
Redford, I. 1981 (Rangers) 6
Reid, B. 1991 (Rangers) 4
Reid, C. 1993 (Hibernian) 3
Reid, M. 1982 (Celtic) 2
Reid, R. 1977 (St Mirren) 3
Reilly, A. 2004 (Wycombe W) 1
Renicks, S. 1997 (Hamilton A) 1
Reynolds, M. 2007 (Motherwell) 9
Rhodes, J. L. 2011 (Huddersfield T) 8
Rice, B. 1985 (Hibernian) 1
Richardson, L. 1980 (St Mirren) 2
Ridgers, M. 2012 (Hearts) 5
Riordan, D. G. 2004 (Hibernian) 5
Ritchie, A. 1980 (Morton) 1
Ritchie, P. S. 1996 (Hearts) 7
Robertson, A. 1991 (Rangers) 1
Robertson, A. 2013 (Dundee U, Hull C) 4
Robertson, C. 1977 (Rangers) 1
Robertson, C. 2012 (Aberdeen) 10
Robertson, D. 1987 (Aberdeen) 7
Robertson, D. 2007 (Dundee U) 4
Robertson, G. A. 2004 (Nottingham F, Rotherham U) 15
Robertson, H. 1994 (Aberdeen) 2
Robertson, J. 1985 (Hearts) 2
Robertson, L. 1993 (Rangers) 3
Robertson, S. 1998 (St Johnstone) 2
Roddie, A. 1992 (Aberdeen) 5
Ross, G. 2007 (Dunfermline Ath) 1
Ross, N. 2011 (Inverness CT) 2
Ross, T. W. 1977 (Arsenal) 1
Rowson, D. 1997 (Aberdeen) 5
Ruddy, J. 2017 (Wolverhampton W) 1
Russell, J. 2011 (Dundee U) 11
Russell, R. 1978 (Rangers) 3

Salton, D. B. 1992 (Luton T) 6

Sammut, R. A. M. 2017 (Chelsea) 3
Samson, C. I. 2004 (Kilmarnock) 6
Saunders, S. 2011 (Motherwell) 2
Scobbie, T. 2008 (Falkirk) 12
Scott, M. 2006 (Livingston) 1
Scott, P. 1994 (St Johnstone) 4
Scougall, S. 2012 (Livingston, Sheffield U) 2
Scrimgour, D. 1997 (St Mirren) 3
Seaton, A. 1998 (Falkirk) 1
Severin, S. D. 2000 (Hearts) 10
Shankland, L. 2015 (Aberdeen) 4
Shannon, R. 1987 (Dundee) 7
Sharp, G. M. 1982 (Everton) 1
Sharp, R. 1990 (Dunfermline Ath) 4
Sheerin, P. 1996 (Southampton) 1
Sheppard, J. 2017 (Reading) 2
Shields, G. 1997 (Rangers) 2
Shinnie, A. 2009 (Dundee, Rangers) 3
Shinnie, G. 2012 (Inverness CT) 2
Simmons, S. 2003 (Hearts) 1
Simpson, N. 1982 (Aberdeen) 11
Sinclair, G. 1977 (Dumbarton) 1
Skilling, M. 1993 (Kilmarnock) 2
Slater, C. 2014 (Kilmarnock, Colchester U) 9
Smith, B. M. 1992 (Celtic) 5
Smith, C. 2008 (St Mirren) 2
Smith, C. 2015 (Aberdeen) 1
Smith, D. 2012 (Hearts) 4
Smith, D. L. 2006 (Motherwell) 2
Smith, G. 1978 (Rangers) 1
Smith, G. 2004 (Rangers) 8
Smith, H. G. 1987 (Hearts) 2
Smith, L. 2017 (Hearts) 3
Smith, S. 2007 (Rangers) 1
Sneddon, A. 1979 (Celtic) 1
Snodgrass, R. 2008 (Livingston) 2
Soutar, D. 2003 (Dundee) 11
Souttar, J. 2016 (Dundee U, Hearts) 6
Speedie, D. R. 1985 (Chelsea) 1
Spencer, J. 1991 (Rangers) 3
Stanton, P. 1977 (Hibernian) 1
Stanton, S. 2014 (Hibernian) 1
Stark, W. 1985 (Aberdeen) 1
Stephen, R. 1983 (Dundee) 1
Stevens, G. 1977 (Motherwell) 1
Stevenson, L. 2008 (Hibernian) 8
Stewart, C. 2002 (Kilmarnock) 1
Stewart, J. 1978 (Kilmarnock, Middlesbrough) 3
Stewart, M. J. 2000 (Manchester U) 17
Stewart, R. 1979 (Dundee U, West Ham U) 12
Stillie, D. 1995 (Aberdeen) 14
Storie, C. 2017 (Aberdeen) 2
Strachan, G. D. 1998 (Coventry C) 7
Sturrock, P. 1977 (Dundee U) 9
Sweeney, P. H. 2004 (Millwall) 8
Sweeney, S. 1991 (Clydebank) 7

Tapping, C. 2013 (Hearts) 1
Tarrant, N. K. 1999 (Aston Villa) 5
Taylor, G. J. 2017 (Kilmarnock) 1
Teale, G. 1997 (Clydebank, Ayr U) 6
Telfer, P. N. 1993 (Luton T) 3
Templeton, D. 2011 (Hearts) 2
Thomas, D. 2017 (Motherwell) 1
Thomas, K. 1993 (Hearts) 8
Thompson, S. 1997 (Dundee U) 12
Thomson, C. 2011 (Hearts) 2
Thomson, J. A. 2017 (Celtic) 1
Thomson, K. 2005 (Hibernian) 6
Thomson, W. 1977 (Partick Thistle, St Mirren) 10
Tolmie, J. 1980 (Morton) 1
Tortolano, J. 1987 (Hibernian) 2
Toshney, L. 2012 (Celtic) 5
Turner, I. 2005 (Everton) 6
Tweed, S. 1993 (Hibernian) 3

Wales, G. 2000 (Hearts) 1
Walker, A. 1988 (Celtic) 1
Walker, J. 2013 (Hearts) 1
Wallace, I. A. 1978 (Coventry C) 1
Wallace, L. 2007 (Hearts) 10
Wallace, M. 2012 (Hudderfield T) 4
Wallace, R. 2004 (Celtic, Sunderland) 4
Walsh, C. 1984 (Nottingham F) 5
Wark, J. 1977 (Ipswich T) 8
Watson, A. 1981 (Aberdeen) 4
Watson, K. 1977 (Rangers) 2
Watt, A. 2012 (Celtic) 9
Watt, M. 1991 (Aberdeen) 12
Watt. S. M. 2005 (Chelsea) 5
Webster, A. 2003 (Hearts) 2
Whiteford, A. 1997 (St Johnstone) 1
Whittaker, S. G. 2005 (Hibernian) 18
Whyte, D. 1987 (Celtic) 9
Wighton, C. R. 2017 (Dundee) 3
Wilkie, L. 2000 (Dundee) 6
Will, J. A. 1992 (Arsenal) 3
Williams, G. 2002 (Nottingham F) 9
Wilson, D. 2011 (Liverpool, Hearts) 13
Wilson, M. 2004 (Dundee U, Celtic) 19
Wilson, S. 1999 (Rangers) 7
Wilson, T. 1983 (St Mirren) 1
Wilson, T. 1988 (Nottingham F) 4
Winnie, D. 1988 (St Mirren) 1
Woods, M. 2006 (Sunderland) 2
Wotherspoon, D. 2011 (Hibernian) 16
Wright, P. 1989 (Aberdeen, QPR) 3
Wright, S. 1991 (Aberdeen) 14
Wright, T. 1987 (Oldham Ath) 1
Wylde, G. 2011 (Rangers) 7

Young, Darren 1997 (Aberdeen) 8
Young, Derek 2000 (Aberdeen) 5

WALES

Adams, N. W. 2008 (Bury, Leicester C) 5
Alfei, D. M. 2010 (Swansea C) 13
Aizlewood, M. 1979 (Luton T) 2
Allen, J. M. 2008 (Swansea C) 13
Anthony, B. 2005 (Cardiff C) 8

Baddeley, L. M. 1996 (Cardiff C) 2
Balcombe, S. 1982 (Leeds U) 1
Bale, G. 2006 (Southampton, Tottenham H) 4
Barnhouse, D. J. 1995 (Swansea C) 3
Basey, G. W. 2009 (Charlton Ath) 1
Bater, P. T. 1977 (Bristol R) 2
Beevers, L. J. 2005 (Boston U, Lincoln C) 7
Bellamy, C. D. 1996 (Norwich C) 8
Bender, T. J. 2011 (Colchester U) 4
Birchall, A. S. 2003 (Arsenal, Mansfield T) 12
Bird, A. 1993 (Cardiff C) 6
Blackmore, C. 1984 (Manchester U) 3
Blake, D. J. 2007 (Cardiff C) 14
Blake, N. A. 1991 (Cardiff C) 5
Blaney, S. D. 1997 (West Ham U) 3
Bloom, J. 2011 (Falkirk) 1
Bodin, B. P. 2010 (Swindon T, Torquay U) 21
Bodin, P. J. 1983 (Cardiff C) 1
Bond, J. H. 2011 (Watford) 1
Bowen, J. P. 1993 (Swansea C) 5
Bowen, M. R. 1983 (Tottenham H) 3
Boyle, T. 1982 (Crystal Palace) 1
Brace, D. P. 1995 (Wrexham) 6
Bradley, M. S. 2007 (Walsall) 17
Bradshaw, T. 2012 (Shrewsbury T) 8
Brough, M. 2003 (Notts Co) 3
Brown, J. D. 2008 (Cardiff C) 6
Brown, J. R. 2003 (Gillingham) 7
Brown, T. A. F. 2011 (Ipswich T, Rotherham U, Aldershot T) 10
Burns, W. J. 2013 (Bristol C) 18
Byrne, M. T. 2003 (Bolton W) 1

Calliste, R. T. 2005 (Manchester U, Liverpool) 15
Carpenter, R. E. 2005 (Burnley) 1
Cassidy, J. A. 2011 (Wolverhampton W) 8
Cegielski, W. 1977 (Wrexham) 2
Chamberlain, E. C. 2010 (Leicester C) 9
Chapple, S. R. 1992 (Swansea C) 8
Charles, J. D. 2016 (Huddersfield T, Barnsley) 9
Charles, J. M. 1979 (Swansea C) 2
Church, S. R. 2008 (Reading) 15

Clark, J. 1978 (Manchester U, Derby Co) 2
Coates, J. S. 1996 (Swansea C) 5
Coleman, C. 1990 (Swansea C) 3
Collins, J. M. 2003 (Cardiff C) 7
Collins, M. J. 2007 (Fulham, Swansea C) 2
Collison, J. D. 2008 (West Ham U) 7
Cornell, D. J. 2010 (Swansea C) 4
Cotterill, D. R. G. B. 2005 (Bristol C, Wigan Ath) 11
Coyne, D. 1992 (Tranmere R) 7
Craig, N. L. 2009 (Everton) 4
Critchell, K. A. R. 2005 (Southampton) 3
Crofts, A. L. 2005 (Gillingham) 10
Crowe, M. T. T. 2017 (Ipswich T) 1
Crowell, M. T. 2004 (Wrexham) 7
Curtis, A. T. 1977 (Swansea C) 1

Davies, A. 1982 (Manchester U) 6
Davies, A. G. 2006 (Cambridge U) 6
Davies, A. R. 2005 (Southampton, Yeovil T) 14
Davies, C. M. 2005 (Oxford U, Verona, Oldham Ath) 9
Davies, D. 1999 (Barry T) 1
Davies, G. M. 1993 (Hereford U, Crystal Palace) 7
Davies, I. C. 1978 (Norwich C) 1
Davies, L. 2005 (Bangor C) 1
Davies, R. J. 2006 (WBA) 4
Davies, S. 1999 (Peterborough U, Tottenham H) 10
Dawson, C. 2013 (Leeds U) 2
Day, R. 2000 (Manchester C, Mansfield T) 11
Deacy, N. 1977 (PSV Eindhoven) 1
De-Vulgt, L. S. 2002 (Swansea C) 2
Dibble, A. 1983 (Cardiff C) 3
Dibble, C. 2014 (Barnsley) 1
Doble, R. A. 2010 (Southampton) 10
Doughty, M. E. 2012 (QPR) 1
Doyle, S. C. 1979 (Preston NE, Huddersfield T) 2
Duffy, R. M. 2005 (Portsmouth) 7
Dummett, P. 2011 (Newcastle U) 3
Dwyer, P. J. 1979 (Cardiff C) 1

Eardley, N. 2007 (Oldham Ath, Blackpool) 11
Earnshaw, R. 1999 (Cardiff C) 10
Easter, D. J. 2006 (Cardiff C) 1
Ebdon, M. 1990 (Everton) 2
Edwards, C. N. H. 1996 (Swansea C) 7
Edwards, D. A. 2006 (Shrewsbury T, Luton T, Wolverhampton W) 9
Edwards, G. D. R. 2012 (Swansea C) 6
Edwards, R. I. 1977 (Chester) 2
Edwards, R. W. 1991 (Bristol C) 13
Evans, A. 1977 (Bristol R) 1
Evans, C. 2007 (Manchester C, Sheffield U) 13
Evans, J. A. J. 2014 (Fulham, Wrexham) 6
Evans, K. 1999 (Leeds U, Cardiff C) 4
Evans, L. 2013 (Wolverhampton W) 13
Evans, P. S. 1996 (Shrewsbury T) 1
Evans, S. J. 2001 (Crystal Palace) 2
Evans, T. 1995 (Cardiff C) 3

Fish, N. 2005 (Cardiff C) 2
Fleetwood, S. 2005 (Cardiff C) 5
Flynn, C. P. 2007 (Crewe Alex) 1
Folland, R. W. 2000 (Oxford U) 1
Foster, M. G. 1993 (Tranmere R) 1
Fowler, L. A. 2003 (Coventry C, Huddersfield T) 9
Fox, M. A. 2013 (Charlton Ath) 6
Freeman, K. 2012 (Nottingham F, Derby Co) 15
Freestone, R. 1990 (Chelsea) 1

Gabbidon, D. L. 1999 (WBA, Cardiff C) 17
Gale, D. 1983 (Swansea C) 2
Gall, K. A. 2002 (Bristol R, Yeovil T) 8
Gibson, N. D. 1999 (Tranmere R, Sheffield W) 11
Giggs, R. J. 1991 (Manchester U) 1
Gilbert, P. 2005 (Plymouth Arg) 12
Giles, D. C. 1977 (Cardiff C, Swansea C, Crystal Palace) 4
Giles, P. 1982 (Cardiff C) 3
Graham, D. 1991 (Manchester U) 1
Green, R. M. 1998 (Wolverhampton W) 16
Griffith, C. 1990 (Cardiff C) 1
Griffiths, C. 1991 (Shrewsbury T) 1
Grubb, D. 2007 (Bristol C) 1
Gunter, C. 2006 (Cardiff C, Tottenham H) 8

Haldane, L. O. 2007 (Bristol R) 1
Hall, G. D. 1990 (Chelsea) 1
Harrison, E. W. 2013 (Bristol R) 14
Hartson, J. 1994 (Luton T, Arsenal) 9
Haworth, S. O. 1997 (Cardiff C, Coventry C, Wigan Ath) 12
Hedges, R. P. 2014 (Swansea C) 11
Henley, A. 2012 (Blackburn R) 3
Hennessey, W. R. 2006 (Wolverhampton W) 6
Hewitt, E. J. 2012 (Macclesfield T, Ipswich T) 10
Hillier, I. M. 2001 (Tottenham H, Luton T) 5
Hodges, G. 1983 (Wimbledon) 5
Holden, A. 1984 (Chester C) 1
Holloway, C. D. 1999 (Exeter C) 2
Hopkins, J. 1982 (Fulham) 5
Hopkins, S. A. 1999 (Wrexham) 1
Howells, J. 2012 (Luton T) 5
Huggins, D. S. 1996 (Bristol C) 1
Hughes, D. 2005 (Kaiserslautern, Regensburg) 2
Hughes, D. R. 1994 (Southampton) 1
Hughes, I. 1992 (Bury) 11
Hughes, L. M. 1983 (Manchester U) 5
Hughes, R. D. 1996 (Aston Villa, Shrewsbury T) 13
Hughes, W. 1977 (WBA) 3
Huws, E. W. 2012 (Manchester C) 6

Isgrove, L. J. 2013 (Southampton) 6

Jackett, K. 1981 (Watford) 2
Jacobson, J. M. 2006 (Cardiff C, Bristol R) 15
James, D. 2017 (Swansea C) 3
James, L. R. S. 2006 (Southampton) 10
James, R. M. 1977 (Swansea C) 3
Jarman, L. 1996 (Cardiff C) 10
Jeanne, L. C. 1999 (QPR) 8
Jelleyman, G. A. 1999 (Peterborough U) 1
Jenkins, L. D. 1998 (Swansea C) 9
Jenkins, S. R. 1993 (Swansea C) 2
John, D. C. 2014 (Cardiff C) 9
Jones, C. T. 2007 (Swansea C) 1
Jones, E. P. 2000 (Blackpool) 1
Jones, F. 1981 (Wrexham) 1
Jones, G. W. 2014 (Everton) 9
Jones, J. A. 2001 (Swansea C) 3
Jones, L. 1982 (Cardiff C) 3
Jones, M. A. 2004 (Wrexham) 4
Jones, M. G. 1998 (Leeds U) 7
Jones, O. R. 2015 (Swansea C) 1
Jones, P. L. 1992 (Liverpool) 12
Jones, R. 2011 (AFC Wimbledon) 1
Jones, R. A. 1994 (Sheffield W) 3
Jones, S. J. 2005 (Swansea C) 1
Jones, V. 1979 (Bristol R) 2

Kendall, L. M. 2001 (Crystal Palace) 2
Kendall, M. 1978 (Tottenham H) 1
Kenworthy, J. R. 1994 (Tranmere R) 3
King, A. 2008 (Leicester C) 11
Knott, G. R. 1996 (Tottenham H) 1

Law, B. J. 1990 (QPR) 2
Lawless, A. 2006 (Torquay U) 1
Lawrence, T. 2013 (Manchester U) 8
Ledley, J. C. 2005 (Cardiff C) 5
Letheran, G. 1977 (Leeds U) 2
Letheran, K. C. 2006 (Swansea C) 1
Lewis, D. 1982 (Swansea C) 9
Lewis, J. 1983 (Cardiff C) 1
Llewellyn, C. M. 1998 (Norwich C) 14
Lockyer, T. A. 2015 (Bristol R) 7
Loveridge, J. 1982 (Swansea C) 3
Low, J. D. 1999 (Bristol R, Cardiff C) 1
Lowndes, S. R. 1979 (Newport Co, Millwall) 4
Lucas, L. P. 2011 (Swansea C) 19

MacDonald, S. B. 2006 (Swansea C) 25
McCarthy, A. J. 1994 (QPR) 3
McDonald, C. 2006 (Cardiff C) 3
Mackin, L. 2006 (Wrexham) 1
Maddy, P. 1982 (Cardiff C) 2
Margetson, M. W. 1992 (Manchester C) 7
Martin, A. P. 1999 (Crystal Palace) 1
Martin, D. A. 2006 (Notts Co) 1
Marustik, C. 1982 (Swansea C) 7
Matthews, A. J. 2010 (Cardiff C) 5
Maxwell, C. 2009 (Wrexham) 16
Maxwell, L. J. 1999 (Liverpool, Cardiff C) 14
Meades, J. 2012 (Cardiff C) 4

Meaker, M. J. 1994 (QPR) 2
Melville, A. K. 1990 (Swansea C, Oxford U) 2
Micallef, C. 1982 (Cardiff C) 3
Morgan, A. M. 1995 (Tranmere R) 4
Morgan, C. 2004 (Wrexham, Milton Keynes D) 12
Morris, A. J. 2009 (Cardiff C, Aldershot T) 8
Moss, D. M. 2003 (Shrewsbury T) 6
Mountain, P. D. 1997 (Cardiff C) 2
Mumford, A. O. 2003 (Swansea C) 4

Nardiello, D. 1978 (Coventry C) 1
Neilson, A. B. 1993 (Newcastle U) 7
Nicholas, P. 1978 (Crystal Palace, Arsenal) 3
Nogan, K. 1990 (Luton T) 2
Nogan, L. M. 1991 (Oxford U) 1
Nyatanga, L. J. 2005 (Derby Co) 10

Oakley, A. 2013 (Swindon T) 1
O'Brien, B. T. 2015 (Manchester C) 8
Ogleby, R. 2011 (Hearts, Wrexham) 12
Oster, J. M. 1997 (Grimsby T, Everton) 9
O'Sullivan, T. P. 2013 (Cardiff C) 15
Owen, G. 1991 (Wrexham) 8

Page, R. J. 1995 (Watford) 4
Parslow, D. 2005 (Cardiff C) 4
Partington, J. M. 2009 (Bournemouth) 8
Partridge, D. W. 1997 (West Ham U) 1
Pascoe, C. 1983 (Swansea C) 4
Pearce, S. 2006 (Bristol C) 3
Pejic, S. M. 2003 (Wrexham) 6
Pembridge, M. A. 1991 (Luton T) 1
Peniket, R. 2012 (Fulham) 1
Perry, J. 1990 (Cardiff C) 3
Peters, M. 1992 (Manchester C, Norwich C) 3
Phillips, D. 1984 (Plymouth Arg) 3
Phillips, G. R. 2001 (Swansea C) 3
Phillips, L. 1979 (Swansea C, Charlton Ath) 2
Pipe, D. R. 2003 (Coventry C, Notts Co) 12
Pontin, K. 1978 (Cardiff C) 1
Poole, R. L. 2017 (Manchester U) 3
Powell, L. 1991 (Southampton) 4
Powell, L. 2004 (Leicester C) 3
Powell, R. 2006 (Bolton W) 1
Price, J. J. 1998 (Swansea C) 7
Price, L. P. 2005 (Ipswich T) 10
Price, M. D. 2001 (Everton, Hull C, Scarborough) 13
Price, P. 1981 (Luton T) 1
Pritchard, J. P. 2013 (Fulham) 3
Pritchard, M. O. 2006 (Swansea C) 4
Pugh, D. 1982 (Doncaster R) 2
Pugh, S. 1993 (Wrexham) 2
Pulis, A. J. 2006 (Stoke C) 5

Ramasut, M. W. T. 1997 (Bristol R) 4
Ramsey, A. J. 2008, (Cardiff C, Arsenal) 12
Ratcliffe, K. 1981 (Everton) 2
Ray, G. E. 2013 (Crewe Alex) 5
Ready, K. 1992 (QPR) 5
Rees, A. 1984 (Birmingham C) 1
Rees, J. M. 1990 (Luton T) 3
Rees, M. R. 2003 (Millwall) 4
Reid, B. 2014 (Wolverhampton W) 1
Ribeiro, C. M. 2008 (Bristol C) 8
Richards, A. D. J. 2010 (Swansea C) 16
Richards, E. A. 2012 (Bristol R) 1
Roberts, A. M. 1991 (QPR) 2
Roberts, C. 2013 (Cheltenham T) 6
Roberts, C. J. 1999 (Cardiff C) 1
Roberts, C. R. J. 2016 (Swansea C) 2
Roberts, G. 1983 (Hull C) 1
Roberts, G. W. 1997 (Liverpool, Panionios, Tranmere R) 11
Roberts, J. G. 1977 (Wrexham) 1
Roberts, N. W. 1999 (Wrexham) 3
Roberts, P. 1997 (Porthmadog) 1
Roberts, S. I. 1999 (Swansea C) 13
Roberts, S. W. 2000 (Wrexham) 3
Robinson, C. P. 1996 (Wolverhampton W) 6
Robinson, J. R. C. 1992 (Brighton & HA, Charlton Ath) 5
Robson-Kanu, K. H. 2010 (Reading) 4
Rodon, J. P. 2017 (Swansea C) 2
Rowlands, A. J. R. 1996 (Manchester C) 5
Rush, I. 1981 (Liverpool) 2

Savage, R. W. 1995 (Crewe Alex) 3
Saunders, C. L. 2015 (Crewe Alex) 1
Sayer, P. A. 1977 (Cardiff C) 2
Searle, D. 1991 (Cardiff C) 6
Sheehan, J. L. 2014 (Swansea C) 12
Shephard, L. 2015 (Swansea C) 2
Slatter, D. 2000 (Chelsea) 6
Slatter, N. 1983 (Bristol R) 6
Smith, D. 2014 (Shrewsbury T) 3
Somner, M. J. 2004 (Brentford) 2
Speed, G. A. 1990 (Leeds U) 3
Spender, S. 2005 (Wrexham) 6
Stephens, D. 2011 (Hibernian) 7
Stevenson, N. 1982 (Swansea C) 2
Stevenson, W. B. 1977 (Leeds U) 3
Stock, B. B. 2003 (Bournemouth) 4
Symons, C. J. 1991 (Portsmouth) 2

Tancock, S. 2013 (Swansea C) 6
Taylor, A. J. 2012 (Tranmere R) 3
Taylor, G. K. 1995 (Bristol R) 4
Taylor, J. W. T. 2010 (Reading) 12
Taylor, N. J. 2008 (Wrexham, Swansea C) 13
Taylor, R. F. 2008 (Chelsea) 5
Thomas, C. E. 2010 (Swansea C) 3
Thomas, D. G. 1977 (Leeds U) 3
Thomas, D. J. 1998 (Watford) 2
Thomas, J. A. 1996 (Blackburn R) 21
Thomas, Martin R. 1979 (Bristol R) 2
Thomas, Mickey R. 1977 (Wrexham) 2
Thomas, S. 2001 (Wrexham) 5
Thompson, L. C. W. 2015 (Norwich C) 2
Tibbott, L. 1977 (Ipswich T) 2
Tipton, M. J. 1998 (Oldham Ath) 6
Tolley, J. C. 2001 (Shrewsbury T) 12
Tudur-Jones, O. 2006 (Swansea C) 3
Twiddy, C. 1995 (Plymouth Arg) 3

Valentine, R. D. 2001 (Everton, Darlington) 8
Vaughan, D. O. 2003 (Crewe Alex) 8
Vaughan, N. 1982 (Newport Co) 2
Vokes, S. M. 2007 (Bournemouth, Wolverhampton W) 14

Walsh, D. 2000 (Wrexham) 8
Walsh, I. P. 1979 (Crystal Palace, Swansea C) 2
Walsh, J. 2012 (Swansea C, Crawley T) 11
Walton, M. 1991 (Norwich C.) 1
Ward, D. 1996 (Notts Co) 2
Ward, D. 2013 (Liverpool) 6
Warlow, O. J. 2007 (Lincoln C) 2
Weeks, D. L. 2014 (Wolverhampton W) 2
Weston, R. D. 2001 (Arsenal, Cardiff C) 4
Wharton, T. J. 2014 (Cardiff C) 1
Whitfield, P. M. 2003 (Wrexham) 1
Wiggins, R. 2006 (Crystal Palace) 9
Williams, A. P. 1998 (Southampton) 9
Williams, A. S. 1996 (Blackburn R) 16
Williams, D. 1983 (Bristol R) 1
Williams, D. I. L. 1998 (Liverpool, Wrexham) 9
Williams, D. T. 2006 (Yeovil T) 1
Williams, E. 1997 (Caernarfon T) 2
Williams, G. 1983 (Bristol R) 2
Williams, G. A. 2003 (Crystal Palace) 5
Williams, G. C. 2014 (Fulham) 3
Williams, J. P. 2011 (Crystal Palace) 8
Williams, M. 2001 (Manchester U) 10
Williams, M. P. 2006 (Wrexham) 14
Williams, M. J. 2014 (Notts Co) 1
Williams, M. R. 2006 (Wrexham) 6
Williams, O. fon 2007 (Crewe Alex, Stockport Co) 11
Williams, R. 2007 (Middlesbrough) 10
Williams, S. J. 1995 (Wrexham) 4
Wilmot, R. 1982 (Arsenal) 6
Wilson, H. 2014 (Liverpool) 8
Wilson, J. S. 2009 (Bristol C) 3
Worgan, L. J. 2005 (Milton Keynes D, Rushden & D) 5
Wright, A. A. 1998 (Oxford U) 3
Wright, J. 2014 (Huddersfield T) 2

Yorwerth, J. 2014 (Cardiff C) 7
Young, S. 1996 (Cardiff C) 5

FA SCHOOLS AND YOUTH GAMES 2016–17

▪ *Denotes player sent off.*

ENGLAND UNDER-16

FRIENDLIES

Buftea, Tuesday 24 August 2016

Romania (1) 1 *(Mitrea 2)*

England (2) 3 *(Matthews 19, Appiah 40, Mola 57)*

England: Ashby-Hammond; Aina, Appiah (Saka 77), Elewa-Ikpakwu, Mola, Doyle, Cottrell, Amaechi, Matthews (Cashman 61), Coyle (Maghoma 61), John-Jules.

Buftea, Thursday 26 August 2016

Romania (0) 2 *(June 71, Bodea 74)*

England (0) 1 *(Saka 80)*

England: Wickens; Daley-Campbell (Doyle 41), Asare, Mola (Aina 41), Saka, Bowden (Matthews 60), Ogbeta (Elewa-Ikpakwu 68), Amaechi (Coyle 41), Maghoma (Cottrell 68), Elliott (John-Jules 68), Cashman.

Teresopolis, Wednesday 23 November 2016

Brazil 3 *(Vitor, Julio Vitor)*

England 4 *(Duncan 3, Amaechi)*

England: Ashby-Hammond; Asare, Williams, Mola, Saka, Doyle, Dixon-Bonner, Longstaff, Coyle, Duncan, Amaechi.
Substitutes: Okonkwo, Anjorin, Alese, Appiah, Maghoma, Cashman, Jones, Glatzel, John-Jules.

Teresopolis, Friday 25 November 2016

Brazil 1 *(Vitor)*

England 0

England: Okonkwo; Asare, Alese, Anjorin, Saka, Dixon-Bonner, Glatzel, Maghoma, Duncan, John-Jules, Appiah.
Substitutes: Ashby-Hammond, Williams, Doyle, Longstaff, Coyle, Cashman, Mola, Amaechi, Jones.

VAL DE MARNE TOURNAMENT

Villejuif, Tuesday 25 October 2016

USA (0) 2 *(Llanez 61 (pen), 80)*

England (0) 1 *(Maghoma 58 (pen))*

England: Ashby-Hammond; Aina, Williams, Mola, Appiah, Maghoma, Cottrell (Dixon-Bonner 62), Matthews (Mumba 60), Jones, Tulloch, Glatzel.

Boissy-Saint-Leger, Thursday 27 October 2016

France (0) 1 *(Taoui 70)*

England (0) 0

England: Seaden; Mumba, Asare, Mola, Devine, Clarkson, Dixon-Bonner, Maghoma, Jones, Johnson, Tulloch.
Substitutes: Ashby-Hammond, Aina, Cottrell, Appiah, Glatzel, Williams, Matthews.

Boissy-Saint-Leger, Saturday 29 October 2016

England (0) 0

Russia (2) 3 *(Sevikyan 10, Kutovojs 29, Markitesov 75)*

England: Ashby-Hammond; Aina, Asare, Williams, Devine, Clarkson, Dixon-Bonner, Cottrell, Matthews, Johnson, Glatzel.
Substitutes: Seaden, Mumba, Mola, Appiah, Maghoma, Jones, Tulloch.

UEFA UNDER-16 DEVELOPMENT TOURNAMENT

Burton, Wednesday 15 February 2017

England 4 *(Cashman, Tulloch 2, Duncan (pen))*

Finland 0

England: Okonkwo; Asare, Saka, Alese, Solanke, Dixon-Bonner, Maghoma, Amaechi, Tahir, Tulloch, Cashman.
Substitutes: Doyle, Anjorin, Longstaff, Duncan, John-Jules, Seaden, Ogbeta, Mola, Jones.

Leek, Friday 17 February 2017

England (0) 1 *(John-Jules 52)*

Spain (2) 5 *(Bayon B 8, Zoubdi 37, Rodriguez 41, Mollejo 54, Camello 80)*

England: Seaden; Asare, Ogbeta, Mola, Anjorin, Doyle, Dixon-Bonner, Longstaff, John-Jules, Jones, Duncan.
Substitutes: Okonkwo, Saka, Alese, Cashman, Tahir, Tulloch.

Burton, Monday 20 February 2017

England 3 *(Duncan 38, 47 (pen), Jones)*

Italy 1 *(Gyabuaa 30)*

England: Okonkwo; Solanke, Saka, Anjorin, Alese, Doyle, Maghoma, Jones, Cashman, Longstaff, Duncan.
Substitutes: Asare, John-Jules, Seaden, Dixon-Bonner, Ogbeta, Mola, Amaechi, Tahir.

MONTAIGU TOURNAMENT

La Chaize le Vicomte, Tuesday 11 April 2017

England 1 *(Johnson)*

Mexico 1 *(Martinez Vidrio)*

England: Seaden; Asare (Binks), Alese, Ogbeta (Shihab), Jasper, Doyle, Kpohomouh, Perry (Johnson), Wright-Phillips (Whittaker), Duncan, Hilton (Maghoma).

La Chaize le Vicomte, Thursday 13 April 2017

England (0) 0

Portugal (0) 3 *(Faustino 48, Embalo 61, Tavares 65)*

England: Wickens; Shihab, Mola, Anjorin, Binks, Maghoma, Kpohomouh, Johnson, Duncan, Whittaker, Cashman.
Substitutes: Seaden, Asare, Doyle, Alese, Ogbeta, Wright-Phillips, Hilton, Perry, Jasper.

La Chaize le Vicomte, Saturday 15 April 2017

China PR 0

England 4 *(Whittaker 3, Jasper)*

England: Seaden; Alese, Ogbeta, Anjorin, Shihab, Perry, Hilton, Wright-Phillips, Johson, Jasper, Whittaker.
Substitutes: Wickens, Asare, Mola, Doyle, Duncan, Maghoma, Cashman, Kpohomouh, Binks.

Mouilleron le Captif, Monday 17 April 2017

Belgium 4 *(Cuypers 9, Berben 36, Suray 38, Sidibe 74)*

England 0

England: Wickens; Perry, Alese, Binks, Ogbeta, Doyle, Mola, Anjorin, Wright-Phillips, Cashman, Whittaker.
Substitutes: Seaden, Asare, Duncan, Maghoma, Shhihab, Hilton, Kpohomouh, Johnson, Jasper.

ENGLAND UNDER-17

FRIENDLIES

Burton, 25 August 2016

England (2) 3 *(Gomes 4, Brewster 40, Eyoma 68)*

Belgium (1) 1 *(Leoni 21)*

England: Anderson; Guehi, Gibson, Skipp, Eyoma, Strachan, Smith-Rowe, Oakley-Boothe, Brewster, Gomes, Poveda.

Burton, 25 August 2016

England (3) 6 *(Sancho 2, Lyons-Foster 13, Loader 24, Foden 60, McEachran 61, Gibbs-White 69)*

Belgium (0) 0

England: McGill; Lavinier, Latibeaudiere, Panzo, Lyons-Foster, Kirby, McEachran, Sancho, Foden, Gibbs-White, Loader.

UNDER-17 CROATIA CUP

Pula, Wednesday 28 September 2016

Croatia (0) 0

England (4) 5 *(Sancho 10, Brewster 12, 31, 62, Gomes 18)* 300

England: Anderson; Wilson (Guehi 52), Latibeaudiere, Panzo, Gibson (Lyons-Foster 52), Gibbs-White (Gibbs-White 59), McEachran■, Foden, Gomes, Sancho (Smith-Rowe 68), Brewster (Hudson-Odoi 68).

Novigrad, Friday 30 September 2016

England (1) 3 *(Loader 30, Smith-Rowe 47, Hudson-Odoi 73)*

Greece (0) 0

England: McGill; Lavinier, Lyons-Foster, Guehi, Gibson, Denny, Gomes (Foden 46), Poveda-Ocampo, Smith-Rowe (Sancho 67), Hudson-Odoi, Loader (Brewster 67).

Pula, Monday 3 October 2016

Germany (1) 1 *(Schlax 12)*

England (6) 8 *(Gomes 4, Sancho 8, Foden 29, McEachran 31, Brewster 34, 37, Hudson-Odoi 59, 76)*

England: Anderson, Wilson, Lyons-Foster (Lavinier 46), Latibeaudiere, Panzo (Gibson 46), Foden (Denny 59), McEachran, Gomes (Poveda-Ocampo 64), Sancho, Hudson-Odoi (Smith-Rowe 64), Brewster (Loader 46).

2017 UEFA UNDER-17 QUALIFYING – GROUP 6

Buftea, Tuesday 25 October 2016

England (2) 2 *(Gomes 16, Sancho 23)*

Azerjaban (0) 0 100

England: McGill; Eyoma, Gibbs-White, Latibeaudiere, Panzo, Foden (Oakley-Boothe 73), McEachran, Gomes (Hudson-Odoi 65), Sancho (Smith-Rowe 65), Gibson, Brewster.

Buftea, Thursday 27 October 2016

Romania (0) 0

England (2) 3 *(Foden 1, 13, Sancho 68)* 450

England: McGill; Eyoma, Latibeaudiere, Panzo (Lyons-Foster 23), Gibson, Oakley-Boothe (Loader 69), McEachran, Gomes, Foden, Hudson-Odoi, Sancho (Denny 72).

Voluntari, Sunday 30 October 2016

Austria (1) 2 *(Ballo 28, 78 (pen))*

England (1) 3 *(Gibson 39, Loader 44, Brewster 65 (pen))* 100

England: Anderson; Lyons-Foster, Denny, Panzo, Gibson, Gibbs-White, Oakley-Boothe, Hudson-Odoi, Loader, Smith-Rowe, Brewster.

2017 UEFA UNDER-17 ELITE ROUND – GROUP 7

Bijeljina, Thursday 23 March 2017

England (3) 5 *(Brewster 9, 46, Foden 11, 66, Gibbs-White 15)*

Czech Republic (2) 3 *(Majka 37, Pechacek 47, Hezoucky 76)*

England: McGill; McEachran, Guehi, Panzo, Foden (Loader 69), Brewster, Hudson-Odoi (Kirby 67), Sancho (Oakley-Booth 72), Gibbs-White, Sessegnon, Wilson.

Bijeljina, Saturday 25 March 2017

England (2) 4 *(Sancho 25, 76, Eyoma 29, Loader 54)*

Slovenia (0) 0

England: Bursik; Eyoma, Gibson, McEachran (Gibbs-White 74), Guehi, Panzo, Foden (Hudson-Odoi 66), Kirby, Brewster (Oakley-Booth 61), Sancho, Loader.

Bijeljina, Tuesday 28 March 2017

Bosnia-Herzegovina (0) 0

England (1) 1 *(Gibson 15)*

England: Bursik; Eyoma, Gibson, Guehi (Panzo 41), Kirby, Hudson-Odoi, Oakley Boothe, Gibbs-White, Sessegnon, Loader, Wilson.

2017 UEFA UNDER-17 FINALS CROATIA – GROUP D

Velika Gorica, Thursday 4 May 2017

Norway (1) 1 *(Guehi 7 (og))*

England (2) 3 *(Brewster 10, 35, Foden 78)*

England: Bursik; Eyoma, Guehi, Panzo, Gibson, Foden (Loader 79), Oakley-Boothe, McEachran, Sancho, Brewster (Griffiths 80), Hudson-Odoi.

Sesveste, Sunday 7 May 2017

England (3) 4 *(McEachran 20, Sancho 36, Barlow 69)*

Ukraine (0) 0

England: Bursik; Eyoma, Gibson, McEachran, Guehi, Panzo, Foden (Loader 59), Oakley-Boothe (Barlow 66), Brewster, Hudson-Odoi, Sancho (Smith-Rowe 74).

Zapresic, Wednesday 10 May 2017

England (1) 3 *(Sancho 23, 48 (pen), Hudson-Odoi 80)*

Netherlands (0) 0

England: Bursik; Eyoma, Gibson, McEachran, Guehi, Panzo, Foden (Barlow 67), Oakley-Boothe, Brewster (Loader 56), Hudson-Odoi, Sancho (Smith-Rowe 62).

QUARTER-FINALS

Zapresic, Tuesday 16 May 2017

England (1) 1 *(Sancho 13)*

Republic of Ireland (0) 0

England: Bursik; Eyoma, Guehi, Panzo, Gibson, McEachran, Foden, Oakley-Boothe, Brewster, Hudson-Odoi, Sancho.

SEMI-FINALS

Zapresic, Tuesday 16 May 2017

Turkey (1) 1 *(Kesgin 40)*

England (2) 2 *(Hudson-Odoi 11, Sancho 37)*

England: Bursik; Eyoma, Gibson, McEachran, Guehi, Panzo, Foden (Smith-Rowe 76), Oakley-Boothe (Denny 26), Brewster, Hudson-Odoi (Loader 69), Sancho.

2017 UEFA UNDER-17 FINAL

Varazdin, Friday 19 May 2017

Spain (1) 2 *(Morey 38, Diaz 80)*

England (1) 2 *(Hudson-Odoi 18, Foden 58)* 8187

England: Bursik; Gibson, McEachran, Guehi, Panzo, Foden (Loader 80), Brewster, Hudson-Odoi (Barlow 77), Sancho (Vokins 80), Denny, Latibeaudiere.
Spain won 4-1 on penalties.

ALGARVE TOURNAMENT

Algarve, Friday 10 February 2017

Portugal (1) 1 *(Embalo 40)*

England (0) 0

England: Anderson; Eyoma (Latibeaudiere 55), Vokins, Guehi (Sessegnon 55), Gibson, Kirby (Harper 41), Denny (Oakley-Boothe 62), Richards, Gomes (Loader 41), Walker, Soule (Brewster 55).

Algarve, Sunday 12 February 2017

Germany (0) 2 *(Malone 70, Mbom 80)*

England (1) 3 *(Sancho 14, Foden 59, Brewster 68)*

England: McGill; Eyoma, Gibson (Gibson 27), Oakley-Boothe, Sessegnon, Latibeaudiere, Foden (Richards 70), Kirby (Denny 70), Brewster (Walker 77), Gomes (Harper 64), Sancho.

Algarve, Tuesday 14 February 2017

Netherlands (0) 0

England (1) 1 *(Walker 9)*

England: Anderson; Wilson, Vokins, Harper, Sessegnon, Latibeaudiere, Denny, Richards, Brewster, Walker, Sancho.
Substitutes: McGill, Eyoma, Gibson, Oakley-Boothe, Guehi, Foden, Kirby, Gomes, Loader, Soule.

ENGLAND UNDER-18

UNDER-18 FA INTERNATIONAL TOURNAMENT

Fleetwood, Thursday 1 September 2016

England (1) 2 *(Mount 37, 73)*

Italy (0) 1 *(Gabbia 69)* 1581

England: Thompson; Williams, Feeney, Kigbu, Bola, Adeniran (McGuane 60), Diallo (Dozzell 60), Leko (Morris 80), Mount, Nelson (Brown 89), Ennis (Hirst 80).

Morecambe, Monday 5 September 2016

England (3) 5 *(Feeney 8, Hirst 43, 45, Nelson 54, Brown 74)*

Israel (0) 1 *(Nadir 59)*

England: Sandford; Williams (Adeniran 46), Feeney, Dinzeyi, Brown, Dozzell (Bola 64), McGuane (Diallo 61), Morris (Ennis 76), Mount, Leko (Nelson 46), Hirst.

FRIENDLIES

Kungsangens, Friday 7 October 2016

Sweden (0) 1 *(Ahmedhodzic 88)*

England (0) 0 1543

England: Balcombe; Tanganga, Brown, McGuane (Adeniran 83), Feeney, Dinzeyi, Leko (Taylor-Crossdale 72), Dozzell, Hirst, Mount, Embleton.

Taby, Sunday 9 October 2016

Sweden (0) 1 *(Ahmedhodzic 47)*

England (2) 2 *(Mount 32, Taylor-Crossdale 40)* 737

England: Sandford; Tanganga (Brown 46), Bola, Uwakwe, Feeney, Kigbu, Leko (Hirst 85), Adeniran, Taylor-Crossdale, Mount (Dozzell 78), Embleton.

Stevenage, Thursday 10 November 2016

England (1) 2 *(Hirst 38, 49)*

Poland (0) 0 2655

England: Balcombe; Bola, McGuane, Feeney, Tanganga, Dinzeyi, Adeniran, Dozzell, Embleton, Hirst, Leko (Ennis 63).

Peterborough, Monday 14 November 2016

England (0) 0

France (0) 0 3084

England: Turner; Tanner, Feeney, Dinzeyi, Brown, Embleton (Taganga 83), Uwakwe (Dozzell 60), Adeniran (McGuane 60), Mount, Leko, Ennis (Hirst 64).
France won 5-4 on penalties.

Doha, Wednesday 22 March 2017

Saudi Arabia (0) 0

England (1) 2 *(Feeney 5, Nketiah 57)*

England: Balcombe; James, Tymon, Diallo, Feeney, Tanganga (Bola 87), Leko (Tanner 77), Embleton (McGuane 83), Nketiah Hirst 83), Dozzell, Nelson (Shashoua 77).

Doha, Friday 24 March 2017

Qatar (1) 1 *(Unknown 45)*

England (1) 2 *(Hirst 15, Shashoua 88)*

England: Turner; Tanner, Bola, McGuane, James, Tanganga, Leko, Nydam, Hirst, Uwakwe, Shashoua.
Substitutes: Schofield, Feeney, Francis, Diallo, Dozzell, Embleton, Nketiah, Tymon.

Doha, Monday 27 March 2017

Qatar (0) 0

England (1) 4 *(Nketiah 14, 53, 63, Tanner 87)*

England: Schofield; Tymon, Francis, Feeney, James, Diallo, Embleton, Nketiah (Tanner 82), Dozzell, Shashoua (McGuane 69), Hirst (Bola 86).

ENGLAND UNDER-19

UEFA EUROPEAN UNDER-19 CHAMPIONSHIP FINALS GERMANY – GROUP B

Heidenheim, Tuesday 12 July 2016

France (1) 1 *(Augustin 33)*

England (2) 2 *(Onguene 3 (og), Solanke 9)* 2344

England: Woodman; Kenny, Moore, Tomori, Connolly Walker-Peters 65), Rossiter, Maitland-Niles, Ojo (Abraham 65), Onomah, Solanke, Brown (Ledson 78).

Ulm, Friday 15 July 2016

Netherlands (1) 1 *(Lammers 10)*

England (1) 2 *(Solanke 36, Brown 90)* 3928

England: Woodman; Oxford, Moore, Tomori, Walker-Peters, Rossiter, Onomah, Maitland-Niles, Abraham, Solanke (Ojo 62), Lookman (Brown 75).

Heidenheim, Monday 18 July 2016

England (2) 2 *(Brown 4, Anocic 10)*

Croatia (0) 1 *(Moro 58)* 7400

England: Woodman; Moore (Maitland-Niles 78), Fry, Oxford, Kenny, Walker-Peters, Onomah, Ledson, Ojo, Lookman, Brown.

SEMI-FINALS

Mannheim, Thursday 21 July 2016

England (0) 1 *(Picchi (og) 85)*

Italy (1) 2 *(Dimarco 27 (pen), 60)* 7412

England: Woodman; Kenny, Oxford, Tomori, Walker-Peters, Onomah, Rossiter, Maitland-Niles, Solanke, Abraham (Ojo 58), Brown.

FRIENDLIES

Telford, Thursday 1 September 2016

England (1) 1 *(Davies 45)*

Netherlands (0) 1 *(Hoogma 84)*

England: Mannion (Pears 46); Alexander-Arnold, DaSilva (Field 61), Davies (Evans 61), Humphreys, Suliman, Holland (Hepburn-Murphy 80), Edun (Sterling 80), Willock (Buckley-Ricketts 80), Nmecha (Green 80), Maddox (Chalobah 61).
England won 9-8 on penalties.

Brussels, Sunday 4 September 2016

Belgium (1) 1 *(Vancamp 40)*

England (0) 0

England: Ramsdale; Sterling, DaSilva (Alexander-Arnold 75), Davies (Edun 75), Johnson, Chalobah, Buckley-Ricketts (Holland 88), Field, Hepburn-Murphy, Evans (Nmecha 62), Green (Willock 75).

Zagreb, Friday 7 October 2016

Croatia (0) 1 *(Majic 51)*

England (1) 3 *(Alexander-Arnold 34, 56 (pen), Mavididi 50)*

England: Ramsdale; Alexander-Arnold, DaSilva, Davies, Johnson, Chalobah, Sterling (Green 88), Edun (Field 88), Mavididi (Buckley-Ricketts 88), Willock (Edwards 70), Sessegnon.

Wycombe, Monday 10 October 2016

England (1) 2 *(Edwards 9, Sterling 90)*

Bulgaria (0) 1 *(Ivanov 70)* 676

England: Pears (Mannion 46); Alexander-Arnold (Chalobah 71), DaSilva, Humphreys (Willock 85), Suliman, Davies (Edun 60), Buckley-Ricketts (Sterling 40), Field, Edwards (Johnson 85), Mavididi, Green (Sessegnon 60).

2017 UEFA UNDER-19 QUALIFYING – GROUP 6

Rhyl, Thursday 10 November 2016

England (1) 2 *(Mavididi 3, Sessegnon 80)*

Luxembourg (0) 0

England: Ramsdale; Alexander-Arnold, Williams, Chalobah, DaSilva, Sterling, Edun, Mavididi (Willock, Davies, Sessegnon (Green 84), Hepburn-Murphy (Nmecha 71).

Bangor, Saturday 12 November 2016

Wales (1) 3 *(Broadhead 34, 74, Harris 60)*

England (0) 2 *(Alexander-Arnold 62, 72 (pen))* 732

Wales: Hale-Brown; Cole, DaSilva, Ampadu, Poole, Woodburn (Harris 57), Smith, Roberts, Broadhead (Evans 86), Lewis, Ovenden.
England: Ramsdale, Alexander-Arnold (Green 81), DaSilva, Davies, Williams, Chalobah, Sterling, Edun, Willock, Sessegnon (Hepburn-Murphy 74), Mavididi (Nmecha 63).

Rhyl, Tuesday 15 November 2016

England (1) 2 *(Arnold 20, Chalobah 63)*

Greece (0) 0 260

England: Ramsdale, Arnold, Suliman, Chalobah, DaSilva, Sterling, Davies, Willock (Nmecha 74), Field, Green (Sessegnon 58), Hepburn-Murphy (Mavididi 80).

2017 UEFA UNDER-19 ELITE ROUND – GROUP 3

Burton, Wednesday 22 March 2017

England (1) 3 *(Mount 33, Edun 46, Field 55)*

Norway (0) 0

England: Ramsdale; Alexander-Arnold (Oxford 66), DaSilva, Chalobah, Sterling (Buckley-Ricketts 67), Field, Nmecha, Mount, Sessegnon (Willock 73), Edun, Suliman.

Burton, Friday 24 March 2017

England (1) 3 *(Alexander-Arnold 9, 64, Willock 86)*

Spain (0) 0

England: Ramsdale; Alexander-Arnold, DaSilva, Davies (Field 80), Chalobah, Oxford, Sterling, Mount, Sessegnon (Willock 74), Edun, Brereton (Buckley-Ricketts 85).

Burton, Monday 27 March 2017

England (2) 5 *(Nmecha 15, Buckley-Ricketts 24, Edwards 57, Willock 61, 74)*

Belarus (1) 1 *(Mukhamedov 5)*

England: Whiteman; DaSilva, Oxford (Alexander-Arnold 66), Sterling (Chalobah 66), Field, Nmecha (Brereton 74), Edun, Willock, Suliman, Edwards, Buckley-Ricketts.

ENGLAND UNDER-20

FRIENDLIES

Burton, Thursday 1 September 2016

England (0) 1 *(Maitland-Niles 83)*

Brazil (1) 1 *(Richarlison 31)*

England: Southwood (Henderson 46); Tafari Moore (Walker-Peters 75), Taylor Moore, Fry, Lowe, Ledson, Tuanzebe (Maitland-Niles 56), Roberts P (Onomah 56), Lookman, Dowell, Armstrong (Calvert-Lewin 75).
Behind closed doors. Brazil won 4-3 on penalties.

Kidderminster, Sunday 4 September 2016

England (0) 1 *(Calvert-Lewin 80)*

Brazil (2) 2 *(Pacqueta 8, Malcolm 26)*

England: Woodman; Walker-Peters, Borthwick-Jackson (Tafari Moore 46 (Tuanzebe 86)), Cook, Oxford (Fry 46), Tomori (Taylor Moore 46), Chapman (Ledson 46), Onomah, Armstrong (Calvert-Lewin 63), Maitland-Niles, Dowell (Lookman 46).
Brazil won 3-2 in penalty shoot-out practice.

U20 INTERNATIONAL TOURNAMENT

Oldham, Wednesday 5 October 2016

England (2) 2 *(Roberts P 6, Armstrong 13)*

Netherlands (0) 0

England: Southwood; Walker-Peters, Tomori, Clarke-Salter, Tafari Moore, Tuanzebe, Dowell, Roberts P, Reed (Cook 75), Chapman (Roberts C 75), Armstrong (Calvert-Lewin 81).

Huddersfield, Friday 7 October 2016

England (2) 3 *(Lookman 14, Calvert-Lewin 23, 72)*

Germany (1) 1 *(Ochs 3)* 2882

England: Henderson; Kenny, Fry, Taylor Moore, Connolly, Cook (Tuanzebe 72), Maitland-Niles, Ejaria, Lookman, Solanke (Chapman 55), Calvert-Lewin.

Rochdale, Monday 10 October 2016

England (0) 2 *(Ejaria 84, Solanke 90 (pen))*

USA (0) 0

England: Henderson (Southwood 46); Walker-Peters (Kenny 46), Oxford, Clarke-Salter (Taylor Moore 46), Connolly (Tafari Moore 63), Maitland-Niles, Reed (Tuanzebe 46), Roberts C (Dowell 63), Roberts P (Armstrong 63), Chapman (Ejaria 76), Solanke.

CONTINENTAL CUP

Suwon, Korea Republic, Wednesday 9 November 2016

England (4) 8 *(Taylor Moore 19, Armstrong 20, 27, 70, Solanke 25, Connolly 46, Roberts P 49, 87)*

Nigeria (1) 1 *(Yusuf 35)*

England: Henderson (Southwood 46); Walker-Peters, Fry, Taylor Moore (Kenny 75), Connolly (Tomori 75), Tuanzebe, Dowell, Roberts P, Solanke (Calvert-Lewin 75), Brown (Lookman 82), Armstrong.

Suwon, Korea Republic, Thursday 10 November 2016

Korea Republic (1) 2 *(Lee 31, 70)*

England (1) 1 *(Ejaria 14)*

England: Woodman; Kenny, Tomori, Clarke-Salter, Tafari Moore, Onomah (Solanke 78), Maitland-Niles, Ejaria (Reed 70), Lookman, Calvert-Lewin, Chapman.

Suwon, Korea Republic, Saturday 12 November 2016

Iran (0) 1 *(Jafari 54)*

England (1) 4 *(Armstrong 32, Solanke 51, 76, Brown 68)*

England: Woodman, Kenny (Tafari Moore 46), Fry (Tomori 46), Clarke-Salter (Taylor Moore 46), Connolly (Walker-Peters 46), Reed, Maitland-Niles (Onomah 46), Dowel (Ejaria 71), Roberts (Brown 46), Chapman (Lookman 46), Armstrong (Solanke 46).

UNDER-20 INTERNATIONAL TOURNAMENT, FOUR NATIONS

Saint-Brieuc, Thursday 23 March 2017

England (2) 2 *(Solanke 22, Roberts 38)*

Portugal (0) 2 *(Ferreira F 65, Ferreira H 90)*

England: Woodman; Kenny, Henry, Cook, Fry, Clarke-Slater (Tomori 83), Lookman (Armstrong 74), Roberts (Tunazebe 83), Onomah (Maitland-Niles 55), Solanke, Dowell.

Saint-Brieuc, Saturday 25 March 2017

France (0) 0

England (0) 1 *(Armstrong 71)*

England: Henderson; Tuanzebe, Tomori, Armstrong (Dowell 88), Connolly, Cook (Lookman 46), Sims (Roberts 67), Ledson, Lowe (Henry 67), Maitland-Niles, Calvert-Lewin (Solanke 58).

Ploufragan, Saturday 28 March 2017

Senegal (0) 0

England (2) 2 *(Calvert-Lewin 6, Solanke 18)*

England: Southwood; Tomori, Clarke-Salter (Fry 75), Henry (Lowe 46), Kenny (Connolly 46), Cook (Tuanzebe 66), Maitland-Niles, Roberts (Armstrong 66), Solanke, Lookman (Dowell 46), Calvert-Lewin (Sims 46).

TOULON TOURNAMENT
(England mixed age group due to U20 World Cup)

GROUP Q

Aubagne, Monday 29 May 2017

Angola (0) 0

England (0) 1 *(Ugbo 46)*

England: Schofield; Worrall, Grant, Tymon, James, Ukwakwe (Brooks 58), Vieira, Mitchell, Kemp (Barnes 58), Embleton, Ugbo (Hirst 75).

Salon-de-Provence, Thursday 1 June 2017

Cuba (1) 1 *(Saucedo 37)*

England (2) 7 *(Barnes 19, 44, Hirst 34, 54, 65 (pen), Brooks 61, Taylor-Crossdale 77 (pen))*

England: Schofield; James (Bolton 55), Grant (Moore 62), Tymon, Worrall, Tanganga, Barnes (Taylor-Crossdale 59), Vieira (Slattery 48), Embleton, Hirst, Brooks.

Toulon, Sunday 4 June 2017

Japan (0) 1 *(Ando 53)*

England (1) 2 *(Hirst 25 (pen), Taylor-Crossdale 72 (pen))*

England: Balcombe; Tymon, Moore, Tanganga, Mitchell, Slattery, Ukwakwe (Embleton 75), Kemp (75), Bolton (James 66), Hirst (Barnes 59), Taylor-Crossdale.

SEMI-FINALS

Fos-sur-Mer, Thursday 8 June 2017

England (1) 3 *(Barnes 7, 65, Embleton 52)*

Scotland (0) 0

England: Schofield; James, Grant, Tymon, Worrall, Barnes, Mitchell, Vieira, Embleton, Brooks (Kemp 67), Ugbo (Hirst 63).
Scotland: Ruddy; Ralston, Iacovitti, McCart, Taylor, McCrorie (Sammut 23 (Maggenis 69)), Holsgrove, Wilson, Wighton (Hardie 54), Frizzell, Burke.

TOULON TOURNAMENT 2017 FINAL

Aubagne, Saturday 10 June 2017

Ivory Coast (0) 1 *(Loba 80 (pen))*

England (1) 1 *(Brooks 14)*

England: Schofield; James, Grant, Tymon (Tanganga 52), Worrall, Barnes, Mitchell (Slattery 77), Vieira, Embleton, Hirst (Ugbo 58), Brooks (Uwakwe 65).
England won 5-3 on penalties.

FIFA U20 WORLD CUP 2017 – KOREA REPUBLIC

GROUP A

Jeonju World Cup Stadium, Saturday 20 May 2017

England (1) 3 *(Calvert-Lewin 38, Armstrong 52, Solanke 90 (pen))*

Argentina (0) 0

England: Woodman; Kenny, Connolly, Cook, Tomori, Clarke-Salter, Onomah (Ejaria 84), Armstrong (Naitland-Miles 66), Solanke, Calvert-Lewin, Dowell (Ojo 73).

Jeonju World Cup Stadium, Tuesday 23 May 2017

England (0) 1 *(Cook 53)*

Guinea (0) 1 *(Tomori 59 (og))*

England: Henderson; Kenny, Tomori, Clarke-Salter, Connolly, Lookman (Calvert-Lewin 73), Cook, Maitland-Niles, Ojo (Dowell 63), Armstrong (Chapman 81), Solanke.

Suwon World Cup Stadium, Friday 26 May 2017

England (0) 1 *(Dowell 56)*

Korea Republic (0) 0

England: Woodman; Kenny, Fry, Tomori, Walker-Peters, Ejaria, Onomah, Dowell, Maitland-Niles (Solanke 28), Lookman (Ojo 85), Calvert-Lewin.

ROUND OF 16

Jeonju World Cup Stadium, Wednesday 31 May 2017

England (1) 2 *(Lookman 35, 63)*

Costa Rica (0) 1 *(Leal 89)*

England: Woodman; Kenny, Fry, Tomori, Walker-Peters, Cook, Onomah (Maitland-Niles 75), Dowell (Chapman 84), Solanke, Lookman, Calvert-Lewin (Armstrong 71).

QUARTER-FINALS

Cheonan Sports Complex, Monday 5 June 2017

England (0) 1 *(Solanke 47)*

Mexico (0) 0

England: Woodman; Kenny, Tomori, Fry, Walker-Peters, Cook, Onomah■, Dowell (Maitland-Niles 90), Solanke, Lookman (Ejaria 75), Armstrong (Calvert-Lewin 70).

SEMI-FINALS

Jeonju World Cup Stadium, Thursday 8 June 2017

Italy (1) 1 *(Orsolini 2)*

England (0) 3 *(Solanke 66, 88, Lookman 77)*

England: Woodman; Kenny, Tomori, Clarke-Salter, Walker-Peters, Cook, Maitland-Niles, Lookman (Konsa 90), Solanke, Dowell (Ojo 54), Calvert-Lewin.

FIFA U20 WORLD CUP 2017 FINAL – KOREA REPUBLIC

Suwon World Cup Stadium, Sunday 11 June 2017

Venezuela (0) 0

England (1) 1 *(Calvert-Lewin 35)*

England: Woodman; Kenny, Tomori, Clarke-Salter, Walker-Peters, Cook, Onomah, Lookman (Maitland-Niles 76), Solanke, Dowell (Ojo 62), Calvert-Lewin.
Venezuela: Farinez; Velasquez, Ferraresi, Jose Hernandez, Ronald Hernandez, Herrera, Lucena, Penaranda (Hurtado 90), Pena, Chacon (Soteldo 52), Cordova (Sosa 72).

SCHOOLS FOOTBALL 2016–17

BOODLES INDEPENDENT SCHOOLS FA CUP 2016–17

**After extra time.*

PRELIMINARY ROUND

Bournemouth Collegiate v Lingfield Notre Dame	3-1
Frensham Heights v Box Hill	3-0
Haberdashers' Aske's v RGS Guildford	5-0
Harrodian v Dover College	7-0
Kingston GS v ACS Cobham	1-4
Merchant Taylors (Crosby) v Grange	3-1
Queen Ethelburga's College v Cheadle Hulme	2-3
Radnor House v Trinity	2-6
RGS Worcester v John Lyon	1-0
Sevenoaks v St John's, Leatherhead	3-0
Sherborne v Berkhamsted	1-3*
St John's College, Southsea v Hurstpierpoint	0-6
Taunton v Bedales	4-3*

FIRST ROUND

Aldenham v Brooke House College	4-3*
Ardingly v LVS Ascot	11-0
Bedford Modern v Alleyn's	0-7
Bede's v Sevenoaks	5-1
Berkhamsted v Trinity	4-3*
Birkdale v Brentwood	1-9
Bolton v Whitgift	0-0*
(Whitgift won 4-1 on penalties)	
Bury GS v Grammar School at Leeds	3-1
Canford v Malvern	4-0
Charterhouse v Latymer Upper	6-2
Frensham Heights v Wolverhampton GS	0-3
Harrodian v RGS Worcester	5-1
Harrow v St Columba's College	6-1
Highgate v Haileybury	5-3*
Hurstpierpoint v Chigwell	1-4
Ibstock Place v Bournemouth Collegiate	3-0
King Edward's Witley v Kimbolton	1-3
King's School, Chester v Manchester GS	2-2*
(King's School won 5-4 on penalties)	
Lancing v ACS Cobham	2-1*
Millfield v Bradfield	2-2*
(Millfield won 5-4 on penalties)	
Norwich v Cheadle Hulme	0-3
Oldham Hulme GS v Hampton	1-7
RGS Newcastle v City of London	1-3
Royal Russell v Colfe's	4-1
Shrewsbury v University College School	5-0
St Bede's College, Manchester v Westminster	4-1
Stockport GS v Merchant Taylors (Crosby)	3-3*
(Merchant Taylors won 5-4 on penalties)	
Tonbridge v Haberdashers' Aske's	4-1
Taunton v Eton	0-10
Truro v Forest	0-6
Wellington v Repton	0-8
Winchester v Dulwich	5-2

SECOND ROUND

Aldenham v Ardingly	4-4*
(Aldenham won 4-2 on penalties)	
Alleyn's v King's School, Chester	2-1
Brentwood v Royal Russell	0-2
Bury GS v Ibstock Place	1-0
Canford v Shrewsbury	5-7*
Cheadle Hulme v Bede's	1-1*
(Cheadle Hulme won 4-2 on penalties)	
City of London v Harrodian	5-4
Eton v Lancing	1-0
Forest v Winchester	4-3
Hampton v St Bede's College, Manchester	6-1
Harrow v Whitgift	3-1
Kimbolton v Berkhamsted	3-2
Millfield v Chigwell	5-1
Merchant Taylors, Crosby v Charterhouse	3-5
Repton v Highgate	5-1
Wolverhampton GS v Tonbridge	1-3

THIRD ROUND

Cheadle Hulme v Royal Russell	1-3
Eton v Harrow	3-0
Forest v Kimbolton	4-1
Hampton v Aldenham	5-1
Millfield v Alleyn's	3-1
Repton v Bury GS	9-1
Shrewsbury v City of London	3-2
Tonbridge v Charterhouse	1-5

FOURTH ROUND

Eton v Millfield	0-4
Forest v Hampton	0-1*
Royal Russell v Charterhouse	1-1*
(Royal Russell won 3-1 on penalties)	
Shrewsbury v Repton	2-1

SEMI-FINALS

Hampton v Royal Russell	0-1
Millfield v Shrewsbury	3-3*
(Millfield won 9-8 on penalties)	

FINAL (at Milton Keynes Dons FC)

Royal Russell 2 *(Pike (og), Obazee)* **Millfield 1** *(Tenientes)*

Royal Russell: L. Greenwood; M. O'Donoghue, R. Norrington-Davies, M. Weller, M. Penn-Kekana, B. Linter, J. Sims, P. Ogunmekan, R. Doherty, S. Johnson, L. Shango.
Substitutes: A. Hewitt, R. Obazee, D. Davis, N. Wilson, D. O'Rourke.
Millfield: M. Price; O. Light, S. Cunningham, C. Pike, M. McGlinchey, T. Tenientes, P. Stein, D. Walker, M. Samuel, H. Ardron, H. Lee.
Substitutes: F. Francis, A. Eckland, C. Leelavichitchai, J. Hunter-Lees, N. Martins.
Referee: Martin Atkinson (Yorkshire).

INVESTEC ISFA U15 CUP FINAL

Whitgift v Forest 3-1
(at Burton Albion FC)

INVESTEC ISFA U13 CUP FINAL

Moorland v Whitgift 1-0*
(at Burton Albion FC)

UNIVERSITY FOOTBALL 2017

133rd UNIVERSITY MATCH

(Sunday 19 March, at The Hive, Barnet FC)

Oxford (1) 3 Cambridge (1) 2

Oxford: Windmill; Stamper, Hale, Brown, Wroe, Wade, Dinneen, Bain, Thelen, Crespo, Feeney, Pilley, Wicker, Urwin, Moneke, Gleeson.
Scorers: Thelen, Salama (og), Crespo.

Cambridge: Warne; Congdon, Gregory, Sears-Black, Salama, Makings, Huybrechts, Wolf, Herring, Rodrigues, Bolderson, Nielsen, Harrison, Saunders, Crease, Burley, Celsus.
Scorers: Bolderson, Nielsen.

Referee: Paul Tierney (Lancashire).

Oxford have won 54 games (2 on penalties), Cambridge 52 games (3 on penalties) and 27 games have been drawn. Oxford have scored 211 goals, Cambridge 207 goals.

WOMEN'S SUPER LEAGUE 2016

FA WOMEN'S SUPER LEAGUE 1 TABLE 2016

			Home					*Away*					*Total*						
		P	*W*	*D*	*L*	*F*	*A*	*W*	*D*	*L*	*F*	*A*	*W*	*D*	*L*	*F*	*A*	*GD*	*Pts*
1	Manchester C	16	6	2	0	18	2	7	1	0	18	2	13	3	0	36	4	32	42
2	Chelsea	16	5	1	2	19	12	7	0	1	23	5	12	1	3	42	17	25	37
3	Arsenal	16	4	1	3	13	7	6	1	1	20	7	10	2	4	33	14	19	32
4	Birmingham C	16	4	2	2	6	8	3	4	1	12	5	7	6	3	18	13	5	27
5	Liverpool	16	3	3	2	10	9	4	1	3	17	14	7	4	5	27	23	4	25
6	Notts Co	16	3	1	4	11	17	1	3	4	5	9	4	4	8	16	26	−10	16
7	Sunderland	16	1	2	5	7	24	1	2	5	10	17	2	4	10	17	41	−24	10
8	Reading	16	0	3	5	5	12	1	3	4	10	14	1	6	9	15	26	−11	9
9	Doncaster R Belles	16	0	0	8	5	27	1	0	7	3	21	1	0	15	8	48	−40	3

FA WOMEN'S SUPER LEAGUE 1 RESULTS 2016

	Arsenal	Birmingham C	Chelsea	Doncaster R Belles	Liverpool	Manchester C	Notts Co	Reading	Sunderland
Arsenal	—	0-0	0-2	2-0	1-2	0-1	2-0	3-1	5-1
Birmingham C	0-0	—	0-4	2-1	2-1	0-2	1-0	0-0	1-0
Chelsea	1-2	1-1	—	4-0	6-3	0-2	2-1	3-2	2-1
Doncaster R Belles	0-5	0-1	1-4	—	1-3	0-4	1-2	1-4	1-4
Liverpool	3-5	1-0	1-2	1-0	—	0-0	0-0	2-0	2-2
Manchester C	2-0	1-1	2-0	6-0	1-1	—	1-0	2-0	3-0
Notts Co	0-2	0-1	1-3	2-1	3-2	1-5	—	2-2	2-1
Reading	1-2	1-1	0-3	0-1	0-1	1-2	1-1	—	1-1
Sunderland	0-4	1-7	0-5	4-0	0-4	0-2	1-1	1-1	—

FA WOMEN'S SUPER LEAGUE 1 LEADING GOALSCORERS 2016

Player	*Team*	*Goals*	*Player*	*Team*	*Goals*
Eniola Aluko	Chelsea	9	Jess Clarke	Notts Co	5
Jane Ross	Manchester C	8	Toni Duggan	Manchester C	5
Caroline Weir	Liverpool	7	Francesca Kirby	Chelsea	5
Danielle Carter	Arsenal	6	Beth Mead	Sunderland	5
Katie Chapman	Chelsea	5	Ji So-Yun	Chelsea	5

FA WOMEN'S SUPER LEAGUE 2 TABLE 2016

			Home					*Away*					*Total*						
		P	*W*	*D*	*L*	*F*	*A*	*W*	*D*	*L*	*F*	*A*	*W*	*D*	*L*	*F*	*A*	*GD*	*Pts*
1	Yeovil T	18	7	1	1	24	6	5	2	2	17	10	12	3	3	41	16	25	39
2	Bristol C	18	7	1	1	19	6	5	2	2	18	10	12	3	3	37	16	21	39
3	Everton	18	5	3	1	21	8	5	1	3	14	10	10	4	4	35	18	17	34
4	Durham	18	6	1	2	14	7	4	2	3	16	12	10	3	5	30	19	11	33
5	Sheffield	18	4	2	3	13	9	3	3	3	12	9	7	5	6	25	18	7	26
6	Aston Villa	18	4	2	3	15	11	3	1	5	11	16	7	3	8	26	27	−1	24
7	London Bees	18	3	2	4	14	21	3	2	4	14	18	6	4	8	28	39	−11	22
8	Millwall Lionesses	18	1	4	4	9	14	2	3	4	15	17	3	7	8	24	31	−7	16
9	Oxford U	18	3	1	5	13	21	1	0	8	7	21	4	1	13	20	42	−22	13
10	Watford	18	2	0	7	9	25	0	1	8	4	28	2	1	15	13	53	−40	7

FA WOMEN'S SUPER LEAGUE 2 RESULTS 2016

	Aston Villa	Bristol C	Durham	Everton	London Bees	Millwall Lionesses	Oxford U	Sheffield	Watford	Yeovil T
Aston Villa	—	2-2	2-0	0-2	1-1	3-1	2-1	1-2	4-0	0-2
Bristol C	2-0	—	1-0	0-1	3-0	2-1	4-1	0-0	4-1	3-2
Durham	3-0	0-0	—	1-3	2-0	2-1	2-1	1-0	3-0	0-2
Everton	2-1	2-3	1-1	—	5-1	1-1	3-0	1-1	3-0	3-0
London Bees	2-1	0-3	2-2	3-4	—	2-1	3-1	0-5	2-2	0-2
Millwall Lionesses	2-2	1-2	0-1	2-2	1-1	—	*	1-1	2-1	0-4
Oxford U	0-1	0-5	1-5	0-1	4-2	3-5	—	1-0	2-0	2-2
Sheffield	1-2	3-1	0-1	1-0	0-1	2-2	2-1	—	3-0	1-1
Watford	0-2	0-2	1-6	2-1	0-5	1-2	3-2	1-3	—	1-2
Yeovil T	4-2	2-0	4-0	1-0	2-3	1-1	2-0	3-0	5-0	—

**Match postponed, Oxford U awarded 3 points without game being played.*

FA WOMEN'S SUPER LEAGUE 2 LEADING GOALSCORERS 2016

Player	*Team*	*Goals*
Ini-Abasi Umotong	Oxford U	13
Jo Wilson	London Bees	13
Sarah Wiltshire	Yeovil T	11
Claire Emslie	Bristol C	10
Millie Farrow	Bristol C	9
Beth Hepple	Durham	9
Bethan Merrick	Aston Villa	9
Ann-Marie Heatherson	Yeovil T	7
Jodie Michalska	Sheffield	7
Ashlee Hincks	Millwall Lionesses	6
Claudia Walker	Everton	6
Katie Wilkinson	Aston Villa	6

WOMEN'S SUPER LEAGUE CONTINENTAL TYRES CUP 2016

**After extra time.*

PRELIMINARY ROUND

Sheffield v Durham	3–1
Oxford U v Millwall Lionesses	1–0
Watford v London Bees	0–2

FIRST ROUND

Aston Villa v Manchester C	0–8
Everton v Liverpool	0–1
Reading v Arsenal	1–3
London Bees v Chelsea	3–3*
London Bees won 4-2 on penalties.	
Sheffield v Bristol C	2–0
Doncaster R Belles v Sunderland	2–1
Oxford U v Birmingham C	0–2
Yeovil T v Notts Co	1–3

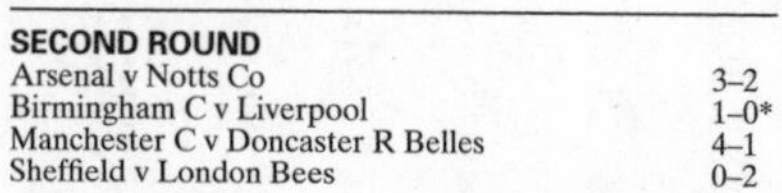

SECOND ROUND

Arsenal v Notts Co	3–2
Birmingham C v Liverpool	1–0*
Manchester C v Doncaster R Belles	4–1
Sheffield v London Bees	0–2

SEMI-FINALS

London Bees v Birmingham C	0–4
Manchester C v Arsenal	1–0

CONTINENTAL TYRES CUP FINAL 2016

Academy Stadium, Manchester,
Sunday 2 October 2016

Manchester C (0) 1 *(Bronze 105)*

Birmingham C (0) 0 4214

Manchester C: Hourihan; Bronze, Houghton, Beattie, Stokes, Walsh, Scott, Christiansen, Parris (Asllani 65), Duggan (Corboz 105), Ross (Middag 84).
Birmingham C: Berger; Sargeant, Carter, Harrop, Ayisi (Linden 105), Linnett (Wellings 75), Hegerberg (Peplow 90), Ewers, Lawley, Westwood, Mannion.
Referee: Rebecca Welch.
aet.

Manchester City's Jill Scott puts City 4-1 up as they beat Birmingham City to win the Women's FA Cup at Wembley Stadium. (Reuters/Paul Childs Livepic)

FA WOMEN'S PREMIER LEAGUE 2016–17

FA WOMEN'S PREMIER LEAGUE NORTHERN DIVISION 2016–17

			Home					Away					Total						
		P	*W*	*D*	*L*	*F*	*A*	*W*	*D*	*L*	*F*	*A*	*W*	*D*	*L*	*F*	*A*	*GD*	*Pts*
1	Blackburn R	20	8	2	0	32	12	9	1	0	27	8	17	3	0	59	20	39	54
2	Middlesbrough	20	6	1	3	27	14	8	0	2	33	17	14	1	5	60	31	29	43
3	Leicester City Women	20	6	2	2	25	20	4	2	4	19	17	10	4	6	44	37	7	34
4	Stoke C	20	4	3	3	18	15	4	3	3	25	22	8	6	6	43	37	6	30
5	Derby Co	20	6	0	4	22	18	3	2	5	17	17	9	2	9	39	35	4	29
6	WBA	20	5	1	4	17	16	3	2	5	16	21	8	3	9	33	37	–4	27
7	Fylde*	20	5	2	3	20	12	3	3	4	16	18	8	5	7	36	30	6	26
8	Bradford C	20	5	1	4	19	13	2	0	8	21	27	7	1	12	40	40	0	22
9	Huddersfield T	20	4	4	2	22	21	1	1	8	15	32	5	5	10	37	53	–16	20
10	Nottingham F	20	3	1	6	18	28	2	2	6	9	21	5	3	12	27	49	–22	18
11	Newcastle U	20	2	0	8	12	33	0	1	9	4	32	2	1	17	16	65	–49	7

**Fylde deducted 3 points.*

FA WOMEN'S PREMIER LEAGUE SOUTHERN DIVISION 2016–17

			Home					Away					Total						
		P	*W*	*D*	*L*	*F*	*A*	*W*	*D*	*L*	*F*	*A*	*W*	*D*	*L*	*F*	*A*	*GD*	*Pts*
1	Tottenham H	20	8	1	1	26	7	9	0	1	32	6	17	1	2	58	13	45	52
2	Coventry U	20	7	2	1	29	7	8	1	1	26	8	15	3	2	55	15	40	48
3	Cardiff C	20	8	0	2	44	8	6	2	2	28	11	14	2	4	72	19	53	44
4	Charlton Ath	20	6	1	3	27	15	7	2	1	28	10	13	3	4	55	25	30	42
5	Crystal Palace	20	5	3	2	28	9	4	3	3	20	14	9	6	5	48	23	25	33
6	C & K Basildon	20	5	1	4	17	17	3	2	5	12	25	8	3	9	29	42	–13	27
7	Lewes	20	4	2	4	19	17	3	2	5	12	19	7	4	9	31	36	–5	25
8	Portsmouth	20	4	0	6	21	29	1	2	7	10	37	5	2	13	31	66	–35	17
9	West Ham U	20	0	4	6	4	27	1	2	7	8	32	1	6	13	12	59	–47	9
10	Swindon T	20	1	1	8	8	27	1	1	8	12	33	2	2	16	20	60	–40	8
11	QPR	20	0	2	8	4	32	2	0	8	7	32	2	2	16	11	64	–53	8

FA WOMEN'S PREMIER LEAGUE NORTHERN DIVISION ONE 2016–17

			Home					Away					Total						
		P	*W*	*D*	*L*	*F*	*A*	*W*	*D*	*L*	*F*	*A*	*W*	*D*	*L*	*F*	*A*	*GD*	*Pts*
1	Guiseley Vixens	22	9	2	0	35	7	10	0	1	37	13	19	2	1	72	20	52	59
2	Liverpool Marshall Feds	22	7	0	4	25	12	6	5	0	41	17	13	5	4	66	29	37	44
3	Hull C	22	6	1	3	27	15	8	0	4	27	23	14	1	7	54	38	16	43
4	Chester-le-Street T	22	7	1	3	33	18	6	1	4	25	24	13	2	7	58	42	16	41
5	Chorley	22	7	0	4	29	25	5	2	4	22	19	12	2	8	51	44	7	38
6	Brighouse T	22	4	3	4	21	21	7	1	3	29	13	11	4	7	50	34	16	37
7	Morecambe*	22	6	2	4	35	23	4	0	6	16	27	10	2	10	51	50	1	29
8	Leeds	22	3	1	7	25	27	4	1	6	26	32	7	2	13	51	59	–8	23
9	Mossley Hill Ath	22	2	0	9	25	43	4	1	6	20	29	6	1	15	45	72	–27	19
10	Crewe Alex	22	3	4	4	18	23	1	2	8	13	36	4	6	12	31	59	–28	18
11	Blackpool Wren R	22	3	2	6	21	28	2	1	8	16	40	5	3	14	37	68	–31	18
12	Tranmere R	22	1	1	9	12	37	0	3	8	7	33	1	4	17	19	70	–51	7

**Morecambe deducted 3 points.*

FA WOMEN'S PREMIER LEAGUE MIDLANDS DIVISION ONE 2016–17

			Home					Away					Total						
		P	*W*	*D*	*L*	*F*	*A*	*W*	*D*	*L*	*F*	*A*	*W*	*D*	*L*	*F*	*A*	*GD*	*Pts*
1	Wolverhampton W	22	9	1	1	35	12	9	1	1	22	6	18	2	2	57	18	39	56
2	Loughborough Foxes	22	10	0	1	54	10	8	0	3	57	21	18	0	4	111	31	80	54
3	Sporting Khalsa	22	8	1	2	40	11	5	1	5	17	22	13	2	7	57	33	24	41
4	Radcliffe Olympic	22	8	0	3	33	12	5	1	5	25	24	13	1	8	58	36	22	40
5	Birmingham & West Midlands	22	7	1	3	29	18	6	0	5	30	27	13	1	8	59	45	14	40
6	The New Saints	22	7	1	3	37	21	5	2	4	28	23	12	3	7	65	44	21	39
7	Long Eaton U	22	6	3	2	35	16	3	0	8	19	29	9	3	10	54	45	9	30
8	Steel City W	22	5	1	5	34	38	4	0	7	12	24	9	1	12	46	62	–16	28
9	Solihull	22	4	3	4	20	18	2	2	7	21	37	6	5	11	41	55	–14	23
10	Leicester City Ladies	22	3	0	8	16	32	2	2	7	11	56	5	2	15	27	88	–61	17
11	Rotherham U	22	3	0	8	23	31	2	1	8	22	39	5	1	16	45	70	–25	16
12	Loughborough Students*	22	0	0	11	10	54	0	1	10	9	58	0	1	21	19	112	–93	0

**Loughborough Students deducted 1 point.*

FA WOMEN'S PREMIER LEAGUE SOUTH EAST DIVISION ONE 2016–17

			Home					Away					Total						
		P	W	D	L	F	A	W	D	L	F	A	W	D	L	F	A	GD	Pts
1	Gillingham	22	9	2	0	57	8	9	1	1	47	6	18	3	1	104	14	90	57
2	Milton Keynes D	22	9	0	2	37	10	7	1	3	26	11	16	1	5	63	21	42	49
3	AFC Wimbledon	22	8	1	2	34	11	5	4	2	23	17	13	5	4	57	28	29	44
4	Cambridge U	22	7	1	3	30	17	6	1	4	25	18	13	2	7	55	35	20	41
5	Luton T	22	6	3	2	25	15	5	1	5	19	24	11	4	7	44	39	5	37
6	Actonians	22	5	3	3	17	14	5	3	3	34	23	10	6	6	51	37	14	36
7	Enfield T	22	5	2	4	20	23	2	2	7	11	28	7	4	11	31	51	–20	25
8	Denham U	22	6	0	5	26	27	2	1	8	12	32	8	1	13	38	59	–21	25
9	Ipswich T	22	3	2	6	15	28	4	2	5	21	30	7	4	11	36	58	–22	25
10	Norwich C	22	2	4	5	11	34	2	0	9	20	47	4	4	14	31	81	–50	16
11	Stevenage	22	2	2	7	14	24	1	4	6	5	21	3	6	13	19	45	–26	15
12	Lowestoft T	22	1	0	10	13	40	1	0	10	8	42	2	0	20	21	82	–61	6

FA WOMEN'S PREMIER LEAGUE SOUTH WEST DIVISION ONE 2016–17

			Home					Away					Total						
		P	W	D	L	F	A	W	D	L	F	A	W	D	L	F	A	GD	Pts
1	Chichester C	20	10	0	0	51	2	9	1	0	49	6	19	1	0	100	8	92	58
2	Plymouth Arg	20	9	0	1	57	12	9	0	1	47	7	18	0	2	104	19	85	54
3	Southampton Saints	20	8	1	1	29	16	4	4	2	23	16	12	5	3	52	32	20	41
4	Keynsham T	20	6	1	3	39	14	6	1	3	32	18	12	2	6	71	32	39	38
5	Larkhall Ath	20	6	2	2	20	16	5	1	4	25	26	11	3	6	45	42	3	36
6	Brislington	20	3	3	4	23	27	3	1	6	21	36	6	4	10	44	63	–19	22
7	Maidenhead U*	19	3	1	5	13	23	2	1	7	13	31	5	2	12	26	54	–28	17
8	St Nicholas	20	3	2	5	21	42	1	1	8	10	32	4	3	13	31	74	–43	15
9	Basingstoke T	20	3	2	5	15	26	0	3	7	14	31	3	5	12	29	57	–28	14
10	Cheltenham T	20	4	0	6	15	26	0	1	9	10	48	4	1	15	25	74	–49	13
11	Exeter C*	19	0	3	7	11	45	0	1	8	5	43	0	4	15	16	88	–72	4
12	Shanklin†	0	0	0	0	0	0	0	0	0	0	0	0	0	0	0	0	0	0

**Maidenhead U v Exeter C (21/5/2017) match postponed. †Shanklin resigned from league, record expunged.*

FA WOMEN'S PREMIER LEAGUE CUP 2016–17

**After extra time.*

DETERMINING ROUND

AFC Wimbledon v Plymouth Arg 3-2
Basingstoke T v Cheltenham T 3-0
Blackburn R v Rotherham U 19-0
Blackpool Wren R v Crewe Alex 5-0
C & K Basildon v St Nicholas 8-0
Cambridge U v Lewes 3-3*
Cambridge U won 4-2 on penalties.
Charlton Ath v Shanklin 8-1
Chichester C v Actonians 6-2
Coventry U v Maidenhead U 9-0
Denham U v Swindon T 2-1*
Derby Co v Steel City W 7-0
Enfield T v Exeter C 3-1
Huddersfield T v Fylde 1-2
Hull C v Guiseley Vixens 3-0
Ipswich T v Cardiff C 0-5
Keynsham T v Crystal Palace 1-2
Long Eaton U v Loughborough Students 13-0
Loughborough Foxes v Leicester City Ladies 9-3
Luton T v Milton Keynes D 1-3
Morecambe v Middlesbrough 0-3
Mossley Hill v Brighouse T 0-5
Newcastle U v Leicester City Women 2-1
Nottingham F v Chorley 3-1*
Portsmouth v Lowestoft T 8-2
QPR v Norwich C 2-3
Southampton Saints v Gillingham 0-4
Sporting Khalsa v Chester-le-Street T 2-4
Stevenage v Larkhall Ath 0-3
Stoke C v Birmingham & West Midlands 13-0
The New Saints v Solihull 3-0
Tranmere R v Liverpool Marshall Feds 0-5
WBA v Bradford C 2-1
West Ham U v Tottenham H 0-10
Wolverhampton W v Radcliffe Olympic 3-2
Forest Green R v Brislington (walkover)
Leeds (walkover) v Nuneaton T

FIRST ROUND

Blackburn R v Nottingham F 3-1
Denham U v Brislington 3-2
Gillingham v Norwich C 8-2
Long Eaton U v Liverpool Marshall Feds 1-1*
Liverpool Marshall Feds won 4-3 on penalties.

SECOND ROUND

Charlton Ath v C & K Basildon 3-2
Hull C v Middlesbrough 3-1
Leeds v Liverpool Marshall Feds 1-4
Loughborough Foxes v The New Saints 10-1
Stoke C v Derby Co 1-2*
Wolverhampton W v Brighouse T 2-2*
Wolverhampton W won 4-2 on penalties.
AFC Wimbledon v Crystal Palace 0-2
Chester-le-Street T v Blackpool Wren R 3-0
Coventry U v Denham U 3-0
Gillingham v Milton Keynes D 2-0
Newcastle U v Blackburn R 0-1
Portsmouth v Cambridge U 3-2
Tottenham H v Enfield T 5-1
WBA v Fylde 2-1*
Basingstoke T v Chichester C 0-5
Cardiff C (walkover) v Larkhall Ath

THIRD ROUND

Blackburn R v Loughborough Foxes 5-0
Cardiff C v Chichester C 7-1
Charlton Ath v Portsmouth 4-2
Chester-le-Street T v Derby Co 2-1
Crystal Palace v Coventry U 1-0
Hull C v Liverpool Marshall Feds 0-4
WBA v Wolverhampton W 1-0*
Tottenham H v Gillingham 4-2

QUARTER-FINALS

Liverpool Marshall Feds v Cardiff C 0-2
Charlton Ath v WBA 1-1*
Charlton Ath won 4-2 on penalties.
Chester-le-Street T v Blackburn R 1-3
Tottenham H v Crystal Palace 4-1

SEMI-FINALS

Tottenham H v Cardiff C 3-0
Charlton Ath v Blackburn R 4-3*

FA WOMEN'S PREMIER LEAGUE CUP FINAL 2017

Stevenage, Sunday 7 May 2017

Tottenham H (0) 0
Charlton Ath (0) 0 544

Tottenham H: Wayne; Leon, Rawle (O'Leary 90), McLean, Green (Pond 100), Baptiste, Martin, Schillaci, Vio, Hector, Humes (Whinnett 70).

Charlton Ath: Baker; Flack (Nash 107), Dixson, Sullivan, Coombs, Clifford, Bergin, Pepper (Lee 66), Graham, Monaghan (Simmons 66), Southgate.

aet; Tottenham H won 4-3 on penalties.

THE SSE FA WOMEN'S CUP 2016–17

**After extra time.*

FIRST QUALIFYING ROUND

South Shields v Gateshead Leam Rangers 2-0
Wigan Ath v MSB Woolton 1-0

SECOND QUALIFYING ROUND

Wallsend Boys Club v Boldon CA Villa 5-2
South Shields v Cramlington U 1-1*
South Shields won 4-2 on penalties.
South Park Rangers (walkover) v Kendal T (withdrawn)
Penrith v Bishop Auckland 1-0*
(0-0 at full time)
RACA Tynedale (walkoveer) v Rutherford (withdrawn)
Workington Reds v Birtley T 2-1
Norton & Stockton Ancients v Carlisle U 7-0
Prudhoe T v Hartlepool U 0-9
Boldon CA v Blyth T Lions 3-1
Ossett Alb v Malet Lambert 1-0
Wakefield v Farsley Celtic 0-7
Bradford Park Avenue v Sheffield U 1-8
Sheffield W v Brighouse Ath 4-0
Accrington Girls & Women v Curzon Ashton 11-2
FC United of Manchester v Bolton W 2-1
CMB v Stockport Co 0-4
Burnley v Wigan Ath 0-7
Merseyrail Bootle v City of Manchester 4-1
Chorltonians v Warrington Wolverines 0-2
Rise Park v Arnold T 0-0*
Arnold T won 4-3 on penalties.
Leicester City Women Development v Winterton Rangers 3-0
Dronfield T v Lincoln Moorlands Railway 4-4*
Lincoln Moorlands Railway won 3-2 on penalties.
Nettleham v Teversal 16-0
Market Warsop v AFC Leicester 5-1
Stourbridge v Stockingford AA Pavilion 2-1
Coundon Court v Bilbrook 9-0
Leamington Lions v Wolverhampton Sporting Community 2-2*
Leamington Lions won 5-4 on penalties.
Bedworth U v Stone Dominoes 7-0
Coleshill T v Coventry Development 0-3
Shrewsbury T v Wyrley 2-4
Bradwell Belles v Shrewsbury Juniors 1-5
Knowle v Leek T 1-2
Crusaders v Gornal 2-2*
Gornal won 4-3 on penalties.
Burton Alb v Lye T 3-1
Rubery v Boldmere St Michaels 2-3*
(2-2 at full time)
Moulton v Histon 2-5
Riverside v Woodford U 9-0
Oadby & Wigston v Roade 2-0
Peterborough U v Cambridge C 0-1
Acle U v Netherton U 2-0
ICA Sports (withdrawn) v Peterborough Northern Star (walkover)
Newmarket T v Wymondham T 2-7
Park v Northampton T 0-14
Kettering T v Thrapston T 4-0
Colchester T v AFC Sudbury 0-3
Brandon T (walkover) v Great Wakering R (withdrawn)
Little Thurrock Dynamos v Brentwood T 1-2*
(1-1 at full time)
Harlow T v Billericay T 2-3
Writtle v Leyton Orient 0-3
Haringey Bor v Chelmsford C 12-0
Bishop's Stortford v Bungay T 1-3
Hertford T (walkover) v Garston (withdrawn)
Houghton Ath v Sherrardswood 2-1
AFC Dunstable v Sandy 8-0
Colney Heath v Royston T 1-3
Hemel Hempstead T v Bedford 2-1
QPR Girls Development v Wargrave 5-0
Marlow v Oxford C 2-4*
(2-2 at full time)
Ascot U v Milton Keynes D 3-2
Newbury v Chinnor 6-2
Brentford v Chesham U 0-8
Carshalton Ath v Aylesford 1-3
Meridian v Eastbourne 2-0
Haywards Heath & Wivelsfield v Cowfold 1-5
Burgess Hill T v Regents Park Rangers 0-4
Long Lane v Fulham Foundation 2-3
Margate v Bexhill U 1-9
Herne Bay v Parkwood Rangers 1-1*
Herne Bay won 3-1 on penalties.
London Corinthians v Victoire 6-0
Abbey Rangers v Crawley Wasps 1-7
Worthing T (walkover) v Rottingdean Village (withdrawn)
Warsash Wasps v Poole T 1-2
Fleet T v Team Solent 6-0
New Milton T v Bournemouth 1-0
Bournemouth Sports v Southampton 0-12
Middlezoy R v Ilminster T 2-2*
Ilminster T won 2-0 on penalties.
AEK Boco v Royal Wootton Bassett T 3-1*
(1-1 at full time)
Buckland Ath (walkover) v Cheltenham Civil Service (withdrawn)
Downend Flyers v Pen Mill 7-1
Keynsham T Development (withdrawn) v Torquay U (walkover)

THIRD QUALIFYING ROUND

Wallsend Boys Club v Wigan Ath 3-2
Norton & Stockton Ancients v FC United of Manchester 2-1
Leeds v South Park Rangers 6-1
Farsley Celtic v Merseyrail Bootle 2-4
Penrith v Boldon CA 4-2
Lincoln Moorlands Railway v Warrington Wolverines 1-6
Crewe Alexandra v Morecambe 3-3*
Crewe Alexandra won 4-2 on penalties.
Steel C W v Sheffield W 1-4
Mossley Hill v Liverpool Marshalls Feds 0-4
Guiseley Vixens v Rotherham U 7-2
Chester-le-Street T v Sheffield U 0-1
Hartlepool U v Ossett Alb 7-1
Accrington Girls & Women v Tranmere R 3-0
Stockport Co v Brighouse T 1-2
Blackpool Wren R v Chorley 2-2*
Blackpool Wren R won 5-3 on penalties.
Hull C v South Shields 4-2*
(2-2 at full time)
Workington Reds v RACA Tynedale 1-5
Wyrley v Radcliffe Olympic 1-6
Leamington Lions v Burton Alb 0-4
Sporting Khalsa v Coundon Court 7-0
Arnold T v Coventry Development 3-3*
Coventry Development won 4-3 on penalties.
Bedworth U v Leicester City Women Development 2-6
Leicester City Ladies v Birmingham & West Midlands 2-3
Loughborough Foxes v Wolverhampton W 2-3
Shrewsbury Juniors v The New Saints 2-6*
(1-1 at full time)
Boldmere St Michaels v Long Eaton U 2-8
Stourbridge v Gornal 1-2
Oadby & Wigston v Solihull 0-6
Market Warsop v Nettleham 3-4
Loughborough Students v Leek T 1-3
Norwich C v Riverside 10-0
Lowestoft T v Enfield T 2-0
Milton Keynes D v Actonians 4-0
Histon v Peterborough Northern Star 0-5
Northampton T v Cambridge C 2-3
Denham U v Ipswich T 4-1
Cambridge U's v Wymondham T 3-0
AFC Sudbury v Luton T 2-3
Kettering T v Brandon T 6-0
Bungay T v Acle U 3-6
Hemel Hempstead T v Herne Bay 2-0
AFC Dunstable v Meridian 4-1
Houghton Ath v Brentwood T 0-3
Haringey Bor v Chichester C 2-8
Crawley Wasps v Oxford C 0-2
Newbury v Hertford T 2-1
Leyton Orient v Ascot U 16-0
Billericay T v Basingstoke T 1-2

Fulham Foundation v QPR Girls Development 0-2
Worthing T v Stevenage 0-15
Cowfold v Aylesford 1-2
Chesham U v London Corinthians 2-1
Bexhill U v AFC Wimbledon 0-6
Royston T v Regents Park Rangers 2-3
Gillingham v Maidenhead U 4-0
Southampton v Fleet T 5-1
Shanklin v St Nicholas 3-2
Buckland Ath v Keynsham T 2-3
Torquay U v Brislington 2-4
Poole T v AEK Boco 3-0
Ilminster T v Plymouth Arg 0-4
Southampton Saints v Downend Flyers 8-2
Larkhall Ath v Cheltenham T 9-1
New Milton T v Exeter C 1-2

FOURTH QUALIFYING ROUND

Sheffield U v Merseyrail Bootle 3-1
Penrith v Norton & Stockton Ancients 0-4
Guiseley Vixens v Nettleham 7-1
Liverpool Marshalls Feds v Warrington Wolverines 7-1
RACA Tynedale v Crewe Alexandra 2-1
Brighouse T v Blackpool Wren R 5-0
Hartlepool U v Accrington Girls & Women 7-1
Hull C v Leeds 6-0
Wallsend Boys Club v Sheffield W 1-2
Sporting Khalsa v Wolverhampton W 2-4*
(2-2 at full time)
Solihull v Burton Alb 3-0
Radcliffe Olympic v Gornal 8-0
Leek T v Leicester City Women Development 1-2*
(1-1 at full time)
The New Saints v Birmingham & West Midlands 2-5
Long Eaton U v Coventry Development 7-1
Acle U v Brentwood T 3-0
Norwich C v Lowestoft T 3-3*
Norwich C won 4-3 on penalties.
Cambridge U's v Stevenage 3-0
Kettering T v Peterborough Northern Star 0-3
Leyton Orient v Cambridge C 3-1
Luton T v Oxford C 6-1
Chesham U v Regents Park Rangers 2-4
Hemel Hempstead T v AFC Dunstable 2-0
AFC Wimbledon v Denham U 4-2
Aylesford v Gillingham 0-7
QPR Girls Development v Milton Keynes D 1-6
Brislington v Poole T 8-0
Southampton Saints v Exeter C 10-0
Larkhall Ath v Newbury 8-1
Plymouth Arg v Basingstoke T 3-1
Shanklin v Southampton 0-3
Chichester C v Keynsham T 1-2

FIRST ROUND

Radcliffe Olympic v Sheffield W 6-0
Sheffield U v Leicester City Women Development 2-0
Bradford C v Blackburn R 0-1
Stoke C v Liverpool Marshalls Feds 1-1*
Liverpool Marshalls Feds won 4-2 on penalties.
Guiseley Vixens v Nottingham F 0-1
Wolverhampton W v Solihull 4-0
Birmingham & West Midlands v Leicester C Women 0-3
Middlesbrough v Hartlepool U 1-0
WBA v Fylde 4-1
Huddersfield T v Derby Co 0-1
RACA Tynedale v Newcastle U 0-3
Norton & Stockton Ancients v Hull C 1-6
Long Eaton U (walkover) v Nuneaton T (withdrawn)
Brighouse T v Peterborough Northern Star 3-2
Southampton Saints v Gillingham 1-7
Acle U v C&K Basildon 0-2
Cardiff C v Larkhall Ath 6-0
Tottenham H v Leyton Orient 1-0
Cambridge U's v QPR 3-1
Milton Keynes D v Hemel Hempstead T 3-1
Plymouth Arg (walkover) v Forest Green R (withdrawn)
Lewes v Brislington 5-0
West Ham U v Coventry U 0-3
Crystal Palace v Charlton Ath 1-2
Luton T v Portsmouth 1-4
Norwich C v AFC Wimbledon 1-4
Southampton v Swindon T 2-0
Regents Park Rangers v Keynsham T 1-6

SECOND ROUND

Long Eaton U v Brighouse T 3-4
Derby Co v Sheffield U 3-2*
(2-2 at full time)
WBA v Radcliffe Olympic 4-0
Nottingham F v Wolverhampton W 4-0
Middlesbrough v Leicester C Women 1-2*
(1-1 at full time)
Blackburn R v Hull C 5-0
Liverpool Marshalls Feds v Newcastle U 1-0
Coventry U v Milton Keynes D 4-0
C&K Basildon v Keynsham T 1-3
Lewes v Cardiff C 2-0
Tottenham H v Gillingham 3-0
Plymouth Arg v AFC Wimbledon 0-3
Cambridge U's v Southampton 4-0
Charlton Ath v Portsmouth 5-0

THIRD ROUND

Blackburn R v Tottenham H 1-2
Charlton Ath v Sheffield 0-2
Aston Villa v Cambridge U's 7-1
Millwall Lionesses v London Bees 1-0
Leicester C Women v Liverpool Marshalls Feds 2-1
Keynsham T v Durham's 0-7
Coventry U v Oxford U 2-0
WBA v Lewes 3-1
Doncaster R Belles (walkover) v Watford (withdrawn)
Derby Co v Nottingham F 0-1
Brighouse T v Everton 1-8
AFC Wimbledon v Brighton & HA 1-4

FOURTH ROUND

Durham's v Everton 2-2*
Everton won 4-3 on penalties.
Coventry U v Aston Villa 0-1
Millwall Lionesses v Nottingham F 3-1
WBA v Leicester C Women 2-1
Tottenham H v Brighton & HA 1-0
Sheffield v Doncaster R Belles 0-1

FIFTH ROUND

Notts Co v Yeovil T 3-2
Liverpool v Everton 2-1*
(1-1 at full time)
Arsenal v Tottenham H 10-0
Sunderland v Aston Villa 3-2
Birmingham C v WBA 2-0
Bristol C v Millwall Lionesses 5-0
Manchester C v Reading 1-0
Chelsea v Doncaster R Belles 7-0

SIXTH ROUND

Birmingham C v Arsenal 1-0
Chelsea v Sunderland 5-1
Bristol C v Manchester C 1-2
Liverpool v Notts Co 2-0

SEMI-FINALS

Manchester C v Liverpool 1-0
Birmingham C v Chelsea 1-1*
Birmingham C won 4-2 on penalties.

THE SSE FA WOMEN'S CUP FINAL 2017

Wembley , Saturday 13 May 2017

Manchester C (3) 4 *(Bronze 17, Christiansen 25, Lloyd 33, Scott 80)*

Birmingham C (0) 1 *(Wellings 73)* 35,271

Manchester C: Bardsley; Bronze, Houghton, Campbell (McManus 78), Stokes, Walsh, Scott, Christiansen, Parris (Stanway 70), Lloyd, Lawley (Duggan 56).
Birmingham C: Berger; Harrop, Mannion, Sargeant, Williams (Stringer 87), Carter, Hegerberg (Peplow 83), Mayling, White, Brazil, Ayisi (Wellings 64).
Referee: Rebecca Welch.

UEFA WOMEN'S CHAMPIONS LEAGUE 2016–17

**After extra time.*

QUALIFYING ROUND

GROUP 1 (CYPRUS)

Apollon v Klaksvikar Itrottarfelag 5-0
PAOK Thessaloniki v Hajvalia 1-1
Klaksvikar Itrottarfelag v PAOK Thessaloniki 1-1
Apollon v Hajvalia 1-0
Hajvalia v Klaksvikar Itrottarfelag 1-1
PAOK Thessaloniki v Apollon 3-3

Group 1 Table	P	W	D	L	F	A	GD	Pts
Apollon	3	2	1	0	9	3	6	7
PAOK Thessaloniki	3	0	3	0	5	5	0	3
Hajvalia	3	0	2	1	2	3	–1	2
Klaksvikar Itrottarfelag	3	0	2	1	2	7	–5	2

GROUP 2 (CROATIA)

Standard Liege v Minsk 1-3
Osijek v Dragon 2014 14-1
Standard Liege v Dragon 2014 11-0
Minsk v Osijek 5-0
Osijek v Standard Liege 1-1
Dragon 2014 v Minsk 0-9

Group 2 Table	P	W	D	L	F	A	GD	Pts
Minsk	3	3	0	0	17	1	16	9
Standard Liege	3	1	1	1	13	4	9	4
Osijek	3	1	1	1	15	7	8	4
Dragon 2014	3	0	0	3	1	34	–33	0

GROUP 3 (WALES)

NSA v Cardiff Met 0-4
Spartak Subotica v Breidablik 1-1
Breidablik v NSA 5-0
Spartak Subotica v Cardiff Met 3-2
NSA v Spartak Subotica 0-2
Cardiff Met v Breidablik 0-8

Group 3 Table	P	W	D	L	F	A	GD	Pts
Breidablik	3	2	1	0	14	1	13	7
Spartak Subotica	3	2	1	0	6	3	3	7
Cardiff Met	3	1	0	2	6	11	–5	3
NSA	3	0	0	3	0	11	–11	0

GROUP 4 (POLAND)

Olimpia Cluj v Parnu Jalgpalliklubi 7-1
Medyk Konin v Breznica Pljevlja 9-0
Olimpia Cluj v Breznica Pljevlja 10-0
Parnu Jalgpalliklubi v Medyk Konin 0-1
Medyk Konin v Olimpia Cluj 3-1
Breznica Pljevlja v Parnu Jalgpalliklubi 2-2

Group 4 Table	P	W	D	L	F	A	GD	Pts
Medyk Konin	3	3	0	0	13	1	12	9
Olimpia Cluj	3	2	0	1	18	4	14	6
Parnu Jalgpalliklubi	3	0	1	2	3	10	–7	1
Breznica Pljevlja	3	0	1	2	2	21	–19	1

GROUP 5 (SLOVENIA)

FC Zurich v Slovan Bratislava 3-1
Pomurje v Vllaznia 6-1
FC Zurich v Vllaznia 3-0
Slovan Bratislava v Pomurje 2-4
Vllaznia v Slovan Bratislava 1-2
Pomurje v FC Zurich 0-5

Group 5 Table	P	W	D	L	F	A	GD	Pts
FC Zurich	3	3	0	0	11	1	10	9
Pomurje	3	2	0	1	10	8	2	6
Slovan Bratislava	3	1	0	2	5	8	–3	3
Vllaznia	3	0	0	3	2	11	–9	0

GROUP 6 (BOSNIA-HERZEGOVINA)

Sarajevo v Ramat Hasharon 1-0
Kharkiv v Rigas FS 2-0
Ramat Hasharon v Kharkiv 1-0
Sarajevo v Rigas FS 3-0
Rigas FS v Ramat Hasharon 0-4
Kharkiv v Sarajevo 2-2

Group 6 Table	P	W	D	L	F	A	GD	Pts
Sarajevo	3	2	1	0	6	2	4	7
Ramat Hasharon	3	2	0	1	5	1	4	6
Kharkiv	3	1	1	1	4	3	1	4
Rigas FS	3	0	0	3	0	9	–9	0

GROUP 7 (REPUBLIC OF IRELAND)

Gintra Universitetas v ARF Criuleni 13-0
BIIK-Kazygurt v Wexford Youths 3-1
BIIK-Kazygurt v ARF Criuleni 3-0
Wexford Youths v Gintra Universitetas 1-2
ARF Criuleni v Wexford Youths 0-0
Gintra Universitetas v BIIK-Kazygurt 0-3

Group 7 Table	P	W	D	L	F	A	GD	Pts
BIIK-Kazygurt	3	3	0	0	9	1	8	9
Gintra Universitetas	3	2	0	1	15	4	11	6
Wexford Youths	3	0	1	2	2	5	–3	1
ARF Criuleni	3	0	1	2	0	16	–16	1

GROUP 8 (FINLAND)

Avaldsnes Idrettslag v Newry C 11-0
PK-35 Vantaa v Benfica 1-2
Benfica v Avaldsnes Idrettslag 1-6
PK-35 Vantaa v Newry 2-0
Newry C v Benfica 0-5
Avaldsnes Idrettslag v PK-35 Vantaa 2-0

Group 8 Table	P	W	D	L	F	A	GD	Pts
Avaldsnes Idrettslag	3	3	0	0	19	1	18	9
Benfica	3	2	0	1	8	7	1	6
PK-35 Vantaa	3	1	0	2	3	4	–1	3
Newry C	3	0	0	3	0	18	–18	0

GROUP 9 (NETHERLANDS)

Konak Belediyespor v Hibernians 5-0
FC Twente '65 v Ferencvaros 2-1
FC Twente '65 v Hibernians 9-0
Ferencvaros v Konak Belediyespor 2-0
Konak Belediyespor v FC Twente '65 2-6
Hibernians v Ferencvaros 0-4

Group 9 Table	P	W	D	L	F	A	GD	Pts
FC Twente '65	3	3	0	0	17	3	14	9
Ferencvaros	3	2	0	1	7	2	5	6
Konak Belediyespor	3	1	0	2	7	8	–1	3
Hibernians	3	0	0	3	0	18	–18	0

ROUND OF 32 – FIRST LEG

BIIK-Kazygurt v Verona 3-1
Medyk Konin v Brescia 4-3
Sarajevo v Rossiyanka 0-0
Breidablik v Rosengard 0-1
Sturm Graz v FC Zurich 0-6
Avaldsnes Idrettslag v Lyon 2-5
Apollon v Slavia Prague 1-1
FC Twente '65 v Sparta Prague 2-0
Athletic Bilbao v Fortuna Hjorring 2-1
Chelsea v Wolfsburg 0-3
St Polten v Brondby 0-2
Hibernian v Bayern Munich 0-6
Minsk v Barcelona 0-3
Lillestrom v Paris Saint-Germain 3-1
Eskilstuna U v Glasgow C 1-0
Manchester C v Zvezda 2005 2-0

ROUND OF 32 – SECOND LEG

		(agg)
Zvezda 2005 v Manchester C	0-4	0-6
Barcelona v Minsk	2-1	5-1
Bayern Munich v Hibernian	4-1	10-1
Wolfsburg v Chelsea	1-1	4-1
Sparta Prague v FC Twente '65	1-3	1-5
Brondby v St Polten	2-2	4-2
Slavia Prague v Apollon	3-2	4-3
Fortuna Hjorring v Athletic Bilbao	3-1	4-3*
FC Zurich v Sturm Graz	3-0	9-0
Rosengard v Breidablik	0-0	1-0
Verona v BIIK-Kazygurt	1-1	2-4
Lyon v Avaldsnes Idrettslag	5-0	10-2
Rossiyanka v Sarajevo	2-1	2-1
Paris Saint-Germain v Lillestrom	4-1	5-4
Brescia v Medyk Konin	3-2	6-6
Brescia won on away goals.		
Glasgow C v Eskilstuna U	1-2	1-3

ROUND OF 16 – FIRST LEG

Bayern Munich v Rossiyanka	4-0
Lyon v FC Zurich	8-0
Barcelona v FC Twente '65	1-0
Manchester C v Brondby	1-0
Brescia v Fortuna Hjorring	0-1
BIIK-Kazygurt v Paris Saint-Germain	0-3
Slavia Prague v Rosengard	1-3
Eskilstuna U v Wolfsburg	1-5

ROUND OF 16 – SECOND LEG

		(agg)
Brondby v Manchester C	1-1	1-2
FC Zurich v Lyon	0-9	0-17
Fortuna Hjorring v Brescia	3-1	4-1
FC Twente '65 v Barcelona	0-4	0-5
Rosengard v Slavia Prague	3-0	6-1
Rossiyanka v Bayern Munich	0-4	0-8
Wolfsburg v Eskilstuna U	3-0	8-1
Paris Saint-Germain v BIIK-Kazygurt	4-1	7-1

QUARTER-FINALS – FIRST LEG

Rosengard v Barcelona	0-1
Fortuna Hjorring v Manchester C	0-1
Bayern Munich v Paris Saint-Germain	1-0
Wolfsburg v Lyon	0-2

QUARTER-FINALS – SECOND LEG

		(agg)
Barcelona v Rosengard	2-0	3-0
Manchester C v Fortuna Hjorring	1-0	2-0
Paris Saint-Germain v Bayern Munich	4-0	4-1
Lyon v Wolfsburg	0-1	2-1

SEMI-FINALS – FIRST LEG

Manchester C v Lyon	1-3
Barcelona v Paris Saint-Germain	1-3

SEMI-FINALS – SECOND LEG

		(agg)
Paris Saint-Germain v Barcelona	2-0	5-1
Lyon v Manchester C	0-1	3-2

UEFA WOMEN'S CHAMPIONS LEAGUE FINAL 2017

Cardiff, Thursday 1 June 2017

Lyon (0) 0

Paris Saint-Germain (0) 22,433

Lyon: Bouhaddi; Renard, Kumagai, Majri, Le Sommer, Marozsan, Hegerberg (Bremer 60), Buchanan, Abily, M'Bock Bathy, Morgan (Thomis 23 (Lavogez 108)).

Paris Saint-Germain: Kiedrzynek; Delannoy, Diallo (Veronica Boquete 57), Cristiane, Lawrence, Paredes, Perisset (Morroni 90), Delie, Formiga, Geyoro, Cruz Trana (Georges, 80).

Lyon won 7-6 on penalties.

Referee: Bibiana Steinhaus (Germany).

UEFA WOMEN'S EURO 2017

PRELIMINARY ROUND

GROUP 1 (MOLDOVA)

Luxembourg v Latvia	4-3
Moldova v Lithuania	2-0
Lithuania v Luxembourg	2-0
Moldova v Latvia	0-1
Luxembourg v Moldova	0-3
Latvia v Lithuania	1-1

Group 1 Table	P	W	D	L	F	A	GD	Pts
Moldova	3	2	0	1	5	1	4	6
Latvia	3	1	1	1	5	5	0	4
Lithuania	3	1	1	1	3	3	0	4
Luxembourg	3	1	0	2	4	8	–4	3

GROUP 2 (MALTA)

Georgia v Faroe Islands	2-0
Andorra v Malta	3-5
Faroe Islands v Andorra	8-0
Georgia v Malta	1-2
Malta v Faroe Islands	2-4
Andorra v Georgia	0-7

Group 2 Table	P	W	D	L	F	A	GD	Pts
Georgia	3	2	0	1	10	2	8	6
Faroe Islands	3	2	0	1	12	4	8	6
Malta	3	2	0	1	9	8	1	6
Andorra	3	0	0	3	3	20	–17	0

QUALIFYING ROUND

GROUP 1

Slovenia v Scotland	0-3
Iceland v Belarus	2-0
Slovenia v Belarus	3-0
FYR Macedonia v Iceland	0-4
Scotland v Belarus	7-0
Slovenia v Iceland	0-6
FYR Macedonia v Scotland	1-4
FYR Macedonia v Belarus	0-2
Scotland v FYR Macedonia	10-0
Scotland v Slovenia	3-1
Belarus v Iceland	0-5
Slovenia v FYR Macedonia	8-1
FYR Macedonia v Slovenia	0-9
Scotland v Iceland	0-4
Belarus v Scotland	0-1
Iceland v FYR Macedonia	8-0
Belarus v FYR Macedonia	6-2
Iceland v Slovenia	4-0
Belarus v Slovenia	2-0
Iceland v Scotland	1-2

Group 1 Table	P	W	D	L	F	A	GD	Pts
Iceland	8	7	0	1	34	2	32	21
Scotland	8	7	0	1	30	7	23	21
Slovenia	8	3	0	5	21	19	2	9
Belarus	8	3	0	5	10	20	–10	9
FYR Macedonia	8	0	0	8	4	51	–47	0

GROUP 2

Finland v Montenegro	1-0
Republic of Ireland v Finland	0-2
Portugal v Republic of Ireland	1-2
Finland v Spain	1-2
Republic of Ireland v Spain	0-3
Portugal v Montenegro	6-1
Spain v Portugal	2-0
Montenegro v Spain	0-7
Montenegro v Republic of Ireland	0-5
Portugal v Spain	1-4
Montenegro v Finland	1-7
Spain v Republic of Ireland	3-0
Finland v Republic of Ireland	4-1
Montenegro v Portugal	0-3
Finland v Portugal	0-0
Republic of Ireland v Montenegro	9-0
Spain v Montenegro	13-0
Portugal v Finland	3-2
Republic of Ireland v Portugal	0-1
Spain v Finland	5-0

Group 2 Table	P	W	D	L	F	A	GD	Pts
Spain	8	8	0	0	39	2	37	24
Portugal	8	4	1	3	15	11	4	13
Finland	8	4	1	3	17	12	5	13
Republic of Ireland	8	3	0	5	17	14	3	9
Montenegro	8	0	0	8	2	51	–49	0

GROUP 3

France v Romania	3-0
Albania v Greece	1-4
Ukraine v Romania	2-2
Romania v Albania	3-0
Ukraine v France	0-3
Greece v Romania	1-3
Albania v France	0-6
Greece v France	0-3
Greece v Albania	3-2
Albania v Ukraine	0-4
Greece v Ukraine	1-3
Ukraine v Albania	2-0
Romania v France	0-1
France v Ukraine	4-0
Albania v Romania	0-3

France v Greece 1-0
Ukraine v Greece 2-0
Romania v Ukraine 2-1
Romania v Greece 4-0
France v Albania 6-0

Group 3 Table	P	W	D	L	F	A	GD	Pts
France	8	8	0	0	27	0	27	24
Romania	8	5	1	2	17	8	9	16
Ukraine	8	4	1	3	14	12	2	13
Greece	8	2	0	6	9	19	−10	6
Albania	8	0	0	8	3	31	−28	0

GROUP 4

Moldova v Sweden 0-3
Sweden v Poland 3-0
Poland v Slovakia 2-0
Denmark v Moldova 4-0
Slovakia v Moldova 4-0
Sweden v Denmark 1-0
Slovakia v Denmark 0-1
Moldova v Poland 1-3
Moldova v Slovakia 0-4
Poland v Denmark 0-0
Slovakia v Sweden 0-3
Slovakia v Poland 2-1
Poland v Sweden 0-4
Denmark v Slovakia 4-0
Sweden v Moldova 6-0
Denmark v Poland 6-0
Sweden v Slovakia 2-1
Moldova v Denmark 0-5
Poland v Moldova 4-0
Denmark v Sweden 2-0

Group 4 Table	P	W	D	L	F	A	GD	Pts
Sweden	8	7	0	1	22	3	19	21
Denmark	8	6	1	1	22	1	21	19
Poland	8	3	1	4	10	16	−6	10
Slovakia	8	3	0	5	11	13	−2	9
Moldova	8	0	0	8	1	33	−32	0

GROUP 5

Turkey v Croatia 1-4
Germany v Hungary 12-0
Croatia v Germany 0-1
Hungary v Turkey 1-0
Germany v Russia 2-0
Germany v Turkey 7-0
Croatia v Hungary 1-1
Turkey v Russia 0-0
Hungary v Russia 0-1
Croatia v Turkey 3-0
Turkey v Germany 0-6
Hungary v Croatia 2-0
Germany v Croatia 2-0
Russia v Hungary 3-3
Russia v Turkey 2-0
Turkey v Hungary 2-1
Croatia v Russia 0-3
Russia v Germany 0-4
Hungary v Germany 0-1
Russia v Croatia 5-0

Group 5 Table	P	W	D	L	F	A	GD	Pts
Germany	8	8	0	0	35	0	35	24
Russia	8	4	2	2	14	9	5	14
Hungary	8	2	2	4	8	20	−12	8
Croatia	8	2	1	5	8	15	−7	7
Turkey	8	1	1	6	3	24	−21	4

GROUP 6

Italy v Georgia 6-1
Georgia v Czech Republic 0-3
Italy v Switzerland 0-3
Georgia v Northern Ireland 0-3
Czech Republic v Italy 0-3
Switzerland v Georgia 4-0
Northern Ireland v Switzerland 1-8
Switzerland v Czech Republic 5-1
Switzerland v Italy 2-1
Czech Republic v Georgia 4-1
Italy v Northern Ireland 3-1
Northern Ireland v Georgia 4-0
Czech Republic v Switzerland 0-5
Georgia v Italy 0-7
Czech Republic v Northern Ireland 3-0
Northern Ireland v Czech Republic 1-1
Georgia v Switzerland 0-3
Northern Ireland v Italy 0-3
Italy v Czech Republic 3-1
Switzerland v Northern Ireland 4-0

Group 6 Table	P	W	D	L	F	A	GD	Pts
Switzerland	8	8	0	0	34	3	31	24
Italy	8	6	0	2	26	8	18	18
Czech Republic	8	3	1	4	13	18	−5	10
Northern Ireland	8	2	1	5	10	22	−12	7
Georgia	8	0	0	8	2	34	−32	0

GROUP 7

Estonia v Serbia 0-1
Estonia v England 0-8
Belgium v Bosnia-Herzegovina 6-0
Bosnia-Herzegovina v Estonia 4-0
Serbia v Estonia 3-0
Bosnia-Herzegovina v Belgium 0-5
Serbia v Bosnia-Herzegovina 0-1
England v Bosnia-Herzegovina 1-0
Belgium v Serbia 1-1
England v Belgium 1-1
Bosnia-Herzegovina v England 0-1
Belgium v Estonia 6-0
Estonia v Belgium 0-5
England v Serbia 7-0
Estonia v Bosnia-Herzegovina 0-1
Serbia v England 0-7
Serbia v Belgium 1-3
England v Estonia 5-0
Bosnia-Herzegovina v Serbia 2-4
Belgium v England 0-2

Group 7 Table	P	W	D	L	F	A	GD	Pts
England	8	7	1	0	32	1	31	22
Belgium	8	5	2	1	27	5	22	17
Serbia	8	3	1	4	10	21	−11	10
Bosnia-Herzegovina	8	3	0	5	8	17	−9	9
Estonia	8	0	0	8	0	33	−33	0

Group 8

Kazakhstan v Austria 0-2
Kazakhstan v Norway 0-4
Austria v Wales 3-0
Israel v Kazakhstan 0-0
Norway v Wales 4-0
Israel v Austria 0-1
Wales v Kazakhstan 4-0
Israel v Wales 2-2
Israel v Norway 0-1
Austria v Kazakhstan 6-1
Austria v Norway 0-1
Kazakhstan v Wales 0-4
Kazakhstan v Israel 1-0
Norway v Austria 2-2
Austria v Israel 4-0
Wales v Norway 0-2
Norway v Kazakhstan 10-0
Wales v Israel 3-0
Norway v Israel 5-0
Wales v Austria 0-0

Group 8 Table	P	W	D	L	F	A	GD	Pts
Norway	8	7	1	0	29	2	27	22
Austria	8	5	2	1	18	4	14	17
Wales	8	3	2	3	13	11	2	11
Kazakhstan	8	1	1	6	2	30	−28	4
Israel	8	0	2	6	2	17	−15	2

PLAY-OFF FIRST LEG

Portugal v Romania 0-0

PLAY-OFF SECOND LEG

Romania v Portugal 1-1
aet; Portugal won on away goals.

Finals in Netherlands July–August 2017.

ENGLAND WOMEN'S INTERNATIONALS 2016–17

▪ *Denotes player sent off.*

WOMEN'S EUROPEAN CHAMPIONSHIP 2017 – QUALIFIERS GROUP 7

Meadow Lane, Thursday 15 September 2016

England (3) 5 *(Carter 9, 17, 56, Scott J 13, Carney 90 (pen))*

Estonia (0) 0 7052

England: Chamberlain; Bronze, Houghton, Potter, Davison (Flaherty 74), Nobbs, Scott J (Moore 62), Carney, Stokes, Parris (Daly 60), Carter.

Leuven, Tuesday 20 September 2016

Belgium (0) 0

England (0) 2 *(Parris 65, Carney 85)*

England: Bardsley; Flaherty, Houghton, Potter, Bronze, Nobbs, Scott J, Carney (Bright 90), Stokes, Parris (Daly 77), Carter (Moore 46).

FRIENDLIES

Doncaster, Friday 21 October 2016

England (0) 0

France (0) 0 7398

England: Bardsley; Bronze, Houghton, Potter, Davison (Scott A 71), Scott J, Moore, Nobbs, Stokes, Carney (Duggan 88), Daly (Parris 58).

Guadalajara, Tuesday 25 October 2016

Spain (1) 1 *(Torrejon 19)*

England (2) 2 *(Torrejon 14 (og), Houghton 17)*

England: Bardsley; Bronze, Houghton, Potter, Davison (Daly 58), Scott J (Christiansen 64), Moore, Nobbs, Stokes, Carney (Williams 74), Parris (Duggan 64).

Tilburg, Tuesday 29 November 2016

Netherlands (0) 0

England (0) 1 *(Taylor 75)*

England: Bardsley; Bronze, Houghton, Potter, Christiansen (Scott A 90), Scott J (Taylor 58), Moore, Nobbs, Stokes, Carney (Williams 81), Duggan (Flaherty 76).

La Manga, Sunday 22 January 2017

England (0) 0

Norway (1) 1 *(Hegerberg 26)*

England: Chamberlain; Bronze, Houghton, Potter, Scott A, Moore, Williams (Bright 62), Stokes, Parris, Taylor (White 62), Duggan.

La Manga, Tuesday 24 January 2017

England (0) 0

Sweden (0) 0

England: Chamberlain; Bonner, Flaherty (Houghton 80), Bright, Daly, Christiansen, Nobbs, Rafferty (Davison 55), Scott J, Williams, Carney (Stokes 70).

Port Vale, Friday 7 April 2017

England (0) 1 *(Taylor 70)*

Italy (0) 1 *(Cernoia 73)* 7181

England: Chamberlain; Bronze, Houghton, Bright, Stokes (Greenwood 69), Nobbs, Moore (Williams 69), Scott J, Carney, Taylor, Duggan (Parris 90).

Milton Keynes, Monday 10 April 2017

England (1) 3 *(White 5, Bronze 67, Christiansen 86)*

Austria (0) 0 6593

England: Chamberlain; Bronze, Houghton, Bassett, Stokes, Nobbs, Bright, Moore, Christiansen (Scott J 87), White (Taylor 74), Duggan (Carney 61).

Biel, Saturday 10 June 2017

Switzerland (0) 0

England (2) 4 *(Nobbs 30, Kirby 40, Taylor 50, 62)*

England: Bardsley (Earps 75); Bronze, Houghton (Bassett 63), Bright (Potter 63), Stokes, Nobbs, Moore (Williams 63), Scott J, Duggan, Taylor (Parris 75), Kirby (Carney 63).

Copenhagen, Saturday 1 July 2017

Denmark (0) 1 *(Harder 66)*

England (1) 2 *(White 44, 76)*

England: Chamberlain (Telford 76); Scott A, Bassett, Stoney, Stokes, Christiansen (Bright 76), Williams (Bronze 88), Potter, Carney (Nobbs 32), Parris (Taylor 76), White.

SHEBELIEVES CUP

Pennsylvania, Wednesday 1 March 2017

England (1) 1 *(Nobbs 32)*

France (0) 2 *(Delie 80, Renard 90)* 8616

England: Bardsley; Bronze, Houghton, Bright, Daly (Scott A 74), Nobbs (Christiansen 87), Moore, Scott J, Stokes, Taylor (Williams 54), White (Parris 74).

New Jersey, Saturday 4 March 2017

USA (0) 0

England (0) 1 *(White 89)* 26,500

England: Chamberlain; Bronze, Houghton, Bassett, Stokes, Nobbs (Moore 90), Williams, Christiansen (Bright 90), Carney (Scott J 63), Duggan (White 75), Parris (Taylor 75).

Washington, Tuesday 7 March 2017

Germany (1) 1 *(Mittag)*

England (0) 0 10,000

England: Chamberlain; Bronze, Houghton, Bassett, Stokes, Williams (Bright 52), Moore (Scott J 73), Nobbs, Carney, Duggan, Taylor (White 63).

ENGLAND WOMEN'S INTERNATIONAL MATCHES 1972–2017

Note: In the results that follow, WC = World Cup; EC = European (UEFA) Championships; M = Mundialito; CC = Cyprus Cup; AC = Algarve Cup. * = After extra time. Games were organised by the Women's Football Association from 1971 to 1992 and the Football Association from 1993 to date. **Bold type** indicates matches played in season 2016–17.

v ARGENTINA

WC2007	17 Sept	Chengdu	6-1

v AUSTRALIA

2003	3 Sept	Burnley	1-0
CC2015	6 Mar	Nicosia	3-0
2015	27 Oct	Yongchuan	1-0

v AUSTRIA

WC2005	1 Sept	Amstetten	4-1
WC2006	20 Apr	Gillingham	4-0
WC2010	25 Mar	Shepherd's Bush	3-0
WC2010	21 Aug	Krems	4-0
2017	**10 Apr**	**Milton Keynes**	**3-0**

v BELARUS

EC2007	27 Oct	Walsall	4-0
EC2008	8 May	Minsk	6-1
WC2013	21 Sept	Bournemouth	6-0
WC2014	14 June	Minsk	3-0

v BELGIUM

1978	31 Oct	Southampton	3-0
1980	1 May	Ostende	1-2
M1984	20 Aug	Jesolo	1-1
M1984	25 Aug	Caorle	2-1
1989	14 May	Epinal	2-0
EC1990	17 Mar	Ypres	3-0
EC1990	7 Apr	Sheffield	1-0
EC1993	6 Nov	Koksijde	3-0
EC1994	13 Mar	Nottingham	6-0
EC2016	8 Apr	Rotherham	1-1
EC2016	**20 Sept**	**Leuven**	**2-0**

v BOSNIA-HERZEGOVINA

EC2015	29 Nov	Bristol	1-0
EC2016	12 Apr	Zenica	1-0

v CANADA

WC1995	6 June	Helsingborg	3-2
2003	19 May	Montreal	0-4
2003	22 May	Ottawa	0-4
CC2009	12 Mar	Nicosia	3-1
CC2010	27 Feb	Nicosia	0-1
CC2011	7 Mar	Nicosia	0-2
CC2013	13 Mar	Nicosia	1-0
2013	7 Apr	Rotherham	1-0
CC2014	10 Mar	Nicosia	2-0
CC2015	11 Mar	Larnaca	1-0
2015	29 May	Hamilton	0-1
WC2015	27 June	Vancouver	2-1

v CHINA PR

AC2005	15 Mar	Guia	0-0*
2007	26 Jan	Guangzhou	0-2
2015	9 Apr	Manchester	2-1
2015	23 Oct	Yongchuan	1-2

v COLOMBIA

WC2015	17 June	Montreal	2-1

v CROATIA

EC1995	19 Nov	Charlton	5-0
EC1996	18 Apr	Osijek	2-0
EC2012	31 Mar	Vrbovec	6-0
EC2012	19 Sept	Walsall	3-0

v CZECH REPUBLIC

2005	26 May	Walsall	4-1
EC2008	20 Mar	Doncaster	0-0
EC2008	28 Sept	Prague	5-1

v DENMARK

1979	19 May	Hvidovre	1-3
1979	13 Sept	Hull	2-2
1981	9 Sept	Tokyo	0-1
EC1984	8 Apr	Crewe	2-1
EC1984	28 Apr	Hjorring	1-0
M1985	19 Aug	Caorle	0-1
EC1987	8 Nov	Blackburn	2-1
EC1988	8 May	Herning	0-2
1991	28 June	Nordby	0-0
1991	30 June	Nordby	3-3
1999	22 Aug	Odense	1-0
2001	23 Aug	Northampton	0-3
2004	19 Feb	Portsmouth	2-0
EC2005	8 June	Blackburn	1-2
2009	22 July	Swindon	1-0
2017	**1 July**	**Copenhagen**	**2-1**

v ESTONIA

2015	21 Sept	Tallinn	8-0
EC2016	**15 Sept**	**Nottingham**	**5-0**

v FINLAND

1979	19 July	Sorrento	3-1
EC1987	25 Oct	Kirkkonummi	2-1
EC1988	4 Sept	Millwall	1-1
EC1989	1 Oct	Brentford	0-0
EC1990	29 Sept	Tampere	0-0
2000	28 Sept	Leyton	2-1
EC2005	5 June	Manchester	3-2
2009	9 Feb	Larnaca	2-2
2009	11 Feb	Larnaca	4-1
EC2009	3 Sept	Turku	3-2
CC2012	28 Feb	Nicosia	3-1
CC2014	7 Mar	Larnaca	3-0
CC2015	4 Mar	Larnaca	3-1

v FRANCE

1973	22 Apr	Brion	3-0
1974	7 Nov	Wimbledon	2-0
1977	26 Feb	Longjumeau	0-0
M1988	22 July	Riva del Garda	1-1
1998	15 Feb	Alencon	2-3
1999	15 Sept	Yeovil	0-1
2000	16 Aug	Marseilles	0-1
WC2002	17 Oct	Crystal Palace	0-1
WC2002	16 Nov	St Etienne	0-1
WC2006	26 Mar	Blackburn	0-0
WC2006	30 Sept	Rennes	1-1
CC2009	7 Mar	Paralimni	2-2
WC2011	9 July	Leverkusen	1-1*
CC2012	4 Mar	Paralimni	0-3
2012	20 Oct	Paris	2-2
EC2013	18 July	Linkoping	0-3
CC2014	12 Mar	Nicosia	0-2
WC2015	9 June	Moncton	0-1
2016	9 Mar	Boca Raton	0-0
2016	**21 Oct**	**Doncaster**	**0-0**
2017	**1 Mar**	**Pennsylvania**	**1-2**

v GERMANY

EC1990	25 Nov	High Wycombe	1-4
EC1990	16 Dec	Bochum	0-2
EC1994	11 Dec	Watford	1-4
EC1995	23 Feb	Bochum	1-2
WC1995	13 June	Vasteras	0-3
1997	27 Feb	Preston	4-6
WC1997	25 Sept	Dessau	0-3
WC1998	8 Mar	Millwall	0-1
EC2001	30 June	Jena	0-3
WC2001	27 Sept	Kassel	1-3

WC2002	19 May	Crystal Palace	0-1
2003	11 Sept	Darmstadt	0-4
2006	25 Oct	Aalen	1-5
2007	30 Jan	Guangzhou	0-0
WC2007	14 Sept	Shanghai	0-0
2008	17 July	Unterhaching	0-3
EC2009	10 Sept	Helsinki	2-6
2014	23 Nov	Wembley	0-3
WC2015	4 July	Vancouver	1-0*
2015	26 Nov	Duisburg	0-0
2016	6 Mar	Nashville	1-2
2017	**7 Mar**	**Washington**	**0-1**

v HUNGARY

WC2005	27 Oct	Tapolca	13-0
WC2006	11 May	Southampton	2-0

v ICELAND

EC1992	17 May	Yeovil	4-0
EC1992	19 July	Kopavogur	2-1
EC1994	8 Oct	Reykjavik	2-1
EC1994	30 Oct	Brighton	2-1
WC2002	16 Sept	Reykjavik	2-2
WC2002	22 Sept	Birmingham	1-0
2004	14 May	Peterborough	1-0
2006	9 Mar	Norwich	1-0
2007	17 May	Southend	4-0
2009	16 July	Colchester	0-2

v ITALY

1976	2 June	Rome	0-2
1976	4 June	Cesena	1-2
1977	15 Nov	Wimbledon	1-0
1979	25 July	Naples	1-3
1982	11 June	Pescara	0-2
M1984	24 Aug	Jesolo	1-1
M1985	20 Aug	Caorle	1-1
M1985	25 Aug	Caorle	3-2
EC1987	13 June	Drammen	1-2
M1988	30 July	Arco di Trento	2-1
1989	1 Nov	High Wycombe	1-1
1990	18 Aug	Wembley	1-4
EC1992	17 Oct	Solofra	2-3
EC1992	7 Nov	Rotherham	0-3
1995	25 Jan	Florence	1-1
EC1995	1 Nov	Sunderland	1-1
EC1996	16 Mar	Cosenza	1-2
1997	23 Apr	Turin	0-2
1998	21 Apr	West Bromwich	1-2
1999	26 May	Bologna	1-4
2003	25 Feb	Viareggio	0-1
2005	17 Feb	Milton Keynes	4-1
EC2009	25 Aug	Lahti	1-2
CC2010	3 Mar	Nicosia	3-2
CC2011	2 Mar	Larnaca	2-0
CC2012	6 Mar	Paralimni	1-3
CC2013	6 Mar	Nicosia	4-2
EC2014	5 Mar	Larnaca	2-0
2017	**7 Apr**	**Port Vale**	**1-1**

v JAPAN

1981	6 Sept	Kobe	4-0
WC2007	11 Sept	Shanghai	2-2
WC2011	5 July	Augsburg	2-0
2013	26 June	Burton	1-1
WC2015	1 July	Edmonton	1-2

v KOREA REPUBLIC

2010	19 Oct	Suwon	0-0
CC2011	9 Mar	Larnaca	2-0

v MALTA

WC2009	25 Oct	Blackpool	8-0
WC2010	20 May	Ta'Qali	6-0

v MEXICO

AC2005	13 Mar	Lagos	5-0
WC2011	27 June	Wolfsburg	1-1
WC2015	13 June	Moncton	2-1

v MONTENEGRO

WC2014	5 Apr	Brighton	9-0
WC2014	17 Sept	Petrovac	10-0

v NETHERLANDS

1973	9 Nov	Reading	1-0
1974	31 May	Groningen	0-3
1976	2 May	Blackpool	2-0
1978	30 Sept	Vlissingen	1-3
1989	13 May	Epinal	0-0
WC1997	30 Oct	West Ham	1-0
WC1998	23 May	Waalwijk	1-2
WC2001	4 Nov	Grimsby	0-0
WC2002	23 Mar	Den Haag	4-1
2004	18 Sept	Heerhugowaard	2-1
2004	22 Sept	Tuitjenhoorn	1-0
WC2005	17 Nov	Zwolle	1-0
WC2006	31 Aug	Charlton	4-0
2007	14 Mar	Swindon	0-1
EC2009	6 Sept	Tampere	2-1*
EC2011	27 Oct	Zwolle	0-0
EC2012	17 June	Salford	1-0
CC2015	9 Mar	Nicosia	1-1
2016	**29 Nov**	**Tilburg**	**1-0**

v NEW ZEALAND

2010	21 Oct	Suwon	0-0
WC2011	1 July	Dresden	2-1
CC2013	11 Mar	Larnaca	3-1

v NIGERIA

WC1995	10 June	Karlstad	3-2
2002	23 July	Norwich	0-1
2004	22 Apr	Reading	0-3

v NORTHERN IRELAND

1973	7 Sept	Bath	5-1
EC1982	19 Sept	Crewe	7-1
EC1983	14 May	Belfast	4-0
EC1985	25 May	Antrim	8-1
EC1986	16 Mar	Blackburn	10-0
1987	11 Apr	Leeds	6-0
AC2005	9 Mar	Paderne	4-0
EC2007	13 May	Gillingham	4-0
EC2008	6 Mar	Lurgan	2-0

v NORWAY

1981	25 Oct	Cambridge	0-3
EC1988	21 Aug	Kleppe	0-2
EC1988	18 Sept	Blackburn	1-3
EC1990	27 May	Kleppe	0-2
EC1990	2 Sept	Old Trafford	0-0
WC1995	8 June	Karlstad	3-2
1997	8 June	Lillestrom	0-4
WC1998	14 May	Oldham	1-2
WC1998	15 Aug	Lillestrom	0-2
EC2000	7 Mar	Norwich	0-3
EC2000	4 June	Moss	0-8
AC2002	1 Mar	Albufeira	1-3
2005	6 May	Barnsley	1-0
2008	14 Feb	Larnaca	2-1
2009	23 Apr	Shrewsbury	3-0
2014	17 Jan	La Manga	1-1
WC2015	22 June	Ottawa	2-1
2017	**22 Jan**	**La Manga**	**0-1**

v PORTUGAL

EC1996	11 Feb	Benavente	5-0
EC1996	19 May	Brentford	3-0
EC2000	20 Feb	Barnsley	2-0
EC2000	22 Apr	Sacavem	2-2
WC2001	24 Nov	Gafanha da Nazare	1-1
WC2002	24 Feb	Portsmouth	3-0
AC2005	11 Mar	Faro	4-0

v REPUBLIC OF IRELAND

1978	2 May	Exeter	6-1
1981	2 May	Dublin	5-0
EC1982	7 Nov	Dublin	1-0
EC1983	11 Sept	Reading	6-0
EC1985	22 Sept	Cork	6-0
EC1986	27 Apr	Reading	4-0
1987	29 Mar	Dublin	1-0

v ROMANIA

EC1998	12 Sept	Campina	4-1
EC1998	11 Oct	High Wycombe	2-1

v RUSSIA

EC2001	24 June	Jena	1-1
2003	21 Oct	Moscow	2-2
2004	19 Aug	Bristol	1-2
2007	8 Mar	Milton Keynes	6-0
EC2009	28 Aug	Helsinki	3-2
EC2013	15 July	Linkoping	1-1

v SCOTLAND

1972	18 Nov	Greenock	3-2
1973	23 June	Nuneaton	8-0
1976	23 May	Enfield	5-1
1977	29 May	Dundee	1-2
EC1982	3 Oct	Dumbarton	4-0
EC1983	22 May	Leeds	2-0
EC1985	17 Mar	Preston	4-0
EC1986	12 Oct	Kirkcaldy	3-1
1989	30 Apr	Kirkcaldy	3-0
1990	6 May	Paisley	4-0
1990	12 May	Wembley	4-0
1991	20 Apr	High Wycombe	5-0
EC1992	17 Apr	Walsall	1-0
EC1992	23 Aug	Perth	2-0
1997	9 Mar	Sheffield	6-0
1997	23 Aug	Livingston	4-0
2001	27 May	Bolton	1-0
AC2002	7 Mar	Quarteira	4-1
2003	13 Nov	Preston	5-0
2005	21 Apr	Tranmere	2-1
2007	11 Mar	High Wycombe	1-0
CC2009	10 Mar	Larnaca	3-0
CC2011	4 Mar	Nicosia	0-2
CC2013	8 Mar	Larnaca	4-4

v SERBIA

EC2011	17 Sept	Belgrade	2-2
EC2011	23 Nov	Doncaster	2-0
EC2016	4 June	Wycombe	7-0
EC2016	7 June	Stara Pazova	7-0

v SLOVENIA

EC1993	25 Sept	Ljubljana	10-0
EC1994	17 Apr	Brentford	10-0
EC2011	22 Sept	Swindon	4-0
EC2012	21 June	Velenje	4-0

v SOUTH AFRICA

CC2009	5 Mar	Larnaca	6-0
CC2010	24 Feb	Larnaca	1-0

v SPAIN

EC1993	19 Dec	Osuna	0-0
EC1994	20 Feb	Bradford	0-0
EC1996	8 Sept	Montilla	1-2
EC1996	29 Sept	Tranmere	1-1
2001	22 Mar	Luton	4-2
EC2007	25 Nov	Shrewsbury	1-0
EC2008	2 Oct	Zamora	2-2
WC2010	1 Apr	Millwall	1-0
WC2010	19 June	Aranda de Duero	2-2
EC2013	12 July	Linkoping	2-3
2016	**25 Oct**	**Guadalajara**	**2-1**

v SWEDEN

1975	15 June	Gothenborg	0-2
1975	7 Sept	Wimbledon	1-3
1979	27 July	Scafati	0-0*
1980	17 Sept	Leicester	1-1
1982	26 May	Kinna	1-1
1983	30 Oct	Charlton	2-2
EC1984	12 May	Gothenburg	0-1
EC1984	27 May	Luton	1-0
EC1987	11 June	Moss	2-3*
1989	23 May	Wembley	0-2
1995	13 May	Halmstad	0-4
1998	26 July	Dagenham	0-1
EC2001	27 June	Jena	0-4
2002	25 Jan	La Manga	0-5
AC2002	5 Mar	Lagos	3-6
EC2005	11 June	Blackburn	0-1
2006	7 Feb	Larnaca	0-0
2006	9 Feb	Achna	1-1
2008	12 Feb	Larnaca	0-2
EC2009	31 Aug	Turku	1-1
2011	17 May	Oxford	2-0
2013	4 July	Ljungskile	1-4
2014	3 Aug	Hartlepool	4-0
2017	**24 Jan**	**La Manga**	**0-0**

v SWITZERLAND

1975	19 Apr	Basel	3-1
1977	28 Apr	Hull	9-1
1979	23 July	Sorrento	2-0
EC1999	16 Oct	Zofingen	3-0
EC2000	13 May	Bristol	1-0
CC2010	1 Mar	Nicosia	2-2
WC2010	12 Sept	Shrewsbury	2-0
WC2010	16 Sept	Wohlen	3-2
CC2012	1 Mar	Larnaca	1-0
2017	**10 June**	**Biel**	**4-0**

v TURKEY

WC2009	26 Nov	Izmir	3-0
WC2010	29 July	Walsall	3-0
WC2013	26 Sept	Portsmouth	8-0
WC2013	31 Oct	Adana	4-0

v UKRAINE

EC2000	30 Oct	Kiev	2-1
EC2000	28 Nov	Leyton	2-0
WC2014	8 May	Shrewsbury	4-0
WC2014	19 June	Lviv	2-1

v USA

M1985	23 Aug	Caorle	3-1
M1988	27 July	Riva del Garda	2-0
1990	9 Aug	Blaine	0-3
1991	25 May	Hirson	1-3
1997	9 May	San Jose	0-5
1997	11 May	Portland	0-6
AC2002	3 Mar	Ferreiras	0-2
2003	17 May	Birmingham (Alabama)	0-6
2007	28 Jan	Guangzhou	1-1
WC2007	22 Sept	Tianjin	0-3
2011	2 Apr	Leyton	2-1
2015	13 Feb	Milton Keynes	0-1
2016	4 Mar	Tampa	0-1
2017	**4 Mar**	**New Jersey**	**1-0**

v USSR

1990	11 Aug	Blaine	1-1
1991	20 July	Dmitrov	2-1
1991	21 July	Kashira	2-0
1991	7 Sept	Southampton	2-0
1991	8 Sept	Brighton	1-3

v WALES

1974	17 Mar	Slough	5-0
1976	22 May	Bedford	4-0
1976	17 Oct	Ebbw Vale	2-1
1977	18 Sept	Warminster	5-0
1980	1 June	Warminster	6-1
1985	17 Aug	Ramsey (Isle of Man)	6-0
WC2013	26 Oct	Millwall	2-0
WC2014	21 Aug	Cardiff	4-0

v WEST GERMANY

M1984	22 Aug	Jesolo	0-2
1990	5 Aug	Blaine	1-3

OTHER MATCHES

v ITALY B

1984	27 Aug	Monfalcone	3-1
M1988	20 July	Riva del Garda	3-0

v USA B

1990	7 Aug	Blaine	1-0

NON-LEAGUE TABLES 2016–17

EVO-STIK NORTHERN PREMIER LEAGUE PREMIER DIVISION 2016–17

			Home			*Away*			*Total*						
		P	*W*	*D*	*L*	*W*	*D*	*L*	*W*	*D*	*L*	*F*	*A*	*GD*	*Pts*
1	Blyth Spartans	46	18	4	1	13	4	6	31	8	7	114	44	70	101
2	Spennymoor T¶	46	15	5	3	10	7	6	25	12	9	96	48	48	87
3	Stourbridge	46	14	4	5	11	6	6	25	10	11	84	51	33	85
4	Workington	46	15	1	7	11	4	8	26	5	15	73	56	17	83
5	Nantwich T	46	11	6	6	12	6	5	23	12	11	86	59	27	81
6	Whitby T	46	13	6	4	10	4	9	23	10	13	64	56	8	79
7	Buxton	46	14	6	3	8	6	9	22	12	12	81	54	27	78
8	Grantham T	46	12	6	5	10	4	9	22	10	14	74	57	17	76
9	Matlock T	46	13	6	4	9	3	11	22	9	15	68	58	10	75
10	Warrington T	46	14	1	8	8	7	8	22	8	16	65	57	8	74
11	Ashton U	46	12	4	7	7	7	9	19	11	16	85	78	7	68
12	Rushall Olympic	46	10	4	9	8	6	9	18	10	18	60	60	0	64
13	Stafford Rangers	46	9	8	6	7	7	9	16	15	15	63	60	3	63
14	Barwell	46	9	6	8	7	8	8	16	14	16	58	53	5	62
15	Hednesford T	46	10	5	8	8	2	13	18	7	21	68	65	3	61
16	Mickleover Sports	46	12	0	11	7	3	13	19	3	24	68	71	–3	60
17	Coalville T	46	7	7	9	8	3	12	15	10	21	71	79	–8	55
18	Marine	46	9	9	5	5	4	14	14	13	19	62	74	–12	55
19	Halesowen T	46	7	7	9	6	5	12	13	12	21	46	70	–24	51
20	Sutton Coldfield T	46	10	6	7	2	5	16	12	11	23	49	79	–30	47
21	Corby T	46	8	7	8	4	3	16	12	10	24	49	72	–23	46
22	Frickley Ath	46	8	2	13	4	1	18	12	3	31	47	97	–50	39
23	Ilkeston	46	5	3	15	2	3	18	7	6	33	31	86	–55	27
24	Skelmersdale U	46	4	2	17	1	7	15	5	9	32	40	118	–78	24

¶Spennymoor T promoted to National League North via play-offs.

EVO-STIK NORTHERN PREMIER LEAGUE DIVISION 1 NORTH 2016–17

		P	*W*	*D*	*L*	*W*	*D*	*L*	*W*	*D*	*L*	*F*	*A*	*GD*	*Pts*
1	Lancaster C	42	14	2	5	13	2	6	27	4	11	73	41	32	85
2	Farsley Celtic¶	42	14	2	5	12	4	5	26	6	10	100	50	50	84
3	Scarborough Ath	42	14	3	4	8	4	9	22	7	13	70	47	23	73
4	Ossett T	42	11	4	6	11	3	7	22	7	13	69	49	20	73
5	Colne*	42	11	3	7	11	4	6	22	7	13	74	50	24	72
6	Trafford	42	8	8	5	10	8	3	18	16	8	80	46	34	70
7	Clitheroe	42	11	5	5	9	5	7	20	10	12	74	54	20	70
8	Glossop NE	42	14	3	4	7	3	11	21	6	15	72	70	2	69
9	Brighouse T	42	8	11	2	9	6	6	17	17	8	66	48	18	68
10	Hyde U†	42	8	10	3	8	4	9	16	14	12	78	58	20	61
11	Bamber Bridge‡	42	11	2	8	5	5	11	16	7	19	59	58	1	54
12	Kendal T	42	9	6	6	5	6	10	14	12	16	61	62	–1	54
13	Droylsden	42	7	6	8	7	6	8	14	12	16	71	77	–6	54
14	Ramsbottom U§	42	9	4	8	7	5	9	16	9	17	64	81	–17	53
15	Colwyn Bay	42	6	8	7	7	3	11	13	11	18	61	57	4	50
16	Prescot Cables#	42	8	7	6	5	4	12	13	11	18	71	81	–10	47
17	Mossley	42	7	1	13	7	3	11	14	4	24	67	87	–20	46
18	Ossett Alb	42	7	2	12	6	4	11	13	6	23	47	78	–31	45
19	Tadcaster Alb	42	8	5	8	3	6	12	11	11	20	57	70	–13	44
20	Radcliffe Bor	42	8	0	13	4	8	9	12	8	22	59	82	–23	44
21	Goole	42	5	6	10	4	3	14	9	9	24	39	83	–44	36
22	Burscough	42	4	2	15	2	4	15	6	6	30	26	109	–83	24

*¶Farsley Celtic promoted via play-offs. *Colne deducted 1pt for fielding an ineligible player. †Hyde U deducted 1pt for fielding an ineligible player. ‡Bamber Bridge deducted 1pt for fielding an ineligible player. §Ramsbottom U deducted 4pts for fielding an ineligible player. #Prescot Cables deducted 3pts for fielding an ineligible player.*

EVO-STIK NORTHERN PREMIER LEAGUE DIVISION 1 SOUTH 2016–17

		P	*W*	*D*	*L*	*W*	*D*	*L*	*W*	*D*	*L*	*F*	*A*	*GD*	*Pts*
1	Shaw Lane AFC	42	18	3	0	14	3	4	32	6	4	104	36	68	102
2	Witton Alb*¶	42	16	4	1	15	2	4	31	6	5	100	41	59	96
3	Spalding U	42	11	4	6	13	3	5	24	7	11	74	42	32	79
4	Stocksbridge Park Steels	42	11	3	7	11	4	6	22	7	13	67	50	17	73
5	AFC Rushden & Diamonds	42	8	8	5	12	3	6	20	11	11	73	52	21	71
6	Basford U†	42	15	4	2	5	9	7	20	13	9	78	53	25	70
7	Newcastle T	42	14	2	5	7	2	12	21	4	17	59	59	0	67
8	Lincoln U	42	11	2	8	8	6	7	19	8	15	67	61	6	65
9	Leek T	42	10	5	6	8	5	8	18	10	14	63	63	0	64
10	Belper T	42	7	8	6	8	5	8	15	13	14	55	55	0	58
11	Bedworth U	42	8	5	8	7	7	7	15	12	15	73	72	1	57
12	Kidsgrove Ath	42	9	2	10	7	5	9	16	7	19	72	66	6	55
13	Romulus	42	8	5	8	6	4	11	14	9	19	65	75	–10	51
14	Market Drayton T	42	11	1	9	5	1	15	16	2	24	60	93	–33	50
15	Sheffield	42	8	3	10	5	6	10	13	9	20	62	60	2	48
16	Stamford	42	7	5	9	6	4	11	13	9	20	62	80	–18	48
17	Chasetown	42	7	5	9	6	3	12	13	8	21	64	75	–11	47
18	Gresley	42	7	4	10	5	5	11	12	9	21	56	83	–27	45
19	Carlton T	42	6	8	7	4	4	13	10	12	20	48	68	–20	42
20	Loughborough Dynamo	42	6	3	12	4	1	16	10	4	28	45	94	–49	34
21	Rugby T	42	3	3	15	5	3	13	8	6	28	44	77	–33	30
22	Northwich Vic‡	42	4	5	12	4	7	10	8	12	22	53	89	–36	26

*¶Witton Alb promoted via play-offs. *Witton Alb deducted 3pts for fielding an ineligible player. †Basford U deducted 3pts for fielding an ineligible player. ‡Northwich Victoria deducted 10pts for entering administration.*

EVO-STIK SOUTHERN LEAGUE PREMIER DIVISION 2016–17

			Home			*Away*			*Total*						
		P	*W*	*D*	*L*	*W*	*D*	*L*	*W*	*D*	*L*	*F*	*A*	*GD*	*Pts*
1	Chippenham T	46	17	4	2	14	6	3	31	10	5	94	47	47	103
2	Leamington¶	46	15	5	3	12	6	5	27	11	8	74	32	42	92
3	Merthyr T	46	15	7	1	10	7	6	25	14	7	92	42	50	89
4	Hitchin T	46	13	7	3	11	7	5	24	14	8	79	45	34	86
5	Slough T	46	15	3	5	11	4	8	26	7	13	84	56	28	85
6	Banbury U	46	13	4	6	11	4	8	24	8	14	67	40	27	80
7	Biggleswade T	46	13	5	5	8	6	9	21	11	14	85	59	26	74
8	Frome T	46	11	8	4	9	6	8	20	14	12	80	67	13	74
9	Kettering T	46	9	7	7	12	3	8	21	10	15	84	66	18	73
10	Weymouth	46	10	8	5	6	10	7	16	18	12	79	58	21	66
11	Chesham U	46	12	6	5	6	4	13	18	10	18	67	62	5	64
12	Basingstoke T	46	11	3	9	7	5	11	18	8	20	65	72	–7	62
13	King's Lynn T	46	9	8	6	5	10	8	14	18	14	60	69	–9	60
14	Stratford T	46	8	7	8	5	10	8	13	17	16	64	66	–2	56
15	St Ives T	46	8	7	8	7	4	12	15	11	20	49	70	–21	56
16	Dunstable T	46	9	4	10	7	2	14	16	6	24	46	65	–19	54
17	Redditch U	46	7	6	10	6	5	12	13	11	22	54	75	–21	50
18	Dorchester T	46	8	9	6	4	3	16	12	12	22	52	80	–28	48
19	St Neots T	46	9	4	10	5	2	16	14	6	26	66	101	–35	48
20	Kings Langley	46	6	5	12	5	9	9	11	14	21	57	72	–15	47
21	Cambridge C	46	7	6	10	5	5	13	12	11	23	46	72	–26	47
22	Cirencester T	46	7	3	13	4	6	13	11	9	26	54	92	–38	42
23	Hayes & Yeading U	46	6	4	13	4	7	12	10	11	25	48	81	–33	41
24	Cinderford T	46	7	2	14	1	1	21	8	3	35	49	106	–57	27

¶Leamington promoted to National League North via play-offs.

EVO-STIK SOUTHERN LEAGUE DIVISION 1 CENTRAL 2016–17

		P	*W*	*D*	*L*	*W*	*D*	*L*	*W*	*D*	*L*	*F*	*A*	*GD*	*Pts*
1	Royston T	42	17	3	1	15	3	3	32	6	4	121	48	73	102
2	Farnborough¶	42	16	3	2	12	3	6	28	6	8	96	51	45	90
3	Barton R	42	11	6	4	12	2	7	23	8	11	91	66	25	77
4	Marlow	42	10	6	5	13	2	6	23	8	11	65	43	22	77
5	Egham T	42	14	4	3	6	10	5	20	14	8	79	51	28	74
6	Kempston R	42	11	4	6	10	6	5	21	10	11	82	61	21	73
7	AFC Dunstable	42	11	4	6	10	4	7	21	8	13	85	53	32	71
8	Bedford T	42	9	8	4	9	5	7	18	13	11	76	58	18	67
9	Potters Bar T	42	8	4	9	8	10	3	16	14	12	71	61	10	62
10	Ashford T (Middlesex)	42	9	3	9	8	5	8	17	8	17	73	71	2	59
11	Kidlington	42	10	2	9	8	3	10	18	5	19	70	79	–9	59
12	Hanwell T*	42	8	6	7	8	4	9	16	10	16	64	67	–3	57
13	Aylesbury U	42	8	2	11	8	5	8	16	7	19	58	68	–10	55
14	Fleet T	42	8	6	7	5	5	11	13	11	18	72	81	–9	50
15	Arlesey T	42	7	3	11	7	5	9	14	8	20	55	69	–14	50
16	Beaconsfield SYCOB	42	6	5	10	7	4	10	13	9	20	81	85	–4	48
17	Uxbridge	42	5	4	12	8	4	9	13	8	21	67	80	–13	47
18	Chalfont St Peter	42	6	4	11	8	1	12	14	5	23	49	77	–28	47
19	Aylesbury	42	6	5	10	6	3	12	12	8	22	54	75	–21	44
20	Northwood	42	5	7	9	4	5	12	9	12	21	57	88	–31	39
21	Histon	42	3	4	14	6	3	12	9	7	26	54	93	–39	34
22	Petersfield T	42	1	1	19	1	2	18	2	3	37	32	127	–95	9

*¶Farnborough promoted via play-offs. *Hanwell T deducted 1pt for fielding an ineligible player.*

EVO-STIK SOUTHERN LEAGUE DIVISION 1 SOUTH & WEST 2016–17

		P	*W*	*D*	*L*	*W*	*D*	*L*	*W*	*D*	*L*	*F*	*A*	*GD*	*Pts*
1	Hereford	42	17	3	1	16	5	0	33	8	1	108	32	76	107
2	Salisbury	42	16	2	3	13	0	8	29	2	11	118	52	66	89
3	Tiverton T¶	42	15	4	2	12	3	6	27	7	8	92	50	42	88
4	Taunton T*	42	15	5	1	12	2	7	27	7	8	114	42	72	85
5	Evesham U	42	12	5	4	12	3	6	24	8	10	88	50	38	80
6	North Leigh	42	12	5	4	10	4	7	22	9	11	84	65	19	75
7	Swindon Supermarine	42	11	3	7	10	6	5	21	9	12	85	57	28	72
8	Mangotsfield U	42	9	5	7	12	2	7	21	7	14	73	69	4	70
9	Shortwood U	42	7	4	10	12	1	8	19	5	18	65	77	–12	62
10	Bideford	42	8	6	7	7	6	8	15	12	15	61	58	3	57
11	Wimborne T	42	11	2	8	6	4	11	17	6	19	67	68	–1	57
12	Didcot T	42	9	4	8	5	8	8	14	12	16	70	71	–1	54
13	Larkhall Ath	42	7	5	9	6	9	6	13	14	15	69	69	0	53
14	Winchester C	42	9	3	9	7	2	12	16	5	21	62	70	–8	53
15	Paulton R	42	9	4	8	6	2	13	15	6	21	62	69	–7	51
16	Bishops Cleeve	42	6	6	9	8	2	11	14	8	20	66	86	–20	50
17	Barnstaple T	42	8	3	10	5	3	13	13	6	23	52	68	–16	45
18	Yate T	42	7	3	11	5	5	11	12	8	22	49	77	–28	44
19	AFC Totton	42	6	4	11	4	5	12	10	9	23	49	86	–37	39
20	Slimbridge	42	7	3	11	3	4	14	10	7	25	47	90	–43	37
21	Wantage T	42	3	3	15	1	6	14	4	9	29	29	110	–81	21
22	Bridgwater T	42	1	2	18	1	2	18	2	4	36	23	117	–94	10

*¶Tiverton T promoted via play-offs. *Taunton T deducted 3pts for fielding an ineligible player.*

RYMAN ISTHMIAN LEAGUE PREMIER DIVISION 2016–17

			Home			*Away*			*Total*						
		P	*W*	*D*	*L*	*W*	*D*	*L*	*W*	*D*	*L*	*F*	*A*	*GD*	*Pts*
1	Havant & Waterlooville	46	15	4	4	13	6	4	28	10	8	88	43	45	94
2	Bognor Regis T¶	46	15	5	3	12	6	5	27	11	8	87	41	46	92
3	Dulwich Hamlet	46	12	4	7	10	10	3	22	14	10	89	55	34	80
4	Enfield T	46	11	8	4	10	5	8	21	13	12	86	57	29	76
5	Wingate & Finchley	46	12	3	8	11	3	9	23	6	17	63	61	2	75
6	Tonbridge Angels	46	12	7	4	9	4	10	21	11	14	66	55	11	74
7	Leiston	46	13	5	5	8	5	10	21	10	15	98	66	32	73
8	Billericay T	46	13	3	7	8	6	9	21	9	16	77	56	21	72
9	Needham Market	46	12	7	4	8	5	10	20	12	14	76	80	–4	72
10	Harlow T	46	13	3	7	7	4	12	20	7	19	76	72	4	67
11	Lowestoft T	46	10	5	8	8	5	10	18	10	18	63	73	–10	64
12	Staines T	46	10	4	9	6	9	8	16	13	17	78	68	10	61
13	Leatherhead*	46	10	8	5	6	4	13	16	12	18	72	72	0	57
14	Worthing	46	8	6	9	8	2	13	16	8	22	73	85	–12	56
15	Folkestone Invicta	46	12	4	7	3	6	14	15	10	21	75	82	–7	55
16	Kingstonian	46	8	3	12	8	4	11	16	7	23	65	73	–8	55
17	Metropolitan Police	46	9	5	9	6	4	13	15	9	22	54	72	–18	54
18	Hendon	46	5	10	8	9	2	12	14	12	20	68	88	–20	54
19	Burgess Hill T	46	10	3	10	4	9	10	14	12	20	59	80	–21	54
20	Merstham*	46	10	6	7	5	5	13	15	11	20	70	72	–2	53
21	Harrow Bor†	46	8	6	9	6	5	12	14	11	21	60	80	–20	53
22	Canvey Island	46	8	4	11	5	9	9	13	13	20	63	92	–29	52
23	AFC Sudbury	46	7	6	10	5	4	14	12	10	24	57	85	–28	46
24	Grays Ath	46	5	4	14	6	1	16	11	5	30	46	101	–55	38

*¶Bognor Regis T promoted to National League South via play-offs. *Leatherhead and Mersham deducted 3pts for fielding an ineligible player. †Harrow Bor reprieved from relegation.*

RYMAN ISTHMIAN LEAGUE DIVISION 1 NORTH 2016–17

		P	*W*	*D*	*L*	*W*	*D*	*L*	*W*	*D*	*L*	*F*	*A*	*GD*	*Pts*
1	Brightlingsea Regent	46	17	3	3	15	4	4	32	7	7	114	57	57	103
2	Maldon & Tiptree	46	20	1	2	9	3	11	29	4	13	107	51	56	91
3	Thurrock¶	46	15	4	4	12	4	7	27	8	11	84	39	45	89
4	AFC Hornchurch	46	12	8	3	12	5	6	24	13	9	78	42	36	85
5	Haringey Bor	46	16	1	6	9	5	9	25	6	15	108	74	34	81
6	Bowers & Pitsea	46	13	4	6	10	5	8	23	9	14	102	66	36	78
7	Aveley	46	14	5	4	7	8	8	21	13	12	75	64	11	76
8	Phoenix Sports	46	9	6	8	13	3	7	22	9	15	71	72	–1	75
9	Norwich U*	46	14	4	5	10	1	12	24	5	17	70	61	9	74
10	Cheshunt	46	9	5	9	11	6	6	20	11	15	85	72	13	71
11	Bury T	46	13	3	7	7	6	10	20	9	17	74	66	8	69
12	Tilbury	46	9	9	5	8	4	11	17	13	16	67	73	–6	64
13	Witham T	46	10	5	8	6	6	11	16	11	19	77	80	–3	59
14	Brentwood T	46	11	0	12	6	5	12	17	5	24	63	77	–14	56
15	VCD Ath	46	10	4	9	5	7	11	15	11	20	53	76	–23	56
16	Romford	46	8	9	6	7	2	14	15	11	20	59	90	–31	56
17	Thamesmead T	46	7	4	12	9	2	12	16	6	24	70	78	–8	54
18	Dereham T	46	7	5	11	8	4	11	15	9	22	70	89	–19	54
19	Soham Town Rangers	46	7	6	10	7	5	11	14	11	21	62	78	–16	53
20	Waltham Abbey	46	9	5	9	5	4	14	14	9	23	57	73	–16	51
21	Heybridge Swifts	46	8	6	9	5	6	12	13	12	21	64	81	–17	51
22	Ware†	46	10	3	10	5	3	15	15	6	25	66	84	–18	51
23	Wroxham	46	4	3	16	2	4	17	6	7	33	42	103	–61	25
24	Great Wakering R	46	2	3	18	4	4	15	6	7	33	49	121	–72	25

*¶Thurrock Promoted via play-offs. *Norwich U deducted 3pts for fielding an ineligible player.*
†Ware reprieved from relegation

RYMAN ISTHMIAN LEAGUE DIVISION 1 SOUTH 2016–17

		P	*W*	*D*	*L*	*W*	*D*	*L*	*W*	*D*	*L*	*F*	*A*	*GD*	*Pts*
1	Tooting & Mitcham U	46	18	3	2	15	3	5	33	6	7	120	54	66	105
2	Dorking W¶	46	18	1	4	15	5	3	33	6	7	103	44	59	105
3	Greenwich Bor	46	16	1	6	14	4	5	30	5	11	102	52	50	95
4	Corinthian-Casuals	46	13	5	5	16	1	6	29	6	11	99	59	40	93
5	Hastings U	46	14	4	5	9	9	5	23	13	10	128	64	64	82
6	Carshalton Ath*	46	14	5	4	10	4	9	24	9	13	106	69	37	78
7	Hythe T	46	10	8	5	13	1	9	23	9	14	87	65	22	78
8	South Park	46	10	1	12	14	3	6	24	4	18	95	80	15	76
9	Lewes	46	11	4	8	12	3	8	23	7	16	88	75	13	76
10	Faversham T	46	14	5	4	8	3	12	22	8	16	89	58	31	74
11	Cray W	46	9	5	9	10	6	7	19	11	16	88	86	2	68
12	Ramsgate	46	9	7	7	9	4	10	18	11	17	79	75	4	65
13	Walton Casuals	46	12	2	9	7	6	10	19	8	19	98	99	–1	65
14	Whyteleafe	46	10	3	10	9	4	10	19	7	20	81	75	6	64
15	Sittingbourne	46	11	4	8	6	7	10	17	11	18	71	86	–15	62
16	Horsham	46	9	5	9	8	5	10	17	10	19	79	80	–1	61
17	Herne Bay	46	8	7	8	5	5	13	13	12	21	74	98	–24	51
18	East Grinstead T	46	6	4	13	8	1	14	14	5	27	82	121	–39	47
19	Molesey	46	7	9	7	4	1	18	11	10	25	61	116	–55	43
20	Chipstead	46	5	4	14	6	4	13	11	8	27	68	99	–31	41
21	Guernsey	46	6	7	10	3	4	16	9	11	26	66	112	–46	38
22	Chatham T	46	2	3	18	5	7	11	7	10	29	57	120	–63	31
23	Three Bridges	46	3	2	18	4	6	13	7	8	31	59	114	–55	29
24	Godalming T*	46	5	0	18	3	3	17	8	3	35	49	128	–79	24

*¶Dorking W Promoted via play-offs. *Carshalton Ath and Godalming T deducted 3pts for fielding an ineligible player.*

THE BUILDBASE FA TROPHY 2016–17

**After extra time.*

PRELIMINARY ROUND

Witton Alb v Brighouse T	5-2
Glossop NE v Tadcaster Alb	2-0
Prescot Cables v Ossett Alb	1-1, 1-0
Colne v Trafford	1-2
Burscough v Kendal T	1-2
Clitheroe v Stocksbridge Park Steels	0-5
Colwyn Bay v Hyde U	1-0
Northwich Vic v Mossley	1-1, 2-3
Shaw Lane Association v Scarborough Ath	2-0
Belper T v Goole	1-2
Radcliffe Bor v Farsley Celtic	1-3
Lancaster C v Droylsden	1-1, 3-1
Ramsbottom U v Sheffield	3-1
Ossett T v Bamber Bridge	0-1
Bedworth U v Rugby T	3-3, 2-0
Stamford v Basford U	1-0
AFC Rushden & Diamonds v Histon	1-1, 6-1
Gresley v Spalding U	4-1
Carlton T v Chasetown	3-1
Newcastle T v Soham T Rangers	1-3
Loughborough Dynamo v Leek T	1-2
Lincoln U v Romulus	2-2, 3-1*
(1-1 at full time)	
Aylesbury v Ware	1-3
Sittingbourne v Bury T	0-2
Maldon & Tiptree v Great Wakering R	3-1
East Grinstead T v Three Bridges	4-0
Witham T v Aveley	2-1
Cray W v Carshalton Ath	3-0
Potters Bar T v Horsham	0-2
Thurrock v Bowers & Pitsea	1-2
Chipstead v Kempston R	3-3, 0-2
Aylesbury U v Chatham T	4-1
Uxbridge v AFC Dunstable	4-0
Lewes v Tilbury	1-1, 3-0
South Park v Guernsey	2-0
Whyteleafe v Cheshunt	1-3
Haringey Bor v Hythe T	1-2
Dorking W v Northwood	3-6
Wroxham v Godalming T	3-0
Norwich U v Tooting & Mitcham U	0-2
Ramsgate v Hastings U	0-3
AFC Hornchurch v Ashford T (Middlesex)	2-3
Molesey v Romford	1-3
Brentwood T v Marlow	1-2
Arlesey T v Chalfont St Peter	2-2, 0-6
Corinthian Casuals v Thamesmead T	2-1
Brightlingsea Regent v Dereham T	2-1
VCD Ath v Greenwich Bor	1-1, 2-1
Royston T v Egham T	3-0
Hanwell T v Bedford T	4-0
Barton R v Herne Bay	0-1
Slimbridge v Swindon Supermarine	1-3
Bridgwater T v North Leigh	2-2, 1-4
Winchester C v Petersfield T	1-1, 3-1*
(1-1 at full time)	
Wimborne T v AFC Totton	2-2, 2-1
Salisbury v Hereford	4-3
Paulton R v Tiverton T	1-6
Bishop's Cleeve v Didcot T	1-0
Mangotsfield U v Yate T	0-2
Farnborough v Barnstaple T	1-5
Fleet T v Bideford	2-1
Kidlington v Wantage T	2-3
Taunton T v Larkhall Ath	6-2
Shortwood U v Evesham U	0-1

FIRST QUALIFYING ROUND

Goole v Blyth Spartans	1-1, 1-7
Spennymoor T v Matlock T	1-2
Warrington T v Nantwich T	0-2
Stocksbridge Park Steels v Lancaster C	2-1
Whitby T v Workington	4-3
Skelmersdale U v Kendal T	1-3
Colwyn Bay v Witton Alb	1-1, 1-3
Mossley v Farsley Celtic	1-3
Ramsbottom U v Prescot Cables	2-1
Bamber Bridge v Trafford	0-2
Buxton v Glossop NE	2-0
Ashton U v Marine	0-4
Shaw Lane Association v Frickley Ath	6-2
Stratford T v Grantham T	2-2, 0-4
Leamington v Mickleover Sports	0-1
Kidsgrove Ath v Soham T Rangers	5-3
Rushall Olympic v Halesowen T	1-2
Ilkeston v Barwell	0-2
Carlton T v St Ives T	1-4
Stourbridge v King's Lynn T	1-2
Corby T v Stafford Rangers	0-2
Kettering T v Market Drayton T	5-1
Redditch U v Cambridge C	3-1
Stamford v Hednesford T	1-4
Leek T v Sutton Coldfield T	2-1
AFC Rushden & Diamonds v Coalville T	1-0
Bedworth U v St Neots T	2-3
Lincoln U v Gresley	4-2
Horsham v Romford	1-3
East Grinstead T v Phoenix Sports	2-3
Kingstonian v Lewes	2-1
Hastings U v Aylesbury U	4-0
Hythe T v Walton Casuals	3-2
Burgess Hill T v Beaconsfield SYCOB	5-1
Leatherhead v Chesham U	2-3
Waltham Abbey v Merstham	0-5
Hanwell T v Bury T	2-1
Metropolitan Police v Brightlingsea Regent	2-6
Needham Market v Wroxham	2-0
Slough T v Bognor Regis T	4-1
Grays Ath v Wingate & Finchley	1-1, 0-2
Worthing v Kempston R	3-1
AFC Sudbury v Bowers & Pitsea	4-0
Tonbridge Angels v Ashford T (Middlesex)	3-3, 4-1
Kings Langley v Heybridge Swifts	1-0
Leiston v Hendon	5-0
VCD Ath v Ware	1-3
Enfield T v Canvey Island	3-2
Tooting & Mitcham U v Dunstable T	2-4
Billericay T v Maldon & Tiptree	2-0
Chalfont St Peter v Corinthian Casuals	3-2
Cray W v Marlow	4-0
Cheshunt v Folkestone Invicta	1-3
Royston T v Northwood	2-2, 4-1
Lowestoft T v Dulwich Hamlet	1-2
Biggleswade T v Witham T	1-0
Faversham T v South Park	3-4
Uxbridge v Harlow T	0-1
Herne Bay v Harrow Bor	2-2, 0-3
Hayes & Yeading U v Hitchin T	0-1
Evesham U v Frome T	1-1, 0-1
Yate T v North Leigh	1-6
Salisbury v Chippenham T	2-3
Taunton T v Swindon Supermarine	5-0
Tiverton T v Wimborne T	0-1
Cirencester T v Havant & Waterlooville	1-2
Merthyr T v Cinderford T	6-1
Banbury U v Bishop's Cleeve	0-1
Fleet T v Winchester C	1-2
Weymouth v Wantage T	4-0
Dorchester T v Barnstaple T	3-1
Staines T v Basingstoke T	1-4

SECOND QUALIFYING ROUND

Nantwich T v Kendal T	2-0
Blyth Spartans v Halesowen T	4-3
Buxton v King's Lynn T	1-3
Marine v St Neots T	1-1, 4-2
Hednesford T v Stafford Rangers	1-1, 1-2*
(1-1 at full time)	
St Ives T v Leek T	2-1
Shaw Lane Association v Whitby T	3-0
Ramsbottom U v Redditch U	4-1
Kidsgrove Ath v Stocksbridge Park Steels	3-5
Barwell v Farsley Celtic	2-3
Grantham T v Matlock T	0-2
Trafford v Mickleover Sports	0-1
AFC Rushden & Diamonds v Lincoln U	3-3, 0-2
Witton Alb v Kettering T	2-1
Kings Langley v Enfield T	1-0
Bishop's Cleeve v Taunton T	0-1
Dunstable T v Weymouth	1-4
Dorchester T v Basingstoke T	0-3

Merthyr T v Slough T 2-2, 0-2*
(2-2 at full time)
Havant & Waterlooville v Billericay T 5-0
Brightlingsea Regent v Harlow T 0-0†, 1-1, 1-2
†First match abandoned (0-0 after 46 minutes) due to floodlight failure
Hanwell T v Frome T 0-1
Chippenham T v Leiston 0-1
Dulwich Hamlet v Chesham U 4-0
Merstham v Hythe T 0-3
Burgess Hill T v Chalfont St Peter 2-2, 1-1*
Burgess Hill T won 8-7 on penalties
Biggleswade T v Hitchin T 1-1, 2-3
Folkestone Invicta v North Leigh 2-3
Royston T v Wimborne T 4-0
Needham Market v Harrow Bor 1-2
Cray W v Worthing 1-2
Phoenix Sports v Winchester C 1-3
Hastings U v South Park 1-1, 2-3
(1-1 at full time)
AFC Sudbury v Romford 4-0
Kingstonian v Tonbridge Angels 1-1, 2-1
Ware v Wingate & Finchley 0-2

THIRD QUALIFYING ROUND

Stocksbridge Park Steels v Stalybridge Celtic 2-2, 3-2
Harrogate T v Salford C 1-0†, 2-2, 3-0
†First match abandoned (1-0 after 45 minutes) due to fog
Witton Alb v Boston U 1-0†, 4-2
†First match abandoned (1-0 after 45 minutes) due to fog
Mickleover Sports v Brackley T 1-1, 1-3
Gainsborough Trinity v Alfreton T 0-0, 1-4*
(1-1 at full time)
King's Lynn T v St Ives T 1-0
Shaw Lane Association (removed) v Nantwich T (walkover)
Altrincham v Blyth Spartans 2-2, 3-2
Ramsbottom U v AFC Telford U 0-2
Matlock T v FC Halifax T 1-1, 3-2
Farsley Celtic v Tamworth 2-2, 4-0
Chorley v Stafford Rangers 1-0
Kidderminster H v Lincoln U 3-1
Curzon Ashton v Worcester C 1-2
FC United of Manchester v Nuneaton T 1-5
Stockport Co v Bradford (Park Avenue) 2-0
Gloucester C v AFC Fylde 2-3
Darlington 1883 v Marine 2-2, 2-3
Ebbsfleet U v Harrow Bor 4-2
Slough T v Wingate & Finchley 2-4
Truro C v Frome T 6-1
Hampton & Richmond Bor v Royston T 0-0, 1-2
Concord Rangers v Welling U 0-1
Kings Langley v AFC Sudbury 1-3
Weston Super Mare v Dartford 2-4
Worthing v Hemel Hempstead T 1-1, 1-0
Hungerford T v Gosport Bor 0-1
Oxford C v South Park 1-2
Bath C v Basingstoke T 2-0
Chelmsford C v Taunton T 1-0
Margate v East Thurrock U 1-1, 0-2
Leiston v Eastbourne Bor 1-1, 2-2*
Leiston won 5-3 on penalties
Poole T v Weymouth 1-1, 0-2
Havant & Waterlooville v Harlow T 1-3
Winchester C v Dulwich Hamlet 0-1
Maidenhead U v Wealdstone 2-2, 1-2
Burgess Hill T v Hitchin T 0-3
Whitehawk v St Albans C 1-1, 1-0
North Leigh v Kingstonian 1-0
Hythe T v Bishop's Stortford 4-2

FIRST ROUND

Gateshead v King's Lynn T 2-0
Farsley Celtic v Southport 0-4
Solihull Moors v Matlock T 1-2
Nantwich T v Lincoln C 1-2
Alfreton T v North Ferriby U 1-0
Kidderminster H v AFC Telford U 4-0
Nuneaton T v Stocksbridge Park Steels 3-1
Harrogate T v Barrow 3-3, 2-4*
(2-2 at full time)
AFC Fylde v Brackley T 1-1, 0-4
York C v Worcester C 3-1
Chorley v Guiseley 0-1
Witton Alb v Chester FC 1-1, 1-2
Wrexham v Tranmere R 0-1
Altrincham v Macclesfield T 1-1, 1-2
Stockport Co v Marine 3-2
Ebbsfleet U v Woking 1-1, 1-0
Chelmsford C v Hitchin T 1-0
Dagenham & Redbridge v Worthing 1-2
Harlow T v Eastleigh 2-0
Whitehawk v Weymouth 2-2, 2-1
Braintree T v Torquay U 2-0
East Thurrock U v Aldershot T 1-1, 4-3*
(3-3 at full time)
Dulwich Hamlet v Royston T 2-2, 1-0
Welling U v Hythe T 8-1
Wealdstone v Wingate & Finchley 2-2, 2-1*
(1-1 at full time)
Dartford v Dover Ath 1-1, 2-1
South Park v North Leigh 1-1, 3-1
AFC Sudbury v Gosport Bor 2-1
Sutton U v Bath C 1-0
Forest Green R v Truro C 1-1, 1-0*
(0-0 at full time)
Boreham Wood v Maidstone U 0-0, 3-2
Bromley v Leiston 1-1, 5-3

SECOND ROUND

Worthing v Sutton U 2-2, 2-3*
(2-2 at full time)
Tranmere R v South Park 4-1
Bromley v Welling U 1-2
East Thurrock U v Braintree T 2-5
Nuneaton T v Guiseley 6-1
Boreham Wood v Alfreton T 2-1
Barrow v Matlock T 3-2
Southport v Wealdstone 1-2
Gateshead v Lincoln C 1-3
Dartford v Chelmsford C 0-1
Kidderminster H v Ebbsfleet U 3-0
Harlow T v York C 1-2
AFC Sudbury v Macclesfield T 1-3
Whitehawk v Dulwich Hamlet 1-4
Chester FC v Forest Green R 0-2
Stockport Co v Brackley T 1-1, 0-2

THIRD ROUND

Welling U v Lincoln C 1-3
Braintree T v Dulwich Hamlet 0-0, 2-5
Barrow v Kidderminster H 1-0
Tranmere R v Chelmsford C 1-1, 4-1
Macclesfield T v Forest Green R 1-0
Wealdstone v Brackley T 1-4
Nuneaton T v York C 0-3
Sutton U v Boreham Wood 0-0, 0-5

FOURTH ROUND

Dulwich Hamlet v Macclesfield T 2-2, 0-2
York C v Brackley T 1-0
Boreham Wood v Lincoln C 0-2
Tranmere R v Barrow 5-1

SEMI-FINALS – FIRST LEG

Macclesfield T v Tranmere R 1-1
York C v Lincoln C 2-1

SEMI-FINALS – SECOND LEG

Tranmere R v Macclesfield T 0-1
Macclesfield T won 2-1 on aggregate
Lincoln C v York C 1-1*
York C won 3-2 on aggregate

THE BUILDBASE FA TROPHY FINAL 2017

Wembley , Sunday 21 May 2017

Macclesfield T (2) 2 *(Browne 13, Norburn 45)*

York C (2) 3 *(Parkin 8, Oliver 22, Connolly 86)*
38,224 (combined with FA Vase)

Macclesfield T: Flinders; Halls, Byrne (McCombe 67), Pilkington, Fitzpatrick, Browne, James, Norburn (Dudley 89), Whitaker, Hancox (Summerfield 87), 9 Holroyd.
York C: Letheren; Parslow, Klukowski (Moke 46), Bencherif, Heslop, Newton, Hall (Connolly 69), Holmes (Rooney 75), Morgan-Smith, Oliver, Parkin.
Referee: Paul Tierney.

THE BUILDBASE FA VASE 2016–17

**After extra time.*

FIRST QUALIFYING ROUND

Bridlington T v Yorkshire Amateur 6-0
Bedlington Terriers v Bishop Auckland 0-3
Albion Sports v Ashington 3-4
Knaresborough T v Silsden 1-2
Stockton T v Eccleshill U 2-0
Blyth T v Ryton & Crawcrook Alb 1-2
Darlington Railway Ath v Barnoldswick T 0-4
Consett v Hebburn T 5-1
Daisy Hill v Garforth T 4-1
Penrith v Durham C 5-3*
(3-3 at full time)
Billingham T v Willington 4-2
West Allotment Celtic v Hall Road Rangers 0-2
Washington v Billingham Synthonia 0-1
Easington Colliery v Thackley 2-1
AFC Darwen v Pickering T 1-2
Nelson v Heaton Stannington 1-2
West Auckland T v Seaham Red Star 3-2*
(2-2 at full time)
Crook T v Esh Winning 1-2
Carlisle C v Team Northumbria 1-2
Brandon U v Chester-le-Street T 0-7
Tow Law T v Norton & Stockton Ancients 1-3
Whickham v Charnock Richard 0-2
Thornaby v Liversedge 1-4
Newcastle Benfield v Alnwick T 8-1
City of Liverpool v Litherland Remyca 1-2
Barton T Old Boys v Grimsby Bor 0-2
Staveley MW v Cheadle T 1-0
Maltby Main v Widnes 0-2
Alsager T v Squires Gate 2-1
Ashton T v Parkgate 4-2
Bootle v Maine Road 4-1
St Helens T v Chadderton 3-5
Runcorn T v Winsford U 4-1
Dronfield T v Glasshoughton Welfare 0-2
Pontefract Collieries v Hemsworth MW 2-4
Irlam v Selby T 1-0
Winterton Rangers v Penistone Church 1-5
Ashton Ath v Athersley Recreation 2-0
Armthorpe Welfare v Congleton T 2-3
Barnton v Harworthy Colliery 5-2*
(2-2 at full time)
Black Country Rangers v Stafford T 1-0
Dudley T v Wellington Amateurs 0-4
FC Oswestry T v Walsall Wood 1-3*
(1-1 at full time)
Coton Green v Kirby Muxloe 1-3
Ashby Ivanhoe v Pelsall Villa 2-1
Whitchurch Alport v Wellington 1-2*
(1-1 at full time)
Highgate U v Lye T 2-0
Bolehall Swifts v Heath Hayes 7-2
Bromyard T v Atherstone T 2-6
Cradley T v Uttoxeter T 1-4
Pershore T v Bewdley T 1-2
Chelmsley T v Studley 3-2
Ellistown & Ibstock U v Bromsgrove Sporting 0-13
Redditch Bor v Rocester 2-5
AFC Bridgnorth v Boldmere St Michaels 0-5
Shawbury U v Heather St Johns 3-1
Shifnal T v Gornal Ath 5-1
Barnt Green Spartak v Cadbury Ath 0-1
Racing Club Warwick v Coventry U 1-3
Malvern T v Tividale 4-1
Bardon Hill v Littleton 1-5
Lutterworth Ath v Stone Old Alleynians 0-2
Brocton v Eccleshall 6-0
Continental Star (withdrawn) v
Wolverhampton Casuals (walkover)
Stourport Swifts v Smethwick 5-1
Ellesmere Rangers v Pegasus Juniors 2-7*
(2-2 at full time)
Clay Cross T v Leicester Road 2-3
Clifton All Whites v Oadby T 7-0
Borrowash Vic v Bottesford T 1-7
Gedling MW v Oakham U 2-3*
(1-1 at full time)
Loughborough University v Arnold T 7-1
Ollerton T v Retford U 2-3
Pinxton v Harrowby U 4-0
Rainworth MW v Heanor T 1-4
Graham St Prims v Kimberley MW 2-5
Teversal v Blidworth Welfare 0-1*
(0-0 at full time)
Aylestone Park v Stapenhill 3-7
Belper U v Radford 0-1
Barrow T v St Andrews 0-3
Long Eaton U v South Normanton Ath 2-0
Brigg T v Harborough T 0-4
Holbrook Sports v Hinckley 0-2
Thetford T v Framlingham T 4-3
Yaxley v Eynesbury R 7-0
Great Yarmouth T v Bourne T 3-0
Wisbech T v Mildenhall T 2-2, 0-4
Ely C v Kirkley & Pakefield 3-2*
(1-1 at full time)
Walsham Le Willows v Deeping Rangers 2-2, 3-3*
Walsham Le Willows won 5-4 on penalties
Gorleston v Wisbech St Mary 2-0
Diss T v Team Bury 3-0
London Bari v Newbury Forest 3-0
FC Clacton v Enfield 1893 0-1
Wivenhoe T v Wadham Lodge 1-2
FC Broxbourne Bor v Cornard U 3-2
Takeley v Tower Hamlets 7-2
Halstead T v Hadley 3-2
Langford v Baldock T 2-2*
Baldock T won 4-3 on penalties
Stansted v Saffron Walden T 1-2
Hadleigh U v Debenham LC 1-0
Burnham Ramblers v London Lions 2-1
Harpenden T v Ilford 1-3*
(1-1 at full time)
Whitton U v Biggleswade U 0-4
Woodbridge T v Hatfield T 4-1
Southend Manor v West Essex 7-0
Hertford T v Clapton 0-0, 2-1
Sporting Bengal U v Stowmarket T 2-1*
(1-1 at full time)
Codicote v St Margaretsbury 0-3
Redbridge v Eton Manor 5-4*
(2-2 at full time)
Raunds T v Northampton ON Chenecks 1-4
Risborough Rangers v Broadfields U 0-3
Winslow U v Rushden & Higham U 6-4
Long Buckby v Hillingdon Bor 1-3
Bedfont & Feltham v Sandhurst T 3-0
Ampthill T v Northampton Sileby Rangers 2-3
Rothwell Corinthians v Burton Park W 8-0
AFC Hayes v Crawley Green 2-2*
Crawley Green won 4-1 on penalties
Kensington Bor v Thrapston T 0-2
Brackley T Saints v Leighton T 3-3, 3-4
Spelthorne Sports v Tring Ath 0-0, 0-2
Cranfield U v Southall 2-2
Replay awarded to Southall – Cranfield U failed to fulfil fixture
Bicester T v Potton U 3-2
FC Deportivo Galicia v Irchester U 0-1
London Tigers v Cogenhoe U 3-1
Daventry T v Windsor 3-1
Stotfold v North Greenford U 2-2, 0-4
Bedford v CB Hounslow U 0-1
Desborough T v Woodford U 10-0
Stewarts & Lloyds Corby v
Wellingborough Whitworths 0-4
Hanworth Villa v Bedfont Sports 0-4
Amersham T v Highmoor Ibis 0-2
AFC Stoneham v Malmesbury Vic 3-0
Buckingham Ath v Binfield 2-3
Hook Norton v Bracknell T 1-5*
(1-1 at full time)
Shrivenham v Abbey Rangers 2-3*
(2-2 at full time)
Ash U v Tytherington Rocks 2-1
Thame U v Tadley Calleva 5-1
Badshot Lea v Farnham T 3-1
Fairford T v Chipping Sodbury T 3-2
Chertsey T v Lydney T 1-2
AFC Portchester v Holyport 3-0
Woodley U v Ardley U 0-4
Cove v Buckingham T 0-4
Tunbridge Wells v Steyning T 4-1
Hailsham T v Lingfield 0-3
Croydon v Loxwood 2-1
Whitstable T v Chichester C 2-2, 2-3

Broadbridge Heath v Crowborough Ath 2-4
Southwick v FC Elmstead 1-2
Bearsted v Pagham 0-1
Cray Valley (PM) v Glebe 0-1
St Francis Rangers v Ringmer 1-2
Raynes Park Vale v Haywards Heath T 1-2
Arundel v Westfield 1-2
Horley T v Hassocks 4-2
Sevenoaks T v Crawley Down Gatwick 3-1
Little Common v Erith T 2-1*
(1-1 at full time)
Redhill v Deal T 1-2
Guildford C v Eastbourne U 2-1
Tie awarded to Eastbourne U – Guildford C removed
Chessington & Hook U v Rochester U 3-3, 1-2
Bexhill U v Holmesdale 2-3
Shoreham v Meridian 8-2
Mile Oak v Erith & Belvedere 2-1
Littlehampton T v Saltdean U 2-0
Worthing U v Peacehaven & Telscombe 2-0†, 0-2
†First match abandoned (2-0 after 70 minutes) due to pitch invasion
Dorking v Beckenham T 1-4
Bridon Ropes v Colliers Wood U 2-1
Langney W v Selsey 4-4, 1-4
Brockenhurst v Ringwood T 5-0
Corsham T v United Services Portsmouth 1-0
Westbury U v Folland Sports 2-1
New Milton T v Horndean 1-5
Oldland Abbotonians v Lymington T 4-0
Whitchurch U v Laverstock & Ford 3-1
Hamworthy U v Amesbury T 3-5
Cowes Sports v Cadbury Heath 4-2*
(1-1 at full time)
Andover New Street v Gillingham T 1-3*
(1-1 at full time)
Hallen v Fawley 3-2
Bournemouth v Verwood T 4-3
Hythe & Dibden v Team Solent 1-2
Bemerton Heath Harlequins v Downton 7-0
Romsey T v Warminster T 3-0
Christchurch v Swanage T & Herston 2-1
Bridport v Cribbs 2-4
Alresford T v Chippenham Park 5-1
Welton R v Ashton & Backwell U 0-3
Liskeard Ath v Portishead T 1-2
Hengrove Ath v Camelford 3-2
AFC St Austell v Crediton U 3-2
Cullompton Rangers v Wincanton T 3-2
Shepton Mallet v Tavistock 1-6
Radstock T v Torpoint Ath 3-6
Wellington v Bishop Sutton 0-1
Keynsham T v Ivybridge T 4-2
Cheddar v Elburton Villa 2-1

SECOND QUALIFYING ROUND

Northallerton T v Jarrow Roofing Boldon CA 0-4
Whitley Bay v Stockton T 0-2
West Auckland T v Padiham 1-2*
(1-1 at full time)
Heaton Stannington v Billingham Synthonia 0-1
Esh Winning v South Shields 0-4
Easington Colliery v Ashington 2-0
Birtley T v Holker Old Boys 2-4
Chester-le-Street T v Norton & Stockton Ancients 3-2
Bishop Auckland v Billingham T 1-2
Ryton & Crawcrook Alb v Sunderland Ryhope CW 0-5
Barnoldswick T v Stokesley SC 7-1
Bridlington T v Daisy Hill 5-2
Newcastle Benfield v Liversedge 3-0
Penrith v Team Northumbria 4-2
Silsden v Hall Road Rangers 3-4*
(2-2 at full time)
Consett v Pickering T 1-3
Harrogate Railway Ath v Charnock Richard 1-3
Westella VIP v Irlam 0-3
Atherton LR v Cammell Laird 1907 3-2
Alsager T v Stockport T 0-3
AFC Liverpool v Abbey Hey 3-2*
(2-2 at full time)
AFC Blackpool v Runcorn T 0-2
Congleton T v Bacup Bor 7-3*
(3-3 at full time)
Ashton Ath v AFC Emley 1-2
Hallam v Nostell MW 8-1
Staveley MW v Grimsby Bor 2-0
Rossington Main v Bootle 0-4
Penistone Church v West Didsbury & Chorlton 3-2*
(2-2 at full time)
Ashton T v Barnton 3-2
Litherland Remyca v Vauxhall Motors 3-1
Widnes v Chadderton 1-4
Glasshoughton Welfare v Hemsworth MW 2-2, 1-1*
Hemsworth MW won 3-2 on penalties
Hanley T v Boldmere St Michaels 2-1
Uttoxeter T v Wellington Amateurs 3-0
Tipton T v Bromsgrove Sporting 0-1
Birstall U v Malvern T 2-2, 2-3*
(2-2 at full time)
Rocester v Black Country Rangers 1-0
Willenhall T v Haughmond 0-3
Walsall Wood v Pegasus Juniors 2-0
Stourport Swifts v Cadbury Ath 0-1
Paget Rangers v Highgate U 2-1
Coventry Copsewood v Atherstone T 2-1
Stone Old Alleynians v Ashby Ivanhoe 1-1, 1-1*
Ashby Ivanhoe won 3-1 on penalties
Coventry U v Wednesfield 2-0
Kirby Muxloe v Littleton 2-0*
(0-0 at full time)
Shawbury U v Coventry Sphinx 3-2
Wolverhampton Casuals v Bilston T 4-2
Brocton v Chelmsley T 0-2
Bolehall Swifts v Shifnal T 0-2
Westfields v Dudley Sports 8-0
Wellington v Lichfield C 2-5
Bewdley T v Wolverhampton SC 1-7
Leicester Road v West Bridgford 4-3
Dunkirk v Bottesford T 1-4
Heanor T v Kimberley MW 2-2, 2-0
Anstey Nomads v Quorn 0-2
Oakham U v Retford U 1-0
Harborough T v Blaby & Whetstone Ath 2-1
Blidworth Welfare v Shirebrook T 2-0
Hucknall T v Eastwood Community 5-0
Pinxton v Loughborough University 4-2
Greenwood Meadows v Hinckley 3-6
Clipstone v Sherwood Colliery 1-3
Stapenhill v Long Eaton U 2-3
Clifton All Whites v Holwell Sports 1-2*
(1-1 at full time)
AFC Mansfield v Radcliffe Olympic 4-2
New Mills v Radford 3-4
St Andrews v Retford 3-0
Yaxley v Newmarket T 4-3*
(2-2 at full time)
Fakenham T v Great Yarmouth T 1-3
Peterborough Northern Star v Blackstones 4-0
Thetford T v Downham T 2-0
Gorleston v March T U 3-2
Ely C v Diss T 4-2
Huntingdon T v Swaffham T 1-4
Mildenhall T v Peterborough Sports 1-3
Boston T v Walsham Le Willows 2-3
Biggleswade U v Woodbridge T 3-0
Colney Heath v Redbridge 2-1
Takeley v Biggleswade 1-2
(1-1 at full time)
Cockfosters v Hadley Wood & Wingate 4-0
Waltham Forest v Hadleigh U 2-1
Sporting Bengal U v Sawbridgeworth T 3-2
Hertford T v Brantham Ath 3-2
Haverhill Bor v Haverhill R 1-0
Wadham Lodge v Enfield 1893 3-1
Long Melford v Baldock T 2-3
Southend Manor v Canning T 0-0*
Canning T won 5-4 on penalties
Halstead T v St Margaretsbury 1-4
London Bari v Barkingside 2-1*
(1-1 at full time)
FC Broxbourne Bor v Saffron Walden T 1-2
Burnham Ramblers v Ilford 0-4
Harefield U v Leverstock Green 0-4
Wembley v Hillingdon Bor 2-1
Daventry T v Edgware T 4-1
London Tigers v Southall 2-5
North Greenford U v Oxhey Jets 1-2
Bicester T v Broadfields U 2-3
Holmer Green v Cricklewood W 3-0
Desborough T v Wellingborough Whitworths 6-3*
(3-3 at full time)
Northampton ON Chenecks v Leighton T 1-0
Bedfont & Feltham v Sun Sports 2-4
Northampton Sileby Rangers v Rayners Lane 5-0
LPOSSA (withdrawn) v Crawley Green (walkover)
Burnham v Highmoor Ibis 2-3*
(2-2 at full time)
Thrapston T v CB Hounslow U 3-1

Winslow U v Tring Ath 1-4
Rothwell Corinthians v Irchester U 2-1
Wellingborough T v Bedfont Sports 0-2
Tuffley R v Ardley U 4-1
Carterton (withdrawn) v Brimscombe & Thrupp (walkover)
Ash U v Milton U 3-1
Frimley Green v Walton & Hersham 0-3
Fleet Spurs v Fairford T 1-3
Alton T v Henley T 4-2
Bashley v Highworth T 0-4
Melksham T v New College Swindon 4-0
Bracknell T v Binfield 2-1
Royal Wootton Bassett T v Thame U 2-4
Buckingham T v Eversley & California 4-3*
(2-2 at full time)
Oxford C Nomads v Abingdon U 2-3
AFC Stoneham v Longlevens 3-1
Abbey Rangers v Badshot Lea 1-0
Lydney T v AFC Portchester 2-0
Rochester U v Beckenham T 1-2*
(1-1 at full time)
Glebe v Deal T 1-1, 3-1
FC Elmstead v AFC Uckfield T 1-0
Ringmer v Sporting Club Thamesmead 2-2, 1-6
Holmesdale v Banstead Ath 1-4
Mile Oak v Croydon 1-3
Oakwood v Shoreham 0-10
Horley T v Selsey 1-0
Chichester C v Sheppey U 3-1
AC London v Littlehampton T 1-1, 5-1
Little Common v Wick 0-2
Crowborough Ath v Gravesham Bor 2-0
Corinthian v Sevenoaks T 3-2
Cobham v Lingfield 0-1
Westfield v Haywards Heath T 0-1
East Preston v Tunbridge Wells 1-4
Bridon Ropes v Rushtall 2-1*
(1-1 at full time)
Eastbourne U v AFC Croydon Ath 2-1
Tooting & Mitcham W v Seaford T 3-1
Canterbury C v Peacehaven & Telscombe 8-0
Pagham v Horsham YMCA 0-1
Westbury U v Cribbs 1-2
Whitchurch U v Amesbury T 0-6
Devizes T v Corsham T 2-1
Portland U v Almondsbury UWE 2-0
Shaftesbury T v Fareham T 5-1
Christchurch v Romsey T 1-3
Hallen v Team Solent 1-3
Bournemouth v Brockenhurst 3-1
Bitton v Gillingham T 0-3
Horndean v Oldland Abbotonians 2-0
Calne T v Roman Glass St George 4-3
Cowes Sports v Alresford T 0-2
Bemerton Heath Harlequins v Longwell Green Sports 3-0
East Cowes Vic Ath v Sherborne T 0-4
Cullompton Rangers v Budleigh Salterton 4-1*
(1-1 at full time)
Keynsham T v Tavistock 0-6
Clevedon T v Cheddar 3-1*
(1-1 at full time)
AFC St Austell v Street 2-3
Exmouth T v Witheridge 1-0
Hengrove Ath v Bishop Sutton 2-1
Wells C v Torpoint Ath 1-2
Ashton & Backwell U v Willand R 0-1
Portishead T v Helston Ath 1-3*
(1-1 at full time)
Brislington v Plymouth Parkway 0-1

FIRST ROUND

AFC Liverpool v Bootle 0-6
1874 Northwich v Billingham Synthonia 1-0
Stockport T v Sunderland Ryhope CW 1-3
Penrith v Easington Colliery 3-1
Guisborough T v Padiham 0-3
Runcorn T v Hallam 1-2
South Shields v Runcorn Linnets 2-1
Charnock Richard v Barnoldswick T 3-1*
(1-1 at full time)
Atherton LR v Chester-le-Street T 0-3
Ashton T v Billingham T 0-4
AFC Emley v Chadderton 3-1
Newcastle Benfield v Irlam 3-1
Atherton Collieries v Jarrow Roofing Boldon CA 5-0
Congleton T v Hall Road Rangers 2-3
Bridlington T v Pickering T 0-1
Holker Old Boys v Stockton T 1-2
Litherland Remyca v Shildon 1-4
Shifnal T v Quorn 1-4
Heanor T v Blidworth Welfare 0-4
St Andrews v Paget Rangers 1-2
Long Eaton U v Coventry U 2-1
Wolverhampton Casuals v Chelmsley T 2-1
Ashby Ivanhoe v Hucknall T 3-4*
(3-3 at full time)
Handsworth Parramore v Shepshed Dynamo 3-4
Bromsgrove Sporting v Cadbury Ath 5-3*
(3-3 at full time)
Westfields v Walsall Wood 6-0
Staveley MW v Pinxton 2-0
Holwell Sports v AFC Mansfield 0-2
Hinckley v Wolverhampton SC 3-1*
(1-1 at full time)
Lichfield C v Shawbury U 2-1
Kirby Muxloe v Hemsworth MW 0-1
Penistone Church v Sherwood Colliery 1-2
Bottesford T v Haughmond 2-0
Malvern T v Worksop T 1-2
Rocester v Oakham U 8-1
Uttoxeter T v Leicester Road 5-4
Radford v Harborough T 3-1*
(1-1 at full time)
Sporting Khalsa v Hanley T 1-0
Coventry Copsewood v Holbeach U 0-2
Northampton Sileby Rangers v Oxhey Jets 1-0†, 5-0
†First match abandoned (1-0 after 15 minutes) due to serious injury to player
Thetford T v Great Yarmouth T 2-1
Wadham Lodge v Hertford T 2-1
Sporting Bengal U v Southall 0-3
Felixstowe & Walton U v Haverhill Bor 4-0
Broadfields U v London Bari 2-1
Highmoor Ibis v Holmer Green 0-1
Peterborough Sports v Swaffham T 6-0
Waltham Forest v Rothwell Corinthians 1-2
Thrapston T v Leverstock Green 3-7
Canning T v Biggleswade 4-5*
(3-3 at full time)
Northampton ON Chenecks v Ely C 1-3
Gorleston v Barking 2-0
Biggleswade U v Baldock T 2-1
Flackwell Heath v Cockfosters 0-3
Walsham Le Willows v Tring Ath 0-1
Crawley Green v Basildon U 1-2
Colney Heath v Hoddesdon T 1-4
Daventry T v Newport Pagnell T 2-3
Godmanchester R v London Colney 0-3
Yaxley v Stanway R 0-1
St Margaretsbury v Ilford 3-2
Peterborough Northern Star v Sun Sports 1-3
Welwyn Garden C v Saffron Walden T 3-1
Wembley v Desborough T 5-2
Banstead Ath v Crowborough Ath 1-3
Wick v Haywards Heath T 0-1
Bedfont Sports v Buckingham T 5-4
Canterbury C v Lydney T 3-1
FC Elmstead v Sporting Club Thamesmead 0-2
Abbey Rangers v Tunbridge Wells 3-0
Hollands & Blair v Ascot U 0-1
Walton & Hersham v Thame U 3-0
Croydon v Bracknell T 4-1
Epsom & Ewell v Bridon Ropes 1-0
Horsham YMCA v Horndean 3-2
Eastbourne U v Horley T 2-0
Shoreham v Glebe 2-3
Beckenham T v Lancing 1-3
Eastbourne T v Tooting & Mitcham W 9-0
AC London v Highworth T 3-3, 0-1†, 1-2
†First replay abandoned (0-1 after 85 minutes) due to serious injury to player
Fairford T v Andover T 1-2
Alton T v Corinthian 0-2
Ash U v Chichester C 0-4
Alresford T v Lingfield 5-3
Lordswood v Newhaven 1-2
Abingdon U v Thatcham T 1-3
Cribbs v Odd Down 1-1, 1-2
Devizes T v Gillingham T 0-3
Amesbury T v Brimscombe & Thrupp 0-1
Helston Ath v Team Solent 1-2
Street v Blackfield & Langley 0-2
Bournemouth v Melksham T 0-3
Calne T v Torpoint Ath 0-2
Tuffley R v Sherborne T 4-0
Cullompton Rangers v Hengrove Ath 1-0
Bemerton Heath Harlequins v Plymouth Parkway 2-2, 3-0

Sholing v Buckland Ath 0-3
Clevedon T v Willand R 4-2*
(2-2 at full time)
Romsey T v Portland U 2-3
Exmouth T v Tavistock 3-2
AFC Stoneham v Shaftesbury T 1-3

SECOND ROUND

Newton Aycliffe v Worksop T 4-0
Pickering T v Shildon 0-5
Padiham v Bootle 0-2
1874 Northwich v Atherton Collieries 0-3
Charnock Richard v Staveley MW 2-4*
(2-2 at full time)
Billingham T v Sunderland Ryhope CW 5-2
Hallam v Morpeth T 0-4
Hall Road Rangers v Bottesford T 0-2
Sunderland RCA v Stockton T 1-0*
(0-0 at full time)
North Shields v Chester-le-Street T 2-0
Dunston UTS v Hemsworth MW 3-1
Newcastle Benfield v Penrith 0-1
South Shields v Marske U 2-0
AFC Emley v Cleethorpes T 1-2
Sleaford T v Leicester Nirvana 4-1
Long Eaton U v Holbeach U 3-2
Wolverhampton Casuals v Nuneaton Griff 1-2
Hucknall T v Rocester 5-1
Blidworth Welfare v AFC Mansfield 1-2
Paget Rangers v Hinckley 1-4
Westfields v Sherwood Colliery 3-2
Alvechurch v Sporting Khalsa 1-2
Radford v Shepshed Dynamo 1-3
Uttoxeter T v Coleshill T 1-3
Bromsgrove Sporting v Lichfield C 3-1
Quorn v AFC Wulfrunians 3-1*
(1-1 at full time)
Wadham Lodge v Ely C 0-3
Rothwell Corinthians v Tring Ath 1-2
Leverstock Green v Welwyn Garden C 1-2
St Margaretsbury v Stanway R 4-2*
(1-1 at full time)
Newport Pagnell T v Broadfields U 2-1
Berkhamsted v Hullbridge Sports 5-2
Gorleston v Northampton Sileby Rangers 2-1
Cockfosters v Wembley 1-2
Peterborough Sports v Biggleswade 5-3
London Colney v Holmer Green 3-0
Biggleswade U v Sun Sports 1-1, 1-1*
Sun Sports won 5-4 on penalties
FC Romania v Ipswich W 2-0
Hoddesdon T v Thetford T 2-0
Basildon U v Felixstowe & Walton U 3-2
Eastbourne T v Ashford U 2-1
Sutton Common R v Sporting Club Thamesmead 2-1
Newhaven v Ascot U 2-1
Bedfont Sports v Haywards Heath T 2-0
Eastbourne U v Crowborough Ath 0-1
Walton & Hersham v Glebe 2-2*
Glebe won 3-1 on penalties
Camberley T v Southall 0-4
Croydon v Andover T 2-1
Corinthian v Alresford T 3-2
Lancing v Horsham YMCA 1-7
Chichester C v Canterbury C 3-1*
(1-1 at full time)
Highworth T v Knaphill 1-3
Epsom & Ewell v Abbey Rangers 2-3
Portland U v Blackfield & Langley 1-2
Shaftesbury T v Team Solent 1-3
Brimscombe & Thrupp v Bradford T 2-2, 0-5
Bristol Manor Farm v Odd Down 2-1
Moneyfields v Thatcham T 0-4
Cullompton Rangers v Bemerton Heath Harlequins 1-1, 2-3
Hartley Wintney v Melksham T 1-2
Gillingham T v Exmouth T 0-1
Buckland Ath v Newport (IW) 1-0
Torpoint Ath v Clevedon T 1-0
Tuffley R v Bodmin T 0-2

THIRD ROUND

North Shields v Shildon 1-2
Newton Aycliffe v Morpeth T 2-3
Cleethorpes T v Bootle 2-1
South Shields v Staveley MW 3-0
Penrith v Atherton Collieries 0-3
Dunston UTS v Sunderland RCA 1-3
Bottesford T v Billingham T 1-2
Hucknall T v AFC Mansfield 1-2
Nuneaton Griff v Bromsgrove Sporting 0-2
Sporting Khalsa v Sleaford T 5-5, 3-0
Coleshill T v Westfields 4-1
Hinckley v Quorn 2-1*
(1-1 at full time)
Long Eaton U v Shepshed Dynamo 2-4*
(2-2 at full time)
Wembley v Peterborough Sports 0-4
FC Romania v Tring Ath 1-1, 1-2
Newport Pagnell T v London Colney 3-1
Gorleston (walkover) v Basildon U (withdrawn) 0-1†
†*First match abandoned (0-1 after 89 minutes) due to serious incident*
St Margaretsbury v Berkhamsted 1-3
Sun Sports v Hoddesdon T 3-1
Welwyn Garden C v Ely C 2-3
Abbey Rangers v Eastbourne T 1-2
Crowborough Ath v Bedfont Sports 2-2, 3-2
Croydon v Glebe 3-2
Knaphill v Southall 1-2
Newhaven v Chichester C 1-3
Sutton Common R v Corinthian 1-4
Horsham YMCA v Buckland Ath 0-3
Bemerton Heath Harlequins v Melksham T 2-3
Team Solent v Bodmin T 1-0
Bradford T v Torpoint Ath 2-0
Bristol Manor Farm v Thatcham T 4-1
Exmouth T v Blackfield & Langley 5-0

FOURTH ROUND

Shildon v Atherton Collieries 1-4
Billingham T v Cleethorpes T 1-2
AFC Mansfield v Sunderland RCA 0-1
South Shields v Morpeth T 2-4†, 4-0
†*First match abandoned (2-4 after 81 minutes) due to floodlight failure*
Gorleston v Coleshill T 0-3
Sun Sports v Bromsgrove Sporting 0-4
Newport Pagnell T v Peterborough Sports 3-2
Sporting Khalsa v Tring Ath 1-0
Ely C v Shepshed Dynamo 3-0
Hinckley v Berkhamsted 5-0
Bradford T v Southall 2-4*
(2-2 at full time)
Bristol Manor Farm v Melksham T 1-1, 5-3
Chichester C v Buckland Ath 1-3
Team Solent v Croydon 3-0
Exmouth T v Corinthian 4-0
Crowborough Ath v Eastbourne T 6-0

FIFTH ROUND

Cleethorpes T v Atherton Collieries 3-2
Southall v Exmouth T 4-2
Bromsgrove Sporting v Bristol Manor Farm 2-1
Crowborough Ath v Coleshill T 3-6
Hinckley v Buckland Ath 3-4*
(3-3 at full time)
Newport Pagnell T v Sunderland RCA 3-2*
(2-2 at full time)
Ely C v Sporting Khalsa 0-3
Team Solent v South Shields 2-5

SIXTH ROUND

South Shields v Newport Pagnell T 6-1
Southall v Cleethorpes T 2-5
Bromsgrove Sporting v Buckland Ath 2-0
Coleshill T v Sporting Khalsa 2-0

SEMI-FINALS – FIRST LEG

Bromsgrove Sporting v Cleethorpes T 1-1
Coleshill T v South Shields 1-2

SEMI-FINALS – SECOND LEG

Cleethorpes T v Bromsgrove Sporting 1-0
Cleethorpes T won 2-1 on aggregate
South Shields v Coleshill T 4-0
South Shields won 6-1 on aggregate

THE BUILDBASE FA VASE FINAL 2017

Wembley , Sunday 21 May 2017

South Shields (1) 4 *(Finnigan 43 (pen), Morse 80, Foley 86, 89)*

Cleethorpes T (0) 0 38,224 (combined with FA Trophy)

South Shields: Connell; Nicholson, Morse, Shaw, Lough, Stephenson (Briggs 55), Arca, Phillips (Smith 83), Cogdon, Finnigan (Richardson 70), Foley.

Cleethorpes T: Higton; Lowe, Bloomer, Coleman (Mascall 70), Winn, Davis (Richardson 73), Dickens, Flett, Oglesby, Cooper (Taylor 61), Robertson.

Referee: Darren England.

THE FA YOUTH CUP 2016–17

**After extra time.*

PRELIMINARY ROUND

Chester-le-Street T v Darlington 1883 2-5*
(2-2 at full time)
Newcastle Benfield v Spennymoor T 3-2
Blyth Spartans v Hebburn T 5-3
Workington v Ryton & Crawcrook Alb 0-4
Skelmersdale U v Hyde U 0-4
FC United of Manchester v Curzon Ashton 3-0
AFC Blackpool v St Helens T 3-4
Prescot Cables v Clitheroe 1-2
Altrincham v Stockport Co 3-2
Irlam v Radcliffe Bor 6-0
Vauxhall Motors v Warrington T 2-1
Nelson (walkover) v Lancaster C (withdrawn)
Abbey Hey v Witton Alb 3-1
Bootle (withdrawn) v West Didsbury & Chorlton (walkover)
Burscough v Ashton Ath 1-4
Mossley v Colne 0-3
Sheffield v Maltby Main 3-0
Harrogate Railway Ath v Hemsworth MW 3-1
Tadcaster Alb v Brighouse T 4-1
FC Halifax T v Staveley MW 4-0
Farsley Celtic v Goole 3-2
Ossett T v Worksop T 5-7
Garforth T v Silsden 3-2
Pontefract Collieries v Ossett Alb 4-2
Hall Road Rangers v Selby T 7-4
AFC Emley v Stocksbridge Park Steels 1-2
Kimberley MW v Bourne T 3-0
Leicester Nirvana v Lutterworth Ath 3-2
Stamford v Ashby Ivanhoe 1-2
Anstey Nomads (withdrawn) v Loughborough Dynamo (walkover)
Boston U v Lincoln U 5-0
Grantham T v Bottesford T 1-2
Leicester Road v Mickleover Sports 3-0
Matlock T v Dunkirk 0-7
Alfreton T v Aylestone Park 3-2
Gresley v St Andrews 0-3
Tamworth v Hednesford T 5-3*
(3-3 at full time)
Wolverhampton Casuals v Highgate U 3-0
Nuneaton Griff v Kidsgrove Ath 1-2
Hereford v Malvern T 8-0
Alvechurch v Sutton Coldfield T 7-1
Stourbridge v Redditch U 3-1
Halesowen T v Coton Green 2-1
Ellesmere Rangers v Rugby T 4-2
Racing Club Warwick v Romulus 1-10
Dudley T v Nuneaton T 2-5
Leamington (walkover) v Paget Rangers (withdrawn)
Coleshill T v Dudley Sports 2-0
Stratford T v Bromsgrove Sporting 1-2*
(1-1 at full time)
Newcastle T v Bilston T 6-0
St Ives T v St Neots T 2-0
Desborough T v Eynesbury R 4-1
Godmanchester R v Northampton ON Chenecks 1-3
Corby T v Brackley T 7-2
Kempston R v Rothwell Corinthians 3-0
Wellingborough T v AFC Rushden & Diamonds 1-5
Cogenhoe U v Rushden & Higham U 0-2
Peterborough Sports v Peterborough Northern Star 1-2
Wroxham v Felixstowe & Walton U 4-1
Needham Market v Great Yarmouth T 4-1*
(1-1 at full time)
Leiston v Hadleigh U 5-3
Mildenhall T v Woodbridge T 0-4
Fakenham T v Newmarket T 3-5
Cornard U v Wisbech St Mary 3-2
Cambridge C v King's Lynn T 2-1
Bury T v Brantham Ath 1-1*
Bury T won 5-4 on penalties
Dereham T v Ely C 1-2
Stowmarket T v AFC Sudbury 0-8
Swaffham T v Walsham Le Willows 1-5
Gorleston (walkover) v Lowestoft T (withdrawn)
Chelmsford C v Waltham Abbey 2-1
Ilford (walkover) v Clapton (withdrawn)
Hullbridge Sports v AFC Hornchurch 3-4
Heybridge Swifts v Brentwood T 2-4
Great Wakering R v St Margaretsbury 2-1
Saffron Walden T v Barking 2-1
Woodford T (not accepted) v Bishop's Stortford (walkover)
Thurrock v Royston T 3-1
Ware v Brightlingsea Regent 6-2
Aveley v Redbridge 4-1
North Greenford U v Hatfield T 4-0
Hendon v Tring Ath 3-6
Potters Bar T v Ashford T (Middlesex) 5-2
Bedfont Sports v Harrow Bor 5-1
Colney Heath v Hitchin T 1-4
Spelthorne Sports v Hadley Wood & Wingate 3-1
Beaconsfield SYCOB v Staines T 3-1
Buckingham Ath v Harefield U 4-3
Hemel Hempstead T v Uxbridge 1-2
Chesham U v Sun Sports 5-0
Hanwell T (walkover) v Welwyn Garden C (withdrawn)
St Albans C v Hayes & Yeading U 4-2
Sporting Club Thamesmead (walkover) v Croydon (withdrawn)
Eastbourne Bor v Margate 4-1
Bridon Ropes v Chipstead 1-0
Tonbridge Angels (walkover) v Whitstable T (withdrawn)
East Grinstead T v Greenwich Bor 1-3
Lewisham Bor (Community) (not accepted) v VCD Ath (walkover)
Meridian v Faversham T 4-1
Thamesmead T v Folkestone Invicta 3-4
Eastbourne T v Ebbsfleet U 0-2
Dulwich Hamlet v Phoenix Sports 1-2
Erith & Belvedere (withdrawn) v Ramsgate (walkover)
AFC Croydon Ath v Lordswood 0-0*
Lordswood won 3-2 on penalties
Ashford U v Glebe 1-0
Carshalton Ath v Dartford 2-3
Chessington & Hook U v Mile Oak 2-2*
Mile Oak won 5-4 on penalties
Pagham v Leatherhead 3-4
Corinthian Casuals v Haywards Heath T 1-4
Worthing v Dorking 7-0
Dorking W v Guildford C 3-2*
(2-2 at full time)
Whitehawk v Burgess Hill T 2-1
Metropolitan Police v Three Bridges 3-1
Camberley T (walkover) v Lancing (withdrawn)
Bognor Regis T (withdrawn) v Knaphill (walkover)
Lewes v South Park 2-1
Chertsey T v Redhill 10-0
Shoreham v Westfield 2-3
Wick (walkover) v Walton & Hersham (withdrawn)
Steyning T v Arundel 3-1
Crawley Down Gatwick v Newhaven 2-6
Ascot U v Carterton 3-0
Hungerford T v Kidlington 5-2
Wantage T v Thatcham T 4-3
Slough T v Andover T 0-6
Didcot T v Shrivenham 3-2
Farnborough v Oxford C 0-3
Fleet T (withdrawn) v Burnham (walkover)
Thame U v Windsor 0-2
Alton T v Highmoor Ibis 3-3*
Alton T won 6-5 on penalties
Maidenhead U v Binfield 2-1
Holmer Green v Marlow 1-6
Salisbury v Wimborne T 4-2
Winchester C v Moneyfields 5-3
Tadley Calleva v Hamworthy U 1-5
Christchurch v Sholing 1-2
Havant & Waterlooville v AFC Stoneham 3-0
Yate T v New College Swindon 3-2
Cirencester T v Oldland Abbotonians 4-2
Chippenham T v Bristol Manor Farm 4-2*
(2-2 at full time)
Bishop Sutton v Portishead T 1-0
Clevedon T v Weston Super Mare 2-4
Bridgwater T v Paulton R 1-4
Odd Down v Bath C 0-1
Radstock T v Brislington 6-2*
(2-2 at full time)

FIRST QUALIFYING ROUND

Blyth Spartans v Durham C 1-8
Shildon v Darlington 1883 1-2

South Shields v Newcastle Benfield 1-2*
(1-1 at full time)
Ryton & Crawcrook Alb (walkover) v Kendal T (withdrawn)
Vauxhall Motors v Altrincham 1-4
St Helens T v Chadderton 2-1
Marine v Abbey Hey 4-1
Ashton Ath v Colne 6-1
Clitheroe v Chorley 1-0
Stalybridge Celtic v AFC Fylde 0-5
West Didsbury & Chorlton v Nantwich T 3-2
Ashton T v FC United of Manchester 2-4
AFC Darwen v Irlam 2-2*
Irlam won 4-2 on penalties
Hyde U v Nelson 1-0*
(0-0 at full time)
Farsley Celtic v Nostell MW 2-3
Rossington Main v Garforth T 0-3
Handsworth Parramore v Cleethorpes T 4-0
FC Halifax T v Stocksbridge Park Steels 1-0
Worksop T v Sheffield 2-4
Harrogate Railway Ath v Hall Road Rangers 0-1
Barton T Old Boys v Harrogate T 6-1
Pontefract Collieries v Tadcaster Alb 3-2
Belper T v Basford U 4-3
Boston U v Leicester Nirvana 1-0
St Andrews v Bottesford T 0-5
Kimberley MW v Leicester Road 2-1
Ilkeston v Dunkirk 1-3
Loughborough Dynamo v New Mills 6-2
Ashby Ivanhoe v Alfreton T 1-6
Boldmere St Michaels v AFC Telford U 4-5
Kidderminster H v Kidsgrove Ath 4-0
Romulus v Leamington 8-0
Coleshill T v Alvechurch 5-3
Stourbridge v Newcastle T 0-1
Rushall Olympic v Leek T 6-0
Ellesmere Rangers (walkover) v Worcester C (withdrawn)
Bromsgrove Sporting v Halesowen T 2-0
Nuneaton T v Lye T 4-3*
(2-2 at full time)
Evesham U v Hereford 0-2
Pegasus Juniors v Bedworth U 2-3*
(1-1 at full time)
Tamworth v Wolverhampton Casuals 3-5
Peterborough Northern Star v Biggleswade T 1-2
Desborough T v AFC Rushden & Diamonds 0-3
Kempston R v Kettering T 0-7
Northampton ON Chenecks v AFC Dunstable 1-2*
(0-0 at full time)
Yaxley v Rushden & Higham U 4-5
St Ives T v Corby T 3-2
Framlingham T v Histon 7-3
Cambridge C v Ely C 0-1
Bury T v Norwich U 4-1
Wroxham v Gorleston 1-2
Newmarket T v AFC Sudbury 1-9
Needham Market v Haverhill R 12-1
Woodbridge T v Cornard U 10-0
Leiston v Walsham Le Willows 2-1
Whitton U v Ipswich W 5-3
Bishop's Stortford v Great Wakering R 3-2
AFC Hornchurch v Tower Hamlets 3-1
Sawbridgeworth T v Ware 1-7
Barkingside v Concord Rangers 3-4
Brentwood T v Cheshunt 2-5
Tilbury v Waltham Forest 9-1
Aveley v Halstead T 4-1
FC Broxbourne Bor v Ilford 2-1
Wadham Lodge v Saffron Walden T 4-2*
(2-2 at full time)
Chelmsford C v Thurrock 2-1
CB Hounslow U v Beaconsfield SYCOB 1-3
Spelthorne Sports v Potters Bar T 1-2
Uxbridge v Flackwell Heath 6-2
Hanwell T v Northwood 5-1
Bedfont Sports v Chesham U 3-2*
(2-2 at full time)
Chalfont St Peter v Wealdstone 0-1
Leverstock Green v Cockfosters 1-6
North Greenford U v London Tigers 10-1
Edgware T v Hitchin T 2-2*
Hitchin T won 3-0 on penalties
St Albans C v Tring Ath 4-2
Wingate & Finchley v Buckingham Ath 5-3*
(3-3 at full time)
Lingfield v Meridian 1-3
VCD Ath (withdrawn) v Bridon Ropes (walkover)
Ebbsfleet U v Dartford 1-0
Ramsgate v Hastings U 0-4
Tonbridge Angels v Phoenix Sports 4-0
Ashford U v Little Common 9-0
Corinthian v Cray W 13-1
Sporting Club Thamesmead v Sevenoaks T 2-0
Tooting & Mitcham U v Greenwich Bor 0-2
Lordswood v Eastbourne Bor 0-0*
Lordswood won 11-10 on penalties
Welling U v Folkestone Invicta 1-3
Metropolitan Police v Dorking W 1-0
Haywards Heath T v Chichester C 2-0
Molesey v Knaphill 8-2
Chertsey T v Westfield 1-4
Worthing v Horley T 6-1
Steyning T v Hampton & Richmond Bor 1-4
Lewes v Wick 6-1
Merstham v Leatherhead 7-1
Newhaven v Whitehawk 0-6
Mile Oak v Camberley T 1-3
Marlow v Basingstoke T 6-0
Didcot T v Hungerford T 1-4
Maidenhead U v Oxford C 3-6
Ascot U v Burnham 5-2
Bracknell T v Windsor 2-2*
Bracknell T won 4-3 on penalties
Andover T v Hartley Wintney 6-2
Wantage T v Alton T 3-2
Fareham T v Team Solent 0-1
Havant & Waterlooville v Winchester C 4-4*
Havant & Waterlooville won 4-1 on penalties
Cove v Poole T 0-10
Salisbury (walkover) v Weymouth (withdrawn)
Gosport Bor v AFC Portchester 2-1*
(1-1 at full time)
Sholing v Ringwood T 1-0
Hamworthy U v AFC Totton 2-2*
Hamworthy U won 4-3 on penalties
Chippenham T v Gloucester C 0-7
Tuffley R v Yate T 1-9
Bradford T v Cirencester T 0-5
Bitton v Malmesbury Vic 3-0
Ashton & Backwell U v Weston Super Mare 0-3
Bath C v Bishop Sutton 9-0
Radstock T v Taunton T 4-1
Cullompton Rangers v Welton R 4-2
Paulton R v Larkhall Ath 2-0

SECOND QUALIFYING ROUND

Darlington 1883 v Clitheroe 2-1
West Didsbury & Chorlton v Irlam 2-9
St Helens T v Newcastle Benfield 1-2
Southport v Altrincham 1-5
Ryton & Crawcrook Alb v Marine 4-0
Tranmere R v Durham C 3-0
FC United of Manchester v Gateshead 3-0
AFC Fylde v Barrow 4-1
Hyde U v Ashton Ath 2-1
Wrexham v North Ferriby U 2-1
York C v Garforth T 6-0
Pontefract Collieries v Hall Road Rangers 4-1
Barton T Old Boys v Handsworth Parramore 2-1*
(1-1 at full time)
Nostell MW v Sheffield 2-0
Guiseley v FC Halifax T 2-3
Belper T v Alfreton T 4-5
Lincoln C v Dunkirk 4-5*
(3-3 at full time)
Boston U v Loughborough Dynamo 3-1
Bottesford T v Kimberley MW 0-2
Solihull Moors v Coleshill T 2-1
Bedworth U v Rushall Olympic 3-3*
Bedworth U won 4-3 on penalties
Newcastle T v Ellesmere Rangers 3-2
Hereford v Bromsgrove Sporting 8-1
Wolverhampton Casuals v AFC Telford U 3-1
Romulus v Kidderminster H 3-1
AFC Rushden & Diamonds v Ely C 1-3
Biggleswade T v St Ives T 3-0
Kettering T v Nuneaton T 3-2
AFC Dunstable v Rushden & Higham U 4-4*
Rushden & Higham U won 4-2 on penalties
Framlingham T v Gorleston 5-4*
(2-2 at full time)
Chelmsford C v Leiston 0-1
Whitton U v AFC Sudbury 0-4
Bury T v Woodbridge T 0-5

Braintree T v Needham Market	1-1*
Braintree T won 3-2 on penalties	
Bishop's Stortford v Ware	1-2
Wadham Lodge v Aveley	1-2
FC Broxbourne Bor v Concord Rangers	3-2*
(2-2 at full time)	
AFC Hornchurch v Tilbury	4-0
Dagenham & Redbridge v Cheshunt	4-1
Boreham Wood v Hanwell T	5-1
St Albans C v Wealdstone	1-3
Bedfont Sports v Cockfosters	1-0
Hitchin T v North Greenford U	1-3
Wingate & Finchley v Beaconsfield SYCOB	2-3*
(1-1 at full time)	
Uxbridge v Potters Bar T	3-2*
(2-2 at full time)	
Maidstone U v Bridon Ropes	6-2
Tonbridge Angels v Dover Ath	3-0
Bromley v Folkestone Invicta	2-3
Greenwich Bor v Ashford U	1-4
Sporting Club Thamesmead v Meridian	2-3
Lordswood v Ebbsfleet U	1-2*
(1-1 at full time)	
Hastings U v Corinthian	2-3
Sutton U v Molesey	5-4*
(3-3 at full time)	
Whitehawk v Worthing	0-1
Westfield v Hampton & Richmond Bor	0-3
Merstham v Lewes	3-0
Camberley T v Woking	2-5
Haywards Heath T v Metropolitan Police	1-8
Wantage T v Bracknell T	1-4
Oxford C v Ascot U	4-4*
Oxford C won 6-5 on penalties	
Hungerford T v Marlow	4-2
Eastleigh v Havant & Waterlooville	3-0
Andover T v Sholing	2-1
Hamworthy U v Poole T	1-7
Team Solent v Gosport Bor	3-4
Aldershot T v Salisbury	0-2
Gloucester C v Cirencester T	4-1
Paulton R v Radstock T	1-2
Cullompton Rangers v Bitton	2-3
Yate T v Bath C	0-7
Forest Green R v Weston Super Mare	6-4*
(3-3 at full time)	

THIRD QUALIFYING ROUND

Altrincham v Tranmere R	1-7
Hyde U v Irlam	2-0
York C v Barton T Old Boys	9-0
Ryton & Crawcrook Alb v Darlington 1883	4-2
Newcastle Benfield v Chester FC	0-8
Pontefract Collieries v Wrexham	0-3
FC Halifax T v AFC Fylde	4-1
Nostell MW v FC United of Manchester	2-3
Romulus v Kettering T	2-1
Kimberley MW v Boston U	0-9
Dunkirk v Alfreton T	2-1
Hereford v Newcastle T	2-1
Wolverhampton Casuals v Solihull Moors	4-3
Ely C v Bedworth U	1-2
Braintree T v Dagenham & Redbridge	2-4*
(2-2 at full time)	
Biggleswade T v Beaconsfield SYCOB	0-2
Woodbridge T v AFC Sudbury	1-2*
(1-1 at full time)	
Uxbridge v North Greenford U	1-3
Aveley v FC Broxbourne Bor	0-3
AFC Hornchurch v Rushden & Higham U	5-0
Framlingham T v Leiston	2-0
Boreham Wood v Wealdstone	4-0
Ware v Bedfont Sports	3-0
Hampton & Richmond Bor v Metropolitan Police	0-1
Ashford U v Folkestone Invicta	0-1
Tonbridge Angels v Maidstone U	5-5*
Maidstone U won 6-5 on penalties	
Sutton U v Corinthian	0-3
Worthing v Meridian	4-0
Merstham v Ebbsfleet U	4-0
Eastleigh v Hungerford T	2-1
Bath C v Gloucester C	0-2
Poole T v Bracknell T	9-0
Woking v Radstock T	4-5
Salisbury v Bitton	3-1*
(1-1 at full time)	
Gosport Bor v Andover T	0-3
Forest Green R v Oxford C	1-2

FIRST ROUND

Bradford C v Hartlepool U	1-0
Chester FC v Fleetwood T	1-0
Sheffield U v Crewe Alexandra	2-1
FC United of Manchester v Carlisle U	0-2
Hyde U v Morecambe	1-4
Wrexham v Accrington S	0-2
Bolton W v Blackpool	2-1*
(1-1 at full time)	
Scunthorpe U v Grimsby T	2-0
Oldham Ath v Bury	2-0
Tranmere R v Doncaster R	3-0
FC Halifax T v York C	2-2*
FC Halifax T won 4-3 on penalties	
Rochdale v Ryton & Crawcrook Alb	7-0
Dunkirk v Coventry C	3-2*
(2-2 at full time)	
Notts Co v Romulus	1-3
Peterborough U v Port Vale	2-0
Shrewsbury T v Wolverhampton Casuals	5-1
Bedworth U v Mansfield T	0-3
Chesterfield v Walsall	3-1
Boston U v Hereford	3-2
Boreham Wood v Northampton T	1-0
Cambridge U v Beaconsfield SYCOB	4-1
Barnet v Luton T	1-3
Southend U v Leyton Orient	0-6
Dagenham & Redbridge v Colchester U	7-3
AFC Sudbury v Framlingham T	2-1
Milton Keynes D v AFC Hornchurch	6-1
Ware v Stevenage	2-4*
(2-2 at full time)	
Charlton Ath v Maidstone U	1-1*
Charlton Ath won 3-1 on penalties	
Millwall v Worthing	6-0
Gillingham v Corinthian	3-1
Folkestone Invicta v Merstham	1-4
AFC Wimbledon v North Greenford U	8-1
Gloucester C v Poole T	0-4
Newport Co v Yeovil T	0-1
Radstock T v Exeter C	0-8
Oxford U v Bristol R	0-2
Andover T v Oxford C	2-3
Cheltenham T v Plymouth Arg	1-5
Salisbury v Swindon T	2-3
Portsmouth v Eastleigh	5-0

Byes: FC Broxbourne Bor, Metropolitan Police

SECOND ROUND

FC Halifax T v Sheffield U	1-5
Rochdale v Shrewsbury T	1-2
Chester FC v Bolton W	2-0
Morecambe v Accrington S	2-2*
Accrington S won 4-2 on penalties	
Mansfield T v Dunkirk	5-2
Chesterfield v Carlisle U	1-2*
(1-1 at full time)	
Bradford C v Boston U	2-1
Scunthorpe U v Tranmere R	2-4
Romulus v Oldham Ath	0-2
Poole T v Leyton Orient	1-7
Swindon T v AFC Sudbury	3-2*
(2-2 at full time)	
Plymouth Arg v Gillingham	2-2*
Gillingham won 4-2 on penalties	
Stevenage v Charlton Ath	2-0
Luton T v Dagenham & Redbridge	4-3*
(2-2 at full time)	
Oxford C v Peterborough U	3-1
Boreham Wood v FC Broxbourne Bor	1-2
Portsmouth v Metropolitan Police	2-0
Cambridge U v Millwall	2-0
Yeovil T v Merstham	2-0
AFC Wimbledon v Bristol R	3-0
Exeter C v Milton Keynes D	3-1

THIRD ROUND

Middlesbrough v Rotherham U	5-0
Liverpool v Crystal Palace	2-2*
Liverpool won 5-4 on penalties	
FC Broxbourne Bor v Chester FC	1-0*
(0-0 at full time)	
Burnley v Bradford C	2-0
Watford v Norwich C	1-5
Gillingham v Oxford C	2-0
Huddersfield T v AFC Wimbledon	1-2
Reading v Manchester C	0-4
Swindon T v QPR	1-3
Shrewsbury T v Accrington S	2-1

Portsmouth v Newcastle U	1-4
Leicester C v Leyton Orient	3-1
Brighton & HA v Derby Co	2-0
Exeter C v Wigan Ath	1-2*
(1-1 at full time)	
Arsenal v Blackburn R	0-1
Preston NE v Sheffield U	1-0
Oldham Ath v Birmingham C	1-4
Swansea C v Wolverhampton W	2-1
Sunderland v Burton Alb	4-1
Fulham v Mansfield T	3-1
Cambridge U v Bournemouth	2-1
Barnsley v Carlisle U	0-1
Chelsea v Cardiff C	5-0
Everton v Tranmere R	2-0
Stoke C v West Ham U	2-2*
Stoke C won 4-2 on penalties	
Nottingham F v Ipswich T	4-2*
(2-2 at full time)	
WBA v Yeovil T	2-3
Hull C v Leeds U	3-2*
(2-2 at full time)	
Tottenham H v Stevenage	10-1
Bristol C v Aston Villa	0-2
Sheffield W v Luton T	4-0
Manchester U v Southampton	1-2

FOURTH ROUND

Preston NE v Everton	0-0*
Preston NE won 7-6 on penalties	
AFC Wimbledon v Hull C	3-0
Stoke C v Nottingham F	4-1
Middlesbrough v Fulham	2-1
Blackburn R v Aston Villa	0-0*
Aston Villa won 7-6 on penalties	
Newcastle U v Swansea C	3-1
QPR v Tottenham H	1-4
Wigan Ath v Southampton	1-2
Manchester C v Liverpool	3-1
Brighton & HA v Cambridge U	2-0
Leicester C v Carlisle U	2-1
Birmingham C v Chelsea	0-5
FC Broxbourne Bor v Yeovil T	1-0
Sheffield W v Gillingham	3-0
Burnley v Norwich C	0-4
Sunderland v Shrewsbury T	3-1

FIFTH ROUND

Manchester C v Southampton	4-0
Chelsea v Sheffield W	4-0
Aston Villa v FC Broxbourne Bor	7-0
Sunderland v Newcastle U	3-4
Tottenham H v Norwich C	2-0
Stoke C v Brighton & HA	2-2*
Stoke C won 4-2 on penalties	
Middlesbrough v Leicester C	0-1*
(0-0 at full time)	
Preston NE v AFC Wimbledon	3-2*
(1-1 at full time)	

SIXTH ROUND

Leicester C v Chelsea	0-1
Newcastle U v Tottenham H	3-5
Preston NE v Stoke C	1-3
Aston Villa v Manchester C	1-2

SEMI-FINALS – FIRST LEG

Manchester C v Stoke C	6-0
Tottenham H v Chelsea	1-2

SEMI-FINALS – SECOND LEG

Stoke C v Manchester C	2-3
Manchester C won 9-2 on aggregate	
Chelsea v Tottenham H	7-1
Chelsea won 9-2 on aggregate	

FA YOUTH CUP FINAL 2017 – FIRST LEG

Tuesday 18 April 2017

Manchester C (0) 1 *(Foden 61)*

Chelsea (1) 1 *(Ugbo 44)* 3392

Manchester C: Muric; Wilson, Francis, Diallo, Duhaney, Foden (Bolton 85), Davenport, Smith, Sancho (Dele-Bashiru 90) Nmecha, Diaz.

Chelsea: Thompson; Guehi, Chalobah, James, Castillo, Uwakwe (Gallagher 90), Maddox, Sterling, Hudson-Odoi, Ugbo (St Clair 86), Mount.

Referee: Oli Langford (Staffordshire).

FA YOUTH CUP FINAL 2017 – SECOND LEG

Wednesday 26 April 2017

Chelsea (2) 5 *(Chalobah 7, Ugbo 24, Hudson-Odoi 60, Sterling 66, Dasilva 87)*

Manchester C (0) 1 *(Nmecha 52)* 5000

Chelsea: Cumming; James, Chalobah, Guehi, Castillo, Uwakwe (McEachran 80), Sterling, Maddox, Ugbo (Taylor-Crossdale 77), Mount, Hudson-Odoi (Dasilva 83).

Manchester C: Muric; Duhaney, Diallo, Francis, Wilson, Davenport (Bolton 46), Diaz (Dele-Bashiru 80), Smith, Nmecha, Foden, Sancho (Gonzalez 77).

Chelsea won 6-2 on aggregate.

Referee: Oli Langford (Staffordshire).

THE FA COUNTY YOUTH CUP 2016–17

**After extra time.*

FIRST ROUND

Nottinghamshire v Manchester	4-2*
(2-2 at full time)	
Lancashire v Isle of Man	2-1
Lincolnshire (withdrawn) v West Riding (walkover)	
Amateur Football Alliance v Oxfordshire	1-3
Devon v Berks & Bucks	1-5
Suffolk v London	4-1
Herefordshire v Essex	0-1

SECOND ROUND

West Riding v Leicestershire & Rutland	1-2
Liverpool v Lancashire	2-4
Sheffield & Hallamshire v Northumberland	3-2*
(2-2 at full time)	
Westmorland v Nottinghamshire	0-1
Birmingham v North Riding	2-3
Cumberland v Cheshire	0-1
Durham v Staffordshire	3-0
Wiltshire v Kent	3-2*
(2-2 at full time)	
Suffolk v Hertfordshire	4-3
Cambridgeshire v Essex	0-3
Bedfordshire v Norfolk	0-1*
(0-0 at full time)	
Gloucestershire v Cornwall	0-7
Northamptonshire v Middlesex	0-3
Oxfordshire v Berks & Bucks	5-3
Jersey v Guernsey	3-1
Somerset v Sussex	1-3

THIRD ROUND

Essex v Sussex	1-2
Oxfordshire v Nottinghamshire	5-1
Jersey v Durham	1-2
Cheshire v Suffolk	2-1
North Riding v Wiltshire	1-0
Leicestershire & Rutland v Norfolk	2-1
Cornwall v Lancashire	5-2
Sheffield & Hallamshire v Middlesex	1-2

FOURTH ROUND

Cornwall v Sussex	2-1*
(0-0 at full time)	
Cheshire v Oxfordshire	0-3
Leicestershire & Rutland v Durham	2-3*
(2-2 at full time)	
Middlesex v North Riding	4-2

SEMI-FINALS

Cornwall v Durham	2-1
Oxfordshire v Middlesex	2-7

FA COUNTY YOUTH CUP FINAL 2017

Barnet, Saturday 1 April 2017

Middlesex (2) 2 *(Haile 8, Watson 44)*

Cornwall (1) 0 *(Penrose 9)* 736

Middlesex: Todd; Watts, Agholor, Kukoyi (Malin), Taylor, Watson, O'Reilly, McGovern (Hadjithemistou), Livingstone (Mooney), Cole, Haile .

Cornwall: Gwilliam; Otto (Rapsey), Roberts (Webber), Allen, Hambly, Turner, Penrose, Harrison, Buchan, Adkins (Soares), Walker.

Referee: Anthony Backhouse.

THE FA SUNDAY CUP 2016–17

**After extra time.*

FIRST ROUND

Thornaby Village (walkover) v
Wrekenton Blue Star (withdrawn) 2-1†
†Match abandoned (2-1 after 45 minutes) due to crowd disturbance
Amble Tavern v Witton Park Rose & Crown 0-2
Northallerton Police (withdrawn) v Burradon & New Fordley (walkover)
Dawdon Colliery Welfare v
Newton Aycliffe Locomotion 1-2
FC Dovecot v Garston 4-1
Oyster Martyrs (walkover) v Nicosia (withdrawn)
Chapeltown Fforde Grene v Mayfair 1-2
Oakenshaw v Ferrybridge Progressive 0-7
Woodman Sports Club v Seacroft WMC 0-3
Neston Nomads v Poulton Royal 3-2*
(2-2 at full time)
West Bowling v Queens Park 2-0
Lobster (walkover) v Seymour (withdrawn)
Olympic (withdrawn) v The Molly (walkover)
Custys v Millhouse 3-1
St John Fisher OB v Pineapple 3-7
Lower Breck v Dengo U 0-3
New Sharlston Welfare (walkover) v Colton (withdrawn)
Thornton U v Kennelwood 5-3*
(2-2 at full time)
AFC Blackburn Leisure v Allerton 1-10
Austin Ex Apprentices v FC Brimington 5-2
Frolesworth U v Alcester T 4-3*
(3-3 at full time)
RHP Sports & Social v Halfway 3-0
Attenborough Cavaliers v Sporting Dynamo 1-0
Wolverhampton Casuals (Sunday) (walkover) v
Thomas Brothers (failed to fulfil fixture)
Enderby Social v OJM 0-1
Birstall Stamford v Carlton Top Spot 4-3
Black Horse (Redditch) v Oadby Ath 3-0
Nuthall v Hampton Blackwood 2-1
Weddington Thistle v Mowmacre & Hoskins 8-2
Olympia v Falcons 0-2
Gym U v Priory Sports 1-0
Omonia v Upshire 2-1
NLO v FC Houghton 3-2*
(1-1 at full time)
Club Lewsey v British Airways HEW 4-2
St Josephs (Luton) (walkover) v
Brache Nation (withdrawn)
Harpole v Doves U 3-2
Broadfields U (Sunday) v North Wembley 2-0
Two Touch v AC Sportsman 2-3
Market Hotel v Broadwater 1-4
Chessington U v London St Georges 2-1
Wickham W v Portland 2-1
Lebeqs Tavern Courage v Southall U 4-2
Black Horse (Chesham) (withdrawn) v
Shire U (walkover)
FC Bengals v AFC Kumazi Strikers 4-2

SECOND ROUND

Burradon & New Fordley v Mayfair 5-3
Custys v Thornaby Village 4-1
Dengo U v Hartlepool Lion Hillcarter 3-3*
Dengo U won 4-2 on penalties
Home & Bargain v Allerton 5-0
Canada v Black Bull 1-5
Newton Aycliffe Locomotion v West Bowling 4-1
Ferrybridge Progressive v Thornton U 4-1
Witton Park Rose & Crown v
New Sharlston Welfare 12-0
Alder v Neston Nomads 0-3
Pineapple v Seacroft WMC 4-0
Oyster Martyrs v Campfield 3-1
Hardwick Social v The Molly 3-1
FC Dovecot v Wallsend New Rising Sun 2-3
Lobster v Leeds C R 1-0
Austin Ex Apprentices v Black Horse (Redditch) 3-2
Wolverhampton Casuals (Sunday) v
Anstey Sports Bar Swifts 3-0
Gym U v Nuthall 3-1
Weddington Thistle v Quorn Royals 2008 4-2
Attenborough Cavaliers v Stanleys 5-2
Frolesworth U v Birstall Stamford 3-4
Harpole v OJM 2-3
RHP Sports & Social v Riverside R 5-0
St Josephs (Luton) v Wickham W 3-2
New Salamis v Belstone (Sunday) 7-1
Falcons v Green Man (Luton) 4-1
NLO v Omonia 2-3
AC Sportsman v FC Bengals 1-5
Shire U v St Josephs (South Oxhey) 0-1
Broadfields U (Sunday) v Club Lewsey 0-3
Broadwater v Lebeqs Tavern Courage 0-2
Barnes Alb v Lambeth All Stars 4-1
Barnes v Chessington U 3-3*
Chessington U on 3-2 on penalties

THIRD ROUND

Wallsend New Rising Sun v Home & Bargain 2-3*
(2-2 at full time)
Lobster v Custys 3-1*
(1-1 at full time)
Witton Park Rose & Crown v
Burradon & New Fordley 2-1
Neston Nomads v Black Bull 1-4
Newton Aycliffe Locomotion v Hardwick Social 0-4
Dengo U v Oyster Martyrs 2-4
Ferrybridge Progressive v Pineapple 3-2
Wolverhampton Casuals (Sunday) v Gym U 4-3*
(2-2 at full time)
RHP Sports & Social v Weddington Thistle 1-4*
(1-1 at full time)
Austin Ex Apprentices v Birstall Stamford 4-0
OJM v Attenborough Cavaliers 3-3*
Attenborough Cavaliers won 5-4 on penalties
Falcons v FC Bengals 2-3
Chessington U v Lebeqs Tavern Courage 1-0
Club Lewsey v Omonia 0-1
New Salamis (walkover) v
St Josephs (South Oxhey) (failed to fulfil fixture)
St Josephs (Luton) v Barnes Alb 0-0*
St Josephs (Luton) won 4-2 on penalties

FOURTH ROUND

Hardwick Social v Lobster 2-0
Ferrybridge Progressive v Oyster Martyrs 1-0
Witton Park Rose & Crown v Black Bull 3-0†
†Match abandoned (3-0 after 70 minutes) due to serious incident – both clubs removed
Attenborough Cavaliers v Home & Bargain 0-4
FC Bengals v Austin Ex Apprentices 2-3
Omonia v St Josephs (Luton) 4-2
New Salamis v Weddington Thistle 4-0
Wolverhampton Casuals (Sunday) v Chessington U 3-0†
Tie awarded to Chessington U – Wolverhampton Casuals (Sunday) removed

FIFTH ROUND

Hardwick Social (walkover)
Home & Bargain v Ferrybridge Progressive 2-1
Austin Ex Apprentices v New Salamis 0-4
Omonia v Chessington U 2-2*
Chessington U won 5-3 on penalties

SEMI-FINALS

New Salamis v Chessington U 6-2
Home & Bargain v Hardwick Social 1-3

THE FA SUNDAY CUP FINAL 2017

Bramall Lane, Sunday 7 May 2017

Hardwick Social (1) 1 *(Coleman 23)*

New Salamis (0) 1 *(MacKenzie 67 (pen))*

Hardwick Social: Arthur; Carter, Bishop (Hannah 79), Poole, Nicholson (Roberts 33), Coulthard, Mulligan, Ward, Coleman (Whittaker 90), Owens, Stockton.
New Salamis: Behcet; Kyriacou, Oujdi, Hervel, Kirby, White, Georgiou R (Georgiou H 57), Kiangebeni, MacKenzie, Mehmet (Portou 116), Karagul (Addai 63).
aet; Hardwick Social won 3-1 on penalties.
Referee: Dean Whitestone.

PREMIER LEAGUE 2 2016–17

PROFESSIONAL UNDER-23 DEVELOPMENT LEAGUE

LEAGUE 1

DIVISION 1	P	W	D	L	F	A	GD	Pts
1 Everton	22	15	3	4	48	21	27	48
2 Manchester C	22	13	6	3	54	33	21	45
3 Liverpool	22	13	4	5	47	27	20	43
4 Arsenal	22	10	3	9	40	32	8	33
5 Chelsea	22	7	9	6	40	32	8	30
6 Manchester U	22	6	8	8	29	38	−9	26
7 Sunderland	22	6	7	9	27	37	−10	25
8 Derby Co	22	6	6	10	31	42	−11	24
9 Leicester C	22	5	8	9	31	42	−11	23
10 Tottenham H	22	6	4	12	33	44	−11	22
11 Reading	22	6	4	12	36	56	−20	22
12 Southampton	22	5	6	11	28	40	−12	21

DIVISION 2	P	W	D	L	F	A	GD	Pts
1 Swansea C	22	17	1	4	43	22	21	52
2 Wolverhampton W	22	12	5	5	42	30	12	41
3 Newcastle U	22	11	4	7	34	30	4	37
4 Fulham	22	10	3	9	39	33	6	33
5 West Ham U*	22	9	6	7	32	26	6	33
6 Blackburn R	22	9	5	8	24	28	−4	32
7 Aston Villa	22	8	6	8	34	32	2	30
8 Brighton & HA	22	7	7	8	20	22	−2	28
9 WBA	22	6	4	12	25	33	−8	22
10 Middlesbrough	22	5	6	11	25	34	−9	21
11 Stoke C	22	4	8	10	25	36	−11	20
12 Norwich C	22	4	5	13	18	35	−17	17

**West Ham U promoted after play-offs.*

PROMOTION PLAY-OFFS – SEMI-FINALS

Wolverhampton W v West Ham U 1-2
Newcastle U v Fulham 2-0

FINAL

Newcastle U v West Ham U 1-2

PREMIER LEAGUE UNDER-23 DEVELOPMENT

LEAGUE 2

NORTH DIVISION	P	W	D	L	F	A	GD	Pts
1 Sheffield W	28	15	5	8	43	28	15	50
2 Hull C	28	15	3	10	51	42	9	48
3 Bolton W	28	13	7	8	53	42	11	46
4 Birmingham C	28	13	7	8	47	39	8	46
5 Crewe Alex	28	13	7	8	53	46	7	46
6 Huddersfield T	28	13	5	10	54	42	12	44
7 Sheffield U	28	12	6	10	49	43	6	42
8 Nottingham F	28	10	5	13	43	39	4	35
9 Barnsley	28	9	4	15	35	50	−15	31
10 Leeds U	28	6	6	16	33	52	−19	24

SOUTH DIVISION	P	W	D	L	F	A	GD	Pts
1 Charlton Ath	28	15	8	5	53	26	27	53
2 Millwall	28	12	6	10	47	33	14	42
3 Cardiff C	28	10	8	10	46	44	2	38
4 Coventry C	28	11	5	12	50	58	−8	38
5 Bristol C	28	10	6	12	45	49	−4	36
6 QPR	28	11	3	14	51	63	−12	36
7 Ipswich T	28	11	2	15	57	54	3	35
8 Colchester U	28	8	9	11	42	56	−14	33
9 Watford	28	9	5	14	42	65	−23	32
10 Crystal Palace	28	8	5	15	26	49	−23	29

Teams play each team in their own division twice, and each team in the other division once.

KNOCKOUT STAGE – SEMI-FINALS

Sheffield W v Millwall 2-1
Charlton Ath v Hull C 3-3
aet; Hull C won 5-4 on penalties.

FINAL

Sheffield W v Hull C 3-1

FA PREMIER LEAGUE 2 LEAGUE CUP

**After extra time.*

GROUP STAGE

GROUP A TABLE	P	W	D	L	F	A	GD	Pts
1 Newcastle U	6	3	1	2	9	6	3	10
2 Swansea C	6	3	1	2	7	6	1	10
3 Southampton	6	3	0	3	7	5	2	9
4 Bristol C	6	2	0	4	7	13	−6	6

GROUP B TABLE	P	W	D	L	F	A	GD	Pts
1 Sunderland	6	3	2	1	9	7	2	11
2 Blackburn R	6	3	1	2	8	3	5	10
3 Burnley	6	2	1	3	10	13	−3	7
4 Cardiff C	6	1	2	3	5	9	−4	5

GROUP C TABLE	P	W	D	L	F	A	GD	Pts
1 Hull C	6	3	1	2	10	7	3	10
2 Colchester U	6	3	1	2	8	9	−1	10
3 Manchester C	6	2	1	3	13	10	3	7
4 Derby Co	6	2	1	3	9	14	−5	7

GROUP D TABLE	P	W	D	L	F	A	GD	Pts
1 Portsmouth	6	3	2	1	11	6	5	11
2 Norwich C	6	3	1	2	13	9	4	10
3 Everton	6	2	1	3	7	9	−2	7
4 Wolverhampton W	6	1	2	3	7	14	−7	5

GROUP E TABLE	P	W	D	L	F	A	GD	Pts
1 Brighton & HA	6	5	0	1	17	3	14	15
2 West Ham U	6	3	1	2	10	9	1	10
3 Nottingham F	6	1	2	3	6	16	−10	5
4 Leicester C	6	0	3	3	5	10	−5	3

GROUP F TABLE	P	W	D	L	F	A	GD	Pts
1 Fulham	6	5	0	1	14	7	7	15
2 Middlesbrough	6	3	0	3	7	10	−3	9
3 Charlton Ath	6	2	2	2	13	11	2	8
4 AFC Wimbledon	6	0	2	4	3	9	−6	2

GROUP G TABLE	P	W	D	L	F	A	GD	Pts
1 Liverpool	6	5	1	0	17	3	14	16
2 Huddersfield T	6	2	1	3	6	11	−5	7
3 WBA	6	1	2	3	3	5	−2	5
4 Ipswich T	6	1	2	3	3	10	−7	5

GROUP H TABLE	P	W	D	L	F	A	GD	Pts
1 Reading	6	4	1	1	16	9	7	13
2 Sheffield U	6	2	2	2	12	13	−1	8
3 Birmingham C	6	2	1	3	7	12	−5	7
4 Stoke C	6	1	2	3	8	9	−1	5

ROUND OF 16

Norwich C v Fulham 5-5*
Norwich C won 3-2 on penalties.
Sunderland v Colchester U 0-1
Brighton & HA v Huddersfield T 3-1
Newcastle U v West Ham U 3-2*
Swansea C v Blackburn R 2-0
Hull C v Liverpool 2-2*
Liverpool won 5-4 on penalties.
Reading v Middlesbrough 4-1
Portsmouth v Sheffield U 1-0

QUARTER-FINALS

Newcastle U v Reading 0-1
Swansea C v Brighton & HA 1-0
Liverpool v Norwich C 0-1
Portsmouth v Colchester U 2-0

SEMI-FINALS

Reading v Norwich C 4-1
Swansea C v Portsmouth 3-0*

FINAL

Swansea C v Reading 2-0

UNDER-18 PROFESSIONAL DEVELOPMENT LEAGUE 2016–17

PREMIER LEAGUE UNDER-18 DEVELOPMENT LEAGUE 1

FIRST LEAGUE STAGE

NORTH DIVISION

	P	W	D	L	F	A	GD	Pts
1 Manchester C	22	17	4	1	70	22	48	55
2 Manchester U	22	14	4	4	63	31	32	46
3 Liverpool	22	14	4	4	50	33	17	46
4 Blackburn R	22	13	5	4	40	27	13	44
5 Everton	22	11	6	5	49	35	14	39
6 Derby Co	22	10	2	10	38	45	–7	32
7 Middlesbrough	22	7	3	12	33	40	–7	24
8 Stoke C	22	7	2	13	34	49	–15	23
9 Newcastle U	22	6	4	12	25	43	–18	22
10 WBA	22	4	6	12	29	42	–13	18
11 Sunderland	22	3	4	15	23	55	–32	13
12 Wolverhampton W	22	2	4	16	30	62	–32	10

SOUTH DIVISION

	P	W	D	L	F	A	GD	Pts
1 Chelsea	22	16	4	2	68	21	47	52
2 Arsenal	22	12	5	5	46	26	20	41
3 Reading	22	12	3	7	51	40	11	39
4 West Ham U	22	10	4	8	37	31	6	34
5 Fulham	22	9	6	7	39	32	7	33
6 Aston Villa	22	9	6	7	31	39	–8	33
7 Tottenham H	22	9	4	9	48	36	12	31
8 Norwich C	22	9	4	9	46	38	8	31
9 Southampton	22	7	5	10	28	41	–13	26
10 Brighton & HA	22	5	8	9	28	51	–23	23
11 Swansea C	22	2	6	14	28	51	–23	12
12 Leicester C	22	2	5	15	17	47	–30	11

SECOND LEAGUE STAGE

GROUP 1

	P	W	D	L	F	A	GD	Pts
1 Chelsea (C)	7	6	0	1	17	7	10	18
2 Arsenal	7	4	2	1	22	13	9	14
3 Manchester C	7	4	2	1	16	11	5	14
4 Manchester U	7	2	2	3	16	18	–2	8
5 Reading	7	2	1	4	10	17	–7	7
6 West Ham U	7	1	3	3	8	13	–5	6
7 Blackburn R	7	2	0	5	11	18	–7	6
8 Liverpool	7	1	2	4	8	11	–3	5

GROUP 2

	P	W	D	L	F	A	GD	Pts
9 Aston Villa	7	5	2	0	15	5	10	17
10 Tottenham H	7	4	2	1	21	13	8	14
11 Norwich C	7	3	2	2	15	15	0	11
12 Derby Co	7	2	3	2	16	13	3	9
13 Fulham	7	1	4	2	15	16	–1	7
14 Stoke C	7	1	4	2	9	13	–4	7
15 Middlesbrough	7	2	0	5	10	16	–6	6
16 Everton	7	1	1	5	4	14	–10	4

GROUP 3

	P	W	D	L	F	A	GD	Pts
17 Wolverhampton W	7	5	1	1	12	5	7	16
18 Swansea C	7	4	1	2	11	6	5	13
19 Leicester C	7	2	4	1	9	9	0	10
20 Newcastle U	7	2	3	2	9	9	0	9
21 Brighton & HA	7	2	2	3	11	9	2	8
22 Southampton	7	1	4	2	8	9	–1	7
23 Sunderland	7	1	4	2	4	6	–2	7
24 WBA	7	0	3	4	5	16	–11	3

FA PREMIER UNDER-18 DEVELOPMENT LEAGUE 2

NORTH DIVISION

	P	W	D	L	GF	GA	GD	Pts
1 Sheffield U	28	19	6	3	68	32	36	63
2 Sheffield W	28	15	4	9	62	46	16	49
3 Nottingham F	28	14	4	10	73	53	20	46
4 Bolton W	28	12	8	8	57	48	9	44
5 Huddersfield T	28	13	3	12	60	49	11	42
6 Crewe Alex	28	12	4	12	56	55	1	40
7 Barnsley	28	9	10	9	51	58	–7	37
8 Leeds U	28	8	8	12	42	49	–7	32
9 Birmingham C	28	7	9	12	40	46	–6	30
10 Hull C	28	7	7	14	39	62	–23	28

SOUTH DIVISION

	P	W	D	L	GF	GA	GD	Pts
1 Coventry C	28	21	2	5	76	30	46	65
2 Charlton Ath	28	19	4	5	67	33	34	61
3 Crystal Palace	28	13	4	11	59	53	6	43
4 Ipswich T	28	13	2	13	54	49	5	41
5 Millwall	28	10	5	13	50	58	–8	35
6 Watford	28	9	5	14	30	40	–10	32
7 Bristol C	28	8	6	14	39	55	–16	30
8 Cardiff C	28	9	3	16	41	73	–32	30
9 Colchester U	28	6	5	17	38	69	–31	23
10 QPR	28	4	5	19	39	83	–44	17

Teams play each team in their own division twice, and each team in the other division once.

KNOCKOUT STAGE – SEMI-FINALS

Coventry C v Sheffield W 3-1
Sheffield U v Charlton Ath 2-0

FINAL

Sheffield U v Coventry C 1-0

CENTRAL LEAGUE 2016–17

NORTH WEST	P	W	D	L	F	A	GD	Pts
1 Walsall	10	8	1	1	19	6	13	25
2 Port Vale	10	5	3	2	22	12	10	18
3 Bradford C	10	5	0	5	10	16	–6	15
4 Burton Alb	10	4	2	4	18	9	9	14
5 Morecambe	10	3	0	7	9	18	–9	9
6 Wrexham	10	1	2	7	9	26	–17	5

NORTH EAST	P	W	D	L	F	A	GD	Pts
1 Grimsby T	10	7	2	1	24	11	13	23
2 Hartlepool U	10	6	2	2	21	16	5	20
3 Rotherham U	10	4	0	6	13	15	–2	12
4 Mansfield T	10	4	0	6	16	25	–9	12
5 York C	10	3	1	6	13	15	–2	10
6 Chesterfield	10	3	1	6	16	21	–5	10

SOUTH EAST	P	W	D	L	F	A	GD	Pts
1 Bournemouth	6	2	4	0	21	11	10	10
2 Peterborough U	6	3	0	3	12	18	–6	9
3 AFC Wimbledon	6	2	2	2	12	11	1	8
4 Southend U	6	1	2	3	13	18	–5	5

SOUTH WEST	P	W	D	L	F	A	GD	Pts
1 Exeter C	8	6	0	2	22	10	12	18
2 Cheltenham T	8	4	2	2	18	10	8	14
3 Bristol R	8	4	0	4	11	19	–8	12
4 Swindon T	8	2	2	4	13	17	–4	8
5 Newport Co	8	2	0	6	12	20	–8	6

Winner of the South division (South East and South West combined) is decided by points per match ratio.

CENTRAL LEAGUE CUP 2016–17

NORTHERN GROUP 1	P	W	D	L	F	A	GD	Pts
1 Sheffield U	4	3	0	1	9	4	5	9
2 Newcastle U	4	2	1	1	13	5	8	7
3 Hartlepool U	4	2	0	2	9	8	1	6
4 Bradford C	4	2	0	2	2	11	–9	6
5 Rotherham U	4	0	1	3	3	8	–5	1

NORTHERN GROUP 2	P	W	D	L	F	A	GD	Pts
1 Chesterfield	4	3	1	0	11	6	5	10
2 Shrewsbury T	4	2	1	1	6	5	1	7
3 Nottingham F	4	2	0	2	8	6	2	6
4 Mansfield T	4	1	0	3	5	8	–3	3
5 Notts Co	4	1	0	3	3	8	–5	3

NORTHERN GROUP 3	P	W	D	L	F	A	GD	Pts
1 Fleetwood T	3	3	0	0	7	1	6	9
2 Wigan Ath	3	2	0	1	10	4	6	6
3 Port Vale	3	1	0	2	6	7	–1	3
4 Morecambe	3	0	0	3	1	12	–11	0

NORTHERN SEMI-FINALS

Fleetwood v Sheffield U 3-2
Chesterfield v Wigan Ath 1-1
Wigan Ath won 5-3 on penalties.

NORTHERN FINAL

Wigan Ath v Fleetwood T 3-1

SOUTHERN GROUP A	P	W	D	L	F	A	GD	Pts
1 Barnet	4	2	1	1	12	6	6	7
2 AFC Wimbledon	4	2	1	1	8	4	4	7
3 Peterborough U	4	2	0	2	8	9	–1	6
4 Southend U	4	2	0	2	6	7	–1	6
5 Colchester U	4	1	0	3	4	12	–8	3

SOUTHERN GROUP B	P	W	D	L	F	A	GD	Pts
1 Bristol C	3	2	0	1	8	2	6	6
2 Portsmouth	3	2	0	1	10	5	5	6
3 Exeter C	3	2	0	1	6	8	–2	6
4 Newport Co	3	0	0	3	4	13	–9	0

SOUTHERN SEMI-FINAL

AFC Wimbledon v Barnet 2-3
Bristol C v Portsmouth 3-1

SOUTHERN FINAL

Barnet v Bristol C 1-2

EFL YOUTH ALLIANCE 2016–17

NORTH WEST	P	W	D	L	F	A	GD	Pts
1 Blackpool	28	19	5	4	75	23	52	62
2 Burnley	28	18	6	4	64	36	28	60
3 Walsall	28	18	4	6	55	31	24	58
4 Rochdale	28	17	4	7	60	33	27	55
5 Port Vale	28	14	5	9	46	40	6	47
6 Bury	28	13	2	13	47	54	–7	41
7 Wigan Ath	28	10	10	8	52	41	11	40
8 Shrewsbury T	28	10	9	9	47	50	–3	39
9 Fleetwood T	28	10	5	13	54	63	–9	35
10 Preston NE	28	7	12	9	44	50	–6	33
11 Carlisle U	28	9	2	17	44	56	–12	29
12 Accrington S	28	8	4	16	34	56	–22	28
13 Morecambe	28	7	3	18	39	57	–18	24
14 Tranmere R	28	4	7	17	21	51	–30	19
15 Wrexham	28	3	8	17	29	70	–41	17

NORTH EAST	P	W	D	L	F	A	GD	Pts
1 Mansfield T	24	16	4	4	41	15	26	52
2 Rotherham U	24	15	1	8	49	25	24	46
3 Oldham Ath	24	13	5	6	47	22	25	44
4 York C	24	12	3	9	34	40	–6	39
5 Burton Alb	24	10	7	7	47	44	3	37
6 Notts Co	24	11	4	9	39	36	3	37
7 Chesterfield	24	9	5	10	46	43	3	32
8 Doncaster R	24	8	6	10	37	35	2	30
9 Hartlepool U	24	8	6	10	38	45	–7	30
10 Scunthorpe U	24	8	5	11	37	33	4	29
11 Grimsby T	24	7	3	14	26	51	–25	24
12 Bradford C	24	6	4	14	33	53	–20	22
13 Lincoln C	24	4	5	15	26	58	–32	17

SOUTH WEST	P	W	D	L	F	A	GD	Pts
1 Exeter C	18	11	2	5	36	26	10	35
2 Bristol R	18	8	4	6	42	38	4	28
3 Swindon T	18	8	4	6	36	34	2	28
4 Plymouth Arg	18	7	5	6	40	35	5	26
5 Newport Co	18	7	5	6	36	33	3	26
6 Portsmouth	18	8	2	8	35	41	–6	26
7 Oxford U	18	7	4	7	40	27	13	25
8 Bournemouth	18	6	4	8	24	23	1	22
9 Cheltenham T	18	6	4	8	37	40	–3	22
10 Yeovil T	18	4	2	12	19	48	–29	14

SOUTH EAST	P	W	D	L	F	A	GD	Pts
1 Leyton Orient	22	18	2	2	59	23	36	56
2 Southend U	22	11	4	7	62	40	22	37
3 Stevenage	22	11	4	7	49	34	15	37
4 Cambridge U	22	9	8	5	46	30	16	35
5 Luton T	22	10	4	8	48	38	10	34
6 Gillingham	22	10	4	8	44	51	–7	34
7 AFC Wimbledon	22	9	5	8	40	30	10	32
8 Northampton T	22	6	6	10	49	61	–12	24
9 Dagenham & R	22	7	3	12	40	65	–25	24
10 Barnet	22	5	5	12	34	50	–16	20
11 Milton Keynes D	22	5	4	13	45	63	–18	19
12 Peterborough U	22	4	5	13	29	60	–31	17

The top 5 teams in South West and top 6 in South East form Merit League 1. The remaining teams form Merit League 2.

MERIT LEAGUE 1	P	W	D	L	F	A	GD	Pts
1 Newport Co	10	9	1	0	22	9	13	28
2 Swindon T	10	5	3	2	25	16	9	18
3 Exeter C	10	4	3	3	20	18	2	15
4 Stevenage	10	4	2	4	22	20	2	14
5 Southend U	10	4	2	4	19	18	1	14
6 Luton T	10	3	4	3	17	11	6	13
7 Leyton Orient	10	3	3	4	19	24	–5	12
8 Gillingham	10	3	2	5	15	19	–4	11
9 Plymouth Arg	10	3	2	5	17	23	–6	11
10 Cambridge U	10	2	3	5	16	21	–5	9
11 Bristol R	10	2	1	7	10	23	–13	7

MERIT LEAGUE 2	P	W	D	L	F	A	GD	Pts
1 Bournemouth	10	7	1	2	24	10	14	22
2 Peterborough U	10	5	5	0	17	11	6	20
3 AFC Wimbledon	10	5	4	1	16	10	6	19
4 Northampton T	10	5	1	4	19	20	–1	16
5 Oxford U	10	4	3	3	16	13	3	15
6 Portsmouth	10	3	3	4	20	17	3	12
7 Barnet	10	3	3	4	17	19	–2	12
8 Milton Keynes D	10	4	0	6	13	21	–8	12
9 Cheltenham T	10	3	1	6	13	17	–4	10
10 Yeovil T	10	1	4	5	12	20	–8	7
11 Dagenham & R	10	1	3	6	15	24	–9	6

IMPORTANT ADDRESSES

The Football Association: Wembley Stadium, P.O. Box 1966, London SW1P 9EQ. *0800 169 1863*

Scotland: Hampden Park, Glasgow G42 9AY. *0141 616 6000*

Northern Ireland (Irish FA): Chief Executive, 20 Windsor Avenue, Belfast BT9 6EG. *028 9066 9458*

Wales: 11/12 Neptune Court, Vanguard Way, Cardiff CF24 5PJ. *029 2043 5830*

Republic of Ireland: National Sports Campus, Abbotstown, Dublin 15. *00 353 1 8999 500*

International Federation (FIFA): Strasse 20, P.O. Box 8044, Zurich, Switzerland. *00 41 43 222 7777. Fax: 00 41 43 222 7878*

Union of European Football Associations: Secretary, Route de Geneve 46, P.O. Box 1260, Nyon 2, Switzerland. *Fax: 00 41 848 00 2727*

THE LEAGUES

The Premier League: M. Foster, 30 Gloucester Place, London W1U 8PL. *0207 864 9000*

The Football League: Shaun Harvey, Unit 5, Edward VII Quay, Navigation Way, Preston, Lancashire PR2 2YF. *0844 463 1888. Fax 01772 325 801*

The National League: D. Strudwick, 4th Floor, Wellington House, 20 Waterloo Street, Birmingham B2 5TB. *0121 643 3143*

FA Women's Super League: Wembley Stadium, PO Box 1966, London SW1P 9EQ. *+44 844 980 8200*

Scottish Premier League: Letherby Drive, Glasgow G42 9DE. *0141 620 4140*

The Scottish League: Hampden Park, Glasgow G42 9EB. *0141 620 4160*

Football League of Ireland: D. Crowther, National Sports Campus, Abbotstown, Dublin 15. *00 353 1 8999 500*

Southern League: J. Mills, Suite 3B, Eastgate House, 121–131 Eastgate Street, Gloucester GL1 1PX. *07768 750 590*

Northern Premier League: Ms A. Firth, 23 High Lane, Norton Tower, Halifax, W. Yorkshire HX2 0NW. *01422 410 691*

Isthmian League: Ms K. Discipline, The Base, Dartford Business Park, Victoria Park, Dartford, Kent DA1 5FS. *01322 314 999*

Eastern Counties League: N. Spurling, 16 Thanet Road, Ipswich, Suffolk IP4 5LB. *07855 279 062*

Essex Senior League: Secretary: Ms. M. Darling, 39 Milwards, Harlow, Essex CM19 4SG. *01279 635740*

Hellenic League: B. King, 7 Stoneleigh Drive, Carterton, Oxon OX18 1EE. *0845 260 6644*

Kent Invicta League: John Moules, 25 Brantwood Avenue, Erith, Kent DA8 1EH. *01322 408 557*

Midland League: N. Wood, 30 Glaisdale Road, Hall Green, Birmingham B28 8PX. *07967 440 007*

North West Counties League: J. Deal, 24 The Pastures, Crossens, Southport PR9 8RH. *07713 622 210*

Northern Counties East: B. Gould, 42 Thirlmere Drive, Dronfield, Derbyshire S18 2HW. *07773 653 238*

Northern League: K. Hewitt, 21 Cherrytree Drive, Langley Park, Durham DH7 9FX. *0191 373 3878*

Spartan South Midlands League: M. Mitchell, 26 Leighton Court, Dunstable, Beds LU6 1EW. *07710 455 409*

Southern Combination League: Ms K. Scott, Llandilo, Old Lane, Crowborough TN6 2AF. *07788 737 061*

United Counties League: Ms W. Newey, 4 Wulfric Square, Bretton, Peterborough PE3 8RF. *01733 330 056*

Wessex League: J. Gorman, 6 Overton House, London Road, Overton, Hants RG25 3TP. *01256 770 059*

Western League: M. Edmonds, Cemetery Lodge, Pennings Road, Tidworth, Wiltshire SP9 7JR. *01980 842 153*

Combined Counties League: A. Constable, 3 Craigwell Close, Staines, Middlesex TW18 3NP. *01784 440 613*

West Midlands League: N.R. Juggins, 14 Badger Way, Blackwell, Bromsgrove, Worcs B60 1EX. *07977 422 362.*

South West Peninsula League: P. Hiscox, 45a Serge Court, The Quay, Exeter, Devon EX2 4EB. *07788 897 706*

Southern Counties East League: T. Day, 87 Blackburn Road, Herne Bay, Kent CT6 7UT. *07789 655 768*

East Midlands Counties League: R. Holmes, 9 Copse Close, Hugglescote, Coalville LE67 2GL. *07826 452 389*

OTHER USEFUL ADDRESSES

Amateur Football Alliance: M. Brown, Unit 3, 7 Wenlock Road, London N1 7SL. *0208 733 2613*

Association of Football Badge Collectors: K. Wilkinson, 18 Hinton St, Fairfield, Liverpool L6 3AR. *0151 260 0554*

British Olympic Association: 60 Charlotte Street, London W1T 2NU. *0207 842 5700*

British Blind Sport (including football): Plato Close, Tachbrook Park, Leamington Spa, Warwickshire CV34 6WE. *01926 424 247*

British Universities and Colleges Sports Association: Karen Rothery, Chief Executive: BUCSA, 20–24 King's Bench Street, London SE1 0QX. *0207 633 5080*

English Schools FA: 4 Parker Court, Staffordshire Technology Park, Stafford ST18 0WP. *01785 785 970*

Fields In Trust: 20 Woodstock Studios, Woodstock Grove, London W12 8LE. *0207 427 2110*

Football Foundation: Paul Thorogood, Chief Executive: Whittinghton House, 19–30 Alfred Place, London WC1E 7EA. *0345 345 4555*

Football Postcard Collectors Club: PRO: Bryan Horsnell, 275 Overdown Road, Tilehurst, Reading RG31 6NX. *0118 942 4448 (and fax)*

Football Safety Officers Association: John Newsham, FSOA Ltd, Suite 17, Blackburn Rovers Enterprise Centre, Ewood Park, Blackburn BB2 4JF. *01254 841 771.*

Institute of Football Management and Administration: Andy Daykin, St George's Park, Newborough, Needwood, Burton on Trent DE13 9PD. *0128 357 6350*

Institute of Groundsmanship: 28 Stratford Office Village, Walker Avenue, Wolverton, Milton Keynes MK12 5TW. *01908 312 511*

League Managers Association: St George's Park, Newborough Road, Needwood, Burton on Trent DE13 9PD. *0128 357 6350*

National Football Museum: Urbis Building, Cathedral Gardens, Todd Street, Manchester M4 3BG. *0161 605 8200*

Professional Footballers' Association: G. Taylor, 20 Oxford Court, Bishopsgate, Off Lower Moseley Street, Manchester M2 3WQ. *0161 236 0575*

Programme Monthly & Football Collectable Magazine: 11 Tannington Terrace, London N5 1LE. *020 7359 8687*

Programme Promotions: 21 Roughwood Close, Watford WD17 3HN. *01923 861 468*
Web: www.footballprogrammes.com

Referees' Association: A.W.S. Smith, 1A Bagshaw Close, Ryton-on-Dunsmore, Coventry CV8 3EX. *024 7642 0360*

Scottish Football Historians Association: John Lister, 5 Balwearie Road, Kirkcaldy, Fife KY2 5LT. *01592 268 718*

Sir Norman Chester Centre for Football Research: Department of Sociology, University of Leicester, University Road LE1 7RH. *0116 252 2741/5.*

Soccer Nostalgia: G. Wallis, Albion Chambers, 1 Albion Road, Birchington, Kent CT7 9DN. *01303 275 432.*

Sport England: 21 Bloomsbury Street, London WC1B 3HF.

Sports Grounds Safety Authority: East Wing, 3rd Floor, Fleetbank House, 2–6 Salisbury Square, London EC4Y 8JX. *0207 930 6693*

Sports Turf Research Institute: St Ives Estate, Harden, Bingley, West Yorkshire BD16 1AU. *01274 565 131*

The Football Supporters' Federation: 1 Ashmore Terrace, Stockton Road, Sunderland, Tyne and Wear SR2 7DE. *0330 440 0044*

The Ninety-Two Club: Mr M. Kimberley, The Ninety-Two Club, 153 Hayes Lane, Kenley, Surrey CR8 5HP.

UK Programme Collectors Club: PM Publications, 38 Lowther Road, Norwich NR4 6QW. *01603 449 237*

FOOTBALL CLUB CHAPLAINCY

Dave worked full-time in the finance section of a large business, but was also a fully qualified referee who formerly officiated in several of the local minor leagues. He was sufficiently well-regarded that, a couple of seasons ago, he began running the line at Football League level.

Dave, and his wife Joy, attend a local church, having initially been invited along by a couple of neighbouring friends. They were delighted to find the church welcoming, and the addresses always brief, usually relevant, and occasionally direct and pointed.

Last autumn, Dave was due to act as linesman at a match on the ground of one of the clubs among the majority to have appointed a Chaplain. Dave was more than pleased about the appointment, because he and Joy had been confirmed, with about a dozen others, by the local Bishop a few weeks earlier and Dave knew that the Chaplain would almost certainly spend some time in the dressing-room area before the game. Dave's intention was to make himself known to the Chaplain and to impart the news of his recent confirmation.

Everything worked out as planned and Dave and Harry (the Chaplain) related well immediately. Both men promised to keep in touch. Dave and Joy were Harry's guests at a match last season at which Harry undertook to become one of the godparents to Dave and Joy's first baby, which arrived a day or two before the FA Cup final.

THE REV

OFFICIAL CHAPLAINS TO FA PREMIERSHIP AND FOOTBALL LEAGUE CLUBS

Aston Villa – Ken Baker
Barnsley – Peter Amos
Birmingham C – Kirk McAtear
Blackburn R – Ken Howles
Blackpool – Michael Ward
Bolton W – Philip Mason
Bournemouth – Co-Chaplains Andy Rimmer and Peter Homden
Bradford C – Andrew Grieff
Brentford – Stuart Cashman
Bristol C – Derek Cleave
Bristol R – Dave Jeal
Burnley – Barry Hunter
Burton Alb – Phil Pusey
Bury – David Ottley
Cambridge U – Stuart Wood
Cardiff C Academy– Keiron Webster
Carlisle U – Alun Jones
Charlton Ath Academy – Tony Dark
Charlton Ath – Matt Baker
Cheltenham T – Malcolm Allen
Chesterfield – Danny Woolf
Crawley T – Steve Alliston
Crewe Alex – Phil Howell
Crystal Palace – Chris Roe
Derby Co – Tony Luke
Doncaster R – Barry Miller
Everton – Harry Ross
Everton Training Ground – Henry Corbett
Fleetwood T – George Ayoma
Fulham – Gary Piper
Gillingham – Chris Gill
Hartlepool U – Chris Stuttard
Huddersfield T – Dudley Martin
Hull C Academy – Martin Batstone
Ipswich T – Kevan McCormack
Leeds U – Dave Niblock
Leicester C – Andrew Hulley
Leyton Orient – Neil Kinghorn
Liverpool – Bill Bygroves
Luton T – Alan West
Manchester C – Pete Horlock
Manchester U – John Boyers
Mansfield T – Ray Shaw
Millwall – Owen Beament
Newcastle U Academy – Glyn Evans
Newport Co – Keith Beardmore
Northampton T – Ken Baker
Norwich C – Co-Chaplains Jon Norman and Bert Cadmore
Nottingham F – John Parfitt
Notts Co – Liam O'Boyle
Oldham Ath – John Simmons
Peterborough U – Co-Chaplains Richard Longfoot and Sid Bridges
Plymouth Arg – Arthur Goode
Port Vale – John Hibberts
Portsmouth – Co-Chaplains Mick Mellows and Jonathan Jeffrey
Preston NE – Chris Nelson
QPR – Co-Chaplains Cameron Collington and Bob Mayo
Reading – Steven Prince
Scunthorpe U – Alan Wright
Sheffield U – Alistair Beattie
Sheffield W – Baz Gascoyne
Sheffield W Academy – Malcolm Drew
Sheffield W Wise Old Owls – David Jeans
Shrewsbury T – Phil Cansdale
Southampton – Andy Bowerman
Southend U – Co-Chaplains Stu Alleway and Mike Lodge
Sunderland – Marc Lyden-Smith
Swansea C – Kevin Johns
Swansea C Academy – Eirian Wyn
Swindon T – Simon Stevenette
Walsall – Peter Hart
Watford – Clive Ross
WBA Academy – Steven Harper
West Ham U – Alan Bolding
West Ham U Academy – Philip Wright
Wolverhampton W – Co-Chaplains David Wright and Steve Davies
Wycombe W – Benedict Musola
Yeovil T – Jim Pearce

WOMEN'S FOOTBALL CLUB CHAPLAINS

Bournemouth – Hannah Rogers
Bristol C – Esther Legg-Bagg
Charlton Ath – Kathryn Sales
Notts Co – Wendy Murphy
Reading – Angy King

The chaplains hope that those who read this page will see the value and benefit of chaplaincy work in football and will take appropriate steps to spread the word where this is possible. They would also like to thank the editors of the Football Yearbook for their continued support for this specialist and growing area of work.

For further information, please contact: Sports Chaplaincy UK, The Avenue Methodist Church, Wincham Road, Sale, Cheshire M33 4PL. Telephone: 0800 181 4051 or email: admin@sportschaplaincy.org.uk. Website: www.sportschaplaincy.org.uk

OBITUARIES

Ernie Ackerley (Born: Manchester, 23 September 1943. Died: Melbourne, Australia, 1 June 2017.) Ernie Ackerley was on Manchester United's books as a youngster and also had a spell with Blackburn Rovers but it was only on dropping down the divisions to play for Barrow that he gained first-team experience. He went on to feature regularly for the Holker Street club, making 55 appearances and finishing as joint-top scorer in 1963–64. He subsequently emigrated to Australia where he enjoyed a lengthy and successful career with South Melbourne Hellas.

Steve Adams (Born: Sheffield, 7 September 1959. Died: 3 March 2017.) Steve Adams was a winger who played in semi-professional football with Gainsborough Trinity and Worksop Town before getting his chance in the Football League with Scarborough at the age of 28. He went on to sign for Doncaster Rovers before returning to play in non-league football with Boston United. He later became a coach and was Community Programme manager at Sheffield Wednesday for a number of years.

Carlos Alberto (Born: Rio de Janeiro, Brazil, 17 July 1944. Died: Rio de Janeiro, Brazil, 25 October 2016.) Carlos Alberto was right-back and captain of the Brazil team which won the 1970 World Cup and scored the fourth goal in their 4-1 victory over Italy in the final. He won a total of 53 caps for Brazil. He began his senior football at Fluminense and then made over 400 appearances for Santos before returning to Fluminense. He finished his playing career in the NASL with New York Cosmos.

Len Allchurch (Born: Swansea, 12 September 1933. Died: Swansea, 15 November 2016.) Len Allchurch was a winger who made his name in the 1950s with Swansea Town, where he was a fixture in the line-up from 1954 until moving on to Sheffield United in March 1961. He later helped Stockport County win the Division Four title in 1966–67, and was a near ever-present for Swansea City when they gained promotion in 1969–70. Len, who was the younger brother of Ivor Allchurch, won 11 caps for Wales.

George Allen (Born: Small Heath, Birmingham, 23 January 1932. Died: Solihull, 13 July 2016.) George Allen was a left-back who established himself in the Birmingham City line-up in November 1958, holding his place in the side until shortly after the start of the 1961–62 season when he fractured his skull. He featured in both legs of the 1958–60 Inter City Fairs Cup final, when Blues went down to Barcelona, later moving on to Torquay United, where he added almost 150 more senior appearances.

Sandy Anderson (Born: Auchtermuchty, Fife, 20 February 1930. Died: July 2016.) Sandy Anderson was snapped up by Southend United in April 1950 and proved excellent value for the Essex club. A steady, reliable defender he was a first-team regular for 12 years and his total of 452 Football League appearances remains an all-time record for the Shrimpers. On leaving senior football he played for Folkestone.

Stan Anslow (Born: Hackney, 5 May 1931. Died: April 2017.) Stan Anslow was a tough and uncompromising full-back who signed for Millwall in March 1951 and went on to make close on 150 league and cup appearances for the club. A regular in the late 1950s, he had a spell at centre-forward in the 1956–57 season with considerable success. His haul of 16 goals made him the club's second-top scorer that term and included a hat-trick against Torquay United and both goals in the 2-1 FA Cup fourth round victory over Newcastle United.

John Arnott (Born: Sydenham, 6 September 1932. Died: 31 March 2017.) John Arnott was an inside-or centre-forward who progressed from the Lewisham Schools team to West Ham United, signing professional forms in July 1954. Mostly a reserve with the Hammers, he moved on to Shrewsbury Town and then Bournemouth where he made over 150 first-team appearances, latterly converting to right-half. He subsequently followed manager Freddie Cox to Gillingham where he was a near ever-present in the team that won the Division Four title in 1963–64. After bringing his career total of senior appearances beyond the 400-mark he moved into non-league football with Dover.

Tommy Asher (Born: Dunscroft, nr. Doncaster, 21 December 1936. Died: Gotham, Notts, 11 March 2017.) An England Schools international, Tommy Asher failed to break into the first team with Wolverhampton Wanderers and was released in January 1954. After a brief spell with Wath Wanderers he signed for Notts County, featuring for the Magpies in their Second Division days. Later he played for Peterborough United in their final season as a non-league club.

Denis Atkins (Born: Bradford, 8 November 1938. Died: 13 September 2016.) Right-back Denis Atkins signed professional terms for Huddersfield Town shortly after his 17th birthday but it was four more years before he broke into the first team. He was a regular at Leeds Road from early 1962 and remained so until the 1966–67 season. At Valley Parade he helped Bradford City win promotion in 1968–69 and took his total of senior appearances beyond the 300-mark before leaving the game.

Dalian Atkinson (Born: Shrewsbury, 21 March 1968. Died: Telford, 15 August 2016.) Dalian Atkinson was a quick and powerful striker who developed in the youth set-up at Ipswich Town. Progressing to a professional contract at the age of 17, he first attracted attention by scoring a hat-trick against Middlesbrough in April 1988. His namesake Ron Atkinson signed him for Sheffield Wednesday in July 1989 where he was capped by England B before moving on to Real Sociedad. He linked up with manager Atkinson again at Aston Villa for what were to be the best years of his career. He scored Villa's first-ever Premier League goal while a tremendous individual effort against Wimbledon earned him Match of the Day's Goal of the Season award for 1992–93. In March 1994 he scored the opening goal as Villa went on to beat Manchester United 3-1 and win the Football League Cup final at Wembley. Injuries and loss of form led to his departure from Villa Park and his career never really picked up thereafter.

Graham Atkinson (Born: Birmingham, 17 May 1943. Died: 5 January 2017.) Graham Atkinson was attached to Aston Villa as a youngster before signing for what was then Headington United as a 16-year-old, scoring on his debut for them in September 1959. The club changed names to Oxford United and he appeared in their first-ever Football League fixture at Barrow in August 1962, scoring their first goal in the competition. Apart from a brief spell with Cambridge United he stayed at Oxford for 15 years and remains the club's all-time leading Football League goal scorer with a total of 77 goals. He played alongside his older brother Ron for most of his career with the U's.

Eddie Bailham (Born: Dublin, 8 May 1941. Died: December 2016.) Eddie Bailham was on the books of Manchester United as a youngster but returned home to Ireland where he enjoyed a useful career with Cork Hibs and then Shamrock Rovers where he developed into a regular goalscorer, netting 18 goals in the 1963–64 season as Shamrock won the League of Ireland title. He was capped for the Republic of Ireland against England in May 1964 but a few months later he crossed the Irish Sea to sign for Cambridge City. He became a prolific scorer in Southern League football for City, Worcester City and Wimbledon over the following seasons.

Larry Baxter (Born: Leicester, 24 November 1931. Died: 24 November 2016.) Larry Baxter was a tall, skilful winger who developed with Northampton Town and Norwich City before signing for Gillingham, where he became a first-team regular. He is best known for a five-year spell at Torquay United, where he made over 150 appearances and featured in the team that won promotion from the old Fourth Division in 1959–60.

Colin Beer (Born: Exeter, 15 August 1936. Died: 13 August 2016.) Colin Beer signed for Exeter City in 1955 initially playing as an amateur in the A team before turning professional. He scored twice on his first-team debut for the Grecians in

September 1956 but mainly appeared for the reserves in the Southern League. He later played for Bideford and Bridgwater, then spent 20 years playing for Devon & Exeter League club Okehampton Argyle retiring at the age of 47.

Albert Bennett (Born: Chester-le-Street, 16 July 1944. Died: 15 December 2016.) Arnold Bennett made his name as an inside-forward with Rotherham United for whom he led the scoring charts in two of the three seasons he was a first-team regular. He was rewarded with an England U23 cap, featuring against Wales in November 1964, and the following summer he was sold to Newcastle United. He was increasingly affected by ankle problems during his time at St James' Park and then moved on to Norwich City, before eventually retiring due to injury having scored a career total of 109 goals in just 271 appearances.

Peter Bennett (Born: Plymouth, 29 November 1939. Died: 27 October 2016.) Peter Bennett was a centre-forward who scored on his senior debut for Exeter City and hit a hat-trick in a 4-2 win over Doncaster Rovers on the final day of the 1959–60 season but made just six first-team appearances for the Grecians. He was later a prolific scorer in non-league football during spells at Falmouth Town, Bideford, Plymouth City and Bodmin Town.

Peter Berry (Born: Aldershot, 20 September 1933. Died: 8 October 2016.) Peter Berry joined the groundstaff at Crystal Palace on leaving school before progressing to the senior ranks at the age of 17. Initially featuring on the right wing, he later played at inside-right and centre-forward for Palace, making over 150 first-team appearances during his stay. He subsequently signed for Ipswich Town, then managed by Alf Ramsey, but an injury suffered in September 1959 effectively ended his career. He was the younger brother of Johnny Berry (Birmingham City, Manchester United and England).

Eunan Blake (Born: Letterkenny, Co Donegal, Circa 1938. Died: Letterkenny, Co Donegal, 10 May 2017.) Eunan Blake made five appearances for the League of Ireland representative team while at Sligo Rovers. He was later a member of the Derry City team which won the Irish Cup in 1964 before concluding his career with Finn Harps, with whom he later had a spell as manager. After his playing career came to an end he had a spell as manager of Finn Harps

Paul Bowles (Born: Manchester, 31 May 1957. Died: 2017.) Paul Bowles was a ball playing central defender who broke into the Crewe Alexandra team at the age of 17 and went on to make close on 200 appearances during his time at Gresty Road. He moved on to Port Vale in October 1979 and then to Stockport County where he suffered an ankle injury in October 1984 which effectively ended his career.

Peter Brabrook (Born: Greenwich, 8 November 1937. Died: Basildon, Essex, 10 December 2016.) Winger Peter Brabrook was a product of the East Ham Schools team and signed for Chelsea, where he was a first-team regular for six seasons. Shortly after the Blues were relegated from the top flight in 1962 he moved across London to sign for West Ham United. He went on to win the FA Cup with the Hammers in 1964 and also featured in the Football League Cup final defeat by West Bromwich Albion in 1965–66. Peter concluded his career with a spell at Orient where he was a near ever-present in the team that won the Division Three title in 1969–70. He won three caps for England, featuring in the 1958 World Cup finals in Sweden.

Arthur Brady (Born: 12 July 1927. Died: 8 July 2016.) Arthur 'Mousey' Brady was an outside-right who was Belfast Celtic's last signing before they disbanded in 1949. He later played for Crusaders for 10 years, split between two spells, and was with Derry City when they won the Irish Cup in 1954. He made one appearance for the Irish League representative side.

Ray Brady (Born: Dublin, 3 June 1937. Died: 15 November 2016.) Ray Brady was a versatile defender who mostly featured at centre-half. He joined Millwall from League of Ireland club Transport and went on to win a Fourth Division championship medal with the Lions in 1961–62. He later played for Queens Park Rangers (1963–66) winning six caps for the Republic of Ireland during his time at Loftus Road. Ray then had two seasons with Southern League club Hastings United before a spell back in Ireland with St Patrick's Athletic.

Jack Bridgett (Born: Walsall, 10 April 1929. Died: 2 November 2016.) Jack Bridgett was on the books of West Bromwich Albion as a youngster but failed to make the first team and in August 1950 he went on to sign for neighbours Walsall where he made over 100 senior appearances. Although mainly a centre-half he was used for a couple of seasons as a centre-forward. Later he spent two seasons with Southern League club Worcester City before switching to the Welsh League with Abergavenny. At the time of his death he was president of Walsall Former Players Association.

Johnny Brooks (Born: Reading, 23 December 1931. Died: Bournemouth, 7 June 2016.) Johnny Brooks was a gifted inside-forward who joined Reading in April 1949. Four years later he was sold to Tottenham Hotspur where he established himself as a first-team player towards the end of the 1954–55 campaign and went on to win three England caps. Later he played for Chelsea, Brentford (where he was a member of the team that won the Division Four title in 1962–63) and Crystal Palace. His son Shaun Brooks played professionally for Crystal Palace, Leyton Orient and Bournemouth.

Steve Browne (Born: Hackney, 21 June 1964. Died: 1 January 2017.) Steve Browne was a midfield player who was still an apprentice when he made his only senior appearance for Charlton Athletic coming on as a substitute against Wrexham in February 1982. He was briefly on the club's books as a professional and went on to forge a useful career in non-league football, notably with Wealdstone, Yeovil Town, Slough Town and Hendon. He later managed several clubs in the Isthmian and Southern Leagues.

Brian Bulless (Born: Hull, 4 September 1933. Died: Hull, 7 December 2016.) Brian Bulless was a wing-half who joined the Hull City groundstaff, progressing to a professional contract shortly after reaching the age of 17. A solid and dependable performer, he enjoyed eight seasons of regular first-team football at Boothferry Park making over 350 first-team appearances before injury led to his retirement.

Tony Byrne (Born: Rathdowney, Co Laois, Ireland, 2 February 1946. Died: Hereford, 13 June 2016.) Tony Byrne was initially a winger at Millwall before being converted to full-back. After a single appearance for the Lions he joined Southampton in August 1964 and in all he made over 100 appearances during a decade with the club before moving on to Hereford where he linked up with his former colleague Terry Paine. He enjoyed one good season with the Bulls before concluding his career at Newport County. He won 14 caps for the Republic of Ireland.

Bobby Campbell (Born: Belfast, 13 September 1956. Died: Huddersfield, 15 November 2016.) Bobby Campbell was a big bustling centre forward who started out with Aston Villa. He struggled to make an impact in the early stages of his career in spells with Huddersfield Town, Sheffield United and Halifax, but came to the fore after signing for Bradford City in December 1979. His most memorable goal gave City a 1-0 League Cup win over Liverpool in August 1980, and in two spells at Valley Parade he established a club record of 121 Football League goals, a total that has yet to be beaten. He twice helped City win promotion and also played for Derby County and Wigan Athletic. He won two caps for Northern Ireland.

Don Campbell (Born: Bootle, 19 October 1932. Died: September 2016.) Don Campbell was a talented youngster who won England Youth international honours and went on to sign professional terms for Liverpool, but in eight seasons at Anfield he was principally a reserve. Joining Crewe Alexandra in July 1958 he was a near ever-present in his first three seasons before concluding his senior career at Gillingham.

Derek Carr (Born: Northumberland, 1936. Died: August 2016.) Derek Carr was a wing-half who was signed by Crook Town in April 1959 as a replacement for the injured Bill Jeffs and after just three appearances turned out for Crook in their FA Amateur Cup final victory over Barnet that year. At the time he was serving in the RAF based at Felixstowe. He turned professional shortly after leaving the RAF and went on to make almost 50 senior appearances for Scottish League club Berwick Rangers between January 1960 and April 1961.

Matt Carragher (Born: Liverpool, 14 January 1976. Died: December 2016.) Matt Carragher developed in the Wigan Athletic youth set-up and was the youngest player to make a century of Football League appearances for the club before he was released at the end of the 1996–97 season. He signed for Port Vale where he moved from right-back to sweeper and captained the team that defeated Brentford to win the LDV Vans Trophy final at the Millennium Stadium in 2001. After leaving Vale Park he had a brief association with Stafford Rangers before concluding his senior career back in the Football League with Macclesfield Town.

Ray Carter (Born: West Hoathly, Sussex, 1 June 1933. Died: 2017.) Centre-forward Ray Carter developed with APV Athletic before moving into senior football with Torquay United in August 1958. Although a regular scorer with the reserves he struggled to break into the Gulls' first team and in October 1960 he moved on to Exeter City. In three seasons at St James Park he scored 54 goals in just 110 first-team games, finishing as top scorer in 1961–62 and 1962–63. He then returned to Sussex, joining Crawley Town in time for their first season of Southern League football.

Ian Cartwright (Born: Brierley Hill, Staffs, 13 November 1964. Died: December 2016.) Ian Cartwright was a midfield player who broke into the Wolverhampton Wanderers first team as an 18-year-old. Wolves won promotion in his first season, but then suffered three consecutive relegations. After just 68 first-team appearances Ian's career was ended due to an ankle injury.

Mel Charles (Born: Swansea, 14 May 1935. Died: Swansea, 24 September 2016.) Mel Charles was a versatile player who appeared at full-back, wing-half and as a forward during his career. He signed for Swansea Town on leaving school and went on to make over 200 appearances before Arsenal paid what was then a club record fee of £40,000 plus two players when he signed for them in March 1959. His time at Highbury was interrupted by injury and he eventually moved on to Cardiff City and then Port Vale. He won 31 caps for Wales and was a member of the team which reached the quarter-finals of the 1958 World Cup. Mel was the younger brother of John Charles and the father of Jeremy Charles who both also appeared for Wales.

Les Cocker (Born: Wolverhampton, 18 September 1939. Died: Newport, Shropshire, 16 February 2017.) Wing-half Les Cocker was a member of the Wolves team which won the 1958 FA Youth Cup final and also captained Staffordshire to victory in the FA County Youth Cup final the same season. He went on to make a solitary first-team appearance for Wolves before moving on to Southern League club Wellington Town and later spent two seasons in South Africa with Arcadia Shepherds before returning home to play for Hereford United.

David Coleman (Born: Colchester, 27 March 1942. Died: Spain, 23 September 2016.) David Coleman was a centre-forward who joined Colchester United from Harwich & Parkeston in November 1961, but in 12 months with the U's he managed just three first-team starts before returning to a lengthy career in non-league football in East Anglia.

Tony Conwell (Born: Bradford, 17 January 1932. Died: May 2017.) Tony Conwell was a tough tackling full-back who made over 300 senior appearances in a 15-year professional career. He featured in top-flight action with both Sheffield Wednesday and Huddersfield Town, but his best seasons were with Derby County, for whom he was an ever-present in the 1960–61 season. He concluded his career at Doncaster Rovers where he came back from a broken leg to regain his place in the line-up.

Ronnie Cope (Born: Crewe, 5 October 1934. Died: September 2016.) Defender Ronnie Cope was capped for England Schools before joining Manchester United. An FA Youth Cup winner in 1952–53, he broke into the first team four seasons later but it was only after the Munich Disaster that he stepped up for a regular place in the side. He retained his place for two more seasons before eventually moving on to Luton Town. After a couple of seasons he returned to the North West, signing for Northwich Victoria.

Russell Coughlin (Born: Swansea, 15 February 1960. Died: Carlisle, 3 August 2016.) Russell Coughlin was a busy, combative midfield player who made over 700 senior appearances in a professional career that spanned almost 20 years. Capped by Wales at Schools and Youth levels, he joined Manchester City as an apprentice but made no headway at Maine Road. He twice gained promotion from the old Third Division, with Carlisle United (1981–82) and Plymouth Argyle (1985–86), while he made over 100 Football League appearances for four clubs (Carlisle, Plymouth, Blackpool and Swansea City) and also appeared for all three Devon League clubs.

Alan Cousin (Born: Alloa, 7 March 1938. Died: September 2016.) Alan Cousin was a talented forward who signed for Dundee as a 17-year-old after representing the Scotland NABC and Youth teams. He was an ever-present when the Dark Blues won the Scottish League championship in 1961–62 and retained his place the following season when the club reached the semi-finals of the European Cup. He made almost 400 first-team appearances in a decade at Dens Park and later appeared for Hibernian and Falkirk. He won representative honours for Scotland U23s and the Scottish League.

Ian Cowan (Born: Falkirk, 27 November 1944. Died: Larbert, Stirlingshire, 8 November 2016.) Ian Cowan was a winger who could play on either flank; he possessed pace as well as being a great crosser of the ball. He began his senior career at Falkirk in 1960, but his best seasons were spent at Partick Thistle where he made over 90 first-team appearances and featured in Fairs Cup action. He went on to play for a number of clubs including St Johnstone, a second spell at Falkirk, Dunfermline Athletic, Southend United and Albion Rovers.

Jimmy Coyle (Born: Dundee, 1937. Died: Dundee, 5 June 2016.) Jimmy Coyle signed for Dundee United at the age of 17 after being a member of the St Mary's Youth Club team which reached the final of the U18 Scottish Amateur Cup in 1955. A winger, he appeared regularly in his first two seasons at Tannadice before dropping down to the reserves.

Corbett Cresswell (Born: Birkenhead, 3 August 1932. Died: 19 May 2017.) Corbett Cresswell was a centre-half who signed for Bishop Auckland from Evenwood Town as a teenager and went on to become a member of the Bishops' team that won three successive FA Amateur Cup finals in the 1950s. He later had a spell with Carlisle United before returning to non-league football with Horden CW. Corbett won 10 caps for England Amateurs. His father Warney had been capped for the full England team in the 1920s.

Ken Currie (Born: Thornton, Fife, 3 September 1925. Died: Glenrothes, 22 March 2017.) Ken Currie was a member of the Bayview Youth Club team which won the Scottish Juvenile Cup in 1942 and went on to play for Hearts in wartime football, featuring regularly in the North Eastern League team in 1944–45. He continued to play in senior football until 1956, making just short of 100 senior appearances in a career that also saw him play for Third Lanark, Raith Rovers, Dunfermline Athletic and Stranraer.

Joe Davis (Born: Glasgow, 22 May 1941. Died: Fenwick, Ayrshire, 5 August 2016.) Joe Davis entered senior football with Third Lanark towards the end of the 1960–61 season and made 79 first-team appearances during his stay. In November 1964 Jock Stein signed him for Hibernian as a replacement full-back for the departed John Park and he went on to establish a new club record for consecutive appearances, being ever-present for four seasons in a row for Scottish League matches. He was also a prolific scorer of penalties during his time at Easter Road. He concluded his career with a spell at Carlisle United before leaving the game.

Lindy Delapenha (Born: Kingston, Jamaica, 20 May 1927. Died: St Andrew, Jamaica, 26 January 2017.) Lindy Delapenha was a talented all-round sportsman at school and initially came to England for a trial with Arsenal. He signed for Portsmouth in April 1948 but struggled to break into the side at Fratton Park. On moving to Middlesbrough he fared much better, establishing himself in the side as a talented winger and becoming one of the great pioneering Black footballers of the 1950s. He made over 250 appearances for Boro' and a further 150 for Mansfield Town then played in non-league football for Heanor Town, Hereford United and Burton Albion. He also played a number of representative games for Jamaica in the 1950s. He was inducted into Jamaica's national Sporting Hall of Fame in 1998.

Peter Denton (Born: Gorleston, Norfolk, 1 March 1946. Died: Luton, 6 October 2016.) Peter Denton was a right winger who was mostly a reserve in four seasons with Coventry City, making 11 appearances in the first team. He moved on to Luton Town in January 1968, but made just a handful of appearances before switching to Southern League football with Canterbury City and Margate.

Eamonn Dolan (Born: Dagenham, 20 September 1967. Died: 20 June 2016.) Eamonn Dolan was a lively, energetic striker whose playing career was often hampered by injuries. As a youngster he featured for the Republic of Ireland team in the 1985 FIFA World Youth (U20) Championship finals. After a playing career with West Ham United, Birmingham City and Exeter City he joined the Grecians' backroom staff. Following a spell as manager he moved on to become manager of Reading's Academy in September 2004. He was still in post at the time of his death which was due to cancer. He was capped for Republic of Ireland U21s.

Dick Donnelly (Born: Dundee, 11 September 1941. Died: Balmullo, Fife, 21 July 2016.) Dick Donnelly was a goalkeeper who graduated from Junior outfit Carnoustie Panmure to sign for East Fife in the summer of 1960. He made over 100 first-team appearances for the Methil club and later had a spell with Brechin City. He subsequently turned to journalism, progressing from covering matches for the *Courier* to reporting for Radio Tay, where he became known as the voice of football on Tayside.

Cammy Duncan (Born: Shotts, 4 August 1965. Died: 1 May 2017.) Cammy Duncan was a goalkeeper who joined Sunderland as a youngster but struggled to break into the team, making just three league and cup appearances. He returned to Scotland in the summer of 1987 and went on to make over 300 senior appearances in the decade that followed. After spells with Motherwell and Partick Thistle he enjoyed the best seasons of his career with Ayr United where he proved to be an effective performer, despite occasional absences through injury. He concluded his senior career with Albion Rovers.

Shay Dunne (Born: Wicklow, 13 April 1930. Died: Dublin, 28 September 2016.) Shay Dunne was a full-back who began his career in Ireland, joining Luton Town after playing for League of Ireland club Shelbourne. He made over 300 first-team appearances for the Hatters helping the team win promotion to Division One in 1955 and also appeared 15 times for the Republic of Ireland, captaining his country on a number of occasions. Shay later played for Yiewsley and Dunstable Town.

Dave Durie (Born: Blackpool, 13 August 1931. Died: Blackpool, 30 August 2016.) Dave Durie began his career as an inside-left for Blackpool, establishing himself in the line-up towards the end of the 1955–56 season and going on to make over 300 appearances for the Seasiders. He subsequently spent three seasons with Chester and then became player-coach and subsequently manager of Fleetwood Town until October 1968.

Don Dykes (Born: Ashby by Partney, Lincs, 8 June 1930. Died: Lincoln, 25 October 2016.) Don Dykes was a versatile player who spent 12 seasons with Lincoln City where he appeared in a number of different positions having made his debut at outside-right, but never established himself as a first-team regular. He made a total of 101 appearances for the Imps before moving on to play for Boston United in the summer of 1959.

Bryan Edwards (Born: Woodlesford, Leeds, 27 October 1930. Died: 21 June 2016.) Bryan Edwards signed professional forms for Bolton Wanderers at the age of 17, and was still a teenager when he made his first-team debut. He quickly established himself in the side, and after missing out on the 1953 FA Cup final he went on to gain a winners' medal in 1958 before taking his career total of appearances for Wanderers to beyond the 500-mark. He subsequently worked on the backroom staff for a number of clubs and was manager of Bradford City between November 1971 and January 1975.

Ugo Ehiogu (Born: Hackney, 3 November 1972. Died: London, 21 April 2017.) Ugo Ehiogu was a big, powerful central defender who began his career as a youngster with West Bromwich Albion. Although he managed just a couple of first-team appearances for the Baggies his career blossomed when Ron Atkinson took him to Aston Villa in the summer of 1991. He played over 300 games for Villa, gaining a League Cup winners' medal in 1996 as well as being an FA Cup runner-up in 2000. He became Middlesbrough's record signing later that year and was a member of the team that won the League Cup in 2004, the club's first major honour. After winding down his career with spells at Rangers and Sheffield United he moved into coaching and was working with Tottenham Hotspur at the time of his death. He won four full caps for England.

Fred Evans (Born: Petersfield, Hampshire, 20 May 1923. Died: Portsmouth, 13 April 2017.) Fred Evans was a centre-forward who did well for Portsmouth in wartime, scoring 19 goals from 27 appearances including a hat-trick in a 9-1 win over Crystal Palace on Boxing Day in 1944. However, he struggled to break into the line-up when football resumed in 1946–47. He moved on to Notts County and then Crystal Palace where he was a near ever-present in the 1951–52 registering a double-figure tally of goals. Fred concluded his career with a season at Rochdale.

Alan Fahy (Born: Liverpool, 27 January 1973. Died: 23 September 2016.) Alan Fahy was a midfield player who appeared for Witton Albion and Barrow in the Northern Premier League before making the step up to join Doncaster Rovers. He made five substitute appearances for Rovers all came in the closing weeks of the 1996–97 season and afterwards moved on to join Droylsden.

Finbarr Flood (Born: Dublin, 1938. Died: Dublin, 24 July 2016.) Finbarr Flood was a goalkeeper who made his name with Shelbourne playing in their 1960 FAI Cup final winning team despite having fractured three fingers in the semi-final. He later signed for Morton where he made 26 first-team appearances in a three-year stay. He subsequently spent four seasons with Sligo Rovers. In later years he was chairman of Shelbourne. The FAI presented him with a Hall of Fame award in 2011 in recognition of his contribution to Irish soccer.

Denis Foreman (Born: Cape Town, South Africa, 1 February 1933. Died: Portslade, Sussex, 23 July 2016.) Denis Foreman was a South African forward who played in his home country for Hibernian of Cape Town before arriving in the UK and signing for Brighton & Hove Albion after a successful trial. He went on to spend a decade at the Goldstone Ground, making over 200 appearances, and was a key player in their team which won the Division 3 South title in 1957–58. Denis was also an accomplished cricketer who played in his native South Africa for Western Province and later for Sussex, making over 100 appearances between 1952 and 1967.

Tommy Forse (Born: Cardiff, 19 October 1916. Died: Llandough, near Penarth, 28 July 2016.) Tommy Forse was a full-back who won two caps for Wales Amateurs in the late 1930s and later made three first-team appearances for Cardiff City during the war years. He was subsequently heavily involved with football administration up to his death which occurred in his 100th year. He was a member of the Welsh League management committee from 1960 until his death and president from 2001, and a member of the FA of Wales Council from 1966, serving as president of the FA of Wales between 1989 and 1992.

Jimmy Frizzell (Born: Greenock, 16 February 1937. Died: July 2016.) Jimmy Frizzell was a tenacious inside-forward who began his senior career with Morton. In the summer of 1960 he was sold to Oldham Athletic for whom he initially proved to be a more than useful goalscorer, topping the club's scoring charts in 1961–62 and 1964–65. He later dropped back to a more defensive role before succeeding Jimmy McIlroy as manager, gaining promotion from the Fourth Division in 1970–71 and then winning the Third Division title in 1973–74. He left Boundary Park after a 22-year association with the club and later worked on the backroom staff at Manchester City for more than a decade, serving as manager from September 1986 to May 1987.

Fred Furniss (Born Sheffield, 10 July 1922. Died: 9 April 2017.) Fred Furniss was a right back who was a regular first-team player for Sheffield United from October 1943 through to 1954 and in total made over 400 first-team appearances for the

Blades. He was a key member of the 1945–46 League North championship winning team and was ever present in 1952–53 when the Second Division title was won. Fred later had a spell on the backroom staff at Chesterfield and continued to play in local Sheffield football to the age of 55 when he took up refereeing.

Paul Futcher (Born: Chester, 25 September 1956. Died: November 2016.) Paul Futcher was a solid, steady and very skilful defender who made his senior debut for Chester whilst still an apprentice. He was just 17 when he became Luton Town's record signing and went on to establish himself for England U21s before being sold to Manchester City, becoming the most expensive defender in English football. Paul enjoyed a lengthy career in the game, making over 800 senior appearances and helping Grimsby Town win promotion from the old Third Division in 1990–91. He also played for Oldham Athletic, Derby County, Barnsley and Halifax Town. Paul was the twin brother of Ron Futcher, younger brother of Graham and father of Ben, all of whom played senior football.

Thomas Gardner (Born: Liverpool, 17 March 1923. Died: November 2016.) Thomas Gardner was a winger who spent a season at Liverpool after service with the Royal Navy. He was unable to break into the first team at Anfield but after moving to Everton he made his only first-team appearance against Wolverhampton Wanderers in October 1947. After leaving Goodison Park he had a brief spell at South Liverpool before his football career was ended by injury.

Roy Gater (Born: Chesterton, 22 June 1940. Died: Bournemouth, 1 May 2017.) Roy Gater was a hard-tackling centre-half who came up through the ranks with Port Vale but struggled to win a place in the first team. In the summer of 1962 he moved on to Bournemouth and by the following March he became a regular in the side. He went on to play for Crewe Alexandra, taking his total of Football League appearances to beyond the 400-mark before moving into non-league football with Weymouth.

Tommy Gemmell (Born: Glasgow, 16 October 1943. Died: 2 March 2017.) Left-back Tommy Gemmell was one of the finest attacking full-backs of the 1960s. The highlight of his career came when he helped Celtic win the 1967 European Cup, scoring the Hoops' first goal as they went on to beat Internazionale 2-1 and become the first British club to win the trophy. Tommy was a key figure in Jock Stein's hugely successful Celtic team which saw him win the Scottish League six times, the Scottish Cup three times and the League Cup on four occasions. He went on to play for Nottingham Forest and Dundee, where he won another League Cup as a member of the team that defeated Celtic in 1973–74. Thereafter he had spells as manager of Dundee (August 1977 to April 1980) and Albion Rovers (January 1986 to November 1987 and April 1993 to January 1994). He won 18 caps for Scotland.

Jim Gillespie (Born: Chapelhall, Airdrie, 13 July 1947. Died: 25 November 2016.) Jim Gillespie was a tall winger with a powerful shot. Capped by Scotland at Junior international level, he had spells with East Stirlingshire and Raith Rovers before joining Dunfermline Athletic in December 1969. He enjoyed the best years of his career at East End Park, making almost 100 appearances and featuring in Fairs Cup action. He later played for Alloa Athletic and was on the coaching staff at Raith and Cowdenbeath.

Chris Glennon (Born: Manchester, 29 October 1949. Died. 10 May 2016.) Chris Glennon was a centre-forward who played for Manchester Boys before joining Manchester City as an apprentice. He went on to sign a professional contract at the age of 18, but struggled to make a breakthrough at Maine Road, making just five first-team appearances. After a spell on loan at Tranmere Rovers he moved into non-league football with Northwich Victoria.

Sylvia Gore, MBE (Born: Prescot, Lancashire, 25 November 1944. Died: September 2016.) Sylvia Gore was a prolific goalscorer who started playing for Manchester Corinthians at a young age before switching to the Sandbach-based Fodens team in 1967. She went on to play in the first official England international in November 1972, scoring her country's first-ever goal. After retiring through injury she turned to coaching and managed the Wales women's team from 1982 to 1989. She was awarded the MBE for services to football in 2000 and in 2014 she was inducted into the National Football Museum Hall of Fame.

Alex Govan (Born: Glasgow, 16 June 1929. Died: Plymouth, 10 June 2016.) Alex Govan was a pacy, skilful winger who won youth international honours for Scotland before moving south to sign for Plymouth Argyle. However, he is best known for his time with Birmingham City where he gained a Division Two champions' medal in 1954–55 and featured in the team that lost out to Manchester City in the FA Cup final at Wembley the following season. Alex became a legendary figure at St Andrew's by introducing the club's anthem, 'Keep Right On' before moving, briefly to Portsmouth and then back to Plymouth.

Gerry Gow (Born: Glasgow, 29 May 1952. Died: 10 October 2016.) Gerry Gow was a tough-tackling Scottish midfield player who made his senior debut for Bristol City as a 17-year-old. He made over 400 appearances in more than a decade at Ashton Gate before moving on to play for Manchester City, Rotherham United and Burnley. Later he was player-manager of Yeovil Town and then manager of Weymouth. He was an ever-present member of the Bristol City team that won promotion to the old First Division in 1975–76 and during his time with Manchester City appeared in the 1981 FA Cup final when City lost to Tottenham Hotspur in a replay.

Mick Granger (Born: Leeds, 7 October 1931. Died: York, 6 November 2016.) Goalkeeper Mick Granger was recruited by York City in the summer of 1951 and spent 10 years on the club's books, mostly serving as a reliable deputy to legendary 'keeper Tommy Forgan, although he made over 80 first-team appearances. He later had spells at Hull City and Halifax Town as back-up 'keeper before joining Midland League club Scarborough.

Bobby Grant (Born: 25 September 1940. Died: Spain, February 2017.) Bobby Grant was a centre-forward who made a single appearance for Rangers towards the end of the 1959–60 season. After spells with St Johnstone and Carlisle he established himself as a goalscorer in Southern League football with Chelmsford City, Cheltenham Town and Gloucester City. He subsequently returned to the Scottish Juniors with Newtongrange Star and spent 1968–69 back in the seniors with Stirling Albion. Bobby continued to play in Junior football for a further decade.

Matt Gray (Born: Renfrew, 11 July 1936. Died: Renfrew, September 2016.) Matt Gray was an inside-forward who spent six seasons with Third Lanark as a member of the free-scoring team of the late '50s and early '60s, netting over a century of goals. He was sold to Manchester City for a club record fee in March 1963 and added a further century of appearances for the Maine Road club before moving to play in South Africa.

Harry Gregory (Born: Hackney, 24 October 1943. Died: 6 June 2016.) Harry Gregory was Leyton Orient's first-ever apprentice and gained England Youth international honours before breaking into the O's first team as a teenager. He was still only 21 when he moved on to Charlton Athletic where he enjoyed four seasons of regular first-team football at The Valley, captaining the side and leading by example. Later he played for Aston Villa before concluding his career at Hereford United.

Reinhard Häfner (Born: Sonneberg, East Germany, 2 February 1952. Died: Dresden, Germany, 24 October 2016.) Reinhard Häfner was a midfield player who was one of the all-time greats of East German (DDR) football in the 1970s and '80s. He played most of his club football with Dynamo Dresden, winning four DDR League titles and four DDR Cup winners' medals. He was an unused substitute for East Germany in the 1972 Olympic Bronze Medal match but played in the 1976 Gold Medal game, scoring his team's third goal in their 3-1 victory over Poland.

Billy Hails (Born: Nettlesworth, Co Durham, 19 February 1935. Died: Watford, 19 March 2017.) Billy Hails joined Lincoln City in March 1953 but was unable to establish himself with the Imps. Moving on to Peterborough United, he was a member of the team that won five consecutive Midland League titles before gaining election to the Football League for the 1960–61 season. He was ever-present for Posh in their first season in the League, when they walked away with the Fourth Division title, and also won promotion with Northampton Town as Division Three champions in 1962–63. He later returned to Peterborough as physio in August 1968 and went on to manage the club from November 1978 to February 1979. He was subsequently physio at Watford between 1979 and 1987.

Cyril Hammond (Born: Woolwich, London, 10 February 1927. Died: Princes Risborough, Bucks, 10 September 2016.) Cyril Hammond was a wing-half who waited six years to become a first-team regular for Charlton Athletic, and eventually went on to make over 200 appearances for the Addicks. He later enjoyed three seasons with Colchester before leaving football.

Robin Hardy (Born: Worksop, 18 January 1941. Died: Worksop, 16 January 2017.) Robin Hardy signed for Sheffield Wednesday as a teenager but apart from a decent run in the side in the closing stages of the 1961–62 season he was mostly a reserve during his time at Hillsborough. A move to Rotherham United was effectively ended when he fell out with the management and he did not play for the club from mid January 1966. He returned to the game in November 1967, signing for Cambridge United. He captained Cambridge's Southern League championship winning teams of 1968–69 and 1969–70 and subsequently appeared in the club's first Football League game against Lincoln City in August 1970.

Graham Hawkins (Born: Darlaston, Staffordshire, 5 March 1946. Died: 27 September 2016.) Graham Hawkins started out as a wing-half with Wolverhampton Wanderers, but played his best football as a centre-half in six seasons at Preston between 1968 and 1974. An ever-present captain for North End when they won the old Division Three title in 1970–71, he gained another Division Three championship with Blackburn Rovers. He wound down his senior career with Port Vale, taking his career total of senior appearances beyond the 500-mark. He was subsequently manager of Wolves (August 1982 to April 1984), leading them to promotion in 1982–83, and then coached in Bahrain. His final post was as head of youth development at the Football League – a position he held for a decade.

David Herd (Born: Hamilton, Lanarkshire, 15 April 1934. Died: 1 October 2016.) David Herd was a centre-forward who made history on his Football League debut as a 17-year-old for Stockport County when he played alongside his 39-year-old father Alec. He was sold to Arsenal in August 1954 and scored over 100 senior goals for the Gunners, but the most successful period of his career came after a move to Manchester United in the summer of 1961. He was a member of the club's 1963 FA Cup-winning team, scoring twice in the final against Leicester City, and featured in two League championship winning teams. After winding down his career with Stoke City and Waterford he had a short spell as manager of Lincoln City (March 1971 to December 1972). He won five caps for Scotland

Brian Hill (Born: Bedworth, Warwickshire, 31 July 1941. Died: 26 October 2016.) Brian Hill became Coventry City's youngest Football League player when he made his debut in their final game in Division Three South at the age of 16 years and 273 days, marking the occasion with a goal. His record as the club's youngest player has since been beaten but he remains Coventry's youngest Football League goalscorer. He began his career as a forward but later switched to a more defensive role and stayed with the Sky Blues as they rose from the Fourth Division through to the old First Division, making over 250 appearances. He concluded his career with two seasons at Torquay United.

Barry Hillier (Born: Redcar, 8 April 1936. Died: 10 December 2016.) Barry Hillier initially signed for Southampton as a groundstaff boy in September 1952 before becoming a professional in April 1953. He was mostly a reserve during his time with the Saints, making just nine first-team appearances, and went on to play for Poole Town, Dorchester Town and Andover. Barry was the son of Joe Hillier, a pre-war goalkeeper, who played in the Football League for Cardiff City, Middlesbrough and Newport County.

John Hope (Born: Shildon, 30 March 1949. Died: Stockton, 18 July 2016.) Goalkeeper John Hope made his first-team debut for Darlington as a 16-year-old apprentice and was soon snapped up by Newcastle United where he spent two years as back-up to Willie McFaul. His best seasons were at Sheffield United where he helped the Blades win promotion from the Second Division in 1970–71, keeping seven consecutive clean sheets. He was the first choice the following season in the top flight then lost his place and eventually moved on to conclude his career at Hartlepool.

Ernie Hudson (Born: Carlisle, 23 November 1926. Died: Carlisle, 28 April 2017.) Wing-half Ernie Hudson developed with Edinburgh Waverley and after completing his National Service he signed for East Fife shortly after the start of the 1948–49 season. He made a handful of appearances for the Methil club before moving south and signing for the then Headington United (later to become Oxford United). He made over 100 appearances for the U's, who were members of the Southern League at the time.

Colin Hutchinson (Born: Lanchester, Co Durham, 20 October 1936. Died: 20 January 2017.) Colin Hutchinson was a forward who joined Stoke City from Consett in November 1953, but his time at the Victoria Ground was disrupted by National Service and then injury and he made few first-team appearances during his stay. He moved on to Stafford Rangers and then Macclesfield, where he helped the Silkmen win the Cheshire League title in 1963–64, before returning to Stafford as player-manager.

Ragnar Hvidsten (Born: Sandar, Norway, 3 December 1926. Died: Sandefjord, Norway, 21 September 2016.) Ragnar Hvidsten was an inside-forward who became the first Norwegian to appear in an FA Amateur Cup final when he played in the Hendon team which was defeated by Bishop Auckland at Wembley in April 1955. He won 21 caps for Norway and played for a number of clubs in his home country including Runar, Sandefjord BK (in two spells) and Skeid Oslo.

Roger Hynd (Born: Falkirk, 2 February 1942. Died: 18 February 2017.) Roger Hynd spent a decade on the books of Rangers, but despite appearing in the European Cup Winners' Cup final against Bayern Munich in May 1967 he was unable to establish himself in the line-up. He fared better when moving south of the Border, enjoying a useful season with Crystal Palace and then making over 200 appearances for Birmingham City. A robust, no-nonsense defender, he was ever-present in 1971–72 when Blues won promotion back to the top flight and reached the FA Cup semi-final. After concluding his playing career at Walsall he returned to Scotland where he had a spell as manager of Motherwell (December 1977 to November 1978).

Anatoli Isayev (Born: Moscow, 14 July 1932. Died: Moscow, 10 July 2016.) Anatoli Isayev was a forward who starred with Spartak Moscow for whom he was a member of four Soviet League championship sides. He was an Olympic Gold Medal winner at the Melbourne Games in 1956 when the Soviet Union defeated Yugoslavia 1-0 to take the title.

Harry Jackson (Born: Shaw, Lancs, 12 May 1934. Died: 2016.) Harry Jackson was a centre-forward who signed for Oldham Athletic as a 17-year-old and spent four seasons at Boundary Park but was mostly a reserve, making 10 first-team appearances. He later had a short spell with Rochdale before going on to play for a number of clubs in the Cheshire League.

Bobby Jeffrey (Born: Ayr, 7 November 1942. Died: 20 May 2017.) Bobby Jeffrey was an outside-left who joined Celtic in October 1961 and made 17 appearances during a two-year stay at Parkhead. After a spell with Airdrieonians he moved south to play for a number of teams including Rhyl and Altrincham before returning to Scotland to conclude his career at Stranraer. He won a single cap for Scotland U23s, scoring in a 2-0 win over Wales in December 1962.

Nick Jennings (Born: Wellington, Somerset, 18 January 1946. Died: 4 June 2016.) Nick Jennings was a tricky winger capable of opening up opposition defences and was a member of the Plymouth team which reached the League Cup semi-finals in 1964–65. He was allowed to move on to Fratton Park at the beginning of 1967 where he proved a useful asset to the team, making over 200 first-team appearances during his stay. Nick concluded his senior career at Exeter, maintaining his record of making over 100 appearances for each of his senior clubs.

Roy Jennings (Born: Swindon, 31 December 1931. Died: 21 October 2016.) Roy Jennings started his career as a full-back but later switched to centre-half. He joined Brighton & Hove Albion in May 1952 and made 297 senior appearances before moving on to Crawley Town in the summer of 1964.

Allan Jones (Born: Paddington, London, 19 September 1940. Died: 27 December 2016.) Centre-forward Allan Jones scored on his debut for Fulham, but despite finding the net regularly for the club's reserve and 'A' teams he struggled to win a place in the first team at Craven Cottage. He went on to become a prolific scorer in Southern League football for Dover, Tonbridge, Canterbury City and Gravesend & Northfleet.

Merfyn Jones (Born: Bangor, Caernarvonshire, 30 April 1931. Died: Bristol, 4 October 2016.) Merfyn Jones was a diminutive outside-left who joined Liverpool from Bangor City in November 1951 but was unable to secure a regular first-team place during his time at Anfield. He moved on to Scunthorpe United, going on to make over 200 appearances for The Iron and featuring in the team that won the Division Three North championship in 1957–58. He subsequently spent time at Crewe Alexandra, Chester and Lincoln City before leaving senior football.

Len Keilt (Born: Falkirk, 27 June 1934. Died: Larbert, Stirlingshire, 23 March 2017.) Len Keilt developed with Denny Boys' Club and Camelon Juniors and had a trial with Falkirk, appearing in their Division C team, before joining Stenhousemuir in November 1956. An inside-left, he featured regularly for the Ochilview club over the next two-and-a-half seasons scoring 14 goals from 69 appearances before leaving senior football.

Ian King (Born: Loanhead, Midlothian, 27 May 1937. Died: 24 July 2016.) Centre-half Ian King signed for Leicester City in June 1957 and within a matter of weeks he was playing first-team football. He went on to form an effective half-back trio alongside Colin Appleton and Frank McLintock, gaining two FA Cup runners-up medals (1961 and 1963) and playing in the side that defeated Stoke City over two legs to win the Football League Cup in 1963–64. After a spell at Charlton Athletic he returned to the East Midlands to become player-manager of Burton Albion.

Noel Kinsey (Born: Treorchy, 24 December 1925. Died: 24 May 2017.) Noel Kinsey was a scheming inside-forward who made a couple of wartime appearances for Cardiff City before signing for Norwich City in the summer of 1947. He went on to play close on 250 games for the Canaries and won international honours for Wales although playing for a Third Division side. In May 1953 he signed for Birmingham City where he enjoyed some of the best years of his career, helping Blues to the Second Division title in 1954–55 and gaining an FA Cup runners-up medal the following season. He concluded his senior career with a spell at Port Vale.

Raymond Kopa (Born: Noeux-les-Mines, France, 13 October 1931. Died: Angers, France, 3 March 2017.) Raymond Kopa was an attacking midfield player who made his name with Stade de Reims, for whom he played in the first-ever European Cup final in 1956 when they were defeated by Real Madrid. Shortly afterwards he was sold to the Spanish club and over the next three seasons he became a key player as they lifted the European Cup on consecutive occasions. In 1958 he received the European Footballer of the Year award and he starred for France as they finished third in that year's World Cup finals. He subsequently returned to Reims to conclude his career. He won a total of 45 caps for France scoring 18 goals.

Gordon Larkin (Born: Hartlepool, 12 October 1958. Died: Hartlepool, 10 December 2016.) Gordon Larkin was a winger who signed for Hartlepools United from Billingham Synthonia in the summer of 1977. However, in three seasons with Pools he was principally a reserve player, starting just six first-team games. He went on to play for Blyth Spartans, Peterlee Town and Crook Town before leaving football.

Tommy Lawrence (Born: 1933. Died: October 2016.) Tommy Lawrence was an England Amateur international centre-forward who was Enfield's all-time record goalscorer. He netted 196 goals in 204 appearances in his five years with the club during which time they twice won the Athenian League. He won 12 caps for England Amateurs and also appeared for Great Britain in the qualifying rounds for the 1964 Olympic Games before his career was ended by a serious head injury.

John Leadbitter (Born: Sunderland, 7 May 1953. Died: Scarborough, 12 September 2016.) John Leadbitter joined Sunderland straight from school and progressed to a professional contract at the age of 17. However, a knee injury hampered his career and he moved on to Darlington where he made 21 appearances during the 1972–73 season before leaving senior football.

Ken Ledger (Born: Stapleford, Notts, 17 August 1924. Died: Nottingham, 19 August 2016.) Ken Ledger was an outside-right who made wartime appearances for Notts County (16A, 7G in 1943–44) and Nottingham Forest (10A, 1G in 1945–46). He remained a professional at Forest for the first three seasons after the war without making any further senior appearances before joining Ilkeston Town.

Peter Leggett (Born: Newton-le-Willows, Lancs, 16 December 1943. Died: Chelmsford, 2 November 2016.) Peter Leggett was signed by Swindon Town in May 1962 but struggled to gain first-team football both at the County Ground and at Brighton, before developing into one of the best wingers in Southern League football in the late 1960s. He won the Southern League title with Chelmsford City (1967–68) and Cambridge United (1968–69, 1969–70) and went on to appear for the U's in their first-ever Football League game in August 1970.

Johnny Little (Born: Calgary, Canada, 7 July 1930. Died: Largs, 18 January 2017.) Johnny Little was a solid full-back who specialised in sliding tackles. He won Scotland Youth international honours and was playing in the first team at Queen's Park whilst still at school before turning professional with Rangers in the summer of 1951. He went on to make over 250 appearances during his time at Ibrox, winning the Scottish Cup twice (1953 and 1960) and the Scottish League on two occasions (1952–53, 1955–56) and then concluded his career with a season at Morton. He won a single cap for Scotland, appearing against Sweden in May 1953.

Bert Llewellyn (Born: Golborne, Lancashire, 5 February 1939. Died: September 2016.) Bert Llewellyn was a slightly built forward who scored on his debut for Everton when he was just 17. He went onto become a prolific goalscorer, topping the seasonal charts for Crewe in 1958–59 and 1959–60, while he netted four hat-tricks during his time with Port Vale between 1960 and 1963. He later had spells with Northampton Town and Walsall before signing for the then Cheshire League club Wigan Athletic.

Willie Logie (Born: Montreal, Canada, circa 1933. Died: Stirling, 20 June 2016.) Left-half Willie Logie spent three seasons with Rangers, with all his first-team appearances coming in the 1956–57 season, sufficient to earn him a League championship medal. Willie also created an unwanted record by becoming the first British player to be sent off in a competitive European match when he was dismissed in the second leg of Rangers' European Cup clash with OGC Nice in October 1956. He later had spells with Aberdeen, Arbroath, Brechin City and Alloa Athletic without ever establishing himself as a first-team regular.

Dick Lowrie (Born: 7 July 1943. Died: 2017.) Dick Lowrie signed for Brentford from Junior club St Roch shortly after the start of the 1961–62 season. He failed to make the first team at Griffin Park, then had two seasons with Morton before eventually making his senior debut on signing for Stenhousemuir. A left-half, he went on to make over 100 first-team appearances for the Warriors before returning to Junior football with Petershill and Cambuslang Rangers.

Bobby Lumley (Born: Leadgate, Co Durham, 6 January 1933. Died: 25 February 2017.) Bobby Lumley was a skilful winger or inside-forward who joined the groundstaff at Charlton Athletic on leaving school. He made just a handful of appearances for the Addicks but saw plenty of first-team action after joining Hartlepools United in February 1955. After helping the side reach runners-up position in Division Three North in 1955–56 he moved on to Chesterfield and then Gateshead, for whom he played in their last-ever Football League game at Carlisle in April 1960 before winding down his career back with Pools.

Jim McAnearney (Born: Dundee, 20 March 1935. Died: 14 March 2017.) Jim McAnearney developed with St Joseph's BC in Dundee before moving south to join his brother Tom at Sheffield Wednesday. A skilful inside-forward with great vision, he gave good service to Wednesday, Plymouth Argyle and Watford and after completing over 300 senior appearances he turned to management and coaching. He was coach under Tommy Docherty at Rotherham United before succeeding him as manager (December 1968 to May 1973) and served on the coaching staff at Leeds United and Sheffield Wednesday.

Jim McCabe (Born: Coatbridge, 27 May 1951. Died: 5 July 2016.) Jim McCabe was a skilful attacking player forward who began his career with Motherwell in 1969–70 before moving on to Stranraer. He was a regular at Stair Park where he came to be regarded as one of the most talented players to appear for the club. Jim later appeared for Albion Rovers before his career was cut short in the summer of 1978 following an ankle injury.

Dan McCaffrey (Born: Omagh, Co Tyrone, 23 November 1929. Died: Omagh, Co Tyrone, 8 June 2016.) Dan McCaffrey won a single cap for Northern Ireland Amateurs against England in September 1954 when he was on the books of Derry City. He turned professional shortly afterwards and turned out for Worcester City, Yeovil Town and Boston United before switching to the League of Ireland. His most successful season came in 1960–61 when his performances for Drumcondra earned him the inaugural Soccer Writers' Association of Ireland Personality of the Year.

Paul McCarthy (Born: Cork, 4 August 1971. Died: 19 February 2017.) Paul McCarthy was a solid central defender; brave, comfortable on the ball and presenting a danger to opposition defences when he moved up to support the attack. After winning schoolboy caps for the Republic of Ireland he became a trainee with Brighton & Hove Albion, going on to make over 200 appearances for the South Coast club. At Wycombe he was a member of the team that reached the FA Cup semi-finals in 2000–01 only to lose to Liverpool. He later played for Oxford United, Hornchurch and Ebbsfleet United, captaining the latter club to victory in the 2008 FA Trophy final. He won representative honours for Republic of Ireland U21s.

Tommy McCready (Born: 19 October 1943. Died: 2016.) Tommy McCready was a determined and strong-tackling defender who represented Scotland Schools before signing professional terms with Hibernian. He did not make the first team during two seasons at Easter Road but made three appearances for Watford after moving south. In the summer of 1964 he became Wimbledon's first full professional signing and spent a decade with the Dons, making over 400 appearances.

Sam McCulloch (Born: 28 February 1959. Died: 23 January 2017.) Sam McCulloch was a big, powerful defender who was one of the key figures in the successful Auchinleck Talbot team of the 1980s and '90s. Sam had a brief association with the seniors, making two appearances as a triallist for Queen of the South in the closing stages of the 1984–85 season.

Tommy McCulloch (Born: 1 March 1934. Died: 10 December 2016.) Tommy McCulloch was a goalkeeper who completed nearly 500 senior appearances for Clyde during 16 years with the club. He appeared for the Bully Wee in their 1958 Scottish Cup final winning team and was a regular until departing in the summer of 1972 to finish his career with half a season at Hamilton Academical.

Ian McGregor (Born: 9 December 1936. Died: Edinburgh, 20 July 2016.) Ian McGregor was a defender who signed for Raith Rovers from Edinburgh Juvenile football and was initially used at right-back. Later he switched to centre-half, making occasional first-team appearances during a four-year spell at Stark's Park. He subsequently spent a season at Cowdenbeath.

Jackie McInally (Born: Ayr, 21 November 1936. Died: 8 July 2016.) Jackie McInally was a powerful inside-forward who helped Crosshill Thistle win the Scottish Amateur Cup in 1959. Twelve months later he was in the Kilmarnock team which lost to Rangers in the final of the Scottish Cup and in 1962 was a member of their team which lost in the final of the League Cup. He was a key member for Killie when they won the Scottish League title in 1964–65 when he missed just two games and finished the season with 11 goals. Later he spent six years at Motherwell before winding down his career at Hamilton Academical, taking his career tally of appearances to more than 550.

Jimmy McIntosh (Born: Forres, 3 August 1936. Died: Denny, Stirlingshire, 2 October 2016.) Jimmy McIntosh was a versatile player who made his debut for Falkirk in September 1955 and went on to make over 200 first-team appearances for the Bairns. Later he was player-manager of Forres Mechanics before leaving football. He won three caps for Scotland U23s.

George McKimmie (Born: Dundee, 19 July 1951. Died: South Africa, 19 October 2016.) George McKimmie was an inside-forward who signed for Dunfermline Athletic as a 16-year-old in April 1968. He spent three seasons with the Pars making 27 first-team appearances before moving to South Africa where he played for a number of clubs including Highlands Park, Arcadia Shepherds and Florida Albion.

Dave Maclaren (Born: Auchterarder, Perthshire, 12 June 1934. Died: Castlemaine, Victoria, Australia, December 2016.) Dave Maclaren was a goalkeeper who began his career at Dundee as cover for Bill Brown before joining Leicester City in January 1957. He established himself with the Foxes before losing his place to a young Gordon Banks. Later he made over 100 appearances for Plymouth Argyle, then had spells with Wolves and Southampton before spending a season in the Southern League with Worcester City.

George McLeod (Born: Inverness, 30 November 1932. Died: Luton, 5 September 2016.) George McLeod was a quick and tricky winger who developed in Highland League football before moving south to join Luton Town in January 1955 and was a regular in the line-up in 1957–58 before losing out to new signing Billy Bingham. George quickly moved on to Brentford for whom he made over 200 appearances and was an ever-present in the team that won the Division Four title in 1962–63. After a spell at Queens Park Rangers he emigrated to South Africa, where he played for Port Elizabeth City.

Charlie McNeil (Born: Stirling, 11 March 1963. Died: Stirling, 11 December 2016.) Charlie McNeil was a winger who spent five seasons with Stirling Albion, making his first-team debut as a 17-year-old. He was used on both flanks and featured in Stirling's record Scottish Cup victory, coming on as a substitute in the 20-0 win over Selkirk in December 1984. After making over 100 appearances he moved on to Junior club Kilsyth Rangers.

Ray Mabbutt (Born: Aylesbury, 13 March 1936. Died: Weston-super-Mare, 2 November 2016.) Ray Mabbutt was a solid, reliable wing-half who signed for Bristol Rovers in August 1956 and went on to make over 400 first-team appearances for the club. He occasionally featured as a forward in the 1967–68 season, scoring six goals in a run of three matches, including a hat-trick in a 5-4 win over Northampton Town. After concluding his senior career at Newport he played for a number of non-league clubs in the West of England including Trowbridge Town and Bath City. He is the father of Gary (Bristol Rovers, Tottenham Hotspur and England) and Kevin (Bristol City and Crystal Palace).

Ludek Macela (Born: 3 October 1950. Died: 16 June 2016.) Ludek Macela was a defender who captained the Czechoslovakia team that defeated East Germany 1-0 to win the Gold Medal at the 1980 Moscow Olympic Games. He played most of his club football with Dukla Prague (1965–82) before concluding his career in West Germany with SV Darmstadt.

Stuart Markland (Born: Edinburgh, 12 February 1948. Died: Edinburgh, 31 March 2017.) Stuart Markland joined Berwick Rangers as a centre-forward in March 1967 but after little more than a season with the Shielfield club he was released. He subsequently signed for Dundee United where he spent five seasons and featured in UEFA Cup action. Later he had two spells with Montrose separated by a period in Australia with Sydney Olympic, taking his total of senior appearances beyond the 300-mark.

Reg Matthewson (Born: Sheffield, 6 August 1939. Died: Malaga, Spain, 29 August 2016.) Reg Matthewson was a steady, solid defender who joined Sheffield United as a teenager, eventually progressing to win a regular slot in the line-up in the second half of the 1963–64 season. He later helped Fulham win promotion back to the Second Division in 1970–71 and then captained the Chester team that won promotion from the Fourth Division and reached the semi-finals of the Football League Cup in 1974–75. In total he made over 400 senior appearances.

John Middleton (Born: Skegness, 24 December 1956. Died: 3 July 2016.) John Middleton was a goalkeeper who completed an apprenticeship with Nottingham Forest before graduating to the senior ranks. He was Forest's regular goalkeeper in 1976–77 when they won the Division Two title and also played in the team that won the Anglo Scottish Cup during the same season. In September 1977 he lost his place to new signing Peter Shilton and soon afterwards moved on to Derby County where he went on to make over 70 top-flight appearances before a shoulder injury led to his retirement. He won three caps for England U21s.

Ron Mitchell (Born: Lancaster, 13 February 1935. Died: Lancaster, 23 January 2017.) Ron Mitchell was a wing-half as a youngster before converting to full-back. He played for Preston North End's junior teams, then switched to Bolton-le-Sands before signing for Morecambe. Ron then moved on to Leeds United but made little impression during his season at Elland Road, making four senior appearances. He subsequently returned to Morecambe where he became a mainstay of the side over the next few seasons, featuring in the successful team of the early 1960s.

Ronnie Moran (Born: Liverpool, 28 February 1934. Died: 22 March 2017.) Ronnie Moran spent almost 50 years at Liverpool both as a player and a member of the club's backroom staff. Signed as a 15-year-old amateur he came up through the ranks and established himself as a regular at full-back during the 1954–55 season. He remained in the side for nearly a decade, contributing to the Division Two championship team in 1961–62 and making over 350 appearances. He also won representative honours for the Football League. He subsequently joined the famous Anfield Bootroom where he stayed until retirement in 1998, twice serving as caretaker manager.

Paul Morrison (Born: Aberdeen, 19 August 1974. Died: Aberdeen, 22 February 2017.) Paul Morrison was a winger who had a brief spell with Arbroath during the 1996–97 season but otherwise spent most of his football career playing in the Highland League and in the Juniors, turning out for Stonehaven, Cove Rangers, Culter and Lewis United.

Jack Moule (Born: Steeton, Yorkshire 4 July 1921. Died: Steeton, Yorkshire 11 October 2016.) Jack Moule was an outside-right who made 21 appearances for Leeds United during the Second World War, making his debut against Huddersfield Town on Christmas Day 1943. He later had a spell with Bradford City, where he appeared for the reserves, and then played in the Lancashire Combination for Morecambe and Barnoldswick.

Bobby Murdoch (Born: Garston, 25 January 1936 . Died: 12 February 2017.) Inside-forward Bobby Murdoch developed with South Liverpool before making a move to Anfield. He had a good run in the first team towards the end of the 1957–58 season but then lost his place and began a somewhat peripatetic career around the North West taking in Barrow, Stockport County, Carlisle United and Southport. He helped Carlisle gain promotion in 1961–62 but eventually left senior football to play for Wigan Athletic.

Eric Murray (Born: Symington, Ayrshire, 12 December 1941. Died: 7 November 2016.) Eric Murray made his debut for Kilmarnock as a centre-forward but was switched to right-half and went on to make almost 200 senior appearances for the club. He was the only ever-present in the Killie team which won the Scottish League title in 1964–65 and remained with the club until the summer of 1968 before finishing his career with St Mirren.

Max Murray (Born: Falkirk, 7 November 1935. Died: Falkirk, 5 September 2016.) Max Murray was still a Falkirk High School student when he made a memorable senior debut at the age of 17, scoring a hat-trick in Queen's Park's 7-1 win over Cowdenbeath in October 1953. He turned professional with Rangers and went on to top their scoring charts in three consecutive seasons, winning League championships in 1956–57 and 1958–59. After his time at Ibrox he was briefly at West Bromwich Albion and later turned out for Third Lanark, Clyde and Distillery. He was capped for Scotland Amateurs and U23s.

Pat Neil (Born: Portsmouth, 23 October 1937. Died: May 2017.) Pat Neil was an England schoolboy international who made his first-team debut for Portsmouth as a 17-year-old amateur in August 1955. He went on to play for Wolves, also as an amateur, and was a Cambridge University Blue in three consecutive seasons. Later he played for Pegasus and Corinthian Casuals before briefly returning to Pompey. He won 10 caps for England Amateurs.

Derek Neilson (Born: Leith, 23 January 1959. Died: 26 May 2017.) Goalkeeper Derek Neilson joined Dundee United as a youngster but his only first-team experience during his time at Tannadice came in loan spells with East Stirlingshire and Meadowbank Thistle. In the summer of 1980 he signed for Brechin City and over the next nine years he made over 280 appearances before moving on to Berwick Rangers where he took his total of senior appearances to more than 450.

David Nicol (Born: Fallin, Stirlingshire, 2 May 1936. Died: Stirling, 29 June 2016.) David Nicol was signed by Falkirk as a winger from Secondary Juvenile outfit Airth Castle Rovers, but in senior football he played as a right-back. Mostly a reserve throughout his career he managed just 10 first-team appearances, also turning out for Cowdenbeath, Airdrieonians and Stirling Albion.

Peter Noble (Born: Newcastle-upon-Tyne, 19 August 1944. Died: 6 May 2017.) Peter Noble was a forward who spent the best part of four seasons on the books at Newcastle United without ever establishing himself in the line-up. Moving on to Swindon Town in January 1968 he became a key figure in the team, playing every game as the Robins won promotion from the old Third Division in 1968–69 and gaining a League Cup winners' medal as they defeated Arsenal to win the trophy that season. Later he made over 200 appearances for Burnley where he captained the team and was a member of the side that won the Anglo Scottish Cup in 1968–69. He finished off at Blackpool, taking his total of senior appearances to just short of 700.

Ken Oakley (Born: Rhymney, 9 May 1929. Died: 2017.) Centre-forward Ken Oakley was principally a reserve in four seasons with Cardiff City, during which time his career was interrupted by a spell of National Service. He fared better in a season with Northampton Town before returning to South Wales where he went on to become a regular scorer for Ebbw Vale in a lengthy spell with the Welsh League club.

Norman Oakley (Born: Stockton, 4 June 1939. Died: 29 November 2016.) Goalkeeper Norman Oakley joined Doncaster Rovers from Wingate Welfare in April 1957, but failed to break into the first team at Belle Vue. However, after joining Hartlepools United he saw regular match action and his total of 193 appearances remains the second-highest by a goalkeeper for the club. He then had spells with Swindon Town and Grimsby Town before moving into non-league football with Boston United.

Anne O'Brien (Born: Inchicore, Dublin, 25 January 1956. Died: Rome, Italy, 29 August 2016.) Anne O'Brien was one of the pioneers of modern women's football in Ireland and went on to achieve great success playing in Europe. She played professionally in France for Rheims and then for several years in Italy. A five times winner of Serie A titles (with four different clubs: Lazio, Trani, Reggiana and AC Milan) she also won two Copa Italias. She is believed to be the first woman from the British Isles to sign for a professional European football team.

Jackie O'Connor (Born: Durham, 12 March 1929. Died: 10 February 2017.) Jackie O'Connor was an outside-left who developed with Bearpark Welfare Juniors and was a member of the Durham team that won the FA County Youth championship in 1946–47. He joined Hartlepools as an amateur in November 1947, signing professional forms the following month. However, he mostly featured in the reserve team in the North Eastern League, deputising on just two occasions in the first team. He later played for Spennymoor United and Consett.

Eddie O'Hara (Born: Glasgow, 28 October 1935. Died: October 2016.) Eddie O'Hara was an outside-left who was capped by Scotland Schools before going on to join Falkirk where he quickly established himself in the first team. He was a key player in the Bairns' team which won the Scottish Cup in 1957 and a year later signed for Everton along with team mate Alex Parker. Eddie went on to play for Rotherham United, Morton and Barnsley, before emigrating to South Africa. He won three caps for Scotland U23s.

Sid O'Linn (Born: Oudtshoorn, Cape Province, South Africa, 5 May 1927. Died: Randberg, South Africa, 11 December 2016.) Sid O'Linn was a winger who came to prominence as a teenager in South Africa before signing for the then First Division club Charlton Athletic in December 1947. He spent a decade at The Valley combining football with a career as a cricketer, playing for Kent in the County Championship between 1951 and 1954 as an opening batsman and stand-in wicket keeper. He played in the Currie Cup for both Transvaal and Western Province and appeared in seven Test matches for South Africa.

John O'Rourke (Born: Northampton, 11 February 1945. Died: Dorset, 7 July 2016.) John O'Rourke was a goalscoring forward who was particularly effective in the air. An apprentice with Arsenal, he joined the professional ranks at Stamford Bridge but his only first-team opportunity for the Blues came in a Football League Cup tie. He moved on to Luton Town in December 1963 where he became a prolific scorer, netting 66 goals from 90 appearances. Later his goals would fire both Middlesbrough (1966–67) and Ipswich Town (1967–68) to promotion. He later played for Coventry City and Queens Park Rangers before concluding his career with a spell at Bournemouth. He won a single cap for England U23s.

Dave Pacey (Born: Luton, 2 October 1936. Died: 6 September 2016.) Dave Pacey played at wing-half for Hitchin Town, signing professional forms for Luton Town in August 1956. After making his debut at Old Trafford on Christmas Day 1957 he quickly became a regular and went on to make over 250 appearances for the Hatters. The highlight of his career came when he gained an FA Cup runners-up medal in 1959, scoring his team's goal in the 2-1 defeat to Nottingham Forest. He won a single cap for England U23s.

Granville Palin (Born: Armthorpe, South Yorkshire, 13 February 1940. Died: 9 September 2016.) Granville Palin developed as a centre-half with Wolverhampton Wanderers' nursery club Wath Wanderers before moving south to sign a contract for the Molineux club. He captained the side that won the FA Youth Cup in 1958, but was unable to break into the first team at Wolves and moved on to Walsall in the summer of 1960. He helped the Saddlers win promotion to the old Second Division in 1960–61 and went on to make over 100 first-team appearances, mostly at right-back.

Bill Park (Born: Gateshead, 23 February 1919. Died: Newton Abbot, Devon, 19 July 2016.) Half-back Bill Park was spotted by Blackpool whilst playing for Felling Red Star and signed on amateur forms at the age of 16. He switched to professional status on turning 17, and made three first-team appearances in the 1938–39 season. During the war he guested for Distillery, Gateshead and Middlesbrough and once peacetime football returned he moved on to spend the 1946–47 season at York City. At the time of his death he was believed to be Blackpool's oldest surviving player.

Ray Paul (Born: 1923. Died: 15 April 2017.) Ray Paul was an inside forward who was on the books of Nuneaton Borough for most of the 1940s. He appeared in wartime football for both Coventry City and Nottingham Forest.

George Peebles (Born: 22 April 1938. Died: Stirling, October 2016.) George Peebles was an outside-right who signed provisional forms with Falkirk in August 1952, but he was never called up by the Bairns and instead signed for Dunfermline Athletic in 1955. He went on to make over 400 senior appearances for the Pars and played in the club's 1961 Scottish Cup winning team when they defeated Celtic in the final replay. He subsequently spent time with Stirling Albion before moving into coaching, and later served as manager of Stirling between December 1986 and March 1988.

Fred Perry (Born: Cheltenham, 30 October 1933. Died: 11 July 2016.) Fred Perry was a full-back who joined Liverpool from Worthing in the summer of 1954. However, in two-and-a-half seasons at Anfield he managed just a solitary first-team appearance, against Blackburn Rovers on New Year's Eve 1955. He later played for Sittingbourne before his career ended tragically after he lost a leg following a car accident.

John Phillips (Born: Shrewsbury, 7 July 1951. Died: March 2017.) Goalkeeper John Phillips developed at Shrewsbury Town under the guidance of manager Harry Gregg before being sold to Aston Villa in October 1969. He was soon on his way again, this time to Chelsea and in a decade at Stamford Bridge he made over 150 appearances, although for most of this period he was only second choice. He later had brief spells at Brighton & Hove Albion and Charlton Athletic. He won four full caps for Wales.

Tony Potrac (Born: Westminster, London, 21 January 1953. Died: 2017.) Tony Potrac was an apprentice with Chelsea, turning professional at the age of 17. His only senior appearance came at outside-right against Huddersfield Town in January 1972. He subsequently moved on to Notts County, where he was unable to break into the first team, then spent two seasons in South Africa with Durban City before returning to play for Bexley United.

Jack Pratt (Born: Workington, 5 May 1916. Died: Grange-Over-Sands, Lancs, 5 August 2016.) Jack Pratt was a goalkeeper who joined Preston North End from Whitehaven Athletic in early 1935 and made a number of reserve-team appearances. He was an emergency signing for Blackburn Rovers in late April 1936 after Rovers' three professional 'keepers were all ruled out through injury. He went on to make eight senior appearances for Rovers and later appeared for North-Eastern League club Workington before going on to feature for Carlisle United during 1939–40. He was Blackburn Rovers' oldest former player at the time of his death.

Derek Presley (Born: Warminster, 8 March 1930. Died: 2016.) Derek Presley was a right-half who joined Bristol City from Warminster Town in March 1950. However, he was mostly a reserve during his time at Ashton Gate and after two seasons he moved on to join Bristol Rovers but failed to break into the first team at Eastville.

Jim Pressdee (Born: Swansea, 19 June 1933. Died: South Africa, 20 July 2016.) Jim Pressdee captained the Wales Schoolboy team and went on to sign for Swansea Town. A full back, he later featured for Wales at youth international level and made a handful of first-team appearances during a five-year spell at the Vetch Field before moving on to Brecon Corinthians and Llanelly. He was much better known for his exploits as a cricketer, making 347 first class appearances for Glamorgan (1949 to 1965) and North-Eastern Transvaal (1965 to Jan 1970), scoring over 14,000 runs and taking 481 wickets as a slow left-arm bowler.

David Provan (Born: Falkirk, 11 March 1941. Died: November 2016.) David Provan signed for Rangers in the summer of 1958 but it was a further five years before he established himself in the line-up, taking over the left-back slot from Eric Caldow. He was a member of the club's treble-winning team of 1963–64 and also won the Scottish Cup in 1963 and 1966 and the League Cup in 1964–65, while he played in the 1967 European Cup Winners' Cup final. On moving south he had a brief and unsuccessful time at Crystal Palace, but did well at Plymouth Argyle where he was the club's Player of the Year for 1971–72. He was manager of Albion Rovers from November 1987 to October 1991, leading the club to the Second Division title in 1988–89. He won five caps for Scotland.

Roy Proverbs (Born: Wednesbury, Staffs, 8 July 1932. Died: 15 February 2017.) Roy Proverbs was a tough and uncompromising defender who signed for Coventry City in April 1956. He featured fairly regularly in the first half of the 1956–57 season but then lost his place and moved on to Bournemouth. Unable to break in to the side at Dean Court he switched to Gillingham where he enjoyed the best years of his career, with four seasons of regular first-team football. He subsequently played for a number of non-league clubs including Canterbury City, Tunbridge Wells United, King's Lynn and Banbury United.

Jack Rawlings (Born: Hackney, 18 June 1923. Died: 21 September 2016.) Jack Rawlings was an amateur inside-forward who made six wartime appearances for Clapton Orient in 1940–41 scoring three goals. He then joined the forces, returning to football in January 1947 when he signed for Athenian League club Enfield. He was capped 12 times for England Amateurs and also played for Great Britain in the 1948 Olympic Games. After leaving Enfield in 1949 he spent six years with Hayes before finishing his career at Hendon.

Martin Reagan (Born: Newcastle-upon-Tyne, 12 May 1924. Died: Kirk Hammerton, North Yorkshire, 26 December 2016.) Martin Reagan was a very pacy winger who played in the York first team as an amateur at the age of 17 and made a number of wartime appearances when on leave from the army. When peacetime football returned he was quickly snapped up by Hull City and then went on to briefly partner Wilf Mannion on the right flank for Middlesbrough. Further moves to Shrewsbury Town and Portsmouth followed before he concluded his senior career at Norwich City having played over 150 senior games. He moved into coaching and in 1979 he was appointed manager of the England women's team which was a post he held until 1991, leading the team to the final of the 1984 European Championships when they lost out to Sweden over two legs.

Fred Richardson (Born: Spennymoor, Co Durham, 18 August 1925. Died: 28 July 2016.) Fred Richardson was a centre-forward who played in the 1946 FA Amateur Cup final for Bishop Auckland and was signed afterwards by Chelsea. He only featured in two senior games during his time at Stamford Bridge but was a prolific scorer for the reserves, netting 41 goals before moving back north in October 1947. He went on to have two spells at Hartlepool United as well as playing for Barnsley, West Bromwich Albion and Chester, making over 250 senior appearances.

John Richardson (Born: Worksop, 20 April 1945. Died: Derby, 21 January 2017.) John Richardson was a right-back who was Derby County's first apprentice professional. He went on to sign full professional forms at the age of 17 and was still a teenager when he made his debut for the Rams. He completed over 100 first-team appearances, but fell out of favour following the arrival of Brian Clough as manager before moving on to sign for Notts County. He made just one senior start for the Magpies plus a couple of brief appearances as a substitute before injury ended his career.

Norman Rimmington (Born: Staincross, Barnsley 29 November 1923. Died: 29 December 2016.) Goalkeeper Norman Rimmington made three wartime appearances for Barnsley in 1944–45 and featured regularly in the first post-war season. Unable to win a place in the side in 1947–48 he moved on to Hartlepools where he quickly established himself in the side and was an ever-present in 1948–49. After leaving Pools he eventually returned to Oakwell, serving the club in a variety of roles over the next 50 years or so and he was awarded (posthumously) the British Empire Medal in the 2017 New Year's honour's list for services to football and the community in Barnsley.

Bob Ritchie (Born: Glasgow, 1 Feb 1920. Died: 5 May 2017.) Inside-forward Bob Ritchie played in army football during the war and then with Rickmansworth Town before joining Watford in February 1948. His only senior appearance came for the Hornets at Port Vale in January 1949. He subsequently played briefly for Margate and then Bury Town.

Tommy Ross (Born: Tain, Ross-shire, 27 February 1947. Died: 18 May 2017.) Tommy Ross joined Ross County as a teenager and developed into a prolific goal scorer. In November 1964, aged just 17, he scored what is believed to be the fastest hat-trick in football, netting three times in just 90 seconds against Nairn County. In the summer of 1965 he signed for Peterborough United but was mostly a reserve in two seasons at London Road. A move to York City brought regular first-team action in 1967–68 when he was second-top scorer. Following this he played in non-league football notably for Wigan Athletic and Scarborough before returning north.

Len Saward (Born: Aldershot, 6 July 1927. Died: 7 March 2017.) Len Saward was an inside-forward who was mostly a reserve during his time with Crystal Palace. Released at the end of the 1950–51 campaign, he spent a season in the Southern League with Tonbridge before joining Cambridge United, then members of the Eastern Counties League. He scored the first goal in United's FA Cup victory over Football League side Newport County and later signed for the South Wales club. He returned to Cambridge in March 1955 and went on to play for Sudbury Town, Newmarket Town and Soham Town Rangers.

Jackie Sewell (Born: Kells, Cumberland 24 January 1927. Died: Nottingham, 26 September 2016.) Jackie Sewell played for Notts County during the war and helped the Magpies to the Division Three South title in 1949–50. When he left Meadow Lane for Sheffield Wednesday in March 1951, his goals tally constituted a club record, as did his transfer fee of £34,500. He helped the Owls win the Second Division title in 1951–52 and was an FA Cup winner with Aston Villa (1957). He visited Canada (1950) and Australia (1951) with FA touring teams and won six caps for England.

Duncan Sharp (Born: Barnsley, 16 March 1933. Died: Penistone, 21 October 2016.) Duncan Sharp developed in the Barnsley junior teams, and was rewarded with a professional contract shortly after reaching the age of 17. He went on to become a powerful no-nonsense centre-half who was a first-team regular for the best part of five seasons, making over 200 first-team appearances before retiring from football at the age of 29.

Dave Shipperley (Born: Uxbridge, 12 April 1952. Died: 21 January 2017.) Dave Shipperley was a huge centre-half who was effective in the air and offered a considerable physical presence in the centre of defence. A product of the Charlton Athletic youth set-up, he made his first-team debut as an 18-year-old. After over 100 appearances he moved on to Gillingham, where he was Player of the Year in 1975–76 before returning for a second spell with the Addicks. After a couple of seasons with Reading he left senior football.

Billy Simpson (Born: Belfast, 12 December 1929. Died: 27 January 2017.) Billy Simpson was an old-fashioned centre-forward who made his name with Linfield before signing for Rangers in October 1950. He enjoyed a successful career at Ibrox, making over 200 first-team appearances and featuring in European Cup action. Billy won three Scottish League championship medals and two Scottish Cup medals before winding down his career with spells at Stirling Albion, Partick Thistle and the then Southern League club Oxford United. He won 12 caps for Northern Ireland, scoring the decisive goal in a 3-2 victory over England at Wembley in November 1957 which was his country's first win against England for 30 years.

Mel Slack (Born: Bishop Auckland 7 March 1944. Died: Cambridge, 6 August 2016.) Mel Slack was a tough-tackling midfield player who spent his formative years with Sunderland but received few senior opportunities on Wearside. He moved to Southend United in August 1965 where he made over 100 first-team appearances and then on to Cambridge United. Mel played in the club's first-ever Fourth Division game against Lincoln City but was released at the end of the 1970–71 season and joined Cambridge City.

Alan Smith (Born: Birkenhead, 8 June 1939. Died: 27 August 2016.) Alan Smith was a centre-half who joined Torquay United from Port Sunlight and went on to make his debut in the final game of the 1957–58 season. It was not until early 1962 that he established himself in the Gulls' line-up, but he then went on to make over 300 first-team appearances for the club. A tough and uncompromising defender his career was ended by injury.

Harry Smith (Born: Wolverhampton, 10 October 1932. Died: Torquay, 23 December 2016.) Harry Smith was a defender who signed for Torquay United in January 1954. By the end of the year he had established himself in the line-up at left-back and he went to make over 200 senior appearances during his time at Plainmoor. His solitary goal came from the penalty spot in his final game for the club at Newport County in April 1961. Following an unproductive season at Bristol City he moved into non-league football, signing for Dorchester Town.

John Smith (Born. circa 1930. Died. Pembury, Kent, 3 August 2016.) John Smith was a wing-half who won Scottish Junior international honours before moving up to the seniors with Stirling Albion in November 1949. He made almost 200 appearances during his time at Annfield then spent two further seasons with Dumbarton where he switched to playing at inside-forward. He subsequently played for Tonbridge in the Southern League before injury ended his career.

Sammy Smyth (Born: Belfast, 25 February 1925. Died: Grand Cayman, Cayman Islands, 19 October 2016.) Sammy Smyth was the last survivor of the Wolverhampton Wanderers team which won the 1949 FA Cup final in which he scored Wolves' crucial third goal to ensure their victory over Leicester City. His career began in Northern Ireland where he won an Amateur international cap and appeared for the Irish League representative team before joining Wolves from Linfield. He made over 100 appearances during his time at Molineux then continued in top flight football with Stoke City and Liverpool before moving back to Northern Ireland to become player-manager of Bangor. He scored twice on his debut for Northern Ireland and won a total of nine caps.

Ray Spencer (Born: Birmingham, 25 March 1933. Died: 2016.) Ray Spencer was capped for England Schoolboys and went on to join the groundstaff at Aston Villa but failed to break into the first team and moved on to Darlington towards the end of 1957–58. A versatile player who appeared across the half-back line and at inside-forward, Ray made over 100 appearances for the Quakers, later spending three seasons with Torquay United before switching to non-league football with Bath City and Bridgwater Town.

Gary Sprake (Born: Winch Wen, Swansea, 3 April 1945. Died: 18 October 2016.) Gary Sprake was a goalkeeper who was capped by Wales Schools and joined Leeds United as an apprentice. He went on to become the club's first-choice 'keeper for a decade, making over 500 appearances. He won a Second Division winners medal in 1963–64, followed by the Football League Cup in 1967–68, a First Division championship in 1968–69, and two Inter Cities Fairs Cup winners' medals (1968 and 1971). He made his international debut for Wales at the age of 18 and went on to win 37 caps for his country. He concluded his career at Birmingham City before injury led to his retirement.

Eric Stevenson (Born: Eastfield, Lanarkshire, 25 December 1942. Died: Dalkeith, Midlothian, 17 May 2017.) Eric Stevenson was a skilful, entertaining winger who left school at 15 and worked down the pit before joining Hibernian in October 1960. He spent 11 years at Easter Road, making over 350 first-team appearances during his stay. He received representative honours for the Scottish League XI before concluding his career with Ayr United.

Rab Stewart (Born: Airdrie, 3 January 1962. Died: 21 August 2016.) Rab Stewart was a striker who developed with Whitburn Bluebell before signing for Dunfermline Athletic in the summer of 1981. After 70 appearances for the Pars he moved on to Motherwell where he was joint-top scorer in the team that won the First Division title in 1984–85. He went on to play for Falkirk and Queen of the South, taking his tally of appearances to just short of 300 before retiring from the game.

David Stride (Born: Lymington, Hampshire, 14 March 1958. Died: 10 July 2016.) David Stride was an apprentice with Chelsea before progressing to the senior ranks in January 1976. He developed into a left-back, later spending time in the United States with a number of clubs before returning to play for Millwall in January 1983. He was a member of the Lions' team that won the Group Cup final in 1982–83 before finishing his career with Leyton Orient.

Roy Summersby (Born: Lambeth, 19 March 1935. Died: Bury St Edmund's, Suffolk, 7 August 2016.) Roy Summersby came up through the ranks with Millwall and made his senior debut shortly after his 17th birthday. A goalscoring inside-forward, his best years were spent at Selhurst Park where he formed an effective striking partnership with Johnny Byrne and netted 25 goals in 1960–61 when the team won promotion from the Fourth Division. He subsequently had an unproductive spell at Portsmouth before switching to the Southern League with Chelmsford City for the 1965–66 season.

Dave Syrett (Born: Salisbury, 20 January 1956. Died: 26 July 2016.) Dave Syrett was capped by England Youths and made his first-team debut for Swindon at the age of 17. He went on to play for Mansfield Town, Walsall, Peterborough United and Northampton Town, making over 350 senior appearances. He was a useful goalscorer for most of his clubs as evidenced by a career tally of 108 goals in senior football; he was most effective when playing off a big strike partner.

Dave Taylor (Born: Rochester, 17 September 1940. Died: 12 March 2017.) Dave Taylor was an inside-forward who started his career with Gillingham and later spent a season at Portsmouth before following his former Pompey manager Basil Hayward to Yeovil Town in the summer of 1960. He went on to establish a post-war record of 284 goals in 436 appearances during his nine years with the Glovers, winning the Southern League title in 1963–64 and the League Cup in 1960–61 and 1965–66.

George Taylor (Born: circa 1930. Died: 2017.) George Taylor was a defender who started out as a right-back before switching to centre-half. He was a regular for Scotland Amateurs in the second half of the 1950s winning 15 caps and captaining Hounslow Town in the 1962 FA Amateur Cup final when they lost to Crook Town after a replay.

Graham Taylor, OBE (Born: Worksop, 15 September 1944. Died: Kings Langley, Herts, 12 January 2017.) Graham Taylor was a neat and tidy full-back who captained both Grimsby and Lincoln City, making over 150 appearances for both clubs before a long-standing injury ended his playing career. In December 1972 he became the Football League's youngest manager at the age of 28 when he was appointed as the Imps' boss. He built the team that enjoyed a record-breaking season in 1975–76 when they won the Fourth Division title, and in the summer of 1977 he moved to Watford. In six seasons he took the Hornets from the basement division to runners-up in the First Division. He enjoyed further success at Aston Villa and from July 1990 to November 1993 he was manager of the England team. His reign ended when they failed to qualify for the 1994 World Cup finals. He returned to club management with Wolverhampton Wanderers, Watford and Aston Villa and later worked as pundit for radio and television.

Harry Taylor (Born: Crawcrook, Gateshead, 5 October 1935. Died: 5 January 2017.) Harry Taylor was a winger who joined Newcastle United as a teenager. However, he never really established himself at St James' Park and his time was interrupted by a spell of National Service in the REME during which he made a number of appearances on loan to Fulham. On leaving the Magpies he played in the Southern League for Chelmsford City and Cambridge United.

John Taylor (Born: Creswell, Derbyshire, 11 January 1939. Died: Brimington Common, Derbyshire, 2016.) John Taylor was a forward who had been on Chesterfield's books as an amateur before signing professional terms for Mansfield Town. He made five appearances for the Stags in the 1959–60 season and then moved on to Peterborough United where he managed just a single outing in the club's first-ever Football League campaign.

John Telfer (Born: Douglas, Lanarkshire, 1933. Died: Ayr, 14 April 2017.) John Telfer signed for Ayr United from Douglas Water Thistle in December 1956. He very quickly established himself in the line-up at left-back and was a regular in the side that won the Second Division title in 1958–59. He remained at Somerset Park until the end of the 1960–61 season, making close on 100 first-team appearances during his time with the club.

Ernie Till (Born: Edinburgh, 28 February 1919. Died: Edinburgh, 22 November 2016.) Ernie Till was a wing-half who joined Raith Rovers shortly after the start of the 1938–39 campaign. He went on to spend 13 seasons on the books of the Kirkcaldy club, but much of this was interrupted by wartime when he appeared for both Rovers and Hibernian. He was a member of the Raith team that won the Second Division title in 1948–49 and concluded his career with spells at Arbroath and Leith. He featured in Leith's final Scottish League fixture, against Falkirk 'A' in April 1953.

Rex Tilley (Born: Swindon, 16 February 1929. Died: Carbis Bay, near St Ives, Cornwall, 14 May 2016.) Inside-forward Rex Tilley joined Plymouth Argyle from Chippenham in March 1951 and enjoyed four good seasons at Home Park making over 100 appearances. He subsequently returned to Wiltshire, adding further appearances for Swindon Town before moving on to Trowbridge Town.

Cheick Tiote (Born: Yamoussoukro, Ivory Coast, 21 June 1986. Died: Beijing, China, 5 June 2017.) Cheick Tiote was a combative defensive midfield player who developed as a youngster with Anderlecht and then with FC Twente. In August 2010 he signed for Newcastle United and he went on to make over 150 first-team appearances during his stay on Tyneside. In February 2017 he signed for Beijing Enterprises and featured regularly until his sudden death at the age of 30. Cheick played more than 50 international games for Ivory Coast.

Laurie Topp (Born: St Pancras, 11 November 1923. Died: 8 January 2017.) Laurie Topp was a right-half who made almost 600 appearances for Hendon during a 17-year career with the club during which he was a member of three Athenian League title-winning teams and also gained an FA Amateur Cup winners' medal in 1960. He played for England Amateurs regularly over a 10-year period winning 32 caps, and also represented Great Britain in both the 1952 and 1956 Olympic Games.

Liam Tuohy (Born: Dublin, 27 April 1933. Died: 13 August 2016.) Liam Tuohy was a skilful winger who made a big impact on the wing for Shamrock Rovers in the 1950s, assisting them to three League of Ireland titles and two FAI Cup wins. He joined Newcastle United in May 1960 and made 42 appearances for the Magpies over the next three seasons before returning to Shamrock as player-manager. He led the Hoops to six consecutive FAI Cup wins from 1964 and later had spells as manager of both Dundalk and the Republic of Ireland national team. As a player he won eight caps for the Republic of Ireland.

Tony Turley (Born: London, October 1945. Died: December 2016.) Tony Turley was a striker who played for a number of clubs including Finchley, St Albans City, Enfield, Barnet and Ilford. Tony made five appearances for England Amateurs and also played for the Athenian League representative team. He appeared in the 1972 FA Amateur Cup final for Enfield and was also in the Ilford team which lost in the last Amateur Cup final in 1974.

Roy Turnbull (Born: Edinburgh, 22 October 1948. Died: 15 May 2017.) Roy Turnbull was an inside-forward who made a single substitute's appearance for Heart of Midlothian in November 1968 before heading south to sign for Lincoln City. However, he was mostly a reserve at Sincil Bank too and his only start in senior football came the following season for Berwick Rangers. He subsequently played for Hawick Royal Albert for a number of seasons.

Francois Van der Elst (Born: Opwijk, Belgium, 1 December 1954. Died: Aalst, Belgium, 11 January 2017.) Francois Van der Elst made his name with Anderlecht, with whom he won the European Cup Winners' Cup in 1976 and 1978. He spent time in the NASL with New York Cosmos, helping them win the 1980 Soccer Bowl before signing for West Ham United in December 1981. He spent 18 months with the Hammers, making over 50 appearances before moving on to KSC Lokeren. He won 44 caps for Belgium.

Harold Waller (Born: 1921. Died: Bempton, nr. Bridlington, 6 December 2016.) Harold Waller was a wartime player for Rotherham United. A winger, he made 17 appearances scoring four goals for the Millers in the emergency competitions in the 1943–44 season.

Tom Wardrop (Born: Dundee, circa 1931. Died: Bonnyrigg, Midlothian, 14 September 2016.) Tom Wardrop was an inside-left who signed for East Fife from Loanhead Mayflower. He played almost exclusively in the reserves during his time at Bayview, with his single senior appearance coming in a goalless draw against East Stirlingshire in November 1958.

Dennis Warner (Born: Rotherham, 6 December 1930. Died: 6 December 2016.) Full-back Dennis Warner spent five seasons on the books of Rotherham United in the mid-1950s, making over 50 appearances. He later had a season at Chesterfield before winding down his career with spells at Gainsborough Trinity and Worksop Town.

Paul Went (Born: Bromley-by-Bow, Middlesex, 12 October 1949. Died: Chelmsford, 4 January 2017.) Paul Went became Leyton Orient's youngest player when he made his senior debut at the age of 15 and developed into a powerful defender, representing England Youths. He went on to make over 500 senior appearances in a career that also saw him play for Charlton Athletic, Fulham, Portsmouth and Cardiff City.

Brian Whitehouse (Born: West Bromwich, 8 September 1935. Died: 16 January 2017.) Brian Whitehouse joined West Bromwich Albion as a teenager but he struggled to gain a regular place in the line-up. He fared better when dropping down the divisions and he made a useful contribution to Wrexham's promotion campaign in 1961–62 while two seasons later he helped Palace win promotion as well. Initially a centre- or inside-forward, he dropped back to defence later in his career, concluding with spells at Charlton Athletic and Leyton Orient. Injury ended his playing days and he subsequently turned to coaching with Luton Town, Arsenal, West Bromwich Albion and Manchester United.

Neil Wilkinson (Born: Blackburn, 16 February 1955. Died: 2 August 2016.) Neil Wilkinson was a full-back who spent four seasons as a professional with Blackburn Rovers in the early 1970s, mostly on the fringes of the first team. After spells with Great Harwood and Port Vale he joined Crewe Alexandra where he was a regular in the 1978–79 and 1979–80 seasons before moving to play in South Africa.

Alan Willey (Born: Exeter, 16 September 1941. Died: April 2017.) Alan Willey was an inside-forward who signed for the then Southern League club Oxford United in December 1960. He featured in the U's debut Football League season and became their first-ever used substitute when he came off the bench against Bristol Rovers in September 1965. After 96 appearances for the U's he spent just over a season at Millwall then went on to play in South Africa for Durban City and Port Elizabeth City.

Alan Williams (Born: Bristol, 3 January 1938. Died: 18 May 2017.) Alan Williams was a brave and solid centre-half who made over 600 senior appearances in a career that spanned the period 1955 to 1972. After joining Bristol City from school he featured regularly from the 1957–58 season before moving on to Oldham Athletic in the 1961 close season. He was an ever-present for the Latics when they won promotion from the Fourth Division in 1962–63 and went on to play for Watford, Newport County and Swansea Town, winning a second promotion with the Swans in 1969–70.

Clarrie Williams (Born: Felling, Gateshead, 13 January 1933. Died: Cleethorpes, 14 January 2017.) Clarrie Williams was a goalkeeper who made over 200 senior appearances for Grimsby Town. He was an ever-present in 1955–56 when the Mariners won the Division Three North championship, setting a club record of 25 clean sheets and not conceding a goal in the final eight games of the season. He finished his playing career at Barnsley before returning to Grimsby to join the backroom staff.

Alex Young (Born: Loanhead, 3 February 1937. Died: Edinburgh, 27 February 2017.) Alex Young was a prodigiously talented football who enjoyed success in club football on both sides of the Border. After joining Heart of Midlothian in September 1954 he went on to gain a Scottish Cup winners' medal in 1956 to which he added two League titles (1957–58, 1959–60) and a League Cup award (1959–60). Midway through the 1960–61 season he was sold to Everton for a substantial fee and he quickly became an object of adoration for the club's supporters. Given the title 'The Golden Vision' he helped the Toffees to the Football League title in 1962–63 and the FA Cup four years later. After losing his place at Goodison he had a brief spell as player-manager of Glentoran then played for Stockport County before injury ended his career. He won eight full caps for Scotland.

Ian Nannestad, Soccer History Magazine
www.soccer-history.co.uk

THE FOOTBALL RECORDS

BRITISH FOOTBALL RECORDS

ALL-TIME PREMIER LEAGUE CHAMPIONSHIP SEASONS ON POINTS AVERAGE

	Team	Season	P	W	D	L	F	A	Pts	Pts Av
1	Chelsea	2004–05	38	29	8	1	72	15	95	2.50
2	Chelsea	2016–17	38	30	3	5	85	33	93	2.45
3	Manchester U	1999–2000	38	28	7	3	97	45	91	2.39
4	Chelsea	2005–06	38	29	4	5	72	22	91	2.39
5	Arsenal	2003–04	38	26	12	0	73	26	90	2.36
	Manchester U	2008–09	38	28	6	4	68	24	90	2.36
7	Manchester C	2011–12	38	28	5	5	93	29	89	2.34
	Manchester U	2006–07	38	28	5	5	83	27	89	2.34
	Manchester U	2012–13	38	28	5	5	86	43	89	2.34
10	Arsenal	2001–02	38	26	9	3	79	36	87	2.28
	Manchester U	2007–08	38	27	6	5	80	22	87	2.28
	Chelsea	2014–15	38	26	9	3	73	32	87	2.28
13	Chelsea	2009–10	38	27	5	6	103	32	86	2.26
	Manchester C	2013–14	38	27	5	6	102	37	86	2.26
15	Manchester U	1993–94	42	27	11	4	80	38	92	2.19
16	Manchester U	2002–03	38	25	8	5	74	34	83	2.18
17	Manchester U	1995–96	38	25	7	6	73	35	82	2.15
18	Leicester C	2015–16	38	23	12	3	68	36	81	2.13
19	Blackburn R	1994–95	42	27	8	7	80	39	89	2.11
20	Manchester U	2000–01	38	24	8	6	79	31	80	2.10
	Manchester U	2010–11	38	23	11	4	78	37	80	2.10
22	Manchester U	1998–99	38	22	13	3	80	37	79	2.07
23	Arsenal	1997–98	38	23	9	6	68	33	78	2.05
24	Manchester U	1992–93	42	24	12	6	67	31	84	2.00
25	Manchester U	1996–97	38	21	12	5	76	44	75	1.97

PREMIER LEAGUE EVER-PRESENT CLUBS

	P	W	D	L	F	A	Pts
Manchester U	962	604	209	149	1856	848	2021
Arsenal	962	525	247	190	1698	912	1822
Chelsea	962	516	241	205	1645	927	1789
Liverpool	962	478	243	241	1601	986	1677
Tottenham H	962	400	247	315	1406	1231	1447
Everton	962	349	277	336	1259	1207	1324

TOP TEN PREMIER LEAGUE APPEARANCES

1	Giggs, Ryan	632	6	Heskey, Emile	516
2	Barry, Gareth	628	7	Schwarzer, Mark	514
3	Lampard, Frank	609	8	Carragher, Jamie	508
4	James, David	572	9	Neville, Phil	505
5	Speed, Gary	534	10=	Ferdinand, Rio and Gerrard, Steven	504

TOP TEN PREMIER LEAGUE GOALSCORERS

1	Shearer, Alan	260	6	Fowler, Robbie	163
2	Rooney, Wayne	198	7	Defoe, Jermain	158
3	Cole, Andrew	187	8	Owen, Michael	150
4	Lampard, Frank	177	9	Ferdinand, Les	149
5	Henry, Thierry	175	10	Sheringham, Teddy	146

SCOTTISH PREMIER LEAGUE SINCE 1998–99

	P	*W*	*D*	*L*	*F*	*A*	*Pts*
Celtic	718	532	105	81	1689	551	1701
Rangers	566	383	103	80	1179	462	1242
Aberdeen	718	277	166	275	897	939	997
Hearts	680	269	168	243	892	827	960
Motherwell	718	252	155	311	903	1094	911
Kilmarnock	718	229	182	307	851	1056	869
Dundee U	680	214	184	282	842	1021	823
Hibernian	568	191	145	232	743	812	718

Rangers deducted 10 pts in 2011–12; Hearts deducted 15 pts in 2013–14; Dundee U deducted 3 pts in 2015–16.

DOMESTIC LANDMARKS 2016–17

AUGUST 2016

9 Manchester United sign Paul Pogba from Juventus for world record transfer fee of £89m, surpassing the £85m paid by Real Madrid for Gareth Bale in 2013.

31 Premier League clubs break the record spend in a transfer window spending over £1.1 billion. Thirteen Premier League clubs exceeded their respective transfer records during the summer transfer window: Bournemouth (Jordon Ibe – £15m), Burnley (Jeff Hendrick – £10.5m), Crystal Palace (Christian Benteke – £32m), Everton (Yannick Bolasie - £30m), Hull City (Ryan Mason – £13m), Leicester City (Islam Slimani – £29.7m), Manchester United (Paul Pogba – £89.3m), Southampton (Sofiane Boufal – £16m), Swansea City (Borja Baston – £15.5m), Watford (Roberto Pereyra – £13m), West Bromwich Albion (Nacer Chadli – £13m), West Ham United (Andre Ayew – £20.5m).

SEPTEMBER 2016

10 Dundee United goalkeeper Cammy Bell saves 3 penalties in the first half of the Scottish Championship match at Dunfermline Athletic. The heroics help Dundee United to a 3-1 victory.

13 Newcastle United equal their record away league winning margin with the 0-6 victory over QPR at Loftus Road in the EFL Championship. The defeat was also QPR's record league defeat.

17 Gareth Barry becomes only the third player to reach 600 Premier League appearances in Everton's 3-1 home defeat of Middlesbrough, scoring his side's first goal. The other players to reach the milestone are Ryan Giggs (632) and Frank Lampard (609).

24 Tony Pulis completes 1,000 games as a manager. His West Bromwich Albion side scored a last gasp equaliser in the 1-1 draw at Stoke City.

OCTOBER 2016

2 Arsène Wenger celebrates 20 years as Arsenal manager with 1-0 win over Burnley at Turf Moor. The disputed winner came in the final minute of injury time from Laurent Koscielny.

18 Leicester City become the first English team to win their first three Champions League games. Their 1-0 home victory over FC Copenhagen followed Group G victories over Club Brugge and Porto.

29 Sunderland make the worst start to a season in Premier League history. Their 4-1 home defeat at the hands of Arsenal equals Manchester City's total of only 2 points from their opening 10 Premier League games, but their inferior goal difference makes their start worse.

NOVEMBER 2016

5 East Kilbride of the Scottish Lowland League surpass Ajax's run of 26 consecutive victories with a 3-1 victory over BSC Glasgow.

24 Wayne Rooney becomes Manchester United's all-time European record goalscorer with his 39th European goal in the 4-0 Europa League Group A win over Feyenoord at Old Trafford.

27 Celtic win their 100th major trophy with a 3-0 victory over Aberdeen in the Scottish League Cup Final at Hampden Park.

29 Ben Woodburn creates Liverpool history by becoming the youngest player to score for the club at 17 years 45 days in the 2-0 League Cup victory over Leeds United at Anfield.

JANUARY 2017

7 Wayne Rooney equals Sir Bobby Charlton's all-time Manchester United top-scorer record with his 249th goal, scoring the first in a 4-0 victory of Reading in the FA Cup 3rd Round at Old Trafford.

21 Wayne Rooney becomes Manchester United's all-time top goalscorer with an injury-time equaliser at Stoke's Britannia Stadium in a 1-1 draw. His 250th goal for the club surpassed Sir Bobby Charlton's 40-year-old record of 249 goals. He also becomes the highest scorer of away goals in Premier League history with 88, passing Alan Shearer's total of 87.

FEBRUARY 2017

11 Manchester United become the first team in Premier League history to reach 2,000 points. Thanks to goals from Juan Mata and Anthony Martial they defeated Watford 2-0 at Old Trafford.

MAY 2017

21 Celtic become the first Scottish top-flight club to go through a whole league season unbeaten since 1899. On the way they also broke the previous points total of 103 by reaching 106 points in the season. A league record 34 wins and a highest goals total of 106 completed a season of records under manager Brendan Rodgers.

27 Arsène Wenger becomes the most successful manager in FA Cup history when his Arsenal side beat Chelsea 2-1 in the 2017 FA Cup final at Wembley. It was his seventh success in the competition as Arsenal produced an excellent all-round performance to defeat the Premier League champions. The previous holder of the record was George Ramsay of Aston Villa, who won it six times between 1887 and 1920.

EUROPEAN CUP AND CHAMPIONS LEAGUE RECORDS

MOST WINS BY CLUB

Real Madrid	12	1956, 1957, 1958, 1959, 1960, 1966, 1998, 2000, 2002, 2014, 2016, 2017.
AC Milan	7	1963, 1969, 1989, 1990, 1994, 2003, 2007.
Bayern Munich	5	1974, 1975, 1976, 2001, 2013.
Liverpool	5	1977, 1978, 1981, 1984, 2005.
Barcelona	5	1992, 2006, 2009, 2011, 2015.

MOST APPEARANCES IN FINAL
Real Madrid 15; AC Milan 11; Bayern Munich 10

MOST FINAL APPEARANCES PER COUNTRY
Spain 28 (17 wins, 11 defeats)
Italy 28 (12 wins, 16 defeats)
England 19 (12 wins, 7 defeats)
Germany 17 (7 wins, 10 defeats)

MOST CHAMPIONS LEAGUE/EUROPEAN CUP APPEARANCES
168 Iker Casillas (Real Madrid, Porto)
157 Xavi (Barcelona)
151 Ryan Giggs (Manchester U)
144 Raul (Real Madrid, Schalke)
144 Cristiano Ronaldo (Manchester U, Real Madrid)
139 Paolo Maldini (AC Milan)
130 Clarence Seedorf (Ajax, Real Madrid, Internazionale, AC Milan)
130 Paul Scholes (Manchester U)
128 Roberto Carlos (Internazionale, Real Madrid, Fenerbahce)
127 Xabi Alonso (Real Sociedad, Liverpool, Real Madrid, Bayern Munich)
124 Andreas Iniesta (Barcelona)
123 Zlatan Ibrahimovic (Ajax, Juventus, Internazionale, Barcelona, AC Milan, Paris Saint-Germain)

MOST WINS WITH DIFFERENT CLUBS
Clarence Seedorf (Ajax) 1995; (Real Madrid) 1998; (AC Milan) 2003, 2007.

MOST WINNERS MEDALS
6 Francisco Gento (Real Madrid) 1956, 1957, 1958, 1959, 1960, 1966.
5 Alfredo Di Stefano (Real Madrid) 1956, 1957, 1958, 1959, 1960.
5 Jose Maria Zarraga (Real Madrid) 1956, 1957, 1958, 1959, 1960.
5 Paolo Maldini (AC Milan) 1989, 1990, 1994, 2003, 2007.

CHAMPIONS LEAGUE BIGGEST WINS
HJK Helsinki 10, Bangor C 0 19.7.2011
Liverpool 8 Besiktas 0 6.11.2007
Real Madrid 8 Malmo 0 8.12.2015

MOST SUCCESSIVE CHAMPIONS LEAGUE APPEARANCES
Real Madrid (Spain) 20 1997–98 to 2016–17.
Manchester U (England) 18: 1996–97 to 2013–14.

MOST SUCCESSIVE EUROPEAN CUP APPEARANCES
Real Madrid (Spain) 15: 1955–56 to 1969–70.

MOST SUCCESSIVE WINS IN THE CHAMPIONS LEAGUE
Barcelona (Spain) 11: 2002–03.

LONGEST UNBEATEN RUN IN THE CHAMPIONS LEAGUE
Manchester U (England) 25: 2007–08 to 2009 (Final).

MOST GOALS OVERALL
106 Cristiano Ronaldo (Manchester U, Real Madrid).
94 Lionel Messi (Barcelona).
71 Raul (Real Madrid, Schalke).
60 Ruud van Nistelrooy (PSV Eindhoven, Manchester U, Real Madrid).
58 Andriy Shevchenko (Dynamo Kyiv, AC Milan, Chelsea, Dynamo Kyiv).
51 Thierry Henry (Monaco, Arsenal, Barcelona).
51 Karim Benzema (Lyon, Real Madrid).
50 Filippo Inzaghi (Juventus, AC Milan).
49 Alfredo Di Stefano (Real Madrid).
49 Zlatan Ibrahimovic (Ajax, Juventus, Internazionale, Barcelona, AC Milan, Paris Saint-Germain).
47 Eusebio (Benfica).
44 Alessandro Del Piero (Juventus).
44 Didier Drogba (Marseille, Chelsea).

MOST GOALS IN CHAMPIONS LEAGUE MATCH
5 Lionel Messi, Barcelona v Bayer Leverkusen (25, 42, 49, 58, 84 mins) (7-1), 7.3.2012.
5 Luiz Adriano, Shaktar Donetsk v BATE (28, 36, 40, 44, 82 (0-7), 21.10.2014.

MOST GOALS IN ONE SEASON
17 Cristiano Ronaldo 2013–14
16 Cristiano Ronaldo 2015–16
14 Jose Altafini 1962–63
14 Ruud van Nistelrooy 2002–03
14 Lionel Messi 2011–12

MOST GOALS SCORED IN FINALS
7 Alfredo Di Stefano (Real Madrid), 1956 (1), 1957 (1 pen), 1958 (1), 1959 (1), 1960 (3).
7 Ferenc Puskas (Real Madrid), 1960 (4), 1962 (3).

HIGHEST SCORE IN A EUROPEAN CUP MATCH
European Cup
14 Feyenoord (Netherlands) 12, KR Reykjavik (Iceland) 2 *(First Round First Leg 1969–70)*
Champions League
12 Borussia Dortmund 8, Legia Warsaw 4 22.11.2016

HIGHEST AGGREGATE IN A EUROPEAN CUP MATCH
Benfica (Portugal) 18, Dudelange (Luxembourg) 0
8-0 (h), 10-0 (a) *(Preliminary Round 1965–66)*

FASTEST GOALS SCORED IN CHAMPIONS LEAGUE

10.2 sec	Roy Makaay for Bayern Munich v Real Madrid, 7.3.2007.
11.0 sec	Jonas for Valencia v Bayer Leverkusen, 1.11.2011.
20.07 sec	Gilberto Silva for Arsenal at PSV Eindhoven, 25.9.2002.
20.12 sec	Alessandro Del Piero for Juventus at Manchester U, 1.10.1997.

YOUNGEST CHAMPIONS LEAGUE GOALSCORER
Peter Ofori-Quaye for Olympiacos v Rosenborg at 17 years 195 days in 1997–98.

FASTEST HAT-TRICK SCORED IN CHAMPIONS LEAGUE
Bafetimbi Gomis, 8 mins for Lyon in Dinamo Zagreb v Lyon (1-7) 7.12.2011

FIRST TEAM TO SCORE SEVEN GOALS
Paris Saint-Germain 7, Rosenborg 2 24.10.2000

MOST GOALS BY A GOALKEEPER
Hans-Jorg Butt (for three different clubs)
Hamburg 13.9.2000, Bayer Leverkusen 12.5.2002, Bayern Munich 8.12.2009 – all achieved against Juventus.

LANDMARK GOALS CHAMPIONS LEAGUE
1st Daniel Amokachi, Club Brugge v CSKA Moscow 17 minutes 25.11.1992
1,000th Dmitri Khokhlov, PSV Eindhoven v Benfica 41 minutes 9.12.1998
5,000th Luisao, Benfica v Hapoel Tel Aviv 21 minutes 14.9.2010

HIGHEST SCORING DRAW
Hamburg 4, Juventus 4 13.9.2000
Chelsea 4, Liverpool 4 14.4.2009
Bayer Leverkusen 4, Roma 4 20.10.2015

MOST CLEAN SHEETS
10: Arsenal 2005–06 (995 minutes with two goalkeepers Manuel Almunia 347 minutes and Jens Lehmann 648 minutes).

EUROPEAN CUP AND CHAMPIONS LEAGUE RECORDS – continued

CHAMPIONS LEAGUE ATTENDANCES AND GOALS FROM GROUP STAGES ONWARDS

Season	*Attendances*	*Average*	*Goals*	*Games*
1992–93	873,251	34,930	56	25
1993–94	1,202,289	44,529	71	27
1994–95	2,328,515	38,172	140	61
1995–96	1,874,316	30,726	159	61
1996–97	2,093,228	34,315	161	61
1997–98	2,868,271	33,744	239	85
1998–99	3,608,331	42,451	238	85
1999–2000	5,490,709	34,973	442	157
2000–01	5,773,486	36,774	449	157
2001–02	5,417,716	34,508	393	157
2002–03	6,461,112	41,154	431	157
2003–04	4,611,214	36,890	309	125
2004–05	4,946,820	39,575	331	125
2005–06	5,291,187	42,330	285	125
2006–07	5,591,463	44,732	309	125
2007–08	5,454,718	43,638	330	125
2008–09	5,003,754	40,030	329	125
2009–10	5,295,708	42,366	320	125
2010–11	5,474,654	43,797	355	125
2011–12	5,225,363	41,803	345	125
2012–13	5,773,366	46,187	368	125
2013–14	5,713,049	45,704	362	125
2014–15	5,207,592	42,685	361	125
2015–16	5,116,690	40,934	347	125
2016–17	5,398,851	43,191	380	125

HIGHEST AVERAGE ATTENDANCE IN ONE EUROPEAN CUP SEASON

1959–60 50,545 from a total attendance of 2,780,000.

GREATEST COMEBACKS

Werder Bremen beat Anderlecht 5-3 after being three goals down in 33 minutes on 8.12.1993. They scored five goals in 23 second-half minutes.
Deportivo La Coruna beat Paris Saint-Germain 4-3 after being three goals down in 55 minutes on 7.3.2001. They scored four goals in 27 second-half minutes.
Liverpool after being three goals down to AC Milan in the first half on 25.5.2005 in the Champions League Final. They scored three goals in five second-half minutes and won the penalty shoot-out after extra time 3-2.
Liverpool three goals down to FC Basel in 29 minutes on 12.11.2002. They scored three second half goals in 24 minutes to draw 3-3.

MOST SUCCESSFUL MANAGER

Bob Paisley 3 wins, 1977, 1978, 1981 (Liverpool);
Carlo Ancelotti 3 wins, 2002–03, 2006–07 (AC Milan), 2013–14 (Real Madrid).

REINSTATED WINNERS EXCLUDED FROM NEXT COMPETITION

1993 Marseille originally stripped of title. This was rescinded but they were not allowed to compete the following season.

EUROPEAN LANDMARKS 2016–17

JUNE 2016

23 Alexis Sanchez made his 100th international appearance for Chile in their 2-0 victory over Colombia in the 2016 Copa America semi-final.

26 Nani made his 100th international appearance for Portugal in their dramatic late victory over Croatia in the round of 16 European Championship match. Ricardo Quaresma headed the winner deep into extra time to send Portugal into the quarter-finals.

SEPTEMBER 2016

18 Real Madrid equalled the record number of consecutive wins in La Liga history with their 16th win in succession with a 2-0 away victory at Espanyol.

OCTOBER 2016

29 Cristiano Ronaldo's 17th minute penalty in Real Madrid's 4-1 victory at Alaves was the 350th league goal of his career.

NOVEMBER 2016

10 Christian Benteke scored the fastest goal in World Cup qualifying history when he scored for Belgium after only 7 seconds against Gibraltar. The Group H qualifier ended Gilbraltar 0 Belgium 6, with Benteke going on to score a hat-trick.

23 Borussia Dortmund defeated Legia Warsaw 8-4 in the highest-scoring Champions League match in history. It was also the first match in Champions League history to see seven goals scored in the first half.

JANUARY 2017

12 Real Madrid set a new Spanish record for unbeaten matches as they drew 3-3 with Sevilla in the Copa del Rey to record their 40th consecutive unbeaten game. It took an injury-time equaliser from Karim Benzema to maintain the unbeaten run.

MARCH 2017

8 Barcelona made Champions League history with a stunning comeback to defeat Paris Saint-Germain 6-1 at the Nou Camp in the Round of 16 second leg tie. They had been 4-0 down from the first leg but recovered to reach the quarter-finals. No team had ever recovered from 4 goals down in Champions League history.

12 Real Madrid set a new word record for scoring in 48 consecutive matches as they defeated Real Betis 2-1 at the Bernabeu. The previous record of 47 by Benfica had stood for 52 years.

12 Fifty-year-old Kazuyoshi Miura broke Sir Stanley Matthews record for the oldest professional goalscorer. He scored the only goal as Yokohama defeated Thespa Kusatsu in the Japanese J-League.

12 Cristiano Ronaldo became the first player to reach 100 Champions League goals when he scored twice in Real Madrid's 2-1 win over Bayern Munich at the Allianz Areana. The 77th minute strike came 4,624 days after his first Champions League goal for Manchester United against Debrecen in 2005.

23 Lionel Messi scored his 500th goal in all competitions for Barcelona. The landmark was achieved with his 92nd minute winner against Real Madrid at the Bernabeau.

24 Gianluigi Buffon made his 1,000th appearance of his professional career in Italy's European Championship qualifier against Albania in Palermo. Buffon kept a clean sheet as Daniele de Rossi and Ciro Immobile scored in Italy's 2-0 victory.

MAY 2017

17 Cristiano Ronaldo breaks Jimmy Greaves' 46-year European scoring record as Real Madrid thrashed Celta Vigo 4-1. His two goals took him to 368 goals overtaking Greaves' tally of 366.

JUNE 2017

3 Real Madrid became the first team to make a successful defence of the UEFA Champions League. The 4-1 Champions League Final defeat of Juventus in Cardiff meant they had won 6 out of 6 Champions League Finals they had appeared in, with a total of 12 European Champions titles. When Ronaldo scored their first goal they became the first club to reach 500 Champions League goals.

3 Cristiano Ronaldo added to his ever-increasing list of records by becoming the first player to score in 3 UEFA Champions League Finals. He scored his 600th professional career goal.

TOP TEN PREMIER LEAGUE AVERAGE ATTENDANCES 2016–17		
1	Manchester U	75,290
2	Arsenal	59,957
3	West Ham U	56,972
4	Manchester C	54,019
5	Liverpool	53,016
6	Chelsea	41,508
7	Sunderland	41,287
8	Everton	39,310
9	Leicester C	31,893
10	Tottenham H	31,639

TOP TEN FOOTBALL LEAGUE AVERAGE ATTENDANCES 2016–17		
1	Newcastle U	51,106
2	Aston Villa	32,107
3	Derby Co	29,085
4	Brighton & HA	27,996
5	Leeds U	27,698
6	Sheffield W	27,129
7	Norwich C	26,354
8	Sheffield U	21,892
9	Wolverhampton W	21,570
10	Huddersfield T	20,343

TOP TEN AVERAGE ATTENDANCES			
1	Manchester U	2006–07	75,826
2	Manchester U	2007–08	75,691
3	Manchester U	2012–13	75,530
4	Manchester U	2011–12	75,387
5	Manchester U	2014–15	75,335
6	Manchester U	2008–09	75,308
7	Manchester U	2016–17	75,290
8	Manchester U	2015–16	75,279
9	Manchester U	2013–14	75,207
10	Manchester U	2010–11	75,109

TOP TEN AVERAGE WORLD CUP FINAL CROWDS			
1	In USA	1994	68,991
2	In Brazil	2014	52,621
3	In Germany	2006	52,491
4	In Mexico	1970	50,124
5	In South Africa	2010	49,669
6	In West Germany	1974	49,098
7	In England	1966	48,847
8	In Italy	1990	48,388
9	In Brazil	1950	47,511
10	In Mexico	1986	46,039

TOP TEN ALL-TIME ENGLAND CAPS		
1	Peter Shilton	125
2	Wayne Rooney	119
3	David Beckham	115
4	Steven Gerrard	114
5	Bobby Moore	108
6	Ashley Cole	107
7	Bobby Charlton	106
	Frank Lampard	106
9	Billy Wright	105
10	Bryan Robson	90

TOP TEN ALL-TIME ENGLAND GOALSCORERS		
1	Wayne Rooney	53
2	Bobby Charlton	49
3	Gary Lineker	48
4	Jimmy Greaves	44
5	Michael Owen	40
6	Tom Finney	30
	Nat Lofthouse	30
	Alan Shearer	30
9	Vivian Woodward	29
	Frank Lampard	29

GOALKEEPING RECORDS

(without conceding a goal)

FA PREMIER LEAGUE
Edwin van der Sar (Manchester U) in 1,311 minutes during the 2008–09 season.

FOOTBALL LEAGUE
Steve Death (Reading) 1,103 minutes from 24 March to 18 August 1979.

SCOTTISH PREMIER LEAGUE
Fraser Forster (Celtic) in 1,215 minutes from 6 December 2013 to 25 February 2014.

MOST CLEAN SHEETS IN A SEASON

Petr Cech (Chelsea) 24 2004–05

MOST CLEAN SHEETS OVERALL IN PREMIER LEAGUE

Petr Cech (Chelsea and Arsenal) 190 games.

MOST GOALS FOR IN A SEASON

FA PREMIER LEAGUE		Goals	Games
2009–10	Chelsea	103	38
FOOTBALL LEAGUE			
Division 4			
1960–61	Peterborough U	134	46
SCOTTISH PREMIER LEAGUE			
2016–17	Celtic	106	38
SCOTTISH LEAGUE			
Division 2			
1937–38	Raith R	142	34

MOST GOALS AGAINST IN A SEASON

FA PREMIER LEAGUE		Goals	Games
1993–94	Swindon T	100	42
FOOTBALL LEAGUE			
Division 2			
1898–99	Darwen	141	34
SCOTTISH PREMIER LEAGUE			
1999–2000	Aberdeen	83	36
SCOTTISH LEAGUE			
Division 2			
1931–32	Edinburgh C	146	38

MOST LEAGUE GOALS IN A SEASON

FA PREMIER LEAGUE		Goals	Games
1993–94	Andy Cole (Newcastle U)	34	40
1994–95	Alan Shearer (Blackburn R)	34	42
FOOTBALL LEAGUE			
Division 1			
1927–28	Dixie Dean (Everton)	60	39
Division 2			
1926–27	George Camsell (Middlesbrough)	59	37
Division 3(S)			
1936–37	Joe Payne (Luton T)	55	39
Division 3(N)			
1936–37	Ted Harston (Mansfield T)	55	41
Division 3			
1959–60	Derek Reeves (Southampton)	39	46
Division 4			
1960–61	Terry Bly (Peterborough U)	52	46
FA CUP			
1887–88	Jimmy Ross (Preston NE)	20	8
LEAGUE CUP			
1986–87	Clive Allen (Tottenham H)	12	9
SCOTTISH PREMIER LEAGUE			
2000–01	Henrik Larsson (Celtic)	35	37
SCOTTISH LEAGUE			
Division 1			
1931–32	William McFadyen (Motherwell)	52	34
Division 2			
1927–28	Jim Smith (Ayr U)	66	38

MOST FA CUP FINAL GOALS

Ian Rush (Liverpool) 5: 1986(2), 1989(2), 1992(1)

SCORED IN EVERY PREMIERSHIP GAME

Arsenal 2001–02: 38 matches

FEWEST GOALS FOR IN A SEASON

FA PREMIER LEAGUE		Goals	Games
2007–08	Derby Co	20	38
FOOTBALL LEAGUE			
Division 2			
1899–1900	Loughborough T	18	34
SCOTTISH PREMIER LEAGUE			
2010–11	St Johnstone	23	38
SCOTTISH LEAGUE			
New Division 1			
1980–81	Stirling Alb	18	39

FEWEST GOALS AGAINST IN A SEASON

FA PREMIER LEAGUE		Goals	Games
2004–05	Chelsea	15	38
FOOTBALL LEAGUE			
Division 1			
1978–79	Liverpool	16	42
SCOTTISH PREMIER LEAGUE			
2001–02	Celtic	18	38
SCOTTISH LEAGUE			
Division 1			
1913–14	Celtic	14	38

MOST LEAGUE GOALS IN A CAREER

FOOTBALL LEAGUE			
Arthur Rowley	*Goals*	*Games*	*Season*
WBA	4	24	1946–48
Fulham	27	56	1948–50
Leicester C	251	303	1950–58
Shrewsbury T	152	236	1958–65
	434	619	
SCOTTISH LEAGUE			
Jimmy McGrory			
Celtic	1	3	1922–23
Clydebank	13	30	1923–24
Celtic	396	375	1924–38
	410	408	

MOST HAT-TRICKS

Career
37: Dixie Dean (Tranmere R, Everton, Notts Co, England)

Division 1 (one season post-war)
6: Jimmy Greaves (Chelsea), 1960–61

Three for one team in one match
West, Spouncer, Hooper, Nottingham F v Leicester Fosse, Division 1, 21 April 1909
Loasby, Smith, Wells, Northampton T v Walsall, Division 3S, 5 Nov 1927
Bowater, Hoyland, Readman, Mansfield T v Rotherham U, Division 3N, 27 Dec 1932
Barnes, Ambler, Davies, Wrexham v Hartlepools U, Division 4, 3 March 1962
Adcock, Stewart, White, Manchester C v Huddersfield T, Division 2, 7 Nov 1987

MOST CUP GOALS IN A CAREER

FA CUP (pre-Second World War)
Henry Cursham 48 (Notts Co)

FA CUP (post-war)
Ian Rush 43 (Chester, Liverpool)

LEAGUE CUP
Geoff Hurst 49 (West Ham U, Stoke C)
Ian Rush 49 (Chester, Liverpool, Newcastle U)

GOALS PER GAME (Football League to 1991–92)

Goals per game	Division 1		Division 2		Division 3		Division 4		Division 3(S)		Division 3(N)	
	Games	Goals	Games	Goals	Games	Goals	Games	Goals	Games	Goals	Games	Goals
0	2465	0	2665	0	1446	0	1438	0	997	0	803	0
1	5606	5606	5836	5836	3225	3225	3106	3106	2073	2073	1914	1914
2	8275	16550	8609	17218	4569	9138	4441	8882	3314	6628	2939	5878
3	7731	23193	7842	23526	3784	11352	4041	12123	2996	8988	2922	8766
4	6229	24920	5897	23588	2837	11348	2784	11136	2445	9780	2410	9640
5	3752	18755	3634	18170	1566	7830	1506	7530	1554	7770	1599	7995
6	2137	12822	2007	12042	769	4614	786	4716	870	5220	930	5580
7	1092	7644	1001	7007	357	2499	336	2352	451	3157	461	3227
8	542	4336	376	3008	135	1080	143	1144	209	1672	221	1768
9	197	1773	164	1476	64	576	35	315	76	684	102	918
10	83	830	68	680	13	130	8	80	33	330	45	450
11	37	407	19	209	2	22	7	77	15	165	15	165
12	12	144	17	204	1	12	0	0	7	84	8	96
13	4	52	4	52	0	0	0	0	2	26	4	52
14	2	28	1	14	0	0	0	0	0	0	0	0
17	0	0	0	0	0	0	0	0	0	0	1	17
	38164	**117060**	**38140**	**113030**	**18768**	**51826**	**18631**	**51461**	**15042**	**46577**	**14374**	**46466**

Extensive research by statisticians has unearthed seven results from the early years of the Football League which differ from the original scores. These are 26 January 1889 Wolverhampton W 5 Everton 0 (not 4-0), 16 March 1889 Notts Co 3 Derby Co 5 (not 2-5), 4 January 1896 Arsenal 5 Loughborough 0 (not 6-0), 28 November 1896 Leicester Fosse 4 Walsall 2 (not 4-1), 21 April 1900 Burslem Port Vale 2 Lincoln C 1 (not 2-0), 25 December 1902 Glossop NE 3 Stockport Co 0 (not 3-1), 26 April 1913 Hull C 2 Leicester C 0 (not 2-1).

GOALS PER GAME (from 1992–93)

Goals per game	Premier		Championship/Div 1		League One/Div 2		League Two/Div 3	
	Games	Goals	Games	Goals	Games	Goals	Games	Goals
0	828	0	1131	0	1074	0	1093	0
1	1782	1782	2580	2580	2580	2580	2629	2629
2	2351	4702	3498	6996	3504	7008	3446	6892
3	2054	6162	2984	8952	3024	9072	2971	8913
4	1449	5796	1903	7612	1924	7696	1812	7248
5	708	3540	1028	5140	1027	5135	949	4745
6	346	2076	458	2748	425	2550	395	2370
7	142	994	154	1078	169	1183	159	1113
8	64	512	49	392	50	400	49	392
9	16	144	8	72	18	162	19	171
10	5	50	5	50	5	50	5	50
11	1	11	2	22	0	0	3	33
	9746	**25769**	**13800**	**35642**	**13800**	**35836**	**13530**	**34556**

New Overall Totals (since 1992)		Totals (up to 1991–92)		Complete Overall Totals (since 1888–89)	
Games	50876	Games	143119	Games	193995
Goals	131803	Goals	426420	Goals	558223

A CENTURY OF LEAGUE AND CUP GOALS IN CONSECUTIVE SEASONS

	League	*Cup*	*Season*
George Camsell			
Middlesbrough	59	5	1926–27
(101 goals)	33	4	1927–28

(Camsell's cup goals were all scored in the FA Cup.)

Steve Bull			
Wolverhampton W	34	18	1987–88
(102 goals)	37	13	1988–89

(Bull had 12 in the Sherpa Van Trophy, 3 Littlewoods Cup, 3 FA Cup in 1987–88; 11 Sherpa Van Trophy, 2 Littlewoods Cup in 1988–89.)

PENALTIES

Most in a season (individual)

Division 1 *Goals* *Season*

Francis Lee (Manchester C) 13 1971–72

Also scored 1 in League Cup and 2 in FA Cup.

Most awarded in one game

Five Crystal Palace (1 scored, 3 missed) v Brighton & HA (1 scored), Div 2 1988–89

Most saved in a season

Division 1

Paul Cooper (Ipswich T) 8 (of 10) 1979–80

MOST GOALS IN A GAME

FA PREMIER LEAGUE

4 Mar 1995 Andy Cole (Manchester U) 5 goals v Ipswich T
19 Sept 1999 Alan Shearer (Newcastle U) 5 goals v Sheffield W
22 Nov 2009 Jermain Defoe (Tottenham H) 5 goals v Wigan Ath
27 Nov 2010 Dimitar Berbatov (Manchester U) 5 goals v Blackburn R
3 Oct 2015 Sergio Aguero (Manchester C) 5 goals v Newcastle U

FOOTBALL LEAGUE

Division 1
14 Dec 1935 Ted Drake (Arsenal) 7 goals v Aston Villa

Division 2
5 Feb 1955 Tommy Briggs (Blackburn R) 7 goals v Bristol R
23 Feb 1957 Neville Coleman (Stoke C) 7 goals v Lincoln C

Division 3(S)
13 Apr 1936 Joe Payne (Luton T) 10 goals v Bristol R

Division 3(N)
26 Dec 1935 Bunny Bell (Tranmere R) 9 goals v Oldham Ath

Division 3
24 Apr 1965 Barrie Thomas (Scunthorpe U) 5 goals v Luton T
20 Nov 1965 Keith East (Swindon T) 5 goals v Mansfield T
16 Sept 1969 Steve Earle (Fulham) 5 goals v Halifax T
2 Oct 1971 Alf Wood (Shrewsbury T) 5 goals v Blackburn R
10 Sept 1983 Tony Caldwell (Bolton W) 5 goals v Walsall
4 May 1987 Andy Jones (Port Vale) 5 goals v Newport Co
3 Apr 1990 Steve Wilkinson (Mansfield T) 5 goals v Birmingham C
5 Sept 1998 Giuliano Grazioli (Peterborough U) 5 goals v Barnet
6 Apr 2002 Lee Jones (Wrexham) 5 goals v Cambridge U

Division 4
26 Dec 1962 Bert Lister (Oldham Ath) 6 goals v Southport

FA CUP

20 Nov 1971 Ted MacDougall (Bournemouth) 9 goals v Margate (*1st Round*)

LEAGUE CUP

25 Oct 1989 Frankie Bunn (Oldham Ath) 6 goals v Scarborough

SCOTTISH LEAGUE

Premier Division
17 Nov 1984 Paul Sturrock (Dundee U) 5 goals v Morton

Premier League
23 Aug 1996 Marco Negri (Rangers) 5 goals v Dundee U
4 Nov 2000 Kenny Miller (Rangers) 5 goals v St Mirren
25 Sept 2004 Kris Boyd (Kilmarnock) 5 goals v Dundee U
30 Dec 2009 Kris Boyd (Rangers) 5 goals v Dundee U
13 May 2012 Gary Hooper (Celtic) 5 goals v Hearts

Division 1
14 Sept 1928 Jimmy McGrory (Celtic) 8 goals v Dunfermline Ath

Division 2
1 Oct 1927 Owen McNally (Arthurlie) 8 goals v Armadale
2 Jan 1930 Jim Dyet (King's Park) 8 goals v Forfar Ath
18 Apr 1936 John Calder (Morton) 8 goals v Raith R
20 Aug 1937 Norman Hayward (Raith R) 8 goals v Brechin C

SCOTTISH CUP

12 Sept 1885 John Petrie (Arbroath) 13 goals v Bon Accord (*1st Round*)

LONGEST SEQUENCE OF CONSECUTIVE DEFEATS

FOOTBALL LEAGUE Division 2	*Team*	*Games*
1898–99	Darwen	18

LONGEST UNBEATEN SEQUENCE

FA PREMIER LEAGUE	*Team*	*Games*
May 2003–Oct 2004	Arsenal	49
FOOTBALL LEAGUE – League 1		
Jan 2011–Nov 2011	Huddersfield T	43

LONGEST UNBEATEN CUP SEQUENCE

Liverpool 25 rounds League/Milk Cup 1980–84

LONGEST UNBEATEN SEQUENCE IN A SEASON

FA PREMIER LEAGUE	*Team*	*Games*
2003–04	Arsenal	38
FOOTBALL LEAGUE – Division 1		
1920–21	Burnley	30
SCOTTISH PREMIERSHIP		
2016–17	Celtic	38

LONGEST UNBEATEN START TO A SEASON

FA PREMIER LEAGUE	*Team*	*Games*
2003–04	Arsenal	38
FOOTBALL LEAGUE – Division 1		
1973–74	Leeds U	29
1987–88	Liverpool	29

LONGEST SEQUENCE WITHOUT A WIN IN A SEASON

FA PREMIER LEAGUE	*Team*	*Games*
2007–08	Derby Co	32
FOOTBALL LEAGUE Division 2	*Team*	*Games*
1983–84	Cambridge U	31

LONGEST SEQUENCE WITHOUT A WIN FROM SEASON'S START

FOOTBALL LEAGUE Division 4	*Team*	*Games*
1970–71	Newport Co	25

LONGEST SEQUENCE OF CONSECUTIVE SCORING (individual)

FA PREMIER LEAGUE
Jamie Vardy (Leicester C) 13 in 11 games 2015–16

FOOTBALL LEAGUE RECORD
Tom Phillipson (Wolverhampton W) 23 in 13 games 1926–27

LONGEST WINNING SEQUENCE

FA PREMIER LEAGUE	*Team*	*Games*
2001–02 and 2002–03	Arsenal	14
FOOTBALL LEAGUE – Division 2		
1904–05	Manchester U	14
1905–06	Bristol C	14
1950–51	Preston NE	14
FROM SEASON'S START – Division 3		
1985–86	Reading	13
SCOTTISH PREMIER LEAGUE		
2003–04	Celtic	25

HIGHEST WINS

Highest win in a First-Class Match
(*Scottish Cup 1st Round*)

Arbroath	36	Bon Accord	0	12 Sept 1885

Highest win in an International Match

England	13	Ireland	0	18 Feb 1882

Highest win in an FA Cup Match

Preston NE	26	Hyde U	0	15 Oct 1887

(*1st Round*)

Highest win in a League Cup Match

West Ham U	10	Bury	0	25 Oct 1983
(*2nd Round, 2nd Leg*)				
Liverpool	10	Fulham	0	23 Sept 1986
(*2nd Round, 1st Leg*)				

Highest win in an FA Premier League Match

Manchester U	9	Ipswich T	0	4 Mar 1995
Tottenham H	9	Wigan Ath	1	22 Nov 2009

Highest win in a Football League Match

Division 2 – highest home win

Newcastle U	13	Newport Co	0	5 Oct 1946

Division 3(N) – highest home win

Stockport Co	13	Halifax T	0	6 Jan 1934

Division 2 – highest away win

Burslem Port Vale	0	Sheffield U	10	10 Dec 1892

Highest wins in a Scottish League Match

Scottish Premier League – highest home win

Celtic	9	Aberdeen	0	6 Nov 2010

Scottish Division 2 – highest home win

Airdrieonians	15	Dundee Wanderers	1	1 Dec 1894

Scottish Premier League – highest away win

Hamilton A	0	Celtic	8	5 Nov 1988

MOST HOME WINS IN A SEASON

Brentford won all 21 games in Division 3(S), 1929–30

RECORD AWAY WINS IN A SEASON

Doncaster R won 18 of 21 games in Division 3(N), 1946–47

CONSECUTIVE AWAY WINS

FA PREMIER LEAGUE
Arsenal 12 games 2012–13, 2013–14.

FOOTBALL LEAGUE
Division 1
Tottenham H 10 games (1959–60 (2), 1960–61 (8))

HIGHEST AGGREGATE SCORES

FA PREMIER LEAGUE

Portsmouth	7	Reading	4	29 Sept 2007

Highest Aggregate Score England
Division 3(N)

Tranmere R	13	Oldham Ath	4	26 Dec 1935

Highest Aggregate Score Scotland
Division 2

Airdrieonians	15	Dundee Wanderers	1	1 Dec 1894

MOST WINS IN A SEASON

		Wins	*Games*
FA PREMIER LEAGUE			
2004–05	Chelsea	29	38
2005–06	Chelsea	29	38
FOOTBALL LEAGUE			
Division 3(N)			
1946–47	Doncaster R	33	42
SCOTTISH PREMIERSHIP			
2016–17	Celtic	34	38
SCOTTISH LEAGUE			
Division 1			
1920–21	Rangers	35	42

FEWEST WINS IN A SEASON

		Wins	*Games*
FA PREMIER LEAGUE			
2007–08	Derby Co	1	38
FOOTBALL LEAGUE			
Division 2			
1899–1900	Loughborough T	1	34
SCOTTISH PREMIER LEAGUE			
1998–99	Dunfermline Ath	4	36
SCOTTISH LEAGUE			
Division 1			
1891–92	Vale of Leven	0	22

UNDEFEATED AT HOME OVERALL

Liverpool 85 games (63 League, 9 League Cup, 7 European, 6 FA Cup), Jan 1978–Jan 1981

UNDEFEATED AT HOME LEAGUE

Chelsea 86 games, March 2004–October 2008

UNDEFEATED AWAY

Arsenal 19 games, FA Premier League 2001–02 and 2003–04 (only Preston NE with 11 in 1888–89 had previously remained unbeaten away) in the top flight.

MOST POINTS IN A SEASON

(three points for a win)

		Points	*Games*
FA PREMIER LEAGUE			
2004–05	Chelsea	95	38
FOOTBALL LEAGUE			
Championship			
2005–06	Reading	106	46
SCOTTISH PREMIER LEAGUE			
2001–02	Celtic	103	38
SCOTTISH LEAGUE			
League One			
2013–14	Rangers	102	36

MOST POINTS IN A SEASON

(under old system of two points for a win)

		Points	*Games*
FOOTBALL LEAGUE			
Division 4			
1975–76	Lincoln C	74	46
SCOTTISH LEAGUE			
Division 1			
1920–21	Rangers	76	42

FEWEST POINTS IN A SEASON

		Points	*Games*
FA PREMIER LEAGUE			
2007–08	Derby Co	11	38
FOOTBALL LEAGUE			
Division 2			
1904–05	Doncaster R	8	34
1899–1900	Loughborough T	8	34
SCOTTISH PREMIER LEAGUE			
2007–08	Gretna	13	38
SCOTTISH LEAGUE			
Division 1			
1954–55	Stirling Alb	6	30

NO DEFEATS IN A SEASON

FA PREMIER LEAGUE
2003–04 Arsenal won 26, drew 12

FOOTBALL LEAGUE
Division 1
1888–89 Preston NE won 18, drew 4
Division 2
1893–94 Liverpool won 22, drew 6

SCOTTISH LEAGUE
Premiership
2016–17 Celtic won 34, drew 4
Division 1
1898–99 Rangers won 18
League One
2013–14 Rangers won 33, drew 3

ONE DEFEAT IN A SEASON

FA PREMIER LEAGUE		*Defeats*	*Games*
2004–05	Chelsea	1	38
FOOTBALL LEAGUE			
Division 1			
1990–91	Arsenal	1	38
SCOTTISH PREMIER LEAGUE			
2001–02	Celtic	1	38
2013–14	Celtic	1	38
SCOTTISH LEAGUE			
Division 1			
1920–21	Rangers	1	42
Division 2			
1956–57	Clyde	1	36
1962–63	Morton	1	36
1967–68	St Mirren	1	36
New Division 1			
2011–12	Ross Co	1	36
New Division 2			
1975–76	Raith R	1	26

MOST DEFEATS IN A SEASON

FA PREMIER LEAGUE		*Defeats*	*Games*
1994–95	Ipswich T	29	42
2005–06	Sunderland	29	38
2007–08	Derby Co	29	38
FOOTBALL LEAGUE			
Division 3			
1997–98	Doncaster R	34	46
SCOTTISH PREMIER LEAGUE			
2005–06	Livingston	28	38
SCOTTISH LEAGUE			
New Division 1			
1992–93	Cowdenbeath	34	44

MOST DRAWN GAMES IN A SEASON

FA PREMIER LEAGUE		*Draws*	*Games*
1993–94	Manchester C	18	42
1993–94	Sheffield U	18	42
1994–95	Southampton	18	42
FOOTBALL LEAGUE			
Division 1			
1978–79	Norwich C	23	42
Division 3			
1997–98	Cardiff C	23	46
1997–98	Hartlepool U	23	46
Division 4			
1986–87	Exeter C	23	46
SCOTTISH PREMIER LEAGUE			
1998–99	Dunfermline Ath	16	38
SCOTTISH LEAGUE			
Premier Division			
1993–94	Aberdeen	21	44
New Division 1			
1986–87	East Fife	21	44

SENDINGS-OFF

SEASON
451 (League alone) 2003–04
(Before rescinded cards taken into account)

DAY
19 (League) 13 Dec 2003

FA CUP FINAL
Kevin Moran, Manchester U v Everton 1985
Jose Antonio Reyes, Arsenal v Manchester U 2005
Chris Smalling, Manchester U v Crystal Palace 2016
Victor Moses, Chelsea v Arsenal 2017

QUICKEST
FA Premier League
Andreas Johansson, Wigan Ath v Arsenal (7 May 2006) and Keith Gillespie, Sheffield U v Reading (20 January 2007) both in 10 seconds
Football League
Walter Boyd, Swansea C v Darlington, Div 3 as substitute in zero seconds 23 Nov 1999

MOST IN ONE GAME
Five: Chesterfield (2) v Plymouth Arg (3) 22 Feb 1997
Five: Wigan Ath (1) v Bristol R (4) 2 Dec 1997
Five: Exeter C (3) v Cambridge U (2) 23 Nov 2002
Five: Bradford C (3) v Crawley T (2)* 27 Mar 2012
**All five sent off after final whistle for fighting*

MOST IN ONE TEAM
Wigan Ath (1) v Bristol R (4) 2 Dec 1997
Hereford U (4) v Northampton T (0) 6 Sept 1992

MOST SUCCESSFUL MANAGERS

Sir Alex Ferguson CBE
Manchester U
1986–2013, 25 major trophies:
13 Premier League, 5 FA Cup, 4 League Cup, 2 Champions League, 1 Cup-Winners' Cup.

Aberdeen
1976–86, 9 major trophies:
3 League, 4 Scottish Cup, 1 League Cup, 1 Cup-Winners' Cup.

Bob Paisley – Liverpool
1974–83, 13 major trophies:
6 League, 3 European Cup, 3 League Cup, 1 UEFA Cup.

Bill Struth – Rangers
1920–54, 30 major trophies:
18 League, 10 Scottish Cup, 2 League Cup

LEAGUE CHAMPIONSHIP HAT-TRICKS

Huddersfield T	1923–24 to 1925–26
Arsenal	1932–33 to 1934–35
Liverpool	1981–82 to 1983–84
Manchester U	1998–99 to 2000–01
Manchester U	2006–07 to 2008–09

MOST FA CUP MEDALS

Ashley Cole 7 (Arsenal 2002, 2003, 2005; Chelsea 2007, 2009, 2010, 2012)

MOST LEAGUE MEDALS

Ryan Giggs (Manchester U) 13: 1993, 1994, 1996, 1997, 1999, 2000, 2001, 2003, 2007, 2008, 2009, 2011 and 2013.

MOST SENIOR MATCHES

1,390 Peter Shilton (1,005 League, 86 FA Cup, 102 League Cup, 125 Internationals, 13 Under-23, 4 Football League XI, 20 European Cup, 7 Texaco Cup, 5 Simod Cup, 4 European Super Cup, 4 UEFA Cup, 3 Screen Sport Super Cup, 3 Zenith Data Systems Cup, 2 Autoglass Trophy, 2 Charity Shield, 2 Full Members Cup, 1 Anglo-Italian Cup, 1 Football League play-offs, 1 World Club Championship)

MOST LEAGUE APPEARANCES (750+ matches)

1,005 Peter Shilton (286 Leicester C, 110 Stoke C, 202 Nottingham F, 188 Southampton, 175 Derby Co, 34 Plymouth Arg, 1 Bolton W, 9 Leyton Orient) 1966–97
931 Tony Ford (355 Grimsby T, 9 Sunderland (loan), 112 Stoke C, 114 WBA, 68 Grimsby T, 5 Bradford C (loan), 76 Scunthorpe U, 103 Mansfield T, 89 Rochdale) 1975–2002
909 Graeme Armstrong (204 Stirling A, 83 Berwick R, 353 Meadowbank Thistle, 268 Stenhousemuir, 1 Alloa Ath) 1975–2001
863 Tommy Hutchison (165 Blackpool, 314 Coventry C, 46 Manchester C, 92 Burnley, 178 Swansea C, 68 Alloa Ath) 1965–91
833 Graham Alexander (159 Scunthorpe U, 150 Luton T, 370 Preston NE, 154 Burnley) 1990–2012
824 Terry Paine (713 Southampton, 111 Hereford U) 1957–77
790 Neil Redfearn (35 Bolton W, 10 Lincoln C (loan), 90 Lincoln C, 46 Doncaster R, 57 Crystal Palace, 24 Watford, 62 Oldham Ath, 292 Barnsley, 30 Charlton Ath, 17 Bradford C, 22 Wigan Ath, 42 Halifax T, 54 Boston U, 9 Rochdale) 1982–2004
788 David James (89 Watford, 214 Liverpool, 67 Aston Villa, 91 West Ham U, 93 Manchester C, 134 Portsmouth, 81 Bristol C, 19 Bournemouth) 1988–2013
782 Robbie James (484 Swansea C, 48 Stoke C, 87 QPR, 23 Leicester C, 89 Bradford C, 51 Cardiff C) 1973–94
777 Alan Oakes (565 Manchester C, 211 Chester C, 1 Port Vale) 1959–84
774 Dave Beasant (340 Wimbledon, 20 Newcastle U, 133 Chelsea, 6 Grimsby T (loan), 4 Wolverhampton W (loan), 88 Southampton, 139 Nottingham F, 27 Portsmouth, 1 Tottenham H (loan), 16 Brighton & HA) 1979–2003
771 John Burridge (27 Workington, 134 Blackpool, 65 Aston Villa, 6 Southend U (loan), 88 Crystal Palace, 39 QPR, 74 Wolverhampton W, 6 Derby Co (loan), 109 Sheffield U, 62 Southampton, 67 Newcastle U, 65 Hibernian, 3 Scarborough, 4 Lincoln C, 3 Aberdeen, 3 Dumbarton, 3 Falkirk, 4 Manchester C, 3 Darlington, 6 Queen of the S) 1968–96
770 John Trollope (all for Swindon T) 1960–80†
764 Jimmy Dickinson (all for Portsmouth) 1946–65
763 Stuart McCall (395 Bradford C, 103 Everton, 194 Rangers, 71 Sheffield U) 1982–2004
761 Roy Sproson (all for Port Vale) 1950–72
760 Mick Tait (64 Oxford U, 106 Carlisle U, 33 Hull C, 240 Portsmouth, 99 Reading, 79 Darlington, 139 Hartlepool U) 1975–97
758 Ray Clemence (48 Scunthorpe U, 470 Liverpool, 240 Tottenham H) 1966–87
758 Billy Bonds (95 Charlton Ath, 663 West Ham U) 1964–88
757 Pat Jennings (48 Watford, 472 Tottenham H, 237 Arsenal) 1963–86
757 Frank Worthington (171 Huddersfield T, 210 Leicester C, 84 Bolton W, 75 Birmingham C, 32 Leeds U, 19 Sunderland, 34 Southampton, 31 Brighton & HA, 59 Tranmere R, 23 Preston NE, 19 Stockport Co) 1966–88
755 Jamie Cureton (98 Norwich C, 5 Bournemouth (loan), 174 Bristol R, 108 Reading, 43 QPR, 30 Swindon T, 52 Colchester U, 8 Barnsley (loan), 12 Shrewsbury (loan), 88 Exeter C, 19 Leyton Orient, 35 Cheltenham T, 83 Dagenham & R) 1992–2016
752 Wayne Allison (84 Halifax T, 7 Watford, 195 Bristol C, 101 Swindon T, 74 Huddersfield T, 103 Tranmere R, 73 Sheffield U, 115 Chesterfield) 1987–2008

† record for one club

CONSECUTIVE
401 Harold Bell (401 Tranmere R; 459 in all games) 1946–55

YOUNGEST PLAYERS

FA Premier League appearance
Matthew Briggs, 16 years 65 days, Fulham v Middlesbrough, 13.5.2007

FA Premier League scorer
James Vaughan, 16 years 271 days, Everton v Crystal Palace 10.4.2005

Football League appearance
Reuben Noble-Lazarus 15 years 45 days, Barnsley v Ipswich T, FL Championship 30.9.2008

Football League scorer
Ronnie Dix, 15 years 180 days, Bristol Rovers v Norwich C, Division 3S, 3.3.1928

Division 1 appearance
Derek Forster, 15 years 185 days, Sunderland v Leicester C, 22.8.1964

Division 1 scorer
Jason Dozzell, 16 years 57 days as substitute Ipswich T v Coventry C, 4.2.1984

Division 1 hat-tricks
Alan Shearer, 17 years 240 days, Southampton v Arsenal, 9.4.1988
Jimmy Greaves, 17 years 308 days, Chelsea v Portsmouth, 25.12.1957

Division 2 hat-tricks
Trevor Francis, 16 years 307 days, Birmingham C v Bolton W, 20.2.1971

FA Cup appearance (any round)
Andy Awford, 15 years 88 days as substitute Worcester City v Boreham Wood, 3rd Qual. rd, 10.10.1987

FA Cup appearance (competition rounds)
Brendan Galloway, 15 years 240 days, Milton Keynes D v Nantwich T, 12.11.2011

FA Cup Final appearance
Curtis Weston, 17 years 119 days, Millwall v Manchester U, 22.5.2004

FA Cup Final scorer
Norman Whiteside, 18 years 18 days, Manchester United v Brighton & HA, 1983

FA Cup Final captain
David Nish, 21 years 212 days, Leicester C v Manchester C, 1969

League Cup appearance
Chris Coward, 16 years 30 days, Stockport Co v Sheffield W, 2005

League Cup Final scorer
Norman Whiteside, 17 years 324 days, Manchester U v Liverpool, 1983

League Cup Final captain
Barry Venison, 20 years 7 months 8 days, Sunderland v Norwich C, 1985

Scottish Premier League appearance
Stephen Thompson, 15 years 150 days, Rangers v Hearts, 12.9.2004

Scottish Football League appearance
Jordan Allan, 14 years 189 days, Airdrie U v Livingston, 26.4.2013

Scottish Premier League scorer
Fraser Fyvie, 16 years 306 days, Aberdeen v Hearts, 27.1.2010

OLDEST PLAYERS

FA Premier League appearance
John Burridge, 43 years 162 days, Manchester C v QPR, 14.5.1995

Football League appearance
Neil McBain, 52 years 4 months, New Brighton v Hartlepools U, Div 3N, 15.3.47 (McBain was New Brighton's manager and had to play in an emergency)

Division 1 appearance
Stanley Matthews, 50 years 5 days, Stoke C v Fulham, 6.2.65

INTERNATIONAL RECORDS

MOST GOALS IN AN INTERNATIONAL

Record/World Cup	Archie Thompson (Australia) 13 goals v American Samoa	11.4.2001
England	Howard Vaughton (Aston Villa) 5 goals v Ireland, at Belfast Steve Bloomer (Derby Co) 5 goals v Wales, at Cardiff Willie Hall (Tottenham H) 5 goals v N. Ireland, at Old Trafford Malcolm Macdonald (Newcastle U) 5 goals v Cyprus, at Wembley	18.2.1882 16.3.1896 16.11.1938 16.4.1975
Northern Ireland	Joe Bambrick (Linfield) 6 goals v Wales, at Belfast	1.2.1930
Wales	John Price (Wrexham) 4 goals v Ireland, at Wrexham Mel Charles (Cardiff C) 4 goals v N. Ireland, at Cardiff Ian Edwards (Chester) 4 goals v Malta, at Wrexham	25.2.1882 11.4.1962 25.10.1978
Scotland	Alexander Higgins (Kilmarnock) 4 goals v Ireland, at Hampden Park Charles Heggie (Rangers) 4 goals v Ireland, at Belfast William Dickson (Dundee Strathmore) 4 goals v Ireland, at Belfast William Paul (Partick Thistle) 4 goals v Wales, at Paisley Jake Madden (Celtic) 4 goals v Wales, at Wrexham Duke McMahon (Celtic) 4 goals v Ireland, at Celtic Park Bob Hamilton (Rangers) 4 goals v Ireland, at Celtic Park Jimmy Quinn (Celtic) 4 goals v Ireland, at Dublin Hughie Gallacher (Newcastle U) 4 goals v N. Ireland, at Belfast Billy Steel (Dundee) 4 goals v N. Ireland, at Hampden Park Denis Law (Manchester U) 4 goals v N. Ireland, at Hampden Park Denis Law (Manchester U) 4 goals v Norway, at Hampden Park Colin Stein (Rangers) 4 goals v Cyprus, at Hampden Park	14.3.1885 20.3.1886 24.3.1888 22.3.1890 18.3.1893 23.2.1901 23.2.1901 14.3.1908 23.2.1929 1.11.1950 7.11.1962 7.11.1963 17.5.1969

MOST GOALS IN AN INTERNATIONAL CAREER

		Goals	*Games*
England	Wayne Rooney (Everton, Manchester U)	53	119
Scotland	Denis Law (Huddersfield T, Manchester C, Torino, Manchester U) Kenny Dalglish (Celtic, Liverpool)	30 30	55 102
Northern Ireland	David Healy (Manchester U, Preston NE, Leeds U, Fulham, Sunderland, Rangers, Bury)	36	95
Wales	Ian Rush (Liverpool, Juventus)	28	73
Republic of Ireland	Robbie Keane (Wolverhampton W, Coventry C, Internazionale, Leeds U, Tottenham H, Liverpool, Tottenham H, LA Galaxy)	68	146

HIGHEST SCORES

World Cup Match	Australia	31	American Samoa	0	2001
European Championship	San Marino	0	Germany	13	2006
Olympic Games	Denmark Germany	17 16	France USSR	1 0	1908 1912
Olympic Qualifying Tournament	Vanuatu	46	Micronesia	0	2015
Other International Match	Libya *Abandoned after 80 minutes as Oman refused to play on.*	21	Oman	0	1966
European Cup	Feyenoord	12	KR Reykjavik	2	1969
European Cup-Winners' Cup	Sporting Lisbon	16	Apoel Nicosia	1	1963
Fairs & UEFA Cups	Ajax	14	Red Boys Differdange	0	1984

GOALSCORING RECORDS

World Cup Final	Geoff Hurst (England) 3 goals v West Germany	1966
World Cup Final tournament	Just Fontaine (France) 13 goals	1958
World Cup career	Miroslav Klose (Germany) 16 goals	2002, 2006, 2010, 2014
Career	Artur Friedenreich (Brazil) 1,329 goals Pele (Brazil) 1,281 goals Franz 'Bimbo' Binder (Austria, Germany) 1,006 goals	1910–30 *1956–78 1930–50
World Cup Finals fastest	Hakan Sukur (Turkey) 10.8 secs v South Korea	2002

**Pele subsequently scored two goals in Testimonial matches making his total 1,283.*

MOST CAPPED INTERNATIONALS IN THE BRITISH ISLES

England	Peter Shilton	125 appearances	1970–90
Northern Ireland	Pat Jennings	119 appearances	1964–86
Scotland	Kenny Dalglish	102 appearances	1971–86
Wales	Neville Southall	92 appearances	1982–97
Republic of Ireland	Robbie Keane	146 appearances	1998–2016

THE FA PREMIER LEAGUE AND FOOTBALL LEAGUE FIXTURES 2017–18

**Sky Sports †BT Sport All fixtures subject to change.*

Community Shield

Sunday, 6 August 2017
Chelsea v Arsenal† (14:00)

Premier League

Friday, 11 August 2017
Arsenal v Leicester C* (19:45)

Saturday, 12 August 2017
Brighton & HA v Manchester C† (17:30)
Chelsea v Burnley
Crystal Palace v Huddersfield T
Everton v Stoke C
Southampton v Swansea C
Watford v Liverpool* (12:30)
WBA v Bournemouth

Sunday, 13 August 2017
Newcastle U v Tottenham H* (13:30)
Manchester U v West Ham U* (16:00)

Saturday, 19 August 2017
Bournemouth v Watford
Burnley v WBA
Leicester C v Brighton & HA
Liverpool v Crystal Palace
Stoke C v Arsenal† (17.30)
Swansea C v Manchester U* (12:30)
Southampton v West Ham U
Fixture reversed.

Sunday, 20 August 2017
Huddersfield T v Newcastle U* (13:30)
Tottenham H v Chelsea* (16:00)

Monday, 21 August 2017
Manchester C v Everton* (20:00)

Saturday, 26 August 2017
Bournemouth v Manchester C* (12:30)
Chelsea v Everton
Crystal Palace v Swansea C
Huddersfield T v Southampton
Manchester U v Leicester C† (17:30)
Newcastle U v West Ham U
Tottenham H v Burnley
Watford v Brighton & HA

Sunday, 27 August 2017
WBA v Stoke C* (13:30)
Liverpool v Arsenal* (16:00)

Saturday, 9 September 2017
Arsenal v Bournemouth
Brighton & HA v WBA
Everton v Tottenham H
Leicester C v Chelsea
Manchester C v Liverpool* (12:30)
Southampton v Watford
Stoke C v Manchester U† (17:30)

Sunday 10, September 2017
Burnley v Crystal Palace* (13:30)
Swansea C v Newcastle U* (16:00)

Monday 11, September 2017
West Ham U v Huddersfield T* (20:00)

Friday, 15 September 2017
Bournemouth v Brighton & HA* (20:00)

Saturday, 16 September 2017
Crystal Palace v Southampton* (12:30)
Huddersfield T v Leicester C
Liverpool v Burnley
Newcastle U v Stoke C
Tottenham H v Swansea C† (17:30)
Watford v Manchester C
WBA v West Ham U

Sunday, 17 September 2017
Chelsea v Arsenal* (13:30)
Manchester U v Everton* (16:00)

Saturday, 23 September 2017
Arsenal v WBA
Burnley v Huddersfield T
Everton v Bournemouth
Leicester C v Liverpool† (17:30)
Manchester C v Crystal Palace
Southampton v Manchester U
Stoke C v Chelsea
Swansea C v Watford
West Ham U v Tottenham H* (12:30)

Sunday, 24 September 2017
Brighton & HA v Newcastle U* (16:00)

Monday, 25 September 2017
Arsenal v WBA* (20:00)

Saturday, 30 September 2017
Bournemouth v Leicester C
Chelsea v Manchester C† (17:30)
Huddersfield T v Tottenham H* (12:30)
Manchester U v Crystal Palace
Stoke C v Southampton
WBA v Watford
West Ham U v Swansea C

Sunday, 1 October 2017
Arsenal v Brighton & HA† (12:00)
Everton v Burnley* (14:15)
Newcastle U v Liverpool* (16:30)

Saturday, 14 October 2017
Brighton & HA v Everton
Burnley v West Ham U
Crystal Palace v Chelsea
Leicester C v WBA
Liverpool v Manchester U
Manchester C v Stoke C
Southampton v Newcastle U
Swansea C v Huddersfield T
Tottenham H v Bournemouth
Watford v Arsenal

Saturday, 21 October 2017
Chelsea v Watford
Everton v Arsenal
Huddersfield T v Manchester U
Manchester C v Burnley
Newcastle U v Crystal Palace
Southampton v WBA
Stoke C v Bournemouth
Swansea C v Leicester C
Tottenham H v Liverpool
West Ham U v Brighton & HA

Saturday, 28 October 2017
Bournemouth v Chelsea
Arsenal v Swansea C
Brighton & HA v Southampton
Burnley v Newcastle U
Crystal Palace v West Ham U
Leicester C v Everton
Liverpool v Huddersfield T
Manchester U v Tottenham H
Watford v Stoke C
WBA v Manchester C

Saturday, 4 November 2017
Chelsea v Manchester U
Everton v Watford
Huddersfield T v WBA
Manchester C v Arsenal
Newcastle U v Bournemouth
Southampton v Burnley
Stoke C v Leicester C
Swansea C v Brighton & HA
Tottenham H v Crystal Palace
West Ham U v Liverpool

Saturday, 18 November 2017
Bournemouth v Huddersfield T
Arsenal v Tottenham H
Brighton & HA v Stoke C
Burnley v Swansea C
Crystal Palace v Everton
Leicester C v Manchester C
Liverpool v Southampton
Manchester U v Newcastle U
Watford v West Ham U
WBA v Chelsea

Saturday, 25 November 2017
Burnley v Arsenal
Crystal Palace v Stoke C
Huddersfield T v Manchester C
Liverpool v Chelsea
Manchester U v Brighton & HA
Newcastle U v Watford
Southampton v Everton
Swansea C v Bournemouth
Tottenham H v WBA
West Ham U v Leicester C

Tuesday, 28 November 2017
Bournemouth v Burnley
Arsenal v Huddersfield T
Brighton & HA v Crystal Palace
Leicester C v Tottenham H
Watford v Manchester U
WBA v Newcastle U (8pm)

Wednesday, 29 November 2017
Chelsea v Swansea C
Everton v West Ham U
Manchester C v Southampton (8pm)
Stoke C v Liverpool (8pm)

Saturday, 2 December 2017
Bournemouth v Southampton
Arsenal v Manchester U
Brighton & HA v Liverpool
Chelsea v Newcastle U
Everton v Huddersfield T
Leicester C v Burnley
Manchester C v West Ham U
Stoke C v Swansea C
Watford v Tottenham H
WBA v Crystal Palace

Saturday, 9 December 2017
Burnley v Watford
Crystal Palace v Bournemouth
Huddersfield T v Brighton & HA
Liverpool v Everton
Manchester U v Manchester C
Newcastle U v Leicester C
Southampton v Arsenal
Swansea C v WBA
Tottenham H v Stoke C
West Ham U v Chelsea

Tuesday, 12 December 2017
Burnley v Stoke C
Crystal Palace v Watford (8pm)
Huddersfield T v Chelsea
Manchester U v Bournemouth (8pm)
Swansea C v Manchester C
West Ham U v Arsenal

Wednesday, 13 December 2017
Liverpool v WBA (8pm)
Newcastle U v Everton
Southampton v Leicester C
Tottenham H v Brighton & HA (8pm)

Saturday, 16 December 2017
Bournemouth v Liverpool
Arsenal v Newcastle U
Brighton & HA v Burnley
Chelsea v Southampton
Everton v Swansea C
Leicester C v Crystal Palace
Manchester C v Tottenham H
Stoke C v West Ham U
Watford v Huddersfield T
WBA v Manchester U

Saturday, 23 December 2017
Arsenal v Liverpool
Brighton & HA v Watford
Burnley v Tottenham H
Everton v Chelsea
Leicester C v Manchester U
Manchester C v Bournemouth
Southampton v Huddersfield T
Stoke C v WBA
Swansea C v Crystal Palace
West Ham U v Newcastle U

Tuesday, 26 December 2017
Bournemouth v West Ham U
Chelsea v Brighton & HA
Crystal Palace v Arsenal
Huddersfield T v Stoke C
Liverpool v Swansea C
Manchester U v Burnley
Newcastle U v Manchester C
Tottenham H v Southampton
Watford v Leicester C
WBA v Everton

Saturday, 30 December 2017
Bournemouth v Everton
Chelsea v Stoke C
Crystal Palace v Manchester C
Huddersfield T v Burnley
Liverpool v Leicester C
Manchester U v Southampton
Newcastle U v Brighton & HA
Tottenham H v West Ham U
Watford v Swansea C
WBA v Arsenal

Monday, 1 January 2018
Arsenal v Chelsea
Brighton & HA v Bournemouth
Burnley v Liverpool
Everton v Manchester U
Leicester C v Huddersfield T
Manchester C v Watford
Southampton v Crystal Palace
Stoke C v Newcastle U
Swansea C v Tottenham H
West Ham U v WBA

Saturday, 13 January 2018
Bournemouth v Arsenal
Chelsea v Leicester C
Crystal Palace v Burnley
Huddersfield T v West Ham U
Liverpool v Manchester C
Manchester U v Stoke C
Newcastle U v Swansea C
Tottenham H v Everton
Watford v Southampton
WBA v Brighton & HA

Saturday, 20 January 2018
Arsenal v Crystal Palace
Brighton & HA v Chelsea
Burnley v Manchester U
Everton v WBA
Leicester C v Watford
Manchester C v Newcastle U
Southampton v Tottenham H
Stoke C v Huddersfield T
Swansea C v Liverpool
West Ham U v Bournemouth

Tuesday, 30 January 2018
Huddersfield T v Liverpool
Swansea C v Arsenal
West Ham U v Crystal Palace

Wednesday, 31 January 2018
Chelsea v Bournemouth
Everton v Leicester C
Manchester C v WBA (8pm)
Newcastle U v Burnley
Southampton v Brighton & HA
Stoke C v Watford (8pm)
Tottenham H v Manchester U (8pm)

Saturday, 3 February 2018
Bournemouth v Stoke C
Arsenal v Everton
Brighton & HA v West Ham U
Burnley v Manchester C
Crystal Palace v Newcastle U
Leicester C v Swansea C
Liverpool v Tottenham H
Manchester U v Huddersfield T
Watford v Chelsea
WBA v Southampton

Saturday, 10 February 2018
Chelsea v WBA
Everton v Crystal Palace
Huddersfield T v Bournemouth
Manchester C v Leicester C
Newcastle U v Manchester U
Southampton v Liverpool
Stoke C v Brighton & HA
Swansea C v Burnley
Tottenham H v Arsenal
West Ham U v Watford

Saturday, 24 February 2018
Bournemouth v Newcastle U
Arsenal v Manchester C
Brighton & HA v Swansea C
Burnley v Southampton
Crystal Palace v Tottenham H
Leicester C v Stoke C
Liverpool v West Ham U
Manchester U v Chelsea
Watford v Everton
WBA v Huddersfield T

Saturday, 3 March 2018
Brighton & HA v Arsenal
Burnley v Everton
Crystal Palace v Manchester U
Leicester C v Bournemouth
Liverpool v Newcastle U
Manchester C v Chelsea
Southampton v Stoke C
Swansea C v West Ham U
Tottenham H v Huddersfield T
Watford v WBA

Saturday, 10 March 2018
Bournemouth v Tottenham H
Arsenal v Watford
Chelsea v Crystal Palace
Everton v Brighton & HA
Huddersfield T v Swansea C
Manchester U v Liverpool
Newcastle U v Southampton
Stoke C v Manchester C
WBA v Leicester C
West Ham U v Burnley

Saturday, 17 March 2018
Bournemouth v WBA
Burnley v Chelsea
Huddersfield T v Crystal Palace
Leicester C v Arsenal
Liverpool v Watford
Manchester C v Brighton & HA
Stoke C v Everton
Swansea C v Southampton
Tottenham H v Newcastle U
West Ham U v Manchester U

Saturday, 31 March 2018
Arsenal v Stoke C
Brighton & HA v Leicester C
Chelsea v Tottenham H
Crystal Palace v Liverpool
Everton v Manchester C
Manchester U v Swansea C
Newcastle U v Huddersfield T
West Ham U v Southampton
Fixture reversed.
Watford v Bournemouth
WBA v Burnley

Saturday, 7 April 2018
Bournemouth v Crystal Palace
Arsenal v Southampton
Brighton & HA v Huddersfield T
Chelsea v West Ham U
Everton v Liverpool
Leicester C v Newcastle U
Manchester C v Manchester U
Stoke C v Tottenham H
Watford v Burnley
WBA v Swansea C

Saturday, 14 April 2018
Burnley v Leicester C
Crystal Palace v Brighton & HA
Huddersfield T v Watford
Liverpool v Bournemouth
Manchester U v WBA
Newcastle U v Arsenal
Southampton v Chelsea
Swansea C v Everton
Tottenham H v Manchester C
West Ham U v Stoke C

Saturday, 21 April 2018
Bournemouth v Manchester U
Arsenal v West Ham U
Brighton & HA v Tottenham H
Chelsea v Huddersfield T
Everton v Newcastle U
Leicester C v Southampton
Manchester C v Swansea C
Stoke C v Burnley
Watford v Crystal Palace
WBA v Liverpool

Saturday, 28 April 2018
Burnley v Brighton & HA
Crystal Palace v Leicester C
Huddersfield T v Everton
Liverpool v Stoke C
Manchester U v Arsenal
Newcastle U v WBA
Southampton v Bournemouth
Swansea C v Chelsea
Tottenham H v Watford
West Ham U v Manchester C

Saturday, 5 May 2018
Bournemouth v Swansea C
Arsenal v Burnley
Brighton & HA v Manchester U
Chelsea v Liverpool
Everton v Southampton
Leicester C v West Ham U
Manchester C v Huddersfield T
Stoke C v Crystal Palace
Watford v Newcastle U
WBA v Tottenham H

Sunday, 13 May 2018
Burnley v Bournemouth
Crystal Palace v WBA
Huddersfield T v Arsenal
Liverpool v Brighton & HA
Manchester U v Watford
Newcastle U v Chelsea
Southampton v Manchester C
Swansea C v Stoke C
Tottenham H v Leicester C
West Ham U v Everton

EFL Championship

Friday, 4 August 2017
Sunderland v Derby Co* (19:45)

Saturday, 5 August 2017
Aston Villa v Hull C* (17:30)
Bristol C v Barnsley
Burton Alb v Cardiff C
Fulham v Norwich C
Ipswich T v Birmingham C
Nottingham F v Millwall
Preston NE v Sheffield W
QPR v Reading
Sheffield U v Brentford
Wolverhampton W v Middlesbrough

Sunday, 6 August 2017
Bolton W v Leeds U* (16:30)

Saturday, 12 August 2017
Barnsley v Ipswich T
Birmingham C v Bristol C
Brentford v Nottingham F
Cardiff C v Aston Villa
Derby Co v Wolverhampton W
Hull C v Burton Alb
Leeds U v Preston NE
Middlesbrough v Sheffield U* (17:30)
Millwall v Bolton W
Norwich C v Sunderland
Reading v Fulham
Sheffield W v QPR

Tuesday, 15 August 2017
Barnsley v Nottingham F
Birmingham C v Bolton W
Brentford v Bristol C
Cardiff C v Sheffield U
Derby Co v Preston NE
Hull C v Wolverhampton W
Leeds U v Fulham
Middlesbrough v Burton Alb
Millwall v Ipswich T
Norwich C v QPR
Reading v Aston Villa
Sheffield W v Sunderland

Friday, 18 August 2017
Burton Alb v Birmingham C* (19:45)

Saturday, 19 August 2017
Aston Villa v Norwich C
Bolton W v Derby Co
Bristol C v Millwall
Fulham v Sheffield W
Ipswich T v Brentford
Nottingham F v Middlesbrough
Preston NE v Reading
QPR v Hull C
Sheffield U v Barnsley
Sunderland v Leeds U* (17:30)
Wolverhampton W v Cardiff C

Friday, 25 August 2017
Bristol C v Aston Villa* (19:45)

Saturday, 26 August 2017
Barnsley v Sunderland
Birmingham C v Reading
Brentford v Wolverhampton W
Burton Alb v Sheffield W
Cardiff C v QPR
Hull C v Bolton W
Ipswich T v Fulham
Middlesbrough v Preston NE
Millwall v Norwich C
Nottingham F v Leeds U* (17:30)
Sheffield U v Derby Co

Friday, 8 September 2017
Derby Co v Hull C* (19:45)

Saturday, 9 September 2017
Aston Villa v Brentford
Bolton W v Middlesbrough
Fulham v Cardiff C
Leeds U v Burton Alb
Norwich C v Birmingham C
Preston NE v Barnsley
QPR v Ipswich T
Reading v Bristol C
Sheffield W v Nottingham F* (17:30)
Sunderland v Sheffield U
Wolverhampton W v Millwall

Tuesday, 12 September 2017
Aston Villa v Middlesbrough
Bolton W v Sheffield U
Derby Co v Ipswich T
Fulham v Hull C
Leeds U v Birmingham C
Norwich C v Burton Alb
Preston NE v Cardiff C
QPR v Millwall
Reading v Barnsley
Sheffield W v Brentford
Sunderland v Nottingham F
Wolverhampton W v Bristol C

Saturday, 16 September 2017
Barnsley v Aston Villa
Birmingham C v Preston NE
Brentford v Reading
Bristol C v Derby Co
Burton Alb v Fulham
Cardiff C v Sheffield W
Hull C v Sunderland
Ipswich T v Bolton W
Middlesbrough v QPR
Millwall v Leeds U
Nottingham F v Wolverhampton W
Sheffield U v Norwich C

Saturday, 23 September 2017
Aston Villa v Nottingham F
Bolton W v Brentford
Derby Co v Birmingham C
Fulham v Middlesbrough
Leeds U v Ipswich T
Norwich C v Bristol C
Preston NE v Millwall
QPR v Burton Alb
Reading v Hull C
Sheffield W v Sheffield U
Sunderland v Cardiff C
Wolverhampton W v Barnsley

Tuesday, 26 September 2017
Barnsley v QPR
Birmingham C v Sheffield W
Brentford v Derby Co
Bristol C v Bolton W
Burton Alb v Aston Villa
Cardiff C v Leeds U
Hull C v Preston NE
Ipswich T v Sunderland
Middlesbrough v Norwich C
Millwall v Reading
Nottingham F v Fulham
Sheffield U v Wolverhampton W

Saturday, 30 September 2017
Aston Villa v Bolton W
Burton Alb v Wolverhampton W
Cardiff C v Derby Co
Hull C v Birmingham C
Ipswich T v Bristol C
Middlesbrough v Brentford
Millwall v Barnsley
Nottingham F v Sheffield U
Preston NE v Sunderland
QPR v Fulham
Reading v Norwich C
Sheffield W v Leeds U

Saturday, 14 October 2017
Barnsley v Middlesbrough
Birmingham C v Cardiff C
Bolton W v Sheffield W
Brentford v Millwall
Bristol C v Burton Alb
Derby Co v Nottingham F
Fulham v Preston NE
Leeds U v Reading
Norwich C v Hull C
Sheffield U v Ipswich T
Sunderland v QPR
Wolverhampton W v Aston Villa

Saturday, 21 October 2017
Aston Villa v Fulham
Barnsley v Hull C
Bolton W v QPR
Brentford v Sunderland
Bristol C v Leeds U
Derby Co v Sheffield W
Ipswich T v Norwich C
Middlesbrough v Cardiff C
Millwall v Birmingham C
Nottingham F v Burton Alb
Sheffield U v Reading
Wolverhampton W v Preston NE

Saturday, 28 October 2017
Birmingham C v Aston Villa
Burton Alb v Ipswich T
Cardiff C v Millwall
Fulham v Bolton W
Hull C v Nottingham F
Leeds U v Sheffield U
Norwich C v Derby Co
Preston NE v Brentford
QPR v Wolverhampton W
Reading v Middlesbrough
Sheffield W v Barnsley
Sunderland v Bristol C

Tuesday, 31 October 2017
Birmingham C v Brentford
Burton Alb v Barnsley
Cardiff C v Ipswich T
Fulham v Bristol C
Hull C v Middlesbrough
Leeds U v Derby Co
Norwich C v Wolverhampton W
Preston NE v Aston Villa
QPR v Sheffield U
Reading v Nottingham F
Sheffield W v Millwall
Sunderland v Bolton W

Saturday, 4 November 2017
Aston Villa v Sheffield W
Barnsley v Birmingham C
Bolton W v Norwich C

Brentford v Leeds U
Bristol C v Cardiff C
Derby Co v Reading
Ipswich T v Preston NE
Middlesbrough v Sunderland
Millwall v Burton Alb
Nottingham F v QPR
Sheffield U v Hull C
Wolverhampton W v Fulham

Saturday, 18 November 2017
Birmingham C v Nottingham F
Burton Alb v Sheffield U
Cardiff C v Brentford
Fulham v Derby Co
Hull C v Ipswich T
Leeds U v Middlesbrough
Norwich C v Barnsley
Preston NE v Bolton W
QPR v Aston Villa
Reading v Wolverhampton W
Sheffield W v Bristol C
Sunderland v Millwall

Tuesday, 21 November 2017
Aston Villa v Sunderland
Barnsley v Cardiff C
Bolton W v Reading
Brentford v Burton Alb
Bristol C v Preston NE
Derby Co v QPR
Ipswich T v Sheffield W
Middlesbrough v Birmingham C
Millwall v Hull C
Nottingham F v Norwich C
Sheffield U v Fulham
Wolverhampton W v Leeds U

Saturday, 25 November 2017
Aston Villa v Ipswich T
Barnsley v Leeds U
Burton Alb v Sunderland
Fulham v Millwall
Hull C v Bristol C
Middlesbrough v Derby Co
Norwich C v Preston NE
Nottingham F v Cardiff C
QPR v Brentford
Reading v Sheffield W
Sheffield U v Birmingham C
Wolverhampton W v Bolton W

Saturday, 2 December 2017
Birmingham C v Wolverhampton W
Bolton W v Barnsley
Brentford v Fulham
Bristol C v Middlesbrough
Cardiff C v Norwich C
Derby Co v Burton Alb
Ipswich T v Nottingham F
Leeds U v Aston Villa
Millwall v Sheffield U
Preston NE v QPR
Sheffield W v Hull C
Sunderland v Reading

Saturday, 9 December 2017
Aston Villa v Millwall
Barnsley v Derby Co
Burton Alb v Preston NE
Fulham v Birmingham C
Hull C v Brentford
Middlesbrough v Ipswich T
Norwich C v Sheffield W
Nottingham F v Bolton W
QPR v Leeds U
Reading v Cardiff C
Sheffield U v Bristol C
Wolverhampton W v Sunderland

Saturday, 16 December 2017
Birmingham C v QPR
Bolton W v Burton Alb
Brentford v Barnsley
Bristol C v Nottingham F
Cardiff C v Hull C
Derby Co v Aston Villa
Ipswich T v Reading
Leeds U v Norwich C
Millwall v Middlesbrough
Preston NE v Sheffield U
Sheffield W v Wolverhampton W
Sunderland v Fulham

Saturday, 23 December 2017
Aston Villa v Sheffield U
Bolton W v Cardiff C
Derby Co v Millwall
Fulham v Barnsley
Leeds U v Hull C
Norwich C v Brentford
Preston NE v Nottingham F
QPR v Bristol C
Reading v Burton Alb
Sheffield W v Middlesbrough
Sunderland v Birmingham C
Wolverhampton W v Ipswich T

Tuesday, 26 December 2017
Barnsley v Preston NE
Birmingham C v Norwich C
Brentford v Aston Villa
Bristol C v Reading
Burton Alb v Leeds U
Cardiff C v Fulham
Hull C v Derby Co
Ipswich T v QPR
Middlesbrough v Bolton W
Millwall v Wolverhampton W
Nottingham F v Sheffield W
Sheffield U v Sunderland

Saturday, 30 December 2017
Barnsley v Reading
Birmingham C v Leeds U
Brentford v Sheffield W
Bristol C v Wolverhampton W
Burton Alb v Norwich C
Cardiff C v Preston NE
Hull C v Fulham
Ipswich T v Derby Co
Middlesbrough v Aston Villa
Millwall v QPR
Nottingham F v Sunderland
Sheffield U v Bolton W

Monday, 1 January 2018
Aston Villa v Bristol C
Bolton W v Hull C
Derby Co v Sheffield U
Fulham v Ipswich T
Leeds U v Nottingham F
Norwich C v Millwall
Preston NE v Middlesbrough
QPR v Cardiff C
Reading v Birmingham C
Sheffield W v Burton Alb
Sunderland v Barnsley
Wolverhampton W v Brentford

Saturday, 13 January 2018
Barnsley v Wolverhampton W
Birmingham C v Derby Co
Brentford v Bolton W
Bristol C v Norwich C
Burton Alb v QPR
Cardiff C v Sunderland
Hull C v Reading
Ipswich T v Leeds U
Middlesbrough v Fulham
Millwall v Preston NE
Nottingham F v Aston Villa
Sheffield U v Sheffield W

Saturday, 20 January 2018
Aston Villa v Barnsley
Bolton W v Ipswich T
Derby Co v Bristol C
Fulham v Burton Alb
Leeds U v Millwall
Norwich C v Sheffield U
Preston NE v Birmingham C
QPR v Middlesbrough
Reading v Brentford
Sheffield W v Cardiff C
Sunderland v Hull C
Wolverhampton W v Nottingham F

Saturday, 27 January 2018
Barnsley v Fulham
Birmingham C v Sunderland
Brentford v Norwich C
Bristol C v QPR
Burton Alb v Reading
Cardiff C v Bolton W
Hull C v Leeds U
Ipswich T v Wolverhampton W
Middlesbrough v Sheffield W
Millwall v Derby Co
Nottingham F v Preston NE
Sheffield U v Aston Villa

Saturday, 3 February 2018
Aston Villa v Burton Alb
Bolton W v Bristol C
Derby Co v Brentford
Fulham v Nottingham F
Leeds U v Cardiff C
Norwich C v Middlesbrough
Preston NE v Hull C
QPR v Barnsley
Reading v Millwall
Sheffield W v Birmingham C
Sunderland v Ipswich T
Wolverhampton W v Sheffield U

Saturday, 10 February 2018
Aston Villa v Birmingham C
Barnsley v Sheffield W
Bolton W v Fulham
Brentford v Preston NE
Bristol C v Sunderland
Derby Co v Norwich C
Ipswich T v Burton Alb
Middlesbrough v Reading
Millwall v Cardiff C
Nottingham F v Hull C
Sheffield U v Leeds U
Wolverhampton W v QPR

Saturday, 17 February 2018
Birmingham C v Millwall
Burton Alb v Nottingham F
Cardiff C v Middlesbrough
Fulham v Aston Villa
Hull C v Barnsley
Leeds U v Bristol C
Norwich C v Ipswich T
Preston NE v Wolverhampton W
QPR v Bolton W
Reading v Sheffield U
Sheffield W v Derby Co
Sunderland v Brentford

Tuesday, 20 February 2018
Aston Villa v Preston NE
Barnsley v Burton Alb
Bolton W v Sunderland
Brentford v Birmingham C
Bristol C v Fulham
Derby Co v Leeds U
Ipswich T v Cardiff C
Middlesbrough v Hull C
Millwall v Sheffield W
Nottingham F v Reading
Sheffield U v QPR
Wolverhampton W v Norwich C

Saturday, 24 February 2018
Birmingham C v Barnsley
Burton Alb v Millwall
Cardiff C v Bristol C
Fulham v Wolverhampton W
Hull C v Sheffield U
Leeds U v Brentford
Norwich C v Bolton W
Preston NE v Ipswich T
QPR v Nottingham F
Reading v Derby Co
Sheffield W v Aston Villa
Sunderland v Middlesbrough

Saturday, 3 March 2018
Aston Villa v QPR
Barnsley v Norwich C
Bolton W v Preston NE
Brentford v Cardiff C
Bristol C v Sheffield W
Derby Co v Fulham
Ipswich T v Hull C
Middlesbrough v Leeds U
Millwall v Sunderland
Nottingham F v Birmingham C
Sheffield U v Burton Alb
Wolverhampton W v Reading

Tuesday, 6 March 2018
Birmingham C v Middlesbrough
Burton Alb v Brentford
Cardiff C v Barnsley
Fulham v Sheffield U
Hull C v Millwall
Leeds U v Wolverhampton W
Norwich C v Nottingham F
Preston NE v Bristol C
QPR v Derby Co
Reading v Bolton W
Sheffield W v Ipswich T
Sunderland v Aston Villa

Saturday, 10 March 2018
Aston Villa v Wolverhampton W
Burton Alb v Bristol C
Cardiff C v Birmingham C
Hull C v Norwich C
Ipswich T v Sheffield U
Middlesbrough v Barnsley
Millwall v Brentford
Nottingham F v Derby Co
Preston NE v Fulham
QPR v Sunderland
Reading v Leeds U
Sheffield W v Bolton W

Saturday, 17 March 2018
Barnsley v Millwall
Birmingham C v Hull C
Bolton W v Aston Villa
Brentford v Middlesbrough
Bristol C v Ipswich T
Derby Co v Cardiff C
Fulham v QPR
Leeds U v Sheffield W
Norwich C v Reading
Sheffield U v Nottingham F
Sunderland v Preston NE
Wolverhampton W v Burton Alb

Saturday, 31 March 2018
Barnsley v Bristol C
Birmingham C v Ipswich T
Brentford v Sheffield U
Cardiff C v Burton Alb
Derby Co v Sunderland
Hull C v Aston Villa
Leeds U v Bolton W
Middlesbrough v Wolverhampton W
Millwall v Nottingham F
Norwich C v Fulham
Reading v QPR
Sheffield W v Preston NE

Monday, 2 April 2018
Aston Villa v Reading
Bolton W v Birmingham C
Bristol C v Brentford
Burton Alb v Middlesbrough
Fulham v Leeds U
Ipswich T v Millwall
Nottingham F v Barnsley
Preston NE v Derby Co
QPR v Norwich C
Sheffield U v Cardiff C
Sunderland v Sheffield W
Wolverhampton W v Hull C

Saturday, 7 April 2018
Barnsley v Sheffield U
Birmingham C v Burton Alb
Brentford v Ipswich T
Cardiff C v Wolverhampton W
Derby Co v Bolton W
Hull C v QPR
Leeds U v Sunderland
Middlesbrough v Nottingham F
Millwall v Bristol C
Norwich C v Aston Villa
Reading v Preston NE
Sheffield W v Fulham

Tuesday, 10 April 2018
Aston Villa v Cardiff C
Bolton W v Millwall
Bristol C v Birmingham C
Burton Alb v Hull C
Fulham v Reading
Ipswich T v Barnsley
Nottingham F v Brentford
Preston NE v Leeds U
QPR v Sheffield W
Sheffield U v Middlesbrough
Sunderland v Norwich C
Wolverhampton W v Derby Co

Saturday, 14 April 2018
Aston Villa v Leeds U
Barnsley v Bolton W
Burton Alb v Derby Co
Fulham v Brentford
Hull C v Sheffield W
Middlesbrough v Bristol C
Norwich C v Cardiff C
Nottingham F v Ipswich T
QPR v Preston NE
Reading v Sunderland
Sheffield U v Millwall
Wolverhampton W v Birmingham C

Saturday, 21 April 2018
Birmingham C v Sheffield U
Bolton W v Wolverhampton W
Brentford v QPR
Bristol C v Hull C
Cardiff C v Nottingham F
Derby Co v Middlesbrough
Ipswich T v Aston Villa
Leeds U v Barnsley
Millwall v Fulham
Preston NE v Norwich C
Sheffield W v Reading
Sunderland v Burton Alb

Saturday, 28 April 2018
Aston Villa v Derby Co
Barnsley v Brentford
Burton Alb v Bolton W
Fulham v Sunderland
Hull C v Cardiff C
Middlesbrough v Millwall
Norwich C v Leeds U
Nottingham F v Bristol C
QPR v Birmingham C
Reading v Ipswich T
Sheffield U v Preston NE
Wolverhampton W v Sheffield W

Sunday, 6 May 2018
Birmingham C v Fulham
Bolton W v Nottingham F
Brentford v Hull C
Bristol C v Sheffield U
Cardiff C v Reading
Derby Co v Barnsley
Ipswich T v Middlesbrough
Leeds U v QPR
Millwall v Aston Villa
Preston NE v Burton Alb
Sheffield W v Norwich C
Sunderland v Wolverhampton W

EFL League One

Saturday, 5 August 2017
Bradford C v Blackpool
Bury v Walsall
Charlton Ath v Bristol R
Doncaster R v Gillingham
Fleetwood T v Rotherham U
Milton Keynes D v Wigan Ath
Oldham Ath v Oxford U
Peterborough U v Plymouth Arg
Portsmouth v Rochdale
Scunthorpe U v AFC Wimbledon
Shrewsbury T v Northampton T
Southend U v Blackburn R

Saturday, 12 August 2017
AFC Wimbledon v Shrewsbury T
Blackburn R v Doncaster R
Blackpool v Milton Keynes D
Bristol R v Peterborough U
Gillingham v Bradford C
Northampton T v Fleetwood T
Oxford U v Portsmouth
Plymouth Arg v Charlton Ath
Rochdale v Scunthorpe U
Rotherham U v Southend U
Walsall v Oldham Ath
Wigan Ath v Bury

Saturday, 19 August 2017
Bradford C v Blackburn R
Bury v Bristol R
Charlton Ath v Northampton T
Doncaster R v Blackpool
Fleetwood T v AFC Wimbledon
Milton Keynes D v Gillingham
Oldham Ath v Wigan Ath
Peterborough U v Rotherham U
Portsmouth v Walsall
Scunthorpe U v Oxford U
Shrewsbury T v Rochdale
Southend U v Plymouth Arg

Saturday, 26 August 2017
AFC Wimbledon v Doncaster R
Blackburn R v Milton Keynes D
Blackpool v Oldham Ath
Bristol R v Fleetwood T
Gillingham v Southend U
Northampton T v Peterborough U
Oxford U v Shrewsbury T
Plymouth Arg v Scunthorpe U
Rochdale v Bury
Rotherham U v Charlton Ath
Walsall v Bradford C
Wigan Ath v Portsmouth

Saturday, 2 September 2017
Blackpool v AFC Wimbledon
Bradford C v Bristol R* (12:30)
Bury v Scunthorpe U
Doncaster R v Peterborough U
Gillingham v Shrewsbury T
Milton Keynes D v Oxford U
Oldham Ath v Charlton Ath
Southend U v Rochdale
Walsall v Plymouth Arg
Wigan Ath v Northampton T

Sunday, 3 September 2017
Blackburn R v Fleetwood T* (12:15)
Portsmouth v Rotherham U* (14:30)

Saturday, 9 September 2017
AFC Wimbledon v Portsmouth
Bristol R v Walsall
Charlton Ath v Southend U
Fleetwood T v Oldham Ath
Northampton T v Doncaster R
Oxford U v Gillingham
Peterborough U v Bradford C
Plymouth Arg v Milton Keynes D
Rochdale v Blackburn R
Rotherham U v Bury
Scunthorpe U v Blackpool
Shrewsbury T v Wigan Ath

Tuesday, 12 September 2017
AFC Wimbledon v Gillingham
Bristol R v Oldham Ath
Charlton Ath v Wigan Ath
Fleetwood T v Bury
Northampton T v Portsmouth
Oxford U v Bradford C
Peterborough U v Milton Keynes D
Plymouth Arg v Blackpool
Rochdale v Doncaster R
Rotherham U v Walsall
Scunthorpe U v Blackburn R
Shrewsbury T v Southend U

Saturday, 16 September 2017
Blackburn R v AFC Wimbledon
Blackpool v Oxford U
Bradford C v Rotherham U
Bury v Plymouth Arg
Doncaster R v Scunthorpe U
Gillingham v Charlton Ath
Milton Keynes D v Rochdale
Oldham Ath v Shrewsbury T
Portsmouth v Fleetwood T
Southend U v Northampton T
Walsall v Peterborough U
Wigan Ath v Bristol R

Saturday, 23 September 2017
AFC Wimbledon v Milton Keynes D
Bristol R v Blackpool
Charlton Ath v Bury
Fleetwood T v Southend U
Northampton T v Bradford C
Oxford U v Walsall
Peterborough U v Wigan Ath
Plymouth Arg v Doncaster R
Rochdale v Gillingham
Rotherham U v Oldham Ath
Scunthorpe U v Portsmouth
Shrewsbury T v Blackburn R

Tuesday, 26 September 2017
Blackburn R v Rotherham U
Blackpool v Rochdale
Bradford C v Fleetwood T
Bury v Oxford U
Doncaster R v Shrewsbury T
Gillingham v Scunthorpe U
Milton Keynes D v Northampton T
Oldham Ath v Peterborough U
Portsmouth v Bristol R
Southend U v AFC Wimbledon
Walsall v Charlton Ath
Wigan Ath v Plymouth Arg

Saturday, 30 September 2017
AFC Wimbledon v Rochdale
Blackburn R v Gillingham
Bradford C v Doncaster R
Bristol R v Plymouth Arg
Bury v Milton Keynes D
Fleetwood T v Charlton Ath
Peterborough U v Oxford U
Portsmouth v Oldham Ath
Rotherham U v Northampton T
Shrewsbury T v Scunthorpe U
Southend U v Blackpool
Wigan Ath v Walsall

Saturday, 7 October 2017
Blackpool v Blackburn R
Charlton Ath v Peterborough U
Doncaster R v Southend U
Gillingham v Portsmouth
Milton Keynes D v Bradford C
Northampton T v Bristol R
Oldham Ath v Bury
Oxford U v AFC Wimbledon
Plymouth Arg v Fleetwood T
Rochdale v Rotherham U
Scunthorpe U v Wigan Ath
Walsall v Shrewsbury T

Saturday, 14 October 2017
Bristol R v Oxford U
Bury v Bradford C
Charlton Ath v Doncaster R
Fleetwood T v Rochdale
Northampton T v AFC Wimbledon
Oldham Ath v Blackburn R
Peterborough U v Gillingham
Plymouth Arg v Shrewsbury T
Portsmouth v Milton Keynes D
Rotherham U v Scunthorpe U
Walsall v Blackpool
Wigan Ath v Southend U

Tuesday, 17 October 2017
AFC Wimbledon v Rotherham U
Blackburn R v Plymouth Arg
Blackpool v Bury
Bradford C v Oldham Ath
Doncaster R v Portsmouth
Gillingham v Wigan Ath
Milton Keynes D v Walsall
Oxford U v Charlton Ath
Rochdale v Northampton T
Scunthorpe U v Fleetwood T
Shrewsbury T v Bristol R
Southend U v Peterborough U

Saturday, 21 October 2017
AFC Wimbledon v Plymouth Arg
Blackburn R v Portsmouth
Blackpool v Wigan Ath
Bradford C v Charlton Ath
Doncaster R v Walsall
Gillingham v Northampton T
Milton Keynes D v Oldham Ath
Oxford U v Rotherham U
Rochdale v Bristol R
Scunthorpe U v Peterborough U
Shrewsbury T v Fleetwood T
Southend U v Bury

Saturday, 28 October 2017
Bristol R v Milton Keynes D
Bury v Doncaster R
Charlton Ath v AFC Wimbledon
Fleetwood T v Oxford U
Northampton T v Blackpool
Oldham Ath v Scunthorpe U
Peterborough U v Shrewsbury T
Plymouth Arg v Rochdale
Portsmouth v Bradford C
Rotherham U v Gillingham
Walsall v Southend U
Wigan Ath v Blackburn R

Saturday, 11 November 2017
AFC Wimbledon v Peterborough U
Blackburn R v Walsall
Blackpool v Portsmouth
Bradford C v Plymouth Arg
Doncaster R v Rotherham U
Gillingham v Bury
Milton Keynes D v Fleetwood T
Oxford U v Northampton T
Rochdale v Wigan Ath
Scunthorpe U v Bristol R
Shrewsbury T v Charlton Ath
Southend U v Oldham Ath

Saturday, 18 November 2017
Bristol R v AFC Wimbledon
Bury v Blackburn R
Charlton Ath v Milton Keynes D
Fleetwood T v Doncaster R
Northampton T v Scunthorpe U
Oldham Ath v Rochdale
Peterborough U v Blackpool
Plymouth Arg v Oxford U
Portsmouth v Southend U
Rotherham U v Shrewsbury T
Walsall v Gillingham
Wigan Ath v Bradford C

Tuesday, 21 November 2017
Blackpool v Gillingham
Bradford C v Scunthorpe U
Bristol R v Rotherham U
Bury v Shrewsbury T
Charlton Ath v Rochdale
Milton Keynes D v Southend U
Oldham Ath v AFC Wimbledon
Oxford U v Blackburn R
Peterborough U v Portsmouth
Plymouth Arg v Northampton T
Walsall v Fleetwood T
Wigan Ath v Doncaster R

Saturday, 25 November 2017
AFC Wimbledon v Walsall
Blackburn R v Bristol R
Doncaster R v Milton Keynes D
Fleetwood T v Blackpool
Gillingham v Oldham Ath
Northampton T v Bury
Portsmouth v Plymouth Arg
Rochdale v Peterborough U
Rotherham U v Wigan Ath
Scunthorpe U v Charlton Ath
Shrewsbury T v Bradford C
Southend U v Oxford U

Saturday, 9 December 2017
Blackpool v Rotherham U
Bradford C v Rochdale
Bristol R v Southend U
Bury v AFC Wimbledon
Charlton Ath v Portsmouth
Milton Keynes D v Shrewsbury T
Oldham Ath v Northampton T
Oxford U v Doncaster R
Peterborough U v Blackburn R
Plymouth Arg v Gillingham
Walsall v Scunthorpe U
Wigan Ath v Fleetwood T

Saturday, 16 December 2017
AFC Wimbledon v Wigan Ath
Blackburn R v Charlton Ath
Doncaster R v Oldham Ath
Fleetwood T v Peterborough U
Gillingham v Bristol R
Northampton T v Walsall
Portsmouth v Bury
Rochdale v Oxford U
Rotherham U v Plymouth Arg
Scunthorpe U v Milton Keynes D
Shrewsbury T v Blackpool
Southend U v Bradford C

Saturday, 23 December 2017
AFC Wimbledon v Bradford C
Bristol R v Doncaster R
Charlton Ath v Blackpool
Fleetwood T v Gillingham
Northampton T v Blackburn R
Oxford U v Wigan Ath

Peterborough U v Bury
Plymouth Arg v Oldham Ath
Rochdale v Walsall
Rotherham U v Milton Keynes D
Scunthorpe U v Southend U
Shrewsbury T v Portsmouth

Tuesday, 26 December 2017
Blackburn R v Rochdale
Blackpool v Scunthorpe U
Bradford C v Peterborough U
Bury v Rotherham U
Doncaster R v Northampton T
Gillingham v Oxford U
Milton Keynes D v Plymouth Arg
Oldham Ath v Fleetwood T
Portsmouth v AFC Wimbledon
Southend U v Charlton Ath
Walsall v Bristol R
Wigan Ath v Shrewsbury T

Saturday, 30 December 2017
Blackburn R v Scunthorpe U
Blackpool v Plymouth Arg
Bradford C v Oxford U
Bury v Fleetwood T
Doncaster R v Rochdale
Gillingham v AFC Wimbledon
Milton Keynes D v Peterborough U
Oldham Ath v Bristol R
Portsmouth v Northampton T
Southend U v Shrewsbury T
Walsall v Rotherham U
Wigan Ath v Charlton Ath

Monday, 1 January 2018
AFC Wimbledon v Southend U
Bristol R v Portsmouth
Charlton Ath v Gillingham
Fleetwood T v Bradford C
Northampton T v Wigan Ath
Oxford U v Milton Keynes D
Peterborough U v Doncaster R
Plymouth Arg v Walsall
Rochdale v Blackpool
Rotherham U v Blackburn R
Scunthorpe U v Bury
Shrewsbury T v Oldham Ath

Saturday, 6 January 2018
AFC Wimbledon v Blackburn R
Bristol R v Wigan Ath
Charlton Ath v Oldham Ath
Fleetwood T v Portsmouth
Northampton T v Southend U
Oxford U v Blackpool
Peterborough U v Walsall
Plymouth Arg v Bury
Rochdale v Milton Keynes D
Rotherham U v Bradford C
Scunthorpe U v Doncaster R
Shrewsbury T v Gillingham

Saturday, 13 January 2018
Blackburn R v Shrewsbury T
Blackpool v Bristol R
Bradford C v Northampton T
Bury v Charlton Ath
Doncaster R v Plymouth Arg
Gillingham v Rochdale
Milton Keynes D v AFC Wimbledon
Oldham Ath v Rotherham U
Portsmouth v Scunthorpe U
Southend U v Fleetwood T
Walsall v Oxford U
Wigan Ath v Peterborough U

Saturday, 20 January 2018
AFC Wimbledon v Blackpool
Bristol R v Bradford C
Charlton Ath v Walsall
Fleetwood T v Blackburn R
Northampton T v Milton Keynes D
Oxford U v Bury
Peterborough U v Oldham Ath
Plymouth Arg v Wigan Ath
Rochdale v Southend U
Rotherham U v Portsmouth
Scunthorpe U v Gillingham
Shrewsbury T v Doncaster R

Saturday, 27 January 2018
Blackburn R v Northampton T
Blackpool v Charlton Ath
Bradford C v AFC Wimbledon
Bury v Peterborough U
Doncaster R v Bristol R
Gillingham v Fleetwood T
Milton Keynes D v Rotherham U
Oldham Ath v Plymouth Arg
Portsmouth v Shrewsbury T
Southend U v Scunthorpe U
Walsall v Rochdale
Wigan Ath v Oxford U

Saturday, 3 February 2018
Bristol R v Shrewsbury T
Bury v Blackpool
Charlton Ath v Oxford U
Fleetwood T v Scunthorpe U
Northampton T v Rochdale
Oldham Ath v Bradford C
Peterborough U v Southend U
Plymouth Arg v Blackburn R
Portsmouth v Doncaster R
Rotherham U v AFC Wimbledon
Walsall v Milton Keynes D
Wigan Ath v Gillingham

Saturday, 10 February 2018
AFC Wimbledon v Northampton T
Blackburn R v Oldham Ath
Blackpool v Walsall
Bradford C v Bury
Doncaster R v Charlton Ath
Gillingham v Peterborough U
Milton Keynes D v Portsmouth
Oxford U v Bristol R
Rochdale v Fleetwood T
Scunthorpe U v Rotherham U
Shrewsbury T v Plymouth Arg
Southend U v Wigan Ath

Tuesday, 13 February 2018
Bristol R v Rochdale
Bury v Southend U
Charlton Ath v Bradford C
Fleetwood T v Shrewsbury T
Northampton T v Gillingham
Oldham Ath v Milton Keynes D
Peterborough U v Scunthorpe U
Plymouth Arg v AFC Wimbledon
Portsmouth v Blackburn R
Rotherham U v Oxford U
Walsall v Doncaster R
Wigan Ath v Blackpool

Saturday, 17 February 2018
AFC Wimbledon v Bristol R
Blackburn R v Bury
Blackpool v Peterborough U
Bradford C v Wigan Ath
Doncaster R v Fleetwood T
Gillingham v Walsall
Milton Keynes D v Charlton Ath
Oxford U v Plymouth Arg
Rochdale v Oldham Ath
Scunthorpe U v Northampton T
Shrewsbury T v Rotherham U
Southend U v Portsmouth

Saturday, 24 February 2018
Bristol R v Scunthorpe U
Bury v Gillingham
Charlton Ath v Shrewsbury T
Fleetwood T v Milton Keynes D
Northampton T v Oxford U
Oldham Ath v Southend U
Peterborough U v AFC Wimbledon
Plymouth Arg v Bradford C
Portsmouth v Blackpool
Rotherham U v Doncaster R
Walsall v Blackburn R
Wigan Ath v Rochdale

Saturday, 3 March 2018
AFC Wimbledon v Charlton Ath
Blackburn R v Wigan Ath
Blackpool v Northampton T
Bradford C v Portsmouth
Doncaster R v Bury
Gillingham v Rotherham U
Milton Keynes D v Bristol R
Oxford U v Fleetwood T
Rochdale v Plymouth Arg
Scunthorpe U v Oldham Ath
Shrewsbury T v Peterborough U
Southend U v Walsall

Saturday, 10 March 2018
AFC Wimbledon v Oxford U
Blackburn R v Blackpool
Bradford C v Milton Keynes D
Bristol R v Northampton T
Bury v Oldham Ath
Fleetwood T v Plymouth Arg
Peterborough U v Charlton Ath
Portsmouth v Gillingham
Rotherham U v Rochdale
Shrewsbury T v Walsall
Southend U v Doncaster R
Wigan Ath v Scunthorpe U

Saturday, 17 March 2018
Blackpool v Southend U
Charlton Ath v Fleetwood T
Doncaster R v Bradford C
Gillingham v Blackburn R
Milton Keynes D v Bury
Northampton T v Rotherham U
Oldham Ath v Portsmouth
Oxford U v Peterborough U
Plymouth Arg v Bristol R
Rochdale v AFC Wimbledon
Scunthorpe U v Shrewsbury T
Walsall v Wigan Ath

Saturday, 24 March 2018
Bradford C v Gillingham
Bury v Wigan Ath
Charlton Ath v Plymouth Arg
Doncaster R v Blackburn R
Fleetwood T v Northampton T
Milton Keynes D v Blackpool
Oldham Ath v Walsall
Peterborough U v Bristol R
Portsmouth v Oxford U
Scunthorpe U v Rochdale
Shrewsbury T v AFC Wimbledon
Southend U v Rotherham U

Saturday, 31 March 2018
AFC Wimbledon v Fleetwood T
Blackburn R v Bradford C
Blackpool v Doncaster R
Bristol R v Bury
Gillingham v Milton Keynes D
Northampton T v Charlton Ath
Oxford U v Scunthorpe U
Plymouth Arg v Southend U
Rochdale v Shrewsbury T
Rotherham U v Peterborough U
Walsall v Portsmouth
Wigan Ath v Oldham Ath

Monday, 2 April 2018
Bradford C v Walsall
Bury v Rochdale
Charlton Ath v Rotherham U

Doncaster R v AFC Wimbledon
Fleetwood T v Bristol R
Milton Keynes D v Blackburn R
Oldham Ath v Blackpool
Peterborough U v Northampton T
Portsmouth v Wigan Ath
Scunthorpe U v Plymouth Arg
Shrewsbury T v Oxford U
Southend U v Gillingham

Saturday, 7 April 2018
AFC Wimbledon v Scunthorpe U
Blackburn R v Southend U
Blackpool v Bradford C
Bristol R v Charlton Ath
Gillingham v Doncaster R
Northampton T v Shrewsbury T
Oxford U v Oldham Ath
Plymouth Arg v Peterborough U
Rochdale v Portsmouth
Rotherham U v Fleetwood T
Walsall v Bury
Wigan Ath v Milton Keynes D

Saturday, 14 April 2018
Blackpool v Fleetwood T
Bradford C v Shrewsbury T
Bristol R v Blackburn R
Bury v Northampton T
Charlton Ath v Scunthorpe U
Milton Keynes D v Doncaster R
Oldham Ath v Gillingham
Oxford U v Southend U
Peterborough U v Rochdale
Plymouth Arg v Portsmouth
Walsall v AFC Wimbledon
Wigan Ath v Rotherham U

Saturday, 21 April 2018
AFC Wimbledon v Oldham Ath
Blackburn R v Peterborough U
Doncaster R v Oxford U
Fleetwood T v Wigan Ath
Gillingham v Blackpool
Northampton T v Plymouth Arg
Portsmouth v Charlton Ath
Rochdale v Bradford C
Rotherham U v Bristol R
Scunthorpe U v Walsall
Shrewsbury T v Bury
Southend U v Milton Keynes D

Saturday, 28 April 2018
Blackpool v Shrewsbury T
Bradford C v Southend U
Bristol R v Gillingham
Bury v Portsmouth
Charlton Ath v Blackburn R
Milton Keynes D v Scunthorpe U
Oldham Ath v Doncaster R
Oxford U v Rochdale
Peterborough U v Fleetwood T
Plymouth Arg v Rotherham U
Walsall v Northampton T
Wigan Ath v AFC Wimbledon

Saturday, 5 May 2018
AFC Wimbledon v Bury
Blackburn R v Oxford U
Doncaster R v Wigan Ath
Fleetwood T v Walsall
Gillingham v Plymouth Arg
Northampton T v Oldham Ath
Portsmouth v Peterborough U
Rochdale v Charlton Ath
Rotherham U v Blackpool
Scunthorpe U v Bradford C
Shrewsbury T v Milton Keynes D
Southend U v Bristol R

EFL League Two

Saturday, 5 August 2017
Accrington S v Colchester U
Carlisle U v Swindon T
Chesterfield v Grimsby T
Coventry C v Notts Co
Crawley T v Port Vale
Crewe Alex v Mansfield T
Exeter C v Cambridge U
Forest Green R v Barnet
Luton T v Yeovil T
Morecambe v Cheltenham T
Stevenage v Newport Co
Wycombe W v Lincoln C

Saturday, 12 August 2017
Barnet v Luton T
Cambridge U v Carlisle U
Cheltenham T v Crawley T
Colchester U v Stevenage
Grimsby T v Coventry C
Lincoln C v Morecambe
Mansfield T v Forest Green R
Newport Co v Crewe Alex
Notts Co v Chesterfield
Port Vale v Wycombe W
Swindon T v Exeter C
Yeovil T v Accrington S

Saturday, 19 August 2017
Accrington S v Mansfield T
Carlisle U v Cheltenham T
Chesterfield v Port Vale
Coventry C v Newport Co
Crawley T v Cambridge U
Crewe Alex v Barnet
Exeter C v Lincoln C
Forest Green R v Yeovil T
Luton T v Colchester U
Morecambe v Swindon T
Stevenage v Grimsby T
Wycombe W v Notts Co

Saturday, 26 August 2017
Barnet v Stevenage
Cambridge U v Morecambe
Cheltenham T v Exeter C
Colchester U v Forest Green R
Grimsby T v Wycombe W
Lincoln C v Carlisle U
Mansfield T v Luton T
Newport Co v Chesterfield
Notts Co v Accrington S
Port Vale v Crewe Alex
Swindon T v Crawley T
Yeovil T v Coventry C

Saturday, 2 September 2017
Cambridge U v Colchester U
Carlisle U v Mansfield T
Cheltenham T v Stevenage
Chesterfield v Coventry C
Crawley T v Yeovil T
Exeter C v Newport Co
Grimsby T v Crewe Alex
Lincoln C v Luton T
Morecambe v Accrington S
Port Vale v Notts Co
Swindon T v Barnet
Wycombe W v Forest Green R

Saturday, 9 September 2017
Accrington S v Carlisle U
Barnet v Cambridge U
Colchester U v Crawley T
Coventry C v Port Vale
Crewe Alex v Chesterfield
Forest Green R v Exeter C
Luton T v Swindon T
Mansfield T v Grimsby T
Newport Co v Wycombe W
Notts Co v Morecambe
Stevenage v Lincoln C
Yeovil T v Cheltenham T

Tuesday, 12 September 2017
Accrington S v Grimsby T
Barnet v Exeter C
Colchester U v Chesterfield
Coventry C v Carlisle U
Crewe Alex v Cambridge U
Forest Green R v Lincoln C
Luton T v Port Vale
Mansfield T v Wycombe W
Newport Co v Cheltenham T
Notts Co v Swindon T
Stevenage v Crawley T
Yeovil T v Morecambe

Saturday, 16 September 2017
Cambridge U v Coventry C
Carlisle U v Barnet
Cheltenham T v Colchester U
Chesterfield v Accrington S
Crawley T v Notts Co
Exeter C v Crewe Alex
Grimsby T v Yeovil T
Lincoln C v Mansfield T
Morecambe v Newport Co
Port Vale v Forest Green R
Swindon T v Stevenage
Wycombe W v Luton T

Saturday, 23 September 2017
Accrington S v Cheltenham T
Barnet v Crawley T
Colchester U v Wycombe W
Coventry C v Exeter C
Crewe Alex v Carlisle U
Forest Green R v Swindon T
Luton T v Chesterfield
Mansfield T v Cambridge U
Newport Co v Grimsby T
Notts Co v Lincoln C
Stevenage v Morecambe
Yeovil T v Port Vale

Tuesday, 26 September 2017
Cambridge U v Forest Green R
Carlisle U v Stevenage
Cheltenham T v Mansfield T
Chesterfield v Yeovil T
Crawley T v Newport Co
Exeter C v Notts Co
Grimsby T v Colchester U
Lincoln C v Barnet
Morecambe v Luton T
Port Vale v Accrington S
Swindon T v Coventry C
Wycombe W v Crewe Alex

Saturday, 30 September 2017
Chesterfield v Cheltenham T
Coventry C v Crewe Alex
Crawley T v Carlisle U
Exeter C v Morecambe
Forest Green R v Accrington S
Grimsby T v Lincoln C
Luton T v Newport Co
Mansfield T v Notts Co
Stevenage v Port Vale
Swindon T v Cambridge U
Wycombe W v Barnet
Yeovil T v Colchester U

Saturday, 7 October 2017
Accrington S v Luton T
Barnet v Coventry C
Cambridge U v Wycombe W
Carlisle U v Exeter C
Cheltenham T v Swindon T
Colchester U v Mansfield T
Crewe Alex v Stevenage
Lincoln C v Chesterfield

Morecambe v Crawley T
Newport Co v Yeovil T
Notts Co v Forest Green R
Port Vale v Grimsby T

Saturday, 14 October 2017
Accrington S v Coventry C
Chesterfield v Morecambe
Colchester U v Carlisle U
Forest Green R v Newport Co
Grimsby T v Crawley T
Lincoln C v Cambridge U
Luton T v Stevenage
Mansfield T v Swindon T
Notts Co v Barnet
Port Vale v Cheltenham T
Wycombe W v Exeter C
Yeovil T v Crewe Alex

Tuesday, 17 October 2017
Barnet v Mansfield T
Cambridge U v Yeovil T
Carlisle U v Wycombe W
Cheltenham T v Grimsby T
Coventry C v Forest Green R
Crawley T v Chesterfield
Crewe Alex v Notts Co
Exeter C v Luton T
Morecambe v Port Vale
Newport Co v Colchester U
Stevenage v Accrington S
Swindon T v Lincoln C

Saturday, 21 October 2017
Barnet v Yeovil T
Cambridge U v Chesterfield
Carlisle U v Notts Co
Cheltenham T v Lincoln C
Coventry C v Colchester U
Crawley T v Luton T
Crewe Alex v Accrington S
Exeter C v Port Vale
Morecambe v Grimsby T
Newport Co v Mansfield T
Stevenage v Forest Green R
Swindon T v Wycombe W

Saturday, 28 October 2017
Accrington S v Barnet
Chesterfield v Carlisle U
Colchester U v Crewe Alex
Forest Green R v Morecambe
Grimsby T v Cambridge U
Lincoln C v Crawley T
Luton T v Coventry C
Mansfield T v Exeter C
Notts Co v Newport Co
Port Vale v Swindon T
Wycombe W v Cheltenham T
Yeovil T v Stevenage

Saturday, 11 November 2017
Barnet v Colchester U
Cambridge U v Accrington S
Carlisle U v Yeovil T
Cheltenham T v Luton T
Coventry C v Mansfield T
Crawley T v Forest Green R
Crewe Alex v Lincoln C
Exeter C v Grimsby T
Morecambe v Wycombe W
Newport Co v Port Vale
Stevenage v Notts Co
Swindon T v Chesterfield

Saturday, 18 November 2017
Accrington S v Newport Co
Chesterfield v Exeter C
Colchester U v Morecambe
Forest Green R v Crewe Alex
Grimsby T v Carlisle U
Lincoln C v Coventry C
Luton T v Cambridge U
Mansfield T v Stevenage
Notts Co v Cheltenham T
Port Vale v Barnet
Wycombe W v Crawley T
Yeovil T v Swindon T

Tuesday, 21 November 2017
Accrington S v Wycombe W
Cheltenham T v Cambridge U
Chesterfield v Forest Green R
Colchester U v Lincoln C
Crawley T v Exeter C
Grimsby T v Swindon T
Luton T v Carlisle U
Morecambe v Crewe Alex
Newport Co v Barnet
Port Vale v Mansfield T
Stevenage v Coventry C
Yeovil T v Notts Co

Saturday, 25 November 2017
Barnet v Grimsby T
Cambridge U v Stevenage
Carlisle U v Morecambe
Coventry C v Crawley T
Crewe Alex v Luton T
Exeter C v Accrington S
Forest Green R v Cheltenham T
Lincoln C v Port Vale
Mansfield T v Chesterfield
Notts Co v Colchester U
Swindon T v Newport Co
Wycombe W v Yeovil T

Saturday, 9 December 2017
Accrington S v Swindon T
Cheltenham T v Crewe Alex
Chesterfield v Barnet
Colchester U v Exeter C
Crawley T v Mansfield T
Grimsby T v Forest Green R
Luton T v Notts Co
Morecambe v Coventry C
Newport Co v Carlisle U
Port Vale v Cambridge U
Stevenage v Wycombe W
Yeovil T v Lincoln C

Saturday, 16 December 2017
Barnet v Morecambe
Cambridge U v Newport Co
Carlisle U v Port Vale
Coventry C v Cheltenham T
Crewe Alex v Crawley T
Exeter C v Stevenage
Forest Green R v Luton T
Lincoln C v Accrington S
Mansfield T v Yeovil T
Notts Co v Grimsby T
Swindon T v Colchester U
Wycombe W v Chesterfield

Saturday, 23 December 2017
Accrington S v Crawley T
Barnet v Cheltenham T
Colchester U v Port Vale
Coventry C v Wycombe W
Crewe Alex v Swindon T
Forest Green R v Carlisle U
Luton T v Grimsby T
Mansfield T v Morecambe
Newport Co v Lincoln C
Notts Co v Cambridge U
Stevenage v Chesterfield
Yeovil T v Exeter C

Tuesday, 26 December 2017
Cambridge U v Barnet
Carlisle U v Accrington S
Cheltenham T v Yeovil T
Chesterfield v Crewe Alex
Crawley T v Colchester U
Exeter C v Forest Green R
Grimsby T v Mansfield T
Lincoln C v Stevenage
Morecambe v Notts Co
Port Vale v Coventry C
Swindon T v Luton T
Wycombe W v Newport Co

Saturday, 30 December 2017
Cambridge U v Crewe Alex
Carlisle U v Coventry C
Cheltenham T v Newport Co
Chesterfield v Colchester U
Crawley T v Stevenage
Exeter C v Barnet
Grimsby T v Accrington S
Lincoln C v Forest Green R
Morecambe v Yeovil T
Port Vale v Luton T
Swindon T v Notts Co
Wycombe W v Mansfield T

Monday, 1 January 2018
Accrington S v Morecambe
Barnet v Swindon T
Colchester U v Cambridge U
Coventry C v Chesterfield
Crewe Alex v Grimsby T
Forest Green R v Wycombe W
Luton T v Lincoln C
Mansfield T v Carlisle U
Newport Co v Exeter C
Notts Co v Port Vale
Stevenage v Cheltenham T
Yeovil T v Crawley T

Saturday, 6 January 2018
Accrington S v Chesterfield
Barnet v Carlisle U
Colchester U v Cheltenham T
Coventry C v Cambridge U
Crewe Alex v Exeter C
Forest Green R v Port Vale
Luton T v Wycombe W
Mansfield T v Lincoln C
Newport Co v Morecambe
Notts Co v Crawley T
Stevenage v Swindon T
Yeovil T v Grimsby T

Saturday, 13 January 2018
Cambridge U v Mansfield T
Carlisle U v Crewe Alex
Cheltenham T v Accrington S
Chesterfield v Luton T
Crawley T v Barnet
Exeter C v Coventry C
Grimsby T v Newport Co
Lincoln C v Notts Co
Morecambe v Stevenage
Port Vale v Yeovil T
Swindon T v Forest Green R
Wycombe W v Colchester U

Saturday, 20 January 2018
Accrington S v Port Vale
Barnet v Lincoln C
Colchester U v Grimsby T
Coventry C v Swindon T
Crewe Alex v Wycombe W
Forest Green R v Cambridge U
Luton T v Morecambe
Mansfield T v Cheltenham T
Newport Co v Crawley T
Notts Co v Exeter C
Stevenage v Carlisle U
Yeovil T v Chesterfield

Saturday, 27 January 2018
Cambridge U v Notts Co
Carlisle U v Forest Green R
Cheltenham T v Barnet
Chesterfield v Stevenage
Crawley T v Accrington S

Exeter C v Yeovil T
Grimsby T v Luton T
Lincoln C v Newport Co
Morecambe v Mansfield T
Port Vale v Colchester U
Swindon T v Crewe Alex
Wycombe W v Coventry C

Saturday, 3 February 2018
Accrington S v Stevenage
Chesterfield v Crawley T
Colchester U v Newport Co
Forest Green R v Coventry C
Grimsby T v Cheltenham T
Lincoln C v Swindon T
Luton T v Exeter C
Mansfield T v Barnet
Notts Co v Crewe Alex
Port Vale v Morecambe
Wycombe W v Carlisle U
Yeovil T v Cambridge U

Saturday, 10 February 2018
Barnet v Notts Co
Cambridge U v Lincoln C
Carlisle U v Colchester U
Cheltenham T v Port Vale
Coventry C v Accrington S
Crawley T v Grimsby T
Crewe Alex v Yeovil T
Exeter C v Wycombe W
Morecambe v Chesterfield
Newport Co v Forest Green R
Stevenage v Luton T
Swindon T v Mansfield T

Tuesday, 13 February 2018
Accrington S v Crewe Alex
Chesterfield v Cambridge U
Colchester U v Coventry C
Forest Green R v Stevenage
Grimsby T v Morecambe
Lincoln C v Cheltenham T
Luton T v Crawley T
Mansfield T v Newport Co
Notts Co v Carlisle U
Port Vale v Exeter C
Wycombe W v Swindon T
Yeovil T v Barnet

Saturday, 17 February 2018
Barnet v Accrington S
Cambridge U v Grimsby T
Carlisle U v Chesterfield
Cheltenham T v Wycombe W
Coventry C v Luton T
Crawley T v Lincoln C
Crewe Alex v Colchester U
Exeter C v Mansfield T
Morecambe v Forest Green R
Newport Co v Notts Co
Stevenage v Yeovil T
Swindon T v Port Vale

Saturday, 24 February 2018
Accrington S v Cambridge U
Chesterfield v Swindon T
Colchester U v Barnet
Forest Green R v Crawley T
Grimsby T v Exeter C
Lincoln C v Crewe Alex
Luton T v Cheltenham T
Mansfield T v Coventry C
Notts Co v Stevenage
Port Vale v Newport Co
Wycombe W v Morecambe
Yeovil T v Carlisle U

Saturday, 3 March 2018
Barnet v Port Vale
Cambridge U v Luton T
Carlisle U v Grimsby T
Cheltenham T v Notts Co
Coventry C v Lincoln C
Crawley T v Wycombe W
Crewe Alex v Forest Green R
Exeter C v Chesterfield
Morecambe v Colchester U
Newport Co v Accrington S
Stevenage v Mansfield T
Swindon T v Yeovil T

Saturday, 10 March 2018
Chesterfield v Lincoln C
Coventry C v Barnet
Crawley T v Morecambe
Exeter C v Carlisle U
Forest Green R v Notts Co
Grimsby T v Port Vale
Luton T v Accrington S
Mansfield T v Colchester U
Stevenage v Crewe Alex
Swindon T v Cheltenham T
Wycombe W v Cambridge U
Yeovil T v Newport Co

Saturday, 17 March 2018
Accrington S v Forest Green R
Barnet v Wycombe W
Cambridge U v Swindon T
Carlisle U v Crawley T
Cheltenham T v Chesterfield
Colchester U v Yeovil T
Crewe Alex v Coventry C
Lincoln C v Grimsby T
Morecambe v Exeter C
Newport Co v Luton T
Notts Co v Mansfield T
Port Vale v Stevenage

Saturday, 24 March 2018
Accrington S v Yeovil T
Carlisle U v Cambridge U
Chesterfield v Notts Co
Coventry C v Grimsby T
Crawley T v Cheltenham T
Crewe Alex v Newport Co
Exeter C v Swindon T
Forest Green R v Mansfield T
Luton T v Barnet
Morecambe v Lincoln C
Stevenage v Colchester U
Wycombe W v Port Vale

Saturday, 31 March 2018
Barnet v Crewe Alex
Cambridge U v Crawley T
Cheltenham T v Carlisle U
Colchester U v Luton T
Grimsby T v Stevenage
Lincoln C v Exeter C
Mansfield T v Accrington S
Newport Co v Coventry C
Notts Co v Wycombe W
Port Vale v Chesterfield
Swindon T v Morecambe
Yeovil T v Forest Green R

Monday, 2 April 2018
Accrington S v Notts Co
Carlisle U v Lincoln C
Chesterfield v Newport Co
Coventry C v Yeovil T
Crawley T v Swindon T
Crewe Alex v Port Vale
Exeter C v Cheltenham T
Forest Green R v Colchester U
Luton T v Mansfield T
Morecambe v Cambridge U
Stevenage v Barnet
Wycombe W v Grimsby T

Saturday, 7 April 2018
Barnet v Forest Green R
Cambridge U v Exeter C
Cheltenham T v Morecambe
Colchester U v Accrington S
Grimsby T v Chesterfield
Lincoln C v Wycombe W
Mansfield T v Crewe Alex
Newport Co v Stevenage
Notts Co v Coventry C
Port Vale v Crawley T
Swindon T v Carlisle U
Yeovil T v Luton T

Saturday, 14 April 2018
Accrington S v Exeter C
Cheltenham T v Forest Green R
Chesterfield v Mansfield T
Colchester U v Notts Co
Crawley T v Coventry C
Grimsby T v Barnet
Luton T v Crewe Alex
Morecambe v Carlisle U
Newport Co v Swindon T
Port Vale v Lincoln C
Stevenage v Cambridge U
Yeovil T v Wycombe W

Saturday, 21 April 2018
Barnet v Newport Co
Cambridge U v Cheltenham T
Carlisle U v Luton T
Coventry C v Stevenage
Crewe Alex v Morecambe
Exeter C v Crawley T
Forest Green R v Chesterfield
Lincoln C v Colchester U
Mansfield T v Port Vale
Notts Co v Yeovil T
Swindon T v Grimsby T
Wycombe W v Accrington S

Saturday, 28 April 2018
Accrington S v Lincoln C
Cheltenham T v Coventry C
Chesterfield v Wycombe W
Colchester U v Swindon T
Crawley T v Crewe Alex
Grimsby T v Notts Co
Luton T v Forest Green R
Morecambe v Barnet
Newport Co v Cambridge U
Port Vale v Carlisle U
Stevenage v Exeter C
Yeovil T v Mansfield T

Saturday, 5 May 2018
Barnet v Chesterfield
Cambridge U v Port Vale
Carlisle U v Newport Co
Coventry C v Morecambe
Crewe Alex v Cheltenham T
Exeter C v Colchester U
Forest Green R v Grimsby T
Lincoln C v Yeovil T
Mansfield T v Crawley T
Notts Co v Luton T
Swindon T v Accrington S
Wycombe W v Stevenage

NATIONAL LEAGUE FIXTURES 2017–18

†BT Sport All fixtures subject to change.

Saturday, 5 August 2017
AFC Fylde v Boreham Wood
Bromley v Eastleigh
Dagenham and R v Barrow
FC Halifax T v Aldershot T
Guiseley v Ebbsfleet U
Hartlepool U v Dover Ath
Maidstone U v Maidenhead U
Solihull Moors v Chester FC
Sutton U v Leyton Orient† (12:30)
Torquay U v Tranmere R
Woking v Gateshead
Wrexham v Macclesfield T

Tuesday, 8 August 2017
Aldershot T v Torquay U
Barrow v FC Halifax T
Boreham Wood v Dagenham and R
Chester FC v AFC Fylde
Dover Ath v Bromley
Eastleigh v Sutton U
Ebbsfleet U v Maidstone U
Gateshead v Guiseley
Leyton Orient v Solihull Moors
Macclesfield T v Hartlepool U
Maidenhead U v Wrexham
Tranmere R v Woking

Saturday, 12 August 2017
Aldershot T v Guiseley
Barrow v Woking
Boreham Wood v Solihull Moors
Chester FC v FC Halifax T
Dover Ath v Wrexham
Eastleigh v Dagenham and R
Ebbsfleet U v AFC Fylde
Gateshead v Torquay U
Leyton Orient v Maidstone U
Macclesfield T v Bromley
Maidenhead U v Hartlepool U
Tranmere R v Sutton U

Tuesday, 15 August 2017
AFC Fylde v Maidenhead U
Bromley v Leyton Orient
Dagenham and R v Ebbsfleet U
FC Halifax T v Dover Ath
Guiseley v Tranmere R
Hartlepool U v Chester FC
Maidstone U v Aldershot T
Solihull Moors v Barrow
Sutton U v Macclesfield T
Torquay U v Boreham Wood
Woking v Eastleigh
Wrexham v Gateshead

Saturday, 19 August 2017
AFC Fylde v Dagenham and R
Boreham Wood v Aldershot T
Bromley v Hartlepool U
Chester FC v Sutton U
Dover Ath v Barrow
Eastleigh v Tranmere R
Gateshead v Macclesfield T
Guiseley v Torquay U
Maidenhead U v Ebbsfleet U
Maidstone U v Wrexham
Solihull Moors v FC Halifax T
Woking v Leyton Orient

Saturday, 26 August 2017
Aldershot T v Chester FC
Barrow v Maidenhead U
Dagenham and R v Bromley
Ebbsfleet U v Gateshead
FC Halifax T v Guiseley
Hartlepool U v AFC Fylde
Leyton Orient v Eastleigh
Macclesfield T v Dover Ath
Sutton U v Maidstone U
Torquay U v Solihull Moors
Tranmere R v Boreham Wood
Wrexham v Woking

Monday, 28 August 2017
AFC Fylde v Barrow
Boreham Wood v Wrexham
Bromley v Sutton U
Chester FC v Macclesfield T
Dover Ath v Ebbsfleet U
Eastleigh v Aldershot T
Gateshead v FC Halifax T
Guiseley v Hartlepool U
Maidenhead U v Leyton Orient
Maidstone U v Dagenham and R
Solihull Moors v Tranmere R
Woking v Torquay U

Saturday, 2 September 2017
Aldershot T v Solihull Moors
Barrow v Boreham Wood
Dagenham and R v Gateshead
Ebbsfleet U v Eastleigh
FC Halifax T v AFC Fylde
Hartlepool U v Maidstone U
Leyton Orient v Guiseley
Macclesfield T v Woking
Sutton U v Maidenhead U
Torquay U v Chester FC
Tranmere R v Dover Ath
Wrexham v Bromley

Saturday, 9 September 2017
AFC Fylde v Bromley
Aldershot T v Dover Ath
Boreham Wood v Leyton Orient
Chester FC v Ebbsfleet U
FC Halifax T v Maidenhead U
Guiseley v Eastleigh
Hartlepool U v Dagenham and R
Maidstone U v Woking
Solihull Moors v Macclesfield T
Sutton U v Gateshead
Torquay U v Wrexham
Tranmere R v Barrow

Tuesday, 12 September 2017
Barrow v Guiseley
Bromley v Torquay U
Dagenham and R v Sutton U
Dover Ath v Boreham Wood
Eastleigh v Maidstone U
Ebbsfleet U v Aldershot T
Gateshead v Chester FC
Leyton Orient v FC Halifax T
Macclesfield T v AFC Fylde
Maidenhead U v Tranmere R
Woking v Solihull Moors
Wrexham v Hartlepool U

Saturday, 16 September 2017
Barrow v Torquay U
Bromley v Solihull Moors
Dagenham and R v FC Halifax T
Dover Ath v Chester FC
Eastleigh v AFC Fylde
Ebbsfleet U v Tranmere R
Gateshead v Aldershot T
Leyton Orient v Hartlepool U
Macclesfield T v Maidstone U
Maidenhead U v Boreham Wood
Woking v Sutton U
Wrexham v Guiseley

Saturday, 23 September 2017
AFC Fylde v Woking
Aldershot T v Leyton Orient
Boreham Wood v Ebbsfleet U
Chester FC v Maidenhead U
FC Halifax T v Bromley
Guiseley v Dover Ath
Hartlepool U v Eastleigh
Maidstone U v Gateshead
Solihull Moors v Dagenham and R
Sutton U v Barrow
Torquay U v Macclesfield T
Tranmere R v Wrexham

Saturday, 30 September 2017
Barrow v Maidstone U
Bromley v Tranmere R
Dagenham and R v Torquay U
Dover Ath v Solihull Moors
Eastleigh v Chester FC
Ebbsfleet U v FC Halifax T
Gateshead v Boreham Wood
Leyton Orient v AFC Fylde
Macclesfield T v Aldershot T
Maidenhead U v Guiseley
Woking v Hartlepool U
Wrexham v Sutton U

Tuesday, 3 October 2017
AFC Fylde v Gateshead
Aldershot T v Dagenham and R
Boreham Wood v Eastleigh
Chester FC v Woking
FC Halifax T v Wrexham
Guiseley v Macclesfield T
Hartlepool U v Barrow
Maidstone U v Bromley
Solihull Moors v Ebbsfleet U
Sutton U v Dover Ath
Torquay U v Maidenhead U
Tranmere R v Leyton Orient

Saturday, 7 October 2017
Barrow v Leyton Orient
Boreham Wood v FC Halifax T
Gateshead v Bromley
Macclesfield T v Ebbsfleet U
Maidenhead U v Aldershot T
Maidstone U v Guiseley
Solihull Moors v Hartlepool U
Sutton U v AFC Fylde
Torquay U v Dover Ath
Tranmere R v Chester FC
Woking v Dagenham and R
Wrexham v Eastleigh

Saturday, 21 October 2017
AFC Fylde v Maidstone U
Aldershot T v Tranmere R
Bromley v Woking
Chester FC v Boreham Wood
Dagenham and R v Wrexham
Dover Ath v Maidenhead U
Eastleigh v Gateshead
Ebbsfleet U v Barrow
FC Halifax T v Torquay U
Guiseley v Solihull Moors
Hartlepool U v Sutton U
Leyton Orient v Macclesfield T

Tuesday, 24 October 2017
AFC Fylde v Wrexham
Aldershot T v Sutton U
Bromley v Maidenhead U
Chester FC v Barrow
Dagenham and R v Macclesfield T
Dover Ath v Woking
Eastleigh v Solihull Moors
Ebbsfleet U v Torquay U
FC Halifax T v Maidstone U
Guiseley v Boreham Wood
Hartlepool U v Tranmere R
Leyton Orient v Gateshead

Saturday, 28 October 2017
Barrow v Aldershot T
Boreham Wood v Bromley
Gateshead v Dover Ath
Macclesfield T v Eastleigh
Maidenhead U v Dagenham and R
Maidstone U v Chester FC
Solihull Moors v AFC Fylde
Sutton U v Ebbsfleet U
Torquay U v Hartlepool U
Tranmere R v FC Halifax T
Woking v Guiseley
Wrexham v Leyton Orient

Saturday, 11 November 2017
Aldershot T v AFC Fylde
Barrow v Macclesfield T
Boreham Wood v Hartlepool U
Chester FC v Wrexham
Dover Ath v Eastleigh
Ebbsfleet U v Leyton Orient
FC Halifax T v Woking
Guiseley v Bromley
Maidenhead U v Gateshead
Solihull Moors v Sutton U
Torquay U v Maidstone U
Tranmere R v Dagenham and R

Saturday, 18 November 2017
AFC Fylde v Torquay U
Bromley v Chester FC
Dagenham and R v Guiseley
Eastleigh v Barrow
Gateshead v Tranmere R
Hartlepool U v Aldershot T
Leyton Orient v Dover Ath
Macclesfield T v Boreham Wood
Maidstone U v Solihull Moors
Sutton U v FC Halifax T
Woking v Maidenhead U
Wrexham v Ebbsfleet U

Tuesday, 21 November 2017
AFC Fylde v Guiseley
Bromley v Aldershot T
Dagenham and R v Dover Ath
Eastleigh v Maidenhead U
Gateshead v Barrow
Hartlepool U v FC Halifax T
Leyton Orient v Chester FC
Macclesfield T v Tranmere R
Maidstone U v Boreham Wood
Sutton U v Torquay U
Woking v Ebbsfleet U
Wrexham v Solihull Moors

Saturday, 25 November 2017
Aldershot T v Wrexham
Barrow v Bromley
Boreham Wood v Woking
Chester FC v Dagenham and R
Dover Ath v AFC Fylde
Ebbsfleet U v Hartlepool U
FC Halifax T v Eastleigh
Guiseley v Sutton U
Maidenhead U v Macclesfield T
Solihull Moors v Gateshead
Torquay U v Leyton Orient
Tranmere R v Maidstone U

Saturday, 2 December 2017
AFC Fylde v Chester FC
Bromley v Dover Ath
Dagenham and R v Boreham Wood
FC Halifax T v Barrow
Guiseley v Gateshead
Hartlepool U v Macclesfield T
Maidstone U v Ebbsfleet U
Solihull Moors v Leyton Orient
Sutton U v Eastleigh
Torquay U v Aldershot T
Woking v Tranmere R
Wrexham v Maidenhead U

Saturday, 9 December 2017
Aldershot T v FC Halifax T
Barrow v Dagenham and R
Boreham Wood v AFC Fylde
Chester FC v Solihull Moors
Dover Ath v Hartlepool U
Eastleigh v Bromley
Ebbsfleet U v Guiseley
Gateshead v Woking
Leyton Orient v Sutton U
Macclesfield T v Wrexham
Maidenhead U v Maidstone U
Tranmere R v Torquay U

Saturday, 23 December 2017
AFC Fylde v Ebbsfleet U
Bromley v Macclesfield T
Dagenham and R v Eastleigh
FC Halifax T v Chester FC
Guiseley v Aldershot T
Hartlepool U v Maidenhead U
Maidstone U v Leyton Orient
Solihull Moors v Boreham Wood
Sutton U v Tranmere R
Torquay U v Gateshead
Woking v Barrow
Wrexham v Dover Ath

Tuesday, 26 December 2017
Aldershot T v Woking
Barrow v Wrexham
Boreham Wood v Sutton U
Chester FC v Guiseley
Dover Ath v Maidstone U
Eastleigh v Torquay U
Ebbsfleet U v Bromley
Gateshead v Hartlepool U
Leyton Orient v Dagenham and R
Macclesfield T v FC Halifax T
Maidenhead U v Solihull Moors
Tranmere R v AFC Fylde

Saturday, 30 December 2017
Aldershot T v Maidstone U
Barrow v Solihull Moors
Boreham Wood v Torquay U
Chester FC v Hartlepool U
Dover Ath v FC Halifax T
Eastleigh v Woking
Ebbsfleet U v Dagenham and R
Gateshead v Wrexham
Leyton Orient v Bromley
Macclesfield T v Sutton U
Maidenhead U v AFC Fylde
Tranmere R v Guiseley

Monday, 1 January 2018
AFC Fylde v Tranmere R
Bromley v Ebbsfleet U
Dagenham and R v Leyton Orient
FC Halifax T v Macclesfield T
Guiseley v Chester FC
Hartlepool U v Gateshead
Maidstone U v Dover Ath
Solihull Moors v Maidenhead U
Sutton U v Boreham Wood
Torquay U v Eastleigh
Woking v Aldershot T
Wrexham v Barrow

Saturday, 6 January 2018
Barrow v Tranmere R
Bromley v AFC Fylde
Dagenham and R v Hartlepool U
Dover Ath v Aldershot T
Eastleigh v Guiseley
Ebbsfleet U v Chester FC
Gateshead v Sutton U
Leyton Orient v Boreham Wood
Macclesfield T v Solihull Moors
Maidenhead U v FC Halifax T
Woking v Maidstone U
Wrexham v Torquay U

Saturday, 20 January 2018
AFC Fylde v Macclesfield T
Aldershot T v Ebbsfleet U
Boreham Wood v Dover Ath
Chester FC v Gateshead
FC Halifax T v Leyton Orient
Guiseley v Barrow
Hartlepool U v Wrexham
Maidstone U v Eastleigh
Solihull Moors v Woking
Sutton U v Dagenham and R
Torquay U v Bromley
Tranmere R v Maidenhead U

Saturday, 27 January 2018
Barrow v Sutton U
Bromley v FC Halifax T
Dagenham and R v Solihull Moors
Dover Ath v Guiseley
Eastleigh v Hartlepool U
Ebbsfleet U v Boreham Wood
Gateshead v Maidstone U
Leyton Orient v Aldershot T
Macclesfield T v Torquay U
Maidenhead U v Chester FC
Woking v AFC Fylde
Wrexham v Tranmere R

Saturday, 3 February 2018
AFC Fylde v Eastleigh
Aldershot T v Gateshead
Boreham Wood v Maidenhead U

Chester FC v Dover Ath
FC Halifax T v Dagenham and R
Guiseley v Wrexham
Hartlepool U v Leyton Orient
Maidstone U v Macclesfield T
Solihull Moors v Bromley
Sutton U v Woking
Torquay U v Barrow
Tranmere R v Ebbsfleet U

Saturday, 10 February 2018
Barrow v Hartlepool U
Bromley v Maidstone U
Dagenham and R v Aldershot T
Dover Ath v Sutton U
Eastleigh v Boreham Wood
Ebbsfleet U v Solihull Moors
Gateshead v AFC Fylde
Leyton Orient v Tranmere R
Macclesfield T v Guiseley
Maidenhead U v Torquay U
Woking v Chester FC
Wrexham v FC Halifax T

Saturday, 17 February 2018
AFC Fylde v Leyton Orient
Aldershot T v Macclesfield T
Boreham Wood v Gateshead
Chester FC v Eastleigh
FC Halifax T v Ebbsfleet U
Guiseley v Maidenhead U
Hartlepool U v Woking
Maidstone U v Barrow
Solihull Moors v Dover Ath
Sutton U v Wrexham
Torquay U v Dagenham and R
Tranmere R v Bromley

Tuesday, 20 February 2018
Aldershot T v Bromley
Barrow v Gateshead
Boreham Wood v Maidstone U
Chester FC v Leyton Orient
Dover Ath v Dagenham and R
Ebbsfleet U v Woking
FC Halifax T v Hartlepool U
Guiseley v AFC Fylde
Maidenhead U v Eastleigh
Solihull Moors v Wrexham
Torquay U v Sutton U
Tranmere R v Macclesfield T

Saturday, 24 February 2018
AFC Fylde v Dover Ath
Bromley v Barrow
Dagenham and R v Chester FC
Eastleigh v FC Halifax T
Gateshead v Solihull Moors
Hartlepool U v Ebbsfleet U
Leyton Orient v Torquay U
Macclesfield T v Maidenhead U
Maidstone U v Tranmere R
Sutton U v Guiseley
Woking v Boreham Wood
Wrexham v Aldershot T

Saturday, 3 March 2018
Aldershot T v Hartlepool U
Barrow v Eastleigh
Boreham Wood v Macclesfield T
Chester FC v Bromley
Dover Ath v Leyton Orient
Ebbsfleet U v Wrexham
FC Halifax T v Sutton U
Guiseley v Dagenham and R
Maidenhead U v Woking
Solihull Moors v Maidstone U
Torquay U v AFC Fylde
Tranmere R v Gateshead

Saturday, 10 March 2018
AFC Fylde v Aldershot T
Bromley v Guiseley
Dagenham and R v Tranmere R
Eastleigh v Dover Ath
Gateshead v Maidenhead U
Hartlepool U v Boreham Wood
Leyton Orient v Ebbsfleet U
Macclesfield T v Barrow
Maidstone U v Torquay U
Sutton U v Solihull Moors
Woking v FC Halifax T
Wrexham v Chester FC

Saturday, 17 March 2018
AFC Fylde v Hartlepool U
Boreham Wood v Tranmere R
Bromley v Dagenham and R
Chester FC v Aldershot T
Dover Ath v Macclesfield T
Eastleigh v Leyton Orient
Gateshead v Ebbsfleet U
Guiseley v FC Halifax T
Maidenhead U v Barrow
Maidstone U v Sutton U
Solihull Moors v Torquay U
Woking v Wrexham

Saturday, 24 March 2018
Aldershot T v Boreham Wood
Barrow v Dover Ath
Dagenham and R v AFC Fylde
Ebbsfleet U v Maidenhead U
FC Halifax T v Solihull Moors
Hartlepool U v Bromley
Leyton Orient v Woking
Macclesfield T v Gateshead
Sutton U v Chester FC
Torquay U v Guiseley
Tranmere R v Eastleigh
Wrexham v Maidstone U

Friday, 30 March 2018
AFC Fylde v FC Halifax T
Boreham Wood v Barrow
Bromley v Wrexham
Chester FC v Torquay U
Dover Ath v Tranmere R
Eastleigh v Ebbsfleet U
Gateshead v Dagenham and R
Guiseley v Leyton Orient
Maidenhead U v Sutton U
Maidstone U v Hartlepool U
Solihull Moors v Aldershot T
Woking v Macclesfield T

Monday, 2 April 2018
Aldershot T v Eastleigh
Barrow v AFC Fylde
Dagenham and R v Maidstone U
Ebbsfleet U v Dover Ath
FC Halifax T v Gateshead
Hartlepool U v Guiseley
Leyton Orient v Maidenhead U
Macclesfield T v Chester FC
Sutton U v Bromley
Torquay U v Woking
Tranmere R v Solihull Moors
Wrexham v Boreham Wood

Saturday, 7 April 2018
AFC Fylde v Sutton U
Aldershot T v Maidenhead U
Bromley v Gateshead
Chester FC v Tranmere R
Dagenham and R v Woking
Dover Ath v Torquay U
Eastleigh v Wrexham
Ebbsfleet U v Macclesfield T
FC Halifax T v Boreham Wood
Guiseley v Maidstone U
Hartlepool U v Solihull Moors
Leyton Orient v Barrow

Saturday, 14 April 2018
Barrow v Ebbsfleet U
Boreham Wood v Chester FC
Gateshead v Eastleigh
Macclesfield T v Leyton Orient
Maidenhead U v Dover Ath
Maidstone U v AFC Fylde
Solihull Moors v Guiseley
Sutton U v Hartlepool U
Torquay U v FC Halifax T
Tranmere R v Aldershot T
Woking v Bromley
Wrexham v Dagenham and R

Saturday, 21 April 2018
AFC Fylde v Solihull Moors
Aldershot T v Barrow
Bromley v Boreham Wood
Chester FC v Maidstone U
Dagenham and R v Maidenhead U
Dover Ath v Gateshead
Eastleigh v Macclesfield T
Ebbsfleet U v Sutton U
FC Halifax T v Tranmere R
Guiseley v Woking
Hartlepool U v Torquay U
Leyton Orient v Wrexham

Saturday, 28 April 2018
Barrow v Chester FC
Boreham Wood v Guiseley
Gateshead v Leyton Orient
Macclesfield T v Dagenham and R
Maidenhead U v Bromley
Maidstone U v FC Halifax T
Solihull Moors v Eastleigh
Sutton U v Aldershot T
Torquay U v Ebbsfleet U
Tranmere R v Hartlepool U
Woking v Dover Ath
Wrexham v AFC Fylde

THE SCOTTISH PREMIER LEAGUE AND SCOTTISH LEAGUE FIXTURES 2017–18

**Sky Sports †BT Sport All fixtures subject to change.*

SPFL Premiership

Saturday, 5 August 2017
Aberdeen v Hamilton A
Celtic v Hearts* (12:30)
Dundee v Ross Co
Hibernian v Partick Thistle
Kilmarnock v St Johnstone

Sunday, 6 August 2017
Motherwell v Rangers* (13:30)

Friday, 11 August 2017
Partick Thistle v Celtic† (19:45)

Saturday, 12 August 2017
Hamilton A v Dundee
Hearts v Kilmarnock
Rangers v Hibernian
Ross Co v Aberdeen
St Johnstone v Motherwell

Saturday, 19 August 2017
Aberdeen v Dundee
Hibernian v Hamilton A
Kilmarnock v Celtic* (12:30)
Motherwell v Ross Co
Rangers v Hearts
St Johnstone v Partick Thistle

Saturday, 26 August 2017
Celtic v St Johnstone
Hearts v Motherwell
Kilmarnock v Hamilton A
Partick Thistle v Aberdeen

Sunday, 27 August 2017
Dundee v Hibernian* (12:30)
Ross Co v Rangers† (15:00)

Saturday, 9 September 2017
Hamilton A v Celtic
Hearts v Aberdeen
Motherwell v Kilmarnock
Rangers v Dundee
Ross Co v Partick Thistle
St Johnstone v Hibernian

Saturday, 16 September 2017
Aberdeen v Kilmarnock
Celtic v Ross Co
Dundee v St Johnstone
Hamilton A v Hearts
Hibernian v Motherwell
Partick Thistle v Rangers

Saturday, 23 September 2017
Hearts v Partick Thistle
Kilmarnock v Dundee
Motherwell v Aberdeen
Rangers v Celtic
Ross Co v Hibernian
St Johnstone v Hamilton A

Saturday, 30 September 2017
Aberdeen v St Johnstone
Celtic v Hibernian
Dundee v Hearts
Hamilton A v Rangers
Kilmarnock v Ross Co
Motherwell v Partick Thistle

Saturday, 14 October 2017
Celtic v Dundee
Hamilton A v Motherwell
Hibernian v Aberdeen
Partick Thistle v Kilmarnock
Ross Co v Hearts
St Johnstone v Rangers

Saturday, 21 October 2017
Hearts v St Johnstone
Kilmarnock v Hibernian
Motherwell v Celtic
Partick Thistle v Dundee
Rangers v Aberdeen
Ross Co v Hamilton A

Wednesday, 25 October 2017
Aberdeen v Celtic
Dundee v Motherwell
Hamilton A v Partick Thistle
Hibernian v Hearts
Rangers v Kilmarnock
St Johnstone v Ross Co

Saturday, 28 October 2017
Aberdeen v Ross Co
Celtic v Kilmarnock
Dundee v Hamilton A
Hearts v Rangers
Motherwell v Hibernian
Partick Thistle v St Johnstone

Saturday, 4 November 2017
Hamilton A v Aberdeen
Hibernian v Dundee
Kilmarnock v Hearts
Rangers v Partick Thistle
Ross Co v Motherwell
St Johnstone v Celtic

Saturday, 18 November 2017
Aberdeen v Motherwell
Dundee v Kilmarnock
Hibernian v St Johnstone
Partick Thistle v Hearts
Rangers v Hamilton A
Ross Co v Celtic

Saturday, 25 November 2017
Celtic v Partick Thistle
Dundee v Rangers
Hamilton A v Hibernian
Hearts v Ross Co
Kilmarnock v Aberdeen
Motherwell v St Johnstone

Saturday, 2 December 2017
Aberdeen v Rangers
Celtic v Motherwell
Hearts v Hamilton A
Partick Thistle v Hibernian
Ross Co v Dundee
St Johnstone v Kilmarnock

Saturday, 9 December 2017
Dundee v Aberdeen
Hamilton A v St Johnstone
Hibernian v Celtic
Kilmarnock v Partick Thistle
Motherwell v Hearts
Rangers v Ross Co

Wednesday, 13 December 2017
Celtic v Hamilton A
Hearts v Dundee
Hibernian v Rangers
Partick Thistle v Motherwell
Ross Co v Kilmarnock
St Johnstone v Aberdeen

Saturday, 16 December 2017
Aberdeen v Hibernian
Dundee v Partick Thistle
Hamilton A v Ross Co
Hearts v Celtic
Kilmarnock v Motherwell
Rangers v St Johnstone

Saturday, 23 December 2017
Celtic v Aberdeen
Hibernian v Ross Co
Kilmarnock v Rangers
Motherwell v Dundee
Partick Thistle v Hamilton A
St Johnstone v Hearts

Wednesday, 27 December 2017
Aberdeen v Partick Thistle
Dundee v Celtic
Hamilton A v Kilmarnock
Hearts v Hibernian
Rangers v Motherwell
Ross Co v St Johnstone

Saturday, 30 December 2017
Aberdeen v Hearts
Celtic v Rangers
Hibernian v Kilmarnock
Motherwell v Hamilton A
Partick Thistle v Ross Co
St Johnstone v Dundee

Wednesday, 24 January 2018
Dundee v Hibernian
Hamilton A v Hearts
Kilmarnock v St Johnstone
Motherwell v Ross Co
Partick Thistle v Celtic
Rangers v Aberdeen

Saturday, 27 January 2018
Aberdeen v Kilmarnock
Celtic v Hibernian
Hamilton A v Dundee
Hearts v Motherwell
Ross Co v Rangers
St Johnstone v Partick Thistle

Wednesday, 31 January 2018
Celtic v Hearts
Hibernian v Motherwell
Kilmarnock v Dundee
Partick Thistle v Rangers
Ross Co v Aberdeen
St Johnstone v Hamilton A

Saturday, 3 February 2018
Aberdeen v Hamilton A
Dundee v Ross Co

Hearts v St Johnstone
Kilmarnock v Celtic
Motherwell v Partick Thistle
Rangers v Hibernian

Saturday, 17 February 2018
Celtic v St Johnstone
Hamilton A v Rangers
Hibernian v Aberdeen
Motherwell v Kilmarnock
Partick Thistle v Dundee
Ross Co v Hearts

Saturday, 24 February 2018
Aberdeen v Celtic
Dundee v Motherwell
Hamilton A v Partick Thistle
Kilmarnock v Hibernian
Rangers v Hearts
St Johnstone v Ross Co

Wednesday, 28 February 2018
Celtic v Dundee
Hearts v Kilmarnock
Hibernian v Hamilton A
Motherwell v Aberdeen
Ross Co v Partick Thistle
St Johnstone v Rangers

Saturday, 10 March 2018
Dundee v St Johnstone
Hamilton A v Motherwell
Hibernian v Hearts
Kilmarnock v Ross Co
Partick Thistle v Aberdeen
Rangers v Celtic

Saturday, 17 March 2018
Aberdeen v Dundee
Hearts v Partick Thistle
Motherwell v Celtic
Rangers v Kilmarnock
Ross Co v Hamilton A
St Johnstone v Hibernian

Saturday, 31 March 2018
Aberdeen v St Johnstone
Celtic v Ross Co
Dundee v Hearts
Hibernian v Partick Thistle
Kilmarnock v Hamilton A
Motherwell v Rangers

Saturday, 7 April 2018
Hamilton A v Celtic
Hearts v Aberdeen
Partick Thistle v Kilmarnock
Rangers v Dundee
Ross Co v Hibernian
St Johnstone v Motherwell

SPFL Championship

Saturday, 5 August 2017
Dumbarton v Greenock Morton
Inverness CT v Dundee U
Livingston v Dunfermline Ath
Queen of the South v Brechin C
St Mirren v Falkirk

Saturday, 12 August 2017
Brechin C v Livingston
Dundee U v Queen of the South
Dunfermline Ath v Inverness CT
Falkirk v Dumbarton
Greenock Morton v St Mirren

Saturday, 19 August 2017
Dundee U v Brechin C
Dunfermline Ath v Falkirk
Inverness CT v Greenock Morton
Livingston v St Mirren
Queen of the South v Dumbarton

Saturday, 26 August 2017
Brechin C v Inverness CT
Dumbarton v Dunfermline Ath
Falkirk v Queen of the South
Greenock Morton v Livingston
St Mirren v Dundee U

Saturday, 9 September 2017
Brechin C v Falkirk
Dundee U v Dumbarton
Livingston v Queen of the South
Greenock Morton v Dunfermline Ath
St Mirren v Inverness CT

Saturday, 16 September 2017
Dumbarton v Brechin C
Dunfermline Ath v St Mirren
Falkirk v Dundee U
Inverness CT v Livingston
Queen of the South v Greenock Morton

Saturday, 23 September 2017
Brechin C v Dunfermline Ath
Dumbarton v Inverness CT
Dundee U v Greenock Morton
Falkirk v Livingston
St Mirren v Queen of the South

Saturday, 30 September 2017
Dunfermline Ath v Dundee U
Inverness CT v Queen of the South
Livingston v Dumbarton
Greenock Morton v Falkirk
St Mirren v Brechin C

Saturday, 14 October 2017
Brechin C v Greenock Morton
Dumbarton v St Mirren
Falkirk v Inverness CT
Livingston v Dundee U
Queen of the South v Dunfermline Ath

Saturday, 21 October 2017
Brechin C v Queen of the South
Dundee U v Inverness CT
Dunfermline Ath v Livingston
Falkirk v St Mirren
Greenock Morton v Dumbarton

Saturday, 28 October 2017
Dumbarton v Dundee U
Inverness CT v Dunfermline Ath
Livingston v Brechin C
Queen of the South v Falkirk
St Mirren v Greenock Morton

Saturday, 4 November 2017
Brechin C v Dumbarton
Dundee U v St Mirren
Falkirk v Dunfermline Ath
Livingston v Inverness CT
Greenock Morton v Queen of the South

Saturday, 11 November 2017
Dumbarton v Queen of the South
Dundee U v Falkirk
Dunfermline Ath v Greenock Morton
Inverness CT v Brechin C
St Mirren v Livingston

Saturday, 25 November 2017
Brechin C v Dundee U
Dunfermline Ath v Dumbarton
Falkirk v Greenock Morton
Inverness CT v St Mirren
Queen of the South v Livingston

Saturday, 2 December 2017
Dundee U v Dunfermline Ath
Livingston v Falkirk
Greenock Morton v Brechin C
Queen of the South v Inverness CT
St Mirren v Dumbarton

Saturday, 9 December 2017
Brechin C v St Mirren
Dumbarton v Livingston
Dunfermline Ath v Queen of the South
Inverness CT v Falkirk
Greenock Morton v Dundee U

Saturday, 16 December 2017
Falkirk v Brechin C
Inverness CT v Dumbarton
Livingston v Greenock Morton
Queen of the South v Dundee U
St Mirren v Dunfermline Ath

Saturday, 23 December 2017
Dumbarton v Falkirk
Dundee U v Livingston
Dunfermline Ath v Brechin C
Greenock Morton v Inverness CT
Queen of the South v St Mirren

Saturday, 30 December 2017
Brechin C v Inverness CT
Dumbarton v Greenock Morton
Falkirk v Queen of the South
Livingston v Dunfermline Ath
St Mirren v Dundee U

Tuesday, 2 January 2018
Dundee U v Brechin C
Dunfermline Ath v Falkirk
Inverness CT v Livingston
Greenock Morton v St Mirren
Queen of the South v Dumbarton

Saturday, 6 January 2018
Brechin C v Greenock Morton
Dumbarton v Dunfermline Ath
Falkirk v Dundee U
Livingston v Queen of the South
St Mirren v Inverness CT

Saturday, 13 January 2018
Brechin C v Livingston
Dumbarton v St Mirren
Dunfermline Ath v Dundee U
Inverness CT v Queen of the South
Greenock Morton v Falkirk

Saturday, 27 January 2018
Dundee U v Greenock Morton
Dunfermline Ath v St Mirren
Falkirk v Inverness CT
Livingston v Dumbarton
Queen of the South v Brechin C

Saturday, 3 February 2018
Dumbarton v Brechin C
Falkirk v Livingston
Inverness CT v Dundee U
Greenock Morton v Dunfermline Ath
St Mirren v Queen of the South

Saturday, 17 February 2018
Brechin C v Falkirk
Dundee U v Dumbarton
Dunfermline Ath v Inverness CT
Livingston v St Mirren
Queen of the South v Greenock Morton

Saturday, 24 February 2018
Falkirk v Dumbarton
Inverness CT v Greenock Morton
Livingston v Dundee U
Queen of the South v Dunfermline Ath
St Mirren v Brechin C

Tuesday, 27 February 2018
Brechin C v Dunfermline Ath
Dumbarton v Inverness CT
Dundee U v Queen of the South
Greenock Morton v Livingston
St Mirren v Falkirk

Saturday, 3 March 2018
Dundee U v St Mirren
Dunfermline Ath v Livingston
Inverness CT v Brechin C
Greenock Morton v Dumbarton
Queen of the South v Falkirk

Saturday, 10 March 2018
Brechin C v Dundee U
Dumbarton v Queen of the South
Falkirk v Greenock Morton
Livingston v Inverness CT
St Mirren v Dunfermline Ath

Saturday, 17 March 2018
Brechin C v Dumbarton
Dundee U v Inverness CT
Dunfermline Ath v Greenock Morton
Livingston v Falkirk
Queen of the South v St Mirren

Saturday, 24 March 2018
Dundee U v Dunfermline Ath
Inverness CT v Falkirk
Greenock Morton v Brechin C
Queen of the South v Livingston
St Mirren v Dumbarton

Saturday, 31 March 2018
Dumbarton v Livingston
Dunfermline Ath v Queen of the South
Falkirk v Brechin C
Inverness CT v St Mirren
Greenock Morton v Dundee U

Saturday, 7 April 2018
Brechin C v St Mirren
Dumbarton v Dundee U
Falkirk v Dunfermline Ath
Livingston v Greenock Morton
Queen of the South v Inverness CT

Saturday, 14 April 2018
Dundee U v Falkirk
Dunfermline Ath v Brechin C
Inverness CT v Dumbarton
Greenock Morton v Queen of the South
St Mirren v Livingston

Saturday, 21 April 2018
Dumbarton v Falkirk
Inverness CT v Dunfermline Ath
Livingston v Brechin C
Queen of the South v Dundee U
St Mirren v Greenock Morton

Saturday, 28 April 2018
Brechin C v Queen of the South
Dundee U v Livingston
Dunfermline Ath v Dumbarton
Falkirk v St Mirren
Greenock Morton v Inverness CT

SPFL League One

Saturday, 5 August 2017
Albion R v Ayr U
Alloa Ath v Raith R
Arbroath v Queen's Park
Forfar Ath v Airdrieonians
Stranraer v East Fife

Saturday, 12 August 2017
Airdrieonians v Arbroath
Ayr U v Forfar Ath
East Fife v Alloa Ath
Queen's Park v Albion R
Raith R v Stranraer

Saturday, 19 August 2017
Albion R v Airdrieonians
Alloa Ath v Queen's Park
Arbroath v East Fife
Raith R v Forfar Ath
Stranraer v Ayr U

Saturday, 26 August 2017
Airdrieonians v Alloa Ath
Ayr U v Arbroath
East Fife v Raith R
Forfar Ath v Albion R
Queen's Park v Stranraer

Saturday, 9 September 2017
Alloa Ath v Forfar Ath
Arbroath v Albion R
East Fife v Queen's Park
Raith R v Ayr U
Stranraer v Airdrieonians

Saturday, 16 September 2017
Airdrieonians v East Fife
Albion R v Stranraer
Ayr U v Alloa Ath
Forfar Ath v Arbroath
Queen's Park v Raith R

Saturday, 23 September 2017
Alloa Ath v Albion R
East Fife v Forfar Ath
Queen's Park v Ayr U
Raith R v Airdrieonians
Stranraer v Arbroath

Saturday, 30 September 2017
Airdrieonians v Queen's Park
Albion R v Raith R
Arbroath v Alloa Ath
Ayr U v East Fife
Forfar Ath v Stranraer

Saturday, 14 October 2017
Ayr U v Airdrieonians
East Fife v Albion R
Queen's Park v Forfar Ath
Raith R v Arbroath
Stranraer v Alloa Ath

Saturday, 21 October 2017
Albion R v Queen's Park
Alloa Ath v East Fife
Arbroath v Airdrieonians
Forfar Ath v Ayr U
Stranraer v Raith R

Saturday, 28 October 2017
Airdrieonians v Albion R
Ayr U v Stranraer
East Fife v Arbroath
Forfar Ath v Raith R
Queen's Park v Alloa Ath

Saturday, 4 November 2017
Albion R v Forfar Ath
Alloa Ath v Airdrieonians
Arbroath v Ayr U
Raith R v East Fife
Stranraer v Queen's Park

Saturday, 11 November 2017
Airdrieonians v Stranraer
Albion R v Alloa Ath
Ayr U v Raith R
Forfar Ath v East Fife
Queen's Park v Arbroath

Saturday, 25 November 2017
Alloa Ath v Ayr U
Arbroath v Forfar Ath
East Fife v Airdrieonians
Raith R v Queen's Park
Stranraer v Albion R

Saturday, 2 December 2017
Airdrieonians v Forfar Ath
Arbroath v Stranraer
Ayr U v Albion R
Queen's Park v East Fife
Raith R v Alloa Ath

Saturday, 9 December 2017
Airdrieonians v Raith R
Albion R v Arbroath
Ayr U v Queen's Park
East Fife v Stranraer
Forfar Ath v Alloa Ath

Saturday, 16 December 2017
Alloa Ath v Arbroath
East Fife v Ayr U
Queen's Park v Airdrieonians
Raith R v Albion R
Stranraer v Forfar Ath

Saturday, 23 December 2017
Airdrieonians v Ayr U
Albion R v East Fife
Alloa Ath v Stranraer
Arbroath v Raith R
Forfar Ath v Queen's Park

Saturday, 30 December 2017
Airdrieonians v Alloa Ath
Arbroath v East Fife
Ayr U v Forfar Ath
Queen's Park v Albion R
Raith R v Stranraer

Tuesday, 2 January 2018
Albion R v Airdrieonians
Alloa Ath v Queen's Park
East Fife v Raith R
Forfar Ath v Arbroath
Stranraer v Ayr U

Saturday, 6 January 2018
Airdrieonians v East Fife
Alloa Ath v Albion R
Ayr U v Arbroath
Queen's Park v Stranraer
Raith R v Forfar Ath

Saturday, 13 January 2018
Arbroath v Queen's Park
East Fife v Alloa Ath
Forfar Ath v Albion R
Raith R v Ayr U
Stranraer v Airdrieonians

Saturday, 27 January 2018
Airdrieonians v Arbroath
Albion R v Stranraer
Alloa Ath v Raith R
East Fife v Forfar Ath
Queen's Park v Ayr U

Saturday, 3 February 2018
Arbroath v Albion R
Ayr U v Alloa Ath
Forfar Ath v Airdrieonians
Queen's Park v Raith R
Stranraer v East Fife

Saturday, 10 February 2018
Albion R v Ayr U
Alloa Ath v Forfar Ath
East Fife v Queen's Park
Raith R v Airdrieonians
Stranraer v Arbroath

Saturday, 17 February 2018
Airdrieonians v Queen's Park
Albion R v Raith R
Arbroath v Alloa Ath
Ayr U v East Fife
Forfar Ath v Stranraer

Saturday, 24 February 2018
Ayr U v Airdrieonians
East Fife v Albion R
Queen's Park v Forfar Ath
Raith R v Arbroath
Stranraer v Alloa Ath

Saturday, 3 March 2018
Airdrieonians v Stranraer
Albion R v Queen's Park
Alloa Ath v East Fife
Arbroath v Ayr U
Forfar Ath v Raith R

Saturday, 10 March 2018
Arbroath v Forfar Ath
Ayr U v Raith R
East Fife v Airdrieonians
Queen's Park v Alloa Ath
Stranraer v Albion R

Saturday, 17 March 2018
Albion R v Arbroath
Alloa Ath v Airdrieonians
Forfar Ath v Ayr U
Raith R v East Fife
Stranraer v Queen's Park

Saturday, 24 March 2018
Airdrieonians v Raith R
Albion R v Alloa Ath
Arbroath v Stranraer
Ayr U v Queen's Park
Forfar Ath v East Fife

Saturday, 31 March 2018
Alloa Ath v Arbroath
East Fife v Ayr U
Queen's Park v Airdrieonians
Raith R v Albion R
Stranraer v Forfar Ath

Saturday, 7 April 2018
Airdrieonians v Ayr U
Albion R v Forfar Ath
Alloa Ath v Stranraer
Arbroath v Raith R
Queen's Park v East Fife

Saturday, 14 April 2018
Airdrieonians v Albion R
Ayr U v Stranraer
East Fife v Arbroath
Forfar Ath v Alloa Ath
Raith R v Queen's Park

Saturday, 21 April 2018
Albion R v East Fife
Alloa Ath v Ayr U
Arbroath v Airdrieonians
Forfar Ath v Queen's Park
Stranraer v Raith R

Saturday, 28 April 2018
Airdrieonians v Forfar Ath
Ayr U v Albion R
East Fife v Stranraer
Queen's Park v Arbroath
Raith R v Alloa Ath

SPFL League Two

Saturday, 5 August 2017
Annan Ath v Peterhead
Berwick Rangers v Clyde
Edinburgh C v Montrose
Elgin C v Cowdenbeath
Stenhousemuir v Stirling Alb

Saturday, 12 August 2017
Clyde v Annan Ath
Cowdenbeath v Edinburgh C
Montrose v Stenhousemuir
Peterhead v Elgin C
Stirling Alb v Berwick Rangers

Saturday, 19 August 2017
Berwick Rangers v Annan Ath
Elgin C v Clyde
Montrose v Cowdenbeath
Stenhousemuir v Peterhead
Stirling Alb v Edinburgh C

Saturday, 26 August 2017
Annan Ath v Montrose
Clyde v Stenhousemuir
Cowdenbeath v Berwick Rangers
Edinburgh C v Elgin C
Peterhead v Stirling Alb

Saturday, 9 September 2017
Edinburgh C v Berwick Rangers
Elgin C v Annan Ath
Peterhead v Montrose
Stenhousemuir v Cowdenbeath
Stirling Alb v Clyde

Saturday, 16 September 2017
Annan Ath v Stenhousemuir
Berwick Rangers v Elgin C
Clyde v Edinburgh C
Cowdenbeath v Peterhead
Montrose v Stirling Alb

Saturday, 23 September 2017
Clyde v Cowdenbeath
Edinburgh C v Peterhead
Elgin C v Montrose
Stenhousemuir v Berwick Rangers
Stirling Alb v Annan Ath

Saturday, 30 September 2017
Annan Ath v Cowdenbeath
Montrose v Clyde
Peterhead v Berwick Rangers
Stenhousemuir v Edinburgh C
Stirling Alb v Elgin C

Saturday, 21 October 2017
Berwick Rangers v Montrose
Clyde v Peterhead
Cowdenbeath v Stirling Alb
Edinburgh C v Annan Ath
Elgin C v Stenhousemuir

Saturday, 28 October 2017
Berwick Rangers v Cowdenbeath
Clyde v Elgin C
Montrose v Edinburgh C
Peterhead v Annan Ath
Stirling Alb v Stenhousemuir

Saturday, 4 November 2017
Annan Ath v Berwick Rangers
Cowdenbeath v Montrose
Edinburgh C v Stirling Alb
Elgin C v Peterhead
Stenhousemuir v Clyde

Saturday, 11 November 2017
Berwick Rangers v Edinburgh C
Clyde v Stirling Alb
Cowdenbeath v Elgin C
Montrose v Annan Ath
Peterhead v Stenhousemuir

Saturday, 25 November 2017
Annan Ath v Clyde
Edinburgh C v Cowdenbeath
Elgin C v Berwick Rangers
Stenhousemuir v Montrose
Stirling Alb v Peterhead

Saturday, 2 December 2017
Annan Ath v Elgin C
Berwick Rangers v Stirling Alb
Clyde v Montrose
Cowdenbeath v Stenhousemuir
Peterhead v Edinburgh C

Saturday, 9 December 2017
Elgin C v Edinburgh C
Montrose v Berwick Rangers
Peterhead v Clyde
Stenhousemuir v Annan Ath
Stirling Alb v Cowdenbeath

Saturday, 16 December 2017
Annan Ath v Stirling Alb
Berwick Rangers v Peterhead
Cowdenbeath v Clyde
Edinburgh C v Stenhousemuir
Montrose v Elgin C

Saturday, 23 December 2017
Annan Ath v Edinburgh C
Clyde v Berwick Rangers
Peterhead v Cowdenbeath
Stenhousemuir v Elgin C
Stirling Alb v Montrose

Saturday, 30 December 2017
Berwick Rangers v Stenhousemuir
Cowdenbeath v Annan Ath
Edinburgh C v Clyde
Elgin C v Stirling Alb
Montrose v Peterhead

Tuesday, 2 January 2018
Clyde v Annan Ath
Edinburgh C v Berwick Rangers
Montrose v Cowdenbeath
Peterhead v Elgin C
Stenhousemuir v Stirling Alb

Saturday, 6 January 2018
Annan Ath v Montrose
Cowdenbeath v Edinburgh C
Elgin C v Clyde
Stenhousemuir v Peterhead
Stirling Alb v Berwick Rangers

Saturday, 13 January 2018
Berwick Rangers v Annan Ath
Clyde v Stenhousemuir
Edinburgh C v Montrose
Elgin C v Cowdenbeath
Peterhead v Stirling Alb

Saturday, 20 January 2018
Annan Ath v Peterhead
Berwick Rangers v Elgin C
Montrose v Clyde
Stenhousemuir v Cowdenbeath
Stirling Alb v Edinburgh C

Saturday, 27 January 2018
Clyde v Peterhead
Cowdenbeath v Berwick Rangers
Edinburgh C v Annan Ath
Elgin C v Stenhousemuir
Montrose v Stirling Alb

Saturday, 3 February 2018
Annan Ath v Cowdenbeath
Clyde v Edinburgh C
Peterhead v Montrose
Stenhousemuir v Berwick Rangers
Stirling Alb v Elgin C

Saturday, 10 February 2018
Berwick Rangers v Clyde
Cowdenbeath v Stirling Alb
Edinburgh C v Peterhead
Elgin C v Annan Ath
Montrose v Stenhousemuir

Saturday, 17 February 2018
Clyde v Cowdenbeath
Elgin C v Montrose
Peterhead v Berwick Rangers
Stenhousemuir v Edinburgh C
Stirling Alb v Annan Ath

Saturday, 24 February 2018
Annan Ath v Stenhousemuir
Berwick Rangers v Montrose
Cowdenbeath v Peterhead
Edinburgh C v Elgin C
Stirling Alb v Clyde

Saturday, 3 March 2018
Berwick Rangers v Stirling Alb
Clyde v Elgin C
Edinburgh C v Cowdenbeath
Montrose v Annan Ath
Peterhead v Stenhousemuir

Saturday, 10 March 2018
Annan Ath v Edinburgh C
Cowdenbeath v Montrose
Elgin C v Berwick Rangers
Stenhousemuir v Clyde
Stirling Alb v Peterhead

Saturday, 17 March 2018
Annan Ath v Clyde
Berwick Rangers v Stenhousemuir
Cowdenbeath v Elgin C
Edinburgh C v Stirling Alb
Montrose v Peterhead

Saturday, 24 March 2018
Berwick Rangers v Edinburgh C
Clyde v Montrose
Peterhead v Annan Ath
Stenhousemuir v Elgin C
Stirling Alb v Cowdenbeath

Saturday, 31 March 2018
Annan Ath v Berwick Rangers
Cowdenbeath v Stenhousemuir
Elgin C v Stirling Alb
Montrose v Edinburgh C
Peterhead v Clyde

Saturday, 7 April 2018
Annan Ath v Elgin C
Berwick Rangers v Peterhead
Cowdenbeath v Clyde
Edinburgh C v Stenhousemuir
Stirling Alb v Montrose

Saturday, 14 April 2018
Clyde v Stirling Alb
Elgin C v Edinburgh C
Montrose v Berwick Rangers
Peterhead v Cowdenbeath
Stenhousemuir v Annan Ath

Saturday, 21 April 2018
Annan Ath v Stirling Alb
Berwick Rangers v Cowdenbeath
Edinburgh C v Clyde
Elgin C v Peterhead
Stenhousemuir v Montrose

Saturday, 28 April 2018
Clyde v Berwick Rangers
Cowdenbeath v Annan Ath
Montrose v Elgin C
Peterhead v Edinburgh C
Stirling Alb v Stenhousemuir

FOOTBALL ASSOCIATION FIXTURES 2017–18

JULY 2017

4 Tuesday UEFA Champions League 1Q(2)
5 Wednesday UEFA Champions League 1Q(2)
6 Thursday UEFA Europa League 1Q(2)
11 Tuesday UEFA Champions League 2Q(1)
12 Wednesday UEFA Champions League 2Q(1)
13 Thursday UEFA Europa League 2Q(1)
16 Sunday UEFA Women's Euros 2017 Commences
18 Tuesday UEFA Champions League 2Q(2)
19 Wednesday UEFA Champions League 2Q(2)
20 Thursday UEFA Europa League 2Q(2)
25 Tuesday UEFA Champions League 3Q(1)
26 Wednesday UEFA Champions League 3Q(1)
27 Thursday UEFA Europa League 3Q(1)

AUGUST 2017

1 Tuesday UEFA Champions League 3Q(2)
2 Wednesday UEFA Champions League 3Q(2)
3 Thursday UEFA Europa League 3Q(2)
5 Saturday The Emirates FA Cup EP
EFL Commences
National League Commences
6 Sunday FA Community Shield
UEFA Women's Euros 2017 Final
8 Tuesday UEFA Super Cup
9 Wednesday Carabao Cup 1
12 Saturday Premier League Commences
15 Tuesday UEFA Champions League Qualifying Play-Off(1)
16 Wednesday UEFA Champions League Qualifying Play-Off(1)
17 Thursday UEFA Europa League Qualifying Play-Off(1)
19 Saturday The Emirates FA Cup P
22 Tuesday UEFA Champions League Qualifying Play-Off(2)
23 Wednesday UEFA Champions League Qualifying Play-Off(2)
Carabao Cup 2
24 Thursday UEFA Europa League Qualifying Play-Off(2)
30 Wednesday Checkatrade Trophy MD1

SEPTEMBER 2017

1 Friday Malta v England – World Cup Qualifier
2 Saturday The Emirates FA Cup 1Q
3 Sunday The SSE Women's FA Cup 1Q
4 Monday England v Slovakia - World Cup Qualifier
The FA Youth Cup P+
9 Saturday The Buildbase FA Vase 1Q
12 Tuesday UEFA Champions League MD1
13 Wednesday UEFA Champions League MD1
14 Thursday UEFA Europa League MD1
16 Saturday The Emirates FA Cup 2Q
17 Sunday The SSE Women's FA Cup 2Q
18 Monday The FA Youth Cup 1Q+
20 Wednesday Carabao Cup 3
23 Saturday The Buildbase FA Vase 2Q
FA Women's Super League Commences
26 Tuesday UEFA Champions League MD2
27 Wednesday UEFA Champions League MD2
28 Thursday UEFA Europa League MD2
30 Saturday The Emirates FA Cup 3Q

OCTOBER 2017

2 Monday The FA Youth Cup 2Q+
4 Wednesday Checkatrade Trophy MD2
UEFA Women's Champions League 32(1)
5 Thursday England v Slovenia – World Cup Qualifier
7 Saturday The Buildbase FA Trophy P
The FA County Youth Cup 1*
8 Sunday Lithuania v England - World Cup Qualifier
The SSE Women's FA Cup 3Q
11 Wednesday UEFA Women's Champions League 32(2)
14 Saturday The Emirates FA Cup 4Q
The FA Inter-League Cup 1*
15 Sunday The FA Sunday Cup 1
16 Monday The FA Youth Cup 3Q+
17 Tuesday UEFA Champions League MD3
18 Wednesday UEFA Champions League MD3
19 Thursday UEFA Europa League MD3
21 Saturday The Buildbase FA Vase 1P
25 Wednesday Carabao Cup 4
28 Saturday The Buildbase FA Trophy 1Q
31 Tuesday UEFA Champions League MD4

NOVEMBER 2017

1 Wednesday UEFA Champions League MD4
2 Thursday UEFA Europa League MD4
4 Saturday The Emirates FA Cup 1P
The FA Youth Cup 1P*
The FA County Youth Cup 2*
8 Wednesday Checkatrade Trophy MD3
UEFA Women's Champions League 16(1)
10 Friday World Cup Qualifying Play-Off (1)
11 Saturday The Buildbase FA Trophy 2Q
The Buildbase FA Vase 2P
12 Sunday The SSE Women's FA Cup 1P
The FA Sunday Cup 2
14 Tuesday World Cup Qualifying Play-Off (2)
15 Wednesday UEFA Women's Champions League 16(2)
18 Saturday The FA Youth Cup 2P*
21 Tuesday UEFA Champions League MD5
22 Wednesday UEFA Champions League MD5
23 Thursday UEFA Europa League MD5
25 Saturday The Buildbase FA Trophy 3Q

DECEMBER 2017

2 Saturday The Emirates FA Cup 2P
The Buildbase FA Vase 3P
3 Sunday The SSE Women's FA Cup 2P
5 Tuesday UEFA Champions League MD6
6 Wednesday UEFA Champions League MD6
Checkatrade Trophy 32

7 Thursday UEFA Europa League MD6
9 Saturday The FA County Youth Cup 3*
10 Sunday The FA Sunday Cup 3
16 Saturday The Buildbase FA Trophy 1P
The FA Youth Cup 3P*
20 Wednesday Carabao Cup 5
23 Saturday The FA Inter-League Cup 2*

JANUARY 2018

1 Monday New Year's Day
6 Saturday The Emirates FA Cup 3P
The Buildbase FA Vase 4P
7 Sunday The SSE Women's FA Cup 3P
10 Wednesday Carabao Cup SF(1)
Checkatrade Trophy 16
13 Saturday The Buildbase FA Trophy 2P
14 Sunday The FA Sunday Cup 4
20 Saturday The FA Youth Cup 4P*
The FA County Youth Cup 4*
24 Wednesday Carabao Cup SF(2)
Checkatrade Trophy QF
27 Saturday The Emirates FA Cup 4P

FEBRUARY 2018

3 Saturday The Buildbase FA Trophy 3P
The Buildbase FA Vase 5P
4 Sunday The SSE Women's FA Cup 4P
10 Saturday The FA Youth Cup 5P*
The FA Inter-League Cup 3*
11 Sunday The FA Sunday Cup 5
13 Tuesday UEFA Champions League 16(1)
14 Wednesday UEFA Champions League 16(1)
15 Thursday UEFA Europa League 32(1)
17 Saturday The Emirates FA Cup 5P
18 Sunday The SSE Women's FA Cup 5P
20 Tuesday UEFA Champions League 16(1)
21 Wednesday UEFA Champions League 16(1)
22 Thursday UEFA Europa League 32(2)
24 Saturday The Buildbase FA Trophy 4P
The Buildbase FA Vase 6P
The FA County Youth Cup SF*
25 Sunday Carabao Cup Final
28 Wednesday Checkatrade Trophy SF

MARCH 2018

3 Saturday The FA Youth Cup 6P*
6 Tuesday UEFA Champions League 16(2)
7 Wednesday UEFA Champions League 16(2)
8 Thursday UEFA Europa League 16(1)
11 Sunday The FA Sunday Cup SF
13 Tuesday UEFA Champions League 16(2)
14 Wednesday UEFA Champions League 16(2)
15 Thursday UEFA Europa League 16(2)
17 Saturday The Emirates FA Cup QF
The Buildbase FA Trophy SF(1)
The Buildbase FA Vase SF(1)
18 Sunday The SSE Women's FA Cup 6P
21 Wednesday UEFA Women's Champions League QF(1)
23 Friday International Friendly
24 Saturday The Buildbase FA Trophy SF(2)
The Buildbase FA Vase SF(2)
The FA Youth Cup SF(1)*
The FA Inter-League Cup SF*
27 Tuesday International Friendly
28 Wednesday UEFA Women's Champions League QF(2)

APRIL 2018

3 Tuesday UEFA Champions League QF(1)
4 Wednesday UEFA Champions League QF(1)
5 Thursday UEFA Europa League QF(1)
7 Saturday The FA Youth Cup SF(2)*
8 Sunday Checkatrade Trophy Final
10 Tuesday UEFA Champions League QF(2)
11 Wednesday UEFA Champions League QF(2)
12 Thursday UEFA Europa League QF(2)
14 Saturday The FA County Youth Cup Final (prov)
15 Sunday The SSE Women's FA Cup SF
21 Saturday The Emirates FA Cup SF
UEFA Women's Champions League SF(1)
22 Sunday The Emirates FA Cup SF
24 Tuesday UEFA Champions League SF(1)
25 Wednesday UEFA Champions League SF(1)
26 Thursday UEFA Europa League SF(1)
28 Saturday National League Ends
The FA Inter-League Cup Final (prov)
UEFA Women's Champions League SF(2)
29 Sunday The FA Sunday Cup Final (prov)

MAY 2018

1 Tuesday UEFA Champions League SF(2)
2 Wednesday UEFA Champions League SF(2)
3 Thursday UEFA Europa League SF(2)
5 Saturday The SSE Women's FA Cup Final
EFL Ends
12 Saturday National League Promotion Final
13 Sunday Premier League Ends
16 Wednesday UEFA Europa League Final
19 Saturday The Emirates FA Cup Final
20 Sunday The Buildbase FA Vase Final
The Buildbase FA Trophy Final
FA Women's Super League Ends
24 Thursday UEFA Women's Champions League Final
26 Saturday UEFA Champions League Final
EFL Championship Play-Off Final
27 Sunday EFL 1 Play-Off Final
28 Monday EFL 2 Play-Off Final

JUNE 2018

14 Thursday 2018 World Cup Commences

The FA Youth Cup Final 1st & 2nd Leg – dates to be confirmed
EFL Play-Off Semi Finals – dates to be confirmed
**closing date of round*
+week commencing

STOP PRESS

Football pays tribute to six-year-old Bradley Lowery who passed away on Friday 7 July. Shirts, flags, flowers and teddy bears were laid outside of the Stadium of Light, home of his beloved Sunderland. The Sunderland and England mascot lost his brave fight with cancer after becoming an inspiration to the whole of football with his infectious smile and special relationship with favourite player and best friend Jermain Defoe. Bradley, we salute you – RIP.

England win UEFA Under-19 European Championship beating Portugal 2-1 in the final in Georgia ... Rangers in humiliating exit from Europa League at the hands of Progrès Neiderkorn from Luxembourg ... Hammers take Hart on loan ... Champion Conte signs improved deal ... Mourinho aims to emulate Sir Alex at United ... Leiva leaves Liverpool for Lazio ... Tiger goalkeeper Jakupovic becomes a fox ... England and Scotland clash at Women's Euro 2017 tournament ... £24m West Ham deal close for Stoke's Arnautovic ... Free-agent Fraizer hired by Hull ... Cassano joins Verona, retires then does U-turn ... Samba and Terry line up as Villa defensive pairing ... Wijnaldum believes Liverpool can win title.

SUMMER TRANSFER DIARY 2017

Reported fees only, otherwise Free or Undisclosed.

June 1: **Danny Andrew** Grimsby T to Doncaster R; **Reece Brown** Birmingham C to Forest Green R; **Gary Deegan** Shrewsbury T to Cambridge U; **Darren Fletcher** WBA to Stoke C; **Alan McCormack** Brentford to Luton T; **Joe Skarz** Oxford U to Bury; **Adam Thompson** Southend U to Bury; **Marley Watkins** Barnsley to Norwich C.

June 2: **Gael Bigirimana** Coventry C to Motherwell; **Dan Gardner** Chesterfield to Oldham Ath; **Hadi Sacko** Sporting Lisbon to Leeds U.

June 3: **Sean Maguire** Cork C to Preston NE.

June 5: **Chey Dunkley** Oxford U to Wigan Ath; **Kyle McClean** Nottingham F to St Johnstone; **Dimitar Mitov** Charlton Ath to Cambridge U; **Moussa Sanoh** RKC Waalwijk to Crawley T; **Craig Tanner** Reading to Motherwell.

June 6: **Cameron Burgess** Fulham to Scunthorpe U; **Sead Kolasinac** Schalke to Arsenal; **Adam Le Fondre** Cardiff C to Bolton W; **Luke O'Neill** Southend U to Gillingham.

June 7: **Curtis Davies** Hull C to Derby Co; **Matt Dolan** Yeovil T to Newport Co; **Callum Paterson** Hearts to Cardiff C; **Charlie Raglan** Chesterfield to Oxford U; **Jordan Williams** Barrow to Rochdale – £100,000; **Gabriel Zakuani** Northampton T to Gillingham.

June 8: **Panutche Camara** Dulwich Hamlet to Crawley T; **Billy Clarke** Bradford C to Charlton Ath; **Ruben Lameiras** Coventry C to Plymouth Arg; **Ederson Moraes** Benfica to Manchester C – £35m; **Eoghan O'Connell** Celtic to Bury; **Bobby Olejnik** Exeter C to Mansfield T; **Deji Oshilaja** Cardiff C to AFC Wimbledon; **Mario Vrancic** Darmstadt to Norwich C; **Billy Waters** Cheltenham T to Northampton T.

June 9: **Tom Elliott** AFC Wimbledon to Millwall; **Jay O'Shea** Chesterfield to Bury.

June 11: **Sean Kelly** AFC Wimbledon to Ross Co.

June 12: **Jon Nolan** Chesterfield to Shrewsbury T.

June 13: **George Baldock** Milton Keynes D to Sheffield U; **Ryan Edwards** Morecambe to Plymouth Arg; **Philipp Hofmann** Brentford to Greuter Furth; **Jason McCarthy** Southampton to Barnsley; **Roderick Miranda** Rio Ave to Wolverhampton W; **Andy Rose** Coventry C to Motherwell; **David Stockdale** Brighton & HA to Birmingham C; **Peter Whittingham** Cardiff C to Blackburn R.

June 14: **Luke Leahy** Falkirk to Walsall; **Victor Lindelof** Benfica to Manchester U – £31m; **Darren Potter** Milton Keynes D to Rotherham U; **Marek Stech** Sparta Prague to Luton T.

June 15: **Harry Beautyman** Northampton T to Stevenage; **Jerome Binnom-Williams** Peterborough U to Chesterfield; **Delial Brewster** Everton to Chesterfield; **Charlie Cooper** Birmingham C to Forest Green R; **Davy Klaassen** Ajax to Everton – £23.6m; **Harry Maguire** Hull C to Leicester C – £17m; **Brendan Moore** Torquay U to Rochdale; **Jordan Pickford** Sunderland to Everton – £25m rising to £30m; **Jordan Sinnott** FC Halifax T to Chesterfield; **Curtis Tilt** Wrexham to Blackpool; **Christoph Zimmermann** Borussia Dortmund II to Norwich C.

June 16: **Rhys Browne** Grimsby T to Yeovil T; **Lee Camp** Rotherham U to Cardiff C; **Joe Garner** Rangers to Ipswich T; **Matt Gilks** Wigan Ath to Scunthorpe U; **Peter Hartley** Bristol R to Blackpool; **Alex Kiwomya** Chelsea to Doncaster R; **Mark Little** Bristol C to Bolton W; **Mark Marshall** Bradford C to Charlton Ath; **Harvey Rodgers** Hull C to Fleetwood T; **Mathew Ryan** Valencia to Brighton & HA; **Terell Thomas** Charlton Ath to Wigan Ath.

June 17: **Jason Cummings** Hibernian to Nottingham F; **Stefan Scougall** Sheffield U to St Johnstone.

June 19: **Adam Chicksen** Charlton Ath to Bradford C; **Tariqe Fosu** Reading to Charlton Ath; **Fiacre Kelleher** Celtic to Oxford U; **Danny Newton** Tamworth to Stevenage.

June 20: **Liam Boyce** Ross Co to Burton Alb; **Rob Lainton** Bury to Port Vale; **Scott Laird** Scunthorpe U to Forest Green R; **Cristian Montano** Bristol R to Port Vale; **Havard Nordtveit** West Ham U to Hoffenheim; **Phil Ofosu-Ayeh** Eintracht Braunschweig to Wolverhampton W; **Declan Rudd** Norwich C to Preston NE; **Richie Smallwood** Rotherham U to Blackburn R; **Ollie Turton** Crewe Alex to Blackpool; **Ryan Williams** Barnsley to Rotherham U.

June 21: **Adam Campbell** Notts C to Morecambe; **Joe Davis** Fleetwood T to Port Vale; **Russell Griffiths** Everton to Motherwell; **Sam Hornby** Burton Alb to Port Vale; **Rory McArdle** Bradford C to Scunthorpe U; **Connor Smith** Plymouth Arg to Yeovil T; **Peter Vincenti** Rochdale to Coventry C.

June 22: **David Ball** Fleetwood T to Rotherham U; **Max Clayton** Bolton W to Blackpool; **Craig Davies** Scunthorpe U to Oldham Ath; **Tom Eaves** Yeovil T to Gillingham; **Jon Guthrie** Crewe Alex to Walsall; **Graham Kelly** Sheffield U to Port Vale; **Liam Lindsay** Partick Thistle to Barnsley; **Cody McDonald** Gillingham to AFC Wimbledon; **Jamie Ness** Scunthorpe U to Plymouth Arg; **Chris Robertson** AFC Wimbledon to Swindon T; **Mohamed Salah** Roma to Liverpool – £36.9m rising to £43m; **Nathan Thompson** Swindon T to Portsmouth.

June 23: **Dean Bowditch** Milton Keynes D to Northampton T; **Nathan Clarke** Coventry C to Grimsby T; **Laurent Depoitre** Porto to Huddersfield T; **Mark Gillespie** Carlisle U to Walsall; **Joel Grant** Exeter C to Plymouth Arg; **Josh Harrop** Manchester U to Preston NE; **Mateusz Klich** FC Twente to Leeds U; **Conor McAleny** Everton to Fleetwood T; **Cameron McGeehan** Luton T to Barnsley; **Alan Power** Lincoln C to Kilmarnock; **Paul Taylor** Peterborough U to Bradford C; **Danny Ward** Rotherham U to Cardiff C.

June 24: **Will Hughes** Derby Co to Watford – £8m.

June 26: **Nick Anderton** Barrow to Blackpool; **Luke Croll** Crystal Palace to Exeter C; **Nicky Devlin** Ayr U to Walsall; **Jake Gray** Luton T to Yeovil T; **Matt Green** Mansfield T to Lincoln C; **Zak Jules** Reading to Shrewsbury T; **Ollie Palmer** Leyton Orient to Lincoln C; **George Saville** Wolverhampton W to Millwall; **Jack Stacey** Reading to Luton T; **Bertrand Traore** Chelsea to Lyon – £8.8m; **Jed Wallace** Wolverhampton W to Millwall; **Stephen Warnock** Wigan Ath to Burton Alb.

June 27: **Maxime Biamou** Sutton U to Coventry C; **Bradley Dack** Gillingham to Blackburn R – £750,000; **Billy Knott** Gillingham to Lincoln C; **Joe Martin** Millwall to Stevenage; **Dean Moxey** Bolton W to Exeter C; **Paul Mullin** Morecambe to Swindon T; **Eros Pisano** Hellas Verona to Bristol C; **Lamar Reynolds** Brentwood to Newport Co; **Erico Sousa** Tranmere R to Accrington S; **Omari Sterling-James** Solihull to Mansfield T; **Robbert te Loeke** Achilles '29 to Plymouth Arg; **Blair Turgott** Bromley to Stevenage.

June 28: **Jake Buxton** Wigan Ath to Burton Alb; **Pelle Clement** Ajax to Reading; **Famara Diedhiou** Angers to Bristol C – £5.3m; **Viktor Fischer** Middlesbrough to Mainz; **Ben Gladwin** QPR to Blackburn R; **Bafetimbi Gomis** Swansea C to Galatasaray; **Emyr Huws** Cardiff C to Ipswich T; **Antony Kay** Bury to Port Vale; **Kyle Lafferty** Norwich C to Hearts; **Olly Lancashire** Shrewsbury T to Swindon T; **Jack Marriott** Luton T to Peterborough U; **Mekhi McLeod** unattached to Accrington S; **Dominic Poleon** AFC Wimbledon to Bradford C; **Ben Purkiss** Port Vale to Swindon T; **Scott Tanser** Port Vale to St Johnstone; **Aaron Taylor-Sinclair** Doncaster R to Plymouth Arg; **Garry Thompson** Wycombe W to Morecambe; **Gregg Wylde** Millwall to Plymouth Arg; **Stephane Zubar** Weymouth to Yeovil T.

June 29: **Kundai Benyu** Ipswich T to Celtic; **Patrick Brough** Carlisle U to Morecambe; **Ousseynou Cissé** Tours to Milton Keynes D; **James Collins** Crawley T to Luton T; **Jermain Defoe** Sunderland to Bournemouth; **Michael Doughty** QPR to Peterborough U; **Kelvin Etuhu** Bury to Carlisle U; **Stephen Hendrie** West Ham U to Southend U; **Hallam Hope** Bury to Carlisle U; **Amine Linganzi** Portsmouth to Swindon T; **Shay McCartan** Accrington S to Bradford C; **Chris O'Grady** Brighton & HA to Chesterfield; **Josh Vickers** Swansea C to Lincoln C; **Conor Wilkinson** Bolton W to Gillingham.

June 30: **Tom Adeyemi** Cardiff C to Ipswich T; **Nathan Ake** Chelsea to Bournemouth; **Will Buckley** Sunderland to Bolton W; **Liam Edwards** Swansea C to Hull C; **Akaki Gogia** Brentford to Dynamo Dresden; **Chris Humphrey** Hibernian to Bury; **Ryan Jackson** Gillingham to Colchester U; **Aaron Mooy** Manchester C to Huddersfield T – £8m; **Kevin O'Connor** Cork C to Preston NE; **Vadaine Oliver** York C to Morecambe; **Henry Onyekuru** Eupen to Everton – £7m; **Ethan Pinnock** Forest Green R to Barnsley; **Mark Randall** Newport Co to Crawley T; **Michael Smith** Peterborough U to Hearts; **Felix Wiedwald** Werder Bremen to Leeds U; **Chris Willock** Arsenal to Benfica.

July 1: **Ethan Ampadu** Exeter C to Chelsea; **Daniel Bachmann** Stoke C to Watford; **Jan Bednarek** Lech Poznan to Southampton; **Willy Caballero** Manchester C to Chelsea; **Barry Douglas** Konyaspor to Wolverhampton W; **Kiko Femenia** Alaves to Watford; **Zeki Fryers** Crystal Palace to Barnsley; **Niall Keown** Reading to Partick Thistle; **Marc Roberts** Barnsley to Birmingham C; **Craig Ross** Macclesfield to Barnet; **Josh Scowen** Barnsley to QPR.

July 2: **Lloyd Isgrove** Southampton to Barnsley; **Jay Rodriguez** Southampton to WBA – £12m.

July 3: **George Boyd** Burnley to Sheffield W; **Marcelo Djalo** CD Lugo to Fulham; **Adam El-Abd** Shrewsbury to Wycombe W; **Jordon Forster** Hibernian to Cheltenham T; **Dan Jones** Chesterfield to Notts Co; **Michael Keane** Burnley to Everton – £25m rising to £30m; **Eddie Nolan** Blackpool to Crewe Alex; **Jamie Proctor** Bolton W to Rotherham U; **Sandro Ramirez** Malaga to Everton – £5.2m; **James Shea** AFC Wimbledon to Luton T; **John Terry** Chelsea to Aston Villa; **Ben Williams** Bury to Blackpool; **Andre Wisdom** Liverpool to Derby Co; **Zhang Yuning** Vitesse to WBA.

July 4: **Jozabed** Fulham to Celta Vigo; **James Bailey** Carlisle U to Yeovil T; **Kirk Broadfoot** Rotherham U to Kilmarnock; **Tom Ince** Derby Co to Huddersfield T; **Yaser Kasim** Swindon T to Northampton T; **Elliot Lee** Barnsley to Luton T; **Florian Lejeune** Eibar to Newcastle U – £8.7m; **Connor Mahoney** Blackburn R to Bournemouth; **Stephen O'Donnell** Luton T to Kilmarnock; **Tom Parkes** Leyton Orient to Carlisle U; **Jake Reeves** AFC Wimbledon to Bradford C; **Brad Walker** Hartlepool U to Crewe Alex.

July 5: **Ade Azeez** Partick Thistle to Cambridge U; **Jack Grimmer** Fulham to Coventry C; **Jack Hendry** Wigan Ath to Dundee; **Cedric Kipre** Leicester C to Motherwell; **Alexandre Lacazette** Lyon to Arsenal – £45m rising to £52m; **Craig MacGillivray** Walsall to Shrewsbury T; **Barrie McKay** Rangers to Nottingham F; **Conor McLaughlin** Fleetwood to Millwall; **Steve Mounie** Montpellier to Huddersfield T – £11.5m; **Ash Taylor** Aberdeen to Northampton T; **Josh Tymon** Hull C to Stoke C.

July 6: **Tom Aldred** Blackpool to Bury; **Vurnon Anita** Newcastle U to Leeds U; **Tyrone Barnett** AFC Wimbledon to Port Vale; **Loic Damour** Bourg-Peronnas to Cardiff C; **Graham Dorrans** Norwich C to Rangers; **Vincent Iborra** Sevilla to Leicester C – £10.5m; **Gavin Massey** Leyton Orient to Wigan Ath; **Roque Mesa** Las Palmas to Swansea C – £11m; **Jonathan Obika** Swindon T to Oxford U; **Stefan O'Connor** Arsenal to Newcastle U; **Jimmy Ryan** Fleetwood T to Blackpool; **Sam Slocombe** Blackpool to Bristol R; **Adam Smith** Northampton T to Bristol R; **Richard Stearman** Fulham to Sheffield U; **Charlie Taylor** Leeds U to Burnley; **Thomas Verheydt** MVV Maastricht to Crawley T; **Josef Yarney** Everton to Newcastle U.

July 7: **Cyrus Christie** Derby Co to Middlesbrough; **Ibrahima Cisse** Standard Liege to Fulham; **Joe Coveney** Manchester C to Nottingham F; **Stephen Darby** Bradford C to Bolton W; **Rene Gilmartin** Watford to Colchester U; **Jonny Howson** Norwich C to Middlesbrough; **Mathias Jorgensen** FC Copenhagen to Huddersfield T; **Michael Kightly** Burnley to Southend U; **Nicky Maynard** Milton Keynes D to Aberdeen; **Kamo Mokotjo** FC Twente to Brentford; **Jerell Sellars** Aston Villa to Cheltenham T; **Wieger Sietsma** Heerenveen to Milton Keynes D; **Jon Walters** Stoke C to Burnley – £3m.

July 8: **Harvey Bradbury** Portsmouth to Watford; **Sam Howes** West Ham U to Watford; **Jak McCourt** Northampton T to Chesterfield; **Ruben Neves** FC Porto to Wolverhampton W – £15.8m.

July 9: **Kaylen Hinds** Arsenal to Wolfsburg; **Wayne Rooney** Manchester U to Everton; **Antonio Rudiger** Roma to Chelsea.

July 10: **Richard Brindley** Colchester U to Barnet; **Romelu Lukaku** Everton to Manchester U – £75m; **Elvis Manu** Brighton & HA to Genclerbirligi; **John Ruddy** Norwich C to Wolverhampton W; **Liam Shephard** Swansea C to Peterborough U.

July 11: **Jack Cork** Swansea C to Burnley – £10m; **Caleb Ekuban** Chievo Verona to Leeds U; **James Husband** Middlesbrough to Norwich C; **Steve Mandanda** Crystal Palace to Marseille; **Will Norris** Cambridge U to Wolverhampton W; **Dominic Solanke** Chelsea to Liverpool; **Mario Suarez** Watford to Guizhou Hengfeng Zhicheng; **Michael Turner** Norwich C to Southend U; **Ron-Robert Zieler** Leicester C to Stuttgart.

July 12: **James Henry** Wolverhampton W to Oxford U; **Adnan Januzaj** Manchester U to Real Sociedad – £9.8m; **Luke McGee** Tottenham H to Portsmouth; **Olivier Ntcham** Manchester C to Celtic – £4.5m.

July 13: **Ezgjan Alioski** FC Lugano to Leeds U; **Martin Braithwaite** Toulouse to Middlesbrough; **Nathaniel Chalobah** Chelsea to Watford; **Rob Hunt** Brighton & HA to Oldham Ath; **Luke James** Peterborough U to Forest Green R; **Glen Kamara** Arsenal to Dundee; **Donal McDermott** Rochdale to Swindon T; **Aiden McGeady** Everton to Sunderland; **Samuel Saiz** SD Huesca to Leeds U; **Markus Suttner** Ingolstadt to Brighton & HA; **Lee Tomlin** Bristol C to Cardiff C – £2.9m; **Enner Valencia** West Ham U to Tigres; **James Vaughan** Bury to Sunderland – £900,000.

July 14: **Sammy Ameobi** Newcastle U to Bolton W; **Jon Dadi Bodvarsson** Wolverhampton W to Reading; **Gerard Deulofeu** Everton to Barcelona – £10.6m; **Marcel Franke** Greuther Furth to Norwich C; **Neal Maupay** St Etienne to Brentford; **George Miller** Bury to Middlesbrough; **Cheikh N'Doye** Angers to Birmingham C; **Brett Pitman** Ipswich T to Portsmouth; **Kyle Walker** Tottenham H to Manchester C – £45m.

July 15: **Tiemoue Bakayoko** Monaco to Chelsea; **Federico Fazio** Tottenham H to Roma; **Tom Huddlestone** Hull C to Derby Co – £2m; **Ben Killip** Norwich C to Grimsby T; **Douglas Luiz** Vasco Da Gama to Manchester C; **Steven Whittaker** Norwich C to Hibernian.

July 16: **George Dobson** West Ham U to Sparta Rotterdam; **Nolito** Manchester C to Sevilla – £7.9m.

July 17: **Ali Al-Habsi** Reading to Al-Hilal; **Britt Assombalonga** Nottingham F to Middlesbrough – £14m; **Harry Cardwell** Reading to Grimsby T; **Courtney Duffus** Everton to Oldham Ath; **Yoan Gouffran** Newcastle U to Goztepe SK; **Cole Kpekawa** Barnsley to Colchester U; **Cuco Martina** Southampton to Everton; **Tom Nichols** Peterborough U to Bristol R.

Compiler's pick: Finley Davies appointed captain of Ashton Boys U12s for 2017–18 season.